D1032119

KENKYUSHA'S

NEW DICTIONARY OF ENGLISH COLLOCATIONS

Edited by

SENKICHIRO KATSUMATA

AN ENTIRELY NEW EDITION

TOKYO KENKYUSHA JAPAN

First edition 1958

PRINTED IN JAPAN

新版の刊行に際して

辞書は語の意義をあきらかにするのがその本領である．わが国における英語を例にとれば，そのために変則的には和訳・和釈による英和辞書があり，正則的には原釈，すなわち英釈による英英辞書がある．

ところが，わたしの『英和活用大辞典』は，これらの英辞書とその類を異にして，語義を示すのではなくて，語が他の語と慣習的に結合して一つの表現単位をなすその姿を広く採集し，これを文法的に排列したもので，その狙いは英語活動態 (English in action) を展示しようとするにある．

こういう観点から編集された辞書は，もちろん，英語にはなく，おそらく他の国語にもないと思う．わたしの辞書が新機軸を出したものであろう．語の意味だけでなく語の結成型を対象にした辞書は，わが国の英語知識が字で生れ，語で立っているだけで，連語 (collocation) によって歩くという域に達していない現状から見て大いに意義ある存在と言えよう．

『英和活用大辞典』は，いまから二十年前（詳しくは昭和十四年四月）に出版されたもので，その内容はわたしが三十年ばかりの間に集めた十二万のコロケーションを収録したものであるが，今回刊行の『新英和活用大辞典』には，その後に採集した資材を加えてあり，コロケーションの数は二十万に近いものになっているであろう．すなわち，前後半世紀にわたるノートブック・ハビットの結晶で，そのためにわたしの目を通した文献はこれを普通のページに直すと何万ページという尨大なものになるのである．で，その文献は主として，いわゆる popular English に属するものであって，文学に属するというより，むしろジャーナリズムに属するものである．というのは，わたしの目標は美辞麗句を集めるのでなく，また特殊の難句を集めることでもなく，達意を主とした英文の姿を集成しようという考えであったからである．

初版の序に，私はこの辞書が「作った辞書」でなく「出来た辞書」であるということを書いたのであるが，ここではこの辞書が「引く」だけではなく，「読む」辞書でもあるということを強調したい．この辞書を一日一ページときめて読めば，わたしが五十年かかって何万ページから拾い集めた何十万というコロケーションを四年ばかりで通覧し，English in action の千容万態のレビューができるのである．この実行を切におすすめする．

本辞書に収めたコロケーションは，これを文法的に言って，名詞と動詞が基本になっている．名詞を基語にしたものの内でも‘他動詞＋目的語’という型を特に注意して集めてある．これはコロケーションの中心をなすからである．名詞にはそれぞれ適当の形容詞が添えてあり，動詞には常用副詞が附記してあり，また名詞・動詞ともに慣用の前置詞が結びつけてある．‘形容詞＋名詞’型 に属すべき‘名詞＋名詞’型 は便宜上別に分類してある．この‘名詞＋名詞’型は初版にはほとんど採録してないのであるが，この新版には相当多数とり入れられてある．これには Q² という見出しがついている．‘動詞＋副詞’型の内，副詞が前置詞ともなるものは idiomatic collocation として広く用いられているので，これを M² として別項に収めることにした．前置詞もそのかかる語の前にくる場合と後にくる場合を区別して，後にくるものは P² として別に分類した．

巻尾の附録は完語，すなわち affix (prefix と suffix) に対し，一語性のある語の compound word の一覧表で，語が他の語とどういうふうに結合して一語を形成するかを示したもので，一語の中のコロケーションとして研究に値いするものである．本辞書の参考として有意義のものであると信ずる．

編集陣について少しく申し上げると，コロケーションは全部わたしが採集した．その取材文献は English-speaking people の書いたものに限定し，漫然記憶などから採ったものを極力避けたかったからである．材料の分類整理は困難を極めたものであるが，これはわたしと佐藤佐市氏が取り扱った．佐藤氏は原稿を印刷するまでの整理を担当され，またコロケーションの一部の翻訳を引き受けられ，残りの分は内藤三介氏と武者金吉氏が翻訳された．なお佐藤氏のほか，田桐大澄，水野清太郎の両氏は編集並びに校正を最後まで丹念にやって下され，大橋進氏は原稿と校正刷の引合せを担当された．わたしは視力減退のため残念ながら校正に与ることはできなかった．

こうした多能なる協力者を得たので本書もここに晴々しく陽の目を見ることができた．上記の諸君に対し謹んで感謝の意を表する．なお小酒井社長に対して一言謝意を述べる．社長は仕事に熱心な方で，この辞書編成の諸方面にわたって，苦心惨憺たるものがあった．お蔭でここに完成を見るに至り，その端麗な外観は使用者の机上を飾るに足るものとなってあらわれたことは，わたしの欣喜に堪えない次第である．

なお，読み難いわたしの手蹟を巧みに捌かれ校正の労を軽減された整版部の方方の労力はわたしが忘れることのできないありがたいサービスであった．

本辞書に不備の点が多々あることと思うが，これらの点については，ご使用の方方のご示教を切にお願いする次第である．

昭和三十三年九月　　　　　　　　　　　　　　編　者

本辞典の使い方

I　本辞典の編集方法について

本辞典は序文で明示された基本方針によって編集されたもので，従来発刊された英和諸辞典とは全くその型が違っている．すなわち，他の辞典のように，一つの単語を引いて，その意義を知るというやり方ではなく，見出し語を中心にした連語がどう結びつくかを明らかにしている．この点，はじめて本辞典を手にされる方に特にご注意申し上げたい．

なお，本辞典の特色を一言につくせば，「引くだけの辞典ではなく読みこなす辞典」ということになる．単語を引いてその語義を調べる辞典ではなく，見出し語の下に配列された語群を吟味して英語の特性を明らかにする辞書という意味である．

したがって，語群の配列には特別の編集法をとっている．次に例によって具体的に解説してみよう．

A　名詞を中心とした配列

たとえば，いま fashion という語を引いてみよう．

fashion, *n.* 流行，流行物；[集合的に] 上流の人士；様式，やり方，風．

V　***create*** a *fashion* 流行を生む．¶***follow*** the *fashion* 流行を追う．（以下略）

V²　*Fashions* ***change*** quickly. 流行はすぐに変る．¶The *fashion* has ***come*** to stay. その流行は一時的のものでなくなった．

Q　live in a ***beggarly*** *fashion* こじきのような生活をする．¶She was dressed after the ***European*** *fashion.* 彼女は洋装していた．(以下略)

Q²　this year's ***beach*** *fashion* 今年の海水着の新型．¶the ***fall*** *fashion* 秋の流行．（以下略）

P　***after*** a *fashion* とも角も，幾分か，どうにかこうにか．【類】He can speak and write French —***after*** a *fashion.*　¶fall ***behind*** the *fashion* 流行に後れる．（以下略）

P²　it is the *fashion* ***for*** gentlemen to ... ...するのは紳士の習いだ．¶be the *fashion* ***of*** the moment. 現在流行している．（以下略）

O　it used to be the *fashion* to ... 以前は...することが流行したものだ．

以上の配列の仕方で，(1) V (Verb 1) は **fashion** という名詞を支配する動詞にはどんなものがあるかを明らかにしたもの．(2) V² (Verb 2) では名詞がどんな述語をとるかを示している．(3) Q (Qualifier 1) では fashion にはどんな修飾語(主に形容詞) がつくか，(4) Q² (Qualifier 2) では同様どんな修飾語(名詞または名詞相当語句)がつくかを示している．(5) P (Preposition 1) では **fashion** という名詞の前にはどんな前置詞がくるか，(6) P² (Preposition 2) では，**fashion** と次の名詞を結ぶ前置詞にはどんなものがあるかを示している．(7) O (Others) では上記の範囲に属しない形式を集めてある．

B　動詞を中心とした配列

ここでは極めて普通の動詞 call を例にとって説明しよう．

call, *v.* 呼ぶ，招く；称する；求める；訪問する；《米》電話をかける．

M　I was *called* ***away*** and scarcely knew what to say. 私は心乱れて何と言っていいのか当惑した．¶*Call* [me] ***back*** later. [電話] 後でまたかけて下さい．‖ be *called* ***back*** to life 生返る．¶*call* ***forth*** all the faculties of the mind 知恵をしぼる．¶He *called* me ***out.*** 彼は僕を呼び出した．¶***preferably*** *called* ... ...と言った方が正しいのだが．（以下略）

M²　He *called* me ***down*** like anything. 彼は私をひどくしかった．¶A doctor was *called* ***in.*** 医者を招(よ)んだ．¶*call* ***off*** a dinner (game, meeting) 晩さん会(など)を中止する．【類】*call* ***off*** negotiations with ....　¶*call* him ***up*** 彼に電話する．

P　*call* ***across*** a river 川向こうに声をかける．¶He *called* ***after*** the children who were fleeing. 彼は逃げて行く子供らを大声で呼んだ．¶We *called* ***for*** beer. われわれはビールを命じた．【類】*call* ***for*** a raise (=rise) in pay (昇給)．/ *call* ***for*** medical (=medicinal) aid.（以下略）

O　I don't *call* that fair. それは公平とは言えない．（以下略）

この例では M と M² という欄がある．M は Modifiers (修飾語)の略で，動詞を限定する意である．そして (1) M は純粋な副詞語句で，preferably とか colloquially, correctly, earthly, familiarly, fancifully, popularly, suddenly, well など，また away, back, forth, out などもっぱら副詞に用いられ普通前置詞にならないものをやはりこのグループに収録した．

(2) M² は副詞・前置詞両様に用いられるものを集めた．すなわち，down, up, in, off, on, along, about, around (round), by 等々である．

C　形容詞を中心とした配列

次に kind と new を例にとってみる．

kind, *a.* 親切な.

M an ***embarrassingly*** *kind* welcome 迷惑するほど丁重な歓迎. ¶He was *kind* ***enough*** to take me over the city. 親切にも市内を案内してくれた. 【類】Be *kind* ***enough*** to hold your tongue (だまる).

P It's very *kind* ***of*** you. どうもご親切ありがとう. ¶Be *kind* ***to*** old people. 老人には親切にせよ. ¶He was *kind* and gentle ***with*** his wife and children. 彼は妻子に親切でやさしかった.

new, *a.* 新しい；新来の.

M He has something ***absolutely*** *new* to say. 彼はある全く新しい考えを持っていてそれを言おうとしている. ¶The United States is a ***comparatively*** *new* country. 米国は比較的新しい国である. ¶This work is ***quite*** *new* to me. 私はこの仕事は全然不案内だ.

P What's *new* [***to*** us]? 何か変ったことでもあるか. ¶a youngster *new* ***at*** the game その仕事に不慣れな若者. ¶a young man *new* ***from*** the country いなかから出たばかりの若者.

以上を読んで見ると，形容詞に副詞のついたものと，前置詞のついたものと二通りあることに気付くであろう．もちろん形容詞は名詞につく場合が圧倒的に多いのであるが，本辞典では名詞修飾の例はすべて名詞の方にまわしてある．たとえば a *kind* (*old*) *teacher* は teacher の項に，a *new mode* of living は mode の項にと言った具合である．be 動詞その他の不完全自動詞につく形容詞はすべて動詞の方にまわしてある．

例: *look* ***alarmed*** (***amazed***) びっくりしたらしい (以下略).

その他 *look* ***angry*** (***better, blue, green, nice, sharp***), etc. ¶*grow* ***angry*** (***faint, fat, hot, cold, late, rich, ripe***), etc.

なお本辞典では特に be の項を新設して 'be＋adj.' の例を多数収録してある.

すなわち本辞典で形容詞を引く場合は，(1) どんな修飾語 (副詞) がつくか，(2) どんな副詞句(前置詞＋名詞の型) が次に続くかを知ろうとする場合である.

例: (1) ***extremely*** *abundant*; ***remarkably*** *fine*; ***mighty*** *good*; ***highly*** *educated*; ***so*** *good.* (2) *high* ***in*** price; *high* ***in*** office; *angry* ***with*** him; *angry* ***at*** one's words; *famous* ***for*** his learning; *noted* ***for*** skill, etc.

(2) の場合も，形容詞は名詞 (price, office, word, learning, etc.) の方に含まれていることが多い.

II 本辞典の活用について

「活用」と銘を打った意味は語と語の結びつき，語群としていかに活動するかを示すことはもちろんであるが，さらにこの辞典を大いに活用して英語の真の姿をつかんでいただきたいという意味も含まれている．そこで本辞典をいかに活用するかにつき，程度によってきまることではあるが，特に次の諸点に留意されたら一層効果的であろう.

A 名詞＋名詞の型

旧版にはなかった本辞典の特色の一つである．この '名詞＋名詞' 型は英語の一大特色で，他の国語に見られない便利な連語形式である．たとえば「彼は州立カリフォルニア大学の一学生である」という意味の英語は 'He is a State University of California student.' と極めて簡明に表現できる [student の項参照]．同様に a 65-year-old U.N. Secretary-General とか a 5-foot, 97-pound, 24-year-old strawberry blonde といった型は英語独特のものである.

次に，この種の例を示してご参考に供する [それぞれの項参照].

1. ***leadership*** *ability* 統率力；***language*** *ability* 語学力；***reading*** (***speaking, writing***) *ability* 読書(など)力. (以下略)
2. the ***behind-the-scenes*** *activity* 暗躍；***black market*** *activity* やみ取引；undergraduates' ***campus*** and ***community*** *activities* 学生の大学内及び学外活動；***espionage*** *activity* スパイ活動. (以下略)
3. the ***anti-administration*** *party* 反対党 (野党)；arrange a ***good-bye*** *party* for ... ...のため送別会の仕度をする；the ***Hitler*** *party* ヒットラー党；a ***weekend beach*** *party* 週末海水浴団. (以下略)
4. an ***easy payment*** *plan* 分割払い；a ***happy-go-lucky*** *plan* 行き当りばったりの計画；the ***pay-as-you-go*** *plan*「代金はお帰りの際」式のやり方. (以下略)
5. the acute ***clothing*** (***housing, food***) *shortage* ひどい衣料(など)不足；in the face of drastic ***labor*** and ***material*** *shortages* 労働力及び物質のはなはだしい不足にもかかわらず；***wartime paper*** *shortage* 戦時の紙ききん. (以下略)
6. ***air-mail*** *service* 航空郵便(制)；***Armed Forces Radio*** *Service*＝AFRS；***radio*** (***television***) [***broadcasting***] *service* 放送事業(など)；***water*** (***gas, light***) *service* 配水(など)；***bus*** (***subway, railway***) *service* バス(など)事業.

B 動詞＋副詞の型

本辞典では特に M, M² という項を設けて '動詞＋副詞' の姿をはっきりさせることに努めた．特に up, down, (out は M¹), on, over, forth などきわめて頻用度の高い副詞を M² として多数追加したのは新版の特色の一つである．これらの実例は come, go, put, call ... などの項にある.

若干の例を示すと，go の項に

go, *v.* ...

M² *go* ***about*** with ... / *go* ***along*** to ... / *go*

down to ... / go ***in*** for ... / go ***off*** / go ***on*** with ... / go ***over*** to ... / go ***under*** / go ***up*** to ...

など二百にものぼる用例が収録されている．さらに，**push** や **put** の項には

push, *v.* ...

M *push* ***apart*** / *push* ***aside*** / *push* ***forward*** / *push* a door ***open*** / *push* ***out*** ...

M² *push* ... ***along*** / *push* ... ***down*** / *push* ***off*** / *push* ***on*** / *push* ... ***through*** / *push* ***up*** ...

put, *v.* ...

M *put* ***apart*** / *put* ***aside*** / *put* ***away*** / *put* ***back*** / *put* ... ***fast*** / *put* ***forth*** / *put* ***forward*** / *put* ***out*** / *put* ***through***

M² *put* ***about*** / *put* ***by*** / *put* ***down*** / *put* ***in*** / *put* ***off*** / *put* ***on*** / *put* ***up*** ...

などはそれぞれ多数の用例をあげてその意義の多様性を明らかにしてある．

そこで，これらの例文はそれぞれ他の語または語群と結びついていくつかの異なった意味を含んでいることに気ずくであろう．たとえば put down には約三十の用例が載っているが，その意味はいずれも必ずしも同じではない．*put* ***down*** one's pen（ペンをおく）と *put* me ***down*** at ...（...で降してくれ）では違うし，*put* ***down*** a strike（ストを止める）と I *put* him ***down*** at 35（三十五歳と見当をつけた）ではずいぶん意味が違う．

以上から，この種の項目は語句を拾い読みしないで，ぜひ通読して，その語義の全般的な変化を会得されんことを希望する．一つ一つの用例は異なっていても必ずやそこには一貫した通則があり，その通則をマスターすることが大切だからである．

C　動詞＋目的語の型

たとえば heart という名詞が胸に浮んだとする．さてこれにはどんな他動詞がついて collocation を形成するか？この疑問は **heart** (*n.*) の項の v 部を見れば解ける．若干の例を示すと

v ***affect*** the *heart* / ***break*** one's *heart* / ***brighten*** one's *heart* / ***captivate*** one's *heart* / ***cry*** one's *heart* ***out*** / ***eat*** one's *heart* ***out*** / ***fix*** one's *heart* on ... / The good news ***filled*** their *hearts* with joy. / ***gather*** *heart* / fear and anxiety ***gnawing*** her *heart* / ***keep*** the *heart* ***beating*** / ***lose*** one's *heart* / ***move*** the *heart* / ***open*** one's *heart* to ... / ***rend*** one's *heart* / ***soften*** one's *heart* / His *heart* was ***thrilled*** with secret pleasure. / ***touch*** one's *heart* ...　(以下略)

など多数の例文や類例が出てくる．これによって自分の求める型を自由に選択できる．

更に，**pocket** (*n.*) の項を見ると

v ***cram*** one's *pocket* with ... / ***enrich*** the *pocket* / ***fill*** one's own *pockets* ... / ***lighten*** one's *pocket* / ***pick*** a [man's] *pocket* / ***search*** one's *pocket* / ***suit*** the *pockets* of these people (以下略)

などの用例が出ている．

D　主語＋述語の型

この型は名詞の v² に収録してある．前記の **heart** (*n.*) を見ると

v² My *heart* ***aches***. / My *heart* ***beats*** high. / My *heart* ***bleeds*** for him. / his *heart* ***broke*** when ... / My *heart* ***pounded*** with expectation. /Our *hearts* ***sank*** low. (以下略)

など名詞 heart の動きが示されている．

なお，**hair** (*n.*) を調べてみよう．

v² Her *hair* is ***coming off***. / Her *hair* ***flows*** in the wind. / *Hair* ***falls out*** (=***off***). / *hair* ***grows*** on ...　(以下略)

なおこの型は Q (形容詞＋名詞) の項とも関係があるから，あわせて通読されたい．

E　前置詞を求める型

本辞典が前置詞を見出し語として取入れていないことは前述の通りである．ではどうして前置詞を求めるかというと，前置詞は元来名詞（または名詞同等語）の前におかれて動詞とか形容詞と結んだり，または名詞と名詞を結合する役をしたりするものであるから，当然主語あるいは目的語である名詞を求めれば出てくるわけである．

たとえば **absence** (*n.*) を引いてみる．

P ***after*** a short *absence* / ***by*** its *absence* / ***during*** the *absence* of ... / ***in*** your *absence* / ***in*** the *absence* of the president, etc.

P² a teacher's *absence* ***from*** classes / *absence* ***from*** school (office) / *absence* ***without*** notice, etc.

また **chair** (*n.*) の項には

P He rose ***from*** his *chair*. / sit ***in*** a *chair* / sit back ***in*** one's *chair* / sit up ***on*** a *chair*, etc.

P² a *chair* ***for*** organic chemistry, etc.

次は動詞から前置詞を求める場合をあげてみよう．

agree (*v.*) を引くとそれには in, on, to, with ... の前置詞がつくことがわかる．

P *agree* ***about*** it / *agree* ***as to*** ... / *agree* ***between*** two persons / *agree* ***in*** chorus / *agree* ***in*** opinion (principle) / *agree* ***on*** some plane of campaign / *agree* ***to*** the terms / *agree* ***to*** one's opinion / I cannot *agree* ***with*** you ***on*** that. / *agree* ***with*** one's pocket / This fish does not *agree* ***with*** me. (僕はこの魚を食べるとあたる).

attend (*v.*) には at, on, to, with などの前置詞がつく．

I *attend* regularly ***at*** church. / *attend* ***on*** the sick (one's sick mother) / *attend* ***to*** one's lesson / be *attended* ***with*** brilliant results ....

belong (*v.*) と名詞の結合：

P they *belong* ***in*** the same class with ... / This book *belongs* ***on*** that shelf. / They *belong* ***to*** respectable families. / This belt *belongs* ***with*** that coat.（このバンドはそのコートの附属品だ）.（以下略）

また **graduate** (*v.*) には from という前置詞を伴なうのが通例だが，試みに graduate の項を引いてみよう．

graduate, *v.* 卒業させる；学位を授ける，卒業する(略).

M （中略）

P He *graduated* ***as*** M.D. ***at*** Edinburgh in 1807. 【類】 He was *graduated* ***at*** Yale in 1920. / He was *graduated* ***from*** grammar school in 1956. =《英》 He completed his grammar school course in 1956. 【類】He *graduated* ***from*** Harvard with the degree of M.A. / be *graduated* ***from*** .... （以下略）

その他 Hellen Keller *graduated* ***with*** honors ***at*** Radcliffe College. という例も見える．

以上から graduate *at*, be graduated *at*; graduated *from*, be graduated *from* の四つの型があることがわかる．一般には be graduated *from* ... が米語用法で，graduate *at* (or *from*) ... が英語用法だといわれているが，必ずしもそうとは言えぬ．なお☞を見ると，“米国では be graduated from ... は文語体でいく分古い用法．口語では graduate from ... が通例”となっている．

listen (*v.*) を引くと at, for, to などの前置詞が出てくる．

listen ***at*** key-holes / *listen* ***for*** a footstep / *listen* ***to*** a lecture / *listen* ***with*** strained ears ....

その他“listen in ***on*** the radio (***to*** the music) ラジオ(の音楽)を聴取する”という例もある．

さらに，もっとも頻用度の高い動詞 come, go, set, put, get, call, look などは副詞か前置詞かの助けを借りていろいろな意味を持たせることが多いのだから当然多数の副詞，前置詞(本辞典では M, M², P の見出しで集録されている)がつく．

たとえば come や go は 7 ページにわたり，put も 5 ページに及び，それぞれ七百から千内外の例文をあげてある．次に形容詞から前置詞を求める例を二三示しておく．

たとえば **angry** (*a.*) を引くと，about, at, for, with などの前置詞が出てくる．

He was *angry* ***about*** it. / He was *angry* ***at*** the dog (words). / He is *angry* ***for*** (=about) trifles. / I'm *angry* ***with*** you ***for*** your conduct.

happy (*a.*) の項を見ると

He is *happy* ***about*** his promotion. / He is *happy* ***among*** his children. / be *happy* ***at*** the news (***at*** hearing that ...) / I am *happy* ***in*** the consciousness that ... / He is *happy* ***over*** his success. / He is *happy* ***with*** his wife (friends).

の例がある．

keen (*a.*) には after, about, of, on など．

He is *keen* ***after*** money-making / He is *keen* ***about*** his game ... / *keen* ***of*** scent (hearing) / He is *keen* ***on*** stamp collecting ...

kind (*a.*) には of, to, toward, with など．

It's very *kind* ***of*** you. / They are always *kind* ***to*** us. / He was *kind* and gentle ***with*** his wife and children.

popular (*a.*) には among, for, in, with など．

He is *popular* ***among*** the students. / be *popular* ***for*** his kindness / He is very *popular* ***with*** the ladies.

F 冠詞の問題

名詞を使う場合，冠詞の用法が一番厄介な問題になる．名詞にはいわゆる countable, uncountable とはっきり定められない borderline case がよく出てくる．次に **accommodation** の項を引いてみる．

辞典では「設備・宿泊」の意では主に（しばしば）複数になることをうたっているが実例ではどうか．

☞ *A.C.D.* には‘(*chiefly pl.*) lodging, or food and lodging’とあり，Webster 大辞典にも‘often in *pl.*; as, the *accommodations* (that is, lodgings and food) at a hotel’とある．

accommodation, *n.* [しばしば *pl.*] 設備，宿泊.

V The hotel ***affords*** luxurious *accommodation* for 400 guests. そのホテルは設備が優秀で四百人の客を収容できる．¶ ***engage*** sleeping *accommodation* 寝台を予約する．¶There travelers may ***find*** *accommodation* at moderate terms.(かっこうの料金で)． ¶ ***get*** *accommodation* for the night. 一泊する． ¶Hotels there ***give*** (=***furnish***) good *accommodations.* そこのホテルは設備がよい．¶ ***reserve*** the *accommodation* in advance 宿泊の予約をする． ¶ ***secure*** *accommodation*[*s*] 宿泊する．（以下略）

Q ***de luxe*** *accommodations* [ホテルなど]特等待遇．¶ ***Rough*** *accommodation* can be had at the local inn. 地方の宿屋で(設備は悪いが)どうにかこうにか宿泊ができる．（以下略）

Q² ***hotel*** *accommodations* / excellent ***hotel*** *accommodations.* ¶ ***rooming*** *accommodations* (貸部屋)（以下略）

以上を通観して accommodation には *pl.* が比較的多いが，しかし絶対的でないことが分る．この例は *an* accommodation という例が皆無であることも注意すべきである．

今一つ **communication** (*n.*) を例にとると，これは *a* communication, communication, communications の三つの形が現われている．a communication は伝言・手紙の意味であり，communication は輸送・通信すること．また communications は通信の制度，(特に軍の)連絡機関，その制度．

☞単数の形は *A.C.D.* では‘a document or a message ...’ *Webster* では‘a verbal or written message’となっている．複数の形については *A.C.D.* は‘**a.** the means of sending military messages, orders, etc., as by telephone, telegraph, radio, couriers. **b.** routes and transportation for moving troops and supplies ....' また, *Webster* も '**a.** A system using signals, couriers, telegraphy, radio ... for communicating information or orders, as in the armed forces. **b.** A system of routes for moving troops, supplies, etc. ...' となっている.

communication, *n.* 通信; 交通; 連絡.

V ***address*** all *communications* to ... すべての通信を...にあてる. 【類】All *communications* should be ***addressed*** to the College, E.C. 4. ¶ ***await*** a *communication* 書信を待つ. ¶ The photograph ***bears*** a *communication.* その写真には通信文が載っている. ¶ ***cut off*** *communications* with ... ...との連絡を絶つ. ¶ ***establish*** wireless *communication* between ... 間に無線を設置する. (以下略)

Q a ***confidential*** *communication* 秘密の情報. ¶ There are ***good*** *communications* to the place. そこへの交通は便利である. (以下略)

Q² ***cable*** *communication* 海外通信. ¶ ***mass*** *communication* 大衆伝達(マスコミ). ¶ ***phone*** *communications* with the outside have been cut off 外部との電話連絡は絶たれた. (以下略)

以上の諸例から communication の用法をほぼ了解できよう.

air や water にはそれぞれ air, air*s*, *the* air; water, water*s*, *the* water などの形が出ている.

air (*n.*) の項を見ると (1)「空気」「空中」の意味では air と the air がある. すなわち

V ***admit*** *air* / ***blow*** *air* into a balloon / ***clear*** the *air* / ***purify*** the *air* / ***sniff*** the *air* (以下略)

V² The *air* ***grows*** colder as we go up. (以下略)

Q The *air* is ***breathless.*** / The *air* is ***crisp*** and ***cool.*** (以下略)

Q² in the ***country*** *air* / the cool ***mountain*** *air* (以下略)

P ***by*** *air* / ***from*** the *air* / ***in*** the *air* / ***on*** the *air* / tread (walk) ***on*** *air* (うちょう天になる)

(2) 「様子」「態度」の意味では an air; airs とある.

V ***assume*** an *air* of superiority / ***carry*** a kingly *air* / ***put on*** high *airs*

Q assume a ***nonchalant*** *air* / with a ***downcast*** *air* / with ***lordly*** *airs* ... / with ***empty*** *airs*

Q² (以下略)

以上から **(2)** は純然たる Common Noun であることが明らかとなる.

water (*n.*) の方はいかなる場合も a water という形は出てこない. ただし ***under*** *water* は無冠詞だが ***in*** *water,* ***in*** the *water*; ***on*** *water,* ***on*** the *water* は二種あり, ***through*** the *water* という例は一つある. これから

「海, 川, 湖水など」の意味では **waters** となる例はいくつもあるが, ***water*** という例はあまりでてこない. これは辞典に (often pl.) Body of water. とあるように, 少くとも文語では waters の形が圧倒的に多いことを示している.

history (*n.*) を例にとってみよう. これも history, a history と二様ある. a ship ***with a history*** (歴史のある船) / a woman ***with a history*** (数奇な運命をたどった女) などが誌されていて, 不定冠詞のつく例がいくつか示されている. もちろん American *history* / learn *history* / *History* shows that ... などは無冠詞である.

次に industry と business を少しく調べてみよう. まず **industry** (*n.*) には「産業」と「勤勉」の意味があることはご承知の通り.「勤勉」の意味では抽象名詞 (無冠詞) だが,「産業」の意味では industry, *an* industry, industrie*s* の例がある. すなわち peace *industry,* peace *industries*; war *industry,* war *industries* など. expand *industry* and commerce (無冠詞) と, open up *a* new *industry* の例が出ている. すなわち, industry, an industry, industries の三つの形があるわけである.

この意味では **business** (*n.*) も同様で, *Business* is declining (improving) とか do *business* with ... は無冠詞だが, establish *a business* of one's own, start (begin) *a business* では普通名詞になっている. また Q² (n.+n.) の部を見ると, a ***hit or miss*** *business* (一か八かの商売)とか a ***touch-and-go*** *business* (けんのんな仕事) など興味ある句も見える. No business is like ***show*** *business.* (ショーほどすてきな商売はない) なども入っている.

cf. This is an age of recession in all *businesses* and *industries.* (今はあらゆる事業産業の景気後退の時代である)—*N. Y. Times.*

rain (*n.*) を引いてみよう.「雨」という意味では rain, *the* rain, *a* rain, *the* rain*s* (雨季) の例が出てくる. すなわち

We shall have *rain.* (雨が降るだろう) / We have *the rains* in early summer. (初夏が雨季だ) / A soft *rain* fell like tears. (静かな雨が涙のようにしとしとと降った) / *Rain* is much needed. (一雨欲しい) / The *rain* is coming down in sheets. (しのつく雨だ) 等々.

修飾語の欄 (Q) を見ると大体形容詞がつくと a ... rain *or* rains となることがわかる. 例: a ***soft*** *rain,* a ***fine*** *rain,* ***heavy*** *rains,* a ***pouring*** *rain,* etc. また in *the* rain という句が多いのは主に口調の関係らしく, in rain という例もある. 例: I was cought in [*the*] rain / in *the* blinding rain (目もあけられない雨中をついて) / a mountain view *in* rain (雨中の山景), etc.

では in a ... rain とは言わないかというと, 次の例もある.

In *a* streaming rain (ざあざあ降る雨の中で).

cloud (*n.*) には *a* cloud, cloud*s*, *the* cloud*s* の例があり, それぞれ用法が出ている.

color, *n.* にも color, *a* color, colors の用例があり，***full*** *color* (極彩色) / ***loud*** *color* (けばけばしい色) / ***solid*** *color* (無地) / ***subdued*** *color* (渋い色) など興味ある例が出ている．

見出し語についての注意

1 連語の見出しについて

New Year Day (New Year's Day) とか post office などは day, office の項を参照されたい．ただし，この場合のようにほとんど合成語的な語句は，独立させ別に項目を設けたものもある．

例：bank note, bank bill, object lesson, etc.

2 be 動詞の項を新設

be 動詞と形容詞や副詞や前置詞との結びつきを示し，その動きと変化を明らかにした．

例：*be* ***badly off*** / *be* ***comfortably off*** / Where *are* you ***off*** to? / about to *be* ***down*** on him / The hour *is* ***up***. / That's ***against*** the law. / He *is* ***at*** . . . again. / The tide *is* ***with*** us. / ***Here*** we *are* !

3 -self の項を新設

これは oneself, itself, myself (yourself, himself, herself, themselves, etc.) を含むいわゆる再帰用法 (Reflexive use) を特に独立させ，その型を示したもの．-self の用法の全貌を知るためには便利であろうと思われる．本辞典では S 部の p. 1139–p. 1157 の 18 ページにわたり約五千の用例を収録してある．

つづりやハイフンについて

本辞典では見出し語は米つづりを主として採用した．本文の例文も可能なかぎり米つづりによっている．ただし，英語特有な表現や，英人 writer から採った例文の中には英語つづりのものも若干含まれている．いずれの場合も，見出し語は colo[u]r; travel[l]er; center, centre; theater, theatre... のように米・英両形を示してある．☞ 詳細は次ページの「米語つづり一覧表」参照していただきたい．

ハイフン語は必ずしも従来の諸辞典と一致しないものもあるが，これは本辞典の性質上，ぜひもないことである．そのため，特に Compound Words の一覧表を付し，その参照の便に当てた．

注： to-day → today, to-morrow → tomorrow, to-night→tonight, war-time→wartime, pre-war →prewar, post-war→postwar, etc.

付録：A List of Compound Words について

この表は *The Compounding and Hyphenation of English Words*—by Alice M. Ball によったものである．なお『大ウエブスター』を参照して，その正確を期した．

この語表の目的は，ハイフン語 (hyphened words) と，結合語 (solid words) の結合の経過を明らかにすることにある．この表では，接頭語 (prefix) や接尾語 (suffix) は省き，一語として完全な形を成す語と語の結びつきだけを表示した．この表には two-noun form ('名詞＋名詞' 型) は含まれていないが，随所に挿入して参考に資してある．

各種記号の解説

1. [ ] (A) 英語では省略し得る語またはつづりを示す．

annex[e], *n.* ... **appal[l],** *v.* ... **colo[u]r,** *n.*

(B) 日本語では訳語の説明及び補足説明を示す．

game, *n.* ..., [比ゆ的に] 作戦, ...

habit, *n.* [婦人用の] 乗馬服．

(C) 用例の中に，

M ***blast out*** a *stone* [雷管などで] 石を吹きとばす．

Q² a ***show*** *boat* [演芸用の] ショーボート．

2. ( ) (A) 訳語の同意語を示す．

bench, *n.* 腰かけ (ベンチ)； **bloc,** *n.* 圏 (ブロック)； **calendar,** *n.* 暦 (カレンダー)．

(B) 修飾語 'noun＋noun' の形で，紙面節約のため異語をはさむ場合．

Q ***front*** (***back***) *benches* [国会の]大もの(陣笠)席．

Q² a ***short***(***long***)***-term*** *bill* 短(長)期の手形．

(C) 訳語補足に．

V ***clear*** a *bill* 手形を(交換して)清算する．

Q² a ***paper*** *boat* 紙艇 (マニラ紙などで製した狩猟または競争用の)．

3. (A) 《 》米・英語 (及び他の外国語)．

《米》,《米口》,《米俗》,《英》,《英口》など．

(B) 〖 〗専門語または語の特別用法を示す．主なものは，法・医・理・工・電・商・株式・野球・音楽・映画・劇・服飾・スポーツ・放送(ラジオ)・植物・諺・文法など．

4. ☞「参考」の意．たとえば **pair** (*n.*) には

☞ a *pair* of ..., two *pair* of ... となり，-s をつけない．ただし，商業英語や口語では複数形にして -s をつけることがある．例：How many *pairs* of socks do you have? / Show me a couple more *pairs*.

また **sure** (*a.*) の項を見ると，

☞ *Sure*, I am. は Yes の感じだが，否定は *Sure*, I am not. となって No の感じ．英語用法は Surely である．

road (*n.*) の米語用法については，次のような説明がしてある．

☞ 米語の road (＝railroad) は英語の line に当る．米国では鉄道の方が州(公)道より先にできたためという．

本辞典使用の米語つづり一覧表

1. [-l《米》——-ll《英》]
council[l]or, dul[l]ness, enrol[l], fulfil[l], instil[l], jewel[l]er, travel[l]er, wool[l]en
注：**instal[l]ment** は，米語用法では **-l-**, **-ll-** の両形．英語は **-l-** だけである．

2. [-or《米》——-our《英》]
colo[u]r, endeavo[u]r, favo[u]r, hono[u]r, labo[u]r, neighbo[u]r, parlo[u]r, vapo[u]r succo[u]r

3. [-er《米》——-re《英》]
center (=centre), fiber (=fibre), luster (=lustre), maneuver (=manoevre), somber (=(=sombre), theater (=theatre)
注：**acre, massacre, mediocre** は米・英共通．

4. [-ize《米》——-ise《英》]
analyze (=analyse), paralyze (=paralyse), realize (=realise)
注：**advertise** は米・英共通で，**advertize** は米語用法．なお advertisement, advertizement; advertiser, advertizer; advertising, advertizing の関係も同様．ただし，現代英語の用法は動詞の語尾 -ise は -ize の方が多く使われる傾向がある．

5. [-se《米》——-ce《英》]
defense (=defence), license (=licence), offense (=offence), pretense (=pretence)
注：**practice** の米語用法は *n.*, *v.* で，英語用法は **practice** *n.*, **practise** *v.* となっている．但し，practise (*v.*) は米でも使うが，英語には practice (*v.*) という用法はない．

6. [in-《米》——en-《英》]
inclose (=enclose), indorse (=endorse), infold (=enfold), inquire (=enquire)
注：現代英語，特に米語では **in-** と **en-** は混用している．

7. [-ction《米》——-xion《英》]
connection (=connexion), inflection (=inflexion), reflection (=reflexion)

8. [-i-《米》——-y-《英》]
cider (=cyder), flier (=flyer), siren (=syren), tire (=tyre)
注：逆に **y→i** となる場合は gayety (=gaiety), gayly (=gaily), Gypsy (=Gipsy). 米語には **dryer, drier** の両形がある．英語は **drier** だけ．

9. [-o-《米》——-ou-《英》]
font (=fount), mold (=mould), moldy (=mouldy), molt (=moult)

10. [-y《米》——-ey《英》]
bogy (=bogey), nosy (=nosey), story (=storey), trolly (=trolley), whisky (=whiskey)

11. [-c, -k, ck《米》——que《英》]
check (=cheque), checkers (=chequers), man[n]ikin (=mannequin), picket (=piquet), cue (=queue)
注：k が c となる例としては，ankle (=ancle), disk (=disc), skeptic (=sceptic).

12. [-er-《米》——-ar《英》]
brier (=briar), peddler (=pedlar)

13. [-i-《米》——-e-《英》]
benzine (=benzene), dispatch (=despatch), gasoline (=gasolene)

14. [-z《米》——-s《英》]
cozy (=cosy), fuze (=fuse), tzar (=tsar), vizor (=visor)

15. [-ed《米》——-t《英》]
burned (=burnt), dreamed (=dreamt), learned (=learnt), leaped (=leapt), leaned (=leant), smelled (=smelt)
注：burnt《米》は主に形容詞に使う．例：a *burnt* child (house).

16. [-e-《米》——-ae-《英》]
medieval (=medaeval), esthetic (=aesthetic), encyclopedia (=encyclopaedia), anemia (=anaemia)

17. [その他]（前が《米》で後が《英》）
draft (=draught), vial (=phial), plow (=plough); program[me], gram[me]; educator (=educationist); diplomat (=diplomatist); jail (=gaol); pajamas (=pyjamas); gray (=grey)
注：**cigaret[te], omelet[te], catalog[ue], dialog[ue], veranda[h]; lik[e]able, lov[e]able, siz[e]able; good-by[e]** は米語では両形とも使っている．

☞ 米国版各辞書で **bazaar** (*n.*) を引いてみると Also **bazar** とあり，両形を認めていることが分る．

各種記号一覧表

1. 英　字

a.	=adjective
ad.	=adverb
conj.	=conjunction
F.	=French
interj.	=interjection
M	=modifiers
n.	=noun
O	=others
P	=prepositions
pa.	=participle
pl.	=plural
pron.	=pronoun
Q	=qualifiers
sing.	=singular
v.	=verb
V	=verbs

2. 邦　字

単	単　数
複	複　数
個	個体名詞
団	団体名詞
米	米語用法
英	英語用法
俗	俗　語
卑	卑　語
古	古　語
雅	雅　語
海	海上語・海軍
空	航空語
陸	陸　軍
法	法律用語
商	商業用語
株	株式用語
理	理学(物・化)
工	工　学
解	解　剖

3. 符　号

=	大体同義の句・文
《 》	英・米語用法
〖 〗	専門語・特殊用語
[ ]	解説及び補足
( )	補足 [英字の場合主に意味徹底のため補訳]
¶	用例の小項目
‖	¶の中に含まれる句・文
【類】	類句・文
/	類句・文の用例
☞	参考・注解
(1) (2)	見出し語の区分
→	「…の項を見よ」の意

☞ V^2, M^2, Q^2 その他については解説参照.

KENKYUSHA'S NEW DICTIONARY OF ENGLISH COLLOCATIONS

A

abacus, *n.* そろばん.
V *use* (=*work*) an *abacus* そろばんをはじく.
P beads ***on*** an *abacus* そろばんの玉 ‖ reckon ***on*** the *abacus* そろばんで計算する ‖ set figures ***on*** the *abacus* そろばんに数を置く.

abaft, *adv.* 船尾に.
M The gale was ***right*** *abaft*. 真うしろの強風だった.

abandon, *n. F.* 放縦.
Q[2] The effects of a spirit of ***wartime*** *abandon* have not run their course. 戦時の捨てばちな気分がまだ残っている.
P scream and guffaw ***with*** *abandon* in dancing halls and restaurants ダンスホールや料理店で盛んにわめいたりばか笑いをしたりする.

abandon, *v.* (**1**) 見捨てる, やめる.
M will most ***probably*** be *abandoned* たいてい放棄されるだろう.
P *abandon* it ***as*** unnecessary それを不必要として捨てる. ¶ *Abandoned* ***by*** one deity and helped by another, that is the beauty of it. 捨てる神あれば助ける神がある, よくしたもんだ. ‖ The ship was *abandoned* ***by*** the crew. 水夫は船を見捨てた. ¶ He came to London to study law, but *abandoned* it ***for*** art. 法律研究にロンドンへやって来たが美術の方へ河岸を変えた. ‖ He *abandoned* her ***for*** another woman. 彼はその女から別の女にくらがえした.
(**2**) まかせる, ゆだねる.
P *abandon* him ***to*** his fate 彼を成行にまかせる ‖ *abandon* oneself ***to*** the pursuit of a pleasure 快楽にふける ‖ *abandon* oneself ***to*** drinking 酒びたりになる. 【類】 *abandon* oneself ***to*** intemperance (不節制) / *abandon* oneself ***to*** despair (pleasures) ‖ *abandon* oneself ***to*** grief 悲嘆に沈む ‖ He *abandoned* the city ***to*** the conqueror. その市を征服者のなすがまゝにした.

abandonment, *n.* 放棄; 委付.
Q a ***complete*** *abandonment* of secular duties and cares 全く浮世を捨てること.
P a notice ***of*** *abandonment* 〖法〗委付の通告.
P[2] *abandonment* ***of*** cargo 積荷の委付 ‖ *abandonment* ***of*** right 権利の放棄.

abase, *v.* 低める, へこませる.
P *abase* oneself ***before*** a superior 長上の前にへりくだる. 【類】 *abase* oneself ***before*** God. ¶ He was *abased* ***by*** misfortune. 不幸のためにいじけた.

abash, *v.* 赤面させる, はにかませる.
M Your kindness ***quite*** *abashed* me. 御親切には全く恐縮しました.
P be *abashed* ***at*** a sight 一目見て恥ずかしがる. ¶ He is *abashed* ***at*** discovery (=detection). 露顕したのを恥じている. ‖ The poor man stood *abashed* ***at*** the display of his wealth. その貧乏人は彼の裕福を見せつけられて恥ずかしい思いをした. ¶ He was quite *abashed* ***before*** the king. 国王の御前で平に恐縮していた. ¶ I feel *abashed* ***in*** the presence of superior goodness and wisdom 優れた善人や知者の前に出るとおもはゆく感じる.

abate, *v.* 減じる; 値引する.
M Demand has ***considerably*** *abated*. 需要が著しく減った. ¶ The weather ***sufficiently*** *abated* to permit landing from the vessel. 天候がすっかり静まったので上陸することが出来た.
P *abate* ***by*** law 法律で禁止する. ¶ *abate* 5 cents ***from*** (=***out of***) the price その値段から五セント引く. ☞ *abate* ... ***of*** は古体. ¶ *abate* ***in*** fury (violence) 激怒(など)が鎮まる. ¶ *abate* ***of*** the fever 熱が下がる.

abatement, *n.* 値引, 減価; 減少, 減退.
V These prices ***admit*** no *abatement*. 値引は少しもできない. ¶ ***make*** (=***effect***) an *abatement* 値引する ‖ Our rule is to ***make*** no *abatement*. 私共では値引をしないことになっています. 【類】 We are obliged to ***make*** these *abatements*.
Q[2] ***noise*** *abatement* 騒音防止.
P[2] *abatement* ***from*** the price asked 呼び値より負けること. ¶ There is no *abatement* ***in*** his temperature. 彼の体温は一向下がらない. ¶ *abatement* ***of*** the fever 熱が下がること ‖ *abatement* ***of*** penalty 減刑.

abbot, *n.* 僧正.
Q[2] a great ***Buddhist*** *abbot* 大師.

abbreviate, *v.* 略する.
P "Sweets" is *abbreviated* ***from*** "sweetmeats." sweets は sweetmeats の略語だ. 【類】 Mathematics is sometimes *abbreviated* ***to*** math. / Young Men's Christian Association is commonly *abbreviated* ***to*** Y.M.C.A.

abbreviation, *n.* 略語.
Q an ***inelegant*** *abbreviation* 俗な省略 (laboratory を lab と略すような). ¶ a ***colloquial*** *abbreviation* 俗語体の略し方 (Japanese を Jap と略すような). ¶ Col. is a ***familiar*** *abbreviation* of Colonel. Col. は Colonel の普通の略し方だ.
P Can't is an *abbreviation* ***for*** cannot. can't は cannot に対する略語.

A B C (=a b c), *n.* 初歩.
P They are only ***at*** the *A B C* of their studies. 彼らは学業のほんの初歩にある. ¶ begin ***with*** the *a b c* of a subject 学科の初歩から始める.
P[2] He does not know even the *A B C* ***of*** philosophy. 彼は哲学の初歩も知らない. ¶ *a b c* ***to*** speculation in stock exchange 相場の手ほどき.

abdicate, *v.* 退位する.
P *abdicate* ***from*** the throne 王位を譲る.

abdomen, *n.* 腹, 腹部.
V ***slash*** the *abdomen* horizontally 腹を切る. ¶ ***slim*** the *abdomen* 腹をほっそりさせる.
Q a ***heavy, pendulous*** *abdomen* during later weeks of pregnancy 臨月の落っこちそうなおなか.
P sleep ***upon*** the *abdomen* 腹ばいに寝る.

abduct, *v.* 誘拐(ゆう)する.
P *abduct* a person ***from*** his home 人を誘拐する.

abeam, *adv.* 真横に.
M ***right*** *abeam* 真横に.
P *abeam* ***of*** ... ...と並んで.

aberration, *n.* 錯乱.
Q suffer from ***mental aberration*** 精神が錯乱している.

abet, *v.* 教唆する.
P *abet* a man ***against*** his master 人をおだててその主人に反抗させる. ¶*abet* a man ***in*** a crime 人を教唆して罪を犯させる. 【類】*abet* a man ***in*** his folly (愚行).

abeyance, *n.* 中絶, 中止.
P It is ***in*** *abeyance.* それは中絶している. ‖ The matter is kept ***in*** *abeyance.* あの件は中止になっている. ¶The right of property cannot be ***in*** *abeyance.* 財産権は無主たることを得ない. ‖ keep ***in*** *abeyance* 中止して置く. ¶fall ***into*** *abeyance* 中止になる. ¶It is in a state ***of*** *abeyance.* それは中止の状態にある.

abhorrence, *n.* 大きらい, 憎悪.
V He ***has*** an *abhorrence* of sin. 彼は罪悪をいみきらう. ¶***show*** *abhorrence* of snakes 蛇をきらう.
Q He has a ***great*** *abhorrence* of medicine. 彼は薬が大きらいだ.
P hold a person ***in*** *abhorrence* 某を忌みきらう. ¶be struck ***with*** *abhorrence* ぎょっとする.
P^2 *abhorrence* ***of*** ingratitude (gambling) 忘恩(など)をきらうこと. ¶It is an *abhorrence* ***to*** his feeling. 彼はそれを忌みきらう.

abhorrent, *a.* いとわしい; 相容れない.
P *abhorrent* ***from*** ...＝[古] abhorrent ***to*** *or* ***of.*** ¶He is *abhorrent* ***of*** excess. 彼は度を過す事がきらいだ. ¶Such an act is *abhorrent* ***to*** my sense of right (my feelings). こうした行為はどうしても僕の道徳観念(など)と相容れない.

abide, *v.* 住む; 服従する; 固守する.
M He *abode* (＝abided) ***faithful.*** 彼は依然忠実であった. ¶*abide* ***faithfully*** by one's promise 約束を忠実に守る. ¶She *abode* ***virgin.*** 彼女は処女で通した.
P *abide* ***at*** a place (house) 某所(など)に宿る. ¶*abide* ***by*** one's first love 初恋を守り通す ‖ *abide* ***by*** one's resolution 決意を翻えさない. 【類】*abide* ***by*** a promise (an agreement) ‖ *abide* ***by*** a judgment 判決に服する ‖ *abide* ***by*** the decision of the majority 多数決に従う. 【類】take their disputes before it and *abide* ***by*** its decisions / *abide* ***by*** the law / *abide* ***by*** the conditions of ... ‖ *abide* ***by*** the consequence 結果に甘んじる. 【類】*abide* ***by*** the event (inevitable) ‖ *abide* ***by*** a friend 友を助ける. ¶*abide* ***for*** a time しばらく住む. ¶*abide* ***in*** a place (house) 某所(など)に住む. 【類】*abide* ***in*** the wooded hills. ¶*abide* ***with*** ... ...と同居する.

ability, *n.* 技倆, 手腕, 才能.
V ***appreciate*** one's *ability* 腕を買う. ¶His condition ***baffles*** the diagnostic *abilities* of medical men. 彼の容態には医師も診断をしかねている. ¶***conceal*** one's *ability* 自分の力量を隠す. ¶***cultivate*** one's natural *ability* 天賦の才能をみがく. ¶***depreciate*** one's *abilities* 人の腕前をけなす. ¶***develop*** special *ability* in ... ...における特殊技倆を発達させる. ¶***display*** one's own *ability* 自分の腕前を発揮する. ¶***doubt*** his *ability* to translate 彼の翻訳に対する能力を疑う. ¶***exhibit*** considerable *ability* 大いに腕前を発揮する. ¶***have*** the *ability* to make a big plan 大計画を立てる能力がある. ¶***improve*** one's conversational *abilities* もっと会話の力をつける. ¶***measure*** one's *ability* その技倆を測る. ¶***overlap*** his *ability* 彼以上の力量を示す. ¶***prostitute*** one's *ability* 自己の能力を濫用する. ¶***show*** *ability* in the dispatch of business 仕事が早いという長所を示す.
Q ***administrative*** *ability* 経営の才. ¶***all-round*** *ability* 円満の才. ¶He shows more than ***average*** *ability* in this direction. 彼のこの方面の手腕は人並以上だ. ¶***diplomatic*** *ability* 外交的手腕. ¶***distinct literary*** *ability* きわ立った文才. ¶a woman of ***distinguished intellectual*** *ability* 抜群の知力を備えた婦人. ¶a man of ***exceptional*** *ability* 異数の手腕家. ¶***executive*** *ability* 経営の才. ¶***financial*** (＝***pecuniary***) *ability* 財力. ¶good ***conversational*** *ability* 座談の才. ¶show ***great*** *ability* 大手腕を見せる. ¶an ***innate*** *ability* 天賦の才能. ¶The Americans are celebrated for their ***inventive*** *ability.* 米国人はその発明の才で名高い. ¶***linguistic*** *ability* 語学の才. ¶a lady of ***marked literary*** *ability* 際立って文才のある婦人. ¶a man of all-round ***mediocre*** *ability* 何でも人並にできる人. ¶a man of ***no*** *ability* 無能の人. ¶***oratorical*** *ability* 弁舌の才. ¶***practical*** *ability* 応用の才. ¶It was achieved with ***praiseworthy*** *ability.* それはあっぱれなできばえだった. ¶He shows ***rare*** *ability* in this direction. 彼はこの方面にはすばらしい技倆がある. ¶a scholar of ***recognized*** *ability* 定評ある学者. ¶***remarkable*** *ability* 非凡の手腕. ¶By ***sheer*** *ability* and force of character, he has acquired the present position. 全く技倆と人格の力とで今日の地位を得た. ¶He speaks English with ***some*** *ability.* 彼はいくらか英語が話せる. ¶He excelled me in ***strategical*** *ability.* 私以上の戦術家であった. ¶***striking*** *abilities* in diplomacy すばらしい外交手腕. ¶men of ***substantial*** *ability* 実力のある人. ¶a scholar of ***undoubted*** *ability* 確かに実力のある学者. ¶His *ability* is ***unquestionable.*** 彼の手腕は疑う余地がない. ¶He won his way to an earldom by his ***warlike*** *ability.* 軍人としての手腕によって伯爵の位をかち得た.
Q^2 He has the ***artist*** *ability* to endow the people of whom he writes with flesh and blood. 作中の人物を生き生き描き出す芸術的才能に恵まれている. ¶show great ***business*** *ability* 偉大な商才を示す. ¶defects in ***language*** *ability* 語学力の欠陥. ¶has ***leadership*** *ability* 統率力がある. ¶***organizing*** *ability* 組織力. ¶***pupil*** *ability* 生徒の学力. ¶***reading*** *ability* in English 英語の読解力. ¶his good ***reasoning*** *ability* 彼のりっぱな推理力. ¶develop one's ***speaking*** *ability* 弁舌の才をのばす. ¶***teaching*** *ability* 教授力. ¶end Germany's ***war-making*** *ability* ドイツの戦争能力を封じる. ¶restore ***working*** *ability* 労働力を回復する. ¶One's ***writing*** *ability* grows by practice. 文章は練習次第でうまくなる.
P ***according to*** their *ability* 彼らの力量に応じて. ¶His appointment is ***from*** sheer *ability.* 彼の任命は全くその手腕が然らしめたのだ. ¶He is wanting ***in*** *ability.* 彼は腕がない. 【類】He is not behind the other students ***in*** *ability.* ¶I will do it to the best ***of*** my *ability.* できるだけよくやりましょう. ‖ a man ***of*** *ability* 敏腕家. ¶***Thanks to*** his *ability,* he has obtained great success. 力量があったために大成功をした. ¶rise ***through*** *ability* 実力で昇進する. ¶do ***to*** one's best *ability* 全力を尽してやる.
P^2 *ability* ***for*** (＝***in***) some work ある仕事にかけての技倆.
O the *ability* to construe Browning ブラウニングを解釈する力. 【類】the *ability* to express oneself on paper (作文) / the *ability* to write a foreign language.

ablaze, *a., ad.* きらきらして.
P a monster emporium *ablaze* ***with*** light 電灯できらきらしている大商店. 【類】The sky is *ablaze* ***with*** flame. / The streets are *ablaze* ***with*** decorations. / The mountain-sides are *ablaze* ***with*** azalea, wistaria, and many other beautiful flowers.

able, *a.* 力ある, ...することのできる.
M He is ***financially*** *able* to establish a home. 家庭を持つだけの余裕がある. ¶be but ***poorly*** *able* to ... どうにかこうにか...をすることが出来る. ¶He is ***quite*** *able* to teach. 彼は十分教えられる. ¶be not ***so*** *able* in ... as expected ...では期待されるほど有能でない.
O I may not be *able* to get back before tomorrow. あすまでは帰れまい. 【類】He will probably be *able* to see you this evening.

ablution, *n.* 沐浴(もくよく).
V ***do*** (＝***perform***) the *ablution* on the hands and the feet 手足を洗う.
Q ***personal*** *ablution* 沐浴.
Q^2 the ***morning*** *ablution* and toilet 朝の沐浴と化粧.

abnormality, *n.* 変則, 変態.
V She has ***shown*** no *abnormality* in intelligence or in disposition. 彼女は知能または気質に何ら常人と変った所が見えない.

aboard, *ad.* 船へ, 船内に.
M ***All*** *aboard!* 皆さんお乗り下さい. ¶***close*** (＝***hard***) *aboard* 舷側に接して.
P He came *aboard* ***of*** my ship. 彼は私の船に乗り込んで来た. ‖ I fell *aboard* ***of*** him. 彼と(感情が)衝突した.

abode, *n.* 住所; 居住.
V They ***established*** their permanent *abode* here. 彼らはここに永住の居宅を構えた. ¶***form*** a fit *abode* for ... ...の住所に適している. ¶He ***has*** no fixed (＝certain) *abode.* 住所不定だ. ¶***make*** one's *abode*＝dwell 居住する. ¶He ***took*** his *abode* in the ruined castle. その荒れはてた城に居を占めた. 【類】He ***took up*** his *abode* in a cave. ‖ She believed that the souls of her dead relations have ***taken up*** their *abode* in those parrots. 彼女は死んだ縁者

の霊魂があのおうむに乗移っていたと信じた.
Q a man of no ***fixed abode*** 住所不定の人.
P² his *abode **at*** the monastery 彼の僧院の住い. ¶one's *abode **in*** the suburbs 郊外の住宅.

abolition, *n.* 廃止.
Q ***total*** *abolition* 全廃. 「せられたとき.
P ***on*** the *abolition* of the feudal system 封建制度が廃止
P² *abolition **of*** the privilege enjoyed by ... ...が享有して
A-bomb, *n.* 原爆. └いた特権の喪失.
V ***explode*** an *A-bomb* by way of experiment 原爆爆発の
abominable, *a.* いやな. └実験をする.
P Any food that savors of onions is *abominable **to*** him. ねぎ臭いものは何でもきらいだ.
abomination, *n.* ...きらい, 憎悪. 「をきらう.
V They ***have*** an *abomination* for heretics. 彼らは異端者
P regard smoking ***with*** *abomination* 喫煙をきらう.
P² Lying lips are *abominations **to*** the Lord.—Bible. いつわりのくちびるはエホバに憎まる. 【類】Sentiment (感傷) is an *abomination **to*** the Japanese people.

abortion, *n.* 堕胎.
V ***bring on*** an *abortion* 流産をもたらす. ¶***cause*** *abortion* 堕胎させる. ¶***have*** an *abortion* 堕胎する. ¶artificially ***induce*** *abortion* 人工的に流産させる. ¶***perform*** (=***practice***) *abortion* on eugenic grounds 優生学上の理由で流産させる. ¶It will ***produce*** (=***procure***) *abortion*. そうすると流産する. 「産.
Q ***criminal*** *abortion* 堕胎罪. ¶***induced*** *abortion* 人工流

abound, *v.* 富む, 充満する.
P This garden *abounds **in*** flowers. この庭園には花が多い. ‖ The place *abounds **in*** legendary lore. その土地は伝説に富んでいる. 【類】The district *abounds **in*** scenic and natural wonders. / This forest *abounds **in*** game (猟鳥). / This country *abounds **in*** products. / His poems *abound **in*** passages of great beauty. / He *abounds **in*** wealth. / *abound **in*** natural resources / Such cases *abound **in*** military history (戦史). / Game (獲物) *abounds **in*** the fields. / The pheasant (きじ) *abounds **in*** Japan. / a lecture *abounding **in*** wise counsel (教訓). ¶feed the swans that *abound **on*** the rivers 川にたくさんいる白鳥に食物をやる. ¶Streams *abound **with*** fish. 川には魚がうようよいる. 【類】This country *abounds **with*** fruit (fine scenery). / This river *abounds **with*** trout. / The ship *abounds **with*** rats. / Japan *abounds **with*** rain. / Italian literature *abounds **with*** good stories. / The Italian tongue *abounds **with*** smooth and liquid sounds.

about-face, *n.* [回れ右から]完全な転換.
P² an *about-face **of*** his stand 彼の立場の百八十度の転換.
abrasion, *n.* 皮膚のすりむけ.
P² an *abrasion **of*** the skin 擦過傷.
abreast, *ad.* 並んで. 「で歩いた.
M They walked ***two or three abreast***. 彼らは二三人並ん
P keep *abreast **of*** progress in science 科学の進歩におくれない. 【類】keep *abreast **of*** the thought of the age. ¶keep *abreast **with*** (=***of***) the times 時代後れにならない
abridge, *v.* 省略する; 奪う. └ようにする.
P It was *abridged **from*** the original work. それは原本の省略だ. ¶*abridge* him ***of*** his rights 彼の権利を奪う.
abroad, *n.* 海外.
P letters ***for*** *abroad* 外国行の手紙. ¶letters ***from*** *abroad* 外国からの手紙 ‖ a watch brought ***from*** *abroad* 舶来の懐中時計. 【類】a teacher engaged ***from*** *abroad* / after his return ***from*** *abroad*.
abroad, *ad.* 戸外に; 方々に.
M You are ***all abroad***. 君はまるで見当違いだ.
P The storm was *abroad **with*** all its thunders. 雷雨が激
abrogation, *n.* 〖法〗失効. └しかった
P² the *abrogation **of*** the leases 借地権の失効.
abscond, *v.* 逃亡する.
P *abscond **from*** a place ある場所を逐電する. 【類】*abscond **from*** his jail / *abscond **from*** his creditors. ¶*abscond **with*** valuables 貴重品を持逃げする.
absence, *n.* 不在, 欠席; 皆無.
V ***mark*** the *absence* of students 学生の欠席の印(しるし)をつける. ¶***miss*** the *absence* of ... ...がないのに気がつく. ¶Its *absence* will never be ***noticed***. それがないことには決して気がつかないだろう.

Q There was a ***complete*** *absence* of information as to how the little fellow met his death. その子がどうして死んだのか一向様子が分らなかった. ¶He presided in the ***enforced*** *absence* of the president. 会長が止むなく欠席したので彼が議長席についた. ¶the ***entire*** *absence* of reason 全然理性の欠けていること. ¶short meetings between ***long*** *absences* 永く間を置いてはちょっと会うこと. 【類】After a ***long*** *absence* her son was coming home. ¶during his ***temporary*** *absence* from Japan 一時日本を留守にしていた(いる)間. ¶revisit Paris after ***ten years' absence*** 十年振りでパリを再訪する. ¶in the ***unavoidable*** *absence*, owing to illness of ... ...が病気のため止むを得ず欠席したので. ¶an ***unexcused*** *absence* in a class 授業時間無断欠席. ¶There was an ***utter*** *absence* of a fixedly honest intention. 一貫したまじめな意図が全然欠けていた.
Q² ***business*** *absences* 用事による不在. ¶return to one's birthplace after a ***seven-year*** *absence* 七年間留守にした後郷里へ帰る. ¶come home after ***war*** *absence* 応召不在の後帰宅する.
P return to one's seat ***after*** a short *absence* 一時席を離れてまた戻る. 【類】***after*** an *absence* of several months in America / ***After*** an *absence* of twenty minutes, he returned. ¶It is conspicuous ***by*** its *absence*. [あるべきものが]ないのでかえって目立つ. ¶***during*** the *absence* of ... ...の不在中. 【類】Please take care of my house ***during*** my *absence* in the country. ¶A good many of the degrees were conferred ***in*** *absence*. 学位の授与式に多数の受領者が欠席した. ‖ He called ***in*** your *absence*. 君の留守に訪ねて来た. ‖ ***In*** the *absence* of the president, vicepresident occupied the chair. 議長不在中副議長が代理を勤めた. ‖ Speak no ill of one ***in*** one's *absence*. 人のかげ口をきくな. ‖ be presumed, ***in*** the *absence* of proof to the contrary 反対の証拠がないので推定する. 【類】I was obliged to accept it as true ***in*** the *absence* of other evidence. / ***in*** the *absence* of such notification (通告) / ***in*** the *absence* of the right article (適当な品) / ***In*** the *absence* of exact data (資料), these discussions are bootless (徒労). ‖ ***in*** the *absence* of a special contract 特に契約がある場合の外. ¶a report ***of*** *absence* 欠席届. ¶***owing to*** his *absence* from school (work, a meeting) 学校(など)を休んでいるので.
P² a teacher's *absence **from*** classes 休講. 【類】your *absence **from*** lectures / *absence **from*** school ‖ Business made my *absence* necessary ***from*** home. 用事でるすにしなければならなかった. ¶*absence **of*** order 無秩序 ‖ His *absence **of*** mind is proverbial. あの男のぼんやりはだれ知らぬものはない. ‖ The *absence **of*** advertisement there is very soothing. そこには広告が見えないので非常に気持がよい. ‖ *absence **of*** vulgarity 脱俗. ¶*absence **without*** notice (=due notification) 無断欠席.

absent, *n.* 不在者.
V ***criticize*** the *absent* かげ口をきく.
absent, *a.* 不在の, 欠席している. 「する.
M be ***unavoidably absent*** 止むを得ぬ事情のため欠席(勤)
P He is *absent **at*** Nagoya. 名古屋に行っている. ¶At times he would be *absent **for*** a couple of days. 彼は時々二三日の欠席(勤)をした. ¶He was *absent **from*** church. 教会に出なかった. 【類】be *absent **from*** school (a meeting) without due notice / He was *absent **from*** home yesterday. / be *absent **from*** Tokyo / I am to be *absent **from*** England till June. / He was *absent **from*** his wife for some years. / be *absent **from*** roll-call (点呼) / He was *absent **from*** his work without leave (無断で). / be *absent **from*** duty ‖ be entirely *absent **from*** one's mind 全く念頭にない. ¶He is *absent **in*** Nikko (Europe, China). 日光(など)に行ってるすだ. ¶be *absent **on*** a tour 旅行中で不在だ. ¶*absent **with*** (***without***) leave 賜暇中(無断欠勤中)の(軍人など).
absent, *v.* 欠席する, るすにする.
P He *absented* himself ***from*** school (work) yesterday. きのう学校(など)を休んだ. 【類】He *absented* himself ***from*** the meeting (lectures). / He frequently *absents* himself ***from*** home. / *absent* oneself ***from*** the city.
absentee, *n.* 欠席者.
Q² a ***long-term*** *absentee* 長期欠勤者.
P *absentees **from*** class 学校の欠席者. ¶an ***absentee***

without leave 無断欠席者.

absenteeism, *n.* 不在; 〖労〗欠勤サボ.

Q *literary absenteeism* 文士が生国をるすにすること, 文士の外国居住.

Q^2 *mass absenteeism* 集団欠席(勤)(多くの者が一度に休むこと).

P^2 *absenteeism from* classes 教場の欠席.

absolution, *n.* 免除, 赦免.

V *give* (=*grant*) *absolution* to ... 〖宗〗〖司祭が〗赦免を与える.

P^2 *absolution from* all sins 〖宗〗すべての罪の赦免.

absolve, *v.* 許す, 解除する.

P *absolve* a person *from* blame 人を許す ‖ He *absolved* me *from* a promise. 彼は僕の約束を解消してくれた. ‖ It *absolves* me *from* the contract. それで僕の契約に対する責任は解除される. 【類】it *absolves* me *from* all responsibility in connection with ... / he must be *absolved from* the charge of ... ☞ be *absolved of* ...はまれ.

absorb, *v.* 吸収する; 心を奪う; 併合する.

P *absorb* moisture *from* the air 空気から水分を吸収する ‖ He is *absorbed in* study. 彼は研究に没頭している. 【類】*absorbed in* thought / become *absorbed in* scientific work (the study of ...) / be *absorbed in* reading (business) ‖ It has been *absorbed in* the recently formed company. それは新設の会社に合併された. ¶*absorb* the small states *into* her empire その帝国に諸小国を併合する ‖ be *absorbed into* the flood 洪水にのまれる ‖ *absorb* it *into* the system through the skin 皮膚を通じてそれを身体に吸収する.

absorber, *n.* 吸収器.

Q^2 a *shock absorber* 緩衝器.

absorption, *n.* 吸収; 一心不乱.

Q *Complete absorption* of light makes a thing appear black. 光を完全に吸収すると物が黒く見える. ¶He sat in *silent absorption.* 彼は無言三昧ですわっていた.

P^2 *absorption in* one's work 仕事への没頭. ¶*absorption of* water *by* the earth 地中への水の吸収. ¶*absorption of* a body *in* a whirlpool 渦中への人体の吸込. ¶the *absorption of* his own nation *into* that of France 自国民とフランス国民との併合.

abstain, *v.* 絶つ, 控える.

P *abstain from* food 断食する ‖ *abstain from* flesh and fish 精進する ‖ *abstain from* luxuries ぜいたくをしない ‖ *abstain from* speaking ill of others 他人の悪口を控える. 【類】*abstain from* quarreling (wine) / *abstain from* voting (棄権).

abstainer, *n.* 節制者, 禁酒家.

Q He is a *total abstainer* from liquors and tobacco. 彼は酒タバコを一切のまない.

P^2 an *abstainer from* alcoholic liquors 禁酒家.

abstinence, *n.* 節制; 禁酒.

V *Abstinence* from all alcoholic beverages should be vigorously *enforced.* 禁酒は大いに励行すべきだ. ¶*practice abstinence* 節制する.

Q *sexual abstinence* 禁欲. ¶*total abstinence* from alcohol 絶対禁酒.

P^2 *abstinence from* food 絶食 ‖ *abstinence from* flesh meat 精進. 【類】*abstinence from* all sorts of comfort in life ‖ a protracted *abstinence from* soap and water 永らく石けんや水に遠ざかっていること.

abstract, *n.* 抽象; 抜粋, 摘要.

Q a *condensed abstract* 摘要.

P consider a subject *in* the *abstract* 問題を抽象的に考える. 【類】The advice, however sound *in* the *abstract* (理論), is always dangerous when applied to practice. ‖ speak *in* the *abstract* 抽象的な言い方をする.

P^2 an *abstract from* a magazine (newspaper) 雑誌(など)からの抜き書き. ¶an *abstract of* official reports (a sermon) 公報(など)の摘要 ‖ an *abstract of* account 摘要計算書 ‖ an *abstract of* contract 摘要契約書 ‖ an *abstract of* a log book 航海日誌摘要.

abstract, *v.* 引離す; 抜粋する.

P *abstract* spirit *from* a substance 物質からエキスを取る. 【類】*abstract* an action *from* its evil effects (結果) ‖ *abstract* the purse *from* the pocket 財布をすり取る. ¶*abstract* a book *into* a compendium 一冊の本の摘要を作る.

abstraction, *n.* 抽象; 放心; 〖美〗抽象(性); 抽出.

Q a picture of *near abstraction* 抽象派に近い絵.

P with an air *of abstraction* ぼう然として.

P^2 *abstraction of* whiteness from white objects 白い物体から純白を抽出すること.

abstractionism, *n.* 〖美術〗抽象派.

Q *pure abstractionism* 純抽象派.

absurd, *a.* 不合理な.

M *highly absurd* 極めて不合理な. ¶It is *manifestly absurd* to call him a fanatic. 彼を狂信者と呼ぶのは明らかにばかげている. ¶Your claim is *quite absurd.* 君の要請は沙汰の限りである. ‖ be *too absurd* to repeat お話しにならない. ¶*utterly absurd* 全くばかげた.

absurdity, *n.* 不合理, 矛盾.

V *declare* the *absurdity* of ... ...のばからしさを言明する. ¶*utter* an *absurdity* ばかげた事を言う.

Q *amusing absurdities* おかしい矛盾. ¶*childish absurdities* 子供っぽい矛盾. ¶*glaring absurdities* 知れきった不合理. ¶a *grotesque absurdity* へんてこな矛盾. ¶*manifest absurdities* 明かな不合理. ¶a *quixotic absurdity* ドン・キホーテ式の没常識. ¶a *rank absurdity* とほうもない不合理. ¶*sheer absurdity* 全くの不合理. ¶This convention has passed into the limbo of *social absurdities.* この慣例は既に社会的矛盾として世間から葬られてしまった.

P the height *of absurdity* 不合理の極.

P^2 the *absurdity of* the thing is still more apparent when we consider that ... ...という点を考えるとそれは実に沙汰の限りである.

abundance, *n.* 沢山, 豊富.

V An *abundance* of instances is *cited.* 沢山の例が挙げてある. ¶He *had abundance* of blessings. 彼は非常に幸福だった. ¶An *abundance* of daylight is *secured.* 採光が十分だ. ¶The apple-tree *yields* an *abundance* of fruit. そのりんごの木から沢山りんごが採れる.

Q there is a *great abundance* of ... ...が沢山ある. ¶They exist in *immense abundance.* それは沢山にある. ¶Maiden-hair spleenworts grow in *rich abundance* in Sicily. くじゃくしだはシシリー島におびたゞしくはえている.

P live *in abundance* 豊かに暮す. 【類】Coal is found *in abundance* here. / We have money *in abundance.* ¶a year *of abundance* 豊年. ¶*with* an *abundance* of gilding 金ぴかの(お寺の仏壇など) ‖ It is illustrated *with* an *abundance* of apt examples. それは適切な例を沢山引いて説明してある.

P^2 an *abundance of* material supplies 豊富な物資 ‖ There is an *abundance of* tonnage in port. 港には船腹は十分ある.

abundant, *a.* 沢山の, 豊富な.

M They are *extremely abundant* on the east coast of North America. それは北米の東海岸に極めて多い.

P The country is *abundant in* (=*with*) natural resources. その国は天然資源に富んでいる. 【類】be *abundant in* marine products (海産物) / *abundant in* mineral resources.

abuse, *n.* **(1)** 弊害, 悪弊.

V *check abuses* 弊害を防止する. ¶*expose* and *correct* contemporary social *abuses* 時弊を暴露し矯正する. ¶*reform abuses* 弊害を改める. ¶*root up abuses* 弊害を根絶する.

Q an exposure of *civic abuse* 市政紊乱(ぶん)の暴露. ¶a *gross abuse* which is being perpetrated in their midst 彼らの間で行われているけしからぬ悪習. ¶a *long existing abuse* 積弊. ¶reform *social abuses* 社会悪を矯正する.

Q^2 *trade abuses* 商業上の不徳義.

P The word can be so used *without abuse.* その語はそういう風に使って差支ない.

P^2 the *abuses of* government 失政 ‖ *abuses of* the age 時弊.

(2) ののしり, 悪口.

V *give* him much *abuse* 彼をひどくののしる. ¶much *abuse* has been *heaped* upon ... ...にひどく毒突いた. ¶*hurl abuse* at ... ...を罵倒(ばう)する.

Q *personal abuse* 人身攻撃.

P Hailstones *of abuse* were pelting him. 散々の悪口を彼にあびせていた.

(3) 濫用, 虐待.

V *prevent abuses* [職権の]濫用を防ぐ.

P subject a child *to abuse* 子供を酷使する.

P^2 *abuse of* one's body 身体の虐待 ‖ *abuse of* confidence 背信.

abut, *v.* 接している.

P Our stable *abuts against* his dwelling. うちのうまやはあの人の家にくっついている. 【類】The building *abuts against* the rock. ¶The building *abuts on* (=*upon*) the highway. その建物は往来に接している. 【類】His land *abuts on* mine. / the streets *abutting on* the park.

abuzz, *a.* 騒然と.

M The world of entertainment is *vigorously abuzz*

modation [ホテルなど]優秀な設備がある. ¶The steamer ***possesses*** berthing *accommodations* for 750 passengers in the first class. あの汽船には一等船客七百五十名分の設備がある. ¶The society ***provides*** *accommodation* for the meeting. その会の方で会場の都合をつける. ¶***reach*** some *accommodation* 何とか話合がつく. ¶name the class of *accommodation* ***required*** [汽車・汽船など]希望の等級を指定する. ¶***reserve*** the *accommodation* in advance 宿泊の予約をする. 【類】*accommodation* can be ***reserved*** at a hotel on payment of ... ¶***secure*** *accommodation[s]* 宿泊する. ¶***supply*** *accommodation* for ... [旅館などが]...を宿泊させる.

Q ***adequate*** *accommodation* for ... ...の適当な設備. ¶has ***capital*** (=***excellent***) *accommodations* りっぱな設備がある. ¶***de luxe*** *accommodations* [ホテルなど]特等待遇. ¶***mutual*** *accommodation* of have-nots 持たざる者同士の融通. ¶The ***present*** *accommodation* of the school is filled to the utmost limit. その学校では現在できるだけ多数の生徒を収容している. ¶provide ***proper*** *accommodation* and convenience for passengers 旅客のために適当の設備をして便宜を計る. ¶***Rough*** *accommodation* can be had (=is procurable) at the local inn. 地方の宿屋で(設備は悪いが)どうにかこうにか宿泊ができる. ¶The *accommodation* is ***small*** and men have little elbow-room. 部屋が狭いのでひじを伸ばす余地もない. ¶***suitable*** *accommodation* 相当の設備. ¶***What*** *accommodations* have you available? どんな部屋が借りられますか.

Q² has no ***cabin*** *accomodation* 船室の設備がない. ¶There is ample ***dock*** (=***docking***) *accommodation* here. ここには十分なドックの設備がある. ¶***dormitory*** *accommodations* 寄宿舎の設備. ¶The ***hotel*** *accommodation* is extremely limited. そのホテルは狭くて幾人も客が止宿出来ない.【類】In the matter of ***hotel*** *accommodations* Milwaukee is hard to beat. / The city has excellent ***hotel*** *accommodations.* ¶a grave shortage of ***housing*** *accommodation* 深刻な住宅払底. ¶***infirmary*** *accommodations* 病院施設. ¶***living*** *accommodation* 住宅施設. ¶lighter and more airy ***office*** *accommodations* 採光通風のもっとよい事務室の設備. ¶The ship has no first-class ***passenger*** *accommodation.* その船には一等船客の設備がない. ¶***rooming*** *accommodations* 貸部屋. ¶The auditorium has ***seating*** *accommodation* for about 1,600 people. その講堂は千六百人を入れる座席がある.【類】a public hall with ***seating*** *accommodations* for 1,000. ¶engage ***sleeping car*** *accommodation* 汽車の寝台を取る. ¶The ***streetcar*** *accommodation* is taxed to the utmost. 電車の台数が極度に不足している. ¶***Storehouse*** *accommodation* is good (poor). 倉庫の設備はよい(よくない).

P The gallery is ***for*** the *accommodation* ***of*** visitors. [国会などで]階上は傍聴者のために設けたのである.

P² The *accommodation* ***at*** the Stadium surpasses anything yet attempted. その競技場の設備のりっぱさは空前のものである. ¶There is *accommodation* ***for*** several thousand spectators. 数千の観衆を入れる施設がある. ¶*accommodation* ***of*** a man ***to*** his surroundings 人が環境に順応すること.

accompaniment, *n.* 伴奏; 付属物.

V ***play*** his *accompaniment* on the *samisen* 三味線で彼の歌の調子をとる ‖ ***play*** an *accompaniment* to ... ...の伴奏をする.

Q Disease is a ***frequent*** *accompaniment* of famine. 病は飢饉につきもの. ¶an ***inevitable*** *accompaniment* to ... ...につきもの. ¶with ***musical*** *accompaniment* 鳴物入りで. ¶an ***ornamental*** *accompaniment* さしみのつま. ¶an ***unpriced*** *accompaniment* [無料の]付品(おとも).

Q² a ***food*** *accompaniment* to drink 酒のさかな. ¶a ***prize*** *accompaniment* 副賞. ¶chant rhymes in a ***sing-song*** *accompaniment* 歌うような節で詩を吟じる.

P She sang it ***at*** ...'s *accompaniment*. 彼女は...の伴奏でそれを歌った. ¶dances performed ***to*** [the *accompaniment* of] *samisen* music 三味線に合わせた舞踊. ¶***with*** music *accompaniment* 鳴物入りで ‖ A Japanese dinner was served ***with*** the *accompaniment* of dancing. 日本料理のごちそうに踊の余興があった.

P² an *accompaniment* ***for*** beer ビールのさかな. ¶Laver is capital *accompaniment* ***to*** *sake.* のりは良い酒のさかなだ.

accompany, *v.* 伴う, 伴奏する.

P She was *accompanied* ***by*** her brother. 彼女は弟を同伴した. ‖ *accompanied* ***by*** a friend (his suite) 友だち(など)を連れて. 【類】*accompanied* ***by*** his dog ‖ be *accompanied* ***by*** violence 暴力を伴う ‖ sing *accompanied* ***by*** piano ピアノに合わせて歌う ‖ The text is *accompanied* ***by*** illustrations. 本文にはさし絵が付いている. 【類】The text is *accompanied* ***by*** glossaries (字解) and textual comment (本文に対する批評). / Each coupon must be *accompanied* ***by*** ten cents to cover the cost of mailing (郵税として). ‖ A decreased income has been *accompanied* ***by*** increased expenditure. 収入が減って入費が増してきた. ‖ *accompany* a present ***by*** a letter 贈物に手紙を添える ‖ a notification *accompanied* ***by*** an explanation and statement of regrets 説明を加え且つ遺憾の意を表わした通知. ¶*accompany* a guest ***to*** the door 客を戸口まで見送る. ¶be *accompanied* ***with*** money 金を添えて. 【類】All orders must be *accompanied* ***with*** cash. ‖ defeat *accompanied* ***with*** disgrace 屈辱を伴う敗北. 【類】rain *accompanied* ***with*** thunder ‖ The operation was *accompanied* ***with*** much pain. 手術は非常な苦痛を伴った. 【類】His speech was *accompanied* ***with*** an appealing gesture (聴衆に訴えるような身振り).

accomplice, *n.* 共犯者.

P² an *accomplice* ***in*** (=***of***) a crime 共犯者. ¶an *accomplice* ***with*** (=***of***) a person ***in*** some crime ある犯罪における某の共犯者.

accomplish, *v.* 仕遂げる, 果たす.

M The prediction was ***literally*** *accomplished.* 予言は文字通り的中した. ¶She thought mistakenly that the infidelity could be *accomplished* ***safely.*** 彼女は不心得にも不義をしても大丈夫だと思った.

P *accomplish* ***by*** force 暴力によって達成する. ¶The task will not be *accomplished* ***in*** one generation. その仕事は一代では成し遂げられぬ. ¶The journey was *accomplished* ***with*** a maximum of comfort and ease and a minimum of discomfort. 非常に愉快に格別不便なこともなく旅行を終えた.

accomplished, *a.* [技芸に]優れた.

P one who is *accomplished* ***in*** some art 一芸に長じた人, 達人.

M ***thoroughly*** *accomplished* in ... ...の名手.

accomplishment, *n.* 芸, 才芸; 業績.

V ***acquire*** an *accomplishment* 一芸に達する. ¶He ***had*** every *accomplishment* except that of making money. 金もうけ以外のことは何でもできた. ¶***use*** an *accomplishment* to advantage ある芸能を利用する.

Q an ***elegant*** *accomplishment* 上品なたしなみ. ¶***light*** *accomplishments* 遊芸. ¶She has ***literary*** *accomplishment* sufficient to secure her an independent income from her pen. 彼女には文筆で独立できるだけの文才がある. ¶Japanese performers of ***no mean*** *accomplishment* なかなか腕のたしかな日本の芸人たち. ¶***polite*** *accomplishments* 上品なたしなみ. ¶a ***poor*** (***substantial***) *accomplishment* 不(好)成績(資金募集など). ¶a pianist of ***rare*** *accomplishment* ざらにはいないピアノの名手. ¶have ***some*** *accomplishments* 芸を身につけている. ¶a man of ***varied*** *accomplishments* 多芸多能の士.

Q² a ***hobby*** *accomplishment* 余技.

P² his *accomplishment* ***as*** a linguist 語学者としての彼の学殖. ¶*accomplishments* ***of*** a physicist 物理学者の業績.

accord, *n.* 一致, 調和.

Q in ***close*** and ***consistent*** *accord* with the principle of ... 終始...主義を厳守して. ¶be in ***full*** (=***perfect***) *accord* with ... ...と全く合致している. ¶I am glad to find myself in ***general*** *accord* with your views. 私の意見が君のと大体あっているので喜んでいる. ¶the establishment of a ***sincere*** *accord* between the ruler and the ruled 治者被治者間の真の調和の確立. ¶be in ***substantial*** *accord* with ... ...と実質的に調和している.

P opinions ***in*** *accord* 一致した意見 ‖ as long as Japan and America are ***in*** *accord* 日米が手を組んでいる間は. ¶I did it ***of*** my own *accord.* 私はそれを自発的にやった. ‖ ***of*** its own *accord* 自然と, ひとりでに. ¶our publicists protest ***with*** one *accord* that ... 政治評論家は一致して...と言い張っている.

P² My views are in *accord* ***with*** his. 私の意見は彼のと一致している. 【類】Such a state of affairs is not in *accord* ***with*** sound international relations.

accord, *v.* 一致する, 合う; 与える.

M ***ill*** (***well***) *accord* with ... ...と調和しない(する).

P They *accorded against* Germany. 彼らは心を一にしてドイツに反対した. ¶They *accorded* him praise *for* his good work (=*accorded* praise *to* him *for* his good work). 彼の善事をほめたゝえた. ¶Most of my friends *accord in* that opinion. 私の大抵の友はその意見に同意している. ¶A cordial welcome was *accorded* [*to*] him. ねんごろに彼を迎えた. ¶*accord with* friends 友と和合する ‖ Your opinion *accords* substantially *with* mine. 君の意見は大体においで私のと一致している. ‖ *accord with* one's feelings 自分の感情に合う ‖ *accord with* reason 理くつに合う. 【類】 *accord with* one's hopes (desires) / It does not *accord with* my wishes.

accordance, *n.* 調和, 一致, 和合.

Q be in *exact* (=*strict*) *accordance* with ... すっかり…と一致している. ¶in *natural accordance* with ... 自然…と一致して.

P be *in accordance* with reason 理に合っている ‖ *in accordance* with custom 慣例に従って. 【類】 *in accordance* with the schedule / Everything has been done *in accordance* with the rules. ‖ The Army and Navy were reformed *in accordance* with Western models (洋式に従って). / This is not *in accordance* with facts. / It is not *in accordance* with the spirit of the law. / *in accordance* with the wishes of the donor (寄贈者) / *in accordance* with my promise to you ... / *in accordance* with the form provided (書式通り).

accordant, *a.* 一致した, 合っている.

M This is *perfectly accordant* with his idea (principles).

P be *accordant to* reason (the law, truth) 理性(など)に合致している ‖ ornaments not *accordant to* Japanese tastes 日本人の趣味に合わない飾り. ¶*accordant with* (=*to*) ... …と一致した, …に合っている.

according, *ad.* 従って.

P *according to* his account 彼の話によれば ‖ *according to* circumstances 模様次第で, ことによると. 【類】 *according to* the N.Y. Times / *according to* him / *according to* the papers / vary *according to* age / *according to* class and locality / An inventor, *according to* Edison, usually lacks the bump of practicality (実地の才). / *according to* custom / *according to* one's income / *according to* instructions ‖ grade pupils *according to* their merit 成績順に生徒を列べる. 【類】 rank guests *according to* seniority / Prices range from ... to ... *according to* quality and size. / *According to* arrangement, the goods were to be delivered by the end of last month. 打合わせでは品物を先月末までに渡すはずであった. ‖ The exhibits were arranged *according to* schools (学校別に). ‖ Cut your coat *according to* your cloth. 〘諺〙布地に応じて服を仕立てよ(身分相応の暮しをせよ). 【類】 arrange ... *according to* color.

O *According* as the demand increases, prices go up. 需要増大に伴って物価は騰貴する. ‖ One is rewarded *according* as one has merits or demerits. 人は功過のいかんによって報いられる. ‖ The plan will succeed or not *according* as it is judiciously managed or not. その計画の成否は処理の適不適によって分れる. 【類】 We have different views of a thing *according* as we are rich or poor.

account, *n.* **(1)** 勘定, 計算; 勘定書, 計算書; 取引.

V *adjust* an *account* 精算する. ¶*audit accounts* 勘定を監査する. ¶*balance accounts* 口座を締切る; 決済する. ¶*cast accounts* 計算する. ¶*cast up accounts* 勘定を締める ‖ *charge* this *account* with ... この勘定を…の借方に回す. ¶*check accounts* 勘定を引き合わせる. ¶*close* one's *accounts* with ... …との勘定を締切る, 取引を止める. ¶*collect accounts* 勘定を取立てる. ¶*consider* an *account* as settled 勘定を棒引きにする. ¶*credit* the *account* 計算書の貸方に記入する. ¶*deliver* an *account* of the cargo 積荷計算書を引渡す. ¶*enter* an *account* 勘定を記入する. ¶*examine* an *account* 勘定を検査する. ¶*falsify* (=*manipulate or cook*) *accounts* 帳じりをごまかす. ¶You must *give in* my *account* once a month. 月に一度ずつ私の計算書を渡してもらいたい. ‖ *hand* an *account* to ... …に計算書を手渡しする. ¶we *have* a small *account* against you for ... …の勘定が少しですが未済になっています ‖ I *have* an (no) *account* with that bank. その銀行と取引がある(取引がない). 【類】 I *had* some *account* to settle with him. ¶*itemize* an *account* 勘定書を件別に作る. ¶*keep accounts* 勘定を整理する; 帳面を付ける; 数を取って置く ‖ *keep* a regular *account* 一々記帳して置く. 【類】 The mistress *keeps* her excellent *accounts*. / *keep* household *accounts*. ¶He didn't *pay* much *account* how time went. 時のたつのに余り注意していなかった. ¶*liquidate* an *account* 清算する. ¶*make out accounts* to date 当日までの勘定書を作る. ¶*make up accounts* 勘定を締切る, 決済する. ¶I am not in a position to *meet* this little *account* at this precise moment. わずかではあるがこの勘定は今直ぐは払えない. ¶*offer* charge *accounts* 掛勘定にする. ¶*open* (=*start*) an *account* at a bank 銀行と取引を始める(口座を設ける). ¶*overdraw* one's *account* [小切手を]振出し過ぎる, 当座借越をする ‖ *overdraw* one's salary *account* 前借が月給をオーバーする. ¶*pay* more *account* to matter than to manner 外形より内容に重きをおく. ¶*present* one's *account* to the cashier 出納方に勘定書を提出する. ¶*put account straight* 帳合のきまりをつける. ¶*render account* for ... semi-annually 年二回の計算書を提出する. 【類】 *render* your *account* (勘定書) up to Christmas / monthly *account rendered* if desired. ¶Tell the butcher, please, to *send* his *account* tomorrow. 肉屋にあす勘定書を出すように話して下さい. ¶*settle* (=*square*) *accounts* with ... …と勘定を決済する ‖ the day for *settling* the *account* 決算日. ¶*take* an *account* of ... …の数を取る ‖ *take account* of stock たなおろしをする.

Q *bad accounts* (=debts) 貸倒れ(こげつき). ¶a *closed account* 決済勘定. ¶a *current account* 当座勘定 ‖ an *account current* 交互計算. ¶a *duplicate account* 勘定書の写し. ¶Japan's *international account* for ... shows a favorable balance of ... …年度における日本の国際収支は…という有利な帳じりを示している. ¶a *joint account* 共同勘定. ¶My tailor has run me up a *long account*. 仕立屋がつけ掛けをした. ¶make *no account* of an objection 苦情を問題にしない. ¶an *open account* 清算勘定 ‖ The balance on the *open account* is to be payable with goods or dollar. 残額は商品またはドル貨決済の取引勘定で行うこと. ¶*outstanding accounts* 未決済勘定. ¶an *account payable* (*receivable*) 支払(受取)勘定. ¶open *separate accounts* for ... …のために個々の口座を設ける. ¶We have a *small account* against you for ... の勘定が少額ながら未済です. ¶*uncollectable accounts* and bills 金のとれない勘定と手形. ¶Your *account* is still *unpaid*. お勘定が済んでいません.

Q² a *bank account* 銀行勘定. ¶a blocked *bank account* 封鎖預金. 【類】 Their funds are tied up in "blocked" *bank account*. ‖ This suggests a snug *bank account*. これから考えると銀行に預金がたくさんありそうだ. ¶open *banking accounts* with ... …と銀行口座を開く. 【類】 He has no *banking account*. ‖ a capitalist with a low-figure *banking account* 銀行預金の乏しい資本家. ¶open a *charge account* in one's name その名義で掛売りを始める. 【類】 refuse a *charge account*. ¶open a *credit account* with ... …と信用取引を開く. ¶a *disbursement account* 立替勘定. ¶be placed in a *dollar account* in one of the banks to the credit of ... …ドル勘定としてある銀行で…の貸方に記帳させる. ¶an *interim account* 中間勘定. ¶have a *ledger account* 掛取引をしている. ¶settlement of *lend-lease accounts* between ... …国間の武器貸与計算の決済. 【類】 a $112 billion *lend-lease account*. ¶recording of *money accounts* 金銭勘定の記録. ¶auditing of *property accounts* 財産帳簿の検査. ¶a *running account* 当座勘定. ¶a *profit* and *loss account* 損益勘定. ¶begin (=start) a *savings account* 銀行貯金を始める. ¶a *suspense account* 仮勘定. ¶How does his *wage account* stand? 彼の給料の勘定はどうなっています.

P He has come *for* his *account*. 彼は勘定を取りにきた. ‖ the repairs are to be *for account* of ... 修理は…支払のはずです ‖ sell ... *for* the *account* and risk of the concerned 関係者の勘定と責任で…を売る. ¶*in account* with ... …と取引勘定のある, …と取引して. ¶balance *of accounts* 勘定帳尻. ¶Received from Mr.—the sum of 20,000 yen *on account*. 内金として二万円正に受け取りました——様. 【類】 a payment *on account* ‖ invest money *on* one's *account* 独力で資金を注ぎこむ ‖ start business *on* one's own *account* 独立して商売をやる ‖ a tailor *on* his own *account* 一本立ちの仕立屋 ‖ The purchase is *on* your *account*. この買入れは君の勘定でやる. ¶charge the amount ***to*** his *account* その金額を彼の勘定につける ‖ Debit the amount ***to*** my *account*. その金額は当方の借方勘定に記入して下さい. ‖ apply time ***to*** profitable *account* 時を有利に使う.

P² an *account **of*** charges 掛売の勘定書.

(**2**) 説明, 解説; 報告, 記事.

V the Asahi ***contains*** a full *account* of ... 朝日新聞には...のくわしい記事が出ている. 【類】 a record dated 1543 ***contains*** an *account* of ... ¶***give*** an *account* of all that has passed 一部始終を述べる. 【類】 ***give*** an *account* of one's experience. ¶The book ***presents*** a faithful *account* of the event. その本はできごとを忠実に伝えている. ¶***provide*** a true *account* of an event 事件の真相を伝える. ¶We ***received*** an excellent *account* of your success as a translator. 我々は君が翻訳者として成功したというすてきな便りを聞いた. ¶***render*** *account* of (=report on) one's mission 使命の結果を報告する(復命する).

Q keep ***accurate*** *accounts* 正確に記録する. ¶That is an approximate *account* of what happened. それがこの事件のあらましだ. ¶an ***authentic*** and ***well-documented*** *account* 権威ありまた諸説を参考にした記事. ¶give (=write) a ***brief*** *account* 手短かに説明する. ¶a ***clear*** and ***factual*** *account* 明瞭でありのままの記事. ¶fail to give a ***coherent*** *account* of ... ...の話は筋が通っていない. ¶a ***comic*** *account* こっけいな記事. ¶give a ***concise*** *account* of ... ...を簡明に述べる. ¶weld it together into a ***connected readable*** *account* うまく接ぎ合わせてちゃんとした記事にまとめる. ¶***earliest extant*** *accounts* 最古の史料. ¶a fairly ***exhaustive*** *account* かなりよく網羅した記事. ¶present a ***faithful*** *account* of ... ...を誤りなく伝える ‖ give a ***fake*** *account* of it それについて事実無根の話を伝える. ¶***falsified*** *accounts* 作りごと. ¶a ***first-hand*** *account* 本人直接の話. ¶a ***first-rate*** *account* 第一流の記事. ¶give a fairly ***full*** *account* of ... ...について相当詳細に書く. ¶give a ***full*** and ***detailed*** *account* of ... ...を詳細に述べる. ¶a ***gloves-off*** *account* 赤裸々な(つくろわない)話. ¶a ***graphic*** *account* of a fire 生々しい火災記事. ¶a ***graphic*** and wholly ***unvarnished*** *account* of the event その事件の生々としたありのまゝの記事. ¶a ***historic[al]*** *account* 歴史上の記録. ¶That is an ***incorrect*** *account* of the matter. それはその事件の誤った報告だ. ¶give an ***interesting*** *account* of ... ...の興味ある記事を書く. 【類】 an ***interesting*** *account* of the rise and growth of the company. ¶give a ***lucid*** *account* 明瞭な記事を書く. ¶a ***mike-side*** *account* 実況放送. ¶an ***oral*** *account* 口頭の報告. ¶give a ***plausible*** *account* of ... ...をもっともらしく言う. ¶the ***popular*** *account* is that ... 俗説にいわく.... ¶a ***prejudiced*** *account* 片よった報告. ¶The report gave an extremely ***satisfactory*** *account* of the progress made up to that date. 報告はその日までの事業進捗の極めて満足な経過を述べている. ¶give a ***short*** *account* of ... ...を簡単に説明する. ¶give a ***statistical*** *account* 統計的に記述する. ¶a ***succinct*** but ***exhaustive*** *account* of ... ...に関する簡にして要を得た記事. ¶a ***succinct*** and ***well-informed*** *account* 簡明でよく事情に通じた説明. ¶give a ***summary*** *account* of ... ...を概説する. ¶give a ***systematic*** *account* of ... ...を系統的に記述する. ¶a very ***thrilling*** *account* 身の毛のよだつような話. ¶provide a ***true*** *account* of an event 事件の真相を伝える. ¶all the ***trustworthy*** *accounts* agree as to ... ...については信頼すべき報告が皆一致している. ¶an ***unbiased*** *account* 公平な報告. ¶an ***unfair*** *account* of what had happened 事件の不公平な報告. ¶an ***unscientific*** *account* 通俗的記事. ¶an ***untechnical*** *account* 専門的でない記述. ¶give a ***vivid*** *account* of his life and fortunes 彼の生涯と運命について真に迫る記述をする. 【類】 a ***vivid*** and ***entertaining*** *account* of a journey. ¶be required to send in a ***written*** *account* of the affair その事件の始末書を取られる.

Q² an ***eye-witness*** *account* 目撃者の談話. ¶a ***full-length*** *account* 長文の記事. ¶Don't believe ***newspaper*** *accounts* especially during a war. 特に戦時は新聞記事を信用するな. ¶***press*** *accounts* and comments 新聞の記事評論. 【類】 according to ***press*** (=newspaper) *accounts*.

P ***according to*** her own *accounts* of it 彼女自身の話によると. ¶***at*** latest *accounts* 最近の記録によれば. ¶***by*** all *accounts* 諸説を総合するに. 【類】 judging ***by*** the *account* of ... ¶***from*** your *account* of him 彼に関するお話によると. ¶***in*** the biblical *accounts* of Paradise 天国を聖書的に説明すれば. ¶the book opens ***with*** an *account* of ... その本は...の話から書き起している.

P² an *account **of*** one's life 伝記 ‖ an *account **of*** travels 旅行記. 【類】 an *account **of*** the life and work of ...

(**3**) 利, 利益, ため.

V ***find*** one's *account* in ... ...で得(とく)をする ‖ don't ***find*** *account* in the work その仕事はわりに合わない.

P mainly ***on*** *account* of economy 主として経費節減のために ‖ ***on*** *account* of his health 保養に ‖ pay ***on*** *account* of another 立替える ‖ ***on*** one's own *account* 自己のために. 【類】 Don't make yourself uneasy ***on*** my *account*. / Pray don't give yourself so much trouble ***on*** my *account*. ¶He turns everything ***to*** [good] *account*. あの人は何でも利用する(ころんでもただは起きない). 【類】 You can turn your time ***to*** better *account*. / turn it ***to*** immediate *account*.

(**4**) 理由, 原因.

P He could not come ***on*** *account* of his illness. 彼は病気で来られなかった. 【類】 resign ***on*** *account* of age (老朽) / neglect her home and family ***on*** *account* of outside work / ***On*** *account* of holiday our store will be closed tomorrow. 【類】 can do nothing ***on*** *account* of the weather ‖ ***on*** all *accounts* どう見ても ‖ It is best to do so ***on*** every *account*. どう見てもそうするのが一番よい. ‖ I will never do such a thing ***on*** any *account*. こんなことは決してすまい. 【類】 Don't tell him ***on*** any *account*. / Do not part with the shares ***on*** any *account*. / Do not sell ***on*** any *account* until further advice. ‖ you must ... ***on*** no *accounts* どんなことがあっても決して...してはならぬ. 【類】 look upon it as one of the sights of London that must ***on*** no *account* be missed (見ずにしまう) / You ought ***on*** no *account* to take part in that. ‖ ***on*** this *account* こんな訳で ‖ ***on*** what *account* どういう訳で. ¶He has already had several cures ***to*** his *account*. 彼の手で既に数人の患者を治している.

(**5**) 重要, 価値; 評価, 考慮.

V ***give*** a good *account* of ... ...をりっぱに成し遂げる(好成績をあげる). 【類】 Such men will ***give*** a good *account* of themselves at the front (戦地). ¶***make*** much (little) *account* of ... ...を重(軽)視する ‖ ***make*** no *account* of difficulties 困難にとん着しない. ¶you need not ***take*** much *account* of ... ...は余り重きを置くに足らない ‖ ***take*** no *account* of ... ...を無視する(気に留めない). 【類】 the statement ***takes*** no *account* of ... ‖ in making the classification, *account* is ***taken*** of the fact that ... 分類にあたって...という事実を考慮に入れる.

Q a matter of ***great*** (***small***) *account* 大(小)事. ¶It is of ***much*** *account* that boys have good companions. 子供は良い友だちを持つことが大切だ. ¶His achievements in letters were of ***little*** *account*. 彼の文学上の業績は大したものではなかった. ‖ a man of ***no*** *account* つまらない人 ‖ a matter of ***no*** *account* 取るに足らぬこと. 【類】 It is of ***no*** *account*.

P take it ***into*** *account* それを勘定に入れる, それをしんしゃくする ‖ This is not a heavy stone, its size being taken ***into*** *account*. 大きさを考えれば別に重い石ではない. ¶leave that factor ***out of*** *account* その要素を度外視する.

account, *v*. 見なす; 説明する; 勘定する.

P *account* it ***as*** (=deem it) unwise それを拙策と見なす. ¶*account* ***for*** ... ...を説明する ‖ That *accounts* ***for*** your always looking so seedy. 道理で君はいつも浮かぬ顔している. 【類】 He is ill; that *accounts* ***for*** his absence. / it is to be *accounted* ***for*** by the fact that ... / Can you *account* ***for*** the delay of the steamer? / cannot *account* in any way ***for*** ... / How do you *account* ***for*** it? / how do you *account* ***for*** the fact that ... / That *accounts* ***for*** his non-attendance. / That *accounts* ***for*** his long silence. ‖ Old age *accounts* ***for*** it. それは年のせいだ. ‖ Transactions are to be *accounted* ***for*** yearly. 取引は一年一年の勘定にする. 【類】 I want you to *account* ***for*** every cent you spent (使途を細かく). ‖ It *accounts* ***for*** 26 per cent of all railway accidents. 鉄道事故の 26 パーセントを占めている. ‖ Police said that 146 persons still are not *accounted* for. まだ 146 名が行方不明だと警察では言っていた. ¶***ac-***

count with (=*to*) the treasurer for money received 受取った金を出納係に勘定して納める.

accountability, *n.* 責任. 「帰すること.

P *accountability* ***for*** result ***to*** ... 結果に関して…に責任を

accountable, *a.* 責任ある.

P Who is *accountable* ***for*** this? この責任者はだれか. ¶We are *accountable* ***to*** him ***for*** the loss. 我々はその損失に関して彼に対し責任がある.

accountant, *n.* 会計係. 「*ant* 公認会計士.

Q a ***public accountant*** 会計士 ‖ a certified ***public account-***

accounting, *n.* 計算; 説明.

V He refused to ***make*** an *accounting* of the funds. 彼は金の処分を明かにすることを拒んだ.

Q^{2} ***cost accounting*** 原価計算.

P It's just one of those strange things ***for*** which there is no *accounting*. それも全く訳の分らぬ不思議なことだ.

P^{2} There is no ***accounting for*** tastes. たで食う虫も好き

accredit, *v.* 信任する; 任命する; …に帰する. ⌊好き.

P *accredit* a minister ***to*** (=***at***) a foreign government 外国政府に公使を派遣する. 【類】 He was ***accredited to*** the English Court to represent Japan (英国駐在日本国大使). ¶They all *accredited* him ***with*** the authorship of this book. 彼らは皆この書を彼の著作だとした. ‖ They *accredited* him ***with*** the remark. この言は彼のものとされている.

accrue, *v.* 生じる.

P Interest ***accrues to*** a man ***from*** loan. 貸金から利子が取れる. ‖ royalty ***accruing from*** ... …から入る印税(特許料など) ‖ A great profit ***accrues to*** government ***from*** the coinage of copper. 政府は銅貨鋳造で巨利を占める.

accumulate, *v.* 積む.

M ***patiently accumulate*** data 苦心して資料を集める. ¶Goods are *accumulating* ***rapidly*** (***slowly***). 滞貨が急に(徐々に)かさみつゝある.

accumulation, *n.* 集積.

Q the exploration of the ***rich accumulations*** of material 豊富な材料を検討する.

P^{2} accumulation ***of*** evidence for a law suit 裁判の証拠固め ‖ my own *accumulation* ***of*** words and phrases 自分の

accuracy, *n.* 正確, 精密. ⌊収集した語句.

V ***attain*** absolute *accuracy* 絶対的正確に達する. ¶***check*** the *accuracy* of ... …が正確か否かを調べる. ¶***doubt*** the *accuracy* of the report that ... …という報道の正確さを疑う. ¶***sacrifice*** *accuracy* to brilliancy of effect おもしろく読ませるために正確さを犠牲にする. ¶***test*** the *accuracy* of the statement 陳述の正確かいなかをためす.

Q measure with ***considerable*** *accuracy* かなり精密に計る. ¶a man of ***general*** *accuracy* in writing 概して正確な文章を書く人. ¶***grammatical*** *accuracy* 文法的正確. ¶***historical*** *accuracy* 史的正確. ¶with ***mathematical*** *accuracy* 数学的正確さで. ¶with ***minute*** *accuracy* 細かい点まで正確に. ¶with ***reasonable*** *accuracy* かなり正確に. ¶with ***remarkable*** *accuracy* ひときわ正確に. ¶with ***satisfactory*** *accuracy* 十分正確に. ¶***scientific*** *accuracy* 科学的正確. ¶with ***strict*** *accuracy* 厳正に, 的確に. ¶***syntactical*** *accuracy* 措辞の正確なこと. ¶with ***technical*** *accuracy* 専門的に正確に. ¶with ***tolerable*** *accuracy* どうやら正確に. ¶His *accuracy* is ***undoubted*** (=***unquestionable***). 彼の正確さは疑いをいれない. ¶predict with ***unerring*** *accuracy* 極めて正確に予言する.

Q^{2} a ***hair's-breadth*** *accuracy* in the choice of words 言葉を選ぶ上の極度の正確さ. ¶the watch of ***railroad*** *accuracy* 鉄道の時間のように正確な時計.

P be ***of*** doubtful *accuracy* 正確のほどが疑わしい. ¶inquire into the matter ***with*** *accuracy* 正確に事件を調査する.

P^{2} speed and *accuracy* ***in*** thought-getting [読書で]思想をつかむことの迅速と正確. ¶*accuracy* ***of*** fire [射撃の]命

accurate, *a.* 正確な. ⌊中精度.

M ***fairly*** *accurate* 相当に正確. ¶***mathematically*** *accurate* 数学的に正確な. ¶try to be ***meticulously*** *accurate* あくまで(やかましい位)正確を期する. ¶***perfectly*** (=***absolutely or strictly***) *accurate* 全く正確な.

P *accurate* ***in*** one's statement (statistics) 陳述(など)の正確な. 【類】 He is *accurate* ***in*** his observation (観察).

O to be *accurate* 正確に言えば.

accusable, *a.* 責むべき.

P He is *accusable* ***of*** being heterodox. 彼は異端のそしり

accusation, *n.* 非難; 告発. ⌊を免れない.

V *Accusation* after accusation was ***brought*** against him. 彼は続々非難をあびせられた. ¶***deny*** an *accusation* 告訴を否定する. ¶***lay*** (=***lodge***) an *accusation* 告発する. ¶triumphantly ***refute*** the slanderous *accusation* したり顔に誹謗(ひぼう)を論ばくする.

Q a ***false accusation*** of theft against ... …に対する窃盗罪の誣告(ぶこく). ¶***formal accusation*** 公式の訴追. ¶an ***impudent accusation*** 図々しい非難. ¶an ***insolent accusation*** 侮辱的な非難. ¶***just*** (***unjust***) *accusation* 正当(不当)の告発. ¶a ***reproachful accusation*** 問責, 非難. ¶an ***unfounded accusation*** 無実の罪. ¶an ***unscrupulous*** and ***lying accusation*** 無法な, しかも事実無根の非難. ¶make ***various accusations*** against ... …を様々に非難する.

P ***under*** a false *accusation* of ... …という無実の罪で. ¶*Accusation* ***of*** theft lay against him. 窃盗の罪は彼にあっ

accuse, *v.* 告発する; 非難する. ⌊た.

M He was ***falsely*** (=***unjustly or wrongly***) *accused* of stealing. 窃盗のぬれ衣を着た. ¶a person ***jointly accused*** 共同被告.

P He was *accused* ***as*** an accomplice. 共犯者として告発された. ¶be *accused* ***in*** an action filed by ... …から告訴される. ¶He *accused* me ***of*** having neglected my work. 彼は僕が仕事を怠けたと言って責めた. ‖ We *accused* him ***of*** immoral conduct towards her. われわれは彼女を裏切った彼の不義を責めた. ‖ He was *accused* ***of*** the practice of magic. 魔法使いと非難された. 【類】 be *accused* ***of*** theft (offenses) / try those who are *accused* ***of*** breaking the laws. / We *accused* him ***of*** taking bribes (収賄). / They *accused* the teacher ***of*** favoritism (えこひいき). / They *accused* me ***of*** an untruth (cowardice, ambition). / He was *accused* ***of*** fraud (=committing a fraud). / He was *accused* ***of*** corruption (stealing, unpatriotism). / He was *accused* ***of*** being a spy.

accused *n.* 被告人. 「*cused* 被告を審理する.

V ***discharge*** the *accused* 罪人を赦免する. ¶***try*** the *ac-*

accustom, *v.* 慣らす.

M be ***fully*** *accustomed* to ... …に十分慣れている.

P *accustom* oneself ***to*** early rising 早起きに慣れる. 【類】 *accustom* a person ***to*** work / I *accustomed* myself ***to*** humble fare (粗食). / I am *accustomed* ***to*** a spare diet (粗食). / They are *accustomed* ***to*** this sort of work (labor, the use of arms (武器)). ‖ In the realm of language we are *accustomed* ***to*** inconsistency. 言語の領域では矛盾は珍しくない. ‖ We became *accustomed* ***to*** it. それに慣れてきた. 【類】 They got *accustomed* ***to*** taking long walks. / grow *accustomed* ***to*** the place / *accustomed* ***to*** the ways of the world (世なれた).

O we are *accustomed* to think of it as ... われわれはそれを…という風に考えてきた.

ace, *n.* (トランプの)一点; 第一人者; 危急存亡の時.

Q^{2} an ***air ace*** 空の第一人者. ¶America's ***flying ace*** アメリカ航空界の第一人者. ¶a ***net ace*** テニスのナンバーワン.

P He was ***within*** an *ace* of his ruin. あやうく没落する所だった. 【類】 He came ***within*** an *ace* of death. / come ***within*** an *ace* of being drowned.

P^{2} an *ace* ***of*** spades スペードのエース; 《俗》末亡人 ‖ an

ache, *n.* 痛み. ⌊*ace of* aces ピカー.

V It seemed almost impossible to ***stand*** the *ache* and the smart without crying. 泣かずに痛みをこらえることはできそうに思えなかった.

P^{2} an *ache* ***in*** one's head 頭痛. 【類】 an *ache in* a tooth. 「どく痛む.

ache, *v.* 痛む.

M My head *aches* ***badly***. 頭痛がする. ¶*ache* ***cruelly*** ひ

P *ache* ***for*** a person (place, one's home) 人(など)にあこがれる. ¶*ache* ***in*** a joint 関節が痛む. ¶*ache* ***with*** longing あこがれる ‖ My whole body *aches* ***with*** weariness. 疲労で全身が痛む.

achieve, *v.* 仕遂げる.

M All this cannot be *achieved* ***overnight***. 一夜でこれを全部やりおわせることはできない. ¶***successfully*** *achieve* an end 首尾よく目的を遂げる.

achievement, *n.* 功績; 成就.

V He praised the flyers as ***adding*** a new *achievement* to the annals of American aviation. 彼は米航空界

の記録に一つの新たな功績を加えたものとして飛行家たちを称揚した. ¶***evaluate*** the *achievements* of pupils 学生の成績を考査する. ¶We have probably not yet ***reached*** the highest possible *achievement* in this matter. われわれは恐らくこのことにはまだ最大の功績を挙げていない. ¶The book ***represents*** the highest *achievement* of the printer's art. その本は印刷技術の最高水準を示す. 【類】 In its combination of thoroughness with exactness, the New English Dictionary ***represents*** the highest *achievement* of modern English scholarship. ¶***stimulate*** *achievement* in industry 産業を振興する. ¶It ***surpasses*** all previous *achievements* in lexicography. 辞書編集上空前の業績だ.

Q an ***academic*** *achievement* 学問上の業績. ¶the ***artistic*** *achievement* of Turner ターナーの美術上の業績. ¶Each poem is a ***complete*** and ***artistic*** *achievement*. 一つ一つの詩が申し分ない芸術作品だ. ¶This is a remarkable ***biographic*** *achievement*. りっぱに完成された伝記だ. ¶a ***brilliant*** *achievement* in a war 赫々たる武勲. ¶a ***creditable*** *achievement* 見事な業績. ¶The medicine is the ***crowning*** *achievement* of chemical science. その薬は化学の最大成功である. 【類】 The painting is one of the ***crowning*** *achievements* of Japanese art. ¶***dazzling*** *achievements* まばゆい程の功績. ¶***diplomatic*** *achievements* 外交上の功績. ¶an ***editorial*** *achievement* of the very high order すばらしい編集上の成功. ¶the ***esthetic*** *achievement* of Japan 日本の美術上の功績. ¶his ***final*** *achievement* 終局の成功. ¶a ***gigantic*** *achievement* 巨大な業績. ¶***glorious*** *achievements* 赫々たる功績. ¶a ***great*** *achievement* in the field of ... ...界における一大功績. ¶a ***heroic*** *achievement* 雄々しい業績. ¶a ***high*** *achievement* 大成功. ¶English literature is one of the noblest of ***human*** *achievements*. 英文学は人間の業績中最高なるものの一つだ. ¶These are too ***insignificant*** *achievements* to be heralded in print. これらはささいなことがらで印刷して伝えるほどのものではない. ¶in the sphere of ***intellectual*** *achievement* 知的業績の範囲で. ¶the ***latest*** *achievement* of science 科学界最近の成功. ¶his latest ***literary*** *achievement* 彼の文学上の近業. 【類】 his chief ***literary*** *achievement*. ¶the story of ***mankind's*** *achievements* in the past hundred years 過去百年間の人類事績の物語. ¶It is no ***mean*** *achievement* それは並々ならぬ業績だ. ¶a ***memorable*** *achievement* 記憶すべき功績. ¶a ***miraculous*** *achievement* 奇蹟的成功. ¶the ***outstanding*** *achievement* of the year 1928 一九二八年の抜群な成績. ¶the ***past*** *achievements* of the Japanese race 日本民族の過去の業績. ¶***scholarly*** *achievement* 学業の成績. ¶***scientific*** *achievements* 科学上の功績. ¶men and women of ***substantial*** *achievement* 実質的に業績を挙げた男女. ¶a ***technical*** *achievement* 技術上の実績. ¶a ***thrilling*** *achievement* ひやりとするような放れ業. ¶a ***worthy*** *achievement* りっぱな仕事.

Q² ¶The tunnel is a great ***engineering*** *achievement*. そのトンネルは工学上の一大成功である. ¶***record*** *achievements* in sport 競技上の新記録. ¶his two outstanding ***screen*** *achievements* 彼の優れた二つの映画作品. ¶***sporting*** *achievements* 競技の記録.

P He was awarded the Nobel prize for *achievements* ***in*** physiology. 生理学上の功績でノーベル賞を授与された.

acid, *n.* 酸.

Q weak ***boracic*** *acid* 希薄なほう酸. ¶***citric*** *acid* くえん酸. ¶***nicotinic*** *acid* ニコチン酸. ¶***Sulfuric*** *acid* is a heavy, colorless, oily, very strong *acid*. 硫酸は重い, 無色, 油質の, 極めて強い酸である.

P It is soluble ***in*** dilute *acids*. それは希酸中に溶解する.

acknowledge, *v.* 認める.

M I *acknowledged* myself ***beaten***. 僕は負けたと言った. ¶***courageously*** *acknowledge* a mistake 男らしく誤りを認める. ¶It is ***generally*** *acknowledged* that ... ...であると一般に認められている. ¶He ***gladly*** *acknowledged* himself to be in the wrong. 彼は喜んで自分の間違っていたことを認めた. ¶***gratefully*** *acknowledge* a favor 恩恵をありがたく思う. ¶He ***openly*** *acknowledged* (=admitted *or* believed) his fault. 自分の過失を公然と認めた. ¶it is ***universally*** *acknowledged* that ... ...ということは一般に認められている.

P I *acknowledge* it ***as*** binding. 私はそれを守るべき義務あるものと認める. ‖ I *acknowledged* him ***as*** my superior. 僕より腕があると認めた. ¶I *acknowledged* his politeness ***with*** a bow. 僕は頭を下げて彼に答礼した.

acknowledgment, *n.* 承認; 感謝.

V an *acknowledgment* is ***expressed*** to ... for ... ...に対して...に感謝の意を表する. ¶***make*** an *acknowledgment* あいさつをする. ¶***make*** one's *acknowledgment* with thanks 感謝の意を表する. ¶I ***owe*** an *acknowledgment* to my uncle. 私は叔父に感謝せねばならぬ. ¶Pray ***receive*** my best *acknowledgment*. 誠にありがとうございます. ¶***return*** one's grateful *acknowledgment* to him 彼に感謝の意を表わす. ¶She ***sent*** her handsome *acknowledgment* to him. 彼女は彼に十分の報酬を送った. ¶I ***tender*** my warmest *acknowledgments* to him for ... 私は...に対して心から彼に感謝する. ¶***wave*** one's *acknowledgment* 帽子を振ってあいさつする.

Q make a most ***cordial*** *acknowledgment* to ... 心から...に感謝する. ¶a ***frank*** *acknowledgment* 率直な認識. ¶in ***grateful*** *acknowledgment* of ... ...を厚く感謝して. ¶an ***ingenuous*** *acknowledgment* of guilt 率直な罪の告白. ¶make a ***public*** *acknowledgment* of one's meritorious service その功績を表彰する. ¶To him I ***feel*** my ***sincerest*** *acknowledgment* to be due. 私は心底から彼に感謝している. ¶as a ***slight*** *acknowledgment* of your services いささかお礼の印までに. ¶a ***small*** *acknowledgment* of kindness received 好意に対するさゝやかな謝礼. ¶wish to extend ***special*** *acknowledgment* to ... 特に...に感謝の意を表したい. ¶in ***thankful*** *acknowledgment* 感謝して. ¶This would be the ***wrong*** *acknowledgment* of the kindness. これはその厚意に報いる道ではあるまい.

P we have ***for*** *acknowledgment* your letter of ... ...日付の貴翰正に拝見致しました. ¶***in*** *acknowledgment* of a present 贈物の返礼に. 【類】 ***in*** *acknowledgment* of your valuable help. ¶print an article ***without*** *acknowledgment* 文を出所を示さないで印刷する.

P² *acknowledgment* ***for*** permission to reprint is extended to ... 転載の許可に対して...に謝意を述べる. ¶*acknowledgment* ***of*** delivery 配達証明.

acme, *n.* 絶頂.

V ***attain*** the *acme* of development 発展の絶頂に達する. ¶***reach*** the *acme* of its prosperity (power) 繁栄(など)の絶頂に達する.

P the *acme* ***of*** happiness and comfort 至幸至楽. 【類】 the *acme* ***of*** perfection (完ぺき) / the *acme* ***of*** luxury and comfort ‖ The stage scene was the *acme* ***of*** realism. そのシーンは真に迫るものがあった.

acquaint, *v.* 知らせる; 知合にさせる.

M be ***little*** *acquainted* with the art of poetry 歌道に暗い. ¶I am not ***personally*** *acquainted* with him. 私は彼と面識がない. ¶be ***really*** *acquainted* with ... 実際...に精通している. ¶He is but ***slightly*** *acquainted* with the art. 彼はその芸術には余り通じていない. ¶We are not ***sufficiently*** *acquainted* with the facts. その事実を十分に理解していない. ¶*acquaint* oneself ***thoroughly*** with the procedure やり方をすっかりのみ込む. 【類】 in order to get ***thoroughly*** *acquainted* with English commerce (=trade) / make oneself ***thoroughly*** *acquainted* with every aspect of the question. ¶He is ***well*** *acquainted* with history. 彼は歴史に明るい.

P I *acquainted* him ***with*** my intention. 僕の考えを彼に知らせた. 【類】 Let me *acquaint* you ***with*** the facts. / I *acquainted* him ***with*** the event. / *acquaint* Western readers ***with*** the present status of the Republic of China / I have got *acquainted* ***with*** him. / How came you to be *acquainted* ***with*** him? / The Japanese became *acquainted* ***with*** Chinese writing in the fifth century, if not earlier. ‖ As if you were *acquainted* ***with*** it! 知りもしないくせに. ‖ be *acquainted* ***with*** the ways of the people 下情に通じている.

acquaintance, *n.* 交際, 知合い; 知識.

V ***acquire*** a closer *acquaintance* with ... ...に一層通暁する. ¶***begin*** an *acquaintance* with ... ...と交際を始める. ¶***compass*** an *acquaintance* with ... ...と近付きになる. ¶***continue*** an *acquaintance* with ... ...と交際を続ける. ¶***contract*** an *acquaintance* with ... ...と知合いになる. ¶I don't want to ***cultivate*** his *acquaintance.* あの人と交際しようとは思わない. 【類】 ***cultivate*** each other's *acquaintance.* ¶***cut*** (=***drop***) an *acquaintance* 絶交する. ¶***enlarge*** our *acquaintance* with ... ...の見聞を広める. ¶***establish*** an *acquaintance* 交際を始める. ¶***extend*** one's *acquaintance* of ... ...の知識を広める. ¶***form*** the *acquaintance* of (=an *acquaintance* with) ... ...と知合になる. ¶I ***gained*** *acquaintance* with ... ...を知った. ¶I ***had*** some previous *acquaintance* with the subject. その学科は前からいくらか知っていた. ‖ He ***has*** an intimate *acquaintance* with English. 彼は英語に通じている. ¶I still ***keep up*** my *acquaintance* with him. 僕はまだ彼と交際している. ¶He ***lacks*** a first-hand *acquaintance* with the country. 彼はその国に行ったことがない. ¶***make*** one's *acquaintance* その知合いとなる ‖ they ***made*** one another's *acquaintance* at ... 彼らは...で知合いになった ‖ he ***made*** the *acquaintance* of and formed friendship with ... 彼は...と知合いになって親しく交った. ¶***obtain*** a practical *acquaintance* with seamanship 海員の仕事を実地に覚える. ¶***pick*** *acquaintance* with ... 偶然...と知合いになる. ¶***possess*** only a slight *acquaintance* with ... ...をちっとばかりかじっている ‖ He ***possesses*** more than a second-hand *acquaintance* with savage life. 彼は蛮人生活をいくらか実地に見ている. 【類】 ***possessing*** a fair *acquaintance* with the facts of ... ¶***renew*** my *acquaintance* with ... ...との旧交を温める. 【類】 ***renew*** our *acquaintance* formed in my former visit to ... ¶I ***resumed*** *acquaintance* with Tokyo after an absence of thirteen years. 十三年ぶりで東京にまたやってきた. ¶***scrape*** an *acquaintance* 紹介なしに知己となる. ¶***seek*** the *acquaintance* of ... ...との交際を求める. ¶I have ***struck up*** an *acquaintance* with him. 僕は彼と親しくなった. ¶***widen*** one's *acquaintance* with literature 文学の知識を広める.

Q an ***adequate*** *acquaintance* with ... ...に対する十分の知識. ¶I made some most ***agreeable*** *acquaintances.* 二三会心の友ができた. ¶***bowing*** *acquaintance* [会えばお辞儀する程度の]一通りの交際 ‖ had a ***bowing*** *acquaintance* with English literature 英文学を少々かじっていた. ¶We are the ***casual*** *acquaintances* of a long railway journey. 私たちは長い汽車の旅での偶然の知合いです. ¶cultivate a ***close*** *acquaintance* with ... ...と親密に交際する. ¶He is entirely innocent of even the most ***elementary*** *acquaintance* with the language. 彼はその国語のごく初歩の知識すら持っていない. ¶He has an ***exhaustive*** *acquaintance* with the works of Shakespeare. シェークスピアの作を残らず読んでいる. ¶He has a ***familiar*** *acquaintance* with authors of whom the ordinary student hardly knows the name. 普通の学生がほとんど名前も知らない作家をよく知っている. 【類】 He has a ***familiar*** *acquaintance* with English literature. ¶make their ***first*** *acquaintance* with the capital of France フランスの首都を始めて見る. ¶a ***fortuitous*** *acquaintance* 偶然近づきになった人. ¶establish ***further*** *acquaintance* 一層親しくする. ¶get a ***general*** *acquaintance* with English classics 英国の古典に一通り目を通す. ¶a ***halfway*** *acquaintance* with English なまかじりの英語. ¶He has an ***international*** *acquaintance* with these matters. 彼はこれらのことがらには世界的に通じている. ¶an ***intimate*** *aquaintance* with pathology in all its branches 病理学の全部門にわたっての造詣の深さ ‖ form an ***intimate*** *acquaintance* with England 英国をよく知る. ¶a ***journalistic*** *acquaintance* 新聞記者の知合い. ¶He has a ***large*** [circle of] *acquaintance.* あの人は交際が広い. ¶He has only a ***limited*** *acquaintance* with the matter. 彼はそのことをほんの少しばかり知っている. ¶have ***little*** *acquaintance* with ... ...を余りよく知らぬ. ¶a ***mere*** *acquaintance* ほんのちょっとの知り合い. 【類】 the ***merest*** *acquaintances.* ¶a ***minute*** *acquaintance* with an author ある著者に対する緻密な認識. ¶I have ***no*** *acquaintance* with him. 私は彼と面識がない. ¶I have more than a ***nodding*** *acquaintance* with him. 彼との間柄は義理一ぺんの交際ではない. ¶as if we were ***old*** *acquaintances* われらは旧友でもあるかのように. 【類】 an ***old*** *acquaintance* of mine. ¶a ***passing*** *acquaintance* 通り一ぺんの知合い. ¶make the ***personal*** *acquaintance* with ... ...と知合になる. ¶a ***pestering*** *acquaintance* 鼻つまみの知人(途中で長話などする). ¶his ***profound*** *acquaintance* with ... ...に関する彼の深い知識. 【類】 have ***profound*** *acquaintance* with his business. ¶books that are my ***recent*** *acquaintances.* 最近読んだばかりの書物. ¶a ***slight*** *acquaintance* with the language その国語に対する少しばかりの知識. ¶make ***some*** *acquaintance* with Shakespeare シェークスピアを少しかじる. ¶He has a ***special*** *acquaintance* with the subject. その問題を特別よく知っている. ¶acquire a ***superficial*** *acquaintance* with ... ...に関する浅薄な知識を得る. ¶a ***thorough*** *acquaintance* with ... ...に関する徹底的の知識. ¶***undesirable*** *acquaintances* 好ましくない知人. ¶his ***wide*** *acquaintance* with the literature on the subject その種の文献に関する彼の該博な知識 ‖ He has a ***wide*** *acquaintance.* 彼は知人が多い(交際が広い). ¶The reading of novels is not only an agreeable but an effective means of getting a ***working*** *acquaintance* with a foreign language. 小説を読むことは単に楽しいだけでなく外国語に親しむ一つの有効な手段でもある. ¶***worldly*** *acquaintance* 世故に通じていること.

Q² a ***chance*** *acquaintance* 偶然の知合い. ¶taking advantage of a ***girlhood*** *acquaintance* with him 少女時代に彼を知っていたのを縁に. ¶I have a ***reading*** *acquaintance* with Russian. ロシア語を読むぐらいの知識がある. ¶have a ***speaking*** *acquaintance* with ... ...とはあいさつするぐらいの知合いである.

P ***from*** my very slight *acquaintance* with the subject, I should say that ... その問題に関するきわめて貧弱な知識から推して私は...と言いたい. ¶a young woman ***of*** my *acquaintance* 私の知人である若い婦人. 【類】 He is the cleverest man ***of*** my *acquaintance.* ¶They married ***on*** brief *acquaintance,* and have lived happily afterward. 彼らは交際を始めて間もなく結婚をしてその後幸福な生涯を送った. ¶a circle ***of*** my *acquaintance* 知合いの連中. ¶I found him, ***on*** a closer *acquaintance,* to be a very fine man. 交際している内にりっぱな人間だということが分った.

P² *acquaintance* ***between*** persons 人と人との交際. ¶Where did you make the *acquaintance* ***of*** this lady? どこでこの婦人を御存知ですか. ¶His *acquaintance* ***with*** French is insufficient to enable him to appreciate the author. 彼のフランス語の知識ではその著者を鑑賞することはできない.

acquaintanceship, *n.* 相識, 交際.

V ***broaden*** and ***deepen*** one's *acquaintanceship* with foreign peoples 外国人との交際を広げかつ深める. ¶a man with whom I can ***claim*** *acquaintanceship* 僕が知人と称し得る人. ¶***promote*** mutual *acquaintanceship* 相互の親睦(ぼく)を計る. ¶***renew*** old *acquaintanceship* [以前知っていた人に会って]旧交を温める. ¶His inquisitive spirit made him ***strike up*** close *acquaintanceship* with the people among whom he lived. 彼のせんさく好きの精神が自然彼を周囲の人々と懇意にさせた.

acquiesce, *v.* 従う, 納得する.

P *acquiesce* ***in*** an arrangement (a proposal) 協定(など)に同意する ‖ *acquiesce* ***in*** the doctrine その教義に服従する ‖ *acquiesce* ***in*** everything 言いなり放題になる. 【類】 The other members *acquiesced* ***in*** his resignation. / He is so uncompromising (鼻いきが荒くて) that he is hardly likely to *acquiesce* ***in*** our request.

acquiescence, *n.* 同意, 服従.

V they went on strike in order to ***enforce*** *acquiescence* in their demand that ... 彼らの...という要求を強いるためストをやった. ¶***express*** a grim *acquiescence* in ... ...に対していやいや同意する.

P ***by*** *acquiescence* or positive agreement 止むを得ず納得するかあるいは進んで同意して. ¶***without*** the *acquiescence* of ... ...の同意を得ないで.

P² *acquiescence* ***in*** the dispensations of life 浮世の習いとあきらめること.

acquire, *v.* 得る, 修得する.

M It can ***easily*** be *acquired.* それは容易に得られる. 【類】 The habit is ***easily*** *acquired* but broken up with difficulty. ¶I desire to *acquire* French ***quickly.*** 手っ取早くフランス語を覚えたい.

P His features are handsome but manly and of a ruddy bronze color *acquired* ***at*** sea. 彼の顔はりっぱで男らしく潮風に吹かれて赤(しゃ)銅色になっている. ¶*acquire* land ***by*** purchase 土地を買受ける ‖ *acquire* ... ***by*** transfer ...を譲り受ける. ¶*acquire* the knowledge ***through*** experience 経験で知る.

acquirement, *n.* 取得, 獲得; 学識.

Q Japanese students' ***English acquirements*** 日本の学生の英語の力. ¶a man of eminent ***scientific acquirements*** 知名の科学者. ¶a man of ***uncommon acquirements*** 博学多才の人.

P² the ***acquirement of*** knowledge (property) 知識(など)の獲得. 【類】 the ***acquirement of*** information from the printed page (印刷した書物).

acquisition, *n.* 所得; 学識.

V ***inspect*** the latest *acquisition* on the subject その問題に関する最近の研究を調査する. ¶Most of the art museums in America are almost entirely dependent upon the gifts of friends for ***making*** new *acquisitions.* 米国の美術博物館の多数はほとんど全部篤志家の寄贈によってその内容の充実を計っている.

Q the formation of character rather than the ***mere acquisition*** of knowledge 知識の獲得よりむしろ人格のとうや. ¶***scholarly acquisition*** 学識. ¶a ***valuable acquisition*** 掘り出しもの.

acquisitive, *a.* 得たがる; 欲の深い.

P a man *acquisitive* ***to*** (=***for***) property 財産を得たがる人.

acquit, *v.* [身を]処する; 放免する.

M The contestants *acquitted* themselves very ***ably.*** 参加競技者たちは有能にやった. ¶*acquit* oneself ***admirably*** in conversation 会話をうまくやる. ¶*acquit* oneself ***bravely (brilliantly)*** 勇敢(りっぱ)に振舞う. ¶*acquit* oneself ***creditably*** in social and business performances 社会的にも仕事の上でも信頼を得るやり方をする. ¶The innocent were ***rightly*** *acquitted.* 無罪者は当然釈放された. ¶The orator *acquitted* himself very ***poorly.*** 弁士ははなはだ不できであった. ¶He *acquitted* himself ***well*** of his task. 彼はその仕事をうまくやってのけた. 【類】 *acquitted* themselves very ***well*** in circumstances of extreme danger and provocation.

P *acquit* oneself ***of*** a debt (duty, an obligation) 負債(など)を済ます ‖ They *acquitted* him ***of*** the charge. 彼らは彼を放免した. ‖ He was *acquitted* ***of*** the crime (blame). 彼は無罪(など)となった. 【類】 He was ***acquitted of*** forgery (fraud, the murder of ...). ¶He *acquitted* himself ***to*** his credit (=with credit). 彼はうまくやってのけた.

acre, *n.* エーカー(四段二十四歩).

V The grounds ***comprise*** (=***contain***) six hundred and thirty-five *acres.* 敷地は六百三十五エーカーある. ¶The playground ***covers*** over an *acre* in extent. 運動場は広さ一エーカー以上ある. ¶The building ***embraces*** over ... *acres.* 建物が…エーカー以上を占めている. ¶The [college] campus ***includes*** three hundred *acres.* 大学の校庭は三百エーカーだ.

P The building stands in nine ***acres of*** ground. 建物は九エーカーの地所に建ててある.

acreage, *n.* エーカー数, 反別.

Q² one's [real] ***estate*** *acreage* 敷地面積. ¶A war decree restricting ***mulberry*** *acreage* was revoked in November. くわ畑の面積を制限する戦時訓令は十一月廃止された. ¶***rice*** *acreage* 稲の作付面積.

acrobat, *n.* 軽業師.

Q a ***tricky*** *acrobat* 手練の軽業師.

acrobatics, *n. pl.* 軽業曲芸.

Q those who are gifted in ***mental*** *acrobatics* 頭がよく働く人々.

act, *n.* **(1)** 行為.

V fail to ***appreciate*** an *act* of kindness 親切を無にする. ¶***commend*** (=***praise***) an *act* of charity 慈善行為を賞賛する. ¶***commit*** a rash *act* 早まったことをする ‖ ***commit*** an *act* of war against ... …に対し戦争行為をなす. 【類】 The *act* was ***committed*** with savage brutality (残忍). ¶***do*** an *act* of charity 慈善を行う. 【類】 ***do*** many *acts* of kindness ‖ He ***did*** another noble *act.* 彼はもう一つりっぱなことをした. ¶***have*** no *act* in ... …に関係していない. ¶***perform*** a plucky *act* 勇ましいことをする. ¶***practice*** a forbidden *act* 禁じられたことをする. ¶This is the most cruel *act* I have ever ***witnessed.*** 私のこれまで見たうちで最も残忍な行為だ.

Q an ***amendatory*** *act* 修正法. ¶commit a ***barbarous*** (=***cruel***) *act* on ... …に残忍なことをする. ¶perform a ***courageous*** *act* 勇ましいことをする. ¶the universal fascination of the ***creative*** *act* その創造的事業が広く一般の人々をとらえた魅力. ¶objects which have ***constituted*** a ***criminal*** *act* 犯罪行為を組成した物. ¶He paid for the ***foolhardy*** *act* with his life. 無鉄砲なことをやって命を取られた. ¶a ***foolish*** *act* 愚行. ¶a ***graceful*** *act* 優雅な行為. ¶a ***gracious*** *act* of condescension 腰の低いしとやかな行為. ¶a ***heroic*** *act* 雄々しい行為. ¶a ***heroic*** but ***sad*** *act* 壮烈だが悲惨な行為. ¶a ***high-handed*** *act* 横暴なやり方. ¶an ***ignoble*** *act* 不らちな行状. ¶an ***illegal*** *act* 不法行為. ¶an ***illicit*** *act* 不正行為. ¶he was guilty of ***immoral*** *acts* and conduct with Mrs. ... 彼は…夫人と不倫な行為があった. ¶an ***impulsive*** *act* 感情にかられた行い. ¶***incriminating*** *acts* 犯罪行為. ¶an ***indecent*** *act* わいせつ行為. ¶an ***indiscreet*** *act* 無分別な行為. ¶with an ***inner*** *act* of homage to the spirit of ... …の霊に黙礼して. ¶the ***judicial*** *acts* and proceedings of a court 裁判所の司法行為と事務. ¶a ***juridical*** *act* 法律行為. ¶a ***kindly*** *act* 親切. ¶a ***laudable*** *act* 奇特な行為. ¶a ***mean*** (=***ignoble***) *act* 卑しい行為. ¶a ***monstrous*** *act* 不らちきわまる行為. ¶a ***noble*** *act* りっぱな行為. ¶commit ***obscene*** *acts* upon ... …にみだらなことをする. ¶an ***official*** *act* 公務上の行為. ¶an ***overt*** (a ***covert***) *act* 歴然たる(隠れた)行為. ¶the Queen's first ***public*** *act* after the coronation 即位式後に女王の執った最初の公的行為. ¶a ***questionable*** *act* うろんな行為. ¶a ***rash*** *act* 軽挙. ¶a ***seditious*** *act* of violence 暴動的行為. ¶a noble ***selfsacrificing*** *act* りっぱな献身的行為. ¶a ***sexual*** *act* 性行為. ¶a ***shameful*** *act* 浅ましい行為. ¶it would be a ***statesmanlike*** *act* on the part of ... to ... …するのは…として政治家らしい処置というべきだ. ¶a ***thoughtful*** *act* 思慮深い行為. ¶grossly ***unconstitutional*** *acts* きわめて非立憲的な行為. ¶an ***unfair*** *act* 不公平の行為. ¶the performance of an ***unlawful*** *act* 不法行為の実行. ¶You have done a ***virtuous*** and ***humane*** *act* in translating that book so well. 君があんなにりっぱにあの本を翻訳したのは実に篤志で親切なことだ. ¶a ***well-justified*** *act* りっぱに弁明のできる行為. ¶a ***wicked*** *act* 非行. ¶do some ***wrongful*** or ***wicked*** *act* 不法なもしくはよこしまな行為をする.

Q² ¶a death-defying ***motor-cycle*** *act* 命知らずのオートバイの曲芸.

P He was caught ***in*** the ***act.*** 現場で(現行中に)つかまった. 【類】 He was taken ***in*** adultery (姦通) ***in*** the very ***act.*** / He was caught ***in*** the ***act*** of stealing.

P² an ***act of*** aggression 侵略行為 ‖ an ***act of*** audacity 無礼 ‖ an ***act of*** bankruptcy 破産行為 ‖ he thought it an ***act of*** charity to ... 彼は…に対する慈悲だと考えた ‖ an ***act of*** clemency [赦免など] 寛大な行為 ‖ an ***act of*** folly 愚行. 【類】 an ***act of*** folly amounting to wickedness ‖ an ***act of*** God 天災, 不可抗力 ‖ an ***act of*** kindness 親切. 【類】 an ***act of*** politeness / an ***act of*** retaliation (報復) ‖ an ***act of*** insulting and disrespectful nature 不敬の行為 ‖ It is the ***act of*** a mad man. 気違いざただ.

(2) 条例, 法令.

V ***frame*** *Acts* of Parliament 《英》 法令を編制する. ¶an *act* was ***passed*** empowering it to ... それに…の権能を賦与する法令が通過した. 【類】 The *Act* was ***passed*** by Congress and went into effect in August, 1950.

Q² the ***Dry*** *Act* 《米》 禁酒法. ¶the ***Cinematograph Films*** *Act* 《英》 映画取締法. ¶***Emergency Powers*** *Act* 非常時強権法. ¶the ***Lend-Lease*** *Act* 武器貸与法. ¶the ***Marriage Law Amendment*** *Act* 結婚法改正法. ¶the ***Mining*** *Act* 鉱業法. ¶the ***National Insurance*** *Act* 国民保険法. ¶a ***quarantine*** *act* 検疫停船法. ¶The ***Selective Service*** *Act* established peace-time conscription for the first time in American history. 徴兵制が出来て米国史上始めて平時徴兵が行われる事になった. ¶a ***Shop*** *Act* 商店法.

P ***by*** *Act* of Parliament 《英》 法令で. 【類】 All water used by the Metropolitan Fire Brigade for fire extinction purposes is supplied free ***by*** *Act* of Parliament. ‖ ***by*** *act* of law 法律に基いて. ¶***under*** this *Act* 本法により.

P² an ***act of*** procedure 訴訟行為.

(3) 幕, 段.

V She ***took*** her *act* to England and her opening performance at the Alhambra was a splendid success. 彼女は芝居をロンドンへ持って行きアルハンブラ座における初興行は大成功だった.

P ***between*** *acts* 幕間に. ¶a play ***in*** two *acts*=a two-act play 二幕もの.

act, *v.* 働く.

M He believed the report and *acted* ***accordingly.*** その

報道を信じそれに基いて行動した. ¶act ***advisedly*** 故意にやる. ¶*act* ***cautiously*** よく気をつけて行う. ¶*act* ***contemptibly*** 卑劣な振舞をする. ¶*act* ***contrary*** to reason 道理に合わぬことをする. ¶Some acids *act* ***corrosively***. 酸によっては腐食性がある. ¶*act* ***cowardly*** in a battle 戦に出て卑怯な振舞をする. ¶*act* ***craftily*** ずるく立ちまわる. ¶*act* ***dastardly*** 卑劣な振舞いをする. ¶*act* ***decisively*** 断然やり切る. ¶I advise you to *act* ***deliberately*** in such an important affair. こんな大切なことは考えてやり給え. ¶*act* ***diplomatically*** 外交的にやる. ¶*act* ***disloyally*** to ... ...に不忠実なことをする. ¶*act* ***disrespectfully*** towards ... ...に無礼なことをする. ¶*act* ***fair and square*** 公明正大に行動する. ¶I admit that I have *acted* ***foolishly*** in what I did. われながらばかな真似をしたものだ. 【類】It is not at all likely that he will *act* so ***foolishly*** as that. ¶*act* ***halfheartedly*** いい加減にやる. ¶*act* ***harshly*** がさつなことをする. ¶*act* ***hastily*** (=***quickly***) 急いでする. ¶*act* ***indiscreetly*** 軽率なまねをする. ¶*act* ***ignobly*** 浅ましい振舞をする. ¶*act* ***injuriously*** on the system 健康を害する. ¶*act* ***judiciously*** よろしきを得た所置をとる. ¶*act* ***justly*** towards ... ...に対して正当なことをする. ¶*act* ***manly*** 男らしくふるまう. ¶*act* ***nobly*** りっぱに行動する. ¶*act* ***precipitately*** 短兵急にやる. ¶*Act* ***promptly*** or the opportunity will be gone. てきぱきやらないと機会をのがしてしまう. ¶*act* ***prudently*** 慎重にやる. ¶To *act* ***rashly*** is a losing game. 軽卒なやり方は結局損だ. ¶*act* ***rightly*** 至当なことをする. ¶*act* ***selfishly*** わが侭をする. ¶*act* ***sensibly*** 賢明にふるまう. ¶*act* ***squarely*** and ***above-board*** 公明正大にふるまう. ¶*act* very ***unadvisedly*** 無分別すぎる振舞をする. ¶*act* ***unexpectedly*** だし抜く. ¶*act* ***unwisely*** まずいことをやる. ¶*act* ***vigorously*** for the eradication of yellow fever 黄熱病撲滅に努力する. ¶*act* ***warily*** in order to detect ... ...を看破するために用心深くふるまう. ¶The medicine *acts* ***well***. この薬はよくきく. ‖ *act* one's part ***well*** 自分の役割をりっぱに勤める. ¶*act* ***wisely*** 賢明にふるまう. ¶I have *acted* very ***wrongly*** toward you. 本当に済まないことをした.

P *act* ***according to*** instructions 指図通りにする. 【類】*act* ***according to*** one's conscience (conviction). ¶*act* ***against*** one's own interest 自分のためにならぬことをする ‖ *act* ***against*** the will of ... ...にさからう ‖ He *acted* ***against*** my advice. 彼は僕の忠告を守らなかった. 【類】I had to *act* ***against*** my own judgment (止むを得ず). ¶*act* ***as*** consultant on problems relating to ... ...問題の顧問を勤める. 【類】*act* ***as*** amanuensis (筆記者) for ... / *act* ***as*** a German spy / *act* ***as*** agents for ... / *act* ***as*** an antidote (解毒剤) to ... / *act* ***as*** a stimulus (刺激) / *act* ***as*** an irritant / stretch ribbons to *act* ***as*** barriers (境界) / *act* ***as*** conductor / *act* ***as*** a buffer (緩衝的な役割) ***against*** ... / *act* ***as*** one's deputy (代理) / *act* ***as*** go-between (仲人) / *act* ***as*** interpreter for ... / *act* ***as*** receptionist (接待掛) / *act* ***as*** umpire ‖ It *acted* ***as*** a talisman to call forth past memories. それが過去の記憶をよび起す御符となった. ‖ Alcohol *acts* ***as*** a poison to a child. アルコールは子供に毒になる. ‖ A corporation is a body formed to *act* ***as*** single person. 法人は一個人同様の仕事をする団体である. ‖ a table to *act* ***as*** pantry, larder and what not 食器室食料置場その他いろいろに使われる調理台. ¶Boys delight to *act* ***at*** being soldiers, horses, and many queer things. 子供というものは兵隊とか馬とかその他種々の変ったことをして遊ぶのが好きなものだ. ¶She *acts* ***before*** the camera and on the stage. 彼女は映画女優もやれば舞台にも立つ. ¶He *acted* ***for*** the Russian Goverment as secret agent. 彼はロシア政府のためスパイをやった. ‖ I *acted* ***for*** him. 彼の代理をした. 【類】He *acted* ***for*** his interest. ¶She *acted* ***from*** jealousy. 彼女はしっと心でやった. 【類】*act* ***from*** impulse (はずみ) / *act* ***from*** instinct (本能) / He *acted* ***from*** caprice (出来心). / *act* ***from*** a sense of duty (義務感) ‖ We should not always *act* merely ***from*** a regard to ourselves. われわれはいつも自己本位でのみ行動すべきでない. ¶He was released on the ground that he was *acting* ***in*** self-defense. 彼は正当防衛の理由で放免された. ‖ *act* ***in*** movies 映画に出演する ‖ *act* ***in*** concert (=unison) with ... ...と一致してやる ‖ *acting* ***in*** collusion 示し合せて. ¶*act* ***like*** one man 一致協力してやる ‖ *act* ***like*** an ostrich 頭隠してしり隠さず, 浅はかな振舞をする ‖ Her refusal to accompany him *acted* ***like*** a wet blanket. 彼女が彼に同行を拒んだのは彼をしょげさせることになった. ¶Acids *act* ***on*** metals. 酸は金属に作用を及ぼす. ‖ He *acted* ***on*** the faith of what he had been told. 彼は言われた通りを信じてやった. 【類】*act* ***on*** the idea / *act* ***on*** another's advice (suggestion, one's principle) / *act* ***on*** impluse (一時の感情) ‖ *act* ***on*** one's behalf 人の代りをする ‖ *acting* ***on*** a previously-determined plan (きまった計画) / *act* ***on*** one's knowledge ‖ Last week the Senate *acted* ***on*** the House measure. 《米》先週上院は下院の案を審議した. ‖ I have *acted* ***on*** the square to them. 私は彼らに対して正当に振舞った. ¶*act* ***out of*** pity. あわれみの心からやる. 【類】I *acted* ***out of*** spleen (腹立ちまぎれ). ¶In this your father is *acting* ***through*** me. これは君のお父さんになり代ってやってるのだ. ¶I will *act* ***to*** the best of my judgment. 僕は十分考えてやりましょう. ¶He *acted* nobly ***towards*** the enemy. 彼は敵に対してりっぱに振舞った. ¶*act* ***under*** the coercion of ... ...に強いられてやる. 【類】*act* ***under*** compulsion (強いられて). ¶*act* ***up to*** a promise 約束を履行する. 【類】*act* ***up to*** one's ideal / *Act* ***up to*** your belief. ¶*act* ***upon*** (=on) a maxim of a wise man 賢人の格言を服膺(ﾖｳ)する. 【類】*act* ***upon*** a rule / *act* ***upon*** your opinion ... / He did not *act* ***upon*** my order. / *act* ***upon*** (=on) one's own judgment ‖ This drug *acts* ***upon*** the nerves. この薬は神経にきく. ¶*act* ***with*** great composure 泰然とやる. 【類】*act* ***with*** vigor / He *acted* ***with*** the most perfect sense (判断). / *act* ***with*** extreme caution (注意深く) ‖ I *acted* ***with*** her in the Sphinx. 私はスフィンクスという劇にあの女と一緒に出演した. ¶*act* ***without*** thought 考えなくやる. 【類】He *acted* ***without*** any thought of the consequence (結果). / *act* ***without*** authority (権限).

acting, *n.* 行為, 所作.

Q ***good*** (***poor***) *acting* of poor (good) plays 悪い(良い)劇の良い(悪い)演出. ¶***psychological*** (=***subjective***) *acting* 腹芸. ¶***successful*** *acting* 当り芸.

Q² ***motion picture*** *acting* 映画俳優の演技.

P² *acting* ***on*** the stage 舞台上の所作.

action, *n.* (**1**) 行動, 動作; 行為.

V ***commence*** *acting* against ... ...に対して行動を始める. ¶***condemn*** the hasty *action* of ... ...の短気な行動を責める. ¶***criticize*** unreservedly the *actions* of public men 公人の行動を遠慮なく批評する. ¶***defend*** my *action* in taking the step 私がその行動に出たことを弁護する. ¶***delay*** *action* 行動を手間どらせる. ¶***deprecate*** hasty *action* 短気な行動をいさめる. ¶I am told you have again ***done*** a mad-brained *action*. 君はまた気違いじみたことをやったそうだね. ¶***emulate*** the virtuous *actions* of great and good men 偉い人たちの徳行にならう. ¶***initiate*** *action* 行動を開始する. ¶***judge*** the *actions* of the past by the moral standard of our own age 現代の道徳標準で過去の行動を批判する. ¶***misrepresent*** an *action* 行為を曲げて伝える. ¶I have tried to recall what ***motivated*** my *action* on this occasion. この場合僕の行動の動機となったものを想起しようと努めた. ¶***obstruct*** the free *action* of ... ...の自由行動を妨げる. ¶***perform*** a friendly *action* 親切なことをする. ¶***suiting*** the *action* to the word, he ... そういうなり彼は ... ¶***take*** *action* (=***act***) on a plan 案を実行する / ***take*** *action* with a view to ... ...の目的で処置を執る. 【類】***take*** *action* with regard to ... / An *action* must be ***taken*** to check this tendency. / ***take*** *action* in a body (一体となって) / slow in ***taking*** *action*. ¶the psychological motive which ***underlines*** the *action* of ... ...の行動の裏面に伏在する心理的動機. ¶***withstand*** the *action* of fire 火に耐える.

V² The *action* seemed rather to ***drag***. [俳優などの]しぐさはちとだれ気味であった.

Q an ***awkward*** *action* 無作法. ¶do a ***bad*** *action* 悪いことをする. ¶require ***careful*** *action* 注意して行動する必要がある. ¶***common*** *action* among nations 列国の共同的行動. ¶take ***concerted*** *action* with the Powers 列強と歩調をそろえる. 【類】A ***concerted*** and ***unified*** *action* is required. ¶***corresponding*** *action* with ... ...と相応じて行動する. ¶a ***criminal*** *action* 犯罪行為. ¶a ***decisive*** *action* 断固たる行動. ¶do a ***dishonest*** *action* 不正を働く. ¶a ***drastic*** *action* 思い切った事. ¶clear thinking and ***due*** *action* in good times 違眼機を見て善処すること. ¶as ***first action*** 第一着に. ¶take ***free action*** 自由行動を取る. ¶stop (=suspend) all ***further action*** for the present 当分これ以上の行動を一切停止する. ¶do a ***good action*** よいことをする. ¶***hasty*** or ***ill-considered action*** 気早のまたは無分別な行動. ¶a ***high-handed action*** 高圧手段. ¶an ***idle*** and ***unworthy action*** 無益なくだらない行為. ¶an ***ignoble action*** 卑劣な行動. ¶an ***illiberal*** and ***arbitrary action*** 偏狭で気ままな行動. ¶take ***immediate*** (=***prompt***) *action* さっそく処置する. ¶take ***independent action*** 自由行動をとる. ¶an ***insistent action*** 押付けがましい行動. ¶a ***kind*** action on the part of ... ...の親切な行為. ¶***legislative*** or ***other actions*** 立法その他の措置. ¶His *action* is ***light*** (***stiff, constrained, overdrawn***). [俳優などの] 所作が軽妙 (生硬, 窮屈, 誇大)だ. ¶a ***never-to-be-forgotton action*** 忘れようのない行為. ¶by ***official action*** 職務上. ¶***political action*** 政治行動. ¶His *action* is ***praiseworthy*** 彼の行は奇特なことだ. ¶***public actions*** 公人的諸行動. ¶***public-spirited action*** 気慨のある行動. ¶take more ***radical action*** against ... ...に対して一層根本的な処置を執る. ¶take ***remedial action*** 救済策を講じる. ¶take ***similar action*** 同様の所置をとる. ¶take ***strong action*** for ... ...に対し強硬な処置をとる. ¶***unchristian actions*** on the part of Christian nations キリスト教国側の非キリスト教的な仕打. ¶take ***united action*** 一致行動をとる. ¶an ***unpatriotic action*** 非愛国的行動. ¶take ***vigorous action*** きびきびやる.

Q^2 a ***bowel action*** every day 一日一回の便通. ¶***Breath*** and ***heart action*** ceased for six minutes. 呼吸と心臓の鼓動が六分間止った. ¶take ***emergency action*** 応急処置をとる. ¶owing to ***enemy action*** 敵の行動のために. ¶***government action*** for social welfare 社会福祉を増進するための政府の処置. ¶***group action*** 団体行動. ¶revolutionary ***mass action*** 革命的集団行動. 【類】through the ***mass action*** of women's organizations. ¶brand a ***police action*** as illegal ある警察行為を違法だと断じる.

P ***after*** an *action* of the bowels 便通後に. ¶judge a person ***by*** his *action* その行為で人物を判断する ‖ Rumanian Jews driven out ***by*** the *action* of the Government 政府の力で放逐されたルーマニアのユダヤ人. ¶They are ready ***for action***. 一同活動の用意ができている. 【類】The time has come ***for action***. ¶Christianity ***in action*** 活動しているキリスト教. ‖ natural forces ***in action*** along the coast 沿岸に働きかける自然力 ‖ like a beast ***in action*** 動作は獣のように. 【類】be quick (slow) ***in action***. ¶put it ***into action*** それを実行する ‖ be crystallized ***into action*** 実行の段どりになる ‖ be persuaded ***into action*** 説きつけられてやる. ¶a man ***of action*** 活動家. ¶put the propaganda ***out of action*** 宣伝をとめる. ¶Say it ***with action***. その心を行動で表現せよ. ☞ "Say it with flowers" 「その心を花で」.

(2) 作用.

V ***exert*** a chemical *action* on ... ...に化学作用を及ぼす. ¶***hinder*** the *action* of soap 石けんの作用を妨げる(利き目を失わせる). ¶It ***resists*** the *action* of fire. それは火力に耐える.

Q by means of ***chemical action*** 化学作用で. ¶It is brought about by the ***combined action*** of several factors. それは幾多要素の総合的作用によって生じる. ¶have an ***injurious action*** on ... ...に有害な作用を及ぼす. ¶by a ***pure reflex action*** 全くの反射作用で(おのずと, 我知らず). ¶by ***reciprocal action*** 交互作用で. ¶the ***stimulant action*** of caviare on the genital organs 生殖器に及ぼすキアビアの刺激作用.

P ***by*** the *action* of an acid 酸の作用により ‖ ***by*** the *action* of the weather 風化作用で. ¶***under action*** of the water 水の作用を受けて.

P^2 ***action of*** rain water ***on*** lead 鉛に及ぼす雨水の作用.

(3) 〖法〗訴訟.

V ***abandon*** an *action* 訴訟を取下げる. ¶***bring*** an *action* against ... ...に対して訴訟を提起する. 【類】***bring in*** an *action* in a court against ... relating to a claim for ... ‖ ***bring*** an *action* at law 裁判沙汰にする. ¶the *action* has been ***decided*** against (in favor of) ... ...の敗(勝)訴となった. ¶***defer action*** 〖法〗所置を延期する. ¶***dismiss*** the *action* against ... ...に対する訴訟を却下する. ¶***file*** an *action* in a court against ... ...に対して訴訟を提出する. ¶***have*** an *action* against ... ...に対し訴訟を起す. ¶the judge ***heard*** the *action* brought by him against ... 判事は...に対して彼の提起した訴訟を調べた. ¶***institute*** an *action* 起訴する. ¶***raise*** an *action* of damages against ... ...に対して損害賠償の訴訟を起す. ¶***renounce*** one's *action* その訴訟を廃棄する. ¶***take*** legal *action* 起訴する ‖ ***take*** any *action* that may be deemed wise and effectual 適当かつ有効と認める措置を執る.

Q ***civil action*** 民事訴訟. ¶the defendant has brought a ***cross action*** demanding back ... 被告は...取戻しの反訴を提起した. ¶***private action*** (=lynching) 私刑. ¶***public action*** 公訴.

P The only redress open is ***by*** an *action* at law. 訴訟によって賠償させる外に手はない.

P^2 an ***action for*** compensation for damage 損害賠償の訴訟 ‖ an ***action for*** divorce 離婚訴訟 ‖ an ***action for*** libel 誹毀(ひ)罪の訴訟.

(4) 戦, 戦闘.

V ***commence action*** 開戦する. ¶***fight*** an indecisive *action* with ... ...と勝敗の決せぬ戦争をする. ¶***witness*** a naval *action* 海戦を見る.

Q^2 ***day action*** 白昼戦.

P He is missing ***in action*** in Korea. 彼は朝鮮戦線で行方不明になっている. ‖ He was killed ***in action*** in France. フランスで戦死した. 【類】The soldier was unfortunate enough to have his nose carried away ***in action*** by a bullet.

activate *v.* 活動的にする.

P ***activated by*** selfish motives 利己的な動機に動かされて.

active, *a.* 活動する.

P He is ***active about*** some business. あることについて活動している. ¶He is ***active for*** an object. ある目的のために活動している. 【類】be ***active for*** her feed (生活のため). ¶He is ***active in*** work. 盛んに働いている. 【類】***active in*** doing good to men / ***active in*** his welfare work (厚生事業) ‖ participles ***active in*** meaning 〖文〗能動態の意味をもつ分詞.

activity, *n.* 活動; 好景気.

V ***acquire*** a healthy *activity* 健全に活動するようになる. ¶***arrest*** its *activity* その活動を妨げる. ¶***assume*** full *activity* 十分に活動し出す. ¶***centralize*** the various *activities* of the theater 劇場の各種にわたる事業の中心を作る. ¶***continue*** one's literary *activity* 引続き文筆を執る. ¶***coordinate activities*** 活動を調整する. ¶***cramp*** the *activities* of ... ...の活動を妨げる. ¶***develop*** an intellectual *activity* 知的活動を発展させる. ¶I have ***devoted*** my whole *activities* to the cause for a quarter of a century. 専心その主義のために四半世紀の間働いてきた. ¶***direct*** one's *activity* against ... ...反対の運動をする. ¶***display*** considerable *activity* 著しい活動ぶりを見せる. ¶Japan is now ***enjoying*** great commercial and industrial *activity*. 日本の商工業は現在大いに活動している. ¶The police is ***exhibiting*** the greatest *activity* in searching for the criminal. 警察は犯罪人の捜索に手を尽している. ¶***extend*** one's *activities* to America and Europe 欧米まで(事業の)手を拡げる. ¶What ***motivated*** this furious *activity?* 何がこの猛烈な活動の動機となったのか. ¶***paralyse*** the *activity* of ... ...の活動力をまひさせる. ¶Business is ***recovering activity***. 景気が直りだした. ¶***repress activity*** 活動を抑える. ¶***restore*** the functional *activity* of ... ...の機能を回復する. ¶The new association has ***started*** its *activities*. 新設の協会は事業を開始した. ¶Theaters temporarily ***stopped*** their *activities* owing to the prevalence of influenza. 劇場は悪性感冒流行のため一時興行を中止した.

Q There was immense ***argumentative activity*** in the newspapers and in the magazines over the question. その問題について新聞雑誌に大議論があった. ¶***baleful activities*** of enemy aliens in England 英国における在住敵国人の有害な活動. ¶this age of ***bustling activity*** このいそがしい時代. ¶What we call thought is only the product of ***cerebral activity***. われらの思想と称するものは脳の活動の産物に過ぎない. ¶He was arrested and placed on trial for ***communistic activities***. 彼は赤化運動でつかまって調べられた. ¶a wife's ***excessive activities*** outside the home 家庭外における人妻の過度の活動. ¶***extra-curricular*** (=***-curriculum***) *activities* in college 大学における課外活動. 【類】take part in ***extra-curricular activities*** /

the multitudinous (多様の) ***extra-curricular*** *activities* which play such a large part in the development of the individual (個性) in the college environment. ¶***feverish*** *activity* 奮励. ¶be in ***full*** *activity* 盛んに活動している. ¶***housewifely*** *activity* 家政. ¶a branch of ***human*** *activity* 一つの事業. ¶***illegal*** *activities* 違法の活動. ¶in the world of ***inner*** *activity* 精神界において. ¶people of ordinary ***intellectual*** *activity* 常人の知能を備えた人. 【類】in nearly every department of ***intellectual*** *activity*. ¶his ***innumerable*** *activities* 彼の多方面の活動. ¶He is widely known as a peace propagandist in addition to his ***many other*** *activities*. 他の多くの活動の外に平和の宣伝者として彼は知れわたっている. ¶the ***many-sided*** *activities* of the firm あの商店の多角的な事業. ¶***mental*** and ***physical*** *activities* 心身の活動. ¶***misdirected*** *activities* 指導宜しきを得ない活動. ¶***organized*** *activities* 統制ある活動. ¶***philanthropic*** *activities* 慈善事業. ¶***poetic*** *activity* 作詩の仕事. ¶a period of ***political*** *activity* 政治的活動の時期. ¶***prewar*** and ***postwar*** *activities* 戦前戦後の事業. ¶***productive*** *activities* 生産方面の活動. ¶***profitless*** and ***wasteful*** *activities* 利益のない不経済な事業. ¶***purposeful*** *activity* 目標のある仕事. ¶his last ***remaining*** *activity* 残務. ¶Communist-led ***subversive*** *activities* 共産党指導による破壊的活動. ¶***terroristic*** *activities* 暴力活動. ¶***un-American*** *activities* of the communists 共産党の非米活動. ¶***united*** *activity* 団体活動. ¶***unremitting*** *activity* 絶間ない活動. ¶a ***third*** *activity* of the company その会社の第三の事業. ¶engage in years of ***useful*** *activity* 多年有益な事業にたずさわる. ¶The volcano burst into ***violent*** *activity*. 火山は突然猛烈な活動を始めた. ¶***worthwhile*** *activities* やりがいのある事業.

Q^{2} ***Army subsistence*** *activities* 兵站(たん)部の活動. ¶***Banking*** *activities* are at standstill. 銀行事業が停止状態になっている. ¶the ***behind-the-scenes*** *activities* 暗躍. ¶a shopkeeper suspected of ***black market*** *activities* 闇取引の疑いある商店主. 【類】stamp out (撲滅する) ***black market*** *activities*. ¶***business, industrial,*** and ***amusement*** *activities* 商業, 産業及び娯楽関係の事業. ¶participate in ***campus*** *activities* 学内活動に加わる ‖ undergraduates' ***campus*** and ***community*** *activities* 学生の大学内及び学外活動. ¶a ***classroom*** *activity* 教室活動. ¶***Communist propaganda*** *activity* 共産党の宣伝工作. ¶***counterpropaganda*** *activities* 逆宣伝工作. ¶***espionage*** *activities* スパイ活動. ¶the so-called "***fifth-column***" *activities* in Europe 欧州のいわゆる第五列活動. ¶commercialized ***gambling*** *activities* 商業化した賭博. ¶***government*** *activities* 政府の事業. ¶enter into ***group*** *activities* with ... ...の集団活動に加わる. ¶***home-room*** *activities* 〖教育〗ホームルーム活動. ¶***lecturing*** *activities* 講演の仕事. ¶choose wholesome ***leisure time*** *activities* 健全な娯楽を選ぶ. ¶the ***life*** *activities* of the vegetation 草木の生態. ¶***Red*** (=***Communist***) *activities* 共産主義活動. ¶the combination of ***retail*** and ***manufacturing*** *activities* 小売と製造の兼業. ¶***school*** *activities* 校内活動. ¶***social service*** *activities* 社会奉仕活動. ¶***spy*** *activities* in the United States 米国内のスパイ活動. ¶***student*** *activities* such as dramatics, publications, and athletics 演劇, 出版, 運動競技などの学生活動. ¶***talking*** and ***writing*** *activities* 舌と筆による活動. ¶be found guilty of ***terrorist*** *activities* 暴動のかどにより有罪と認められる. ¶[labor] ***union*** *activities* [労働]組合運動. ¶Such teaching does not come within the sphere of ***university*** *activity*. こうした授業は大学教育の中には入らぬ. ¶the cessation of ***war*** *activities* 休戦.

P^{2} his *activities* ***as*** a broadcaster ラジオ放送者としての彼の活躍. ¶*activity* ***in*** trade 商売の好景気. ¶the *activity* ***of*** a volcano 火山の活動 ‖ one of the *activities* ***of*** the Y.M.C.A. キリスト教青年会の事業の一. ¶*Activity* ***with*** mistakes is better than indolence without mistakes. なまけていて失策しないよりも活動して失策する方がましだ.

actor, *n.* 俳優.

V The *actor* was ***applauded***. 役者はかっさいされた. ¶The *actor* was ***called*** before the curtain. [アンコールで]役者は幕前に呼出された. ¶***cast*** an *actor* for a part 俳優に役を振当てる. ¶The *actor* was ***encored***. 役者はアンコールを受けた. ¶The *actor* was ***hissed***. その俳優はやじられた.

V^{2} This *actor* will ***appear*** in the charactor of Hamlet. この役者はハムレットの役を勤める. ¶A good *actor* ***draws***. 一人よい役者がいると入りが違う.

Q a very ***celebrated*** *actor* 大評判の俳優. ¶the ***first*** *actor* of the part その役を最初に勤めた俳優. ¶a company of ***itinerant*** *actors* 旅役者の一行. ¶He is a ***good*** *actor* as *actors* go nowaday. 今日の俳優並から言えば彼は相当な役者だ. ¶a ***versatile*** and ***finished*** *actor* 多芸で円熟した俳優.

Q^{2} a ***character*** *actor* 性格俳優. ¶a ***film*** (=***movie***) *actor* 映画俳優. ¶a topnotch ***film*** *actor* 一流の映画俳優. ¶***minor role*** *actors* 端役. ¶an ***Oscar*** *actor* (*actress*) 〖映〗オスカー(アカデミー)賞を受けた俳優. ¶a ***part-time*** *actor* and the master of ceremonies on a show 臨時俳優兼ショウの司会者. 【類】The ***screen*** (=***movie***) *actor* returned to the stage after a fifteen year absence. ¶a ***stage*** *actor* of eminence 有名な舞台俳優. ¶a ***star*** *actor* 花形役者.

P^{2} an *actor* ***of*** female rôles 女形.

actress, *n.* 女優.

Q She thrilled with delight on seeing her ***favorite*** *actress*. 好きな女優を見てうれしさに胸がわくわくした. ¶an ***undistinguished*** *actress* 名の売れていない女優.

Q^{2} an American ***comedy*** *actress* 米国の喜劇女優. ¶a ***motion-picture*** and ***radio*** *actress* 映画と放送に出る女優. ¶a ***stage*** and ***screen*** *actress* 舞台と映画に出演する女優.

P^{2} an *actress* ***in*** comedy = a comedienne 喜劇女優.

actuate, *v.* 活動させる, 駆る.

P *actuated* ***by*** public spirit 公共精神に燃えて ‖ *actuated* ***by*** intense patriotic avidity 憂国の至情に燃えて. 【類】*actuated* ***by*** the highest ideals / A great statesman is *actuated* ***by*** love of his country, not by love of power (権力). / I have been *actuated* ***by*** the best intentions in addressing you these few lines (短かい手紙). / *actuated* ***by*** higher ideas. ¶He was *actuated* ***to*** the crime by revenge. 復しゅう心にかられてその罪を犯した.

acumen, *n.* 鋭敏, 洞察力.

V ***display*** great *acumen* in doing ... ...に大手腕を示す. ¶The critic and the metaphysician ***require*** unusual *acumen*. 批評家と哲学者には非凡の英知が必要だ.

Q ***critical*** *acumen* 批評眼. ¶***legal*** *acumen* 法律の才.

Q^{2} ***business*** *acumen* 商才.

acupuncture, *n.* 鍼(り)術.

V ***apply*** *acupuncture* はりを打つ.

ad, =advertisement, advertising, *n.* 広告.

V ***insert*** *ads* in a magazine 雑誌に広告をのせる. ¶the ***circus*** *ads* in the subways 地下鉄の曲馬団の広告.

Q^{2} a ***want*** *ad* in a daily 日刊紙の「求む」広告.

adage, *n.* 諺.

V ***fulfilling*** the *adage* that ... ...のたとえにもれず.

Q as in the ***homely*** *adage* 俗諺にもある通り. ¶the ***oft-referred*** *adage* of ... ...というよく持出される諺.

P ***according to*** an old *adage* 古諺によれば.

adapt, *v.* 適応させる.

M It is ***admirably*** *adapted* for a school prize. これは学校の賞品用にうってつけだ. ¶accommodation ***best*** *adapted* for the requirements of travelers 旅客の要求によく適した設備. 【類】the calling (職業) ***best*** *adapted* to one's taste. ¶goods ***especially*** *adapted* for gift 特に贈答向きの品. ¶***freely*** *adapted* from ... ...を大分変更してつづった. ¶streets ***ill*** *adapted* for the residence of wealthy persons 富豪連の住居には向かない街. ¶*adapt* oneself ***rhetorically*** to one's surroundings 人を見て法を説く. ¶***well*** *adapted* to local conditions 土地の状態に適合している.

P She is not *adapted* ***for*** such work. あの女はこんな仕事には向かない. ‖ boilers *adapted* ***for*** burning wood まき兼用のボイラー. ‖ an opera *adapted* ***for*** the English stage by ... ...氏が英国の舞台向きに翻案した歌劇. 【類】books *adapted* ***for*** Japanese students / a course of practical physics (応用物理学) *adapted* ***for*** elementary students ‖ The house was *adapted* ***for*** occupation. その家ははいれるように改造された. ¶*adapt* ***from*** a well-known book (author) 有名な本(など)から翻案する. 【類】abridged and *adapted* ***from*** the original. ¶*adapt* ***to*** (=for) a purpose 目的に適合させる. 【類】*adapt* oneself ***to*** circumstances (environment) ‖ The region is well *adapted* ***to*** apple culture. その辺はリンゴの栽培に適してい

る. ‖ The matter is *adapted* ***to*** the understanding of American readers. 内容はアメリカの読者に分るようにしてある. 【類】become more *adapted* ***to*** a new position.

adaptability, *n.* 適応性.

V ***show*** great *adaptability* for ... ...に大いに適していることを示す.

Q² ***business*** *adaptability* 仕事に対する適応性.

P² the *adaptability* ***of*** an organism ***to*** its surroundings 生物の外界に対する順応性.

adaptation, *n.* 適応; 改作.

Q² ***light*** (***dark***) *adaptation* 明(暗)適応. ¶stage plays suitable for ***screen*** *adaptation* 上映に適した劇.

P² an *adaptation* ***from*** another work 他書からのやき直し. ¶an *adaptation* ***of*** the "Garden City" system 田園都市制の応用. ¶a wise *adaptation* ***of*** means ***to*** end 巧みに手段を目的に適応させること.

add, *v.* 加える.

M *add* ***a good deal*** to the appearance of the town 大いにその都市の外観をよくする. ¶The index *adds* ***appreciably*** to the usefulness of the book. その本は索引が付いているために際立って役に立つ. ¶This *added* ***considerably*** to his experiences. このことは彼にとって大いに経験になった. 【類】It *adds* ***considerably*** to the effect (効果). / The beautiful plates (挿画) *add* ***considerably*** to its attractiveness. / This *adds* ***considerably*** to the flavor (風味) of the dish. ¶*add* ***constantly*** to one's knowledge 絶えず知識を増す. ¶It will *add* ***greatly*** to the cost. そのために大いに入費が増すだろう. 【類】*add* ***greatly*** to our knowledge and understanding of ... / That *added* ***greatly*** to the gaiety (にぎやかさ) of the occasion. / *add* ***greatly*** to the charm of the room / *add* ***greatly*** to the interest of the exhibition / *add* ***greatly*** to the prestige of ... ¶That *adds* ***heavily*** to the difficulty of my position. それで僕の立場が非常に苦しくなる. ¶This *adds* ***immensely*** to its interest. このためにそれが大変興味を増す. ¶The lake *adds* ***much*** to the beauty of the landscape. 湖水が大いに風景を美しくする. 【類】*add* ***much*** to one's knowledge and one's taste. ¶The statistics *add* ***not a little*** to the value of the publication. 統計がすくなからずその出版物の価値を増す. ¶***parenthetically*** we may *add* that ... ちなみに言う. ¶He *added* ***philosophically.*** 悟り顔に言葉を添えた. ¶*add* ***steadily*** to one's stock of words 語彙の数をだんだんふやす. ¶*add* ***together*** these figures これらの数字を合計する.

M² There is an error in *adding* ***up*** 寄せ方が違っている. 【類】*Add* ***up*** these figures and see if the sum is correct.

P *added* (=in addition) ***to*** this (these) おまけに ‖ to *add* ***to*** their infamy あまつさえ ‖ Electric illuminations *add* ***to*** the attraction at night. 電気のイルミネーションが夜景に美を添える. 【類】The gorgeous (豪華な) costume *added* ***to*** the brilliance of the dance. / *add* ***to*** complication (複雑) / inventions which *add* ***to*** our daily comfort / It *added* ***to*** the enjoyment of my visit. / *add* ***to*** the interest (general utility) of the book / It *added* ***to*** the hilarity (陽気さ) of the excursion. / *add* ***to*** one's income / His enforced separation from his beautiful young wife *added* ***to*** the pathos of the tragic situation (一層悲惨を深める). / *add* ***to*** the bitterness of life / These new features will *add* ***to*** the personal pleasure of spectators. / *add* ***to*** one's travel pleasure / *add* ***to*** the picturesqueness of the place / *add* ***to*** its popularity as a pleasure resort (歓楽境) / He *added* ***to*** the power and dignity of his kingdom (国威を宣揚した) by conquest. / *add* ***to*** the glory of the realm (その国) by ... / *add* ***to*** his responsibilities / The work *added* ***to*** his reputation. / *add* ***to*** the bright tone (明るい調子) of the poem / Children *add* ***to*** the weight of the struggle for existence of their parents. / *add* ***to*** one's store of information (見聞) / *add* ***to*** her stock of knowledge of her favorite study / *add* ***to*** the sum of human knowledge / *add* ***to*** the terror ‖ insult *added* ***to*** injury けがをさせた上に加えた侮辱(ふんだりけったり) ‖ He is *adding* ***to*** his house. 彼は家を建増している. 【類】is *added* ***to*** the day's work / Discovery has been *added* ***to*** discovery. ‖ Twenty-five *added* ***to*** fifteen is equal to forty. 十五に二十五を加えれば四十だ. ‖ to *add* ***to*** the fun さらに興味あることは ‖ to *add* ***to*** one's misfortunes 泣きっつらにはちで. 【類】to *add* ***to*** the grief of a person.

addict, *n.* たんでき者.

Q² ***alcohol*** *addicts* 酒飲み. ¶an ***antiques*** *addicts* 骨とう道楽の人. ¶an ***opiate*** *addict* アヘン常用者. ¶***cafe society*** *addicts* よくカフェーに出入する人たち. ¶***shore*** or ***mountain*** *addicts* 好んで海や山へ行く人.

addict, *v.* ふけらせる.

M He was ***passionately*** *addicted* to skating. 彼はスケートに熱中した. ¶He was ***unduly*** *addicted* to study. 彼は過度に勉強した.

P He was *addicted* ***to*** gambling. 彼は賭博にふけった. 【類】He was *addicted* ***to*** drunkenness. / He was *addicted* ***to*** all sorts of vice. / He is *addicted* ***to*** low company (下等な連中). / He *addicted* himself ***to*** drinking. / *addict* oneself ***to*** the use of alcoholic stimulants (酒) / be *addicted* ***to*** drugs ‖ be *addicted* ***to*** ill speaking 口がわるい.

addiction, *n.* たんでき.

P resulting ***from*** *addiction* to the bottle 酒にひたるのが「原因で.

addition, *n.* 増加.

V This ***brought*** an *addition* of ¥... to the original estimate. このために予算が...円ふえた. ¶we may ***expect*** *addition* to our knowledge of ... ...に関する我々の知識を一層増す事ができるものと見てよい.

Q He had ***another*** *addition* to his family. あの人の所にまた一人子供がふえた. ¶The book is a most ***desirable*** *addition* to the library of every business man. それはどの実業家の書斎にもぜひあってほしい書である. ¶an ***important*** *addition* to the already voluminous literature of Hearn ハーンに関する多大の既刊文献の中に加えるべき重要な新刊書. ¶an ***indispensable*** *addition* to every sporting library スポーツ関係書の中にぜひ加えるべき書. ¶an ***interesting*** *addition* to the literature of the subject その方面の文献に対する一つの興味ある追加. ¶***late*** *additions* to the zoological gardens 動物園へ近ごろ来た動物 ‖ the ***latest*** *addition* to this number 以上の数に最近加えられたもの. ¶a ***much-to-be-welcomed*** *addition* to ... ...中に大いに歓迎さるべきもの. ¶There should be no ***needless*** *addition* to the making of books. これ以上無益な著作を公にすべきでない. ¶the ***newest*** *addition* to the fleet of the N.Y.K. 日本郵船会社最近の新造船. 【類】the ***newest*** *addition* to the American Navy. ¶an ***outstanding*** *addition* to the literature of the subject その方面の文献に対する一大貢献. ¶The work will doubtless prove a highly ***popular*** *addition* to the list of schoolbooks. この本はきっと非常に受けのよい教科書となるでしょう. ¶The new ship is a ***valuable*** *addition* to the British Navy. その新造艦は英海軍の威力を一段と増すものである. ‖ make a ***valuable*** *addition* to the literature of the subject その部門に属する文献に含まるべき貴重な書を一つ加える. 【類】a most ***valuable*** *addition* to our legal literature. ¶a ***welcome*** *addition* to historical literature 歴史の文献に属する新良書 ‖ The careless, slovenly writer is not a ***welcome*** *addition* to the staff of any paper. ずぼらな記者はどの新聞社にも歓迎されない.

P I met some friends and other people ***in*** *addition.* 私は数人の友だちとなおほかの人たちにも会った. ‖ ***in*** *addition* to this そこへもって来て. 【類】***in*** *addition* to his salary / ***in*** *addition* to the order previously sent (前に出した注文).

P² *addition* ***of*** revenue to the national exchequer 国庫歳入の増加.

address, *n.* (**1**) 演説, 式辞.

V ***deliver*** an *address* to a large number of educators 多数の教育家に向って演説する. ¶***draft out*** an *address* 演説の草稿を作る. ¶***follow*** an *address* with interest and appreciation 興味を持ち, 味わいながら演説を聴く. ¶***give*** an impressive *address* 人を感動させるような演説をする. ¶***hear*** an *address* from him 彼の演説を聴く. ¶President Wilson ***made*** an *address* on the occasion. その折にウイルスン大統領が式辞を述べた. ¶***present*** one's *address* [書いた]式辞を捧呈する. ¶***propagate*** inflammatory *address* throughout the country 全国に檄(げき)を飛ばす. ¶he ***read*** an *address* of welcome on behalf of ... ...を代表して歓迎の辞を朗読した.

Q a ***baccalaureate*** *address* [米国大学における]告別演説. ¶a ***complimentary*** *address* 賀表. ¶a ***congratulatory*** *address* 祝辞. ¶an ***inaugural*** *address* 就任のあいさつ. ¶an *interesting* and *informing address* 興味ある有益な演説. ¶Of these articles the first and last were ***presidential*** *addresses* before the American Sociological Society. これら論文の内最初と最後の分は米国社会学会での会長就任講演であった. ¶a ***public*** *address* 公開演説.

Q[2] a ***broadcast*** (=***radio***) *address* 放送演説. ¶a ***commencement*** *address* 《米》卒業式の演説. ¶a ***convocation*** *address* 評議会開会の辞. ¶make a ***farewell*** *address* 送別の演説をする. ¶the President's "***fireside***" *address* to the nation 大統領の炉辺談話. ¶deliver a ***moving*** *address* 人を動かす演説をやる. ¶give an ***opening*** (***closing***) *address* 開(閉会)の辞を述べる. ¶a ***parting*** *address* 告別演説. ¶make the ***presentation*** *address* 贈呈の辞を述べる.

P[2] an *address* ***of*** congratulation 祝辞. 【類】an *address* ***of*** welcome / an *address* ***of*** thanks. ¶General ...'s *address* ***to*** his army ...将軍の部下への訓示. 【類】an *address* ***to*** the audience (聴衆).

(**2**) 名あて, 所書, 宿所.

V those who wish to ***change*** their *addresses* 転居しようとする人々. ¶he ***gave*** his *address* as ... 彼は住所は...だと言った. 【類】Can you ***give*** me the *address* of Mr....? ¶He ***has*** my *address*. 彼は僕の住所を知っている. 【類】Please let me ***have*** your *address* as soon as you are settled. ‖ find out if they ***have*** an *address* to go to 頼って行く先があるかどうか(移民などに)尋ねる. ¶***leave*** one's new *address* at the post-office, so that letters may be forwarded 書状の転送ができるように新規の所書を郵便局に置いて行く(転居の場合). ¶***look up*** one's *address* in the telephone book 電話帳で住所を捜す. ¶***note*** his new *address* 彼の新規の住所を書留める. ¶I cannot ***obtain*** his *address*. 彼の住所が分らない. ¶I ***want*** his *address*. あの人の住所を知りたい.

Q the ***above*** *address* 上記肩書の所. ¶give a ***false*** *address* 住所を偽る. ¶of no ***fixed*** *address* 住所不定の. ¶An agency has been opened at the ***following*** *address*. 次の肩書の所に代理店を開いた. ¶an ***insufficient*** *address* 不十分な所書. ¶am sending this to your ***old*** *address*, trusting that the postal authorities will know where to find you. これは古い所書にして出しますが郵便局の方で転送してくれると存じます. ¶a ***permanent*** *address* 本籍. ¶How long have you been living at the ***present*** *address*? 今の番地の所にどの位お住いですか. ¶one's ***private*** *address* 私宅の所書. ¶This is a ***sufficient*** *address* for letters to reach me. この所書で出せば私の所に結構手紙が着きます. ¶a ***temporary*** *address* 仮の住所. ¶call at the ***wrong*** *address* 門違いをする.

Q[2] use an ***accommodation*** *address* of one's letters [自宅でなく]別の所書にして手紙を出す. ¶***business*** *address* 営業所の居所. ¶a ***cable*** *address* 海外電信略号. ¶a ***code*** *address* 電信略号. ¶a ***delivery*** *address* 品物引渡し先. ¶an ***envelope*** *address* 封筒の所書. ¶a ***forwarding*** *address* 送り先. ¶his ***home*** *address* is at ... あの人の自宅は...です. ¶the ***mail*** *address* of Mr. M. M 氏の郵便送り先. ¶***office*** and ***home*** *address* 勤務先と自宅の所書. ¶an ***out-of-date*** *address* 古い(以前の)住所. ¶one's ***residence*** *address* 自宅の名あて. ¶There is no ***return*** *address* on this letter. この手紙には返事を出すあて先が書いてない. ¶a ***summer*** *address* 避暑地の宿所. ¶Send the newspaper to my ***vacation*** *address*. 新聞を休暇中の宿所へ送って下さい.

P She was employed ***at*** the above *address* as typist. 上記肩書の所でタイピストに雇われていた. ‖ Apply ***at*** the following *address*. 左の所へ御申込下さい. ¶He is still ***in*** the same *address*. あの人はまだ同じ所にいる. ¶forward a letter ***to*** a new *address* 手紙を新住所に転送する.

P[2] the *address* ***on*** a letter 書状に記載のあて名.

(**3**) 請願, 上奏.

P[2] an *address* ***to*** Parliament 議会への請願書 ‖ an *address* ***to*** the Throne 上奏文 ‖ an *address* ***to*** the soul of the dead 祭文.

(**4**) 言寄り, 愛の言葉.

V He ***paid*** his *addresses* to a young lady of considerable attractions. 彼は愛きょうたっぷりの若い婦人に言寄った.

(**5**) 手ぎわ, 熟練.

P He managed the affair ***with*** *address*. 彼は事件をうまく処理した. 「際.

P[2] *address* ***in*** dealing with opponents 相手を操縦する手

(**6**) 話ぶり, 応対ぶり.

Q a man of an ***awkward*** *address* 応対ぶりのまずい人. ¶a man of ***good*** *address* 応対ぶりのよい人. ¶a man of ***pleasing*** *address* 気持の好い応対ぶりの人.

address, *v*. (**1**) 演説する.

P He *addressed* the audience ***in*** an eloquent speech. 彼は弁舌さわやかに演説した. ¶I have the honor of introducing to you Mr. Ando, who will *address* you ***on*** his recent tour abroad. 諸君に安藤君を御紹介致します, 同君は先ごろ海外漫遊中見聞されたことにつきお話をされます.

(**2**) 話掛ける, 呼び掛ける.

P *address* him ***as*** John Smith ジョン・スミスといって彼に話掛ける. ¶He was always *addressed* ***by*** his surname with the prefix of "Mr." 彼はいつもその苗字に「さん」を付けて話掛けられた. ‖ *addressed* ***by*** one's Christian name (姓でなく名前で). ¶I was *addressed* ***in*** English ***by*** a passer-by. 通行人に英語で話し掛けられた. ¶papers *addressed* ***to*** different audiences 各層の読者に呼びかける新聞. ¶*address* an intruder ***with*** indignation 乱入者をしかりつける ‖ *address* ***without*** a title of honor 呼捨てにする.

(**3**) あて名を書く, あて名を書いて送る.

M ***properly*** (***wrongly***) *address* a letter ちゃんと(誤って)手紙にあて名を書く.

P *Address* me ***as*** above. 私の所へは上の所書で手紙を出して下さい. ¶He *addressed* his friend ***on*** the subject. 彼はその事を(口頭または手紙で)友人に持出した. ¶*address* ***to*** care of ... ...気付に(郵便などを)出す ‖ a letter *addressed* ***to*** ... ...あての手紙. 【類】*address* a letter ***to*** a friend / The letter was *addressed* ***to*** the wrong house (誤配された). ‖ *Address* your mail ***to*** street and number. 郵便物には町名番地を明記すること.

(**4**) 請願する, 建白する.

P *address* oneself ***to*** the proper authority その筋に請願する ‖ *address* a memorial ***to*** the Diet 議会に建白する.

(**5**) 身をゆだねる, 力を注ぐ.

P *address* oneself ***to*** the work その仕事に着手する.

adept, *n*. 名人, 老手.

P an *adept* ***at*** lying うそつきの名人 ‖ *adepts* ***at*** the subject その問題に通じた人たち ‖ He is *adept* ***at*** figures. 計算がうまい. ¶an *adept* ***in*** diplomacy (flattery, magic, all the tricks of the trade) 外交(など)のベテラン. 【類】be *adept* ***in*** stage performance (演技).

adept, *a*. 巧妙な.

P He is unusually *adept* ***in*** mathematical calculations. 非常に計算が達者だ.

adequate, *a*. 適当な, 十分な.

P *adequate* ***for*** the purpose 目的に適当した ‖ a remedy *adequate* ***for*** the disease その病の適薬. ¶His income is not *adequate* ***to*** his needs. 彼の収入はその所要を満たすに足りない. 【類】The supply is not *adequate* ***to*** the demand. / He is *adequate* ***to*** a great work. / the power *adequate* ***to*** a great work / be *adequate* ***to*** the demand / Though a bit too old, he is still *adequate* ***to*** the work. / be not *adequate* ***to*** the occasion (situation) / *adequate* ***to*** requirements (条件) of... ‖ The means is not *adequate* ***to*** the end. 手段が目的につり合わない.

adhere, *v*. 固守する, 守る; 付属する; 付着する.

M He *adheres* too ***closely*** to the regulations あの人は余りにその規則に拘泥しすぎる. ¶***consistently*** *adhere* to the original plan 終始一貫原案を固執する. ¶He ***rigidly*** *adhered* to his old habits. 彼は旧習を固守した. ¶***slavishly*** *adhere* to his order 彼の命令に屈従する. ¶***strictly*** *adhere* to a rule 規則を厳守する. 【類】The specification (仕訳書) must be ***strictly*** *adhered* to. ¶*adhere* ***strongly*** to a decision 決議を固守する. ¶***stubbornly*** *adhere* to the original plan 最初の計画を固守する. ¶***tenaciously*** *adhere* to ... あくまで...を守る. ¶The face powder *adheres* ***well*** to the skin. そのおしろいははだに付きがいい.

P *adhere* ***to*** Buddhism 仏教を捨てぬ. 【類】He *adhered* ***to*** the religion of his forefathers (祖先). / those who profess to *adhere* ***to*** the teachings of Christ / The old calendar (旧暦) is still *adhered* ***to*** in many country places. ‖ Wax *adheres* ***to*** the finger. 蠟(ろう)は指にくっつく. ‖ the rights that *adhere* ***to*** man 人間固有の権利 ‖ *adhere* ***to*** neutrality 中立を守る. 【類】*adhere* ***to*** ancient customs (one's resolution) / *adhere* ***to*** the old ways (旧慣).

adherence, *n*. 固執, 固守; 加盟.

v ***give*** (=***send***) ***in*** one's *adherence* (=adhesion) to a treaty (party) 条約(など)に加盟の旨を表明する.

Q a ***consistent*** *adherence* to ... 終始一貫…を守ること. ¶a ***firm*** *adherence* to the doctrines その教義の固守. ¶a ***nominal*** *adherence* to a religion ある宗教に対する見てくれの信仰. ¶***patriotic*** *adherence* to the things which made us what we are today われらをして今日あらしめたものの死守. ¶a ***rigid*** *adherence* to duty 本分を堅く守ること. ¶a ***slavish*** *adherence* to ... …への屈従. ¶by the ***strict*** *adherence* to this rule この規則を固守して.

adherent, *n.* 固執者；信奉者.

v This view has never entirely lost its ground, and still ***counts*** *adherents* in this country. こういう意見は全然その地歩を失ったのではなくこの国にもまだこれを信じている者がいる. ¶The new faith ***found*** *adherents* among princes and scholars. その新しい宗旨が王侯や学者に信奉された. ¶The theory is steadily ***gaining*** *adherents*. その学説は着着信奉者がふえて来る. ¶The scheme ***has*** many influential *adherents*. その計画には多数の有力な賛成者がある. 【類】The newly-risen religion (新興宗教) ***has*** its numerous *adherents*.

Q a ***devoted*** *adherent* 熱心な信者 ‖ a ***devoted*** and fanatically ***faithful*** *adherents* of the Tsar ロシア皇帝の忠実にして熱誠なる臣民. ¶***earnest*** and ***ardent*** *adherents* 熱烈な味方(賛同者). ¶an ***enthusiastic*** *adherent* of the theory その学説の熱心な信奉者. ¶The new faith has gained a ***few*** *adherents* only. 新宗教が抱込んだ信者はほんの少数だ. ¶***fresh*** *adherents* to the theory この学説を新たに奉ずる人人. ¶***nominal*** *adherents* of a creed 名ばかりの信者. ¶an ***obstinate*** *adherent* of the Zen sect 禅宗にこりかたまった人. ¶***staunch*** *adherents* of ... のこり屋.

P² the *adherents* ***of*** the new faith 新宗教の信奉者. 【類】Over 200,000,000 people are *adherents* ***of*** Hinduism (インド教). / the *adherents* ***of*** Methodism (メソジスト派) / *adherents* ***of*** Luther ‖ the *adherents* ***of*** the reform 改革派の人々. ¶*adherents* ***to*** a cause (=principle) 主義の固執者.

adherent, *a.* 執着する.

P He was *adherent* ***to*** Luther. 彼はルーテルに味方した. ‖ a lobule *adherent* ***to*** the cheek 貧乏耳.

adhesion, *n.* 粘着；加入, 同意.

V He ***gave in*** his *adhesion* to the Liberal Party. 彼は自由党参加を表明した. 【類】Germany ***gave in*** its *adhesion* to the treaty.

Q ***voluntary*** *adhesion* 心服.

P² *adhesion* ***between*** two things 二物の粘着. ¶*adhesion* ***by*** signature to the declaration 署名による宣言への賛成. ¶letters of *adhesion* ***to*** the scheme その計画に賛意を表する手紙.

adhesive, *a.* 固執する.

P remain *adhesive* ***to*** the cause その主義を固執する.

adieu, *n.* 告別.

V I ***bade*** (=***said***) *adieu* to my colleagues. 同僚に別れをつげた. 【類】***bid*** a respectful *adieu* to ... ¶They ***bowed*** their *adieus*. 彼等はお辞儀をして別れた. ¶I ***made*** my *adieu* to ... 私は…に別れを告げた. ¶I ***received*** the *adieus* of my friends. 僕は友人たちの告別を受けた. ¶***take*** one's *adieu* 告別する ‖ ***take*** fond *adieu* of ... …との別れを惜しむ.

adjacent, *a.* 接した.

P a room *adjacent* ***to*** the hallway 廊下に接した部屋. 【類】a field *adjacent* ***to*** the highway / The house is *adjacent* ***to*** a graveyard.

adjective, *n.* 〖文法〗形容詞.

V ***merit*** the same *adjective* 同じ形容詞を付ける価値がある. ¶***use*** too many *adjectives* 形容詞を使いすぎる.

Q ***derivative*** *adjectives* 他品詞から転じた形容詞. ¶a ***stereotyped*** *adjective* 紋切型の形容詞. ¶use ***an unguarded*** *adjective* 不用意(不穏当)な形容詞を使う.

adjoin, *v.* 接する.

M a yard ***immediately*** *adjoining* the house 家続きの庭.

P The field *adjoins* ***to*** the highway. 野良は街道に接している.

adjourn, *v.* 延期する；休会する；会場を移す.

M *adjourn* ***sine die*** (=without day) 無期延期にする. ¶foreign nationals ***temporarily*** *adjourning* in the United States 米国に一時滞在している外国人. ¶The meeting *adjourned* ***upstairs***. 会場が二階に移った.

P The meeting *adjourned* ***at*** four o'clock. 集会は四時に散会した. ¶*adjourn* ***for*** dinner [会を]中止して晩餐に移る ‖ The session was *adjourned* ***for*** the morning. 午前の会議はこれで閉会となる. ‖ The inquiry was *adjourned* ***for*** a month. 調査は一カ月間延期された. 【類】After further evidence the hearing (公判) was *adjourned* ***for*** a week. / The Congress *adjourned* ***for*** the day. ¶They *adjourned* ***from*** day ***to*** day. その日その日と休会を続けた. ¶The meeting *adjourned* ***in*** confusion. 集会は混乱裡に散会となった. ¶They *adjourned* ***over*** the holidays. 休暇に際して休会になった. ¶The enquiry was then *adjourned* ***till*** Monday. 調査は月曜日まで延期になった. ¶After discussing some other minor points, the party *adjourned* ***to*** lunch. 他のささいな点を二三討議してから会は中食に移った. ‖ *adjourn* ***to*** the specified day or hour 指定の日または時間まで散会する. 【類】After dinner the party *adjourned* ***to*** the drawingroom. / The audience were invited to *adjourn* ***to*** another room.

adjournment, *n.* 散会.

V An *adjournment* was then ***made*** to a restaurant. 会は閉じて料理屋に席を移した.

Q² ***lunch*** *adjournment* 昼食のための閉会.

adjudge, *v.* 授与する；宣告する.

M He has been *adjudged* ***bankrupt***. 彼は破産を宣告された.

P *adjudge* a prize ***to*** a victor 勝利者に賞品を授与する ‖ *adjudge* a criminal ***to*** death 罪人に死刑を宣告する.

adjudicate, *v.* 判決する.

M The court *adjudicated* him [to be] ***guilty*** (***bankrupt***). 裁判所は彼を有罪(破産)と判決した.

P The court *adjudicated* ***upon*** the case. 裁判所でその件を判決した.

adjudication, *n.* 〖法〗判決.

Q ***formal*** *adjudication* 主文.

adjunct, *n.* 付属物；〖文法〗修飾語.

Q Publication forms an ***essential*** *adjunct* to broadcasting. 出版は放送には欠くべからざるものだ. ¶The dictionary is an ***indispensable*** *adjunct* to the means of study. 辞書は勉学に欠くべからざる付属物だ. ‖ an ***indispensable*** *adjunct* of research for all persons engaged in ... …に従事するすべての人にとって必要欠くべからざる研究の道具. ¶The international congress is a ***necessary*** *adjunct* of a progressive, co-operating world. 万国会議は進歩協力の世界には必要な付属機関だ. ¶a ***mere*** *adjunct* to ... …のほんのお添えもの. ¶Massage is an exceedingly ***useful*** *adjunct* to a treatment. マッサージは治療には非常に有益なつきものだ.

P an *adjunct* ***to*** the verb 〖文法〗動詞の修飾語. ‖ With what anxiety is the weather watched—that great *adjunct* or drawback ***to*** every festivity! 天気が心配だ, 天気次第で興も添えれば妨げともなるから. ‖ a naval officers' training school to be established in California as an *adjunct* ***to*** the Naval Academy カリフォルニアに新設される海軍大学付属海軍士官研修所 ‖ Our learning is but an *adjunct* ***to*** ourselves. 学問は我々のアクセサリーに過ぎない.

adjunct, *a.* 付属の.

P *adjunct* ***to*** a man 人間に付属している(性質など).

adjust, *v.* 合わせる.

M ***properly*** *adjust* ... to the eye …を目に正しく合わせる.

P *adjust* it ***to*** a standard それを標準に合わせる. ‖ *adjust* itself ***to*** external changes 外界の変化に適合させる ‖ See through the telescope till *adjusted* ***to*** your eyes. 目に合うまで望遠鏡をのぞきなさい.

adjustment, *n.* 調節；調停.

V ***make*** *adjustment* to ... …を調節する ‖ ***make*** very good *adjustment* 折合がきわめてよい. ¶An *adjustment* was ***reached***. 調停が成立した.

Q capable of ***amicable*** *adjustment* 和解のできる. ¶a ***delicate*** *adjustment* of these directly opposite necessities この相反する必要に対する巧妙な調節. ¶find a ***peaceful*** and ***satisfactory*** *adjustment* of the questions now at issue between the two nations 両国民間の目下の係争問題に関し平和的で満足な調停法を見出す.

Q² ***labor-management*** *adjustment* 労使関係の調整. ¶the ***Labor Relations*** *Adjustment* Act 労働関係調整法. ¶***liquidation*** *adjustment* 残務整理. ¶***price*** *adjustments* 物価調節. ¶a ***rate*** *adjustment* 料金の調整.

P² *adjustment* ***of*** science ***to*** practice 科学の実地への適応.

administer, *v.* 助ける；宣誓させる；管財する.

P *administer* ***to*** the comforts of passengers 旅客の便利を計る ‖ Health *administers* ***to*** peace of mind. 健康は心の

平和を助ける. ‖ *administer* an oath *to* him 彼に宣誓させる. 【類】*administer* the oath *to* the witness (目撃者). ¶*administer upon* an estate 遺産を管理する. ¶be *administered under* the laws of ... ...の国法の下に施政を行う.

administration, *n.* 政治; 内閣; 管理, 経営.

V an *administration* ***captained*** (=***headed***) by Mr. Balfour バルフォア氏を首班とする内閣. ¶***decentralize*** *administration* 地方分権にする. ¶The new *Administration* has been ***opposed*** in Parliament. 新政府は(英国)議会で反対された. ¶***reorganize*** the *administration* 行政組織を改める.

Q the ***chief*** *administration* of a company 本社. ¶introduce ***civil*** *administration* at Hankow 漢江に民政を布く. ¶***compulsory*** *administration* 強制管理. ¶***internal*** *administration* 内政. ¶***Lord North's*** *administration* ノース卿内閣. ¶***mandatory*** *administration* 委任統治. ¶***military*** *administration* 軍政. ¶***municipal*** *administration* 市政. ¶changes in the ***political*** *administration* of the country その国の政変.

Q² ***business*** *administration* 事業経営. ¶***city*** *administration* 都市行政 ¶the ***Eisenhower*** *Administration* 《米》アイゼンハワー政府. ¶***food*** *administration* 食料管理. ¶a ***fusion*** *Administration* 連立内閣. ¶questions of ***home*** *administration* 内政上の諸問題. ¶***labor*** *administration* 労働行政. ¶***library*** *administration* 図書館管理. ¶General MacArthur's ***occupation*** *administration* マッカーサー元帥の占領行政. ¶***office*** *administration* 業務管理. ¶***personnel*** *administration* 人事管理. ¶***public health*** *administration* 国民保健行政. ¶***school business*** *administration* 学校経営. ¶a ***shadow*** *administration* (=cabinet) 《英》[野党の]準備内閣. ¶a member of two ***successive*** *administrations* 二代にわたる内閣の閣僚. ¶***union*** *administration* 組合管理.

P ***during*** the Jackson *administration* ジャクソン内閣の時代に. 【類】***During*** his *administration* the company attained its highest prosperity. ¶It is ***under*** Japanese *administration.* それは日本の統治下にある. ‖ The company developed ***under*** his wise *administration.* 彼の賢明な統率の下にその会社は発展した.

P² the *administration* ***of*** charities 慈善事業の経営. ¶an *administration* ***under*** Count Okuma 大隈内閣.

administrator, *n.* 管理者; 行政官.

Q² a ***concentration camp*** *administrator* 俘虜収容所長. ¶a ***foundation*** *administrator* 財団の管理者. ¶a ***price*** *administrator* 物価管理者. ¶a ***school*** *administrator* 主事. ¶a ***trust*** *administrator* 信託管理人. ¶a ***university*** *administrator* 大学監(理)事.

admirable, *a.* 見事な.

P The work is *admirable* ***for*** the vast labor it involved. その著作は巨大な労力を要した点で称賛すべきものである.

admiration, *n.* 嘆賞, 驚嘆.

V ***arouse*** the *admiration* of the public 公衆に嘆賞の念を起させる. ¶***attract*** the *admiration* of many a lover of nature 自然愛好者の多くを感嘆させる. ¶***await*** the *admiration* of the passing throngs [公園の花などが]通行人の嘆美を待っている. ¶***call forth*** the *admiration* of the beholder 見る人を感嘆させる. ¶For him I have long ***cherished*** a despairing *admiration.* 私は久しく彼にはとても及ばぬものと畏敬していた. ¶***claim*** our highest *admiration* われわれを大いに感嘆させる ‖ his work ***claims*** the *admiration* of ... あの人の作品は...からほめられる価値がある. ¶His piety towards God ***commands*** my *admiration.* あの人の敬神は感服の至りだ. 【類】His argument ***commands*** *admiration* by its ability. / It must undoubtedly ***command*** real *admiration.* / ***command*** the *admiration* and the deepest gratitude of... ¶It ***compels*** *admiration* instantly. たちまち感服させる. ¶I ***conceived*** the highest *admiration* for his talents and energy. 彼の才能と精力とには極度に感服した. ¶***demand*** *admiration* 感服させる. ¶***deserve*** *admiration* 感嘆に値いする. ¶***elicit*** the *admiration* of the world 世界の賞賛を博する. ¶***evoke*** the *admiration* of the beholder 見る人の賞賛を博する. ¶This ***excited*** so much *admiration.* これが大いに感嘆の念を起させた. 【類】It is human nature to take delight in ***exciting*** *admiration.* ¶***express*** great *admiration* for ... ...に対して大いに感嘆する. 【類】I cannot refrain from ***expressing*** my warm *admiration* for ... ¶***feel*** *admiration* for people who ... ...いう人々には敬服する. ¶He ***has*** a great *admiration* for Japan. 彼は大いに日本を敬慕している. ¶***invite*** his *admiration* 彼の賞嘆の念を誘発する. ¶***maintain*** one's *admiration* for ... 相変らず...を称賛する. ¶***merit*** our *admiration* われらの称賛に値いする. ¶***secure*** *admiration* 称賛を博する. ¶***win*** wide-spread *admiration* 広く賞賛を博する. ¶The reader cannot ***withhold*** his interest and *admiration.* 読者は三嘆おく能わずである.

Q ***blind*** *admiration* 盲目的感服. ¶a ***deep*** *admiration* for ... ...に対する深い感服. ¶a ***heartfelt*** (=***hearty***) *admiration* for ... ...に対する心からの感服. ¶cherish a ***passionate*** *admiration* for ... ...を非常に敬慕している. ¶a ***profound*** *admiration* for ... ...に対する深い嘆美. ¶***respectful*** *admiration* 敬服. ¶a feeling of ***secret*** *admiration* 心ひそかに景慕するの情. ¶in ***sheer*** *admiration* 全く感服して. ¶he has a very ***sincere*** *admiration* for ... 彼は...を心から景慕している. ¶I have a very ***small*** *admiration* for him. 彼にはあまり感心しない. ¶an ***unbounded*** *admiration* for ... ...に対する限りなき景慕. ¶***unconscious*** *admiration* in the form of hatred for a person's intellectual superiority 人の知的優秀に対する憎悪という形式の無意識的嘆美. ¶excite (=awaken) ***universal*** *admiration* あまねく賞賛の念を起させる.

P lost ***in*** *admiration* 見ほれて ‖ with mouth open ***in*** *admiration* 感心の余り口あんぐりで ‖ ***in*** *admiration* of ... ...に感心して. ¶***through*** *admiration* for his bravery その勇気に感じて. ¶I was struck ***with*** *admiration.* 感心した.

P² *admiration* ***at*** an unexpected event 意外の事件に対する驚嘆. ¶his *admiration* ***for*** the poet 彼の詩人に対する景慕. ¶He won for him the *admiration* ***of*** the world. 彼は世界の賞賛を博した.

admire, *v.* 嘆賞する, 驚嘆する.

M I have always *admired* him ***extravagantly.*** 私はこれまでいつも彼を激賞した. ¶*admire* ***ignorantly*** 盲目的にほめる. ¶The work of Edgar Allan Poe has been ***long*** and ***deeply*** *admired* in France and England as well as in his own land. エドガー・アラン・ポーの作品は自国のみならず英仏両国で長年の間大いに嘆賞されて来た.

P *admire* a person or a thing ***as*** a fine one りっぱなものだと感心する. ¶I *admire* ***at*** your fortune. 君の運のよいには驚く. ¶*admire* him ***for*** what he has done 彼の仕事に対して彼を嘆美する.

admirer, *n.* 嘆美者, 景慕者, ファン.

V The pretty girl ***attracted*** many *admirers.* あの美人は大勢からちやほやされた. ¶It still ***finds*** *admirers* in every land. それは今もってあらゆる国に礼賛者がいる.

Q an ***ardent*** (=***intense, enthusiastic*** *or* ***fervent***) *admirer* of the West 西洋心酔者. ¶a ***blind*** *admirer* 盲目的(無批判的)な心酔者. ¶a ***discerning*** *admirer* 眼識ある礼賛者. ¶his ***enthusiastic*** *admirer* 彼の熱烈なファン. ¶her ***gallant*** *admirer* 彼女に言い寄る男. ¶a ***great*** *admirer* of Burns バーンズの愛読者. ¶the most ***infatuated*** *admirer* of ... ...にうつつを抜かしている人. ¶a ***prodigious*** *admirer* of ...法外に...を景慕する人. ¶a ***sincere*** *admirer* 真の景慕者. ¶a ***staunch*** *admirer* of English political institutions 英国の政治上の制度を熱烈に嘆美する人. ¶an ***unconditional*** *admirer* of ...あくまで...を嘆美する人. ¶a flock of ***Wagnerian*** *admirers* ワグネル崇拝者の一団. ¶***warm*** *admirers* of Japan 熱心な親日家連 ‖ his ***warmest*** *admirers* 彼のもっとも熱心なファン(礼賛者).

P He has his host ***of*** *admirers.* 彼には沢山のファンがある.

admissibility, *n.* 〘法〙認容.

P² *admissibility* ***of*** evidence 証拠能力.

admissible, *a.* 承認すべき.

M ***otherwise*** *admissible* それ以外は結構なのだが.

P be *admissible* ***as*** evidence against ... ...に不利な証拠と認められる. ¶*admissible* ***for*** the sake of argument 議論のために許容される. ¶persons *admissible* ***in*** evidence 証人として入場させてもよい人々. ¶people *admissible* ***to*** office (=position *or* employment) 就職資格のある人々.

admission, *n.* (**1**) 入会, 入学, 入場(入学)許可, 入場料.

V *Admissions* will be ***allotted*** in order of application. 入学(会)は申込順に許可する. ¶*Admission* can be ***attained*** gratuitously by the ticket. その切符で無料入場ができる. ¶***deny*** *admission* to an applicant 志願者の入会(学)を拒む. ¶***gain*** (=***get***) *admission* into a club (association) クラブ

(など)への入会を許される.【類】Early application is necessary to ***gain admission*** to the school. ¶***give up*** one's *admission* to a school 入学許可を棄権する. ¶***grant*** free *admission* to students 学生を無料で入場させる. ¶***obtain*** (=gain) *admission* to a school 入学を許可される. ¶***pay*** *admission* 入場料を払う. ¶***prevent*** the *admission* of wind 風が入らないようにする. ¶***receive*** prompt *admission* 直ちに入会を許可される. ¶***secure*** *admission* to … …に入ることを許される.

Q ***selective*** *admission* to a university 大学の選抜入学許可.

Q² approximately 20 per cent of ***hospital*** *admissions* 入院許可数の約二割.

P applicants ***for*** *admission* 入会(学)志望者. ‖ apply ***for*** *admission* to (=into) a school 入学を出願する ‖ the price ***for*** single *admission* 一回の入場料.

P² *admission* ***by*** card 招待状での入場. ¶*admission* ***into*** (=to) a school 入学許可. ¶*admission* ***of*** a candidate ***into*** a school 志願者の入学許可. ¶*Admission* ***to*** … is difficult to obtain. …へ入るのはむずかしい.【類】*Admission* ***to*** … is open to all. / *admission* ***to*** students only / *admission* ***to*** a theater by ticket / *admission* ***to*** a literary club (文学会) ‖ *admission* ***to*** the exhibition, … yen 展覧会入場料…円 ‖ *Admission* ***to*** the lectures free. [掲示]聴講無料. ‖ *Admission* ***to*** the lectures will be by ticket only. 聴講券所持者に限り聴講を許す. ‖ *admission* ***to*** the privilege 特権の付与 ‖ prepare for *admission* ***to*** the bar 弁護士試験の準備をする. ¶*admission* ***upon*** certificate 卒業証書による無試験入学. ¶*admission* ***within*** a circle 仲間入り.【類】*admission* ***within*** an enclosure (構内).

(2) 承認, 自白.

V ***extract*** an *admission* from him that … 彼に…ということを強いて承認させる. ¶He ***made*** full *admission* of his crime (=guilt). 彼はきっぱりその罪に服した.

Q a ***damaging*** *admission* 不利な承認. ¶***magnanimous*** *admission* 寛大な承認. ¶a ***reluctant*** *admission* しぶしぶの承認.

P I knew it ***on*** his own *admission*. 彼自身の告白でそれを知り得た.

P² an *admission* ***of*** guilt 服罪.

admit, *v.* (1) 入れる, 通す; 許す.

M The passage *admits* two ***abreast***. この廊下は二人並んで通れる. ¶we ***cheerfully*** *admit* that … 快く…を認める. ¶I *admit* as ***much***. そこまでは認める. ¶This seems quite ***generally*** *admitted*. このことは極めて普通になっているらしい.

P He was *admitted* ***as*** a partner. 彼は社員に加えられた. ¶*admit* a person ***into*** the office (place) 人を任命する. ‖ *admit* a person ***into*** our residence (a society) 人を住宅(など)に入れる.【類】He opened the door and *admitted* me ***into*** the house. / He was *admitted* ***into*** the company (仲間) of a samurai. ‖ I was *admitted* ***into*** his intimacy. 彼の親交を辱うした.【類】Japan was fully *admitted* ***into*** the fellowship (仲間) of European nations. / He was *admitted* ***into*** their fullest confidence. ‖ He was *admitted* ***into*** the Imperial presence. 拝謁を仰せつけられた. ‖ The study was *admitted* ***into*** the university curriculum. その学科が大学の課程に加えられた. ¶It was too clearly proved to *admit* ***of*** denial (dispute). 立証が余りに明瞭なので否定(など)をはさむ余地がなかった. ¶*admit* ***of*** no exception 例外が許されない.【類】The dream *admits* ***of*** realization. / The evidence cannot *admit* ***of*** doubt. / *admit* ***of*** no explanation / an axiom *admitting* ***of*** no dispute / *admit* ***of*** no defense / Such conduct *admits* ***of*** no excuse. / English adjectives *admit* ***of*** no change. / *admit* ***of*** the use of … / The sentence *admits* ***of*** several interpretations (色々な解釈). / The word *admits* ***of*** no other meaning in this case. / The sentence is so formed as to *admit* ***of*** no other construction. ‖ The price quoted will not *admit* ***of*** any allowance. 申し上げた値段は割引はいたしません. ‖ It is too apparent to *admit* ***of*** discussion. 明々白々で議論の余地がない. ¶*admit* ***on*** tickets 入場券で入れる. ¶*admit* one ***to*** its membership 入会を許す.【類】He was *admitted* ***to*** citizenship. / The ticket *admits* you ***to*** one lecture (一回聴講). / My companions *admitted* me ***to*** their councils (相談仲間). ‖ He has had a painting *admitted* ***to*** the Royal Academy. 彼の絵は王立美術協会の展覧会に入選した. ‖ He was *admitted* ***to*** the bar in 1930. 一九三〇年に弁護士の資格を与えられた. ‖ This gate *admits* ***to*** the grounds. この門から場内に行かれる. ‖ He was *admitted* ***to*** bail. 保釈を許された. ¶*admit* … ***within*** a fortification 要塞内に…の入るのを許す.

(2) 認める.

M *admit* oneself ***beaten*** 降参したという. ¶***frankly*** *admit* that … いさぎよく…を認める. ¶***freely*** *admit* that there is some measure of truth in it その内に幾分の真理があることをあからさまに認める. ¶it is ***generally*** (=***universally***) *admitted* that … …は一般に認められている. ¶***readily*** *admit* it 快くそれを認める. ¶***reluctantly*** *admit* it それをしぶしぶ認める. ¶He *admits* the charge ***to be founded*** (***groundless***). その告発を根拠ある(ない)ものと認めている. ¶He *admits* the statement ***to be true***. この話を事実と認めている.

P He *admitted* his mistake ***with*** a good grace. 快く自分の誤りを認めた.

admittance, *n.* 入場, 入場許可.

V ***gain*** (=have) *admittance* to membership 入学(会)を許される. ¶***give*** *admittance* 入ることを許可する. ¶They ***had*** free *admittance*. 彼等は無料で入場した. ¶They ***refused*** him *admittance*. 彼らは彼の入場を拒んだ.【類】I have been ***refused*** *admittance* for want of room (収容の余地がないので).

Q *Admittance* ***free*** to students only. [掲示]学生に限り入場無料. ¶***No*** *admittance* to outsiders. 係員のほか入るべからず. ‖ ***No*** *admittance* except on business. [掲示]無用の者入るべからず.

P² *admittance* ***into*** the church 教会員たる許可. ¶*admittance* ***of*** the public ***to*** the entertainment by ticket 入場券で公衆を演芸場に入れること.【類】*admittance* only ***to*** adults (成人) ‖ *Admittance* ***to*** the room is gained through a door. 戸口を通って室にはいれる.

admittance-fee, *n.* 《米》入場料.

P² There is an *admittance-fee* ***of*** a dime ***for*** adults and five cents ***for*** children. 入場料は大人十セント子供五セント.

admixture, *n.* 混和.

P there still lingers the delusion—with a sufficient *admixture* ***of*** truth to keep it alive—that … 今も…という迷想が残っているがそれにはそれを持続させるだけの十分な真理が交っている. ¶*admixture* of sulfur ***with*** alum 明礬(みょうばん)と硫黄との混和.

admonish, *v.* さとす; 警告する.

P He was *admonished* ***against*** doing wrong (a fault). 彼は曲った事(など)をせぬようにさとされた. ¶*admonish* him ***for*** his fault (idleness) 過失(など)に対して彼を責める. ¶*admonish* him ***of*** a fault 彼の過失を戒める ‖ He was *admonished* ***of*** his duty. 彼はその義務をさとされた.【類】He *admonished* me ***of*** the danger of trusting strangers.

admonition, *n.* 訓戒.

Q an ***excellent*** *admonition* ありがたい訓戒.

ado, *n.* 騒ぎ.

V We ***had*** much *ado*. 大騒ぎをした. ‖ I ***have*** much *ado* to keep out of debt. 借金せずにいるのはなかなか骨だ. ¶***make*** much *ado* about nothing から騒ぎをする.【類】What is the use (効果) of ***making*** so much *ado* about nothing? / ***make*** *ado* about trifles.

P ***with*** much *ado* 大騒ぎをして. ¶I dismissed the maid ***without*** any more *ado*. その上とやかく言わずに女中を解雇してしまった.

adopt, *v.* 採用する; 養子にする.

M *adopt* ***eclectically*** all that is best in other nations 他国民の良い所は何んでも折衷して採る. ¶a ***legally*** *adopted* son 法律上の手続をした養子. ¶*adopt* a resolution ***unanimously*** 異議なく決議を採択する. ¶Japan has *adopted* Christmas ***whole-heartedly***. 日本ではクリスマスを心から祝うようになった. ¶be more ***widely*** *adopted* もっと広い範囲に採用される.

P *adopt* teaching ***as*** a profession 教師を職業にする ‖ *adopt* him ***as*** a pupil 彼を弟子にする. ¶*adopt* a bill ***in*** its integrity 議案をそのまま可決する. ¶He was *adopted* ***into*** a respectable family. 彼は相当の家へもらわれた. ¶*adopt* a violent attitude ***towards*** … …に対して乱暴な態度を取る.

O *adopt* a method just as it is 方法をそのまま採る.

adoption, *n.* 採用; 可決.

V ***move*** the *adoption* of a report [会議などで]報告の可決

を動議する. ¶He could *secure* the *adoption* of his plans. 彼の考案を採用させた. 「英語になっている.
P The word is now English *by adoption*. その語は今では

adoration, *n*. 礼拝, 崇拝.
P fall down *in adoration* before an idol 偶像を伏し拝む. ‖sing *in adoration* 唱歌で賛美する.
P² the *adoration of* the cross 十字架礼拝.

adore, *v*. 崇拝する.
P They *adore* her *as* a living goddess. 彼らは彼女を生神様として崇拝している. ¶*adore* God *with* true devotion 心から神を崇拝する.

adorn, *v*. 飾る.
M *lavishly adorned* やたらに飾り立てた.
P *adorn* a speech *by* appropriate action 適当な身振りをして演説に光彩を添える. ¶She *adorned* herself *with* jewels. 彼女は宝玉で飾り立てた. 【類】His room is *adorned with* Japanese pictures. / The book is *adorned with* numerous and excellent illustrations. / The book is *adorned with* the author's portrait. / The hall was *adorned with* a great variety of flags. / Her character is *adorned with* many virtues.

adornment, *n*. 装飾.
Q the *personal adornment* of a woman befitting those under her age 女の若造り. ¶*tasteful adornment* 渋い飾り. ¶furnish a room without *unnecessary adornment* むだな飾りをせずに部屋の設備をする.

adrift, *ad*. 漂って.
P The boat went *adrift from* the moorings. ボートは繋留場から漂い出した. ¶The ship was *adrift on* unknown seas. 船は見知らぬ海上に漂っていた.

adroit, *a*. 巧みな.
P a person *adroit in* (=*at*) some feat あるわざに巧みな人.

adroitness, *n*. 巧妙.
V *display* a great *adroitness* in it それに大手腕を示す.
P *with* an *adroitness* which a conjurer might envy 手品師もうらやむほどの鮮かさで.

adulation, *n*. うぬぼれ.
Q *self adulation* うぬぼれ.

adult, *n*. 成人.
Q *dependent adults* 扶養されている成人. ¶*young adults* 青壮年.

adulterate, *v*. 混ぜる.
P *adulterate* wine *with* water ぶどう酒に水を混ぜる. 【類】*adulterate* a language *with* slang (卑語).

adultery, *n*. 姦通.
V *commit adultery* with ... ...と姦通する.
Q *double adultery* かん通 (双方既婚) ¶*single adultery* かん通 (片方既婚).

advance, *n*. (**1**) 前進, 行進; 進歩; 昇進; 予約.
V *accelerate* the *advance* of the army 軍の前進を便にする. ¶*check* the *advance* of the enemy 敵の前進を阻止する. ¶*further* national *advance* 国民の進歩を助長する. ¶*harass* the *advance* of the enemy 敵の前進を妨げる. ¶Civilization has *made* [a] great *advance*. 文明が大いに進歩した. 【類】countries where medical education has *made* least *advances* / *make advances* in mechanical industry. ¶*mark* a great *advance* in the progress of photography 写真術の一大進歩を画する. 【類】*mark* new *advances* upon its predecessors. ¶*resist* the *advance* of an army 軍の前進を食いとめる. ¶*show* a remarkable *advance* on ... ...に比し著しい進歩を見せる. ¶The *advance* was *sounded*. 前進のラッパが鳴った.
Q the *constant advance* in ... ...における不断の進歩. ¶follow to its certain goal the path of *constitutional advance* 憲政の目標に到達することを期する. ¶show a very *decided advance* upon ... ...に比し顕著な進歩を示す. ¶a *definite advance* 歴然たる進歩. ¶a *distinct advance* 明らかな進歩. ¶the *educational* and *moral advance* of Japan 日本の教育上および道徳上の進歩. ¶There is something about him that discourages *friendly advances*. あの人にはどこか親しめない所がある. ¶the *general advance* of society 社会一般の進歩. ¶a discovery that marks a most *important advance* 極めて重大な進歩を示す発見. ¶show a *marked advance* 著しく進歩の跡が見える. ¶the *material advance* of the age 時代の物質的進歩. ¶make *rapid advance* towards ... ...の方に急速の進歩をする. 【類】The forces made *rapid advances* in three directions, east, north and west. / the *rapid advance* of the world in knowledge and achievement. ¶*recent advances* in ... ...における近年の進歩. ¶a *steady advance* 着々の進歩. ¶a *substantial advance* has been made in ... ...が実質的に進歩した. ¶*swift advance* (軍隊などの)急進. 【類】make *swift advances* to the summit of learning. ¶*tremendous advances* have been made in the realm of ... ...の方面にすばらしい進歩が見られた.
Q² with the pretext of *future advance* 将来の昇進を口実に. ¶a *headlong advance* 向うみずな前進.
P *during* the *advance* 進軍中に. ¶His idea is *in advance* of the time. 彼の思想は時世に先んじている. 【類】His policy was *in advance* of his times. / His ideas were *in advance* of those of his people. / The express train reached Kobe two minutes *in advance* of its schedule time. ‖We are *in advance* (=ahead) of England in ... われわれは...にかけては英国よりも進んでいる. 【類】He is far *in advance* of his class. / He is far *in advance* of the other pupils. / French railway time is 4 min. 2 sec. *in advance* of England. ‖march *in advance* 先頭に立って進む ‖I shall go a few steps *in advance* of you. 一足お先に. ‖thank *in advance* 予め礼をいう. 【類】an arrangement made *in advance* / Please accept our thanks *in advance* for the favor of a reply. / *in advance* of the day of publication ‖Reservations far *in advance* are necessary to secure desirable quarters. [ホテルなどの]よい部屋をうるにはずっと前に予約して置くことが必要だ.
P² *advance in* medical science 医学の進歩. ‖his *advance in* knowledge 彼の知識の進歩. ¶the German *advance into* Russia ドイツのロシアへの進出. ¶an *advance of* health 健康の増進. 【類】*advance of* learning / *advance of* a people in learning. ¶an *advance on* ... (場所)への進出; ...以上の進歩 ‖an *advance on* view (theory, doctrine) 見解(など)の進歩. ¶a marked *advance over* last year 去年に比し著しい進歩. ¶an *advance upon* the former method 旧方法に加えた進歩. 【類】It is an *advance upon* the author's previous books.

(**2**) 騰貴.
V They *asked for* an *advance* in their wages. 彼らは賃金の引上げを要求した. ¶*bring about* a great *advance* in freight 船の運賃の大高騰を来す. ¶*cause* an *advance* in price 騰貴させる. ¶*check* the *advance* in the price of rice 米価の騰貴を阻止する. ¶*follow* the *advance* in prices 物価の騰貴に続いて起る.
P They can sell these goods today *at* enormous *advances*. 今日ではこの品は非常に高く売れる. ‖The order can only be repeated *at* an *advance* of ... その注文は...の値上げによってのみ追加ができる. ¶The prices are *on* the *advance*. 物価は騰貴している. 【類】Silk is *on* the advance.
P² an *advance in* price 物価の騰貴. 【類】5 per cent *advance in* wages. ¶an *advance on* the prime cost of goods 原価の騰貴 ‖an *advance on* cottons 綿布の値上げ ‖an *advance on* the cost of production.

(**3**) 前金, 前払い, 前貸し; 立替金.
V *give* him an *advance* upon his allowance 手当の前貸をする. ¶*make advances* to ... ...に資金を貸与する ‖*make* an *advance* of ... on a ring 指輪をかたに...融通する ‖*make* an *advance* on a contract 請負の前払いをする. 【類】an *advance made* upon a wage account (賃金勘定). ¶endeavor to *obtain* an *advance* of ... の前貸をしてもらおうと努める. 【類】*obtain* an *advance* on one's salary. ¶*pay* an *advance* 前貸の金を支払う.
Q He has made some *heavy advances* to ... ...に彼は大分多額の金を先に渡していた. ¶make only *small advances* ほんのちょっぴり前貸しをする.
P borrow (lend) money *in advance* 前借(貸)する ‖loan money with interest reduced *in advance* 利息天引きの借金 ‖receive one month's salary *in advance* 一カ月の給料を前借する ‖pay the rent *in advance* 家賃を前納する.
P² the *advance of* money 前貸し. ¶an *advance on* wages 賃金の前貸し. 【類】make *advances on* mortgages (抵当) / an *advance on* one's first week's wages.

(**4**) *pl*. 申込, 提案; *pl*. 手出し.
V *encourage* one's *advances* 誘いの水を向ける. ¶*make advances* to a woman 女に言い寄る ‖*make advances* to-

wards one's superior 上役に取入る. ¶***reject*** his *advances* 彼の持ちかけた件をはねつける.

P[2] *advances* ***from*** a person 申し出.

advance, *v.* **(1)** 進める; 進む, 前進する; 進歩する.

M have not *advanced* ***materially*** in ... ...において大した進歩を遂げなかった. ¶*advance* ***rapidly*** 急速に進む. ¶*advance* ***slowly*** but ***steadily*** ゆっくりだが着実に進む.

P *advance* ***against*** (=on) the capital 都に攻入る ‖ *advance* ***against*** the enemy 敵に向って進撃する. ¶The commander *advanced* ***before*** the squadron. 指揮官は隊の先頭に立って進んだ. ¶*advance* ***by*** strides 長足の進歩をする. ¶He *advanced* ***in*** stature. 彼は背が延びた. 【類】 as the world *advances* ***in*** civilization / *advance* ***in*** knowledge (wisdom) / as they *advance* ***in*** age (=years) / *advance* ***in*** one's position (=station) / *advance* steadily ***in*** esteem and popularity (尊敬と人望). ¶The army *advanced* ***into*** the enemy's country. 軍隊が敵国に進入した. ¶They *advanced* ***on*** each other with drawn revolvers. 彼らは拳銃をケースから抜いて詰寄った. ¶The troops *advanced* ***to*** the river. 軍隊は河まで進出した. ‖ Units *advance* ***to*** tens. 単位は十位になる. ¶They *advanced* ***towards*** the castle. 彼らは城の方に進んだ. ¶*advance* ***upon*** the enemy 敵を攻撃する. ¶*advance* ***within*** a few feet of ... ...を去る数フィートのところまで進む.

(2) 騰貴する; 高くする.

M Prices *advanced* ***rapidly***. 値段がずんずん上がった. ¶*advance* ***sharply*** [値段など] 際立って上がる. ¶The market *advanced* ***suddenly***. 市況が突然活気づいた. ¶The season is not ***sufficiently*** *advanced*. 季節がまだ早い.

P *advance* prices ***by*** 10% 一割方値段を上げる. ¶*advance* ***in*** price 物価が上がる.

(3) 昇進させる; 昇進する.

P *advance* a person ***from*** a tutorship to a professorship 助教授から教授に昇進させる. ¶*advance* ***in*** office 昇進する ‖ *advance* ***in*** one's position 地位が上がる.

(4) 前貸しする, 前渡しする.

P *advance* money ***on*** wages 賃金の前貸しをする ‖ Can you *advance* me one thousand yen ***on*** my salary? 千円だけ月給の前借ができませんか. ¶*advance* wages to ... ...に賃金の前貸しをする.

advanced, *pa.* 年を取った.

M a man ***far*** (=***well***) *advanced* in years 余程(かなり)年配の人. ‖ people ***far*** *advanced* in life (=years) 大分のお年寄たち. 【類】 ***well*** *advanced* in technique (技術).

advancement, *n.* 進歩; 発達, 増進.

V ***gain*** *advancement* 進級する. ¶We shall ***witness*** further *advancements* in the near future that will outshine anything in the past. われらは近い将来過去の何物にもまさる進歩を見るでしょう.

Q The ***moral*** and ***intellectual*** *advancement* of the people of India インド国民の道徳的, 知的向上. ¶for ***professional*** *advancement* 腕をみがくために. ¶***rapid*** *advancement* 迅速な発達. ¶***social*** *advancement* 社会の進歩.

P ***for*** the *advancement* of geographical science 地理学の発達のために ‖ opportunities ***for*** *advancement* in life 出世の機会. ¶***with*** the *advancement* of closer international relations 国際親善の増進につれて.

P[2] *advancement* ***in*** knowledge 知識の進歩. ¶the *advancement* ***of*** learning (knowledge, science) 学問(など)の進歩.

advantage, *n.* 利益, 便益.

V ***claim*** many *advantages* for a newly introduced article 新輸入品の幾多の長所を並べ立てる. ¶***combine*** the *advantages* of a club with lectures, concerts, and other attractions 講演・演奏会やショーなどのできるクラブの特色を備えている. 【類】 The location ***combines*** *advantages* of country and city. ¶***consider*** one's own *advantage* first まず第一に自己の利益を考える. ¶***consolidate*** the *advantages* gained in war 戦争で得た利権を確立する. ¶***counterbalance*** the *advantage* その利益を殺(そ)ぐ. ¶***derive*** lasting *advantage* 永久の利益を得る. ¶***discuss*** the *advantages* and disadvantages of ... ...の利害得失を論じる. ¶***draw*** much *advantage* from ... ...から多大の利益を得る. ¶***enjoy*** the *advantages* of city life 都会生活の便益を受けている. 【類】 ***enjoy*** substantial *advantage* (実質的な便宜) over ... / ***enjoy*** educational *advantages* under one's care (指導). ¶***find*** one's *advantage* in ... ...に利益のあることを知る. ¶***gain*** (=obtain *or* reap) an important *advantage* from ... ...から多大な便宜を得る ‖ He ***gained*** the *advantage* in the game. 彼は有利にゲームを進めた. ‖ ***gain*** (=***get***) an *advantage* over a person ある人よりもさらに優位に立つ. ¶He at once ***grasped*** the *advantages* of the situation. 直ちに形勢の利をつかんだ. ¶it ***has*** an enormous *advantage* in that ... それは...という点において非常に便利な所がある. 【類】 He ***had*** the *advantage* of a good education, received at the Westminster. / in the preparation of the present volume the author has ***had*** the *advantage* of the scholarship (学識) of ... / He never ***had*** the *advantage* of any school training. / Earthenware ***has*** an *advantage* over wood in being more easily kept clean. ‖ he has ***had*** the *advantage* of the assistance of ... 彼には...の加勢という強味があった ‖ It ***has*** (=***possesses***) certainly one great *advantage* to commend it. それには確かに推賞するに足る一大長所がある. 【類】 Each ***has*** *advantages* and disadvantages. / You ***have*** an *advantage* over me. / He ***had*** the *advantage* of his antagonist. ‖ You ***have*** the *advantage* of me. 貴君はどなたですか(お見それ申しました). ¶***impart*** a twofold *advantage* 二重の便益を与える. ¶***make*** one's *advantage* of ... ...を利用する, ...につけ込む. ¶***obtain*** an *advantage* 利益を得る. ¶***offer*** many *advantages* to ... ...に幾多の便宜を与える. ¶***offset*** an *advantage* 利点を喪失させる. ¶***possess*** the *advantage* of ... ...という利点を持っている. 【類】 ***possess*** a great *advantage* over ... ¶***present*** the triple *advantage* of ..., ..., and ... ...と...と...との三重の利益があることを示す. ¶***procure*** commercial *advantages* 貿易上の便益を得る. ¶***reap*** the full *advantage* of ... ...から十分の利益を収める. ¶***secure*** an *advantage* 利益する. ¶***see*** the *advantage* of ... ...を有利と見る. 【類】 He ***saw*** his *advantage*, and shaped the course accordingly. ¶***show*** superior *advantages* of it over ... ...以上にそれが勝れていることを示す. ¶***take*** *advantage* of odd minutes 余暇を利用する. 【類】 ***take*** *advantage* of a situation (circumstance) / I ***took*** *advantage* of the opportunity of visiting the sights of Paris. / ***take*** due (full) *advantage* of the columns of the public press / Full *advantage* has been ***taken*** of the researches of recent writers—French, German, American, and English. ‖ The occasion was ***taken*** *advantage* of. その機会に乗じた. ‖ the determination not to ***take*** *advantage* of the weakness of other countries 他国の弱味につけ込まないという決意. 【類】 It would be ***taking*** an unfair (=mean) *advantage* of him. / They ***took*** *advantage* of the disturbance. ‖ *advantage* was ***taken*** of the day to hold a bazaar in aid of ... ...のバザーの開催にその日を利用した ‖ The master's absence was ***taken*** *advantage* of by the servants. 奉公人たちは鬼のいぬ間の洗たくをやった. ¶***weigh*** *advantages* and disadvantages 利害を比較考量する.

Q ***climatic*** and scenic *advantages* 気候と風景の利. ¶It has its ***compensating*** (=***counterbalancing***) *advantages*. それには埋合せになるだけの利益がある. ¶An adequate knowledge of English is a ***considerable*** *advantage* in getting on in the world. 相当英語を知っていれば出世するに余程の利がある. ¶There are some ***contingent*** *advantages*. ある付帯的の利益がある. ¶***Corresponding*** *advantages* are offered. それ相応の利益が提供されている. ¶the ***cultural*** *advantages* of a great city 大都市の教養上の便益. ¶a ***decided*** *advantage* with ... ...にとって断然優利. have a ***decided*** *advantage* over ... ¶It has the ***distinct*** *advantage* of ... それには...というはっきりした利益がある. ¶enjoy ***domestic educational*** *advantages* over other children 他の子供以上に家庭教育の利益を受ける. ¶It has a ***double*** *advantage*. それには二重(一石二鳥)の利益がある. ¶a ***doubtful*** *advantage* 疑わしい(不確実な)利益. ¶thanks to its ***geographical*** *advantage* 地の利を得ているために. ¶***Great*** *advantages* would thereby accrue to science. そのために科学は大なる利益を受けることになるだろう. ‖ His works on the subject have been consulted with ***great*** *advantage*. そのことに関する彼の著作は大いに参考になった. ¶take ***gross*** *advantage* of his ignorance 大いに彼の無知につけ込む. ¶to an ***immeasurable*** *advantage* 測り知れぬ利益をもたらして. ¶***immense*** *advantages* 莫大な利便. ¶***manifold*** *advantages* 種々様々の利益. ¶take ***mean*** *advantage* of a weaker opponent ひきょうにも相手の弱身につけ込む. ¶a ***minor*** *advantage* 些細な利益. ¶for ***mutual*** *advantage* 相互の利益のため. 【類】It will be to our ***mutual*** *advantage*. ¶***natural*** *advantage* 天恵. ¶***personal*** *advantage* 容姿の利(美貌) ‖ alter a check to one's ***personal*** *advantage*=raise a check 自分に都合のいいように小切手を[高額に]改ざんする. 【類】gain some ***personal*** *advantage* (私利). ¶turn it to one's ***private*** *advantage* それを私欲に振り向ける. ¶of ***questionable*** *advantage* 利益があるかどうか疑わしい. ¶***relative*** *advantage* of ... and ... ...と...との便不便. ¶***tangible*** *advantages* 実利. ¶It has a ***twofold*** *advantage*. それには二重の利益がある. ¶It will be to Japan's ***ultimate*** *advantage*. それは結局日本の利益になろう. ¶take ***undue*** *advantage* of ... ...を利用し過ぎる ‖ an ***unfair*** and ***unlawful*** *advantage* 不正非合法の利益. ¶have ***unique*** *advantages* 無類の利益がある. ¶***unquestionable*** *advantage* 分り切った利益. ¶***vocational*** *advantages* 就職上の利.

Q² "***factory-to-consumer***" *advantages* [中間業者の手を経ずに直接]工場から消費者へという利益. ¶The ***showmanship*** *advantages* of the wide screen are undisputed, when properly applied. 適当に用いられればワイド・スクリーンが興行上有利なことは明らかだ.

P It is ***at*** a decided *advantage*. 確かに好都合だ. ‖ buy ***at*** an *advantage* 安く買う ‖ take it ***at*** *advantage* 利用する(往々不正の意味を含む). ¶He negotiated ***for*** my *advantage*. 彼は私の得になるように談判した. 【類】Whether it be ***for*** his *advantage* or detriment. ¶It is ***of*** *advantage*. それは役に立つ. ‖ It is ***of*** great *advantage* to them. それは彼らにとって大利益である. ¶It is seldom made use of ***to*** *advantage*. めったに利用されていない. ‖ turn it ***to*** *advantage* 利用する ‖ Several days may be spent here ***to*** *advantage*. ここで数日を送るのもまた興味がある. 【類】use (=employ) ... ***to*** the best *advantage* / show it off (引きたたせる) ***to*** *advantage* / It is ***to*** the world's *advantage*. ‖ It proved ***to*** his *advantage*. 結局あの人の利益になった. / It will be ***to*** the *advantage* of all concerned (関係者全体). / it would be ***to*** your *advantage* as well as mine if ... / It is not at all ***to*** his *advantage* that ... / I heard of something ***to*** my *advantage*. / you will find it ***to*** your *advantage* to ... ‖ It proved (=turned out) ***to*** his *advantage*. 結局それは彼の得になった. ‖ That dress sets her figure off ***to*** *advantage*. あの着物を着ると彼女の姿が引立つ. ‖ The blooming cherry-tree is seen ***to*** the best *advantage* by moonlight. 咲いた桜は月明りで見るのが一番いい. ¶***with*** *advantages* to all concerned 関係者全体に有利に. ¶***without*** the slightest counterbalancing *advantage* 埋合せになるような利益は少しもなく.

P² derive an *advantage* ***from*** ... ...から利益を得る. ¶*advantage* ***in*** argument (ability, number) 議論(など)における有利. 【類】*advantage* ***in*** position ‖ There is no *advantage* ***in*** doing. やってもだめだ. ¶the *advantage* ***of*** ground 地の利 ‖ the *advantage* ***of*** a good constitution 体格がよいという強味 ‖ The four best *advantages* ***of*** riches are leisure, travel, reading, and conversation. 富の四大便益は閑暇・旅行・読書および会話である. ¶the *advantages* ***of*** the theater ***over*** the movies 演劇の映画にまさる点. 【類】secure an *advantage* ***over*** another in argument.

advantageous, *a.* 便利な; 有利な.

P It will be found *advantageous* ***to*** any one. それはだれにも便利だと認められるだろう. ‖ be detrimental to us and *advantageous* ***to*** the enemy 味方にとって不利で敵には有利である.

advent, *n.* 現出, 到来.

V ***hasten*** the *advent* of this period この時期の到来を促進する. ¶A little baby ***made*** his *advent* upon earth. 赤ん坊が誕生した.

P ***at*** the *advent* of the railway train (steam, electricity) 汽車(など)の始まった時に ‖ ***at*** the *advent* of the coldest season 寒の入りに. ¶***on*** the *advent* of fair weather 天気が好くなると. ¶***with*** the *advent* of the New Year 新年にはいってから.

P² the *advent* ***of*** spring 立春. 【類】the *advent* ***of*** the dog-days (土用). ¶the *advent* ***to*** power of Hideyoshi 秀吉の勃興(天下を取ったこと).

adventure, *n.* 冒険; 奇談, 珍事.

V ***give*** the *adventure* 一かばちかやって見る. ¶I ***had*** a singular *adventure*. 一珍事に遭遇した. ¶He ***loves*** *adventure*. 冒険が好きだ.

Q a ***blood-curdling*** *adventure* ぞっとするような冒険. ¶a ***bold*** *adventure* 思い切った冒険. ¶one of the most ***boldly-conceived*** and ***boldly-executed*** *adventures* the world has ever seen 考案実行ともに今までにない最も思い切った試みの一つ. ¶a ***dangerous*** (=***perilous***) *adventure* はなはだしい冒険. ¶tales of ***exciting*** *adventures* 血わき肉おどる冒険談. ¶a ***first*** *adventure* into the world of letters 文学界への初陣. ¶without any ***further*** *adventures* それからは無事で. ¶***gallant*** *adventures* 勇壮な冒険. ¶after many ***miraculous*** *adventures* [名器など]数奇な運命をたどった後. ¶one of the ***pleasantest*** *adventures* I ever met with in my life 私が一生の中で出会った最もおもしろい事件の一つ. ¶***romantic*** *adventures* 小説的な冒険. ¶his ***sad-ending matrimonial*** *adventure* 彼の悲劇に終った結婚沙汰. ¶have a ***serious*** *adventure* 重大事件にぶつかる. ¶***singular*** *adventures* 変った出来事. ¶a ***tame*** *adventure* 平凡な試み. ¶bristle with ***thrilling*** *adventures* ぞっとするような冒険に満ちている. ¶***various strange*** *adventures* 色々な不思議な事件.

Q² a ***hairbreadth*** *adventure* 危機一髪の冒険. ¶a ***pioneer*** *adventure* into the field of ... ...界の草分け. ¶***smuggling*** *adventure* 密貿易.

P He employed all his capital ***in*** *adventures*. 彼は金を残らず投機に使った. ‖ embark ***in*** (=***on***) *adventure* 冒険に乗出す.

P² the *adventures* ***of*** Robinson Crusoe ロビンソン・クルーソーの漂流奇談. ¶an *adventure* ***on*** sea 海上の冒険. ¶an *adventure* ***with*** pirates 海賊相手の冒険.

adventure, *v.* 冒険する.

P *adventure* ***in*** the unknown, uncertain fields 未知な不確実な方面で一つやって見る. ¶*adventure* ***on*** unknown seas 未知の海洋に(冒険的に)乗出す. ¶The king *adventured* his crown ***upon*** the issue. 国王はその事に王位を賭した.

adventurer, *n.* 冒険者.

Q ***dauntless*** *adventurers* 大胆な冒険者. ¶the zeal of the ***ecclesiastical*** *adventurers* 宗教的冒険者の熱心. ¶***political*** *adventurers* 政界の策士連. ¶that ***Western*** (=***w-***) *adventurer* in the East, Marco Polo 東洋における西洋の冒険家マルコ・ポーロ.

Q² ***merchant*** *adventurers* (十六世紀ごろの)政商.

adverb, *n.* 〚文法〛副詞.

Q an ***interrogative*** *adverb* 疑問副詞. ¶a ***negative*** adverb 否定副詞. ¶a ***relative*** *adverb* 関係副詞.

adversary, *n.* 敵手.

Q a ***subtle*** (=***wily or crafty***) *adversary* 狡猾(こう)な敵手. ¶a ***violent*** *adversary* 猛烈な敵手.

P² an *adversary* ***of*** (=***to***) a person 人の敵.

adverse, *a.* 反対の.

P *adverse* ***to*** his interest 彼の利益に反する ‖ He is *adverse* ***to*** letting his "left hand know what his right hand doth." 彼は「右の手のなすことを左の手に知らしめる」ということに反対である.

adversity, *n.* 逆境, 不運.

Q the ***deepest*** *adversity* 大困難.

P He is steeled ***against*** *adversity*. 彼は苦難に耐えられる. ¶He has been a good friend to me ***in*** *adversity* or in prosperity. 彼は逆境にも順境にも私の善い友人であった. 【類】cheerful ***in*** *adversity*. ¶He is patient ***under*** *adversity*. 彼は苦難によく堪える. ¶struggle ***with*** *adversity* 逆境と戦う.

advert *v.* 注意を向ける.

P *advert* ***to*** a statement (circumstance) 陳述(など)に意を注ぐ. 【類】the Government was compelled to *advert* ***to*** ... / He only *adverted* ***to*** some leading points of the arguments. / The King's illness was *adverted* ***to*** in the House of Commons. 国王の御不例は下院の日程に上った.

advertise, *v.* 広告する, 公告する.

M *advertise* ***energetically*** 熱心に広告する. ¶*advertise* ***extensively*** 盛んに広告する. ¶*advertise* ***freely*** 金を惜しまず広告する. ¶***heavily*** *advertise* in local papers 地方新聞にうんと広告する.

P *advertise* a child ***as*** lost 迷子の広告をする. ¶*advertise* ***by*** handbills ビラで広告する. 【類】*advertise* ***by*** outcry (口上で). ¶*advertise* goods ***for*** sale 売物の広告をする ‖ *advertise* ***for*** contracts to construct a bridge 橋梁架設工

事の請負を広告で求める ‖ *advertise* ***for*** a servant (house, situation) 召使(など)入用の広告をする. ‖ *advertise* ***for*** tenders for repairs 修理の入札を広告する. ¶I saw it *advertised* ***in*** today's papers. それを今日の新聞広告で見た. ¶I *advertised* him ***of*** my intention. 僕の所存を彼に告げた. ‖ *advertise* ***of*** (=concerning) a matter ある事件について広告する. ¶*advertise* ***on*** a bulletin-board 掲示板に出す. ¶*advertise* ***through*** the press 新聞で広告する. ¶*advertise* ***with*** the voice 声で宣伝する(ふれ回る). ‖ concerns *advertising* ***with*** us われわれの刊行物に広告する諸商店.

advertisement, *n.* 広告.

V ***answer*** an *advertisement* in a newspaper 新聞広告に応じる. ¶The prosecution ***gave*** that book a great *advertisement.* 検事の告発は大いにその本の広告になった. ¶***place*** an *advertisement* in a newspaper 新聞に広告を出す. ¶A New York paper ***prints*** this *advertisement.* ニューヨークの一新聞にこの広告が出ている. ¶***put in*** (=***insert***) an *advertisement* in a magazine 雑誌に広告を出す. ¶***withdraw*** one's *advertisement* 広告を撤回する.

Q an ***enticing*** *advertisement* 人の気を引く広告. ¶It proved a ***fine*** *advertisement.* 好い広告になった. ¶act as a ***good*** *advertisement* 好い広告になる. ¶***objectionable*** *advertisements* いかがわしい広告. ¶a ***matrimonial*** *advertisement* 結婚の告知. ¶for ***personal*** *advertisement* 自己宣伝のため. ¶the company was given a ***thunderous*** *advertisement* by ... ...が会社の大々的広告になった. ¶put a ***timid*** *advertisement* into his local weekly 地方の週刊新聞にちっぽけな広告を出す. ¶an ***unclean*** *advertisement* わいせつな広告. ¶***walking*** *advertisement* [ちんどん屋のするような]街頭広告. ¶a ***well-designed*** (=***ingenious***) *advertisement* 気のきいた広告.

Q² a ***color*** *advertisement* 色刷りの広告. ¶a ***fullpage*** [***newspaper***] *advertisement* 一ページ大の新聞広告. ¶a ***magazine*** *advertisement* 雑誌の広告. ¶a ***neon-light*** *advertisement* ネオンサイン広告. ¶***outdoor*** *advertisement* 屋外広告. ¶a ***patent medicine*** *advertisement* 売薬の広告. ¶***self*** *advertisement* 自己宣伝.

P buy things ***from*** *advertisements* 広告を見て物を買う. ¶the columns ***of*** *advertisements* 広告欄. ¶a notice appears among the *advertisement* ***in*** the Shanghai papers saying that ... 上海諸新聞の広告に...という告示が出ている.

advertiser, *n.* 広告主.

Q ***help-wanted*** *advertisers* 求人の広告主.

advertising, *n.* 広告.

V ***cut off*** *advertising* 広告を縮少する. ¶***display*** *advertising* 誇大な広告をする.

Q a firm which does ***big*** *advertising* 大々的な広告をする商社. ¶***extensive*** *advertising* 大規模な広告. ¶***gigantic*** *advertising* 大々的広告. ¶***outdoor*** *advertising* 屋外広告. ¶***successful*** *advertising* 効果的な広告.

Q² ***poster*** *advertising* ポスター広告. ¶***sandwich-board*** *advertising* サンドイッチマンによる広告法. ¶***window*** *advertising* 飾窓の広告. ¶***word of mouth*** *advertising* 口頭の広告.

P ***by*** clever *advertising* 巧みな広告によって. ¶***through*** skilful *advertising* 巧妙な広告で.

advice, *n.* **(1)** 忠告, 助言, 勧告, 意見.

V haughtily decline to ***accept*** *advice* ごう然と忠告をはねつける. 【類】He is not at all disposed to ***accept*** *advice.* ¶***ask*** *advice* of him for ... ...につき彼の助言を求める. ¶***carry out*** *advice* 勧告通りに実行する. ¶***contemn*** (=***despise***) the *advice* of ... ...の意見を軽べつする. ¶***disregard*** *advice* 勧告を無視する. ¶He ***followed*** his friend's *advice* literally. 彼は忠実に友人の勧めに従った. 【類】If they ***follow*** this *advice,* there is no telling how happy they would be. ‖ ***follow*** *advice* ***out*** to the letter 文字通りに忠告を実行する. ¶***furnish*** *advice* about ... ...につて助言を与える. ¶***give*** legal *advice* on questions pertaining to ... ...の問題に関する法律上の意見を述べる. 【類】I gave up ***giving*** her any *advice.* / I want to ***give*** you a little *advice* on ... ‖ The doctor ***gives*** *advice* every day at home. 彼は毎日宅診する. ‖ The old often ***give*** good *advice* to the young. 老人は若い人によい助言をすることがよくある. ¶***improve*** *advice* 助言を利用する. ¶***laugh*** the *advice* to scorn 忠告を一笑に付する. ¶This is because you ***neglected*** his *advice.* これは君があの人の忠告をおろそかにしたためだ. ¶***obtain*** medical *advice* 医師に診(み)てもらう. ¶***offer*** expert *advice* on all matters pertaining to ... ...の問題一切に関する専門家の意見を述べる. ¶***proffer*** *advice* 助言をする. ¶***provide*** skilled *advice* to ... ...に熟練家の意見を聞かせる. ¶***reject*** his *advice* 彼の忠告をはねつける. ¶***seek*** the *advice* of an expert regarding ... ...について専門家の意見をたゝく. 【類】***seek*** *advice* with respect to ... / ***seek*** *advice* from ... / ***seek*** the *advice* of acknowledged authorities (権威者) in various countries on points of ... / my *advice* was ***sought*** by ... about ... / ***seek*** the *advice* of a competent surgeon. ¶***solicit*** *advice* 助言を懇請する. ¶***spurn*** the *advice* of ... ...の忠告を一蹴する. ¶He ***took*** my *advice* as to what he should do. 彼は身の振方について私の意見に従った. 【類】He ***took*** my *advice* in good part (快く). / ***take*** *advice* from ... / ***Take*** my *advice* for your good. / Japan is the one Asiatic nation which has ***taken*** the Western *advice* so freely given to all Asiatic nations. / after ***taking*** the *advice* of ... ¶It is no easy matter to ***tender*** *advice* upon such a subject. こういう問題に参考として意見を述べるのは容易なことではない. ¶I ***want*** your *advice* on the matter. この事で御意見を伺いたい.

Q This is very ***common*** *advice* to the novice. これは初心者にとってごく普通の忠告だ. ¶***critical*** *advice* 批判的忠告. ¶***customary*** *advice* 通り一ぺんの忠告. ¶he gave me ***earnest*** *advice* ... 彼は私に...せよと切に勧めた. ¶No doubt this is ***excellent*** *advice.* たしかにこれは絶好の勧告だ. ¶***expert*** *advice* 専門家の意見. ¶give ***frank*** *advice* 苦言を呈する. ¶a piece of ***friendly*** *advice* 友人としての忠告. 【類】Take my ***friendly*** *advice* and do as I say. ‖ ***friendly*** *advice* on girls' problems 女子問題に関する親切な助言. ¶He gave me ***good*** *advice.* 私に善い事を勧めてくれた. ‖ waste ***good*** *advice* on ... ...は忠告してもむだだ. ¶***helpful*** *advice* 有益な助言. 【類】find a great deal of ***helpful*** *advice* on... ¶It is very ***homely*** *advice* to say. それは極めて平凡な忠告である. ¶***judicious*** *advice* 宜しきをえた助言. ¶You had better have ***legal*** *advice* before acting. 訴訟を起す前に弁護士に相談した方がよい. ¶give him a ***little*** *advice* on ... ...に関しいさゝか彼に忠告する. ¶seek ***medical*** *advice* 診察してもらう. 【類】Skilled ***medical*** *advice* should be at once sought. ¶***moderate*** *advice* おだやかな助言. ¶***negative*** *advice* (...するなという)消極的忠告. ¶***pithy*** *advice* 要領をえた助言. ¶***platitudinous*** (=***flat or commonplace***) *advice* 平凡な助言. ¶***practical*** *advice* 実際的な助言. ¶***professional*** *advice* 専門家の意見. ¶some ***sensible*** *advice* on this point is given by ... この点について...が筋の立った助言をしている. ¶***sound*** *advice* もっともな忠告. ¶require the ***supplementary*** *advice* その助言を更に補足する必要がある. ¶***Unasked*** *advice* is not, as a rule, acceptable. 余計な口だしは概して喜ばれないものだ. ¶***uncalled-for*** *advice* いらぬ差出口. ¶give ***unpleasant*** but ***kind-hearted*** *advice* 苦言を呈する. ¶give ***unpalatable*** but ***wholesome*** *advice* 苦言を呈する. ¶give ***verbal*** *advice* on ... ...について口頭で勧告する. ¶***well-put*** *advice* うまく持ちかけた忠告. ¶***well-weighed*** *advice* 熟考の上の助言. ¶***wholesome*** *advice* 健全な忠告. ¶really good ***workable*** *advice* ほんとうに良い実行のできる忠告. ¶***written*** *advice* 勧告書.

Q² ***expert*** *advice* 専門家の助言. 【類】do under reliable ***expert*** *advice.* ¶***expert travel*** *advice* 専門家の旅行に関する注意.

P ***against*** my *advice* 私の言うことを聴かないで ‖ act ***against*** *advice* 忠告にそむく. 【類】***against*** the *advice* of all his friends. ¶take this step ***at*** the *advice* of ... ...の勧告に従ってこの手段を取る. ¶***by*** his doctor's *advice* 彼のかかりつけの医師の勧めで ‖ It was only ***by*** his *advice* that he had given up the idea. その考えを捨てたのは全く彼の忠告があったからだ. ¶I came to you ***for*** *advice.* 君の意見を聞きに来た. ‖ convene an advisory board ***for*** *advice* in respect to ... ...に関する諮問の協議会を開く. ¶a word ***of*** *advice* 一言の忠告. 【類】a piece ***of*** *advice.* ¶It was done ***on*** my *advice.* 僕の考えでやった. 【類】***on*** the *advice* of his physicians (closest friends) / He has given up smoking ***on*** medical *advice.* ‖ acting ***on*** the *advice* of ... ...の忠告に従って. ¶***with*** the *advice* of ... ...の助言によって.

P^2 some *advice* ***about*** ... ...についてのある助言. ¶*advice* ***for*** a youth 一青年への訓戒. ¶his *advice* ***to*** young men on ... ...に関して青年に与えた彼の訓示. 【類】*advice* ***to*** students about to leave college / my *advice* ***to*** you as a ⌊friend is ...

(**2**) 通知, 案内, 報道.

V ***await*** *advice* from a buyer 買手からの通知を待つ. ¶***receive*** *advice* from abroad 外国よりの通知に接する. ‖ *advice* has been ***received*** that ... ...という通知に接した.

Q^2 receive ***cable*** *advice* from ... ...から海底電信で通知が来る.

P It is revised ***according to*** the latest *advices*. 最近の報道によって改訂した. ¶***as for*** our *advice* of ... ...日の通知通り. ¶***by*** the last *advices* from England 最近英国よりの報道によって. ¶***pending*** *advice* ***from*** him その人から通知があるまで. ¶Do not sell on any account ***until*** further *advice*. 当分(重ねて通知があるまでは)決して売ってはな⌊らぬ.

P^2 *advice* ***of*** shipment 出荷通知.

advisability, *n.* 得策, 可否.

V ***consider*** the *advisability* of ... ...の可否を考慮する. ¶I ***doubt*** the *advisability* of ... 私には...するのは得策でないように思われる. ¶I ***question*** its *advisability*. それは果して得策だろうか. ¶I would ***suggest*** the *advisability* of an effort being made to ... 私は...するように努力することをお勧めしたい.

advisable, *a.* 得策な.

M It is not absolutely necessary, but ***highly*** *advisable*. それは是非必要だというのではないが非常に望ましいことだ. ¶I thought it ***most*** *advisable* to ... ...するのが一番得策だと思った. ¶It is ***seldom*** *advisable*. それは滅多に勧められない.

P would it not be *advisable* ***for*** him to ...? ...するのは彼にとって得策ではないでしょうか.

advise, *v.* (**1**) 勧める, 忠告する.

M he is ***best*** *advised* to ... 彼は...するに若(し)くはない. ¶*advise* ***fervently*** 熱心に勧める. ¶act as ***legally*** *advised* 弁護士の助言通りにする. ¶I can ***safely*** *advise* you to buy it. それなら買っても大丈夫です. ¶I ***strongly*** *advise* you to ... ...することをたってお勧めする. ¶be ***urgently*** *advised* to ... 是非...なさい. ¶you are ***well*** *advised* to ... 君は...するがよい. 【類】the beginners will be ***well*** *advised* to.

P *advise* one ***against*** wrong 悪い事をしないように戒める. ‖ In cases of diabetes, physicians *advise* ***against*** the use of sugar. 糖尿病の場合には医者は砂糖をとらないようにと言う. ¶Be *advised* ***by*** me. = Let me advise you. 僕の言う事を聴き給え.

Q I *advised* him to be cautious. 気をつけるよう彼に注意した. ¶I *advised* him to do it himself. 自分でするように⌊勧めた.

(**2**) 通知する.

M be ***duly*** *advised* 正式の通知を受けている. ¶until ***further*** *advised* (=notice) 重ねて通知があるまで(当分). ¶be *advised* ***officially*** 公式に通告される. ¶as ***previously*** *advised* 既に通知の通り. 【類】at prices ***previously*** *advised*. ¶Keep me ***well*** *advised* of the progress of the matter. 事件の進行を漏れなく知らして下さい.

P I *advised* him ***of*** my whereabouts. 私は彼に居所を知らせた. ‖ I wish to be *advised* ***of*** ... ...の件を御通知下さい. 【類】I will keep you *advised* ***of*** the state of the market ⌊(市況).

(**3**) 相談する, 商議する.

P *advise* ***with*** one's pillow 一晩寝て考える ‖ *advise* ***with*** friends 友人と相談する ‖ The President *advised* ***with*** the Cabinet. 大統領は閣議に諮った.

advisement, *n.* 勘考.

P have ***under*** *advisement* 勘考中.

adviser, *n.* 顧問, 相談役.

V ***call in*** the best *advisers* 最良の顧問を聘(へい)する. ¶***employ*** foreign *advisers* 外人顧問を招聘する.

Q a ***competent*** *adviser* 敏腕の顧問. ¶***confidential*** *advisers* 秘密の相談に預る人. ¶an ***itinerant*** *adviser* 巡回相談相手. ¶a ***legal*** *adviser* 法律顧問. ¶He is ***medical*** *adviser* for the New York Society for the Protection of Children. 彼はニューヨーク児童保護協会嘱託医です. ¶a ***military*** *adviser* 軍事顧問. ¶Dr. G. E. Morrison, the ***political*** *Adviser* to the President of the Chinese Republic 中華民国大総統政治顧問モリソン博士. ¶a ***technical*** *adviser* 技術顧問. ¶a ***spiritual*** *adviser* 宗教顧問.

Q^2 a ***desk*** *adviser* 座右の参考書. ¶a ***full-time*** *adviser* 専任顧問. ¶a ***student*** *adviser* 学生の相談相手. ¶***vocation*** *advisers* 職業指導者.

P^2 an *adviser* ***in*** sericulture 養蚕顧問. ¶an *adviser* ***on*** legal affairs (=legal adviser) ***to*** the Siamese Government シャム政府法律顧問.

advising, *n.* 助言.

Q^2 effective ***faculty*** *advising* 教授(学校側)の効果的な指導.

advocacy, *n.* 弁護; 唱道, 鼓吹.

V His *advocacy* of it was heartily ***endorsed***. 彼のその唱道⌈は大賛成をえた.

Q an ***open*** *advocacy* of ... ...を公然唱道すること. ¶***strenuous*** *advocacy* of the right 熱烈な権利の主張. ¶***zealous*** *advocacy* of the defence of the country against foreign aggression 熱心な国防鼓吹.

P use these facts ***in*** *advocacy* of ... ...の弁護にその事実を⌊利用する.

P^2 *advocacy* ***of*** peace 平和の鼓吹.

advocate, *n.* 弁護者, 擁護者; 鼓吹者, 唱道者.

V the work ***found*** an *advocate* in the person of ... ...がその事業に賛成した.

Q The paper is an ***able*** *advocate* of the laborers. その新聞は労働者の有力な味方である. ¶a ***blind, headlong*** *advocate* 盲目的で軽卒な鼓吹者. ¶an ***earnest*** *advocate* of the work of ... ...の事業の熱心な擁護者. 【類】an ***earnest*** *advocate* of this idea. ¶a ***keen*** *advocate* of it その熱烈な唱道者. ¶a ***misled*** and ***overhasty*** *advocate* of social equality 社会的平等の脱線的性急な擁護者. ¶a ***powerful*** *advocate* for free love 自由恋愛の有力な唱道者. ¶a ***sincere*** *advocate* of a phonetic orthography 表音綴字法の真剣な唱道者. ¶one of the most ***strenuous*** *advocates* of socialism 最も熱心な社会主義の唱道者. ¶a ***theoretical*** and ***practical*** *advocate* ***of*** ... ...の理論的及び実際的の唱道者. ¶an ***unhesitating*** *advocate* of orthographic reform 果断なる綴字改良論者. ¶a ***vigorous*** *advocate* of well-made highways 有力な道路改良者. ¶a ***warm*** *advocate* of (=for) a cause ある主義の熱心な唱道者.

Q^2 a ***birth control*** *advocate* 産児制限の主唱者. ¶a ***temperance*** *advocate* 禁酒論者.

P^2 a warm *advocate* ***for*** Japan 熱心な日本の弁護者. 【類】an *advocate* ***for*** the weak and oppressed (弱者と被圧制者). ¶an *advocate* ***of*** truth 真理の擁護者.

advocate, *v.* 擁護する, 弁護する; 主張する.

M ***firmly*** *advocate* ... 堅く...を擁護する. ¶*advocate* ***militantly*** 猛烈に主張する. ¶***strongly*** *advocate* ... 強く...を主張する.

P *advocate* ***with*** passionate eloquence 熱弁を振って弁護⌈する.

aegis, *n.* 庇護.

P the unchallenged supremacy of Britain ***under*** the *aegis* of the Crown 国王の庇護の下にある押しも押されもせぬ英国の覇権. 【類】It flourished ***under*** the Imperial *aegis*. / ***under*** the *aegis* of that lady.

aeroplane, *n.* 飛行機 =airplane.

V ***fly*** an *aeroplane* 飛行機を飛ばす. ¶***pilot*** an *aeroplane* 飛行機を操縦する.

P travel to Paris ***by*** *aeroplane* 飛行機でパリへ旅行する. ¶He flew a mile a minute ***in*** his *aeroplane*. 彼は一分に一マイル飛行した. ¶***on*** an *aeroplane* 飛行機に乗って.

afar, *ad.* 遠く.

P He came ***from*** *afar* to see the sight. 彼ははるばるそれを見物に来た. 【類】It is seen ***from*** *afar*. ‖ worship ***from*** ⌊*afar* 遥拝.

affability, *n.* 愛想のよいこと.

P ***with*** *affability* 愛想よく.

affable, *a.* 愛想のよい.

P *affable* and courteous ***in*** manner 愛想よくいんぎんな態度で. ¶He is *affable* ***to*** his guests. 彼は客に愛想がよい.

affair, *n.* 事柄; 事務; 事件.

V ***administer*** the *affairs* of the university 大学の事務を管理する. ¶go home to ***arrange*** his *affairs* 家事整理のため帰家する ‖ ***arrange*** (=settle) an *affair* amicably 円満に事件を解決する. ¶***break off*** an *affair* 事件を破談にする. ¶***close*** an *affair* 事件を落着させる. ¶***conduct*** state *affairs* (=the affairs of state) 国政を執る. ¶The *affair* has been ***covered up*** (=***hushed up***). あの一件はもみ消されてしまった. ¶She ***directs*** the *affairs* of her neighbors. その国が隣国の政治を指導する. ¶***discuss*** the *affairs* of the nation 国事を談じる. ¶Edison has had the gift of picking the right men to ***handle*** his *affairs*. エディソンは彼の仕事をやらせる適材を選ぶことに妙を得ていた. 【類】*han-*

dle the *affairs* of State (国務). ¶One of the directors went out to India in order to ***investigate*** the *affairs*. 理事者の一人が実情調査のためにインドに赴いた. ¶He is quite able to ***manage*** his own *affairs*. あの人は自分のことは結構自分でやって行ける人だ.【類】You cannot expect him to ***manage*** his *affairs* satisfactorily. ¶***Mind*** your own *affairs*. 大きなお世話だ. ¶***mismanage*** the whole *affair* すっかりやりそこなう. ¶***neglect*** worldly *affairs* 俗事から遠ざかる. ¶***open*** the whole *affairs* to ... 一部始終を...に打ち明ける. ¶I shall be happy to give you all my aid in ***promoting*** your *affairs*. 喜んで貴下が好成績を挙げられるように御援助致します. ¶***put*** one's *affairs* into another's hands 自分の事を人に任せる. ¶Events have ***reshaped*** human *affairs*. 新しいでき事で世の中が一変した. ¶***settle*** one's *affairs* 諸事を整理する. ¶***straighten out*** the *affairs* of an all but ruined bank つぶれかかった銀行の財政を整理する. ¶***take*** the *affair* in his own hands その事件を引き受ける. ¶a great revolution that has ***transformed*** human *affairs* 人事を一変させた一大改革. ¶If you will ***undertake*** the *affair* I shall be very grateful. 貴下が御引受け下さるならこの上もないことです. ¶***wind up*** the *affairs* of a business 店をしまう.

V² How are *affairs* ***looking***? 形勢はどうか. ¶We discovered how *affairs* ***stood***. どういう実情にあるかが分った.

Q in ***all*** *affairs* of life 人生万事万端. ¶an ***annual*** *affair* 年中行事. ¶The function proved a very ***beautiful*** *affair*. その宴会は実に盛んなものだった. ¶a ***big*** *affair* 大事件. ¶***civil*** *affairs* 民事. ¶a ***clumsy*** *affair* 不出来なもの. ¶a very ***complicated*** *affair* ごく込み入った事件. ¶***culinary*** *affairs* 炊事. ¶***current*** *affairs* 時事. ¶a ***cut-and-dried*** *affair* 紋切形(演説など). ¶It was a most ***democratic*** *affair*. 極めて平民的な催しだった. ¶a ***disastrous*** *affair* 惨事. ¶***domestic*** *affairs* 家事 ‖ Russian ***domestic*** *affairs* ロシアの国情. ¶The party was a ***dull*** *affair*. 会はつまらなかった. ¶The race turned out to be an ***exciting*** *affair*. その競走は見物人を興奮させた. ¶She has had some ***family*** *affair*. 彼女は何か家に用事があった. ¶Japan now played an important part in ***Far Eastern*** *affairs*. 日本は今や極東の大立者であった. ¶the ***financial*** *affairs* of a company 会社の財政. ¶a ***framed*** (=***got-up***) *affair* 八百長. ¶The machine is a ***grand*** *affair*. あの機械は大したものだ. ¶a ***hackneyed*** *affair* ありふれた事. ¶carry on ***household*** *affairs* 家計をたてる. ¶in literature, as in all other ***human*** *affairs* 他の人事と同様に文学上でも.【類】In all ***human*** *affairs*, fertile periods are succeeded by periods comparatively sterile (不況時代), to be followed in their turn by periods of abundance (盛況時代). ¶The luncheon was strictly an ***informal*** *affair*. 午餐は全く略式なものだった. ¶***international*** *affairs* 国際事情. ¶The dispute is a ***long*** *affair*. あの争議は久しいものだ. ¶a well-known writer on ***military*** *affairs* 著名な軍事記者. ¶***monetary*** *affairs* 財務. ¶a ***much-talked-of*** *affair* 有名な事件. ¶***mundane*** *affairs* 俗事.【類】the vanity of ***mundane*** *affairs* and the certainty of death to all. ¶earnest students of ***municipal*** *affairs* 市政の熱心な研究者. ¶***national*** *affairs* 国政. ¶***naval*** and ***military*** *affairs* 軍事. ¶It is ***no*** *affair* of ours. そりゃわれわれの知った事じゃない. ¶in the ***ordinary*** *affairs* of life 日常の事で[は]. ¶interfere in ***other men's*** *affairs* 人の事に干渉する. ¶The exhibition will be a ***petty*** *affair*. その博覧会は小規模のものだろう. ¶the course of ***political*** *affairs* in ... ...における政治上の方針. ¶The river is a ***poor*** *affair*. ちっぽけな川だ. ¶illustrations taken from the ***practical*** *affairs* of everyday life 日常生活の実際から取った例証. ¶a ***private*** *affair* 私事. ¶a very ***provoking***, ***vexatious*** *affair* 腹の立つ厄介な事. ¶***public*** *affairs* 公務. ‖ men of ***public*** *affairs* 公人. ¶The wedding was a ***quiet*** *affair*. その結婚式は質素であった. ¶a ***sanguinary*** *affair* 流血騒ぎ. ¶***secular*** *affairs* 俗事. ¶a ***serious*** *affair* 一大事. ¶His anger is a very ***small*** *affair*. 彼が怒ったって少しも驚くに足らない. ¶I am asked to more ***social*** *affairs* than I have time to attend. 出席しきれないほど沢山のパーティーに招待を受けている. ¶His funeral will be a very ***swell*** *affair*. あの人の葬儀は定めしりっぱなものでしょう. ¶a ***tragic*** *affair* 惨事. ¶the ***transient*** *affairs* of this life 浮世のはかない物事. ¶a ***trifling*** *affair* ささいな事. ¶act as a settler in an ***unpleasant*** *affair* おもしろくない事のしりぬぐい役を買って出る. ¶*Affairs* at present are very ***unsettled***. 目下の事態は極めて安定を欠いている. ¶The building is not an ***unsightly*** *affair*. あの建物は目ざわりにならない. ¶forget the ***whole*** *affair* そのことをすっかり忘れる. ¶***worldly*** *affairs* 俗事.

Q² on ***business*** *affairs* 商用で. ¶the ***China*** *Affair* シナ事変. ¶***city*** *affairs* 市内の状況. ¶an ***everyday*** *affair* 日常茶飯事.【類】Sleep, though in the strictest sense an ***everyday*** *affair*, is still the strangest and most wonderful of the phenomena of existence. ¶***family*** *affairs* 家事. ¶***home-front*** *affairs* 銃後の事情. ¶handle one's ***household*** *affairs* 家事を処理する. ¶Some novelists make ***love*** *affairs* their stock-in-trade. ある小説家は恋愛事件を商売道具にしている.【類】She has had some ***love*** *affair*. ¶It has become a ***neighborhood*** *affair*. 近所で知らぬ者はない. ¶an important ***state*** *affair* 重大な国務.【類】His funeral will be made a ***state*** *affair*. ¶a ***tripod*** *affair* 写真撮影. ¶with the ***world*** *affairs* in their present state 現状のような世界情勢では.【類】discuss ***world*** *affairs* in an address (演説で) / a student of ***world*** *affairs*.

P He was mixed up ***in*** the *affair*. 彼はその事件に関係するようになった. ‖ ***in*** the *affairs* of men 人事において ‖ He helped me ***in*** the recent *affair*. 先日の件であの人の世話になった. ¶What an alarming state ***of*** *affairs*! 実に恐るべき事態だ.【類】in the present state ***of*** *affairs* ‖ a man ***of*** *affairs* 事務家. ¶He is much occupied ***with*** *affairs* of state. 彼は国事に没頭している.

P² Good writing is partly an *affair* ***of*** the ear, and the ear can best be trained through oral reading. りっぱな文を書くということは一部は耳の問題でその耳の練習は音読によるのが一番いい.【類】The *affairs* ***of*** the enterprise went from bad to worse. / War is more and more an *affair* ***of*** money. / an *affair* ***of*** great importance (重大) / an *affair* ***of*** love = a love *affair* ‖ an *affair* ***of*** honor = a duel 決闘 ‖ *affair* ***of*** everyday life 世の常の事 ‖ The journey from Tokyo to Kyoto, which was formerly an *affair* ***of*** 12 or 13 days on foot, is now reduced to as many hours. 東京から京都への旅行はもとは十二三日かかったものだが今では十二三時間に短縮された.

affect, *v.* (1) 影響する.

M ***adversely*** *affected* by it それにわざわいされて. ¶***directly*** *affect* the living of the people 国民の暮しの上にすぐ響く. ¶local questions that *affect* them ***closely*** 密接に彼等に影響する地方問題. ¶***hypocritically*** *affect* coyness ねこをかぶって恥ずかしそうにする. ¶*affect* ***indirectly*** 間接に影響する. ¶*affect* ***materially*** 実質的に影響する. ¶He is ***mentally*** *affected*. 気が変だ. ¶be ***seriously*** *affected* by... ...のために重大な影響を受けている.【類】The change has ***seriously*** *affected* my income. ¶The crop was more or less ***severely*** *affected* by the recent heavy frost. その作は最近の霜害を多かれ少なかれ受けた. ¶*affect* it ***unfavorably*** それに害がある. ¶matters ***vitally*** *affecting* his interests 彼の利害に重大の影響を及ぼす事柄.

P I am *affected* ***by*** the climate. 私は気候の影響を受けた. ‖ Are your interests *affected* ***by*** it? それが君の利害に影響するか. ‖ persons *affected* ***by*** the purge directive パージに引っかかる人々.【類】be *affected* ***by*** various conditions / Thousands of people were *affected* ***by*** the floods. ¶He was *affected* ***in*** character by the environment. 彼はその環境のために品性に影響を受けた. ¶be *affected* ***in*** health ***by*** the environment. 環境の影響を受けて健康を害している. ¶business *affected* ***with*** a public interest 公共の利益を図る仕事.

(2) 感動させる.

M The audience was ***deeply*** *affected*. 聴衆は深く感動した. ¶he was ***strongly*** *affected* with the wish to ... 彼はぜひ...したがっていた.【類】be ***strongly*** *affected* by the sufferings of ...

P He was *affected* ***at*** the news. 彼はその話に感動した. ‖ He was *affected* ***at*** seeing it. ¶I was deeply *affected* ***by*** your words. 私はあなたのお言葉に非常に感動しました.【類】*affected* ***by*** kindness. ¶*affected* ***with*** pity (=compassion) 哀れみの気持に動かされて.【類】He was *affected* ***with*** awe (sorrow, joy).

(3) 感染する, 冒す.

P persons *affected by* the disease その病に冒された人々 ‖ He was *affected* ***by*** the heat. 彼は暑さにあたった. 【類】The throat is *affected* ***by*** a cold. / The patient is possessed with the idea that the entire organism is *affected* ***by*** an incurable disease. ¶those *affected* ***with*** tuberculosis 結核患者. 【類】In France alone, more than a million people are *affected* ***with*** some form of mental ailment (精神病).

affectation, *n.* 気取り. 「る.

V ***make*** an *affectation* of one's learning 学問を鼻にかけ

Q His *affectations* are ***insufferable***. あいつのきざなことったら鼻もちならん. ¶***mincing*** *affectation* おつに気取ること ‖ with ***mincing*** *affectation* いやに気取った言い方で. ¶a ***snobbish*** *affectation* 俗っぽい気取り.

P ***with*** an *affectation* of *sang-froid* 平気を装って. ¶***without*** *affectation* 気取らずに.

P^2 an *affectation* ***of*** sincerity (scholarship, virtue, great wealth, wit) 誠実(など)を装うこと.

affected, *a.* 気どった; きざな.

M a girl ***awfully*** *affected* いやにぶっている女.

P a young lady very *affected* ***in*** manner いやに気取った

affection, *n.* (**1**) 愛情, 愛. 【若い女.

V ***alienate*** *affection* between friends 友人を離間させる. ¶***appreciate*** the *affection* he has won 彼がかちえた愛情を喜ぶ. ¶he ***cherished*** the deepest *affection* for ... 彼は...に対して深甚の愛情を懐いていた. ¶she ***conceived*** a great *affection* for ... 彼女は...を非常に愛していた. ¶***cultivate*** the *affections* of the young lady one is in love with ほれている若い女の愛をえようと努める. ¶***devote*** her *affection* on some one ある人に彼女の愛情を捧げる. ¶***feel*** much *affection* for ... ...を非常に愛する. ¶He tried every way he knows to ***gain*** her *affection*. 彼は彼女に愛されようと百方試みた. ¶***have*** an *affection* for children (one's parents, a woman) 子供(など)を愛する. 【類】I ***have*** deep *affection* for the memory (遺名) of ... ¶All his *affection* was ***heaped*** on his grandson. 彼は孫をこの上もなくかわいがった. ¶***keep*** one's *affection* of ... ...を愛し続ける. ¶He has ***killed*** her *affection*. 女から愛想をつかされた. ¶***reciprocate*** the *affection* of ... ...の愛に報いる(...と相思の仲となる). ¶He ***retained*** a tender *affection* for his wife to the end of his life. 彼は終生その妻に対し優しい愛情を失わなかった. ¶He ***returned*** her *affection*. 彼は彼女の愛に報いた. ¶He ***set*** his *affections* on it. 彼はそれを愛した. ¶He took an ignominious position to ***share*** her *affection* with another. 二人の男が同時に彼女を愛するという肩身の狭い立場に彼はおかれた. ¶***show*** *affection* for... ...に対して愛情を示す. ¶His *affections* were ***turned*** from his wife. 彼は妻に愛想をつかした. ¶He ***won*** her *affections*. 彼は彼女の愛をかち得た. 「て来た.

V^2 Her husband's *affection* ***waned***. 夫の愛情に秋風が立っ

Q the ***benevolent*** *affections* 慈愛. ¶he has a ***deep*** *affection* for (=towards) ... 彼は...を深く愛する. ¶***deep-seated*** *affection* 根強い愛情. ¶indulge in ***demonstrative*** *affection* in public 人前で遠慮なく愛情を表明する. ¶cherish ***great*** *affection* for ... ...に対し多大の愛を持つ. ¶a ***keen*** *affection* 切なる愛. ¶a ***mawkish*** *affection* めめしい愛情. ¶She has a ***mother's*** (=***motherly***) *affection* for her pupils. 彼女の生徒を愛すること慈母のようだ. ¶***mutual*** *affection* 相思. ¶cherish a strictly ***platonic*** *affection* for ... ...に対して極めて清純な愛情を抱く. ¶***reciprocal*** *affection* 相思. ¶***spurious*** *affection* 偽りの愛. ¶a ***strong*** *affection* for ... ...に対する強い愛情. ¶Remember me with the ***tenderest*** *affection* to your children. お子様方へくれぐれもよろしく. ¶***unrequited*** *affection* 失恋(片思い).

P She married ***from*** *affection*. 彼女は愛の結婚をした. ¶love each other ***with*** an undying *affection* 末永く愛し合う ‖ She was reared ***with*** the utmost care and *affection*. ちょうよ花よと育てられた. ¶She married ***without*** *affection* and from pure necessity. 彼女は愛のない全く止むを得ない情実結婚をした.

P^2 *affection* ***between*** the sexes 男女の情. ¶His *affection* ***for*** (=***towards***) his wife continued unabated. 妻に対する彼の愛情は少しも変らなかった. ¶the *affection* ***of*** a parent for a child 子に対する親の愛情 ‖ the *affection* ***of*** parent and child 親子の愛情.

(**2**) 疾患.

Q ***bacterial*** *affections* 細菌性の病気. ¶Tremor of the hands is a common symptom in many ***nervous*** *affections*. 手の震えるのは多くの神経病の普通の症状だ. ¶a ***painful*** *affection* of the knee ひざの痛み.

Q^2 relieve ***chest*** *affections* 胸の病気をなおす.

P^2 an *affection* ***of*** the lungs 肺患 ‖ *affections* ***of*** the skin 【皮膚病.

affectionate, *a.* 愛情の深い.

P He is *affectionate* ***to*** (=toward) her. 彼は彼女を愛している. 【類】They are *affectionate* ***to*** each other. ¶I feel increasingly *affectionate* ***towards*** Tokyo. ますます東京が

affianced, *pa.* 婚約して. 【好きになる.

P He is *affianced* ***to*** her. 彼は彼女と婚約をしている.

affidavit, *n.* 〖法〗宣誓口供書.

V ***make*** an *affidavit* 宣誓する. ‖ ***make*** *affidavit* of it それに基く調書を作製する. ¶***swear*** an *affidavit* 口供書に誤りのないことを宣誓する. ¶The judge ***took*** the *affidavit*. 判事は[宣誓]口供書を取った.

affiliate, *n.* 支部, 加盟国.

Q^2 a ***U.N.*** *affiliate* 国連加盟国.

P^2 an *affiliate* ***of*** the International Typographical Union 国際印刷連盟支部. 「する.

affiliate, *v.* 仲間に入れる; 併合する; 《米》親しくする; 帰

P The two banks were *affiliated* ***by*** a common ownership of stock. 両銀行は株を共有している点で関係があった. ¶She *affiliated* her child ***to*** (=***on or upon***) him. 彼女はその子(私生児)の父親は彼だと言った. ¶*affiliate* oneself ***with*** (=to) a political party 政党に加入する. ‖ He is *affiliated* ***with*** good fellows. 《米》彼はいい友だちをもっている. ‖ The hospital is *affiliated* ***with*** (=to) the University of Oxford. あの病院はオクスフォード大学に付属している. 【類】a parent (母体たる) society ***with*** which others are *affiliated* / The express companies (運送会社) are private corporations *affiliated* ***with*** the railroad companies. / be *affiliated* ***with*** the Liberal Party / be *affiliated* ***with*** Communist-front organization (共産党前衛組織).

affiliation, *n.* 提携; 関係.

V ***choose*** one's *affiliation* wisely 入会先の選択を誤らない. ¶***form*** an *affiliation* with ... ...と提携する. ¶***have*** no *affiliation* with ... ...とは何の関係もない. ¶The screen actress ***made*** a new picture *affiliation*. その映画女優はある映画会社と新たに契約ができた.

Q^2 ***business*** *affiliation* 事業上の関係. ¶the unions with ***Communist*** *affiliations* 共産党に関係のある組合. ¶Lemon and fish are natural ***food*** *affiliations*. レモンと魚はよく調和する. ¶without any ***party*** *affiliations* 政党とは一切関係なく ‖ The Economist has no ***party*** *affiliation* but is generally considered conservative. エコノミスト誌は全く党派に関係がないが一般に保守的と見なされている. ¶***political*** or ***labor*** *affiliations* 政党もしくは労働組合との

P hospitals ***in*** *affiliation* 附属病院. 【関係.

affinity, *n.* 密接な関係; 和合性; 〖化〗親和力.

V It ***has*** an *affinity* for water. それは水と親和する. ¶Oil and water ***lack*** natural *affinity*. 水と油は自然の親和力を欠いている.

P^2 the *affinity* ***between*** congenial spirits 気の合った同士の和合性. 【類】There is an *affinity* ***between*** English and German. / There is mutual *affinity* ***between*** the magnet and iron. ¶the *affinity* ***of*** oxygen ***for*** hydrogen 酸素と水素との親和力. ¶English has a very close *affinity* ***to*** French. 英語はフランス語に密接な関係がある. ¶Music has much *affinity* ***with*** poetry. 音楽は詩によく似ている.

affirm, *v.* 断言する, 主張する.

M *affirm* ***categorically*** 明確に断言する. ¶from my own experience, I ***confidently*** affirm that ... 私は私自身の経験から自信を以て...と断言する. ¶*affirm* ***peremptorily*** 断固として主張する. ¶we can ***safely*** *affirm* that ... ...と言っても差支えない. 【類】it may ***safely*** be *affirmed* that... ¶***unhesitatingly*** *affirm* ちゅうちょせずに断言する.

P The witness *affirmed* ***to*** the fact. 証人はそれが事実だと

affirmation, *n.* 確認, 〖法〗証言. 【断定した.

V ***make*** an *affirmation* 確認(証言)する.

affirmative, *n.* 肯定, 是認.

V ***take*** the *affirmative* [討論等で]賛成側に立つ.

P He was ***for*** the *affirmative*. 彼は賛成の方だった. ¶answer (=reply) ***in*** the *affirmative* そうだと答える(うんと返

affix, *v.* つける, はる, [印を]おす. 【事をする).

Q *affix* the eye ***on*** a person 人に目をつける. ¶*affix* a stamp ***to*** a letter 手紙に切手をはる. 【類】*affix* a seal ***to*** an instrument (証書) / *affix* a syllable ***to*** a word.

afflict, *v.* 悩ます, 苦しめる.

M He is ***grievously*** *afflicted.* 彼は非常に悩まされている. ¶He is ***sorely*** *afflicted* with the gout. 彼は痛風でひどく悩んでいる.

P He was ***afflicted at*** seeing it. 彼はそれを見て心を痛めた. 【類】He is ***afflicted at*** that circumstance (the failure). ¶He was ***afflicted with*** the rheumatism. 彼はリューマチスに悩まされた. 【類】He was ***afflicted with*** persecution (迫害). ¶a young woman ***afflicted with*** a serious hysteria 重いヒステリーをわずらっている若い女 ‖ *afflict* oneself ***with*** illness 病気で苦しむ. 【類】***afflicted with*** lung [heart] diseases / *afflict* a land ***with*** plagues (疫病) / I am ***afflicted with*** suffering. / I am ***afflicted with*** anxiety on the subject of ...

affliction, *n.* 苦難.

Q a ***treacherous*** *affliction* 始末の悪い病.

P He bore up ***under*** *affliction.* 彼は苦難を耐え忍んだ.

affluence, *n.* 富裕.

V ***reach*** *affluence* 富裕の身となる.

P He lived ***in*** *affluence.* 彼は裕福に暮した.

P² *affluence* ***of*** words (thoughts) 言葉(思想)の豊富.

affluent, *n.* 支流.

P The city is situated ***on*** the *affluent* of a river. その都市は支流の河畔にある.

affluent, *a.* 富んでいる.

P a land *affluent* ***in*** minerals 鉱物に富む土地. ¶be *affluent* ***with*** Saturday's wages 土曜の給料で懐中があたたかい.

afford, *v.* …する余裕がある; 与える; 耐える.

M can *afford* it ***financially*** 経済的にその余裕がある. ¶can ***hardly*** *afford* to neglect 投げやりにしておけない. ¶I can ***ill*** *afford* to pay 1st class. 一等は払いかねる. ‖ We can ***ill*** *afford* to spare it. それは手離しかねる. ‖ His purse could ***ill*** *afford* any but the simplest fare. 彼の収入では粗食しかできない. 【類】I can ***ill*** *afford* the time (money). / the death of two men which it could ***ill*** *afford* to lose ‖ those whom the nation can ***ill*** *afford* to spare 国家有用の人材. ¶can ***scarcely*** *afford* to be without ... なしではちょっと済ませない. ¶can ***well*** *afford* to ... …しても一向差支えない. 【類】items (事項) for which we can ***well*** *afford* to be grateful ‖ I can ***well*** *afford* the expense 十分入費に堪えられる.

P It has *afforded* great satisfaction ***to*** me. 私は大いに満足した. ¶dress as well as one can *afford* ***upon*** one's income 収入の許す限り服装を良くする. ¶No one who studies English can *afford* ***without*** it. それは英語研究者にはなくてならぬものだ.

Q Do not be cross with the child; you cannot *afford* it. 子供に対して意地悪くしてはいけない. それは損だ. ¶I'm not rich enough to *afford* an automobile. 自動車を置くだけの余裕がない. 【類】We can *afford* to sell them cheap. / Few can *afford* to buy luxuries. / I cannot *afford* to have you idle. / You cannot *afford* to get discouraged. ¶He could *afford* to die. 彼としては死んでもよかったのだ. ¶I cannot *afford* to be critical. あれこれ言いたくない.

affright, *n.* 驚き, 恐怖.

P be ***in*** *affright* こわがっている.

affright, *v.* 驚かす.

P I was ***affrighted at*** (=***by***) the sight. 私はその光景にびっくりした. / be ***affrighted at*** (=***by***) a vision (幻影). ¶*affright* him ***from*** his purpose 彼をおどしてその目的を断念させる. ¶*affright* a person ***with*** (=by) threats 人をおどす.

affront, *n.* 侮辱.

V ***offer*** an *affront* to (=***put*** an *affront* upon) ... …に無礼を加える. ¶***pocket*** the *affront* 辱(はずか)しめを忍ぶ.

Q a ***deadly*** *affront* 致命的侮辱.

P² It is an *affront* ***to*** understanding (common sense, good taste). それは理解力(など)に対する侮辱だ. 【類】*affront* ***to*** the King.

affront, *v.* 怒らせる.

P be *affronted* ***at*** his conduct 彼の不都合を怒る.

aflame, *ad.* 燃えて; 輝いて.

M The city was ***all*** *aflame.* 市は火に包まれていた.

P The cliff is *aflame* ***with*** the crimson maple. がけは紅葉したかえでで赤一色になっている. 【類】The street is *aflame* ***with*** lamps. ‖ He was *aflame* ***with*** indignation (= wrath). 彼はかんかんに怒っていた. 【類】I am all *aflame* ***with*** curiosity. / Her face was *aflame* ***with*** blushes.

afloat, *a., ad.* 浮んで; 浸水して; ぐらついて.

M The firm is ***again*** *afloat.* 会社は赤字がなくなった. ¶The meadows are ***all*** *afloat.* 草原は一面浸水している. ‖ Our affairs are ***all*** *afloat.* われわれの仕事はぐらついている.

P The rumor is *afloat* ***about*** me. 僕に関してそういう風説が立っている.

afraid, *a.* 恐れている.

M She seems ***awfully*** *afraid* of losing her lover. 彼女は愛人に逃げられはしないかと大いに心配しているようだ. ¶Napoleon was ***deadly*** *afraid* of a razor. ナポレオンはひどくかみそりをこわがった. ¶I am ***dreadfully*** *afraid* it will ... 私はそれが ... することを非常に恐れている. ¶I was ***half*** *afraid* of bathing there. 私はそこで水に入ることがちょっと恐ろしかった. ¶I am ***intensely*** *afraid* of thunder. 雷が大きらいだ. ¶Will the patient recover?—I am *afraid* ***not.*** 病人は治りましょうか—ちょっとむずかしい. ¶I am ***really*** *afraid* of presuming upon your kindness. あなたの御親切に甘え過ぎることになりはしまいかと本当に心配しています. ¶I am *afraid* ***so.*** そうかも知れぬ. ¶he is ***weakly*** *afraid* of ... 彼は心ひそかに…を恐れている.

P He is *afraid* ***of*** death. 彼は死を恐れている. 【類】He is *afraid* ***of*** the results. / You need not be *afraid* ***of*** being late. / He is *afraid* ***of*** punishment. / I am so *afraid* ***of*** the sea. / He is not *afraid* ***of*** being called a communist.

O He is *afraid* to die. 彼は死ぬのをこわがっている. ¶We were *afraid* lest we [should] hurt him. われわれは彼を傷つけ(おこらせ)てはならぬと心配した. ¶I am *afraid* [that] it will happen. 私はもしやそんなことがありはしないかと心配している. 【類】I am *afraid* he won't come.

after, *ad., prep.* 後に; …を尋ねて; …に次ぐ.

M ***immediately*** *after* 間もなく; すぐ後に. ¶***shortly*** *after* three o'clock 三時少し過ぎに. ¶***soon*** *after* ほどなく. ¶It happened ***twenty years*** *after.* それは二十年後に起った.

P ***from*** *after* (=behind) 後から.

O the most influential politician *after* ... …に次いで一番勢力のある政治家. ¶I am *after* you. 君を探していた. ¶Several people have been here *after* you today. きょう幾人もあなたを尋ねて来ました.

aftercare, *n.* 補導; 病後の手当.

P² the *aftercare* ***of*** the prisoners 免囚保護 ‖ the *aftercare* ***of*** a mother in childbirth 産後の手当.

aftereffect, *n.* 余波.

V ***cause*** (=***produce***) no harmful *aftereffects* [薬など]副作用を起さない. ¶have ***bad*** *aftereffect* 後がたたる.

P² *aftereffects* ***of*** drinking=《米》a hang-over 二日酔い.

afterglow, *n.* 夕焼.

V ***display*** an *afterglow* of death 死花を咲かす.

afterhour, *n.* 引け時間.

P They play tennis ***in*** their *afterhours.* 引けてからテニスをやる.

afternoon, *n.* 午後.

V ***sacrifice*** an *afternoon* 午後を犠牲にする. ¶***spend*** an interesting *afternoon* there そこでおもしろく午後を送る.

V² as the *afternoon* ***advances*** 午後の時間が立つにつれて.

Q What a ***delightful*** *afternoon* it is after the rain! 雨が降ってから気持のよい午後になったこと. ¶in the ***late*** *afternoon* 午後おそく. ¶It is a ***pleasant*** *afternoon.* 気持の好い午後だ. 【類】spend a ***pleasant*** *afternoon.* ¶a ***sleepy*** *afternoon* 眠たい午後. ¶***social*** *afternoons* 社交に当てた午後.

Q² on a ***summer Saturday*** *afternoon* 夏の土曜日の午後に.

P ***during*** the *afternoon* 午後中. ¶It can be done ***in*** an *afternoon* 午後を使えばできる. ‖ early ***in*** the *afternoon* 午後早々. 【類】four o'clock ***in*** the *afternoon* / I am always at home ***in*** the *afternoon.* ¶It is my habit to play tennis ***of*** an *afternoon* 僕はいつも午後にテニスをやる. ¶I stayed at home ***on*** the *afternoon* of that day. その日の午後は在宅でした. 【類】***on*** an *afternoon* in May = on a May afternoon / ***on*** Monday *afternoon* / ***on*** spring *afternoons.*

P² the *afternoon* ***of*** life 晩年.

afterthought, *n.* 後思案.

Q as a ***happy*** *afterthought* 後からの思いつきで.

afterward[s], *ad.* 後に.

M *shortly afterward[s]* 程なく.

again, *ad.* もうそれだけ.

O It is as ***large again*** as that. あれの二倍も大きい. 【類】 as ***long*** (***many, much, tall***) ***again*** as ... ‖ It is half as ***large again*** as that. あれよりももう半分ほど大きい(一倍半). 【類】 The grouse is about half as ***large again*** as a partridge. ¶half as ***much*** (***many***) ***again*** as ... ...の一倍半. ¶***once again*** 今一度. ¶Read it ***over again***. もう一度お読みなさい. 【類】 ***over*** and ***over again***.

against, *prep.* ...に反対して; ...と向い合って; ...にもたれかかって.

M he declared himself ***dead against*** ... 彼は...に断然反対であると述べた. ¶The house is ***over against*** the church. 家は教会の向いだ. 【類】 He sat backwards ***over against*** me. ¶He was leaning ***right against*** the wall. 彼はまともに壁にもたれかかっていた.

age, *n.* (**1**) 年齢, 年.

V a woman who ***accepts*** middle ***age*** 中年とあきらめ年齢相応の化粧などする婦人. ¶***approach*** adult ***age*** 成年に近づく. ¶He ***asked*** my ***age***. 彼は私の年を聞いた. ¶He has ***attained*** the ***age*** of eighty years. 彼は八十になった. 【類】 ***attain*** (=live to) old ***age*** ‖ Orange-trees ***attain*** a great ***age***. ¶He ***bears*** (=***carries***) his ***age*** well. 彼は[年の割合に]若く見える. ¶a woman who ***combats*** middle ***age*** 中年とあきらめ兼ね年不相応の化粧などする婦人. ¶***defer*** old ***age*** 年を取らない. ¶She refuses to ***divulge*** her ***age***. 彼女は中年を明かさない. ¶***enjoy*** a calm old ***age*** 老後を穏かに送る. ¶***estimate*** the ***age*** of the skull at 100,000 years その頭がい骨の年代を十万年と見積る. ¶***exceed*** the ***age*** of three score and ten 七十の坂を越す. ¶***expect*** a happy old ***age*** 老後の幸福を期する. ¶He ***looks*** his ***age***. 彼は年齢相応に見える. ¶***pass*** middle ***age*** 中年を越す ‖ ***pass*** the ***age*** of boyhood 成人する. ¶***raise*** the ***age*** to ... 年齢の制限を広げる. ¶He has ***reached*** the ***age*** of three score and upwards. 彼は六十余歳に達した. 【類】 The carp may ***reach*** an (=the) ***age*** of 200 years. ¶***respect*** (=***revere***) old ***age*** 老人を敬う. ¶***retard*** old ***age*** 年が寄らぬようにする. ¶She ***told*** me her ***age***. 彼女は私に年をあかした. ‖ In ***telling*** him her ***age*** she sank a year upon him. 彼女は年を一つ若く言った. ¶Women are disposed to ***understate*** their ***ages***. 女はとかく年齢を若く言いたがる.

V^2 ***Age*** has not ***softened*** his stubbornness. 年はとっても一向彼のがん固さは直らない.

Q reach an ***adult age*** 成年に達する. 【類】 at an ***adult age***. ¶at an ***advanced age*** 高齢で. ‖ nobody with ***advancing age*** finds it necessary to ... だんだん年よりになるとだれも...の必要を感じなくなるだろう. ¶the traditional ***Biblical age*** of threescore years and ten 伝統的な聖書記載の七十才の寿命. ¶children of ***certain ages*** ある年齢の子供たち. ‖ a woman of a ***certain age*** (老年に近く)言わぬが花の年ごろになった女. ¶women at a ***critical age*** 厄年の婦人. ¶He died at the ***early age*** of forty-two. 彼は四十二の年若で死んだ. 【類】 die at the comparatively ***early age*** of 61 ‖ at an ***early age*** 若いころ. ¶men of ***full age*** 成年の人々. ¶He is a ***good old age***. 彼は高齢だ. 【類】 the ***good age*** of eighty. ‖ be of a ***good age*** 相当年をとっている. ¶in spite of his ***great age*** 高齢にもかかわらず ‖ women of ***ages greater*** than 55 五十五才以上の婦人 ‖ live to be a ***great age*** 長生きする. ¶***indicate*** great ***age*** 古い時代のものである事が分る ¶a ***green old age*** 矍鑠(かくしゃく)たること. ¶The sage is the instructor of a ***hundred ages***. 聖人は百代の師なり. ¶marry at a ***late age*** おそく結婚する. ¶the ***late marital age*** of men and women おくれた男女の結婚年齢. ¶My ***age*** is ***less*** than yours. 私の方があなたより若い. ¶reach a ***marriageable age*** 結婚適齢になる. ¶a man of ***mature age*** 分別盛りの人. ¶be of a ***mental age*** of feeble boys about thirteen 薄弱な十三才位の子供と同じ精神年齢である. ¶a man past ***middle age*** 中年を過ぎた人. 【類】 after ***middle age*** / He is of ***middle age*** just running 50 (五十の坂を越したばかりの). / arrive at ***middle age***. ¶amuse readers of ***most ages*** 老若を問わず読者を楽しませる. ¶***Old age*** is creeping on us apace. 年を取るのは早いもの. ‖ in ***old age***=when old 年を取ると. ‖ common in ***old age*** 老人にありがちな. ¶***oncoming age*** 寄る年波. ¶die at the ***premature age*** of twenty-two 二十二の若さで死ぬ. ¶***premature old age*** 早老. ¶at a ***proper age*** 適当の年齢で. ¶boys of ***readin', writin'***, and ***wrestlin' age*** 読み書きすもうにいそがしい年ごろの子供たち. ¶He died at the ***ripe age*** of eighty-six. 彼は八十六の高齢で死んだ. 【類】 enjoy a ***ripe old age***. ¶He is the ***same age*** as you. 彼は君と同年だ. ¶***serene old age*** 平穏な老後. ¶children of ***tender age*** 幼い子供ら. ¶a lady of ***uncertain age*** 年齢不詳の女. ¶men of ***various age*** 様々な年齢の人たち. ¶a ***venerable age*** 高齢. ¶a ***vigorous old age*** 老いて益々盛んなこと.

Q^2 after a child gets past the " ***bib*** " age 小児がはなったらし時代を過ぎてから. ¶students of ***college age*** 大学へ通う年齢の学生. ¶the ***conscription age*** 徴兵適齢. ¶be over ***draft age*** 徴兵適齢を越えている. ¶in ***early adult age*** 成年期の初めに. ¶the ***homeweaning age*** 家庭から巣立つ年ごろ. ¶little ones of ***kindergarten age*** 幼稚園へ通う年ごろの子供たち. ¶the ***minimum age*** of employment 雇用の最低年齢. ¶children of ***pre-school age*** 学齢未満の児童. 【類】 children from ***pre-school*** to ***high school age***. ¶children under ***school age*** 学齢前の子供たち. ¶the raise of ***school-learning age*** 小学校修了年齢の延長. ¶at ***teen age*** 十代で / girls of ***teen age***. ¶citizens of ***voting age*** 選挙資格のある公民 ‖ reduce the legal ***voting age*** 法令で定められた投票年齢を引下げる. ¶youths of ***working age*** 働き盛りの青年たち.

P provide ***against age*** 老後に備える. ¶***at*** the ***age*** of fourteen 十四歳で ‖ ***at*** an ***age*** when... ...の年ごろに. 【類】 ***At*** your ***age*** you should be wiser. ¶the boys ***between*** the ***ages*** of twelve and twenty 十二から二十までの間の少年. ¶He was advanced ***beyond*** the ***age*** of mere childhood. 彼はもう子供ではなかった. ¶dotage caused ***by age*** 年のせいのもうろく ‖ Wine is softened ***by age***. ぶどう酒は年月で熟する. ¶He is very strong, ***considering*** (=***for***) his ***age***. 年の割によほど強い. 【類】 She looks young ***for*** her ***age***. ¶make provision ***for*** old ***age*** 老後に備える. 【類】 He scraped together (ためた) some money ***for*** his old ***age***. ‖ He has no respect ***for age***. 少しも老人を敬わない. ¶He began the study of English ***from*** the ***age*** of ten. 十歳から英語を習い始めた. ‖ the book yellowed ***from age*** and dog-eared from use 古いので黄色くなりよく読んだのでページの折れた本. ¶He is much older in mind than ***in age***. 彼は年よりも頭の方が進んでいる. ‖ a superior ***in age*** 年長者. 【類】 He worked hard ***in*** his old ***age***. ‖ ***in spite of*** (=***notwithstanding***) his advanced ***age*** 高齢にもかかわらず. ¶those ***near*** your ***age*** あなたと同じ年かっこうの人々. ¶people ***of*** all ***ages*** and both sexes 老若男女 ‖ He has become (=come) ***of age***. 成年に達した ‖ come ***of age*** 成年になる. ‖ They are just ***of*** an ***age***. ちょうど同年だ. ‖ He is ***of*** an ***age*** to know better. もっと分別があってよい年だ. ‖ children ***of*** all ***ages*** 年齢不同の子供ら ‖ boys ***of*** his ***age*** 彼と同年配の少年 ‖ when I was [***of***] your ***age*** 君ぐらいの年だった時 ‖ He is ***of*** middle ***age***. 彼は中年だ. ‖ He died ***of*** old ***age***. 彼は老死した. ‖ He is now past sixty years ***of age***. 彼はもう六十の上だ. ‖ All the children above six years ***of age*** must go to school. 六歳以上の子供はすべて学校へ行かねばならぬ. ¶He is ***over age***. 成年以上だ. ¶He lived [on] ***to*** [be] an extreme old ***age***. 非常に長生きをした. ¶He is still ***under age***. まだ成年に達しない. ‖ boys ***under*** military ***age*** 未成年者 ‖ He is sinking ***under age***. 彼は老い込んだ. ¶***up to*** the ***age*** of thirty 三十まで. ¶records, yellow and worn ***with age*** 年数が経って黄色くなりすれ損じた記録 ‖ Wines get better ***with age***. ぶどう酒は古くなるほど良くなる. ‖ Her eyesight got weaker ***with age***. 年のせいで視力が衰えた 【類】 an old woman a little bowed (少し腰の曲った) ***with age***. / His back is bent ***with age***. / His eyes are dim (目がかすんで) ***with age***. / a man hoary (白髪になった) ***with age*** / He is infirm (弱って) ***with age***. ‖ be ***within*** (=under) ***age*** まだ成年に達していない.

P^2 the ***age at*** death 行年. ¶the ***age of*** admittance ranged from ... to ... 入学年齢[の制限]は...から...まで ‖ ***age of*** maturity 成熟年齢 ‖ ***age*** (=years) ***of*** discretion 分別のつく年齢 ‖ this grand old man, who is still hale, at the ***age of*** ninety 九十歳にして依然矍鑠(かくしゃく)たる老偉人 ‖ the ***age of*** a tree 樹齢 ‖ the ***age of*** a house 建築年齢.

(**2**) 時代.

V ***judge*** the ***age*** of an antique 古物の時代を鑑定する.

Q in ***after** ages* 後世において. ¶the "***analytic***" *age*「分析」時代. ¶a ***barren** age* 産出の少い時代. ¶a ***bloodstained** age* 血なま臭い時代. ¶an affair of ***bygone** age* 過ぎし日の事. ‖ in ***bygone** ages* 過去の時代に. 【類】an old monument of ***bygone** ages*. ¶He says that this was ***commercial** age*, and that beauty could not be permitted to interfere with business.「現代は商業時代だから美のために商売が妨げられてはならぬ」と彼はいっている. ¶the ***Dark** Ages* 暗黒時代(欧州中世期の). ¶the ***dim** ages* of antiquity 上古のもうろうたる時代. ¶in the ***early** ages* of the world 大昔. ¶That cannot be thought of in this ***enlightened** age*. この文化の進んだ時代にそんな事は思いもよらぬ. ¶in a ***far-gone** age* 遠い昔に. ¶a savage of some ***far-off** age* 遠い昔の野蛮人. ¶this ***fast-moving** age* このテンポの早い時代. ¶the nineteenth century, the ***golden** age* of Russian literature ロシア文学の黄金時代と称すべき十九世紀. 【類】The eighteenth century was the ***golden** age* of the English engravers (彫刻家). ¶a ***heroic** age* 英雄時代. ¶the ***horseless** age* 馬を使わない時代. ¶It is somewhat voluminous for a ***hurried** age*. その本はこのいそがしい世の中にはちょっと大部過ぎる. ¶this ***hurry-worry** age* このせわしない世の中. ¶***immemorial** age* 遼遠なる太古. ¶in this "***individual***" *age* of ours 個人主義の今の世に. ¶a ***later** age* 後世. ¶a ***learned** age* 学術隆盛の時代. ¶an extremely ***loose** age* 道徳退廃の時代. ¶in this ***materialistic** age* この物質主義の世の中に. ¶in the ***Middle** Ages* 中世に. ¶the ***primitive** ages* 原始時代. ¶this ***progressive** age* 今の進歩時代. ¶from ***remote** ages* 遠い昔から. ¶a ***revolutionary** age* 革命時代. ¶this ***scientific** age* この科学の世の中. ¶a ***stormy** age* 旋風時代. ¶***this** age* of third rate novels 三流(大衆)小説の持てはやされる今日. ¶a ***transitional** age* 過渡期. ¶This is an ***unpoetical** age*. 今日は無風流な時代だ. ¶in ***warlike** ages* 戦国時代に.

Q² the ***air** age* 航空時代. ¶with the advent of the ***cement** age* セメント時代の出現と共に. ¶Generally a ***Copper*** or ***Bronze** Age* preceded the ***Iron** Age* in Egypt, Western Asia, and Europe. 概してエジプト・西部アジアおよび欧州では銅器時代が鉄器時代に先立った. ¶a "***jazz***" *age* ジャズ時代. ¶the ***machine** age* 機械時代. ¶We have come to the ***Picture** Age*. 今や映画時代が到来した. ¶the ***rush** age* テンポの早い時代. ¶the ***stone axe** age* 石斧(せきふ)時代. ¶the ***Tokugawa** age* 徳川時代.

P ***across*** all the *ages* and countries of the world 古今東西を通じて. ¶***At*** that *age* of the world the sum was far more valuable than in our own day. その金高はあの時代には今日におけるよりもはるかに価値があった. ¶thought ***before*** the *age* 時代より進んだ思想. ¶It is stigmatized as being ***behind*** the *age*. それは時代後れという非難を受けている. ¶It was an act to be praised ***by*** all *ages*. それはいつの世にも称賛せらるべき行為であった. ¶***during*** countless *ages* [幾代となく]長い間. ‖ ***During*** the middle *ages*, Sado was used as a place of exile for criminals. 中世にあっては佐渡は罪人の流刑地に使用された. ¶His name shall endure ***for*** *age*. 彼の名は永久に伝わるだろう. ‖ ***for*** *ages* (=an *age*) 長らく, 久しい間 ‖ ***for*** *ages* eternal 永遠に ‖ ***for*** all *ages* 万世にわたって. 【類】***for*** many *ages* / an act too brutal ***for*** the present *age* of refinement (文化の今日). ¶***from*** *age* to age 代々 ‖ ***from*** a very early *age* 往古から. ¶***in*** an *age* nearer our own さらに降っては ‖ We live ***in*** an *age* when the picture is rivalling the written word. 今は絵画と文字の競争時代だ. 【類】It is the same ***in*** all *ages* and in all nations. ‖ ***in*** every *age* of the world 古今を通じて. 【類】***in*** the Elizabethan *age* / ***in*** this *age* of haste / ***in*** this busy *age* / ***in*** this *age* of mechanical genius (機械の天才). ¶***since*** the *age* of the God 神代より. ¶***through*** all *ages* 古今を通じて ‖ ***through*** untold *ages* 数えられないほど長い間.

P² in an *age* ***like*** our own 今日のような世の中では. ¶This is an *age* ***of*** business. 今日は商業の時代だ. 【類】This is the *age* ***of*** specialists (専門家). ‖ The sixteenth century was specially the *age* ***of*** tapestries (かけ毛氈). ‖ this *age* ***of*** testimonials 推薦状が物をいう今の世 ‖ the *age* ***of*** chivalry 騎士道時代 ‖ the "*Age* ***of*** Wars," 400 years ago 四百年前のいわゆる戦国時代. ¶*ages* ***upon*** ages 時代に時代を重ねて(幾代となく).

age, *v.* 年とる. ふける.

M He has *aged* ***considerably***. 彼は目立って年をとった. ¶He has *aged* very ***much*** since then. 彼はあれ以来大層年を取った. ¶Women *age* ***rapidly***. 婦人はずんずんふける. ¶He has *aged* ***visibly***. 彼は目に見えて年をとった.

aged, *pa.* 年をとっている.

M a lady *aged* ***50 years*** 五十歳の婦人. ¶the ***most*** *aged* of the three 三人の最年長者.

P He is *aged* probably ***between*** 35 and 40. 彼は多分三十五と四十の間だろう. ¶people of both sexes *aged* ***from*** fourteen years upwards 十四歳以上の男女.

age-limit, *n.* 年齢制限.

P ***beyond*** (***within***) the *age-limit*.

agency, *n.* 代理(権); 代理店; 機関; 力, 作用.

V ***accept*** the *agency* of a firm 商会の代理を引受ける ‖ cannot ***accept*** the *agency* on your terms お申し入れの条件で代理店を引受けることは出来ない. ¶***establish*** an *agency* 代理店を設ける. ¶***grant*** a person *agency* …を代理店にする. ¶The firm ***holds*** the *agency* of a well-known English company. その店は有名な英国会社の代理店となっている. ¶I ***offer*** you the *agency* for your district. 貴地方の代理店をあなたにお任せしたい. ¶***organize*** *agencies* for human betterment 人類の向上機関を設ける. ¶please endeavor to ***procure*** me the *agency* of … …の代理店を私にやらせてもらえるよう御尽力下さい. ¶***withdraw*** an *agency* 代理権を撤回する.

Q a ***detective** agency* 私立探偵所. ¶the cinema as an ***educational** agency* 教育機関としての映画. 【類】the value of examination as an ***educational** agency*. ¶give an ***exclusive** agency* for … …の一手販売権を与える. ¶brought about by ***human** agency* 人間の力でやった. ¶Electricity is a ***mysterious** agency*. 電気は不可思議な力だ. ¶the ***national** agencies* affecting higher education 高等教育に影響のある国家機関. ¶***natural** agency* 自然作用. ¶the railroad and the printing press, the two ***potent*** and ***indispensable** agencies* in our modern civilization 近代文明に欠くべからざる二大利器である鉄道と印刷機. ¶the ***sole** agency* of our company in Japan わが社の日本一手代理店.

Q² an ***advertising** agency* 広告代理業. ¶a ***buying** agency* 買付代理店. ¶a ***clipping** agency* [新聞・雑誌の]切抜通信社. ¶a ***construction** agency* 建設機関. ¶an ***employment** agency* 職業安定所. ¶a domestic ***employment** agency* 家庭雇用周旋所. ¶a ***fact-finding** agency* 実情調査機関. ¶a ***forwarding** agency* 運送店. ¶***Government** agencies* 諸官庁. ¶the competent ***Government** agency* 当該官庁. ¶the Japanese ***Government Overseas** Agency* 日本政府の海外機関. ¶a semi-independent ***government** agency* 半官半民の政府機関. ¶***health** agencies* 保健所. ¶***housing** agencies* 家屋周旋業. ¶laxity of ***law-enforcement** agencies* 法律施行機関の事務緩慢. ¶a ***lending** agency* 金融機関. ¶the personnel of the ***Marine Safety** Agency* 海上保安庁の職員. ¶a ***news** agency* 通信社. ¶***off-campus** agencies* 校外の機関. ¶A reputable ***opinion-testing** agency* recently conducted a private poll of workers. ある評判のよい世論調査機関が最近労働者の非公開民間投票を行った. ¶an ***outpost** agency* 出先機関. ¶dissolve formal ***purge** agencies* 正式の追放機関を解消する. ¶***police*** (=policing) *agency* 警備機関. ¶a ***sales*** (=***selling***) *agency* 販売代理店. ¶Tass, the official ***Soviet news** agency* ソ連国営通信社タス. ¶a ***student employment** agency* 学生求職会. ¶a ***tourist** agency* 観光社. ¶***trade*** and ***market survey** agencies* abroad 海外貿易市場調査機関. ¶***welfare** agencies* 厚生機関.

P Creation is ***by*** divine *agency*. 創造は神力の致す所. ‖ ***by*** an invisible *agency* 目に見えぬ作用で. ¶***through*** (=by) his *agency* 彼の周旋(斡旋)で ‖ ***through*** human *agency* 人手で ‖ ***through*** the *agency* of various funds 各種の基金から支出して. 【類】***through*** the *agency* of rapid transportation and cold storage. ¶transact business by the *agency* ***of*** a broker 仲買人の手を経て取引をする.

agenda, *n. pl.* 会議事項.

V It will ***head*** the *agenda*. それが議事の筆頭になるだろう.

P an item ***in*** the *agenda* 会議事項中の一項目. ¶the first business ***on*** the *agenda* 会議事項第一. ‖ There is a motion ***on*** the *agenda* of the conference. その会議の日程に動議が入っている. ‖ The item was placed ***on the agenda***. その事項が上程された.

agent, *n.* 代理人(商); 事務官; 動作者; 作因, 動因.
V *appoint* an *agent* 代理人を任命する. ¶*employ agents* 代理人を使用する.
Q *acting agents* 臨時代理人. ¶his duly *authorized agents* 彼の受権代理人. ¶a *canvassing agent* (新聞・雑誌等の)拡張係. ¶a *chemical agent* 〖化学〗化学的作因. ¶a *commercial agent* 商務官. ¶a *confidential agent* 密使. ¶a *consular agent* 代理領事. ¶*dramatic* and *musical agents* 劇・音楽の周旋業者. ¶a *Dutch agent* at Nagasaki 長崎オランダ館長. ¶the theater as an *educational agent* 教育機関としての劇場. ¶*exclusive Japanese agents* 日本一手代理店. ¶a *first agent* 主動者. ¶a *general agent* 総代理人. ¶an *immunizing agent* 予防薬. ¶a *managing agent* 支配人. ¶natural forces as a *mechanical agent* 機械の動力としての自然力. ¶a *medical agent* 薬剤. ¶a *morbific agent* 病根. ¶a *natural agent* 自然力. 【類】Rains and frosts are *natural agents* that wear away rocks. ¶a *patent agent* 弁理人. ¶*political agents* 政治運動員. ¶a *powerful agent* 偉大な力を持つもの. ¶a *prophylactic agent* 予防剤. ¶a *responsible agent* [学生等の]保証人. ¶a *secret agent* 秘密代理人. ¶a *social agent* 社会の原動力. ¶as a *sole agent* for Japan 日本一手販売業として. ¶think him a very *suitable agent* 彼を適当の代理人と思う. ¶*therapeutic agents* 薬剤.
Q² an *ad* (=*advertising*) *agent* 宣伝係; 広告業者. ¶a *bargaining agent* 交渉委員. ¶a *book agent* 書籍販売人(委託による). ¶a *business agent* 《米》商業上の管理人. ¶a *buying agent* 買付代理人. ¶his *campaign agent* 彼の遊説員. ¶a *cleaning* and *polishing agent* つや出し剤. ¶a *collective bargaining agent* 団体交渉の代表者. ¶a *commission agent* 委託仲買人(商). ¶a *Communist agent* 共産党の手先. ¶a *drying agent* 乾燥剤. ¶an *enemy agent* 敵のスパイ. ¶an *estate agent* 土地家屋周旋業者. ¶*FBI agents* 《米》連邦検察局員 (G メンのこと). ¶a *forwarding agent* 運送業者. ¶a *Government agent* 政府委員. ¶a *house agent* 差配人; 家屋周旋業者. ¶an *insurance agent* 保険代理業. ¶a *land agent* 土地周旋業者. ¶a *leavening agent* ふくらし粉(の類). ¶a *liaison agent* 連絡員. ¶a *lecture agent* 講演周旋業者. ¶a *press* (=*newspaper*) *agent* 新聞取次業者. ¶a *propaganda agent* 宣伝係. ¶a *publicity agent* 宣伝業者. ¶a *purchasing agent* 買付代理人. ¶a *recruitment agent* 募集人. ¶a *road agent*=a highwayman 《米》追いはぎ. ¶a *sales agent* 販売係. ¶a *secret service agent* 機密(情報)部員. ¶a *security police agent* 公安委員. ¶a sole *selling agent* 一手販売人. 【類】We desire to act for you as *selling agent* in Japan for your goods. ¶a *shipping agent* 回漕問屋. ¶a *station agent* 《米》=a station master 《英》駅長. ¶a *ticket*[*-selling*] *agent* 《米》出札係. ¶a *transmitting agent* of disease 病気伝染の媒介物.
P the value of legislation *as* an *agent* in human advancement 人類進歩の一要因としての立法の価値.
P² an *agent* here *for* Messrs. Thompson & Co. トムソン商会の当地の代理店. ‖ *agents for* the sale of books published by ... ...発行の書籍販売代理店. ¶the company's *agent in* the East 東洋における同社の代理店. 【類】sole *agents in* Japan *for* ... & Co. 【類】Messrs. Dodwell & Co. are the *agents in* Japan *for* the Underwood typewriting machines. ¶*agents of* a company *for* selling ... 会社の...販売人.

ager, *n.* 若者.
Q *pre-school agers* 未就学児.

aggravate, *v.* 激させる.
P He was *aggravated at* a thing. ある事に対してじれていた. ¶His disease was *aggravated by* anxiety. あの人の病気は心配で悪化した. ¶He was *aggravated with* a person. ある人に対して憤慨していた.

aggregate, *n.* 総計.
P taking them *in* the *aggregate* (=as a whole) 全体として見て ‖ $50,000 *in* the *aggregate* 総計五万ドル. 【類】amounted *in* the *aggregate* to ...

aggress, *v.* 侵す.
P *aggress upon* the public property 公有財産を侵害する.

aggression, *n.* 侵入. 「外部からの侵略.
Q an *armed aggression* 武力侵略. ¶*external aggression*
Q² repel *Communist* (=*Red*) *aggression* 共産軍の侵略を撃退する. ¶oppose *Soviet* (*Nazi*) *aggression* ソ連(ナチ)の侵略に対抗する. ¶halt *totalitarian aggression* 全体主義の侵略を阻止する.
P an *aggression upon* (=*on*) another's estate (rights) 他人の所有地(権利)の侵害. ¶be guilty *of aggression* 侵略の罪を犯している.

aggressive, *a.* 積極的な.
P very *aggressive in* pursuing the policy of ... ...の方針遂行に大いに積極的な.

aggressor, *n.* 侵略者.
P a nation branded [*as*] an *aggressor* 侵略者のらく印を押された国民.

aggrieved, *pa.* 不平満々の.
P feel *aggrieved at* it それに対して不満を抱く.

aghast, *a.* 唖然として.
P He stood *aghast at* (=on hearing) the news. その話を聞いてびっくりした.

agitate, *v.* かき乱す; 運動する, アジる.
P He was *agitated by* (=*with*) grief. 悲しみで心が乱れた. ¶*agitate for* reform (a strike, a repeal of the business tax) 改革(など)の運動をする. ¶*agitate* water *into* froth 水をかきまわしてあわを立てる.

agitation, *n.* 騒動; 激昂; 動揺, 運動, 扇動.
V *conduct agitations* 騒動を指揮する. ¶*create agitation* 騒ぎを起す. ¶*excite* public *agitation* 騒動を起す. ¶*raise* considerable *agitation* against it それに対し相当強力な反抗運動を起す. ¶an *agitation* has been *set on foot* (=*started*) by ... against (for) ... ...に反対(賛成)して...が運動を開始した.
V² A great *agitation arose* against the system. その制度に対して一大反対運動が起った.
Q Small shopkeepers carried on a *long agitation* against large department stores. 小売商人が長期にわたってデパート反対運動を行った. ¶*open agitation* 露骨な扇動. ¶a *revolutionary agitation* for ... ...に対する革命運動. ¶*secret agitation* 暗躍. ¶sanity in *social agitation* 社会運動の堅実性.
Q² *anti-slavery agitation* 奴隷廃止運動. ¶the "*barbarian-expelling*" *agitation* 攘夷運動. ¶*Communist agitation* 共産党のアジ. ¶*expulsion agitation* 排斥運動. ¶*mob agitation* 暴民の騒乱. ¶*nationalist agitation* 国家主義者の運動. ¶*student agitation* 学徒の運動.
P be *in agitation* ごたついている ‖ pace about a room *in* uncontrollable *agitation* 非常に激昂して部屋をあちこち歩く. ¶*with agitation* 激昂して.
P² an *agitation against* high prices 値下げ運動. ¶an *agitation for* the exclusion of Japanese 日本人排斥運動. ‖ an *agitation for* the extension of the franchise 選挙権拡張運動. 【類】an *agitation for* the suffrage (参政権) of women. ¶an *agitation on* the surface of water 水面の波立ち.

agitator, *n.* 扇動家, 運動者.
V *relegate* an *agitator* beyond the city limit 扇動者を市外に追放する.
Q *political agitators* 政治運動者.
Q² *anti-vivisection agitators* 動物生体解剖反対論者. ¶*communist* (*Nazi*) *agitators* 共産主義(ナチ)扇動者. ¶a *labor agitator* スト扇動者. ¶*socialist agitators* 社会主義の運動者.

aglow, *ad.*, *a.* 真赤になって.
M Her cheeks were *all aglow*. ほおが真赤になっていた.
P His face is *aglow with* enthusiasm. 彼の顔が熱意で紅潮している.

ago, *ad.* 以前に.
M *ages ago* 何代も前に. ¶*a fortnight ago* 二週間前に. ¶*a long time ago* 久しい前 ‖ It was a *long time ago* now. もう随分古い話だ. 【類】I knew him as *long ago* as the year 1900. ¶*a long while ago* 久しい前. ¶barely *a week ago* 一週間になるかならないか前のこと. ¶*a while ago* さっき. ¶*three nights ago* 一昨々夜.

agog, *a.*, *ad.* 夢中になって; 浮立って.
M The city was *all agog*. 市中は沸き立っていた. ¶He was *quite agog* to see (=for *or* on) the comet. 彼は彗星(ほうき)を見ようと夢中になっていた.
P The boy was all *agog for* mischief. 子供は何かいたずらをしようとうずうずしていた. ¶He was *agog with* excitement. 彼は興奮して夢中になっていた.

agony, *n.* 苦痛, 苦もん; [感情の]極致.
V *experience* the hot *agony of* shame 赤恥をかく.
Q The *last agony* was over. 断末魔の苦もなくなっていた. ¶*mental agony* 煩もん. ¶*untold agony* 口に言えない苦痛.
Q² *death agony* 死の苦しみ.
P bite *in agony* 苦しまぎれにかむ. 【類】die *in* great

agony. ¶***in*** an *agony* of joy 狂喜して ‖ ***in*** the *agonies* of death 断末魔の苦もんの中で.【類】We found him ***in*** the *agonies* of death.

P² an *agony* ***of*** despair 絶望の悩み.

agree, *v*. 一致する, 合う；同意する.

M this *agrees* ***closely*** with ... これは ... とぴったり合う. ¶He *agreed* ***entirely*** with me. 彼は私と全く同意見だった. ¶I ***fully*** *agree* with him that ... ...は彼と完全に私の意見が合う. ¶it was ***generally*** *agreed* that ... ...では大体一致していた. ¶With this I *agree* ***heartily***. この事は大いにわが意を得たものだ. ¶I ***quite*** *agreed* with him on that point. その点は彼と全く同感だった. ¶I cannot ***readily*** *agree* with you. 僕はにわかに君に同意はできない. ¶***reluctantly*** *agreed* to assume the responsibility for ... ...の責任を負う事を不承不承承諾した. ¶The Members of the League ***severally*** *agree* that ... 連盟国は各自...なることを承認する. ¶I *agree* ***substantially*** in their findings. 彼らの決定には大体賛成です. ¶All the accounts ***sufficiently*** *agree*. 勘定が皆十分に合う. ¶be ***unanimously*** *agreed* to by the members thereof 会員全部の同意を得る.【類】It was ***unanimously*** *agreed* that some active measure be adopted to improve the situation. ¶it is ***universally*** *agreed* that ... ...は一般に異論がない. ¶*agree* ***unreservedly*** 全く同意する. ¶*agree* very ***well*** with him 彼と意気がよく合う.

P They *agreed* ***about*** it. 彼らはその事につき同意した.【類】Buyers and sellers cannot *agree* ***about*** price. ¶They *agreed* ***among*** themselves on the subject. その問題について彼ら同士同意した. ¶opinions *agree* ***as to*** ... に関しては意見が一致している. ¶*agree* ***between*** two persons 二人の間に話がまとまる. ¶*agree* ***in*** chorus 一斉に同意する.【類】*agree* ***in*** opinion / *agree* ***in*** principle / all religions *agree* ***in*** asserting that ... / They were unable to *agree* ***in*** their choice. / There is one point ***in*** which they all *agree*. ¶all parties *agee* ***on*** ... 一同...に同意している ‖ try to *agree* ***on*** an agenda 日程に関して意見が一致するようにする.【類】They *agreed* ***on*** some plan of campaign (作戦計画). / They *agreed* ***on*** the terms of a contract (契約の条件). / *agree* ***on*** (=***upon***) a statement of principles (主義の声明) / That is *agreed* ***on*** by all. ‖ Terms of reconciliation were readily *agreed* ***on***. ¶If you can *agree* ***to*** the proposal, the business will no doubt be settled. 君がその申出に同意できれば事件の解決は疑いない. ‖ Do not *agree* ***to*** the conditions named. 先方の条件に同意するな. ‖ *agree* ***to*** the terms proposed 提供条件に同意する.【類】*agree* ***to*** arbitration (仲裁) / I do not *agree* ***to*** your opinion. / Come, come! I can't *agree* ***to*** that. / *agree* ***to*** the conditions / I *agree* to the terms of payment (支払条件). ‖ The motion was *agreed* ***to*** without opposition. その動議は反対なしに成立した. ¶Gentlemen of the jury, have you *agreed* ***upon*** your verdict? 陪審官諸君, 諸君の御意見はまとまりましたか. ‖ at a price *agreed* ***upon*** 折合った値段で.【類】fail to *agree* ***upon*** a price. ‖ the day *agreed* ***upon*** for ... ...のために打合せた日.【類】The committee *agreed* ***upon*** the following articles (左記の条項). ‖ I *agree* ***with*** you in thinking that ... ...の考えは同感です.【類】I *agree* ***with*** you in your views. / I cannot *agree* ***with*** you ***on*** that. / I *agree* ***with*** neither side. / My opinion *agrees* ***with*** yours. / He complains that it does not *agree* ***with*** the original arrangements. / not every one will *agree* ***with*** him that ... ‖ The price does not *agree* ***with*** my pocket. その値段では私は買いかねる. ‖ Paris did not *agree* ***with*** her. パリは彼女には適しなかった.【類】The work does not *agree* ***with*** every constitution (体質). / I don't *agree* ***with*** the sea. ‖ The picture does not *agree* ***with*** the original. この絵は原物に似ていない. ‖ The medicine *agrees* ***with*** the patient. 薬が病人に合っている. ‖ This fish does not *agree* ***with*** me. 僕はこの魚を食べるとあたる.【類】Do these dishes *agree* ***with*** you?

agreeable, *a*. 気持のよい；適合する；...に従って.

M I am ***quite*** *agreeable* with your views. 君と全く同意見だ.

P *agreeable* ***in*** manner 動作の気持のよい. ¶*agreeable* ***to*** the ear 音の好い.【類】*agreeable* ***to*** the smell (taste) ‖ *agreeable* ***to*** the palate 口あたりのよい ‖ *agreeable* ***to*** the custom of those days 当時の慣例に従って.【類】*Agreeable* ***to*** my promise I have come. ‖ *agreeable* ***to*** nature 自然に順応して(無理のない) ‖ The terms are *agreeable* ***to*** me. その条件は私に都合がよい.【類】Would this arrangement (取極) be *agreeable* ***to*** you? ‖ make oneself *agreeable* ***to*** ... ...のきげんを損じないようにする. ‖ Her manners and person were *agreeable* ***to*** each other. 彼女の動作は人(ﾋﾄ)相応のものであった.

agreeably, *ad*. 従って.

P *agreeably* ***to*** your request (instructions, established usage²) 御依頼(など)通り.

agreement, *n*. 協定, 契約, 約束；一致, 同意.

V ***annul*** (=***break off*** *or* ***cancel***) an *agreement* 契約を取消す. ¶***break*** one's *agreement* with ... ...との約束を破る. ¶faithfully ***carry out*** an *agreement* 忠実に契約を履行する. ¶before ***concluding*** the *agreement* 契約を結ぶ前に. ¶***confirm*** an *agreement* 契約を確認する. ¶***draw up*** an agreement 契約書を作製する. ¶***establish*** a mutual *agreement* in ... ...の打合せをする. ¶***find*** an *agreement* of views 意見が一致を見る. ¶***fix up*** an *agreement* 契約を極める. ¶***fulfil*** an *agreement* 契約を履行する. ¶***get*** a written *agreement* 契約書を取る. ¶***have*** a special *agreement* with ... ...と特別の契約がある. ¶***keep agreements*** 約束を守る. ¶***maintain*** an *agreement* 約束を守る. ¶***make*** an *agreement* with ... ...と契約を結ぶ. ‖ ***make*** a written *agreement* with ... ...と契約書を取交わす. ¶***reach*** an *agreement* with him as to (=with regard to) ... ...について彼と話合いがつく.【類】no *agreement* was ***reached*** on ... / England and Russia have ***reached*** an *agreement* regarding ... / failed to ***reach*** a final *agreement*. ¶... shall ***require*** the *agreement* of ... ...は...の同意が必要. ¶He will not ***sign*** the *agreement* in its present form. 現在のままでは契約書に調印しないだろう. ¶***violate*** an *agreement* 契約を破棄する.

V² the present *agreement* ***ceases*** to be operative upon ... 現在の協約は...に対して効力を失う.

Q an ***amicable*** *agreement* 円満妥結. ¶a ***collective*** *agreement* 団体協約. ¶a matter of ***common*** *agreement* 一般に認めている事 ‖ by ***common*** *agreement* 話合いで. ¶arrive at a ***complete*** *agreement* 完全の一致を見る.【類】it is in ***complete*** (=***precise***) *agreement* with ... ¶a ***conditional*** *agreement* 条件付同意. ¶in ***cordial*** *agreement* with ... ...と心(ｼﾝ)から折合って. ¶I have his ***definite*** *agreement* about it. その事は彼ときちんとした約束ができている. ¶in ***essential*** (=***substantial***) *agreement* with ... ...と本質的に(大体)一致して. ¶without any ***formal*** *agreement* 黙諾の形で. ¶there seems to be a ***general*** *agreement* that ... ...には大体意見が一致しているらしい.【類】It was, by ***general*** *agreement*, one of the best seen in recent years. ¶enter into some form of ***gentlemen's*** *agreement* 一種の紳士協約を結ぶ. ¶in ***hearty*** *agreement* 心から同意して. ¶an ***international*** *agreement* 国際協定. ¶by ***mutual*** *agreement* 合意で(相談ずくで).【類】We separated by ***mutual*** *agreement* and in a friendly spirit. ¶an ***oral*** *agreement* 口約. ¶I am in ***partial*** *agreement* with ... 私は...に多少同感だ. ¶as if by ***previous*** *agreement* 言い合わしたように. ¶a ***private*** *agreement* 内約. ¶under a ***provisional*** *agreement* 仮契約の下に. ¶a ***secret*** *agreement* 密約. ¶make a ***special*** *agreement* 特別の契約を結ぶ. ¶a ***tacit*** *agreement* existed between ... and ... ...と...との間には黙契が成立していた. ¶a ***temporary*** *agreement* with opinions 人の説にその場の相づちを打つこと. ¶an ***undisclosed*** *agreement* 黙契. ¶There is nearly ***universal*** *agreement* on this point. この点に関してはほとんど全般的に意見が一致している. ¶a ***verbal*** *agreement* to that effect そういう主旨の口頭契約.

Q² an ***armistice*** *agreement* 休戦協定. ¶a ***ceasefire*** *agreement* 停戦協定. ¶an ***employment*** *agreement* 就職契約書. ¶a ***four-point*** *agreement* 四カ条協定. ¶win ***management*** *agreement* 幹部の同意を得る. ¶a ***master*** *agreement* 主たる協約. ¶a ***non-intervention*** *agreement* 不干渉協定. ¶the ***Potsdam*** *Agreement* ポツダム協定. ¶on lines with which it has ***ticket*** *agreements* その会社の切符の協定のある線で(鉄道など). ¶negotiate ***trade*** *agreements* with ... ...と取引契約の交渉をする ‖ bilateral ***trade*** *agreements* 双務労働契約. ¶a ***truce*** *agreement* 休戦協定.

P ***according*** to the *agreement* entered into by him with

…彼と…の間に締結された協約によって. ¶That's ***against*** the *agreements*. それじゃ話が違う. ¶***by agreement*** 同意の上. ¶We are not all ***in*** *agreement* on this point. われわれはこの点で皆が一致してはいない. ‖ ***in*** *agreement* with … …と一致して(…の通りに) ‖ Notning is said about that ***in*** the *agreement*. その事は契約書には何とも言ってない. ¶enter ***into*** an *agreement* not to … …しないと協定する. ¶I took the house ***on*** a simple *agreement* for three years. 三年の単純契約で家を借りた. ¶come ***to*** an *agreement* 折合がつく(話がまとまる) ‖ He acted up ***to*** his *agreement*. 彼は約束を守った. ¶***under*** an *agreement* made with … …と締結した契約の下に. ¶comply ***with*** an *agreement* 契約に同意する.

P² an *agreement* ***for*** exchange of prisoners 捕虜交換協定. ¶***agreement in*** writing＝paper ***agreement*** 書面による協約. ¶There is no probability of coming to (＝reaching) an *agreement* ***on*** the matter. この事件はまとまりそうもない. ¶be under an *agreement* ***with*** him to … 彼と…するという協定がある. ‖ enter into an *agreement* ***with*** … …と契約する.

agriculture, *n.* 農業.

Q have ***flourishing agriculture*** 農業が盛んだ.

ague, *n.*〘病〙おこり.

V I ***had*** the *ague* last year. 昨年おこりにかかった.

ahead, *ad.* 真先に；前方に；まっしぐらに.

M He is ***far ahead*** of his class in English. 彼は英語では級中で一頭地を抜いている. ¶We saw a boat ***right ahead***. ちょうど向うに一隻のボートが見えた. ¶She was clever enough, so she was ***soon ahead*** of the other girls in the class. 彼女は利口なのでじきにクラスで他の生徒を追い越した. ¶***somewhat ahead*** in the art of … …の技術にかけては少し上である. ¶He pushed ***straight ahead*** with his plans. 自分の計画を提げて敢然猛進した.

P The steamer left ***ahead of*** time. その汽船は時間前に出発した. 【類】one lesson ***ahead of*** his pupils / The steamer slided some hours ***ahead of*** time. / people who are ***ahead of*** their time (＝the times) / get ***ahead of*** others in … / The prediction (予言) was made 24 hours ***ahead*** of the event. ‖ I noticed a piece of paper lying on the grass ***ahead of me***. 私の前の草の上に一枚の紙が落ちていたのに気がついた. 【類】He was a class ***ahead of*** me in the University at B. / a Stanford man, a couple of classes ***ahead of*** him (二年上級の) ‖ You got a call from Miss White a little ***ahead of*** noon. 正午少し前にホワイト嬢から電話がありましたよ. ¶Go ***ahead with*** your work. 君の仕事をどんどんやれ.

aid, *n.* 助け, 扶助, 補助金.

V ***administer*** (＝***afford***) the first *aid* to employees in case of accident or sudden illness けがまたは急病の場合には従業員に応急手当を施す. ¶***call in*** (＝***ask***) the *aid* of … …の援助を求める. ¶They did not ***disdain*** his *aid*. 彼らはいさぎよく彼の扶助を受けた. ¶***enlist*** the *aid* of … …の助けを借りる. ¶***furnish*** *aid* to deserving students 然るべき学生を補助する. ¶***give aid*** to the enemy of one's country 敵軍に援助を与える ‖ willing to ***give aid*** unstinted 惜しまず援助する. ¶***implore*** the *aid* of Heaven 天佑を祈る. ¶***invoke*** the *aid* of the Almighty 神の加護を祈る. ¶***invoke*** the *aid* of the law if necessary 心要の場合には法律の助けを仰ぐ. 【類】Those engaged in marine occupations (航海業) constantly resort there, to ***invoke*** the *aid* of, or to return thanks to, the deity. ¶***lend*** their *aid* to this end この目的達成に力を致す. ¶***obtain*** medical *aid* 医者にみてもらう. ¶***offer*** pecuniary *aid* 金銭上の援助を与えようと言う. ¶it should ***prove*** a valuable *aid* to … それはりっぱに…の助けになるべきはずだ. ¶the book ***provides*** *aids* for those who are in search of information about … その本は…について調べたいという人には参考になる. ¶The hospital ***receives*** no State *aid* and is entirely dependent upon voluntary support. その病院は少しも政府の補助を受けず全然有志の寄付で維持している. ¶***render*** first *aid* 応急の手当をする. ¶***request*** *aid* from … …の補助を請う. ¶***secure*** another's *aid* 他人の力を借りる. ¶before ***seeking*** outside *aid* 外部の補助を求める前に. ¶***solicit*** *aid* of … …の助けを懇望する. ¶***summon*** medical *aid* 医者を呼ぶ.

Q ***associative aids*** 連想の助けとなるもの. ¶his ***chief aid*** 彼の主要助力者. ¶***divine aid*** 神助. ¶***efficacious aids*** to research 研究のために大いに助けとなること. ¶call in ***efficient medical aid*** たしかな医者にかかる. ¶***excellent aids*** in preparing for school examinations 受験準備のすぐれた参考書. ¶***first aid*** to the injured けが人の応急手当. ¶***friendly aid*** 親切な援助. ¶be beyond the reach of ***human aid*** 人力の及ばない. ¶***important aid*** has been received from … …から重要な援助を受けた. ¶be of ***invaluable aid*** to them あの人たちにとってこの上もない助けになる. ¶give ***material aid*** to … …に物質的援助を与える. ¶give all ***moral*** and ***material aid*** in its power … …にできうる限り有形無形の援助を与える. ¶***mechanical aids*** 機械の助け. ¶seek ***medical aid*** 医者にみてもらう. ¶***mutual aid*** 相互の助力. ¶give ***pecuniary*** and ***other aid*** to … …に金銭その他の援助を与える. ¶a ***powerful aid*** to health 大いに健康に益あるもの. ¶a ***prompt aid*** 即座の援助. ¶a ***staple aid*** to national prosperity 国民繁栄の一要素. ¶a ***timely aid*** 時宜をえた補助. ¶without their ***unflagging*** and ***efficient aid*** 彼らの有力な不断の援助なくては. ¶a ***valuable aid*** in teaching (historical studies) 教授(など)において貴重な参考となるもの. ¶a ***visual aid*** to understanding 視覚による理解補助.

Q² ***arms aid*** 武器援助. ¶***beauty aids*** 化粧品. ¶***emergency aid*** for Europe 欧州に対する緊急援助. ¶be under ***government*** *aid* 政府の援助を受けている. 【類】The industry enjoys a ***government aid*** to the extent of … ¶a battery for a ***hearing aid*** 補聴器用電池. ¶an ***interim aid*** 臨時雇. ¶***learning aids*** 勉強の手引き. ¶in ***lend-lease aid*** 武器貸与の一環として. ¶grant a ***State aid*** 国庫補助金を与える. 【類】Some form of ***State aid*** must be granted. / by ***State aid***.

P I was encouraged ***by aid***. 助勢された. ‖ master a foreign language ***by aid*** of a grammar and dictionary 文法書と辞書をたよりに外国語を修める ‖ ***by*** the ***aid*** of scientific knowledge 科学的知識の助けで. ¶I lean upon you ***for aid***. 私は貴君にすがっている. ¶state grants ***in aid*** of disabled soldiers 傷病兵扶助のための政府の補助金 ‖ a bazaar ***in aid*** of … …の後援のために催される慈善市. 【類】give a performance of a dance called "Winds" ***in aid*** of charity / The garden party was given ***in aid*** of the British and Belgian wounded (負傷兵). / ***in aid*** of the fund for … ¶it is ***of*** especial ***aid*** それは大いに役に立つ. ¶***Through*** your ***aid*** I may succeed. 君の助力で僕は成功ができましょう. ¶In France silk is grown ***under*** the ***aid*** of bounties. フランスでは絹糸産業は奨励金を受けている. ¶***with*** the ***aid*** of a megaphone メガフォンを使って ‖ ***with*** the ***aid*** of English capital 英国の資本で. ¶***without aid*** from … …の力をからずに. 【類】***without*** the ***aid*** of a glass / ***without*** the ***aid*** of a single note (註釈).

P² physical ***aids for*** mental culture 精神修養のための体育 ‖ an ***aid for*** solving problems 問題解決の一助. ¶apply ***for aid from*** the scholarship funds 奨学資金給与を申請する. ¶***aids in*** practical geology 応用地質学のしるべ ‖ ***aid in*** a fraud 詐欺の幇助 ‖ regard literature as a useful ***aid in*** learning English 文学を英語学習の有益な助けと見なす. ¶an ***aid to*** memory (pronunciation) 記憶(など)の助け ‖ a decided ***aid to*** beginners 初心者にとっての明かな助け ‖ ***aids to*** facial beauty 化粧品 ‖ ***aids to*** English composition 英作文の参考 ‖ ***aids to*** navigation 航路標識.

aid, *v.* 助ける, 手伝う.

M it ***aided materially*** in developing … それは…を発展させる上に大いに力があった.

P ***aid*** a person ***against*** an enemy 敵に反抗して人に助勢する. ¶He was ***aided by*** an accomplice. 彼は共犯者に幇助された. ‖ ***aided by*** the stethoscope 聴診器を用いて. ¶I ***aided*** him ***in*** the enterprise. 彼の事業を援助した. 【類】***aid*** a person ***in*** the work of … ¶***aid*** a person ***to*** success 人を助けて成功させる. ¶I ***aided*** him ***with*** money and advice. 僕は彼に金をやりまた助言もした.

aide, *n.* 助手.

Q² ***Cabinet aides*** 内閣補佐官. ¶use students as ***election aides*** 選挙応援に学生を使う.

aide-de-camp, *n.* 副官.

Q the ***chief aide-de-camp*** 侍従武官長.

P² the ***aide-de-camp to*** the Crown Prince 東宮武官 ‖ an ***aide-de-camp to*** the Sovereign 侍従武官.

ailment, *n.* 疾病.
V *cure* a certain *ailment* 一定の疾病を癒(い)やす.
Q a *common ailment* 普通の病気. ¶*kindred* (*allied*) *ailment* 類似の疾病. ¶*minor ailments* 微恙(びよう), 軽症. ¶*sudden ailments* 急病. ¶*trifling ailments* 軽症. ¶*women's ailments* 婦人病.
Q^2 die of a *brain ailment* 脳病で死ぬ. ¶a *heart* (*kidney*) *ailment* 心(腎)臓病. ¶suffer from a *stomach* (*skin*) *ailment* 胃(皮膚)病で苦しむ.
P^2 *ailment of* pregnancy 妊娠に伴う病気.

aim, *n.* (**1**) 目的; 計画.
V *achieve* one's *aim* 目的を達する. ¶to *accomplish* that *aim* その目的を果たすために. ¶*defeat* the true *aims* of education 教育の真の目的にそむく ¶*divert* the *aim* of a teacher from the instruction of his pupils to preparing them for passing the examination 教師の目的を生徒の教育ということから試験通過の準備ということに転向させる. ¶*execute* (=*carry out*) one's *aims* 目的を決行する. ¶*fulfil* its high *aims* その大きな目的を果たす. ¶*further* their special *aims* 彼らの特殊の計画をはかどらせる. ¶*have* a high *aim* in life 人生に大きな目的を持っている. ¶*pursue* an *aim* 計画通りやる. ¶*set out* (=*forth*) the *aims* and objects of ... ...の趣旨を表明する.
Q the *central aim* of its work その事業の中心目的. ¶make it the *chief aim* to ... ...を主目的とする. ¶They united in one *common aim*, that, namely, of making a living. 彼らは一つの共通の目的即ち生計を立てて行くという点で一致した. ¶make it one's *consistent aim* to ... 終始一貫して... ¶make it my *first aim* to ... ...することを私の第一の目的とする. ¶supply *fixed aims* to popular aspiration 一般の向上心に一定の目標を示す. ¶a *leading* aim おもな目的. ¶*lofty aims* 高遠な目的. ¶a *noble aim* 高尚な目的. ¶attain the *original aim* 初志を貫く. ¶the *primary aim* in teaching 教授の主要目的. ¶for the attainment of *selfish aim* and purpose 利己的な目的を達せんがために. ¶a man with a *single narrow aim* of money-getting 金もうけというたった一つのちっぽけな目的を持っている人. ¶the *true aims* of life 人生の真の目的. ¶the *ultimate aim* 究極の目的.
Q^2 *dollars-and-cents aim* in education 教育における打算的目標. ¶*war aims* 戦争目的.
P an organization having *for* its *aim* ... ...を目的とする団体. ¶*with* this high *aim* in view この大きな目的を目指して. 【類】*with* the *aim* of ... ¶*without aim* 目当てなく.
P^2 one of the *aims of* the organizers of the exhibition その博覧会発起人の目的の一つ.
(**2**) ねらい, 標的.
V *have* a right *aim* よくねらう. ¶*miss* one's *aim* ねらいが狂う. 【類】The pistol *missed* its *aim*. ¶*take aim* at ... ...にねらいをつける. ‖ *Take* a good *aim* with your rifle. 君のライフル銃でよくねらえ. ‖ *take aim* with a gun 鉄砲でよくねらう.
Q taking *accurate aim* 正確なねらいをつけて. ¶take *careful aim* よくねらいをつける. ¶take *deliberate aim* at=draw a bead on ... ...にじっとねらいをつける. ¶taking a *good aim* ねらいを定めて. ¶take *quick aim* す早くねらいを定める. ¶take a *steady aim* しかとねらいをつける. ¶take *sure aim* 確かなねらいをつける. ¶with *unerring aim* ねらいあやまたず.

aim, *v.* ねらう; 志ざす.
M *aim chiefly* to ... 主として...を志す. ¶*aim high* 志を高くする. ¶*aim solely* at ... 専ら...を志ざす. ¶be *aimed specifically* at ... 主として...が目指される. ¶*aim vigorously* at perfection あくまで完全を期す. ¶*aim wrongly* at ... ...のねらいを誤る.
P *aim at* a mark 的をねらう ‖ He *aimed at* honors. 彼は名誉を得ようとした. ‖ in no case can one who *aims at* ... lay claim to be ... ...を目的とする者は断じて...と主張する事はできない / *aim at* promotion of international understanding and maintenance of world peace ‖ *aim at* raising men to a higher level, socially and spiritually / He *aims at* accuracy (正確) / *aim at* greater proficiency (熟達) in the art / *aim at* practical utility (実益) / *aim at* the downfall of the Cabinet (倒閣) ‖ He *aimed* the pistol *at* me. 彼は私にピストルを向けた. ‖ the object *aimed at* 目的. 【類】measures *aimed at* ... ¶*aim for* the highest result 最大の効果を挙げようと努める. ¶*aim with* one eye 片目でねらいをつける.

air, *n.* (**1**) 空気; そよ風; 空中; 戸外; 流布.
V *admit air* 空気を入れる. ¶*beat* the *air* 空を打つ, むだ骨を折る. ¶*blow air* into a balloon 風船に空気を吹込む. ¶*breathe* foul *air* 不潔な空気を呼吸する. ¶*claw* the *air* 空をつかむ. ¶*clear* the *air* 気分を新たにする, 空気を一掃する. ¶*draw* the fresh *air* 新鮮な空気を吸入する. ¶*enjoy* the cool *air* 涼む. ¶The apple blossoms *filled* the *air* with their fragrance. りんごの花の芳香があたり一面に立ちこめていた. ¶*foul* (=*vitiate*) the *air* 空気を悪くする. ¶*lose* the *air* 制空権を失う. ¶*navigate* the *air* in an aeroplane 航行機で空を飛ぶ. 【類】The first vehicles to *navigate* the *air* were balloons. ¶Plum blossoms *perfume* the *air* with delicious odors. 梅の花が芳香を放つ. ¶*purify* the *air* of a room 室内の空気を浄化する. ¶*put air* in the tire タイヤに空気を入れる. ¶Shouts of joy *rent* the *air*. 歓呼の声は空に響いた. ‖ The exclusive *air* of the place was *rent* with the hum of voice. その静寂の別天地にざわざわと人声がした. ¶*sniff* the *air* かぎつける(陰謀などを). ¶The story has *taken air*. その話が世間に広まった. ‖ *take* the *air* 運動に出る. ¶*take in* salt *air* 潮風を吸込む. ¶*win* the *air* 制空権を握る.
V^2 The *air* of morning *drifted in*. 朝の空気が流れ込んだ. ¶The *air grows* colder as we go up. [登山の際など]登るに従って空気は段々冷くなる. ¶The *air resounds* with the cries of boys. 大気は子供らの叫びで鳴り響く.
Q in the *bracing air* of the Southern Ocean 南洋の爽快な空気に. ¶The *air* was *breathless*. 少しも風がなかった. ¶the *chilly* and *foggy air* of the North 北地のひやひやする霧深い空気. ¶The *air* is *close*. むしむしする. ¶*compressed air* 圧搾空気. ¶open windows and let in *cool air* 窓をあけて涼風を入れる. ¶The *air* is *crisp* and *cool*. 清々しく涼しい. ¶the *dense air* of a deep mine 深い坑内の濃密な空気. ¶in *dry air* 乾燥した空気中で. ¶The *air* was *electric* with the impending danger. 差迫る危険で人人は緊張していた. ¶This *fine air* will do you good. こんなよい空気は君の体によい. ¶*flower-fragrant air* 花の香のただよう空気. ¶That *fresh air* feels great. あの新鮮な空気はすてきだ. ¶The *air* is *heavy* with the perfume of flowers. 空気は花の香を濃厚に含んでいる. ¶The *air* is now at its *hottest*. 今暑い盛りだ. ¶*impure* and *vitiated air* 不潔な汚れた空気. ¶The *air* is *keen* and *bright*. 身にしみるようなさえた空気だ. ¶*liquid air* 液体空気. ¶The *air* is *mild*. のどかな陽気だ. ¶in *moist air* 湿った空気中に. ¶have exercise in the *open air* 戸外で運動する. 【類】preach in the *open air* / I love *open air* and outdoor life. ¶open to the *outside air* 外気にさらされて. ¶*pure* and *invigorating air* 澄んでさわやかな空気. ¶the *rarefied air* of high mountains 高山の希薄な空気. ¶The *air* is *relaxing*. 体のだるくなるような陽気だ. ¶The *air* is *soft*. なごやかな陽気だ. ¶*stagnant air* よどんだ空気 ¶the *stuffy air* むっとする陽気. ¶the *sultry air* むしむしする陽気.
Q^2 Children thrive (=grow strong) in the *country air*. 子供はいなかで育つと丈夫になる. ¶The sound of joyous laughter rose on the fresh *morning air*. 楽しい笑声が新鮮な朝の空気にふっと起った. 【類】take a walk in the fresh *morning air* / the crisp *morning air* in autumn (さわやかな朝の空気). ¶the cool *mountain air* すがすがしい山気. ¶Through the open windows snatches of melody float on the *night air*. 明けはなした窓からとぎれとぎれの旋律が夜の空気に乗って漂って来る. 【類】damp *night air*. ¶*sea air* 海風.
P traveling *by air* 空の旅. 【類】the conquest of the Atlantic *by air*. ¶During the great war London was attacked *from* the *air*. 大戦中ロンドンは空襲を受けた. ‖ It was a big thrust *from* the *air*. それは大がかりな空襲だった. ¶aloft *in* the *air* 空高く ‖ float *in* the *air* 空中に漂う ‖ fly *in* the *air* ‖ hover *in* the *air* 空中に舞う. 【類】There was dampness *in* the *air*. ‖ There is a nip *in* the *air*. ぴりっと寒い. ‖ a project *in* the *air* 覚束ない計画 ‖ build the castles *in* the *air* 空中楼閣を描く ‖ Baseball is very much *in* the *air* just now in England. 野球は今英国で非常に盛んである. 【類】When the fall comes football is *in* the *air*. ‖ there is a rumor *in* the *air* that ... ...と

いう風説が立っている. 【類】rumors of ... are already *in* the *air*. ¶fly up *into* the *air* 空中高く上がる. 【類】rise *into* the *air* / spout water *into* the *air*. ¶There is not a breath *of air* here. ここには風がそよとも吹かない. ‖ take a change *of air* and scene 転地する. ¶There was a fresh scent *on* the *air*. さわやかな香が漂っていた. ‖ feel as if one's body disappeared and one walked *on air* 体が消えて空中を歩いているような気がする ‖ The NBC has only one outstanding function to give what you want *on* the *air*. NBC にはただ一つの役目, 即ち聴取者の期待するものを与えるという一つのりっぱな役目がある. 【類】a comic opera *on* the *air* / What's *on* the *air* (ラジオの番組) today? / a visit into a studio while a program is *on* the *air* ‖ The letter was sent *on* the *air* (=by air). その手紙は航空郵便で出した. ¶The swallows darted *through* the *air*. つばめは空中をかすめて飛んだ. 【類】travel *through* the *air*. ¶The tube was filled *with air*. チューブには空気が一杯詰っていた.

(**2**) 様子, 態度, 振り.

V *assume* a triumphant *air* 得意になる ‖ *assume* an *air* of superiority (great dignity) えらそう(など)にする ‖ *assume* the *air* of a scholar 学者ぶる. ¶It *bears* a truly rural *air*. そこには真に野趣がある. ¶*carry* a kingly *air* 王者の貫禄を備えている. ¶*give* an *air* of coolness to the room 部屋に涼しげな趣を添える ‖ *give* an *air* of reality to ... ...を本当らしく見せる. 【類】introduce a few breakages and repairs to *give* forgeries an *air* of antiquity (にせ物を古物らしく見せる) ‖ *give* oneself *airs* いばる ‖ *give air* to one's view 意見を公表する. ¶She *has* an *air* of languor about her. どこかしおれているような所がある. ‖ The town *has* a European *air*. この町にはヨーロッパ風の所がある. 【類】The word *has* a foreign *air* about it. ‖ *have* the *air* of a scholar. 学者タイプだ. ¶It *lends* an *air* of gravity to the proceedings. そのために議事が重要性を持つ. ¶*preserve* an *air* of studied hauteur 殊更横柄な態度をしている. ¶*put on airs* 気どる. ¶"It is I" sounds to me like "*putting on airs*." It is I というといかにも気取っているように聞える. ‖ *put on* high *airs* with one's learning 学問を鼻に掛ける. ¶*take on* a patronizing *air* 親分ぶった様子をする. ¶*wear* an *air* of lofty dignity えらくりきみかえる.

Q He had an *abstracted air*. 彼はぼんやりした様子をしていた. ¶a *cheerful air* 快活な態度. ¶with a *downcast air* がっかりした様子で. ¶with *empty airs* 気取って. ¶an *exotic air* 異国情調. ¶put on *fearful airs* 恐ろしい楯幕になる. ¶a *graceful air* しとやかな態度. ¶He had an *injured air*. 彼は気を悪くしたようだった. ¶He has an *innocent air*. 彼は無邪気な様子をしている. ¶a *kingly air* 王者の風. ¶with a *knowing air* 知ったかぶりで. ¶assume *live air* 活気を帯びる(市場など). ¶with *lordly airs* ごう然と構えて. ¶a *melancholy air* 陰気な様子. ¶assume a *nonchalant air* 何食わぬ顔をする. ¶with a *pained air* 苦しそうな様子をして. ¶her *patrician air* 彼女の貴族的な態度. ¶with a *pedantic air* 物知り顔に. ¶he all of a sudden assumed a *strange* and *cool air* toward ... 彼は急に...に対してよそよそしい冷淡な態度を取った. ¶put on *superior airs* えらそうに構える. ¶His judgment has an *unmistakable air* of authority. 彼の見解はたしかに権威あるものと思わせる.

Q^2 a "*Hey-my-pal*" air「おい兄弟」といった様子. ¶with an "*I-told-you-so*" *air*「いわないこっちゃない」といったような顔をして. ¶He has a "*look-who-I-am*" *air* about him. あの人には「おれをだれだと思う」といったような所がある.

P *with* an *air* of importance (=superiority) もったいぶって ‖ *with* an *air* of perfect nonchalance 何食わぬ顔をして ‖ *with* an *air* of profound respect かしこまって ‖ *with* an *air* of triumph したり顔に.

P^2 an *air of* cheerfulness 快活な態度 ‖ This house has an *air of* comfort. この家は住み心地がよさそうだ. 【類】The town has an *air of* prosperity. / have an *air of* sadness / there is an *air of* seediness (貧乏たらしい).

(**3**) 歌曲, 歌調.

V *hum* an air 小歌を歌う. ¶An organ-grinder was *murdering* an *air* from *La Cencrentola*. 手まわしオルガンひきがラ・サンクラントラの一節のめちゃくちゃな演奏をしていた. ¶The band *played* martial *airs*. 楽隊が軍楽を奏した. ¶The band *struck up* a sprightly *air*. 楽隊が陽気な曲を演奏し始めた.

Q the *latest popular airs* of the day 最近の流行歌. ¶play a succession of *lively airs* 続けざまに陽気な曲を演奏する. ¶a *national air* 国民愛唱の歌. ¶The military band played *operatic airs*. 軍楽隊は歌劇の曲を奏した. ¶*thrilling patriotic airs* 血が沸くような愛国の歌.

aircraft, *n.* 航空機.

Q *nuclear aircraft* 原子力航空機. ¶overflights of Japanese territory by *unidentified aircraft* 国籍不明の飛行機の日本領土上空飛行.

Q^2 bring down five *enemy aircraft* 敵機五機を撃墜する. ¶*fighting* (*bombing*) *aircraft* 戦闘(爆撃)機.

airing, *n.* 散歩.

V *get* an evening *airing* after office hours 執務時間後に夕方の散歩をする.

Q^2 *summer airing* 土用干し.

airlift, *n.* 空中輸送.

Q the greatest *peace-time airlift* in history 平時における史上最大の空輸.

air-line, *n.* 一直線.

P fly *air-line to* ... ...に一直線に飛ぶ.

airliner, *n.* 定期旅客機.

Q^2 a *London-to-Paris air-liner* ロンドン・パリ間定期旅客機.

airplane, *n.* 《米》飛行機.

V *pilot* an *airplane* 飛行機を操縦する. ¶*drive* an *airplane* 飛行機を操縦する. ¶*fly* an *airplane* 飛行機を飛ばす. ¶*operate* five *airplanes* on its Pacific route 太平洋航空路に五台の飛行機を就航させる. ¶*stop airplanes* 飛行停止する.

Q an *atom-driven* (=*atomic*) *airplane*, a plane which could fly anywhere on earth without refueling 原子力飛行機即ち給油せずに地球上いかなる地点にも飛行しうる飛行機. 【類】An *atomic airplane* could travel enormous distances powered by a lump of uranium no bigger than a man's fist.

Q^2 *combat airplanes* 戦闘機. ¶*fighter airplanes* 戦闘機. ¶"*flying coffin*" *airplanes* 棺おけ飛行機(神風特攻機のこと).

air-raid, *n.* 空襲.

Q *massed air-raids* 大空襲.

aisle, *n.* 座席間の通路.

Q^2 the *side aisles* of a theater 《米》劇場内の座席両側の通路.

akin, *a.* 似ている, 近い.

V *closely akin* to ... ...に酷似している.

P A buffalo is *akin to* an ox. 水牛は雄牛に似ている. ‖ it needs something *akin to* genius to ... ...することは天才といったものでなくてはできない. 【類】Spanish is *akin to* Latin. / It evoked something *akin to* consternation in the Diplomatic Corps (外交団).

alacrity, *n.* 快活.

V *show alacrity* はきはきする.

P *with alacrity* 快活に, はきはきと.

alarm, *n.* (**1**) 驚がく, 騒ぎ.

V *awaken* anxiety and *alarm* 憂慮と驚がくの念を喚起する. ¶It need *cause* no *alarm*. それは心配には及ばぬ. 【類】The news *caused* great *alarm*. ¶It need not *create* any great *alarm*. それは大した心配にはおよばない. ¶*display* one's *alarm* ぎょっとした様子をする. ¶*excite* great *alarm* in the minds of ... 大いに...に驚がくの念を起させる. ¶*express alarm* at the news その報を得てびっくりする. ¶*Alarm* was *felt* in the camp. 陣中大騒ぎになった. ¶His present condition *gave* his friends the deepest *alarm*. 彼の現状は大いにその友だちを驚かした. ¶*raise* an *alarm* 悲鳴をあげる. ¶He *took alarm* at the prospect. 先のことを考えて大いに悲観した.

P There is no ground *for alarm*. 少しも騒ぐことはない. ¶exclaim *in* great *alarm* びっくりして叫ぶ. ¶He was struck *with alarm*. 彼は仰天した. ¶*without alarm* 落着いて.

(**2**) 警報, 合図.

V *beat* an *alarm* on a gong ドラを鳴らして急を知らせる. ¶*display* an *alarm* 警報信号を掲げる. ¶The *alarm* was *given* for a fire. 出火の警報が発せられた. ¶*raise* an *alarm* of fire 出火の警報をする. ¶The clock *rings* the *alarm*. 時計が目覚しのベルを鳴らす. ¶*send in* an *alarm* 急を報じる. ¶*set* the *alarm* to go off at 6 六時に鳴るように目覚しを掛ける. ¶*set* the *alarm* at rest 安心させる. ¶*shout* the *alarm* 大声で急を告げる. ¶*sound* the *alarm* 非常合図を鳴らす. ¶*taking* the *alarm* 危険と気が付いて.

V^2 The *alarm **spread*** rapidly. 警報がたちまち広まった.

Q an ***electric** alarm* 電鈴, 電気警鈴. ¶a ***false** alarm* [火事などの]無根の警報 ‖ turn in (=sound) a ***false** alarm* 火災報知器にいたずらする.

Q^2 an ***air** alarm* 空襲警報. ¶ring up a ***burglar** alarm* in the kitchen of one's home 台所の強盗報知器を鳴らす. ¶The ***fire** alarm* sounded. 半鐘(火災報知器)が鳴った. ¶a ***gas** alarm* 毒ガス警報.

alarm, *v.* 驚かす.

M I was *alarmed **beyond measure*** at ... 私は...に非常に驚いた. ¶they were ***much** alarmed* when they saw ... 彼らは...を見てひどく驚いた. ¶I was ***quite** alarmed* last night at the cry of "fire." 昨夜火事だと叫ぶのを聞いて実に驚いた. ¶I was ***terribly** alarmed*. 私はひどく驚いた.

P People began to feel *alarmed **about*** the cholera. コレラで世間が騒ぎ出した. ¶be *alarmed **at*** the prospect of ... ...の前途を悲観する ‖ I am *alarmed **at*** your rashness. 君の乱暴には驚いた. 【類】I was much *alarmed **at*** the news (sight, report). / He was *alarmed **at*** what he had just heard. / He was not *alarmed **at*** receiving the telegram. ¶They were *alarmed **by*** a sudden attack. 不意の襲撃で仰天した. ¶become *alarmed **over*** a situation 形勢を見てびっくりする.

album, *n.* アルバム.

Q a ***commemorative** album* 記念帖. ¶a ***photographic** album* 写真帖.

Q^2 ***autograph** albums* 署名収集帳.

P photographs, framed or ***in** albums* 額にしたりアルバムにはったりした写真.

alcohol, *n.* アルコール.

Q^2 ***grain** alcohol*=***ethyl** alcohol* [穀類から採った]エチルアルコール. ¶***wood** alcohol*=***methyl** alcohol* メチルアルコール.

alcoholism, *n.* アルコール中毒.

Q ***chronic** alcoholism* 慢性アルコール中毒.

alcove, *n.* 床の間.

P an ornament ***in** the alcove* 床の間の飾り物.

ale, *n.* ビール.

Q ***bottled** ale* びん詰めビール.

alert, *n.* 見張り.

P be ever ***on** the alert* いつも油断せずにいる. ¶He was instructed to be ***on** the alert* for any indications of battle. 彼は開戦の徴候に気を付けているように命令された. 【類】They were constantly ***on** the alert* not to be taken by surprise (不意を打たれぬよう).

alert, *a.* 油断のない.

M be *alert **mentally*** 緊張している. ¶be ***ever** alert* to making money 金もうけにかけては抜け目がない.

P was *alerted **for*** Korean duty 朝鮮に出動を命ぜられていた.

alertness, *n.* 機敏さ.

Q Stimulants increase ***mental** and **physical** alertness*. 刺激は心身を敏活にする.

alias, *n.* 変名.

V ***take** an alias* 変名する.

Q a ***high-sounding** alias* 仰々しい変名.

alibi, *n.* 不在証明.

V ***establish** an alibi* 不在証明を確立させる. ¶***prove** an alibi* 不在証明を実証する.

alien, *n.* 外国人.

Q Japanese arts and crafts owe a good deal to ***skilled** aliens*. 日本の美術工芸は技芸に長じた外国人に負う所が多い. ¶***undesirable** aliens* 好ましくない外人.

Q^2 ***Communist** aliens*=*alien* Communists 外人の共産党員. ¶***enemy** aliens* 敵である外国人. ¶***pauper** aliens* 貧窮の外人.

P^2 *aliens **among*** our people わが国民間に在住する外人. ¶*aliens **in*** our land わが国在住の外人.

alien, *a.* かけはなれている.

M Cruelty is ***quite** alien* to his nature. 彼の性質には少しも残忍なところがない.

P be *alien **from*** my thought 私の本意に反している. 【類】This style is *alien **from*** genuine English. ‖ Nothing human is *alien **from*** him. 人間に関する事であれば人ごととは思わぬ. ‖ principles *alien **from*** our religion われわれの宗教とは異った教義. ¶Luxury is *alien **to*** his nature. ぜい沢は彼の性に合わない.=be *alien **to*** her feelings その感じは彼女にはわからない. 【類】*alien **to*** his character (heart, taste, the climate^2). / A Latin construction (構文) is *alien **to*** the genius (特質) of the English language.

alienate, *v.* 遠ざける.

P He was *alienated **from*** his friends. 友だちに見捨てられた.

alienation, *n.* 錯乱; 離反; 譲渡.

Q ***mental** alienation* 精神錯乱.

P^2 *alienation **from*** a friend 友人との疎遠. 【類】*alienation **of*** affection ***from*** a friend 友人に愛想をつかされること. ¶*alienation **of*** mind 精神錯乱. ‖ *alienation **of*** property 財産の譲渡.

alight, *v.* 降りる, 下る; 偶然出会う.

P *alight **from*** a carriage 馬車から降りる. 【類】on *alighting **from*** the train. ¶The birds *alighted **on*** the ground (field, roof). 鳥は地上(など)に降りた. 【類】The butterfly *alighted **on*** a flower (tree, branch). ‖ He *alighted **on*** a rare plant. 彼は珍らしい植物を見付けた. ‖ The blow *alighted **on*** his head. 彼は頭をなぐられた. ‖ *alight **on*** feet [地上に落ちたとき]足で立つ.

alight, *a.* あかあかとした.

P The room is *alight **with*** many lamps. へやには沢山のランプが煌々(こう)とついている.

alignment, *n.* 整列線.

Q The result of it was a ***new** alignment* in the International. その結果インターナショナル党は改組した.

P be ***in** alignment* 一直線を成している.

alike, *a., ad.* 等しい, 相似ている.

M We are ***all** alike* concerned in religion. われわれはひとしく宗教に関係している. ¶They are ***exactly** alike*. それらはうり二つだ. ¶The houses in this row are ***just** alike*. こちら側の家は全く同じだ. ¶They are ***much** alike* in character. 彼らは性格がよく似ている. ¶The two words, though ***phonetically** alike*, are written with different ideographs. この二字は音は同じだが形が違う. ¶They are ***somewhat** alike*. 彼らは幾分似ている.

P *alike **in*** character (kind) 性質(など)が等しい ‖ *alike* only ***in*** appearance 似て非なる. ¶escape sins *alike **of*** omission and of commission in compiling 編集上の脱漏と誤謬を免れる. ¶They are all *alike **to*** me. 彼らは私から見れば皆同じだ(その間に甲乙がない).

alive, *a.* 生きている; にぎやかな; 活気のある; 敏感な.

M The city was ***all** alive* when he arrived. 彼が着いた時は町はほんとににぎやかだった. ‖ The company were ***all** alive*. 一行は皆元気だった. ¶The Americans are ***far more** alive* to the importance of good teeth than the English. 米人は英人よりも歯の衛生の重要なことをずっとよく知っている. ¶The authorities are ***fully** alive* to the danger of it. 当局はその危険を百も承知している. ¶He is ***just** alive*. 彼は生きているというだけだ. ¶***keenly** alive* to the responsibilities of one's position 職責を痛感して ‖ be ***keenly** alive* to the best interests of ... 出来るだけ...のためになるように抜目なくやっている. ¶I fear he is ***no longer** alive*. 彼はもう死んだかも知れない. ¶He is *alive **still***. 彼はまだ生きている. ‖ His love is ***still** alive*. 彼の愛情はいまも続いている. ¶he is *alive **to the full*** that ... 彼は...ということを十分に承知している. ¶while he is ***yet** alive* 彼の存命中に.

P He is *alive **in*** every nerve. 彼は元気おう盛である. ¶He is *alive **through*** all his being. 元気が全身にみなぎっている. ¶He is *alive **to*** pain. 彼は苦痛に感じやすい. ‖ he is *alive **to*** the necessity of ... 彼は...の必要をよく知っている. 【類】*alive **to*** the value of ... / He is *alive **to*** his interests. 彼は自利にさとい. / *alive **to*** dangers facing him (身に迫る危険). ¶be *alive **to*** the feelings of honor 恥を知っている. ¶He is *alive **with*** fervor (hope, resolve). 情熱(など)に燃えている. ‖ The woods are *alive **with*** birds. 森は鳥でにぎやかだ. 【類】The harbor is *alive **with*** sailing craft of every conceivable kind (ありとあらゆる帆船). / The hive is *alive **with*** bees. / The lake is *alive **with*** fish (魚がうようよ).

all, *n.* のこらず, 全部.

V I have ***done** all* that man can do. 人事を尽した. ‖ I ***did** all* I could. できるだけのことはした. ¶He ***knows** all* about Japanese history. 彼は日本史に精通している. ¶He has ***lost** his all*. 彼は財産を皆失った. ¶She puts *all* she ***earns*** on her back. あの女はもうけた金は皆着てしまう. ¶I have ***said** all* there is to be said about it 言うだけのことは言った. ¶I will ***take** all* of it. 全部もらおう.

V^2 *All* are ***agreed***. 一同同意だ. ¶when *all **comes*** to all 結局.

P ***Above** all* beware of idleness. 殊に怠惰を慎しめ. ¶***After*** *all* it is not so hard as it looks. 結局思うほどはむずかしくはない. 【類】Grain crops are only a kind of grass *after all*. ¶I was surprised at his coming *at all*. そもそも彼が来るというのが既に意外だった. ‖ if undertaken *at all* やるからには ‖ Whatever is worth doing *at all* is worth doing well. いやしくもやる価値のある事ならよくやる価値があるものだ. ‖ That hat does not suit you *at all*. あの帽子は少しも君に似合わない. ‖ No good *at all*. てんでなっていない. 【類】It will not do *at all*. / It is not *at all* likely that he will come. / I did not *at all* expect that he would come. / Buy a good one if you buy *at all*. ¶*before all*. 何はさておき, まず第一に. ¶*beyond all* 第一に, 真先に. ¶He will not trust you *for all* that you may say in your defense. 君が何と申訳しても彼は信じまい. 【類】He may do so *for all* [that] I care. ‖ He may be a lunatic *for all* I know. あの人は気違いかも知れない. ‖ I tell you once *for all* this noise must cease. やかましいから静かにしろ分かったか. ‖ I say this once *for all*. このことははっきりいっておく. ‖ He worked *for all* he was worth. あの人はやりがいのある事のためには何でもした. ¶*From all* we hear he is mad. どうも彼は狂人らしい. ¶There are twenty teachers *in all*, including the Director. 校長を入れて皆で二十人教師がいる. ¶That is the common opinion *of all*. それが一般の説です. ‖ He came first *of all*. 彼が真先に来た.

P² I have forgotten *all about* it. 私はすっかり忘れていた. ‖ I'll let you know *all about* it. 万事お話しします. ‖ *All About* Dogs 畜犬全書(書名). ¶*all along* the road 沿道一帯に. ¶*All at* once I heard a peal of thunder. 突然雷鳴を聞いた. ¶And this ends forever *all between* us. これで(この手紙限り)絶交する. ¶He was *all but* drowned. 彼はほとんど溺死していた. ‖ *all but* ten years ほとんど十年 ‖ *All but* one were present. 一人の外皆出席した. 【類】*All but* the morning star have disappeared. ¶She is *all in* all to him. 彼女は彼に取っては掌中の玉だ. 【類】The fleet of England is her *all in* all. / Grammar is not *all in* all. ‖ Trust me *all in* all, or not at all. 私を信じるなら何もかも, 信じてないならきっぱりと. ¶*All of* the children died young. 子供は皆早死した. 【類】*All of* us were present, except the servants. ‖ *all of* a sudden 突然 ‖ *all of* one's life 一生を通じて. ¶*all over* the country 国内至る所. 【類】*all over* the world. ¶go *all round* the world 世界中を一周する. ¶*all save* one 一つの外全部. ¶*all through* his life 彼の生涯中. ¶It is *all* one *to* me. 僕にはどれも一つ事だ. ¶*all without* exception 一つ残らず.

allegation, *n.* 主張, 申立.

V *retract* an *allegation* 主張を撤回する. ¶*scout* the *allegation* that ... …という申立を取上げない.

Q *inaccurate allegations* 不正確な申立て.

P *on* the *allegation* that ... …を主張して.

allege, *v.* 言立てる.

P it is *alleged against* his character that ... …という彼にとって聞えの悪いことが挙げられている.

allegiance, *n.* 忠順, 恭順.

V *acknowledge* no *allegiance* to ... …に対して何ら忠順の義務を認めない. ¶*bear* true *allegiance* to ... …に対して真に忠順の念を懐く. ¶*demand allegiance* 忠順を求める. ¶*display* willing *allegiance* to ... …に対して進んで恭順を示す. ¶*forsake allegiance* そむく. ¶He *offered* me his *allegiance*. 彼は私に臣事すると言い出した. ¶*owe allegiance* to that country (a monarch) その国(など)に臣従の義務を負う. 【類】*owe allegiance* to Britain's sovereign (英国王) / the country to which the foreigner *owes allegiance*. ¶*pay* but a nominal *allegiance* to ... …に対して名目だけの恭順を致す. ¶*pledge* our *allegiance* to these principles その主義に忠実ならんことを誓う. ¶They *renounced allegiance* to Spain (the Pope). 彼らはスペイン(法王)にそむいた. ¶*repudiate* one's *allegiance* 臣従の義務を否認する. ¶*strengthen* one's *allegiance* to one's native land (=the country of one's birth) 母国に対する恭順の念を強くする. ¶*swear* one's lasting *allegiance* to ... 末永く…に臣事する事を誓う. ¶*throw off allegiance* そむく. ¶*yield* one's *allegiance* to ... …に臣事する.

Q I trust you will favour us with your *continued allegiance*. 私は貴下がわれわれのために相変らずお尽し下さることを信じます. ¶*divided allegiance* of American-born Japanese 米国生れの日本人が日米両国に臣従すること. ¶*double allegiance* 二重に臣従の義務を負うこと.

Q² *party allegiance* [所属]政党への忠誠.

P² The government has a right to *allegiance from* the citizen. 政府は国民に忠順を求める権利がある. ¶*allegiance of* the citizen to the government 政府に対する国民の忠順. ¶*allegiance to* a sovereign (one's country) 元首(など)への忠誠. 【類】pacify and win back the revolting natives to *allgiance to* Spanish rule.

alley, *n.* 小路.

Q a *blind alley* 袋小路. ¶a *back alley* 裏通り.

alliance, *n.* 同盟, 提携; 縁組.

V *abrogate* an *alliance* 同盟を廃止する. ¶*arrange* an *alliance* with ... against ... …に対抗して…と提携する. ¶*conclude* (=*contract*) an *alliance* with ... …と同盟を結ぶ. ¶*declare* one's *alliance* to ... …に某の提携を声明する. ¶*form* an *alliance* with the man of her choice 意中の男と縁組する. ¶*maintain* an *alliance* 同盟を継続する. ¶*make* an *alliance* with ... …と同盟を結ぶ. ¶*renounce* an *alliance* 同盟を廃棄する.

V² This *alliance makes* for peace. この同盟は平和を助成する.

Q the *Anglo-Japanese alliance* 日英同盟. ¶a *dual* (*triple*) *alliance* 二(三)国同盟. ¶a *lop-sided alliance* 不平等同盟. ¶form a *matrimonial alliance* with ... …と夫婦の縁を結ぶ. ¶form an *offensive* and *defensive alliance* with ... …と攻守同盟を結ぶ ‖ a *secret alliance* 秘密同盟.

Q² a *defense alliance* against ... …を目標とした防衛同盟. ¶a students' *purity alliance* 学生純潔連盟. ¶the *tripartite Axis Alliance* 枢軸三国同盟.

P wage war with the Prussians *in alliance* with the French フランスと同盟してプロシヤと戦う. ¶ruined in health *through alliance* with libertines [無垢の婦人などが]放とう者と縁組して体をだいなしにされる.

P² a yellow *alliance against* the white races 白色人種に対抗する黄色人種の同盟. 【類】*alliance against* the common enemy. ¶an *alliance among* nations 国民間の同盟. ¶an *alliance between* church and state 宗教と政治との合体. ¶an *alliance for* offense and defense 攻守同盟. 【類】*alliance for* the common cause (共同の目的). ¶an *alliance with* a neighboring people 隣邦との同盟.

allocation, *n.* 割当.

Q² receive a *budget allocation* of ... for ... …のために…の予算割当を受ける. ¶*food allocation* 食糧の割当て. ¶*materials allocation* 資材の割当て. ¶*petroleum allocation* to ... …の石油割当. ¶*priority allocation* 優先割当制度. ¶commodities needed for *ration allocations* 食糧配給に必要な物資.

P² *allocations of* newsprint 新聞用紙の割当.

allot, *v.* 割当てる.

P *allot* a plot of ground *for* a cemetery 一区画の地所を墓地に当てる ‖ He returned to the study, which had been *allotted for* his use. 自分にあてがわれた書斎に戻った. ¶the time *allotted to* sleep 睡眠に当てた時間 ‖ Fifty years are *allotted to* man. 人生五十年. 【類】Two hours a week are *allotted to* instruction in English. / A share (分前) was *allotted to* each.

allotment, *n.* 割当.

Q Forty-five minutes is the *ordinary allotment* for lunch at Macy's. メーシー百貨店では普通四十五分の昼休を与えている.

Q² *steel allotments* to the automobile industry 自動車産業への鋼鉄の割当. ¶extend *time allotments* 時間の割当を多くする.

allow, *v.* 許可する; 差引く.

M No smoking *allowed here*. [掲示]禁煙. ¶The prisoners were *allowed out* on bail. 囚人は保釈出所を許された. ¶be *readily allowed* to be superior to ... …に優っている事はすぐ分る. ¶Admission is *seldom allowed* to outsiders. 局外者はめったに入場を許されない. ¶*willingly allow* 快諾する.

P It is *allowed by* the law. それは法律で許されている. ¶Between the hours of teaching, ten minutes are *allowed for* play or rest. 授業時間の間に十分間遊戯または休息の時が与えられている. ‖ Two hours and a half *allowed for* this paper. この問題の解答時間を二時間半とす. ‖ They are *allowed* a certain space *for* their sports. 彼らは一定の運動場を与えられている. ‖ *allow for* circumstances 実情を酌量する ‖ allowing for his youth 若いにしても ‖ allow for discrepancy 差を計算に入れる ‖ allow one tenth for shrinkage 減量(めべり)として一割を差引く ‖ the period allowed for appeal 控訴期間. ¶allow oneself in such a course of life こんな人生に甘んじる. ¶be allowed in a graduate course 大学院に入学を許可される. ¶allow a person into a house (room) 家(など)の中へ人を入れる. ¶Such conduct allows of no excuse. こんな行為は言訳が立たない. ‖ too wicked to allow of palliation 余り悪いので言訳が立たない. 【類】It is certain that the American manufacturer cannot cut his prices 50 per cent to allow of competition with the Japanese. / They are sold on terms which will not allow of discount. ¶No scribbling allowed on the wall. [掲示]壁に落書せぬこと. ‖ what interest is allowed on fixed deposits? 定期預金の利子はいかほどですか.

O I allow that I was wrong. 私は自分が間違っていたことを認めます. ¶You must allow yourself to be in the wrong. 君は君が間違っていることを認めねばならぬ. ¶I allowed him to depart. 彼を出立させた. ¶Can I be allowed to see it? それを拝見できましょうか. ¶if I may be allowed to talk about myself 自分の事を申上げて何ですけれど. ¶I will not allow such things to be done. こんな事はさせない. 【類】It is not allowed to enter in clogs (下駄). / I am not allowed to mention it.

allowable, *a.* 許すべき.

P it is allowable to (=for) some one to ... 人によっては...することを許すべきだ.

allowance, *n.* 扶持(ふち), 手当; 酌量; 割引.

V draw feudal allowance 扶持をもらう. ¶You got your allowance only yesterday. お小使いをきのうあげたばかりよ. ¶give him but a stinted allowance すずめの涙ほどの手当を給する. 【類】I will give you an allowance of 20 dollars a month. ¶grant an allowance 手当を給する ‖ No allowance will be granted. 割引は一切しない. ¶My father makes me an allowance. 父が私に衣食を与えてくれる. ‖ We must make a liberal allowance for unforeseen circumstances. 不慮のでき事を十分に見越して置かなければならぬ. ‖ make allowance[s] for one's youth 年若の点を酌量する ‖ Don't you make any allowance? 少しも割引をしないのか. 【類】make an allowance of 10% for cash payment (現金払).

Q daily allowance 日給. ¶making a due allowance 話半分に聞いても. ¶extra allowance 加俸. ¶draw a feudal allowance 扶持をもらう. ¶a fixed allowance あてがい扶持. ¶A free allowance of 56 lbs. is granted. [手荷物など]五十六ポンドまで無料. ¶make a generous allowance off the price 代価から大割引をする. ¶a handsome allowance 沢山の手当. ¶a heavy allowance 大割引. ¶make just allowance 正当な酌量をする. ¶make large allowance for ... ...を大いに酌量する. ¶This is the last allowance I can afford for the month. 今月のお小使いはこれが最後ですよ. ¶miscellaneous allowances 雑手当. ¶a monthly allowance 月々の手当(仕送り) ¶a reasonable allowance 相当の手当. ¶have a regular allowance for one's personal expenses 一定の小使い銭をもらう. ¶sea allowance 航海加俸. ¶be kept on short allowance of food 食物の減配を受けている. ¶a slight allowance わずかの割引. ¶a small allowance 少額の手当. ¶sundry allowances 諸手当. ¶weekly allowance 週給. ¶a yearly allowance of 200,000 yen 二十万円の歳費.

Q[2] free baggage allowance 手荷物の無料取扱. ¶clothing (=outfit) allowance 被服手当. ¶coal allowance 石炭手当. ¶cost-of-living allowances 生活費手当. ¶family allowance 扶養手当. ¶field allowance 〖軍〗戦時手当. ¶payable holiday allowance 有給休日手当. ¶get their household allowances from husbands 亭主から家計の費用をもらう. ¶mileage allowance マイルを標準とした旅費. ¶overtime allowance 時間外手当. ¶a fair retiring allowance 相当の退職手当. 【類】live on one's retiring allowances. ¶severance allowances to servicemen demobilized 復員した軍人の解職手当. ¶sick time allowances and benefits 疾病手当と給付. ¶subsistence allowance 生計手当. ¶specific duty allowance 特別勤務手当. ¶time allowance 時間の特典(競技の際の). ¶travel[ling] allowance 旅費.

P plunder at no allowance 遠慮なく略奪を試みる. ¶by your allowance 失礼して, 御免をこうむって. ¶with an allowance for board and lodging まかないとへや付で.

P[2] an allowance for housekeeping 家計手当 ‖ allowance for defects きずに対する割引(商品などの) ‖ allowances for employed foreigners やとい外国人の給与 ‖ allowance for tare or leakage 風袋または漏量を差引くこと ‖ allowance for office expenses 事務所費. ¶allowance from invoice price 送り状値段の割引. ¶allowance in price of ... ...の代価の割引. ¶an allowance of food 食物の給与. ¶allowance of expenses to him 彼への雑費給与 ‖ allowance to part-time service employees 非常勤職員手当.

alloy, *n.* 合金.

P[2] an alloy of silver and copper 銀と銅との合金. ¶an alloy of copper with nickel 銅と白銅との合金.

alloy, *v.* 合金する, まぜる.

P alloy gold with silver 金に銀を合金する ‖ alloy pleasure with misfortune 不幸で快楽を殺(そ)ぐ.

allude, *v.* 言及する.

P allude to the subject その事に説きおよぶ. 【類】The subject was never alluded to. / It is alluded to in several passages of the Old and New Testaments. / What were you alluding to just now? / Whom do you allude to? / He often alluded to his poverty (貧乏).

allure, *v.* そゝのかす, 誘惑する.

M He was allured back to the country. いなかへだまして連れ戻された.

P allured by one's promises 約束に釣込まれて. 【類】allure a person by hopes 人を希望で釣る. ¶allure a person from religion (righteousness, fidelity) 宗旨(など)から人を誘い出す ‖ allure a person from evil to good 人を善導する. ¶allure a person into a place (snare, party) 場所(など)に人を誘い込む. ¶allure a person toward a place ある場所へ人を誘い出す.

allurement, *n.* 誘惑; 魅力.

Q the artistic allurement of its architecture その建築の豊かな芸術味. ¶hold out (=offer) countless allurements 無数の誘惑を持出す. ¶the world and its many allurements 世間とそのおびただしい誘惑. ¶sexual allurement 性的魅惑.

allusion, *n.* 言及, 暗示.

V He made no allusion to you. 彼は君の事を何とも言わなかった.

Q the book contains only a brief allusion to ... その書物には...のことはちょっとしか載せてない. ¶make a distant allusion 遠まわしにほのめかす. ¶there is not the faintest allusion to ... ...の事には少しも触れていない. ¶a far-fetched allusion こじつけ. ¶There are many humorous allusions to human foibles in the drama. その劇には人間の欠点をおもしろくほのめかした個処が沢山ある. ¶Make no personal allusions in speaking. 話中に個人的のことを言うな. ¶trite and beaten allusions 陳腐なよく使われる故事の引用.

P the name in allusion to ... ...を指す名称. ¶an allusion to one's misconduct 人の非行への言及.

ally, *n.* 同盟者, 同盟国; 味方.

V make an ally of ... ...を味方にする. ¶seek in England an ally 英国を同盟国にしようとする.

Q The climate is his faithful ally. (げた屋・かさ屋などには)この(多雨の)気候がその忠実な味方である. ¶a faithful and gallant ally of ... ...の忠実にして勇敢なる同盟者. ¶our Japanese allies われらの同盟日本人. ¶her potent (=powerful) ally 有力なる同盟国. ¶our staunch allies わが忠実なる同盟諸国. ¶stout allies 剛勇なる同盟諸国. ¶found a valuable ally in ... ...は大切な同盟国となった. ¶domesticated animals and their wild allies 飼養動物とその野生種.

Q[2] Atlantic Pact allies 大西洋条約加盟国. ¶Russia and her Iron Curtain allies ロシアとロシアの鉄のカーテン内の同盟国. ¶Soviet Russia and its satellite allies ソ連とその衛星国. ¶her war[-time] allies その戦時の同盟国.

P[2] the allies of our nation against the enemy 敵国に対するわが同盟諸国.

ally, *v.* 連合させる; 縁組させる; 類する.

M banking is closely allied to ... 銀行業は...とは密接な関係がある.

P She was allied to Mr. X rather romantically. 彼女はX氏とロマンチックな結婚をした. ‖ animals most nearly *allied* ***to*** man 最も人間に近似した動物. ¶Common interests *allied* Holland ***with*** the Protestant German states. 共通の利害がオランダとドイツの新教諸邦を連合させた.

almanac, *n.* 暦.

Q a ***nautical*** *almanac* 航海暦. ¶a ***prophetic*** *almanac* [身上判断などの]迷信的な暦. ¶a ***scientific*** *almanac* 科学的な暦.

alms, *n.* [単・複同型] 施し, 喜捨.

V ***beg*** *alms* from door to door 戸毎にこじきして歩く. ¶***collect*** pious *alms* 浄財を集める. ¶***give*** *alms* to a beggar こじきに施しをする. ¶***solicit*** *alms* 施しをこう.

P They lived ***by*** *alms*. 彼らは施しで暮していた. ¶He begged us ***for*** *alms*. 彼はわれわれに施しをこうた. ¶give money ***in*** *alms* 金を施す. ¶spend money ***in*** *alms* ***to*** the needy 貧民への施しに金を費す.

alms-giving, *n.* 施し.

V judiciously ***exercise*** *alms-giving* 思慮深い施しをする.

Q ***indiscriminate*** *alms-giving* 無分別な施し.

alone, *a., ad.* ひとりの; ひとりで.

M ***all*** *alone* たったひとり. ¶He was ***almost*** *alone* in that opinion. その説を持っているのはほとんど彼ばかりであった. ¶as soon as we were ***conveniently*** *alone* [内談の際]都合よく二人きりになると.

P I am not *alone* ***in*** this opinion. この説を持つ者は僕ばかりでない. ¶*alone* ***with*** the moon ひとり月に対して ‖ when [I was] *alone* ***with*** ... [私が]...と二人きりの時.

along, *ad., prep.* 沿って; 一緒に; 前方に; ...の故に.

M He intended to deceive me ***all*** *along*. 始めから私をだまそうとしていたのだ. ¶Come ***right*** *along*. すぐ来い(一緒に出かける時). ¶He walked ***right*** *along* without replying. 返事もせずにずんずん歩いた.

P walk *along* ***by*** a hedge (river) 生垣(など)に沿って歩く. ¶It is [all] *along* ***of*** you that I failed. 僕の失敗したのは君のせいだ【類】This is [all] *along* ***of*** your meddling (干渉). ¶I will go *along* ***with*** you. 御同伴しましょう.【類】He came *along* ***with*** some friends. ‖ I sent them *along* ***with*** the other things. 私は他の物と共にそれを送った.【類】The body must be developed *along* ***with*** the mind. ‖ something to eat *along* ***with*** rice 飯のおかず.

alongside, *ad.* 相並んで; 横着けに.

P I sat *alongside* ***of*** him. 私は彼と並んですわった. ‖ A boat came *alongside* ***of*** the wharf. 一隻のボートが波止場へ横着けになった.

aloof, *ad.* 離れて.

P I sat *aloof* ***from*** them. 私は彼らから離れてすわった. ‖ Keep *aloof* ***from*** such fellows. あんなやつらと付合うな.

aloofness, *n.* 疎遠.

V ***maintain*** a respectable *aloofness* 敬遠する.

P a misanthropic *aloofness* ***from*** life 厭世.

alphabet, *n.* エー・ビー・シー, 字母.

V He is still to ***learn*** his *alphabet*. 彼はまだいろはも知らない.

Q ***God's*** *Alphabet* 神のいろは(即ち音楽). ¶a ***manual*** *alphabet* 点字. ¶a ***phonetic*** *alphabet* 音標文字. ¶the ***Romic*** (=***Roman***) *alphabet* ローマ字. ¶a ***telegraphic*** *alphabet* 電信文字, モールス符号.

Q^2 a ***deaf-and-dumb*** *alphabet* 指話文字. ¶a ***finger*** *alphabet* [ろうあ者の]指字母. ¶a ***typewriter*** *alphabet* for China 中国で使用するタイプ用漢字字母.

P the first letter ***in*** (=***of***) the English *alphabet* 英語字母の第一字.

Alps, *n.* アルプス.

P ***Beyond*** the *Alps* comes Italy. アルプスの向うがイタリアだ.

altar, *n.* 祭壇.

P offer one's life ***on*** the *altar* of one's country 国家(の祭壇)に生命を捧げる ‖ sacrifice ***on*** the *altar* of speed [船など]スピードを早くするために他の点を犠牲にする.

alter, *v.* 変える; 変る.

M The weather *alters* almost ***daily***. 天候がほとんど毎日のように変る. ¶His conduct has ***greatly*** *altered*. 身持が大分改まってきた. ¶***materially*** *alter* 著しく変る. ¶Conditions of trade here ***radically*** *altered*. 商況ががらりと変った.

P *alter* ***for*** the better (worse) 善い(悪い)方へ変る. ¶*alter* ***from*** the first design 始めの計画と違う ‖ *alter* the date ***from*** Wednesday to Saturday 日取を水曜日から土曜日に変える.【類】*alter* it ***from*** the original ***to*** a new design. ¶*alter* a house ***into*** a barn 家屋を物置に改造する. ¶The suburbs have *altered* almost ***out of*** recognition. 郊外がほとんど見違える位変った. ¶*alter* it ***to*** a circular form それを円形に変える.

alteration, *n.* 変更.

V ***effect*** (=***make***) *alterations* on ... ...を変更する. ¶***have*** *alterations* in one's dress (house, garden) 衣服(など)の改造をする.【類】***make*** some *alteration* / no *alteration* whatever is ***made*** to ... ¶***procure*** an *alteration* of the existing law 現行法律を変更する.

Q after ***considerable structural*** *alterations* 大改築の後. ¶make ***costly*** *alterations* in the building 多額の出費をして建物を改造する. ¶make the ***necessary*** *alteration* 必要な変更をする. ¶a ***verbal*** *alteration* 語句の変更.

Q^2 ***price*** *alterations* 値段の変更.

P ***with*** some slight *alterations* and additions 少し改訂増補を施して.

P^2 an *alteration* ***in*** one's plan 計画の変更. ¶an *alteration* ***to*** a building 改築.

altercation, *n.* 論争.

V to ***avoid*** an *altercation* 論争を避けるために.

Q a ***lively*** *altercation* between ... and ... ...と...の激しい口論.

P^2 an *altercation* ***between*** two men 二人間の論争. ¶an *altercation* ***with*** him 彼との論争.

alternate, *v.* 交替する.

P He *alternates* ***between*** constipation and outbreaks of diarrhoea. 便秘したり下痢したりする.【類】He *alternates* ***between*** joy and grief. ¶He *alternates* ***from*** one extreme ***to*** another. 極端から極端に走る. ¶*alternate* joy ***with*** (=***by***) grief 喜びに次ぐに悲しみを以てする. ¶The flood and ebb tides *alternate* ***with*** each other. 満潮と干潮とは互に交替する.【類】Day *alternates* ***with*** night.

alternation, *n.* 交替, 循環.

Q a ***systematic*** *alternation* of work and recreation 仕事と娯楽との規則正しい交替.

P^2 the *alternation* ***of*** day and (=with) night 昼夜の循環 ‖ *alternation* ***of*** generations 〘生〙 世代の交番.

alternative, *n.* 二者の一, 採るべき策.

V cheerfully ***accept*** the *alternative* [選ばねばならぬ二者のうち]どちらか一方を喜んで取る. ¶***adopt*** the former *alternative* [二者のうち]前者の方を採る. ¶***embrace*** heroic *alternative* [退くか進むかという場合に]勇ましい方を選ぶ. ¶***finding*** no other *alternative* しょうことなしに. ¶he was ***given*** the *alternative* of ... or ... 彼は...か...かの選択を許された. ¶***have*** the *alternative* of ... or ... ...か...のいずれか一つを選ぶ事ができる. ¶I ***had*** no *alternative* but to ... 私は...するより外に道がなかった. ¶it ***leaves*** me no *alternative* but to ... 私には...するより外に道がない.

Q He had to work harder or to be sent away from school, and he chose the ***first*** *alternative*. 今までよりもっとよく勉強するかさもなくば学校から追出すぞといわれて前者を選んだ. ¶there was ***no*** *alternative* but to yield to ... ...に降服するより外に道がなかった. ¶There is ***no other*** *alternative* left. 外に策がない. ¶with it as an ***occasional*** *alternative* 時々それを合の手として. ¶as the ***only*** *alternative* しょうことなしに.【類】There is ***only one*** *alternative* left. ¶Two *alternatives* are ***open***. 二つの取るべき手段がある. ¶the ***only remaining*** *alternatives* are ... 後に残る策というのは...だけである. ¶a ***third*** *alternative* [あれもいかぬこれもいかぬという場合に]第三に採るべき道.

P ***as*** an *alternative* to ... ...に代る手段として. ¶He was forced to fall back ***upon*** the other *alternative*. 彼はもう一つの手段を取らねばならぬ仕儀となった.

P^2 The *alternative* ***of*** surrender is death. 降服しなければ死ぬ外はない.

alternative, *a.* 二者その一を選ぶべき.

M These statements are not ***necessarily*** *alternative*. これらの説は両立しないこともない.

altitude, *n.* 高さ, 高度.

V begin to ***lose*** *altitude* 〘空〙 降下[墜落]し始める.

Q the ***absolute*** *altitude* 〘空〙 絶対高度. ¶***high*** *altitudes* 高所. ¶The *altitude* was so ***great*** that I breathed with difficulty. 呼吸困難を覚えるほどの高さだった.

P ***at*** an *altitude* of ... feet ...フィートの高所で ‖ ***at*** great *altitudes* 非常な高所で. ¶***from*** a high *altitude* 高所から. ¶sojourn ***in*** a high *altitude* 高所に泊る.

altogether, *n.* 《口語》 裸体.

P ***in*** the *altogether*=stark naked 身に一糸もまとわず.

alumnus, *n.* 卒業生.

V The College has ***had*** (=***turned out***) many famous

alumni. この大学は多数の有名な卒業生を出した.

Q the most ***distinguished living alumnus*** of … …の同窓中現今最も有名な人. ¶***returning alumni*** 母校訪問の校友. ***out-of-town*** *alumni* 地方の校友. ¶a ***virgin alumnus*** 未婚の校友.

P² an *alumnus **of*** the University of Georgia of the class of 1919 一九一九年度ジョージア大学卒業者.

amalgamate, *v*. 汞和(こう)する; 合同する.

M Mercury ***easily*** *amalgamates* gold. 水銀は金と合金になりやすい.

P it was *amalgamated **as*** the Nisshin Mining Company with … それは…と合同して日清鉱業会社となった. ¶*amalgamate **into*** a single church [多数の宗派などが]連合して一教会となる. ¶become *amalgamated **with*** … …に合併する.

amalgamation, *n*. 混汞(こう)法.

P mix metals ***by*** *amalgamation* 混汞法で金属をまぜる.

amass, *v*. 蓄積する.

P *amass* money ***by*** industry 勤労によって金をためる. ¶*amass* money ***for*** oneself 自分の為に金をためる. 【類】*amass* money ***for*** a purpose ¶*amass* riches ***with*** great labor 大いに働いて富を作る.

amateur, *n*. しろうと.

Q a ***mechanical*** *amateur* しろうと機械師.

P² an *amateur **in*** engineering しろうと技師. 【類】an *amateur **in*** philosophy 哲学道楽の人.

amaze, *n*. 驚がく.

P He stood ***in*** *amaze* at the scream. その叫び声に驚いて立っていた.

amaze, *v*. 驚かす.

P I was *amazed **at*** the idea of his trial. 彼が試みるとは(やって見ると聞いて)あきれた. 【類】We are *amazed **at*** his industry. ¶I was *amazed **by*** the proposal (his audacity). その提案(など)には驚いた.

amazement, *n*. 驚がく.

V It ***excites*** my *amazement*. がく然たらしめる.

Q He looked at me in ***blank*** *amazement*. 彼はぼう然と私を見詰めた. ¶in ***mute*** *amazement* 唖然(あぜん)として. ¶in ***open-mouthed*** *amazement* ぼう然として. ¶make the reader sit up in ***startled*** *amazement* 読者をびっくり起直らせる. ¶in ***utter*** *amazement* あっと驚いて.

P ask ***in*** *amazement* 驚いて尋ねる. 【類】He held up his hands ***in*** *amazement*. / gaze at him ***in*** *amazement*. ¶The news struck me ***into*** *amazement*. その知らせでびっくりした. ¶stare ***with*** *amazement* 驚いて見つめる ‖ he was dumb (=struck) ***with*** *amazement* at… 彼は…に驚いて物も言えなかった.

P² *amazement **of*** people ***at*** … …に対する人々の驚き ‖ The juggler was the *amazement **of*** the whole city. その奇術師は全市の絶賛する所であった.

ambassador, *n*. 大使.

Q an *ambassador* ***extraordinary*** 特命大使. ¶a ***one-time*** *ambassador* to the United States かつては駐米大使であった人. ¶an ***ordinary*** (=a ***resident***) *ambassador* 弁理大使. ¶an *ambassador* ***plenipotentiary*** 全権大使.

Q² a ***doll*** *ambassador* of goodwill 親善人形使節.

P² the British *Ambassador **at*** Tokyo 東京駐在英国大使. ¶*Ambassador **from*** Great Britain 英国大使. 【類】*Ambassador **from*** Chile to the United States. ¶He was British *Ambassador **in*** Portugal and Spain during the Peninsular war. 彼は半島戦争中ポルトガルおよびスペイン駐在の英国大使だった. ¶An author of international reputation is a sort of *ambassador **of*** ideas. 海外に名声を博する著作家は言わば思想の大使である. ¶the Japanese *Ambassador **to*** the Court of St. James 駐英日本大使. 【類】the ex-U.S. *Ambassador **to*** Japan. ¶*Ambassador **at large*** 無任所大使.

amber, *n*. 琥珀(こはく).

Q² ***imitation*** *amber* 人造琥珀.

ambiguity, *n*. あいまい.

V to ***avoid*** *ambiguity* 意義を明瞭にするために ‖ the *ambiguity* is ***avoided*** by …ing …すればあいまいでなくなる. ¶***clear up*** *ambiguity* 明瞭にする. ¶***produce*** (=***create***) *ambiguity* あいまいを来たす. ¶***remove*** all *ambiguity* あいまいでないようにする.

P It is ***above*** all *ambiguity*. 少しもあいまいな点がない.

ambiguous, *a*. あいまいな.

P be *ambiguous **between*** two ideas 二つの観念のうちいずれを指すかが不明瞭である. ¶*ambiguous **in*** sense 意味の紛らわしい.

ambition, *n*. 野心, 望; 名誉心.

V ***awaken*** a burning *ambition* to … …しようとする勃々たる野心を起させる. ¶***check*** (=***thwart***) *ambition* 野心を抑える. ¶After leaving the diplomatic service he ***developed*** Parliamentary *ambitions*. 外交官をやめてから彼は国会議員になろうという望を起した. ¶He ***disavows*** any political *ambitions* on his part. 彼には何ら政治的野心がないと言う. ¶***fire*** the *ambition* of … …の野心をたきつける. 【類】It ***fired*** his *ambition* to write poetry. ¶***frustrate*** one's *ambition* 人の望みをくじく. ¶***fulfil*** one's *ambition* その野望を遂げる. ¶***further*** the *ambitions* of … …の野心を助長する. ¶***harbor*** great territorial *ambition* 領土併合の野心を抱く. ¶***have*** no *ambition* whatever 何ら野心はない ‖ ***have*** no *ambition* beyond it それ以上の野心はない. ¶***immolate*** *ambition* on the altar of duty 義務のために野心を犠牲にする. ¶***lose*** all *ambition* through disappointment in a woman 失恋のために総ての望みを失う. ¶I have always ***nourished*** the *ambition* to … 私は…しようという望を常に抱いていた. ¶***pique*** *ambition* 野心をそそる. ¶***sacrifice*** one's own *ambition* on the shrine of one's country's best interests 邦家最大の利益のため一身の野心を犠牲にする. ¶***stimulate*** *ambition* 名誉心をあおる.

Q an ***audacious*** *ambition* 不敵な野心. ¶at the expense of his own most ***cherished*** *ambition* その宿望を捨てて. ¶his ***chief*** *ambition* was …彼の主なる望は…であった. ¶a ***commendable*** *ambition* りっぱな望. ¶a ***disappointed*** *ambition* 当ての外れた望. ¶the ***domineering*** *ambition* of German diplomacy ドイツ外交の主たる志望. ¶achieve a ***global*** *ambition* 世界的野望を遂げる. ¶entertain a ***high*** *ambition* 大望を抱く. 【類】He has very ***high*** *ambitions*. / a ***higher*** *ambition* than that of worldly honors (俗界の名誉) / his ***highest*** *ambition* is to … ¶he has the ***honorable*** *ambition* to … 彼には…たらんとする大望がある. ¶***illimitable*** (=limitless) *ambition* 飽く事を知らぬ野望. ¶an ***inordinate*** *ambition* 過分の望. ¶an ***insatiable*** *ambition* 飽くなき望. ¶some of the young men and women with ***journalistic*** *ambitions* 新聞記者たらんとする一部の青年男女. ¶a ***laudable*** *ambition* あっぱれな望. ¶a ***legitimate*** *ambition* 当然の望. ¶his ***life-long*** *ambition* 彼一生の念願. ¶men and women with ***literary*** *ambitions* 文学志望の男女. ¶***lofty*** (=***noble***) *ambition* 高尚な望. ¶a ***long-standing*** *ambition* 宿望. ¶Russia's ***naval*** *ambition* ロシアの海軍の野心. ¶equipped with a ***political*** *ambition* 政治上の野心のある. ¶a struggle between ***rival*** *ambitions* 二つの野心の煩悶. ¶become the ***ruling*** *ambition* of one's life 生涯の主な望となる. ¶***territorial*** *ambition* 領土的野心. ¶a ***thwarted*** *ambition* 失敗した野心. ¶His *ambition* is ***unbounded***. 彼の野心は止まる所を知らない. ¶a ***universal*** *ambition* 万人の野心. ¶an ***unrealized*** *ambition* 達成できなかった大望. ¶a lady with ***unsatisfied social*** *ambitions* 社交界に活動したいという望みのかなわない淑女. ¶set out with a ***vaulting*** *ambition* 大野心を抱いて打って出る. ¶a ***vulgar*** *ambition* 低俗な望. ¶people with ***writing*** *ambitions* 文士になろうという志のある人々.

P Be moderate ***in*** *ambition*. 分外の望を起すな. ¶***out of*** *ambition* to excel 卓越を望む心から. ¶***with*** all his *ambitions* crushed 一切の望をくじかれて ‖ he burns ***with*** an *ambition* to … 彼は…たらんとする野心に燃えている ‖ ***without*** *ambition* 野心もなく.

P² *ambition **for*** distinction 功名心 ‖ I have no *ambition **for*** riches. 私は富貴は一向望まない. ¶his *ambition **of*** the crown 王者たらんとする彼の野心.

ambitionist, *n*. 野心家.

Q² a ***fiction*** *ambitionist* 小説家志望者.

ambitious, *a*. 野心をいだいている; 熱望する.

M he is *ambitious **enough*** to … 彼は…たらんことを望んでいる.

P He is *ambitious **after*** wealth. 富貴を望んでいる. ¶He is *ambitious **for*** power. 権勢に恋々としている. ¶He is *ambitious **of*** distinction. 彼は栄達に恋々たるものがある. 【類】He is *ambitious **of*** success in his enterprise. / be *ambitious **of*** having their works read by foreigners as well as their compatriots.

ambush, *n*. 待伏せ.

V ***make*** (=***lay or construct***) an *ambush* 伏兵を設ける.

P lie ***in*** *ambush* for … …を待伏せする. 【類】He concealed himself *in ambush*.

ameliorate, *v.* よくなる.

P *ameliorate in* health 健康がよくなる.

amelioration, *n.* 改善.

Q ***gradual** amelioration* of the station 次第に向上する地位. ¶***social** amelioration* 社会の改善.

P^2 *amelioration **of*** working conditions 労働条件の改善.

amen, *n.* アーメン.

V Surely all the people will ***say** amen* to that. たしかに皆がそれに賛成するだろう.

amenable, *a.* 服従すべき.

M He is ***easily** amenable* to flattery. あの人はすぐおだてに乗る.

P *amenable **to*** the law (authority, reason) 法(など)に従って. 【類】*amenable **to*** arguments (advice).

amenably, *ad.* 服従して.

P live *amenably **to*** reason 道理にかなった生活をする.

amend, *v.* 改める.

P be *amended **as*** follows 左の通り改正する. ¶The regulations are *amended **to*** the 1st of September, 1918. 該条例は一九一八年九月一日までの改正を含む.

amendment, *n.* 改正; 改善; 修正案.

V ***make** (=**bring forward**) an amendment* 修正案を提出する. ¶***put forward** an amendment* 修正説を唱える.

Q The assent of three fourths of the states is required to adopt a ***constitutional** amendment*. 憲法を改正するには州の四分の三の同意が必要である. ¶the ***following** amendment* is made to ... ...中左の通り改正する.

P^2 *amendment **of*** health 健康の改善. ¶an ***amendment to*** the Press Law (a bill) 新聞紙条例(など)の改正 ‖ ***amendments to*** this Covenant 本規約の改正.

amends, *n.* つぐない, 賠償.

V ***accept** amends* 賠償を受ける. ¶***make** amends* for ... ...の埋合せをする. 【類】***make*** ample ***amends*** for the loss. ¶***tardy** amends* 支払いが滞る.

P^2 *amends **for*** some fault ある過失に対する補償. ¶make *amends **to*** the sufferers ***for*** injuries 被害者に対して賠償をする.

amenity, *n.* 歓楽.

Q a place with ***many** amenities* 歓楽郷. ¶the ***material** amenities* of life 人生の物質的快楽. ¶The ***usual** amenities* of a club are found there. そこに一通りクラブの設備ができている.

amerce, *v.* 罰を課する.

P The court *amerced* him ***in*** the sum of 5,000 yen. 法廷は彼を五千円の罰金に処した. ¶*amerce* a person ***of*** a month's salary 一カ月分の罰俸処分にする.

America, *n.* アメリカ.

Q ***tropical** America* 熱帯アメリカ. ¶***two** Americas* 南北アメリカ.

American, *n.* アメリカ人.

Q^2 a ***second-generation** American* 二世アメリカ人.

Americanism, *n.* 米語; 米国風.

V to ***use** Americanism* 米国風に言えば.

Q ***exotic** Americanism* 異国的の米国風. ¶a ***vile** Americanism* 下品なアメリカ風[の言い方].

P^2 an *Americanism **for*** ... ...に対する米語.

amiability, *n.* 愛きょう.

Q men of ***boundless** amiability* 愛きょうこぼれるばかりの人.

amiss, *a.* 誤りのある, 工合のわるい, 不正の.

P it would not be *amiss **for*** them to consider that ... 宜しく...すべきである. ¶There is something *amiss **in*** his accounts. 彼の勘定には何か間違がある. ¶There is something *amiss **with*** (=***of***) him (the engine). 彼(など)はどうかしている. ‖ What is *amiss **with*** it? 何が工合が悪いのか. 【類】Nothing is *amiss **with*** him.

amity, *n.* 和親, 親ぼく.

Q an ***international** amity* 国際間の和親. 【類】Desire to see ***international** amity* prevails throughout the world.

P He lived ***in** amity* with his neighbors. 隣人と仲よく暮した. 【類】live ***in** amity* side by side (共に) / They parted ***in** amity*.

P^2 the *amity **between*** monarchs (neighboring countries) 国王(など)間の和親. ¶*amity **with*** surrounding nations 周囲の諸国との親善.

ammunition, *n.* 弾薬.

Q^2 ***sporting** ammunition* 狩猟用の弾薬.

amnesty, *n.* 大赦.

V ***grant** an amnesty* to political transgressors 政治犯人の大赦を行う.

Q a ***general** amnesty* 大赦. ¶***special** amnesty* 特赦.

P They were favored ***with** amnesty*. 彼らは赦免された.

P^2 an *amnesty **to*** all the insurgents (反乱者) for all offenses.

amorous, *a.* 好色な, ほれた.

M one of the ***most** amorous* of all Western stories 西部もの中でもっとも好色な小説.

P He is *amorous **of*** that lady. 彼はあの婦人に恋をしている.

amount, *n.* 数, 量, 額.

V ***allow** a* fair *amount* for his trouble 彼の骨折に対して相応の金額を給与する. ¶Any *amount*, great or small, will be ***appreciated***. 金額は多少にかかわらずありがたくお受けします. ¶***bring together*** an immense *amount* of scattered data 散在しているおびただしい材料を収集する. ¶***carry*** the *amount* to the credit of ... その金額を...の貸方へ転記する. ¶***cause*** some *amount* of damage 若干の損害を生じる. ¶***claim*** an *amount* against ... ...にある金額を請求する. ¶***debit*** the *amount* to ... その金額を...の借方に記入する. ¶He ***enjoyed*** a certain *amount* of prosperity. 彼は相当に栄えた. ¶sign one's name and ***enter*** the *amount* of one's subscription 署名の上寄付金額を記入する. ¶***expend*** a certain *amount* of moral indignation on ... ...に対していささか憤慨する. 【類】a very great *amount* of study has been ***expended*** on ... ¶***figure out*** the exact *amount* 正確な数を算出する. ¶***find*** the total *amount* 合計する. ¶***fix*** the *amount* to be raised 調達する金高をきめる. ¶***lavish*** an astonishing *amount* of compliments むやみにお世辞を浴びせかける. ¶It ***means*** an immense *amount* of outlay. 大変な入費を要することになる. ¶***pass*** an *amount* to the credit of ... 金額を...の貸方に繰入れる. ¶***pay*** the *amount* due 不足を払う. 【類】***pay*** the *amount* in full (全額). ¶***place*** (=***put***) an *amount* to the credit of ... 一定の金額を...の貸方に記入する. ¶***raise*** a sufficient *amount* 十分の金を調達する. ¶***reach*** a very large *amount* 巨額にのぼる. ¶It ***requires*** an incalculable *amount* of patience. 多大の忍耐がいる. 【類】***require*** a certain *amount* of pluck (度胸). ¶I will ***subscribe*** the same *amount* to the relief fund. 私も救援基金中へ同額の寄付を致しましょう. ¶***trim*** the *amount* 金額を削減する.

Q an ***aggregate** amount* 総額. ¶take no ***appreciable** amount* of time 大して時間がかからない. ¶***approved** amount* 承認額. ¶an ***approximate** amount* 概算額. ¶He has more than ***average** amount* of common sense. 普通以上の常識を持っている. ¶a ***broken** amount* 端銭(はせん). ¶a ***considerable** amount* of money 巨額の金 ‖ sustain a ***considerable** amount* of damage. ¶a ***definite** amount* 一定の(金)額. ¶only a few dollars of the ***desired** amount* 希望金額中のほんの数ドル. ¶A ***fair** amount* of rain has fallen. 雨がかなり降った. ¶an ***extravagant** amount* ばく大な(金)額. ¶a ***fixed** amount* 一定の(金)額. ¶a ***huge*** (=***immense***) *amount* 巨額. ¶in continually ***increasing** amounts* 絶えず量(数・額)を増して. 【類】spend an ***increased** amount* of money in forest service. ¶do an ***infinite** amount* of good to ... ...に数限りない利益を与える. ¶a ***large** amount* of original matter connected with ... ...と関連のある多量の根本材料. ¶There was but a ***moderate** amount* of traffic. 往来は余り交通ひん繁ではなかった. ¶leaving a ***net** amount* of ... ...の正味を残して. ¶He contributed a ***nice** amount* of money to the fund. あの人はその基金に多額の金を寄付した. ¶***No** amount* of washing will remove them. いくら洗っても取れまい. ¶an ***outstanding** amount* 未払い高. ¶a ***proper** amount* of exercise and sleep 適当な運動と睡眠. ¶the ***relative** amounts* of ... in ... ...の中に含まれている...の相対量. ¶the ***required** amount* approved 承認要求額. ¶***respectable** amount* 相当の金額. ¶the ***same** amount* as ... ...と同額. ¶a ***surprising** amount* 巨額. ¶a ***total** amount* 総額. 【類】an annual output to the ***total** amount* of ... ¶a ***tremendous** amount* of ignorance 驚くべき無知. ¶***trifling** amounts* わずかな額. ¶an ***undue** amount* of work 不当な分量の仕事. ¶a ***usual** amount* of ... ...の通常額. ¶save a ***vast** amount* of time (information) ばく大な時間(など)の節約になる. ¶***What** amount* of purchase-money is required? 手付金は幾らですか.

Q^2 the ***face** amount* 額面金額.

P more than £10 ***in** amount* 締めて十ポンド以上 ‖ ***in*** great or small *amounts* 大小の数(量・額)に ‖ rival ... ***in** amount* of ... ...の額(量・数)においては...に匹敵する.

P^2 *amounts **in*** figures 字で示した数量 ‖ *amounts **in*** words 語で示した数量. ¶the *amount **of*** a claim 要求額 ‖ No *amount **of*** good facts will make a good story. どんなにおもしろい事実を並べてもおもしろい物語にはならない.

amount, *v.* …になる; …に達する.

M it ***annually*** *amounts* to … 年額…になる. ¶*amount **approximately*** to … …総計約…に上る. ¶That ***practically*** *amounts* to a fraud. それじゃりっぱな詐欺だ. ¶the subscription will ***probably*** *amount* to … 予約の数が恐らく…に達するだろう. ¶it *amounted, **roughly**,* to …総計およそ…に上った. ¶*amount **roundly*** to … およそ…の総計になる.

P the company's reserve fund now *amounts **to*** … 会社の積立金は今総額…に達している. 【類】expenses already incurred (負担した費用) *amount **to*** about … / It does not *amount **to*** a paltry three-hundred yen (わずか三百円). / It *amounted **to*** little short of 2,000 yen. (ほとんど二千円). ‖ a noble whose assessment *amounted **to*** 10,000 *koku* and upwards 知行高一万石以上の大名 ‖ *amount **to*** upwards of … …以上に達する ‖ What he has done does not *amount **to*** much. 彼のした事は大したことはない. 【類】It may *amount **to*** nothing. / These attempts *amounted **to*** no great things. / disinclination *amounting **to*** repugnance (反感) ‖ Excess of virtue may in certain cases *amount **to*** a fault. 美点も度を過ごすと時に欠点になる. 【類】admiration *amounting **to*** worship / My gratification *amounted **to*** jubilation (欣喜雀躍). / It *amounted **to*** a threat. / His talents *amount **to*** genius. / Dislike of grandeur (晴の場) *amounts **to*** a passion. / make to it contributions which *amount **to*** collaboration (共著と言ってもよいくらいの) ‖ it *amounts **to*** saying that … …というに等しい / *amount **to*** rudeness (impoliteness).

amour, *n.* 情事.

V ***have*** an *amour* with … …と情を通じる.

P He is given up ***to*** *amours.* 女色にふけっている. ‖ take ***to*** *amour* 浮気をする.

ample, *a.* 広々としている; 十分な.

P *ample **for*** the purpose その目的には十分な. ¶a building *ample **in*** dimensions 広々とした建物.

amplifier, *n.* 拡声器.

P make the sound fuller and more extensive ***through*** an *amplifier* 拡声器の音を大きくする.

amplify, *v.* 敷衍(ふえん)する.

P He *amplified* the matter ***by*** illustrations. 例を挙げてその事を説明した. 【類】*amplify* the sense ***by*** a paraphrase. ¶*amplify **on*** (=*upon*) the topics 論旨を敷衍する.

amplitude, *n.* 広さ.

Q ***seismic*** *amplitude* 〚地震〛震幅.

ampoule, *n.* 〚医〛アンプル.

P^2 *ampoules **of*** a scrum 血清のアンプル(注射液を入れる密閉した小ガラス管).

amputate, *v.* 切断する.

P *amputate* a leg ***at*** the knee ひざ頭で足を切断する.

amputee, *n.* [手・足を]切断された人.

Q a ***quadruple*** *amputee* 四肢を切断された者.

Q^2 a ***single arm*** *amputee* 片腕を切断された者.

amputation, *n.* 切断.

V ***perform*** *amputation* of a leg 足を切断する.

amulet, *n.* 護身符.

P^2 an *amulet **against*** … …よけのお守り.

O an *amulet* to ward off evils 災難よけのお守り.

amuse, *v.* 喜ばせる, 楽しませる.

M *amuse* him ***hugely*** (=***vastly***) えらく彼を喜ばせる. ¶I was ***mildly*** *amused.* ちょっとおもしろいと思った. ¶He was ***much*** *amused* at the child's remarks. 子供の言うことを聞いて非常におもしろがった. ¶I was ***quite*** *amused.* 実におかしかった. ¶I was ***rather*** *amused* at the idea. 私にはその考えがちょっとおかしく感じた.

P I was *amused **at*** his appearance (the joke). 彼の風さい(など)がおもしろかった. 【類】I was *amused **at the sight*** (おかしく思った). / *amused **at*** his antics (おどけた動作) / I was much *amused **at*** the children's remarks. / be *amused **at*** an incident (a person's simplicity). ¶*I amuse* myself ***by*** (=with) reading. 読書を楽しみにしている. ‖ I was *amused **by*** a funny man. おかしなやつがいて愉快だった. 【類】I was *amused **by*** his account (話). / *amuse* them ***by*** telling a story. ¶Some *amuse* themselves ***in*** folly. ばかなことをやっておもしろがる者もある. ¶How do you *amuse* yourself ***in*** rainy weather? 雨の日は君は何をして遊ぶか. ¶I *amused* myself ***on*** the seashore. 海岸へ出て遊んだ. 【類】How do you *amuse* yourself ***on*** board [a steamer]. ¶I *amused* children ***with*** stories (toys). 話をして(おもちゃで)子供らを喜ばせた. 【類】Children are *amused **with*** a picturebook. / I was *amused **with*** the scenery. / We were *amused **with*** (=at) the joke (his remarks).

O I'm *amused* to learn that … …と知ってうれしくなった.

amusement, *n.* 娯楽.

V ***afford*** them endless *amusement* 彼らに無限の娯楽を与える. ¶***cut off*** (=***avoid***) all *amusement* 一切の娯楽をさける. ¶***derive*** much *amusement* from … …から多大の娯楽を得る. ¶***direct*** their *amusements* into proper channels 彼らの娯楽を適当な方向に仕向ける. ¶***excite*** much *amusement* 大いに興味を起させる. ¶***find*** *amusement* in … …をおもしろがる. 【類】Millions of men, women and children ***find*** their chief *amusement* in the films. ¶It ***procured*** me *amusement.* それが私の娯楽となった. ¶***provide*** *amusement* for … …に娯楽を与える. ¶***run*** public *amusements* 公衆娯楽機関を経営する. ¶***take*** their *amusement* at home 家庭で楽しむ. ¶blue laws ***suppressing*** public *amusements* 公衆の娯楽を禁止する厳法.

Q an ***aristocratic*** *amusement* 貴族的な娯楽. ¶afford a ***cheap*** and ***healthy*** *amusement* to thousands of people 数千の人に安価で健全な娯楽を与える. ¶***demoralizing*** *amusement* 人を堕落させる娯楽. ¶***elegant*** *amusements* 優雅な娯楽. ¶***empty*** *amusements* くだらない娯楽. ¶***fashionable*** *amusements* 流行の娯楽. ¶He found his ***favorite*** *amusement* in reading. 読書が道楽であった. ¶***harmless*** *amusements* 無害な娯楽. ¶afford ***huge*** *amusement* to … …を非常に楽しませる. ¶***hurtful*** *amusements* 害になる娯楽. ¶***innocent*** *amusements* 罪のない道楽. ¶an ***obstreperous*** *amusement* 騒がしい遊び. ¶***outdoor*** *amusements* 戸外遊戯. ¶***popular*** *amusements* 大衆的娯楽. ¶places of ***public*** *amusement* 公衆の娯楽場. ¶***rural*** *amusements* いなかの娯楽. ¶***sensuous*** *amusements* 肉体の娯楽.

Q^2 ***group*** *amusements* 集団娯楽. ¶***street*** *amusements* [子供の]街頭遊び. ¶***winter*** *amusements* 冬の娯楽.

P a film just good ***for*** *amusement* 娯楽映画 ‖ I tried traveling ***for*** *amusement.* 楽しみに旅行をした. ¶a popular place ***of*** *amusement*=an amusement center 大衆娯楽場. ¶watch it ***with*** *amusement* 興味をもってそれに注目する. ¶The report was received in well-informed circles ***with*** considerable *amusement.* その報道は消息通の間ではとんでもないおかしなことに感ぜられた.

P^2 *amusements **for*** the rich (the poor) 金持(貧乏人)の楽しみ. 【類】*amusements **for*** lowbrows (ミーハー族). ¶*amusement **in*** mathematics 数学の遊戯.

amusing, *a.* おもしろい.

M a sight ***agreeably*** *amusing* ほゝえましい光景. ¶***highly*** *amusing* 非常におもしろい.

P It was *amusing **to*** me. それはおもしろかった.

anachronism, *n.* 時代錯誤.

Q an ***absurd*** *anachronism* とんでもない時代錯誤.

P^2 an *anachronism **in*** the twentieth century 二十世紀における前代の遺物. 「来時代錯誤的なものとなろう.

O War may become an *anachronism* in future. 戦争は将

anaesthetic, *n.* 麻酔薬.

V ***administer*** *anaesthetic* 麻酔をかける.

Q under a ***general*** *anaesthetic* 全身麻酔を施して.

P ***under*** an *anaesthetic* 麻酔を施されて.

analogous, *a.* 似ている.

P *analogous **to*** one another 互いに似た. 【類】Sleep is *analogous **to*** death. 睡眠は死に似ている.

analogue, *n.* 類似物.

V^2 a useful compilation, to which no *analogue **exists*** in English 英書には類のない有益な編集物.

analogy, *n.* 類似.

V the difference ***bears*** an *analogy* to that existing between … and … その相違は…と…との間の相違に似ている. ¶***draw*** an *analogy* between … and … …と…との類似を説く. ¶it ***has*** some *analogy* with … それは…に幾らか似ている. ¶it ***offers*** the closest *analogy* with … それは…に非常によく似ている. ¶***show*** a very close *analogy* 非常によ

く似ている.

Q there is a ***close*** *analogy* between ... and ... ...と...とはよく似ている. ¶***euphonic*** *analogy* 音調(語呂)の類似. ¶have ***much*** *analogy* with ... ...に非常に似ている. ¶the ***striking*** *analogy* between ... and ... ...と...との間の著しい類似. ¶merely a ***superficial*** *analogy* 単に皮相の類似.

P ***after*** the *analogy* of ... ...の例にならって. ¶It was explained ***by*** *analogy*. それは類推で説明された. ‖ ***by*** the *analogy* of ... ...にならって. ¶***on*** the *analogy* of this これにならって. 【類】 form a new word ***on*** the *analogy* of words already in use.

P² an *analogy* ***between*** two things 二物の類似 ‖ There is an *analogy* ***between*** the human heart and a pump. ¶the *analogy* ***of*** A ***to*** (=***with***) B 乙と甲との類似. 【類】 the *analogy* ***of*** sound ***to*** light / a family has some *analogy* ***with*** (=***to***) a state.

analysis, *n.* 分析.

V ***attempt*** an *analysis* 分析を試みる. ¶***elude*** *analysis* 分析しにくい. ¶***defy*** (=***resist***) *analysis* 端倪(ﾀﾝｹﾞｲ)すべからざるものがある. ¶***make*** a previous *analysis* of it それを予め分析する. ¶***push*** the analysis further, and you will see that ... この筆法で行くと結局...ということになる.

Q a ***careful*** *analysis* of all the factors of a problem 問題の各要素の丹念な分析. ¶***chemial*** *analysis* 化学的分析. ¶a ***cold*** *analysis* [問題などの] 冷静な解剖. ¶The writer's culture for force, therefore, is in its ***deepest*** *analysis* a culture of character. 従って力ある文章を作り習うことは結局品性の養成ということになる. ¶in its ***final*** (=the ***last***) *analysis* つまるところ, 所詮. ¶He believes that, ***on*** the last *analysis*, all property is theft. 結局一切の財産所有は盗みであると彼は信じている. ¶an ***intelligent*** and ***clarifying*** *analysis* 賢明な釈明的な分析. ¶a ***powerful*** and ***subtle*** *analysis* 力強く鋭敏な解剖. ¶***qualitative*** (***quantitative***) *analysis* 定性(量)分析. ¶a ***scientific*** *analysis* of a subject 問題の科学的解剖. ¶***statistical*** *analysis* 統計的分析. ¶All real education is, in the ***ultimate*** (=last) *analysis*, self-education. すべて本当の教育は結局自己教育ということになる. 「内容の検討).

Q² ***job*** *analysis* 職業分析. ¶***press*** *analysis* 新聞分析(新聞

P ***At*** (=***in*** *or* ***on***) the last *analysis*, working for others should be the keynote of all business. 結局他人のために働くということが一切の商業の基調であるべきである. 【類】 ***on*** *analysis* it proved to be ... / you will find, ***on*** *analysis*, that ... / ***On*** *analysis*, it gave the following results.

P² the *analysis* ***of*** character 性格の分析.

analyst, *n.* 分析家.

Q a ***political*** *analyst* 政論家.

analyze, *v.* 分析する, 分解する. 「部分を除く.

M *analyze* ***away*** unnecessary elements 解剖して不要の

P *analyze* water ***into*** oxygen and hydrogen 水を酸素と水素に分解する. 【類】 *analyze* it ***into*** its elements (元素) ‖ *analyze* ***out of*** existence 分析してその存在を失わせる.

anathema, *n.* 〖宗〗呪い.

P the *anathema* of the church ***upon*** (=***against***) the sacrilegious 神を冒とくした者に対する教会の呪い.

ancestor, *n.* 先祖.

V a ceremony of ***honoring*** one's *ancestors* 先祖の祭. ¶I can ***trace*** my *ancestors* back through fourteen generations. 十四代前まではすっかり先祖の調べがつきます. 【類】 Queen Mary could ***trace*** her *ancestors* back to about 900 years ago.

Q be derived from a ***common*** *ancestor* 共通の祖先から出ている. ¶the ***direct*** *ancestor* of the present company 今の会社の前身. ¶our ***prehistoric*** *ancestors* われらの有史以前の祖先. ¶***prehuman*** *ancestors* 人間以前の祖先. ¶man's ***primitive*** *ancestor* 人類の始祖. ¶His ***primordial*** *ancestor* was an owl: he is so fond of working late at night. あの人の先祖はふくろうだ, それであの人は夜おそく働くのが好きなのだ. ¶man's ***remote*** *ancestors* 人類の遠い昔の先祖. ¶the ***wild*** *ancestor* of a domesticated animal 家畜の祖先である野獣.

Q² be inherited from our ***animal*** *ancestors* われわれの祖先たる動物から伝承している. 「がある.

P He is sprung ***from*** noble *ancestors*. 彼にはりっぱな先祖

P² he was *ancestor* ***to*** (=***of***) ... 彼は...の先祖だった.

ancestry, *n.* 系統, 系図.

V Those features ***show*** his Indian *ancestry*. あの顔を見れば彼がインド人の血を引いていることが分る. ¶They ***trace*** their *ancestry* from Genghis Khan. 彼らはジンギスカンの子孫だ. ‖ ***trace*** a person's *ancestry* back to ... 人の系図を...までさかのぼって調べる.

Q citizens of ***foreign*** *ancestry* 外国系の国民. ¶have ***honorable*** *ancestry* 名門である. ¶Schiller came from ***humble*** *ancestry* both on his father's and on his mother's side シルレルの系図は父方も母方も身分がいやしかった. ¶Hawaiians of ***Japanese*** *ancestry* 日系ハワイ人. 【類】 Nearly half the population of Hawaii is of ***Japanese*** *ancestry*. / American citizens of ***Japanese*** *ancestry*. ¶their ***lineal*** and ***collateral*** *ancestry* 彼らの直系および傍系の先祖. ¶come of a ***long-lived*** *ancestry* 長生きをした祖先の血を引いている. ¶He is of ***mixed Irish*** and ***English*** *ancestry*. 彼の系統にはアイルランド人とイングランド人との血が混っている. ¶an individual of ***neuropathic*** *ancestry* 神経病の系統を引いた人.

P He takes great pride ***in*** his *ancestry*. 彼は系図をえらく自慢する. ¶He is born ***of*** good *ancestry*. 彼は名門の出 「だ.

anchor, *n.* 錨(ｲｶﾘ).

V ***back*** an *anchor* 副錨を投じる. ¶***cast*** *anchor* at Kobe 神戸に投錨する. 【類】 The sailors ***cast*** *anchor* for the night, and set sail again next day. ¶***drag*** its *anchor* (船が)錨を引きずる. ¶We ***dropped*** (=***let go***) our *anchor* at 4.45. 船は四時四十五分に投錨した. ‖ the ship ***dropped*** *anchor* off ... その船は...沖に投錨した. ¶***fish*** the *anchor* 収錨する. ¶***heave up*** the *anchor* 錨を揚げる. ¶The ship ***let fall*** her *anchor*. その船は投錨した. ¶***slip*** *anchor* 錨を解く. ¶***sweep*** [***for***] an *anchor* 海底の錨を捜す. ¶***weigh*** (=***raise*** *or* ***pull up***) *anchor* 抜錨する, 出帆する. 【類】 ***weigh*** its *anchor*.

V² The *anchor* ***bites***. 錨が地に食い込む. ¶The *anchor* ***drags***. 錨がずれる.

P lie (=ride) ***at*** *anchor* 停泊している. 【類】 whilst lying ***at*** *anchor* / be fouled (衝突する) whilst ***at*** *anchor* ‖ ships ***at*** *anchor* 停泊船. ¶come ***to*** *anchor* at some distance out in the offing 少し離れて沖合に投錨する.

anchor, *v.* 停泊する; 繫留する.

M so ***loosely*** *anchored* as to be easily carried away たやすく運び去られるような不完全な繫留で.

P *anchor* ***along*** [the] shore 海岸に沿って停泊する. ¶We *anchored* ***at*** Uraga. われわれは浦賀に停泊した. ¶*anchor* ***by*** the stern 錨を船尾に投じて停泊する. ¶*anchor* ***in*** a harbor 港に停泊する. ¶*anchor* ***off*** the shore 沖に停泊する. 【類】 *anchor* ***off*** Bristol. ¶A cruiser painted in curious sooty black was *anchored* ***to*** a red buoy. 妙なすすけた黒色に塗った巡洋艦が赤い浮標につながれていた.

anchorage, *n.* 停泊; 錨地.

V The bay ***affords*** a good *anchorage* and a safe station for ships. 湾は船舶のよき停泊所でありまた安全なたまり場である. ¶Ships of the largest class ***find*** safe *anchorage* here. 最も大型の船もここでは安全に停泊ができる. ¶Such a belief ***has*** no *anchorage* in truth. こんな信念には実際何らのより所もない. ¶***provide*** a safe *anchorage* in rough weather 暴風の時安全な停泊場になる.

Q a ***clear*** *anchorage* 安全な錨地. ¶a ***snug*** *anchorage* 安全錨地(風波をしのぎやすい投錨地).

P² He was the *anchorage* ***of*** my hopes. 彼は私の望の綱 「であった.

anecdote, *n.* 逸話, 奇聞.

V ***tell*** characteristic *anecdotes* about him 彼の面目躍如たる逸話を語る. ¶***use*** this *anecdote* as an illustration of ... この逸話を...の説明に使う.

Q an ***amusing*** *anecdote* is told of ... ...についておもしろい逸話がある. ¶***historical*** *anecdotes* 歴史上の逸話. ¶***literary*** *anecdotes* of the nineteenth century 十九世紀文壇の逸話. ¶***off-the-record*** *anecdotes* 記録にない逸話. ¶a ***personal*** *anecdote* 私行上の逸事. ¶***trifling*** *anecdotes* of famous characters 有名な人物のちょっとした逸話. ¶a ***well-told*** *anecdote* おもしろく書いた逸話.

P² an *anecdote* ***of*** (=***about, concerning*** *or* ***in regard to***) him 彼に関する異聞. ¶an *anecdote* ***relative to*** ... ...に関する逸事.

anesthesia, *n.* 〖医〗麻酔(法).

Q² be under ***cocain*** *anesthesia* コカイン麻酔にかかってい 「る.

anesthetize, *v.* 麻酔をかける.

V *anesthetize **locally*** 局部麻酔をかける.

angel, *n.* 天使.

V He who is overdesirous of ***playing*** the *angel*, plays the beast. 余り天使らしくしようとすると畜生らしくなるものだ.

Q a ***fallen*** *angel* 落ちた天使(街の女). ¶a ***guarding*** *angel* 守護の天使. ¶a ***recording*** *angel* 人間の罪禍を記録する天使.

Q² ***street*** *angels* 夜(やみ)の女.

P² He is an *angel **of*** a man. 彼はほんとに善人だ.

anger, *n.* 怒り.

V ***abide*** (=***face***) his *anger* 彼の怒りに直面する. ¶***aggravate*** one's *anger* 一層立腹させる. ¶Nothing will ***allay*** his *anger*. 何物も彼の怒を和らげることはできまい. ¶***appease*** the *anger* of the gods 神々の怒を鎮める. ¶***calm*** his *anger* 彼をなだめる. ¶***cause*** his *anger* 彼を怒らせる. ¶***checking*** his rising *anger* 腹の虫を殺して. ¶***control*** one's *anger* 怒を抑える. ¶***deprecate*** his *anger* 彼をなだめる. ¶***hold back*** rising *anger* 腹のたつのを抑える. ¶***incur*** the *anger* of one's superiors 上官の怒に触れる. ¶***quell*** one's *anger* 怒を鎮める. ¶***refrain*** one's *anger* 怒を慎む. ¶***repress*** *anger* 怒を抑える. ¶***show*** *anger* 怒を色に現わす. ¶***vent*** one's *anger* 怒りをもらす ‖ to ***vent*** his *anger* 腹いせに. ¶***wreak*** one's *anger* upon ... ...に当り散らす.

V² His *anger **blazed forth***. かんかんになって怒った. ¶*Anger **burned*** in him. 彼はかっと怒った. ¶their *anger **flamed*** at ... 彼らは...をかっと怒った.

Q in ***great*** (=***hot***) *anger* 非常に怒って. ¶***simmering*** *anger* じっとこらえている怒り.

P He was excited ***by*** *anger*. 立腹した. ¶give cause ***for*** *anger* 怒らせる. ‖ He could not contain himself ***for*** *anger*. 怒らずにはいられなかった. ¶We parted ***in*** *anger*. 怒ったまま別れた. 【類】He shouted ***in*** *anger*. / He left home ***in*** *anger*. ‖ more in sorrow than ***in*** *anger* 腹がたつより悲しくなって. ¶the ebullitions ***of*** *anger* 怒の爆発. ¶He wept ***through*** *anger*. 憤激の余り泣いた. ‖ ***through*** (=in) the *anger* of the moment 一時の腹たちまぎれに. ¶He was roused ***to*** *anger*. 怒り出した. ‖ give vent ***to*** one's *anger* 怒り出す. ¶He is beside himself ***with*** *anger*. 怒って逆上している. 【類】He is quivering (身を震わせて) ***with*** *anger*. / burn ***with*** *anger* / shaking ***with*** *anger* / swollen (むくれて) ***with*** *anger* / speak ***with*** *anger* / He foamed ***with*** *anger*.

P² *anger **against*** a person 人に対する憤怒. ¶*anger **at*** the insult 侮辱に対する憤り. ¶*anger **toward*** the offender 罪人に対する憤怒.

anger, *v.* 怒る.

P They were *angered **at*** the measures. 彼らはその処置を怒った.

angle, *n.* 角(かく), 角度.

V ***form*** an *angle* of 45° with ... ...と四十五度の角をなす. ¶***have*** a right *angle* 直角をなす. ‖ ***have*** their own *angle* of observation あの人たちはそれぞれ観察に独特の角度がある. ¶***make*** a right *angle* with ... ...と直角をなす. ¶***measure*** an *angle* 角度を測る. ¶***take*** the *angle* 角度を測る.

Q an ***acute*** *angle* 鋭角. ¶a ***blunt*** *angle* 鈍角. ¶view life from a ***different*** *angle* 違った角度から人生を見る. ¶at a ***high*** *angle* 高角度に. ¶view from his own ***individual*** *angle* 彼自身独特の見地から見る. ¶an ***interior*** *angle* 内角. ¶at a ***moderate*** *angle* 適度の角をなして. ¶from a ***new*** *angle* of vision あらたな見地から ‖ approach a topic from a ***new*** *angle* ある問題に対し新しい見方をする. ¶a ***right*** (***acute, obtuse***) *angle* 直(鋭・鈍)角 ‖ These lines are at ***right*** *angles* [to each other]. この線は直角をなしている. ‖ One line cuts another at ***right*** *angle*. 一線が他線を直角に切る. 【類】Two lines cross at ***right*** *angles*. / the track (線路) turns an abrupt ***right*** *angle* and proceeds to ... ¶at a ***sharp*** *angle* 鋭角を成して. ¶a figure with ***six*** *angles* 六角の図形. ¶Seen at ***such*** an *angle*, I got an entirely different viewpoint on my troubles. そうした観点から見ると自分の労苦なるものが今までとは全然違って見えた. ¶view the subject solely from the ***technological*** *angle* 専ら工業的見地から問題を観測する. ¶from ***various*** *angles* (=standpoints, viewpoints *or* angles of vision) 種種の見地から. ¶a ***vertical*** *angle* 〘幾何〙対頂角.

P ***at*** an *angle* of 90° 九十度の角で. 【類】inclining ***at*** an *angle* of fifty degrees ‖ ***at*** *angles* with ... ...と角をなして. ¶viewed ***from*** this *angle* この角度から見て. ¶an ornament ***on*** the *angles* of spires 尖塔の角(かど)の飾り. ¶It was ***with*** *angles*. それは角(かど)ばっていた.

P² an *angle **of*** vision 観点. ¶The streets run at right *angle **with*** each other. 往来は互に直角をなしている.

angle, *v.* 釣る; 誘い出す.

P *angle **for*** fish in a brook 小川で釣をする. 【類】*angle **for*** trout ‖ *angle **for*** praise (compliments) ほめられるように仕向ける ‖ *angle **for*** a man 人の意中を釣り出す. ¶*angle **with*** an artificial fly 擬餌針で釣をする ‖ *angle **with*** the silver hook 魚を買う(釣らずに); わいろを使う.

angler, *n.* 釣師.

Q² a ***lady*** *angler* 女の釣師.

angling, *n.* 釣.

P² *angling **from*** the bank (a boat) 土手(など)からの魚釣. ¶*angling **on*** the river 河畔の魚釣.

anglist, *n.* 釣師.

Q a ***scientific*** *anglist* 科学的な釣師.

angry, *a.* 怒っている.

M When I said so, he grew ***doubly*** *angry*. 私がそういったらますます腹をたてた. ¶He became ***furiously*** *angry*. 猛烈に怒った. ¶be *angry **outwardly*** 怒りを顔に出す. ¶He got ***very*** *angry*. 彼は大いに怒った.

P He was *angry **about*** it. その事を怒っていた. 【類】What is he *angry **about***? ¶He was *angry **at*** the dog. 犬のことを怒っていた. 【類】He was *angry **at*** (=about) the hurt. / I ought to be *angry **at*** being made a fool of. / He grew *angry **at*** my words. ¶He is *angry **for*** trifles. 彼はつまらない事を怒っている. ¶I am *angry **with*** you. 私は君に対して怒っている. 【類】I am *angry **with*** you for your conduct. / He was *angry **with*** me for saying so. / I shall be very *angry **with*** you if you pull that flower.

O He was *angry* to hear it. 彼はそれを聞いて怒った.

anguish, *n.* 悲痛, 苦悩.

V ***acclaim*** a person's *anguish* 人の苦悩を見て快哉を叫ぶ. ¶***cause*** mental *anguish* 心を苦しめる. ¶She ***felt*** *anguish* at the idea. そのことを思って悲しんだ. ¶She ***vented*** the *anguish* of her heart in bitter tears. さめざめと泣いて心の苦悩を漏らした.

P She cried out ***for*** *anguish* at parting. 彼女は別れのつらさに泣いた. ¶***in*** *anguish* 悲しんで. ¶the *anguish **of*** despair 失望の苦痛.

angularity, *n.* 角立ち.

V ***soften down*** (=***round off***) awkward *angularities* [文章や人間などの]角を取る.

animadversion, *n.* 批評, 非難.

P *animadversion **on*** (=***upon***) a subject ある問題に対する批判.

animadvert, *v.* 非難する.

P *animadvert **on*** a person's faults 人の過失を非難する.

animal, *n.* 動物, 獣.

V ***chain*** [***up***] an *animal* 動物を鎖でつなぐ. ¶***domesticate*** *animals* 動物を飼いならす. ¶***keep*** domestic *animals* 家畜を飼って置く. ¶***kill*** *animals* for food 動物を殺して食用とする. ¶***raise*** domestic *animals* 家畜を飼養する. ¶***tame*** *animals* for domestic use 動物をならして家畜とする.

Q The deer is an ***agile*** *animal*. しかはすばしっこい動物だ. ¶***amphibious*** *animals* 両生動物. ¶an ***aquatic*** *animal* 水生動物. ¶a ***bathy-benthal*** *animal* 深海動物. ¶a ***bovine*** *animal* 牛科の動物. ¶***brute*** *animals* 畜生, 獣. ¶a ***carnivorous*** *animal* 肉食動物. ¶***cold-blooded*** *animals* 冷血動物. ¶***compound*** *animals* 群生動物. ¶***domesticated*** (=***domestic***) *animals* 家畜. ¶***dumb*** *animals* 口のきけぬ動物. ¶a ***ferocious*** *animal* 猛獣. ¶Man is a ***gregarious*** (***sociable***) *animals*. 人は群生(社会的)動物だ. ¶a ***herbivorous*** *animal* 草食動物. ¶a ***higher*** *animal* 高等動物. ¶a ***lower*** *animal* 下等動物. 【類】*animals* much ***lower*** than man. ¶a ***nocturnal*** *animal* 夜行性動物. ¶***performing*** *animals* 芸をする動物. ¶***pet*** *animals* 手飼いの動物. ¶Aristotle's definition of man as a "***political*** *animal*." アリストテレスが下した「政治的動物」という人間の定義. ¶a ***sagacious*** *animal* 利口な動物. ¶Man is a ***sociable*** *animal*. 人間は社交的動物だ. ¶a ***stray*** *animal* 迷子になった動物. ¶a ***tame*** *animal* 人になれた動物. ¶a ***warm-blooded*** *animal* 温血動物. ¶***wild*** *animals* of the chase 狩猟用の野獣. 【類】A zoo is a place where ***wild*** *animals* are kept to be seen.

Q^2 a ***baby*** *animal* 生れたての動物. ¶a ***bottom*** *animal* 底生動物. ¶a ***deep-sea*** *animal* 深海産動物. ¶a ***draught*** *animal* 駄獣(馬車馬のような). ¶a ***farm*** *animal* 耕作用の動物. ¶a ***food*** *animal* 食用動物. ¶a ***fresh-water*** *animal* 淡水産動物. ¶The elephant is the largest ***land*** *animal.* 象は最大の陸生動物である. ¶***meat*** *animals* 食肉用動物. ¶a ***sea*** *animal* 海産動物. ¶a ***toy*** *animal* おもちゃの動物. ¶***water*** *animals* 水生動物.

P^2 *animals* ***below*** mammals 哺乳類以下の[下等]動物. ¶an *animal* ***of*** draught 駄獣. ‖an *animal* ***of*** monkey kind さる類の動物 ‖an *animal* ***of*** prey 肉食獣.

animate, *v.* 励ます, 活気づける.

P *animated* ***by*** jealousy しっと心にあおられて. ‖He was *animated* ***by*** examples to noble deeds. 彼はりっぱな行いをするように手本で激励された. 【類】The dogs were *animated* ***by*** the horns and voices of the hunters. / He was *animated* all his life ***by*** love of his country. ¶*animate* a person ***with*** fresh hope 新しい希望で人を活気づける. 【類】be *animated* ***with*** a true zeal for holiness / They are *animated* ***with*** a spirit peculiar to the Japanese. ‖The body is *animated* ***with*** the soul. 肉体は精神で生きている. ‖He is *animated* ***with*** good feelings toward you. 彼は君に好感をもっている.

animation, *n.* 生気, 活気; 〔映〕漫画制作.

V ***restore*** *animation* by artificial respiration 人工呼吸で(でき死者などを)正気づかせる. ¶He ***showed*** great *animation.* 彼は非常に活発だった.

Q ***bodily*** *animation* in speaking 話す時のからだの活動. ¶***suspended*** *animation* 仮死状態.

Q^2 ***cartoon*** *animation* =production of animated cartoons 漫画制作.

P He spoke ***with*** great *animation.* 彼は勢よく話した.

animosity, *n.* 怨恨; 敵がい心.

V ***arouse*** the *animosity* of … …の怨恨を激発させる. ¶***exasperate*** race *animosities* 民族的敵がい心を激発させる. ¶help to ***keep alive*** *animosities* which were much better allowed to die 忘れさせた方がよい怨恨をそのままにしておく事になる. ¶***rouse*** the *animosity* of my countrymen わが国民の敵がい心を喚起する.

Q ***international*** *animosities* 国際間の悪感情. ¶***religious*** *animosity* 宗教上の反感.

P^2 *animosity* ***against*** a person (country) 人(など)に対する反感. ¶*animosities* ***between*** classes 階級間の反目. ¶the *animosity* ***of*** one class ***toward*** (=against) another 階級が他階級に対する敵意. ¶*animosity* ***to*** (=toward) an opponent 敵に対する怨恨.

animus, *n.* 悪意.

P *animus* ***against*** the teachings of socialism 社会主義の趣旨に対する反感.

ankle, *n.* くるぶし, 足くび.

V ***sprain*** (=***strain or wrench***) one's *ankle* by a fall 倒れてくるぶしをくじく. ¶***twist*** one's *ankle* くるぶしを違える.

Q a ***sprained*** *ankle* くじいた足首.

annalist, *n.* 歴史家.

Q^2 a ***college*** (***war***) *annalist* 大学(など)の歴史を書く人.

annals, *n.* 歴史.

Q make him immortal in ***industrial*** *annals* 産業界の歴史に不朽の名を留める.

Q^2 The World Almanac has been for many years the most widely circulated general ***reference*** *annals* in America.「世界年鑑」は数年前から最も普及している米国出版の年鑑である.

P unique ***in*** the *annals* of diplomacy 外交の歴史にその類例を見ない.

annex[e], *n.* 別館; 補遺.

Q^2 a ***hotel*** *annex* 旅館の別館.

P^2 an *annex* ***to*** a house (hotel, main building) 別館, はなれ ‖an *annex* ***to*** a document (law) 文書(など)の補遺 ‖the *Annex* ***to*** this Covenant 本規約付属書.

annex, *v.* 併合する; 付加する.

P it was *annexed* ***by*** … それは…に併合された. ¶It was invented by … or *annexed* ***from*** abroad. それは…の発明によるかまたは海外から輸入されたものだ. ¶*annexed* ***to*** the main building 本館に附属した. 【類】The Hawaiian Islands were *annexed* ***to*** the United States by act of Congress, July 7, 1898. / Malta was *annexed* ***to*** the British Crown in 1814. / *annex* notes (註) ***to*** a book / *annex* privileges ***to*** the peerage (貴族).

annexation, *n.* 併合; 併合地.

Q ***Japanese*** *annexations* 日本への併合領土.

P^2 *annexation* ***of*** a territory ***to*** a state 一国に一領土を合併すること. ¶*annexation* ***with*** … …との合併.

annihilation, *n.* 全滅, 絶滅.

V ***suffer*** *annihilation* 全滅する.

Q^2 ***mass*** *annihilation* 大虐殺.

P^2 the *annihilation* ***of*** atomic war 原子戦による殺りく.

anniversary, *n.* 周年祭, 記念祭.

V She ***attained*** the sixty-third *anniversary* of her birthday. 彼女は六十三の誕辰に達した. ¶***celebrate*** the second centennial *anniversary* of Mozart モーツァルトの二百年祭を行う ‖***celebrate*** the 80th *anniversary* of one's birthday 八十歳の誕辰を祝う ‖***celebrate*** the 20th *anniversary* of its existence 創立第二十周年祭を挙行する. ¶an exhibition at Columbia University to ***commemorate*** the one hundredth *anniversary* of the birth of Lewis Carrol コロムビヤ大学におけるルーイス・カロル百年誕辰記念の展覧会. ¶The University is going to ***have*** an *anniversary.* 同大学は記念祭を挙げるはず. ¶***honor*** the *anniversary* of His Majesty's august birth 陛下の御誕生を祝する. ¶***keep*** the *anniversary* of his birth 彼の誕生日を祝う. ¶***observe*** the 50th *anniversary* of … …の五十年祭を挙げる. ¶The newspaper ***reached*** the one hundredth *anniversary* of the publication of its first number. その新聞紙は創刊百周年に達した.

Q a ***fiftieth*** *anniversary*=a jubilee 五十年祭. ¶the ***one hundredth*** *anniversary* of his death 彼の百年忌. ¶the ***tenth*** *anniversary* of his reign 在位十年記念式典. ¶the ***third*** *anniversary* of the founding … 創立三周年. ¶the ***25th*** *anniversary* of his professorship 同教授在職二十五年.

Q^2 a ***surrender*** *anniversary* 降伏記念日. ¶announce their ***twenty-fifth wedding*** *anniversary* 銀婚式の通知を出す.

P ***at*** the 100th *anniversary* of … …の百年記念祭に. ¶***on*** the nineteenth *anniversary* of the existence of the Hakluyt Society ハクルート会創立十九年祭に. ‖***on*** the *anniversary* of his death 彼の命日に.

P^2 the *anniversary* ***of*** one's birth 誕生日. 【類】the 50th *anniversary* ***of*** the opening of Yokohama to foreign trade / the 30th *anniversary* ***of*** the promulgation of the Imperial Constitution / This day is the *anniversary* ***of*** my arrival in Japan / the fiftieth *annivarsary* ***of*** his first appearance on the stage.

annotate, *v.* 註解する.

M a book ***elaborately*** (=***copiously***) *annotated* 詳註を施した本. ¶The book is ***usefully*** *annotated.* その本には有益な註が入っている.

annotation, *n.* 詳解.

Q contain ***copious*** *annotations* 詳註が付いている.

announce, *v.* 発表する; 知らせる.

M as ***already*** (=***previously***) *announced* 予告通り. ¶***formally*** *announce* 正式に発表する. ¶be *announced* ***forthwith*** 即刻発表される. ¶It was ***informally*** *announced.* それが非公式に発表された. ¶it is ***officially*** *announced* that … …と正式に発表される. ¶***publicly*** *announce* 公表する. ¶***respectfully*** *annouce* 謹告する. ¶it has been ***semi-officially*** *announced* that … …と準公式に発表された.

P *announced* ***as*** … …というふれ込みで. ¶It was *announced* ***by*** loud beating of the drum. 太鼓をどんどんたたいて知らせた. ¶The ceremony was *announced* ***for*** 9 a.m. 式は午前九時と発表された. ‖Messrs Methuen *announce* ***for*** September the biography of … 来る九月…伝が出版されるとメシュエン会社が予告している. 【類】The inauguration of President Clarence M. Dunnelly, of Kentucky Wesleyan College, is *announced* ***for*** Friday, January 3. ¶the death was *announced* ***of*** Mr. … …氏の死去が報ぜられた. ¶*announce* ***to*** the public 公衆に告示する ‖*announce* an event ***to*** the family by telegraph 電報で家族に事件を知らせる.

O This soil *announces* the article to have been long exposed in the shop. こんなによごれているのは店ざらしの証拠だ.

announcement, *n.* 通知, 告示, 発表.

V ***knell*** the *announcement* of the death of … …の死去を鐘を打って知らせる. ¶***make*** public *announcement* of … …を公表する. 【類】an *announcement* has been ***made*** by the Government that ... ¶*place* (=*post*) an *announcement* on a notice(=bulletin)-board 掲示板で告示する.

Q a *formal announcement* 正式の発表. ¶*Further announcement* will be made within a few days. 後報が二三日中に発表されるはず. ¶bald "*official*" *announcements* いわゆるお役所式の殺風景な告示 ‖ *official announcement* was made that ... ...と公式の発表があった. ¶a *preliminary announcement* 予告.

Q² a *bargain announcement* 割引販売広告. ¶*spot announcement* 〖ラジオ〗スポット・アナウンス (番組の間にはさむもの). ¶make a *surprise announcement* 突然発表する.

P *on* the *announcement* of ... ...が発表されると.

announcer, *n.* 放送員, アナウンサー.

Q² a *lady* (=*woman*) *announcer* 婦人アナウンサー. ¶an *NBC announcer* NBC 放送員. ¶a *radio announcer* ラジオ放送員. ¶a [*railway*] *station announcer* 駅の放送係.

annoy, *v.* 困らせる.

M *constantly annoyed* at the thought that ... 絶えず...を苦にして. ¶I am not *easily annoyed* at trifles. 私はちょっとした事ぐらいには滅多にいらいらしない.

P I was *annoyed* ***about*** the matter. 私はその事には困った. ¶I am *annoyed* ***at*** his behaviour. 彼の行動は困ったものだ. 【類】I was *annoyed* ***at*** his remark. / I was *annoyed* ***at*** his intrusion (出しゃばり). / be much *annoyed* ***at*** the tone of a person's letter (手紙の書き振り) ‖ You will be *annoyed* ***by*** complaints. 泣言を言われて困るだろう. 【類】He *annoyed* me ***by*** jest. ‖ is *annoyed* ***by*** what Mrs. Grundy says とかく世間の口がうるさい. ¶I am *annoyed* ***with*** applications for an interview. 諸方から面会を申込まれるので困っている. 【類】I am *annoyed* ***with*** him for doing what I do not like. / You must pardon me for *annoying* ***with*** this matter. / be *annoyed* ***with*** complaints made from outside (外部からの不満).

O I am *annoyed* to find that ... ...なので困っている. ¶I am *annoyed* to hear that. それを聞いて困っている.

annoyance, *n.* 迷惑.

V *cause annoyance* to ... ...に迷惑をかける. ¶*give annoyance* to ... ...に迷惑をかける. ¶That may *save* some *annoyance*. それでいくらか厄介が省けるかも知れない.

Q *exasperating annoyance* 腹立たしい迷惑. ¶to my *extreme annoyance* 実に困ったことには. ¶a matter of *great annoyance* やっかいな事件. ¶put on him too *much annoyance* 彼に大迷惑を掛ける. ¶with carefully *repressed annoyance* 迷惑を少しも顔に出さないで.

Q² *family annoyances* 家庭のわずらい.

P much ***to*** my *annoyance* 大いに困ったことには.

P² *annoyance* ***to*** the neighborhood 近所迷惑.

annoying, *pa.* うるさい.

M That is *distinctly annoying*. そいつは全くうるさい. ¶the mosquitoes were so *terribly annoying* that ... 蚊がばかにうるさいので...した.

P It is *annoying* ***to*** me. うるさい.

annual, *n.* 一年草.

Q *fall-blooming* (*winter-flowering*) *annuals* 秋(冬)咲の一年草.

annuity, *n.* 年金.

V *grant* an *annuity* 年金を給与する. ¶*pay* an *annuity* 年金を払う. ¶*settle* an *annuity* on him 彼に給与する年金をきめる.

Q He has a *considerable annuity* to live on. 大分年金が付いているからそれで暮していける. ¶grant a *terminable annuity* 有期年金を与える.

Q² a *life annuity* 終身年金.

P He lives ***on*** his *annuity*. 年金で暮している. ¶an *annuity* ***of*** ... yen ***for*** life ...円の終身年金.

annulment, *n.* 解除.

V *obtain* the *annulment* of the ban その禁止を解除される.

anoint, *v.* 油を塗る.

P *anoint* one's body ***with*** cocoanut oil やし油で身体を清める.

anomaly, *n.* 異常.

Q *magnetic anomaly* 〖物理〗地磁気異常. ¶*mental anomaly* 精神異状. ¶present *psychic anomalies* 精神異状を呈する. ¶there is a *strange anomaly* in ... ...には妙に変った所がある.

anonymity, *n.* 匿名, 無名.

V *keep* the *anonymity* 匿名にして置く. ¶She *maintained* her *anonymity* for many years. 彼女は永い間その本名を秘していた.

Q He lost himself in the *willing anonymity* of freshman year in college. 彼はすすんで大学一年生という無名の状態に身をかくした.

another, *pron.* 今一つの物.

Q and *many anothers* そして多数のこれに類するもの. ¶*such another* この手で別の物.

answer, *n.* 回答, 返事; 解答.

V He *avoided* a direct *answer*. 即答をさけた. ¶*Bring* an *answer*. 返事をもらって来い. ¶Shall I *bring back* an *answer?* 返事をもらって参りましょうか. ¶I think that *constitutes* the *answer*. それで返答になると思う. ¶*decide* one's *answer* 何と返事するかきめる. ¶*deign* an *answer* 返事をよこして下さる. ¶I *expect* an affirmative *answer*. 賛成の返事が来ると思う. ¶I cannot *find* the *answer*. 返答しかねる. ¶be unable to *furnish* an answer 返事をあげられない. ¶*get* an *answer* 返事をもらう. ¶He will not *give* me a decided *answer*. 確答はしないだろう. 【類】He *gave* me no *answer*. ¶We shall *have* an *answer* by tomorrow evening. 明晩までに返事が来るだろう. 【類】We shall *have* an *answer*, yes or no. ‖ I will let you *have* an *answer* after mature consideration. 熟考の上御返事しよう. ¶*know* the *answer* to a puzzle 考え物が解ける. ¶*make* an *answer* to a question 質疑に応答する. 【類】He *made answer* with tears. / She *made* him no *answer*. ‖ He is not in a position to *make answers* straight off. 彼としては即答しかねる. ¶I *received* no *answer*. 何の返事もなかった. 【類】He *received* no *answer* to his knock. ¶Does this letter *require* an *answer?* この手紙には返事がいりますか. ¶An evasive *answer* was *returned*. 逃げ口上を言ってよこした. 【類】*return* no *answer* to a question. ¶Please *send* me an *answer* at your earliest convenience. なるべく早く御返事を願います. 【類】I *sent* an *answer* to the effect that ... (...という内容の). / Please *send* me an *answer* by return of post (折返し). / I will *send* you an *answer* by telephone. ¶*supply* an *answer* to the question 質疑に解答する. ¶I shall *take* no *answer* until then. その時になって御返答を承りましょう. ¶I *want* a distinct *answer* to my question. 私の質問にはっきり答えて下さい. ¶Immediately on receipt of it I *wrote* an *answer*. それを受取るとすぐ返事を書いた. 【類】I *wrote* the *answer* myself. ¶*write back* an *answer* 返事を書いて出す.

Q an *affirmative answer* 応諾の返答. ¶a *brief* and *unsatisfactory answer* 簡単で要領を得ない返事. ¶a *categorical answer* 確答. ¶a decidedly *clever* and *effective answer* 至極巧妙で要領を得た返事. ¶a *curt answer* そっけない返事. ¶give no *definite answer* to ... ...に確答しない. 【類】I must have a *definite* answer, yes or no. ¶a *disconcerting answer* 当惑させる返事. ¶a *dubious* (=an *undecisive*) *answer* あやふやな返事. ¶give an *evasive answer* 言抜けをする. ¶make a *false answer* ***to*** ... ...に虚偽の返事を出す. ¶a *favorable answer* 色よい返事. ¶a *flippant answer* ぞんざいな返事. ¶His *answer* was very *guarded*. 彼の返事ははなはだ慎重なものであった. ¶Give an *immediate answer*, Yes or No. 否か応か即答しろ. 【類】letters requiring *immediate answer*. ¶an *impertinent answer* 失敬な返事. ¶an *indefinite* and *unsatisfactory answer* 不得要領の返答. ¶"..." was the *injured answer* ...という腹を立てたような返事をした. ¶get an *instant answer* すぐ返事をもらう. ¶*irrelevant answers* 見当違いの返答. ¶a *laconic answer* 簡潔な返答. ¶a *negative answer* 否定の返答. ¶There is *only one answer* to that. そりゃもうわかっている. ¶a *poor answer* へたな返事. ¶give a *positive answer* きっぱり返事をする. ¶a *prevaricating answer* 一時逃れの返事. ¶He consented with a *ready answer*. 二つ返事で承知した. ¶*shrewd* and *relevant answers* 抜目のない適切な返答. ¶a *shuffling answer* 逃げ口上. ¶A *soft answer* turned away his wrath. やさしく受け流したので相手の立腹はおさまった. ¶a *succinct answer* 簡明な返答. ¶a *sufficient answer* to one's question 質問に対する十分な解答. ¶a *thoughtless* (=*heedless*) *answer* かるはずみの返答. ¶an *unwilling answer* 不本意の返答. ¶a *vague answer* ばく然たる答. ¶*What answer* can you make? なんと返答ができますか. ¶a *witty answer* 気のきいた(しゃれた)返事.

P He was taken aback ***at*** the unexpected *answer*. 意外の

返答にあきれていた. ¶I was perplexed ***for*** an *answer.* 返事に困った. ‖ ***For*** *answer* came a chuckle. 返事もせずにくすっと笑った. ‖ What did you have ***for*** the *answer?* 返事はどうでした? ¶***in*** *answer* to the question その質疑に答えて. 【類】 ***In*** *answer* to his request for help, I gave him a dollar. / What have you to say ***in*** *answer* to the charge (非難)? / write ***in*** *answer* / ***In*** *answer* to my "Come in," a young man came into my room. ‖ ***in*** *answer* to my look of inquiry 僕が不思議そうな顔をしていたので. 【類】 He rose to speak ***in*** *answer* to his name. (指名されて). ¶I am ready ***with*** an *answer.* 僕には返答の用意がある.

P² an *answer* ***about*** ... ...についての返事. ¶an *answer* ***by*** word of mouth 口頭の返事. ¶an *answer* ***for*** a question 質疑に対する応答. ¶insist on a definite *answer* ***from*** him 彼に必ず確答せよと言い張る. ¶an *answer* ***in*** writing 書面での返事. ¶Give me the *answer* ***of*** this puzzle. このなぞを解いて下さい. ¶*answers* ***to*** puzzles なぞの解答. 【類】 an *answer* ***to*** his letter / *answers* ***to*** examination papers. ‖ That is no *answer* ***to*** my question. それはてんで返答になっていない. ‖ an *answer* ***to*** travelers' prayer 旅行者の切望に応えたもの.

answer, *v.* **(1)** 答える, 解く, 解答する.

M *answer* ***back*** 口返答をする. ¶*answer* ***bitterly*** にがにがしい返答をする. ¶*answer* ***coldly*** (=curtly) すげなく答える. ¶The fundamental question of it has not been ***definitely*** *answered* by biology. その根本問題は生物学ではきっぱり解かれていない. ¶He *answered* ***frankly*** and ***truthfully*** all my questions. 彼は私の質問にみな腹蔵なく正直に答えてくれた. ¶I have ***fully*** *answered* by letter. 委細手紙で返事をした. ¶I am unable to *answer* ***offhand.*** 私には即答はできない. ¶*answer* ***orally*** 口頭で答える. ¶*answer* ***philosophically*** 冷静に答える. ¶*answer* ***promptly*** てきぱきと答える ‖ Inquiries by mail ***promptly*** and ***courteously*** *answered.* 郵便での問合せは即時丁重にお答え致します. ¶*answer* ***relevantly*** つじつまの合った返答をする. ¶*answer* ***sensibly*** うまく答える. ¶"No I cannot!," I *answered* ***sharply.*** 「いや僕にはできん」とはっきり答えた. ¶*answer* ***sheepishly*** きまり悪るそうに答える. ¶*answer* ***shortly*** (=***briefly***) 簡単に答える. ¶*answer* ***shortly*** and ***huffily*** つっけんどんに返答する. ¶*answer* ***snappishly*** がみがみ答える. ¶*answer* ***tartly*** 皮肉たっぷりに答える. ¶***truthfully*** *answer* 正直に答える.

P *answer* the question ***by*** saying that ... ...といってその質問の答えとする. ¶I *answered* ***in*** the affirmative. そうだと答えた. ¶*answer* ***to*** one's name 名を呼ばれて返事する. 【類】 *Answering* ***to*** their names, they came forward one by one. ‖ She *answers* ***to*** the name of "Dora." 彼女は名をドラという. 【類】 The dog *answered* ***to*** the name of "Grip." ¶*answer* ***with*** an unhesitating negative 断固として否と答える.

(2) 間に合う.

M It *answers* ***admirably.*** それで結構. ¶It *answers* very ***well.*** それで結構(十分目的に適う).

P This tool best *answers* ***for*** my purpose. この道具は一番私の目的に適っている.

(3) 責を負う, 保証する.

P I will *answer* ***for*** him. 彼のことは私が引受ける. 【類】 I will *answer* ***for*** his honesty. / I *answered* ***for*** it with my life. / You will have to *answer* ***for*** your carelessness. / He will apologize to you for his conduct, I *answer* ***for*** it. ¶You will have to *answer* ***to*** me ***for*** it. 君はそれに対し僕に責任を負わねばならない.

(4) 一致する, 符合する.

P This does not *answer* ***to*** the description given. これは当方の注文と合わない. 【類】 a man *answering* ***to*** the description (人相書) / It *answered* ***to*** a great popular need (大衆の切なる希望).

answerable, *a.* 責任ある; 相応している.

P He is *answerable* ***to*** me ***for*** his conduct. 彼はその行為に対して僕に責任がある. 【類】 I am *answerable* ***to*** no one ***for*** its loss. ‖ Its thickness is *answerable* ***to*** the height. その厚さは高さに釣合っている. 【類】 His fame is *answerable* ***to*** his success.

antagonism, *n.* 反対, 反抗, 敵対.

V His speech did not ***arouse*** any particular *antagonism* on the part of the press. 彼の演説は格別新聞紙の反対を買わなかった. ¶considerable *antagonism* was ***displayed*** by ... ...がかなり反対の気勢を揚げた. ¶***engender*** bitter *antagonism* between labor and capital 労資間に激烈な敵意をかもす. ¶***lay*** to rest an *antagonism* 反目を和げる. ¶***maintain*** an uncompromising *antagonism* against ... ...に対してがん強な反対を持続する.

V² *antagonism* ***grew up*** between ... ...間に反対運動が起った.

Q ***active*** *antagonism* 大反対. ¶the ***deadly*** *antagonism* between France and Germany 仏独間の激烈なる反抗気分. ¶a ***deep*** (=***profound***) *antagonism* 深刻な対立. ¶in ***direct*** *antagonism* in it それに直接反抗して. ¶It met with most ***vehement*** *antagonism* from the world at large. 一般社会からの猛烈な反対を受けた.

P ***in*** *antagonism* with ... ...に反抗して.

P² one's *antagonism* ***against*** (=to) a rival 競争相手に対する反抗. ¶the *antagonism* ***between*** two persons (parties, rivals) 二人(など)の間の反抗気分. ¶the *antagonism* ***of*** one race to another 一民族と他民族との対立. ¶*antagonism* ***to*** the doctrine 教義に対する反抗. ¶come into *antagonism* ***with*** ... ...に敵対する.

antagonist, *n.* 敵, 相手.

V ***foil*** one's *antagonist* 敵をくじく.

Q a ***formidable*** *antagonist* 強敵. ¶a ***wily*** *antagonist* 奸智(かんち)にたけた敵手.

P² the *antagonist* ***of*** our teammate ***in*** the contest 競技で味方の敵手.

antagonistic, *a.* 相いれぬ.

M ***irreconcilably*** *antagonistic* 氷炭相いれない.

P ideologies *antagonistic* ***to*** each other 氷炭相いれない観念論. 【類】 Truth is *antagonistic* ***to*** error. / bitterly *antagonistic* ***to*** the existing order of things (現状).

antagonize, *v.* 反対する.

M Buddhism was ***violently*** *antagonized.* 仏教は猛烈な反対を受けた.

antecedent, *n.* 素性(すじょう), 経歴; 先行詞.

V If he had ***known*** that girl's *antecedents,* he would never have married her. 彼があの女の素性を知っていたら結婚はしなかったろう.

Q a woman of ***doubtful*** *antecedents* 怪しい素性の女. ¶a man of ***irreproachable*** *antecedents* 申分のない経歴の人. ¶a man of the ***vilest*** *antecedents* ごく素性の悪い男. ¶a person of ***unknown*** *antecedents* どこの馬の骨かわからない者.

P inquire ***into*** one's *antecedents* 経歴を調べる. ¶the *antecedent* ***to*** 'it' it の先行詞.

antecedent, *a.* 以前の.

P The event is *antecedent* ***to*** the French Revolution. それはフランス革命以前のことだ.

antedate, *v.* 先立つ.

M at a time ***far*** *antedating* Christianity キリスト教(の開基より)ずっと前に. ¶it ***long*** *antedates* ... それは...よりずっと前だ.

P it is *antedated* only ***by*** ... それより設立の古いのは...だけだ. 【類】 his predecessor, ..., who had *antedated* him ***by*** nearly fifty years.

O China has a civilization that *antedates* any other in the world. 中国の文化は世界中いずれの国よりも古い.

anterior, *a.* 以前の.

P ages *anterior* ***to*** the Flood ノアの洪水以前の時代 ‖ be assigned to a date *anterior* ***to*** that by some years それより数年以前の年月が指定されている.

anthem, *n.* 頌歌(しょうか).

Q While the Marine Band was rendering the ***national*** *anthem,* the crowd began to melt away. 海軍軍楽隊の国歌奏楽中に群衆は解散し始めた.

antic, *n.* [しばしば *pl.*] おどけ.

Q ***droll*** *antics* [子犬などの]ふざけ.

Q² ***animal*** *antics* 動物のおどけた身振り. ¶a ***schoolboy*** *antic* 学童のわるふざけ.

P² the *antics* ***of the*** clown 道化師のおどけた所作. 【類】 the *antics* ***of*** a kitten with a feather or a reel of thread (糸まき).

anticipate, *v.* 予期する.

M ***confidentially*** *anticipate* 確信をもって予期する. ¶the suggestion was long ***previously*** *anticipated* by ... その説はずっと以前に...が述べている.

P *anticipate* ***with*** much pleasure 大喜びで期待する.

anticipation, *n.* 予想, 予期, 先駆.

V Their *anticipation* were not ***realized.*** 彼らの予想は実現

しなかった. ¶The result ***surpassed*** the highest *anticipations* of the promoters of the scheme. 発起人のとても予想しない好成績だった.

Q ***Eastern anticipations*** of modern medical science 近世医学の東洋における先駆. ¶in ***happy*** and ***eager anticipation*** of the morrow あすの事を楽しく熱心に予想して. ¶await ... with ***keen anticipation*** ...を大いに当てにして待つ.

P ***by anticipation*** あらかじめ. ¶order ***in anticipation*** of a rise 値上りを見越して注文する. 【類】Sell ***in anticipation*** of a fall. / ***in anticipation*** of your success (前祝に) / 【類】***in anticipation*** of Sales at Christmas / thanking you ***in anticipation*** of your reply. ¶business in war risks at insurance offices has largely increased ***upon*** the *anticipation* of war with ... 保険会社の戦時保険契約は...との戦争を見越して大分ふえた. ¶look forward ***with*** the keenest *anticipation* to ... 鋭意...を期待する. ¶an ***anticipation of*** the present linotype machine 現在のライノタイプのさきがけ.

antidote, *n.* 解毒剤.

V ***administer*** an *antidote* 解毒剤を飲ませる. ¶***apply*** an *antidote* to a disease (poison) 病気(など)に解毒剤を用いる.

Q a ***powerful antidote*** 強い解毒剤. ¶a ***strong antidote*** 有効な解毒剤. ¶a ***sure antidote*** 効能確実な解毒剤. 【類】a ***sure antidote*** for melancholy (憂うつ).

P an ***antidote against*** infection 伝染予防薬.

P² The cat is the best ***antidote for*** the plague. ねこはこの上もないペスト除けだ. 【類】Prosperity is a good ***antidote for*** political unrest (政局不安定). ¶an ***antidote to*** poisons 解毒剤. 【類】There is an ancient notion that the burnt hair of a dog is an ***antidote to*** its bite.

antipathy, *n.* 反感; 生来の嫌悪; 性の合わぬこと.

V freely ***air*** one's *antipathy* 遠慮なくいやだと言う. ¶***arouse antipathy*** 反感を呼び起す. ¶Oil and water ***have*** an *antipathy*. 油と水とは相いれない. ‖ ***have*** an *antipathy* to snakes (spiders) へび(など)をきらう. ¶I cannot ***overcome*** my antipathy. いやでたまらない. ¶***provoke antipathy*** 反感をそそる. ¶***take*** an *antipathy* to ... ...をきらう.

Q I have a ***natural antipathy*** toward it. 生来それがきらいだ. ¶he has no ***rooted antipathy*** to ... 彼は...に対して根深い反感は持っていない. ¶he had a ***strong antipathy*** to ... 彼は...に対して強い反感を持っていた.

P² a mutual *antipathy* ***between*** two persons 二人間の反感. 【類】*antipathy* ***to*** (=***toward, for or against***) a person or a thing / *antipathy* ***to*** (=***against***) a political boss (政界の顔役).

antipode, *n.* 正反対.

P ***at antipode*** with ... ...と正反対に. ‖ Australia is ***at*** the *antipode* of England. 豪州は英国の対せき地にある. ¶***in*** the very *antipodes* of ... 丁度...の対せき地に.

antiquary, *n.* 古物愛好者.

P It is known only ***to*** the *antiquary*. 好古趣味の人だけが知っている.

antiquate, *v.* 古くする.

P be *antiquated* ***in*** ideas 頭が古い.

antique, *n.* 古物, 古器.

Q ***fake antiques*** にせの古物. ¶***genuine antiques*** 本物の古器. ¶***Greek antiques*** ギリシアの古物. ¶***spurious antiques***

Q² ***imitation*** *antiques* 模造古物. 擬造古物.

antiquity, *n.* (**1**) 古いこと; 上古, 古代.

V ***claim*** an *antiquity* of 3,000 to 5,000 years for ... ...は三千年ないし五千年以前のものと主張する. ¶***trace*** the *antiquity* of the hen 鶏の由来を調べる.

Q in ***classical antiquity*** ギリシア・ローマの古代において. ¶It is of ***considerable antiquity***. よほど古いものだ. ¶there was a time in ***dim antiquity*** when ... 茫漠(ぼう)たる上古にあっては...のような時代もあった. ¶Wrestling, as a game strict to special rules, is of ***great antiquity***. すもうは特殊の法則に支配される競技として非常に古いものだ. ¶of ***high*** (=great) *antiquity* 非常に古い ‖ Babylon was a city of the ***highest antiquity***. バビロンは一番古い都市であった. ¶from a ***hoary antiquity*** 太古から ‖ boast of a ***hoary antiquity*** 古いのを誇る ‖ a ***hoary antiquity*** is claimed for ... ...は非常に古い物だといわれる. ¶from ***immemorial antiquity*** 太古から. ¶the ***immense antiquity*** of the Chinese silk industry 中国の絹糸工業の非常に古いこと. ¶in very ***remote antiquity*** 太古に. ¶object of ***remote antiquity*** 上代の器物(など). 【類】Beer is a beverage of the most ***remote antiquity***. ¶It is of a very ***respectable antiquity***. 随分古いものだ. ¶***unknown antiquity*** 茫漠(ぼう)たる太古. ¶Its origin dates back to a ***venerable antiquity***. その起原は遠い昔にさかのぼる.

P Glazes had been used ***from*** high *antiquity* in Egypt. エジプトでは大昔からうわぐすりを使った. ¶***of antiquity*** 昔の ‖ Many religious customs are ***of*** great *antiquity*. 宗教上の慣例には太古からのものが多い. ‖ a family ***of*** great *antiquity* 系図の非常に古い家.

P² *antiquity* ***of*** man 人類の由来.

(**2**) 古物, 古器.

V ***forge antiquities*** 古物を擬造する.

Q ***spurious Egyptian antiquities*** エジプトの模造古器.

P² *antiquities* ***from*** Egypt エジプト渡来の古物.

antiseptic, *n.* 防腐剤.

Q a ***safe antiseptic*** 安全な防腐剤.

P It is largely used ***as*** an *antiseptic*. それは広く防腐剤として用いられている.

antithesis, *n.* 正反対.

Q the ***direct antithesis*** of ... ...と正反対. ¶the ***exact antithesis*** of ... ...の正反対. ¶the ***very antithesis*** of that conjured up by the popular imagination 世人の想像の正反対. ¶a ***violent antithesis*** between ... ...間の著しい対照.

P² the *antithesis* ***to*** theory and fact (=between theory and fact) 理論と実際の対照 ‖ was in several respects the *antithesis* ***of*** Professor B 幾つもの点で B 教授の意見と正反対であった. ¶an *antithesis* ***to*** ... ...の対照物.

anus, *n.* 〖解〗こう門. ¶***through*** the *anus* 同上.

P emit wind ***from*** the *anus* 放ひする. ¶vent wind

anvil, *n.* かなとこ.

P It was hammered ***on*** *anvil*. かなとこの上で打たれた. ‖ He has now ***on*** (=***upon***) the *anvil* another scheme. 彼は今別の計画を考慮中だ. 【類】The scheme was then still ***on*** the *anvil*.

P² It was like an *anvil* ***upon*** a hammer. それはまるでハンマーにのせたかなとこだった(主客転倒だった).

anxiety, *n.* 不安, 心配; 渇望.

V ***allay*** the *anxiety* of ... ...の不安を軽減する. ¶***appease*** *anxiety* 気安めに言う. ¶it ***aroused*** (=***caused***) *anxiety* to ... それは...に心配を掛けた ‖ His condition continues to ***cause*** *anxiety*. あの人の容体は引続き憂慮すべき状態にある. ¶***display*** *anxiety* 心配を色に出す. ¶***drown*** one's *anxiety* in ... ...で気を紛らす. ¶Producers ***evince*** more *anxiety* to sell. 製造家は売りあせりをしている. ¶***experience*** *anxiety* 心配をする. ¶He ***expressed*** his *anxiety* for his son's welfare. 息子の幸福を願っていると言った. ¶***feel*** horrible *anxiety* ばかに心配する. ¶***leave*** an *anxiety* from a person 人の心配を一掃する. ¶a considerable *anxiety* is ***manifested*** here regarding ... このへんでは...に関してよほど憂慮されている. ¶It ***occasioned*** me much *anxiety*. それで大層心配になった. ¶***undergo*** *anxiety* 心配する.

V² *anxiety* constantly ***deepened*** いよいよ募った不安.

Q a source of ***constant*** *anxiety* 不断の心配の種. ¶***domestic*** *anxiety* 家事上の心づかい. ¶live in a condition of ***dreadful*** *anxiety* concerning... ...について戦々きょうきょうとして暮す. ¶***grave*** *anxiety* has been felt by ... on account of ... ...のために一方ならず心を悩ました. ¶with ***palpitating*** *anxiety* 不安に胸をとどろかせて. ¶***pecuniary*** *anxiety* 金銭上の心配. ¶cause ***terrible*** *anxiety* to ... ...に恐ろしく心配をかける. ¶I know an ***undefined, lurking*** *anxiety* about ... ...では私はばくとした心の悩みを覚えている. ¶That's an ***unnecessary*** *anxiety*. そんな心配はいらない. ¶***well-founded*** (=***well-grounded***) *anxiety* 正当の理由ある(無理もない)心配. ¶***wide-spread*** *anxiety* 世人一般の人々の憂慮.

P have no reason ***for*** *anxiety* 心配する理由がない. 【類】There is no ground ***for*** *anxiety*. ¶I was relieved ***from*** an *anxiety*. [心配がなくなって]ほっと一息ついた. ¶***in*** my *anxiety* to do so そうしたいと思って. ¶It gave me a great deal ***of*** *anxiety*. それが私によほど心配をかけた. ¶fall a prey ***to*** *anxiety* 心配の犠牲になる. ¶he is afflicted ***with*** *anxiety* on the subject of ... 彼は...の問題を心配している. ‖ wait ***with*** *anxiety* for a doctor to come 医者の来るのを待ちわびる. 【類】***with*** great *anxiety*. ¶***without*** *anxiety* 心配なしに.

P^2 *anxiety* ***about*** (=***in regard to or concerning***) the future 未来の心配 ‖ give oneself *anxiety* ***about*** … …につい て心配する ‖ full of *anxiety* ***about*** … …について非常に心配して. ¶*anxiety* ***for*** the future 将来の心配.【類】*anxiety* ***for*** any one's safety ‖ His *anxiety* ***for*** knowledge deserves our praise. あの人の知識欲は賞賛に値する.

anxious, *a.* 心配する, 気になる; 切望する.

P I am very *anxious* ***about*** the result of the examinations. 試験の結果が非常に気になる.【類】I am *anxious* ***about*** his health (welfare, safety). / His extravagance makes me feel *anxious* ***about*** him. / I am so *anxious* ***about*** my wife and children. ¶We are really *anxious* ***for*** peace. われわれは真に平和を希望している.【類】I am *anxious* ***for*** the prize. / I am *anxious* ***for*** a change. ¶He was *anxious* ***on*** the tariff question. 彼は税率問題を気にしていた. ¶Parents are *anxious* ***to*** (=***for***) the welfare of their children. 両親は子供たちの幸福を切望している.

O He was *anxious* to do his duty. 彼は義務の履行に腐心していた.【類】He is *anxious* to gain your confidence. / I am *anxious* to know the result.

anybody, *n.* だれか.

V He seems trying to ***ape anybody*** he thinks great and wonderful. 彼はだれでも偉い人すばらしい人と見るとまねをしようとするようだ.

Q some ***unknown*** (***obscure***) *anybodies* 名もない連中.

anything, *pron., n., ad.* 何か.

V he refused to ***do anything*** further with … 彼はそれ以上…と関係しない. ‖ I shall not ***do anything*** of the kind. そんな事は決してしない. ‖ Can I ***do anything*** for you this morning, sir? 何を差上げげましょうか(店員など). ‖ he cannot ***do anything*** with … 彼は…を持て余している.【類】I would ***do anything*** in the world for your sake. ¶He ***gets*** me ***anything*** I like. あの人は何でも私が欲しいものを買ってくれる. ¶He declined to ***have anything*** to do with the affair. 彼はその件に関係することは断った. ‖ ***Have*** you *anything* to say to me? 何か私に言うことがあるか. ¶Do you ***know anything*** about astronomy? 天文学のことは御存じですか. ¶***make anything*** out of … …から得を取る. ¶Do you ***remember anything*** about the affair? あの件について何か覚えているか. ¶No one will ***say anything***. だれも何とも言いやしない. ¶I don't ***see anything*** of him. 彼はどこへ行ったかさっぱり見当らない.【類】Really I don't ***see anything*** dishonorable in the procedure.

P ***before anything*** else 何はさておき. ¶***for anything*** and everything どうしても ‖ ***for anything*** I know 私の知っている所では. ¶***like*** (=***as***) ***anything*** 大いに.【類】He praised me ***like anything***. ¶cannot write English ***with anything*** like credit ろくに英文も書けない.

P^2 Was there ***anything about*** it in the newspaper? それが新聞に何とか出ていたか. ¶Did he give you ***anything besides*** the letter? 手紙の外に何か渡したか. ¶It is ***anything but*** cheap. 安いどころではない.【類】His manners are ***anything but*** pleasant. / He is ***anything but*** a chatterbox. (おしゃべり). ‖ I will do anything for you ***but*** that. その外の事なら何んでもして上げる. ¶He does not like ***anything like*** labor. 彼は少しでも骨の折れることをいやがる. ¶If he is ***anything of*** a gentleman, he will pay the money. いやしくも紳士なら払うだろう.

apart, *a., ad.* 離れて; 離して, 別として.

M He stood ***far apart*** from me. 僕からずっと離れて立っていた. ¶It was set up about ***six feet apart***. 六フィート離して建てられた. ¶***widely apart*** in ability 能力の点で段違い ‖ He had a pair of gray eyes, set ***widely apart*** あの人の目は灰色で間がひどく離れている.

P live ***apart from*** other people 他の人々と別居する ‖ consider a question ***apart from*** others 一問題を他問題と離して考える.【類】They have a hobby ***apart from*** their ordinary work. ‖ ***apart from*** this このことは別として.【類】***apart from*** joking=joking apart (=aside) / ***Apart from*** his imprudence (無分別), he has been very unfortunate. / Our greatest foe, ***apart from*** indifference, is ignorance.

apartment, *n.* [一戸分の]アパートの室; 《英》貸部屋; *pl.* アパート.

V ***hang*** an *apartment* with pictures (drapery) 絵画(など)を室にかける. ¶***hire*** a furnished *apartments* 家具付のへやを借りる. ¶***take*** (=***engage***) an *apartment* 間借りを約束する.

Q ***palatial*** *apartments* 壮麗なアパート. ¶a ***roomy*** *apartment* 手広いアパートのへや. ¶a ***sleeping apartment*** 寝室. ¶***furnished*** or ***unfurnished*** *apartments* 造作付あるいは造作なしのアパート. ¶an ***apartment to let*** 貸間.

Q^2 a ***hotel apartment*** ホテル式アパートのへや.

P a suite ***of*** *apartments* 続きべや.

P^2 "*Apartments* ***for*** Rent"《米》「貸室あり」(アパートの). ¶an *apartment* ***on*** the first floor《英》二階のへや;《米》一階のアパートのへや.

apathy, *n.* 冷淡.

V ***throw off*** their *apathy*, and show renewed interest in … 冷淡な態度を捨てて…に一層興味を持つ.

Q ***political*** *apathy* 政治に対する冷淡.

Q^2 ***election*** *apathy* 選挙に対する無関心.

P^2 The *apathy* ***of*** the people ***toward*** the war worried the Government. 政府は国民が戦争に無関心であることを苦慮した. ¶He has an *apathy* ***to*** food. 食物を欲しがらない. ¶*apathy* ***toward*** good 善に対する無関心.

ape, *n.* さる.

Q^2 He's a ***Minnesota*** *ape*. あいつはミネソタの山ざるさ.

aperture, *n.* 穴.

P^2 an *aperture* ***for*** admitting light 明り取り.

apex, *n.* 頂上.

P^2 the *apex* ***of*** earthly honor 現世栄誉の極み ‖ the other *apex* ***of*** the triangle その三角関係のもう一人の相手.

aping, *n.* 真似事.

Q ***mere*** *aping* ほんのまねごと.

apologist, *n.* 弁護者.

P^2 an *apologist* ***for*** slavery 奴隷制度擁護論者.

apologize, *v.* 言訳する, わびる.

M *apologize* ***civilly*** for … 丁寧に…をわびる. ¶***deeply*** *apologize* 幾重にもおわびをする. ¶***humbly*** *apologize* to you for … …ことはまことにすまない. ¶He *apologized* ***unreservedly***. 彼はひら謝りに謝った.

P *apologize* ***for*** rudeness (fault, mistake) 無礼(など)を謝する.【類】I must *apologize* ***for*** my lateness. ‖ They set the meal before him *apologizing* ***for*** its quality. 何にもありませんがと申訳をしながら食事を出した.【類】I must *apologize* ***to*** you ***for*** not soon replying to the letter. ¶I must *aplogize* ***to*** you ***for*** coming so late. ¶*apologize* ***with*** a good (bad) grace いさぎよく(渋々)わびる.

apology, *n.* 言訳, わび, 謝罪; 弁解.

V ***accept*** the *apologies* tendered わびを容れる ‖ I cannot ***accept*** the *apology*. 承知できない. ¶***demand*** an *apology* from … …の謝罪を要求する. ¶in writing to ***express*** his *apologies*, he said … わび手紙の中に彼は…と述べた. ¶***give*** an *apology* for a dinner ほんの申訳の食事をすゝめる. ¶She ***has*** an *apology* for a nose. 彼女にはほんの申訳ばかりの鼻がついている. ¶I ***made*** an *apology* for my lateness. 遅刻をわびた.【類】he ***made*** no *apology* for … / Even if it is a mistake it is proper that he should ***make*** an *apology*. ¶little *apologies* are ***needed*** for … …に対して弁解の必要がほとんどない. ¶***offer*** an *apology* to … …にわびを入れる. ¶I ***owe*** you an *apology*. 貴下に申訳がない. ‖ ***owe*** my *apologies* to … for … …した事は…に対して相済まない. ¶***tender*** a profuse *apology* しきりにわびる.

Q tender my ***heartfelt*** *apologies* 心からおわび致します. ¶make a ***humble*** *apology* 低頭平身してわびる. ¶make an ***immediate*** *apology* さっそくわびる. ¶a ***lame*** *apology* つじつまの合わぬ言訳. ¶a ***mere*** *apology* for a dinner ごちそうとは名ばかりのもの.【類】a ***mere*** *apology* for soup. ¶There is ***no*** *apology* needed. 別段わびることはない. ¶a ***polite*** *apology* 丁寧なわび. ¶a ***poor*** *apology* for a painting 絵とは名ばかりのもの. ¶demand a ***public*** *apology* [新聞広告による]謝罪を要求する. ¶This is a ***sad*** *apology* for a hat. これはひどい帽子だ. ¶offer one's ***sincere*** *apology* for … …に対して心からわびる. ¶a ***written*** *apology* わび状.

P ***in*** *apology* he pleaded that … 申訳に彼は…と弁解した. ¶a letter ***of*** *apology* わび状. ¶***with*** *apology* to … …にははなはだ済まないが ‖ ***with*** many *apologies* 色々申訳をしながら.

P^2 an *apology* ***for*** one's fault 過失のおわび ‖ *apologies* ***for*** absence were received from … …から欠席の申訳を

言って来た ‖ Otherwise there is no *apology* ***for*** its being. さもなくばその存在の理由がない. 【類】only an *apology* ***for*** the real thing. ¶an *apology* ***to*** the guest for ... ...に対する客への申訳.

apoplexy, *n.* 卒中.

Q ***cerebral*** *apoplexy* 脳いっ血. ¶***simple*** *apoplexy* 卒中.

Q² ***heat*** *apoplexy* 熱射病.

P He had a fit ***of*** *apoplexy.* 彼は卒中を起した. ‖ a stroke ***of*** *apoplexy* 卒中.

apostasy, *n.* 〖宗〗背教.

P² *apostasy* ***from*** the Christian faith キリストからの離脱.

apostate, *n.* 背教者.

P² an *apostate* ***from*** faith 背教者. ¶an *apostate* ***from*** Christianity ***to*** Buddhism キリスト教から仏教への転教者.

apostate, *a.* 背教した.

P a man *apostate* ***from*** a creed 信教にそむいた人.

apostatize, *v.* 信教にそむく.

P *apostatize* ***from*** Christianity キリスト教にそむく. ¶He *apostatized* ***to*** Islam. 回教に転教した.

apostle, *n.* 使徒; 主義宣伝者.

P² a great *apostle* ***of*** plain living and high thinking 生活は質素に思想は高尚にという生活の大使徒(実行者). 【類】an *apostle* ***of*** temperance (禁酒).

apostrophe, *n.* アポストロフィ; 〖修辞〗頓呼(とんこ).

P² an *apostrophe* ***to*** physicians 医師連への檄(げき). 【類】an *apostrophe* ***to*** the duty (virtue).

appal[l], *v.* 驚かす.

P I was *appalled* ***at*** the sight of ... ...を見てびっくりした. 【類】He was *appalled* ***at*** the prospect.

apparatus, *n. sing & pl.* 器械, 装置.

V ***install*** wireless *apparatus* on board 船内に無線電信(または電話)機を備え付ける.

Q a ***chemical*** *apparatus* 化学器械. ¶disturbances of the ***digestive*** *apparatus* 消化器の故障. ¶simple experiments requiring only ***inexpensive*** *apparatus* 費用のかからぬ装置で出来る簡単な実験. ¶an ***electric*** *apparatus* 電気装置.

Q² a ***cooling*** *apparatus* 冷房装置. ¶***diffusion*** *apparatus* 蔗糖搾出器. ¶***distilling*** *apparatus* 蒸留装置. ¶a ***drying*** *apparatus* 乾燥器. ¶an ***electric lighting*** *apparatus* 電燈装置. ¶a ***feeding*** *apparatus* 給水器. ¶a ***fire[-fighting]*** *apparatus* 消火器. ¶***gasmaking*** *apparatus* ガス製造装置. ¶a ***heating*** *apparatus* 暖房装置. ¶***lifesaving*** *apparatus* 救命用具. ¶liners equipped with ***long-distance wireless*** *apparatus* 長距離無線装置のある定期船. ¶a ***radio receiving*** *apparatus* ラジオの受信機. ¶a ***record-making*** and ***record-playing*** *apparatus* 録音兼用プレーヤー. ¶a ***sterilizing*** *apparatus* 殺菌装置. ¶a ***ventilation*** (=***ventilating***) *apparatus* 換気装置.

apparel, *n.* 衣服, 服装.

V ***discard*** one's *apparel* 衣服を脱ぎ捨てる.

Q ***glistening*** *apparel* きらめく衣裳. ¶appear in ***striking*** *apparel* 奇抜な服装で出る.

Q² ***maternity*** *apparel* 妊産婦服. ¶***sports*** *apparel* 運動着. ¶the ***gala spring*** *apparel* for outings 春の外出用の晴着. ¶***men's wearing*** *apparel* 男の衣類. 【類】cheap articles of ***wearing*** *apparel.* ¶the ***wedding*** *apparel* of animals 動物の婚礼衣裳(交尾期が近づいて体色が美しくなりつやを増した状態).

P ***in*** decent *apparel* 見苦しからぬ服装をして.

apparel, *v,* 装う, 着衣させる.

M a person ***gaily*** *appareled* はでな服装をした人. ¶He is ***gorgeously*** *appareled.* 華美な服装をしている.

P ships *appareled* ***for*** sea 艤装した船. ¶He is *appareled* ***in*** white (silk). 彼は白(など)の衣服を着ている. ¶trees *appareled* ***with*** flowers 花を着けた樹木 ‖ *apparel* one ***with*** gorgeous dress 華美な衣服を着せる.

apparent, *a.* 明白な; 皮相の.

M ***incontestably*** *apparent* 論をまたずして明白な. ¶The difficulty is ***more*** *apparent* than real. その困難は想像であって実際にはないのだ. ¶***strikingly*** *apparent* 明々白々な.

P His guilt is *apparent* ***in*** every act to all observers. すべての行いから見てあの男の有罪はだれの目にもハッキリ分る. ¶This is a fact which is *apparent* ***to*** any one. これは何人にも明白な事実だ. ‖ Prince Humbert, the heir *apparent* ***to*** the throne of Italy イタリア皇太子ウムベルト一殿下.

appeal, *n.* 控訴, 上告; [世論などへの]訴え; 哀訴.

V ***address*** an *appeal* to ... ...に訴える. ¶***disregard*** the most pitiful *appeals* of the human soul 人類の最もいたましい哀訴を無視する. ¶An *appeal* may be ***had*** to ... ...に訴えてよい. ¶***hear*** criminal *appeals* on matters of law 法律問題に関して刑事[問題]の訴えを聴く. ¶***institute*** an *appeal* 控訴する. ¶I ***lodged*** (=***entered***) an *appeal* against the decision. 判決に対して控訴した. ¶***make*** a great *appeal* to ... ...に大変受ける ‖ ***make*** an *appeal* to arms (force, violence) 武力(など)に訴える. 【類】An *appeal* should be ***made*** to common sense (charity). / ***make*** an *appeal* to a higher court ‖ the magazine ***making*** its *appeal* to a popular rather than purely literary audience その雑誌の対象は純文学的読者よりもむしろ一般大衆だ ‖ ***make*** an *appeal* for contributions 寄付金を募る. 【類】An *appeal* is ***made*** for £100,000 to erect new engineering laboratories for the University. / An *appeal* is being ***made*** for funds to restore the grave, which is in a very dilapidated (破損) state. / ***make*** an *appeal* for sufferers by flood. ¶The Red Cross Fund *appeal* was ***oversubscribed*** by 22.5 per cent. 赤十字の基金募集が 22.5 パーセントだけ申込超過になった. ¶The work ***presents*** an irresistible *appeal* to people of all shades of political thoughts. その本はそれぞれ政見を異にしている人々が読んで非常におもしろい. ¶***resist*** the *appeals* of his appetite (飲酒家などが)食欲を制する. ¶***take*** an *appeal* from a lower to a higher court 下級裁判所から上級裁判所へ控訴する. ¶The *appeal* has been ***thrown out.*** 控訴は棄却になった.

Q a ***direct*** *appeal* 直訴(じきそ). ¶a strong ***dramatic*** *appeal* 強く劇的に人心に訴えること. ¶the ***esthetic*** and ***artistic*** *appeal* of skyscrapers 摩天楼の審美的芸術的魅力. ¶The play can make but a ***faint*** *appeal* to Western minds. その劇は西洋人には余り受けない. ¶have ***feminine*** *appeal* 女に受ける. ¶the ***final*** *appeal* 最後の手段. ¶make a ***friendly*** *appeal* to ... ...の友誼に訴える. ¶This is my ***humble*** *appeal* to the nation at large. これは一般国民に対する私の謙虚な訴えです. ¶made an ***immediate*** *appeal* to the fancy of the novelty-loving Parisian 新奇を好むパリ人の気持にぴったり投合した. ¶an ***incidental*** *appeal* 《法》附帯上訴. ¶Al Jolson, a singer of ***international*** *appeal* 世界的に人気のある歌手アル・ジョルソン. ¶its ***irresistible*** *appeal* to the senses その五感への強い訴え. 【類】an ***irresistible*** *appeal* to mountaineers. ¶make only a ***languid*** *appeal* 迫力が乏しい. ¶The career of the merchant is the one that has the ***largest*** *appeal* to him. 彼は何でも実業家になろうと考えている. ¶be of ***little*** *appeal* to the present-day audience 現代の聴衆に訴える力が弱い. ¶The music has not ***much*** *appeal* for me. その音楽は私には余りぴんと来ない. ¶in ***mute*** *appeal* 無言の中に哀願をこめて. ¶a ***pathetic*** (=***touching***) *appeal* いじらしい哀願. ¶make ***personal*** *appeal* to several men of wealth 数名の資産家に直接哀願する. ¶it rivals ... in ***popular*** *appeal* それは一般の受けでは...に負けない. ¶A ***public*** *appeal* was made for funds. 資金を公けに募った. ¶an ***urgent*** *appeal* made by ... ...からの切なる依頼. ¶a ***whining*** *appeal* 泣声の哀願. ¶a book of ***wide*** *appeal* 広く受ける書物. ¶a subject of ***wide-spread*** *appeal* 広く人気を呼んでいる問題. ¶make a ***worldwide*** *appeal* 満天下に訴える.

Q² the "***box-office*** *appeal*" of a film 映画の興行(収入)価値. 【類】The play has no ***box-office*** *appeal.* ¶an ***eye*** *appeal* 目から見た魅力. ¶It has a ***heart*** *appeal* to every person of humanity and sympathy. その中には慈悲深い同情心のある人々の心に訴えるものがある. ¶a ***radio*** *appeal* ラジオを利用して世間に訴える事. ¶***sales*** *appeal* 販売の面から見た魅力. ¶emanate a ***sex*** *appeal* 性的魅力を発散する ‖ have strong ***sex*** *appeal.*

P ***by*** *appeal* to her reason 彼女の理性に訴えて. ¶heartily respond ***to*** an *appeal* 心から哀願に応じる ‖ in response ***to*** the *appeal* for contributions 寄付金募集に応じて. ¶***without*** an *appeal* to arms 武力に訴えずに.

P² an *appeal* ***for*** aid 援助の依頼 ‖ set the *appeal* ***for*** argument 上訴事件を弁論に付する. 【類】an *appeal* ***for*** mercy / an *appeal* ***for*** money / an *appeal* ***for*** funds for a memorial / There is no *appeal* ***from*** its verdict (裁決). ¶There is no *appeal* ***from*** the decision of the Supreme Court. 最高裁判所の判決は上告ができない. ¶an *appeal* ***in*** first instance 控訴.

appeal, *v.* 訴える；控訴する，上告する；請う．

M *earnestly* ***appeal*** to ... いちずに...に訴える． ¶***forcibly*** *appeal* to ... 力強く...に訴える，非常に...の気に入る． ¶it *appealed* ***irresistibly*** to ... それがばかに...の気に入った． ¶*appeal* ***powerfully*** to the imagination 感興をそゝる，血を沸かす． ¶a sentiment which *appeals* ***profoundly*** to every Japanese heart どの日本人にも深い感動を与える感情． ¶*appeal* ***strongly*** to the popular imagination.

P *appeal* ***against*** a sentence (judgment, arbitration, decision) 宣告(判決，仲裁裁判，裁決)が不服で控訴する ‖ *appeal* ***against*** the decision of the lower court 下級裁判所の判決に対して控訴を起す．【類】The decision of the Supreme Court shall not be *appealed* ***against***. ¶*appeal* ***for*** the co-operation of all who are interested in the scheme その計画に共鳴する一般人士の協力を求める ‖ *appeal* ***for*** mercy (charity) 泣きを入れる ‖ *appeal* ***for*** funds 資金を募る ‖ *appeal* ***for*** redress 賠償の訴を起す． ¶*appeal* ***to*** a higher court 上級裁判所に訴える．【類】*appeal* ***to*** the Supreme Tribunal (最高裁判所) / *appeal* ***to*** the law ‖ *appeal* ***to*** arms (force) 武力(腕力)に訴える．【類】*appeal* ***to*** the sword / *appeal* ***to*** the eye / *appeal* ***to*** one's conscience / *appeal* ***to*** our fancy (想像力) ‖ *appeal* as often ***to*** the heart as ***to*** the head 知に訴えると同じくらい情にも感動を与える．【類】The book will *appeal* only ***to*** a very limited public. ‖ *appeal* ***to*** the best and not the worst in us われわれの劣情でなく最高の心情を動かす ‖ ***To*** them no good cause *appeals* in vain. いやしくも善事であればあの人たちは賛成する．【類】*appeal* ***to*** public opinion / *appeal* ***to*** the clemency of ... (...のなさけ) ‖ *appeal* less ***to*** the European sense of beauty 欧州人の美感には大して訴えない ‖ particularly *appeal* ***to*** the palate of foreigners とりわけ外人の口に合う．【類】*appeal* ***to*** low tastes / *appeal* ***to*** the vulgar taste (俗受け) ‖ The job rather *appeals* ***to*** me. かなりその仕事が好きだ． ‖ They *appealed* ***to*** him in vain ***for*** help. 彼に助けを求めてもむだだった．【類】The prisoner *appealed* ***to*** the judge for mercy. / *appeal* ***to*** the people ***for*** support.

appear, *v.* 見える，現われる，出る；世に出る；出頭する；...らしい．

M *appear* ***anonymously*** [新聞の小説などが]匿名で出る． ¶*appear* ***creditable*** 本当らしい． ¶*appear* ***far*** in the distance はるか遠方に現われる． ¶The magazine will *appear* ***fortnightly***. その雑誌は隔週発行される． ¶A few words of explanation *appear* ***necessary***. 少しく説明の必要があるようだ． ¶We expected him, but he ***never*** *appeared*. 彼を待っていたが来なかった． ¶These novels ***originally*** *appeared* in daily and monthly numbers. これらの小説はもと新聞雑誌に連載されたものだ． ¶It *appears* very ***plausible***. 至極もっともらしい． ¶They *appear* ***ragged***. 見すぼらしい． ¶it would *appear* quite ***reasonable*** that ... ...は実にもっともらしい． ¶after *appearing* ***serially*** in the magazine 雑誌に連載されてから． ¶*appear* ***strange*** to ... ...には変に見える． ¶Saleswomen are expected to *appear* ***well***. 女店員は服装をよくすることが期待されている． ¶He *appears* ***wise***. 彼は利口らしい．

P *appear* ***above*** the clouds 雲の上に現われる． ¶He will *appear* ***against*** me in court. 彼は私の反対側の弁護に出廷する． ¶*appear* ***among*** the first 一流の人物と伍す． ¶*appear* ***as*** Hamlet ハムレットに扮して登場する． ¶*appear* ***as*** witness 証人として出頭する．【類】The work *appeared* first ***as*** a serial in a newspaper (新聞に連載された). ¶The flag *appeared* ***at*** the masthead 旗が檣頭に掲げられた． ‖ *appear* ***at*** the door (meeting, lecture, the front) 戸口(など)に出る． ¶*appear* ***before*** the audience 演壇に立つ．【類】*appear* ***before*** the public / *appear* ***before*** the court (出廷) / *appear* ***before*** the footlights (脚光). ¶*appear* ***below*** the surface 表面下に現われる． ¶it *appears* ***by*** (=***from***) ancient records that ... 古い記録によれば...らしい ‖ as *appears* ***by*** (=***out of***) these records この記録で分る通り． ¶*appear* ***for*** the ceremony 式に列なる ‖ *appear* ***for*** the defendant 被告弁護のために出廷する． ¶it would *appear* ***from*** this that ... ...がこれで分るだろう． ¶*appear* ***in*** public 世間に出る ‖ My name does not *appear* ***in*** the list. 私の名が名簿の中に見えない． ‖ *appear* ***in*** person 自身出頭する ‖ *appear* ***in*** a court to answer a charge 訴訟の答弁に出廷する ‖ The artist did not *appear* ***in*** the field until several years later. その芸術家は数年後まで世間に出なかった．【類】articles *appearing* ***in*** the current issue ‖ The desire to *appear* well ***in*** the eyes of their fellows is a fundamental motive in all classes of the human race. 他人から好く見られたいというのが総ての階級の人間の根本動機をなしている． ‖ *appear* ***in*** print for the first time 始めて印刷になる(出版される). 【類】It has never *appeared* ***in*** print before. / The advertisement did not *appear* ***in*** yesterday's Nippon Times. / The article *appeared* pseudonymously (匿名で) ***in*** The Tatler. / This work *appears* ***in*** parts (分冊で). ‖ *appear* ***in*** an examination 試験に出る ‖ *appear* ***in*** full dress 正装で出る． ¶*appear* ***in behalf of*** ... ...に代って出頭する ‖ *appear* ***on*** the stage (platform) 舞台(など)に立つ ‖ *appear* ***on*** the scene (=spot) 現場に現われる ‖ so far as it *appears* ***on*** the surface 表面に現われたところでは ‖ *appear* ***through*** the mist 霧の中に見える． ¶St. Peter *appeared* ***to*** him on the eve of his feast. 聖ペテロがその節会の前夜に彼の前に現われた． ‖ He *appeared* ***to*** me ***in*** a dream. 彼は私の夢まくらに立った．【類】*appear* ***to*** him in a vision (まぼろし) ‖ *appear* ***to*** the eye 目に見える．【類】The Virgin *appeared* ***to*** a peasant girl. ‖ *appear* ***to*** a summons charging him with having ... ...罪の告発による召喚に応じて出廷する． ¶a ship *appearing* ***under*** the lee 風下に見える船． ¶*appear* ***upon*** the scene of history 史上に現われる．

O there *appears* to be no doubt about ... ...は疑いのないことらしい．【類】The plan *appears* to be a good one. / He *appears* to be ignorant of the fact. / He *appears* to be satisfied. / He *appears* to be well (ill, hot, cold). / He *appears* to have caught cold.

appearance, *n.* **(1)** 出現；発刊；出場，登場；出頭．

V ***delay*** its *appearance* for a twelvemonth その発行を十二カ月間延長する． ¶***enter*** an *appearance* 出頭する． ¶***make*** one's *appearance* 出頭する． ¶The journal ***makes*** its *appearance* once every two months. この雑誌は二カ月に一回出る．【類】He ***made*** his *appearance* as a historian. / when electricity ***made*** its first *appearance* in the realms of power and light (動力と光の世界に). ¶He failed to ***put in*** an *appearance*. 彼は顔を出さなかった．【類】He never ***put in*** an *appearance* again. / It was not long before he ***put in*** an *appearance*.

Q her ***farewell*** *appearance* [芸人などの]名残の出場． ¶The magazine ***made*** its first *appearance* in 1806. 同誌は 1806 年に創刊号を出した．【類】The Times made its ***first*** *appearance* in 1785 as the Daily Universal Register. / he made his ***first*** *appearance* in a volume entitled ... / made his ***first*** *appearance* (初お目見得) before the American public / he made his ***first*** *appearance* in journalism on the staff of ... ¶There is ***no*** *appearance* of him yet. 彼はまだ見えない． ¶the ***one thousandth*** *appearance* (=issue) of Blackwood ブラックウッド誌の第一千号発行． ¶***personal*** *appearances* in movie theaters [映画俳優の]映画館ごあいさつ． ¶He made his first ***professional*** *appearance* in musical comedy. 彼は初めて喜歌劇の本舞台を踏んだ． ¶***public*** *appearances* 公開の席への出頭． ¶Christianity made its ***second*** *appearance* in Japan shortly before the Restoration of Meiji. キリスト教は明治維新のちょっと前に再び日本に現われた． ¶The singer made her ***successful*** *appearance* at ... その歌手は...で評判をとった． ¶The policeman made a ***timely*** *appearance*. 折よく巡査がその場に来た．

Q[2] She made her first ***stage*** *appearance* in London. 彼女はロンドンで最初に舞台を踏んだ．

P Diseases ***at*** their first *appearance* are easily cured. 病気は治療が早いと容易になおる． ‖ ***at*** the *appearance* of the enemy 敵が現われると． ¶***on*** the first *appearance* 初めて現われるとき．

P[2] the *appearance* ***of*** his first book 彼の処女作の発刊 ‖ the *appearance* ***of*** a new power among the nations 列国間に新強国の出現．

(2) 外観；形勢，情況；容貌；体裁；現象．

V ***assume*** an outward *appearance* of happiness 表に幸福を装う． ¶***change*** the *appearance* of things 新生面を開く． ¶***fear*** the *appearance* of danger あぶなそうなのを恐れる ¶to ***give*** it the *appearance* of age 時代を付けるために，古く見せるために ‖ It ***gives*** the *appearance* of bronze.

青銅のように見える. ¶It has all the appearance of leather. 全く革のように見える.【類】The relic has an appearance of great age. / The streets have a gay appearance. / This monument has a fine appearance. ‖ He has an appearance of youthfulness below his age. 彼は年よりも若若しく見える. / He has the appearance of a rustic fellow (いなか者). ¶to impart an ancient appearance [骨とう品などを]古く見せるために. ¶improve the appearance of one's schoolroom 教室をきれいにする. ¶injure its appearance その体裁を損じる. ¶keep up appearances 人前を繕う; うわべを飾る.【類】keep up an appearance of good health. ¶liken his appearance to that of ... 彼の風采(ふう)を…に似ているとする. ¶trousers which have lost their trim appearance 形がくずれたズボン. ¶maintain the appearance of a gentleman 紳士の体面を維持する. ¶present a seedy or slovenly appearance みすぼらしく見える ‖ present a very attractive appearance 至極見てくれがよい ‖ present a most striking appearance 非常に目に付きやすい. ¶to produce the appearance of ... …と見せかけるために. ¶put on the appearance of honesty 正直らしく見せかける.【類】He put on the appearance of innocence (知らぬ顔). ¶ruin the appearance of ... …の美観を損じる. ¶save appearances 世間体をつくろう.

V^{2} Appearance belies one. 見かけは判断を誤る. ¶So far as the appearances go, things are prosperous. 見た所では万事好都合にいっている. ¶appearances indicate that ... …の模様(形勢)がある.

Q to give it an appetizing appearance うまそうに見せるために. ¶an artistic appearance 芸術的な外観. ¶an attractive appearance 美しい外観. ¶present a rather awkward appearance ちょっとぎこちない(困った)様子をする. ¶The streets have a busy appearance. 街(まち)はにぎやかに見える. ¶An armchair gives the study a comfortable appearance. 安楽いすは書斎を居心地よく見せる. ¶a man of commanding appearance 堂々たる風采(ふう)の人. ¶Appearances are often deceitful. 見掛けというのは余り当てにならない. ¶this deceptive appearance of robust health 見掛け倒しの壮健. ¶of dignified appearance 威厳のある様子の. ¶doubtful appearances 疑わしい形勢. ¶There is every appearance of rain. どうも降りそうだ. ¶in external appearance 外観は. ¶a life of false appearances いんちきの生活 ‖ assume a false appearance 見せ掛ける. ¶favorable appearance 首尾がよさそうな情勢. ¶at first appearance 最初見た所では. ¶gay appearance はでな様子. ¶general appearance 大体見た所. ¶genteel appearance 優雅な風情. ¶make a good appearance 身なりをととのえる.【類】a man of good appearance / good appearance—a step toward success. ¶a grotesque appearance 奇怪な風貌. ¶handsome appearance 美貌. ¶have a healthy appearance 健康そうに見える. ¶a woman of imposing appearance 押出しのりっぱな婦人. ¶mellow appearance 古色. ¶natural appearance 自然現象. ¶neat appearance 清楚(そ)な風采 ‖ give the room a neat appearance へやをきちんと見せる. ¶There is no appearance of fine weather (rain). 天気がよく(悪く)なりそうな模様は更にない. ¶a man of noble appearance 風采の高雅な人. ¶present an odd appearance 変に見える. ¶put in an opportune appearance 折よく顔を出す. ¶though a woman in outward appearance 見た所では女のようだが ‖ judge ... from outward appearance …を外観で判断する ‖ to all outward appearance どう見ても. ¶a gem of pearly appearance 真珠のように見える玉. ¶be attentive to one's personal appearance 身だしなみがいい. ¶present a picturesque appearance 絵のように美しい. ¶a ship of pleasing appearance 見て気持のよい船. ¶He made a poor appearance at the meeting. 集会の席で彼は不体裁だった. ¶according to present appearances 現在の形勢によると. ¶a man of the most pretentious appearance ばかに気取った風の男. ¶a man of respectable appearance きちんとした(見苦しくない)身なりの人. ¶clothes having a shabby appearance 見すぼらしく見える衣服. ¶a shapely appearance 良いかっこう. ¶give a slipshod appearance だらしなく見える. ¶smart appearance 気のきいた体裁.【類】The hat gives the wearer a much smarter appearance. ¶a sorry appearance あわれな姿. ¶a gentleman of stylish appearance しゃれた紳士. ¶when appearances are suspicious 見掛けが怪しいと. ¶tardy appearance おくればせの出頭. ¶threatening appearance けわしい形相(天候など). ¶present a rather ugly appearance 少し体裁が悪い. ¶His appearance is uncouth. 風采が無骨だ. ¶be of undignified appearance 風采があがらない. ¶unfavorable appearances 不利な形勢. ¶present a very untidy appearance 非常にだらしなく見える.

Q^{2} the business appearance 真剣な(抜目のない)態度.

P the reality which lies behind appearances 外観の背後に存する実在.

P^{2} appearance from the back 後姿 ‖ From the appearance of matters, I am inclined to think that things will turn out unfavorable to us. こんな情況から推すと形勢が結局われわれに不利になると考えたくなる. ¶In appearance it is a very strong building. 見た所堅固な建築だ. ‖ different in appearance 外観の違った.【類】elegant in appearance / He has improved in appearance. / He is like a wolf in appearance. / His wife is ordinary in her appearance. (きりょうは十人並). ‖ not prepossessing in appearance 見た所人好きのしない. ¶To all appearances, he is healthy. どう見ても彼は健康体だ.

P^{2} He has the appearance of an Italian. 彼はイタリア人らしい. ‖ have the appearance of being half-starved 餓死でもしそうに見える ‖ This gives the appearance of probability to rumor. これから察するとうわさがもっともらしく思われる. ‖ it has every appearance of being ... どう見ても…らしい ‖ It has all appearance of leather. 見たところ本物の皮と変らない.

appease, *v.* なだめる.

P appease a person by kindness 深切で人をなだめる. ¶appease a person with the present 贈物で人をなだめる.

appellation, *n.* 名称.

V He obtained for him the well-merited appellation of the Prince of Booksellers. 彼が書林王の名を得たのは当然だ. ¶Japan has received many poetical appellations. 日本は色々な詩的名称を付けられた. ¶On account of its wealth of art collections, Dresden has won for it the appellation of the "German Florence." 美術収集品に富んでいるのでドレスデンは「ドイツのフロレンス」という異名をとった.

Q a posthumous honorific appellation 戒名.

P under some appellation ある名称のもとに.

append, *v.* 添える, 付ける.

M we append below a list of ... 次に…の表を添える.

P append an M.D. to one's name 名に「医学博士」の肩書を付ける ‖ append notes to a book 本に注を付ける.【類】append an index to a book / append a seal to a document (書類) / append a tag (荷札) to a trunk.

appendage, *n.* 付属物.

P^{2} an appendage of an integral part 全体の一部. ¶an appendage to a book 本の付録.【類】These museums are appendages to universities and colleges.

appendant, *a.* 付属の.

P appendant to something ある物に付帯する.

appendix, *n.* 付録.

V add an appendix to a book 本に付録を付ける.

P with an appendix on verbs 動詞に関する付録を加えて.

P^{2} appendices to a dictionary 辞書の付録 ‖ printed as an appendix to the present volume 本書の付録として印刷に付した.

appertain, *v.* 属する.

P a house and everything appertaining to it 家屋ならびに一切の付属物.

appetite, *n.* 食欲, 肉欲; 欲望; 好み, 趣味.

V appease the appetite of a baby 赤ん坊の空腹をとめる. ¶arouse an appetite in a person for ... …に対する欲望を起させる. ¶diminish the appetite 食欲を減じる. ¶feel an appetite 空腹を感じる. ¶A brisk walk will give you an appetite. 急いでお歩きになれば腹がへるでしょう. ¶have no appetite 食欲がない. ¶improve the appetite 食欲を増進する. ¶He indulged his appetites. 彼は我欲をほしいままにした. ‖ indulge one's appetite to excess 過食する. ¶lack appetite 食欲がない. ¶lose one's appetite 食欲を失う. ¶moderate appetites for ... …に対する欲望を和げる. ¶pamper one's appetite 飽食する. ¶prepare the appetite for dinner ごちそうをいただくために腹をすかしておく. ¶provoke the appetite 食欲を起させる. ¶quicken the ap-

petite 食欲を進める. ¶***satisfy*** one's *appetite* 食欲を満足させる. ¶***sharpen*** (=***stimulate or excite***) the *appetite* 食欲を促す. ¶***subdue*** the *appetite* 情欲を制する. ¶***take away*** the *appetite* 食欲を失わせる. ¶***tempt*** lazy summer *appetite* 夏のだらけた食欲をそそる. ¶***whet appetite*** 食を進める ‖ ***whet*** his *appetite* for stamp collecting 彼の切手収集欲を強める. ¶***work up*** (=excite) an *appetite* 食欲を促す.

V² *My appetite* ***fails***. 食欲がない. ¶His *appetite* ***fell off***. 彼の食欲は減退した. ¶The *appetite* ***improves***. 食欲が増して来る.

Q have a ***bad*** (=***poor or dull***) *appetite* 食が進まない. ¶provoke the ***carnal*** *appetite* 性欲を起させる. ¶have a ***delicate*** (=***feeble or weak***) *appetite* 食欲が少ない. ¶the control of ***fleshly*** *appetites* and desires 肉欲の抑制. ¶***Gargantuan*** *appetites* 旺盛な食欲. ¶He has a ***gigantic*** *appetite* and eats gigantic meals. あの男は大食家でものすごく食う. ¶I wish you a ***good*** *appetite*. 十分召上れ. ¶the ***grosser*** *appetite* of the body みだらな肉欲 ‖ the satisfaction of one's ***grosser*** *appetites* 劣情の満足. ¶I had a ***hearty*** *appetite* for ... ...が食べたくてたまらなかった. ¶He had an ***insatiable*** *appetite* for the marvellous. 彼は非常に珍らし物好きだ. ¶a sort of cayenne to a ***jaded*** *appetite* 食欲不振に対する一種の薬味. ¶I had a ***keen*** *appetite*. 食欲が旺盛だった. ¶***moderate*** *appetite* for ... ...に対する欲望を和らげる. ¶I had ***much*** *appetite*. 大分腹が減っていた. ¶have a ***sharp*** *appetite* for ... ...は大好物だ. ¶The *appetite* is ***small***. 食欲が少ない. ¶He has a ***strong*** *appetite*. 彼は食欲が盛んだ. ¶a giant of ***vast*** *appetite* 大食家. ¶He has a most ***voracious*** *appetite* for knowledge. 彼は知識欲が旺盛だ.

Q² ***sea*** *appetite* 船に乗ると増す食欲.

P loss ***of*** *appetite* 食欲喪失. ¶a man ***with*** a small *appetite* 少食の人 ‖ He ate it ***with*** the *appetite* of sturdy health. 彼は盛んに平げた. 【類】***with*** the *appetite* of a shark ‖ eat ***with*** a hearty *appetite* うまがって食べる.

P² *appetite* ***for*** food 食欲 ‖ an *appetite* ***for*** arts (knowledge) 芸術(知識)欲 ‖ as a historian, with an *appetite* ***for*** facts 歴史家の立場から事実の正確を求めて ‖ an *appetite* ***for*** scandal 人の悪口に対する興味. 【類】his *appetite* ***for*** writing. ¶have the *appetite* ***of*** a shark ふかのような食欲がある ‖ the *appetite* ***of*** sex=sexual appetite 性欲 ‖ the *appetite* ***of*** young people ***for*** English literature 英文学に対する青年の興味.

applaud, *v.* ほめそやす; 拍手かっさいする.

M be ***heartily*** *applauded* 感心してかっさいされる. ¶He was ***loudly*** *applauded*. 彼は盛んに拍手かっさいされた. ¶He was ***vociferously*** *applauded*. やんやと拍手かっさいされた.

P He was *applauded* ***by*** the audience. 彼は聴衆に拍手かっさいされた. ¶We *applauded* him ***for*** his courage. われわれは彼の勇気を賞賛した. ¶*applaud* ***with*** the hands 拍手する.

applause, *n.* かっさい, 賞賛.

V Generous (=unstinted) *applause* was ***accorded***. 盛にかっさいされた. ¶***ensure*** (=win) *applause* of the world 世界の賞賛を勝ち得る. ¶***excite*** (=***elicit, draw forth, evoke, catch or command***) *applause* かっさいを博する. ¶***give*** *applause* かっさいする. ¶***receive*** much *applause* 多大の賞賛を博する. ¶***seek*** popular *applause* 大衆の賞賛を得んと努める. ¶***shout*** *applause* 大声でかっさいする. ¶*Applause* was ***showed*** upon him. 彼はかっさいを浴びせられた. ¶***win*** *applause* かっさいを博する.

V² The *applause* ***thundered forth***. かっさいは雷のように響き渡った.

Q His speech elicited ***enthusiastic*** *applause*. 彼の演説は熱烈な喝かっさいを博した. ¶The performance met with ***general*** *applause*. 演技は満場のかっさいを博した. ¶the ***ignorant*** *applause* of the multitude 民衆の盲目的賞賛. ¶***subdued*** *applause* 控え目にしたかっさい. ¶He retired after ***tumultuous*** (=***loud or thunderous***) *applause*. わくが如きかっさいを博して退場した. ¶amid ***uproarious*** *applause* 大かっさい裡に. ¶a ***vociferous*** *applause* 盛んなかっさい. ¶receive ***warm*** *applause* after each number 一番終るごとに熱烈なかっさいを受ける. ¶The curtain was rung down amidst ***whirling*** *applause*. わくが如きかっさい裡に幕が下りた.

Q ***amid*** wild *applause* 割れるような拍手かっさいのうちに. 【類】The curtain fell ***amid*** the *applause* of the audience. ¶a burst ***of*** *applause* にわかに起ったかっさい ‖ The speech was received with hearty rounds ***of*** *applause*. 聴衆はその演説に対し繰返し繰返し熱心にかっさいした. ‖ a shout ***of*** *applause* 歓声 ‖ There was a storm ***of*** *applause*. かっさいわくが如くであった. ¶greet (=receive) him ***with*** *applause* かっさいして彼を迎える ‖ The hall echoed ***with*** *applauses*. 満場割れるような拍手かっさいだった.

apple, *n.* りんご.

V The *apples* have been ***acclimatized*** in this country. りんごの木はこの国の風土に馴化した. ¶***bite*** an *apple* between them 一つのりんごを二人で食べ合う. ¶***deserve*** the *apple* for beauty 美人コンテストで王座を占める価値がある. ¶***halve*** an *apple* りんごを半分に割る. ¶***pare*** an *apple* りんごの皮をむく. ¶He ***pocketed*** some *apples*. あの男はりんごを二つ三つポケットにねじ込んだ.

Q ***cooked*** *apples* 焼きりんご. ¶***green*** *apple* 未熟のりんご. ¶a ***measly-looking*** *apple* 赤いはん点のあるりんご. ¶a beautiful ***red*** *apple* 美しい赤りんご. ¶***red-cheeked*** *apples* 真赤なりんご. ¶***sour*** *apples* すっぱいりんご. ¶***windfallen*** *apples* 落ちたりんご. ¶***withered*** *apples* しなびたりんご.

Q² ***cider*** *apples* りんご酒用のりんご. ¶***cooking*** *apples* 料理用りんご. ¶***eating*** *apples* 食用りんご.

P² She was brought up like the *apples* ***of*** my eye. 彼女を掌中の玉と育てた.

appliance, *n.* 器具, 設備; 応用.

Q ***delicate*** *appliance* of science 科学用の精密機械類. ¶The building is equipped with the latest ***fire-extinguishing*** *appliances*. その建物には最新の消火器が備え付けてある. ¶***mechanical*** *appliances* 機械. ¶the use of ***modern*** *appliances* 現代式器具の使用. ¶***sanitary*** *appliances* 衛生用具. ¶***scientific warlike*** *appliance* 科学応用の兵器. ¶***space-destroying*** *appliances* 場所を取る器具.

Q² ***fire-fighting*** *appliances* 消防器具. ¶***first-aid*** *appliances* 応急手当用具. ¶***gas defense*** *appliances* 防毒器具. ¶***household*** *appliances* 家庭用品. ¶***labor-saving*** *appliances* 労力節約器具 ‖ ***labor-saving household*** *appliances* 労力を省く家庭用品. ¶***life-saving*** *appliances* 救命諸用具. ¶***paper-making*** *appliances* and machinery 製紙用品及び機械. ¶***safety*** *appliances* 安全用具. ¶***salvage*** *appliances* 海難救助用具. ¶a ***timesaving*** *appliance* for ... ...のための時間節約用品.

P The hotel is fitted up ***with*** modern *appliances*. そのホテルの設備は現代式だ.

P² the *appliances* ***of*** science ***for*** the purpose その目的への科学の応用. ¶the *appliance* ***of*** chemistry ***to*** manufacture 工業における化学の応用.

applicable, *a.* 適用される.

P That regulation is not *applicable* ***to*** this case. その規則はこの場合に適用されない. 【類】the same remark is *applicable* ***to*** ...

applicant, *n.* 志願者; 研究家.

V ***winnow*** *applicants* for admission 入学志願者を考査する.

Q a ***close*** *applicant* 熱心な研究家. ¶***rejected*** *applicants* はねられた志願者. ¶There are ***several*** *applicants* for the agency. 代理店志望者が数人ある.

Q² a ***job*** *applicant* 求職者. ¶***screen*** *applicants* 志願者を選衡する.

P² *applicants* ***for*** membership 入会志願者 ‖ *applicants* ***for*** office 就職志願者.

application, *n.* (1) 申込, 志願; 申込書, 願書.

V The school is now open for ***accepting*** *applications* from students. その学校は目下生徒募集中である. ¶*applications* should be ***addressed*** to the Secretary of ... 願書は…幹事あてに提出すべし. ¶***file*** a formal *application* for permission 正式の願書を提出する ‖ *Applications* are ***filed*** in order of their receipt. 申込書は受付順にとじ込んである. ¶***fill out*** (=***in***) an *application* 願書に書入れをする. ¶***grant*** an *application* 申込を容れる. ¶***hand in*** written *applications* 願書を差出す. ¶***invite*** *applications* for the professorship of ... ...教授の職に対し人を招聘(しょうへい)する. ¶***lodge*** an *application* with ... ...に願書を提出する. ¶***make*** *application* for membership 入会を申込む ‖ An *application* has been ***made*** to the Government for an official sanction. 政府に許可を出願した. 【類】***make*** *application* either in writing or by word of mouth (文書か口頭で) / I hereby ***make*** *application* to you for .... / *Applications* are to be ***made*** in writing. ¶Applicants wishing to sit together should ***pin*** their *applications* ***together.*** 席を並べる希望の方は申込書をピンで留めて置いて下さい. ¶***postpone*** its *application* その適用を延期する. ¶The university is prepared to ***receive*** *applications* for admission. 大学は入学志願の取扱を開始した. ¶***refuse*** an *application* 申込を拒む. ¶He ***sent in*** his *application* to the office. 彼は事務所へ願書を出した. ¶*applications* may be ***sent in*** up to ... 申込は...日までは受付ける. ¶***sign*** an *application* for a place 採用願に署名する.

Q You are advised to make ***early*** *application.* 申込は早い方がよい. ¶for ***external*** *application* [薬の]外用. ¶a ***formal*** *application* 正式の申請. ¶His *application* is ***hopeless.*** 彼の申込は望みがない. ¶I made ***immediate*** *application.* 早速申込んだ. ¶***indiscriminating*** *application* of a rule しゃくし定規. ¶be of ***limited*** *application* 応用の範囲が限られている. ¶the ***local*** *application* of a remedy 局所治療. ¶Science has a wealth of ***practical*** *application.* 科学は多くの方面に応用がきく. ¶***successful*** *application* of constitutional government 憲政運用の妙. ¶an ***unsuccessful*** *application* for a raise (=rise) in pay 昇給要求の不成立. ¶send in a ***written*** *application* 願書を提出する.

Q² ***Membership*** *applications* may be obtained on request from the secretary. 入会申請書は幹事に請求すればもらえる.

P ***by*** *application* to ... ...へ申込んで, ...に頼んで ‖ it may be obtained ***by*** personal *application* at ... ...へ自身申込めばもらえる. ¶a form ***of*** *application* 出願書式. ¶it may generally be obtained ***on*** *application* at ... 普通...へ申込めばもらえる. 【類】A list of publications is sent free ***on*** *application* at the office or to the Secretary of the Museum. 出版目録は事務所または博物館主事へ申込めば無料で送付される ‖ Estimates free ***on*** *application.* 見積りは申込により無料で作製する. 【類】A prospectus (規則書) will be forwarded ***on*** *application.* ¶we are ***under*** *application* from ... for it ...からその申込を受けている. ¶***upon*** the *application* of ... ...の請求あり次第. 【類】It can be renewed ***upon*** a new *application.*

P² make *application* ***at*** the British Consulate 英国領事館に出願する. 【類】by *application* ***at*** the Custom House. ¶*application* ***for*** employment 就職の申込 ‖ an *application* ***for*** a loan of ... ...の借用申込 ‖ Early *application* ***for*** a passage should be made. 乗船申込は早いがよい. 【類】100 *applications* ***for*** one position (=vacant place) / *application* ***for*** permission to compete must be made on or before June 1, on forms that be obtained from ... / *application* ***for*** aid ‖ *application* ***for*** enrollment in a school 入学出願 ‖ *Application* ***for*** second class entry is pending. 第二種郵便認可出願中. ¶in response to *application* ***from*** ... ...よりの請求に応じて. ¶An *application* ***to*** that effect will be filed with the ... office. その旨の出願は...局あてに提出すべし.

(**2**) 応用, 適用; 貼(ちょう)用.

V ***justify*** the literal *application* of the term この語の文字の適用を正当とする. ¶***limit*** the *application* to be made of it その適用の範囲を制限する. ¶***maintain*** a uniform *application* of the regulations 規則を平等に適用するようにする.

O a medicine for ***external*** *application* 外用薬. ¶a rule of ***general*** *application* 一般適用の規則. ¶***internal*** *application* [薬の]内服用. ¶a ***judicious*** *application* of praise and blame 賞罰の適用よろしきを得ること. ¶a ***poor*** *application* of a good method 良法の応用よろしきを得ないこと. ¶make a ***practical*** *application* of the principles その原理を実地に応用する. 【類】***practical*** *applications* of research / make ***practical*** *application* of one's knowledge. ¶Give your skin a ***thorough*** *application.* すっかり皮膚に塗付けなさい. ¶No rules of ***universal*** *application* can be given. 一般的応用の法則は挙げられない. ¶It is of very ***wide*** *application.* 応用が極めて広い. ¶He made a ***wrong*** *application.* 適用を誤った.

P The pain was removed ***by*** this *application.* この薬をつけたので痛みが取れた. ¶It is true ***in*** a far wider *application.* それはもっと広汎な応用の場合に当てはまる. ‖ universal ***in*** *application* 応用の広い. 【類】It is wanting ***in*** *application.* ¶a broadening ***of*** its *application* [蓄音機などの]応用範囲が広くなること.

P² *application* ***of*** a principle ***to*** practice 原理の実地応用. 【類】the *application* ***of*** science ***to*** industry / The Philosophy of Science is an *application* ***of*** the scientific method ***to*** philosophy. / the *application* ***of*** natural forces ***to*** the service of man (自然力の利用) through machines.

(**3**) 勤勉, 努力.

Q a man of ***close*** *application* 努力家 ‖ a student of ***close*** *application* せっせと勉強する学生. ¶the ***diligent*** *application* of national energies to peaceful pursuits 国民精力の平和. ¶***intense*** *application* to study 熱心な研究. ¶***mental*** *application* 精神的努力. ¶***persistent*** (=***steady, earnest*** or ***untiring***) *application* 不断の勤勉. ¶He has ***wonderful*** *application.* 驚くべき努力家だ.

P ***By*** *application* to his work he got a better job. 仕事に精出したので位置が上がった. ¶diligent ***in*** *application* 勤勉な. ¶A registration fee of 10*s.* 6*d.* must be sent ***with*** the *application* for admission to the course. 10シリング6ペンスを同科入学の登録料として送付されたい.

P² *application* ***of*** justice in society 社会正義を行うこと.

apply, *v.* (**1**) 当てはまる; 適用する, あてる.

M *apply* ***aptly*** よく当てはまる. ¶a word ***commonly*** *applied* to ... 通例...に用いられる言葉. ¶the term is ***contemptuously*** *applied* to ... この言葉は軽蔑的に...に適用される. ¶these words ***fitly*** *apply* to ... これらの言葉はぴったり...に当てはまる. ¶words *applied* ***literally*** 文字通りに用いられた言葉. ¶be *applied* ***opprobriously*** to ... 侮辱の意味で...に用いられる. ¶the word is ***popularly*** *applied* to ... その語は通常...に適用される. ¶be ***satirically*** *applied* to ... 諷刺的に...に用いられる. ¶a person to whom the following description could be ***truthfully*** *applied* 次の人相書きがぴったり当てはまる人. ¶*apply* ***unerringly*** 間違なく適用する. ¶It *applies* very ***well*** in this case. この場合によく当てはまる.

P English *applied* ***in*** technical writing 専門方面の文に用いる英語. ¶*apply* it ***to*** the ear それを耳にあてる ‖ It does not *apply* ***to*** this case. それはこの場合には当てはまらない. ‖ the same *applies* ***to*** ... ...の場合も同様だ. 【類】*apply* a word ***to*** an idea different from common sense / *apply* a rule ***to*** ... / streamline (流線形) *applied* ***to*** ... / *apply* it ***to*** various (practical) uses ‖ He *applied* the money ***to*** his own use. その金を自分用にあてた. 【類】It was *applied* ***to*** the payment of debts. ¶*apply* money (=funds) ***toward*** ... 金銭を...にあてる. ¶this *applies* ***with*** special force in the case of ... これは...の場合に特に当てはまる. ¶if mechanically *applied* ***without*** reference to varying circumstances 種々の事情に関係なく機械的に適用すれば.

(**2**) 申込む, 出願する.

M I ***hereby*** *apply* for the enrolment of my name on your books. 小生氏名の御記帳のことここに申込みます(入会の時など). ¶This house is to let; *apply* ***next door.*** 貸家一御用の方は隣家にお申込下さい. ¶*Apply* ***personally.*** 自身お申込下さい. 【類】*apply* either ***personally*** or in letter. ¶*Apply* ***within.*** 当家にお申込下さい.

P For further particulars, *apply* ***at*** the following address. 詳細は次の場所に申込まれたい. 【類】*Apply* ***at*** the office. / *apply* ***at*** the address given. ¶*Apply* ***by*** letter. 書面にてお申込下さい. ¶*apply* ***for*** admission to ... ...へ入会(または入学)を申込む. 【類】About 100 persons have *applied* ***for*** the appointment (=position). / *apply* ***for*** the post of private secretary ‖ *apply* ***for*** the right to use the New York Public Library ニューヨーク公立図書館の使用許可を申請する ‖ *apply* ***for*** the authority to issue a loan 公債発行を当局に申請する. 【類】*apply* ***for*** payment / *apply* ***for*** membership in a society ‖ Accommodations should be *applied* ***for*** as much in advance as possible. へやはなるべく前約になさるがよい. ‖ *Apply* ***in*** your own handwriting. 自筆にてお申込ありたい. ‖ *Apply* ***in*** person. 自身お申込下さい. ‖ You should *apply* ***in*** the proper quarter. その筋へ申込なさい. ‖ *Apply* ***to*** the address given above. 上記の宿所へお申込下さい. 【類】*apply* ***to*** the agent. ¶*apply* ***to*** ... ***for*** aid ...に補助を依頼する. 【類】I *applied* ***to*** him ***for*** information. / *apply* ***to*** the Consul ***for*** a passport.

(**3**) 当てる, 塗る.

M *apply* mentholatum ***liberally*** (=***freely***) メンソラを十分に塗る.

P *apply* it ... *as* a poultice それをあん法薬として...塗る. ¶*apply* a match *to* gunpowder 火薬にマッチをつける ‖ *apply* the hand *to* the ear 耳に手を当てる ‖ *apply* the varnish *to* the surface 表面にニスを塗る.

(**4**) 身を入れる, 専心する.

M He *applied* himself ***closely*** to the study of English. 英語の勉強に専心した. ¶He *applied* himself ***diligently*** to classics. 彼は孜々(し)として古典研究に没頭した. 【類】 *apply* oneself ***perseveringly*** to the task of ... 一生懸命...の仕事に専心する. ¶*apply* oneself ***wholly*** and ***indefatigably*** to ... うまずたゆまず...に全精力を打込む.

P *apply* oneself (=one's mind) *to* one's studies 研究に没頭する.

appoint, *v.* (**1**) 任命する; 指名する; 指定する.

M ***officially*** *appointed* 政府の定めた; 正式に任命された. ¶***temporarily*** *appointed* as ... ...として臨時に任命される.

P He was *appointed* ***as*** one of the committee. 彼は委員に挙げられた. 【類】 he has been *appointed* ***as*** the agent ***for*** the sale of ... / has been *appointed* ***as*** representative ***for*** ... / it is for the time being *appointed* ***as*** substitute for (の代りに)... ‖ ... was *appointed* ***as*** the day ***for*** the conference [何月何日]を会議の日に決めた. ¶The member was *appointed* ***by*** the Emperor. その議員は勅選である. ¶His intended bride died on the morning *appointed* ***for*** the wedding. 彼の新婦となるはずだった人は結婚式当日の朝死んだ. ‖ *appoint* a place and time ***for*** the meeting 会合の場所と時日を取りきめる ‖ time *appointed* ***for*** making tenders 入札期日 ‖ A judicial officer is *appointed* ***for*** life. 法官は終身官である. ¶He was *appointed* professor ***in*** the University. その大学の教授に任ぜられた. ¶was *appointed* ***on*** the Atomic Bomb Casualties Commission 原爆傷害調査委員に任ぜられた. ¶He was *appointed* ***over*** his contestants. 彼は競争者を追いのけて任命された. ¶They *appointed* him ***to*** a high office. 彼を高官に任じた. 【類】 He was *appointed* ***to*** this post. / the post ***to*** which each man is *appointed* / He was *appointed* ***to*** a university chair.

O They *appointed* Nelson admiral. ネルソンを海軍大将に任じた. 【類】 He was *appointed* Mayor of Tokyo. ¶He *appointed* me to come at one o'clock. 彼は私に一時に来るように言った.

(**2**) 設備する.

M In all respects the hotel is most ***elegantly*** and ***comfortably*** *appointed*. そのホテルは設備万端雅味豊かに気持よくできている. ¶a room ***finely*** *appointed* 設備のよいへや. ¶a ***luxuriously*** (=***lavishly***) *appointed* hotel 設備のぜいたくなホテル. ¶a ***magnificently*** *appointed* (=equipped) laboratory 設備の完備した実験所(室). ¶The house is ***miserably*** *appointed*. この家の設備はなっていない.

appointment, *n.* (**1**) 任命; 職; 指定.

V ***accept*** (=***agree to***) the *appointment* 任命を受諾する. ¶The Ambassador Hotel System ***announced*** the *appointment* of Mr. ... as manager of the Hotel Alexandria, Los Angeles, from the first of May, 1920. アムバサダー・ホテル系では一九二〇年五月一日より...氏をロスアンジェルスのアレキサンダー・ホテル支配人に任命の由を発表した. ¶***approve of*** the *appointment* to the office of ..., vacant by the resignation of ... ...氏辞職のため欠員になっていた...職に任命の件を認可する. ¶***decline*** an *appointment* 任命を辞退する. ¶***distribute appointments*** それぞれの位地に人を分配する. ¶***get*** an *appointment* 任命される, 就職する. 【類】 He ***got*** a good *appointment* in the civil service (文官). / I ***got*** an *appointment* through his good office (彼のつてで). ¶He was constrained by ill health to ***give up*** this *appointment*. 病気のため止むを得ずこの職を辞した. ¶He ***has*** an *appointment* in the Foreign Office at present. 今外務省に勤めている. 【類】 He ***has*** a small *appointment* about the Palace (宮中で). ¶He ***holds*** an *appointment* under Government. 彼は官職に在る. 【類】 He ***held*** that *appointment* for two years. / He successfully ***held*** the *appointment* as a treasurer. / He ***holds*** his *appointment* for life (終身官). / He ***holds*** an interim (=a temporary) *appointment* (臨時雇). / ***hold*** the *appointment* of secretary. ¶***lose*** one's *appointment* 免職される. ¶The following *appointments* have been ***made*** at the Home Office. 内務省で次の任命があった. ¶***obtain*** an *appointment* 就職する. 【類】 He ***obtained*** his *appointment* at Waseda. / increase your chances of ***obtaining*** a junior *appointment* (下級社員) with a good business house. ¶he ***received*** an *appointment* in the public service, as consul at ... ...領事を拝命した. 【類】 ***receive*** an *appointment* from his alma mater (母校) ‖ ***received*** the *appointment* of Gifford Lecturer to the University of Edinburgh for 1899–1901. 1899年から1901年までエディンバラ大学ギッフォード講師に任ぜられた. ¶He has ***resigned*** his *appointment* as the city engineer of Leeds. リーズ市技師の職を辞した. ¶He ***secured*** the *appointment* of professor of English literature in the University. その大学の英文学教授に任命された. ¶***take up*** an *appointment* 就任する. ¶***throw up*** one's *appointment* 職をなげうつ. ¶***withdraw*** an *appointment* 任命を取消す.

Q His first ***diplomatic*** *appointment* was that of Minister to France. 彼の最初の外交方面の任命はフランス公使であった. ¶The ***following*** *appointments* have been made at the Foreign Office. 外務省で次の任命があった. ¶He has a ***good*** *appointment* in a firm. 某社でりっぱな役を勤めている. ¶get a ***handsome public*** *appointment* りっぱな公職に就く. ¶a ***highly paid*** *appointment* 高給の職. ¶a ***lucrative*** *appointment* 身入りの好い役. ¶a ***misfit*** *appointment* 不適当な役. ¶he held a ***similar*** *appointment* for years with Mr. ... 彼は数年...氏と同役だった. ¶an undersecretary of ***special*** *appointment* 理事官. ¶The *appointment* is quite ***suitable***. それは適任だ.

Q² a poorly paid ***government*** *appointment* 薄給官吏の職. ¶a ***life*** *appointment* 終身官.

P ***according to*** *appointment* 命により. ¶A. & F. Pears Ltd., soapmakers ***by*** *appointment* to Their Majesties the King and Queen 王室御用石けん製造業ペアーズ商会. ¶Several candidates presented themselves ***for*** an *appointment*. 数名が採用を願い出た. ¶The Rev. Robert Morrison, ***under*** *appointment* by the London Mission, reached Canton in September, 1808. ロンドン伝道会から任命されたモリスン師は一八〇八年九月広東に着いた. ¶***without*** an *appointment* 無任所.

P² his *appointment* ***to*** the professorship 彼の教授拝命 ‖ an *appointment* ***to*** the Foreign Office 外務省入り.

(**2**) 約束.

V ***break*** an *appointment* 約束通りに来ない. ¶***fix*** an *appointment* 会合の時と所を決める. ¶He ***followed*** my *appointment*. 僕の言付けを守った. ¶***fulfil*** an *appointment* punctually 几帳面に会見約束を果す. ¶***keep*** one's *appointment* with ... ...と会合の約束を守る ‖ No sign of him yet! I do like a man to ***keep*** an *appointment*. 彼はまだやって来ない, 僕は約束を守る人が好きなんだ. ¶***lose*** one's *appointment* by the delay of train 汽車が遅れたので約束の時間に後れる. ¶I ***made*** an *appointment* to see him [on] Sunday. 日曜に彼と会う約束をした. 【類】 They ***made*** an *appointment* for the second day of March. / I ***made*** an *appointment* to see him in my office at a certain hour. / An *appointment* was ***made*** for the following morning. / ***make*** an *appointment* with a friend. ¶***Remember*** your *appointment* at the dentist's tomorrow. あす歯医者へお出でになる約束をお忘れないように.

Q reminders of ***daily appointments*** 日々の約束の心覚え. ¶seek an interview without ***previous*** *appointment* 打合せをしておかないで会見を求める.

Q² have a ***business*** *appointment* 商売上の会見の約束をしている. ¶keep a ***speaking*** *appointment* [会見などの]口約束を守る.

P I called ***by*** *appointment* at the home of ... あらかじめ打合せをして...氏宅を訪問した. 【類】 ***by*** *appointment* in advance ‖ a meeting ***by*** *appointment* 約束の会合 ‖ Private lessons ***by*** *appointment*, ¥3,000 per hour. 時間指定の個人教授一時間三千円のこと.

P² I have an *appointment* ***for*** five in the evening. 今夕五時に会合の約束がある.

O *Appointments* to wait upon customers will receive prompt attention. 御用の節は時間を御指定下されば間違なく参上致します(洋服屋など).

(**3**) 装備, 設備.

Q ***sumptuous appointments*** 豪しゃな調度.

Q² ***hotel appointments*** ホテルの施設. ¶***table appointments*** 食卓用具.

apportion, *v.* 分配する.

P *apportion* ... ***according to*** numbers 数に応じて…を分配する. ¶*apportion* the property ***among*** the heirs 財産を相続人に分配する. ¶*apportion* ... ***between*** two claimants 二人の請求者に…を分配する. ¶*apportion* ***to*** each a fair amount 銘々に応分の額を分配する.

apposite, *a.* 適切な. 「場合に適切だ.
P This argument is *apposite* ***to*** the case. この議論はこの

apposition, *n.* 〖文法〗同格.
P² This noun is in *apposition* ***to*** the foregoing. この名詞は先の名詞と同格だ. ¶a noun in *apposition* ***with*** a pronoun 代名詞と同格の名詞.

appositive, *n.* 〖文法〗同格.
P² be an *appositive* ***of*** ... …の同格語である.

appraise, *v.* 評価する.
P *appraise* property (land) ***at*** ... 財産(など)を…と評価する. 【類】this estate is *appraised* ***at*** ...

appraiser, *n.* 鑑定人.
Q² a ***jewelry*** *appraiser* 宝石鑑定人.

appreciable, *a.* 判別できる.
P a difference *appreciable* ***to*** the eye 目で判別できる差異.

appreciate, *v.* (**1**) ありがたく思う; 鑑識する; 評価する.
M we would have *appreciated* it ***better*** if ... had ... ... が…して下さったならもっとありがたかったろう. ¶I ***deeply*** *appreciate* your kindness. 御親切に大いに感謝しております. ¶It can only be ***fully*** *appreciated* on the spot. そこへ行って初めて十分の鑑賞ができるのだ(記事や写真ではなかなか描写することはできない). ‖ do not *appreciate* ***fully*** what he means あの人のいう事のありがた味がよく分っていない. ¶Any suggestions you may make will be ***gratefully*** *appreciated*. どんな御注意でもありがたく存じます. ¶***highly*** *appreciate* his assistance 彼の助けをしみじみありがたく思う. ¶***keenly*** *appreciate* 非常にありがたく思う. ¶We have now ***much*** *appreciated* the gifts offered. もらった贈物を今では非常にありがたく思っている. ¶be ***rightly*** *appreciated* 正しく評価される. ¶They do not ***sufficiently*** *appreciate* their own country. あの人たちは自分の国のよい点がよく分っていない. ¶His great ability was ***universally*** *appreciated*. 彼の大手腕は一般に認められた. ¶be ***well*** *appreciated* 高く買われる.
P *appreciate* ... ***at*** its true value その真価で…を評定する. 【類】*appreciate* ... ***at*** its proper (full, just) value. ¶The ancients *appreciated* all knowledge ***by*** a high standard. 古人は知識をすべて高い標準で評価した. ¶I *appreciate* your kindness ***to*** the full. 御親切はしみじみありがたい.
(**2**) 騰貴する.
M Since the building of the new railway, real estate has ***rapidly*** *appreciated*. 鉄道ができてから不動産の値が急に出

appreciation, *n.* 鑑識; 認識; 鑑賞; 感謝. 「てきた.
V ***cultivate*** the *appreciation* of good music りっぱな音楽の鑑賞力を養う. ¶***deepen*** one's *appreciation* of ... …に対する認識を深くする. ¶truly ***deserve*** our warm *appreciation* 真にわれわれの深い感謝に値いする. ¶The reply ***evinces*** a shrewd *appreciation* of the circumstances. 返書の文面で先方が事情をよく了解していることが分る. ¶I wish to ***express*** my deep *appreciation* for ... …に対して深い感謝の意を表したい. 【類】I desire to ***express*** my *appreciation* of the numerous courtesies extended to me by ... / ***express*** my *appreciation* of the assistance rendered me by ... / take this opportunity to ***express*** our high *appreciation* of ... ¶He ***has*** a keen *appreciation* of a joke. しゃれの味がよく分る人だ. ¶***mark*** the *appreciation* of ... by ... …して…に対する感謝の意を表示する. ¶***promote*** the *appreciation* of Japanese arts and letters in the United States of America 北米合衆国における日本の美術及び文学に対する鑑識を助長させる. ¶desire to ***record*** my *appreciation* of ... …に対する感謝を記録にとめて置きたい. ¶***show*** one's *appreciation* of ... …に対する感謝の意を表する ‖ by way of ***showing*** *appreciation* 感謝の意を表する意味で ‖ The audience ***showed*** its *appreciation* by frequent bursts of laughter. 聴衆はそれがよく分り時時どっと笑った. ¶***voice*** one's *appreciation* 称賛する ‖ His speech ***voiced*** the *appreciation* of the guests of the day. 彼は当日の来賓側の満足を表明する演説をした.
Q his ***aesthetic*** *appreciation* of our literature 国文学に対する彼の審美的鑑識. ¶a ***better*** *appreciation* of the beauties of the country その国の美点の一層深い認識. ¶come to a ***full*** *appreciation* of its value その価値を十分に認めるようになる. ¶the ***growing*** *appreciation* which is steadily received 益々高まる好評. ¶a ***hearty*** *appreciation* 心からの鑑賞. ¶***honest*** *appreciation* いつわらざる鑑賞. ¶a ***keen*** *appreciation* of its importance その重要性のはっきりした認識. 【類】He has a ***keen*** *appreciation* of the students' needs. ¶***literary*** *appreciations* 文芸作品の鑑賞. ¶a ***nice*** *appreciation* of shades of meaning 意味の微妙な点の認識. ¶have a ***proper*** *appreciation* of ... …を本当に認めている. ¶It is meeting with the ***public*** *appreciation*. 一般に認められつつある. ‖ supported by ***public*** *appreciation* 公衆の認識に力を得て. ¶I deserve the most ***respectful*** *appreciation* 大いに認められる価値がある. ¶a ***sound*** *appreciation* of the facts of history 史実に対する正しい鑑識. ¶a ***true*** *appreciation* of ... …に対する真の認識. ¶a ***wider*** and more ***adequate*** *appreciation* of Japanese culture abroad 海外での一層広くかつ一層十分な日本文化の認識. ¶receive ***wider*** and ***better*** *appreciation* 一層広く一層よく認識される. ¶a ***wide-spread*** *appreciation* of his public services 一般が認める彼の国家·社会に尽した功労.
Q² a programme of ***music*** *appreciation* 音楽鑑賞の番組. ¶some ***press*** *appreciations* 新聞雑誌の賛辞二三.
P ***in*** sincere *appreciation* of his efforts to ... 彼の…に対する努力を心から認めて. ¶a letter ***of*** *appreciation* 感状. ¶His lecture was received ***with*** much *appreciation*. 彼の講演は大いに受けた. ‖ people ***with*** an *appreciation* of literature 文学の鑑識力を有する人々.

appreciative, *a.* 眼識のある. 「を知っている.
M they are ***deeply*** *appreciative* of ... 彼らはよく…の真価
P He is always *appreciative* ***of*** kindness. 彼は人から受ける親切をいつでも感謝の気持で受取っている.

apprehend, *v.* 会得する, 悟る.
M ***readily*** *apprehend* ... …を容易に会得する.
P It was *apprehended* ***at*** a glance ***by*** everyone. だれにも

apprehension, *n.* (**1**) 懸念, 不安. 「一目で分った.
V It might ***allay*** some of his worst *apprehensions*. それで幾分彼の最も深刻な不安が和らげられるかも知れぬ. ¶some *apprehension* was ***caused*** by ... …のため幾分不安に思われている. ¶***entertain*** *apprehensions* 懸念する. ¶It ***excited*** no little *apprehension*. それが少なからず不安の念を起させた. ¶***express*** grave *apprehension* as to ... …について大いに心配する. ¶grave *apprehension* ***is felt*** about ... …について大に心配している. ¶***have*** no *apprehension* of ... …を少しも心配しない. ¶***remove*** (=***dispel***) all *apprehensions* regarding ... …に関する一切の懸念を晴らす.
P he was ***in*** no small *apprehension* for ... 彼は…を少なからず心配した. ¶I was ***under*** great *apprehensions*. 私は非常に心配していた. ‖ ***under*** the *apprehension* that ... …せぬかと気づかって. 【類】***under*** no *apprehensions*.
P² *apprehension* ***of*** danger 危険がありはしまいかという
(**2**) 理解, 理解力. 「不安.
Q a ***correct*** *apprehension* 正解. ¶an ***intelligent*** *apprehension* 明察.
P It is ***beyond*** all *apprehension*. 一向訳が分らぬ. ¶***in*** our *apprehension* われらの見る所では. ¶a man ***of*** dull *apprehension* 理解力の鈍い人 ‖ quick ***of*** *apprehension* 理解力の鋭敏な.

apprehensive, *a.* 恐れている, 気づかっている.
P I am *apprehensive* ***for*** his safety. 彼の安否が気づかわれる. ¶He is *apprehensive* ***of*** danger. 彼は危険を恐れている. ‖ inmates who are *apprehensive* ***of*** committing violence or suicide 暴力や自殺の恐れのある収容者.
O he is *apprehensive* lest ... [should] ... 彼は…しないかと

apprentice, *n.* 徒弟, 見習生. 「懸念している.
V ***serve*** one's *apprentice* to literature 文士の下げいこをする. ¶***take*** *apprentice* 徒弟(内弟子)を置く.
Q a ***joiner's*** *apprentice* 建具屋の弟子. ¶a ***judicial*** *apprentice* 司法見習生.
P work ***as*** *apprentice* for ... …の弟子となる.
P² an *apprentice* ***in*** handicraft 手工業の徒弟. ¶*apprentices* ***to*** a printer 印刷屋の小僧. 【類】He is *apprentice* ***to*** a carpenter. / He was bound *apprentice* ***to*** a

apprentice, *v.* 徒弟にする, 見習に出す. 「merchant.
P He was *apprenticed* ***to*** an engraver. 彼は彫刻家の弟子になった. 【類】When he had finished his schooling at

twelve, he was *apprenticed to* a carpenter.

apprenticeship, *n.* 年期奉公, 見習, 弟子入り.

V ***commence*** one's *apprenticeship* to the art of angling 魚釣を始める. ¶***offer*** a good *apprenticeship* for a young author 青年作家には好い勉強になる. ¶She has ***served*** an *apprenticeship* to a milliner. 彼女は婦人帽子屋に年期奉公をした. 【類】***served*** his *apprenticeship* at a bookseller's / Japan ***served*** her *apprenticeship* to the older civilization of China. ¶He has not ***served out*** his *apprenticeship*. 彼は未だ年期が済まない. ¶He has ***undergone*** an *apprenticeship* of full seven years. 彼は満七年の年期を入れた. ¶How long will his *apprenticeship* ***last***? 彼の年期は何年か.

P ***after*** an *apprenticeship* on the staff of a newspaper office ある新聞社で下級記者を勤めた後. ¶He is not ***out of*** his *apprenticeship*. 彼の年期はまだすまない. ¶He is ***through*** his *apprenticeship*. 彼は年期が明けた. ¶the master ***under*** whom he served his literary *apprenticeship* 彼が文学の弟子入りをした先生. ¶He served his *apprenticeship* ***with*** a certain artist. ある画家の内弟子になっした.

apprise, *v.* 知らせる, 告げる.

P *apprise* him ***of*** his peril その人に危険を告げる. 【類】He *apprised* the general ***of*** the approach of the enemy. / I shall not fail to *apprise* ***of*** his arrival.

approach, *n.* 近寄り, 近接; 近似; 親近; 進路, 入口, とっつき; 言寄り.

V Heralds with trumpets ***announced*** the *approach* of His Excellency. らっぱを持った伝令使が間もなく閣下の臨場せられることを知らせた. ¶***begin*** one's *approaches* 渡りをつける. ¶a faint blush, that ***heralded*** the *approach* of dawn 黎明(れいめい)近しと知らせるかすかな赤らみ. ¶He ***made*** the first *approaches*. 彼の方から切出した. ¶***realize*** the *approach* of old age 老いの至るを覚える. ¶I ***repelled*** his *approaches*. 私は彼が持掛けて来るのをしりぞけた. ¶I ***saw*** his swift *approach*. 彼がぐんぐん近寄って来るのを見た.

Q make an ***amorous*** *approach* to ... ...に求愛する, 言寄る. ¶a ***fair*** *approach* to accuracy 正確に近いもの. ¶There are signs of a ***gradual*** *approach* to that ideal state of things. あの理想の状態に漸次接近する形勢が見える. ¶on a ***nearer*** *approach* it is discovered that ... もっと近寄ると...が分った ‖ the ***nearest*** *approach* to ... ...に一番よく似ているもの. ¶a ***scientific*** *approach* to the subject その問題の科学的考究. ¶make a ***sexual*** *approach*=court 口説く. ¶the ***stealthy*** *approach* of old age 知らぬ間に来た老いの坂. ¶a ***tactful*** *approach* 如才のない接近(依頼の件など).

Q^2 an ***impressionist*** *approach* 印象派的態度.

P ***at*** the *approach* of summer 夏が近づいたので. ¶He is difficult ***of*** *approach*. 彼は近づきにくい. ¶***on*** the *approach* of mild weather そろそろ時候がよくなると. 【類】***On*** the *approach* of death, he discovered the vanity of all human grandeur. ¶***with*** the *approach* of winter 冬の近づくにつれ ‖ I cannot foretell ***with*** any *approach* to accuracy. とても正確な予言などはできない.

P^2 the *approach* ***by*** road 道路による進入. ¶the *approach* ***of*** the traveller ***to*** the village 旅人の村への接近. ¶I never heard an *approach* ***to*** a murmur. 不平らしいことは何も聞いたことがない. ‖ live in some *approach* ***to*** decency どうやらこうやら人間らしい暮しをする ‖ an *approach* ***to*** perfection ほとんど完全なこと ‖ an *approach* ***to*** the human type [猿など]人間への近似. ¶an *approach* ***to*** the villa 別荘の入口. 【類】the *approach* ***to*** the city ‖ the *approach* ***to*** a bridge 橋のたもと ‖ Our *approach* ***to*** the general ***for*** an armistice ended in unconditional surrender on our part. 休戦の目的でその将軍に交渉を打ち込んだが結局当方の無条件降服になった.

approach, *v.* 近よる, 接近する; 近い, ほぼ等しい; [人に]近づく, 面接する.

M *approach* the history ***backward*** その歴史を倒叙する(年代を逆に). ¶I cannot pretend to *approach*, even ***distantly***, to the rapidity and accuracy with which he worked. 彼の働き方の迅速で正確なのには足許にもおっつけない. ¶The king was ***easily*** *approached*. 国王にたやすく拝謁ができた. ¶*approach* ***nearest*** to the requirements of the standard 規格の条件に一番近い.

P The monument is *approached* ***by*** steps. 記念碑へは階段を昇って行く. ¶*approach* him ***for*** information (advice, suggestion) 彼に問い合わせる(など). 【類】Owing to the death of his daughter, he could not be *approached* ***for*** an interview. ¶*aproach* ...***from*** the rear 背面から...に近づく. ¶I shall *approach* him ***in*** the matter. この事を彼に掛合いましょう. ¶The cat *approaches* ***to*** the tiger. ねこはとらに似ている. 【類】It *approaches* ***to*** excellence. ‖ He *approached* himself ***to*** the stove. 彼はストーヴに近寄った. ¶I saw a figure *approaching* ***toward*** me. だれか私の方へ近寄って来るのが見えた. ¶*approach* him ***with*** a request for ... ...の依頼のため彼に面接する ‖ He *approached* me ***with*** stealthy steps. 彼は抜足さし足で寄って来た. ‖ Those officials were *approached* ***with*** bribes. あの役人どもは鼻薬でその話を持込まれた.

O She is *approaching* womanhood. 彼女はもうじき大人だ.

approbation, *n.* 是認, 賛成, 得心.

V the scheme ***earned*** the *approbation* of ... その案は...の賛成を得た. ¶All present ***expressed*** their *approbation* of the work and promised assistance. 出席者全部この事業に賛意を表して助力を約した. ¶The actor ***gained*** hearty *approbation*. その役者は大受けだった. ¶They ***gave*** their enthusiastic *approbation*. 彼等は熱心にそれに賛成した. ¶he refused to ***grant*** his *approbation* of ... 彼は...を承知しなかった. ¶The proposal ***met*** his *approbation*. その提案は彼の賛成を得た. ¶***nod*** one's *approbation* 承知したとうなずく. ¶***secure*** public *approbation* 社会一般から認められる. ¶***win*** the *approbation* of ... ...の同意を得る.

P It was received ***with*** *approbation*. それは是認された.

P^2 *approbation* ***of*** conscience 良心の満足.

appropriate, *v.* 私用する, 流用する; 充当する.

P *appropriate* it ***for*** one's own use それを専有する(横領する). ¶*appropriate* money ***for*** an enterprise ある事業に金を支出する ‖ a spot of ground *appropriated* ***for*** a garden 庭にあてた一区域. ¶be *appropriated* ***from*** the national treasury 国庫から支出する. ¶The whole sum was *appropriated* ***to*** the support of his widow. 全額彼の未亡人の扶助料にあてられた. ‖ *appropriate* money ***to*** oneself 金を横領する ‖ *appropriate* public money ***to*** private purpose (=use) 公金を私消する.

appropriate, *a.* 適当の, 適切な.

M articles ***particularly*** *appropriate* for Christmas gifts クリスマスの贈答にはあつらえ向きの品. 【類】***particularly*** *appropriate* to the season. ¶***singularly*** *appropriate* 極めて適切な.

P a position *appropriate* ***for*** him あの人にうってつけの勤め口. ¶*appropriate* ***to*** (=***for***) the occasion その場合に適した. 【類】behavior *appropriate* ***to*** time and place.

appropriation, *n.* 支出, 経費.

V ***grant*** an annual *appropriation* of ... for 10 years 十年間年...の支出を承認する. ¶an *appropriation* of ... yen has been ***made*** by the city for ... 市は...に...円を支出した. 【類】A certain *appropriation* is ***made*** every year for public purposes. ¶***necessitate*** the *appropriation* of a sum of ... 金...円の支出を要する.

Q has no ***budgetary*** *appropriation* 予算がない. ¶***humanitarian*** *appropriations* 博愛事業としての支出(ヨーロッパの救済費). ¶***No*** *appropriation* for it can be made from the budget. 予算がない.

Q^2 increase ***advertising*** *appropriations* 広告費の支出を増額する. ¶***budget*** *appropriations* 予算支出. ¶urgent ***deficiency*** *appropriation* 緊急不足額支出. ¶a ***State*** *appropriation* of ... ...の国庫支出費. ¶$3,000,000,000 ***Treasury*** *appropriation* 30 億ドルの国庫支出.

P *appropriation* ***for*** schools 諸学校経費.

approval, *n.* 是認, 賛成, 嘉納.

V ***compel*** the *approval* of American public opinion 米国の世論をして賛同せざるを得ないようにする. ¶***conquer*** scientific *approval* 科学的に承認される. ¶***deserve*** *approval* 賞賛に値する. ¶***express*** one's *approval* for ... ...に賛意を表する. ¶The custom does not ***find*** much *approval*. この慣習は余り喜ばれない. ¶***gain*** the *approval* of ... ...の賛成を得る. ¶The association has ***given*** its official *approval* to the balls. 協会はその(テニスなどの)球を公認した. ¶We ***had*** his hearty *approval*. われわれは彼の熱心な賛成を得た. ¶The book continues to ***merit*** the *approval* awarded to former editions. この新版は旧版同様推奨に値する. ¶***nod*** one's *approval* 承認したとうなずく.

¶***obtain*** an *approval* 認可になる. ¶***put*** his *approval* in these words 次の言葉でその賛意を述べている. ¶***receive*** *approval* of ... …の賛成を得る ‖ ***receive*** universal *approval* 広く賛成される. ¶***seek*** the *approval* of one's own conscience 自分の良心に承認を求める. ¶***show*** one's *approval* toward ... …に対して賛意を示す. ¶***stamp*** *approval* on a programme 計画を承認する. ¶I am personally pleased to ***voice*** my *approval*. 私は個人として喜んで賛意を表明する. 【類】The president received many telegrams ***voicing*** *approval* of his new policy. ¶***win*** public *approval* 一般民衆の賞賛を博する. 【類】***win*** the enthusiastic *approval* of his hearers. ¶***withdraw*** *approval* from the revolutionary sentiments and measures 革命的思想ならびに方策に対する賛成を撤回する.

Q *conditional* *approval* 条件付承認. ¶We have sent you these goods on ***five day's*** *approval*. 品を御覧に入れますからお気に召しましたら五日間以内にお買上を願います. ¶win ***general*** *approval* 大衆の賞賛を博する. ¶It won ***high*** *approval*. それは非常に歓迎された. ¶meet with the ***hearty*** (=***warm***) *approval* 心からの賛成を受ける. ¶The new play won ***immediate*** *approval* from critics and audiences. 新作狂言は直ちに批評家および観客の賞賛を博した. ¶give ***official*** *approval* to ... …に正式の認可を与える. ¶win ***passing*** *approval* 一時的の賞賛を博する. ¶***popular*** *approval* 一般民衆の賞賛. ¶give a ***silent*** (=***tacit***) *approval* to ... …を黙認する. ¶view ... with ***strong*** *approval* ひどく感心して…を見る. ¶with a ***unanimous*** *approval* 満場一致で. ¶The goods met with ***unequivocal*** *approval*. その品は大好評を博した. ¶express one's ***unqualified*** *approval* 無条件に賛成する.

Q^2 ***House*** *approval* is expected this week. 今週国会の承認がありそうだ.

P forward documents ***for*** *approval* before signature 調印に先だって文書を送付する. ¶***on*** *approval* 点検売買の条件で ‖ sale ***on*** *approval* 点検売買(実物を見た上での売買). 【類】I send this to you ***on*** *approval*. ¶They are subject ***to*** your *approval*. ご覧の上御取きめを願いたい. ¶***with*** the *approval* of the Faculty Council 教授会の議を経て ‖ ***with*** the *approval* of the majority of ... …の過半数の同意を得て. ¶I hope this article will meet ***with*** your *aproval*. この品がお気に召せばよろしいと存じます. 【類】The new opera meets ***with*** general *approval*. ‖ The scheme did not meet ***with*** complete *approval*. その案は決定的賛成を得るに至らなかった.

P^2 *approval* ***of*** conscience 良心の満足.

approve, *v.* 賛成する, 是認する, 認可する.

M I can ***hardly*** *approve* of it. 賛成し兼ねる. ¶***heartily*** *approve* 衷心より賛成する. ¶I ***highly*** *approve* of it. 大いにわが意を得たりである. ¶***thoroughly*** *approve* of the aims of the association 会の目的には満腔(ｺｳ)の賛意を表する. ¶***unanimously*** *approve* 満場一致で賛成する.

P The policy was *approved* ***by*** the thought of the time. 当時の思想はその政策を是認した. ¶I *approve* ***of*** your choice. 御選定は結構です. ‖ Justice will not *approve* ***of*** it. それでは名義が立たない. 【類】I do not *approve* ***of*** your going out with him. ‖ Do you *approve* ***of*** ladies learning to dance? 婦人がダンス習うのをよいと思いますか. 【類】I affected to *approve* ***of*** the plan although I disliked it. / The French Government have *approved* ***of*** thoroughly modernizing the Paris telephone system (電話系統の現代化) at a cost of £400,000.

approximate, *a.* 近い.

M a statement ***closely*** *approximate* to a falsehood 全くうそに近い声明.

approximate, *v* …に近い.

M Olefiant gas ***closely*** *approximates* air. オレフィアントガスは空気によく似ている.

P The number *opproximates* ***to*** one thousand. その数は一千に近い.

approximation, *n.* 接近, 近似.

Q a ***close*** *approximation* 密接. ¶Only a ***rough*** *approximation* is required. ほんの概算だけでよい.

P estimate ***with*** some *approximation* to reality 幾分実際に近い見積をする.

P^2 *approximation* ***of*** the vegetable to the animal 植物と動物との類似. ¶*approximation* ***to*** the truth 真理への接近.

April-fool, *n.* 四月ばか.

V ***make*** an *April-fool* of ... …に四月ばかのいたずらをする.

apron, *n.* 前掛, 前だれ.

V ***wear*** an *apron* 前だれを掛ける.

Q a ***waterproof*** *apron* 防水エプロン.

Q^2 a ***shop*** *apron* [くつ屋などの]職人前掛.

P ***in*** *apron* 前だれ掛けで ‖ What have you ***in*** your *apron?* 前だれの中に何がはいっているの.

apropos, *ad.* 適切に, 都合よく.

M You speak ***quite*** *apropos*. 君の言うことは全く当を得ている. ¶He arrived ***very*** *apropos*. 大変都合よく彼は着いた.

P *apropos* ***of*** (=***to***) that affair その件に関して.

apt, *a.* 適当な; 適切の; …しやすい; 敏い.

M be ***dangerously*** *apt* to mislead beginners 初心者を誤らせる危険が大である. ¶It is a ***very*** *apt* remark. うまい言葉だ. ‖ they will be ***very*** *apt* to ... 彼らはとかく…し勝ちだ.

P He is *apt* ***at*** (=in) mathematics. 数学が得手だ. 【類】be *apt* ***at*** skating (fencing, martial arts) / He is *apt* ***at*** devising means / *apt* ***at*** learning=teachable. ¶He is *apt* ***for*** feats of strength. 力わざに適している. ‖ The ground is *apt* ***for*** the plow. この地は耕作に適する. ¶He is very *apt* ***in*** his studies. 非常に学問ができる. ¶He is *apt* ***with*** his instruments. 彼は道具の使い方がうまい.

Q He is *apt* to forget. 忘れっぽい. 【類】He is *apt* to catch cold. / He is very *apt* to learn. ¶He is the most *apt* of all pupils. 生徒中で一番できる.

aptitude, *n.* 適性; 傾向, たち; 才能.

V ***develop*** one's *aptitude* 適性を発揮させる. ¶he ***evinced*** an *aptitude* for ... 彼は…への適性を示した. ¶He ***found*** no *aptitude* to carry on the work of his father. 彼は父の業を継ぐに適していなかった. ¶Oil ***has*** an *aptitude* to burn. 油には燃える性質がある. 【類】He ***has*** an *aptitude* for language by nature. / ***have*** an *aptitude* for literary work / ***have*** no *aptitude* in that direction / He ***has*** little *aptitude* for a business career. ¶***possess*** a natural *aptitude* for ... 生来…に適している. ¶He ***showed*** an *aptitude* for mathematics. 彼には数学の才があった.

Q He possessed an ***extraordinary*** *aptitude* for calculation. 非常に計算の才があった. ¶combine the ***intellectual*** *aptitudes* of the bookworm with the physical vigor and athletic tastes that are desirable in soldiers 読書家という知的適性と軍人に望ましい体力と運動趣味を兼ね備える. ¶***mathematical*** *aptitude* 数学の才. ¶his ***natural*** *aptitude* for organization 彼の組織力. ¶he has a ***special*** (=***peculiar***) *aptitude* for ... 彼は特に…に長じている. ¶measure ***specific*** *aptitudes* of students 学生の特殊能力を調べる. ¶***vocational*** *aptitude* 職業適性.

Q^2 ***employment*** *aptitude* 職業上の適否.

aptness, *n.* 適合; 傾向, 素質.

P^2 *aptness* ***of*** things ***to*** their end その目的に対する事物の適性 ‖ *aptness* ***of*** iron ***to*** rust 鉄のさびやすい性質 ‖ *aptness* ***to*** vice 悪に染まりやすいこと.

Arab, *n.* 浮浪児.

Q^2 a ***street*** *Arab* 浮浪少年.

arbiter, *n.* 仲裁人; 裁決者.

Q the ***last*** *arbiter* 最後の裁決者(神).

P He acted ***as*** *arbiter*. 彼が仲裁をした. ¶an *arbiter* ***between*** the contending parties 紛争者間の調停者.

P^2 an *arbiter* ***of*** the dispute 紛議の調停者 ‖ God is the *arbiter* ***of*** our fate. 神がわれわれの運命を握っている.

arbitrate, *v.* 仲裁する.

P *arbitrate* ***between*** two persons 両人の仲裁をする. ¶He will *arbitrate* ***in*** this matter. 彼がこの件を調停するでしょう.

arbitration, *n.* 仲裁.

P It was settled ***by*** *arbitration*. それは仲裁で決った. ¶I asked ***for*** his *arbitration*. 彼に仲裁を頼んだ. ¶The matter will go ***to*** *arbitration*. その事件は仲裁に付することになるだろう. ‖ It was submitted ***to*** *arbitration*. それは仲裁に付された.

arbor, *n.* あずまや.

Q^2 a ***grape*** *arbor* ぶどうだな付園亭.

P girls ***under*** a wistaria *arbor* 藤だなの下の少女たち.

arcade, *n.* [屋根のある]商店街.

Q^2 a ***penny*** *arcade* 安物販売の商店街.

arch, *n.* アーチ.

P It is rested ***on*** 18 *arches*. 十八のアーチの上に乗っている. ¶The house is roofed ***with*** an *arch*. その家屋の屋根はアーチ状になっている.

arch, *v.* アーチ状にする; 弓形になる.

M The sky *arches overhead.* 空は頭上にアーチ状をなしている.
M² a road *arched over* with green branches 緑の枝のトンネルになっている道.

archaism, *n.* 古体.
V *archaisms embedded* in proverbs or well-known quotations ことわざや有名な引用句に残っている古文体.
Q *imitative archaism* [文章などの]擬古体.
P *Thou* and *ye* are now regarded *as archaism.*

archer, *n.* 弓の射手.
Q² one of the nation's *top women archers* その国で一流の婦人弓道家の一人.

architect, *n.* 建設者; 建築技師.
Q the *chief architect* of public opinion 世論の主たる建設者 ‖ Mr. Dulles was the *chief architect* of Japan's Peace Treaty. ダレス氏は日本の平和条約の生みの親だ.
Q² the *city architect* 市の建築技師. ¶a *landscape architect* 造園技師. ¶a *naval architect* 造船技師.
P² Man is the *architect of* his own future. 人間は自分の将来を自分で築き上げる者だ.

architecture, *n.* 建築; 建築術.
V *practice architecture* 建築業を営む.
Q *civil architecture* [軍事などに対し]普通建築. ¶*domestic architecture* 住宅建築. ¶*marine architecture* 造船術. ¶*military architecture* 築城術. ¶*molten architecture*=music 音楽. ¶*naval architecture* 造船術. ¶*secular architecture* [寺院などに対し]普通建築. ¶*wooden architecture* 木造建築.
Q² *Buddhist architecture* 寺院建築. ¶built in *foreign style architecture* 洋風建築の. ¶*landscape architecture* 造園術. ¶*Renaissance architecture* ルネサンス式建築.

archive, *n.* 公文書.
V *grub up archives* never ransacked before これまで手を着けていない公文書を研究する.
P Records of each meeting are made for file *in* the Club's *archives.* 会ごとに記録を作ってクラブの書類中に保存する. 【類】The *archives of* the Department are stirred to the bottom. その省の文書を残りなく詮索した.

archway, *n.* 拱(きょう)道.
V Venerable oaks *form* a sylvan *archway.* 神々しいオークの樹で森の拱道ができている.

ardor, *n.* 熱情, 熱心, 鋭気.
V *awake* one's *ardor* 熱意を喚起する. ¶It has not *cooled* his *ardor* in the cause of the people. それは人民の味方としての彼の熱情をさましはしなかった. ¶*damp* one's *ardor* 気をくじく. ¶This *destroyed* or at least *chilled* his *ardor* for further effort. このためにそれ以上努力しようとする彼の熱意を全然なくさせてしまうとまでは行かなくとも少くとも冷却させた. ¶*fire* the *ardor* of youth 青年の血を沸かす. ¶eager to do something to *show* the *ardor* of their faith 彼らの信仰の熱情を見せるような事をしたい気持でいっぱい. ¶*whet* the *ardor* of ... ...の熱情をあおる.
Q an *inextinguishable ardor* 抑えがたい熱心. ¶*missionary ardor* 布教熱. ¶*patriotic ardor* 愛国的熱情. ¶*strenuous,* even *ludicrous, ardor* 精力的でばかげたといってもよい位の熱心. ¶*youthful ardor* 年少の鋭気.
P take up a pursuit *with ardor* 身を入れて仕事を始める ‖ *with* all the *ardor* of the youth. 若さから来る情熱を傾けて.
P² *ardor for* glory 強い名誉心.

area, *n.* 地面, 場所; 地域, 地区; 地坪, 面積.
V The work *covers* an *area* of ten acres. この工場は十エーカーの面積を占めている. ¶It *encloses* an *area* of nearly twenty acres. それは約二十エーカーの面積がある. ¶Budgets tend to *follow* the *areas* of greatest recognized need. 予算は必要と認められた最大限に従う傾向がある. ¶*reforest* a desolated *area* 荒地を再び森林に仕立てる. ¶The building covers an *area measuring* 43×707 feet. この建物は縦四十三フィート横七百七フィートの面積を占めている. ¶it covers a *total area* of ... それは総面積...を占めている. ¶a *vast uncultivated area* 広大な未耕地.
Q changes in the boundaries of the *administrative areas* 行政区画の組替え. ¶*cultivated area* 開墾した地域. ¶proceed to the *disturbed area* (=scene of disturbance) [暴動などで]不穏の現場へ出向く. ¶an *earthquake-stricken* (=*earthquake-devastated, quake-ridden or quake-stricken*) *area* 震災地. ¶an *epicentral area* 震源地. ¶a *flood-affected area* 水害地. ¶troops in the *forward areas* 前線の軍隊. ¶at other times and in other *geographical areas* 別の時代に別の地方で. ¶an *immense* (=vast) *area* 広漠たる地域. ¶an *industrial area* 工業地. ¶the most *industrialized area* 最も工業化した地域. ¶an *insanitary area* 不健康地域. ¶in a *jurisdictional area* of a city, town, or village 市町村の区域内. ¶Though the *area* is *limited,* there is no want of variety. 面積は狭いが変化に乏しくはない. ¶the Tokyo *metropolitan area* 東京都全域. ¶the *neighboring areas* 隣接地域. ¶an *occupied area* 占領地域. ¶the great *Pacific area* 大太平洋地域. ¶a *planted area* 作付面積. ¶a *prohibited area* [立入]禁止地域. ¶a *railed-off area* 横木で仕切られた区域. ¶*residential areas* 住宅区域. ¶a *restricted area* 禁止地域. ¶a *requisitioned area* 接収区域. ¶in *rural areas* いなかでは. ¶*scenic areas* 風致地区.
Q² the *amusement areas* of Asakusa and Shinjuku 浅草や新宿の興行街. ¶in far *battle areas* 遠方の交戦地域. ¶a *buffer area* 緩衝地域. ¶the *city areas* 市域. ¶*combat areas* 戦闘地域. ¶a *concentration areas* 密集地域. ¶*country areas* いなか. ¶a *danger area* 危険地域. ¶a *second defense area* 第二防衛地域. ¶irrigate *desert areas* さばく地をかんがいする. ¶a *drainage area* 流域. ¶*evacuation areas* 疎開区域. ¶European *famine areas* 欧州の飢餓地域. ¶a *fighting area* 交戦地域. ¶a *floor area* (=space) 建坪. ¶a *food-surplus* (*food-deficit*) *area* 食糧過剰(欠乏)地域. ¶be in a *gas area* [家庭に利用できる]ガスのある地域にある. ¶a *goal area* 主陣地. ¶the Burmese living in *hill areas*山地に住むビマル人. ¶a *housing area* 宅地 ‖ a dependent *housing area* [軍などの]家族住宅地域 ‖ a community *housing area* 集団住宅地域. ¶heavy *industry areas* 重工業地区. ¶a *labor market area* 労働市場区域. ¶the *mid-town area* 都市の中心地域. ¶*occupation areas* 占領地域. ¶an "*off limits*" *area* 出入禁止区域. ¶*overseas market areas* 海外市場地域. ¶a *parking area* 自動車置場. ¶the "*peace*" *areas* in North China 北中国の無戦地域. ¶in the *periphery areas* 周辺地域に. ¶outside the *price control area* 物価統制地区外. ¶a *resort area* 盛り場. ¶a *rice surplus area* 米穀余剰地域. ¶a *riot area* 暴動地域. ¶the *service area*『テレビ・ラジオ』利用地域. ¶countries outside the *sterling area* スターリングブロック地域外の国々. ¶the *Tokyo-Yokohama* (*Shanghai-Nanking*) *area* 京浜(上海・南京)地域. ¶Japan's *trading area* 日本の通商地域. ¶the greatest *travel area* 旅行が最も盛んな地域. ¶a *war area* 戦争地域. ¶the *western addition area* of the city 市の西部の新開地.
P *in area* 坪数において ‖ take a photograph *in* a prohibited *area* 禁止地区で写真を撮る.
P² an *area of* a triangle 三角形の面積 ‖ an *area of* production 産地 ‖ this *area of* work 職域 ‖ What is the *area of* this garden? この庭は幾坪か. ¶the *area under* poppy cultivation けし栽培の面積.

arena, *n.* 闘技場; 活舞台, 場面.
V *enter* the commercial *arena* 商業界に入る.
Q He had not an *adequate arena* for the exercise of his talents. 彼は天分を伸ばす場所がなかった. ¶the *literary arena* 文壇. ¶the *poetical arena* 詩壇. ¶the *political arena* 政界.
Q² a *sports arena* 競技場.
P *in the arena* of warfare 戦闘場裡に. 【類】*in the arena* of world diplomacy. ¶*on the arena* of ... ...の舞台に.
P² the *arena* (=theater) *of* war 戦地.

argue, *v.* 論じる; 論破する; 議論する.
M *ably argue* 巧みに弁じる. ¶*argue acrimoniously* 痛烈に論じる. ¶I must *argue away* (=*off*) his misunderstanding. 彼を論破して誤解を一掃しなければなるまい. ¶*forcibly argue* 力強く論じる. ¶there can be no *further arguing* of ... ...はこれ以上議論してもむだだ. ¶*argue heatedly* 熱心に弁じる. ¶*argue out* their differences 意見の相違を議論で決する. ¶I will have to *argue* this *out* with you another time. いつか君とこの議論の結末をつけなければならない. ¶*plausibly argue* that ... もっともらしく...と論じる. ¶*sensibly argue* 物のわかった議論をする. ¶*shrewdly argue* 抜かりなく弁じる. ¶one may *so argue* そうも言える. ¶*vehemently argue* 猛烈に論じる.
P *argue about* a trifle ささいな点について議論する. ¶*argue against* injustice 不正を論駁(ばく)する. ¶*arguing along* these lines こういう風に論じて来ると. ¶*argue for* the

right 正義のために弁じる. ¶You are *arguing from* entirely false premises. 君の議論は全然前提を誤っている. 【類】*argue from* insufficient information ‖ *argue from* a cause *to* an effect 原因から結果に論及する. ¶*argue in* a circle どうどうめぐりの議論をする ‖ *argue in* the closet 密談する ‖ *argue in* the dark 盲目的に議論する ‖ *argue in* favor of ... ...のために弁じる ‖ if you *argue* [*in*] that way そんなことを言えば. ¶*argue* a person *into* the belief that ... ...を信じるように説き伏せる. 【類】*argue* a person *into* a course of action (ある行動を取るように). ¶It is useless to *argue on* suppositions. 想像で論じるのは無益だ. ‖ *argue on* a subject (question) ある題目(など)について論じる. ¶I *argued* him *out of* doing it. それをやめるように彼を説き伏せた. 【類】be *argued out of* one's action / He was *argued out of* his opposition. ¶*argue over* a matter ある事に関して論じる. ¶No use *arguing with* him about the matter. その事はあいつと議論したってだめだ. 【類】There is no *arguing with* him. / Such people should not be *argued with.* ‖ we were *arguing with* each other about the justice of the war ‖ it has been *argued with* considerable force that ... ...と盛んに論じられた / *argue with* great heat.

argument, *n.* 議論, 立論, 論拠, 論点.

v his observation appears to me to *add* a very substantial *argument* in favor of ... 彼の言は...に有利な実質的論拠を付加するもののように思われる. ¶*adduce arguments* for and against ... ...に関する賛否の議論を挙げる. 【類】*Arguments* are constantly *adduced* on both sides. ¶Such is the line of *argument adopted* by our contemporaries. 同業新聞紙はこんな風に論じている. ¶*advance* an *argument* 説を述べる. ¶this same *argument* can be *applied* to ... この議論はそのまま...に当てはまる. ¶*balance arguments* 議論の違いを調整する. ¶They *base* their *arguments* against socialism on Darwinism. 彼らはその社会主義反対論の基礎を自然淘汰説に置いている. 【類】*base* an *arguments* on false premises (誤った前提). ¶whatever the *arguments* that may be *brought forth* for or against it それに関する賛否の議論は何であろうと. ¶*bring forward arguments* to demonstrate the justice of ... ...の正義を弁明する. ¶*build up* an *argument* 議論を立てる. ¶he *clinched* (=*clenched*) his *argument* by saying that ... ...と論じて彼の議論を結んだ. ¶let us *consider* the *argument* in the light of ... その議論は...によって考慮して見よう. ¶*draw* one's *arguments* from ... ...に基づいて論じる. ¶*drive home* the *arguments* 議論を徹底させる. ¶*enforce* one's *arguments* with one's fist[s] こぶしを振って自説を強調する. ¶*fortify* (=*strengthen*) one's *argument* by adding more evidence さらに証拠を挙げて論拠を固める. ¶He *founds* his *argument* upon it. 彼は論拠をそこに置いている. ¶*get up* an *argument* 議論をする. ¶he *had* a heated *argument* with ... 彼は...と激しく論じ合った. ¶*heap argument* on *argument* to prove to ... that ... ...に...を立証するために色々と論じる. ¶to *illustrate* this *argument* この論点を説明するために. ¶*invalidate* the *argument* その議論を無効にする. ¶He *made* a very persuasive *argument.* 極めて説得力のある議論をやった. ¶In a democratic nation, assuredly *argument* should always be *met* with argument. 民主主義の国では当然言論に対しては言論をもってこれに対抗すべきである. ¶It is so obvious that it *needs* no *argument.* それは論ずるまでもないほど明白だ. ¶*open up argument* 議論を始める. ¶*present* one's *arguments* in an orderly way 秩序正しく議論を述べる. ¶*press* one's *argument* upon ... ...に自説を押しつける. ¶*prove* one's *argument* 自説を立証する. ¶*putting aside* an *argument* 議論はしばらくおき. ¶*put forward* an *argument* 議論を持ち出す. 【類】doubt the seriousness of the people who have *put forward* those *arguments.* ¶*refute* (=*repudiate*) his *argument* 彼の議論を論駁(ばく)する. ¶the *argument* has been *repeated* that ... ...という議論はたびたび出た. ¶It is too obvious to *require* any *argument.* 明白で議論を要しない. ¶*set* (=*put*) *forth* an *argument* 議論を述べる. ¶*shelve* an *argument* 議論をたな上げする. ¶Modern events have *silenced* the *argument.* 近代のでき事が論より証拠だ. ¶*start* an *argument.* 議論を始める. 【類】*start* new *arguments* against. ¶*Argument* should never be *stifled* by forces. 議論は実力で圧迫すべきものでない. ¶*sum up* one's *argument* 議論を概括する. ¶*support* one's *argument* 自分の申立を証明する. ¶*understand* one's *argument* その論旨を理解する. ¶*urge arguments* against the measure その案に反対の説を主張する ‖ *urge* every possible *argument* in one's favor 極力自己のために弁ずる. ¶*use* the same *argument* 同一論法を用いる. 【類】*use* this *argument* against ... / He *used* all the *arguments* he could imagine to dissuade me. ‖ *using* traditional *argument* 伝統的な論法で行けば. ¶he *weakens* his *argument* by ignoring ... 彼は...を無視しているのでその論拠が薄弱である.

v² this *argument applies* with still greater cogency to ... この議論は一層痛切に...に当てはまる. ¶That *argument* will not *hold.* その議論は立たない. ¶The *argument sounds* a bit forced. その議論は少し無理だ. ¶This *argument weighs* with me. この論は私に取って相当の価値がある.

Q the *ablest argument* that has been made against ... ...の反対論中最も有力な議論. ¶a *clinching argument* 決定的議論. ¶a *cogent argument* 有力な議論. ¶The average American citizen pays little attention to *communistic arguments.* 概して米国民は共産主義的議論にはほとんど耳を傾けない. ¶a *conclusive argument* 決定的な議論. ¶with *convincing argument* he shows that ... 彼は適確な論法で...を証明している. ¶a *counter argument* 反対論. ¶a *crushing argument* ぎゃふんとまいらせる(ぐうの音も言わさぬ)議論. ¶a *dubious argument* 怪しげな議論. ¶*elaborate* and *ingenious arguments*, advanced to show that ... ...を示すために提出した綿密で巧妙な議論. ¶a *fallacious argument* 謬論(びゅう). ¶a *false argument* 誤った議論. ¶a *flimsy argument* 貧弱な議論. ¶a *forcible argument* 力のある議論. ¶It is a *fruitless argument.* それは水掛論だ. ¶This is a *good argument* to silence him. これは彼を閉口させるに足る議論だ. ¶a *groundless argument* 根拠のない議論. ¶during a discussion of it, a very *heated argument* arose as to ... その審議中に...に関して激論が起った. ¶*impregnable arguments* 歯の立たぬ議論. ¶prove by *indisputable argument* 明白な議論で立証する. ¶give many *ingenious arguments* to support his theory that ... という自説を支持するために多くの巧妙な論証をする. ¶prove by *invincible argument* 反駁(ばく)を許さない論法で立証する. ¶*irrefutable* and *just argument* 正々堂々たる立論. ¶It can be proved by *logical argument.* それは筋の通った論法で証明できる. ¶There has been *much argument* in recent years about it. 近年それについてなかなか議論があった. ¶Let's not start that *old argument* again. その古くさい議論のむし返しはやめよう. ¶an *opposing argument* 反対論. ¶it would be sufficient, without any *other argument*, to show that ... ...を証明するためにはこれ以上議論をしないでもよかろう. ¶a *powerful argument* against ... ...に対する有力な反対説. ¶after a *prolonged argument* 長時間にわたる論議の後. ¶a *question-begging* (=an *insatiable*) *argument* 不徹底の議論. ¶it offers a *ready argument* to those who ... それは...の人々にすぐ役に立つ論拠になる. ¶a *sane, sober,* and *convincing argument* 穏健で冷静で人を信服せしめるに足る議論. ¶a *sound argument* 堅実な議論. ¶You should not be taken in by his *specious argument.* もっともらしい口振りに言いくるめられてはいけない. ¶a *stock argument* put forward by the opponents of ... ...の反対論者常用の議論. ¶a *strong argument* in favor of ... ...に極めて有利な議論. ¶a *subtle argument* 微妙な点を突いた議論. ¶a *supporting argument* 賛成説. ¶advance *telling arguments* in favor of ... ...のために有効な議論を提出する. ¶a *trumpery argument* 浅薄な議論. ¶an *unending argument* 水掛け論. ¶The *argument* is *unsound.* その議論は不確実だ. ¶His *argument* is *untenable.* 彼の議論は受取りがたい. ¶The *argument* is *valid.* その議論は有力だ. ¶a *weak argument* 薄弱な議論. ¶a *wild argument* 暴論. ¶a *wordy* and *weedy argument* 文句は沢山だが内容の貧弱な議論.

Q² make good *sales arguments* for ... ...に対し販売上巧みに説明する.

P *after* vain *argument* with ... ...と無益な議論を戦わした後. ¶attack *by argument* 論難する. ¶It is no longer a matter *for argument.* もはや議論にならない. ‖ give proofs *for* an *argument* 議論の証拠を示す ‖ He was a Marxist *for argument.* 彼は議論となるとマルクス主義的だった. ¶There is a fallacy *in* the *argument.* その論旨に誤りがあ

る. ‖ sound ***in*** *argument* 論旨の正しい ‖ corner a person ***in*** *argument* 人をやり込める. ¶get ***into*** an *argument* with … …と議論をする. ¶the drift ***of*** an *argument* 論旨 ‖ some facts in support ***of*** my *argument* 僕の議論の根拠になる若干の事実. ¶the thread ***of*** *argument* 議論の筋道. ¶***on*** a priori *argument* 演繹(えき)的論法で. ¶impregnable ***to*** *argument* 議論をはさむことができない. ¶***without*** further *argument* それきり論は打切って.

P^2 The above *argument* ***against*** it at once falls to the ground. それに反対の上述の議論はたちまち立たなくなる. ¶The *argument* ***for*** and ***against*** the use of tobacco is ceaselessly waged. 喫煙の可否の議論は絶えず続行されている. ¶These are *arguments* ***in*** favor of this hypothesis. 以上はこの仮説に対する論拠である. ‖ various *arguments* ***in*** its favor 種々の賛成説. ¶his *arguments* ***on*** the case その事件に関する彼の論告. ¶There is no need for *arguments* ***over*** it. その事については論じる必要がない.

argumentation, *n.* 議論.

Q if my *argumentation* be ***sound*** 私の議論が正しいとすれば.

arise, *v.* 起る, 興る, 生じる; 起き上がる; 起(た)つ, 蜂起する; 退散する.

P The people *arose* ***against*** the ruler. 人民は君主に対して反乱を起した. ¶A revolt has *arisen* ***among*** the people. 謀叛(ほん)が人民の間に起った. ¶the question *arose* ***as to*** … …に関して問題が起った. ¶*arise* ***at*** the summons 召集に応じる ‖ The court *arose* ***at*** 4 o'clock. 裁判所は四時に閉廷した. ¶*arise* ***from*** slumber 眠りから覚める ‖ *arise* ***from*** one's seat 席から立上がる. 【類】men who have *arisen* ***from*** poverty ***to*** affluence / the new Europe which has *arisen* ***from*** the ashes of the old (灰じんの中から). 【類】the new city that has *arisen* phoenix-like (不死鳥のように) ***from*** the ruins of the old laid low by fire and earthquake / *arise* ***from*** a cause / the dispute *arises* ***from*** … / the expense *arising* ***from*** … / fears *arising* ***from*** … / it *arises* ***from*** the fact that … ‖ His illness *arose* partly ***from*** want of food. 彼の病気の一因は食物の欠乏という点にもあった. ‖ we are not responsible for delay *arising* ***from*** … …から起る遅延に対し当方は責を負わない ‖ The English army has now many officers who have *arisen* ***from*** the ranks. 英国の現軍隊には兵から昇進した将校が沢山いる. ¶Difficulties *arose* ***out of*** the affair. 色々めんどうな事がその事件から起った. 【類】questions *arising* ***out of*** the situation / the treaty *arose* ***out of*** the conference held in … on the question. ¶*arise* ***to*** duty 義務につく. ¶*arise* ***with*** the lark 朝早く起きる.

aristocracy, *n.* 貴族; 貴族風; 一流の人々.

Q an ***arrogant*** *aristocracy* 高慢な貴族連. ¶His *aristocracy* was very ***pronounced.*** 彼は貴族臭さが目立った. ¶the ***true intellectual*** *aristocracy* of a nation 国民中の真の知識階級.

Q^2 ***codfish*** *aristocracy* 《米俗》成金族.

P ladies and gentlemen ***of*** the *aristocracy* 男女の貴族.

P^2 the *aristocracy* ***of*** intellect (birth, wealth) 知識(など)の点で一流の階級.

aristocrat, *n.* 貴族; 貴族的な人.

Q a ***born*** *aristocrat* 生れつき貴族的な人. ¶***impecunious*** *aristocrats* 貧乏華族. ¶***white-handed*** *aristocrats* 骨折仕事を知らない貴族.

Q^2 ***spendthrift*** *aristocrats* 金使いの荒い貴族ら.

arithmetic, *n.* 算術.

Q ***commercial*** *arithmetic* 商業算術. ¶***mental*** *arithmetic* 暗算. ¶***simple*** *arithmetic* indicates that … ちょっと計算すれば…が分る.

P a problem ***in*** *arithmetic* 算術の問題.

arm, *n.* 腕; 力.

V ***bare*** one's *arms* 腕をまくる. ¶***break*** one's *arm* 腕をくじく. ¶***brown*** their *arms* in the sun 腕を日焼けさせる. ¶He had to ***carry*** his *arm* in a sling for some weeks. 数週間腕につり包帯を掛けて置かなければならなかった. ¶***clutch*** each other's *arms* 互に腕をつかみ合う. ¶***extend*** open *arms* of welcome to a guest もろ手を広げて客を歓迎する. ¶***flinging*** his little *arms* round my neck その小さな腕で僕の首根っこにかじり付いて. ¶***fold*** our *arms* and trust to … われわれは腕組をして…に頼る. ¶a French soldier who ***gave*** both *arms* to his country in the World War 欧州大戦で国家に一身を捧げた一フランス兵. ¶The bride left the church ***holding*** her husband's left *arm*. 新婦は新郎の左腕を取って教会を出た. ¶***lean*** one's *arms* on the table テーブルに両腕をもたせかける. ¶***lend*** one's *arms* 腕を貸す. ¶***lock*** *arms* with each other お互いに腕(スクラム)を組む ‖ ***lock*** one's *arms* around another's neck 首っ玉にかじりつく. ¶***make*** a long *arm* 腕を伸ばす. ¶***offer*** one's right *arm* to a lady 婦人に右腕を貸す. ¶***open*** wide inviting *arms* 愛想よく両手を広げる ‖ We ***opened*** our *arms* to each other. 私らは互に腕を広げて迎えた. 【類】He ***opened*** his *arms* wide. ¶His left *arm* was ***paralyzed.*** あの人の左腕が麻痺(ひ)した. ¶He ***put*** his *arms* round my neck. 彼は僕の首にしがみついた. ¶***raise*** the *arms* 両手を挙げる. ¶***set*** the *arms* akimbo 両手を腰に当ててひじを張る. ¶He ***slipped*** an *arm* around her. 彼女をそーっと片手で抱いた. ¶***sprain*** one's *arm* 腕をくじく. ¶He ***stretched*** his *arm* ***out*** toward it. その方に片腕を差伸べた. ¶***swing*** one's *arms* 腕を振る. ¶She ***threw*** her *arms* round his neck. 彼の首を抱きしめた. ¶He ***took*** my *arm*. 僕の手を取った. ¶***toss up*** one's *arms* in the air in despair 絶望の余り両手を高く突き上げる.

Q with ***bare*** *arms* 腕をあらわにして. ¶with ***dimpled*** *arms* bare to the elbow 肥ってくぼみのある腕をひじまでまくり上げて. ¶We can reach you with the ***long*** *arm* of the Post Office. 郵便局があるから(別れても)こちらの消息を知らせることができる. ¶welcome him with ***open*** *arms* もろ手を広げて彼を歓迎する. ¶That big tree would take seven men to encircle it with ***outstretched*** *arms*. あの大木は七人で抱えるほどあるだろう. ¶one's ***right*** *arm* [右腕から]股肱(こう), 片腕. ¶a ***strong*** *arm* 強力, 暴力手段 ‖ only the ***strong*** *arm* of law has … 法律上の強硬手段のみが…である. ¶the ***upper*** (***lower***) *arms* 上(下)膊(はく).

Q^2 Watch the ***cross*** *arms* on a post. 柱に取り付けた十字交通標に注意せよ. ¶The pitcher had a ***glass*** *arm*. 投手は腕が疲れていた. ¶a ***signal*** *arm* 信号器の腕.

P He caught the robber ***by*** the *arms*. 盗賊の両腕をつかまえた. 【類】He took me ***by*** the *arm*. ¶go arm ***in*** *arm* 手に手を取って歩く ‖ clasp (=hold *or* take) it ***in*** one's *arms* それを抱きしめる ‖ He was wounded ***in*** the right *arm*. 彼は右手に負傷した. ‖ A bullet has lodged ***in*** his *arm*. 弾丸が腕にささった. 【類】The baby fell asleep ***in*** his *arms*. / a woman with an infant ***in*** *arms* ‖ toss a baby fondly ***in*** the *arms* 赤ん坊をかわいがって抱きゆすぶる ‖ her face beautiful even ***in*** the *arms* of death 死んだ後まで美しい彼女の顔 ‖ He was up ***in*** *arms* against the accusation. その言いがかりに対して憤然として立上った. ¶He lifted a child ***into*** his *arms*. 子供を抱き上げた. ‖ She threw herself ***into*** my *arms* 彼女は私の両腕に身を投げた. ¶The bride entered ***on*** the *arm* of her brother. 新婦は兄の腕にすがって入って来た. ‖ I have a sore place ***on*** my *arm*. 腕に痛い所がある. ‖ He got a shot ***on*** (=***in***) the *arm*. 《俗》腕に注射を一本した(モルヒネなど). ‖ The wasp stung me ***on*** the *arm*. はちが腕を刺した. ‖ with deep ***crepe*** bands ***on*** their *arms* その腕には幅広のちりめん喪章を着けて. ¶with a band ***round*** his *arm* to indicate that … 彼の腕には…の腕章を巻いて. ¶He was shot ***through*** the *arm*. 腕を射抜かれた. ¶with an English dictionary (a bunch of paper) ***under*** his *arm* 英語の辞書(など)を小わきにはさんで. 【類】with an umbrella ***under*** one's *arm*. ¶walk ***with*** one's *arm* round another's waist 他の人の腰に片手をまわして歩く. ‖ ***with*** folded *arms* 手をこまぬいて ‖ ***with*** *arms* akimbo ひじを張って ‖ receive him ***with*** open *arms* 両手を広げて彼を迎える.

P^2 the *arm* ***of*** the law 法律の力 ‖ Fortunately the "*Arm of* the Law" is not often needed. 幸い"法網"(法律での取締り)の必要は余りない.

arm, *v.* 武装する.

M ***fully*** *armed* for warfare 十分戦闘準備を整えて. ¶***heavily*** (***lightly***) *armed* soldiers 重(軽)装備兵.

P *arm* ourselves in time ***against*** danger 危険を予想して武装をする. ¶He is *armed* ***at*** all points. どこからどこまで武装している. ¶He is *armed* ***from*** top ***to*** toe. 頭からつま先まで(完全)武装している. ¶*armed* ***to*** the teeth 十分に武装して. ¶*arm* a person ***with*** a weapon 武装させる. 【類】He was *armed* ***with*** bow and arrows. / He was *armed* ***with*** a coat of mail (鎖かたびら). 【類】a fort *armed* ***with*** 5 guns ‖ trees *armed* ***with*** prickles とげのある木 ‖ He is *armed* ***with*** a pair of spectacles. 眼鏡を掛けている. ‖ a man *armed* ***with*** an evil tongue 毒舌家. 【類】people *armed* ***with*** patience.

armada, *n.* 艦隊.
 Q the ***Invincible Armada*** [スペインの]無敵艦隊.
 Q^2 the coming of the ***Mongol Armada*** 蒙古艦隊の襲来,元寇(げんこう).

armament, *n.* 軍備; 備砲, 砲数.
 V ***cut*** *armaments* 軍備を縮小する. ¶***increase*** *armaments* 軍備を拡張する. ¶***limit*** *armaments* 軍備を制限する. ¶***put aside*** the *armaments* 軍備を撤廃する. ¶***reduce*** *armaments* 軍備を縮小する.
 Q ***auxiliary*** *armament* 補助砲. ¶***Competitive*** *armaments* lead to war. 軍備の競争はその結果として戦争を招くことになる. ¶***heavy*** *armament* 巨砲. ¶***main*** *armament* 主砲.
 Q^2 ***land*** and ***sea*** *armaments* 陸海軍備. ¶reduce ***world*** *armaments* 世界諸国の軍備を縮小する.
 P competition ***in*** *armament* 軍備の競争. ¶an expansion ***of*** *armaments* 軍備拡張. ¶a warship ***with*** an *armament* of sixteen guns 大砲十六門を備えた軍艦.

armful, *n.* [片・両]腕一杯.
 P^2 an *armful* ***of*** wood (books) 一抱えの薪(など).

armistice, *n.* 休戦.
 V An *armistice* was ***declared.*** 休戦が布告された. ¶***denounce*** an *armistice* 休戦終了を告示する. ¶after the *armistice* was ***signaled*** 休戦協定の調印後に.
 P a proposal ***for*** an *armistice* 休戦の提議.

armor, *n.* よろい; 武装.
 V ***buckle on*** one's *armor* よろいを身にまとう. ¶***don*** (=put on) their *armor* and come forth to battle よろいを着て戦に出る. He ***wore*** *armor* over his clothes. 着物の上によろいを着けていた. 【類】men ***wearing*** samurai *armor.*
 Q ***protective*** *armor* 護身武装.
 P a samurai (warrior) ***in*** *armor* よろいを着けた侍. 【類】a soldier ***in*** full *armor* ‖ He was clad (=clothed) ***in*** *armor* from top to toe (頭からつま先まで). / He was equipped ***in*** *armor.* ‖ the knee-piece ***in*** *armor* よろいのひざ当て.
 P^2 a piece of *armor* ***for*** the throat のど当て.

armor, *v.* 武装する.
 M ***heavily*** *armored* 堅固に武装して.

armpit, *n.* 腋(わき)の下.
 P the glands ***in*** the *armpit* 腋の下の腺. ¶hair ***under*** the *armpit* 腋毛(わきげ).

arms, *n.* [*pl.* まれに *sing.*] 武器(小形の銃など); 記章, 紋章.
 V able to ***bear*** *arms* 武器の執れる, 軍役に服すことができる. 【類】In case of need, we must ***bear*** *arms.* ¶Alexander ***carried*** his victorious *arms* to the northward beyond the Jaxartes. アレキサンダーはジャキザーテスを越えて北方にその勝利を誇る軍勢を進めた. ¶***lay down*** (=***ground***) one's *arms* 降服する. ¶***Pile*** *arms!* 組め銃(つつ)! ¶The soldiers ***presented*** *arms.* 兵士は捧げ銃をした. ¶***Reverse*** *arms!* [銃口を下にして]返せ銃! ¶***Shoulder*** *arms!* になえ銃(つつ)! ¶***stack*** *arms* 叉銃する. ¶***take up*** *arms* against the king 国王にそむいて兵を挙げる ‖ ***take up*** *arms* in their defense 防御のために武器を執る. 【類】***take up*** *arms* and fight for one's faith (信仰) and liberty. ¶***throw down*** their *arms* and ask for quarter 降服して和睦(むつ)を請う.
 Q ***small*** *arms* 小銃.
 Q^2 the Navy's ***air*** *arm* 海軍の航空兵器. ¶surrendered ***fire*** *arms* 引渡された火器.
 P apt ***at*** *arms* 武芸に長じた ‖ feat ***at*** *arms* 武勲. ¶it is a barbarous way to extend dominion ***by*** *arms.* 武力で領土を拡張するのは野蛮な行為である. ¶They were up ***in*** *arms* against French aggression. 彼らはフランスの侵入に抗して武装していた. ‖ He is up ***in*** *arms* against the accusation. 彼はその非難にすこぶる激昂している. ‖ comrades ***in*** *arms* 戦友. 【類】a nation ***in*** *arms.* ¶by force ***of*** *arms* 武力で ‖ They numbered about 12,000 ***of*** all *arms.* 各種兵科を通じてその数約一万二千を算した. ‖ 100 stands ***of*** *arms* 武器百組. ¶He was bred ***to*** *arms.* 彼は軍人教育を受けた. ¶The troops were ***under*** *arms.* 兵士は武装していた. 【類】marines (陸戦隊) ***under*** *arms* / keep troops ***under*** *arms.*

army, *n.* 陸軍; 軍, 軍隊; 大群.
 V ***accompany*** an *army* 従軍する. ¶***array*** an *army* against an enemy 敵軍を前に戦闘隊形をとる. ¶The *army* was ***beaten.*** 軍が不利であった. ¶***build up*** a modern *army* and navy 現代的の陸海軍を築き上げる. ¶***collect*** an *army* 軍勢を募る. ¶***create*** new model *armies* and navies armed and trained and organized in the Western way 洋式に武装し訓練し編成した現代的な陸海軍を創設する. ¶***defeat*** an invading *army* 侵入軍を破る. ¶***demoralize*** an *army* 軍の士気をくじく. ¶***disband*** an *army* 軍隊を解散する. ¶The *army* was ***disorganized.*** 軍隊は乱れてしまった. ¶***draw out*** an *army* 軍隊を繰出す. ¶The *army* was ***drawn up*** in battle array. 軍隊は戦闘隊形に入った. ¶***enter*** the *army* 軍人になる, 入営する. 【類】persons desiring to ***enter*** the *army.* ¶***equip*** an *army* 軍隊を武装する. ¶***join*** the *army* 入隊する ‖ ***join*** the *army* in a war 従軍する. 【類】***join*** the *army* as a volunteer (志願兵). ¶***launch*** a mighty *army* against ... ...に大軍を向ける. ¶He ***led*** his *army* against the city. 軍を率いて市を攻撃した. 【類】He ***led*** an *army* into Egypt. / ***lead*** his *army* to victory ¶***leave*** the *army* 除隊になる. ¶***maintain*** an *army* for home defence 国防のために軍隊を維持する. ¶The *Army* and Navy are ***manned*** by youths drawn from throughout the country. 陸海軍は全国から徴発した青年によって組織される. ¶***mobilize*** an *army* of something like three million of men on the war footing 戦時編成の兵約三百万を動員する. ¶***organize*** an *army* 軍隊を編成する. ¶***raise*** a large *army* 大軍を起す. 【類】The *army* is ***raised*** by conscription (徴兵制度). ¶***reorganize*** an *army* 軍を再編する. ¶He ***served*** the *Army* during the World War. 彼は世界大戦に参加した. ¶Financial depression ***swells*** the *army* of the unemployed. 不景気で失業者がふえる. 【類】***swell*** the *army* of female suicides.
 V^2 The *army* ***marched off*** with a flourish of trumpets. 軍隊がらっぱを吹奏して行軍した. ¶The *army* ***met*** with a check. 軍隊が食止められた.
 Q an ***advancing*** *army* 前進軍. ¶a ***besieging*** *army* 包囲軍. ¶a ***conquering*** *army* 戦勝軍. ¶***contending*** *armies* 対抗する両軍. ¶The ***Emperor's*** *army* if you win; a rebel *army* if you lose. 勝てば官軍, 負ければ賊軍. ¶an ***expeditionary*** *army* against ... ...遠征軍. ¶a ***great*** (=***large or vast***) *army* 大軍. ¶those who are employed in our great ***industrial*** *armies* わが大工場で働いている人々. ¶the ***innumerable*** *army* of magazine-readers 無数の雑誌購読者. ¶defeat a ***large*** *army* 大軍を破る. ¶a ***little*** (=***small***) *army.* 小軍. ¶***opposing*** *armies* 相対峙(じ)する両軍. ¶a ***regular*** *army* 正規軍. ¶an ever ***victorious*** *army* 常勝軍.
 Q^2 an ***occupation*** *army* 占領軍. ¶the ***industrial rescue*** *army* 産業予備軍(失業労働者を指す). ¶the ***Salvation*** *Army* 救世軍. ¶a ***standing*** *army* 常備軍. ¶a census of ***world*** *armies* 世界の軍備情勢調査.
 P He is qualifying himself ***for*** the *army.* 陸軍の受験資格を造っている. ¶He retired ***from*** the *army.* 陸軍を退役した. ¶My elder brother is ***in*** the *army.* 僕の兄は陸軍にいる. 【類】an officer ***in*** the *army* / a surgeon ***in*** the British *army* / serve ***in*** the *army.* ¶the general placed ***over*** the *army* 全軍の統帥. ¶He is ***with*** the *army.* 陸軍に勤めている. ‖ ***with*** a mighty *army* in the background 背後に大軍を控えて / advance ***with*** an *army* ten thousand strong (一万の軍勢).
 P^2 the *Army* ***as*** a career 職業としての陸軍. ¶an *army* ***of*** locusts いなごの大群 ‖ an *army* ***of*** voters 多数の選挙人. ¶the British *army* ***under*** Havelock ハヴロク旗下の英軍.

aroma, *n.* 芳香, におい.
 V ***develop*** the *aroma* of coffee by roasting 炒(い)ってコーヒーの香を出す. ¶***diffuse*** a savory *aroma* うまそうな香を散布する. ¶***inhale*** the *aroma* 香を吸う. ¶The cigarettes ***possess*** a most delicate *aroma.* その巻煙草は非常にかおりがよい. ¶try to ***recall*** the *aroma* of the days when ... ...当時の情趣を思い出そうと努める.
 Q the ***pungent*** *aroma* of onions たまねぎの鼻をつくにおい. ¶the ***pure Parisian*** *aroma* きっすいのパリ人のにおい(情趣). ¶the ***sweet*** *aroma* of flowers 花の芳しい香.
 P^2 the *aroma* ***of*** poetry 詩のかおり(妙味).

around, *ad.* まわりに.
 M I heard noises ***all*** *around.* あたりに声が聞えた.

arouse, *v.* 起す; 励ます.
 M Public attention is ***thoroughly*** *aroused* as to its importance. その重要性が世間から非常に注目されるようになった.
 P I was *aroused* ***from*** a sound sleep by ... よく寝ていたのを...で起された. ¶I was *aroused* ***out of*** a sound sleep. ぐっすり寝込んでいたのを起された. ¶*arouse* him ***to*** action 彼を活動させる. 【類】*arouse* a person ***to*** anger.

arraign, *v.* 審問する；告訴する.

M *publicly arraign* 訴追する.

P *arraign* a criminal ***at*** the bar 法廷で罪人を調べる. ¶*arraign* a person ***before*** the tribunal 法廷で人を審問する. ¶He was *arraigned* ***for*** high treason. 彼は国事犯で訴えられた. ¶*arraign* a person ***of*** (=for) a crime 犯罪で人を告訴する. ¶He was *arraigned* ***on*** (=***upon***) an indictment. 彼は起訴によって調べられた.

arrange, *v.* 整える；排列する；調停する；取り決める；取りまとめる；手配をつける.

M It is ***all*** *arranged.* すっかりきまりがついた. ¶*arrange* ***alphabetically*** エービーシー順に排列する. ¶*arrange* matters ***amicably*** 穏便に事をまとめる. ¶*arrange* ***beforehand*** 前もって手配をする. ¶His hair was ***carefully*** parted and *arranged.* 彼の髪は丁寧に分けてなでつけてあった. ¶agents of Lloyd's ***geographically*** *arranged* 地方別にしたロイド代理店. ¶You must *arrange* ***immediately*** or it is useless. 君はすぐに取り決めないとだめだ. ¶They are classified and ***methodically*** *arranged.* 分類ができて整然と排列してある. ¶unless ***otherwise*** *arranged* 別に取り決めがなければ. ¶*arrange* everything ***satisfactorily*** to both parties 万事双方都合のよいように取まとめる. ¶They were ***tastefully*** *arranged* on silver dishes. ていさいよく銀のさらに盛ってあった. ¶They are *arranged* ***topically.*** 題目別に排列してある. ¶***well*** *arranged* for ... …のためによく手配ができている.

P *arrange* guests ***according to*** seniority 来賓を年齢順に列べる. 【類】be *arranged* ***according*** to size (大小の順に). ¶*Arrange* the matter ***at*** your own convenience. その事は御都合のよいように取り決めて下さい. ¶we *arranged* ***between*** us to ... われわれは…のことに相談をきめた. 【類】The meeting was *arranged* ***between*** the two parties (両当事者間で). ¶It has been *arranged* satisfactorily ***by*** (=***through***) the mediation of friends. 友だちの仲裁で首尾よく落着した. ‖ The cards are *arranged* ***by*** author and subject. カードは著者と題目別になっている. ¶*arrange* ***for*** an excursion 遠足の手はずをする. 【類】*arrange* ***for*** any difference that may arise / He went to England to *arrange* ***for*** his boy's education. ‖ The meeting has been *arranged* ***for*** Thursday evening. 会は木曜日の夕刻と決まった. 【類】The first four meetings of the series *arranged* ***for*** the winter months 1953 have now been held. ‖ *arrange* troops ***for*** battle 戦闘準備として軍容を整える ‖ *arrange* ***for*** a special car to convey us by rail われわれを鉄道で輸送するために特別車両の手はずをする. ¶*arrange* them ***in*** order それをきちんと整える ‖ a list *arranged* ***in*** ABC order エービーシー順に排列した表 ‖ they may be *arranged* ***in*** three classes as follows: 次の三綱目に排列される. 【類】They are *arranged* ***in*** kinds (=sorts). ¶*arrange* food ***on*** a dish 食物をさらにならべる ‖ *arrange* ... ***on*** sound principles 健全な原則に基いて…を処理する ‖ The exhibits are *arranged* ***on*** a historical basis. 陳列品は年代順に排列されている. ¶*arrange* ... ***with*** respect to size 大小別に…を並べる ‖ *arrange* ***with*** creditors 債権者と示談にする. 【類】*arrange* ***with*** the buyers (manufacturers) / *arrange* a journey ***with*** a friend / *arrange* the terms of a bargain (売買条件) ***with*** a seller.

O as *arranged* 予定通り. ¶*arrange* as deemed best 最善と考えられるように取計らう. 【類】Everything has been *arranged* as you wished.

arrangement, *n.* (**1**) 協定, 妥協, 打合せ.

V ***alter*** the *arrangements* made 協定を変更する. ¶an *arrangement* has been ***arrived at*** between them for ... 彼らの間に…の協定が成立した. ¶***cancel*** *arrangements* 協定を取消す. ¶***carry out*** the *arrangements* satisfactorily 円満に協定を遂げる. ¶***complete*** *arrangement* to ... …する打合せを完了する. ¶the *arrangement* that he has ***concluded*** with me for the purchase of ... 彼が私と取りきめた…購入の協定. ¶***countermand*** *arrangements* 協定を取消す. ¶He was called in to ***effect*** an amicable *arrangement* between the two parties. 両当事者示談のために彼を招いた. ¶To ***facilitate*** *arrangements* your prompt answer is requested. 早く話をまとめるために速答を希望します. ¶The *arrangement* was ***kept*** secret. 協定は極秘に付せられた. ¶***make*** *arrangements* with him 彼と打合せをする ‖ special *arrangements* have been ***made*** with him for ... 彼と特別…の協定をした. 【類】we have ***made*** *arrangements* by which it is enabled to ... ‖ if agreeable to you I should like to ***make*** the following *arrangement*: 一御差支えなければ次の契約を取交わしたい. ¶***propose*** an *arrangement* 相談を持出す.

V[2] The *arrangement* has ***broken down.*** 協定が破れた. ¶The *arrangement* has ***expired.*** 協定の期限が切れた. ¶Our *arrangement* ***stands*** (=***holds***) good. われわれの協定は効力を有している.

Q by ***advance*** *arrangement* with him 彼と前もって打合せをして. ¶make ***advantageous*** *arrangements* with publishers 出版者と有利な契約をする. ¶It resulted in an ***amicable*** *arrangement.* 示談になった. ¶***conditional*** *arrangements* 条件つきの協定. ¶by some ***diplomatic*** *arrangement* 何か外交的協定によって. ¶He has an ***exclusive*** *arrangement* with us. 彼はわれわれと独占協定を結んでいる. ¶suit the ***existing*** *arrangements* 現在の取りきめに適する. ¶make ***further*** *arrangements* 更に打合せをする. ¶***musical*** *arrangements* 音楽の催しの打合わせ. ¶by a ***preconcerted*** *arrangement* 前から打合せをしておいて. ¶according to a ***previous*** *arrangement* 予定通りに. ¶***private*** *arrangements* 秘密協定. ¶make ***special*** *arrangements* with ... …と特約を結ぶ. 【類】unless under a ***special*** *arrangement* for that purpose. ¶it is a rather ***strange*** *arrangement* of nature that ... …は妙な天の配剤である. ¶make some ***temporary*** *arrangement* 仮協定を結ぶ. ¶a very ***wise*** *arrangement* はなはだ賢明な協定.

Q[2] the ***inter-library loan*** *arrangements* between the colleges of the United States 米国大学間の図書館共用協定. ¶make ***money*** *arrangements* with ... …と金銭上の打合せをする. ¶***pre-election*** *arrangement* 選挙前の打合せ. ¶***price*** *arrangements* 価格協定.

P ***according to*** *arrangement* 打合せ通り. ¶***by*** *arrangement* made by me with him 私は彼と打合せをして ‖ ***by*** agreed *arrangement* 打合せをしておいて ‖ a quarrel ***by*** *arrangement* 八百長のけんか. ¶pave the way ***for*** an *arrangement* まとまりの付きやすいように前ごしらえをする. ¶He has entered ***into*** an *arrangement* to purchase that building lot. 彼はあの建物の敷地を買う契約を結んだ. ¶***through*** [an] *arrangement* with ... …と打合せの上. ¶come ***to*** an *arrangement* with him about ... …につき彼と話がまとまる ‖ Foreign orders will be subject ***to*** special *arrangements.* 外国からの注文は特別の協定にまたねばならぬ. ¶We are ***under*** *arrangement* with him. 当方は彼と打合せができている. ‖ ***under*** these *arrangements* 前記協定により ‖ ***under*** *arrangements* entered into by us with ... われわれと…とで取結んだ協定により.

P[2] What are the *arrangements* ***for*** payment? 支払の取りきめはどうなっているか.

(**2**) 手はず, 支度; 設備.

V ***alter*** existing *arrangements* 現在の手はずを変える. ¶*arrangements* have been ***completed*** to ... …する手はずがついた. ¶***dislocate*** (=***disturb***) existing *arrangements* 現在の手はずを狂わせる. ¶all *arrangements* in connection with it can be ***made*** at ... それに関する手続は全部…でできる ‖ *arrangements* are being ***made*** for ... …の手配が進行中だ. ¶***upset*** *arrangements* 番狂わせをする. 【類】***upset*** all household *arrangements* by one's late hours in the morning.

Q ***complete*** *arrangement* with him for ... 彼と取り決めた…に関する申分のない手はず. ¶make ***elaborate*** *arrangements* to ... 入念に…の手はずをする. ¶***initial*** *arrangements* 最初の手はず. ¶***mutual*** *arrangements* have been made to ... …の相互の手はずをつけた. ¶make ***necessary*** *arrangements* for mountaineering 登山に必要な準備をする. ¶The ***sanitary*** *arrangements* are antiquated and imperfect. 衛生設備は旧式で不完全だ. 【類】provide for proper ***sanitary*** *arrangements* / ***Sanitary*** *arrangements* have been carefully attended to.

P[2] *arrangements* ***in*** connection with it それに関する手はず. ¶make ***satisfactory*** *arrangements* for a reception 十分接待の準備をする.

Q[2] comfortable ***landing*** *arrangements* alongside the pier 桟橋における便利な上陸設備. ¶the ***seating*** *arrangement* for the ceremony その式典のための座席の配置.

(**3**) 整理, 排列, 排列法.

V this *arrangement* is also ***adopted*** by ... この排列法は...でも採用した. ¶I am going to ***change*** the *arrangement* of the household for economic reasons. 一つ家計切りつめの整理をやろうと思う. ¶***departmentalize*** the *arrangement* of news 新聞記事を部門別にする.

Q an ***awkward*** *arrangement* of words in a sentence 文中の語の拙劣な配置. ¶in ***handy*** *arrangement* 便利に排列して. ¶a ***happy*** *arrangement* of phrases 句の巧妙な配置.

P The *tanka* contains thirty-one syllables ***in*** 5-7-5-7-7 syllabic *arrangement*. 短歌は五七五七七の三十一文字である.

P² *arrangement* ***by*** subjects 題目別. ¶the *arrangement* ***of*** the place of ceremony 式場内の配置 ‖ the *arrangement* ***of*** words in a sentence 文中の語の排列.

(**4**) 制度.

Q the ***postal*** (=***post-office***) *arrangements* 郵便制度.

array, *n.* (**1**) 整列, 排列.

V ***display*** a formidable *array* of teeth 恐ろしく歯をむき出す. ¶***make*** an *array* 勢ぞろいをする.

Q march on in ***brave*** *array* 勇ましい整列行進をする. ¶a ***brilliant*** *array* of heroes りっぱな豪傑ぞろい. ¶a ***gallant*** *array* of nobles and cavaliers 威風りりしい貴族と騎士の列座. ¶***martial*** (=***battle***) *array* 陣立, 戦列. ¶present "lessons" in ***orderly*** *array* 学課を秩序正しく排列する. ¶in ***proud*** *array* 堂々とそろい立って. ¶He has a ***splendid*** *array* of wearing apparel. 彼は衣類がりっぱにそろっている. ¶a ***whole*** *array* of proofs ありたけの証拠.

Q² a ***window*** *array* ショーウィンドーの陳列.

P set ***in*** *array* 排列する. ¶The army was drawn up ***in*** battle *array*. 軍隊は戦列を布いていた. ¶***with*** an appalling *array* of studies 学課目が盛沢山にならべてあって.

(**2**) 服装.

Q a baby in ***full*** *array* 着飾った赤ん坊. ¶ladies in their ***lightest*** *array* 至極軽装の婦人たち. ¶fix oneself up in ***rich*** *array* 盛装する.

array, *v.* 整列する; 装う.

P The army was *arrayed* ***against*** the enemy. 軍隊は敵に向って整列させられた. ‖ Ridicule and contempt were *arrayed* ***against*** him. 嘲弄(ちょう)と軽べつを真向から浴びた. ¶The army was *arrayed* ***before*** the commander. 軍隊は司令官の前に整列させられた. ¶The army was *arrayed* ***in*** the open field. 軍隊は野外に整列した. ‖ The army was *arrayed* ***in*** order of battle. 軍隊を戦闘隊形に並べた. ‖ She *arrayed* herself ***in*** a silken robe. 絹の衣装を着けていた. 【類】*array* a cat ***in*** doll's clothing. ¶Even Solomon in all his glory was not *arrayed* ***like*** one of these [flowers]. 〖聖〗ソロモンの栄華だにその装いこの花の一つにもしかざりき. ¶She was *arrayed* ***with*** splendid trappings. 彼女は美しく着飾っていた.

arrear, *n. pl.* 未払金; 延滞, 未済, 後れ.

V try to ***catch up*** the *arrears* in answering letters 手紙の返事遅れを片づけようとする. ¶He failed to ***pay*** *arrears*. 滞納金を払わなかった.

P His rent (subscription) was more than twelve months ***in*** *arrear*[*s*]. 彼の家賃(など)は一年以上も滞っていた. 【類】payment ***in*** *arrears* / In this we are much ***in*** *arrear*[*s*] of Europe. この点われわれは大いに欧州に後れている. ¶His studies have fallen ***into*** *arrears*. 彼は勉強が後れた. ¶interest ***on*** *arrears* 延滞利子.

P² *arrears* ***of*** pay (rent, taxes) 給料(など)の未払. ¶He is in *arrear* (=is back) ***with*** his rent. 彼は家賃の滞りがある. 【類】He is in *arrears* ***with*** the repayment of the money. / cut off the gas from the house of a person who is in *arrears* ***with*** his payments.

arrest, *n.* 拘引, 拘留.

V ***anticipate*** *arrest* by flight 捕まらない先に高飛びする. ¶***effect*** his *arrest* 彼を捕縛する. ¶Some 300 *arrests* were ***made*** with only 14 convictions. 約三百名が拘留されたが十四名だけしか服罪しない.

V² *Arrest* soon ***followed***. その結果間もなく逮捕された.

Q ***Several*** *arrests* have been made. 数件の検挙があった.

Q² a ***house*** *arrest* 自宅拘禁. ¶a ***surprise*** *arrest* 抜打ちの検挙.

P put a person ***under*** *arrest* ...を拘引する. ¶The offender is ***under*** *arrest*. 犯人は拘留中だ. ‖ He was placed ***under*** *arrest*. 彼は拘引された. ¶*arrest* ***with*** (***without***) a warrant 令状による(よらない)逮捕.

arrest, *v.* 拘引する, 捕縛する.

P He was *arrested* ***by*** the police by warrant of the judge. 彼は判事の令状で警察の手に捕縛された. 【類】a robber who was *arrested* ***by*** the authorities for theft. ¶He was *arrested* ***for*** high treason. 国事犯で逮捕された. 【類】be *arrested* ***for*** a minor offense (軽犯罪). ¶He was *arrested* ***in*** the king's name. 王の名で捕縛された. ¶He was *arrested* ***on*** suspicion. 嫌疑で捕縛された. ‖ He was *arrested* ***on*** a charge of having infringed the Election Law. 選挙法違反で逮捕された. ‖ have one's attention *arrested* ***by*** it その方に気を取られる.

arrester *n.* 防止装置.

Q² a ***lightning*** *arrester* 避雷器(避雷針とは別). ¶a ***spark*** *arrester* 火の粉止め.

arrival, *n.* 到着; 到着者, 到着品.

V His wife is ***expecting*** the *arrival* of a new member of the family. 彼の妻は近々赤ん坊を生む. ¶Our *arrival* was ***hailed*** with unusual demonstrations of pleasure by them. 私たちの来着を彼らは非常に歓迎した. ¶They "***sign in***" their *arrival* upon a sheet. 表に出勤の署名をする. ¶They ***timed*** their *arrival* to an hour. 彼らは到着の時を何時という所まで決めた.

V² *Arrivals* ***continue*** to be abundant (scarce). 着荷が引続き多い(少い).

Q ***belated*** *arrival* 延着. ¶***dilatory*** *arrival* of goods 貨物の延着. ¶He was among the ***early*** *arrivals* in the meeting. 早い来会者の一人であった. ¶***heavy*** *arrivals* おびただしい着荷. ¶He was the ***first*** *arrival*. 一番先に着いた. ¶***new*** (=***fresh***) *arrivals* 新来者; 新入荷品. 【類】There were a lot more ***new*** *arrivals* expected at the meeting. ¶The *arrival* of the steamer is considerably ***overdue***. 汽船の到着が大分遅れている. ¶Nobody can guarantee the ***punctual*** *arrival* of the train in such foggy weather. こんな濃霧では列車の定刻到着はだれにもうけ合えない. ¶a ***recent*** *arrival* ignorant of the English language 英語を知らない新来者. ¶There have already been ***scattering*** *arrivals*. [来遊の客など]到着した者がちらほらいる.

Q² ***air*** *arrivals* from ... ...からの飛行機到着数. ¶evening departure from Seattle or Portland; third ***morning*** *arrival* in Chicago シアトルもしくはポートランドから夜の出発; シカゴに三日目の朝到着(航海日程).

P I cannot find his name ***among*** the *arrivals*. 来着者名簿中に彼の名が見えない. ¶***on*** *arrival* 到着次第. 【類】***on*** the ship's *arrival* / ***On*** my *arrival* I will give you an interview.

P² our *arrival* ***at*** the station われらの停車場到着. 【類】telegraph me her *arrival* ***at*** your port ‖ *arrival* ***at*** a conclusion 結論への到達. 【類】There was a long debate, but no *arrival* ***at*** any agreement. ¶*Arrivals* ***from*** Hongkong are now admitted to free pratique. 香港よりの到着者は陸上との自由交通を許されている. ¶his recent *arrival* ***in*** London 彼の最近のロンドンへの到着. 【類】Now this man with his family was a recent *arrival* ***in*** this city. ¶*Arrivals* ***of*** goods from the interior are very poor (heavy). 内地からの着荷は非常に少ない(多い).

P² since his *arrival* ***on*** (=***upon***) American soil 彼の着米以来 ‖ their *arrival* ***on*** our shores 彼らの来朝.

arrive, *v.* 到着する; 到達する.

M We *arrived* ***at last***. とうとう着いた. ¶*arrive* ***back*** in Paris from ... ...からパリに帰着する. ¶*arrive* ***home*** in the evening 夕刻に帰宅する. ¶They *arrived* ***late*** for their lessons. 遅刻して授業に間に合わなかった. ¶He *arrived* ***long ago***. とっくに着いた. ¶*arrive* ***safely*** at the destination 無事目的地に着く. ¶The goods *arrived* "***short***." 荷物は入手のとき品が不足していた. ¶He will *arrive* ***shortly***. 間もなく着くでしょう. ¶Produce is *arriving* very ***slowly***. 製品の到着が非常におそい.

P He *arrived* ***after*** me. 私の後で着いた. ‖ He *arrived* ***after*** dark. 暗くなってから着いた. ¶He *arrived* ***at*** San Francisco. サンフランシスコに着いた. 【類】He will *arrive* ***at*** his end this afternoon. ‖ *arrive* ***at*** manhood. 大人になる. 【類】*arrive* ***at*** years of maturity (壮年) / *arrive* ***at*** man's estate (成年) / *arrive* ***at*** puberty (思春期) ‖ *arrive* ***at*** the blissful state 成仏する ‖ *arrive* ***at*** a conclusion 結論に達する / the conclusion we *arrived* ***at*** was that ... / *arrive* ***at*** a correct conclusion / quick to *arrive* ***at*** decision / *arrive* ***at*** an early decision / *arrive* ***at*** the goal /

arrive at some arrangement ‖ All efforts to ***arrive at*** an understanding have failed. 折合おうと色々骨を折って見たがどうもうまく行かなかった. 【類】It is necessary to ***arrive at*** understanding with him. ‖ ***arrive at*** its perfection 完全の域に達する. 【類】***arrive at*** no result ‖ ***arrive at*** some knowledge ある知識を得るようになる ‖ ideas ***arrived at*** intuitively (empirically) 直覚的に(経験的に)到達した観念 ‖ things have ***arrived at*** such a pitch that ... 事態が...という所まで進展した ‖ I have not yet ***arrived at*** an opinion. まだ意見がまとまらない. ‖ A new baby ***arrived at*** the Johnsons. ジョンソンさんの宅で赤ちゃんが生れた. ‖ He has not yet ***arrived at*** the power of managing his own estate. 彼にはまだ自分の財産を管理するだけの権利がなかった. ¶He ***arrived before*** me. 私より先に着いた. ‖ He ***arrived before*** dark. 暗くならない内に着いた. ‖ ***arrive by*** the noon train 正午の列車で着く. 【類】He ***arrived by*** the six o'clock train. ¶A letter ***arrived for*** you yesterday evening. ゆうべ君の所へ手紙が来た. ¶the steamer which ***arrived from*** Kobe 神戸から来た船. ¶The steamer ***arrived in*** harbor last night. 汽船は昨夜入港した. ‖ He ***arrived in*** town. 彼は着京した. 【類】***arrive in*** England (a country, a city). ¶***arrive on*** the American coasts 米海岸に到着する ‖ foreigners ***arriving on*** our shores 来朝の外人. 【類】The party ***arrived on*** the race-course (競馬場). ¶Sense cannot ***arrive to*** the inwardness of things. —Dr. H. More. 感覚では物の本質は分らない. ¶***arrive upon*** the spot (=scene) 現場に着く.

arrogance, *n.* 尊大, ごう慢.

V I cannot ***brook*** his *arrogance*. 彼のごう慢は我慢ができない.

P² *arrogance* ***of*** the nobility ***toward*** the common people 平民に対する貴族のごう慢.

arrogant, *a.* ごう慢な.

P He is *arrogant* ***toward*** us. われわれに対してごう慢だ.

arrogate, *v.* 僭(せん)称する, 僭取する.

P *arrogate* power ***to*** (=***for***) oneself 権力を僭取する ‖ She *arrogated* ***to*** herself a certain importance. えらそうに振舞った.

arrow, *n.* 矢.

V ***aim*** the *arrow* at ... ...に矢のねらいをつける. ¶The man who scrambles to the top of tree naturally ***attracts*** the *arrows* of criticism. 喬木風多し. ¶***discharge*** (=***let fly***) an *arrow* 矢を放つ. ¶***fledge*** an *arrow* 矢に羽根をつける. ¶***make*** *arrows* 矢をはぐ. ¶carefully ***notch*** one's *arrow* 念入りに(弦に)矢をつがえる. ¶***shoot*** (=***send***) an *arrow* into the air 空中に矢を射る. ¶He ***shot*** an *arrow* into the animal. その獣を射止めた. 【類】He ***shot*** *arrows* one by one, but each missed. ¶***slip*** an *arrow* 矢を放つ.

P shoot an *arrow* ***at*** ... ...をねらって矢を射る.

art, *n.* 技術, 技芸; 芸術, 美術; 人為, 技巧.

V ***acquire*** the *art* of adjusting oneself to new situation 新たな境遇に善処する術を会得する. ¶***choose*** *art* as a career 芸術で身を立てることにする. ¶Art lies in ***concealing*** *art*. 技巧は技巧を隠すことに存する. ¶***cultivate*** the *art* of story-telling 話しかたを修行する. ¶He ***discovered*** the *art* of making dynamite. ダイナマイトの製法を発見した. ¶The landscape ***eluded*** the painter's *art*. その風景には画家も筆を投じた. ¶***follow*** *art* as a profession 芸術を職業とする. ¶***foster*** the *arts* 諸芸術を奨励する. ¶He ***has*** the *art* of imparting his knowledge attractively. 彼には知っていることを巧に人に伝える手腕がある. ¶He ***knows*** the *art* of making money. 金もうけの術を心得ている. ¶the physician who ***loves*** his *art* 医術を愛する医師. ¶***master*** the *art* of flower arrangement 生け花のこつを修得する. ¶***practice*** the *art* of composition 作文を習練する. ¶The cylinder press has ***revolutionized*** the *art* of printing. 輪転機は印刷術を革新した. ¶The Korean craftsmen ***took*** this *art* with them into Japan. 朝鮮の工人はこの技術を日本に伝えた. ¶She ***understands*** the *art* of being well dressed. 着物の着こなし方を心得ている. 【類】The people ***understood*** the potter's *art* (製陶術). ¶They ***used*** *art* and intrigue in promoting or accomplishing their purposes. 彼らはその目的を助成しまたは達成させるのに陰謀術策をめぐらした.

Q geology, mining, metallurgy, and the ***allied*** *arts* 地質学・採鉱・冶金およびこれに関連する技術. ¶***ceramic art*** 製陶術. ¶a masterpiece of the ***chef's art*** 庖丁(料理)の傑作. ¶the ***culinary art*** 料理法. ¶a ***dead art*** 滅びた製法(技術). ¶***decorative art*** 装飾美術. ¶Translation is a ***difficult art***. 翻訳はむつかしい技術だ. ¶the ***divining art*** 占術, 易断. ¶***domestic arts*** [料理裁縫などのような]家庭諸芸. ¶the true nature of ***dramatic art*** 演劇の本質. 【類】Human voice plays a tremendous part in ***dramatic art***. ¶***exquisite art*** 入神の技. ¶The *art* is now ***extinct***. その技術は今日では滅びてしまった. ¶a mistress of all the ***feminine arts*** 女性の技芸百般に通じた女. ¶***fictile art*** 製陶術. ¶***fine arts*** 美術 ‖ ***fine*** and ***applied art*** 美術工芸. ¶cubism and other ***freak art*** 立体派などの変態芸術. ¶the ***gentle art of*** keeping young 年を取らない法 ‖ the ***gentle art of*** good talking 話術. ¶***graphic arts*** 印刷芸術. ¶in the language of ***histrionic art*** it is termed ... 舞台芸術の言葉では...という. ¶***imitative arts*** 模造芸術(絵画彫刻など). ¶master the very ***important art*** of being interesting 人をおもしろがらすというきわめて重要な技術に熟達する. ¶***industrial arts*** 工芸. ¶***liberal arts*** [語学・哲学・音楽などの]教養学芸; 教養学科. ¶a ***living art*** 現存の技術. ¶Conversation is now nearly a ***lost art***. 話術は今はほとんど滅びた芸術である. ¶the ***magnificent*** and ***undying art*** of Mme. Sarah Bernhardt サラ・ベルナール夫人の堂々として不滅の芸術. ¶***martial*** (=***military***) ***arts*** 武術. ¶***national arts*** 国民芸術. ¶Line-engraving is now practically an ***obsolete art***. 筋彫りは今は事実上すたれた芸術である. ¶Pottery is the ***oldest art*** in the world. 陶器製造は世界最古の技術である. ¶an appreciator of ***Oriental art*** 東洋美術の理解者. ¶the ***pictorial art*** 絵画芸術. ¶***plastic arts*** 造形美術. ¶a ***practical art*** 実用的技芸. ¶a ***primitive art*** 原始芸術. ¶the important ***social art*** of communication in writing 文通という重要な社交術. ¶Simplicity, sincerity, naturalness are all lost in the ***studied art*** of workmanship. 素ぼく・率直・自然というものが皆こった技巧のために死んでしまった. ¶a ***technical art*** 工芸. ¶the ***textile art*** 紡織術. ¶the ***twin*** (=***sister***) ***arts*** 相関芸術. 【類】typewriting and shorthand are ***twin arts***. ¶***useful arts*** 有用な技芸. ¶the ***wedded arts*** of engraving and printing 相関芸術たる彫刻と印刷. ¶the ***Western art*** of war 西洋の戦術.

Q² English 17th ***century art*** 十七世紀の英国芸術. ¶***costume art*** 衣裳芸術. ¶the sciences that underlie the ***healing art*** 医術の基礎を成す諸科学. ¶***household arts*** 家庭諸芸. ¶***language arts*** 語学の諸技術. ¶***motion-picture arts*** 映画製作技術 ‖ the Academy of ***Motion-picture Arts*** and Sciences 〖映〗アカデミー映画賞審査委員会. ¶***peasant art*** in Roumania ルーマニアの民芸. ¶***Renaissance art*** 文芸復興期の芸術. ¶the technics of the ***ship-building art*** 造船技法. ¶the ***telephone art*** 電話の技術. ¶***theater arts*** 舞台芸術.

P an abortion (=a miscarriage) produced ***by*** *art* 人工流産. ¶I have a great taste ***for*** *art*. 私には大いに美術に対する趣味がある. ¶one skilled ***in*** a fine *art* 一芸術に長じている人. ¶objects ***of*** *art* 美術品 ‖ a man ***of*** *art* 美術家 ‖ He is a good judge ***of*** *art*. 眼識のある美術批評家だ. ‖ works ***of*** *art* 美術作品 ‖ He is an authority ***on*** Japanese *arts*. 日本美術に関する権威だ. ¶a smile ***without*** *art* すなおな微笑.

P² He admits that "*art* ***for*** man" is an even higher doctrine than "*art* ***for*** art." 彼は"人間のための芸術"は"芸術のための芸術"よりも一層高尚な説だと認めている. ¶*art* ***from*** the kilns 陶芸. ¶There is no *art* ***in*** doing it. それをするに別に面倒はない. ¶the *art* ***of*** floral oration (arrangement) 生け花 ‖ the *art* ***of*** living 生活技芸 ‖ master the "*art* ***of*** omission" 「省略のこつ」を会得する ‖ the *art* ***of*** defense with a sword=fencing 剣道 ‖ the *art* ***of*** medicine 医術 ‖ the *art* ***of*** trickery 手品 ‖ the *art* ***of*** character-painting 性格描写の技術 ‖ the *art* ***of*** correspondence 商用文の書き方 ‖ the *art* ***of*** expression 表現法 ‖ the *art* ***of*** health 健康法 ‖ the *art* ***of*** pleasing 人を喜ばせる法 ‖ the *art* ***of*** wealth 利殖法 ‖ the *art* ***of*** writing 文筆のわざ ‖ Literature is the *art* ***of*** words. 文学は言葉の芸術だ. 【類】the *art* ***of*** making friends.

Artemis, *n.* 女神アルテミス.

Q² the chaste ***goddess*** *Artemis* 純潔な女神アルテミス.

arteriosclerosis, *n.* 〖病理〗動脈硬化.

Q ***senile*** *arteriosclerosis* 動脈硬化.

artery, *n.* 動脈; 脈路, 大道.

V ***rupture*** an *artery* 動脈を破裂させる.

Q the *great artery* of traffic between the City and the West End ロンドン市区とウエストエンド間の交通要路. ¶Liverpool is the *main artery* of Great Britain's overseas trade. リヴァプールは大英国海外貿易の大動脈だ.【類】a *main artery* for traffic between the North and the South of the Metropolis. ¶The *artery* becomes *plugged*. 動脈が閉塞(ぷ)する.

Q² *traffic arteries* 交通上の動脈(要路).

article, *n.* (1) 文, 論文.

V it *contains* an important *article* by ... それに...の重要寄稿が載っている. ¶He *contributed* an *article* to the November issue. 十一月号に一文を寄せた. ¶*dash off articles* at midnight 真夜中に(新聞雑誌などの)原稿のなぐり書きをする. ¶It *deserves* an *article* to itself. そのことだけで一文を草する価値がある. ¶The paper *devotes* its leading *article* to the subject. その新聞はその問題について社説を載せている. ¶*head* an *article* with the words, "..." ... という見出しを記事に付ける. ¶*publish* an anonymous *article* concerning it それに関する匿名の文を公にする. ¶*put in* an *article* on ... in a magazine 雑誌に...に関する文を載せる. ¶*See* the *article* printed in the Outlook for October 30. 十月三十日のアウトルック誌に出たその記事を見よ. ¶*submit articles* to the censor before publication 記事を発表前に検閲官に見てもらう. ¶*write* an *article* on a portable typewriter 携帯用タイプライターで原稿を作る.

Q Several *able articles* on the subject have appeared in the periodicals. その問題を扱った色々のすぐれた記事が雑誌に出た. ¶a magazine full of *bright* and *topical articles* 時事問題に関するおもしろい記事を満載した雑誌. ¶a *copyrighted article* in a paper 新聞掲載の版権所有記事. ¶write *editorial articles* of astonishing worth りっぱな社説を書く. ¶*fresh, bright, light articles* 清新ではなやかで軽妙な記事. ¶do *hack articles* for ... ...のために下らぬものを書く. ¶the paper contains an *important article* by ... その新聞には...の書いた重要な文が載っている. ¶an *impressive article* 感動させる文. ¶publish an *incentive article* 扇動的な論文を発表する. ¶*inflammatory articles* 扇動的な記事. ¶a very *instructive article* きわめて教訓的な文. ¶The Times devotes a *leading article* to the subject. タイムス紙はその問題を社説で取扱っている. ¶*notable articles* in the number その号に載っている著しい独立記事. ¶*pointed articles* 痛烈な論文. ¶write a *powerful article* on ... ...について力のこもった論文を書く. ¶a *readable article* おもしろい記事. ¶he exposed the secret mercilessly in his *scathing article* on ... 彼は...に関する激越な文章で容赦なく秘密をすっぱぬいた. ¶a *signed article*=《米》a byliner 署名入の記事. ¶a *solid article* 充実した文. ¶*topical articles* on politics 政治に関する時事論文.

Q² a *city article*《英》[新聞の]商況欄. ¶*fact articles* 事実記事, 実話. ¶*money market articles* 金融市場記事. ¶a *newspaper* (*magazine*) *article* on ... ...関係の新聞(雑誌)記事.【類】clip out (切抜く) a *newspaper article*. ¶*periodical* (=*magazine*) *articles* 雑誌記事. ¶the *star article* in the current issue of the magazine その雑誌の今月号に出ているピカーの記事. ¶a *three-column article*〘新聞〙三段にわたる記事.

P *in* an *article* to appear next month in *Asia* 来月発行の「アジア」誌への寄稿中に.

P² write friendly *articles about* the country その国について好意ある文を書く. ¶an *article in* the Times タイムス紙の記事. ¶an *article on* it would not be complete without a reference to ... それに関する論文は...に言及しなくてはまとまりがつくまい.【類】an *article on* Whitman's place in American literature.

(2) 品物, 物品.

V British cotton flannel is *displacing* the Japanese *article* at Canton. 広東では英国製の綿フランネルが日本品を圧倒している. ¶*redeem* a pledged *article* 質受けをする. ¶*trace* (=*search out*) a missing *article* 紛失品を捜索する. ¶*sell* a person an *article* for so much ある品をいくらいくらで人に売る. ¶*supply* the *article* ordered 注文品を供給する.

Q a *bad article* 粗製品. ¶*chief articles* of our export trade with America 対米主要輸出品.【類】one of the *chief articles* of food. ¶patented *commercial articles* 特許商品. ¶*competing articles* 競争品. ¶*crude articles* at high speed 粗製濫造品. ¶a newly *devised article* 新案商品. ¶a *domestic article* 家庭用品. ¶*duty-paying articles* 課税品. ¶Milk is an *essential article* of diet. 牛乳は必需食品だ. ¶*fancy articles* 小間物類. ¶*finished articles* 完成品. ¶*hazardous articles* 有害物. ¶buy *home-produced articles* 国産品を買う. ¶find a *lost article* 遺失物を見つける. ¶ready-made clothing and other *made-up articles* 衣服及び他の製品. ¶*principal articles* of domestic produce 主なる国産品. ¶*second-hand articles* for sale 売物の中古品. ¶*seized articles* 押収物. ¶*shop-soiled articles* たなざらしの品物. ¶*small articles* of convenience 細かい調法な品. ¶a *staple article* of diet 日常食料品. ¶a *superior article* 上等品. ¶*used articles* of furniture 古手の家具. ¶*useful articles* 役に立つ品物. ¶*window-soiled articles* たなざらしの品.

Q² *comfort articles* 慰問品. ¶*gift articles* 贈り物用品. ¶common *household articles* 一般の家庭用品. ¶the *necessity article* for daily life 日常生活の必需品. ¶pearls and *pearl articles* 真珠及び真珠製品. ¶*toilet articles* (=cosmetics) 化粧品類. ¶*trade articles*=commodities of commerce 商品.

P the value of birds *as articles* of food 食料品としての鳥類の価値. ¶We are *out of* the *articles* at present. ただ今品切れです.

P² *articles at* an exhibition 陳列品. ¶*articles for* Christmas presents クリスマス用贈答品 ‖ a set of *articles for* the toilet-table 化粧用品一そろい. ¶an *article in* brass 真ちゅう製品. ¶an *article of* clothing 衣類 ‖ an *article of* commercial importance 重要商品 ‖ an *article of* food 食品.【類】an *article* (=piece) *of* furniture / an *article of* export / *articles of* commerce (=merchandise) / *articles of* taste / *Articles of* tortoise shell are a speciality of Nagasaki. べっこう細工は長崎の名物です. ‖ *articles of* utility 実用品 ‖ *articles of* value 金目のもの.

(3) 箇条; 約款, 規約.

V having *served* one's *articles* 年期が明けてから. ¶*sign* and *seal articles* of agreement 契約書に署名・調印する. ¶*take up* the *articles* seriatim 逐条審議する.

Q the *foregoing article* 前条.

Q² *marriage articles*=a marriage contract 婚姻契約書. ¶*memorandum articles* 覚書箇条.

P *under Article* 10 第十条によって ‖ He was *under articles* to an attorney. 弁護士の書生をしていた.

P² *articles of* incorporation [会社の]定款. ¶The *article upon* the school appropriation was lost. 学校経費の議題は否決された.

(4)〘文法〙冠詞.

V The word *takes* no *article* before it. その語には冠詞をつけない.

article, *v.* 年期奉公に出す.

P He *articled* his son *to* a carpenter. 息子を大工の所に年期奉公に出した.

articulate, *v.* 関節でつなぐ.

P It is *articulated to* the spine. それは背骨に関節でつながっている.

articulation, *n.* 発音.

Q a *distinct articulation* 明確な発音.

artifice, *n.* 奇計.

V *use* every *artifice* to ... ...するためにあらゆる奇計を用いる.

Q by a *clever artifice* 奇計を用いて. ¶a *sly artifice* 狡(こう)計.

P escape (avoid) *by artifice* 狡計を用いて逃れる(避ける). ¶*without artifice* 奇計を用いずに.

artificial, *a.* 人工的な.

M *highly artificial* はなはだしく不自然な.

artillery, *n.* 砲兵隊.

Q² *anti-aircraft artillery* 高射砲隊.

artist, *n.* 芸術家, 美術家; 技芸家.

V It would *take* a literary *artist* to properly describe it. それを正しく記述するには文芸家の筆が必要だ.

Q a *consummate literary artist* りっぱな文芸家. ¶a *culinary artist*=a cook 料理人. ¶illustration from drawings by *Dutch artists* オランダの画家の絵を複製したさし絵. ¶the *first artists* of the day 当代一流の芸術家. ¶*glyptic artists* in jade 玉(ぎょく)の彫刻家. ¶a production of a true *literary artist* 真の文芸家の作品. ¶a *music[al] artist* 音楽家. ¶really great *national artists* 真に偉大な国民的芸術家たち. ¶Mr. Ihei Kimura, well-known Japanese *photographic artist* 日本写真芸術の大家木村伊兵衛氏.

¶a ***talented*** *artist* 手腕のある芸術家.

Q² younger ***avant-garde*** *artists* of recognition 世に認められている青年前衛画家たち. ¶a group of ***concert*** *artists* オーケストラ団. ¶an ***escape*** *artist* 脱獄の名人. ¶a ***flagstone*** *artist* 大道画家. ¶a ***lady*** *artist* 婦人画家. ¶a ***lightning*** *artist* 早描きの画家. ¶a ***lightning sketch*** *artist* 大道の似顔絵描き. ¶***motion picture*** *artists* 映画関係技術家たち. ¶a ***movie make-up*** *artists* 映画俳優のメーキャップ技術者. ¶a ***muscle*** *artist* 筋肉を思うままに動かせる人. ¶***music-hall*** *artists* 寄席芸人たち. ¶a ***pavement*** *artist* 《英》舗道に絵を描いて金をもらう画家. ¶a ***poster*** *artist* ポスター画工. ¶a ***publicity*** *artist* 宣伝関係の画家. ¶***radio*** *artists* 放送芸能人. ¶a ***sand*** *artist* 砂絵を描く人. ¶a ***sleight-of-hand*** *artist* 奇術師. ¶a ***spare-time*** *artist* 余暇に絵をかく人. ¶***stage show*** *artists* ショーに出る芸能人. ¶a ***street*** *artist* 街を流す芸人. ¶a ***typewriter*** *artist* タイプライターで器用な図案などを造るタイピスト. ¶***variety show*** *artists* 寄席芸人たち. ¶***Walt Disney*** *artists* ディズニーものの画家. ¶***woman*** *artists* 婦人画家.

P He ranks high ***as*** an *artist*. 彼は技工としては第一流だ. ¶a picture ***by*** a famous *artist* 知名な某大家の絵.

P² He is an *artist* ***at*** the work. 彼はその仕事が上手だ. ¶a celebrated *artist* ***in*** lacquer 有名な漆芸家 ‖ an *artist* ***in*** words 名文家. ¶an *artist* ***of*** genius 天才はだの美術家.

artiste, *n.* 芸人.

V a ***quick-change*** *artiste*「早変り」芸人.

ascend, *v.* 登る, 昇る; さかのぼる.

P *ascend* ***against*** a rushing stream 激流をさかのぼる. ¶*ascend* ***in*** a balloon 気球で上昇する. ¶with a representation of dragons rising from the angry waves of the sea and *ascending* ***into*** the clouds 竜が怒濤から出て雲に登る図柄の. ¶Christ *ascended* ***to*** (=into) heaven. キリストは昇天した. ‖ These inquiries *ascend* ***to*** the remotest antiquity. これらの研究は太古にさかのぼる. ¶Tens *ascend* ***to*** hundreds. 数十から数百に増加する.

ascendant, *n.* 優位, 優勢.

P At that period the star of France was definitely ***in*** the *ascendant*. 当時フランスはたしかに国運が隆盛であった. ‖ He is again ***in*** the *ascendant*. 再び優位に立っている. ‖ My star is ***in*** the *ascendant*. 僕の運勢は上り坂だ(有卦(うけ)に入る). 【類】in days when heraldry (紋章学) was ***in*** the *ascendant*.

ascendency, ascendancy, *n.* 優勢.

V ***attain*** its highest *ascendency* 全盛をきわめる. ¶***gain*** an *ascendency* at a court 朝廷で大いに羽振がきく ‖ ***gain*** (=***get*** *or* ***obtain***) the *ascendency* 優位に立つ. ¶***have*** an *ascendency* over him 彼にまさる. ¶***lose*** its *ascendancy* 衰える.

Q ***commercial*** and ***industrial*** *ascendancy* 商業と産業の隆盛.

Q² Tokimasa was the founder of the ***Hojo*** *ascendancy*. 時政は北条氏執権の創立者である.

P The king was completely ***under*** the *ascendancy* of his wife. 王は全然王妃のしりに敷かれていた.

P² the *ascendency* ***over*** the surrounding nations 衛星国に対する指導権.

ascension, *n.* 上昇.

Q² a ***balloon*** *ascension* 気球の上昇.

P² *ascension* ***to*** the throne 登位 ‖ *ascension* ***to*** glory 光栄獲得.

ascent, *n.* 上昇; さかのぼること; 上り坂, こう配.

V He ***accomplished*** the first *ascent* of Mt. Robson. 彼はロブソン山の初登頂をなし遂げた. ¶***attempt*** a guideless *ascent* of a high mountain 高山を強力なしに登ろうとする. ¶***carry out*** the *ascent* of Fuji 富士登山を実行する. ¶The road ***has*** an *ascent* of about five degrees. この道路のこう配は五度位だ. ¶the place from which the *ascent* is ***made*** 登山口 ‖ He ***made*** the *ascent*, the first by a foreign traveler. 彼は外人として最初の登山をした. ‖ It is possible to ***make*** the *ascent* and the descent of the mountain in one long day. その山は日山ができる. ¶***undertake*** a laborious *ascent* up ... 骨の折れる…登山を試みる. ¶***venture*** the *ascent* その登山を試みる.

Q The mountain is an ***easy*** *ascent*. その山は登るのに楽だ. ¶an ***experimental*** *ascent* of a military balloon 軍用気球の試揚. ¶make one's ***first*** *ascent* [気球・山などの]初乗(初登山)をする. ¶a ***gentle*** (=gradual) ascent ゆるやかなのぼり. ¶make a ***midwinter*** *ascent* of Mount Fuji 富士の寒中登山をする. ¶a ***regular*** *ascent* 段々登り. ¶He has achieved one of the most ***speedy*** and ***spectacular*** *ascents* to international fame as a writer. 彼は一朝にしてみごと世界的文名をかち得た. ¶a ***steep*** *ascent* 急坂. ¶The first ***successful*** *ascent* to the summit of Mont Blanc was made in August 1786 by Paccard. 始めてモン・ブランの絶頂を極めたのはパッカールで 1786 年 8 月のことだった. ¶a ***toilsome*** *ascent* 難儀な登り.

P² an *ascent* ***of*** a balloon 気球の上昇. ¶the *ascent* ***of*** vapors ***from*** the earth 地上からの水蒸気の上昇. ¶an *ascent* ***to*** antiquity 古代研究. ¶*ascent* ***toward*** civilization 文明開化.

ascertain, *v.* 確かめる; 決定する.

M *ascertain* ***confidentially*** 秘密に確かめる. ¶*ascertain* ***experimentally*** 実験によって確かめる. ¶*ascertain* ***statistically*** 統計によって決定する.

P *ascertain* it ***from*** the company's agents 同会社の代理店に照会してその事件を確かめる ‖ Please *ascertain* ***from*** whom the inquiry emanated. その質問がだれから出たのか確かめて下さい.

asceticism, *n.* 禁欲主義.

V ***practice*** the severest *asceticism* 厳重な禁欲生活を行う. 【類】a famous Indian priest and hermit—Daruma—***practiced*** *asceticism* until his lower limbs rotted off.

ascribable, *a.* 帰せらるべき.

P His failure is *ascribable* ***to*** incompetence. 彼の失敗はその無能に帰すべきだ.

ascribe, *v.* 帰する.

M The picture is ***traditionally*** *ascribed* to Sesshu. その絵は雪舟の作と伝えられている.

P *ascribe* it ***to*** a cause それをある原因の結果であるとする ‖ *ascribe* losses ***to*** imprudence 損害を不用意に帰する. 【類】*ascribe* all the glory ***to*** God ‖ the poem is *ascribed* ***to*** the pen of ... その詩は…の作とされている.

ash, *n.* 灰; *pl.* 遺骸, 遺骨.

V It has been decided by his family and the Foreign Office that his *ashes* shall be ***buried*** in Batavia. その人の遺骨はバタビヤに埋葬されることに遺族と外務省で打合せた. ¶***collect*** the *ashes* in an urn つぼに(火葬後の)遺骨を収める. ¶***knock off*** the *ashes* of one's cigar into the stove 葉巻の灰をストーヴの中へ払い落す. ¶This coal ***leaves*** little (much) *ash*. この石炭は灰が出ない(出る). ¶***rake up*** *ashes* 灰をかき立てる. ¶Under the tomb ***rest*** his *ashes*. この墓の下に彼が葬ってある.

Q² shower "***death*** *ash*" over ... …に「死の灰」を降らす. ¶drop ***cigar*** (***cigarette***) *ash* on the mat タバコの灰をマットにおとす. ¶***wood*** (***straw***) *ashes* 木(わら)灰.

P lie ***in*** *ashes* [燃えて]灰になっている. ¶Peace ***to*** his *ashes!* 彼の霊よ安らかなれ(南無阿彌陀仏)! ‖ The building was burned (=reduced) ***to*** *ashes*. 建物は烏有(うゆう)に帰した.

P² the *ashes* ***of*** his cremated corpse 火葬にした彼の遺骸の灰.

ashamed, *pa.* 恥じている, 赤面している.

M feel ***deeply*** *ashamed* 汗顔の至り. ¶He is ***deliberately*** *ashamed* of it. 深くそれを恥じている. ¶I am ***half*** *ashamed* to confess it. それを自白するのはいささかはずかしい. ¶I am ***heartily*** *ashamed* of it. それを心から恥じている. ¶be very ***much*** *ashamed*. ¶I am ***utterly*** *ashamed* of you. 君のことでは赤恥もんだ.

P He was *ashamed* ***at*** being unable to give answer. 答えられないので赤面した. ¶They are *ashamed* ***for*** having treated you so. 彼らは君に対してあんなことをしたのを恥じている. ¶I am *ashamed* ***of*** your conduct. 君の行いには赤面する. 【類】be *ashamed* ***of*** one's child / She was asked if she was not *ashamed* ***of*** herself. / There is nothing to be *ashamed* ***of***. / What is there to be *ashamed* ***of*** in confessing one's errors? / I am *ashamed* ***of*** having done so.

O I am *ashamed* to do such a thing. そんな事をするのははずかしい.

ashore, *ad.* 浜へ, 陸へ.

P The ship was *ashore* ***on*** the Awa coast. 船は阿波海岸で擱坐(かくざ)した. ‖ The ship was (=got *or* went) *ashore* ***on*** a rock (shoal). 船は暗礁(など)に乗上げた.

asiatic, *n.* アジア人.

Q ***upstart*** *Asiatics* 新興のアジア人.

aside, *n.* わきぜりふ.

P ***in*** an *aside*, he muttered that ... 彼はわきぜりふで…とつぶやいた.

aside, *ad.* 離れて.

P it is *aside* ***from*** our present aims to ... …するのはわれわれの現在の目的にはずれる. 【類】it is *aside* ***from*** the main purpose of this paper to discuss ... ‖ That is *aside from* the subject. それは問題外です.

ask, *v.* 請う, 求める; 尋ねる; 要求する; 招く.

M I *asked* him **civilly** what he wanted. 何の御用ですかと丁寧に尋ねた. ¶ *ask* **earnestly** for your forgiveness 切に御勘弁を願う. ¶ He **hospitably** *asked* me to step in and have a talk. 彼はちょっと入ってお話なさいと親切に言ってくれた. ¶ **impertinently** *ask* なまいきに尋ねる. ¶ He *asked* me **in**. 私におはいりなさいと言った. ¶ **lightly** *ask* ちょっと尋ねる. ¶ Don't *ask* so **loud**. そんなに大きな声で尋ねるな. ¶ *ask* him **out** (=invite him) to tea 彼をお茶に招く. 【類】 *ask* students **out** to one's home. ¶ *ask* a question **pertinently** 適切な質問をする. ¶ *ask* **pointblank** 無遠慮に尋ねる. ¶ **politely** *ask* 丁寧に頼む(尋ねる). ¶ He will **probably** *ask* me over for tea some afternoon. そのうち午後のお茶によんでくれるだろう. ¶ *ask* **savagely** 乱暴な聞き方をする. ¶ *ask* **sharply** 鋭い質問をする. ¶ You *ask* **too much.** 値が高すぎる; 要求がひど過ぎる. ¶ *ask* **sternly** きっとなって尋ねる. ¶ *Ask* the gentleman **upstairs.** 二階へ御通し申せ. ¶ You may **well** *ask* that. それはごもっともなご質問です. ¶ *ask* **wistfully** なつかし気に尋ねる.

P I *asked* him **about** his business. 彼の用向を尋ねた. 【類】 I *asked* him **about** the matter. / I came to *ask* you **about** my boy. ¶ *ask* **after** one's health ご機嫌伺いをする ‖ I *asked* **after** my sick friend. 病気の友人を見舞った. ‖ *ask* **after** his trade 商売の景気を尋ねる. ¶ I *ask* you **as** a favor to ... お願いですから...して下さい. ¶ *ask* (=inquire) **at** [Scot.] (=of) ... ...に尋ねる. ¶ How much do you *ask* **for** this? これはいくらか. ‖ beggars *asking* **for** charity 施しをこうこじき. 【類】 *ask* a person **for** advice / He never *asked* **for** any favors for himself. / *ask* him **for** employment (採用) in his office / We must *ask* **for** indulgence in this respect. / *ask* **for** a revision of salaries (昇給) / *ask* **for** his opinion regarding ... / *ask* **for** a night's lodging / *ask* **for** information (情報) / *ask* **for** a compensation (代償) of ... / *ask* **for** a contribution (寄付) / *ask* **for** a loan of money (金の融通) / *ask* **for** a postponement (猶予) / without *asking* **for** reward (報酬) ‖ I *asked* **for** the hand of his daughter in marriage. 彼の娘を妻にもらいたいと申込んだ. ‖ *ask* **for** one's bill 勘定書を請求する ‖ *ask* **for** another course [食物の]お代りをする ‖ *ask* **for** a lift [自動車に]同乗させてくれと頼む ‖ *ask* **for** a recount [投票などの]再調を要求する ‖ It's like *asking* **for** trouble. わざわざ禍を招くようなものだ. ‖ *ask* **for** it by name 名ざしでそれ(商品)を買いたいという ‖ *ask* **for** an additional tip また酒手を請求する ‖ *ask* **for** a "yes or no" answer on ... ...に関して諾否の返事を求める ‖ the newspaper *asked* **for** a vote of its subscribers as to their nominee for the office of ... その新聞は...の職にだれを任命すべきかという読者の希望投票を募集した ‖ It is hardly worth *asking* **for**. 頼む価値がないほどだ. ¶ *ask* a thing **from** a person 人に物を求める. ¶ He *asked* me **in** surprise. 彼はびっくりして私に尋ねた. ¶ *ask* bread **of** a person 人にパンをこう ‖ I *asked* a favor **of** him. 彼に頼んだ. 【類】 *ask* **of** him the favor of a loan / I wish to *ask* a favor **of** you. / May I *ask* a question **of** you? / what he *asks* **of** them (頼み事). ¶ I *asked* merely **out of** curiosity. ちょっと伺って見たいと思っただけです. ¶ *ask* him **to** dinner 彼を晩さんに招く. 【類】 *ask* persons **to** one's party.

O I *asked* him to come in. 彼におはいりと言った.

asker, *n.* 尋ねる人.

Q an **indefatigable** *asker* of questions 盛んに質問する人.

asking, *n.* 求めること.

P it may be had **for** the *asking* at ... それは...へ申込めば手にはいります. 【類】 All our catalogues are free **for** the *asking*.

asleep, *a., ad.* 眠って.

M He fell **fast** *asleep*. 彼はぐっすり寝込んだ. ¶ He lay **half** *asleep*. 半ば眠っていた. ¶ He is **sound** *asleep*. 彼はよく眠っている.

P fall *asleep* **in** one's seat 居眠りをする. 【類】 The regiment were *asleep* **in** the tents. ¶ I have been *asleep* **to** it. 私はそれに無関心だった.

aspect, *n.* 面相; 外観, 形勢, 様子, 局面; 見方, 観, 相; 方向, 方面, 向き.

V That **alters** the *aspect* of the case. そうなると形勢が変って来る. ¶ Depressing thoughts disappear and life **assumes** a smiling *aspect*. 心配などなくなって世の中がおもしろくなる. ‖ Things are **assuming** a serious *aspect*. 形勢不穏になりつつある. 【類】 The situation is **assuming** a more serious *aspect*. ¶ The city **bears** a decidedly Flemish *aspect*. その市はフランダ風の所を多分に持っている. ¶ **change** *aspect* 様子を変える. 【類】 **change** the entire *aspect* of a city / The mountain **changes** its *aspect* at every turn (一歩一歩). ¶ **give** the affair another *aspect* 事態に新生面を開く. ¶ This house **has** a bad *aspect*. この家は向きが悪い. 【類】 His house **has** a southern *aspect*. ‖ Serious situations often **have** a humorous *aspect*. 重大な事態にも往々こっけいなことがある. 【類】 The question **has** important *aspects*. ¶ Its presence **imparts** a very bright and cheerful *aspect* to the place. それがあるのでそこにきわめて陽気な朗かな気分を出している. ¶ **open** new *aspects* on it それに新生面を開く. ¶ The event has **put** a very different *aspect* upon the situation. その事件のため形勢が一変した. ¶ The city has **regained** its prewar *aspect*. その市は戦前の姿に回復した. ¶ The situation has **taken on** a new *aspect*. 形勢が一変した.

Q Facts have a habit at times of bearing a not altogether **agreeable** *aspect*. 事実は余りおもしろくないと思わせる事がよくある. ¶ The *aspect* of the mountain is very **beautiful.** その山の景色(姿)は実に好い. ¶ study a question in its **broader** *aspects* その問題を大局から研究する. ¶ Everything had a **cheerful** *aspect*. 何もかも朗らかに見えた. ¶ Streets at New Year assume a **decorated** *aspect*. 新年の街々は飾りを着ける. ¶ The question has taken on an entirely **different** *aspect*. その問題は局面ががらっと変った. ¶ **diverse** *aspects* of human life 人生の諸相. ¶ the **economic** *aspects* of a subject 一問題の経済的方面. ¶ **eternal** and **enduring,** rather than **topical** or **transitory,** *aspects* of human life 人生の一時的または過渡的な方面よりむしろ永久的かつ恒常的なそれ. ¶ its **financial** *aspect* その財政上の面. ¶ It has a **full south** *aspect*. それは真南向きだ. ¶ He said it with a very **gracious** *aspect*. ごくやさしい面持でそう言った. ¶ But there are other and much **graver** *aspects* of this question. しかしこの問題には他の一層重大な方面がある. ¶ a crippled wretch of **hideous** *aspect* 悪相をしたびっこの男. ¶ the **humorous** *aspects* of life 人生のユーモラスな面. ¶ the **international** *aspects* of a situation 局面の国際的関係. ¶ **knowing** *aspect* 知った風. ¶ the **legal** *aspect* of sport 競技の法律的方面. ¶ The scenery appears here in its **loveliest** *aspect*. ここでその景色の一番よい所が見られる. ¶ a **mild** *aspect* 温容. ¶ the **moral** *aspect* of a case 一事件の道義上の関係. ¶ open **new** *aspects* on the utilization of heavy crude oil 重油利用に新生面を開く. ¶ one **other** *aspect* of the society's work その協会の事業のもう一つの方面. ¶ a man of **owl-like** *aspect* ふくろうのような(まじめくさった)顔つきの男. ¶ the **physical** *aspect* of the country その国の地勢. ¶ a **piteous** *aspect* of woe 災禍の惨状. ¶ The society is assuming a **political** *aspect*. その協会は政治的色彩を帯びて来た. ¶ its **practical** *aspect* その実際的方面. ¶ of **repellent** *aspect* いやなようすの. ¶ the **routine** *aspect* of research 研究の型にはまった方面. ¶ the **sentimental** *aspect* of a case 事件の感情的方面. ¶ at length the matters assumed one day so **serious** an *aspect* that ... やがてその問題はある日...ほど重大な様相を示すに至ったので.... ¶ the **solemn** *aspect* of a judge 裁判官のいかめしい顔つき. ¶ with a **south-eastern** *aspect* 東南向きの. ¶ a house with a **sunny** *aspect* 日当りのいい家. ¶ a **third** *aspect* of the question その問題の今一つ別の方面. ¶ Her face has a **tired** *aspect*. 疲れが顔に見えている. ¶ add to the **tragic** *aspect* of the affair 事態の悲劇味を増す. ¶ the question in its **true** *aspect* その問題の真相. ¶ The subject may be viewed from **two** *aspects*. その問題は二つの方面から見ることができる. ¶ vice in its **ugliest** *aspect* 醜悪極まる罪悪. ¶ **various** *aspects* of national life 国民生活の諸相. 【類】 One had better see life in its **various** *aspects* when young.

P discuss it **in** all its *aspects* (=bearings) その問題をあらゆる方面から論じる. 【類】 crime **in** all its *aspects* ‖ serious **in** *aspect* 顔付の厳粛な. 【類】 a house **with** a warm southern *aspect* (南向).

P² the *aspect* **of** affairs is black for ... 形勢が...にとって不利である ‖ *aspects* **of** the same problem 同一問題の諸方

面 ‖ *aspects of* nature＝physical features 地形 ‖ an *aspect of* grandeur 壮観.

asperity, *n.* 無愛相.

P *with asperity* 無愛想に, つっけんどんに.

aspersion, *n.* 誹謗(ひぼう).

V *cast aspersions* on him 彼を誹謗する. ¶*make aspersions* upon ... ...を誹謗する.

Q *invidious aspersions* 悪感を抱かせる誹謗.

aspirant, *n.* 志望者, 熱望者.

Q *literary aspirants* 文学志望者. ¶*young aspirants* after fame 青雲の志ある青年.

P a crowd (＝multitude) *of aspirants* 数多の熱望者.

P² *aspirants after* literary honor 文名にあこがれる者. ¶the *aspirants for* literary reputation 文名を得ようとするもの. ¶a young *aspirant to* the art of fiction 小説を書こうという文学青年 ‖ *aspirants to* screen careers 映画俳優を希望する人々.

aspiration, *n.* 大望, 抱負, 熱望.

V *hamper aspiration* 志望を阻害する. ¶They *have* intense *aspirations* toward liberty. 彼らは自由に対する熱望を持っている. ¶*kindle aspirations* 大望を起させる. ¶His father *opposed* his collegiate *aspiration*. 父は彼の大学に進もうという志望に反対した. ¶*realize* one's *aspiration* 望みを遂げる. ¶*thwart* one's *aspirations* 志望を阻害する.

Q *dynastic aspirations* 王朝を隆盛にしようとする大望. ¶not *ignoble aspirations* 卑しからぬ願望. ¶*legitimate aspirations* 正当の欲望. ¶*lofty aspirations* 高邁(こうまい)な抱負. ¶its *national aspirations* その国民的欲望. ¶a *sublime aspiration* 崇高な望み. ¶have *vice-presidential aspirations* 副大統領たらんとする下心がある.

P a man *of* noble *aspirations* 高尚な望みを持つ人.

P² a fervent *aspiration after* better things さらに優良なものを得ようとする熱望 ‖ *aspirations after* virtue 徳に対するあこがれ. ¶I have no *aspiration for* (＝after) fame. 名誉は望まない. 【類】an *aspiration for* the beautiful. ¶the *aspiration of* the Filipinos *toward* liberalism and modern life and progress フィリッピン人の自由と近代的生活と進歩とに対する欲望.

aspire, *v.* 高きを望む, 熱望する; そびえ立つ.

M a tower *aspiring heavenward* 天高くそびえる塔.

P *aspire after* greatness 大きな抱負を抱く ‖ *aspire after* supremacy in the Far East 極東の覇権(はけん)を握ろうとする. ¶noble trees *aspiring to* the sky 高く天にそびえる大木 ‖ an author who *aspires to* the first rank in his profession 一流たらんとする作家. 【類】*aspire to* literary success ‖ The more modern buildings *aspire to* the skyscraper class. もっと新しい建物は摩天楼式に(高く)建てる. 【類】*aspire to* such a position (地位) / *aspire to* high honors / *aspire to* something higher and greater in life. ¶*aspire toward* something perfect 一層完全なものを欲する.

ass, *n.* うさぎうま; ばか.

V *call* an *ass* a cow うさぎうまを牝牛と呼ぶ. ¶*make* an *ass* of oneself ばかなまねをする. 【類】Don't *make* an *ass* (＝a fool) of me.

assail, *v.* 攻撃する, 襲う; 非難する.

M *bitterly assail* 手ひどく攻撃する. ¶*openly assail* 公然と非難する. ¶*assail recklessly* and *indiscriminately*＝run amuck 相手かまわず乱暴を働く. ¶*unjustly assail* 正当の理由なくして攻撃する. ¶*vehemently assail* 猛烈に攻撃する.

P The ship was *assailed by* a severe storm. 船は猛烈な暴風に襲われた. ‖ I was *assailed by* a shower of stones. ばらばらと石を投げつけられた. ¶be *assailed from* all sides by criticism and abuse 四方八方から酷評と悪口を浴せられる. ¶He was *assailed with* abuse (reproaches). 彼は罵詈(ばり)(など)を浴びた. 【類】*assail* a man *with* blows.

assassination, *n.* 暗殺.

Q² a piece of *character assassination* 人身攻撃の一例.

assault, *n.* 襲撃, 攻撃; 強襲.

V *commit* an *assault* upon him 彼を襲撃する. ¶*make* an *assault* on a fort 堡塁(ほうるい)を攻める. ¶*meet* the *assault* of foreign ideologies 外国の思想戦に対抗する.

Q an *all-out assault* 総攻撃. ¶a *brutal assault* 残虐な襲撃. ¶a *dastardly assault* 卑怯な襲撃. ¶a *hooligan assault* よた者の襲撃. ¶an *indecent assault* わいせつ行為. ¶commit an *unprovoked assault* on ... 故なくして...を襲撃する. ¶a *violent assault* 猛襲.

Q² make a *night assault* upon ... ...を夜襲する.

P take a town *by assault* 襲撃して市を占領する. ¶The one-time splendid decorations of the temples have succumbed *to* the *assaults* of time and are now devoid of beauty. かつては金ぴかの寺院の装飾も 時の手に荒されて今は見る影もない).

P² an *assault against* prejudice 偏見に対する攻撃. ¶an *assault upon* a fortress 城砦(じょうさい)の強襲. 【類】the *assaults of* the enemy *upon* our works (施設). ¶an *assault with* a weapon 武器での攻撃 ‖ an *assault with* intent to kill ...を殺す目的での襲撃.

assault, *v.* 襲撃する.

M *improperly assault* a girl 女子に暴行を加えようとする.

P He was *assaulted with* stones. 彼は石で襲撃された.

assemblage, *n.* 会合; 群集, 集団.

V The scenery *represents* the most striking *assemblage* of figures and colors in nature. その風景は自然界における最も著しい形並に色の集団である.

Q a *brilliant assemblage* 名士の会合. ¶a *motley assemblage* 多彩(色々の方面の人)の集会.

P I was one *of* the *assemblage*. 私も群集に交じっていた.

assemble, *v.* 集まる; 組立てる.

M *assemble together* 寄り合う.

P *assemble* parts *into* a unit 部分品を組立てて単一の機械にする.

assembler, *n.* 組立工.

Q² a *machine assembler* 機械組立工.

assembly, *n.* 集会, 会合.

V *address* a large *assembly* 多数の聴衆に向って演説する. ¶*call* an *assembly* of ... ...議員を召集する. ¶They *form* a strange and motley *assembly*. それらが変った雑然たる一集団を成している. ¶*hold* an *assembly* 集会を開く. ¶The orator *swayed* the *assembly*. その弁士は会衆を圧倒した.

Q an *august assembly* of banking, industrial, and commercial magnates 銀行・産業・実業界の大立物を集めた一大会合. ¶a *deliberative assembly* 議会. ¶in the *full Assembly* 本会議で. ¶a *national assembly* 国民議会(フランスの). ¶a *periodic assembly* 定期の会合. ¶an instance of extreme bashfulness, or lack of presence of mind, before a *public assembly* 公開の席での極端な臆し方, つまり落着きのなさ, の一例.

Q² the second Annual *Alumni assembly* 第二回校友会年会.

P He presided *at* the *assembly*. 彼が司会した.

P² an *assembly of* eminent men 名士の集り.

assemblyman, *n.* 議員.

Q a *prefectural assemblyman* 県会議員.

Q² a *State assemblyman* 《米》州議会の下院議員. ¶a *ward assemblyman* 区会議員.

assent, *n.* 同意, 承諾; 裁可, 協賛.

V *command* the *assent* of ... 当然...の同意を得る. 【類】He may fail at times to *command assent*. ¶*compel assent* to one's exorbitant demand 法外の要求を強制的に承諾させる. ¶They *enforced assent* to their demands. 彼らは無理やりに自分らの要求を承諾させた. ¶*give* one's *assent* to a plan 計画に賛成する. 【類】reluctantly *give* one's *assent*. ¶*have* his *assent* 彼の同意を得る. ¶*nod assent* to ... ...にうなずいて承諾の意を示す. ¶*obtain* the *assent* of our reason 理性の満足を得る. ¶He *read* my *assent* in my eyes. 私の承諾を顔色で察した. ¶*receive* the King's *assent* 王の裁可を受ける. 【類】The Bill *received* Royal *assent*. / It has never *received* the *assent* of those who are qualified to judge. ¶*refuse assent* 承諾を断る. ¶*signify assent* to ... ...に同意を表する. ¶*win assent* 承諾を得る.

Q give a *ready assent* 快諾する. ¶The *Sovereign's assent* is given to bills which have passed both Houses. 両院を通過した議案に対し君主は裁可を与える.

P *with* one *assent* 満場一致で.

P² the *assent* and consent *of* the Diet 議会の協賛. ¶*assent to* a proposal (resolution) 提議(など)への協賛.

assent, *v.* 同意する, 賛成する.

M *amiably assent* 快く承知する. ¶*cordially assent* 快諾を与える. ¶*obligingly assent* あいづちを打つ. ¶He *assented readily* when asked to help. 彼は援助を求められたとき快くこれに応じた.

P I *assent to* your views. 君の意見に同意する. 【類】I *assent to* that. / He *assented to* the statement. ‖ *Assenting to* the premises, we reject the conclusion. 前提は認めるが結論は反対だ.

assert, *v.* 断言する, 言張る.
M *boldly assert* 大胆に断言する. ¶*assert* ***emphatically*** 強調する. ¶*assert* most ***positively*** 断固として主張する. ¶***proudly*** *assert* ごう然言放つ. ¶it may be ***safely*** *asserted* that ... ...と言って差支なかろう.
P *assert* ***with*** emphasis 力説する ‖ *assert* ***with*** confidence 自信をもって言う.
assertion, *n.* 断言, 言明; 主張.
V carefully ***ascertain*** all the *assertions* 言明について一々丁寧に確かめる. ¶***explode*** the oft-repeated *assertion* その常套(とう)の説を打破する. ¶***hazard*** the *assertion* that.... ...と臆断する. ¶***make*** an *assertion* 言明する.
Q ***ancient physiognomical*** *assertions* 人相に関する昔の説. ¶***baseless*** *assertions* 根拠のない所説. ¶a ***bold*** *assertion* 大胆な主張. ¶a ***calm*** *assertion* 冷静な陳述. ¶a ***false*** *assertion* 偽の申立. ¶a ***mendacious*** *assertion* 虚偽の申立. ¶***self*** *assertion* 自己の権利主張. ¶a very ***sweeping*** *assertion* きわめて概括的な(十ぱ一からげ的な)言明. ¶a totally ***unfounded*** *assertion* 全然根拠のない言明. ¶make ***unguarded*** *assertions* うっかりしたことを言う. ¶an ***unqualified*** *assertion* 資格のない人の所説. ¶***unsubstantiated*** *assertions* 根拠薄弱な言明. ¶They are only a mass of ***unsupported*** *assertions.* それはどれもこれもずさんな断定に過ぎない.
assess, *v.* 割当てる, 賦課する.
P *assess* a fine of ... ***against*** him for ... ...に対して彼から...の科料を徴収する. ¶*assess* the members ***for*** expense 入費に当てるために会員に会費を課する. ¶*assess* a tax ***on*** (=***upon***) land 土地に税を課する ‖ A tax *assessed* ***upon*** property is a property tax. 財産に課する税を財産税という. 【類】*assess* a fine (科料) ***upon*** him.
assessment, *n.* 賦課.
V He felt that he had reason to ***dispute*** the *assessment* of his income. 彼は自分の所得税の決定に対して不服を唱える理由があると感じた.
Q² ***party*** *assessments* 政党の割付金.
P² the *assessment* ***of*** damage 損害保償額.
assessor, *n.* 評価人.
Q² an ***expert*** *assessor* 老練な財産評価人.
asset, *n.* 資産, 財産.
V ***gain*** mental *assets* by travel 旅行をして思想を豊富にする.
Q Youth is the most ***attractive*** *asset* of the revue. 若さこそレビュー最大の魅力である. ¶He is a very ***big*** *asset* to the house. 彼はその社の宝である. ¶Good climate is her ***chief*** *asset* and almost a monopoly. 気候の良いということがその国の主な財産でほとんど独占している. ¶a ***cultural*** *asset* 文化財. ¶***external*** *assets* 在外資産. ¶The Cockerell workshops were among the best in Europe and their activities formed one of Belgium's greatest ***industrial*** *assets.* コックレルの工場は欧州最良のものであり, その事業はベルギーの産業界において最大勢力の一つを成している. ¶an ***intangible*** *asset* 無形の財産. ¶***invisible*** *assets* 無形の諸財産. ¶Knowledge is a ***moral*** *asset.* 知識は精神的財産である. ¶He has become the most valuable ***national*** *asset* of the country. 彼はその国の最も貴重な国宝となった. ¶scholars whose names are among the ***noblest*** *assets* of the country 国宝的学者. ¶Style is a greater ***social*** *asset* than beauty. 社交上美装は美貌(ぼう)よりもさらに重大な財産である. ¶Abundance of water power is one of the most ***valuable*** *assets* of a country. 水力の豊富なのは一国の最も貴重な財産の一つである. 【類】Personality (人物) is a ***valuable*** *asset* in business.
Q² ***enemy*** *assets* 敵国の財産.
P² The festival is regarded as an *asset* ***for*** innkeepers and postcard vendors. その祭典は旅館や絵はがき屋の金もうけの種になっている. ¶The country has in its superb climate an *asset* ***of*** rare worth. その国は実に気候がよいという点がりっぱな取柄だ. ¶The child is an *asset* ***to*** the state. 子供は国の宝だ. ‖ a great *asset* ***to*** a business 商売上有用の人材. 【類】He will become a better worker and a greater *asset* ***to*** his employer. / The gleam of water is a great *asset* ***to*** a landscape. / He is expected to be a valuable asset ***to*** the work. / A pretty and charming woman, neatly dressed, is an *asset* ***to*** any office.
assiduity, *n.* 勤勉.
P ***with*** *assiduity* 精出して. ¶work ***with*** unremitting *assiduity* 孜々(し)として怠らぬ.
assiduous, *a.* 勤勉な.
P be *assiduous* ***at*** one's studies 学業を励む. ¶He is *assiduous* ***in*** his studies. 彼は精出して勉強する. 【類】*assiduous* ***in*** one's occupation / *assiduous* ***in*** performance of duty. ¶He is *assiduous* ***over*** his visitor. 彼は来訪者に対してご愛想をする.
assign, *v.* 指定する; 帰する.
P *assign* a day ***for*** a meeting 会合の日を指定する ‖ the vessel *assigned* ***for*** the expedition 遠征に選定された船. ¶That duty was *assigned* ***to*** him. その義務が彼に課された. ‖ The fire is *assigned* ***to*** various causes. その火災は種々の原因に帰せられている. ‖ *assign* odd behavior ***to*** ill health 奇異な挙動を不健康のせいにする ‖ be *assigned* ***to*** the bench 〖野〗[投手などが]交替させられる ‖ a sergeant *assigned* ***to*** K. P. 炊事担当の軍曹 ‖ The Buddhists of Burma and Ceylon *assign* Gautama's birth and death ***to*** 623 and 543 B.C. respectively. ビルマ及びセイロンの仏教徒は釈迦の誕生と入滅をそれぞれ西紀前 623 年及び 543 年としている.
assignment, *n.* 指定, 割当.
V I am correspondent for the New York Herald Tribune and ***have*** a special *assignment* to get a story in Israel. 私はニューヨーク・ヘラルド・トリビューンの通信員でイスラエルについて書くように特命を受けている. ¶He always takes care to ***prepare*** his *assignments.* 研究課題をやるようにいつも心掛けている. ¶He ***received*** *assignments* from a number of publications. 若干の刊行物から寄稿の依頼を受けた.
Q return from ***overseas*** *assignments* of soldiers 軍の海外派遣軍からの帰還. ¶The City Editor sent reporter and cameraman out on special ***rush*** *assignment.* 社会部長は緊急用務に関し記者とカメラマンを派遣した.
Q² ***date*** (***hour***) *assignment* 日(時間)割. ¶***study*** *assignments* [生徒への]研究題目の割当. ¶***work*** *assignment* 作業充当.
P come to Japan as correspondent ***on*** *assignment* from Life ライフ誌から指名されて通信員として日本に来る. ¶***under*** *assignment* by ... ...からの指定で.
P² an *assignment* ***of*** errors 誤りの指摘書.
assimilate, *v.* 同化する; たとえる.
P *assimilate* our law in this respect ***to*** the law of Scotland この点についてわが法律をスコットランドの法律に準拠させる ‖ By living with the Indians, he was *assimilated* ***to*** them in thinking and actions. インデアンと生活を共にしていたので彼は考え方も行動もインデアン風になっていた. ¶one substance *assimilating* ***with*** another 他の物質と同化する一物質 ‖ *assimilate* a conqueror ***with*** (=***to***) a robber 征服者を盗賊にたとえる.
assimilation, *n.* 同化.
P² Japan's *assimilation* ***of*** Western influence 日本の西洋文明同化.
assist, *v.* 助ける, 手伝う; 列席する.
M ***ably*** *assisted* by ... ...によって有力な援助を与えられて. ¶***materially*** *assist* a person ...に物質的援助をする. ¶*assist* a lady ***out*** from a car 手を貸して婦人を車から降ろす. ¶*assist* ***pecuniarily*** 金銭上の補助を与える.
P The man ***at*** whose treat we are to *assist* is a collector of Japanese color prints. われわれをごちそうによんでくれる人というのは日本の錦絵収集家である. ‖ All his friends *assisted* ***at*** the ceremony. 友人たちは皆その式に列した. 【類】*assist* ***at*** the solemnity (entertainment). ¶I *assisted* him ***from*** the saddle. 手を貸して彼を鞍から降ろしてやった. 【類】*assist* a lady ***from*** a car. ¶*assist* ***in*** the work of rescue 救助作業を助ける ‖ *assist* ***in*** child delivery 助産役をつとめる. 【類】He *assists* me ***in*** editing the paper. / *assist* ***in*** getting a living. ¶*assist* him ***to*** his feet 彼に手を貸して立たせてやる ‖ Graduates are *assisted* ***to*** positions. 卒業生には(学校で)就職の世話をする. ¶He *assisted* me ***with*** good counsel and encouragement. 彼はよい忠告と奨励の言葉で私に力をつけてくれた. ‖ *assist* a gentleman on ***with*** his coat 手伝って紳士にオーバーを着せる.
assistance, *n.* 援助, 補助.
V He generously ***afforded*** us *assistance.* 彼は惜気なくわれわれを援助してくれた. ¶***call*** medical *assistance* to his little son その小さい息子のために医者を呼ぶ. ¶***decline*** *assistance* 援助の申出を辞退する. ¶***derive*** *assistance* from ... ...から援助を受ける. ¶***employ*** his *assistance* 彼の力を借りる. ¶***engage*** his *assistance* 彼の援助を得る. ¶***extend*** *assistance* to ... ...に援助を与える. ¶***give*** *assistance* 援助する. ¶***have*** the *assistance* of ... ...から援助してもらう.

¶***invoke*** the *assistance* of the police 警察の援助を求める. ¶***lend*** *assistance* 力を貸す. ¶***obtain*** *assistance* from others 人手を借りる.【類】***obtain*** the *assistance* of ... ¶***offer*** *assistance* 援助を申出る. ¶***promise*** military *assistance* 軍事上の援助を約束する. ¶***receive*** great *assistance* from ... ...から大いに援助を受ける.【類】***receive*** an improper (不正の) *assistance* during an examination.【類】A tug (ひき船) proceeded to ***render*** *assistance*. ¶***require*** no outside *assistance* 外部からの補助を要しない. ¶***secure*** his *assistance* 彼の援助を得る. ¶***seek*** medical *assistance* 医者にかかる.

Q have command of ample ***clerical*** *assistance* 部下に十分の補助員を有している. ¶offer ***cordial*** *assistance* 誠意ある援助を申出る. ¶***courteous*** and ***invaluable*** *assistance* 鄭重できわめて貴重な援助. ¶the most ***esteemed*** and ***valued*** *assistance* きわめて重要にして貴重な援助. ¶offer ***financial*** *assistance* 財政上の援助を申出る.【類】lend ***financial*** *assistance* to ... ¶be unable to render ***further*** *assistance* これ以上の援助は不可能である. ¶***generous*** and ***hearty*** *assistance* 惜気なく誠意のある援助. ¶It is of ***great*** *assistance* to him. それは大いに彼の助けになる. ¶***heavenly*** *assistance* 天佑(ゆう). ¶require ***immediate*** *assistance* 即時の援助を要する. ¶***important*** *assistance* 重要な援助. ¶render a person ***material*** *assistance* 人に物質上の援助をする. ¶***mutual*** *assistance* 相互援助. ¶render ***necessary*** *assistance* to ... ...に必要な援助をする. ¶I express my gratitude for the ***obliging*** *assistance* thus rendered to me. こうして私に与えられた好意ある援助に対して感謝する. ¶a ***pecuniary*** (=***monetary***) *assistance* 金銭上の援助. ¶be of ***practical*** *assistance* to ... ...にとって実際上助けになる. ¶***prompt***, ***generous***, and ***effectual*** *assistance* さっそくの, 惜しみない, 効果的な援助. ¶I am not competent to carry it through without ***technical*** *assistance*. 私には専門家の助力を仰がずにそれを完成するだけの力がない. ¶receive most ***valuable*** *assistance* ***from*** ... ...からきわめて貴重な援助を受ける.

Q^{2} ***American dollar*** *assistance* アメリカのドル資金援助. ¶***emergency*** *assistance* 危急な場合の援助. ¶***employment*** *assistance* 就職あっ旋. ¶the ***expert*** *assistance* of ... ...という専門家の助力. ¶***relief*** *assistance* to the people of countries devastated by war 戦禍を受けた国民に対する救済援助. ¶***priority*** *assistance* 優先援助制度. ¶The industry receives ***state*** *assistance*. その産業は政府の補助を得ている.

P It is seconded ***by*** government *assistance*. それには政府の補助がある. ¶He cried out ***for*** *assistance*. 彼は助けを呼び求めた. ¶Would it be ***of*** any *assistance* to you? それが何かお役に立つでしょうか. ¶I succeeded ***through*** (=***by***) your *assistance*. おかげで成功しました. ¶bring him ***to*** my *assistance* 手伝いに連れて来る. ¶***with*** his *assistance* 彼の援けを借りて ‖ it was carried out ***with*** the *assistance* of an endowment given by ... それは...の寄付で実行された.

P^{2} with *assistance* ***from*** ... ...から援助されて. ¶*assistance* ***in*** a vendetta かたき討の助だち. ¶It is of *assistance* ***to*** me. それは私の助けになる.

assistant, *n.* 助手.

Q an ***able*** *assistant* 手腕のある助手. ¶a ***capable*** *assistant* 敏腕の補助者. ¶a ***four-legged*** *assistant* 四ツ足(馬など)の補助者. ¶an ***unpaid*** *assistant* 無給助手.

Q^{2} a ***business*** *assistant* 事務員. ¶a ***laboratory*** *assistant* 研究室助手. ¶a ***maternity*** *assistant* 助産手. ¶a ***shop*** *assistant* 店員. ¶her ***women*** *assistants* 彼女の女助手たち.

P^{2} *assistants* ***in*** trades 職工見習. ¶an *assistant* ***of*** the surgeon in the operation その手術の際の外科医の助手. ¶an *assistant* ***to*** a physician 代診.

associate, *n.* 友だち, 仲間.

V He ***has*** such rude *associates* at school, and they influence him in the wrong direction. 学校に乱暴な友だちがいるので悪い感化を受ける.

Q one's ***close*** *associates* ...の側近筋. ¶a ***congenial*** *associate* 会心の友. ¶***evil*** *associates* 悪友たち. ¶my ***scholarly*** *associate* at Waseda, Professor ... 早稲田での学友である...教授.

P^{2} one's *associates* ***at*** school 学校での友人. ¶an *associate* ***in*** a crime 共犯者 ‖ Mr. X, his younger *associate* ***in*** the British diplomatic service 英国外交界で彼の後進同僚であるＸ氏. ¶He is the *associate* ***of*** the leader in the enterprise. 彼はその事業経営者の女房役である.

associate, *v.* 連想する, 連結する; 提携する, 交わる.

M He is ***closely*** *associated* with Japan. 彼は日本と密接な関係がある. ¶his name will ***ever*** be *associated* with ... 彼の名はいつまでも...と連想されるであろう. ¶Girls are allowed to *associate* ***freely*** with men. 女子は男子と自由に交際する事が許されている. ¶***indelibly*** *associated* with ... ...と切っても切れない縁のある. ¶The name of Marquis Okuma is ***indissolubly*** *associated* with Waseda University. 大隈侯の名は早稲田大学と密接な関係がある. ¶the name most ***prominently*** *associated* with it is that of Mr. ... それと一番縁の深い人は...氏である.

P a pair of lovers who are *associated* ***for*** a lifelong union 一生のちぎりを結んだ夫婦. ¶He is *associated* ***in*** partnership with his son as a publisher. 彼は彼の息子と共同して出版事業をやっている. ¶I don't care to *associate* ***with*** him. あの人と交際したくない. ‖ *associate* one thing ***with*** another 甲のものから乙のものを連想する.【類】His name is *associated* ***with*** it. / the word can be remembered by *associating* it ***with*** ... / All over Europe red hair is *associated* ***with*** treachery and deceitfulness. / objects *associated* ***with*** the life of ... / *associate* oneself ***with*** a political movement ‖ *associate* ***with*** him in business 彼と共同で事業をやる ‖ articles *associated* ***with*** ... ...に関係のある品物 ‖ long *associated* ***with*** the firm その会社に永年関係して ‖ His very name is *associated* ***with*** awe. その名を聞いただけでも畏怖(い)を覚える.

association, *n.* (**1**) 連想; 交際; 関係.

V ***bring up*** *associations* of ... 色々...の連想を起させる. ¶He ***has*** no *association* with foreigners. 彼は外人との交際がない. ¶Those words have ***lost*** slangy *associations*. それらの語は俗語という色彩を失った. ¶the *associations* the word ***recalls*** その語が喚起する連想. ¶***stir up*** the *association* of ... ...の連想を起させる.

V^{2} Historical *associations* ***cluster*** richly around it. 色々歴史上の連想がそれにつきまとっている. ¶An *association* of ideas ***wells up***. 色々連想がわいて来る.

Q It is said to have belonged to Robert Burns, and is precious because of that ***assumed*** *association*. それはロバート・バーンズの所有品であったという仮定の縁故から貴重品になっている. ¶its ***chief*** *association* is with ... その主なる連想は...に関連している. ¶On account of his ***constant*** *association* with youth, he rejoices in unusual vitality. 若いものと絶えず接触しているので彼は非常に元気だ. ¶***evil*** *association* 悪友との交際. ¶beautiful scenery and ***historic*** *association* 風景の美と歴史的連想.【類】The sight calls up in my mind a host of ***historical*** *associations*. ¶He has made many ***interesting*** *associations* in the club. あの人はそのクラブで多数のおもしろい人物と交際した. ¶Religion had an ***intimate*** *association* with alchemy during the Middle Ages. 宗教は中世紀において錬金術と密接な関係があった. ¶places that have definite ***literary*** *associations* はっきりした文学的連想のある場所. ¶the ***literary*** and ***historical*** *associations* of these beauty spots これら形勝の地の文学的歴史的連想. ¶so many ***old*** *associations* clustered about ... が...のまわりに纏綿(めん)している往時への数々の連想. ¶The word has ***unpleasant*** *associations*. その言葉には不愉快な連想がある. ¶***venerable*** *associations* 色々の崇敬的連想.

Q^{2} The place is rich in ***old-world*** *associations*. その所は昔の思い出が多い.

P You will learn much ***from*** *association* with him. あの人と交際すると色々なことを覚える. ¶I had been ***in*** close *association* with him many years. 多年彼と親密に付合って来た. ¶It is interesting ***on account of*** its historical *associations*. それは歴史的連想のために興味がある. ¶***through*** *association* with ... ...との連想から. ¶a spot ***with*** its old *association* 古跡.

P^{2} the *association* ***of*** Mr. ... as a new official of the company ...氏の役員としての新入社. ¶the name is so well known in *association* ***with*** ... その名は...と関連してよく知られている ‖ Be kind in *association* ***with*** one's fellows. 同輩と親切につき合え.【類】In commemoration of its *association* ***with*** Goethe's youth the town of Strassburg erected a statue of the "Young Goethe (「若き日のゲーテ」)."

(2) 会, クラブ.

V form an association under the name of …という名称の協会を組織する.

Q an athletic association 運動会. ¶a cooperative association 協同組合. ¶a fraternal association 同胞組合. ¶a house-renters' association 借家人組合. ¶an industrial association 産業団体. ¶the Women's National Patriotic Association 愛国婦人会. ¶a supporters' association 後援会.

Q² an alumni association 校友会. ¶a banking association 銀行協会. ¶a building loan association 建築資金組合. ¶a credit association 信用組合. ¶the Judicial Rehabilitation Association 司法保護協会. ¶member associations of a federation or labor 総同盟下部の組合. ¶a mutual aid (=benefit) association 共済会. ¶the neighborhood association 隣保会. ¶a parent-teacher association=P.T.A. ¶a pilgrim association 講(中). ¶the spelling reform association つづり字改良会. ¶a superannuation fund association 退職基金協会. ¶a trade association 貿易協会. ¶a trade protection association 貿易擁護協会. ¶a village improvement association 村落改善協会.

P² an association of banks and bankers 銀行(及び銀行家)協会 ‖ an association of scholars for the advancement of knowledge 学術振興協会 ‖ an association of producers 演出家協会.

assort, *v.* 類別する.

P assort them into groups それらを分類する.

assortment, *n.* 種類, 口分け.

Q mineral specimens in great assortment (=variety) 種類の豊富な鉱物標本. ¶a large (=rich) assortment of goods 各種大口の品物. ¶have a small assortment of facial expressions [演じうる]顔面表情の種類が少ない.

P² an assortment of patterns 色々な柄.

assuage, *v.* 静める.

P assuage it by treatment 治療でそれを静める. ¶assuage it with remedies 医薬でそれを静める ‖ assuage one's anger with gentle words 温和な言葉で人の怒りを静める.

assume, *v.* 仮定する.

M hastily assume 速断する. ¶it may safely be assumed that … …と見なして差支なかろう. ¶tacitly assume 口には出さぬがそれと推定する. ¶unceremoniously assume a person to be … 人を…だと無遠慮に仮定する.

P assume it as a standard 仮にそれを標準にする.

O it is reasonable to assume that … …と見なしても無理はしない.

assumption, *n.* 装うこと; 仮定; 受任; 昇天.

V put on an assumption of ignorance 知らぬ振りをする.

Q an absurd assumption 不合理な仮定. ¶hypothetical assumptions 仮定的推断. ¶It is mere assumption, resting on no authority whatever and contradicted by all the evidence. それは何ら根拠なく反証がいくらでも挙げられる一個の純然たる推定に過ぎない. ¶probable assumption 真実性のある推定. ¶it is a safe assumption that … …というのは間違のない推定である. ¶a strong assumption of superiority 強い優越感. ¶a tacit assumption 沈默の推定. ¶unwarranted assumptions of power on the part of the shogun 将軍側の越権.

P on the assumption that … …と想像して ‖ it was based on the assumption that … それは…という仮定に基づいていた.

P² the assumption of an office 就任 ‖ the Assumption of the Virgin into heaven マリアの昇天.

assurance, *n.* 確信; 保証.

V Please convey to Madam the assurance of my esteem. 奥様にどうぞよろしく. ¶give assurance that … …ということを保証する.【類】he gave me an assurance that … ¶I have an assurance that … …を保証されている. ¶make assurance doubly sure 念には念を入れる. ¶obtain an assurance from him that … 彼から…という保証を取る. ¶indications offer reasonable assurance that … 情勢が…に相当確実性があるということを示している. ¶receive assurances from … …から保証される ‖ I received many assurances of good wishes from him. 彼から情のこもったあいさつを送られた. ¶You may take my assurance that I will see to it myself. 私が自分でその事に当ることを貴方に対して言明します.

Q speak with a calm assurance 冷静に落着きはらって話す. ¶I have full assurance of its safety. それは少しも危険がないと保証を得ている.

Q² stage assurance 舞台での落着き.

P speak with assurance 自信を持って語る ‖ He tried to set my heart at rest with the assurance. 彼はそのことを保証して僕を安心させようとした. ‖ meet danger with assurance 泰然として危難に処する.

assure, *v.* 保証する; 確信する.

P I assured myself against losses. 損害の保険を付けた. ‖ He is assured of life. 彼は生命を保証されている. ‖ Visitors to the shop are assured of a gracious reception and a sympathetic understanding of their requirements. 御来店のお客様は必ず丁重にお取扱致し親切にご用命をお伺い致します. ‖ I'm fully assured of your success. 私はあなたの成功を十分確信する.【類】He assured me of his assistance. / I am assured of his honesty (innocence). / I assure you of its truth. / be assured of getting a livelihood ‖ As far as the industry is concerned, we are perfectly assured of the future. その工業に限り将来に対して少しも心配する必要がない. ¶He assured his life with (=in) this company. 彼はこの会社に生命保険を付けた.

asterisk, *n.* 星標.

V put (=set) an asterisk against the name その名に星印を付ける.

astir, *a.* 起きている; 活動して.

P We were astir with the dawn. 私たちは夜の明けると同時に起きた. ‖ The whole town was astir with the news. 町中がそのニュースでざわめいていた.

astonish, *v.* 驚かす.

M It fairly astonished me. それには全く驚いた. ¶I was much astonished. 非常にびっくりした.

P be astonished at the sight それを見て驚く. ¶I am astonished at your conduct. 君のやり口には驚いた. ¶He was astonished by his mother's appearance. 彼は母が見えたのでびっくりした. ¶You must have been astonished on seeing him. あの人を見たときはさぞ驚いたことでしょう.

O Why, you astonish me! こりゃ驚いた. ¶I am astonished to hear it. それを聞いて驚いた.

astonishing, *a.* 驚くべき.

M It was really astonishing. 全く驚くべきことであった.

P It was astonishing to every one. だれも皆驚いた.

astonishment, *n.* 驚がく, 仰天.

V express astonishment that he should … あの人が…したのかと驚く. ¶look one's astonishment 驚きを顔に表わす.

Q in bewildered astonishment あっけにとられて. ¶in mute astonishment あっけに取られて. ¶in naive astonishment 無邪気な驚きを見せて. ¶in open-mouthed astonishment 口あんぐりで. ¶to his no small astonishment 彼の少なからず驚いたことには. ¶in undisguised astonishment ありありと驚きを示して.

P cry in astonishment びっくりして大声を出す.【類】gaze in astonishment ‖ He stared at me in silent astonishment. 彼はあっけに取られて私を見つめた. ¶I was thrown into astonishment. 僕はあっと驚いた. ¶to his utter astonishment 彼の仰天したことには.【類】he learned to his astonishment that … ¶be struck dumb with astonishment 驚いて声も出ない ‖ listen with open-mouthed astonishment to … あっけにとられて…を聞く.

P² he was filled with astonishment at seeing … 彼は…を見てびっくり仰天した.

astound, *v* びっくりさせる.

P He was perfectly astounded at the intelligence. その報に接して彼はほんとにたまげた.

astride, *ad.* またがって.

P seat oneself astride of a horse 馬に乗る ‖ get astride of a fence 垣にまたがる.

O sit astride a horse 馬にまたがる.

asylum, *n.* 庇護所, 避難所.

V gain an asylum on shore [船員などが]陸に避難する. ¶I offered him an asylum in my own dwelling. 私は彼を自分の家にかくまってやろうと申出た. ¶seek asylum in the United States 米国へ逃避する.

Q proprietary asylums 営利的静養所. ¶Holland was once a sure asylum for all persecuted and oppressed foreigners. オランダはもと迫害や圧制を受けた外国人の安住のできる場所であった.

P² an asylum for the aged 養老院 ‖ an asylum for lepers らい患者収容所.

atheist, *n.* 無神論者.

Q a professed atheist 公然の無神論者.

athlete, *n.* 運動選手.

Q² the Tenth ***Olympiad Athletes*** 第十回オリンピック出場選手たち. ¶***track*** (***field***) ***athletes*** トラック(フィールド)の競技者.

athletics, *n. pl.* 競技.

Q² ***track*** (***field***) ***athletics*** トラック(フィールド)諸競技.

O *Athletics* is one of the major interests in college life. 陸上競技は大学生活の大きな関心事の一つである.

Atlantic, *n.* 大西洋.

V ***cross*** the *Atlantic* 大西洋を横断する.

atmosphere, *n.* 空気; 雰(ふん)囲気.

V ***breathe*** an impure and dust-laden *atmosphere* 不純なほこりだらけの空気を吸う. ¶***create*** the *atmosphere* of the times of Queen Anne アン女王時代の気分を造り出す ‖ ***create*** an *atmosphere* of cheerfulness 朗らかな気分を造る. 【類】***create*** an *atmosphere* that will cool down a fiery argument (激しい議論). ¶His family ***has*** a Christian *atmosphere*. 彼の家庭はキリスト教徒的だ. ¶***impregnate*** the *atmosphere* of a room with the smell of charcoal 炭のにおいをへやに充満させる. ¶***preserve*** the Oriental *atmosphere* 東洋的気分を保存する. ¶***produce*** the churchly *atmosphere* 教会的気分を造り出す. ¶***vitiate*** the *atmosphere* 空気を悪くする.

Q a ***bracing*** *atmosphere* of high regions 山地のさわやかな空気. ¶a ***clear*** *atmosphere* 透明な空気. ¶The *atmosphere* is ***cloudless***. 空気が曇っていない. ¶a ***comfortable homely*** *atmosphere* 快適で家庭的な雰囲気. ¶a ***congenial*** *atmosphere* 打ちとけた雰囲気. ¶an ***English atmosphere*** 英国的雰囲気. ¶create a ***friendly*** *atmosphere* 友好的な空気を醸し出す. ¶a ***pro-British*** *atmosphere* 親英気分. ¶a highly ***rarefied*** *atmosphere* きわめて希薄な空気. ¶***smoke-laden*** *atmosphere* 煤煙に曇った空気. ¶the ***stuffy*** *atmosphere* [室内の]息づまるような空気. ¶a ***subdued*** *atmosphere* 沈滞した空気. ¶create a ***suitable*** *atmosphere* 気分を出す. ¶the ***sweltering*** *atmosphere* of the towns and cities of the plains 平地の都市におけるうだるような暑気. ¶in a ***sympathetic*** *atmosphere* 同情のある雰囲気の中で. ¶The *atmosphere* was ***uncomfortable***. 雰囲気がいやだった. ¶The *atmosphere* is ***uncongenial***. 環境がおもしろくない. ¶The ***warm, stuffy*** *atmosphere* in the theater made her feel faint. 劇場の中の暖い息づまるような空気のために彼女は気が遠くなった.

Q² the ***conference*** *atmosphere* その会議の雰囲気. ¶a ***pleasant family*** *atmosphere* 楽しい家庭的気分. ¶a ***wholesome home*** *atmosphere* 健全な家庭的気分. ¶a town with an ***old-world*** *atmosphere* 旧世界の気分のする町.

P He was reared ***in*** an *atmosphere* of freedom. 彼は自由の空気の中で育った. 【類】Some plants grow best ***in*** cold *atmosphere*.

P² An *atmosphere* ***of*** peace pervaded the place. 平和の空気がそこにあふれていた. ‖ An *atmosphere* ***of*** friendliness and mutual consideration prevails. 友愛と思いやりの空気がみなぎっている.

atoll, *n.* 環礁.

Q² a tiny ***coral*** *atoll* 小さいさんご環礁.

atom, *n.* 微分子; 〖理〗原子.

P ***physical*** (***chemical***) *atoms* 分(原)子. ¶The edifice was blown ***to*** *atoms*. [爆発などで]建物が粉砕された.

P² There is not an *atom* ***of*** truth in the rumor. そのうわさは全然うそっぱちだ.

atone, *v.* 償う.

P *atone* ***for*** a crime 罪滅しをする. 【類】*atone* ***for*** all past neglect ‖ *atone* ***for*** the wrong she had done 彼女自身の罪滅しをする. ¶He *atoned* his sin ***with*** life. 彼は死をもってその罪をあがなった.

atonement, *n.* あがなうこと.

V ***make*** *atonement* for ... …をあがなう.

P ***as*** an *atonement* for ... …の罪滅しのため. ¶***in*** *atonement* for ... …の弁償として.

atrocity, *n.* 暴行; 大間違い.

V ***commit*** a horrible *atrocity* 恐るべき暴行をする. ¶the *atrocities* ***perpetrated*** in the name of commerce and expansion 商業の発達と国力進展の名の下に行われた残虐. ¶***practice*** *atrocities* on ... …に暴行を加える.

Q ***dreadful*** *atrocities* 凶行. ¶commit all kinds of ***grammatical*** *atrocities* 色々とひどい文法上の間違いをやる.

Q² ***war*** *atrocities* 戦争中の色々な残虐行為.

attach, *v.* (**1**) 愛着させる.

M *attach* oneself ***dearly*** to ... …を深く愛する. ¶He is ***deeply*** *attached* to his wife. 彼は大の女房思いだ. ¶***devotedly*** *attached* to ... …に愛情を傾けて. ¶grow ***fondly*** *attached* to ... …を恋しがるようになる. ¶the death of his mother, to whom he was ***tenderly*** *attached* 彼が深く愛していた母の死. ¶She is ***warmly*** *attached* to her mother. 彼女は大の母思いだ.

P He was very much *attached* ***to*** his brothers and sisters. 彼は大の兄弟思いだった.

(**2**) 付属させる; 付ける.

M all rights *attached* ***thereto*** これに付帯する一切の権利.

P be *attached* by a chain ***to*** ... …に鎖でつないである ‖ a civilian *attached* ***to*** the Army (Navy) 軍属 ‖ be *attached* ***to*** a staff ある部局に付属している. ¶the Lake Laboratory at Otsu, *attached* ***to*** the Kyoto University 大津の京都大学付属湖沼研究所. 【類】The school is *attached* ***to*** the Higher Normal School. / the cemetery *attached* ***to*** a temple / a list *attached* ***to*** the document ‖ Is there a dining car *attached* ***to*** the train? 汽車に食堂が付いていますか. ‖ the remuneration *attached* ***to*** the chair [教授などの]講座給 ‖ *Attach* ***to*** the answer, in each case, the number and letter used in the printed paper. 答案には一々試験問題の番号と記号 (A, B, C など)とを付記すべし. ‖ *attach* importance ***to*** the fact その事実に重きをおく ‖ He *attached* himself ***to*** the party. その仲間にはいった. ‖ Is the company *attached* ***to*** the telephone system? あの会社には電話がありますか.

(**3**) 差押える.

P *attach* property ***for*** a debt 負債のかたに財産を差押える.

attache, *n.* 大(公)使随行員.

Q a ***commercial*** *attache* 商務官. ¶a ***legal*** *attache* 法律関係担当随員. ¶a ***naval*** (***military***) *attache* to an Embassy 大使館付海軍(陸軍)武官.

Q² ***hospital*** *attaches* 病院の職員等. ¶a ***press*** *attache* at an embassy 大使館付新聞係事務官.

attachment, *n.* 愛着; 付属品; 〖法〗差押え.

V ***form*** an *attachment* for a woman ある女を愛するようになる. ¶***show*** no *attachment* to ... …を愛するようすが見えない.

Q an ***ardent*** *attachment* for ... …に対する強い愛着. ¶his ***intense*** *attachment* to his country 彼の熱烈な愛国心. ¶strengthen (=solidify) the ***mutual*** *attachment* between them その二人の間の互いの愛着を強める.

Q² His ***family*** *attachments* are close. 彼は家族を深く愛している. ¶a phonograph with a ***headphone*** *attachment* イヤホーンのついた蓄音機. ¶a government bond with ***lottery*** *attachment* 抽せん付勧業債券. ¶her ***love*** *attachment* to ... あの婦人の…に対する恋慕.

P an order ***of*** *attachment* 差押命令.

P² form a strong *attachment* ***for*** ... …を熱愛するようになる. ¶*attachments* ***to*** sewing machine ミシンの附属品. ¶He formed a lasting *attachment* ***to*** the lady. 彼はその女を末永く愛するようになった. ‖ an *attachment* ***to*** a chief for his valor 武勇に心服しての上長に対する愛着.

attack, *n.* 攻撃; 襲来.

V ***bring on*** an *attack* 発病などさせる. ¶***deliver*** (=***make***) fierce *attacks* against the enemy 敵に猛撃を加える. ¶***disarm*** further *attacks* この上攻撃をできなくする. ¶***foil*** an *attack* 撃退する. ¶He ***had*** an *attack* of fever (gout, illness, influenza). 彼は熱病(など)にかかった. ¶***invite*** *attack* from ... …からの攻撃を誘発する. ¶***launch*** an *attack* against (=on) ... …の攻撃を始める. ¶***make*** an *attack* upon ... …を攻撃する. ¶***open*** (=***initiate***) an *attack* against (=on) ...に対して攻撃を開始する. ¶An inoculation is liable to ***produce*** a slight feverish *attack*. 注射すると少し熱が出がちである. ¶***push*** the *attack* unflinchingly 仮借なく攻撃を進める. ¶***repel*** an *attack* 撃退する. ¶***repulse*** the *attack* of ... …の侵入を撃退する. ¶***resist*** the *attacks* of ... …の攻撃を撃退する. ¶***turn*** his *attack* against ... …に攻撃の矢を向ける. ¶***ward off*** an *attack* 攻撃をそらす. ¶***withstand*** an *attack* from ... …の攻撃に耐える.

V² when the *attack* ***passes off*** 病気が治ると.

Q a very ***acute*** *attack* of indigestion 猛烈な不消化 ‖ suffer from an ***acute*** *attack* of delirium tremens 急性アルコール中毒にかかる. ¶launch an ***all-out*** *attack* 総攻撃を開始する. ¶He had a ***bad*** *attack* of "flu." 彼はひどい流感にかかった. ¶a ***blistering*** *attack* 手きびしい攻撃. ¶a

bitter** attack* 手ひどい攻撃. ¶a ***convulsive** attack* けいれん. ¶Three robbers made a most ***daring** attack* on a French mail train near Paris. 三人の泥棒がパリーの近傍で仏国郵便列車にきわめて大胆な襲撃をした. ¶a ***decisive** attack* 決定的攻撃. ¶He made a ***determined** attack* on me. 彼は堅い決心を見せて僕を攻撃した. ¶A ***feverish** attack* laid me up for a few days. 僕は発熱して二三日寝ていた. ‖ Vaccination produces a slight ***feverish** attack.* 種痘は微熱を起す. ¶the ***first and ***opening** attack* 第一回の攻撃. ¶a ***flank** attack* 側面攻撃. ¶a ***frontal** attack* 正面攻撃. ¶a ***grand** attack* 大攻撃. ¶She merged into a ***hysterical** attack*. 彼女はヒステリーの発作を起した. ¶make an ***indiscriminate** attack* on ... ...を無茶苦茶に攻撃する. ¶make a ***joint** attack* on ... ...に一斉攻撃を加える. ¶The Emperor Hwang Ti built the Great Wall to protect the Chinese people from the ***marauding** attacks* of the Hiong Nu (=Huns). 秦の始皇帝は匈奴の侵入を防ぐために万里の長城を築いた. ¶make an ***open** attack* on ... ...を公然攻撃する. ¶***overbold** attacks* on the Government 政府に対する過激な攻撃. ¶a ***perfidious** attack* だまし打ち. ¶He stood by his theory despite the ***persistent*** and ***virulent** attacks* of the medical press. 医学雑誌の執拗(ょう)かつ劇烈な攻撃にもかゝわらず彼はその説を棄てなかった. ¶***personal** attack* on ... ...に対する人身攻撃. ¶a ***powerful*** and ***trenchant** attack* on ... ...に対する力強い勇敢な攻撃. ¶a ***scientific** attack* 科学的攻撃. ¶make a ***scurrilous** attack* on ... ...を口汚なくののしる. ¶He had a ***second** attack* of the disease. 彼の病気が再発した. ¶He suffered from a ***sharp** attack* of intermittent fever. 彼は間歇(けつ)熱のひどいのにやられた. ¶make a ***slashing** attack* 猛烈に攻撃する. ¶He had a ***slight** attack* of insanity. 彼はちょっと精神に異状をきたした.【類】a ***slight** attack* of fever. ¶a ***spirited** attack* 手きびしい攻撃. ¶a ***stinging** attack* 手ごたえのある攻撃. ¶make a ***strong** attack* upon ... ...に対して手ごわい攻撃をする. ¶make a ***three-pronged** attack* on ... ...に三叉攻撃をする. ¶an ***unjustifiable** attack* on the liberty of the Press 言論の自由に対する不当の攻撃. ¶Kublai's ***unsuccessful** attack* upon Japan in 1281. 1281 年の忽必烈の不成功に終った日本攻撃. ¶a ***vigorous** attack* 猛攻. ¶The dog made a ***violent** attack* on the man. 犬が猛烈にその人を襲った. ¶He had a ***virulent** attack* of the disease. 彼はその病気の重いのにかかった.

Q² be destroyed by ***air** attacks* 空襲で破壊される. ¶a ***blitz** attack* 電撃. ¶a ***bomb** attack* from ... ...からの爆撃. ¶stage a mock ***bomb[ing]** attack* 模擬爆撃を行う. ¶his sudden passing from a ***heart** attack* 心臓病による彼の急死.【類】die of a ***heart** attack*. ¶launch a ***mass** attack* against ... ...に対して総攻撃を開始する.【類】a ***mass** attack* of about 150 planes. ¶a ***mob** attack* 暴民の襲撃. ¶resistant to ***insect** attack* 虫害に対して抵抗力のある. ¶a ***newspaper*** (=***press***) *attack* of the Government's foreign policy 新聞の政府の外交攻撃. ¶a treacherous ***night** attack* 陰険な夜襲. ¶a ***resistance** attack* 反撃. ¶a ***sabotage** attack* 怠業攻勢. ¶the Pearl Harbor ***sneak** attack* 真珠湾の潜行攻撃. ¶a ***surprise** attack* 不意打ち.【類】capture a town in a ***surprise** attack* / launch (=make) a ***surprise** attack* against ... ¶a ***torpedo** attack* upon ... ...に対する雷撃. ¶a ***two-way** attack* 二方面からの攻撃. ¶***vilification** attacks* on ... ...に対する誹謗(ぼう).

P They were alarmed ***by*** a sudden *attack*. 彼らは不意打で仰天した. ¶He looks quite cheerful and happy ***notwithstanding*** *attacks* of insomnia. 不眠症にかかっていながらいたって元気に見える.

P² an *attack* ***from*** the sky 空襲. ¶an *attack* ***in*** the darkness やみ打ち. ¶An *attack* ***of*** paralysis seized him. 彼は中風にかかった. ¶an *attack* ***on*** the government 政府攻撃.【類】*attacks* ***on*** competitors / an *attack* ***on*** a city / make an *attack* ***on*** an enemy's camp.

attack, *v.* 攻撃する.

M ***fiercely*** (=***furiously***) *attack* ... ...を猛烈に攻撃する. ¶He was ***harshly** attacked* by critics. 彼は批評家からひどく攻撃された. ¶He was ***personally** attacked* by an ignorant mob. 訳のわからない弥次馬たちに暴行を加えられた. ¶***savagely** attack* ... ...を手ひどく攻撃する. ¶***sharply** attack* ... 鋭く...を攻撃する. ¶be *attacked* ***unexpectedly*** in the rear 背後から思わぬ攻撃を受ける. ¶*attack* ... ***vehemently*** 躍起となって...を攻撃する. ¶*attack* ... ***vigorously*** for the steps taken その処置に出たことに対して盛んに...を攻撃する.

P The fort was *attacked* ***by*** an enemy with cannon. 要塞は敵に大砲で攻撃された. ‖ He was *attacked* ***by*** argument. 彼は議論ぜめに合った. ‖ The enemy *attacked* the camp ***by*** surprise. 敵は陣営を不意打ちした. ‖ be *attacked* ***by*** a disease 病気にかかる. ¶*attack* ... ***from*** a secret road 間道から...を攻める. ¶*attack* the enemy ***in*** the rear 敵の背後を突く. ¶*attack* the enemy ***with*** fire weapons 火器で敵を攻撃する.【類】*attack* a person ***with*** a stick (sword) ‖ He has been *attacked* ***with*** influenza (scarlet fever). 彼は流感(など)にかかった.

attain, *v.* 達する.

P The cultivation of an international mind helps to *attain* ***to*** a world consciousness. 国際心の養成は世界的自覚を得る助けとなる. ‖ *attain* ***to*** man's estate 一人前になる.【類】He *attained* ***to*** a flourishing condition. 彼は隆盛になった. ‖ *attain* ***to*** greatness えらくなる ‖ *attaining* ***to*** Buddhahood 成仏.【類】*attain* ***to*** the first rank / *attain* ***to*** great age / *attain* ***to*** maturity (成熟期) / *attain* at one leap (一躍して) ***to*** ... / *attain* ***to*** manhood / *attain* ***to*** perfection in ... / *attain* ***to*** a state of independence.

O *attain* the crown of success 成功の栄冠を獲得する ‖ *attain* one's end (=aim) 目的を達する.

attainment, *n.* 達成; 学識.

V ***further** attainment* of that end その目的の達成を助ける.

Q with ***artistic** attainments* 芸能を身につけた. ¶***educational** attainments* 学業. ¶a philosopher and poet of ***humble** attainments* 哲学も詩も造詣の浅い人. ¶His *attainments* are ***large*** and ***varied***. あの人は万能だ. ¶possess the ***liberal** attainments* that distinguish the gentleman 紳士に特有な高等教育を身につけている. ¶***linguistic** attainments* 語学の力. ¶a scholar of ***rare** attainments* まれに見る学識の高い人. ¶It promised more ***ready** attainment* of his ends. そうすれば一層容易に目的が達成されそうであった. ¶***scientific** attainments* 科学の造詣. ¶***scholastic** attainments* うん蓄. ¶a higher plane of ***spiritual** attainment* 一段高い精神修養の達成. ¶men of ***superior mental** attainments* 博学な人々. ¶***warlike** attainments* 武芸.

P Such a lofty object is ***beyond** attainment*. そんな高尚な目的は達せられぬ.【類】The task has hitherto appeared ***beyond** attainment*. ¶He is well fitted for that post ***by*** character and *attainment*. 彼は人格と学識とでその地位に最もよく適している. ¶***in*** the *attainment* of his object 彼の目的を達するために. ¶a man ***of*** great *attainments* 博識の人. ¶Their objects are not ***worth*** the *attainment*. 彼らの目的は達成する値打がない.

P² *attainment* ***in*** scholarship 学力.

attempt, *n.* 試み, 企図.

V We had to ***abandon*** the *attempt* as hopeless. われわれはその企ては成功の見込ないものとして放棄しなければならなかった. ¶the difficulties ***attending*** the *attempt* to ... ...する試みに伴う困難. ¶Being idle and obstinate he ***defies*** any *attempt* of correction. 怠けもので強情だから始末におえない. ‖ The door ***defies*** all *attempts* to open it. その戸はどうしても開かない. ¶His productions ***elude*** all *attempts* to imitate. 彼の作品は他の追随を許さない.【類】These ceramic wares ***elude*** all *attempts* at classification. ¶the *attempt* was ***foiled*** (=***frustrated***) chiefly by ... その試みは主に...のために失敗に終った. ¶***give up*** an *attempt* 企てを放棄する. ¶The weather was sufficiently good to ***justify*** an *attempt*. 仕事にかかってもよいほどに好天気だった. ¶***make*** an *attempt* at suicide 自殺をしようとする.【類】***make*** an *attempt* at "fine writing" (「美文」) ‖ He ***made*** no *attempt* to carry it into practice. / No *attempt* is ***made*** for embellishment (文の修飾). ‖ two *attempts* were ***made*** on the life of ... 二度も...の殺害を図った. ¶He ***meditates*** a fresh *attempt*. 彼には新規の企てがある. ¶***vitiate*** an *attempt* 試みを無効にさせる.

V² if the *attempt* ***fails*** その試みが失敗に終ったら.

Q The *attempt* proved completely ***abortive***. その試みは全然不成功に終った. ¶a ***bold** attempt* 大胆な試み. ¶a ***brave** attempt* at rescue 勇ましい救命の試み. ¶***brilliant*** but ***fruitless*** *attempts* 竜頭蛇尾の試み. ¶He was caught in a ***burglarious*** *attempt*. 押し入ろうとした所を捕縛された. ¶***conciliatory*** *attempts* 仲裁的努力. ¶make a ***conscientious*** *attempt* to ... 良心的に...をやろうとする. ¶a ***daring*** *attempt* to escape 大胆な逃走の企て. ¶a ***deliberate*** *attempt* 熟考した企て. ¶make a ***determined*** *attempt* to... 断然...しようとする. ¶These pictures are specimens of his ***early*** *attempts*. これらの絵は彼の習作時代のものだ. ¶a ***frantic*** *attempt* 熱狂的な試み. ¶a ***fruitless*** *attempt* 徒労. ¶A ***further*** *attempt* will be made. さらにそのことが試みられるであろう. ‖ All ***further*** *attempts* at salvage have been abandoned. 遭難船救助のためそれ以上手を尽すことは一切断念された. ¶make a ***futile*** *attempt* 無益な試みをする. 【類】after several ***futile*** *attempts* to ... ¶a ***gallant*** *attempt* to save an elderly man from being burnt to death 老人を焼死から救うというあっぱれな行為. ¶***half-hearted*** *attempts* to ... ...に対するなま半可な試み. ¶a ***heroic*** *attempt* 壮挙. ¶an ***honest*** *attempt* 誠意ある試み. ¶***immoral*** *attempts* on young girls 少女に対するみだらな行為. ¶***impracticable*** *attempts* 実行性のない試み. ¶an ***ingenious*** but ***hazardous*** *attempt* 着想は良いが危険な試み. ¶he made a ***last despairing*** *attempt* to ... 彼は...せんとする最後の絶望的な試みをした. ¶a ***maiden*** *attempt* 始めての試み. ¶a ***murderous*** *attempt* 殺害しようとする企て. ¶a ***plucky*** *attempt* to save the life of ... ...の命を救おうというけなげな試み. ¶a ***praiseworthy*** *attempt* 感心な試み. ¶make a ***premature*** *attempt* 早まる. ¶A final success will be made after ***repeated*** *attempts*. 何度も試みるうちには成功するだろう. ¶make a ***resolute*** *attempt* to ... 敢然として...を試みる. ¶make a ***serious*** *attempt* 真剣にやる. ¶a ***silly*** *attempt* 愚かな試み. ¶The ***single*** *attempt* at decoration in the room was a framed print. へやの装飾と言っては版画の額が一つあるだけ. ¶a ***slavish*** *attempt* to imitate others 奴隷的な人まね. ¶there had been ***sporadic*** *attempts* at organizing a similar association before, but ... それ以前同種の協会を組織しようという試みがぽつぽつあったが... ¶a ***successful*** *attempt* 成功した試み. ¶a ***suicidal*** *attempt* 自殺未遂. ¶He spent many months of the year in various watering places in a ***vain*** (=***unfruitful***, ***unsuccessful*** *or* ***futile***) *attempt* to restore his health. 一年の内数カ月色々湯治に出かけたがきき目がなかった. ¶A ***systematic*** *attempt* has been made to improve one's health. 組織だった健康増進法をやってみている. ¶***various*** *attempts* were made to ... ...しようと色々苦心を払った. ¶a ***well-meant*** *attempt* 善意の試み.

Q² a ***comeback*** *attempt* 出直し. ¶***pioneer*** *attempts* to ... ...しようとする前人未踏の試み. ¶a ***suicide*** *attempt* 自殺の企図.

P ***after*** several futile *attempts* to ... 数回...しようとして失敗したあげく. ¶It was successful ***from*** his very first *attempt*. 最初からうまく行った. ¶He perished ***in*** the *attempt* to swim across. 向う側へ泳ぎ着こうとして死んだ. ¶***without*** any *attempt* at classification 分類には一切手をふれないで.

P² an *attempt* ***against*** one's life 人を殺害しようとする企て. ¶Mr. Morton's *attempt* ***at*** the simple life is one of the most heroic of which we have heard. モートン氏の試みた簡易生活が今までの内で一番思い切ったやり方だ. 【類】another of the *attempts* ***at*** self-advertisement (自己宣伝) / an *attempt* ***at*** suicide. ¶Despair drove him to an *attempt* ***on*** his own life. あの人は絶望の余り自殺を企てた. ‖ the author of the *attempt* ***upon*** (=***on***) the life of ... ...殺害計画の張本人. 【類】the *attempt* ***upon*** the King of Spain.

attempting, *n.* 試みること.

P Wait till the car has stopped ***before*** *attempting* to get on or off. 乗り降りは車が止まるまで待つこと ¶The work is ***worth*** *attempting*. その仕事はやって見る値打がある.

attend, *v.* (**1**) 出席する; 見物する.

M ***clandestinely*** *attend* a race こっそり競馬を見に行く. ¶The classes are ***eagerly*** *attended*. 学生が熱心に授業に出席する. ¶The meeting was ***fairly*** *attended*. 会は相当出席があった. ¶It was ***far better*** *attended* than the preceding night. 前夜よりずっと出席が多かった. ¶The funeral was ***largely*** *attended*. その葬式は多数会葬者があった. ¶The gathering was most ***numerously*** *attended*. 会には非常に多数の人が出席した. ¶The meeting was ***poorly*** *attended*. 会は出席者が少なかった. ¶***regularly*** *attend* its meetings その会に欠かさず出席する. ¶The theater was ***well*** *attended*. 芝居はかなり入りがあった.

P I *attend* regularly ***at*** church. 僕はきちょうめんに教会へ出席する. 【類】He *attended* only one year ***at*** high school. ¶*attending* ***in*** a ***body*** (=en masse) 総見物.

(**2**) 注意する; 仕える, 勤める.

M ***carefully*** *attend* to this point この点に念を入れる ‖ Your request will be ***carefully*** *attended* to. 御申出の件は十分考慮致します. ¶*attend* ***closely*** to one's classwork クラスの勉強を熱心にやる. ¶He *attended* ***diligently*** to business. 勤勉に事務を執った. ¶***faithfully*** *attend* to one's duties 忠実に職務を執る. ¶*attend* ***immediately*** さっそく着手する. ¶Business is ***properly*** *attended* to. きちんと事務を執る. ¶*attend* ***scrupulously*** to ... ...を念入りにやる. ¶those who *attend* ***seriously*** to the subject 真剣にその問題と取組む人々.

P *attend* ***on*** the sick (one's sick mother) 看護する ‖ He has only one servant to *attend* ***on*** him. 彼は一人だけ召使を雇っている. ¶*attend* ***to*** one's lesson 学課をまじめにやる. 【類】*attend* ***to*** one's duty / *attend* ***to*** business / *attend* ***to*** money affairs ‖ All things are *attended* ***to***. 万事注意が届いている. ‖ *attend* ***to*** one's wounds 傷の手当をする ‖ a sick child *attended* to ***by*** a physician 医者にかかっている病児 ‖ *attend* ***to*** one's wants 給仕する. 【類】Orders by post and telephone are *attended* ***to*** at once. ‖ *attend* ***to*** the call of nature [大小便などの]用を足す. ¶*attend* ***upon*** ... ...に侍する.

(**3**) 伴う; 付添う.

P The work was *attended* ***by*** signal success. その仕事は大成功を収めた. 【類】The work was *attended* ***by*** every difficulty. / It was *attended* ***by*** the most momentous (重大な) results. ‖ the Sovereign, *attended* ***by*** the Court 朝臣たちを従えた君主. ¶The situation is *attended* ***with*** difficulty and danger. 事態は困難と危険を伴っている. 【類】The disaster was *attended* ***with*** great loss of life. / It was *attended* ***with*** many advantages. ‖ The attempt was *attended* ***with*** no results. 企画は功を奏さなかった. 【類】The treatment was *attended* ***with*** brilliant results.

attendance, *n.* (**1**) 出席; [団] 出席者.

V ***attract*** a large *attendance* 多数の聴衆を引き付ける. ¶***check*** *attendance* 出席をとる. ¶An increase in admission prices ***diminished*** the *attendance* of the public. 入場料の値上をしたので一般の入りが減じた. ¶We ***expect*** a large *attendance*. 多数出席者のある見込み. ¶The school ***has*** an *attendance* of about 800 students. 同校にはおよそ八百人の通学生がある. ¶***secure*** his *attendance* 彼が出席してくれる.

V² *Attendance* frequently ***exceeds*** 500. 出席は往々五百を越える. ¶The *attendance* has ***fallen off***. 出席が減った. ¶the *attendance* ***included*** ... 来会者の中に...もいた.

Q an ***aggregate*** *attendance* 総出席者. ¶***alternative*** *attendance* of vassals at Shogun's court 参勤交代. ¶an ***average*** *attendance* of students 学生の平均出席数. ¶a ***crowded*** *attendance* 多人数の出席. ¶The ***daily*** *attendance* at the New York Aquarium averages 4,000. ニューヨーク水族館の来観者は一日平均四千人. ¶an ***erratic*** *attendance* of students 学生出席の不同. ¶There was a ***good*** *attendance*. 出席は相当にあった. ¶***high*** *attendance* of voters at the polls 多数選挙人の投票. 【類】The *attendance* was ***high***. ¶A ***large*** *attendance* is hoped for. 多数来会者があることを希望している. ¶a ***lax*** *attendance* at church 教会への出席不成績. ¶Our class (committee) has ***perfect*** *attendance* today. きょうはわれわれのクラス(など)は全員出席だ. ¶There was a ***poor*** (***fair***) *attendance* at the meeting. 会は出席者が少なかった(かなりあった). 【類】There was a ***poor*** *attendance* at the concert. ¶***pre-time*** *attendance* 早出. ¶a very ***slim*** *attendance* ごく少ない入り. ¶a ***small*** *attendance* 出席少数. ¶The *attendance* of members was very ***thin***. 会員の出席がきわめて少なかった.

Q² increase ***church*** *attendance* 教会出席者をふやす. ¶***office*** *attendance* 出勤. ¶***one hundred percent*** *attendance* for a lesson ある学課における全員出席. ¶check ***school*** *attendance* 生徒の出席を取る.

P He was suspended ***from*** *attendance* at school for three months. 彼は三カ月停学させられた ‖ be ***in*** *attendance* at

[a] school 在学している. ¶Mr. X was also ***in attendance***. X 氏も出席していた. ‖ He is not regular ***in*** his *attendance* at his office. 社への出勤が不規則だ. ‖ a failure ***in attendance*** 不参.

P² *Attendance* ***at*** the conference is open to all who wish to come. 有志の会議への出席は自由である. 【類】 children's *attendance* ***at*** motion pictures.

(**2**) 奉仕, 付添.

V He is always ***dancing*** *attendance* on you. 彼は始終君に追従している. ¶Does the two pounds a week ***include*** *attendance?* 一週二ポンドというのは給仕料もはいっているのか. ¶***provide*** medical *attendance* 医療を施す.

Q ***bad*** *attendance* at a hotel ホテルの悪いサービス. ¶The *attendance* in this hotel is very ***remiss***. このホテルははなはだサービスが悪い.

P Please have some one ***in*** *attendance* to look after him. [世話をするために] だれかあの人に付けて下さい. ‖ Have you a good doctor ***in*** *attendance?* 良いお医者におかかりですか. ‖ maids ***in*** *attendance* 腰元たち.

P² a man in *attendance* ***at*** a bathing-place 海水浴場の見張人. ¶in *attendance* ***on*** ... ...に付添って ‖ be in *attendance* ***on*** (=***upon***) Royalty 高貴の方に供奉(ぐぶ)する.

attendant, *n.* 出席者; 付添人, 随員; 随伴物.

Q the examination system and its ***inevitable*** *attendant* —cramming 試験制度と必然的にこれに付随する詰込み. ¶He served as a ***personal*** *attendant* on Her Majesty. 彼は皇后陛下の御付役を務めた. ¶A maid of honor is the ***principal*** *attendant* on a bride at the wedding ceremony. メード・オヴ・オナーというのは結婚式で花嫁のおも立った付添である. ¶***regular*** *attendants* 定連. ¶a ***uniformed*** *attendant* at the door 制服姿のドアマン.

Q² a ***bath*** *attendant* 湯番. ¶a ***check room*** *attendant* 携帯品預り係. ¶a regular ***church*** *attendant* 教会によく出る人. ¶a ***gas-station*** *attendant* ガソリンスタンドの係. ¶a ***lift*** *attendant* エレヴェーター係. ¶a ***mess*** *attendant* 食堂給仕人. ¶a ***parking-lot*** *attendant* 駐車場の世話係. ¶a ***rink*** *attendant* 屋内スケート場の係. ¶a ***table*** *attendant* [食卓の]給仕人. ¶a ***traveling*** *attendant* 旅行付添人.

P a train ***of*** *attendants* 随員一行.

P² *attendants* ***in*** livery そろいの服の供 ‖ an *attendant* ***in*** a gathering 集会の給仕人. ¶an *attendant* ***of*** the king 王の侍従 ‖ an *attendant* ***of*** the service 式の参列者. ¶the *attendant* ***on*** a bridegroom at his marriage 新郎付添人. ¶*attendants* ***to*** an ambassador 大使の随員たち.

attendant, *a.* 付添う; 伴う.

P an officer *attendant* ***on*** the general 大将付の士官. 【類】 the gentlemen *attendant* ***on*** (=***upon***) their lord ‖ the suffering *attendant* ***on*** war 戦争に伴う災害. ¶circumstances *attendant* ***to*** ... ...の行きがかり.

attention, *n.* (**1**) 注意.

V ***absorb*** public *attention* 世人の注意をひく. ¶***accord*** special *attention* to ... ...に特に注意する. ¶***accumulate*** *attention* on ... ...に注意を集中する. ¶***add*** special *attention* to ... 特に...に注意を加える. ¶The question has begun to ***arouse*** considerable *attention* on the part of the government. その問題は政府から大分注目されるようになり出した. 【類】 Public *attention* is thoroughly ***aroused*** as to its importance. ¶***arrest*** *attention* 注意をひく. ¶***attract*** the *attention* of ... ...の目にとまる. 【類】 The subject has lately ***attracted*** considerable *attention*. / a book of extraordinary interest that is bound to ***attract*** wide *attention* / The *attention* of the police was never ***attracted*** to the matter. / what ***attracted*** my *attention* most were ... / ***attracted*** much *attention* in the newspaper. ¶***awaken*** all my *attention* 大いに私の注意を喚起する. ¶a friend of mine on whom you deigned to ***bestow*** your *attention* 御配慮下さった私の友人 ‖ he next ***bestowed*** his *attention* on the question of ... 彼は次に...の問題を論じた. ¶***bring*** his *attention* to ... 彼の注意を...に向ける. ¶***bring back*** his *attention* to ... 彼の注意を...へ引戻す. ¶***call*** *attention* to ... ...に注意を向ける. 【類】 our *attention* has been ***called*** to the fact that ... / *attention* may specially be ***called*** to ... / the two points to which I wish to ***call*** your *attention* are ... ¶my *attention* was ***called off*** to ... 僕の注意が...の方に転じた. ¶***capture*** the *attention* of ... ...の注意を捕える. ¶***catch*** (=***arrest***) the *attention* of ... ...の注意をひく. ¶one's *attention* is ***chained*** to ... に注意を引きつけられる. ¶***challenge*** their *attention* by its novelty or strangeness 目新しく変っているので必ず彼らの注意をひく. ¶places of interest which may ***claim*** the *attention* of the traveler 旅行者の注意すべき遊覧地. ¶***command*** public *attention* 自然世人の注意をひく. ¶***compel*** *attention* 注意を余儀なくする. ¶***concentrate*** *attention* upon ... ...に注意を集中する. ¶***confine*** one's *attention* to ... [それ以外の事にわたらないで]...に注意を限定する. ¶***control*** the *attention* and concentrate it upon one subject 注意をそらさないで一つの題目に集中する. ¶It seemed to ***court*** *attention*. 見てくれと言わんばかりに見えた. ¶The complaint appears to be well founded and ***demands*** immediate *attention*. 苦情は十分根拠のあるもので早速処理する必要がある. ¶***deserve*** the careful *attention* of ... ...が大いに注意する値打がある. 【類】 The book ***deserves*** wide *attention*. / a point which ***deserves*** our *attention*. ¶***detract*** *attention* from ... ...から注意をそらせる. ¶***devote*** *attention* to ... ...に注意を向ける. 【類】 special *attention* has been ***devoted*** to ... / ***devote*** as much *attention* to ... as to ... ¶in this place *attention* will be ***directed*** to only ... ここでは...の事だけを論じることにする. ¶***distract*** the *attention* of ... ...の気をそらす. 【類】 ***distract*** public *attention* from ... ¶***divert*** his *attention* from ... ...から彼の気をそらす. ¶The theater ***divided*** *attention* with the picture house. 客が劇場と映画と両方に引かれた. ¶Our *attention* has been ***drawn*** to the fact that ... われわれは...という事に気が付いた. 【類】 first to ***draw*** Japanese *attention* to this field of study. ¶***dull*** (=***lazy***) *attention* にぶい関心. ¶***enchain*** the *attention* of ... ...の注意をそらせない. ¶The subject is now ***engaging*** our *attention*. その問題は目下われわれが研究中である. 【類】 ***engage*** the *attention* of men of science / It is now ***engaging*** the *attention* of the engineering world. / ***engage*** the keenest *attention* of ... ¶to ***ensure*** prompt *attention* 必ず迅速の取扱を受けるために. ¶It ***escapes*** the *attention* it deserves. その事は注意されるべきであるのに注意されずにいる. 【類】 one result which is apt to ***escape*** *attention*. ¶It ***excited*** considerable *attention* at the time. それは当時大いに注意を喚起した. 【類】 not striking enough to ***excite*** special *attention*. ¶***fix*** (=***fasten***) one's *attention* on ... よく...に注意する. ‖ I could not ***fix*** my *attention*. 精神統一ができなかった. 【類】 I often find that my mind is so wearied that even a sensational novel fails to ***fix*** my *attention*. ¶Much *attention* is now ***focused*** on the island. その島は目下多大の注意を集めている. 【類】 our chief *attention* should be ***focused*** upon ... ¶***force*** public *attention* upon ... いやでも応でも世間の人を...に注意させる. ¶should ***gain*** *attention* 注意されていいわけである. ¶To this we have already ***given*** *attention*. この点はすでに論じた. 【類】 I am too ill to ***give*** *attention* to anything in your letter at present. / I will ***give*** *attention* to the business on condition that ... ¶***grasp*** and ***retain*** the reader's *attention* 読者の注意を捕えて逃さない. ¶It still ***grips*** public *attention*. それはまだ世間から注目されている. 【類】 ***grip*** the *attention* and compel the sympathy of his readers. ¶***have*** the *attention* of a surgeon 外科医にかかっている ‖ May I ***have*** your *attention*, please? 皆さん御注意申上げます. ‖ Your wish shall ***have*** every *attention* of ours. 御希望に添うよう十分考慮致します. 【類】 Your proposal is ***having*** every *attention*. ¶***hold*** the complete *attention* of the audience 完全に聴衆の注意を捕える. 【類】 ***hold*** the *attention* of all who heard him / ***hold*** the *attention* like a novel / ***hold*** the undivided *attention* of every student in the class. ¶***intrigue*** one's *attention* ...の注意をそそる. ¶***invite*** the *attention* of ... to the fact that ... ...の注意を...に向ける. ¶***keep*** an unflagging *attention* to ... ...に対してゆるみない注意を続ける. ¶From beginning to end he never ***loses*** the *attention* of his readers. 始めから終りまで彼は決して読者の注意をそらさない. ¶The utterance ***merits*** no *attention*. その説は何ら注意する価値がない. 【類】 hardly ***merit*** the *attention* of ... ¶***need*** special *attention* 特に注意を要する. ¶***occupy*** the *attention* of ... ...の注意をひく. 【類】 The subject has recently ***occupied*** considerable public *attention*. ¶***pay*** close *attention* to

… …に細心の注意を払う. 【類】Don't ***pay*** any ***attention*** to me. / ***pay*** due ***attention*** to one's duties / ***pay*** strict ***attention*** to one's lessons / ***pay*** chief ***attention*** to … / ***pay*** no special ***attention*** to … / ***pay attention*** exclusively (もっぱら) to …. ¶***proffer*** small ***attention*** 余り注意しない. ¶***provoke*** the ***attention*** of the whole civilized world 文明国全体の注意を喚起する. ¶Your letter of … is to hand and ***receiving attention*** …の御手紙落手, 御申出の件考慮中であります. 【類】The matter is ***receiving attention.*** / ***receive*** considerable ***attention*** / ***receive*** due ***attention*** from … / In secondary schools, games ***receive*** great ***attention.*** ¶***relax*** one's ***attention*** 注意をゆるめる. ¶It will well ***repay*** his ***attention.*** それに注意すれば十分の益が彼にある. ¶I ***request*** your ***attention*** to the matter. この件に御注意を請う. ¶***require*** very little ***attention*** ほとんど手がかからない ‖ a matter ***requiring*** immediate ***attention*** 急務. ¶***rivet*** one's ***attention*** on … …にじっと目を留める. 【類】the ***attention*** of all was suddenly ***riveted*** upon … / ***rivet*** the ***attention*** of the reader. ¶***secure attention*** 注意を得る. ¶I shall consider any ***attention shown*** to Mr. … as a personal favor. …へのご厚情は私から感謝します. ¶for the sake of ***stimulating attention*** 注意を促すために. ¶***strain*** one's ***attention*** かたずをのむ. ¶***sustain*** the ***attention*** of one's pupils 生徒の注意をそらさぬようにする. ¶***took*** his entire ***attention*** 彼を専心ならしめた ‖ ***take*** one's ***attention off*** … …から注意をそらす. ¶***turn*** [one's] ***attention*** to … …に注意を向ける. 【類】***turn*** one's ***attention*** in another direction / ***turn*** one's chief ***attention*** toward …. ¶***usurp*** the ***attention*** of … …の注意を奪う. ¶***weary*** the ***attention*** 注意力を疲らす. ¶***win*** its ***attention*** by the public それが世間から注意されるようになる. ¶***win*** and ***hold*** the ***attention*** of one's hearers 聴衆の関心をしっかり握ってはなさない.

V[2] public ***attention*** is beginning to ***center*** on … 世人の注意が…に集まりつつある.

Q give ***active attention*** to … 進んで…に配慮する. ¶give ***added attention*** to … なお一層…に注意する. ¶I was ***all attention.*** 私は一所懸命に注意していた. ¶This will receive ***ampler attention*** later. これは後章で詳論する. ¶Your application will have the ***best attention.*** お申込はせいぜい考慮します. ¶with ***breathless attention*** かたずをのんで. ¶***careful attention*** to the rules of duty よく本分を守ること. 【類】deserve ***careful attention*** / Your inquiries will receive our most ***careful attention.*** ¶his ***characteristic attention*** to accuracy 彼の持前の正確に対する用意. ¶pay ***close attention*** to … …に細心の注意を払う. ¶give ***close*** and ***unremitting attention*** 切実不断の注意を加える. ¶***considerable attention*** has been devoted to … 大いに…に注意した. 【類】It has attracted ***considerable attention*** in the scientific circles. ¶I regard this as a ***delicate attention*** on your part. これはあなたの優しいお心尽しだと思います. ¶with ***devout attention*** 恭しく. ¶devote ***disproportionate attention*** to … …に必要以上の注意を払う. ¶have ***due attention*** 当然受くべき注意を受ける. ¶Your letter shall have (=receive) our ***earliest attention.*** 手紙の件はさっそく手配いたします. ¶give ***earnest attention*** to … …に対し心を込めた取扱いをする. ¶He stood gazing with ***entranced attention*** on the scene before him. 彼は眼前の光景をじっと見入っていた. ¶Your proposal is having ***every attention.*** ご提案は慎重に考慮しています. ¶his ***filial attention*** to his mother's wants 母親の望みに対する子としての心づかい. ¶demand our ***first attention*** 真先に処理する必要がある. ¶devote one's ***full attention*** to … …に十分尽力する. 【類】catch one's ***full attention*** of … / give one's ***full attention*** to a project (計画). ¶pay ***further attention*** to … …に一層注意する. ¶It is now attracting ***grave attention.*** それは目下慎重な注意を引きつつある. ¶Please give your ***immediate attention*** to the business I wrote to you the other day. 先だってお願いの件をさっそくご配慮下さい. ¶devote ***increased attention*** to … …に益々注意する. ¶attract ***increasing attention*** from … …から益々注意される. ¶A teacher cannot give ***individual attention*** to his pupils if his class is large. 受持学級の生徒数が多いと教師は銘々の世話をする事ができない. 【類】Students receive more ***individual attention*** in a small than a larger institution (大きな学校より小さい学校). ¶attract ***instant attention*** たちまち注意をひく. ¶***international attention*** is being directed to … 各国の注意が…に向けられつつある. ¶pay ***keen attention*** to … 大いに…に対して注意を払う ‖ engage our deepest interest and our ***keenest attention*** われわれの最も深甚な興味と最も切実な注意をひく. ¶I thank you for your ***kind attention.*** 御清聴を感謝する. ¶it has received ***little attention*** beyond … それは…以上に余り注意されていない. ¶The injured were given ***medical attention.*** けが人は医者にかけた. ¶receive the ***merited attention*** 当然受くべきはずの注意を受ける. ¶***meticulous attention*** 細かすぎる注意. ¶***much attention*** has been devoted, during the last few decades, to … 過去二三十年間に…に対して大いに注意が与えられた. ¶***particular attention*** is drawn to … 特に…に注意を促す. 【類】***particular attention*** must be given to the fact that … ¶It is worthy of more than ***passing attention.*** それは大いに考慮すべきだ. ‖ devote only ***passing attention*** to … …にちょっと触れる (詳説せずに). ¶give ***personal attention*** 自身が直接事に当る. ¶enlist ***popular attention*** 一般民衆の注意をよぶ. ¶***prolonged attention*** to a single subject 一つの問題の長期研究. ¶Your order will receive our ***prompt attention.*** ご注文は敏速にお取扱い致します. ‖ The matter needs ***prompt*** and ***thorough attention.*** その件は至急徹底的に処理する必要がある. ¶give ***proper attention*** to … …に適当な注意を加える. ¶The subject commands much ***public attention.*** その問題は大分世間から注意されている. 【類】gain considerable ***public attention.*** ¶He listened with ***rapt attention.*** 聞きほれていた. ¶deserve ***respectable attention*** 敬聴の価値がある. ¶His opinions received, and deserved, ***respectful attention,*** irrespective of party or politics. 彼の説は政党や政見のいかんに係らず敬意を表されまたそうされる値打があった. ¶a ***rigid attention*** to the tasks of the day 一日の仕事を厳格に(きちんきちんと)やって行くこと. ¶gaze with ***riveted attention*** upon … …をじっと見入る. ¶The subject hitherto has received but ***scant attention.*** その問題はこれまで余り研究されていない. ‖ pass it over with ***scant attention*** ろくに注意もしないでそれを見過ごす. 【類】The theories are given but ***scant attention*** today. ¶***Scientific attention*** is being directed to the universal language proposed by Prof. Piano. ピアノ教授の新案になる世界語は学者間に研究されている. ¶recommend it to the ***serious attention*** of … …の慎重な注意を促す. 【類】pay ***serious attention*** to … / has attracted ***serious attention*** in many quarters (多くの方面で) by … ¶deserve ***some attention*** 幾分注意する値打がある. ¶I should like to draw ***special attention*** to … …に特にご注意願いたい. 【類】deserve the ***special attention*** of … ¶***spontaneous attention*** 自然の注意. ¶by ***steady attention*** to … …に絶えず注意して. ¶The whole company listened with ***strained attention.*** 一同かたずをのんで傾聴した. ¶The question does not receive ***sufficient attention*** from the authorities. その問題は当局者からあまり注意されていない. ¶attract his ***suspicious attention*** 彼に怪しいと見られる. ¶give ***undivided attention*** to one's lesson 学課に専心する ‖ with ***undivided attention*** 余念なく. 【類】She gave me her ***undivided attention.*** / The teacher must hold the ***undivided attention*** of every student in the class during the entire hour. ¶give ***unflagging attention*** to … …に不断の注意を加える. ¶His ***attention*** is ***unremitting.*** 彼は絶えず注意している. ¶hold one's ***unwavering attention*** たえず注意をさせる. ¶with ***unwearied attention*** 鋭意. ¶***vigilant attention*** 細心の注意. ¶***voluntary attention*** 自発的な注意. ¶give plants ***watchful attention*** against frost 植木に十分寒さの手当をしてやる. ¶attracted ***widespread attention*** throughout the country 全国にわたって広く注意を喚起した. ¶attract ***world-wide attention*** 世界的注意を喚起する.

Q[2] have ***newspaper attention*** 新聞記者の注意を引いている. ¶come to ***police attention*** 警察の手にかゝるようになる ‖ The case is now receiving ***police attention.*** その事件は目下警察の手で調査中である. ¶with ***world attention*** focused on … 世界の視聴が…に集中されて.

P stand ***at attention***「気を付け!」の姿勢を取る. ¶It is ***beneath*** the ***attention*** of serious critics. それはまじめな批評家の注意に値しない. ¶***by*** careful ***attention*** to … …に

細心の注意を払って. ¶*in* rapt *attention* 聞きほれて. ¶recommend it ***to*** the best *attention* of ... それを...がとくと考慮せられんことを望む. ¶have the matter forced ***upon*** one's *attention* ...を見せつけられる. ¶The result will be watched ***with*** close *attention*. その結果は刮(かつ)目して待たれることであろう. ¶***without*** minute *attention* to ... 細かに...に注意を払わないで.

P² divert *attention* ***from*** ... ...から注意をそらす. ¶*attention* ***of*** a student to study 学生が意を学業に用いること. ¶I beg to call your *attention* ***to*** the fact that ... ...にご注意を願う.

(2) [しばしば *pl.*] 礼儀; 愛情.

V ***bestow*** polite *attentions* upon ... ...を丁重に取扱う. ¶***encourage*** *attentions* [女の方から]持かける. ¶***pay*** amorous *attentions* (=make love) to ... ...に愛を寄せる. ¶She ***welcomed*** his *attentions*. 彼の愛を迎えた.

Q pay ***assiduous*** *attention* to a lady 女に情を尽す. ¶pay ***courteous*** *attention* to a guest 来客を丁重に扱う. ¶***embarrassing*** *attentions* 迷惑な親切. ¶pay a lady ***marked*** *attentions* 婦人に特別いんぎんにする. ¶***officious*** *attentions* おせっかい. ¶***undesired*** *attentions* of ... ...から寄せられるうれしくない好意. ¶the ***unobtrusive*** *attention* of all employees 全店員のうるさくない程度の愛きょう.

P² His *attentions* ***to*** her have become so marked of late. 彼女に対する彼の心尽しは最近非常に目立って来た.

attentive, *a.* 注意深い; ねんごろな.

M ***deeply*** *attentive* of ... ...に深く留意する. ¶be ***eagerly*** *attentive* 熱心に傾聴している. ¶be ***too*** *attentive* to women 女にでれでれしている.

P a man *attentive* ***to*** dress (fashion) 服装(など)に注意する人. 【類】be *attentive* ***to*** the speaker's words (one's work, duties) / He is very *attentive* ***to*** his parents.

attentiveness, *n.* 注意深いこと.

Q an ***eager*** *attentiveness* 熱心な注意.

attest, *v.* 証明する. 「証明される.

M it is ***abundantly*** *attested* by ... それは...によって十分に

P *attest* ***to*** a fact 事実を証明する ‖ This *attests* ***to*** his industry. これが彼の勤勉を証明する.

attire, *n.* 服装.

V ***wear*** female *attire* 女装する.

Q naval officers in ***civilian*** *attire* 私服の海軍士官. ¶in ***gorgeous*** (=***splendid***) *attire* 盛装をして. ¶in ***light*** *attire* 軽装で. ¶a girl in ***male*** *attire* 男装の少女. ¶He was clad in ***objectionable*** *attire* 悪趣味な服装をしていた. ¶in [one's] ***ordinary*** *attire* ふだん着で. ¶in ***proper*** *attire* ちゃんとした身なりで. ¶in ***woman's*** *attire* 女装して.

Q² in ***everyday*** *attire* ふだん着で. ¶in ***night*** *attire* 寝巻で. ¶***sport*** *attire* スポーツ服. ¶in their ***Sunday*** (***holiday***) *attire* 晴着を着て. ¶in ***wedding*** *attire* 婚礼の衣裳を

attire, *v.* 装う. 「つけて.

M ***fashionably*** *attired* 時好の服装をして. ¶***irreproachably*** *attired* 一点非の打ちようのないなりをして. ¶***neatly*** *attired* きちんとした風をして. ¶***shabbily*** *attired* みすぼらしい風をして. ¶***smartly*** *attired* in Army uniform スマートな軍服姿で.

P She was *attired* ***as*** a man. 彼女は男装していた. ¶*attired* ***in*** Japanese dress 和服すがたで. 【類】*attired* ***in*** black (黒衣) / *attired* ***in*** his school uniform ‖ *attired* ***in*** purple (white) 紫衣(など)を着て.

attitude, *n.* 態度; 姿勢.

V ***adopt*** a violent *attitude* 乱暴な態度に出る. ¶***ascertain*** the *attitude* of ... ...の態度を確かめる. ¶***assume*** a hostile *attitude* 反抗的態度に出る / ***assume*** an *attitude* of superiority (優越感). ¶***change*** one's *attitude* 態度を変える. ¶***cultivate*** a charitable *attitude* of mind 寛容の態度を取るように努める. ¶He ***had*** a ghastly *attitude*. 物すごいけんまくだった. ¶***maintain*** the present *attitude* 現在の態度を維持する. 【類】***maintain*** an *attitude* of scepticism (懐疑) toward ... ¶***make*** one's *attitude* ***clear*** 自分の態度を明かにする. ¶***modify*** one's *attitude* on the question その問題に対する態度を少し変える. ¶if this unreasoning *attitude* be ***persisted*** この不合理な態度が持続されるならば. ¶***preserve*** an *attitude* of cynical indifference 皮肉な無関心的態度を持する. ¶***retain*** a cautious and sceptical *attitude* 細心な懐疑的態度を持続する. ¶***revise*** our *attitude* toward it われわれのそれに対する態度を改める. ¶***show*** an *attitude* of indifference 無関心な態度を示す. ¶***strike*** an *attitude*=pose for effect 気どる. ¶***take*** a more modest *attitude* 一層謙虚な態度を取る. ¶***take up*** *attitude* of antagonism to it それに対して反対の態度を取る.

V² His *attitude* ***stiffened***. その人の態度が硬化した.

Q an ***adamant*** *attitude* 断固たる態度. ¶a ***bold*** *attitude* 大胆な態度. ¶in a ***broader*** and a more ***tolerant*** *attitude* 一層宏量でかつ寛容な態度. ¶a ***broad-minded*** *attitude* 宏量な態度. ¶adopt a ***businesslike*** *attitude* てきぱきした態度をとる. ¶a ***calm*** and ***determined*** *attitude* 落着きのある断固とした態度. ¶buyers' ***cautious*** *attitude* 買手の控目. ¶encounter a ***choosy*** *attitude* より好みをする(気むずかしい)態度であしらわれる. ¶It is high time that a ***clearer*** *attitude* were adopted. もう旗幟(し)を鮮明にしてもいい時分だ. ¶assume a ***compromising*** *attitude* 折れて出る. ¶a ***conciliatory*** *attitude* 譲歩的態度. ¶a ***cool, impartial***, and ***open-minded*** *attitude* 冷静で公平で腹蔵のない態度. ¶a ***cosmopolitan*** *attitude* 世界人的態度. ¶a ***critical*** *attitude* of mind 批評的態度. ¶a ***defensive*** *attitude* 防衛的態度. ¶assume a ***defiant*** *attitude* けんか腰になる. ¶a ***dignified*** *attitude* 貫禄のある態度. ¶a ***docile, passive*** *attitude* 従順な受身の態度. ¶an ***earnest*** *attitude* 真剣な態度. ¶an ***easy*** and ***graceful*** *attitude* 悠揚迫らざる態度. ¶the ***editorial*** *attitude* of a newspaper 新聞社説の態度. ¶an ***energetic*** *attitude* 強硬な態度. ¶his ***habitual*** *attitude* 彼の常習的態度. ¶resent being addressed on the "***hail-fellow-well-met***" *attitude* なれなれしく話しかけられて憤然とする. ¶an ***indulgent*** *attitude* 手ぬるいな態度. ¶The *attitude* of the general public is ***interrogatory***, if not ***respectful***. 公衆は丁重というのでないにしても疑問的態度である. ¶***inward*** *attitude* 精神的態度. ¶He was standing in an ***irresolute*** *attitude* for a few minutes. 彼は二三分間決し兼ねたていで立っていた. ¶adopt a more ***liberal*** *attitude* 一層の雅量を示す. ¶in a ***listening*** *attitude* 傾聴の態度で. ¶a ***lukewarm*** *attitude* toward ... ...に対するなまぬるい態度. ¶the rise of ***modern*** *attitude* toward life 人生に対する近代的態度の始まり. ¶his ***moral*** *attitude* 彼の道徳上の態度. ¶a ***noble*** *attitude* 見上げた態度. ¶a strictly ***objective*** *attitude* 厳正な客観的態度. ¶an ***optimistic*** *attitude* 楽観的態度. ¶assume a ***patronizing*** *attitude* 先輩づらをする. ¶a ***pessimistic*** *attitude* 悲観的態度. ¶a ***pro(anti)-foreign*** *attitude* 対外軟弱(強硬)態度. ¶a ***psychic*** *attitude* 心情(状). ¶He stood in a ***pugilistic*** *attitude*. 拳闘の身構えで立った. ¶a ***questioning*** *attitude* 疑問的態度. ¶a ***religious*** *attitude* 敬けんな態度. ¶its ***repressive*** *attitude* toward all independent thinking すべての自由思想に対する圧迫的態度. ¶a ***resolute*** *attitude* 断固たる態度. ¶with ***respectful*** *attitude* 恭しく. ¶a ***saner*** *attitude* based on realities 現実に則した一層堅実な態度. ¶a ***scientific*** *attitude* of mind 科学的態度. ¶a ***self-approving*** *attitude* 独善的な態度. ¶a ***self-pitying*** *attitude* 自己をあわれむ態度. ¶a more ***sensible*** *attitude* 一層賢明な態度. ¶a ***sincere*** and ***friendly*** *attitude* 真実な友誼的態度. ¶His *attitude* was ***statuesque***. 彼の姿勢は立像のようであった. ¶in a ***stiff*** *attitude* 堅苦しい態度で. ¶adopt a ***stoic*** *attitude* in the presence of sufferings 苦難に面して忍従的態度を持する. ¶kneel in a ***supplicating*** *attitude* 哀願の姿勢でひざまずく. ¶approach with a ***sympathetic*** *attitude* 同情的態度で接する. ¶a ***terrifying*** (=***threatening***) *attitude* 恐ろしい剣幕. ¶strike a ***theatrical*** *attitude* 気取る. ¶in a ***threatening*** *attitude* すごんで. ¶a ***tyrannical*** *attitude* 暴君的態度. ¶He maintained an ***uncertain*** *attitude*. 彼はあいまいな態度を続けた. ¶adopt an ***unfriendly*** *attitude* toward ... ...に対して反抗的態度に出る. ¶an ***unhistorical*** and ***uncritical*** *attitude* 史実や批判を重んじない態度. ¶an ***unscientific*** *attitude* 非科学的態度. ¶a ***virulent*** *attitude* 激越な態度. ¶a ***weak*** *attitude* 弱腰.

Q² a more ***commonsense*** *attitude* 一層常識的な態度. ¶a ***cover-up*** *attitude* 臭いものにふた的な態度. ¶a ***do-nothing*** *attitude* 無為の態度. ¶a "***get-tough***" *attitude* toward ... ...に対するがん固な態度. ¶in an ***I-told-you-so*** *attitude* それ見たことかといわんばかりに. ¶show a "***no-comment***" *attitude* 「意見なし」的(無関心な)態度を示す. ¶his ***pro-central Government*** *attitude* 彼の中央政府に迎合する態度. ¶the ***sales appeal*** *attitude* 売らんかなの態度. ¶a ***watch and wait*** *attitude* 静観的態度. ¶the "***yellow***

***journal*" *attitude* toward Japan 日本に対する「デマ新聞」的(扇情的)な態度.

P the contrast ***in*** the British and the German *attitude* toward science 科学に対する英国とドイツの態度の相違 ‖ The director read the Imperial Rescript on Education ***in*** an *attitude* of devotion. 校長は恭しく教育勅語を朗読した. 【類】***in*** the *attitude* of prayer.

P² one's *attitude* ***of*** mind toward ... ...に対する心構え. 【類】the white race's *attitude* ***of*** arrogant superiority toward all non-white peoples ‖ an *attitude* ***of*** proud reticence いばってむっつりした態度. ¶Russia's *attitude* ***on*** the subject has undergone no modification. その問題に対するロシアの態度は少しも変っていない. ¶his *attitude* ***to*** Christianity キリスト教に対する氏の態度. ¶the author's *attitude* ***toward*** life 著者の人生観. 【類】briefly review the transformations (変化) in the *attitude* ***toward*** ... ¶become less rigid in father's *attitude* ***toward*** an unfilial son 不孝息子に対する父親の気がゆるむ.

attorney, *n.* 代理人, 弁護士.

Q² a ***defense*** *attorney* 被告の弁護士. ¶a ***district*** *attorney* 地方検事 (D.A. と略す). ¶a ***state*** *attorney* 検事.

P He acted ***as*** *attorney* for me. 私の代理人となった.

P² an *attorney* ***at*** law 弁護士. ¶the *attorney* ***for*** the defendant 被告側の弁護士. ¶an *attorney* ***in*** the spiritual court 宗教裁判所の弁護人.

attract, *v.* 引く, 誘う.

M He was ***irresistibly*** *attracted* by her charm. 彼女の魅力に思わず引付けられた.

P my attention was *attracted* ***by*** ... ...に気を取られた. ¶*attract* a person ***to*** virtue (evil) 人を善行(悪事)に誘う ‖ have one's attention *attracted* ***to*** it その方に気を取られる. 【類】*attract* another's attention ***to*** oneself / It *attracted* many visitors ***to*** the place.

attraction, *n.* 引力, 引きつける物.

V ***feel*** no sexual *attraction* to the opposite sex 異性に対して何ら魅力を感じない. ¶The existence of an extensive view ***forms*** a great *attraction*. 見晴らしが大いに利くので非常によい. 【類】***form*** the best *attraction*. ¶It ***has*** no *attraction* for me. それには僕は興味がない. 【類】Politics will always ***have*** an *attraction* for young men. / Women ***have*** no *attraction* for him. ¶The town ***held out*** no *attractions* to him. その市は彼には何の興味も与えなかった. ¶a subject which ***offers*** *attractions* to every cultured mind 教養ある人ならだれにでも興味のある題目. ¶it ***owes*** its chief *attraction* to ... それが人目を引くのは主に...のためだ. ¶They ***possess*** *attractions* of person. 彼らは美貌(ぼう)の持主である. 【類】***possess*** the *attraction* of novelty or the charm of beauty / Of all subjects of study, it may be safely admitted that grammar ***possesses*** as a rule the fewest *attractions* for the youthful mind. ¶This will ***provide*** an added *attraction*. これをやると一段とおもしろ味が加わる. ¶He could not ***resist*** the *attraction* of the footlights. 彼は脚光(舞台)の魅力に勝つことができなかった.

Q These are ***additional*** *attraction*. これは錦(にしき)上さらに花を添えるものである. ¶***chemical*** *attraction* 化学親和力. ¶the ***chief*** *attraction* 呼物, 取柄. ¶the ***crowning*** *attraction* of the exhibition 展覧会の呼物. ¶***engrossing*** *attraction* 何とも言えぬおもしろみ. ¶***ever-appealing*** *attraction* いつも変らない魅力. ¶offer ***exceptional*** *attractions* to the foreign tourist 外来観光客に対して特に興味を感じさせる. ¶She possessed ***extraordinary personal*** *attractions*. 非常な美人であった. ¶one of Central Park's ***favorite*** *attractions* セントラル・パークの見ものの一つ. ¶the center of ***feminine*** *attraction* 女性魅力の中心. ¶Life had no ***further*** *attraction* for her. 彼女はもう世の中がいやになった. ¶The ***great*** *attraction* of the circus was a python. そのサーカスの大呼物は大へびであった. ¶***magnetic*** *attraction* 磁力 ‖ a ***magnetic*** *attraction* I was powerless to resist 抗しがたい強い魅力. ¶***mental*** and ***spiritual*** *attraction* 知的及び精神的魅力. ¶This has always had a ***peculiar*** *attraction* for me. 僕は以前からこれに対して特に興味を持っていた. ¶a ***popular*** *attraction* 呼物. ¶What are the ***principal*** *attractions* of the evening? 当夜の呼物は何か. ¶***scenic*** *attractions* 風景の美. ¶attract ***world-wide*** *attraction* 世界的注意を喚起する.

Q² a top ***box-office*** *attraction* 興業的に最大の魅力. ¶a ***star*** *attraction* 人気スターが出演するショーなど. ¶***tourist*** *attractions* 観光客にとって興味ある事物.

P It is now a center ***of*** *attraction* of the Tokyo people. それに今東京人の興味が集っている. ¶They are not ***without*** their *attraction*. それらにも人を引付ける所がないでもない.

P² *attraction* ***between*** two objects 二物間の引力. ¶Beauty has an *attraction* ***for*** all. 美にはすべての人を引付ける力がある. 【類】The magnet has *attraction* ***for*** iron. ¶*attraction* ***of*** gravitation 重力, 引力. ¶*attraction* ***to*** (= ***towards***) anything 何物かに引付けられること ‖ They have natural *attraction* ***to*** each other. 二人は気が合ってお互に引付けられる.

attractive, *a.* 人目を引く.

M ***physically*** *attractive* 肉体的に魅力がある. ¶a man not ***sexually*** *attractive* to women 女から見て性的魅力のない男.

P The journey by the route is *attractive* ***by*** its picturesqueness. その経路による旅行は風景の美に富んでいる. ¶every variety of dish *attractive* ***to*** the eye and appetizing to the taste 見て美しく食べてうまいさまざまの料理.

attractiveness, *n.* 人の目を引くこと.

V ***lessen*** the *attractiveness* of ... ...の魅力をそぐ. ¶unmarried female teachers who have ***passed*** their physical *attractiveness* 肉体の美が衰えた未婚の女教師.

Q ***personal*** *attractiveness* 容姿の魅力.

attributable, *a.* 帰せられる.

M it is ***directly*** *attributable* to ... ...が直接その原因になっている. ¶***distinctly*** *attributable* to ... 確かに...から起った.

P be *attributable* ***to*** his encouragement 彼の激励のたまものだ.

attribute, *n.* 属性.

Q a ***divine*** *attribute* 神の属性. ¶Eyesight is a ***valuable*** *attribute* of the physically perfect man. 視覚は肉体的に完全な人の貴重な資性である.

P² an *attribute* ***of*** God 神の属性.

attribute, *v.* 帰する, 嫁する.

M The image of Buddha is ***traditionally*** *attributed* to the chisel of Kobo Daishi. その仏像は弘法大師の作と言われている. ¶The book (picture) is ***wrongly*** *attributed* to him. その本(絵)を彼の作とするのは誤りである.

P He *attributed* his success ***to*** good luck. 彼はその成功を僥倖(ぎょうこう)だと考えた. ‖ ***to*** this cause, more than to any other, must be *attributed* ... ...は第一にその原因をこれに帰せなければならぬ / *attribute* evil motives (邪念) ***to*** others. 【類】watercolor drawings *attributed* ***to*** ... / the remark *attributed* ***to*** Macaulay, that ... / the book is *attributed* ***to*** the authorship of ...

attrition, *n.* 摩擦.

P² The *attrition* ***of*** undergraduate mind ***on*** undergraduate mind is an important factor of the educational process. 学生同士の切磋琢磨(せっさたくま)こそは教育上の一大要素である.

attune, *v.* 調子を合せる.

P *attune* ***to*** music on the radio ラジオの音楽に調子を合せる. ¶*attune* the voice ***to*** a harp 声をたて琴に合せる.

auction, *n.* 競売.

V the *auction* is ***held*** (***postponed***, ***withdrawn***) 競売が行われる(延期される, 取止めになる).

V² When will the *auction* ***take place***? 競売はいつ行われますか.

Q a ***Dutch*** *auction* 次第にせり下げる競売.

P goods to be sold ***at*** *auction* 競売に付すべき品物 ‖ put ... up ***at*** *auction* ...を競売に掛ける. ¶sell ***by*** *auction* = 《英》sell ***at*** *auction* 競売に付する. ¶a sale ***by*** auction 競売 ‖ His library was sold ***by*** *auction*. 彼の蔵書は競売にされた. ¶His collection was put up ***to*** *auction*. 彼の収集は競売に付せられた.

audacity, *n.* 大胆, 厚顔.

V He ***had*** the *audacity* to pick pockets in broad daylight. 大胆にも白昼すりをやった.

Q with ***confident*** *audacity* 傍若無人に. ¶***presumptuous*** *audacity* 鉄面皮.

P an act ***of*** *audacity* 大胆不敵の振舞. ¶***with*** *audacity* = audaciously 大胆にも.

audience, *n.* (**1**) [団] 聴衆; 観客; 読者.

V ***address*** an *audience* of about 4,000 およそ四千人の聴衆に向って演説する. 【類】He ***addressed*** *audiences* on his speaking tour. ¶The *audience* was deeply ***affected***. 聴衆は深く感動した. ¶He is gifted with the knack of ***arousing*** an *audience* to enthusiasm for noble causes.

彼は聴衆の義憤に訴えることに妙を得ている. ¶He knows how to ***attract*** an *audience*. 彼は聴衆の引付け方を知っている. ¶***befuddle*** one's *audience* 聴衆を酔わす. ¶He ***carried*** his *audience* with him from beginning to end. 彼は始めから終りまで聴衆を飽きさせなかった. ¶He is so successful as a lecturer that he ***commands*** a growing *audience*. 彼は講演者としては大成功でますます多数の聴衆を得つつある. ¶The *audience* was ***composed*** almost entirely of ladies. 聴衆はほとんど全部婦人連であった. ¶The actor ***delighted*** the Japanese *audience* during some 40 years. その俳優はおよそ四十年間日本の観客を喜ばした(日本で成功的舞台生活を送った). ¶The lecture ***drew*** a large *audience*. その講演者は多数の聴衆を引付けた. ‖ The show is ***drawing*** but a meager *audience*. その興行は入りがない. ¶The *audience* were ***enraptured***. 聴衆は狂喜した. ¶***face*** a large *audience* 多数の聴衆に向う. ¶***gather*** large *audience* 多数の聴衆を集める. ¶He skillfully ***handled*** the uncertain and highly skittish *audience*. 彼はその浮いた極めて変りやすい聴衆を巧みに操った. ¶His lecture ***had*** a crowded *audience*. 彼の講演には多数の聴衆があった. ¶He ***held*** the *audience* spellbound for three quarters of an hour with one of the best speeches I have ever heard. 彼は私の聴いた中では最もできばえのよい演説をやって四十五分間聴衆を酔わした. ¶***move*** an *audience* to laughter (tears) 聴衆を笑わす(泣かす). ¶The lecturer ***obtained*** a huge *audience* of many thousands. 講演者は数千人に及ぶ多数の聴衆を得た. ¶***reach*** a wider *audience* 一層広い聴衆を相手にする. ¶***remind*** the *audience* that ... 聴衆に...を想起させる. ¶***rouse*** (=***move***) his *audience* to enthusiasm 聴衆をやんやと言わせる. ¶The *audience* was deeply ***stirred***. 聴衆は深く感激した. ¶The orator ***swayed*** his *audience*. 弁士は聴衆を感動させた. ¶This ***threw*** the *audience* into paroxysms of laughter. これで聴衆は腹を抱えて笑った. 【類】***threw*** the *audience* into convulsions by saying ... ¶***touch*** the *audience* deeply 聴衆を感動させる. ¶***turn*** the *audience* inside out 聴衆をどっと笑わせる.

V² The *audience* ***dropped off***. 聴衆は次第に立去った. ¶The *audience* ***hissed***. 聴衆は野次った.

Q He had an ***appreciative*** *audience*. 彼は話の分る聴衆を得た. 【類】Actors are stimulated by ***appreciative*** *audiences*. ¶an ***enormous*** *audience* 大変な数の聴衆. ¶an ***imaginary*** *audience* 仮定上の聴衆. ¶an ***intelligent*** *audience* インテリの聴衆. ¶The presence of a very ***large*** *audience* stimulated the speaker. 聴衆が多いので弁士は興奮した. 【類】a moderately ***large*** (かなり大入の) *audience* / She gave her first performance in the city to a ***large*** and ***enthusiastic*** *audience* (多数の熱心な観客). / The book will find a ***large appreciative*** *audience* (多数の目の高い読者). ¶There is a very ***limited*** *audience* for the magazine. 同誌の読者は極めて少数だ. ¶perform to a ***packed*** *audience* 大入の聴衆の前で演じる. ¶address a ***popular*** *audience* 大衆を相手に演説をする. ¶a ***responsive*** *audience* 手答のある聴衆. ¶a rather ***scanty*** *audience* 余り多くない聴衆. ¶a ***small*** but ***enthusiastic*** *audience* 少数ながら熱心な聴衆. ¶a ***stimulating*** *audience* 励みをつけてくれる聴衆. ¶***unreflecting*** *audiences* 無思慮な聴衆. ¶a radio broadcaster and his ***unseen*** *audience* ラジオ放送者とその目に見えぬ聴衆. ¶The book will not command a very ***wide*** *audience*. その本はあまり多くは読まれまい. ¶the famous author and his ***world-wide*** *audiences* 有名な著者と彼の世界各国の読者.

Q² a ***bumper*** *audience* 満員(演説会など). ¶The musicals are playing to ***capacity*** *audiences*. その喜歌劇は引き続き満員を取っている. 【類】Obviously drawn by curiosity, ***capacity*** *audiences* saw the film. ¶a ***film*** *audience* 映画の観客. ¶the ***first-night*** *audience* 初日の観客. ¶a ***gallery*** *audience* entering a music-hall 演芸場に入場する桟敷の聴衆. ¶a ***magazine*** *audience* 雑誌の読者. ¶a ***radio*** *audience* ラジオ聴取者. ¶The book should have as wide a ***reading*** *audience* as possible. その本はできるだけ広範囲の読者に読ますべきだ. ¶a ***soldier*** *audience* 兵士の聴(観)衆. ¶a ***theater*** *audience* 劇場の観客. ¶a ***TV*** (=***television***) *audience* テレビ聴視者. ¶face (=address) a ***world*** *audience* 世界に呼びかける.

P He was ***among*** the *audience*. 彼も聴衆の中にいた. ¶The play was produced in New York ***before*** an *audience* of 1,000 persons. その狂言はニューヨーク市で一千人の観客を前にして上演された. 【類】She is considered to be the most talented of the native pianists now ***before*** London *audiences*. ¶he had ***for audience*** Prince ... Lord ..., etc. ...公...卿らが彼の講演を聴いた. ¶There were at least three hundred persons ***in*** the *audience*. 聴衆は少くも三百人はいた. ‖ a child ***in*** the *audience* 聴衆の中の一人の子供.

P² an *audience* ***at*** a theater (concert) 劇場(など)の観客. ¶an *audience* ***of*** a hundred thousand persons 十万人の聴衆.

(2) 会見, 引見.

V ***grant*** an *audience* to ... ...に拝謁を賜う. ¶***have*** the *audience* of the Emperor 天皇陛下に拝謁する. 【類】He ***had*** an *audience* of the King of England. ¶***secure*** a favorable *audience* with ... ...と有利な会見を遂げる. ¶***seek*** an *audience* with ... ...に会見を求める.

Q² a ***farewell*** *audience* 告別の謁見.

P ***at*** my first *audience* 最初面会の時. ¶he has received ... ***in audience*** 彼は...を引見した. 【類】He was received ***in*** an *audience* by the Emperor. ¶He had his *audience* ***of*** (=***with***) the Emperor. 皇帝に拝謁した.

auditorium, *n.* 《米》講堂.

Q a ***main*** *auditorium* 大講堂.

Q² a tiered ***horse-shoe*** *auditorium* 階段式馬蹄(てい)形の講堂. ¶a ***lecture*** *auditorium* 大講堂.

aught, *n.* 何かある物.

P it is necessary ***before*** *aught* (=anything) else to ... 何はさておき...しなくてはいけない. ¶***for*** *aught* I know to the contrary 反対説を考慮して見ても(やはり) ‖ He may die ***for*** *aught* I care. あいつが死んだってかまうもんか.

augur, *v.* 占う.

M It *augurs* extremely ***well*** for the future. それは誠にめでたい前兆である.

P *augur* a result ***from*** all circumstances 情勢を総合して結果を推定する. ¶It *augurs* ill ***of*** the enterprise. その計画はよくなさそうな気がする.

augury, *n.* 前兆.

Q It was begun among ***happy*** *augury*. それは幸先よく始められた.

P It is ***of*** good *augury* for the future of the company. それはその会社の将来の有望を約束するものである.

P² an *augury* ***of*** good 吉兆.

aunt, *n.* 伯(叔)母.

Q a ***sour-tempered*** *aunt* ひねくれ者の叔母.

Q² one's ***old maid*** *aunt* ...の老嬢の伯母.

auspices, *n. pl.* 保護, 主催, 後援.

V ***take*** the *auspices* 占う.

Q studies made under the ***joint*** *auspices* of the Social Science Research Council and the American Geographical Society 社会科学研究会と米国地理学協会との連合後援の下に進められた研究. ¶under the ***kind*** and ***cordial*** *auspices* of ... ...の親切な誠意ある後援の下に. ¶under his ***protecting*** *auspices* 彼の後援を得て.

Q² under ***Government*** *auspices* 政府の後援のもとに. 【類】The bureau has been organized and conducted under ***Government*** *auspices*. ¶form a coalition Cabinet under ***Socialist*** *auspices* 社会党支持の連立内閣を組織する.

P published ***under*** the *auspices* of the ... Society. 【類】a show given ***under*** its *auspices* / The magazine is published ***under*** the *auspices* of a Commission of Direction (指導委員会).

austerity, *n.* 耐乏, 緊縮.

Q a ***greater*** *austerity* in the living of the British people 英国人の一段深刻な耐乏生活.

Q² ***wartime*** *austerities* 戦時の耐乏生活.

P an English life characterized ***by*** *austerity* 英国の耐乏生活.

authenticate, *v.* 確証する.

M a certified copy ***duly*** *authenticated* 正式の謄本.

authenticity, *n.* 確実.

V ***give*** *authenticity* to ... ...に真実性を与える. ¶***question*** (=***challenge***) the historical *authenticity* (=creditability) of ... ...の歴史的真実性を疑う. 【類】***question*** the *authenticity* of a legend.

Q its ***admitted*** or ***suspected*** *authenticity* その認められたまたは疑われたる真実性. ¶of ***dubious*** *authenticity* 確実と思われない. ¶lack ***historical*** *authenticity* 史実を欠く. ¶of ***unquestionable*** *authenticity* まぎれもない確実な.

P² *authenticity* ***of*** a document 文書の真正.

author, *n.* 著者, 著作物; 創始者.

V *assist* necessitous *authors* 窮乏の作家を援助する. ¶*expurgate* (=*bowdlerize*) an *author* 一著作を删(え)修する. ¶*follow* the *author* to the end 著作を読了する ‖ We *follow* the *author* into a pleasant wood. われわれは(本の中で)著者に連れられて楽しい林にはいって行く. ¶I *haven't* any pet *author*, but I like his works pretty well. 私には特に好きな作家というものはないがあの作家の著作はかなり好きだ. ¶Men who *read* French *authors* with ease are at sea when they come to express their simplest wants in that language. フランスの作家をらくに読める人でもさて仏語で簡単な用事をたすということになると困ってしまう. ¶The publisher is often certain to *rob* the *author*. 出版者が著者を搾取する事は往々にして事実である. ¶*trace* the *author* of a report そのうわさの出所を探る.

Q an *anonymous author* 匿名(無名)作家. ¶the most illustrious of *Canadian authors* カナダの作家中で最も著名な人. ¶*classic authors* 古典的作家. ¶*contemporary authors* 現代の作家. ¶a *fair author* 女流作家. ¶*authors, full fledged* or *embryo* 一人前の作家連や作家の卵たち. ¶a *globe-trotting author* 世界をまたにかける作家. ¶*professional authors* (=bookmakers) who write to sell 売るために書く職業作家. ¶a *prolific author* 多作家. ¶a *recondite author* 難解な作家. ¶a *reviving*, not "*disappearing*," *author* 消えるのではなく返り咲く作家. ¶a *rising author* 新進作家. 【類】a *rising young author*. ¶a *scholarly* and *conscientious author* 学識あり且つ良心的な著者. ¶*self-obliterating author* 没我の著作家. ¶a *talented author* 手腕ある作家. ¶a *young and untried author* 若い未熟な著作家. ¶a *would-be author* 作家志望者.

Q² the *brother authors* 兄弟作家. ¶*English-writing authors* of high rank 一流の英文作家. ¶a *gift-book author* 進物用図書の著者. ¶be *part author* with his brother, ..., of ... 兄(弟)と共著として...を出している. ¶a *textbook author* 教科書編集者.

P² the *author of* many learned books 多数の学術書の著者. 【類】the *author of* several notable poems ‖ Who is the *author of* the phrase? この句を始めて使ったのはだれですか. ‖ an *author of* great permanence 永久に読まれる作家. 【類】the *author of* that plan / the *author of* the rumor / We are most often the *authors of* our own troubles. ‖ the *author of* a fault 罪科の犯人.

authoress, *n.* 女流作家.

Q an *accomplished authoress* 円熟した女流作家.

authoritative, *a.* 権威のある.

Q be *absolutely* (*completely*) *authoritative* 絶対的[完全]に権威がある.

authority, *n.* 権能, 権威; [通例 *pl.*] 当局(者); 典拠; 大家.

V *abuse authority* 職権を濫用する. ¶*accept* the *authority* of ... ...の権威を認める. ¶*assert* one's *authority* 権力を主張する. ¶*bring* the *authorities* to account 当局者を責める. ¶*centralize authority* 中央に集権する. ¶*cite authorities* 出典を示す. ¶*consult* the *authorities* 諸大家の説を参考する. ¶*defy* the *authority* of ... ...の権威を無視する. ¶*deny* the *authority* of ... ...の権威を否認する. ¶*dispute* the *authority* of ... ...の権威に対して疑をはさむ. ¶openly *disregard* the *authority* of ... の権威を公然無視する. ¶*exercise authority* over ... ...に対して権力をふるう. ¶*exert* one's *authority* 権威をふるう. ¶I can *find* no *authority* for the statement. 私はその言明に対して何ら根拠を認めることができない. ¶*follow* the *authority* of a good dictionary in writing compounds 複合語を書くのに良い辞書に準拠する. ¶*give* in detail the *authorities* for every statement 一々出典を明示する. 【類】No *authority* for the statement was *given*. ‖ *give* a person an *authority* to ... ...に...する権能を与える. ¶I *have* his *authority* for saying that ... 私がこういうのは彼の説によったものである. 【類】if I *had authority* (権力) to make a law and the power to enforce it I should ... / He *has* no *authority* to settle the question. / *have* no *authority* (権限) whatever to act as ... ¶still *hold* the *authority* of ... 今でも...の権能がある. ¶*has authority* with ... ...ににらみがきく. ¶*ignore* the *authority* of ... ...の権威を無視する. ¶I *leave authority* in your hands until advised to the contrary. 権限を撤回するまでは君に権限を預けておく. ¶citations to *lend authority* to one's statement 所説に権威を添えるための引用. ¶I have *named* my *authority* for my statement. 私は私の陳述に対してその根拠を明らかにした. ¶*overstep* one's *authority* 職権を濫用する. ¶*possess* a written *authority* to do so そうする認可証を持っている. ¶*question* the *authority* of ... ...の権威に対して疑をはさむ. ¶*resist authority* 官憲に反抗する. ¶His *authority* is not *respected*. 彼はにらみがきかない. ¶*ridicule* the *authority* of ... ...の権威を愚弄(ろう)する. ¶Applicants must *satisfy* the University *Authorities* that their previous training has been suitable. 志望者は大学当局が適当なる予備教育を受けていると認めたものに限り入学を許可する. ¶*secure* their *authority* 彼らの認可を得る. ¶*Authority* must be *sent* immediately. さっそく当事者を派遣しなければならない. ¶*use authority* 権威を示す. ¶*usurp* the *authority* 権威をさん奪する. ¶*vest* a world *authority* in the League of Nations 国際連盟に世界的権力を賦与する. ¶*violate* the *authority* of court 法廷の尊厳を犯す. ¶*weaken the authority* 権力を弱める. ¶*wield* a certain *authority* ある権威をふるう. ¶*withdraw* an *authority* to buy (fix, close, sign) 購入する(確定する, 止める, 調印する)権能を取上げる.

V² *authorities differ* (=*do not agree*) as to ... ...については権威者の間に意見の一致を見ていない. ¶some *authorities state* that ... ...という説もある.

Q have *absolute authority* 絶対権限を有する. ¶an *accepted authority* 認められた権限. ¶an *acknowledged authority* 一般に認められている権威. ¶*administrative authority* 行政権. ¶according to the *best authorities* 最高権威の意見によれば. ¶the *central authority* 中央の権力. ¶the *chief English authority* on this question この問題に対する英国の最高権威. ¶a very *competent military authority* 極めて敏腕な軍事専門家. 【類】R. Strange is said to be "a most *competent authority* as regards the subject of feminine beauty (女性美)." ¶the *authorities concerned* 当局(その筋). ¶The dictionary is a *conclusive authority* for the English-speaking people. その辞典は英語を話す人々にとって決定的典拠である. ¶a *distinguished authority* on Chaucer チョーサー研究の一大権威者. ¶an expression of *doubtful authority* 典拠のいかがわしい言葉使い. ¶*eminent authorities* on the subject その問題に対する知名の権威. ¶one of the soundest of *European authorities* on the subject その事に関する最も確かなヨーロッパの権威者の一人. ¶be sanctioned by *excellent authorities* 堂々たる権威者に認められている. ¶the *executive authorities* 行政官庁. ¶the *first living authority* on ... ...に関する現代最高権威. ¶a *first-rate authority* on all Japanese subjects 日本の諸問題に関する一流権威者. ¶the *foremost authority* on this subject この方面の最高権威. ¶he has *full authority* to ... 彼は...する権能をりっぱに持っている. 【類】Do not operate without *full authority*. ‖ Browning left his son *full authority* to do what he pleased with his love letters. ブラウニングは自分の恋文を適当に処理して一向差支えないと息子に言い残した. ¶I have *good authority* for stating that ... ...と言明するには確かな根拠があります. 【類】be unable to find *good authority* for such usage of the word. ¶a *great authority* on epitaphs and sepulchral lore 碑銘並びに墳墓文献に関する一大権威. 【類】Dr. George Carpenter, a *great authority* on the disease of childhood. / unchallengeably one of the *great authorities* 押しも押されもしないその道の権威 / He is pronounced to be the *greatest living authority* on Japan. ¶a *high authority* on finance 財政の権威. 【類】a *high authority* on the subject of old maps / we have it on the *high authority* of Mill that ... / we are recommended, on *high authority*, to ... / a *higher authority* than myself / His work was for many years the *highest authority* on Greek art. ‖ For years Professor Moore has been regarded as being probably the *highest living authority* concerning (=on) the history of American diplomacy. 以前からムア教授はまず米国外交史の現存最高権威ということになっている. ‖ be of *high* and *supereminent authority* 卓絶した権威者である. ¶have *international authority* or influence 世界的に権威または勢力がある. ¶be quoted universally as a *leading authority* 一大権威者として広く認められている ‖ the world's *leading authority* on ... ...に関する世界的大権威者. ¶a highly

learned German authority 学識の高いドイツの権威者. ¶it has ***literary authority*** in ... ...にその出典がある. ¶The use has been challenged, but has abundant ***literary authority***. その語の用法については異議をはさむものもあるが十分文学的な根拠がある. ¶He is the first ***living authority*** on the art of fortification. 築城の術にかけて現存第一人者である. ¶the ***managing authorities*** 当局者. ¶a leading ***medical authority*** 目ぼしい医学の権威者. ¶***municipal authorities*** 市の当局者. ¶a historian of ***no authority*** 権威のない歴史家 ‖ There is ***no authority*** for such a proceeding. そんな事をして良いという訳はない. ¶according to ***one authority*** 一説によれば. ¶on one's ***own authority*** 自分の勝手で, 独りぎめで. 【類】He is a Doctor of Philosophy on his ***own authority*** (自称). ¶***parental authority*** 親権. ¶the extension of ***Portuguese authority*** beyond seas 海外におけるポルトガルの国威の拡張. ¶***postal authorities*** 郵便当局者. ¶challenge ***presidential authority*** 大統領の権力に挑戦する. ¶a ***profound authority*** on the subject その道の大家. ¶submit a statement to the ***proper authorities*** 該当官庁に声明書を提出する. ¶a ***recognized authority*** of high standing 定評ある大権威者. 【類】***recognized authorities*** in special fields / be the ***recognized authority*** on commerce. ¶a ***reliable authority*** 信頼すべき権威. ¶we had been assured, on ***respectable authority***, that ... 確かな筋から...という言明を得た. ¶The ***royal authority*** totters. 王権がゆるぐ. ‖ a ruler acting with ***royal authority*** 帝王の権力をもって当る支配者. ¶the ***ruling authorities*** of colleges and universities 大学の統治者. ¶we also learn, on the ***same authority***, that ... なお同書に...という事が述べてある. ¶The report rests on ***slender authority***. その報道は根拠が薄弱だ. ¶I can speak with ***some authority*** about ... ...のことについては幾分の権威をもって申上げられる. ¶the book is the ***standard authority*** on ... その本は...の権威書である. 【類】The book ranks as the ***standard authority*** on Japanese financial and economic questions. ¶hold ***supreme authority*** over ... ...に対し絶大の権威を持つ. ¶***trustworthy authorities*** 信頼するに足る権威者. ¶He wielded almost ***undisputed authority***. 彼はほとんどだれも疑うもののない権威を持っていた. ¶an ***undoubted authority*** on ... ...に対する押しも押されもせぬ大家. ¶***unimpeachable authorities*** 申分のない権威者. ¶He speaks with ***unquestioned authority***. 彼の言うことは絶対に信をおくに足る. ¶it is said, on ***unquestionable authority***, that ... 断固として...といわれる. ¶an ***unsurpassed authority*** 第一人者. ¶a ***well-known authority*** on economic affairs 経済学の認められた権威. ¶a ***world-wide authority*** on the subject of ... ...の世界的権威. 【類】a publication of ***world-wide authority***. ¶require ***written authority*** 認可証を必要とする.

Q² the ***Allied occupation authorities*** 連合国占領軍当局. ¶***approval authority*** 承認の権能. ¶in the opinion of ***business authorities*** 実業界の権威筋の説では. ¶the ***city authorities*** of New Jersey ニュジャージーの市当局. ¶The goods were seized by ***customs authorities*** その貨物は税関吏に差押えられた. ‖ The ***customs*** (=***custom house***) ***authorities*** have sold all goods salved from the wreck. 税関の役人どもが難破船から引上げた貨物を売却した. ¶This pronunciation has now ***dictionary authority***. この発音は今では辞書が認めている. ¶***education authorities*** 文教当局. ¶a ***fashion authority*** 流行に関する権威者. ¶Rebel troops continued to challenge ***Government authorities***. 反乱軍は政府への反抗を続けた. ¶***health authorities*** 保健当局. ¶When any question arises as to the meaning of any instructions issued, the interpretation of the ***issuing authority*** shall be final. 発せられたる指令の意義について疑義ある場合には発令当事者の解釈をもって決定的のものとする. ¶***legation authorities*** 公使館員. ¶the ***library*** (***museum***) ***authorities*** 図書(博物)館当局者. ¶the United States ***Military Government authorities*** 米軍政部当局. ¶turn down the wage increase recommendations by the ***National-Personnel Authority*** 人事院の賃上げ勧告を拒否する. ¶***Pentagon authorities*** 米国軍部. ¶usurp ***police authority*** 警察権を奪う. ¶***port authorities*** 港湾当局者. ¶The Attorney General is designated as the sole ***rule-making authority*** 法務長官は法規制定の唯一権威者として任命されている. ¶exert the ***sovereign authority*** 君主の権力を揮う. ¶***town authorities*** 町役場の当局者. ¶His researches have made him a ***world authority*** on the subject. 彼は研究によってその問題に関する世界的権威になった. ‖ consult ***world authorities***, the encyclopedia 百科辞典という世界の権威に相談する.

P The permit is issued ***by authority*** of the Minister of Education. その許可証は文部大臣の名で発行する. 【類】***by*** the ***authority*** of the king (law) / The locution (句法) is sanctioned ***by*** the ***authority*** of the best writers. ‖ be forbidden ***by*** authority その筋から禁止されている. ‖ ***By*** whose ***authority*** do you act? だれに言付けられてするのか. ¶***by virtue of*** his ***authority*** 彼の権能で. ¶I have heard ***from*** good ***authority*** that ... ...ということを信頼するに足る筋から聞込んだ. 【類】our correspondent learns ***from*** good ***authority*** that .... ¶consult others higher ***in authority*** 一層権威のある人々の意見を聞く ‖ be ***in authority*** over people 人々の上に立っている. 【類】one ***in*** high ***authority*** / a letter from some one ***in authority*** ‖ one who is placed ***in authority*** 主宰者. ¶opinion ***of authority*** 権威ある説. ¶I acted ***on*** my own ***authority***. 僕一個の量見でやった. ‖ I will accept it ***on*** your ***authority***. 君が言うのだから真(ま)に受ける. ‖ ***On*** what ***authority*** do you say so? どんな根拠があってそんな事を言うのだ. ‖ ***on*** the ***authority*** of Plato プラトンを典拠として. 【類】***On*** whose ***authority*** (だれの命令で) did you dismiss him? / I am glad to be able to announce, ***on*** the ***authority*** of a Government report (官報によって), that ... 【類】I give these statements ***on*** the ***authority*** of the World and other papers. / Unless he has it ***on*** good ***authority***, it is not worth believing. / I heard it stated ***on*** good ***authority*** that .... ¶They are all ***under*** the ***authority*** of the War Department. 彼らはみな陸軍省の管轄下に在る. ‖ ***under*** one ***authority*** 一統の下に ‖ ***under*** what ***authority*** だれから許されて. ¶a statement made ***upon*** (=***on***) good ***authority*** たしかな根拠のある言明. ¶he is invested ***with*** full ***authority*** to ... 彼は...の全権を与えられている ‖ I can speak ***with authority***. 私は権威をもって申上げられます. ¶***with***-the ***authority*** of that book その本に述べてある所によって. 【類】No man is better qualified to speak ***with authority*** on the subject. / On this subject I am entitled to write ***with*** the ***authority*** of one who knows. ¶he acted ***without*** the ***authority*** of ... ...の許可を受けずにやった. 【類】***without*** the ***authority*** of law.

P² His ***authority as*** a manager is withdrawn. 彼の支配人としての権能は解除された. ¶the ***authorities at*** the Museum = the Museum authorities 博物館の当事者. ¶Mr. ... is the ***authority for*** the following:— 次に述べることは...氏によったものである. 【類】Is there any ***authority for*** the word ... used in this sense? / Who is the ***authority for*** your statement? ¶a written ***authority from*** one person authorizing another to transact certain business for him 委任状. ¶an ***authority in*** the particular field その方面の大家. 【類】an ***authority in*** his subject (own particular field, optical science) / although a great ***authority in*** divinity / ***authorities in*** usage (語の用法). ¶Mr. A. J. Daniels, an ***authority of*** note ***on*** English boxing. ダニエル氏は英国式拳闘の著名な権威者だ. ‖ The prestige and ***authority of*** Johnson was unchallenged for a century after the appearance of his dictionary in 1755. 1755年にこの辞書が出た後一世紀間はジョンソンの声価と権威に対しだれも異論を唱えるものはなかった. ¶the book is ***authority on*** ... その本は...の権威(重要著作)である ‖ he is admittedly an ***authority on*** ... 彼は押しも押されもしない...の権威である ‖ the highest of all ***authorities on*** ... ...に関する大家中の大家. 【類】Professor ..., an ***authority on*** China (South African problems, questions of the Far East). / an ***authority on*** the subject of ... and kindred (関連した) subjects. ¶A father possesses ***authority over*** his children. 父は子に対して権威を持っている.

authorization, *n.* 許可.

V ***obtain*** official ***authorization*** 政府の許可を得る.

Q receive the ***exclusive authorization*** of Ruskin's heirs. ラスキンの相続人から独占的許可を受ける.

P except ***on*** the ***authorization*** of ... ...の許可がなくては. ¶***without authorization*** 許可なしに, みだりに.

authorize, *v.* 許可する, 認可する; 権を授ける.

M be *legally authorized* to ... 法律上…する権限を与えられている. ¶*properly authorized* officials 正当に権限を与えられた役員.

P he is *authorized by* law to ... 彼は…することを法律上許されている. ¶It is *authorized by* usage. それは慣例で認められている.

O They were not *authorized* to do it. 彼らにはその権能がなかった.

authorship, *n.* 著述.

V *attribute* the *authorship* to ... その本は…の著作だとする. ¶*claim* the *authorship* of ... …の著作者であると名乗る. ¶He *denied* the *authorship* of the poem. その詩は自分の作でないと言った. ¶*put* the *authorship* of the term on ... その言葉を作ったのは…だとする.

Q *creative authorship* 創造的著作. ¶of *dubious authorship* 著者不詳の. ¶suggest *feminine authorship* 作者が女ではないかと思わせる. ¶plays of distinction of *native authorship* 本国人の作った名脚本. ¶The *original authorship* of the book is in doubt. その本の原作者はだれであるか不明である. ¶It is of *uncertain authorship.* それは著者が不明. ¶lines whose *authorship* is *unknown* 読人知らずの詩歌.

P books *of* English *authorship* 英国人の著書.

auto, *n.* 自動車 =automobile.

V *drive* an *auto* in the street 街で自動車を運転する.

Q a *high-powered auto* 動力の大きい自動車.

P He took me to my house *in* his *auto.* 彼は自分の自動車で私を家まで送ってくれた.

auto-addresser, *n.* 名あて印刷器.

Q a *standard auto-addresser* 標準式自動名あて印刷器.

autobiography, *n.* 自叙伝.

P an *autobiography by* Herbert Spencer スペンサー自伝.

autocracy, *n.* 専制政治.

Q the *Fujiwara autocracy* 藤原氏の専制政治.

autograph, *n.* 自署.

V *sign* one's *autograph* 自筆で署名する.

Q² *celebrity autographs* 名士の筆跡.

autographing, *n.* 自署すること.

Q² *book autographing* 書物の自署.

automation, *n.* オートメーション.

P² The cost of production is considerably saved *by automation.* オートメーションによって大いに生産費が節約される.

automobile, *n.* 自動車.

V *drive* an *automobile* 自動車を運転する(駆る). ¶*hire* an *automobile* 自動車をやとう. ¶*keep* an *automobile* 自動車を置く. ¶*own* an *automobile* 自動車を所有する. ¶There are always several *automobiles parked* about his residence. 彼の邸宅にはいつも数台の自動車が来ている(来客が多い). ¶*present* one's *automobile* for inspection 自動車の検査を受ける.

V² *Automobiles whiz by.* 自動車がさっと通る.

Q an *expensive automobile* 高価な自動車.

Q² a *six-cylinder automobile* 六汽筒自動車.

P *by automibile* 自動車で. ¶an adventurous trip around the world *in* an *automobile* 自動車世界冒険旅行.

autonomy, *n.* 自治権.

V Russia is at present a Federative Republic of Soviets, each of which *enjoys* the greatest possible local *autonomy.* ロシアは目下ソビエト連邦共和国であって連邦の各自が最大の自治権を持っている. ¶*give* the country its *autonomy* その国に自治権を与える. ¶*receive autonony* 自治権を付与せられる.

Q *absolute autonomy* 絶対自治権. ¶*economic autonomy* 経済自治(権). ¶Japan regained her *full autonomy* with the signing of a peace treaty. 日本は平和条約調印と共に完全な自治権を回復した. ¶a vigorous agitation in favor of *national autonomy* 国民自治権を主張する盛んな運動.

Q² *Philippine autonomy* フィリピンの自治権.

autopsy, *n.* 検死解剖.

V *hold* an *autopsy* on the remains of ... …の死体を解剖に付する.

autosuggestion, *n.* 〖心理〗自己暗示.

V *soothe* unhealthy *autosuggestions* 不健全な自己暗示を静める.

Q a victim of *foolish autosuggestions* ばかげたことを思い込んでいる人.

autumn, *n.* 秋.

Q the *coming autumn* 今年の秋.

P early (late) *in autumn*=in early (late) *autumn* 初(晩)秋.

auxiliary, *n.* 補助物.

Q *useful auxiliary* [役に立つ]補助者(物). 【類】Esperanto is a *useful auxiliary* to languages.

P oil as an *auxiliary to* coal 石炭の補助品としての石油. 【類】They are used as *auxiliaries to* the present and past perfect tenses.

avail, *n.* 利益.

Q It is of *little avail.* それは余り役に立たない. ¶be not of *much avail* 余り役に立たない. ¶It is of *no avail* to say such a thing now. 今さらそんなこと言ってみたって始まらない. 【類】All his efforts proved of *no avail.* ¶it may be of *some avail* in ...ing ... …の場合幾分役に立つでしょう.

P *Of* what *avail* is it? 何の役に立つか. ¶but *to* no *avail* しかし何のかいもなく. ¶but *without avail* (=effort) しかしそのかいもなく.

avail, *v.* 利用する; 役に立つ.

M I *gladly avail* myself of your kind offer. 折角のお申出故喜んでお願致します. ¶Eloquence will *avail* you *little* or *nothing* in such a case. こんな場合君には弁舌なんかほとんど全く役にも立ちはしない. ¶That will not *avail much.* それはあまり役に立つまい. ¶*willingly avail* oneself of another's kind offer 進んで他の厄介になる.

P He *availed* himself *of* the first opportunity to visit America. 彼は最初の機会を利用して渡米した. 【類】I will *avail* myself *of* your help. ‖ be *availed of* for political gain 政争の具に供する.

available, *a.* 役に立つ, 有効な.

M "*not available*" [原稿など]「不採用」. ¶a special offer *available only* until ... …日限りの特別提供. ¶be made *readily available* for reference 参考に便利になっている.

P The coupon is *available at* (=*to*) any hotel in this country. そのクーポンはどのホテルにも適用する. ¶Statistics are not *available for* the purpose. その材料になる統計が得られない. 【類】It is not *available for* the present purpose. / The ticket is *available* (=good) *for* one month. / Two tennis courts and a swimming pool are *available for* the members. ¶The ticket is *available to* Dec. 25,1914. その切符は一九一四年十二月二十五日まで通用. ‖ There was no sleeping accommodation *available* [*to* us] for the night. その晩とまる場所がなかった. ¶this ticket is *available to* and *from* ... この切符は…までの往復に通用する.

avalanche, *n.* なだれ.

V *receive* an *avalanche* of letters from ... …からどっと手紙が殺到する.

avaricious, *a.* どん慾な.

P be *avaricious of* gain 欲張っている. ¶He is *avaricious of* power. 彼は権力に汲々としている.

avenge, *v.* 復しゅうする.

M be *amply avenged* 存分に恨みを晴らす.

P be *avenged by* ... …にかたきを討ってもらう. 【類】*avenge* a murder *by* bringing the criminal to trial. ¶*avenge on* him the murder of father 彼に対して父のかたきを取る. 【類】*avenge on* the Portuguese the massacre (虐殺) of Macao / He swears that he will be *avenged on* you sooner or later. ¶*avenge* (revenge) oneself *upon* ... …に対して仕返しする.

O *avenge* one's sister (妹)の仇(あだ)をうつ. ¶*avenge* a deed ある行為のかたき打ちをする.

avenue, *n.* 並木路; 《米》大通り; 方法.

V *open* [a] new *avenue* of trade 貿易の新方面を開拓する. 【類】*open* a new *avenue* for medicine. ¶*open up* new *avenues* of use for a material 原料品の新用途を開く.

Q an *imposing avenue* of fine buildings りっぱな建物の並んだ堂々たる大通. ¶a *magnificent avenue* of giant cryptomeria trees 杉の巨木のすばらしい並木道. ¶a *stately avenue* of cryptomerias りっぱな杉の並木道. ¶*tree-lined avenues* 並木道.

Q² a *palm avenue* やしの並木道.

P² *avenue of* success 成功の道. ¶*avenue to* honor 栄達の道.

average, *n.* 平均.

V *keep up* their *average* 平均を持続する. ¶It is difficult to *strike averages.* 中庸を得るのはむずかしい. ¶the *average works out* at roundly ... 平均はおよそ…に当る.

Q a *fair average* 普通なみ. ¶a *normal average* 普通平均.

Q² has a .271 *batting average* 平均打率は 0.271.

P The rice crop this year is 20 per cent. *above* the *average.* 本年の米作は平年の二割方増収. ‖ far *above* the *average* 優に平均以上. ¶we get 3.5 *as average* 平均 3.5 という数が出る. ¶it may be put *as* an *average* of ... それは

...平均と見られる. ¶His mental faculties fall somewhat *below* the *average*. 彼の知能は少し平均を下まわる. 【類】Our crop is *below* the *average*. ¶*beyond* the *average* 平均以上. ¶The school is attended *by* an *average* of 300 to 450. その学校は平均四百五十人に対する三百人という出席率を示している. ¶*on* the (=an) *average* 平均して. 【類】The United States has been engaged in war *on* an *average* of every twenty-nine years. / Medical men, *on* an *average*, die sooner than other professional men. ¶The crops are quite *up to* the *average*. 農作はたしかに平年並.

P^2 Their lives have had more than the *average of* human sorrow and danger. 彼らの生涯(がい)は人生の悲哀や危難を並以上に含んでいる. 【類】An *average of* 650 readers daily repair (行く) to the British Museum Reading-Room to draw upon a store of 1,000,000 volumes.

averse, *a.* きらっている.

P He is *averse to* hard working (study, writing). 彼は骨を折る事(など)がきらいだ. 【類】No cat is *averse to* fish. / The Chinese are *averse to* having their world-ancient customs ridiculed.

aversion, *n.* 大きらい.

V *bear aversion* to ... ...をきらう. ¶*contract* an *averison* for ... ...がきらいになる. ¶*exhibit* an *aversion* to ...をいやがる. ¶*feel* an *aversion* to war 戦争をきらう. ¶He *has* an *aversion* for women. 彼は女ぎらい.

Q He felt a *decided aversion* to that mode of life. そういう生活ぶりを彼はあくまできらった. ¶Gambling is his *chief aversion*. 彼はばくちが何よりきらいだ. ¶a *deep [-rooted] aversion* 根深い嫌悪(けんお). ¶Motoring is his *greatest aversion*. 彼は自動車が大きらいだ. ¶He feels an *invincible aversion* to snakes. へびが大きらい. ¶Idleness in any form is his *pet aversion*. なまけることは一切彼はきらいだ. ¶feel (=experience) a *profound aversion* to ... ...をひどくきらう. ¶He has a *strong aversion* to work. 彼は仕事が大きらいだ. ¶It is my *utter aversion*. それは大きらいだ.

avert, *v.* そらす; 防ぐ.

P *avert* the eyes *from* an object ある物体から目をそむける. 【類】*avert* danger *from* a man 人の危険を防止する.

aviation, *n.* 飛行.

Q *civil aviation* in Japan 日本の民間飛行. ¶*commercial aviation* 商業飛行.

Q^2 *transport aviation* 輸送飛行.

aviator, *n.* 飛行家.

Q a *civil[ian] aviator* 民間飛行家. ¶a *daring aviator* 果敢な飛行家.

avid, *a.* むさぼって.

P be *avid for* gold (gain) 黄金(利益)に目がない. ¶those *avid of* (=*for*) the exotic 異国趣味に耽溺(たんでき)する人々.

avidity, *n.* どん欲.

V *have* an *avidity* to know ... ...を切に知らんとする. ¶*raise* the *avidity* of the landlords 地主の利欲心を高める.

P read *with avidity* 耽読(たんどく)する ‖ seek *with avidity* せっせと探す ‖ eat *with avidity* がつがつ食べる ‖ fall upon it *with avidity* やっきとなってそれを攻撃する.

avocation, *n.* 副業; 《口語》職業.

V *follow* one's *humble avocation* つまらぬ仕事に従事する.

Q those engaged in *honest* and *decent avocations* かたぎのりっぱな職業の人々. ¶pursue a *lawful avocation* in a lawful manner 合法的な方法で合法的な職業に従事する.

P a botanist *by avocation* 植物学の研究を道楽にやっている人 ‖ He is by vocation a journalist and a man of letters only *by avocation*. 本職は新聞記者で文士の方は副業に過ぎない.

avoid, *v.* 避ける.

M a thing to be *carefully avoided* 大禁物. ¶be *scrupulously avoided* 細心の用意をもって回避される. ¶*strictly avoid* あくまで避ける. ¶*studiously avoid* つとめて避ける.

avoidable, *a.* 避けられる.

M it is *hardly avoidable* that ... ...は避けがたい.

avoidance, *n.* 回避.

Q *studious avoidance* of self-advertisement つとめて自己宣伝を避けること.

avouch, *v.* 保証する.

P *avouch for* the quality 品質を保証する.

avow, *v.* 公言する; 認める.

M I can most *conscientiously avow* that ... 私は極めて良心的に...を誓う事が出来る.

P He *avowed* the little child *for* his son. その小さな子を自分の息子と認めた. ¶He *avowed* himself *in* the wrong. 自分の非を認めた.

avowal, *n.* 公言; 自白.

Q a *frank avowal* 正直な自白.

await, *v.* 待つ.

M the *long awaited* summer vacation 待ちに待った夏休み. ¶The two great crews now *tensely awaited* the gun. 二組のボートの選手たちは息を殺して出発の号砲を待っていた.

P The result is *awaited with* interest. その結果は興味をもって待たれる.

awake, *a.* 覚めている.

M he was *scarcely awake* when he heard ... あの人が...を聞いた時にはまだよく目が覚めていなかった. ¶after getting *thoroughly awake*, however, he realized that ... しかし意識がはっきりしてから...ということがよくわかった. ¶He is *wide awake* to the need of improvement in various directions. 彼は種々の改善を要するということをよく知っていた. 【類】I am *wide awake* to his weak points. ‖ I was *wide awake* half the night. 半夜眠らなかった.

P^2 he is ever *awake to* the necessity of ... 彼は常に...の必要を悟っている.

awake, *v.* 目を覚まさせる; 目が覚める.

M be *suddenly awaked* to the sense of folly 愚かな行為だったと突然悟る.

P be *awaked by* low cries 低い声に目をさます. ¶I *awoke from* (=*out of*) sleep. 目を覚ました. 【類】The noise *awoke* me *from* my sleep (ecstasy, revery). ¶*awake* a man *to* a sense of sin 人に罪を自覚させる. ¶when Japan was just beginning to *awake to* the glow of Western civilization 日本がわずかに西洋文化の光に目覚めて来た時. 【類】*awake to* the need for ... / *awake to* the truth (fact) that ... ¶I *awoke with* a start. 跳び起きた.

awaken, *v.* 覚まさせる; 覚める.

P I was *awakened by* a singular sound. 妙な音で目を覚ました. ¶a giant *awakening from* a heavy sleep 熟睡から目覚めつつある巨人. ¶I was *awakened out of* my sleep by a fire-bell. 僕は半鐘で目を覚ました. ¶the public has *awakened to* the fact that ... 公衆が...という事に気が付いた. 【類】be *awakened to* new needs (新時代の要求) / be already *awakened to* the fallacy (誤り) of ...

awakening, *n.* 目覚め.

V *experience* an *awakening* of the erotic impulse 性の目覚めを感じる.

Q With the improved means of communication came the *economic awakening* of the district. 交通の便が開けると共にその地方の経済的勃興が起った. ¶*intellectual awakening* of the masses 大衆の知識への目覚め. ¶*sudden awakening* of a sleeping lion by ... ...による眠れる獅子の突然の目覚め.

P *upon awakening* 目が覚めると.

award, *n.* 賞与; 審判, 審査.

V The medal of the first class *carries* with it an *award* of $1,000. 一等賞には千ドルの賞金が付く. ¶*gain* an *award* 賞を得る. ¶*hand out awards* to ... 賞を...に与える. ¶*make* an *award* to ... ...に賞を贈る ‖ The *award* of judges will be *made* on February 1. 審査員の決定は二月一日に発表します. 【類】the *award* of the oratorical contest was *made* by a jury of nine professors headed by ... ¶*present awards* 賞を贈呈する. ¶The company *received* (=*obtained*) *awards* from various exhibitions. その会社は諸方の博覧会から賞を授与された. ¶He *won* the third *award* of $250. 彼は二百五十ドルの三等賞を得た. ¶*withhold* an *award* 授賞を差控える.

Q It is the custom of this academy to make an *annual award* for outstanding research in chemistry. 本学会では毎年傑出した化学の研究に授賞する例になっている. ¶The firm is in possession of many *high awards*, received at international exhibitions and national fairs. その会社は内国並に万国博覧会で多数の賞を授与された. ¶a *literary award* 文学賞.

Q^2 The film won the *Academy Award* for 1955. その映画は1955年のアカデミー賞を獲得した. ¶an *arbitration award* 仲裁裁判の判決. ¶a *cash award* 賞金. ¶conferring of *merit awards* for achievements in ... ...の功績による褒賞授与. ¶encourage good writing by *prize awards* 賞をかけて作文を奨励する. ¶a *reparation award* 賠償裁決. ¶a distinguished service to *safety award* 安全に対する抜群の功績賞. ¶a *trophy award* トロフィー(優勝杯など).

P^2 the *award by* the arbitrator 仲裁裁判官の判決. ¶the Nobel *award in* medicine 医学に対するノーベル賞. ¶a medal of the first class carrying with it an *award of* $… …ドル賞金付一等メダル. ¶*awards to* Japanese exhibition at St. Louis セント・ルイスにおける日本の陳列品に対する賞.

award, *v.* 授与する.

P A prize of ¥50,000 is *awarded for* the best essay in English. 英文の最も優秀なものには五万円の賞金を贈呈する. 【類】The prize was *awarded* me *for* excellence in French. ¶The degree of B. A. was *awarded to* him. 文学士の称号が与えられた. 【類】A medal was *awarded to* the best speller (つづり字の最も正しい生徒) in the class.

aware, *a.* 知っている.

M *aware **enough*** of the fact that … …は百も承知. ¶I conceived him to be ***fully** aware* of his weight in society. 彼はその社会上の貫禄を十分に自覚していると私は思った. ¶be ***painfully** aware* of … …に気がついて苦痛を感じる. ¶he was ***quite** aware* of the consequence of … 彼は…の結果をよく知っていた.

P He became *aware **of*** it. 彼はそれに気が付いた. ‖ before one is *aware **of*** it 知らない間に. 【類】I am *aware **of*** the matter (his intentions, his being so rich). / The man, *aware **of*** his mistake, ran away. / He is *aware **of*** his danger. = He is *aware* that there is a danger to him.

away, *ad.* あちらへ, 離れて.

M ***a mile** away* 一マイル隔って. ¶***An hour** away* I started. 一時間たって出発した. ¶How ***long*** will you be *away?* いつまでお出掛けの予定ですか. ¶***right** away* 即刻.

P He is *away **for*** the vacation (weekend). 彼は休暇(週末)旅行中だ. ¶He is *away **from*** Japan. 日本にはいない. 【類】He is never happy, *away **from*** home. ‖ That is *away **from*** the question. それは問題外だ. 【類】He talked *away **from*** the subject (脱線した). ¶He is *away **on*** a trip. 彼は旅行に出ている. 【類】He is *away **on*** leave of absence (公休). ¶*away **to*** the north ずっと北方に. 【類】He is *away **to*** Nagoya. ¶*Away **with*** the thought! 飛んでもない. ‖ *Away **with*** you! 出て行け! ‖ That saucy fleer I cannot *away **with***. そんな無礼な嘲弄(ちょうろう)は我慢できぬ.

awe, *n.* 畏敬.

V ***rouse*** superstitious *awe* in … …に迷信的恐怖の念を懐かせる.

Q with a sense of almost ***reverent** awe* 畏敬に近い念をもって. ¶with a ***shuddering** awe* 戦々兢々(きょうきょう)として.

P hold (=keep) a man *in **awe*** of … 人をして…を畏敬せしめる ‖ stand *in awe* of … …ではっと立ちすくむ. ¶be lost *in awe* おそれおののきわれを忘れる. ¶inspire a man *with awe* 人を恐れさせる. 【類】I was struck *with awe*.

awe, *v.* 恐れさせる.

P One is *awed **by*** the majesty of "the deep." 我々は「深海」の荘厳に打たれる. ¶*awe* any one ***into*** obedience 威嚇して人を服従させる, …を威圧する. 【類】They *awed* him ***into*** doing it.

awkward, *a.* まずい, 不器用な.

P He is *awkward **at*** the business. 彼は仕事がまずい. 【類】be *awkward **at*** handling tools. ¶be *awkward **in*** action (one's manner, one's movements) 動作(など)がぎごちない. 【類】You are so very *awkward* (不器用) ***in*** doing a thing.

awkwardness, *n.* 不器用.

V ***experience*** a certain *awkwardness* 幾分ぎごちなく思う.

ax, axe, *n.* おの.

V ***grind*** an *ax* おのをとぐ. ¶The magazine ***has** no axe* to grind. その雑誌は何のおもわくも持っていない.

Q² a ***meat** axe* 獣肉処理用のおの.

P chop wood ***with*** an *ax* おので木を切る.

axiom, *n.* 公理.

V ***lay down*** the *axiom* that … …という公理を樹立する.

Q an ***accepted** axiom* 認識された公理. ¶the ***first** axiom* of foreign policy 外交策の第一義. ¶We often hear the remark, "Exchange is no robbery," quoted as a ***legal** axiom*. 「交換は強奪でない」ということは法律上の公理として往々引用されるのを耳にする. ¶If he is right, it is certain that our ***political** axioms* need a good deal of revision. 彼の説が正しければ われわれの政治に関する公理は大いに改めなければならぬ. ¶a ***social** axiom* 社会に関する公理. ¶accept it as a ***sound** axiom* それを堅実な公理として認める. ¶It is a ***well-known** axiom* in psychiatry that all subjects of hallucinations are dangerous patients. 幻影を見る精神病者は すべて危険な患者であるということは精神病学上の公理である.

axis, *n.* 軸.

Q² the ***Rome-Berlin** Axis* ローマ・ベルリン枢軸.

P it is the *axis **around*** which … revolves それは…の中枢になっている. ¶turn around ***on*** its *axis* 自転する. 【類】the rotation of the earth ***on*** its *axis* (自転) / make a revolution ***on*** the earth's *axis*.

B

babble, *v.* 片言を言う, べちゃべちゃしゃべる.

P The crowd *babbled **of*** the hero. 群集がその勇士の事をしゃべっていた. 【類】The sick man *babbles **of*** his home.

babble, *n.* 片言; おしゃべり.

P² the *babbles **of*** a crowd 群集のがやがや声.

babe, *n.* 《米俗》若い女.

Q He seems getting off with that ***cute little*** babe. 彼はあのきれいな娘っ子に参ってるらしい.

babel, *n.* 雑然たる人声.

P The words were heard clearly ***above*** the *babel*. がやがやしている人声の中にその言葉だけはっきり聞取れた.

P² a *babel **of*** tongues [色々な言葉が入り混じる]言語の混乱. ¶A *babel **of*** voices was heard from a classroom. 教室からがやがや声が聞えて来た.

baby, *n.* 赤児, 赤ん坊.

V ***baptize*** a *baby* 赤ん坊に洗礼を施す. ¶Japanese mothers ***carry** babies* ***pick-a-back***. 日本では母親が赤ん坊を背におぶって歩く. ¶***cheer*** a *baby* with a toy おもちゃで赤ちゃんをあやす. ¶***christen*** a *baby* 赤ん坊に(洗礼のとき)名を付ける. ¶My dog ***dropped*** three *babies*. うちの犬は三匹子を生んだ. ¶My mother was ***expecting*** another *baby* at the time. その時また赤ちゃんが母に生れる所であった. ‖ eight weeks before the *baby* is ***expected*** 赤ん坊が生れるまでの最後の八週間. ¶***feed*** a *baby* on cow's milk = 《米》feed cow's milk to a baby 赤ん坊を牛乳で育てる. ¶She is going to ***have*** a *baby*. お産が近い. ¶***hold*** one's *baby* in one's arms 赤ん坊を抱く. ¶***hug*** a *baby* 赤ん坊をしっかり抱く. ¶***hush*** a *baby* to sleep 赤ん坊をだまして寝かしつける. ¶***lift*** a *baby* [***up***] from the bed 赤ん坊を寝床から抱きあげる. ¶***lull*** a *baby* to sleep 赤ん坊を寝かしつける. ¶People ***make*** a *baby* of him. 人が彼を子供扱いにする. ¶I'll have Willie ***mind*** the *baby*. ウィリーに赤ん坊を見させましょう. ¶***nurse*** a *baby* at the breast 赤ん坊に乳をやる. ¶***play*** the *baby* to … …に甘える. ¶try to ***please*** a *baby* 赤ん坊をあやす. ¶***quiet*** a *baby* 泣く赤ん坊をだまらせる. ¶***rear*** a *baby* at the breast 赤ん坊を母乳で育てる. ¶***rock*** a *baby* to sleep 赤ん坊をゆすって寝かしつける. ¶***sing*** the *baby* to sleep 歌を歌って赤ん坊を寝かしつける. ¶***stop*** a *baby* from crying 赤ん坊を泣き止ませる. ¶a mother ***sucking*** a *baby* 赤ん坊に乳を飲ましている母親. ¶***take up*** a *baby* in one's arms 赤ん坊を抱っこする.

Q an ***abandoned** baby* 捨て児. ¶a ***bottle-fed** baby* 牛乳で育った赤ん坊. ¶a ***clear little pink** baby* かわいらしい桜色をした赤ん坊. ¶lull a ***crying** baby* 泣く赤ん坊をだまらせる. ¶a ***cute** baby* 《口語》かわいい赤ちゃん. ¶a ***few-weeks-old** baby* 生れて二三週間たった赤ん坊. ¶one's ***first** baby* 始めての赤ん坊. ¶My *baby* is ***fretful***. 私の赤ん坊は気むずかしい. ¶a ***grown-up** baby* 大きな赤ちゃん(大人). ¶the ***Imperial** Baby* 幼い皇子. ¶while he was yet a ***mere** baby* 彼がまだほんの赤ん坊のころ. ¶We have had a ***new** baby **at*** our house. うちでは赤ちゃんが生れた. ¶a ***new-born** baby* 生れたばかりの赤ん坊, 新生児. ¶a ***squalling** baby* ぎゃーぎゃー泣く赤ん坊.

Q² a ***boy** (**girl**) baby* 男(女)の赤ん坊. ¶a ***GI** baby* 《米》[占

領地でつくった]兵隊の子供. ¶a ***war*** *baby* = a GI baby.

P since he was a *baby* ***in*** arms 彼がちのみ子の時から.

baby, *v.* 赤ん坊扱いにする.

P She was *babied* ***by*** all hands. 彼女はみんなからあまやかされた.

bachelor, *n.* 独身男; 〘学位〙学士.

Q an ***elderly*** *bachelor* かなり年を取った独身男. ¶a very ***eligible*** *bachelor* 結婚相手として極めて好ましい独身男. ¶a ***hardened*** *bachelor* どうしても結婚しない独身男. ¶an ***old*** *bachelor* 年を取った独身男.

Q² a ***summer*** *bachelor* 避暑地(だけ)の独身者.

P² *Bachelor* ***of*** Arts 文学士. ‖ *Bachelor* ***of*** Medicine (Science) 医(理)学士.

bacillus, *n.* 細菌.

V a dead rat ***containing*** plague *bacillus* ペスト菌保有の死んだねずみ.

Q ***malignant*** *bacilli* 有害な細菌.

Q² ***comma*** *bacillus* = the ***cholera*** *bacillus* コレラ菌. ¶***tubercle*** *bacillus* 結核菌.

back, *n.* 背; 背面, 裏面.

V Now we have ***broken*** the *back* of the work. もう仕事はあらまし片づいた. ¶***curve*** one's *back* like a button-hook くの字に背を曲げる. ¶She ***gave*** me her *back*. 彼女は私を見捨てた. ¶This carpet ***has*** a *back* of a strong linen fabric. このじゅうたんは強いリンネル裏が付いている. ¶***lean*** one's *back* against the wall 壁に背をもたせかける. ¶The cat ***set*** its *back* ***up***. ねこは背を立てた. ¶***shove*** one's *back* against the wall その背中をかべに押しつける ‖ ***shove*** a person off the sidewalk 人を歩道から押し出す. ¶***show*** the *back* to ... ...から逃げ出す. ¶***turn*** one's *back* on the sun 太陽に背を向ける ‖ ***turn*** one's *back* upon civilization 文明に背を向ける, 文明国を去って蛮地に向かう ‖ ***turning*** your *back* on ... you have before you ... ...を後ろにして行くと前方に...があります ‖ ***turn*** one's *back* to nobody 誰にもひけを取らぬ ‖ ***turn*** one's *back* towards ... ...の方に背を向ける. 【類】no sooner was his *back* ***turned*** than ... ¶a coat with ***unlined*** *back* 背抜きの上衣.

P He has the idea ***at*** the *back* of his mind. 彼は心の奥底にその考えを持っている. ‖ has ... ***at*** his *back* [比ゆ的に]背後に...がついている ‖ a seat for servants ***at*** the *back* of a carriage 馬車の後部にある召使の座席 ‖ The sound is produced ***at*** the *back* of the palate. その音は口蓋(ｺｳｶﾞｲ)の後部で発声される. ¶You will only get laughed at ***behind*** your *back*. 君はかげで笑われるばかりだ. 【類】Never has a depreciatory (非難の) word been uttered about him ***behind*** his *back*. / speak ill of a man ***behind*** his *back*. ¶an appendix printed ***in*** the *back* of the book その本の末尾にある付録 ‖ a glossary ***in*** the *back* of a reader 読本の巻末にある用語解 ‖ what is ***in*** the *back* of one's mind 心の奥底で思っている事. 【類】He was not aware of this, but it was ***in*** the *back* of his mind. ¶My coat was taken ***off*** my *back*. 上衣を脱いだ. ¶an advertisement ***on*** the *back* of a magazine 雑誌の裏表紙にある広告. ‖ He has a knapsack ***on*** his *back*. 彼は背のうを背負っている. ‖ ***on*** the *back* of a winged steed 天馬に乗って ‖ throw her shawl over ***on*** her *back* ショールを背に掛ける ‖ Which is the best position for a child when sleeping—***on*** his *back*, or on his side? 子が眠る時の最もよい姿勢はあお向きか横向きか. ‖ roll over ***on*** one's *back* あお向けにごろっと引っくり返る ‖ a fall ***on*** *back* あお向きの倒れ. 【類】lie ***on*** one's *back* / He lay dead on the floor ***on*** his *back*. / swim ***on*** one's *back*. ¶No animal, but man, ever lies ***upon*** its *back* unless it is dead. 人間以外の動物は死なないと決してあお向けに寝ることはない. ¶***with*** one's *back* to the wall [比ゆ的に]窮地に落入って.

P² the *back* ***of*** a hand 手の甲.

back, *a., ad.* 後ろに; 戻って.

M ***far*** *back* in history 遠い昔に ‖ as ***far*** *back* as the third century 三世紀の昔 ‖ He is ***far*** *back* on his rent. 彼は家賃が大分滞っている. ¶credit a simile to that writer who is the one ***farthest*** *back* in point of time ある直喩(ﾁｮｸﾕ)について最も古く使った作家に功を帰する. ¶I will be *back* ***in a moment***. すぐ帰って来ます. ¶He will be *back* ***soon***. 彼はすぐ戻る.

P I will be *back* ***at*** four o'clock at latest. 遅くも四時には帰って来る. ¶He will be *back* ***before*** evening. 夕刻前に戻って来るでしょう. ¶He will be *back* ***by*** four o'clock. 四時までには戻って来るでしょう. ‖ I went to Shinagawa and *back* ***by*** bicycle. 品川へ自転車で往復した. ‖ He is *back* ***from*** the country. いなかから帰った. ¶He will be *back* ***in*** Tokyo ***by*** the early part of October. 十月始めまでに帰京するでしょう. ¶*back* ***in*** the 60's of the last century 前世紀の(一八)六〇年代に. ¶*back* ***of*** ... (《米口》)...の背後に. 【類】a hill *back* ***of*** the town ‖ issues of the magazine *back* ***of*** 1920 その雑誌の一九二〇年以前の旧号 ‖ There is something *back* ***of*** his words. 彼の言葉には何か含むところがある. ¶be *back* ***on*** the job [ストの後など]以前通り就業している. ¶Things will then be *back* ***to*** normal condition. その時になると常態にかえっているでしょう. 【類】Things are *back* ***to*** normalcy. ‖ My house is *back* ***to*** back with his. 僕の家は彼の家と背なか合せになっている. 【類】He sat *back* ***to*** back with a girl. ¶*Back* ***with*** you at once. たった今引きさがれ.

back, *v.* 後援する; 裏をつける.

M He was to go with me, but *backed* ***out*** (=declined) at the last moment on the plea of illness. 彼は僕と一しょに行くことになっていたがいよいよという時に病気を口実に断った. ‖ We're in too deep to *back* ***out***. 深入りしすぎて後へは退けぬ. ¶*back* ***out in*** the Imperial presence 後じさりして御前を引き下がる.

M² *back* ***down*** from ... ...から後じさりする; ...から手を引く. ¶*back* ***off*** (=***out of***) a danger 危険を避ける. ¶*back* a person ***up*** by cheerful expenditure 喜んで金を出してくれる者がある. 【類】*back* ***up*** a friend financially / *back* ***up*** the Chiang regime / *back* ***up*** one's view ‖ *back* it ***up*** with their lives 生命をかけてそれを守る ‖ *back* ***up*** their protest with force 力ずくで抗議を押しつける ‖ *back* ***up*** second base 〘野球〙二塁をバックアップする.

P facing the sea and *backing* ***against*** the mountain 海に面し山を負い. ‖ I'll *back* him ***against*** all the others. みんなと反対の彼の立場を支持する. ¶a Buddhist image *backed* ***by*** a beautifully carved and gilded mandala 美しく刻まれて金色のまんだらのある仏像 ‖ *backed* ***by*** father's influence 父の威光で ‖ a vote *backed* ***by*** a pure heart 清き一票. ¶He *backed* his car ***into*** the garage. 彼は自分の車を後進させて車庫に入れた. ‖ easily *back* ***out of*** a scrape やすやすと難関を突破する. ¶He is *backed* ***with*** a fair knowledge of the English language. 彼はかなりよく英語を知っている.

backbone, *n.* 背骨.

V ***give*** the *backbone* to the party 党に筋金を入れる. ¶***strain*** one's *backbone* through farm work [骨の折れる]野良仕事で骨を折る.

P a Britisher ***to*** the *backbone* 生っ粋の英国人. 【類】a progressive ***to*** the *backbone*.

P² Young people are the *backbone* ***of*** a country. 青年は一国の中堅である.

backer, *n.* 後援者; 騎手.

Q ***financial*** *backers* 財政上の後援者. ¶***professional*** *backers* on the turf 競馬の本職騎手.

background, *n.* 背景; 裏面; 〘ラジオ〙音楽効果.

V I read widely to ***build up*** a *background* of useful information. 私は有益な知識の背景を築き上げるために広く読書する. ¶The mountain ***forms*** the beautiful *background* of the scene. その山が風景の美しい背景をなしている. ‖ This will ***form*** (=***make***) a suitable *background*. これは適当な背景になるだろう. ¶a city that ***has*** a historic *background* 歴史的背景のある都市. ¶It ***provides*** a *background* for the intelligent study of ... ...を本当に研究するためのした地となる.

Q one's ***academic*** *background* 学校の背景(出身学校). ¶the ***biological*** *background* to women's history 女性史に対する生物学上の背景. ¶form a ***brilliant*** *background* to it それに対してりっぱな背景をなす. ¶tales with an old ***Celtic*** and ***pagan*** *background* 古代ケルト族や異教徒の背景をもつ物語. ¶He has a ***high cultural*** *background*. 彼にはりっぱな教養の素地がある. ¶There is something lacking in one's ***educational*** *background* when one does not know at least one foreign language. 外国語を少くとも一つは知らなければ教養の基礎に幾分欠ける所がある. ¶afford ***fitting*** *background* for... ...に対しよいした地となる. ¶Kyoto is rich in ***historical*** *background* and natural beauty. 京都は歴史的背景と自然美に富んでいる. ¶form a ***picturesque*** *background* 絵のような美しい背景をなす. ¶He has no ***scientific*** *background*. 彼には科学的な下地がない. ¶the ***social*** *background* of early Christianity 初期キリスト教の社会的背景.

Q² with a ***college*** *background* 大学出身という経歴で. ¶a townsman without ***country*** *background* いなかに何の関係

も持っていない都会人. ¶with a good ***family*** *background* 毛並のよい. ¶***radio*** *background* [擬音・音楽など]ラジオの音響効果. ¶***stage*** *background* 舞台の背景.

P set in vivid relief ***against*** its *background* of ... …を背景にしてくっきりと浮彫りされて. ¶keep (=put) the matter ***in*** the *background* その事を表面に出さずに置く ‖ though other motives may have lurked ***in*** the *background*, he was chiefly inspired by ... 他の動機もかげに潜んでいたかもしれないが彼は主として…に感激した ‖ ***In*** the *background* churches and palaces lift their ghostly domes and towers into the air. 後方には教会や宮殿があり, その円屋根や塔はぼうっとかすんで空に浮んでいる. ¶the fire hydrant sign, the blue "H" ***on*** a white *background* [ロンドンの]白地に青で H を出した消火栓の記号. ¶He could do his work in life efficiently ***with*** a *background* of domestic comforts. 彼は家庭的安楽という背景を持って能率的に一生の仕事をやることができた.

P² It is replete with beautiful scenery and a *background* ***of*** history and romance. 美しい景色や歴史・伝奇の背景に富んでいる. ¶a *background* ***to*** English literature and life 英文学と英人の生活に対する背景.

backing, *n.* 後援. 「る.

V the plan ***has*** the *backing* of ... その計画は…の後援があ

Q Alfred Nobel went to Paris to secure ***financial*** *backing* for the invention. アルフレッド・ノーベルはこの発明の助成金を得ようとパリへ行った.

Q² ***Communist*** (=***Red***) *backing* 共産党の支持.

backlog, *n.* 残高.

Q dispose of the ***large*** *backlog* of the cares remaining from World War II 第二次大戦から続いている数多くの懸

backset, *n.* 妨害. 」案の処理.

V ***give*** a *backset* to ... …を妨害する.

backward, *a.* 進歩のおそい.

M He is ***intellectually*** *backward*. 知能が遅れている.

P The child is *backward* ***in*** many studies. その子は不成績の学科が多い. 【類】*backward* ***in*** development (civilization) / This country is not *backward* ***in*** its appreciation (鑑賞) of art. ‖ He is *backward* ***in*** giving people his views. 人前で自分の意見を述べたがらない.

backwardness, *n.* 不進歩, 後進性. 「す.

V ***regain*** (=***recover***) *backwardness* in ... …の遅れを取戻

Q the ***general*** *backwardness* of middle class society 中流社会一般の遅れ.

P² *backwardness* ***in*** ... …の点での遅れ. ¶the *backwardness* ***of*** public opinion on the subject この問題に関する世

backwater, *n.* 沈滞, スランプ. 」論の時世後れ.

Q be in an ***intellectual*** *backwater* 知的スランプに落入っている(頭が働かない).

P I live ***in*** a *backwater* in this small village. この小村の活気のない環境の中にくすぶっている.

P² a *backwater* ***of*** civilization 文明に取残された片いなか.

backyard, *n.* 裏庭.

Q ***untidy*** *backyard* とり散らしてある裏庭.

bacteria, *n. pl.* 細菌.

Q ***dangerous*** *bacteria* 危険なバクテリヤ. ¶***harmless*** *bacteria* 無害のバクテリヤ. ¶***pathogenic*** *bacteria* 病原菌. ¶***noxious*** *bacteria* 有害なバクテリヤ. ¶***virulent*** *bacteria* 毒性バクテリア.

Q² the ***soil*** *bacteria* 土壌のバクテリア.

bad, *a.* 悪い; 拙劣な.

M ***deucedly*** *bad* とても悪い. ¶***downright*** *bad* からっきしだめ. ¶It is *bad* ***enough*** to have one's own house burnt. 自分の家を焼出されることは随分つらいことだ. ¶it is not ***exactly*** *bad*, but ... 悪いという訳でもないが. ¶It is ***extremely*** *bad*. 実によくない. ¶It is ***not altogether*** *bad*. 満更すてたもんでもない. ¶***not half*** *bad*=rather good 《口語》捨てたもんでもない. ¶***not so*** *bad* それほど悪くもない. ¶It's ***pretty much*** *bad*. 相当に悪い. ¶It's ***too*** *bad* of you to desert her in trouble. 彼女の困ってる時見すてるとはひどい. ‖ be ***vastly*** *bad* とっても悪い.

P He is *bad* ***at*** playing baseball (handwriting). 野球(など)が不得手だ. ‖ boys who are *bad* ***at*** their books (classwork) 勉強ができない男の子 ‖ He is not *bad* ***by*** nature. あの男は性質(たち)は悪くはない. ¶It is *bad* ***for*** one's health (eyes). それは健康(など)によくない. ‖ It would be *bad* ***for*** morale. 士気をそそうさせるだろう. 【類】It was *bad* ***for*** discipline to have his ignorance known to his subordinates. ¶It is *bad* ***in*** quality. それは質が悪い. ‖ though *bad* ***in*** appearance 外観はよくないが ‖ It is very *bad* ***of*** you to leave him. 君が彼を後に残して行くのははなはだ不親切だ. ¶Things are *bad* ***with*** me. どうも万事うまく行かない. ‖ The actor got in *bad* ***with*** the audience. その俳優は観客の受けが悪い. 【類】That will certainly get you in *bad* ***with*** his master.

bad, *n.* 悪いこと; 悪人.

P His business is going ***from*** *bad* to worse. 彼の商売は左り前になって来た. ¶go ***to*** the *bad* 破滅する ‖ It has gone ***to*** the *bad* from being so long neglected. 手入れをしないので悪くなった. 【類】The drunkard is going ***to*** the *bad*. ‖ I am ten pounds ***to*** the *bad*. こっちは十ポンドの赤字だ(借りになっている).

badge, *n.* 記章, バッジ.

V ***carry*** *badges* 記章を付けている. ¶a guide ***wearing*** a distinctive *badge* それと知れる記章を付けた案内者.

Q with the ***distinguishing*** *badge* on each arm めいめいの腕に目だつ記章を付けて. ¶***numbered*** *badges* 番号付き記章. ¶an ***ornamental*** *badge* 装飾用のバッジ.

Q² a ***class*** *badge* クラスのバッジ ‖ a ***good conduct*** *badge* 善行章. ¶an ***identification*** *badge* (=tag) 〖軍〗[身分・所属を表わす]認識票. ¶a ***merit*** *badge* 功労記章. ¶wear a ***mourning*** *badge* 喪章をつける. ¶***school*** (***college, club***) *badge* 学

badness, *n.* 悪い状態. 」校(など)のバッジ.

P² the *badness* ***of*** the times 不景気.

baffle, *v.* 失敗させる. 「ない神秘.

M mysteries that *baffle* us ***completely*** てんで想像もつか

P I was completely *baffled* ***in*** my search for ... …を捜したが全然失敗に終った. ¶This *baffled* him ***out of*** his design. これで彼の計画が破れた.

bag, *n.* 袋(バッグ).

V Many good *bags* were ***got*** (=obtained). 獲物がどっさりあった. ¶He ***made*** a bad *bag*. 獲物が少なかった. ¶The largest *bag* was ***obtained*** by him. 彼が一番猟があった. ¶***pop*** a paper *bag* 紙の袋をぽんと破る. ¶***secure*** good *bags* in shooting 大猟を占める. ¶***zip up*** (***unzip***) a *bag* バッグのチャックをしめる(あける).

Q a good ***second-hand*** *bag* 結構役に立つセコハンのかばん. ¶a ***sinister*** *bag* 怪しい袋. ¶***watertight*** *bags* 防水袋. ¶You're the ***weariest*** *bag* of bones I've ever seen. 君の長っ尻には参った.

Q² an ***earth*** *bag* 土のう. ¶a ***Gladstone*** *bag* ボストンバッグ. ¶a ***brown paper*** *bag* ハトロン紙の袋. ¶a ***burlap*** *bag* [黄麻(ジュート)製の]南京袋. ¶a ***carpet*** *bag* カーペット製旅行カバン. ¶a ***comfort*** *bag* 慰問袋. ¶a ***garment*** *bag* 衣しょう袋. ¶a ***golf*** *bag* ゴルフ用具袋. ¶a ***gunny*** *bag* ズックの袋. ¶a ***hot water*** *bag* ゴム製の湯たんぽ. ¶a ***laundry*** *bag* 洗たく袋. ¶***leather*** *bags* 革製の袋. ¶a ***money*** *bag* がま口. ¶a ***nose*** *bag* [馬の]かいば袋. ¶a ***plastic-film*** *bag* [キャンデーなどを入れる]薄いビニールの袋. ¶a ***sleeping*** *bag* [登山家の]寝具. ¶a ***string*** *bag* 網袋. ¶a ***travel***[***ing***] *bag* 旅行用か

P put it ***into*** a *bag* それを袋に入れる. 」ばん.

P² a *bag* ***of*** money 一袋の金 ‖ a *bag* ***of*** bones やせっぽち.

bagatelle, *n.* つまらないもの. 「かな金.

Q a ***mere*** *bagatelle* to a rich man 金持にとってほんのわず

baggage, *n.* 《米》手荷物.

V ***book*** one's *baggage* through to ... …まで手荷物を預ける. ¶***check*** *baggage* to destination 目的地まで荷物をチッキで預ける ‖ *baggage* ***checked*** on a ticket 切符を見せて預けた(鉄道)荷物. ¶***clear*** *baggage* through the customs 荷物の通関手続を済ませる. ¶***deliver*** *baggage* at a station 停車場で荷物を渡す. ¶***leave*** *baggage* behind 手荷物を置き忘れる. ¶I have not ***unpacked*** my *baggage* yet. 荷物はまだほどいていない.

Q be assessed as ***excess*** *baggage* 超過手荷物として料金を徴収される. ¶***light*** (***heavy***) *baggage* 軽い(重い)手荷物 ‖ take necessary ***light*** *baggage* 必要な手回り品を少し持って行く. ¶take ***little*** *baggage* with a person 余り手荷物を持って行かない. ¶trace ***missing*** *baggage* 紛失した手荷物の行方を調べる. ¶***personal*** *baggage* 手回り品.

Q² ***pool*** *baggage* 組合せ手荷物(一人分の制限を越えないように同行者の荷物を組合せる).

P for each piece ***of*** *baggage* 手荷物一個につき.

bail, *n.* 保釈, 保釈保証人.

V ***accept*** *bail* 保釈を許す. ¶***go*** *bail* for … …の保釈保証人となる；…を保証する. ¶***save*** one's *bail*〘法〙保釈中の被告が出廷する. ¶***take*** *bail* for … …を保釈に付する.

P The prisoner was allowed out ***on*** *bail*. 囚人は保釈金を入れて出所を許された. 【類】let him get out ***on*** *bail* / He was liberated ***on*** *bail* to the amount of 100,000 yen. / release a prisoner ***on*** *bail* / be released ***on*** *bail* of 20,000 rupees / He is held ***on*** $100,000 bail.

bail, *v.* くみ出す.

M ***bail out*** a boat ボートのあか[水]をくみ出す ‖ ***bail*** water ***out*** 水をかい出す ‖ ***bail out*** from a flying plane 飛行中の航空機から落下さんで降下する ‖ It is, as it were, to try to ***bail out*** the ocean. 大海の水をくみ出そうとするようなものだ.

bait, *n.* 餌(ᵉ).

V ***swallow*** a *bait* 餌をのみ込む. ¶***take*** a *bait* 餌を食う.

Q^2 ***ground*** *bait* 寄せ餌(釣の). ¶***paste*** *bait* ねり餌.

P fish with artificial flies ***as*** *bait* 蚊ばりで釣る. ¶It is much used ***for*** *bait* by fishermen. それは漁師が盛んに餌に使う.

bake, *v.* 焼く.

P bricks *baked* ***by*** the sun or fire 日または火力で焼いたれんが. ¶*bake* bread ***in*** an oven かまどでパンを焼く.

balance, *n.* 権衡, 釣合；差引 残高；貸借平均.

V to ***acquire*** *balance* and to maintain stability 平衡を得て安定を保つために. ¶***adjust*** the *balance* 権衡をとる. ¶This will ***alter*** the whole *balance* of power between the two countries. これで両国間の均勢は全く一変するだろう. ¶***ascertain*** exact *balance* 差引高をはっきりと確める. ¶***carry forward*** a *balance* of about £8,000 約八千ポンドの差引残高を繰越す. ¶***collect*** the *balance* from … …から差額を集金する. ¶***destroy*** the *balance* in her favor その国が優位に立つので均勢が破れる. ¶***disturb*** the *balance* of power 勢力の均衡を乱す ‖ ***disturb*** the metabolic *balance* 新陳代謝の調節を乱す. ¶***draw*** the *balance* to nothing [預金]残額全部を引出す. ¶I ***have*** still a *balance* at my bank. 銀行にまだ預金が残っている. ‖ The country ***has*** a *balance* (=an excess) of imports over exports every year. この国は毎年輸入超過だ. 【類】We ***had*** a very favorable international trade *balance* last year. ¶***hold*** the *balance* [二大勢力の間にあって]バランスをとっている, 決定権を握っている. ¶He found it advantageous to ***keep*** *balances* (=accounts) with (=at) the Bank of England. イングランド銀行と取引するのが有利だとさとった. ¶***lack*** mental *balance* 心の平衡を欠いている. ¶this ***leaves*** a *balance* of … これで…の残金となる. ¶***lose*** one's *balance* 権衡を失う(倒れる) ‖ ***lose*** the *balance* of power 力の均衡が破れる. ¶Health is best preserved by ***maintaining*** an adequate *balance* between work and play. 健康は仕事と遊楽を適当に調節することによって最もよく保たれる. ¶***make*** the *balance* (=rest) of the journey on foot 最後の旅程は徒歩でやる. ¶I will ***make up*** the *balance*. 私が不足額を出す. ¶***overcome*** the adverse *balance* of trade 貿易の逆調を乗切る. ¶***overturn*** a *balance* 平衡をくつがえす. ¶***pay*** the *balance* of his account 彼の勘定の差額を支払う. ¶***recover*** one's mental *balance* 冷静にかえる. ¶***redress*** the *balance* 平均を得るように直す. ¶***refund*** the *balance* 差額を戻す. ¶***remit*** *balance* to … …へ残金を回送する. ¶***restore*** (=***regain***) the *balance* 平衡を回復する. ¶My mind had ***retained*** its *balance*. 私は心を乱さなかった. ¶nature has ***righted*** the *balance* by … 自然は…によって平衡を保つようにした. ¶this will ***show*** a net *balance* of … これで…の正味差額を示すことになる. ¶***strike*** a *balance* 貸借を差引する, 清算する. ‖ equitably ***strike*** the *balance* 公平に清算する. ¶***tip*** the *balance* in favor of … …に有利に動く. ¶***transfer*** the *balance* to … 残高を…に繰越す. ¶This ***turned*** the *balance* and decided the course of events. これで局面が一変して事態の成行を決した. ‖ ***upset*** balance 権衡をやぶる.

V^2 finally the *balance* ***inclined*** toward … 遂に…が優位に立つようになった. ¶The *balance* ***standing*** to your credit is 1,000 yen. 君の貸方になっているのが千円ある. ‖ On the 31st December the trial *balance* of the Books ***stood*** as follows. 十二月三十一日の帳じりは次のようであった. ¶No one could certainly predict how the *balance* would ***sway***. どちらが優位に立つようになるかだれにも断言はできなかった.

Q The victory depended long in ***doubtful*** *balance*. 勝敗いかんは永い間分らなかった. ¶Tourist expenditure is an important element in ***international*** *balances* of payments. 観光客の落す金は国際貸借勘定の一大要素をなしている. ¶recover (upset) one's ***mental*** *balance* 心の動揺を静める(心の平静をくつがえす). ¶a man of ***unusual*** *balance* of mind 非常にバランスのよく取れている精神の持主.

Q^2 an ***automation*** *balance* 自動貨幣分類機. ¶the ***bank*** *balance* 銀行預金の残高. 【類】The best friend I've got in the world is my ***bank*** *balance*. ¶***cash*** *balance*〘簿記〙現金借方の差引残頭. ¶a ***credit*** *balance* 貸越. ¶a ***debit*** *balance* 借越. 【類】What is meant by saying that an account has a ***debit*** *balance*? ¶affect the ***power*** *balance* between … …の力の均衡を失わせる. ¶have an unfavorable ***trade*** *balance* of several hundred million dollars 数百万ドルの輸入超過となる. ¶turn the ***world*** *balance* of power against us 世界の力の均衡がわれわれに不利となる. 【類】the importance of the ***world*** *balance* of power to the United States.

P weigh it ***in*** the *balance* それを天びんにかける ‖ The fate of the bill hung ***in*** the *balance*. 議案の運命はどうなるか分らなかった. 【類】Victory is hanging ***in*** the *balance*. / The issue (成行) now hangs ***in*** the *balance*. ‖ The fate of Italy was then trembling ***in*** the *balance*. 当時イタリアの運命は危急に迫っていた. ¶He is mentally ***off*** *balance*. 気が違っている. ¶There is a slight loss of value ***on*** *balance*.〘相場〙差引少し下落している.

P^2 have *balance* ***against*** (***in favor of***) … …にとって赤(黒)字になている. ¶*balance* ***between*** two accounts, income and expense 収入支出勘定の差額. ¶He was absent the *balance* ***of*** the day.《俗》その日それから後彼は不在であった. ¶There is a *balance* ***to*** your credit of $1,000. 君の受取勘定は千ドルだ.

balance, *v.* 釣合わせる；釣合う；ためらう.

M mentally (physically) ***well balanced*** 心(身体)の均勢がよく取れている.

P *balance* commendable qualities ***against*** small shortcomings 美点によって小さな欠点を補う ‖ The tale is well *balanced* ***between*** comedy and pathos. この物語はうまく喜劇味と哀感の釣合が取れている. ¶*balance* one thing ***by*** (=***with***) another 乙で甲との釣合を取る. ¶food *balanced* ***for*** egg production 鶏卵増産の助けとなるように調整した食料. ¶*balance* ***in*** one's choice 選択に迷う. ¶a boy *balancing* ***on*** a rope 綱渡りの子供. ¶The penalty does not *balance* ***with*** the offense. 刑罰が罪科と釣合わない.

balancing, *n.* 平衡.

Q^2 ***budget*** *balancing* 予算の均衡を得させること.

balcony, *n.* 中二階, バルコニー.

Q a ***mezzanine*** *balcony* [劇場・デパートなどの]中二階.

P address a large crowd ***from*** a *balcony* バルコニーから大群集に呼びかける.

bald, *a.* はげた.

P a man *bald* ***on*** the head=a baldpate 頭のはげた人.

M be ***slightly*** *bald* 少しはげている.

baldness, *n.* はげ.

Q ***complete*** *baldness* まるはげ.

balk, *n.* 妨害；あてはずれ.

P^2 a *balk* ***to*** one's plans 計画の妨害 ‖ It was a great *balk* ***to*** him that you did not comply with my request. 君が僕の頼みをきかなかったので彼は大いに当てがはずれた.

balk, *v.* 立往生する.

P The Russian plenipotentiaries *balked* ***at*** payment of indemnity. ロシアの全権らは賠償金支払の段になって二の足を踏んだ. ¶He *balked* ***in*** his speech. 演説中に立往生した. ‖ He *balked* ***in*** a love affair (business scheme). 恋愛関係(など)で失敗した. ¶*balk* him ***of*** his object 彼の目的をくじく.

ball, *n.* まり, ボール；弾丸.

V ***balloon*** the *ball*〘野球〙小飛球を飛ばす. ¶***bang*** a *ball* 球をかーんと打つ. ¶***bat*** a *ball* 球をバットで打つ. 【類】***bat*** the *ball* hard. ¶***bounce*** a *ball* まりをつく ‖ ***bounce*** a *ball* against the wall ボールをかべに当てる. ¶fail to ***catch*** a *ball* ボールを受けそこなう. ¶***extract*** the *ball* from a pistol ピストルから弾丸を抜きとる. ¶***fumble*** a *ball* 球をとりそこなう. ¶***hit*** a *ball* with a bat バットでボールを打つ. ¶a trained seal that ***juggles*** a *ball* on the end of its nose 鼻の先で球を巧にあしらう芸をするあざらし. ¶***kick*** a *ball* with one's foot 足でボールをける. ¶***pitch*** the first *ball* 始球を投げる. ¶***play*** *ball* 球戯をする；野球を開始する.

¶He *set* the *ball rolling*. 彼が口切をやった(外の人はこれにならった). ¶*shoot* a *ball* まりを投げる; 〘野球〙シュートボールを投げる. ¶*swat* a *ball* into outfield 〘野球〙ボールを外野にかっとばす. ¶*throw* a *ball* to (at) … …に(を目がけて)ボールを投げる ‖ *throw up* a *ball* ボールを投げあげる. ¶*toss* a *ball* to a second baser 〘野球〙[遊撃手から]二塁手へボールをトスする.

Q a *curved ball* 〘野球〙曲球. ¶miss a *fair ball* 好球を見逃す. ¶*no ball* 〘野球〙規則違反の投球.

Q[2] become perceptible in the polished *crystal balls* of many government economists 多くの政府の経済専門家の目から見るとはっきり分る. ¶a *cue ball* 〘玉突〙突き球. ¶*fern balls* 〘植〙シノブ. ¶a *golf ball* ゴルフボール. ¶a *ground ball* (=a grounder) 〘野球〙匍(ほ)球(ごろ). ¶a *knuckle ball* 〘野球〙ナックル・ボール. ¶*moth balls* [ナフタリンなど]虫よけ玉. ¶a *smoke ball* 〘野球〙快速球. ¶Here comes my *superspeed ball*. そら行くぞ僕の超速球が! ¶a *time ball* 時報球 ☞ 英は一時に, 米は正午に測候所でさおからおろした. ¶The *16-pound ball* is rolled down a narrow 60-foot-long polished floor. 十六ポンドの球が狭い六十フィートのみがかれた床上を転がって行く.

P strike *at* a *ball* 球を打とうとする.

P[2] a *ball of* fire=a fire ball《俗》[火の玉のような]せっかち.

O The *ball* is with you. 打球は君の番だ.

ball, *n*. 舞踏会.

V *give* a *ball* 舞踏会を開く. ¶How did you *enjoy* the *ball*? 夜会はおもしろかったか. ¶*open* a *ball* 舞踏を開始する ‖ He was the first to *open* the *ball* (=begin a dispute). 彼の方から議論のほこ先を向けた. ¶The *ball* has been *postponed*. 夜会は日延べになった. ¶When does the *ball come off* (=*take place*)? 舞踏会はいつあるか. ¶The *ball proved* a great success. 舞踏会は大成功だった. ¶The *ball went off* well. 舞踏会は盛会であった.

Q a *masked ball* 仮面舞踏会.

Q[2] a *carnival ball* カーニバル(謝肉祭)の舞踏会.

P I met him *at* the Premier's *ball*. 首相招待の夜会で彼に会った.

ball, *v*. かたまる.

M clouds rapidly *balled up* 雲はどんどんかたまった. ¶He got *balled up* in his speech.《米口》演説はしどろもどろだった.

ballad, *n*. 民謡.

V *chant* a *ballad* 民謡を歌う. ¶*drone* a plaintive *ballad* 悲しげな小歌を低い声で歌う. ¶*hum* lightly some *ballad* from the opera オペラの民謡をふんふんと鼻で歌う. ¶*sing* tender love *ballads* 情緒こまやかな恋の俗謡を歌う.

Q make the incident into a *beautiful ballad* そのできごとを美しい民謡に織込む. ¶*martial ballads* 軍歌.

Q[2] a *folk ballad* 民謡.

P[2] the *ballad of* war and Empire 戦争と帝国の物語詩.

ballast, *n*. 底荷.

V *discharge* her *ballast* [船の]脚荷(バラスト)をおろす. ¶He *lacks ballast*. [比ゆ的に]彼にはどっしりした所がない.

Q[2] *ship ballast* 船の脚荷.

P The ship arrived in harbor *in ballast*. 船は底荷ばかりで(積荷がなく)港に着いた. ¶leave *in ballast* [船が]空荷で出る. ¶*without ballast* 底荷なしに.

ballast, *v*. バラスを入れる.

M the roadbed is *poorly ballasted*. 〘鉄道〙路床には十分バラスが入っていない.

baller, *n*. 〘野球〙投手.

Q[2] a *knuckle baller* ナックル投手.

ballon d'essai, *F*. 試用気球.

V *fly* a *ballon d'essai*=throw out a feeler 瀬踏みをする, さぐりを入れる.

balloon, *n*. 気球; 風船玉.

Q a *captive balloon* 繋留気球. ¶a *non-rigid dirigible balloon* 軟式飛行船. ¶a *rigid dirigible balloon* 硬式飛行船.

Q[2] hoist an *ad* (=*advertising*) *balloon* 広告球(アドバルーン)をあげる. ¶a *barrage balloon*=a balloon barrage 阻塞気球. ¶an *observation balloon* 〘気象〙観測気球. ¶put out a *pilot balloon* (=trial balloon) さぐりを入れる. ¶send up a *trial balloon* in the form of … …という風にさぐりを入れる. ¶a *war balloon* 軍用気球.

P ride *in* a *balloon* 気球に乗る. 【類】ascend *in* a *balloon*.

ballot, *n*. 投票紙, 投票.

V *cast ballots* 投票する ‖ *cast* a *ballot* for … …に一票を投じる. ¶*demand* a new *ballot* 投票の仕直しを要求する. ¶*hold* a *ballot* 投票を挙行する. ¶*take* a *ballot* for … …を投票で決める.

Q *open ballot* 記名投票. ¶by *postal ballot* 郵便投票で. ¶*by secret single ballot* 単記無記名投票で.

Q[2] a *blanket* (=*long*) *ballot* [選挙の]連記制投票用紙. ¶Decision is reached by *majority ballot*. 多数票で決定される.

P elect *by ballot* 投票で選挙する ‖ determine (=decide) *by ballot* 票決する. 【類】voting was done *by ballot*. ¶The result *of* the *ballot* for the election of the council was announced. 議員選挙の投票結果が発表された.

P[2] A *ballot for* the election of members will be taken. 会員選挙の投票が行われる. ¶submit to a *ballot of* the committee 委員会の投票に付す.

ballot, *v*. 投票する.

P *ballot for* (*against*) a resolution 決議案に賛成(反対)の投票をする.

balloting, *n*. 投票.

Q Japan's *postwar balloting* 戦後日本の選挙投票.

ballplayer, *n*. 野球選手.

Q[2] a *star ballplayer* 野球の花形選手.

ballyhoo, *n*.《米俗》うかれ騒ぎ.

V *received* much *ballyhoo* as a land of golden opportunities すばらしい好機に満ちた国と大いに騒がれた.

ballyhoo, *v*.《米俗》うかれ騒ぐ.

M[2] *ballyhoo* it *up*《米俗》どんちゃん騒ぎの宣伝をやる.

ban, *n*. 禁制; 非難.

V *cancel* a *ban* 解禁する. ¶*lay* [a] *ban* on … …を禁止する. ¶*lift* the *ban* on foreign travel for pleasure and recreation 遊覧保養のための海外旅行に対する禁止を解く. 【類】*lift* a press *ban* (新聞掲載禁止). ¶The Government *placed* a *ban* on its export. 政府はその輸出を禁止した. ¶*put* a *ban* on luxuries ぜいたく品を禁止する. 【類】*put* the *ban* to tango and other questionable dances. ¶*remove* the *ban* [検閲などでの]禁を解く ‖ The *ban* of entering Yosemite Valley with automobiles has been *removed*. ヨセミテ谿谷(けいこく)自動車乗入れの禁令が解かれた.

Q[2] *parking ban* 駐車禁止. ¶in contravention of a *two-century ban* against femininity 二世紀にわたる女人禁制の伝統を破って. ☞ Princeton 大学で軍人の妻にその campus に居住を許した. ¶The *wartime ban* on (=against) dancing has been lifted 戦時のダンス禁制は解除された.

P The anarchism is *under* the *ban* in every country of Europe. 無政府主義は欧州各国で禁止されている. ‖ You will be put *under* the *ban* of public opinion. 君は世論の攻撃を受けるだろう. 【類】The practice was placed *under* the *ban*. / The film came *under* the *ban* of the censor.

P[2] the withdrawal of the *ban against* foreign books in 1720 外書に対する一七二〇年の禁止解除. ¶It falls under the *ban of* the English law. それは英国法に触れる. ¶a *ban on* exportation (smoking, drinks) 輸出(など)に対する禁止.

band, *n*. 群, 隊; 楽隊(バンド).

V *call* one's *band* of men 部下を寄せ集める. ¶Let us go to *hear* the *band* playing at Hibiya. 日比谷のバンドを聞きに行こう. ¶*hire* a *band* バンドを雇う. ¶During the intervals the *band played* selections. その合間にバンドは選曲を奏した. ¶The town *band sailed by* at the head of a torch-light procession. 町の楽隊がたいまつ行列の先頭に立って堂々と通って行った. ¶The *band struck up* "Kimigayo." 音楽隊は「君が代」の奏楽を始めた.

Q Preceded by a *full band* the procession moved through the streets. 大吹奏楽隊を先頭に立てて行列は町を進んで行った. ¶a *marine* (=*naval*) *band* 海軍軍楽隊. ¶a *military band* 陸軍軍楽隊. ¶listen to a *music band* 音楽隊を聴く. ¶a *picked band* of artisans 選り抜きの職人. ¶a *predatory band* 略奪者の一群. ¶*wandering bands* of Tartars 遊牧のタタール族の群.

Q[2] an *amateur string band* 素人弦楽隊. ¶a *brass band* 吹奏楽団(ブラス・バンド). ¶a *guerrilla band* ゲリラ部隊. ¶a *jazz band* ジャズ・バンド. ¶a *negro band*=color-boys' band 黒人バンド. ¶a *pilgrim band* [寺社参りの]講の連中. ¶a *silver band* [銀色管楽器による]吹奏楽団. ¶to the accompaniment of a *string band* 弦楽隊の伴奏に合わせて. ¶a *terrorist band* 暴力団.

P[2] A *band of* military music was stationed near. 陸軍軍楽隊がそばに配置してあった. ‖ a *band of* able writers 腕き

き作家のグループ.

band, *n.* 縛るもの, バンド.

Q² wear an ***arm band*** 腕章をつける. an ***iron band*** 鉄輪. ¶a ***leather band*** on a travel bag 旅行カバンについている皮バンド. ¶numbered ***leg bands*** for distinguishing chicks ひよっ子を区別するため脚につけた番号づきのバンド. ¶a ***rubber band*** 輪ゴム. ¶a ***steel band*** on a chest 箱についた鋼鉄の帯金. ¶a ***spring band*** 弾性帯金.

P stick it ***in*** the *band* of his hat それを帽子のリボンにはさむ.

band, *v.* 団結する.

M a body of men *banded* ***together*** by common interests 共通の利害によって結ばれたグループ. 【類】They are *banded* ***together*** closely by ties of mutual interests. ‖ *band* themselves ***together*** and organize a committee 一団となって委員会を作る.

P *band* themselves ***against*** a person (the enemy) 結束して人(など)に当る. ¶*band* themselves ***into*** an association (a club) 団結して協会(など)を組織する. ¶*band* ***with*** ... ...と団結する.

bandage, *n.* 包帯; 目隠し.

V ***apply*** a *bandage* 包帯をかける. ¶***change*** *bandage* 包帯を換える. ¶Justice ***has*** a *bandage* over her eyes. 正義の女神は(不公平のないように)目隠しをしている. ¶***make*** *bandages* for the Red Cross 赤十字の包帯を作る. ¶***put*** a *bandage* over one's eyes 目隠しをする. ¶***remove*** a *bandage* 包帯をとる. ¶***roll*** *bandages* 包帯を巻く. ¶***wear*** a *bandage* round one's wrist 腕首に包帯する.

Q At the end of eight months the ***last*** *bandages* were removed. 八カ月経って傷が全治して包帯をとった. ¶a ***surgical*** *bandage* 外科用包帯. ¶a ***suspensory*** *bandage* つり包帯.

Q² a ***foot*** *bandage* 足部の包帯. ¶a ***starch*** *bandage* 包帯をした後のりをつけてこれを堅くしたもの. ¶a ***tar*** *bandage* 防腐用包帯. ¶a ***venesection*** *bandage* 放血用包帯.

P with his head ***in*** *bandages* 頭に包帯して ‖ ***with*** a *bandage* on his eyes and a gag in his mouth 目隠しされさるぐつわをはめられて.

bandage, *v.* 包帯する.

P *bandage* ***with*** a soft linen cloth 柔かなリンネルで包帯する ‖ *bandage* ***with*** a piece of cotton cloth 木綿きれで包帯をする ‖ He was *bandaged* ***with*** cold water. 冷罨(あん)法を施された.

bandit, *n.* 盗賊, 追はぎ.

Q a ***mounted*** *bandit* 馬賊. ¶a ***rapacious*** *bandit* 追いはぎの山賊.

Q² a ***bank*** *bandit* 銀行破り(強盗). ¶a ***bathhouse*** *bandit* 板の間かせぎ. ¶a ***mail train*** *bandit* 郵便列車専門の強盗.

P² a gang ***of*** *bandits* 盗賊の一味.

bandleader, *n.* 楽隊長(バンドリーダー).

Q² a ***Navy*** *bandleader* 海軍軍楽隊長.

bandstand, *n.* 音楽堂.

P people listening to music ***at*** the *bandstand* 奏楽堂で音楽を聴いている人々.

bandy, *v.* [話・議論を]交わす; 打合いをする.

M² *bandy* a story ***about*** 話をそれからそれへと伝える.

P *bandy* blows (words) ***with*** ... ...となぐり合い(口げんか)をする. ¶*bandy* greetings (compliments) ***with*** ... ...とあいさつ(など)を交わす.

bane, *n.* 有害物.

P² Sectarianism is the *bane* ***of*** religion. 宗閥は宗教のがんである. 【類】Drink is the *bane* ***of*** his life. ¶Avarice is a *bane* ***to*** happiness. どん欲は幸福に害がある.

bang, *n.* どんと鳴る音.

P shut a door ***with*** a *bang* ばたんと戸を閉める. ¶It burst ***with*** a great *bang*. 大きな音を立てて破れた.

bang, *v.* どんと打つ.

M The hunters *banged* ***away*** at the deer. 猟師たちはしかを目がけてずどんずどんと打ちまくった. ¶*bang* ***out*** a tune [音楽を]じゃんじゃん奏する ‖ The kitchen clock *banged* ***out*** twelve. 台所の時計が十二時を打った ‖ *bang* (=fight) it ***out*** あくまで戦う. ¶*bang* a door ***shut*** ドアをばんと閉める.

M² Don't *bang* the furniture ***about***. 家具を乱暴に取扱うな. ¶be *banged* ***up*** to the eyes (=be drunk) 酔う.

P He *banged* the butt-end of his musket ***against*** the door. 銃の台じりをどんと戸に打ちつけた. ¶He *banged* the door ***behind*** him. 戸をどしんと閉めて表へ出た. ¶He *banged* the door ***to*** us. 彼はわれわれの目の先でドアをばたんと閉めた(中に入れなかった). ¶The speaker *banged* the table ***with*** his fist. その弁士はテーブルを拳でごつんと打った.

banish, *v.* 追放する, 追いやる.

P He was *banished* ***from*** the land. 彼は国外に放逐された. ¶*banish* a person ***to*** an islet 島流しにする.

banishment, *n.* 追放, 流刑.

P The king lived ***in*** *banishment*. 王は配所で暮した.

P² a *banishment* ***for*** manslaughter 殺人罪での流刑. ¶*banishment* ***of*** care ***from*** the mind 気晴らし. ¶a *banishment* ***to*** Siberia シベリアへの追放.

banjo, *n.* 〖楽器〗バンジョー.

V ***pick*** a *banjo* バンジョーをひく.

bank, *n.* (1) 堤, 岸.

V One of the gutters ***burst*** its *banks*. みぞの一つがあふれ出した. ¶The willows ***lined*** the *banks*. 柳が土手の両側に並んでいた. ¶The river was threatening to ***overflow*** its *banks*. 川が今にも氾濫(はんらん)せんとしていた.

Q² the ***cherry*** *banks* at Koganei 小金井の桜堤. ¶The ***cloud*** *banks* lay low against the shore. 雲の堤が海岸に低くたな引いた. ¶the ***fishing*** *banks* of Newfoundland ニューファウンドランドの漁場. ¶a break of a ***river*** bank 河堤の崩壊. ¶a ***sand*** *bank* 海岸の砂堤.

P walk ***along*** a river's *bank* 川の土手伝いに歩く. ¶The richest and most continuous civilization yet studied is that which grew up ***by*** the *banks* of the Nile. これまで研究された最も豊富にしてかつ最も永続的な文明はナイル河の沿岸に発達した文明である. ¶a little town ***on*** the *banks* of the Avon エーヴォン河畔の小さな町. 【類】The town stands ***on*** the left *bank* of the river. ¶The river has run ***over*** its *banks*. 河水が土手からあふれた.

P² a *bank* ***of*** snow 雪の吹だまり. 【類】a *bank* ***of*** cloud.

(2) 銀行; 貯金箱.

V ***manage*** (=***carry on***, ***conduct or direct***) a *bank* 銀行を経営する.

V² That *bank* has ***failed***. その銀行は破産した.

Q shake the ***baby's*** *bank* for carfare おもちゃの貯金箱を振って電車賃を出す. ¶a ***baby-managed*** *bank* 経営の悪い銀行. ¶a ***commercial*** *bank* 商業銀行. ¶a ***national*** *bank* 国立銀行. ¶an ***official*** *bank* 公立銀行. ¶get the money out of my ***piggy*** *bank* 私の子豚の[形をした]貯金箱から金をとり出す.

Q² a ***blood*** *bank* 血液銀行. ¶a ***business*** (=***commercial***) *bank* 商業銀行. ¶a ***credit*** *bank* 貸付銀行. ¶***deposit*** *banks* 預金銀行. ¶an ***export-import*** *bank* 輸出入銀行. ¶an ***investment*** *bank* 投資銀行. ¶an agricultural ***loan*** *bank* 農業貸付銀行. ¶a ***member*** *bank* 加盟銀行. ¶a ***penny*** *bank* [銅貨を入れる]安っぽい貯金箱. ¶drop pennies into a little ***toy*** *bank* 小さいおもちゃの貯金箱に銅貨を入れる. ¶a ***savings*** *bank* 貯蓄銀行. ¶a ***school*** *bank* 学校銀行. ¶a ***wildcat*** *bank* → wildcat banking.

P There is ¥5,000 standing on deposit in his name ***at*** the *bank*. その銀行に彼の名前の預金が五千円ある. ‖ make a loan ***at*** a *bank* 銀行から金を借りる ‖ a bill payable ***at*** the *bank* その銀行渡しの手形 ‖ place ¥... on deposit ***at*** a *bank* 銀行に...円を預ける. ¶draw money ***from*** the *bank* 銀行から金を引出す. ¶He has much money ***in*** *bank*. 銀行にどっさり預金している. 【類】I keep my money ***in*** the Yasuda *Bank*. / lodge (=deposit) a large sum of money ***in*** a *bank* ‖ He is employed ***in*** a *bank*. 彼は銀行に勤めている. 【類】He is an employee ***in*** a *bank*. ‖ These unenterprising people have money lying idle ***in*** *bank*. こうした企業心のない連中は銀行に金を遊ばして置く. ¶I transact business ***through*** the *bank*. その銀行を通して取引している. ¶I have an account ***with*** the *bank*. 私はその銀行と取引している.

P² *banks* ***of*** issue 紙幣発行銀行.

bank, *v.* 堤を築く.

M² *bank* ***up*** a stream 堤をきずいて流をせき止める.

bank, *v.* (1) 銀行と取引する.

M ***Where*** do you *bank?* どこへ預金するか.

P *bank* ***with*** a banker 銀行家と取引する.

(2) 《俗》頼る.

P You can *bank* (=trust) ***on*** his honesty. 彼は正直に違いない. ¶*bank* ***on*** Japan to go along the highway of democracy 日本が民主々義の途を歩むことを期待する.

bank bill, 《英》銀行手形; 《米》紙幣.

Q a *one hundred pound bank bill* 百ポンド銀行手形.
P a wad ***of*** *bank bills* 《米》 札束.

banker, *n.* 銀行家.
V References are a worry to many men who ***have*** no *banker*. 照会先を指名するのは銀行と取引がない多数の人に取っては厄介なことである.
Q a ***distinguished*** *banker* 著名銀行家. ¶She married a ***rich*** *banker*. 彼女は金持ちの銀行家に嫁した.
Q^2 a ***millionaire*** *banker* 百万長者の銀行家.

banking, *n.* 銀行業.
Q^2 ***wildcat*** *banking* 《米》 山ねこ銀行業 ☞ 西部において条例の不備に乗じ無資本で兌換券を乱発した銀行または個人の営業振を評した語.

bank note, 《英》 紙幣.
V ***change*** a *bank note* into gold 札を金貨に替える.
Q ***crisp*** *bank notes* 手の切れそうな札(さつ).
P Will you have the money ***in*** *bank note?* 紙幣で宜しいですか.

bankrupt, *n.* 破産者.
V ***adjudicate*** a *bankrupt* to ... ...に破産を宣告する. ¶***play*** the *bankrupt* 破産する.
Q an ***undischarged*** *bankrupt* 債務を果さない破産者.
P It will send him ***into*** *bankrupt*. そのために彼は破産するだろう.

bankrupt, *a.* 破産した.
V ***go*** *bankrupt* 破産する.
P a brain *bankrupt* ***of*** its store of energy 疲れ果てて役に立たなくなった頭脳.

bankruptcy, *n.* 破産.
Q ***fraudulent*** *bankruptcy* 不正手段による破産. ¶those exhausted persons who are on the threshold of ***physiological*** *bankruptcy* 生理的破たんにひんしている疲労しきった人々.
P a petition ***in*** *bankruptcy* 破産の申請. ¶go ***into*** *bankruptcy* 破産に陥る. ¶The company is on the verge ***of*** *bankruptcy*. 会社は破産せんばかりだ.
P^2 *bankruptcy* ***of*** statesmanship 政治の貧困.

banner, *n.* 旗.
V He should be ***awarded*** the "*banner*" for his presence of mind. 彼の沈勇に対して表彰すべきだ. ¶In Denmark not a city or hamlet but what the national *banner* is ***flung*** to the breeze on this day of celebration. デンマークではこの祝日に当って国旗を掲揚しない町や村は一つもない. ¶***follow*** (=***join***) the *banner* of ... ...の旗下に加わる. ¶The book now ***holds*** the *banner*. 今の所その本が一番良い. ‖ ***hold*** aloft the *banner* of ... ...の旗を高く掲げる. ¶***hold up*** a *banner* of a holy principle 神聖な主義の旗をかざす. ¶They first ***planted*** the Portuguese *banner* on the Moorish coast. 彼らはムーア人の海岸に初めてポルトガルの旗を立てた. ¶They ***unfurled*** the new *banner*. 彼らは旗上げをした.
Q with a ***large*** *banner* on which were the words "..." "..."と記した大きな旗を立てて. ¶a ***defiant*** *banner* 反旗. ¶***processional*** *banners* 行列の旗. ¶the ***triumphal*** *banner* for the season そのシーズンの優勝旗.
Q^2 a ***church*** *banner* 宗教上の儀式に用いる旗. ¶a ***party*** *banner* 党旗. ¶a ***school*** *banner* 校旗. ¶a ***trophy*** *banner* 優勝旗.
P march ***beneath*** the *banner* of ... ...の旗の下に進軍する. ¶the loyal army that serves ***under*** the *banner* of ... ...の旗下に仕える忠義な軍隊 ‖ fight ***under*** the same *banner* 同じ旗下で戦う. 【類】 gather together ***under*** the *banner* of the Crusade (十字軍). ¶***with*** a large *banner* 大旗をかざして.

banquet, *n.* 饗(きょう)宴.
V ***eat*** a *banquet* ごちそうをたべる. ¶We ***gave*** him a farewell *banquet*. われわれは彼のために送別の宴を張った. 【類】 a *banquet* was ***given*** in Tokyo by ... to ... ¶***serve*** a handsome *banquet* りっぱなごちそうを出す. ¶A *banquet* was ***spread*** before the guests. 来客のために饗宴が張られた. ¶The people of the city ***tendered*** him a *banquet*. 市民は彼のために饗宴を張った.
V^2 as the *banquet* ***closed*** 饗宴が終った時に.
Q give a ***complimentary*** *banquet* to ... ...に敬意を表するための饗宴を催す. ¶a ***congratulatory*** *banquet* on the conclusion of alliance with Japan 日本との同盟締結を祝賀するための饗宴. ¶set before them a ***delicious*** *banquet* 彼らの前においしいごちそうを並べる. ¶give an ***elaborate*** *banquet* in honor of ... ...を招待して大饗宴を催す. ¶A very ***handsome*** *banquet* awaited them. 非常にりっぱなごちそうが彼らを待っていた. ¶a ***literary*** *banquet* 文学関係(作家など)の宴会. ¶a most ***magnificent*** *banquet* given in honor of ... ...を招いて催された実に盛大な饗宴. ¶a ***public*** *banquet* 公けの饗宴. ¶a ***swank*** *banquet* 豪華な宴会. ¶a ***sumptuous*** *banquet* ぜいたくな宴会.
Q^2 The ***fellowship*** *banquet* is covered by the cost of registration. 懇親会の会費は入会金に含まれている. ¶a ***midday*** *banquet* 午餐会. ¶a ***seven-course*** *banquet* 七品付きのごちそう.
P He was entertained ***at*** a farewell *banquet* in the Imperial Hotel. 帝国ホテルの送別会に招かれた. ‖ speak ***at*** a *banquet* 饗宴の席で演説する.

banter, *v.* ひやかす; ふざける.
P *banter* him ***on*** (=***about***) the subject その問題に関して彼をからかう. ¶*banter* ***with*** ... ...と冗談を言いあう(ふざける).

banzai, *n.* 万歳.
V Three *banzai* were ***given*** with enthusiasm. 万歳が熱心に三唱された.
Q a ***loyal*** and ***hearty*** *banzai* 忠君熱誠の万歳. ¶***three lusty*** *banzai* were given for the Emperor at the instance of ... ...の発声で元気よく陛下の万歳を三唱した.
P^2 *Banzai* ***for*** the Empire (Navy, Japanese nation, Allies). 帝国(など)万歳.

baptism, *n.* 洗礼.
V ***accept*** Christian *baptism* キリスト教の洗礼を受ける. ¶***administer*** *baptism* to ... ...に洗礼を施す. ¶***receive*** Christian *baptism* キリスト教の洗礼を受ける ‖ He ***received*** his *baptism* of fire. 彼は実戦の経験を持っている.
P Christian names are those one receives ***at*** (=***in***) *baptism*. クリスチャン・ネームは洗礼の時に受ける名だ. ¶a sponsor ***in*** *baptism* 洗礼の時の名親.

baptist, *n.* バプテスト派の人.
Q ***hard-shell*** *Baptists* 《俗》 こちこちのバプテスト.

baptize, *v.* 洗礼を施す.
P *baptize* ... ***by*** immersion ...に洗礼を施す. ¶He was *baptized* ***into*** the Christian faith 彼は洗礼を受けてキリスト教に入った. ¶He seems to have been *baptized* ***of*** his mother's church, the Church of England. 彼は母親の教会たる英国教会の洗礼を受けたらしい. ¶He was *baptized* ***with*** sorrow. 悲哀を体験した.

bar, *n.* (**1**) 弁護士, 弁護士業; 法廷; 被告人席.
V He ***chose*** the *bar* for his profession. 彼は弁護士を職業に選んだ. ¶***give up*** the *Bar* 弁護士を廃業する.
P Let the matter be tried ***at*** the *bar* of enlightened public opinion. その事件を賢明なる世論の批判にゆだねよ. ¶a prisoner ***at*** the *bar* 刑事被告人. 【類】 he stood ***at*** the *bar* of justice (法廷) to be tried for the murder of ... ‖ when he was a young man ***at*** the *Bar* 彼が若い弁護士であった時分. 【類】 practice ***at*** the *bar*. ¶He was brought up ***for*** the *bar* 弁護士の教育を受けた. 【類】 He was qualifying himself ***for*** the *bar*. ¶He went ***from*** the *bar* to the bench. 彼は弁護士から判事になった. 【類】 He retired ***from*** the *bar*. ‖ a veteran member ***of*** the Tokyo *bar* 在京法曹(そう)界の元老. ¶He was called ***to*** the *bar* at thirty. 三十歳で弁護士になった.

(**2**) 障害, 邪魔; 制裁.
V ***let down*** the *bars* to success 成功への障害を除く.
Q^2 a liberal interpretation of the ***color*** *bar* 異民族に対する偏見の少ない見方. ¶a relaxation of ***immigration*** *bars* 障害となる移民法の緩和.
P ***before*** the *bar* of conscience 良心の制裁を受けて ‖ Popular opinion is not the *bar* ***before*** which the question is to be decided. この問題は世論に付して決せられるべき性質のものではない. 【類】 ***before*** the *bar* of civilization (modern science).
P^2 a *bar* ***to*** success (progress) 成功(など)の邪魔もの ‖ become a *bar* ***to*** marriage 結婚の邪魔になる.

(**3**) 酒場(バー).
V ***operate*** (=***run***) a luncheon *bar* 軽食堂を経営する. ¶***tend*** a *bar* 酒場で働く.
Q^2 a ***cocktail*** *bar* カクテルバー. ¶a "***quart-ale***" *bar* 《英俗》 一クォート四ペンスの安酒場. ¶an ***oyster*** *bar* かき料理のバー. ¶a ***refreshment*** *bar* 軽食食堂. ¶a ***saloon*** *bar* 酒場. ¶a ***snack*** *bar* for soldiers and civilian clerks 兵隊・軍属のための軽食バー.
P a waiter ***at*** the *bar* 酒場の給仕.

(**4**) 棒, 金棒; *pl.* 鉄窓.
Q^2 a ***candy*** *bar* 《米》 チョコレート・キャンデー(ヌガー式のもの) ‖ Here's a ***candy*** *bar* to cheer you up. そらチョコレー

ト, 泣くんじゃないよ. ¶a ***chocolate*** *bar* 板チョコ. ¶an ***iron flat*** *bar* 平鉄棒(資材). ¶an ***iron round*** *bar* 丸鉄棒. ¶set up a ***mosquito*** *bar* (=net) 蚊帳をつる. ¶***parallel*** *bars* 〘体操〙平行棒. ¶a ***side*** *bar*「ちなみに記す」的の記事. ¶a ***steel channel*** *bar* みぞ付き鋼棒. ¶***steel flat*** (***round, square***) *bars* 鋼鉄平(など)棒.

P He spent a night ***behind*** [the] *bars*. 鉄窓の下に一夜を明かした. ¶have him ***behind*** *bars* 彼を鉄窓に閉じ込めておく. ¶brass (copper) ***in*** *bar* 棒状真ちゅう(など) ‖ metals ***in*** *bar* 棒状の金属. ¶be shut up ***within*** the *bars* of a prison 鉄窓に閉じ込められる.

P² a *bar* ***of*** soap (chocolate, iron, metal) 棒石けん(など).

(5)〘音楽〙縦線, 小節.

V He ***played*** the first few *bars* of "God Save the King." 彼は英国歌の最初の数小節を演奏した. ¶***single*** (***double***) *bars*〘音楽〙単(複)縦線.

bar, *v.* 禁制する, 妨げる; しまを付ける.

P The country was jealously *barred* ***against*** foreign intercourse. この国は外国との交際を厳禁していた. ¶*bar* a person ***from*** some action (place, right) 人がある行動をなすこと(など)を妨げる. ¶The east was *barred* ***with*** light. 東には暁の光のしまが見えていた. ¶be *barred* ***from*** permanent residence in the country 国内永住を禁ぜられている.

barbarian, *n.* 野蛮人.

V ***repel*** the *barbarians* 野蛮人を追い払う.

Q They're ***real*** *babarians*, I can tell you. あいつらは野蛮だよ, 全く.

barbarism, *n.* 蛮風, 蛮行.

Q be considered as ***provincial*** *barbarism* 地方的な蛮風と見なされている.

Q² ***Fascist*** *barbarism* ファシストの蛮行.

P People are living ***in*** *barbarism* in some parts of Africa. アフリカのある地方では住民は野ばんな生活をしている.

barbarity, *n.* 蛮行.

Q ***hideous*** *barbarities* ひどい蛮行. ¶The garden is disfigured by certain ***modern*** *barbarities*. その庭は殺風景な近代味が加えられて台なしになった. ¶*barbarities* too ***shocking*** to be told 口には出せないほど惨酷な蛮行.

barbarous, *a.* 野蛮な.

M an ***atrociously*** *barbarous* people 言語道断な野蛮な国民.

barber, *n.* 理髪師.

V These people look to have been studiously ***evading*** the *barber*. この人たちは床屋になるべく行かないようにしていたらしい(大分顔が見苦しくなっている).

P have a shave ***at*** the *barber's* 床屋でひげをそる.

bard, *n.* 詩人.

Q a ***liberal*** *bard* 自由詩人. ¶a ***patriotic*** *bard* 愛国詩人.

bare, *v.* 裸にする.

P *bare* it ***of*** its covering その覆いをとり去る. 【類】*bare* a person ***of*** his clothing.

bare, *a.* 裸の.

P I am *bare* ***in*** purse. ふところがさびしい. ‖ The garden looks *bare* ***in*** winter. 庭は冬になると木が裸になって殺風景だ. ¶The hill is *bare* ***of*** trees. 山に木がない. ‖ cloth *bare* ***of*** thread 糸筋のあらわれている布. 【類】walls *bare* ***of*** pictures / a small room *bare* ***of*** furniture / trees *bare* ***of*** leaves / The merchant is *bare* ***of*** stocks. / He is *bare* ***of*** money. ¶He is *bare* ***to*** the elbow. 彼はひじまではだを出している. ‖ There stood a solitary house *bare* ***to*** the blast. 木枯の吹きすさぶにまかせた一軒家があった.

bareness, *n.* 裸なこと.

V These pines ***relieve*** the *bareness* to the bald rockery. むき出しの築山だがその松があるので見られる.

bargain, *n.* 約定, 取引; 売買; 買物; 格安品.

V ***beat*** a *bargain* 値切る. ¶***clench*** the *bargain* 約定を取極める. ¶***close*** a *bargain* 取引を済ます. ¶***conclude*** a *bargain* 契約を締結する(手を打つ). ¶I hope you will ***drive*** a good *bargain* with him. 君が彼と割のよい取引をすればよいが. ¶***get*** a dead *bargain* すてきに安い買物をする. ¶The old Tower of London is ***having*** a *bargain* or a remnant sale. 古いロンドン塔では安売や整理品販売をやっている. ¶He ***left off*** his *bargain*. 約束を放棄した. ¶No woman who ***loves*** a *bargain* is stoical enough to ignore these goods. 格安品を買いたがる女がどうしてこれを見過すことができよう. ¶I'll ***make*** a *bargain* with you. あなたと取引しましょう. ¶After thirty-five minutes of parleys the *bargain* was ***made***. 商談三十五分の後約定がまとまった. 【類】They ***made*** a *bargain* that they would not forsake each other. ¶***pick up*** a cheap *bargain* 掘出し物をする. ¶***strike*** a *bargain* with ... ...と商談をまとめる. ¶one of my best *bargains* ***fell*** to me when ... ...の時に良いもうけ仕事にぶっつかった.

Q She soon found that she had made a ***bad*** *bargain*. やがて自分が貧乏くじを引いたことに気が付いた(悪い夫を持った場合など). ¶try to make a ***better*** *bargain* もっと有利な取引をしようとする. ¶***big*** *bargains* in great books 名著の大安売. ¶She is a good hand at making a ***cheap*** *bargain*. 彼女は格安品を手に入れるのが上手だ. ¶and the *bargain* is ***complete*** それで商談がまとまった. ¶a ***Dutch*** *bargain* 不公平な取引(値段は高くて量目は少ない). ¶It is an ***exceptional*** *bargain*. これは取分け安い品です. ¶a ***great*** *bargain* in choice articles 上等品の大見切. ¶drive a ***hard*** *bargain* ひどく値切る. ¶a ***mervelous*** *bargain* 驚異的安売. ¶a ***onesided*** *bargain* 一方だけに有利な取引. ¶a ***real*** *bargain* 本当の掘出物. ¶a ***record-breaking*** *bargain* 破天荒の安い買物. ¶***special*** *bargains* in ... ...の大廉売. ¶a ***tempting*** *bargain* 買い気をそそる格安品.

Q² a ***remainder*** *bargain*〔書籍などの〕特価本; 残品整理.

P Those goods are offered ***at*** a *bargain* それは廉売品です. 【類】buy a thing ***at*** a *bargain*. ¶I have a headache and a toothache and a cough ***into*** the *bargain*. 頭痛で歯痛でおまけにせきが出る. ¶He had the best ***of*** the *bargain*. その取引でうまい事をした. ¶I cannot close ***with*** such a *bargain*. そんな契約には応じられない.

P² *bargains* ***in*** ribbons リボンの安売. ¶He made a *bargain* ***with*** me, but he is trying to back out of it. 約束して置きながらそれを取消そうとしている.

O The *bargain* is off. それは破談になった. ¶Quite a *bargain*, isn't it? 全く掘出し物じゃないか.

bargain, *v.* 掛合う; 約定する; 予期する.

M *bargain* ***away*** one's estate その土地を安く売渡す.

P *bargain* ***for*** fish 魚を買う約束をする ‖ This bad weather is more than I *bargained* ***for***. 予期した以上に悪い天気だ. ¶I *bargained* ***with*** the producer for a constant supply of the articles. 製造元から絶えず品物を送らせるように話をつけた. 【類】He *bargained* ***with*** his editors for so much a line (一行いくらで). / Italian porters expect to be *bargained* ***with***. / *bargain* ***with*** the vegetable seller.

bargainer, *n.* 売買約定者.

Q a ***hard*** *bargainer* しつこく値切る人.

bargaining, *n.* 値切ること.

Q ***collective*** *bargaining*〘労〙団体交渉. ¶***direct*** *bargaining* じか談判. ¶***individual*** *bargaining* 個人交渉. ¶***sole*** *bargaining* 単一交渉.

P do business ***by*** *bargaining* 値切って取引をする.

P² *bargaining* ***in*** darkness やみ取引.

barge, *n.* 荷船.

V ***employ*** [=***hire***] *barges* はしけをやとう. ¶***load*** a *barge* with grain 荷揚船に穀物を積む. ¶***unload*** *barges* of coal 荷船の石炭を降ろす.

P ***with*** a *barge* in tow はしけを引き船して.

bark, *n.* 木の皮.

Q India paper is made from the ***inner*** *bark* of the bamboo. インデアン紙は竹の内皮で作られる.

P a man ***with*** the *bark* on《米》山男.

bark, *n.* ほえ声.

Q a dog's long ***deep*** *bark* 犬の遠ぼえ. ¶give a ***short*** *bark* かみつくようにほえる.

bark, *v.* ほえる.

M *bark* ***furiously*** 猛烈にほえる. ¶*bark* ***noisily*** at ... ...に向ってやかましくほえる. ¶The dogs *barked* ***savagely*** at imaginary burglars. 犬どもがいもしない泥棒に向って猛烈にほえた. ¶*bark* ***shrilly*** or ***fussily***=yap きゃんきゃんあるいはうるさくほえる.

M² Your attack is *barking* ***up the wrong tree***. 君の攻撃は見当違いだ.

P *bark* ***against*** (=***at***) the moon いたずらに騒ぎ立てる. ¶*bark* ***at*** a person (beggar, robber, thing) 人(など)に向ってほえる.

barker, *n.*《米》呼込人.

Q a ***Coney Island*** *barker* コーニーアイランド(歓楽郷)の客引き. ¶a ***merry-go-round*** *barker* 回転木馬の呼込人.

barley, *n.* 大麦.

V ***pound*** *barley* in a mortar 大麦をうすでつく.

Q ***patent*** *barley* 玉麦粉.

barmaid, *n.* バーの女給.
Q a ***prostitute barmaid*** いんちき酒場の女(青線区域の女給 ⌊など).

barn, *n.* 納屋;《米》車庫.
V The wind ***unroofed*** a *barn.* 風で納屋の屋根をはがれた.
Q² a ***cow barn*** 牛舎. ¶an ***electric-car barn*** 電車庫. ¶an ***engine barn***〖鉄道〗機関車庫. ¶a ***tin-plate barn*** トタン ⌊張りの小屋.

barometer, *n.* 晴雨計.
V The *barometer* has ***risen*** in N.E. Japan and ***fallen*** in all other stations. 東北地方では晴雨計が昇ったがその他の場所ではどこも下った.
Q Building activity is always a ***fair barometer*** (=index =indicator) of business conditions. 建築界の活動は常に商況を知る確かなバロメーターである. ¶The ***financial*** *barometer* is rising in Japan. 日本の財界は景気がよくなりつつある. ¶The arrival of the seagulls serves as a ***living*** *barometer.* かもめがやって来るのが生きた晴雨計になる.
Q² as the ***trade barometer*** falls 不景気になると

baron, *n.* 貴族;《米》豪商, 大立者.
Q ***feudal barons*** 諸大名. ¶a ***modern industrial baron*** 近代工業界の大立物.
Q² a ***labor baron*** 労働者のボス. ¶a ***land*** (an ***oil***) ***baron*** 大地主(など). ¶a ***paper baron*** (=lord) 一代限りの爵位(など)を有する人. ¶a ***movie baron*** 映画界の大立物.

barrack, *n.* [通例 *pl.*] 兵営.
V ***break barracks*** 脱営する.
Q ***naval barracks*** 海兵団.
Q² ***army barracks*** 兵舎.
P living ***out of barracks*** 営外居住; 外泊.

barrage, *n.* 弾幕; 圧倒的多数.
Q² a ***balloon*** *barrage*=a barrage balloon 阻塞(ｿｻｲ)気球. ¶direct a heavy ***propaganda barrage*** against ... ...に向け猛烈な宣伝戦の火ぶたを切る.
P² a ***barrage of*** questions 質問の雨あられ.

barrel, *n.* たる.
V ***barrels hooped*** with plaited bamboo 竹のたがを掛けた ⌈たる.
Q ***tight*** (=***watertight or airtight***) ***barrels*** or casks [水・空気漏れのない]密封したたる.
P² a ***barrel of*** beer (flour, gunpowder) ビール(など)一た ⌊る.

barren, *a.* 不妊の; 不毛の.
P often ***barren of*** success しばしば失敗して ‖ be ***barren of*** trade 霜枯れ時である. ¶The literature is ***barren of*** works on this important subject. この重要な問題に関する文献がない. ‖ She was ***barren of*** children. 彼女は子がなかった. 【類】they rendered their marriage ***barren of*** children (避妊法) ‖ ***barren of*** results 成績のあがらない. 【類】a story ***barren of*** interest.

barrenness, *n.* 不毛.
V ***mitigate*** the wretched *barrenness* of our railroad embankments わが鉄道線路の殺風景を緩和する(植樹などで).
Q our higher education and the ***singular barrenness*** of its results わが国の高等教育とその不思議なほど貧弱な効 ⌊果.

barricade, *n.* バリケード.
Q² ***Barbed-wire barricades*** blocked off streets in the principal cities. 有刺線のバリケードで主要都市への街路を ⌊ふさいだ.

barrier, *n.* 障壁.
V ***abolish*** the *barrier* between classes 階級間の障壁を撤廃する. ¶***break down*** the *barrier* which separate them それを分離する障壁を打破する. 【類】***break down*** the *barrier* of self-consciousness (自我意識). ¶***build*** (=***set up***) a *barrier* 障壁を築く. ¶***constitute*** an insuperable *barrier* to ... ...に対して越え難い障壁となっている. ¶***demolish*** *barriers* 障害物を打破する. ¶***disrupt*** all human *barriers* of nation, race, religion, age, class and caste 国家・人種・宗教・時代・階級等のあらゆる人事的障害を打ち砕く. ¶***drop*** trade *barriers* 貿易の障壁を撤廃する. ¶***erect*** *barriers* between nations 国民間に障壁を築く. ¶***form*** a *barrier* against ... ...に対して障壁を築く. 【類】Language ***forms*** a *barrier* between nations. ¶lower the ***immigration barriers*** 移民法の障壁を緩和する. ¶***pile up*** an insurmountable *barrier* 越え難い障壁を築き上げる. ¶*Barriers* between nations are ***reared*** by slow and infrequent communication. 国民間の障壁は交通が緩慢でひん繁ならざるがために築かれる. ¶***remove*** foreign trade *barriers.* 外国貿易上の障害を除去する. ¶***tear*** class *barriers* ***down*** 階級間の障壁を打破する.
Q The expansion of Japan's export trade depends on the lowering of the ***artificial*** *barriers* to trade. 日本の外国貿易振興は人為的な障害を少なくすることにある. ¶an ***ideologic*** *barrier* 思想的防壁. ¶an ***impenetrable barrier*** 貫通し難い障壁.
Q² ***artificial trade barriers*** such as tariffs, preferences, and embargoes 人為的貿易障害例えば関税, 特恵, 禁制品目など. ¶set up ***customs barriers*** between the Saar and the rest of Germany ドイツのザール地方とその他の地方との間に関税の障壁を設定する. ¶let down ***immigration barriers*** 移民に対する障壁を撤廃する. 【類】stricter ***immigration barriers.*** ¶break down ***impassable class barriers*** between ... ...間の越え難い階級的障害を打破する. ¶the eradication of ***international trade barriers*** 国際貿易障害の根本的な除去. ¶brush aside (=remove) the ***language barrier*** 言語の障壁を除く. ¶erect high ***tariff barriers*** 高い関税の障壁を設ける.
P² erect *barriers* ***against*** commerce 商業に対して障壁を築く. ¶a *barrier* ***between*** nations and races 国家民族間の障壁. ¶the *barrier* ***of*** language 言語という障害. ¶a ***barrier to*** progress (development) 進歩(など)に対する障害. 【類】Poor health and lack of money are ***barriers to*** edu- ⌊cation.

barrister, *n.*《英》法廷弁護士.
Q ***disbarred barristers*** 弁護士の資格を失った法律家. ¶He was a ***rising*** *barrister,* much employed in commercial cases. 彼は新進の弁護士で商業関係の仕事が大分あった.

barrow, *n.* 手押車.
V ***push*** a *barrow* through the streets 手押車を押して町を通る. ¶***roll*** his *barrow* to a night fair 縁日へ手押車をこ ⌊ろがして行く.
Q² a ***hand barrow*** 手押し車.

barter, *n.* 交易(バーター).
V ***carry on*** *barter* 交易を行う.
P received ***in barter*** with ... ...とのバーターで受取った(食 ⌈料など).

barter, *v.* 交易する.
M ***barter away*** one's honor (freedom, position) 欲に目がくらんで名誉(自由・地位)を手放す.
P ***barter*** rice ***for*** cloth 織物と米を交易する. ¶***barter with*** the islanders その島の土人と物々交換をする.

base, *n.* 基礎;〖軍〗基地; ふもと;〖野球〗塁.
V ***clear*** the *bases*〖野球〗ランナーを一掃する. ¶***establish*** a naval *base* 海軍根拠地を設置する. ¶The railroad ***skirts*** the *base* of Mt. Fuji. その鉄道は富士山のすそ野をめぐっている.
Q use Japan as a ***military base*** 日本を軍事基地として使用する. ¶The harbor forms an important ***naval base.*** 同港は重要な海軍根拠地をなしている.
Q² an ***air base*** 空軍基地. ¶a ***center base*** of Japan's commercial operations in ... ...における日本の商業活動の中心地 ‖ a ***center base*** of Japan's commercial operations in the South Seas 南洋における日本の商業活動の中心地. ¶an ***Edison base***〖電気〗ねじ込口金. ¶Hongkong as a ***fleet operating base*** 艦隊作戦基地としてのホンコン. ¶tin-plate with an ***iron base*** トタン板. ¶former Japanese ***island bases*** in the Pacific 太平洋上の旧日本基地. 【類】strategic ***island bases.*** ¶a ***relay base*** 中継基地. ¶***sea*** and ***air bases*** 海空軍基地. ¶establish ***security bases*** in the Pacific islands 太平洋上に安全保障の基礎を築く. ¶the "***stepping stone***" *bases* the United States conquered on the road to Tokyo 米軍が東京への途上で征服した飛び石基地. ¶a ***squadron base*** 補給基地. ¶a ***swan base***〖電気〗さし込み口金. ¶***United States*** *bases* in the Far East 極東における米軍基地. ¶an ¥8,000 ***wage base*** 八千円賃金ベース.
P This lies ***at*** the *base* of national life. これが国民生活の根底を成している. 【類】Misunderstanding is ***at*** the *base* of most international troubles. ‖ ***at*** the *base* of a mountain ふもとに ‖ cut down the tree close ***at*** the *base* その木を根元から切倒す. ¶***from*** *base* ***to*** summit ふもとから頂上まで ‖ It is a covenient *base* ***from*** which trips and excursions radiate. そこに腰をすえてあちこち小旅行をすると便利だ. ¶The runner was ***off*** his *base.*〖野球〗ランナーは塁を離れていた. ¶a column standing ***on*** a *base* 土台の上に立つ一本の柱 ‖ act ***on*** the *base* of ... ...に基いて行動する ‖ with T ***on*** second *base*〖野球〗二塁に T がいて.
P² a *base* ***for*** the company's operations 会社の策源地. ¶taking it as a *base* ***of*** comparison それを比較の基礎として. ¶a *base* ***of*** operations 作戦基地 ‖ A *base* ***of*** agreement was arrived at. 協定の基準条件が確立された. ‖ BC is

the *base of* a triangle. 〖幾何〗BC は三角形の底辺である.

base, *v*. 基づかせる.

P These charges are *based* ***on*** misunderstanding. こうした攻撃は誤解に基づいている. 【類】this is *based* ***on*** information furnished by ... ‖ form a Cabinet *based* ***on*** a parliamentary majority in the Diet 国会における議員多数派を基盤に内閣を作る. 【類】be *based* ***on*** the theories of specialists / a society *based* ***on*** private property in land and capital ‖ *based* ***on*** the Chinese model 中国に範を取って ‖ The inference is *based* ***on*** wholly false premises. その推論は前提が全然間違っている. ‖ classification *based* ***on*** color 色による分類 ‖ These prices are *based* ***on*** the normal exchange of Frs. 25–Swiss to the £. この値段は一ポンド二十五フラン(スイス)という普通の為替相場を基準としてきめたものである. 【類】a wage *based* ***on*** cost of living / *based* ***on*** a superstitious belief common among all people that ... / an alliance between the two countries *based* not only ***on*** policy, but ***on*** genuine friendship / The legend is *based* ***on*** fact. ¶a political philosophy *based* ***upon*** force and deception 力と偽まんを骨子とする政治哲学. 【類】This dread is *based*, however, ***upon*** a misconception. / the theory is *based* ***upon*** the notion that ... / This conviction is *based* ***upon*** experience. / *based* ***upon*** insufficient grounds ‖ The generalization is *based* ***upon*** insufficient data. その総括論は資料が不十分だ.

baseball, *n*. 野球.

V ***play*** *baseball* 野球をやる.

P That school is prominent ***in*** *baseball*. あの学校は野球で有名だ.

baseman, *n*. 〖野球〗塁手.

V ***spike*** a *baseman* [ランナーが]塁手をスパイクでける.

Q a ***first*** *(**second, third**) baseman* 一(二, 三)塁手.

bash, *v*. 《俗》強く打つ.

M² *bash* ***in*** car windows with stones 車窓のガラスを石を投げてこわす.

P *bash* one's head ***against*** a tree 木に頭をひどくぶっつける.

bashful, *a*. はずかしがる.

P She is *bashful* ***in*** doing (=to do) anything. 彼女は何をするにもはずかしがる.

bashfulness, *n*. はじらい, はにかみ.

V Men of great ability so often ***feel*** *bashfulness* in addressing a large assembly. 非凡の才能がある人も大勢に向って話す時ははずかしがることが往々ある. ¶***outgrow*** one's *bashfulness* 年をとってはずかしがらなくなる. ¶***overcome*** *bashfulness* 内気でなくなる.

Q ***maiden*** *bashfulness* 乙女のはじらい. ¶his ***modest*** *bashfulness* 彼のつつましやかな内気.

basin, *n*. 洗盤.

V ***empty*** a *basin* 洗面器の水をあける. ¶***fill*** a *basin* 洗面器に水を入れる.

Q² a ***catch*** *basin* [下水のはけ口にある]目ざら. ¶a ***collecting*** *basin* 集水地. ¶an ***ocean*** *basin* 〖地〗海盆. ¶a ***river*** *basin* 河床. ¶a ***tide*** *basin* 潮待繫船池. ¶a ***wash*[*-hand*]** *basin* 手洗いばち.

basis, *n*. 基礎, 根拠; 原則.

V This ***affords*** a sound *basis* for the statement. これがその陳述の確かな根拠になる. ¶when the scheme ***assumes*** a practice *basis* その計画実行の段になると. ¶***establish*** a *basis* of improved international relations 国際親善関係の基礎を樹立する. 【類】***establish*** a *basis* for practical measures. ¶The farmers ***form*** the *basis* of a nation. 農夫は国の本. ‖ This ***forms*** a *basis* for judgment. これが判定の根拠となっている. ¶***furnish*** a satisfactory *basis* for study 研究に満足な根拠を与える. 【類】Berlin shall ***furnish*** the *basis* of our discussion. ¶It ***gave*** a *basis* for reasoning. それが推論の根拠をなした. ¶***implant*** the *basis* of commercial interests 商売の基礎を築く. ¶be ***made*** the *basis* of frequent oral and written drill 口頭及び筆記の練習の基本になる. ¶***provide*** a *basis* for a fuller work to follow これに次ぐさらに十分な研究への根拠を与える.

Q schools established and conducted on a ***Christian*** *basis* キリスト教主義に基いて設立しかつ経営されている学校. ¶The philanthropic institution has been put on a thoroughly sound ***commercial*** *basis*. その博愛事業は十分引き合う商業的基礎ができた. ‖ make transactions on a ***commercial*** *basis* 商業採算で取引をする. ¶on a ***conservative*** *basis* of appraisement 内輪に評価して. ¶If you desire to purchase on a ***deferred*** *basis* we invite you to open a charge account. 延べ払いでお買上の御希望ならば掛勘定になさることをお勧め致します. ¶Schools there are placed on an ***English*** *basis*. そこの学校は英語で教育をしている. ¶on the most ***equitable*** *basis* もっとも公平なやり方で. ¶on an ***equivalent*** *basis* with ... …と対等に. ¶on a firm ***financial*** *basis* 確固たる財政的基礎に立って. ¶put the finance of the company on a ***firm*** *basis* 会社の財政を確立させる. 【類】The popularity of the work (作品) is established on a ***firm*** basis. ¶share profits on the ***following*** *basis* 次の方法で利益を分配する. ¶place their relationship on a ***friendly*** and ***amicable*** *basis* 戦争の関係を親善友好的なものにする. ¶evaluate it on an ***impersonal*** *basis* それを(個人的でなく)一般的な基準によって評価する. ¶a vast edifice established upon an ***insecure*** *basis* 砂上に築かれた大楼閣. ¶The report has been prepared upon an ***insufficient*** *basis* of fact and observation. その報告は事実と観察が十分でない. ¶an association organized on ***international*** *basis* 国際的精神に基いて組織された協会. ¶incorporate a society on ***legal*** *basis* 会を法人組織にする. ¶It has no ***logical*** *basis*. それは論理的基礎を有していない. ¶on a ***nation-wide*** *basis* 全国的な規模で. ¶the ***physical*** *basis* of life 人生の物理的原則. ¶Germany has already brought her commerce back to a ***prewar*** *basis*. ドイツは既にその商業を戦前の状態に復した. ¶The belief has no ***scientific*** *basis* whatever. その信念には何ら科学的根拠がない. 【類】It was put on a really ***scientific*** *basis*. 【類】the ***scientific*** *basis* of morality. ¶The business is conducted on a perfectly ***secure*** *basis*. その事業は全く安全な経営をやっている. ¶put it on a ***sound*** *basis* それを確固たる基礎に置く. ¶on a ***voluntary*** *basis* 自由意志に基づいて. ¶remodel ... on a ***Western*** *basis* …を西洋式に改造する.

Q² All sales are on an ***as-is*** *basis*, with no returns. 販売はすべて現状を基とし, 返品はできないことになっている. ¶arrange food imports on the ***barter*** *basis* 食料品の輸入をバーター方式にする. ¶The organization is conducted upon a purely ***business*** *basis*. その団体は純然たる営利的事業である. ¶Everything is on a "***business as usual***" *basis*. 万事が平常通り行われている. ¶do business on a ***cash*** *basis* 現金主義で商売をする. ¶Business is conducted on a ***commission*** *basis*. 仕事は手数料制度でやっている. ¶use white labor on a ***contract*** *basis* 契約制度で白人労働者を使う. ¶Our prices are made on a ***direct-to-consumer*** *basis* which permits of no discounts except quantity discounts. 手前共ではお値段は直接販売の方式でやっておりますので大量お買上げ以外は一切値引きを致しません. ¶a night club run on a "***dry***" *basis* 排酒主義で経営している夜間クラブ. ¶on an ***escrow*** *basis* 〖商〗間接取引の方式で(売買契約が成立するまで第三者に証書を寄託する方式). ¶be on a ***five-day-week*** *basis* 一週五日の勤務制になっている. ¶hold a job on a ***full-time*** *basis* 終日勤務の仕事をやっている. ¶Our currency is on a ***gold*** *basis*. わが国の通貨は金本位に基く. 【類】The rise in prices is partly due to the fact that our money has no longer got a real ***gold*** *basis*. ¶on a ***long-range*** *basis* 長期計画で. ¶Many of these factories are operating now on little more than a ***maintenance*** *basis*. これら工場は現在では作業が続けられればいいといった程度である. ¶turning out on a ***mass-production*** *basis* 大量生産で. ¶promotion on a ***merit*** *basis* 能率制による昇進. ¶It is sold on a ***money-back guarantee*** *basis* それは「品物ご不満の節は返金」の保証がいつている. ¶Only occasionally a student meets the members of the faculty on a ***non-classroom*** *basis*. 学生が打解けて教授たちと会合するのはほんのたまのことである. ¶restore it to a ***peacetime*** *basis* それを平和時の常態に復帰させる. ¶a student earning on a ***part-time*** *basis* ¥3,000 a month アルバイトで一月三千円かせぐ学生. ¶put it on a ***percentage*** *basis* それを百分率で示す. 【類】distribute on a ***percentage*** *basis* / employees working on a ***percentage*** *basis*. ¶be on a ***permission*** *basis* 許可制になっている. ¶The work is paid for on a ***piece-work*** *basis*. その仕事はでき高払いである. ¶allocate coal on a ***priority*** *basis* 石炭を重点主義で割当てる. ¶on a ***profit-sharing*** *basis* 利益配当ということで. ¶on a ***rental*** *basis* 損料で. ¶have a book published on a ***royalty*** *basis* 印税方式で本を出版させる ‖ be paid on a strictly ***royalty*** *basis* はっきり印税方式で支払われる. ¶employed on a ***salary*** *basis* 月給制で雇われている. ¶on ***self-sufficiency*** *basis*

自給自足の方式で. ¶on a ***self-supporting basis*** 自給自足主義で. ¶a magazine on a ***subscription basis*** 予約購読制の雑誌. ¶factories working on a ***two-shift basis*** 二部交替制で作業する諸工場. ¶Japanese economy is not yet on a ***world trade basis***. 日本経済はまだ世界貿易の水準に達していない. ¶on a ***50-50 basis*** 五分五分で(利益分配など).

P take it ***as*** a *basis* in compiling a book それを著作の台本にする ‖ ***as*** a *basis* to work upon 労作の根底として.【類】It is important ***as*** the *basis* of many other studies. ¶neglect what lies ***at*** the very *basis* of all learning あらゆる学問の根底となるものを軽視する.【類】Erotic affairs (恋愛事件) lie ***at*** the *basis* of social life. ¶He took it ***for*** the *basis* of his work. 彼はそれを研究材料に使った. ¶Wages are fixed ***on*** a *basis* of ten hours per day. 賃銀は一日十時間の割で決められている. ‖ ***on*** the *basis* on the terms submitted 提出の条件をもととして.【類】***on*** the *basis* of these figures (数字), it is evident that ... ‖ It does not rest ***on*** a scientific *basis*. それには科学上の根拠がない. ‖ the grading of milk ***on*** the *basis* of bacterial content 細菌含有量による牛乳の等級別 ‖ buying ***on*** the *basis* of quality 品質本位での買入 ‖ The official intercourse was to be ***on*** a *basis* of equality. 正式通商は均等の立場に立ってやることになっていた.【類】***on*** the *basis* of these facts, it may be inferred that ... / a general election ***on*** the *basis* of universal suffrage (普通選挙法) ‖ The inter- est is calculated ***on*** the *basis* of 360 days to the year. 利息は一年三百六十日の割で計算される. ‖ a bond ***on*** a yield *basis* of 4% 四分の利回りの債券 ‖ He was willing to contribute to the fund ***on*** the *basis* of his personal regard for the man. 彼はその人を個人として尊敬していたので喜んで基金に寄附した. ‖ social organization ***on*** the *basis* of property right, specially in lands 財産特に土地所有権に基く社会組織.【類】He was a great English scholar, and ***on*** that *basis* his ultimate fame must rest. ‖ mark examination papers ***on*** the *basis* of 100 百点満点で答案を採点する ‖ promotion ***on*** the *basis* of merit 成績による昇進 ‖ ***On*** what *basis* can we get a contract? どんな条件で請負契約ができますか. ¶bring down ***to*** a same *basis* 同一基準に下げる. ¶Essays shall be judged ***upon*** the *basis* of the following points. 論文は次の点を考慮の上考査する事になっている.

P² The subject supplies us with an admirable *basis* ***for*** discussion. その題目はわれわれが意見を交換する絶好の基点になる.【類】This will be a *basis* ***for*** further researches. / be the *basis* ***for*** employment for a large section of the population. ¶There is no *basis* ***in*** fact whatsoever. 全く事実無根だ. ¶the *basis* ***of*** a claim 請求の基礎 ‖ a *basis* ***of*** comparision 比較の基準.

bask, *v.* 日なたぼっこをする.

P *bask* ***in*** the sun 日なたぼっこをする ‖ *bask* ***in*** the heat 暖まる ‖ *bask* ***in*** the Imperial favor 聖恩に浴する ‖ *bask* a few moments ***in*** the smile of one's love しばし愛人の微笑に浴する.

basket, *n.* かご(バスケット).

V ***weave*** a *basket* of grass and rushes 草やいぐさでかごをつくる.

Q² an ***all-purpose*** *basket* 万能バスケット. ¶a ***baby*** *basket* 小型のかご. ¶The Middle West is America's "***bread*** *basket*" 中西部はアメリカの小麦の宝庫である. ¶a ***food*** *basket* 食料かご. ¶a ***market*** *basket* 市場買い出しかご. ¶a ***picnic*** [***lunch***] *basket* ピクニック用の弁当かご. ¶a ***shopping*** *basket* 買物かご. ¶a ***waste***[***-paper***] *basket* 紙くずかご.【類】***waste-paper*** *basket* of meshed wire (金あみ製の) / throw (=toss) it into a ***waste-paper*** *basket*. ¶***akebi vine*** and ***willow*** *baskets* (アケビのつるや柳で作った)かご.

P² a *basket* ***of*** fruits (food) 果物(など)一かご ‖ two *baskets* ***of*** lunch 弁当の入ったかご二つ.

basketful, *n.* バスケット一杯.

P² a *basketful* ***of*** apples (grapes) かご一杯のりんご(など).

bass, *n.* 低音;〖音〗バス.

Q It (=The voice) was ***deep, beautiful*** *bass*. その声は太い美しいバスだった.

P sing ***in*** *bass* バスで歌う.

bat, *n.*〖野球〗バット.

V ***cross*** *bats* with ... …と野球の試合をする. ¶those who once ***swung*** a *bat* 野球をやったことのある人々.

Q² You can buy anything there from baby pants to ***baseball*** (=***ball***) *bat*. 赤ん坊のパンツ(短いずぼん)から野球のバットに至るまで何でも買える.

P the side ***at*** *bat* [野球の]攻撃側 ‖ a player ***at*** *bat* バッターボックスに立った打者.

batch, *n.* 一回分の数量.

Q Here comes a ***fresh*** *batch* of visitors. また客が一組来た.

P² a *batch* ***of*** bread 一かま分のパン ‖ I have a *batch* ***of*** letters to answer. 返事未済の手紙が一たばある.

bath, *n.* 入浴, 水浴, 風呂(ふ); 浴槽.

V ***enjoy*** frequent *baths* しばしば入浴する ‖ ***enjoy*** a *bath* in the sea (=a sea bath) 海水浴をする. ¶***give*** a baby a *bath* 赤ん坊にお湯を使わせる. ¶***have*** a *bath* 入浴する.【類】***have*** a *bath* at home. ¶***heat*** the *bath* 風呂をたてる. ¶***prepare*** the *bath* バスの仕度をする, 風呂をわかす. ¶For want of something to do I thought I would ***take*** a *bath*. しょざいがないので湯にでも入ろうかと思った.【類】***take*** frequent *baths* / He ***takes*** two *baths* a day, night and morning. ‖ ***take*** a hasty *bath* からすの行水をやる. ¶He ***tried*** the *baths* there for an internal malady. 彼は内科の病気でそこの温泉で湯治をした. ¶***use*** the *bath* first まず入浴する.【類】***use*** *baths* several times daily.

Q take a ***cold*** (***hot***) *bath* 冷水浴(入浴)をする. ¶***electric*** *baths* 電気風呂. ¶the ***first*** charming *bath* 産湯. ¶a ***full*** *bath* 全身浴. ¶***local*** *baths* 局部浴. ¶a ***medicated*** bath 薬湯. ¶a ***perfumed*** *bath* 香水風呂. ¶a ***solar*** *bath* 日光浴. ¶a ***swimming*** *bath* pools [プールなどでの]水泳浴. ¶a ***tepid*** *bath* 微温浴. ¶a ***Turkish*** *bath* トルコ風呂. ¶a ***warm*** *bath* 温浴.

Q² an ***air*** *bath* 空気浴. ¶***brine*** *baths* 塩湯. ¶a ***brush*** *bath* 筆洗. ¶***douche*** *baths* 注水浴. ¶Fowls take great delight in a ***dust*** *bath*. にわとりは土にもぐるのが大好きだ. ¶an ***electric light*** *bath* 電光浴(陽光ランプの). ¶an ***open-air*** *bath* 野天風呂. ¶a ***milk*** (***salt-water***) *bath* 牛乳(塩水)ぶろ. ¶***mud*** *baths* 泥風呂. ¶***peat*** *baths* 泥炭風呂. ¶a ***plunging*** *bath* とび込み水浴. ¶a child's ***porcelain*** *bath* 小児用磁器浴器. ¶a ***radiation*** *bath* 放熱浴. ¶***sand*** *baths* 砂風呂. ¶***sea***[***-water***] *baths* 海水浴. ¶a ***shower*** *bath* 注水浴. ¶***spray*** *baths* 水沫浴. ¶take a ***sun*** *bath* a la nude 裸体で日光浴をする. ¶a ***thunderstorm*** *bath* 雷雨浴. ¶***vapor*** (=***steam***) *baths* 蒸風呂.

P a woman ***at*** her *bath* 入浴中の婦人. ¶go ***for*** a *bath* to the sea or a river 海または川へ浴びに行く. ¶I have derived groat benefit ***from*** the *baths* in the hot spring. 大分温泉がきいた. ¶when ***in*** his *bath* 入浴している時に.

P² A *bath* ***in*** the hot spring and bed finished the day. その日は温泉で一あびして寝てしまった. ¶a *bath* ***of*** water as cold as snow 雪の様に冷たい水浴.

bathe, *v.* 入浴させる; 入浴する.

M *bathe* ***promiscuously*** in all the abandon of perfect nudity まっぱだかで混浴する. ¶*bathe* ***together*** 混浴する.

P *bathed* ***in*** perspiration 汗びっしょりになって ‖ *bathe* ***in*** sweat (blood) 汗(など)にまみれる ‖ *bathe* ***in*** the surf 荒いそで浴びる ‖ *bathe* ***in*** nice warm water 丁度よい湯加減の風呂にはいる ‖ Let us go and *bathe* ***in*** the river. 川へ水浴びに行こう. ¶*bathe* a horse ***with*** water 馬を水で洗ってやる ‖ *bathed* ***with*** blood 血を浴びて.

bather, *n.* 水浴する人.

Q² a ***sun*** *bather* 日光浴をする人.

bathing, *n.* 入浴.

V It ***affords*** good sea *bathing*. そこは海水浴によい.【類】Owing to its fine stretch of clean, firm sand, it ***affords*** safe *bathing*. ¶I ***enjoy*** *bathing*. 水浴びは好きだ.

Q ***cold*** *bathing* in a river 川での水浴び. ¶***promiscuous*** *bathing* of the sexes 男女混浴. ¶***warm*** *bathing* 温浴.

Q² ***air*** (***sun***) *bathing* 空気(日光)浴. ¶***shore*** (=***sea***) *bathing* 海水浴. ¶***spa*** *bathing* 鉱泉浴. ¶***surf*** and ***still-water*** *bathing* 波のある海や波の静かな海の海水浴.

P² *bathing* ***in*** the sea=sea bathing. ¶a *bathing* ***with*** warm water 温浴.

bathrobe, *n.* 浴衣(バスローブ).

P ***in*** my *bathrobe* and straw slippers 浴衣とわらぞうりをはいて.

baton, *n.* 指揮棒.

V ***wield*** a good *baton* 巧妙に合奏を指揮する.

P a splendid orchestra of eighty performers ***under*** the *baton* of ... …氏指揮下の八十人から成るりっぱな管弦楽団.

batter, *n.*〖野球〗打者.

Q a ***heavy*** (=***powerful***) *batter* 強打者. ¶a ***leading*** *batter* 一流打者.

batter, *v.* 連打する; 使いへらす.

M an old hat ***well battered*** いゝ加減損じた古帽子.

M^{2} *batter **down*** the doors ドアをたたきつぶす.

P The boat was *battered **against*** the rocks by heavy surf. ボートは大浪のために岩に打ちつけられた. ¶*batter **at*** the door for admittance 案内をこうて戸をたゝく. ¶*batter* one's face ***into*** a mummy 顔をめちゃめちゃに打つ. ¶*batter* the door ***with*** stones 石を戸に投げる.

battery, *n.* 砲台.

V ***build*** (=***construct, erect, establish*** *or* ***form***) a *battery* 砲台を築く. ¶***change*** one's *battery* 攻撃の方向を変える. ¶***mount*** a *battery* 砲台を装備する. ¶***silence*** a *battery* 砲台を沈黙させる.

Q an ***obsolete*** *battery* 旧式砲台.

Q^{2} ***shore*** *batteries* 海岸砲台.

battle, *n.* 戦, 戦闘.

V ***accept*** *battle* 応戦する. ¶***deliver*** *battle* 攻撃する. ¶***do*** *battle* with the world 世界を相手に戦う. ¶The *battle* was ***fought*** early in the morning. その戦は早朝のことであった. ‖The veterans ***fought*** their *battles* over again in their talks. 老兵たちは戦争の手柄話をした. ‖She ***fought*** the *battle* of a husbandless life bravely. 彼女は未亡人の辛い生活とりっぱに戦った. ¶***gain*** a *battle* 勝利を得る. ¶He ***gave*** *battle* to the Russian fleet. 彼はロシアの艦隊と戦った. 【類】go forth and ***give*** *battle*. ¶***join*** *battle* with ... ...と戦う. ¶His troops ***lost*** the *battle*. 彼の兵は敗戦した. 【類】***lose*** *battle* after battle. ¶sally forth and ***offer*** *battle* 進み出て戦をいどむ. ¶***provoke*** a *battle* 戦をいどむ. ¶it was ... that ultimately ***turned*** the *battle* in favor of ... それは結局その戦闘を...に有利に転回させた原動力であった. ¶***venture*** a *battle* 開戦の挙に出る. ¶***wage*** a *battle* of words 論戦をする. ¶***win*** a *battle* 戦いに勝つ.

Q the ***age-old*** *battle* against cancer 多年にわたるがんとの闘病. ¶bring on an ***all-out*** *battle* over the issue その問題で全面的な戦闘となる. ¶a ***bloody*** *battle* 血戦. ¶No one will attempt to deny that the naval victory in the Sea of Japan was one of the ***decisive*** *battles* of the world. 日本海の海軍大勝利は世界の大決戦だったことを否定しようとする者はなかろう. ¶a ***drawn*** *battle* 勝負なしの戦. ¶fight a ***fair*** *battle* 正々堂々と戦う. ¶A ***fierce*** *battle* is raging between the two peoples. その二国民は猛烈な戦争中である. ¶a ***glorious*** *battle* はなばなしい戦. ¶A ***great*** *battle* has taken place. 大激戦が起った. ¶That is ***half*** the *battle*. そうなればもう占めた(こっちの)ものだ. ¶a ***hand-to-hand naval*** *battle* 舷々相摩する戦. ¶fight a ***hard*** *battle* 苦戦する. 【類】a 24-hour ***hard*** *battle*. ¶a ***hard-fought*** *battle* 悪戦苦闘. ¶an ***indecisive*** *battle* 勝敗のはっきりしない戦. ¶have long been a ***losing*** *battle* 永いこと負け戦を続けて来た. ¶a ***lost*** *battle* 負け戦. ¶a ***maiden*** *battle* 初陣. ¶a ***mimic*** *battle* 模擬戦. ¶a ***mock*** *battle* 擬戦. ¶a ***modern*** *battle* 近代戦. ¶a ***murderous*** *battle* 血戦. ¶a ***naval*** *battle* 海戦. ¶a ***pitched*** (=***regular***) *battle* 予め計画した対戦. ¶a ***stubborn*** *battle* がん強な戦. ¶No school truly performs its duty that does not fit all its pupils for a ***successful*** *battle* against life's temptations. 人生の誘惑に打勝つように生徒を教育しない学校は真にその任務を果しているとは言えない. ¶He fought some ***valiant*** *battles* in behalf of civic improvement and advancement. 彼は市政の改善進歩のために勇敢に戦った. ‖a ***valiant*** *battle* with the slum 細民救済の勇ましい活動.

Q^{2} an ***air*** *battle* 空中戦. ¶a ***cops-and-robbers gun*** *battles* 警官と盗賊の射撃戦. ¶a ***kite*** *battle* たこ揚げ合戦. ¶a big ***land*** *battle* 大規模の陸戦. ¶a ***land*** and ***sea*** *battle* 陸海戦. ¶fight a ***life-and-death*** *battle* 食うか食われるかの死闘をやる. ¶a ***street*** *battle* 市街戦. ¶a ***word*** *battle* 舌戦.

P He gained a brilliant victory over the ... ***at*** the *battle*. その戦役で...軍に対して赫々たる勝利を得た. ¶Have you ever been ***in*** a *battle*? 実戦の経験がありますか. 【類】distinguish oneself ***in*** a *battle* / He was killed ***in*** *battle*. / He fell (=died) ***in*** *battle* at the siege of Port Arthur (旅順). / There are a great many casualties ***in*** a *battle*. ¶go ***into*** *battle* 戦を開始する. ¶The general led the army ***to*** *battle*. 将軍は軍を率いて戦におもむいた.

P^{2} a *battle **against*** time 時間との競争(大急ぎでやる仕事). ‖he fell in *battle **against*** ... ...との戦で倒れた. ¶a *battle **between*** land and sea 陸海間の戦. 【類】a *battle **between*** armies. ¶a *battle **for*** the possession of a territory 領土獲得のための戦. 【類】fight a good *battle **for*** ... ‖a *battle **for*** life 命がけの戦 ‖a *battle **for*** living 生活戦. ¶a *battle **of*** water against fire 消防戦 ‖a *battle **of*** blades 真剣勝負 ‖a *battle **of*** revenge 葬い合戦. ¶a *battle **to*** the death 決死の戦. ¶do *battle **with*** ignorance 無知と(啓蒙のために)戦う.

battle, *v.* 戦う.

P *battle **against*** invaders 外敵と戦う ‖ *battle **against*** heavy odds 寡を以て衆と戦う. 【類】*battle* fearlessly ***against*** the current opinion of the day. ¶*battle **for*** the free expression of new ideas 新思想の自由表現のために奮闘する ‖In her love and womanly pride were *battling* ***for*** mastery. 彼女の心の中で愛と女性の誇とが互に優位を争っていた. ¶*battle **with*** an enemy 敵と戦う. 【類】*battle **with*** poverty and rise triumphantly in life.

battle-cry, *n.* ときの声, 喊声(かんせい).

V ***raise*** the *battle-cry* ときの声をあげる. ¶***shout*** the *battle-cry* of freedom 自由のときの声をあげる.

battlefield, *n.* 戦場.

Q the ***old*** *battlefields* of the Somme ソムの古戦場.

P The nations have never stood against one another ***in*** the *battlefield*. これら国民はかつて干戈(かんか)を交えたことがなかった. ¶die ***on*** the *battlefield* 戦死する. 【類】He was slain ***on*** the *battlefield* (=in battle). ¶bivouac ***upon*** the *battlefield* 戦場の露営.

battlefront, *n.* 戦地.

P ***on*** a *battlefront* 戦地で.

battleground, *n.* 戦場.

V The subject ***furnished*** a *battleground* for much controversy and inconclusive speculation in the past. その題目は過去において幾多の論争と未解決の考察とを引起した.

Q the ***chief*** *battleground* of theological controversy 神学上の議論を戦わす主なる論点. ¶a ***famous*** *battleground* 有名な戦場.

bawl, *v.* 叫ぶ.

M^{2} *bawl **about*** 呼び回る. ¶*bawl **out*** どなる.

P *bawl **at*** ... ...を大声でどなる. ¶*bawl **for*** any thing one wants 自分の欲しいものを大声で求める.

bay, *n.* 湾.

V Here an indentation in the coast ***forms*** a beautiful *bay*. 海岸が入込んでここに美しい湾ができている. ¶Riverborne deposits ***silt up*** *bays*. 川の運んだ沈でん物で湾が埋まる.

Q coastline with ***deep*** *bays* and good harbors 深い湾と良い港のある海岸線. ¶a ***land-locked*** *bay* 陸地に深く入込んだ湾. ¶a ***sail-flecked*** *bay* 白帆の点在する湾.

P The ship anchored ***inside*** the *bay*. 船は湾内に停泊した. ¶a city ***on*** a *bay* 湾頭の一都市 ‖yachting (boating) ***on*** the *bay* その湾内でのヨット(など)遊び.

bay, *n.* 窮地.

P hold a person ***at*** *bay* 窮地に陥れる ‖In his case age kept ***at*** *bay*. 彼は年を取らなかった(若く見えた). ‖The stag was ***at*** *bay*. 雄じかは追詰められた. ‖stand ***at*** *bay* 追詰められる. 【類】have a fox ***at*** *bay*. ¶drive it ***to*** *bay* それを追詰める ‖turn ... ***to*** *bay* ...を絶体絶命の境地に陥れる.

bay, *n.* ほえ声.

Q hear the ***distant*** *bay* of the hounds 猟犬の遠ぼえが聞える.

bay, *v.* ほえる.

P *bay **at*** a person 人にほえつく. 【類】A dog was *baying* ***at*** the moon.

bayonet, *n.* 銃剣.

V ***fix*** (***unfix***) *bayonets* 銃剣を付ける(はずす).

P They fell ***beneath*** (=***under***) the Japanese *bayonets*. 彼らは日本軍の銃剣に倒れた. ¶govern ***by*** the *bayonet* 武断政治を行う. ¶***with*** fixed *bayonets* 銃剣つきで. ¶charge ***with*** *bayonets* 銃剣で突撃する.

bazaar, 《米》 **bazar,** *n.* バザー, 慈善市; 勧工場.

V ***hold*** a *bazaar* in aid of the society その会を後援するバザーを開く.

Q an ***industrial*** *bazaar* 勧工場.

Q^{2} a ***charity*** *bazaar* 慈善市. ¶an ***infant welfare*** *bazaar* 小児厚生募金バザー. ¶a ***U.S. used clothing*** *bazar* アメリカ輸入古着市.

P her stall ***at*** the *bazaar* バザーの彼女の売店.

be, *v.* [am, are, is, etc. の原形].

M He *is* himself ***again***. [病気が直って]元の身体になる. ¶I *was* then ***away*** in Germany. 当時私はドイツにおった. ‖He has ***been away***, has he not? 彼は留守だったんだろう. ¶He will ***be back*** home in a couple of weeks. 氏は二三週間で

帰宅(国)するでしょう. ‖ He *was back* again for the umbrella he had left. 忘れもののかさを とりに戻られた. ‖ Stay here. I'll *be back* with you in a few minutes. ここで待ってくれ. 二三分したら戻ってくるから. ¶ We shall not *be badly off*. われわれがまずく行くようなことはなかろう. ¶ People in general *are* slightly *better off* than they were a year ago. 人々は一年前よりはいくらか暮しが楽だ. ¶ His family *is comfortably off*. 彼の家族は安楽に暮している. ¶ You ought to *be fairly up* in it as you have studied it for ten years. 十年も勉強したんだから当然相当できるはずだ. ¶ The ideal may yet *be far off*. 理想にはまだ遠い. ¶ I'*m* full *up* with work till late to night. 今晩は遅くまで仕事で一杯だ. ¶ Things *are* very *hard* upon us. 世の中の風は荒い. ¶ He *is* very *hard up*. 非常に困っている. ¶ *Here* I *am!* さあ着いた(ただ今). ‖ *Here* it *is* (*or Here* they *are*). はいここにおきますよ; はいあげるよ. ‖ *Here* we *are* home! さあうちに着いた(ただ今). ‖ *Here's* your money. = *Here's* money for you. そらお金をあげる. ‖ *Here* you *are!* = *Here* it *is* (*or* they *are*)! そらあげるよ. ¶ I have *never* (*once, twice*) *been* there. 一度もそこに行ったことはない(一度,二度行ったことがある). ¶ *Officially* it has *been* spring for several weeks. 暦の上では春になって数週間たっている. ¶ were it *otherwise* もしそうでなかったら. ¶ School *is out*. 学校は終りだ. ‖ before the year *is out* 年が明けない中に. 【類】 before the week *was out* ‖ *be out* late at the club 遅くまでクラブに出かけている ‖ *be out* for peace at any price どんな犠牲を払っても 平和を唱える ‖ My luck *is out* today. きょうは運が悪い. ‖ All lights have to *be out* by eleven. 十一時までには全部消灯しなければならぬ. ¶ this *being so* そういう訳で. ¶ All *is well* with the government. 天下泰平.

M² I didn't like to say anything while your man *was about*; but the fact is ... あの彼氏がいる間は何事も言いたくなかったんだが実際のところ...である. ¶ He *is down* there for a speech. 彼は一席ぶちに出かけている. ¶ The manager will soon *be down* here to meet you. 支配人はすぐ参ります. ‖ He *is down* with flu. 流感でふせっている. ‖ He *was* rather *down* (=depressed) to hear it. それを聞いて少しがっかりしていた. ‖ I'll *be* right *down*. じきに降りて行くよ(二階から). ‖ It *is* not *down* in the Club Directory in New York. それはニューヨークのクラブ名簿に出ていない. ¶ They were about to *be down* on (=upon) him. 彼らはまさに彼に食ってかかろうとした. ‖ They *were down* on their luck. 彼らは苦境に立っていた. ¶ The train *was in* right on time. 列車は時間通り入って来た. ‖ I *am* fairly *in* for it (=launched into it) now. せっかく乗出した船だ(比喩的). ¶ Let's *be off*. さあ出かけよう. ‖ Where *are* you *off* to? どちらへお出かけです. ¶ One of my coat buttons *is off*. 上衣のボタンが一つとれている. ‖ He *is off* on a five days vacation trip. 彼は五日間の休暇旅行中です. ¶ The saddle *is on*. [馬に]くらがおいてある. ‖ The light *is on*. 電灯がついている. 【類】 The large chandeliers of glistening crystals make the room beautiful when the lights *are on*. ‖ That trend has *been on*. その傾向は続いている. ‖ The Hamlet *is on*. ハムレットがかかっている. 【類】 while the war *was on* / The *battle is on* in earnest. ¶ The war *is* officially *over*. 戦争は正式に終戦となった. ¶ The mailman hasn't *been round* yet. 郵便屋はまだ回って来ない. ¶ I'm *through* with her. 彼女とは手を切った. ‖ I'll *be through* with this in a few minutes. もうじきこれはおしまいだ. ¶ The moon will *be up* soon. 月がじきに上る. ‖ Milk *is up* 32 per cent. 牛乳の値段が三十二パーセント上っている. ¶ He has *been up* all night. 彼は一晩中起きていた. ‖ The hour *is up*. 時間が切れた. 【類】 before the afternoon *was up* / Time *is* nearly *up*. ‖ what I'*m up* against 私が直面しているもの ‖ The whole country *was up* against the enemy. 全国民は立上って敵にぶっつかった. ‖ The issue of ... *was up* for solution. ...の問題は解決を待っていた. ‖ The plan *is up* for our consideration. その計画はわれわれの考慮すべきものである. 【類】 The measure *is* not *up* for formal consideration. / the case *was up* for the final decision in the Supreme Court. / The issue *is* now *up* for debate before the assembly. / The whole issue of labor-management relations (労使関係) *is up* for reexamination. ‖ The bird *is up* in the tree. その鳥は木の上にいる. ‖ What have you *been up* to? [今まで]何をしていたんだい. ‖ it *is up* to us to ... ...するのはわれわれの責任である. 【類】 It's *up* to you, boys. / The problem *is up* to the Japanese themselves. / I never once suspected what he *was up* to. ‖ if you would *be up* to the minute with the latest news of the world 君が今までの世界の最近ニュースに精通したいならば ‖ It's all *up* (=*over*) with us. 万事休すだ.

P That's *against* [the] law (etiquette). それは法(エチケット)に反する. ‖ The arbitration *is against* us (in our favor). 仲裁はわれわれに不利(有利)だ. ¶ *be among* those ... ...に属する. ¶ He *is at* it again. またやっている. ‖ He doesn't know where he *is at*? 《米俗》 彼は自分の立場をご存じない. ‖ Some one must *be at* the back of this. この後ろ(黒幕)はだれかおるに違いない. ¶ if it had not *been for* him もし彼がいなかったら ‖ decide whether one *is for* or *against* another 向背を決する. ¶ Pansies *are of* many colors. パンジイ(三色すみれ)には色々変った色がある. ¶ The scars *are* still *on* me. 傷あとがまだ残っている. ‖ There is nothing like *being on* your guard. 要心にしくはなし. ‖ He *is on* trial for murder. 彼は殺人容疑で公判中. ¶ He has *been to* high school. 彼は高校をやった. ¶ Westerners who have *been to* the Orient 東洋を訪れた西欧人. 【類】 He had not *been to* school enough to know how to spell some very common words. ¶ The wet (dry) season *is* now *upon* us. もうじき雨(乾)季になる. ‖ Xmas *is* just *upon* us. クリスマスはもうすぐだ. ¶ I *am with* those who hope that ... ...という希望をもっている人々とは私は同じ意見だ. ‖ The tide *was with* us. 情勢はわれわれに有利であった. ‖ I wish I might *be with* you. 一しょに行ってたらよかった. ‖ I'*m with* you on that. その点では君に賛成だ. ¶ I can *be without* it. それなしでもやれる.

beach, *n.* いそ, 浜.

V The waters of the Pacific *wash* the *beach*. 太平洋の波が海岸を洗っている.

Q on a *rock-strewn beach* on the Cornish coast コーンウォールの海岸の岩石多い浜辺に. ¶ a *sandy beach* 砂浜. ¶ a *shingly beach* 砂利の多い浜.

Q² a fine *bathing beach* 好い海水浴場. ¶ a *pleasure beach* in Hawaii ハワイの海水浴場(ワイキキなど). ¶ a *sea beach* 海浜.

P walk *along* the *beach* 浜伝いに散歩する. ¶ He was drowned while swimming *at* the *beach*. 浜辺で水泳中でき死した. ¶ take a walk *in* (=*on*) the *beach* 浜辺を散歩する. ¶ a day *on* the *beach* 海岸の一日 ‖ a cottage *on* the *beach* 海辺の家. ¶ the rippling of the sea *upon* the *beach* 浜辺に寄せるさざ波.

beach, *v.* 浜に引きあげる.

P a small vessel *beached at* ... ...の海辺に引きあげられた「小船.

beacon, *n.* 警標.

Q² a *radio beacon* 〚通信〛 ラジオ・ビーコン(無電標式).

P it acted *as* a *beacon* to ... それが...にとって警標の用をなした. ¶ His error was a *beacon to* others. 彼の過失は他の人たちの戒めとなった.

bead, *n.* じゅず玉; ビーズ.

V *count* (=*bid or number*) *beads* じゅずをつまぐる. ¶ *draw* a *bead* to (=take aim at)... ...にねらいをつける. ¶ *recite* (=*say or tell*) the *beads* 念仏(祈りの言葉)を唱える.

Q² *negligee beads* 首飾りなどに用いるさんご形の珠.

P² Great *beads of* sweat (=perspiration) stood on his forehead. 彼の額は玉なす汗であった. 【類】 *beads of* dew.

beam, *n.* (**1**) [船の]真横; はかりざお.

P *abaft* the *beam* 真横後に.

P² The *beam of* the balance tipped to this side. 天びんのさおがこちらへ傾いた.

(**2**) 電波.

V *fly* the *beam* 〚航空〛 信号電波に乗って飛ぶ.

Q² shift the *radio beam* from ... to ... ラジオのダイヤルを...から...に変える.

P ¶ *on* the *beam* 電波に乗って; [比喩的] 軌道に乗って ‖ a man *on* the *beam* 時の人.

P² a *beam from* a distant lighthouse 遠くの灯台からの光線 ‖ a *beam of* moonlight 月の光 ‖ a *beam of* hope 希望の光り. 【類】 the *beam of* youth.

beam, *v.* 輝く; にっこりする.

M The sun *beamed* (=shone) *brightly*. 太陽がきらきら輝いた.

M² From a sky of untarnished blue the sun *beamed down* upon London and surrounding areas. こんぺきの空から太陽はロンドン市内外に明るい光を投げていた.

P *beam at* a person 人を見て笑顔をつくる. ¶ *beam upon*

(=*on*) a person 人に微笑を送る. ¶with a countenance *beaming with* intellect 理知の光を満面にたたえて. 【類】 his face *beaming with* compassion (同情) / *beam with* satisfaction ‖ Her face *beamed with* joy. 彼女の顔は喜色にあふれた. 【類】 Her blue eyes *beamed with* the wild joy of living.

bean, *n.* 隠元豆.

V *parch* some *beans* 豆をいる.

Q *broad beans* そら豆. ¶*kidney beans* いんげん豆. ¶*snap beans*=string beans さやえんどう.

bear, *n.* くま.

V *impersonate* a *bear* くまに扮する.

Q a *polar bear* 北極ぐま(白くま). ¶a *regular bear* くまみたいな男. ¶a *wee little bear* かわいい小ぐま.

Q² ¶a *father* (*mother*) *bear* 父(母)ぐま. ¶the baby's toy *Teddy bear* 赤ん坊のおもちゃの小ぐま.

bear, *v.* (**1**) 運ぶ; になう.

M *bear away* the prize 賞品を獲得する ‖ *borne away* by an impulse 一時の衝動に駆られて. ¶sing the old world words that *bear* us *back* to the days of … …の当時をしのばしめる古い歌詞を歌う. ¶a responsibility *too heavy* for a person to *bear* にない切れない重い責任.

M² *bear off* the palm 栄冠を獲得する.

P a bridge which *bore* us *across* the crevasse われわれに氷河の裂目を越させてくれた橋. ¶the part *borne by* the Dutch in the discovery of Australia 豪州発見におけるオランダ人らの役割. ¶*bear* a thing *on* one's shoulder 物を肩にかつぐ. ¶a hansom *bore* us swiftly *to*… 二輪馬車がわれわれを乗せて迅速に…に向った ‖ He was *borne to* prison. 刑務所に送られた.

(**2**) 帯びる, 付ける.

P *bear* a revolver *at* one's side 拳銃(ピストル)を帯びる. ¶*bear* a sword *by* one's side 剣を帯びる. ¶*bear* a badge *on* a coat lapel 上衣のえりにバッジを付ける.

(**3**) 忍ぶ, 耐える.

M I cannot *bear* it *any longer*. もう耐えられない. ¶*bear* … *bravely*, and with courage 勇敢に…を忍ぶ. ¶*heroically bear* 勇敢に忍ぶ. ¶*bear manfully* 男らしく堪える. ¶*bear* this *out* これを堪え抜く. ¶*patiently bear* burdens 重荷をじっと堪える. 【類】 *bear* one's disappointment *patiently*. ¶*bear philosophically* 冷静に我慢する. ¶*bear stoically* 泰然と忍ぶ.

M² *Bear up, bear up*! しっかりしっかり. ‖ It is particularly difficult to *bear up* against the midsummer heat. 真夏の暑さはまた格別だ. ‖ He *bore up* bravely the affliction (grief). 彼は苦難(など)を受けたがよく堪え忍んだ. ‖ *bear up* against misfortune (trouble) 不幸(など)に負けない ‖ How could I *bear up* and live in this destitution? どうしてこの困窮が切抜けられよう.

P *bear with* patience よく我慢する ‖ It will be better for you to *bear with* him up to a certain extent. ある程度まで彼のやり口を我慢するのが君のためだ.

(**4**) 処する, 振舞う.

M She *bears* herself *gracefully*. 彼女は立居振舞がしとやかだ. ¶He *bore* himself *nobly*. あっぱれな振舞をした.

P *bear* oneself *like* a gentleman 紳士のように振舞う.

(**5**) 果実を結ぶ; 子を産む; 産する.

M be *untimely born* 早産する. ¶The peach trees are not going to *bear well* this year. 今年は桃のなり年ではないらしい.

P the heroes *borne by* ancient Greece 古代ギリシアの産んだ英雄. 【類】 He was *borne by* an English woman. ☞ bear (生む)が by という前置詞を伴う時に限り borne となる. ¶a child *born from* healthy parents 健康な両親から生れた子. ¶What year was he *born in*? 彼は何年生れですか. ‖ The idea was *born in* the minds of three enterprising Japanese. その考は三人の企業心に富んだ日本人の頭から出た. ‖ an art *born in* the man, not acquired 習い覚えたものでなくその人に生れつきの芸能. ¶No man is *born into* this world whose work is not born with him —James Russel Lowell. 人がこの世に生れたのは何かの仕事を持って来ているのだ. ¶Aphrodite, the Greek goddess of love, is fabled to have been *born of* the foam of the sea. ギリシアの恋愛の女神アフロディテは海のあわから生れたという伝説がある. 【類】 Christ is regarded by all orthodox Christians as divinely *born of* Mary. / He was *born of* fairly well-to-do parents. かなり裕福な家に生れた. / He was *born of* this second marriage. / being *born of* a concubine (妾腹の出) / He was *born of* German parents. / He was *born of* humble parentage. / He was *born* of poor fisherfolk in Holland. / He was *born of* a samurai (wealthy, noble) family. / Their friendship had been *born of* curious accident (不思議な縁). ‖ He speaks with the conviction *born of* experience. 彼は経験から得た確信をもって話した. ‖ confidence *born of* first-hand knowledge 直接その事を知っているという事情から来た確信. 【類】 with a calm confidence *born of* superior knowledge ‖ Love is *born of* heart, not mind.—Browning. 恋愛は思考から出ず感情から発する. 【類】 It was *born of* Edison's brain (=invented by Edison) in 1877. ‖ *born out of* wedlock 庶子として. ¶a man *to* whom she *bore* three children その間に三人の子供ができた男. 【類】 Mark Twain was *born to* Samuel Langhorne Clemens, in Florida, Mo., November 30, 1835. / Two children were *born to* them. ‖ She was *born to* the purple; diamonds suited her. 高貴の家に生れたのでダイヤが彼女に似合った. ‖ Though *born to* some other language, they speak English. 生れは外国だが彼らは英語が話せる. ¶It is *born with* a man. それは人に生れつくのだ(先天的のものだ). ‖ be *born with* a good memory 生れつき記憶がよい.

O. His parents are foreign *born*. 彼の両親は外国生れだ.

(**6**) いだく, 心に持つ.

P *bear* a grudge *against* … …に恨みを抱く ‖ it is good to *bear in* mind that … …と心得えて置くとよい. 【類】 This fact can't be too strongly *borne in* mind. / it has to be *borne in* mind, however, that … / another point to be *borne in* mind is … / I will endeavor to *bear* your criticism *in* mind. ‖ It was *borne in* upon me that … 私は…と確信するに至った. ‖ A sense (=feeling) of … is *borne in* upon him. 彼は…と思い込んでいる. ‖ I could never bring my recollection to *bear upon* those days. 当時の記憶はどうしても浮んで来なかった.

(**7**) 関係を有する.

M Education should *bear directly* upon life. 教育は人生に即して施さるべきだ.

P The argument does not *bear on* the subject. この議論はその問題に関係はない. ‖ It *bears* directly *on* our topic. それは直接にわれわれの話題に関する. 【類】 all the facts *bearing on* the case / works *bearing on* religion ‖ *bear on* the caption (手紙など)首題に関係している. ¶the proportion with … *bears to* … …が…に対する割合. ¶The prosperity of Europe *bears upon* that of America. 欧州の繁栄はアメリカの繁栄に関係がある.

(**8**) 支持する; 確める.

M The famine *bore heavily* on the settlers. 飢饉は痛く植民を苦しめた. ¶*bear out* (=*confirm*) an evidence 証拠を確認する. 【類】 *bear out* one's statement / *bear out* a theory ‖ *bear out* a matter by fact (proof) 事実(など)によってある事を確める. 【類】 The assertion is not *borne out* by the facts. ‖ He will *bear* me *out* in what I advance. 彼は私の意見の肩を持ってくれるだろう. ‖ This view, plausible as it may appear, is not *borne out* by facts. この見解はまことしやかだが事実が証明していない.

P *bear* witness *to* one's innocence 人の無罪を証言する.

(**9**) 推す, 圧する.

M A policeman *bore back* the crowd. 一警官が群衆を制した. ¶The weight of taxation *bears hard* on the poor. 重い税金が貧民を圧迫する.

M² He *bears down* on the scales at 376 pounds. 彼は三百七十六ポンドの体重がある. ‖ He *bore down* everything before him. 彼の向う所敵なしだった. ‖ *bear down* all opposition あらゆる反対を圧服する ‖ *bear down* on … like a hawk on a chicken たかがひな鳥に襲いかかるように…を急迫する. 【類】 *bear down* upon the enemy ‖ The branches were *borne down* with the weight of the fruit. 枝は果実の重みでたわんでいた. ¶*bear upon* the center of the enemy's line 敵の中心部を突く.

beard, *n.* あごひげ.

V *grow* (=*cultivate or wear*) a *beard* ひげをはやす. ¶a man *having* a *beard* ひげのある人. ¶a *beard left* on the chin あごさきに残してあるひげ. ¶*pluck out* one's *beard* ひげをむしりとる. ¶*shave* [*off*] the *beard* ひげをそる. ¶*stroke* one's *beard* ひげをしごく. ¶*trim* the *beard* ひげの手入れをする. ¶He *wears* a heavy *beard* and mustache. 彼はあごひげも口ひげも多い.

V[2] A *beard* is one that ***grows*** on the chin. ビアドはあごさきにはえるひげをいう. ¶His *beard* hadn't ***had*** the barber's care for weeks. 彼は何週間もひげの手入れを怠っていた.

Q a ***blond beard*** 金色のひげ. ¶with ***chestnut brown beard*** 赤ひげをはやした. ¶a ***dark beard*** 黒ひげ. ¶a ***dense beard*** 濃いひげ. ¶a ***false beard*** 付けひげ. ¶a ***full beard*** 房々としたひげ. ¶He has a ***gray beard***. 彼のひげは白い. ¶a ***harsh beard*** あらいひげ. ¶a long ***gray beard*** 長い白いあごひげ. ¶a ***long iron-gray beard*** 長い鉄かっ色のひげ. ¶a ***matted beard*** むしゃくしゃなひげ. ¶a ***scanty beard*** ちょんぼりひげ. ¶He has a ***shaggy beard***. 彼のひげはむしゃくしゃしている. ¶a ***sparse beard*** 薄いひげ. ¶his ***straggling gray beard*** 彼のまばらな白ひげ. ¶a ***stubborn beard*** こわいひげ. ¶a ***thick*** and ***short beard*** 濃くて短いひげ.

Q[2] a ***snappy Vandyke beard*** and mustache ぴんと先のはねたバンダイク型のあごひげと口ひげ.

P take one ***by*** the *beard* ひげをつかまえる. ¶a man ***with*** a venerable white *beard* りっぱな白ひげをはやした人.

bearded, *pa.* ひげのある.

M a ***heavily bearded*** man ひげ男 ‖ He was ***heavily bearded***, apparently unshaved for weeks. 彼は何週間もそらないらしくもじゃもじゃひげを生やしていた.

bearer, *n.* 所有者, 持参人; かごかき; 果実を結ぶ樹.

V this ticket ***admits*** *bearer* to ... この切符を持って行くと...に入場ができる. ¶***exchange*** the *bearers* of the palanquin かごかきを取替える.

Q This persimmon-tree is a ***good*** *bearer*. この柿はよくなる.

Q[2] a ***fur*** *bearer* 毛深い動物. ¶the ***standard*** *bearer* of ... ...の旗頭. ¶a ***stretcher*** *bearer* たんか運搬夫.

P The cheque is payable ***to*** *bearer*. この小切手は持参人払いだ.

P[2] the *bearers* ***of*** these names こういう名の人々.

bearing, *n.* **(1)** 態度, 風姿.

V ***preserve*** a gentlemanly *bearing* 紳士的態度を持する.

Q His *bearing* was ***admirable***. 彼の態度はあっぱれなものだった. ¶***decorous*** *bearing* 端正な態度. ¶***gentlemanly*** *bearing* 紳士的態度. ¶a man of ***good*** *bearing* 風采のよい人. ¶He preserved his ***grave*** and ***dignified*** *bearing*. 彼はその重々しい貫録のある態度を失わなかった. ¶He has a ***haughty*** *bearing*. 彼の態度は横柄だ. ¶her ***kindly*** *bearing* 彼女のやさしい物腰. ¶a man of ***military*** *bearing* 軍人風の人. ¶a man of ***noble, dignified*** *bearing*. りっぱな威厳のある態度の人. ¶***polite*** *bearing* ていねいな物腰. ¶***slovenly*** *bearing* だらしのない態度. ¶***soldierly*** *bearing* 軍人らしい態度.

P a man agreeable ***in*** *bearing* 態度の気持のよい人. ¶He is possessed of dignity ***of*** *bearing*. 彼の態度には威厳がある. ¶China's *bearing* ***toward*** Japan and Russia 日露に対する中国の態度.

(2) 関係.

V It ***has*** some *bearing* on this subject. それはこの題目に幾分関係がある. 【類】They ***have*** no *bearing* upon real life.

Q ***collateral*** *bearing* 側面関係. ¶It has ***direct*** *bearing* upon the subject. それはその問題に直接関係がある. ¶its ***economic*** *bearing* その経済的関係. ¶consider the problem in its ***financial*** *bearings* その問題の財政的関係を考察する. ¶It has an ***important*** *bearing* on the relations of Japan to the United States. それは日米間の諸問題に重要な関係を持っている. 【類】has necessarily very ***important bearing*** upon the case ‖ in its ***important*** *bearings* その重要な方面において. ¶The motion picture has an ***intimate*** *bearing* on education. 映画は教育に密接な関係を持っている. ¶subjects on a school curriculum that have ***little*** bearing on life ほとんど世の中と無関係な学科目. 【類】These details have ***little*** *bearing* upon the main issue. ¶the ***political*** *bearings* of the subject その題目の政治的関係. ¶It has a ***remote*** *bearing* on this. それはこの事に薄いけれど縁がある. ¶has a ***vital*** (***weighty***) *bearing* on ... ...とはきわめて重大な(大いに)関係がある.

P consider it ***in*** all its *bearings* 各方面の関係から考察する. 【類】discuss the question ***in*** all its *bearings*.

P[2] the *bearing* ***of*** logic on education in general 論理学の教育全般との関係. ¶What is the *bearing* ***of*** this on the argument? これはその議論にどんな関係があるか. ¶evolution and its *bearing* ***on*** religion 進化とその宗教に対する関係. ¶details having little *bearing* ***upon*** the main issue 根本問題に余り関係のないこまかい点.

(3) 方角, 位置.

V ***find*** one's *bearings* in a new place 初めての場所で自分の居所の見通しをつける. 【類】With the aid of a good map the traveler can ***find*** his *bearings*. ¶The climbers ***lost*** their *bearings*. 登山家たちは方角がわからなくなった. ¶***mistake*** one's *bearings* 見当ちがいをやる. ¶***obtain*** *bearing* 方角を確める. ¶***take*** *bearings* 方角を見定める. 【類】The *bearings* of a ship at sea must be often ***taken***.

P bring a person ***to*** his right *bearings* 人材を適所におく.

(4) 忍耐.

P ***beyond*** *bearing* 堪え切れない. 【類】***beyond*** all *bearing*. ¶Such hardships are ***past*** *bearing*. こんな困難には堪えられない.

(5) 結実.

P a tree ***in*** full *bearing* なりざかりの樹. ¶a tree ***past*** *bearing* 結実期を過ぎた樹.

(6)〖機械〗ベーアリング.

Q[2] a ***ball*** *bearing* ボールベアリング. ¶a ***roller*** *bearing* ローラー・ベアリング.

beast, *n.* 獣; 獣性; 人非人.

V He ***has*** the *beast* in him. 彼の心はけだものだ. ¶this method of "***taming*** the *beast*" この懐柔策. ¶***trace*** a wild *beast* 野獣の跡をつける.

V[2] The *beast* in him ***came up*** (=rose). 獣性が頭をもたげ出した.

Q ***Clumsy*** *beast!* 気を付けろ[人に足を踏まれたときなどの用語]. ¶a ***drunken*** *beast* 泥酔者, 大とら. ¶The lion is a ***noble*** *beast*. ししは気高い獣である. ¶The ox is a ***patient, plodding*** *beast* of burden. 牛は辛抱強く歩みの遅い運搬用の獣である. ¶***poor dumb*** *beasts* 哀れな口のきけない獣. ¶a ***raving*** *beast* 荒狂うけだもの. ¶He was saved from those ***savage*** *beasts* by a narrow margin. その猛獣どもにすんでのことでやられる所だった. ¶a ***wild*** *beast* 野獣.

Q[2] ***store*** *beasts* 屠殺のために飼養する獣.

beat, *n.* **(1)** 巡回区域.

V ***cover*** their *beats* 受持区域を巡回する. ¶a policeman ***patrolling*** a *beat* 巡回中の警官.

Q a ***milkman's*** beat 牛乳配達人の配達区域. ¶a ***policeman's*** *beat* 警官の持区域.

P a constable (=patrolman) ***on*** his *beat* 巡回中の警官 ‖ There is a policeman in every man's conscience; you may not always find him ***on*** the *beat*.—Punch. だれの良心の中にもおまわりさんがいる, ただ, このおまわりさんは時にいねむりしていることがある. ¶English grammar is ***out of*** my *beat*. 英文法は僕の畑ではない.

(2) 時計の音, 拍子; どうき.

V ***quicken*** the heart *beat* 心臓の動悸を早める. 【類】The heart *beats* ***become*** stronger and quicker.

Q[2] strong and quick ***heart*** *beats* 強く早い胸の鼓動.

P The ticking of the clock is ***in*** (***out of***) *beat*. 時計の音の調子がそろっている(いない).

(3)〖新聞〗特種, ねた.

V ***gain*** (=***obtain***) a *beat* for one's paper ねたを手に入れる.

Q[2] go out on the ***City Hall*** *beat* 市役所に種取りに行く.

P The alert and jaunty newsman was intent ***on*** his *beat*. その抜け目のない快活な記者は特種さがしに熱心だった.

P[2] I secured a "*beat*" ***for*** my paper. わが社のためのいわゆる特種を見つけた.

beat, *v.* **(1)** 打つ; さがす; 値切る; 打勝つ; 打寄せる; どうき打つ.

M This *beats* me ***altogether***. これは全く私の手におえない. ¶***beat back*** the sword into the plowshare 戦争がすんで帰農する. ¶He ***beat*** the boy ***black and blue***. 彼は子供をあざになるほどなぐった. ¶The rain ***beat pouringly*** (=very hard) outside. 外では猛烈に雨が降っていた. ¶The opponent was one who is not to be ***easily beaten***. 相手もさるものだった. ¶Her heart ***beat fast*** with joy. 彼女の胸は喜びでどきどきした. ¶The rain ***beat hard*** against the windows. 雨がひどく窓を打った. ¶His two daughters ***beat*** him ***home*** from church. 二人の娘がお父さんより先に教会から戻って来た. ¶My heart ***beats high***. 動悸がはげしい. ¶The long journey ***quite beat*** him. (俗) 彼は長途の旅行でへたばった. ¶His pulse ***beats slow*** (***fast***). 彼の脈の打方が遅(早)い. ¶He got ***soundly beaten***. 彼はしたたか打たれた. ¶***beat together*** 棒で(液体を)混ぜる.

M[2] ***beat about*** the whole length of the country for ... ...を求めて国中をさがし回る(草の根をわけてさがす). ¶The sailboat ***beats along*** the coast. 帆船は海岸に沿うて曲りく

ねって進む. ¶The sun *beat* ***down*** upon us. 太陽が僕たちの頭へ照付けた. ‖ I tried to *beat* him ***down***. 値を引かせようとした. 【類】 *beat* ***down*** the price to five yen ‖ *beat* a person ***down*** 言いこめる ‖ *beat* it ***down*** to bedrock その真相をきわめる. ¶*beat* ***off*** an attack 撃退する. 【類】 *beat* ***off*** the enemy / The dogs were *beaten* ***off***. ¶*beat* ***up*** (=whip) eggs 卵をかきまぜる ‖ *beat* ***up*** for recruits (talent) 兵(など)を求める. ¶*beat* ***up*** subscribers to a scheme 計画への賛成(後援)者を募る ‖ The ship *beat* ***up*** against a monsoon 船は季節風(モンスーン)を切って進んだ. ¶*beat* ***up*** and ***down*** for ... ...を求めてあちこちかけ回る.

P *beat* ***about*** the bush 遠まわしに言う ‖ *beat* ***about*** for ... ...をさがし回る. ¶The rain *beats* ***against*** the windows (rocks). 雨が窓(など)に当たる. ‖ *beat* one's head ***against*** the wall 頭をかべに打ちつける. 【類】 The air *beats* ***against*** the face. / The sea *beat* ***against*** the rocky coast. ¶The tattoo *beat* ***at*** 8 o'clock. 門限の太鼓が八時をつげた. ¶Their team *beat* ours ***by*** a large score. 相手方のチームはわれわれの方を大差で負かした. ¶The boy was *beaten* ***for*** disobedience. 子供は言う事をきかないので打たれた. ¶the heart *beat* ***in*** sympathy with ... 胸の鼓動が...に同情して打った ‖ I *beat* him ***in*** a match. 試合で彼を負かした. 【類】 *beat* a person ***in*** argument. ¶He *beat* his sword ***into*** a plowshare. 剣を収めて帰農した. ‖ I *beat* him ***into*** submission. 彼を打って降参させた. ‖ *beat* ... ***into*** the head 頭に...をたたきこむ ‖ *beat* gold ***into*** a [gold] leaf 金をのばして金箔にする ‖ *beat* an idea ***into*** a definite plan 思付をはっきりした計画にまとめ上げる ‖ *beat* a person ***into*** insensibility (=unconsciousness) 人をなぐって気絶させる. ¶*beat* a person ***on*** the head 人の頭を打つ ‖ He was *beaten* ***on*** his shin bones. 彼は向うずねをかっ払われた. ¶I could not *beat* it ***out of*** his head. 彼にその非を悟らせることができななかった. ¶*beat* a path ***through*** the snow 踏んで雪道を作る. ¶*beat* ***to*** a mummy めちゃめちゃになぐる ‖ *beat* a fish ***to*** a jelly 魚肉を打ってべとべとにする ‖ *beat* it ***to*** powder 打って粉にする ‖ *beat* a person ***to*** nothing ぎゅうの目にあわす ‖ *beat* a person ***to*** death なぐり殺す ‖ They were *beaten* ***to*** their knees. 彼らを降参させた. ¶The surf *beat* ***upon*** the cliffs. 波ががけに打寄せた. ‖ The sound *beats* ***upon*** our ears. その音が耳に迫って来る. ‖ *beat* ***upon*** the pavement with one's stick つえで舗道を打つ. ¶*beat* a table ***with*** one's fist テーブルをこぶしでたたく.

(2) 〚航海〛 間切る.

M² The steamer put back, having been unable to *beat* ***up*** against the storm. 風が強いので進航ができず船が戻って来た.

P A ship *beats* (=tacks) ***against*** the wind. 船が風を間切って行く. ¶*beat* a ship ***to*** windward 船を風下に進める.

beater, *n.* かくはん器.

Q² a rotary ***egg*** *beater* 回転式鶏卵かくはん器.

beating, *n.* 打つこと; どうき.

V My heart for a moment almost ***ceased*** its *beating*. 一瞬間私の心臓はほとんど鼓動を止めた. ¶He ***got*** a good (=painful) *beating* (=thrashing *or* licking). 彼はひどく打たれた. ¶The child is ***receiving*** (=***undergoing***) a *beating*. 子供が打たれている.

Q give a boy a ***good*** *beating* 男の子をひどく打つ. ¶the ***loud*** *beating* of one's heart 高鳴る心臓の鼓動 ‖ It was announced by ***loud*** *beating* of the drum. 太鼓を強く打ってそのことを知らせた. ¶give him a ***sound*** *beating* 思い切り彼を打つ. 「*beating* 細君せっかん.

Q² ***carpet*** *beating* [ちりを除くため]毛せん打ち. ¶***wife***

P Why not say so at once? Why all this *beating* ***about*** the bush? なぜ率直にそう言わないか, なんでそんなに遠まわしに言うのか.

beautician, *n.* 《口語》 美容師.

Q an ***expert*** *beautician* 熟練した美容師.

beautiful, *a.* 美しい.

M ***bewitchingly*** *beautiful* 魅惑的に美しい. ¶She was ***distractingly*** *beautiful*. 彼女はたまらなく美しかった. ¶It is ***too*** *beautiful* for words. 言うに言われぬほど美しい.

P It is *beautiful* ***beyond*** description. 何とも言えないほど美しい. ¶*beautiful* ***in*** appearance (spirit) 容貌(など)の美しい. ¶*beautiful* ***of*** aspect 容貌の美しい. ¶*beautiful* ***to*** the eye 見た目に美しい.

beautify, *v.* 《口語》 美化する.

P *beautify* life ***by*** art 人生を芸術で美化する. 【類】 *beautify* city streets ***by*** planting trees.

beauty, *n.* 美; 美人.

V ***add*** *beauty* to the landscape 風景の美を増す. ¶***accentuate*** the *beauty* of the eyes 目の美を強調する. ¶An artist ***associates*** *beauty* with any subject he takes up. 芸術家はどんな題目でもそれを美と結び付ける. ¶***brighten*** *beauty* by contrast 対照によって美をはっきりさせる. ¶***bring out*** the *beauty* of the wood by polishing みがいて木の持味を出す. ¶***bring out*** its *beauty* to the best advantage その美を十二分に発揮させる. ¶***complement*** feminine *beauty* 女性美を補う. ¶***cultivate*** one's *beauty* [婦人などが]よそおいを凝らす. ¶No human language can ***describe*** the terrific *beauty* of that chasm. その山峡の偉容は人間の言葉では言い表わし得ない. ¶***destroy*** the scenic *beauty* of the place その地の風景美を害する. ¶***enhance*** the *beauty* of ... ...の美を増す. ¶***enjoy*** the *beauties* of life 人生の美を楽しむ. ¶the life that is past ***gains*** *beauty* 過ぎし昔は美しく見える. ¶***get*** the most *beauty* out of ... ...の美を十分に発揮させる. ¶***injure*** the *beauty* of a city 都市の美を傷つける. ¶Banks of cloud ***lend*** a fantastic *beauty* to the scenery. たな引く雲が風景に一種夢幻的な美を添える. ¶not to ***mention*** her *beauty* その麗人であることは言うまでもなく. ¶Translation that seeks to ***preserve*** the *beauty* of manner as well as the matter of the original is one of the most difficult of literary tasks. 原文の内容の美と共に文体の美を伝えようとする翻訳は文芸中最も困難な仕事の一つである. ¶So treated flowers will ***retain*** their fresh *beauty* for a long time after gathering. そうすると切った後いつまでも花がその新鮮美を失わないでいる. ¶I ***seek*** the *beauty* of being second, instead of the glory of being first. 僕は二と言って一と上らないという主義だ. ¶Leafless stems ***take*** a new *beauty* when they are clothed with blossoms of hoarfrost. 葉の落ちた幹は真白な霜の衣を着るとまた格別な美しさを見せる. ¶The trees ***throw*** into relief the *beauty* of architecture. 樹木が建築美をくっきりと浮立たせる.

Q one of the ***acknowledged*** *beauties* of the screen キネマ界で評判のスターの一人. ¶a temple of great ***architectural*** *beauty* 建築美の豊かな寺院. 【類】 one of the few ***architectural*** *beauties* of London. ¶I became enamoured of her ***artless*** *beauty*. 僕は彼女の巧まぬ美しさにほれた. ¶the ***crowning*** *beauty* 白眉. ¶***delicate*** and ***quiet*** *beauty* たおやかで静かな美. ¶landscapes of ***enthralling*** *beauty* 魅惑的な美景. ¶her ***extraordinary*** *beauty* 彼女のたぐいまれな容色. ¶Banks of cloud lend a ***fantastic*** *beauty* to the scenery. 層雲のため景色は夢のような美しさを現わす. ¶a feature of ***feminine*** *beauty* 女性美の一面. ¶The city is in its ***fullest*** *beauty* at Christmas. その市はクリスマスの時が一番美しい. ¶a girl of ***great*** *beauty* 美貌の麗人(べっぴん). ¶the ***leafy*** *beauties* of springtime 春季に見る木の葉の美しさ. ¶the ***literary*** *beauty* of a poem 詩の文学的な美. ¶the ***great*** *beauty* of his personal character 彼の非常に美しい人格. ¶There is no definite standard of ***male*** *beauty*. 男性美には一定の規準がない. ¶***manly*** (***womanly***) *beauty* 男(女)性美. ¶the ***marvelous*** *beauty* of her womanhood 成熟した彼女のすばらしい美しさ. ¶a ***modest*** and ***bashful*** *beauty* 謙そんで内気な美人. ¶*beauty*, ***natural*** and ***man-created*** 天然と人工の美. ¶of ***overwhelming*** *beauty* あっというほど美しい. ¶a woman of ***peerless*** *beauty* 絶世の美人. ¶a man of great ***personal*** *beauty* 非常に容貌の美しい人. ¶***physical*** *beauty* 形体美. ¶Their ***poetic*** *beauty* is the despair of the artist. その詩的美には画家も筆を投げる. ¶astonished at her ***radiant*** *beauty* 彼女のまばゆい美貌に圧倒されて. ¶***ragged*** *beauty* 取りつくろわぬ美. ¶She is a ***regular*** *beauty*. 彼女は本当の美人だ. ¶a ***reigning*** *beauty* 美の女王. ¶***rustic*** *beauty* 野趣美. ¶unsurpassed for ***scenic*** *beauty* 風景の美なること天下無比の. 【類】 The summer resort is famed for its healthfulness and ***scenic*** *beauty*. ¶*Beauty* is only ***skin deep***. 美というもほんの皮一重. ¶women remarkable for their ***stately*** *beauty* 気品があって美しいので有名な婦人たち. ¶***strong virile*** *beauty* 強い男性美. ¶the ***successive*** *beauties* of the year 四季折々の美. ¶a spot of ***unparalleled*** *beauty* 絶景. ¶a ***voluptuous*** *beauty* 肉感的な美人 ‖ the ***voluptuous*** *beauty* and richness of Keats's verses キーツの詩の艶麗美と豊かさ. ¶a ***wide-eyed*** *beauty* 目のぱっ

ちりした美人. ¶*wild beauty* of nature 野趣満々の天然美. ¶the *willowy beauties* of Genroku days 元禄時代のきゃしゃな美人. ¶a scene of *wonderful beauty* 絶景.

Q² *bathing beauties* for the contest《米》コンクールに出場の水着姿の美人たち. ¶a *budding beauty* of seventeen 年も十七つぼみの美人. ¶a *society beauty* 社交界の花. ¶There the *spring beauty* is specially alluring. そこでは春の美が特に魅力的だ. ¶a *village beauty* 村の小町娘.

P I am not so unwise as to choose a wife *for* her *beauty* only. 容色のみで妻を選ぶような愚は学ばない. ¶It is unequalled *in beauty*. 無二の美だ. ¶A thing *of beauty* is a feast to the eye. 美しい物は目の保養だ. ‖ a figure *of* great *beauty* 非常に美しい姿. ¶She was endowed *with beauty*. 彼女は美しく生れた. ‖ He was struck *with* the *beauty* of scenery. 風景の美に打たれた.

P² *beauty in* woman 女性美 ‖ *beauty in* the landscape 山水の美. ¶the *beauties of* the English language 英語の美点 ‖ the *beauty of* the imperfect 未完成の美 ‖ the *beauties of* symmetry 均斉美 ‖ She was the *beauty of* the ball. 彼女は舞踏会の花形だった. ‖ The *beauty of* the apparatus is its simplicity. その器具は簡単な所が美点である. ‖ The *beauty of* the game lies in its liveliness. その競技の取柄は活発な点にある.

because, *conj.* …の故に.

M not *merely because* 単に…の故のみならず. ¶*simply because* 全く…のために.

P He is good, not *because of* any virtue, but *because* he is too much of a coward to be bad. 美徳があるから善いのではなくてあまりに臆病で悪人になり得ないから善いのだ. 【類】I could not leave the house *because of* a snowstorm (吹雪).

beck, *n.* うなずき, 手招き.

P He is *at* your *beck* and call. 彼は君の命のまゝになる. 【類】have him *at* my *beck* ‖ yield *at* the first *beck* of attraction 一目で参ってしまう. 【類】The Countess sits resplendent at the head of the table, the butler *at* her *beck* behind her.

beckon, *v.* さし招く.

M *beckon eagarly* to … …をしきりに手招きする.

P *beckon for* a man to approach 人を手招きよせる. 【類】He *beckoned for* me to sit down. ¶*beckon* one's hand *to* him to be home 帰って来いと彼に手招きする.

become, *v.* 成る; 似合う.

M *become abstracted* 考え込む. ¶*become accustomed* to … …に慣れる. ¶How did you *become acquainted* with him? どうしてあの人と懇意になったのか. ‖ on *becoming* better *acquainted* もっとよくわかって来ると. ¶He has *eventually become* a statesman. 彼は遂に政治家となった. ¶*How* did he *become* a favorite? 彼はどうしてお気に入りになったか. ¶It would *ill become* you to do such a thing. こんなことをするのは君に似合わしくないだろう. ‖ I *became ill*. 病気した. ¶*become irksome* 退屈する. ¶these possessions *became joined* to … これらの領土は…に併合された. ¶*become known* 有名になる. ¶The boy *rapidly becomes* a man. 子供はすぐ大人になる. ¶He will *soon become* eighty. もうやがて八十になる. ¶*become steady* 堅人になる. ¶Money will *undoubtedly become* cheaper soon. たしかに金の価値はすぐ下るだろう. ¶This dress (hat, color) *becomes* her very *well*. この着物(など)は彼女によく似合う.

P *become* (=come) *of* age 成年に達する. ‖ What has *become of* him? 彼はどうなったか. 【類】I wonder what has *become of* him. / What shall *become of* us, if the war breaks out? ¶*become to* a mother 母にふさわしい.

O as *becomes* a good Christian 善良なキリスト教徒にふさわしく. ¶It does not *become* a gentleman to tell a lie. うそをつくのは紳士らしくない. ¶He *became* King of England. 英国の王となった. 【類】He has *become* a soldier (doctor, merchant).

becoming, *a.* 適した, 似合った.

M a hat *well becoming* to the wearer かぶってる人にぴったりする帽子.

P Such conduct is *becoming in* him. かような行は彼には相当している. 【類】It's not *becoming in* a man of your experience. ¶The dress is *becoming to* her. 着物が彼女に似合っている.

bed, *n.* 寝台(ベッド); 苗床; 河床; [石炭などの]層.

V *fold* a *bed* 床をたゝむ. ¶They *get* ' *bed* and board ' at his house. 彼らはあの人の家に下宿している. ¶He is ill and *keeps* his *bed*. 病気で寝ている. 【類】He is now a great deal better and does not *keep* his *bed*. ¶*leave* one's *bed* [病気回復して]床離れする. ¶*make* a *bed* 床をとる ‖ *Make* a *bed* whenever you're up. 起きたら寝台をちゃんと整とんしておきなさいよ. ¶*make* one's [own] *bed*〘比ゆ〙自ら不幸を招く. ¶He *offered* me a *bed*. 彼は私にとまれと言った. ¶*share* a *bed* with … …と一緒に寝る. 【類】I *shared* his *bed*. ¶*take* a *bed* 産褥(じょく)につく. ¶*take up* the *bed* 床をあげる. ¶*trim up* the *bed* with sheets and counterpane 敷布や上掛でベッドをきちんとする. ¶The child often *wets* the *bed*. その子は時々寝小便をする.

Q a *comfortable bed* 寝心地のよいとこ. ¶a *double* (*single*) *bed* ダブル(シングル)ベッド. 【類】sleep together in a *double bed*. ¶a *dry bed* 河原. ¶an old-fashioned *four-posted bed* 旧式な四本柱の寝台. ¶a *hard bed* 堅い床. ¶Cheap " dance halls " are *hot beds* of immorality. 安っぽいダンスホールは桃色行為の養成所だ. ¶an *inviting bed* ごろっと横になりたくなる寝台. ¶the *narrow bed* 墓. ¶the eldest son of his *second bed* 後妻にできた長男. ¶On his *sick bed* his mind turned strongly to religion. 病床にあって彼の心は強く宗教に向いた. ¶She left her *sleepless bed*. 一睡もせずに起きてしまった. ¶I cannot sleep well in a *strange bed*. 床が変るとよく眠れない.

Q² a *camp bed* キャンプ用の軽便ベッド. ¶a *coal bed* 炭層. ¶at one's *death bed* その死に際に. 【類】lie on one's *death bed* (臨終). ¶a *double-decker bed* [船・汽車・旅客機などの]上下になっているベッド. ¶a *feather bed* 羽ぶとん. ¶a *flower bed* 花壇. ¶a green-enameled *day bed* グリーンのエナメル塗りのソファー兼用ベッド. ¶a *garden bed* 庭床(花壇など). ‖ a *hospital bed* 病院のベッド. ¶a *marriage bed* 結婚初夜のベッド. ¶a *rose bed*=a bed of rose ばらの床; [比ゆ的に]安楽な身分. ¶a *nursery bed* 子供べやのベッド. ¶The *river bed* is considerably raised by silting. 河床は泥で大分あがっている. ¶a *road bed* 路床(舗装前の)「の]路床 ‖ a *seed bed* 苗床 (=seed plot). ¶one of the *twin beds* 対になっているベッドの一つ.

P sit *by* the *bed* 枕辺に侍する. ¶He rose *from* his *bed*. 彼は起床した. ¶die *in* one's *bed* 定命で死ぬ(横死に対して) ‖ One must lie *in* the *bed* one has made.〘諺〙自業自得(身から出たさび). ‖ He lay *in bed* beyond his usual hour. 彼は平常より長く寝ていた. 【類】He lies *in bed* till nine. / He had to lie *in bed*. / I found him ill *in bed*. / read *in bed* / I prefer to remain *in bed* and dream on undisturbed. / sit up *in bed* / He stayed *in bed*. / He is still *in bed*. ¶just as you get *into bed* 寝しなに. 【類】have breakfast *in bed* / be sick *in bed* with a cold ‖ die *of* a *bed* of honor. ¶put clean sheets *on* a *bed* 敷布のきれいなのを床に敷く ‖ A bolster and pillows are used *on* a *bed*. くくりまくらや西洋まくらは寝台に付属するのである. ‖ repose *on* a *bed* of down (=flowers *or* roses) 安楽に暮す ‖ lie *on* a *bed* of thorns つらい立場にある. ¶I told him the story *on bed*. 彼に寝物語に話した. ‖ lay him down *on* the *bed* 彼を床の上に寝かす. 【類】lie *on* one's *bed* / turn uneasily *on* one's *bed* いらいらして寝返りを打つ ‖ He spent the vacation unhappily *on* a sick *bed*. 休暇を詰らなく病床で暮した. ¶jump *out of bed* 床から飛起きる. 【類】He got *out of bed*. ¶a narrow curtain *over* a *bed* 床の上の狭いカーテン. ¶She was brought *to bed*. 彼女はお産をした. ‖ He is confined *to bed* by age (an attack of fever, with a cold). 彼は老衰(など)で寝た切りになっている. ¶get *to bed* 床につく. 【類】We got *to bed* early. / I am going *to bed*. ‖ go *to bed* between blankets 毛布の間にもぐり込む ‖ put children *to bed* 子供たちを寝かせる. ¶He was concealed *under* the *bed*. 彼は寝台の下に隠れていた. ‖ a *bed of* dust 墓.

P² a *bed of* coal=a coal bed ‖ the *bed of* gravel [舗装用

bed, *v.* 植付ける.

M *bed out* 花壇に苗を移し植える.

M² tulips *bedded in* rich soil 肥えた土地に植えてあるチューリップ. ¶*bed up* for planting seedlings 苗つけをするためのうねを作る ‖ ridge or " *bed up* " the land〘農〙うねあげ即ち植付床を作る.

bedaub, *v.* 塗付ける; くどくどと飾り立てる.

P It was *bedaubed with* paint. それはペンキで塗り立てられた. ‖ Her dress was *bedaubed with* cheap finery. 彼女の衣裳はごてごて安ぴか物で飾ってあった.

bedclothes, *n. pl.* 寝具類(シーツ, 毛布など).

V ***turn down*** the *bedclothes* 寝具をたたむ.

bedding, *n.* 苗床作り; *pl.* 寝具類.

V ***air*** *beddings* when used 使ったら寝具に風をあてる.

Q² ***summer*** *bedding* 夏の花床作り.

P Straw is used ***as*** *bedding* for cows and horses. 牛や馬のとこにはわらが用いられる.

bedeck, *v.* 飾る.

P The mother *bedecked* her daugther ***with*** silk and jewels. 母は絹物や宝石で娘を飾った.

bedew *v.* ぬらす.

P Her face was *bedewed* ***with*** tears. 彼女の顔は涙にぬれていた.

bedroom, *n.* 寝室.

V I ***shared*** my friend's *bedroom.* 友人と一しょの室に寝た.

bedside, *n.* 枕頭.

P She was unable to be ***at*** his *bedside* when he died. 彼女は彼の死目に会えなかった. ‖ ***at*** [the] *bedside* of a sick person 病人のまくらべに. ¶I ***sit by*** one's *bedside* そのまくらべにすわる ‖ I watched ***by*** her *bedside.* 彼女の病床に付添っていた.

bedtime, *n.* 就寝時.

Q² a ***ten o'clock*** *bedtime* 十時就寝.

P take a medicine ***at*** *bedtime* 寝しなに服薬する.

bee, *n.* みつばち; 《米》集会.

V ***line*** *bees* 野ばちの飛ぶあとをつけてその巣をさぐる.

V² *Bees* ***hum*** (=***buzz***). はちがぶんぶんいう. ¶*Bees* ***fly*** straight (=in a bee line). はちは直線に飛ぶ.

Q² a ***husking*** *bee* とうもろこしの皮むきの集り. ¶***sea*** *bees* 《米》海蜂部隊. ¶a ***spelling*** *bee* つづり字(スペリング)当てゲームの集り. ¶a ***spinning*** *bee* はた織りの集り ‖ a ***worker*** *bee* 働きばち.

P He was stung ***by*** a *bee.* はちに刺された. ¶a cluster (=swarm) ***of*** *bees* はちの群.

beef, *n.* 牛肉.

Q a slicc of ***cold*** *beef* 一片の冷牛肉 ‖ There is ***cold*** *beef* going. 今午の冷肉のごちそうが出ます. ¶***corned*** *beef* コンビーフ. ¶***dried*** *beef* くん製牛肉. ¶***honest*** *becf* 本物の牛肉. ¶***jerked*** *beef* ほし牛肉. ¶Is this *beef* too ***rare*** for you? この牛肉は少しなま焼けでしょうか.

Q² ***roast*** *beef* 焼肉.

beeline, *n.* 直線.

V ***make*** a *beeline* from ... to ...から直線に飛ぶ(走る, 航海する).

P fly ***in*** a *beeline* 真一文字に飛ぶ.

beer, *n.* ビール.

V ***cool*** the *beer* ビールを冷やす. ¶***drink*** *beer* ビールを飲む. ¶***sip*** *beer* ビールをちびりちびり飲む.

Q ***dark*** *beer* 黒ビール. ¶***homely*** *beer* 薄いビール. ¶***pale*** *beer* 薄いビール. ¶a draught (=draft) of ***icy cold*** *beer* 氷のように冷したビールの一飲み. ¶***near*** *beer* 水っぽいビール. ¶This *beer* is ***small*** (=***weak or watery***). このビールは薄い. ¶This *beer* is ***stale.*** この ビールは気が抜けている. ¶***thick*** *beer* 濁ったビール.

Q² ***draft*** *beer*=beer on draft たる入りの生ビール. ¶***March*** *beer* 三月醸造のビール.

M This *beer* is ***up.*** ビールが吹いた.

P a froth ***on*** *beer* ビールのあわ. ¶have (=take) a draft ***of*** *beer* ビールをぐいとやる.

P² *beer* ***from*** the wood なまビール. ¶Have you any of this *beer* ***on*** draught (=from the cask)? このビールのなまがありますか.

beet, *n.* かぶ, 大根.

Q a big ***red*** *beet* 大きな赤かぶ. ¶a ***sugar*** *beet* 砂糖大根.

befall, *v.* 起る.

P A misfortune *befell* [***to***] him. 不幸が彼にふりかかった.

beforehand, *ad.* 前以て, あらかじめ.

M for ***many months*** *beforehand* 何カ月も前に.

P He has been *beforehand* ***with*** me. 彼は僕の先を越した. 【類】He knew the value of being *beforehand* ***with*** an enemy. / He was *beforehand* ***with*** the world. / I was going to buy it, but he was *beforehand* ***with*** me.

befriend, *v.* ...の味方になる.

P *befriend* him ***against*** all attacks あらゆる攻撃に対して彼を助ける.

beg, *v.* 請う; こじきする.

M He *begged* ***importunately.*** 彼はしつこく頼んだ. ¶I *beg* ***respectfully*** to say that ... 謹んで...と申し上げたい.

M² *beg* ***off*** from doing it しり込みする. 【類】He promised at first to go with us, but he has since *begged* ***off.***

P He *begged* ***for*** food (money, water). 彼は食物(など)をくれと言った. 【類】*beg* ***for*** mercy (alms, peace) / I *beg* ***for*** your kindly help. / May I *beg* you ***for*** a subscription (寄付)? ‖ *beg* ***for*** quarter 命ごいをする. ‖ *beg* ***for*** shelter 宿をこう ‖ May I *beg* ***of*** you to do it? それをして戴けましょうか.

O I *beg* to be excused. 御免をこうむりたい. ¶He *begged* me to accompany him. 彼は僕に一しょに来てくれと言った. ¶I *beg* to inform you that ... ...の件を御知らせ申上ます. 【類】He *begged* to inquire whether he might go home.

begetting, *n.* 産むこと.

P² the *begetting* ***of*** children 子供を産むこと.

beggar, *n.* こじき.

V ***follow*** the *beggar* to his lodgings こじきのねぐらまでついて行く.

Q an ***importunate*** *beggar* あつかましいこじき. ¶a ***plausible*** *beggar* まことしやかなこじき. ¶***professional*** *beggars* 本職のこじき.

P Be on your guard ***against*** *beggars.* こじきに用心せよ. ¶a resort (=haunt) ***of*** *beggars* こじきの巣くつ.

begging, *n.* 請うこと.

V To give money to beggars sometimes amounts to ***encouraging*** *begging.* こじきに金をやるのは時にこじきを奨励することになる.

P live ***by*** *begging* こじき生活をする.

begin, *v.* 始まる, 始める.

M You must *begin* ***afresh.*** 君はやり直さなければならぬ. ¶The fishing season *began* most ***auspiciously.*** 漁期は極めて幸先がよかった. ¶It is probable that the fatal disease *began* ***insidiously*** months ago. その命取りの病気は数カ月前知らぬ間に始まったらしい. ¶Everything had to be *begun* ***over again.*** 一切新規まき直しにしなければならなかった. ¶His new novel *began* ***serially*** in Windsor Magazine. 彼の新作小説はウインザ誌に続き物として載り始めた. ¶He *begins* school ***today.*** きょうから通学する. ‖ We are to have four holidays *beginning* ***today.*** きょうから四日休める. ¶***When*** did you *begin* to learn English? 君はいつ英語を習い始めたか.

P *began* life ***as*** a newspaper reporter 最初は報道記者としてスタートを切った. ¶*Beginning* ***as*** a fishing village, it has grown to be a prosperous town. 一漁村が発展して繁華な市となった. ¶The bidding *began* ***at*** ¥100 and rose up to ¥1,000. せりは百円に始まって千円まで上った. 【類】It *began* ***at*** fifty guineas and reached eight hundred and fifty. ‖ ***At*** what time does the show *begin?* ショーの始まりは何時ですか. 【類】The meeting *begins* ***at*** 3 p.m. on Friday, the 26th inst. ‖ *begin* ***at*** (=***with***) the beginning 最初から始める. ¶Charity *begins* ***at*** home, but should not end there. 慈善は先ず家庭からだが, そこで止ってはいけない. ¶he *began* ***by*** scolding us, saying ... 彼はまず手始めに...と言ってしかった. ‖ He *began* the New Year ***by*** saluting the sun. 彼は年が明けるとまず太陽を拝した. ¶He *began* Latin ***from*** (=***at***) the age of ten. 十歳からラテン語を始めた. ‖ His reception days will *begin* ***from*** next Thursday. 彼の面会日は今度の木曜日から始まる. 【類】The Christian Era *begins* ***from*** the birth of Christ. ¶Armenian literature *begins* ***in*** 400 A.D. アルメニア文学は西暦四百年に始まる. 【類】Your subscription *begins* ***in*** the Christmas number and ends in November, 1912. / It *begins* ***in*** (=***with***) February, running on to August or September. ¶It *begins* ***on*** October 12. それは十月十二日に始まる. ‖ *begin* ***on*** page four 四ページから始める ‖ *begin* ***on*** a job 仕事に取りかゝる. ¶he *began* ***with*** a salary of ... 彼は月給...が振出しだった. ‖ He *began* ***with*** entreaties and ended with threats. 始めは嘆願の態度に出たがしまいには恐喝になった. ‖ *beginning* ***with*** ..., gradually proceed to ... ...から始めて順次...に至る ‖ The continent *began* ***with*** the "little grain of sand." 大陸も始まりは一握の砂である. 【類】English written literature *begins* ***with*** Beowulf and the poems of Cædmon. / The nineteenth century *began* ***with*** the first day of 1801. / My enjoyment of books *began* and will end ***with*** Boswell's Life of Johnson—Leslie Stephen. / Education, in the largest sense, *begins* ***with*** a man's birth and does not end until he dies. / You had better *begin* ***with*** this book. / The ocean *began* ***with*** the little drops of water. / Which shall I *begin* ***with***? / The gigantic oak *began* ***with*** the acorn (どんぐり). / He *began* his talk ***with*** an apology. ‖ He is very rich, to *begin* ***with.*** 第一彼は非常な金持だ.

beginner, *n.* 初学者.

V a few hints that will ***aid biginners*** 初心者の助けになる二三の注意. ¶There are several points that tend to ***puzzle*** ***beginners***. 初心者を迷わしそうな点が五つ六つある.

Q an ***absolute beginner*** 全くの初心者. ¶a ***mere beginner*** ほんの初心者. ¶***promising beginners*** 前途有望な初学者. ¶a ***raw*** (=***mere***) ***beginner*** ほんの初心者.

P The book is ***beyond beginners***. その本は初心者には歯が立たない.

P[2] the ***beginner in*** French フランス語の初学者.

beginning, *n.* 初め.

V ***feel*** the ***beginnings*** of love 恋のきざしを感じる. ¶The discovery of America ***forms*** the ***beginning*** of a new period, both in modern history and in modern geography. アメリカ発見は近代歴史及び地理上新紀元の発端をなしている. ¶***give beginning*** to a new era 新時代を始める. ¶This industry ***had*** its ***beginning*** in 1864. この産業の起原は一八六四年である. ‖ the case ***had*** its ***beginnings*** in the killing of ... 事件のそもそもの起りは...の殺人である. ¶***lay*** the ***beginning*** of a new social order 新しい社会組織の基礎を据える. ¶School teaching, however good, can only ***make*** a ***beginning*** and create a desire for further advance. 学校教育はどんなに善くても教育の端緒を開き更に進歩せんとの念願を生ぜしむるに過ぎない. ‖ Only a ***beginning*** has been ***made*** in this direction. この方面にはほんの端緒が開かれただけだ. ¶***mark*** the ***beginning*** of a new era (=epoch) 新時代の紀元を画す. 【類】an event that ***marks*** the ***beginning*** of ... / ... will, we hope, ***mark*** the ***beginning*** of better times / ***mark*** the ***beginning*** of one's fall (堕落). ¶***took*** its ***beginning*** from the Ching dynasty 清朝から始まった. ¶***trace*** the ***beginning*** of one's illness back to a certain date 発病の日にさかのぼる.

Q It is not an ***auspicious beginning*** if a young woman loses her wedding ring on her wedding tour. 若い女が新婚旅行で結婚の指輪をなくしたとするとそれは縁起のよいことではない. ¶***Bright beginning*** and dull finish. 竜頭蛇尾. ¶make an ***excellent beginning*** すべり出しはすこぶる好調だ. ¶make a ***favorable beginning*** 出だしは好調だ. ¶A ***good beginning*** has been made. すべり出しがよい. ‖ make a ***good beginning*** with the Three R's. 読み書き算術でしっかり基礎を造る. ¶His life reached its earthly end and its ***heavenly beginning***. 彼は浮世の生活を終り天国の生活を始めた. ¶the ***hopeful beginnings*** さい先のよい出発. ¶It often happens that ***little beginnings*** have great endings. 小事に始まり大事に終ることがしばしばある. ¶its ***modest beginning*** それの微々たる出発. 【類】This hospital whose ***beginnings*** were very ***modest*** is now second to none in London for the skill of its medical, surgical, and nursing staff. ¶has made a ***promising beginning*** 大いに幸先がよい. ¶It is not of ***recent beginning***. それは昨今始まったことじゃない. ¶The play has a ***sad beginning***, but ends in a comedy. この劇は悲劇で始まって喜劇で終っている. ¶make a ***small beginning*** 小さく始める. 【類】Like most great enterprises, the University had a ***small beginning*** and developed gradually, through successive stages. ¶He has made a ***successful beginning***. 彼は始めからうまく行った. ¶make a ***suitable beginning*** すべり出しは順調である. ¶He made an ***unpromising beginning***. やり始めがまずかった. ¶***unrecorded beginnings*** 記録のない大昔. ¶It was the ***very beginning*** of the affair. それがそもそも始まりであった.

P ***about*** the ***beginning*** of autumn 初秋のころ. ¶Adverbial phrases are emphasized by being placed ***at*** the ***beginning***. 副詞句は文頭に置かれると意味が強くなる. ¶***After beginning*** with *he*, the writer lapsed into *I*. (自分を三人称にして) he と書き出したがやがて I になってしまった. ‖ ***at*** the very ***beginning*** ごく最初に ‖ It is ***at the beginning*** that the greatest difficulty is encountered. 最大の困難に会うのは創業時においてである. 【類】***at*** the ***beginning*** of the New Year, 1544 / ***at*** the ***beginning*** of the historic period / ***at*** (=***in***) the ***beginning*** of July (1900, the present week, the Christian era) / ***at*** the ***beginning*** of next week / ***at*** the ***beginning*** of the chapter. ¶***from*** the ***beginning*** of time 太古から. 【類】***from*** the very ***beginning*** / I knew right ***from*** the ***beginning*** that it would not pay. ‖ The principle is pernicious ***from beginning*** to end. その主義は徹頭徹尾有害である. ¶as I said ***in*** the ***beginning*** 最初私が言った通り. 【類】You will find it rather difficult ***in*** the ***beginning***. / You will think it rather difficult ***in*** the ***beginning***, but you will soon get accustomed. / ***in*** the ***beginning*** of the disease / ***in*** the ***beginning*** of the T'ang dynasty (唐朝) / ***in*** (=***at***) the ***beginning*** of the eighteenth century / ***in*** the ***beginning*** of 1928 / ***in*** the ***beginning*** of summer / ***in*** the ***beginning*** of life. ¶***since*** (=***from***) the ***beginning*** of the world 開闢(ｶｲﾋﾞｬｸ)以来. 【類】***since*** the ***beginning*** of human existence on the earth.

P[2] make a ***beginning in*** efficient language teaching 能率のあがる語学教授の端緒を開く. ¶The novel was the ***beginning of*** his fame. その小説が氏の出世作であった. 【類】... was the ***beginning of*** his career ‖ It was the ***beginning of*** the end of his prosperity. それから彼は下り坂になった. ‖ the ***beginnings of*** Greek culture ギリシア文化の始まり. 【類】The ***beginnings of*** Japanese art, as of almost all things Japanese excepting cleanliness, can be traced to China through Korea.—Chamberlain. / This Weekly Register might almost be described as the ***beginning of*** modern journalism in England.

beguile, *v.* 欺く; まぎらす.

P I was ***beguiled into*** consenting. 私は釣込まれて賛成した. ‖ ***beguile into*** a trap 人をわなにかける ‖ ***beguile*** a person ***into*** believing that ... 人を[だまして]...と信じさせる. ¶They ***beguiled*** him ***of*** his right by false pretence. 彼らは虚偽の口実で彼の権利を奪った. ¶He ***beguiled*** the child ***with*** tales. 彼は話をして子供をすかした. ‖ ***beguile*** weary hours ***with*** jest 冗談を言って退屈をまぎらす. 【類】I ***beguiled*** my journey ***with*** conversation. / Our train journey was ***beguiled with*** pleasant talk.

behalf, *n.* 利益, ため.

P I thank you for all the trouble you have taken ***in*** my ***behalf***. 色々と私のためにお骨折下さいましてありがたく存じます. ‖ People go to shrines and temples to influence the gods ***in*** their ***behalf***. 人は御利益を得ようとして神社仏閣へ参詣する. 【類】This request is made to you ***in behalf*** of my son. / Public sympathy was active ***in*** his ***behalf***. /***In behalf*** of Yale University I am giving myself the pleasure of sending felicitations to its oldest living graduate on the completion of his ninety-fourth year. ¶***On behalf*** of the German Government I have the honor to make to you the following communications. ドイツ政府に代って私は次のことを御通知申し上げます. ‖ a person empowered to act ***on*** his ***behalf*** 彼の代理たる権利のある人. 【類】The lawyer spoke convincingly ***on behalf*** of his client (弁護依頼人) / the business which he is engaged ***on behalf*** of his master / ***On*** his ***behalf***, as well as for myself, I thank you. / My client (弁護を依頼した人) cannot come, and I appear ***on*** his ***behalf***. / ***on*** his own ***behalf*** and in the name of ... / attend a meeting ***on*** another's ***behalf*** / He put himself to much trouble ***on*** my ***behalf***. / plead ***on behalf*** ***of*** a great cause (大義) / He rendered many services ***on behalf*** of justice and freedom.

behave, *v.* 振舞う.

M He ***behaves*** [himself] ***badly*** (***well***). 彼の挙動がよくない(よい). ¶***behave better*** in future 将来行状を慎む. ¶***behave chivalrously*** to ... ...に対して義侠的行動を取る. ¶***behave*** oneself ***decently*** 行儀正しく振舞う. ¶***behave disgracefully*** 恥ずべき行動をする. ¶He ***behaved filially*** by his mother. 彼は母に孝行をした. ¶***behave flippantly*** 軽率な行動をする. ¶He ***behaved*** himself ***gallantly***. 彼は男らしく行動した. ¶***behave handsomely*** to ... ...に対しりっぱに(男らしく)行動する. ¶***behave harshly*** 粗暴な事をする. ¶***behave honorably*** 恥しくない行動をする. ¶***How*** did he ***behave*** [himself]? 彼のやり口はどんなだったか. ¶***behave hysterically*** ヒステリックな行動をする. ¶***behave ignobly*** 卑しい振舞をする. ¶***behave mannerly*** at table 食卓で行儀よくする. ¶***behave properly*** 場合に適した行動をする. ¶***behave nobly*** りっぱにふるまう. ¶He ***behaves respectfully*** toward his superiors. 長上に対して丁重だ. ¶I am sorry that he ***behaved*** so ***rudely*** to you. 彼が貴方にあんな失礼な事をしてお気の毒です. ¶It is impossible for her to ***behave sensibly*** about money. 彼女は金を利口に使うことはできない. ¶***behave shamefully*** toward ... ...に対して恥かしい行動をする. ¶He ***behaved*** very ***strangely***. 彼の様

子ははなはだ変であった. ¶ *behave* ***unkindly*** to one's wife 妻に不親切にする. ¶ He *behaved* ***well*** in spite of his misfortunes. 彼は身の不幸にもかゝわらず良くやっていた. ¶ He *behaves* ***worse*** than ever. 彼の挙動はこれまでよりな お悪い.

P *behave* ***as*** a gentleman (lady) 紳士(など)らしく振舞う. ¶ He *behaved* ***in*** a becoming manner. 適当に振舞った. ‖ He *behaved* ***in*** a questionable manner toward her. 彼女にけしからぬ振舞をした. ¶ *behave* ***like*** "slackers" ずるけ者のようなやり方をする. 【類】Nobody will want you if you *behave* ***like*** this. / He *behaved* himself ***like*** a man. ¶ She *behaved* ***toward*** him as a mother. 彼女は彼を我子のように取扱った. ¶ He *behaved* ***with*** great composure. 彼の挙動は非常に落着いていた. ‖ how to *behave* ***with*** a burglar 泥棒に入られた場合の処置法.

behavio[u]r, *n.* 振舞, 挙動, 態度.

V He ***observed*** a quiet *behavior*. 彼は静粛にしていた. ¶ ***report*** a person's *behavior* 人の操行を知らせる. ¶ I could not ***understand*** her enigmatic *behavior*. 彼女のなぞのような態度がわからなかった.

Q ***barbaric*** *behavior* 野蛮な行動. ¶ I was on my ***best*** *behavior*. 僕は謹んで(行状に細心の注意を払って)いた. ¶ indulge in ***delinquent*** *behavior* 不良を働く. ¶ ***eccentric*** *behavior* 一風変った挙動. ¶ He has been rewarded for his ***gallant*** *behavior* in saving their lives. 彼らの生命救助に当っての勇敢な振舞に対して彼は表彰された. ¶ cases of ***heroic*** *behavior* 勇敢な行動の例. ¶ his ***furtive*** *behavior* こそこそした彼の行動. ¶ ***girlish*** *behavior* 少女らしいふるまい. ¶ a ***high-handed*** *behavior* 高飛車なやり口. ¶ his ***merciful*** *behavior* toward the enemy 彼の敵に対するなさけある仕打. ¶ his ***physical*** *behavior* on the platform 氏の壇上における動作(演説ぶり). ¶ ***rough, wild*** *behavior* 粗暴で無作法. ¶ I shall call him to account for his ***shameful*** *behavior*. 彼の不都合千万な態度の申開きをしてもらおう. ‖ ***shameless*** *behavior* 恥知らずの態度. ¶ ***sluggish*** *behavior* のろのろした動作. ¶ Noting his ***strange*** *behavior*, I asked him the meaning of it. 不思議な態度だと気が付いて彼にその理由を尋ねた. ¶ His ***sullen*** *behavior* showed that he was displeased. 彼のしかめ面を見るときげんの悪いことが分った. ¶ ***uncouth*** *behavior* ぶざまな振舞. ¶ ***unbecoming*** *behavior* 似つかわしくない態度. ¶ ***ungentlemanlike*** *behavior* 紳士にあるまじき振舞. ¶ ***unpatriotic*** *behavior* 非国民的行為.

Q² ***group*** *behavior* 団体行動.

P I am disgusted ***at*** his *behavior*. 彼の仕打には胸くそが悪くなった. ¶ He is like a beast ***in*** *behavior*. 彼の行動は獣のようだ. ¶ He was ***on*** his best *behavior*. 彼は実におとなしくしていた. ‖ He was put ***on*** his good *behavior*. 彼は謹慎を申付けられた.

P² his *behavior* ***before*** the multitude 群集の前での彼の挙動. ¶ his *behavior* ***in*** the church 教会における彼の振舞. ¶ the *behavior* ***of*** the lord toward his people 君主の人民に対するやり方. ¶ the *behavior* ***of*** the teacher ***to*** (=***toward***) his pupils 子弟に対する教師の態度. ¶ his *behavior* ***on*** (=***upon***) the streets 街上での彼の振舞. ¶ His *behavior* ***toward*** me was shameful. 彼の私に対する態度は恥ずべきものであった. ¶ His *behavior* ***with*** the godly as well as ***with*** the worldly was faultless. 来世に対してまた現世の事に対しても彼の態度には欠点がなかった.

behead, *v.* 斬首する.

P He was *beheaded* ***for*** high treason. 彼は国事犯で斬首された. ¶ He was *beheaded* ***with*** the guillotine. 彼は断頭台で斬首された.

behind, *ad., prep.* 後れて, 後ろに.

M He is ***always*** *behind* time. 彼はいつも遅刻する. ¶ The houses are ***often*** *behind* on their orders for the most popular goods. 一番よく売れる品の注文はよく品渡しがおくれる. ¶ I am ***much*** *behind* with my work. 仕事が大分後れている.

P push a cart ***from*** *behind* 車をあとから押す ‖ He came out ***from*** *behind* the door. 彼は戸の後ろから出て来た. ‖ goad him onward ***from*** *behind* 後から彼をつっつき出す. ¶ He is *behind* ***in*** his rent (payment). 彼は家賃(など)を遅らしている. ‖ He is *behind* ***in*** fulfilling his obligation. 債務の履行を怠っている. ¶ He is *behind* ***with*** his work. 彼は仕事が後れている.

behindhand, *a., ad.* 後れて, 滞って.

P He is *behindhand* ***in*** his circumstances. 身代が左前になっている. ¶ He is *behindhand* ***with*** his payment (rent). 支払(など)が滞っている.

behold, *v.* 見る.

P *behold* ... ***with*** envy ...を嫉視する.

behoof, *n.* ため, 利益.

P Keep these documents ***for*** (=***in, on*** *or* ***to***) my *behoof*. 僕のためにこの書類を取って置いて下さい. 【類】It was ***for*** the *behoof* of my children.

being, *n.* 存在; 生存物, 生きもの.

V ***has*** its *being* 存在する. 【類】One cannot detach a statesman from the political world in which he ***has*** his *being*. ¶ the achievements of the geniuses to which those sciences ***owe*** their *being* これらの科学の生みの親である天才たちの偉業. ¶ All her *being* was ***stirred***. 彼女は心から感動した.

Q an ***angelic*** *being* 天使. ¶ ***created*** *beings* [神の]創造物. ¶ He became a ***different*** *being*. 彼は別人のようになった. ¶ ***exalted*** *beings* 高貴の人々. ¶ a very thin ***glossy*** *being* 薄っぺらなもの. ¶ those ***hapless*** *beings* それらの不幸な人人. ¶ ***human*** *beings* 人間. ¶ an ***immaterial*** *being* 霊的な存在. ¶ ***inanimate*** *beings* 無生物. ¶ In primitive conceptions animals are not ***inferior*** *beings* separated from man by a great gulf. 原始人の考えでは動物は人間と非常に懸隔のある劣等物ではない. ¶ What an ***insupportable*** *being!* 何んと言ういやなやつだろう. ¶ ***living*** *beings* 生物. ¶ ***male*** and ***female*** *beings* 男女. ¶ Man is a ***moral*** *being*. 人は道徳的な動物である. ¶ ***mortal*** *beings* 浮世の人々. ¶ a ***reasoning*** *being* 理性のある動物(人間). ¶ Man is a ***sentient*** *being*. 人木石にあらず. ¶ ***sentient*** and ***nonsentient*** *beings* 有情無情. ¶ ***supernatural*** *beings* 超自然的なもの. ¶ He was a ***new*** *being*. 彼はそれで生れ変った. ‖ A war makes millions of ***unoffending*** *beings* suffer. 戦争は何百万と言う何の罪もない人々を苦しめる.

P the fleet ***in*** *being* 現存海軍. ¶ before the railway came ***into*** *being* 鉄道ができる以前には ‖ call ***into*** *being* 生み出す ‖ come ***into*** *being* 成立する; 現われる.

bejewel, *v.* 宝石で飾る.

M The crown is ***richly*** *bejewelled*. 王冠はりっぱに宝玉で飾ってある.

belch, *v.* 噴出する.

M *belch* ***forth*** fire 火を噴き出す.

P smoke *belching* ***from*** a funnel 煙突から吐き出す煙.

belie, *v.* 裏切る, ざん言する.

P He has *belied* me ***to*** my friend. 彼は僕の友人に僕のざん言をした.

O His acts *belie* his words. 彼は言行が一致しない.

belief, *n.* 信仰, 信念.

V ***abjure*** one's *belief* in the doctrine その教義に対する信仰を放棄する. ¶ ***carry*** their *belief* into the practice of life 彼らの信仰を実際生活に取入れる. ¶ ***confess*** unalterable *belief* 堅い信仰を告白する. ¶ ***confirm*** the *belief* that ... ...という信念を堅くする. ¶ ***corroborate*** one's *belief* 自己の信念を強固にする. ¶ ***declare*** one's *belief* that ... ...と自己の信念を言明する. ¶ ***discard*** (=***give up***) a *belief* 信念を捨てる. ¶ ***dispel*** a *belief* 信念を打破する. ¶ ***entertain*** (=***cherish***) the *belief* that ... ...と言う信念を懐く. ¶ ***eradicate*** the *belief* in ... ...の信仰を根絶する. ¶ These old *beliefs* are now ***exploded***. これらの古い信仰はもう一掃されてしまった. ¶ ***express*** one's *belief* in Christianity キリスト教の信仰を言明する. ¶ He worked diligently to ***extend*** the *belief* of his church. 彼はその教会の信仰の宣伝に努めた. ¶ ***foster*** a *belief* that ... ...という信念を育てあげる. ¶ he ***founds*** his *belief* on the fact that ... 彼は...という事実に基いてそう信じている. ¶ ***harbor*** an inveterate *belief* in the existence of ghosts 幽霊が存在しているとあくまでも信じる. ¶ he ***had*** much *belief* in ... 彼は...を大いに信じていた. ¶ we ***hazard*** the *belief* that ... あえて...と思う. ¶ ***hold*** a firm *belief* that ... ...とを堅く信じる. 【類】The *belief* ***held*** by him is not supported by any substantial evidence. ¶ ***hug*** a *belief* that ... ...ということに執着する. ¶ the report is colored by a desire to ***impress*** a *belief* that ... その報道は...と思わせたい念願から多少色が付けてある. ¶ ***instill*** Christian *belief* in the minds of the people 民衆の心にキリスト教の信仰を注入する. ¶ These observations fully ***justify*** this ancient *belief*. これらの言説によってこの古代信仰の正しいということがわかる. ¶ ***lose*** one's *belief* in ... ...に対する信念を失う. ¶ ***maintain*** one's *belief* 自己の信念を持続する. ¶ ***nurse*** the *belief* that … …という信念を養う. ¶Some *beliefs* once deemed idle have now been ***reinstated*** in the regard of science. かつては空想と思われた信念も今や科学のために復活した. ¶***relinquish*** a *belief* 信念を捨てる. 【類】No criticism, no abuse has ever ***shaken*** his *belief* in himself. ¶they ***share*** my *belief* that … 彼らは私同様…という信念を持っている. ¶***spread*** the *belief* that … …という所信を広める. ¶***strike*** one's *belief* 自分の信念を述べる. ¶***strengthen*** the *belief* that … …という信念を強める. ¶***support*** a *belief* ある信念を支持する. ¶It ***surpasses*** *belief* (=is incredible). それは信じられない. ¶I ***won*** his *belief* in my innocence. 私に罪のないことを彼に信じさせた.

Q a widely ***accepted*** *belief* 広く認められた信仰. ¶There was an ***ancient*** *belief* that … …という古い信仰があった. ¶these ***antique*** *beliefs* これら古風の信仰. ¶***bygone*** *beliefs* 過去の信仰. ¶attack people's ***cherished*** *beliefs* 人の心に抱く信念を攻撃する. ¶contrary to a ***common*** *belief* 一般世人の所信と反対に. ¶it is the hope and the ***confident*** *belief* of … それが…の希望でありかつ確信である ‖ in the ***confident*** *belief* that … …ということを確信して. ¶They share the ***contemporary*** *belief* that … 彼らは…という現代人の信仰を持っている. ¶the ***current*** *belief* among … …の間に行われている信念. 【類】the once ***current*** *belief* that … ¶the ***customary*** *belief* that … is a fallacy …という従来の信仰は誤っている. ¶a ***deep-rooted*** *belief* 深く根ざした信仰. ¶a ***fanatic*** *belief* 狂信. ¶A ***firm*** *belief* that … exists among seamen. 海員の間には…という確信がある. 【類】It is my ***firm*** *belief* that knowledge is power. / with the ***firm*** *belief* that … ‖ I can give it my full *belief*. 私はそれは大丈夫間違いなしと思っている. ¶He bought it in the ***full*** *belief* that it was genuine. 彼はそれを本物とばかり思込んで買取った. ¶the ***general*** *belief* was that … 一般の信じる所は…であった. ¶there is ***growing*** *belief* that … …という考えが高まって行く. ¶an ***inveterate*** *belief* in … …に対する抜きがたい信仰. ¶the Ganges, the hallowrd river of ***Hindu*** *belief* インド教の聖河ガンジス. ¶That *belief* is ***long*** since exploded. その信念はとっくの昔に解消した. ¶in the ***mistaken*** *belief* that … …と思い違って. ¶a ***monotheistic*** *belief* 一神教の信仰. ¶Some natives retain their ***old*** (=***oldtime***) ***religious*** ***belief***. 土人の中にはこの古い信仰を今以て奉じているものもある. ¶I may venture to give my ***personal*** *belief* that … …という私一個の所信を思い切って申しましょう. ¶a study of ***popular*** *beliefs* 民間信仰の一考察. ¶there is a very ***prevalent*** *belief* among many people that … …という信仰が極めてひろく流布している. ¶a generally ***received*** *belief* 一般に受入れられた信仰. ¶the decay of ***religious*** *beliefs* 信仰心の衰微. 【類】the ***religious*** *beliefs* of the known races of men. ¶a ***rooted*** *belief* 根強い信仰. ¶a ***similar*** *belief* is held by … 同様の信仰が…によって奉ぜられている. ¶***sincere*** *belief* in the principles of democracy, peace and freedom 民主主義, 平和, 自由の原則に対する衷心よりの信念. ¶the ***supernatural*** *beliefs* of the people 人民の超自然的な信仰. ¶an old ***superstitious*** *belief* 古い迷信. 【類】there is a ***superstitious*** *belief* that … ¶confess an ***unalterable*** *belief* 不変の信仰を告白する. ¶He had an ***unshakable*** *belief* in democracy. 彼の民主主義に対する信念はゆるがなかった. ¶a ***vulgar*** *belief* 俗説. ¶a ***wide-spread*** *belief* has prevailed that … …という信仰が広く流行した. 【類】there is a ***widespread*** *belief* that … ¶abjure a ***wrong*** *belief* 誤れる信念を捨てる.

Q² ***folklore*** *beliefs* 古くから地方に伝わっている信仰.

P ***according*** ***to*** popular *belief* 世人の信じる所によれば. ¶It is ***beyond*** ***belief***. それは信じられない. 【類】***beyond*** all *belief* / almost (altogether) ***beyond*** ***belief***. ¶***from*** a popular *belief* that … …という世人の信仰から. ¶*belief* ***in*** God 神の信仰 ‖ he acted ***in*** the *belief* (=believing) that … 彼は…と信じてやった. 【類】he is working hard ***in*** the *belief* that … ‖ things sacred ***in*** popular *belief* 世人の神聖と信じている物. ¶lead one ***into*** a *belief* that … 人を…という信仰に導き入れる ‖ They deceived him ***into*** this *belief*. 彼らは彼をだましてこう信じさせた. ¶This is easy ***of*** *belief*. これは信じやすい. 【類】It is hard ***of*** *belief*. ‖ To the best ***of*** my *belief* there is no difficulty. 私はあくまで少しも困難ではないと信じる. ‖ it goes far to dispose ***of*** the *belief* that … それは…という説をくつがえすに足りる ‖ a man worthy ***of*** *belief* 十分信をおける人. ¶he acted ***on*** the *belief* that … 彼は…という所信に基いてやった. ¶***under*** the *belief* that … …という所信の下に.

P² folk *beliefs* ***about*** … …に関する民間信仰. ¶*beliefs* ***among*** the natives 土人間の信仰. ¶*belief* ***in*** the existence of God 神があるという信仰. 【類】[a] firm *belief* ***in*** these doctrines / I have strong *belief* ***in*** my religion. ‖ I have no *belief* ***in*** extreme measures 僕は極端な手段を良いとは思わない. 【類】I have no *belief* ***in*** my servant's honesty. ¶a *belief* ***upon*** testimony 証拠に基いた信念.

believe, *v.* 信じる.

M as it is ***commonly*** ***believed*** 普通信ぜられるごとく. ¶it is ***confidently*** ***believed*** that … …という事は確信されている. ¶***firmly*** ***believe*** 堅く信じる. ¶***fully*** ***believe*** 確信する. ¶The report is ***generally*** ***believed***. その報告は一般に信ぜられている. ¶I could ***hardly*** ***believe*** my eyes. 自分の目を信じることができないほどだった. ¶***scarcely*** ***believe*** ほとんど信じない. ¶***sincerely*** ***believe*** 心から信じる. ¶***thoroughly*** ***believe*** 十分に信じる. ¶it is almost ***universally*** ***believed*** that … …ということはほとんど一般に信じられている.

P I now *believe* ***beyond*** all doubt that … 今はどこまでも…と確信する. ¶those who *believe* ***in*** Him 神を信じる人 ‖ *believe* ***in*** the efficacy of prayer 祈りの効果を信じる. 【類】I *believe* ***in*** Buddhism (Christianity, education, future life, God, immortality, miracles, the Bible). ‖ So you *believe* ***in*** ghosts? じゃ君は幽霊があると思うのか. ‖ When I am ill, I *believe* more ***in*** diet than ***in*** drugs. 僕は病気にかゝると薬よりも食物の方で療治をする. 【類】*believe* ***in*** the truth of the theory / They *believe* ***in*** the philosophy of "Eat, drink, and be merry, for to-morrow we die." / I don't *believe* ***in*** this man. / He did not *believe* ***in*** what I was talking about. 彼は私の言うことを信じなかった. ¶He *believed* it ***on*** insufficient evidence. 彼はそれを十分な証拠がなくて信じた. ¶I *believe* ***with*** him that … 彼同様僕も…と信じる.

O I *believed* the man insane. あの男を気違いだと思った. 【類】We *believe* him mistaken. ¶I *believe* him to be dead. 彼は死んだと思った. 【類】He is *believed* to be mad. ¶I *believed* it to be a fact. 事実だと信じた. ¶He made *believe* to hand it to her. それを彼女に渡すふりをした.

believer, *n.* 信者.

V He ***found*** most *believers* among the farming population. 農民の間に最も多数の信徒を得た.

Q an ***ardent*** *believer* 熱心な信者. ¶a ***confirmed*** *believer* in the possibility of … …の可能性を堅く信じている人. ¶a ***devout*** *believer* in Herbert Spencer 大のハーバート・スペンサー礼賛者. ¶a ***devout*** and ***earnest*** *believer* 熱心でまじめな信者. ¶a ***fanatic*** *believer* in the Hokke sect 法華のこりかたまり. ¶a ***firm*** *believer* in the theory その説を堅く信じる人. ¶a ***great*** *believer* in the power of the people 民力を堅く信じる人. ¶an ***out-and-out*** *believer* in "yellow journalism" 扇動的新聞を徹頭徹尾礼賛する者. ¶a ***penitent*** *believer* in Jesus 悔悟してイエスを信じるに至った人. ¶a ***sincere*** *believer* まじめに信じる人. ¶reassure many a ***timid*** and ***distressed*** *believer* 多くの気の小さい逆境に立つ信者を安心させる. ¶There are still ***warm*** *believers* in its efficacy. その効能を今でも熱心に信じている人がある.

P² a *believer* ***in*** Christianity (Buddhism, spiritualism) キリスト教(など)を信じる人 ‖ He is not a *believer* ***in*** corporal punishment. 彼は体罰の効果を信じていない. 【類】Are you a *believer* ***in*** astrology (占星術)? ‖ I am a great *believer* ***in*** sleep. 僕は睡眠が何より薬だと思っている.

bell, *n.* 鐘, 鈴, ベル.

V ***answer*** the *bell* 呼鈴に応じる. ¶Of all angling, taking salmon with the fly ***bears*** the *bell*. 凡そ釣では蚊ばりでさけを捕るのが王座だ. ¶***bear*** ***away*** the *bell* [競争などに]勝つ, 賞品を獲得する. ¶***cast*** a *bell* 鐘を鋳造する. ¶***chime*** *bells* 鐘楽を奏する. ¶***crack*** a *bell* 鐘を打ってひびを入らせる. ¶***found*** a *bell* 鐘を作る. ¶I ***hear*** the *bells* from the village church. 村の教会から鳴り響いて来る鐘の音が聞える. ¶***jingle*** a little *bell* 小さな鈴をりんりん鳴らす. ¶***press*** the *bell* ベルを押す. ¶Please ***pull*** the *bell*. ひもを引いてベルを鳴らして下さい. ¶***ring*** a *bell* 鐘を鳴らす ‖ ***ring*** the *bell* for … 鈴を鳴らして…を求める. 【類】***ring*** two *bells*= ring twice / A *bell* was ***rung*** in warning. ¶***sound*** the *bell* rapidly 鐘を乱打する. ¶Who's it that'll ***tie*** a ***bell*** around the cat's neck? だれがねこの首に鈴をつける役をするのか. ¶***tinkle*** a ***bell*** 鈴をちんちん鳴らす. ¶***toll*** a ***bell*** 入相(葬式)の鐘を鳴らす. ¶***touch*** an electric *bell* 電鈴を鳴らす.

V² the *bells* ***ceased*** 鐘の音が止んだ. ¶The *bells* are ***chiming***. [教会などの]鐘が鳴っている. ¶Suddenly a *bell* ***clangs***. It is the dinner hour. 突然鐘の音が響き渡る. 食事の時間だ. ‖ The loud *bell* ***clangs*** its warning to the traffic. けたたましいベルの音が往来の人に警戒を与える. ¶There ***goes*** the *bell!* そらベルが鳴ってる. ‖ The *bell* ***has gone***; it is time to cease work. 鐘が鳴った, 休み時間だ. ‖ The *bell* ***went*** for the end of school. ベルが終業を報じた. ¶Merry *bells* were ***jingling*** on the horse. 馬についてる鈴が気持ちよくじゃらんじゃらん鳴っていた. ¶The *bell* ***pealed*** from the village temple. 村の寺から鐘が聞えた. ¶*Bells* ***pealed out***. 鐘が殷々(いんいん)と鳴り響いた. ¶The *bells* are ***ringing*** for church. 教会へ行く鐘が鳴っている. ¶The *bell* ***rang out*** in celebration of the occasion. その祝賀の鐘が鳴渡った. ¶The *bell* is ***tolling***. 入相の鐘が鳴っている.

Q ***clamorous bells*** 騒々しい鐘. ¶a ***cracked bell*** ひびの入った鐘. ¶A ***deep-toned bell*** tolled the hour. ぼーんと時の鐘が鳴った. ¶The ***funeral bell*** tolled solemnly. とむらいの鐘がおごそかに鳴った. ¶The ***heavy bell*** of St. Paul's tolled for the death of another day. 真夜中を告げるセント・ポール寺院の巨鐘が鳴り出した. ¶a ***loud-sounding bell*** 殷々(いんいん)と鳴り響く鐘. ¶The ***mighty bells*** are deep-toned and vibrating and affect one strangely. Centuries seem to roll back. 大鐘はその音深沈として震え一種異様の感を与える. 幾百年の昔にさかのぼるような気持になる. ¶the ***oldest-dated bell*** in existence 現存中最古の年号の印刻のある鐘. ¶a ***richly-toned bell*** 音色のよい鐘.

Q² an ***alarm bell*** 警鐘. ¶The ***cathedral*** *bells* are tolling. 大きな寺院の鐘が鳴っている. ¶hear ***church bells*** chiming きんこんかんと鳴る教会の鐘を聞く ‖ The ***church bell*** rang out eleven. 教会の鐘が十一時を報じた. 【類】***Church bells*** rang all over. ¶the ***evening bell*** of Miidera 三井寺の晩鐘. 【類】the distant sound of an ***evening bell***. ¶answer the ***front-door bell*** 玄関先の呼りんに答える. ¶The ***fire bell*** is clanging. 半鐘がじゃんじゃん鳴っている. ¶a ***hand bell*** 手に持って鳴らす鈴(呼りん). ¶a ***minute bell*** つり鐘(喪を表わすため一分間ごとに鳴らす鐘). ¶a ***monster bell*** 巨大な鐘. ¶***nine o'clock bells*** 九時の鐘. ¶The ***sleigh bells*** jingle as we ride on. そりの鈴が進むにつれてちりんちりんと鳴る. ¶a hanging ***temple bell*** 寺の釣鐘.

P ***at*** eight *bells* 八点鐘の時 ‖ A boy answered his ring ***at*** the *bell*. ベルを鳴らしたら少年がこれに応じた. 【類】There came a ring ***at*** the *bell*. ¶a chime ***of*** *bells* [教会などの]鐘の奏楽音. ¶He entered the class-room ***with*** the *bell*. 彼はベルと共に教場にはいった. ¶hear the *bell* ***from*** the village church tower 村の教会の塔から鳴出す鐘の音を聞く.

bell, *v.* 鈴をつける; らっぱ形に広がる.

M trousers with thier bottoms ***belled out*** らっぱずぼん.

O ***bell*** the cat at a crisis 進んで難局に当る.

belle *n.* 美女. 「社交界の花.

Q² the ***area*** *belle* その地区の美女(…小町). ¶a ***society belle***

bellow, *v.* ほえる, どなる. 「ンがうなった.

M The wounded lion ***bellowed out***. その傷ついたライオ

M² When he was about to utter words, he was ***bellowed off***. 何か言おうとしたらどなりつけられた.

P *bellow* ***at*** a servant 召使をどなりつける.

bellows, *n.* [単・複同型] ふいご.

V ***work*** (=***blow***) the *bellows* ふいごを使う.

P a pair ***of*** *bellows* ふいご一個.

belly, *n.* 腹.

V ***rip up*** the *belly* 切腹する.

Q a ***capacious belly*** 大きな腹. ¶We're miners without jobs, and our *bellies* are ***empty***. おれたちは失業した坑夫だ. 腹がへってる. ¶A ***hungry belly*** has no ears.—Proverb. 空腹には(道理を聞く)耳がない. ¶the ***lower belly*** 下腹.

P full ***in*** the *belly* 懐妊して. ¶crawl (=creep *or* move) ***on*** the *belly* 腹ばいをする.

bellyful, *n.* 腹一杯.

V ***eat*** one's *bellyful* 腹一杯に食べる. ¶He ***had*** a *bellyful*. 彼は腹一杯に食べた.

P² do a *bellyful* ***of*** fighting 思う存分戦う.

belong, *v.* 属する.

M the blue sky that *belongs* ***equally*** to us all 万人の所有物である青空. ¶this idea *belongs* ***exclusively*** to … この思想は…の独創である. ¶*belong* ***indisputably*** to … 正に…のものだ. ¶She doesn't *belong* ***here***. 彼女はこんな所にいるべき女ではない. ¶The potato plant ***properly*** *belongs* to South America. ジャガイモは南米が本場. ‖ The study of the subject *belongs* ***properly*** to the domain of another science. この問題の研究は本来他の科学の領域に属すべきものである. ¶***rightly*** *belong* to … 当然…に属すべきものだ. ¶things or people *belonging* ***together*** グループになっている人あるいは物.

P they *belong* ***in*** the same class with … それらは…と同種に属する 【類】These all *belong* ***in*** a different classification. / *belong* ***in*** the same category as … ‖ Those words do not *belong* ***in*** modern dictionaries. それらの語は現代辞書に採録さるべきものでない. ¶This book *belongs* ***on*** that shelf. この本はその本だなに入れることになっている. ‖ He *belongs* ***on*** a university faculty. 彼は大学の先生だ. ¶He *belongs* ***to*** the Foreign Office. 外務省の役人だ. / They *belong* ***to*** the dramatic profession (=are actors or actresses). ‖ You should *belong* ***to*** the club. 会に入会し給え. 【類】They *belong* ***to*** respectable families (良家). ‖ Bacteria *belong* ***to*** the vegetable kingdom. 細菌は植物である. ‖ land *belonging* ***to*** the Government 官有地. 【類】as he happened to *belong* ***to*** that nationality / Discussion of these problems *belongs* ***to*** the next section. / Many of his best works *belong* ***to*** this period. / They *belong* ***to*** a special class. / It *belongs* ***to*** the province of practical politics. ‖ ***to*** him *belongs* the credit of … …は彼の手柄だ ‖ *belong* ***to*** nobody 主がない ‖ ***To*** the victor *belong* the spoils of the defeated. 《米》敗者のものは勝者のもの. ☞ 勝者が政権を握れば官職は思いのままである. ‖ Some pieces of wreck supposed to have *belonged* ***to*** her has been picked up. 同船のものと想像される破船のかけらが拾い上げられた. ‖ It is more than doubtful if they *belong* ***to*** the original work. それが果して原作にあったかどうかはすこぶる疑わしい. ‖ The letter is misdated by him May 17, and really *belongs* ***to*** June 17, 1798. 彼はその手紙の日付を間違えて五月十七日としているが一七九八年の六月十七日が本当である. ‖ We *belong* ***to*** each other now—for life or for death. 今はお互に偕(かい)老同穴の仲だ. ¶This belt *belongs* ***with*** that coat. このバンドはそのコートの附属品だ. 【類】Poetry *belongs* ***with*** music and dancing, and is opposed to the arts of painting, sculpture, and architecture. ‖ A bondsman was one who *belonged* ***with*** land and sold with it. 農奴は土地に付随し, 土地と一しょに売られた. ‖ If a question mark *belongs* ***with*** the quotation, it goes inside final quotes. 疑問符が引用文(句)に伴うときは最後の引用符の内側につける.

belonging, *n.* 所有物.

V I will ***carry*** all my *belongings* with me. 僕は持物を皆持って歩く. ¶***gather up*** one's *belongings* 身のまわりの品を取りまとめる.

Q With all his ***earthly*** *belongings* he couldn't make his life any longer. あらゆる現世の財産をもってしても定命を延ばすことはできなかった. ¶tags to identify ***personal*** *belongings* 手荷物の所有主を明かにする荷札. ¶their ***scanty*** *belongings* 彼らのわずかばかりの所有物.

P He came here ***with*** all his *belongings*. 彼は持物を残らず持って来た.

beloved, *pa.* 愛せられている.

P He is *beloved* ***of*** all. 彼は皆にかわいがられている.

belt, *n.* 帯(バンド), ベルト; 地帯.

V ***put*** one's *belt* around one's waist バンドをしめる. ¶***tighten*** the *belt* 腹をこしらえる(空腹に食物を取る). ¶He ***wears*** a *belt* round his waist. 彼は腰に帯をしめている.

V² This *belt* won't ***meet*** round my waist. この帯は腰にはまわりそうもない.

Q ***abdominal*** *belts* for corpulent men 肥満の人の用いる腹帯. ¶a ***green*** *belt* 緑地帯.

Q² the ***black*** *belt* 《米》黒人地帯. ¶a ***championship*** *belt* 選手権ベルト; 横綱. ¶a ***conveyor*** *belt* 流れ作業ベルト. ¶the ***corn*** (***cotton***) *belt* 《米》とうもろこし(など)地帯. ¶a ***forest*** *belt* 森林地帯. ¶the city's ***night club*** *belt* 都市のキャバレー街(花柳界). ¶the western New York ***fruit*** *belt* 西部ニューヨーク州の果樹園地帯. ¶a ***full-dress*** *belt* 正剣帯. ¶a ***health*** *belt* 腹帯. ¶***judo*** *belts* 柔道階級ベルト

(white: beginners; brown: intermediates; black: experts). ¶The rich ***black-soil belt*** of the Ukraine. ウクライナ州の肥沃な黒土地帯. ¶the southern California ***citrus*** *belt* 南カリフォルニヤの柑橘(かんきつ)地帯.

P In those days, people wore a *yatate* ***at*** their *belts*. その時代には人々は矢立を腰に差していた. ¶They carried a pair of swords ***in*** their *belts*. 彼らは腰に両刀をたばさんでいた. 【類】A revolver was ***in*** his *belt*.

belting, *n.* 〘機〙ベルト.

Q² ***leather*** *belting* 皮製ベルト.

bemoan, *v.* なげき悲しむ.

M *bemoan* oneself ***deeply*** over the death of ... ...の死を深くなげき悲しむ. ¶He sat down and *bemoaned* himself most ***lamentably***. 彼は腰を下して悲嘆にくれた.

bench, *n.* 腰掛(ベンチ); 裁判官席.

Q ***front*** (***back***) *benches* 〘政〙[国会の]大もの(陣笠)席. ¶***hard wooden*** *benches* 堅い木の腰掛. ¶***ministerial*** *benches* 与党席. ¶***red blanketed*** *benches* 赤毛布を敷いた腰掛.

Q² the ***Government*** *benches* in Congress 国会の政府側席. ¶***opposition*** *benches* 野党席. ¶a ***work*** *bench* [職人の]作業台.

P serve a practical apprenticeship ***at*** the *bench* 裁判官の実習をやる. ¶men ***on*** the *bench* 裁判官 ‖ ball-players ***on*** the *bench* 〘野球〙ベンチの控え選手 ‖ sit ***on*** the *benches* awaiting their turn いすに腰掛けて順番を待つ. ¶He was elevated ***to*** the *bench*. 裁判官に昇進した.

bend, *n.* 屈曲, 屈曲部; 意向.

V He was allowed to ***follow*** his own *bend*. 彼には好きな事をさせて置いた. ¶He ***has*** a *bend* of the back. 彼は背が曲っている. ¶***make*** a *bend* at a street corner 町の角を曲る. ¶***round*** the *bend* of a race course 競馬場の曲り角をまわる. ¶Here the river ***takes*** an abrupt *bend* to the west. 川はここで急に西に曲っている.

Q There is a ***sharp*** *bend* on the road. 道路が急カーブしている. ¶I greeted him with a ***slight*** *bend* of the head. ちょっと頭を屈めて彼に会釈した.

P The task is ***above*** (=***beyond***) my *bend*. 《俗》その仕事は僕の手に余る. ¶angle ***at*** a *bend* in a river 川の曲り目の所で釣をする. ¶***on*** the *bend* 《俗》こっそりと. ¶The vehicle disappeared ***round*** a *bend* in the road. 乗物は路の曲り角をまわって見えなくなった.

bend, *v.* 曲げる, 向ける; 曲る.

M The lobster's body is *bent* ***double***. えびの体は折れ曲っている. ¶The old man trudged *bending* ***forward***. その老人は前こごみになってとぼとぼと歩んだ. 【類】*bend* ***forward*** to listen to ... ¶***reverently*** *bend* their heads down to the ground うやうやしく地上に平伏する. ¶The road *bends* there ***sharply*** to the right. 道路はここで右に急カーブしている. ¶*bend* ***slightly*** forward 少し前かがみになっている.

P Willows *bent* ***above*** (***over***) the little river. 柳が小川にたれ下っていた. ‖ *bend* ***before*** a person 人に屈服する. ¶We cannot *bend* him ***from*** his purpose. 彼の目的を変えさせることはできない. ¶*bend* a piece of wire ***into*** a ring 針金を曲げて環にする ‖ be *bent* ***into*** a U-shape U-字型に曲っている. ¶He *bent* his eyes ***on*** it. 彼はそれに目を向けた. ‖ He is fully *bent* ***on*** the project. 彼はその計画に本腰を入れている. ‖ a pine branch that *bends* ***over*** a pond 池の面にさし出ている松の枝 ‖ *bend* ***over*** one's work at desk 机に向い体をかがめて仕事をする. 【類】*bend* pityingly ***over*** a dying dog. ¶*bend* one's mind ***to*** (=***on***) one's study 研究に没頭する ‖ *bend* ***to*** the oars 烈しくこぐ ‖ *bend* ***to*** his will 彼の意に従う. 【類】*bend* ***to*** fate (necessity) ‖ *bend* ***to*** the west (right, left) 西(など)へ曲る. ¶*bent* his course ***toward*** ... ...の方へ歩みを向けた.

beneath, *prep.* 下に.

M They are ***far*** *beneath* the average in intelligence. 彼らは知能の点ではるかに普通の人に劣っている.

P He took it ***from*** *beneath* his coat. 上衣の下からそれを取出した.

benediction, *n.* 祝禱(しゅくとう).

V The pastor ***pronounced*** the *benediction*. 牧師が祝禱を述べた.

Q the ***nuptial*** *benediction* 結婚祝禱.

P² the *benediction* ***of*** the preacher ***upon*** the congregation 会衆に対する牧師の祝禱.

benefaction, *n.* 恩恵, 寄付.

V The University gratefully ***accepts*** this munificent *benefaction*. 本大学はこの豊かな恩恵をありがたくお受けする(講座新設などに対する基金の寄付を受けた時など).

P² the *benefaction* ***of*** the wealthy ***to*** the church 教会への金持の寄付.

benefactor, *n.* 恩人.

V ***pose*** a *benefactor* 恩に着せる.

Q a ***great*** *benefactor* of humanity (learning) 人類(など)の大恩人. ¶a ***public*** *benefactor* 社会の恩人.

P² a *benefactor* ***of*** learning 学問の恩人. ¶a *benefactor* ***to*** the race その民族の恩人. 【類】They were *benefactors* ***to*** science and ***to*** the human species.

beneficence, *n.* 慈善.

P² *beneficence* ***to*** the poor 貧乏人への慈善.

beneficent, *a.* 慈悲深い.

P He was *beneficent* ***to*** the poor. 貧乏人に慈悲深かった.

beneficial, *a.* 有益な.

M ***highly*** *beneficial* 非常に有益な.

P It is *beneficial* ***for*** sufferers from rheumatism, gout, and kidney complaints. リューマチス・痛風・腎臓病患者にとってきき目がある. ¶These birds are *beneficial* ***to*** man. これらの鳥は益鳥である. 【類】*beneficial* ***to*** health / It is *beneficial* ***to*** the patient in various diseases.

benefit, *n.* 利益; 恩典.

V ***confer*** a *benefit* upon ... ...に恩恵を施す. ¶I read the book many times in order to ***derive*** the full *benefit* from its pages. 僕は十分な利益を収めるためにその本を数回繰返して読んだ. ¶***do*** a public *benefit* 公益を図る. ¶I ***enjoyed*** the *benefit* of his instructions concerning the matter. 私はその件について彼の指導を仰いだ. ¶***extend*** the *benefits* of the treaty to ... 条約の利益を...に及ぼす. ¶***get*** the *benefit* of rise in the market 市価の上昇で利益を得る. ¶He ***gave*** me the *benefit* of his advice. 彼は私に忠告してくれた. 【類】He ***gave*** me the *benefit* of his valuable criticism. / ***gave*** us the *benefit* of their special knowledge in their respective fields / The jury ***gave*** the prisoner the *benefit* of the doubt (しばらく判定を延ばした). / ***give*** one's children the *benefit* of a foreign education / He ***gave*** me the *benefit* of his experience and scholarship. / I will ***give*** you the *benefit* of my knowledge of it. ‖ He is kind enough to ***give*** my store the *benefit* of his patronage. あの方は好意を持って僕の店の品を買って下さる. 【類】He ***gave*** me one evening the *benefit* of a talk all to myself on the subject. ¶The delinquent was ***granted*** the *benefit* of conditional freedom or of pardon. 違犯者は条件付放免または免罪を許された. ¶I should like to ***have*** the *benefit* of your advice. 御助言を仰ぎたいものです. 【類】***have*** the *benefit* of wise counsel and guidance. ¶justly ***lose*** the *benefit* of law 当然法律の恩恵に浴しない. ¶it ***promises*** fruitful *benefit* for ... それは...に好成績をもたらす見込がある. ¶***reap*** the *benefit* of ... ...の利益を収める. 【類】***reap*** some direct *benefit* from their English studies. ¶***receive*** the *benefits* 恩を受ける ‖ to ***receive*** the *benefit* of their criticism 彼らの批評を仰ぐために. 【類】The article has ***received*** the *benefit* of his correction. / ***receive*** the *benefit* of rains / ***receive*** the *benefit* of a reduction in the subscription price ‖ He ***received*** no *benefit* from the medicine. 彼にはその薬のきき目がなかった. ¶***repay*** a *benefit* 恩を返す. ¶***secure*** a double *benefit* 二重の利益を得る. ¶***see*** *benefit* in joining the association その会の会員になると得になることが分る.

V² *benefits* ***accruing*** to ... from ... ...から...へ及ぼす利益.

Q result in ***far-reaching*** *benefit* to mankind 人類に広範な利益を与える結果となる. ¶reap the ***full*** *benefit* of ... ...の利益を十分に収める. 【類】get the ***full*** *benefit* of the sunshine. ¶***Half*** the *benefit* of a virtue disappears when we advertise it. 折角の美徳も広言するとその功徳が半減する. ¶He doubts "civilization" as a ***human*** *benefit*. 彼はいわゆる「文明」が果して人間のためになるかを疑っている. ¶confer an ***inestimable*** *benefit* upon ... ...に無限の恵みを与える. ¶***lasting*** *benefit* 永久の利益. ¶be of ***material*** *benefit* in ... ...において顕著な利益となる. ¶***maximum*** *benefit* 最大利益. ¶It will prove of ***mutual*** *benefit* to all concerned. それは関係者一同のためになるだろう. 【類】work for the ***mutual*** *benefit* of the members. ¶for the ***national*** *benefit* 国家のために ‖ A cheap edition of this masterpiece is a ***national*** *benefit*. この傑作の廉価版は国益になる. ¶We do not derive any ***pecuniary*** *benefit* from the work. 私たちはその事業から何等金銭上の利益を得ていない. ¶for the ***spiritual*** *benefit* of ... …の精神的利益のために. ¶for the ***spiritual***, ***moral***, and ***physical*** *benefit* of ... …という精神的, 道徳的, かつ身体的な利益のために. ¶a ***substantial*** *benefit* 実質上の利益. ¶produce ***unspeakable*** *benefits* to the public 口では言われないほどの利益を一般大衆に与える.

Q^2 workman's ***compensation*** *benefits* [社会保険による]勤労者の補償金給付. ¶***insurance*** *benefit* 保険給付. ¶***retirement*** *benefit* 退職資金給付. ¶***sickness*** and ***death*** *benefits* [健康保険制度による]病気死亡の補償給付. ¶pay ***strike*** *benefits* 〖労〗ストによる生活補償金を支払う. ¶the enjoyment of ***treaty*** *benefits* 条約による特典を受けること. ¶the fair distribution of ***welfare*** *benefits* 厚生施設による恩恵を公平に施すこと.

P ***by*** the *benefit* of ... …の恩義によって. ¶The handbook has been prepared mainly ***for*** their *benefit*. その便覧は主として彼らのために編集されたものだ. 【類】***for*** the *benefit* of all concerned / ***for*** the *benefit* of a charity / ***for*** the *benefit* of the civilization of the world / ***for*** the *benefit*, or supposed benefit, of ... / He traveled ***for*** the *benefit* of his health. / ***for*** the *benefit* of posterity / The money is given ***for*** the *benefit* of the Scholarship Fund (奨学資金のため). / ***for*** the *benefit* of the war fund (軍資金) ‖ ***for*** the general *benefit* of the community 社会一般の利益のために. ¶participate ***in*** the *benefit* of a club クラブの利益を受ける. ¶get the last ounce ***of*** *benefit* out of one's university 在学している大学からできるだけの利益を得る ‖ It proved ***of*** great *benefit* to him. それが彼にとって大きな利益となった. 【類】it would be ***of*** little *benefit* to ... / The voyage was ***of*** much *benefit* to me. ¶It would be ***to*** his *benefit* to do so. そうするのが彼の利益になるだろう. ¶Oblige me ***with*** the *benefit* of your advice. 貴下の御意見を伺いたい. ¶***without*** *benefit* 便益なしに.

P^2 the *benefit* ***from*** reading aloud 音読の利益. ¶the *benefit* ***of*** clergy (peerage) 僧侶(など)の特典. 【類】the *benefit* ***of*** study to the pupil. ¶it is of mutual *benefit* ***to*** ... それは…にとって相互の利益となる.

benefit, *v.* 利する, 利益を得る.

P I have *benefited* ***by*** the labor of others. 他人の努力から得る所があった. ¶university extension work for those who are unable to *benefit* ***from*** the university 大学の利益に与ることのできないもののための校外教育. ¶He is *benefited* ***in*** every way. いろいろの点で利益を受けている.

benevolence, *n.* 博愛.

V The Rockefeller Foundation is a fund by which Mr. Rockefeller has ***organized*** his *benevolence*. ロックフェラー基金は氏の社会奉仕を組織化した基金である.

Q ***inadvertent*** *benevolence* 思慮を欠いた慈善行為. ¶A whole village sunk still in misery and despair by their ***well-meant*** but ***unwise*** *benevolence*. 心は賞すべきもやり方のまずい慈善のために村中のものが未だに悲嘆と失望の中に沈んでいる.

P^2 *benevolence* ***from*** the wealthy 金持からの慈善. ¶*benevolence* ***of*** the wealthy 金持の慈善. ¶*benevolence* ***on*** the part of the wealthy 金持の慈善. ¶*benevolence* ***to*** (=***toward***) the poor 貧民への慈善.

bent, *n.* 好み, 性癖.

V ***ascertain*** the vocational *bent* of a child 子供の適性検査をする. ¶***follow*** one's own *bent* 心の向く所に従う. 【類】***follow*** the natural *bent* of one's genius. ¶***give*** one's humor the true *bent* ほんとうに気の向いたようにやる. ¶Early he ***showed*** a strong mechanical *bent*. 子供の時から彼は機械が大好きであった.

Q follow one's ***artistic*** *bent* 好きな芸術の道を進む. ¶on ***holiday-making*** *bent* 享楽(遊山)気分で. ¶His ***natural*** *bent* was toward books and reading. 彼は生来読書好きだった. ¶follow the ***natural*** *bent* of one's genius. 【類】have a ***natural*** *bent* for study. ¶follow one's ***personal*** *bent* in the choice of an occupation 職業は自分の性格に合うものを選ぶ.

Q^2 be on ***cricket*** *bent* クリケットをやりたい. ¶on ***pleasure*** *bent* 快楽を追うという気分で.

P Science was ***out of*** his *bent*. 科学は彼の性に合わなかった. ¶a young man ***with*** a literary *bent* 文学青年.

bent, *pa.* 心を向けている; 曲った.

P The boy is *bent* ***on*** mischief. 彼はいたずら小僧だ. ‖ He is *bent* ***on*** becoming a sailor. 彼は船乗になりたがっている. 【類】They seem to be *bent* ***on*** making the most of their childhood, which is but a short one. / be *bent* ***on*** gains (=profit) もうけ事に熱心だ / He is *bent* more ***on*** selling than ***on*** buying. ¶He was *bent* ***over*** the task. その仕事に熱中していた. ¶he is *bent* ***upon*** opposing ... 彼は…に反対と意気込んでいる. ¶*bent* double ***with*** age 取る年で体がくの字に曲って.

benumbed, *pa.* しびれて.

P My hands are *benumbed* ***with*** cold. 私の手は寒さでかじかんでいる.

bequeath, *v.* 遺す, 伝える.

P *bequeath* property ***to*** one's heirs 財産を相続人に遺す ‖ *bequeath* it ***to*** a museum それを博物館に寄贈する ‖ the swords *bequeathed* ***to*** them by their forefathers 先祖伝来の刀.

bequest, *n.* 遺産, 遺贈.

V ***administer*** his *bequest* 彼の遺産を管理する. ¶***leave*** a *bequest* 財産を遺す. ¶***make*** many *bequests* to ... …に多くの遺産を贈る.

Q ***charitable*** *bequests* 慈善事業への遺産. ¶***munificent*** *bequests* 社会事業の遺贈.

P ***by*** *bequest* 遺志により.

P^2 a *bequest* ***to*** the Smithsonian Institution for the investigation of the properties of the upper air 上層空気の性質研究のためスミソニア学会への遺贈.

bereave, *v.* 奪う, 失わす.

P He must have been *bereft* ***of*** his senses. 気が変になっていたに相違ない. ‖ persons *bereft* ***of*** sense 気違になった人々 ‖ those who are *bereft* ***of*** hearing 耳の聞えなくなった人たち. 【類】those who are *bereft* of reason / be *bereft* ***of*** half the pleasure / He is *bereft* ***of*** all hope. / An accident *bereft* me ***of*** my leg. / They were *bereft* ***of*** the pillar of their family (一家の支柱). / Death *bereaved* us ***of*** our children. / Mr. Gray, *bereaved* ***of*** mother, wife, child ‖ be *bereft* ***of*** every particle of shame てんとして恥を知らない.

bereavement, *n.* 喪失.

Q a ***sad*** *bereavement* 不幸.

Q^2 on account of some ***family*** *bereavement* 家に不幸があるので.

P convey one's sympathy with him and his family ***in*** their *bereavement* 彼の家族の不幸に弔意を述べる.

berry, *n.* 漿果(しょう)(いちごなど).

V ***pick*** *berries* いちご(など)をつむ.

Q^2 ***coffee*** *berry* コーヒーの種子. ¶***mistletoe*** *berry* やどり木の実.

P^2 the *berry* ***of*** grains 穀物の粒.

berth, *n.* **(1)** [汽車・汽船の]寝台; 停泊所.

V ***allot*** *berth* 停泊地を指定する. ¶be ***allowed*** a *berth* to No. 4 buoy 泊地を四番浮標に指定される. ¶***book*** a *berth* at the commencing station 始発駅で寝台を取って置く. ¶***give*** a wide *berth* to ... …を避ける ‖ The ship ***gave*** the other a wide *berth*. 船は衝突しないように他船と十分の間隔を置いて通った. ‖ You had better ***give*** a wide *berth* to such a dangerous man. / When we meet a tipsy man (酔っぱらい), we ***give*** him a wide *berth*. ¶The steamer ***has*** a *berth* at the quay. 汽船が埠頭(ふ)に着いている. ¶I recommend you to ***keep*** a wide *berth* of him. あまり彼に近づかないようにお勧めする. ¶Serpentines of confetti floated from the decks when the ship ***left*** her *berth*. 停泊地から船が出るとデッキから投げた紙テープが長蛇のように流れた. ¶***reserve*** a steamer *berth* 汽船の寝台を予約する. ¶I ***secured*** a *berth* on board the Hakone Maru bound for London. ロンドン行箱根丸の寝台を取って置いた. ¶The ship ***shifted*** its *berth*. 船がその繋船所を変えた. ¶***take up*** a *berth* 停泊する.

Q a ***good*** *berth* 良好の投錨(びょう)地.

Q^2 Rooms contain two single beds and a ***sofa*** *berth*. へやにはシングルベッドが二つとソファー兼用ベッドが一つある. ¶***sleeping*** *berths* are provided, on application, in the first class cars of any of the express trains. 一等急行列車では希望によって寝台が設備される.

P Is there any steamer ***on*** the *berth* for America? アメリカ行の汽船が停泊しているか. 【類】vessels ***on*** the *berth*.

P^2 *Berths* ***on*** steamships can be booked a long while in advance. 汽船の寝台はずっと前から取って置ける.

(2) 地位, 職.

V He has ***got*** a good *berth* at last. やっと好い仕事にありついた. ¶***leave*** one's *berth* 辞職する. ¶He ***lost*** his *berth* through drink. 酒のために職を失った.

P be ***out of*** a *berth* 浪人する, 失業する.

beseem, *v.* 似合う.

M It *ill beseems* you to complain. 泣言を言うとは君にも似合わない.

beset *v.* 包囲する; ちりばめる.

P The task was *beset **with*** difficulties. その仕事は幾多の困難が伴っていた. 【類】The undertaking is *beset **with*** danger (perils). / The city dweller's life is *beset **with*** little worries. / The river is *beset **with*** ice and snow. ‖ *beset **with*** gold and jewels 黄金や宝石をちりばめた.

beside, *prep.* かたわらに.

P He was *beside* himself ***with*** rage (fear, joy). 彼は激怒(など)のあまり気も狂わんばかりであった.

besiege, *v.* 包囲する; 押寄せる.

P He was *besieged **by*** visitors. 訪問者に取巻かれた. ¶He was *besieged **with*** enquiries. 質問の包囲攻撃に会った.

besieger, *n.* 包囲者.

V They successfully ***resisted*** the *besieger* for many months. 数カ月間攻囲軍に対抗し得た.

besmear, *v.* なすりつける.

P They *besmeared* him ***with*** tar. 彼らは彼にタールをぬたくり付けた. ‖ cloth *besmeared **with*** oil 油で汚れた布. 【類】He is *besmeared **with*** blood (mud).

bespangle, *v.* ぴかぴかした物で飾る.

P sentence thickly *bespangled **with*** exclamation points 感嘆符をやたらに付けた文章. 【類】The heavens are *bespangled **with*** stars.

bespatter, *v.* はねかける.

P white trousers *bespattered **with*** mud 泥がはねかかった白ズボン.

besprinkle, *v.* 注ぐ; 振りかける.

P It was *besprinkled **with*** flour. 粉を振りかけてあった. 【類】The flowers were *besprinkled **with*** morning dews.

best, *n.* 最善; 全力.

V ***claim*** the *best* of the fight 闘争の勝者であると主張する. ¶***do*** the *best* possible 最善をつくす ‖ with a determination to ***do*** one's *best* 腕によりをかけて. 【類】He has ***done*** his *best* in every way. / ***do*** the *best* that is in one 全力を尽す ‖ Humanity has, at any rate, ***done*** its *best* to answer this question. 人類はこの質問に答える(問題を解決す)べくとにかく全力を尽した. ‖ He ***did*** his level *best* to appear as unconcerned as possible. できるだけ平静を装った. ¶***draw out*** the *best* that is in him 彼の持っている最善を引出す(発揮させる). ¶He ***got*** (=***had***) the *best* of it. 勝負に勝った. ¶He ***had*** the *best* of the bargain. 有利に取引をまとめた. ‖ He ***had*** the *best* of the argument. 彼は議論で勝った. ¶endeavor to ***look*** one's *best* せいぜい美しく(りっぱに)見せようとする ‖ She is bent on ***looking*** her *best*. 彼女はおつくり(美容)に腐心している. ¶I had to ***make*** the *best* of it. それで間に合わせるより外なかった. ‖ ***make*** the *best* of a bad job (=bargain) おもしろくない事態に精々善処する ‖ how to ***make*** the *best* of life 処世の道 ‖ ***make*** the *best* of mothers for ... …のために最善の母親としてつくす ‖ ***make*** the *best* of the situation 措置よろしきを得る ‖ ***make*** the *best* of one's way 成るべく道を急ぐ. ¶***require*** the *best* of care 最大の注意を要する. ¶***see*** the *best* of a city 町の一番美しい所を見る. ¶***sing*** one's *best* 一番得意な歌を歌う. ¶***Try*** your *best* to secure the business. 全力を尽してその仕事を手に入れるようにせよ. ‖ "society" where humanity is ***trying*** its poor *best* to wear a mask 人々がうまく行かぬが一生懸命になって仮面を被ろう(外面を繕ろおう)と努めているいわゆる交際場裡.

Q do one's ***level*** *best* to ... …しようと真に全力を尽す. ¶the ***next*** (=***second***) *best* 次善. ¶He says that incubators are ***second*** *best* and hens are first. 彼の説では孵卵器が次善でめんどりが一番よいのである. ¶I will do my ***poor*** *best* to do so. 及ばずながら全力を尽しましょう. ¶the ***third*** *best* 三番目に善いもの. ¶one of the ***very*** *best* 最善の一つ ‖ This is the ***very*** *best*. これが本当の最上です.

Q² all in their ***Sunday*** *best* みんなそろって晴着を着て.

P He is a fool ***at*** [the] *best*. よく言っても彼はばか者だ. ‖ Life is short ***at*** *best*. どう考えても人生は短い. ‖ The flowers are ***at*** their *best*. 花は見ごろだ. ‖ Art was then ***at*** its *best*. 当時美術は全盛であった. ‖ ***at*** the *best* of it せいぜい ‖ The place is ***at*** its *best* just now. そこへ行くのは今が一番良い時だ. ‖ He was ***at*** his *best* this morning. けさの彼の容体は非常に良かった. ‖ shows the author ***at*** his *best* この作家の最高のできばえを示している ‖ The author will be read ***at*** his very *best* in ... この作家のものを読むなら…という最高の作品のがよい. ‖ The story-teller was ***at*** his *best* in the imitation of Danjuro's voice. その落語家は団十郎の声色が一番よくできた. ¶He managed everything ***for*** the *best*. 彼は万事うまく行くように処理した. 【類】I meant it ***for*** the *best* of your nephew. ‖ I don't know what to do ***for*** the *best*. どうしたら良いのか分りません. ¶I was ***in*** the *best* of health and spirits. 体も気持も申分がなかった. ¶he is ***on*** the *best* with ... 彼は…とごく親密だ. ¶try ***to*** the *best* of one's ability (=power) to ... 力の及ぶ限り…しようとする ‖ All the statements are perfectly correct ***to*** the *best* of his belief. その陳述全部が徹頭徹尾正しいと彼は堅く信じている. ‖ He declared that ***to*** the *best* of his judgement, it was genuine. それはたしかに本物と鑑定すると彼は断言した. ‖ ***to*** the *best* of my knowledge 私の知っている限りでは ‖ The foregoing is, ***to*** the *best* of my knowledge and belief, a true statement in all particulars. 右の通り相違ありません. 【類】***to*** the *best* of my memory (=recollection *or* remembrance). ¶She went out ***in*** her *best*. ¶***with*** the *best* of care 最大の注意を払って, 念には念を入れて.

P² It is the *best* ***for*** the general reader. それは一般読者にとって最良のものである. ¶***Best of*** luck! お元気で(告別のときのあいさつ). ‖ The *best* ***of*** the joke was that my friend never saw it. 一番おかしかったのは僕の友人にそのしゃれが分らなかった事だ. ‖ This is the *best* ***of*** its kind now in our hand. これが手前どもにある品では一番上等の品です.

bestir, *v.* 奮起させる.

M *bestir* oneself very ***satisfactorily*** りっぱにやりおおせる.

bestow *v.* 与える; しまっておく; 泊める.

M We are grateful for the benefits which nature has so ***bountifully*** *bestowed* upon us. 自然が豊かに与えた恩恵に対して私たちは感謝する. ¶I hope for a continuance of the patronage which was so ***liberally*** *bestowed* upon us. 一方ならぬお引立に預りましたがなにとぞ引続き御愛顧を賜わりますようお願い致します. ¶He was well deserving of the applause ***ungrudgingly*** *bestowed* upon him. 彼に浴せかけられた絶讃を彼はりっぱに受ける値打があった.

P *bestow* travelers ***for*** the night 旅人を一泊させる. ¶*bestow* something ***on*** (=***upon***) a person 人に何物かを与える. ☞古くは "to" または "of" を用いた. ‖ the labor he has *bestowed* ***on*** ... …につくした彼の努力 ‖ I sincerely thank you for the favors you have *bestowed* ***on*** me. お世話になって誠にありがとう存じます. 【類】He *bestowed* a gift (kindness) ***on*** me. ¶I hardly deserve such benefit as was *bestowed* ***upon*** me. 身にあまる御恩を受けました. 【類】I do not deserve all the praise that is *bestowed* ***upon*** me. ‖ Poet Laureate, the highest honor England can *bestow* ***upon*** her poetical sons 英国がその国の詩人に授与しうる最高の名誉たる桂冠(けいかん)詩人. ¶*bestow* (=deposit) ... ***with*** a friend …を友達に預けて置く

bestowing, *n.* 贈与.

P a lavish *bestowing* ***upon*** ... …への惜しげもない贈り物.

best seller, ベスト・セラー.

Q² ***drugstore*** *best sellers* 最も好評な売薬.

P² one of the *best sellers* ***for*** 1956 一九五六年度のベストセラーの一つ.

bet, *n.* かけ, かけ事.

V ***accept*** a *bet* かけの申出に応じる. ¶***call off*** a *bet* かけをやめる(撤回する). ¶I ***declare*** the *bet* ***off***. そのかけはやめた. ¶Let us ***have*** a *bet* on the result of the ball game. その野球試合でかけをしよう. ¶I will ***lay*** you a *bet*. 君とかけをしよう. ¶***lay*** a *bet* on ... …にかける. ¶***lose*** a *bet* かけに負ける. 【類】The *bet* was ***lost***. ¶***make*** a *bet* as to who would be the first to ... だれが…の一番になるかについてかけをする ‖ ***make*** a *bet* of 1,000 yen with him on ... …について彼と千円のかけをする. 【類】a *bet* was once ***made*** that ... ‖ He ***made*** a *bet* that he would reach the summit before any of the others. 彼は一番がけに頂上に着くことは大丈夫とうけ合った. ¶***win*** a *bet* on a horse 馬にかけて勝つ(馬券が当る).

P I lost 3,000 yen ***in*** one *bet*. 一度のかけで三千円をなくした.

bet, *v.* かける.

M² ***bet round*** 《俗》[競馬で]総ての馬に万べんなくかける(大損害を避けるために).

P ***bet against*** another person 他人とかけをする. ¶***bet on*** horse races 競馬にかける. 【類】I'll *bet* ten dollars ***on*** the black horse. / ***bet on*** the result of a race / Americans ***bet on*** horseraces, prize-fights, baseball and football games and even on the election. / *bet* money ***on*** (=***upon***) some future event. ¶I offered to *bet* ***with*** him that Rikkyo would win. 立教が勝つということでかけをしようと彼に持ち掛けた.

O I will *bet* a couple of oranges and a pineapple or two that ... 僕は...ということをみかん二つとパイナップルを一つか二つをかけて保証する. ¶*bet* a man one thousand dollars that ... きっと...だと千ドルをかけて保証する. ¶I *bet* he's right. たしかに彼が正しいよ.

betake, *v.* 身を委ねる.

P He *betook* himself ***to*** arms. 武器に訴えた. ‖ His threats proving of no avail, he *betook* himself ***to*** entreaties. おどしが利かないので今度はすかして見た. ‖ He *betook* himself ***to*** a friend for aid. 彼は友に助けを求めた. ‖ The stag *betook* himself ***to*** the thicket. 雄じかは茂みの中へ入って行った. ‖ *betake* oneself ***to*** submission 投降する ‖ *betake* himself ***to*** his heels (=legs) 逃走する ‖ He *betook* himself ***to*** an inn. 旅館に投宿した. 【類】He *betook* himself ***to*** teaching. / He *betook* himself ***to*** a study of law.

bethink, *v.* 思う; 思い出す.

M then ***suddenly bethinking*** himself 突然気が付いて.

P He *bethought* himself ***of*** an excellent plan. 彼に妙案が浮んだ. ☞古くは "of" の代りに "on" または "upon" を用いた.

betray, *v.* 裏切る; 敵の手に渡す; あざむく.

M *betray* oneself ***easily*** by ... ...でたちまち化の皮をあらわしてしまう. ¶He ***soon*** *betrayed* his ignorance. 自分の無学をすぐ暴露した.

P *betray* one's character ***by*** the manner 態度で人格の卑しさを暴露する. 【類】He *betrayed* his intention ***by*** his behavior. ¶*betray* a person ***into*** the enemy's hands 人を裏切って敵の手に渡す ‖ I was *betrayed* ***into*** folly. だまされてばかをやった. 【類】His thoughtlessness *betrayed* him ***into*** foolish alliance. / He was *betrayed* ***into*** great extravagance by a woman. / He was *betrayed* ***into*** a snare. ¶*betray* a secret ***to*** a person 秘密を人に漏らす.

betrayal, *n.* 裏切; 密告.

P² She was a victim of *betrayal* ***by*** men. 彼女は男たちにもてあそばれた. ¶*betrayal* ***of*** a secret 秘密の内通をすること.

betroth, *v.* 婚約する, いいなずけにする.

P He *betrothed* a woman ***for*** his wife. 彼はある女と婚約した. ¶He *betrothed* his daughter ***to*** my son. 彼は娘を私の息子の嫁にくれる約束をした. 【類】She was *betrothed* ***to*** John.

better, *n.* 一層よいこと; 優勝; 長上.

V you can ***do*** no *better* than to ... ...するに越したことはない. ¶***get*** the *better* of one's opponent 相手を負かす(議論で) ‖ I always ***get*** the *better* when I argue alone. 僕は頭の中で議論する時はいつも自分の説に理があると思う. ‖ curiosity ***got*** the *better* of him and he asked ... 好奇心に動かされて...と尋ねた. ¶I always ***had*** the *better* of the play (=game). 僕はいつも競技に勝った.

P ***before*** one's *betters* 長上の前で. ¶The patient has taken a turn ***for*** the *better*. 病人は良い方へ向いた. 【類】This is a change ***for*** the *better*. / My fortune has changed ***for*** the *better*. ‖ ***for*** *better* or [for] worse よくとも悪くとも. ☞Prayer Book には "for better for worse" とある. 【類】The partner he took in contract, ***for*** *better* or for worse, turned out for worse. ¶despise the advice ***of*** one's *betters* 長上の忠告を侮る ‖ There is no hope ***of*** *better* left for him. 彼にはもう善い事のある見込みはない. ¶give place ***to*** one's *better* 自分より腕のある人に地位を譲る. ¶came out ***with*** no *better* than a tie 勝負なしに終った.

better, *a., ad.* 一層よい.

M The patient is now ***a degree*** *better*. 病人は今いくらかよい. ¶He is ***a little*** (=***rather***) *better* this morning. 彼は今朝は少しよい. ¶He is not ***any*** *better* as yet. 彼はまだ一向よくない. ¶it is ***decidedly*** *better* not to ... ...しない方が断然いい. ¶This is ***much*** *better*. この方がよっぽどいい. ¶He is ***no*** *better* than an idiot. 彼はどうしてもばかだ. ‖ You could have done ***no*** *better*. そうしたのが一番よかった. ¶be *better* ***off*** 裕福にやっている ‖ He is rather *better* ***off*** than I am. 彼は私より暮しが楽な位だ. ¶He is ***something*** *better*. 彼は幾分よい. ¶Well, if so, so much ***the*** *better* for him. そうならあの人にとってなおよい.

O You had *better* be quiet. 静かにした方がよい. ¶You had *better* do so. そうする方がよい(未来にいう). 【類】You had *better* not be doing so. / You had *better* not have done so. ¶Theoretically, it is *better* to be right and beaten than to be wrong and win. 理屈から言って負けて正しい方が, 勝って間違っているよりはよい.

betterment, *n.* 改善.

V things that ***need*** *betterment* 改善を要するもの.

Q ***civic*** *betterment* 市政の改善. ¶He organized agencies for ***human*** *betterment*. 彼は人生改善のために諸種の機関を組織した.

Q² ***race*** *betterment* 民族の向上.

betting, *n.* かけごと.

Q ***away-from-the-track*** *betting* on the horses 場外競馬券の賭け.

Q² ***street*** *betting* 街頭でのかけごと.

P² *betting* ***on*** horse racing 競馬でかけること.

between, *prep.* 間.

P ***from*** *between* 間から. ¶trees planted with the space of 100 yards ***in*** *between* 百ヤードの間隔をおいて植えた木.

O This [matter] is *between* ourselves. これは内々だ. 【類】Let this be *between* ourselves.

beverage, *n.* 飲料.

Q ***alcoholic*** *beverages* アルコール飲料. ¶***cooling*** *beverages* 清涼飲料. ¶Coffee is a ***fragrant*** *beverage*. コーヒーは芳香のある飲物である. ¶Aerated water is a ***pleasant*** and ***invigorating*** *beverage*. 炭酸水は気持がよく元気をつける飲み物である. ¶a ***popular*** *beverage* 大衆的飲料.

Q² a ***summer*** *beverage* 夏季飲料. ¶beer and other ***table*** *beverages* ビールその他食卓用飲料.

bevy, *n.* 群.

P² a *bevy* ***of*** maidens (fair women) 乙女(美女)の群. ¶a *bevy* ***of*** pheasants きじの群.

beware, *v.* 用心する.

P *Beware* ***of*** fire. 火の用心. ‖ *Beware* ***of*** the savage dog! 〖掲示〗猛犬注意. 【類】*Beware* ***of*** pickpockets (dangers, imitations). / *Beware* ***of*** falling into their evil ways. ‖ *Beware* ***of*** a man of one book.—St. T. Aquinas 専門家との論争は避けるがよい.

bewilder, *v.* 当惑させる.

M He was ***so*** *bewildered* that he did not know what to do. 彼は面くらってどうすることもできなかった.

P be *bewildered* ***at*** the sight (news) of ... ...を見て(聞いて)あわてふためく.

bewilderment, *n.* 当惑.

P in ***some*** *bewilderment* ちょっとあっ気に取られて. ¶***in*** huge *bewilderment* 大いに面くらって. ¶***with*** a foolish *bewilderment* ばかげたたまげ方で.

bewitch, *v.* 魅する, ばかす.

M She has ***quite*** *bewitched* ***him***. 彼女は全く彼を悩殺した.

P He was *bewitched* ***by*** a fox. 彼はきつねにばかされた. ‖ He has been *bewitched* ***by*** some evil spirit. 彼は悪霊に取りつかれた.

beyond, *prep.* 越えて, 以上に.

M He lives ***five doors*** *beyond* the church. 彼は教会から五軒先に住んでいる. ¶This book is ***quite*** *beyond* me. この本は僕にはとても分らない. 【類】He is ***quite*** *beyond* recovery.

P He came ***from*** *beyond* the sea. 彼は海の彼方から来た.

bias, *n.* 片寄り, 偏見, 偏執; 〖服飾〗バイヤス.

V ***give*** a *bias* to one's actions 不公平な事をする. ¶They ***have*** a strong *bias* in that direction. 彼らは非常にその方に偏している. ¶***root out*** a *bias* 偏見を根絶する.

Q a ***personal*** *bias* 自分一個の偏見. ¶a ***religious*** *bias* 宗教的偏見. ¶He wrote under ***strong*** *bias*. 強い偏見にとらわれて執筆した.

Q² an ***anti-English*** *bias* 排英思想. ¶a ***party*** *bias* 党人的偏見.

P He is free ***from*** *bias*. 彼には偏見がない. ¶cut cloth ***on*** the *bias* 布をバイヤスに切る. ¶He could not possibly be ***under*** any *bias*. 決して何らの偏見にもとらわれていない. ¶He writes ***with*** a little *bias* on some points. ある点は少し筆を曲げて書いている.

P² a *bias* ***to*** (=***toward***) a thing or person 物事または人への偏見. ¶Strong love is a *bias* ***upon*** the thoughts. 強い愛は思想を片寄ったものにする.

bias, *v.* 偏せしめる.

P The judgment is often *biased* ***by*** interest. 判断は往々利害関係から片寄ったものになる. ¶He was *biased* ***into*** a belief in its justice. 彼は偏見からそれが正しいと信じるに至った.

bias, *a.* 〖服飾〗バイヤスの.

O cloth cut *bias* バイヤスに切った布.

Bible, *n.* 聖書.
Q^2 a ***family*** *Bible* 家庭用聖書(一家の生・死・結婚などを記入するようになっている). ¶a ***reference*** *Bible* 引照付き聖書.
bibliography, *n.* 書籍解題; 書籍目録.
V ***attempt*** a comprehensive *bibliography* 広範な書史編集を試みる. ¶a *bibliography* ***bearing*** on ... ...に関する文献目録.
Q an ***exhaustive*** *bibliography* 遺漏のない図書目録. ¶an ***extensive*** *bibliography* of phonetic literature 発音学に関する書籍の広はんな目録. ¶a ***formidable*** *bibliography* 驚くほど広はんな図書目録. ¶a ***polyglot*** *bibliography* 数カ国語にわたる図書目録. ¶a ***selective*** *bibliography* 要書目.
P^2 a *bibliography* ***of*** cremation 火葬に関する図書目録. 【類】a *bibliography* ***of*** George Meredith / a *bibliography* ***of*** the subject. ¶a *bibliography* ***on*** the nineteenth century 十九世紀に関する図書目録.
bibliomaniac, *n.* 蔵書狂.
Q a ***rational*** *bibliomaniac* 合理的愛書家.
bicker, *v.* 口論する; 揺れる.
P Withered leaves were *bickering* (=quivering) ***in*** a fresh breeze. 枯葉が涼風に揺れていた. ¶*bicker* ***with*** ... ...
bickering, *n.* 口論. Lとけんかをする.
Q ***petty*** *bickerings* つまらない口論.
bicycle, *n.* 自転車.
V ***coast*** a *bicycle* 《米》[ペダルを踏まずに]自転車で坂路を降りる. ¶***hire*** a *bicycle* by the hour 時間ぎめで自転車を借りる. ¶***ride*** a *bicycle* =cycle, *v.* 自転車に乗る. 【類】***ride*** one's *bicycle* to the post office ‖ while ***riding*** a *bicycle*(=as ... was cycling) 自転車で走っている間に. ¶I ***walked*** my *bicycle* back with Prof. X. 帰りは X 教授と一しょに自転車を手で引いて歩いた.
V^2 The *bicycle* ***swerved*** at the corner and upset. 自転車が角でそれて転覆した. 「*bicycle* 二人乗自転車.
Q a ***convertible*** *bicycle* 男女兼用の自転車. ¶a ***duplex***
Q^2 a ***motor*** *bicycle*=《米》an autobicycle (=autobike) オートバイ. ¶a ***pedal*** *bicycle* [ペダルで動かす]自転車. ¶a ***racing*** *bicycle* 競輪用の自転車.
P The doctor pays calls ***astride*** a *bicycle*. その医者は自転車に乗って回診する. ¶He traveled ***by*** *bicycle* the whole way. 全行程を自転車で旅行した. 【類】He came to school ***by*** *bicycle*. ¶He lost control ***of*** his *bicycle*. 自転車のかじをとりそこなった. ¶the seat ***on*** a *bicycle* 自転車のサドル. 【類】an adventurous ride ***on*** a *bicycle* through the desert of Asia ‖ Over the Alps ***on*** a *Bicycle* [書名] 自転車でアルプス越え. ‖ I set off ***on*** my *bicycle* to see it. 自転車に乗ってそれを見に出掛けた. 【類】round the world ***on*** a *bicycle* / ***on*** foot or *bicycle* ‖ coast down ***on*** a *bicycle* 自転車で坂道を滑走する. ¶He was ***upon*** a *bicycle* pedaling with energy. ペダルを勢いよく踏みながら自転車を走らしていた. ¶see off ***with*** my *bicycle* to ... 私の自転車で
bicycler, *n.* 自転車乗り. L...まで見送る.
Q^2 a ***career*** *bicycler* [曲馬・競輪など]職業自転車乗り.
bid, *n.* 付け値; 入札.
V We are prepared to ***entertain*** *bids*. 入札を受理します. ¶The article did not ***get*** a *bid*. のそ品には値をつけるものがなかった. ¶***make*** a *bid* for ... [入札で]...に値をつける; ...で人気を得ようとする ‖ I ***made*** the largest *bid* for the article. 私がその品に一番高い値をつけた. ¶*Bids* have been ***opened*** in the Navy Department, under the appropriation of $4,100,000 for the purchase of 100 planes. 飛行機百台の購入に対して見積価格四百十万ドルの入札が海軍省で行われた. ¶ask dealers to ***submit*** *bids* (=make competitive offers) 商人から入札を募る. ¶***tender*** *bids* 入札する. ¶***write*** one's *bid* on a slip of paper 入札の札を書
Q the ***highest*** *bid* 最高の付値. Lく.
P it was sold ***on*** the first *bid* made to the auctioneer by ... それは...の付けた最初の指し値で落ちた.
P^2 The first *bid* ***for*** the picture was five guineas. その絵の寄り付き値は五ギニーであった. ¶The figure rose by *bids* ***of*** £500. 値は五百ポンドずつ呼値が上って行った.
bid, *v.* 命じる; 述べる; 値を付ける, 入札する; 招待する.
M *bid* him ***depart*** 彼に去れと命じる. ¶The plan *bids* ***fair*** to succeed その計画は成功の見込がある. ¶How ***much*** did you *bid*? いくらに値をつけたか. ¶We *bade* him ***welcome***. 彼に歓迎のあいさつを述べた. 「ととせり上げる.
M^2 *bid* ***up*** [値を]せり上げる ‖ *bid* ***up*** successively あとあ

P We offered £60, but another man *bid* ***against*** us. 六十ポンドに値を付けたが別の男がもっと高く付けた. ¶*bid* ***at*** auction 競売で値を付ける. ¶*bid* ***for*** the construction of a battleship 軍艦建造の請負入札をする ‖ *bid* ***for*** (=***on***) a new building 新らしい建物の入札をする. ¶He was *bid* (=*bidden*) ***to*** the feast. 彼は宴会に招かれた.
bidder, *n.* 入札者.
Q sell one's services to the ***highest*** *bidder* 一番高給を出す人に雇われる. ¶a ***successful*** *bidder* 落札人.
P^2 a *bidder* ***for*** a contract 請負仕事の入札者.
bidding, *n.* 命令; 入札.
V ***await*** the *bidding* of the home office 本社の命を待つ. ¶attendants ready to ***do*** his *bidding* 彼の命に従おうと待構えている従者. ¶the *bidding* ***fell*** to ... at ... with ... as the under bidder 次札は誰々で入札は幾ら幾らで...の手に落ちた. ¶the *bidding* ***started*** (=***began***) at 100 guineas and rose up to ... せりは百ギニーが寄り付きで...までせり上げられた.
Q ***competitive*** *bidding* 競争入札. ¶At the sale there was some ***sensational*** *bidding* for Carot's picture, "Orpheus and Eurydice." その売立でカロー筆「オーフュースとユーリディス」の絵は突飛な高値が付けられた.
P ***at*** his *bidding* 彼の命に応じて. ¶They undertook the task ***without*** his *bidding*. 彼の命を待たずに彼らはその仕事
P^2 *bidding* ***for*** ... ...に対する入札. Lを始めた.
big, *a.* 大きい.
M a fruit ***as*** *big* as an apple りんご位の大きさの果物. ¶This coat is ***too*** *big* for me. この上衣は私には大き過ぎる. ¶He talks ***very*** *big*. 大口をたたく.
P She is *big* ***with*** child (=pregnant). 彼女は妊娠している. ‖ His heart is *big* (=full) ***with*** grief (joy). 彼の胸は悲哀(など)で一杯であった. ‖ be *big* ***with*** pride 傲(ごう)然として
biggest, *a.* 最大の. Lいる.
P America is always ***for*** the *biggest*. アメリカは最大が好
bigoted, *a.* 凝り固まって. Lきだ.
P He is *bigoted* ***to*** (=***in***) his opinion. 彼は自説を固執している. ‖ be *bigoted* ***in*** religion (politics) 宗教(など)の考えが偏狭である ‖ He is *bigoted* ***to*** ancient customs. 旧慣がと
bill, *n.* (**1**) 手形; 証券; 《米》紙幣. Lれない.
V ***accept*** a *bill* for the honor of the drawer 振出人の顔を立てて手形を引受ける. ¶***back*** a *bill* for a friend 友人のために手形の裏書をする. ¶***clear*** a *bill* 手形を(交換して)清算する. ¶***cover*** a *bill* 為替手形の支払資金を準備する. ¶***date*** *bills* 手形に支払期日を記入する. ¶***discount*** a *bill* 手形を割引く. ¶***dishonor*** a *bill* 手形の支払を拒絶する. ¶***do*** a *bill* 手形を現金に替える. ¶***draw*** one's *bill* for the amount of ... 金額...の手形を振出す ‖ ***draw*** a *bill* on ... ...に手形を振出す. ¶I refuse to ***honor*** your *bill*. 貴下の手形を支払う事はお断りします. ¶I advise you not to ***make*** a *bill* on ... ...への手形振出しは控えた方がよろしい. ¶***meet*** *bills* 手形を支払う. ¶***negotiate*** a *bill* on ... ...の手形を割引する. ¶***palm off*** a forged *bill* にせ手形をつかませる. ¶***present*** a *bill* at a bank 銀行に手形を提示する. ¶***protest*** a *bill* [約束]手形の支払を拒絶する. ¶***renew*** *bills* 手形を書替える. ¶***retire*** a *bill* 手形(紙幣など)を回収する. ¶***take up*** (=honor) a *bill* 引受けて手形を支払う.
V^2 The *bill* will soon ***fall*** due. すぐ手形の支払日になる.
Q a ***dishonored*** *bill* 不渡手形. ¶a ***duplicate*** *bill* of lading 鉄道荷為替(証券)の写し. ¶a ***foreign*** *bill* 外国為替. ¶***gilt-edged*** *bills* 信用のある手形. ¶The *bill* is ***overdue***. 手形の期日が過ぎている. ¶This *bill* is ***payable*** to bearer. この手形は持参人払である. ‖ a *bill* ***payable*** on demand 要求払の手形 ‖ a *bill* ***payable*** at sight 一覧払手形. ¶a ***short*** (***long***) *bill* 短(長)期の手形.
Q^2 ***accommodation*** *bill* 融通手形. ¶a ***document*** *bill* 荷為替手形. ¶a ***dollar*** *bill* 《米》一ドル紙幣. ¶an ***exchequer*** *bill* 大蔵省証券. ¶a crisp ***five-dollar*** *bill* 手の切れるような五ドル札. ¶an ***inland*** *bill* 内国為替. ¶a ***short-term*** (***long-term***) *bill* 短(長)期証券. ¶draw his ***sixty-day*** *bill* on the London bank with shipping documents attached 六十日後払の荷為替をロンドンの銀行に振出す.
P He paid part of the sum ***in*** *bills* and the rest in silver. 金額の一部は手形で残部は銀貨で支払った. ¶the interest ***on*** *bills* 手形の利子.
P^2 a *bill* ***at*** sight 一覧払手形. ¶a *bill* ***of*** exchange 外国為替手形 ‖ a *bill* ***of*** credit 〖商〗信用状 ‖ make out (=up) a

bill of lading 貨物引換券(船荷証券)を作成する. ¶a *bill* **on** London for £100 ロンドンの銀行へ振出した百ポンドの為替手形.

(**2**) 議案;〖法〗訴状.

V ***adopt*** a *bill* 議案を採択する. ¶***bring*** [***in***] a *bill* before Parliament 法律案を議会に持出す ‖ The *bill* was ***brought*** to a vote and defeated. その案は表決に付され否決された. ¶***burke*** a *bill* 議案を握りつぶす. ¶The *bill* has been ***carried.*** 法律案が可決された. ¶The *bill* was ***defeated*** by 379 against 149. その案は一四九対三七九で否決になった. ¶***deposit*** a *bill* in Parliament for the next session 法律案を次の議会に提出する. ¶***draw up*** a *bill* 議案を起草する. ¶***ignore*** the *bill* 訴状を否認する, 不起訴とする. ¶***introduce*** *bills* before the Board of Aldermen at Chicago シカゴ市参事会に議案を提出する. 【類】the *Bill* was ***introduced*** in the House of Lords by ... / ***introduce*** a *Bill* into Parliament. ¶***lay*** a *bill* before the Diet 法案を国会に提出する. ¶The *Bill* was ***OK'd.*** 法案は通過した. ¶***pass*** a *bill* 議案を通過する. ¶***present*** a *bill* in Congress (the state legislature) 議会(など)に法律案を提出する. 【類】***present*** a *bill* to Parliament. ¶A *Bill* will be ***promoted*** in the next session of Parliament to give effect to this arrangement. この打合せを有効ならしめるため次の議会で一つの法律案の通過が謀られるだろう. ¶***push*** a *Bill* in Parliament 法律案の議会通過に努力する. ¶***quash*** a *bill* 議案を握りつぶす. ¶***race*** a *bill* through the House 一しゃ千里に議案を通過せしめる. ¶***railroad*** a *bill* through a legislature《米》議案を急速力で通過さす. ¶***read*** a *bill* 議案を読会に付す. ¶***reject*** a *bill* 法案を排斥する. ¶***shelve*** a *bill* 議案をたな上げする. ¶***submit*** a *bill* to the Diet 法案を国会に提出する. ¶The *bill* was ***thrown aside.*** 議案は棄却された. ¶Parliament ***threw out*** the *bill.* 議会は同案を棄却した. 【類】The *bill* was ***thrown out*** after a brief discussion. ¶***water down*** *bill* 議案を骨抜きにする.

V² The *bill* ***fell through.*** その議案は不成立に終った.

Q² a ***Diet*** *bill* 国会提出の法案. ¶an ***omnibus*** *bill* 二箇以上の問題を一束にした議案.

P They were ***for*** (***against***) the *bill.* 彼らは議案に賛成(反対)だった.

P² a *bill* ***of*** particulars 罪状項目書 ‖ a *bill* ***of*** exception 抗告状. ¶a *bill* ***for*** a vote on nonconfidence 不信任の決議案.

(**3**) 勘定書; 費用.

V I ***bought*** a *bill* of goods from ... ...から商品を一口買った. ¶***collect*** *bills* due to him once a month 月に一度かけを集める. ¶***cut down*** coal *bills* 石炭費を切詰める. ¶***fill*** the *bill*《口語》要求に応じる, 条件を充す. ¶***foot*** a *bill*《米口語》勘定を支払う ‖ help ***foot*** the *bill* for ... ...に対して収支相償うようにさせる. ¶*Bills* must be ***itemized*** and ***rendered*** monthly. 勘定書は明細書にして月々出さねばならぬ. ¶***keep down*** gas *bills* ガス代を節約する. ¶***Make out*** one *bill* for both of us. [ホテルなどで]二人一しょに勘定してくれ給え. ‖ Will you please ***make out*** my *bill* while I wait? 待っている間につけを出してもらいたい. ¶bring home a little dough every day to the wife to ***meet*** our *bills* with 諸勘定支払の金を毎日少し持って来ては妻に渡す ‖ ***pay*** one's *bill* at a hotel ホテルの止宿料を払う. 【類】***pay*** a *bill* in cash. ¶***put in*** (=***submit***) a *bill* for one's work 仕事に対し支払請求を出す. ¶I will ***receipt*** your *bill.* 勘定書を受取に致しましょう. ¶***render*** a *bill* in duplicate 勘定書を二通出す. ¶Kindly ***return*** *bill* receipted and oblige. 勘定書を受取にして御返送下さい. ¶City attractions tempt students to ***run up*** *bills* beyond their means. 都会のおもしろ味が学生を誘惑して財布を空っぽにさせる. ‖ ***run up*** *bills* at grocer's 八百屋の払をかさ張らせる. ¶I use a hairclipper and ***save*** barber's *bill.* 僕はバリカンを使って理髪料を浮かせる. ¶The hotel *bill* is not yet ***settled.*** 宿の勘定はまだ済んでいない.

V² His *bill* ***comes*** to £20. 勘定が合計二十ポンドになる.

Q ***uncollectible*** *bills* 取れない勘定.

Q² pay ***doctor*** and ***hospital*** *bills* 診察料および入院料を支払う. ¶Her ***dress*** *bills* are ridiculously large. 彼女の着物の払いはばかに多い. ¶a heavy ***electric lighting*** *bills* 多額の電灯料金. ¶***Food*** *bills* run high. 食糧費がかかる. ¶pay a ***gas*** *bill* ガス代を払う. ¶pay one's ***hotel*** *bill* ホテル代を払う. ¶In summer we have a large ***ice*** *bill.* 夏は氷代がかゝる. ¶save (=except) ***repair*** *bills* 修繕費を除いて. ¶***utility*** *bills* ガス, 電気, 水道の払い. ¶a huge ***war*** *bill* ぼう大な戦費.

P² a *bill* ***for*** a coat 上衣の払い. ¶a *bill* ***from*** a restaurant 料理屋からよこした勘定書. ¶a *bill* ***of*** sale 売渡し請求書(つけ).

(**4**) はり札, ビラ.

V ***paste*** [***up***] a *bill* ビラをはりつける ‖ ***Paste*** no *bills*〖掲示〗はり紙無用. 【類】A *bill* was ***pasted*** on the outside of the gate. ¶***stick*** (=***paste up***) *bills* ビラをはりつける.

P he was ***on*** the *bill* with ... 彼(芸人)は...と同じ興行に出たことがあった. 【類】We worked ***on*** the same *bill* several times.

(**5**) 番組, 証明書; メニュー.

V The show ***tops*** the *bill* [of entertainment]. 番組の最初がそのショーだ.

Q The vessel has a ***clean*** *bill* of health. 同船は完全な健康証明書をもっている. ¶issue a ***foul*** *bill* of health 不正な健康証明書を発行する. ¶a ***suspected*** *bill* of health 疑わしい健康証明書.

Q² a ***theater*** *bill* 劇場や音楽会のプログラム.

P assign ***by*** *bill* of sale ... 商品納入書によって...[の品]を収める. ¶He was once ***on*** the *bill* with us. 彼はわれわれと同じ興行に出たことがある.

P² a *bill* ***of*** fare《米》献立表, メニュー. 【類】a printed *bill* ***of*** fare. ¶a *bill* ***of*** entry 税関申告書 ‖ a *bill* ***of*** clearance (entry)〖航海〗出(入)港届 ‖ a *bill* ***of*** costs 費用明細書 ‖ a *bill* ***of*** mortality 死亡統計表 ‖ a *bill* ***of*** parcels 小荷物の送り状.

bill, *n.* くちばし.

P The dove brings an olive-branch ***in*** her *bill.* はとがオリーヴの木の枝をくわえて来る.

bill, *v.* 勘定書に記入する; ビラをくばる.

P *bill* us ***for*** ... ...の勘定は当方へ書出す.

O You may send the Journal of Educational Sociology, a journal for progressive school men and women, for one year and *bill* me $ 3.00. 進歩的男女教育家の雑誌教育社会学雑誌を一年間お送り下さい, 代金三ドルは小生へお書出し下さい. ¶*bill* a circus (new business) サーカス(開店)のビラ宣伝をする.

billboard, *n.* 掲示板.

Q ***walking*** *billboards* サンドイッチマン.

P ***on*** the *billboard* I found such notices as ... 掲示板に...という掲示が出ていた.

billet *n.*〖軍〗宿舎.

Q an ***offcers'*** *billet* 将校宿舎.

Q² a ***US Army*** *billet* 米陸軍の宿舎.

billet *n.*〖冶金〗ビレット.

Q² an ***iron*** *billet* [資材]鉄棒. ¶a ***steel*** *billet* [資材]鋼鉄.

billet, *v.* 宿泊させる.

P The soldiers were *billeted* ***on*** the inhabitants. 兵士たちは民家に宿営した.

billiards, *n.* 玉突.

P play ***at*** *billiards* 玉突をする ‖ set a new record ***at*** *billiards* 玉突の新記録を作る.

billiardist, *n.* 撞(どう)球家.

Q ***professional*** *billiardists* 職業撞球家.

billow, *n.* 大浪.

V ***calm*** the *billows* 波を静める.

Q ***angry*** *billows* 怒濤(とう).

bin *n.* 箱, 袋.

Q an ***ash*** (=a ***dust***) *bin*《英》ごみ箱. ¶a ***canvas*** *bin* ズックの袋. ¶a ***coal*** *bin* (=coalbin) 石炭入れ. ¶a ***zinc*** (***wood***) *bin* とたん(木製)のごみ箱.

bind, *v.* 縛る, くくる; とじる, 結びつける; 固める; 束縛する; 奉公にやる; とざす; 製本する.

M ***closely*** *bound* [***up***] with ... ...と緊密な間柄である. ¶They *bound* him ***hand and foot.*** 彼を手足とも縛った. ¶These volumes are ***handsomely*** *bound* in blue cloth. これらの本は青色のクロースでりっぱに装ていされている. ¶be ***inseparably*** *bound* together by the tie of brotherhood 友情のきずなで固く結ばれている. ¶be *bound* ***loosely*** with a straw rope わらなわでゆるく縛ってある. ¶be *bound* ***out*** to service 奉公に出される. ¶a book ***sumptuously*** *bound* in green and gold 緑や金色で豪華に装ていされた本 ‖ *bind* ***together*** into a corporate unity 法人組織にする ‖ Kindness is the golden chain by which society is *bound* ***together.*** 親切は社会を結合する黄金の鎖である.

M² *bind* ***up*** a wound 傷を包帯する ‖ They were *bound* ***up*** by a cordial friendship. 肝胆相照らす仲であった. 【類】Wireless is now *bound* ***up*** with the daily life of the community. ‖ They are the names which suggest how closely the career of this great school is *bound* ***up*** with the history of our country. それらの名前はこの偉大な学校の歴史がいかに密接にわが国の歴史と関係しているかを暗示す

るものである. ‖ Her life was *bound up* in her lad's life. 彼女はその息子の成長に没頭している.

P *bind* the wreath ***around*** (=***about or round***) her head 彼女の頭に花輪を巻付ける. ¶ be ***bound as*** an apprentice to ... ...にでっち奉公している. ¶ The twigs are ***bound at*** both ends and in the middle. 小枝は両端と真中で結ばれている. ¶ They ***bound*** his arms ***behind*** the back. 彼らは彼をうしろ手に縛った. ¶ They are not ***bound by*** vows of celibacy. 彼らは独身生活の誓を立てているわけではない. ‖ He is ***bound by*** a promise (contract). 彼は約束(など)に縛られている. 【類】 being ***bound by*** no traditions / ***bound by*** affection ‖ he is ***bound by*** honor to ... 体面上...せざるを得ない ‖ *bind* gravel ***by*** cement セメントで砂利を固める ‖ *bind* one ***by*** writing ***to*** the fulfilment of terms 文書によって約束履行の義務を負わせる. ¶ be ***bound for*** ... to ... に対して...をする責を負う. ¶ *bind* twigs ***in*** (=***into***) faggots 小枝を束にする ‖ He is ***bound in*** duty to obey. 彼には従う義務がある. 【類】 He is ***bound in*** gratitude. ‖ books ***bound in*** boards (cloth, roan, lamb-skin, calf, vellum, morocco, flexible leather) 厚紙(など)装ていの本. 【類】 be ***bound in*** the red cover 赤い表紙で装ていされている ‖ a book ***bound in*** Japanese style 日本式にとじた本 ‖ four poles ***bound in*** red and white and slanting a little inward at the four corners of the arena 紅白の布を巻いて土俵の四すみの所で少しく内側に傾いている四本柱 ‖ The lake was ***bound in*** ice. 湖は氷にとざされた. ‖ He ***bound*** himself ***in*** marriage. 婚約をした. ¶ be ***bound into*** books 製本される. ¶ be ***binding on*** ... ...が遵守する義務がある. ¶ *bind* him ***to*** a pillar 彼を柱に縛りつける. 【類】 Attraction (引力) *binds* the planets ***to*** the sun. ‖ He stood erect there with his arms ***bound to*** the sides. 彼は両手をきちんと両わきにつけて直立した. ‖ *bind* a person ***to*** secrecy 人に秘密を守らせる ‖ He is much ***bound to*** her. 彼は彼女から離れない(子供が母親から). ‖ *bind* a person ***to*** a date [でき上りなど]日付でしばる ‖ I am ***bound to*** my wife. 妻に二世を契った. ‖ He is ***bound*** as apprentice ***to*** a carpenter. 彼は大工へ年期奉公に出ている. 【類】 I have ***bound*** him ***to*** a shoemaker. ‖ ***bind*** ... ***to*** a service ...に任務を負わす ‖ They are ***bound*** up ***to*** hard work. 彼らははげしい労働にしばられている. ¶ One is ***bound under*** a penalty to fulfil a contract. 契約を履行しないと罰せられる. ¶ A splint is ***bound upon*** a limb. 腕(脚)にそえ木がつけてある. ¶ *bind* them ***with*** a rope それらをなわで縛る ‖ It was ***bound with*** bamboo hoops. それには竹のたがが掛けてあった. 【類】 *bind* a wound ***with*** a handkerchief / *bind* a man ***with*** (=***in***) chains ‖ The book is ***bound with*** another. その本はもう一つの本と合冊になっている.

O I was not *bound* to believe allhis wonderful stories. 彼の不思議な物語をことごとく信じなければならない義務は私にはなかった. ‖ The new discovery is *bound* to be of great service to science. この新発見は科学上非常に役立つに相違ない. ‖ He is *bound* to succeed in his enterprise. 彼はきっとその事業に成功する.

binder, *n.* とじ込み表紙.

Q^2 a ***loose-leaf*** *binder* ルースリーフ式のとじ込み表紙. ¶ a ***ring*** *binder* 輪付とじ込み表紙.

binding, *n.* 装てい, 製本.

Q ***attractive*** *binding* 美しい装てい. ¶ ***durable*** *binding* 丈夫な製本. ¶ ***handsome*** *binding* 美麗な製本. ¶ The *binding* is ***sober*** and ***solid***. 製本は地味で堅牢だ. ¶ books in ***superb*** *bindings* りっぱな装ていの本. ¶ ***tasteful*** *binding* 凝った製本.

Q^2 books in ***leather*** *bindings* 革装の本. ¶ ***library*** *binding* 図書館用製本.

P a book ***in*** elegant *binding* 装ていの優美な本. ¶ What sort ***of*** *binding* do you want? どんな装ていが好きですか.

binding, *a.* 義務を負わせる.

P These regulations shall be *binding* ***on*** them without exception. これらの規則は一様に彼らに適用さるべきものである. ‖ a contract (an agreement) *binding* ***on*** a person 人の履行すべき契約(など).

binoculars, *n.* 双眼鏡.

Q ***high-powered*** *binoculars* 高度の双眼鏡.

biography, *n.* 伝記.

V people famous enough to ***justify*** *biography* 当然伝記に書かれるほど有名な人々.

Q an ***anecdotal*** *biography* 逸話的伝記. ¶ a ***brief*** *biography* 略伝. ¶ a ***critical*** *biography* 評伝. ¶ by far the ***fullest*** *biography*, in existence 現存するものの中では最も詳しい伝記. ¶ write a ***personal*** *biography* 自伝を書く. ¶ a ***rationalized*** *biography* of Kōbō Daishi [伝説的な部分を除いた]弘法大師の実伝. ¶ a ***vivid*** *biography* 躍如たる伝記.

Q^2 a ***screen*** *biography* 伝記映画.

P He deserves a place ***in*** the *biography* of self-made men of the Meiji Era. 明治年間における立志伝中の人と言って差支えない.

biology, *n.* 生物学.

Q^2 ***plant*** *biology* 植物生物学(特に動物生物学に対して).

bioscope, *n.* 活動写真.

P Egypt ***on*** the *bioscope* 映画上のエジプト.

birch, *n.* かば(の木).

Q the ***silver*** (=***white***) *birch* 白樺.

P The mischievous boy was ordered six strokes ***with*** the *birch*. その悪太郎は六度打の罰を受けた.

bird, *n.* 鳥.

V ***breed*** *birds* 鳥を飼う. ¶ ***hear*** a *bird* sing 内報に接する. ¶ a chance to ***kill*** two *birds* with one stone 一石二鳥の好機. ¶ ***pluck*** a *bird* 鳥の羽をむしる. ¶ ***stuff*** a *bird* 鳥をはく製にする. ¶ ***train*** a *bird* to sing 鳥を慣らしてさえずらせる.

V^2 The *birds* ***chirp*** merrily. 鳥がおもしろくさえずる. ¶ *Birds* ***hop***. 小鳥がぴょいぴょいと跳ぶ. ¶ *Birds* are ***singing*** merrily. 小鳥は楽しく歌っている. ¶ *Birds* ***twitter***. 小鳥がさえずる. ¶ a little *bird* has ***whispered*** to me that ... ...と良い人から(風の便りで)聞いた.

Q a ***chattering*** *bird* やかましくさえずる鳥. ¶ ***chirping*** *birds* ちゅっちゅっとさえずる鳥. ¶ an ***early*** (a ***late***) *bird* 朝早く起きる(夜ふかしする)人 ‖ emulate the ***early*** *bird* 小鳥に負けず朝早く起きる. ¶ A ***little*** *bird* has told it. すゞめから聞いた話だが. ¶ ***mythical*** *bird* [ほうおうなどの]霊鳥. ¶ a ***mythological*** *bird* 神話に出る鳥. ¶ The eagle is the ***national*** *bird* of America. わしは米国民を代表する鳥である. ¶ The goose is a ***pompous*** *bird*. がちょうはもったいぶった鳥だ. ¶ ***predacious*** (=***predatory***) *birds* and mammals 肉食の鳥獣. ¶ The turkey is a large ***proud*** *bird*. 七面鳥は大きな鳥でいばってる. ¶ English sparrows are ***pugnacious*** *birds*. 英国すゞめはけんか好きだ. ¶ An American robin is a ***red-breasted*** *bird*. アメリカつぐみは胸毛の赤い鳥だ. ¶ a ***red-throated*** *bird* のどの赤い鳥. ¶ In the Tokugawa period the crane was preserved as a ***royal*** *bird*. 徳川時代には鶴は名鳥として禁猟されていた. ¶ a ***sacred*** *bird* 霊鳥. ¶ a ***wading*** *bird*=a wader (さぎのような)脚の長い鳥. ¶ ***yarded*** *birds* 庭に放し飼いの鳥.

Q^2 a ***baby*** *bird* ひな鳥. ¶ a ***cage*** *bird* 飼い鳥. ¶ a ***call*** *bird* おとり. ¶ the ***first-prize*** *bird* [共進会などで]一等賞をとった鳥. ¶ ***father*** (***mother***) *bird* 父(母)鳥. ¶ a ***game*** *bird* 猟鳥(かも・きじなど). ¶ a ***general-purpose*** *bird* 用途の広い鳥. ¶ a ***jail*** *bird* 《米口》囚人; 前科者. ¶ a ***parent*** *bird* 親鳥. ¶ feed for ***show*** *birds* 鳥を共進会に出すように仕込む. ¶ ***song*** *birds*=songsters 鳴禽(きん).

P^2 *Birds* ***of*** a feather flock together. 同気相求む; 牛は牛連れ. 【類】 These meetings enabled *birds* ***of*** a feather to flock together at least once a week. ‖ a *bird* ***of*** the same kind 同種の鳥 ‖ a *bird* ***of*** passage 渡り鳥; 渡り者 ‖ a *bird* ***of*** prey 肉食鳥 ‖ a *bird* ***of*** the year 鳥の一年子.

birth, *n.* 出生, 出産.

V His wife ***gave*** *birth* to a son. 細君が男の子を産んだ. 【類】 ***give*** *birth* to twin girls / She died soon after ***giving*** *birth* to him. / The town ***gave*** *birth* to (=produced) great men. ‖ This spring ***gives*** *birth* to a river that is navigable for steamers. この泉が流れて汽船の航行できる川となっている. ¶ European civilization first ***had*** its *birth* in these lands. これらの国々は欧州文明発祥の地である. 【類】 It was in Asia that civilization began and the world's greatest cultures and religions ***had*** their *birth*. ¶ ***predate*** the *birth* of Christ 時はキリスト誕生の以前である. ¶ His mother did not ***survive*** his *birth*. 彼の母親は彼を産み落して死んだ. ¶ It is the custom of the world to ***value*** *birth* above accomplishment. 習得した学芸以上に家柄を重んじるのが世の習わしである.

Q men of ***American*** *birth* アメリカ生れの人. ¶ a ***difficult*** *birth* (=delivery) 難産. ¶ He was of ***gentle*** *birth* and lived amid refined surroundings in his early years. 彼は紳士階級に生れ幼年時代はりっぱな生活をしていた. ‖ be utterly unworthy of a lady of ***gentle birth*** 姫御前のあられもない. ¶E. Berliner, the inventor of the gramophone, was a naturalized American citizen of ***German birth.*** 蓄音機の発明家E・バーリナーはドイツ生れの米国帰化人であった. ¶a woman of ***high birth*** 上流婦人. ¶a man of ***ignoble birth*** 微賤から身を起した人. ¶children of ***illegitimate birth*** 私生児. ¶in spite of her ***illustrious birth*** 彼女は名門の出にもかかわらず. ¶men of British blood, whether of ***insular birth*** or of the homes beyond the seas 本土または海外出生の英国人. ¶a ***live*** (***dead***) ***birth*** 新生(死産)児. ¶a ***new birth*** of national life 国民生活の更新. ¶be of ***noble*** (***mean***) ***birth*** 高貴(下賤)の生れである. ¶a man of ***obscure birth*** 素性の卑しい人. ¶Her ***patrician birth*** colors her doings. 彼女は貴族の生れであるからする事が貴族的だ. ¶a ***plural birth*** 複産 (twins, triplets, quadruplets, quintuplets, etc.). ¶a ***premature*** (=an ***untimely***) ***birth*** 早産. ¶one of a ***quadruple birth*** 四つ子の一人. ¶a ***single birth*** 単産. ¶have a ***still birth*** 死産をする. ¶four women who were the fruit of two ***triple births*** 二組の三つ子の中の四人の女. ¶the ***virgin birth*** [マリヤの]処女生誕.

Q^2 a school teacher of ***London birth*** ロンドン子の先生.

P ***At birth,*** he was very small. 生れた時非常に小さかった. 【類】The child weighed 19 pounds ***at birth.*** ‖ four young at ***a birth*** 一腹に四匹の子 ‖ Six ***at a birth*** is the largest accredited number on record. 六つ児が記録の上では信頼のできる最大のものである. ‖ Chinese customs ***at*** (=***surrounding***) the ***birth*** of a child 子供の誕生にまつわる中国の習慣. ‖ ***at*** their ***birth*** 彼らの誕生に際し ‖ born ***at*** the same ***birth*** 同時に生れて. ¶a Londoner ***by birth*** きっすいのロンドン子. 【類】He is a Japanese ***by birth*** and American by training. / a gentleman (poet) ***by birth*** ‖ ***by birth*** or naturalization 出生もしくは帰化することによって. 【類】be entitled to ... ***by birth.*** ¶She has been blind ***from birth.*** 彼女は生れつき盲目だ. ‖ ***from birth*** till death 生れてから死ぬまで. ¶I am beneath him ***in birth.*** 私の生れは彼より家柄が低い. ‖ The baby was strangled ***in birth.*** 赤ん坊が出産の時に窒息した. ¶Japan is the land ***of*** his ***birth.*** 日本は彼の生国. 【類】the date ***of*** the ***birth*** of Buddha / since the day ***of*** his ***birth*** ‖ Of the applicants 53 per cent were ***of*** Irish ***birth.*** 出願者中五割三分がアイルランド生れだった. ‖ a man ***of birth*** 由緒ある家柄の人 ‖ a man ***of*** no ***birth*** [家柄のない]平民. ¶bring it ***to birth*** それを産み出す ‖ trace a thing ***to*** its ***birth*** 事物の起源を調べる.

P^2 the ***birth of*** New Japan 新日本の誕生 ‖ the ***birth of*** a son (daughter) 男(女)児出生. 【類】***birth of*** Confucius, 551 B.C. / the ***birth of*** Darwinism ‖ It is well known that the ***birth*** (=delivery) ***of*** boys is in general more difficult than the ***birth of*** girls. 男児は女児の場合よりも概して分娩が困難だとは周知の事実だ.

birthday, *n.* 誕生日.

V ***attain*** his eightieth ***birthday*** 八十歳の誕生日を迎える. ¶***celebrate*** one's ***birthday*** 誕生日を祝う. 【類】the nation ***celebrates*** its ***birthday*** on ... / ***celebrate*** one's 82nd ***birthday.*** ¶***complete*** one's 30th ***birthday*** 三十回の誕生日を終える(満三十歳になる). ¶***commemorate*** the seventieth ***birthday*** of ... ...の第七十回誕辰を記念する. ¶***keep*** (=***observe***) a ***birthday*** 誕生日を祝う. ¶September, 1928, ***marked*** the sixth ***birthday*** of the Oregon State College Honor System. 一九二八年九月はオレゴン州立大学の学生自治制度創設第六週年に相当した.

V^2 The Cunard Line's ***birthday,*** like that of the United States, ***occurs*** on July 4. キューナード汽船会社の創立は米国の建国同様に七月四日である.

P age ***at*** last ***birthday*** この前の誕生日の年齢. ¶***on*** the Emperor's ***birthday***=on the birthday of his Majesty 天皇誕生日に. 【類】***on*** his next ***birthday.*** ¶***since*** his last ***birthday*** この前の誕生日以来.

P^2 the ***birthday of*** a nation 建国記念日.

birthplace, *n.* 出生地.

V He ***has*** his ***birthplace*** near the town. 彼はその市の近所で生れた.

P^2 Asia is the ***birthplace of*** the great religions of the world. アジアは世界大宗教の発祥地である. 【類】Shrewsbury is the ***birthplace of*** Charles Darwin. / Britain is the ***birthplace of*** liberalism.

birthrate, *n.* 出生率.

Q an ***exuberant birthrate*** 旺盛な出産率. ¶a ***falling birthrate*** 減少しつゝある出産率. ¶a ***high birthrate*** 高い出産率.

biscuit, *n.* ビスケット; 《米》焼きパン.

Q The ***American biscuit*** is a kind of bread baked in small soft cakes. アメリカのビスケットは柔かいケーキの形に焼いた小形のパンである. ¶***assorted biscuits*** 組合わせビスケット.

Q^2 ***meat biscuit*** 肉ビスケット(肉スープと麦粉とを混ぜてビスケット形に焼いたもの).

bit, *n.* 一片; [馬の]くつわ.

V At a meeting, one should ***add*** one's ***bit*** to the give-and-take of conversation or to the general entertainment. 会に出席したら人と語り人と共に楽しむという風にすべきである. ¶***do*** a ***bit*** of figuring on an abacus ちょっとそろばん玉をはじく ‖ ***do*** one's ***bit*** for America 米国のためにひとはだ脱ぐ. 【類】***do*** one's ***bit*** in adding to Japan's prestige (国威). ¶***give*** a ***bit*** of one's mind うちつけに言う.

Q Stop ***a bit.*** ちょっと止れ. ¶Wait ***a bit.*** ちょっと待て. ‖ He is ***a bit*** too stiff-necked.—Yes, quite ***a bit.*** 彼は少しがんこ過ぎるよ.—まったく相当のもんだ. ‖ "Do you mind smoking?" "No, not ***a bit.***" 「たばこを吸っても構いませんか」「ちっとも構わない」. 【類】He is not ***a bit*** like his elder brother. ¶His claim is ***every bit*** as good as yours. 彼の主張はどう見ても君のに劣らず正当だ. 【類】He is ***every bit*** a gentleman.=He is a gentleman, ***every bit*** of him. ¶He was not the ***least bit*** upset. 彼は一向困らなかった. ¶Just a ***little bit,*** please. ほんのちょっぴり. ¶a ***nice*** (=***good***) ***bit*** of ... かなり沢山の... 【類】have a ***nice bit*** of money. ¶a very ***successful bit*** of work きわめて好成績の仕事. ¶Shall I lengthen it a ***tiny bit?*** 心持ち(ほんの少し)長くしましょうか. ¶I'm a ***mere bit*** tedious. 少し退屈だ.

P ***by bits*** 少しずつ ‖ bite ***by*** small ***bits*** かじる ‖ bit ***by bit*** 少しずつ, 段々. ¶I will go back to my home ***for*** a ***bit.*** ちょっと家へ帰ります. ¶a slip of paper torn ***to bits*** こまかく引きさいた紙片.

P^2 a capital ***bit of*** land 絶好な地所. 【類】a ***bit of*** paper / a ***bit of*** water / a ***bit of*** fun ‖ There is not a ***bit of*** difference. ちっとも違っていない. ‖ bring a ***bit of*** Japan to San Francisco 日本的のものをサンフランシスコに移植する ‖ in that ***bit of*** woods あの森の一ケ所で. 【類】The phrase is a ***bit of*** Japanese English. / He learned a ***bit of*** Latin at Eton. / be a ***bit of*** a coward ‖ live in a ***bit of*** a cottage 小屋みたいな所に住む ‖ He has (=There is) a ***bit of*** a humorist about him. 彼にはちょっとユーモラスな所がある.

bit, *n.* [くつわの]はみ; きり.

V ***draw bit*** 手綱を引いて馬を制御する; 速度をゆるめる ‖ ***put*** a ***bit*** on a horse 馬にくつわをはめる. ¶***take*** the ***bits*** [馬が]はみを受ける ‖ ***take*** (=***get***) the ***bit*** between one's (=the) teeth [馬が]逃げ出す; [比喩的に]取締が利かない, 手におえない.

Q^2 a ***coal-boring bit*** きりの一種(炭層などを掘りくずすもの). ¶a ***plug-center bit*** 円筒ぎり(金属に穴をあけるもの).

bite, *n.* かむこと; [釣りの]あたり; 一口.

V ***get*** a ***bite*** at it それを一口食べる ‖ I think I've ***got*** a ***bite.*** あたりがある. ¶Let's ***have*** a ***bite*** [for lunch]. 《米俗》食事をしよう. ¶***put*** a ***bite*** into one's mouth 一口食べる. ¶Please ***take*** a ***bite.*** ちょっと一口召上って下さい. 【類】The poor tramp (ルンペン) has not ***taken*** a ***bite*** all day. ‖ ***take*** a good ***bite*** of her lip くちびるをぐっとかむ.

Q I had a ***powerful bite.*** 良いあたりを見た[釣師が].

Q^2 an ***insect bite*** [のみや蚊の]ひとくい. ¶a ***mosquito bite*** 蚊のひとさし.

P^2 just the thing for hasty luncheons and "***bites between*** meals" 急ぎの弁当やおやつには丁度あつらえ向の品. ¶a ***bite from*** a snake へびの一かみ. ¶a ***bite of*** a dog 犬の一かみ.

bite, *v.* かむ.

M Barking dogs ***seldom bite.*** ほえる犬はめったにかみつかない.

M^2 The cat ***bit off*** the mouse's tail. ねこがねずみのしっぽをかじりとった. ‖ ***bite*** meat ***off*** the bone 肉を骨からかじりとる. ¶The puppy ***bit up*** the hem of a mat. 小犬がマットの端をかじりとった.

P ***bite at*** a hook (cake, an apple) 釣針(など)に食いつく ‖ ***biting at*** the chance offered 渡りに船と. 【類】They are too knowing (利口) to ***bite at*** such a bait. ¶Remorse ***bites into*** one's heart. 後悔の念が胸を刺す. ¶No fish ***bites on*** the fly today. きょうはこの蚊ばりに一向当りがない. ‖

bite on the bridle 非常に難儀する ‖ I was *bitten* ***on*** the leg by a dog. 犬にすねをかまれた. ¶*bite* ***with*** a mouth (the teeth) 口(など)でかむ ‖ He was completely *bitten* ***with*** the angling mania. 彼はすっかり釣マニヤになってしまった.

bitter, *n.* 苦味.

V ***take*** the *bitter* with the sweet 清濁合せのむ.

P² the sweets and the *bitters* ***of*** life 人生の苦楽.

bitter, *a.* にがい.

P He was *bitter* ***against*** the plan. その計画をおもしろく思わなかった. ‖ He was *bitter* ***against*** the authorities. 当局者をにがにがしく思った. ¶be *bitter* ***in*** his condemnation of … …を容赦なくやっつける. ¶*bitter* ***to*** taste (=mouth) に

bitterness, *n.* にがさ；辛さ. └がい.

P ***in*** the *bitterness* of the heart いまいましく思って. ¶speak it up ***with*** *bitterness* にがにがし気に言い放つ.

bivouac, *n.* 露営.

P pass the night ***in*** *bivouac* テントで夜を明かす.

bivouac, *v.* 野営する.

P They *bivouacked* ***for*** the night. 彼らは野宿した.

black, *n.* (**1**) 黒色；黒衣.

V ***wear*** *black* 喪服を着ける.

Q ***inky*** *black* 真っ黒.

Q² ***animal*** *black*=boneblack 骨炭. ¶***carbon*** *black* is a component of tires 炭素はタイヤの一成分である. ¶***lamp*** *black* 油煙；黒い絵具. ¶dressed in sober ***schoolboy*** *black* 地味な学生服を着て.

P put down ***in*** *black* and white はっきりと書下す. 【類】I must see the contract ***in*** *black* and white. ‖ a drawing (picture) ***in*** *black* and white 墨絵 ‖ a motion picture ***in*** *black* and white [色彩映画に対し]白黒映画 ‖ The box is lacquered ***in*** *black*. 箱は黒塗りだ. ‖ a woman clad all ***in*** *black* (white) 黒(白)ずくめの婦人 ‖ Being in mourning, he was dressed ***in*** *black*. 喪中で彼は黒を着ていた. ‖ a severe-looking lady ***in*** rusty *black* さび色がかった黒服を着たき (**2**) 《米》黒字. └りっとした顔の婦人.

P The business is ***in*** [the] *black*. 商売は黒字だ. ¶The balance is going ***into*** the *black* (red). 経営が黒(赤)字になりつつある. 【類】We undertook the task of taking the National Treasury out of the red and put it back ***into***

black, *a.* 黒い；険悪な. └the *black*.

P He was *black* ***in*** the face. 血相をかえていた. ¶He was *black* ***with*** rage. 彼は怒気満面にあふれていた. ‖ The pavements are *black* (=alive) ***with*** people. 歩道は黒山の人.

O Things look *black*. 形勢不穏だ.

black, *v.* 黒く塗る.

M The articles were *blacked* ***out*** by the censor. その記事は検閲官に抹殺された. ‖ This block was *blacked* ***out*** for hours last night. この町内は昨晩何時間も停電(灯管)だった.

black-board, *n.* 黒板.

V ***clean*** [***off***] the *black-board* 黒板をふく.

P write music notes with chalk ***on*** (=***upon***) the *black-board* 白墨で黒板に音符を書く. 【類】chalk down music notes ***on*** a *black-board*.

blacken *v.* 黒くする. 「やすすで黒ずんでいる.

P The room is *blackened* ***with*** smoke and soot. へやが煙

black-list *n.* ブラックリスト, 黒表.

P put him ***on*** the *black-list* 彼を黒表に載せる ‖ a man ***on*** the *black-list* 注意人物.

blackmail *n.* ゆすり. 「おどして金銭を取る.

V ***levy*** *blackmail* on … …をゆする ‖ ***levy*** one's *blackmail*

blackness, *n.* 黒いこと.

V Her hair ***approaches*** *blackness* in color. 彼女の髪は黒

blackout, *n.* 灯火管制；停電. └に近い.

V A strong blast of snowstorm ***caused*** a *blackout* in places. 吹雪のためあちこち停電となった.

Q the ***intellectual*** *blackout* in Germany ドイツにおける知識の喪失. 「ひんぱんな地域停電.

Q² ***news*** *blackout* 報道管制. ¶frequent ***section*** *blackouts*

bladder, *n.* 膀胱(ぼう).

V ***empty*** the *bladder* before retiring 寝る前に小便をする.

Q present oneself with a ***full*** *bladder* [検尿のために]尿を

blade, *n.* 刃；葉. └ためて来る.

V ***make*** dull the *blade* 刃を鈍くする. ¶***nick*** the *blade* of a sword 刀の刃を欠く. 「全かみそりの刃.

Q² a ***propeller*** *blade* プロペラーの一翼. ¶a ***razor*** *blade* 安

P The rice plants are still ***in*** the *blade*. まだ稲の穂が出ない. ¶a sword ***with*** a broad *blade* 刃の広い刀, だんびら.

blamable, *a.* 非難すべき.

M be not ***necessarily*** *blamable* あながち悪いともいえな

blame, *n.* 非難；罪, とがめ. └い.

V the *blame* is to be ***ascribed*** to … 罪は…に帰すべきである. ¶***assume*** to oneself all the *blame* 全責任を一身に引受ける. ¶***attach*** *blame* to … …に罪をきせる ‖ There is no *blame* ***attached*** to his life. 彼の生がいには一点の非の打ち所もない. ¶***bear*** the *blame* of another's 他人に代って責を負う ‖ ***bear*** *blame* due to others ぬれぎぬを着る. 【類】***bear*** the *blame* for the mistakes of others / gladly ***bear*** all the *blame* ‖ He ***cast*** (=***charged***) all the *blame* on me. 彼はみな僕のせいにした. ¶***deserve*** *blame* 非難に値する. ¶***divide*** the *blame* between you and me 貴下と私と二人で責任を負う. ¶***fix*** the *blame* on the wrong party 無実の罪をきせる. ¶they ***heaped*** all the *blame* for it on … 彼らはその罪を一切…にきせた. ¶***incur*** (=***bring on oneself***) a *blame* 非難を招く. ¶***lay*** the *blame* at the door of another 人のせいにする. 【類】***lay*** the *blame* at the proper door (当然受くべき人) / ***lay*** all the *blame* on … ¶the *blame* should be ***placed*** upon … 責は…が負うべきだ. ¶***put*** *blame* upon others 他人のせいにする. ¶***shift*** the *blame* from … to … …の責任を…に転嫁する. 【類】***shift*** a *blame* on to another. ¶***take*** all the *blame* to oneself 自ら全責任を負う. ¶***take*** the *blame* for … …の責を負う ‖ ***throw*** the *blame* upon … …に責任を転嫁する.

V² No *blame* ***attaches*** to you. 君には何のとがめもない. ¶All the *blame* ***falls*** upon him. みな彼のせいだ. ¶I know where the *blame* ***lies***. その責任者は私には分っている.

Q It is ***small*** *blame* to you that the plan did not work well. 計画が失敗したのは君だけの責任じゃない. ¶an ***undeserved*** *blame* 無実の罪. ¶He said he would take the ***whole*** *blame*. 彼は全責任を負うと言った.

P He is free ***from*** *blame*. 彼にはとがめる所はない. ¶Much was said ***in*** *blame* of him. いろいろ非難された.

O The *blame* is his. 責は彼にある.

blame, *v.* 非難する, とがめる；責を負う.

M they are not to be ***hastily*** *blamed*, because of their …彼らが…であるからといってにわかに非難すべきではない. ¶to be ***highly*** *blamed* もっての外である. ¶*blame* a person ***squarely*** for … …の件を正面から非難する. ¶He was ***unfairly*** *blamed*. 無実の罪を受けた. ¶*blame* ***unjustly*** 罪もないのに非難する.

P Movies have been *blamed* ***for*** the crime wave. 映画は罪悪を激発するものとして非難されてきた. ‖ The conductor is *blamed* ***for*** the accident. その事件は車掌に責任があると言われている. 【類】*blame* a person ***for*** a fault (mistake) / You should be *blamed* ***for*** that. ‖ Nobody is to *blame* ***for*** it. これはだれが悪いのでもない. 【類】It isn't very fair to *blame* me ***for*** that. ¶the incident was *blamed* ***on*** … 事故の責任は…にあるとされた.

blanch, *v.* 白くする；白くなる.

P *blanch* ***with*** fear 青くなる.

blank, *n.* 余白, 空所；《米》書込用紙；からくじ.

V ***draw*** a *blank* からくじを引く ‖ The angler ***drew*** a *blank*. 釣師はあぶれた. 【類】Such attempts have ***drawn*** *blanks*. ¶The present [work] is an attempt to ***fill*** that *blank*. 本書はその欠陥を補わんとの試みである. ¶***fill in*** a *blank* 空白を満たす. ¶***fill out*** *blanks* 空所に文字を記入する. ☞《米》fill out a blank=《英》fill up a form 用紙に記入する. ¶Please ***fill up*** *blanks* in their order sheet. どうぞこの注文用紙の空所に書入れて下さい.

Q My mind became a ***complete*** *blank*. 何もかも忘れてしまった. ¶The war has caused a ***great*** *blank* in her modern history. 戦争のため同国の現代史に大きな空白ができた. ¶a means of collecting data in the form of a definite series of questions on ***printed*** *blanks* 書込み式アンケートという資料収集の方法.

Q² an ***application*** *blank* 申込用紙, 願書用紙. ¶an ***entry*** *blank* 入会申込書. ¶an ***order*** *blank* 注文用紙. ¶a ***subscription*** *blank* 申込用紙. ¶employ a ***suggestion*** *blank* [投書箱の]投票用紙を使う. ¶a ***telegraph*** *blank* 電報頼信紙.

P² a *blank* ***in*** one's memory 記憶の空白 ‖ The bill of lading was made out ***in*** *blank*. 船荷証券は空白式に作製された. ¶His funds amount ***to*** *blank*. 彼は結局金がないことになる. ¶a *blank* ***for*** the renewal of subscriptions 購

読継続申込用紙. ¶a *blank in* a document 書類の空欄 ‖ a *blank in* a forest 林間の空地. ¶a *blank on* a page ページの余白.

blanket, *n.* 毛布.

V I *laid* a *blanket* over him. 彼に毛布を掛けた. ¶*spread* a *blanket* over (=on) the grass 草の上に毛布を敷く. ¶*throw* a cold *blanket* over a plan ある計画にけちを付ける.

Q the children cuddled up under a *thick warm blanket* 子供たちは厚地のあったかい毛布に抱き合って寝た.

Q^2 an *army* (a *navy*) *blanket* 陸(海)軍用毛布. ¶a *rubber blanket* ゴム製の覆い.

P I was wrapped *in* a *blanket*. 毛布にくるまった. ¶It was covered *with* a *blanket*. それに毛布をかぶせた.

blaspheme, *v.* 不敬の言を吐く.

P *blaspheme against* God 神を冒瀆(ぼうとく)する.

blast, *n.* 一吹き; 一陣の風.

V *blow* a shrill *blast* on a pocket-whistle 小笛をするどくぴりぴりと吹く. ¶*give* three *blasts* on a horn 角笛を三度吹く. ¶The trumpeters *sounded* a *blast*. らっぱ手は吹奏した.

Q through drenching rain and *biting blast* しのつく雨と身を切る風を冒して. ¶be in *full blast* 盛んに活躍している; 熔鉱炉が盛に吹いている ‖ a party going on in *full blast* どんちゃん騒ぎの連中. ¶The factory people are at work at *full blast*. 工場は大車輪でやっている. 【類】The industries of the country are kept going at *full blast*. ¶*icy blasts* 氷のように冷い風. ¶a *strong blast* of snowstorm 吹雪の突風 ‖ give two or three *strong blasts* on a bugle らっぱを二三度強く吹奏する. ¶a *wintry blast* 木枯し.

Q^2 fire three *shotgun blasts* into his body 彼の身体に銃弾を三回打ち込む.

P *at* a *blast* from a conch-shell ほら貝を吹くと ‖ *at* first *blasts* of the trumpet らっぱの第一声で. ¶The factories are *out of blast*. 工場は休業中. ¶His arrival was heralded *with* bugle *blasts*. 彼が来着するのでらっぱの吹奏で先触をした.

P^2 the *blast of* a hurricane 吹きすさむ大風. ¶a *blast of* wind 一陣の風. ¶a *blast on* the horn ホルンのひと吹き.

blast, *v.* 吹きとばす.

M *blast out* stone [雷管などで]石を吹きとばす ‖ be *blasted out* by charges of dynamite ダイナマイトの数回の爆発で破壊される.

blaze, *n.* 火焔; 光輝.

V A few dry sticks *afforded* us a cheerful *blaze*. 少しのかわいた木片で心地よい火ができた.

V^2 To heaven the *blaze uprolled*. 火焔は天に巻き上った.

Q emerge into the *full blaze* of the sun 太陽の赫々たる光の中に出る. ¶A *lively blaze* was under way when it was first discovered. 最初発見された時盛に燃えていた.

P The whole house was soon *in* a *blaze*. たちまち火が家中に広がった.

P^2 a *blaze of* fire 火焔 ‖ a *blaze of* fury 激怒 ‖ I saw a *blaze of* a cheerful fire through the window. 窓を通して心地よげに火が赤々と燃えているのが見えた.

blaze, *v.* 輝かす; 輝く.

M *blaze away* 盛んに砲撃する. ¶*blaze furiously* 盛に燃える. ¶The fire *blazed high* into the air. 火柱が高くあがった. ¶*blaze out* 燃え上る. ¶Their fame *blazed suddenly* upon the world. 彼らの名声はたちまち揚った.

M^2 *blaze up*=burst into flame *or* passion 燃え上がる; かっとなる. 【類】His anger *blazed up* furiously (=hotly).

P It was *blazed with* ornaments of gold, silver, and precious stones. それは金銀及び宝石でまばゆいほど飾ってあった. ‖ The store fronts *blazed with* flowers and brilliant colored lights. 店先は花や華麗な色電燈でさん然と輝いた. ‖ a garden *blazed with* flowers 燃え立つような花園. ‖ He *blazed with* fury (=rage). 烈火の如く怒った.

blazer, *n.* 燃え上るもの.

Q Like all *trail blazers*, he is a martyr. 多くの先駆者と同様に, 彼もまた殉教した者の一人だった.

bleacher, *n.* 《米》外野観覧席.

Q comfortable *steel bleachers* かけ心地のよい鉄製の外野スタンド.

bleat, *v.* [羊・こやぎが]めえと鳴く.

M *bleat out* めえと鳴く; 弱々しい声で話す.

P *bleat about* their sorrows and the burden of life 人生の苦労をかこつ.

bleed, *v.* 出血する.

M *bleed away* one's life 出血で命を取られる. ¶*bleed badly* 激しく出血する. ¶*bleed freely* 盛に出血する. ¶I cut my finger and it *bled profusely*. 指を切って大層血が出た.

P You are *bleeding at* the nose. 鼻血が出ている. ¶He *bled for* a righteous cause. 正義のために血を流した. ‖ My heart *bleeds for* him. 彼のために心痛に堪えない. ¶*bleed* profusely *from* a wound on the head 頭の傷から盛んに出血する. ¶*bleed to* death 出血して死ぬ.

bleeding, *n.* 出血.

V *cause bleeding* 出血の原因となる.

Q *copious bleeding* 多量の出血. ¶*profuse bleeding* 大出血.

P *without bleeding* 出血なしに.

blemish, *n.* 欠点, 汚点.

V *eliminate blemishes* 欠点を除く. ¶*obviate* this *blemish* この欠点を除去する. ¶Many engravers have *removed blemishes* in the work of the painter while retaining the best features of his work. [版画の製作で]画家の作品の美点を保存すると同時に欠点を除去した版画師が多い.

Q a *natural blemish* 生れつきのきず. ¶a *small* (=*slight*) *blemish* 小さなきず. ¶But these are *trivial blemishes*. しかしこれらは些々(さ)たる欠点である. ¶*typographical* and *other blemishes* 印刷上やその他の欠点.

P lead a life pure *from* any *blemish* 完全無欠な生活を送る.

P^2 It is quite a *blemish in* him. それは彼の大きな欠点だ. ¶It is a *blemish on* his book. それは彼の本のきずだ.

blench, *v.* ひるむ.

P *blench at* the scene その光景を見てぞっとする.

blend, *n.* 混合.

Q This is the *best* coffee of our own *blend*. 当店自慢のコーヒーです.

P^2 This coffee is a *blend of* Java and Brazil. このコーヒーはジャバとブラジルのミックスです. 【類】These cigarettes are a *blend of* the best tobaccos.

blend, *v.* 混合する.

M majesty and simplicity most *happily blended* together うまく調和した尊厳と単純. 【類】yesterday and today (今昔) *happily blended* ‖ They are *so blended* that it is often difficult to say where the one ends and the other begins. 徐々に混和しているので, 初めと終りの境目を見分けることが難しい. ¶The colors are not *blended well*. 色がよく混っていない.

P The colors *blended into* one. 色がとけ合って一色になった. ¶a drama *blended of* comedy and tragedy 悲喜劇を織りまぜた狂言. ¶The song *blended* so well *with* the whispering of the leaves. 歌は木の葉のささやきとよく調和した.

blending, *n.* 混合, 融合.

Q The city is a *happy blending* of town and country. その市は都会と田園との美しい融合を示している. ¶He is a case of an *unusual blending* of virtues and vices. 彼は善と悪を一身に備えた珍しい例である.

P^2 the *blending of* the two worlds of the East and the West in one 東西両洋を打って一丸とすること.

bless, *v.* 祝福する; 恵む.

P How I *blessed* them *for* disturbing my slumber! せっかくの睡眠を妨げられて私はどんなに彼らをのろったろう! ☞ blessed を反語に用いた例. ¶*bless* God (=the Lord) *for* a gift 賜物に対し神に感謝する. ¶*bless* oneself *from* danger 危険から身を避ける ‖ *Bless* me *from* all evils! 諸々の禍をはらい給え. ¶God *blessed* him *with* good health. 彼は健康に恵まれていた. 【類】Our country is *blessed with* natural resources (天然資源). / Harvard is *blessed with* financial resources (財力), which provide teachers on relatively generous salaries and a generous ratio of teachers to students (学生の数に対して教師の数が多い). / He is *blessed with* a good son. / be *blessed with* a treasure of children (子宝) / The union (結婚) has been *blest with* no children. / *blessed with* a sense of beauty ‖ hot springs *blessed with* healing virtue よくきく温泉 ‖ He is *blessed with* an unusually thick skin. 彼は特別心臓が強い.

blessedness, *n.* 幸福.

Q live in *single blessedness* のんきな独身生活を送る. 【類】be happy enough in *single blessedness*.

blessing, *n.* 天恩, 幸福.

V *ask* God's *blessing* 天恩を垂れ給わんことを祈る. ¶*call down* a *blessing* 神に願をかける. ¶a charm to *call forth blessing* 幸運のお守り. ¶She is a barren woman and her husband *desires* the *blessing* of issue. 女に子供ができない

ので夫が子を欲しがっている. ¶***invoke*** the *blessing* of the gods on its labors その努力に神々の恵みあらんことを祈る. 【類】***invoke*** a *blessing* upon the next day's fishing. ¶***seek*** the *blessings* of the gods 神々の恵みを求める. ¶The *blessing* is ***shared*** by all. 万人がその恩典に浴している. ¶***shower*** *blessings* upon ... …に恵みを雨と降らせる.

Q invoke the ***divine*** *blessing* upon this effort この努力に対する天佑を祈る. ¶A comfortable fire is a ***great*** *blessing* in cold weather. あったかい火は寒い日には何よりだ. ¶a ***mingled*** *blessing* 一喜一憂. ¶a ***mixed*** *blessing*, perhaps a curse in disguise あやふやな幸福, 恐らく一皮むけば不幸かも知れぬ. ¶May the ***richest*** *blessings* of our Heavenly Father be upon you and this institution. 天の父の豊かな恵みの諸君とこの協会の上にあらんことを. ¶an ***unlooked-for*** *blessing* 思いがけぬ幸福. ¶It is not an ***unmixed*** *blessing*. それは完全な幸福ではない. ¶an ***unqualified*** *blessing* 申分のない幸福. ¶The storm is over, ***what*** a *blessing!* 暴風が静まって何とありがたいことだろう. ¶a ***wonderful*** *blessing* 非常な幸福.

P ***by*** God's *blessing*, he may be permitted to ... 神の恵みによって彼は…することができよう. ¶The pastor raised his hands ***in*** *blessing*. 牧師は祝禱(ﾄｳ)のために手を挙げた. ¶***through*** God's *blessing* 神の恵みによって. ¶***under*** the Divine *blessing* 神の恵みの下に.

P^2 It is a *blessing* ***for*** him. それは彼にとって幸福である. This is a *blessing* ***from*** Heaven. これは天与の恵みである. the *blessing* ***of*** health 健康の幸福. ¶This, however, proved a *blessing* ***in*** disguise. しかしこの不幸は実は幸福であった. ¶an inestimable *blessing* ***to*** the world (society) 世界(など)にとって計り知れないほど貴い幸福.

blight, *n.* 障害.

P a *blight* ***on*** one's honor (family) 人の名誉(など)の毀損.

blind, *n.* 日よけ, 目かくし; 盲人.

V ***draw*** (=***pull***) *blinds* 日よけを上げる. ¶Would you object to my ***drawing up*** the *blinds?* 日よけを上げてもいいですか. ¶***lower*** (=***draw down or let down***) a *blind* 日よけをおろす.

Q a ***rolling*** *blind* 巻きすだれ. ¶***Venetian*** *blinds* 板すだれ.

P It was done ***for*** a *blind*. それは人目をごまかすためにやったものだ.

P^2 an institution ***for*** the *blind* 盲人院.

blind, *a.* 盲目の.

M He is ***as*** *blind* as a bat. 全然目が見えない. ¶***half*** *blind* 半盲の. ¶***nearly*** *blind* めくら同然な. ¶***totally*** *blind* まるっきり盲目の. ¶***utterly*** *blind* to ... …には全然盲目な.

P a man *blind* ***from*** *birth* 生れつきの盲人 ‖ be *blind* ***in*** the right eye 右の目が見えない. ¶He is *blind* ***of*** (=***in***) one eye. 片目だ. ‖ *blind* ***of*** both eyes 両眼とも見えない. ¶He is *blind* ***to*** his own defects. 彼には自分の欠点が見えない. 【類】He was *blind* ***to*** the consequences (his own interests). / I am not *blind* ***to*** the evils of alcoholic liquors (酒の害). / be *blind* ***to*** fine arts. ¶He is *blind* ***with*** anger (rage, fury, love). 怒(など)で目がくらんでいる.

blind, *v.* 盲目にする.

M He was ***accidentally*** *blinded* of one eye. けがで片目を失った.

P *blinded* ***by*** passion 激情にわれを忘れて ‖ be *blinded* ***by*** prejudice 偏見にとらわれている. ¶Patriotism cannot *blind* us ***to*** it. いかに愛国の目で見ても見逃す訳にはいかぬ. 【類】this should not *blind* us ***to*** the fact that ... / Neither ... nor ... should *blind* us ***to*** the fact. ¶Our eyes are often *blinded* ***with*** passion. 折々は感情のために目のくらむことがある.

blindness, *n.* 盲目.

V *Blindness* ***prevails*** in Japan to a greater extent than in any other country. 日本にはどこの国よりも盲人が多い.

Q I am too old not to know such ***wilful*** *blindness*. わざと分らないふりをしているのに気付かぬような若僧ではない.

Q^2 ***color*** *blindness* 色盲. ¶He has ***night*** *blindness*. 彼は鳥目だ. ¶***red*** *blindness* 赤色盲. ¶***snow*** *blindness* 雪めくら(雪の反射で起る).

P^2 *blindness* ***to*** one's own faults 自分の欠点に気の付かない事.

blink, *v.* 目をしばたたく.

M The boy *blinked* ***up*** at me in some surprise. 少年は驚いて目をぱちくりしながら僕を見た.

P The light *blinked* ***through*** darkness. その灯火がやみの中でまたたいた. ¶*blink* ***with*** astonishment 仰天して目を白黒させる.

bliss, *n.* 天福, 至福.

Q No one can ***appreciate*** the *bliss* of health until he loses it. 健康は失って始めてそのありがた味が分る. ¶the religious promise of ***celestial*** *bliss* as a reward for the privations suffered in this life 現世で受けた苦労の報酬として宗教が約束する天国の至福. ¶***domestic*** *bliss* (=happiness) 家庭の幸福. ¶a rapture of ***wedded*** *bliss* 結婚の歓喜.

blister, *n.* 水疱(ﾎｳ).

V ***raise*** a *blister* on (=blister) one's palm 手の平に水疱ができる.

blizzard, *n.* 吹雪.

V ***encounter*** the *blizzards* of Siberia シベリアの吹雪に会う.

Q^2 a freezing ***mountain*** *blizzard* 凍りつく山の大吹雪. ¶a ***winter*** *blizzard* 冬の大吹雪.

bloat, *v.* ふくらす; 慢心させる.

P He is *bloated* ***with*** pride. 慢心しきっている. ‖ a dog *bloated* ***with*** overeating 食い過ぎで肥った犬.

bloater, *n.* くん製にしん.

V ***toast*** a *bloater* at the fire くん製にしんを火であぶる.

bloc, *n.* 圏(ブロック).

Q ***regional*** *blocks* 地方ブロック.

Q^2 the countries of the ***Communist*** *bloc* 共産ブロックの国々. ¶the ***Slav*** *bloc* スラブ民族圏. ¶the ***Soviet*** *bloc* ソビエト・ブロック. ¶the creation of a "***sterling*** *bloc*" ポンド地域の設定. ¶the ***12-nation*** *bloc* 十二カ国ブロック.

block, *n.* **(1)** 片, 塊; 台, 斬首台; 型; 版木; 〘建築〙ブロック材.

V ***cut*** *blocks* with a razor 何にもならぬ事に頭や金銭を使う, いらぬ事に頭を悩ます.

Q a ***barber's*** *block* 理髪店のかつら. ¶a ***large*** *block* of wood [建築用]大型角材. ¶***mosaic*** *blocks* モザイク用の木(石)片. ¶hats of the ***newest*** *block* (=pattern) 最新型の帽子. ¶a picture printed in colors from ***wooden*** *blocks* 色ずりの木版画.

Q^2 ***alphabet*** *blocks* 教育文字合せ. ¶***building*** *blocks* [遊戯の]積木; 〘建築〙[コンクリートの]ブロック材. ¶***concrete*** *blocks* 工事用のコンクリート製ブロック材.

P sell ***in*** a *block* ひとまとめにして売る ‖ Three bills were brought ***in*** *block* for discussion. 三議案が一括上程された. ¶Hats are made ***on*** a *block*. 帽子は型で作る. ¶He was sentenced ***to*** the *block*. 死刑の宣告を受けた.

P^2 a *block* ***of*** marble (wood, limestone) 大理石(など)のブロック材. ¶The house is built of *blocks* ***of*** stone. 家は石造だ.

(2) 《米》街区.

V a building which ***covers*** two *blocks* 二街区を占める建物 ‖ Its façade ***covers*** one city *block*. その正面が市の一角を占めている. ¶a building which ***occupies*** an entire *block* 一街区全部を占める建物.

Q The station is ***five*** *blocks* away. 停車場は五丁先きだ. ¶You'll see a bar on your right about ***three*** *blocks* down there. その先三丁ほどのところ右側にバーがあります. ¶Walk ***two more*** *blocks* east. 東の方へもう二丁ほどいらっしゃい.

P American towns are built ***in*** *blocks*. 米国の都市は町が碁盤目にできている. ‖ It consists of about 4,000 acres ***in*** one *block*. それは面積四千エーカーの一区画を成している.

P^2 a *block* ***of*** houses 一区画の家屋.

block, *n.* 障害物, 閉塞.

Q a ***single*** (***double***) *block* 単(複)滑車.

Q^2 the major ***stumbling*** *block* 主な障害物. 【類】a ***stumbling*** *block* to the progress of human civilization.

P I have been detained ***by*** a *block* in the streets. 街が混雑して通れなかったので遅くなった.

P^2 a *block* ***on*** a railway=a railway block 〘鉄道〙閉塞式による一閉塞区間.

block, *v.* 封鎖する, 妨止する.

M *block* ***out*** スケッチする; 概略の計画を立てる. ¶He had some hand in *blocking* ***out*** this republic. 彼はその共和国の建設に幾分参加していた.

M^2 The harbor was *blocked* ***in*** by heavy masses of ice. 港は大氷塊で閉塞された. ¶*block* ***up*** the passage (way, street) 通路(など)をふさぐ ‖ A severe snowstorm *blocked* ***up*** railroads. ひどい吹雪のため鉄道の運転は休止となった. 【類】The river is *blocked* ***up*** with ice (=blocked by ice).

P The river is *blocked* ***by*** pleasure boats. 川は遊覧船で埋まっている. ¶The harbor is *blocked* ***from*** the rest of the world. その港は他の世界との交通を封鎖されている. 【類】The canal is *blocked* ***on account of*** a vessel being aground (座礁). ¶The street is *blocked* ***to*** traffic. その街

は通行止になっている. ¶The alley was *blocked with* crowds (people, carriages, snow). その小路は群集(など)のために通れなかった.

blockade, *n.* 封鎖.

v ***break*** a *blockade* 封鎖線を突破する. ¶***enforce*** a *blockade* 封鎖を強行する. ¶*Blockade* has been ***established*** here. ここは交通がしゃ断されている. ¶***lift*** a *blockade* 封鎖を解く. ¶No *blockade* is ***mainstaind*** here. ここには封鎖線が布いてない. ¶***raise*** a *blockade* 封鎖を解く. ¶***run*** the *blockade* 封鎖線を突破する. 【類】The steamer has been captured in ***running*** the *blockade*.

v² the *blockade* will not ***cease*** until ... 封鎖は...までは「除去されない.

Q A very ***strict*** *blackade* is maintained here. ここには厳重な封鎖線が布かれている.

Q² a ***long distance*** *blockade* 長距離の封鎖線. ¶It is nothing more than a ***paper*** *blockade*. 紙上の封鎖に過ぎない.

blood, *n.* 血, 血統.

v ***aerate*** *blood* 血液に酸素を供給する. ¶It will ***bring*** the *blood* to their faces (=make them flush). そうすると彼らは赤面するだろう. ¶***cause*** the *blood* to tingle 血を沸かせる. ¶***congeal*** *blood* 血を凝結させる. ¶The war ***cost*** so much British *blood*. その戦争で英国人が大分血を流した. ¶***cough*** *blood* せきをしながら血を吐く. ¶***curdle*** one's *blood* 肝を冷させる. ¶***donate*** *blood* for ... ...に(自分の血を)輸血する. ¶***draw*** *blood* from ... ...から血を取る ‖ a maiden sword, which has not yet ***drawn*** *blood* まだ血を見たことのない新刀. ¶***eject*** *blood* 吐血する. ¶***emit*** *blood*=bleed 出血する. ¶They ***have*** Jewish *blood* in their veins. 彼らはユダヤ人の血を受けている. ¶***inflame*** the *blood* of the patriotic people 憂国の士の血をわかす. ¶***let*** *blood* 血を取る. ¶It ***makes*** my *blood* boil. 腹が立ってたまらない. ‖ It ***makes*** my *blood* run cold. それは私の心胆を寒からしめる. ‖ Such places as these will ***make*** the fishermen's *blood* tingle. かような釣場は釣師をうずうずさせる. 【類】***make*** the *blood* tingle in one's cheek. ¶***pump*** the *blood* 血液を吸いあげる. ¶***purify*** the *blood* 血を清める. ¶***regenerate*** the *blood* 血液を若返らせる. ¶***run*** *blood* =bleed 出血する. ¶***see*** *blood* 血を見る. ¶***shed*** one's *blood* for one's country 国のために血を流す. ¶The stirring news of our Naval victory ***set*** the *blood* dancing in my veins. 海軍勝利の快報は私の血を躍らした. ‖ This insult ***set*** his *blood* on fire. この侮辱が彼をかっとさせた. ¶He ended his career by turning traitor to the cause for which he had ***shed*** his *blood*. かつてはその主義のために血をも流した彼は遂に裏切者となって一生を終った. ‖ without ***shedding*** *blood* 血を流さず平和裡(り)に. ¶They ***spilled*** his *blood*. 彼らは彼を殺害した. ¶***spit*** [***up***] *blood* 血を吐く. ¶a wound ***spouting*** *blood* 血がほとばしる傷. ¶***squeeze out*** the life's *blood* of the people 人民の膏(こう)血を絞る. ¶***stir*** one's *blood* 激昂(こう)させる, 血を沸かす. ¶***stop*** the *blood* 血を止める. ¶***suck*** the *blood* of the people 人民の膏血を絞る. ¶***suck up*** *blood* 血を吸う. ¶***transfuse*** one's *blood* into another 輸血する.

v² The *blood* ***circulates*** through the body. 血は体内を循環する. ¶My *blood* ***coursed*** merrily through vessels. ほがらかになった. ¶In his veins ***dances*** the *blood* of the son of Yamato. 彼の血管には大和男子の血が躍る. ¶The best *blood* of England ***flows*** in his veins. 彼には英国貴族の血が通っている. ‖ bite the hand till the *blood* ***flows*** 血が出るまで手をかむ. ¶My *blood* ***froze***. ぞっとした. ¶*blood* ***oozes*** from ... ...から血がにじみ出る. ¶*Blood* ***rained down*** from a deep gash in his forehead. 額の深手から血がだらだらと流れた. ¶*Blood* ***runs*** (=***flows***). 血が流れる. ‖ a collection of people in whose veins ***runs*** the best blue (=aristocratic) *blood* of every nation 各国の名門のお歴々の会合. ¶The *blood* ***rushed*** into my head. のぼせた. ¶His *blood* ***spurted*** on all sides. 彼の血はあたりにほとばしった. ¶claw an itch till *blood* ***starts*** 血が出るまでかゆい所をつめでかく. ¶*Blood* ***streams down***. 血が流れ落ちる. ¶Dull indeed must be that man whose *blood* does not ***tingle*** with anticipation. 期待に血をわかさないような男はよくよく鈍感な人だ. ¶*Blood* ***trickled down***. 血がだらだら流れた.

Q his affection for the sea—the one thing inborn of his ***ancestral*** *blood* 祖先からの唯一の遺伝である海に対するあこがれ. ¶He is of ***alien*** *blood*. 彼は外国人の血統だ. ¶The ***best young*** *blood* has gone abroad in search of fortune. 最も優秀な青年が運命を開拓すべく海外へ向った. ¶men of birth and breeding, or "***blue*** *blood*," as it was once called 名門教養の人, 古い言葉で言えば碧(へき)血(貴族の血統)の人々. ¶There is some ***caked*** *blood* on his coat. 彼の上衣に血の塊が付いている. ¶think it over in ***cold*** *blood* 冷静にその事を考える ‖ They are shot down in ***cold*** *blood*. 彼らは計画的に(出来心でなく)射殺された. ¶***full*** (***half***) *blood* 同親血縁(腹または種違いの兄弟・姉妹). ¶of ***gentle*** (=***honorable***) *blood* 名門の出の. ¶youths of ***hot*** *blood* 血気にはやる青年たち. ¶a prince of *blood* ***Imperial*** (***Royal***) 皇(王)族. ¶Much ***innocent*** *blood* was shed (=spilled). 幾多無垢(く)の血を流した. ¶a man of ***mixed*** *blood*, English and Sicilian 英人とシシリー島人の合の子. ¶infuse ***new*** *blood* into old policies 古い政策に新しい血液を注入する. ¶He has ***Oriental*** *blood* in his veins. 彼には東洋人の血が流れている. ¶The horse is of the ***purest Arab*** *blood*. この馬は完全な純アラビヤ種だ. ¶He has ***royal*** *blood* in his veins. 王族の血を引いている. ¶people of ***Spanish*** *blood* スペイン系の人々. ¶***venous*** and ***arterial*** *blood* 静脈及び動脈血. ¶He committed the murder in ***warm*** *blood*. かっとなってその殺人をやった. ¶***young*** *blood* 若い人々.

Q² spend one's ***life*** *blood* 身命を堵する. ¶persons with ***Negro*** *blood* in their veins 黒人の血が流れている人々.

P a brother ***by*** *blood* 血を分けた兄弟. 【類】a prince ***by*** *blood* ‖ Collateral relations ***by*** *blood* up to the third degree inclusive are forbidden by law to intermarry. 傍系三等親までは法律によって結婚を禁ぜられている. 【類】relationship (親戚関係) ***by*** *blood*. ¶The clothes were dyed ***in*** *blood*. 着物は血に染まっていた. 【類】It was written ***in*** *blood* (血書). ‖ He lay weltering ***in*** *blood*. 彼は血にまみれてのたくっていた. ‖ those near ***in*** *blood* 近親の人々 ‖ The disease runs ***in*** the *blood*. その病気は血統を引いている. ¶A wounded man lay in a pool ***of*** *blood*. けが人が血みどろになって横たわっていた. ‖ He is ***of*** foreign *blood*. 外人系である. ¶a prince (princess) ***of*** the *blood* 直系の宮様(王子・王女). ¶Mosquitoes feed ***on*** *blood*. 蚊は血を吸って生きている. ¶be ***out of*** *blood* 意気消沈している. ¶a cloth stained ***with*** *blood* 血に染まった布.

P² [with] *blood* ***in*** his eyes 殺気立って.

blood pressure, 血圧.

v He ***has*** a high *blood pressure*. 彼は血圧が高い. ¶***raise*** the *blood pressure* 血圧を高める.

Q ***high*** *blood pressure* 高血圧. ¶***low*** *blood pressure* 低い血圧. ¶***rising*** (***falling***) *blood pressure* 上向き(下向き)の血圧.

blood-relationship, *n.* 血縁.

v a family which ***claims*** *blood-relationship* with ... ...と血族関係があると称する家族.

bloodshed, *n.* 流血.

Q The mutiny of prisoners was put down without ***serious*** *bloodshed*. 囚人の反乱は大した流血もなく鎮圧された.

P The question was settled ***without*** *bloodshed*. 問題は流血のさんを見ずに解決がついた.

bloodstain, *n.* 血痕.

v try to ***efface*** the *bloodstains* from the boarded floor 板床から血のしみをふきとろうとする.

blood-vessel, *n.* 血管.

v He ***burst*** a *blood-vessel* in a fit of coughing. 彼は急に激しくせきがでたので血管が破れた. ¶***distend*** the *blood-vessels* 血管を膨張させる.

bloom, *n.* 花, 開花; 盛り; [ほおの]桜色; ろう粉.

v These fruits ***have*** a *bloom* upon them. この果物は粉がふいている. ¶those women who have ***lost*** the first *bloom* of youth 色がうつろい始めた彼女たち(うば桜). ¶***take*** the *bloom* off it その新鮮味または美観を殺ぐ.

Q handsome boys with the ***fresh*** *bloom* in the cheeks 紅顔の美少年 ‖ the ***fresh*** *bloom* of a glossy new-laid egg 生みたての玉子の真新しいつや. ¶The cherrytrees are in ***full*** *bloom*. 桜が満開だ. ¶She is in the ***lovely*** *bloom* of health. 彼女は健康美がみなぎっている. ¶a country girl with the ***ruddy*** *bloom* of health ほおの赤い, 見るからに健康そうないなか娘. ¶in ***youthful*** *bloom* 年は二八の花盛りの.

Q² ***zinc*** (***lead, tin, iron, steel, cobalt***) *bloom* 亜鉛(など)華.

P The apple tree is ***in*** *bloom* for the second time this season. そのりんごは返り咲をしている. 【類】The trees are clad ***in bloom*** (花盛り). ‖ young men ***in*** the ***bloom*** of adolescence 青春期の若人. 【類】a woman ***in*** the ***bloom*** of youth (=young womanhood) (若盛り). ¶The roses have come ***into bloom***. ばらが咲いた. ¶The cherry-trees are all ***out of bloom***. 桜はすっかり盛りが過ぎた. ¶The trees are clothed (=covered) ***with bloom***. 樹は花盛りだ.

bloom, *v.* 花咲く.

M These flowers *bloom* ***all the year round***. これらの草花は年中咲く. ¶The rose *bloomed* ***beautifully***. そのばらは美しく咲いた. ¶flowers *blooming* ***gaily*** はでに咲いている花.

P Flowers were *blooming* all ***along*** the valley. 谷一帯に花が咲いていた. ¶*bloom* ***into*** a prima donna 花形歌手に出世する.

blossom, *n.* 花, 開花.

V The cherry-trees began to ***put forth*** their *blossoms*. 桜の花が咲き始めた. ¶blooming cherry-trees ***snowing*** *blossoms* 花を雪と降らす桜.

Q ***full-blown*** *blossoms* 満開の花. ¶Manila is again enjoying almost the same exuberance of ***literary*** *blossoms* which so perfumed the air in the days of the Empire. マニラは帝政時代とほとんど同様なけんらんたる文華を再び現出している. ¶cherry trees of ***single*** and ***double*** *blossoms* 一重と八重の桜.

Q[2] a ***fruit*** *blossom* 果樹の花. ¶the ***moonlight*** *blossom* 月下の花. ¶a wreath of ***orange*** *blossom* オレンジの花の花冠.

P I suppose plum trees are ***in*** *blossom* now. 梅はもう咲いたろう. ‖ flowers ***in*** full *blossom* 満開の花. ¶spring ***into*** *blossom* 咲きだす. ¶decorate ***with*** *blossoms* 花で飾る.

blossom, *v.* 花咲く.

P *blossom* ***in*** thought and fruit in action 思想の花と咲き実行の果と実る. ¶That lonely, remote settlement *blossomed* ***into*** a charming little city. あのさびしい遠隔の植民地も追々発展して魅力のある小さな町になった. ‖ He has *blossomed* ***into*** a statesman. 彼はりっぱな政治家になった. ¶His industry has made the barren land *blossom* ***like*** a rose. 彼の努力でその荒野の地がばらのように花咲く土地となった.

blot, *n.* 汚れ.

V His misbehavior ***cast*** a *blot* on our name. 彼の非行でわれわれの名誉が傷つけられた. ¶I can't ***get out*** these *blots*. このしみは取れない. ¶I have ***made*** a *blot* on my paper. 紙にしみを付けた. ¶***put*** a *blot* on the nation 国家に汚点をつける. ¶***remove*** a foul *blot* from it それから汚名を取り除く. ¶***wipe out*** a *blot* 汚点をぬぐい去る.

Q a ***great*** *blot* of his career 彼の生涯の一大汚点. ¶the most ***serious*** *blot* in its history その歴史における一大汚点. ¶a ***slight*** *blot* さ細の汚点. ¶an ***ugly*** *blot* on his reputation 彼の名声に対する一大汚点.

P It is a lamentable (=sad) *blot* ***on*** his fame (fair name, character, honor). それは彼の名声(など)の一大汚点だ. ‖ It was a *blot* ***on*** the color-scheme. それで折角の色調を台なしにした. ¶a *blot* ***upon*** American history 米国史上の一汚点. 【類】a *blot* ***upon*** the applicant's escutcheon / The great *blot* ***upon*** musical London today is the overtraining of the unfit, the exploitation of the unworthy.

blot, *v.* 汚す; 消す; おおう.

M *blot* it ***out*** ふき消す, 除く; 《俗》殺す ‖ *blot* ***out*** one's name from the list 除名する ‖ His sins are all *blotted* ***out***. 彼の罪は皆ぬぐわれた. ‖ The sky is *blotted* ***out*** by clouds. 空は雲でおおわれている.

P I tried hard to *blot* the matter ***from*** my memory. どうにかしてそのことを忘れようとした.

blouse, *n.* 労働服.

P He was working ***in*** a *blouse* (=with a blouse on). 彼は労働服で働いていた.

blow, *n.* 開花.

P Apple-trees are ***in*** full *blow*. りんごは花盛りだ.

blow, *n.* 打撲, 打撃.

V I ***aimed*** a *blow* at his head with my cane. つえで彼の頭に一本参ろうとした. ¶***deal*** a *blow* at a dog 犬に一撃を食わせる ‖ The Opposition ***dealt*** a deadly *blow* at the Government. 野党は政府に致命傷を与えた. ¶***deliver*** a telling *blow* at (=against) the enemy 敵に手ごたえのある打撃を与える. ¶***dodge*** a *blow* 打撃をよける. ¶***exchange*** *blows* なぐり合をする. ¶This remark of his ***fetched*** a *blow*. 彼はこういったために拳骨を食わされた. ¶I ***gave*** him a *blow* upon the middle finger of the right hand. 彼の右手の中指を打った. 【類】He ***gave*** a strong *blow* to his dog. ¶***hit*** a clear *blow* 十分に打つ. ¶***impart*** a *blow* to it それに打撃を与える. ¶***inflict*** a crushing *blow* 致命的打撃を与える. ¶He ***received*** a severe *blow* by the death of his righthand man. 彼は右腕と頼む人に死なれて非常な打撃をこうむった. 【類】***received*** its death *blow* from ... ¶***return*** a *blow* with interest 利息をつけて仕返しをする. ¶***shower*** (=***rain***) *blows* on ... …にげん骨の雨を降らせる(乱打する). ¶***strike*** a hard *blow* はげしく打つ ‖ ***strike*** a *blow* against ... …に抵抗する ‖ ***strike*** a mortal *blow* at the vitals 急所に致命的一撃を加える ‖ The army retreated without ***striking*** a *blow*. 軍は一撃も加えずに退却した. ‖ ***strike*** a *blow* for freedom (against slavery) 自由擁護のため(奴隷制度に反対して)火の手をあげる ‖ He ***struck*** me a *blow* in the face. 彼は僕の顔を打った. ¶***suffer*** an irreparable *blow* 取返しの付かない打撃を受ける. ¶She held up her hand as though to ***ward off*** a *blow*. 彼女は打撃を受け止めようとするかのように手を挙げた.

V[2] A *blow* still more bitter ***followed***. 続いてひとしおきびしい一撃が下された. ¶*Blows* ***rained*** down upon him. 彼の上に乱打が雨と降った(めちゃくちゃになぐられた).

Q receive a ***bitter*** *blow* 大打撃を受ける. ¶strike a ***critical*** *blow* at ... …に徹底的な攻撃を与える. ¶a ***deadly*** (=***fatal***) *blow* 致命的打撃. ¶The war struck a ***decisive*** *blow* at Russia in East Asia. その戦役は東アジアにおけるロシヤに止めをさした. ¶a ***deplorable*** *blow* 悲しむべき打撃. ¶deal a ***discouraging*** (=***crushing***) *blow* to ... …に徹底的な一撃を加える. ¶The criminal screamed at ***every*** *blow*. 打たれるたびに罪人はわめいた. ‖ ***Every*** *blow* told. 打込みにむだがなかった. ¶that would be a ***fatal*** *blow* to ... …にとって致命的打撃であろう. ¶give the ***finishing*** *blow* 止めをさす. ¶strike the ***first*** *blow* 先手を打つ, 攻勢にでる. ¶is a ***great*** *blow* to ... …にとって大打撃である. ¶a ***hard*** *blow* 痛打. ¶give a ***hard-dealt*** *blow* to ... …に鉄拳をお見舞申す. ¶A ***heavy*** *blow* at him was struck by the Press. 諸新聞によって激しい攻撃が彼の上に加えられた. ¶deal a ***mortal*** (=***death***) *blow* to him 彼に致命的打撃を与える. ¶His loss is a ***national*** *blow*. 彼の死は国家的打撃である. ¶strike him a ***powerful*** *blow* in the face 彼の顔をいやというほど打つ. ¶Her head split and almost severed by ***repeated*** *blows* from an axe. おのでめった打ちにされ彼女の頭は裂けほとんどわれかかっていた. ¶The bereavement was a ***sad*** *blow* to his family. 彼の死は家族にとって悲しむべき打撃であった. ¶The failure of the bank proved a ***serious*** *blow* to the depositors. 銀行の破産は預金者にとって手痛い打撃となった. ¶strike a ***severe*** *blow* at ... …をはげしく打つ. ¶strike a person a ***sharp*** *blow* 人を手ひどく打つ. ¶a ***smart*** *blow* 鋭い打撃. ¶He dealt me a ***sudden*** *blow* 彼は僕をだし抜けに打った. ¶a ***terrible*** *blow* 大打撃. ¶receive a ***terrific*** *blow* from a telephone pole [汽車の窓から頭を突だしなどして]いやというほど頭を電話線の柱に打つける. ¶strike a ***treacherous*** *blow* at ... …にひきょうな攻撃を加える. ¶He struck her several ***violent*** *blows* on the head and hands with a big stick. 彼は太いステッキで彼女の頭や手を続けざまにはげしく打った. 【類】I struck him a ***violent*** *blow* on the head.

Q[2] a ***death*** *blow* 致命的打撃. ¶a ***knockout*** *blow* 一発必中の強打. ¶land a person a ***K.O.*** *blow* on the upper jaw 上あごに KO パンチを一発食わせる.

P The executioner cut off his head ***at*** one *blow*. 首切り役人は一刀のもとに彼の首を切り落した. ‖ His library was scattered ***at*** a *blow* of the hammer. 彼の蔵書は競売に付せられて四散した. ‖ The enemy was expelled ***at*** the first *blow*. 敵は最初の一撃で退却した. ¶He answered not by word but ***by*** *blow*. 彼は口で答えないで鉄拳で応じた. ¶He died ***from*** a *blow*. 打たれたのが原因で死んだ. ¶At last they came ***to*** *blows*. あげくの果がなぐり合になった. ¶He slayed the beast ***with*** one *blow*. 彼はそのけだものを一打ちに殺した.

P[2] strike a *blow* ***at*** class difference 階級的闘争を攻撃する ‖ It dealt another *blow* ***at*** British prestige and enterprise in the East. それもまた東洋における英国の威信と企業に取っての打撃であった. ¶He struck her a heavy *blow* ***in*** (=***on***) the face. 彼は彼女の顔をはげしく打った. ¶a *blow* ***to*** their pride of race 彼らの優秀人種という誇りに対する一痛打 ‖ It was a great *blow* ***to*** the company. それは会社に取って一大打撃であった.

blow, *n.* 吹くこと.

V ***give*** the fire a *blow* with the bellows ふいごで火をふーっと吹く. 【類】***give*** a hard *blow* on a whistle (口笛).

blow, *v.* 吹く, 吹きつける; 言いふらす; 慢心させる; 爆裂する; [鼻を]かむ.

M The ship was at last *blown* ***ashore.*** 船はとうとう岸に吹き上げられた. 【類】The tempest *blew* the ship ***ashore.*** ¶*blow* ***away*** 吹き飛ばす. ¶The wind was *blowing* ***gently*** (***hard***). 風がそよそよ(烈しく)吹いていた. ¶It *blew* ***heavily*** during our voyage. 航海中風がひどく吹いた. ¶The wind *blew* ***hard.*** 風が強く吹いた. ¶*blow* ***hot and cold*** 冷熱常ならず; 定見がない (気が変りやすい), 御都合次第 ‖ These people can *blow* ***hot and cold*** out of the same mouth to serve purposes. この連中は都合次第で言を二にする人たちだ. ¶The wind was *blowing* ***northerly*** (***southerly***). 風が北(南)から吹いていた. ¶*blow* ***out*** the candle ろうそくを消す ‖ *blow* ***out*** the spark of life 息の音を止める ‖ It *blew* itself ***out.*** 風が止んだ. ‖ *blow* ***out*** one's brains with a pistol ピストルで頭を撃ち抜く. 【類】I'll *blow* your brains ***out.*** ‖ *blow* ***out*** the gas ガスを爆発させる. 【類】*blow* ***out*** a tire (balloon) / The fuse *blew* ***out*** with a snap (ぱちっと). / have a tire *blown* ***out.*** ¶The wind *blew* ***strong*** with a heavy sea. 風が強く波が荒かった. ¶He had not long been at sea, before the wind began to *blow* ***tempestuously.*** 海に出て間もなく風があらしになりだした. ¶It *blows* ***tremendously.*** すさまじい風だ. ¶a rumor ***widely*** *blown* about 広く言ふらされた風聞.

M² *blow* ***down*** a lamp to extinguish it ランプを消そうと吹く ‖ trees and fences were *blown* ***down*** [あらしで]木や垣が倒された. ¶I expect him to *blow* ***in*** next Sunday. 今度の日曜あたり彼はひょっこり顔を出すんじゃないかと思っている. ‖ The fresh air *blew* ***in*** from (=at) the open window. 新鮮な空気が窓から入って来た. ¶*blow* ***off*** one's hat 風で帽子を飛ばす ‖ The house had its roof *blown* ***off.*** 家は屋根をはがされた. ‖ He had his leg *blown* ***off*** by a dynamite bomb. 彼は爆弾で片足取られた. 【類】The ship's bow was *blown* ***off*** by a mine (機雷). ¶the lid *blew* ***off*** this week when ... 今週にはいると間もなく... ¶The wind has *blown* ***over*** a boat. 風で小舟がてんぷくした. ‖ The storm had *blown* ***over.*** 暴風が止んだ. ‖ The present disturbances will soon *blow* ***over.*** 今のこの騒ぎはまもなく静まるだろう. ‖ The incident will be *blown* ***over*** in course of time. その事件はその中忘れられるだろう. ¶*blow* ***up*** a soap balloon シャボン玉を吹上げる ‖ *blow* ***up*** a mine 雷管(機雷)を爆発させる. 【類】*blow* ***up*** a ship by setting fire to the magazine (火薬庫に点火して) ‖ The wreck will have to be *blown* up. 破船は爆破せねばならない. ‖ *blow* ***up*** a bridge with gun-powder 橋を爆破する ‖ Your father will *blow* you ***up*** if you don't behave better. おとなしくしないとお父さんにしかられるよ. ‖ *blow* ***up*** one's spirits 元気をつけてやる ‖ A storm suddenly *blew* ***up.*** 突然あらしが起った. ‖ *blow* ***up*** a person with flattery おだてあげる.

P The wind *blows* ***against*** the sail. 風が帆に向って逆に吹いている. ¶*blow* ***at*** a candle ろうそくを吹き消そうとする. ¶The whistle *blew* ***for*** the end of the day's labor. その日の終業を告げる汽笛が鳴った. ¶The wind *blew* stiffly ***from*** the north-east. 北東の風が強く吹いていた. ‖ The wind *blew* a roof ***from*** a house. 風が家の屋根を吹きめくった. ¶There was a chilly wind *blowing* ***in*** our faces. 冷い風がわれわれの顔にあたっていた. 【類】A little breeze is *blowing* ***in*** the window. ‖ The wind *blew* ***in*** fitful gusts. 風が急に吹いたり止んだりした. ¶The rock was *blown* ***into*** fragments with dynamite. 岩石はダイナマイトでみじんに爆破された. ‖ *blow* one's nose ***into*** a handkerchief ハンケチで鼻をかむ. ¶The force of the wind nearly *blew* me ***off*** my feet. 風は私の足をさらうほど強かった. 【類】Fruits *blown* ***off*** a tree by the wind were seen scattering on the ground. ¶*blow* ***on*** pipes 笛を吹く. ¶*blow* ***through*** a pipe (shell horn) 笛(ほら貝)を吹く. 【類】The whistle (呼笛) makes a noise when you *blow* ***through*** it. ‖ The wind *blew* ***through*** the forest. 風が森を吹き通した. ¶It was *blown* ***to*** atoms. 粉みじんに爆破した. ‖ *blow* a person ***to*** a drink 人をおだてて一杯おごらせる. ¶*blow* ***upon*** one's face 人の顔をよごす; 人の信用を失わせる.

O It is *blowing* a gale. あらしだ. 【類】It has *blown* a gale all day. ¶It *blows* great guns. 大風だ. ¶*blow* a ***whistle*** (***flute, trumpet***) 呼笛(など)を吹く.

blowout, *n.* 破裂, パンク.

V we ***had*** two *blowouts* on our auto trip to ......までのドライブに二回パンクした.

P² the *blowout* ***of*** a fuse ヒューズがとぶこと.

blowtorch, *n.* 〘機〙トーチ・ランプ.

V ***use*** a *blowtorch* in plumbing work 鉛管工事にトーチ・ランプを使う.

blue, *n.* 青色; 青空.

V ***get*** (=***win***) one's *blue* [英国の大学などで]対校競技の選手となる.

Q ***light*** (***dark***) *blue* 明(濃)青色. ¶***Prussian*** *blue* 紺青色.

Q² ***Alice*** *blue* 薄紺(え)色. ¶famous ***Cambridge*** "*blue*" 有名なケンブッリジ大学の短艇選手. ¶The sea was of a ***lapis lazuli*** *blue.* 海は紺青(こん)に色どられていた. ¶***navy*** *blue* 紫紺色. ¶***rugger*** (***rowing***) *blue* ラグビー(ボート)の選手. ¶***turquoise*** *blue* 青緑色.

P² be dressed ***in*** *blue* 青服を着ている. ¶like a bolt ***out of*** the *blue* 突如.

blue, *a.* 青い.

P He turned *blue* ***in*** the face. 彼は(驚いて)青くなった. ¶He was *blue* ***over*** his dismissal. 彼は解雇されてふさいでいた. ¶My hands are *blue* ***with*** cold. 寒さで手の血色がなくなっている.

blues, *n.* 憂うつ; 《米》ブルース.

V ***have*** the *blues* ふさぎこんでいる. ¶*Blues* is a type of folk song, ***originated*** among negroes. ブルースは黒人の間で始められた民謡の一種だ.

bluff, *n.* 《米》威かく.

V ***detect*** a *bluff* おどしだとみてとる. ¶He ***made*** a *bluff* at hitting me. 僕を打つと言っておどかした.

P No use ***of*** your *bluff.* からいばりしてもだめ.

bluff, *v.* 《米》虚勢を張る.

M *bluff* ***off*** a dun うるさい借金取りを威勢よく追い払う.

blunder, *n.* 間違い, 失策.

V ***commit*** an egregeous *blunder* 途方もない間違いをする. ¶***make*** *blunders* 失策をやる.

Q an ***astounding*** *blunder* 飛んでもない間違い. ¶a ***capital*** (=***colossal, gross*** or ***huge***) *blunder* 大間違い. ¶a ***costly*** *blunder* (犠牲を払うので)手痛い間違い. ¶a ***glaring*** *blunder* 目立った間違い. ¶a ***grave*** *blunder* 由々しい失策. ¶a truly ***ludicrous*** *blunder* 全くばかばかしい間違い. ¶one of the gravest ***political*** *blunders* which have ever been committed 政治上にあらわれた最も由々しい失策の一つ. ¶a ***queer*** *blunder* おかしな失策. ¶a ***sad*** *blunder* 悲しむべき失策. ¶It is indeed a very ***serious*** *blunder.* 実に重大な失策だ. ¶***technical*** *blunders* 技術上の間違い.

P ***by*** some *blunder* [or other] どう間違ったか.

blunder, *v.* 失策する

M He *blundered* ***away*** his fortune. 彼はへまをやって財産をなくしてしまった. 【類】He is not likely to *blunder* ***away*** the interests of his country. ¶*blunder* ***out*** a secret うかつに秘密をもらす.

M² They *blundered* ***on*** hopelessly through the unknown country. 彼らは当てもなく不案内の土地をまごつき歩いた.

P *blunder* ***against*** each other お互いにぶっつかる. 【類】A large fish *blundered* ***against*** our boat. ¶*blunder* ***in*** reading (writing) 読み方(など)を間違える. ¶He *blundered* ***into*** a sense. 彼はけがの功名でうまいことを言った. ¶He *blundered* ***on*** a new fact. 彼は間違って新発見をした. ¶*blunder* ***through*** an affair どうかこうか(曲りなりに)やってのける.

blunt, *a.* 無骨(ぶ)な, 露骨な.

P He is very *blunt* ***in*** his bearing (manner, speech) 彼の態度(など)はすこぶる無骨だ.

bluntness, *n.* 無骨.

Q the captain, with the ***rough*** *bluntness* of a sailor, peremptorily told them that ... 船長は海員らしい無骨さで...するよう厳然と彼らに命じた.

blur, *n.* 曇り, かすみ.

Q ¶There was ***no*** *blur* on the mirror. 鏡中には一点のくもりもなかった.

P² There was a *blur* ***in*** his voice. 声がかすれていた. ¶The object was a *blur* ***to*** her sleeping eyes. その物は彼女の眠い目にはぼんやりかすんで見えた.

blur, *v.* よごす; ぼやけさせる.

M *blur* ***out*** distinctions between races and nations 人種, 国家間の差別を除去する.

M² *blur* ***over*** scandals 不正事件をもみ消す.

P *blur* a page *with* ink ページをインキでよごす.

blurt, *v.* 口走る, うっかりしゃべる.

M *blurt out* a secret 秘密を口走る ‖ without being questioned by me, she *blurted out* the fact that ... 問わず語りに彼女は...の事実を口走った.

blush, *n.* 赤面; 一べつ, 一見.

V This *brought* the *blush* of shame to his face. こう言うと彼は赤面した. ¶*check* the *blush* by sheer force of will 全然意志の力で赤面を防ぐ. ¶*raise* a *blush* of girlish modesty on the cheeks 恥かしくてうぶなほおが赤くなる. ¶*Spare* my *blushes.* そうおだてられてはずかしいよ. ¶peaches that have *stolen blushes* from maidens 乙女のほおを思わせるほの赤い桃.

Q *bashful blushes* しゅうちの赤面. ¶It seems natural at *first blush.* 一応もっともである. ¶at *first blush,* it might seem (appear) that ... 一見...と思われるだろう. 【類】At *first blush* the scheme promises well. / It may not be obvious at *first blush.* ¶a *telltale blush* 隠しても出る恥じらいの色.

P It was an instance of that trumpeting anger with which young men regard injustices *in* the first *blush* of youth. 世間ずれのしない(純情の)青年が不正行為を見るとやっきとなって怒るものだがこの場合もそれだった. ¶He was put *to* the *blush.* 彼は赤面した. ¶*with* a *blush* ちと顔を赤くして.

blush, *v.* 赤面する.

M *blush confusedly* まごついて赤面する. ¶*blush deeply* ひどく赤面する. ¶*blush hotly* 顔を真赤にする. ¶It made her *blush scarlet.* それで彼女は顔を真赤にした. ¶He *blushed up* (=reddened *or* colored up) to the temples (eyes, root of the hair). 彼は耳(など)まで真赤になった. ¶*blushing violently* all over 顔を真赤にして.

P He *blushed at* her. 彼女を見て顔を赤くした. ‖ I *blush at* my own faults (folly). 失策にわれながら赤面する. ¶*blush for* shame 恥かしくって赤くなる ‖ I *blush for* your degraded conduct. 君の不品行ははずべきことだ. ‖ We need *blush for* your reputation (good name). われわれは君の名誉のためにそれを恥ずべきことと考えざるを得ない. ‖ I *blush for* you. 君には赤面する. ¶She *blushed like* a full-blown peony. 彼女は顔に紅葉を散らした. ¶come to *blush with* shame (mortification) 恥辱(など)で赤面するようになる ‖ hills *blushing with* roses ばらの花で赤らんでいる小山.

O I *blush* to own it. 白状するさえはずかしい. ¶I *blushed* to hear it. それを聞いて赤面した.

blushing, *n.* 赤面すること.

Q *spontaneous* (=*involuntary*) *blushing* 自然に出る赤面.

bluster, *v.* どなる; 吹きすさむ.

M *bluster out* a threat すご文句をならべる. ¶The storm *blusters without.* 暴風は戸外に吹きすさむ.

M² The wind *blustered round* the house. 風は家の回りをびゅうびゅう吹きまくった.

P He *blustered at* them. 彼は彼らをどなりつけた.

board, *n.* (**1**) 板; 台; 掲示板; 厚紙.

V They *put up* a little *board* marking his tomb. 彼の墓のしるしに小さな板を立てた. ¶*saw* a *board* 板をのこぎりで切る.

Q a *knotless board* 節なし板. ¶a *terminal board* 端子盤. ¶pieces of *well-seasoned board* よくからした板.

Q² an *academy board* 画学用紙. ¶a loud *advertisement board* 大々的な広告板. ¶a *bulletin board* 告知板. ¶a *chip board* [紙箱用]パルプボールの一種. ¶a book with *cloth boards* クロース表紙の本 ‖ This pure journalism is masquerading between *cloth boards.* これは新聞記事を単行本にしただけのものだ. ¶a *destination board* [列車などの]方向板. ¶the *edict boards* against Christianity were not taken down until 1872 キリシタン禁令掲示は一八七二年になってようやくはずされた. ¶an *ironing board* アイロン台. ¶a *kneading board* [パン粉の]こね板. ¶a *lap board* ひざ板(仕立師の). ¶a *message board* [駅などの]伝言板. ¶Post this message on the *notice* (=*bulletin*) *board* so that all interested may read. この便りを掲示板に掲げてみんなに読まして下さい. ¶*sandwich boards* [sandwich manが前後にたれて歩く]広告板. ¶a *shuffle board* 玉転ばし台. ¶a *spring board* at a swimming pool 水泳場の飛込板. ¶a *sound[-ing] board* 反響盤; 防音板. ¶a *switch board* [電気の]配電盤; 交換台.

P He left a note *on* the bulletin *board* on the platform. 彼はプラットホームの掲示板に短信を書いておいた. ‖ moves *on* the Asiatic chess *board* アジア政局の動き. ¶bore *through* a *board* きりで板をもみ抜く.

(**2**) 食卓; まかない.

V These delicacies often *adorn* the festive *boards* of English households. これらの美味は英国の家庭でよくお祝いの食卓に上される. ¶They *charge* only a nominal *board.* ほんの名ばかりの食費を徴収する. ¶*give board* 食事を出す ‖ We *give* no *board.* [間貸だけで]食事は出しません.

Q They feasted at a *festive board.* 彼らは祝賀の宴を張った. ‖ She gives *good board.* [しろうと下宿の]おかみがうまいものを食わす. 【類】You can find *good board* for as little as $5 a week. ¶a *groaning board* [食卓に盛った]たくさんの御ちそう. ¶I dined at his *hospitable board.* 彼の家で御ちそうになった. ¶*part board* [下宿などの]一部食事付.

P I sat *at* the *board* with him. 彼と食卓をともにした. ‖ Many prominent men were seated *at* the banquet *boards.* 幾多知名の士がきょう宴の席に列していた. ¶I pay weekly *for* my *board* and lodging. 毎週食料と間代を払う. ¶The room rent is $50 *with board.* へやはまかないつきで五十ドルです.

(**3**) 委員会, 局.

Q He is a member of the *advisory board.* 彼は相談役だ. ¶He was on the *executive board.* 彼は実行委員の一人であった.

Q² an *adjustment board* 〘労〙調停委員会. ¶the *Appeal Board* of Accident Compensation 労働者災害補償審査委員会. ¶an *appraisal board* 評価委員会. ¶an *arbitration board* 仲裁委員会. ¶the *Construction Board* 建設局. ¶an *editorial board* 編集局. ¶the *Education Board* 教育委員会. ¶He is one of the *examining board* 彼は試験委員だ. ¶a *fact-finding board* 実情調査委員会. ¶a *food allocation board* 食料割当委員会. ¶a member of the *governing board* of the school 学校管理者の一人. ¶a *health board* 保健局. ¶a *joint board* 共同委員会. ¶a *policy-making advisory board* 政策審議会. ¶a *price-fitting board* 物価設定委員会. ¶a *referee board* 審査委員. ¶a *seven-man policy making board* 政策七人委員会. ¶the *Social Security Board* 社会保障局. ¶a *tourist board* 観光局. ¶the *Treasury Board* 《英》国家財務委員会. ¶a *trial board* 諮問委員会.

P It is best to be *above board* in everything. 何事も公明正大が一番だ. 【類】His conduct is quite *above board.* / He is fair and *above board.* ¶He is *on* the *board* of directors. 彼は重役だ. ‖ resign one's position *on* the *board* of directors 理事(重役)の職を辞する.

P² The school is managed by a *board of* eight directors. 同校は八人の理事会が管理している. ‖ a *board of* trade=《英》a chamber of commerce 商業会議所. ☞英国の the Board of Trade は「商務省」‖ a *board of* arbitration 《米》調停委員会.

(**4**) 船内, 船側; 《米》列車(飛行機)内.

V *keep board* 船内に留まる; 秘密にする.

P goods landed in this city *from on board* the S.S. "..." 汽船...号から当市に陸揚した荷物. ¶go (=get) *on board* 《英・米》乗船する; 《米》列車(飛行機など)に乗る. 【類】The passenger has come *on board.* ‖ a life *on board* [a] ship 船の生活 ‖ He sprang *on board,* sword in hand. 彼は剣を手にして船におどり込んだ. 【類】jump *on board* the train ‖ free *on board* (=f.o.b.) 本船渡し ‖ board *on* (=*to*) *board* げんげん相摩して ‖ He is *on board* [of] the ship. 彼は乗船している. 【類】A prince (皇族) is *on board* one of those ships. / serve *on board* a warship / A dinner was given *on board* the flagship. / In 1620 the "Mayflower," a ship of 180 tons, sailed from Southampton, England, with 101 Puritans *on board.* ‖ We were *on board* an 18-hour train for Chicago. 《米》われわれはシカゴまで十八時間列車に乗っていた.

(**5**) *pl.* 舞台.

V She decided to *tread* the *boards* once more. 彼女は舞台生活に戻ろうと決心した.

P Our greatest actors appeared *on* its *boards.* その舞台にはわが梨園(りえん)の名花たちが姿を現わした. ‖ The play is now *on* [the *boards*] at Kabuki-za. その狂言は目下歌舞伎座で上演中である.

board, *v.* 板で囲う；下宿する，食事する；上船する；《米》列車(飛行機)に乗る.

M *board out* 外食する；[板じきりで]交通をしゃ断する.

M² a portion *boarded off* with the word "private" on the door「事務用」とドアに張出し仕切ってある部分(デパートなどの). ¶*board up* a road 板で道路をしゃ断する ‖ *board up* a home 家の周囲に板を張る.【類】*board up* a flock of chickens.

P I *board at* his house. 私はあの人の家に下宿している. ‖ *board at* a hotel ホテルで食事をとる. ¶*board by* the month 月ぎめで下宿する ‖ He is *boarded* and lodged *by* the principal. 彼は校長の所に下宿している. ‖ be *boarded by* pirates [船が]海賊に押寄せられる. ¶How much will you *board* me *for*? いくらでまかなってくれるか. ¶*board in* a farm house in summer 夏期農家に下宿する. ¶He is *boarding with* us. 彼はわれわれの家に下宿している.

O *board* oneself 自すいする. ¶*board* a train (Clipper) 列車(など)に乗る.

boarder, *n.* 下宿人.

V *take* (*in*) *boarders* 下宿人を置く.

Q *monthly boarders* at a hotel 旅館にいる月ぎめの下宿人.

Q² a *day boarder* 半寄宿人；食事だけの下宿屋. ¶her *star boarders* 下宿屋の女主人の最高級の寄宿人. ¶take [in] *summer boarders* 夏季だけ下宿人を置く.

P² a *boarder at* a public school 《英》パブリック・スクールの寄宿生.

boast, *n.* 自慢.

V he *flung* at me a *boast* that ... 彼は私に…と言って大ぶろ敷を広げた. ¶*fulfil* one's proud *boast* that ... …という自慢通りに実行する. ¶*make* a *boast* of being a spendthrift 金使いの荒いのを自慢する.

Q an *empty boast* から自慢. ¶it is their *favorite boast* that ... 彼らは好んで…と自慢する. ¶it is no *idle boast* of ours that ... …というのは決してわれわれのから自慢じゃない. ¶a *loud boast* 大言壮語. ¶a *proud boast* 大自慢.【類】it is his *proudest boast* that ... ¶a *racial boast* 民族的誇り. ¶he really made us *vain boast* when he claimed that ... …と言ったのは実は空いばりだったのである. ¶a *vapid boast* つまらない自慢. ¶It is no very *wild boast* to say so. そう言ってもあまり途方もない自慢ではない.

P² He was the *boast of* his age. 氏はその時代の誇りであった.

O he made it his *boast* to ... 彼は…を誇りとした.

boast, *v.* 自慢する.

M he *laughingly boasted* that ... 彼は笑いながら…と自慢を言った. ¶*vainly boast* of ... うぬぼれて…を口にする.

P *boast about* one's own country お国自慢をする. ¶*boast of* one's deeds (success, ancestors, learning, cleverness, skill) 自己の業績(など)を自慢する.【類】a nation *boasting of* its practical common-sense (実際的常識) ‖ I can *boast of* many influential men as sponsors. 後援者として幾多有力な人士をもっている. ‖ We can *boast of* Imperial patronage. 手前どもは宮内省の御用をうけたまわっています. ‖ This proverb can *boast of* a hoary antiquity. このことわざは非常に古いものだ. ‖ They can all *boast of* unnumbered crimes. 彼らは皆無数の罪悪を重ねている. ‖ It's not a thing one can well *boast of*. あまり自慢にはならないことだ.

O The society *boasts* among its membership two greatest names in contemporary letters. その会員の中に現文壇の巨匠二人を有している.【類】The city *boasted* a good school. / He *boasts* a first edition of Shakespeare.

boastful, *a.* 自慢する.

P He is *boastful of* his wealth. 彼は金持が自慢だ.

boasting, *n.* 自慢.

Q *empty* (=*vain*) *boastings* 空自慢. ¶*modest* (*immodest*) *boasting* 内輪(大げさ)な自慢. ¶*vain boasting* からいばり.

P I think I may say, *without boasting*, that ... 私が…と言っても必ずしも自画自賛ではなかろう.

boat, *n.* 小舟，ボート；船.

V *board* a *boat* at Kobe 神戸で乗船する. ¶*cast off* a *boat* from its moorings ボートを繋留所から離す. ¶*catch* a *boat* at Kobe 出帆間際に神戸で乗船する. ¶*engage* a whole *boat* 船を借切る. ¶*get* one's *boat* on the water ボートを水におろす ‖ *get* a *boat* out of (into, in) a boathouse 艇庫から(へ)ボートを出す(納める). ¶*hire* a *boat* to see the fireworks 花火見物にボートをやとう. ¶*Boats* can be *had* for hire. 貸ボートがある. ¶*hoist* a *boat* ボートを引揚げる. ¶Do you *keep boats* for hire? 貸ボートがありますか. ¶*launch* a *boat* 船を進水させる. ¶*lower* a *boat* ボートをおろす. ¶*man* a *boat* 船に乗組員を乗り込ます. ¶*man* and *arm* a *boat*〘海〙船を軍装する. ¶*manage* a *boat* ボートを操縦する. ¶The *boat* was *overloaded* and *upset*. 船は荷が過ぎて転覆した. ¶*overturn* (=*turn over*) a *boat* ボートを転覆さす. ¶*patronize* N.Y.K. *boats* 日本郵船の船の常得意になる. ¶*pole* a *boat* 船にさおさす. ¶*pull* a *boat* ボートをこぐ. ¶a *boat put off* from the ship その船から出されたボート. ¶*row* a *boat* on a river 川でボートをこぐ. ¶*run* one's *boat aground* 小舟を坐礁させる. ¶*sail* a *boat* 船を帆走させる. ¶*send away boats* to the rescue 救助に小舟を出す. ¶*set* a *boat adrift* 小舟をただよわす(漂流させる). ¶*steer* a *boat* with a rudder かじをとって舟を進める. ¶He *stroked* the Cambridge *boat* this year. 彼は今年は(オックスフォード対ケンブリジボート・レースで)ケンブリジの整調だった. ¶*swamp* a *boat* ボートをくつがえす. ¶We *took* a *boat* at Kobe. われわれは神戸で船に乗った. ¶*untether* "duty *boats*" 当番艇を繋鎖から離す. ¶The *boat* was *upset* (=*blown over*) by a squall. ボートは突風のために転覆した. ¶*upturn* (=*topple*) a *boat* ボートを転覆させる.

V² *Boat* after boat *arrived*. 船が続々着いた. ¶The *boat canted* and *upset*. 船がかたむいて転覆した. ¶The *boat capsized*. ボートが転覆した. ¶The *boat measures* twenty feet long. 船の長さは二十フィートある. ¶The *boats ran foul* of each other. 船がぶつかり合った. ¶The *boat sails* over the river. 船は川の上を帆走する. ¶The *boat tipped up* (=*toppled over*). 船が転覆した.

Q an *abandoned boat* 廃船. ¶We are all in the *same boat*. われわれは皆同じ境遇(状態・運命)だ. ‖ he is said to be in the *same boat* with ... 彼は…と同船しているそうだ. ¶by *slow boat* 汽船で(飛行機に対し). ¶a *staunch boat* 堅固なボート. ¶a *swift boat* 快速船. ¶The *boat* is *water-tight*. このボートは水が通らない.

Q² a *coast guard patrol boat* 沿岸防備船. ¶a *collier boat* 石炭船. ¶a *diver boat* 潜水夫乗組船. ¶operate *ferry boats* to ... and from ... 連絡船を…間に運転する. ¶a *flying boat* [水上]飛行艇. ¶a *fighting boat* 軍装艇. ¶a *guard* (=*picket*) *boat* 警備艇. ¶an *ice-breaking boat* 砕氷船. ¶a *life boat* 救助艇. ¶a *light-draught boat* 吃水の浅い船. ¶a *light boat* 灯台船. ¶a *look-out boat* 監視船. ¶a *mail boat* 郵船. ¶a *paper boat* 紙艇(マニラ紙などで製した狩猟または競争用の). ¶a *passenger boat* 客船. ¶a *pearling boat* 真珠採取船. ¶a *pirate boat* 海賊船. ¶a *pleasure boat* 遊覧船. ¶a *rescuing boat* 救助艇. ¶a *river police boat* 警備用川ボート. ¶a *row boat* 漕艇. ¶a *rubber boat* [救助用]ゴムボート. ¶a *show boat* [演芸を見せる]ショーボート. ¶a *toy boat* おもちゃのボート.

P He came *by boat*. 彼は船で来た. ¶They were conveyed *in* a *boat*. 彼らは船で運ばれた. ‖ We crossed a stream *in* a *boat*. われわれは船で川を渡った.【類】proceed *in* one's *boat* down a river. ¶*on* (=*in*) the same *boat* there were ... 同じ船に…がいた ‖ What *boat* are you *on* now, may I ask? 今どの船に乗っておいでですか.

boating, *n.* ボート(船)遊び.

V *enjoy boating* on the lake 湖水で船遊びをする.

Q² *ice boating* 氷上ヨットでの滑走.

P go to ... *for boating* ボート遊びに…に行く. ¶pass a day *in boating* ボート遊びで一日を過す.

boat race, ボート・レース.

V The *boat race* will be *held* (=*rowed*) on Sunday. ボート・レースは日曜に催される.

Q an *inter-university* (=*inter-collegiate*) *boat race* 大学対抗ボート・レース.

P We took part (=rowed) *in* the *boat race*. 僕たちはそのボート・レースに参加した.

bob, *v.* あざむく.

M You can not *bob* me *off* with such payment. そんなわずかな金で私をごま化そうとしてもそうは行かない.

P *bob* it *of* (=*out of*) ... それを…からあざむき取る.

bode, *v.* 前兆する.

M There was a superstition that omens seen on the left *boded ill*. 前兆を左方に見ると縁起が悪いという迷信があった. ¶This *bodes well* for your success. これは君が成功する吉兆だ.

P This *bodes* evil (well) *to* the state. 国家の凶(吉)兆だ.

body, *n*. 身体；死体；団体；主体；実質.

V *bare* the *body* はだを脱ぐ. ¶ *bend* the *body* こごむ. ¶ ***build up*** one's *body* 身体をこしらえる.【類】***build up*** a healthy *body*. ¶ ***commit*** the *body* to the deep 水葬にする. ¶ ***cremate*** the *body* 火葬にする. ¶ *Bodies* were ***dug out***. 死体が発掘された. ¶A feather bed ***enervates*** the *body* of a child. 羽根ぶとんは子供の体を弱くする. ¶ ***entomb*** the *body* of ... ...の死体を葬る. ¶ ***exercise*** the *body* and the mind 身心を鍛錬する. ¶ ***fatigue*** one's *body* 身体を疲労させる. ¶ ***give*** the *body* a decent burial 死体を丁重に葬る. ¶The mind ***governs*** the *body*. 精神が肉体を支配する. ¶He ***has*** a sound, strong *body*. 彼は体がしっかりして丈夫だ. ¶The lubricating oil ***holds*** its *body* under extreme heat. 機械油は極度の熱にあっても変質しない. ¶ ***identify*** a dead *body* 死体の身もとをはっきりさせる. ¶ ***invigorate*** the *body* 体を丈夫にする. ¶ ***keep*** the *body* at least two feet away from ... ...から少くとも二フィート体を離す. ¶ ***keep*** the *body* and soul ***together*** 命をつなぐ. ¶ ***mutilate*** the *body* of a victim 犠牲者の体を不具にする. ¶ ***nourish*** the *body* 身体を養う. ¶ ***offer*** her *body* to an indiscriminate sexual intercourse with men だれ彼の区別なく男たちに身を任せる. ¶He does not even ***own*** his *body*. 彼は自分の体さえ自由にならない. ¶ ***prostitute*** her *body* for hire 売春する. ¶ ***reassume*** one's proper *body* 正体を現わす. ¶ ***rebuild*** the *body* 身体を改造する. ¶ ***rejuvenate*** the *body* からだを若返らす. ¶women who have fallen so low that they will ***sell*** their *bodies* 肉を売るほどに堕落した女たち. ¶ ***slash*** open one's *body* 切腹する.

Q an ***advisory*** *body* 顧問団. ¶a ***celestial*** *body* 天体. ¶a ***charitable*** *body* 慈善団体. ¶The chamber of commerce is an important ***commercial*** *body*. 商業会議所は重要な商業団体である. ¶a thoroughly ***conservative*** *body* きわめて保守的な団体. ¶a legally ***constituted*** *body* 法人団体. ¶a ***dead*** *body* 死体. ¶a ***deliberative*** *body* 審議機関. ¶the ***diplomatic*** *body* (=corps diplomatique) 外交団. ¶She belongs to a rapidly ***disappearing*** *body* of street caterers. 彼女はどんどん影が薄くなって行く屋台店に働いている. ¶an address presented to him by a ***distinguished*** *body* of signatories, headed by ... ...を主班とする著名署名者団体から氏に提出された建白書. ¶the opinion of the organization as an ***entire*** *body* その機構全体としての意見. ¶a ***foreign*** *body* [直接縁のない]外来物. ¶wine of ***good*** *body* こくのあるぶどう酒. ¶the ***governing*** *body* of the institution consists of ... その会の幹部は...である ‖ the ***Governing*** *Body* of the International Labor Office 国際労働事務局理事会.【類】the ***governing*** *body* (理事会) of the public library / the idea (意向) of the ***governing*** *body* is that ... ¶A ***healthy*** *body* is one of the firmest foundations of happiness. 健全な肉体は最も確実な幸福の一要素. ¶the visible ***heavenly*** *bodies* 肉眼で見える天体. ¶The university has the ***largest*** *body* of undergraduate students. その大学は学生数が一番多い. ¶Congress is a ***legislative*** *body*. 国会は立法機関である. ¶ ***lifeless*** *bodies* in the battlefield 戦場にある死がい. ¶the ***main*** *body* of an army 一軍の主力 ‖ the ***main*** *body* (=hull) of a ship 船体の主要部分 ‖ be incorporated in the ***main*** *body* of the dictionary 辞書の本文に組入れてある. ¶All ***material*** *bodies* tend to fall toward the earth. すべての物体は地上に落下する傾向がある. ‖ The angels have no ***material*** *bodies* at all. 天人は全然肉体がない. ¶a ***narrow*** (***large***) *body* of water 河(湖・海). ¶The association is becoming a ***numerous*** and ***powerful*** *body*. 同会は会員も多く有力な団体となりつつある. ¶an ***opaque*** *body* 不透明の物体. ¶an ***over-grown*** *body* 太り過ぎた体. ¶a ***picked*** *body* of men 選抜された一団の人. ¶a ***powerful national*** *body* 強力な国民団体. ¶a very ***prosperous*** *body* きわめて盛大な団体. ¶a ***public*** *body* 公共団体. ¶a ***religious*** *body* 宗教団体. ¶a ***rigid*** *body* 〘理〙剛体. ¶a ***sick*** *body* 病身. ¶a ***small*** *body* of men 男性だけの小団体 ‖ rally round us a ***small*** *body* of enthusiasts われわれの周囲に...の小数の熱心家が集まる. ¶A sound mind in a ***sound*** *body*. 〘諺〙健康な身体に宿る健全な精神. ¶a ***sponsoring*** *body* 開催母体. ¶They have square heads and ***thick-set*** *bodies*. 彼らは角頭でずんぐり肥っている. ¶a ***transparent*** *body* 透明な物体. ¶a ***tubby***, ***solid*** *body* ずんぐりがっちりした身体. ¶an ***unidentified*** *body* だれのとも知れない死体. ¶the ***whole*** *body* of mankind 人類全体.

Q^2 an ***appointing*** *body* [委員など]指命団体. ¶an ***arbitration*** *body* 調停団体. ¶a ***bargaining*** *body* 交渉団体. ¶ ***examining*** *bodies* 試験委員団. ¶a ***fact-finding*** *body* 実情審査委員会. ¶The commission is a ***five-member*** *body* 同委員会は五人の委員から成っている. ¶The Caspian Sea is the largest ***inland*** *body* of water in the world. カスピ海は世界最大の内海である. ¶a ***labor*** *body* 労働団体. ¶a ***non-profit-making*** *body* 非営利団体. ¶a ***nude*** *body* 裸体. ¶its ***parent*** *body* その母体, 本部.【類】The Security Council of the U.N. is the ***parent*** *body* of the United Nations Atomic Energy Commission. ¶a ***policy-making*** *body* 政策立案の団体. ¶a ***propagandist*** *body* 宣伝機関. ¶a ***research*** *body* 研究団体. ¶its sedate ***sister*** *body* その落着いた姉妹団体(米国下院に対し上院を指す). ¶a ***streamline***[*-d*] *body* 流線形の車体. ¶the faculty and the ***student*** *body* of a college 大学の教授団と学生団 ‖ the size of a ***student*** *body* 学生数. ¶The State Council is the ***supreme policy making*** *body* in China. 中国では省議会が最高立法府である. ¶an ***underground*** *body* 地下組織.

P take them ***as*** a *body* それらを一団(体)として考える. ¶Though absent ***in*** *body*, I am with you in spirit. たとえからだは離れていても心は君と一しょにいる. ‖ He is sound ***in*** *body*. 彼は身体健全だ. ‖ They acted ***in*** a *body*. 彼らは一体となって活動した.【類】The Cabinet resigned ***in*** a *body* (総辞職). / The class will attend his funeral ***in*** a *body*. ‖ Every bone ***in*** my *body* seems to ache. からだ中の骨が痛むようだ. ‖ the largest gland ***in*** the *body* 体の一番大きな腺 ‖ wheather ***in*** the *body* or out of it 生きていても死んでも. ¶a disorder ***of*** (=in) the *body* 肉体の病. ¶carry it ***on*** the *body* それを身に着ける ‖ keep the belt ***on*** one's *body* 帯を解かずにいる. ¶Spread it all ***over*** the *body*. それをからだ中に塗れ. ¶The assassin's sword ran ***through*** his *body*. 刺客の刀が彼の肉体を突き通した.

P^2 The *body* ***of*** the people are opposed to the measure. 人民の大部分はその方策に反対している. ‖ a *body* ***of*** laws 一括の法典 ‖ the *body* ***of*** a book 本の主要部(序文や索引などを除いた) ‖ in the *body* ***of*** a letter (treaty) 手紙(など)の本文において ‖ the *body* ***of*** a type 〘印刷〙活字のボデ(脚).

body, *v*. 形づくる.

M Imagination *bodies* ***forth*** the forms of things unknown. 想像によって未知のものをあれこれと作りあげる.

bodyguard, *n*. 護衛.

Q^2 ***plaincloth*** *bodyguards* 平服の用心棒.

bog, *v*. 泥にはまる；停とんする.

M *bog* ***down*** progress 進行を停とんさせる ‖ The scheme *bogged* ***down***. 計画は中絶した.【類】It *bogged* ***down*** from two and a half years of warfare. / get *bogged* ***down*** in efficiency.

P a pig *bogged* ***in*** the mud 泥水にはまった豚.

boggle, *v*. しり込みする.

P *boggle* ***at*** a word 言葉を聞いてしり込みする(二の足を踏む).

Bohemian, *n*. 自由放縦な生活をする人(ボヘミヤン).

Q a ***noble*** *Bohemian* 貴族出の自由人.

boil, *n*. 煮沸.

V ***give*** it a *boil* それを煮る.

P keep the kettle ***on*** (=***at***) the *boil* かまの湯を沸かして置く. ¶when it comes ***to*** the *boil* それが沸騰したとき ‖ bring it ***to*** a *boil* それを沸騰させる.

boil, *v*. わかす；煮える, わく.

M *Boiled* ***again***! またやられた. ¶The water *boiled* ***away***. 水は沸とうして蒸発した. ¶The water is *boiling* ***briskly***. 湯が煮えくり返っている. ¶The mouth of a fool *boils* ***forth*** follies. ばかものの口からはばかな文句がとび出す. ¶These potatoes are not *boiled* ***enough***. このじゃがいもは煮が足りない. ¶ ***fairly*** *boil* with activity 全く大車輪の活動振りを示す. ¶ *boil* it ***gently*** 静かに沸かす. ¶The rice is not ***thoroughly*** *boiled*. ご飯にしんがある. ¶Meat *boils* ***hard***. 肉は煮えると堅くなる. ‖ *boil* an egg ***hard*** 卵を堅くゆでる. ¶potatoes ***plain*** *boiled* しらゆでにしたじゃがいも. ¶ ***soft*** *boiled* eggs 半熟の卵.【類】*Boil* me an egg ***soft***.

P Eggs *boil* ***by*** the heat of the spring. 温泉の熱で卵が煮える. ¶ *boil* lotus-roots ***in*** milk (soy, water) れんこんを牛乳(など)で煮る. ¶The robber was *boiled* ***to*** death. その盗賊はかまうでにされた. ¶He *boiled* ***with*** rage (=anger). 彼はかんかんに怒った.【類】My blood *boils* ***with*** indignation (憤激). ¶My blood *boiled within* me. 腹が立ってたまらなかった.

M² *boil down* beef 牛肉を煮つめる ‖ *boil down* to its essence 煮つまってエキスになる ‖ *boil down* ... into a syrup ...を煮つめてシロップにする ‖ information and advice *boiled down* to bare essentials ほんの要点だけに約めた報道 ‖ to *boil down*, the question is whether ... せんじつめると問題は...となる. 【類】 *boil* it *down* to something concrete (具体化する). / *boil down* an article to a few sentences / *boil down* to the simplest form possible / It all *boils down* to one thing—human nature. ¶He was *boiling over* with rage at finding himself ignored. 彼は自分が無視されたので非常に憤慨していた. ‖ The pot is *boiling over*. なべが煮えこぼれている. 【類】 The water in the kettle is *boiling over*. ¶*boil up* 煮え立つ. 【類】 Paste is ready for use as soon as it has once *boiled up*.

boiler, *n.* 汽罐(ｶﾝ).

V The ship *burst* her *boiler*. 船の汽かんが破裂した.

V² The *boiler cracked*. ボイラーにひびが入った.

Q *coal(oil)-fired boiler* 石炭(石油)をたく汽かん. ¶a *leaky* and *defective boiler* 水がもる不完全なボイラー.

Q² a *marine engine boiler* 船舶用エンジンボイラー. ¶a *pot boiler*=a potboiler 生活のための売文作者. ¶a *rag boiler* [製紙用]ラグ・ボイラー. ¶a *water-tube boiler* 水管式汽かん.

boiling, *n.* 煮沸.

P cook potatoes *by boiling* じゃが芋を煮たきする.

bold, *a.* 大胆な.

M be *bold enough* to ... ...だけの度胸がある. ¶Let me be *so bold* as to ask you. 失礼ながらお尋ね致します.

P It is very *bold on* us to venture to do so. われわれがそうするのははなはだ大胆だ.

boldness, *n.* 大胆.

V He *had* the *boldness* to approach the man with the request. 思い切ってその人に頼んで見た. 【類】 He *had* the *boldness* to ask for more money.

Q *bluff boldness* ぶっきら棒.

P *with* great *boldness* 大胆に.

bolster, *v.* 支持する.

M *bolster up* the weaker 弱者を支持する.

bolt, *n.* (**1**) 電光, いなずま.

V The *bolt fell* close by. 雷が近くに落ちた.

Q *lightning bolts* shot from her eyes 彼女の目から突然発したきらめき.

P² It came like a (=the) *bolt from* the blue. それは青天のへきれきであった. 【類】 The news was like a *bolt from* the blue. ¶a *bolt of* lightning in a thunderstorm. 雷雨のときの電光.

(**2**) 〘機〙 ボールト.

Q² a *copper bolt* 銅製のボールト. ¶a *holding-down bolt* [線路などの]しめつけボールト. ¶a *machine bolt* 機械用ボールト. ¶a *railroad track bolt* 軌条しめボールト. ¶a *roller bolt* 車両しめボールト. ¶a *square-head* (*button-head*, an *oval-head*) *bolt* 角頭(など)ボールト.

bolt, *v.* 逐電する; 飛込む, 飛出す; [ドアなどを]閉め切る.

M be *bolted out* from a house 家から閉め出される. ¶a tale that *bolted* one's hair *upright* 髪を逆立たせた(ぞっとする)話.

M² *bolt* a person *in* 人を閉じ込める. ¶*bolt up* all the openings of a building 建物の出口窓口を全部閉め切る.

P *bolt from* a party (an association) 突然仲間(など)から抜ける. ¶He *bolted into* the room. 彼は部屋にかけ込んだ. ¶*bolt out of* the house いきなり表へ飛出す. ¶The burglar *bolted through* the back-door. 盗賊は裏戸から逃げ出した. ¶He *bolted with* all his master's money. 彼は主人の金を持ち逃げした.

bomb, *n.* 爆弾.

V A fanatic *threw* a *bomb* at his coach. 凶漢が彼の馬車に爆弾を投げつけた.

Q an *incendiary bomb* 焼夷弾.

Q² an *atom* (=*atomic*) *bomb*=an A-bomb 原子爆弾(原爆). ¶a *balloon bomb* 風船爆弾. ¶face the *blitz* and *buzz bombs* 電撃的音響爆弾に出会う. ¶a *dummy bomb* [演習用]擬弾. ¶a *cobalt bomb*=a C-bomb コバルト爆弾. ¶a *demolition bomb* 高性能の大型爆弾. ¶a *depth bomb*=a depth charge 爆雷. ¶a *flare* (=*light*) *bomb* 照明弾. ¶a *hydrogen bomb*=an H-bomb 水素爆弾(水爆). ¶a *leaflet bomb* [宣伝用の]紙弾. ¶a *liquid-flame bomb* 火焔爆弾. ¶a *nitrogen bomb*=an N-bomb 窒素爆弾. ¶an *oil bomb* 油脂焼夷弾. ¶a *tear-gas bomb* 催涙弾. ¶a *time bomb* 時限爆弾. ¶a *uranium bomb*=a U-bomb ウラン爆弾.

bomb, *v.* 爆撃する.

M people *bombed out*=bombed-out people [空襲で]焼け出された人々.

bombard, *v.* 砲撃する.

P The actress has been *bombarded with* offers of engagements. 女優は婚約申出の包囲攻撃を受けた. ‖ Her fans *bombarded* her *with* letters. ファンは彼女を手紙攻めにした. ‖ *bombard* a person *with* questions 質問を浴びせる.

bombardier, *n.* 爆撃手.

Q² a *B-29 bombardier* B-29 の爆撃手.

bombardment, *n.* 砲(爆)撃.

Q *light* (*medium, heavy*) *bombardment* 軽(中, 重)爆(砲)撃.

Q² *air bombardment* 空爆. 【類】 The city of Essen suffered 272 *air bombardments* during the war. ¶The troops advanced under cover of a heavy *artillery bombardment*. 部隊は重砲火援護の下に進撃した. ¶a *long-range bombardment* 長距離爆(砲)撃.

bomber, *n.* 爆撃機.

Q² *enemy bombers* 敵の爆撃機. ¶a *long-range bomber* 長距離爆撃機. ¶a *torpedo bomber* 雷撃機. ¶a *two-seat bomber* 両座式爆撃機.

bombing, *n.* 爆撃.

Q *Allied bombings* 連合軍の爆撃. ¶*strategic bombing* 戦略爆撃.

Q² *around-the-clock bombing*=round-the-clock bombing 二十四時間連続空爆. ¶*terror bombing* 恐怖爆撃. ¶*wartime bombing* 戦時空爆.

bond, *n.* (**1**) 結束物, きずな; 約束.

V *bind* more closely *together* the *bonds* which unite them 彼らの関係を一層緊密にする. ¶*break* the *bonds* of convention 因襲のきずなを切る. ¶*create* a sympathetic *bond* between two countries 両国間に同情の機縁を造る. ¶*dissolve* the *bonds* of matrimony 結婚を解消する. ¶Common tastes *form* a *bond* of union. 趣味が同じだと気が合う. ¶These circumstances *knit* the *bonds* of the alliance. これらの情勢が同盟の縁を結んだ. 【類】 *knit bonds* of sympathy (同情のきずな) betweem classes. ¶*loosen* the *bonds* of ... ...の関係をそ遠にする. ¶*strengthen* the *bonds* of affection that bind the two nations together 二国民の親善を深める. 【類】 gradually, but surely, *strengthen* the *bonds* of union between them. ¶*tighten* the *bonds* 結束を固める.

Q a *spiritual bond* 精神的結束. ¶A common language is the greatest of all *unifying bonds* that bind the peoples of the United States and Britain. 共通の言語が米英を結びつけるすべての結束力の中で最も強固なものである.

Q² the sanctity of the *marriage bond* 結婚の神聖.

P They have by daily association become knit together *in bonds* of mutual good-will. 彼らは毎日の交際でお互に好意を持つ仲となった. ¶enter *into* a *bond* 契約する. ¶He is free (=out) *on bonds*. 彼は保釈中である.

P² a *bond between* two men (par ties, countries) 二人(など)間の結束. ¶the *bond of* union among ... ...間の結合のきずな ‖ the *bond of* friendship which binds the two nations 二国民を結びつける友情.

(**2**) 国(公)債; 証券; 証書.

V *Buy bonds* for victory. 〘掲示〙 勝利のために国債を買いなさい. ¶*redeem bonds* for payment on March 24 this year 本年三月二十四日支払の債券を償還する. ¶*retire bonds* by maturity 支払期日の来た証券を回収する. ¶*sign* a *bond* 証書に調印する.

Q an *active* (*inactive*) bond 花形(不況)債券. ¶the *Commercial* and *Industrial Bond* 商工債券. ¶a *consolidated bond* 整理公債. ¶a *high-grade bond* 高値の公債. ¶a *public bond* 公債. ¶*registered bonds* 記名公債.

Q² a *baby bond* 小額国債. ¶*bail bond* 保釈に対する保証書. ¶a holder of the *bottomry bond* 〘海法〙 船舶抵当借入証書の所有者. ¶issue *development bonds* 開発債券を発行する. ¶*government* (*municipal*) *bonds* 国(市)債. 【類】 a *Government bond* with its lottery attachment (富くじ付). ¶a *lottery bond* 福引券付債券. ¶issuance of *low-interest bonds* 低利債券の発行. ¶a *peace bond* [囚人の]善行保証. ¶Each bidder must pay $100,000 as *performance bond*. 各入札人は参加保証金として十万ドル支払わねばならない. ¶a *treasury bond* 《米》 財務省の短期借入公債. ¶assimilate *war bonds* 戦時国債を消化する. 【類】 $ 15,000 in *war bonds*. ¶a ***winning*** *bond* 当り債券.

P I have forwarded the baggage ***in*** *bond* to destination. 手荷物を保税倉庫あずけで先方へ送り出した. ‖ The goods are ***in*** *bond*. 品物が保税倉庫あずけになっている. ¶On paying the duty you can get the goods ***out of*** *bond*. 関税を払えば品物を引取れる.

P² a *bond* ***for*** the performance of a contract 契約履行の ⌊約定書.

bondage, *n.* 束縛.

P He is ***in*** *bondage* to his ambition. 彼は野心の奴隷になっている. ‖ be held (=kept) ***in*** *bondage* とらわれの身となっている; 奴隷となっている.

P² the *bondage* ***of*** custom 習慣のきずな.

bone, *n.* 骨; 争因.

V ***break*** a *bone* 骨をくじく. ¶No *bones* ***broken***! 大した事はないよ. ¶***dislocate*** a *bone* 脱臼する. ¶***fracture*** a *bone* 骨をくじく. ¶I ***have*** a *bone* to pick with you. 君に文句を言わなければならないことがある. ¶Many a soldier ***left*** his *bone* on (=upon) the moor. 多数の兵士が骨を荒野にさらした. ¶***make*** no *bones* 遠慮しない, 平気でする. ¶***make*** dry *bones* ***alive*** 枯骨に活を入れる; 枯木に花を咲かす. ¶***rest*** one's *bones* 骨休めをする. ¶***saw away*** (=***off***) a *bone* 骨を切断する. ¶***set*** a broken *bone* 骨を接ぐ. ¶***show*** *bones* 骨張っている. ¶***spare*** *bones* 骨惜みをする. 【類】***spare*** no *bones*. ¶A *bone* has ***stuck*** in his throat. 骨がのどに立った.

Q ***bleached*** *bones* 白骨. ¶***cranial*** *bones* 頭がい骨. ¶a heap of ***dry*** *bones* 白骨の山. ¶***Lazy*** *bones* that you are! このなまけ者め. ¶my ***old*** *bones* わが老躯(く).

Q² a ***rib*** *bone* あばら骨. ¶***soup*** *bone* スープ種のあら.

P His love of research was bred ***in*** the *bone*. 彼は天性研究好きであった. ¶The sword (wound, ulcer) penetrated ***to*** the *bone*. 刀(など)が骨に通った. ‖ I was chilled ***to*** the *bones* (=*bone*). 寒さが骨にしみた.

P² a *bone* ***of*** contention among the nations 国際紛争の種 ‖ He is a bag ***of*** *bones*. 彼は骨と皮だ. ¶a *bone* ***to*** the ⌊bone 徹底した硬骨漢.

bonfire, *n.* かがり火.

V ***feed*** a *bonfire* かがり火にまきをくべる. ¶***make*** a *bonfire* かがり火をたく ‖ ***make*** a *bonfire* of books (rubbish) 書籍(ごみ)を焼き捨てる. 【類】Rioters ***made*** a huge *bonfire* of the building. ⌈り火.

Q² a sea of ***victory*** *bonfires* 海のように拡がった勝利のかが

bonnet, *n.* ボンネット[型].

Q a ***motor-car's*** *bonnet* (=hood) 《英》自動車の前部機関の覆い. ⌈コップ型の帽子.

Q² a ***scoop*** (=coal scuttle) *bonnet* [救世軍女子のかぶる]ス

bonus, *n.* 特別手当(ボーナス).

V ***distribute*** an extra *bonus* of 100% in shares 株券で十割の臨時配当をする.

Q² a ***cost-of-living*** *bonus* of ... ...の生活特別手当. 【類】a starting pay (初任給) of $2,900, plus a $750 ***cost-of-living*** *bonus*. ¶a ***dismissal*** *bonus* 退職手当. ¶***food*** *bonuses* put on miners 鉱夫に与える食費手当. ¶a 25 percent ***overseas*** *bonus* 二割五分の海外勤務手当. ¶a ***production*** *bonus* 生産手当. ¶an extra ***cash*** *bonus* 現金支給の特別手当. ¶a ***year-end*** *bonus* 年末賞与.

P² a *bonus* ***on*** a job 仕事の配当.

bonze, *n.* 坊主.

Q ***tonsured*** *bonzes* in yellow robes 黄色の法衣を着た円頭 ⌊の坊主.

book, *n.* (**1**) 書物, 本.

V ***abridge*** a *book* 本を抄略する. ¶***arrange*** *books* in order 書籍をきちんと排列する. ¶*books* ***banned*** in America 米国で発売禁止の本. ¶The *book* is ***bound*** in crimson morocco. その本は深紅色のモロッコ皮で製本してある. ¶***besprinkle*** a *book* with marginalia 本に書き込みをする. ¶the *book* I now ***bring forward*** 私が今出版する本. ¶***bring*** a *book* ***out*** opportunely 好い時機に本を出版する. ¶Out of the material thus accumulated he has ***built*** a *book*. かく集めた材料をまとめて彼は本を書いた. ¶***burke*** (=***suppress***) a *book* 書物の発行または発売を禁止する. ¶***catalogue*** *books* 書籍の目録を作る. ¶***close*** a *book* 本を閉じる. ¶***collect*** *books* 本を集める. ¶***conduct*** (=***see***) a *book* through the press 著書の印刷中校正をする. ¶***dedicate*** (=***inscribe***) a *book* to ... 著書を...に献呈する(冒頭にそのむねを印刷して). ¶***devote*** a *book* to the subject その問題に関する一書を著す. 【類】a *book* ***devoted*** to the study of sociology (社会学). ¶***disfigure*** a *book* by pencil marks 鉛筆の書入で本を汚す. ¶***draw*** *books* from a library 図書室から書物を借り出す. ¶***expurgate*** (=***bowdlerize***) a *book* [本の]削除版を作る. ¶The articles which ***form*** this *book* have already appeared in a magazine. 本書の内容をなす記事は既にある雑誌に載ったものである. 【類】We ***get*** *books* to read from the library. ¶I sincerely hope you will be able to ***get*** your *book* ***out*** soon. 遠からず貴著の刊行を見ることを切望する. ¶He ***got up*** a *book* to teach how to write letters. 彼は手紙の書き方を教える本を作った. ¶***give*** the *book* to the public その本を世に送る. ¶Please let me ***have*** the *book* I lent you the other day. 先日お貸しした本をお返し下さい. ¶I shall ***have*** the new *book* ***out*** in due course. 私の新著はその中出版の運びになるでしょう. ¶***introduce*** a *book* to the public 一書を広く紹介する. ¶***issue*** a *book* upon the war 戦争に関する一書を刊行する. ¶Do you ***keep*** French *books*? フランス語の本をお持ちですか. ¶I found it hard to ***lay*** the *book* ***down*** until the final page is reached 最後のページまで読み続けないではいられなかった. ¶***lay*** one's *book* ***face downwards*** in one's lap ひざの上に本を伏せる. ¶***lend out*** *books* to ... ...に書籍を貸す. ¶***license*** a *book* to be published 本の出版を許可する. ¶How do you ***like*** this *book*? この本をどうお考えになりますか. ¶***master*** a *book* 書物を十分に会得する. ¶The *book* may have been ***misplaced*** somewhere else. その本はどこかとんでもないとこにあるよ. ¶surreptitiously ***mutilate*** *books* こっそりと書物を切り取る. ¶***open*** a *book* 本を開く. ¶I ***ordered*** some new *books* from Maruzen. 丸善へ新刊書を数冊注文した. ¶I ***picked up*** some rare *books*. 珍本を見付けた. ¶***pirate*** a *book* ひょう窃する; 偽版を出す. 【類】His *books* ***were pirated*** in places. ¶***pore over*** one's *book* at night 夜書物をたん読する. ¶***prepare*** one's *book* for [the] press 自分の本の出版を準備する ‖ ***prepare*** a briefer *book* on the same plan 同じ方針でさらに簡略な本を作る. ¶***produce*** a *book* 本を出す. ¶***publish*** (=***issue***) a *book* 書物を刊行する. ¶Compositors ***put*** *books* into type. 植字工は著書を活字に組む. ‖ The *book* should be ***put*** in the hands of every thinking man. その書物は心ある人に一人残らずぜひ読んでもらいたい. ¶***put together*** (=***compile***) a little *book* 小著を編む. ¶I have ***read*** your *book* with pleasure. 貴著をおもしろく拝見しました. 【類】He ***read*** the book at a sitting (一気に) without laying it aside. / finish ***reading*** a *book*. ‖ ***read*** a *book* ***through*** 本を通読する. ¶***redust*** and ***reread*** old *books* 古本のほこりを払って読み直す. ¶***reprint*** a *book* 本を複刻する. ¶I ***require*** *books* to read. 何か読む本が欲しい. ¶***reset*** a *book* 改版する. ¶I ***return*** you the *book* you lent me. 拝借の本を御返しします. ¶***review*** a *book* 本の批評をする. ¶***revise*** a *book* 本を改訂する. ¶***rewrite*** a *book* ***all through*** 本を全面的に書き直す. ¶***skim*** a *book* 本にざっと目を通す. ¶I've ***skipped*** the *book* ***through***. その本をとびとびに読んだ. ¶Can you ***spare*** this *book* for a little while? この本をちょっと拝借できますか. ¶***slam*** a *book* on a desk 机の上に本をばたりと置く. ¶I ***studied*** the *book* from fly-leaf. その本を始めから終まで精読した. ¶*books* I would ***take*** to sea 私が航海に持って行きたい書物. ¶***take out*** *books* from a library 図書室から本をとり出す(借り出す). ¶***talk*** *books* 学者ぶる. ¶***tear*** one's *book* 本を破る. ¶***transcribe*** *books* 書物を筆写する. ¶He ***translated*** that *book* into English. 彼はその本を英訳した. ¶learn how to ***use*** *books* and how to study 書物の用法と研究法を学ぶ. ¶He ***wrote*** a *book* on the experiences of his tour. 彼は旅行の経験を書物に書いた.

V² This *book* ***deals*** with (=handles *or* treats of) an important social problem. この本は重要な社会問題をとり扱っている. ¶The *book* ***fell*** flat on the market. この本は売行が悪かった.

Q an ***authoritative*** *book* 権威ある書. ¶a ***brilliant*** *book* すばらしい本. 【類】a most delightfully ***brilliant*** and ***refreshing*** *book*. ¶a ***bulky*** *book* ぼう大な本. ¶Its history is a ***closed*** *book*. その歴史は一向分っていない. 【類】Chemistry is a ***closed*** *book* to me. / These feelings are a ***closed*** *book* to me. ¶a ***comic*** *book* 漫画本. ¶***companionable*** *book* 座右に置くべき本. ¶the most ***complete*** *book* on the subject issued (in existence) その問題に関する現存著書中最も完全なもの. ¶a ***copyrighted*** *book* 版権のある本. ¶***dirty*** (=***foul, indecent, naughty*** *or* ***lewd***) *books* わい本. ¶***dry-as-dust*** *books* 乾燥無味な本. ¶the ***earliest*** *book* of its kind in the English language この方面では

英語で書かれた最初の本. ¶a writer of successful ***educational*** *books* 成功した教科書の著者. ¶Malthus's Essay on Population is an ***epoch-making*** *book*. マルサスの人口論は新紀元を画した書である. ¶an ***exciting*** and ***absorbing*** *book* 刺激性に富んで感興をわかす本. ¶a too ***far-fetched*** *book* ありもしないような(不自然な)ことが書いてある本. ¶a ***fascinating*** *book* 非常におもしろい本. ¶a ***favorite*** *book* for family (home) readers 家庭向きの読物. ¶***Fewer*** and ***better*** [出版の標語]量は少なく質は良く. ¶a ***fine*** *book* on Japan 日本に関する良書. ¶a ***first*** *book* in psychology (English) 心理学(など)入門 ‖ A ***first*** *Book* on the Bible 〘書名〙 聖書入門書. ¶the ***first*** and ***only*** *book* of its kind in the English language 英語で書かれたこの種の本としては最初で唯一のもの. ¶a ***flashy*** *book* つまらない本. ¶***forthcoming*** *books* 近刊書. ¶a ***fresh***, ***unconventional***, and ***fascinating*** *book* ざん新で伝統を破った魅力ある本. ¶I am not in his ***good*** *books*. 〘比ゆ〙 私はあの人に気に入られていない. ¶a ***handwritten*** *book* 手写本. ¶***handy*** *books* 便利な本, 便覧. ¶It is one of the ***hardest*** *books* to construe in the language. それはその語での最も難解の本である. ¶***helpful*** *books* 参考になる本. ¶Che-wan-te ordered to destroy thousands of ***historical*** and ***philosophical*** *books*. 始皇帝は数千の歴史・哲学に関する書物を破棄することを命じた. ¶an ***idiotic*** *book* 愚にもつかない本. ¶an ***illustrated reading*** *book* for children 子供向きの絵入読物. ¶an ***informative*** and ***instructive*** *book* 有益でためになる本. ¶the most ***important*** *book* of its kind that has appeared for a decade この十年間に現われたその種の本としては最も重要なもの. ¶an ***inspiring*** *book* 感激させる本. ¶an ***instructional*** *book* 教本. ¶an invaluable *book* of reference 非常に価値のある参考書. ¶a ***juvenile*** *book* 少年少女[向]の読物. ¶read a ***light*** *book*, one that is not overstimulating, not too dry 刺激も強過ぎず余り無味乾燥でもない軽い本を読む. ¶This problem we shall examine in this ***little*** *book*. この問題をこの小著で検討することにする. ¶a ***long*** (***short***) *book* 厚い(薄い)本. ¶This *book* is ***longwinded***. この本はくどい. ¶a ***low-priced*** *book* 廉価本. ¶a ***nonpartisan*** *book* 片寄らない(公平な)本. ¶***old*** *books* in new binding 新装した古本. ¶the ***only*** *book* on the subject この題目に関する唯一の本. ¶***out-of-the-way*** *books* 一風変った本. ¶a ***popular*** *book* 通俗書, 大衆本. ¶in this ***present*** *book* この著作で. ¶a good ***practical*** *book* 実用的の良書. ¶The *book* is fairly ***readable***. その本はかなりおもしろい. ¶***rare*** *books* 珍本. 【類】 a ***rare, old*** *book*. ¶a ***reading*** *book*＝a reader 読本. ¶a ***recreational*** *book* 娯楽本. ¶***reliable*** *books* 信用のできる本. ¶Her past is a ***sealed*** *book*. 彼女の過去はだれにも分らない. ‖ Our destiny is a ***sealed*** *book* to us. われわれの運命は不可解だ. 【類】 The future is a ***sealed*** *book*. / Philosophy is a ***sealed*** *book* to most people. / It remains a ***sealed*** *book*. ¶a ***secret*** *book* 秘伝書. ¶a "***sexy*** *book*" エロがかった本. ¶***shelfworn*** (＝***shopworn***) *books* たなざらし本. ¶a ***single*** *book* of reference 一冊物の参考書. ¶a ***single-sewed*** *book* ミシンでとじた本. ¶a ***slim*** *book* 小冊子. ¶I am not a reader of novels, but of more ***solid*** *books*. 私は小説でなくもっと堅い本を読む. ¶a ***standard*** *book* of reference 標準参考書. ¶The *book* is very ***suggestive***. この本は暗示に富んでいる. ¶a *book* ***suitable*** for a Xmas present クリスマスの贈物に適した本. ¶a ***sumptuous*** *book* 豪華本. ¶a ***thick*** *book* of nearly 800 pages 約八百ページの厚い本. ¶a ***thought-provoking*** *book* 考えさせられる本. ¶a ***timely*** *book* 時宜に適した本. ¶wrote a very ***tolerable*** *book* on ethics 倫理に関するかなりの良書を書いた. ¶***trashy*** *books* 下らない本. ¶the most ***uncalled-for*** *books* もっとも売れの遠い本. ¶an ***uncut*** *book* ふちの切ってない本. ¶an ***unknown*** *book* 秘密. ¶an ***unopened*** *book* 折ったままになっている本. ¶The *book* is ***unpretending***. この本はまじめだ. ¶The future is not an ***unwritten*** *book*. それが将来どういうことになるか察するに難くはない ¶a highly ***useful*** *book* of reference 非常に有益な参考書. 【類】 This is one of the ***useful*** *books* on books ever compiled (既刊書の中で). ¶Mr. H.L. Mencken has written a ***valuable*** and ***read able*** *book* on the subject of the American Language. メンケン氏は米語に関する有益で興味のある本を書いた. ¶a ***voluminous*** *book* 浩かんな書. ¶a ***weighty*** *book* on the subject その問題に関する重要な本. ¶***well-bound*** *books* 装ていのりっぱな本. ¶a ***well-thumbed*** *book* 手あかで汚れた本. ¶a ***wonder-stirring*** *book* 驚きに打たれる本.

Q² an ***Appleton*** (***Iwanami***) *book* アップルトン出版社刊行(岩波)本. ¶a ***campaign*** *book* 《米》 政党の綱領・政策などを説明した小冊子. ¶a ***class*** *book* 教科書. ¶foreign reprints of ***copyright English*** *books* 版権のある英書の翻刻版. ¶a useful ***cram*** *book* 《口語》 役に立つ虎の巻. ¶a ***crime*** [***-story***] *book* 犯罪小説本. ¶a ***desk*** *book* 座右宝典. ¶use the volume as a ***desk*** or ***table*** *book* 卓上便覧としてその本を使う. ¶a ***detective story*** *book* 探偵もの. ¶make up a ***dummy*** *book* 〘製本〙 型見本を作る. ¶a ***fact*** *book* 事実を集めた本. ¶It constitutes a delightful ***gift*** *book*. その本はすばらしい贈物になる. ¶a ***flasher*** *book* 俗本, 赤本. ¶a ***geography*** (***language***) *book* 地理(語学)書. ¶***Gladstone*** *books* グラドストーン関係の書物. ¶a ***guide*** *book* 案内書. ¶***highbrow*** (***lowbrow***) *books* インテリ(ミーハー)向きの本. ¶a ***history*** *book* 歴史の本. ¶a ***how-to*** *book* 製法を説いた本. ¶an ***instruction*** *book* 教授書. ¶recent ***Japan*** *books* on ... …に関する最近の日本関係の図書. ¶the ***Japan Year*** *Book* 日本年鑑. ¶a ***jest*** *book* 滑けい集. ¶a ***lounging*** *book* 肩の凝らない本. ¶a ***Mazarine*** *Book* 活字印刷の最初の聖書. ¶a ***mystery*** [***story***] *book* 探偵小説の類. ¶a ***nonfiction*** *books* 小説以外の本(エッセイなど). ¶a ***pattern*** *book* 〘洋裁〙 パタン・ブック. ¶a ***picture*** *book* 絵本. ¶a ***question-answer*** *book* 問答体の本. ¶a handy ***reference*** *book* to all questions of the day 今日のあらゆる問題に対する便利な参考書. 【類】 a pocket ***reference*** *book* to be consulted on every occasion of difficulty and uncertainty. ¶a ***school*** *book* 教科書. ¶a ***six-penny*** *book* 六ペンス本. ¶a ***skin*** *book* 皮紙に書いた本. ¶a ***source*** *book* 資料書. ¶a ***seven day*** *book* [図書館で]最も読手の多い本. ¶a ***true story*** *book* 実話本. ¶a ***two-volume*** *book* 二巻もの. ¶a ***westernstyle*** *book* 洋書.

P a man of letters ***among*** his *books* 書斎裡の文士. ¶He is well-off ***for*** *books*. 彼は蔵書に富んでいる. ¶He looked up ***from*** his *book*. 彼は本から目を離して見上げた. ¶He is buried ***in*** his *books*. 彼は読書に没頭している. ‖ He is learned (＝well versed) ***in*** *books*. 彼は博く本を読んでいる. ‖ He defends his doctrine ***in*** his new *book*. 彼は新刊書で自説を弁護している. ¶I will make you a present ***of*** this *book*. この本を進上します. ‖ a review ***of*** a *book* 本の批評 ‖ a set ***of*** four *books* 四冊一組の本. ¶He is asleep ***over*** his *book*. 彼は本を前に置いてい眠りをしている. ‖ Do not linger too long ***over*** your *books*. ぐずぐず本を読むな. ‖ I glanced ***over*** the *book*. その本にざっと目を通した. ¶I skimmed ***through*** (＝***over***) the *book*. その本を飛々に読んだ. ¶He cheated me, but I brought him ***to*** *book*. 僕をだましたのでとっちめてやった. ¶a sermon delivered ***without*** *book* [原稿なしに]暗記でやった説教. ‖ He is ready to assert anything ***without*** *book*. 彼はよく典拠もなしに断定する.

P² the best *books* ***about*** (＝on) Japan 日本に関する最良の本. ¶*books* ***at*** [the] press 印刷中の本. ¶a *book* ***for*** the beginner in English 英語初学者用の本 ‖ *books* ***for*** the household 家庭向の書籍 ‖ *books* ***for*** pleasure as well as ***for*** wisdom and knowledge 知識と娯楽の本 ‖ a *book* ***for*** all tastes だれの趣味にも合う本. ¶a catalogue of *books* ***from*** the library of W University W大学図書館図書目録. ¶a *book* ***in*** English 英語で書いた本 ‖ *books* ***in*** the press 印刷中の本 ‖ *books* ***in*** print 印刷本 ‖ *books* ***in*** paper covers 紙表紙の本 ‖ a *book* ***in*** several volumes 数冊からなる一部の本. ¶a *book* ***of*** reference on Japan travel 日本旅行の参考書 ‖ a *book* ***of*** travel 旅行記 ‖ a *book* ***of*** pictures 絵本. 【類】 a first *book* ***of*** geometry / an ancient *book* ***of*** poetry / a *book* ***of*** recitations (暗記用). ¶his *book* ***of*** *books* 彼の愛読書. ¶*books* ***on*** French フランス語に関する書籍. 【類】 a *book* ***on*** arithmetic (China, the English language) / Montaigne gives a list of ancient classical lost *books* (逸書) ***on*** love. / a *book* ***on*** nature study / *books* ***on*** electronics (電子工学). ¶a *book* ***out of*** print 絶版本. ¶a *book* ***with*** prints さし絵のある本.

O There are *books* to read and *books* to look at. 読む本と見る本がある.

(2) 帳簿, 通帳; 練習帳; 報告書.

V ***audit*** the *books* 帳簿を検閲する. ¶***close*** the *books* 帳簿を締切る. ¶He ***keeps*** my *books*. 彼はうちの帳簿係だ. 【類】

Books (=Records) must be ***kept*** according to a prescribed form (一定の形式で). ¶we found on ***looking through*** our *books* that ... 帳簿を調べて見て...が分った. ¶***sign*** the Visitors' *Book* 参観者名簿に記名する.

V^2 The *books* ***balanced*** exactly. 帳じりがきちんと合った.

Q I am in the ***good*** (=***bad or black***) *books* of him. 私は彼と仲が良(悪)い.

Q^2 ***account*** *books* 種々の会計簿. ¶an ***association*** *book* (=copy) 名士手沢(しゅたく)本. ¶an ***autograph*** *book* 署名帳. ¶***bamboo*** *books* 竹簡書(中国古文書). ¶a ***Bismarck*** *book* ビスマルクに関する著書. ¶a "***black letter***" *book* ゴシック活字の(古い)書物. ¶a ***blank*** *book* 未記入の帳簿. ¶He knew his ***botany*** *books* backward. 彼は植物学の書は実によく読んでいる. ¶the ***Buff*** *Book*=a classified Telephone Directory 分類式電話帳. ¶a ***care*** *book* [医師の]病状記入簿. ¶a petty ***cash*** *book* 小使帳. ¶a ***check*** *book* 小切手帳. ¶a ***chit*** *book* 印判取帳. ¶a ***clothing*** *book* 衣料切符帳. ¶inspection of ***company*** *books* 会社帳簿の検査. ¶The ***company*** *books* or records are kept on a fiscal year basis. 会社帳簿または記録は会計年度制になっている. ¶a passengers' ***complaint*** *book* 船客申告簿. ¶a ***composition*** *book* 作文帳. ¶a ***cookery*** *book* 料理の本. ¶a ***copy*** *book* 習字帳; 複製記入帳. ¶a ***fact-finding*** *book* 事実調査の報告書. ¶a ***memorandum*** *book* 備忘録. ¶a ***national treasure*** *book* 国宝台帳. ¶Edison's "***notion***" *books* エジソンの発明の経路を示した本人の控. ¶look up a number in the ***phone*** *book*. 番号を電話帳でさがす. ¶consult a ***phone*** *book* for addresses 住所を電話帳でさがす. ¶a ***ration*** *book* 配給通帳. ¶a ***rice*** *book* 米穀通帳. ¶a ***ring*** *book* 輪とじの帳簿. ¶a ***subscription*** *book* 寄付帳. ¶a ***stamp*** *book* 切手帳. ¶a ***telephone*** *book* =a phone book.

P make false entries ***in*** the company's *books* 会社の帳簿に不正の記入をする. ¶The trade mark is registered ***on*** the *books* of the Patent Office. 商標は特許局の登録になっている. ‖ customers ***on*** the company's *books* 会社の帳簿に載っている顧客.

P^2 a *book* ***for*** signatures of visitors 来観者署名簿. ¶a *book* ***of*** tickets=a ticket book 回数券のつづり込み.

book, *v*. 切符を買う; 予約する; 当て込む.

M^2 I *booked* the luggage ***through*** to Paris. 私の手荷物をパリ受けにしてチッキにした. ¶Cargoes may now be *booked* ***through*** to it without transhipment at ... as hitherto. 今は船荷はこれまでのように...で積替の必要なくそこへ託送ができる. ¶I shall *book* ***through*** to Paris. パリまでの通し切符を買おう.

P *book* ***at*** A station to B and change at C A 停車場で B までの切符を買って C で乗換える. ¶He *booked* himself ***for*** the following day's bus. 彼はその翌日のバスの切符を買った. ‖ *book* ***for*** the play 芝居の切符を買う ‖ You are *booked* ***for*** the tenth of September. 貴下は九月十日の予約になっています(劇場の座席など). ¶*book* through ***from*** A ***to*** B second-class return A から B までの二等往復切符を買う. ¶My luggage is *booked* ***to*** London. 私の荷物はロンドン行として預けた. ‖ The ship was *booked* ***to*** her full capacity. 船は満員であった.

book form, 単行本.

P These lectures are to be published ***in*** *book form* later on. これらの講演は他日単行本にしてでる予定である.

booking, *n*. 予約, 切符発売.

Q ***cheap*** *bookings* by fast trains 急行列車による割引切符の発売[遊覧切符など]. ¶*Bookings* are ***obtainable*** from railway and tourist agents. 切符は鉄道および観光案内所で求められます.

Q^2 ***advance*** *bookings* of hotel rooms 旅館の客室予約. ¶"***capacity***" *booking* [劇場など]貸切り予約.

bookkeeper, *n*. 帳簿係.

Q a ***75-a-week*** *bookkeeper* 週給七十五ドルの記帳係.

P^2 a *bookkeeper* ***in*** an office 会社の帳簿係.

book-keeping, *n*. 簿記.

Q ***double*** *book-keeping* 帳簿の二重記入, 二重帳簿.

P^2 *book-keeping* ***by*** single (double) entry 単式(複式)簿記.

booklet, *n*. 小冊子.

Q a ***mere*** *booklet* ほんの小冊子.

book-lover, *n*. 愛書家.

Q valued possessions of ***ardent*** *book-lovers* 熱心な愛書家の珍蔵.

book-marker, *n*. しおり.

V ***put*** a *book-marker* between the leaves ページとページの間にしおりをはさむ.

Q^2 a ***ribbon*** *book-marker* リボンのしをり.

bookseller, *n*. 書店(人).

P You can get it ***through*** any *bookseller* (***or at*** *bookseller's*). それはどの書店にもあります.

bookshelf, *n*. 本だな.

Q a ***built-in*** *bookshelf* 作りつけの本だな.

bookshop, *n*. 本屋.

Q ***second-hand*** *bookshops* 古本屋.

bookstall, *n*. 本売台.

P The new magazine has not yet appeared ***on*** *bookstalls*. その新刊雑誌は未だ本屋の店頭にでていない.

boom, *n*. にわか景気.

V The country is ***having*** a great *boom* in industry. この国では今工業が大好況を示している. ¶a ***postwar*** *boom* in suburban areas 戦後の郊外の発展. ¶the ***postwar*** *boom* in higher education 戦後にわかに活気づいた高等教育.

Q the ***recent*** *boom* in rubber 近ごろのゴムのにわか景気. ¶the "***Russian***" *boom* ロシヤ熱.

Q^2 postwar ***building*** *boom* 戦後の建築景気. ¶The "***build-it-yourself***" *boom* 「手製の家」式の建築景気. ¶steel increases in demand as Britain's ***heavy industries*** *boom* 英国重工業景気が出ると鋼鉄需要が増す. ¶***inflation*** *boom* レンフレ景気. ¶keep the ***trade*** *boom* going 貿易景気を持ち続ける. ¶***war*** *boom* 戦争景気. 【類】the so-called "Korean ***war*** *boom*."

P^2 a *boom* ***in*** bar silver 銀塊の暴騰. ¶a *boom* ***in*** real estate 家屋・地所の値上り. 【類】There is sure to be a *boom* ***in*** land there. ‖ a *boom* ***in*** shipbuilding 造船界の活況 ‖ The *boom* ***in*** Japanese imports started to slump. 日本品輸入の好景気はがら落に向いた. 「る.

boom, *v*. にわか景気がでる, 物価が騰貴する; ぼんぼんと鳴る.

M The clock *boomed* ***out*** twelve. 大時計が十二時を打った. 【類】The temple bell *boomed* ***out*** the hour.

P He is just *booming* ***as*** a writer. 彼は今作家として売出している. ¶Every market was *booming* ***during*** the war. 戦時中はどこの市場も好景気だった.

boom, *v*. 〚海〛帆げた(ブーム)で帆を張る.

M *boom* ***out*** a sail ブームで帆を張る.

M^2 *boom* ***off*** 船を岸壁から推し出す.

boon, *n*. 恩恵, 賜物.

V ***confer*** a *boon* on the traveling public 一般旅行者の便利になる. ¶His captivity ***yielded*** him one priceless *boon*. 捕われの身となったので彼は一つの得がたい収穫を見た.

Q a ***distinct*** *boon* to ... ...にとって特別の恩恵. ¶***prove*** a great *boon* to ... ...にとって福音となる. ¶It will prove an ***inestimable*** *boon* to him. それは彼にとってこの上もなく貴い利益となるであろう. ¶a ***priceless*** *boon* 非常に貴い賜物. ¶a ***valuable*** *boon* to students 学生にとっての大福音. ¶a ***veritable*** *boon* 本当の恩恵.

P^2 What a *boon* ***for*** the poorer classes! 貧民に取って何という幸福だ. ¶the *boon* ***of*** freedom 自由という恩恵. ¶a great *boon* ***to*** mankind (the public, a nation) 人類(など)にとっての一大恩恵. 【類】This public garden is a precious *boon* ***to*** the citizens. / a *boon* ***to*** suffering humanity (悩む人々).

boost, *n*. 《米俗》押上げること.

Q^2 a ***fare*** *boost* [電車・バス]料金の値上げ. ¶wage increases that would force ***price*** *boosts* 必然的に物価高騰をもたらす賃金の引上げ. ¶a ***salary*** *boost* on a big scale 大規模な給料引上げ. ¶a substantial ***wage*** *boost* 大幅の賃金引上げ. 【類】a $4 weekly ***wage*** *boost* / a 25-cent hourly ***wage*** *boost*.

P an eight-hour day and a 50 per cent. *boost* ***in*** salary 八時間労働と月給五割の引上げ.

boost, *v*. 押上げる.

P *boost* one ***over*** a fence 押上げて垣を越させる. ¶*boost* ***up*** production 生産を向上させる. 【類】*boost* [***up***] prices.

boot, *n*. くつ; 《米》長ぐつ.

V ***discard*** *boots* and stockings くつやくつ下を用いない(はだしになる). ¶***get*** the *boot* 《俗》お払箱になる. ¶I cannot ***get*** my *boots* ***on***. くつがはけない. ¶I ***gave*** him the *boot*. 《俗》彼を首にした. ¶***have*** one's *boots* ***stretched*** くつをゆるめてもらう. ¶***reheel*** a *boot* くつのかかとをつけ直す. ¶***patch up*** one's *boots* くつをつくろう. ¶***polish*** (=***clean***) one's *boots* くつをみがく. ¶***pull*** (=***take***) ***off*** one's *boots*

くつをぬぐ. ¶***put*** the ***boot*** on the wrong leg 〖比ゆ〗賞罰その宜しきを得ない. ¶***put on*** one's ***boots*** くつをはく. ¶***try on*** ***boots*** くつをはいて見る. ¶***unlace*** one's ***boots*** くつのひもをはずす. ¶***wipe*** one's ***boots*** くつをぬぐう.

Q ***brown boots*** with white buckskin uppers 上は白しか皮の赤長くつ. ¶***elastic-sided*** ***boots*** [側面にゴム布を付けた]深ゴムくつ. ¶***high*** ***boots*** 長くつ. ¶***high-heeled*** ***boots*** かかとの高いくつ. ¶***munition*** ***boots*** 兵隊くつ. ¶***nailed*** ***boots*** 裏にびょうを打ったくつ. ¶We wipe our ***soiled*** ***boots*** on a mat before entering a house. 家に入る前に汚れたくつをマットでふく. ¶***strong*** and ***well-tried*** ***boots*** 使って見て丈夫だと分ったくつ. ¶My ***boots*** are too ***tight***. くつがきつ過ぎる. ¶***worn, misshapen*** ***boots*** いたんで形のくずれたくつ.

Q^2 the ***seven-league*** ***boots*** [おとぎ話に出る]長くつ(このくつをはくと一ぺんに二十一マイル飛ぶという). ¶***Wellington*** ***boots*** 《英》[前ひざ上にかぶさる]長くつ.

P Napoleon was always ***in*** ***boots***. ナポレオンはいつも長くつをはいていた. ¶a pair ***of*** ***boots*** くつ一足. ¶He lost his purse and his watch ***to*** ***boots*** (=into the bargain). 金入をなくしおまけに時計までなくした. ¶He came ***with*** long ***boots*** on. 彼は長くつをはいてきた.

booth, *n.* 露店; 室.

Q^2 a ***broadcasting*** ***booth*** 放送室. ¶a ***cashier*** ***booth*** 会計室. ¶an ***information*** ***booth*** 案内(受付)室. ¶a ***night-fair*** ***booth*** for selling goods 縁日の夜店. ¶a ***phone*** (=***telephone***) ***booth*** 電話室. ¶a ***polling*** ***booth*** 投票所. ¶a ***screen projector*** ***booth*** 〖映画〗映写室. ¶a ***street*** ***booth*** 露店. ¶a ***voting*** ***booth*** 投票所.

booty, *n.* 獲物.

V He ***returned*** his ***booty***. 彼は獲物を手に収めた.

Q^2 a ***war*** ***booty*** 戦利品.

P He returned laden ***with*** ***booty***. 彼は獲物を持って帰ってきた.

border, *n.* 境界, 国境; ふち, へり.

V The Soviets ***crossed*** the ***border*** far into the Manchurian territory. ソ連軍は国境を越えて中国領土深く侵入した. ‖ He is always polite, and never ***crosses*** the ***border*** to familiarity. 彼はいつでもていねいで無遠慮にわたるようなことは決してしない. ¶***enlarge*** the ***borders*** of knowledge 知識の領域を拡大する. ¶***put*** a ***border*** to (=on) it それにへりを付ける.

Q^2 surrounded by a ***gold*** ***border*** 金ぶちの. ¶a ***lace*** ***border*** round a handkerchief ハンカチの回りについているレースのふち. ¶the ***Pakistan-India*** ***borders*** パキスタンインド国境. ¶Europe of the ***Soviet*** ***border*** ソ連と隣接する欧州.

P He fled ***across*** the ***border***. 彼は国境を越えて逃げた. ¶***at*** an international ***border*** 国境で. ¶protect the edge ***by*** a ***border*** ふちを付けてへりを丈夫にする. ¶He was brought back ***from*** the ***borders*** of the Beyond. 彼は死線を越えかかったが(心づくしの看護で)命を拾った. ¶***in*** (=***within***) the ***borders*** of ... …の領地内で. ¶thirty-six states ***on*** the Chinese ***border*** 西域三十六カ国. ¶***on*** the ***borders*** of Hida and Shinano 飛弾と信濃の国境に. 【類】 Buddha was born ***on*** the ***borders*** of Nepal about 563 B.C. ¶***out of*** ***borders*** 国境外に. ¶***over*** the ***border*** 境界を越えて. ¶decorate it ***with*** a ***border*** それにふち飾りを付ける. ¶***within*** its ***borders*** その領地内に. 【類】 ***within*** her own ***borders***.

border, *v.* 接する, 界する; ふち取る.

P His age ***borders on*** fifty. 彼はもう五十に近い. ¶it ***borders on*** the northern frontier of ... それは…の北境に接する. 【類】 the countries ***bordering on*** the Pacific [Ocean]. ‖ He was left on the spot in a condition ***bordering on*** the grave. 彼はひん死の状態でその場に残された. ‖ Such a proceeding ***borders on*** folly. そんなやり口は愚に近い. ‖ those who are of so low a degree of intelligence that they ***border on*** feeble-mindedness 非常に低能で精神薄弱に近い人々 ‖ The results ***bordered*** almost ***on*** the miraculous. その結果はほとんど奇跡的であった. 【類】 ***bordering on*** insanity (hysterics) / They are left in a state ***bordering on*** destitution (窮乏). ¶***bordering upon*** the railway line 線路にそった ‖ the countries ***bordering upon*** and adjacent to the Pacific Ocean 太平洋に臨む国々. 【類】 Russia has a frontier line (国境線) of six thousand miles ***bordering upon*** China. ¶a street ***bordered with*** trees 並木街 ‖ The whole coast is ***bordered with*** splendid sands and offers ideal and perfectly safe bathing facilities. 沿岸はことごとく素敵な遠浅で理想的できわめて安全な海水浴場をなしている.

borderland, *n.* 境界地.

V ***extend*** the ***borderland*** of knowledge 知識の領域を広げる.

Q^2 that ***twilight*** ***borderland*** between what is conscious and what is subconscious in our minds われわれの意識と潜在意識とのもうろうたる中間識域.

P Hungary is the ***borderland between*** the West and the Orient. ハンガリーは欧州と東洋との境界地である. ¶***on*** the ***borderland*** of ... …の境に立って ‖ They are ***on*** the ***borderland*** of insanity. あの手合は狂人の親類みたいなものだ.

borderline, *n.* 境界線.

Q an ***indefinable*** ***borderline*** [動植物など]はっきり区別できない境界線.

P be ***on*** the ***borderline*** of crime 法網すれすれの線にある. ¶***on*** the ***borderline*** between A and B AB 間の境界線に.

P^2 words which seem to be on the ***borderline between*** two parts of speech 両品詞のいずれとも決定し難い語. 【類】 the ***borderline between*** love and friendship.

bore, *n.* うるさい人(もの), たいくつな人(もの); 銃腔.

Q a ***dreadful*** (=***confounded or terrible***) ***bore*** 恐ろしくうるさいやつ. ¶an ***exasperating*** ***bore*** しゃくにさわるほど厄介なやつ. ¶It is a ***great*** ***bore*** to have a poet read his own verses. 詩人が自作の詩を読むのを聴かされるのは実に閉口だ. ¶a ***perfect*** ***bore*** 鼻つまみ. ¶a ***smooth, unrifled*** ***bore*** すべすべして旋条のない銃腔. ¶He always stays long; he is a ***tedious*** ***bore***. あの男は長っちりで鼻つまみだ. ¶an ***unspeakable*** ***bore*** 話にならないうるさ型.

bore, *v.* 困らす, 退屈させる.

P I am ***bored by*** his tedious talk. 彼のおもしろくもない長談義にはうんざりする. ¶He ***bores*** me ***to*** death. あいつうるさくってたまらん. ¶Picture men are ***bored with*** beauty. 映画の男優は美人にはあきあきしている.

bore, *v.* うがつ; 押分ける.

P ***bore*** a hole ***through*** the board 板に穴をもみ明ける ‖ ***bore*** one's way ***through*** a crowd 群衆を押分けて行く. ¶***bore*** a plank ***with*** a rifle-ball 小銃弾で厚板を射抜く.

boredom, *n.* 退屈.

V to ***escape*** ***boredom*** 退屈を避けるために. ¶***relieve*** ***boredom*** 退屈をまぎらす.

V^2 when ***boredom comes*** upon 退屈に悩むときに.

born, *pa.* → bear.

borough, *n.* 区画; 独立区.

Q a ***parliamentary*** ***borough*** 選挙区.

Q^2 a ***brewers pocket*** ***borough*** 醸造業者の牛耳っている都市. ¶***Greater New York*** ***boroughs*** 大ニューヨーク市の独立区.

borrow, *v.* 借りる.

P I ***borrowed*** some money ***from*** (=***of***) him. 彼に金を少し借りた. ¶words ***borrowed into*** English ***from*** French 仏語から借用した英語. ¶He ***borrowed*** money ***on*** his furniture. 家具を担保に金を借りた. 【類】 He ***borrowed*** money ***on*** credit (信用で).

bosom, *n.* 胸, 懐; 内部.

V ***heave*** the ***bosom*** [息を吸込んで]胸をふくらます. ¶***speak*** one's ***bosom*** freely 遠慮なく胸中を語る. ¶It ***struck*** her ***bosom***. それがひどく彼女の胸に応えた.

Q a ***heaving*** ***bosom*** [深呼吸で]ふくらむ胸. ¶***pendulous*** ***bosoms*** 垂れ乳.

P He drew the papers ***from*** his ***bosom***. 彼は懐から書類を取出した. ¶a child ***in*** the ***bosom*** 抱いた子 ‖ It is implanted ***in*** his ***bosom***. 彼はそれを心に銘じた. ‖ a waterfall ***in*** the ***bosom*** of a mountain 山奥の滝 ‖ He spent his holidays ***in*** (=***within***) the ***bosom*** of his family. 彼は家庭でしんみり休暇を送った. ¶a wife ***of*** one's ***bosom*** 恋女房. ¶***on*** the ***bosom*** of the ocean 大洋のまっただ中に.

P^2 the ***bosom of*** the earth 地球の内部 ‖ the ***bosom of*** a shirt ワイシャツの胸部.

boss, *n.* 頭, 長, ボス.

Q a ***political*** ***boss*** 政治ボス. ¶a ***powerful*** ***boss*** 有力なボス.

Q^2 a ***gang*** ***boss*** 組頭, 職長. ¶a communist ***labor*** ***boss*** 共産党員の労働者のボス. ¶a ***party*** ***boss*** 政党のボス. ¶a ***straw*** ***boss*** 職[工]長代理.

boss, *v.* 《米俗》威張る.

P ***boss*** it ***over*** other people 人に威張り散らす.

botany, *n.* 植物(学).

Q ***geographical*** ***botany*** 植物地理学.

P^2 the ***botany of*** North America 北米の植物. ¶the ***botany of*** deciduous trees 落葉樹の生態.

botch, *n.* 不手ぎわ, へま.

Q His baking was a ***complete botch***. 彼のパンの焼き方は全くなっていなかった.

bother, *n.* めんどう, やっかい.

Q a ***needless bother*** かけなくとも済むめんどう.

P^2 It is a *bother* ***to*** me. そいつはやっかいなことだ.

bother, *v.* わずらわす, 悩ます; 悩む.

M He is ***always bothering*** me. あの男は始終私に迷惑を掛けている. ¶He comes *bothering* me ***day after day***. 彼は毎日うるさくやって来る.

P I am too busy to *bother* ***about*** such trifles. いそがしくてそんなつまらないことに気を使っていられない. ‖ Please don't *bother* ***about*** me. どうぞ私におかまいなく. ¶He *bothered* me ***for*** money. 彼は私に金をねだった. ¶He *bothered* me ***with*** questions. 彼は私にうるさく質問をした. 【類】I was *bothered* ***with*** constipation (便秘).

O Oh, *bother* you! ああ, うるさい.

bottle, *n.* びん.

V ***crack*** a *bottle* びんの口を開けて飲む. ¶Let us ***drain*** a *bottle* or two. 一二本平らげようじゃないか. ¶We ***drank*** six *bottles* of wine. ぶどう酒を六本飲んだ. ¶***fill*** a *bottle* with hot water びんに湯を詰める. ¶***punish*** three *bottles* of beer ビールを三本平げる. ¶***release*** *bottles* for the purpose of studying the growth and distribution of fishes 魚類の成長と分布を研究するためにびんを放流する. ¶***rinse*** a *bottle* びんをゆすぐ. ¶***rinse out*** a *bottle* びんをゆすぐ. ¶I ***stood*** him a *bottle* of beer. 《口語》私は彼にビールを一本おごった. ¶slowly ***tip*** a ***bottle over,*** till the ink runs out インクの出るまでびんを静かにかしげる. ¶***uncork*** a *bottle* びんのコルクを抜く.

V^2 This ***bottle leaks***. このびんは漏る.

Q an ***empty*** *bottle* あきびん. ¶the ***bottle is half-filled*** with ... びんに...が半分残っている.

Q^2 a ***carbide*** *bottle* 火焔びん. ¶a ***feeding*** ***botte*** 哺乳びん. ¶a molded ***glass bottle*** [型に入れて作った]ガラスびん. ¶a ***round*** (***square***) ***shoulder bottle*** 丸(角)びん. ¶a warmed ***sake bottle*** かんをしたお銚子. ¶a ***stone bottle*** 小形の水さし. ¶a "graybeard" ***stoneware*** *bottle*「白ひげ」とくり(首部に白ひげ翁の模様のある). ¶a ***thermos*** *bottle* (=flask) 真空びん(魔法びんなど). ¶have a ***hot water*** *bottle* at one's *feet* 足下に湯たんぽを入れる.

P sell it ***by*** the *bottle* それを一びん幾らで売る. ¶sell it ***in*** *bottles* それをびん詰めにして売る. ¶pour water ***into*** a *bottle* びんに水を注ぐ. ¶the directions ***on*** a *bottle* びんに張ってある用法書. 【類】the label (レッテル) ***on*** a *bottle* ‖ The baby was brought up ***on*** the *bottle*. その赤ん坊は牛乳で育った. ¶They talked merrily ***over*** a (=the) *bottle*. 彼らは酒を飲みながら陽気に話し合った. 【類】We discussed the matter ***over*** a *bottle* of wine.

P^2 a *bottle* ***of*** whisky (beer, milk) 一びんのウイスキー(など).

bottle, *v.* びん詰にする.

M *bottle* ***off*** beer ビールをびん詰にする ‖ get (wine in) a barrel and *bottle* it ***off*** oneself ぶどう酒をたるで買って自分でびんに詰める. ¶*bottle* ***up*** one's wrath 怒を抑える ‖ *bottle* ***up*** the harbor mouth 港口を閉塞する.

bottleneck, *n.* [比ゆ的に]隘路(あいろ).

V ***break*** *bottlenecks* in Japanese production 日本の生産の隘路を打開する.

Q the ***financial*** *bottleneck* 金融の隘路.

Q^2 uncork the ***production*** *bottleneck* 生産の隘路を切り開く. ¶break the ***transport*** *bottlenck* 輸送の隘路を除く.

P^2 The *bottleneck* ***in*** transportation. 輸送上の隘路.

bottom, *n.* 底; 船底.

V ***clean*** the ship's *bottom* 船底を掃除する. ¶The anchor ***found*** *bottom*. いかりが底に着いた. ¶I am only sad that my purse ***has*** a *bottom*. ただ私は金持でないから十分買えないのが残念だ. ‖ His energy ***has*** no *bottom*. 彼の精力は無尽蔵だ. ¶He wants to ***know*** the *bottom* of everything. 彼は何でも徹底的に知りたがる. ¶***reach*** the *bottom* 〚相場〛底を入れる. ¶***rotate*** the *bottom* (=posterior) しりを振る. ¶Prices go down and down without ***striking*** any *bottom*. 底なしに値段がどんどん下る. ¶The facts have ***taken*** (=***knocked***) the *bottom* out of the theory. 事実が理論を覆えした. ¶The vessel ***took*** the *bottom*. 船が沈没した. ¶It seems to me that the prices have now ***touched*** *bottom*. もう値段は底をついたらしい.

Q a vessel with a ***false*** *bottom* あげ底の入れもの.

Q^2 The tidal waves were caused by a great earthquake on the ***ocean*** *bottom* near Alaska. その津波はアラスカ付近の大洋の海底に起った大地震に基くものであった. ¶a shortage of ***shipping*** *bottoms* 船腹不足.

P ***at*** the *bottom* of the stairs 階段の上り口で. ¶The principle ***at*** *bottom* is the same. 根本の理屈に変りはない. 【類】a good man ***at*** *bottom* / ***At*** *bottom* they are one and the same. / He is, ***at*** *bottom* (腹は), an honest man. / "Universal history", says Carlyle, "is ***at*** *bottom* the history of the great men who have worked here." ‖ Pearls lie ***at*** the *bottom*. 真珠は水底にある. ‖ ***at*** the *bottom* (=in the depth) of one's heart 心の奥底に ‖ a note ***at*** the *bottom* of a page 脚註. 【類】***at*** the *bottom* of the sea / He is ***at*** the *bottom* (びり) of his class. ‖ We must try to get ***at*** the *bottom* of the affair (trouble). 事件(など)の真相を調べ上げなければならない. ‖ Jealousy is ***at*** the *bottom* of it. しっとがもとだ. ‖ Somebody must be maneuvering ***at*** the *bottom* of this affair. この事件の陰にはだれかが糸を引いているに違いない. 【類】He is ***at*** the *bottom* of this affair. ‖ the principle ***at*** the *bottom* of a movement (社会)運動の根本原理 ‖ He is mistaken ***at*** the *bottom* in thinking so. そう考えるのがそもそもの間違いである. ¶I thank you ***from*** the *bottom* of my heart for your telegram of congratulation. 御祝電に対し衷心より感謝致します. ‖ raise a sunken ship ***from*** the *bottom* of the harbor 沈没船を港の海底から引き上げる. ¶The foreign commerce of the United States was largely carried on ***in*** foreign *bottoms* (=vessels). 米国の外国貿易は主として外国船によって行われた. ‖ consigned ***in*** one *bottom* (=a single ship) ただ一隻の船で託送された ‖ They treated me to a cup of Russian tea with the strawberry jam ***in*** the *bottom* of the cup. 彼らはコップの底にいちごジャムを入れたロシア風の茶を一杯私に出してくれた. ¶The ship has sunk and is ***on*** the *bottom*. 船は沈んで海底についている. ‖ stand ***on*** one's own *bottom* 一本立になる, 独立する ‖ stand ***on*** the *bottom* in water 足を水底につけて立つ. ¶The house must be repaired from top ***to*** *bottom*. この家は土台から修繕しなければならない. ‖ drain the cup ***to*** the *bottom* 杯を飲みほす ‖ The ship was sent ***to*** the *bottom*. 船を沈没させた. 【類】The boat went (=sank) ***to*** the *bottom*. ‖ The ship sustained damage ***to*** her *bottom*. 船底が破損した. ‖ search (=probe) the matter ***to*** the *bottom* その件を徹底的に調べる. ¶a ship ***with*** double *bottom* 二重底の船.

O *Bottoms* up, gentlemen! みなさん, ぐっとほして下さい(乾杯して下さい).

bough, *n.* 木の枝.

Q ***slender*** *boughs*, bent down with the weight of the terminal bunches of fruit 端に実った果物の房の重みで垂れ下っている細枝.

P ***beneath*** the *bough* of a tall pine 高い松の木の下で.

bounce, *n.* 跳躍.

V The fish ***gave*** a *bounce* in the basket. 魚がびくの中でぴょんとはねた.

P ***on*** the *bounce* ぴょんぴょんと, 飛びはねて.

bounce, *v.* 飛ぶ, はねる; 飛ばす; しかる.

M *bounce* ***back*** with allegations that ... ...という論証で逆襲する. ¶Business *bounced* ***back*** to prewar levels. 商業が戦前の状態に戻った.

M^2 *bounce* ***about*** はね回る. ¶Striking a rock the bullet *bounced* ***off***. 岩に当って弾丸がはね返った. ¶*bounce* a child ***up and down*** こどもを揺り上げ揺り下ろす.

P The clerk was well *bounced* ***for*** his carelessness. 番頭はさんざんその不注意をしかられた. ¶The ball *bounced* ***into*** a room. 球が部屋へ飛び込んだ. ¶The tiger *bounced* ***on*** (=***upon***) its prey. とらはその獲物にとびかかった.

bound, *n.* 限界, 境界.

V Scientists ***advance*** the *bounds* of knowledge. 科学者は知識の領域を進展せしめる. ¶I ***burst*** the *bounds* of all convention あらゆる慣習の障壁を打破する. ¶***exceed*** the *bounds* 度を過ごす. ¶the desire to ***extend*** the *bounds* of one's knowledge 新知識増進の欲望. ¶***have*** *bounds* 限りがある. ¶The fertility of his invention ***knew*** no *bounds*. 彼の発明の才は無限に発揮された. 【類】Avarice (欲) ***knows*** no *bounds*. / His happiness (delight, rage) ***knew*** no *bounds*. ¶He often ***oversteps*** the *bounds* of propriety. 彼の言動はしばしば穏当を欠くことがある. ¶***pass*** the *bounds* of common sense 常軌を逸する ‖ The fellow's impudence ***passed*** all *bounds*. そいつの厚かましさは全く度はずれであった. ¶***set*** *bounds* to (=restrict) it それを制

限する. ¶never ***transcend*** the *bounds* of decency 決してぶしつけにわたらない.

Q get beyond all ***reasonable bounds*** 常軌を逸する, 度を越す. 【類】overstep the ***reasonable bounds.*** ¶overstep the legally ***prescribed bounds*** of its constitutional power 憲法に明示してある範囲を逸脱する. ¶the ***utmost bounds*** of the west 西の果.

P ***beyond*** the *bounds* of the country 国境外に. ¶It is not ***beyond*** the *bounds* of possibility to do so. それは必ずしも不可能ではない. 【類】It is ***beyond*** the *bounds* of reason (hope, patience). / He has gone ***beyond*** the *bounds* of moderation (politeness, prudence). / The sensation was ***beyond*** [all] *bounds.* ¶It is ***out of*** the *bounds* of possibility. それはあり得ないことだ. ‖ be ***out of*** *bounds* (=off limits) to ... ...は入場を禁じている. ¶be ***outside*** the *bounds* of literature 文学の圏外にある. ¶keep it ***within*** *bounds* それが限度を越えないようにする. 【類】It is ***within*** the *bounds* of reasonable probability. ‖ it is ***within*** the *bounds* of reason to ... ...するのは不合理でない.

P² the *bounds* ***of*** all European countries 欧州の各国の境界.

bound, *v.* 限る; 界する.

P Our ideas are *bounded* ***by*** our experience. われわれの思想はその経験に制限される. ¶The Pacific Ocean *bounds* the United States ***on*** the west. 太平洋は西に米国に界している. 【類】The United States is *bounded* ***on*** the north by Canada. / The country is *bounded* ***on*** three sides by the sea. / The building is *bounded* ***on*** its four sides by A, B, C, and D streets.

bound, *n.* 飛ぶこと.

P Few men rise to eminence ***at*** one *bound.* 一躍して群を抜くものは少い. 【類】He jumped it ***at*** a *bound.* / Of course we cannot expect to attain our desires ***at*** a single *bound.* ¶He made progress in English ***by*** leaps and *bounds.* 彼は英語がずんずん進歩した. ¶strike a ball ***on*** its first *bound* 球を最初のバウンドの時打つ. ¶***With*** one *bound,* I reached the hatch. 一飛びで艙口の所へ行った. ‖ Australia has sprung ***with*** a *bound* into a film producing country. 豪州は一躍して映画製作国の仲間入をした.

bound, *v.* 飛ぶ.

M A ball *bounds* ***back*** when it is thrown on the pavement. ボールを舗道に投げるとはね返る.

P *bound* ***from*** ... ***to*** ... ...から...にはずんで飛ぶ. ¶Lawn tennis *bounds* ***into*** favor once again. またにわかにテニスの人気が出てきた. 【類】he *bounded* ***into*** fame (一躍名を成した) as the author of ... / The place is rapidly *bounding* ***into*** fame as one of the popular mountain resorts (山の遊場) of the coast.

bound, *a.* ...行きの.

M a ship ***homeward*** *bound* from ... ...から帰航中の船.

M² the steamer was *bound* ***in*** from ... その汽船は...から帰航中であった. ¶an ***outward*** (***a homeward***) *bound* steamer 往(帰)航の汽船. ¶***Where*** is the ship *bound?* 船はどこ行きですか.

P The ship is *bound* ***for*** Europe. この船は欧州行だ. 【類】Ships *bound* ***for*** Europe touch at Hongkong. / a freight train *bound* ***for*** Ueno / Their day's work was done and they were *bound* ***for*** home. ‖ the town ***for*** which we are *bound* 目的地たる町. ☞ *bound* ***to*** ... は古体. ¶a steamer *bound* ***from*** here ***for*** ... ここから...行きの汽船. ¶They are *bound* ***on*** (=***upon***) a journey (an expedition). 彼らは旅行(など)の途上にある.

bound, *pa.* → bind.

boundary, *n.* 境界.

V ***advance*** the *boundaries* of knowledge 知識の領域を拡張する. ¶The oil field ***bestrides*** the *boundary* between Persia and Iraq. その油田はペルシヤとイラクの国境にまたがっている. ¶***define*** *boundaries* 境界を定める. ¶***enlarge*** (=***extend***) the *boundaries* of human knowledge 知識の領域を広げる. ¶***expand*** its political *boundaries* その政治上の領域を拡大する. ¶***extend*** the *boundaries* of our trade わが貿易の範囲を拡張する. ¶the river ***forms*** the *boundary* between ... and ... その川が...と...の境界になっている. ¶countries ***having*** a common *boundary* 隣接する国々. ¶***overstep*** the *boundary* between freedom and license 自由と放縦をはき違える. ¶***push forward*** (=***advance***) the *boundaries* of knowledge 知識の領域を拡大する.

Q an ***international*** *boundary* 国境. ¶Because of the lack of surveys there will be ***overlapping*** *boundaries* and hiatuses 地測不完全のため重複している境界線や空間があるだろう. ¶***readjusted*** *boundaries* 再整理された境界線.

P ***within*** the *boundary* of ... ...の区域内に.

P² the *boundary* ***between*** neighboring territories 隣接領土間の境界線. ¶the *boundary* ***between*** two countries 二国間の境界. ¶the *boundary* ***of*** a country 国境.

bountiful, *a.* 気前のよい.

P He is *bountiful* ***of*** gifts. 彼は惜気もなく物をくれる.

bounty, *n.* 恩恵, 賜物; 補助金.

V ***distribute*** one's *bounty* 恵与品を分配する. ¶***give*** *bounties* upon exported sugar 輸出砂糖に補助金を与える. ¶***grant*** a *bounty* 助成金を下付する.

P² a *bounty* ***for*** poor clergyment 貧しい牧師への支給. ¶a *bounty* ***from*** the Government 政府の補助金. ¶a *bounty* ***on*** exports 輸出品に対する補助金.

bouquet, *n.* 花束.

V It has dodged many brickbats, ***caught*** many *bouquets.* 幾多の非難を免れ, 幾多の賞賛を博した. ¶*bouquets* ***presented*** to the representative members of a mission 使節団の代表者に贈られた花束.

bourgeois, *n.* 中産市民.

Q an ***old, unregenerate, soft-centered*** *bourgeois,* masquerading in a red tie 赤いネクタイをつけその本性を押し隠した道楽もので, 裕福な市民の軟派老人.

bourgeoisie, *n.* 中流社会; 有産階級.

Q the ***moneyed*** *bourgeoisie* 金のある中流階層.

bourse, *n.* 取引所, 金融市場.

P in spite of all-round denials, the rumor persists ***on*** the local *Bourse* that ... 世間が否定しているにも拘らず...という風説がこの土地の取引所仲間にこびり付いている ‖ transactions ***on*** the *bourse* 取引所の取引.

bout, *n.* 一勝負; 酒宴.

V I'll ***have*** a *bout* with you. 君と一勝負やろう. ¶***hold*** a grand drinking *bout* 大酒宴を張る. ¶***win*** a *bout* 勝負に勝つ.

V² After the *bout* has ***started,*** the first wrestler who touches the ground with any part of his body except his feet is the loser. 力士が立上ってから足以外体のどこか最初に地についた方が負である.

Q² a ***boxing*** ***bout*** 拳闘試合. ¶a heavy ***drinking bout*** 大量の酒合戦. ¶a ***fencing bout*** フェンシング試合. ¶a ***wrestling bout*** レスリング試合. ¶a ***10-round bout*** 十回戦.

P ***at*** one *bout* 一勝負で.

bow, *n.* 弓; ちょう結び.

V ***bend*** a *bow* 弓を引絞る. ¶***draw*** a *bow* 弓を引く ‖ ***draw*** a *bow* at a venture でたらめを言う ‖ ***draw*** the long *bow* 針小棒大に言う, ほらをふく. ¶She ***had*** a *bow* of red ribbon in her hair. 彼女は頭に赤いリボンをかけていた. ¶***string*** a *bow* 弓に弦を張る. ¶***untie*** a *bow* ちょう形ネクタイ(ちょう結び)を解く.

Q² a ***violin bow*** バイオリンの弓.

P An arrow is shot ***by*** a *bow.* 矢は弓で射る. ¶like an arrow ***from*** a *bow* 弓を離れた矢のように. ¶A ribbon is tied ***in*** a *bow.* リボンをちょう形に結ぶ. 【類】tie a shoe-lace ***in*** a *bow.* ¶A violin is played ***with*** a *bow.* ヴァイオリンは弓でひく.

bow, *n.* お辞儀.

V ***exchange*** *bows* 互にお辞儀を交す. ¶He ***gave*** her a *bow* for it. 彼はそれに対して体をこごめて彼女にあいさつをした. ¶***make*** one's *bow*=retire 引き下がる, 舞台を降りる ‖ ***make*** one's first *bow* to ... ...に初見参する. 【類】He ***made*** his first *bow* in Paris in 1783. ‖ a new process ***makes*** its *bow* nearly every week in the year ほとんど毎週のように年中新しい製法が出現する ‖ ***make*** one's *bow* to ... ...にお辞儀をする ‖ ***make*** two *bows* 二度お辞儀をする ‖ The book ***made*** *bow* to the public three years after. その本はその後三年たって世に公にされた. ¶I ***received*** a slight *bow* of recognition from him. 私は彼からちょっと会釈を受けた. ¶The teacher ***returned*** the *bow* (=bowed in return). 先生が答礼をした.

Q He made a very ***civil*** *bow* to me. 彼はきわめてていねいに私にお辞儀をした. ¶with a ***courteous*** *bow* てい重なお辞儀をして. ¶with a ***deep*** (=***low***) *bow* 頭を低く下げて. ¶make one's ***final*** *bow* and retire from the stage of life 最後の暇(いとま)を告げてこの世を去る. ¶a ***graceful*** *bow* しとやかなお辞儀. ¶with ***gracious*** *bows* of thanks いんぎ

んに感謝のお辞儀をして．¶make a ***polite bow*** to ... ...にていねいにお辞儀をする．¶make a ***profound bow*** 最敬礼をする．¶make a ***respectful bow*** 丁寧なお辞儀をする．¶make a ***slight bow*** 軽くお辞儀をする．¶a ***stiff bow*** ぎごちないお辞儀．¶a ***sweeping bow*** 居並ぶ人に行渡るようなお辞儀．

Q² a ***parting bow*** 別れのお辞儀．

P He greeted me ***with*** a *bow* 彼は頭を下げて私にあいさつした．‖ He ushered us upstairs ***with*** a *bow*. 一寸おじぎをしてからわれわれを階上に案内した．

bow, *v.* お辞儀する；腰をかがめる；腰を曲げる，屈服する．

M *bow* ***deeply*** (＝*low*) at ... ...に丁寧にお辞儀をする ‖ *bow low* to the ground 最敬礼する．¶I *bowed* ***meekly*** to his order. 私はおとなしく彼の命令通りにした．¶*bow* a person ***out*** おじぎして人を送り出す．【類】In April, 1946, the League of Nations *bowed* ***out*** (発展的解消をした) in favor of the United Nations. ¶*bow* ***pleasantly*** 快活にお辞儀をする．¶He *bowed* ***politely***. 彼は丁寧にお辞儀をした．¶*bow* ***profoundly*** 最敬礼をする．¶*bow* ***respectfully*** before the spirit of the man その人の霊前にうやうやしくお辞儀をする．

M² *bow* ***down*** to the ground 平身低頭する．【類】They *bowed* ***down*** to the idol. / *bow* ***down*** in admiration [驚嘆のあまり] before it ‖ *bow* ***down*** upon one's knees ひざまずく ‖ He was *bowed* ***down*** with years. 彼は取る年で腰が曲った．‖ *bow* ***down*** one's ear 自らひくうして人に聴く．

P *bow* ***before*** the inviolable laws of the universe 厳然たる宇宙の法則に服従する ‖ *bow* ***before*** the Great Buddha in the temple 仏殿の中の大仏を拝する．【類】They *bowed* ***before*** our Emperor's picture. ¶*bow* ***on*** (＝***upon***) one's knees ひざまずいてお辞儀をする．¶He *bowed* me ***out of*** the room. 彼はお辞儀して私を部屋から引下がらした(体よく追払った)．¶*bow* ***to*** each other お互いにお辞儀をする．【類】*bow* ***to*** him / Who was that that *bowed* ***to*** you just now? ‖ There seemed nothing to be done but to *bow* ***to*** the storm till it passed over. 暴風が通過するまで頭を下げているより仕方がなかった(主人のかんしゃくなど)．‖ *bow* ***to*** one's authority (wishes, command) その権威(など)に従う．【類】He was politic enough to *bow* ***to*** the force of circumstances. / We must *bow* ***to*** the universal law (the inevitable). ‖ I *bowed* ***to*** the fates by divorcing my wife. 運命だとあきらめて妻を離縁した．¶*bow* ***towards*** the Imperial Palace 皇居に向って礼拝する．¶an old man *bowed* ***with*** age 年のせいで腰が曲った老人 ‖ a heart *bowed* ***with*** grief (care) 悲しみ(心労)で気力を失った心．

bowel, *n.* 腸．

V ***clear*** [***out***] the *bowels* by a full enema or by irrigation 十分なかん腸剤またはかん注法で通じをつける．¶***empty*** (＝***evacuate***) the *bowels* 通じをつける．¶***evacuate*** the *bowels* and bladder 大小便の通じをつける．¶It is important to ***keep*** the *bowels* ***loose*** with a moderate dose of salts. 塩剤を適当に服(の)んで通じをよくするのが大切だ．‖ ***keep*** the *bowels* ***open*** and regular 便通を整調する．¶***loosen*** the *bowels* 便通をつける．¶***move*** the *bowels* 通じをつける．¶***relax*** the *bowels* 腸をゆるめる．¶***relieve*** one's *bowels* 通じをつける．¶***rip open*** one's own *bowels* 切腹する．

V² The *bowels* ***move***. 通じがある．

P deep down ***in*** the *bowels* of the earth 地下の深部に於て．

bower, *n.* あずまや，休息所．

Q² a ***wistaria*** *bower* 藤だなの休息所．

bowl, *n.* 〘遊戯〙ボーリングの木球．

V ***throw*** *bowls*＝play bowling ボーリングをやる．

V² The *bowl* ***tumbled*** down on the floor. ボーリングの球が床上をころがって行った．

bowl, *n.* はち(ボール)．

Q² a ***china*** *bowl* どんぶり，茶わん．¶a ***fire*** *bowl* [茶の湯などの]風炉(ふろ)．¶Indo-China, Thailand and Burma—the so-called ***rice*** *bowl* of Asia インド・シナ，タイ，ビルマーいわゆるアジアの米びつ．¶a ***sugar*** *bowl* 砂糖つぼ．

bowl, *v.* 倒す，アウトにする．

M I was ***completely*** *bowled* out by the news. そのニュースで気も転倒した．¶*bowl* ***out*** (＝***down***) 〘クリケット〙打者をアウトにする．

M² Our car *bowled* ***along*** the smooth country road. われわれの車は平たんな田舎道をすべって行った．

P Germans *bowled* ***over*** France. ドイツ軍はフランスを席巻した．

bowlful, *n.* ボール(はち)に一杯．

P² have a *bowlful* ***of*** vermicelli そばをどんぶり一杯で食べる．【類】a *bowlful* ***of*** water (milk, wine).

bow-shot, *n.* 矢の到達距離．

P ***within*** *bow-shot* of it そこから矢が届くぐらいの所に．

box, *n.* 箱；御者台；特別席；贈物．

V How many times a day is this *box* ***cleared***? この郵便箱は一日に何度開けますか．¶I have ***engaged*** (＝***taken***) a *box* in the Imperial Theater. 帝劇に特別席を取って置きました．¶***mount*** the *box* 御者台に乗る．¶***open*** a Pandora's *box* of political issues やぶへびを出す．¶***pack*** a *box* with books 箱に本を詰め込む．¶***pass*** a *box* for the band 楽隊をやらせるので寄付箱を(乗客などの間に)回す．¶a pretty ***plush*** *box* きれいなフラシ天の箱(宝石屋の)．¶I have ***turned*** the *box* ***upside down***. 箱をひっくりかえした．

Q check ***applicable*** *box* 該当する四角囲いの所に印をつける．¶an ***introductory*** *box* [食糧品などの]宣伝用の見本箱．¶A ***japanned*** *box* 漆塗の箱．¶a ***strong*** *box* 《俗》金庫．¶a ***water-tight*** *box* 防水箱．

Q² a ***ballot*** *box* 投書箱．¶a ***cardboard*** *box* 厚紙の容器．¶a ***carton*** *box* 段ボール包装箱．¶a ***chow-chow*** *box* [遊山用]べんとう箱．¶a ***Christmas*** *box* [召使などへの]クリスマスの贈りもの．¶a ***collection*** *box* 寄付金箱．¶a ***document*** *box* 書類箱．¶an ***economy*** *box* [食品などの大きい]徳用箱．¶goods shipped in ***fiber*** *boxes* ファイバー包装箱の積荷．¶a ***fire alarm*** *box* 火災報知器．¶the ***first aid*** *box* 急救箱．¶the blare of hasting ***turned-on-juke*** *boxes* いそいでかけた自動電蓄のがあがあという鳴り音．¶rifle ***mail*** *boxes* ポストに手を入れて(郵便物を)盗む．¶a ***make-up*** *box* 役者の化粧箱．¶a ***music*** *box*＝《英》a musical box オルゴール．¶set up (＝place *or* fix) a ***nest*** *box* on a tree 木の上に巣箱を作る．¶an ***omnibus*** *box* 舞台に通じる高土間．¶the ***press*** *box* atop the Stadium 競技場の高い場所に備えつけた記者席．¶a ***seed***[***ing***] *box* 苗入れ箱．¶a ***shoe*** *box* くつ箱．¶a ***shipping*** *box* [輸送用の]発送箱．¶A ***suggestion*** *box* is provided. 投書箱が設けてある．¶a ***tool*** *box* [大工の]道具箱．¶a ***window*** *box* 植木箱(窓の下わくの上におく)．

P He is ***in*** a *box*. 彼は苦しい羽目におちいっている．【類】He and I are ***in*** the same *box*. ‖ a driver ***in*** his *box* 御者台の御者．

P² a *box* ***of*** colors 絵具箱．

box, *n.* 拳骨．

V He ***got*** a *box* on the ear. 彼は横面をはられた．¶I ***gave*** him a *box* on the ear. 彼の横面をはった．¶***administer*** him a *box* on the ear 横っつらをがんとぶんなぐる．

box, *v.* 箱に詰める；閉じこめる．

M² *box* ***about*** in a yacht ヨットであちこち遊び回る．¶*box* ***off*** [へやを]仕切る．¶*boxed* ***up*** in a small room 狭いへやに押し込められて．

P be *boxed* ***for*** gift-giving 贈答用箱入になっている．

box, *v.* 拳で打つ．

M *box* it ***out*** あくまで殴り合う．

P *box* a person ***on*** the ear 耳に一発くわせる．¶*box* ***with*** the hands 手で打つ．

boxer, *n.* 拳闘家(ボクサー)．

V The *boxer* was ***downed*** at a blow. そのボクサーは一撃でダウンとなった．

boxful, *n.* 箱に一杯．

P² a *boxful* ***of*** apples 箱に一杯のりんご．

box-holder, *n.* [買切りの]御常連．

Q² ***season*** *box-holders* [野球など]一シーズン座席買切りの常連．

boy, *n.* 少年，小僧．

V ***apprentice*** one's *boy* to a trade 息子を職業の見習にだす．¶***domineer*** and ***bully*** younger *boys* 年下の少年に威張り散らしたり乱暴に振舞ったりする．¶***fit*** *boys* for a business life 少年に実務教育を施す．¶***reclaim*** *boys* from an evil life 不良少年を矯正する．¶***send*** a *boy* to school 子供を学校に上げる．¶***withdraw*** a *boy* from school 子供を学校から下げる．

V² He was affectionate and considerate as *boys* ***go***. 子供にしては愛情があって思いやりが深かった．¶The *boy* is ***shooting up***. 子供がずんずん大きくなる．

Q ***backward*** *boys* 知能の遅れている男の子たち．¶***beardless*** *boys* まだひげのない若僧．¶You are a ***big*** *boy* now. 大きくなったね．¶***bright*** *boys* 頭の良い少年．¶a ***cheeky*** *boy* 《俗》生意気な少年．¶a ***clear-cut*** *boy* すっきりした少年．¶***clever*** *boys* 賢い少年．¶***dirty-minded*** *boys* 心の汚れた少年．¶***dull*** *boys* 頭の悪い少年．¶Stop it and be a ***good*** *boy*. 好い子だからおよし．‖ That's a ***good*** *boy!* まあ

いい子だこと. ‖ Can't you sit still like a ***good*** *boy?* いい子だからちゃんとおすわりしてるんですよ. ¶a ***green*** *boy* 青二歳. ¶***growing*** *boys* 伸び盛りの少年. ¶a ***grown-up*** *boy* 成人した男の子. ¶a ***husky*** *boy* 《米》大きくてがっちりした若人. ¶an ***impertinent*** *boy* 生意気な男の子. ¶a ***lean*** *boy* やせっぽちの少年. ¶a ***mere*** *boy* まだほんの子供. ¶a ***mischievous*** *boy* いたずら小僧. ¶***Naughty*** *boys* are a plague. いたずらっ子には困る. ¶a ***nice*** (=***cute***) ***little*** *boy* 愛らしい子供. ¶The *boys* are ***noisy***. 子供たちはやかましい. ¶***older*** *boys* of sixteen years of age and over 十六歳以上の比較的年長の少年たち. ¶an old "***young*** *boy*"=a youth with hoary hair 気の若い老人. ¶a ***parlous*** *boy* 恐るべき少年. ¶He has the ***perpetual*** *boy* in him. 彼はいつも気が若い. ¶a ***red-faced chubby*** *boy* りんごのほおをした丸ぽちゃの少年. ¶a ***reserved*** *boy* 内気な少年. ¶That would be placing a ***round*** *boy* in a square hole. そんなことをしたらあの子に不向の仕事をさせることになる. ¶Then came a ***second*** *boy.* 次で次男が生れた ‖ the ***second*** *boy* in the line その系列では次男. ¶a ***sweet*** *boy* かわいい少年. ¶a ***tall, heavy, muscular*** *boy* せいが高く, 肥って筋骨たくましい少年. ¶a ***tall, light-haired*** *boy* のっぽで金髪の少年. ¶Put out that ***troublesome*** *boy.* あのいたずらっ子を追出してしまえ. ¶a ***virgin*** *boy* 童貞の少年. ¶***wayward*** *boys* and girls 不良の少年少女. ¶a ***weakly*** *boy* 弱々しい少年.

Q² a ***baby*** *boy* 男の赤ん坊. ¶a ***bell*** *boy* [ホテル]接客係のボーイ. ¶***Carter*** *boys* カーターという人の男の子たち. ¶a ***city*** *boy* 都会の少年. ¶an undersized ***color*** *boy* 背の低い黒人少年. ¶a ***copy*** *boy* 〖新聞〗校正運びの給仕. ¶a ***delivery*** *boy* 配達係の少年. ¶an ***elevator*** *boy* エレベーターボーイ. ¶her "***fancy*** *boy*" 彼女の若いつばめ. ¶a ***farm*** *boy* =a farm hand 農園の手伝い. ¶a ***fisher*** *boy* 少年漁夫. ¶***football pin-up*** *boys* on the wall かべにピンで止めてある写真のしゅう球選手. ¶a ***ginger bread*** (=***flimsy***) *boy* 弱弱しい少年. ¶a ***high-school*** *boy* 男子高校生. ¶an ***idiot*** *boy* のろまな男の子. ¶a ***junior high*** *boy* 男子の中学生. ¶a ***mail*** *boy*=mailman 《米》郵便配達人. ¶a ***messenger*** *boy* メッセンジャーボーイ. ¶Charles Stratton, a pretty ***midget*** *boy*, two feet high チャールス・ストラトンという二尺ぐらいの美少年. ¶That ***office*** *boy* is never here when wanted. あの給仕ときたら用事のある時いたためしがない. ¶an ***orphan*** *boy* 孤児(片親または両親のない). ¶a ***Roosevelt*** *boy* ルーズベルト家の男の子. ¶a ***sixth form*** boy 六年生の男児. ¶a ***shoe-shine*** *boy* くつみがき少年. ¶jolly ***soldier*** *boys* 愉快な兵隊たち. ¶The London ***street*** *boy* is terribly undersized. そのロンドンの浮浪児はおっそろしく小びとだ. ¶***teenage*** *boys* 十代の少年. ¶a ***wool-hat*** *boy* 毛の帽子をかぶった男の子.

P He is tall ***for*** a *boy* of his age. 子供としてはせいが高い.

P² a *boy* ***of*** ten [years] 十歳の少年. 【類】a *boy* [***of***] about your age.

boycott, *n.* 不買同盟.

V ***declare*** a *boycott* against ... ...に対し不買同盟を声明する. ¶***institute*** a *boycott* of Japanese goods 日本品の不買同盟を始める. ¶***launch*** a *boycott* 不買同盟を始める. ¶***lift*** the present *boycott* of Indian raw cotton 現在の印度棉花不買同盟を撤回する.

Q an ***economic*** *boycott* 経済的不買同盟. ¶prohibition of ***secondary*** *boycott* 第二次ボイコットの禁止.

Q² ***examination*** *boycott* 受験拒否.

boycott, *v.* 拒否する.

M His lecture has been *boycotted* ***twice*** so far. 彼の講義はこれまで二回(学生に)拒否された.

boyhood, *n.* 少年時代.

V His *boyhood* was ***passed*** there. 彼は少年時代をそこで過した.

Q² in his greedily ***ambitious*** *boyhood* 野心で燃えている少年時代に.

P ***from*** his *boyhood* [upwards] 幼少の時から. ¶***in*** early *boyhood* ほんの子供のころ. ¶***since*** his *boyhood* 幼少より. ¶He was in the country ***through*** all his *boyhood.* 彼は幼少の時ずっといなかにいた.

brace, *n.* [単・複同型] 一番(㋡つ).

Q a ***few*** *brace* of ducks 二三つがいのかも. ¶***five*** *brace* of geese (pheasants) 五つがいのがちょう(きじ).

P² a *brace* ***of*** dogs 一つがい(二頭)の犬 ‖ a *brace* ***of*** birds 一つがいの鳥.

brace, *v.* ふんばる.

M *brace* oneself ***up*** 奮起する ‖ *Brace* ***up***, America! アメリカよ, 頑張れ! ‖ *brace* ***up*** the whole system 全身をひきしめる(緊張させる). ¶*brace* oneself ***against*** a champion 奮起してチャンピオンに挑戦する ‖ *brace* oneself ***up*** for a fight 戦おうと緊張する.

P *brace* one's foot ***in*** the stirrup あぶみをふんばる.

bracer, *n.* 刺激剤.

Q² a ***skin*** *bracer* [アストリンゼン式の]皮膚強壮化粧水.

bracket, *n.* 括弧; 腕木; 一定の階層(の人々).

Q those in the ***higher*** *brackets* 成績(など)優良なもの.

Q² be within the ***age*** *bracket* of 30 三十という年令制限内にある. ¶ex-soldiers in the ***lower-income*** *bracket* 下級の旧軍人たち. ¶those in ***middle-income*** *bracket* 中流階層に属する人々. ¶In the language of printers, the term "bracket" denotes ***square*** *brackets.* 印刷用語でブラケットというと角括弧のことである.

P put words ***between*** *brackets* 語を括弧に入れる. 【類】the figure ***between*** *brackets* indicates ... ¶a shelf supported ***by*** *brackets* 腕木で支えられているたな. ¶telegraphic addresses shown ***in*** *brackets* 括弧内に示した電信のあて名. ¶enclose a remark ***within*** square *brackets* 言葉を角括弧に入れる.

bracket, *v.* 括弧で包む; 同順位(階層)の人々.

P those *bracketed* ***for*** the prize 受賞者として挙げられている人々(入選者). 【類】the names of those two boys are *bracketed* ***for*** the first prize.

brag, *n.* 自慢.

V He ***made*** a great *brag* of it. 彼はそれが大自慢だった.

P He is full ***of*** *brag.* 彼は自慢ばかり言う.

brag, *v.* 誇る, 自慢する.

P It is not in good form to *brag* ***about*** (=***of***) your gifts (ability, learning, success). 自分の才能(など)を自慢するのは感心したことではない. ‖ *brag* ***about*** what one would have done 自分ならこうやったんだと自慢する. ¶*brag* ***of*** one's accomplishments (achievements, deeds, talent, ancestors) 自分の芸能(など)を自慢する.

braid, *n.* べん髪; モール.

Q² cuffs covered with ***gold*** *braid* 金モールの巻いてあるそで口. ¶of ***straw*** *braid* 麦かんさなだ製の.

P girls wearing their hair ***in*** *braids* 髪をおさげにした少女たち.

braid, *v.* 編む.

P *braid* one's hair ***into*** a crown 束髪に結ぶ. 【類】She *braided* her hair ***into*** tresses.

brail, *v.* 帆をしぼる.

M *brail* ***up*** 絞帆する.

brain, *n.* 脳, 頭; *pl.* 知能.

V ***addle*** one's *brains* 頭を悪くする(思想を鈍らす). ¶***beat*** one's *brains* for an idea 知恵を絞る. ¶Such a book serves only to ***bewilder*** (=***confuse***) the *brains* of the unhappy learner. こんな本はいたずらに学習者の頭を混乱さすだけだ. ¶***blow out*** his *brain* with a pistol ピストルで彼の脳天を射ち貫く. 【類】I'll ***blow*** your *brains* ***out***! ¶Don't ***bother*** your *brain* about that! そんなことに気を使うのはやめ給え. ¶Their thought ***burned*** their *brains.* 彼らの思想は胸中に燃えていた. ¶***cram*** the *brain* with facts and figures 事実や数字を頭に詰め込む. ¶***cudgel*** one's *brains* over ... ...に脳みそをしぼる. 【類】***cudgel*** one's *brains* to understand how on earth such a thing could happen. ¶***dash out*** one's *brains* 脳天を割る. ¶His *brain* is ***debilitated*** by alcohol. 彼の頭はアルコールでばかになっている. ¶***dull*** one's *brain* through (=by) smoking 喫煙で頭をにぶくする. ¶He ***had*** *brains* to see it. 彼にはそれがわかるだけの頭があった. ‖ He ***has*** no *brains.* 彼は頭がない. ¶It so ***irritated*** his *brains* that he could not sleep. 彼はそのためあまり神経がいらだって眠られなかった. ¶***lack*** (=***want***) *brains* 脳味噌(知恵)が足りない. ¶I ***knocked*** my *brains* against German as hard as I could. 一生懸命にドイツ語を勉強した. ¶***muddle*** the *brain* 頭を混濁させる. ¶***overtax*** one's *brains* 頭を酷使する. ¶***put*** one's *brains* at another's service 人の仕事に知恵を貸す. ¶***puzzle*** one's *brains* about it そのことに頭を悩ます. 【類】***puzzle*** the *brains* of the students. ¶I ***racked*** my *brains* for his name. 彼の名を思い出そうとして骨を折った. 【類】I ***racked*** my *brains* for a plan (way of escape). / ***rack*** his *brains* for ideas that obstinately refuse to come at his bidding / ***rack*** one's *brains* over a question / ***rack*** one's *brains* to devise some scheme to ... / ***rack*** one's *brains* trying to .... ¶***shoot*** one's *brains* ***out*** ピストルで脳天を射抜いて自殺する. ¶***tax*** one's *brains* 頭を悩ます.【類】*tax* the *brains* of scholars. ¶***turn*** one's *brain* 慢心させる; 頭を変にさせる. ¶***Use*** your *brains!* 頭を働かせろ(気のきかないやつだ).【類】He is a great guy who can ***use*** the *brains* of others to carry on his work.

V^2 The *brain* began to ***reel***. 頭がふらふらし出した. ¶My *brain* ***turns***. 目が回る. ¶I thought and worried till my *brain* ***whirled***. 頭がぐらぐらするまで考え悩んだ.

Q The *brain* became ***addled***. 頭がはっきりしなくなった. ¶persons of ***average*** *brains* 普通の頭脳の人々. ¶Her ***busy*** *brain* was shaping pictures of what might have been. 彼女は(取返しのつかないことを)こうもあったろうかと空想にふけっていた. ¶***capable*** *brains* 有能な頭. ¶develop a ***clear-thinking*** *brain* 明析な頭を作る. ¶a great ***criminal*** *brain* 犯罪上の天才. ¶persons with more or less ***disordered*** *brain* 多少頭の変になった人間. ¶his ***drink-muddled*** *brain* 飲酒で濁った頭. ¶a product of his ***fertile*** *brain* 彼の豊富な頭の産物. ¶a ***highly strung*** *brain* 緊張し切った頭脳. ¶an ***inventive*** *brain* 発明の才. ¶the fifty-first production of her ***kaleidoscopic*** *brain* その多彩な頭から出た五十一番目の所産. ¶He has a ***mathematical*** *brain*. 彼は数理的の頭脳を持っている. ¶Bobby had the most ***remarkable*** *brain* of any dog in my long experience. ボビは私の長い畜犬の経験から言ってもっともすばらしい頭のある犬だった. ¶mobilize the ***scientific*** *brains* of America アメリカ中の科学者を動員する. ¶The child believed so in his ***seven-year-old*** *brain*. 子供はその七歳の頭でそう信じていた. ¶***skilled*** *brains* 熟練した頭(才能). ¶a ***strong*** and ***powerful*** and ***capacious*** *brain* 健全で力があって規模の大きい頭. ¶the ***teeming*** (=***prolific***) *brains* of Mr. H.G. Wells ウエルズ氏の豊富な頭脳. ¶a ***weary*** *brain* 疲れた頭.

Q^2 a ***railway*** *brain* 鉄道事故に基く一種の神経病.

P Ideas flittered ***across*** his *brain*. 考えがちらちらと彼の頭に動いた. ¶Much that Charles Dickens wrote came ***from*** the *brain*, still more from the heart. チャールス・ディッケンズの描いたものは理知の産物も多いが感情から出たものが一層多い. ¶suffusion of blood ***on*** the *brain* 脳充血. ¶His appeal was ***to*** the *brain* not to the feelings. 彼は感情に訴えずに道理に訴えたのだ. ¶a writer ***with*** *brains* 頭のある作家. ¶***with*** a reeling *brain* 目が回って.

P^2 a laborer working ***with*** his *brain*=a brain worker 頭脳労働者.

brain-truster, *n.* 頭脳委員会の一員.

Q^2 a ***Roosevelt*** "*brain-truster*" ルーズベルト大統領付き政策顧問団の一人.

brain-worker, *n.* 頭脳労働者.

Q ***hard*** *brain-workers* 勤勉な精神労働者. ¶an ***impoverished*** *brain-worker* 貧窮している頭脳労働者(作家など).

brake, *n.* 制動機.

V ***apply*** (=***put on***) the emergency *brake* 応急制動機をかける. ¶***put*** one's *brakes* ***on*** suddenly 突然ブレーキをかける.

Q^2 an ***air*** *brake* 空気制動機. ¶a ***hand*** (***foot***) *brake* 手(足)動制動機. ¶a ***vacuum*** *brake* 真空制動機.

bran, *n.* ふすま.

Q^2 ***rice*** *bran* 米ぬか, ふすま.

branch, *n.* 枝; 分科, 部門; 支店, 支部.

V ***adopt*** some *branch* of literature as a profession (hobby) 職業(道楽)として文学の方の仕事をする. ¶The *branch* carried on at 140 Strand was ***closed*** [***down***]. ストランド街一四〇番地で営業していた支店は閉鎖した. ¶***develop*** provincial *branches* 地方の支店をふやす. ¶***erect*** a *branch* of our house in Paris パリに当店の支店を設置する. ¶***establish*** a *branch* 支店をつくる. ¶The company has ***formed*** a British *branch* in London. 会社はロンドンに英国支店を設けた. ¶***lop off*** a *branch* 枝を切取る. ¶***open*** [***up***] *branches* at several places 所々に支店を開く. ¶***organize*** a *branch* 支店をつくる. ¶trees ***sending forth*** *branches* 枝を延す木. ¶the *branch* I have ***specialized in*** 私が専門にやった部門. ¶***start*** a *branch* in Canada カナダに支店を置く. ¶***wind up*** (=***close***) a *branch* 支店を閉じる.

Q junior members or ***collateral*** *branches* of a family ある家族の傍系. ¶a ***drooping*** *branches* 垂れ下る枝. ¶a ***dry*** *branch* of a family 一門の断絶した分家. ¶an old pinetree with ***gnarled*** *branches* 節だらけの枝が出ている古い松の木. ¶an ***important*** *branch* of the government 政府の重要な一部分. ¶***intertwining*** *branches* 錯綜する枝. ¶one of the most ***neglected*** *branches* of psychology 心理学で最も等閑に付せられた一部門.【類】a ***neglected*** *branch* of Alps literature (アルプス文学). ¶Poultry is a ***profitable*** *branch* of farm work. 養鶏は農家の有利な事業の一つだ. ¶a tree with ***shapely*** *branches* 枝振りのよい木. ¶one particular ***specialized*** *branch* 専門化した一部門. ¶the twelve ***terrestrial*** *branches* 十二支. ¶the ***two*** *branches* of the English race 英国民族の二支流. ¶scholars and experts in ***various*** *branches* of knowledge 各方面の学者および専門家. ¶a ***worthy*** *branch* of learning 一つのりっぱな学問.

Q^2 a ***Cabinet*** *branch* 内閣の一部局. ¶open a ***Japan*** *branch* 日本に支店(部)を開設する. ¶The ***olive*** branch is the symbol of peace. オリーヴ樹の枝は平和の象徴である. ¶an ***overseas*** *branch* 海外支店(所). ¶Uguisu in ***plum*** *branches* singing their welcomes to spring. 春を迎えてさえずる梅のうぐいす.

P Monkeys leap ***from*** *branch* to *branch*. さるが枝から枝へ飛ぶ. ¶the growth of journalism ***in*** all its *branches* 各部門における新聞事業の発達.【類】the Civil Service (文官) ***in*** all its *branches* ‖ He is well versed ***in*** the higher *branches* of military knowledge. 彼は高級な軍事知識に通暁している. ‖ spread out ***in*** *branches* like a tree 木のように枝の広がる.

P^2 establish a *branch* ***for*** the special accommodation of ... 特に...のために支部を設ける. ¶a *branch* ***of*** the Oyama family 小山家の分家 ‖ an important *branch* ***of*** instruction in schools 学校の重要な一教科目 ‖ in every *branch* ***of*** human endeavor 人間活動のあらゆる部門において. ¶*branches* ***of*** learning 学問の分科. ¶His speciality was psychology—one important *branch* ***on*** the great tree of knowledge. 彼の専門は知識という大木の大切な一枝である心理学であった.

branch, *v.* 分岐する.

M *branch* ***away*** to the left 左方へ分岐する. ¶The tree *branches* ***forth*** (=***out***) in spring. この木は春に枝を出す. ¶*branch* ***out*** 枝を出す; 岐路に入る ‖ *branch* ***out*** one's business 商売を新方面に拡張する ‖ *branch* ***out*** into a long extempore dissertation わき道に入ってその場の思いつきで長々と論じる.

M^2 *branch* ***off*** from the main road (line) 本道(など)から分岐する ‖ *branch* ***off*** in all directions [鉄道線路などが]八方に分岐する.【類】*branch* ***off*** from the trunk line / The street *branches* ***off*** at this point.

brand, *n.* (**1**) 商標, 印(しるし); 品質.

V The most bearish and crusty of man grows affable and optimistic when ***smoking*** the *brand* he loves. くまのように粗暴で無愛想な人間でも自分の好きなタバコをすっていると愛想よく楽天的になるものだ.

Q an ***approved*** *brand* 一般に認められた商標(品). ¶We use only the ***best*** *brand* of wine and spirits. こちらではぶどう酒や酒類は最優良品だけ使っています. ¶a ***famous*** *brand* of safety razor 名の通っている印の安全かみそり. ¶one's ***favored*** *brands* いつも使う商品. ¶the most ***popular*** *brand* on the market その種の中で最も人気のある商品. ¶The ***previous*** *brand* is obliterated. 前の焼印は消してある. ¶a ***standard*** *brand* 標準の品. ¶a ***wellknown*** *brand* 有名品(メーカーもの).

Q^2 a popular ***cigarette*** *brand* 一般向きのシガレット.

P a tin of condensed milk ***of*** a *brand* which has a bear for trade-mark くま印のコンデンス・ミルク一かん.

P^2 There are two *brands* ***of*** the article on the market (=in the trade). その品は市場に二種出ている.

(**2**) 燃えさし.

P^2 a *brand* ***from*** the fire 火の燃えさし.

brand, *v.* らく印を押す; 印をつける.

M He may be ***justly*** *branded* as a coward. 彼はおく病者だと言われても仕方がない.

P He is *branded* ***as*** an impostor (traitor). 彼は世間から詐欺師(裏切者)とされている. ‖ We *branded* him ***as*** a Shylock. われわれは彼にシャイロック(強欲者)というあだ名を付けた.【類】*brand* a person ***as*** a seditious man. ¶That is *branded* ***in*** my memory. それは私の記憶に染込んでいる. ¶He was *branded* ***with*** infamy. 彼は汚名をきせられた ‖ goods *branded* ***with*** the name ... ...の名の付いている商品.

brandish, *v.* 振り回す.

P *brandish* a weapon ***over*** one's head 武器を頭上に振りかざす.

brass, *n.* 真ちゅう；吹奏楽器；《米俗》将軍連.

Q² *Army (Navy) brass* 将軍(提督)連. ¶*sounding brass* 吹奏楽器.

P articles *in brass* 真ちゅう製の品. ¶engrave *on brass* 真ちゅうに刻む.

brat, *n.* 小僧, ちび.

Q a *disgusting little brat* 小なまいきな(いまいましい)小僧. ¶a *skinny brat* やせこけたちび.

brave, *v.* 冒す.

M *brave* death *a hundred times* 数限りなく死線を越える. ¶*brave* the matter *out* その件を敢然とやり通す.

brave, *a.* 勇敢な.

P He is *brave by* nature. 彼は生来勇敢だ. ¶She is *brave for* a woman. 女にしては勇敢だ. ¶He was *brave in* defense. 彼の守備はりっぱだった. ¶the bravest *of braves* 勇者中の勇者. ¶*brave to* recklessness 無鉄砲な.

bravery, *n.* 勇敢.

Q *personal bravery* 一個人としての勇敢さ.

P He is unrivalled *in bravery.* 彼は勇敢無比である.

bravo, *n.* 凶漢.

Q an *Italian bravo* イタリア人の暴漢.

brawl, *n.* けんか, 殴り合い.

Q² a *bar brawl* 酒屋でのけんか. ¶a *street brawl* 街上のけんか.

P go *for* a *brawl* 殴り合いを始める.

bray, *v.* どなる.

M *bray forth* insults 大声でののしる. ¶*bray out*＝utter loudly and harshly 大声をあげる, どなる.

brazen, *v.* 厚かましくやる.

M I'm resolved to *brazen* it (＝the business, affair *or* matter) *out.* 心臓を強くしてその仕事をやり通そうと決心している.

M² *brazen* it *through* どこまでもやり通す.

brazier, *n.* 火ばち.

Q² a *charcoal brazier* 火ばち.

P Warm your hands *over* the *brazier* a bit. 火ばちでちとお手をおあぶり下さい.

breach, *n.* 破れ口, 破壊；違犯；不和.

V This *caused* (＝*produced*) a *breach* of friendship between them. これで二人は仲違いになった. ¶*cause* a breach of the peace by shouting in the street 外で大声を張上げて治安妨害となる. ¶*commit* a *breach* of international practice 国際的慣習を破る. ¶*heal* the *breach* 仲違いを直す. ¶The battery had *made* a *breach* in the wall. 砲兵中隊は城壁を一箇所打破った. ¶He was the first to *mount* the *breach.* 彼が城壁の破れ口の一番乗をした. ¶Thus was the schism originated which steadily *widened* the *breach* between the two rivals. かくしてその二人の競争者の間に不和を生じそのすきまが益々拡大した.

Q The sea made a *clear breach* over the vessel. 波浪が見事船を越した. ¶it was a *flagrant breach* of their solemn treaty obligations to ... それは...に対する彼らの厳かな条約上の義務をふみにじったものであった. ¶a *grave breach* of discipline 重大な規律違反. ¶The *breach* appeared to be *practicable.* 城壁を打破ることはできそうに見えた. ¶an *unpardonable breach* of etiquette けしからぬ無礼の振舞.

Q² The *East-West breach* widened. 東西間の離反が大きくなった.

P stand *in* the *breach* 攻撃の矢面に立つ.

P² a *breach between* friends (two parties) 友人(など)の間の不和. ¶a *breach in* a garment 着物のほころび. ¶a *breach of* the Constitution (law) 憲法(など)違反. 【類】a *breach of* the rule (regulation) / a *breach of* the Copyright Act (著作権法) / a *breach of* duty / a *breach of* promise / a *breach of* contract ‖ a *breach of* trust 背任 ‖ a *breach of* prison 破獄 ‖ a *breach of* public peace 治安妨害 ‖ a *breach of* courtesy 失礼. 【類】It's a *breach of* etiquette. ‖ There is no *breach of* confidence involved. 何ら不信の意味は含まれていない. ¶a *breach upon* kingly power 王権の侵害. ¶the *breach within* party ranks 党内陣がさ連のあつれき.

bread, *n.* パン, 食物；生計.

V *bake bread* パンを焼く. ¶I could have *begged* my *bread* with him all over the world. あの人となら世界中こじきをして回ることもできた. ¶He has *broken bread* with me. 彼は私と同じかまの飯を食った男だ. ¶*butter* one's *bread*＝spread bread with butter *or* spread butter on bread パンにバターを塗る ‖ He knows on which side his *bread* is *buttered.* 彼は自分の利益になることを心得ている(現金だ). ¶The *bread* is *cut up.* パンが小さく切ってある. ¶*earn* one's *bread* by the sweat of one's brow 稼いで生計を立てる. 【類】*earn* one's daily *bread.* ¶*eat* the *bread* of idleness 座食する. ¶he *gained* his *bread* as ... 彼は...として生計を立てた. ¶succeed in *making* one's *bread* 生計の道にありつく. ¶*spread bread* with butter パンにバタを付ける. ¶*take* the *bread* out of one's mouth 生活手段を奪う. ¶*toast bread* パンをトーストにする.

Q *brown bread* 黒パン. ¶a slice of *buttered bread* 一切のバタパン. ¶*clammy* (＝*heavy or doughy*) *bread* ねばねばするパン. ¶earn their *daily bread* 彼らの日々のパンをもうける. ¶*eucharistic bread* 聖さんのパン. ¶My cook bakes *excellent bread.* 家のコックは良いパンが焼ける. ¶a poor woman who earns very *hard bread* indeed by mending of stockings くつ下の修繕をして実際細い生活を立てる貧しい女. ¶The *bread* is *stale.* このパンは古い. ¶*unleavened bread* イースト菌を入れないパン. ¶*toasted bread* トーストパン. ¶*white* (*brown*) *bread* 白(など)パン. ¶*whole-meal bread* [最も栄養価のある部分を含めた] 全粉製パン.

Q² *raisin bread* [干]ぶどうパン. ¶*rye bread* 裸麦のパン. ¶*whole-wheat bread* 全小麦粉のパン.

P Man shall not live *by bread* alone. 人はパンのみにて生くるものに非ず. ¶a loaf *of bread* 一塊のパン ‖ a slice (＝piece) *of bread* 一片のパン ‖ a crust *of bread* 一片のパンの皮 ‖ The breaking *of bread* together is an expression of friendship. 食事をともにするのは友情の表われである. ¶I like jelly *on* my *bread.* 私はパンにジェリをつけたのが好きだ. ¶He is *out of bread.* パンにあぶれている(失業している).

breadth, *n.* 幅.

Q *four breadths* of silk 四幅の絹布. ¶to a *hair's breadth* 寸分の違いなく ‖ miss the target by a *hair's breadth* ほんのちょっとのとこで的がはずれる ‖ tend even by a *hair's breadth* to advance this art ほんのちょっぴりでもこの技能を延ばそうとする ‖ be within a *hair's breadth* of starving (drowning) 餓(溺)死寸前にある. ¶a *hand's breadth* 手だけの幅.

P The house is forty feet *in breadth.* その家は間口が四十フィートある.

P² a *breadth of* cloth 一幅の布. ¶a proof of his *breadth on* mind 彼の心の広さの証拠.

breadwinner, *n.* 稼ぎ手.

Q² *women breadwinners* 婦人の稼ぎ手.

P² the *breadwinner for* ... ...に取っての財源.

break, *n.* 破損；休息；破壊；中断；ぼっ発；ブレーキ；《米》運；〚玉つき〛連続得点；《米》失策, へま.

V *commit* a *break* of etiquette 不行儀なことをする. ¶The cinema director discovered the actress and *gave* her a *break.* その映画監督がその女優を発見して始めて彼女に役を割り振った. ¶Let's *have* a *break.* 《口語》一休みしよう. ¶The prisoner *make* a *break* for freedom. 囚徒が脱獄した. ‖ He *made* a *break* of 23,769. 〚玉つき〛彼は一キュー二万三千七百六十九出した.

Q This is an *agreeable break* in the ordinary routine. これがきまりきった仕事の間にはさまる一つの変った仕事でうれしい. ¶There was an *awkward break* in delivery. 演説中不体裁な絶句をした. ¶make a *bad break* 《米》へまをやる. ¶represent a *complete break* with an old tradition 古い伝統と完全に絶縁する. ¶A *delightful break* in the voyage across the Pacific is the stop at Honolulu. 太平洋航海中の愉快な中休みはホノルル寄航である. 【類】a *delightful break* in the train journey (途中下車). ¶a *diplomatic break* 国交断絶. ¶an *even break* 五分五分のチャンス. ¶*Interesting breaks* in the journey may be made at several points. その旅行中数カ所で愉快な途中下車ができる. ¶There was *no break* in the rains. 雨の止み間がなかった.

Q² a *mass prison break* 囚人の大挙脱獄. ¶a *news break* (＝release) ニュース提供.

P *at* [the] *break* of day 夜明けに. ¶*during* a *break* in the official duties 忙中閑を得て. ¶We started *with* the *break* of day. 僕らは夜が明けるなり出発した. ¶The line continued for ten generations *without* a *break.* その血統は十代連綿と続いた. ‖ He has been staying in Japan over 25 years *without* a *break.* 彼は一度も帰国しないで二十五年以上日本に住んでいる. 【類】I travelled to London *without* a *break.*

P² There was a *break in* the conversation. 話がちよっと途切れた. ‖ There was a *break in* the programme. [会・興行などにおける] 進行に支障があった(舞台に穴があいた). ‖ a *break in* a levee 堤防の決壊. ¶a *break in* the continuity 『ラジオ』放送劇の切れ目(説明個所・音楽など). ¶at the *break of* June 六月の初めに ‖ *breaks of* passion 情熱の燃え上がり ‖ a *break of* voice 声変り ‖ a *break of* diplomatic relations 国交断絶. ¶It was a *break with* tradition. それは新例を開いたものであった. ¶a *break with* the past 過去の清算.

break, *v.* 破る; 馴らす; 分ける; 破れる; ぱっ発する; 衰弱する; 離散する.

M They *broke away* the bars which kept him prisoner. 彼が入獄している刑務所(鉄格子)を破った. ‖ *break away* from home 突然家出する. ¶*break away* from the old conventions 古来の伝統を破る.【類】*break away* entirely from its traditions / *break away* from a friend (絶交する). ¶A cry *broke forth*. 泣声が突然聞えた. ‖ He *broke forth* into a martial air. 彼は急に軍歌を歌いだした.【類】Their applause *broke forth* with enthusiasm. ‖ The plum *broke forth* in green. 西洋すももの木に青葉が出て来た. ¶*break free* from a prison 脱獄する. ¶*break* the news *gently* その知らせを(びっくりしないように)除々に打明ける. ¶The dog has *broken loose*. 犬が抜けだした. ‖ She *broke loose* from America's leading strings. その国は手を引いてもらっていた米国を(独立独歩のために)振り切った. ¶The locked case was *broken open*. 錠のおりている箱をこじ明けた.【類】He has *broken open* the door. / A riot *broke out*. / fighting (violence) *broke out* / The strife *broke out* afresh. / A revolution *broke out*. ¶Cholera has *broken out*. コレラが発生した. 【類】A storm (fire) *broke out*. ‖ A rebellion (An insurrection) *broke out*. 反乱(暴動)が起った.【類】War *broke out*. / Fire *broke out* in the banker's (at the pier). ‖ The whole meeting *broke out* in cheers. 一同が破れるばかりのかっさいをした.【類】The audience *broke out* into jubilant applause (盛んなかっさい). / *break out* into an exclamation ‖ He is liable to *break out* into furious passions. 彼はすぐかっとなる. ‖ *break out* into open rebellion 大っぴらに謀反する ‖ The measles *break out* in the skin. はしかは皮膚にでる. ‖ His face *broke out* into ulcers. 彼の顔にかいようが吹きだした. 【類】Rashes (吹出物) *broke out* on his chest. ‖ Beriberi *broke out* in the Siamese Navy. シャムの海軍内で脚気が出た. ‖ Trees are *breaking out* into buds. 木が芽をふきだした. ‖ *break out* into a cold sweat 冷汗をかく ‖ Her face *broke out* with pimples. 彼女の顔に吹出物がでた. ‖ Poetry *broke out* into a flowering time. 詩歌がけんらんを競う時代に入った. ‖ He did this to prevent it from *breaking out* into violence. 彼はそれが表面化した暴力にならないように努力した. 【類】Typhus (チブス) threatens to *break out* through the flood-devastated area. ¶The band will *break out* with the strains of "Auld Lang Syne." そのバンドはまず「なつかしのふるさと」の曲から始める. ¶An alarm of fire in the adjoining building caused the play at the theater to be *broken short off*. 隣が火事だという警報で芝居が中止になった.

M² The power generator *broke down*. 発電機がこわれた. ‖ *break down* the barriers of racial bias (discrimination) 人種的偏見(差別)のかきねをとり去る. 【類】*break down* economic barriers / *break down* the *barrier* between ... and ... / *break down* the old prejudice (偏見) ‖ The plan has *broken down*. 計画は失敗に終った. ‖ He has completely *broken down* [in health]. 彼はすっかり身体をこわした. ‖ He is *broken down* in disappointment. 彼はすっかり落胆している.【類】His health *broke down* because his business broke up. / quite *broken down* with sorrow ‖ The argument *broke down*. その議論は立たなかった. ‖ *break down* to one's naked personal merits 裸一貫になる. ¶*break in* while others are speaking 人の話の中に割込む ‖ *break in* with a jest 横合から冗談口をたたく ‖ Thieves had *broken in* during the night. 夜中に盗賊が押入った.【類】*break in* by the window. ¶*break in* on the thoughts of ... 突然...という考えが浮ぶ. ¶The booming of cannon occasionally *broke in* upon the singing of the psalms. 大砲のどんという音が賛美歌の歌い声を時々消した. ‖ The hooting of an owl *broke in* upon the quiet of the place. ふくろうの声がその地の静寂を不意に破った. ‖ Her pastoral quiet (牧師生活の静けさ) was sometimes *broken in* by the excitement of a visit to New York. ‖ *break in* animals to labor 動物をならして労役につかせる. ¶He is *broken in* to the work. 彼はその仕事になれている. ‖ *break in* a new pair of shoes 新調のくつを足に慣らす. ¶*break off* the old usage of ... ...という古い慣習を打破する.【類】*break off* one's habits ‖ *break off* all relations with her 彼女とは一切手を切る. 【類】*break off* diplomatic relations with ... ...との外交的関係を断絶する.【類】*break off* one's writing of a letter / The speaker *broke off* a few seconds till he found proper words to make his idea clearer. / *break off* one's studies and hurry back to ... ‖ The handle is *broken off*. ハンドル(手)がとれている. ‖ *break off* from ... ...から脱け出す ‖ The conference *broke off* at noon. 会議は正午に散会した. ‖ The ship *broke off* from her moorings. 同船は停泊所から[あらしなどで]流された. ‖ resuming now where I *broke off* in my last, I am in my way to remark to you that ... この前の続きを申し上げますが... ‖ I *broke off* the conversation. 話を途切らした. 【類】*break off* one's remarks / *break off* laughing (crying) ‖ He *broke off* a branch of the tree. 彼は一枝折った. 【類】*break off* a twig with a snap (ぽきんと) ‖ The engagement has been *broken off*. 婚約が破れた.【類】*break off* a match (marriage) ‖ *break off* with him 彼と絶交する ‖ *break off* one's engagement with a person 人との約束を破談にする. ¶The crowd *broke up*. 群集は四散した. ‖ The meeting was *broken up* by the police. 会合は警官の手で解散させられた.【類】Our school *breaks up* (休みになる) about three weeks hence. / The assembly *broke up* ten p.m. / The conference *broke up* on Oct. 1. / The garden party *broke up* at 6 p.m. / The conference *broke up* resultless. ‖ *break up* the blackmarket やみ市場を解散させる ‖ Let us have a class meeting before we *break up* for the vacation (=holidays). 休暇で散らばる前に一度クラス会をやろうじゃないか. ‖ The old man is *breaking up*. 老人は大変弱くなった. ‖ The earth is *breaking up*. 土割れしている. ‖ *break up* into small fractions 小党に分裂する ‖ families that have been *broken up* by war 戦争でめちゃめちゃになった家族. 【類】homes *broken up* by separation or divorce ‖ Labor troubles are constantly *breaking up*. 労働争議は絶えず起っている. ‖ Difference of opinion *broke* the party *up* into camps. 意見の相違で党が数派に分れた. ‖ He is quite *broken up*. 彼はひどく弱っている. ‖ *break up* crust of the soil 耕地の堅い上層を打ちくだく ‖ *break up* monotony 単調を破る ‖ The steamer will be *broken up* for scraps その汽船は解体してスクラップになる. ‖ *break up* a business 廃業する ‖ *break up* housing bottlenecks 住宅問題の隘路(あい)を切り開く ‖ *break up* old industrial combines 古い企業合同体を解体する. ¶*break up* a household 世帯を畳む ‖ try to *break up* picket lines 『労』ピケラインを突破しようとする ‖ New suckers *break up* from the roots. 新しい球根が根から分出する. ‖ *break* it *up* into its component parts それをその成分に分析する.【類】*break* the sentence into separate thoughts in the interest of clarity and ease of reading.

P *break* a bamboo stick *across* one's knee 竹の棒をひざに当てて折る. ¶She christened the ship *breaking* the ceremonial bottle of wine *against* her side. 彼女は儀式用のぶどう酒びんを舷側に打ち当ててこわし船の命名式をやった. ‖ waves *breaking against* the shore (rocks) 岸(など)にぶつかって砕ける波. ¶The exchange value of the yen finally *broke below* the $20 level Wednesday morning. 水曜日の朝には円の為替がいよいよ二十ドル台を割った. ¶Its white, glittering surface was *broken by* a black spot. その白いぴかぴかした表面に一つの黒斑が現れていた. ¶*break from* a prison 脱獄する ‖ *break from* a party (an alliance) 党派(など)から脱退する. ¶He is *broken in* health. 彼は健康を損じている. ‖ Their faces *broke in* ripples of mirth. 彼らの顔に笑いの小波が立った. ‖ The dish was *broken in* three pieces. さらが三つに破れた.【類】*break in* fragments (砕片) / The ship was *broken into* two pieces. / The mirror *broke into* splinters (かけら). ¶Thieves *broke into* his house. 泥棒が彼の家にはいった. 【類】The store was *broken into*. ‖ *break into* smithereens (=a thousand atoms) 粉みじんに破れる.【類】The bottle was *broken into* several (small, a dozen) pieces. ‖ She *broke into* a smile. 彼女はにっこり笑った. ‖ *break into* exclamations of wonder あっと嘆声をあげる. 【類】

These pretty girls, at the slightest provocation, *break into* dimples, into smiles, into silvery peals of laughter. ‖ The entire audience *broke into* loud and uncontrolled laughter. 満場どっと笑いくずれた. ‖ He *broke into* a desultory chat with me over his business affairs. 彼の仕事のことについて私と雑談に入った. ‖ *break into* a conversation 会話を始める ‖ *break into* tears (sweat, a wail) 涙(など)をだす ‖ *break into* a quarrel upon trifling things つまらないことでけんかを始める ‖ a wave *breaking into* foam 砕けて白泡となる ‖ My face *broke into* perspiration. 顔に汗がでた. ‖ The horse *broke into* a gallop. 馬がかけ足になった. ¶ *break* oneself *of* the practice その習慣を打破する ‖ *break* a child *of* a habit 子供の習慣を破る. ¶ surf *breaking on* the shore 岸に砕ける波. ¶ *break* a bottle of wine *on* her bow [船の命名式で]ぶどう酒のびんを船首に当てて割る ‖ The scene *broke on* his sight. 突然その光景が見えて来た. ¶ *break out of* prison (=jail) 脱獄する. 【類】 The horse *broke out of* the stable. ¶ A heavy sea *broke over* her aft. 荒波が船尾に打つかって砕けた. 【類】 Waves mountain-high *broke over* the reef. ¶ A skater *broke through* the ice. 氷が割れてスケートをやっていた人が落ちた. ‖ *break through* the enemy's line 敵の戦線を突破する ‖ *break through* the cordon of police 非常線を潜る. 【類】 The mounted policeman *broke through* the throngs of people. / The river *broke* through its banks, and flooded the country for many miles around. ¶ wild horses *broken to* saddle or harness 乗馬用・馬車用に馴らした荒馬 ‖ It has *broken to* atoms. みじんになった. 【類】 The vase has *broken to* pieces. ‖ I *broke* this bad news *to* him. この悪い知らせを彼にもらした. ¶ The horse *broke under* weight. 馬は重荷にたえずへたばった. ¶ He *broke upon* my seclusion. 彼は僕の閑居を不意に訪問した. ‖ *break* in *upon* one's privacy 独りで室にいる所へ無断で立入る ‖ *break with* a friend 友人と絶交する. 【類】 She should have *broken with* him altogether. / *break with* the army ‖ his philosophy *breaks* decisively *with* ... 彼の哲学は...と全然行き方を異にしている ‖ *break with* all the old traditions あらゆる古い伝統を捨てる. 【類】 Great geniuses *break with* the past.

breakage, *n.* 破損.

V be more apt to *cause breakage* 破損を生じやすい.

P[2] the *breakage in* the water main 水道本管の破損個所.

breakdown, *n.* 衰弱; 停止; 破壊.

V No *breakdown* of the number is *given*. その総数の小わけは示されていない.

Q in case of an *electric* or *mechanical breakdown* 停電または機械破損の場合に. ¶ have a *nervous breakdown* 神経衰弱にかかっている. ¶ *physical* and *nervous breakdown* 肉体的精神的障害.

P[2] *breakdown from* overwork 過労からの身体の衰弱. ¶ since his *breakdown in* health 彼が健康を害してから. ¶ a *breakdown in* negotiation with ... ...との交渉の決裂 ‖ a *breakdown of* machine 機械の破損. 【類】 the *breakdown of* modern civilization ‖ the *breakdown of* the total is this その合計の内訳は次の通りである. ¶ the *breakdown of* the transportation system 交通網の支障. ¶ owing to a nervous *breakdown through* overwork 過労からきた神経衰弱により.

breaker, *n.* 破る物; くだけ波.

Q[2] an *ice breaker* (=icebreaker) 砕氷船. ¶ a *jail* (=*prison*) *breaker* 牢破り. ¶ a *law breaker* 違法者. ¶ a *peace breaker* 平和かく乱者. ¶ a *record breaker* in exhibitions 展覧会中のレコード破り. ¶ a *strike breaker* スト破り.

P *breakers on* the beach (rocks) いそ波(岩にくだける波).

breakfast, *n.* 朝食.

V *eat breakfast* 朝食を食べる. ¶ I have *finished* my *breakfast*. 朝食を済ました. ¶ I have not yet *had* my *breakfast*. まだ朝飯を食べない. ¶ *Serve breakfast* immediately. すぐ朝飯を出してくれ. ¶ She had to *snatch* her *breakfast* standing. 彼女は大急ぎで朝飯を立食しなければならなかった. ¶ I *swallowed* my *breakfast*. 朝飯をかっ込んだ. ¶ *take breakfast* 朝飯を食べる.

Q after an *early breakfast* 朝飯を早く食べてから. ¶ have a *hasty* (=*hurried*) *breakfast* 急いで朝飯を食う. ¶ *plain breakfast* 簡単な朝飯. ¶ after a *substantial breakfast* しっかり朝飯を食べてから.

Q[2] *meat breakfast* 肉付の朝飯.

P I always drink tea *at breakfast*. 朝飯のときはいつも茶を飲む. ¶ I did some work *before breakfast*. 朝飯前に少し仕事をした. ¶ I take an egg *for breakfast*. 私は朝飯に卵を食べる.

breakfast, *v.* 朝飯を食う.

P I *breakfasted on* poor coffee and bread. まずいコーヒーとパンで朝飯を済ました. 【類】 *breakfast on* fish.

breaking, *n.* 破ること, 砕けること.

Q[2] *jail breaking* 脱獄. ¶ *law breaking* 違法.

breakup, *n.* 瓦解(がかい).

P[2] until the recent *breakup of* the feudal system 最近の封建制度の瓦解まで.

breast, *n.* 胸; 乳房.

V The idea *crossed* his *breast*. その考が彼の胸に浮んだ. ¶ He *felt* her *breast* against his chest. 彼は彼女の乳房が自分の胸に当るのを感じた. ¶ These feelings *filled* his *breast*. その感想で胸が一杯になった. ‖ His *breast* was *filled* with the highest ideals. 彼の胸には至高の理想を宿していた. ¶ She *gave* the *breast* to her baby. 彼女は赤児に乳をのませた. ¶ His *breast swelled* with pride. 彼は得意にそり身になった. ¶ The thought of his mother *swelled* his *breast*. お母さんのことを考えて胸が一杯になった. ¶ The baby *took* (=*sucked*) the *breast*. 赤児が乳を飲んだ. ¶ *thrill* one's *breast* 心臓の高鳴るを覚える.

Q float on the *azure breast* 青海原に浮ぶ. ¶ He made a *clean breast* of the secret. 彼はきれいさっぱり秘密を打明けた. ‖ make a *clean breast* of past errors of judgment 過去の考え違いを清算する. ¶ mother's *dry breast* 母親の乳の出ない乳房. ¶ a *firm* and *elastic breast* 堅い弾力のある乳房. ¶ *flabby* (=*sagged*) *breasts* ぐんにゃりと垂れた乳房. ¶ The baby is suckled at her *mother's breasts*. 赤ん坊は母の乳を飲んでいる. ¶ a *padded breast* 乳バンドを入れた胸. ¶ *pendulous breasts* (=bosoms) 垂れ乳.

P an infant *at* the *breast*=a suckling 乳飲児. 【類】 a middle-aged (中年の) lady with a child *at* the *breast* ‖ I suckled her *at* this *breast*. 私は彼女をこの乳で育てました. ‖ The child was reared *at* the *breast*. その児は母乳で育った. ¶ He received the bullet *in* the *breast*. 彼は胸に銃弾を受けた. ‖ Her heart was beating violently *in* her *breast*. 彼女の心臓は激しくどうきがしていた. ‖ I have a pain *in* my *breast*. 私は胸が痛む. ¶ stab a person *on* the *breast* 胸を刺す ‖ a soldier with a decoration worn *on* his left *breast* 左の胸に勲章を下げた軍人 ‖ His head sank *on* his *breast*. 彼は頭を垂れた. ¶ He shot the man *through* the *breast*. 彼は銃でその人の胸部を撃ち抜いた.

breast, *v.* 対抗する; 胸につける.

M[2] They gradually forced ahead, *breasting aside* the floes. われわれは水面の氷を排除して推進した.

P He *breasted* himself *to* danger. 彼は雄々しく危険に対抗した. ¶ a veteran general *breasted with* medals and ribbons 多くの勲章を胸にさげた老将軍.

breasting, *n.* 対抗.

Q No success is worthy of the name unless it is won by honest industry and *brave breasting* of the waves of fortune. およそどんな成功も正直な努力で運命の波を勇敢に押し切って得たものでなければその名に値しない.

breast-line, *n.* 胸の線.

Q a rich *curvaceous breast-line* 突き出た豊かな胸の線.

breast-milk, *n.* 母乳.

V children *receiving breast-milk* 母乳を飲む子供たち.

breath, *n.* 息, 呼吸; 微風.

V *bate* one's *breath* 息を殺す. ¶ *blow* one's *breath* against a candle ろうそくをぷっと吹く. ¶ *breathe* the *breath* of liberty 自由を生命とする ‖ *breathe* one's last [*breath*] 息を引取る ‖ The "chivalry" *breathed* her last [*breath*] with the termination of the Middle Ages. 武士制度は中世時代の終結とともに終を告げた. ¶ I *caught* my *breath*. はっとした. ‖ We have all *caught* our *breath*. われわれは皆息を殺した. 【類】 The story is full of surprises which cause the reader to *catch* his *breath*. ¶ stop speaking to *draw breath* 息継ぎに話を切る ‖ *draw* a deep *breath* 息を深くつく. ¶ It was a long time before he could *fetch* his *breath*. 大分たってから彼は息を吹き返した. ¶ *gather* (=*take*) *breath* 息をつく. ¶ I could not *get* my *breath* anyhow. どうしても息をつけなかった. ¶ *give out* (*take in*) *breath* 息を出す(吸う). ¶ *hold* one's *breath* 息を殺す. ¶ *hold* one's *breath* in admiration (wonder, surprise, fear) あっと思わず息をのむ. ¶ I write this to advise him (and others) to "*keep* their *breath* to cool their porridge." 僕は彼(および他人)に向って余計な口をたたかないことをここに勧告する次第である. ¶*lose* one's *breath* in running 走って息を切らす. ¶*perfume* the *breath* 息の香りをよくする. ¶*recover* one's *breath* 息をつく. ¶I trust I have not *spent* (=*wasted*) *breath*. 言ったことがむだにならなかったと信ずる. ¶*sweeten* one's *breath* 息をさわやかにする. ¶I *took breath* when I got my head above the water. 水から首を出して息をついた. ¶It *took* my *breath away*. はっと思った. 【類】It was a sight which nearly *took away* my *breath*. ‖ You *take* my *breath away*. 驚きましたね.

Q He has *bad breath*. 彼は息が臭い. ¶He heard the news with *bated breath*. 彼は息を殺してその知らせを聞いた. ‖ watch with *bated breath* 息を殺して見守る. ¶she was protesting with her *dying breath* that ... 彼女は息を引取るときに...と言い張っていた. ¶He has a *fetid breath*. あの人は息が臭い. ¶the *foul* (=*offensive or bad*) *breath* of heavy smokers 大喫煙家の臭い息. 【類】His *breath* is *foul*. ¶draw (=take) a *full* (=*deep*) *breath* 深く息を吸う. ¶a *hard* and *jerky breath* はげしくてせわしい息づかい. ¶take a *long breath* 深く息を吸う. ¶but in the *next breath* said that ... しかし舌の根の乾かないうちに...と言った. ¶contrive in the *same breath* to extol ... ...も同時にほめ称えようとする. ¶The locality figures in ancient classics as a cherry blossom paradise mentionable in the *same breath* with Yoshino. この地方は吉野と肩を並ぶべき桜の名所として古典に誌されている. 【類】The two cannot be mentioned in the *same breath*. ¶I have *short breath*. 息切れがする. ¶Opposition is the *very breath* of his nostrils. 反対は彼の生命だ. 【類】That ideal is the *very breath* (生命そのもの) of national life.

P *after* [taking] a *breath* 一息ついてから. ¶scream all *in* a *breath* 異口同音にさけぶ ‖ He condemned *in* one *breath* what he approved in another. 彼は善いというそばから悪いといった. ¶I am sometimes short *of breath*. 時々息が切れる. ¶a sailor with evidences of liquor *on* his *breath* 酒臭い息をする水夫. ¶He is *out of breath*. 彼は息をきらしている. 【類】He ran himself *out of breath*. ¶He said *under* his *breath* (=in a whisper). 彼は小声で言った. 【類】talk (sing, laugh) *under* one's *breath*. ¶*with* a whisky *breath* ウイスキー臭い息をして.

P² There was not a *breath in* the air. 少しも風がなかった. 【類】Not a *breath of* wind stirred the surface of the sea. ‖ I had not a *breath of* fresh air all day. 終日新鮮な空気を吸わなかった. ‖ Singularity seems in contemporary art to be the very *breath of* life. 特異性が現代美術の生命その物と考えられる. ¶Coal is indeed the *breath of* life to the shipping industries. 石炭は実に海運業にとって生命そのものである.

breathe, *v.* 息をする.

M *breathe* in *deeply* 深い呼吸をする. ¶*breathe fast* 呼吸が早い. ¶*breathe forth* 息を吐き出す. ¶Everyone *breathed freely* once more. だれもかも安心した. 【類】I did not *breathe freely* (まくらを高くして寝る) until ... ¶He *breathed hard*. 彼ははげしい息使いをした. ¶he *breathed out* reproaches 彼は烈しく非難した. ¶be *still breathing* まだ息がある.

M² *breathe in* (*out*) 息を吸いこむ(吐き出す).

P Once again I *breathed as* a free man. 再び自由の身となった. ¶*breathe into* his hearers a contagious fire 彼の聴衆に燃える熱誠を吹き込む. ¶*breathe on* (=*upon*) window panes (a mirror) 窓ガラス(など)に息を吹き掛ける. ¶*breathe through* the nostrils 鼻で呼吸する ‖ The purity of tone and ardent love of country *breathe through* the book. 純潔な調子と熱烈な祖国愛とが全篇にみなぎっている. ¶*brethe with* difficulty 苦しい息使いをする.

breather, *n.* 一息き.

V pause to *take* a *breather* 一息入れる.

breathing, *n.* 呼吸.

V *cease breathing* 呼吸を止める, 死ぬ.

Q *abdominal breathing* 腹式呼吸. ¶*deep* (*shallow*) *breathing* 深(浅)い呼吸. ¶*irregular breathing* 不規則な呼吸. ¶*labored breathing* 苦しい息づかい.

breathing place, いこいの場所.

Q a *happy breathing place* 絶好のいこいの場所.

breathing space, 休む暇.

Q get a *little breathing space* ちょっと一休みする.

breeches, *n.* もも引.

Q² *knee breeches* 半ズボン.

P a tumbler *in* red *breeches* 赤もも引の軽業師.

breed, *n.* 品種, 種.

V *originate* a *breed* 〘植・動〙新種を作り出す.

Q greyhounds of the *best breed* 最良種の猟犬. ¶a dog of *mixed breed* 雑種の犬. ¶canaries of *various breeds* 各種のカナリヤ.

Q² a *general-purpose breed* 一般向きの品種.

P² a *breed of* pigeons はとの一種.

breed, *v.* 産む; 育てる; はん殖させる.

M *breed out* and *out* 異種交配によって増殖する. ¶Rabbits *breed rapidly*. うさぎは盛んに殖える. 【類】*breed solely* to the beauty standard. ¶be *bred true* to the business その仕事にぴったりするように仕込まれる.

M² *breed in* and *in* 同種交配によって増殖する.

P a man *bred at* a university=a university-trained man 大学出. ¶He was *bred for* the church. 彼は聖職(牧師)に教育された. ¶*breed* animals *from* a stock ある種(たね)から動物を繁殖させる. ¶men *bred in* the most cultivated society 最も文化的な社会に育った人々. 【類】He was born and *bred in* London. / He was *bred in* luxury (poverty). ‖ His love of drink is *bred in* the bone. 彼の酒好きは遺伝だ. ¶He was *bred to* arms. 彼は軍人に育った. ‖ *bred to* the standard 標準に達するように養育されて(共進会出品の鶏など). 【類】What was the trade he was *bred to*?

breeder, *n.* 飼養者.

Q² a *poultry breeder* 養鶏家. ¶a *stock breeder*=stock-breeder 家畜飼養家.

breeding, *n.* 繁殖; 教養, 育ち.

V Hogs *commence breeding* when they are from nine to twelve months old. 豚は生れて九カ月から十二カ月になると子を産み始める.

Q a lady of *good breeding* りっぱな教養のある婦人. ¶of *high* (*low*) *breeding* 育ちのよい(よくない). 【類】One of the most certain evidences of a man of *high breeding* is his simplicity of speech.

Q² the awkwardness and simplicity of *country breeding* いなか育ちの洗練されないぼくとつさ.

P He is English *in* blood and *breeding*. 彼は氏も育ちも英国だ. ¶He is a man *of breeding*. 彼は育ちの良い人だ.

breeze, *n.* 微風, 軟風.

V *enjoy* the cool *breeze* that comes from the water 水の面を渡って来る涼しい風に当る.

V² a pleasant *breeze* was *blowing* from the west. 西から気持の好い風が吹いていた. ¶A *breeze came up*. 風が出てきた. ¶The *breeze died away*. 風が止んだ. ¶A very strong *breeze sprang up*. 随分強い風が吹き出した. ¶The *breezes swept* over the lake. 軟風が湖面をかすめた.

Q enjoy the *cool breeze* 涼む. ¶a *cool, refreshing breeze* 涼しいさわやかな微風. ¶a *fitful breeze* 気まぐれな微風. ¶*a friendly breeze* 順風. ¶a *gentle* (=*soft*) *breeze* 軟風. ¶an *icy breeze* 冷風. ¶a *knife-edged breeze* ripping in straight from the sea 海からまともに吹いて来る身を切るような風. ¶a *light breeze* 軽い風. ¶the *mild breeze* of summer 夏の微風. ¶a *pleasant breeze* 快い風. ¶a *rattling breeze* やかましい風. ¶enjoy a *refreshing breeze* in summer 夏のそよ風を楽しむ. ¶a *soft breeze* that was little more than a whisper ささやくといいたいような軟風. ¶a *stiff breeze* 相当のきつい風. ¶a *wanton breeze* 気まぐれな風.

Q² a *morning breeze* 朝風. ¶the smell of whiffs of the *salt sea breeze* 塩気のある海の軟風のにおい. ¶a fresh *sea breeze* さわやかな海風.

P a ship scudding hither and thither *before* the *breeze* 風に追われてあちこち走る船. ¶trees fanned *by* the evening *breeze* 夕風にあおられる木々. 【類】The leaves were scattered *by* the *breeze*. ¶The tree trembles *in* a slight *breeze*. 樹はそよ風にわななく. ¶The smell of roses and the murmur of voices were wafted to me *on* the *breeze*. ばらの香や人々のささやきが微風に乗って私の方へただよってきた. 【類】The salt smell of the ocean is *on* the *breeze*. / All the bunting (旗) in the town was *on* the *breeze* to welcome him.

P² A *breeze from* the hills is refreshing. 山からのそよ風は気持がよい. ¶*breezes with* a distinct briny flavor 海の香が高い風.

brethren, *n. pl.* → brother.

brevity, *n.* 簡潔; 短時間.
V *cultivate brevity* in style 文体の簡潔を心掛ける. ¶*study brevity* 簡潔を学ぶ.
Q *Editorial Brevities* 片々録. ¶say with *epigrammatic brevity* 警句的簡潔さで言う. ¶comment on with *laconic brevity* 春秋の筆法をもってすれば. ¶*luminous brevity* in business communication 商業文の明快な簡潔さ.
P It was omitted *for brevity*. それは長いので略された. ‖ *For brevity* the Committee on Intellectual Cooperation is called C.I.C. 知識協力委員会は略して C.I.C. といっている. 【類】*For brevity* the Western Association of Motion Picture Advertisers is called WAMPAS.
P² the *brevity of* human life 人生の短さ.
brew, *n.* 醸造.
V *have* a few *brews* ビールを二三杯引っかける.
Q an *excellent brew* 上等の酒. ¶the *first brew* of tea お茶の出花. ¶the *poor brew* of tea (coffee) 紅茶(コーヒー)の出のよくないこと.
brew, *v.* 醸造する; (悪事などが)たくらまれる.
P A plot is *brewing against* the government. 反政府的陰謀が企まれている. ¶*brew* beer *for* home use 自家用にビールを醸造する. ¶Sake is *brewed from* rice. 酒は米で醸造する.
briar, *n.* ブライア・パイプ.
V Will you *have* a *briar* or a weed? パイプになさいますか葉巻になさいますか.
bribe, *n.* わいろ.
V *accept* (=*take*) a *bribe* 収賄する. ¶*give* a *bribe* 贈賄する. ¶*offer* a *bribe* わいろを提供する. ¶*promise* a *bribe* 贈賄を約束する. ¶*receive* a *bribe* 収賄する.
bribe, *v.* 贈賄する.
P *bribe* him *by* costly presents 彼を高価な贈物で買収する. ¶He could not be *bribed from* the path of virtue. 彼は正道を曲げるように買収されなかった. ¶*bribe* one *into* silence (secrecy, doing something) 人にわいろを使って沈黙(など)を守らせる.
bribery, *n.* 贈賄, 収賄.
V *practice bribery*=bribe 贈賄する. ¶*use bribery* わいろを使う.
P He is proof *against bribery*. 彼には収賄の気づかいがない. ¶He was charged *with bribery*. 彼は収(贈)賄で訴えられた.
brick, *n.* れんが.
V *bake* (=*burn or make*) *bricks* れんがを焼く. ¶*deliver* a *brick* at ... れんがを...にぶつける. ¶*hit* the *bricks* 罷業に加わる. ¶*lay bricks* れんがを積む. ¶Jobless graduates *throw bricks* at their alma mater. 就職のできない卒業生は母校を悪く言う.
Q a *dressed brick* 化粧れんが. ¶*Flemish bricks* 鋪装れんが. ¶*red* (*yellow, white, blue*) *bricks* 赤(など)れんが. ¶crumbling *sun-dried bricks* ぼろぼろになる日で焼いたれんが.
Q² *fire* (*wood*) *bricks* 耐火(木)れんが. ¶a *gold brick* 《米俗》怠け者, 仮病使い.
P a building *in brick*=a brick building れんがの建物. ¶a house built *of brick* れんがの家屋. ¶build it *with bricks* それをれんがで建てる.
brick, *v.* れんがで囲う; れんがで作る.
M *brick over* れんがを被せる. ¶*brick up* a wall れんがでかべを作る, れんがでかべのへりをとる.
brickbat, *n.* れんが片.
V *throw brickbats* (bouquets) at ... ...を非難(賞賛)する.
P² a *brickbat at* a politician ある政治家に対する攻撃.
bride, *n.* 花嫁, 新婦.
V The *bride* is *going away* from home. 花嫁が里の家から出かけるところだ.
Q a fully *bedizened bride* 飾り立てた花嫁.
Q² a *picture bride* 写真結婚による花嫁. ¶a *war bride* 戦争花嫁.
bridge, *n.* 橋.
V *build*(=*construct or throw*) a *bridge* over a river 川に橋をかける ‖ The *bridge* is *built* on twenty-eight arches. その橋は二十八個のアーチで支えてある. ¶The *bridge* was *carried* (=*swept or washed*) *away* by the swollen river. 橋は増水で流された. ¶*cross* a *bridge* that spans a river 川にかけてある橋を渡る. ¶*erect* (=*lay or stretch*) a *bridge* across a river 川に橋をかける. ¶The *bridge* was *opened* in 1935. 橋は一九三五年に開通した. 【類】The *bridge* is now *opened* for traffic (交通). ¶*put up* a temporary *bridge* 仮橋をかける. ¶The old *bridge* has been *taken down*. もとの橋は取りこわされた.
V² a *bridge arching* over a river 川の上にアーチを形造る橋. ¶a *bridge spanning* a stream (moat) 小川(など)にかかっている橋.
Q a *cross-over bridge* 跨(こ)線橋. ¶The railway crosses the Tamagawa on a *long bridge*. 汽車の線路は長い橋の上を通って多摩川を越す. ¶"*Low bridge*." 橋に御注意(川船などで低い橋下を通る人への注意). ¶a *natural bridge* 天然橋. ¶*rustic bridges* いなか風の橋. ¶They say this *bridge* isn't *safe*. この橋は安全でないそうだ. 【類】determine whether a *bridge* is *safe* or not before they attempt to cross it.
Q² a *bottom-road bridge* 底路橋. ¶a *brick bridge* れんが橋. ¶a *cast-iron bridge* 鋳鉄製の橋. ¶a *draw bridge* はね橋. ¶a *foot bridge* 徒歩橋(かちばし). ¶a *girder bridge* 〚鉄道〛ガード(鉄橋). ¶lay a *gold* (=*silver*) *bridge* for flying enemy. 退却する敵によい逃げ道を作ってやる. ¶the famous *half-moon bridge* at Kameido 亀戸の有名な半月(太鼓)橋. ¶an *occupation bridge* 鉄道線路または溝渠(きょ)の左右にある農場または所有地をつなぎ合わす橋. ¶an *overroad bridge* 架道橋. ¶a *railway bridge* 鉄橋. ¶a *road bridge* 陸橋. ¶a *suspension bridge* つり橋. ¶a *steel arch bridge* アーチ形の鉄橋. ¶a *stone bridge* 石橋. ¶a *swing bridge* [ワイヤの]つり橋. ¶*a toll bridge* 通行料を取る橋. ¶a *toproad* (=*deck*) *bridge* 頂路橋. ¶a *truss bridge* トラス(構)橋. ¶iron work for a *wood bridge* 木橋の鉄製の部分.
P go *along* (=*across or over*) a *bridge* 橋を渡る. ¶The water of the Thames *at* London *Bridge* is about thirty feet deep. テムズ川のロンドン橋の所は深さ三十フィートある. ¶about a mile *below* the *bridge* 橋から一マイルばかり川下に. ¶cross a moat *by* (=*on*) a *bridge* 橋を渡って堀の向うへ行く ‖ The river is crossed *by* a *bridge*. 川に橋がかかっている. ¶pass *over* (=*on*) a *bridge* 橋を渡る. 【類】a tram passing *over* a *bridge*. ¶The boat is *under* a *bridge*. ボートが橋の下にある. 【類】The boat is passing *under* a *bridge*. ¶span a river *with* a *bridge* 川に橋をかける.
P² a *bridge above* rapids 急流にかかる橋. ¶There are three *bridges across* the river. その川に橋が三つある. ¶The Dutch acted as a *bridge between* Japan and the outer world. オランダ人は日本と外国との橋渡しを勤めた. ¶the 53-arch *bridge on* the Grand Canal near Soochow 蘇州付近の大運河に架した五十三アーチ橋. ¶a *bridge over* a mountain torrent 渓流にかけた橋. 【類】There is a *bridge over* (=*across*) the river.
bridge, *v.* 橋をかける.
P *bridge over* the chasm of ... ...のギャップを埋める ‖ *bridge over* difficulties 困難を切り抜ける.
bridle, *n.* 手綱.
V *give* a horse the *bridle*=lay the bridle on a horse's neck 馬の自由に任せる. ¶*put* a *bridle* on one's tongue 口を慎む. ¶*seize* the *bridle* of a runaway horse 逃げた馬の手綱をとらえる.
P break a horse *to* the *bridle* 馬をならして乗馬にする.
bridle, *v.* 頭をもたげる.
M² Everybody *bridled up* at this remark. この言葉を聞いて一同憤然たる態度を示した.
brief, *n.* (1) 要約, 約言; 〚法〛訴訟趣意書.
V *draw up* a *brief* for a speech 演説の心覚えを作る. ¶*hold* a *brief* for ... ...に対して弁護の役を勤める. ¶*take* a *brief* 事件を引受ける.
Q² *skeleton* (=*outline*) *briefs* 文の骨組(大要).
P This, *in brief* (=to be brief), is the answer to the argument. つまりこれがその議論に対する答弁である. ‖ comments *in brief* 寸評 ‖ News *in Brief*. 短信(新聞の欄名) ‖ the city *in brief* 市井小観.
(2) 《米》ズロース.
Q² a *leg brief* =panties [またのない]ズロース.
brief, *a.* 簡潔な.
P He is *brief of* speech. 彼は寡言だ. ¶to be *brief with* you 手短かに言うと.
brief case, [書類入れの]折かばん.
P papers *in* his *brief case* 彼のカバンの中に詰めこまれている書類.
brier, *n.* いばら.
P He is *in* the *briers*. 彼は悩んでいる
brigade, *n.* 旅団; 隊.
Q a *mixed brigade* 混成旅団.
Q² a *fire brigade* 消防隊.
bright, *a.* 輝ける; りこうな; 晴々した.

M He is not very *bright* ***intellectually***. 彼はあまり頭がよくない.
P She is *bright* ***beyond*** her years. 彼女は年以上に知恵が回る. ¶She is *bright* ***in*** the eye. 彼女は目がぱっちりしている. ¶The garden is *bright* ***with*** sunshine. 庭に日が照っている.
O [as] *bright* as a lark ほがらかな.

brighten, *v*. 明るくする.
M *brighten up* dull moments (one's prospects) たいくつな一とき(その将来)を明るくする.
P a garden *brightening* (=blazed) ***with*** flowers 花が一面咲いている庭.

brightest, *n*. 一番陽気.
P This popular resort is ***at*** its *brightest* at night. この盛り場は夜が一番にぎやかだ.

brightness, *n*. 光明, 光輝.
Q ***dazzling*** *brightness* まばゆい輝き. ¶The sun shines with ***subdued*** *brightness* through the dim veil. 太陽が薄雲を通してやわらかに照っている.

brilliancy, brilliance, *n*. 光輝.
V here and there he ***revealed*** the *brilliancy* of his natural gifts 氏の天才のひらめきが所々にうかがわれた. ¶***subdue*** the *brilliancy* of one's genius 天才のひらめきを隠す.
Q ¶***dazzling*** *brilliancy* 目もくらむほどのきらめき. ¶shine out with ***great*** *brilliancy* さん然と輝く. ¶***pyrotechnic*** *brilliance* 花火のようなさんらんたる美しさ. ¶in recognition of services of ***special*** *brilliancy* in the field 抜群の武勲に対して. ¶human butterflies of ***tropical*** *brilliancy* 熱帯の色彩美を持つ人間のちょうちょう.
P The magazine is distinguished ***for*** the *brilliance* of its contributors. その雑誌は大家ぞろいの寄稿で有名である. ¶the electric sign shines ***with*** a 4,000,000 watt *brilliance* その電光広告は四千キロの強力な光を投げる.
P[2] her *brilliance* ***at*** the piano 彼女のピアノの巧みさ.

brilliant, *a*. 異彩を放つ, めざましい.
P She is *brilliant* ***at*** language. 彼女の語学は素敵だ. ¶a child *brilliant* ***in*** some respect ある点ではすばらしい才能を示す子供. ¶At night these streets are *brilliant* ***with*** a pearly radiance of electricity. 夜間はこの辺の通りは真珠色の電光がきらめいてまばゆいほどだ.

brim, *n*. ふち.
P a glass filled ***to*** the *brim* なみなみと注いだコップ. 【類】fill glasses up ***to*** the *brim*. ¶a vase ***with*** a broad *brim* ふちの広い花びん.

brim, *v*. なみなみと注ぐ; いっぱいになる.
M with eyes *brimming* ***over*** with tears 両眼に一杯涙をためて.
P The river *brimmed* ***over*** its banks. 河水が両岸からあふれ出た. ¶*brim* a cup ***with*** wine ぶどう酒をコップになみなみと注ぐ. ‖ To the student of history, Ghent *brims* over ***with*** memories of great men and great events. 歴史の研究者にとってはゲントは偉人・大事件の思い出豊かな土地である. 【類】This book *brims* over ***with*** interest (興味). ‖ Her eyes were *brimming* ***with*** tears. 彼女は目に一杯涙を浮べていた.

brimful, *a*. あふれるばかり.
P a cup *brimful* ***of*** wine ぶどう酒のなみなみと注いであるコップ ‖ This book is *brimful* ***of*** information on the subject. この本はその問題に関する記事を満載している. 【類】a book *brimful* ***of*** interest ‖ He is *brimful* ***of*** enthusiasm (new ideas).

brine, *n*. 海水.
Q The "***Black Brine***" 黒潮. ¶the ***foaming*** *brine* 荒海.

bring, *v*. 持って来る, もたらす.
M *bring* a child ***abed*** 床に就かせる. ¶What shall I *bring* you ***back*** as a present? どんなおみやげがいいかね. ‖ *Bring* them ***back*** when you are through. 済んだら返して下さい. ¶*bring* a person ***back*** to life 生き返らせる ‖ That has *brought* the whole story ***back*** to me. それで話が全部思い出された. 【類】She labored to *bring* her husband ***back*** to a truer life (真人間にさせる). / be *brought* ***back*** to the former shape ‖ Much booty was *brought* ***back*** by the conquerors. 多くの戦利品が勝利者によって持来された. ‖ *bring* a hysteric person ***back*** to truth from a state of self-deception ヒステリ患者の迷想を是正して自己の本然に引戻す. ¶*bring* the East and West ***closer together*** 東西両洋を一層親密ならしめる. ¶be ***constantly*** *brought* into contact with ... 絶えず...と接触するようになる. ¶*bring* it ***forcibly*** to his notice それについて大いに彼の注意を呼び起す. 【類】It was *brought* ***forcibly*** to my mind by him. ¶*bring* ***forth*** (=produce) young (fruit) 子を産む(実を持つ) ‖ *bring* ***forth*** good results 好結果をもたらす ‖ Idleness and luxury *bring* ***forth*** poverty and want. 怠惰とぜいたくは貧乏のはじまり. ‖ *bring* ***forth*** the usual crop of rumors regarding ... ...について例の通り色々のうわさを生む. 【類】The advance in prices will *bring* ***forth*** increased supplies. ‖ A mountain in labor has *brought* ***forth*** a mouse. 大山鳴動してねずみ一匹. ‖ *bring* it ***forth*** to one's consideration それについて考慮を促す. ‖ *bring* ***forth*** convincing evidence to show that ... 納得のいく証拠を出して...ということをはっきりさせる. ¶*bring* ***forward*** a matter (question) at a meeting 会合の席に事件(など)を持出す. ¶*bring* ***forward*** views 意見を持ち出す ‖ *bring* ***forward*** a case 一例をあげる. 【類】*bring* ***forward*** for comparison a case in which ... / *bring* ***forward*** evidence on the question / many arguments *brought* ***forward*** in favor of ... / *bring* ***forward*** reasons in favor of the view that ... / *bring* ***forward*** an objection (苦情) / *bring* ***forward*** a number of questions / *bring* ***forward*** much evidence in confirmation of his view. ¶it was *brought* ***home*** to me forcibly that ... ...ということが私にはっきり分った ‖ Its importance has been *brought* ***home*** to me very strongly. その重要性は切実に私の胸を打った. ‖ a good way of *bringing* this ***home*** to them is ... このことを彼らに徹底せしめる良い方法は...することである. 【類】*bring* ***home*** to the public mind the practical importance of ... ¶those who are *brought* ***low*** by misfortune 災難にあって落ちぶれた人々. ¶*bring* ***out*** its beauty to the best advantage その美点を十分に発揮させる ‖ add ... to *bring* ***out*** the flavor 味付けに...を入れる 【類】*bring* ***out*** one's genius ‖ *bring* ***out*** fresh demand 新しい要求をもち出す. 【類】*bring* ***out*** a book privately (非売品として) / *bring* ***out*** a translation of a book / *bring* ***out*** a new edition / *bring* ***out*** books within the orbit of any budget (どんな収入の人でも買えるような) ‖ It justifies the publisher in *bringing* it ***out*** again. そういう事情があるのだから出版屋がそれを再版したことはもっともなことである. ‖ I am *bringing* ***out*** a magazine. 私は雑誌を発行しようとしている. ‖ This warm sunshine will soon *bring* ***out*** the flowers. このあったかい陽気ですぐ花が開くだろう. ¶That will *bring* ***out*** what is good in the author. この書によって著者の長所がはっきりするであろう. ‖ *bring* ***out*** sentiment in favor of their party その党に好感を懐かせる ‖ This will *bring* ***out*** more production and more money. これでさらに生産はあがり, 金ももっともうかるだろう. ¶*bring* ***out*** the meaning of ... ...の意味を明かにする ‖ *bring* ***out*** a contrast very strongly 対照をきわめてはっきり感じさせる. 【類】This purple shade (色彩) *brings* ***out*** both black and white in striking relief (はっきりと). ‖ *bring* ***out*** clearly what one intends to convey 自分の言わんとする所をはっきり述べる ‖ *bring* ***out*** facts from darkness into light 世間に知れていない事実を明らかにする. 【類】*bring* ***out*** all the facts ‖ *bring* ***out*** the latent possibilities of developments 進歩の潜在的可能性を発揮させる ‖ the shapely figure of Mt. Fuji *brought* ***out*** in sharp relief against the clear autumn sky 晴れた秋の空にくっきりと浮出した富士の美容 ‖ The biography *brings* ***out*** into clear view all the salient features of his career. その伝記は彼の経歴の荒筋をあきらかにしている. ¶A good doctor and careful nursing alone will *bring* him ***right***. よい医者と行きとどいた看護によってのみ彼の病気は回復するだろう. ¶They *brought* him ***safe*** to land. 彼らは彼を無事に水から陸(おか)へ救い上げた. ¶*bring* all those ***together*** in a (=one) volume これらを一巻にまとめる ‖ *bring* ***together*** a great deal of evidence 数多くの証拠を集める. 【類】*bring* ***together*** a mass of data / *bring* ***together*** many interesting references bearing on ... / *bring* ***together*** evidence pointing in this direction. ¶Fate *brought* them ***together***. 運命が彼らを結びつけた. 【類】*bring* the people ***together*** socially / The book is not scholarly in its methods, but *brings* ***together*** a large mass of interesting information. ¶The waitress is really the geisha modernized and *brought* more ***up-to-date***. 女給は実は近代化して一層時勢に適応せしめた芸妓である. 【類】*bring* theaters ***up to date*** / *bring* them ***up to date*** on world topics. ¶The importance of it was *brought* ***vividly*** home to me. その重要性が私にまざ

まざと感ぜられた. ¶circumstances which have *brought* them ***where they are*** 彼らの今日あるを得しめた事情.

M[2] *bring* ***about*** these results こういう結果をもたらす. 【類】*bring* ***about*** a great advance / *bring* ***about*** a cure / *bring* ***about*** good luck / *bring* ***about*** a good result / *bring* ***about*** a settlement / *bring* ***about*** stability / *bring* ***about*** an amicable solution (友好的な解決) / *bring* ***about*** a better understanding of ... / *bring* ***about*** a genuine improvement (真の改善) / *bring* ***about*** a sweeping change (全面的な変革) / *bring* ***about*** a revolution (革命) in ... / *bring* ***about*** revolutionary changes in all human affairs (革命的な変化) / *bring* ***about*** a great advance in education / It may *bring* ***about*** a change of the Cabinet. / His folly has *brought* ***about*** his ruin. ‖ *bring* ***about*** a truce in the arms race 軍拡競争を停止させる / It failed to *bring* ***about*** the desired effect. / *bring* ***about*** a state of affairs that works to his disadvantage / *bring* ***about*** an unfavorable (better) state of affairs / *bring* ***about*** the consummation of the individual (個人の完成) / *bring* ***about*** the neccessity for ... / *bring* ***about*** a resumption of negotiations (交渉の再開) / *bring* ***about*** the defect of ... / It will *bring* ***about*** a cut in taxes (減税). ¶The news *brought* ***about*** a reversal of feeling in the wheat market. そのニュースで小麦相場に反対の気勢が起った. ¶the failure was *brought* ***about*** by speculation in ... ...への投機は失敗だった ‖ the use of authority to *bring* ***about*** like-mindedness in the people 国民が心を一にするための権力行使 ‖ *bring* ***about*** the wreck of one's hopes 希望を破壊させる ‖ *bring* ***about*** order [議場など]静粛にする ‖ *bring* ***about*** (=realize) a radical reform 根本的に改革する. 【類】*bring* ***about*** closer relationship between ... / fail to *bring* ***about*** an agreement / *bring* ***about*** a hot argument (火を吐く激論). ¶*bring* it ***along*** with him それをいっしょに持って来る. ¶*bring* ***down*** a curtain 幕をおろす ‖ hit and *bring* ***down*** an airplane 飛行機を撃墜する ‖ *bring* ***down*** the game [鳥などの]獲物を射落す. 【類】He fired ten shots, and not one of them *brought* ***down*** a bird. ‖ *bring* the government ***down*** 政府を打倒する ‖ Good harvest will *bring* ***down*** the prices. 豊作のため値が下るだろう. ‖ *bring* it ***down*** to the same basis それ(賃金など)を同じベースにまで引きさげる. ‖ *bring* one ***down*** into the dust 人を倒す, 滅ぼす ‖ *bring* a sword (stick) ***down*** upon one's skull (=head) 頭に一刀(など)を浴びせる ‖ The statistics are *brought* as nearly ***down*** to date as is possible. 統計はできるだけ最近のところまで載せてある. ‖ The book is *brought* ***down*** to the present day. その本は現代まで書きおよんである. ‖ *bring* ***down*** the gallery (=house) 大向うをうならせる ‖ *bring* ***down*** on it the wrath of the God そのことが神の怒りに触れる. ¶*bring* ***in*** a measure 議案を提出する ‖ *bring* ***in*** tea things 茶道具を持ち出す. ‖ *bring* ***in*** a new order 新体制を布く. ‖ *bring* a thing ***in*** from another place よそから物を移入する ‖ A really good article will *bring* ***in*** (=fetch) a handsome remuneration. 本当によい文章だと好い報酬が得られる. 【類】The disposal of the property will *bring* him ***in*** several thousand dollars. / *bring* ***in*** the money due (受取るべき金) ‖ *brought* ***in*** its train ... それに続いて...が起った ‖ *bring* ***in*** a verdict of ... [陪審員が]...という評決を下す. 【類】*bring* ***in*** its verdict of acquittal (釈放) ‖ *bring* ***in*** a law suit against ... ...を告訴する. ¶*bring* ***off*** a major change in the ... ...に大変動を起す ‖ They *brought* ***off*** the passengers on the wrecked ship. 彼らは船客を破船から救い出した. ¶*bring* ***on*** a disaster / *bring* ***on*** an abortion (流産) / *bring* ***on*** a disease ‖ *bring* ***on*** (=cause) an attack of madness 狂乱の発作を起させる ‖ He has *brought* ***on*** an illness by overwork. 彼は働き過ぎて健康を害した. ‖ The poison he took *brought* ***on*** great agony. 彼は飲んだ毒でひどく苦しんだ. 【類】He got his feet wet and this *brought* ***on*** a bad cold. / *bring* ***on*** the miseries of civil war (内戦) / *bring* ***on*** suspicion (discussion) / *bring* ***on*** (=cause) trouble ‖ *bring* ***on*** eruption of the skin 皮膚に吹出もの(発しん)が出来る. ¶*bring* it ***over*** to ... それを...に招来する ‖ It was *brought* ***over*** from China to Japan. それは中国から日本へ伝わった. ‖ *bring* ***over*** passengers in a boat 客を舟で渡してやる ‖ *bring* others ***over*** to one's way of thinking 人を自分の考えに同調させる. 【類】He was *brought* ***over*** to our side. ¶Then coffee was *brought* ***round***. それから一同にコーヒーが出された. ‖ *bring* one's opponent ***round*** 相手を説伏せる(納得させる) ‖ I'll try to *bring* him ***round*** to your views. 君の考えに同調するように説いて見ましょう. ‖ He *brought* ***round*** the conversation to his favorite topics (得意な問題). ‖ The doctor will *bring* him ***round*** all right. 大丈夫あの医者の手で意識を回復する. ¶I am sure the doctor will *bring* him ***through***. 先生はきっと(病人を)なおして下さる. ¶He will soon be *brought* (=come) ***to***. まもなく正気に返るだろう. ¶*bring* him ***under***=subdue him *or* reduce him to obedience 彼を屈服させる. ¶*bring* him ***up*** as a business man (soldier) 彼を実業家(など)に仕込む ‖ *bring* him ***up*** as one's own child 自分の子として育てあげる ‖ children *brought* ***up*** in English 英語で育った子供 ‖ He was *brought* ***up*** in the mountains. 彼は山家に育った. ‖ be *brought* ***up*** in luxury (simplicity, old ways) ぜい沢(など)に育てられる. 【類】those who have been *brought* ***up*** in the idea that ... / be *brought* ***up*** in the most happy surroundings / He was *brought* ***up*** on the farm. ‖ He was *brought* ***up*** in the greatest poverty. 彼は洗うがごとき赤貧の中に育った. 【類】*brought* ***up*** in Christian civilization ‖ *bring* ***up*** large numbers of the fallen to the path of duty 多数の堕落したものを正道に立帰らせる ‖ *Bring* them ***up***, won't you? あれを持って来てくれ. ‖ *bring* ***up*** peace 平和をもたらす ‖ *bring* ***up*** a ship 船を回航する ‖ The troops were *brought* ***up*** in time to repel the enemy from their country. 敵軍を国外に撃退すべく間に合うように軍隊が派遣された. ‖ *bring* ***up*** a subject=introduce a subject to notice 問題を提起する ‖ It was *brought* ***up*** for discussion. それが討議に上った. 【類】The question will be *brought* ***up*** again in the next meeting. ‖ be *brought* ***up*** to light 明るみに持出される ‖ be *brought* ***up*** to justice 正邪を明かにされる ‖ For what crime has he been *brought* ***up***? 彼は何の犯罪であげられたのか. ‖ *bring* him ***up*** to her mark 彼を彼女の思うつぼにはめる ‖ *bring* ***up*** the rear of the procession 行列のしんがりを勤める. 【類】His troops *brought* ***up*** the rear. ‖ *bring* it ***up*** to the standard attained in America それをアメリカの水準まで引き上げる.

P *bring* an action ***against*** ... ...を相手取って訴訟を提起する ‖ evidence *brought* up ***against*** the accused 提出された被告に不利な証拠. 【類】he is the judge to hear charges *brought* ***against*** ... ¶*bring* it prominently ***before*** the public それを公衆の目を引くようにする ‖ be *brought* ***before*** court 裁判ざたになる ‖ He was *brought* ***before*** a court martial. 彼は軍法会議に掛けられた. 【類】These items were *brought* ***before*** the meeting as matters requiring attention / *bring* a question (bill) *before* a meeting (Parliament) ‖ *bring* the matter ***before*** the eyes of the country そのことを国民に示す. 【類】These films will serve to *bring* ***before*** the eyes of the world the natural beauties and picturesque sights of Japan. ¶It has been *brought* ***from*** abroad. それは外国品だ. ‖ He *brought* his wife a very handsome present ***from*** America. 彼は細君に大層りっぱなみやげを米国から持って帰った. ‖ *bring* a sum of money ***from*** the previous account (term) 金額を前勘定(など)から繰越す. ¶The author has revised the book so as to *bring* it ***into*** accordance with recent advances in the science. 著者は該科学における近年の進歩を考慮してその著作を改訂した. ‖ *bring* the question ***into*** the arena of practical politics その問題を実際的政治の舞台に上す(政治上の実際問題とする) ‖ be *brought* ***into*** being (=shape) 具体化される; [本など]出版される ‖ *bring* materials collected ***into*** more manageable shape 集めた材料を整理する ‖ *bring* ***into*** being a peace which will be lasting 永久的な平和を招来する ‖ *brought* him ***into*** association with ... 彼を...の仲間に入れた ‖ She was *brought* ***into*** chance contact with him. 彼女は偶然彼と交際するようになった. 【類】be *brought* ***into*** contact with ... / the girl with whom I was *brought* ***into*** conversation ‖ be *brought* ***into*** close and friendly relations with ... ...と親密な間柄になる. 【類】*bring* us ***into*** the society of agreeable and interesting men ‖ The subject was *brought* ***into*** a condition of hypnotism. 相手は催眠状態に入った. ‖ be *brought* ***into*** court 裁判ざたになる ‖ be *brought* ***into*** currency by ... ...によって一般化する ‖ *bring* it ***into*** disrepute (不評判) ‖ Your influence will materially help to *bring* the plan *into* effect. あなたのお力があればその計画もうまく行くでしょう. ‖ *brought* a person *into* eminence (=prominence) 人に名を成させる. 【類】*bring* a club *into* existence (創立する) ‖ Such a sad story *brings* tears *into* one's eye's. こんな悲しい話を聞くと涙が出て来る. ‖ *bring* it *into* the focus of public attention それを世人注視の焦点に持って来る. 【類】*bring* it *into* fashion (流行) ‖ I have endeavored to *bring* my book *into* harmony with the results of the investigations of recent times. 私は私の著作に最近調査の結果を加味するように努力した. ‖ We must *bring* him *into* our interest. 彼をわれわれの仲間に引入れねばならぬ. ‖ This *brought* it *into* international reputation. このためにそれが世界的名声を博するに至った. ‖ *bring* it *into* line with ... それを…と歩調をそろえさす ‖ This *brought* him *into* unpleasant notoriety. このために彼におもしろからぬ評判が立った. 【類】*bring* it (=put) *into* operation (実施する)... ‖ Five streams of water were *brought into* play. 五本の水流が放出された. ¶ Swimming *brings into* active play nearly all the muscles of the body. 水泳はほとんど全身の筋肉を活動させる. ¶ *bring* [out] *into* strong relief the fact that ... …という事実を強調する ‖ *bring* him *into* the world=give birth to him 彼を生む ‖ *bring into* subjection (repentance) 服従(など)させる ‖ The opening of these art exhibitions *brings* the autumn season *into* full swing. これら美術展覧会が開会されたので美術の秋も正に色深しというべきだ. ‖ *bring* it *into* the service of man それを人間の役に立たせる ‖ *bring* what is in my mind *into* fully effective touch with the mind of the reader 自分の考えを十分読者に貫徹させる ‖ the knowledge he *brings into* the task of ... 彼が…の仕事に活用する知識. 【類】*bring* the peoples *into* better understanding / *bring into* use one's knowledge of English. ¶ *bring* misfortune (trouble, shame) *on* ... 不幸(など)を…にもたらす ‖ be *brought on* trial on spy charges スパイ嫌疑で裁判される. ¶ be *brought to* the attention of ... …の注目を引く ‖ He was *brought to* the verge of bankruptcy. すんでのことに破産する所だった. ‖ be *brought* (=driven) *to* bay 窮地に追いつめられる ‖ *bring to* his bearings 人をそれ相当の地位におく; 人をへこます ‖ His wife was *brought to* bed twenty-one times. 彼の細君は二十一回お産をした. ‖ *bring* it *to* the boil それを役立てる ‖ It *brought* a blush *to* her cheeks. これには彼女も赤面した. ‖ So the gathering was *brought to* a close. かくして散会になった. 【類】The war has been *brought to* a close with the complete triumph of the Allies. / This *brought* that day's examination *to* a close. / *bring* armed aggression *to* an end ‖ To linger at the gate is sweet, and difficult to *bring to* an end. [愛人の]門に低徊するのは楽しいものでちょっと切上げ憎いものだ. ‖ He did his best to *bring to* completion (=fruition) the policy which he had announced. 彼は自分が発表した政策を完成させるために最善をつくした. ‖ *bring* a person *to* disgrace 人の面目を失わせる ‖ A shriek *brought* him *to* the door. 叫び声がしたので彼は戸口へやってきた. 【類】*bring to* our minds the fact that ... ‖ *bring* them *to* their feet 彼らを立たせる ‖ The matter has been so much *brought to* the fore. このことは大いに世人の注目を引くようになった. ‖ *bring* a person *to* grief その人に不覚を取らせる ‖ His library was *brought to* the hammer (=sold at auction). 彼の蔵書は競売に付された. ‖ *bring* a motor-car *to* a halt (=stop) 自動車を止める. 【類】The train was *brought to* a sudden halt. ‖ He was *brought to* court for forgery. 彼は文書偽造の罪科で裁判に回された. ‖ *bring* a criminal *to* justice 犯人を裁判にかける. 【類】be *brought to* judgment ‖ *bring* Germany *to* her knees ドイツを降服させる. 【類】The striker *brought* the employers *to* their knees. ‖ *bring to* his knowledge 彼に知らせる ‖ *bring* a person *to* reason 人に道理をさとらせる ‖ be *brought to* life 生き返らせる ‖ *bring* an interesting relic *to* light 興味ある遺物を発掘する ‖ He threatened to *bring* the matter *to* light. 彼はそのことを明るみへ出すとおどかした. 【類】investigations have *brought to* light the fact that ... / The plot (陰謀) was *brought to* light. ‖ *bring to* life a half-drowned victim of a wreck 海難でおぼれ死かかった者を生きかえらせる ‖ if *brought to* life again この世に生れ返って来たら ‖ *bring* him *to* his senses (=reason) 彼の目をさます ‖ *bring* the patient *to* a sense of conviction that she would be cured 彼女は直るということを確信させる ‖ He tried to *bring* me *to* myself by several means. 彼は私に正気を付けようとして色々手を尽した. ‖ *bring to* nought (=nothing) plans (hope, prospects) ... 計画(など)を水泡に帰せしめる ‖ He *brought* it *to* my notice. 彼はそれを私の耳に入れた. ‖ A striking instance was *brought to* my notice the other day. 先日驚くべき一例が私の注目を引いた. 【類】*bring* it *to* public notice ‖ *bring* it *to* perfection それを完成する ‖ *bring* water *to* the boiling point 湯を沸騰点に達せしめる ‖ be *brought to* ruin 没落する ‖ *bring* one *to* a recollection of ... …をしのばせる ‖ *bring* it *to* the service of ... それを…の用に当てる ‖ *bring* it *to* a speedy conclusion それを速かに終了する ‖ *bring* ... *to* submisson …を征伐する ‖ The author *brings to* his subject a thorough scholarly knowledge and an ability to make his material vivid and amusing. 著者は深遠な学識と材料を生かしておもしろく読ませる才筆をもってその問題を取扱っている. ‖ The revolution *brought* him *to* the surfcae. 彼はその革命で表面に現われた人物であった. ‖ *bring to* terms 従わせる, 意を貫く ‖ The war has been *brought to* a termination (=close *or* an end). 戦争は終った. ‖ be *brought to* trial 裁判にかけられる ‖ Their thrift may be said to be often *brought to* the verge of absolute miserliness. 彼らの節約は全くしみったれとも見られるものが往々ある. ‖ Another hour's ride *brought* me *to* the village. あと一時間(汽車など)に乗ってから村に着いた. ‖ I will have him *brought* up *to* some profession. あれをなにか[頭の方の]職業に仕込んでもらおう. ¶ *bring* land *under* cultivation 土地を開墾する ‖ He was *brought under* suspicion. 彼は嫌疑をかけられた. ‖ *bring* it *under* the notice of ... それを…の目(耳)に入れる ‖ He first *brought* the system *under* my attention. 彼が最初この方法を私の耳に入れた. ‖ be *brought under* review (著書など)批評される. ¶ *bring* discredit and suspicion *upon* one 不信用と嫌疑を自分に招く. ¶ What did you *bring with* you? 何を持ってきたか. 【類】*Bring* your friend *with* you. ¶ This will *bring* London *within* four days of Egypt. これでエジプトから四日間でロンドンに行かれるようになる. ‖ reduce the price so as to *bring* them *within* the reach of all students 一般学生の手にはいるように値を下げる.

O I cannot in any way *bring* myself to eat them. どうしても食べる気にはなれない. ¶ I have *brought* him to see his error. 彼の心得違いをさとらせた.

brink, *n.* ふち, きわ.

P stand *on* a valcano's *brink* 噴火口のふちに立つ ‖ *on* the *brink* of starvation (death, ruin) 飢(など)にひんして. 【類】The country is *on* the *brink* of a serious disaster (災禍).

brisk, *v.* 歩調を早める.

M² The woman *brisked up* to him as if she would fight him. その婦人はまるでけんかを仕かけるかのように彼のそばにばたばたやって来た.

bristle, *v.* 逆立てる, 逆立つ, 剛毛を逆立てる, 林立する.

M² a cock *bristling up* his crest とさかを逆立てている雄鶏 ‖ His hair *bristled up.* 彼の髪が逆立った. ‖ He *bristled* himself *up.* 彼はふん然たる態度をとった. ‖ She *bristled up* as if I had been assaulting her. 私が暴力でも振ったかのように彼女はふん然とした.

P Printers' errors *bristle from* every page. 誤植がどのページにも見える. ¶ the difficulties which *bristle in* these works こうした事業に集まる困難 ‖ *bristle in* anger 怒って顔をふくらす. ¶ The town *bristles with* chimneys (towering buildings). その市には煙突(など)が林立している. 【類】a port *bristling with* thousands of masts / a job *bristling with* technical difficulties / books *bristling with* incorrect statements (間違いだらけ) / The volume *bristles with* misinformation (間違った記事).

Briton, *n.* 英国人.

Q *beef-eating* and *beer-bibbing Britons* 牛肉を食いビールを飲む英国人. ¶ *true-born Britons* きっすいの英国人.

brittle, *n.* カルメ焼.

Q² a *peanut brittle* ピーナッツのカルメ焼.

broad, *a.* 広い.

M The river is *a mile broad* here. 川幅はここでは一マイルある. ¶ I've found the street *much broader* than before. 通りは以前よりずっと広くなっている. ¶ This room is fifteen feet long and *ten broad*. この室は縦が十五フィート横が十フィートある.

P a man *broad in* the beam かっぷくのよい人. ¶He is *broad of* face (chest). 彼は顔(など)幅が広い.

broadcast, *n.* 放送.

V *deliver* over a national hook-up a weekly *broadcast* upon foreign affairs 全国中継で毎週一回海外事情に関する放送をする. ¶*exchange broadcasts* 無電放送を交換する. ¶*have* a *broadcast* from England 英国からの放送を聞く. ¶These *broadcasts* will be able to be *heard* in most parts of the world. この放送は世界中大概の所で聴取ができる.

Q an *international broadcast* 国際放送. ¶a *nation-wide broadcast* on ... …に関する全国向け放送. ¶*sponsored* (*unsponsored*) *broadcasts* スポンサーづき(スポンサーなしの)放送.

Q² a *foreign language broadcast* 外国語放送. ¶a *half-hour broadcast* of the day's news 三十分の当日ニュースの放送. ¶an *overseas broadcast* 海外放送. ¶in a *radio broadcast* ラジオ放送で. ¶a *short-cast broadcast* 短波放送. ¶a *wartime propaganda broadcast* 戦時宣伝放送.

P² *broadcast by* radio=radio broadcast.

broadcasting, *n.* 放送.

V *use broadcasting* for advertising purposes 放送を広告に利用する.

Q *wireless* (=*radio*) *broadcasting* ラジオ放送.

Q² *shortwave broadcasting* 短波放送.

broaden, *v.* 広くなる.

P as one *broadens in* experience 経験を積むにつれて.

broadside, *n.* 片舷(ぱん)斉射.

V *fire* a *broadside* 片舷斉射を行う.

brocade, *n.* にしき.

P dressed *in brocade* にしきを着て.

brocade, *v.* にしきで飾る.

P Hazlitt's prose is as richly *brocaded with* imagery. ハズリットの散文もそれと同様詞藻(しそう)が花やかに織出だされている.

brochure, *n.* 小冊子.

Q a handsomely *got-up brochure* りっぱに装ていを施した小冊子.

Q² a *campaign brochure* (=book) 《米》政党の綱領政策を説明した小冊子.

brogue, *n.* なまり.

Q She spoke with a slight *Irish brogue*. 彼女はちょっとアイルランドなまりがあった.

broil, *v.* 焼(や)く.

P *broil on* coals (a gridiron) 火(など)で焼く. ¶*broil with* salt 塩をつけて焼く.

broken, *pa.* → break.

broker, *n.* 仲買人, ブローカー.

Q² a *blackmarket broker* やみブローカー. ¶a *curb-stone broker* もぐり仲買人. ¶an *exchange broker* 両替屋. ¶a *custom-house broker* 税関手続代弁人. ¶an *insurance broker* 保険周旋人. ¶a *real estate broker* 不動産ブローカー. ¶a *ship broker* 船舶仲買人.

brok[er]age, *n.* 仲買口銭.

Q² *marriage brokage* 結婚媒妁(しゃく)業; 結婚媒妁料.

P² *brokerage on* bills 手形仲買の手数料.

bronze, *n.* 青銅.

Q *phosphorous bronze* in ingot りん青銅棒材.

P cast it *in bronze* それを青銅で鋳る ‖ a statue *in bronze* =a bronze statue 銅像.

bronze, *v.* 青銅色にする.

P His face was *bronzed by* the sun. 彼の顔は日に焼けて黒くなった.

brooch, *n.* ブローチ.

V *wear* a *brooch* ブローチをつける.

Q² a *badge brooch* バッジ形のブローチ.

brood, *n.* 一腹のひな.

V A hen *gathered brood* under her wings. 雌鳥がつばさの下にひなを集めた. ¶The silkworm *produces* six or seven *broods* a year. かいこは一年六七回産卵する.

P² a *brood of* chickens 一腹のひな ‖ a widow with a *brood of* daughters 数人の娘を抱えた未亡人.

brood, *v.* 苦に病む; 考え込む; ひなを抱く.

P *brood over* one's wrongs 自分の非行をつくづく考えてみる. ¶He *broods over* his misfortunes (troubles, ill-fated destiny). 彼は自分の不運(など)をくよくよ思いつめている.【類】*brood over* past grievances (苦難). ¶be *brooded under* hens めんどりに抱かれる.

brook, *n.* 小川.

Q In every *babbling brook* he finds a friend. さらさら流れる小川にも彼は親しみを感じる. ¶a *lazy brook* とろ流れの小川. ¶a *shallow brook* 浅い小川. ¶a *willowy brook* 柳の多い小川.

broom, *n.* ほうき.

Q² a *bamboo broom* 竹ぼうき. ¶a *hair broom* 毛製のほうき.

P sweep *with* a *broom* ほうきで掃く.

broth, *n.* スープ.

Q² *chicken broth* 鶏のスープ.

brothel, *n.* 娼家, 遊女屋.

V *visit* (*frequent*) a *brothel* 娼家に登楼する(通う).

brother, *n.* 兄弟, 同胞.

V *beseech* one's *brother* for ... 兄(弟)の…を欲しがる. ¶*cherish* one's *brother* 弟をかわいがる. ¶I have no *brother* or sister. 私には兄弟がない. ¶*make brothers* with ... …と兄弟の契りを結ぶ.

Q one's *big brother* その兄. ¶my *dear brother* 私の親愛する兄. ¶a *full* (=*whole*) brother [両親を同じくする]兄弟. ¶*gallant brothers* in arms 勇敢な戦友. ¶a *half brother* 異父(母)兄弟. ¶All the men on earth are *human brothers*. 世界の人間はすべて同胞である. ¶one's *little brother* 小さい弟.【類】This is my *littlest brother*. ¶an *older* (*elder*) *brother* 兄.【類】my *oldest brother*. ¶*professional brothers* 同業者(医師など). ¶Language is a characteristic that distinguishes man from his *quadruped brethren*. 言語は人間が獣類と異なる一つの特徴である. ¶a *sworn brother* 盟友. ¶*uterine brothers* or sisters 異父兄弟.

Q² a *blood brother*=a *brother by* blood 血を分けた兄(弟). ¶*cousin brothers* (sisters) 男のいとこ. ¶*fighting brothers* 戦友. ¶*fraternity brothers* 《米》フラト・クラブの会員仲間. ¶one's *kid brother* 《米》小さい弟. ¶*triplet brothers* [男ばかりの]三つ児. ¶a *twin brother* 男子双生児の一人.

P² *brothers in* arms 戦友 ‖ a *brother in* misfortune 苦難をともにする友 ‖ *brothers in* Christ キリストの信者仲間. ¶a *brother of* the half blood 異父(母)兄弟 ‖ a *brother of* the quill 文士. ¶he is *brother to* (=a brother of) ... 彼は…の兄弟だ.

O Harpers & *Bros.* ハーパーズ兄弟商会.

brotherhood, *n.* 兄弟の関係.

V *promote* the *brotherhood* of nations 世界国民の親交を増進する.

Q *International brotherhood* 国際的友情 ‖ the *International Brotherhood* 国際友の会 ‖ the promotion of *international brotherhood* 国際親善の増進. ¶work for the sake of a *universal brotherhood* of man and a lasting peace 世界同胞主義と永久の平和のために働く.

Q² *world* (=*universal*) *brotherhood* 四海同胞.

P² a *brotherhood of* nations 世界国民の親善.

brougham, *n.* 箱馬車.

Q² a *single-horse brougham* 一頭立箱馬車.

brow, *n.* ひたい; まゆ.

V *draw* the *brow* together まゆをひそめる, しかめつらをする. ¶*knit* (=*wrinkle or bend*) the *brows* ひたいにしわを寄せる. ¶*mop* one's *brow* with one's handkerchief ハンカチでひたいをぬぐう. ¶*sweat* one's *brow* 汗みずくになって働く.

Q *arched, well-defined brows* アーチ形の鮮かなまゆ. ¶a pallid student with a *bulging brow* ひたいの突き出た青ざめた学生. ¶a *furrowed brow* しわの寄ったひたい. ¶with a *gloomy brow* 憂うつそうな顔をして. ¶with *knitted brows* ひたいにしわをよせて. ¶mop the *perspiring brow* ひたいの汗をぬぐう. ¶a *protruding* (=*projecting*) *brow* おでこ. ¶*stubby brows* 立毛のまゆ. ¶her "*airy brows*" 彼女の上品なまゆ.

Q² a *beetle brow* [老人などの]飛び出しまゆ毛, 長寿まゆ. ¶a *mountain brow* 山の端.

P put wrinkles *in* his *brow* ひたいにしわをよせる. ¶a kerchief tied *over* the *brow* はち巻. ¶A heavy cloud came *upon* his *brow*. 彼は顔をひどく曇らせた. ‖ A cold perspiration started out *upon* his *brow*. 彼のひたいに冷汗(ひやあせ)が出た. ¶*with* an anxious *brow* 心配げな顔をして.

browbeat, *v.* おどしつける.

P He *browbeat* me *into* accepting the proposal. 彼は威圧的に私にその提案を承諾させた.

brown, *n.* かっ色.

Q The pie had become a *lovely brown*, and it was steaming hot. そのパイは美しいきつね色に焼けてぽかぽか

湯気が出ていた. ¶The water was of a ***muddy brown.*** 水は泥でにごっていた.

brown, *a.* かっ色の.

P a man *brown* ***in*** complexion 渋紙色の顔をした人.

browse, *v.* 新芽を食う.

M² *browse* ***around*** (=***about***) [牛馬が]若草を求めて歩き回る.

P *browse* ***amongst*** the best sellers and thrillers to be found at the bookstall 本屋で一番評判の良い本や大衆小説などを漁(あさ)る. ¶*browse* ***in*** its pages その本の拾い読みをする. ¶*browse* ***on*** young leaves [牛などが]若葉を食う.【類】cattle *browsing* ***on*** the meadow / *browse* ***on*** the green sward (芝生). ¶*browse* ***upon books*** 本を拾い読みする.

bruise, *n.* 打撲傷.

P² a *bruise* ***on*** one's leg (arm) 脚(など)の打撲傷.

brunt, *n.* 衝, 攻撃; 鋭ほう.

V ***bear*** the *brunt* of an attack 攻撃の衝(矢面)に立つ ‖ ***bear*** the *brunt* of criticism やり玉に上げられる.【類】***bear*** the *brunt* of battle (戦闘). ¶***take*** the *brunt* 矢面に立つ.

V² the *brunt* of the system ***falls*** upon ... その制度でばかを見るのは...である.

brush, *n.* はけ, ブラシ; 筆.

V Her face will ***delight*** the painter's *brush.* 彼女の顔は画家が好んで描くだろう. ¶***give*** one's hat a *brush* 帽子にブラシをかける.

Q Give the shoes ***another*** *brush.* くつにもう一度ブラシをかけてくれ. ¶Turner's ***magic*** (=***magical***) *brush* ターナーの霊筆. ¶a ***tapering, pointed*** *brush* 毛筆. ¶use his ***vigorous*** *brush* to paint nature 風景画に雄こんな筆を振う.

Q² a ***boot*** (=***shoe***) *brush* くつブラシ. ¶a ***laundry*** *brush* 洗たく用ブラシ. ¶a ***paint*** *brush* 絵筆. ¶a ***scrub*** (=***scrubbing***) *brush* [泥などをとる]洗いたわし. ¶a ***shaving*** *brush* and kit ひげ剃り用のブラシと道具一式. ¶a ***wire*** *brush* for suede shoes [けばのある]スエード皮用の針金ブラシ. ¶a ***writing*** *brush* 毛筆.

P crush ***at*** a *brush* 一撃で倒す ‖ ***at*** the first *brush* 最初の攻撃で. ¶canvases ***from*** the *brush* of that world-master その世界的巨匠の筆になる油絵.【類】a picture ***from*** the same *brush* / one of six works ***from*** his *brush* / ***from*** the *brushes* of the most eminent contemporary (現代の) artists. ¶The picture was dashed ***with*** a *brush.* この絵は一気呵成に描いたのだ. ‖ make a stroke ***with*** a *brush* 一筆揮う ‖ paint ... ***with*** the *brush* of a lover of Ireland アイルランドを愛する目で...を描く.

brush, *v.* はけではらう; ふれる.

M Their opinions cannot lightly be *brushed* ***aside.*** 彼らの意見は軽々しく片付けてしまうことはできない.【類】He *brushes* ***aside*** all objections (difficulties, oppositions, suggestions). ‖ *brush* ***away*** (=***off***) the dust ほこりをブラシで払う.【類】*brush* ***away*** dirt with a few whisks of the brush / *brush* ***away*** tears with one's sleeve.

M² *brush* ***off*** one's coat / *brush* the snow ***off*** ‖ *brush* the whole matter ***off*** 問題を最初から再検討する. ¶*brush* a person ***over*** with brandy 人にブランデーを一杯飲ませる. ¶*brush* ***up*** [on] one's English 英語にみがきをかける(やり直す) ‖ My English has got rusty; I must *brush* it ***up.*** 英語が下手になったから少しみがきをかけなければならない. ‖ *brush* ***up*** (=refresh) one's memory 記憶を新たにする.【類】I *brushed* ***up*** my recollections of the map of England. / *brush* ***up*** one's acquaintance with another.

P I was *brushed* ***against*** by cyclists. 自転車に乗って走る人たちが私のそばをすれすれに通った. ¶*brush* tears ***from*** one's face 顔から涙をはらいのける. ¶*brush* ***through*** a crowded street 通りの人込みの中を疾過する.

brushing, *n.* はけではらうこと.

V ***give*** trousers a good *brushing* ズボンをはけでよくはらう.

brutality, *n.* 残忍.

Q ***intelligent*** *brutality* 効果的と考えた残忍.

Q² ***concentration camp*** *brutality* [敵国人]収容所内の残虐行為.

brute, *n.* 畜生, 野獣的な人.

V ***have*** the *brute* 獣性を持っている.

Q He is a ***degraded*** *brute* あいつは畜生にも劣る奴だ. ¶a ***heartless*** *brute* 冷酷な人間. ¶a ***hideous*** *brute* 人間と思われぬ残虐な人.

P² He is a *brute* ***of*** a man. 薄情なやつだ.【類】a *brute* ***of*** a husband ‖ He is a *brute* ***to*** his children. 彼は子供に残酷だ.

bubble *n.* あぶく; 詐欺.

V ***blow*** *bubbles* シャボン玉を吹く. ¶***prick*** a *bubble* シャボン玉を突いて破る; [比ゆ的] ばけの皮をひんむく. ¶***puncture*** any evilly blown *bubbles* of ... ...の悪宣伝をすべて撃破する. ¶The *bubble* has ***burst.*** シャボン玉が破裂した; ばけの皮があらわれた.

Q² ***air*** *bubbles* 気泡(きほう). ¶a ***soap*** *bubble* 石けんの泡.

P rise ***in*** *bubble* 泡立つ. ¶vanish ***like*** a *bubble* 泡のように消える.

P² a *bubble* ***in*** water 水中の泡.

bubble, *v.* 欺く, だます.

M² when one's blood *bubbles* ***up*** to the brim 血沸き肉おどる時.

P *bubble* a person ***into*** ... 人をだまして...させる. ¶*bubble* him [out] ***of*** his money だまして彼の金を取る. ¶The huge crowd was *bubbling* ***over*** with excitement. 大群集が興奮で沸き立っていた.

buck, *v.* 振落す; 抵抗する.

M The horse *bucked* ***off*** his rider. 馬が乗手をはね落した.

P *buck* ***against*** one's fate 運命に反抗する(逆流にさおをさす).

bucket, *n.* バケツ.

Q a ***wooden*** *bucket* 木製バケツ.

Q² a ***fire*** *bucket* 消防用バケツ. ¶a ***honey*** *bucket* 《米俗》こやしおけ.

bucketful, *n.* バケツに一杯.

Q the ***first*** *bucketful* of the New Year's water バケツに一杯の若水.

P² a *bucketful* ***of*** cow milk バケツに一杯の牛乳.

buckle, *n.* しめ金, バックル.

Q² a ***brass*** (***gold***) *buckle* on a leather belt 皮バンドの真ちゅうのバックル. ¶a ***shoe*** *buckle* くつのしめ金.

buckle, *v.* 専心従事する.

M² *buckle* ***down*** to a hard job 鋭意困難な仕事に当る. ¶*buckle* ***up*** [しめ金で]しめ上げる.

P *buckle* ***on*** one's armor よろいを締め金でしめる.

bud, *n.* 芽, つぼみ.

V ***put forth*** (=***shoot out***) *buds* 芽をふく. ¶trees ***unfolding*** their *buds* 新緑の木々.

Q ***withering*** *buds* しおれかかったつぼみ(孤児などにいう).

Q² ***flower*** *buds* つぼみ. ¶***leaf*** *buds* 木の芽.

P a beauty ***in*** the *bud* 美少女 ‖ The plot has been nipped ***in*** the *bud.* 陰謀を芽生えのうちにつみ取った(未然に防いだ).

bud, *v.* 芽を出す.

M *bud* ***out*** into popularity [芸能人など]売出す.

Buddhahood, *n.* 正覚(しょうがく), 悟り; 仏性.

V Gautama ***attained*** *Buddhahood* at 35. 釈迦は三十五歳で正覚の境地に達した. ¶All living beings ***have*** *Buddhahood.* 生類には一切仏性が備わっている.

Buddhism, *n.* 仏教.

V *Buddhism* was first ***taught*** in China in 65 A.D. 仏教は紀元六五年に初めて中国に布教された.

Buddhist, *n.* 仏教信者.

Q a ***fanatical*** *Buddhist* 熱狂的仏徒. ¶a very ***fervent*** *Buddhist* きわめて熱心な仏徒.

budget, *n.* (1) 予算, 経費.

V ***balance*** the *budget* 出費の予算が不足のないようにする ‖ wives who can't ***balance*** household *budgets* 家計に赤字を出す細君. ¶***cut down*** home (=family) *budgets* 家庭の予算を切りつめる. ¶***enlarge*** *budgets* 予算額を多くする. ¶***increase*** (=***add to***) one's family *budget* 家庭の予算を増す. ¶***make*** a *budget* 予算を立てる. ¶***open*** the *budget* 議会に予算を提出する. ¶The charity work ***requires*** a *budget* of ¥50,000,000 a year. その慈善事業は年五千万円の経費が要る. ¶***strain*** the family *budget* 家庭の予算を狂わせる. ¶***submit*** a *budget* 予算案を提出する. ¶***vote*** the *budget* 予算を票決する. ¶carefully ***work out*** an expense *budget* 出費予算を入念に作る.

Q raise an ***adequate*** *budget* 予算を適当に増額する. ¶the 1956 ***fiscal year*** *budget* 一九五六年度予算. ¶With a ***limited*** *budget* the society is handicapped in its operations. 限りある予算で会は十分活動ができない. ¶the ***main*** *budget* 本予算. ¶The trip will not strain a ***modest*** *budget.* その旅行は収入の少ない人でも大して無理しなくてもできましょう. ¶the ***revised*** *budget* 修正予算.

Q² The main items in a ***family*** *budget* 家計予算の主要項目. ¶a ***household*** *budget* 家庭の入費. ¶the ***State*** *budget* 国家予算. ¶a ***war*** *budget* 戦費の予算. ¶the ***working*** *budget* 実行予算.

P keep ***within*** its *budget* その予算を越えないようにする.

P² a *budget* ***for*** next year 来年度の予算.

(2) 一束の物.

P² a *budget* ***of*** letters 一束の書信 ‖ a *budget* ***of*** news 彙報(いほう).

buff, *n.* 裸身.

P [all] *in buff*=naked 丸はだかで. ¶strip a person *to* the buff《口語》[人を]すっぱだかにする.

buffer, *n.* [列車の緩衝器から]緩衝国.

P act *as buffers* between the Western and the Eastern camp 東西両陣営の緩衝国の役割を演じる.

buffet, *v.* 打つ; …と戦う.

M He *bravely buffeted* misfortune's billows. 彼は勇ましく不幸の波浪と戦った.

M^2 He was *buffeted about* from pillar to post. 彼は運命にほんろうされた.【類】I have been *buffeted about* in the world.

buffoon, *n.* 道化師.

V *play* the *buffoon* おどけ役をやる, おどける.

bug, *n.* 虫; …狂.

Q^2 a *potato bug*《米》いもむし. ¶a *shutter bug* 写真狂; カメラファン.

buggy, *n.* 四(二)輪馬車.

Q^2 a *baby buggy* 乳母車. ¶a *doll buggy* 人形を乗せるおもちゃのうば車.

bugle, *n.* らっぱ.

V *blow* (=*sound*) the *bugle* らっぱをふく.【類】At 5 o'clock a *bugle* was *sounded*.

V^2 the *bugle rang out* commanding … …を命じるらっぱが鳴り渡った.

Q^2 a *conch-shell bugle* ほら貝.

P give (=blow) a strong blast *on* one's *bugle* らっぱを高らかに吹く.【類】He gave two or three loud notes (音) on his *bugle*.

bugler, *n.* らっぱ手.

V^2 *Buglers sounded* "God Save the King." らっぱ手は英国の国歌を吹奏した.

build, *n.* 構造; 体格.

Q of *blocky* (=*stocky*) *build* ずんぐり肥った. ¶vessels of *European* (*Japanese*) *build* 西洋(日本)型の船. ¶men of *greater build* and height もっとがらの大きい背の高い人. ¶a man of *heavy build* どっしりした体格の男. ¶He is of *large build*. あの人はかっぷくが好い. ¶of *lighter build* 体重のもっと軽い. ¶of *muscular build* 筋肉たくましい. ¶of *medium build* 中背の. ¶of *robuster build* 一層がん丈な. ¶of *slender* (=*slight*) *build* すらっとした体格の. ¶a man of *stalwart build* 体格のがっしりした人. ¶of *stout build* でっぷりした. ¶of a *sturdy build* がっしりした. ¶of *thin* (=*slim*) *build* やせ型の. ¶a *trim, muscular build* 均整のとれた男らしい体格.

build, *v.* 建てる, 組立てる.

M women who are *powerfully built* and in good health がっしりして健康な女. ¶*slimly built* ほっそりした. ¶*thickly builded*-over parts of London ロンドンの家込になっている方面. ¶He was *well built*. 彼はがっしりした体格であった.

M^2 *build up* vitality while you sleep すい眠によって活力を回復する ‖ *build up* one's body 身体を作る.【類】*build up* one's wasted body (弱り切った身体) ‖ *build up* an educated public opinion 教養ある世論を作り上げる.【類】*build up* the power of inhibition / It has done so much to *build up* the honor and prosperity of the firm. ‖ those who have *built up* a trade in licentiousness there そこに売笑業を始めた人々 ‖ *build up* a record that the voters will like 投票者も満足するような記録を作る.【類】*build up* a ditch between … / *build up* fabulous fortunes / *build up* her defenses against possible attack / *build up* the country as a cultural state / *build up* a fund / *build up* their *business* / *build up* good-will / *build up* a great barrier between / *build up* a modern army and navy / *build up* a powerful navy / *build up* a permanent reputation / *build up* reputations through sound and sober observation ‖ *build up* a story around an incident ある事件についてうわさを立てる ‖ *build up* the wave of national resentment 国民の怒りをかき立てる ‖ *build up* the Army morale by … …によって陸軍の士気を高揚する ‖ *build up* one's sentence『文法』文を作る. ¶know-how of *building up* suspense in a narrative 物語にスリルをもるこつ ‖ *build up* a progressive vocabulary 語彙を益々増大する. ¶The place is very much *built up* now. その場所は今は随分建て込んでいる. ¶Just as France is *built up* on Protection, so England is constituted by Free Trade. 丁度フランスが保護貿易の上に立っていると同様に英国は自由貿易に基づいている.

P It was *built after* a European model. それはヨーロッパ風に造られた. ‖ *built after* a design by … …の設計に基いて造られた.【類】*built after* the European model. ¶*built by* the company at its provincial factory その会社が地方の工場で造った. ¶automobiles *built for* service in the Far East 極東向けに造った自動車 ‖ He is too slightly *built for* hard work. ほっそりしたからだで荒仕事には適しない. ¶*built from* (=*to*) the designs of a famous architect 有名な建築家の設計に基いて造った. ¶*build* castles *in* the air (=Spain) 空中楼閣を描く ‖ *built in* (=*with*) brick and stone れんがと石で造った. ¶*built of* stone (brick, wood, concrete, steel) 石(など)で造った ‖ *built* largely *of* American material 主としてアメリカの材料で造った. ¶*built on* (=*upon*) a solid foundation 堅固な基礎の上に建った ‖ The house was *built on* a knoll. その住宅は丘の上に建っていた.【類】The science has been *built on* the foundations of those who have gone before. ‖ *built on* the model of … …を手本にして造った ‖ Modern civilization is *built on* power. 動力は近代文明の基底をなしている. ‖ The new building, *built on* the site of the one destroyed by fire, is one of the largest office buildings in the world. 焼跡にできた新造の建物は世界で最も大きい会社用建築の一つである. ‖ *build* our hopes *on* air われわれの希望を空中に描く(空想する).

builder, *n.* 建設者; 建築家.

Q^2 prospective *home builders* 近く家庭を作ろうとする人人. ¶a *master builder* 棟梁; 建築技師. ¶an *organ builder* パイプ・オルガンの製作者. ¶a *road builder* [道路建設の]土木技師. ¶*ship builders* and repairers 造船および船舶修理の技師(受負業者). ¶a *utopia builder* 理想郷を夢みる人.

P^2 a *builder in* stone 石材建築家. ¶one of the *builders of* the society その協会創立者の一人.

building, *n.* 建物; 建設.

V Don't you *admire* that *building*? あの建物をいいと思いませんか. ¶*alter* the *building* to suit the machinery 機械設置に都合のよいように建物を一部改造する. ¶*amortize* a *building* 建築費を割賦償却する. ¶*burn down* a *building* 建物を焼く. ¶they have yet to *commence* the *building* of … まだ…の建築にかかっていない. ¶It will take some months to *complete* the *building*. その建築が落成するまでには数カ月かかる. ¶The church *building* was *consecrated* in 1900. その教会の建物は一九〇〇年に奉献された. ¶*demolish* (=*pull down or tear down*) an old *building* 古い建物を取こわす. ¶*erect* (=*put up*) a new *building* 新築する. ¶The *building* has been *evacuated* for the use of the Occupation Forces. その建物は進駐軍に明け渡した. ¶They have a nearly *finished building*. 建築はほぼ完成した. ¶The fire *gutted* the *building*. 火事で建物の内部だけ焼けた. ¶*overhaul* the entire *building* その建物全部にわたって手入れをする. ¶The tornado *overthrew* many *buildings*. その旋風で多数の建物が倒壊した. ¶*relinquish* a requisitioned *building* 接収建物を返還する. ¶*renovate* a *building* 建物を若返らせる. ¶*share* a *building* 一軒家に相世帯で住む. ¶*shore* (=*prop*) *up* a *building* with timbers 建物に支柱を施す. ¶The *building* was *taken over* by the Occupation. その建物は進駐軍に接収された. ¶*buildings thrown down* by an earthquake 地震で倒壊した建物.

V^2 The *buildings cover* more than 2,000 tsubo. その建物の地坪は二千坪ある. ¶The *buildings housing* New York banks are more magnificent than palaces pictured in stories of the Arabian Nights. ニューヨーク市にある銀行の建物はアラビアン・ナイトの物語に描かれた宮殿よりもさらに豪華である. ¶a *building* that *occupies* an entire block 一街区を全部占める建物. ¶*Buildings* are *springing up* 家屋がどんどんできる.

Q The flames caught the *adjoining building*. 火が隣の建物にうつった. ¶A hondo is the *chief building* of a monastery and residence of the abbot. 本堂は寺の主な建物で住職の住いである. ¶*civic buildings* 市の建物. ¶a *cloud-kissing building* 雲つく高層建築物. ¶a *comely building* 見掛のよい建物. ¶a *dilapidated building* あばら家. ¶a *dingy building* うすぎたない建物. ¶*dull, prosaic-looking buildings* 栄えない平凡な建物. ¶a *handsome building* しゃれた建物. ¶*high* (=*tall or lofty*) *buildings* 高い建物 ‖ the world's *highest building* 世界最高の建物. ¶lecture-visits to *historic buildings* 歴史的建物への講演行脚. ¶*imposing*, and withal *graceful building* 堂々たるしかも優美な建物. ¶a *building known* as No. 681 Fifth Avenue 五番街六八一番地にある建物. ¶the *main building* of a business company 会社の本館. ¶a *model building* of the kind その種の模範的建物. ¶It would be hard, indeed, to imagine a more ***neglected-looking building***. これほどほったらかしのままになってる建物も珍しいだろう. ¶a ***new*** and ***well-appointed building*** 新しくて造作一切完備した建物. ¶a ***noble building*** 高くてりっぱな建物. ¶***Occupation-used Japanese buildings*** 進駐軍で使った日本の建物. ¶***palatial buildings*** 宏壮な建物. ¶a ***permanent building*** 本建築. ¶***public buildings*** and business premises 官庁と会社商店の建物. ¶a ***ramshackle building*** ぼろ家. ¶***reinforced concrete buildings*** 鉄筋コンクリートの建物. ¶a ***spacious building*** of two floors 二階建の広い家. ¶a ***steel-constructed, stone-fronted building*** 鉄骨石装の建物. ¶***steel-framed*** concrete ***buildings*** 鉄筋コンクリートの建物. ¶a ***tall building*** 縦長の建物. ¶a ***tumble-down*** (=***dilapidated***) ***building*** 荒れ果てた建物. ¶a ***venerable building*** 古雅な建物. ¶a ***war-battered building*** 戦火に痛められた建物.

Q² an ***administration building*** 事務所のある建物, 本部. ¶an ***apartment building*** アパート. ¶a ***big-money building*** 巨額の建築費を要した建物. ¶a work of ***character building*** 修養に関する著作. ¶the ***Diet building*** 国会議事堂. ¶a ***factory building*** 工場の建物. ¶a ***fifty-six story office building*** 五十六階の高層貸ビル. ¶***four-story buildings*** 四階建. ¶a ***frame building*** 木造の建物. ¶a ***Government building*** 庁舎. ¶***lath*** and ***plaster buildings*** 木ずりとしっくいで造った建物. ¶***new extension buildings*** 新たに増築した建物. ¶massive ***office buildings*** どっしりした貸ビル(事務所のある建物). 【類】The Empire State is the world's tallest ***office building***. ¶a one-story ***plant building*** 平家の工場建物. 【類】a ***plant building*** and its extension (付属建物). ¶a ***power-house*** (=***power-station***) ***building*** 発電所の建物. ¶Smoking is prohibited in the ***school buildings***. 校舎内では喫煙を禁じている. ¶a ***skyscraper building*** 高層建築物. ¶a ***steel skeleton building*** 鉄骨の建物. ¶the ***State capitol building*** = the Statehouse 《米》州議事堂. ¶A pyramid is a ***stone building***. ピラミッドは石でできている. ¶a ***store building*** 《米》商店の建物. ¶The ***War Ministry building*** was the nerve center of Japan's war efforts. 陸軍省が日本の戦争遂行の中枢であった.

P Flags were displayed ***at*** all ***buildings***. 建物にはすべて旗が掲げてあった. ‖ The police are on guard ***at*** that ***building***. 警察官がその建物を警護している. ¶It has been forty years ***in building***. その建物は工事を始めてから四十年になる. ‖ The fire started ***in*** the ***building***. 火事はその建物から出た. ‖ There are too few windows ***in*** that ***building***. その建物には窓が少なすぎる. ¶Flags are displayed ***on*** all Government ***buildings***. 諸官庁は総て旗を出している. 【類】"flares" (点滅電飾) ***on*** theaters and other public ***buildings***.

O One of the ***buildings*** is of the old frame sort while the other is of the newer concrete type. 建物の内一つは旧式の木造のもので一つは新しいコンクリート様式のものである.

bulb, *n.* 球; 電球.

Q a ***clear bulb*** 透明電球. ¶an ***electric bulb*** 電球. ¶an ***electric-light*** (=***-lamp***) bulb 電球. ¶a ***flash bulb*** 〖写真〗せん光電球. ¶a ***frosted bulb*** つや消し(曇り)電球. ¶pull a long, dangling string to switch on an ***unshaded bulb***. 長いぶら下ったひもを引っぱってはだか電灯をつける.

Q² plant a ***lily bulb*** ゆりの球根を植える.

bulge, *n.* 膨張.

V ***eliminate*** several ***bulges*** of Germany into Holland オランダ国境内へのドイツのはみ出しを除去する.

bulge, *v.* ふくれる.

P His eyes ***bulged*** nearly ***out of*** their sockets. 目が眼窩(がん)からほとんどとび出ていた. ¶pockets ***bulged with*** apples and candy りんごやキャンデーでふくらんだポケット.

bulk, *n.* 大きさ, かさ; 大半; 体躯.

V ***break bulk*** 船荷をおろす. ¶the miscellaneous articles which ***fill*** the ***bulk*** of the paper ページ数を増すための雑記事. ¶It ***forms*** the huge ***bulk*** of our exports. それがわが輸出品の大部分をなしている. ¶The great ***bulk*** (=The major portion) of British silver is ***obtained*** from lead ores. 英国では銀の大部分を鉛鉱から採る. ¶***secure*** the ***bulk*** of the trade その貿易の大部分を手に収める. ¶To include all will ***swell*** the ***bulk*** of the book too much. 皆収めるということになると本のかさが張り過ぎる.

Q a ship of ***great bulk*** 大きな船. ¶works of far more ***important bulk*** and pretension もっとずっと大部の著作. ¶a man of ***large*** (=***great***) ***bulk***=a stout person 肥った人. ¶amalgamate the content of several volumes into a single volume of ***reasonable bulk*** 数巻の内容を圧縮して適当な大きさの一巻にまとめる. ¶Gold and silver possess great value in ***small bulk***. 金銀はかさは小さくても大なる価格を有している. ¶a package of ***unwieldy bulk*** かさばって扱いにくい包み.

P ***by bulk*** or by weight かさか目方で. 【類】Do they charge carriage (運賃) ***by bulk?*** ¶sell goods ***in bulk*** 船貨を一船まとめて売る ‖ laden ***in bulk*** (穀類など船に)ばらで積んだ ‖ read Stevenson ***in bulk*** スチーブンソンものをまとめて読む ‖ We do not believe that men, taken ***in bulk***, are irreligious. 人間は全体として考えると非宗教的であるとは信じられない. ¶a package ***of bulk*** かさばった包み.

P² ***bulk for*** bulk 容積を比較していうと. ¶the ***bulk of*** a debt 負債の大部分. 【類】the ***bulk of*** the land / the ***bulk of*** population (the inhabitants).

bulk, *v.* 大きく見える; ふくれる.

M ***bulk large*** in one's eyes 大きく(重要に)見える ‖ The fact ought to be of special interest at the present moment when that country ***bulks*** so ***largely*** in international politics. その国が世界政治にかくも関係の深い現時においてその事実は特に興味がある.

M² ***bulk up*** かさばる.

bulky, *a.* かさ張った.

M be ***unwieldily bulky*** 始末が悪いほどかさばっている.

bull, *n.* 雄牛; 教書.

V boldly ***take*** the ***bull*** by the horns in the matter of ... ...に関して英断的処置を取る.

V² ***Bulls roar***. 雄牛はもーと鳴く.

Q the ***Pope's Bull*** on the subject その題目に関するローマ教皇の教書.

bullet, *n.* 弾丸.

V ***drive out*** a ***bullet*** 弾丸を発射する. ¶***fire*** a ***bullet*** through a board 板を弾丸で打ち抜く. ¶He ***received*** a ***bullet*** in the wrist. 彼は手くびに弾丸を受けた. ¶***send*** a ***bullet*** through one's brain 脳天を打ち抜く.

V² ***Bullets*** suddenly ***hissed*** about our ears. 突然われわれの耳の辺でひゅーっという弾丸の音がした. ¶As the ***bullet lodged*** near the skin, the pain was intense. 弾丸が膚に近く止まったので苦痛が激しかった. 【類】A ***bullet*** has ***lodged*** in his arm. ¶The ***bullet missed*** her by one inch. たまがちょっとの差で彼女に当らなかった. ¶The ***bullet went wild***. 弾丸がひどくそれた.

Q ***random bullets*** めくら打の弾丸. ¶He was hit by a ***stray bullet***. 流弾にあたった.

Q² a ***dumdum bullet*** ダムダム弾. ¶be killed by a ***machinegun bullet*** 機関銃にやられる. ¶a ***pistol bullet*** ピストルのたま.

bulletin, *n.* 告示, 報告; 公報; 報告書.

V ***issue*** a ***bulletin*** 公報を発行する. ¶***put out*** a ***bulletin*** giving ...を告げる公報を出す.

Q the ***annual bulletin*** of a club 会の年報. ¶put out a ***special bulletin*** on ... ...に関する特別公報を出す.

Q² a ***news bulletin*** [放送]ニュース.

P ***According to bulletins*** given out (=issued) by the physicians, the patient is passing beyond the crisis. 医師の発表した容体報告によれば病人は危機を遠ざかりつつある.

P² the daily ***bulletin on*** the condition of a patient 毎日の患者容体報告.

bull's-eye, *n.* [圏的の真中の]黒点, 正鵠(こく).

V ***hit*** (=***make***) the ***bull's-eye*** 金的を射る. 【類】***hit*** the ***bull's-eye*** of her heart / ***hit*** the ***bull's-eye*** of success with the first shot.

bully, *n.* 弱い者いじめ.

V ***play*** the ***bully*** 弱い者いじめをする.

O treat him ***bully*** 彼をひどい目に会わす.

bulwark, *n.* とりで, 砲台; 保障.

Q an ***impregnable bulwark*** 難攻不落の砲台. ¶an ***unassailable bulwark*** 要害堅固のとりで.

P² a ***bulwark of*** public liberty 公衆の自由を保障するもの ‖ a ***bulwark of*** security to the state 国家の干城.

bump, *n.* 衝突; こぶ; 才能, 能力.

V He ***has*** no ***bump*** of music. 彼には音楽の才がない.

Q We had good confidence in the ***driver's bump*** of locality. 御者が道に迷うようなことは万なかろうと思っていた.

P He was not well endowed ***with*** the ***bump*** of locality. 彼には場所を記憶する能力が乏しかった.

P² The ***bump on*** my head has subsided. 頭のこぶは引込んだ.

bump, *v.* 突き当てる.

M² be *bumped off* a train 列車にはね飛ばされる. ¶*bump up* against the imposed ceiling 制限高の頭をつく.

P *bump* one's head *against* a wall (lamp-post) 壁(など)に頭をどんとぶっつける ‖ *bump against* each other お互いに突きあたる. ¶The car *bumped along* the rough road. 車はでこぼこ道をがたごとやって行った. ¶*bump into* a man 人に突きあたる. 【類】The blind man *bumped into* me. ‖ *bump into* a stone 石につまずく.

bumpkin, *n.* かぼちゃ; 《俗》いなかっ平.

Q a *monster bumpkin* of 40 pounds 四十ポンドというばけ物かぼちゃ.

Q² a *country bumpkin* 《俗》いなかもの.

bunch, *n.* 束, ふさ; 群; こぶ.

P Grapes grow *in bunches*. ぶどうは房になって実がなる.

P² a *bunch of* cattle 一群の牛 ‖ a *bunch of* 16 bananas 十六ついたバナナの一房. 【類】a *bunch of* flowers / a *bunch* (一房) *of* grapes / a *bunch* (一束) *of* keys / a *bunch of* children. ¶a *bunch on* the face 顔面のこぶ.

bunch, *v.* 群がる.

M be *bunched together* 一団になる; 群生する.

bund, *n.* 海岸通り.

P Situated in the first position *on* the *Bund*, the hotel commands an unbroken view of the harbor and Tokyo Bay. 海岸通りの首位に位していてそのホテルは港と東京湾がくまなく眺められる.

bundle, *n.* 束, 包み.

V *make up* a *bundle* of ... ...を一束にする. ¶*untie* a *bundle* 包みをほどく.

Q in a *big* (*small*) *bundle* 大(小)束にして.

Q² a *handkerchief bundle* [船員のふろ敷代用の]ハンケチの包み.

P New Year post-cards were delivered all *in* a *bundle*. 年賀の端書が一束になって配達された. ‖ sell them *in* a *bundle* 束で売る ‖ tie them up *in* a *bundle* 一束にしばる ‖ the biggest rascal *in* the *bundle* ギャング中で一番の悪漢. ¶a blanket made *into* a *bundle* 束ねた一枚の毛布.

P² I have a *bundle of* letters to answer. 返事を出す手紙が山とある. ‖ a *bundle of* bank-notes 札たば. 【類】*a bundle* (一包) *of* old clothes / a *bundle of* sticks / a *bundle of* superstitions.

bundle, *v.* 束ねる; 無造作に取扱う.

M *bundle out*=expel suddenly いきなり追出す. ¶*bundle* a person *out* 人をいそいで追い出す ‖ *bundle* them *out* in quick order それらをさっさと運び出す.

M² The children were *bundled off* to bed. 子供らをさっさと寝床につかした. ¶it was *bundled up* with ... それは...と一緒に一束にした ‖ They *bundled* themselves *up* in the corner of the room. みなへやの片すみに丸まって寝た.

P She *bundled* him *into* the hut. 彼女は彼を小屋にほうり込んだ. ‖ All are *bundled into* one group. 十ぱ一からげにした. ¶I *bundled* him *out of* doors. 彼を戸外にほうり出した.

bung, *v.* ふさぐ.

M² His pipe was *bunged up*. パイプの穴がつまった.

bungle, *n.* 手ぬかり, 失策.

Q make a *pretty bungle* of ... ...にへまをやる. ¶make a *stupid* (=*bad*) *bungle* へまをやる.

bunk, *n.* ごま化し.

Q It's *all* the *bunk*. うその皮だ.

bunker, *n.* 石炭庫.

V *fill* their *bunkers* with coal [汽船が]石炭庫に石炭を入れる.

buoy, *n.* 浮標(うき).

Q² an *anchor buoy* いかりの浮標. ¶a huge *gas buoy* 〘航〙巨大な圧縮ガスの入った浮き袋. ¶a *life buoy* 救命用浮袋.

buoy, *v.* 浮かす, 元気づける.

P He is *buoyed* up *by* good news. 彼は吉報に浮立っている. 【類】I was *buoyed* up *by* the hope that ...

buoyancy, *n.* 浮力; 快活.

P² *buoyancy of* youth 青春の快活さ.

burden, *n.* 荷, 重荷; 負担, 責任.

V *alleviate* (=*lighten*) the *burden* imposed on ... ...の重荷を軽くする. ¶*bear* their *burdens* lightly 彼らの重荷を苦にしない. 【類】Life was a *burden* which he could no longer *bear*. ¶*carry* an irksome *burden* on one's back 骨の折れる重荷を背負う. ¶*cast* (=*pass*) our *burden* on ... われわれの負担を...に課す. ¶equitably *distribute* a *burden* 負担を不公平のないように課する. ¶after she has *dropped* her *burden* [お産をして]身軽になってから. ¶*endure burden* 重荷に堪える. ¶He *found* the *burden* of the empire too great for his failing health. 彼は帝国の重責を担うことは病弱の身に取って過重だと考えた. ¶*impose* (=*lay*) a *burden* on him 彼に負担させる ‖ the economic *burden imposed* on society by prostitution (売笑). ¶*lay down* life's *burden* 人生という重荷をおろす(死ぬ). ¶*lessen* the *burden* of toil 労苦を軽くしてやる ‖ *lessen* household *burdens* 主婦の負担を軽くする. ¶*lighten* the *burden* 負担を軽くする. ¶*relieve burden* from ... ...の重荷をおろしてやる. ¶*share* the *burden* その重荷を分担する. ¶*shift* a *burden* on to the weaker 弱い者にしわ寄せする. 【類】an *uguisu shifting* her light *burden* (=load) of song from tree to tree. ¶*shoulder* the *burden* of heavy responsibilities 重い責任を引受ける. 【類】She has borne her husband's breakdown (没落) and *shouldered* all the *burdens*. ¶*take up* the *burdern* with cheerful courage きん然として重荷を背負う.

V² its *burden falls* on ... その責任が...の身にふりかかる.

Q relieve the *crushing burdens* of naval and military establishments 陸海軍建設の過重な負担を軽減する. ¶shoulder the *financial burden* 財政を負担する ‖ The nation can face this *financial burden* without flinching. 国民は平気でこの不況に当れる. ¶be relieved of *heavy burdens* 重責から解放される. 【類】a *heavy burden* of taxation laid on the people. ¶lighten *housekeeping burdens* 家事の手数を省く. ¶an *intolerable burden* 堪え難い重荷. ¶carry *irksome burden* on one's shoulders やっかいな重責を担う. ¶With a slender income the family to him is *no light burden* to support. 収入の少ない彼にとって家族を養うのは容易ならぬ重荷である. ¶a *severe burden* on one's memory 人の記憶力に対する一大負担. ¶a *sweet burden* [苦にならない]うれしい重荷. ¶an *unbearable burden* 堪え難い重荷. ¶a *useless burden* on the community 社会にかける無益な負担. ¶a *weighty burden* 重責. ¶He took it upon himself to bear the *whole burden*. 彼は全部自分で負担した.

Q² ease the *occupation burden* 進駐軍の負担を緩和する. ¶ease the *tax burden* 税負担を軽減する. ¶the rickshawmen and their *whiteman burden* 白人を乗せた車夫. ¶a ship of 12,000 *tons burden* 積載量 12,000 トンの船.

P a beast *of burden* 労役または運搬に使う動物 ‖ He was relieved *of* the *burden*. 彼は重荷を下した(気が楽になった). ¶groan *under* intolerable *burdens* of taxation 堪え難い課税の重荷に悩む. ¶*with* a *burden* on his back 荷物を背負って. 【類】The ship was laden *with* a heavy *burden*.

P² Ever since the days of the *Kaitakushi*, Hokkaido has been a *burden in* the central treasury. 開拓使時代からずっと北海道は国庫のやっかいであった. ¶the *burden of* the criticism has been directed against ... 批評の主力が...に向けられた ‖ the *burden of* life 生活苦 ‖ the *burden of* taxation 税の負担 ‖ a *burden of* sin (sorrow, tax, care) 罪(など)の重荷 ‖ the *burden of* her talk is ... 二言目には...と言うのが彼女のくせ. ¶a *burden on* others 他人のやっかいもの. 【類】a *burden on* one's father / a *burden on* society (the state). / The *burden on* his back seemed crushing him to the earth. ¶an intolerable *burden to* society 社会に対する忍び難いやっかいもの. 【類】become a *burden to* the community / a *burden to* a person (one's shoulder) / The theater has for long been a *burden to* the owners. ‖ Life was made a *burden to* him. 彼は世の中がいやになった. ‖ Taxes were so high that they became a great *burden to* the people. 課税は非常に重く人民にとって大なる負担となった.

burden, *v.* ...に重荷を負わせる, わずらわす.

P *burden* a nation *with* taxes 国民に納税の義務を負わす ‖ *burden* an animal *with* a load 動物に荷を負わせる ‖ He is *burdened with* a heavy debt. 彼は負債をうんと背負っている. ‖ They are not *burdened with* families. 彼らは世帯を持っていない. 【類】He is *burdened with* a wife and three children. / Professors in private universities are too heavily *burdened with* teaching to engage in research work. / be *burdened with* the function of ...

burdensome, *a.* わずらわしい, 荷やっかいな.

P Life is *burdensome to* me. 世の中がいやになった.

bureau, *n.* 局, 部, 事務所.

Q an *extra-ministerial bureau* 外局. ¶an *intra-ministerial bureau* 内局. ¶a *matrimonial bureau* 結婚媒介所. ¶a *vocational bureau* 職業安定所.

Q² the *Administration Litigation Bureau* 行政訟務局. ¶the *Civil Affairs Bureau* 民事局. ¶the *Civil Liberties Bureau* 人権擁護局. ¶an *employment bureau* 職業安定所. ¶a kind of "*enquire within*" *bureau* for … …に対する一種の案内所. ¶the *Data* and *Statistics Bureau* 資料統計局. ¶the public *information bureau* attached to our publicity department 当社の宣伝部に属する情報室. 【類】The university is far more than an *information bureau*. ¶the *Judicial Affairs Bureau* 司法事務局. ¶the *Juvenile Correction* and *Rehabilitation Bureau* 少年矯正局. ¶a *marriage guidance bureau* 結婚相談所. ¶a *placement bureau* 職業配置局.

P² the *Bureau of* Decoration 賞勲局. ¶the *Prison Affairs Bureau* 行刑局. ¶a *registration bureau* for the unemployed 失業者の登録局. ¶a *student employment bureau* [大学の]学生職業周旋所. ¶a *suggestions bureau* (会社などの雇員からの)思付き受付所. ¶the *Weather Bureau* 《米》[商務省]気象局; [一般に]測候所 (a weather bureau).

bureaucracy, *n.* 官僚主義.

Q² *Washington bureaucracy* ワシントンの官僚主義.

bureaucrat, *n.* 官僚主義者.

Q² an *old-school bureaucrat* 旧派の官僚主義者.

burglar, *n.* 夜盗, 押込み.

V² *burglars broke* into a house occupied by … …の家に夜盗が入った.

Q an *expert burglar* 本職の夜盗.

burglary, *n.* 夜盗, 押込み.

V A *burglary* was *committed* in her house. 彼女の所に夜盗が入った. ¶*see* a *burglary* 夜盗行為を見る.

Q an *extraordinary burglary* 変り種の夜盗事件. ¶There were *many burglaries* last night. 昨夜は諸所に夜盗が押入った.

burial, *n.* 埋葬.

Q the *provisional burial* 仮葬.

Q² cave habitations and *cave burials* of primitive men 原始人の穴居生活と洞穴埋葬. ¶*church burial* 教会の儀式による埋葬.

P² a *burial at* sea 水葬.

burn, *n.* やけど.

V He *had* three *burns* on the right arm. 彼は右腕三カ所にやけどのあとがあった. ¶*produce* a deep *burn* ひどくやけどをする. ¶*suffer burns* やけどをする.

Q a *serious burn* はげしいやけど. ¶a *small burn* from tobacco たばこの焼こげ.

Q² *cigar burns* in a rug 敷物についてる葉巻の焼こげ.

P three *burns on* the right arm 右腕に三個所のやけどきず.

burn, *v.* 焼く, やけどさせる; 焼ける, 燃える.

M He was *burned alive*. 彼は焼殺された. ¶The child *burnt* himself *badly*. 子供がひどいやけどをした. ¶He was *burned* quite *black* by the sun. 彼は日に焼けて真黒になった. ¶The lamp did not *burn brightly*. ランプが明るくともらなかった. ¶Fire is *burning briskly*. 火が盛んに燃えている. ¶*burn cheerfully* 気持ちよく燃える. ¶The midnight oil *burns dim*. 深夜の灯火がほのぐらくともる. ¶*burn dull* (=*dully*) どんより燃える. ¶*burn easily* 燃えやすい. ¶It is *burning furiously*. 猛烈に燃えている. ¶The place was *burning fast*. その家はどんどん燃えていた. ¶The boiler fires are *burning low*. 汽罐の火が消えそうになっている. ¶He was *burned out* in a fire. 彼は焼だされた. ‖ It was *burned out* by the fire of 1906. それは一九〇六年の火事で焼失した. ¶Any electric light *bulb* will eventually *burn out*. どんな電球でも結局は焼け切れる. ¶Flames *burned out* the adjoining houses. 火焔が隣近所の家を焼きつくした. 【類】The match is *burned out*. / The heater coil (熱コイル) is *burnt out*. / *burn out* with the oil ‖ Thousands of people were *burned out* and made homeless overnight. 数千の人が焼け出され一夜で宿なしになった. ¶*burn quietly* とろとろ燃える. ¶He was *severely burnt* about the face. 彼の顔のあたりをひどくやけどした. ¶*burn together* 溶接する. ¶*burn vigorously* 火が燃えさかる.

M² be all (partly) *burned down* 全(半)焼する ‖ *burn down* a *building* 建物を焼失する ‖ The city was *burned down* by the enemy. その市は戦火で焼失した. ¶*burn off* gently (rapidly) 除々に(急速に)燃え切る. ¶The books were *burned up*. 書物が焼捨てられた. ¶The house *burned up*. =《英》The house was *burnt down*. 家が焼失した. 【類】The whole block *burned up* in war flames. / The fire *burned up* more than $50,000 worth of antiques (古物). / The filament of an incandescent light (白熱灯) cannot *burn up* (焼け切れない) because the bulb in which it is enclosed contains no air.

P *burn* aloes-wood *as* a perfume 沈香をたく. ¶He was *burned at* the stake. 彼は焼殺された. ‖ The ship has been *burnt at* sea. 同船は海上で燃えた. ¶Incense was *burnt before* his tomb. 彼の墓の前で香をたいた. ¶He *burns for* utterance. 彼は口をききたくてむずむずしている. ¶The potatoes were *burned in* the fire. じゃがいもを火にくべて焼いた. ‖ with a certain anger and rebellion *burning in* his heart 怒りと反抗ではらわたが煮え返って ‖ be *burned* (=baked) *in* a kiln (=oven) [パンなど]かまどで焼く. ¶*burn into* one's memory 記憶に焼きつく ‖ The thought *burned into* his mind (=soul). その思想が彼の心にしみ込んだ. ‖ The student's lamp was kept *burning* far *into* the night. その学生は夜の更けるまで勉強を続けた. ¶Most of the dead were *burned on* the hands and feet and blackened all over. 死者の大部分は手足を焼かれて全身真黒になっていた. 【類】He *burned* his hand *on* a hot stove. ¶He was *burned out of* house and home. 彼は焼け出された. ¶*burn through* the skin 皮膚を焼き通す. 【類】*burn through* the roof. ¶The house was *burned to* ashes. 家が灰になった. 【類】Some of the bodies were *burned to* the bone (骨まで). / The fish *burned to* a crisp (黒っこげに). / He was horribly *burned to* death by a fire. / The building was *burned to* the ground. / He found his cabin *burned to* the ground. ‖ *burn* it *to* powder それを焼いて粉にする. ¶he had it *burned upon* his mind that … …ということを彼の肝に銘じた. ¶She was *burning with* love. 彼女は愛に燃えていた. 【類】I fairly (全く) *burned with* love for her. / He *burned with* anger (ambition, curiosity, devotion, hope, jealousy, envy, ardor, rage, wrath). ‖ The patient *burned with* fever. 病人は熱が高かった. ‖ *burn* it *with* a caustic (hot iron) それを腐食剤(など)で焼く ‖ *burn with* flames 炎を立てて燃える. 【類】*burn with* a purple flame / *burn with* scarcely any flame / *burn with* a glaring light (きらきらと).

burner, *n.* 焼く人.

Q² a *brick burner* れんが工. ¶*Bunsen burner* ブンゼン式燈口. ¶The hibachi or open *charcoal burner*, is the universal heating plant in a Japanese home. 日本の家庭では火ばちが一般に暖房設備になっている. ¶a *perfume burner* 香炉.

burrow, *v.* 穴を掘る.

P *burrow in* the mud (ground, wood) 泥(など)に穴を掘る ‖ *burrow in* archives 文書をあさる. ¶Worms *burrow into* fruits (twigs). 虫が果物(など)に穴をあける. ‖ *burrow into* documents for oneself 書類を自分で綿密に調べる.

burst, *n.* 破裂; 一奮発; 一気呵成.

V With Chaucer English literature had *made* a *burst*. チョーサーが出てイギリス文学は一躍ぼつ興した.

Q The swimmer won the contest with a *splendid burst* of speed at the end. 最後に素晴しいスピードを出して水泳選手は競技に勝った. ¶There was a *wild burst* of applause. われんばかりの拍手かっさいだった.

P *at* a (=one) *burst* 一挙に, 一気(呵成)に. ¶*in* the *burst* of anger 憤然と. ¶*with* a little *burst* of laughter くすっと笑って. 【類】The statement was received *with* a *burst* of laughter. / His appearance on the platform was greeted *with* a *burst* of applause.

P² The place is a *burst of* roses. 見渡す限りのばらの花.

burst, *v.* 破裂する; ぼっ発する, 突発する.

M The crowd *burst away* in no time. 群集はたちまち四散した. ¶They *burst boisterously* into the room. 彼らはどかどかっと部屋に押かけた. ¶The sun *burst forth* again. 太陽は再び輝き出した. 【類】The cherry blossoms *burst forth* in all their beauty. ‖ They *burst forth* in music and dancing. にわかに音楽と舞踊が始まった. ¶*burst* the door *open* ドアをばたんとあける. 【類】The gate was *burst open*. ¶*burst out* crying (weeping, laughing) 泣き(など)出す. 【類】She *burst out* into a flood of tears. 急に涙がぼろぼろあふれ出てきた. ‖ *burst out* into an exclamation 感激の声をあげる. 【類】*burst out* into a roar of laughter (豪傑笑い) ‖ *burst out* into the open air 表へとび出す.

P *burst from* a prison 刑務所から脱走する ‖ "Banzai" *burst from* a thousand throats. 万歳の声が一千の口からほ

とばしった. ¶*burst in* the seam ほころびる. ¶trees *bursting into* leaf 新緑にもえ出る木々. 【類】cherry trees *bursting into* bloom (=blossom) ‖ *burst* [out] *into* song 歌いだす ‖ The crowd *burst into* prolonged cheering. 群衆のかっさいはしばし鳴りもやまなかった. 【類】*burst into* applause / *burst into* a loud fit of laughter / *burst into* laughter (rage) ‖ The smouldering embers *burst* (out) *into* flames. いぶっていた燃えさしがぱっと燃え立った. 【類】Resentment among ... is *bursting into* flame. ¶*burst into* a frenzy of vilification 気違いのようにののしる ‖ *burst into* fragments 粉々にくだける ‖ The volcano *burst into* eruption with great rumbling. 火山がごう然爆発した. ‖ *burst into* (*out of*) the room 室へ飛込む(室から飛出す) ‖ The poor girl *burst into* tears when she heard the sad news. その悲報を聞いてかわいそうに少女はわっと泣きだした. 【類】*burst into* weeping. ¶*burst on* the eye (ear) 急に見え(聞え)る. ¶The moon *burst through* the clouds. 月光が雲間をもれだした. ¶*burst upon* the country その国に侵入する ‖ *burst upon* one's ears 耳に響く ‖ A splendid view *burst upon* us. たちまちりっぱな景色が見えて来た. ‖ Summer-like weather has *burst upon* us unexpectedly. 急に夏らしい陽気になった. ¶*burst with* a noise like thunder 雷のような音をして破裂する ‖ *burst with* laughter どっと笑いだす. 【類】*burst with* envy (delight) ‖ The hall was *bursting with* people. ホールは人ではち切れんばかりだった.

bursting, *n*. 破裂.

P² the *bursting of* a blood vessel of the brain 脳の血管の破裂.

bury, *v*. 埋める, 葬る.

M He was *buried alive*. 彼は生埋めにされた. ¶He is *buried deep* under the ground. 彼は地下に深く埋葬されている. ¶He was *reverently buried*. 丁重に葬られた.

P He was *buried before* his time. [仮死を]本当に死んだものと思って埋められた. ¶He is *buried beneath* this stone. 彼はこの石の下に葬ってある. ‖ He was *buried beneath* the debris. 彼はくずれた石の下敷となった. ¶*bury* a person *from* a church 教会から葬式を出す. ¶be *buried in* the potter's field 共同墓地に埋葬される ‖ be *buried in* one's home town 故郷で埋葬される ‖ He is *buried in* his books. 彼は読書にふけっている. 【類】He is *buried in* business (study). / He remained *buried in* thought for some time. ‖ Here we've been three years *buried in* the country. この片いなかに引込んで三年暮した. ‖ *bury* it *in* the ground (=earth) それを地中に埋める ‖ *bury* one's head *in* one's hands 頭を抱える ‖ The town was already *buried* in sleep. 町は既に眠りに落ちていた. ‖ He is *buried in* oblivion. 彼は忘れられた. 【類】*buried in* the ruins (debris) ‖ *bury* oneself *in* solitude (one's work, the country) 孤独(など)に埋まる. ¶be *buried under* 11 inches of snow 十一インチの雪の中に埋められる. ¶He was *buried under* the landslide (debris). 彼は山くずれ(など)の下に埋まった. ¶those who have been *buried without* identification 身もと不詳のまま埋葬された人々.

bus, *n*. 乗合馬車; 乗合自動車(バス).

V *board* a *bus* 《米》 バスに乗る. ¶I could *catch* the last *bus*. 最終の乗合自動車に乗れた. ‖ He's just *made* a *bus*. 《米》 彼は丁度バスに間に合った.

V² The *bus pulled in* at the curb. バスが街路のふち石のところに止った. ¶Loaded *buses rattled* into the village. 人を乗せた乗合馬車ががたごとと村へ入って行った. ¶The *bus* was *speeding up*. バスがスピードをあげていた.

Q a *double-decked bus* 二階乗合自動車.

Q² a *diesel bus* ディーゼル・エンジンのバス. ¶a *motor bus* モーター・バス. ¶a *penny bus* 一ペンスで乗れるバス. ¶a *school bus* 通学用バス. ¶a *sight-seeing bus* 遊覧バス. ¶a *special services bus* 特別仕立てのバス. ¶a new *streamline bus* 新型流線形のバス. ¶a *trolley bus* トローリーバス.

bush, *n*. やぶ.

V without any more *beating about* the *bush* 遠回しの話は切上げて.

Q² a *berry bush* 木いちごの木. ¶a flowered *rose bush* 花の咲いているばらの木.

P a clump *of bushes* かん木林, 叢林(そうりん).

bushel, *n*. ブッシェル(ます目).

P They sell corn *by* the *bushel*. 穀物を一ブッシェルいくらで売る. ‖ measure another's corn *by* one's own *bushel* 自己の尺度で人をはかる. ¶*under* a *bushel* 秘密に, 人目を忍んで.

P² a *bushel of* corn 穀物一ブッシェル.

bushman, *n*. ブッシュ・マン(オーストラリヤの原住民).

Q an *Australian bushman* オーストラリアの原住民.

busiest, *n*. 多忙の最中.

V The election is now *at* its *busiest*. 選挙は今がたけなわだ.

business, *n*. 事務, 仕事; 営業, 商売; 店.

V We have *absorbed* the *business* of the old company under the above heading. 旧会社は(この便箋の)頭書通りの商号で弊社と合併しました. ¶I can *accept business* only on terms already proposed. 前申上げた条件でなければ仕事は引受けられません. ¶A *business* which is not a good business should not be *advertised*. りっぱな商売でなければ宣伝すべきでない. ¶It *affects* our *business*. それはわれわれの仕事に影響する. ¶He is of no *ascertained business* or calling. 彼は何ら定った商売とか職業とかいうものがない. ¶*begin* (=*commence or start*) a *busineess* 一つの仕事を始める. ¶*boom* (=*push or promote*) a *business* 商売の景気をつける. ¶The money was paid by them to *boost* their *business*. その金は彼らの商売を助長するために彼らが支出したのだ. ¶*break up* (=*discontinue*) one's *business* 廃業する. ¶It will *bring in* more *business*. そうするとますます注文が取れるだろう. ¶*build* a *business* to gigantic proportions 非常に大きく商売を広める. ¶merchants and others in Japan who may be interested in *building up business* with Hawaii ハワイと商取引をすることに関心を持つ日本の商人やその他の人々 ‖ They have *built up* a steadily prosperous *business*. 彼らの事業は基礎ができてますます繁昌している. 【類】*build up* a good Oriental *business*. ¶*buy out* a *business* 店を買収する. ¶*cancel* the *business* その取引の件を取消す. ¶*carry on* the *business* of baker パン屋の商売を営む. 【類】*carry on business* as a timber merchant / *carry on* a book-binding *business* (製本業) / *carry on* a large *business* with a small capital / He *carries on* a prosperous *business*. ¶*cede* our *business* to ... ...に商売を譲る. ¶The firm *closed business* for the Christmas holiday. 会社はクリスマスで休業だった. ¶Unless you hear from me to the contrary, you may *close* the *business*. こっちから別にさたがなければ取引の話をまとめても差支えない. ¶his net capital at the time of *closing business* 廃業当時における彼の正味の資本金. ¶He *commenced business* as a bookseller and publisher 彼は書籍商兼出版業を開始した. ‖ the amount of his investment on *commencing business* 商売を始めた当時の彼の投資額. ¶*complete* the *business* as soon as possible できるだけ早くその仕事を完成する. ¶*conduct* a mercantile *business* 商業を営む. 【類】*conduct* one's *business* in an approved manner (手際よく) ‖ a woman who is *conducting* great *business* 大きな商売をやっている女性. 【類】*conduct business* on a cash basis (現金主義で) / For many years he *conducted* his *business* from his private house. / For the next thirteen years the *business* was *conducted* from No. 14 Charles Street, Haymarket. ¶His *business* is *confined* to a single branch. 彼は営業科目を一つだけにしている. ¶I *consider* the *business* safe (unsafe). その取引を安全(不安)と思う. ¶*consummate* business 取引をすます. ¶After the death of his father, the *business* was *continued* by his son. 父の死後商売はその息子によって継続された. ¶He is in the *contracting business*. 彼は請負業である. ¶The company *controls* all the electric lighting *business* in the city. 会社は同市の電灯業を一手に引受けている. ¶The war has *curtailed* my *business*. 戦争で私の商売は減った. ¶I must *decline* the *business* on account of ... ...の理由でその取引はお断りをしなければならない. ¶*discharge business* connected with ... ...に関係の用向を果す. ¶*discontinue business* 廃業する. ¶Belgium, Scotland, England, Germany and the Scandinavian countries have *divided* the *business*. ベルギー, スコットランド,英国, ドイツおよび北欧諸国はその造船などの仕事を分担した. ¶*do business* together 協同事業をやる ‖ *do* (=*transact*) *business* through another house 他店で取引をする. 【類】continue to *do* the *business* as hitherto (従来通り) / He *does business* in his wife's name (名義). / Naples *does* a great *business* in fish and in coal and sponges. / We hope that we may in the future have the pleasure of *doing business* with you. / *do business* with France / foreign companies *doing business* in Japan / refuse to *do business* / a concern (店) *doing* a *business* of over a quarter of a million dollars annually /

he is in the habit of (始終) ***doing business*** with ... / I decline to ***do business*** with your representative (代表者). / I am glad to ***do business*** for a small pittance (わずかの利). ‖ In England, for instance, wireless messages can be sent or received through any post office ***doing*** telegraphic *business*. 例えば英国では無線電報は電信事務を取扱う郵便局ならどこでも受付ける. ‖ The store ***does*** a ***business up*** in the millions monthly. その店は毎月数百万台の取引をしている. ¶cannot ***encourage*** the *business* その商売は奨励できない. ¶***enter*** one's father's *business* 父の業を継ぐ. ¶the company is formed with the object of ***establishing*** the *business* of ... 同社は…業を開始する目的をもって組織された. 【類】 ***establish*** coal *business* ‖ ***estabilish*** a *business* of one's own 独立して商売をする. ¶***execute*** (=***carry out***) a *business* 仕事をやり遂げる. ¶***expand business*** 商売を拡張する. ¶obtain the funds necessary to ***extend*** the *business* 事業拡張に必要な資金を調達する. ¶***finish*** a *business* 用向をすます. ¶***follow*** the *business* of ... …業に従事する. ¶He ***founded*** the *business* in that street in 1811 彼は一八一一年にその町に店を開いた. ¶***give up*** the *business* 廃業する. 【類】 clearance sale on ***giving up business***. ¶seriously ***hamper*** (=***interrupt***) *business* はなはだしく商売のさまたげになる. ¶***hand over*** the *business* 店を譲る. ¶***handle*** the *business* at a better profit もっともうかるように経営をやる ‖ ***handle*** your *business* expeditiously and satisfactorily 御用を敏速に且つ満足に取扱う. 【類】 He knows how to ***handle*** his *business*. ¶I ***have business*** with the firm. 手前どもはその店と取引がある. ‖ He ***has*** a thriving *business*. 彼は繁昌する店を持っている. ‖ I ***have*** *business* with him. あの人に用がある. ‖ You ***have*** no *business* to absent yourself from office without leave. 無届で欠勤するという法はない ‖ ***have*** the *business* in the hands of ... 商売を…の手に任せる. 【類】 I ***have*** my *business* to attend to. / You ***have*** no *business* to do it so roughly as this. / I ***have*** some *business* which prevents me from going out this evning. ¶In 1919 the *business* was ***incorporated*** (=***formed***) as (=into) a limited company. 一九一九年にその店は有限責任会社になった. ¶***increase*** *business* with China 対華取引を盛んにする. ¶***keep*** one's *business* going 自分の商売を続ける ‖ ***keep*** the *business* ***well*** in hand 得意を他に取られないようにしっかりやる. ¶a man who "***knows*** his own *business*" いわゆるその道の達人 ‖ I ***know*** the *business* inside out. 私はその仕事は何から何まで心得ている. ¶those important little things which ***link*** all *business* with the different points of law 一切の商業が法律と何か関係を持つ細かいことではあるが重要な諸点. ¶It may cause us to ***lose*** the *business*. それで仕事(注文)が取れなくなるかも知れない. ¶***make*** a *business* of photography 写真術を業とする ‖ ***make business*** of athletics 運動で身を立てる ‖ He ***makes business*** a pleasure. 彼は仕事を楽しんでいる. ‖ to ***make*** the *business* a success there must be mutual co-operation between ... この商売の成功には…間の協調が必要だ ‖ ***make*** the *business* to ... …するのを本職にする. ¶Do not think he ***means business***. 彼が本気で言っていると思ってはいけない. 【類】 He really ***means*** *business* (真剣). / Prompt means must be taken if you ***mean business*** (ものにしようという気なら). ¶***Mind*** your own *business*. 余計な御世話だ. ‖ May I ask you to ***mind*** your own *business?* 余計なことはしないようにして頂けませんか. ¶Don't ***mix business*** with pleasure. 仕事と遊びをいっしょにしちゃいけない. ¶***monopolize*** the local *business* その地方の商売を独占する. ¶he ***moved*** (=***removed***) his *business* to ... あの人の店は…へ引越した. ¶He ***neglects*** his own *business* to look after other people's. あれは自分の仕事をたなにあげて人の仕事の世話をやく男だ. ¶***negotiate*** the *business* through you あなたのおせわで取引の交渉をする ‖ utterly ***neglecting*** his proper *business* (=main occupation) 本業をそっちのけにして ‖ According to the laws of Japan, in those days Nagasaki was the only place for ***negotiating*** foreign *business*. 当時日本のおきてによると長崎は外国の事務を取扱う唯一の場所であった. ¶***open*** *business* 開業する ‖ ***open*** *business* (=accounts) with ... …と取引を開始する. ¶***operate*** the express *business* upon the railway 鉄道の運送業を経営する. 【類】 ***operate*** a jewelry *business*. ¶***organize*** a *business* 商店を組織する. ¶He ***owns*** a fine *business*. 彼は良い店を持っている. ¶***paralyse*** *business* 商売を沈滞させる. ¶***pass*** the *business* on to ... 注文を…に回す. ¶successfully ***pilot*** the *business* ***through*** その仕事をうまくやってのける. ¶***place*** the *business* in the hands of ... 仕事を…の手に委ねる. ¶***promote*** tourist *business* 観光業を振興させる. ¶We can ***put*** the following *business* in your hands. 次の注文を貴店に出すことができる. ‖ He has ***put*** his *business* into the hands of our opponents. 自分の商売をわれわれの商売がたきの手に渡した. ¶***quit*** *business* to enjoy one's wealth 商売をやめて楽に暮す. ¶***reduce*** the *business* 商売を縮小する. ¶***resume*** *business* 仕事を再び始める. ¶It will ***ruin*** my *business*. そうすると私は身代限りになる. ¶If there were no people who wear hats, the hat dealer's *business* would be ***ruined***. 帽子をかぶる人がいなくなったら帽子屋はあがったりだ. ¶***run*** one's *business* 商売をやってゆく. 【類】 In a democracy the citizens themselves choose the men who ***run*** the *business* of the government. ¶***rush*** one's *business* 仕事を大急ぎでやる. ¶Competitors will ***secure*** the *business*. 競争者にその仕事を取られるだろう. ‖ endeavor to ***secure*** the *business* その仕事を手に入れようと努力する. ¶expect to ***see business*** improve shortly 近く景気がよくなるだろうと思う. ¶***sell out*** (=***dispose of***) a *business* to ... …へ店を譲る. ¶***set up*** a private detective *business* 私立探偵事務を開設する. ¶The *business* will no doubt be ***settled***. その件は確かに解決する. ¶We ***shut up*** *business* at five. 五時に店を仕舞う. ¶his *business* (=store =place of business) is ***situated*** in ... 彼の店は…にある. ¶***solicit*** *business* 仕事を求める. ¶***speed up*** (=***expedite***) *business* 事務を敏速にする. ¶***stammer out*** one's *business* to ... …用事をどもりながら言う(はっきり言わない). ¶***start*** a *business* of one's own=start one's own business 独立して商売を始める. ¶***start*** a *business* in a small way 小商売を始める ‖ ***start*** one's *business* on a shoestring《米》小資本で商売を始める. 【類】 ***start*** *business* on one's own account (独立して) / He ***started*** a small *business* with fancy and silk goods. ¶be precise in ***stating*** one's *business* はっきり自分の用向きを述べる. ¶All *business* is ***stopped*** by strikes. ストで仕事が全部停止している. ¶all *business* will be ***suspended*** during (until)... …中(まで)業務一切を停止します. ¶He ***took*** the *business* in hand. 彼はその仕事を引受けた. ‖ He succeeded in ***taking*** much *business* from his competitor. 彼は競争者の顧客を大部分自分の方へ取ってしまった. ¶***take over*** the *businesss* of ... …の店を譲り受ける. ¶***talk*** *business* with ... …と商談をする. ¶refuse to ***transact*** the *business* その取引を拒絶する. 【類】 ***transact*** their *business* privately / ***transact*** *business* in Spanish ‖ ***transact*** *business* at a meeting 会議する. ¶be competent to ***transact*** *business* 議事の能力がある(法定定数があるので). ¶he has ***transferred*** his *business* as a printer to ... 彼は印刷屋の店を…へ譲渡した ‖ The *business* of the company has been ***transferred*** to more commodious premises at ... 同社はもっと手広な…に移転した. ¶retire and ***turn*** the *business* ***over*** to ... 引退して店を…に譲渡する. ¶Are you willing to ***undertake*** the *business?* その仕事を引受けて下さいますか. ‖ provided you will ***undertake*** the *business* あなたがその仕事をお引受け下さるなら. ¶***upset business*** 仕事を混乱させる. ¶His *business* was ***wrecked***. 彼は商売に失敗した.

V^2 ***Business brightens up***. 商売が立直る. ¶This *business* ***bristles*** with difficulty. この仕事は大変だ. ¶The *business* of the day ***commences***. その日の商売が始まる. ¶Our *business* is ***dealing*** in flour and grain. 手前どもは麦粉と穀類をあきなっています. ¶*Business* is ***declining***. 景気が段段悪くなる. ¶*Business* ***dropped off*** in the retail stores at an alarmin grate. 小売店の客足がどんどん落ちて行った. ¶*Business* ***extends*** (=***expands*** or ***enlarges***). 商売が広まる. ¶*Business* is ***going on*** as usual. 商売は平常通りやっている. ¶*Business* is apparently ***improving***. 景気が段々直ってくるらしい. ¶when *business* ***lags*** 不景気のとき. ¶This *business* ***pays*** well. これは結構引合う商売だ. ¶*Business* is ***picking*** (=***looking*** or ***perking***) ***up***. 景気が見直して来た. ¶His *business* has ***prospered*** well. 彼の商売はなかなか繁昌した. ¶*Business* is ***reviving***. また景気が出てきた. ¶The *business* is steadily ***shrinking***. その商売は衰える一方だ.

Q It is ***bad business***. それはやり方が悪い. ‖ It is a very ***bad*** *business*. 実に困ったことだ. ¶He does a ***big*** *business* among foreigners. 彼は外人相手に手広く取引している. 【類】They handle a *big business.* ¶the prosperous ***book-publishing** business* 景気のよい出版業. ¶be doing a ***booming** business* in … …は商売繁昌である. ¶the ***chief** business* of the teacher 教師の本領. 【類】make it their ***chief** business* to … ¶a ***clean** business* かたぎの商売. ¶on ***commercial** business* 商用で. ¶transact the ***common** business* of life 日常の用務を取扱う. ¶He does a ***conservative** business.* 彼は手がたい営業をしている. ¶a ***creditable** business* 正しい行為. ¶a ***crooked** business* 不正な行為. ¶keep off ***dirty** business* 汚い商売には手を出さない. ¶a ***disreputable** business* 不名誉な行為. ¶do a ***double** business* 売上が倍になる. ¶*Business* is ***dull.*** 不景気だ. ¶***executive** business* 監理の業務. ¶do an ***extensive** business* with country customers いなかを相手に手広く営業する. ¶do ***fair** (**foul**) business* 正しい(不正な)商売をする ‖ He is doing a ***fair** business.* 相当な商売をやっている. ¶the ***first** business* of life 人生の第一目的. ¶the beginner's ***first** business* is … 初心者の第一にすべきことは…である. ¶The place is doing a ***flourishing** business.* その店は商売が繁昌している. ¶build up a ***foreign** business* 外国に得意を作る. ¶do a ***good** business* 一もうけする. ¶find it ***good** business* to buy … …を買うことは結構いい商売になる. ¶He does very ***good** business* in rubber goods. 彼はゴム製品で大分もうけている. ¶War is a ***grim** business.* 戦争は真剣なことだ. ¶he does an ***immense** business* in … 彼は…を非常に手広く営業している. ¶have more ***important** (**urgent**) business* to attend to than … それどころじゃないもっと大事な(急を要する)仕事がある. ¶*Business* is ***inert.*** 商況が不活発である. ¶the ***infamous** business* 泥水商売. ¶do an ***international** business* 国際的商売を営む. ¶heads of ***large** businesses* 大会社の社長連 ‖ a ***large** business* has been done in … …の大口の取引があった ‖ The retail business is the ***largest** business* in the United States. 米国では小売業が最大の商売だ. ¶a ***legitimate** business* 合法的な商売. ¶do a ***lucrative** business* もうかる商売をやる. ¶his ***main** business* in life is … 彼が人生の重なる目的としているのは…である ‖ be not one's ***main** business* 本職じゃない. ¶a ***moderate** business* そこそこの商売. ¶***No** business* on account of holiday. 休日に付休業. ‖ You have ***no** business* to do it so roughly as this. そんな乱暴な事ってない. ¶a ***non-routine** business* 一風変った商売. ¶on ***official** business* 公務で. ¶I was obliged to be absent from school on ***particular** business.* 余儀ないことで学校を休んだ. ¶a ***paying** business* 引き合う商売. ¶a ***poor** business* 割の悪い仕事(商売). ¶on very ***pressing** business* 至急の用事で. ¶Here's a ***pretty** business!* これは飛んでもないことだ. ¶give more chances to ***private** business* to go prosperous 個人企業が景気づくような機会をもっと与える. ¶a ***profitable** business* もうかる商売. ¶He built up a ***prosperous** business* in a mechanical line. 彼は機械の方面の商売で成功した. ¶a ***protracted** business* 長びく仕事. ¶the transaction of ***public** business* 公務の処置. ¶*Business* is ***quiet.*** 景気が悪い. ¶a ***reckless** business* 向う見ずの商売. ¶clear up the ***remaining** business* 残務を整理する. ¶a pretty ***risky** business* かなり危険な商売. ¶handle the ***routine** business* 定り切った仕事をやる. ¶have a ***rushing** business* 商売繁昌だ. ¶***secular** business* 俗務(聖務に対して). ¶Study is ***serious** business.* 研究ってまじめな仕事だ. ¶*Business* is ***slack.*** 景気が悪い. ¶start a ***small** business* with fancy and silk goods. 洋品や絹ものを扱う商売を小さく始める. ¶I have ***some** business* with you. 君にちょっと用事がある. ‖ make a ***special** business* of … …を専業にする. ¶be made a ***special*** or ***exclusive** business* 特別のあるいは専門の仕事になっている. ¶a ***speculative** business* 投機的事業. ¶do ***square** business* 公正な取引をする. ¶***stagnant** business* 不景気. ¶A ***steady** business* is being done in freights at present. 現在貨物輸送事業は確実に行われている. ¶It proved a ***successful** business.* その事業は成功であった. ¶It is a ***teacher's** business* to help his pupils. 生徒を教えるのは先生の仕事だ. ¶a very ***tedious** business* はなはだ退屈な仕事. ¶he does a ***thriving** business* in the sale of … …の販売で商売が繁昌している. 【類】enjoy a ***thriving** business* / *build* a ***thriving** business* at … ¶a ***troublesome** business* やっかいなこと. ¶on ***unavoidable** business* やむを得ない用事で. ¶But there's still some ***unfinished** business* to settle. しかしまだ未解決の仕事がある. ¶I was suddenly called home on ***urgent** business.* 私は突然急用で故郷に呼び寄せられた. 【類】I have some ***urgent** business* to attend to. ¶***wholesale** business* おろし売業.

Q[2] the ***agency** business* 代行業務; 代理業. ¶my thirty years of service in the ***amusement** business* 私の興行界における三十年の仕事. ¶transact (=conduct) a general ***banking** business* 一般銀行事務を取扱う. ¶Hotels did a ***capacity weekend** business.* ホテルは週末客で大入満員だった. ¶We do a strictly ***cash** business.* 手前どもでは現金に限り取引を致しております. ¶conduct a ***commission** business* ブローカーをやる. ¶***communications*** and ***transportation** business* 通信輸送の業務. ¶rebuild Japanese ***cotton textile export** business* 日本の綿製品輸出事業を再建する. ¶the ***entertainment** business* 興行界の事業. ¶conduct (=handle) one's ***everyday** business* 毎日の業務を取扱う. ¶the ***export** business* 輸出業. ¶succeed to the ***family** business* 家事を受継ぐ. ¶be dispatched on ***government** business* 公用で派遣される. ¶***high volume** business* is now being done in … …では大量の仕事が処理されている. ¶be largely a ***hit or miss** business* 大体あてずっぽうである. ¶open an ***import-export** business* [輸出入]貿易事業を始める. ¶the technique of the ***lecture** business* 講演商売のこつ. ¶the ***leg** business*=ballet-dancing 《俗》バレエ. ¶the ***mail-order** business* 通信販売事業. ¶An extensive ***manufacturing** business* is carried on by … in the building of cars. 車両製造業が…によって手広く営まれている. ¶the ***money-lending** business* 金貸業. ¶start into poultry raising as ***moneymaking** business* 営利事業として養鶏を始める. 【類】It is not merely a ***moneymaking** business.* ¶It is a ***must** business* for radio. それは放送にはどうしても必要な事である. ¶The post office does not transfer ***money-order** business.* その郵便局では為替を扱わない. ¶a ***one-man** business* 個人営業. ¶He was wise enough to mind no more of ***other people's** business* than he could help. 彼は賢明なるべく他人の仕事には気を使わなかった. ¶do a large ***overseas** business* on a cashand-carry basis 現金自国船主義で大きな外国貿易をやる. ¶the ***pawnbroking** business* 質屋経営. ¶the ***publishing** business* was purchased by … その出版社は…の手に買取られた. ¶The Eastern carriers do roughly 40 per cent of the nation's ***rail transport** business.* 東部の運送店だけで大体全米鉄道輸送の四割の仕事をやっている. ¶The big movie houses did a ***record** business.* 一流映画館は記録的大入りを続けた. ¶***retail** business* 小売業. ¶they have ***rush** business* with …で商売がいそがしい. ¶the ***shoeshine** business* くつみがきの仕事. ¶No business is like ***show** business.* ショーほどすてきな商売はない. ¶a ***stop-gap** business* 臨時の仕事. ¶a ***touch-and-go** business* けんのんな仕事. ¶handle a ***trading** business* 貿易を行う. ¶put a ***worth while** business* back on its feet やりがいのある仕事を再び独立させる.

P I sent my servant ***about*** his *business.* 召使を解雇した. ¶I have to be ***at** business* by nine. 私は九時までに店へ出なければならない. ¶I was prevented ***by business.*** 用事で差支えた. ‖ I have been pressed ***by business.*** 私は非常に急がしかった. ‖ I have lost money ***by*** the *business.* その商売で損をした. ¶He has a good head ***for business.*** 彼は商才がある. ‖ ***for** business* or pleasure 商売のためまたは娯楽のために. 【類】I have been too busy to get to Tokyo except ***for** business* now and then. ¶He is now ***in business.*** 彼は今は商売をしている. ‖ a man ***in** business* 実業人. 【類】He has been ***in*** this *business* for three years. / a man ***in*** such *business* / men ***in*** the *business* (その道の) / The firm is now more than sixty years ***in** business.* / He is ***in** business* for himself (独立して). ‖ He is buried ***in business.*** 彼は仕事に没頭している. ‖ competition ***in business*** 商売の競争 ‖ be connected ***in** business* with … …と取引関係がある ‖ He is ***in** business* with his father. 彼は父と共同事業をやっている(父子商会を作っている). ‖ There is a lull ***in business.*** 商売には小やみがある; 景気がちょっと落ちている. ‖ There is not much to gain ***in*** that *business.* あの商売は余りもうからない. 【類】He takes a leading part ***in*** the *business.* / He has made great strides ***in*** this *business.* ¶He has gone ***into business.*** 彼は実業界に入った. ‖ I must see ***into*** the *business.* 業務の検査をしなければならな

い. ¶volume ***of*** *business* 取引量(高). ¶I have charge ***of*** the *business.* 私が営業を管理している. ‖ depression ***of*** *business* 不景気 ‖ a man ***of*** *business* 実務家 ‖ It's none ***of*** your *business.* お前の知ったことじゃない. ‖ I wash my hand ***of*** the whole *business.* 僕はそれと全然関係を断つ. ¶He is away ***on*** *business.* 用事でよそへ行っている. ‖ ***on*** *business* best known to himself 彼だけに判っている何かの用事で ‖ No admittance except ***on*** *business.* 無用の者入るべからず. ‖ ***on*** the company's *business* 社用を帯びて. 【類】I was suddenly called to Kobe ***on*** *business.* / go abroad ***on*** Government *business* (官用で) / ***on*** *business* of the country (公用) / I saw him ***on*** *business* of importance (大切な) / ***On*** what *business* did he come here this morning? ¶He is ***out of*** *business.* 彼は廃業している ; 失業中. ‖ go ***out of*** *business* 廃業する. 【類】Depression has put many merchants ***out of*** *business.* ¶In my daily walk ***to*** *business* I frequently meet a certain gentleman. 私は毎日店へ歩いて行くときある紳士によく出会う. ‖ attend ***to*** one's *business* 用事に着手する ‖ He has taken ***to*** *business.* 彼は商売をやるようになった. ¶Let's be square ***with*** our *business.* 取引は五分五分と行こう. ¶***with*** no particular *business* in hand 別に用事がないので. ¶He has done (= He is through) ***with*** his *business.* 彼は仕事を片づけた.

P² *business* ***about*** (=***concerning*** *or* ***in regard to***) certain property ある財産に関する用務. ¶*business* ***in*** coal 石炭業. ¶the *business* ***of*** a druggist 薬種業 ‖ the *business* ***of*** travel 観光事業 ‖ It is no *business* ***of*** yours. いらないお世話だ. ¶Have you *business* ***with*** me? 私に用事ですか. ‖ He has done *businees* ***with*** us for years. あの人は長年手前どもと取引している.

O It is my *business* to see you all going the right way. みんなが正しい道を行くように気をつけるのが私の役目だ. 【類】We shall make it our *business* to make the public fully aware of the real situation they are in. ¶*Business* is at a standstill. 商売は停止状態だ.

businesslike, *a.* 事務的な.

M be ***very*** *businesslike* てきぱきしている.

bust, *n.* 胸像 ; 胸部(特に女性の).

V ***measure*** one's *bust* バストを計る.

Q² a ***life-like bronze*** *bust* 青銅作りの等身大の胸像. ¶a ***plaster*** *bust* 石こう製の胸像. ¶a ***stone*** *bust* of Dickens ディケンスの石の胸像.

bustle, *n.* 雑とう ; 騒ぎ.

P be ***in*** a *bustle* さわいでいる ; 雑とうしている.

bustle, *v.* 騒ぐ.

M² *bustle* ***about*** さわぎ回る. ¶*bustle* ***up*** さわぎ立てる.

busy, *a.* 急がしい.

M be ***frightfully*** *busy* ばかにいそがしい. ¶I'm ***too*** *busy* now to attend to anything else but my work. 今はとてもいそがしいから自分の仕事以外はとても手が回らぬ. ¶He was then so ***tremendously*** *busy* handling piles of desk work. 彼は山のような事務を片づけるのでおっそろしく多忙だった. ¶They are now ***very*** *busy* with the harvest. 彼らは今取入れで大多忙だ.

P He is *busy* ***about*** (=***over*** *or* ***with***) his task. 彼は自分の仕事で急がしい. ‖ be *busy* ***about*** trifles 雑事で急がしい. ¶He is *busy* ***at*** work. 彼は仕事で急がしい. ¶I was *busy* ***in*** packing up to go home. 帰郷するので荷ごしらえに急がしかった. 【類】He is *busy* ***in*** canvassing for the election (選挙運動). ‖ he is *busy* ***in*** preparing for ... 彼は...の準備で急がしい ‖ We are *busy* ***in*** making arrangement for Christmas. われわれはクリスマスの準備で急がしい. ¶You're *busy* ***with*** nothing to do, aren't you? 君はひま過ぎて困ってるんだろう. ‖ The factory is *busy* ***on*** Government work. 工場は官庁の仕事で急がしい. ‖ He is *busy* ***with*** social functions. 彼は会に出席するので急がしい. ‖ He was *busy* ***with*** his camera. 彼は盛んにカメラで写真を取っていた. 【類】one who is busy ***with*** family cares (家庭の雑事) ‖ He is *busy* ***with*** the picture for next year's Academy (アカデミーに出品). / She is *busy* ***with*** her make-up (お化粧) before a mirror. / She is always *busy* ***with*** her needle and thread. / They are *busy* ***with*** their knitting needles (編みもの). / I am too *busy* ***with*** this work to think any more about it myself.

O I found him *busy* packing his trunk. 私が見たとき彼はしきりにトランクの荷造りをしていた. ¶I am *busy* preparing for the examination. 僕は試験準備で急がしい.

busy, *v.* 急がしくする.

P I do not *busy* myself ***about*** (=***with***) such affairs. 私はそんなことには係り合わない. ¶*busy* oneself ***over*** papers and documents 書類の調査に没頭する. ¶He is *busied* ***with*** (=***in*** *or* ***about***) studies. 彼は研究に急がしい.

butt, *n.* 標的, 的.

Q a ***favorite*** *butt* of ... ...がよくやり玉にあげるもの.

P² a *butt* ***for*** laughter (ridicule) 笑い(など)の的. ¶the *butt* ***of*** the company 一座の笑いもの ‖ make him the *butt* ***of*** ridicule 彼を笑いの的にする.

butt, *n.* [銃の]台じり ; 吸いさし.

Q² retrieve the ***cigarette*** *butts* from the pavement 鋪道から巻きタバコの吸いさしを集める. ¶the ***gun*** *butt*=the butt of a gun 銃の台じり. ¶be beaten with ***rifle*** *butt* 銃の台じりで殴られる.

P² the *butt* ***of*** a spear やりの石突き.

butt, *v.* 突く ; 口を出す.

P *butt* a person ***in*** the stomach 人の横腹を突く ‖ Don't *butt* ***in*** while others are speaking. 人の話している時口を出すな.

butter, *n.* バター.

Q ***fresh*** *butter* 新鮮なバター. ¶***rancid*** *butter* 腐ったバター.

Q² ***cocoa*** (***peanut***) *butter* ココア(ピーナッツ)バター.

P fry it ***in*** *butter* それをバターで揚げる. ¶spread bread ***with*** *butter*=spread butter on bread パンにバタを塗る.

butterfly, *n.* ちょう.

V ***break*** the *butterfly* on the wheel 赤ん坊の手をねじるようなことをする. ¶*Butterflies* were ***seen*** fluttering from flower to flower. 花から花へとちょうが飛び回っていた.

Q a ***social*** *butterfly* あちこちとび回る社交ずきの女(浮気女).

buttocks, *n. pl.* しり.

V ***protrude*** one's uncovered *buttocks* しりをまくって突き出す.

button, *n.* ボタン.

V ***press*** (=***touch***) the electric *button* 電気ボタンを押す. ¶***push*** the *button* for the elevator エレベーター用のボタンを押す. ¶***sew*** a *button* on a coat 上着にボタンを縫い付ける. ¶***sew on*** all the *buttons* that have come off とれたボタンを全部縫い付ける. ¶***turn*** [***back***] a *button* [電灯を点滅するときなどに]ボタンを引く(戻す). ¶***undo*** a *button* ボタンをはずす.

V² A *button* has ***come off*** (=is ***torn off***). ボタンが取れた.

Q a man of ***brass*** *buttons* 金ボタン(制服)の人. 【類】a uniform with ***brass*** *buttons.* ¶a ***fancy*** *button* 変りボタン. ¶a ***lapel*** *button* えりき章. ¶a ***shell*** *button* 貝ボタン. ¶a ***union*** *button* 組合記章.

P I held him ***by*** the *button.* 彼を引留めて長話をした. ¶a boy ***in*** (=***of***) *buttons* 少年給仕. ¶We are ready ***to*** the last *button.* もうすっかりこっちの用意はできています.

P² *buttons* ***on*** a sweater (shirt) セーター(など)のボタン. ¶a *button* [***on*** a coat] is off [上衣の]ボタンがとれている.

button, *v.* ボタンで止める, ボタンをかける.

M These shoes *button* ***easily.*** このくつはたやすくボタンが掛けられる. ¶*button* up ***tightly*** しっかりボタンをかける.

M² *button* ***up*** one's coat 上衣にボタンをかける. ¶*button* ***up*** the lips=silence だまらせる ‖ *button* ***up*** one's pantaloons ずぼんのボタンをかける. 【類】I'll *button* you ***up.***

buttonhole, *v.* 引留める.

M I was ***abruptly*** *buttonholed* by ... 突然...に引留められた.

buy, *n.* 《俗》買いもの.

Q the world's ***best*** *buy* in motor trucks 貨物自動車では世界一の品. ¶It is not a ***good*** *buy.* それは好い買いものではない.

buy, *v.* 買う.

M I *bought* it ***back.*** 私はそれを買戻した. ¶*buy* ***cautiously*** 用心して買う. ¶You can *buy* the article ***cheaper*** at that shop. その品はあの店で安く買えます. ¶I will *buy* it, ***dear*** or ***cheap.*** 高くも安くも(値に拘らず)買いましょう. ¶It was ***dearly*** *bought.* それは高買だった. ¶*buy* ***elsewhere*** よそで買う. ¶*buy* ***freely*** どんどん買う. ¶Do not *buy* too ***hurriedly.*** あまり急いで買うな. ¶*buy* ***moderately*** 控えめに買う. ¶You can *buy* it ***nowhere else.*** それはよそでは売っていない. ¶*buy* ***secondhand*** 古で買う. ¶*buy* her ***out*** 彼女を受けだす. ¶I *bought* it ***ready-made.*** でき合いで買った. ¶*buy* ***sensibly*** 上手に買う. ¶*buy* ***wholesale*** instead of retail 小売でなくおろしで買う.

M² *buy* ***in*** bonds 債券を買込む ‖ *buy* ***in*** everything at hand 手あたり次第に買込む. ¶*buy* a person ***off*** by bribery 人を買収する ‖ *buy* ***off*** some members of the House 議員を買収する. ¶He had *bought* the jury ***over*** to a man. 彼は陪審官を残らず買収した. ‖ He had *bought* the soldiers in a body ***over*** to the invaders. 兵隊を買収して侵略軍の方に渡した. ¶*buy* ***up*** all the goods 品物を全部買占める ‖ *buy* ***up*** the latest equipment 最新型の設備を買取る.

P I have had to *buy* ***against*** you in consequence of goods not arriving in time. 品物の到着が間に合わなかったのであなたの意に反して買わなければならなかった. ¶I *bought* it ***at*** Maruzen. 私はそれを丸善で買った. 【類】*buy* it ***at*** a shop (street-stall) ‖ I *bought* them ***at*** low prices. それを安く買った. 【類】*buy* ... [***at***] so much a piece (一個いくらで). ¶I *bought* this ***at*** a sale. これを売立てで手に入れた. ‖ *buy* it ***at*** a bargain sale それを廉価で買う ‖ *buy* (***at***) retail 小売で買う ‖ *buy* [***at***] second hand 古で買う. ¶we *buy* ... ***by*** weight ...を目方で買う ‖ *buy* ***by*** the pound (box, yard) 一ポンド(など)幾らで買う. 【類】They are cheap ***by*** the hundred (百とまとめて). ‖ It was *bought* ***by*** some other person. だれか外の人に買われた. ¶I *bought* it ***for*** cash (=ready money). それを現金で買った. ‖ It can be *bought* ***for*** a few thousand yen. それは二三千円で買える. ‖ I *bought* this ***for*** under half its value. 私はこれを半値以下で買った. 【類】It cannot be *bought* ***for*** gold (=money). / I *bought* it ***for*** its weight in gold. ‖ *buy* it ***for*** one's account=buy it for account of ... ...の勘定で買う ‖ I *bought* it ***for*** my own use. 自家用に買った. ‖ It was *bought* ***for*** a certain collector. それは某収集家の内意を受けて買取ったものであった. ‖ *buy* lumber ***for*** manufacture 木材を製作原料として買う ‖ I *bought* it ***for*** little more than a song. 私はそれをほとんど二束三文で買った. ¶I *bought* it ***from*** him for cash. 彼から現金で買った. ‖ I *bought* it ***from*** New York. それをニューヨークから取り寄せた. ¶My wood was *bought* ***of*** farmers near town. 私の薪は市外の百姓から買った. 【類】You can *buy* it ***of*** any bookseller's. ¶*buy* it ***on*** credit それを掛けで買う ‖ *buy* it ***on*** speculation その投機買をする ‖ *buy* it ***on*** time それをのべで買う ‖ I *bought* this much ***on*** trial. 試しにこれだけ買った. 【類】*buy* (sell) ***on*** commission of ... per cent. ¶I *bought* it ***under*** a pound. 一ポンド以下で買った. ¶We cannot *buy* happiness ***with*** money. 幸福は金では買えない. ‖ *buy* another's favors ***with*** flattery おべっかで他人の恩顧を買う.

buyer, *n.* 買手.

V can ***find*** *buyers* for ... ...の買手を見つけられる ‖ ***find*** quick *buyers* 早く買手がつく. ¶The prices do not ***tempt*** *buyers*. その値段では買手はつかない.

Q an ***American*** (***European***) *buyer* アメリカ(欧州)のバイヤー. ¶The country is a ***heavy*** *buyer* of Japanese goods. その国は日貨の顧客だ. ¶the ***only*** *buyers* for ... ...の唯一の買手. ¶***prospective*** *buyers*=《米》prospects 買いそうな客. ¶*Buyers* are ***wary***. 買手は手控えしている.

Q² a ***blackmarket*** *buyer* やみ屋のバイヤー. ¶a prospective (=potential) ***home*** *buyer* 買いそうな国内のバイヤー.

P² he figured in the great art sales of the time as a *buyer* ***for*** ... 彼は当時の美術品売立で...から内意を受けた買手として活動した.

buying, *n.* 購買.

V ***cease*** *buying* for the present 目下の処買入れをやめる. ¶***Do*** your *buying* now. 今買込みをし給え.

Q ***preclusive*** *buying* 先回りの買い方. ¶***speculative*** *buying* おもわく買い. ¶***unwise*** *buying* まずい買い方.

Q² ***credit*** *buying* 信用買い. ¶***quantity*** *buying* 大量の買入れ. ¶on suspicion of ***vote*** *buying* 投票買収の疑いで.

buzz, *v.* [はちなどが]ぶんぶんいう.

M The machine is *buzzing* ***busily*** on the job. 機械がさかんにぶんぶん運転している.

M² *buzz* ***about*** いそがしく動き回る.

P The place is quiet enough on week days, but *buzzes* ***with*** life on Sunday. そこは普通の日は随分静かだけれど日曜は大分人出がある.

O A plane was seen *buzzing* close over tree-tops. 飛行機がこずえすれすれに飛んでるのが見えた.

buzzer, *n.* ブザー.

V ***ring*** (=***sound***) *buzzer* ブザーを鳴らす.

V² A *buzzer* ***vibrates*** when a train passes. 列車が通過する際ブザーが鳴りひびく.

buzzing, *n.* はちなどの出す音.

P² the *buzzing* ***in*** the ears 耳鳴り.

bylaw, *n.* 内規.

Q² ***village*** *bylaws* 村のおきて.

P² the *bylaws* ***of*** a club (company, an office) 会(など)の内規.

by-line, *n.* 《米》[新聞・雑誌記事の]署名 (by ...より).

P carry an article ***with*** a *by-line*=carry a by-liner 署名入り記事をのせる.

by-product, *n.* 副産物.

V It ***represents*** merely a *by-product* of a mind whose main activities lie in a sphere highly technical in nature. それは主としてきわめて専門的な研究をしている人の副産物たるにすぎない.

Q Pleasure is a very ***important*** *by-product* of education. 興味は教育の重要な副産物である.

P² a *by-product* ***from*** the oil extraction 油しぼりからの副産物.

bystander, *n.* 傍観者.

V ***send away*** the *bystanders* 傍観者を追払う.

Q as an ***impartial*** *bystander* 公平な第三者として.

C

cab, *n.* 一頭立ての馬車; タクシー.

V ***hire*** a *cab* 馬車(タクシー)を頼む.

Q² a ***hansom*** *cab* 二頭引の辻馬車.

P go ***in*** a *cab* 馬車(タクシー)で行く.

cabaret, *n.* キャバレー.

Q² an ***all-night*** *cabaret* 終夜営業のキャバレー.

cab-driver, *n.* 御者; タクシーの運転手.

Q² a ***London*** *cab-driver* ロンドンの辻馬車の御者.

cabin, *n.* 船室; 小屋.

Q Both ***first*** and ***second-class*** *cabins* are fitted in quite a luxurious style. 一二等船室ともにぜいたくな設備がしてある. ¶a ***squalid*** *cabin* 見すぼらしい小屋.

Q² a ***log*** *cabin* 丸太小屋.

P What is the charge ***in*** the first *cabin?* 一等船賃はいくらですか.

cabinet, *n.* (**1**) 内閣.

V The new *cabinet* has been ***constructed*** (=formed) as follows: 新内閣の顔ぶれは次の通りである. ¶***form*** a *Cabinet* based on a Parliamentary majority in the Diet 国会の多数与党により内閣を組織する.

V² The *cabinet* ***fell***. 内閣が倒れた.

Q² James Ramsay MacDonald formed the first ***Labor*** *Cabinet* of Great Britain in 1924. ジェームス・ラムゼー・マクドナルドは 1924 年大英帝国最初の労働党内閣を組織した. ¶form a ***coalition*** *cabinet* 連立内閣を組織する. ¶a ***single-party*** *cabinet* 単独内閣. ¶a ***war*** *cabinet* 戦時内閣.

P go ***into*** the *cabinet* 入閣する. ¶the breakup ***of*** a *cabinet* 内閣の瓦解 ‖ a change ***of*** the *cabinet* 内閣の更迭 ‖ He is a supporter ***of*** the *cabinet*. 現内閣の支持者だ.

P² the *Cabinet* ***under*** Premier ... (=the ... Cabinet) ...内閣.

(**2**) 用だんす.

Q² a ***bathroom*** *cabinet* 浴室のたんす. ¶a ***bedroom*** *cabinet* 寝室のたんす. ¶a ***china*** *cabinet* 陶器飾りだな. ¶a ***curio*** *cabinet* 骨とう品飾りだな. ¶a ***filing*** *cabinet* 書類整理だんす. ¶a ***kitchen*** *cabinet* ねずみ入らず. ¶a ***music*** *cabinet* 楽譜入. ¶a ***pigeonhole*** *cabinet* [書類用]区画戸だな. ¶a ***school*** *cabinet* 学校の便所. ¶a ***silence*** *cabinet* 声が外に漏れない室. ¶a ***utility*** *cabinet* 用だんす.

cable, *n.* 海底電線, 海外電報.

V ***build*** (=***lay***) a submarine *cable* 海底電線を敷設する.

Q² ***electric lighting*** and ***power*** *cables* 電灯および動力用架

空電線. ¶*electric-telegraph* cable 海底(地下)電線. ¶by *letter cable* (=lettergram) 間送電報で. ¶a *low-tension cable* 低圧電線. ¶an *overseas cable* 海外電線. ¶send a *protest cable* 抗議の外電を打つ.

P a reply *by cable* 海外電報による回答. 【類】The messages have come *by cable*.

cable, *v*. 海底電信で通信する.

P I *cabled in* reply. 返電を送った. ¶he *cabled* his condolence *to* … …に弔電を送った.

cablegram, *n*. 海外電報.

V *send* a *cablegram* home 海外電報を本国に送る.

cabman, *n*. =cab-driver.

Q a smartly *uniformed cabman* スマートな制服姿の御者 L(運転手).

cad, *n*. 下卑た奴.

Q a *heartless cad* 残忍な悪漢.

cadet, *n*. 士官学校の生徒.

Q² a *revenue cadet* of the revenue-cutter service 税関巡ら船見習士官. ¶*West Point cadets*=West pointers ウェスト・ポイント士官学校生徒たち.

café, *n*. 料理店; コーヒー店.

V *use* the *café* as a club その料理店をクラブに使う.

Q *gilded cafés* 高級(金ぴか)料理店.

cage, *n*. 鳥かご; わく細工.

Q² a *bathing cage* [船などの]海水浴用仕切り. ¶a *bird cage*

P² a *cage for* birds=a bird cage. L鳥かご.

caisson, *n*. ケーソン(潜函).

Q² *dock-gate caissons* ドックの入口を構築するための潜函.

cajole, *v*. 甘言でだます.

P He could not be *cajoled from* his avowal. 彼は何とだましてもその誓言を捨てるようなことはしなかった. ¶*cajole* a person *into* consent (agreement, doing …) 人を丸め込んで承諾(など)させる ‖ I am not about to *cajole* you *into* the reception of my view. 僕は君をだまして僕の意見を入れさせようとするのではない. ¶The populace are not to be *cajoled out of* a ghost story by any of these plausible explanations. 世人はこんなもっともらしい説明を聞いたって幽霊談を信じなくなるものではない. ‖ He *cajoled* a knife *out of* a child. 子供をだましてナイフを取った.

cake, *n*. 菓子; 固形物.

V *brown* a *cake* 菓子をきつね色に焼く. ¶You cannot *have* the *cake* and eat it. 二つ良いことはないもの(一得一失). ¶get things for her to *make cakes* with 彼女が菓子を造る材料を調える. ¶*Pass* the *cake* to Mr. T. [食卓で]菓子をTさんへ回して下さい. ¶*put* a *cake* in the oven to bake 焼くために菓子を焼きがまに入れる. ¶I hope you will *sample* this *cake*. It is home-made. この菓子を一つあがって見てください. 手製ですが. ¶It is the Japanese custom to *set cakes* and tea before visitors. 客に菓子と茶を出すのは日本の習慣である.

Q a *hot cake* ホット・ケーキ. ¶*light cakes* 淡白な菓子. ¶*rich cakes* こってりした菓子. ¶a *round* (*square*) *cake* 円(角)形の菓子.

Q² a *birthday cake* 誕生日の菓子. ¶a *chocolate cake* チョコレート菓子. ¶a *Christmas cake* クリスマス用菓子. ¶a *cup cake* カップ・ケーキ(紙製のコップに入っている菓子). ¶a *fancy cake* for Christmas クリスマス用のデコレーション・ケーキ. ¶*oil cakes* 油かす. ¶a *pound cake* パウンド・ケーキ. ¶*sponge cakes* with currants in them ほしぶどう入りのカステラ. ¶a *tea cake* 茶菓子.

P soap made up *in cakes* 丸いかたまりにした石けん. ¶press … *into cakes* …を押してかたまりにする. ¶ornament icing *on* a *cake* 菓子にかけた美しい糖衣. ¶Please help yourself *to* the *cake*. 菓子を御自由に召上ってください.

P² a *cake of* soap 石けん一個 ‖ a *cake of* ice 氷塊. 【類】*cakes of* ice rolling down the flood.

calamitous, *a*. 悲惨な.

M It means nothing *nationally calamitous* or discreditable. それは国民にとって不幸なことでもなく不名誉なことで Lもない.

calamity, *n*. 災難, 不幸.

V *avert* a *calamity* 災難を避ける. ¶*suffer* a *calamity* 災難に会う. ¶*ward off calamities* 厄よけをする.

V² A dire *calamity* here *befell* us. ここで恐ろしい災難がわれわれの身にふりかかった. ¶I fear that some *calamity* will *happen*. 何か災難が起りはしないかと心配だ.

Q a victim of *crushing calamities* 大災禍の犠牲. ¶a *domestic calamity* 家庭の災難. ¶War is a *frightful calamity*. 戦争は恐ろしい災禍である. ¶an *individual calamity* 個人の災難. ¶a *national calamity* 国難. ¶a *natural calamity* 天災. ¶a *real calamity* to the nation 国民にとり真の災難. ¶a *social calamity* 社会的災厄. ¶an *unavoidable calamity* 天災.

Q² a *war calamity* 戦禍. ¶a *water calamity* 水害.

P² The loss of the ship was a *calamity to* the Navy. あの船を失ったことは海軍にとっての一大不幸であった.

calculate, *v*. 数える; 考量する; 当て込む; 見込む.

M He presented his case in the light which he thought would be *best calculated* to win for it sympathetic attention. 彼はその事件を提示するに当って世間の同情的な関心を最もよく引きうると思われた方法を取った. ¶nothing would be *better calculated* to convince him of her sincerity than … …ほどに彼女の誠実さを彼に確信させうるものはなかろう. ¶It was *ill calculated* to serve the purpose at which he aimed. それは彼が企図した目的に添いそうにも思われなかった. ¶The population of the country is *calculated roughly* at 90,000,000. 同国の人口は九千万と概算されている. 【類】*Calculating roughly*, it will cost one thousand yen. ¶be *very calculating* そろばん高い. ¶Claudius Smith was a born leader of men (天才的な指導者), and *well calculated* to command the rough and dangerous band (乱暴で危険な連中の党) he had gathered around him. ¶I must have *calculated wrongly*. 私は勘定違いをやったに相違ない.

P The room is not *calculated for* such uses. このへやはこんな事に使うようには造られていない. 【類】The school is *calculated for* poor students. ¶*calculate on* (=*upon*) success 成功を当てにする ‖ *calculate on* fine weather 好天気と見込む. ¶*calculate to* a nicety 精算する.

O I *calculate* to go on a journey. 《口語》旅行をしようと L思う.

calculation, *n*. 計算; 予想.

V *baffle* one's *calculations* 人の予想を狂わせる. ¶*base* the *calculation* on the latest statistics 最近の統計に基づいて計算する. ¶*confound* the *calculations* of … …の番狂わせになる. ¶*defy calculation* 計算がしきれない(ほど多量). ¶*do* a rapid mental *calculation* とっさに暗算をやる. ¶*make* a *calculation* 計算する. ¶*perform* mathematical *calculations* 数学上の計算をやる. ¶*require* a troublesome *calculation* 面倒な計算を要する. ¶*upset* the *calculations* 予想を裏切る. ¶The *calculation* must be *worked out*. それをすっかり計算しなければならぬ.

Q a *hasty calculation* 軽率な予想. ¶*mental calculation* 暗算. ¶on a *moderate* (*liberal*) *calculation* 内輪の(大ざっ

Q² *profit-and-loss calculation* 損益計算. Lぱな)計算で.

P The result is *beyond calculation* at present. 結果は今の所見込が立たない. ¶I have made a mistake *in* my *calculation*. 私は計算違いをやった. ¶be way *off calculation* 予想が大分はずれる. ¶One thousand yen will be enough *on* a *calculation*. 見積たっところ千円で足りる.

calculator, *n*. 計算する人.

Q² a *lightning calculator* 暗(速)算の上手.

calendar, *n*. 暦(カレンダー).

V All the dates given in this story *follow* the Old *Calendar*. この物語中の日付はすべて旧暦による. ¶*keep* a *calendar* hung up before one's desk 机の前にカレンダーを掛けておく. ¶*Mark* your *calendar* now! (思出せるように)暦のその日の所に印をおつけなさい. ¶*turn back* the *calendar* for forty years 年代を四十年さかのぼる.

Q the third of the third month by the *ancient calendar* 旧暦で三月三日. ¶adoption of the *Gregorian calendar* in 1874 千八百七十四年の太陽暦採用. ¶a *hanging calendar* 掛け暦. ¶the *lunar calendar* 陰暦. ¶the *solar calendar* 太陽暦.

Q² *daily pad calendar* 日めくり. ¶The Lord Mayor's Show maintains its position year after year as one of the most popular festivals in the *London calendar*. 市長行列はロンドンの最も人気ある年中行事の一つとして毎年行われている. ¶one of the greatest events of the *racing calendar* 競馬界の最大行事の一つ. ¶a *strike calendar* ストライキの経過. ¶an advertising "*throw-away*" (=*free*) *calendar* 広告用のロハ・カレンダー.

P *in* the old *calendar* 旧暦で ‖ celebrate the day of every saint *in* the *calendar* 暦に載っているすべての聖者の日を祝う. ¶put a bill *on* the *calendar* (=agenda=order of the day) 議案を日程にのぼす. 【類】The judge will hear the next case (次の訴訟) *on* the *calendar*. ¶*under* old *calendar* 旧暦によると.

calf, *n.* 子牛.

V One great masterful bull, out of twenty bulls in a herd of a hundred cows, may easily *sire* twenty or thirty *calves*. 百頭の雌牛群中にいる二十頭の雄牛の中で一頭の大きな大将株の雄牛は容易に二三十頭の子牛の親となりうる.

Q a *bawling calf* 大きく叫ぶ子牛.

Q² *tree calf* 樹の幹および枝に似せて造った製本用子牛皮.

caliber, calibre, *n.* 口径; 才幹, 器量.

Q Their works are entirely of *different caliber* to those of mine. 彼らの作品は私のとは全然その選を異にしている. ¶guns of *fourteen inch caliber* 口径十四インチの砲. ¶a man of *great caliber* 大器. ¶a statesman of the *highest caliber* 最も優れた力量の政治家. ¶a man of his *intellectual caliber* 彼ほどの知力の優れた人. ¶The president of a railroad should be a man of *large caliber*. 鉄道会社の社長は才幹の秀でた人物でなければいけない. ¶a man of *small calibre* 器(き)が小さい人. ¶These schools are distinguished for *superior mental caliber* of their students. これらの諸学校はその学生が優秀な頭を持っているのが特徴である.

P a singer *of* Mr. ...'s *caliber* ...氏ほどの大声楽家. ‖ officers *of* the *caliber* of Lord Kitchener キッチナー卿級の軍人.

calisthenics, *n.* 柔軟(美容)体操.

Q² *mass calisthenics* 団体柔軟体操.

call, *n.* 呼声; 召出; 招へい; 訪問; 通話; 〘商〙当座貸付(コール); 〘株〙払込請求.

V He has *accepted* the *call* to the chair of physics in that university. 彼は同大学の物理学講座への招へいに応じた. ‖ He *accepted* a *call* to the presidency of the College. 彼はその大学の学長への招へいに応じた. ¶He hurried to *answer* the *call*. 彼は(電話の)呼声に急いで応じた. ‖ *answer* the *call* for volunteers 義勇兵の募集に応じる. 【類】Nobly and cheerfully he *answered* the *call* of duty and fought the brave fight and the supreme sacrifice (名誉の戦死). ‖ *anwer* the *call* of the blood 血の呼掛に応じる(白人は白人に同情するなど). ¶The doctor *attended* a professional *call*. その医者は患者から呼ばれて訪問した. ¶*await* the *call* of duty 本分を尽すための呼掛け(召集)を待つ. ¶The professor *declined* a *call* to another university. 同教授は他の大学の招へいを断った. ¶You *got* a *call* from Miss White. ホワイトさんからお電話でしたよ. ¶I won't fail to *give* you a *call*. きっとお訪ね致します. ‖ *give* a long *call* 長時間の訪問をする. ¶I've just *had* a *call* from that friend of yours, Mr. T. 貴下の友人のあのTさんから丁度訪問(電話)を受けた所です. ‖ *have* a *call* to the ministry 牧師職に召される ‖ You *have* no *call* to blush. 君は赤面するには当らない. ‖ Heifers *had* the *call* of the market at £17 to £20 each. 一頭十七ポンドないし二十ポンドという所で雌の子牛の需要が非常にあった. ‖ *have* a *call* of nature 大(小)便を催す. ¶*head* the *call* of honor beyond the call of race 名誉の呼掛を民族の呼掛以上に顧慮する. ¶*issue* a *call* for a meeting to be held at ... ...において開催される会合への案内状を発する. 【類】*issue* a *call* to him to attend ... ‖ *issue calls* to the colors 軍隊への召集令状を発する ‖ The newspaper *issued* the first *call* for aid. その新聞が救済募集の第一声をあげた. ¶*make* a *call* on ... ...を訪問する ‖ *make* a *call* at ... ...の家を訪ねる. 【類】*make calls* at chief ports (寄港する) on the Pacific coast ‖ *make* a *call* over the telephone 電話をかける ‖ Sunday is not the proper day for *making calls*. 日曜は本来人を訪問すべき日ではない. ‖ A *call* of ... per share has been *made*. 一株に付...の払込催告があった. ¶I was very sorry to *miss* your *call*. お出で下さったのにるすで誠にすみません. ¶The steamer *omitted* a *call*. 汽船は寄航を見合わせた. ¶Mind, you *owe* me a *call* now. いいかね, 今度は君が僕を訪問する番だよ. ¶*pay* a *call* on shares 株の払込をする. ¶He *received* his *call* as a poet in a dream. 彼は夢の中で詩人として世に立つの使命を受けた. ‖ The General has spent the day in *receiving* and *returning calls* from his colleagues. 将軍はその日は同僚から訪問を受けたりまた訪問を返したりして暮した. 【類】You must *return* promptly a *call* made upon you. ¶A personal *call* is *solicited*. 直接の面談を希望する.

Q *bridal calls* 新婚あいさつの訪問. ¶a *brief call* 短時間の訪問. ¶receive *ceremonial calls* 正式の訪問を受ける. ¶It was a *close call*. 《米》あやうく難をのがれた. ¶a *congratulatory call* 祝賀の訪問. ¶make a *domiciliary call* at one's house 家宅捜索をする. ¶pay a *formal call* 正式の訪問をする. ¶make *frequent* (*several*) *calls* on a person 人を度々(数回)訪問する. ¶make a *fruitless call* むだ足をする. ¶make *further calls* その後度々訪問する. ¶a *greater call* (=demand) for ... ますますふえる...の需要. ¶That was his *last call*. それっきり訪ねて来ない. ¶*local calls* 市内電話. ¶a *maiden call* at Dover ドーヴァ港への処女寄航. ¶there are *many calls* for ... ...を欲しがるものが多い. ¶We make *New Year's call* on our customers. お得意先へ年始回りをする. ¶There is *no call* to blush. 何も赤面することはない. ¶I have *one more* (=*another*) *call* to make. もう一軒訪ねる家がある. ¶make a *personal call* 自身訪問をする. ¶a *short call* 短時間の訪問. ¶pay *social calls* 社交上の訪問をする. ¶a *third call* of 50 yen 第三回の払込金五十円. ¶an *uncalled-for call* 余計な訪問. ¶have an *urgent call* from ... ...から急用で呼ばれる. ¶the *wordless call* of these mountains これらの山の無言の呼びかけ.

Q² an *afternoon call* 午後の訪問. ¶put in an *alarm call* from the nearest signal box 一番近い信号所から非常信号を伝達する. ¶sound the *bugle call* 召集らっぱを吹鳴らす. 【類】*bugle calls* are sounded for ... ¶make a *business call* 商用で人を訪ねる. ¶*closing time call* 閉店時間の知らせ. ¶make a *courtesy call* on ... ...に儀礼的訪問をする. ¶clap for a *curtain call* 幕前あいさつに呼出すために拍手する. ¶The stars took *curtain calls* in answer to round after round of applause. 次ぎ次ぎに起るかっさいに答えてスターたちは幕前に現われた. 【類】Thunderous applause (割れるようなかっさい) brought the actors to the front for repeated *curtain calls*. / respond to five *curtain calls*. ¶a *draft call* of the Army 軍隊の分遣隊召集. ¶answer a *distress call* from a ship 船舶からの遭難信号に応信する. ¶an *emergency call* 非常警鈴. 【類】*emergency calls* on the telephone. ¶a *farewell call* 暇ごい. ¶make *house-to-house calls* for orders 戸別訪問的に注文を取る. ¶receive a *long-distance* [*phone*] *call* 長距離電話の呼出を受ける. ¶make a *morning call* 朝の訪問をする. ¶a *person call* 通話者指定通話. ¶receive a *phone call* from ... ...からの電話呼出を受ける. ¶answer *phone calls* 電話呼出に応答する. ¶make *P.P.C. calls* 告別訪問をする. ¶a *return call* 答礼訪問. 【類】make a *return call* on ... ¶answer a *roll call* 点呼に答える ‖ line up for the morning *roll call* 朝の点呼のために整列する. ¶issue a *strike call* 罷業の声明を発する. 【類】revoke (取消す) a *strike call*. ¶get a [*tele*]*phone call* 電話がかかる. ¶had a [*tele*]*phone call* from ... ...から電話の呼出しがあった ‖ make a *telephone call* to ... ...に電話をかける ‖ pester with *telephone calls* and letters 電話と手紙で悩ます(投稿など) ‖ incoming and outgoing *telephone calls* 受ける電話と掛ける電話 ‖ an anonymous *telephone call* threatening to ... ...すると脅迫する掛け主不明の電話呼出 ‖ the handling of *telephone calls* 電話呼出しの受付. ¶the *trumpet call* of action 戦闘開始の集合らっぱ.

P awake *at* the *call* 呼ぶ声に目をさます ‖ come *at* his *call* 彼に呼ばれたので来る ‖ rise *at* our country's *call* 祖国の危機を見て立つ ‖ *at* the *call* of the Emperor 陛下の御召に応じて. 【類】Meetings of the Executive Committee shall be held *at* the *call* of the Chairman. ‖ *at* the *call* of duty =at duty's call 本分の呼掛に応じて ‖ *at* the first *call* to arms 軍隊への召集があり次第 ‖ loans *at call* コール貸付け. ¶*by* a *call* for the ayes and noes 可否の採決によって. ¶I suppose you have quite a round *of calls* to make! あなたはたくさん回る(訪問する)所がおありのようですね. ¶go to the relief of a distressed ship *on* wireless *calls* 無線電信に接して遭難船の救助に出向く ‖ money *on call* 当座貸付金. ¶*under* a three months' *call* 三箇月の召集で. ¶There are plenty of police *within call*. 呼べば声の届く所に警官が大勢いる. 【類】*within* telephone *call* of ...

P² a *call before* the curtain=a curtain call. ¶a tradesman's *call for* orders 御用聞きの訪問 ‖ a *call* (=demand) *for* articles 品物の需要 ‖ a *call for* rescue 救いを求める声.

call, *v.* 呼ぶ, 招く; 称する; 求める; 訪問する; 《米》電話をかける.

M Then I'll *call again*. ではまたあがりましょう; ではもう

一度お呼出しをしましょう. ‖ I hope you will *call* ***again*** soon. すぐまたお訪ね下さい. ¶a short-barrelled firearm ***anciently*** *called* a dragoon 昔はドラグーンと呼んだ銃身の短い鉄砲. ¶I was *called* ***away*** and scarcely knew what to say. 私は心乱れて何と言っていいのか当惑した. ‖ *call* Congress ***back*** 《米国》議会を再開する ‖ *call* ***back*** to … …の呼び声に答える ‖ *Call* [me] ***back*** later. [電話]後でまたかけて下さい. ‖ be *called* ***back*** to life 生返る ‖ He would like to *call* you ***back*** as soon as he is free. 彼は手があき次第また電話に出てもらいたいと言っています. ¶*call* him ***back*** to life 彼をよみがえらせる. ¶it is *called* ***colloquially*** "…" それは俗に…と呼ばれている. ¶it is ***commonly*** *called* "…" いわゆる「…」. ¶be ***corruptly*** *called* … なまって…となっている. ¶it is ***derisivelly*** *called* … それはばかにして…といわれている. ¶Please *call* me ***early*** tomorrow. あした早く起して下さい. ¶We *call* it … ***euphemistically***. われわれはそれを遠曲に…と呼ぶ. ¶The Institute of Foreign Travel is ***familiarly*** *called* I F T in these days of alphabetical enthusiasm. 海外旅行協会は略語ばやりのこのごろでは IFT と言っている. ¶it is ***fancifully*** *called* … それには…というしゃれた名がついている. ¶It is ***fitly*** *called* the most beautiful of cities. それは最も美麗な都市と言われるのも当然だ. ¶*call* ***forth*** clamours of indignation けんけんごうごうたる憤激を惹起する ‖ *call* ***forth*** spirits by magic 魔術で亡霊を呼出す ‖ *call* ***forth*** no response in his breast 彼の心情に少しも応えない ‖ *call* ***forth*** a flush of shame (triumph) 赤面(得意に)させる ‖ *call* ***forth*** all the faculties of the mind 知恵をしぼる. 【類】 *call* ***forth*** a sense of indignation / *call* ***forth*** one's reminiscences / His address *called* ***forth*** applause. ‖ *call* ***forth*** denunciation of … …だと非難を招く. ¶*call* ***frequently*** 度々訪問する. ¶The British Ambassador was *called* ***home***. 英国大使は帰国を命ぜられた. ¶***How*** (= ***What***) do you *call* that? それは何という名ですか. ¶*call* ***imperatively*** for a reform ぜひ改革を要する. ¶it might not ***improperly*** be *called* … それを…といっても差支えないだろう. ¶the "Chief", as they ***lovingly*** *call* Croker クローカー氏を親しんで呼ぶ彼らのいわゆる「隊長」. ¶He *called* ***out*** for help. 彼は大声で助けを求めた. ‖ He *called* ***out*** for his wife. 彼は大声で妻を呼んだ. ‖ distinctly *call* ***out*** the names of stations 駅名をはっきり呼ばわる ‖ *call* ***out*** from the head of the stairs はしご段の上から怒鳴る ‖ He *called* ***out*** with pain. 彼は痛いので大声をあげた. ‖ He *called* ***out*** in his sleep. 彼は眠っていて声を掛けた. ‖ *called* ***out*** to … …に声をかけた ‖ He *called* me ***out***. 彼は僕を呼出した. ‖ *call* ***out*** reservists 予備兵を召集する ‖ *call* ***out*** them together 彼らを呼び集める ‖ The military has been *called* ***out***. 軍隊が召集された. ‖ *call* … ***out and out*** …としきりに叫ぶ. ¶He *called* on me ***personally***. 彼は自身私を訪問した. ¶Will Hays is ***popularly*** *called* the "Tzar" of Hollywood. ウイル・ヘイズはハリウッドではツァー(大御所)で通っている. ¶***preferably*** *called* … …と言った方が正しいのだが. ¶It is ***rightly*** *called* … …と言われるのももっともだ. ¶He may ***safely*** be *called* the best writer of English in Japan. 彼は日本の英文家として第一人者であると言ってさしつかえあるまい. ¶they ***slightingly*** *call* it … 世人は軽べつしてそれを…と言う. ¶***so*** *called* because … その名がつけられた訳は… ‖ Political economy, properly ***so*** *called*, has grown up almost from infancy since the time of Adam Smith.—John Stuart Mill. 本当の意味の経済学はアダム・スミスの時代からほとんど新規に発達したものである. 【類】 The Waverley novels are a series of historical novels (歴史小説の双書) by Sir Walter Scott: ***so*** *called* from the first book of the series. / it is ***so*** *called* on account of … / It is euphemistically (遠曲に) ***so*** *called*. ¶I was ***suddenly*** *called* home on urgent business. 突然急用で帰宅した. ¶It was Bonaparte who ***tauntingly*** *called* the English "a nation of shopkeepers." 英国人をあざけって「商売国民」と言ったのはナポレオン・ボナパルトであった. ¶be ***variously*** *called*, "a …, or …; or…" 「…あるいは…あるいは…」と色々の呼び方がある. ¶it has ***well*** been *called* … それが…と呼ばれてきたのももっともなことである. ¶***What*** do you *call* such conduct? このていたらくは君どうしたというのか.

M² He *called* me ***down*** like anything. 彼は私をひどくしかった. ¶He *called* ***down*** a blessing on her head. 彼は彼女の上に天恵の天降らんことを祈った. ‖ *call* ***down*** the curse of Heaven on … …の上に天ののろいを呼びおろす. 【類】 *call* ***down*** the vengeance of Heaven (天罰) upon … ¶*call* ***in*** at a port 寄港する ‖ A doctor was *called* ***in***. 医者を招(よ)んだ. 【類】 A physician was *called* ***in*** for advice (診察に). / Military advisers were *called* ***in*** from France. / *call* ***in*** police to restore order. / *call* ***in*** the aid of … …の手を借りる ‖ *call* ***in*** money lent 貸金を取立てる ‖ *call* ***in*** the services of … …の尽力を頼む ‖ *call* ***in*** loans on real estates 不動産を抵当の貸出しを回収する ‖ *call* ***in*** a person to his assistance …の力を借りる. ¶*call* ***off*** a dinner (game, meeting) 晩餐会(など)を中止する ‖ The dog was *called* ***off*** when about to bark at a pussy. その犬はねこにほえ付こうとして止められた. 【類】 *call* ***off*** the hounds (猟犬を) / *call* ***off*** their meeting / *call* ***off*** his regular press conference / *call* ***off*** negotiations with … / *call* ***off*** one's engagement (婚約) / *call* ***off*** a festival / *call* ***off*** a party / *call* ***off*** walkouts (スト) / *call* ***off*** general strike (ゼネスト) / *call* ***off*** a revolt (反乱) ‖ Imperative and unexpected business made me *call* ***off*** our engagement. 急にやむを得ない用事ができて約束を守る事ができなかった. ¶The officer *called* ***over*** the names of his men. 士官は部下の姓名を声高く読み上げた. ¶*call* ***up*** spirits, good or bad 善または悪の亡霊を呼出す ‖ *call* him ***up*** 彼に電話する. 【類】 I will *call* you ***up*** on the telephone. / I will *call* you ***up*** later and tell you all about it. ‖ be *called* ***up*** for military service 召集される ‖ The division was *called* ***up*** to active duty. その師団は出動命令を受けた. 【類】 *call* them ***up*** to their daily labor / Hired men on the farms were *called* ***up***. / *call* ***up*** reservists (予備兵).

P *call* ***across*** a river 川向こうに声をかける. ¶I *called* ***after*** you, but you did not hear. 君のうしろから呼んだのだが聞えなかった. ‖ He *called* ***after*** the children who were fleeing. 彼は逃げて行く子供らを大声で呼んだ. ‖ She was *called* Sophia ***after*** her mother. 彼女は母親の名をとってソフィアと命名された. 【類】 They *called* him ***after*** the illustrious (有名な) Washington. ¶he is not *called* or considered ***as*** a scholar unless … …でなければ学者とはいわれないあるいは考えられない. ¶*call* ***at*** one's house (home, residence, office, hotel) 人の家(など)を訪問する. ‖ The liner *called* ***at*** Hongkong. その汽船は香港に寄港した. 【類】 This boat *calls* ***at*** intermediate ports (中間諸港) on the way. ‖ I will *call* ***at*** the post office and enquire whether the ship is in. 郵便局へ行ってその船が入港しているかどうか尋ねよう. ¶by *calling* him ***at*** 23-3137 彼を電話 23-3137 番で呼び出して. ¶He was *called* ***before*** the manager (judge, committee). 彼は支配人(など)の前に呼び出された. ¶*call* a person ***by*** name その人の名前を呼ぶ ☞ call a person names 悪口を言う. 【類】 *call* a person ***by*** name without using a title of courtesy (敬称をつけずに) ‖ *call* a person ***by*** his last name only 姓を呼捨てにする. 【類】 People *call* him ***by*** the name of John. / He is *called* ***by*** the name of Paul. / *call* reporters ***by*** their first (=Christian) names (なれなれしく) ‖ see things as they are and *call* things ***by*** their proper names 事物をありのままに見, 本来の名称でこれを呼ぶ ‖ as it is *called* ***by*** its detractors 悪口でそう言われるように ‖ *Call* a spade ***by*** no other name than a spade. 卒直に言いたまえ. ¶I will *call* ***for*** you at your house. あなたをお宅までお誘いに上ります. 【類】 *Call* ***for*** me on your way to the station. / tradesmen (商人) *calling* ***for*** orders ‖ To be [left till] *called* ***for*** =《仏》*poste restante*. 郵便局留置. 【類】 This parcel is to be left till *called* ***for***. ‖ We *called* ***for*** beer. われわれはビールを命じた. ‖ *call* ***for*** medical (=medicinal) aid 医者にかかる. 【類】 *call* ***for*** a raise (=rise) in pay / The meeting is *called* ***for*** Monday. ‖ *call* ***for*** cheers for … …の万歳を唱える音頭を取る ‖ It is too ovbious to *call* ***for*** comment. それはあまりにも明白なことで註釈はいらない. 【類】 Being self-explanatory, it *calls* ***for*** no further comment from us. / *call* ***for*** an explanation ‖ The occasion *calls* ***for*** a cool head. この場合は冷静に考える必要がある. ‖ There is nothing much to *call* ***for*** special remark. 特にいうべきほど大したこともない. ‖ a question *calling* ***for*** serious consideration 真剣な考慮を要する問題. 【類】 It *called* ***for*** reflection (慎重な反省). / Explanation is *called* ***for***. / *call* ***for*** such a publication / be *called* ***for*** encores (アンコー

ル) / *call **for*** further consideration ‖ if a second edition is *called **for*** 再版の要求があったら ‖ It *calls **for*** the highest commendation. それは絶賛する値打がある. ‖ *call **for*** the expenditure of ¥…. …円の出費を要する ‖ thoughts *called **for*** by his death 彼の死によって呼起される感想 ‖ Every crime *calls **for*** punishment. 犯罪はすべて罰する必要がある. ‖ *call **for*** a meeting 会を開催する ‖ *call **for*** help 声をあげて救いを求める. 【類】 *call **for*** a cab (=taxi) ‖ *call **out for*** one's wife 妻を呼ぶ ‖ What *calls **for*** this merriment? なぜ笑うか. ‖ *call **for*** public airing 発表する必要がある ‖ *call **for*** a three-power conference to discuss the question その問題を論議するために三大国会議を要請する. ¶was so *called **from*** the name of … …の名に因んでそういう名が付けられた. ¶His integrity has never been *called **in*** question. 彼の清廉はいまだかって疑われた事がない. ‖ pronunciations *called **in*** question 問題になった発音. ¶The plant was *called **into*** being by war requirements. 同工場は戦争の影響で出現したものだ. ‖ A combination of these circumstances *called* the British Empire ***into*** being. これらの情勢が重なって英帝国を現出させた. 【類】 the circumstances under which the society (協会) was *called **into*** being ‖ *call* it ***into*** service それを持ち出して使う ‖ *call* it ***into*** existence それを現出させる ‖ *call **into*** existence an abundant crop of literature おびただしい文献の出版を見る. 【類】 books *called **into*** being by the … centenary (百年祭) ‖ I *call **into*** doubt the correctness of the statement. 私はその記事の正確さを疑う. 【類】 I *call* its validity (真実性) ***into*** doubt. ‖ *call* it ***into*** question それを問題にする ‖ *call* one ***into*** a room (house) 人を室(など)に呼び入れる. ¶I shall *call **on*** you tomorrow. 明日あなたをお訪ね致しましょう. ‖ *call **on*** a person for … 人に…するよう求める. 【類】 They *called **on*** him for aid. / He was unexpectedly *calling **on*** me for a speech! / be *called **on*** for explanation / be *called **on*** to perform some stunt (隠し芸など) / The teacher *called **on*** him to answer. ‖ *call **on*** shares 株の払込を催告する ‖ She will not *call **on*** this voyage ***at*** … 船は今度の航海では…に立寄らない. ¶He was *called **out of*** town. 彼は用があって町から出た. ¶She raised her voice to *call **to*** her sister. 彼女は声を張り上げて妹を呼んだ. 【類】 I *called **to*** him and heard him answer. / *call **to*** a person to stop / He *called* me ***to*** his side. ‖ The bell *called **to*** dinner. 食事のベルが鳴った. ‖ He *called **to*** me ***for*** help. 私に助けを求めた. ‖ *call* it ***to*** mind それを思い出す ‖ I cannot this minute *call* it ***to*** mind. ちょっとど忘れした. ‖ He is *called **to*** the ministry. 伝道に従事している. ‖ be *called **to*** the head (=home) office 本社詰になる ‖ He was *called **to*** the company's service. その会社に招へいされた. ‖ *called **to*** office by the confidence of the President of the United States 米大統領の信頼で任用された ‖ The member was *called **to*** order by the Speaker. 同議員は議長に静粛を命ぜられた. 【類】 The meeting was *called **to*** order by the chairman. ‖ I *call* heaven ***to*** witness. 天の照覧を祈る. ‖ *call* him ***to*** account 彼をけん責する ‖ He was *called **to*** the bar. 彼は弁護士になった. ‖ be *called **to*** the stand … 証人台に立つことを要請される ‖ be *called **to*** the colors by their government 召集される. ¶I *called **upon*** him for aid in the solution of the problem. その問題の解決について彼の知恵を借りた. 【類】 *call **upon*** one's wife to … 妻に…させる / be *called **upon*** to speak (=make a speech) / be *called **upon*** to pay down (現金払) / be *called **upon*** to do so many things / The country *called **upon*** us to defend her. / The teacher *called **upon*** him (あてた) to read. ‖ if *called **upon*** to do so ‖ they are *called **upon*** to swear that … 彼らは…を誓約することを求められる ‖ *call **upon*** God to witness … 神に…を御照覧あらんことを願う. 【類】 *call **upon*** heaven to aid us ‖ Please do not hesitate to *call **upon*** us at any time that we can be of assistance to you. お役に立つような時はご遠慮なくいつでもお出で下さい. ‖ The law was *called **upon***. 法律に訴えた.

O Must I *call* you a liar as well as a thief? お前は泥棒をした上にうそまでつくのか. ¶This is what I *call* real coffee—it's the most delicious I've ever tasted. これが本当のコーヒーというものだ—こんなおいしいコーヒーは飲んだことがない. ¶I don't *call* that fair. それは公平とは言えない.

callable, *a.* 請求によって支払われる.

P *callable **at*** a day's notice 一日の予告で支払の請求ができる.

caller, *n.* 訪問者.

V I ***have*** a *caller*. 来客がある. ¶I personally ***received*** 300 *callers* in one week. 一週三百人の訪問者に親しく接した.

Q[2] an ***afternoon*** *caller* 午後の来訪者. ¶an expert ***bird*** *caller* 鳥寄せの名人. ¶receive ***office*** *callers* 事務所へ来る人の応対をする.

P[2] a *caller **at*** one's house (home, hotel) 家(など)への訪問者 ‖ *callers **at*** this office 当事務所への来訪者.

calligraphy, *n.* 能書; 筆跡.

Q in ***rude*** *calligraphy* 金くぎ流で.

P He possessed astonishing skill ***in*** *calligraphy*. 彼は驚くほど書に巧みであった.

calling, *n.* 職業; 点呼.

V ***betray*** one's *calling* お里が知れる. ¶those who ***follow*** the *calling* その職業に従事する人たち. 【類】 ***follow*** another *calling* in addition (副業). ¶His *calling* ***laid aside***, he lived at ease. 彼は商売をやめて気楽に暮した. ¶***pursue*** one's *calling* as an engraver 彫版師としての職業に従事する. 【類】 Fishermen ***pursue*** their *calling* in constant difficulty and danger.

Q follow a ***certain*** *calling* 一定の職につく. ¶follow the ***homely*** *calling* of a chimney sweep 煙突掃除という卑しい職業に従事する. ¶a ***humble*** *calling* 卑しい家業. ¶engaged in the pursuit of a ***legitimate*** (=***respectable***) *calling* 正業についている. ¶The emoluments of the ***literary*** *calling* 文筆業者の報酬. ¶a list of ***little-known*** *callings* 世に知られぬ職業の数々. ¶the ***main*** *calling* 本職. ¶Among the Greeks the acting profession was looked upon as a ***noble*** *calling*. ギリシア人の間では俳優はりっぱな職業と見なされていた. ‖ A man of letters follows the ***noblest*** *calling* which any man can pursue.—Thackeray. 文学者の仕事は世に最も気高いものである. ¶***odd*** *callings* for women 女が片手間にできる仕事. ¶a ***precarious*** *calling* 不安定な職業. ¶one's ***regular*** *calling* 本職. ¶a ***sacred*** *calling* 神聖な職業. ¶an ***unattractive*** *calling* 人好きのしない職業. ¶follow ***useful*** *callings* 有益な職業に従事する.

P ***By*** *calling*, he is a carpenter. 彼の職は大工だ. 【類】 I was a ferry-man (渡し船の船頭) ***by*** *calling*.

P[2] the *calling **of*** a roll 氏名点呼.

calling-place, *n.* 寄港地.

P[2] a *calling-place **for*** liners 定期船の寄港地.

callous, *a.* 無感覚な.

P He is perfectly *callous **to*** ridicule (rebuke). 彼はあざけり(など)に対して全く無感覚だ. 【類】 grow *callous **to*** it because accustomed.

callousness, *n.* 無感覚, 無神経.

Q astounding ***moral*** *callousness* and blindness 驚くべき道徳上の無神経・盲目ぶり.

calm, *n.* 静穏, 無風.

Q a ***dead*** *calm* 大なぎ. ¶He paid for ***external*** *calm* with an internal struggle. 彼は上べは平静を装っていたが心は煩もんしていた. ¶He said so with ***forced*** *calm*. 平静を装ってそう言った. ¶eye one with ***frosty*** *calm* 冷静に人の顔を見る. ¶with ***imperturbable*** *calm* 落ちつき払って.

Q[2] an ***evening*** (a ***morning***) *calm* 夕(朝)なぎ.

P The storm was followed ***by*** a great *calm*. あらしの後は大なぎになった.

calm, *a.* 静かな.

P It is *calm **of*** him to expect me to do so. 私にそれをしてもらおうと思うなんて彼も随分虫がいい.

calm, *v.* 静める; なだめる.

M[2] *calm **down*** an angry man 怒っている人をなだめる.

calmness, *n.* 冷静さ.

Q ***philosophic*** *calmness* 哲学者流の冷静.

calory, *n.* カロリー(熱量の単位).

V ***furnish*** 35 to 40 *calories* per bodyweight per diem 毎日体重に対し三十五ないし四十カロリーを供給する.

calumny, *n.* 中傷, ざんぼう.

V ***heap*** *calumny* upon … …にざんぼうを浴びせかける. ¶***ward off*** *calumnies* ばりざんぼうをはねつける.

Q It was a ***mere*** *calumny*, not a shadow of proof. それは単なる中傷であってちっとも証明にはならなかった.

P they actively propagated all sorts of *calumnies **against*** … 彼らは…に対しありとあらゆるざんぼうを盛んにふりまいた.

camel, *n.* らくだ.

Q^2 a *slaughter camel* 屠(と)殺用のらくだ.

P^2 The reindeer is the *camel of* the desert of snow. となかいは雪のさばくのらくだだ.

camera, *n.* (**1**) 写真機.

V ***call*** the *camera* to one's aid 写真機の力を借りる. ¶***click*** the *camera* カメラをパチリとやる. ¶Shy film stars ***dodge*** *cameras.* 気の小さい映画スターはカメラを避ける. ¶***grind*** a *camera* [撮影のため]カメラを回す. ¶***level*** the *camera* at ... ...にカメラを向ける. ¶***load*** a *camera* 写真機にフィルムを入れる. ¶***snap*** the *camera* at ... ...にカメラを向けてパチリと写す.

V^2 The *camera* ***started*** turning. [映画の]カメラを回し(撮影を)始めた.

Q a ***collapsible*** *camera* じゃ腹式写真機.

Q^2 a ***motionpicture*** *camera* (=projector) 映写機(映画の). ¶a ***movie*** *camera* 映写機(おもに小型の). ¶face the ***news-reel*** *cameras* ニュース映画カメラで撮影される. ¶a ***vest-pocket*** *camera* 小型カメラ.

P an incessant fire ***of*** *cameras* 絶え間ないカメラの攻撃.

(**2**) 判事の私室; 非公開.

P The details of the trial were heard ***in*** *camera.* その公判の詳細は傍聴禁止で尋問された. ¶The caucus is a meeting of political leaders usually to be held ***in*** *camera.* 幹部会は一般に非公開の政党幹部の会合である.

cameraman, *n.* 撮影技師(カメラマン).

V ***take*** a *cameraman* along カメラマンを連れて行く.

Q^2 an "***ace***" *cameraman* ピカーのカメラマン. ¶a ***motion-picture*** *cameraman*=a cinematographer 映画撮影技師.

camouflage, *n.* 偽装.

V ***wear*** *comouflage* 偽装する.

camp, *n.* 陣営, 露営.

V ***break up*** (=***strike***) a *camp* 露営を解く. ¶***make*** a *camp* 陣取る ‖ ***make*** *camp* under the shade of trees 樹陰に露営する. ¶***pitch*** *camp* (=bivouac) 露営する. 【類】***pitch*** one's camp at ...

Q a ***fortified*** *camp* 防御工事をした陣地. ¶a ***hunter's*** *camp* 猟師の仮小屋.

Q^2 an ***aviation*** (=***flying***) *camp* 航空隊駐とん所. ¶a ***base*** *camp* 基地陣営. ¶a ***clearance*** *camp* for refugees 避難者処理所. ¶the ***Communist*** *camp* 共産陣営. ¶clap them in ***concentration*** *camps* 彼らを俘虜(ふょ)収容所にぶち込む. 【類】a prisoner-physician (俘虜の医師) in a German ***concentration*** *camp.* ¶a ***detention*** *camp* 抑留者収容所. ¶a ***DP*** (=***displaced persons***) *camp* 戦争流民収容所. ¶an ***internment*** *camp* 敵国人抑留所. ¶an ***isolation*** *camp* 隔離所. ¶a ***labor*** *camp* 労働者のたまり場. ¶a Soviet ***labor*** *camp* ソ連の労働陣営. ¶a ***lumber*** *camp* 仮伐木所. ¶a ***mining*** *camp* 仮採鉱所. ¶the Hirohata ***POW*** ***Camp*** 広畑俘虜収容所. ¶a ***prison*** *camp* 俘虜収容所. ¶the commander of a ***prisoner-of-war*** *camp* 俘虜収容所所長. ¶a ***refugee*** *camp* 避難民収容所. ¶a ***repatriation*** *camp* 帰還者収容所. ¶a ***training*** *camp* for recruits 新兵訓練所 ‖ a military ***training*** *camp* 軍事訓練所. ¶a ***war felon*** *camp* 戦犯収容所. ¶a ***youth correction*** *camp* 感化院.

P be found ***in*** the same *camp* 味方同志である.

camp, *v.* 野営する.

M *camp out* 野営する(キャンプをする).

campaign, *n.* 戦役; 運動.

V ***begin*** a *campaign* against ... ...と戦争を始める. ¶***carry on*** a *campaign* against the rival forces under ... ...指揮下の敵軍と対戦する. 【類】***carry on*** a *compaign* for educational reform / ***carry on*** a vigorous *campaign* for enlarging the influence of the society (協会). ¶***conduct*** (=carry on) a *campaign* of advertising 宣伝の火ぶたを切る ‖ ***conduct*** a *campaign* for the fund of a new school building 校舎新築の資金募集を行う. ¶An energetic *campaign* was ***inaugurated.*** 盛んな運動が開始された. ¶***initiate*** a powerful *campaign* to boost British films 英国製映画を後援する有力な運動を開始する. 【類】***initiate*** a strenuous (奮闘的) *campaign* in favor of ... ¶***intensify*** a *campaign* 運動を強化する. ¶the magazine ***launched*** a *campaign* for ... その雑誌が...の運動を開始した. ¶***make*** a speaking *campaign* 遊説する. ¶***map out*** a *compaign* 作戦計画の概略を書く. ¶***organize*** a publicity *campaign* 宣伝計画を立てる. ¶***plan*** a *compaign* 作戦計画をする. ¶the *campaign* is ***sponsored*** by ... その運動は...が後援している ‖ the committee ***started*** an active *campaign* for funds for ... 委員は...資金募集のため盛んな運動を開始した. ¶***undertake*** a *campaign* against the rat ねずみ退治を始める. 【類】***undertake*** a *campaign* for a twenty million dollar endowment fund for research in pure science (純粋科学研究のため). ¶It is continually ***waging*** an intensive *campaign* to rouse the country to the peril. それは国家をその危険を悟らせるよう絶えず猛烈な運動をやっている.

Q begin an ***active*** *campaign* in the encouragement of ... ...奨励の活発な運動を開始する. ¶start a ***chauvinistic*** *campaign* against ... ...の向うを張って愛国運動をやる. ¶surrender a large part of the fruits of a brilliantly ***conducted*** *campaign* 赫々たる戦勝の結果を大部分放棄する. ¶an ***effective educational*** *campaign* 効果的教育運動. ¶an ***evangelistic*** *campaign* 福音宣伝. ¶a ***heated*** *campaign* 熱烈な運動. ¶the ***Japanese*** *campaign* against Russia 日露戦役. ¶the ***late victorious American*** *campaign* 先ごろの米出征軍の勝利. ¶the recently ***launched*** *campaign* against outdoor advertising 近ごろ始まった戸外広告反対運動. ¶a ***nation-wide*** *campaign* 全国的な運動. ¶an ***oratorical*** *campaign* 遊説. ¶promote a ***political*** *campaign* 政治運動を促進する. ¶a ***sober*** *campaign* against war 真剣な反戦運動. ¶made an ***unsuccessful*** *campaign* for Congress in 1920 一九二〇年の(米国)国会議員選挙運動に失敗した. ¶***vigorous educative*** *campaigns* 盛んな教育運動.

Q^2 an ***anti-Japanese press*** *campaign* 新聞による排日宣伝. ¶an ***anti-tuberculosis*** *campaign* 結核撲滅運動. ¶conduct ***advertising*** *campaigns* 宣伝戦を行う. 【類】plan an ***advertising*** *campaign* / a nation-wide ***advertising*** *campaign* ‖ Japan's national ***advertising*** *campaign* to bring more tourists and travelers to her shores. ¶an ***air*** *campaign* 飛行機を利用した宣伝. ¶an ***all-out selling*** *campaign* 蔵払い大売出し. ¶launch ***annihilation*** *campaigns* against ... ...に対し殲(せん)滅戦を開始する. ¶an ***anti-crime*** *campaign* 犯罪撲滅運動. ¶initiate a "***back-to-normalcy***" *campaign* to reduce prices 物価を引下げるために"常態に戻せ"運動を始める. ¶a ***clean-up*** *campaign* 掃蕩(とう)戦; [政界などの] 粛正運動. ¶a "***don't buy***" *campaign* 「不買」運動. ¶an ***election*** *campaign* 選挙運動. ¶a "***Buy-war-bond***" *campaign* "戦時債券購入勧告"運動. ¶Gandhi's ***civil disobedience*** *campaigns* ガンジーの武力によらぬ反抗運動. ¶a Presidential ***Election*** *campaign* 大統領選挙運動. ¶***electioneering*** *campaign* 選挙運動. ¶conduct a ***follow-up*** *campaign* to ... ...の波状運動をやる. ¶a ***fund-raising*** *campaign* 基金募集運動. ¶begin an ***inoculation*** *campaign* 予防注射運動を始める. ¶a ***membership*** *campaign* 会員募集運動. ¶a ***motion-picture*** *campaign* 映画での宣伝. ¶the secret of Gandhi's strength in his ***nonresistance*** *campaign* against the power of the British government 英国政府の権力に対するガンジーの無抵抗運動の強みの秘訣. ¶a ***poster*** *campaign* ポスター宣伝. ¶a ***pre-election*** *campaign* 事前運動. ¶the party's promises in its ***pre-general election*** *campaign* 予選運動に関する党の公約. ¶through ***press*** *campaigns* 新聞宣伝によって. 【類】There was a ***press*** *campaign* against the bill. ¶start (=launch) a ***propaganda*** *campaign* 宣伝戦を始める ‖ intensify *campaign* 宣伝を強化する. ¶organize a ***publicity*** *campaign* 宣伝を組織化する. 【類】a concentrated ***publicity*** *campaign.* ¶an extensive nation-wide ***recruiting*** *campaign* 広汎な全国的の募兵運動. ¶a ***safety movement*** *campaign* 安全運動. ¶conduct a ***sales*** *campaign* 売出宣伝をやる. ¶the German "***Strength through Joy***" *Campaign* ドイツの"歓喜力行"運動. ¶a ***student*** political *campaign* 学生の政治運動. ¶a ***subscription*** *campaign* 予約勧誘. ¶***travel publicity*** *campaigns* 旅行宣伝.

P The college is now engaged ***in*** a *campaign* for a million and a half dollars. 同大学は目下百五十万ドルの寄付金募集をやっている. 【類】he met with sad reverses (大敗北) ***in*** his *campaign* against ... ‖ the screens of America should be used ***in*** a *campaign* of information relative to ... アメリカ映画は...に関する情報の宣伝に用いるべきものだ. ¶the plan ***of*** *campaign* 作戦計画.

P^2 a *campaign* ***against*** malaria (a disease) マラリヤ(など)撲滅運動 ‖ the *campaign* ***against*** mosquitoes in the East Indies 東インドにおける蚊撲滅運動. ¶a *campaign* ***for*** contributions (members) 寄付金(など)募集 ‖ during the *campaign* ***for*** the mayoralty 市長選挙運動中.

camper, *n.* キャンプする人.
Q² a ***summer camper*** 夏季キャンプ生活をする人. ¶ ***vacation campers*** 休暇でキャンプ生活をする人たち.

campus, *n.* 校庭.
Q² a ***college campus*** 大学の校庭. ¶on the ***Columbia campus*** コロンビヤ大学の構内で. ¶the first of her sex to teach on the ***Princeton campus*** プリンストン大学で女性として始めて教壇に立った人. ¶his home on the ***university campus*** 大学の構内にある彼の家.
P In extension classes, texts are the same as or similar to those provided ***on*** the *campus.* 大学公開講義では教材は校内と同様かまたは類似のものを使用する.【類】He has few friends ***on*** the *campus* (学校). / guidance and welfare organizations (指導ならびに厚生施設) ***on*** the *campus.*

can *n.* かん.
Q² an ***ash can*** 《米》ごみ入れ. ¶a ***coffee can*** コーヒーのかん. ¶a ***garbage can*** 《米》廃物容器. ¶ ***key-opening cans*** ついているかぎで開けるかん. ¶an ***oil can*** 油差し. ¶a ***tin can*** ブリキかん ‖ a ***tin can*** of corn かん入りとうもろこし.
P² a ***can with*** a cover ふたつきのかん.

canal, *n.* 河溝, 運河.
V The *canal* is ***blocked.*** その運河は閉塞(ﾍｲｿｸ)されている. ¶ ***close*** a *canal* to merchant ships for military reasons 軍事上の理由で商船の運河通過を禁止する. ¶ ***cut*** (=***make***) a *canal* through ... ...に運河を開さくする. ¶ ***drive*** a *canal* across the Isthmus of Panama パナマ地峡に運河を開さくする.
Q the ***alimentary canal*** 食道. ¶ ***evil-smelling canal*** 悪臭のある堀.
P a boat used ***on canals*** 運河で用いる舟.
P² a *canal* ***for*** irrigation (navigation) かんがい用(など)の堀わり.

canard, *n.* 虚報.
V ***explode*** a *canard* 虚報であることを暴露する. ¶ ***start*** an idle ***canard*** つまらない虚報をねつ造する.
Q an ***absurd*** and ***harmful canard*** ばかげた有害な虚説. ¶a ***pure canard*** 全くの虚報.

canary, *n.* カナリヤ.
V ***breed canaries*** in large numbers カナリヤをたくさん飼育する. ¶ ***raise canaries*** カナリヤを飼育する.
Q² a ***roller canary*** ローラー・カナリヤ.

cancel, *v.* 抹殺する;〖数〗約する.
P Nine and twelve *cancel* ***by*** three. 九と十二は三で約せる. ¶ *cancel* one's order ***for*** ... ...の注文を取消す. ¶ *cancel* ***with*** a mark 印を付けて消す.

cancer, *n.* がん(癌).
V ***get cancer*** がんにかかる.
Q² ***breast cancers*** 乳がん.

candid, *a.* 公平な, 公明な.
P *candid* ***about*** (=***in regard to***) the matter その事に公平な. ¶be *candid* ***in*** debate 議論が公平である. ¶He is *candid* ***to*** (=***toward***) his opponents. 彼は敵に公平だ. ¶to be *candid* ***with*** you 打明けて話すが ‖ be *candid* ***with*** friends or foes 敵味方に公平である.

candidacy, *n.* 候補資格.
Q² an ***Eisenhower candidacy*** アイゼンハワーの立候補.
P A dissertation was submitted to the Faculty of the Graduate School of Arts and Literature ***in candidacy*** for the degree of Doctor of Philosophy, University of Chicago, August, 1922. 一九二二年八月シカゴ大学哲学博士の候補として同大学院文学部に学位請求論文が提出された.
P² *candidacy* ***for*** the mayoralty of the city of New York ニューヨーク市長立候補. 【類】his *candidacy* ***for*** president (会長) of the club.

candidate, *n.* 候補者; 志願者.
V ***boom*** a *candidate* 候補者の人気をあおる. ¶ ***boost*** a *candidate* 候補者のしり押をする. ¶ ***examine candidates*** in four subjects 志願者に四学科の試験を行う. ¶ ***nominate*** a *candidate* 候補者を指名する. ¶ ***prepare candidates*** for entrance examinations 入学志願者に試験準備をしてやる. ***put up*** a *candidate* 候補者を立てる. ¶ ***run candidate*** at ... ...で立候補する. ¶ ***support*** a *candidate* 候補者を後援する. ¶ ***test*** a *candidate* for employment 就職志願者を試験する. ¶ ***train candidates*** for an examination 受験生に準備教育を施す.
Q a ***defeated candidate*** 落選候補; 不合格者. ¶a ***failed candidate*** 落選者; 不合格者. ¶ ***intending candidate*** for the post of ... ...の地位志望者. ¶a ***presidential candidate*** 大統領候補者. ¶ ***rejected candidates*** 落選者. ¶ ***selected candidates*** 選抜された志願者. ¶a ***strong candidate*** 有望な候補者. ¶a ***successful candidate*** 当選(合格)者. 【類】This class prepared 70 ***successful candidates*** for the examinations last year. ‖ an ***unsuccessful candidate*** 落選(不合格)者. ¶a ***victorious candidate*** 当選(合格)者.
Q² a ***bread-and-butter candidate*** 衣食のための志願者. ¶a ***compromise candidate*** 中道(一方に偏しない)候補者. ¶an ***election candidate*** 選挙に打って出た候補. ¶an ***examination candidate***=a candidate for examination 受験志願者. ¶The ***Liberal candidate*** is safe to win the election. 自由党候補者の当選は確実である. ¶a ***Lower House candidate*** 衆議院議員候補. ¶a ***mayoralty candidate*** 市長候補者. ¶a ***Progressive candidate*** 改進党候補.
P He came out ***as*** a *candidate.* 彼は候補者として打って出た. ‖ He has sent up (=in) his name ***as*** a *candidate.* 彼は候補者として届け出た. ¶I shall vote ***for*** this *candidate.* 僕はこの候補者に投票しよう.
P² become a *candidate* ***for*** the next Presidency 次期大統領に立候補する ‖ a *candidate* ***for*** admission 入学(会)志願者. 【類】*candidates* ***for*** President (=Presidency) in the 1928 campaign / a *candidate* ***for*** Parliament / *candidates* ***for*** members of the House of Representatives / *candidates* ***for*** election / *candidates* ***for*** examination / a *candidate* ***for*** elective office (公選職) / *candidates* ***for*** the prize / a *candidate* ***for*** the Democratic nomination (民主党の指名) for President in 1928 ‖ There were over three hundred *candidates* ***for*** the appointment. その就職口は三百人以上志願者があった. ‖ a *candidate* ***for*** office 就職希望者. 【類】a *candidate* ***for*** the post (=situation) ‖ a *candidate* ***for*** membership 入会希望者. 【類】*candidates* ***for*** the army / a *candidate* ***for*** teachers' licences ‖ a *candidate* ***for*** death ひん死の人 ‖ Such a person would be deemed a *candidate* ***for*** the lunatic asylum. こんな人は精神病院に行った方がよい.

candidature, *n.* 立候補.
Q ***parliamentary candidature*** 国会議員立候補.

candle, *n.* ろうそく.
V ***blow out*** a *candle* ろうそくを吹き消す. ¶ ***burn candles*** to see by 照して見るためにろうそくをつける ‖ ***burn*** a *candle* at both ends. 精力(金銭)を浪費する. ¶ ***extinguish*** (=***put out***) a *candle* ろうそくを消す. ¶ ***hold*** a *candle* to another 他人の手助けをする ‖ He is not fit to ***hold*** a *candle* to his rival. 彼はとうてい敵にはかなわない. ¶ ***light*** a *candle* ろうそくをともす. ¶ ***make*** (=***mold***) *candles* ろうそくを製造する. ¶ ***put candles*** on one's birthday cake 誕生祝いのケーキの上にろうそくを立てる.
V² The *candle* ***burns*** quickly. ろうそくがずんずん燃え進む. ¶ *Candles* ***flicker.*** ろうそくの火がゆらめく. ¶A *candle* ***goes out.*** ろうそくが消える.
Q a ***flickering candle*** ちらちらと燃えるろうそく. ¶a ***lighted candle*** ともっているろうそく. ¶The game does not appear to be ***worth*** the *candle.* その競技はつまらなそうだ.
Q² ***wax candles*** set in chandeliers シャンデリヤ(枝形燈架)に立てたろうそく.
P hold up an egg ***before*** a *candle* 卵をろうそくの光にすかして見る.

candor, *n.* 公正; 率直さ.
Q ***childlike candor*** 子供のような率直さ. ¶ ***openminded candor*** 公正無私. ¶ ***scientific candor*** 徹底的な率直さ.
P ***with*** much *candor* きわめて公正に.

candy, *n.* キャンデー, チョコレートのかかったヌガー式のもの.
Q a box of ***delicious candy*** おいしいキャンデー一箱. ¶ ***mixed candies*** 取合せたキャンデー.
P² Here is a *candy* ***for*** you. そらキャンデーをあげるよ.

cane, *n.* つえ, ステッキ; 砂糖きび.
V ***flick*** a *cane* つえを急に振う. ¶He was taking a walk, ***sporting*** his *cane.* ステッキをもてあそびながら散歩をしていた. ¶ ***twirl*** a *cane* つえを振り回す.
Q² tasseled ***sugar cane*** 穂の出たさとうきび. ¶a ***sword cane*** 仕込みづえ.
P An old man was walking ***with*** a *cane.* 老人がつえをついて歩いていた.

canner, *n.* 《米》かん詰業者.
Q² a ***meat canner*** 肉かん詰製造者.

cannery, *n.* 《米》かん詰製造所.
Q² a ***fish cannery*** 魚類のかん詰製造所. ¶a ***floating [crab] cannery*** かに工船.

P The output ***of*** the *cannery* goes all over the globe. 同かん詰製造所の製品は世界中に行き渡っている.

cannibalism, *n.* 人食いの風習.

V *practise cannibalism* 人を殺して食う.

cannon, *n.* [*pl.* **-s** *or* (集合的に) **cannon**] 大砲.

V ***captured*** thirty *cannons* 大砲三十門を分捕った. ¶***fire*** (=***shoot off***) a *cannon* 大砲を発射する.

V^{2} A *cannon* ***booms***. 大砲がどーんと鳴る. ¶The *cannon* are ***firing***. 大砲を打っている. ¶The *cannon* ***thundered***. 大砲がとどろいた.

P attack it ***with*** *cannon* それを砲撃する. ¶the report ***of*** a *cannon* 大砲の音.

P^{2} *cannons* ***from*** forts and warships boomed as she sailed into the gateway of ... 同艦(船)が...の入口に入ると要塞および軍艦から大砲がとどろいた. ¶the booming of *cannon* ***on*** board the men-of-war in the harbor and in the forts that guard its approach 在港軍艦上の大砲と港の入口をまもる要塞の大砲のごう音.

canon, *n.* 法典, 法規.

P sin ***against*** the *canons* of taste 趣味の原則にそむく.

P^{2} The *canons* ***of*** the church are few and its beliefs are simple. 同教会の教会法は少数でその信仰箇条は簡単だ.

canonize, *v.* 聖徒に列する.

P He was *canonized* ***for*** a saint. 彼は聖徒の列に加えられた.

canopy, *n.* 天がい, 空.

Q^{2} a ***range*** *canopy* (ガス)レンジ用の天がい.

P The two cannot live together ***under*** the *canopy* of heaven. 二人は不倶戴天の間柄だ.

cant, *v.* 傾く.

M *cant* ***over*** to the left side 左側に傾く.

canteen, *n.* 酒保; 筒.

Q^{2} a ***cellophane*** *canteen* セロファン筒(特殊の飯ごう).

P Soldiers buy food, drinks, etc. ***at*** their *canteen* (now officially called post exchange). 兵士は酒保(今は正式にはPX)で食物, 飲物などを買う.

canter, *n.* なみかけ足.

P The dog came ***at*** a *canter*. 犬はちょこちょこ走ってきた. ¶win ***in*** a *canter* (=easily) 楽に勝つ.

canvas, *n.* 帆布, 画布(カンバス).

V ***stretch*** a *canvas* on a frame カンバスをわくに張る.

Q require a ***large*** *canvas* 大形のカンバスを必要とする. ¶In this ***tiny*** canvas, all his virtues meet. この小さい画布に彼の長所が遺憾なく発揮されている. ¶His *canvas* is ***vast***. 彼の作(小説など)は規模が大きい. ¶***waterproof*** *canvas* 防水帆布.

Q^{2} ***chess-board*** *canvas* 市松形厚織綿ししゅう地.

P This parcel should be sewn up ***in*** *canvas*. この荷物はズックに入れて縫付けるといい. ¶I will introduce you to some of our family ***on*** *canvas*. 家族の肖像画を少し御覧に入れましょう. ‖ as if it were traced ***on*** *canves* 絵にかいたように. ¶be ***under*** *canvas* 露営する ‖ a camp ***under*** *canvas* 天幕露営. 【類】He passed his first night in Africa ***under*** *canvas*. ‖ The steamer broke her screw at sea and was compelled to return ***under*** *canvas* to the port. その汽船は航海中推進機を損じたので帆で帰港せねばならなかった.

canvass, *n.* 運動, 遊説.

V The *canvass* was ***pushed*** vigorously ***forward***. その運動は極力推進された.

Q^{2} make a ***house-to-house*** *canvass* 戸別運動をする.

canvass, *v.* 運動する, 遊説する.

M They are *canvassing* ***everywhere***. 彼らは至る所で運動している.

P^{2} *canvass* ***among*** students ***for*** contributions 学生間に寄付金を募集する. ¶*canvass* ***for*** (=***on behalf of***) a candidate 候補者のために運動する. 【類】*canvass* ***for*** subscriptions ‖ *canvass* ***for*** votes 投票獲得運動をする ‖ He is very busy in *canvassing* ***for*** the election. 彼は選挙運動にいそがしい. ¶*canvass* ***in the interest of*** ... ...のために運動をやる.

canvassing, *n.* [選挙]運動.

Q^{2} ***house-to-house*** *canvassing* 戸別訪問運動. ¶***insurance*** canvassing 保険勧誘.

cap, *n.* 帽子; ふた.

V He ***carried*** my *cap* clean off my head. 私のかぶっていた帽子をすーっと持って行った. ¶***lift*** one's *cap* slightly 軽く帽子を上げる. ¶***pull*** the *cap* well over one's eyes 帽子を目深にかぶる. ¶The average English boy hates to ***take off*** his *cap* in greeting you and does it awkwardly. 普通の英国少年はあいさつの時に帽子を取るのをいやがりまた取るにしても不器用な取り方をする. ¶***wave*** one's *cap* above one's head 帽子を頭上で振る. ¶***wear*** a peaked *cap* and brass buttons 三角帽子をかぶり真ちゅうボタンのついた制服を着る.

V^{2} My *cap* ***tumbled*** from the hook. 私の帽子は帽子かけから落ちた. ¶the *cap* ***fits*** 評語がぴったり当てはまる.

Q soldiers' ***visored*** *caps* 軍人のひさし付帽子.

Q^{2} a ***college*** *cap* 大学の制帽. ¶a ***dunce*** *cap* のろま帽子(学校で覚えの悪い生徒に冠らせる円すい形の紙の帽子). ¶a ***garrison*** *cap* 守備隊帽. ¶a ***golf*** *cap* ゴルフ帽. ¶the ***metal*** *cap* of a bottle びんの口金. ¶a ***mortarboard*** *cap* 角帽. ¶an ***outing*** *cap* ハイク用帽子. ¶a ***regulation*** *cap* 制帽. ¶a ***skull*** *cap* おわん形帽子. ¶a ***square college*** (=***four-cornered***) *cap*=a mortarboard 大学生の角帽. ¶a ***work*** *cap* 作業帽.

P boys ***in*** official school *caps* 制帽の少年. ¶wear a badge ***on*** one's *cap* 帽子に記章を付けている.

capability, *n.* 能力, 手腕.

P It is quite ***above*** (=***beyond***) his *capabilities*. それは全く彼の手に余ることだ.

P^{2} his *capability* ***in*** selecting the right man 適材を選ぶ彼の手腕.

capable, *a.* ...しうる; ...に堪える.

M He is ***hardly*** *capable* of executing such a difficult work. 彼はこういう難事を遂行する手腕に乏しい. ¶***most*** *capable* of leadership 最も指導者たる手腕のある.

P The subject is one *capable* ***of*** almost indefinite expansion. その題目はほとんど無限に敷衍(えん)することができる. ‖ He is *capable* ***of*** being taught. 教育を受ける能力がある. 【類】He is *capable* ***of*** great things. / be *capable* ***of*** self-government / These vehicles are each *capable* ***of*** carrying 20 persons. / He is *capable* ***of*** fulfilling all the promises. ‖ be arranged so as to be *capable* ***of*** easy enlargement at a future date 将来容易に拡張のできるように設計してある ‖ not *capable* ***of*** reproduction in our alphabet われわれの国の文字ではその音が出せない. 【類】He is *capable* ***of*** most unscrupulous acts.

capacity, *n.* 量, 容量; 力量, 手腕; 資格.

V ***ascertain*** the navigable *capacities* of a harbor 港湾の船舶収容力を確かめる. ¶***decrease*** the *capacity* for intellectual and manual labor 頭と手の労働能率を低下する. ¶***develop*** the reasoning *capacities* 推理力を発達させる. ¶***draw out*** and ***train*** a boy's potential *capacities* 少年の潜在能力を引出して練磨する. ¶***gauge*** the linguistic *capacity* of a student 学生の語学力をテストする. ¶***hamper*** its *capacity* その能力を妨げる. ¶The theater ***has*** a *capacity* of 600. その劇場は600人の収容力がある. ¶He ***has*** a great *capacity* for mathematics. 非常に数学の才がある. ‖ He ***has*** the *capacity* for great achievement. 彼は大事業を成しうる. ¶They ***illustrate*** the Anglo-Saxon *capacity* for making the best of things. 彼らは精々事物を利用するアングロ・サクソン特有の性能を例示するものだ. ¶***increase*** one's earning *capacity* 収入を多くする道を講じる. ¶***obtain*** the entire *capacity* of one steamer 一船買切る. ¶They ***recognized*** his *capacities* as a man of business. 実業家としての彼の手腕を認めた. ¶Christmas mails ***tax*** the *capacity* of his Majesty's post office almost to the point of the last straw. クリスマス郵便は英国郵便局のほとんど手に余るほどの数量である. ¶***undermine*** his *capacity* for work 彼の仕事をする能力を破壊する.

Q immense energy and admirable ***administrative*** *capacity* 絶大な精力とすぐれた経営の才. ¶work in an ***advisory*** *capacity* 顧問の資格で働く. 【類】act in an ***advisory*** *capacity* with ... on ... ¶the ***automobile-producing*** *capacity* of the country その国の自動車生産能力. ¶act in ***both*** *capacities* 両方の資格で行動する. ¶employment with the Army in a ***civilian*** *capacity* 文官の資格で軍への勤務. ¶***directive*** *capacity* 首領の材. ¶his ***dual*** *capacity* of shop keeper and manager of a post-office 店主と郵便局長と二重の資格. ¶an ***earning*** *capacity* insufficient for the family needs 家族を養うに足らぬ収入 ‖ The company has an ***earning*** *capacity* of forty millions a year. 同社は一年に四千万円の収益をあげる能力がある. ¶his ***enormous*** *capacity* for study 彼の非凡な研究力. ¶develop one's ***full*** *capacity* 全能力を出す ‖ a person of ***full*** *capacity* 能力者. ¶a man of ***great*** *capacity* 大手腕家. ¶a task beyond ***human*** *capacity* 人間わざでおよばぬ仕事. ¶in one's ***individual*** *capacity* 個人の資格で. ¶It was the result of the most prosaic of all the attributes of genius—namely, the *infinite capacity* for taking pains. それは天才の属性の中最も平凡なもの, 即ち, 刻苦に耐える無限の力の結果であった. ¶*initiative capacity* 創業の才. ¶a man of great *intellectual capacity* 非常に知力のある人 ‖ A nation's *intellectual capacity* is the ultimate spring of distinctive achievement. 国民の知力は結局目ざましい偉業の源泉である.【類】the *intellectual capacity* of women / determine the *intellectual capacity* of students / Do you find the *intellectual capacity* of the yellow race equal to that of the white race? ¶the *magnifying capacity* of a lens レンズの倍率. ¶*mental capacity* 知能. ¶in their *official capacity* 官吏たる資格で. ¶in my *personal private capacity* 私一個人の資格で. ¶in his *private* and *public capacity* 公私両方の資格で. ¶*productive capacity* 生産能力. ¶in a *professional capacity* 商売上(商人として). ¶work in a *public capacity* 公人の資格で働く. ¶He has a *remarkable capacity* for lying. よくもあんなうそが言えたものだ. ¶a premature exhaustion of the *reproductive capacity* 生殖能力の早期減退 ‖ the *reproductive capacity* of the memory 記憶の再現力. ¶in a *semi-official capacity* 半官半私の資格で. ¶the *testing capacities* of examination 受験能力. ¶has an *unbounded capacity* for enjoyment あくまで快楽を追求する力を持っている. ¶The auditorium was crowded to its *utmost capacity*. 聴衆席は超満員であった. ¶serve in *various capacities* 色々な資格で勤める. ¶In *what capacity* was he employed? 彼はどんな資格で雇われたか.

Q² He has excellent *business capacity*. りっぱな実務の才がある. ¶*carrying capacity* 運搬量. ¶be not up to *classroom capacity* 教室の収容力以下である. ¶a vessel's *deadweight capacity* for cargo 船舶の従量載貨トン数. ¶lessen its *holding capacity* その収容力を減じる. ¶the *laying capacity* of domestic birds 家禽の産卵能力. ¶*litigation capacity* 訴訟能力. ¶be deficient in *lung capacity* 肺活量が不足している. ¶a vessel's *measurement capacity* for cargo 船の積荷収容力. ¶the *passenger-carrying capacity* of an ocean liner 定期船の船客輸送能力. ¶*payment capacity* 仕払能力. ¶operate at *peak capacity* 最大能力を出して経営する ‖ has a *peak capacity* of 43 passengers 最大収容能力乗客四十三人. ¶expand *plant capacity* 工場の生産力を拡大する. ¶with a *production capacity* of ... ...の生産能力で. ¶British filmmakers have small *production capacity*. 英国の映画製作者は生産能力が低い. ¶the *seating capacity* of a theater 劇場の観客収容力. 【類】The auditorium has a *seating capacity* of 1400. / The theater does not have enough *seating capacity*. ¶*storage capacity* 貯蔵能力. ¶*skull capacity* 頭蓋容積. ¶the *training capacity* of a school 学校の訓育能力. ¶deteriorate *transportation capacity* 輸送能力を低下させる. ¶his *wage-earning capacity* after the disability 廃疾後の彼の賃金獲得能力.

P The factory is running *at* full *capacity*. 工場が全能力を挙げて操業している. ¶All the hotels were filled *beyond* their *capacity*. どの旅館も収容力以上に一杯であった. ‖ it is far *beyond* the *capacity* of ... それはとうてい...のよくする所でない. ¶*in* the *capacity* of director 理事の資格で. 【類】He travelled *in* the *capacity* of a guide (案内者). ¶The hall was packed *to capacity*. 会館は満員であった. ¶work up *to capacity* 力一杯に仕事をする ‖ Lodging may be had at ... *to* the *capacity* of the building. その建物の許す限り宿泊の便を計ります. ¶buses *with* a seating *capacity* of 90 persons each 各々九十人の座席のあるバス ‖ a theater *with* a *capacity* of 6,700 seats 六千七百人の座席を備えた劇場.【類】a steamer *with* a seating *capacity* for 50 first-class passengers.

P² the *capacity for* doing good and rapid work on a typewriter タイプライターを正確迅速に扱いうる力 ‖ *capacity for* assuming responsibility for illegal act 不法行為責任能力 ‖ his *capacity for* organization 彼の組織力 ‖ Japan's *capacity for* progress 日本の進歩力.【類】He has no *capacity for* improvement. ‖ the *capacity for* self-expression the students command 学生が駆使しうる自己表現力 ‖ a *capacity for* heat (moisture) 熱(など)の導引性. ¶a *capacity of* 20 gallons 二十ガロンの容量.【類】the *capacity of* the filter (ろ過器) is ... gallons per hour / a *capacity of* 20 horse-power ‖ *capacity of* parties 当事者能力 ‖ *capacity of* will 意思能力.

cap-and-gowner, *n.* 大学卒業者.

Q² the *'48 cap-and-gowner* 1948 年度大学卒業者.

capital, *n.* (**1**) 首府.

V beautify Tokyo so that it may *befit* the *capital* of Japan 日本の首都にふさわしいように東京を美化する. ¶*found* a *capital* 首都を建設する. ¶*shift* (=*remove, transfer or transplant*) the *capital* to ... 首都を...へ移す.

Q Cracow, the *ancient capital* of Poland ポーランドの昔の首都クラコウ. ¶Irkutsk, the *eastern capital* of Siberia シベリアの東の首都イルクーツク. ¶the *mightiest capital* the world has ever seen 世界最大の首都. ¶Kamakura, the *military capital* of the Middle Ages 中世期の軍都だった鎌倉. ¶Washington, D.C., the *national capital* [米国の]国都ワシントン府.

Q² the *Communist capital* of Yen'an 中共の首都延安. ¶Manchester is the *cotton capital*, the so-called "Cotton opolis" of England. マンチェスターは英国綿糸業の中心地いわゆる「綿都」である. ¶Paris, the *fashion capital* 流行の首都パリー. ¶Hollywood, the *film capital* 映画の都ハリウッド. ¶Kyoto was a *one time capital* of Japan. 京都はかつて日本の首府だった. ¶Simla, the *summer capital* of India インドの夏季の首府シムラ. ¶a *wartime capital* 戦時の首府 ‖ China's interim *wartime capital* 中華民国の戦時臨時首府. 【類】Chungking, China's *wartime* national *capital*. ¶London and other *world capitals* ロンドンおよび他の世界的首都.

P He is now staying *in* the *capital*. 今在京中である. ¶the establishment *of* the *capital* at Tokyo 東京に首都の創設.

(**2**) 資本; [団] 資本家.

V They managed to *gather capital* from great financiers for various schemes. 諸種の計画に当てるため大資本家からどうにか資金を集めた. ¶The company *has* a *capital* of $40,000. その会社の資本は 40,000 ドルだ. ¶*invest* one's *capital* to the best advantage 最も有利に投資する.【類】*invest* much *capital* in a business. ¶You can *make capital* of your knowledge of English. 君の英語の知識をもと手に(利用)することができる. ¶He was able to *persuade capital* to adopt his plans. 彼は資本家を説き伏せて自分の計画を採用させた. ¶*raise* the necessary *capital* to carry on a scheme ある計画を実行するために必要な資金を募集する. ¶*redeem* a *capital* invested 投下資本を回収する. ¶It *represents* a *capital* of about eight millions of money. それには約八百万の資本金が出してある.【類】the industry *represents* an invested *capital* of ... ¶The enterprise *requires* much *capital*. その事業は多大の資本金を要する.【類】it is estimated that the project will *require* a *capital* of ... ¶*sink* a *capital* in ... ...に投資する ‖ The *capital sunk* in it is fabulous in amount. それに投じた資金はばく大なものである. ¶*socialize capital* 資本を一般社会の所有にする. ¶*tie up capital* 資本を固定させる.

Q it represents an *aggregate capital* of ... それは資本金総額...に該当する. ¶an *authorized capital* 公称資本. ¶*circulating capital* 流通資本. ¶a *corporeal capital* 物的資本. ¶*dead capital* 不生産的資本. ¶invest *enormous capital* 巨額の投資をする. ¶*floating* (=*circulating*) *capital* 流動資本. ¶an inflow of *foreign capital* 外資流入 ‖ the induction (=introduction) of *foreign capital* 外資導入. ¶with the assistance of *foreign-borrowed capital* 外債の助けを借りて. ¶He has some *idle capital*. 彼は少し遊金がある. ¶The business represents many millions of *invested capital*. その事業には何百万という資金が投ぜられている. ¶merchants with *limited capital* 小資本の商人. ¶*Much capital* is required to run a newspaper. 新聞を経営するには多額の資金が必要である. ¶raise the *necessary capital* to carry out the scheme その計画遂行のために必要な資本を募集する. ¶*net capital* 純資金. ¶*outstanding capital* 未払込資本金. ¶make *political capital* on the price issue 物価問題を政治上に利用する. ¶*private capital* 個人資本. ¶with a *small capital* 小資本で. ¶a *subscribed capital* 公募資本. ¶*surplus capital* 過剰資本. ¶*unemployed capital* 遊休資本. ¶He faced the world with a *working capital* of only five yen. 彼はわずか現金五円を元手にして商売を始めた.

Q² a *loan capital* 借入資本. ¶The company has been formed with a *share capital* of $1,350,580. その会社は

1,350,580 円の株資本で組織された.

P He is credited with controlling eight billion marks ***of capital***. 彼は八十億マルクの資金を運用しているということである. ¶start a business ***upon*** borrowed *capital* 借金で商売を始める. ¶start ***with*** a *capital* of £... ...ポンドの資本で始める ‖ a company organized ***with*** a *capital* of one million yen in ... shares ...株で百万円の資本で組織した会社.

capitalism, *n.* 資本主義.

Q ***modified capitalism*** 修正資本主義.

Q² ***monopoly capitalism*** 独占資本主義. ¶***state capitalism*** 国家資本主義.

capitalist, *n.* 資本家.

Q a ***budding capitalist*** 新進の資本家. ¶***foreign capitalists*** 海外資本家. ¶***theatrical capitalists*** 興行資本家. ¶a ***millionaire capitalist*** 百万長者の資本家.

Q² a ***mammoth capitalist*** 大資本家.

capitalization, *n.* 資本投下.

V the company ***has*** a *capitalization* amounting to ... 同会社の資本金は...に上る.

Q ***sufficient*** (***insufficient***) ***capitalization*** (不)十分な出資.

capitalize, *v.* 資本化する.

P The concern ***capitalizes at*** $50,000,000. 同商会は五千万ドルの資本を持っている.【類】The Bank of Mexico, ***capitalized at*** $50,000,000, is the only bank authorized (認可された) to issue paper money.

caprice, *n.* 気まぐれ.

Q ***Divine caprice*** 神様の気まぐれ. ¶a ***sudden caprice*** ほんのでき心.

P ***at*** the *caprice* of his master 彼の主人のその時その時の気分で. ¶He acted ***from caprice***. 気まぐれでやった.

P² the *caprice* ***of*** the moment 一時の気まぐれ.

capstan, *n.*〘機〙車地(しゃ), キャプスタン.

V ***man*** the *capstan* 車地に配員する. ¶***pawl*** the *capstan* 車地に歯止めを掛け(て止め)る. ¶***surge*** the *capstan* 車地(に巻いた索)をゆるめる.

capsule, *n.* 小容器(カプセル).

Q² a ***time capsule*** 永久埋没箱(ある時代の実状を後世に伝えるため記念物を入れて地下に埋める).

captain, *n.* 首領, 隊長, 船長.

V The *captain* of the ship has ***deserted***. その船の船長が脱走した.

Q the ***greatest captain*** of industry 工業界の第一人者.【類】the three ***great captains***, Nobunaga, Hideyoshi, and Iyeyasu. ¶one of the most ***prominent captains*** of commerce in Germany ドイツ商業界における巨頭の一人.

Q² an ***air forces captain*** 空軍の隊長. ¶a ***merchant captain*** 商船長. ¶a ***plane captain*** 機長. ¶a ***sea captain*** 船長, 艦長. ¶a ***ship captain*** 船長.

P² *captains* ***in*** the mercantile marine 商船の船長. ¶*captains* ***of*** industry and commerce 商工業界の巨頭連. ¶the *captain* ***of*** the commissariat department [ピクニックなどの]食料部長.

captainship, *n.* 統率.

P a baseball team ***under*** the *captainship* of ... 主将...の率いる野球団.

caption, *n.* 表題, 見出し.

V an editorial ***bearing*** the above *caption* 上記の見出しの社説. ¶***put*** a *caption* on an article 記事に見出しをつける.

P he addressed ***under*** the *caption* "..." 彼は「...」という演題で話をした. ¶He refers to it in the course of an article ***with*** the *caption* "..." 「...」という題の文の中でその事に説きおよんでいる.

caption, *v.* 見出しをつける.

M re the matter ***above captioned*** 頭書の件につき.

captivate, *v.* 魂を奪う, 悩殺する.

P He was *captivated* ***by*** an actress. 彼は一女優に迷った. ‖ I was *captivated* ***by*** the cordiality of your people. お国の方々の御親切にはすっかり参ってしまいました. ¶He was *captivated* ***with*** (=***by***) her beauty. 彼女の美貌のとりこになってしまった.

captive, *n.* 捕虜(ほりょ).

Q a ***life-long captive*** 終身捕虜.

captivity, *n.* とらわれの身, 監禁.

P Orangs are delicate ***in captivity***, seldom living as long as two years. しょうじょうは手飼いでは弱くってめったに二年と生きていない.【類】wild animals ***in captivity*** ‖ These animals thrive ***in captivity***. これらの動物は飼育して弱らない. ‖ He was held ***in captivity***. 捕虜になった. ‖ Black rats will not breed ***in captivity***. 黒ねずみは飼って置くと子を産まない.

capture, *n.* 捕獲.

V The bandits ***defy capture***. 匪(ひ)賊は容易につかまらない. ¶***evade capture*** 捕縛を免れる.

Q They will then become liable to ***hostile capture***. そうすると彼らは敵につかまる恐れがある. ¶make a ***long-delayed capture*** ようやくのことで逮捕する.

P marriage ***by capture*** 略奪結婚.

P² *capture* ***of*** a city 都市の奪取. ¶the *capture* and condemnation ***of*** ships 船舶のだ捕および捕獲.

capture, *v.* 分捕る.

M ***treacherously capture*** 謀略を用いて捕獲する.

P be *captured* ***by*** pirates 海賊にだ捕される ‖ *Captured* ***by*** the enemy, the soldiers were in danger of being shot. その兵士は敵に捕えられ, 銃殺されるおそれがあった. ¶*capture* it ***from*** the enemy (rival) 敵(など)からそれを分捕る.

car, *n.* 電車;《米》列車の車両;《口語》自動車.

V ***back*** a *car* out of a garage 自動車を車庫からバックさせる. ¶Seeing the danger, the driver ***brought*** the *car* to a standstill. 危険と見て運転手は電車をぴったり止めた. ¶***change cars at*** ... ...で汽車を乗換える. ¶run to ***catch*** a *car* 電車に乗り遅れないように走る. ¶***drive*** a *car* ***forward*** 車を前方へ進める ‖ ***drive*** a *car* down to ... ...までドライブをやる. ¶***engage*** a motor *car* at an exorbitant rate 自動車を法外な賃金で雇う. ¶***enter*** a *car* 車に乗る. ¶***get off*** a *car* backward 電車の進行と反対の方へ降りる. ¶The *car* was ***jammed*** (=***crowded***) full.《米》電車は満員だった. ¶***leave*** a *car* 車を乗りすてる ‖ ***leave*** the *cars*《米》列車から降りる. ¶***lock*** one's *car* ...の自動車に錠を下ろす. ¶Cafe *cars* are ***operated*** on trains by the Railway. その鉄道では喫茶列車を運転している. ¶She ***parked*** her *car* before a beauty saloon. 美容院の前に自動車をとめておいた. ¶A locomotive without steam cannot ***pull*** a *car*. 蒸気のない機関車は車を引けない. ¶***pull up*** a *car* 車を止める. ¶***put on*** more *cars* to accommodate the traffic 交通を緩和するため運転車両数を増す. ¶Extra *cars* will be ***run*** on the day. その日は平常より余計に電車を運転する. ¶***stop*** a *car* 車をとめる. ¶It is his duty to ***switch*** *cars* from one track to another. 車両を他の線路へ移す(転轍する)のが彼の仕事だ. ¶***take*** *car* to ... ...へ電車で行く. ¶***use*** electric *cars* 電車を乗用する.

V² The *car* ***shot out*** into the light of day again. 電車は射るがごとくに(トンネルから)再び明るみに出た.

Q a ***closed car*** 有蓋自動車. ¶a fully equipped ***electric car*** 整備電車 ‖ Many delightful excursions to near-by points can be made on ***electric cars*** from ... at a nominal expense. ...からは電車でその付近数箇所へわずかな費用で愉快な遠足ができる. ¶a ***mortor-driven car*** 自動車. ¶***used cars*** 中古自動車 ‖ slightly ***used cars*** of the '52 model 五十二年型の中古自動車.

Q² a ***baggage car***《米》荷物車. ¶a ***box car*** 有蓋車. ¶a ***cable car*** ケーブル・カー(索条車). ¶a ***cattle car*** 家畜用貨車. ¶a ***chill car*** 冷蔵車. ¶a ***clinic car*** 医療車. ¶a ***combat car***〘軍〙装甲車. ¶a ***command car***〘陸〙指揮[官]車. ¶a ***dining car***=a diner 食堂車.【類】There is no ***dinner car*** on this train. ¶a ***drawing-room car*** 特別客車. ¶a ***family car*** 中型自家用車. ¶a ***flat car*** 無蓋貨車. ¶a ***freezer car*** 冷凍車(汽車の). ¶a ***freight car***《米》貨車. ¶a ***general-purpose car***—jeep 何にでも使える車—ジープ. ¶a ***gondola car*** 無蓋貨車. ¶a ***horse car*** 鉄道馬車. ¶a ***midget car*** 小型自動車. ¶a ***news car*** 報道車. ¶an ***observation car*** 展望車. ¶an ***overage car*** 使い古した自動車. ¶a ***parlor car***《米》特等客車. ¶a ***passenger car*** 客車; 乗用車. ¶a ***pleasure car*** 行楽自動車. ¶a ***press car*** 新聞記者自動車. ¶a ***Pullman car*** プルマン式寝台車. ¶a ***push*** [***man***] ***car*** 手押車. ¶a ***radio car*** 走る通信車. ¶a ***railroad car***《米》客車. ☞英語は a railway carriage. ¶a ***restaurant car*** 食堂車. ¶a ***refrigeration car*** 冷凍車. ¶an iced ***refrigerator car*** 氷使用冷凍車. ¶a ***sleeping car***=a sleeper 寝台車. ¶a ***seven-thousand-dollar car*** 七千ドルの自動車. ¶a [***street***] ***surface car*** 路面電車. ¶a ***tank car*** for oil 石油運搬用タンク車. ¶a ***touring car*** 回遊自動車. ¶an air-conditioned ***train car*** 空気調節客車. ¶a ***tramway car***《英》市内電車. ¶run ***trial cars*** over a new section 新区間に試乗車を運転する. ¶a ***trolley car***=a streetcar《米》市内電車. ¶a ***south-bound trolley car***《米》南方行きの電車. ¶take a ***tunnel car*** 地下鉄に乗る.

P go ***by car*** 車で行く. ¶alight ***from*** (=get off) a *car* 車から降りる. ¶Articles lost ***on*** the *cars* are turned in at these offices. 車内の遺失物はこれらの役所に回される. / Crowds of people were ***on*** the *car*.【類】he accosted (話し掛けた) me ***on*** a *car* and asked, "Sir, ...?"

P² a *car* ***for*** private use 自家用車.

caravan, *n.* [団]隊商；ほろ馬車.

Q² a ***gipsy*** (***circus***) *caravan* ジプシー(など)のほろ馬車.

P² a *caravan* ***of*** forty pilgrims traveling through the great desert of Arabia アラビアの大さばくを横断する四十人の巡礼の一隊.

carbon, *n.* 炭素.

Q ***activated*** *carbon* 活性炭.

card, *n.* 厚紙札；カルタ(トランプ)札；名刺；はがき.

V ***cut*** *cards* トランプを切る. ¶***deal*** *cards* トランプ札をくばる. ¶***deposit*** a visiting *card* on a small silver tray 名刺を小さな銀の盆に入れる. ¶***discard*** a *card* カルタ札を捨てる. ¶***divide*** *cards* カルタを分ける. ¶***exchange*** *cards* 名刺を交換する. ¶***file*** *cards* カードをとじ込む. ¶Could you please ***give*** me your *card?* 御名刺をいただけませんか. ¶***leave*** one's *card* at the door 玄関に名刺をおいて来る. ¶I have ***misplaced*** his *card.* 彼から受取ったはがきをしまいなくした. ¶***pack*** *cards* ごま化す. ¶***play*** a *card* カルタ札を出す‖***play*** *cards* トランプをする‖The candidate ***played*** his *cards* well (badly) 同候補者(志願者)はしっかり(へたに)やった‖***play*** one's last *card* 奥の手を出す. ¶he ***presented*** his *card* of introduction from ... 彼は...からの紹介の名刺を出した. ¶***send in*** one's *card* to the person one wishes to see 面会したい人に刺を通じる. ¶One does not ***send*** one's *card* ***up*** unless one calls on some commercial business. 商用で訪問する以外は名刺を出さない. ¶I'll make him ***show*** his *card.* 彼の手(計略)を見てやろう. ¶***shuffle*** *cards* カルタ札を混ぜる‖The *cards* are ***shuffled*** afresh for a new deal with fortune. 新規まき直しをやる. ¶***turn down*** *cards* カルタ札を伏せる.

Q Please reply on the ***accompanying*** *card* by Saturday, January 5th. どうぞ一月五日の土曜日までにこの往復はがきの返信用紙で御返事ください. ¶the ***attached postal*** *card* 往復はがきの返信用. ¶a ***blank*** *card* 白紙のカード. ¶a ***congratulatory*** *card* 賀状. ¶It is not good form to send acknowledgement of a gift on a ***postal*** *card.* 進物の礼をはがきで述べるのは礼儀にはずれる. ¶a big ***printed*** *card* 大きな印刷したカード. ¶a ***sure*** *card*＝a sure thing《俗》大丈夫, 間違いなし(のもの).

Q² an ***advertising*** *card* 広告はがき‖a bus or car ***advertising*** *card* バスあるいは電車内の広告ビラ. ¶an ***application*** *card* 申込カード. ¶a ***bed*** *card* 寝台券. ¶a ***business visiting*** *card* 商売用の名刺. ¶an ***embarkation*** *card* 乗船券. ¶an "***ex libris***" *card* 蔵書票. ¶a "***flash***" *card* ちょっと見せて裏返しにする語学教授用のカード. ¶a ***greeting*** *card* あいさつ状. ¶one's ***identity*** *card* 身分証明書‖present their official ***identity*** *cards* 職員身分証明書を示す. ¶a ***letter*** *card* 書簡はがき. ¶a ***membership*** *card* 会員カード. ¶a ***permit*** *card* 許可証. ¶a ***playing*** *card* カルタ(一枚). ¶fill out the enclosed ***pledge*** *card* 封入した誓約カードに書入れる. ¶require them to carry ***police*** *cards* 警官証の携帯を要求する. ¶a fancy ***post*** *card* 意匠を凝らしたはがき. ¶a ***press*** *card* 新聞記者証. ¶a ***probation*** *card* 人物試験カード. ¶a ***race*** *card* 競馬の番付. ¶present their rice ***ration*** *cards* as a means of identification 身分の証明に米穀通帳を示す‖The masses have not seen a ***ration*** *card.* 配給制が布かれていない. ¶a ***report*** *card* (学校から家庭への)通信簿. ¶a special ***reservation*** *card* 特別予約カード(ホテルなどの). ¶a ***score*** *card* 点数記録カード. ¶a ***seat reservation*** *card* 座席予約カード ¶a ***show*** *card* 店頭の広告用ポスター. ¶a tobacconists' ***show*** *card* たばこ屋の店頭ポスター. ¶a ***streetcar*** *card* 電車内広告用ポスター. ¶a ***student*** *card* 学生証. ¶a ***study*** *card* [半学期の聴講科目選定用]聴講カード. ¶a ***talkie*** *card* 発声絵葉書. ¶a ***town*** *card* 横二インチ縦三インチの札. ¶a ***transfer*** *card* 転勤カード. ¶hold a ***trump*** *card*〚トランプ〛切札を持つ.‖He had one ***trump*** *card* left, however. も一つ出す手があった. ¶a ***union shop*** *card* 組合加盟カード. ¶Until the sixteenth century, ***vising*** *cards* were unknown in Europe. 十六世紀までは名刺は欧州になかった. ¶official ***voting*** *cards* 正式の投票券. ¶a ***wedding*** *card* 結婚通知状. ¶hold all the ***winning*** *cards* 勝札を皆手に握っている. ¶a ***withdrawal*** *card* 退職カード.

P while ***at*** *cards* トランプ勝負中‖Shall we have a game ***at*** (＝***of***) *cards?* トランプをしようか.‖play ***at*** *cards* カルタ(トランプ)をする‖gamble ***at*** *cards* カルタでかけをやる. 【類】how to win ***at*** *cards.* ¶admission ***by*** *card* 招待状での入場. ¶send one's regret ***on*** a post *card* 葉書で断る‖of course, it is ***on*** the *card* that ... もち論...ということははっきり分っている.

cardigan, *n.*〚服飾〛カーディガン(セーター).

Q² an ***all-wool*** *cardigan* 純毛のカーディガン.

care, *n.* 心配；世話；注意, 用心.

V ***assume*** the *care* of children in their mother's absence 母親の不在中子供たちの世話をする. ¶Much *care* has also been ***bestowed*** on the illustrations. さし絵に対しても同様多大の注意を加えてある. ¶***borrow*** *care* [from tomorrow] 取越苦労をする. ¶There are men who ***carry*** their *care* to bed every night of their lives. 毎晩寝床についてまで心配事を考えている人がある. ¶***cast*** *care* ***aside*** 心配を忘れる. ¶Such a matter ***demands*** special *care.* そんな事は特に注意を要する. ¶*Care* has been ***devoted*** to it. それに注意を払った. ¶special *care* has been ***directed*** to ... ...に特に力を入れた. ¶to ***drown*** their *cares* they often resort to alcohol あの人たちはしばしば酒を飲んで憂さを晴らす. ¶The most laborious *care* has been ***employed*** in securing accuracy. 正確を期するためには最大の苦心が払われた. ¶Great *care* should be ***exercised*** in future. 今後大いに注意しなければいけない. ¶He ***expended*** great *care* in doing it. 彼はそれをやるのに非常な注意を払った. 【類】much *care* has been ***expended*** upon ... ¶The trousers hanger recommends itself to all men who ***give*** *care* to their apparel. ズボン掛けは服装に注意を払う人にはだれにでも必要だ. 【類】great *care* should be ***given*** to ... ¶He ***has*** the *care* of two younger students. 彼は二人の学生を世話している. 【類】***have*** the *care* of horses.‖***Have*** a *care! Have* a *care!* 気を付けて！気を付けて.‖***have*** a *care* not to ... ...しないように気をつける. 【類】He ***has*** a great many *cares.* ¶The author ***lavished*** much *care* on that work. 著者はその本に大層力を入れた. ¶***need*** medical *care* 医者に掛かる必要がある. ¶***receive*** painstaking *care* from ... 一方ならず...の世話になる. ¶The patient ***requires*** much *care* and experienced nursing. 病人は非常な注意と熟練した看護を要する. ¶***soothe*** the *cares* 苦労をなぐさめる. ¶I shall ***take care*** it does not occur again. 二度とそんなことのないように注意しましょう. 【類】great *care* must be ***taken*** not to ...‖Will you ***take care*** to thank him for me? 私に代ってお礼を言って下さいませんか.‖***Take care*** that the quality is satisfactory. 品質をよくするようにせよ.‖Please ***take care*** of my home for me while I am away. るす中私の家の世話をして下さい.‖Matters can not be left to ***take care*** of themselves. そのまま放っておくことはできない.‖until the children grow up and can ***take care*** of themselves 子供たちが成長して自分の世話ができるようになるまで. ¶a woman who can not ***take care*** of herself だらしのない女‖***Take care*** of the pence, and the pounds will ***take care*** of themselves. 小事をゆるがせにせざれば大事はおのずから成る.‖He is well ***taken care*** of. 彼は行届いた世話を受けている.‖May I ***take care*** of your bag? おかばんをお預りしましょうか. 【類】I have ***taken care*** (手掛けた) of nervous people for more than twenty years. ¶***use*** all possible *care* あらゆる注意を加える‖*care* should be ***used*** to ... ...するように注意すべきだ.

Q take the ***best*** *care* of ... ...にできる限り注意する. ¶They should take ***better*** *care* of themselves. 彼らはもっと気を付けなければいけない. ¶neglect of ***bodily*** *care* からだに対する不注意. ¶show ***conscientious*** *care* 真心こめて面倒を見る. ¶***daily*** *cares* of life 日々の心配. ¶He thanked his physician for his ***devoted*** *care.* 彼は医師の心尽しに対して感謝した. ¶***diligent*** *care* has been taken to ... 精を出して...の世話をした. ¶He is constantly under a ***doctor's*** *care.* 彼は絶えず医者のやっかいになっている. ¶***domestic*** *cares* 家事の世話. ¶exercise ***due*** *care* よく注意する. ¶it must needs be studied with ***earnest*** *care* by ... ...が是非力を入れて研究しなければいけない. ¶***especial*** *care* has been taken to ... ...するよう特に注意した. ¶***extreme*** *care* must be taken to ... ...するように十二分の注意を払わなければいけない. ¶***fatherly*** *care* 父親(ほど)の心配. ¶take ***good*** *care* of one's sight 目を大切にする‖I will take ***good*** *care* of him. 彼のことは十分注意します. 【類】take ***good*** *care* not to ... ¶very ***great*** *care* is bestowed upon ... 多大の注意が...に加えられている. ¶***heavy*** *cares* of the family 家族たちの非常な気苦労. ¶lack of ***hygienic*** *care* 不衛生.

¶be placed under the ***kindly*** *care* of a friend 友人に親切に世話をしてもらうように頼む. ¶give ***medical*** *care* to a wounded man 負傷者の手当をする. ¶***meticulous*** *care* is required in ... ...に関しては細心の注意が必要だ. ¶take ***motherly*** *care* of ... 母親のように...世話をする. ¶too ***much*** *care* cannot be exercised in ... ...にはいくら注意してもし過ぎるということはない. ¶much *care* is ***necessary*** in ... ...について大いに注意する必要がある. ¶The work was executed with the ***nicest*** *care*. 仕事はきわめて綿密な注意を払って行われた. ¶take ***one*** *care* from the shoulders of ... ...の肩の荷を一つおろしてやる. ¶use ***ordinary*** *care* 普通の注意を払う. ¶with ***painstaking*** *care* 刻苦精励して. ¶***particular*** *care* has been devoted to ... ...に特別の注意を払った. ¶with ***paternal*** *care* 父親のような心尽しで. ¶I will take every ***possible*** *care* that it shall not happen again. 以後そんなことのないようできるだけ注意します. ¶lack of ***proper*** *care* 適当の注意を欠くこと. 【類】take ***proper*** *care* of borrowed books. ¶with the most ***punctilious*** *care* きわめて周到な注意を払って. ¶with ***scrupulous*** *care* 細心の注意を払って. ¶***special*** *care* should be taken not to ... 特に...せぬように注意すべきである. ¶***studied*** *care* 周到な注意. ¶***thousand*** *cares* and worries by day and by night 夜となく昼となく数多い心配と苦労. ¶***tomorrow's*** *cares* あすの心配. ¶***unremitting*** *care* and vigilance 間断のない注意と警戒. ¶the ***utmost*** *care* must be taken in ... ...に最大の注意を払わなければいけない. ¶guard with ***watchful*** *care* 十分注意して警戒する. ¶***worldly*** *cares* 俗事.

Q² ***business*** *cares* 商売上の用務. ¶***health*** *cares* 養生. ¶***household*** (=***family***) *cares* 家事. 【類】the exhaustion and worry of ***household*** *cares*.

P The king was weighed down ***by*** *cares* of state. 王は国事に心を痛められた. ¶leave one's valuables (children) ***in*** [the] *care* of ... 貴重品(など)を...にあずける. 【類】leave one's children ***in*** the *care* of ... ‖ kindly ship the goods to ..., in bond, ***in*** *care* of our shipping agent ... 品は保税倉庫あずけで当社関係の回漕店気付で送り出して下さい. 【類】Address all letters to Dr. John L. Haney, ***in*** *care* of The Ladies' Home Journal, Philadelphia. / For further information he may be addressed ***in*** *care* of Yale University. / address me ***in*** *care* of ... Company, 225 Fifth Avenue, New York City. ¶He came ***into*** my *care*. 私が彼を世話することになった. ¶He is full ***of*** *care*. 彼は注意深い. ¶send the letter ***to*** (=***in***) the *care* of Mr. ... ...氏気付で手紙を出す ‖ I committed my son ***to*** his *care*. 子供の世話を彼に頼んだ. ¶These children are ***under*** his *care*. この子供たちは彼の世話になっている. ‖ He is sinking ***under*** *cares*. 彼は心配でめいっている. ¶a technician ***with*** more *care* for style than for substance 内容よりも文章に一層心を用いる文章家 ‖ encumber his mind ***with*** *cares* 彼に心配させる ‖ I entrusted him ***with*** the *care* of my property. 財産の管理を彼に頼んだ. ¶He is ***without*** a *care* in the world. 彼には何の心配もない.

P² exercise the reasonable *care* ***against*** fires 相当火災の用心をする. ¶Take *care* ***for*** the future (=in future). 今後気を付けなさい. ¶exercise *care* ***in*** selecting ... ...の選択に注意する. 【類】He takes little *care* ***in*** the choice of his words (用語). ‖ *care* ***of*** the body 身じまい. ¶*care* ***of*** state 政事. ¶the *cares* ***of*** business 商売上の気配り ‖ the *care* ***of*** the household 家事の世話 ‖ *care* ***of*** the house 家の手入れ ‖ A letter addressed to me "*care* ***of*** ..., Yokohama" will always reach me. 手紙は横浜...方として出して下されば必ず着きます. 【類】Letters sent *care* ***of*** this Agency will be forwarded (回送される).

care, *v.* 心配する, 懸念する; 世話する.

M What music do you *care* for ***best***? あなたの一番お好きな音楽は何ですか. ¶I don't *care* ***a bit*** (=***straw, pin or snap of the fingers***) what people say. 世間のいうことなんか少しも気にしない. ¶***How*** do you *care* for bowling? ボーリング(球戯)はお好きですか. ¶I don't *care* very ***much*** for going to the theater. 私は余り芝居に行きたくはない. 【類】You don't appear to *care* ***much*** for (=about) music. ¶They *cared* ***nothing*** for the orders of the Peking administration. 彼らは北京政府の命令なんか何とも思っていなかった. ¶***tenderly*** and ***properly*** *care* for ... ...をやさしく, 行届いた世話をする. ¶The children are ***well*** *cared* for. 子供らはよく世話をしてもらっている.

P I don't *care* ***about*** the matter. 私はそのことは何んとも思わない. 【類】She does not *care* ***about*** him in the least. ‖ those who do not *care* ***about*** expense, if they get efficiency 能率が上がるなら出費にはとんちゃくしない人々. ¶He always *cares* ***for*** my interest. 彼はいつも私のためを思ってくれる. 【類】I don't *care* ***for*** that. / *care* ***for*** some one's welfare / Nobody will *care* ***for*** you so long as you remain selfish. / He thinks and acts without *caring* ***for*** opinion of the world. / Father earns money to *care* ***for*** his children. / I *care* more ***for*** my honor than my money. ‖ I was too tired to *care* ***for*** anything but bed. あまりに疲労したので寝るほかは何も考えなかった.

O If you *care* to come along [on] Thursday evening, I shall be glad to see you. 木曜日の晩お出でくださるなら喜んでお会い致します. ¶I don't *care* to run the risk. その危険をおかす気はない. ¶Will you come along with us? —I don't *care* if I do. 僕たちと一緒に行かないか—行ってもいい(行きたい).

careen, *v.* 傾く.

P *careen* ***in*** the wind 風で(船が)かしぐ. ¶*careen* ***to*** port 左舷にかしぐ. ¶*careen* ***under*** sail 帆で(船が)かしぐ.

career, 経歴, 生涯; 進行.

V She ***abandoned*** her stage *career*. 彼女は舞台生活をやめた. 【類】He ***abandoned*** a *career* of promise (有望な地位) as a lawyer and in politics to devote himself to the interests of the next generation. ¶***begin*** one's *career* as a newsman 新聞記者として人生のスタートを切る. ¶***blast*** one's *career* 一生を棒に振る. ¶***build*** a *career* 世に立つ道を開く. ¶***carve out*** one's *career* 運命を開拓する. ¶His early *career* was ***chequered***. 彼の青年時代は波瀾に富んでいた. ¶***choose*** wisely a life *career* 一生の仕事を賢明に選ぶ. ¶***close*** one's *career* 生涯を終える. ¶Spain ***commenced*** her *career* as a colonial power by the acquisition of the Canary Islands in the middle of the fifteenth century. スペインは十五世紀の中葉にカナリー諸島を獲得して植民国たるの緒についた. ¶His *career* was abruptly ***cut*** short by his death in 1729. 一七二九年における彼の死によって突然彼の生涯に幕が下りた. ¶This ***determined*** his *career* for the rest of his life. これで今後彼が人生をいかに送るべきかが決定した. ¶He has long ***directed*** the *career* of that famous journal. 彼は長年その有名な雑誌の経営をして来た. ¶***embrace*** the *career* of art 芸術家として世に立つ. ¶Thus the hotel ***ended*** its *career*. こういうわけでそのホテルは廃業することになった. ‖ He ***ended*** his *career* at the hands of an assassin. その人は刺客の手にかかって生涯を終えた. ¶May the Club ***enjoy*** a long and prosperous and useful *career*. 願わくばクラブが永く栄えて有益な事業を続けられんことを. ¶He ***followed*** his *career* with much interest. 彼は大いに身を入れて自分の仕事に当った. ¶He is still young enough to ***have*** a very great *career* before him. 彼はまだ年が若いから今後大いに有望だ. ‖ The vessel has ***had*** a *career* of 27 years. 同船はすでに二十七年間就役している. ¶This ***imperiled*** his whole future *career*. このことのために彼の将来は危機に陥った. ¶This success ***opened*** his *career* as a poet. この成功が詩人として彼が世に立つ機縁になった. ¶This ***opened up*** a brilliant *career* for her. これで彼女は輝かしい生涯に入った. ¶***outline*** his *career* 彼の経歴を略説する. ¶There are girls who ***plan*** a "*career*," and do not look forward to marriage. 世間には自活の道を立てようとして結婚を考えていない若い女がいる. ¶I ***prophesy*** a bright *career* for you. 君の明るい将来を予言する. ¶***pursue*** a *career* in journalism 新聞記者として働く ‖ The university will long ***pursue*** her *career* of usefulness. その大学は末永くその有益な事業を継続することであろう. ¶This ***ruined*** his screen *career*. これで彼の映画俳優としての生活は葬られてしまった. ¶briefly ***sketch*** his *career* 彼の経歴を簡単に語る. ¶He ***sought*** a *career* in the movies. 彼は映画界に進出しようとした. ¶***start*** his business *career* at fifteen 十五歳で商業界に入る ‖ ***start*** one's *career* all over 振出しから始める ‖ He ***started*** his *career* as a reporter on the Philadelphia Press. フィラデルフィア・プレスの探訪記者として世に立った. ¶***wreck*** a *career* 前途をぶちこわす.

Q His ***academic*** *career* was undistinguished. あの人の学者としての経歴は平凡だった. ¶an ***astonishing*** *career* 驚くべき経歴. ¶have a ***brilliant*** *career* in politics 政界で光輝

ある経歴を持つ. 【類】open up a ***brilliant career***. ¶after a ***brilliant academic*** *career* 優秀な成績で学業を終えて後. ¶He has had a very ***chequered career***. 彼は多彩の生涯を送った. 【類】a ***chequered*** and ***romantic*** (小説的) *career*. ¶boys being trained for a ***commercial career*** 商業教育を受けている少年たち. ¶***diplomatic*** *career* 外交家としての生涯. ¶He has had a ***distinguished*** *career* as a diplomat. 彼は外交官として抜群の経歴を持っている. ¶when my imagination was in ***full career*** 私が想像をたくましくしていたとき. ¶The school collaborates with parents in choosing each boy's ***future career***. 学校は各生徒将来の職業選択について両親と協力する. ¶He has a ***great career*** before him. 彼は実に前途有望である. ¶Teaching is an ***honorable*** *career*. 教師はりっぱな職業である. ¶begin one's ***literary*** *career* 文筆生活に入る. ¶the ***meteoric*** *career* of Napoleon ナポレオンの流星のような生涯. ¶His idea is to follow a ***military*** *career*. 彼は軍人になる考えだ. ‖ He has had a distinguished ***military*** *career*. 軍人として抜群であった. ¶His ***mortal*** *career* came to a premature termination. 春秋に富む身であったが生涯は終りを告げた. ¶Public competitive examinations admit to an ***official*** *career*. 公開の競争試験に合格すると官吏になれる. ‖ He started his ***official*** *career* as a diplomat. 彼は外交官出身である. ¶prepare oneself for a ***pedagogical*** *career* 教育家になる準備をする. ¶early in his ***political*** *career* 彼の政治家生活の初めに. ¶a ***professional*** *career* 職歴 ‖ enter upon a ***professional*** *career* 専門の仕事にはいる. ¶He bids fair to have a ***prosperous*** *career*. 彼は将来栄達の見込がある. ¶his ***public*** *career* as an author and a statesman 作家兼政治家としての彼の公的生涯. ¶a ***reproachful*** *career* 恥ずべき経歴. ¶She began her ***theatrical*** *career* by entering the ballet. 彼女は舞台生活の皮切にバレエ団に入った. ¶his ***turbulent*** *career* 彼の波瀾重畳の生涯. ¶She has had a ***varied*** *career*. 彼女は多彩な経歴の持主だ. 【類】a singularly ***varied*** *career*. ¶one's ***wartime*** *career* ... の戦争中の経歴.

Q[2] He began his ***business*** *career* as a cowboy. 彼は牛飼として実生活に入った. ‖ He has had a long and honorable ***business*** *career*. 長らくりっぱな実業家として世に立って来た. ‖ She combines motherhood and a full-time ***business*** *career*. 彼女はお母さんでありまた職業婦人でもある. ¶In some cases a good marriage ends the ***butterfly*** *career*. 良縁を得て浮いた生活から足を洗うような例もある. ¶a successful ***engineering*** *career* 成功した技術家としての生涯. ¶go into the teaching profession for a ***life*** *career* 一生の仕事として教職につく. ¶begin one's ***newspaper*** *career* 新聞記者生活を始める. ¶a ***picture*** (=***movie*** *or* ***film***) *career* 映画人としての経歴. ¶resumption of a ***school*** *career*=re-entrance to school (復学). ¶follow a ***screen*** or a ***stage*** *career* 映画または舞台生活にはいる. ¶a ***seafaring*** *career* [職業としての]海上生活. ¶in the early part of my ***student*** *career* 私の学生生活の始めに. ¶his ***undergraduate*** *career* at Oxford オクスフォードにおける彼の大学生活.

P He passed away ***after*** an exceptionally busy and useful *career*. 並はずれて多忙でまた有益な生涯を終えて彼は世を去った. ¶***during*** his military *career* 彼の軍職にあった間. ¶withdraw absolutely ***from*** his public *career* 公生活から全く退く. ¶early ***in*** my *career* as a writer 私の作家として立った初めに ‖ He is getting on well ***in*** his *career*. りっぱにその仕事をやっている. ¶start ***on*** one's *career* 実生活に踏み出す.

P[2] It was on the way from Paris that her *career* ***as*** an actress really began. 女優としての彼女の経歴が本当に始まったのはパリからの帰途であった. ¶during his student *career* (=days) ***at*** Waseda 早稲田での学生生活中. ¶"*careers*" ***for*** women 女の職業. ¶He began his public *career* ***in*** the Ministry of Justice. 彼は司法省(法務省)でその官吏生活に入った.

career, *v.* 疾走する.

M *career* ***away*** 疾走し去る. ¶*careering* ***gaily*** over the waves 楽しげに波上を疾走して.

P a gentleman wildly *careering* ***among*** the traffic ***after*** his hat 人通りの中を夢中になって帽子を追いかける一紳士.

careful, *a.* 注意深い, 用心深い.

M if one is not *careful* ***enough*** 用心してかからないと. ¶be ***extremely*** *careful* about cleanliness 非常にきれい好きである. ¶be ***overly*** *careful* あまりに注意深い. ¶be ***very*** *careful* about ... ...についてはなはだ用意周到である.

P He is *careful* ***about*** his appearance (health, dress). 彼は風采(など)に注意する. 【類】Be *careful* ***in*** money matters (speech). / be very *careful* ***in*** doing ... / be *careful* ***in*** one's diet (食事) / Tell him to be *careful* ***in*** the future. ¶*careful* ***in regard to*** one's diet 食事に注意する. ¶He is *careful* ***of*** his health (money). 彼は健康(など)を大事にする. 【類】He is *careful* ***of*** the rights (feelings, welfare) of others. / be *careful* ***of*** small things. / Be *careful* ***of*** what you are doing. ¶Be very *careful* ***with*** fire. 火の元に十分注意しなさい.

O I was *careful* to notify in good time. 私は時を失せず告知するようにした. ¶Be *careful* never to use bad language. 決して悪い言葉を使わぬように気を付けなさい.

careless, *a.* 不注意な, 無とん着な.

M be *careless* ***enough*** to ... 不覚にも...する.

P He is *careless* ***about*** his dress (appearance). 彼は服装(など)に無とん着だ. 【類】He is *careless* ***about*** future. / He is *careless* ***about*** (=***of***) the consequences (結果). / be *careless* ***about*** one's appearance. ¶*careless* ***in*** morals 身持が悪い. 【類】He is *careless* ***in*** everything (his health, work, writing). ¶He is *careless* ***of*** his money (health, reputation, what people say). 彼は金銭(など)に無とん着だ. 【類】He is *careless* ***of*** his own safety.

carelessness, *n.* 不注意.

V *carelessness* ***engendered*** by too much supervision 監督の行き過ぎから生じた不注意.

Q ***rank*** *carelessness* 大変な不注意.

P You will have to answer ***for*** your *carelessness*. 君は不注意の責任を負わなければならない. ¶I used this word ***from*** *carelessness*. うっかりこの言葉が出た. ¶***In*** his *carelessness* he has evidently overlooked it. 彼が不注意からそれを見落したのはたしかだ. ¶***through*** *carelessness* with fire 火の用心を怠ったので ‖ The fire occurred ***through*** *carelessness* with fire. その火事は火の不始末から出た.

P[2] a Bohemian *carelessness* ***in*** matters of money 金のことにかけて豪傑流の無とん着.

caress, *v.* 愛撫(ぶ)する.

P be *caressed* ***at*** court 宮中でちょう愛される. ¶The boy was *caressed* ***by*** (=***with***) the hand. 少年は手でなでられた.

cargo, *n.* 船荷, 積荷.

V ***carry*** *cargo* 荷を積んでいる ‖ a steamer ***carrying*** a *cargo* of boards to ... 板材を積んで...へ行く汽船. ¶***discharge*** her *cargo* その積荷を荷上げする ‖ ***discharge*** *cargo* into lighters 荷物をはしけにおろす. ¶***engage*** *cargo* (passengers) for the vessel その船に貨物を積込む(船客を載せる)契約をする. ¶The steamer ***got*** a *cargo* in Kobe. 汽船は神戸で荷を積んだ. ¶The ship ***has*** a *cargo* of about 800 tons. その船は約八百トンの荷を積んでいる. ¶***land*** a *cargo* 積荷を陸揚する. ¶***load*** a *cargo* of rice 米を積み込む. ¶***purchase*** a return *cargo* 帰り荷(復航貨物)を買う. ¶***secure*** a return *cargo* 帰り荷を獲得する. ¶***ship*** *cargo* 船に荷物を積む. ¶***stow*** *cargo* 船荷を積む. ¶***take*** a *cargo* to and from alongside 船側から荷の積おろしをする. ¶***take in*** a *cargo* of fish 魚を積み込む. ¶***take on*** (=***in***) *cargo* at the port その港で船荷を積込む. ¶***transfer*** a *cargo* to ... 船荷を...積替える. ¶***unload*** her *cargo* 船の荷をおろす.

Q ***damaged*** *cargo* 海上でいたんだ貨物. ¶remove the ***entire*** *cargo* 船荷をことごとく取去る. ¶cannot make up a ***full*** *cargo* 十分の船荷が得られない. 【類】secure a ***full*** *cargo* for ... ¶a ***general*** *cargo* 一般船荷. ¶an ***inward*** *cargo* 輸入船荷. ¶***lighter*** *cargoes* 軽い船荷. ¶a ***miscellaneous*** *cargo* 雑多な船荷. ¶an ***outward*** *cargo* 輸出船貨物. ¶take a ***return*** *cargo* of coal 帰り荷に石炭を積込む. ¶a ship heavily laden with a ***rich*** *cargo* 高価な荷物を満載した船. ¶a ***saved*** *cargo* 損失を免かれた船荷. ¶She has never carried ***similar*** *cargo* before. その船は同種の船荷を運んだことはない.

P load a ship ***with*** *cargo* 船に荷を積む.

caricature, *n.* 漫画, 風刺画.

V ***draw*** *caricatures* 漫画をかく.

Q a ***bold*** *caricature* 大胆な戯画. ¶a ***harsh*** *caricature* しんらつな漫画. ¶***hideous*** *caricatures* 見るもいやな戯画. ¶a ***manifest*** *caricature* 紛れもない漫画(写実的でなく誇張した絵). ¶an ***offensive*** *caricature* of ... ...のいやらしい漫画.

P the picture is *in caricature* of ... その絵は…を漫画化したものである.

caricaturist, *n.* 漫画家, 風刺画家.

Q a *facile caricaturist* 筆の達者な漫画家.

carnation, *n.* カーネーション.

V People *wear carnations* on Mother's Day in honor of motherhood. 母の日には母性を称えてカーネーションを付ける.

Q *perpetually-flowering carnation* 四季咲きのカーネーション.

carnival, *n.* 謝肉祭, お祭騒ぎ.

V *hold* a high *carnival* どんちゃん騒ぎをやる.

P² a *carnival of* bloodshed 血まみれ騒ぎ.

carouse, *v.* 大酒を飲む.

P a group of men *carousing at* an inn のみ屋で底抜け騒ぎをしている団体. ¶They had been all aboard, *carousing to* each other's health. 彼ら一同は乗船してお互いの健康を祝して大いに飲んだ.

carp, *v.* 口やかましく言う, 難癖をつける.

P *carp at* one's errors 誤りをやかましく言う.

carpet, *n.* じゅうたん, 敷物.

V *lay* (=*put down*) a *carpet* じゅうたんを敷く. ¶The *carpet* must be *taken up* and *beaten*. じゅうたんを上げてたたかないといけない.

P put some straw *beneath* the *carpet* じゅうたんの下にわらを入れる. ¶upset the ink and make a mess *on* the *carpet* インキをこぼして敷物を台なしにする ‖ have a servant *on* the *carpet* 《俗》召使をしかる. ¶walk *over* the *carpet* じゅうたんの上を歩く.

carpet, *v.* じゅうたんを敷く.

P The garden is *carpeted with* a mass of multicolored flowers. 庭は色とりどりの一むれの花で敷き詰められている. 【類】The valley is *carpeted with* verdure (wild flowers).

carriage, *n.* (1) 馬車; 乗物; 《英》客車.

Q a *horse-drawn carriage* 馬車.

Q² *railway carriages*=《米》railroad cars 鉄道の車両(主に客車).

(2) 運送料; 運送.

V *charge carriage* by bulk (weight) 容積(重量)によって運賃を取る. ¶I sent the parcel "*carriage paid*." 運賃前払いでその小包を送った.

V² What does the *carriage* of the parcel *come to*? 小荷物の運賃はいくらになるか.

P free *of carriage*=carriage free 運賃無料.

P² the *carriage of* goods *by* rail (boat, land, water, air) 鉄道(など)での運送. ¶*carriage on* goods 運賃.

(3) 風采, 姿勢; 動作.

V *give* a gracious and graceful *carriage* to the body 身体に優美な風姿を添える. ¶Dancing *improves* the *carriage*. ダンスは動作を美しくする. ¶*preserve* one's dignified *carriage* 威厳のある態度をくずさないようにする.

Q He has a *conceited carriage*. 彼は気取ったようすをする. ¶an *erect carriage* and manly bearing 真直ぐな姿勢と男らしい態度. ¶a *free* and *easy carriage* ゆうよう迫らぬ態度. ¶She has a *graceful carriage*. あの婦人は動作が優美である. ¶a man of *haughty carriage* ごう然たる態度の人. ¶her *imperious carriage* 彼女の堂々たる身のこなし. ¶She has a thoroughly *masculine carriage* and habits. 彼女の態度や習慣は全く男のようだ. ¶the *proper carriage* of the body 上品な身のこなし. ¶He has a *proud carriage*. 威張ったようすをする. ¶He has a *smart carriage*. 動作がスマートだ.

carrier, *n.* 運搬人; 集配人.

Q *public carriers* 運送業者.

Q² *mail carriers* 郵便集配人.

P² Flies and mosquitoes are *carriers of* infectious diseases. はえや蚊は伝染病の媒介物だ.

carrot, *n.* 人参.

V *plant carrots* in one's garden 菜園に人参を植える.

Q a dish of *diced carrots* さいの目に切った人参一さら.

carry, *v.* 運ぶ, 携行する; かち得る.

M Love for art *carried* him *abroad*. 彼は芸術が好きで海外に行った. ¶This rifle *carries* nearly *a mile*. この小銃の射程は約一マイルだ. ¶His passion *carried* him *astray*. 彼は情に迷わされた. ¶He was *carried away* by the plague. 疫病に命を取られた. ‖ The bridge was *carried away* by the flood (torrent). 橋が洪水(など)で流された. ‖ *carried away* by her feelings 彼女はその感情にかられて. 【類】*carried away* by one's [own] enthusiasm ‖ be so *carried away* by her wounded pride as to ... その婦人は誇りを傷けられたために…をするほど逆上していた. ¶we shall *carry away* a pleasant and lasting recollection of ... …の楽しい, いつまでも消えない追憶がわれわれの心に残ることであろう. ¶*carry* the stone *back* to its place その石をもとの所へ運び返す ‖ *carry* one's thought *back* 回顧する ‖ *carry* us *back* in imagination to ... われわれは想像で…の過去にさかのぼる ‖ His words *carried* me *back* to the old time. 彼の言葉で昔を思い出した. 【類】I feel certain that all of us will *carry back* to our homes and countries a lively recollection (生き生きした追憶) of ... ‖ *carry* oneself *defiantly* under suspicion or blame=fight it out 疑惑あるいは非難の目で見られながら反抗的に振舞う. ¶*carry* the matter so *far* 『比喩』そこまでこぎつける ‖ Conservatism is *carried* too *far*. 保守主義にしてもそれでは行きすぎだ. ¶*carry forward* to next year account 来年の勘定に繰越す. 【類】have a balance of ... to *carry forward* to next quarter (次の四半期に) ‖ A sum of ... is *carried forward* to next account. …の金額を次の勘定に繰越す. ‖ *carry forward* an enterprise 事業を推進する ‖ *carry forward* the tradition of good will toward ... …に対して伝統的な好意を示す. ¶It is needless to *carry* this illustration *further*. この説明をこれ以上する必要はない. ¶If I take any more, I fear I shall be unable to *carry* myself *home*. この上頂戴すると家へ帰れなくなります. ¶*carry* trade *inland* 奥地と交易をする. ¶The waves *carried* it *out* to sea. それは浪にさらわれた. ¶It was *carried out* with wisdom and discretion. それは賢明にかつ慎重に実行された. 【類】*carry out* one's intention (mission, order, plan, policy) / The proceedings (議事) were *carried out* in style. / unflinchingly (ひるまず) *carry* it *out* / *carry* it *out* systematically (組織的に) / has been *carried out* over a two-year period (二年の期限以上にわたって) / failure to *carry out* some of the provisions of a contract (契約のある条項) / strictly *carry* it *out*. ¶The heavy stocks *carried over* from last year have now gone into consumption. 昨年から持越したたくさんの在庫品ももうさばけ切った. ¶The regulation is *perfunctorily carried* out. その規定はお座なりに施行されている. ¶not *properly carried* out 適当に実行されていない. ¶He was *carried shoulder-high* by his classmates. 彼は同じ組の生徒から胴上げをされた. ¶be *successfully carried out* 見事に実行される. ¶The decision was *carried unanimously*. その決議は満場一致で可決された. ¶He *carries* his eighty years *well*. 彼は八十歳でもしっかりしている.

M² I *carry about* with me some volume or other. 私は何かしら本を持って歩く. ‖ *carry* them *about* for sale それを売り歩く. 【類】*carry about* favorite authors 好きな著者の本を持って行く. ¶His hat was *carried along* by the wind. 彼は帽子を風に持って行かれた. ¶A purse is convenient for *carrying* money *around* with one 財布は金銭を携帯するために便利だ. ¶The sinking ship *carried down* with her the captain and a large number of passengers. 沈みかけている船と共に船長および多数の船客が海にのまれた. ‖ be *carried off* by a thief 盗賊に持って行かれる. 【類】The soldiers seized two young men and *carried* them *off*. ‖ *carry off* prizes 賞品を勝ち得る. 【類】*carried off* the first class gold medal (一等金牌) for painting at a Paris exhibition ‖ They were *carried off* by cholera. コレラで死んだ. ‖ *carry off* the palm 勝利を博する. ¶*carry on* a long conversation 長話をする. 【類】*carry on* a conversation with a foreigner in his own language (自国語で) ‖ *carry on* speech with ... …と話をする ‖ This pair of lovers were *carrying on* an ardent correspondence. この恋人同志は情熱的な文通をしていた. 【類】*carry on* a correspondence under a fictitious name (仮名で) ‖ be *carried on* by tradition 昔からの慣例によって行う ‖ *carry on* their campaign against ... …反対運動をする ‖ they *carried on* so sturdily their warfare against ... 彼らは非常にがん強に…と戦った. 【類】*carry on* a desperate fight / *carry on* the war to the bitter end (あくまでも) ‖ *carry on* active occupational activities 占領活動を活発に進める ‖ he *carried on* business for many years at ... 彼は…で多年営業していた ‖ *carry on* the business of the Association 協会の事務を執る. 【類】*carry on* business by upright methods (正しい方法で) / *carry on* business in an up-to-date way / *carry on* all kinds of professions / *carry on* a retail iron mongery business (金物小売商) / *carry* ***on*** a trade in silks (絹織物業) / *carry* ***on*** a lucrative trade (割のよい取引) with ... / *carry* ***on*** more advanced studies / laboriously *carry* ***on*** researches ... / *carry* ***on*** the work of his father / was *carried* ***on*** uninterruptedly for 81 years / *carry* work ***on*** by candle-light ‖ The department *carries* ***on*** a busy life. その部局は仕事がいそがしい. ‖ *carry* ***on*** prostitution 売春行為をする ‖ *carry* ***on*** the fund until a sufficient sum should be collected for ... ...のために十分の金額が集まるまで基金の募集を続ける ‖ *carry* ***on*** nation-wide investigations of ... ...の全国的調査を行う ‖ These meetings are *carried* ***on*** entirely in English. これらの会合は全部英語で行われる. ‖ *carry* ***on*** sex relations with ... ...と性的に関係する ‖ The millers are confident that they can *carry* ***on*** with volunteer labor. 各工場主は有志労働者の手でやって行けると確信している(同盟罷業の場合など). ¶*carry* us ***on*** from 1864 to 1874 1864 年から 1874 年まで続く ‖ Stockraising is actively *carried* ***on.*** 畜産業が盛んに行われている. ¶*carry* it ***over*** to next quarter 次ぎの四半期まで持ち越す ‖ The case was *carried* ***over*** to the next term of court. その事件は次期の裁判に持越された. ¶I am certain he will *carry* it ***through.*** きっとそれをやり通すだろう. ‖ *carry* it ***through*** to its logical extremes それを徹底的にやる. 【類】 *carry* ***through*** an enterprise (a work) / *carry* a project (計画) ***through*** / *carry* a fight ***through*** ‖ This courage will *carry* him ***through.*** あの人は勇気でやってのけるだろう. 【類】 can get the business *carried* ***through.***

P He always *carries* some money ***about*** him. 彼は始終いくらか金を身に着けている. ¶*carry* it ***across*** the street それを持って街を横切る ‖ *carry* it ***across*** one's shoulders それを肩に掛けて持って行く. ¶*carry* two swords ***at*** (=in) the girdle 大小を腰にたばさむ. ¶He *carried* everything (=all) ***before*** him. 彼の向う所敵なしであった. ¶*carry* a thing ***by*** hand (cart) 手(など)で物を運ぶ ‖ It is *carried* ***by*** goods-train. 貨物列車で運ぶ. ‖ *carry* a motion ***by*** a large majority (a majority of five) 大多数(など)で動議を可決する ‖ There is a strong connection between the wealth of a nation and the amount of life insurance *carried* ***by*** its citizens. 国民の富と国民の生命保険の金額との間には深い関係がある. ¶*carry* it ***in*** one's pocket (bag, hand, arms) それを懐(など)に入れて持歩く ‖ *carry* goods ***in*** a vehicle 貨物を車で運ぶ. ¶*carry* a person ***into*** a room 人を室内に連れ込む ‖ *carry* a law ***into*** effect (=execution=operation) 法律を実施する ‖ *carry* a project ***into*** execution 計画を実現する ‖ *carry* it ***into*** practice それを実行する ‖ The case was *carried* ***into*** court. 同事件は法廷に持ち出された. ‖ This novel *carries* me ***into*** the tenderest scenes of domestic life. この小説を読むと家庭生活の最も温い光景がしのばれる. ‖ *carry* the war ***into*** Africa アフリカに攻め入る ‖ *carry* an account ***into*** ledger 勘定を元帳に移す ‖ *carry* the amount of money ***into*** the next term その金額を次期へ繰越す. ¶*carry* it ***on*** one's back (shoulder) それを背(など)に担って行く. 【類】 *carry* a baby ***on*** one's back / *carry* a wounded soldier ***on*** a stretcher (担架) ‖ *carry* it ***on*** the body それを身に着けている ‖ The broadcast was *carried* ***on*** national network. その放送は全国に流された. ¶He was *carried* ***out of*** himself. 彼は無我夢中になった. ¶*carry* it ***over*** one's shoulder それをかついで行く ‖ It was *carried* ***over*** the bridge. 橋を通ってそれを運んだ. ¶*carry* ***over*** winter lettuce and cabbage ちさやキャベツを越冬させる. ¶*carry* a sash ***round*** and ***round*** the waist without tying the ends 帯をぐるぐる巻きにする. ¶*carry* a work ***through*** the press 著作の印刷を進行させる ‖ His voice *carried* ***through*** the hall. 彼の声は満場に行渡った. ‖ Grace will *carry* us ***through*** all difficulties. 温雅な態度で向えばどんな困難にも打ち勝つことができる. ¶It is walking *carried* ***to*** fatigue. それでは散歩が過ぎて疲れる. ‖ Things are not yet *carried* ***to*** that extent. まだそれまではやっていない. 【類】 if *carried* ***to*** an excess(過度) / be *carried* ***to*** the extreme (極端) / Even good habits may be *carried* ***to*** harmful extreme. ‖ The work was *carried* ***to*** completion. その仕事が完成した. ‖ be *carried* ***to*** its logical conclusion 論理的結論に達する ‖ *carry* it ***to*** success やり通す ‖ He *carried* the news ***to*** his wife. 彼はそれを妻の所へ行って知らせた. ‖ Her husband was *carried* ***to*** prison. 彼女の夫は刑務所に入れられた. ¶*carry* it always ***upon*** one's person それを始終身に着けている. ¶The privileges *carry* ***with*** them great responsibilities. その特権は大なる責任を伴う. ‖ He *carried* it ***with*** him as a constant companion. 彼はいつもそれを身に付けていた. ‖ *carry* one's own ***with*** └an air 気取る.

carrying-out, *n.* 実行.

P² enforce the *carrying-out* ***of*** the contract 契約の実行 └を強請する.

carry-over, *n.* 持越し.

P² *carry-over* ***on*** farms 保有(米).

car-stop, *n.* 停留所.

Q a ***temporary*** *car-stop* 臨時電車停留所.

cart, *n.* 荷車.

V The *cart* was ***drawn*** by horses. その車を馬が引いた. ¶***get*** a *cart* up a hill 坂に車を押す. ¶***pull*** a *cart* 荷車を引く. ¶***push*** a *cart* uphill 坂に荷車を押上げる. ¶That is a case of ***putting*** the *cart* before the horse. それではあべこべだ. ¶***upset*** one's apple *cart* 〖比喩〗人の計画をひっくり返す.

V² *Carts* were ***creaking*** through the streets. 荷車が町をきしりながら通っていた. ¶All through the night the market *carts* have been ***jogging*** into town. 夜通し市場行の荷車がことんことんと通っていた. ¶A *cart* ***lumbers along.*** 荷車が重そうに通って行く. ¶There is procession of *carts* and waggons that ***lumber up*** and ***down.*** 手車や荷馬車が列をなして重そうに右往左往している. ¶The *cart* ***stuck*** fast in the mud. 車が泥の中にはまり込んだ. ¶The *cart* ***tipped up.*** 車が転覆した. ¶*carts* ***waddling*** slowly のろのろとよろめきながら行く車.

P convey it ***in*** a *cart* それを車で運ぶ.

cart, *v.* 車で運ぶ.

M *cart* ***away*** 車で運ぶ. ¶*cart* ***off*** 車で運び去る ‖ *cart* garbage ***off*** to ... 台所のごみを...に運んで行く.

cartful, *n.* 車一杯.

P² a *cartful* ***of*** water (coal, fuel) 車一杯に積んだ水(など).

cartload, *n.* 一車(分).

P² a *cartload* ***of*** fuel 車一台分の燃料.

carton, *n.* ボール箱.

P² a *carton* ***of*** cigarettes (assorted chocolates) 巻たばこ包(など)の入った大箱.

cartoon, *n.* 漫画.

V ***execute*** a *cartoon* 漫画を描く.

Q ***animated*** *cartoons* 漫画映画(動画). ¶a ***powerful*** and ***caustic*** *cartoon* 力のある辛らつな漫画. ¶a ***scurrilous*** *car-* └*toon* 下品な漫画.

cartridge, *n.* 弾薬筒, 薬きょう.

Q a revolver containing three ***spent*** and two ***live*** *cartridges* 三弾は発射し二弾は未発の連発拳銃.

Q² a ***fire blank*** cartridge 空弾(弾丸のない薬きょう).

P load a gun ***with*** *cartridges* 銃に薬きょうを装塡する.

carve, *v.* 彫る, 刻む.

M *carve* ***out*** one's career 運命を開拓する. ¶***richly*** *carved* in a scroll pattern 唐草模様が花やかに彫刻してある.

P *carve* ***for*** one's self 自分の思うままに振舞う. ¶*carved* ***from*** ivory 象牙に彫った. ¶*carve* an image (a figure) ***in*** wood (marble, metal, stone) 像を木(など)に彫る ‖ a Buddha *carved* ***in*** wood 木彫の仏像. 【類】 an inscription (銘) *carved* ***in*** stone / a piece of wood *carved* ***in*** the shape of a fish. ¶*carve* marble ***into*** a statue 大理石で像を作る. 【類】 the ivory was *carved* ***into*** the shape of ... ¶rude pictures *carved* ***on*** bone by prehistoric artists 有史前の芸術家が骨に彫刻した素ぼくな絵. 【類】 a stone ***on*** which is *carved* the information (告示) that ... ¶*carve* it ***out of*** wood (marble) 木(など)でそれを刻む. 【類】 *carve* it ***out*** └***of*** a potato.

carver, *n.* 彫刻家.

P² a *carver* ***in*** wood=a wood carver 木彫家.

carving, *n.* 彫刻, 彫り物.

P² *carving* ***in*** wood and ivory 木や象げの彫り物.

case, *n.* (**1**) 場合, 立場; 状態; 実例; 問題.

V Only one more *case* shall be ***adduced*** in illustration. 参考に例をも一つだけ挙げよう. ¶This does not ***alter*** the *case.* そうだとしても局面は変らない. ‖ The *case* is ***altered.*** 話が別になる. ¶***bring forward*** numerous *cases* in illustration. 説明のため多数の例を持ち出す. 【類】 in this connection I may ***bring forward*** a *case* which ... ¶***cite*** *cases* illustrative of ... ...を証明するような例を引く. 【類】 As an example, I may ***cite*** a *case* from my own experience. ¶These *cases* of longevity are now ***considered*** mythical.

これら長寿の例は今日では神話じみると思われている. ¶*contrast* his *case* with that of mine 彼の場合を私の場合と対照する. ¶it *covers* the *case* to say that ... ...というのは要を得ている ‖ a rule to *cover* every *case* すべての場合に当てはまる規則. ¶*embrace* all *cases* すべての場合を包括する. ¶This *case* is *exaggerated*. この件は誇張されている. ¶*give cases* in point それに当てはまる例を示す. ¶We recently *had* a *case* in point. 近ごろそれに該当する例があった. ¶A very simple example will *illustrate* the *case*. きわめて簡単な例でその場合を説明しうる. ¶*instance* a *case* of ... ...の一例を挙げる. ¶I *know* a *case* where ... 私は...の例を知っている. 【類】 *cases* are (=have been) *known* where ... ¶if he wishes to *maintain* his *case* 彼が自分の立場を維持したいと思うなら. ¶He *made* a very good *case* for me. 彼は非常に私に有利のように取扱ってくれた. ‖ If you do so, you will *make* your *case* worse. そうすると君の立場が一層悪くなるだろう. ¶There is no reserve fund to *meet* such *cases*. こうした場合に当てるべき予備金がない. ‖ *cases* are often *met with*, which ... ...という場合にしばしば出会う. ¶I wish to *mention* a *case* in point. 適例を一つ挙げて見たい. ¶*present* Japan's *case* to the English-speaking world 英語国に向って日本の立場を明かにする. ¶should that unfortunately *prove* the *case* 不幸にしてそれが事実となって現われるとしたら. ¶someone has wittily *put* the *case* in this way: ある人がその場合をおもしろくこう言っている ‖ to *put* the *case* very mildly 内輪に言っても ‖ he *puts* the *case* pithily when he says ... 彼が...と言っているのは要を得ている. ¶the *case* has been *recorded* of a man who ... という人の例が記録にある. ¶had the *case* been *reversed* それと反対の場合であったら. ¶*state* the *case* with clearness その件をはっきり述べる. ¶This little colloquy (=conversation *or* dialogue) *sums up* the real *case*. このちょっとした対話でその真相が尽されている. ¶Let us *suppose* (=put) a *case* 一つの場合を仮定して見よう. ¶*take* a *case* in point 適例を持って来る ‖ let me *take* another *case*, that of ... も一つ...の例を挙げて見よう. 【類】 to *take* only one *case* / *take* one *case* out of many / Let me *take* the *case* of Japan and the United States as illustrating what I mean. ‖ *talk* the *case* over with ... その件について...と相談する.

V² no *cases* have as yet *arisen* in which it has been found necessary to ... ...する必要が起った例は今までにない. ¶a *case cropped up* in which ... ...というある事が起った. ¶if a similar *case happens* again 同じようなことがまた起ったら. ¶*cases* not unfrequently *occur* in which ... ...ということはよくおこる. ¶As the *case stands*, you must leave tonight. そういう事情だから君は今夜立たなくてはいけない.

Q Prevention is here, as in *all cases*, the best cure. どの場合でもそうだがこの場合も予防が最善の療法である. ¶cite *analogous cases* 類例を挙げる. ¶in *another case* 別の場合に. ¶in *any case* ともかく. ¶a *classic case* よく引かれる昔の例. ¶a *clear case* of "putting the cart before the horse" 明かに本末を転倒した例. ¶a most *complicated case* 非常にも複雑な例. ¶a *concrete case* 具体的の例. ¶But the *case* is not so *desperate* after all. しかし事態は結局それほどに行詰ってはいない. ¶the *case* is *different* with ... ...の場合は話が違う ‖ Those are two *different cases*. それとこれとは話が違う. 【類】 This is a *different case*. ¶in *disputed* and *doubtful cases* 議論のあるかつ疑わしい場合は. ¶in that *dread case* その恐ろしい場合には(開戦など). ¶in *either case* どっちにしても. ¶in *every case* あらゆる場合に ‖ in *every possible case* ありとあらゆる場合に. ¶an *extraordinary case* 非常の場合. ¶an *extreme case* 極端な場合. ¶*few cases* are known where ... ...という例はほとんどない. 【類】 there are not *a few cases* in which ... ¶Reply in *first case* to "Z.Y." care of the "Japan Times" Office. ジャパン・タイムス社内 Z.Y. あてに至急御返事ください. ¶There is something almost uncanny in the *following case*. 次に申上げるのは実に不思議な因縁話です. ¶He is in *good case* (=well off). 彼はらくに暮している. ‖ Have legal assistance if you have a *good case*. りっぱないい分があるなら法律の助けをお借りなさい. ‖ make out a *good case* for one's theory ...の理論をりっぱに証明する. ¶His is a *hardened case*. 彼の場合は病すでにこう盲に入っている. ¶*illustrative cases* 具体例. ¶*individual cases* 個々の場合. ¶an *interesting case* in point それに当る興味ある事例. ¶These are not *isolated cases*. これらは特殊の(一般的でない)例ではない. ‖ except possibly in *isolated cases* 恐らく特殊の場合は別として. 【類】 It is not an *isolated* or even an *uncommon case*. ¶*like* (=*similar*) *cases* 同様の場合. ¶in *most cases* 大ていの場合に. ¶never, in *no cases* 金輪際...ない. ¶in *numerous cases* 多くの場合に. ¶be only an *ordinary case* 普通の場合に過ぎない. ¶So far as known there is no *parallel case* on record. われわれの知っている限りではその類例は記録にない. ¶in *particular cases* 特殊の場合において. ¶What shall be done in the *present case?* 現在の場合どうしたらよろしいか. ¶the most *pronounced cases* 最も顕著な例. ¶in *rarer cases* 一層まれな場合には. ¶a *reversed case* 反対の例. ¶in *several cases* 種々の場合に. ¶to take a very *simple case* きわめて簡単な例を挙げれば. ¶in *some cases* ある場合に. ¶in *sorry case* 情けない状態で. ¶What is the practice in *such cases?* こうした場合の慣例はどうなっていますか. ¶It is not a *supposable case*. それはあり得べからざることである. ¶in *that* (*this*) *case* この場合には. 【類】 Even in *that case*, he might send a letter of excuse anyhow. ¶a fairly *typical case* 先ず代表的な例. 【類】 a *typical*, not *exceptional* (異例の), *case*. ¶His *case* is *untenable*. 彼の立場は弁護の余地がない. ¶in the *worst case* 最悪の場合には.

Q² *childbirth cases* 出産件数. ¶meet *emergency cases* 非常事態に対処する. ¶This is a *test case*. これは試験的なものだ.

P take it *as* a *case* in point それをこの場合当てはまる例と見なす. ¶*in case* of danger (emergency, doubt, failure, difficulty, need, necessity) 危険(など)の場合は ‖ *in cases* of accidents (urgent need) ちん事の起った(など)場合は. 【類】 *in case* (=in the event) of war / mediate (調停する) / *in case* of dispute / *in* the *case* of your consent / *in case* of my absence / *in case* of his being absent / *in case* of a disagreement between judges (審判者) / in *cases* of doubt / *in case* of any such aggression (侵略) / It is as well to have more than one *in case* of loss. ‖ *In case of* rain, I have an umbrella. 雨が降ってもかさがある. ‖ *in* the *case* of unsold goods 売れ残った品の場合には ‖ *in case* of default 履行しない場合は ‖ *in case* there should be any delay 万一遅れた場合には. 【類】 *in cases* where (=in which) such a step (処置) is advisable / *In case* you give me leave (許可), I will start at once. / *In case* I am prevented from coming, please excuse me. ‖ It doesn't hold *in* my case. 僕の場合とは違う. ‖ *In* no *case* have I noticed that. いつにもそれに気が付いたことはない. ‖ as it is likely *in* his *case* あの人のことだから. ‖ *in* nine *cases* out of ten 十中八九は. 【類】 *in* 99 *cases* out of 100. ¶This may be applicable *to* most *cases* of ours. これはわれわれの場合にも大体当てはまる.

P² It is a *case between* ourselves. これはないしょだが. ¶Here is a *case in* point. ここにその実例を一つ挙げる. 【類】 A *case in* point came under my observation (目撃した) only last week. / Such is also the *case in* Japan. 日本でも同様なのです. ¶This is a *case of* conscience. これは良心の問題だ. ‖ It is a *case of* fools rushing in where angels fear to tread. それは俗に言うめくらへびにおじずである. ‖ a *case of* a badman's prosperity 悪運が強い一例 ‖ a *case of* fact stranger than fiction うそのような本当の話 ‖ It is considered a *case of* no importance. それは重きを置くに足らぬ事件と考えられている. ‖ His is a *case of* old age deferred. あの人は年を取らない. ‖ a *case of* suffering from not letting well alone やぶへびの例 ‖ a *case of* a wish anticipated 願ったりかなったり ‖ a *case of* poor work 不手際の一例 ‖ a *case of* appearances being deceitful 見かけ倒しの一例 ‖ a *case of* new wine in old bottles 古いびんに入れた新しいぶどう酒の一例 ‖ a *case of* the unconscious lie 無意識的なうその例 ‖ a *case of* "what oft thought, but ne'er so well expressed" 「よく胸に浮ぶがかくも適切に言い表わされたことがなかった」と感じる一例. ¶It is also the *case with* my friend. 私の友人も同様だ. 【類】 Such is also the *case with* him. / the same is the *case with* ... / especially is this the *case with* ...

O such being the *case*, it seems to us that ... こういう訳なのでわれわれは...と思われる. ¶the reverse is the *case* in ... ...においてはちょうどその正反対である. ¶This is a *case* where "Familiarity breeds contempt." これはことわざに言う「慣れると軽く見るようになる」という一例だ. ‖ *cases* are on record where ... ...という例が記録にある. ¶it is often the *case*, I regret to say, that ... ...ということは遺憾ながら事実だ. ¶as was the *case* last year 昨年もそうであったが. 【類】as is too (不幸にして) frequently (=often) the *case*. ¶even if that were the *case* よしんばそれが事実だとしても. ¶I have found it the *case* that ... ...ということが事実だと知った.

(**2**) 〘法〙訴訟事件; 事件; 〘法〙申し立て.

V ***allow*** the *case* to be settled out of court その事件を法廷外できまりをつけるようにする. ¶***appeal*** a *case* 上訴する. ¶***bring***(=file) a *case* against ... ...を相手取って訴訟を起す. ‖ Such *cases* are seldom ***brought*** before court. こういう事件はめったに法廷に持ち出されない. ¶My *case* will be ***brought on*** to-morrow. 私の事件はあす裁判になるでしょう. ¶The judge ***decided*** the *case* for me. 裁判官は私に有利にその事件を裁決した. ¶The *case* was ***dismissed.*** その訴訟は却下された. ¶***explain*** the *case* その事件を説明する. ¶***file*** a *case* in a court 事件を裁判ざたにする. ¶He ***gained*** his *case*. 彼は訴訟に勝った. ¶***get*** the *case* ***withdrawn*** その訴訟を却下してもらう. ¶The judge ***has*** three *cases* to try today. その裁判官が調べる公判がきょうは三件ある. ¶***hear*** a *case* 訴訟事件を審理する. ¶***lose*** one's *case* 訴訟に負ける. 【類】I have ***lost*** that *case* after all. ¶The *case* was ***misrepresented.*** その事件は誤り伝えられた. ¶***overstate*** a *case* 事件を大げさに述べる. ¶***present*** one's *case* to the court 事件を法廷に持出す. ¶I ***put*** the *case* in the hands of the police. 私はこの事件を警察の手にまかした. ¶***refer*** the *case* to ... for an amicable settlement その件を...に委任して円満解決をはかる ‖ ***refer*** a *case* back to ... 訴訟事件を...に差戻す ‖ ***report*** one's *case* to the police その事件を警察に届ける. ¶He ***took*** the *case* into the courts and won it. 彼はその事件を数回法廷に持出して勝った. ¶a *case* ***tried*** in a country court いなかの法廷で裁判された事件. 【類】In what court will the *case* be ***tried***? ¶The advocate has ***undertaken*** my *case*. その弁護士が私の事件を引受けてくれた. ¶***win*** a *case* against ... for $3,000 ...との三千ドル損害賠償事件に勝つ.

V² The *case* is now ***dragging*** its way through the court. この事件は目下法廷でだらだらと審理中だ.

Q Nine ***additional*** *cases* were docketed. 追加九件が公判日程に載った. ¶an ***aggravated*** or ***flagrant*** *case* 一層重いまたは悪質の事件. ¶***alarming cases*** 意外な事件. ¶a ***civil*** *case* 民事訴訟事件. ¶***connected cases*** 関連事件. ¶the ***criminal*** *case* at hand 今取扱っている刑事事件. ¶a ***strong*** *case* can be made out of ... ...は十分主張のできる事件になりうる. ¶a ***ticklish*** *case* 扱いにくい事件. ¶an ***unsolved*** *case* of murder 未解決の殺人事件.

Q² Several ***court*** *cases* are being prepared. 目下数件の訴訟準備中. ¶a ***court-martial*** *case* 軍法会議事件. ¶an ***extradition*** *case* 犯罪人引渡し事件. ¶a ***fraud*** *case* 詐欺事件. ¶a ***murder*** *case* 殺人事件. 【類】a frightful ***murder*** *case* ‖ ***Murder*** and ***burglary*** *cases* are increasing. 殺人と夜盗罪が増加している. ¶an authentic ***police*** *case* 認証された警察事件. ¶a ***purge*** *case* 追放事件. ¶a ***rape*** *case* 強かん事件. ¶a ***traffic*** *case* 交通事故.

P put down ***as*** a *case* of suicide 自殺と判定する. ¶***in*** the *case* of Sibley Walter シブレー対ウォールターの訴訟事件で.

P² a *case* ***against*** ... ...を相手取った訴訟事件. ¶the *case* ***for*** the defendant 被告側の申立て. ¶a *case* ***of*** murder ⌊=a murder case.

(**3**) 病状, 容態; 患者.

V a *case* ***abandoned*** by physicians 数人の医者がさじを投げた病人. ¶***diagnose*** a *case* 病人を打診する. 【類】***diagnose*** one's *case* as malaria ... ¶***isolate*** *cases* 患者を隔離する. ¶He ***laid*** his *case* before the doctor. 彼は自分の病気について医者に相談した. ¶A very few *cases* of cholera are now ***reported.*** 目下のところコレラ患者の数は極めて少ない. ¶The patient ***stated*** his *case*. 患者は自分の病状を述べた. ¶***treat*** fever *cases* 熱病患者を診療する.

V² several *cases* of cholera ***occurred*** in ... コレラ患者が...に数名出た. 【類】Plague (疫病) does not appear to be very extensive, but *cases* are still ***occurring.***

Q ***acute*** and ***severe*** *cases* 急性の重患. ¶In ***advanced*** *cases* of beri-beri the patient is too weak to stand on his legs. 病勢が進んだのになると脚気患者は衰弱して立てなくなる. ¶His *case* is ***alarming.*** 彼は容易ならぬ容態だ. ¶***chronic*** and ***milder*** *cases* 慢性の軽い病気. ¶There were three ***fatal*** *cases*. 患者が三人死んだ. ¶a ***fresh*** *case* of influenza 流感の新患者. ¶a ***hopeless*** *case* 回復の見込のない病人; 見込みのないこと. 【類】His *case* is ***hopeless.*** ¶His is a ***mental*** *case*. 彼は精神病患者である. ¶***pronounced*** *cases* 症状の著しい患者. ¶a very ***serious*** *case* 重症患者. ¶***sporadic*** *cases* 特発性の病気. ¶***suspected*** *cases* of the plague 疑似ペスト患者. ¶***well-authenticated*** *cases* of cure 確実に直った病気の実例. ¶a ***well-marked*** *case* それにまぎれのない病気の一例.

Q² ***dysentery*** *cases* developed after the food was given to Navy personnel 海軍の人員に食糧を支給した後それが元で発生した赤痢患者. ¶***hospital*** *cases* of cholera 入院中のコレラ患者. 「れらの病人は皆全治した.

P ***In*** all these *cases* complete cures have been made. こ

P² a *case* ***of*** cholera (measles) コレラ(など)患者.

(**4**) 〘文法〙格.

Q the ***ablative*** *case* 奪格. ¶the ***accusative*** *case* 対格. ¶the ***dative*** *case* 与格. ¶the ***genitive*** *case* 属格. ¶the ***locative*** *case* 位置格. ¶the ***nominative*** *case* 主格. ¶the ***objective*** *case* 目的格. ¶the ***oblique*** *case* 斜格. ¶the ***possessive*** *case* 持格. ¶the ***vocative*** *case* 呼格.

case, *n.* 箱, 入れもの.

V ***pack*** a *case* with ... ケースに...を詰める. ¶***tilt*** the *case* to one side 箱を一方にかしげる. 「箱.

Q ***airtight*** *cases* of sterilized ... 殺菌した...を入れた密閉の

Q² a ***cartridge*** *case* 薬きょう. ¶a ***clippings*** *case* 新聞の切抜入れ. ¶a ***display*** *case* 陳列箱. ¶a ***filing*** *case* 書類整理たんす. ¶a ***handkerchief*** *case* ハンカチ入れ. ¶***leather*** *cases* lined with silk or satin 絹またはしゅす裏張の革箱 ‖ a velvet-lined ***leather*** *case* ビロード内張りの革箱. ¶a ***packing*** *case* 荷箱. ¶a ***pillow*** *case* まくらおおい. ¶a ***shell*** *case* 薬きょう(留散弾の). ¶a ***show*** *case* 陳列箱. ¶a ***window*** *case* 窓わく. 「bottles.

P pack wine bottles ***into*** a *case*=pack a case with wine

P² a *case* ***for*** books=a bookcase 本箱. 【類】a *case* ***for*** containing letters. ¶a *case* ***of*** wine (whisky) ぶどう酒(ウイスキー)一ダース入りの箱.

case, *v.* 箱に入れる.

M All the goods have been *cased* ***up.*** 品は皆箱詰にした.

P *case* ***with*** copper 銅をかぶせる.

cash, *n.* 現金, 正金.

V ***cost*** hard *cash* 現なまがかかる. ¶please send me for *cash* ***enclosed*** ... 代金を封入しましたから...を送って下さい. ¶The dealer confessed that he ***needed*** *cash* badly. その商人は手もとに現金がなくって大いに困っていると白状した. ¶He always ***pays*** *cash* for his purchases. 彼はいつも現金買をする. ¶***pay*** *cash* ***down*** 即金で支払う. ¶***receive*** *cash* 現金を受取る. ¶But little *cash* is being ***signed*** for whatever is purchased. [船内では]何を買うにも伝票や切符に署名するので現金はほとんど使わない. ¶***squander*** one's hard-earned *cash* on drink 骨折ってもうけた金を酒に浪費する.

Q in ***hard*** *cash* 現金で ‖ write more for ***hard*** *cash* than for the advancement of learning 学問の進歩のためよりもむしろ金もうけのために執筆する. ¶***net*** *cash* 正味(割引なしの)現金払い. ¶***petty*** *cash* 小口出納金. ¶***prompt*** *cash* 即金. ¶have no ***ready*** *cash* at hand 現金の持合せがない. ¶I have a certain amount of ***spare*** *cash*. 遊金を少し持合している.

Q² avoid creating new "***inflation*** *cash*" またもや「通貨膨張」になる事を回避する. ¶***net spot*** *cash* 無割引即金.

P Payment may be made either ***by*** *cash* or monthly instalments. 支払は現金でも月賦でも差支えありません. ¶We make it a rule to sell only ***for*** *cash*. 現金売を店の立前としております. 【類】purchase (=buy) it ***for*** *cash* / Do you allow any discount ***for*** *cash?* ‖ He is straitened (=hard up) ***for*** *cash*. 彼は現金に困っている. ¶pay ***in*** *cash* 現金で払う ‖ donate $1,000 ***in*** *cash* to ... ...へ現金一千ドルを寄付する ‖ Twenty thousand bucks ***in*** *cash* is a lot of money. 現金二万両は大金だ. ¶convert (=turn) it ***into*** *cash* それを現金に換える. ¶He is short ***of*** *cash*. 彼は手もとに現金が乏しい. ¶I am ***out of*** *cash* just now. 今現金が

手もとにない.

P² *cash **before** delivery* 引渡し前の現金払い ‖ *cash **in*** one month 一カ月後現金仕払い. ¶*cash **in*** hand 手もとの現金 ‖ *cash **on*** arrival 到着払い ‖ *cash **on*** delivery 引換払 ‖ *cash **on*** shipment 積込の際現金払い. ¶be payable, *cash **with*** order 支払方法は現金注文のこと.

cash, *v.* 正金にする, 正金と引換える.

M *cash **down*** 即金で支払う.

cask, *n.* おけ, たる.

V ***hoop*** a *cask* おけにたがをかける. ¶The *cask* was ***knocked in***. たるをぶち明けた. ¶A *cask* of wine was ***washed up*** by the sea. ぶどう酒のたるが海岸に打上げられた.

P² twenty *casks **of*** beer ビール二十たる.

casket, *n.* 宝石箱.

Q² an ***ebony*** *casket* 黒檀製の宝石箱.

cast, *n.* (**1**) 投げ; 型, 性質; 痕跡; べつ見, 目つき.

V ***give*** a *cast* with one's eye 一べつする. ¶She ***has*** a *cast* in her eye.=She is cross-eyed. 彼女はすがめだ. ¶The *cast* he ***threw*** fell on a goose. すごろくで投げたサイががちょうの上に乗った.

Q a man of a ***liberal*** *cast* of mind 自由主義の人. ¶He is somewhat of a ***serious*** *cast*. 彼はいくらかまじめな方の人だ. ¶within a ***stone's*** *cast* (=throw) of ... ...から投石距離に.

Q² a ***plaster*** *cast* of ... ...の石こう模型 ‖ first in a ***plaster*** *cast* and then in splints 始め石こうの型で包み, その後は添え木をあてて.

P ***with*** one *cast* of an eye 一べつして.

P² a *cast **of*** dejection 気落したようす ‖ a *cast **of*** feature 顔形 ‖ a *cast* (=frame) ***of*** mind 心だて ‖ a *cast **of*** Venus ヴィナスの塑像.

(**2**) 〔映画〕役割; [全体の]配役.

V ***head*** the *cast* 主役を演じる.

Q in the ***original*** *cast* of the play were ... 初興行の時の役割は...であった.

Q² an ***all-star*** *cast* 権威者ぞろい; 〔映〕スター総出演.

P juvenile stars ***in*** the *cast* 役割中の少年俳優たち. ¶the head ***of*** *cast* of a film 映画劇の主演者.

P² the *cast **of*** characters 役割.

cast, *v.* 投げる; 鋳造する; 工夫する; 〔映〕配役する.

M He was *cast **ashore*** (=***on shore***) with two companions. 彼は二人の仲間と一緒に海岸に打上げられた. ¶*cast* it ***aside*** それを放棄する. 【類】*cast ... **aside*** as useless. ¶*cast **away*** 捨てる; 難破する ‖ The ship was *cast **away*** (=wrecked) on the coast of Africa. その船はアフリカの海岸で難破した. ¶*cast **back*** さかのぼる; 回想する. ¶*cast **back*** for hundreds of years 数百年の昔にさかのぼる. ¶*cast **behind*** all the others [レースで]他を引き離す. ¶be *cast **out*** 追い出される ‖ In computing interest it is usual to *cast* cents of principal ***out*** when less than fifty. 利息計算では普元金五十セント通以下の端数は切り捨てる. ¶The picture is ***well cast***. その映画は配役がよい.

M² He *cast **about*** for a method to ... and hit upon a plan. 彼は...の方法を求めて一案を得た. 【類】*cast **about*** for ways and means (資金) to establish a university / *cast **about*** for some settled employment (一定の職) ‖ *cast **about*** in one's mind for a plan 立案に頭を悩ます ‖ Do not be so *cast **down***. そうがっかりするな. 【類】He was *cast **down*** by misfortune. / be exceedingly *cast **down*** ‖ with her eyes modestly *cast **down*** つつましやかに伏目になって ‖ The national pride was grievously *cast **down*** by the humiliating defeats. 国民の自尊心は屈辱的敗北によって哀れにも地に落ちた. ¶*cast* [***in***] a bone between ... ...の間に不和をかもす ‖ *cast **in*** one's lot with ... ...と運命を共にする. ¶*cast **off*** fear (prejudice) / *cast **off*** as waste 廃物として捨てる. 【類】*cast **off*** one's timidity (しり込み) / *cast **off*** (=give up) one's idea of going abroad / children *cast **off*** (=abandoned) by their parents / He was *cast **off*** (勘当された) by his family. / be *cast **off*** by God / Children were *cast **off*** like old rags. ‖ *cast **off*** clothes 衣服を脱ぎすてる. ‖ The antlers are *cast **off*** yearly. しかの角は年々脱落する. ‖ *cast **off*** the Assyrian yoke アッシリヤのきづなを脱する ‖ *cast **off*** a boat from its moorings 船のともづなを解く. 【類】*cast* oneself ***off*** from traditions. ¶*cast **over*** burden on ... ...に負担を負わせる ‖ I have been *casting **over*** in my head what you said. 君の言った事を思いめぐらしていた. ¶Since then they have been *cast **together*** several times. その後二人は数回(映画などで)共演をやった. ¶*cast **up*** an account 勘定を締める.

P² She *cast* her arms ***about*** me. 彼女は私に抱きついた. ¶M-G-M *cast* her ***as*** Marthy. エム・ジー・エム社は彼女をマーセーに配役した. ¶*cast* a glance ***at*** ... ...をちらと見る ‖ He *cast* sheep's eyes ***at*** her. 彼は彼女に秋波を送った. ¶They have been *cast **for*** disabilities. 彼らは無能のため追出された. ‖ an actor *cast **for*** the part (=rôle) あの役を振当てられた俳優. ¶a statue *cast **from*** the cannon taken in the victories of Waterloo ウォータールーの戦勝で分捕った大砲で鋳造した銅像 ¶It is *cast **in*** bronze (gold, silver). 青銅(など)の鋳物だ. ‖ be *cast **in*** the same mold 同じ鋳型で鋳る; 同じタイプである ‖ He was *cast **in*** a different mold from his father. 彼は父親と異った型の男であった. ‖ He is *cast **in*** too fine a mold for worldly success. 彼はあまり上品な男だから俗世間的成功は収められない. ¶*cast* metal ***into*** coins (a bell) 金属を貨幣(など)に鋳造する ‖ *cast* it ***into*** a systematic shape それを組織立った形に整理する ‖ His brilliant success *cast* the others ***into*** the shade. 彼の大成功は他をして顔色なからしめた. ‖ *cast* a person ***into*** prison 投獄する ‖ *cast* him ***into*** the sea 彼を船員にする. ¶with her look *cast **on*** the ground うつむいて ‖ *cast* light ***on*** the subject その問題に光明を投げる. 【類】The moon *cast* a shadow ***on*** the wall. ‖ It will *cast* a reflection ***on*** him. それは彼の不名誉になるだろう. 【類】*cast* a spell (のろい) ***on*** a person / *cast* a slur (汚点) ***on*** one's reputation. ¶The sad news *cast* a gloom ***over*** the mansion. その悲報が同邸に暗影を投じた. ¶*cast* it ***to*** the ground ***from*** a tower 塔からそれを地に投下する ‖ be all *cast **to*** a standard 千篇一律になる. ¶The boat was *cast **upon*** an island. 小舟は島に打上げられた. ‖ *cast* one's eyes (=a glance) ***upon*** ... ...を一べつする.

caste, *n.* 階級, 身分.

V Since the last scandal, he has ***lost*** *caste* with educationists. この前のスキャンダルがあってから彼は教育家の間に信用を落してしまった. 【類】Really Shanghai has ***lost*** *caste* as an emporium of intelligence (報道の中心). / He ***lost*** *caste* by wearing a (同一の) collar for a week.

Q² a ***warrior*** *caste* 武士階級.

P Once born ***in*** his father's *caste*, he can never get out of it. 一旦この世に生れたら最後, その父親の階級から脱け出すことはできない.

caster, *n.* 小車, 足車.

P furniture mounted ***on*** *casters* 移動式小車付家具.

casting, *n.* 鋳込み.

Q² ***steel*** *castings* 鋼鉄鋳込み.

castle, *n.* 城, 楼閣.

V ***build*** *castles* in the air 空中ろう閣を築く, 皮算用をする. ¶***invest*** a *castle* 城を囲む. ¶The *castle* was ***taken*** by storm. 城が奇襲で占領された.

V² The *castle* ***stands out*** against the sky. 城は空にそびえている.

Q A ***ruined*** *castle* stands on a hill. 古城の残がいが丘の上にある. ¶a ***floating*** *castle* 浮城. ¶an ***imposing temple-like*** *castle* 堂々たる寺院風城郭.

P² a *castle **in*** Spain (=the air) 空中楼閣.

casualty, *n.* 死傷者; 不慮の災難.

V No *casualties* are ***reported***. 死傷者なし.

V² Many *casualties* ***occurred*** during the hurricane. 具風で多数の死傷者を出した.

Q ***heavy*** *casualties* 多数の死傷. 【類】*Casualties* were exceedingly ***heavy***. ¶***serious*** *casualties* 多数の死傷者. ¶The French *casualties* were ***slight***. フランス側の死傷者は少数であった.

Q² ***automobile*** *casualties* 自動車事故による死傷. ¶suffered over 47,000 ***battle*** *casualties* 戦争による死傷は47,000人を越えた. ¶***United Nations*** *casualties* in the hospitals throughout Japan 日本全国の病院に入院中の連合国負傷兵. ¶He is a ***war*** *casualty*. あの人は傷痍(い)軍人だ.

P a list ***of*** *casualties*=a casualty list 死傷者表.

P² There were a great many *casualties* ***in*** the battle. その戦には死傷者が非常に多かった. 【類】Our *casualties* ***in*** this engagement were 277 all ranks (士卒を通じて). ¶*casualties* ***to*** petroleum vessels 石油船の遭難.

cat, *n.* ねこ.

V ***caress*** a *cat* ねこをかわいがる. ¶***fondle*** a *cat* ねこをなでてかわいがる. ¶***keep*** a *cat* ねこを飼う. ¶***let*** the *cat* out of the bag 秘密を漏らす. ¶There is no room to ***swing*** a *cat*. せまくて窮屈だ.

V² A *cat **mews*** (=***miaows***). ねこがにゃあにゃあ鳴く. ¶A

cat pounces on a mouse. ねこがねずみに飛びつく. ¶*Cats purr.* ねこがのどを鳴らす.

Q her *favorite cat* 彼女の愛猫(びょう). ¶a *stray cat* 迷いねこ. ¶a *wild cat* 野良ねこ.

Q^2 a *family cat* 飼いねこ. ¶a *pussy* [*cat*] ねこの愛称.

cataclysm, *n.* 大変動.

Q a *financial cataclysm* 財界の大変動. ¶In September, 1923, Tokyo was smitten by one of the *greatest cataclysms* in its history. 一九二三年九月東京は有史以来の一大災禍の打撃を受けた.

catalogue, *n.* 目録, 型録.

V *compile* a *catalogue* of ... ...の目録を編さんする. ¶to *crown* the whole pleasant *catalogue* 愉快なことが重なった上へ持ってきて; [反語的に] 泣きつらにはちで. ¶*issue* a priced *catalogue* 価格明示の商品カタログを発行する. ¶This will *make up* (=*produce*) a formidable *catalogue*. そうすると恐ろしく長い表ができ上るだろう.

Q These are only a *brief catalogue* of his duties. 以上は彼の関係している仕事を略記したに過ぎない. ¶a *duplicate catalogue* 控えの目録. ¶The biography is little short of an *elaborate catalogue* of his virtues. その伝記は彼の美点を詳細に列記したものと見て大して誤りはない. ¶An account of his public gifts would produce an *endless catalogue*. 彼の公共事業の寄付を一々列記したら果てしがないだろう. ¶He made a *formidable catalogue* of good resolutions at New Year. 彼は新年にどえらい数の決心を書き記した. ¶an *illustrated catalogue* 絵入目録. ¶a man who married a *long catalogue* of women 妻を何度も取りかえた男.

Q^2 a *card catalogue* カード式目録. ¶a *card-index catalogue* カード索引目録. ¶issue *price catalogues* 値段表を発行する. ¶a *sale catalogue* 販売用型録. ¶a *school catalogue* 学校一覧. ¶gayly covered *seed catalogues* はでな表紙の種子カタログ. ¶a *star catalogue* 星座表.

P He was accosted by his unfriendly critics of every crime *in* the *catalogue*. 彼は反対側の批評家からありとあらゆる悪名を浴びせられた. ‖ place (=put) it *in* (=*on*) a *catalogue* それを目録に載せる. ¶a copy *of* our new *catalogue* 弊店の新カタログ一部.

P^2 a *catalogue of* names (=a directory) 名簿.

catalogue, *v.* 目録に載せる.

P *catalogue* it *with* ... ...それを...の部類に入れる.

cataract, *n.* 瀑布, 大滝; 大雨.

V a carp *climbing* a *cataract* こいの滝上り.

P The rain came down *in cataracts*. 雨が滝をなして降った.

P^2 *cataracts of* rain 豪雨.

catastrophe, *n.* 大災害, 災変; 大団円.

Q an *awful* (=a *terrible*) *catastrophe* 恐ろしい災禍. ¶a *heart-rending catastrophe* 大惨事. ¶a *tremendous catastrophe* 非常な大災厄.

Q^2 a *war catastrophe* 戦禍.

P^2 the *catastrophe of* a play 劇の大団円 ‖ the *catastrophe of* a siege 包囲攻撃の惨禍. ¶a *catastrophe to* a person ある人に起った災難.

catcall, *n.* ねこの鳴き声; やじり.

V It would be *courting* the critical *catcall*. いたずらにやじ評を招くだけのことだ. ¶*sound catcall* 口笛など吹いてやじる(半畳を入れる).

catch, *n.* 捕捉; 〘野球〙捕球(キャッチボール); 獲物; 故障; 陥穽(かんせい).

V He *got* a great *catch* of her. 彼は飛んでもない女を妻にもらったものだ. ¶fail to *hold* a *catch* at cricket クリケットで捕球しそこなう. ¶*keep* their *catch* on ice 彼らが捕った魚を氷で保たせる. ¶The angler *made* a good *catch*. 釣師は獲物が多かった. ¶*play catch* キャッチボールをやる. 【類】*play catch* with their passports (パスポートをボール代りにして). ¶the *catch* of trout *taken* from the lake 湖水から捕れたます.

Q a *good catch* 豊漁. ¶a *nice catch* of the lake その湖での大漁. ¶a poor *catch* 不漁. ¶the *total catch* of mackerel in this season 当季節におけるさばの総漁獲高.

Q^2 a *miracle catch* 難球捕球.

P stand for a moment *with* a *catch* in the throat これはこれはとしばしあっけに取られる.

P^2 a *catch in* the voice 音声の故障 ‖ There is some *catch in* your question. 君の質問にはかまが掛けてある. ¶a *catch of* fish 魚の獲物.

catch, *v.* 捕える, つかまえる; 追いつく; (病気など)にかかる; 引掛ける.

M Salmon are *abundantly caught* in the river during the season. さけはその季節中その川で沢山とれる. ¶The fox was *caught alive*. きつねは生捕られた. ¶*catch* cold *easily* じきに風邪を引く. ¶He was *fairly caught*. 彼はうまくひっつかまった(例えば生徒がいたずらなどした場合). 【類】He was *fairly caught* in the act of shoplifting (万引の現場). ¶I could *hardly catch* the train. すんでのことで汽車に乗り遅れるところだった. ¶be *nearly caught* in a shower すんでの事で夕立に遭うところ. ¶*catch out* 〘野球〙捕殺する. ¶Does the bolt *catch properly*? 錠前は具合よく掛かるか. ¶I didn't *quite catch* what he said. 彼の言った事がよく分らなかった. ¶*catch* him *red-handed* 彼を現行犯で捕える. ¶be *caught short* ろうばいする. ¶The lock will not act; it *catches somewhere*. 錠がきかない, どこかに引掛る.

M^2 The play *caught on* well. 《俗》その芝居は評判がよかった(大当りだった). ‖ The craze has *caught on* dreadfully here. 《米俗》当地(ち)ではそれが流行して大したものだ. ‖ "Physical deterioration" is a term that has "*caught on*."「肉体的退化」ははやり言葉になった. ¶*catch up* one's hat and start for the door 帽子をおっ取って戸口に向う ‖ *catch up* ... in its mouth (犬などが)口で受止める ‖ You go on, I will *catch* you *up*. どんどん行き給え, 後から追付くから. ¶The phrase was *caught up* and immediately became popular. その句はそれからそれへと伝わりたちまち一般の流行となった. ‖ My kite's *caught up* on Mrs. M's roof. 私のたこが M 夫人の家の屋根に引掛った. ‖ *catch up* on sleep 眠りにはいる ‖ At birth boys are on the average 1cm. longer than girls; but during puberty the female sex *catches up* to the male in height, or even surpasses it. 生れた時男子は平均一センチメートル女子よりたけが高いが思春期には女の方が男に追付き追越すことさえある. 【類】Prices will fall as soon as production *catches up* to demand. ‖ I ran to *catch up* with him. 彼に追付こうとしてかけた. 【類】*catch up* with the swimmer leading in a race / *catch up* with the rest of the world / *catch up* with production lost in strikes / until production *catches up* with demand / General supply of goods has not yet *caught up* with general demand. / *catch up* with the exceptionally heavy demand generated by years of war production ‖ Rebuilding has a long way to go to *catch up* with the homeless. 家のない人々がなくなるまで住宅再建が進捗するのはまだまだ先のことだ. ‖ The "pros" have been *catching up* with the "cons."「賛成」側が「反対」側とせり合っている. 【類】We must endeavour to *catch up* with Europe and America in this matter.

P A drowning man *catches at* a straw. おぼれる者はわらをもつかむ. ‖ *catch at* the ball その球を捕えようとする ‖ *catch at* an opportunity 機会を捕えようとする. ¶He was *caught between* two fires. 彼は抜差しができなくなった. ¶She rose quickly, and *caught* him *by* the arm. 彼女は急に立って彼の腕を捕えた. ‖ *catch* a person *by* the collar (button, sleeve). 人のえり(など)をつかまえる ‖ *catch* a sword *by* the handle 刀のつかをひっつかまえる ‖ The thief was *caught* and secured *by* the police. 泥棒が警察につかまった. 【類】The fish was *caught by* a hook. ‖ Her flowing robe was *caught by* the breeze. 彼女のゆるやかにたれている着物が風にひらひら. ‖ She was *caught by* the camera at Ueno Park. 彼女は上野公園でカメラに収められた(写真をとられた). ‖ *Caught by* reverie, she sat before the fire in her dressing-gown, her change of garb unfinished. 夢想にふけって彼女は着かえも終えず化粧着のまま煖炉の前にすわった. ¶You'll *catch* it *for* this. お目玉を食うぞ. ¶a fire which *caught from* another fire もらい火 ‖ The nurse *caught* the disease *from* a patient. 看護婦に患者の病気がうつった. ‖ It has been *caught from* life. それは写生だ. ¶be *caught in* a hurricane 具風に見舞われる ‖ be *caught in* mischief 悪いたずらをしているのを見付けられる. ¶*catch* it *in* one's cap それを帽子で受ける. ‖ He *caught* her hand *in* his. 彼は自分の手に彼女の手をにぎった. ‖ She *caught* her foot *in* her robe. 彼女の足が着物に引っ掛った. 【類】be *caught in* the middle 中にはさまる / get *caught in* a trap / be *caught in* a wave / The horns of the deer (鹿の角) *caught in* the branches of a tree. / His feet were *caught in* the ropes. ‖ A bone got *caught* (=stuck) *in* my throat. 骨がのどに引っ掛った. ‖ The kite *caught* ***in*** a tree. たこが樹に引っ掛った. ‖ I *caught* him ***in*** a lie. うそをつくのをつき留めてやった. ‖ I *caught* him ***in*** his own words. 揚足を取ってやった. ‖ I was *caught* ***in*** the rain (=a rain; heavy rain, the storm) yesterday. きのう雨(など)に会った. ‖ *catch* it ***in*** a net 網でそれを捕える. 【類】The corpse was *caught* ***in*** a fisherman's net. / He was *caught* ***in*** some machinery. / The pickpocket was *caught* ***in*** the act. ¶*catch* a person ***off*** his guard 不意打を食わせる. ¶The bull, *catching* the wolf ***on*** his horn, disembowelled it. 雄牛はおおかみを角にひっ掛けてはらわたをぬき出した. ¶He was *caught* ***under*** (=run over by) a motor truck. 彼は貨物自動車にひかれた. ¶*catch* a ball ***with*** the left hand 左手で球をつかむ ‖ He is a shrewd man; he is not to be *caught* ***with*** chaff. 彼は利巧な男だ, 無造作にだまされなんかしない.

catcher, *n.* 捕える者.

Q² a ***bird*** *catcher* 鳥追い. ¶a ***rat*** *catcher* ねずみ取り[屋]. ¶a ***screen eye*** *catcher* 映画界の妖星. ¶***train*** and ***tram*** and ***bus*** *catchers* to the suburbs 大急ぎで列車, 都電, バスに乗って郊外へ帰って行く人々.

catching, *n.* 捕えること.

Q There was a ***general*** *catching* of the breath. 皆のものが息を殺して見守っていた.

catchpenny, *n.* かねもうけ主義の商品.

Q a ***mere*** *catchpenny* [ほんの銭取り主義の]ごまかし物.

catch-phrase, *n.* 人気取の文句.

P a popular *catch-phrase* ***on*** political platforms 政治演説に用いる人気取の警句.

catchword, *n.* 標語.

P² "War to end war" was the *catchword* ***of*** the nation. 「戦争をなくするための戦争」というのが同国民の標語だった.

category, *n.* 部類, 種類, 種目.

V These ***form*** a *category* apart. これらは別に一種目を形成する.

Q belong in (=to) a ***different*** *category* その趣を異にする. 【類】They should be placed in a ***different*** *category*. ¶form an ***independent*** *category* 独立の種目をなす. ¶His ***medical*** *category* was C. 彼の体格検査は丙であった. ¶a carpenter in the ***top*** *category* who fulfils his norm ノルマ(標準の仕事)を遂行する第一級の大工.

Q² one of the most rapidly rising items in the ***food*** *category* 食糧部門で最も急激に騰貴している品の一つ. ¶those who may come under the "***G***" *category* of the purge order 追放命令の「G」項 該当者たち.

P place it ***in*** the same *category* as ... それを…と同一部類に入れる. 【類】it is unfair to place it in the same category with ... ¶come ***into*** the *category* of ...の部に入る. ¶fall (=come) ***under*** this *category* この部類に入る. 【類】They can be brought ***under*** three chief *categories*. / arrange them ***under*** *categories*. ¶come ***within*** the *category* この部に入る.

cater, *v.* 賄う, 満足を与える.

P *cater* ***for*** varying tastes 多方面の趣味に訴える ‖ *cater* ***for*** the tourist traffic 旅行者のためあっせんする ‖ *cater* ***for*** their interests 彼らの利益を計る ‖ categories of staff members *catered* ***for*** in service training 研修せしめる係員の種類. ¶*cater* ***to*** their needs 彼らの必要に応じる ‖ These hotels vie with each other in *catering* ***to*** the comfort of their patrons. これらのホテルは互に競争してお客の気に入るようにする. 【類】hotels *catering* (相手にする) especially ***to*** Europeans / *cater* ***to*** customers (people, the public, people's amusement) / These hotels *cater* ***to*** (を得意にする) high-class tourists.

cathedral, *n.* 大寺院.

V ***consecrate*** a *cathedral* 寺院を奉献する. ¶***enlarge*** a *cathedral* 寺院を取り拡げる. ¶***remodel*** a *cathedral* 寺院を造り替える. ¶***restore*** a much-dilapidated *cathedral* 非常に荒廃した寺院を修理する.

catholic, *n.* 天主教徒.

Q a ***devout Roman Catholic*** 熱心な天主教徒.

catholicity, *n.* 普遍性.

Q a ***wide*** *catholicity* of taste はばの広い趣味.

cat's-paw, catspaw, *n.* 人の手先.

P² make oneself a *catspaw* ***of*** ... ...の手先に使われる.

cattle, *n.* 牛[団]; 家畜.

V ***pasture*** *cattle* 牛に草を食わせる. ¶***rear*** *cattle* 家畜を飼う. ¶***round up*** the scattered *cattle* 散らばった牛を集める.

V² *Cattle* ***feed*** on grass. 牛が草を食う. ¶The *cattle* are ***grazing***. 牛が草を食っている. ¶*Cattle* ***low***. 牛が鳴く.

Q ***domestic*** *cattle* 家畜. ¶***horned*** *cattle* 角のある家畜. ¶***short-horned*** *cattle* 短い角のある家畜. ¶***These*** *cattle* are mine. この牛は私のだ.

Q² ***beef*** (=***feeder***) *cattle* 肉牛. ¶***dairy*** *cattle* 乳牛.

P an inflammatory disease ***in*** *cattle* 家畜のかかる炎症 ‖ He trades (=deals) ***in*** *cattle*. 家畜を売買する. 【類】He carries on a trade ***in*** *cattle*. ¶a herd ***of*** *cattle* 一群の牛.

P² "*Cattle* ***with*** Landscape" [画題]風景と家畜.

caucus, *n.* 部会, 幹部会.

Q a ***primary*** *caucus* 予選会.

Q² call a ***party*** *caucus* 政党幹部会を召集する.

caught, *v.* catch を見よ.

cause, *n.* (**1**) 原因, 理由.

V ***adduce*** the *causes* of ... ...の理由を挙げる. ¶***analyze*** the *causes* of failure 失敗の原因を解剖する. ¶***ascertain*** the real *cause* 真の原因を確かめる. ¶***attribute*** the *cause*, in part, to ... その原因を一部...に帰する. ¶***clear up*** the *cause* 原因を明らかにする. ¶***confuse*** cause and effect 原因と結果を混同する. ¶***correct*** the *cause* 原因を矯正する. ¶***determine*** the *cause* of ... ...の原因を決定する. ¶The *causes* of these were ***divided*** as follows: これらの原因は次のごとく分類された. ¶The *cause* of the explosion has not been ***explained***. この爆発の原因はまだ説明されていない. ¶***fathom*** the *cause* of ... ...の原因を探る. ¶Perhaps our remote posterity might ***find*** *cause* to crown with flowers the statues of the spelling reformers of to-day. 恐らく遠い後世の人々は今日のつづり字改良家たちの功績を認めてその像に花を捧げることであろう. 【類】***find*** *cause* to lament over ... ¶***form*** the determining *cause* 決定的原因となる. ¶see deeply enough to ***get*** the *cause* behind the effect 結果の裏面にある原因をどう察する. ¶It ceased to ***give*** *cause* for further anxiety. そのことはもう心配がなくなった. ¶You ***have*** no *cause* for worry. 君は心配するには当らない. 【類】***have*** no *cause* for complaining / Everything that happens ***has*** a *cause* and an effect. ¶***investigate*** *causes* 原因を調査する. ¶***ponder*** the *causes* of ... ...の原因をよく考える. ¶It ***presented*** no special *cause* of anxiety. それは特に心配すべきことではなかった. ¶***remove*** its *causes* その原因をのぞく. ¶***set forth*** *causes* of grievance of ... against ... ...に対する...の苦情の原因を開陳する. ¶***show*** *cause* why ... ...の原因を示す. ¶***trace*** its *causes* その原因にさかのぼる.

V² when any *cause* for complaint ***arises***, apply to ... 一切苦情は...にお申出で下さい. ¶Many other *causes* ***conspired*** toward the same result. 他に幾多の原因が重なってその結果を生じた. ¶*causes* ***contributing*** to the making of ... ...の構成に関係ある原因. ¶the *causes* ***leading*** to a result ある結果をもたらす原因. ¶the *cause* ***underlying*** ... ...の根底に横たわる原因. ¶several other *causes* ***united*** to ... 他に数個の原因が重なって...に至った.

Q an ***adequate*** *cause* for war 開戦してもよいだけの理由. ¶***adventitious*** *causes* 外来的原因. ¶an ***aggravating*** *cause* 益々悪化させる原因. ¶without ***appreciable*** *cause* これという原因もなく. ¶without any ***assignable*** *cause* 何らこれという理由なしに. ¶the ***basic*** *cause* of the present war 今度の戦争の根本原因. ¶***collective*** *causes* 総合的原因. ¶a ***contributory*** *cause* of ... ...を助成する原因. 【類】chief contributing *causes* / a strong ***contributory*** *cause* / act as ***contributory*** *causes* (導因). ¶There are unquestionably ***deeper*** *causes* too. たしかにもっと深い原因もある. ¶one of the most ***deep-rooted*** *causes* of international discord 国際紛争の最も根深い原因の一つ. ¶a ***determining*** *cause* 決定的原因. ¶without any ***discoverable external*** *cause* 何ら具体的な外因もなしに. ¶a ***double*** *cause* 二重の理由. ¶one of the ***effective*** *causes* 有力な原因の一つ. ¶***etiological*** *cause* 病原. ¶one of the ***exciting*** *causes* of the war 戦争誘因の一つ. ¶from a ***financial*** *cause* 財政上の理由で. ¶a ***frequent*** *cause* of perprlexity to novices 初心者がしばしば困ること. ¶without ***good*** *cause* 正当の理由なくして. 【類】there is ***good*** *cause* to believe that ... ¶It was one of the ***immediate*** *causes* of the war. それはこの戦争の直接原因の一つであった. 【類】There is no ***immediate*** *cause* for anxiety. ¶without ***just*** *cause* 正当の理由なく. 【類】We shall give no people a ***just cause*** to make war upon us. / He has ***just cause*** for complaint (苦情). ¶a ***leading cause*** 主なる原因. ¶for ***little*** or ***no cause*** ほとんどあるいは全く原因なしで. ¶the ***main cause*** of the dissatisfaction 不満の主なる原因. 【類】the ***main cause*** of the decline (衰微) of one's fortune. ¶some ***mysterious cause*** is at work 何か分らぬものがその原因となっている. ¶happen from ***natural causes*** 自然に起る. ¶a ***potent cause*** 有力な理由. ¶whatever may be the ***precise cause*** 本当の理由が何であろうと. ¶***predisposing causes*** towards the disease その病気にかかりやすい原因. ¶a ***pregnant cause*** for ... ...という結果をはらむ原因. ¶***preventable causes*** 予防しうる原因. ¶the ***principal cause*** of it is to be sought in ... それは主として...による. ¶***primary causes*** 根本原因. ¶a ***probable cause*** 相当の理由. ¶a ***provoking cause*** of a disease ある病気を誘発させる原因. ¶a ***proximate*** (=immediate) ***causes*** 近因. ¶attribute it to ***psychic causes*** それを心理的原因に帰する. ¶gladness without ***real cause*** ぬか喜び. ¶go to war without ***reasonable causes***. 正当の理由なしに戦争する. ¶***remote causes*** of a war 戦争の諸遠因. ¶***secondary causes*** 二次的原因. ¶the ***self-same cause*** それと全く同じ原因. ¶Diphtheria was one of the most ***serious causes*** of death among children. ジフテリヤは小児死亡の最も重大な原因の一つであった. ¶present no ***special cause*** of anxiety 特に心配する必要はない. ¶***supplementary causes*** 二次的原因. ¶a ***triple cause*** of rejoicing 喜ぶべき三つの理由. 【類】Its ***ultimate cause*** has not been determined. ¶***unavoidable causes*** 避け難い原因. ¶the ***underlying cause*** 根本の原因. ¶from ***unknown cause*** 何かの理由で. ¶The collision had a very ***unusual cause***. その衝突はきわめてまれなことが原因だった. ¶Carelessness is the ***usual cause*** of fires. 通例油断が火事のもとだ. ¶It is due to ***various preventable causes***. それは種々の予防しうべき原因にもとづいている.

Q^2 the ***root causes*** of labor unrest 労働不穏の根本諸原因 ‖ one of the ***root causes*** of the nation's plight 国民の窮状を来した根本原因の一つ ‖ its ***root cause*** goes back to ... その根本理由は...にさか上る.

P The illness was not brought about ***by*** natural *causes*. 病気は自然に起ったものではなかった. ¶***for*** one *cause* or another 何かの原因で ‖ ***For*** what *cause* do you object to the agreement? 何故にその協定に反対するのか. ¶***from*** this *cause* この理由で. 【類】***from*** various *causes* ‖ deduce ***from*** *causes* to effect 原因から結果を推す. ¶***with*** other *causes* 他の原因もあって. ¶***without*** *cause* 故なく. ‖ No effect ***without*** *cause*. 原因のない結果はない. 【類】***without*** any just *cause* / ***without*** any known *cause*.

P^2 There is no *cause* ***for*** alarm. 驚き騒ぐにはあたらない. 【類】There can be no *cause* ***for*** complaint. / Is there any *cause* ***for*** this delay? / There is great *cause* ***for*** the suspicion. ‖ You have given *cause* ***for*** anger to him. 君は彼を怒らせるだけの事をやった. ‖ No *cause* ***for*** a suicide could be imagined. 自殺した訳が分らない. ‖ We have much *cause* ***for*** thankfulness. われわれには大いに感謝すべき理由がある. 【類】a *cause* (種) ***for*** anxiety (fear, regret). ¶I am sorry that I have been the *cause* ***of*** so much trouble to you. 大変ご迷惑をかけまして済みません. 【類】the *cause* ***of*** this delay (your illness) / a *cause* ***of*** anger (complaint, quarrel) / the *cause* ***of*** a disaster (an accident) / be the *cause* ***of*** much fighting (盛んな論争).

(2) 味方; 正義, 主義, 大義; 運動.

V ***advance*** the *cause* of education (peace, Christianity) 教育(など)の促進運動をする. 【類】***advance*** the *cause* in which we are so deeply interested (関心を持っている) / ***advance*** the suffrage *cause*. ¶***advocate*** a *cause* 主義を唱道する. ¶always anxious to ***aid*** a good *cause* 常に正義に組することを心がける ‖ ***aid*** the royal *cause* 勤王の道に志す. ¶***back*** a *cause* ある主義を後援する. ¶***champion*** the *cause* of the poor country folk あわれむべき農村民のためにひとはだ脱ぐ. 【類】***champion*** the *cause* of the liberation of women (婦人開放運動) / strenuously ***championed*** the *cause* of free speech (言論の自由) / ***champion*** the *cause* of truth. ¶***defend*** his *cause* against the vigorous onslaught of a critic ある批評家の猛烈な攻撃に反抗して自己の主張を弁護する. ¶***desert*** a *cause* 主張を放棄する. ¶those who ***embrace*** the *cause* of ... ...に味方する人々. ¶I admire the zeal with which you ***espouse*** your father's *cause*. あなたが熱心に父君の肩を持つのは感心です. 【類】vigorously (鋭意) ***espouse*** the *cause* of ... / ***espouse*** the *cause* of the unfortunate (不幸な人々). ¶***forward*** the *cause* of scientific management 科学的管理法の宣伝をする. 【類】***forward*** the *cause* of better English teaching. ¶***further*** the *cause* of ... ...の主張を助長する. ¶***have*** this *cause* at heart ひそかにこの主義をいだく ‖ ***have*** the *cause* of British Imperial expansion at heart 心に大英帝国膨張主義を懐いている. ¶***help*** (***hinder***) a worthy *cause* りっぱな主義を助け(妨げ)る. 【類】***help*** the *cause* of Christ (キリスト教の宣伝) in Japan. ¶***make*** common *cause* with ... ...と共同一致する. ¶It is the business of a lawyer to ***plead*** the *cause* of his client. 依頼人のために弁護するのは弁護士の本務である. 【類】He ***pleaded*** my *cause* so admirably (eloquently). ¶***prejudice*** the *cause* of ... ...の主張を傷つける. ¶***promote*** the *cause* of general peace (temperance, justice) 一般平和(など)の主義を唱道する. 【類】has done more than any man living to ***promote*** the *cause* / ***promote*** the *cause* of cremation (火葬) / ***promote*** the *cause* of industrial chemistry (化学工業) in this country. ¶***put*** the *cause* of ... before the public ...の主張を提げて公衆に臨む. ¶***safeguard*** and ***advance*** the *cause* of ... ...の主義を擁護しかつ唱道する. ¶***serve*** the *cause* of humanity (truth, freedom, Christ, peace and human brotherhood) 人道(など)のために尽す. 【類】***serve*** the *cause* of knowledge and truth by promoting liberal education (高等教育). ¶***support*** the *cause* of religion 教義を支持する ‖ ***support*** the *cause* of ... against ... ...反抗して...の肩を持つ. ¶***take up*** the *cause* of the modern European movement in drama 近代ヨーロッパの演劇運動を擁護する ‖ ***take up*** the *cause* of the poor 貧者の肩をもつ. 【類】***uphold*** the *cause* of the country. ¶***vindicate*** the *cause* of the oppressed しいたげられた者を擁護する. ¶***win*** the *cause* of internationalism for Japan 日本における国際主義の勝利を実現する.

Q with a zeal worthy of a ***better cause*** もっとよいことのために捧げてもよいほどの熱心さで. ¶a ***better*** and ***holier cause*** さらによくさらに神聖な事業. ¶engage in a ***common cause*** 共同の主義のために尽す. 【類】help the ***common cause*** of humanity / work in a ***common cause*** ‖ make ***common cause*** with the citizens in attacking the mayor 市民とともに市長攻撃の共同戦線を張る. ¶defend a ***dying cause*** 滅びかけている主義を擁護する. ¶The ***final cause*** of law is the welfare of society. 法律の窮極の目的は社会の幸福である. ¶put down one's money in ***good cause*** 善事に金を出す. ¶a group of impressive buildings devoted to the ***great cause*** of education 教育の大道に捧げられた印象深い建物の一群 ‖ fight for a ***great cause*** 大義のために戦う. ¶Oxford has been styled "the home of ***lost causes***." オクスフォードは破れた主張の本家と言われている. ¶***momentous causes*** 重大な主張. ¶advance the ***national cause*** 国益を図る. ¶***No finer cause*** could be found than that of supporting it. それを支持することほどりっぱな仕事は他にない. ¶a ***noble cause*** りっぱな主義. ¶to the ***public cause*** 公衆のために. ¶The World War was waged for the ***sacred cause*** of justice and the freedom of the world. 世界大戦は正義と自由の世界という神聖な主張のもとに戦われた. ¶boost a ***worth-while cause*** 働きがいのある主義のちょうちんを持つ. ¶A most appropriate way to leave money to a ***worthy cause*** is in the form of a bequest to a well-known institution of learning. りっぱな目的に金を残すきわめて適当な方法は有名な学校に遺贈の形で寄付することである. 【類】uphold the ***worthy cause*** for which one stands / a *cause* well ***worthy*** of our support.

Q^2 adherents of the ***Stuart*** *cause* スチュアート党.

P a heroic fighter ***for*** the *cause* of democracy 民主主義の勇敢な闘士 ‖ Such a missionary does more harm than good ***for*** the *cause* of Christianity. こうした宣教師はキリスト教のために害あって益がない. 【類】He has done so much ***for*** the *cause* of peace and goodwill (親善) among nations. / ***for*** a common *cause* (共同の主義) / fight ***for*** a great *cause* (大義のために) / They fought ***for*** the Buddhist *cause* (仏教のために) / write books ***for*** the *cause* of truth, not for money / He suffered a great deal

(多大の犠牲を払った) *for* a noble *cause*. ¶***in*** the *cause* of humanity 人道擁護のために ‖ unwearied workers ***in*** the *cause* of ... ...の運動をする不屈不とうの労働者.【類】He is an enthusiastic worker ***in*** the *cause* of the blind. / lay down our lives (命を捨てる) ***in*** the *cause* of duty / He was created a Baron for services rendered ***in*** the *cause* of Japan's trade and commerce. / work ***in*** the *cause* of charity (humanity) / risk life and limb (身命) ***in*** the *cause* of one's country / co-operate (協力する) ***in*** the *cause* of human progress ‖ the king ***in*** whose *cause* they went to death 彼らが命を捨てて尽した国王. ¶serve ***to*** the *cause* of peace 平和のために尽す ‖ can do no greater service ***to*** the *cause* it represents than to ... ...するのがそのために尽す最大の奉仕である ‖ He rendered unexampled services ***to*** the *cause* of freedom and humanity. 彼は自由と人道のためにかつて比類のない奉仕をした.【類】in recognition of (を表彰して)his services ***to*** the *cause* of ... / The institution confers a great benefit ***to*** the *cause* of English study in Japan. ¶He has great sympathy ***with*** the *cause* of education. 彼は大いに教育の振興に力を入れている.

P^2 the great *cause* ***of*** International Understanding and Goodwill 国際的理解と親善の大道 ‖ The *cause* ***of*** letters owes an immense debt to him. 文学界は彼に負う所すこぶる大である.【類】The *cause* ***of*** temperance has made good progress.

(3)〖法〗訴訟事実(理由); 申立て.

V ***carry*** a *cause* by appeal from ... to ... 上告によって訴訟を...から...へ移して行く. ¶***has*** no *cause* for action 訴訟を起す理由がない. ¶***plead*** a *cause* 訴訟の理由を申立てる. ¶***try*** *causes* 事件を裁判する. ¶***undertake*** his *cause* その訴訟を引受ける.

P^2 a *cause* ***of*** action 訴訟の原因 ‖ within three years from the time the *cause* ***of*** action occurs 訴因発生の時から起算して三年以内に.

cause, *v*. ひき起す; 生ぜしめる.

M The accident was ***maliciously*** *caused*. この事件は悪意でやったものだ.

P fright *caused* ***by*** a fire 火事のために起った恐怖 ‖ diseases *caused* ***by*** microbes 微生物に起因する病気 ‖ calamity suddenly *caused* ***by*** nature 突発的天災事変 ‖ His ruin was *caused* ***by*** those faults. そうした過失が彼の破滅の元となった. ¶It *caused* much inconvenience ***to*** merchants. それは商人に非常な不便を与えた.

O He *caused* a new house to be built. 彼は新宅を建てさせた.

caution, *n*. 用心, 慎重; 警告.

V This will ***banish*** *caution*. こうすると警戒する必要がなくなる. ¶***disregard*** a *caution* 警告を無視する. ¶***employ*** the greatest *caution* できる限り用心をする. ¶***exercise*** *caution* 注意を加える ‖ ***exercise*** a judicious *caution* 賢明な注意を払う ‖ Due *caution* should be ***exercised*** in discriminating between the two. 相当の注意を払って二者の区別をなすべきである. ¶a *caution* is ***needed*** against the idea that ... ...という考えに陥らない用心が必要だ. ¶***observe*** great *caution* in doing it それを大いに注意してやる. ¶***offer*** useful *cautions* 有益な注意を与える. ¶***suggest*** one *caution* 注意を一つ暗示する. ¶***Take*** every *caution* against error. 間違いのないようによくよく用心しなさい. ¶***urge*** *caution* 用心を促す. ¶***use caution*** 大事をとる.【類】the greatest *caution* must be ***used*** in ...

Q ***Abundant*** *caution* does no harm. 用心にしくはなし. ¶act with ***great*** *caution* 十分注意して行動する.【類】The report was taken with ***great*** *caution*. ¶act with the ***utmost*** *caution* できるだけ用心深く行動する.

Q^2 take ***emergency*** *cautions* 急場の注意をする.

P ***by*** prudent *caution* 思慮深い注意によって. ¶I say this ***by way of*** *caution*. 念のために申上げる. ¶There is no need ***for*** *caution*. 用心するにおよばない. ¶A word ***of*** *caution* may be timely here. ここで一言注意を述べることが時宜に適したことと思う. ¶The police dismissed the charge ***with*** a *caution*. 警察は将来を戒めて罪を許した.

P^2 exercise *caution* ***against*** the sudden change of weather 天候の急変を警戒する. ¶a *caution* ***to*** one's friend 友人への注意.

caution, *v*. 注意する, 警告する.

P They *cautioned* him ***against*** the danger. 彼らは危険に陥らぬよう彼に注意した. ‖ the public is *cautioned* ***against*** ... 公衆に...がないよう注意する.

cautious, *a*. 用心深い, 慎重な.

M be ***extremely cautious*** 念に念を入れる. ¶be ***very cautious*** 用心深い.

P they are *cautious* ***in*** their use of ... 彼らは...の使用に用心深い. ¶He is *cautious* ***of*** telling secrets. 彼は警戒して容易に秘密を明かさない. ‖ He is *cautious* ***of*** giving offence to others. 彼は注意して人の感情を害さないようにする. ¶You must be *cautious* ***with*** the razor. かみそりは使用に注意しなければならない.

cavalry, *n*. 騎兵隊.

P an officer ***in*** the *cavalry* 騎兵隊の士官. ¶a troop ***of*** *cavalry* 一隊の騎兵.

cavalryman, *n*. 騎兵.

Q^2 a ***police cavalryman*** 騎馬巡査.

cave, *n*. 洞穴.

V ***pick*** a *cave* for their night camp 夜営するために洞穴を掘る.

Q^2 a ***bone*** *cave* 骨窟(くつ)(亡びた動物の骨や, 時として人類の骨, 遺物のある洞穴).

cave, *v*. 陥没する.

M^2 *cave* ***in*** 陥没する;《口語》降参する ‖ The mine roof *caved* ***in***. 坑道の天井が落ちた(落盤した).

cavern, *n*. 洞穴.

Q a ***rocky*** *cavern* 岩窟(くつ).

cavil, *n*. とがめ立て, へりくつ.

Q settle the dispute beyond ***reasonable*** *cavil* 筋の通った理屈では反ばくできないように論争を解決する.

P It is proved ***beyond*** all *cavil*. へりくつをつける余裕のないほどに証明された.【類】It is demonstrated ***beyond*** *cavil*. ¶state simply and ***without*** *cavil* 率直にへりくつ抜きに述べる ‖ They pay ***without*** *cavil* nothing less than the half-guinea scale to hear such a company. 彼らはこうした一座の興行を聞くのに半ギニーという相当高い入場料を文句も言わずに払う.

P^2 the *cavils* ***of*** critics 批評家のへりくつ.

cavil, *v*. とがめ立てする, へりくつを言う.

P He *cavils* ***at*** everything. 彼は何にでもへりくつを言う. ¶He who *cavils* ***at*** other's faults does not see his own. 他人のあら探しをする人間には自分のあらは見えない. ‖ It is unreasonable to *cavil* ***at*** an error of a few pence in an acount of some thousands of pounds. 数千ポンドの勘定の中で数ペンスの誤りに難癖をつけるのは不合理だ.

cavity, *n*. 穴, 腔(こう).

Q the ***uterine*** *cavity* 子宮腔.

P^2 the *cavity* ***in*** a tooth 虫歯の穴.

cease, *v*. やむ; やめる; なくなる.

P *cease* ***from*** strife (labor, work) 争い(など)をやめる. ¶The publication of the magazine *ceases* ***with*** the September number. 同誌は九月号で廃刊する. ‖ His influence *ceased* ***with*** his death. 彼の勢力はその死とともに解消した.

O The law has *ceased* to be operative. その法律は無効になった.【類】He has never *ceased* to regret. ¶*Cease* fire! 打ち方止め.

ceasing, *n*. 止めること.

P ***without*** *ceasing* ひっきりなしに.

cede, *v*. 譲る, 割譲する.

P *cede* all claims to a disputed right or territory ***to*** ... 紛争を起した権利または領土をはっきりと...に譲与する ‖ Hongkong was then *ceded* ***to*** England. 香港はその時英国に割譲された.

ceiling, *n*. 天井, (価格賃金の)最高限界.

V ***abolish*** price *ceilings* 物価の天井(最高限度)をはずす. ¶***board*** a *ceiling* 天井を張る. ¶This room ***has a*** very low *ceiling*. このへやの天井は低い. ¶***take*** the *ceiling* ***off*** 制限を撤廃する. ¶***whitewash*** the *ceiling* 天井を白く塗る.

Q a ***coved*** *ceiling* 弓(アーチ)形天井. ¶a ***smoky*** *ceiling* くすぶった天井.

Q^2 the ***OPA*** *ceilings* 物価管理局規定の物価最高限度 (OPA は Office of Price Administration の略字). ¶no ***price*** *ceiling* on ... ...の値段の最高限度がきまっていない ‖ set new ***price ceilings*** on retail meat 小売食肉に新たに価格の最高限度を設ける.【類】the reimposition of ***price ceilings*** on essential commodities / maintain the ***price ceilings*** / the removal (撤廃) of ***price ceilings***. ¶the ***production*** *ceiling* on basic materials 基本的材料の生産最高限度. ¶lift ***rent*** *ceiling* 最高家賃制を除去する.【類】the $80 ***rent ceiling***.

P The lamp hangs ***from*** the *ceiling*. ランプが天井から下っている. ¶hang a lamp from a hook ***in*** the *ceiling* ランプを天井のかぎにつるす ‖ the trap-door ***in*** the *ceiling* 天井の揚げぶた. ¶Few people probably know what it is that enables flies to walk ***on*** the *ceiling*. はえが天井を歩けるのはどうした訳かを知っている者は恐らく少ないだろ

う. 【類】 There are many flies ***on*** the *ceiling*.

P^2 a *ceiling* 20 ft. ***above*** the floor 床上 20 フィートの天井.

celebrate, *v.* 祝う; [儀式・祭典などを]挙行する.

M They ***justly*** *celebrated* the occasion. その日を祝ったのはもっともなことである. ¶ *celebrate* rather ***riotously*** 少しくお祝いの乱ちき騒ぎをする. ¶ ***solemnly*** *celebrate* ... 厳かに...を祝賀する. ¶ They ***successfully*** *celebrated* the victory. 彼らは盛大に戦勝を祝した. ¶ They ***warmly*** *celebrated* the festival. 彼らは熱心に祭典を挙行した.

P He was *celebrated* ***above*** his companions. 彼はその同輩以上に有名であった. ¶ He was *celebrated* ***amid*** (=***among***) his contemporaries. 彼は同時代の人の間に有名であった. ¶ *celebrated* ***as*** a scholar 学者として有名な. ¶ The occasion was *celebrated* ***at*** many schools ***by*** a holiday. 当日は大概の学校は休業して祝意を表した. ¶ *celebrate* a birthday ***by*** a banquet きょう宴を催して誕生日を祝う. 【類】 The event was *celebrated* ***by*** poets and historians. / The Cobden centenary (コブデン百年祭) was *celebrated* on Saturday ***by*** numeral meetings. / The victory was *celebrated* ***by*** the people. ¶ The god is *celebrated* ***for*** answers to prayers. その神様は御利益があるので名高い. 【類】 He is *celebrated* ***for*** his courage (ability). / The place is *celebrated* ***for*** its scenery (hot-springs). / *celebrated* ***for*** the gorgeousness of his style (華美な文体). The battle was *celebrated* ***in*** verse (song, music). その戦役は詩(など)に歌われた. ¶ *celebrate* the day ***with*** appropriate ceremonies しかるべき式を挙げて当日を祝う.

celebration, *n.* 祝典, 祝賀.

V ***carry through*** a *celebration* 式典を挙げる. ¶ ***hold*** a *celebration* on the occasion 当日式典を挙げる. 【類】 ***hold*** a *celebration* of the armistice (休戦) / ***hold*** *celebrations* in honor (ために) of a person. ¶ ***join*** a *celebration* 祝賀に参加する. ¶ the *celebration* is ***sponsored*** by ... その祝典は...の主催である.

Q the Protector's ***Centenary*** *celebration* 摂政の百年記念祝典 ‖ the 26th ***centenary*** *celebrations* of Japan's national founding 日本建国二千六百年記念祝典. ¶ at its ***centennial*** *celebration* その百年祭に. ¶ Tokyo's ***civic*** *celebration* of the Allied victory [第一次大戦の際の]東京市民の連合軍戦勝祝賀会. ¶ a ***Communist-sponsored*** *celebration* 共産党主催の祝典. ¶ a ***cordial*** *celebration* 誠意ある祝賀. ¶ Altogether it has been a very ***happy*** *celebration*. 大体から見てそれは非常な盛典であった. ¶ an ***impressive*** *celebration* 印象深い式典. ¶ two ***joyous*** *celebrations* 二つのお目出度い祝典. ¶ make it a day of ***national*** *celebration* それを国祭日とする. ¶ an ***official municipal*** *celebration* 公式の市の祝典. ¶ a ***public*** *celebration* 公式の祝典. ¶ a ***sane patriotic*** *celebration* まじめな愛国的祝典.

Q^2 a ***diamond jubilee*** *celebration* [ヴィクトリア女王即位]六十年記念祝典. ¶ the ***Fourth of July*** *celebration* 七月四日(米国独立)の祝典. ¶ at the ***Jubilee*** *celebration* of the founding of ... ...創立五十年祭で. ¶ ***V-E Day*** *celebrations* V-E デー祝典 (Victory in Europe の略, 連合軍が欧州で勝利を得た記念日).

P in his address ***at*** the *celebration* of the semi-centennial of the school その学校の創立五十年記念祭における彼の演説中に. ¶ ***in*** *celebration* of the occasion 当日を祝って. 【類】 ***in*** *celebration* of the greatest Chinese festival of the year / ***in*** *celebration* of this event (できごと) / ***in*** *celebration* of the Jubilee (創立五十年) of the Manchester Public Library / illumination of the building ***in*** *celebration* of ...

P^2 a *celebration* ***at*** the end of fifty years 五十年目の終に行う祝典. ¶ a *celebration* ***in*** honor of ... ...のための祝賀. ¶ the *celebration* ***of*** the Emperor's Birthday 天長節の祝. 【類】 the *celebration* ***of*** King Edward's coronation ‖ a thoroughly sane *celebration* ***of*** a national holiday おごそかな祭日の祝賀. ¶ They made a great *celebration* ***over*** the event. そのできごとを大いに祝賀した.

celebrator, *n.* 祝う人.

Q^2 ***Yuletide*** *celebrators* キリスト降誕祭を祝う人々.

celebrity, *n.* 有名, 名声; 有名人.

V ***acquire*** *celebrity* by its discovery その発見によって名声を博する. 【類】 In modern times the Venetians first ***acquired*** *celebrity* for the beauty of their glass manufactures (ガラス製品). ¶ He ***attained*** *celebrity* as a rising novelist. 新進作家として有名になった. ¶ He well ***deserves*** his *celebrity*. 彼には名声を博するだけの価値がある. ¶ The temple of Miyajima ***enjoys*** great *celebrity*. 宮島神社は非常に有名だ. ¶ He ***gained*** great *celebrity*. 彼は非常な名声を博した. 【類】 ***gain*** much *celebrity* from ... ‖ The Imitation of Christ by Thomas a Kempis ***has*** a *celebrity* in the Christian world second only to that of the Bible. トマス・ア・ケムピスの「キリストにならいて」はキリスト教界において聖書に次ぐ名声を博している.

Q enjoy ***deserved*** *celebrity* それだけの実があって名声を博する. ¶ ***ephemeral*** *celebrities* 一時的名声のある人々. ¶ acquire ***great*** *celebrity* 非常に有名になる. ¶ the ***leading*** *celebrities* of the English stage 英国の演芸界における一流俳優たち. ¶ He became a ***learned*** *celebrity*. 彼は有名な学者になった. ¶ ***literary*** and ***artistic*** *celebrities* 文学芸術界知名の士. ¶ ***national*** *celebrities* 国内の名士. ¶ Nikko and other ***scenic*** *celebrities* of Japan 日光その他日本における景勝の地. ¶ an actor of ***some*** *celebrity* 相当名のある役者. ¶ names of ***world-wide*** *celebrity* 世界的に知られた名前. 【類】 great works (著作) of ***world-wide*** *celebrity*.

Q^2 ***Hollywood*** *celebrities* ハリーウッドのスターたち. ¶ ***movie*** *celebrities* 映画スターたち. ¶ ***world*** *celebrities* 世界の名士たち.

celibacy, *n.* 独身, 独身生活.

V bonzes ***practicing*** *celibacy* 独身生活の僧りょたち.

cell, *n.* 細胞; 独房; 電池.

Q a ***dry*** *cell* 乾電池. ¶ the fusion of the ***male*** and ***female*** *cells* 雌雄両細胞の融合. ¶ a ***voltaic*** (=***galvanic***) *cell* 電池.

Q^2 be imprisoned in a ***one-room*** *cell* 独房に監禁される. ¶ a ***torture*** *cell* 拷問室.

P^2 the *cells* ***of*** a honeycomb 蜂の巣のみつ房.

cellar, *n.* 穴蔵; 地下室.

V He ***keeps*** a good *cellar*. 彼はぶどう酒をたくさん貯蔵している.

Q ***dark yawning*** *cellars* 暗く口を開いている穴蔵.

Q^2 a ***storage*** *cellar* 貯蔵用地下室.

P The hotel was crowded ***from*** *cellar* to attic. そのホテルは地階から屋根裏まで一杯だった. ¶ Our team is ***in*** the *cellar*. われわれのチームは最下位だ.

Celt, *n.* ケルト人.

Q the ***ancient*** *Celts* of Gaul ゴール地域の古代ケルト民族.

cement, *n.* セメント.

Q ***Roman*** *cement* 天然セメント.

Q^2 ***Portland*** *cement* ポートランド・セメント(現在では人造セメントの総称).

cement, *v.* 結合する.

P friendship *cemented* ***by*** time 時と共に深まった友情.

cemetery, *n.* 墓地.

P His remains lie (=repose) ***in*** the *cemetery*. 彼の遺骸はその墓地に葬られている.

censer, *n.* 香炉.

Q^2 a ***bronze*** *censer* 青銅の香炉.

censor, *n.* 検閲官; 批評家.

Q ***prominent*** *censor* of public morals 知名の公衆道徳批評家.

censorship, *n.* 検閲官の職; 検閲.

V ***establish*** a rigid *censorship* 厳格な検閲を開始する. ¶ they have to ***pass*** the *censorship* of ... ...の検閲を経なければならない. ¶ ***remove*** the *censorship* on cablegrams 海外電報の検閲を廃止する.

Q ***rigid*** *censorship* over the press 厳重な新聞検閲.

Q^2 introduce ***film*** *censorship* 映画検閲制を採用する. ¶ protest the ***press*** *censorship* 新聞検閲に抗議する. 【類】 extend their ***press*** *censorship* to such books as ...

censurable, *a.* 責めるべき.

P He is *censurable* ***for*** some faults. 彼に幾分責めるべき点がある.

censure, *n.* 非難, しっ責, けん責; 批判.

V ***escape*** *censure* けん責を免れる. ¶ ***hint*** *censure* of ... ...を風刺する. ¶ They ***spared*** their *censures* on this head. 彼らはこの項目に関する非難をさしひかえた.

Q a ***tacit*** *censure* 暗々裡の非難. ¶ become an object of ***general*** *censure* 一般の非難の的となる. ¶ The ***public*** *censure* passed upon each party. 世間では双方を非難した.

P take care not to lay oneself open ***to*** *censure* again 再び非難を受けないように注意する.

censure, *v.* しっ責する, 非難する.

M He *censured* me ***bitterly*** for what I had done. あの人は私のした事をひどく非難した. ¶ *censure* ***severely*** 激しくしっ責する. ¶ ***strongly*** *censure* 手きびしく非難する. ¶ *censure* ***unreservedly*** 遠慮なくやっつける.

P *censure* a person *as* selfish (unpatriotic) 人を利己的(など)とけなす. ¶*censure* him *for* his fault (error, selfishness, idleness) 彼の欠点(など)を責める.

census, *n.* 国勢調査, 戸口調査, 人口調査.

V *carry out* a *census* 戸口調査を行う. ¶*take* the *census* 国勢調査をする ‖ *take* a *census* of the amount of venereal disease among men 男子の性病調査を行う.

P *according to* the *census* of 1930 一九三〇年の国勢調査では. ¶*At* the 1890 *census* there were sixteen gold pen factories in the United States. 一八九〇年の調査では合衆国に十六の金ペン製造工場があった. 【類】The population of the United States was over ninety million *at* the last *census*.

P² *census of* manufacture 製造業調査.

cent, *n.* セント.

Q Don't I tell you I haven't a *beastly cent?* びた一文だってないって言ってるじゃないか ‖ There was not a '*red cent*' on his person or among his belongings. 彼は鋼銭一枚も身につけていなかったしまたその所持品の中にもなかった. ¶not a *single cent* びた一文もなく.

P *without* a *cent* of remuneration 報酬は一文もやらずに.

centenary, *n.* 百年間, 百年祭.

V The society has just *attained* its *centenary.* その協会は丁度創立百年に達した. ¶*celebrate* the *centenary* of ... ...の百年祭を祝う. ¶He *reaches* (=*has*) his *centenary* on March 21. 彼は三月二十一日に丁度百歳になる.

P² this year is the *centenary of* the birth of ... 今年は...の誕生第百年祭に当る. 【類】the *centenary of* the founding of the company.

center, *n.* 中心, 中央; 中心点, 起点.

V *create* a *center* of higher learning 学術研究の中心地をつくる. ¶The flower-pot *forms* a table *center.* 植木ばちが食卓の中心をなしている. ¶*shift* the *center* of gravity of it from ... to ... その重心を...から...へ移す. 【類】*shift* the *center* of interest (興味).

Q the *busy center* of the herring industry にしん漁業の盛んな中心地. ¶the *chief center* of social intercourse for the Irish in London ロンドン在住アイルランド人の主なる社交の中心. 【類】the *chief centers* of civilization in the West (西洋). ¶a *civic center* 大都会. ¶a *collecting* and *distributing center* 物資集散地. ¶a busy *commercial center* 繁華な商業区域. ¶the great *cultural centers* of Europe ヨーロッパ文化の大中心. ¶the most *cultured* and *refined centers* of European civilization 欧州文明の最も文化的で洗練された中心. ¶a *distributing center* 集散地. ¶Seville was an *early* and *important center* of the potter's craft in Spain. セヴィリアは昔スペインの陶器業の重要な中心地であった. ¶other *Far Eastern centers* of civilization 極東における他の文化の中心. ¶London is the *financial center* of the world. ロンドンは世界金融の中心である. ¶a *free medical center* 無料診療所. ¶a *gay center* of pleasure 歓楽の中心地. ¶all the *great centers* of English civilization 英国文明のあらゆる大中心地. ¶a *harmonizing center* 調停機関. ¶*hygienic centers* 衛生上の中心. ¶The earth revolves round the sun as an *immovable center.* 地球は不動の太陽を中心としてその周囲を回転する. ¶be an *important center* of traffic (transit) 輸送の要衝に当る. ¶*industrial centers* 産業中心地. ¶Mecca, an *inspiring spiritual center* 敬神家の霊地メッカ. ¶It may be that New York is going to be America's *literary center,* as London is the literary center of England. ロンドンが英国文芸の中心であるように, 今やニューヨークが米国文芸の中心になろうとしているようである. ¶a *manufacturing center* 工業中心地. ¶a *natural commercial center* 天成の商業中心地. ¶*populous centers* 人口稠密な都会. ¶the *principal centers* of population 大都会. ¶a *productive center* 生産地. ¶*provincial centers* 地方の大都市. ¶a *seismic* (=an *earthquake*) *center* 震源地. ¶*significant centers* of culture 文化の重要都市. ¶The hotel is a great *social center* of the capital. そのホテルは首都における社交上の一大中心を成している. ¶The I.R.E.T. is a *stimulating* and *effective center* of union for teachers of English in Japan. 英研(英語教授研究所)は日本の英語教師の協力を刺激しかつ効果的ならしめる中心機関である. ¶New York is the *theatrical center* of the American people. ニューヨークはアメリカ人観劇の本場である. ¶Jeres de la Frontera, of Spain, is the premier *wine producing center* of the world. スペインのヘレス・デ・ラ・フロンテラは世界の主要ぶどう酒産地である. ¶Charing Cross Station, key of the Continent, a *world's center* to which all nations gravitate 大陸ののどで世界各国民の一集合地たるチャリング・クロス停車場.

Q² New York is the *amusement center* of the world. ニューヨークは世界の歓楽郷だ. ¶the *art centers* of the world 世界芸術の中心. ¶*business centers* 商業の中心地. ¶Genoa is a *Communist center.* ゼノアは共産主義の中心地だ. ¶a *community center* 《米》[市・区の]公民館. ¶a *concentration center* 俘虜収容所. ¶an *education center* 教育会館. ¶a *flight-test center* 試験飛行場. ¶Barber shops, in France or America, for instance, are *gossip centers.* 例えばフランスあるいはアメリカの理髪店は世間話に花を咲かせる所である. ¶an important *grain-shipping center* 重要な穀物積出港. ¶a public *health center* 公衆保健所. ¶a *hotel center* ホテルの多い市区. ¶an *intelligence center* 情報部. ¶the Kodokan, foremost *judo training center* in Japan 日本における第一流の柔道道場たる講道館. ¶London is the largest and most important *library center* in the world. ロンドンは世界最大かつ最重要な図書館の中心だ. ¶Paris threatens London as *male fashion center.* パリは男子の流行の中心としてのロンドンに脅威を与える. ¶a great *money center* 金融の一大中心地. ¶a *motoring center* 自動車製造の中心地. ¶a popular *movie center* 人気のある映画街. ¶The news room is the *nerve center* of the newspaper. ニュース室は新聞の神経中枢である. 【類】The mile-square City of London was the *nerve center* of national and empire commerce. / The Emperor system was the *nerve center* of imperialism. ¶an *orientation center* [外国人学生のための]再教育訓練所. ¶a *publishing center* 出版中心地. ¶a great *purchasing center* 一大買入れ市場. ¶a *railroad* (=*railway*) *center* 鉄道の要路. ¶a *recreation center* 娯楽場. ¶a consolidated *refugee center* 統合避難民収容所. ¶a *relocation center* 再配置集合所. ¶a *research center* 学術研究の中心. ¶a *rest center* 休養所. ¶*separation centers* for servicemen to be discharged 解除される軍人の隔離所. ¶a *service center* 物資供給所. ¶the best *shopping center* away from noise of traffic 交通のけん騒がなく気持よく買物のできる区域. ¶a *slaughtering center* と殺場. ¶a *sports center* スポートの中心地. ¶Paris was the *storm center* of the revolution. パリは革命のしゅらの巷であった. ¶a political *storm center* 政界風波の根源地. ¶Uji is the famous *tea growing center* of Western Japan. 宇治は西日本の有名な茶の産地である. ¶London is the greatest *trade centre* of the world. ロンドンは世界最大の商業中心地である. ¶an exhibition to "boost" Hongkong as a *tourist center* 香港への観光熱を「あおり立てる」ための展示会. ¶a *wartime segregation center* 戦時隔離所. ¶a *world center* of information 情報収集の世界的中心地. 【類】Chicago is a *world center* of mechanical civilization (機械文明). / In those days Frankfort was the *world center* for books.

P with a lecture hall *as* its *center* 中央に講堂があって. ¶*at* the *center* 中央に. ¶radiate *from* a common *center* 共通の中心から放射する. ¶right *in* the *center* of ... ...の真中に. ¶step right *into* the *center* of it その真中に歩み入る. ¶He parted his hair *on* the *center* of his forehead in the form of a Norman arch. 彼はノルマンのアーチ型に頭髪を真中で分けていた. ‖ revolve *on* its *center* それを中心として回転する. ¶draw a circle *round* a given *center* 与えられた点を中心に円を描く.

P² a *center for* commerce (industry, porcelain manufacture) 商業(など)の中心. 【類】Charing Cross Road is a *center for* the second-hand book trade. ¶a *center of* business activity 商業の中心 ‖ a *center of* attraction 人を引付ける場所 ‖ the *center of* the celebration その式場 ‖ Paris, a *center of* brilliant social life 花々しい社交生活の中心パリ. 【類】a *center of* club life / a *center of* culture. ¶the *center of* operations 策源地. ¶the *center of* his teaching 彼の教えの核心 ‖ a *center of* communication 四通八達の地. 【類】The bank has now extended its ramification into every *center of* commercial activity in the country. / a *center of* very important industry / a *center of* packing industry (かん詰業) / a *center of* intellectual light (学校) / a *center of* moral life and spiritual power (教会) ‖ Luxor, the *center of* interest for Egyptologists エジプト考古学者の興味の中心地たるラキソル. 【類】 Seville, the *center of* Spanish commerce / the *center of* the company's operations (会社経営) ‖ the shifting of the *center of* gravity from ... to ... [世人の注意など]重心の...から...への移動.

center, *v.* 中心におく, 中心に集ま(め)る.

P Christianity is the outgrowth of the life and work of Jesus Christ and *centers* ***about*** his personality. キリスト教はイエス・キリストの生活および活動の成果であってその人格を中心としている. 【類】 much of the romantic interest *centers* ***about*** ... ¶Brahmanism *centered* ***around*** the performance of an elaborate ritual. ばら門教は複雑な儀式がその中心になっていた. ¶Most of the American and Japanese trade in China *centers* ***at*** Shanghai. 中国における日米の商業は上海を中心にしている. ¶interest in him chiefly *centers* ***in*** the fact that ... 世人が彼に関心を持つのは主として...という事実にもとずく. 【類】 the interest of the story is *centered* mainly ***in*** ... ¶*center* ***on*** a point (person, thing) 一点(など)に集まる ‖ *center* one's hopes ***on*** ... ...の希望を...に集中する. 【類】 Public sympathy was *centered* ***on*** him. / Public interest *centered* ***on*** the peace proposal (平和の提議). ¶Scottish life in London *centers* ***round*** this spot. ロンドンにおけるスコットランド人の生活はここを中心として営まれている.

central, *n.* 《英口》 中央電話局.

V ***ring up*** the "*central*" 電話で本局を呼び出す.

century, *n.* 百年, 一世紀.

V those who ***lived out*** the 19th *century* 十九世紀を越して二十世紀に入った人々 ‖ These songs will ***live out*** the *century*. これらの歌は今世紀の後までも伝わるだろう.

V² The eighteenth *century* ***opened.*** 十八世紀の幕が開いた. ¶Another *century* has ***rolled away.*** また一世紀が過ぎ去った.

Q the absolute illiteracy of the people in ***bygone*** *centuries* 昔の人の全然無学文盲なこと. ¶***countless*** *centuries* ago 幾百年前だか分らない古い時代に. ¶It has come down to us from ***early*** *centuries*. それは昔からわれわれの間に伝わってきた. ¶close upon ***half*** a *century* ago かれこれ五十年ほど前 ‖ in the ***half*** *century* previous to ... ...より前の半世紀に. ¶in the forties and fifties of the ***last*** *century* 前世紀の四十年から五十年代にわたって. ¶the ***later eighteenth*** *century* 十八世紀の後期. ¶the ***mid-nineteenth*** *century* 十九世紀の中ごろ. ¶The last two decades of the ***nineteenth*** *century* 十九世紀の終りの二十年. ¶in ***our own*** *century* 現世紀において. ¶in the ***past*** *century* 前世紀に. ¶a genuine piece of Korean pottery of the ***XVI*** *century* 十六世紀の正銘の朝鮮陶器. ¶the ***sixth*** and ***fifth*** *centuries* B.C. 紀元前第六および第五世紀. ¶***twenty-one*** *centuries* have flown and with them has flown ... 二千百年の歳月が流れた, そしてその歳月と共に...も流れ去った. ¶for ***unnumbered*** (=***untold***) *centuries* 幾世紀となく. 【類】 through ***untold*** *centuries.*

Q² during the ***last quarter*** *century* 過去二十五年間に.

P arrange the list ***by*** *centuries* その表を世紀順に配列する. ¶***during*** the *centuries* immediately following it 直ぐ次の数世紀間に. ¶***for*** *centuries* past (ahead) 過去(今後)数世紀にわたって. 【類】 ***for*** some *centuries* / ***for*** the single *century* from ... to ... / ***for*** a *century* or two. ¶***from*** the third *century* onwards 三世紀以来 ‖ It dates ***from*** the first *century* of the Christian era. 西暦紀元の第一世紀から始まる. 【類】 ***from*** the 13th *century* ***to*** the 17th *century*. ¶***in*** this twentieth *century* of civilization and humanity この文明と人道主義の二十世紀に ‖ early ***in*** the thirteenth *century* 十三世紀の初期に. ¶as late as the end ***of*** the 14th *century* 十四世紀の終りまで ‖ the latter part ***of*** the fifteenth *century* 十五世紀の後半 ‖ a quarter ***of*** a *century* preceding him 彼に先立つ二十五年 ‖ three quarters ***of*** a *century* ago and more 七十五年ないしそれ以前に ‖ for about a third ***of*** a *century* およそ一世紀の三分の一にわたって. ¶***over*** a few *centuries* 数世紀にわたって. ¶ever ***since*** the third *century* 三世紀以来絶えず. ¶***through*** *centuries* 数世紀の間. ¶down ***till*** the 16th *century* 降って十六世紀まで. ¶it was not ***until*** the fourteenth *century* that ... 十四世紀になって始めて ... ¶***within*** a *century* 一世紀以内に.

P² in the second *century* ***after*** Christ 西暦紀元第二世紀に. ¶*centuries* ***of*** oppression 数世紀間の圧制.

cereal, *n.* 穀類, 穀物.

V ***eat*** *cereal* for breakfast 朝食に穀物を食べる.

Q ***miscellaneous*** *cereals* 雑穀.

ceremonial, *n.* 儀式, 式典, 礼儀.

V ***abridging*** the *ceremonial* 堅苦しいこと(儀式)はあっさり片づけて. ¶I was to ***undergo*** a *ceremonial* of initiation. 私が入会するについてはその式を経なければならなかった.

Q with ***appropriate*** *ceremonial* 相当の儀式をもって. ¶Some great ***national*** *ceremonial* of historic import is about to be celebrated. ある歴史的重要性のある国民の大祝典が今執行されようとしている. ¶***ritualistic*** *ceremonials* しゃちこばった儀式. ¶dedicate in ***solemn*** *ceremonial* a memorial to ... 厳粛な式を挙げて記念碑を...に奉献する.

Q² ***marriage*** *ceremonials* 結婚式.

P ***with*** the usual *ceremonial* 例によって式を挙げて.

ceremony, *n.* 儀式, 礼式; 虚礼; 遠慮.

V ***abandon*** all *ceremony* 打とける, 無礼講にする. ¶***hold*** a *ceremony* 式を挙げる. ¶They ***made*** the *ceremony* coincide with the President's visit to Paris. その式は大統領のパリ訪問と同時に挙行するようにされた. ¶***observe*** a *ceremony* with great respect うやうやしく式を挙げる. ¶Some imposing *ceremony* will be ***organized*** in honor of the event. その記念として大祝典が挙行される. ¶***perform*** the *ceremony* of formally opening a new school 新設学校の開校式を挙行する. 【類】 ***perform*** a religious *ceremony*. ¶***use*** (no) *ceremony* 儀式ばる(打とける).

V² The *ceremony* ***took place*** in [the] presence of the Emperor. 陛下の御前で式を挙げた.

Q Why ***all*** the *ceremony* tonight? 今夜はなぜみんな改まっているのか. ¶The new building was formally opened with ***appropriate*** *ceremonies* by the President of the United States. 新築の建物はアメリカ合衆国大統領によって正式の開場式が挙行された. ¶with ***becoming*** *ceremony* ふさわしい儀礼をもって. ¶a ***civil*** (***religious***) *ceremony* 社会的(宗教的)の儀式 [結婚などの場合]. ¶a ***congratulatory*** *ceremony* 祝賀式. ¶***dedicatory*** *ceremonies* 奉献式. ¶the ***formal concluding*** *ceremony* of an exhibition 博覧会の正式閉会式. ¶his ***funeral*** *ceremony* 彼の葬式. ¶without ***further*** *ceremony* それ以後は無礼講で(打ちとけて). ¶***hymeneal*** *ceremonies* 結婚式. ¶The *ceremony* was ***lengthy*** and ***elaborate***. その式は長くて念入のものだった. ¶the ***matrimonial*** *ceremony* uniting ... and ... ...と...の結婚式. ¶with appropriate ***military*** *ceremonies* 相当な軍隊の礼式をもって. ¶the ***nuptial*** *ceremony* 結婚式. ¶with ***proper*** *ceremonies* 相当の儀式を挙げて. ¶Very ***quaint*** are the *ceremonies* observed on the occasion. 当日の儀式ははなはだ奇異なものである. ¶***religious*** *ceremonies* 宗教的諸儀式. ¶What ***ridiculous*** *ceremony!* なあんだ堅苦しい. ¶be rejected with ***scant*** *ceremony* すげなく断る. ¶a ***stately*** and ***moving*** *ceremony* 荘厳で印象の深い儀式.

Q² an ***awarding*** *ceremony* 表彰式. ¶a ***conferment*** *ceremony* 授与式. ¶an ***enshrining*** *ceremony* 神体を社に祭る式. ¶a ***flag-rising*** *ceremony* [国]旗掲揚式. ¶He received the Emperor's prize at the last ***graduation*** *ceremony* of the University. 彼はその大学の去年の卒業式で陛下の恩賜賞をいただいた. ¶the ***inauguration*** *ceremony* of a park 公園開園式. ¶the ***naming*** *ceremony* of a vessel 船の命名式. ¶perform the ***opening*** *ceremony* 開会式を行う ¶a ***presentation*** *ceremony* 贈呈式. ¶***tea*** *ceremony*=ceremonial tea 茶道. ¶at the ***unveiling*** *ceremonies* on behalf of the Jack London bust ジャック・ロンドンの胸像除幕式で. ¶the ***wine*** *ceremony* [アイヌが一年に三回]酒を醸して神に供える大祭.

P his speech ***at*** the *ceremony* 彼の式辞 ‖ preside ***at*** a *ceremony* 式を司る ‖ He was present ***at*** the *ceremony* and the reception following. 彼は儀式とそれに続く接待に列席した. ¶fix a day ***for*** the *ceremony* その式日をきめる. ¶at a place where people are ***on*** *ceremony* with each other 皆が互に儀式張っているような場所では ‖ Please don't stand ***on*** *ceremony*. どうぞ御遠慮なく. ¶The stadium was opened ***with*** *ceremony*. スタジアムは開場式を行って開かれた. ¶Help yourself ***without*** *ceremony*. 遠慮なく召上って下さい. 【類】 ***without*** the slightest *ceremony*.

P² the *ceremony* ***of*** presenting it was performed on ...

その贈呈式が何月何日に行われた. 【類】 the *ceremony of* conferring (授与) graduation certificates ‖ the *ceremony of* prostration called kotow by the Chinese 中国人が叩頭と称する平伏の礼.

certain, *a.* たしかな；確信している；一定した.

M it is ***absolutely certain*** that ... ...は全く確かなことである. ¶it is ***almost certain*** that ... ...はほとんど確実である. ¶I am ***as certain*** as if I had seen it. 見たも同然に確かだと思っている. ¶it is not ***at all certain*** that ... ...は一向分らない. ¶it is ***by no means certain*** that ... ...は決して確実なことじゃない. ¶it is ***morally certain*** that ... ...ということは万間違いないと思う. ¶it is ***more or less certain*** that ... ...は多少(事実に)当っている. ¶It may be regarded as ***pretty certain***. それはまず確かと見てよい. 【類】 it is ***pretty certain*** that ... ¶it is ***quite certain*** that ... ...ということは十分確かである. ¶it is ***reasonably certain*** that ... ...ということは相当確かである. ¶it is ***tolerably certain*** that ... ...ということはかなり確かである. ¶He was ***too certain*** of it to be deceived. 彼はそのことを余りよく知っているのでだまされなかった. ¶it is ***well-nigh certain*** that ... ...ということはほとんど確かなことだ. ¶It is not ***yet certain*** who will succeed him. だれが彼の後継者になるかまだ分らない.

P No one knows ***for certain*** when it will take place. いつそれが起るかだれもしかとは知らない. ‖ I don't know ***for certain***. しかとは存じません. 【類】 I hear ***for certain*** that ... / I could not say ***for certain***. / it is known ***for certain*** that ... ¶it is far ***from certain*** that ... ...は一向判然しない.

P² Are you ***certain of*** that? それは確かですか. ‖ I am ***certain of*** success (victory). 僕は成功(など)疑いなし. ‖ I got up at six so as to be ***certain of*** being in time. きっと間に合うように六時に起きた. ‖ In order to be ***certain of*** it I asked him myself. 間違のないように自分で尋ねた. 【類】 I cannot be ***certain of*** the facts of the case, unless they are ... / I am not ***certain of*** the truth of the matter.

O He was ***certain*** he would succeed. 彼は成功すると信じていた. ¶He is ***certain*** to come. 彼はきっと来る. ‖ The thief is ***certain*** to be caught in time. 盗賊はきっとその内に捕(ﾂｶ)まる.

certainly, *ad.* 確かに, 確実に.

M ***most certainly*** 絶対に間違いなく.

certainty, *n.* 確実, 確実性；確信.

V ***reach*** the ***certainty*** that ... 確かに...という見きわめがつく.

Q an ***absolute certainty*** 絶対的確実なこと. ¶for (=to) a ***dead certainty*** 必ず(疑いなく). ¶We may at least conjecture with ***fair certainty*** that the negotiations will be successful. われわれは交渉が大抵まとまるだろうということの推測がとにかくできる. ¶with the ***highest*** (=***utmost***) ***certainty*** きわめて確実に. ¶It is a ***moral certainty***. それはまず間違いのないことだ. ¶with ***reasonable certainty*** 相当確かに.

P be in a position to announce the plan ***as*** a ***certainty*** その計画は確実だと発表することができる. ¶I know ***for*** a ***certainty*** that ... ...をしかと知っている. ¶I lent it to him ***in*** the ***certainty*** that he will return it. 返すと確信して彼にそれを貸した. ¶***to*** (=for) a ***certainty*** 確かに. ¶testify ***with certainty*** that ... ...ということを確実に証明する ‖ I cannot speak ***with certainty*** as to ... ...については断言はできない ‖ Of his personal history, little or nothing is known ***with certainty***. 彼の履歴についてははっきりしたことはほとんど知れていない. 【類】 The date of its first importation cannot be established ***with*** any ***certainty***. / It cannot be determined ***with certainty***.

P² ***certainty about*** the matter そのことに関する確実性.

certificate, *n.* 証明書, 認可証, 免許状.

V ***award certificates*** 証明書を与える. ¶***confer certificate*** on persons 証明書(など)を人に与える. ¶***draw up*** a ***certificate*** 証明書をしたためる. ¶***gain*** a ***certificate*** 免許状を得る. ¶***grant*** (=***give***) ***certificates*** of proficiency 熟練証明書を下付する ‖ ***grant certificates*** to successful candidates 合格者に証明書を与える. ¶***hold*** a ***certificate*** 証明書を所持する. ¶***issue certificates*** for courses completed 修了学科の証明書を出す. 【類】 A ***certificate*** will be ***issued*** to each student successfully passing the examination. ¶***obtain*** a ***certificate*** of incorporation 法人設定の認可証を得る. ¶***reissue*** a ***certificate*** 免許状を再下付する. ¶***rewrite*** a ***certificate*** 免許状を書換える. ¶The driver's ***certificate*** has been ***suspended*** for ... months. 運転免許証が...カ月間停止された.

Q ***medical certificates*** 診断書. ¶a ***provisional certificate*** 仮証書. ¶a ***clearing-house certificate*** 精算所証明書. ¶a ***high-school teaching certificate*** 高校教員免許証. ¶issue an ***import*** (***export***) ***certificate*** 輸入(輸出)許可証を出す. ¶a ***living aid certificate*** 生活援助証明書. ¶a ***military payment certificate*** 軍票. ¶a ***passenger certificate*** 船客証明書. ¶a ***share certificate*** 株券. ¶attend a university for one's ***teaching certificate*** 教員免状をもらうために大学へ通う. ¶a ***transport certificate*** 運送認可証. ¶a ***typhus immunization certificate*** チブス免疫証明書.

Q² an ***allotment certificate*** [株式または債券の]割当証明書.

P² ***certificates for*** middle-school teachers 中等教員免許状. ¶The university issues ***certificates in*** journalism. 同大学は新聞学の修了証書を授与する. ¶a ***certificate of*** commendation 賞状 ‖ a ***certificate of*** examination 受験証(票) ‖ a ***certificate of*** origin (discharge, birth, marriage, death) 身元(解雇, 出生, 結婚, 死亡)証明書 ‖ a ***certificate of*** efficient study 学業優等証 ‖ a ***certificate of*** good conduct 善行証 ‖ a ***certificate of*** seaworthiness (船の)耐航性証明書 ‖ A ***certificate of*** naturalization is granted only to those foreigners who have lived in the United Kingdom for a term of not less than 5 years. 帰化証明書は五ケ年以上英本国に居住した外人にのみ与えられる.

certificate, *v.* 証明する.

M I do ***hereby certificate*** that ... ここに...なることを証明します.

certify, *v.* 証明する；保証する.

M I ***hereby certify*** that ... ...なることを証明します.

P ***certified*** him ***of*** the fact. その事実たることを彼に保証した. ¶***certify*** the fact ***to*** him 彼にその事実たることを証明する ‖ I can ***certify to*** his character. 私は彼の人物を保証することができる.

O ***certify*** it as correct その正確を証明する.

cessation, *n.* 停止, 中止, 断絶.

Q a ***temporary*** (***final***) ***cessation*** of hostilities 一時的の(最後の)休戦. ¶a ***simultaneous cessation*** of work 同時操業中止.

P ***after*** the ***cessation*** of hostilities 終戦後.

P² ***cessation from*** work 休業. ¶the rule of Sunday ***cessation of*** labor 日曜休業の規定 ‖ ***cessation*** of friendship 絶交.

chafe, *n.* いらだち.

P be ***in*** a ***chafe*** いらいらしている.

chafe, *v.* こする, こすれる；じれる, 怒る.

P The rope ***chafes against*** the branch. なわが木の枝ですれる. ‖ The caged bear ***chafes against*** the bars. おりの中のくまが鉄ごうしに体をこする. ‖ The currents ***chafe against*** the rocks. 流れがはげしく岩に当る. ¶He ***chafes at*** (=under) rebuke. 彼は非難されると怒る. 【類】 ***chafe at*** an injustice (insult, a slight, an affront). ¶The rope snapped, having been ***chafed by*** the rough surface. そのざらざらした面ですれたので綱が切れた. ¶The horse ***chafes under*** the check-rein. 馬が手綱で引止められていらだつ. ¶***chafing with*** impatience じれて.

chaff, *n.* もみがら；廃物.

V ***offer chaff*** for grain まがいものをつかませる. ¶***separate*** the ***chaff*** from the wheat 小麦ともみがらを分ける. ¶***sift*** the whole ***chaff*** to find a few grains 〘比ゆ〙わずかの利益を得ようと大骨を折る.

P I am too old ***for chaff***. だまされるような青二才じゃない. ¶An old bird is not caught ***with chaff***. 〘比ゆ〙年の功を積んだ者は容易にだまされない.

P² That is old ***chaff for*** such as we. おれたちなんかその手は食わない.

chaff, *n.* 《俗》からかい.

V They have the pluck to ***stand*** the ***chaff*** of their companions. 彼らには仲間のからかいを忍ぶだけの勇気がある.

chaffer, *v.* 値切る.

P ***chaffer about*** (=***of***) the price 値切る. ¶They never ***chaffer with*** tradespeople. 彼らは決して商人を値切らない.

chagrin, *n.* 残念.

V ***had*** the ***chagrin*** of failing to ... ...する事ができなかったのが口惜しかった.

P much ***to*** my ***chagrin*** 心外なことには.

P² feel ***chagrin at*** the sight of ... ...を見て残念に思う. 【類】 He felt deep ***chagrin at*** his failure.

chagrin, *v.* 残念がらせる.

P He was *chagrined at* his failure (disappointment). 彼は失敗(など)を残念がった.

chain, *n.* 鎖, 連鎖; 束縛.

V ***build up*** a ***chain*** of stores (=chain stores) 連鎖店をつくる. ¶***burst*** the ***chain*** of conversation 話を途切らせる. ¶***run*** a ***chain*** of stores (hotels) 連鎖式の商店(など)を経営する. ¶***undo*** the ***chain*** 鎖を解く.

Q a ***mysterious*** and ***inexplicable chain*** of events 不思議な説明しがたい事件の連続.

Q² an ***Albert chain*** アルバート鎖(時計の). ¶the ***Kurile chain*** 千島列島. ¶***mooring chains*** 繋船鎖. ¶carry one's gold watch ***on*** (=***upon***) a ***silver chain*** 銀鎖をつけた金時計を携帯する. ¶hang it on a ***watch chain*** それを時計の鎖に下げる ‖ He wears it at his ***watch chain***. 彼はそれを時計の鎖につけている.

P a pier supported ***by chains*** 鎖で支えてあるさん橋. ¶prisoners ***in chains*** 鎖につながれた囚人たち ‖ books ***in chains*** (中世紀の)鎖でつないだ書物 ‖ He was ***in chains*** and disgrace. 彼は縛(ばく)と屈辱の身であった. ‖ They were brought to the police station ***in chains***. 彼らは鎖につながれて警察へひっぱられた. ‖ a link ***in*** the ***chain*** of evidence 連鎖をなす証拠中の一つ. ¶a bridge suspended ***on chains*** 鎖式のつり橋.

P² a ***chain of*** hills (mountains) 山脈 ‖ a ***chain of*** thoughts 次々と浮ぶ考え. 【類】a ***chain of*** events (accidents).

chain, *v.* 鎖でつなぐ; 束縛する.

M² They ***chained*** him ***down***. 彼らは彼を鎖でつないだ. ¶***Chain up*** the dog! 犬を鎖でつないでおけ.

P ***chain*** a dog ***to*** a post 犬を柱につなぐ ‖ He is ***chained to*** his work. 彼は仕事にしばられている.

chair, *n.* いす; 講座; 議長席, 議長.

V The speaker ***abandoned*** the ***chair***. 議長は辞職した. ¶They ***drew*** their ***chairs*** about the fire. 彼らは炉辺へいすを進めた. 【類】***draw*** the ***chair*** nearer. ¶***draw up*** a ***chair*** to the hearth 炉辺にいすを進める. 【類】Please ***draw*** your ***chair up*** to the fire. ¶***establish*** the ***chair*** of Japanese Literature and Life at our Alma Mater われわれの母校に日本文学の講座を設ける. 【類】***establish*** a Shinto ***Chair*** in the Imperial University / ***establish*** a ***chair*** of French, to be called the Marshal Foch Professorship of French Literature. ¶***filled*** the ***chair*** of English literature in the Imperial University 帝国大学英文学の講座を担当した. 【類】***fill*** the ***chair*** of Astronomer Royal (王立科学協会天文台長の職) / the ***chair*** of the President, made vacant by the death of..., was ***filled*** by ... ¶the ***chair*** was ***founded*** by a gift of the late Mrs. ... その講座は故…夫人の寄付によって創設したものである. ¶Go and ***get*** a ***chair*** for him. あの方のお掛けになるいすを持っておいで. ¶***Have*** your ***chair***. [いすに]お掛けなさい. ¶He ***holds*** the ***Chair*** of Sanscrit. サンスクリットの講座を担当しておられる. 【類】He ***held*** a ***chair*** in industrial geography (産業地理). ¶***hunt*** a new ***chair*** 新らしい口(職)をさがす. ¶He still ***kept*** his ***chair***. 彼はいすから立たないでいた. ¶***leave*** (=***resign***) the ***chair*** of editorship 主筆のいすを去る. ¶***obtain*** the ***chair*** of medicine in a university 大学で医学の講座を受持つことになる. ¶***occupy*** the presidential ***chair*** of the university その大学総長のいすをしめる ‖ He ***occupies*** the ***Chair*** of Comparative Philology at the University of Oxford. 彼はオクスフォード大学で比較言語学の講座を受持っている. 【類】he ***occupies*** the ***chair*** of mathematics at the University of ... ‖ He will ***occupy*** the ***chair*** much better than I have done. 彼は僕よりもはるかによく講義をやるだろう. ¶***offer*** a person a ***chair*** 人に席を勧める ‖ He was ***offered*** the ***chair*** of natural science. 彼は自然科学の講座担当の申入れを受けた. ¶Janitors had to ***put*** extra ***chairs*** in the aisles of my lecture room. [聴衆が多いので]小使たちが私の講義室の通路に余分のいすを入れなければならなかった. ¶He ***received*** a ***chair*** at the Berlin University. 彼はベルリン大学の講座に招へいされた. ¶***resign*** one's ***chair*** 講座(または役)を辞する. ¶***take*** the ***chair*** 議長席につく; 議事を始める. 【類】He has ***taken*** the ***chair*** at the conference. ¶***take*** the ***chair*** of presidency 総長(社長)のいすに着く ‖ ***take*** the ***chair*** for the Italian **language** イタリア語の講座を受持つ. ¶***twirl*** a ***chair*** いすを(コマのように)回す.

Q Mr. A. Barton Hepburn, a New York banker, gave 100,000 yen for establishment of an ***American chair*** in the Imperial University of Tokyo. ニューヨークの銀行家エー・バートン・ヘプバーン氏は東京帝国大学に米国講座創設のため十万円を寄贈した. ¶an ***auxiliary*** (=***extra***) ***chair*** 補助いす. ¶a ***cozy chair*** かけ心地のよいいす. ¶***creaking chairs*** きーきー音のするいす. ¶***easy chairs*** worthy of their name 名実備った安楽いす(地位). ¶the ***editorial chair*** 主筆の職. ¶send a culprit to the ***electric chair*** 罪人を電気いすに送る(死刑に処する). ¶an ***empty chair*** 空(から)いす. ¶***folding chairs*** 折畳式いす. ¶the holder of an ***endowed chair*** in the University 同大学で寄付による講座の保持者. ¶sit in a ***low chair*** 低いいすに腰掛ける. ¶a ***professor's*** (=***professorial***) ***chair*** 講座. ¶a restful ***reclining chair*** 安楽なより掛りいす. ¶a ***rickety chair*** ぐらぐらするいす. ¶a ***revolving chair*** 回転いす. ¶a ***rocking chair*** 揺りいす. ¶a ***shaky chair*** しっかりしないいす. ¶There is a ***special Chair*** of Seismology in the University of Tokyo. 東京大学に地震学の特別講座がある. ¶I want a ***steady chair*** to sit upon. しっかりしたいすが欲しい. ¶a ***stuffed*** (=***upholstered***) ***chair*** つめものをしたいす. ¶This ***chair*** is ***unsteady***. このいすはしっかりしていない.

Q² be seated in an ***arm chair*** ひじ掛けいすに掛けている. ¶a little ***baby chair*** 小さい赤ん坊いす. ¶a ***bath chair*** 病人用車輪付いす. ¶a ***beach chair*** 海浜用いす. ¶a ***bent-wood chair*** 曲木細工のいす. ¶a ***camp chair*** キャンプ用いす. ¶a ***cane chair*** とういす. ¶a ***cane-bottom chair*** 座部を籐(とう)で作ったいす. ¶a ***comfort chair*** 安楽いす. ¶a ***deck chair*** 甲板のいす. ¶a ***divan chair*** 長いす. ¶a ***kitchen chair*** 台所いす. ¶settle down in a ***lounge chair*** 寝いすに横たわる. ¶***operating chairs*** 手術いす. ¶The ***philosophy chair*** is vacant. 哲学の講座が欠員になっている. ¶a ***sedan chair*** かご. ¶a ***spring-seat chair*** 発条(ばね)付いす. ¶a ***swivel chair*** 回転いす. ¶a ***weighing chair*** 秤量いす. ¶a ***wheel chair*** 車つきのいす. ¶brought to the ***witness chair*** 証人として出廷する.

P He rose ***from*** his ***chair***. 彼はいすから立上がった. ‖ They dismissed him ***from*** his ***chair*** at the University. 大学における彼の職を解いた. ¶sit ***in*** a ***chair*** いすに掛ける. 【類】Sit down ***in*** this ***chair***, please. / sit back (そり身になって) ***in*** one's ***chair*** / Are you comfortable ***in*** that ***chair?*** ‖ A meeting was held, Lord Lytton ***in*** the ***chair***. リットン卿が座長席について開会した. 【類】with Mr.— ***in*** the ***chair***. ¶sink ***into*** a ***chair*** いすにぐったり身を沈める ‖ sit ***into*** a ***chair*** 深くいすにかける. ¶He fell ***off*** the ***chair***. 彼はいすから落ちた. ¶He is ***on*** the ***chair***. 彼はいすに掛けている. ‖ stand ***on*** a ***chair*** いすの上に立つ ‖ sit [down] ***on*** a ***chair*** いすに腰掛ける ‖ sit up ***on*** a ***chair*** いすにきちんとすわる. ¶He was nominated ***to*** the ***chair*** of Philosophy. 彼は哲学講座担任を命ぜられた.

P² He was appointed to a ***chair for*** organic chemistry. 彼は有機化学の講座担任を命ぜられた. ¶a ***chair of*** oak かしのいす.

chairman, *n.* 議長, 座長.

V The commission ***elects*** a ***chairman*** from its members. 委員会は議長を互選する.

Q² a ***bank board chairman*** 銀行理事長. ¶a ***commission chairman*** 調査委員長. ¶a ***committee chairman*** 委員会の議長. ¶a ***deputy chairman*** 議長代理. ¶an ***ex officio chairman*** of ... …の職権による議長. ¶a ***parade chairman*** 街頭行列の指揮者. ¶a ***Party chairman*** 党首.

P He was ***chairman of*** the meeting. 彼はその会の座長であった. ‖ the ***chairman of*** the science department (大学の)理学部長.

chairmanship, *n.* 議長格; 議(座)長の職.

V ***accept*** the ***chairmanship*** of a congress 会議の議長たることを受諾する.

Q one's ***four years' chairmanship*** 四年にわたる議長の地位.

P ***under*** the ***chairmanship*** of ... = with ... in the chair ... を議長として ‖ create a committee ***under*** the ***chairmanship*** of ... …を委員長にして委員会を設ける.

chalk, *n.* チョーク, 白墨.

V ***walk chalks*** 甲板を歩く(デッキに白墨で二線を引きその中を歩かせて船員が酔っているかどうかを試験するための).

P write ***in*** red ***chalk*** 赤チョークで書く. 【類】a blackboard covered with writings ***in chalk***. ¶a piece ***of chalk*** チョーク一本. ¶mark ***with chalk*** 白墨で記号をつける.

chalk, *v.* 白墨で書く.

M ***chalk out*** チョークで輪郭を描く; 設計する.

M² *chalk* ***down*** on the blackboard 黒板にチョークで書く. ¶*chalk* ***up*** 信用貸をする(白墨で壁上に計算記号を記すところから来た句).

P *chalk* it ***on*** a board それを白墨で板の上に書く.

challenge, *n.* 挑戦, 決闘状; 請求; 要求.

V ***accept*** a *challenge* 挑戦に応じる ‖ ***accept*** a *challenge* for £50 五十ポンドのかけに応じる. ¶***give*** a *challenge* 戦をいどむ. ¶***issue*** a public *challenge* offering money to anyone who can prove it 懸賞で一般からその証明を求める ‖ ***issue*** one's *challenge* to the world 世間に対して挑戦状を発する. ¶in his anger he ***sent*** a *challenge* to ... 激怒のあまり…に決闘を申込んだ. ¶***take up*** the *challenge* 挑戦に応じる.

Q Into her eyes had come a ***hostile*** *challenge*. その時敵対のそぶりが彼女の目に現われていた. ¶***peremptory*** *challenge* 専断的忌避権.

P be ***beyond*** *challenge* 文句がつけられない. ¶***on*** a *challenge* of £50 五十ポンドのかけで ‖ I'll take you up ***on*** that *challenge*. お相手仕ろう. ¶She looked at me ***with*** *challenge*. 彼は挑発的に私を見やった.

P² *challenge* ***to*** jurors 陪審員に対する忌避 ‖ a *challenge* ***to*** a duel 決闘の挑戦.

challenge, *v.* 挑戦する; 誰何(すいか)する.

P *challenge* him ***for*** lying うそをついたかどで彼にけんかを吹き掛ける ‖ *challenge* ***for*** the Davis Cup デ杯戦に出場する. ¶*challenge* a person ***to*** a fight (combat, game, duel) 人に戦い(など)をいどむ. ¶The sentinel *challenged* us ***with*** 'Who comes there?' 番兵は「だれだ」といってわれわれに詰問した.

chamber, *n.* へや, 室.

Q a ***black*** *chamber* 機密室. ¶the ***lower*** (***upper***) *chamber* 下(上)院. ¶a ***secret*** *chamber* 秘密室, あかずの間. ¶a ***sick*** *chamber* 病室.

Q² an ***audience*** *chamber* 謁見室. ¶a ***death*** *chamber* 死者のいる室. ¶a ***presence*** *chamber* 謁見室. ¶a ***torture*** *chamber* 拷問べや.

P² the *chamber* ***of*** commerce 商業会議所 ‖ the *Chamber* ***of*** Councillors 参議院 ‖ the *Chamber* ***of*** Deputies 《フランス》国民議会.

champ=champion.

Q² a ***golf*** *champ* ゴルフの優勝者. ¶a amateur ***sumo wrestling*** *champ* 素人ずもうの優勝者.

champion, *n.* 戦士, 闘士, 勇士; [優勝]選手.

Q an ***able*** and ***unselfish*** *champion* 腕ききで無欲の勇士. ¶a ***bold*** *champion* 大胆な闘士. ¶a ***fearless*** *champion* of reform 大胆な革命の闘士. ¶an ***honorary*** *champion* 張出し大関. ¶***loud*** *champions* of the traditional principles of loyalty and filial piety 忠孝両道の勇敢な闘士. ¶a ***zealous*** *champion* 熱心な闘士.

Q² a ***table-tennis*** *champion* ピンポンの(優勝)選手.

P² a *champion* ***against*** oppressor (injustice) 圧制者(など)と戦う勇士. ¶a *champion* ***for*** people (justice) 民衆(など)のために戦う勇士. ¶a *champion* ***in*** quality (low price) 品質(など)の大関 ‖ the *champion* ***in*** baseball 野球の優勝チーム. ¶a heroic figure of the *champion* ***of*** the oppressed people しいたげられた人々の雄々しい擁護者. 【類】a *champion* ***of*** liberty ‖ He was *champion* ***of*** the show. 彼は一座の花形であった.

championship, *n.* 選手権.

V ***gain*** (=***win***) a *championship* 選手権を得る. ¶He ***holds*** the tennis *championship* to the school. 彼は同校の庭球選手権を保持している. 【類】He ***holds*** the British *championship*. ¶***lose*** a *championship* 選手権を失う. ¶***regain*** a *championship* 選手権を再び獲得する. ¶***retain*** a *championship* 選手権を保持する. ¶***wrest*** the world's *championship* from ... …から世界選手権を奪い取る.

Q² capture the Intercollegiate ***baseball*** *championship* for 1955 一九五五年度の大学対抗野球選手権を獲得する. ¶win the world's ***speed typewriter*** *championship* タイプライター競技の世界選手権を得る. ¶the free-style wrestling ***world*** *championship* 自由型レスリング世界選手権.

chance, *n.* 偶然, ぎょうこう; 勝算, 見込, 機会.

V ***claim*** the *chance* その機会を要望する. ¶***diminish*** the *chance* of ... …する機会を少くする. ¶whenever I ***get*** a *chance* 機会さえあれば. ¶***give*** him a *chance* for ... 彼に…の機会を与える ‖ It will ***give*** me a *chance* to get even. それで私が返報する機会が得られる. 【類】didn't ***give*** him a *chance* to say a word. ¶Personality ***has*** *chance* against "pursenality." 人格は財布より勝ち目がある(語ろにおもしろ味がある). ‖ He may ***have*** a *chance* to become the principal. 彼が校長になるかも知れない. 【類】He still ***has*** a *chance* of success. / when I ***have*** a *chance* ‖ I ***have*** no *chance* against him. 彼にはとても勝てそうもない. ¶The movement ***holds out*** a fair *chance* of ultimate success. その運動は最後に成功しうる見込が結構ある. ¶A good knowledge of English will ***improve*** their *chances* of employment. 英語がよくできると彼らが就職する機会を増すことになるだろう. ¶His excellent result at school ***increased*** his *chance* of appointment. 彼の学校における成績が就職に有利であった. ¶***let*** the *chance* ***go*** その機会を逃がす. 【類】***let go*** a good *chance*. ¶The *chance* is ***lost*** of his going abroad. 彼の洋行の機会はなくなった. ¶He ***missed*** his *chance* for a niche in the Temple of Fame. 不朽の名誉を残す機会を失った. ‖ I cannot afford to ***miss*** the *chance*. この機を逸するわけにはいかない. ¶It ***offers*** little *chance* of success. それはほとんど成功の見込がない. ¶***reduce*** the *chances* of ... …の見込が薄らぐ. ¶***risk*** a *chance* 一か八かやって見る. ¶***run*** the *chance* of ... …の運だめしをやって見る. ¶He ***saw*** his *chance*. 彼はやるなら今だと思った. ‖ I ***see*** no *chance* of its success. それはうまく行きそうもない. ‖ Run the blockade if you ***see*** any *chance*. 機会を見つけたら封鎖を突破しなさい. ¶***sound out*** his *chances* of election 彼に当選できるかどうか探りを入れる. ¶Just what sort of girl ***stands*** the best *chance* in pictures today? 今日の映画界でどんな女が一番成功の見込がありますか. ‖ in order to ***stand*** some *chance* against ... …と対立して幾分有利となるために ‖ If you want to ***stand*** a *chance* in competition with people of such training, you must look to your own equipment. そうした訓練を経た人たちと競争して勝ちたいなら君自身の実力養成を心がけなくてはならない. 【類】***stand*** a good *chance* of carrying off (獲得する) the prize / This ideal ***stands*** a good *chance* of realization. ¶***take*** their *chance* in the Civil Service 文官の方面に進出して見る ‖ ***take*** a *chance* [一か八か]やって見る ‖ Don't ***take*** *chances!* 危ないことはするな. ‖ I will ***take*** my *chance* of finding him at home. いるかどうか一つ行って見よう. ‖ He ***took*** his *chance* of gaining admission into one of them. 彼は両天びんをかけてどっちか(の学校)に入ろうとした. ¶***throw away*** one's *chance* 機会を放棄する. ¶He ***tried*** his *chance*. 彼は運試しをした. ¶***widen*** your *chance* of appointment 君の就職の機会を増す. ¶***wreck*** one's *chances* in life 出世の見込をぶちこわす.

V² if happy *chances* ***serve*** 運がよければ.

Q cut them off from ***all*** *chance* of retreat 彼らの退路をしゃ断する. ¶by ***any*** *chance* ひょっとして, 万一. 【類】if by ***any*** *chances* ... ¶A poor boy has by far the ***best*** *chance* of becoming a millionaire. 貧しい少年は富豪になるためのはるかによい機会がある. ¶Patients have a far ***better*** *chance* of recovery when treated in that way. 患者はそういう治療を受けるとずっと回復の見込がつく. ¶a matter of ***blind*** *chance* 全くの運. ¶a ***capital*** *chance* 絶好のチャンス. ¶There is no ***earthly*** *chance* for her to recover. 彼女が回復する望みは絶体にない. ¶here is an ***excellent*** *chance* for you to... 今こそ君が…する絶好の機会だ. ¶Give him a ***fair*** *chance*. [発言など]公平な機会を与えてやれ. ‖ Through illness I had not a ***fair*** *chance* in the examination. 病気のため私は試験に及第する十分の見込がなかった. 【類】with ***fair*** *chance* of success. ¶They have no ***fighting*** *chance* of victory. 彼らには勝味がない. ¶a ***fine*** *chance* for American money and enterprise 米国が投資して事業をするには好機会. ¶by a ***fortunate*** *chance* 運よく. ¶offer a ***good*** *chance* to ... …に好機会を与える. 【類】This is a ***good*** *chance* for me to practice speaking. ‖ The custom has a ***good*** *chance* of surviving. その風俗は存続する見込みがある. ¶not once in a ***hundred*** *chances* 百度の中一度も. ¶by ***ill*** *chance* 運悪く. ¶I see very ***little*** *chance* of the railway being opened till Feb. 1. 二月一日までに鉄道が開通する見込はないと思う. ¶a ***lucky*** *chance* has made it possible for me to ... 運が好かったので僕は…することができた. ‖ trust to a ***lucky*** *chance* 万一を頼む ‖ by [a] ***lucky*** (***unlucky***) *chance* 運よく(悪く). ¶He was looking after the ***main*** *chance*. 彼はうまい機会をねらっていた. ¶Our meeting was a ***mere*** *chance*. われわれが出会ったのは全く運が好かったのだ. ‖ by ***mere*** (=***pure***) *chance* ふとした拍子で. 【類】by the ***merest chance***. ¶Among the Alfuras it is the man who has the largest number of heads to show who has ***most chance*** of winning the object of his love. アルフュラ族の間では恋人をわがものとする一番勝味の多いのは最も多数の首(どくろ)を持っている者である. ¶It is ***nine chances*** out of ten against us. 十中の八九勝つ見込がない. ¶have ***no chance*** to ... ...する見込が全然ない. 【類】There is ***no chance*** of his becoming a scholar. ¶He has only ***one chance*** in fifty to make it a success. 彼がそれを成功させることは覚束ない. 【類】it is ***one chance*** in a thousand that ... ¶his ***only chance*** 彼の唯一の機会. ¶by an ***opportune chance*** 拍子よく. ¶He has a ***poor chance*** of getting a promotion. 彼が昇進する見込はとぼしい. ¶The machinery has had no ***proper chance*** to do its work. その機関はこれまでその本領を発揮する機会がなかった. ¶a ***prospective chance*** 前途の見込. ¶There is not the ***remotest chance*** of your catching him up. 君はとても彼に追付けません. ¶I have ***scant chance*** of being picked up. 僕が選抜される見込は少ない. ¶by a ***singular chance*** 偶然. ¶have a ***slender chance*** to ... ...する事は覚束ない. 【類】The *chances* of seeing it published are ***slender***. ¶There is a ***slim chance***, if any, for his success. 彼の成功する見込はまずない. ¶He has ***small chance*** of election. 彼は当選しそうもない. ¶He has ***some chances*** of success. 彼が成功する見込はある. 【類】There is ***some chances*** of his being elected. ‖ by ***some chance*** [or other] ひょっとして, 何かのはずみで. ¶it was a ***thousand chances*** to one that he should ... 彼が...することはまず絶対狂いはなかった.

Q² the ***vote-getting chances*** of candidates 候補者の得票見込.

P He is ***beyond*** a *chance* of recovery. 彼は回復の見込がない. ¶***by chance*** 偶然 ‖ if you, ***by*** any *chance*, know it ひょっとして君がそれを知っておれば. 【類】I met him ***by*** *chance* (ひょっくり). ¶I bought it ***on chance***. 山(一か八か)で買って見た. ‖ ***on*** the *chance* of ... うまく行けば...ということになるので. ‖ I offer the information ***on*** the *chance* that it may prove useful. 何か御参考になりはしないかと存じましてこれを申上げるのです. 【類】I mention this ***on*** the *chance* that it may be of some value. / I append (添える) the results ***on*** the *chance* that they may be of some use. / I came ***on*** the *chance* that I might find you at home. / I waited at the station ***on*** the *chance* of meeting him. ¶***owing to*** a lucky *chance* 運がよかったので. ¶***through*** sheer *chance* 全くのぎょうこうで. ¶leave nothing ***to*** *chance* 万全を期する. ¶He has undertaken the work ***with*** some *chance* of success. 彼は幾分成功の見込があってその仕事をやり出した.

P² Here is a *chance* ***for*** you. 君にはこれは好い機会だ. ‖ His *chances* ***for*** recovery are favorable. 彼は回復する見込がある. ‖ Do you think there might be a *chance* ***for*** me in Hollywood? ハリウッドで何か私にやれるでしょうか. ¶the *chance* ***of*** winning 勝つ見込み. 【類】*chances* ***of*** success or failure are affeced by the fact that ...

O a *chance* to see foreign countries 外国を見物する機会. ¶The *chances* are that he will fail. 多分彼は失敗するだろう. ‖ The *chances* that he will succeed are at least fifty to one. 彼には少なくも一に対する五十の成功率がある.

chance, *v*. 偶然起る; 運任せにやる, 万一をあてにする.

M Should I ***ever chance*** to have another, I will give you one. 万一もう一つ手に入れたら一つ君にあげよう.

P *chance on* (=*upon*) a passage in a book 書物の中である文句に偶然出くわす ‖ *chance* ***on*** a beautiful woman 偶然美人に会う.

O should there *chance* to be a fire tonight もし今夜火事があったら. ¶I *chanced* to be there. 僕は偶然そこに居合わせた. 【類】I *chanced* to meet (=fell in with) him.

chancellor, *n*. 《英》大官; [ドイツの]首相.

P the *Chancellor* of the Exchequer 大蔵卿. ¶Konrad Adenauer, *Chancellor* of Western Germany. 西独首相コンラート・アデナウアー.

chandelier, *n*. シャンデリヤ.

Q² a ***crystal*** *chandelier* クリスタルガラス製のシャンデリヤ.

change, *n*. (**1**) 変化, 運動, 変遷; 乗換; 更衣; 転地.

V Momentous *changes* have been ***accomplished***. 重大な改変が実行された. ¶***bring about*** *changes* 変動を生じる. 【類】***bring about*** great *changes*. ¶***carry out*** *changes* 変更を実行する. ¶It ***caused*** a sudden *change* of feeling in financial circles. それが財界に急激な感情の変化を引起した. ¶many *changes* have been ***effected*** in ... ...に幾多の変化をきたした. 【類】It will ***effect*** no *change* of importance. / ***effect*** a *change* of government (政変). ¶It ***entailed*** such *changes*. そのためにかかる変化が生じた. ¶the *change* will be ***hailed*** with delight by ... この変化は...によって喜び迎えられるだろう. ¶***inaugurate*** a great *change* 一大改革を行う. ¶***initiate*** a *change* 変更する. ¶***introduce*** a *change* 改変を行う. ¶***make*** a *change* at a junction 乗換場(分岐点)で乗換える ‖ Here a *change* is ***made*** into a connecting train. ここで連絡する列車に乗換える. ‖ ***make*** a *change* in a schedule (program) 計画(など)の一部変更をする ‖ ***make*** a *change* for the worse 悪変する. 【類】it will ***make*** no *change* in ... / ***make*** a *change* in the system of ... ¶Here is one hundred yen, never ***mind*** the *change*. 百円置いて行く, 釣銭は要りません. ¶***notify*** a *change* of address 住所の変更を通知する. ¶When a *change* of address is ***ordered***, both the new and the old address must be given. 住所変更を通知せられる場合には必ず新旧住所を併記して下さい. ¶A great *change* will certainly be ***produced*** in the world's communications. 世界の交通に大変動をきたすに相違ない. ¶The *change* will soon be ***put*** into effect. その変更は近々実施されるでしょう. ¶***require*** *change* 釣銭がいる. ¶***ring*** the *changes* [一そろいの鐘の]それぞれの音色を出す; 同一のことを色々に説く(色々なやり方をする). ¶***seek*** a *change* of climate from the raw air of ... ...の冷湿な空気を避けて転地しようとする. ¶a map ***showing*** recent boundary *changes* 最近の国境変更を示す地図. ¶***start*** *changes* 変化を起す. ¶***suffer*** a *change* 変化を受ける. ¶***take*** a *change* of air for one's health 保養のため転地する. ¶This town has ***undergone*** great *changes*. この町は大層変った. ‖ ***undergo*** a *change* of heart 心変りがする. ¶***view***, in retrospect, the *changes* during the past thirty years 過去三十年間の変遷を回顧する. ¶***want*** *change* for a dollar 一ドルだけ小銭が欲しい ‖ She ***wants*** a *change* of scene. 彼女は転地する必要がある. ¶The twentieth century has ***witnessed*** a remarkable *change*. 二十世紀には顕著な変化があった. ¶***work*** radical *changes* in social and political life 社会および政治生活に根本的改革をきたす. ¶the *changes* ***wrought*** in ... ...に及ぼす変化 ‖ He ***wrought*** a great *change* in the spirit of his age. 彼は時代精神に一大革新を与えた. ¶***work out*** social *changes* 社会的革新を実行する.

V² A *change* is now ***coming*** over public feeling in regard to the abortionist. 堕胎者への世人の感情に今や変動が起りつつある. ¶the *changes* which have ***taken place*** in the intervening years その間に起った変化.

Q an ***abrupt*** *change* in weather 天候の急変. ¶It wrought ***amazing*** (=***astounding***) *changes*. それは驚くべき変化を招来した. ¶make scarcely ***any*** *changes* in the personnel 職員はほとんど変らない. ¶undergo a ***complete*** *change* 全く一変する. ¶undergo a ***considerable*** *change* 著しい変化をこうむる ‖ A ***considerable*** *change* has come on his behavior. 彼の様子が大いに変って来た. ¶a ***cultural*** *change* between ... ...間の文化の交流. ¶a ***dark*** *change* (舞台の)暗転. ¶The weather has made a ***desirable*** *change*. 天気が好い方へ変った. ¶Such a ***drastic*** *change* as this must have far-reaching effects. こういう激しい変化はその影響が広はんにわたるに相違ない. ¶revolutions and ***dynastic*** *changes* in China 中国の革命や王朝の改変. ¶an ***economic*** *change* for the better 経済上の好転. ¶an ***entire*** *change* 全般にわたる変化. ¶The bill was passed without ***essential*** *change*. その案は根本的の改変なしに通過した. ¶There is a ***favorable*** (an ***unfavorable***) *change* in the market (weather). 市況(など)が好い(悪い)方に向った. ¶***fitful*** *changes* 気まぐれの変更. ¶the ***fourth*** *change* in the programme. 四の替りの出し物. ¶a most ***grateful*** *change* after ... ...の揚句実にありがたい変化. ¶This is one of the ***greatest*** *changes* that characterize New Japan. これは新日本の特性を表わす最大改変の一つである. ¶This effected (=produced) an ***instant*** *change*. このためにたちまち変動が生じた. ¶***kaleidoscopic*** *changes* 百色眼鏡のような(目まぐるしい)変化. ¶it has seen ***many*** *changes* of owners since ... それは...以来持主が何度も変った. ¶a ***marked*** *change* 顕著

な変化. ¶a ***mighty*** *change* 一大変化. ¶a ***ministerial*** *change* 内閣の更迭. ¶make a ***momentous*** *change* 重大な改変を行う. ¶produce ***much*** *change* 非常な変化をきたす. ¶bring about the ***necessary*** *changes* 必要な変革をきたす. ¶***No*** *change* to report. 別条なし. ¶a ***political*** *change* 政変. ¶***quick*** *changes* of temperature 気温の急変. ¶a ***radical*** *change* in the system of government 政治組織の根本改革. ¶a ***rapid*** *change* of weather 天候の急変. ¶***refreshing*** *change* すがすがしい変化(更). ¶find a ***restful*** *change* from work and worries 仕事や心配を離れて落着いた休息を得る. ¶a ***salutary*** (=***wholesome***) *change* 健全な(危険性のない)変化. ¶a ***slight*** *change* 小変化. ¶***undergo*** ***substantial*** *changes* 大変化を来す. ¶a ***sudden*** *change* in the weather 天候の急変. ¶***sweeping*** *changes* in local governorships 地方官の大更迭. ¶***three*** *changes* of dress (=raiment) 三通りの着替. ¶a ***violent*** *change* from ... to ... ...から...への激変. ¶a ***welcome*** *change* 喜ばしい変化. ¶a ***world-historic*** *change* 世界史上に特筆すべき変化.

Q² a ***border*** *change* 境界の変更. ¶a ***Cabinet*** *change* 内閣更迭. ¶***color*** *change* 色彩の変化. ¶a ***currency*** *change* 通貨の変更. ¶by a ***last-minute*** *change* of program 間際になって番組を変更して. ¶effect a ***lightning*** *change* in ... 抜き打ち的に...を変更する. ¶a ***location*** *change* of ... from ... ...から...への移転. ¶a ***name*** *change* 改名. ¶a ***personnel*** *change* 職員変更. ¶Cargos suffer a ***sea*** *change*. 船荷は海運のいたみが出る. ¶***summer address*** *change* 夏季の住所変更. ¶a ***surface*** *change* 表面の変化. ¶interim ***wage*** *change* 暫定賃金変更. ¶a ***wind*** *change* 風の変り.

P ***after*** several *changes* of residence 五六度居住を変えた揚句に. ¶women ***at*** the *change* of life 更年期の女 ‖ ***at*** the *change* of seasons 陽気の替り目に. ¶***by*** a *change* of wind 風が変ったので. ¶go ***for*** a *change* of air 転地する ‖ I ordered buckwheat just ***for*** a *change*. 今日はちょっといつもと変えてそばを注文した. ‖ We have ridden for an hour; let us walk ***for*** a *change*. 一時間乗ったから今度は歩こう. ¶***On*** *change* of residence, members will oblige by giving notice thereof to the secretary. 会員各位ご移転の節はそのむね当会幹事まで御通知下さい. ¶***with*** no (=without any) *change* of clothes (=garments) 着物も着替えずに ‖ ***with*** *change* of names sufficient to disguise them 身分を他人に知られないように変名して. ¶***without*** *change* of cars 乗換えずに.

P² a *change* ***by*** oxidation 酸化作用による変化. ¶a *change* ***for*** the better 好転. 【類】a great *change* ***for*** the better (worse). ¶the *change* ***from*** winter ***to*** spring 冬から春への推移. 【類】the *change* ***from*** wealth ***to*** poverty swiftly made / the *change* ***from*** steam operation ***to*** electric traction (電力牽引) / the *change* ***from*** heat ***to*** cold. ¶a *change* ***in*** policy (management, address) 政策(など)の変化. 【類】a *change* ***in*** one's personal condition (一身上) / a *change* ***in*** the cover design (表紙の意匠) of a magazine ‖ a *change* ***in*** judges 判事の更迭. 【類】the *change* ***in*** the ownership (所有権) of ... / *changes* ***in*** personnel (職員) / a *change* ***in*** a plan / Telegraph wherever there is a *change* ***in*** the market. / a *change* ***in*** administration (内閣) / *changes* ***in*** temperature (the weather). ¶There will be a *change* ***of*** Cabinet after his return from abroad. 彼の帰朝後に内閣の更迭があろう. 【類】a *change* ***of*** popular sentiment (民衆の感情) in England ‖ *change* ***of*** entry (帳簿記入の)更正 ‖ *change* ***of*** pace 〘野〙球速変化 ‖ *change* ***of*** proprietors 代替り. 【類】a *change* ***of*** diet (食物) ‖ a *change* ***of*** carriages 乗換 ‖ The *change* ***of*** life, sometimes briefly called "the change," occurs from forty-five or fifty or thereabout. 時に略して「変化」といっている人体の変化(更年期)は四十五ないし五十歳ごろに起る. 【類】a *change* ***of*** life—for example, a happy marriage / *change* ***of*** seasons ‖ He is in need of *change* ***of*** scene and interest. 彼は場所や気持を転換させる必要がある. ¶the *change* ***of*** water ***into*** steam 水の蒸発.

(2) 釣銭, 小銭.

V ***count out*** the *change* 釣を数えて出す. ¶Please ***examine*** your *change* before leaving the counter. 勘定台で釣銭をお調べ下さい. ¶***get*** *change* 釣銭をもらう. ¶***Give*** me the *change* in notes (silver). 札(など)で釣を下さい. ‖ No *change* ***given***. 釣銭御断り. ¶***give back*** the *change* 釣銭を出す. ¶***Keep*** the *change*. つりはいらない. ¶Here is ten yen. Never ***mind*** the *change!* はい十円. つりはいらない. ¶***return*** the proper *change* 釣銭を間違いなく出す.

Q in ***small*** *change* 小銭で ‖ ***small*** *change* in copper and silver 銅貨や銀貨の小銭. 【類】I have no ***small*** *change*. / Everyday phrases are a very handy kind of conversational ***small*** *change*.

Q² give a person ***fifty yen*** *change* 五十円釣銭を出す.

P He is ***above*** small *change*. 彼は少しのつりなど目もくれない. ¶I received fifty yen ***in*** *change*. おつりに五十円受取った. 【類】give 25 yen ***in*** *change* to ... ¶Can you give me *change* ***for*** a 1,000-yen note? 千円札でおつりがもらえますか.

change, *v.* 変える, 改める; 変る, 改まる; 交換する; 乗換える.

M *change* ***back*** into ... ...に逆戻りする. ¶Public speaking has *changed* ***considerably*** in method during the last two decades. この二十年の間に公開演説のやり方は著しく変った. ¶*change* ***here*** for ... ...行きはここで乗換える. ¶*change* ***markedly*** in color 色彩が著しく変る ‖ be *changed* ***noticeably*** 著しく変る. ¶The railways between Florence and Naples have *changed* ***over from*** steam ***to*** electricity. フロレンス・ナポリ間の鉄道は電化した. ¶*change* ***radically*** 根本的に変る. ¶*change* ***there*** for another train そこで乗りかえる.

P *change* (carriages) ***at*** a rail-junction 連絡駅で乗換える. 【類】*change* ***at*** ... for (行きは)... / Passengers for Takasaki *change* ***at*** Oyama. / *change* ***at*** ... into another train (別の汽車に). ¶The place has *changed* ***beyond*** recognition. その土地は見分けがつかないほどに変った. ¶The policy has *changed* ***by*** the course of events. その方針が世の中の推移で変った. ¶*change* (clothes) ***for*** dinner 食事のために着替えをする ‖ *change* banknotes ***for*** silver 紙幣を銀貨に替える ‖ She *changed* Miss ***for*** Mrs. 彼女は奥様になった. ‖ *change* shillings ***for*** (=***into***) pounds シリングをポンドに換算する ‖ *change* a home toilet ***for*** a street dress 平常着を外出着に着換える ‖ The weather has *changed* ***for*** the better (worse). 天気は持ち直した(悪くなった). 【類】My fortune has *changed* ***for*** the better. ¶a *change* ***from*** city life 都会生活からの逃避(息抜き) ‖ *change* ***from*** one shape ***into*** another ある形状から他の形状に変る ‖ She *changed* ***from*** gray ***to*** grave. 白髪の老婆となって亡くなった. ¶*change* ***from*** a caterpillar ***to*** (=***into***) a butterfly 毛虫からちょうに変る. 【類】His hair *changed* ***from*** black ***to*** white in a single night. / *change* ***from*** inefficiency ***to*** efficiency ‖ Our address has been *changed* ***from*** ... ***to*** ..., and I would appreciate it if you would change your mailing list accordingly. 私たちの住所は...から...へ変更致しましたから貴方の郵送名簿を御変更おきくだされば幸甚に存じます. 【類】*change* one's name ***from*** ... ***to*** ... ¶*change* ***into*** a Ryogoku car 両国行電車に乗換える. 【類】*change* ***into*** an electric car for ... (...行きの電車) ‖ I *changed* ***into*** flannels. 私はフランネルに着替えた. ‖ *change* one's yen ***into*** dollars 円をドルに両替する ‖ had power to *change* ***into*** different shapes 変化できた ‖ *change* ***into*** a woman 女に化ける. 【類】A caterpillar (毛虫) *changes* ***into*** (=to) a butterfly. / Water is *changed* ***into*** steam by heat. ‖ A fox *changed* itself ***into*** a human form. きつねが人間に化けた. ¶*change* ***like*** the leopard's spots ひょう変する. ¶The meeting has been *changed* ***to*** Monday. 会は月曜日に変更になった. ‖ the name has been *changed* ***to*** ... 名が...に変った ‖ During the night the rain *changed* ***to*** snow. 夜の間に雨が雪に変った. ¶*change* ***to*** a higher class car 上級乗換えする ‖ *change* ***to*** another ship 他の船に乗換える ‖ *change* sentences ***to*** indirect discourse 〘文法〙文を間接話法に変える. 【類】*change* the passive voice ***to*** the active. ¶*change* ***with*** the season 季節(時)の移り変りと共に変る ‖ *change* ***with*** the times (=ages) 時勢に順応する. 【類】Times change and we should *change* ***with*** them. ‖ *change* places (things) ***with*** a person 人と場所(など)を取替える ‖ *change* letters ***with*** a foreign friend 外国の友人と手紙のやりとりをする ‖ *change* old ***with*** new 古きを捨て新しきを採る.

change-over, *n.* 転換.

V ***complete*** the *change-over* 引継を完了する.

P the *change-over* ***from*** ... ***to*** ... ...から...へ引継ぎ. ¶a sudden *change-over* ***in*** foreign policies 外交政策の急転

換. ¶Since the *change-over **to*** the wide screen, the cameraman's job has become harder. ワイド・スクリーンになってから撮影技師の仕事が一層むずかしくなった.

channel, *n.* 流床; 水路; 通路; 方面.

V ***approach*** a *channel* to a dock ドックへの水路に近づく. ¶He ***crossed*** the *Channel.* 彼は(英国から)大陸に渡った. ¶***cut*** a *channel* 水路を開さくする. ¶it ***forms*** a *channel* of communication between ... and ... それは...と...との間の交通路をなしている. ¶Business has ***resumed*** its old *channels.* 商売がもと通りになった. ¶***trace*** the *channels* of purchase 買入れのルートを探る.

Q obtain ... through ***illegal*** *channels* 非合法的手段で...を手に入れる. ¶work through ***institutional*** *channels* [直接行動に出ず]それぞれの機関を経て行動する. ¶***legitimate*** *channels* of purchase 買入れの正常ルート. ¶obtain information through ***official*** (***private***) *channels* 官庁(民間)方面を通じて報道を得る ‖ return import and export procedures to ***private*** *channels* 輸出入を元通り個人の手に戻す. ¶They received notice of their peril through some ***secret*** *channel* or other. 彼らは内密に自分らの危険の通告を受けた.

Q² the ***black-market*** *channels* of foreign goods 外国物資のやみルート. ¶through official ***rationing*** *channels* 正規の配給ルートによって. ¶through ***trade*** *channels* (=channels of trade) 正式ルートから. 【類】The Sucz Canal is the main ***trade*** *channel* between East and West. / go into illicit ***trad****channels.* ¶the total amount of wheat normally entering ***world trade*** *channels* 正規の手続をふんで世界の貿易ルートに乗る小麦の総量.

P our neighbors ***across*** the *channel* 海峡の彼方の国民(英国からフランスを見た場合など). ¶He had the strength to break out ***into*** new *channels.* 彼には新生面を開く元気があった. ¶***through*** hidden *channels* 秘密に ‖ We have taken care to make the circulars go ***through*** the best *channels.* その(宣伝用の)回状が最も有効な方面に行渡るように心を用いた. ¶I advised him to direct his energy ***to*** some other *channel.* 彼の精力を何か他の方面に転換させたらよかろうと勧めた.

P² a *channel* ***of*** command 指揮系統 ‖ a *channel* ***of*** communication 交通路. ¶*channels* ***of*** shady transactions やみルート.

channel, *v.* 水路を開く.

P a river *channels* its course ***through*** the rocks.

chanter, *n.* 歌い手.

Q² an amateur ***joruri*** *chanter* 素人義太夫語り.

chaos, *n.* 混乱, 混とん.

Q ***economic*** *chaos* 経済界の混乱. ¶This is the age of ***political*** *chaos.* 今は政界混乱時代だ. ¶***primal*** *chaos* 天地未だ分れず混とんたる状態. ¶It's ***quite*** a *chaos.* 全くてんやわんやだ.

Q² ***world*** *chaos* 世界的混乱.

chap, *n.* 《俗》やつ, 男.

Q Here's a ***new*** *chap!* What an ass he looks! 新入りか! ばかづらしてら! ¶***old*** *chap* 大将(親しい人への呼掛). ¶a ***smart*** *chap* 利口なやつ.

chap, *n.* =chop.

Q² ***pork*** *chaps* ポーク・チョップ(骨付豚肉).

chap, *v.* ひびが切れる.

P My lips *chap* ***in*** winter. 私の口びるは冬ひびわれる.

O *chapped* hands (skin) ひびの切れた手(など).

chaperonage, *n.* 付添い.

P He met Dr. Johnson ***under*** Boswell's *chaperonage.* 彼はボズウェルに付添われてジョンソン博士に面会した.

chapter, *n.* 章, 節.

V ***attack*** the last *chapter* first (本の研究に)最後の章を真先に読始める. ¶This ***closes*** one *chapter* of my life. これが私の生涯の一段落です. ¶The author ***devotes*** an important *chapter* to the subject. 著者は重要な一章をその問題にあてている. 【類】***devote*** separate *chapters* (別々の章) to ... ¶His career ***forms*** a *chapter* of life stranger than any piece of fiction. 彼の経歴はどの小説よりも更に奇なる人生の一章をなしている. ¶***give*** a separate *chapter* to it 別に一章をそれに当てる.

Q The period makes one of the most ***captivating*** *chapters* in the history of Japan. その期間は日本歴史において最も魅力ある一節をなす. ¶The invention forms an ***interesting*** *chapter* in the progress of civilization. その発明は文明の進歩における興味ある一節をなす. ¶an ***introductory*** *chapter* 序論. ¶this ***marvellous*** *chapter* of the world's history 世界史上のこの驚嘆すべき一節. ¶a ***meaty*** *chapter* 内容充実した一章. ¶in the ***opening*** *chapter* 開巻第一章に. ¶the ***second*** *chapter*=chapter two=chapter the second 第二章. ¶A ***special*** *chapter* is devoted it. 特に一章をそれに当てている. 【類】treat it in a ***special*** *chapter.* ¶a ***weighty*** *chapter* 力のある(重要な)一章. ¶***What*** *chapter* shall we begin with? どの章から始めましょうか.

P a story ***in*** three *chapters* 三章から成る物語. ¶***in*** this *chapter* of his life 彼の生涯のこの時期において. ¶Some acquaintances to the end (***of*** the *chapter*). 知人の中には(真の友人とならずに)最後まで知人で終る者もある. ¶Further discussion of ... will be found ***under*** *chapter* on ... ...についての一層突込んだ議論は...に関する章に記してある.

P² he says in the *chapter* ***on*** advertisement that ... 広告を論じた一章で彼は...と言っている. 【類】a *chapter* ***on*** health and pleasure resorts (保養地や遊覧地).

char, *n.* 炭.

V ***wipe*** *char* from wick [石油ストーヴなど]心(しん)からばい煙をぬぐう.

character, *n.* (**1**) 性質, 品性, 性格, 人格; 身分; 評判; 人物; 配役; 《口語》変り者.

V Houses of ill fame ***advertise*** their *character* by red light. あいまい屋は紅灯でその性格を示す. ¶***assume*** (=***acquire***) the *character* of ... ...の性質を帯びる ‖ The situation has ***assumed*** a dangerous *character.* 形勢が不穏になってきた. 【類】***assume*** a more European *character* / began to ***assume*** an international *character* (国際的性質). ¶***bear*** the *character* of ... ...の性質を帯びる ‖ He ***bears*** a good *character* among his friends. 友人間で評判がよい. ¶***build*** [***up***] one's *character* 人格を作る, 品性を陶冶する. ¶The *characters* were well ***cast.*** 配役がよかった. ¶***change*** its *character* その性格を変える. ¶***clear*** one's *character* 身の明りを立てる. ¶***combine*** the *characters* of ... ...の性質を併有する. ¶I cannot ***decipher*** these faded *characters.* この薄れている字は判読ができない. ¶***degrade*** national *character* 国民性を堕落せしめる. ¶***delineate*** (=***describe***) *characters* 人物を描写する ‖ To specifically ***describe*** his *character* would be merely to sum up almost all that is divine in human nature. 彼の性格を一々描写しようとするならそれは全く人間性における神聖なるもののほとんどすべてを総括することになるだろう. ¶***develop*** *character* enough to subdue rebellious impulse 反逆的衝動(邪念)を抑えるまでに修養を積む. ¶rejoice over the thwartings and buffetings of circumstances that ***develop*** and ***strengthen*** and ***deepen*** his *character* 己が品性を陶冶し強固にし練磨してくれる逆境・苦境を歓迎する. ¶George Eliot ***drew*** her *characters* from rural persons. ジョージ・エリオットはいなか者をその作中に取扱っている. ‖ His *characters* are well ***drawn.*** 彼の作中に現われる人物はよく描かれている. ¶***elevate*** the *character* of a paper 新聞の品位を高める. ¶***epitomize*** the national *character* of the English 英国人の国民性を要約する. ¶to ***evolve*** the child's *character* than to overtax the child's mind; to bring out rather than to bring to the faculties of the child 児童の心に重荷を課するよりはその品性を開発する; すなわち児童の能力に付加することを為さずして却ってこれを発揮させる. ¶***form*** the *character* of the young 青年の品性を作り上げる. ¶The religion of a people both ***forms*** and ***indicates*** the national *character.* 一国民の宗教はその国民性を作ると同時にこれを指示するものである. ¶He has ***gained*** the *character* of a miser. 彼はけちん坊の異名をとった, けちで有名だ. ¶***get*** a bad *character* 悪評を得る. ¶They ***gave*** him a bad *character.* 彼らは彼を非難した. ‖ a piece of furniture which ***gives*** *character* to the whole room 室全体がそのために特異性を持つようになる一個の家具. 【類】The presence of many foreigners ***gave*** an international *character* to the meeting. ¶be unable to ***grasp*** his *character* あの人の性質はつかめない. ¶He ***has*** the *character* of being a good deal of a humorist. 彼はユーモリストたる所を多分に持っているという評判だ. ‖ His action in that picture ***has*** *character.* あの映画での彼の演技は性格が出ている. ¶A few specimens will ***illustrate*** their general *character.* 二三の例を挙げるとそれらの一般性質がよく分る. ¶The beautiful lake ***imparts*** a charming *character* to this spot. その美しい湖水がここの魅力を成している. ¶***impersonate*** a *character* ある人物にふんする. ¶***improve*** one's *character* 人格を向上させる. ¶***injure*** one's *character* 人の人格を傷ける. ¶***introduce*** a revolutionary *character* into the struggle この闘争に革命的性質を帯びさせる. ¶The book is well calculated to ***keep up*** the *character* of the series to which it belongs. その本は所属全双書の声価を維持するに足りる. ¶I ***like*** your *character* very much. 君の性質が非常に気に入った. ¶She has ***lost*** her *character* of a genial hostess. 彼女は(招待された者から見て)感じの好い主婦だという評判を落した. ¶***lower*** or ***injure*** one's *character* 評判を悪くしまたは傷つける. ¶The new edition of the manual is so creditably edited as to ***maintain*** its *character* as a reliable manual of reference. 便覧の新版はその編集が行届いて信頼するに足る参考書たるの名声を落さない. ¶There is no way of ***mending*** his *character*. あの男の性格を治す道はない. ¶***mold*** (=shape) one's *character* 人物を造る. ¶She ***pecked*** his *character* to pieces. 彼女は彼の人柄を散々にこきおろした. ¶Garbo makes you feel that she is the *character* she is ***playing***. ガルボはそのふんする人物その者であるという感を与える. ¶***polish*** the *character* 人物をみがく. ¶The author ***portrays*** his *characters* to the life. その作家は人物を生き生きと描写してる. 【類】the screen *character* (映画の役) she has ***portrayed***. ¶***possess*** an independent *character* 個性を有する. ¶***preserve*** the *character* of ... ...の性質を維持する. ¶***purify*** one's *character* 品性を浄化する. ¶***read*** *character* from handwriting 筆蹟で人物を判断する ‖ ***read*** *character* in the face 人相を見る. ¶The fact that national *character* is ***reflected*** in national speech has long been recognized. 国民性は国語に反映するとは長い間認められてきた事実である. 【類】It was one of those simple acts that ***reflect*** a man's *character*. ¶***regain*** one's *character* 評判を回復する. ¶***reveal*** *character* 性格を現わす. ¶Many experts consider street environment the vital factor in ***shaping*** the boy's *character*. 児童の性格を築き上げるのに市街の環境がきわめて重要なることは多数専門家の認める所である. ¶***show*** one's true *character* 化けの皮をはがす. ¶***show up*** the *character* of a man 人の特性を発揮させる. ¶***soil*** one's *character* 人格を汚す. ¶The writer ***sums up*** his *character* thus. 筆者は彼の性格をこう概説している. ¶***take on*** the *character* ***of*** a festival お祭の性質を帯びる. ¶***tell*** *characters* and fortunes by the stars 星で性格や運勢を占う. ¶***train*** one's *character* 品性を陶冶(とう)する. ¶***weaken*** moral *character* 徳性を薄弱にさせる.

Q of ***abandoned*** *character* 自堕落な. ¶***abject*** *character* いやしい品性. ¶***acquired*** *characters* 後天的性格. ¶Much of the teaching there is of an ***advanced*** *character*. そこの教育は大部分程度の高いものである. ¶an ***agreeable*** *character* いや味のない性質(の人). ¶He is a ***bad*** *character*. 彼は人物が悪い. ‖ a woman of ***bad*** *character* 素性のよくない女 ‖ be of the ***best*** *character* 最上級のものである. ¶The magazine is of a ***bilingual*** *character*. その雑誌は二国語で編集してある. ¶He is of ***coarse*** (=***rough*** *or* ***rude***) *character*. 彼は粗暴な性質だ. ¶the ***commercial*** *character* of the whole enterprise その事業全体の商業的色彩. ¶These instances go to show that the British Isles do occasionally produce men of ***cosmopolitan*** *character*. これらの例を見れば英国がときに世界魂を持つ人物を蘐出することがよく分る. ¶thieves and other ***dangerous*** *characters* 盗賊やその他の危険人物. ¶a ***debauched*** *character* 堕落した人. ¶He is of a very ***determined*** (=***decided*** *or* ***resolute***) *character*. 彼は果断家である. ¶take on a ***different*** *character* 違った性格を帯びてくる. ¶a woman of ***disreputable*** *character* 評判のよくない女. ¶it has a ***distinct*** *character*, in that ... それは...という点に於て性質を異にしている. ¶a man of ***distorted*** *character* ねじけた性質の人. ¶be of quite ***diverse*** *character* 性格が全く違っている. ¶a ***dubious*** *character* いかがわしい人物. ¶the ***ephemeral*** *character* of literary fame 一時的の文名. ¶of ***exalted*** *character* りっぱな品性の. ¶He has an ***excellent*** *character* for honesty. 彼は正直者として定評がある. ¶of ***exotic*** *character* 異国人風の. ¶has drawn his ***female*** *characters* admirably 女の登場人物を巧みに描写している. ¶***fictitious*** *characters* 仮想人物. ¶a man of ***fine*** *character* りっぱな人格者. ¶assume a more ***finite*** *character* その性質が一層明かになる. ¶a man of ***firm*** *character* 意志強固な人. ¶men of ***first*** *character* 一流の人々. ¶of a ***formal*** (an ***informal***) *character* 正(略)式の. ¶sentiments, beliefs, and notions which constitute ***French*** *character* フランス人の性格を構成する情操, 信仰, および観念. ¶the ***generic*** *character* 〘生物〙属性. ¶fundamental traits of the ***German national*** *character* ドイツ国民性の根本的特色. ¶a man of ***good*** *character* 善良な性質の人 ‖ He has always had the ***good*** *character* in that way. あの方は信用のできる人であった. ‖ His illness assumed a very ***grave*** *character*. 彼は重態に陥った. ¶a man of ***great*** *character* 大人物. ¶a man of ***hard*** and ***selfish*** *character* 冷酷で利己主義な人. ¶Discussion at the meeting appears to have been of an extremely ***heated*** *character*. この会の討議はきわめて劇烈なものであったらしい. ¶an inmate of a well-known resort of ***high*** *character* 有名な高級喫茶店などの女 ‖ a man of ***high*** *character* 高潔な人格者. 【類】a man of the ***highest*** *character* and undeniable capacity (すばらしく有能). ¶a man not only of great ability, but of the ***highest personal*** *character* ただに偉才を抱くのみならずまたきわめて高潔な人格の持主. ¶Caesar is a great ***historical*** *character*. シーザーは偉大な歴史上の人物だ. ¶a person who understands ***human*** *character* 人間性に理解のある人. ¶a girl of ***impeccable*** *character* 純な性格の少女. ¶***inherent*** *character* 生得の性格. ¶***inherited*** *character* 先天的性格. ¶***insular*** *character* 島国根性. ¶stories of a most ***interesting*** *character* 非常におもしろい話. ¶be of an ***international*** *character* 国際的な性質の. 【類】The exhibition will have an ***international*** *character*. / Sports have an ***international*** *character*. ¶a man of ***irreproachable*** *character* 非の打ちようのない人. ¶a ***leading*** *character* 大立者, 主役 ‖ The play has a potter for its ***leading*** *character*. その劇の主人公は陶工だ. ¶a ***life-like*** *character* 真に迫った(小説中の)人物. ¶of ***like*** *character* 同種の. ¶men of ***loose*** and ***dissipated*** *character* 締りのない放とう者. ¶a ***lovable*** *character* 愛きょうのある人. ¶a set of persons of a ***low*** or ***disreputable*** *character* 下劣なあるいは評判の悪い性質の人間(たち)の一団. ¶an ideal of ***maidenly*** *character* 処女性の一つの理想. ¶diseases of a ***malignant*** *character* 悪性の病. ¶All education forms *character*, ***mental*** and ***moral***. 教育はすべて精神的および道徳的品性を陶冶(とう)する. ‖ fail to establish good ***moral*** *character* 善良な道徳的品性を造り上げられない. ¶assume a ***morbid*** *character* 病的性質を帯びる. ¶The population of the United States is of a ***motley*** *character*. アメリカの住民は多種多様である. ¶a ***mythical*** *character* 神話的人物. ¶a man of ***no*** *character* 人格ゼロの人 ‖ a face with ***no*** *character* 特徴のない顔(平凡な顔). ¶a woman of ***noble*** *character* 高潔な品格の女. ¶The paper is of a professedly ***non-partisan*** *character*. その新聞は断然不偏不党だ. ¶a ***noted*** *character* 名高い人物. ¶a man of ***notorious*** *character* 名評の高い人. ¶an ***odd*** *character* 変人. ¶documents of an ***official*** or ***quasi-official*** *character* 公的または準公的性質を帯びた書類. ¶an ***officious*** *character* おせっかいな人. ¶have an ***Oriental*** *character* 東洋風の色彩がある. ¶***picturesque*** *character* 絵画的性質. ¶assume a ***political*** *character* 政治的色彩を帯びる. ¶of a mere ***pretentious*** *character* ほんの見せ掛けの. ¶the ***principal*** *character* 主役. ¶his ***private*** *character* 彼の素行. ¶the beauty of woman, a ***prominent secondary sexual*** *character* 顕著な第二次的な性的特徴たる女の美貌. ¶a ***public*** *character* 公人 ‖ a strong ***public*** *character* [政界などの]権力ある公人. ¶assume a ***quasi-revolutionary*** *character* 准革命的性質を帯びる. ¶He frequents places of ***questionable*** *character*. 彼はいかがわしい場所に出入する. ¶He is ***quite*** a *character*. 《口語》あいつは変りものだ. ¶a ***real*** *character* [仮想でない]実在の人物. ¶literature of an avowedly ***religious*** *character* 断然宗教的色彩のある文学. ¶gatherings of a ***religious*** or ***superstitious*** *character* 宗教的または迷信的性質の会合. ¶a ***remarkable*** *character* 顕著な人物. ¶of ***respectable*** *character* 相当りっぱな性格の. ¶It has a ***sacred*** or ***ritual*** *character*. それは神聖な祭祀的色彩を有する. ¶of ***saintly*** *character* 聖人のような. ¶owing to the ***serious*** *character* of the political news その政治報道の重要性のために. ¶***shady*** *characters* of all kinds あらゆる種類のいかがわしい人物. ¶people of a ***similar*** *character* 同様な性格の人々. ¶a man of ***small*** *character* 小人物. ¶a man of ***sound*** *character* たしかな人. ¶a ***staid*** *character* 沈着な人物. ¶a man of ***stainless*** *character* 純潔な性格の人. ¶***steadfast*** *character* しっかりした人. ¶a ***steady, constant*** *character* しっかりした節操のある人物. ¶a ***strange***, but ***lovable*** *character* 変っているが愛すべき人物. ¶He has a ***strong*** *character*. 彼はしっかりした性格をもっている. ¶a ***sturdy*** *character* しっかりした人物. ¶a ***suspicious*** *character* 注意人物. ¶surgical instruments of a highly ***technical*** *character* 非常に専門的な外科用手術器具. ¶the ***tentative*** *character* of his conclusion 彼の結論の暫定性. ¶a ***tough*** *character* ねばり強い人. ¶the ***true*** *character* of the present industrial condition 産業現況の真相 ‖ That is the ***true*** *character* of that man. それがあの人の地金だ. ¶a man of ***unblemished*** *character* 高潔な人. ¶The result so far arrived at is of a very ***undecided*** *character*. 今日までの結果ははなはだあいまいな性質のものである. ¶certain reports of an ***unfavorable*** *character* are being circulated with regard to ... ...についておもしろくないうわさが立っている. ¶the ***unphonetic*** *character* of English spelling 英語のつづり字の非表音的性質. ¶an ***unpleasant*** *character* 人好きのしない性格. ¶a man of ***upright*** *character* 正しい人. ¶obtain a loan in order to finance certain public works of an ***urgent*** *character* ある緊急な公共事業を援助するため資金を調達する. ¶The dividends of that company's shares are of a very ***variable*** *character*. 同会社の株式配当金ははなはだ不定なものである. ¶a man of ***vehement*** *character* 熱烈な性格の人. ¶a woman of ***vicious*** *character* 素性(すじょう)の悪い女. ¶a man of ***vigorous*** *character* 男らしい人. ¶He has a ***virile*** and ***sturdy*** *character*. 彼は男性的なしっかりした性格を持っている. ¶The novelist draws a ***vivid*** and ***life-like*** *character*. その小説家は鮮明な写実的な性格を描く. ¶***vulgar*** *characters* 粗野な人物. ¶a ***weak*** *character*=a man of weak character 意志薄弱な人物. ¶***well-known*** *characters* from fiction or romance 小説または伝奇物語からよく引合に出される人物. ¶a ***worthless*** *character* 価値のない人物.

Q² ***Bible*** *characters* 聖書中の人物. ¶courses of the "***bread-and-butter***" *character* きまりきった(料理の)献立. ¶***comic strip*** *characters* 連続漫画の配役. ¶give a ***cyclopedia*** *character* to the work その著作に百科事典的性質を帯びさせる. ¶***miscast*** *character* 配役を誤った俳優. ¶a ***screen*** (=***movie***) *character* 映画に出て来る人物. ¶a ***street*** *character* 街頭でよく見る人物. ¶the ***title*** *character* (=rôle) of a drama 劇の外題に当る配役(ハムレット劇中のハムレットなど). ¶an ***underworld*** *character* 暗黒街の人物.

P He was well fitted for that post ***by*** *character* and attainments. 彼は品性学識の上から最適任であった. ‖ He has won golden opinions ***by*** (=***through***) his high *character*. 彼は品性がりっぱなので評判が高くなった. ¶satisfactory both ***in*** *character* and in capacity 性格においても手腕においても申分のない ‖ He is firm ***in*** *character*. 彼はしっかりしている. 【類】be similar (dissimilar) ***in*** *character* / They are different ***in*** *character*. ‖ some serious defects ***in*** his *character* 彼の品性上の大欠点. ‖ The treasurer also serves ***in*** the *character* of secretary. その会計係はまた秘書の役もかねている. ‖ made a speech ***in*** his (=the) *character* of Ambassador 大使の資格で演説をした ‖ portraits of actors ***in*** *character* 演技中の俳優の似顔 ‖ ***in*** *character* [役柄など]ぴったりした. 【類】His new role is ***in*** *character*. ‖ He appears ***in*** the *character* (=plays the part) of Hamlet. 彼はハムレットにふんする. 【類】We have hitherto regarded him only ***in*** the *characters* of orator, scholar, sportsman, and political "leaper in the dark." (「向う見ず」の政治家) ‖ it is identical ***in*** *character* with ... それは...と同じ性質のものだ. ¶strength ***of*** *character* 意志の強固 ‖ He has firmness ***of*** *character*. 彼は意志が堅い. ‖ ***of*** this *character* この種の. ¶the formation (=upbuilding) ***of*** *character* 人格の陶冶(とうや) ‖ by his force ***of*** *character* 彼の人格の力で ‖ display great force ***of*** *character* 偉大な人格の力を示す ‖ a man ***of*** *character* 人格者 ‖ works ***of*** the *character* of *belles-lettres* 純文学に属する作品 ‖ ***of*** a more or less international *character* 多少国際的性質の. 【類】purely ***of*** national *character*. ¶It is a sad blot ***on*** his *character*. それが彼の品性の一大汚点だ. ‖ cast a stain ***on*** his *character* 彼の名声を傷つける ‖ Farce depends on plot, comedy ***on*** *character*. 茶番劇は筋が, 喜劇は人物が大切. ¶go ***out of*** *character* 柄にないことをする. 【類】His office is ***out of*** *character*.

P² He is a *character* ***above*** suspicion. あの人は疑う余地のない人物だ. ¶her *character* ***as*** a daughter 娘としての彼女の品格 ‖ in his *character* ***as*** (=of) ambassador 大使の資格で. ¶his *character* ***as regards*** honesty, industry and sobriety 正直・勤勉・まじめという点から見た彼の性格. ¶He has a *character* ***for*** honesty. 彼は正直という評判だ. ¶*characters* ***in*** a novel (play, story) 小説(など)中の人物. 【類】*characters* ***in*** a Shakespeare's comedy. ¶the *character* ***of*** an applicant 出願者の人物. 【類】the *character* ***of*** a people (nation) ‖ the *character* ***of*** the country 地方色 ‖ the *character* ***of*** customers 客種 ‖ the *character* ***of*** the Siberian plains シベリヤ平原の様相. ¶The gateway should be in *character* (=keeping) ***with*** the house. 門は家と調和しなくてはいけない. ¶a face ***without*** any *character* 平凡で何の特徴もない顔.

(2) [人物]証明書, 推薦書.

V ***give*** one a written *character* 人に品行証明書を与える ‖ His former employer ***gave*** him a very good *character*. 彼の前雇主は彼に非常にりっぱな勤務証明書を与えた.

Q a servant with a ***good*** (***excellent***) *character* よい(すばらしい)推薦状をもった使用人. ¶a ***ten years'*** *character* 十年勤続証書.

P a servant ***without*** a *character* 推薦(証明)書のない使用人.

(3) 文字.

V *characters* ***cut out*** on stones 石に彫りつけた文字. ¶*characters* ***formed*** with six strokes 六画の漢字. ¶Chinese *characters* ***invented*** in Japan 和製の漢字. ¶***trace*** some *characters* upon the sand 砂の上に文字を書く.

Q ***alphabetic*** *characters* アルファベットの文字. ¶***Arabic*** *characters* アラビア文字. ¶The bell bears an inscription in embossed ***Chinese*** *characters*. その鐘には浮出した漢字の銘がある. 【類】the introduction of ***Chinese characters*** into Japan. ¶a sentence of a ***colloquial*** *character* 口語体の文. ¶***cuneiform*** (=***arrowheaded***) *characters* くさび形文字. ¶He writes ***elegant*** *characters*. 彼は雅致のある字を書く. ¶Can you read a book in ***Greek*** *characters*? ギリシア文字で書いた本が読めますか. ¶The book is printed in a ***large*** *character*. その本は大型文字で印刷してある. ¶***musical*** *character* 楽譜. ¶a writing in ***secret*** *character* 秘密文字の文書. ¶write in ***small*** (***large***) *characters* 細(大)字で書く. ¶in ***sprawling*** *characters* ぶざまにのびた文字で(草書など).

Q² Few typewriters are equipped with ***bracket*** *characters*. 括弧割印のあるタイプライターはほとんどない. ¶write in ***grass*** *characters* 草書で書く.

P² the Chinese *character* ***for*** "tiger" 「虎」という漢字.

character-drawing, *n.* 性格描写.

Q ***delicate*** *character-drawing* 精緻な性格描写.

characteristic, *n.* 特性, 特色, 特徴.

V ***bear*** all the *characteristics* of ... ...の特質をことごとく備える. ¶***display*** many Oriental *characteristics* 幾多東洋人の特色を発揮する. ¶***exhibit*** this national *characteristic* この国民性を発揮する. ¶They ***had*** (=***possessed***) one *characteristic* in common. 彼らは一つの特徴を共通に持っていた. ¶It has ***lost*** its *characteristics*. それは特徴を失った. ¶***preserve*** its ancient *characteristics* 昔ながらの特色を失わない. ¶The dance which reigns at a given epoch almost always ***reflects*** some *characteristic* of that epoch. ある時代に流行する舞踏はほとんど総ての場合その時代のある特質を反映する. ¶He ***united*** with himself the *characteristics* of two distinct persons. 彼は二人の全く異った特色を一人で具えていた.

Q one of the ***charming*** *characteristics* of his style 彼の文体の魅惑的な特徴の一つ. ¶Combination has been the ***chief*** *characteristic* of industry all over the world. 合同は世界を通じて産業の主なる特徴であった. ¶***distinctive*** *characteristics* 特徴. ¶***distinguishing*** *characteristics* of man 人類の特異性. ¶a ***dominant*** *characteristics* 顕著な特色. ¶***facial*** *characteristics* 顔の特徴. ¶***individual*** *characteristics* 個性. ¶Longevity is an ***inheritable*** *characteristic*. 長命は遺伝する特質だ. ¶***leading*** *characteristics* 主なる特徴. ¶the ***main*** *characteristic* of an invention 発明品の主な特徴. ¶The love of money has always been a ***marked*** *characteristic* of the Egyptian. 金銭を愛することは終始一貫してエジプト人の著しい特性であった. ‖ Intense and concentrated energy was one of his most ***marked*** *characteristics.* 熱烈で物にこるのが彼の最も著しい特性の一つであった. ¶***mental*** *characteristics* 精神的特徴. ¶***national*** *characteristics* 国民性. ¶the ***outstanding*** *characteristics* of the people その国民の目立った特色. ¶the ***physical*** and ***psychic*** *characteristics* of ... ...の肉体的及び精神的特徴 ‖ the influence of ***physical*** *characteristics* on the character of a nation 国民性におよぼす地理的特質の影響. ¶a ***predominant*** *characteristic* 目立った特徴. ¶Well, I must say modesty is not your ***prominent*** *characteristics.* 一体君は少し出しゃばり過ぎる. ¶***salient*** *characteristics* 顕著な特質. ¶the ***strongest*** *characteristic* of a nation 一国民の最も著しい特質. ¶***well-marked*** *characteristics* 明白な特徴.

Q² ***body*** *characteristics* 肉体の特徴.

characteristic, *a.* 特質を示す, 独特の. 「をなしている.

M be ***specially*** *characteristic* of the age その時代の特徴

P it is *charactristic* ***of*** the Chinese mind that ... ...ということは中国人の特質を示している ‖ Sympathy is the feeling *characteristic* ***of*** mankind. 同情は人類特有の感情である. ‖ the pronunciation and usage of words *characteristic* ***of*** Americans 米人特有の語の発音と用法.

characterization, *n.* 特徴表示.

Q ***personal*** *characterization* 人物評. ¶The "summer playground of America" is a ***true*** *characterization* of the great Pacific northwest. 「米国の夏季遊園地」は広漠たる西北太平洋によくあてはまる句だ.

characterize, *v.* 特性を表わす.

M *characterize* ***aptly*** in a word or two all the essential features of situation 一二語で情勢の本質的特色を手際よく言い表わす. ¶He may be ***briefly*** *characterized* as a man of hobbies. 彼は一口に言えば趣味の人だ. ¶be ***facetiously*** *characterized* as ... おどけて...といわれる.

P It must be *characterized* ***as*** a failure. それは失敗と断定を下さねばならない. ‖ It is *characterized* ***as*** one of the greatest piece of engineering work in the world. それは世界における最大工事の一つと言われている. ¶The concluding years of the last century were *characterized* ***by*** the discovery of several forms of radiant energy. 数種の輻射エネルギー発見が十九世紀末葉の特色だ. ‖ His style is *characterized* ***by*** verbiage. 冗長が彼の文体の特徴だ.

charcoal, *n.* 木炭.

V ***add*** more *charcoal* 炭をつぐ. ¶***burn*** *charcoal* 炭をやく.

Q a bed of ***live*** *charcoal* [うなぎを焼く時など]平らにならべた炭火.

P feed the fire ***with*** *charcoal* 火に炭をつぐ.

charge, *n.* (**1**) 負担; 費用, 料金; 課税.

V ***bear*** *charges* 費用を負担する. ¶***collect*** *charges* for ... ...の料金を取立てる. ¶a price that ***covers*** all *charges*=an all-round price 諸掛りを含めた. ¶***debit*** all *charges* to ... 掛りは全部...の借方に記入する. ¶greatly ***increase*** the *charge* of ... 大いに...の掛りをたかめる. ¶No *charge* is ***incurred*** without business result. 手数料は商談がまとまった場合のみ頂きます. ¶These courses ***involve*** extra *charges.* [学校で]以上の科目は別に料金を徴する. ¶***Keep*** the *charges* as economical as possible. 掛りをできるだけ節約せよ. ¶***levy*** a *charge* upon commodities 商品に課税する. ¶***lower*** the postal *charge* on newspapers 新聞の郵税を下げる. ¶***make*** a *charge* for admission 入場料を取る ‖ ***make*** an extra *charge* of ... ...だけ余分の料金を取る. 【類】No extra *charge* is ***made*** for packing (荷造費). / No *charge* is ***made*** for this service. / a *charge* of ¥200 is ***made*** for ... ¶*Charges* or fees ***paid*** on goods landed from a vessel 陸あげ船荷に対し支払われた掛りや料金. ¶***strike off*** a *charge* in an account 勘定から掛りの一項目を除く.

Q make a small ***additional*** *charge* 余分の料金を少し取る. ¶***binding*** and ***overhead*** *charges* of books 書物の装ていその他諸掛込値段. ¶pay ***customary*** *charges* 慣例の費用を払う. ¶an ***extortionate*** *charge* 法外の料金. ¶at an ***extra*** *charge* of ... 余分に...の料金を出して. 【類】All ***extra*** *charges* are to be paid by you. / without ***extra*** *charge.* ¶make a ***fair*** *charge* 相当の料金を取る. ¶***forwarding*** *charges* 送料. ¶***heavy*** *charges* 多額の諸掛り ‖ The *charge* is too ***heavy*** to be shouldered. その料金では負担が重過ぎる. ¶make ***invidious*** *charges* 差別的な金の取り方をする. ¶***light*** *charges* 少額の諸掛り. ¶with a ***minimum*** *charge* of 25 yen 二十五円という最低の料金で. ¶at ***moderate*** (***reasonable***) *charges* 安い(相当の)料金で. ¶There is ***no*** *charge* whatever for this service. これは全然無料奉仕です. 【類】There is ***no*** *charge* for admission. ¶at ***nominal*** *charges* ほんの名ばかりの(僅少な)料金で. 【類】A ***nominal*** *charge* is made for such a service. ¶at a ***prepaid*** *charge* of ... ...の前払料金で(汽車用のまくらを借りる場合など). ¶The *charge* is ***reasonable.*** 料金は高くない. ¶***rental*** *charges* 家賃. ¶These may be had on hire at a ***small*** *charge.* これらはわずかな(僅少の)料金で借いりることができる. 【類】a ***small*** *charge* is made for ... ¶Licensed porters, distinguished by scarlet caps, are in attendance at large stations, and carry parcels for a ***small fixed*** *charge.* 公認の赤帽が大きな駅に控えていて僅少の一定料金で荷物を運んでくれる. ¶make a ***special*** *charge* 特別料金を取る. ¶Never does time mean money so terribly as in a film studio with its ***terrifying overhead*** *charges.* 目玉の飛び出るような掛りのする映画製作所ぐらい時は金なりという感を切実に起させるものはない. ¶at a ***trifling*** *charge* わずかな料金で. ¶subject to the ***usual*** *charges* 普通諸掛りの条件で.

Q² ***burial*** *charges* 埋葬料. ¶***carrying*** *charges* 運賃. ¶***collection*** *charges* 取集め料. ¶***dinner*** *charges* 晩餐料. ¶be subject to a ***demurrage*** *charge* 滞船料を払わねばならぬ. ¶establishment *charges* 店費. ¶***landing*** *charges* (=rates) 貨物陸揚税あるいは賃. ¶***lighterage*** *charges* はしけ賃. ¶***port*** *charges* (=dues) 港税. ¶***railway*** *charges* 汽車旅行の諸掛り. ¶***rooming*** and ***boarding*** *charges* 間代および食費. ¶on ***stowaway*** *charges* 密航のかどで. ¶transportation *charges* 運賃. ¶He made me bear all ***traveling*** *charges.* 彼は旅費全部を私に出させた. ¶a ***10c.*** *charge* 十セントの料金. ¶***10 per cent service*** *charge* 一割のサービス料.

P ***at*** a *charge* of ... extra on single tickets 片道切符の場合は...の料金を余分に加えて ‖ He came to Japan ***at*** his own *charges* in the hope of beginning Christian work among the natives. 彼は日本人間にキリスト教伝道の仕事を始めようとして自費で日本へやってきた. ‖ Tramways connect all parts of the town ***at*** the *charge* of a penny. 一ペニの料金でその町のどの方面にも電車で行かれる. ¶free ***of*** *charge* 無料で. ¶It can be obtained ***on*** very reasonable *charges.* それは少しも高くない料金で手に入れられる. ¶The aquarium is open to the public ***without*** *charge.* その水族館は一般人に無料で公開している. 【類】The gallery (美術館) is open to the public ***without*** *charge* three days in each week. / Members receive the Journal (雑誌) ***without*** *charge.* / ***without*** any *charge* whatever.

P² the *charge* ***for*** admission (=admittance) 入場料. 【類】What is your *charge* ***for*** board and lodging? ‖ the *charge* ***for*** tuition 授業料 ‖ the *charge* ***for*** the service 手間代 ‖ the *charge* ***for*** a consultation 診察料 ‖ *charges* ***for*** parcel post 小包郵便料金 ‖ What is the *charge* ***for*** a day at the hotel? あのホテルは一日何ほどですか. ‖ We make no *charge* ***for*** it in the bill. それは勘定に入れません(代金をいただきません). ‖ The *charge* ***for*** a three minutes' conversation is now 10 yen. 三分間の現在通話料金は十円です. ¶the *charge* ***of*** a doctor (lawyer, teacher) 医者(など)への礼 ‖ the *charge* ***of*** a hotel 宿泊料. ¶a *charge* ***on*** the State 国家の負担 ‖ the *charge* ***on*** goods 品物に対する諸掛り. ¶Is there any *charge* ***to*** the Gallery? その美術館は入場料を取りますか.

(**2**) 委任, 預り物; 責任; 監督, 世話.

V ***assume*** the *charge* of a home 一家の世話を引受ける ‖ He started to ***assume*** *charge* in the Madras branch. 彼はマドラス支店長として赴任した. 【類】***assume*** *charge* of the administration of the country (国政) / ***assume*** responsible *charge* (責任ある仕事). ¶We ***gave*** him *charge* of our children. 彼に子供たちの世話を頼んだ. ¶***hand over*** *charge* of an office to ... 事務所の監督を...に引継ぐ. ¶He ***has*** *charge* of the branch. 彼はその支店長です. ‖ He ***has*** *charge* of the fifth-year class. 彼は五年級の主任です. 【類】***have*** *charge* of a contest / ***has*** *charge* of the investigation. ¶He ***resigned*** his *charge* at the university. 彼は同大学学長の位置を辞した. ¶Mr. T will ***take*** *charge* during my absence. 私の留守中はT氏が世話をして下さる. ‖ ***take*** *charge* of one of the children 子供の一人のめんどうを見る. ¶***undertake*** the *charge* of his future 彼の今後の監督を引受ける.

Q an official in ***actual physical** charge* [名誉職でなく]実際監督に当る役員. ¶be in his ***direct** charge* 彼が直接管理している. ¶he has ***entire** charge* of ... 彼は...全部の監督に当っている. ¶a schoolmistress and her ***fair** charges* 女教員とその女子の教え子. ¶have ***general** charge* of ... ...全般の管理をする. ¶One out of every four persons who die in London dies in ***public** charge*. ロンドンで死亡する毎四人中の一人は公衆の厄介になって死亡する. ¶He is in ***sole** charge* of the matter. 彼は一手にそのことを引受けている. ¶a ***troublesome** charge* 世話の焼けるもの.

Q² little mothers with their ***baby** charges* 赤ん坊のお守をする小さい母親.

P He is ***in** charge* of the investigation. 彼はその調査の主任をしている. ‖ He is ***in** charge* of the third-year class. 彼は三年級を受持っている. 【類】Dr. N is ***in** charge* of this ward (病室). / a class ***in*** her *charge* / He is ***in** charge* of the books (帳簿). ‖ I was left ***in** charge* of the house. 僕は留守番だった. ‖ He was placed ***in** charge* of the department. 彼はその部長になった. ‖ a person ***in** charge* 主任 ‖ an officer ***in** charge* 担当役員 ‖ a person ***in** charge* of its affairs 業務担当者 ‖ place it ***in** charge* of a caretaker それに番人をつける ‖ the meeting was ***in** charge* of ... その会合の座長は...だった ‖ the physician ***in** charge* 主治医 ‖ put him ***in** charge* of a mill 彼に工場を監督させる. ¶men ***under*** his *charge* 彼の部下 ‖ pupils ***under*** his *charge* 彼の受持っている生徒. 【類】the hospital ***under*** his *charge* ‖ a pilgrimage ***under*** the *charge* of a well-informed guide 博識の案内者付の巡礼旅行 ‖ I have him ***under*** my *charge*. 私は彼の世話をしている. ¶nurse-maids ***with*** their young *charges*. 子供の守をしている子守たち.

P² She is a *charge* ***on*** her old mother. 彼女は老母のやっかいになっている.

(3) 告訴, 告発, 罪, 科(とが).

V do not ***admit*** the *charge* その罪を認めない. ¶The court summons the debtor to appear and ***answer*** the *charges*. 裁判所が出廷して告訴に答弁するため債務者を召喚する. ¶in order to ***avoid*** the *charge* of exaggeration 誇張のそしりを免れるため. ¶***bring*** [***forward***] a *charge* against ... ...を告発する. 【類】***bring*** a *charge* before a court against the murderer of ... ¶***deny*** the *charge* brought against him 彼に被せた罪を否認する. ¶try to ***disprove*** or ***palliate*** the *charge* 非難を反ばくしまたは緩和しようと努める. ¶A *charge* of burglary was ***entered*** against him. 彼は夜盗罪に問われた. ¶He failed to ***establish*** his *charge*. 彼は罪証を挙げ得なかった. ¶***face** charges* of disturbing the peace 治安妨害の罪科で調べを受ける ‖ ***face** charges* of espionage for Russia ロシヤのスパイの嫌疑を受ける. ¶a *charge* of sedition was ***instituted*** against ... ...は扇動の罪科で訴えられた. ¶***lay*** many false *charges* to ... ...に幾多の無実の罪をきせる ‖ ***lay*** the *charge* at the door of ... 罪を...に着せる. ¶***level*** *charges* of dishonesty against ... ...の不正直を非難する. 【類】The *charge* of "social dumping" has at times been ***levelled*** against Japanese industry. ¶***lodge*** a *charge* of infringement of copyright against ... ...に対して著作権侵害の告訴をする. 【類】***lodge*** a *charge* at a police station. ¶***make*** a *charge* against ... ...を告発する ‖ ***make*** a false *charge* 無根のことを訴える. ¶***place** charges* with ... ...に訴える. ¶***prefer*** (=bring forward) a *charge* against ... ...に対して訴訟を提起する. ¶the difficulty of ***proving*** the *charge* その罪を立証することの困難. ¶The judge ***quashed*** the *charges* against the prisoner and set him free. 裁判官は告訴を破棄して囚人を放免した. ¶***relinquish*** a *charge* 告訴を中止する. ¶***repudiate*** the *charge* 罪科を否認する. ¶***retract*** a *charge* 告訴を撤回する. ¶***withdraw*** one's *charge* against him 彼に対する告訴を撤回する.

Q The *charge* is altogether too ***absurd*** to refute. この非難はばか気きっていて反ばくする気になれない. ¶on a ***criminal** charge* 刑事上の罪科で ‖ prisoner under a ***criminal** charge* 刑事犯の囚人. ¶They made a ***false** charge* against him. 彼らは彼にぬれぎぬを着せた. ¶Two ***further** charges* of a similar character were preferred against him. 同様な性質の告訴がさらに二つ彼に対して提起された. ¶the ***general** charge* against ... ...に対する一般の非難. ¶***graver** charges* もっと重い罪科. ¶a ***heavy** charge* 重罪. ¶He was ruined by an ***unjust** charge* of theft. 彼は窃盗というぬれぎぬを着せられて一生を棒に振った. ¶on an ***unproved** charge* of ... ...という証拠不十分のかどで.

Q² bring ***assault** charges* against ... ...を暴行殴打で訴える. ¶on ***atrocity** charges* 凶行のかどで. ¶on a ***burglary** charge* 夜盗のかどで. ¶a ***counter** charge* 原告に対する反訴. ¶be arrested on ***espionage** charges* スパイのかどで逮捕される. ¶be jailed on a ***forgery** charge* 偽造のかどで収監される. ¶on ***gambling** charge* 賭博のかどで. ¶on ***murder** charges* 殺人罪で. ¶be held on ***robbery** charges* by police 強盗のかどで警官に逮捕される ‖ on an armed ***robbery** charge* 持凶器強盗のかどで. ¶await trial on ***war crimes** charges* 戦犯の審問を待つ.

P he is wanted ***on*** a *charge* of ... 彼は...したというかどでお尋ね者になっている ‖ ***on*** a *charge* of burglary (larceny) 夜盗(など)の罪科で. 【類】He was arrested ***on*** a *charge* of murdering the waitress. / be re-arrested (再び逮捕される) ***on*** a *charge* of ... / He was arrested ***on*** a *charge* of having forged several private letters (私書偽造). / a man convicted ***on*** the *charge* of ... ¶They laid the fault ***on*** his *charge*. 彼らはその過失を彼に被せた.

P² a *charge* ***against*** him 彼に対する告訴. ¶A *charge* ***of*** assault was preferred by him against the man. 殴打という罪科でその人を告訴した.

(4) 進撃, 攻撃; 進撃譜.

V he was killed while ***leading** charge* at the battle of ... 彼は...の戦の先頭に立って進撃中戦死した. ¶***rebut*** a *charge* 反撃する. ¶***sound*** the *charge* 進撃譜を奏する.

Q² a ***bayonet** charge* 突貫.

P a *charge* ***of*** cavalry 騎兵の突撃 ‖ the *charge* ***of*** a judge to a jury 判事の陪審員に対する指令.

charge, *v.* **(1)** 賦課する, 負わす; 委任する; 代金(勘定)を取る; ...の借または貸に付ける.

M *charge* ***double*** for ... ...の値を倍にいう. ¶He *charges* ***extravagantly***. 彼はばかに高く吹掛ける. ¶He was *charged* ***heavily*** for it. 彼はそれに対して高い金を払わせられた. ¶*charge* ***high*** for goods 品物の代金を高く取る.

M² *charge* ***down*** upon ... ...に掛ける. ¶A reasonable amount should always be annually *charged* ***off*** for the depreciation of equipment. 備品の減価償却分として相当の金額を年々準備すべきである. ¶*charge* it ***up*** to ... 勘定は...になる ‖ The loss is *charged* ***up*** against the producer. 損害は全部生産者の負担になる.

P *Charge* these ***against*** me. これは私の勘定につけてくれ. ‖ *charge* ***against*** the purchaser of goods 購入者に掛ける ‖ *charge* a payment ***against*** the reserve fund account 支払を積立金勘定の借方に記入する. ¶How much do you *charge* a month ***for*** room and board? 間代と食費で一カ月いくらですか. 【類】How much do you *charge* ***for*** these? / Doctors and lawyers *charge* a fee ***for*** their service. ¶*charge* ***at*** $3.00 a year 一年三ドルを徴収する ‖ *charge* coal ***at*** $5 a ton 一トン五ドルで石炭を売る. ¶Do they *charge* carriage ***by*** bulk or ***by*** weight? 運賃はかさで取るのか目方で取るのか. 【類】Do you *charge* ***by*** the game or ***by*** the hour? (玉突). ¶Admission will be *charged* ***for*** as follows: 入場料は次の通りいただきます. ‖ fee *charged* ***for*** gambling てらせん(賭博の場代). ¶Storage will be *charged* ***on*** each piece of baggage remaining at stations over 24 hours. 二十四時間以上停車場に荷物を受取らずに置くと一個ごとに保管料を徴収します. ¶*charge* ***to*** the account of ... ...の勘定につける ‖ *charge* expense (a thing bought) ***to*** his credit (=account) 費用(など)を彼の口座につける. 【類】*charge* a sum ***to*** him ‖ State universities in America *charge* little or no tuition ***to*** students from the particular State. 米国の州立大学は大学所在の州の学生に対してほとんどあるいは全く授業料を取らない. ¶a *charge* ***upon*** the government 政府の負担. ¶He is *charged* ***with*** the task. 彼はその仕事を任されている. ‖ He is *charged* ***with*** heavy responsibilities. 彼は重任を負わされている. 【類】He was *charged* ***with*** the supervision (監督) of all the military schools. / be *charged* ***with*** an important commission (重要任務) ‖ He was *charged* ***with*** a courtesy greater than he had deserved. あの人としては身分不相応に丁重な扱いを受けた. ‖ I am *charged* ***with*** a message for you. あなたに伝言を頼まれました. ‖ mules *charged* ***with*** large hampers 大かごを負わされた「らば」‖ *charge* one's memory ***with*** some facts ある事実を記憶に留める ‖ *charge* a person ***with*** goods 品物を人に保管させる.

(**2**) 罪を帰する，非難する.
M *falsely charged* ... 無実の罪を受けて.
P They *charged* treason (a crime, delinquency) ***against*** him. 彼は反乱罪(など)に問われた. ¶He was *charged* ***in*** an action of waste. 彼は浪費したと非難された. ‖ The Russians *charged* the United States ***in*** converting Japan into a military bridgehead of the USA in the Far East. ロシアは合衆国が日本を極東の軍事橋頭堡にしているといって非難した. ¶Do you mean to *charge* the guilt ***on*** (=***upon***) me? その罪を僕にきせる積りか ‖ *charge* a crime (sin, blunder) ***on*** him 彼に罪(など)を着せる. ¶He *charged* the accident ***to*** (=***against***) me. 彼はその事故は僕に責任があるとした.【類】He *charged* the calamity (災禍) ***to*** my carelessness. ¶prisoners *charged* ***with*** military offenses 軍事犯を以て問われた捕虜 ‖ abscond, *charged* ***with*** murder 殺人罪に問われて逃亡する.【類】He has been *charged* ***with*** offenses of every imaginable kind. / They *charged* him ***with*** dishonesty. / What is the prisoner *charged* ***with***? / the defects ***with*** which he *charged* them.
(**3**) 詰め込む；満たす.
P *charge* a gun ***with*** powder and ball 銃に弾薬を装填する ‖ a brush *charged* ***with*** black ink 墨の付いている筆 ‖ the atmosphere *charged* ***with*** spray 水気を含んでいる大気 ‖ *charge* water ***with*** carbon dioxide 水に二酸化炭素を飽和させる.
(**4**) 突進する.
P *charge* ***across*** the field 戦場を横断して突進する. ¶The elephant *charged* ***at*** the tree with terrific violence. 象は恐ろしい勢でその樹に向って突進した.

chargeable, *a*. 課せられるべき；負わされるべき.
P a fault *chargeable* ***on*** (=***upon***) a man 人に負わさるべき罪.【類】a duty (税) *chargeable* ***on*** wine. ¶The support of children is *chargeable* ***upon*** parents. 子供を養う義務が両親にはある. ¶He is *chargeable* ***with*** a fault or neglect. 彼は過失または怠慢を以て問わるべきものだ.

chariot, *n*. 馬車，二輪戦車.
Q a ***south-seeking*** *chariot* 指南車.
P[2] a *chariot* ***for*** the race 競走用の馬車.

charitable, *a*. 慈悲深い，慈善的な.
P He is *charitable* ***to*** (=***toward***) the poor. 彼は貧民に慈悲深い.

charity, *n*. 慈悲，仁慈，慈善，施し物.
V ***ask*** (=***beg***) *charity* 施しを請う. ¶***bestow*** *charity* 仁慈をたれる. ¶***distribute*** *charity* 施しを分ち与える. ¶The true way to gain influence over fellowmen is to ***have*** *charity* toward them. 仲間を動かす真の方法は彼らに情をかける事だ. ¶***practice*** *charity* 施しをする. ¶He will not ***tolerate*** *charity*. 彼は人から恵みを受けることを喜ばないでしょう.
Q an exhibition of ***heroic*** *charity* [疫病撲滅に努めるなど] 勇敢な慈善的行為の一例. ¶***indiscriminate*** *charity* 慎重さを欠く慈善行為. ¶contribute freely to ***organized*** *charities* 慈善団体へ盛んに寄付する. ¶The hospital depends upon ***public*** *charity* for its support. その病院は一般の寄付で支えている.
P He is noted ***for*** his *charities*. 彼は慈善で有名だ. ¶***for the sake of*** *charity* 慈善のため. ¶I am ***in*** (***out of***) *charity* with ... 私は...に対して好意(悪意)を持っている. ‖ He gives money freely ***in*** *charity*. 彼は惜まず金を施す ‖ something given ***in*** *charity* 施し物. ¶an act ***of*** *charity* 慈善行為 ‖ It is a very great piece ***of*** *charity* in you. 実に御親切なことです. ¶He lives (=depends=is dependent) ***on*** *charity*. 彼は施しを受けて暮している. ¶I employ him ***out of*** *charity*. 彼をあわれんで使ってやっている.【類】He did it solely ***out of*** *charity*. ¶He is given ***to*** *charity*. 彼は慈善に心を傾けている.
P[2] *charity* ***for*** the weak and erring 弱き者や身を誤れる者のための慈善. ¶*charity* ***to*** (=***toward***) all men すべての人に対する慈悲.

charlatanism, *n*. 知ったかぶり.
P[2] *charlatanism* ***in*** psychology いんちき心理学.

charm, *n*. (**1**) 魅力；妙味；愛きょう.
V ***add*** *charm* to the surrounding country 周囲の土地に風致を添える ‖ An ornamental flower vase ***adds*** a *charm* to drawing-rooms. 美しい花びんは応接室を引立たせる. ¶***break*** the *charm* 幻滅を感じさせる. ¶try to ***catch*** the elusive *charm* of the original in translation 翻訳すると失われやすい原文の美点を捕えようと努力する. ¶***contemplate*** the *charms* of a girl 少女の美ぼうに見とれる. ¶Women should ***cultivate*** mental *charms* as well as physical ones. 女は容ぼうの美と同時に精神の美を養うべきである. ¶***destroy*** the *charms* of a pretty face 美しい顔の魅力を損う. ¶***dispel*** the *charm* 興ざめがする. ¶***display*** female *charms* 女性美を発揮する. ¶***enhance*** the *charm* of a trip to ... 旅行者から見ての...の魅力を増す. ¶***give*** an additional *charm* ... ...に一段の美を添える. ¶The fireside ***has*** great *charms*. 暖炉のそばは実によい. ¶***heighten*** the *charm* of her complexion 彼女の血色の美を増す. ¶***lend*** a great *charm* to ... ...に大なる魅力を添える. ¶Those members of the third sex have ***lost*** the *charms* of womanhood. こういう第三の性の女たちは女としての魅力を失っている. ¶When in flower the lotus plant ***makes*** the greatest *charm* of the garden. 花のころははすがその庭で一番の見物(みもの)である. ¶it ***owes*** much of its *charm* to ... その魅力は主として...から来る. ¶The collection of autographs ***possesses*** a peculiar (=special) *charm* for many people. 筆蹟の収集は非常に多くの人に取って一種独特の魅力がある. ¶***practice*** that *charm* on ... ...にその魅力を働かす. ¶***retain*** their original *charm* 本来の魅力を失わない. ¶***sell*** her *charms* 愛を売る. ¶To my taste the word ... ***spoils*** the *charm*. 私に言わせると...という語はこの場合つや消しだ.
Q give an ***additional*** *charm* to ... ...に一層魅力を与える. ¶***artistic*** *charm* 芸術的妙味. ¶***bodily*** *charm* 肉体美. ¶their ***budding*** *charms* 彼女らの花も二八のあで姿. ¶constitute one of the ***chief*** *charms* of ... ...の主なる魅力の一つを成す. ¶Daintiness is the very essence of ***feminine*** *charm*. 優雅は女性美の真髄である. ¶his ***great*** *charm* of manner 彼の非常に優美な物腰.【類】Precision (正確) is one of the ***great*** *charms* of composition. ¶***hidden*** *charms* 目に見えない情味. ¶an ***inalienable*** *charm* 他に移し得ない妙味. ¶It has an ***indescribable*** *charm*. それには筆舌に表わし得ない妙味がある. ¶an ***intangible*** *charm* 言うに言われぬ妙味. ¶The *charm* is ***irresistible***. その美しさには降参せざるを得ない. ¶short stories of no ordinary ***literary*** *charm* 非常に文学的魅力のある短篇小説.【類】His style is full of ***literary*** *charm*. ¶the ***magnetic*** *charm* of personality 人格という，人を引きつける力 ¶the ***naive*** *charm* of folk art 民芸品の素朴な味. ¶a ***nameless*** *charm* 言い知れない妙味. ¶***pastoral*** *charm* 田園美. ¶The pagoda adds a ***peculiar*** *charm* to the landscape. その塔は風景に一種独特の美観を添える. ¶***personal*** *charms* 容色. ¶***rhythmical*** *charm* 韻律の美. ¶He does not cultivate any ***particular*** *charm* of style. 彼の文体には特殊な妙味は見られない. ¶its ***quaint, quiet, old-fashioned*** *charm* その珍奇な，落ついた，古風な味. ¶***rustic*** *charm* 素朴な味. ¶a man of ***social*** *charm* 社交的魅力のある人. ¶a smile full of ***subtle*** *charm* 微妙な魅力に満ちた微笑. ¶***unfailing*** *charm* 尽きない魅力. ¶the *charm* of it is so ***winning*** that ... その魅力は非常なもので...
Q[2] the old ***world*** *charm* of Elizabethan drama エリザベス時代の劇の古風な魅力.
P a city ***with*** the *charm* of yesteryear 昔の名残を留めた都市.
P[2] There is a *charm* ***about*** his manner. 彼の動作には魅力がある. ¶a *charm* ***in*** a woman ある女の持つ魅力. ¶the *charms* ***of*** nature 自然の魅力.【類】the *charms* ***of*** oratory (弁舌) / her *charm* ***of*** manner (動作) / His writings have a *charm* ***of*** style (文体). / This is the *charm* (=beauty) ***of*** it.
(**2**) まじない；護符.
V ***wear*** a *charm* to bring in good fortune and keep off bad fortune.
Q a ***life*** *charm* 命の守札.
P ***as*** a *charm* against bad luck 厄よけのおまじないに. ¶This acted ***like*** a *charm*. これがまじないのようにきいた.
P[2] a *charm* ***against*** barrenness in women 子宝の授かるお守札. ¶Formerly cauls were popularly believed to be a sure *charm* ***against*** death at sea by drowning. 昔は胎児膜は確かに溺死除けの護符になると一般に信ぜられていた.【類】a *charm* ***against*** evils (災難) / a *charm* ***against*** forgetfulness (忘れないための).
O a *charm* to call forth blessing 福を招くまじない.

charm, *v*. 魅する；まじないをかける.
M *charm* ***away*** the whooping-cough 百日ぜきをまじないでなおす.【類】Laughter *charmed* ***away*** his troubles.
M[2] *charm* ***off*** a disease 病魔をはらう.
P The serpent was *charmed* ***by*** the music. へびが音楽に

魅せられた. 【類】I was *charmed* **by** this lavish display of paternal love (父性愛). / *charmed* **by** your friendship. ¶*charm* him **from** (=**out of**) melancholy 彼のゆううつを追払う. ¶He was *charmed* **with** the beauty and grandeur of the scenery. 彼はその風景の美と壮大に見とれた.【類】I was *charmed* **with** his conversation. / I felt *charmed* (聞きほれた) **with** the music of birds.

charming, *a.* 愛きょうのある, うっとりさせる.
P *charming* **in** manner 動作に人を引き付ける所のある. ¶She is *charming* **to** all. 彼女はだれにでも愛きょうがある.

chart, *n.* 海図, 図, 表.
V **consult** a *chart* 海図を調べる.
Q a **genealogical** *chart* 系図. ¶a **general** *chart* 総図. ¶a **graphic** *chart* グラフ図. ¶**statistical** *charts* 統計表.
Q^2 a **grammar** *chart* 文法図表. ¶a **temperature** (=**fever**) *chart* 体温表. ¶a **weather** *chart* 天気図.
P It is shown **on** (=**in**) *Chart* 7. それは第七図に出ている. 【類】the curves (曲線) **on** *Chart* 11.

charter, *n.* 免許状, 特許状, 契約書.
V **cancel** a *charter* (party) 免許証(会合)を取消す. ¶**effect** a *charter* 用船契約をする. ¶**receive** a *charter* 特許状を受ける.
Q^2 a **city** *charter* 市で発行する許可証. ¶an organization with a **State** *charter* 州政府認可団体. ¶the ship is under **time** *charter* with ... その船は...と時間賃貸契約がついている.【類】secure a steamer on **time** *charter*. ¶the **United Nations** *Charter* 国際連合憲章.
P the steamer is **under** *charter* by ... to ... 同汽船は...によって...行きのことに用船契約ができている.

charter, *v.* 契約で借りる.
P *charter* a ballpark **for** the season シーズン中野球場を契約で借りる. 【類】a vessel *chartered* **for** the season. ¶*charter* a vessel **with** the government 船を政府から借りる.

chase, *n.* 追求, 追撃; 追われる物; 猟.
V The squadron immediately **gave** *chase* to the enemy's fleet. 艦隊は直ちに敵艦を追撃した. ¶**give up** the *chase* 追撃をやめる.
Q in **full** *chase* 一生懸命に追いかけて. ¶The *chase* was **hot** after him. 彼を追跡することはなはだ急であった. ¶a **losing** *chase* 追いつく見込の無い追撃. ¶Honor is the **noblest** *chase*. 名誉は最も高尚な追求物である.
Q^2 a **wild-goose** *chase* 果しのない仕事, むだな努力.
P one **in** *chase* of the other 一方が他方を追いかけて ‖ The implement is used **in** the *chase*. この道具は狩で用いる. ¶spoils **of** the *chase* 狩の獲物. ¶gain **on** the *chase* 追迫する.
P^2 a *chase* **after** butterflies ちょう採集. ¶the *chase* **for** honors 名誉の追求. ¶*chase* **of** pleasure (profit) 快楽(など)の追求.

chase, *v.* 追う.
M *chase* **away** phantoms 妖怪を追払う.
M^2 The fox was *chased* **off** into the woods. きつねが森の中へ追立てられた.

chase, *v.* 彫刻を施す, [模様など]打ち出す.
P *chased* **in** high relief くっきりと模様を浮出しにした. ¶*chased* **with** birds and foliage 鮮やかに鳥や木の葉を彫刻した.

chaser, *n.* 彫刻師; 追撃する人(者).
Q^2 an **ambulance** *chaser* 《米》三百代言(交通事故などの負傷者を種に鉄道会社などに損害賠償の掛合をするなど).
P^2 a *chaser* **in** metals 金属の彫刻師.

chasm, *n.* 割目, 間隙(かんげき); 分裂, 不和.
V **bridge** the *chasm* between gown and desk 大学における師弟の関係を一層密接にする. ¶**bridge over** the *chasm* その間隙の橋渡しをする. ¶a *chasm* is **opened** between ... and ... ...と...との間に間隙が生じた. ¶**widen** the *chasm* between ... ...の間のみぞを深くする. ¶the linguistic *chasm* **dividing** the two peoples 両国民を隔離する言語のみぞ.
P^2 a *chasm* **in** the earth 地の割目.

chasten, *v.* きたえる, こらしめる.
P a spirit *chastened* **by** adversity (trials and sorrows) 艱難(など)にきたえられた精神. ¶*chasten* a son **with** a rod むち打って息子をこらす ‖ He was *chastened* **with** pain. 彼は痛い目にあった.

chastise, *v.* こらす.
P *chastise* a man **for** his fault 過失のかどをもって人をこらす. ¶*chastise* him **with** blows (a whip) 打って(むちで)彼をこらす.

chastisement, *n.* 折かん, 懲罰.
P **by** mild *chastisement* 穏かなせっかんで. ¶cries of the child **under** *chastisement* せっかん中の子供の泣声.

chastity, *n.* 貞操; 高潔.
V **cultivate** a strict *chastity* of thought and feeling きわめて高潔な思想と感情をかん養する. ¶**defend** her *chastity* 彼女の貞操を守る. ¶**lose** one's *chastity* その純潔を失う.

chat, *n.* 閑談, 雑談.
V I **enjoyed** an animated *chat* with a friend. 友人との話に花が咲いた. ¶**have** a comfortable *chat* 愉快に雑談する.
Q we enjoyed a **friendly** *chat* about ... われわれは...について懇談した. ¶an **intimate** and **friendly social** *chat* 親しい打ちとけた話. ¶have a **long** *chat* 長話しをする. ¶a **moment's** *chat* ちょっとの雑談. ¶Let's have a **nice little** *chat*. 少しおもしろい話でもしようじゃないか. ¶a **pleasant** *chat* 愉快な談笑.
Q^2 give a **fireside** *chat* 炉辺談話をする. ¶a **society** *chat* 社交話, 世間話.
P go **into** *chat* with ... ...と雑談を始める. ¶I began a little *chat* **about** my journey. 少し旅行の話を始めた. ‖ He has too much *chat* **about** him. 彼は余り自慢しすぎる. ¶a *chat* **over** their old Cambridge days 彼らのケンブリッジ大学時代の昔をしのぶ雑談.

chat, *v.* 談笑する, 雑談する.
M *chat* **charmingly** 愉快に話す. ¶*chat* **genially** in groups 三々五々寄合って快談する. ¶We *chat* **together** sometimes. われわれはときどき寄って話す.
P *chat* **about** ... ...について閑談する. ¶We *chatted* **of** old times. われわれは昔を語り合った. ¶*chat* discursively **on** a variety of topics 漫談をやる. ¶We were busy *chatting* **over** our cigars. われわれは葉巻をくゆらしながら盛んに語り合った. ‖ *chat* **over** tea (wine) 茶(など)を飲みながら談ずる. 【類】*chat* **over** the wine cup. ¶*chat* **with** friends **about** our affair われわれの仕事について友だちと話す.

chattels, *n. pl.* 家財.
Q **personal** *chattels* 私有動産.

chatter, *n.* おしゃべり, むだ話.
Q the **idle** *chatter* of the crowd 群集のむだ話.
Q^2 their **magpie** *chatter* 彼らの雑談.

chatter, *v.* しゃべる; がたがた震える.
P *chatter* **about** (=**of**) a matter あることについてぺちゃぺちゃしゃべる. ¶*chatter* **at** (=**to**) a person 人にぺちゃぺちゃ話し掛ける. ¶They were *chattering* **over** their needlework. 彼らは縫物をしながらしゃべっていた. ¶His teeth were *chattering* **with** cold. 彼は寒いので歯ががたがたしていた.
M *chatter* **gaily** 快談する. ¶*chatter* **noisily** やかましくしゃべる.

chatterbox, *n.* おしゃべり屋.
Q She is a **fearful** *chatterbox*. 彼女は大変なおしゃべりだ.

chattering, *n.* おしゃべり.
Q **idle** *chattering* むだ話.
P^2 No *chattering* **over** work. 勤務中雑談無用.

chauffeur, *n.* 自動車の運転手.
Q^2 a **gentleman** *chauffeur* 自分で運転する自動車の持主.
P work **as** *chauffeur* for the vacation 休暇中運ちゃんをやる.

cheap, *a.* 安い, 低廉な; そまつな.
M It was **by no means** *cheap*. それは決して安くなかった. ¶Novels are **dirt**-*cheap* in America. 小説は米国ではめちゃに安い. ¶be *cheap* **enough** to be accessible to every student どんな学生にも買えるほど安い. ¶be **fairly** *cheap* かなり安い. ¶**phenomenally** *cheap* めっぽう安い.
P *cheap* **at** that rate それでは割安である. 【類】If this painting is genuine, it is *cheap* even **at** one thousand yen. ¶It is *cheap* **for** ten yen. 十円では安い. ¶*cheap* **in** make 粗製の.
O feel *cheap* はじる, しょげる. ¶*cheap* entertainment おそまつな余興.

cheap, *ad.* 安く, 廉価に.
M I got these vases **dog** *cheap*. これらの鉢はめちゃ安(やす)に買った. ☞ dog cheap は good cheap のなまりという説がある.
P sell *cheap* **for** cash 現金なら安く売る.

cheapness, *n.* 廉価.
Q **relative** *cheapness* 比較的廉価.

cheat, *n.* ぺてん師.
Q a **notorious** *cheat* 名うてのペテン師.

cheat, *v.* あざむく, ごまかす; 不正を行う.
P *cheat* **at** (=in) one's examinations (lessons) カンニングをやる ‖ *cheat* a person **at** cards カルタ遊びで人をごまかす. 【類】*cheating* **at** cards. ¶*cheat* him **by** false

pretenses (flattery) 詐偽(など)で彼をだます ‖ ***cheated by*** appearance 外見にだまされて. ¶***cheat in*** a contest 競争で不正行為をやる ‖ ***cheat*** a person ***in*** trade 取引で人をだます. ¶They ***cheated*** him ***into*** industry. 彼らは彼をだまして働かした. 【類】 ***cheat*** her ***into*** marrying / ***cheat*** a person ***into*** the belief that ... ¶***cheat*** him [***out***] ***of*** his money 彼をあざむいて金を取る ‖ ***cheat*** a man [***out***] ***of*** his due 人をあざむいて当然受けるべきものを与えない. ¶***cheated with*** counterfeit coin にせ銭をつかまされて.

check, cheque, *n.* 小切手; [チッキの]合札; 阻止, 検束; 〖将棋〗王手.

V ***cash*** a ***check*** 小切手を現金に替える. ¶***cross*** a ***check*** 小切手を横線にする. ¶***draw*** a ***cheque*** to one's order 指図式小切手を振出す. ¶***deposit*** a ***check*** 小切手をあずける. ¶***draw*** a ***check*** 小切手を振出す ‖ ***checks drawn*** on banks 銀行に振出した小切手 ‖ ***checks*** should be ***drawn*** to the order of ... 小切手は…の指図人あてに振出すべし. ¶***enclose*** a ***check*** in a letter 小切手を手紙に封入する. ¶***endorse*** a ***check*** 小切手の裏書をする. ¶***give*** one's ***check*** to the cashier つけ(伝票)を現金掛りに出す(喫茶店などで) ‖ I ***gave*** ***check*** with my bishop. [西洋将棋の]ビショップで王手を差した. ¶***impose*** some legal ***check*** upon ... …に法律の手を回す. ¶***make out*** the required ***check*** 要求された小切手を作成する. ¶***pass*** a bogus ***check*** 偽造小切手を渡す. ¶A large ***check*** was ***paid*** into his account. 大金が小切手で彼の口座に払い込まれた. ¶***place*** a ***check*** on ... …を抑圧する. ¶***present*** a ***check*** 小切手を呈示する. ¶***raise*** a ***check*** 小切手の金額を高額に改ざんする. ¶***receive*** a ***check*** 阻止される. ¶***remit*** a ***check*** for £300 三百ポンドの小切手を送る. ¶***send*** a ***check*** to ... …に小切手を送る. ¶He is noted for his fearlessness in ***signing checks***. 彼は金の出し惜みをしないので有名だ. ¶***stop*** a ***check*** 小切手の支払を止める. ¶***suffer*** a ***check*** 抑制を受ける. ¶***write out*** a ***check*** 小切手を書く.

Q an ***altered check*** 改ざんした小切手. ¶a ***baggage check*** 荷物の合札. ¶a ***blank check*** 白地式小切手. ¶a ***dishonored check*** 不渡り小切手. ¶a ***duplicate check*** for baggage 荷物の片方の合札. ¶impose an ***effective check*** on ... …を十分に防止する. ¶***numbered checks*** 番号付合札.

Q² a ***bank check*** 銀行小切手. ¶a ***bed check*** 寝台券. ¶a ***claim check*** 預り票. ¶a ***gift check*** 贈答用小切手(銀行の). ¶***paper*** (***metal***) ***checks*** 紙(金属)製の引合せ札. ¶a ***pawn check*** 質札. ¶make an ***on-the-spot check*** of ... …の即時払小切手を作成する.

P hold the enemy ***in check*** 敵を食い止める. ¶get the cash ***on*** his ***check*** 彼の小切手で現金を受ける. ¶***under*** proper ***checks*** and restraints 適当の抑制を加えて. ¶***without check*** or restraint 抑制せずに.

P² a ***check for*** my baggage 私の荷物の合札 ‖ a ***check for*** 300 yen 三百円の小切手 ‖ a ***check for*** a wheel 車の輪止め. ¶my ***check on*** you (a bank) 貴殿(など)あて小生振出しの小切手. ¶a ***check to*** some action (movement) ある行動(など)に対する抑制 ‖ ***Check to*** your king! [将棋]王手! ¶letters of credit or ***checks upon*** a well-known London banking firm ある有名なロンドンの銀行に対して振出した信用状または小切手. ¶The enemy met ***with*** a ***check***. 敵は食い止められた.

check, *v.* 《米》阻止する; 《米》チッキにする; 引合わせる.

M ***check out*** 《米》支払を済ましてホテルを出る; 記入済のしるしをつける. ¶***check out*** deposit from a bank 銀行から預金を小切手で引き出す.

M² ***check in*** 《米》ホテルにとまる. ¶***check off*** 引合せまたは記入済の印をつける. ¶***check up*** one's record 《米》成績(経歴)を調べる. 【類】 ***check up*** one's physical record (体格検査証) ‖ ***check up*** on a statement 報告書を調べる.

P be ***checked against*** ... …と引合せる. ¶The advance was ***checked by*** the river. 前が川で進めなくなった. ‖ be ***checked*** for accuracy ***by*** specialists 正確にするために専門家が対照して調べる. ¶***check*** the number ***with*** a mark 印をつけて数を調べる ‖ baggage ***checked with*** the railroad 鉄道でチッキにした荷物 ‖ ***check*** a horse ***with*** reins 手綱で馬を止める ‖ The merchandise does not ***check with*** invoice. 商品が送状と合わない. ‖ You'd better ***check*** it up ***with*** the original. 原文と対照する方がいい.

checking, *n.* 照合, 引合わせ.

V ***effect checking*** with the main register 台帳との照合を「行う.

Q² ***spot checking*** 現場引合せ.

check-off, *n.* 天引き.

P² ***check-off of*** union dues 組合費天引.

cheek, *n.* ほお; 鉄面皮.

V ***blush cheeks*** ほおを赤くする. ¶***have*** the ***cheek*** to ask for more 鉄面皮にもその上をねだる. ¶She ***laid*** her ***cheek*** against mine. 彼女はほおを私のほおにすり寄せた. ¶***pinch*** one's ***cheek*** till it bleeds 血の出るまでほおをつねる. ¶The trumpeter ***puffs out*** his ***cheeks***. らっぱ手がほおをふくらます. ¶***rouge*** their ***cheeks*** and lips 彼女らのほおやくちびるにべにを塗る. ¶***sour*** one's ***cheeks*** にがい顔をする. ¶***stroke*** a child's ***cheeks*** 子供のほおをなでる. ¶Her ***cheeks*** were ***suffused*** with blushes. 彼女は顔に紅葉を散らしていた. ¶He is a man who believes in ***turning*** the other ***cheek*** to violence. あの人は暴力に対して他のほおを向ける事を(無抵抗主義が)よいと信じている人だ. 「にした.

V² His ***cheeks blushed*** with a deep scarlet. 彼は顔を真赤

Q ***bloated cheeks*** ふくれたほお. ¶***burning cheeks*** 燃えるように真赤なほお. ¶***buxom cheeks*** まるぽちゃのほお. ¶***chubby cheeks*** 丸ぽちゃ. ¶***dimpled cheeks*** えくぼのあるほお. ¶***florid cheeks*** 花のようなほお. ¶***flushed cheeks*** 赤らんだほお. ¶***high-colored cheeks*** まっかな(日に焼けた)ほお. ¶***hollow cheeks*** くぼんだほお. ¶***lily-white cheeks*** ゆりのように白いほお. ¶***pale cheeks*** そう白なほお. ¶***pink cheeks*** もも色のほお. ¶a girl with ***plump cheeks*** 丸ぽちゃの少女. ¶***puffed*** [***up***] ***cheeks*** ふくらましたほお, 自慢顔. ¶***purple cheeks*** むらさき色のほお. ¶***red cheeks*** 赤いほお. ¶the ***rosy cheeks*** of maidenhood 処女のばら色のほお. ¶***rosy-hued cheeks*** ばら色のほお. ¶***round cheeks*** 丸ぽちゃ. ¶***ruddy cheeks*** 赤らんだほお. ¶***sunk cheeks*** くぼんだほお. ¶***swollen cheeks*** ふくれたほお. ¶***wan cheeks*** 青ざめたほお. ¶***well-fleshed cheeks*** ふくよかなほお.

P Tears streamed (＝ran) ***down*** her ***cheeks***. 涙が彼女のほおを流れ落ちた. ¶A tear stole ***down*** her ***cheek***. 彼女はほろりと涙を流した. ¶kiss her ***on*** the ***cheeks*** 彼女の両ほおに接ぷんする ‖ I hit (struck, slapped) him ***on*** the ***cheek***. 彼のほおを打った. ‖ that very delicate bloom ***on*** her ***cheeks*** あの美しい彼女のほおのもも色 ‖ He wears whiskers ***on*** his ***cheeks***. 彼はほおひげをはやしている. ¶boys and girls ***with*** the rosy ***cheeks*** and happy looks ばら色したほおと愉快そうな顔した少年・少女たち ‖ a man ***with*** the coolest ***cheeks*** imaginable この上もなく図々しい顔をした男.

P² My house stands ***cheek by*** jowl with a hardware shop. 私の家は金物屋と並んでいる.

cheer, *n.* かっさい, 歓呼; 元気.

V ***acknowledge*** the ***cheers*** of the crowd by saluting 答礼して群集の歓呼に応じる. ¶***evoke cheers*** かっさいをよび起す. ¶***give*** him a farewell ***cheer*** 彼に告別の歓呼を送る. ¶Let's ***give*** him some ***cheers***. 彼を少し応援してやろう. ‖ I led the lads in ***giving*** three ***cheers*** for the King and the Empire. 少年たちの音頭を取って王および帝国の万歳を三唱した. 【類】 We ***gave*** three ***cheers*** of "Banzai" for the Imperial Navy. / His health was drunk (彼の健康のために乾杯し) and three ***cheers*** for him were ***given***. ¶He ***proposed*** three ***cheers*** for the President. 彼は大統領のために万歳三唱を発議した. ¶The crowds ***raised*** a ***cheer*** such as Paris had not heard for years. 群集はパリ市において数年聞いたこともないほどの歓呼の声をあげた. ¶He ***recieved*** a hearty ***cheer*** from the audience. 彼は聴衆から熱心なかっさいを受けた. ¶***send up*** rousing ***cheers*** もりあがる歓呼の声をあげる.

Q amid ***deafening cheers*** 耳もろうせんばかりのかっさい裡に. ¶lost in a round of ***derisive cheer*** 引続いて起るあざけりの叫びにぼう然自失して. ¶reply with ***enthusiastic cheers*** 熱心な歓呼で応じる. ¶Be of ***good cheer***. 元気を出せ. ‖ be in ***good cheer*** はしゃいでいる. ¶A ***hearty cheer*** was raised. 熱心なかっさいが発せられた. ¶***loud cheers*** 高い歓呼. ¶with ***lusty cheers*** 熱心にかっさいして. ¶A ***ringing cheer*** of "Banzai" went up from the crowd. 鳴り響く万歳の叫びが群集から起った. ¶encouraged by the ***sustaining cheer*** of seeing his work well received 自分の著作が歓迎されるのに力を得て. ¶The crowd gave ***three cheers***, "Hip, hip, hurrah!" 群集は「ヒップ・ヒップ・フラー!」と歓呼を三唱した. ¶***vociferous cheer*** とどろく歓呼, 盛んなかっさい.

Q² a ***Christmas cheer*** クリスマスの歓呼.

P *amid* the *cheers* of the crowds of spectators 群がる見物人のかっさい裡に ‖ The game was recommenced *amid* hearty (=great) *cheers.* 競技は歓呼のうちに再び始まった. 【類】The curtain was drawn *amid* loud *cheers.* ¶a round *of cheers* 一しきり鳴渡るかっさい. ¶We received him *with cheers* and clapping of hands which lacked nothing in spontaneity and warmth. われわれは少しも不自然な所がなくまた十分の熱誠をこめた歓呼と拍手をもって彼を迎えた. ¶looks *without cheer* 元気のない顔.

P^2 Cheer *after cheer* followed his appearance on the platform. 彼が演壇に立つとしきりにかっさいが起った. ¶Three *cheers for* the King! 国王万歳. ¶*cheers from* the crowds 群集のかっさい. ¶*cheers over* the victory 勝利へのかっさい.

cheer, *v.* 歓呼する, かっさいする；喜ばす.

M *cheer frantically* 熱狂的に歓呼する. ¶He was *heartily cheered* by the large crowd which had assembled at the station. 彼は停車場に集まっていた群集によって熱心に歓呼された. ¶Men *cheered* themselves *hoarse.* 人々は声をからしてかっさいした. ¶*cheer lustily* 盛んに歓呼する. ¶*cheer vociferously* はげしくかっさいする. ¶They were *warmly cheered.* 彼らは熱心に歓呼された. ¶*cheer wildly* 狂喜かっさいする.

M^2 *cheer down* a speaker 弁士をやじり倒す. ¶*cheer up* ...の元気をつける, 鼓舞する；しっかりする. ¶*cheer up* our spirits われわれを元気づける ‖ He *cheered up* at once when I promised to help him. 私が力を添えると言ったらたちまち元気づいた.

P The success was loudly *cheered by* the crowd. その成功は群集によって盛んにかっさいされた. ‖ He was *cheered by* the good news. 彼はその吉報で元気付いた. 【類】be *cheered by* the hope that ... ¶*cheer for* a good player 上手な俳優(競技者, 演奏者など)にかっさいを送る. ¶*cheer over* the victory 勝利を得て歓呼する. ¶He was *cheered with* singing. 歌で彼の気を引立たした.

cheerful, *a.* 元気のよい.

P He is *cheerful in spite of* his illness. 病気でも元気がいい.

cheerfulness, *n.* 愉快.

V He *gave cheerfulness* to the feast by pleasant talk. 彼はおもしろい座談で御ちそうに興を添えた.

cheering, *n.* 歓呼, かっさい.

V as the *cheering died* かっさいが止むと.

Q *full-throated cheering* 満腔(こう)のかっさい.

P amid outbursts of *cheering from* the crowd 群集からのわれるようなかっさい裡に.

cheese, *n.* チーズ.

Q *ripe cheese* 食べごろのチーズ.

Q^2 *damson cheese* チーズ形の砂糖づけ.

chef, *n. F.* コック長.

Q^2 the cooking of *expert chefs* 腕っこきのコック長の料理.

P restaurants famous *for* their *chefs* りっぱなコック長を使っているので有名な料理店.

chef-d'oeuvre, *n.* 傑作.

P^2 the *chef-d'oeuvre of* the day その時代の傑作.

chemise, *n.* シュミーズ.

V She appeared, wearing a bathrobe and *carrying* a *chemise* over her shoulder. 彼女は浴衣を着, シュミーズを肩に掛けて出て来た. ¶*lay* (=*take*) *off* a *chemise* シュミーズをぬぐ. ¶*wear* a *chemise* シュミーズを着る.

chemist, *n.* 薬剤師.

Q a *manufacturing chemist* 製薬家.

chemistry, *n.* 化学.

Q *physical chemistry* 物理的化学. ¶*warfare chemistry* 兵器用化学.

cheque, *n.* =check.

cherish, *v.* 愛撫する, かわいがる；[希望・うらみなど]いだく.

P opinions *cherished among* them 彼らのいだいている意見. ¶They have *cherished* the child *as* one of their own. 彼らはその子供を自分らの子として愛育した. ¶I *cherish for* you the most lively feelings of affection and gratitude. 諸君に対し愛情と感謝の最も力強い感情をいだいています. ¶She *cherishes* his memory still *in* unforgetting affection. 彼女はいまだに忘れ得ない愛着をもって彼を心ひそかに慕っている. 【類】These proofs of kindness and generous feeling will forever be *cherished in* my memory. ‖ *cherish* the religion *in* the heart その宗教を心ひそかに信奉する.

cherry, *n.* さくらんぼ.

V The kid *swallowed* a *cherry*, stone and all. その子供がさくらんぼを種ごと丸のみにした.

V^2 *Cherries vary* in color from almost black to yellow. さくらんぼは黒っぽいのから黄色まで色々ある.

cherry-tree, *n.* 桜の木.

V He *cut down* the *cherry-tree* with the new hatchet. 彼はその新しいおので桜の木を切り倒した. ¶*intersperse cherry-trees* among the willows 桜を柳の間に植える. ¶*transplant cherry-trees* into Louisiana ルイジアナに桜の木を移植する.

chess, *n.* 西洋将棋.

V *play chess* with ... ...と将棋をさす.

P win a game *at chess* 将棋に勝つ ‖ move a man *at chess* 将棋で駒を動かす. ¶men (=pieces) *in chess* 将棋の駒.

chessboard, *n.* 西洋将棋盤.

Q the *political chessboard* 政界の局面.

Q^2 a *traveling chessboard* 旅行用将棋盤.

chest, *n.* (**1**) 胸.

V *expand* the *chest* 胸を張る. ¶*expand* and *strengthen* the *chest* 胸郭を拡げかつ強壮にする. ¶He *puffed out* his *chest* with pride. 得意になって胸をふくらました. ¶*throw out* one's *chest* 胸を突出す.

Q *man's chest* and woman's breast 男の胸と女の胸. ¶He has been rejected as a soldier for his *narrow chest.* 彼は胸囲が不十分なため徴兵にはねられた. ¶She has a *weak chest.* 彼女は胸が弱い. 【類】His *chest* has been *weak* from his youth.

P I have a pain *in* the *chest.* 胸が痛い. 【類】He was shot *in* the *chest.* ‖ keep one's temper more *in chest* 胸に収めてじっと我慢する ‖ suffer from disease *in* (=*of*) the *chest* 胸の病をわずらう. ¶He struck me a blow *on* the *chest.* 彼は僕の胸を打った. ¶He measures 36 inches *round* the *chest.* 彼は胸囲が三十六インチある.

(**2**) 箱, たんす.

Q be locked up in *water-tight chests* 防水の箱の中に入れて錠をおろされる.

Q^2 the *community chest* 共同募金. ¶a *linen chest* リンネル物(下着)の箱. ¶a *medicine chest* 薬箱. ¶a *treasure chest* 宝箱. ¶an AFL (=American Federation of Labor) political *war chest* アメリカ労働総同盟の軍用金.

P^2 a *chest of* clothes たんすに一杯の着物 ‖ a *chest of* drawers たんす.

chestnut, *n.* 栗.

Q a *toasted chestnut* 焼栗.

Q^2 a *horse chestnut* とちの木の一種.

chew, *n.* かむこと.

V *have* a *chew* of gum=chew gum ガムをかむ.

chew, *v.* かむ.

M^2 I felt as if I could *chew* him right *up.* 彼をいきなりペシャンコにすることができるような気持がした.

chic, *n. F.* 粋, いき.

Q an *undefinable chic* 言うに言われない粋な点.

chic, *a. F.* 粋な, いきな.

M it is considered *very chic* to ... ...することがはなはだ粋だとされている.

chicane, *v.* ごまかす.

M *chicane away* ずるく免れる.

chick, *n.* ひよこ.

V *hatch out chicks* ひよこをかえす. ¶The hen *gathers* her *chicks* under her feathers. めんどりがひなを翼の下に抱える. ¶*give chicks* to a hen to brood ひなをめんどりに抱かせる.

V^2 *Chicks come* out of eggs. ひなは卵からかえる.

Q He is *one chick* to her. 彼はあの女のひとりっ子だ. ¶the *hen-hatched* and *hen-mothered chick* めんどりがかえし育てたひな.

Q^2 a *baby chick* ひよっこ. ¶a brood of *incubator chicks* 孵(ふ)卵器でかえした一回分のひな. ¶*machine chicks* 孵卵器でかえしたひな.

chicken, *n.* ひよこ；《米》にわとり；鶏肉.

V *hatch chickens* ひよこをかえす. ¶*raise chickens* and hogs 鶏と豚を飼う. ¶*singe* a plucked *chicken* 毛をむしったひな鳥の残り毛を焼く.

Q This *chicken is tender.* この鶏肉(にく)は柔い.

Q^2 *sea chicken* [かん詰になった]マグロの肉.

P a brood *of chickens* 一腹のひな.

chicky, *n.* ひよっこ.

Q *Little chickies* are peeping. ひよっこがぴよぴよ鳴いている.

P run *after chickies* ひよっこを追っかける.

chide, *v.* しかる.

M *chide* children ***away*** 子供たちをしかって追っ払う.
P The pupil was *chid* by the teacher ***for*** his fault. その生徒は過失のため先生にしかられた. 【類】*chide* him ***for*** his delay / The boy was *chidden* by his father ***for*** his fault.

chief, *n.* 長, 頭, 首領.
Q Japanese ***feudal*** *chiefs* had power of life and death over subjects. 日本の封建時代の主君は家来に対して生殺(与奪)の権を持っていた. ¶a ***low-born*** *chief* 微賤から身を起した首領.
Q² a ***branch*** *chief* 支店長. ¶a ***business section*** *chief* 営業部長. ¶a ***copy*** *chief* 〘新聞〙整理部長. ¶a ***deputy*** *chief* of the engineering section 技術課長代理 ‖ The ***deputy*** *chief* of the U.S. military government. 米国軍政府長官代理. ¶an ***intelligence*** *chief* 情報部長. ¶a ***laboratory*** *chief* 研究所長. ¶a ***party*** *chief* 政党の首領. ¶a ***pirate*** *chief* 海賊の頭. ¶a ***racketeer*** *chief* 暴力団の団長. ¶a ***section*** *chief* 課(部)長. ¶a ***secret service*** *chief* ... 《米》機密検察部長. ¶a ***training-unit*** *chief* 教育部長.
P ***as*** *chief* to ... …の長として. ¶The mayor is the city official ***in*** *chief*. 市長は市吏の長である.
P² *chief* ***among*** them are ... 彼らの中の主だった者は…である. ¶the *chief* ***of*** the Naval General Staff 海軍軍令部長 ‖ the *Chief* ***of*** Staff 《米》陸軍参謀本部長. ☞ a chief of staff は「参謀長」‖ the *chief* ***of*** the Metropolitan Police Board 警視総監 ‖ the *chief* ***of*** a police station 警察署長 ‖ the *Chief* ***of*** the Committee of Reception 接待委員長 ‖ the *chief* ***of*** a family 家長 ‖ the *chief* ***of*** his tribe 彼の属する部落のしゅう長.

chieftain, *n.* 首長, 族長.
Q ***feudal*** *chieftains* 藩主. ¶a usurping ***military*** *chieftain* 強奪を事とする武将. ¶***warring*** *chieftains* 互いに戦を構える族長たち.
Q² a ***labor*** *chieftain* 労働団体の首領. ¶a ***union*** *chieftain* 組合長.

chilblain, *n.* しもやけ.
V You will ***have*** fearful *chilblains* if you do so. そうするとひどいしもやけになりますよ.

child, *n.* 小児, 子供; 子孫; 産物.
V Meanwhile a fourth *child* was ***added*** to his family. そうこうする中に彼の家庭に四番目の子が生れた. ¶*Children* in arms not ***admitted***. [掲示]乳幼児は入場御断り. ¶***amuse*** *children* 子供たちを楽ませる. ¶Never ***awake*** a healthy *child* from his sleep to dress him, etc. 丈夫な寝ている子供を起して着物を着せたりなどしてはいけない. ¶***bear*** *children* and rear them 子供を産んで育てる. 【類】It is the duty of a woman to marry and ***bear*** *children*. / She ***bore*** (=gave birth to) eleven *children*. / She was divorced after she had ***borne*** him three *children*. / her husband to whom she had just ***borne*** a *child* ‖ a woman who is ***bearing*** a *child* by the man she deeply loves かわいい男のたねを宿した女 ‖ leave her to ***bear*** her *child* in shame 彼女が不義の子を産むに任せる. ¶***beget*** *children* 子供を持つ(男にいう) ‖ ***beget*** healthy, strong, and perfect *children*, wholly free from any hereditary taint 遺伝的な(悪い)影響を全然受けない丈夫で強くて申分のない子供を産む. ¶It is the business of a midwife to ***bring*** *children* into the world. 子供を産み落させるのが助産婦の役目だ. ¶***bring forth*** (=***out***) a *child* 子を生む. ¶***bring up*** one's *child* 自分の子供を育てる. 【類】In ***bringing up*** *children*, we must never run into extremes (極端に走る). ¶***bundle*** the *children* ***off*** to school 子供をさっさと学校へ追いやる. ¶***caress*** a *child* 子供の頭をなでる. ¶***carry*** the *child* on one's back 子供を背負う. ¶Mother ***clasped*** her *child* to her bosom. 母親はその子を胸に抱きしめた. ¶***clothe*** *children* in silk 子供たちに絹物を着せる. ¶***conceive*** a *child* of ... …のたねを宿す. ¶***dance*** a *child* on one's knees 子供をひざの上であやす. ¶***educate*** one's *children* 子供を教育する. ¶***entertain*** *children* 子供たちを楽しませる. ¶***feed*** a *child* on milk 牛乳で子供を育てる ‖ Love ought to make it a pleasure to ***feed*** the *child* from the mother body. 母体で(授乳して)子供を育てるのは親の愛情として当然のことだ. ¶*children* have not been ***forgotten***, and ... [百貨店など]子供のためにも設備がしてあって… ¶***get*** *children* 子供をこしらえる ¶the *children* these Portuguese ***had*** with their Japanese wives これらのポルトガル人が日本人を妻としてできた子供たち ‖ ***have*** a *child* by him あの人の子供を生む. 【類】women who are very anxious to ***have*** *children* / those who ***have*** *children* to bring up (育てる子供) / They ***have*** eight *children* to support (養育する子供). ‖ She ***had*** a *child* in her arms. 彼女は子供を抱いていた. ¶***humor*** a *child* 子供をあやす. ¶You ***idolize*** that *child*. あなたはそのお子さんを大層大事になさいますね. ¶***ill-treat*** their *children* 子供たちを虐待する. ¶He ***indulges*** his *children* too much. 彼は子供らをあまやかし過ぎる. ¶***lead*** a *child* to and from school 子供の通学の送り迎えをする. ¶He ***left*** no *children*. 彼は子供を残さずに死んだ. ¶***lift*** a *child* into one's arms 子供を抱き上げる. ¶He knows how to ***manage*** his *children*. 彼は子供の扱い方を心得ている. ¶***marry*** one's *children* above one 子供たちを自分より身分の上の者と結婚させる. ¶***nurse*** *children* 子供たちの守をする. ¶Some fathers ***outlive*** their *children*. 子供たちより長生きする父親もある. ¶***pamper*** a *child* 子供をあまやかす. ¶***place*** a *child* in his bed 子供を床に寝かす. ¶***procreate*** (=beget) *children* 子をもうける(男にいう). ¶***produce*** no more *children* than they can conveniently maintain 楽に育てられる限度以上に子供をつくらない. ¶***put*** a *child* [***down***] to sleep 子供を寝かせつける ‖ ***put*** a new-born *child* to the breast 生れたての子供に乳を飲ませる. ¶***put out*** a *child* to nurse 子供を里に出す. ¶***rear*** a *child* at the breast 母乳で育てる. ¶***rock*** a *child* to sleep 子供をゆすって寝かせる. ¶***segregate*** Japanese *children* [米国の小学校などで]日本人の子供を分離する. ¶Don't ***set*** the *child* to crying. 子供を泣かすな. ¶***space*** *children* 子供を間引く. ¶***spoil*** a *child* 子供をあまやかす. ¶***suckle*** her *children* 彼女の子供らに乳を飲ます. ¶***tease*** *children* 子供をいじめる. ¶***train*** *children* 子供をしつける. ¶The *children* are ***tucked up*** in bed. 子供らは床の中へくるまった.
V² The *children* did nothing but ***cry***. 子供は泣いてばかりいた. ¶The *child* has started ***going*** on all fours. その子供ははいはいをしだした. ¶Your *children* must be ***growing up*** fast. お子様たちはどんなに大きくおなりになったことでしょう. ¶I think the *child* is ***teething***. その子は歯が生えだすころだと思う. ¶*Children* ***thrive*** in this climate. この気候では子供は丈夫に育つ.
Q a *child* ***about-to-be-born*** 近々生れる子供. ¶***artificially fed*** *children* 人工(牛乳など)で育った子供. ¶a ***backward*** *child* 奥手の子供 ‖ The *child* was ***backward*** in learning to walk. あの児は歩き始めが遅かった. ¶a ***breast-fed*** *child* 母乳で育った子供. ¶a ***chubby*** *child* 丸々肥った子供. ¶a ***cute[-looking]*** *child* 《米俗》愛くるしい子供. ¶mentally ***deficient*** *children* 低能児. ¶a ***delicate*** *child* 虚弱な子供. ¶***dependent*** *children* 扶養している子供. ¶a ***disobedient*** *child* いうことをきかない子供. ¶They had their ***first*** *child*. 彼らは初児をもうけた. ¶The *child* is ***forward*** for his years. この児は年の割にませている. ¶a ***frail*** *child* ひ弱い子供. ¶The ***frightened*** *child* gripped its mother's arm. びっくりした子供が母親の腕を固くつかんだ. ¶***frowzy*** *children* きたならしい子たち. ¶***Full-healthed***, ***bright-eyed***, and ***happy-hearted*** *children* are the true wealth of the nation. 丈夫で, 目のぱっちりした元気な子供は本当に国民の宝である. ¶education of ***gifted*** *children* 優良児教育. ¶Be a ***good*** *child*. おとなしくなさい. ¶a ***handicapped*** *child* 不利な条件のついている子供(私生児・混血児・不具の子など). ¶bear ***healthy*** *children* 丈夫な子供を産む. ¶an ***illegitimate*** *child* 私生児. ¶***ill-treated*** *children* 虐待されている子供たち. ¶an ***impish-looking*** *child* やんちゃな子供. ¶an ***infant*** *child* 幼な児. ¶an ***ingenuous*** *child* がんぜない子供. ¶the ***latest*** *child* of the inventor 同発明家最近の発明. ¶a ***legitimate*** *child* 嫡子. ¶a ***lively*** *child* 元気のよい子供. ¶***London born*** *children* of Irish parents アイルランド人を両親に持つロンドン生れの子供. ¶a ***lost*** *child* 迷子. ¶a ***mere*** *child* in knowledge 知識の点ではほんの子供. ¶a ***naughty*** *child* いたずらっ子. ¶***necessitous*** (=***needy***) *children* 貧困な子供たち. ¶***Noisy*** *children* are a nuisance. やかましい子供は迷惑だ. ¶an ***obedient*** *children* 素直な子供たち. ¶He has an ***only*** *child*. 彼にはたった一人の子がある. 【類】the ***only*** *child* of ... ¶a ***pert*** *child* こましゃくれた子供. ¶a ***plump little*** *child* 丸々肥った子供. ¶a ***posthumous*** *child* 父の死後に生れた子供. ¶***preadolescent*** *children* 青年期前の子供たち. ¶***precocious*** *children* ませた子供. ¶a vocabulary study of ***pre-school*** *children* 学齢前の子供の単語教育. ¶a ***pretty, fair-haired, toddling*** *child* きれいな毛髪の美しいよちよち歩きの子供. ¶a ***ragged*** *child*

ぼろを着た子供. ¶a ***restless child*** 落着かない児. ¶***rosy-cheeked children*** ばら色のほおをした子供. ¶a ***seven-month-old child*** 生後七カ月の子. ¶A ***sick child*** is often fussy. 病児はよくむずかる. ‖ The ***sick child*** tumbled restlessly in his bed. 病児が寝床の中で気ぜわしくころげ回った. ¶a ***sickly child*** 病身の子供. ¶a ***small child*** 小さな子供. ¶a ***spoilt child*** だだっ子. ¶His wife was prematurely delivered of a ***still-born child***. 彼の妻は死産をした. ¶a ***stray child*** 迷い子. ¶a ***strong child*** 丈夫な子供. ¶a ***stubborn child*** きかん坊. ¶a ***sun-brown child*** 日に焼けた子供. ¶a ***supposititious child*** すりかえ子. ¶***Children*** are ***terrible***. 子供は正直(飛んでもないことを言う). ¶a ***thankless child*** 不孝な子. ¶a ***toddling child*** よちよち歩く子供. ¶***town-bred children*** 都会育ちの子供. ¶a ***troublesome child*** 世話のやける子. ¶an ***undernourished child*** 栄養不良の子供. ¶an ***unmanageable child*** 手に余る子供. ¶an ***unruly child*** 始末に負えない子供. ¶an ***unweaned child*** 乳離れしない子供. ¶an ***unworthy child*** of his worthy parents 不肖の子. ¶a ***wanton child*** 茶目公. ¶a ***wayward child*** やんちゃん. ¶avoid bringing a ***weakly child*** into the world ひ弱い子供を産まないようにする. ¶***weak-minded children*** 精神薄弱児. ¶a ***winsome child*** 愛きょうのある子供.

Q² the ***brain children*** of scientists 科学者の頭脳の所産. 【類】The music is his ***brain child***. ¶the ***Connors children*** コナース家の子供たち. ¶A ***girl child*** was born. 女の子が生れた. ¶***idiot children*** 白痴の子供たち. ¶a ***love child*** 私生児. ¶***orphan children*** 孤児. ¶***orphan*** and ***waif children*** 孤児や浮浪児. ¶a "***problem child***" who ran away from school 学校から逃げ出した「問題の子供」. ¶the feeding of ***school children*** 学童給食. ¶a ***vagabond child*** 浮浪児. ¶a ***wonder child*** 神童.

P I have known him ***from*** a ***child*** (=since childhood). 子供の時分からあの人を知っている. 【類】***From*** a ***child*** he was fond of study. ¶The support ***of*** his ***children*** is another burden. その外に彼の子供を養って行かねばならない厄介がある. ‖ a troop ***of children*** 子供のむれ ‖ a gang ***of children*** 《米》子供のむれ. ¶she is ***with child*** by ... 彼女は…のたねを宿している ‖ She was found ***with child***. 彼女は妊娠していた. ¶women ***without children*** 子なし女.

P² our children and their ***children after*** them われわれの子供とその子供の子供. ¶the noise of ***children at*** play 遊んでいる子供らの声. ¶He had ***children by*** his concubine. 彼はめかけに子があった. 【類】He had no ***children by*** his first wife. ¶a ***child in*** arms 抱かれている子. 【類】the ***child in*** her arms ‖ a ***child in*** the bosom 抱いた子 ‖ the ***children in*** that family あの家の子供ら ‖ He is a ***child in*** these matters. 彼はこういうことにかけては赤ん坊だ. ¶a ***child of*** fortune 好運児 ‖ ***children of*** a marriage 結婚によって生れた子供たち ‖ a ***child of*** nature 野育ちの子供 ‖ a ***child of*** poverty 貧家に生れた人 ‖ a ***child of*** illegitimate birth 私生児 ‖ ***children of*** a larger growth=adults, grownups 大人 ‖ ***children of*** school age 学齢児童 ‖ the true ***children of*** the soil 素ぼくないなか者 ‖ Confucius, like Franklin, was the ***child of*** his father's old age. 孔子はフランクリンと同様に父が年をとってからの子供であった. ‖ ***Children of*** twelve years of age and over, full fare. [掲示] 十二歳以上は大人料金 ‖ The general rule is that a little more than a third of a city's prostitutes are ***children of*** the city. 概して都市の売春婦の三分の一余はその都市で生れたものである. ‖ Disease is the ***child of*** intemperance. 病気は不節制の産物だ. ¶a ***child on*** the back おぶった子 ‖ I have a sick ***child on*** my hands. 私には病気の子がある. ¶***Children over*** five are charged half. 五歳以上の子供は半額. ¶***Children under*** five years of age are not charged. 五歳未満の小児は無料.

child-bearing, *n.* 出産.

Q *Child-bearing* is most ***frequent*** in women between the ages of 20 and 40. 女が子を産むのは二十歳ないし四十歳の間が最も多い.

childbed, *n.* 産じょく.

P She was ***in childbed***. 彼女はお産をした. 【類】She died ***in childbed***.

childbirth, *n.* 出産.

P ***after*** *childbirth* 産後に. ¶She died ***in*** *childbirth*. 彼女はお産で死んだ. ‖ a woman ***in*** *childbirth* 産婦 ‖ women ***in, before,*** and ***after*** *childbirth* 分娩中, 分娩前, 分娩後の女.

childhood, *n.* 幼年時代.

V the then remote country village where my *childhood* was ***passed*** 私が幼年時代を送った当時は片いなかの村. ¶Her *childhood* was ***spent*** in Paris. 彼女は少女時代をパリーで過した. 【類】We all love the place where we ***spent*** our *childhood*. ¶***survive*** one's *childhood* 幼年時代をすぎる.

Q since ***early*** *childhood* 幼少のころからずっと. ¶***later*** *childhood* 幼年時代の末期. ¶***middle childhood*** 幼年時代の中ごろ. ¶He is now in his ***second childhood***. 彼はもうもうろくしている. 【類】Old age is called ***second childhood*** (第二次の幼年時代).

P friends ***from childhood*** 竹馬の友 ‖ ***from*** early ***childhood*** 幼少のころから. 【類】***from*** earliest ***childhood*** / ***from*** his ***childhood*** upward. ¶***In*** my ***childhood***, I was delicate. 子供のときは弱かった. 【類】He lost his parents ***in*** his ***childhood***. ¶***since childhood*** 幼少のときから.

childish, *a.* 子供くさい.

P be ***childish with*** age ぼける.

chill, *n.* さむけ, 悪寒; 寒さ.

V ***cast*** (=***dampen or depress***) a *chill* over ...をぞっとさせる, 意気そそうさせる. ¶***catch*** a *chill* 風を引く. ¶I ***felt*** a *chill* creep over me. 体がぞくぞくした. ¶I have ***got*** (=***caught***) a *chill*. 風を引いた. ¶***send chills*** up the spine 背中がぞくぞくする ‖ The sight ***sent*** a *chill* to my heart. それを見て私はぞっとした. ¶***strike*** a *chill* to the heart of an American 米人をぞっとさせる. ¶***take*** a *chill* さむけがする ‖ You should ***take*** the *chill* off the water before you bathe. 浴びる前に湯を差すとよい. ¶Red wines should be served with the *chill **taken off***. 赤ぶどう酒は少しかんをして出すがいい.

V² A *chill **came*** over me. 寒気がした.

chill, *v.* 冷す, 興をさます.

P *chilled **to*** the bone in soaking clothes 着物がびしょぬれになったので寒気が骨に徹して ‖ The most dreadful sight caught his eyes and *chilled* him ***to*** the core (=marrow). いとも恐しい光景に接して彼は骨の髄までぞっとした.

P² I was *chilled **with fear***. 恐ろしさが身にしみた.

chilly, *a.* うすら寒い.

M ***somewhat*** *chilly* うすら寒い.

P feel *chilly* ***in*** the cold wind 寒風にさらされてはだ寒い.

chime, *n.* 一組の鐘.

V² The *chimes* ***pealed out*** merrily. 一組の鐘が陽気に鳴り出した.

chime, *v.* 鳴って促す; 鳴る; 調和する.

M The church clock *chimed* ***four***. 教会の時計が四時を報じた. ¶The bells *chimed* him ***home***. 鐘が鳴って彼の帰りを促した.

M² "Yes, she is," Mrs. W *chimed **in***. 「えーそうなんです」W 夫人は相づちを打った. ‖ The softening voice *chimed **in*** with the echo of the music. やわらかな声が音楽の共鳴の中に溶け込んだ. ¶He *chimed **in*** with the speaker. 彼は弁士の相づちを打った.

chimney, *n.* 煙突.

V The *chimney* was not ***protected*** by a lightning-rod. その煙突には避雷針がついていなかった. ¶***sweep*** a *chimney* 煙突を掃除する.

V² The *chimney* is ***giving off*** volumes of black smoke. その煙突からは黒煙がもうもうと出ている. ¶The *chimney **smokes***. 煙突が煙る.

Q a ***tall*** *chimney* 高い煙突.

chin, *n.* あご, あごさき.

V ***cup*** one's *chin* in one's hands 両手にあごをのせる. ¶He ***gashed*** his *chin* badly when shaving. 顔をそっているときにあごに深きずを付けた. ¶***rest*** his *chin* on (=in) his hand ほおづえをつく. ¶***rub*** one's *chin* あごをなでる.

Q a ***cleft*** *chin* みぞのあるあご ¶a ***dimpled*** *chin* くびれたあご. ¶with a ***dirty*** (=***unshaven***) *chin* あごをそらずに. ¶a man with a ***double*** *chin* 二重あごの男. ¶a ***receding*** *chin* 後屈あご. ¶A ***shaven*** *chin* and upper lip were exacted from French servants of good class until a few years ago. 数年前までは一流のフランス人召使はぜひあごひげと口ひげをそらねばならなかった. ¶an ***underhung*** *chin* たれ下ったあご.

Q² a ***sandpaper*** *chin* [剃った跡の]ざらざらしたあご.

P The beard grows ***on*** the *chin*. ひげはあごに生える. 【類】a beard left ***on*** the *chin*.

China, *n.* 中国.

Q ***New*** *China* 新中国. ¶***Red*** *China* 中共.

Q² ***Communist*** *China* 中共. ¶***Nationalist*** *China* 国民政

府の支配下にある中国.

P the People's Republic *of China* 中華人民共和国.

china, *n.* 磁器.

Q² *egg-shell china* (=porcelain) 薄手の磁器.

Chinaman, *n.* 中国人.

Q an *almond-eyed Chinaman* アーモンド色の目をした中国人.

Chinese, *n.* 中国人, 中国語.

Q *Classical Chinese* 漢文. ¶She is a *halfcaste Chinese.* 彼女は中国人と外国人の合の子だ.

chip, *n.* 木片, 薄片.

Q² a *brother chip* 同業者(古くは仲間の大工). ¶*ice chips* 氷の薄片. ¶*potato chips* じゃがいもを薄く切って油で揚げたもの.

P be burned *to* a *chip* かりかり焼ける.

chip, *v.* 削る.

M² *chip in* 《口語》[けんかなどに]割込む; 《米》寄付をする ‖ They all *chipped in* to buy it. 一同それを買うための金を出し合った. ¶*chip off* そぎ落す.

chisel, *n.* のみ.

Q a *blunt chisel* きれないのみ.

chisel, *v.* 刻む, のみで彫る.

P the bust was *chiseled by* ... その胸像は...の作だ. ¶a bust *chiseled from* a rock 石で刻んだ胸像. ¶very archaic inscriptions deeply *chiseled in* the rock 深く岩に刻んだきわめて古風の銘. ¶*chisel* a block of wood (marble) *into* a statue 木(など)の材料からのみで像を作る. ¶The rock was *chiseled with* the figures of divinities. 岩には神体が彫ってあった.

chit, *n.* 伝票.

P buy goods *on chit* 伝票で品物を買う.

chit-chat, *n.* 雑談.

Q spend time in *common chit-chat* ありふれた雑談をして時を過ごす.

chloroform, *n.* クロロフォルム.

V *administer chloroform* for surgical purposes 外科手術のためにクロロフォルムをかがせる. ¶*apply chloroform* クロロフォルムを掛ける.

P place a patient *under chloroform* 患者をクロロフォルムでまひさせる.

choice, *n.* 選択; 選択物; 選択権.

V he is *allowed* a free *choice* in ... 彼は...を自由に選べることになっている. ¶*bias* the *choice* その選択を片よらせる. ¶*Choice* must be *determined* by merit. 価値で選択を決せねばならない. ¶*exercise* a *choice* 選択する ‖ can *exercise* little *choice* 選択をする余地がほとんどない. ¶*explain* one's *choice* 選んだ理由を説明する. ¶*give* first *choice* to ... ...を真先に選ぶ. ¶*guide* our *choice* われわれの選択を指導する. ¶he *has* his *choice* between ... and ... 彼にはその二つの中一つを選ぶ権利がある. 【類】He *has* his *choice* of two roads (=routes). / I *have* no *choice* between them. ‖ I *have* no *choice* in this affair. この件では私は選択権がない. ‖ If I *have* the *choice,* I would rather have it undone. なろうことならもと通りにしていただきたい. ‖ We *had* no *choice* left. 外に仕方がなかった. ¶It *influenced* his *choice*. それが彼の選択に影響した. ¶set forth all opinions and *leave* the *choice* to the pupils あらゆる意見を提供してその選択は生徒に任せる. 【類】I *leave* the *choice* to you. 【類】There is often no *choice left* to us. ¶*make* one's *choice* 選択する ‖ *make* a *choice* among ... ...の内から選ぶ ‖ *make* a *choice* from a list of names 人名表の中から人選をする ‖ *make* a second *choice* when ordering 注文するとき品切の場合の分も書き添える. 【類】*make* a good (bad) *choice*. ¶he was *offered* the *choice* of ... or ... 彼は...の中一つを選ぶように言渡された. ¶*regret* one's *choice* 自分の選択を後悔する. ¶*require* a *choice* between ... and ... ...と...といずれかを選べと要求する. ¶The *choice* is *restricted* between two. 二つから選択することになっている. ¶You may *take* (=make) your *choice*. よりどりしてよろしい.

V² The *choice fell* upon him. 彼がその選に当った.

Q an *abundant choice* of dress-goods お好み次第のたくさんの洋服地. ¶be the *alternate choice* どっちにするかという選び方だ. ¶make the *best choice* of ... ...を最も賢明に選ぶ. ¶make a *careful choice* 注意して選ぶ. ¶make a *deliberate choice* 慎重に選択する. ¶We have the *first choice*. われわれに最初選択の権利がある. ¶Let him have the *first choice*. 彼に先にとらせろ. ‖ Russian is spoken as *first choice* by no more than 90,000,000 of the 180,000,000 citizen of the U.S.S.R. ロシア語はソビエット連邦国民一億八千万の中わずかに九千万によって第一選択として話されている. ‖ make a *first* and a *second choice* 第一と第二と二通りに選ぶ. ¶by his own *free choice* 自分の勝手な選択で ‖ Did he give you a *free choice?* 彼は君が勝手に選んでもよいと言ったか. ¶He belonged to the very small minority, who, with a *full choice* before them, went into teaching because they wanted to. 彼は職業を自由に選択ができる身でありながら好んで教育界に身を投じたはなはだ少数の人の一人であった. ¶There is a *good choice* of steamship services. 船は色々な会社のがあって十分選択ができる. ¶The *choice* was a *happy* one. それは上手な選択であった. ¶Vice has never been *her choice*. 彼女はこれまで好きで浮いた商売をしたのではない. ¶leave to *individual choice* 銘々の勝手に任す. ¶an *intelligent choice* 賢明な選択. ¶a *judicious choice* of material 材料の賢明な選択. ¶The store has a *large choice* to new-look hats. その店には新型帽子の優良品が沢山ある. ¶The *choice* of leaders is very *limited.* 指導者を選ぶとなると少いものだ. ‖ Only a *limited choice* of foreign food can be obtained at the inn. その旅館でできる洋食の品数は余計ない. ¶*masterly choice* of words 優れた用語の選択. ¶There isn't *much choice*. どっちにしても大した変りはない. ‖ there may not be *much choice* between ... ...の二者何れを選ぶも大差はなかろう. ¶the *nation's choice* 国民の選良. ¶a *sorry choice* まずい選択(物). ¶I have no *special choice*. 別に自分の好みはない. ¶a *successful choice* 上手な選択. ¶make one a *suitable choice* for a position 自分に適した勤め口を選ぶ. ¶A big store can offer you a more *varied choice*. 大きな店へ行くともっと沢山の品の中から選択ができる. ¶*vocational* and *occupational choices* 職業上の選択. ¶a *wide choice* of colors and materials 範囲の広い色彩と材料の選択. 【類】There is a *wide choice* in the kind of music which may be used at the home wedding. / For the general literature of the subject the reader has a *wide choice*. ¶he made a *wise choice* in taking ... 彼が...を選んだのは賢明であった. ¶make a *wrong choice* 選択を誤る.

P I live here *by choice*. 僕は好きでここに住んでいる. 【類】not *by choice*, but by compulsion (強制的に). / books read *by* their own *choice*. ¶bright blue or purple *for choice* 成ろうことなら鮮かな青または紫. ¶I will take French *for choice*. 選択課目として仏語を取る. ‖ Brangwyn is a masterly interpreter of architecture, the Romanesque, *for choice*. ブラングウィンは建築特にローマ風建築の大家である. ¶adopt it *from choice* 好みでそれをとる ‖ live in a garret *from choice*. 好んで屋根裏べやに住む. ¶He is scrupulous *in* the *choice* of words. 彼は語の選択に慎重だ. ¶I did it of necessity, not *of choice*. やむなくしたので好んでやった訳ではない. ‖ *of* her own [free] *choice* 彼女の好き勝手で ‖ a matter *of choice* 銘々の好き好き ‖ the girl *of* his *choice* 彼の好きな女. 【類】He married the woman *of* his *choice*.

P² we gave him his *choice between* ... and ...彼に二者その一を選ばせた. ¶a *choice by* lot (vote) くじ(など)での選定. ¶You may take your *choice for* 25 cents. よりどり二十五セントです. ¶a *choice from among* (=*out of*) many たくさんの中からの選択. ¶a *choice of* an occupation 職業の選択 ‖ the *choice of* the woman of taste 趣味のある婦人の愛用品 ‖ the *choice of* his troops 彼の部下の精鋭 ‖ his *choice of* Dryden as a model of style 彼の文体の模範としてドライデンを選択したこと.

O This pattern is my *choice*. この型は私の選んだものだ.

choice, *a.* 気むずかしい.

P He is *choice of* his food. 彼は食物にやかましい. ‖ He is *choice of* money. 彼は金銭にこまかい.

choir, *n.* 唱歌隊; [天使などの]組, 隊.

V² *Choirs* of exultant seraphs *circle* in the air. 歓喜にあふれた天使たちの数組が空中に舞う.

P a singer *in* a *choir* 唱歌隊の歌手.

choke, *v.* 息を詰める, 窒息させる.

M I *nearly choked* myself in swallowing it. それをのみ込む時息が詰りそうになった. ¶*choke back* (=*down or out*) 無理に抑える(感情などを).

M² *choke off* opposition 反対を抑圧する. 【類】*choke off* discussion (argument) ‖ impose drastic economic controls to *choke off* inflation インフレを抑えるために思い切った経済統制を加える. ¶The pump is *choked up*. ポンプが詰っている. ‖ The harbor is being *choked up* with silt. そ

の港は泥でふさがりかけている.

P They were *choked* (=offended) ***at*** his words. 彼らは彼の言葉に感情を害した. ¶He was *choked* ***by*** smoke (tears). 彼は煙(など)にむせた. ‖ He was *choked* ***by*** a piece of meat. 肉がのどにつかえた. ‖ He was *choked* ***by*** a ruffian. 悪漢にのどをしめられた. ¶*choke* a person ***into*** unconsciousness 人ののどをしめて気絶させる. ¶I *choked* ***on*** a bone (rice cake). 私は骨(など)をのどにひっかけて息が詰った. ¶*choke* the life ***out of*** a person 人をしめ殺す. ¶He was *choked* ***with*** smoke (dust). 彼は煙(など)でむせた. ‖ His voice was *choked* ***with*** emotion (rage). 感きわまって(など)声が出なかった. ‖ rivers *choked* ***with*** ice. 氷に閉ざされた川. 【類】The pump is *choked* ***with*** mud. / The pipe was *choked* ***with*** smoke. / The chimney is almost *choked* [up] ***with*** soot (すす).

cholera, *n.* コレラ.

Q² ***chicken*** *cholera* 鶏コレラ.

P His life was cut short ***by*** *cholera.* 彼はコレラで命をとられた. ¶an epidemic ***of*** *cholera* コレラの流行 ‖ He died ***of*** *cholera.* 彼はコレラで死んだ. ¶He was infected (=smitten) ***with*** *cholera.* 彼はコレラにかかった.

choose, *v.* 選ぶ, 選択する.

M ***carefully*** *choose* 厳選する. ¶***deliberately*** *choose* 熟考した上に選ぶ. ¶The hours of practice are ***ill*** *chosen.* [ピアノなど]練習時間の選び方が悪い. ¶*choose* ***judiciously*** 賢明に選ぶ. ¶*choose* ***out*** 選出する; 抜てきする. ¶*choose* ***wisely*** 賢明に選択する. 【類】if ***wisely*** *chosen.*

P *choose* one ***among*** many 多数の中から一つを選ぶ. ¶*choose* him ***as*** president (head) 彼を総裁(など)に選ぶ ‖ I have *chosen* ***as*** heading for this article the title of "…" 私はこの論文の頭書に"…"という表題を選定した. ¶a sample *chosen* ***at*** random 手当り次第選り出した見本. ¶*choose* death ***before*** dishonor 不名誉をこうむる位ならむしろ命を捨てる. 【類】He *chose* this ***before*** all others. ¶We must *choose* ***between*** death and dishonor. 死か不正かどっちかを選ばなければならない. 【類】if I were to *choose* ***between*** the two evils, I would … / The judge allowed him to *choose* ***between*** a fine and imprisonment (罰金と禁固). ¶*choose* ***by*** voting 投票で選出する. 【類】He was *chosen* ***by*** election. ¶*choose* a wife ***for*** her beauty only 容姿だけで妻をえらぶ. 【類】She *chose* him ***for*** her husband. ‖ "…" is the name he has *chosen* ***for*** his new novel 「…」は彼が自分の新作につけるために選んだ名前だ ‖ Dogs are *chosen* ***for*** scent and speed. 犬は鼻のきくのと足の早いのをもって可とする. ¶*choose* a book ***from among*** many 多数の中から一冊選ぶ. ¶*choose* happiness ***instead of*** riches 富よりは幸福を選ぶ. ¶*choose* five ***out of*** the number その数の中から五つを選ぶ.

O I cannot *choose* but attend the party. 会には出席するほかはない. ¶It was hard *choosing* (=to choose). その選択はむずかしかった.

choosing, *n.* 選択.

Q be governed by men of their ***own*** *choosing* 彼らの選んだ人々に支配される.

P Neither the subject nor the title of this lecture is ***of*** my own *choosing*. この講演の主題も題名も私が自分できめたのではない.

chop, *v.* 切る, 刻む, 打割る, 切り開く.

M *chop* ***away*** the vines つる草を切り払う. ¶*chop* ***thinly*** (***thickly***) 薄く(厚く)切る. ¶meat *chopped* ***together*** 小間切れ.

M² *chop* ***down*** a tree 樹を切り倒す. ¶*chop* (=*cut*) ***in*** 突然じゃまをする, わって入る. ¶*chop* one's head ***off*** (=***away***) 首をちょん切る. ¶*chop* it ***up*** それを切り刻む.

P *chop* ***at*** a tree 木を切りかける. ¶The wood was *chopped* ***in*** pieces. 木を切々に切った. ¶*chop* meat ***into*** small pieces 肉を細かく切る. ¶*chop* … ***on*** (=***upon***) the block …を台の上で切る. ¶*chop* a path ***through*** a forest 森の木を切って道を作る. ¶*chop* it ***with*** an ax in (=into) pieces それをおので細かく切り刻む. 【類】*chop* twigs ***with*** an ax.

chopper, *n.* 切る人(もの).

Q² a ***food*** *chopper* 食物細断器. ¶a ***meat*** *chopper* 肉切ほうちょう. ¶a ***ticket*** *chopper* 《米》〖鉄道〗集札係; 集札箱.

chopping, *n.* 切ること.

Q ***wood*** *chopping* 伐木.

chord, *n.* 絃; 感情, 情緒.

V It ***awakens*** no *chord* of sympathy in us. それは僕たちに何ら同情心を呼び起さない. 【類】The word ***awakened*** no responsive *chord* in my mind. ¶***strike*** a responsive *chord* in the breast of … …の胸を打つ ‖ ***strike*** a *chord* of feeling in the heart of … …の心の琴線にふれる. ¶The picture does not ***touch*** any *chord* in my heart. その絵は感銘を与えない. ‖ ***touch*** the right *chords* 琴線にふれる.

Q strike the ***sensitive, responsive*** *chords* of the soul 感じ易い感応し易い心の琴線にふれる. ¶strike no ***sympathetic*** *chord* in the hearts of the readers 読者の胸底の琴線にふれない.

chores, *n.* 小仕事.

V care for the furnace, rake and tend the lawn, and ***do*** odd *chores* 炉に気を付けるとかくま手を使って芝の手入をしたりその他雑用をする ‖ ***do*** the evening *chores* 夕方の用事をする(食事の仕度など).

Q ***domestic*** *chores* 家庭の雑用.

chorus, *n.* 合唱団; 合唱句; 斉唱.

V All joined in to ***swell*** the *chorus.* 合唱の音量を高めるため皆が加わった.

P a *chorus* ***for*** men's (=male) voices 男声合唱曲. ¶join ***in*** a *chorus* コーラスに加わる. 【類】One sang a piece and the others jointed ***in*** *chorus.*

P² There was a *chorus* ***of*** replies in the affirmative. 一同「賛成」と答えた. ‖ "O.K.!" yelled a *chorus* ***of*** four. 四人が一斉に「オーケー」と言った.

Christ, *n.* キリスト.

P Confucius lived about 500 years ***before*** *Christ* (=B. C.). 孔子は西暦紀元前約五百年の人だ. ¶believe ***in*** *Christ* and his teachings キリストとその教えを信じる.

christen, *v.* 命名する.

P He was *christened* … ***after*** his grandfather. 彼は祖父の名をとって…と命名された.

christening, *n.* 命名式.

V ***perform*** *christening* 命名式を行う.

Christian, *n.* キリスト教徒.

Q a ***devout*** *Christian* 敬けんなキリスト教信者. ¶an ***earnest*** *Christian* 熱心なキリスト教信者. ¶***fervent*** and ***conscientious*** *Christians* 熱心でまじめなキリスト教信者. ¶***fervent*** and ***steadfast*** *Christians* 熱烈でしかも堅実なキリスト教信者.

Christianity, *n.* キリスト教.

V The Armenians were the first nation to ***accept*** *Christianity.* アルメニア人はキリスト教を受け容れた最初の国民であった. ¶***embrace*** *Christianity* キリスト教を信奉する. ¶***plant*** *Christianity* キリスト教を植付ける. ¶***preach*** a very broad *Christianity* はなはだ見解の広いキリスト教を伝道する. ¶***profess*** *Christianity* キリスト教を公然信仰する. ¶***propagate*** *Christianity* キリスト教を宣伝する. ¶***proscribe*** *Christianity* キリスト教を禁止する. ¶***stamp out*** (=***eradicate or uproot***) all *Christianity* キリスト教を全く撲滅する. ¶***tolerate*** *Christianity* キリスト教を黙許する.

Q ***muscular*** *Christianity* 筋肉キリスト教(体育・徳育・信仰を兼行するキリスト教).

Q² ***Latin*** *Christianity* ラテン・キリスト教.

Christmas, *n.* キリスト降誕祭.

V We ***had*** a splendid *Christmas.* われわれはすばらしいクリスマスをやった. ¶***keep*** *Christmas* クリスマスを祝う.

V² *Christmas,* the day of Christ's birth, ***occurs*** on the 25th day of December. クリスマス即ちキリストの誕生日は十二月二十五日だ.

Q A "***green*** *Christmas*" means that the ground is not white with snow.「緑のクリスマス」とは地面が白雪でおおわれていないという意味だ. ¶a ***jolly*** *Christmas* 楽しいクリスマス. ¶A merry *Christmas* ***to*** you. クリスマスおめでとう. ‖ Don't wish your friends "a ***merry*** *Christmas*"—give it them. 友達に「クリスマスおめでとう」と口で言うだけではいけない—クリスマスの楽しみをみんなにわかちなさい.

Q² ***Father*** *Christmas* クリスマスのおじいさん.

P an edition *de luxe* for presentation ***at*** *Christmas* クリスマス贈答用物に好適の豪華版.

chronic, *a.* 慢性の.

P Neuralgia (asthma) is *chronic* ***with*** him. 神経痛(など)は彼の持病だ.

chronicle, *n.* 記録.

Q He is a ***living*** *chronicle* of the company. 彼はその会社の生き字引だ.

chronicling, *n.* 記録.

Q The greater part of this book suffers from too ***faithful*** a *chronicling* of unimportant matters. 本書は大部分重要ならざることがらを余り細々記しているのでその価値を落している.

chrysanthemum, *n.* 菊, 菊属.

V ***grow*** (=***raise or cultivate***) *chrysanthemum* 菊を植える.

Q the ***Imperial sixteen-petalled*** *chrysanthemum* 十六花べ

んの菊花御紋章.

chuck, *v.* 放り出す；止める.

M *chuck* ***away*** an empty box 空箱を放り出す.

M² *chuck* (=jack) ***up***=give in *or* surrender《俗》屈する, 降参する ‖ *chuck* ***up*** one's job 仕事を放り出す.

P *chuck* a visitor ***out of*** a room 来客をへやから追い出す.

chuckle, *n.* くすくす笑うこと.

V ***give*** a *chuckle* to ... ...をくすくす笑う.

chuckle, *v.* くすくす笑う.

M *chuckle* ***out*** くすくす笑いながら言う.

P *chuckle* ***at*** the sight それを見てくすくす笑う. ¶she *chuckled* in glee ***over*** the fact that ... 彼女は...ということを喜んでくすくす笑った. ¶He was *chuckling* ***to*** himself ***over*** what he was reading. 彼は読みながらひとりでくすくす笑った. ¶He *chuckled* ***with*** delight. 彼は悦に入ってふくみ笑いをした.

chug, chug-chug, *n.* ぽっぽっ.

P² the *chug-chug* ***of*** a motorboat (an engine) モーターボート(エンジン)のぽっぽっという音.

chug, *v.* ぽっぽっという.

M *chug* ***away*** ぽっぽっと出て行く.

M² The train *chugged* ***along***. 列車はぽっぽっと進んで行った.

chum, *n.* 同窓生, 親友.

Q an ***intimate*** *chum* of mine 僕の親友.

Q² her ***girlhood*** *chum* 彼女の娘時代のお友だち. ¶an old ***school*** *chum* of mine 僕の古い学友の一人.

P² his *chum* ***in*** college 彼の大学の同窓.

chum, *v.* 同室にいる；親しむ.

P *chum* [up] ***with*** a person 人と仲好くする.

chunk, *n.* 厚切れ.

P² a *chunk* ***of*** wood (bread, meat) 木(など)の厚切れ.

church, *n.* 教会, 会堂.

V ***attend*** *church* regularly きちんと教会に出席する ‖ The *church* is very well ***attended***. その教会は出席がはなはだ良い. ¶***consecrate*** a *church* 教会を献堂する. ¶The *church* was ***crammed***. 教会は人で一杯だった. ¶He ***gave up*** the *church* for the army. 彼は僧職を辞して陸軍に入った. ¶***join*** the *church* 聖職に就く. ¶***talk*** *church* 抹香(ｶｳ)臭い話をする.

Q an ***Anglican*** *church* 英国国教派の教会. ¶the ***Established*** *Church* 国教. ¶the ***Jewish*** *Church* ユダヤ教会. ¶the ***most numerously attended*** *church* 出席者の一番多い教会. ¶the ***Presbyterian*** *Church* 長老教会. ¶the ***primitive*** *church* 初期のキリスト教会. ¶the ***Roman Catholic*** *Church* 天主教会. ¶erect (=rear) a ***splendid*** *church* on that spot その場所に素晴らしい教会を建てる. ¶a ***stately*** *church* 堂堂たる教会. ¶a ***trinity*** *church* 三位一体(を教義とする)教会.

Q² the ***mother*** *church* 本山.

P ***after*** *church* 礼拝後に. ¶He was ***at*** *church* last Sunday. 彼はこの前の日曜日に礼拝に出た. ¶***between*** *churches* 礼拝時間の間に. ¶The bells are ringing ***for*** *church*. 礼拝へ出る鐘が鳴っている. ‖ study ***for*** the *church* 聖職試験の準備をする ‖ leave the bar ***for*** the *church* 弁護士をやめて聖職に就く. ¶I stayed away ***from*** *church* as I was ill. 私は病気で教会を休んだ. ¶listen to a sermon ***in*** (=***at***) *church* 教会で説教をきく. 【類】conduct a prayer meeting ***in*** a *church*. ¶go ***into*** the *church* 聖職に就く. ¶go ***to*** *church* 礼拝に行く.

O *Church* ***is*** over. 礼拝が済んだ.

church-goer, *n.* 礼拝に出る人.

Q an ***ardent*** *church-goer* 熱心な教会出席者.

chute, *n.* すべる斜面, すべり台.

V ***chute*** (=***shoot***) the *chutes* [遊園地などで]すべり台をすべる.

Q² a ***laundry*** *chute* 洗たく物の落し口(洗たく物を一所に集めるための).

cigar, *n.* 葉巻(シガー).

V ***Have*** a *cigar?* 一本どうです [シガーをすすめるとき]. ¶***light*** one's *cigar* at ... ...で葉巻に火をつける. ¶***light*** [***up***] a *cigar* 葉巻に火をつける. ¶***smoke*** a *cigar* 葉巻をくゆらす ‖ ***smoke*** a quiet *cigar* くつろいで葉巻をくゆらす.

Q a ***big*** *cigar* 大きな葉巻. ¶throw aside one's ***half-smoked*** *cigar* 半分すった葉巻を投げ捨てる. ¶***heavy*** (***light***) *cigars* 強い(軽い)葉巻. ¶a ***medium*** *cigar* 中位の葉巻. ¶a ***mild*** *cigar* 強くない(あまい)シガー. ¶***nefarious*** *cigars* てんでのめない葉巻. ¶a ***rank*** *cigar* 香の悪い葉巻.

Q² an ***after-dinner*** *cigar* 食後の葉巻.

P He is slowly puffing ***at*** his *cigar*. 彼は葉巻をくゆらしている. ¶a fine quality ***of*** *cigar* 上等の葉巻. ¶***with*** *cigar* in one's mouth 口に葉巻をくわえて.

cigaret[te], *n.* 巻タバコ, シガレット.

V ***enjoy*** a *cigarette* in the smoking-room 喫煙室でタバコをすう. ¶***hold*** a *cigarette* between one's lips 巻タバコを口にくわえる. ¶start to ***light*** a *cigarette* 巻タバコに火をつけようとする. 【類】May I ***light*** a *cigaret* [for you]! ¶***puff*** *cigarettes* タバコをふかす. ¶***puff away*** a *cigarette* after another タバコを次から次と何本もくゆらす. ¶***roll*** a *cigarette* 巻タバコを巻いて作る. ¶***smoke*** *cigarettes* 巻タバコをすう.

Q a ***cork-tipped*** *cigarette* コルク口付巻タバコ. ¶a ***lighted*** *cigarette* 火のついている巻タバコ.

P puff ***at*** a *cigarette* 巻タバコをくゆらす. ¶a package (=pack) ***of*** *cigarettes* 巻タバコ一個.

cinder, *n.* 灰.

P Many houses crumbled ***into*** *cinders*. 多数の家が灰になった. ¶The meat was burnt ***to*** a *cinder*. 肉が黒こげになった.

cinder-path, *n.* 石炭がらを敷きつめた小道.

P The qualities needed for success ***on*** the *cinder-path* are equally useful in the longer and sterner race for the prizes of life. 石炭がら道の競争での成功に必要な資質はもっと長くって激烈な人生の競争場裡においてもひとしく役に立つ.

cinema, *n.* [集合的に]映画；映画館.

Q There are few ***fine*** *cinemas* in the city. その市にはりっぱな映画館は少ない.

P How do you care ***for*** the *cinema?* 映画はお好きですか. ¶go ***to*** the *cinema* 映画を見に行く.

cinematograph, *n.* 映画.

P Queen Victoria's life ***on*** the *cinematograph* ヴィクトリヤ女王御一代記の映画 ‖ "Hamlet" ***on*** the *cinematograph* 「ハムレット」の映画劇.

cipher, *n.* 零；暗号文字.

Q He is a ***mere*** *cipher*. 彼はつまらない人間だ.

P write ***in*** *ciphers* 暗号文字で書く.

circle, *n.* 円, 円周；仲間, 社会；範囲；循環.

V ***describe*** a *circle* 円を描く ‖ ***describe*** a sinuous *circle* 曲りくねった円を描く. ¶***draw*** a *circle* with ... for its center ... を中心として円を描く ‖ ***draw*** a *circle* round a given center 与えられた中心のまわりに円を描く. ¶***enter*** the *circle* of ... ...の仲間に入る. ¶***extend*** the *circle* of operations 仕事の手(範囲)を拡げる. ¶Let us ***form*** a *circle*. 輪になろうじゃないか. ¶***join*** the *circle* of ... ...の仲間に入る.

V² The *circle* of acquaintance is ever ***widening***. 知人の範囲が絶えず広がって行く.

Q ***aeronautic*** *circles* 飛行界. ¶win a ***brilliant*** *circle* of friends りっぱな友だち仲間ができる. ¶in ***commercial*** and ***financial*** *circles* 商業・金融界で. ¶in the ***diplomatic*** *circles* of Japan 日本の国内で. ¶both in ***domestic*** and in ***social*** *circles* 家庭および社交界で. ¶***economic*** *circles* 経済界. ¶***educational*** *circles* 教育界. ¶*Circles* generally supposed to be ***exclusive*** and ***select*** could not be bought for money. 少数の上流名士の社交界には金の力では仲間入ができない. ¶She was one of a ***fashionable*** and ***worthy*** *circle* in New York. 彼女はニューヨークにおける社交界知名の一人であった. ¶in ***high*** *circles* 上流社会で. 【類】in the ***higher*** *circles* in London / in the ***highest*** *circles* of society. ¶***industrial*** *circles* 工業界. ¶according to ***informed*** *circle* here 当地の消息通の言う所によると. ¶among the ***innermost*** *circle* of his advisers 彼の側近の間では. 【類】admitted to the ***innermost*** *circles* of the Court (宮中の奥深く). ¶have a ***large*** *circle* of acquaintance 顔が広い ‖ The novel has reached a ***large*** *circle* of readers. その小説は広範囲の読者を得た. ¶whirl around in the same ***limited*** *circle* 同一の狭い範囲でぐるぐる回る. ¶He occupies a prominent position in ***literary*** *circles* in the capital. 彼は首都における文学界で卓越した地位を占めている. ¶in ***maritime*** *circles* 海運界で. ¶a ***narrow*** *circle* of friends せまい交友範囲 ‖ the ***narrow*** *circle* of one man's experience 一人の経験という狭い範囲. 【類】the poet's ***narrow*** *circle* of admirers (ファンたち). ¶in ***non-official*** *circles* 民間で. ¶outside of ***official*** *circles* 官界以外で. 【類】in ***official*** *circles* it is declared that ... / the general feeling (一般の空気) in ***official*** *circles* in India is that ... ¶there has been much gossip in ***political*** *circles* as to ... ...について政界にずい分うわさがあった. ¶***religious*** *circles* 宗教界. ¶a ***select*** *circle* of intelligent friends 選り抜きの知的な友だち. ¶***social*** *circles* 交際社会 ‖ These words, although of low, vulgar origin, have ascended in scale and are now received in the best ***social*** *circles*. これらの言葉は，その起りは野卑なものだが，今では

昇格して最上の交際社会でも用いられている. ¶it is popularly believed in ***some*** *circles* (=quarters) that ... ある方面で一般に...と信じられている. ¶in the ***upper*** *circles* of society 社会の上流に. ¶in the ***uppermost*** *circles* of society 社会の最上層に. ¶a ***vicious*** *circle* of prices and wages 物価と賃金の悪循環 ‖ So the present position is the good old ***vicious*** *circle*. それで現在の所例のいたちごっこという訳さ. 【類】There is thus established a ***vicious*** *circle*. / There is a ***vicious*** *circle* going on—prosperity, surplus, depression. / break the ***vicious*** *circle* of war-victory-peace-war. ¶***well-bred*** *circles* 上流社会. ¶there is a rumor in ***well-informed*** *circles* that ... 消息通の間に...といううわさが立っている. 【類】The news is discredited in ***well-informed*** *circles*. ¶touch a ***wide*** *circle* of subjects 広範囲の題目に触れる ‖ The magazine has a ***wide*** *circle* of readers. その雑誌は広い読者層を持っている. 【類】He has a ***wide*** *circle* of friends.

Q^2 ***army*** *circles* 軍人社会. ¶people well known in ***art*** *circles* 芸術界知名の士. ¶financiers prominent in ***banking*** *circles* 銀行界で傑出した財政家. ¶***bookselling*** and ***book-buying*** *circles* 出版界と読者層. ¶***business*** *circles*=the business world 実業界. ¶in ***capital*** *circles* 資本家仲間で. ¶***church*** *circles* 宗教界. ¶a ***dress*** *circle*〘劇〙二階正面桟敷. ¶in the ***family*** *circle* and in society at large 家庭および一般社会で ‖ Marquis O in his ***family*** *circle* [写真などの説明]家族に囲まれた O 侯爵. ¶rest and isolation from the ***family*** *circle* 家族よりの隔離と休養. ¶making of a ***family*** *circle* of nations, each contributing her share to the welfare of the whole world 八紘為宇. 【類】Quiet down and keep their troubles within the ***family*** *circles* 紛争を荒立てないで外に漏れないようにする. ¶***foreign trade*** *circles* report that ... 海外貿易方面の報じる所では... ¶***Government*** *circles* said that ... 政府筋では...といった. ¶Her ***home*** *circle* includes three brothers. 彼女の家庭には三人の兄弟がいる. ¶in ***industry*** *circles* 産業界で. ¶***music*** *circles* 音楽界. ¶a ***reading*** *circle* 読書会. ¶in ***sporting*** *circles* スポーツ界では. ¶a ***stone*** *circle* 環状列石. ¶a ***study*** *circle* 研究グループ. ¶***Washington*** *circles* say ... ワシントン筋での話では...

P ***among*** the aristocratic *circles* in Berlin ベルリンの貴族社会の間に. ¶It is ***beyond*** the *circle* of foresight. それは予想がつかない. ¶Mr. ... will be sorely missed ***by*** a *circle* of personal friends. ...氏の友人たちは痛く氏の帰国を惜むであろう. ¶sit (fly) ***in*** a *circle* 輪になってすわる(飛ぶ) ‖ a dancing ***in*** a *circle* 環状の踊 ‖ reason ***in*** a *circle* 循環的論法の議論をする. ¶***with*** a *circle* of coolies round him 人足どもに取巻かれて. ¶***within*** its *circle* その範囲内に.

P^2 a *circle* ***of*** hills 環状を成す丘陵群 ‖ the *circle* ***of*** the seasons 四季の循環.

circle, *v*. 回る.

M^2 *circle* ***round*** from the right 右巻きに回転する.

circuit, *n*. 一周, 一巡; 巡回; (電)回路.

V ***break*** (=***open***) an electrical *circuit* 電流を阻止する. ¶***close*** (=***complete or make***) a *circuit* 電流を自由に通じるようにする. ¶The judge ***goes*** the *circuit* twice a year. 判事は一年に二回巡回する. ¶***make*** the *circuit* of a meadow 牧草地を一周する ‖ ***make*** a *circuit* of the crater その噴火口を一周する ‖ ***make*** (=***take***) a long *circuit* 迂(う)回する.

Q make a ***complete*** *circuit* of ... ...をぐるっと一周する. ¶a ***judicial*** *circuit* 巡回裁判区.

Q^2 This film has not yet been offered to a major ***cinema*** *circuit*. この映画はまだ大きい映画配給系統には提供されていない. ¶a ***foxhole*** *circuit*《米》前線慰問興業. ¶a ***high (low)-tension*** *circuit* 高(低)圧電路. ¶a ***vacuum tube*** *circuit* 真空管回路.

P an accidental leak ***in*** an electric *circuit* 漏電 ‖ The Hall of Hotei at Tennoji is Number two ***in*** the *circuit* of Osaka's halls of the Seven Gods of Luck. 天王寺の布袋殿は大阪七福神詣での二番札所になっている. ¶The judges are ***on*** *circuit*. 判事が巡回中だ. ¶a film ***on*** the ... *circuit* ...系公開映画.

circular, *n*. 回状, 通知状.

V ***address*** a *circular* to large number of persons 多数の人々に当てて回状を出す. ¶***issue*** a *circular* announcing that ... ...通知の回状を出す. ¶***send*** *circulars* of inquiry to ... ...に質問書を送る. ¶***send out*** *circulars* concerning ... ...に関する回状を発送する.

Q ***Descriptive*** *circular* mailed upon request. 説明書は請求されれば郵送致します.

P^2 a *circular* ***in*** the form of questions 質問形式の回状.

circulate, *v*. 言触らす, 流布する; 広まる.

M The paper is *circulated* ***gratuitously*** through clubs and associations. 同紙はクラブや協会の間に無料で配付されている. ¶The rumor *circulated* ***rapidly***. うわさがたちまち広まった. ¶The secret was ***widely*** *circulated*. 秘密が広く知れ渡った. ¶the most ***widely*** *circulated* of all the magazines あらゆる雑誌の中で最も発行部数の多いもの.

P *circulate* ***about*** the neighborhood 近隣に広まる. ¶*circulate* ***among*** the people 人々の間に広まる. ¶*circulate* ***through***[***out***] a town (country) 町(など)中に伝わる.

circulation, *n*. 循環; 流布; 発行, 発行高.

V The book ***attained*** a wide *circulation*. その本は広く流布した. ¶It has ***caused*** the *circulation* of many stories. それで色々うわさが伝わった. ¶The magazine is ***enjoying*** a wide *circulation*. その雑誌は広く売れる. ¶***give*** a very large *circulation* to the word (information) ある語(情報)を非常に広く流布させる. ¶The bulletin ***has*** a *circulation* of 3,000 copies per issue. その会報は発行ごとに三千部出る. ¶***increase*** its *circulation* その発行部数を増す. ¶The rumor ***obtained*** wide *circulation*. そのうわさがもっぱら広まった. 【類】The treatise ***obtained*** wide *circulation* and influence. ¶***prohibit*** the *circulation* of the book on the ground that ... ...のかどでその本の頒布(はんぷ)を禁止する. ¶***promote*** the *circulation* of a newspaper 新聞の発行高を増すようにする. ¶***stimulate*** the *circulation* of blood 血液の循環をよくする.

Q The magazine has an ***enormous*** *circulation*. この雑誌ははばく大な売行だ. ¶That book obtained ***general*** *circulation*. その書物は広く一般に売れた. ¶The newspaper has a ***good*** *circulation*. その新聞は発行高が多い. ¶I hope the book will have a ***huge*** *circulation* among all classes. その本はすべての階級に猛烈に読まれるだろうと思う. ¶It has an ***immense*** *circulation*. それはばく大な発行部数に上っている. ¶How ***large*** is its *circulation*? その発行部数は幾らか. ¶The magazine has a ***limited*** *circulation*. その雑誌は発行部数が少ない. ¶the ***mammoth*** *circulation* of the London Press ロンドン新聞の驚異的な発行部数. ¶weeklies of ***national*** *circulation* 国内に広く読者を有する週刊紙(誌) ‖ The paper has a ***national*** *circulation*. 同紙は国中に広く読まれている. ¶It has achieved a ***net-paid*** *circulation* of far more than a million. その有料発行部数が百万をはるかに突破した. ¶a book printed for ***private*** *circulation* 同好の間に分配する私版の本. ¶a ***sluggish*** *circulation* of blood 緩慢な血液循環. ¶The news had a ***speedy*** *circulation*. そのことは直ちに世間に伝わった. ¶"Red" literature in ***surreptitious*** *circulations* 秘密に配布される赤色文献. ¶It has a ***wider*** *circulation* than its sister magazine *Newsweek*. それは姉妹誌ニューズ・ウィークより発行部数が多い.

Q^2 reduction of ***currency*** *circulation* 流通貨の縮小. ¶reduce ***note*** *circulation* 紙幣の流通を縮小する.

P paper money ***in*** *circulation* 流通紙幣 ‖ put new coins ***in*** (=***into***) *circulation* 新貨幣を流通させる. ¶the size ***of*** *circulation* [新聞などの]発行高. ¶a monthly magazine ***with*** a *circulation* of 100,000 発行部数十万の月刊雑誌.

P^2 cause a free *circulation* ***of*** the blood 大いに血液の循環をよくする.

circumference, *n*. 円周, 周囲.

V the tree ***has*** a *circumference* of ... この木は周囲...ある.

P a lake about two miles ***in*** *circumference* 周囲約二マイルの湖. 【類】a trunk of only 8 feet ***in*** *circumference*. ¶a point ***on*** the *circumference* 円周上の一点.

circumlocution, *n*. 遠回し, えん曲.

V ***use*** *circumlocution* 遠回しに言う.

Q mincing metaphors and ***affected*** *circumlocution* おつに気どった隠喩ときざな遠回し. ¶an ***awkward*** *circumlocution* まずい遠回し. ¶***cumbrous*** *circumlocutions* 不手際な遠回し. ¶***tortuous*** *circumlocutions* 大変な遠回し.

P ***without*** *circumlocution* 率直に, 赤裸々に.

circumscribe, *v*. とり巻く, 外接させる; 制限する.

P *circumscribe* a circle ***about*** a polygon 多角形に外接する円を描く. ¶The king's prerogative was *circumscribed* ***by*** the Constitution. 国王の特権は憲法によって制限された. ‖ *circumscribe* ***by*** (=***with***) a line 線で巻く. ¶*circumscribe* ... ***within*** narrow bounds ...を狭い範囲内に制限する.

circumspection, *n.* 用心, 慎重.

V It will ***require*** *circumspection.* それは慎重を要する.

Q ***social*** *circumspection* 社交上の心づかい.

P move ***with*** the greatest *circumspection* 最大の注意を払って行動する.【類】***with*** more *circumspection.*

circumstance, *n.* 事情, 情勢; 境遇; 委曲; 仰々しさ.

V ***aggravate*** *circumstances* 情勢を一層悪化する. ¶He ***detailed*** the *circumstance* as they had happened. 彼は事情をありのままに詳説した. ¶The *circumstances* must not be ***disregarded.*** この事情を看過してはならない. ¶***explain*** *circumstances* which led to ... ...に立至った事情を説明する. ¶The method best ***fits*** the *circumstance.* その方法が一番よくこの場合に適応する. ¶his closest friend, who ***knew*** the *circumstances* その事情を知っている彼の最も親しい友. ¶***make*** known the *circumstance* which led to his deed 彼の行動を誘致した事情を公表する. ¶***master*** one's *circumstances* 自己の境遇に打ち勝つ. ¶A friend of his ***narrated*** the *circumstances* to me. 彼の友人が私にその事情を打あけた. ¶***relate*** the *circumstances* 事情を話す. ¶the *circumstance* was ***reported*** to ... その事情は...に報告された. ¶do not ***suit*** their *circumstances* 彼らに都合が悪い. ¶***take*** every *circumstance* into consideration あらゆる事情を考慮する.

V² if *circumstances* ***allow*** (=***permit***) あわよくば. ¶the *circumstances* ***attending*** ... ...に伴う事情. ¶The *circumstances* ***changed*** when he was thirty years old. 三十才になったら情勢が変った. ¶many *circumstances* ***combined*** to ... 種々の事情が重なって...するに至った. ¶*circumstances* that ***conduced*** to the success of ... ...を成功せしめた事情. ¶as *circumstances* ***demand*** 必要に応じて. ¶if *circumstances* ***favor*** 都合よければ. ¶subsequently, *circumstances* ***occurred*** which rendered it necessary that he should ... その後になって彼が...しなければならない事情が起った. ¶so far as *circumstances* ***permit*** 事情の許す限り. ¶whenever *circumstances* ***require*** it その必要があればいつでも.

Q by some ***accidental*** *circumstance* 偶然. ¶***advantageous*** *circumstances* 有利な情勢. ¶***adverse*** *circumstances* 逆境. ¶***aggravating*** *circumstances* 酌量すべき余地のない情状. ¶an ***ameliorating*** *circumstance* 有利な事情(訴訟などで). ¶under ***appropriate*** *circumstances* 適当な事情では. ¶He is in ***bad, distressed*** *circumstances.* 彼はひどく窮迫している. ¶through ***certain*** *circumstances* ある事情のために. ¶an old friend in ***changed*** *circumstances* 昔と変った境遇にある旧友. ¶a lady in very ***comfortable*** *circumstances* 何不足ない婦人. ¶absent oneself under ***compelled*** *circumstances* よんどころなく欠席する. ¶There are ***complicated*** *circumstances* behind the matter. 裏面に複雑な事情がある. ¶be in ***easy*** *circumstances* 生活は楽である.【類】He is in fairly ***easy*** *circumstances.* ¶owing to ***exceptional*** *circumstances* やむを得ない事情のため. ¶in the ***existing*** *circumstances* 目下の情勢では. ¶There are sometimes ***extenuating*** *circumstances.* 酌量すべき事情のある場合もある. ¶***financial*** *circumstances* 財政状態. ¶the ***foregoing*** *circumstances* 以上の事情. ¶***fortuitous*** *circumstances* 予期しない事情. ¶He lives in ***good*** *circumstances.* 彼は楽に暮している. ¶born in ***humble*** *circumstances* 卑賤に生れて. ¶even under these ***inauspicious*** *circumstances* he formed an opportunity to ... かゝる不利の境涯にありながら彼は...する機会を見出した. ¶in ***indigent*** *circumstances* 貧乏な境涯に. ¶according to the difference in the ***local*** *circumstances* 地方の事情に応じて. ¶in case of ***mitigating*** *circumstances* 状情酌量すべき場合は. ¶***narrow*** *circumstances* 窮境. ¶be in ***needy*** (=reduced) *circumstances* 暮しに困っている. ¶under ***no*** *circumstances* どうあっても(...してはならない).【類】In ***no*** *circumstances* must a soldier leave his post. ¶one ***noteworthy*** *circumstance* is that ... 一つの注目すべき事情は...だ. ¶under ***obscure*** *circumstances* その事情がはっきりせずに. ¶a ***poignant*** *circumstance* ある辛い事情. ¶students in ***poor*** *circumstances* 貧乏な暮しの学生. ¶in ***present*** *circumstances* 目下の事情では. ¶if ***propitious*** *circumstances* present themselves 折よくば. ¶in ***prosperous*** *circumstances* よい暮しをして. ¶find himself in ***reduced*** *circumstances* 落ちぶれる.【類】He has left his family in ***reduced*** *circumstances.* ¶Such sentences would be used by an Englishman under ***similar*** *circumstances.* 同様の場合に英人もこんな文句を使うだろう. ¶except under ***special*** *circumstances* 特別な場合の外は. ¶get into ***straitened*** *circumstances* 窮境に陥る.【類】in spite of his ***straitened*** *circumstances.* ¶as always happens in ***such*** *circumstances* こうした場合にいつもそうなるように ‖ the *circumstances* were ***such*** as to ... ...するといったような事情であった. ¶if ***surrounding*** *circumstances* would tend to show that ... 周囲の事情が...を示す傾向ありとすれば. ¶He left his wife in ***tolerable*** *circumstances.* 後に残った妻がどうにか暮して行けるようにした. ¶He was killed under ***tragic*** *circumstances* in a railway accident. 彼は鉄道事故で悲惨な死に方をした.【類】his death in ***tragic*** *circumstances.* ¶under certain ***trying*** *circumstances* あるつらい事情で. ¶in that year ***two*** *circumstances* occurred which held out a prospect of ... その年二つの事情が起って...の見込が立った. ¶from (=through) ***unavoidable*** *circumstances* やむない事情で.【類】owing to ***unavoidable*** *circumstances.* ¶in ***uncongenial*** *circumstances* 不如意の境遇にあって. ¶in the event of ***unforeseen*** *circumstances* 予知しない事情の起った時には. ¶those whose *circumstances* are ***unhappy*** 不幸な境遇にある人々. ¶***untoward*** *circumstances* 不利な事情. ¶taking the ***whole*** *circumstances* into consideration, I think they can best be explained by the conclusion that ... すべての事情を綜合して考えると...と結論を下したなら最もよく説明がつくと思う.

Q² owing to ***family*** *circumstances* 家庭の事情で.

P I may go or not, ***according to*** *circumstances* 僕の行く行かないは事情によりけりだ. ¶calmness of demeanor ***amid*** *circumstances* of embarrassment or danger 困却や危険の場合における冷静な態度. ¶forced ***by*** *circumstances* 事情に迫られて. ¶rise ***from*** the humblest *circumstances* to the height of fame 最も卑賤な境遇から身を起して著名になる. ¶He is straitened ***in*** his *circumstances.* 彼は窮地に立っている. ‖ absolutely dauntless ***in*** other *circumstances* 他の場合ではあくまで大胆な ‖ ***In*** the *circumstances,* he could not have acted otherwise. 場合が場合だから彼としては外にしようがなかったろう.【類】***In*** these *circumstances* only three courses are open to us. / ***In*** these *circumstances* it might reasonably be supposed that ... ¶***owing*** to *circumstances* beyond one's control やむを得ない事情のため ‖ ***owing to*** unforeseen *circumstances* of which you shall be the judge 予想し得ない事情で, ただしそのいかんは貴下の御判定に任せるが. ¶take photographs ***under*** *circumstances* of great difficulty 非常に困難な撮影をする ‖ ***under*** peculiar *circumstances* 特殊な事情のもとに ‖ ***under*** any *circumstances* he must ... ぜひ彼は...せねばならない ‖ ***Under*** some *circumstances* defeat is honorable. 場合によっては敗けても恥でない.【類】***under*** these *circumstances.* ¶It entirely depends ***upon*** *circumstances.* それは全く事情によって決定される. ¶It was told ***with*** much *circumstances.* そのことが細かに述べられた ‖ hard struggles ***with*** *circumstances* 周囲の事情との苦闘. ¶***without*** *circumstances* 儀式張らずに.

P² the *circumstances* ***of*** his case 彼の場合のこみ入った事情 ‖ *circumstances* ***of*** the dispute 紛争事情.

circumstanced, *pa.* ある事情の下にある.

M those who are ***differently*** *circumstanced* 境遇を異にしている人々. ¶be ***so*** *circumstanced* that ... ...という羽目になる.

circus, *n.* サーカス; 円形の広場.

V ***put up*** (=***pitch***) a *circus* サーカスの小屋をかける. ¶***run*** (=***operate***) a *circus* サーカスの興業をやる.

Q² How to put on an ***Amateur*** *Circus* [書名]しろうと曲馬の演出法. ¶a ***flea*** *circus* のみの芸当. ¶***Piccadilly*** *Circus.* [英国]ピカデリー広場. ¶a ***traveling*** *circus* 地方回りのサーカス.

P see the elephants and the clowns ***at*** the *circus* 曲馬団で象と道化師を見る.

citation, *n.* 引用, 引用句; 感状.

Q ***apt*** *citations* and poetic gems to adorn one's speeches 演説を飾るための適切な引用句と美しい詩句. ¶The date of the ***earliest*** *citation* of the word in the OED is 1868. その語が OED (Oxford English Dictionary) に引用されている一番古い年代は 1868 年である. ¶a ***personal*** *citation* 個人感状.

P² a *citation* ***for*** one's war merits (one's bravery in action) 感状. ¶The *citation* ***of*** authority for a word. あ

る語に対する用法の典拠挙示.

cite, *v.* 引用する, 挙示する; 召喚する.

P *cite ... as* instance ...を例に引く.【類】I hope that she may pardon my *citing* her ***as*** an example of ... ¶***cite at*** second-hand from ... ...から孫引する. ¶*cite* a man ***before*** the court 人を法廷に召喚する. ¶***cite from*** the Bible 聖書から引用する.【類】*cite* passages ***from*** books. ¶*cite* a fact ***to*** a person ある事実を人に挙示する.

citizen, *n.* 市民, 公民.

Q ***American*** *citizens* and British subjects 米市民と英国民. ¶an ***eminent*** *citizen* of that city その市の名士. ¶an ***energetic*** and ***public-spirited*** *citizen* 活動的な公共心のある一国民. ¶***law-abiding*** *citizens* 法律を守る公民. ¶a ***native-born*** *citizen* of U.S. 米国生れの市民. ¶a ***naturalized American*** *citizen* 米国帰化人. ¶a ***patriotic*** *citizen* 愛国者.【類】be the duty of every ***patriotic*** *citizen* of every country to ... ¶***peace-loving*** *citizens* 平和を愛する国民. ¶a just ***plain*** *citizen* 役付でない市民(平民). ¶a ***private*** *citizen* 私人である一市民. ¶one of the most ***prominent*** *citizens* of New York ニューヨークの最も卓越した市民の一人. ¶***reputable*** *citizens* 評判のよい(りっぱな)公民. ¶a ***respectable*** *citizen* ちゃんとした(かたぎの)市民. ¶be expelled from the community as an ***undesirable*** *citizen* 好ましからぬ国民として社会から追放される. ¶***young*** *citizens* 小国民.

Q^2 one's ***fellow*** *citizens* 同胞. ¶a ***United States*** *citizen* 合衆国市民. ¶a ***woman*** *citizen* with vote 投票権のある女. ¶a ***world*** *citizen* 世界市民.

P^2 a *citizen* ***of*** the world=a world citizen ‖ He was born a *citizen* ***of*** London. 彼はロンドンの市民に生れた.

citizenship, *n.* 公民権, 市民権; 国籍.

V ***acquire*** *citizenship* 公民権を得る. ¶***derive*** *citizenship* 市民権を得る. ¶***develop*** good *citizenship* りっぱな国民の資格を造り上げる. ¶***elect*** Japanese *citizenship* 日本の国籍の方を選ぶ. ¶***give up*** their Japanese *citizenship* 彼らの日本国民たる資格を放棄する. ¶***grant*** *citizenship* to ... ...に公民権を与える. ¶***lose*** *citizenship* through marriage to aliens 外国人との結婚により国籍を失う. ¶***re-acquire*** (=***regain***) *citizenship* 市民権を取戻す. ¶***renounce*** his Australian *citizenship* and British nationality 豪州の市民権と英国の国籍を放棄する. ¶***revoke*** one's *citizenship* 市民権を取消す. ¶***take*** the Hungarian *citizenship* ハンガリー人になる.

Q ***dual*** *citizenship* 二重国籍. ¶***good*** and ***efficient*** *citizenship* 善良にして有能な公民の資格.

Q^2 ***town*** *citizenship* 市民権(都市の). ¶***United States*** *citizenship* 米国市民権. ¶education in ***world*** *citizenship* 国際的市民に関する教育.

P the admission ***to*** *citizenship* by naturalization 帰化による公民権付与.

city, *n.* 市, 都会.

V He ***adopted*** that *city* as his residence. その市を彼の居住地と定めた. ¶***distress*** a *city* into surrender 都市を苦しめて降服させる. ¶***do*** the *city* その市の見物をする. ¶***dust*** a *city* 都市の清掃をする. ¶***found*** a *city* 都市を建設する. ¶***plan*** a *city* 都市計画をする. ¶***sack*** a *city* [***off***] 都市を略奪する. ¶***sanitate*** *cities* 都市に衛生設備をする.

Q in the ***capital*** *city* 首都で. ¶Ireland and its ***capital*** *city* アイルランドおよびその首都. ¶***cathedral*** *cities* 大寺院のある都市. ¶the ***chief*** *city* 首都. ¶Shanghai was once a ***cosmopolitan*** *city*. 上海はかつて国際都市だった. ¶a ***grey old*** *city* 古色蒼(そう)然たる古都. ¶such a ***high-priced*** *city* as Hollywood ハリウッドのような物価の高い都市. ¶one of the ***key*** *cities* in the territory その地方の主要都市の一. ¶a ***large*** and ***flourishing*** *city* of 750,000 inhabitants 人口七十五万の繁栄する大都会. ¶Indianapolis is the capital and the ***largest*** *city* of Indiana. インディアナポリスはインディアナ州の首府でかつ最大の都市だ. ¶a ***medium-sized*** *city* 中都市. ¶a ***new-old*** *city* 新旧織り交ぜた(古い所も新しい所もある)都市. ¶an ***overpopulated*** *city* 人口過剰の都市. ¶the most ***populous*** *city* 最も人口の多い都市. ¶in ***principal*** *cities* of the world 世界の主要都市で. ¶a ***progressive*** *city* 進歩的都市. ¶***provincial*** *cities* 地方の都市. ¶a ***quiet little manufacturing*** *city* of 13,000 人口一万三千の静かな小工業都市. ¶the culturally ***rich*** *city* of Philadelphia 文化的に発達しているフィラデルフィア. ¶a ***sea-born*** *city* (Venice のように)海のために興った都市. ¶a ***sizable*** *city* 相当の都市. ¶a ***two-decked*** *city* [地下地上]二重都市. ¶a ***walled*** *city* 城壁をめぐらした都市.

Q^2 Glasgow, essentially a ***business*** *city* 本質的に商業都市たるグラスゴー. ¶a ***coal mining*** *city* 炭坑都市. ¶a ***coast*** *city* 海岸都市.【類】an ***east coast*** *city*. ¶a ***floating*** *city* 大船. ¶a ***garden*** *city* 田園都市. ¶The ***Granite*** *City*. スコットランドのバディーン市(みかげ石造りの家が多い). ¶Nikko, famous ***Japanese shrine*** *city* 有名な日本の神社都市日光. ¶***lake*** and ***river*** *cities* 湖畔および河畔の都市. ¶***New York*** *City*=the City of New York. ¶a ***phantom*** *city* 幻の市. ¶a ***port*** (=***seaport***) *city* [海]港市. ¶the ***twin*** *cities* of Moji and Shimonoseki 門司・下関の双子都市. ¶a ***world*** *city* 世界的都市.

P I live ***in*** a great *city*. 大都会に住んでいる. ¶the dwellers ***of*** a *city*=city dwellers 市の住民 ‖ a crowded district ***of*** a *city* 市の人口ちゅう密な方面 ‖ the poorer quarters ***of*** the *city* 市の貧民くつ. ¶A river flows ***through*** the *city*. 川が市中を流れている.

P^2 a fine *city* ***of*** stone and brick buildings with a population of considerably over ... 人口...をはるかに越える石やれんがの家屋からなるりっぱな都会 ‖ any one *city* ***of*** its size in the country その国にある他のそれと同じ位の大きさの都市.

civics, *n.* 市政.

Q^2 ***community*** *civics* 市政.

civies, *n.* 《米》平服, 背広.

P soldiers ***in*** *civies* 背広の軍人たち.

civil, *a.* 丁寧な.

P He is *civil* ***to*** strangers 彼は他人に丁寧だ.

civilian, *n.* 一般市民; 軍属.

Q ***interned*** *civilians* 抑留者たち.

P^2 *civilians* ***in*** the Army (Navy) 軍属.

civility, *n.* 丁寧, いんぎん.

V ***do*** *civility* 礼儀を尽す. ¶***offer*** *civilities* 礼遇する. ¶***proffer*** trifling *civilities* 微細の点に好意を示す. ¶***show*** *civility* to a guest 来客をいんぎんに遇する.

Q take up an air of ***affected*** *civility* 気どったいんぎんの様子を示す. ¶***scant*** *civility* at the customs 税関における(官吏の)無作法.

P I could not ***in*** *civility* refuse him. 礼儀として断わるわけにいかなかった. ¶after an interchange ***of*** *civilities* あいさつの言葉を取り交わした後. ¶behave ***with*** more *civilities* to ... ...に対して一層丁寧に振舞う.

P^2 the *civilities* ***of*** life 世間の義理.

civilization, *n.* 文明, 文化, 教化.

V ***adopt*** foreign *civilization* 外国文明を採り入れる. ¶***attain*** a high *civilization* 高級の文明に達する. ¶ideas which can aid in ***building up*** her new *civilization* その国の新文明を建設するに役立つような考え. ¶***carry*** *civilization* to the remotest parts of the globe 文明を世界のすみずみまで行きわたらせる. ¶the advanced races that are ***creating*** the *civilization* of the future 将来の文明を創造しつつある先進国民 ¶Assyria ***derived*** its *civilization* from Babylonia. アッシリアの文明はバビロニアから由来した. ¶***develop*** a *civilization* of its own 独自の文明を開発する. ¶Modern trade ***discloses*** *civilization* in its acutest form. 近代商業は最も鋭い角度の文化を示している. ¶***establish*** a better and safer *civilization* さらにすぐれかつ安全性のある文明を建設する. ¶***found*** a great *civilization* upon a modern basis 近代的基礎の上に一大文化を建設する. ¶They ***have*** a long *civilization* behind them. 彼らの背後に古い文化を有している. ¶***introduce*** Western *civilization* 西欧文明を輸入する. ¶Missionaries ***planted*** *civilization* among savages. 宣教師が蛮人の間に文化を移植した. ¶***reach*** *civilization* [未開の状態から]文明状態に達する. ¶***rebuild*** *civilization* 文化を再建する.

V^2 as *civilization* ***advances*** 文化の進むにつれて. ¶*Civilization* ***progresses***. 文明が進む. ¶*Civilization* ***retrogrades***. 文明が退歩する. ¶*Civilization* ***stagnates***. 文明が沈滞する.

Q the Far East, with its ***ancient semibarbaric*** *civilizations* 昔ながらの半未開の文化を持っている極東. ¶a ***backward*** *civilization* 進歩の遅れた文化. ¶in ***certain*** *civilizations* ある種の文化に於ては. ¶***elder*** *civilizations* さらに古い文化. ¶The ***English*** *civilization* is a complex of many civilizations that have preceded it. 英国文明は先進諸国文明の集合体である. ¶countries of ***European*** *civilization* 西欧文明国. ¶the ***Greco-Roman*** *civilization* ギ

リシア・ローマ文明. ¶people of ***high civilization*** 高度の文明国民. ¶the old language of ***Hellenic civilization*** 古代ギリシア文明の古語. ¶Los Angeles, one of the jazziest parts of the rather thoroughly ***jazzed up civilization*** of present-day America 現代アメリカのあまりにもジャズ化した文化の中で最もジャズ的な地方の一たるロスアンジェルス. ¶***material civilization*** 物質文明. 【類】a nation with the highest ***material civilization.*** ¶adjuncts of ***modern civilization*** 近代文明の付属物. 【類】a product of ***modern civilization.*** ¶a ***moribund civilization*** ひん死の文明. ¶an ***old, slow civilization*** 古くって進歩のかん慢な文化. ¶***pre-radio civilization*** ラジオ以前の文化. ¶***primitive civilizations*** 原始諸文化. ¶a ***vanished civilization*** 消失した文化. ¶a people with a ***venerable civilization*** 古いりっぱな文化を持っている国民. ¶the ***white man's civilization*** 白人文化.

Q² ***capitalist civilization*** 資本主義文明. ¶***city civilization*** 都市文明. ¶the ***English-speaking civilization*** 英語国民の文明. ¶the ***Inca civilization*** in Peru ペルーのインカ文明. ¶a ***machine civilization*** 機械文明. ¶her ***veneer civilization*** その国の薄っぺらな文明.

P advance (retrograde) ***in civilization*** 文明が進む(退歩する). ¶raise (lower) the level ***of civilization*** 文明の標準を高める(下げる). ¶a march ***toward civilization*** 文明の進歩.

clad, *v.* [clothe の過去および過去分詞].

M be ***poorly clad*** 身なりがよくない. ¶be ***smartly clad*** 身なりがきちんとしている(スマートだ).

P be ***clad in*** rags ぼろをまとっている.

claim, *n.* 要求, 主張; 要求権; 〖商〗苦情.

V ***accept*** a ***claim*** for compensation 損害賠償の要求に応じる. ¶I do not ***admit*** the ***claim.*** 私はその要求は認めない. ¶***advance*** (=***put forward***) a ***claim*** 要求を提出する. ¶No ***claims*** are ***allowed*** for breakage. 破損に対する苦情は一切許されない. ¶***base*** one's ***claims*** to its superiority upon these points これらの点でその優秀性を主張する. ¶***bear out*** the ***claim*** その要求権を支持する. ¶***bring forward*** a ***claim*** to ... ...の要求を持出す. ¶endeavor to ***compromise*** a ***claim*** 要求を示談で解決しようと努める. 【類】I think the ***claim*** can be ***compromised.*** ¶***dismiss*** the ***claim*** of ... on the ground that ... ...の理由で...の要求を却下する. ¶***dispute*** a ***claim*** 要求について論争する. ¶***drop*** (=***lay aside or waive***) one's ***claim*** 自分の要求を放棄する. ¶***enforce*** the ***claim*** immediately 直ちに要求を強制する. ¶***entertain*** a ***claim*** 請求を受理する. ¶***establish*** one's ***claim*** to rank with the Great Powers 強国と肩を並べうる権利を確立する. 【類】It has ***established*** its ***claim*** upon our respect and attention. ¶allow the opposing parties to ***fight out*** their ***claim*** between themselves 反対両党をしてたがいにその主張をあくまで戦わせる. ¶***file*** a ***claim*** on merchandise 商品に対するクレーム(苦情)を提出する. ¶He ***found*** the ***claims*** of music too strong to be resisted. 好きでとうとう楽人となった. ¶***forfeit*** all ***claims*** to confidence 全然信用を失う. ¶Amid the turmoil of affairs he did not ***forget*** the ***claims*** of letters. テンヤワンヤの中にあっても文学のおもしろみを忘れなかった. ¶***hand in*** a ***claim*** 要求を提出する. ¶***give up*** a ***claim*** to ... ...に対する要求権を放棄する. ¶anyone who ***has*** any ***claim*** against the estate of the late ... 故...の財産に対する一切の権利者 ‖ He ***has*** the ***claim*** on (=against) me. 彼は私に対してこの要求権がある. ‖ He ***has*** the best ***claim*** to be appointed to the post. 彼はその地位を占めるに最も適している. ‖ He ***has*** a ***claim*** to be known as an authority on the subject. 彼にはその道の権威と称せられるだけの実力がある. ‖ ***has*** no ***claim*** to scholarship 学者だなどとは言われたものじゃない. 【類】***have*** no ***claim*** to longevity, being only seventy-six. ¶No ***claim*** was ***incurred.*** 何ら要求を受けなかった. ¶***institute*** a ***claim*** for damages suffered 損害賠償を要求する. ¶***invalidate*** a ***claim*** 請求を無効にする. ¶I ***lay*** no ***claim*** to original research. 独創的な研究をやろうとは思わない. 【類】no ***claim*** has yet been ***laid*** to ... ‖ He can justly ***lay claim*** to this distinction. 彼は当然この名誉を担(にな)う資格がある. ‖ The list ***lays*** no ***claim*** to being complete. この表は決して完全とは言い得ない. 【類】in taking up this subject I cannot ***lay*** any special ***claim*** to a deep knowledge of ... ¶***lodge*** a ***claim*** before the British Consul 英国領事にある要求を提出する ‖ ***lodge*** a ***claim*** for repayment 弁償の要求を提出する. 【類】***lodge*** a ***claim*** for compensation (損害賠償) against ... ¶***lose*** all its ***claim*** to respectability 全くその体面を失う. ¶I ***make*** no ***claim*** to originality in this book. 私はこの著作が独創的だとはあえて主張しない. ‖ ***make*** a ***claim*** against an express company 通運会社に対しクレームを出す. ¶***meet*** a ***claim*** for damages 損害賠償の請求に応じる. ¶agree to ***pay*** a ***claim*** 賠償する事を承諾する. ¶The book ***possesses*** no ***claim*** to originality. その著作には何ら独創的な所はない. ¶***press*** one's ***claim*** on ... ...に自分の主張を押しつける. ¶***put forward*** the ***claim*** that ... ...ということを主張する ‖ ***put forward*** a ***claim*** to exhaustiveness あくまで主張する. ¶***put*** (=***send***) ***in*** a ***claim*** of damages 損害賠償を請求する. 【類】***put in claims*** for possession (所有権) of ... / ***put in claims*** for a share in the spoil (獲物). ¶I cannot ***recognize*** any ***claim.*** いかなる要求も認められない. ¶***reject*** one's ***claim*** その要求を拒絶する. ¶***relinquish*** (=***withdraw***) a ***claim*** 要求を撤回する. ¶***renounce*** one's ***claim*** to money 金銭上の要求を放棄する. ¶***resist*** a ***claim*** 要求をはねつける. ¶***rest*** (=base) his ***claims*** to it upon ... 彼のその要求に対し...を根拠とする. ¶unless the ***claim*** is ***satisfied*** 要求が満足されなければ. ¶***set off*** two ***claims*** against one another 相互の権利を相殺する ¶***claims*** were ***set up*** on behalf of Germany by ... ドイツのための要求が...によって持ち出された. ¶***settle claims*** out of court 賠償事件を内済にする. ¶***substantiate*** his hitherto doubtful ***claims*** to ... これまではっきりしてなかった彼の...に対する権利を確実にする. ¶***verify*** one's ***claim*** 要求を履行する. ¶***waive*** (=give up) one's ***claim*** for ... ...に対する要求を放棄する. ¶***withdraw*** a ***claim*** 要求を撤回する.

Q He has the ***best claim*** to the honor. 彼がその名誉を受けるに最も適している. ¶reconcile the ***conflicting claim*** of ... ...の対立する要求を和解させる. ¶a ***correct claim*** 正しい要求. ¶***empty claims*** 不当な要求. ¶an ***excessive claim*** 過大な要求. ¶It is a ***fair claim*** that printing is the most important single mechanical revolution in human history. 印刷が人類の歴史における最大な一つの機械的革命であるというのは公平な見解である. ¶It has the ***first claim*** to consideration. これは第一に考慮すべきことだ. ¶present a ***fraudulent claim*** against ... 虚構の賠償要求を提出する. ¶a ***heavy claim*** 多大な要求. ¶an ***importunate claim*** うるさい要求. ¶an ***indefeasible claim*** 動かしがたい要求. ¶a ***just claim*** 正当な要求. ¶***Later claims*** could not be considered. その後の要求は提出されても取合わない. ¶a ***legal claim*** on an estate 財産に対する法律上の要求権. ¶make ***little claim*** to originality in method 手法においてほとんど独創性を示していない. ¶their ***Messianic claims*** 救世主であるという彼らの声明. ¶has ***more claims*** on admiration than it is possible to mention 記述する事ができないほど賞賛される資格がある. ¶His personality is his ***only claim*** to remembrance. 彼が記憶されているのはただただその人格のためだ. ¶an ***outstanding claim*** 未解決の要求. ¶He has a ***particular claim*** to be considered. 彼には特に考慮してもらわねばならない権利がある. ¶its ***principal claim*** to originality consists in ... その主なる独創性は...の点に存する. 【類】its ***principal claim*** to history is that it ... ¶My order has ***prior claims*** on your time. 私の註文の方が先口だ. ¶The matter has ***reasonable claim*** to consideration. 当然考慮を払うべきである. ¶my appreciation of their ***respective claim*** to literary repute 彼らの文学上の価値に対する私の評価. ¶set up ***rival claims*** 対立的要求を持出す. ¶the ***scientific claims*** of eugenics 優生学の科学的根拠. ¶I have some ***slight claim*** of acquaintance. ほんのちょっと知っているというだけのこと. ¶It has a ***special claim*** to remembrance. 特に記憶されるだけの価値がある. ¶a ***specious claim*** もっともらしい要求. ¶a ***substantiated claim*** 正当な要求. ¶a ***trifling claim*** ささいな要求. ¶an ***unjustified claim*** せん越な要求. ¶an ***unreasonable claim*** 不当な要求. ¶a more ***weighty claim*** 一層重大な要求. ¶***What claim*** has he to the property? その財産に対して彼にはどんな要求権があるか.

Q² a ***compensation claim*** 損害賠償の要求. ¶pay ***war-damage claims*** 戦災賠償要求を支払う. ¶a shorter ***work-week claim*** 週日操短要求.

P ***despite*** the ***claims*** of a busy life 多忙の身でありながら.

P² a ***claim against*** a company for compensation 会社に対する賠償要求. ¶a ***claim by*** right of descent 世襲権によ

る要求. ¶a *claim* ***for*** compensation 賠償の要求. 【類】a *claim* ***for*** damages / a *claim* ***for*** short delivery (数量不足) ‖ The *claim* ***for*** salvage has been compromised. 海難救助に対する要求は示談になった. ¶his *claim* ***of*** priority in the invention その発明に彼が先べんをつけたという主張 ‖ a *claim* ***of*** justice 正義の主張. ¶I have no *claim* ***on*** him. 僕は彼に対して要求権がない. ‖ I have lots of *claims* ***on*** my time. 色々な用事で余暇がない. ¶*Claims* ***on*** cargo not lodged with agents by 19th inst. at 5 p.m. cannot be entertained. 今月十九日午後五時までに運送店に申出ない船荷引渡しの請求は受理致しません ‖ his *claim* ***of*** fame is that ... 彼が名声を博しうるのは...であるからだ. 【類】his *claim* ***of*** fame rests chiefly upon the invention of ... ‖ his *claim* ***to*** distinction rests on the fact that ... 彼が卓越しているのは...という点にある ‖ a *claim* ***to*** indemnities 賠償金請求[権]. 【類】his *claim* ***to*** literary recognition rests on his great work ... / Wycliffe's *claim* ***to*** the title of "founder of English prose-writing" is entirely due to political causes. / their *claim* ***to*** descent in the direct line (直系) from ... ¶a warmer appreciation of their *claim* ***upon*** our sympathy 彼らがわれわれの同情を受ける資格があるということに対する一層深い認識.

claim, *v.* 主張する; 要求する.

M can ***fairly*** *claim* to have ... ...を持つことを正当に要求できる. ¶the gift which he *claims* ***uniquely*** for himself 自分独得のものと誇る技能.

P *claim* a large amount ***against*** him 彼に対して多額の金額を請求する. ¶*claim* the estate ***by*** right of descent 世襲権によって財産を要求する. ¶advantages *claimed* ***for*** this machine この機械の長所. ¶*claim* payment ***from*** ... ...から支払を要求する. ¶*claim* ¥... ***from*** him ***for*** injuries suffered 損害賠償として彼から...円を要求する.

claimant, *n.* 主張者.

Q the ***newest*** *claimants* of the buyer's money 新規売出し品. ¶To the honor of being the birth-place of alchemy, India and China are ***rival*** *claimants.* 錬金術の発祥地についてはインドと中国との二説がある.

P rival *claimants* ***to*** ... ...に対する主張者同志.

clamber, *v.* はう.

P *clamber* ***into*** a car 自動車にはい込む. ¶As soon as a girl begins to earn something honestly, there is hope that she may *clamber* ***out of*** the mire. 何か堅気の商売にありつきさえすれば少女は泥水商売から足を洗う望みがある.

clammy, *a.* ねばねばする.

P *clammy* ***with*** sweat (=perspiration) 汗でべとべとになって.

clamorous, *a.* 騒々しい, やかましい.

P They are *clamorous* ***against*** lower pay. 彼らは賃金値下げ反対で騒いでいる. ¶They are *clamorous* ***for*** better pay. 彼らは賃金値上げを叫んでいる.

clamo[u]r, *n.* けん騒, わいわい騒ぎ.

V It ***called forth*** *clamors* of indignation. それで怒号がまき起った. ¶***make*** a foolish and futile *clamor* about ... ...について愚かなかつむだな騒ぎをする.

Q an ***irresponsible*** *clamor* 無責任なわいわい騒ぎ. ¶***popular*** *clamor* 民衆の叫び.

P^2 the *clamor* ***of*** the press やかましい新聞紙の騒ぎ立て.

clamo[u]r, *v.* 騒ぐ; 促す.

P *clamor* ***against*** the measure その手段に反対して騒ぐ. ¶a problem that *clamors* ***for*** solution 速かに解決を要する問題 ‖ *clamor* ***for*** admission わいわい言って入場を求める ‖ *clamor* ***for*** higher wages 賃銀値上を叫ぶ. 【類】His landlord is *clamoring* ***for*** the rent. ¶*clamor* ***in*** fury 怒って騒ぎ立てる.

clamo[u]ring, *n.* けん騒.

V ***heed*** the *clamorings* of the multitude 群集のけん騒を顧慮する.

clamp, *v.* どしんどしんと踏む.

M^2 *clamp* ***down*** on ... ...を弾圧する; ふみつける. 【類】*clamp* ***down*** on gangsters / *clamp* ***down*** on the floor.

clamp, *v.* 締め金でしめる; 弾圧する.

M^2 *clamp* ***down*** restrictions on ... ...に対し弾圧を加える ‖ *clamp* ***down*** on excessive Communist activities 行き過ぎた共産党運動に鉄ついを加える.

P *clamp* restraints ***on*** labor strike ストに弾圧を加える.

clan, *n.* 閥, 藩; 党.

Q the ***anti-Tokugawa*** *clans* 勤王党. ¶a samurai of the ***Choshu*** *clan* 長州藩のさむらい. ¶a ***dominant*** *clan* 優勢な派. ¶the ***whole*** *clan* of Macdonalds マクドナルド家一門.

clang, *n.* がらんという音.

Q a voice that has a ***metalic*** *clang* 金属性のひびきをもつ声.

P ***with*** a *clang* がらん(かちん)と鳴って.

clansman, *n.* 藩士.

Q^2 an ***Aizu*** *clansman* 会津藩士.

clap, *n.* たたき; ごう声.

V ***give*** a *clap* on the shoulder 肩をたたく.

Q^2 a ***thunder*** *clap* 雷鳴.

P ***at*** a *clap* 一撃で. ¶shut a book ***with*** a *clap* ぴしゃっと本を閉じる.

P^2 a *clap* ***of*** thunder 一しきりの雷鳴.

clap, *v.* ぽんとたたく; ぱたと置く; 閉じこめる.

M^2 *clap* ***up*** a bargain with ... ...との取引を済ます.

P *clap* one ***into*** a bedlam 人を精神病院にぶちこむ. ¶*clap* a friend ***on*** the back 友の背をたたく. ¶*clap* a board ***over*** a pit 板ぶたでおとし穴をぱたりと閉じる. ¶*clap* the hand ***to*** the mouth 手を口にぱたりと当てる ‖ He *clapped* the door ***to.*** ドアをぴしゃりと閉めた.

clapper, *n.* 拍子木.

V ***strike*** *clappers* 拍子木を打つ.

Q ***wooden*** *clappers* 拍子木.

clapping, *n.* 拍手.

Q There wasn't ***much*** *clapping* heard. あまり拍手の音も聞えなかった.

clarification, *n.* 明徴, 明証.

V ***offer*** some *clarification* on a controversy ある論争に対して解明を下す.

clarion, *n.* 〘楽器〙 クラリオン.

Q^2 toot one's ***silver*** *clarion* 銀のクラリオンを吹き鳴らす.

clarity, *n.* 清明, 透明.

Q state with ***astonishing*** *clarity* 驚くべき明快さで述べる. ¶add ***great*** *clarity* to ... ...を非常に明りょうにする.

P see ***with*** *clarity* はっきり見てとる.

clash, *n.* 衝突; がちゃんと相打つ音.

V ***avert*** a *clash* 衝突を避ける.

Q the fear of a ***coming*** *clash* of arms 将来戦争をするようになる恐れ. ¶***Incessant*** *clashes* occur between them. 絶え間ない衝突が彼らの間に起る. ¶a ***serious*** *clash* 本式の衝突.

P It came down ***with*** a *clash.* それががたんと落ちてきた.

P^2 a *clash* ***between*** students and police 学生と警官隊との衝突. ¶a *clash* ***of*** interests 利害の衝突. ¶And a *clash* ***of*** arms ensued. 次いで戦いが起った.

clash, *v.* がちゃがちゃと鳴る; 衝突する.

P *clash* ***against*** armor よろいにがちゃがちゃと打ちあたる. ¶*clash* ***on*** how to ... ...のやり方についての意見が衝突する. ¶*clash* a little ***with*** ... ...と少しく矛盾する ‖ *clash* ***with*** a person over ... ...のことで人と衝突する ‖ *clash* ***with*** his interests 彼の利害と衝突する. 【類】Japan's interests in the Pacific *clash* ***with*** America's.

clasp, *n.* しめ金.

Q^2 a "***gem***" ***letter*** *clasp* 小形の状ばさみ.

clasp, *v.* 抱く, しかと握る.

M He *clasped* her ***hard*** in his arms. 両腕で彼女を固く抱き締めた. ¶*clasp* one's hands ***together*** 両手を堅く組む.

P He *clasped* me ***round*** the neck. 彼は私のくびを抱いた. ¶She *clasped* his child ***to*** her bosom. 彼女は子供を胸に抱き締めた.

class, *n.* (**1**) 種類, 部門.

V It ***constitutes*** a *class* by itself. それだけで一部門をなしている. ¶They ***form*** a *class* by themselves. 彼らだけで一種類をなす ‖ ***form*** a *class* apart (=by itself) 別に一部門をなす.

Q a ***cheap*** *class* of boiler 安価なボイラー. ¶a journal of ***high*** *class* 一流新聞. ¶a ***kindred*** *class* of ... ...に類する種類. ¶They form a very ***numerous*** *class.* その種類が非常に多い. ¶books of the ***same*** *class* 同種類の本. ¶travel [in] ***second*** *class* 二等で旅行する. ¶There is ***some*** *class* about her. 彼女のスタイルは中々すてきだ. ¶of ***superior*** *class* 種類のすぐれた. ¶one of the ***unruly*** *class* 手におえぬ種類の人間.

Q^2 small magazines of the "***Here today and gone tomorrow*** *class*" 三号雑誌. ¶homes in the ***$6,000*** *class* 6,000ドル級の家屋.

P taking them ***as*** a *class* 彼らを一団として考えて. ¶It is ***in*** a *class* by itself. それだけで一部門をなしている. ‖ a man ***in*** the $75,000,000 *class* 七千五百万ドル級の人(財産家) ‖ place it ***in*** the *class* of ... それを...の部に入れる. ¶be ***of*** this *class* この種類に属する. ¶***Under*** what *class* does this

fall? これは何の部に入るか. ‖ *Under* this *class* comes … …はこの部に属する. 「海草.
P² a *class of* men 一種の人 ‖ a *class of* seaweeds 一種の
(**2**) 階級, 社会; *pl.* 上流階級.
V *contrast* the *classes* and the masses 上層階級と下層階級を対照する. ¶He *entered* the criminal *class* in its upper ranks through politics. 彼は政治家として高級犯罪者の中に入れられることになった. ¶*level classes* 階級を打破する. ¶They *represent* a very different social *class*. 彼らは一つのはなはだ異った社会階級を形成している.
Q representatives of *all classes* of society 社会全階級の代表者 ‖ an event in which *all classes* and all ages are interested 貴賤老若共に関心を持つ事件. ¶*arm-bearing classes* 武人階級. ¶*commercial* and *professional classes* 商業および学術的職業階級. ¶the most *cultured classes* 最も教養の高い社会. ¶the *educated class* 知識階級. ¶men belonging to *every class* of society and men of every type 社会のすべての階級に属する人々とあらゆる型の人々. ¶What is the poverty of the *farming classes* due to? 農民階級の貧困は何が原因か. ¶the *feudal fighting class* 武士階級. ¶the less *fortunate classes* それほど幸福でない階級. ¶the *governing class* 支配階級. ¶farmers of the *humbler class* 貧農. ¶two most *important classes* of public servant—the policeman and the pedagogue 社会に奉仕するきわめて重要な二階級, すなわち警官と学校教師. ¶the *industrial classes* 産業階級. ¶the *intermediate class* 中流階級. ¶women of the *laboring classes* 労働階級の女. 【類】 the growing power of the *laboring classes* / the solidarity (団結) of the *laboring classes*. ¶*leisured classes* 有閑階級. ¶girls of *low social class* (=stratum) 下層階級の少女たち. 【類】 English people of *lower class*. ¶the *middle educated class* 教育ある中流社会. ¶the *middle* and *upper classes* 中流および上流社会. ¶the *military class* 武人階級. ¶the *moneyed classes* 資産階級. ¶a *new rich class* 新興富裕階級. ¶the *official classes* 役人階級. ¶*poor* and *hardworking classes* 貧乏で労苦する階級. ¶belong to the *poorer, laboring class* 一層貧乏で労苦する階級に属する. ¶*professional* and *trading classes* 知識職業および商人階級. ¶the *propertied class* 有産階級. ¶the *ruling classes* 支配階級. ¶women of *good social class* 身分のある婦人. ¶The most *spending classes* in Europe is the English gentry. ヨーロッパで一番金を使う階級は英国の紳士階級である. ¶Russians of the *suspicious class* いかがわしい階級のロシア人. ¶among the *upper classes* of society 上流社会の間に. 【類】 in the *upper, well-to-do classes*. ¶The jargons of the *various classes* and occupation. 様々の階級および職業で使う特殊な言葉. ¶women of the *well-to-do class* 相当暮し向きのよい階級の女. ¶the *working classes* 労働階級.
Q² oppression and extermination of the *bourgeois classes* 資本家階級の抑圧と根絶. ¶the *capitalist class* 資本家階級. ¶of the *coolie class* 苦力(クーリー)社会の. ¶the *land-owning class* 地主階級. ¶the *leisure class* 有閑階級. ¶among the *student class* 学生間に. ¶the moderately prosperous members of the *tradesman class* 商人階級の相当にやっている人たち. ¶the *warrior class* 武士階級.
P the false, disastrous notion prevailing *among* all *classes* of society that… 社会のあらゆる階級に浸潤している…という誤った危険思想. ¶*as* a *class* 全体としては. ¶both *by* the scholarly *class* and the general public 学者階級によってもまた一般社会によっても. ¶*of* all *classes* すべての階級の中で ‖ men *of* their own *class* 同社会層の人々.
P² women who belong to the *classes of* prostitutes 売春婦階級に属する女 ‖ all *classes of* the community 社会のあらゆる階級.
(**3**) 学級, (クラス); 授業.
V *Classes* are *assembled* and *dismissed* by the bugle-calls. 授業の始めと終りはらっぱで合図をする. ¶*attend classes* at the Imperial University 帝国大学で講義を聞く ‖ *attend classes* under Mr.… …先生の授業に出る. ¶I always felt sleepy when the *class* in grammar was *called*. 文法の時間になるといつも眠くなった. ¶He *conducts* an English *class* for Japanese students. 日本学生のために英語のクラスを設けている. 【類】 *conduct* private *classes* / *conduct* a *class* in English literature / *conduct* a new *class* at a college. ¶*cut* the English *class* 英語を欠課する. ¶*dismiss* [a] *class* 欠課する. ¶*handle classes* クラスを操縦する. ¶Do you *have* the G *class?* 君は G クラスを受持っているか. ‖ They *have classes* in judo. 柔道科がある. ¶He *heads* his *class*. 彼はクラスの首席. ¶The school *holds classes* for immigrants. その学校には移民科がある. 【類】 *hold classes* in the English language / *hold classes* in the open air / *Classes* are *held* morning, afternoon, and evening. ¶*institute* special *classes* for … …のために特にクラスを設ける. ¶*mass* (=*combine*) two *classes* 二組を合併する. ¶I cannot *meet* my *classes* this afternoon. 今日午後の授業を休みます. ‖ *meet* the *class* two hours a week 毎週二時間授業する. ¶*open classes* in shorthand 速記のクラスを設ける. ¶*organize* a *class* in German ドイツ語のクラスを設ける. ¶*classes run* under its auspices その主催の下に行われる授業. ¶*start* a *class* for instructing them in the work of rendering first aid 応急手当を彼らに教え込むクラスを始める. ¶*classes* are *suspended* in the colleges and universities until … 大学の授業は…まで休業になる. ¶Do you *take* the A *class?* 君は A クラスを教えているか.
V² ¶The *classes began* on the 16th of the same month in the new school. その新設学校の授業は同月十六日から始まった. ¶The *classes* of our university have *closed* for the winter holidays. われわれの大学は冬休みで休業している. ¶*Classes convene*. クラスの生徒が集まる. ¶*Classes meet* for fifty minutes daily at the hour stated. 各クラスとも毎日一定の時間に五十分間授業を受ける. 【類】 The *class met* at eight o'clock in the morning. / The *class meets* once or twice a week. ¶The teacher reads a phrase, the *class says* it in concert, then a pupil is called on to say the same phrase. 先生が一句を読みクラスがそれを一しょに読み次に一生徒が指名されて同じ句を述べる.
Q an *advanced class* 高等科. ¶a *beginners' class* 初等科. ¶a *fidgety* (=*restless*) *class* 落ちつかぬクラス. ¶a member of a *graduating class* 卒業クラスの学生. ¶the [*graduating*] *class* of 1955 一九五五年度の卒業クラス. ¶an *intermediate class* 中等科. ¶a *large class* 多人数のクラス. ¶There are *no classes* on Saturday. 土曜日は休校. ¶put him in the *same class* with … 彼を…と同級に編入する. ¶a *senior* (*junior*) *class* [米大学]最高(三年)のクラス. ¶a *small class* 小人数のクラス.
Q² an *art class* 手芸などのクラス. ¶*baby classes* 幼年組. ¶hold *Bible classes* 聖書の講義をやる. ¶a *continuation class* 補習科. ¶a *cooking class* 料理のクラス. ¶a *correspondence class* 通信クラス. ¶a *day* (*evening*) *class* 昼(夜)間学級. ¶*day* (*evening*) *session class* 《米》昼間(夜間)学期のクラス. ¶hold *demonstration classes* 授業実演をやる. ¶students at *evening classes* at various technical schools 各種工業学校の夜間部生徒. ¶an *exercise class* 運動のクラス. ¶the *first-year class* 初年級. ¶a member of the *Freshman* (*Sophomore*) *class* 《米》一(二)年級の学生. ¶No *German class* will be held today. ドイツ語の授業は今日は休みです. ¶I attended the *lecture class* held in Japan of Mrs. M. M 夫人が日本で開いた講義に出席した. ¶a *music class* 音楽のクラス. ¶the "*pioneer class*" 1890 一八九〇年の「一期生」. ¶*science classes* 理科の授業. ¶in these times of crowded *university classes* 大学のクラスの学生数の多い今日では.
P He did not report *at* his *class* yesterday. 彼はきのうクラスに出なかった. ‖ technical knowledge gained *at* the *classes* 教室で学んだ専門の知識. ¶*between classes* [授業の]休み時間に. ¶He graduated from Waseda *in* the *class* of 1918. 彼は早稲田を一九一八年に卒業した. ‖ Foreign language cannot be learned *in class* alone. 外国語は教室だけでは学ばれない. 【類】 sit obediently *in class* and attend to one's lessons / discuss *in class*.
P² a *class for* shorthand 速記術のクラス ‖ an evening *class for* English 夜の英語の組. ¶The *class in* business English meets in Room 7. 商業英語の授業は第七教室で行う. 【類】 a *class in* English (history) ‖ have two *classes in* charge 二学級担任する.
O He was a *class* ahead of me at Yale. 彼はエール大学では私の一年先輩だった.

class, *v.* 類別する, 分類する; 部に入れる.
M Medicines are *broadly classed* as internal or external

ones from their method of use. 薬はその使用法からして内服薬外用薬の二種に大別される. ¶may be *conveniently classed* under the three classes, A, B, and C 便宜上A, B, Cの三種に類別することができる. ¶It is *classed high* in literature. それは文学上の名著とされている. ¶can not be *properly classed* in the category of ... 本来からいうと...の部門に属するものではない. ¶They may be *roughly classed* under two heads. それを大略二項目に分類することができる. ¶He *classed* two specimens *together*. 彼は二つの標本を同じ部類に入れた.

P *class ... among* "fiction" "小説" の部に入れる. 【類】The islands off the coast of Oshu, collectively known as Matsushima, or the Pine Islands, are *classed among* the three most beautiful sights in Japan. ¶North Carolina is *classed as* an agricultural state. 北カロライナ州は農業州となっている. 【類】They are *classed as* Germans. / At what age is one to be *classed as* "old"? / Of those fires three were *classed as* "serious." / be *classed as* seconds. / be *classed as* "normal" (「正常」) ‖ may be *classed as* such それとして分類する事ができる. ¶*in* this category may be *classed* ... この部類に...を入れてよい. 【類】may be *classed in* five groups. ¶*class* it *under* (= with) this name この名目の部にそれを入れる ‖ Opium is *classed under* the head of narcotics. アヘンは麻酔剤の部に入る. ¶an English lady, by no means to be *classed with* the "learned" 決して学識があると言えない一英国婦人 ‖ be *classed with* those who ... ...の人々と同類に見なされる ‖ may conveniently *classed with* "particles" 便宜上"不変語"と同じ部に入れる. 【類】he refused to be *classed with* ... / Blumenbach *classes* the Chinese *with* the Mongolian race. / be *classed with* the great modern writers / American Indians ought to be *classed with* the Orientals (東洋人).

class-consciousness, *n.* 階級意識.

V *develop class-consciousness* among ... ...間に階級意識を生ぜしめる.

classic, *n.* 古典.

Q *ancient* and *modern classics* 古今の名著. ¶an *eternal classic* 不朽の古典. ¶The Manifesto of the Communist Party is one of the *greatest classics* of history. 「共産党宣言」は文献として最大傑作の一である. ¶an *immortal classic* 不朽の名著. ¶Macmillan's "Library of *English Classics* マクミラン社の「英国古典文庫」. ¶*musty classics* かび臭くなった古典.

Q² *short story classics* 短篇傑作集.

P² *classics for* the million 百万人の(読むべき)古典. ¶a *classic in* sea literature 海洋文学の傑作. 【類】It is a *classic in* the field. / one of the *classics of* Japanese literature / *classic of* fishing literature / *classics of* travel.

classification, *n.* 分類, 類別.

V a *classification based* upon ... ...に基いた分類. ¶*formulate* a *classification* 分類の方法を決定する.

Q a *broad classification* 広い分類. ¶The *fourfold classification* [地水火風などの]四分法. ¶No *hard* and *fast classification* can be given. 厳密の分類はできない. ¶the *social classification* of citizens into the samurai, or military and professional men, the tillers of the soil, the artisans and lastly the merchants 士農工商四階級に国民を分類したこと.

Q² *job classification* 職階[制]. ¶*position classification* 職階. ¶a *three-way classification* 三分法.

classify, *v.* 分類する.

M *classify apart* 別の部に分類する. ¶In a library books are *usually classified* by subjects. 図書館では通例題目で本の分類をする.

P books *classified according to* subjects 題目によって分類された本 ‖ *classify ... according to* structural resemblances 構造の類似によって ... を分類する ‖ *classify* men *according to* skill and assign them suitable work 技能によって職員を類別してこれに適当な仕事を割当てる. ¶Tungsten is *classified among* the metals. タングステンは金属の部に分類される. ¶be *classified as* ... ...として分類される. ¶Stars are *classified by* brilliance as of the first, sixth, etc. magnitude. 星は光度によって一等星・六等星などと分類されている. ‖ Time table for last electric cars *classified by* destination 行先別終電車発車時刻表. 【類】*classified by* sex (age, nationality, locality, prefecture, country, year) / *classify* accidents *by* cause / *classified by* subjects (nationality, color). ¶*classify* them *in* (= divide them into) two large groups それらを二大別にする ‖ *classify* it *in* the first rank それを第一級の部に編入する. 【類】*classify* them *in* three categories (=groups). ¶can be *classified into* three great divisions (=groups) これを三大別にすることができる. 【類】be broadly *classified into* three groups. ¶They are *classified under* the general term of "..." それは...と総称されている. ‖ We may *classify* them *under* two large groups それを二大別にすることができる. ¶*classify* quails *with* poultry うずらを家禽(きん)の部に入れる.

O documents *classified* A 〖軍〗A 級の機密文書.

classmate, *n.* 同級生.

Q² a *college classmate* 大学の同級生.

P² *classmates at* [a] college 大学の同級生.

classroom, *n.* 教室.

Q² a *chemistry classroom* 化学教室. ¶an *unwarmed classroom* 暖房装置のない教室.

clatter, *v.* がたがた(かちかち)音を立てる.

M. Typewriters *clatter away*. タイプライターがかちかち音を立てる. ¶A truck *clattered noisily* down the pavement トラックが鋪道をやかましい音を立てて行った.

clause, *n.* 箇条, 条項, 項目.

V *add* in a contract a *clause* to the effect that ... 契約書に...という意味の条項を加える. ¶*alter* a *clause* 条項を変更する. ¶*condense clauses* 条項を簡約にする. ¶*erase* a *clause* 条項を削除する. ¶What *clause* do you *require* in the contract? その契約にはどんな条項を必要としますか. ¶*waive* a *clause* 一項をやめる.

Q the *anti-Japanese discriminatory clause* of the new American Immigration Law 米国新移民法の差別的排日条項. ¶a *customary clause* 慣例的条項. ¶insert the *following clause* in the contract 契約書に次の条項を入れる. ¶The *relevant clause* of the Indenture runs as follows: 契約書の当該条項は次の通り. ¶a *saving clause* 除外例規定条項.

Q² a *contract clause* 契約条項. ¶an *execution clause* 執行文. ¶a *labor agreement clause* 労働協約条項. ¶the *most favored nation clause* 最恵国条款. ¶a "*no strike*" *clause* 「スト禁止」条項. ¶eliminate the discriminatory Oriental *exclusion clause* 差別的東洋人排斥の条項を削除する. ¶a *peace clause* 平和条項.

P *in* a *clause* 一つの条項で.

P a *clause in* the treaty 条約中の一項.

claw, *n.* つめ.

V *cut* (=*clip or pare*) the *claw* of ... ...の武器を奪う, ...を無害にする. ¶*draw in* (one's) *claws* つめを隠す. ¶*hide* one's *claws* ねこをかぶる. ¶Lobsters are able to *reproduce claws* when these are torn off. えびははさみをもぎ取られても再生する能力がある.

P escape *from* the *claws* of one's enemy 敵手からのがれる. ¶We are *in* (=*within*) his *claws*. われわれは彼の手中にある.

clay, *n.* 粘土.

V *bake clay* 粘土を焼く.

Q² *virgin clay* 新土(器物をこわして得た粘土でない). ¶*modeling clay* 塑造用粘土.

clean, *v.* きれいにする, 片づける.

M *clean away* (=off) 清める, ぬぐい去る. ¶*clean out* 一掃する, きれいに片づける. 【類】*clean out* one's desk drawers.

M² *clean off* a blackboard 黒板の字を消す. ¶*clean up* the controversy 議論の片をつける ‖ *clean up* political scandals 政界の腐敗を一掃する.

clean, *a.* 清い, 清潔な.

M *immaculately clean* 清純な. ¶*scrupulously clean* いかにも清潔な. ¶Everything seemed *spotlessly clean* and in perfect order. 何もかも非常にきれいでちゃんとしているように思われた. ¶keep a machine *thoroughly clean* 機械をよくきれいにしておく.

P *clean of* (=*from*) stain よごれのない.

cleaner, *n.* 掃除人(器).

Q² a *street cleaner* 街路掃除人. ¶a *vacuum cleaner* 真空掃除器. ¶a *window cleaner* 窓ふき. ¶*windshield cleaners* for motorcars=defrosters 自動車用風よけふき.

cleaning, *n.* 掃除, 洗たく.

V *give* it thorough *cleaning* それを十分に掃除する. ¶My watch *wants cleaning*. 僕の時計は掃除しないといけない.

Q the year-end *domestic* (=*household*) *cleaning* 家庭の年末大掃除. ¶*personal cleaning* 体の清潔.

Q^{2} *beat-and-sweep cleaning* 打ったり掃いたりの清潔法. ¶*ditch cleanings* どぶさらい.

cleanliness, *n.* 清潔, 潔白.

Q *internal cleanliness* 体内部の清潔.

cleanse, *v.* 清潔にする.

P *cleanse* the heart ***from*** (=of) stain (sin) 心の汚れ(など)をきよめる. ¶He *cleansed* the garden ***of*** weeds. 彼は庭の草を取った. ¶The room was *cleansed* ***with*** soap and water. 部屋を石けんと水で清潔にした.

cleanser, *n.* クレンザー. 「ンザーを使う.

V ***use*** a *cleanser* for washing and cleaning. 水洗いにクレ

cleansing, *n.* 清潔にすること.

Q^{2} ***soap*** and ***hot water cleansing.*** 「する.

clear, *v.* 取除ける, 空虚にする; 潔白にする; 晴れる; 出港

M *clear* ***away*** dishes and leftovers さらと残りものを片付ける ‖ Sunday *clears* ***away*** the rust of the past week. 日曜日は過去一週間のさびを落す. 【類】*clear* ***away*** obstacles (障害) / *clear* ***away*** misconceptions (誤解) / *clear* ***away*** the wreckage of the war (戦争の残がい) / *clear* ***away*** stenches (悪臭) / *clear* ***away*** the ancient prejudices and superstitions surrounding ... (...に付きまとう古代の偏見と迷信) / The fox has *cleared* ***away.*** ‖ The rubbish must be *cleared* ***away.*** がらくたを片付けなければならない. ¶It is *clearing* ***gradually.*** 段々晴れてくる. ¶The mist has *cleared* ***off*** (=***away***). 霧がはれた. ‖ *clear* ***off*** the table テーブルの上のものを片付ける. ¶The ship will *clear* ***out*** (=***outward***) from the harbor tomorrow. その船は明日出港する. ‖ A considerable ejection of ashes occurred, which *cleared* ***out*** the crater. 多量の灰が噴出され, そのために火口がきれいになった. 【類】The goods have been entirely *cleared* ***out.*** ‖ *clear* ***out*** all war criminals 戦犯全部を一掃する. 【類】*clear* ***out*** Communists from ... ‖ a ship that *cleared* ***out*** from the Thames テムズ川から出帆した商船. ¶***softly*** *clear* the throat 軽くせき払いをする.

M^{2} It *cleared* ***off*** and the sun came bright. 空が晴れて日が照って来た. ‖ The fog has *cleared* ***off.*** 霧が晴れた. ¶*clear* ***up*** ambiguity 不審を晴らす. 【類】*clear* ***up*** a point of obscurity ‖ *clear* ***up*** matters 色々な事件を片付ける ‖ That *clears* it all ***up.*** それですっかり分る. 【類】*clear* ***up*** uncertainties with regard to ... / *clear* ***up*** the truth / *clear* ***up*** obscurity (=obscure points) ‖ It is likely to *clear* ***up.*** 晴れそうだ. ‖ The weather won't *clear* ***up*** until the rainy season is over. 雨季が終るまで空は晴れまい. ‖ It is *clearing* ***up.*** 晴れてきた. 【類】The weather has *cleared* ***up.*** ‖ The difficulty has been *cleared* ***up.*** その困難が片付いた.

P A Chinese steamer *cleared* today ***for*** Tientsin laden with arms and ammunitions. 中国の汽船が本日武器・弾薬を積載し天津に向って出帆した. 【類】The steamer *cleared* ***for*** London today. ‖ *clear* ***for*** action [船などが]戦闘準備をする. ¶He was *cleared* ***from*** the charge brought against him. 彼は晴天白日の身となった. ‖ *clear* things ***from*** the table 食卓のものを片付ける. 【類】*clear* cobwebs (くもの巣) ***from*** the ceiling ‖ *clear* the snow ***from*** the pavement=*clear* the pavement ***of*** snow 鋪道の除雪をする. 【類】*clear* a person ***of*** his suspicion / a tract of land *cleared* ***of*** trees and bushes ‖ He was *cleared* ***of*** entanglements (difficulties, harm, danger). 彼は紛争(など)から脱した. ‖ *clear* oneself ***of*** a charge けんぎを晴らす ‖ We are *cleared* ***of*** all stock. 在庫品全部売切. ‖ The place was *cleared* ***of*** enemy troops. その所の敵兵は全部撃退させた. ‖ *clear* the city ***of*** the great snowfall 市の大雪の後始末をする ‖ In a generation Norway *cleared* the country ***of*** lepers. ノルウェー国は一代(三十年)で自国のらい病患者を一掃した. ¶*clear* ***out of*** (=vacate) a house 家を明渡す ‖ *clear* it ***out of*** one's way その邪魔物を取除ける ‖ They *cleared* me ***out of*** twenty guineas. [とばくなどで]私は二

clear, *a.* 明白な; 潔白な. 十ギニーとられた.

M make it ***abundantly*** *clear* それを十分明白にする. ¶It is ***as*** *clear* as crystal (=day *or* noonday). それは明々白々だ. ¶The day was ***beautifully*** *clear.* その日は気持よく晴れていた. ¶***fairly*** *clear* 十分明白な. ¶My conscience is ***quite*** *clear.* 少しも後ろめたいことはない. ¶is not made ***sufficiently*** *clear* 十分明白にされていない.

P I am not *clear* ***about*** it. そのことははっきりと私にわかっていない. ¶it is *clear* ***from*** the fact that ... それは...の事実から見て明かだ. ¶He is *clear* ***in*** his language. 彼の言葉ははっきりしている. ‖ I am *clear* ***in*** this matter. これはあやふやではない. ¶a man who is *clear* ***of*** (=from) a crime 青天白日の身となった人 ‖ *clear* ***of*** offense to ... ...の不興を買うようなことなく ‖ The ship passed *clear* ***of*** the rock. 船は岩を避けて通った. ¶It is *clear* ***to*** me 私にははっきり分っている. ¶It is *clear* ***to*** my mind. それは私にははっきり分っている.

clearance, *n.* 通関手続; 許可; 切開いた土地.

V I have ***got*** *clearance* from my superior to release the information. 私は上官から発表の許可を得た. ¶***make*** a *clearance* of stored goods 在庫品を一掃する(処分する). ¶***undertake*** the *clearance* of baggage [通訳などが]荷物の通関手続を引受ける.

Q^{2} ***custom*** *clearance* 通関手続. ¶***government*** *clearance* 政府の許可. ¶land acquisition for ***slum*** *clearance* 貧民くつを取払うにつき(住民を移すための)土地取得.

P^{2} a *clearance* ***in*** the forest 森林中の(伐採した)空所.

clearing, *n.* 除去. 「こと.

P^{2} *clearing* ***of*** the ground [樹木などを]地面から除去する

clearness, *n.* 明りょう, 明せき.

V ***aid*** *clearness* 一層明りょうにする. ¶***blur*** the *clearness* of a picture 絵の鮮明を損じる. ¶***combine*** *clearness* with conciseness 明りょうと簡潔を兼ねる. ¶***impart*** *clearness* to expression 表現を明りょうならしめる. ¶***promote*** *clearness* 一層明りょうにさせる. ¶***sacrifice*** *clearness* to terseness 簡潔にするため明りょうさを犠牲にする.

P ***with*** sufficient *clearness* 十分明りょうに.

P^{2} *clearness* ***of*** thinking 頭脳の明せき.

cleavage, *n.* 裂開.

V^{2} A sharp *cleavage* has ***developed*** between them. 彼らの間に激しい破たんを生じた.

P^{2} The *cleavage* ***between*** rich and poor grows deeper and wider. 貧富の差が益々深くかつ広くなって行く.

cleave, *v.* 裂く, 割る, 切る; 割れる, 押分けて進む.

M *cleave* it ***asunder*** それを切れ切れに裂く.

M^{2} *cleave* a tree (***down***) 木を切り倒す.

P The ground *cleaves* ***by*** frost. 地面が凍ってわれる. ¶*cleave* it ***in*** two それを二つに割る. ¶*cleave* the society ***into*** sections 同協会を数課に分ける. ¶We *cleft* a way ***through*** the wilderness. われわれは荒野の路を踏み分けた. 【類】A ship *cleaves* her way ***through*** the strait. ‖ *cleave* ***through*** the throng 群衆を押分けて行く.

cleave, *v.* 結合する; 愛着する.

M *cleave* ***together*** 堅く結合する.

P *cleave* (=adhere) ***to*** a cause (party) 主義(など)を捨てない ‖ Her tongue *clove* ***to*** the root of her mouth. [彼女の]舌がひっつれた.

clergy, *n.* [集合的]聖職者.

Q ***secular*** *clergy* 修道院に入らない聖職者.

clerk, *n.* 事務員, 書記; 番頭.

Q a ***chief*** *clerk* 書記長. ¶a ***junior*** *clerk* 雇員. ¶a ***mercantile*** *clerk* 番頭. ¶a ***municipal*** *clerk* 市の書記. ¶a ***poorly-paid*** *clerk* 薄給の事務員. ¶a ***railway postal*** *clerk* 鉄道郵便係員. ¶a ***senior*** *clerk* 書記. ¶a ***simple*** *clerk* 平の事務員. ¶a ***superintending*** *clerk* 係長.

Q^{2} an ***army*** *clerk* 軍属書記. ¶a ***bank*** *clerk* 銀行員. ¶a ***cipher*** *clerk* 暗号係. ¶a ***code*** *clerk* 暗号係. ¶a ***correspondence*** *clerk* 通信係. ¶a ***counter desk*** *clerk* 帳場係. ¶a ***court*** *clerk* 裁判所書記. ¶a ***delivery*** *clerk* 引渡し係. ¶a ***desk*** *clerk* 内勤社員. ¶a ***disbursing*** *clerk* 支出係. ¶a ***file*** *clerk* 文書係. ¶a ***floor*** *clerk* [ホテル]各階専属の接客サービス係員. ¶a ***girl*** (=***lady***) *clerk* 女事務員. ¶a ***government*** *clerk* 官吏. ¶a ***pay*** *clerk* 支払係員. ¶a ***payroll*** *clerk* 給与[台帳]係員. ¶a ***post office*** (=***mail***) *clerk* 郵便局員. ¶a ***reception*** *clerk* 接待係. ¶a ***sales*** *clerk*=a salesclerk 男子店員. ¶a ***shipping*** *clerk* 発送係. ¶a ***store*** *clerk* 店員. ¶a ***tally*** *clerk* 計算係. ¶a ***telephone*** *clerk* 電話係. ¶a ***town*** *clerk* 町役場書記.

P^{2} a *clerk* ***for*** a firm (=company *or* concern) 会社員. ¶a *clerk* ***in*** a foreign firm 外国商会の事務員. 【類】a *clerk* ***in*** the post office. ¶George Hooper, a *clerk* ***to*** Mr. Andrew アンドルー氏の書記ジョージ・フーパー.

clerkship, *n.* 書記(事務員)の職, 番頭の職.

V I ***obtained*** a *clerkship* in ... 私は...で事務員の職につい

た.【類】I *obtained* a *clerkship* for him with the banking house of ...

Q a *mercantile clerkship* 番頭の職.

Q² obtain a *government clerkship* 官吏になる.

clever, *a.* 上手な, 利口な.

P He is so *clever at* everything of this kind. 彼は何でもこんなことは器用だ.【類】She is *clever at* household management (家政). / He is *clever at* English (mathematics, translation). ¶ *clever in* making excuses 言抜けの上手な.【類】be *clever in* reply. ¶ It was *clever of* me, wasn't it? どうだ, うまくやってのけたろう. ¶ He is *clever with* his fingers. 彼は指先が器用だ.【類】She is *clever with* the needle. / He is *clever with* his pen (筆が立つ). / He is *clever with* his pencil (絵が上手).

O He is the *cleverest* of all. 彼は皆の中で一番利口だ.

cleverness, *n.* 利口さ.

Q *fiendish cleverness* 悪魔のような利口さ. ¶ *Gallic cleverness* ゴール人的な利口さ.

client, *n.* 訴訟依頼人; 顧客.

V *book clients* in advance [汽船など] 客に前切符を売る. ¶ one of those lawyers who knowingly *defend* guilty *clients* 有罪と知っていながら頼まれて弁護する法律家の仲間. ¶ We *route* our *clients* over the companies' lines. われわれの顧客にその(鉄道)諸会社の線によるように案内する. ¶ The attorney did all he could to *whitewash* his *client.* 弁護士は彼の依頼人のえん罪をそそぐことに全力を尽した.

clientele, *n.* [団] 顧客, 定連.

V Advertising through our magazine will enable you to *reach* the *clientele* you wish to reach. われわれの雑誌に広告すると貴下が希望する方面の購買層を獲得することができる.

P² The *clientele of* the police court is largely drawn from the slums and alleys of East London. 警察裁判所の御得意連は主としてロンドン東区の貧民くつや裏町通りの者である.

cliff, *n.* 断がい, 絶壁.

V *scale* a *cliff* 絶壁をよじ登る.

Q *bold cliffs* by the shore 海岸べりの断がい. ¶ a *craggy* (=*rugged*) *cliff* 峨々(がが)たる絶壁. ¶ a *mural cliff* (直立した)けわしい絶壁. ¶ a *sharp-cut cliff* 鋭い絶壁. ¶ a *vertical cliff* 切り立った絶壁.

P It hung just *over* the *cliff.* それはがけの真上に下っていた.

P² the *cliff above* the river 川岸にそびえる絶壁.

climate, *n.* 気候, 風土; 地方, 国.

V The island *has* a cold *climate.* この島は気候が寒い. ¶ How do you *like* (=*find*) the *climate* of Japan? 日本の気候はどうお思いです. ¶ No country in Asia, it is said, *possesses* a better *climate* than Manchuria. アジアで満州ほど気候の良い国はないそうだ.

Q an *arctic climate* 北極の気候. ¶ a *baneful climate* 有害な気候. ¶ a *benign climate* 温暖な気候. ¶ a *bracing climate* さわやかな気候. ¶ a *congenial climate* 気持ちのよい気候. ¶ a *damp climate* 湿気の多い気候. ¶ the *death-dealing climates* of East and West Africa 東西アフリカの殺人的気候. ¶ The *climate* is *depressing.* 気候がうっとうしい. ¶ the *dry climate* of Egypt エジプトの乾燥した気候. ¶ The *climate* is *dry, mild, equable,* and very *salubrious.* そこの気候は雨量少く温暖でむらがなくかつ非常に健康に適している. ¶ In the opinion of many, Australia has the *first climate* in the world. 多数の人の考えによると豪州の気候は世界で最も良い. ¶ a *foreign climate* 慣れない土地の気候. ¶ a *genial climate* 快適な気候. ¶ a *harsh climate* 厳しい気候. ¶ has a *healthful climate* その気候が健康によい. ¶ a *hot climate* 暑い気候. ¶ a *humid climate* 湿気のある気候. ¶ an *insular climate* 島国的気候. ¶ a *malignant climate* 悪い気候. ¶ in *mild climates* 気候温和な土地で. ¶ The region enjoys on the whole a *mild* and *salubrious climate.* その地方はがいして温暖で健康に適した気候である. ¶ a *moist climate* 湿気の多い気候. ¶ a *relaxing climate* だらけさす気候. ¶ a *rigorous climate* 厳しい寒さの気候. ¶ a *soft* and *delightful climate* 温和で心地よい気候. ¶ He was born in a *southern climate.* 彼は南国に生れた. ¶ a *stern climate* 厳しい気候. ¶ a *temperate climate* 温和な気候. ¶ the *treacherous climate* of the tropics 熱帯地方の油断のならない気候. ¶ residents in *tropical climates* 熱帯地方の居住者. ¶ *unhealthy climates* 不健康地. ¶ a *vile climate* 悪い気候. ¶ in a *warm climate* like Hongkong 香港のような暖い地方に.【類】move to a *warm climate.*

P I would rather live in France *for climate.* 気候で言えばフランスに住みたい.

climax, *n.* 頂点; 最高潮.

V *cap* the *climax* 極端に走る, けた外れなことをする ‖ to *cap* the *climax* つけ加えて ‖ *cap* the *climax* of his infamy by ... ...によって恥の上塗をする. ¶ the great movement for freedom which *had* its *climax* in the French Revolution 終にフランス革命を見るに至ったかの自由を求める大運動. ¶ This *marked* the *climax* of his popularity. これで彼の人気が頂点に達した. ‖ Ascot (the most fashionable English race-meeting) *marks* the *climax* of London Season. アスコット(英国の最も高級な競馬)はロンドン社交シーズンの頂点を示す. ¶ The heat of summer has *reached* its *climax.* 夏の暑さが頂点に達した.【類】The town has *reached* the *climax* of its prosperity and splendor.

Q a *dramatic climax* 劇の最高潮に達した場面. ¶ a *thrilling climax* 血わき肉おどるの頂点.

P He was then *at* the *climax* of his fortunes. 当時彼は全盛だった.【類】Woman as wife and mother stands *at* the *climax* of her existence.

P² the *climax of* the crisis 危機の「やま」‖ the *climax of* misfortune 不幸のどん底.

climb, *n.* 登はん, 登山; 坂路.

V *make* a reconnaissance *climb* for the purpose of determining our route われわれの路線を決定する目的で瀬踏み登山をやる.

Q The pass is an *easy climb.* そのとうげは楽だ. ¶ a *hard climb* 難儀な坂路. ¶ The *long climb* made her heart throb. 長時間の登山で彼女の胸がどきどきした.【類】feel tired at the end of a *long climb.* ¶ a *steep* and *toilsome climb* 急で骨のおれるな坂路. ¶ a *stiff climb* up the mountain その山の難儀な登はん. ¶ an *uphill climb* 坂登り.

Q² a *mountain climb* 登山.

P *on* the *climb* 登り路に.

P² a *climb in* the Diamond Mountains 金剛山の登はん. ¶ a *climb of* 40 minutes 四十分の登り.

climb, *v.* よじ上る, 登る.

M the mountain may be *conveniently climbed* from ... その山は...から登るのが便利だ. ¶ *climb hand over hand* 手を代る代るさしのばしてよじ上る.

M² *climb down* (=descend) from a mast 帆柱から降りる ‖ *climb down* from one's cab [からだをかがめて]タクシーから降りる. ¶ *climb up* a tree 木登りをする ‖ *climb* [*up*] into a tree [葉の繁った]木に登る ‖ *climb up* on a tall stool 高い腰掛にはい登る. ¶ *climb up* a mountain for a view 景色を眺めに山に登る.

P *climb from* the bottom of the ladder to the top はしごの下から上まで登る. ¶ *climb in* zigzag fashion くの字なりに登る. ¶ The aviator *climbed into* his machine. 飛行士は機にとう乗した. ‖ *climb* wearily *into bed* 疲れて床にもぐり込む. ¶ Some roses *climb on* frames. ばらが垣にまつわる ‖ *climb on* the rocks 山登りをする. ¶ *climb over* a fence かきを乗り越す. ¶ *climb to* a bank 土手に登る ‖ a balloon used for *climbing to* very great heights 非常な高空に上昇するための気球.【類】*climb to* a height of 12,000 feet above sea level (海抜) / *climb to* the top of a tree (the roof) ‖ He *climbed to* the head of his class. 彼は首席になった.

climber, *n.* 登山家.

Q an *Alpine climber* [アルプス, または一般の]登山家. ¶ a *good* (*bad*) *climber* 登山の名手(下手な人).

Q² a *mountain climber*=a mountaineer *or* an Alpinist 登山家.

clinch, *n.* つかみ;〖拳闘〗クリンチ.

V *get* a good *clinch* of an antagonist 敵手をうまくつかまえる.

P boxers *in* a *clinch* クリンチしている拳闘家.

clincher, *n.* 《俗》とどめをさす言葉(議論).

Q It was an *absolute clincher* for him. それで彼はぎゃふんと参った.

cling, *v.* すがり付く; 執着する.

M *cling persistently* to ... うるさく付きまとう. ¶ *cling tenaciously* to ... ...をねばり強く固守する.

P *cling to* the feeling that we are equal to the task われわれはこの仕事を為しうるという気持をあくまで捨てない ‖ *cling to* one in an embarrassing way うるさく付きまとう.【類】*cling to* one's hope (purpose) / he *clings to* the opinion that ... / *cling to* the old method / *cling to* a custom (tradition) / *cling to* the old unworthy method (昔ながらのむだなやり方) ‖ The ivy *clings to* the wall. つたが壁にか

らみつく. 【類】This cat *clings to* my dress. / The little boy ran and *clung to* his mother's skirts. / Some seamen *clung to* some wreckage (難破船の破片に). / *cling to* a street-car strap (電車のつり革に). ¶They were *clinging to* life by a thread as slender as that we unwind from the cocoon. 彼らは丁度まゆから紡ぐような細い一本の糸で生命にしがみついていた.

clinic, *n.* 診療所.

Q² an *animal clinic* 動物診療所. ¶a *speech clinic* 言語矯正所.

clip, *n.* [羊毛の]一季ばさみ.

Q The wool sent out of the State of Victoria represents 35 per cent of the *total* "*clip*" of Australia. ヴィクトリア州から送り出す羊毛は豪州全産額の三割五分に当る.

P Rockefeller gave away a hundred million dollars "*at a clip.*" ロックフェラーはぽんと一億ドルも出した.

clip, *n.* クリップ.

Q² a *paper clip* 紙挟み. ¶a *tie clip* ネクタイどめ.

clip, *v.* はさみ切る.

M have one's hair *clipped short* 髪を短く刈る.

P *clip* articles *from* a newspaper 記事を新聞から切抜く.

clipper, *n.* はさみ, バリカン; 理髪師; 《米》旅客機.

V The Air Lines *flies* five *clippers* on its Pacific route. その航空会社は太平洋航空路に五機の快速旅客機を運航している.

Q² a *flying clipper* 快速飛行機. ¶*hair clippers* バリカン. ¶a *nail clipper* つめ切り. ¶a *toenail clipper* 足のつめ切り.

clipping, *n.* 切抜き.

V *have* the *clippings pasted* in books 書物にその切抜きを張り付ける.

Q² a *newspaper clipping* 新聞切抜き.

P² *clippings from* a newspaper＝newspaper clippings.

clique, *n.* 徒党, 一味.

Q *bureaucratic cliques* 官僚. ¶a *military clique* 軍閥. ¶*petty cliques* and jealous busybodies 徒党を組む小人やしっと深いおせっかいたち.

Q² the *army clique* 陸軍閥. ¶a *money clique* 財閥.

cloak, *n.* 外とう, マント; 仮面, かこつけ.

V *button* [*up*] one's *cloak* 外とうのボタンを掛ける. ¶He *drew* his *cloak* around him. 彼はマントをからだにまといつけた. ¶*reverse* the *cloak* マントを裏返しにする. ¶*throw* a *cloak* over one's shoulders 外とうを着る.

Q Pride may dwell under a *threadbare cloak.* ぼろはまとっていても自尊心は失っていないかも知れない.

P He was muffled *in* a *cloak.* 彼はすっぽりマントにくるまっていた. ¶*under* the *cloak* of snow 雪におおわれて ‖ *under* the *cloak* of charity (folly) 慈善(など)を装って ‖ hide *under* a *cloak* of ... ...の仮面をかぶる ‖ They masquerade *under* the *cloak* of lawyers. あれらはもぐり代言だ.

P² ice-cream shops which are merely *cloaks for* indecency 表面はアイスクリーム屋で実はあいまい屋 ‖ a *cloak for* vice 悪徳を隠すもの.

clock, *n.* 時計, 掛時計, 置時計.

V *advance* the *clock* one hour 時計を一時間進める. ¶*put back* the *clock* a few minutes 時計を二三分後らす. ¶*put* the *clock on* 時計を進める. ¶*put* the *clock right* 時計を合わせる. ¶*regulate* a *clock* 時計を調節する. ¶*set* a *clock* by the radio time signal ラジオの時報で時計を合わせる. ¶*set ahead* a *clock* 時計を進める. 【類】*set* a *clock* five minutes *ahead.* ¶*set back* the *clock* one hour 時計を一時間後らす. ¶Can you *tell* the *clock?* 何時ですか. ¶Can the *clock* be *turned back*? 時を戻すことができるものか. ¶*wind* [*up*] a *clock* 時計を巻く.

V² The *clock gains.* この時計は進む. ¶My *clock* has *gone wrong.* 僕の時計は狂っている. ¶The *clock loses.* この時計はおくれる. ¶The *clock points* to ten minutes past midnight. 時計は夜の十二時十分を示している. ¶What does the *clock say*? 今何時ですか. ¶The *clock struck* eleven. 時計は今十一時を打った. ¶The *clock* has *stopped* (＝*run down*). 時計が止まった. ¶The *clock ticked on*—he had been gone half an hour. 時計はかちかちと時を刻んだ—彼が出かけてから半時間経っていた.

Q a *big-faced clock,* now indicating 11.45 丁度11時45分を指している大時計. ¶a *derelict clock* 不良時計. ¶an *electric clock* 電気時計. ¶a *flora's* (＝*flower*) *clock* 花時計(花壇内の花の開閉によって時間を示すもの). ¶a *grandfather's clock* 旧式分銅時計. ¶My *clock* is *out of order.* 僕の置時計は狂っている. ¶The *clock* is *slow* (*fast*). この時計はおくれて(進んで)いる.

Q² an *alarm clock* 目覚時計. ¶a *chimney-piece clock* 炉だなの置時計. ¶an *eight-day clock* 八日巻きの時計. ¶a *pendulum clock* 振子時計. ¶a *tower clock* 屋上時計. ¶a *turret clock* 時計台の時計.

P work *around* the *clock* 四六時中働く. ¶It was just five *by* the station *clock* when he arrived. 彼が着いた時は停車場の時計で丁度五時であった. ¶Noon was just striking *on* the *clocks.* 時計は丁度正午を打っていた. ‖ the hand which shows the hour *on* a *clock* 時計の時針.

clockwork, *n.* 時計仕掛.

P move *by clockwork* 時計仕掛で動く. ¶work *like clockwork* [時計のように]正確に働く.

clod, *n.* 土塊.

V *break* the *clods* 土塊を砕く.

clog, *n.* げた, 木ぐつ; 障害物.

Q a pair of *wooden clogs* げた一足.

P enter the school *in clogs* 木ぐつで校舎にはいる. ¶the clatter *of clogs* からころというげたの音. ¶*on* one's wooden *clogs* げたばきで.

P² a *clog upon* industry 産業上の障害物.

clog, *v.* 邪魔する, 妨げる, ふさぐ.

P The export trade is *clogged by* conditions. 輸出貿易は種々の事情に妨げられている. ¶*clog* commerce *with* restrictions 制限を設けて商業の発展を阻害する ‖ The streams are *clogged with* ice. 川は氷でふさがっている. 【類】The road was *clogged with* automobiles.

cloister, *v.* 隔離する.

P an innocent maiden *cloistered in* her home 箱入娘, 深窓に育てられた娘.

close, *n.* 終り, 結末.

V He was *approaching* the *close* of his Prime Ministership. 彼は首相としての任期が終ろうとしていた. ¶The book *marks* the *close* of the series. その本で同双書は完結する.

Q The negotiations came to an *amicable close.* 交渉は円満に局を結んだ. ¶a *complimentary close* [手紙の]敬意を表する末尾.

P as soon as possible *after* the *close* of this year 来年早早. ¶*at* the *close* of each chapter (section). 各章(など)の終りに. ¶High buildings, *at* the *close* of business, pour streams of people into traffic. 高層の建物がひけ時に往来へ人の流れをはき出す.【類】*at* the *close* of the meeting a collection (募金) was made for ... / *at* the *close* of the day ＝at the day's close / *at* the *close* of last year / *at* the *close* of the present academic year (本学年) / *at* the *close* of the day's work (一日の仕事) / *at* the *close* of the seventeenth century / *at* the *close* of his life (晩年) / be served *at* the *close* of a meal / *at* the *close* of the fiscal year (会計年度) / *at* the *close* of the Franco-Prussian War (普仏戦争) / immediately *at* the *close* (直後) of the war. ¶The letter should be mailed in time to reach this office *before* the *close* of the month. 手紙はその月の中に当所に届くように郵送されたし. ¶*from* the *close* of his reign 彼の治世の終りから. ¶draw *near* a *close* 終りに近づく. ¶*since* the *close* of the war 戦争終結以来. ¶The year was drawing *to* a *close.* その年も暮れかかっていた. 【類】The exhibition was brought *to* a *close* last week. ¶*toward* (＝*about*) the *close* of the nineteenth century 十九世紀の終りごろに. 【類】*towards* the *close* of his life / *toward* the *close* of a game / *toward* the *close* of the afternoon (the month, the year). ¶*with* the *close* of the war 戦争終結と同時に.

close, *a., ad.* 親しい; 目のこまかい; 接近して.

P This session (examination) is *close at* hand. 会期(など)が迫ってきた. ‖ finding the pursuer *close at* his heels 追手がすぐ後からつけて来るのを見て. ¶I took up my lodgings *close by* the school. 学校のすぐそばに下宿した. ¶The wood is *close in* the grain. この木は木目がこまかい. ‖ be *close in* meaning 意味がそれに近い. ¶I feel hot and *close in* this room. このへやはむし暑い. ¶It was *close on* daybreak. 夜明け間近かだった. 【類】*close on* noon / He is *close on* (＝upon) sixty years of age. / There are now in Chicago *close on* two hundred rinks, all of which are doing very successful business. ‖ One misfortune followed *close on* another. 不幸が引続いて起った. ‖ *close on* the heels of the sailing of ... ...が出帆したすぐ後. ¶those *close* ***to*** him 彼の側近者 ‖ translate it *close* ***to*** the original 原文に忠実にそれを翻訳する ‖ *close* ***to*** the station 停車場の近くに. 【類】We have a car-stop (停留所) *close* ***to*** us. / It is *closer* ***to*** fact. ‖ *close* ***to*** the feet 足もとに ‖ Moss grows *close* ***to*** the ground. こけは地面にくっついてはえる ‖ get *close* ***to*** nature 自然に親しむ ‖ *Close* ***to*** 500 planes were flying in formation. 約五百機が編隊を組んで飛行していた. 【類】*close* ***to*** a million dollars / live *close* ***to*** death (生死の間を往来する) for two years. ¶*close* ***upon*** midnight 真夜中近く ‖ The number of the students is *close* ***upon*** five thousand. 学生の数は五千に近い. 【類】The sum was *close* ***upon*** 60,000 francs, or £2,400 in English money. / Today *close* ***upon*** 3000 pupils attend its class. ¶I am *close* (=intimate) ***with*** him. 私は彼と親密にしている. ‖ He is *close* ***with*** his money. 彼はけちん坊だ.

close, *v.* 閉じる; 終える; 包囲する; 取組む; 締(め)る; 同意する.

M At his death the business was *closed* ***out.*** 彼が死んだので商売を止めた. ¶A fist is the hand *closed* ***tightly.*** げんことは握り固めた手である. ¶The wrestlers *closed* ***together.*** 相撲が取組んだ. ¶The season is ***virtually*** *closed.* 季節は過ぎたも同然だ. ¶The door *closes* ***well.*** 戸がよくしまる.

M² *close* ***about***=encompass 取囲む. ¶*close* ***down*** a mine 鉱山を閉鎖する ‖ be forced ***to*** *close* ***down*** their plants 止むを得ず工場を閉鎖する ‖ *close* ***down*** the hatches of a ship in a storm 暴風雨で船のハッチをしめ切る. 【類】Many small industrial plants are *closing* ***down*** for lack of fuel. 燃料欠乏のために多くの小工場が閉鎖しつゝある. / The institute (学会) had to *close* ***down.*** ¶as winter *closed* ***in*** on us 冬が近づいた時 ‖ The enemy was *closing* ***in*** on our position. 敵はわが陣地に肉迫しつつあった. ‖ when the evening *closed* ***in*** 夕やみ迫るころ. 【類】The night has quite *closed* ***in.*** 夜が迫って来た. ‖ *close* ***in*** windows 窓を内側に引いてしめる ‖ *close* ***in*** with... ...と妥協する, ...と接触する ‖ gladly *close* ***in*** with callers 喜んで訪問者に会う. ¶The account was *closed* ***off,*** and the balance brought forward. 勘定を仕切って残金は繰越すことになった. ¶Silence, oblivion, like the waves, have *closed* ***over*** them and no one can tell the story of their ends. 沈黙忘却が波のように彼らをおおい隠してその終りはだれにも分らない. ¶The shade of evening began to *close* ***round.*** 暮色が四方から迫ってきた. ‖ Darkness *closed* me ***round.*** あたり一面暗くなった. ¶*close* ***up*** shop 店を畳む ‖ *close* ***up*** an opening 穴をふさぐ ‖ The business was *closed* ***up*** 廃業した. ‖ *close* ***up*** one's stomach with ... ...を腹に詰め込む.

P He pushed the door open, went in, *closing* it ***after*** him. 彼は戸を押し明けて中に入り後から戸をしめた. ¶The river is *closed* ***against*** net fishing. その河は網漁は禁止されている. ‖ professions and occupations *closed* ***against*** women 女子を採用しない職業 ‖ The churchyards are *closed* ***against*** all further interments. その墓地は今後の埋葬は一切断っている. ¶The shop is *closed* ***for*** a week. その店は一週間休業. ¶*Closed* ***for*** the present. 当分休業. 【類】Navigation (航行) in the river is now *closed* ***for*** the season. ‖ *Closed* ***for*** summer season; will be reopened early in September. 〚掲示〛夏季中休業九月早々開場. 【類】The bridge is *closed* ***for*** repairs. ¶We *closed* the door ***on*** (=***against***) him. 私たちは彼にしめ出しを食わした. ‖ We cannot now *close* ***on*** the previous terms offered. 今では前の条件ではお引受できません. ¶*close* one's eyes ***to*** the fact that ... 目をつぶって...という事実を見ぬふりをする ‖ The banks will be *closed* ***to*** business on ..., a Japanese national holiday. 日本の公休日たる...日には銀行は休業する. ‖ employments *closed* ***to*** the woman 女性しめ出しの業務 ‖ The historical mansion is *closed* ***to*** public view. その由緒ある邸宅は公衆に縦覧させない. ‖ The grounds are *closed* ***to*** the public. その境内は公衆の入場を禁じている. 【類】Mt. Fuji will be *closed* ***to*** pilgrims after August 10. / countries *closed* ***to*** outside nations / Japan was *closed* ***to*** all foreigners except the Chinese and the Dutch. / The arsenal (兵器工場) is *closed* ***to*** sightseers (foreigners, visitors). / The harbor is *closed* ***to*** navigation. / The bridge is *closed* ***to*** traffic. ‖ His purse is never *closed* ***to*** them. 彼らに金を与えることを惜しまない. ¶The exercises *closed* ***with*** the singing of "America" which was heartily joined in by the entire attendance. 式は列席者一同の熱心なる「アメリカ」の合唱をもって終了した. ‖ He *closed* ***with*** telling me that ... 最後に彼は...と語った. 【類】The proceedings (式) were *closed* ***with*** the singing of "Kimigayo." ‖ I am willing to *close* ***with*** your terms. お申出での条件で取きめてよろしゅうございます. 【類】He did not *close* ***with*** the offer made to him. ‖ *close* a wound ***with*** stitches 傷を針で縫う.

closeness, *n.* 近接.

P² the *closeness* ***of*** relationship between ... ...間の密接な関係.

closet, *n.* 物置, 戸だな.

Q² a ***china*** *closet* 陶器戸だな. ¶a ***clothes*** *closet* 衣類戸だな. ¶a low ***cistern*** *closet* 低位式浄水槽便所. ¶a ***tipper*** *closet* 覆転式便器. ¶a ***water*** *closet*=a lavatory《英》便所.

closing, *n.* 終了.

Q ***early*** *closing* 早仕舞. ¶***postwar*** *closing* of aircraft plants and shipyards 戦後の飛行機工場および造船所の閉鎖.

Q² ***Sunday*** *closing* in London, though rigorously paraded, is rarely strictly observed. ロンドンの日曜休業は表向きは厳重だが厳守される事はまれだ.

P ***after*** the *closing* of the theater 芝居がはねてから. ¶***from*** the *closing* of the session of the conference 会議終了後. ¶a word ***in*** *closing* 終りにのぞんでの一言.

closure, *n.* 終了, 討論終結.

V ***apply*** the *closure* 討論終結を行う. ¶The *closure* was ***declared*** (=Time was called) at 5.20 p.m. [討論など]午後五時二十分に終了を告げた. ¶***introduce*** a *closure* 討論終結を提起する.

clot, *n.* 血の塊.

Q² a ***blood*** *clot* in one's brain 脳の血管閉塞.

P² a *clot* ***of*** blood 凝血.

cloth, *n.* 布, 織物, 反物; テーブル掛.

V ***color*** the *cloth* 布に着色する. ¶The maid came in to ***lay*** the *cloth* for supper. 女中が夕飯の食卓準備のために入ってきた. ‖ ***lay*** the *cloth* for four 四人前の食事準備をする. ¶***after*** the *cloth* was ***removed*** (=***taken away***) 食事が終ってから. ¶***sew*** *cloth* 裁縫する. ¶***wash*** *cloth* 布を洗たくする. ¶a *cloth* ***worn*** round the neck くびに巻いた布. ¶***weave*** *cloth* 布を織る.

V² This *cloth* ***wears*** well. この布は持ちがよい.

Q ***coarse*** *cloth* あらい生地. ¶a ***damp*** *cloth* 湿布. ¶***fadeless washable*** *cloth* 色があせないで洗たくのきく生地. ¶of ***khaki*** *cloth* カーキー地の. ¶***plain*** *cloth* 無地の生地. ¶***rich*** *cloth* 高価な布. ¶***rough*** *cloth* 粗い布. ¶Satin is a smooth ***silk*** *cloth.* しゅすはすべすべした絹地だ. ‖ Velvet is a soft ***silk*** *cloth.* びろうどは柔い絹地だ. ¶***thick strong*** *cloth* 厚い丈夫な生地. ¶Gauze is a very ***thin, light*** *cloth,* easily seen through. ガーゼはきわめて薄い軽い生地ですき通る. ¶***water-proof*** *cloth* 防水布. ¶***woolen*** *cloth* らしゃ. ¶This *cloth* ***is worth*** the price. この反物は値段だけのことはある.

Q² ***composition*** *cloth* 防水布. ¶***corduroy*** *cloth* コール天地. ¶unbleached rough ***cotton*** *cloth* 漂白しない生(き)木綿. ¶***double-width*** *cloth* 大巾反物. ¶***emery*** *cloth* 銀引砂布. ¶***Empress*** *cloth.* 女皇織(婦人服地の一種). ¶a ***face*** *cloth* 死者の覆面布. ¶***glossy silk*** *cloth* つやのある絹布. ¶a very ***hard-wearing*** *cloth* 丈夫で持ちのよい生地. ¶***Jersey*** *cloth* ジャージー織(毛編みの). ¶wear a ***loin*** *cloth* ふんどしをしめる. ¶***paper*** *cloth* 紙のクロース(表紙). ¶***rubber*** *cloth* ゴム引布; ゴム板. ¶***satin*** *cloth* サテン地. ¶a ***tray*** *cloth* 盆に敷く布. ¶***twine*** *cloth* より糸織りの上綿布(リンネルに代用する). ¶***wire*** *cloth* 細金網(貯肉用またはろ過用の).

P remove the stains ***in*** the *cloth* 織物のしみを抜く. ¶a roll ***of*** *cloth* 巻布 ‖ a strip ***of*** *cloth* 布きれ. ¶a landscape ***on*** *cloth* 織物の風景画 ‖ raise a nap ***on*** *cloth* 布にけばを立てる. 【類】embroidery (縫いとり) ***on*** *cloth.*

clothe, *v.* [衣服を]着せる, 装う.

M A woman can ***fully*** *clothe* herself on $... a year. 婦人は一年...ドルで十分自分の衣服代がある ¶He was ***humbly*** *clothed.* 彼は粗末なきものを着ていた. ¶***insufficiently*** or ***improperly*** *clothed* like a performer of Salome dance サロメ・ダンスの演技者のようにはだを露出したり不体裁な服装をして. ¶***Poorly*** *clad* in winter, he never reveals it by his looks. 冬には薄着だが彼は決して寒そうな顔はしない. ¶He is more ***richly*** *clad* and better housed than his brothers. 彼は兄弟たちよりも服装もりっぱだし住んでいる家もりっぱだ. ¶***scantily*** *clad* ろくにきものも着ないで. ¶be

thickly clad 厚着をしている. ¶He was always ***thinly clad*** in his poor cotton dress. 彼はいつも薄着で粗末な綿服を着ていた. ¶be ***warmly clothed.*** 温かな服装をしている.

P ***clothed by*** statute ***with*** the powers of ... 法規によっての権限を付与されて. ¶***clothe*** her ***in*** beautiful garments 彼女に美しいきものを着せる ‖ savages ***clothed in*** skins 皮を着ている蛮人. 【類】He was ***clothed in*** armor from top to toe. / ***Clad in*** rags, he appears almost like a beggar. / ***clothed in*** silk (cotton, satin, splendid attire) / a soldier ***clad in*** a khaki uniform ‖ ***clothed in*** purple (white) 紫衣(など)をまとって ‖ The field is ***clothed in*** its winter garb of snow. 野は冬の雪ごろもをまとっている. ‖ He was ***clothed in*** a garment of flame. 一面の火にかこまれた. ‖ The hills are ***clad in*** verdure. 山は青葉でおゝわれている. 【類】When the weather is fine, the mountains are ***clothed in*** blue and purple. ‖ We ***clothe*** thought ***in*** (=with) language. われわれは言葉で思想を装う. 【類】What Marx had to say on that subject was ***clothed in*** most incomprehensible verbiage. ¶***clothe*** flesh and blood ***upon*** the bare skeleton がい骨に肉と血を着せる(やせこけること). ¶He was ***clothed with*** seedy (=shabby) garments. 彼はみすぼらしい衣服を着ていた. ‖ a dog ***clothed with*** hair in profusion 毛がもじゃもじゃ生えている犬. 【類】The hills are ***clothed with*** trees. / The mountain slopes are ***clothed with*** rich and varied vegetation. ‖ He was ***clothed with*** shame (power, authority, rights). 彼は恥辱(など)を与えられた.

clothes, *n. pl.* 服, きもの.

V ***borrow*** another's ***clothes*** 他人のきものを借りる. ¶***cast*** (=***discard***) ***clothes*** きものを捨てる ‖ ***cast*** (=***throw***) ***off*** one's ***clothes*** きものをぬぎ捨てる. ¶***change clothes*** 着替えをする. ¶It's unkind to ***criticize*** his ***clothes.*** きものをとや角いうのは不しつけだ. ¶***fold*** one's ***clothes*** きものをたたむ. ¶Moths ***fret*** (=spoil) ***clothes.*** 衣蛾(しみ)がきものをいためる. ¶Where did you ***get*** your ***clothes made***? どこできものを作らせたか. ¶***get*** one's ***clothes singed*** きものをこがす. ¶***hang out*** the ***clothes*** [for the sun and the air] きものを掛けてかわかす. ¶The ***clothes*** were ***hung up*** to dry. きものを掛けてかわかしてあった. ¶***have on*** Japanese ***clothes*** 和服を着ている. ¶***huddle on*** one's ***clothes*** きものを引掛ける. ¶She helped me to ***hurry on*** my ***clothes*** in an instant. 彼は私が大急ぎできものを着るのを手伝った. ¶***iron clothes*** きものにアイロンをかける. ¶***lay*** the ***clothes away*** きものをしまう. ¶***lay off*** one's ***clothes*** 服をぬぐ. ¶***lift up*** one's ***clothes*** きものをまくる. ¶***make clothes*** きものを仕立てる. 【類】My ***clothes*** have been ***made*** to order (あつらえ). ¶***mend*** (=***patch up***) ***clothes*** きもののつくろいをする. ¶The boy has ***outgrown*** his ***clothes.*** その子はきものが少さくなった(成人した). ¶***pack up*** one's ***clothes*** 衣類を包装する. ¶The film artist has to ***provide*** his own ***clothes.*** 映画俳優はきものは自分持だ. ¶***put on*** one's ***clothes*** きものを着る. ¶***ruin*** one's ***clothes*** きものを台なしにする. ¶***scent*** one's ***clothes*** with musk きものにじゃ香の香をつける. ¶***send on*** (=***out***) one's ***clothes*** for laundry きものを洗たくに出す. ¶***sew clothes*** with thread 糸できものを縫う. ¶***slip on*** one's ***clothes*** きものを引っかける. ¶***spoil*** one's ***clothes*** きものを損じる. ¶***starch*** the ***clothes*** きものにのりを付ける. ¶The salesgirl ***straightens*** her ***clothes*** before going to the counter. 女店員は売場へ行く前にきちんと服装を正す. ¶***strip off clothes*** きものをぬぐ. ¶***take off*** one's ***clothes*** きものをぬぐ. ¶***throw on*** ones ***clothes*** きものを引っかける. ¶***try on*** new ***clothes*** 新調のきものを着てみる. ¶***wash clothes*** きものを洗たくする. ¶***wear clothes*** according to the style of London and Paris ロンドンやパリ風の衣服を着る ‖ ***wearing*** practically no ***clothes*** 申しわけ程度にきものを着て(ほとんど裸体で). ¶***wear out*** one's ***clothes*** きものを着ふるす.

V² He is very much fallen away, so that his ***clothes hang*** loosely on him. 彼は非常にやせ衰えたのできものがだぶだぶになっている.

Q ***cast-off clothes*** 古着. ¶put on ***clean clothes*** さっぱりしたきものを着る. ¶***comfortable clothes*** 着心地のよいきもの. ¶send ***dirty clothes*** to wash よごれたきものを洗たくに出す. ¶***expensive clothes*** 高価な衣服. ¶wear very ***extreme clothes*** 非常に風変りなきものを着る. ¶***fine clothes*** りっぱなきもの ‖ No ***fine clothes*** can hide the clown. 馬子にも衣しょうとも言えない. ¶How do you think he looks in ***foreign clothes?*** 彼が洋服を着たらどんなもんでしょう. ¶***indecent*** (=***immodest***) ***clothes*** 不体裁なきもの. ¶***loose-fitting clothes*** きちんと合わないきもの. ¶a handsome woman going about in ***man's clothes*** 男装の麗人. ¶I like ***plain clothes.*** 私は無地の着物が好きだ. ‖ appear in ***plain clothes*** 平服を着て出る. 【類】a policeman in ***plain clothes*** ‖ She knows how to wear ***plain clothes*** with elegance. 彼女は平凡なきものを上品に着こなす. ¶***ragged clothes*** ぼろ服. ¶Hardly anybody above the poorer classes wears ***ready-made clothes*** in England. 英国では貧民階級以上の者はほとんど既製服は着ない. ¶***re-made clothes*** 仕立直した服. ¶***second-hand clothes*** 古着. ¶***seedy clothes*** 着古したきもの. ¶***shabby clothes*** ぼろ服. ¶***sumptuous clothes*** ぜい沢なきもの. ¶***tailored-to-order clothes*** for men あつらえの男子服. ¶wear ***tattered clothes*** ぼろ服をまとっている. ¶***unbecoming clothes*** 似合わないきもの.

Q² spurn off the ***bed clothes*** 夜具をけとばす. ¶***between-season clothes*** あい着. ¶***body clothes*** 胴衣, 下着; 馬の胴衣. ¶smart ***career clothes*** 女のスマートな職業服. ¶***European-style clothes*** 洋服. ¶We wear ***evening clothes*** at a ball. 舞踊会では夜会服を着る[事になっている]. ¶in his ***everyday clothes*** ふだん着で. ¶in their ***holiday clothes*** 晴着で. ¶"***Misses***" ***size clothes*** 少女形の着物. ¶in ***night clothes*** ねまき姿で. ¶***school clothes*** 学校服. ¶***sports clothes*** スポーツ服. ¶take off one's ***street clothes*** よそ行きをぬぐ. ¶shiver in winter in ***summer clothes*** 冬に夏服を着てふるえる. ¶***swaddling clothes*** うぶ着 ‖ while the university was yet in ***swaddling clothes*** 同大学がまだ創立後日なお浅かったころ. ¶a fashion show of ***travel clothes*** 旅行服の流行展示会. ¶don ***work*** (=***working***) ***clothes*** 作業衣を着る. ¶***workaday*** (=everyday) ***clothes*** 平常服. ¶rough artisans in their ***working clothes*** 作業服を着た荒くれ職工.

P He has now grown too big ***for*** the ***clothes.*** 体が大きくなってそのきものが着られなくなった. ¶two suits ***of clothes*** 服二着. ¶stains ***on*** one's ***clothes*** きものについたよごれ. ¶***with*** his ***clothes*** streaming wet びしょぬれになって ‖ ***with*** only the ***clothes*** he stood up in 着のみ着のまゝで.

P² ***clothes for*** misses and juniors ジューニア向きの衣服. ¶the ***clothes of*** men (women) 男(女)服. ¶***clothes on*** a hanger 衣もんかけにかかっている衣服.

clothier, *n.* 衣服商.

Q a ***ready-made clothier*** 出来合服商.

clothing, *n.* きもの, 衣服.

V ***leave off*** winter ***clothing*** 冬服を着かえる. ¶***pack*** [***up***] one's ***clothing*** 衣類を包装する. ¶They ***wear*** very little ***clothing.*** 彼らはほとんどきものというものをまとわない.

Q dress in ***borrowed clothing*** 借着をする. ¶***insufficient*** (=***scanty***) ***clothing*** はだのあらわれるようなきもの. ¶dogs in fine ***male clothing*** 毛なみのよいおす犬. ¶put girls in ***man's clothing*** up to the age of fifteen 女の子に十五歳まで男物を着せる. ¶***mean clothing*** みすぼらしいきもの. ¶a manufactory of ***military clothing*** 陸軍被服廠. ¶Otherwise ***ordinary clothing*** will suffice. その他は普通の服装で差支えない. ¶I was in my nightgown and hastened to find some more ***presentable clothings.*** 僕はねまきを着ていたので急いで何か体裁のよいものを身に着けようとした. ¶***ready-made clothing*** 既製衣類. ¶***shabby unkept clothing*** ぼろぼろで手入のしてないきもの. ¶***used clothing*** 古着. ¶***warm clothing*** for the winter 暖い冬着.

Q² wear ***luxury clothing*** ぜい沢なきものを着る. ¶articles of ***silk clothing*** 絹の衣類.

P I am well-off ***for*** winter ***clothing.*** 冬着はたくさんある. ¶a wolf ***in*** sheep's ***clothing*** ねこかぶり. ¶She has rich stock ***of clothing.*** 彼女はきものはたくさん持っている. ‖ articles ***of clothing*** 衣類. 【類】A coat is an article ***of clothing.*** ¶They are well provided ***with clothing.*** 彼らは着る物は豊富だ.

cloud, *n.* 雲; 大群; 暗雲; はん点; 汚点.

V ***blow*** the ***clouds*** 《俗》喫煙する. ¶***blow away*** (=***off***) the ***clouds*** 雲を吹き散らす. ¶***dispel*** the ***cloud*** of the eastern skies 東方の空をおびやかす暗雲を飛散させる. ¶The ***clouds*** have now been ***dissipated.*** 雲はもう皆散ってしまった. ¶The darkest ***cloud*** has been ***lifted*** from the future. 将来にかかる最も暗たんたる疑雲が一掃された. 【類】

It *lifted* the *cloud* which had weighed heavily upon the country. ¶The summit ***pierces*** the *clouds*. 頂上は雲をつらぬいている. ¶***reach*** the *clouds* 雲をつく.

V² The *clouds* are ***breaking*** overs there! It may clear. あそこに雲切れがある. 晴れるだろう. ¶The *clouds* have begun to ***clear away***. 空が晴れてきた. ¶The *clouds* have ***come up*** a good deal. 大分雲が出てきた. ¶A white *cloud* ***floated*** in the sky. 白雲が空に漂った. ¶*clouds* ***gathering*** before a storm 暴風雨の前の暗雲.【類】*Clouds* ***gathering*** on the horizon. ¶where the *clouds* ***hang*** low 暗雲低くたれる所に. ¶He sat forlornly upon the bench, while *clouds* of black despair ***settled*** over him. 彼はやるせない思いで腰掛にすわった, 絶望の暗雲にとざされて.

Q I see a ***big*** *cloud* in the sky. 空に大きな雲が見える. ¶a ***blood-red*** *cloud* 血のように真赤な雲. ¶German activity in the Near East is a ***dark*** *cloud* upon the Russian horizon. 近東におけるドイツの飛躍はロシアにとっては一まつの暗雲である. ¶a ***fleecy*** *cloud* 白雲. ¶a ***fleeting*** *cloud* 流れる雲. ¶a ***flying*** *cloud* 飛雲. ¶dissipate the ***heavy black*** *cloud* which was hanging over the situation 時局をおおう暗雲を消散させる. ¶a ***mysterious*** *cloud* ふしぎな雲. ¶***radioactive*** *clouds* 放射能雲. ¶The moon is obscured by ***threatening*** *clouds*. 月は険悪な雲におゝわれている. ¶***tousled*** *clouds* 乱雲.

Q² mottled "***mackerel***" *clouds* まだらのさば雲(巻積雲). ¶blow off ***rain*** *clouds* 雨雲を吹きとばす. ¶masses of ***storm*** *clouds* 幾層もの乱雲. 【類】a sky in which the ***storm*** *clouds* were hastening forward. ¶***summer*** *clouds* floating feathery overhead 頭上に羽根のようにただよっている夏雲. ¶The ***war*** *cloud* has dispersed. 戦雲が消散した. 【類】***war*** *clouds* still hanging over Asia / The ***war*** *cloud* in South America is becoming threatening.

P rise ***above*** the *clouds* 雲にそびえる ‖ The plane was flying ***above*** the *clouds*. その飛行機は雲の上を飛んでいた. ¶***among*** the *clouds* 雲間に. ¶The moon was dimmed ***by*** *clouds*. 月は雲でかすんでいた. ‖ The sky is blotted out ***by*** *clouds*. 空が雲で見えない. ¶Concentrated moisture falls in rain ***from*** the *clouds*. かたまった湿気が雲から雨となって降る. ¶***from above*** the *clouds* 雲の上から. ¶The dust is rising ***in*** *clouds*. ちりがぱっと立っている. ‖ raise the dust ***in*** thick *clouds* 黄じんを立てる ‖ His mind is ***in*** the *clouds*. =He has his mind ***in*** the *clouds*. 空想にふけっている. 【類】She has lost herself ***in*** the *clouds*. ‖ those cradled ***in*** the *clouds* 雲上人. ¶a bank ***of*** *cloud* 層雲. ¶The moonbeam breaks ***through*** rifted *clouds*. 月光が雲間をもれる. ¶***under*** *cloud* of night 夜陰に乗じて ‖ be ***under*** a *cloud* 疑いを受けている, 具合がわるい. 【類】He was ***under*** a *cloud* (=discredited *or* out of favor) because of his dishonesty. ‖ a ship ***under*** a *cloud* of canvas 帆を張った船. ¶The moon is covered ***with*** a *cloud*. 月が雲におゝわれている. 【類】The sky is darkened ***with*** *clouds*. / The night is dark ***with*** *clouds*. ‖ a marble ***with*** dark *clouds* 黒いはん点のある大理石. ¶a sky ***without*** *clouds* 雲のない空.

P² a *cloud* ***of*** arrows 雨あられと飛ぶ弓矢 ‖ a *cloud* ***of*** dust (sand) 塵(など)煙 ‖ a *cloud* ***of*** flies (locusts) 無数のはえ(など) ‖ a *cloud* ***of*** sorrow 愁雲. 【類】a *cloud* ***of*** suspicion / a *cloud* ***of*** war / The *clouds* ***of*** doubt rolled away. ¶a *cloud* ***on*** one's brow 愁眉 ‖ a *cloud* ***on*** one's happiness (spirits) 幸福(など)に暗い影. ¶heavy *clouds* ***over*** our heads 頭上の暗雲. ¶a *cloud* ***upon*** one's reputation 名誉の汚点.

cloud, *v*. 曇らせる.

M The origin is ***somewhat*** *clouded* ***in*** obscurity. その起源はやや不明である.

M² The day is *clouding* ***over*** (=***up***). 曇って来た. 【類】The sky is beginning to *cloud* ***over***.

P a face *clouded* ***with*** anxiety 心配に曇った顔.

clove, *n*. ちょうじの木(実).

Q² ***mother*** *cloves* 乾製ちょうじ.

clover, *n*. クローバ.

Q a ***four-leaved*** *clover* 四つ葉のクローバ.

clown, *n*. 道化役者.

V ***act*** the *clown* 道化たまねをする.

Q² a ***circus*** *clown* 曲馬団の道化師.

cloy, *v*. あきあきさせる.

P The child is *cloyed* ***with*** sweets. あの児は菓子にあきている. 【類】be *cloyed* ***with*** luxury (pleasure).

club, *n*. **(1)** 会, クラブ.

V ***disband*** a *club* クラブを解散する. ¶***form*** (=***organize***) a *club* クラブを組織する. ¶***join*** a *club* クラブに加入する. ¶The restaurant ***messes*** our *club*. その料理屋が僕らのクラブの仕出しをしている. ¶The store will ***start*** Christmas *clubs* among their customers. その店は顧客の間にクリスマス(買物の積立)クラブを始める.

Q an ***athletic*** (=a ***sporting***) *club* 運動クラブ. ¶an ***exclusive*** *club* 《米》上流階級のクラブ(会員資格のやかましい). ¶a ***ladies'*** *club* 婦人クラブ. ¶a ***literary*** (***military, naval, social***) *club* 文学(など)クラブ. ¶The *club* is ***nonsectarian*** and ***non-political***. そのクラブは宗教にも政治にも関係していない. ¶a ***political*** *club* 政治クラブ.

Q² an ***automobile*** *club* 自動車クラブ. ¶a ***book*** *club* 読書会. ¶a ***camera*** *club* 写真クラブ. ¶a ***cricket*** (***football, golf***) *club* クリケット(など)クラブ. ¶a ***crime*** *club* 犯罪クラブ. ¶a ***cyclists' touring*** *club* 自転車旅行会. ¶The mushrooming of new professional ***ball*** *clubs*. [雨後のたけのこのような]新しい職業的舞踏クラブの急増. ¶join a ***book*** *club* 読書会に加入する. ¶a ***clothes*** *club* 被服クラブ(衣料費節約のための). ¶a ***country*** *club* カントリ・クラブ(テニス・ゴルフ場などのある). ¶the ***eating*** *club* at an American college アメリカ大学の会食クラブ. ¶the ***Fine Arts*** *Club* 美術クラブ. ¶a ***glee*** *club* 《米》学生合唱団. ¶a ***goose*** *club* 《英》クリスマス用がちょうに対する積立てクラブ. ¶a ***night*** *club* ナイト・クラブ. ¶a men's ***recreation*** *club* 男子レクリエーション・クラブ. ¶a ***rural youth*** *club* 農村青年クラブ. ¶a ***study*** *club* 研究会.

P I will meet you ***at*** my *club*. 僕のクラブでお目にかかろう. ¶He takes a leading part ***in*** the *club*. 彼はクラブを牛耳っている.

(2) こん棒; 〘ゴルフ〙クラブ.

V ***brandish*** *clubs* こん棒を振り回す.

Q² a ***golf*** *club* ゴルフ・クラブ(棒または団体).

club, *v*. **(1)** 団結する.

M *club* ***together*** for ... 出し合って...を買う ‖ They *clubbed* ***together*** for the purpose. 彼らはその目的で団結した. 【類】They all *clubbed* ***together*** to help the defenders against the enemy.

(2) 棒で打つ.

P *club* one ***to*** death 人を撲殺する.

clue, *n*. 手掛り, 心当り.

V ***afford*** a *clue* for ... ...の足がつく. ¶He ***found*** a *clue* to the mystery. 彼はその怪事件の手掛りを得た. ‖ A *clue* has been ***found*** that will lead the way to important developments in the future. 将来重要な発展をなすべき手掛りが見つかった. ¶***gain*** some *clue* as to ... ...について幾分の手掛りを得る. ¶***get*** a *clue* to ... ...の手掛りを得る. ¶Can you ***give*** me some *clue* to it? 何か手掛りがありますか. ¶The police ***has*** no *clue* to his identity. 警察は彼の身元の手掛りを全然つかめない. ¶***leaving*** no *clue* to guide the eager searchers 熱心な捜査隊の頼りになる何らの手掛りをも残さずに. ¶That ***supplied*** a *clue* and the criminal was arrested. それから足がついて犯人がつかまった.

Q an ***important*** *clue* 有力な手掛り. ¶There is ***no*** *clue* to the perpetrator of the outrage. 暴行犯人の手掛りが全くない. ¶a ***promising*** *clue* 有望な手掛り. ¶a ***substantial*** *clue* 確かな手掛り.

P ***from*** *clue* (=clew) ***to*** earing 隅から隅まで, 徹底的に. ¶***with*** this *clue* to go upon これを手掛りに.

P² a *clue* ***for*** solving a problem 問題を解く手掛り. ¶No *clue* ***to*** his whereabout[s] has been found. 彼の所在はまだ一向心当りがない.

clump, *n*. 木立; かたまり.

Q² a ***turf*** *clump* ひとかたまりの芝生.

clump, *v*. 重い足どりで歩く.

P The blind preacher *clumped* up ***into*** the pulpit. 盲目の牧師が説教壇に重い足どりで上った.

clumsy, *a*. へたな, 不器用な.

P He is *clumsy* ***at*** cricket. 彼はクリケットがへただ. ¶I am *clumsy* ***in*** speaking (writing). 僕は話(など)がへただ. ¶He is *clumsy* ***with*** his hands. 彼は手先が不器用だ.

cluster, *n*. 房; 群.

Q ***flower*** *cluster* 群れ咲く花.

Q² an ***embryo egg*** *cluster* [雌鶏などの]胎内の卵塊. ¶a

P grow ***in*** *clusters* 房になって生じる.

P² a *cluster* ***of*** bees (islands, stars) みつばち(など)の群 ‖ a *cluster* ***of*** berries (grapes) ベリー(ぶどう)の房.

cluster, *v*. 群がる, 集まる.

M people ***thickly*** *clustered* along the sides of the road to gaze on ... ...を眺めようと黒山のような人が道の両側に集まった.　「先生の回りに集った.

M^2 The pupils *clustered about* their teacher. 生徒たちは

clutch, *n.* 捕捉, 把握, 掌握.

V *loose* one's *clutch* つかんだ手を放す. ¶*make* a *clutch* at the military force 兵権を握ろうとする.

Q It grips ... in its *death-like clutch*. それは...をその死のように恐ろしい手でつかむ.

P I have him *in* my *clutches*. 彼は僕の掌中にある. ¶fall *into* the *clutches* of an enemy (poverty) 敵(など)に捕えられる. ¶*within clutch* つかまえられて.

P^2 the *clutch of* a usurer 高利貸の魔手.

clutch, *v.* ぎゅっと握る, しかとつかむ.

M *clutch* it *desperately* それを死にものぐるいでつかむ.

P *clutch at* a person (thing, shadow) 人(など)につかみかかる ‖ *clutch at* a straw [おぼれる者が]わらをもつかもうと

coach, *n.* 四輪大馬車; [列車の]客車.　└する.

V *drive* a *coach* 馬車を駆る.

V^2 The *coach rattled* briskly *by*. 馬車はがらがら走って行った.　「する団隊.

Q groups travelling in *chartered coaches* 借切馬車で旅行

Q^2 an *all-steel coach* 総鋼鉄客車. ¶a *baby coach* (=carriage) うば車. ¶an outing on a *four-horse coach* 四頭立の馬車での遠乗り. ¶a *four-in-hand coach* 四頭立の馬車. ¶a *passenger coach* 客車. ¶The *third-class coach* was full almost to overflowing. 三等客車はほとんど満員であった.

P We traveled a great deal *by coach*. われわれは馬車で大いに旅行した. ¶take a seat *in* a *coach* 馬車の席に着く. ¶fall *off* a *coach* 馬車から落ちる.

coach, *n.* 〚スポーツ〛コーチ.

Q^2 a *football coach* しゅう球のコーチ. ¶a *swimming coach*

coach, *v.* 予習してやる; 訓練する.　└水泳のコーチ.

P *coach* a student *for* an examination 学生に試験準備をしてやる ‖ *coach* a boat's crew *for* a race 短艇選手を競漕のために訓練する. ¶*coach* a new hand *in* his duties 新入りの人に仕事を教える.

coaching, *n.* 予習, 訓練.

P *private coaching* 個人教授.

coagulation, *n.* 凝固.

V^2 If *coagulation* did not *take place* after a cut or wound, the wounded might bleed to death. 切傷あるいは負傷の後凝血が起らなかったら, 負傷者は出血が止まらない

coal, *n.* 石炭; *pl.*《英》燃料用の石炭.　└で死ぬだろう.

V *burn coal* in the furnace 炉で石炭をたく. ¶*cut* (=*mine*) *coal* 採炭する. ¶*lay in coals* for the winter 冬仕度に燃料用の石炭を仕込む. ¶*prepare coal* for the market 選炭をする. ¶*put on* some *coal* 石炭をくべる. ¶*ship coal* 石炭を積み出す. ¶*shovel coal*[*s*] 石炭をシャベルで投入れる. ¶The ship stopped at Suez to *take* [*in*] *coal*. 船は石炭積込にスエズに寄った. ¶*trim coal* 積込んだ石炭を整える.

Q *bituminous coal* れき青炭. ¶*black coal* 黒炭(れき青炭). ¶*blind coal* 無煙炭. ¶*brown coal*=lignite 亜炭. ¶*burning coals* 燃える石炭. ¶a *cold coal* to blow at. 成就の見込ない仕事. ¶*hard coal* 硬炭. ¶A *heated coal* fell on the carpet. 熱い石炭(のかけら)がじゅうたんに落ちた. ¶*lignite* [*coal*] かっ炭. ¶a *live coal* 燃えている石炭. ¶*small coal* 粉炭. ¶*soft coal* 軟炭. ¶the "*white coal*" (=*houille blanche*) of France and Italy フランスやイタリアの水力電気.

Q^2 *bunker coal* 自家用燃料炭. ¶*steam coal* 蒸気用炭.

P broil meat *on coals* 火で肉を焼く. ¶cook it *over* hot *coals* 火にかけてそれを料理する.

coal, *v.* 石炭を積込む.

P *coal at* a port 港で石炭を積込む.

coalesce, *v.* 合体する.

P The colonies *coalesced into* a new nation. 植民地が合併して新しい一国となった.

coaling, *n.* 給炭.

V *complete coaling* 石炭積込を終える.

coalition, *n.* 合同, 提携.　「携.

Q^2 the *Socialist-Communist coalition* 社会共産両党の提

P^2 a *coalition against* a common enemy 共通の敵に対する団結. ¶a *coalition between* two parties 二党の提携. ¶a *coalition of* former opponents *with* one another 以前の

coarse, *a.* 粗野な.　└敵同志の提携.

P He is *coarse in* manner (speech). 彼は態度(など)が粗野

coarsen, *v.* 粗雑にする.　└だ.

P prostitutes who have been *coarsened by* their profession 職業ずれのした売春婦たち.

coast, *n.* 海岸, 沿岸地.

V *defend* our *coasts* わが国の海岸を防御する. ¶*finding* the *coast* clear 敵または障害物なしと見て. ¶I took care to *have* the *coast clear* for the reception of him. 彼と接見するとき人に見られないように気を配った. ¶The *coast* is *indented* by tiny bays. 海岸は小湾が多くのこぎり歯状になっている. ¶The Russians *insulted* our *coasts*. ロシア人がわが沿岸を侵した. ¶In the sixteenth century Japanese pirates *raided* the *coast* of China. 十六世紀に和寇(わこう)が中国の沿岸を侵した. ¶The Hokurikudo *skirts* the Japan Sea *coast*. 北陸道は日本海海岸に沿うて走る. ¶A great tidal wave *swept* the *coast* at Iwate, Japan. 大つなみが日本の岩手県海岸を洗い去った.

Q an *exposed coast* 風波にさらされた海岸. ¶off the *French coast* フランス海岸沖で. ¶the fishing grounds on the *Pacific coasts* 太平洋沿岸の漁場. ¶a *rock-bound coast* 岩石に囲まれた海岸. ¶a *rocky coast* 岩石の多い海岸. ¶an *unfortified coast* 無防備の海岸.

Q^2 a *cliff coast* 絶壁の海岸. ¶the *sea coast* 海岸. ¶Winds of gale velocity raked the *West Coast*. 《米》強風が西部海岸を吹きまくった.

P a ship steaming *along* a *coast* 沿海航行船 ‖ The wreckage is strewn *along* the *coast*. 難破船の漂着物が海岸に散らばっている. ¶*from* the *coast to* the interior 海岸から内地まで. ¶The ship foundered *off* the *coast* of Tosa. その船は土佐沖で沈没した. 【類】an island *off* the east *coast* of Africa. ¶The town lies *on* the *coast*. その町は海岸にある. ‖ a common fish *on* the British *coast* 英国沿海に多い魚. ¶The mineral is found *on* south *coast* of England. その鉱物は英国の南海岸に産する. ‖ a rough sea *on* a rocky *coast* 岩浜に打寄せる荒波. ¶a trip *to* the *coast* for sea-bathing 海水浴のため海岸への旅行 ‖ the village lies *to* the immediate *coast* of ... その村は...続きの海岸にある.

coast, *v.* 沿岸を旅行する.

P pedestrian travelers *coasting along* the lake その湖畔

coast-line, *n.* 海岸線.　└を旅行する徒歩客.

V bays *indenting* the *coast-line* 海岸線をのこぎり歯状にきざむ湾. ¶a *serpentine coast-line* 曲りくねった海岸線.

Q a *crooked* and *broken coast-line* 曲って出入の多い海岸線.

Q^2 the *Shantung coast-line* 山東省の海岸線.

coat, *n.* 上着; 被せ, 塗り.

V *button* a *coat* 上着のボタンをはめる. ¶The tailor has *cut out* my *coat* very well. 仕立屋が僕の上着を上手に仕立てた. ¶*draw on* a *coat* 上着を引掛ける. ¶He *gave* the wall two *coats* of whitewash. 壁に白い塗料を二度塗った. ¶He *had* a *coat on*. 彼は上着を着ていた. ‖ The cat *has* a *coat* of fur. ねこは毛皮の上着を着ている. ¶I must *have* (=*get*) a new *coat made*. 上着を新調しなければならない. ¶*lay off* one's *coat* 上着を脱ぐ. ¶My *coat* must be *let out*. 上着はゆるくしないといけない. ¶This cloth will *make* me a *coat*. この布で僕の上着ができる. ‖ The tailor *made* my *coat* in a week. 仕立屋は私の上着を一週間でこしらえた. ¶The *coat* requires to be *mended*. この上衣は直さなければならない. ¶The child has *outgrown* its *coat*. 子供が成長して上着が着られなくなった. ¶My *coat* must be *patched up*. 僕の上着はつくろわなければならない. ¶He *pulled off* his *coat*. 彼は上着を急いでぬいだ. ¶*put on* (*off*) one's *coat* 着物を着る(ぬぐ). ¶The house *received* a fresh (=new) *coat* of paint. その家はペンキの塗り替えをした. ¶He *slipped on* (*off*) his *coat*. 彼はするりと上着を引掛けた(ぬいだ). ¶My *coat* is too wide; it must be *taken in*. 上衣が大き過ぎるからつめなければならない. ¶*take off* one's *coat* to work 上着をぬいで仕事にかかる. ¶I have *torn* my *coat*. 上着を破った. ¶*try on* a *coat* 上着を着て見る. ¶*turn* one's *coat* 変節する, 寝返りを打つ ‖ *turn* one's *coat outside in* (=inside out) 上着を裏返しにする ‖ *turn* a *coat over* for alteration 上着を裏返して仕立直す. ¶*unbutton* a *coat* 上着のボタンをはずす. ¶*wear* a *coat* 上着を着る.

V^2 My *coat* does not *come up* to my expectations. 僕の上着はどうも気に入らない. ¶This *coat fits* me well (=like a glove). この上着はよく合う. ¶The *coat reaches* below the knees. この上着はひざの下までである. ¶His *coat smells* of tobacco. 彼の上着はタバコ臭い. ¶This *coat wears* well. この上着はよく保(も)つ.

Q a ***black coat***＝blackcoat 黒の服;《俗》僧;《英俗》サラリーマン. ☞ a blakcoat worker ともいう. 米の a white color [worker] に対する語. ¶A ***cheap coat*** makes a cheap man. 人は衣装次第, 馬子にも衣装. ¶He came back with ***deep rich coats*** of tan. 彼は(海水浴で)良い色が着いて帰ってきた. ¶a ***fur-lined coat*** 毛皮裏の上着. ¶assume a ***new coat*** 換羽(かん)する(家禽など). ¶a ***ragged coat*** 着古した上着. ¶a ***swallow-tailed coat*** えん尾服. ¶gentlemen in ***tail[ed] coats*** モーニングを着た紳士方. ¶My *coat* is too ***tight*** (***loose***). 僕の上着はあまりきゅう屈(など)だ. ¶a ***warm coat*** 暖い上着. ¶This *coat* is ***worn-out.*** この上衣は着古しだ. ¶a ***zip-lined top coat***＝a zipliner チャック裏付外とう.

Q² a ***blue-serge coat*** こんサージの上着. ¶in ***full-dress coat*** 正装して. ¶a ***fur coat*** 毛皮の上着. ¶a ***mink coat*** てんの毛皮で作った(婦人用)外とう. ¶a "***pea coat***" [米国水夫の]空色コート. ¶a ***Prince Albert*** [***coat***]《米》フロックコート. ¶a ***rayon gabardine coat*** レーヨンギャバジンの上着. ¶a ***roughing-in coat*** 上塗りのあら壁. ¶a ***rubber coat*** ゴム製上着. ¶a ***sharkskin coat*** シャークスキン地で作った上着. ¶a light ***summer coat*** 薄い夏の上着. ¶boys in Eton jackets or ***tail coats*** イートン校服即ちえん服を着た少年. ¶a general ***utility coat*** 一般向実用服. ¶the building's ***wartime coat*** of olive drab そのビルの濃緑かっ色戦時塗装. ¶a heavy ***winter coat*** 厚い冬の上着.

P Please measure me ***for*** a new *coat*. 新調の上着の寸法を取ってくれ. ¶wear a flower ***in*** one's *coat* 上着に花をつける. ¶The cloth has been made ***into*** a *coat*. この生地を上着にした. ¶There is a stain ***on*** my *coat*. 上着によごれが付いている. ¶a man ***with*** a purple *coat* on 紫衣を着た人 ‖ an apple ***with*** a rough *coat* 皮のざらざらしたりんご.

P² a *coat **with*** trousers to match ズボンとよく釣合う上着.

coat, *v.* 着せる, かぶせる.

M The car was ***thickly coated*** with dust. 車は厚くごみをかぶっていた.

P They are of base metals *coated **with*** precious metals. それらは貴金属をきせた卑金属で作ってある. 【類】iron *coated **with*** zinc / be *coated **with*** gold ‖ The pond is *coated **with*** thin ice. 池に薄氷が張っている. ‖ The verandah is *coated **with** dust.* ヴェランダがほこりだらけ. ‖ The paper is *coated **with*** glossy wax. その紙にはつやのあるろうが引いてある. ‖ a cake *coated **with*** sugar 砂糖がけの菓子 ‖ The chimney is *coated **with*** lampblack. ほやは油煙で黒くすすけている.

coating, *n.* 上塗り, ころも.

Q a ***fur-like coating*** on the tongue 毛皮のような舌苔(ぜつ). ¶a ***thin coating*** on fried fishmeat フライにした魚肉の薄いころも.

coax, *v.* 甘言でまるめこむ.

M *coax **away*** ろう絡し去る. ¶*coax* him ***back*** to ... 彼をだまして…へ連れ戻る. ¶*coax **forth*** information 話を釣り出す.

P *coax* a person ***into*** compliance with a wish 人をすかしてこっちの思うつぼにはめ込む ‖ *coax* a person ***into*** doing ... 人を口車に乗せて…をやらせる. ¶*coax* a thing ***out of*** a person 人から物を詐取する.

cobweb, *n.* くもの巣; じゃま物.

V to ***clear away*** the *cobwebs* from my weary brain 疲れた頭の気晴しに. ¶Spiders ***spin*** their *cobwebs* out of threads that look like silk. くもは絹のように見える糸でその巣を張る. ¶***sweep down*** the *cobwebs* くもの巣を払い落す.

cock, *n.* 雄鶏;《英》のみ口.

V They ***fight cocks*** for a business. 商売に闘鶏をやる. ¶***turn on*** (***off***) a *cock* のみ口をひねってあける(しめる).

V The *cock **crows***. 鶏がときをつくる.

P The faucet is turned ***on*** full (half) *cock*. じゃ口は十分(半分)出るようにひねってある.

cock, *v.* ぴんと立つ.

M² *cock **up*** the ears 耳をぴんとあげる ‖ *cock **up*** one's head ふんぞり返る.

P *cock* one's eye ***at*** ... 上目使いに…を見る.

cockcrow, *n.* 鶏のとき.

P ***at*** *cockcrow* 鶏がときをつくる時.

cocktail, *n.* カクテル.

V ***prepare*** *cocktail* カクテルを作る.

Q² a ***tomato-juice*** *cocktail* トマト・ジュース・カクテル.

cocoon, *n.* まゆ.

V Silkworms ***spin*** their *cocoons*. 蚕はまゆを作る.

Q² a ***silkworm cocoon*** 蚕のまゆ.

cod, *n.* たら.

Q² ***night cods*** 夜釣りだら. ¶***school cod*** 群生たら.

code, *n.* 法典; 信号; 電信暗号.

V ***decipher*** (＝***decode***) a *code* 電信暗号を翻読する. ¶***formulate*** a better *code* of newspaper ethics 新聞道徳のさらによい規範を作る. ¶***frame*** a *code* 法典を編成する. ¶***lay down*** a *code* of practice 実行上の規則をたてる. ¶***offend*** the social *code* 風紀をぶん乱する. ¶***set up*** a moral *code* for themselves 彼ら自身のために道徳律を設ける.

Q ***civil code*** 民法. ¶***contrasting codes*** of morality 氷炭相入れない道徳律. ¶***criminal*** (＝***penal***) ***code*** 刑法. ¶a ***doubtful code*** of morals いかがわしい道徳律. ¶the need of an ***equal code*** of morals for both sexes 男女両性に対し平等な道徳律の必要. ¶an ***ethical code*** 道徳律. ¶a ***lofty code*** of morals 高い道徳律. ¶the ***moral code*** 道徳律. 【類】Shinto has no ***moral code***. ¶by a ***pre-arranged code*** of signals 前もって打合わせておいた信号によって. ¶a ***social code*** of manners 礼儀作法. ¶a ***telegraphic code*** 電信符号. ¶the ***unwritten code*** of the English gentleman 英国紳士の不文律. 【類】an ***unwritten*** *code* of moral conduct (礼儀作法).

Q² ***building codes*** (＝ordinances) 都市の建築条令. ¶a ***cipher code*** 暗号電信帳. ¶a ***figure code*** 数字式暗号. ¶the ***Morse code*** モールス式電信符号. ¶the ***press code*** 新聞綱領. ¶mines where the regulatory ***safety code*** is not being met 安全規定が守られていない鉱山 ‖ a ***traffic safety code*** 交通安全規定. ¶the ***schoolboy code*** of life and honor 学童間の道義. ¶a ***word code*** 語による暗号(数字に対し).

P Goods bear a price ***in*** *code*. 商品には符ちょうで値段がつけてある. ‖ a telegram (cablegram) ***in*** *code* (海外)暗号電報.

P² a *code **of*** signals 信号法 ‖ the *code **of*** Christian morality キリスト教の道徳律.

coefficient, *n.* 係数.

Q² ***absorption coefficient*** 〘光学〙[スペクトル]吸収率.

coerce, *v.* 強いる.

P *coerce* one ***into*** submission (obedience, consent) しいて人を服従(など)させる.

coercion, *n.* 強制.

V ***apply*** *coercion* to make him forgo ... 強制的に彼に…を控えさせる. ¶***exert*** a *coercion* on him to ... …すべく彼を強制する.

coeval, *a.* 同時代の, 同年代の.

P *coeval **with*** the world 開びゃく以来存在する.

coexist, *v.* 同時に存在する.

M can *coexist **together*** 同時に存在しうる.

P *coexist **with*** ... …と同時に存在する.

coexistence, *n.* 共存.

Q ***inconsistent*** *coexistence* of old and new 矛盾した新旧の共存.

P² *coexistence **with*** another 他[人]との共存.

coextensive, *a.* [時間・空間で]同じ広がりのある.

P *coextensive **with*** ... …と同空(時)間を占める.

coffee, *n.* コーヒー.

V *Coffee* is ***brought round***. コーヒーが出た. ¶***Have*** some more *coffee?* コーヒーもう少しいかがですか. ¶***make*** *coffee* コーヒーを入れる ‖ ***make*** the *coffee* a little stronger コーヒーをもう少し濃くする. ¶***stir*** one's *coffee* with a spoon さじでコーヒーをかきまわす. ¶***strain*** *coffee* コーヒーをこす. ¶***take*** *coffee* コーヒーを飲む. ¶I will ***try*** your *coffee* before buying any. 味をみてからコーヒーを買いましょう. ¶Let's ***warm up*** some *coffee* and have sandwiches. コーヒーを暖めてサンドイッチを食べよう.

Q ***fresh coffee*** 出したてのコーヒー. ¶***strong coffee*** 濃いコーヒー. ¶***washy coffee*** 水っぽいコーヒー. ¶***weak coffee*** 薄いコーヒー.

Q² Ten Latin American countries ***export coffee*** ラテン・アメリカの十カ国がコーヒーを輸出する. ¶***Mocha coffee*** モッカコーヒー.

P entertain a person ***at*** *coffee* コーヒーで人をもてなす. ¶Do you take (＝have) sugar ***in*** your *coffee?* あなたはコーヒーに砂糖をお入れになりますか. ¶a can ***of*** *coffee* コーヒー一かん ‖ Have a cup ***of*** *coffee*. コーヒーを一つ召上れ. ¶I am ***out of*** *coffee*. コーヒーが切れた. ¶Will you take sugar ***with*** your *coffee?* コーヒーに砂糖を入れましょうか.

coffin, *n.* 棺.

Q² a ***lead coffin*** 鉛色の棺.

cogency, *n.* 適切.

P the same argument applies ***with*** even more *cogency* (=even more obviously) to ... その議論はさらに適切に…に当てはまる.

cogitate, *v.* もくろむ.

P He is *cogitating* mischief ***against us***. 彼はわれわれにいたずらをしようともくろんでいる. ¶He sat *cogitating* ***upon*** some means of revenge. 彼は腰を落付けて復しゅうの手段を考えた.

cognac, *n.* コニャック.

Q^2 the ***appellation*** (=***term***) "*Congnac*" コニャックという名称.

cognate, *a.* 同類の.

M "Sing" and "song" are ***etymologically cognate***. sing と song の語原は同じだ.

cognizance, *n.* 認識, 認知.

V I ***have*** *cognizance* of his misdemeanor. 僕は彼の不行跡には気がついている. ¶***take*** *cognizance* of a crime 犯罪を認める ‖ Little *cognizance* is ***taken*** of these events. これらの事件は一向顧みられない. 【類】*cognizance* is also ***taken*** of ... / ***take*** no *cognizance* of the act.

Q have ***personal*** *cognizance* 自分で気がついている.

P ***beyond*** (=***out of***) his *cognizance* 彼に認識できない. ¶It has come ***into*** his *cognizance*. それは彼に知れた. ¶come ***under*** the *cognizance* of the law as a crime 法律上罪悪と認められる. ¶***within*** one's *cognizance* その人に認識されて.

cognizant, *a.* 認識している.

P He was *cognizant* ***of*** the truth. 彼は真相を知っていた. 【類】I was not *cognizant* ***of*** the fact. / Japan is *cognizant* ***of*** the need of ...

cohabit, *v.* 同居する, 同せいする.

P *cohabit* ***with*** a man without being married 結婚せずに男と同せいする.

coheir, *n.* 共同相続人.

P the *coheir* ***with*** John ***to*** the property ジョンとの共同相続人.

coherence, *n.* 一貫性.

V The argument ***lacks*** *coherence*. 議論に筋が通っていない.

Q^2 violate ***sentence*** *coherence* 文の首尾一貫を破る.

P^2 the *coherence* ***of*** an argument (a discussion) 議論(など)の一貫性.

coherent, *a.* 密着した; 一致した.

M ***partly*** *coherent* to ... …に部分的に一致した.

P *coherent* ***with*** (=***to***) each other お互いに密着している.

cohesion, *n.* 結合.

Q ***national*** *cohesion* 国民の団結.

coign, *n.* 外角, すみ.

Q ***Every*** *coign* of vantage was crowded with spectators. 高所という高所は見物人で一杯であった.

P ***from*** its *coign* of vantage その有利の地点から.

coil, *n.* 輪; とぐろ巻き.

P wind up a rope ***in*** a *coil* ロープをぐるぐる輪に巻く ‖ a snake lying ***in*** a *coil* とぐろを巻いているへび.

P^2 a *coil* ***of*** rope ロープのとぐろ巻き.

coil, *v.* とぐろを巻く.

M The snake was found *coiling* itself ***up*** in the cave. へびが洞くつの中でとぐろを巻いていた.

coin, *n.* 貨幣, 硬貨.

V ***circulate*** counterfeit *coins* 偽造貨幣を行使する. ¶***counterfeit*** *coin* 貨幣を偽造する. ¶***debase*** *coin* 硬貨の品位を落す. ¶***drop*** a *coin* to a slot 銭を自働機に入れる. ¶***flip*** a *coin* on the counter 勘定台の上で硬貨をはじく. ¶***issue*** *coins* 貨幣を発行する. ¶***mint*** (=***strike***) *coins* 貨幣を鋳造する. ¶***palm off*** a spurious *coin* upon a dealer にせがねを商人につかませる. ¶***pass*** (=***utter***) base *coin* 品質劣悪の硬貨を使う. ¶He ***slipped*** a *coin* into the beggar's hand. 彼はそっとこじきに銭をやった. ¶***sweat*** gold *coins* (金粉を売却するために)金貨をすり減らす. ¶***toss*** [***up***] a *coin* 銭を投上げて順番を定める.

V^2 Hardly a *coin* ***comes*** in his way. 一銭だって彼の手にはいってこない位だ. ¶This *coin* will not ***pass***. この銭は通用しない. ¶This *coin* ***rings true***. この金(銀)貨は本ものの音がする.

Q ***antique*** *coins* 古銭. ¶a ***battered*** *coin* 使い減らした銭. ¶the ***commonest*** *coins* of speech きわめて普通の言葉. ¶passers of ***counterfeit*** *coin* にせ金使い. ¶The *coin* is no longer ***current***. その銭は今通用していない. ¶a ***debased*** *coin* 悪貨. ¶a ***false*** *coin* にせ金. ¶a vendor of ***illicit*** *coin* がん造貨幣の売主. ¶a ***light*** *coin* 摩滅した貨幣. ¶a ***spurious*** *coin* がん造貨幣.

Q^2 ***gold*** (***silver, copper***) *coins* 金(銀・銅)貨.

P pay ***in*** *coin* 硬貨で払う ‖ I paid him back ***in*** his own *coin*. 僕は彼にしっぺい返しをした. ¶the character (figure, stamp, motto) ***on*** a *coin* 貨幣面の文字(など).

coin, *v.* 新造する.

P The word "blurb" was *coined* ***by*** G. Burgess. "blurb" という語はバーゼスの造った語だった.

O *coin* a new word 新語を造る.

coinage, *n.* 貨幣鋳造; [語の]新造.

V These are ***new coinages***. これらは新語である. ¶***garble*** *coinage* 貨幣を選り分ける.

Q Words of ***recent coinage*** comprise another group not found fully represented in dictionaries. 新造の言葉の中にはまだ十分辞書に収録してないものがある.

Q^2 ***word coinage*** 言葉の新造.

coincide, *v.* 一致する, 暗合する.

M *coincide* ***fortuitously*** with ... たまたま…と一致する. ¶Appearance ***seldom*** *coincides* with reality. 外観と事実と一致することはめったにない.

P The judges did not *coincide* ***in*** opinion. 裁判官たちは意見が一致しなかった. ‖ *coincide* ***in*** opinion ***with*** ... …と意見が一致する. ¶His views *coincide* ***with*** mine. 彼の意見は私と一致する. 【類】I do not *coincide* ***with*** you in politics. / The rise of the church *coincides* ***with*** the decline of the Roman Empire. / The ideal and the actual will never *coincide* ***with*** each other. ‖ make the ceremony *coincide* ***with*** President Wilson's visit to Paris 大統領ウィルソンのパリ着と同時にその式を挙行するように手はずをする ‖ The Fourth of July *coincides* this year ***with*** the rejoicings for a peace which means more to the world than any peace recorded in history. 今年の七月四日は(独立祭)有史以来いずれの平和よりも世界にとって有意義な平和の日と重なる.

coincidence, *n.* 一致, 符合, 暗合.

V ***bring about*** a curious *coincidence* 不思議な暗合を招来する. ¶***confuse*** mere *coincidence* with lineal derivation [言語の比較研究などで]ほんの暗合と系統的伝来とを混同する.

Q by a ***curious*** *coincidence* 妙な回り合わせで. ¶by a ***happy*** *coincidence* 運よく. ¶by an ***interesting*** *coincidence* おもしろい回り合わせで. ¶a ***mere*** *coincidence* ほんの偶然. ¶by an ***odd*** *coincidence* ゆくりなくも. ¶a ***remarkable*** *coincidence* 珍しい暗合. ¶a ***sad*** *coincidence* 悲しい回り合わせ. ¶a ***startling*** *coincidence* 珍しい回り合わせ. ¶a ***strange*** *coincidence* 奇縁. ¶an ***undesigned*** *coincidence* 思いもうけない暗合.

Q^2 ***chance*** *coincidence* 偶然の一致.

P ***by*** a *coincidence* of fate 運命の回り合わせで ‖ ***by*** a *coincidence* of singular interest 実に不思議な回り合わせで.

P^2 the *coincidence* ***between*** dreams and events 夢と事実の暗合.

coincident, *a.* 一致する, 符合する.

P Your opinion is *coincident* ***with*** mine. 貴説は私の考えと一致している.

coiner, *n.* [新語などの]案出者.

Q the ***original*** *coiner* of the phrase "race suicide"「人種的自殺」という句の案出者.

coke, *n.* コークス.

V ***use*** *coke* for fuel コークスを燃料にする.

cold, *n.* (1) 寒気.

V ***apply*** *cold* over the site of the pain 痛みの個所を冷す. ¶***feel*** the *cold* 寒気がする. ¶***keep out*** *cold* 防寒をする. ¶I can not ***stand*** (=***bear***) the *cold*. 寒さに耐えられない.

V^2 The *cold* has ***decreased*** in severity. 寒気がゆるんだ.

Q in the ***biting*** *cold* 身を刺す寒さに. ¶***bitter*** *cold* 厳寒. ¶***intense*** *cold* 厳寒. ¶***lingering*** *cold* 余寒. ¶***still*** *cold* 風がない寒さ. ¶The *cold* this year is quite ***unprecedented***. 今年の寒さはまた格別だ.

P He is shivering ***from*** (=***with***) *cold*. 彼は寒さに震えている. ¶be kept out ***in*** the *cold* 寒い時に外に出して置かれる. ‖ He was left outside ***in*** the *cold*. ‖ leave one out ***in*** the *cold* (=overlook one=neglect one) 人を無視する. ¶My hands are benumbed ***with*** *cold*. 寒さで手がかじかんでいる. ‖ He died ***with*** *cold*. 彼はこごえ死んだ.

P^2 the *cold* ***in*** Hokkaido 北海道の寒さ. ¶the *cold* ***of*** a Manchurian winter 満州の冬の寒さ.

(2) かぜ.

V ***catch*** *cold* very easily すぐかぜを引く ‖ ***catch*** *cold* in one's head 鼻かぜを引く ‖ those who are predisposed to ***catching*** *colds* かぜを引きやすい人々. 【類】One ***catches*** *cold* more often in summer than in winter. ¶In so doing he ***contracted*** a *cold* which caused his death. そうやって彼はかぜを引いてそれがもとで死んだ. ¶You are ***courting*** a *cold* by going about so thinly clad. そんな薄着で歩き回ってはわざとかぜを引こうとするようなものだ. ¶I have ***got*** a bad *cold*. ひどいかぜを引いた. ¶You've ***given*** me your *cold*. 君は私にかぜをうつした. ¶Most people ***have*** two or three *colds* a year. 大概の人は年に二三度はかぜを引く.【類】He ***had*** a *cold* that seemed to linger. ¶I cannot ***shake*** (=***throw***) ***off*** my *cold*. かぜが抜けない. ¶***suffer*** a severe *cold* ひどいかぜにかゝる. ¶easily ***take*** a *cold* すぐかぜを引く. ¶***withstand*** the *cold* かぜを押す.

Q catch a ***bad cold*** ひどいかぜを引く. ¶I have got a ***fresh*** *cold*. かぜを引き直した. ¶have a ***perpetual cold*** 始終かぜを引いている. ¶contract a ***severe cold*** ひどいかぜを引く. ¶I am suffering from a ***slight*** *cold*. ちとかぜを引いている.

Q^2 a ***head*** *cold* 鼻かぜ. ¶that old American institution, the ***spring*** *cold* (=fever) 昔からアメリカにある春のかぜ.

P I was confined to my house ***by*** a bad *cold*. ひどいかぜで引きこもっていた. ¶This is a good thing ***for*** a *cold*. これはかぜに良い. ‖ a medicine ***for*** the *cold* かぜ薬. ¶He is confined to bed ***with*** a *cold*. 彼はかぜで寝ている.

P^2 a *cold* ***from*** exposure 風雨にさらされたためのかぜ. ¶I have a *cold* ***in*** my (=the) head. 鼻かぜを引いた; かぜで頭が痛い. 【類】a *cold* ***in*** [the] nose. ¶a *cold* ***on*** the lungs (stomach, chest) せき(など)かぜ.

cold, *a.* 寒い, 冷たい; 冷淡な, 冷酷な.

M His feet were ***as cold*** as stone. 彼の足は石のようにつめたかった. ¶The weather is ***biting*** *cold*. 天候は身を刺すように寒い. ¶***Bitterly*** *cold*, isn't it? ひどく寒いじゃないか. ¶It looks like snow.—It is not *cold* ***enough*** for that. 雪になりそうだ.—それほどは寒くはない. ¶It is never ***excessively*** *cold* in winter there. そこは冬ひどく寒いことは決してない. ¶***extremely*** *cold* 非常に寒い. ¶It is ***rather*** *cold* today. きょうはかなり寒い. ¶be ***slightly*** *cold* うすら寒い. ¶His heart is ***stone*** *cold*. 彼は石のように冷酷だ. ¶***What*** *cold!* 何という寒さだろう.

P The patient is apt to be *cold* ***at*** the extremities. 病人はとかく手足が冷える. ‖ He is *cold* ***at*** heart. あの男は冷酷だ. ‖ I was struck *cold* ***at*** heart. 私はぞっとした. ¶He is *cold* ***by*** nature. 彼は冷酷なたちだ. ¶He is *cold* ***in*** death (=dead cold). 彼は死んで冷くなっている. ‖ He is *cold* ***in*** disposition. 彼は冷酷な男だ. ‖ a picture *cold* ***in*** tone 色調の寒い(青色など)絵. ¶She is *cold* ***to*** her husband. 彼女は夫に対して冷淡だ. ‖ It was *cold* ***to*** the touch. さわるとひやっとした. ¶The girls are *cold* ***towards*** men. あの娘などは男に対して冷淡だ. ¶I was *cold* ***with*** fear. 僕は恐怖のためにふるえた. ‖ His blood grew *cold* ***with*** fear. 恐ろしさにぞっとした.

O She looks *cold*, doesn't she? 彼女は寒そうじゃないか.

cold-hearted, *a.* 薄情な, 冷酷な.

M He was *cold-hearted* ***enough*** to forsake a friend in need. あれは困っている友人を見捨てるほど薄情な男だった.

coldness, *n.* 冷酷.

Q with ***cruel*** *coldness* 冷酷無情にも.

P^2 *coldness* ***in*** the extremities 手足の冷え.

collaborate, *v.* 共同して働く, 合作する.

P *collaborate* ***in*** the work その事業に協力する. ¶*collaborate* ***on*** a novel 小説を合作する. ¶*collaborate* ***with*** … on a book …と本を合作する.

collaboration, *n.* 合作, 共同作業.

V They ***lent*** their cheerful *collaboration* to the huge task. 彼らはその大事業に快く力を貸した. ¶***require*** the *collaboration* of specialists 専門家の協力を必要とする.

Q an ***international*** *collaboration* of scientists 科学者の国際共同研究. ¶a ***wonderful*** *collaboration* of European scholars 欧州学者たちの驚くべき共同研究.

P prepared ***in*** *collaboration* ***with*** … …と協力して作られた. ¶***with*** *collaboration* from (=of) … …の協力を得て.

collapse, *n.* 崩解; [健康の]急衰弱.

V^2 his *collapse* ***came*** when … 彼は…の時に没落した.

Q cause ***economic*** *collapse* 経済的崩壊を来す. ¶because England is afraid of its ***financial*** *collapse* 英国はその経済的崩壊を恐れているので. ¶a ***periodic*** *collapse* 周期的なくずれ.

Q^2 Miners are sometimes entombed owing to ***roof*** *collapses* in a mine. 落盤のために時に坑夫が生埋めになることがある. ¶a ***price*** *collapse* 値段の暴落.

P^2 a *collapse* ***of*** food prices 食料品の値段下落 ‖ the *collapse* ***of*** morale 士気そそう ‖ the *collapse* ***of*** money market 金融市場のがら. 【類】the *collapse* ***of*** one's health.

collapse, *v.* つぶれる; つぶす.

M be ***entirely*** *collapsed* 全く意気そそうしている.

P *collapse* ***like*** a house of cards almost without a struggle ボール紙の家のようにほとんどひとたまりもなくつぶれる. ¶*collapse* ***under*** the weight of … …の重さでつぶれる.

collar, *n.* えり, カラー; 首輪.

V The dog ***has*** a *collar* around his neck. その犬は首輪をしている. ¶***put*** a *collar* around the neck of a dog 犬の首に首輪をはめる. ¶***put on*** a clean *collar* きれいなカラーを着ける. ¶***turn up*** one's *collar* [上着の]えりを立てる. ¶***wear*** one's clerical *collar* 僧服を着る.

Q wear a ***brandnew*** *collar* 真新しいカラーをつけている. ¶a ***colored*** *collar* 着色カラー. ¶an ***immaculate*** *collar* [少しも汚れのない]真白いカラー. ¶be in a ***high*** *collar* 高いカラーを付けている. ¶a ***soft*** *collar* ソフト・カラー. ¶a ***stand-up*** *collar* 立てえりカラー. ¶a ***starched*** *collar* のり付カラー. ¶a ***turn-down*** (=***turnover***) *collar* 折えり. ¶***two dozen*** *collars* カラーを二ダース.

Q^2 a ***sailor*** *collar* 水兵服のえり.

P It is working ***against*** the *collar* for that boy to study. その少年は勉強は苦手だ. ¶drag a dog ***by*** (=***at***) the *collar* えり首をつかんで犬を引きずる.

collate, *v.* 照し合わせる; 牧師に推挙する.

P a book *collated* ***by*** … …氏の校訂本. ¶He *collated* his clerk ***to*** the church. 彼はその書記を教会に推挙した. ¶*collate* the later ***with*** the earlier edition 新版を旧版と対照する.

collateral, *n.* 〖商〗見返品.

Q Import is not permitted without ***proper*** *collateral*. 輸入は適当な見返品ある場合に限り許される.

collateral, *a.* 照応の; 〖商〗見返りの.

P put up good security ***as*** *collateral* for a loan. 貸付に対し適当の担保を提供する. ¶The English version is to be *collateral* ***with*** the Japanese on the opposite page. 英文記載事項は対応ページの日本文に照応するものとする.

collation, *n.* 手軽な食事.

V A cold *collation* will be ***served*** at 7.30 p.m. 冷たい夜食が午後七時半に出る.

colleague, *n.* 同僚.

Q^2 our ***language*** *colleagues* 語学の同僚たち.

P work ***as*** one's *colleague* 同僚として働く.

collect, *ad.* 集金して, 代金引換えで.

P There's sixty-five cents *collect* ***on*** that telegram. あの電報は 65 セントいただきます. ‖ Two dollars *collect* ***on*** this package for you. この小包の代金二ドルいただきます.

collect, *v.* 集める; 集まる.

M the materials were ***assiduously*** *collected* by … 資料は…が丹念に集めたものだ. ¶*collect* ***unfairly*** and spend wisely 不正な集め方をしてうまく使う.

M^2 Some typical examples are *collected* ***below***. 若干の代表的実例を次に掲げる.

P The paper-theater man *collected* a crowd of children ***about*** (=***around***) him. 紙芝居の小父さんは大勢の子供を集めた. ¶*collect* students ***at*** (=***in***) a place ある所に学生を集める. ¶*collect* ***by*** purchase …を買い集める. ¶*collect* rent ***from*** tenants 借家人から家賃を取立てる. 【類】The data have been *collected* ***from*** many sources. ¶The lectures are *collected* ***in*** a pamphlet. 講演は小冊子になっている. ¶*collect* fallen leaves ***into*** a heap 落葉を集めて山と積上げる. 【類】be *collected* ***into*** a group (=body) ‖ *collect* essays ***into*** a single volume 論文を一冊にまとめる. 【類】*collect* materials ***into*** a volume / *collect* magazine articles ***into*** volume form (単行本). ¶The pier rates are *collected* ***on*** the quantity of cargo delivered or received. 桟橋料は受渡し船荷の分量によって徴収する. ‖ There is twelve dollars to *collect* ***on*** it. その代を十二ドルいただきます. ¶essays *collected* ***under*** the title of … …の表題下に集められた諸論文 ‖ *collect* them ***under*** one cover 一冊に集める.

collecting, *n.* 収集.

Q^2 ***book*** *collecting* 書籍収集. ¶***signature*** *collecting* 署名運動. ¶***stamp*** *collecting*=philately 郵便切手収集.

collection, *n.* (**1**) 収集(コレクション); 集団.

V A *collection* which was ***assembled*** on that occasion

numbered 426 pieces. その(展覧)会に集まった出品は四百二十六点であった. ¶***catalogue*** a *collection* of pictures 絵の収集目録を作る. ¶After his death the *collection* was ***dispersed.*** 彼の死後その所蔵品は散逸した. ¶***enrich*** one's *collection* with a few choice examples of works 若干の精選した作品をその所蔵に加える. ¶He has ***formed*** a very interesting *collection* of ancient pottery, which consists of 144 pieces. 彼は百四十四点にのぼる興味ある古陶器を収集した. ¶The *collection* is ***housed*** in a fine building. 収集品はりっぱな建物に収められている. ¶***make*** a *collection* of proverbs (stamps, specimens) ことわざ(など)を集める. ¶*collections* ***kept*** by them 彼らに保管されている収集品. ¶***start*** a *collection* 収集を始める. ¶***take up*** *collections* to buy presents for departing employees 退職する職員に贈物をするための寄付を募る.

V² as the *collection* ***grows*** 所蔵品がふえるにつれて.

Q a ***choice*** *collection* of ... ...の精選. ¶make a ***complete*** *collection* of ... ...をもれなく集める. ¶a ***confused*** *collection* of things 雑然と集めた物. ¶an ***extensive*** *collection* of Japanese color prints にしき絵の大コレクション. ¶a ***fine*** *collection* of paintings 絵画のりっぱな収集. ¶an ***immense*** *collection* of ... ...の一大コレクション. ¶an ***interesting*** *collection* of antiquities 興味ある古物の収集. ¶He has a ***large*** *collection* of curios. 骨とうを沢山集めている. ¶a ***magnificent*** *collection* すてきな収集品. ¶a ***motley*** *collection* of individuals hailing from every part of the country この国の各地からやってきた色とりどりの人たち.

Q enrich one's ***private*** *collection* 個人の収集をふやす. ¶a ***rich*** *collection* 豊富な収集. 【類】The Avery Library of Columbia University is the ***richest*** *collection* in the United States of works on architecture and the allied arts. ¶***scientific*** *collections* 科学的収集. ¶a ***small*** *collection* わずかな収集. ¶a ***unique*** *collection* of books 他に比類なき集書. ¶a ***valuable*** *collection* of literature on geology 地質学に関する貴重な文献の収集. ¶a ***vast*** *collection* of poems 一大詩集. ¶a ***well-selected*** *collection* 精選した収集. ¶a ***wonderful*** *collection* 驚くべき収集. ¶his ***world-famous*** *collection* 彼の世界的に有名な収集.

Q² indigenous ***food*** *collections* and imports 国産食糧の供出と輸入. ¶***garbage*** *collection* ちゅう芥のかき集め. ¶These are some of the valuable specimens that have been separated from the ***parent*** *collection.* これらは始めの収集家の手を離れた珍品の二三である. ¶***Quota*** *collections* improved vastly. 割当の供出が非常によくなった. 【類】***rice quota*** *collection* ‖ a ***scratch*** *collection* of western paintings 洋画のかき集め. ¶make a ***Shakespeare*** *collection* シェークスピアに関する収集をやる.

P It is ***in*** the writer's *collection.* それはこの文の筆者の収集中にある. ¶from a rare print ***in*** the *collection* of Mr. M M 氏珍蔵の版画から. ¶one of the great prizes ***of*** the *collection* その収集中の珍品の一つ ‖ the size ***of*** a *collection* ある収集の数量 ‖ the pick ***of*** the *collection* 収集中の逸品.

P² a *collection* ***of*** antiques (paintings, works of art) 古物(など)の収集. 【類】a *collection* ***of*** archives (公文書) ‖ a *collection* ***of*** objects illustrating the folklore of Mexico メキシコの民俗に関する参考品の収集.

(2) 集金, 寄付金; 徴収.

V ***make*** a *collection* among passengers 旅客の間に寄付金を募る ‖ ***make*** *collections* in order to defray the cost of ... ...の費用を支払うために義えん金を募る ‖ A *collection* will be ***made*** for the fund. その資金のために寄付金が募集されるであろう. ¶***organize*** the *collection* of funds for the British sufferers by the Transvaal War トランスバール戦争のために英国避難民を助ける目的で資金募集をやる. ¶***start*** a *collection* 収集を始める. ¶At the end of the concert a *collection* was ***taken,*** the proceeds being given to various charities. 音楽会の終りに募金があってその上り高は各種慈善事業に寄付された. ¶***take up*** a *collection* in aid of Red Cross hospitals 赤十字病院援助の寄付金を募る.

Q take a ***private*** *collection* おぼしめしをもらう(見世物師などが見物人から金を集める).

P² *collection* ***of*** fines and penalties 罰金および過料の徴収 ‖ the *collection* ***of*** taxes 税の徴収.

collector, *n.* 収集家; 集金人; 収電器.

Q an ***antique*** *collector* 骨とう収集家. ¶an ***ardent*** *collector* of literary document 文学関係文書の熱心な収集家. ¶***bogus*** *collectors* いんちき寄付募集員. ¶a ***botanical*** *collector* 植物採集家. ¶a ***humble*** *collector* 小収集家. ¶an ***intelligent*** *collector* そう明な収集家.

Q² an ***art*** *collector* 美術品収集家. ¶a ***bill*** *collector* 集金人. ¶an ***expert*** *collector* 集収のくろうと. ¶a ***Hearn*** *collector* ラフカディオ・ハーン関係品の収集家. ¶a ***pantograph current*** *collector* パンタグラフ (収電器). ¶a ***rare-book*** *collector* 稀覯(きこう)書収集家. ¶a ***ticket*** *collector* 集札係.

P² a *collector* ***for*** a company ある会社の集金人. ¶a *collector* ***of*** curios 骨とう品の収集家.

college, *n.* 大学; 協会.

V Thousands of farm boys and girls in every State of the Union are today ***attending*** *college* to fit themselves for better and fuller lives as farmers and farm women. 米国のどの州でも今日何千という農場の青年男女が将来農夫・農婦として一層りっぱな充実した生活を送るための準備として大学に通っている. ¶***enter*** a *college* at 18 十八歳で大学に入る. ¶***leave*** *college* 大学を出る. ¶***pass through*** a *college* 大学を卒業する. ¶***quit*** *college* 大学を去る.

Q the ***Agricultural*** *College* at Komaba 駒場の農科大学. ¶his ***beloved*** and ***venerated*** *college* 彼の敬愛する大学. ¶a ***junior*** *college* 短期大学. ¶a ***medical*** *college* 医科大学. ¶a ***naval*** *college* 海軍大学. ¶a ***women's*** *college* 女子大学.

Q² an ***all-girl*** *college* [男女共学でない]女子大学. ¶The ***City College*** of New York ニューヨーク市立大学. ¶a ***liberal arts*** *college* 文科大学. ¶***New York University Medical*** *College* ニューヨーク大学医学部. ¶a ***teachers*** *college* 師範大学, 師範学部. ¶a ***training*** *college* 《英》教員養成所, 師範大学 ‖ a domestic subjects ***training*** *college* 家政大学. ¶a ***university*** *college* 大学の分科(学部).

P ***after*** *college* 大学卒業後. ¶a student ***at*** *college*＝a college student 大学生 ‖ a freshman ***at*** *college* 大学の一年生 ‖ They were classmates ***at*** *college.* 彼らは大学では同級生であった. ‖ a fresh term ***at*** *college* 大学の新学期. 【類】when ***at*** *college* / He neglected his study ***at*** *college,* and in after life always regretted it. / He was educated ***at*** [a] *college.* ¶He is ***in*** *college.* 彼は大学在学中だ. 【類】a professor ***in*** a French *college* / since I was ***in*** *college.* ¶He has been thirty years ***out of*** *college.* 彼は大学を出てから三十年になる. ‖ He is ***out of*** (＝***through***) *college.* 彼は大学を出た. ¶go ***through*** *college* 大学をやり通す. ¶Every man should go ***to*** *college* to find out how little college-men really know. 大学生の知識が実際いかに貧弱かは大学に入るとよく分る.

P² a *college* ***of*** agriculture (music) 農業(など)大学 ‖ the *College* ***of*** Engineering of Tokyo University 東京大学工学部.

collide, *v.* 衝突する.

P The boat *collided* ***against*** a rock. ボートが岩に衝突した. ¶*collide* ***with*** an iceberg 氷山と衝突する. 【類】The steamer *collided* ***with*** a sailing vessel (帆船).

collie, *n.* コリー(犬).

Q² a giant ***auburn-and-snow*** *collie* 雪白に赤かっ色のまだらのあるコリー種の大犬.

collision, *n.* 衝突.

V ***avoid*** a *collision* with ... ...との衝突を避ける. ¶***ward off*** a *collision* with ... ...との衝突を避ける.

V² A sanguinary *collision* ***took place*** between the students and the police. 学生と警官との間に流血的衝突が起った.

Q a ***head-on*** *collision* between freight and passenger trains 貨物列車と旅客列車とが正面衝突. ¶It brought him into ***immediate*** *collision* with the enemy. それで彼はたちまち敵と衝突した.

Q² a ***railway*** *collision* on the Tokaido line 東海道線の列車衝突. ¶a ***train-bus*** *collision* 列車とバスの衝突.

P has been ***in*** *collision* and foundered 衝突して浸水沈没した. ‖ The ship sank after being ***in*** a *collision.* 船は衝突後沈没した. 【類】A great liner with 600 souls on board was reported to have been ***in*** *collision* and to have gone down rapidly. ‖ the ship was ***in*** *collision* with ... その船は...と衝突した. ¶The two trains came ***into*** *collision.* 列車と列車が衝突した. ¶the ship sank ***through*** a *collision* with ... その船は...との衝突のために沈没した.

P² a *collision* ***against*** ... ...との衝突. ¶a *collision* ***of*** (＝***between***) two cars (trains) 車(など)の衝突 ‖ a *collision* ***of*** sentiments 感情の衝突 ‖ a *collision* ***of*** one object ***with*** another 二物の衝突.

collocation, *n.* 排列.

Q *non-normal collocation* of words 語の異例の排列.

colloquialism, *n.* 口語体.

Q *American* slang and *colloquialism* アメリカ語法の俗語と口語. ¶"No more than I can help" is a *favorite colloquialism.*「まずまずというところ」はよく会話に使われる句である.

collusion, *n.* なれあい, 共謀.

Q in *dishonest collusion* with ... ...とぐるになって.

P act *in collusion* with ... ...としめし合わせて行動する.

P² *collusion between* the police and the criminal=*collusion of* the police *with* the criminal 警官たちと罪人とのなれあい ‖ *collusion between* the seeming opponents 敵対すると見える二人の間の八百長.

colon, *n.* 〖解〗結腸.

V *flush* the *colon* 結腸を洗う.

colonization, *n.* 植民.

P² the *colonization by* Great Britain of North America, Australia, and South Africa 北米・豪州および南アフリカにおける英国の植民.

colonize, *v.* 植民する, 移住させる.

P The Hebrides were *colonized from* Norway in the 9th century. ヘブリディーズ群島民は九世紀にノルウェーから移住したものだ.

colony, *n.* 植民地; 〖生態〗群生, 群落.

V *cede* a *colony* to ... 一植民地を...に割譲する. ¶*develop colony* 植民地を開発する. ¶*establish* (=*settle*) a *colony* 植民地を樹立する. ¶*found* a *colony* 植民地を建設する. ¶*plant* a *colony* in ... ...に植民地を設ける ‖ The *colonies planted* by England. 英国が設けた植民地. ¶*rear colonies* 植民地を造る. ¶*send out* a *colony* to ... ...へ移民を送る.

Q *mandated colonies* 委任統治植民地. ¶a *self-governing colony* (カナダなどの)自治領植民地. ¶*self-sustaining colony* 自立の植民地.

Q² Hollywood, the *cinema colony*. 映画の都ホリウッド. ¶a *Crown Colony* 英領植民地. ¶a *bee colony* みつばちの群生. ¶a *leper colony* らい患者収容所. ¶a *nudist colony* 裸体主義者の村. ¶a *summer colony* 避暑に集った人の集団.

P A man going out *to* the *colonies* must be prepared to work very hard for his living. 植民地に出かせぎに行く者は生活のため大いに骨を折る覚悟でなくてはならない.

P² a *colony of* ants (plants) あり(など)の群生 ‖ a *colony of* artists 画家の集団住宅.

colo[u]r, *n.* (**1**) 色, 色彩; 絵具; 仮面, 風(ふう).

V Gaily-dressed ladies *added color* and variety to the scene. 盛装した婦人がその場の光景に色彩と変化を添えた. ¶Leaves *change color* in autumn. 木の葉は秋色が変る. ‖ *change color* at ... ...を見て顔色を変える. ¶The sky *assumed* pink *color*. 空が桃色をおびた. 【類】The forests were *changing color*. ¶The high tensile strength of silk and the permanence of *colors dyed* upon it are strong points in favor of its use for wear and ornament. 絹織物は非常に耐伸力を有しそれを染めた色彩が永久性を持っているので服装や装飾に適する. ¶*fix* the *colors* 色止めをする. ¶*give color* to this view この見解に強味を添える ‖ *give* some *color* to the story その話を潤色(して本当らしく)する ‖ Some poet has said that he would *have* no *color* in chrysanthemums but yellow and white. ある歌人が菊は黄と白以外の色はなくもがなと言った. ¶*heighten* (*dull*) *color* 色彩を強(弱)くする. ¶*lend color* to the supposition その想像に確実性を添える. ‖ Some *color* is *lent* to the report that ... ...という報告に色つやをつける. ‖ *lend color* to the theory held by some scientists that ... ある科学者たちが持っていた...という説を有力ならしめる. 【類】*lend* further *color* to the idea that ... ‖ *lose color* 青ざめる. ¶*make color* run 色を落す. ¶*match* the *color* of the cloth 織物の色をそろえる. ¶*obtain* local *color* by ... ...によって地方色を出す. ¶Partisan newspapers *put* a *color* on the events they report. 政党新聞はその報道する事件に勝手な色彩をつける. ¶*put in colors* to outline pictures デッサンに着色する. ¶*restore* the *color* of gray hairs in one's head 頭に生えた白髪を黒くする. ¶The light is said to *show color* almost as well as daylight. その光は日光とほとんど変らないそうだ. ¶This carpet does not *suit* the *color* of the wall paper. このじゅうたんは壁紙の色と調和しない. ¶*take* the *color* of the night 墨染になる. ¶The cloth can *take* no other *color*. その地は他の色には染められない. ¶Maple-leaves *take on* a magnificent red *color* before falling in autumn. かえでの葉は秋の落葉前真紅に色づく.

V² The *color becomes* you. その色は君に似合う. ¶The *color comes off*. その色ははげる. ¶The *color* will not *come out* in the wash. 洗たくしても色は落ちない. ¶Her *color came* and *went* as she listened. 聞き入るうちに彼女の顔色は赤くなったり青くなったりした. ¶Is this *color fade-proof*? この色はさめないか. ¶Those *colors* do not *harmonize*. その色合は調和しません. ¶Her *color heightened* in her cheeks as she answered "Yes."「そうです」と答えた彼女のほおは赤くなった. ¶*Color left* his face. 顔色が青ざめた. ¶His *color rose*. 彼は顔を赤くした. ¶The *colors* don't *run* (=fade). 色はさめません. 【類】The *colors run* in the wash or *fade* when exposed to the sun. ¶This *colour* will *stand*. この色はもつ. ¶I fear the *color* will not *wash*. この色は洗たくがきゝそうもない.

Q of *another color* 異った性格の. ¶*artists' colors* 図画用絵具. ¶in *blazing color* 燃えるような色で. ¶pictures with *bright colors* さえた色の絵. ¶This fall the maples are turning such *brilliant colors*. この秋の紅葉はすてきにいゝ色がついた. ¶afford a *certain color* of justification to ... 幾分...の弁護に強味を与える. ¶U.S. *certified color* アメリカの食用染料. ¶depict the outlook in very *dark colors* 局面に対してきわめて悲観的な書き方をする ‖ *dark brown color* 濃かっ色. ¶be of a *deep red color* 濃紅色だ. ¶be shown by means of *different colors* 様々な色を使って示されている. ¶a *durable color* 持ちのいゝ色. ¶schools that are sailing under *false colors*. 羊頭を掲げて狗肉(くにく)を売る学校. ¶a *fashionable color* 流行色. ¶The cloth has *fast colors*. その生地の色は変らない. ¶his *favorite color* 彼の好みの色. ¶illustrations in *full color* 極彩色のさし絵. 【類】be reproduced (複製する) in *full color*. ¶*gay colors* はでな色. ¶paint its possibilities in *glowing colors* その将来性をきわめて有望と説く. ¶It has a *good* (=*high*) *color*. 色彩が強い. ¶like *heavy, bright* and *deep colors* 強いはっきりしたこい色を好む. ¶*heavy, oppressive color* しつこい色. ¶I don't like that *hectic color* she always has. あの女が始終赤い顔をしているのが(胸の病気を思わせて)いやだ. ¶I saw the *hot color* surge into her beautiful face. 彼女の美しい顔の紅潮するのが目についた. ¶prefer *light* and *delicate colors* 薄いやわらかな色を好む. ¶*literary color* 文学的色彩. ¶travel in search of "*local color*" for one's novel 小説の地方色のある材料を探しに旅行する ‖ obtain *local color* by dialect 方言で地方色を出す. ¶a *loud color* はでな(けばけばしい)色 ‖ love *loud, glaring, contrasting colors* 強いぎらぎらした目立つ色を好む. ¶*loose color* 変色しやすい色. ¶the *losing* (*winning*) *color* [競技] 負けた(勝った)組. ¶*low color* 調子の弱い色. ¶*lugubrious color* 憂色. ¶Poppies are of *many colors*. けしの花の色は様々だ. ¶No picture can reproduce the *marvellous color* of the sea. どんな絵も海の驚歎すべき色彩は出せない. ¶a temple lovely in the *mellow color* of centuries 幾百年の古色を帯びて美しい寺. ¶a photograph (illustrations, motion pictures) in *natural colors* 天然色写真(など). ¶*noisy colors* けばけばしい色. ¶afterward painted in *on-glaze colors* [陶磁器など] 後で上絵を描いた. ¶Green is the *predominant color*. 緑が圧倒的の(最も著しく目立つ)色だ. ¶the most *prevalent colors* in dress 最も流行するきものの色. ¶painted in the *primary colors* 原色で描いた. ¶I endeavoured to draw from him some hints as to the *probable color* of the answer I should receive. どんな風の返事があるか何か手掛りを彼から得ようと努めた. ¶a *quiet* (*somber, flat*) *color* 落着いた(くすんだ, 単調な)色. ¶The custom has a *religious color*. その風俗には宗教的色彩がある. ¶*smoky color* すすけた色. ¶a *subdued color* 渋い色. ¶be of a *tawny color* きつね色をしている. ¶He will come out in his *true color* shortly. 彼は間もなく本性をあらわすだろう. ‖ see a thing in its *true color* 物の真相をみる. ¶depict in *vivid colors* the scenes and manners of ... ...の風物を生き生きした色彩で描写する. ¶give a *wrong color* to facts 事実を曲解させるようにする.

Q² a *bronze color* 青銅色 ‖ His features are handsome but manly and of a ruddy *bronze color* acquired at sea.

彼の顔だちは美しいが男らしく潮風に吹かれて赤銅色をしている. ¶a ***cherry color*** 桜色. ¶***japan*** (=***coach***) ***colors*** 車体塗装用塗料. ¶as bright as ***rainbow colors*** にじの色のように明るく. ¶sketches in ***water colors*** 水彩絵具で描いたスケッチ.

P pictures ***in colors*** 色彩画 ‖ a moving picture ***in colors*** 色彩映画 ‖ a postcard ***in colors*** 色彩絵はがき ‖ photography ***in colors*** 色彩写真術 ‖ painted ***in colors*** 彩色した.【類】attractively printed ***in colors*** / bright ***in color*** ‖ They vary ***in color***. それらは多種多様の色をしている. ‖ engravings of great technical beauty ***in colors*** 優れた着色技術の美を発揮した版画 ‖ ***in*** (=***with***) all the ***colors*** of the rainbow にじ色全部で.【類】***in*** half the ***colors*** of the rainbow. ¶***of*** a purple ***color*** 紫色の ‖ There are countless shades ***of color***. 色の種類は限りがない. ¶I had a short time of feeling ***off color***. ちょっとの間からだの具合が悪かった. ¶***under*** [the] ***color*** of inquiring for something 何かさがしている振りをして ‖ ***under*** the ***color*** of religion 宗教の仮面をかぶって.【類】He cheated me ***under color*** of friendship. ¶Answer me directly ***without color***, whether it be so or not. そうかそうでないかありのまゝに速答しなさい.

P² the ***color of*** night ぬばたまのやみ夜 ‖ some ***color of*** truth いく分の真実味.

(**2**) [主に *pl.*] 旗, 軍旗.

V The political adventurer ***changed*** his ***colors*** 政治屋が変節をした. ¶***desert*** the (=one's) ***colors*** 脱営する. ¶***dip*** their ***colors*** and fire a salute of twenty-one guns 軍艦旗を降ろして二十一発の皇礼砲を発射する. ¶***haul down*** (=***lower***) the ***colors*** 旗を降ろす. ¶***join*** the ***colors*** 入隊する.【類】leave their homes to ***join*** the ***colors***. ¶***present*** new ***colors*** to a regiment 連隊へ新しい軍旗を下賜せられる. ¶***raise colors*** 軍旗を揚げる. ¶***salute*** the ***colors*** 軍旗に敬礼する. ¶Rear-Admiral Nebogatoff ***struck*** his ***colors*** and surrendered with 3,000 of his men as prisoners of war. ネボガトフ少将は旗を巻いて降参し部下三千の士卒とともに捕虜となった. ¶***unfurl*** the American ***colors*** on the battlefield 戦場に米国の軍旗を翻す(米国軍隊が戦争に参加する).

Q The enemy marched under ***false colors***. 敵は偽旗を掲げて進軍した. ‖ They are fighting under ***false colors***. 彼らは主義を偽って闘争をやっている. ¶with ***flying colors*** 旗を翻して; 意気揚々と ‖ He came off with ***flying colors***. 大手を振って及第した.【類】He took a diplomatic examination and passed with ***flying colors***. ¶hoist ***national colors*** 国旗をかかげる. ¶***regimental colors*** 連隊旗.

Q² ***battle colors*** 戦闘旗.

P ***at*** morning ***colors*** 軍艦旗掲揚のとき ‖ ***at*** evening ***colors*** 軍艦旗降下のとき. ¶a ship ***under*** British ***colors*** 英国国旗をかかげた船. ¶serve ***with*** the ***colors*** 現役を勤める.【類】seven years ***with*** the ***colors*** and five in the reserve (予備役) / They have already passed two years ***with*** the ***colors***. ‖ The entrance was decorated ***with*** British ***colors***. 入口は英国の国旗で飾られていた.

colo[u]r, *v.* 彩色する.

M a yolk too ***highly colored*** 色の濃すぎる卵黄. ¶a conversation ***pleasantly colored*** with wit and anecdote 機知や珍談をうまく織込んだ会話. ¶***color prodigiously*** ごてごて着色する. ¶***color*** a meerschaum ***properly*** 海泡石のパイプにきれいに着色する. ¶a ***violently colored*** shirt どぎつい色のシャツ.

M² She ***colors up*** when any one addresses her. 彼女はだれにでも話しかけられると顔を赤くする.

P The facts were ***colored by*** his prejudices. 事実は彼の偏見のためにゆがめられていた. ¶***colored in*** different tints 様々に着色した.

colo[u]ring, *n.* 着色, 彩色; 特色.

V ***give coloring*** to ... ...に色彩を施す ‖ Darwinism and all that it stood for ***gave*** a new ***coloring*** to Continental thought. 進化論およびその主張は欧州の思想に新生面を開いた.

Q the ***autumnal colorings*** of the maples and other trees かえでなどいろいろの樹木の秋色. ¶The picture has too much ***dead coloring***. その絵はあまりに沈んだ色を使っている. ¶***personal coloring*** 個人の特色. ¶a society destitute of any ***political coloring*** 何ら政治的色彩を帯びない協会. ¶***rich coloring*** 極彩色. ¶She is fresh-looking, with a ***vivid, youthful coloring***. 彼女は生々した若々しい血色をしていて水々しい.

colt, *n.* 若馬.

Q² a ***baby colt*** 小馬.

column, *n.* 〘新聞〙欄; 柱; 縦隊.

V ***add*** a ***column*** of figures 数字を寄せ(加算す)る. ¶We cannot ***allow*** our ***columns*** to become the arena of its discussion. 本紙をその問題討議のために提供することはできない. ¶***crowd*** the ***columns*** of the newspapers 新聞の紙面をにぎわす.【類】Announcements of new publications ***crowd*** the advertising ***columns*** (広告欄). ¶The newspaper ***devotes*** its ***columns*** to the discussion of the problem. その新聞は紙面をその問題の討議にささげている. ¶***emit*** a ***column*** of smoke 煙を吹上げる. ¶The story ***fills up*** a ***column*** of a newspaper. その記事は新聞の一欄を埋めている. ¶***make*** a ***column*** and a half out of it その記事で一欄半を埋める. ¶***open*** its ***columns*** to correspondents to discuss the question 投書家のために紙面を開放してその問題を討議させる.【類】***open*** its ***columns*** to a free and impartial discussion (自由公平な論議). ¶The paper ***publishes*** a daily ***column*** of English. その新聞は毎日英文欄を出す. ¶The geyser ***throws*** a ***column*** of boiling water and spray nearly a hundred feet into the air. その間欠泉は熱湯と湯煙を空中約百フィートの高さに吹上げる. ¶***use*** its ***columns*** for the utterance of their views on ... ...に関する彼らの意見を発表せんがためその欄を用いる.

Q ***classified columns*** 〘新聞〙雑事欄(求人・求職など). ¶the ***enquiry column*** of a journal 新聞の案内欄. ¶the ***fifth column*** 第五列(軍事スパイ団). ¶***matrimonial columns*** 結婚広告欄. ¶a ***mobile column*** 機動部隊. ¶arranged in ***parallel columns*** [英文和文などを] 対照するように列べて. ¶the ***personal column*** 〘新聞〙人事欄. ¶throw up a ***steamy column*** 蒸気の柱を吹き上げる. ¶pages in ***triple columns*** 三段組のページ.

Q² the ***agony column*** [新聞の]人事広告欄(尋ね人などの). ¶***correspondence columns*** of a newspaper 新聞の投書欄. ¶***ice columns*** 霜柱. ¶***society columns*** [新聞の]社交界欄. ¶***sports columns*** スポーツ欄. ¶the "***wants***" ***columns*** 求人求職欄. ¶a ***water column*** 水柱.

P We republish a useful table ***from*** the ***columns*** of ... 有益な表を一つ...の紙面から転載する. ¶***in*** a ***column*** headed ... ...という見出しの欄に ‖ lately mentioned ***in*** our ***columns*** 本紙で最近言及した.【類】follow from day to day the developments in China and Manchuria ***in*** the ***columns*** of the press / The article totally unfit to appear ***in*** journalistic ***columns***. ‖ march ***in column*** of fours 四列縦隊で行進する. ¶***through*** the ***columns*** of the "New York Tribune"「ニューヨーク・トリビューン」紙を通じて.【類】inform the public ***through*** your ***columns*** (貴紙) that ...

P² a ***column of*** smoke (steam, water) 煙柱(など).

columnist, *n.* 〘新聞〙特別寄稿家, [特別欄]担当記者.

Q² The unusual incident provided a field day for ***gossip columnists*** その珍しい事件のために雑報記者は大多忙であった. ¶a ***newspaper columnist*** 新聞特約寄稿家. ¶a ***sports*** (***health***) ***columnist*** 運動(保健)欄担当記者.

comb, *n.* くし; 《米》波がしら.

Q a ***jeweled comb*** 宝石をちりばめたくし.

P² the ***comb*** (=crest) ***of*** a wave 波がしら.

comb, *v.* くしけずる, くしをかける.

M ***comb out*** her long black tresses 長い黒髪をくしけずる.

M² ***comb down*** くしでなでつける. ¶***comb off*** [頭髪からごみなどを]すいてとる.

combat, *n.* 格闘, 戦闘.

V a ***combat fought*** breast to breast 接戦.

Q face each other in ***mortal combat*** 命のやり取りをする. ¶a ***personal combat*** 格闘. ¶Goliath was slain by David in a ***single combat***. ゴリアテは一騎打でダビデに殺された.

M² a ***kite combat*** たこ合戦.

P death and life ***in combat*** 生死の瀬戸際.

P² a ***combat between*** a lion and a tiger ライオンととらの戦. ¶he was worsted in his ***combat with*** ... 彼は...との戦に負けた ‖ a ***combat with*** difficulties (wind and waves, an enemy) 困難(など)との戦.

combat, *v.* 戦う, 争う.

P ***combat for*** a noble cause (freedom of speech) りっぱな目的(など)のために戦う. ¶***combat with*** a person ***for*** one's right 自己の権利のために人と争う.

combination, *n.* 組合わせ, 結合, 兼備; 化合; 錠の組合わせ符号.

V *express* a *combination* of ideas by a single word, which otherwise require a circumlocution 長々と遠回しにいわねばならない一連の観念をただの一語で言い表わす. ¶*use* a certain *combination* to open a safe 金庫を開くために一定の組合わせ符号を用いる.

Q a *golden combination* of qualities—forbearance, gentleness, fearlessness りっぱな資質の兼備—すなわち忍耐・温厚・大胆. ¶a *happy combination* of good lucks 重なる幸運 ‖ a *happy combination* of lines and form and proportion 線と形と釣合との巧みな調和. ¶by a *happy combination* of circumstances 回り合わせがよく. ¶*idiomatic combinations* of the English language 英語の慣用句. ¶a scene which is an *impressive combination* of order and disorder 整とんと乱雑を巧みに結び付けている場面. ¶The information found in the newspaper is expressed in a *motley combination* of colloquial, literary, technical, and scientific words. 新聞の報道は慣用語・文語・術語および科学的語句をごったまぜにした文でなされる. ¶a *mysterious combination* of the sublime and the ridiculous 尊厳とこっけいとの不可思議な結合. ¶*new combinations* of old material 古い材料の新しい組合わせ. ¶a *pleasant combination* 気持のよい組合わせ. ¶a *rare combination* of gifts 天才のまれな結合.【類】a *rare combination* of talent and industry. ¶by a *strange combination* of circumstances どうした風の吹き回しか.

Q² *color combinations* 色の配合.

P Most private institutions of higher education are supported *by* a *combination* of income from endowments and fees from students. 大ていの高等の私立学校は寄付金からの収入と学生の月謝と両方で維持している. ¶*due to* a *combination* of causes 色々な原因のために. ¶carry on the work *in combination* with ... ...と共同で経営する.

P² a *combination of* elements *into* a compound 一つの化合物をなす種々の元素の結合. ¶a *combination of* carbon *with* a metal 金属と炭素の化合.

combine, *n.* 《米》合同; 《米》[農具]コンバイン.

Q² a *distributing combine* 配給合同. ¶a *producing combine* 生産合同.

Q They employ a *great combine* to cut, thresh and clean the grain while moving over the field. 彼らは畑を運転しながら穀物を刈ったり脱穀したり, 片づけたりする大型コンバイン(複式収穫機を)使用する.

combine, *v.* 結合する, 連結する; 化合させる.

M envy the somnambulist who can so *happily combine* sleep and exercise 睡眠と運動をいかにも都合よく結び合わすことのできる夢遊病者の身分をうらやむ. ¶*combine well* with ... ...とよく結び付く(語ろがよい).

P *combine in* one book ... 一冊の本にまとめる ‖ The acid and alkali are *combined in* a salt. 酸とアルカリは化合して塩(えん)となる. ¶*combine* the factions *into* a party 分派を合同して一党とする. ¶go to ... for pleasure *combined with* business 用事を兼ねて遊びに行く ‖ *combined with* the fact that ... ...にかてて加えて. ¶a building which *combines* great strength *with* elegance of appearance 堅固と優美とを兼備する建物 ‖ strength *combined with* lightness [建築材料など]軽くて強いこと. 【類】films which best *combine* education *with* recreation / *combine* completeness *with* brevity / *combine* conservatism *with* progressiveness /*combine* clearness *with* conciseness / simplicity *combined with* accuracy (正確) / *combine* artistic distinction *with* practical utility ‖ contrive so as to *combine* the maximum of production *with* the minimum of exertion 最小限度の労力をもって最大限度の生産をなすように工夫する ‖ Japan *combines* Oriental romance *with* Occidental comforts. 日本は東洋的幻想と西洋の文化的快適とを兼備している. ‖ *combine* theory *with* practice 理論と実際とを調和させる ‖ *combine* on a large scale the destruction of dust and refuse *with* the production of electricity ごみの焼却に依る電力獲得を大規模にやる ‖ In that hotel we have comfort and luxury *combined with* a moderate tariff. あのホテルでは格好な料金で安楽とぜいたくが二つながら得られる. 【類】went there on business *combined with* pleasure. ‖ The Youth's Companion (established in 1827) *combined with* The American Boys. (一八二七年創刊の)「青年の友」は「アメリカ少年」と合併した. ‖ Hydrogen *combines with* oxygen to form water. 水素は酸素と化合して水となる. ‖ The acid *combines with* the alkali. 酸はアルカリと化合する.

O The charming scenery and the hot spring baths *combine* to make the traveler's stay there most enjoyable. 美しい景色と温泉とが相まって旅人の滞在をきわめて愉快なものにする. ‖ one of the many characteristics that *combine* to make up what it is そのもの本来の形を作るためにいろいろな役立つ特徴の一つ.

combing, *n.* [髪を]すくこと.

Q² *hair combings* 髪すき.

combustion, *n.* 燃焼.

V *accelerate* (=*quicken*) *combustion* 燃焼を促進する. ¶*attain* a complete *combustion* 完全に燃焼する. ¶drugs, oil, and grease liable to *cause combustion* or ignition 発火または引火のおそれある薬品油脂類.

Q *complete combustion* 完全燃焼. ¶*spontaneous combustion* 自然燃焼.

P reduce it to ashes *by combustion* それを燃やして灰にする.

come, *v.* 来る, 至る; 起る; なる; 発芽する.

M *come aboard* 船に乗込む. ¶The food was poor; but to a hungry man nothing *comes amiss.* 食物は貧弱であったがひもじい者にはまずい物がない. ‖ it may not *come amiss* for ... ...に取っては悪いことはなかろう. ¶*come ashore* 上陸する. ¶I *came away* sadly. 私はつらい思いで別れた. ‖ The branch *came away.* 枝が折れた. ‖ The wheat is *coming away* very well. 小麦の発育は上々だ. ¶when I *come back* for the holiday 休暇で帰るとき ‖ *come back* to one's work [ストの後など]自分の仕事にもどる. 【類】He *came back* to Japan. / *come back* to his old ways (またもとの癖に) / *come back* from abroad / *come back* to one's former position ‖ *coming back* to the subject of ... ...の本題に戻るが ‖ *come back* to power 再び政権を握る ‖ *come back* from the grave 生き返る ‖ if he were to *come back* to life 彼が蘇生するとすれば ‖ The very names are *coming back* to him. その人たちの名前がありありと思出されてくる. ‖ The party has *come back* into power. その政党は再び政権を握った. ‖ *come back* empty-handed 空手で戻る. ¶Nearly everything that we eat or wear *comes directly* or *indirectly* from the soil. われわれが食ったり着たりする物は殆どすべて直接間接に土から生じる. ¶Your esteemed favor has *duly come* to hand. 貴翰正に落手致しました. ¶It is very kind of you to *come* so *far* out of your way. 遠路わざわざお出でくださって誠に有難う存じます. ¶This *comes first.* これが先決問題だ. ‖ *First come,* first served. 早い者勝ち. ¶Black smoke *came forth* at every crevice. 黒煙がすべての割目からふき出した. ‖ The leaves and blooms *come forth* upon the tree. 木々に葉や花が見えて来る. ¶*come forward* when named 名前を呼ばれて進み出る. ¶quickly *come forward* in life ずんずん出世する ‖ Buyers *come forward* freely. 買手がどんどん出てくる. 【類】Supplies will *come forward* rapidly. / Orders (goods) are *coming forward* very scarcely. ¶*gradually come* to see that ... だんだん...が分るようになる. ¶*Here comes* Prof. J. J 教授がやって来る. ‖ Who is *coming here* tonight? 今夜だれが来るか. ¶*come home* late 遅く帰宅する ‖ *come home* to roost ねぐらに帰る; むくいが来る ‖ This *comes* closer and closer *home* to me each year. このことが私に年ごとにはっきりと解って来る. ¶*come honestly* by a fortune 正直にかせいで身代をつくる. ¶*How* did you *come* to Tokyo? どうやって(交通機関)東京へ来たか. ‖ *How came* you to know him? どうして彼を知るようになったのか. ‖ *How come?*=How did it come out? 《口語》どうなったか. 【類】*How comes* it that you know him? / *How came* you to be so intimate with him? ¶The authorities *came immediately* to the spot. 係りの役人が直ちに現場にきた. ¶I am *just coming.* 今行きます (youに対して). ☞Yes, I'm *coming* はいただ今. ¶You are very *late coming* this evening. 今夜はおそいね. ‖ *come late* to work (school, class) 仕事(学校, 教室)に来るのがおそい. ¶*come more* and *more* into publicity 益々世間から知られるようになる. ¶Talking does not *come naturally* to a man. 談話は人に生れついたものではない. ¶*come near* to being run over すんでの事でひかれるところだった ‖ I *came* very *near* to writing to his parents. よっぽど親の所へ知らせてやろうかと思った.

【類】 I *came* very ***near*** to giving it up ‖ Xmas is *coming* ***nearer*** to us. クリスマスが近づく. ¶Who *comes* ***next***? 次にだれが来るか. 【類】 Spring *comes* ***next*** to winter. ¶The magazine *comes* ***out*** once a week. その雑誌は毎週一回出る. 【類】 The magazine has not yet *come* ***out.*** ‖ *come* ***out*** in the papers 新聞に出る. 【類】 What paper did it *come* ***out*** in? / The rain stopped and the sun *came* ***out.*** / The moon *came* ***out*** suddenly from behind the clouds. / The cherryblossoms *come* ***out*** early in April. ‖ The sweat *came* ***out*** on his forehead. 額に汗がにじんだ. ‖ *come* ***out*** in relief 浮彫になって(くっきり)出る ‖ Won't you *come* ***out*** for a game of billiards this evening? 今晩玉突にお出かけになりませんか. ‖ The stain will not *come* ***out.*** そのしみは抜けない ‖ The word doesn't *come* ***out*** clear. [タイプや印刷で]その語ははっきり出ない. 【類】 This photograph does not *come* ***out*** clear. ‖ The color has *come* ***out*** well. 色がよく出た. ‖ You *come* ***out*** well in this photo. 君はこの写真によくとれている. ‖ *come* ***out*** top of his form 級の首席になる. 【類】 That is the student who *came* ***out*** first in the examination. ‖ Well, how did it *come* ***out***? そこで(事件・ゲームなど)どうなったか. ‖ *come* ***out*** all right in the end 末は上首尾に行く ‖ Everything *came* ***out*** all right with him. 彼は万事うまく行った. 【類】 Things are *coming* ***out*** fairly well. / The firm was in difficulties some time back and *came* ***out*** very well (badly). ‖ then it *came* ***out*** that ... そこで…ということがわかった ‖ *come* [***out***] true (false) 真実(虚偽)という事が判明する ‖ I tried to write "swing," but it *came* ***out*** in type "sewing." "swing" と書いたつもりだったが, タイプは "sewing" となっていた. ‖ he *came* ***out*** in print and said a good word for ... 彼は出版物で…をほめた. ‖ Words *come* ***out*** quite smoothly. 言葉がすらすら出る. ‖ It will *come* ***out*** in two volumes. 二巻本にして発行される. ‖ *come* ***out*** into the field 出陣する ‖ *come* ***out*** at the little end of the horn 不首尾に終る; 大失敗する ‖ It *came* ***out*** just as I had expected. 私が予期した通りになった. ‖ *come* ***out*** on strike ストで休む. ¶I will *come* very ***punctually.*** きっと時間通りに参ります. 【類】 *come* ***punctually*** at 6:30. ¶Mr. Withers has during the past few years *come* ***rapidly*** to the forefront as one of the finest cellists of Great Britain. ウィザーズ氏はこの数年間に英国の最も優れたチェロ弾奏者の一人としてめきめき売出した. ¶It ***rarely*** *comes* into the market. それは滅多に売物に出ない. ¶Other examples of it *comes* ***readily*** to mind. それに関する他の例がひょこひょこ思い浮ぶ. ¶We'll see what he says when he ***really*** *comes* to. [今は病気だから]元気になったら彼の言分を聞いて見よう. ¶***sheepishly*** *come* [びくびくして]小さくなって来る. ¶Misfortunes never *come* ***single.*** 不幸は重なる. ¶I ***soon*** *came* to remark (=notice) that ... やがて…に気が付いた. ¶*come* ***straight*** back home 道草を食わないで家に帰る ‖ He *comes* here ***straight*** from his university. 大学を出て直ぐここへやって来た(就職した). ¶*come* ***suddenly*** to life 突然生返る. ¶a turn *came* ***thick*** on the back of another 変化がやつぎばやに起った. ¶Snow is *coming* ***thicker.*** 雪が大降りになって来た. ¶They *came* ***together*** by twos and threes. 彼らは二三人ずつ来た. ¶The dream *came* ***true.*** 夢が本当になった. 【類】 He prophesied some things, which have since *come* ***true.*** ¶The name of ... will *come* quite ***unfamiliarly*** to English ears. ...という名は英国人には全く耳なれない. ¶***Yonder*** *comes* a man. 向うの方から人が来る.

M² so it *comes* ***about*** that ... そこで…ということになる ‖ How did it *come* ***about***? どうしてそうなったか. ‖ Do you know how the phrase *came* ***about***? その句の由来を知っていますか. 【類】 the whole situation *came* ***about*** because ... / it often *comes* ***about*** that ... ‖ What changes have *come* ***about*** in a half-century! わずか半世紀の間に随分変ったものだ. ‖ Well, then, it *came* ***about*** in this way. 実はこういう訳なんです. ¶*Come* ***along***! ついて来給え. 【類】 *Come* right ***along.*** / *Come* ***along*** with me, please. / He *came* ***along*** with some friends. ‖ Buses *came* lumbering ***along*** in strings of hundreds and thousands. 何百台何千台のバスがあとからあとからと並んでやって来た. ‖ if a burglar *comes* ***along*** もし泥棒が入ったら. ¶*come* ***around*** 回ってくる; 気がつく; 元気になる. 【類】 The leap year *comes* ***around*** once in four years. / when Xmas *comes* ***around*** / when the next day *comes* ***around*** / He got faint, but soon *came* ***around.*** ¶He happened to *come* ***by.*** 彼がたまたまやって来た. ¶The custom has *come* ***down*** to us from the past. その風俗は昔からこの国にあったものだ. 【類】 The tales had *come* ***down*** from the old heathen times. / which has *come* ***down*** to us from the past ‖ I will *come* ***down*** in the price a little. 少々お引きしましょう. / *come* ***down*** to less than 20 dollars / *come* ***down*** on the tea to ... ‖ Every hit *comes* ***down*** plump on the head of the nail. 一打ちごとにくぎの頭にかちんと当る. ‖ He *came* ***down*** in the argument. 彼は議論に負けた. ‖ The machinery will have to *come* ***down*** again to be refitted. 機械は調節のため分解しなければなるまい. ‖ *come* ***down*** in torrents [雨が]滝となって流れ落ちる ‖ The water *came* ***down*** in a flood. 水が洪水となって押寄せて来た. ‖ *come* ***down*** on a person 人を攻撃する ‖ The enemy *came* ***down*** upon a sleeping village. 敵は眠っている村を猛烈に攻撃した. ¶Go and ask him to *come* ***in.*** あの方にお入り下さいと言いなさい. ‖ *come* ***in*** at the front door 表口からはいる. 【類】 *Come* right ***in,*** and sit down. / He *came* ***in*** with a laugh (笑いながら). / What you told me *came* ***in*** at one ear and went out at the other. ‖ Tide *came* ***in.*** 潮がさして来た. ‖ *come* ***in*** first in a race 競走で第一着になる ‖ Let us wait here till the train *comes* ***in.*** 汽車が着くまでここで待ちましょう. ‖ How are arrivals *coming* ***in*** from the interior? 地方からの着荷はどんな工合ですか. ‖ Subscriptions are *coming* ***in*** quickly (slowly, fairly well). 予約申込がどんどん(ちらほら, 相当)来る. ‖ I thought that the money would *come* ***in*** handy some day when I stand more in need of it than now. その金は他日私が今より困るときに役立つだろうと思った. ‖ it *comes* ***in*** very handy in ...ing それは…するに至極便利だ ‖ That's where it *comes* ***in*** useful. それはそういう場合重宝だ. ‖ Silken garments did not *come* ***in*** till late. 絹の着物は近ごろまで用いられなかった. ‖ but here *comes* ***in*** the question of ... それで…という問題が起る ‖ the thought *came* ***in*** to his mind that ... という考えがその頭に浮んだ ‖ *come* ***in*** for a lot of competition with ... …と角逐する ‖ Accounts are *coming* ***in*** very slowly just now. 勘定の支払が目下一向はかばかしくない. ‖ He *came* ***in*** for the train. 彼はその汽車に間に合った. ‖ He *came* ***in*** for the profit from the sale. 彼はその販売による利益の分前にあずかることになった. ¶The strike *came* ***off.*** ストが実行された. 【類】 The examination *came* ***off*** yesterday. / The marriage *came* ***off*** last week. / Do you know when the University regatta's *coming* ***off***? 大学のボートレースはいつ行われるかご存知ですか. ‖ The experiment will *come* ***off*** satisfactorily. 実験はうまく行くだろう. ‖ The expected chance failed to *come* ***off.*** 期待した機会がやって来なかった. ‖ before the particular chance *comes* ***off*** そのチャンスが逃げない中に. 【類】 It *came* ***off*** one morning in the way he had imagined. ‖ The match *came* ***off*** last week. 仕合は先週催された. ‖ He *came* ***off*** with honours. 彼はりっぱにやってのけた. ‖ I was half afraid you would not *come* ***off*** roundly. 君がうまく行くか知らんと心配した. ‖ *come* ***off*** with flying colors. りっぱにやってのける. ¶*come* ***off*** victorious (a victor) 勝を占める. 【類】 I remember that I never seemed to *come* ***off*** so well as my brothers with regard to Christmas presents. ‖ We have a great many local gaieties *coming* ***off*** during the next six weeks. この六週間もり沢山の地方的な華やかな催しがある. ‖ Oh, *come* ***off***! おい, よせやい(相手が冗談など言ったとき). ‖ The weather *came* ***off*** pleasant. よい時候になった. ‖ Meat ceilings *came* ***off.*** 肉の価格制限が設けられた. ‖ On that occasion the Japanese *came* ***off*** with relatively little loss. その時日本軍は割に損害を出さずに済んだ. ‖ He *came* ***off*** (=escaped) without a scratch. 彼は少しもけがをしないで逃げた. ‖ *come* ***off*** blue (=badly). 首尾が悪い. ‖ Won't the color *come* ***off***? 色がさめないだろうか. ¶as soon as the warm weather *comes* ***on*** 陽気が暖くなって来るとじき ‖ The summer is *coming* ***on.*** 夏がやって来る. ‖ Darkness (=Night) was *coming* ***on.*** 暗くなりかかっていた. 【類】 Storm *came* ***on*** suddenly. ‖ It *came* ***on*** to blow a gale toward evening. 夕方近くあらしになった. 【類】 It has *come* ***on*** to rain hard. ‖ If it should *come* ***on*** to blow tonight we shall not be able to enter the harbor. ‖ Trial is *coming* ***on*** in a day or two. 公判が一両日に迫っている. ‖ The case *came* ***on*** for hearing before Judge ... その訴訟は...

裁判官の審理を受けることになった. ‖ The attack *came* ***on*** during sleep. 睡眠中に発病した. ‖ sale does not *come* ***on*** until ... ...までは売出さない ‖ The business *comes* ***on*** well. 商売が繁昌する. ‖ *Come* ***on***! さーこい[いどむ時など]. ¶ *Come* ***on*** in. さあお入り. ‖ *Come* ***on*** over. ここへ来たまえ. ¶ I will *come* ***over*** to see you this evening. 今晩御うかがいします. ‖ Please *come* ***over*** here and wash your hands. こちらにお出でになってお手をお洗い下さい. 【類】 He is *coming* ***over*** to see us. / When he comes back, I'll *come* ***over***. / He *came* ***over*** from America. / He wants me to *come* ***over***. ‖ *come* ***over*** on our side われわれの方に加わる. 【類】 He has *come* ***over*** for the government. ‖ The change *came* ***over***. 変化が起った. 【類】 It was an indication (証拠の一つ) of the change that had *come* ***over*** the country. ¶ as spring *comes* ***round*** 一陽来復すると ‖ His birthday *came* ***round***. 彼の誕生日がやって来た. 【類】 till Christmas *comes* ***round*** once more ‖ This date *came* ***round***, but ... その日が来たが. ‖ *come* ***round*** to the opinion that ... ...説をなすに至る. ¶ He has *come* ***round*** to the side of the right. 彼は正義にくみするようになった. ‖ On second thought he will forget his anger and *come* ***round***. 後で気を取直して仲直りをするだろう. ‖ he *came* ***round*** to the view (=opinion) that ... 彼は...という意見に変った. ‖ *come* ***round***=come around ‖ I hope he'll *come* ***round*** (=get well) in a few days. 二三日したら治ると思う. ‖ The convulsion *came* ***round***. けいれんがまた起った. ¶ He *came* ***through*** almost unscathed. 彼はほとんど無きずで済んだ. ¶ *come* ***to***=come around (=round) 気がつく. ¶ *come* ***up*** to a place (person) ある場所(人のもと)に来る ‖ Plants *come* ***up*** again every spring. 草木は春が来る度に芽生える. ‖ A snow storm was *coming* ***up*** as if to meet the morning sun. まるで朝日を迎えるように明方になって吹雪がやってきた. ‖ One *came* ***up*** smiling and ready for the next round. 一方はえみを含み次のラウンド(一試合)の支度して進み出た. ‖ The question will probably *come* ***up*** at the conference next year. その問題は多分来年の会議に上るだろう. ‖ problems that will *come* ***up*** for discussion at the conference 同会議に持出される諸問題. 【類】 At meeting of the London Council on Tuesday the proposed technical high school *came* ***up*** for discussion. / The bill *came* ***up*** for consideration on the floors of Congress. / The bill will *come* ***up*** for a vote (票決) about mid-May. / The bill *came* ***up*** for action (討議) last Tuesday. / *come* ***up*** for final approval at the general assembly's next meeting in September. / The measure *came* ***up*** for final decision. / the question that *comes* ***up*** first / The question *came* ***up*** in the House of Commons. ‖ *come* ***up*** for trial 裁判される ‖ The case *came* [***up***] before the local court. その訴訟が地方裁判所に持ち出された. ‖ The goods failed to *come* ***up*** to the required standard. その品は規格に達しなかった. 【類】 Every candidate for entry has to *come* ***up*** to a certain physical standard (一定の体格標準). / These goods do not *come* ***up*** to the mark. / *come* ***up*** to the same level ‖ the total *comes* [***up***] to ... 総額...になる ‖ Only a few *come* ***up*** to the sample. 見本通りのはほんのわずかである. 【類】 *come* ***up*** to a measure of success (ある程度の成功) / *come* ***up*** to requirements (必要条件) ‖ Several lots failed to *come* ***up*** to specifications. 仕わけ書にあわないものが数々あった. ‖ The water *came* ***up*** as far as his chin. 水が彼のあごについた. ‖ Macarthy soon *came* ***up*** to support Hamilton. 間もなくマッカーシーはハミルトンを後援するに至った. ‖ He is *coming* ***up*** to this university next term. 彼は来学期この大学に入学する ‖ *come* ***up*** to town 《英》 上京する ‖ before the railway *came* ***up*** into being 鉄道敷設以前には ‖ *Come* ***up*** to the fire. 火のそばへお寄りなさい. ‖ by the time the next issue *comes* ***up*** 次号が発行されるまでに ‖ That's a school subject that's *come* ***up*** since my day. それは私の若い時分から始まった学科です. ‖ *come* ***up*** to the scratch 〚競走〛 出発線に立つ ‖ *come* ***up*** with him 彼に追い付く ‖ *come* ***up*** to the chalk=come to the scratch 〚競走〛 出発線に立つ.

P I *came* ***across*** a very curious book (rare plant). 珍本(など)を見付けた. ‖ *come* ***across*** him 彼に会う. 【類】 *come* ***aross*** the material for it ‖ The recollection *came* ***across*** my mind. 昔のことが胸に浮んだ. ‖ *come* ***across*** the sea 海外から来る. ¶ What President *came* ***after*** Abe Lincoln? リンカンの次の大統領はだれですか. ‖ keep a dog till his owner *comes* ***after*** him 犬をその持主が取りに来るまで飼って置く. 【類】 You can have the book, if you will *come* ***after*** it. ‖ I will *come* ***after*** you. 僕が誘いに来る. ‖ He *came* ***after*** his father. 彼は父の跡を継いだ. ¶ It *came* ***as*** a real blow. それは一大打撃であった. ‖ It *came* ***as*** an immense surprise. それは実に意外のできごとであった. 【類】 His going abroad *comes* ***as*** a suprise to most friends of his. / The news of his marriage *came* as a surprise to many of his friends. / his death *came* ***as*** a shock to the literary world (文壇). ¶ We prize most those which are hardest to *come* ***at***. われわれは最も得難い物を最も珍重する. ‖ *come* ***at*** a true knowledge of oneself 真に己を知るに至る ‖ We shall see how this was to *come* ***at***. どうしてこうなったかは後で申しあげる. ¶ The question *came* ***before*** the Improvements Committee. その問題は改善委員に回された. ‖ The bill will probably *come* ***before*** Parliament next session. 同法律案は恐らく次期議会に上程されるであろう. 【類】 *come* ***before*** the conference for final decision ‖ Such a book has not yet *come* ***before*** the public. そんな本はまだ出版されていない. ‖ here he *comes* ***before*** us as ... ...としてそら彼がやってきた. ¶ Some coldness *came* ***between*** them. 二人の間がきまずくなった. ‖ He tried to *come* ***between*** us. 彼はわれわれの間に割込んできた(じゃまをした). ¶ I *came* ***by*** boat (train, steamer). 船(など)できた. ‖ How did you *come* ***by*** (=acquire) your knowledge of French? 君はどうしてフランス語を覚えたか. ‖ How did you *come* ***by*** this money? どうしてこの金を得たか. ‖ He *came* ***by*** data from various sources. 種々の方面から材料を採った. 【類】 But how *came* you ***by*** the knowledge of all these things? / I *came* ***by*** it honestly. / The power to concentrate the mind (精神を統一する力) is an acquirement very hard to *come* ***by***. ¶ *come* (=go) ***down*** stairs 階下に行く. 【類】 *come* ***down*** the mountain (hill). ¶ I have *come* ***for*** you. 君を迎えにきた. ‖ I've *come* ***for*** yes or no. イエースかノーかをききに来た. 【類】 I have *come* ***for*** the parcel. ‖ Did any letters *come* ***for*** you (=Did you get any letters) by today's mail? 今日の郵便で君に手紙がきましたか. ¶ *come* back ***from*** a visit (trip) 外出(旅行)先から帰って来る ‖ It *comes* ***from*** laziness. それはぶしょうのせいだ. ‖ it *comes* ***from*** the pen of ... それは...の著である ‖ Red blood *came* ***from*** the cut. 切傷から赤い血が出た. 【類】 Pork meat *comes* ***from*** pigs. / I do not know what this expression *comes* ***from***. ‖ He *comes* ***from*** an intelligent family. 彼は知識階級の家庭に生れた. 【類】 He *comes* ***from*** a middle-class home. ‖ The mode or style of fashion *comes* ***from*** Hollywood today. 今では流行はホリウッドから来る. ‖ the picture *comes* ***from*** the collection of ... この画は...の所蔵だ. 【類】 The word *comes* ***from*** Greek. ‖ The English word *million* has *come* ***from*** the Latin through the French. million という英語はフランス語を介してラテン語から来た. 【類】 Words *come* trippingly (すらすら) ***from*** the tongue. / The words seemed to *come* ***from*** the head and not from the heart. / Many books on the subject have lately *come* ***from*** the press (=been published[4]). / Great men do not *come* ***from*** dull boys. ‖ a wisdom *coming* ***from*** knowledge of worldly affairs 世故にたけた所から来る知恵. 【類】 knowledge that *comes* ***from*** personal experience / the contentment that *comes* ***from*** useful work well done / the skill which *comes* ***from*** thorough training ‖ wondering where the next meat was *coming* ***from***=living from day to day その日暮しをして ‖ That disease usually *comes* ***from*** infection. その病気は普通伝染による. ¶ He has *come* ***from beyond*** the seas. 彼は海外からやってきた. ¶ He *came* ***from within*** the house. 彼は家の中から出てきた. ¶ Halloween *comes* ***in*** October. 万聖節前夜は十月だ. ‖ A high mountain *came* ***in*** sight. 高い山が見えてきた. ‖ We *came* ***in*** sight of a peak. 峰が見える所に来た. ‖ and all that *came* ***in*** its train 及びこれに付属する一切のもの ‖ all who *come* ***in*** contact with him 彼と接触するすべての人々. 【類】 those with whom he *comes* ***in*** contact ‖ At present the custom is *coming* ***in*** vogue. 目下それが流行しかけている. ‖ I had not expected that he should *come* ***in*** person. よもやあの男が自分でやって来ようとは思わなかった. ¶ whilst *coming* ***into*** harbor 入港中. ¶ A new country *came into* being. 新しい国が出現した. 【類】The society (会) *came into* being on March 8, 1698. ‖ *come into* competition with ... ...と競争する ‖ by the time the peace treaty *comes into* effect 講和条約が発効する時までに. 【類】The regulations have *come into* effect. ‖ the new time-table *comes into* force from ... 改正時間割は...から実施になる ‖ The law *came into* force (=operation) immediately after its passing. その法律は通過後直ちに実施された. 【類】the date of the *coming into* force of this treaty / the law which *came into* operation in January last ‖ Such a society has not *come into* existence. こんな協会は未だかつて存在したことがない. 【類】The Czechoslovak Republic *came into* existence after the collapse of the Austro-Hungarian Empire. ‖ The idea *comes into* conflict with conventional opinion. その思想は従来の考え方と衝突する. 【類】Such a deed *comes into* conflict with the law of the country. / *come into* collision with the police ‖ Scenes drawn from life are so painful, often so hideous, that they do not *come into* the domain of art at all. 実生活そのまゝの風景は非常に痛ましくまたしばしば非常に醜悪であるので全然芸術の分野に入らない. ‖ *come into* fashion (=vogue) 流行になる ‖ *come into* his favor 彼の気に入る ‖ *come into* bearing 実を結ぶ ‖ Color *came into* (=appeared in) her face. 顔を赤らめた. ‖ though *coming into* the field lately その方面の新参ではあるが ‖ *come into* flowers 花をつける ‖ *come into* his hands 彼の手に帰する ‖ say the first thing that *comes into* one's head 出まかせを言う ‖ This is a business that has *come* largely *into* the hands of the French. これはフランス人が広く営むに至った商売である. ‖ Such strange ideas *came into* my head. こんな妙な考えが私の頭に浮んだ. ‖ those whose hands this volume *comes into* この本を手に入れる人々. 【類】They *came into* our language by borrowing from some other language. ‖ These trees *come into* leaf in the beginning of February. これらの木は二月始めに葉が出る. ‖ An offense made in the past *comes into* light. 旧悪露見に及ぶ. ‖ He first *came into* the lime-light last year. 彼は去年始めて世間から知られるようになった. ‖ Youth has everywhere *come into* its own, and has ousted old age and middle age into the background. 至るところ青年が自立するようになって老人や中年のものに取って代るようになった. ‖ He has *come into* his own. 彼は一本立になった. ‖ The two peoples have *come into* full understanding. 両国民は十分理解し合うようになった. ‖ *come into* inheritance 相続する ‖ He has just *come into* a legacy (遺産を相続). ‖ *come into* one's fortune 財産を得る. 【類】He has *come into* a large fortune. / He *came into* a fair sum of money through his father's death. / The widow has *come into* £15,000, and has already another husband in view. ‖ That fire could be produced through friction finally *came into* the knowledge of man. ついに摩擦によって火を起すことを人間は知るようになった. ‖ They rarely *come into* market. 売物に出るのはまれだ. ‖ *come into* (=*in*) contact with ... ...と接触する. 【類】*come into* personal contact with the greatest literary minds in England (英国最高の文豪たち) / it is unlikely that he ever *came into* personal contact with ... ‖ *come into* touch with the spirit of Japan 日本精神に触れる ‖ In the intervals opera-glasses *came* freely *into* play. 幕合に双眼鏡が盛んに用いられた. ‖ His imaginative power *came into* play. 彼の想像力が働いた. ‖ I have *come*, no matter how, *into* possession of ... とに角, 私は...を手に入れた. 【類】The United States *came into* possession of Louisiana by purchase from France. ‖ *come into* office 就任する ‖ *come* again *into* power 再び政権を握る ‖ The seventy-ninth Congress *came into* power on Jan. 3, 1945. 第七十九議会が 1945 年 1 月 3 日に成立した. ‖ *come into* political (literary) prominence 政界(文壇)で著名になる ‖ *come into* repute 評判になる ‖ There is a tendency for women to *come into* rank with men in this respect. この点において女子が男子と肩を並べるに至る傾向がある. ‖ He is liked by all those who *came into* relation with him. 彼は彼と関係を持つに至る者はだれにも好かれる. ‖ Cucumbers are just *coming into* season. もうそろそろきゅうりの季節だ. ‖ The island *came into* view to the N.E. 島が東北に当って見えてきた. ‖ When we are unhappy, the tears sometimes *come into* our eyes. われわれが悲しむときに涙が目に出て来ることがある. ‖ A new lighthouse *came into* use at ... a week ago. ...の新しい燈台が一週間前使用されるに至った. 【類】new terms that have *come into* use ‖ It ought to *come* more *into* use. もっと使用されて然るべきだ. 【類】Electricity was *coming* more and more *into* use for lighting. / Steam *came into* use as a motive power (動力). / Before cannons *came into* use, it must have been an almost impregnable place (難攻不落の場所). / words which have only recently *come into* frequent use / It is rapidly *coming into* general use (一般化). / *come into* popular use / *come into* practical use (実用化) ‖ since the United States *came into* the war 合衆国が戦争に参加して以来 ‖ The child *comes into* the world with no habits, good or bad. 子供は善悪何れの習慣も持たずに生れ出る. ‖ other things *coming into* the way 色々事故があって ‖ The adoption of English as our national language once *came into* question. われわれが国語に英語を採用することが問題となったことがある. ¶He *came near* falling into the pit. 彼はすんでのことに穴へ落ちる所だった. ‖ I *came* very *near* telling him as much. よっぽどそう言ってやろうかと思ったが. 【類】He *came* very *near* being run over by a motor-car. / I once got into a serious trouble with the school authorities which *came near* resulting in my expulsion (追放). / often *came near* starving ‖ No others could *come near* him. 他のものはそばえも寄れなかった(群を抜いていた). ¶Germany *comes next* on the list with ... ドイツは...という数字で二番目になる. ¶She *comes of* an old family on her father's side. 彼女は父方では旧家の出である. 【類】She *comes of* a good family. / He *came of* good New England stock. ‖ His family has *come of* the peerage. 彼の家は貴族の出だ. ‖ Though not richly *come of*, he was in a position to enjoy a Cambridge career. 家に金はなかったが彼はケンブリジ大学の生活を送ることのできる境遇にあった. ‖ Nothing *came of* the plan. その計画はお流れになった. ‖ This *comes of* your not listening to me. 僕の言うことをよく聞かないものだからこんなことになる. 【類】This *comes of* not taking heed. ‖ This *comes of* carelessness. 不注意からこういうことになる. ‖ skill that *comes of* practice 練習から来る熟練 ‖ The quarrel *came of* trifling. そのけんかはささいなことから起った. ‖ Harm may *come of* it, but good never can. それは害があろうとも決して益はない. ‖ What has *come of* Mr. Tanaka? 田中君はどうなったか. ‖ *come of* age 成年に達する ‖ *come of* marriageable age 結婚年齢に達する ‖ *come of* military age 徴兵適齢になる. ¶This year's tea is *coming on* the market. 新茶がもう市場に出ている. ‖ *come on* the tapis 議題に上る ‖ The last of one show is no sooner swept away than another begins to *come on* the scene. 一つの展示会が済むとすぐに次ぎが始まる. ‖ Leaves *come on* the trees in the spring. 春は木の葉が茂る. ¶He *came out of* Yale in 1908. 彼は一九〇八年にエール(大学)を出た ‖ smoke *coming out of* the chimney 煙突から出る煙 ‖ A butterfly *comes out of* a cocoon. ちょうは繭から出る. ‖ One would think it *came out of* the Ark. 神代からのものかも知れない. ‖ an epileptic *coming out of* a trance 失神状態から覚めるてんかん持ち ‖ *come out of* chloroform (a dream) 麻酔(など)から覚める ‖ *Out of* the evil *comes* good. 禍転じて福となる. ‖ *Out of* Plato *come* all things that are still written and debated among men of thoughts. 今なお思想家間で記述したり論じたりする事はことごとくプラトンから出ている. ‖ He *came out of* the ordeal with his life. 彼はその災難から身をもって免れた. ‖ *come out of* the affair with credit 巧にその事件を切り抜ける ‖ *come out of* the small-pox 天然痘がなおる. ¶*come over* (=traverse) a field 野を横切る ‖ A smile that seemed all light *came over* his face. いかにも晴れやかな笑が彼の顔に現われた. 【類】A look of surprise *came over* his face. / A sorrowful look *came over* her. ‖ A change has *come over* him. 彼の身の上に一つの変化が起った. 【類】A great change *came over* his life. / Certain misgivings *came over* me. / a change is now *coming over* public feeling in regard to ... ‖ *come over* her with compliments 彼女をお世辞でだます. ‖ You can't *come round* me with such yarns. そんな話に乗るものか. ¶Skill *comes through* practice. 熟練は練習によって得られる. ‖ He *came* successfully *through* the ordeal.

彼は苦難をりっぱに切抜けた. ‖ Will you understand that the business shall ***come through*** me only? その仕事は私だけでやるという事を御承知願えますか. ¶He soon ***came to*** [his senses]. 彼はじきに正気づいた. ‖ ***come to*** oneself (=one's senses) 正気づく ‖ ***come to*** business 成約を見るに至る ‖ we could not ***come to*** an agreement with ... ...との話がまとまらずじまいになった ‖ ***come to*** the aid of ... ...を助けにやって来る. 【類】 ***come to*** the rescue of ... ‖ expect ... to ***come to*** his assistance 助けに来てくれるとあてにして...を待つ ‖ ***come to*** birth, live, and die 生れ, 生活し, そして死ぬ ‖ A new race is ***coming to*** birth. 新しい民族が生れかかっている. ‖ ***come to*** blows (words) over the matter その事で殴り合い(口論)になる ‖ ***come to*** a breathing place 一休みする場所に来る ‖ So you have ***come to*** civilization. 君都へ出てきたね. ‖ Matters ***came to*** a climax. 事態は頂点に達した. ‖ ***come to*** the conclusion that ... ...という結論に達する ‖ The dispute ***came to*** a deadlock. その争議はデッドロックに乗上げた. ‖ The deceased ***came to*** his death (=lost his life) by cholera. 故人はコレラで死んだ. ‖ The occasion was one on which I experienced the nearest that I ever ***came to*** death. 私が今までに死線を越えたと思うのはその折であった. ‖ ***came to*** the decision that ... ...という事に決った. 【類】 ***come to*** a definite decision. / has ***come to*** no decision ‖ The family has ***come to*** destitution. その家族は貧困に陥った. ‖ ***come to*** dinner 晩さんに招かれて来る ‖ ***come*** by chance ***to*** the ear of ... 偶然...の耳に入る. 【類】 He supposed that this would not ***come to*** my ear[s]. ‖ The god ***came to*** earth. その神が天下った. ‖ The airman safely ***came to*** earth. その飛行士が無事に着陸した. ‖ ***come to*** a close 終結を告げる. 【類】 before this year ***comes to*** a close / The league ***came to*** an end. / The Tokugawa Shogunate ***came to*** an end in 1868. ‖ He ***came to*** an untimely end by an accident. 彼は不慮の死をとげた. ‖ The bus ***came to*** a halt. 乗合自動車が停まった. ‖ everything that ***comes to*** my eye 僕の目にうつるあらゆるもの ‖ ***come to*** flower 花が咲く ‖ our country is ***coming to*** the fore in the production of ... わが国は...の生産で一流どころになりつつある ‖ The question is again ***coming to*** the fore (=front). その問題はまたやかましくなってきた. 【類】 The society (会) is again ***coming to*** the fore. ‖ The contest ***came to*** foul. その競技は中止になった. ‖ The idea has at last ***come to*** fruition. その考えはついに実を結んだ. ‖ ***come to*** one's full estate 男一人前になる ‖ ***come to*** grief 不結果に終る, 悲しい目に会う ‖ They ***came to*** grips with each other. 彼らはつかみ合いになった. ‖ ***come to*** grips with realities (a knotty problem) 現実(など)と四つに組む ‖ His collection ***came to*** the hammer at Christie's. 彼の収集はクリスティーの店で競売に付された. ‖ Your letter has ***come to*** hand. お手紙を受取りました. ‖ before your instructions ***came to*** hand あなたの指令を受取る前に ‖ The newspaper is ***coming to*** hand very irregularly. 新聞の配達がはなはだ不規則だ. ‖ The goods ***came to*** hand deficient. 荷物が不足して届いた. ‖ A swelling has ***come to*** a head. 頭にこぶができた. ‖ He has ***come to*** great honors. 彼は大なる光栄に浴した. ‖ The idea ***came to*** him in a dream. その考えを彼は夢で得た. ‖ We'll have to ***come to*** it eventually. 結局そこへ落ちつくことになるだろう. ‖ He shall ***come to*** you tomorrow. 彼をあす御宅へうかがわせます. ‖ ***coming to*** the topic of ... 今度は...に話題を変えて ‖ the fact ***coming to*** their knowledge 彼らに分ってきたことがら. 【類】 in one instance which has ***come to*** my knowledge ‖ It has ***come to*** my direct knowledge. 私はそれをじかに聞いた. ‖ A drooping plant ***comes to*** life again in water. しおれている植物が水の中で元気づく. 【類】 This old industry has ***come to*** life. ‖ The fraud ***came to*** light. その詐欺が露顕した. ‖ Other factors will some day ***come to*** light. 他の原因は他日明かになるだろう. ¶Those efforts have ***come to*** naught (=nothing). それらの努力は水泡に帰した. 【類】 The enterprise ***came to*** little. / I don't think it will ***come to*** much. ‖ ***come to*** maturity 成熟する. 【類】 ***come to*** full adult maturity ‖ the first that ***comes to*** mind 第一に頭に浮ぶもの. 【類】 There are instances that ***come*** most readily ***to*** mind. / It is the picture which always ***comes to*** mind as most characteristic of him in the olden days. ‖ We have ***come to*** a new realization of our place in the world. われらは世界におけるわれらの立場を新たに認識するようになった. 【類】 The scheme ***came to*** nothing. ‖ first ***coming to*** general notice 始めて世間から注意されるようになって ‖ now that things have ***come to*** such a pass 事態がこうなったからには ‖ ***come to*** the point 要点に触れる ‖ when it ***comes to*** the point いざ実行となると ‖ ***come to*** poverty 貧乏する ‖ when it ***comes to*** the question of ... ...の段になると. ‖ It was he who first ***came to*** reason. 一番先に悟ったのは彼であった. 【類】 I am willing to wait till they ***come to*** reason. ‖ ***come to*** a nice (=pretty) pass 困ったことになる ‖ things have ***come to*** a pretty pass (=critical position) when ... ...するにおよんでやっかいなことになってきた ‖ I try to profit by criticisms that have ***come to*** my notice. 私は自分の目に付いた批評によって利益を得ようと努力する. ‖ Our expense for the journey, lodging, and meals ***came to*** £10 each. われわれの旅行・宿泊・食事の費用は銘々十ポンドに達した. ‖ I will ***come to*** a quarrel. けんかなら来いだ. ‖ ***come to*** one's recollection 思い出す ‖ I told him to his face that he would ***come to*** ruin. 今に困るぞと面と向って言ってやった. ‖ at last he ***came to*** speech and said ... やがて彼は口を開いて...といった. ‖ The train ***came to*** a standstill. 列車が立往生した. ‖ A little way on, and they ***came to*** a stream. 少し進むと流れに出た. ‖ Such cases frequently ***come to*** surface of history. こういう例はひんぴんと歴史に出て来る. ‖ ***come to*** an anchor in a harbor 港に停泊する ‖ The color picture has ***come to*** stay. 色彩映画はりっぱに地盤を得るに至った. ‖ The stallion ***came to*** a stop and stood trembling under his masterful rider. 雄馬ははたと立止まって名騎手のあん下にふるえていた. ‖ His activity ***came to*** a full stop. 彼の活動は全く停止した. 【類】 when the car ***came to*** a stop ‖ The work has ***come to*** a standstill for lack of funds. その事業は資金難で行詰った. ‖ So that's why you didn't ***come to*** supper. それで君は夕食に来なかったのだね. ‖ ***come to*** terms privately 内済ですます. 【類】 try to ***come to*** terms with him / Very sorry we cannot ***come to*** your terms. ‖ She is ***come to*** term. 臨月になった ‖ Any way, I don't know why my opinion isn't as valuable as his, when you ***come to*** that. とに角その段になると僕の意見が彼のほど重要でない理由が分らない. ‖ Will it not ***come to*** the same thing if I pay afterward? 後払いにしても同じ事にならないだろうか. ‖ It was the first word that ***came to*** my tongue. その言葉が最初に私の舌に上った. ‖ The negotiations have ***come to*** an ultimate end. 交渉がいよいよ終局に達した. ‖ we ***came to*** an understanding in regard to ... ...は話がついた. 【類】 ***come to*** an understanding with ... ‖ Cream ***comes to*** the top of the milk クリームは牛乳の上に浮く. ‖ They lost when the question ***came to*** a vote. 採決となると彼らの負けとなった. ¶***come under*** his notice 彼の目に止まる ‖ the most absurd specimen of mistranslation to ***come under*** my observation 最もばからしいと気づいた誤訳の例 ‖ a case which ***came under*** my own personal observation 私が目撃した事件 ‖ ***come under*** its rule その領土となる ‖ ***come under*** the authority of ... ...の支配下に属する ‖ His library ***came under*** the hammer at Christie's, London. 彼の蔵書はロンドンのクリスティー店で競売に付された ‖ ***come under*** this class この部に属する. 【類】 ***come under*** this classification (分類) / Tea and sugar ***come under*** the head of groceries (乾物の部類). ‖ ***come under*** the general heading of Gift Books 贈答用本という中に総括される ‖ does not ***come under*** the designation of ... ...という性質のものではない ‖ ***come under*** the last of his criticism やり玉に上げられる. ¶***come up*** a river 川をさかのぼる ‖ They ***came*** thundering ***up*** stairs. 皆がどかどかっと階段を上ってきた. ¶Spring has ***come upon*** us. 春がきた. ‖ the idea ***came upon*** me that ... ...という考えが私の胸に浮んだ ‖ I ***came upon*** a friend in the park. 公園で友だちに出会った. ‖ ***come upon*** a critical period 危期に際会する ‖ ***come upon*** the scene その場に来る ‖ if war were to ***come upon*** us in the East もしわれわれが東洋で戦争することになったら ‖ A misfortune ***came upon*** him. 不幸が彼の身に起った. ‖ She ***came upon*** the parish with all her children. 彼女とその子供全部が教区の扶養を受けた. ¶I feel confident that success will ***come with*** practice. 練習で成功が得られると確信する. ‖ Despatch ***comes with*** practice. 迅速は練習によって得られる. ‖ Wisdom ***comes with*** age. 亀の甲より年の功. ‖ Robins *come with* the spring. こま鳥は春になるとやって来る. 【類】a new difficulty that *comes with* the new day ‖ *come* to stay *with* people in the country いなかの人たちの所へ滞在に行く. ¶*come within* this category この部類に入る. 【類】*come within* the classification of … ‖ *come within* its province その領域内に入る ‖ The subject does not *come within* the scope of the present article. その問題は本論文の範囲外だ. 【類】*come within* the sphere of … / *come within* one's range of vision (視界) ‖ *come within* a hair (=straw) of succeeding もう少しで成功する所まで行きそうになる. 【類】*come within* a hair's breath of drowning (starving). ¶*come via* Suez スエズ経由で来る.

O Such a phrase has *come* to be a mere compliment—a piece of mock humility. こんな句はほんのお世辞すなわちけんそんのまねごとになってしまった. ‖ when the history of the present war *comes* to be written この戦争の歴史が書かれる段になると ‖ I have *come* to believe that … 私は…と信じるようになった. ‖ when one *comes* to look more closely into the question one is surprised to discover that … その問題をさらにしさいに調べると…であると分って驚くのである ‖ by extension the word has *come* to mean … 広義になってその語は…という意味を持つようになった ‖ A morning dream always *comes* to pass. 明け方の夢は正夢(ベンガルの迷信). ‖ it may *come* to pass that … …ということになるかも知れない ‖ how did you *come* to …? どういう風にして君は…するようになったか. ¶Then we *come* to regret it. そこでわれわれは後悔するようになる. ¶there is no one to surpass him when it *comes* to … …となると彼にかなうものはない.

comeback, *n.* 復旧; カムバック.

V The city ***made*** a splendid *comeback.* 市はりっぱに復活した. ¶***plan*** a *comeback* 再挙を企てる.

Q have a ***fine comeback*** すばらしい立直りをする ‖ make a ***splendid*** *comeback* りっぱにカムバックする.

comedian, *n.* 喜劇俳優.

Q² a ***radio (TV)*** *comedian* ラジオ(テレビ)喜劇俳優.

comedy, *n.* 喜劇.

Q the score of a ***musical*** *comedy* 喜歌劇の楽譜. 【類】the vaudeville (寸劇) and the ***musical*** *comedy.* ¶please children with ***up-to-date*** *comedies* 現代的な喜劇で子供たちを喜ばせる.

Q² a ***farce*** *comedy* 茶番劇. ¶a ***slapstick*** *comedy* どたばた喜劇. ¶a ***two-reel*** *comedy* 二巻ものの喜劇映画.

comer, *n.* 来者, 来客.

Q a ***late*** *comer* 遅参者. ¶a ***new*** *comer* 新参者. ¶a ***new*** *comer* to pictures 映画界の新人. ¶a ***self-invited*** *comer* 招かれないのに来た人.

comet, *n.* すい星.

V A *comet* ***blazed*** in the sky. すい星が天に現われた.

comfort, *n.* 慰安, 快楽.

V ***administer*** spiritual *comfort* 精神的慰安を与える. ¶***bring*** *comfort* to her grief-laden heart 彼女の悲しむ胸に慰安をもたらす. ¶***derive*** *comfort* from … …によって慰安を得る. 【類】***derive*** *comfort* from the fact that … ¶***enjoy*** *comforts* of life 人生の快を楽しむ. 【類】We now ***enjoy*** these *comforts* of which formerly we had only heard. ‖ ***enjoy*** the *comforts* of a good fire よく燃える火にあたる. ¶***find*** *comfort* in one's children (religion) 子供(ら)を慰安とする. 【類】***find*** *comfort* in the fact that … ¶***offer*** one *comfort* 人に慰安を与える ‖ Those hotels ***offer*** plain *comforts.* それらのホテルは一通りの設備があるだけだ. ¶It ***possesses*** every modern *comfort.* そこにはあらゆる近代的設備がある. ¶***seek*** *comfort* from a person 人から慰安を求める. ¶***speak*** *comfort* to a person 人を慰める. ¶The company carefully ***studies*** the *comfort* of passengers. 会社は大いに旅客の便利を計る. ¶***take*** *comfort* (=consolation) from (=in) the fact that … …という事実によって慰められる. 【類】***take*** *comfort* from reading / he ***takes*** little *comfort* from …

Q It is ***cold*** *comfort* to be told that others suffer as much as we do. 他の人も自分たち同様苦しんでいるのだと聞かされてもあわい慰めにしかならない. ¶live in ***decent*** *comfort* 不自由なく暮す. ¶***Dutch*** *comfort* (もっと悪くなくてよかったと考えて自ら慰めること). ¶live in merely ***fair*** *comfort* 一応安楽に暮す. ¶not for ***genuine*** *comfort* but for fashion and display 真の安楽のためではなくて流行と外見のために. ¶***material*** *comfort* 物質的慰安. ¶At the Lygon Arms there is an undeniable atmosphere of Old and Merrie England, combined with ***modern*** *comfort.* リゴン・アームズには古代英国のゆかしさと近代設備とをつきまぜた一種のふん囲気のあることはだれでも認めなければならない. ¶be able to buy ***ordinary*** *comfort* 普通の慰安品は買うことができる. ¶***plain*** and ***simple*** *comfort* 地味で単純な慰安. ¶pity is but ***poor*** *comfort* when … …の場合にかわいそうだというだけではどうにもならない. ¶such ***simple*** *comforts* as cigarettes, chocolates, sandwiches, and daily papers 巻タバコ・チョコレート・サンドイッチ・日日の新聞というような単純な慰み. ¶real ***solid*** *comfort* 本当の充実した快楽. ¶On Sundays some of them attend this sanctuary to get ***spiritual*** *comfort.* その人たちの中には日曜にこのお寺に行って精神的慰安を求める者もある. ¶***substantial*** *comfort* 本当に楽しめる慰安. ¶judged by a general improved standard of ***urban*** *comfort* 都会における一般に向上した慰安生活の標準によって判断すると.

Q² increase ***travel*** *comfort* 一層気持よく旅行ができるようにする. ¶such ***winter*** *comforts* as overcoats 外とうなど冬の身仕度. ¶***20th century*** *comforts* 二十世紀の慰安品.

P live ***in*** ease and *comfort* 安楽に暮す. ¶a great source ***of*** *comfort* 慰安の一大源泉. ¶These are languages I cannot read ***with*** any *comfort.* これらは私がらくに読み得ない国語である.

P² *comfort* ***in*** adversity 逆境における慰安. ¶She is a great *comfort* ***to*** her parents. 彼女は両親にとって非常に慰めになる.

comfort, *v.* 慰める.

M be *comforted* ***externally*** 肉体的に満足する.

P *comfort* him ***for*** the loss その損失に対して彼を慰める. ¶*comfort* oneself ***with*** a thought that … …と思って自ら慰めるだろう.

O he will be *comforted* to learn that … 彼は…と知って安心するだろう.

comfortable, *a.* 安楽な, 気持のよい.

M Take this seat. This is ***more*** *comfortable* [to sit on]. こちらへおかけ. この方がすわり心地がいいから.

P I am quite *comfortable* ***at*** this hotel. この宿屋はまことに気持がよい. ¶He is *comfortable* ***in*** circumstances. 彼は暮しむきが楽だ. ‖ Are you *comfortable* ***in*** this seat? このいすは掛け心地がようございますか.

comic, *n.* [続き]漫画・漫文類.

V Children like ***reading*** *comics* (=funnies). 子供らは漫画が好きだ.

comic, *a.* こっけいな.

M ***irresistibly*** *comic* 断然こっけいな.

coming, *n.* 到来, 来着.

V ***Excuse*** my *coming* so late. 遅刻して済みません. ¶***herald*** the *coming* of spring 春の先ぶれをする.

Q ***late*** *coming* [to work] [職場への]遅刻.

P ***at*** the *coming* of every new spring 初春の来るごとに. ¶He is long ***in*** *coming.* 彼は仲々来ない. ‖ He is slow ***in*** *coming.* 彼は来るのがおそい. ‖ I've been late ***in*** *coming.* おそくなりました. ¶***with*** the *coming* of daylight 夜が明けるにつれて.

coming-of-age, *n.* 成年期到達.

V The Girl Guides Association of England ***celebrated*** its *coming-of-age* a few weeks ago. 英国の女子青年団は数週前その創設二十週年を祝賀した.

comity, *n.* 友誼, 厚誼.

V ***cultivate*** *comity* between nations 国際間の信誼を高める. ¶***enter*** the *comity* of European nations. ヨーロッパ国家群の仲間入りをする. ¶***join*** the *comity* of nations 各国と親善を結ぶ.

comma, *n.* 〚文法〛コンマ(句点).

V ***use*** a *comma* between clauses 節の間にコンマを打つ.

Q a word appearing within ***inverted*** *commas* 単引用符で囲んだ語(卑語などを仮に使ったという意味を含めて).

command, *n.* 指揮, 命令; 支配権; 運用力; 見晴し.

V ***acquire*** *command* of English 英語を自由に使いこなす. 【類】***acquire*** a fluent *command* of good English. ¶***assume*** *command* of an army 軍隊の指揮をする. ¶We ***await*** your *command.* われわれは貴下の御指図を待っています. ¶***give*** a *command* 命令する ‖ Such training will ***give*** a literary *command* of French. こんな風に教えるとフランス語を自由に読み書きすることができるようになる. ‖ It ***gives*** you *command* of the entire countryside. そこから一帯の村落を一ぼうの中に収められる. ¶He ***had*** *command* of the whole army in that battle. 彼はその戦で全軍の司令権を握っていた ‖ ***have*** *command* of metaphors 比ゆが自由

に使える ‖ he ***has** command* of the compilation of … 彼が…の編集長をしている ‖ ***Have*** you any *commands,* Sir? 何か御用がございませんか. ‖ He ***has*** no *command* of himself. 彼は 自分の始末ができない. ¶ He ***held** command* of a cruiser squadron. 彼は巡洋艦隊を指揮した. ¶ ***issue*** a ***command*** 命令を発する. ¶ She cried, having ***lost*** all *command* of herself. 彼女は我を忘れて泣いた. ¶ He ***obtained*** the *command* of very considerable sums. 彼は巨額の金を自由にできるようになった.【類】Once the *command* of the air is ***obtained*** by one of the contending armies, the war must become a conflict between a seeing host and one that is blind.—H.G. Wells. ¶ He ***ordered*** the *command* to halt. 彼は停止を命じた. ¶ ***regain*** the lost *command* of the sea 一度失った制海権を取戻す. ¶ I ***repeated*** my *command* more sternly. 私は命令をさらに厳粛に繰返した. ¶ ***secure*** (=***win***) the *command* of the sea 制海権を握る. ¶ ***take** command* of a paper 新聞の経営を引受ける ‖ He ***took*** the *command* of the Russians. 彼がロシア軍を指揮した. ¶ ***take over*** the *command* at Cape Town ケープタウンの指揮を引継ぐ. ¶ ***turn over*** (=***deliver***) the *command* to the officer next in rank 次席の将校に指揮権を渡す. ¶ Anyone who ***violates*** this *command* shall pay for it with his head. 何人を問わずこの命令を破る者は死刑に処す. ¶ ***withdraw*** a *command* 命令を撤回する.

Q He has ***better** command* of English than myself. 彼は僕より英語ができる. ¶ He is in ***chief** command.* 彼が主幹である. ¶ an ***emphatic** command* 力強い命令. ¶ the ***Far Eastern** Command* 極東軍司令部. ¶ He has ***fluent** command* of English. 彼は英語を流ちょうに話す. ¶ await your ***further** commands* 貴下の次の御指示をお待ちします(商人が買手の返事を待つときなど). ¶ have a ***good** command* of English 英語が自由自在だ. ¶ at ***heaven's** command* 天の命で. ¶ He rose to a ***high** command* in the army. 彼は陸軍で[最高]指揮官に昇進した. ‖ a ***high** command* 〚軍〛[最高]司令部. ¶ by ***Imperial** command* 勅命で. ¶ have a ***masterly** command* of the art of advertising 広告技術を完全に修得している ¶ a ***peremptory** command* 絶対命令. ¶ their ***poor** command* of English 彼らの貧弱な英語の力. ¶ a ***productive** command* 生産力. ¶ have, at ***ready** command,* … …を用意している ‖ opponents with ***ready** command* of language 口の達者な相手側. ¶ a ***stern** command* 厳命. ¶ His *command* of language is not yet ***strong.*** 彼は語学の素養がまだ十分でない. ¶ the ***Supreme** Command* 最高司令部 ‖ The President has the ***supreme** command* of the army and navy. 大統領は陸海軍を統率する.【類】The captain has ***supreme** command* on board. ¶ hold almost ***undisputed** command* in … …に覇を唱える. ¶ He has ***unlimited*** *command* of money. 彼は幾らでも金が自由にできる. ¶ He has a ***wonderful** command* of language. 彼は驚くほど語学が達者だ.

Q² the ***Communist*** high *command* 共産党本部. ¶ the ***Soviet*** high *command* in North Korea 北鮮におけるソ連最高司令部. ¶ the ***United Nations** Command* 国連軍司令部.

P the means ***at*** his *command* 彼の自由になる資産.【類】The money is ***at*** his *command* (=disposal). / He introduced improvements in the office, as far as the scanty capital ***at*** his *command* would permit. / America has ample resources (豊富な資源) ***at** command.* ‖ She has also ***at*** her *command* Italian and French. 彼女はまたイタリア語およびフランス語を自由にあやつる.【類】It has been stated that the uneducated person has only three or four hundred words ***at*** his *command.* / He assisted me in every way ***at*** his *command.* / use all the eloquence ***at*** one's *command* ‖ the latest information ***at*** my *command* states that … 私の入手した最近の情報によれば…である ‖ the library facilities ***at** command* 図書使用の便 ‖ in the short time ***at*** our *command* it has been impossible to … われわれはわずかな時間しか得られなかったのであるから…することは不可能であった. ¶ ***by*** the King's *command* 王の命によって.【類】***by** command* (=order) of his master. ¶ Who is the officer ***in** command?* 指揮官はだれか.【類】General Nogi was ***in** command* of the army. / the officer ***in** command* of the landing company (上陸隊) ‖ ***in** command* of the English squadron (Russian fleet) / the troops were ***in** command* of Colonel … / the Shunyo Maru of the Toyo Kisen Kaisha, ***in** command* of Captain William Filmer / The chief officer (一等航海士) has been placed ***in** command.* ‖ They are deficient ***in*** their *command* of English. 彼らは英語の力が欠けている. ¶ be ***under*** the *command* of … …の指揮下にある.【類】with only some three or four men ***under*** his *command* / The ship was ***under** command* of Admiral … in the operations. ¶ a Japanese teacher ***with*** a good *command* of English 英語を自由に使える日本人の先生. ¶ ***without*** a special *command* from … …からの特別の命令を待たずに.

P² *command **of*** one's temper 怒りの抑制. ¶ *command **over*** a person 人に対する権威.

command, *v.* 命令する.

M The brain, the king of our organs, ***imperiously** commands* the whole army of muscles. 身体諸機関の王たる頭脳は筋肉全軍に厳命を下す.

P be *commanded **by*** the Queen to thank … for … 女王の命により…に…という点で感謝の意を表する. ¶ *command **with*** authority 権威をもって命じる.

commandeer, *v.* 徴発する.

P All of the vessels of the trans-Pacific fleet of the Canadian Pacific Railway Company were *commandeered **by*** the British Admiralty. カナダ太平洋鉄道会社の太平洋航路の全船舶は英国海軍省によって徴発された.

commandeering, *n.* 徴発.

Q² ***government** commandeering* 政府徴用.

commander, *n.* 指揮者, 司令官.

Q a ***naval** commander* 海軍司令官. ¶ a ***personal** commander* [代理でない]本人の司令官. ¶ fill Gen. A's shoes as ***Supreme** Commander* A 将軍の後任として最高司令官になる. ¶ a ***victorious** commander* returning from the seat of war 戦地からがい旋する司令官.

Q² ***Army theater** commanders.* 陸軍戦区司令官たち. ¶ a ***corps** commander* 兵団長. ¶ a ***division** commander* 師団長. ¶ an ***ex-POW camp** commander* 前捕虜収容所長. ¶ the local ***occupation force** commander* 占領軍地区司令官. ¶ ***overseas theater** commanders* 海外戦区司令官たち. ¶ a ***prison camp** commander* 捕虜収容所長. ¶ a ***task force** commander* 遊撃隊長; [海軍の]機動艦隊司令官. ¶ a ***unit** commander* 部隊長.

commandment, *n.* 戒律.

V ***violate*** the Seventh *Commandment* 第七(かんいん)戒律を破る ‖ a propensity to ***violate*** the eighth *commandment* 第八戒律を破る(窃盗をやる)癖.

commemoration, *n.* 記念; 祝典.

Q a gift from him in ***congratulatory** commemoration* of the wedding of … …の結婚祝賀記念として彼からの贈物.

P ***in** commemoration* of friendship formed during … …中に結んだ友情の記念に ‖ We caused a medal to be struck ***in** commemoration* of this discovery. この発明の記念にメダルを造らせた.【類】This monument has been erected ***in** commemoration* of the victory. / a monument ***in*** *commemoration* of …

commemorative, *a.* 記念の.

P a stamp *commemorative **of*** the Wedding of the Crown Prince 東宮御成婚記念の郵便切手.【類】*commemorative **of*** the day that witnessed the event.

commence, *v.* 始める; 始まる; 成る.

M be ***forthwith** commenced* 即刻始められる. ¶ has ***hardly*** yet *commenced* まだ始まったか始まっていないかである. ¶ Work will be *commenced **today.*** 今日から仕事を始める.

P I *commenced* life ***as*** a business man. 実業家として世に立った. ¶ We *commenced **at*** the beginning. われわれは始めからやりだした. ‖ *commencing **at*** 3 o'clock 三時に始まって ‖ The salary *commences* usually ***at*** 6,000 yen a month. 給料は大抵月六千円が振出しだ. ‖ He *commenced* M.A. ***at*** Oxford. 彼はオクスフォードで文学士になった. ¶ he *commenced **by*** remarking that … 彼は…と言って口を切った. ¶ The performances will *commence **from*** 6.30 p.m. 演芸は午後六時半に始まる. ‖ Students can *commence* their course ***from*** any date. 学生はいつからでも入学することができる. ‖ *commencing **from*** date 今日以後. ¶ The rainy season *commences **in*** June. 梅雨は六月に始まる.【類】The first term *commences **in*** April. ¶ The holidays *commence* ***on*** Saturday. 休暇は土曜から始まる. ¶ *commence* (=begin) a sentence ***with*** a capital letter 頭文字で文を書き始める ‖ We will *commence **with*** this work. この仕事から始めましょう. ‖ *Commencing **with*** the issue for this month the subscription will be raised. 本月号から購読料を値上げします。

commencement, *n.* 始まり, 起源; (米)〔大学の〕卒業式.

V A *commencement* will be ***made*** next year with the construction of the railway bridge. その鉄橋架設工事は来年開始する.

Q² He got away to the ***Harvard Commencement.*** 彼はハーバード大学の卒業式に出かけた.

P ***at*** the *commencement* of the nineteenth century 第十九世紀の始めに ‖ The boat upset ***at*** the very *commencement* of the storm. 舟は暴風が始まるやいなやひっくり返った. ¶ ***before commencement*** of a contract 契約の開始前に. ¶ ***from*** the *commencement* 最初から. ¶ ***since*** the *commencement* of the Meiji era 明治時代の始めから.

P² about the *commencement* ***of*** the eighth century 八世紀の初めごろ ‖ June is the month ***of*** brides and *commencements* here. 当地では六月は花嫁と卒業式の月だ.

commend, *v.* 推薦する, 称賛する.

M be ***highly*** *commended* 大いに推賞される. ¶ a saying that *commends* itself ***strongly*** to the approval of the manly-minded men 男らしい人たちになるほどと思わせる強い言葉. ¶ may be ***warmly*** *commended* to the general reader 一般読者に心から推薦できよう.

P He *commended* them ***for*** their enthusiasm. 彼は彼らの熱心を称賛した. ‖ *commend* a person ***for*** his bravery 人の勇敢をほめる. ¶ *commend* a man ***to*** one's friends 友人を人に推挙する ‖ The book doesn't *commend* itself ***to*** me. その本は私の気に入らない. ‖ I *commend* it ***to*** your notice (= attention). そのことを御注意申しあげます. 【類】 *commend* ***to*** the attraction of students.

commendation, *n.* 推挙, 称賛.

V His work ***called forth*** the highest *commendation.* 彼の作品が最高の称賛を博した. ‖ The book ***deserves*** *commendation* for its clear and pleasant print. その本は印刷が鮮明で気持のよいのはうれしい. ¶ His conduct ***merits*** the highest *commendation.* 彼の行動は最高の称賛を受ける価値がある.

Q terms of ***high*** *commendation* 推賞の言葉. ¶ ***mild*** *commendation* ほどほどの称賛. ¶ select it for ***special*** *commendation* それを特に推奨する. ¶ ***unbiased*** and ***intelligent*** *commendations* from the highest sources 最高権威からの公平にして且つ賢明なる推賞. ¶ the ***warmest*** *commendation* 最も熱心な推賞.

commensurable, *a.* 相応した. 「労力に相応した.

P *commensurable* ***with*** the trouble taken in … …に費した

commensurate, *a.* 適応した, 相応した.

P His salary is not *commensurate* ***to*** his worth. 彼の月給は彼の腕に相応しない. ¶ The work bore no fruit *commensurate* ***with*** the efforts. その仕事は努力相応の効果を生じなかった. ‖ a profit *commensurate* ***with*** the outlay for its production その生産費相応の利益. 【類】 His contribution represented a sum *commensurate* ***with*** his position in the commercial world. / *commensurate* ***with*** the importance of their duties / receive the pay *commensurate* ***with*** the work one has done.

comment, *n.* 註釈, 評註; 評論, 批評.

V ***add*** *comments* or explanations 註釈または説明を加える. ¶ she is being seen, quite often enough to ***arouse*** *comment,* with … 彼女は余りたびたび…と一緒なのでうわさが立っている. 【類】 ***arouse*** animated *comment.* ¶ ***bar*** all *comments* あらゆる批判を差止める. ¶ There are several other points in the Chancellor of the Exchequer's speech that ***call for*** *comment.* 大蔵大臣の演説には釈明を要する点が他に数件ある. ¶ He is ***carrying*** much *comment* and surprise with him. 彼はどこへ行っても非難と驚きの的になっている. ¶ I was afraid of ***causing*** *comment.* 何とか言われるのがこわかった. 【類】 Residents can walk to and from their houses in bathing wraps (浴衣) without ***causing*** any *comment.* ¶ It ***created*** wide *comment* in the Japanese press. そのことが日本の新聞に盛んに書きたてられた. ¶ The reason is so apparent to all that it hardly ***deserves*** *comment.* その理由はだれにも明りょうで註釈を要しない. ¶ ***elicit*** many *comments* from … …から色々批判を受ける. ¶ The incident ***evoked*** some *comments* in the press. その事件がちと新聞に書きたてられた. ¶ ***excite*** considerable *comment* 大分問題にされる. 【類】 It has grown so common as hardly to ***excite*** *comment.* / It ***excited*** little or no *comment.* ‖ ***excite*** *comment* and gossip かれこれうわさの種となる. ¶ Some scathing *comments* were ***heard*** from visitors. 訪問者が皮肉な言をろうした. ¶ ***interpolate*** a *comment* 批評をはさむ. ¶ ***invite*** *comment* 問題を起す. ¶ ***make*** such *comments,* either openly or inwardly 口に出すか腹の中でそんな批評をやる ‖ He ***makes*** this amusing *comment.* 彼はこういうおもしろい評を下している. ‖ ***make*** *comment* wedgewise 横やりを入れる. ¶ It ***needs*** no *comment.* それは説明を要しない. 【類】 It is too manifest to ***need*** *comment.* ¶ ***offer*** *comment* 批評を下す. ¶ I remember *comment* being ***passed*** occasionally on … 折々…に対して批評が加えられたことを思い出す. ¶ ***provoke*** most *comment* on … …が一番問題を起す. ¶ ***publish*** *comments* on … …に関する論評を公けにする. ¶ ***quote*** an illuminating *comment* from him 彼の明快な評語を引用する. ¶ too well-known to ***require*** *comment* あまりにも有名で説明を要しない.

Q make ***adequate*** *comment* upon … …に対して十分な説明を加える. ¶ ***adverse*** *comments* 反対の批評. ¶ They made ***audible*** *comments* on his speech. 彼らは彼の演説を聞えよがしに批評した. ¶ It is too important a subject to be dismissed by any ***brief*** *comment.* それはきわめて重大問題だから簡単に片付けてしまうことはできない. 【類】 with a ***brief*** *comment.* ¶ ***caustic*** *comment* 皮肉な批評. ¶ ***current*** *comments* 時事問題の解説. ¶ It became a matter of ***cynical*** *comment* among the neighbors. そのことについては近所の人の口がうるさくなってきた. ¶ ***disjointed*** *comment* すじ道の立たない論評. ¶ ***editorial*** *comments* 新聞の論説. ¶ He made some ***encouraging*** *comment.* 彼は激励の言葉を述べた. ¶ ***explanatory*** *comments* 解説. ¶ produced so much ***favorable*** *comment* from the Press 諸新聞からは大いに好評を博した. ¶ make ***frivolous*** *comment* 茶々を入れる. ¶ a matter of ***general*** *comment* 一般のうわさの種. ¶ ***hostile*** or ***malicious*** *comments* 敵意または悪意のある論評. ¶ a ***humorous*** *comment* かいぎゃくに富んだ批評. ¶ ***ill-natured*** *comment* 意地の悪い批評. ¶ an ***illuminating*** *comment* 明快な評論. ¶ make an ***interesting*** *comment* on … …について興味ある論評をする. ¶ ***no*** *comment* 意見なし (アンケートなどに記入する言葉). ¶ some ***outspoken*** *comment* on … …に関する無遠慮な批評. ¶ a ***passing*** *comment* ついでの評語. ¶ ***ribald*** *comments* 下がかった話. ¶ ***scathing*** *comment* on … …に対する酷評. ¶ ***scornful*** *comment* 侮辱的批評. ¶ ***sensible*** and occasionally ***shrewd*** and ***suggestive*** *comment* 物のわかったそして時々突込んだ示唆に富む批評. ¶ require ***special*** *comments* 特別の解説を要する. ¶ the object of ***strong*** *comment* 激しい批評の的. ¶ Some of their *comments* were ***trenchant.*** 批評の中には手厳しいものもあった. ¶ It has excited ***wide*** and ***approving*** *comment.* それは広く世人の賛意を受けた. ¶ It has aroused ***widespread*** *comment.* それが広くうわさの種になった. ¶ make ***uncalled-for*** *comment* 余計な事をしゃべる.

Q² a ***chance*** *comment* 行き当りばったりの批評. ¶ ***Newspaper*** *comments* on cases *sub judice* are prohibited. 審理中の事件に対する新聞の論議は禁止されている. ¶ ***Press*** *comment* generally is distinctly favorable. 新聞の論調はがいして明らかに有利である.

P ***in*** current *comment* 昨今言いはやされている. ¶ He listened quietly and ***without*** *comment.* 彼は静かにかつ何とも言わずに傾聴した. ‖ ***without*** further *comment* それ以上批評を加えずに.

P² a *comment* ***from*** the Atlantic Journal アトランティク誌の評. ¶ *comments* ***on*** events 時事評論 ‖ His conduct is the best *comment* ***on*** his declaration. 彼の行いが何よりもよく彼の言明を説明している. ‖ *comments* ***on*** foreign policy 対外政策に対する批評. ¶ All history is a *comment* ***upon*** that great truth. すべての歴史はその真理の一解説だ.

comment, *v.* 註解する; 論評する.

M ¶ be ***adversely*** *commented* upon by … …によって反ばくされる. ¶ *comment* ***favorably*** upon his ability 彼の才能に好評を下す. ¶ The newspapers *commented* ***languidly*** on it. 諸新聞はそれについて微温的な(お座なりの)批評をした.

P *comment* ***on*** current events 時事評論を行う. 【類】 *comment* ***on*** a subject (an author) / while I am at it I wish to *comment* ***on*** … / *commenting* ***on*** this, he says … ‖ To *comment* ***upon*** this would be to paint the lily. この論評は

おそらく蛇足であろう. ¶The function of the novelist of this present day is to *comment **upon*** life as he sees it.—Frank Norris. 現代小説家の任務は人生を如実に評論することである. ‖ It is much *commented **upon*** editorially. それは大分新聞で論評されている.

commentary, *n.* 註釈, 評註.

V It ***affords*** a striking *commentary* on the limitations of our present knowledge. それはわれわれの今の知識が貧弱なことを明かに物語っている.

Q a ***parenthetical*** *commentary* 括註. ¶keep up a ***running*** *commentary* on ... ...に関し連続論評を加える.

Q^2 ***news*** *commentaries* 時事諸評論.

P^2 a *commentary* ***on*** the whole Old Testament 旧約聖書全部の註釈.

commentator, *n.* 解説者; 評註者.

Q a ***calm*** and ***unafraid*** *commentator* 平静にして恐れる所のない評論家.

Q^2 a ***radio*** [***news***] *commentator* ラジオの時事解説者.

P^2 a *commentator* ***on*** Shakespeare シェイクスピアの評註者 ‖ a *commentator* ***on*** current events 時事解説者.

commerce, *n.* 商業, 通商, 貿易.

V These rivers ***carry*** a *commerce.* これらの川は通商の仲立をする. ¶Foreign *commerce* is ***carried on*** principally through the ports of Yokohama, Kobe, and Osaka. 海外貿易は主に横浜・神戸・大阪の諸港を通して行われる. ‖ ***carry on*** *commerce* with ... ...と取引をする. ¶***develop*** *commerce* 商業を発展させる. ¶***enlarge*** the foreign *commerce* of the country その国の海外貿易を拡張する. ¶***expand*** (=***extend***) foreign *commerce* 外国貿易を拡張する. ¶***handicap*** the *commerce* of this country わが国の商業を妨害する. ¶a ***legitimate*** *commerce* まともな商売. ¶***open*** *commerce* with Japan 日本と通商を開く. ¶***promote*** *commerce* 商業を促進する. ¶Germans ***push*** their *commerce* into all ports of the globe. ドイツ人は商業を世界至る所に進展させる.

V^2 *Commerce* has ***stagnated.*** 商業が沈滞した.

Q ***internal*** (=***domestic***) *commerce* 内国通商.

Q^2 ***air*** *commerce* 空路による交易. ¶carry on ***living*** *commerce* with God 交霊する. ¶***ocean*** *commerce* 大洋貿易. ¶***overseas*** *commerce* 海外貿易 ‖ steel, wood, composite, and concrete vessels for ***overseas*** *commerce* 貿易のための鋼鉄, 木材, 鉄骨およびコンクリート製の船. ¶***river*** *commerce* 河川貿易. ¶Great Britain had a huge ***sea*** *commerce.* 英国は大規模な海上貿易をやった. ¶vast ***sea-borne*** *commerce* 広い海外貿易. ¶***water*** *commerce* 水路交易. ¶expand ***world*** *commerce* 世界貿易を進展させる.

P make one's fortune ***by*** *commerce* 商売で財産を作る. ¶goods packed in boxes ***for*** *commerce* 発売のために箱づめにした品物. ¶He is engaged ***in*** *commerce.* 彼は商業に従事している. ‖ it is known ***in*** *commerce* under the name of ... それは商人の間に...の名で通っている. ¶Carbonate of potash is the pearl-ash ***of*** *commerce.* 炭酸カリウムは商業の方では真珠灰という.

P^2 *commerce* ***between*** two countries 二国間の通商. ¶*commerce* ***by*** sea 海外貿易. ¶*commerce* ***in*** money 金銭上の取引. ¶There has always been a noble *commerce* ***of*** ideas between the races. 世界各国民の間には常に高尚な思想の交通というものがあった.

commerce, *v.* 交通する, 交際する.

P *commerce* ***with*** a country 国と交際する.

commercial, *n.* 〖ラジオ〗広告放送番組.

O A sponsored radio program is called "*commercial.*" スポンサー付きのラジオ番組を「商業放送」という.

commercial, *a.* 商売本位の.

M ***painfully*** *commercial* 恐ろしく商売本位な.

commingle, *v.* 混合する.

M Fact is ***inextricably*** *commingled* with fiction. 本当とうそが区別しにくいように混ざり合っている.

commingling, *n.* 混合.

Q a ***curious*** *commingling* of things old and new 新品と古物とのおかしな組合わせ. ¶the ***strange*** *commingling* of divergent civilizations 異種文明の異様な合流.

commiserate, *v.* ふびんに思う.

P *commiserate* a person on his misfortune 人の不幸に同情する.

commiseration, *n.* あわれみ.

Q a ***misplaced*** *commiseration* 間違った同情.

commissar, *n.* 〖ソ連〗人民委員.

Q the Council of ***people's*** *Commissars* 〖ソ連〗人民委員会議(内閣に当る).

Q^2 a ***Soviet*** *Commissar* of Foreign Affairs ソ連外相.

commissary, *n.* 〖軍〗酒保.

Q an ***air-base*** *commissary* 航空基地にある物資配給所.

commission, *n.* (**1**) 委任, 委任状; 委員会; 任命; 就役.

V The Government has ***appointed*** a *commission* to investigate the subject in all its aspects. 政府はその問題を徹底的に調査すべく委員を任命した. ¶He came ***bearing*** no *commission* from our Government. 彼はわが国の政府から何ら任命を受けずにきた. ¶***carry out*** a *commission* successully 使命をりっぱに果す. ¶***constitute*** a *commission* under Mr. So-and-So to investigate ... ...を調査すべく某を長とする委員会を組織する. 【類】***constitute*** a *commission* of inquiry (審理委員会). ¶***establish*** a permanent *commission* consisting of ... ...からなる常任委員会を設ける. ¶The artist ***executes*** a *commission* for the Queen. その芸術家は女王の御用をうけたまわっている. ‖ faithfully ***execute*** *commissions* for auction sales 競売の委託を忠実に実行する. ¶***forgo*** one's *commission* 自分の職務を捨てる. ¶***give*** him a *commission* to negotiate 彼に談判を委任する. ¶I ***have*** a high *commission* to execute. 私には遂行すべき大切な任務がある. ¶He ***holds*** a *commission* from the Government to do it. あの人は政府からその委任を受けている. ¶the manufacturers have ***received*** *commissions* for ... from ... その製造所では...から...の註文を受けた. 【類】the artist ***received*** a large number of *commissions* from ... ‖ They ***received*** a *commission* as officers. 彼らは士官に任命された. 【類】He ***received*** the *commission* of lieutenant. ¶The officer ***resigned*** his *commission.* 将校はその職を辞した. ¶He is willing to ***undertake*** the very smallest *commissions* for customers. 彼はお客のためにどんなわずかな御用でも喜んで引受ける.

Q the ***Far Eastern*** *Commission* 極東委員会. ¶a ***secret*** *commission* 秘密委員会. ¶a ***truant*** *commission* 開店休業の委員会.

Q^2 a Russian representative on the ***Allied control*** *commission* for Germany ドイツ管理委員会のソ連代表. ¶a ***battle-field*** *commission* 戦場における軍の任務. ¶the ***Civil Liberties*** *Commission* 人権擁護委員会. ¶the ***Fair Trade*** *Commission* 公正取引委員会. ¶a ***five-man*** *commission* 五人委員会. ¶a ***five-power investigation*** *commission* 五国調査委員会. ¶an important ***Government*** *commission* 重要な政府委員会. ¶an ***inquiry*** *commission* 調査委員会. ¶the United Nations Balkans ***investigating*** *commission* 国連バルカン調査委員会.

P a naval officer ***in*** *commission* 現役海軍士官. ¶I am sitting ***on*** a Royal *Commission* on the Coal Supply of Great Britain. 私は王立英国石炭供給調査委員会に席を持っている. ‖ He serves ***on*** the Historical Manuscript *Commission.* 彼は史料調査委員会に関係している. ‖ retain one's seat ***on*** the *commission* 委員会に席を留保する ‖ ***on*** *commission* from one's home government 本国政府からの使命を帯びて. ¶a war vessel ***out of*** *commission* 予備(廃)艦. 【類】put (=place) a warship ***out of*** *commission.* ¶***under*** a *commission* from ... ...の命を奉じて. 【類】he came to Japan ***under*** *commission* from ... ¶He went out ***upon*** this *commission.* 彼はこの使命を帯びて行った. ¶go to America ***with*** a *commission* from the Department その省の用務を帯びて米国に行く ‖ he sent me ***with*** a *commission* to ... 彼は...という用命で私を使いに出した.

P^2 the *commission* ***of*** authority to him 彼への権限の委任. ¶a *commission* ***of*** enquiry 審理委員会.

(**2**) 口銭, 手数料.

V ***allow*** a *commission* on services supplied 仕事に対して手数料を払う ‖ ***allow*** a *commission* of 20 per cent on sales 売上に対して二割の手数料を出す. ¶***charge*** a small *commission* on a transaction 取扱に対してわずかの手数料を取る. 【類】No *commission* is ***charged*** unless business results. ¶***deduct*** a *commission* and remit the net amount 手数料を差引いて純残高を送金する. ¶***divide*** *commission* with another 手数料を人と分ける. ¶This price does not ***include*** my *commission.* この価格には私の手数料ははいっていません. ¶Will you undertake to ***pay*** me a *commission* of 15 per cent. in the matter? その件に対し一割五分の口銭を私にお払い下さいますか.

Q I will give you a ***fair*** *commission* on the transaction. 君に相当のコンミッションを上げる. ¶the ***usual*** *commission* in such cases こうした場合常例になっている手数料.

P *at* (=*for or on*) a *commission* of ... on sales 売上に対する...の手数料で. ¶sell *by commission* from the producers 生産者からの委託販売をする. ¶profit *in commission* 手数料のもうけ. 「をとる.

Q^2 charge *ten per cent* (=10%) *commission* 一割の手数料

P work *on* a small *commission* わずかの口銭で働く. ¶sell *on commission* 委託販売をやる ‖ sell goods *on commission* 委託で販売する ‖ Agents have goods *on commission.* 取次店は委託品を取扱う. ‖ publishing *on commission* 委託出版 ‖ *on commission* of ... per cent ...パーセントの手数料.

P^2 a *commission for* goods bought or sold 売買した品物に対する手数料. 【類】My *commission for* doing the business is ... per cent.

(**3**) 犯行.

P *on* the second *commission* of the offense 再犯で. ¶be charged *with* the *commission* of murder 殺人罪に問われる ‖ He was charged *with* the *commission* of a crime against the laws. 彼は犯罪のかどで起訴された.

P^2 the *commission of* a theft 窃盗行為.

commission, *v.* 使命を与える, 依頼する.

P I was *commissioned by* him to paint his picture. 彼から肖像画を描いてくれと頼まれた. ‖ claim to have been *commissioned by* heaven *to* ... ...するようにという天からの使命を持っていると主張する.

commissioner, *n.* 事務官.

Q a *chief commissioner* 事務長官 ‖ the *chief commissioner* of the Metropolitan Police 警視総監. ¶a *high commissioner* 高等弁務官.

Q^2 a *civil service examination commissioner* 文官試験委員. ¶the *City Commissioner* of Buildings 都(市)建築監督官. 【類】a *New York City Police Commissioner.* ¶a *fire commissioner* 消防総監. ¶a *jury commissioner* 陪審委員. ¶Valentine is New York's former crack *gang-busting police commissioner.* バレンタイン氏はニューヨークのギャング取締りの元締である前警察長官である.

commit, *v.* (**1**) ゆだねる, 委託する; あずける; 行う.

P *commit* a crime *against* ... ...に違反した罪を犯す. ¶He was *committed for* trial. 彼は裁判に付された ‖ be *committed for* fraud 詐欺罪に問われる. 【類】be *committed for* public trial (公判) / be *committed for* narcotics violations (麻薬取締法違犯). ¶He was *committed to* the care of an aunt, his mother's sister. 彼は母の妹に当る叔母さんにあずけられた. ‖ I *commit* my son *to* you (your care). 息子を君にお委せする. 【類】*commit* this *to* your care. ‖ *commit* the estate *to* the custody of ... 財産を...の保管にゆだねる ‖ *commit* a body *to* the earth (=ground=grave) 死体を埋める. 【類】*commit* the body *to* the keeping of the deep (水葬) ‖ *commit* ... *to* the flames (=fires) ...を焼く ‖ I *committed* it *to* a friend for safe-keeping. それを友人に保管させた. ‖ He was *committed to* a lunatic asylum 彼は精神病院に入れられた. ‖ *commit* it *to* memory それを記憶する ‖ *commit* it *to* writing それを書き記す ‖ *commit* observation (reflection) *to* paper 感想(など)を筆記する ‖ *commit* it *to* print それを印刷に付する ‖ *commit* a criminal *to* prison (=jail) 罪人を投獄する. 【類】*commit* them *to* a short term of imprisonment.

commitment, *n.* 委託; 公約, 言質.

Q an *all-out commitment* 全面的な約束. ¶give *precipitate commitment* 軽率な言質を与える.

Q^2 faithfully observe their *surrender commitments* その降服条件を忠実に守る.

committal, *n.* 〘法〙犯行.

V refuse to *admit* the *committal* of a crime 犯行を否認する.

committee, *n.* 〘団〙委員, 委員会.

V *appoint* a *committee* of inquiry 調査委員を任命する. 【類】*appoint* a *committee* to inquire into ... / *appoint* a *committee* to deal with the subject. ¶The *committee* was *called.* 委員が召集された. ¶*call in* a strong *committee* including ... to determine ... ...を決定すべく(某)をふくむ有力な委員を召集する. ¶a *committee composed* of ... ...からなる委員会. ¶They *constitute* the *committee.* 彼らが構成委員となっている. ¶*discharge* a *committee* 委員会を解散する. ¶*form* a *committee* to take the matter in hand その事件を取扱う委員会を組織する. ¶the *committee* is *made up* of ... 委員会は...からなる. ¶*name* a special *committee* charged with the duty of ... ...の任務に当る特別委員を指名する. ¶*organize* a *committee* 委員会を組織する. ¶the *committee set* in the spring of this year 本年春に設置された委員会.

V^2 The *committee differ* as to what report they shall make. 委員はその報告すべき事項について意見を異にしている. ¶The *committee meets* in the town-hall. 委員は市会堂に会集する.

Q an *advisory committee* of twenty-five persons 二十五人から成る諮問委員会. ¶a *consultative committee* of seven persons 七人からなる協議委員会. ¶a *disciplinary committee* 懲罰委員会. ¶an *executive committee* 実行委員. ¶a *financial committee* 財政委員会. ¶a *joint committee* 両院合同委員会. ¶a *political committee* 政治委員会. ¶a *provisional committee* 仮設委員会. ¶a *representative committee* 代表委員. ¶a *select committee* of inquiry 特別審査委員会.

Q^2 an *anniversary committee* 年祭委員会. ¶serve on the *award* (=*awarding*) *committee* of a competition 競技の審査委員となる. ¶a *budget committee* 予算委員会. ¶a *coordinating committee* 調整委員会. ¶a *Diet fact-finding committee* 国会実情調査委員会. ¶a *deliberation committee* 審議会. ¶a *dispute committee* 争議委員会. ¶a *draft[ing] committee* 徴用(兵)委員会. ¶an *election committee* 選挙委員会. ¶an *entertaining committee* 演芸(余興)係. ¶a *foreign affairs committee* 外務委員会. ¶set up a "*Good Offices*" *Committee* 「親切」委員会を設ける. ¶a *grievance committee* 苦情委員会. ¶the *hanging committee* [美術]審査選択委員会. ¶an *inquiry committee* 審査委員会. ¶an *investigation committe* 調査委員. ¶a *membership committee* 会員資格審査委員会. ¶The *Military Staff Committee* is the "high command" of the UNO. 軍事作戦委員会は国連内の高級司令部である. ¶a *nominating committee* [役員]指命委員会. ¶a *one-man committee* 一人委員会. ¶an *organization committee* 組織委員会. ¶an *organizing committee* 創立(組織)委員会 ‖ the *organizing committee* for the XII Olympic Games 第十二回オリンピック大会の組織委員会. ¶a *police committee* 警察委員会. ¶a *policy planning committee* 政策委員会. ¶a *price picketing committee* 価格統制委員会. ¶a *program[me] planning committee* 番組編成委員会. ¶the *Public Office Qualification Committee* 公職適格審査委員会. ¶He is on the *reception committee.* 彼は接待委員の一人である. ¶a *qualification screening committee* 資格審査委員会. ¶a *research committee* 調査委員. ¶a *reviewing committee* 審査委員. ¶a *selection committee* [作品などの陳列についての]審査委員会. ¶a *shop commmittee* 職場委員会. ¶a *standing committee* 常任委員. ¶a *steering committee* 運営委員. ¶a *three-man committee* 三人委員会. ¶a *vigilance committee* [民間の]警防団. ¶a *visiting committee* [他国からの]訪問委員. ¶a *welcome committee* 歓迎委員.

P a bill modified *in committee* 委員会で修正された議案. ¶The session went *into committee* 会は委員会に移った. 【類】For the first time a woman was elected *into* the *committee.* ¶gentlemen *on* the *committee* 委員となっている諸君 ‖ The school is represented *on* the *committee.* その学校から委員を出している. ¶The Bill is *out of committee.* 該案は委員の手を離れた. ¶The Bill has passed *through* the *committee.* 同案は委員会を通過した.

P^2 a *committee for* the compilation of a history of the Restoration 維新史編集委員. ¶a *committee of* inquiry= an inquiry committee ‖ a *committee of* invitation and reception 接待掛 ‖ a *committee of* eminent scholars 著名の学者からなる委員会. ¶a *committee on* arrangements [展覧会など催すときの]交渉委員. 【類】a *committee on* discipline (hygiene, literature, publication) / the *committee on* organization of International Electrical Congress. ¶a *committee with* Mr. ... as chairman ...氏を委員長とする委員会.

commodity, *n.* 商品, 物品.

Q a distribution agent of *daily commodities* 必需物資配給所. ¶the increase in the *essential commodities* of life 生活必需品の増加. ¶a *marketable commodity* 売口のよい商品. ¶a *perishable commodity* 破損しやすい品物. ¶Sometimes water becomes a *precious commodity.* 水も高価な商品になることがある. ¶a *staple commodity* 主要産物 ‖ The *staple commodity* of London conversation is the weather. ロンドンの主なる話題は天候である. ¶*vital commodities* 大切な日用品.

Q² *farm commodities* 農産物. ¶*shipping commodities* 《米》積荷. ¶The most important of her ***trading** commodities* are grain and cotton. その国の最も重要な商品は穀物と綿である. ¶Sugar now ranks with wheat and cotton as a ***world** commodity*. 砂糖は今や世界的商品として小麦および綿と同列に位する.

P² *Commodities **for*** export have continued to pile up. 輸出物資は引続き停滞している.

common, *n.* 共同, 共通, 普通.

P He is a man ***above*** the *common*. 彼は非凡な人だ. ¶bathing of the sexes ***in** common* 混浴 ‖ The English and the Russian nations have many traits of character ***in** common*. 英ソ両国民は共通な特質を多分に持っている. ‖ the possession of a language ***in** common* 同一国語の共用 ‖ a forest owned ***in** common* 共有森林地 ‖ He believed, ***in** common* with the majority, that it was true. 大多数がそうであったように彼もそれが事実だと信じていた. 【類】He was blamed ***in** common* with the rest. ‖ They have something (nothing) ***in** common* with each other. 彼らはたがいに似通った所がある(ない). 【類】I wonder what he has ***in** common* with those people. / The Japanese have little ***in** common* with the Chinese. ¶It is something ***out of*** (＝above) the *common*. それは珍品だ.

common, *a.* 普通の, 共通の.

M Bad eyesight is ***less** common* in this part. この辺では目の悪い人は少ない. ¶be ***quite** common* ありふれている. ¶It's ***too** common* to mention. きまり切った話だ. ¶be ***very** common* ざらにある.

P an error *common **among*** scholars 学者にありがちな間違い. ¶a defect *common **between*** the two 二者に共通な欠点. ¶a flower *common **in*** the field 野によくある草花. ¶moss *common **on*** British coasts 英国の海岸に多いこけ. ¶Nothing is *commoner **than*** that. それほどありがちなことはない. ¶The desire to make money is *common **to*** most men. 金をもうけたいという欲は大抵の人にあるものだ. 【類】The word "caviare" is *common **to*** most European languages. / The garden is *common **to*** the two houses. / He has some faults *common **to*** all Japanese. / be *common **to*** all ages (あらゆる年代に) / The enjoyment of flowers is *common **to*** all Japanese. ¶*common **with*** the others (＝rest) その他のものと共通な.

commoner, *n.* 平民.

Q Hara was the ***first** commoner* to hold the position of premier. 原は最初の平民宰相であった.

Q² a ***fellow** commoner* 特待校友と食事を共にした外種々の特権を与えられたオクスフォード大学の自費生. ¶a ***gentleman** commoner* オクスフォードやケンブリッジ大学最高クラスの自費生.

commonplace, *n.* 平凡なこと, 陳腐の語.

Q It's a ***mere** commonplace*. 陳腐な言い草だ. ¶Conversation on such an occasion is not expected to soar above ***polite** commonplace*. こんな場合の談話は体裁のよいきまり文句以上に出ることは望まれない. ¶use ***tasteful** commonplaces* for every occasion いつもあり来りだが気のきいた文句を用いる. ¶a ***trite** commonplace* respecting ... ...に関する陳腐な言葉.

O it is a *commonplace* to say ... ...などということはだれでも知っていることだ.

commonplaceness, *n.* 平凡.

V ***hate** commonplaceness* 平凡をきらう.

common sense, 常識.

V ***exercise** common sense* 常識を働かす. ¶we ***have*** too much *common sense* to believe that ... ...と信じることはわれわれの常識が許さない. ¶lack of *common sense* is ***shown*** in ... ...に非常識さが現れている. ¶Here as everywhere, *common sense* must be ***used***. この場合も例の通り常識で行かなければならない.

Q contain much ***robust** common sense* 健全な常識を多分に含む.

P² *common sense **in*** export management 輸出経営上の常識.

commonwealth, *n.* 国家.

Q the ***British** Commonwealth* of Nations 英連邦. ¶a ***non-capitalist** commonwealth* 非資本主義的国家.

commotion, *n.* 騒動; 動揺, 波らん.

V The discovery ***caused*** a tremendous *commotion* in the scientific world. その発見は科学界に非常な動揺をまき起した. ¶***create*** a *commotion* 動揺を引き起す. ¶***excite*** a terrible *commotion* 恐ろしい騒動を激発させる. ¶It ***made*** quite a *commotion* in a small way. それはちょっと大騒ぎだった. ¶The *commotion **subsided*** a bit. 騒動は少し静まった.

Q It is nothing more than a ***petty** commotion*. それは一小波らんに過ぎない.

commune, *v.* 談合する.

P *commune **with*** nature 自然に親しむ ‖ *commune **with*** oneself (＝one's own heart) 沈思默考する.

communicable, *a.* 伝えられる.

M The secret is not ***directly** communicable*. その秘決は(自得しうるだけであって)直接伝授ができない.

P be *communicable **by*** words 言葉で伝えうる.

communicate, *v.* 通知する; 通ずる.

M A side-door of the pavilion ***immediately** communicated* with it. 仮屋のわき戸から直接にそこへ出入ができた. ¶***officially** communicate* to ... ...へ公式に通達する.

P *communicate **by*** letter (post, telephone, wireless) 手紙(など)で知らせる. ¶The Pacific Ocean *communicates **by*** Bering Strait ***with*** the Arctic Ocean on the north. 太平洋は北はベーリング海峡によって北極洋に通じている. 【類】The lake *communicates **with*** the sea ***by*** means of a canal. ¶*communicate* a news (fact) ***to*** ... 消息(など)を...に知らせる. ¶*communicate **to*** a person the fact that ... ...という事実を人に知らせる ‖ The fire *communicated **to*** an adjoining house. 火事は隣家へ燃え移った. ‖ a letter *communicated* (＝sent) ***to*** ... from ... ...から...へ送った手紙. ¶one room *communicating **with*** another 次の部屋に行ける部屋. 【類】The bedroom *communicated **with*** my study. ‖ I immediately *communicated **with*** the police. すぐ警察に知らせた. ‖ We *communicated **with*** the firm regarding the matter. その件で会社と通信した. ‖ *communicate* direct[ly] ***with*** ... ...と直接文通する. 【類】I have no foreign friends to *communicate **with***. / *communicate **with*** a ship by signals / *communicate **with*** him by mail ***about*** the matter.

communication, *n.* 通信; 交通; 連絡.

V ***address*** all *communications* to ... すべての通信を...にあてる. 【類】All *communications* should be ***addressed*** to the College, E. C. 4. ¶the pass ***affords** communication* with ... とうげを越せば...へ行かれる. ¶***await*** a *communication* 書信を待つ. ¶The photograph ***bears*** a *communication*. その写真には通信文が載っている. ¶Steam *communication* is ***carried on*** by the Osaka Shosen Kaisha. 大阪商船会社の汽船が通っている. ¶***cut off** communications* with ... ...との連絡を絶つ. ¶please ***direct*** all *communications* to ... 通信はすべて...あてに願います. ¶***dislocate*** telephone and telegraph *communication* 電話電信の通信を狂わす. ¶***disrupt** communication* 通信を乱す. ¶***establish*** wireless *communication* between ... ...間に無線を設置する. ¶***form*** (＝***establish** or **open up***) direct telegraphic *communication* with ... ...と直通電信を開く. ¶I ***had** communication* from ... ...から便りがあった. ¶***have*** no *communication* with ... ...とは文通していない. ¶***hold** communication* with the spirit world through the medium of superstitious practices 迷信的行為によって霊界と交通する. ¶Telegraphic *communication* is ***interrupted***. 電信に故障を生じた. ¶***keep up*** rapid *communication* between ... and ... ...間は直ちに通信できるようにしておく. ¶***lodge*** a *communication* with ... ...に書信を差出す. ¶***maintain*** regular *communication* between ... and ... ...間に定期交通を続ける. ¶***open*** [***up***] *communication* with Japan 日本と交通を開く. ¶***receive*** a *communication* from ... ...から書信を受ける. 【類】***receive*** a *communication* that ... ¶We cannot undertake to ***return*** rejected *communications*. 没書は御返送致しかねます. ¶***send** communications* to a conference 会議に通信する. 【類】***send*** all *communications* to ... ¶All *communication* was ***stopped*** by the floods. あらゆる通信は洪水のためとだえた.

Q ***Anonymous** communications* cannot be considered, but the names of correspondents will be withheld when so desired. 匿名の通信は没書になりますが通信者の希望があれば御名前は他に漏らしません. ¶a ***confidential** communication* 秘密の情報. ¶in ***constant** communication* with Europeans ヨーロッパ人と絶えず通信して. ¶stand in ***direct** communication* with ... ...と直通している. ¶the scientific and engineering aspects of ***electrical** communication* 電気による通信の科学的および工業的方面. ¶an ***external** communication* 外界との交通. ¶an ***extraordinary*** *communication* 異常な通信. ¶In winter the steam *communication* is less ***frequent***. 冬期は汽船の交通が少くなる. ¶There are ***good*** *communications* to the place. そこへの交通は便利である. ¶He pretended to have ***immediate*** *communication* with the gods. 彼は神々と直接霊交しているようなふりをした. ¶have ***numerous*** *communications* from ... about ... ...に関する無数の情報がある. ¶***oral*** *communication* 口頭による通報. ¶a ***personal*** *communication* 親展の書信. ¶in our ***previous*** *communication* 前回通信の際. ¶a ***private*** *communication* from ... ...からの私信. ¶***privileged*** *communications* 特権事項. ¶the town has no ***telephonic*** *communication* with ... その市は...と電話の連絡がない. ¶***Telegraphic*** *communication* has entirely been stopped (been seriously impeded). 電信が全くとだえた(など). ¶this ***typewritten*** *communication* このタイプの手紙. ¶***wireless telegraphic*** *communication* has been opened with ... ...との無線電信が開通した. ¶***world-wide*** *communication* 世界への通信. ¶a ***written*** *communication* 文書による通報.

Q² a ***business*** *communication* 商用通信. ¶***cable*** *communication* 海外通信. ¶***cipher*** *communication* 暗号通信. ¶The ship is in constant ***land*** *communication* by wireless telegraph and telephone installations, powerful enough to reach Italy from New York. 同船はニューヨークからイタリアに達するほどに強力なる無線電信・電話機によって絶えず陸上と通信している. ¶The transmission of the address was one of the finest examples of ***long-distance*** *communication*. [送信局からの]あて先を知らせる送波は長距離通信のきわめてよい例の一つだった. ¶***mass*** *communication* 大衆伝達(新聞・ラジオなど). ¶***phone*** *communications* with the outside have been cut off 外部との電話連絡は絶たれた. ¶dispatch ***radio*** *communication* 無線による電報(電話)通信を発する. ¶the importance of the ***road*** *communication* between towns and villages 町村間道路交通の重要性. ¶there is constant ***steam*** *communication* between ... and ... ...間には絶えず汽船が通っている. 【類】has a regular ***steam*** *communication* with ... / There was no regular ***steam*** *communication* with ... in those days. / There is ***steam*** *communication*, twice daily, between Aomori and Hakodate, the distance of 56 miles, taking 5 hours. ¶***Telegraph*** *communication* was broken off. 電報通信がとだえた. 【類】***Telegraph*** *communication* has been restored. ¶have ***telephone*** *communication* with ... ...との間に電話が通じている. ¶it is in ***water*** *communication* with ... ...と水路の便がある. ¶establish direct ***wireless*** *communication* 直通無線を創設する. ¶uncertain ***wire*** *communications* 不確実な有線通信 ‖ ***Wire*** *communications* were torn down. 電信(話)線があちこち切れた(暴風などで).

P cut off the island ***from*** *communication* with the outside world その島を外界との交通からしゃ断する. ¶The Governor is ***in*** *communication* with the Central Government on the subject. 同知事はこの問題に関して中央政府と打合わせ中である. ¶What means ***of*** *communication* are there? そこにはどんな通信機関があるか. ¶a famous Scandinavian explorer who has been ***out of*** *communication* in Central Asia for nearly a year. 中央アジアで約一年間消息を絶っている有名なスカンジナヴィアの探検家.

P² a *communication* ***by*** letter (telegraph) 手紙(など)の便り ‖ it is in *communication* ***by*** the air with ... ...と航空路の便がある. ¶a *communication* ***from*** a man signing himself ... ...と自署した通信文. ¶*communication* ***in*** writing 文書による通信. ¶*Communication* ***over*** the new cable line was started the same afternoon. その新海底電線の通信が同日午後開始された. ¶The Government had *communication* ***with*** several countries. 政府は五六カ国と交渉した. ‖ get (=enter) into *communication* ***with*** ... ...と通信を始める ‖ shut off from *communication* ***with*** the outer world except by telegraph 電信による外は外界との交通をしゃ断されて.

communicative, *a.* 打解けた, 話ずきの.

P He was not *communicative* ***about*** himself. 彼は自分のことは打明けなかった. ¶He is *communicative* ***in*** [the] company of the fair. 彼は婦人と同席だと口が軽くなる. ¶He is very *communicative* ***with*** me. 彼は私にはよく打明け話をする.

communion, *n.* 親交.

V ***hold*** *communion* with nature 自然と親くし交わる.

Q a ***religious*** *communion* 宗教団体. ¶be of the ***same*** *communion* 同じ教派に属する.

P² the *communion* ***of*** heart ***with*** heart 以心伝心. ¶*communion* ***with*** the Invisible 霊界との接触.

communist, *n.* 共産主義者; [C-] 共産党員.

Q a ***half-boiled*** *communist* 桃色共産主義者.

Q² the real ***dyed-in-the-wool*** *Communists* 筋金入りの共産党員.

communistic-minded, *a.* 共産主義的傾向の.

M These people are ***more or less*** *communistic-minded*. これらの人々は多かれ少かれ共産主義かぶれしている.

community, *n.* 共同体; [the c-] 社会; 共通; 共有.

V the best ways of ***benefiting*** the *community* 社会を益する最善の方法. ¶We ***have*** a *community* of tastes. われわれは趣味が一致している. 【類】He ***had*** no *community* of tastes with his father. ¶best ***serve*** the *community* 最も社会のためになる.

Q a ***civilized*** *community* 文明社会. ¶The city is a ***cosmopolitan*** *community*. その都市は世界人の集団である. ¶a well-known member of the ***foreign*** *community* of Yokohama 横浜在住外人中知名の士. ¶The town is a thriving ***industrial*** *community*. その町は繁昌する工業地である. ¶the ***mercantile*** *community* 商業社会. ¶***populous*** *communities* 繁華な都会. ¶a ***poverty-stricken, ill-fed*** *community* 困苦と栄養不足の社会. ¶even in the best ***regulated*** *community* 最善の秩序を保っている社会においてすら. ¶a ***religious*** *community* 宗教団体. ¶a ***rural*** *community* 田園部落. ¶an ***urban*** *community* 都市.

Q² an idol of the ***Edo*** *community* 江戸時代の崇拝の的. ¶a ***one-industry*** *community* 単一産業市. ¶***town*** and ***village*** *communities* 町村公共体. ¶build citizenship in a ***world*** *community* 国際社会の構成員たる資格を確立する ‖ a democratic state in the ***world*** *community* of nations 国際社会の民主主義国.

P a remarkable figure ***in*** the foreign *community* of Japan 在日外人中の著名な人物.

P² the *community* ***of*** goods 物資共有 ‖ *communities* ***of*** common interest 共通の利害を有する諸団体. 【類】a recognition of *community* ***of*** interest among the employers and the employed / the restoration of Japanese independence and the return of Japan into the *community* ***of*** nations.

commutable, *a.* 換えられる.

P The sentence of imprisonment is *commutable* ***by*** a fine. 禁固刑は罰金をもってかえることができる.

commutation, *n.* 減刑.

P² *commutation* ***of*** punishment 減刑 ‖ *commutation* ***of*** the death penalty ***to*** penal servitude 死刑の懲役への減刑.

commute, *v.* 取換える; 減刑する; 《米》回数(定期)乗車券を買う.

P *commute* pain ***for*** pleasure 苦痛を変じて快楽とする. ¶The sentence of death was *commuted* ***into*** imprisonment for life. 死刑は終身禁固に減刑された. ¶*commute* a death sentence ***to*** life imprisonment 死刑を終身禁固に減刑する ‖ *commute* ***to*** a place 《米》ある地点までの回数乗車券を買う; [電車・列車などで]ある地へ通う.

commuter, *n.* 《米》回数(定期)券使用者.

Q² a ***rail*** *commuters* 鉄道利用の通勤者.

P² a *commuter* ***between*** ... and ... ...間の回数(定期)乗車券使用者.

compact, *n.* 約定, 契約.

V ***make*** a *compact* by which ... 契約をなしそれによって...する.

P² a *compact* ***between*** parties (individuals, states) 党派(など)間の契約. ¶come into a *compact* ***with*** Russia ロシアと契約する.

companion, *n.* 仲間, 伴りょ, 相手.

V It ***forms*** a *companion* to the present volume. それは本書の姉妹篇だ. ¶***make*** *companions* of books 書籍を友とする. ¶Here's the glove for my left hand but I can't ***find*** its *companion*. 左手の手袋はここにあるんだが, 右手の方が見つからない.

Q an ***agreeable*** *companion* おもしろい相手. ¶an ***agreeable talking*** *companion* たのしい話し相手. ¶***bad*** *companions* 悪い仲間. ¶his ***boon*** *companion* 彼の飲み仲間 ‖ an inimitable ***boon*** *companion* とても愉快な飲み友だち. ¶his ***brave*** *companion* in arms 彼の勇敢なる戦友. ¶***chance-met*** *companions* on life's highways ひよっとしたことで知り合った友. ¶a ***charming*** *companion* このましい友. ¶***congenial*** *companion* 意気投合した友. ¶make a dictionary one's ***constant*** *companion* 辞書を常用する. 【類】his ***constant*** *companion* in illness. ¶***daily*** *companions* 日々の友.

¶a ***delectable*** (=***delightful***) *companion* 会心の友. ¶his ***dissolute*** *companions* 彼の放とう仲間. ¶his ***duller*** *companions* in class 教室で彼より成績の悪い仲間. ¶be led astray by ***evil*** *companion* 悪友に誘惑される. ¶She is a ***faithful*** *companion* for fifty long years. 彼女は[われわれにとって]五十年の長い歳月間の好伴りょだ. ¶The pony is his ***favorite*** *companion*. 彼のいつもの連れは小馬だ. ¶a ***fit*** *companion* 適当な相手. ¶a ***gentlemanly*** *companion* 紳士らしい友. ¶an ***indispensable*** *companion* to students 学生必携の参考書. ¶his ***inseparable*** *companion* 切っても切れない友. ¶a most ***jovial*** *companion* とても愉快な仲間. ¶a ***lifelong*** *companion* 一生の伴りょ. ¶***ruffianly*** *companions* 悪党の仲間. ¶a ***teacher's*** *companion* to ... ...の教師用. ¶shake off (=get rid of) an ***undesirable*** *companion* 好ましくない交友と絶交する. ¶a ***worthy*** *companion* りっぱな友人.

Q² his ***boy*** *companions* 彼の少年のころの友だち. ¶a ***chance*** *companion* 遇然連れになった人. ¶a ***dinner*** *companion* 食い仲間. ¶his ***life*** *companion* 彼の一生の伴りょ ‖ She chose her ***life*** *companion*. 彼女は夫を持った. ¶one's ***seat*** *companion* in a street-car 都電内の座席で隣り合わせた人. ¶a ***student*** *companion* of ... ...の虎の巻. ¶a ***study*** *companion*=a reference book 参考書. ¶a ***travel[ing]*** *companion* 旅の連れ. ¶a good ***walking*** *companion* よい散歩づれ.

P He was led away ***by*** bad *companions*. 彼は悪友に引きずり込まれた. ¶Keep ***from*** (=***off***) bad *companions*. 悪友を避けよ. ¶***with*** five *companions* 五人仲間を連れて.

P² a *companion* ***at*** (=***in***) arms 戦友. ¶a *companion* ***for*** life=a life companion. ¶a *companion* ***in*** crime 共犯者 ‖ *companions* ***in*** folly 放とう仲間.【類】*companions* ***in*** idleness / their *companions* ***in*** misfortune ‖ a *companion* ***in*** his revels 彼の飲み仲間 ‖ a *companion* ***of*** fools ばか者同志 ‖ *companions* ***of*** his pleasures 道楽仲間 ‖ a *companion* ***of*** a picture 双幅画の一. ¶She longs to be his *companion* ***through*** life. 彼女は彼と一生をともにしたいと願っている. ¶a *companion* ***to*** Higher English Grammar「高等英文典」の虎の巻.

companion, *v.* 交わる.

P *companion* ***with*** fools ばか者と交わる.

companionship, *n.* 伴りょたること, 交際.

V ***enjoy*** the *companionship* of ... ...と同席してうれしく思う.【類】***enjoy*** the *companionship* of books. ¶***lacking*** *companionship* 相手欲しやで. ¶I had to change car and ***lost*** the *companionship* of a pretty young lady. 乗換えなければならなかったので乗合わせていた若い麗人と別れた. ¶He ***needed*** the *companionship* of a family. 彼は家族のものと一緒にいることを欲していた. ¶***seek*** the *companionship* of ... ...との交際を求める.

Q ***bad*** *companionship* 悪友との交際. ¶***congenial*** *companionship* 気の合った同志の交友. ¶He loves the book and wants its ***constant*** *companionship*. 彼はその本を愛し座右から放さずにいる. ¶***feminine*** *companionship* 女性との交際 ‖ seek the ***friendly*** *companionship* of ... ...との交際を求める. ¶The couple have lived together in ***happy*** *companionship* for fifty years. 夫婦は五十年間楽しくつれ添ってきた. ¶the ***low*** *companionship* which a drunkard keeps のんべいのやる上品でない連中とのつきあい. ¶the freer ***mutual*** *companionship* of the sexes 男女の一層自由な相互的交際. ¶***pleasant*** *companionship* 愉快なつれ. ¶with the ***sole*** *companionship* of books 書籍を唯一の友として.

P His life has been spent ***in*** the *companionship* of the sea. 彼は海を友として一生を過した.

company, *n.* (**1**) 仲間, 交際, 来客; 一行; 中隊.

V ***amuse*** *company* with singing 歌で客をもてなす. ¶***avoid*** the *company* of strangers 知らない人との交際を避ける. ¶I want some one to ***bear*** me *company*. だれか相手が欲しい. ‖ I cannot ***bear*** his *company* 彼と同席はがまんができない. ¶They ***broke*** *company*. 彼らは別れた. ¶***choose*** (***select***) one's *company* well 友をよく選ぶ. ¶I do not ***enjoy*** the *company* of the opposite sex. 私は異性との交際を好まない. ¶***entertain*** *company* with music 音楽で客をもてなす. ¶the present *company* ***excepted*** この席の方々は例外として(何か差障りのあることを言う場合など). ¶I'm glad to ***have*** her *company*. 彼女と同席できてうれしい. ‖ when I ***have*** *company* 来客があると.【類】They cannot come with us, they ***have*** *company* tonight. ¶***invite*** *company* to tea 茶の会に客を招く. ¶He ***joined*** *company* with us. 彼はわれわれの仲間に入った. ¶***keep*** *company* with ... ...と交際する ‖ ***keep*** her *company* 彼女のお相手をする.【類】I will ***keep*** you *company* as far as ... ¶***love*** the *company* of children 子供を相手にするのが好き. ¶***meet*** *company* on the road 途中で友だちに会う. ¶***part*** *company* from him 彼と別れる ‖ And there I am obliged to ***part*** *company* with him. でその点僕は彼と説を異にする. ‖ ***part*** *company* with the creed of one's childhood 子供時代の信条を捨てる ‖ let us, in ***parting*** *company*, ... 終りに臨んで(筆をおくに当って)...しましょう. ¶***receive*** much *company* 来客が多い. ¶He ***sees*** no *company*. 彼は面会謝絶だ. ‖ She is not used to ***seeing*** *company*. 彼女は人に会いつけていない. ‖ The ... *company* will be ***seen*** at the Imperial Theatre next week. 来週...の一座が帝劇にかゝる. ¶***seek*** the *company* of ... ...との交際を求める. ¶***shun*** *company* 交際を避ける. ¶He exclaimed that, to ***start*** the *company*, he would sing himself. 彼は皆の前座に自分が最初に歌を歌うとさけんだ. ¶***treat*** the *company* with his speech 一座の人々に演説をする.

V² after the *company* ***breaks up*** 一座がお開きになってから. ¶The *company* ***dispersed*** by twos and threes. 一座は三々五々散じた. ¶The *company* ***dropped*** away. 来会者はぼつりぼつり帰った.

Q keep ***bad*** company 悪友と交る.【類】unwisely keep ***bad*** *company* ‖ be fond of ***bright*** *company* 明朗な連中が好きだ. ¶a ***brilliant*** *company* お歴々の方々. ¶a ***concert*** *company* 楽団. ¶a ***congenial*** *company* 気のあった同志 ‖ a ***decent*** *company* 上品な連中. ¶He is lazy and fond of ***evil*** *company*. 彼はなまけ者で悪友と交わるのが好きだ. ‖ We have done so in ***good*** *company*. 私たちと同じようにそうした人は有名な人の中にもある(悪い事をした時などの言訳). ¶He is ***good*** *company* [to keep]. 彼は付合ってよい男だ. ¶keep ***idle*** *company* なまけ者と交わる. ¶a good dinner and ***jolly*** *company* りっぱな御ちそうと愉快な仲間. ¶a ***merry*** *company* 陽気な連中. ¶I was of the ***privileged*** *company* who assembled on Saturday afternoon at ... 幸い私は土曜の午後...に集った人たちと一しょにいた. ¶He belongs to this ***select*** *company*. 彼はこの選り抜きの仲間の一人だ. ¶Some of the big cinema firms now have five or six actors in their ***stock*** *company*. 今では大映画会社の中には五六人の専属俳優をもっているのがある. ¶a ***theatrical*** *company* 演芸一座. ¶He joined Madame Albani's ***world-touring*** *company* of last season. 彼はこの前の興行季節にアルバニ夫人の世界周遊一座に加わった.

P know a man ***by*** his *company* 人はその仲間でわかる. ¶go with him ***for*** *company* おつき合いに彼と一緒に行く ‖ weep ***for*** *company* もらい泣をする.【類】with only a dog ***for*** *company*. ¶travel ***in*** his *company* 彼と一緒に旅行する ‖ tour England ***in*** *company* with ... ...と一緒に英国を漫遊する ‖ I found him ***in*** *company* of ... 彼が...と一緒にいるのを見た. ‖ ***In*** *company* of women, he feels very small and bashful. 彼は女の前へ出ると小さくなって恥かしがる. ‖ hate to be seen ***in*** *company* 人中に出るのをきらう.【類】You must behave well ***in*** *company*. / spend an hour ***in*** one's own *company* / She was ***in*** his *company* for an hour. ‖ He is ***in*** bad *company*. 彼は悪い友だちを持っている. ‖ If I am wrong, I have erred ***in*** very good *company*. 私が悪いなら世間のりっぱな人も私の仲間だ. ‖ In this respect he sinned ***in*** good *company*. この点では彼ばかりとがむべきでない. ¶I get ***into*** bad *company* 悪友の仲間にはいる. ¶I fell ***into*** *company* with him. 偶然彼と一緒になった. ¶He keeps ***to*** his own company. 彼は人と交際しない. ¶There is not much enjoyment in going out for a walk ***without*** *company*. ひとりで散歩に出掛けるのはあまりおもしろくない.

P² one's *company* ***at*** a dinner 食卓での相手. ¶a *company* ***of*** distinguished scholars 著名学者の一団 ‖ a *company* ***of*** foot 歩兵一中隊 ‖ He is fond of the *company* ***of*** profligate men. 彼は放とう者と交際するのが好きだ.

(**2**) 会社.

V ***amalgamate*** *companies* 会社を合併する. ¶a ***bogus*** *company* 幽霊会社. ¶***boom*** a *company* 《米》大いに会社の景気をよくする. ¶The new *company* will be ***capitalized*** at ... yen. 今度の会社は資本金...円になる. ¶***enter*** a *com* *pany* 入社する. ¶*float* (=*launch*) a *company* with a capital of ... yen ...円の資本で会社を起す. ¶*form* (=*establish*) a *company* 会社を設立する. ¶The *company* is now *housed* in fine premises at 15 North Andley Street, Mayfair. 同会社は今メーフェーア市北アドンレー街十五番地のりっぱな建物に収まっている. ¶a new *company* has just been *incorporated* in London called ... ...という新会社が丁度ロンドンに設立された所だ. 【類】The Pacific Mail Steamship *Company* was *incorporated* in New York on April 12, 1848, with a capital of $500,000. ¶*join* an accident insurance *company* 傷害保険会社に入社する. ¶*liquidate* (=*wind up*) a *company* 会社を解散する. ¶*organize* a *company* 会社を組織する. ¶*serve* a *company* with scrupulous fidelity きわめて忠実に会社に勤める. ¶*start* a bogus *company* いかさま会社を始める. ¶*sue* a *company* for damages 会社を相手取って損害賠償の訴訟を提起する.

V² The *company failed.* 会社は破産した. ¶The *company laid off* 100 hands. その会社は百人首を切った. ¶This *company pays* well. この会社はりっぱに立って行く.

Q a *fat company* すっかりもうけた会社. ¶a *collateral company* 会社の分身. ¶a *mercantile company* 商事会社. ¶They branded it as a *pure swindling company.* 世間ではそれを純然たるいんちき会社と判断した. ¶a *subsidiary company* 傍系会社. ¶a *young company* 創立日なお浅い新設会社.

Q² *affiliate companies* 傘下(さんか)の諸会社. ¶an *aviation manufacturing company* 航空機製作会社. ¶a *bubble company* 泡沫会社. ¶a *business company* 商社. 【類】a radio program sponsored by a *business company.* ¶*cable companies,* wire or wireless 有線・無線海外電信諸会社. ¶a *carrying company* 運送会社. ¶a *cooperative building company* 共同建築会社. ¶a *construction company* 土建会社. ¶a big *drag company* 大型貨物輸送会社. ¶an *export* (*import*) *company* 輸出(輸入)会社. ¶an *express company* 《米》運送会社. ¶the splitting up of the *family holding companies* 個人持株信託会社の分裂. ¶a *fire company* 消防団; 《英》火災保険会社. ¶the dissolution of *holding companies* 持株会社の解散. ¶a file clerk in the office of an *insurance company* 保険会社の文書整理係. ¶a *joint-stock company* 株式会社. ¶a *limited liability company* 有限責任会社. ¶a *limited joint stock company* 株式合資会社. ¶a *lumber company* 木材会社. ¶*member companies* 連盟諸会社. ¶a *merger company* 合同会社. ¶a *motor-vehicle manufacturing company* 自動車製作会社. ¶a *mutual insurance company* 相互保険会社. ¶a *mutual loan company* 無尽会社. ¶a *navigation company* 船(航空)会社. ¶a major *oil company* 大石油会社. ¶a *paper products company* 紙製品会社. ¶a *parcels-delivery company* 小運送会社. ¶*parent companies* and their subsidiaries 親会社とその子会社. ¶a *public utility holding company* 公益事業持株会社. ¶a *shipping company* 船会社. ¶a *sister company* 姉妹会社. ¶a *stock company* 株式会社. ¶a *trading company* 商事会社. ¶a *transfer company* 《主に米》運送会社. ¶a *transportation company* 運送会社. ¶the "Big Three" *vehicle producing companies* 三大自動車製作会社.

P He is employed *in* a *company.* 彼はある会社に勤めている.

comparable, *a.* 比較できる.

M an instance only *remotely comparable* to this わずかにこれと比較しうる事例.

P There is no book *comparable to* this in Japan. 日本にこれに匹敵する本はない. ‖ No other power is *comparable to* that of the printed word. その勢力において印刷した言葉に匹敵するものはない.

compare, *n.* 比較, 比類.

P abundant *beyond compare* 比類なく豊富な. 【類】precious jewels *beyond compare.*

compare, *v.* 比較する; たとえる.

M it can be *compared advantageously* with ... それは...と比べてまさる位だ. ¶*compare favorably* with ... in this respect この点において...に比して劣らない. 【類】*compare favorably* in quality (strength) with ... ¶*compare* very *poorly* with ... ...に比して大いに見劣りする. ¶*compare unfavorably* with ... ...と比べると見劣りがする.

P He *compares* it *to* the headlong descent from the height of a wounded eagle. 彼はそれを手負いのわしが高所から真っさかさまに墜落するのにたとえている. ‖ Man's life is often *compared to* a candle. 人間の一生はよくろうそくにたとえられる. ‖ Many poets have *compared* women *to* April weather. 多くの詩人は婦人を四月の陽気にたとえた. 【類】In the Bible, Christians are *compared to* sheep, evil persons to goats, and the use of wine to serpents. / *Compared to* the sun the earth is small, but some of the other planets *compare* favorably in size with the sun. ¶The French *eu* is sometimes *compared with e* in *her*, but is, if anything, a little longer than that sound. 仏語の *eu* はときに *her* の中の *e* と対比されるが *e* 音よりはどちらかと言うとやゝ長い. ‖ nothing can *compare with* ... ...におよぶものはない ‖ He *compared* my hand writing *with* my father's and preferred mine. 彼は僕の筆跡と僕の父のとを比較して僕の方が良いと言った. ‖ *Compared with* what it was, it has improved greatly. それは以前と比べると非常によくなった. ‖ as (when) *compared with* ... ...に比べて.

comparison, *n.* 比較; 類似.

V *bear comparison* with ... ...に匹敵できる ‖ *bear* a very favorable *comparison* with ... ...に比して優に勝る ‖ how do they *bear comparison* with ...? ...と比較して優劣いかん. 【類】will *bear comparison* with the best of ... / can hardly *bear comparison* with ... ¶*carry back* the *comparison* to 1892 比較を一八九二年に持って行く. ¶They boldly *challenge comparison* with their predecessors. 大胆にそれら以前のものとの比較をいどむ(その優秀をほこる). ‖ It may safely *challenge comparison* with any work on the subject. その問題に関するどの著作と比べても決して劣りはしない. ¶It *defies* all *comparison.* それとはとても比較にならない. ¶*draw comparsion* 比較する. ¶*establish* a *comparison* between ... ...間に比較を立てる. ¶*facilitate comparison* 比較を容易にさせる. ¶need not *fear comparison* with ... ...と比較しても劣る心配はない. ¶it *has* no *comparison* with ... それは...と比べ物にならない. ¶*institute* a *comparison* 比較をする. 【類】*institute* a *comparison* between ... and ... ¶*making* a *comparison* between ... and ..., I consider ... ...と...を比べて見ると私は...と思う ‖ it *makes* a very good *comparison* with ... ...と比較して非常によい. ¶*permit* ready *comaprison* 容易に比肩しうる. ¶*stand* (=bear) *comparison* with ... ...と比肩し得る. 【類】cannot *stand* (=*sustain*) *comparison* with ... / cannot *stand* a moment's *comparison* with their New York rivals / the only one of its kind which can *stand comparison* with similar institutions ‖ easily *stands comparison* with ... ...と較べて少しも劣らない.

Q a *critical comparison* of Carlyle and Emerson カーライルとエマースンの比較研究. ¶It is not a *fair comparison.* それは公正な比較ではない. ¶a *fanciful comparison* おもしろい比較. ¶a *far-fetched comparison* 見当はずれの比較. ¶a *humorous comparison* こっけいな比較. ¶draw *invidious comparisons* 不快な比較をする. ¶make a *minute comparison* of their merits 彼らの長所を精密に比較する. ¶tabulated for *ready comparison* 比較の便利のために表にした. ¶*rough comparisons* 大まかな比較. ¶a *tabular comparison* 比較表. ¶It is an *unkind comparison.* その比較は酷だ.

P It is *beyond* all *comparison.* それは全然比較にならない. ‖ This one is superior *beyond comparison.* この方が比較にならぬほど優秀だ. ¶All other crimes are virtues *by comparison.* それに比べると他の罪悪はすべて美徳のようなものだ. 【類】make it seem tame (つまらない) *by comparison* / seem rather weak *by comparison* ‖ fade into insignificance *by comparison* 他と比べると価値のないものになってしまう ‖ it does not suffer *by comparison* with ... それは...と比較して劣らない ‖ The size of this stone can be gauged *by comparison* with the man shown on the right in the quarry. この石の大さは石山の右方に表わしてある人と比較して知ることができる. ¶make it seem like a shadow *in comparison* 他と比べるとそれは影のようなものに思われる. 【類】it is quite insignificant (微々たるもの) *in comparison* with ... ¶the basis *of comparison* 比較の根拠. ¶It is *out of* (=beyond) all *comparison.* それは全く無類だ. ¶in the countries *under comparison* ここに比較をしている国々において ‖ it serves as a standard of *comparison with* which to measure ... それは...測定にお

いて比較の標準になる. ¶*without* (=beyond) *comparison* 比較にならないほど.

P² *comparison* ***between*** nature and art 自然と芸術との比較. 【類】some *comparisons* ***between*** the Latin and the Anglo-Saxon genius / a *comparison* ***between*** the past and the present. ¶a *comparison* ***of*** different types of steam turbines 各種蒸気タービンの比較 ‖ *comparison* ***of*** hands 筆跡の比較. ¶The *comparison* ***of*** the heart ***to*** a pump is a very common one. 心臓をポンプにたとえることは極めて普通のことである.

compartment, *n.* 一区画; 一室.

Q two ***communicating*** *compartments* 相通じている二室.

Q² be accommodated only in the ***baggage*** *compartment* [満員で]手荷物室の方に入れられる. ¶a ***non-smoking*** *compartment* 禁煙室 ¶share a ***railway*** *compartment* with ... ...と鉄道で同車する. ¶did not shy at traveling in a ***third-class*** *compartment* of a train 旅行は堂々と三等車でやった. ¶a ***water-tight*** *compartment* [船の]阻水室 ‖ The weakness of these newspapers is that they work in ***watertight*** *compartment*. これら新聞記者の欠点は密閉した部屋の内ばかりで(足を使わないで)書くことにある.

P² a *compartment* ***for*** ladies (列車などの)婦人室.

compass, *n.* (**1**) 限界, 範囲; 羅(⁵)針盤.

V ***box*** the *compass* 羅針盤の方位を順次に挙示する.

Q it is impossible within a ***brief*** *compass* to ... ...することは簡単に片付けられない. ¶pack into ***small*** *compass* an immense amount of information as to ... ...に関する大量の知識を小さいスペースに詰め込む. ¶It is known that the Chinese had a ***south-seeking*** *compass* for steering their ships nearly 2,000 years ago. 中国人は約二千年前彼らの船を操縦するに指南車(南方を指す羅針盤)を持っていたことが分っている. ¶a ***standard*** *compass* 〚航海〛標準羅針盤.

P We cannot go into detail ***in*** the small *compass* of a primer. 入門書のせまい範囲では詳細な記述はできない. ¶the points ***of*** the *compass* 羅針盤の方位. ¶***with*** the *compass* of a brief review 小論文では十分のスペースがないので. ¶Such a wide range of information has not hitherto (=heretofore) been accessible ***within*** the *compass* of a single volume. かく広範囲にわたる事項は今までただ一冊の本で知ることはできなかった. 【類】I cannot ***within*** the *compass* of this paper (論文) deal adequately with ... ‖ The fundamental principle is ***within*** the *compass* of the mind of a boy of ten. その根本原則は十歳の少年の頭で理解される.

(**2**) *pl.* 両脚規(コンパス).

Q ***universal*** *compasses* 自在コンパス.

P a pair ***of*** *compasses* コンパス一個. ¶measure ***with*** *compasses* コンパスで測る. 【類】draw a circle ***with*** *compasses*.

compassion, *n.* 同情, あわれみ.

V We ***excited*** the *compassion* of every one. われわれはあらゆる人々の同情を呼び起した. ¶***feel*** *compassion* for (= toward) ... ...に対して気の毒に思う. ¶I ***had*** *compassion* on him. 私は彼をかわいそうに思った. 【類】He could not help ***having*** *compassion* for the poor creature. ¶We ***took*** *compassion* on the poor widow (his solitary condition). われわれは気の毒な未亡人(など)をあわれんだ.

P ***in*** *compassion* to ... ...に同情して. ¶tears ***of*** *compassion* あわれみの涙. ¶***out of*** *compassion* あわれみの気持から. ¶He was moved ***with*** *compassion*. 彼はあわれを催した.

P² *compassion* ***for*** him 彼への同情. ¶*compassion* ***of*** the benevolent for the poor 慈悲深い人の貧者に対する同情. ¶*compassion* ***on*** him 彼に対する同情.

compassionate, *a.* あわれみ深い.

P He is *compassionate* ***to*** the helpless. 彼はか弱き者にあわれみ深い.

compatibility, *n.* 両立性.

P the *compatibility* ***of*** manual labor with intellectual life 筋肉の労働と知的生活との両立性.

compatible, *a.* 適合する; 両立する.

P It is *compatible* ***with*** reason. それは理に適っている. ‖ It is *compatible* ***with*** his temper. それは彼の気質にあう. ‖ as far as [it is] *compatible* ***with*** ... ...を妨げない範囲内で. 【類】His interests are not *compatible* ***with*** mine. ‖ Accuracy is not always *compatible* ***with*** haste. 正確は必ずしも迅速とは一致しない(急がば回れ).

compeer, *n.* 匹敵.

P ***without*** a *compeer* たぐいなく.

compel, *v.* 強いる, 余儀なくする.

M unless ***absolutely*** *compelled* 万止むを得ない場合を除いて. ¶be very ***reluctantly*** *compelled* to refuse まことに不本意であるが断わらざるを得ない.

P be *compelled* ***for*** a living to ... 生活のために止むなく...をする. ¶we were *compelled* ***to*** a reluctant admission that ... われわれは不本意ながら ... ということを認めるの余儀なきに至った. 【類】*compel* him ***to*** desertion (逃亡).

O Nothing can *compel* me to do such a thing. どうあっても僕にはそんなことはできない. ¶I was *compelled* to do so by absolute necessity. 僕はやむを得ない訳でそうするようになった.

compendium, *n.* 要約[もの].

Q The book is a ***modest*** *compendium*. その本は手ごろの解説書だ.

P² a most useful *compendium* ***for*** ... ...に対して非常に有益な要約もの. ¶a *compendium* ***of*** literature 文学の綱領. ¶the best *compendium* ***on*** the subject その問題に関する最善の要約.

compensate, *v.* つぐなう, 報いる.

M ***fully*** *compensate* a reader for his effort 読者は骨を折って読むだけの労力は十分に報いられる.

P *compensate* one's loss ***by*** labour 損害を労力でつぐなう. ¶*compensate* ***for*** one's indebtedness 恩を返す. ¶I must *compensate* you ***for*** your services. 僕は君の尽力に対し報いなければならない. 【類】You must *compensate* me ***for*** this loss. ‖ The losses are balanced or *compensated* ***for*** by the gains. そのもうけによって損失も埋めあわせがつく. ‖ Employers have to *compensate* their workmen ***for*** injuries. 雇主は使用人の負傷に対し補償しなければならない. ¶I *compensated* his loss ***with*** money. 僕は彼の損害を金銭でつぐなった.

compensation, *n.* 補償; 《米》報酬.

V We do not ***allow*** any *compensation*. われわれは一切補償をしない. ¶***demand*** (=***claim***) *compensation* for ... ...に対して補償を要求する. ¶***Get*** what *compensation* you can. できるだけの補償を得よ. ¶***give*** *compensation* to ... ...に補償を与える. ¶Some *compensation* must be ***made***. 幾分の補償はせねばならない. ‖ ***make*** full *compensation* for ... ...を十分に償う. ¶***obtain*** a large *compensation* for ... ...に対して多額の補償を得る. ¶What *compensation* is ***offered***? どんな補償が提供されたか. ‖ What *compensation* can you ***offer*** for my service? 私の仕事に対しいくらいただけますか. 【類】No *compensation* is ***offered*** (***claimed***). ¶***pay*** £500 *compensation* for the loss of ... ...の損害に対し五百ポンドの補償金を出す. ¶***refuse*** any *compensation*, pleading ... ...を理由に報酬を拒絶する. ¶Will it ***require*** a heavy *compensation*? 巨額の補償が要るだろうか.

Q for lack of ***adequate*** *compensation* 補償額が少いので. ¶This will be an ***ample*** *compensation*. これで十分な報酬になるだろう. 【類】claim ***ample*** *compensation*. ¶an ***extra*** *compensation* 余分の補償. ¶a ***fair*** *compensation* 相当な補償. ¶Will a ***heavy*** *compensation* be required? 多額の補償が要るであろうか. ¶a ***liberal*** *compensation* たくさんの補償. ¶a ***partial*** *compensation* for the shortcomings その欠点に対する幾分のうめ合わせ. ¶a ***pecuniary*** *compensation* 金銭上の報酬. ¶a ***reasonable*** *compensation* 相当な報酬. ¶a ***satisfactory*** *compensation* 満足な報酬. ¶a ***slight*** *compensation* 軽少な報酬. ¶get ***substantial*** *compensation* for ... ...に対して十分な報酬を得る. ¶a ***suitable*** *compensation* 適当な報酬.

Q² ***accident*** *compensation* 災害補償. ¶***disability*** *compensation* 身体傷害補償. ¶***expiry*** *compensation* 補償打切り. ¶receive ***unemployment*** *compensation* 失業手当を受ける.

P pay ***as*** *compensation* 報酬として支払う. ¶***by way of*** *compensation* 報酬として. ¶put (=send) in a claim ***for*** *compensation* 補償の請求をする ‖ The demand ***for*** *compensation* has been ignored. その補償の要求は無視された. ¶Whatever else may be done ***in*** *compensation*? その外にどんな補償がなされるのか. ¶an amount ***of*** *compensation* 補償額. ¶serve ***without*** *compensation* 無報酬で勤める.

P² *compensation* ***for*** a loss 損害補償 ‖ *compensation* ***for*** public service accidents 公務災害補償費. 【類】I will give you something in *compensation* ***for*** your loss. / £19,028 *compensation* ***for*** damages.

compete, *v.* 競争する.

M ***actively*** *compete* with ... ...と盛んに競争する. ¶***honest-***

ly compete 正直に競争する. ¶*compete* ***successfully*** with ... ...と競争して優勢である.【類】*compete* ***successfully*** for positions in the Government service (官職). / These circumstances have enabled us to *compete* ***successfully*** in the open markets of the world.

P *compete* ***against*** each other with visionary rhetoric たがいに空疎な美辞の羅列をし合う ¶*compete* ***for*** a prize (medal, trophy) 賞品(など)を得ようと競う.【類】*compete* ***for*** leadership (championship) / The prize was *competed* ***for*** by all graduates. / *compete* ***for*** the post (appointment, office, scholarship) / *compete* ***for*** patronage (愛顧) / *compete* ***for*** prizes ‖ Many buyers *compete* ***for*** the blue-ribbon specimen. 多数のバイヤーがブルーリボン賞クラスの品物を買い争う. ‖ contestants *competing* ***for*** the title, Miss America ミス・アメリカの称号の競争者. ¶the school team has been entered to *compete* ***in*** the baseball match at ... ...における仕合にその学校のチームの参加が認められた ‖ *compete* ***in*** price (quality) 値段(など)の競争をする.【類】*compete* ***in*** a race / *compete* ***in*** trade against Great Britain / His battle-pictures will never be able to *compete* ***in*** force and picturesqueness ***with*** those of Carlyle. ¶Woman cannot *compete* ***with*** man on purely physical and intellectual planes. 女は純然たる体と頭の仕事では男と競争ができない. ‖ *compete* ***with*** other rivals to win the love of a girl 女を張る.【類】*compete* ***with*** a rival ***for*** a prize.

competence, competency, *n.* 能力; 相当の資産.

V ***acquire*** a *competence* かなりの財産を作る. ¶***amass*** a *competency* 相当の資産を貯える. ¶***earn*** a handsome *competency* 小金をためる. ¶***exceed*** one's *competence* 自分の力を越える. ¶He ***has*** a certain *competency*. 彼には幾分の資産がある. ¶***lay up*** *competence* 相応の資産を貯える. ¶He has been ***left*** some small *competence* by his father. 少いながらも資産を父から譲られた. ¶***save*** a moderate *competence* 相当の蓄財をする.【類】He has wisely resolved to defer (延ばす) the ceremony until he has ***saved*** the *competency* necessary to support a family.

Q have ***scholarly*** *competence* 学力がある. ¶***social*** *competence* 社交能力. ¶***technical*** *competence* 技術上の手腕. ¶***English*** *competency* 英語力. ¶***literary*** *competency* 文才.

P² his *competency* ***as*** a workman 労働者としての彼の能力. ¶There is no doubt of his *competence* ***for*** the task. 彼にはたしかにその仕事をやれるだけの腕がある. ¶his great *competency* ***in*** all maritime questions あらゆる海事問題についての彼の大手腕.

competent, *a.* 能力ある; 適当な.

M a ***highly*** *competent* teacher 非常に手腕のある教師. ¶be ***quite*** *competent* to ... りっぱに...するだけの能力がある. ¶a ***thoroughly*** *competent* lawyer りっぱな手腕のある弁護士.

P He is *competent* ***for*** teaching. 彼はりっぱに教師になれる. ¶He is not *competent* ***to*** the task of teaching English. 彼には英語は教えられない.

O I am not *competent* to criticize it. 私には解らないから批評はできない. ‖ He is *competent* to do it. 彼にはそれができる.

competition, *n.* **(1)** 競争.

V ***avoid*** ruinous *competition* by price arrangement 値段の協定によって共倒れの競争を避ける. ¶The steamers are ***carrying on*** a spirited *competition* with the railways. 汽船が鉄道と盛んに競争をやっている. ¶These circumstances have ***constituted*** *competition*. このために競争が起った. ¶***defy*** all *competition* いかなる競争も恐れない. ¶***encounter*** *competition* 競争に出会う. ¶The *competition* was ***entered*** by 3,500 competitors. その競争には三千五百人が参加した. ¶***face*** keen *competition* from ... in the markets of China 中国の市場における...からの烈しい競争に対抗する. ¶If quality is considered, we ***have*** no *competition*. 品質の点では他店の追随を許さない. ¶***intensify*** the *competition* among ... ...間の競争を激化させる. ¶***kill*** the English *competition* 英国の競争力を殺ぐ. ¶***maintain*** *competition* 競争を維持する. ¶***meet*** *competition* successfully 首尾よく競争に勝つ ‖ in order to ***meet*** their *competition* 彼らの競争に備えるため. ¶***renew*** *competition* 競争を再び始める. ¶***restrain*** *competition* 競争を抑える.

Q after ***bitter*** *competition* はげしい競争の後で. ¶***cut-throat*** *competition* between rival dealers 商売がたき仲間の死物狂いの競争. ¶after ***fierce*** *competition* 猛烈な競争の後. ¶The ***foreign*** *competition* is getting yearly more and more acute. 外国との競争は年々益々激しくなっている. ¶***free*** *competition* 自由競争. ¶There is ***great*** *competition* in the cotton market. 棉花市場に大競争が行われている. ‖ a ***great*** *competition* for public favor 人気とりの大競争. ¶carry on a ***hot*** *competition* against ... ...と激烈な競争を行う. ¶***keen*** *competition* in business 商売上の激しい競争.【類】There was ***keen*** *competition* among the candidates for Diet membership. / *Competition* is getting ***keener.*** ¶There was very ***little*** *competition* between ... ...間には大して競争はなかった. ¶in ***open*** *competition* 公然の競争で.【類】by ***open*** *competition.* ¶***ruinous*** *competition* 共倒れの競争. ¶***serious*** *competition* in the world market 世界市場における激しい競争. ¶***severe*** [***sharp***] *competition* 激しい競争. ¶***strenuous*** *competition* 熱心な競争. ¶There is ***strong*** *competition* in the business. その商売には盛んに競争が行われている. ¶***vehement*** *competition* 激烈な競争.

Q² ***trade*** *competition* between ... ...間の貿易競争.【類】vigorous ***trade*** *competition* in the South Asian Market. ¶enter ***world*** *competition* 世界的競争に加わる.

P ***after*** keen *competition* with ... ...との激しい競争の後. ¶put it up ***for*** *competition* それを競争させる. ¶***in*** *competition* for the Emperor's trophy 天皇杯の競争で ‖ Suffragism demands that woman should enter politics ***in*** *competition* with man. 婦人参政主義は婦人も男子に伍して政治に参与すべきことを主張する. ¶get (=enter) ***into*** *competition* with ... ...と競争する ‖ bring them ***into*** *competition* 彼らに競争させる. ¶the sharpness ***of*** *competition* 競争の激烈さ.

P² *competition* ***among*** nations 国家間の競争. ¶The *competition* ***between*** buyers caused prices to advance. 買手のせり合いで値があがった.【類】*competition* ***between*** two parties (nations). ¶*competition* ***from*** abroad 外国からの競争 ‖ *competition* ***from*** foreign cement 輸入セメントから受ける競争. ¶*competition* ***in*** armament 軍拡競争 ‖ probable development of Chinese *competition* ***in*** the iron trade 製鉄業における中国の競争が将来起るべき可能性. ¶the *competition* ***of*** proprietary schools ***for*** students 私立学校の学生争奪戦. ¶*competition* ***with*** ... ...との競争. ¶*Competition* ***within*** the industry will be intensified. 該事業内部の競争は激しくなるであろう.

(2) 競技, 懸賞.

V ***attempt*** a *competition* 競技を試みる. ¶***enter*** a *competition* 懸賞に参加する.【類】about fifty manuscripts of plays (脚本原稿) ***entered*** the *competition* for a prize of ... offered by ... ¶rules ***governing*** the *competition* 懸賞の規約. ¶***hold*** a *competition* 競技会を催す.【類】The magazine sometimes ***holds*** prize *competitions* for such work. ¶***launch*** (=***open***) a *competition* for a prize 懸賞を催す. ¶a *competition* ***organized*** (=***staged***) by a newspaper 一新聞社が企てた懸賞. ¶***put forward*** a *competition* 懸賞を催す.

V² The *competition* ***closes*** on January 15, 1900. 懸賞は一九〇〇年一月十五日に締切る.

Q This *competition* is not ***open*** to any reader over fifteen years of age. この懸賞には十五歳以上の読者は参加できません.

Q² the winner of a children's ***beauty*** *competition* recently held at ... 先般...で催された美少年美少女コンクールの入賞者.【類】She ***won*** a beauty *competition.* ¶Karl Schäfer, 1936 Olympic victor in the ***figure-skating*** *competition* for men. 一九三六年度オリンピック大会の男子フィギュアスケートの優勝者であるカール・シーファー. ¶a ***guessing*** *competition* あてっこ. ¶"Morning Snow" was that year's theme of the New Year's ***Imperial poem*** *competition.* 「朝の雪」というのがその年の新年の勅題であった. ¶a ***leg-beauty*** *competition* 脚線美コンクール. ¶a ***novel*** *competition* ざん新な懸賞. ¶organize a ***prize*** *competition* for the most compelling poems 懸賞によってもっとも迫力のある詩作を募集する. ¶a ***speed*** *competition* in the operation of the Japanese typewriter 邦文タイプライターのスピード競技. ¶a ***swimming*** *competition* 水泳競技.

P take part ***in*** a *competition* 競技に加わる ‖ the second prize ***in*** the *competition* その懸賞の二等賞 ‖ offer a thesis ***in*** *competition* 懸賞論文を出す. ¶the closing day ***of*** a *competition* 懸賞締切の日 ‖ the conditions ***of*** a *competition* 懸賞の条件.

P^2 an exhibition of cattle in *competition* ***for*** prizes 懸賞付の家畜共進会.

competitor, *n.* 競争者.

V ***distance*** all *competitors* in the contest その競技においてあらゆる競争者を引離す. ¶***drag*** their *competitors* down to their level 彼らの競争者を倒す. ¶He had to ***face*** extraordinary *competitors*. 彼は手ごわい競争者に対抗しなければならなかった. ¶The Dictionary of Political Economy ***has*** no *competitor* of the same scope in the English language.「経済学辞典」ほど大じかけな同種の英語辞書は類がない. ¶*Competitors* are ***invited*** to send in their entries. 志願者はその希望を申出て下さい. ¶***outdistance*** all *competitors* 競争者をぐっと引き離す. ¶***outdo*** a *competitor* 競争者を追抜く. ¶She ***outshone*** her male *competitors*. 彼女は男子競争者を顔色なからしめた. ¶***undersell*** all *competitors* in foreign markets 海外市場において総ての競争者より安く売る.

V^2 Many *competitors* have ***entered*** for the examination. その試験に競争者がたくさん出た. ‖ Some 27 *competitors* ***entered*** [the lists]. およそ二十七人の競争者がその競技に応じた.

Q I found in him a ***dangerous*** *competitor*. 彼は恐ろしい相手だと思った. ¶a ***formidable*** *competitor* to ... ...に対するあなどり難い競争相手. ¶our ***greatest*** *competitor* われわれにとって一番の大敵. ¶his ***highest*** *competitor* 彼の最大敵手. ¶I have a ***lively*** *competitor* in ... 私には...という好敵手がある. ¶it has a ***near*** *competitor* in ... それには...というほとんど匹敵のできる位の品がある. ¶a ***powerful*** *competitor* 強力な競争相手. ¶a ***successful*** (an ***unsuccessful***) *competitor* 競争の勝利(敗北)者. ¶a ***worthy*** *competitor* あっぱれな競争者.

P liquid fuel ***as*** *competitor* for coal 石炭の競争品としての液体燃料

P^2 *competitors* ***at*** a game 競技の参加者. ¶*competitors* ***for*** the prize その賞を得んと争う人々. ¶*competitors* ***in*** a race 競走の参加者. ¶*competitors* ***in*** business 商売敵.

compilation, *n.* 編集; 編集もの.

Q an ***erudite*** *compilation* りっぱな編集. ¶an ***invaluable*** *compilation* 非常に貴重な編集物.

P data ***for*** the *compilation* of a history book 史書編集の材料. ¶complain of the poor work ***in*** a *compilation* 編集のできが悪いので文句を言う.

P^2 a *compilation* ***from*** various sources 種々の方面から編集したもの. 【類】a *compilation* ***from*** treatises (論文) of much earlier date. ¶the *compilation* ***of*** the budget 予算編成. 【類】the *compilation* ***of*** an index (索引) to a book.

compile, *v.* 編集する.

M a ***carefully*** *compiled* book 綿密な編集ぶりの本.

P *compiled* ***after*** the model of ... ...を手本にして編集されて. ¶tables *compiled* ***from*** actual observations 実地の観察に基いて編集した表 ‖ *compile* a book ***from*** various sources 種々の材料から書物を編集する. ¶*compile* materials (=data) ***into*** a book 材料を編集して一書にまとめる.

complain, *v.* 不平を鳴らす; 訴える; 病む.

M He *complained* ***bitterly*** of his bad memory. 彼は記憶が悪いといってひどくこぼした. ¶one cannot ***honestly*** *complain* that ... ...と苦情を言ってもそれは至当なことではない. ¶You *complain* ***incessantly*** of the heat. 君はしょっちゅう暑いのを苦にしている. ¶*complain* ***loudly*** against ... 盛んに...をこぼす.

P *complain* ***about*** a person (thing, matter) 人(など)に関して不平を鳴らす. 【類】He is aways *complaining* ***about*** something. ¶He *complained* ***against*** me for that. 彼はそれに対して僕に苦情を言った. ¶*complain* ***before*** the court 法廷に訴える. ¶*complain* ***of*** the delay その遅滞に対して苦情をいう ‖ *complain* ***of*** goods not being as represented 見本の品と違うと文句を言う. 【類】He *complained* ***of*** (=about) ill-treatment (overwork). / *complain* ***of*** a person to his father ‖ *complain* ***of*** headache caused by overwork 過度の仕事がもとで頭痛を病む. 【類】Lately he has been *complaining* ***of*** insomnia (不眠症) and headache. / He *complained* ***of*** pains in his stomach (腹痛). / He *complains* ***of*** hunger (indisposition, pains in the head, a toothache, stomach trouble) ‖ Three passengers are reported to have *complained* ***of*** slight injures. 三人の乗客が軽傷を受けたということである.

complaint, *n.* (**1**) 苦情; 告訴.

V ***bring*** a *complaint* against him about some debt 負債の件で彼を訴える ‖ a *complaint* was ***brought*** against him about ... ...について彼に対する文句がつけられた. ¶No *complaints* will be ***considered*** unless made immediately after receipt of goods. 苦情はすべて品物入手後すぐでないと考慮致しかねます. ¶***direct*** one's bitter *complaint* against ... ...に対してひどい小言を言う. ¶***echo*** the *complaints* made by ... ...の苦情に対して同感を持つ(共鳴する). ¶***file*** a *complaint* against ... ...を訴える ‖ ***file*** a *complaint* at an office 事務所に苦情を持ち出す ‖ *complaints* ***filed*** with the police 警察に持ち出した苦情. ¶I ***have*** no *complaint* to make about ... ...については私に文句はありません. ¶*complaints* are being ***heard*** on all sides about ... ...について不満の声が至る所に聞えている. ¶The police, ***heeding*** neighborhood *complaints*, decreed the closing of the establishment. 警察では近所からの苦情を考慮してその商売家に閉鎖を命じた. ¶***ignore*** a *complaint* 苦情を無視する. ¶A *complaint* was immediately ***laid*** before the police. すぐに警察に訴え出た. ¶***lodge*** a *complaint* against ... ...を告訴する. 【類】he ***lodged*** a *complaint* with the court, in which he accused Mr. ... / keep on file (つづり込みにして置く) the *complaints* ***lodged*** with the Police Department. ¶***make*** a *complaint* to ... ...に対して苦情を述べる. 【類】*complaints* have been ***made*** by ... respecting (=regarding) ... / a great deal of *complaint* is being ***made*** by them against ... ¶***meet*** a *complaint* as best one can できうるだけ苦情に応じる. ¶***murmur*** *complaint* 不平を鳴らす. ¶it ***occasioned*** considerable *complaint* from ... そのことで...から随分苦情が起った. ¶*Complaints* ***poured in*** from all quarters. 諸方から苦情の投書が舞い込んだ. ‖ listen to the *complaints* ***poured*** into their ears 彼らの耳に入った不平の声を聞く. ¶***put in*** one's *complaint* 不平を持ち込む. ¶No *complaints* have been ***received*** so far. 今までのところ何らの苦情も出ていない. ¶***receive*** and ***redress*** *complaints* 苦情を受入れて補償する. ¶I cannot ***recognize*** any *complaint*. 何らの苦情を申立てる理由を認めることができない. ¶***register*** *complaints* against the store in the book provided for the purpose 申告簿にその店に対する苦情を記入する. ¶*Complaints* were ***rushed in*** about the weather forecast. 天気予報に文句をつける投書がどっと押寄せた. ¶***ventilate*** a *complaint* 苦情のはけ口をつくる. 【類】a place where *complaints* are ***ventilated***. ¶***voice*** a similar *complaint* 同じ不平を漏らす.

Q make ***bitter*** *complaint* 手厳しく訴える ‖ we heard ***bitter*** *complaints* on the subject of ... ...の問題に関してやかましい苦情を耳にした. ¶The ***commonest*** *complaint* we hear about the journalism of today is that ... 今日の新聞に対する最も一般的の苦情は...である. ¶***constant*** *complaints* 絶え間ない不平. ¶make a ***feeble*** *complaint* 泣言を言う. ¶lay ***formal*** *complaint* against ... ...に対して正式の訴訟を提起する. ¶***immediate*** *complaint* 〖法〗即時抗告. ¶there are ***loud*** *complaints* among them regarding ... ...に関し彼らの間に不平の声が高い. 【類】*complaints* were ***loud*** against ... ¶have ***numerous*** *complaints* about ... ...については沢山の苦情を受けている. ¶lodge a ***serious*** *complaint* 厳重に抗議を申込む. ¶a ***shrill*** *complaints* 耳もつんざくような不平. ¶a ***stock*** *complaint* おきまりの苦情.

P ***on*** *complaint* of ... ...からの訴えにより. ¶accept ... ***without*** *complaint* ...を甘んじて受ける.

P^2 *complaints* ***about*** telephone service 電話事務についての苦情. ¶He brought a *complaint* ***before*** the magistrate ***against*** the neighbor. 彼は隣人のことを役人に訴えた. ¶a *complaint* ***from*** ... ...からの苦情. ¶a *complaint* ***of*** irregularity in postal service 郵便事務の不規律に対する不平. 【類】the *complaint* ***of*** the people ***against*** the government. ¶a *complaint* ***of*** nuisance ***to*** the authorities 当局者に持出した妨害の訴え. ¶*Complaints* ***on*** the matter are mounting. その件の苦情が高まって来ている.

(**2**) 病気.

V Do you ***consider*** my *complaint* dangerous? 私の病気は重症でしょうか. ¶***get*** a *complaint*=contract a disease 病気にかかる. ¶I ***have*** a *complaint* in the chest. 私は胸に故障がある.

Q a ***chronic*** *complaint* 慢性病. ¶a ***constitutional*** *complaint* 持病.

Q^2 suffer from a ***heart*** *complaint* 心臓が悪い. ¶a ***liver***

complaint 肝臓病. 「気にかかっている.
P He is suffering *from* a serious *complaint*. 彼はひどい病

complaisance, *n.* 丁寧, いんぎん.
Q ever ***ready** complaisance* いつも変らぬいんぎんさ.
P I find it hard to bear ***with** complaisance*. いい顔をしていられない.

complement, *n.* 補足, 補足物; 〚文法〛補語; 定員.
V experience great difficulty to ***secure*** the *complement* of their cargoes 船荷の全数量を確保することの困難さを経験する.
Q an ***indispensable** complement* to ... …に対して欠くべからざる補足物. ¶The ***natural** complement* of the house is the garden. 庭園は当然住宅につきものである. ¶the ***necessary** complement* of ... …の一部として欠くべからざるもの.
P supply the deficiency ***in*** the *complement* of lieutenants on board 艦内尉官の定員を補欠する ‖ the moon ***in*** her *complement* 満月.
P² They are the *complement **of*** each other. 彼らは両々相まって完ぺきをなしている. ‖ a great liner with its *complement **of*** three to four thousand souls 三千ないし四千人の乗組員を有する一大定期船 ‖ the *complement **of*** an angle 〚数〛余角. ¶One man was the *complement **to*** the other. 一人が他方の不足を補った. ‖ the *complement **to*** this verb 〚文法〛この動詞の補語.
O Love and justice are *complements* each of the other. 愛と正義は両々相まって完全になる.

complementary, *a.* 補いの, 補充の.
M ***mutually** complementary* 互いに補足しあって.
P *complementary **to*** each other 相補って. ¶*complementary **to*** the text [条約など]本文の補則として.
O They serve as *complementary* one to the other. 彼らは互いに補いになっている.

complete, *v.* 完成する, 落成する. 「落成した.
M The building (railway) is ***now** completed*. 建築(など)が
P the ship will be *completed **for*** sea ***by*** ... 船は…までに航海ができるように完成される. ¶a work to be *completed **in*** three volumes 三巻本. ¶*Complete **with*** the correct word. [試験問題]適当な語をそう入せよ.

complete, *a.* 十分な, 完全な.
M be ***nearly** complete* ほぼ完成している. ¶The year is ***now** complete*. 今年ももう終った. ¶not ***sufficiently** complete* まだ十分と言えない.
P a bill *complete **in*** form 形式上手落ちのない手形 ‖ It is to be *complete **in*** two volumes. それは二冊で完成するはず. 【類】The work is *complete **in*** twenty volumes.

completeness, *n.* 完全, 完備.
V ***attain** completeness* of artistic achievement 至高の芸術の域に達する. ¶to ***give** completeness* to the book その書物を完成するために. 「する.
P detail ***with*** exhaustible *completeness* 細大もらさず詳説

completion, *n.* 完成, 落成.
V It is rapidly ***approaching** completion*. それはぐんぐん完成に近づいている. ¶***celebrate*** the *completion* of 25 years' service 勤続二十五年を祝賀する. ¶it was erected to ***commemorate*** the *completion* of ... それは…の完成を記念すべく建てられた. ¶It is steadily ***nearing** completion*. それは着々完成に近づいている. 【類】plans are rapidly ***nearing*** *completion* for ... ¶He didn't live long enough to ***see*** the *completion* of the work. その著作の完成を見ずして死んだ.
Q ***logical** completion* 論理的補足. ¶it moves onward smoothly toward its ***successful** completion* それは支障なくりっぱな完成に向てっ進んでいる.
Q² ***quota delivery** completion* 供出の完了.
P ***after** completion* of the order その注文ができ上った後. 【類】***after*** the *completion* of a contract (契約). ¶a vast engineering project that will take thirty years ***for*** its *completion* 完成に三十年を要するぼう大な土木計画. ¶***on*** *completion* of five years' service as ... …として五年の勤務を満了した後に ‖ be payable ***on** completion* 完成後払いである. ¶The railway has been brought ***to** completion*. その鉄道は完成した. ¶The enterprise is only half-way ***toward** completion*. この事業はまだ半分しか完成していない. ¶afford a certificate ***upon** completion* of one's course of study 全課程修了後に証書を与える.

complex, *n.* 複雑; 〚心理〛複合, [無意識的]潜在心理.
Q through some ***baffling** complex* of circumstances あるむずかしい複雑した事情のために.
Q² ***crime** complex* 犯罪心理. ¶***inferiority*** (***superiority***) *complex* 劣等(優越)感 ‖ have an ***inferiority** complex* 気が引ける. ¶***jealousy** complex* しっとによるヒステリー症状. ¶***leader** complex* 指導者心理.

complex, *a.* 複雑な. 「は述べつくされない.
P it is too *complex **for*** our space あまり複雑でこの紙上で

complexion, *n.* 顔色; 様子, 形勢.
V The differences are ***assuming*** a critical *complexion*. その紛争は容易ならない形勢を示しつゝある. ¶***beautify*** the *complexion* 顔のはだを美しくする. ¶She ***has*** a beautiful *complexion*. 彼女は色つやがよい. ¶***improve*** the *complexion* 顔色をよくする. ¶The fact ***places*** a very different *complexion* on the position. その事実で局面が一変する. ¶anxiously ***shield*** their *complexions* beneath umbrellas or parasols 彼らの顔を大事(日に焼けないよう)にこうもりや日がさでおゝう. ¶Things were ***wearing*** a dangerous *complexion*. 事態が険悪な様相を帯びていた.
Q a ***blooming** complexion* 花のかんばせ. ¶a beauty of ***clear** complexion* 晴やかな顔をした美人. ¶a ***dark, sallow*** *complexion* あさ黒く血色の悪い顔. ¶a ***fair*** (=***clear***) *complexion* 色白の顔. ¶people with ***florid** complexions* 花のような顔色をした人々. ¶a ***good** complexion* よい血色. ¶a ***healthy** complexion* 健康そうな血色. ¶a ***light** complexion* 明るい血色. ¶with ***olive** complexion* 小麦色の顔をした. ¶a ***pale** complexion* 青ざめた顔色. ¶regardless of chanegs in the ***political** complexion* of the administration 内閣の党色変更に関係なく. ¶She has a ***pretty** complexion*. 彼女はきれいな顔をしている. ¶a ***rosy** complexion* 桜色の顔. ¶a ***ruddy** complexion* 赤ら顔. ¶a ***swarthy** complexion* 浅黒い顔色. ¶a [***sun***]***tanned** complexion* 日焼けし顔色. ¶a ***wan** complexion* 青ざめた顔色. ¶a ***youthlike*** *complexion* of an old man 童顔の老人.
P a little brownish ***in** complexion* 少しとび色がかった顔色の. ¶a man ***with*** a dark *complexion* 色の黒い男.

complexity, *n.* 複雑, 繁雑. 「複雑している.
V The situation ***presents*** great *complexity*. 事態は非常に
V² The *complexity* of life ***increases*** from year to year. 人間生活の複雑さは年々増して行く.
P Inter-racial situations are increasing ***in** complexity* throughout the world. 民族間の情勢は世界中益々複雑にな
P² the *complexities **of*** life 人生の複雑さ. 」りつゝある.

compliance, *n.* 服従, 承諾.
V ***bribe*** her *compliance* 金で彼女にうんと言わせる. ¶***enforce** compliance* with money 金にものをいわせる. 【類】***enforce** compliance* with demands made on ... ¶***obtain*** *compliance* by earnest request 拝み倒す. ¶he ***refused*** *compliance* on the ground that ... 彼は…という理由で拒絶した. ¶***secure*** his *compliance* 彼の承諾を得る.
Q an ***easy** compliance* 容易な承諾.
P ***in** compliance **with*** the demand (duty) その要求(など)に応じて. 【類】***in** compliance **with*** the wishes of his father. ¶The powers forced China ***into** compliance*. 列強は無理に中国を承服させた. ‖ talk one ***into** compliance* 人を説得する.
P² His *compliance **with*** my request gave me much pleasure. 私の要請に応じてくれたので非常にうれしかった.

complicate, *v.* 複雑にする, 紛争させる.
P *complicate* the matter ***by*** needless additions だ足を加えて事態を複雑にする ‖ a headache *complicated **by*** eye trouble 眼病でなおひどくなった頭痛. 【類】The matter was *complicated **by*** his sudden illness.

complicated, *pa.* 入組んだ. 「あ.
M Life is ***so** complicated*, you know. 人生は複雑だからな
P It is much *complicated **in*** structure. それは構造が大分

complication, *n.* 複雑, 紛争; 併発症. 」入り組んでいる.
V It is impossible to ***avoid** complication*. 紛争を避けることはできない. 【類】so as to ***avoid*** unnecessary *complications*. ¶***cause*** further *complication* さらに紛争をきたす. 【類】very likely to ***cause** complication*. ¶It will ***produce*** political *complications*. それは政界の紛争を産むだろう.
V² Further *complications* would ***arise***. さらに紛争が起るだろう. 【類】should any *complication **arise*** ‖ All *complication* has ***ended***. 紛争が全く止んだ.

Q The wound healed without ***dangerous*** *complications*. 傷はひどくとがめずなおった. ¶Here is a ***further*** *complication*. さらにことが面倒になってきた. 【類】a ***further*** *complication* is added by the fact that ... ¶***intercurrent*** *complications* 併発症. ¶There is ***no*** *complication* whatever. 何らめんどうがない. ¶***Serious*** *complications* arose. 厄介なことが持ち上がった. ¶It may lead to ***unpleasant*** *complications*. それがもとで不愉快なごたつきが起るかも知れない.

P^2 *complications* ***between*** two parties (countries) 二党(など)間の紛争. ¶a *complication* ***of*** diseases 病の併発. ¶*complications* ***on account of*** ... ...故の紛争. ¶*complications* ***with*** heart and ear 心臓と耳の併発病.

complicity, *n.* 共謀.

P They were accused ***of*** *complicity* in the so-called rice riots. 彼らはいわゆる米騒動に共謀したというかどで起訴された.

P^2 on the charge of *complicity* ***against*** the life of ... ...の謀殺事件に連座したかどで. 【類】*complicity* ***in*** a crime (theft, murder). ¶*complicity* ***with*** him ***in*** the crime その犯罪で彼との共謀.

compliment, *n.* あいさつ; 賛辞; 伝言.

V Please ***add*** my *compliments* in postscript. どうぞ追伸に私からよろしくとつけ加えて下さい. ¶Please tell him when he comes home that Mr. Kato called and ***desired*** his *compliments* to him. あの方がお帰りになったら加藤が訪ねてきてよろしくと言い置いたと伝えて下さい. 【類】He ***desired*** his *compliments* to you when you came home. ¶***echo*** the *compliment* 一せいにほめる. ¶***exchange*** *compliments* あいさつを交わす. ¶***Give*** my *compliments* to your father. お父上によろしく. ¶He ***made*** me many *compliments*. あの人は色々私にお世辞を言った. ¶***overdo*** the *compliments* ほめ過ぎる. ¶***pass*** *compliments* on ... ...をほめる ‖ he was good enough to ***pass*** a similar *compliments* to ... 彼は同様な賛辞を...にも与えてその好意を示した. ¶***pay*** a person many *compliments* 人を色々ほめそやす ‖ I called to ***pay*** my *compliments*. あいさつに行った. ‖ ***pay*** one the *compliments* of the season 季節のあいさつを述べる. ¶***present*** one's *compliments* to ... ...に宜しく言う ‖ ***presents*** his *compliments* to ... and has the honor to ... ...に敬意を表し, あわせて...することの光栄を有する. 【類】***Present*** him my *compliments!* / Mr. M ***presents*** his best *compliments* to Mr. and Mrs. Y. ¶***return*** the *compliment* of ... ...に答礼する. ¶***say*** a *compliment* 賛辞を呈する. ¶I ***sent*** him my *compliments*. 彼のもとへよろしく言ってやった. ¶***sprinkle*** *compliments* 愛きょうをふりまく. ¶I ***wish*** you the *compliments* of the season. (年始などで)お芽出とう. 【類】***Wishing*** you the *compliments* of the approaching season.

Q He could ask no ***better*** *compliment*. 彼にとってこれ以上の賛辞はあるまい. ¶***condolatory*** *compliments* くやみのあいさつ. ¶a ***courteous*** *compliment* いんぎんなあいさつ. ¶I drew from him the ***delightful*** *compliment*, "..." 彼から「...」というられしい賛辞を受けた. ¶it is a ***distinct*** *compliment* to him that ... ...ということは彼にとって明かな名誉である. ¶a ***double-edged*** *compliment* よくも悪くもとれるお世辞. ¶***doubtful*** *compliments* お世辞にならないようなお世辞. ¶an ***empty*** *compliment* から世辞. ¶it is a ***fine*** *compliment* to ... それは...に対してりっぱな名誉だ. ¶a ***fitting*** *compliment* to him 彼にとって適切な賛辞. ¶***fulsome*** *compliments* もりだくさんのお世辞. ¶pay a ***graceful*** *compliment* to ... ...にしとやかなあいさつをする. ¶pay him a ***great*** *compliment* 彼に丁寧なあいさつをする. ¶pay a ***high*** *compliment* to ... ...に大いに賛辞を呈する. 【類】He paid you a ***high*** *compliment* within my hearing. ‖ we cannot pay him a ***higher*** *compliment* than by saying ... ...というのがわれわれとしては最高のほめ方だ. ¶***honeyed*** *compliments* 口のうまいお世辞. ¶plaster one another with ***insincere*** *compliments* たがいに心にもないお世辞を取り交す. ¶a ***jocular*** *compliment* ユーモアーたっぷりなほめ言葉. ¶too ***lavish*** *compliments* あまりに安売のお世辞. ¶***lefthanded*** *compliments* 皮肉なほめ方. ¶***like*** *compliments* 似たような賛辞. ¶***long-winded*** *compliments* 長たらしいお世辞. ¶pay a ***merited*** (=***deserved***) *compliment* to ... ...をその功にふさわしいほめ方をする. ¶a ***neat*** *compliment* さっぱりしたあいさつ. ¶a ***pretty*** *compliment* to ... ...に対する上手なお世辞 ‖ We paid them the ***pretty*** *compliment* of hoisting the Stars and Stripes. われらは米国々旗を掲揚して彼らに対し美しい敬意を表した. ¶I mean this for a ***sincere*** *compliment*. これは私の心からの賛辞のつもりです. ¶a ***smooth-spoken*** *compliment* うまいお世辞. ¶a ***unique*** *compliment* 人のまねのできないようなほめ方.

P Thank you ***for*** your *compliment*. おほめに預って恐縮です. ¶they gave a splendid ball ***in*** *compliment* to ... 彼らは...に対する礼としてはなやかな舞踏会を催した ‖ the town changed its name ***in*** *compliment* to the victor of ... その町は...の勝利者に敬意を表して名を変更した. 【類】Captain Cook named them the Sandwich Islands ***in*** *compliment* to John Montagu, Fourth Earl of Sandwich and First Lord of the Admiralty (海相). ¶We called the yacht the London, ***out of*** *compliment* to our capital. われらの首府の名にちなんでそのヨットを「ロンドン」と命名した. ‖ ***out of*** *compliment* for ... ...に敬意を表して. ¶I will see that he gets it ***with*** your *compliments*. あなたからよろしくとの御伝言とともにそれを先方にお届けするように取計らいます. 【類】I am to present you ***with*** their *compliments*. ‖ The book was presented to me ***with*** the author's *compliments*. その本は著者から私に寄贈された. ‖ ***with*** the *compliments* of the author [贈本の際]著者の敬意を表して ‖ ***with*** the *compliments* of the season [クリスマスなどの]「おめでとう」というあいさつを添えて.

P^2 Many *compliments* ***from*** Mamma. 母よりくれぐれもよろしく. ¶a *compliment* ***to*** the whole profession of letters 文学界全体の名誉.

compliment, *v.* あいさつする, お世辞を言う, ほめる.

P. I am all the more *complimented* ***by*** your acceptance. お受けくだすって何より有難く存じます. ¶Let me *compliment* you very much ***for*** your attention. ご清聴を感謝します. 【類】He is to be *complimented* ***for*** ... ¶They are *complimented* ***in*** the public press. 彼らは新聞でほめられている. ¶They *complimented* her ***on*** her beautiful shoulders. 皆彼女の美しい肩をほめた. ‖ *compliment* him ***on*** the birth of a son 男子誕生について彼に祝辞を述べる. 【類】*compliment* ***on*** her skill in English. / *compliment* him ***on*** the manner in which he has so successfully carried it out. ¶*compliment* him ***upon*** his achievements 彼の功績をほめる. ¶*compliment* a person ***with*** a present 人に進物を贈って好意を表する. 【類】He *complimented* me ***with*** tickets for the exhibition.

comply, *v.* 応じる, 従う.

M ***fully*** *complied* with the surrender terms 降服条件に全面的に従った. ¶***unhesitatingly*** *comply* with a request 依頼を快諾する. ¶***willingly*** *comply* with instructions 喜んで指図に従う.

P *comply* ***with*** the rules and regulations 諸規則を守る ‖ *comply* ***with*** the standard fixed by Government 政府の定めた標準に従う. 【類】I cannot *comply* ***with*** your terms of payment (支払条件). / I regret that your wish cannot be *complied* ***with***. / They are not willing to *comply* ***with*** your proposal (demand). / He *complied* ***with*** my request. / *comply* at once ***with*** the wishes of ... / *comply* ***with*** all her whims (気まぐれ) / *comply* ***with*** the following instructions / *comply* ***with*** all the requirements (あらゆる条項) of law.

component, *n.* 構成分子.

Q ***civilian*** *components* of the United States Army Forces in Japan 駐日米陸軍の軍属構成人員.

comport, *v.* 適合する.

M *comport* oneself ***gracefully*** (***manly***) 優美に(男らしく)ふるまう.

P Your behavior does not *comport* ***with*** your rank. 貴下のふるまいは御身分にふさわしくない.

compose, *v.* 組立てる; 落着かせる, 安静にする; (詩や文を)作る.

M Japanese houses are ***chiefly*** *composed* of wood. 日本の家屋は大体材料は木だ. ¶I am now *composed* ***enough*** to speak. ようよう気が落ち付いて話ができるようになった. ¶The song was *composed* ***extempore***. その歌は即席に作られた. ‖ be ***largely*** *composed* of ... ...が主成分を成している. ¶The writer *composes* ***slowly***. その作家は遅筆だ.

P The music was *composed* ***by*** Beethoven. それはベートーベンの作曲だ. ¶The poem is *composed* ***in*** Alexandrines. その詩はアレキサンダー格でできている. ‖ be *composed* ***in*** mind 落着きはらっている. ¶a board of judges *composed* ***of*** ... ...から成る審査委員会 ‖ a commission *composed of* Congressmen and business representatives 代議士および民間代表を以て組織する委員会. ¶a ribald mob *composed of* the dregs of the populace 人間のくずのような口ぎたない暴民. 【類】an expedition *composed of* ... / It was *composed* entirely *of* mercenary troops (傭兵). / It is *composed of* fibers. ‖ English weather is *composed of* samples. 英国の天気は変化が多い. ‖ her charm was partly *composed of* shyness, partly of gaiety, but chiefly of ... 彼女の魅力は幾分は内気·幾分ははでな所にもあったのだが主なる点は...にあった ‖ a preparation *composed of* camphor and quinine しょう脳とキニーネの調合剤. 【類】Water is *composed of* hydrogen and oxygen. ¶*compose* a novel (an essay) ***on*** (=***at***) the typewriter タイプライターに打って小説(など)を作る. ¶*compose* poems ***to*** the god of wine 酒の神に詩を寄せる.

composer, *n.* 作者.

Q a ***renowned*** *composer* of *haikai* 有名な俳人.

Q² a ***dance*** *composer* ダンス曲作曲家. ¶a ***poem*** (***song***) *composer* 作詩(など)家.

P² a *composer* ***of*** great genius 天才作曲家.

composite, *n.* 組成物.

Q that great ***racial*** *composite*, the American people あの巨大な各国人種の寄り合世帯たるアメリカ国民.

composition, *n.* 組成; 作文.

V ***build up*** a *composition* 文を組立てる. ¶***impair*** the *composition* of ... ...の組織をこわす. ¶***learn*** *composition* at school 学校で作文を学ぶ. ¶***make*** a *composition* on that subject その題で文を書く. ¶***punctuate*** *compositions* 作文に句読点を施す. ¶***write*** a *composition* 文を書く.

Q The whole of the underwater portion of the hull is painted with ***anti-fouling*** *composition*. 船体の水中にある部分は全部よごれ止めが塗ってある. ¶the art of ***dramatic*** *composition* 劇作法. ¶an ***epistolary*** *composition* 書かん文. ¶***floral*** *composition* 生け花. ¶a ***literary*** *composition* of great brilliance and originality 非常にけんらんたる独創に富んだ文芸作品. ¶The concern of printers is not with ***literary*** but with ***typographical*** *composition*. 印刷者の関心事は文章の作り方ではなくて活字の組み方である. ¶an ***original*** *composition* 創作. ¶a ***short*** *composition* 短篇. ¶in these days of ***slipshod*** *composition* 今日のようにだらしない文を書く時代に. ¶a subject for ***voluntary*** *composition* 自由作文題. ¶***youthful*** *compositions* 若い時分の作文.

Q² a writer of ***business*** *compositions* 商業文を書く人. ¶a practice book in ***English*** *composition* 英作文の練習書. ¶a ***flower*** *composition* 一つの生け花. ¶a ***landscape*** *composition* 日本式庭園. ¶***music*** *composition* 作曲. ¶the writing of ***prose*** *composition* in English 英作文. 【類】the greatest masters of the art of ***prose*** *composition*.

P a subject ***for*** *composition* 文題. ¶He has a touch of madness ***in*** his *composition*. 彼の性質にはちょっと気ちがいじみたところがある. ¶in verses ***of*** his own *composition* 自作の韻文で.

P² a *composition* ***for*** high schools 高等学校用作文書. ¶a *composition* ***in*** verse 韻文の作品. ¶a *composition* ***of*** bread ***with*** sugar, etc. 砂糖などをまぜたパン ‖ the *composition* ***of*** a picture 構図. ¶a *composition* ***on*** a timely subject 時宜に適した題の作文.

compositor, *n.* 植字工.

Q an ***inky-aproned*** *compositor* インキだらけの前かけをしめた植字工.

composure, *n.* 平静, 沈着, 落着き.

V ***lose*** one's *composure* どぎまぎする ‖ ***lose*** *composure* of mind あがる. ¶***maintain*** *composure*=keep one's countenance 沈着を失わない. ¶***obtain*** (=***gain***) a *composure* of mind 度胸を据える. ¶***preserve*** one's *composure* 落着いている. ¶I went to her room to ***recover*** the *composure*, which had been shaken by ... ...によってかき乱された気を落着けるため彼女の部屋に行った. ¶She soon ***regained*** her *composure*. やがて彼女は気が落ちついた.

Q ***complete*** *composure* 泰然自若. ¶my lack of ***facial*** *composure* and my inability to look people in the eye 顔負けして人を真正面に見ることができないこと ‖ He accepted the punishment with ***grave*** *composure*. 彼はその罰を真面目な落ちついた態度で受けた. ‖ He behaved with ***great*** (=***marked***) *composure*. 彼は落着き払って振舞った. ¶with ***perfect*** *composure* 少しも動ぜず.

P I startled him ***out of*** his *composure*. 彼をびっくりさせた. ¶He replied ***with*** *composure*. 彼は落着いて答えた. ‖ No mind could face such a risk ***with*** *composure*. だれもこんな危険に対して平気ではいられまい.

compound, *n.* (1) 構内, 境内.

Q² in the ***Customs*** *compound* 税関の構内に. ¶leave the ***prison*** *compound* 刑務所から外に出る. ¶a ***shrine*** (***school***) *compound* 神社境内(学校構内). ¶in a ***temple*** *compound* 寺の境内に.

P ***in*** a *compound* adjoining the museum 博物館に隣接する構内で. 【類】the Constitution Commemoration Hall (憲法記念館) ***in*** the *compound* of the Meiji Shrine at Yoyogi. ¶***inside*** the *compound* of a school 学校の構内に.

(2) 化合物; 〚文法〛複合語.

Q² a ***self-explaining*** *compound* 説明を要しない複合語.

P² a *compound* ***of*** carbon ***with*** a metal 金属と炭素との化合物. 【類】Water is a *compound* ***of*** hydrogen and oxygen.

compound, *v.* 混ぜあわす; 和解する.

P *compound* this and that ***for*** ... これとあれと調合して...を作る. ¶*compound* ***for*** ... with one's creditors ...で債権者と話合いをつける. ¶*compound* a medicine (=drug) ***from*** ... ...で調剤する. ¶various dishes *compounded* ***of*** snake meat へびの肉で作った色々の料理 ‖ The word is *compounded* ***of*** a preposition and a verb. その語は前置詞と動詞の組合わせだ. ‖ a character *compounded* ***of*** Cecil Rhodes and Samuel Smiles セシル·ローズとサミュエル·スマイルズをつき交ぜた人物. 【類】a character *compounded* ***of*** good and evil qualities.

comprehend, *v.* 包括する.

P be *comprehended* only ***by*** a few 理解しているものは二三に過ぎない. ¶the states *comprehended* ***in*** the Austrian Empire オーストリア帝国に含まれた州.

comprehensible, *a.* 解しうる.

P It is *comprehensible* ***to*** ordinary minds. それは普通の頭でわかる.

comprehension, *n.* 理解, 会得.

V It ***baffles*** (=passes) my *comprehension*. それは僕には分らない. ¶It ***eludes*** *comprehension*. それは会得しにくい. ¶***gain*** a clearer *comprehension* of this brilliant period. この華美けんらんたる時代を一層よく理解する. ¶***nod*** *comprehension* わかったとうなずく. ¶It ***passes*** human *comprehension* what the one hundred-thousandth of an inch really means. 一インチの十万分の一とは実際どれほどなのか人間の頭にはわからない.

Q The aid of the picture to the visualizing of things, and hence to their ***better*** *comprehension*, will not be denied. 絵画が事物を眼前にほうふつたらしめ, これによって理解を一層容易ならしめることを否定するものはなかろう. ¶It is quite past my ***shallow*** *comprehension*. それは私の浅薄な頭ではとても理解ができない. ¶people of ***slow*** *comprehension* 頭の鈍い人.

P This is quite ***above*** (=***past or beyond***) my *comprehension*. これは僕にはとてもわからない. ‖ It is ***beyond*** the *comprehension* of the ordinary man. それは常人には理解できない. 【類】for some reason ***beyond*** our *comprehension* / a mystery ***beyond*** our *comprehension* ‖ It is productive of good ***beyond*** *comprehension*. それから計り知れないほどの利益が生れる. ¶It is a nice little story-book, quite ***within*** the *comprehension* of boys and girls. それは少年少女によくわかる結構な小物語本である.

compress, *n.* 湿布.

V ***apply*** a *compress* to an affected part 患部にあん法を施す.

Q a ***cold*** (***hot***) *compress* 冷(温)湿布.

P² a *compress* ***to*** an affected part 患部への湿布.

compress, *v.* 縮小する, 簡約する.

P *compress* about two months' work ***into*** one 約二カ月の仕事を一カ月につめる ‖ be *compressed* ***into*** less than a hundred pages 百ページ以内に圧縮してある ‖ Here is *compressed* ***into*** a nutshell the moral situation of Japan today. これが現代日本の道徳的状態を要約したものである.

compressor, *n.* 圧搾器.

Q an ***air*** *compressor* 空気圧搾器.

comprise, *v.* 含む.

P A number of separate states were *comprised* ***in*** (=***within***) the German Empire. ドイツ帝国には別々の国が多数含まれていた. ‖ it is *comprised* ***in*** (=***under***) the name of ... それは...の名称の下に包括されている ‖ the properties *comprised* ***in*** the sale are ... 売却に含まれた物件は...である. ¶A number of separate states were then *comprised* ***in*** the United States of America. 米国にはいくつかの別々の州があった.

compromise, *n.* 妥協, 示談; 折衷.

V *arrange* a *compromise* 妥協する. ¶*effect* a *compromise* between ... and ... ...間に示談を成立させる. ¶*make* a *compromise* 歩み合う, 妥協する. 【類】*make* no *compromise* / He is one of those who can *make compromises* with their conscience (融通の利く人). ¶a *compromise reached* by mutual concessions お互いが歩みよってできた妥協.

Q a *satisfactory compromise* 満足な妥協. ¶a *weak compromise* 効果不十分な(骨抜の)譲歩.

P We arrived *at* some *compromise*. ある程度の妥協に到達した. ¶I agreed *to* a *compromise*. 私は妥協を承知した. ¶He did it *without compromise* of his dignity. 彼は面目を損ぜずにそれをやった.

P² a *compromise between* two measures 折衷案 ‖ a *compromise between* Japanese and foreign styles 和洋折衷 ‖ A mule is a *compromise between* a horse and an ass. らばは馬とろばとの雑種だ.

compromise, *v.* 妥協する; [疑惑・危険を]こうむらせる.

P *compromise* one's reputation *by* one's own folly 自分の愚行で名声を害する. ¶*compromise with* him 彼と妥協する ‖ *compromise with* a principle 一つの主義と妥協する. 【類】endeavor to *compromise with* creditors.

compulsion, *n.* 強制.

Q *moral compulsion* 道徳的拘束権.

Q² *state compulsion* 国権による強制.

P *by compulsion* 強制的に. ¶*of compulsion* しいられて. ¶He acted *under compulsion*. 彼は強制されて(心ならずも)やった. ‖ All civilization is the product of toil pursued *under compulsion*. すべて文明はしいられてやった勤労の産物である. 【類】sign a treaty *under compulsion*.

compunction, *n.* 悔恨, 後悔.

V I *feel* no *compunction* in doing ... 私は...しても一向悪いと思わない. ¶I *have* little *compunction* in doing it. 私はそうしても特に悪いとは思わない.

P kill *without* the least *compunction* 少しも容赦なく殺す ‖ *without* any *compunction* 平気で.

computation, *n.* 計算, 推測.

Q at a *moderate computation* 内輪に計算して.

Q² unofficial *Government computations* 政府の非公式計算.

P *according to* recent *computation* 先ごろの計算によると. ¶It is *beyond computation*. それは推測ができない. ¶it amounts, *on* the lowest *computation*, to ... それはごく低く見積っても...に達する.

compute, *n.* 計算.

P It is *beyond compute*. それは計算ができない.

compute, *v.* 数える, 推測する.

P *compute* the distance (sum, amount, loss) *at* ... 距離(など)を...と測定する ‖ it is *computed at* something like ... 約...と計算されている.

comrade, *n.* 仲間, 戦友.

V I *lost* my *comrade* in the crowd in Asakusa Park, and returned home alone. 私は浅草公園の混雑の中で仲間にはぐれて一人で帰った.

Q their *fallen comrades* 彼らの戦歿戦友. ¶a *genial comrade* 気の合った仲間. ¶an *old comrade* 昔なじみ. ¶a *surviving comrades* 生残った同僚.

P² a *comrade in* arms 戦友.

comradeship, *n.* 親交.

Q his *genial comradeship* 彼との意気投合. ¶*good comradeship* 美しい友情. ¶a *life-long comradeship* 終生の親交. ¶enjoy their *young comradeship* 子供らを相手に遊ぶ.

conceal, *v.* 隠す, 包み隠す, おおう.

P *conceal* a thing *about* one's person 身の回りに物を隠す ‖ *conceal* oneself *about* the premises 屋敷のあたりに身を隠す. 【類】*conceal* oneself *among* the rock / carry a dangerous weapon (凶器) *concealed about* one's person. ¶*conceal* oneself *behind* the trees (some bushes) 木かげ(など)に隠れる. ¶be *concealed by* the smoke 煙におおわれて. 【類】The moon is *concealed by* the cloud. ¶I put it where it is *concealed from* view. 私はそれを見えない所へ置いた. ‖ It was *concealed from* notice. それは見られないようにしてあった. 【類】I did not *conceal* anything *from* him. / He *concealed from* me what his plans were. ¶*conceal* (=hide) it *in* the cellar それを地下室に隠す. 【類】*conceal* oneself *in* a wood / *conceal* oneself *in* (=*within*) a house ‖ have a dagger *concealed in* one's breast 九寸五分をふところに忍ばせる ‖ a sword *concealed in* a walking stick 仕込みずえ. ¶*conceal* oneself *under* the leaves 葉かげに身を隠す. 【類】*conceal* oneself *under* a bed ‖ *conceal* one's hysterics *under* a smile ヒステリーを笑いにまぎらす.

concealment, *n.* 隠匿.

P hide (=lie) *in concealment* 潜伏する. ¶his place *of concealment* 彼の隠れ場所. ¶*without concealment* 包み隠さずに.

P² a place favorable to *concealment from* the eyes of their pursuers 追っ手の目をくらますに都合の好い場所. ¶*concealment of* offenders 犯人隠匿.

concede, *v.* 認める, 容れる, 譲歩する.

M This is *generally conceded* to be the best edition of ... 本書は...の最良版だと一般に認められている.

P *concede* a point (game) *to* a person 議論(など)を人に譲る. 【類】*concede* many privileges *to* foreign residents / *concede to* his demands.

O *concede* as true 真実として認める.

conceit, *n.* うぬぼれ, 自慢; 思いつき; 理解.

V He *has* an enormous *conceit*. 彼は恐ろしくうぬぼれている.

Q a *foolish conceit* 愚かな自負. ¶It is a *happy conceit* that has suggested the celebration of ... by them. 彼らが...を祝賀しようと考えたのはうまい思いつきである. ¶a *quaint conceit* 変った思いつき. ¶a man of *ready conceit* すぐいい気になる人. ¶His *conceit* is *unbearable*. 彼のうぬぼれときては鼻もちがならない. ¶*vain conceit* から自慢. ¶some *worthless little conceit* つまらぬうぬぼれ.

P He is a wise man *in* his own *conceit*. 彼は利口者だとうぬぼれている. ¶I am quite *out of conceit* with myself (my work). 自分(など)に愛想がつきた.

P² a man inflated *with conceit* 自信満々の人. ¶a man puffed up *with* a large *conceit* of himself うぬぼれの強い人. ¶*without conceit* うぬぼれずに. ¶He was a *conceit of* his own importance. あの人はえらがり屋だった.

conceive, *v.* はらむ; (考えを)抱く; (計画を)思いつく; 言い表わす.

P *conceived in* plain terms (language) 平易な言葉で言い表わして. ¶*conceive of* ... as the author of the story ...をその物語の著者だと思う ‖ I can't *conceive of* your idea. 君の考えは一向分らん. ‖ It is impossible to *conceive of* anything better. これ以上いい考えは浮ばない. 【類】I cannot *conceive of* your allowing a child to go so far alone. / I cannot *conceive of* such a thing happening again.

concentrate, *n.* 〖冶金〗精鉱, 濃縮鉱.

Q² 20 per cent *uranium concentrate* 20 パーセント濃縮ウラン.

concentrate, *v.* 集中する; 集合する.

P *concentrate* energies *against* the enemy's position 敵の陣地に対して兵力を集中する. ¶*concentrate* troops *at* a strategic point 要害の地に軍隊を集中する. ¶*concentrate* troops *in* a place 兵を某地区に集中する. ¶*concentrate* one's energies (thoughts) *on* some subject ある問題に精力(など)を集中する. ¶He is unable to *concentrate upon* his academic work. 彼は学業に専心することができない.

concentration, *n.* 集中, 専念; 濃縮.

V *cultivate* mental *concentration* 精神の統一を養う.

Q read with *deep concentration* 夢中になって読む.

Q² the *business concentration* in Lower Manhattan 南部マンハッタンにおける商業の集中.

P² *concentration of* thought 精神統一.

concept, *n.* 概念.

V *grasp* the *concept* of words as symbols for experience and ideas 経験や考えを表わす記号としての言葉の概念をつかむ. ¶It was alleged that Western films were ruining Indian culture and *injuring* their moral *concepts*. 西洋の映画がインド人の文化を破壊し彼らの道徳感を害しているという説があった.

Q a *high ethical concept* 高い道徳感. ¶an *important concept* 重要な概念 ‖ some of the more *important concepts* of bookkeeping 簿記のもっと重要ないくつかの意味. ¶the changing *social concepts* of the present era 変り行く現代の社会通念.

Q² the *Communist concept* of economics 共産主義者の経済学の理念. ¶a *constitution concepts* borrowed from western political philosophy 西欧政治哲学から借りた憲法の概念.

conception, *n.* 概念; 意見; 想像; 妊娠.

V Zola *enlarged* the *conception* of the function of the novel, sublimating it into a powerful and far-reaching instrument for social and moral propagandism. ゾラは小説の役目に対する概念を拡張しこれを社会的並に道徳的宣伝の非常に力強い普遍性のある道具として高く評価した. ¶I am unable to ***form*** a *conception* as to ... ...については概念が得られない.【類】***form*** a clear *conception* of ... ¶the value of the education of a nation by a study of its own literature in ***fostering*** the highest *conceptions* of patriotism and citizenship 愛国心および公民資格についての最高理念を養成するために自国文学を研究させる国民教育の価値. ¶***grasp*** firmly the *conception* of ... ...の概念を確実につかむ. ¶***have*** no *conception* (=idea) of ... ...はさっぱり分らない. ¶***prevent conception*** 避妊する. ¶***promote conception*** 妊娠を促す. ¶The *conception* has ***grown*** enormously in the past few years. その思想は過去数年間に非常に発達した.

Q an ***accurate*** *conception* 正確な概念. ¶cannot form an ***adequate*** *conception* of ... ...の正しい概念が得られない. ¶The heroine in the novel is a ***beautiful*** *conception*. その小説の女主人公は好い思いつきだ. ¶the ***British*** *conception* of feminine beauty 英人の女性美観. ¶***changing*** *conceptions* of education 変り行く教育の概念. ¶a ***clear-cut*** *conception* きわめて明白な考え. ¶gain a ***clearer*** *conception* of ... ...のもっとはっきりした概念を得る. ¶gain a ***clearer*** and ***firmer*** *conception* of ... について一層明りょうにして確実な概念を得る. ¶a ***clever*** *conception* うまい考え. ¶a ***cloudy*** *conception* of a subject ある問題についてのぼんやりした考え. ¶the ***Copernican*** *conception* of the universe コペルニクスの宇宙観. ¶This is not a ***correct*** *conception* of the matter. これはそのことに関する正しい見方ではない. ¶They have no ***definite*** *conception* of their duties as citizens. 彼らは公民としての義務についてはっきりした考えがない. ¶a ***distinct*** *conception* はっきりした考え. ¶her ***distorted*** *conception* of the world 世間に対する彼女のゆがんだ見方. ¶a ***divergent*** *conception* of welfare 福利についての異った概念. ¶an ***empty*** *conception* barren of all thought 全然思想のない空虚な概念. ¶I cannot form even the ***faintest*** *conception* of ... 私は...のことは一向見当がつかない. ¶a ***false*** *conception* 間違った考え. ¶the ***general*** *conception* of ... was so hazy that ... ...に対する一般観念が非常にぼんやりしていたので... ¶a man of ***grand*** *conception* 雄図を抱いた人. ¶the ***immaculate*** *conception* of the Virgin Mary 聖母マリヤの無原罪の御(お)宿り(懐妊). ¶ordinary ***legal*** *conceptions* 一般法的概念. ¶the ***materialistic*** *conception* of history, which is better known as "economic determinism"「経済的決定論」という方が通りがよい唯物史観. ¶***mistaken*** *conception* 間違った考え. ¶It is moving toward the ***modern*** *conception* of a university. それは近代的意義の大学という目標に向って進みつつある. ¶in the ***monistic*** *conception* 一元論から言うと. ¶controlled by a ***noble*** *conception* of ethical obligation りっぱな道徳的義務の観念に支配されて. ¶Science has overturned many ***old*** *conceptions* of life. 科学は幾多の古い人生観をくつがえした. ¶It did not occur as an ***original*** *conception*. 最初はそうは思わなかった. ¶some abstruse ***philosophical*** *conception* 深遠な哲学的概念といったもの. ¶The *conception* is ***poetic,*** but does it correspond to the reality? その考えは詩的ではあるが現実と合致しているだろうか. ¶contrary to ***popular*** *conception* 世間の考えとは逆に. ¶I have only a ***remote*** *conception* of what he is saying. 私には彼が言っていることはおぼろげにしか分っていない. ¶Their ***social*** *conceptions* are primitive. 彼らの社会観念は幼稚だ. ¶get a ***true*** *conception* of ... ...の真意をつかむ. ¶the ***wrong*** *conception* of patriotism 愛国心についての誤解.

P It is ***beyond*** our *conception*. それはわれわれの想像におよばない. ¶***in*** my *conception* 私の考えでは.

P^2 my *conception* ***of*** life 私の人生観.

concern, *n.* (**1**) 懸念, 関係, 利害関係; 重要なこと; 事務.

V ***arouse*** *concern* in some quarters ある方面に注意を呼び起す ‖ ***arouse*** the *concern* of the authorities 当事者を動かす. ¶The situation in Russia is ***causing*** very grave *concern* here. ロシアの国情は当地に重大な関心を引き起しつゝある.【類】His illness ***causes*** us considerable *concern*. / Great *concern* was ***caused*** in the city by the news. ¶***entertain*** a lively *concern* for ... ...に対して強い関心を示す. ¶***express*** *concern* over ... ...に対しての懸念を述べる. ¶***feel*** *concern* 懸念する ‖ they ***feel*** no *concern* about ... 彼らは...に対して無関心だ. ¶***give*** oneself *concern* about ... ...について心配する.【類】***give*** all one's *concern* to reflections on what would be the consequence of (結果がどうなるか)... ¶all who ***have*** any *concern* with (=are interested in) printing いやしくも印刷に関係している人々.【類】it ***has*** no *concern* whatever with ... ‖ Others who ***had*** no *concern* with the original dispute were forced to join in the fray. もともと関係のなかった者までも無理にけんかに引きずり込まれた.【類】You know what *concern* I ***have*** for your happiness. ¶***Mind*** your own *concern*. 余計なことをするな. ¶He ***showed*** the greatest *concern* over the situation. 彼は形勢に対して非常に憂慮した.【類】***show*** one's deep *concern* / He does not ***show*** much *concern* about it.

Q his ***chief*** (=***main***) *concern* 彼の大きな心配. ¶the ***central*** *concern* 本領. ¶The situation in the Far East is causing ***grave*** *concern* here. 極東の現状は当地では重大な関心を持たれている. ¶It is an ***important*** *concern*. それは大切な件だ. ¶in matters of ***international*** *concern* 国際的に利害関係ある事項について. ¶It should be regarded as a matter of grave ***national*** *concern*. それは国家の重大事と見るべきである. ¶It is ***no*** *concern* of mine. それは私の関することではない.【類】it is ***no*** *concern* of a university to ... ‖ That is ***no*** *concern* of grammar. それは文法と関係はない. ¶It is of ***no small*** *concern* to him. それは彼に取っては容易ならない件だ. ¶interfere with his ***personal*** *concerns* 彼一身上のことに干渉する. ¶the ***petty*** *concerns* of their daily life 彼ら日常生活の小さなことがら. ¶***practical*** *concerns* of life 人生の俗事. ¶our ***primary*** *concern* should be to ... われわれの第一に憂慮すべきことは...することであるべきだ. ¶***private*** *concerns* 私事. ¶matters of ***public*** *concern* 公事. ¶a matter of ***serious*** *concern* 一大事. ¶a ***supreme*** *concern* of the State 国家の大問題.

Q^2 ***everyday*** *concerns* (=affairs) 日常の仕事. ¶accept the cinema as a matter of ***Government*** *concern* 映画を政府関係の事業と認める. ¶a matter of ***world*** *concern* 世界的関心事.

P People watched ***with*** deepest *concern* the sick-bed of the English King. 人民は英国王の御不例をいとも深く心痛していた. ¶it is impossible to think ***without*** deep *concern* of ... ...のことを思うと深い憂慮にたえない.

P^2 *concern* ***about*** his affairs 彼のことについての心配. ¶*concern* ***at*** his misfortune 彼の不幸に対する心配. ¶a *concern* ***for*** his safety 彼の安全を思う心づかい ‖ Have a *concern* ***for*** your health! 健康に注意して下さい. ¶I have no *concern* ***in*** this business (the crime). 私はこのこと(など)には関係がない. ¶the *concerns* ***of*** the nation 国事.

(**2**) 商会; 商売; 《俗》建物.

V He succeeded in ***building up*** a flourishing *concern*. 彼は繁栄会社をつくり上げることに成功した. ¶***float*** a *concern* for the purpose of ... ...の目的で会社を設立する.

Q a ***dividend-earning*** (=***money-making***) *concern* 営利会社. ¶continue as a ***going*** *concern* その商社としので存在を保つ ‖ He purchased the business as a ***going*** *concern*. 彼はその商館を居抜きのまゝ引受けた. ¶***great*** *concerns* 大会社銀行. ¶a ***large*** *concern* 大会社. ¶a ***large*** and ***powerful*** *concern* 有力な大会社. ¶We are the ***oldest established*** and ***largest*** *concern* in the trade. この商売では私たちのが最古で最大な会社です. ¶a very ***paying*** *concern* 利潤の大いにあがる商売. ¶a ***prosperous*** (=***thriving***) *concern* 繁昌する会社. ¶It was then, as now, the greatest ***publishing*** *concern* in the world. それは当時すでに今日のごとく世界最大の出版会社であった. ¶a ***rickety old*** *concern* 《俗》ぼろ建物. ¶a ***vast commercial*** *concern* 巨大な商事会社.

Q^2 a ***business*** *concern* 商社. ¶a ***mail-order*** *concern* 通信販売会社. ¶a ***mammoth*** *concern* with a quarter of a million employes 二十五万の使用人を有する巨大な会社.

concern, *v.* 関係する; 心配する.

M The book is *concerned* ***chiefly*** with ... その本は主として...を取扱っている. ¶You are ***deeply*** *concerned* in this. 君はこのことに大関係がある. ‖ He was ***deeply*** *concerned* at the news. 氏はそのニュースにひどく心を痛めていた. ¶be ***egoistically*** *concerned* with ... ...についての心配も自己本位である. ¶He was ***greatly*** *concerned* at the advance that his enemy was making. 彼は敵軍の進撃状況に大いに

心を悩ました. ¶it is ***largely*** *concerned* with the fortunes ... それは...の運命に大いに関係する. ¶I am ***much*** *concerned* for his safety. 彼の安否を非常に心配している. ¶be *concerned* ***primarily*** with ... 元来...と関係がある. 【類】The four powers ***primarily*** *concerned* in the Pacific are the U.S.A., Japan, China, and the British Empire. ¶begin to be ***really*** *concerned* 真剣に関心を持ち始める. ¶be ***vitally*** *concerned* with ... ...と非常に重要な関係がある.

P *concern* oneself ***about*** (=with) what people say 人の言うことを気にかける. 【類】I am (=feel) much *concerned* ***about*** his illness. / Everybody is *concerned* ***about*** the future of his country. ¶He was *concerned* ***at*** the condition of his sick friend. 彼は友人の容体を気づかっていた. ¶We are all *concerned* ***for*** his happiness. われわれは皆彼の幸福を願っている. ¶all *concerned* ***in*** it その件の関係者一同 ‖ those who are in any way *concerned* ***in*** ... ...に何らかの形で関係している人々. 【類】He is *concerned* ***in*** the affair (business, matter, company, undertaking, enterprise, crime, plot). ‖ the firm is *concerned* ***in*** the failure of ... その店は...の破産の巻き添えを食った. ¶A good ruler *concerns* himself ***in*** the happiness of his subjects. 仁徳ある君主は臣下の幸福を念じられる. ‖ the parts *concerned* ***in*** digestion 消化に関係ある諸器管. ¶those who are *concerned* ***over*** the problems of the investment of their surplus funds 剰余資金の投資問題に関心をもつ人々. ¶Don't *concern* yourself ***with*** other people's affairs. 他人の問題に口ばしを入れるな. 【類】I am *concerned* ***with*** your welfare. ‖ the present part of this monograph is thus *concerned* ***with*** ... 従って本論文のこの部分は...を題目として取扱う ‖ I am not *concerned* here ***with*** the question whether ... 私は...かどうかの問題を今この文で論じようとするのではない. ‖ We are not here *concerned* ***with*** the moral side of education. ここでは教育の道徳的方面には触れない. 【類】chapters which are *concerned* ***with*** ... ‖ We are here *concerned* ***with*** auto-suggestion (自己暗示).

concert, *n.* 音楽会, 演奏会; 一致.

V ***attend*** a *concert* 音楽会に出席する. ¶The *concert* will be ***cancelled*** in case of rain. その演奏会は雨天の場合は取消しになります. ¶***enjoy*** an open-air *concert* 野外演奏を聞いて楽しむ. 【類】How did you ***enjoy*** the *concert?* ¶The band will ***give*** a *concert*. その楽団の演奏があるでしょう. ¶A *concert* was ***played*** by the University Band while the audience assembled. 聴衆が集まる間同大学の楽団が演奏をした.

V² The *concert* did not ***come up*** to my expectations. 音楽会は思ったほどでなかった. ¶The *concert* ***went off*** without a hitch (successfully, badly). 演奏会は滞りなく(など)済んだ. ¶The *concert* ***passed*** (=***went***) well. 演奏会はうまく行った.

Q an ***al-fresco*** *concert* 野外演奏会. ¶a ***complimentary*** *concert* 歓迎演奏会. ¶an ***impromptu*** *concert* on deck by a touring college band 旅行中の大学生バンドの即席船上演奏会. ¶an ***instrumental*** *concert* 器楽演奏. ¶a ***vocal*** *concert* 声楽コンサート.

Q² A ***band*** *concert* will be given by the Naval Band. 海軍軍楽隊の演奏があるはず. ¶a grand ***benefit*** *concert* 慈善音楽大会. ¶a ***cafe*** (***saloon***) *concert* 喫茶店(など)の演奏. ¶a ***charity*** *concert* at the Academy of Music 音楽学校の慈善音楽会. ¶a ***farewell*** *concert* 送別演奏会. ¶a ***prom*** *concert* 《米》[大学の]舞踏音楽会. ¶organize a ***smoking*** *concert* 《英》[演奏中喫煙を許す]喫煙演奏会を組織する. ¶a ***Sunday afternoon*** *concert* 日曜午後の演奏会. ¶a ***symphony*** *concert* 交響楽演奏会. ¶royalty attending a ***village*** *concert* 村演奏会臨席の王族方.

P a seat ***at*** the *concert* 音楽会の席 ‖ There was a good attendance ***at*** the *concert*. 演奏会は大入りだった. ‖ He is ***at*** a *concert*. 彼は演奏会に行っている. ¶engage (=book) seats ***for*** a *concert* 音楽会の座席を予約する. ¶work ***in*** *concert* with ... ...と協力する. 【類】The whole nation acted ***in*** *concert*. / I acted ***in*** *concert* with them. ¶subscribe ***to*** a *concert* 演奏会の座席を申込む.

concession, *n.* 譲歩; 許可; 居留地; 利権.

V ***exact*** *concession* 譲歩を強要する. ¶***expropriate*** a *concession* 土地を収用する. ¶reluctantly ***grant*** (=make) a *concession* いやいやながら譲歩する ‖ ***grant*** a *concession* for the construction of a railway 鉄道敷設の許可を与える. ¶***make*** mutual *concessions*=compromise, meet halfway 互いに譲り合う. 【類】The matter was settled because they ***made*** mutual *concessions*. ¶***obtain*** a *concession* for ... ...の許可を得る. 【類】***obtain*** *concessions* from the customs, postal and railway authorities. ¶***solicit*** a *concession* 譲歩を求める. ¶***wring*** *concessions* out of China 中国から(鉄道敷設などの)利権を奪取する.

Q a ***graceful*** *concession* 上品な譲歩. ¶a ***heavy*** *concession* 大譲歩. ¶a very ***humiliating*** *concession* はなはだ屈辱的な譲歩. ¶***mutual*** *concessions* 相互の譲歩. ¶a ***painful*** *concession* 苦しい譲歩. ¶the ***Russian*** *concession* at Hankou 漢口のロシア人居留地.

Q² an ***oil*** *concession* 石油採掘権(地区).

P ***at*** remarkable *concessions* from regular prices 定価の「大々的割引で.

P² substantial *concessions* ***by*** the company ***to*** the strikers' demand 罷業者の要求に対する会社の大譲歩. ¶make certain *concessions* ***in*** ... ...においてある譲歩をする. ¶make a *concession* ***to*** a demand 要求に対して譲歩する.

conciliate, *v.* なだめる.

P *conciliate* a child ***with*** a present 子供をおみやげでだま「す.

conciliation, *n.* 調停.

Q ***international*** *conciliation* 国際的調停.

Q² ***labor trouble*** *conciliation* 争議調停.

conciliator, *n.* 調停者.

Q² a ***labor*** *conciliator* 労働調停官.

concise, *a.* 簡潔な.

M be ***admirably*** *concise* 感服するほど簡約してある.

conciseness, *n.* 簡潔.

V *Conciseness* is ***served*** when the sentence is so corrected. その文をこう直すと簡潔になる.

Q ***excessive*** *conciseness* and reliance on the content of Chinese 漢文のあまりに簡潔で前後の関係によりすぎている「こと.

conclave, *n.* 秘密会議.

P meet ***in*** *conclave* 秘密会議を開く.

conclude, *v.* 決定する, 推断する; 終結する.

M I may ***fitly*** *conclude* my article with ... ...という言葉でこの論文を結ぶのが適当であろう. ¶not to be ***hastily*** *concluded* にわかに(そうと)断言できない. ¶we may, therefore, ***reasonably*** *conclude* that ... 故に...と結論を下すのが妥当であろう. ¶it is sometimes ***superficially*** *concluded* that ... ...という皮相な結論が下されることもある.

P *conclude* a treaty ***between*** countries (parties) 二国(など)間に協約を結ぶ. ¶*conclude* ***by*** remarking (=saying) that ... と言って結ぶ. 【類】I beg to *conclude* this letter ***by*** saying that ... ¶I can *conclude* ***from*** my experience that ... 私の経験によって...と断言できる. ‖ it should not be *concluded*, however, ***from*** what has been said above, that ... しかし, 以上述べたことで...という結論を下すべきではあるまい ‖ The article is *concluded* ***from*** yesterday. 昨日から続きのこの文は本日をもって完了. ¶The meeting was *concluded* (=came to an end) ***with*** the college song. 校歌を合唱して閉会した. ‖ *conclude* a treaty ***with*** the country その国と条約を結ぶ. 【類】*conclude* an agreement ***with*** a person. / let me *conclude* my speech ***with*** the remark that ...

O He *concluded* not to come. 彼は来ないことにきめた. ¶As there was nobody around in the hall, I *concluded* that the meeting had been postponed. 会場にはだれもいなかったので会合は延びたものと断定した.

conclusion, *n.* 結論; 断案, 断定; 終結.

V ***accept*** his *conclusions* 彼の決論を受入れる. ¶***adduce*** one's own *conclusion* 自己の断案を例証する. ¶***adopt*** the contrary *conclusion* 反対の断案を採用する. ¶in this conflict of authorities it would be highly presumptuous if I were to ***assert*** any definite *conclusion*, but ... かく諸説が矛盾しているのに私が断案を下すとしたらはなはだせん越でしょうが... ¶I can hardly ***avoid*** the *conclusion* that ... ...という断定を下さざるを得ない. ¶***base*** his *conclusions* largely on ... 氏の結論は主に...に基礎をおいている. ¶***build up*** *conclusions* on insufficient evidence 不十分な証拠で結論する. ¶***confirm*** the *conclusion* that ... ...という断定を確実ならしめる. ¶***deduce*** *conclusions* from premises 前提から断案を下す. ¶***derive*** one's own *conclusion* 自己独特の結論を下す. ¶***draw*** a *conclusion* from facts 事実によって断定する. 【類】***draw*** an erroneous (a false ***or*** a wrong) *conclusion* from ... / ***draw*** the following *conclusion* from ... ¶we cannot ***escape*** the *conclusion* that ... ...と結論せざるを得ない. ¶***force*** a *conclusion* one way or the other 強いていずれかに決定させる. ¶***form*** a *conclusion* 結論する‖***form*** one's own *conclusions* 独自の結論を下す. ¶these opinions ***fortify*** my *conclusion* that ... これらの意見に徴しても...という私の結論の確実なことが明かである. ¶***found*** a *conclusion* upon ... ...にもとずいて結論を下す. ¶***frame*** one's own *conclusions* 独自の結論を作る. ¶You would be disposed to ***hazard*** the *conclusion* that ... おそらく君なら...と無理にも結論を下したい気になるかも知れないが. ¶***justify*** the *conclusion* that ... ...という結論の正確さを示す. ¶***leave*** the *conclusion* of this part of research in abeyance 研究のこの部分を未定のままにしておく. ¶It is premature to ***make*** that *conclusion.* にわかにそうとは断言できぬ. ¶He ***offers*** no *conclusion.* 彼は結論を下さない. ¶***proffer*** a *conclusion* 結論を持ちだす. ¶***reach*** (=***arrive at***) a *conclusion* on a reasonable basis 正当な根拠にもとずいて結論に到達する. 【類】I have ***reached*** the *conclusion* that the least rewarded of all the professions is that of the teacher in our higher educational institutions.—Andrew Carnegie. / ***reach*** the same *conclusion.* ¶***reconsider*** one's *conclusion* 決論を再考する. ¶***summarize*** the general *conclusions* of the assembly 会議の一般決議を約説する. ¶***support*** the *conclusion* that ... ...という結論に賛成する. ¶These facts ***warrant*** such a *conclusion.* これらの事実はかゝる結論の正しきことを証明する.

V^2 The *conclusion* will ***follow*** from the premises. その前提からこの結論が生れるであろう.

Q an ***assailable*** *conclusion* 攻撃しうる結論. ¶reach a ***different*** *conclusion* 異った結論に達する. ¶draw a quite ***erroneous*** *conclusion* that ... ...という全く誤った決論を引出す. ¶Such lack of knowledge will lead to an ***erroneous*** *conclusion.* かゝる認識不足は結論を誤らせるであろう. ¶a ***fallacious*** *conclusion* 不合理な結論. ¶Victory was a ***foregone*** *conclusion.* 勝利は当然のことであった.‖it is a ***foregone*** *conclusion* that ... ...ということは既定の事実である. 【類】The result was a ***foregone*** *conclusion.* ¶form a ***hasty*** *conclusion* 早のみこみする, 速断する. ¶a ***hastily drawn*** *conclusion* 軽率な結論. ¶an ***inexorable*** *conclusion* 思いきった断案. ¶a ***just*** *conclusion* 公正な結論. ¶the ***latest*** *conclusions* of the specialists in all fields of science 科学のあらゆる分野における専門家最近の断案. ¶a ***legitimate*** *conclusion* 正しい決論. ¶carry out the measure to its ***logical*** *conclusion* その案を徹底的に実行する‖it would seem to be a ***logical*** *conclusion* that ... ...ということが合理的な結論であると思われるのである. 【類】This is the only ***logical*** *conclusion.* / the ***logical*** *conclusion* of this is ... ¶the ***majority*** (***minority***) *conclusion* 多(少)数の決論. ¶the ***opposite*** *conclusion* 反対の結論. ¶a very ***rash*** *conclusion* はなはだ早計な結論. ¶arrive at a ***rational*** *conclusion* 合理的結論に到達する. ¶come to a ***right*** and ***final*** *conclusion* 正しい最後の断案に達する. ¶It is not a ***safe*** *conclusion* to make. そうきめるのは安全な断定ではない. ¶It would be impossible to bring it to a ***satisfactory*** *conclusion.* おそらく満足にはおさまらないだろう. ¶the attainment of ***sound*** *conclusions* 確実な結論への到達. ¶be compelled to ***strong*** *conclusions* by the overwhelming force of facts 事実の力が圧倒的であっていや応なしに強い結論に達せざるを得なくなる. ¶achieve the merit of ***successful*** *conclusion* 有終の美をなす. ¶The *conclusion* seems ***tenable.*** その断案は論ばくにたえうると思われる. ¶the ***ultimate*** *conclusions* 究極的断案. ¶an ***unshakable*** *conclusion* 動かない結論. ¶an ***unsound*** *conclusion* 不確実な結論. ¶reach a ***wrong*** *conclusion* 誤った結論に到達する.

P ***at*** the *conclusion* of the ceremony 式の終りに. 【類】***at*** the *conclusion* ***of*** his studies / Formosa was ceded to Japan in 1895, ***at*** the *conclusion* of the victorious war with China. ‖You should not jump ***at*** a *conclusion.* 速断すべきでない. 【類】the *conclusion* we arrived ***at*** was ... ¶***by way of*** *conclusion* 終りに臨んで. ¶Let me say this ***in*** *conclusion* 終りに臨んでこのことを申上げます. 【類】I will ***in*** *conclusion* say a few words about ... / ***In*** *conclusion,* I will briefly summarize the chief propositions (意見) maintained in this paper. ‖they were unanimous ***in*** the *conclusion* that ... 彼らは異議なく...と決定した. ¶***on*** the *conclusion* of peace 平和締結の暁に. ¶We have come ***to*** this *conclusion.* われわれはこの断案を得た. 【類】gradually come ***to*** (=reach *or* arrive at) the *conclusion* that ... ‖I am led ***to*** the *conclusion* that ... ...と断定せざるを得ない. ¶***upon*** the *conclusion* of a peace treaty 平和条約締結の暁は. ¶***upon*** the *conclusion* of the course 課程終了の上.

concoct, *v.* でっち上げる; 作上げる.

M Children are ***merrily concocting*** some queer messes in the yard. 子供らはお庭で楽しそうに妙なごちそうを作っている. ¶*concoct* a story ***offhand*** 話を即席に作る.

concoction, *n.* 調理品.

Q^2 Vodka is a ***potato*** *concoction.* ウオッカはじゃが芋から造る.

concomitant, *n.* 随伴物.

Q An exact and extensive vocabulary is an ***important*** *concomitant* of success. 正確で豊富な語彙(ごい)は成功への重大な要素である. ¶The cherry dance has become an almost ***indispensable*** *concomitant* of the cherry season. 桜おどりは桜の季節にはほとんどなくてはならないものになった. ¶A high pulse is an ***invariable*** *concomitant* of fever. 高い脈はくは必ず発熱にともなう. ¶***necessary*** *concomitants* of community life 団体生活に必ずつくもの.

P^2 a *concomitant* ***of*** virtue 道徳につきもの. ¶a *concomitant* ***to*** greatness 偉大性につきもの.

concord, *n.* 一致.

Q^2 carry out the ***Potsdam Concord*** ポツダム協定を実行する.

P ***in concord*** with ... ...と一致して.

P^2 the *concord* ***of*** husband and wife 夫婦の和合.

concordance, *n.* 要語索引.

P^2 Clarke's *Concordance* ***to*** Shakespeare クラークのシェクスピア要語索引.

concourse, *n.* 群集, 集合.

V ***make*** a *concourse* 群をなす.

Q There was a ***great*** (=***large***) *concourse* of people. 人がたくさんに寄っていた. ¶an ***immense*** *concourse* of the population 人々の大群集. ¶An ***innumerable*** *concourse* of people lined the road. 路には無数の群集が並んでいた.

concrete, *n.* 具体物.

P He has no idea of poverty ***in*** the *concrete.* 彼には貧乏の味が本当に分っていない.

concrete, *a.* 具体的な.

M to be ***more*** *concrete* 早い話が.

concubine, *n.* めかけ.

V ***keep*** a *concubine* 二号を囲う. ¶***take*** to oneself a *concubine* めかけを持つ.

P He had children ***by*** his *concubine.* 彼は二号との間に子があった.

concur, *v.* 同意する, 一致する.

M I ***cordially*** *concur* in this opinion. 私はこの意見に心から同意する. ¶***entirely*** *concur* with your views (=opinion) あなたの御意見に全く同意する. ¶*concur* ***fully*** in one's views その意見に全く同意する. ¶I ***heartily*** (=***enthusiastically***) *concur* with his opinion that ... 私は...という彼の意見に大賛成である. ¶I ***strictly*** *concur* with him in his criticism of ... 私は彼の...の批評に全然賛成だ.

P Authorities *concur* ***in*** this view. この見解には諸大家の意見が一致している. 【類】*concur* ***in*** one's judgment / He and I *concurred* ***in*** opposing the policy of the board (委員会). / The other directors did not *concur* ***in*** his proposal to extend the works (工場拡張案). ¶*concur* ***with*** you ***in*** this opinion この意見では私は貴方と一致する. 【類】*concur* ***with*** Carlyle ***in*** considering that ... / I earnestly hope you will *concur* ***with*** me ***in*** it.

concurrence, *n.* 同意, 賛同; 同時発生.

V ***obtain*** the *concurrence* of all the Government Departments concerned 関係諸官省の同意を得る.

Q have the ***full*** *concurrence* of ... ...から全面的に同意される.

P ***with*** the *concurrence* of ... ...の同意(賛同)を得て. ¶***without*** the *concurrence* of ... ...の同意なくしては.

P^2 *concurrence* ***in*** a proposal 提議に対する賛同. ¶It is supported by a *concurrence* ***of*** evidence. それは証拠の一致によって支持されている. ‖a *concurrence* ***of*** events (circumstances) 事件(事情)の同時発生.

concurrent *a.* 同時発生の.

P *concurrent* (=simultaneously) ***with*** an event ある事件発生と同時に.

condemn, *v.* 罪を宣告する; とがめる, 責める, 非難する; 用に適しないと言渡す.

M ***emphatically*** *condemn* 激しくとがめる. ¶*condemn* ***indiscriminately*** 見さかいなく(やたらに)こきおろす. ¶*condemn* ***most strongly*** こっぴどく責めつける. ¶*condemn* *offhand* 頭からとがめる. ¶He was ***rather condemned*** than extolled. 彼はほめられるどころかむしろとがめられた. ¶They were *condemned* ***root and branch.*** 彼らは徹頭徹尾非難された. ¶cannot so ***sweepingly*** *condemn* そう一概に悪くは言えない. ¶***summarily*** *condemn* 一概に悪く言う. ¶He was ***unjustly*** *condemned.* 彼はぬれぎぬを着せられた. ¶***unsparingly*** *condemn* 容赦なくとがめ立てをする.

P The provisions were *condemned* ***by*** the commissary. その食料品は糧食部から食用に適しないむね告示された. ¶He was *condemned* ***by*** all ***for*** (=***on account of***) his conduct. その不行跡をみんなに非難された. ‖ *condemn* a person ***for*** murder 人に殺害罪を宣告する ‖ *condemn* a person ***for*** bad conduct 非行に対して人を非難する. ¶*condemn* a guilty man ***to*** harakiri 罪人に切腹を宣告する ‖ He was *condemned* ***to*** penal servitude. 彼は懲役を宣告された. 【類】He was *condemned* ***to*** death (exile, hard labor, three months' imprisonment, the gallows). / He was *condemned* ***to*** one hundred days' imprisonment in his own house (自宅謹慎). / be *condemned* ***to*** death ***for*** treason (反逆罪) ‖ It has been *condemned* ***to*** oblivion. それは世間から忘れられた. ‖ be *condemned* ***to*** tramping from coast to coast [アメリカの]各州を放浪するよう運命づけられる. 【類】He was *condemned* ***to*** touring the whole country for a living.

O *condemn* him to pay a fine 彼を罰金に処する. 【類】They *condemned* him to be hanged. ¶be *condemned* as dangerous 危険とレッテルをはられる ‖ *condemn* a person as illiterate ある人を無学者ときめつける. ¶The meat was *condemned* as unfit for human food (=consumption). その肉は食用にはならないと決められた. ¶She was ***condemned as*** unseaworthy. その船は使用にたえないと決定された.

condemnation, *n.* 罪の宣告; 非難.

V ***make*** a sweeping *condemnation* いちがいに悪く言う. ¶He ***merits*** every *condemnation.* 彼はどう非難されても仕方がない.

Q ***social*** *condemnation* 社会の非難. ¶make a ***sweeping*** *condemnation* 頭ごなしにする. ¶a ***wholesale*** *condemnation* 全面的非難, 頭こなし.

P² a *condemnation* ***against*** ... ...に対する非難. ¶*condemnation* ***from*** acids 酸の厳禁. ¶*condemnation* ***to*** exile 遠島の処刑.

condensation, *n.* 凝結.

P² the *condensation* ***of*** the moisture in the air 空中の湿気の凝結. 【類】the *condensation* ***of*** steam into water.

condense, *v.* 凝縮する; 簡約にする.

P *condense* ***by*** cold ***into*** a liquid 寒さのために凝縮して液化する. ¶be *condensed* ***into*** thick soup [煮つまって]どろどろのスープになる. 【類】*condense* a gas ***into*** a liquid / Steam *condenses* ***into*** water when it touches a cold surface. ‖ *condense* a statement ***into*** a few words 陳述を数語に縮める ‖ *condense* a report ***into*** the smallest compass 報告をできるだけ簡約にする.

condescend, *v.* 卑下する; 譲る.

M He ***never*** *condescended* to help his wife with the housework. 彼は細君の仕事を自分の方から手伝ってやろうとは決してしなかった.

P He had to *condescend* ***to*** the meanest hack work in order to keep the wolf from the door. 生きんがためにはどんなつまらぬ仕事でも忍んでやらねばならなかった. ‖ We are not going ***to*** *condescend* upon particulars. 自分は細かい点まで立入ろうとする考えはない.

O *condescend* to accept a bribe [節を捨てて]わいろを受け取る.

condition, *n.* (**1**) 地位, 身分; 情勢, 状態.

V ***ameliorate*** the *conditions* of women (the poor) 婦人(など)の地位を改善する. 【類】In every human being there is a wish to ***ameliorate*** his own *condition.* ¶***amend*** *conditions* 事態を改善する. ¶gradually ***assume*** an abnormal *condition* しだいに変調をきたす. ¶***better*** the *condition* of the industrial workers 産業労働者の生活状態を改善する. 【類】***better*** the *conditions* of manual workers (筋肉労働者) / ***better*** their *condition* in life (生活状態) / the problem of ***bettering*** the *condition* of all mankind. ¶the *conditions* are further ***complicated*** by the fact that ... ...という事実によって事態はさらに複雑化している. ¶***congest*** traffic *conditions* 交通を混雑させる. ¶***correct*** the *condition* 状態を改める. ¶tend to ***create*** a *condition* inconsistent with ... ...と一致しない一つの状態を作りだしがちである. ¶***equalize*** the *conditions* of men 人々の生活状態を平等化する. ¶***improve*** the *condition* of the poor. 貧民の生活状態を改善する. ¶visit the scene and ***investigate*** the *conditions* on the spot 現場を視察して実地調査を行う. ¶***lift up*** (=***elevate***) the *conditions* of women's lives 女子の生活状態を向上させる. ¶***observe*** *conditions* 情況を観察する. ¶***overturn*** the present *conditions* 現状をくつがえす. ¶***present*** these *conditions* こういった状態を呈する. ¶by ***recognizing*** the changed *conditions* of this age 時勢を認識して. ¶***remedy*** a faulty *condition* 誤った状態を直す. ¶He ***reviewed*** the *condition* of things in the crispest words. 彼はきわめてきびきびした言葉で一般情勢を論評した. ¶***study*** the *condition* of the laboring classes 労働階級の生活状態を研究する. 【類】***study*** *conditions* primarily in China and also in Korea. ¶***worsen*** the *conditions* of ... ...の事態を悪化する.

V² The *condition* is rapidly ***changing.*** 事情は急速に変りつゝある. ¶*conditions* ***favoring*** 好調であれば. ¶His *condition* is speedily ***improving.*** 彼の健康はどんどん回復しつゝある. ¶*conditions* ***influencing*** ... ...に影響をおよぼす事情. ¶if the *condition* ***requires*** 事態がそれを必要とするならば.

Q This *condition* is ***abnormal.*** かゝる状態は変調である. 【類】assume an ***abnormal*** *condition.* ¶the ***actual*** *conditions* seen in ... ...に見られる実状. 【類】the ***actual*** *condition* of native life in China. ¶under such ***adverse*** *conditions* かゝる逆境にあって. ¶adapt oneself to ***altering*** *conditions* 周囲の事情の変化に順応する. ¶The American environment and ***American*** *conditions* of life. アメリカ的環境とアメリカ的生活状態. ¶under ***ancient*** *conditions,* when communications were poor 往時交通機関の不備だった時代には. ¶the ***atmospheric*** *conditions* 気象状態(天気都合). ¶***attendant*** *conditions* 付帯事情. ¶The city is in a ***backward*** *condition.* その市は時代後れになっている. ¶owing to the ***bad*** *condition* of the trade 商業不振のため. ¶in ***beautiful*** *condition* [新品と変らず]美しく. ¶***changed*** *conditions* of society 変った社会状態. 【類】meet (対応する) ***changed*** *conditions.* ¶The ***climatic*** *conditions* of Japan vary from semi-tropical to almost sub-arctic. 日本の気候は半熱帯の気候からほとんど亜北極の気候にわたる. ‖ under all ***climatic*** *conditions* どのような気候状態にも. 【類】in order to obtain the most favorable ***climatic*** *conditions.* ¶lie in a ***comatose*** *condition* こんすい状態におち入っている ‖ The state remains in a ***comatose*** *condition.* その国はこんすい状態におち入っている. ¶***commercial*** *conditions* abroad 海外の商況. ¶close observation and study of ***commercial*** and ***industrial*** *conditions* in the Orient 東洋における商工業の綿密な観察と研究. ¶under the ***complicated*** *conditions* of modern life 複雑化した近代生活においては. ¶***conjugal*** (=***marital***) *condition* (未婚・既婚・離婚などの)結婚状態. ¶His *condition* is reported to be ***critical.*** 彼は重態であるとのことである. 【類】The patient is in a ***critical*** *condition.* ¶be received in ***damaged*** *condition* 破損したまま受取る. ¶His *condition* is ***dangerous.*** 彼の病状は危険だ. ¶She is in a ***delicate*** *condition.* 彼女は懐妊している. ☞ 英口語では She is in the family way. ¶Business is in a very ***demoralized*** *condition.* 商業は一向振わない. ¶the present ***deplorable*** *condition* 現今の悲しむべき状態. ¶a ***diseased*** *condition* of trees 樹の病的状態. ¶help forward this ***desirable*** *condition* この改善を助長する. ¶He is in a ***dying*** *condition.* 彼はひん死の状態にある. ¶***economical*** *condions* 経済状態. ¶in the present ***embryonic*** *condition* of eugenic study 今日のごとく優生学研究がきわめて幼稚な状態では. ¶good ***environmental*** *condition* 良好の環境. ¶people of ***every*** *condition* 貧富上下. 【類】in ***every*** *condition* of life. ¶***existing*** *conditions* in (=the present position of) the Far East 極東における現下の情勢. 【類】maintain the ***existing*** *conditions* of society. ¶The crew were brought ashore in an ***exhausted*** *condition.* 船員たちはみんなへとへとになって陸にあげられた. ¶better ***faulty*** *conditions* 不完全な所を改善する. ¶under the most ***favorable*** *conditions* もっとも有利な状態の下に. ¶He was brought up in exceptionally ***favorable linguistic*** *conditions.* 彼は語学の修得上特に都合のよい境遇に育った. ¶the ***feverish*** *condition* of the commercial world 商業界の乱調. ¶The company is not in a thoroughly sound ***financial*** *condition*. 同会社は財政状態が全く安全という風にはなっていない. ¶These used stamps are in ***fine*** *condition*. これら古(郵便)切手はよごれていない. ‖ wheat brought into a very ***fine condition*** 細粉化した小麦. ¶It is in ***first-class*** *condition*. 完全(状態)になっている. ¶be in a ***florid*** *condition* はなやかになっている ‖ Political *conditions* are very ***fluid*** in China. 中国の政局ははなはだ不安定である. ¶bring it back to its ***former*** *condition* 復旧させる. ¶a ***good*** *condition* of health 身体の好調 ‖ The roads are in ***good*** (***bad***) *condition*. 道路はりっぱに(ひどく)なっている. ‖ Our crop is in ***good condition***. われわれの作物は実りがよい. ‖ The cargo was delivered in ***good condition***. 船荷はいたみなしで引渡された. ¶such a ***gross*** *condition* of affairs そんなひどい状勢. ¶The trade is in a ***healthy*** *condition*. 商売が健全な状態にある. ¶The vessel is in a ***helpless*** *condition*. 同船は絶望状態である. ¶The horse is in ***high*** *condition*. この馬は申分がない. ¶in a somewhat ***hilarious*** *condition* (酒などで)大分上気げんで. ¶place working women under ***hygienic*** *conditions* during their term of maternity 妊娠した婦人労働者のために衛生的設備をする. 【類】 labourers under bad ***hygienic*** *conditions*. ¶in ***ideal weather*** *conditions* 理想的な天気模様で. ¶***ignominious*** *conditions* 恥ずべき状態. ¶The three ***important*** *conditions* are fulfilled. 三拍子そろっている. ¶suit one's ***individual*** *conditions* それぞれの状態に適合させる. ¶***inhuman*** *conditions* of life 非人間的生活状態. ¶compel his employees to labor long hours in *conditions* ***inimical*** to life 彼の雇人をしいて健康上有害な状態の下に長時間働かせる. ¶the ***intellectual*** *condition* of our Japanese students today 今日わが日本学生の知的状態. ¶***intermediate transitional*** *conditions* 過渡期における中間状態. ¶this ***intolerable*** and ***scandalous*** *condition* この赦し難い醜悪な状態. ¶in the ***irate*** *condition* of his thoughts 思想が激した時には. ¶a ***lethargic*** *condition* こんすい状態. ¶He rose suddenly from a ***low*** *condition*. 彼は低い地位から急に出世した. ¶***modern*** *conditions* of living 近代の生活状態 ‖ under (=in) ***modern*** *conditions* 現状では. ¶be in a ***musty*** *condition* かびくさくなっている. ¶books in ***new*** *condition* at reduced prices 減価提供の新本. 【類】 The books are in ***new*** *condition* as published. ¶Honor and shame from ***no*** *condition* rise. 栄辱由って来る所がある. ¶under ***normal*** *conditions* 常態では ‖ Things are beginning to assume something like ***normal conditions***. 事態はやゝ正常に復しかけている. 【類】 be back to ***normal*** *conditions* / The ***normal*** *conditions* seem to have been restored. / until the return of ***normal*** *conditions* / War was a ***normal condition*** in those days. ¶in a perfectly ***nude condition***=stark naked 真裸で. ¶under the ***old*** *conditions* 以前[の状態で]は. ¶The ***opposite*** *conditions* prevail. 目下はそれと反対情勢である. ¶Under ***ordinary*** *conditions*, lead is always soft. 普通鉛は必ずやわらかなものだ. ¶all in its ***original*** *condition* すべて元のままで. ¶***outward*** *conditions* 外界の事情. ¶the ***physical*** *condition* of the Japanese 日本人の体格 ‖ I am in the best of my ***physical*** *condition*. 私のからだの調子は上乗です. 【類】 It is every man's duty, these days, to be in good ***physical*** *condition*. ¶a ***piteous*** *condition* あわれな状態. ¶The ground is not in a ***playable*** *condition*. 競技場は使用のできる状態になっていない. ¶the ***political*** *conditions* of the time 現時の政局. ¶The trade of Vienna has suffered severely from ***postwar*** *conditions* ウィンナの商況は戦後の事情でひどく不振になった. ¶Business (The bank) is in a ***precarious*** *condition*. 商売(など)は不安の状態にある. ¶under ***predisposing*** *conditions* [病気など]発生しやすい状態に. ¶under ***present*** *conditions* 現時の状態では. 【類】 during the ***present*** *condition* of the market. ¶under our ***present social*** *conditions* わが国現時の社会状態では. ¶owing to the ***prevailing economic*** *conditions* 時節柄(経済界の現状によって). ¶a return to ***prewar*** *conditions* 戦前の状態への復帰. ¶The roads are in ***prime*** *condition*. 道路は上乗だ. ¶In a ***primitive*** *condition* of society, the female was merely a chattel. 原始社会においては婦人は一つの物品に過ぎなかった. ¶his ***psychological*** *condition* 彼の心理状態. ¶fulfilling the three ***requisite*** *conditions* 三拍子そろえて. ¶under the ***right*** *conditions* 正しい状態では. ¶a very ***rotten*** *condition* 話にならない(ひどい)状態. 【類】 The goods were delivered in ***rotten*** *condition*. ¶improve ***sanitary*** *conditions* 衛生状態を改善する. 【類】 keep the kitchen in a ***sanitary*** *condition*. ¶in a ***semiconscious*** *condition* 意識もうろうとして. 【類】 sink into a ***semiunconscious*** *condition*. ¶in a ***serious*** *condition* 重態で. ¶The affairs of that firm are in a very ***shaky*** *condition*. あの店ははなはだ財政不安の状態にある. ¶***sickly*** *condition* 病気の状態. ¶under ***similar*** *conditions* こういった場合には. ¶be in a ***sinking*** *condition* [船が]今にも沈みそうである. ¶under existing ***social*** *conditions* 今日の社会状態では. ¶His body is in the ***soundest*** *condition*. 彼の体は申分がない. ¶under the ***strenuous*** *conditions* of the modern world 近代世界の激しい生存競争状態の下に. ¶a purely ***temporary*** *condition* 純然たる一時的現象. ¶He was rescued in an ***unconscious*** *condition*. 彼はこんすい状態で救助された. ¶leave it in an ***undecided*** *condition* うやむやのうちに葬る. ¶under the ***unfavorable*** *condition* of trade 商売不振で. ¶excessive labor carried on under most ***unhealthy*** *conditions* 全く不健康な状態のもとに行われる過度な労働. ¶the ***unsettled*** *conditions* in North China 北支における不穏の形勢. ¶The whole system is in a ***weak*** and ***debilitated*** *condition*. 全組織が衰弱した状態になっている. ¶because of the ***weakened*** *condition* of the industry その産業が弱体化しているから.

Q[2] be under ***battle*** *condition* 戦闘中である. ¶the industrial world under ***boom*** *conditions* 好況の産業界. ¶forecast ***business*** *conditions* 市況を予報する. ‖ encouraged by improved ***business*** *conditions* 好景気に刺激されて. ¶exercises, under simulated ***combat*** *conditions* 戦闘演習. ¶better ***farming village*** *conditions* 農村の現状を改善する. ¶The ***foodstuff*** *condition* is at present very precarious. 現在の食料事情はすこぶる不安である. ¶under the old ***foot-and-horse*** *conditions* 昔の徒歩や馬旅行の時代では. ¶under ***greenhouse*** *conditions* 温室育ちで. ¶improve ***housing*** *conditions* 住宅問題を改善する. ¶***inclement weather*** *conditions* 険悪な天候. ¶unsettled ***labor*** *conditions* 不安定の労働情勢 ‖ ***labor*** *conditions* being as they are 現在のような労働情勢では. 【類】 The ***labor*** *conditions* of his time (当時の). ¶***life*** *conditions* 生活状態. ¶The ***living*** *conditions* of modern women. 近代女性の生態. ¶unsanitary ***living*** *conditions* 不衛生な生活状態. 【類】 better (=improve) ***living*** *conditions* / ***Living*** *conditions* since the end of the war have become increasingly difficult. / ease the wretched ***living*** *conditions* (みじめな生活状態) / Modern inventions have changed ***living*** *conditions* and quickened the tempo of the times. ¶as ***market*** *conditions* now stand 市場の現況では ‖ ***Market*** *conditions* remain unchanged and money is still very easy. 市況は変らず, 金融はなおすこぶる緩慢. ¶a knowledge of ***outside-world*** *conditions* 外界事情の知識. ¶under ***peacetime*** *conditions* 平和時には. ¶straighten out the badly congested ***railroad traffic*** *conditions* ひどくこむ鉄道輸送状況を正常化する. ¶The jeeps were guaranteed to be in ***running*** *condition*. ジープ車はいつでも運転できる状態にあることが保証された. ¶to improve ***shipping*** and ***mail*** *conditions* 輸送および通信状況改善のために. ¶bad ***short-wave receiving*** *conditions* 短波受信の不良状況. ¶have good ***soil*** *conditions* 土壌は好状態にある. ¶The ship was in "***spick and span***" *condition*. 船は真新らしい状態にあった. ¶speak on the ***trade*** *conditions* of China 中国の商況について語る ‖ Owing to present ***trade*** *conditions*, quotations for a year ahead are still not possible. 現在の商況では一年先の相場はまだ立たない. ‖ The market has come to a normal ***trade*** *condition*. 市場が常態に戻ってきた. 【類】 ***Trade*** *conditions* everywhere are improving. ¶alleviate the congested ***traffic*** *condition* 交通混雑の状態を緩和する. ¶***travel*** *condition* in Japan 日本の旅行状況. ¶be totally inapplicable to ***twentieth century*** *conditions* 二十世紀の現状には全く合わない. ¶on (=under) ***war*** *conditions* 戦時状態では. 【類】 under present ***war*** *conditions*. ¶***wartime*** *conditions* 戦時状態. ¶because of ***weather*** *conditions* 天候状態のため ‖ braving adverse ***weather*** *conditions* 悪天候を冒して ‖ affected by ***weather*** *conditions* 天候に左右されて. 【類】 depend on ***weather*** *conditions* / report ***weather*** *conditions* / prevailing ***weather*** *conditions*. ¶under present ***world*** *conditions* 現時の

世界状勢下では. 【類】everchanging *world conditions* / *world* economic *conditions* ‖ as soon as *world conditions* permit 世界の情勢が許す限り速かに.

P The value, *according to condition*, is from ... yen upward each. [古切手など] 価額は品次第で一枚...円以上である. ‖ 1 or 2 tablets *according to condition* 容態によって一粒ないし二粒. ¶ low *in condition* 地位の低い ‖ *in* a *condition* (=state) of absolute ignorance of the subject その問題は全然知らない(白紙の)状態で ‖ He is *in* a *condition* of utter helplessness. 彼は実にあわれな状態だ. ‖ I am not *in* [a] *condition* (=position) to ... 僕には...しかねる. ¶ He fell *into* a melancholy *condition*. 彼はふさぎ込んでしまった. ¶ a man *of condition* 身分のある人. ¶ The horse is *out of condition*. この馬は弱っている. ‖ I've been terribly busy lately, so I'm rather *out of condition* now. 最近ばかにいそがしいので, ちと健康を害している. ¶ *under condition* of civilization 文化生活において ‖ He had to work very hard *under conditions* of great weakness and ill-health. 彼は非常に衰弱した体で一生懸命働かねばならなかった. ‖ *under* no *conditions* should they be allowed to ... いかなる事情があろうとも彼らは...することは許されない. 【類】*Under* no *conditions* will we not be disturbed.

P² What would be my *condition before* the law if I were to ...? 私が...するとしたら法律上どんなことになるだろう. ¶ the present *condition of* affairs 現状 ‖ The *condition* (=state) *of* affairs here remains unchanged. 一般の状態には何らの変化もない. 【類】The *condition of* one's health. ‖ This *condition of* things is not encouraging to ... この事態は...にとってかんばしいものではない.

(**2**) 条件.

V *accept conditions* 条件を受け入れる ‖ can *accept* no *conditions* whatever どんな条件にも応じ得ない. ¶ *alter conditions* 条件を(一部)変更する. ¶ *approve* the *conditions* その条件に賛成する. ¶ *enforce* rigid *conditions* upon ... に対して厳重な条件を押付ける. ¶ exactly *fulfil* the *conditions* laid down 定められた条件を正確に果たす. ¶ *give* better *conditions* 一層よい条件を許す. ¶ *impose* the *condition* that ... shall ... ...は...すべしという条件を課す. ¶ *make* the *conditions* as easy as possible 条件をできるだけ楽にする. ¶ *meet* the *conditions* (=requirements) 条件に合する. ¶ *modify conditions* 条件を変更する. ¶ I cannot *obtain* your *condition*. 君の希望通りに取計らえない. 【類】if my *conditions* cannot be *obtained*. ¶ The place *offers* every *condition* conducive to a happy vacation. そこには休暇を愉快に過せるようなあらゆる設備ができている. ¶ *perform conditions* 条件を実行する. ¶ *propose* the following *conditions* 次の条件を提出する. ¶ The machine will *satisfy conditions* which have never before been met. この機械はこれまで満たされなかった欠陥を補足するであろう. 【類】*satisfy* the necessary *conditions*. ¶ *violate conditions* 条件を破る. ¶ *waive conditions* mentioned 提起した条件を撤回する.

Q on *certain conditions* ある条件で. ¶ under *easy conditions* 楽な条件で. ¶ *entrance conditions* 入会(入学)条件. ¶ one of the *essential conditions* of peace 平和の必須条件の一. ¶ a combination of *favorable conditions* 都合のよい条件が重なること. ¶ the *first condition* of success 成功の第一条件. ¶ on the *fixed condition* of ... ...という確定条件で. ¶ *liberal conditions* 寛大な条件. ¶ *moderate conditions* 中位の条件. ¶ *necessary* (=*required*) *conditions* 必要条件. ¶ *unfavorable conditions* 悪条件.

Q² improvement (=betterment) of *working conditions* 労働条件の改善. 【類】cry for better *working conditions*.

P He was admitted to go to Europe *on condition* that he should return at the end of three years. 彼は三年たって帰国するという条件付でヨーロッパに行くことを許された. ‖ I will do it *on condition* that I shall be paid. 報酬があるならやろう. 【類】we can accept only *on condition* that ... / peace (平和条約) was concluded *on* the *condition* that ... ‖ *on condition* of sharing in ... ...の分配に預るという条件で ‖ *on* the *conditions* of this contract この契約の条項により. ¶ the *conditions under* which they work 彼らが働く条件. ¶ *upon* such *conditions* as ... may deem just ...の正当と認むる条件で. ¶ *with* the *condition* that they should ... 彼らが...するという条件で ‖ I can not comply *with* the *condition* of the agreement. 協約の条項に応じることはできない. ¶ *without condition* 無条件で.

P² *conditions of* success 成功の必須条件. 【類】Ability is one of the *conditions of* success. ‖ the *conditions of* sale 販売条件. 「する.

O make it a *condition* that ... ...ということを一つの条件と

condition, *v.* 条件とする, 条件をつける; 《米》仮進級させる.

P It was *conditioned between* them that ... 彼らの間で...という条件が定められた. ¶ The size is *conditioned by* the requirements. 大きさは御希望でどうにでもなる. ¶ He was *conditioned in* history and geography. 彼は歴史と地理は追試験ということで仮進級させられた. ¶ It is *conditioned on* the Goverment's approval. 政府の許可いかんを条件としている. ¶ He *conditioned* his going *upon* the weather. 彼は天気がよければ出掛けることにした.

conditional, *a.* 条件付の.

P It is *conditional on* (=*upon*) your ability. そこは君の力量次第だ.

conditioner, *n.* 調節器.

Q² an *air conditioner* 空気調節器.

conditioning, *n.* 調節.

Q² *Air conditioning* is operating. Close the door, please. 空気調節施行中. ドアをお閉め下さい. 【類】a room comfortably cooled by *air conditioning*.

condole, *v.* くやみを述べる, 弔慰する.

P *condole* a person *in* sorrow 悲しみにくれている人を慰める. ¶ *condole on* his affliction 彼の不幸に対して見舞を述べる. ☞ *condole for* や *over* はまれ. ¶ *condole with* his family *upon* his unexpected death 彼のとん死に対しその家族を弔慰する ‖ *condole with* her *on* her bereavement 彼女に(死の)不幸に対して弔詞を述べる.

condolence, *n.* くやみ, 弔慰.

V *Accept* my sincere *condolence*. 衷心からおくやみ申上げます. ¶ *convey condolence* to ... with regard to the fire in that city その市の火事について...を慰問する. ¶ *express* one's *condolences* くやみを述べる. ¶ *condolences extended* to him on the death of ... ...の死に対し彼に呈した弔詞. ¶ I *offered* my *condolence* to him on the sad event. その悲しいできごとに対して彼におくやみを申述べた. ¶ I *send* my *condolence* to ... ...に私の弔詞を呈する. ¶ We beg to join many friends of his in *tendering* our heartfelt *condolence* to the bereaved relations. 数多い彼の友人同様私たちは御遺族一同に対し衷心よりおくやみを申述べたいと存じます.

P my *condolence with* him 彼に対する私のくやみ.

conduce, *v.* ...に資する.

P it will *conduce to* lucidity to ... ...と文意が明りょうになるであろう ‖ *conduce to* happiness (growth, health, development, peace, success, welfare) 幸福(など)に資する.

conducive, *a.* 資する, 益がある.

P *conducive to* long life (health, success, sleep) 長命(など)に益のある ‖ *conducive to* Anglo-American friendship 英米の親善を助長する. 【類】This sport will be very *conducive to* the physical development of children.

conduct, *n.* 行為, 行動; 品行, 行状.

V *amend* one's *conduct* その行を改める. ¶ *command* one's *conduct* その行動を抑制する. ¶ *guide* one's *conduct* by lofty moral principles 高い道徳律で行為を指導する. ¶ *interrupt* the *conduct* of [mercantile] business 営業を妨害する. ¶ *reform* one's *conduct*=mend one's ways 自己の行いを改める. ¶ *regulate* one's *conduct* upon the maxim その格言にもとずいて行動する. ¶ *square* one's *conduct* with one's principle 自分の行為を主義と一致させる. ¶ I cannot *suffer* (=*tolerate*) such *conduct*. かゝる行為は捨てておけない.

V² His *conduct* does not *harmonize* with his preaching. 彼の行動は口で言うりっぱなことと一致しない.

Q a man of very *bad conduct* 非常に不身もちの人. ¶ He is guilty of *base* (=*low*) *conduct*. 彼は行が卑しい. ¶ *courteous conduct* of the company's employees その会社員の丁寧な行動. ¶ *chivalrous conduct* 騎士的行為. ¶ *degrading conduct* 恥ずべき行為. ¶ *dishonorable conduct* 恥ずべき行為. ¶ *disorderly conduct* 乱暴な行為. ¶ *dubious* and *faithless conduct* 疑わしい誠意のない行為. ¶ for the *efficient conduct* of ... ...の事務遂行のため. ¶ judging from his *everyday conduct* 彼の日々の行動から察すると. ¶ forces that make *good conduct* 善行を誘致する諸原動力 ‖ a girl of *good conduct* 品行のよい娘. ¶*highhanded conduct* 高圧的行動. ¶*human conduct* 人間の行為. ¶*humane conduct* 人情味のあるやり口. ¶*impertinent conduct* 無礼な行為. ¶his wife's *improper conduct* 彼の妻の道ならない行状. ¶*intemperate conduct* 乱行. ¶a man of *irreproachable conduct* 品行方正の人. ¶a man of *loose conduct* 放らつの人. ¶the *magnificent conduct* of all concerned 全関係者のりっぱな行為. ¶supervision over his *moral conduct* 彼の徳行に対する監督. ¶right *municipal conduct* 市政上正しい行為. ¶*obscene conduct* わいせつ行為. ¶*overbearing conduct* ごう慢な仕打. ¶learn *proper* and *decorous conduct* 作法の正しい上品さを学ぶ. ¶his *public conduct* 彼の公的行為. ¶*rational conduct* 合理的な(無理のない)行為. ¶*scandalous conduct* 恥ずべき行為. ¶His *conduct* is *shocking*. 彼の行いにはぞっとする. ¶*unconstitutional conduct* 非立憲的行動. ¶*unethical conduct* 不道徳な所業. ¶*unmanly conduct* on the campus 校庭におけるめめしい行動. ¶*unscrupulous conduct* ふらちな行為. ¶*unseemly conduct* during prayers お祈り中見苦しい挙動. ¶*unstudentlike conduct* 学生にあるまじき行為. ¶a policeman dismissed from the force for *unworthy conduct* 不都合な行為で免職になった巡査. ¶*uproarious conduct* ろうぜき. ¶*violent conduct* 暴行. ¶*wrong conduct* 非行.

P He is quite ***above*** such *conduct*. 彼はそんなことをする人でない. ¶I was shocked ***by*** (=***at***) his *conduct*. 彼の行は実に案外であった. ¶He was cashiered ***for*** *conduct* injurious to the reputation of a soldier. 彼は軍人の体面を汚す行為があったので免官になった. ¶be scrupulous ***in*** *conduct* 行いが注意深い. ¶dissolute ***in*** *conduct* 身持の悪い ‖ transportation necessary ***in*** the *conduct* of war 戦争遂行上必要な輸送. ¶give him a lecture ***on*** his *conduct* 彼の品行について小言をいう. ¶I can testify ***to*** his good *conduct*. 彼の品行方正は証明ができる.

P² Nelson's *conduct* ***as*** a husband 夫としてのネルソンの行状. ¶it is quite bad *conduct* ***for*** students to ... 学生が...するとは実にけしからん. ¶his *conduct* ***toward*** his brothers 彼の兄弟に対する仕打.

conduct, *v*. 案内する, 導く; 演奏指揮をする; 振舞う.

M He *conducted* himself ***nobly***. 彼はりっぱに振舞った. ¶The attempts were ***scientifically*** *conducted*. その試みは科学的に行われた. ¶*conduct* oneself ***wisely*** 賢明に行動する.

P I was *conducted* ***into*** the presence of the president. 私(訪問者)は社長の所へ通された. ¶*conduct* visitors ***over*** a building 案内して訪問客に建物の中を見せる. 【類】I was *conducted* ***over*** a school (camp, hospital, factory). ¶I was *conducted* ***through*** the various departments of the vessel. 同船をあちらこちら案内された. ¶*conduct* him ***to*** the place 彼をその所へ通す(案内する). ¶*conduct* oneself ***without*** any reserve whatever 無遠慮に振舞う.

O Who's *conducting* [the symphony]? だれが指揮者か.

conductor, *n*. 案内者; 取扱者; 導体; 経営者; 《米》車掌.

Q a ***good*** (***bad***) *conductor* 良(不良)導体. ¶***smartly-uniformed*** *conductors* スマートな制服を着た案内者.

Q² a ***girl bus*** *conductor*=a bus conductress バスの女車掌. ¶a ***lightning*** *conductor* 避雷針. ¶a ***streetcar*** *conductor* 市電車掌. ¶a [***train***] *conductor* 《米》列車車掌. ☞《英》a [railway] guard.

P² the *conductors* ***of*** "Blackwood's Magazine" ブラックウッド誌の経営者.

conduit, *n*. 水管, 管.

Q ***All*** the *conduits* of my blood froze up. 私の血管は全部凍りついた(かと思うほどびっくりした).

Q² a ***tile*** *conduit* 陶管. ¶a ***sewer*** *conduit* 下水溝, 溝渠(こうきょ).

cone, *n*. 円すい(形), 松かさ.

Q² a ***five-cent*** icecream *cone* コーンに入れた五セントのアイスクリーム. ¶a ***pine*** *cone* 松かさ.

P icecream ***in*** a *cone* コーンに盛ったアイスクリーム.

P² a *cone* ***of*** a volcano 円すい形の火山.

confection, *n*. 菓子.

Q ***molded*** *confection* だ菓子. ¶***tasty*** *confections* うまい菓子.

Q² a ***millet*** *confection* あわおこし.

P indulge ***in*** *confections* 盛んに菓子を食べる.

confectioner, *n*. 製菓[販売]業者.

Q a ***manufacturing*** *confectioner* 製菓業者.

confectionery, *n*. 菓子.

Q² ***sugar*** *confectionery* 砂糖菓子.

P deal ***in*** *confectioneries* 菓子類を扱う.

confederacy, *n*. 同盟, 徒党.

V ***form*** a *confederacy* 徒党を組む.

P ***by*** *confederacy* with ... ...と共謀して.

confederate, *n*. 共謀者.

P² a *confederate* ***in*** a robbery 強盗の共犯 ‖ one's *confederates* ***in*** crime その共謀犯人ら.

confederate, *v*. 同盟する.

P *confederate* ***with*** a person (state) 人(など)と同盟する ‖ *confederate* ***with*** other colonies ***for*** mutual safety 相互の安全のため他の植民地と同盟する ‖ *confederate* oneself ***with*** ... ...と共謀する.

confer, *v*. 授与する, 贈る; 相談する.

M The senior (junior) grade of the third court rank was ***posthumously*** *conferred* on him. 氏に正(従)三位の贈位があった.

P The degree of A.B. is to be *conferred* ***by*** the college. エイ・ビーの称号は大学で授与する. ¶The University *conferred* ***on*** him the title of LL.D. 同大学は法学博士の学位を彼に授けた. ‖ *confer* franchise and eligibility ***on*** women for municipal elections 婦人に市会議員の選挙権および被選挙権を与える ‖ *confer* a benefit (favor, gift, an honor, rank) ***on*** a person 人に恩典(など)を与える ‖ The Duke *conferred* a kiss ***on*** the lady. 公爵はその婦人に接ぷんを賜わった. ‖ *confer* ***on*** (=***about***) it ***with*** him そのことについて彼と相談する. ¶*confer* ***upon*** matters of mutual concern 相互関係の事務について相談する ‖ *confer* citizenship ***upon*** ... ...に帰化を許す. ¶*confer* ***with*** him ***about*** (=on) the matter そのことについて彼と相談する.

conference, *n*. 相談; 会議.

V ***assemble*** a *conference* 会議を召集する. ¶A great many people ***attended*** the *Conference*. 多数の人がその会議に出席した. ¶***boycott*** a *conference* 会議に参加しない. ¶***call*** a *conference* at Honolulu ホノルルにおいて会議を召集する. 【類】***call*** a *conference* of the leading bankers to devise ways and means of ... / ***call*** a *conference* to discuss the question / at the *conference* ***called*** in San Francisco September 25th and 26th. ¶France ***concluded*** a *conference* with Soviet Russia. 仏・ソ協商が成立した. ¶***convene*** a *conference* on the subject その問題に関して会議を召集する. ¶***convoke*** an international *conference* 国際会議を召集する. ¶he ***had*** a long *conference* with ... 彼は...と長時間の会談をとげた. 【類】I'll ***have*** a *conference* with the president. / He ***held*** *conferences* with his staff (幹部) until late into the night. ¶***inaugurate*** a *conference* 相談会を起す. ¶***invite*** *conference* with the members of the trade 同業者との会談を勧誘する. ¶The *conference* was ***summoned*** by the British Government. その会議は英国政府によって召集された. ¶The *conference* is now ***meeting*** in London. その会議は目下ロンドンで開催中である.

Q an ***animated*** *conference* 活気を呈した会議. ¶an ***annual*** *conference* 年会. ¶a ***city-wide*** *conference* 全市民大会. ¶an ***informal*** *conference* 非公式の会議. ¶an ***Inter-American*** *Conference* 米州会議. ¶the ***International*** *Conference* on Safety of Life at Sea 海難救済国際会議. ¶a ***joint*** *conference* 連合会議. ¶they had ***many*** *conferences* with reference to ... ...に関し何回も会議を開いた. ¶a ***momentous*** *conference* 重要会議. ¶a ***national*** *conference* 国民会議. ¶***private*** *conference* with a teacher 教師との私的の相談.

Q² an ***English-speaking*** peoples' *conference* on Infant Mortality 幼児死亡率に関する英語国人の会議. ¶a ***cards-on-the-table*** *conference* 腹蔵のない話し合い. ¶a ***career*** *conference* 職業相談. ¶a ***civil air*** *conference* 民間航空会議. ¶a ***cloak room*** (=***lobby***) *conference* 《米》議会控室の会談. ¶meet in ***emergency*** *conference* to consider ... 緊急会議を開いて...を審議する. ¶The ***family*** *conference* was called. 親族会議が召集された. ¶a "***hush-hush***" *conference* 秘密会談. ¶an ***inter-party*** *conference* 各党の合同会議. ¶a ***joint House-Senate*** *conference* [米国]上・下両院協議会. ¶a ***joint labor-management*** *conference* 労使協議会. ¶have a ***luncheon*** *conference* with ... ...と昼食をとりながら会談をやる. ¶a ***management*** *conference* 経営協議会. ¶a ***news*** *conference* 記者会見. 【類】a White House ***news*** *conference*. ¶it was the scene of a reception given by ... for the delegates to the ***Peace*** *Conference* それは平和会議代表のため設けられた接待会の会合であった. ¶hold a ***press*** *conference* 新聞会見をやる. 【類】the President's ***press** conference*. ¶convene a ***roundtable** conference* of ... …の円卓会議を召集する. ¶a ***staff** conference* 幹部会. ¶a ***Student Christian Federation** conference* 学生キリスト教連盟会議. ¶the Indo-Japanese ***Trade Conference*** 日印通商会議. ¶a ***two day** conference* 二日間にわたる会議. ¶the ***Washington** Conference* in the limitation of armament ワシントン軍縮会議.

P ***at** conference* with his closer associates 彼の一層親密な仲間との相談で. ¶we have been ***in** conference* with ... われわれは…と相談を重ねてきた ‖ among the bodies which met ***in** conference* were ... 会議に集まった団体中に…があった ‖ sit ***in** a conference* 会議に参加する. 【類】English teachers ***in** conference*.

P² *conference* ***about*** (=***concerning** or **regarding***) a matter ある事柄に関する相談. ¶a *conference* ***before*** the Emperor 御前会議. ¶The *conference* ***between*** them has been futile. その人たちの会見は無効に帰した. ¶a *conference* ***of*** prefectural police chiefs 警察部長会議. ¶a *conference* ***on*** public morality 公衆道徳に関する会議. 【類】a *conference* ***on*** communications and transportation.

confess, *v.* 自白する, 自供する; 承認する.

M ***candidly** confess* つつまず白状する. ¶I must ***frankly** confess* that ... 私は率直に…と自白せねばならない. 【類】I ***frankly** confess* that I have not much respect for that. ¶he ***openly** confessed* that ... 彼はあからさまに…と白状した. ¶***sorrowfully** confess* that ... 悲しみのうちに…と告白する.

P I must *confess* ***to*** some doubt as to the accuracy of ... 遠慮なく言うが私は…の確実性を幾分疑っている. ‖ Most people *confess* ***to*** a bad memory. 大概の人は自分の記憶が悪いことを認める. ‖ I must *confess* ***to*** some surprise at this step. 実の所私はこのやり方には少々驚いている. ‖ people who are too prudish to *confess* ***to*** pleasure in modern police reports 上品にかまえて現代警察事故の報道をおもしろいとは言わない人々. 【類】*confess* ***to*** a crime / I *confess* ***to*** a dread of spiders. / He *confesses* ***to*** a weakness for confectionery (甘党). ‖ Many, asked what money they have, *confess* ***to*** twenty or thirty shillings as their entire fortune. お金がいくらあるかと聞かれて二三十シリングが全財産だと白状する連中が多い. ‖ I *confess* ***to*** no employment. 私は何の職業もない. ‖ I *confess* ***to*** being astonished at this unexpected statement. 実はこの思いがけない申立にはびっくりした. 【類】I *confess* ***to*** being a worshipper at that shrine.

confession, *n.* 自白, 自供; 自認.

V ***bring about** a confession* 白状させる. ¶***elicit** confession* 自白させる. ¶***extort** confession* 無理に自白させる. ¶***make** confession* 自白する ‖ ***make*** one's full *confession* to ... …に思いのたけを打明ける. ¶we ***obtained*** a *confession* from ... of ... …から…についての自白を得た. ¶We failed to ***produce** confession*. 自白させ得なかった. ¶***wring*** a *confession* from an alleged criminal 犯罪容疑者に自白をしいる.

V² The most dire *confessions* ***ensued***. 最も恐ろしい自白がそれに続いてなされた.

Q ***auricular** confession* 〘宗教〙秘密ざんげ. ¶***forced** confession* 無理じいの告白. ¶make a ***frank** confession* of the fact that ... …という事実を明らさまに告白する. ¶a ***humiliating** confession* 屈辱的自白. ¶a ***manly** confession* of failure 男らしい失敗談. ¶a ***naive** confession* むじゃ気な自白. ¶make a ***spurious** confession* of some notable crime 恐ろしい罪を犯したと虚構の自白をする.

P go ***to** confession* 〘宗教〙ざんげする.

confidant, *n.* 腹心の友.

V He ***made*** a *confidant* of me. 彼は秘密を私に打明けた.

confide, *v.* 打明けて話す, 信任する.

P I *confided* ***in*** his honor, and he has kept the secret. 私は彼の名誉を信頼し, そして彼は秘密を守った. 【類】Why should I not *confide* ***in*** those that have been so kind to me? ¶the patient *confided* ***to*** his care 彼にあずけられた患者 ‖ *confide* a task ***to*** a person 人を信用して仕事を任せる. 【類】I *confide* this book ***to*** your keeping. / *confide* something secret ***to*** a person / I *confided* ***to*** him the secrets of my life. ‖ *confide* oneself ***to*** God わが身を神に委ねる ‖ *confide* a trust ***to*** him 彼を信じて頼みごとをする.

confidence, *n.* 信用, 信頼; 自信, 秘密.

V ***abuse*** the trust and *confidence* which he puts in me 彼の私に対する信任を悪用する. ¶He ***betrayed*** my *confidence* in him. 彼は私の信任を裏切った. ¶***capture*** the patient's *confidence* 病人の信用を得る. ¶***cherish*** complete *confidence* in ... …をどこまでも信用する. ¶***command*** the *confidence* and respect of ... …の信用と尊敬を博する. 【類】fail to ***command*** the *confidence* of his men. ¶these things tend to ***confirm** confidence* that ... …という自信を強める傾きがある. ¶***continue*** one's *confidence* in the future 将来に対する希望を絶たない. ¶***create** confidence* 自信を持たせる. ¶***deserve*** their entire *confidence* 彼らに十分信頼される価値がある. ¶He ***enjoys*** the fullest *confidence* of his master. 彼は主人に十分信用されている. ¶***establish** confidence* 信用を確立する. ¶***exchange** confidences* with ... …と秘密の通信を取り交わす. ¶***express*** one's *confidence* that ... …という自信を表明する. ¶***forfeit** confidence* 信用を失う. ¶***gain** confidence* in one's own ability 自分の能力に対する自信がつく. 【類】***gain*** the *confidence* and admiration of ... ¶scholars in whom I ***have** confidence* 私が信用している学者たち ‖ I ***have** confidence* in the justice of his position on labor questions. 私は労働問題に対する彼の立場が正しいと信じている. 【類】Recommend some one in whom you ***have** confidence*. / He ***had*** no *confidence* in himself when facing his audience. ‖ He ***had*** the *confidence* to deny it. 彼は大胆にもそれを否認した. ¶***inspire** confidence* 自信を起させる. ¶***kill*** one's *confidence* 自信を失わせる. ¶***lack** confidence* in our own strength 自分の力量に対する自信を欠く. ¶***lose** confidence* in ... …に信用をおかなくなる. 【類】The patient has ***lost*** all *confidence* in his physician. ¶***misplace*** one's *confidence* 信用すべからざる人を信用する. ¶***obtain*** the *confidence* of ... …の信用を得る. ¶***place*** (=put) some (no) *confidence* in ... …をいく分信用する(全然信用しない). ¶***possess*** the complete *confidence* of ... …に十分信任されている. ¶***put*** our *confidence* to shame 信任にそむいてわれわれを失望させる. ¶***regain*** the *confidence* of ... …の信用を回復する. ¶I ***repose*** every *confidence* in his acting justly. 私は彼が正しく行動することを確信する. ¶***retain*** one's *confidence* in him 彼に対する信任を持続する. ¶My *confidence* in his discretion was severely ***shaken***. 彼が分別ある男だという私の確信がひどくぐらついた. ¶***undermine** confidence* 信用を落す. ¶***win*** the *confidence* of others 他人の信用を得る. ¶***withdraw*** one's *confidence* from ... …に対する信用を撤回する.

Q repose ***absolute** confidence* in ... …を絶対的に信用する. ¶one thing at any rate I can prise with ***complete** confidence*, and that is ... 私が確信してほめることのできる少くとも一つのことがある. でそれは... ¶He has my ***entire** confidence*. 彼は私の全信任を受けている. ¶be worthy of ***every** confidence* 十分信頼できる ‖ it is therefore with ***full** confidence* that ... だから…は十分確かなことである. 【類】place ***full** confidence* in ... / I can declare with ***full** confidence* that ... ¶He has an ***immovable** confidence* in himself. 動かしがたい自信をもっている. ¶he had the most ***implicit** confidence* in ... 彼は…を厚く信任した. 【類】have ***implicit** confidence* in their leaders. ¶On this point I speak with comparatively ***little** confidence*. この点では私はあまり確信をもって申上げられない. ¶the spirit of ***mutual** confidence* 相互信頼の念. ¶He can be recommended with ***perfect** confidence*. 彼は十分安心して推薦ができる. ¶***public** confidence* was badly shaken by ... 世人の信用が…のためひどくぐらついた. ¶The information communicated by him is held in ***strict** confidence*. 彼の通信は厳秘に付してある. 【類】He told me of his intention in ***strict** confidence* (ごく内々で). ¶***unbounded** confidence* 無限の信頼感. ¶I have ***unshaken** confidence* in ... 私は…をかたく信頼している. ¶with ***unwavering** confidence* 不動の確信をもって.

P I give this advice ***in** confidence*. 君に内々忠告する. 【類】I may tell you this ***in** confidence*. ‖ ***in*** the *confidence* that ... …と信じて. ¶I took him ***into*** my *confidence*. 彼に私の秘密を漏らした. ¶A hearty vote ***of** confidence* in the Government was passed. 政府信任案は大賛成で可決された. ‖ He spoke ***with*** great *confidence*. 彼は大いに自信をもって話した. 【類】may be trusted ***with** confidence*.

P² There is a want of *confidence* ***between*** the parties. 両者

間に信頼の念が欠けている. ¶ *confidence* ***in*** one's own capacity (=ability *or* power) その能力に対する自信 ‖ My *confidence* ***in*** medicine has been completely shaken. 私の薬に対する信頼は全くぐらついてしまった.

confident *a.* 確信している, 自信のある.

M we are ***hopefully*** *confident* that ... われわれは...ということを十分確信している. ¶ I feel ***quite*** *confident* that everybody will do his duty. 各人がその本務を尽すことを十分信じている. ¶ ***serenely*** *confident* of his own power 彼自身の力を信じて動ぜずに.

P I am *confident* ***in*** him. 彼を信用している. ¶ we are *confident* ***in*** saying that ... われわれは自信をもって...と言う. ¶ We are *confident* ***of*** our success (victory). われわれは成功(など)を確信している.

confidential *a.* 腹心の, 極秘の.

M be considered ***strictly*** *confidential* 厳秘の事項と考えられる.

P It is not always good to get *confidential* ***with*** strangers. 始めての人との打明け話は時にぐあいが悪いことになる.

configuration, *n.* 形状, 地形.

Q the ***natural*** (=***topographical***) *configuration* of the country その国の地形.

confine, *n.* 境界, 限界.

V ***extend*** the *confines* of knowledge 知識の限界を拡げる.

Q within its ***narrow*** *confines* その狭い場所で.

P ***beyond*** the *confines* of ... ...の範囲を越えて ‖ ***on*** the *confines* of the town その町の境界に ‖ ***on*** the *confines* of night and day=at twilight 夜と昼との境に ‖ All human clamor dies away ***on*** the *confines* of this beautiful park. この美しい公園にはいるとやかましい人声はことごとく消えて行く. ¶ ***out of*** the *confines* of ... ...の範囲外に. ¶ ***within*** the *confines* of the capital 首都の圏内に.

P² the *confines* ***of*** France フランスの国内.

confine, *v.* 閉込める, 引こもらす; 境を接する.

M Sales are ***chiefly*** *confined* to ... 販売は主に...に限られている. ‖ *confine* oneself ***chiefly*** to ... [著作の内容など]範囲を主に...に限る. ¶ *confine* oneself ***completely*** in a cottage 小屋から外へ一歩も出ない. ¶ I will *confine* myself almost ***entirely*** to this phase of the subject. 私は私の議論を大体問題のこの方面に局限する. ¶ *confine* oneself ***strictly*** to the subject 厳重にその問題だけに止める(他に論及しない).

P He is *confined* ***at*** hard labor. 彼は苦役に服している. ¶ be *confined* ***by*** an inclosure [垣や壁で]囲まれている. ¶ He is *confined* ***in*** a lunatic asylum. 彼は精神病院に入っている. 【類】 The thief is *confined* ***in*** jail (=prison). ¶ She was *confined* ***of*** a girl. 彼女は女の子を産んだ. ¶ *confine* (=border) ***on*** a country ある国と境を接する. ¶ The edition is *confined* ***to*** 200 copies. それは二百部の限定版だ. ¶ He was *confined* ***to*** his bed by a slight illness (cold). 彼は軽い病気(など)で臥床していた. 【類】 He has been *confined* ***to*** his home by sickness. / He is *confined* ***to*** his house with flu. / He is *confined* ***to*** his berth by seasickness. / In the olden days women's activities in Japan were *confined* ***to*** the household. / He *confined* himself ***to*** the study of modern language. ‖ The taste for collecting autographs is not *confined* ***to*** modern times. 筆跡収集の趣味は昔もあった. 【類】 Could you not *confine* yourself ***to*** that subject? ‖ These recent developments in philosophy are so far *confined* ***to*** the pages of philosophical journals. 哲学界のこれら最近の発展はまだ哲学雑誌に発表されているだけである(単行本とはなっていない). ¶ He is *confined* ***within*** doors. 彼は家の中に引きこもっている. ‖ Business is *confined* ***within*** very narrow limits. 商売はごくせまい範囲に限られている.

confinement, *n.* 幽閉, 監禁; 制限; お産.

V women who are ***approaching*** *confinement* 分べん期に近づいている女. ¶ No prisoner ever ***survived*** *confinement* in Acca longer than three months. アッカに監禁された囚徒で三カ月以上生き得た者はかつて一人もない.

Q ***associate*** *confinement* 雑居拘禁. ¶ At twenty-eight years she had a rather ***difficult*** *confinement*. 彼女は二十八のときにちょっと難産をした. ¶ a very ***difficult first*** *confinement* すこぶる難産である初産. 【類】 at the time of his wife's ***first*** *confinement*. ¶ ***solitary*** *confinement* 独房監禁.

P The prisoner spent about nine years ***in*** *confinement*. 囚徒は禁固で約九年を過した. ‖ chicks grown ***in*** *confinement* [放し飼いでなく]囲いの中で育ったひよっ子. ¶ My wife is ***near*** her *confinement*. 妻は近々お産をする.

P² He was sentenced to *confinement* ***in*** his own house. 彼は自宅拘禁を申付けられた. ¶ *confinement* ***of*** a man ***to*** his own house 自分の家に閉じこもっていること. ¶ a long *confinement* ***to*** bed 長らく病床にあること ‖ *confinement* ***to*** a prescribed diet [医師からの]特別の食餌(じ)指定.

confirm, *v.* 確かめる; 堅める.

P It is *confirmed* ***by*** experience. それは経験の確証する所だ. ‖ this view is *confirmed* ***by*** the fact that ... ...の事実はこの説を確かめている. 【類】 *confirm* a statement ***by*** testimony. ¶ This only *confirmed* them ***in*** bad habits. これがかえって彼らをますます悪習慣に深入りさせることになった. ‖ this *confirms* me ***in*** the view that ... これで私の...という見方が確実になる ‖ be *confirmed* ***in*** one's belief that ... ...の信念をいよいよ堅くする. 【類】 he was *confirmed* ***in*** his impression (opinion) that ... ‖ He has been *confirmed* ***in*** the rank. 彼は心得から本官になった.

confirmation, *n.* 確定, 確証.

V Enquiries made have failed to ***elicit*** either a *confirmation* or a denial of the rumor. そのうわさを調査して見たが真否のほどは分らなかった. ¶ The report ***lacks*** *confirmation*. その報道には確証がない(うわさの程度だ). ¶ It ***lends*** apparent *confirmation* to this view of the question. その問題に対するこの見解がそのために一見確実なものと思われるようになる. 【類】 Recent events ***lend*** considerable *confirmation* to the belief. ¶ This old truth has ***received*** scientific *confirmation*. この昔からの事実に科学的確証が与えられた.

Q a ***strong*** *confirmation* 確証.

P ***for*** *confirmation* 念のため. ¶ ***in*** *confirmation* of this view he says that ... この見解を確証するため彼は...と言っている. 【類】 ***in*** *confirmation* of the foregoing view.

confirmatory, *a.* 確かめる.

M ***strongly*** *confirmatory* of ... 大いに...を確かめる.

conflagration, *n.* 大火; 災禍.

V ***cause*** an international *conflagration* 国際的大変災を引き起す. ¶ The *conflagration* has been ***got under***. その大火は鎮火した. ¶ The accidental overturning of a lamp ***originated*** the *conflagration*. その大火は誤ってランプをひっくりかえしたのが原因であった.

V² the *conflagration* that ***raged*** through this quarter of the city 市のこの方面を焼き払った大火災.

Q ***accidental*** *conflagration* 失火. ¶ a ***disastrous*** (=***great***) *conflagration* 大火災.

conflict, *n.* 闘争; 衝突.

V ***avoid*** a *conflict* as far as possible できるだけ衝突を避ける. ¶ ***precipitate*** a *conflict* 衝突を激成する. ¶ ***prevent*** an armed *conflict* between two great nations of the globe 世界二大国の交戦を防止する.

V² No *conflict* ***occurred***. 一向闘争が起きなかった. 【類】 whenever *conflicts* ***occur*** between them.

Q the ***age-old*** *conflict* between China and other powers 中国と他の列強間の昔からの衝突. ¶ An ***armed*** *conflict* is at present unavoidable. 戦争は今の所避けられない. ¶ a ***bloody*** *conflict* 血戦. ¶ a ***domestic*** *conflict* 家庭の不和. ¶ ***economic*** *conflicts* 経済上の衝突. ¶ the ***eternal*** *conflict* of the dual nature in man 人間のもつ二重性格の永遠の闘争. ¶ the ***familiar*** *conflict* between the extremists and the moderates 例の過激派と穏健派の闘争. ¶ this ***fundamental*** *conflict* in point of view この根本的な見解の衝突. ¶ engage in a ***hand-to-hand*** *conflict* with ... ...と接戦する. ¶ ***industrial*** *conflict* 産業界の紛争. ¶ an ***irreconcilable*** *conflict* 和解し得ない争闘. ¶ in ***manifest*** *conflict* with ... ...と明かに衝突して. ¶ undergo a ***mental*** *conflict* はんもんする. ¶ the ***Russo-Japanese*** *conflict* of 1904-05 一九〇四年から五年にかけての日露戦役. ¶ a ***sharp*** and ***bloody*** *conflict* 激しい流血騒ぎ. ¶ The most ***signal naval*** *conflict* of a hundred years resulted in a brilliant victory for the Japanese 過去百年間史上に最も顕著なこの海戦は日本のかくかくたる勝利に帰した. ¶ ***spiritual*** *conflict* between the external laws of life and the needs of the inner being 人生の外面的法則と内面的生活の要望との間に起る精神的闘争. ¶ the ***Titanic*** *Conflict* in Europe 欧州大戦. ¶ a ***tremendous*** *conflict* is still raging at ... 激戦はなお...で続行中. ¶ ***Warlike*** *conflicts* are impending. 戦いがさしせまっている.

Q² *class conflict* 階級闘争. ¶the *East-West conflict* 東西[両陣営]のあつれき. ¶*race conflict* 人種闘争.

P it is flatly *in conflict* with … それは…とまともに衝突している(氷炭相いれない) ‖ It is *in conflict* with the provisions of the existing treaties. 現行条約の条項にふれている. ‖ He was wounded *in* the *conflict*. 彼はその戦いで負傷した. ¶come *into conflict* with … …と衝突する.

P² a *conflict among* believers *about* doctrines 教義に関する信奉者間の衝突. ¶a *conflict between* old and new faiths 新旧信仰の衝突. 【類】 a *conflict between* the two nations / a *conflict between* two companions (armies, parties, champions) / the *conflict between* religion and science. ¶a *conflict concerning* … …に関する争闘. ¶a *conflict of* authorities 諸説の不一致. 【類】 a *conflict of* thoughts (ideas, opinions). ¶a *conflict with* the enemy 敵との衝突.

conflict, *v.* 闘争する, 衝突する, どう着する.

P impassioned love *conflicting with* the dictates of morality and convention 道徳および慣習と矛盾する熱烈な恋. ¶This *conflicted with* his father's plans for his son's career. これは彼の父が息子の将来を思ってたてた計画と一致しなかった. 【類】 *conflict with* English interests in the Orient.

confluence, *n.* 合流.

P *at* the *confluence* of the two rivers 二川の合流する所に. ¶a *confluence of* a river *with* the sea 川と海との合流.

conform, *v.* 一致させる; 順応する, 一致する.

M *hardly conform* to the genius of the language その国語の性質とはほとんど一致しない.

P *conform to* the changing needs of successive generations 時代時代で推移する要求に順応する. 【類】 *conform to* local customs / *conform to* the usage of society (社会の習慣) ‖ *conform to* all the requirements of good taste and propriety すべて高尚な趣味と礼儀作法の教える所に従う ‖ try to *conform to* the ways of the community in which one lives 自分の住む社会の風習に従おうと努める. 【類】 *conform to* directions (指示) / *conform to* the fashion (laws) of the country ‖ *conform* conduct *to* a rule 規範に従って行動する ‖ Let me advise you to *conform* your courses *to* his counsel. 君の進路は彼の助言通りに行動することをお勧めしたい. ¶*conform with* (=*to*) the rules 規則に従う.

conformable, *a.* 一致する.

P *conformable to* reasons 理屈にかなった ‖ A subtle, refined policy was *conformable to* the genius of the Italians. きめの細かい洗練された政策はイタリア人の気質にぴったり合ったものであった.

conformably, *ad.* 一致して.

P He came *conformably to* (=*with*) his promise. 彼は約束通り来た.

conformance, *n.* 適合, 順応.

P *in conformance* with … …に順応して.

conformation, *n.* 適合, 順応.

P² *conformation of* a thing *to* another 甲と乙の適合.

conformity, *n.* 適合, 一致.

P *in conformity* to (=with) a law 法律に従って ‖ *in conformity* with the established usage 既存の慣例に従って. 【類】 *in conformity* with your instructions (指令) / *in conformity* with generally accepted accounting principles (会計の原則) ‖ *in conformity* with the popular wish 一般の希望に従って ‖ *in* strict *conformity* with … …を厳守して.

P² *conformity between* physical and mental states 心身の一致. 【類】 *conformity between* the two opinions. ¶*conformity in* shape 形態の相似. ¶*conformity to* custom (conscience, the wish of others) 習慣(など)に対する服従. ¶*conformity with* his views 彼と意見の一致.

confound, *v.* 当惑させる.

M This difficulty *quite confounded* me. 私はこの難問題に全く当惑した. ¶The accusation *utterly confounded* him. 彼はこの言いがかりには大いに面食った.

P he was *confounded at* (=*by*) … 彼は…で驚いた. ¶*confound* means *with* end 目的と手段をはき違える ‖ *confound* public affairs *with* private ones 公私を弁えない.

confront, *v.* 向い合わせる; 対決させる.

P He was *confronted by* a constable at the gate. 彼は門の所で警官にでっくわした. ¶I was *confronted with* a problem (difficulty). 僕はある問題(など)に遭遇した. 【類】 be *confronted with* competition / The new system will be *confronted with* great difficulties at the start. ‖ *confront* the accused *with* his accuser or witnesses 被告と原告または証人とを対決させる.

confuse, *v.* 混雑させる, 混同する; 面食らわす.

P It was *confused among* many objects. それは色々の品とごっちゃになっていた. ¶He was *confused at* his error. 彼は自分の間違いに当惑した. ¶He was *confused by* his guilt. 彼は自己の罪でどぎまぎした. ¶He is *confused in* mind. 彼は頭が混乱している. ¶Don't *confuse* liberty *with* license. 自由と放縦を混同するな. ‖ He *confused* me *with* a deluge of polite words. 彼は丁重な言葉を浴びせて私をまごつかせた. ‖ You are *confusing* me *with* somebody else. 私をだれかと感違いしてますね.

confusion, *n.* 混乱, 混雑; ろうばい.

V *add* unnecessary *confusion* 不必要な混乱を増す. ¶*aggravate* the *confusion* 混乱をいよいよひどくする. ¶to *avoid confusion* let there be clearness with respect to … 混乱を避けるため…の点を明りょうにしておきたい. ¶*cause* unnecessary *confusion* いたずらに混乱をひき起す. ¶*clear away* much *confusion* 大混乱を一掃する. ¶to *conceal* a momentary *confusion* arising from … …のてれ隠しに. ¶*end* further *confusion* これ以上の混乱を阻止する. ¶*enjoy* the offender's *confusion* その無礼者がろうばいするのを見て痛快に感じる. ¶*introduce confusion* into … …を混乱させる. ¶*occasion* great *confusion* 大混乱を来たす. ¶to *prevent confusion* 混雑を避けるために. ¶*save confusion* with … …の混雑を緩和する.

V² A *confusion arose* between them. その間に混乱を生じた.

Q in *bewildering confusion* ぼう然となるような混乱状態で. ¶a *charming confusion* 魅惑的混乱(女のへやなど). ¶make a *complete confusion* between … …を全く混同する. ¶Everything was thrown into *dire* (=*terrible*) *confusion*. 何もかも恐ろしい混乱に陥った. ¶The cargo is in *dreadful confusion*. 船荷は手のつけられぬほど乱雑になっている. ¶The *confusion* was *general*. どこもかしこも大混雑だった. ¶*hopeless confusion* 始末に負えぬ混乱. ¶…are mixed up together in *picturesque confusion* …がまざりあって美しい絵を織り出している. ¶because of the general *postwar confusion* 一般的の戦後の混乱から. ¶hang one's head in *shame-faced confusion* どぎまぎして恥ずかしそうにうなだれる. ¶a scene of *utter confusion* 全くひどい混乱の光景. ¶*wild confusion* 大混乱.

Q² an example of *dream confusion* 夢はとりとめもないものという一例.

P *in confusion* 当惑して ‖ All is *in confusion*. てんやわんやである. ‖ They hurried off *in* great *confusion*. 彼らは大あわてにあわてて立ち去った. ‖ put … *in confusion* …を混乱させる ‖ disappear *in* the *confusion* その混雑に紛れて姿を消す ‖ stammer *in confusion* めんくらって口がどもる. ‖ The meeting adjourned *in confusion*. 会は混雑裡に散会となった. ‖ *in* the *confusion* of the occasion どさくさまぎれに. ¶be thrown *into confusion* 混乱状態に陥る.

P² Let there be no *confusion about it*. それを間違え(混同し)ないようにしたい. ¶*confusion between* … and … …と…との間の混乱. ¶*confusion from* shame 恥じてのろうばい. ¶*confusion of* terms (ideas, objects) 言葉(など)の混乱.

congé, *n. F.* 解雇.

V *give* him his *congé* 彼を解雇する. ¶*receive* (=*get*) one's *congé* 解雇される.

congenial, *a.* 同性質の; 気に合った.

P He found the work not *congenial to* his taste. その仕事は彼の気に合わなかった. 【類】 He was *congenial to* company. ¶To know God, we must have something within ourselves *congenial to* Him. 神を知るにはわれわれ自身の中に神と一致するものを持っていなければならない. ¶*congenial with* … …と同趣味の.

congested, *pa.* 込合っている.

M The street is *much congested*. 街は非常に雑とうしている.

P a place *congested with* things (people) 品物(人)の込合う場所.

congestion, *n.* 群集, 込合; 充血.

V *clear up* traffic *congestion* 交通の混雑を除く. ¶*relieve* the *congestion* of traffic 交通の混雑を緩和する

Q the *great congestion* of cable messages 海底電信の大幅輳(ふく). ¶owing to the *heavy congestion* on the railways at that time 当時鉄道輸送が非常に輻輳していたので.

Q² reduce *city congestion* 都市の雑とうを緩和する. ¶*street congestion* 通りの混雑. ¶because of increasing *traffic congestion* 交通が益々雑とうするので. 【類】 as a

means of helping to relieve the city's ***traffic congestion***.
P ***owing to*** the *congestion* of traffic 乗客殺到のため.
P² *congestion **of*** the brains 脳充血.

congratulate, *v*. 祝う, 慶賀する.

M I *congratulate* you very ***heartily***. 衷心からお喜びを申上げます. ¶we most ***respectfully*** *congratulate* your Excellency on your visit to ... 閣下が...にお出でになったことを謹んでお喜び申上げます[歓迎の辞など]. ¶he is to be ***sincerely*** *congratulated* upon ... 彼は...で本当におめでたい. ¶They are to be ***warmly*** *congratulated* on their success. 彼らの成功を大いに慶賀すべきである.

P. He is to be *congratulated **for*** his success. 彼の成功を慶賀すべきである. 【類】he is to be *congratulated **for*** his valuable contribution to the advancement of knowledge in ... / *congratulate* the American legislators (立法者) ***for*** frankness and courage in effecting the temperance reform (禁酒改革). ¶This city should be *congratulated **in*** having such a brilliant man to head its schools. 当市がその諸学校の首脳者としてかくもりっぱな人物をいただくのは慶賀すべきことである. ¶*congratulate* a clergyman ***on*** the excellence of his sermon 説教がりっぱでしたと牧師にお喜びを言う ‖ May I *congratulate* you ***on*** the present issue, which is a particularly fine one? 今月号は特にりっぱなできばえでお喜び申上げます. ‖ letters from persons unknown *congratulating* us ***on*** ... 未知の人から来た...に対するわれわれへの祝賀状 ‖ I *congratulated* him ***on*** (=***upon***) the birth of his son. あの人に男子出生のお祝いを述べた. 【類】He is to be *congratulated **on*** his excellent book. ‖ He cannot be *congratulated **on*** his powers of prediction. 彼には先見の明がなかった(予言がはずれたなど). 【類】He *congratulated* himself ***on*** his foresight. / The editors are to be *congratulated **on*** the completion of their arduous efforts. / ... is to be *congratulated **on*** the self-restraint (自制) which he has exercised ‖ Mrs. X who trained the boys is to be *congratulated **on*** the success of her efforts. (学生英語劇などで)学生をりっぱに訓練した X 夫人の功労に対して祝辞を述べるべきである. ¶We *congratulated* him ***upon*** his attainment to so great an age. われわれは彼がかく長寿を全うされたことを慶賀した. 【類】*congratulate* a friend ***upon*** a successful achievement (成功) / he is to be *congratulated **upon*** having succeeded in ...

congratulation, *n*. 祝賀; *pl*. 祝詞.

V ***Accept*** my *congratulations* on the beauty of the volume as an excellent example of the bookbinder's art. 同書は装ていの美において製本術の優れた一標本であることをうれしく思います. 【類】Please ***accept*** my sincere *congratulations* on your recovery from illness (病気回復). ¶he ***acknowledged*** the *congratulations* that were showered upon him by ... 彼は...によってわが身に雨とふりかけられた祝辞に対し感謝の意を表した. ¶***cable*** him the most enthusiastic *congratulations* 海外の彼に最も熱意のこもった祝電を送る. ¶***convey*** him our most respectful *congratulations* われわれの最も丁重な祝辞を彼に伝える. ¶***deserve*** much *congratulation* on ... ...に対し大いに祝賀される価値がある. ¶***extend*** one's *congratulations* to ... ...祝意を表する. 【類】***extend*** a most hearty *congratulation*. ¶Indeed! you ***have*** my hearty *congratulations*. そりゃ本当におめでとうございます. ¶*congratulations* are ***heard*** all round on ... ...について至る所に祝賀の声が聞かれる. ¶***offer*** (=tender) him *congratulations* on his deed その行為に対して彼に祝詞を呈する ‖ I beg to ***offer*** my *congratulations* on the New Year. 新年おめでとうございます. 【類】We ***offer*** our *congratulations* to him on his success in a most difficult role (困難な役割). ¶I ***received*** the following *congratulations* from ... 私は...から次の祝辞を受けた. ¶I am glad to ***send*** *congratulations* to the Japan Times on the completion of fifty years of successful journalism. ジャパン・タイムスが創業五十周年を迎えられるに当って祝詞を呈します. ¶***telegraph*** my *congratulations* to ... ...に祝電を送る. ¶***tender*** my heartiest *congratulations* 私の衷心からの祝詞を呈する.

V² From all over the world *congratulations* ***streamed in*** on Mr. Chamberlain at Highbury, Birmingham, yesterday, his seventy-third birthday. 昨日バーミンガムのハイベリなるチェォンバレン氏が七十三回の誕生日を迎えられるに当り世界中から祝詞がひっきりなしに届いた.

Q deserve ***earnest*** *congratulations* on ... ...については心からの祝福を受ける価値がある. ¶***kind*** *congratulations* 親切な祝詞. ¶I wish to convey him my most ***respectful*** *congratulations* on ... 私は彼に対し...について心からの尊敬と祝意を表したいと思う. ¶Please accept my ***sincere*** *congratulations*. 私の心からの喜びをお受け下さい. ¶***warm*** *congratulations* are due to ... ...に熱心な祝詞を呈すべきである. 【類】our ***warmest*** *congratulations* and good wishes to ...

P a subject ***for*** hearty *congratulation* 衷心から祝賀すべきこと. ‖ it is a matter ***for*** *congratulation* that ... ...はめでたいことだ. ¶***in*** *congratulation* of ... ...の祝いに.

P² send *congratulations **after*** one's birth その誕生の祝詞を述べる. ¶*congratulations* ***by*** mail (telegraph, telephone) 郵便(など)による祝詞. ¶These cards are *congratulations **for*** the New Year. これらのはがきは新年の賀状である. ‖ *congratulations **for*** his recovery 彼の全快祝. ¶*congratulations **upon*** the excellence of his work 彼の作の優秀さに対する祝詞.

congregation, *n*. 会衆, 集団.

V ***address*** a *congregation* 会衆に説教する. ¶His sermons ***attract*** a crowded *congregation*. 彼の説教には人が大勢集まる. ¶They soon ***formed*** a fervent *congregation* of converts. 彼らは間もなく熱心な改宗者の一団となった.

Q A sermon was delivered to an ***overflowing*** *congregation*. 満堂にあふれる会衆に向って説教をした.

congress, *n*. 集会, 会議; [C-] 米国議会.

V the National Film *Congress* recently ***called*** in Italy 先般イタリアで開催された国民映画会議. ¶***hold*** a *congress* 会議を開く.

Q a ***medical*** *congress* 医師大会. ¶The ***Seventeenth International*** *Congress* of Medicine met in London. 第十七回万国医学会議はロンドンで開催された.

Q² a ***party*** *congress* 党大会.

P ***in*** the 63rd *Congress* 第六十三回米国議会に. ‖ ***in*** *Congress* and out [米国]議会の内外に. ¶He was elected to the Sixty-fifth, Sixty-sixth, and Sixty-seventh Congresses, and re-elected ***to*** the Sixty-eighth *Congress*. 彼は第六十五・六十六・六十七(米国)議会に議員として当選しまた第六十八議会に再選された.

P² a *congress **on*** Christian work キリスト教伝道事業に関する会議.

congruous, *a*. 適した.

P The work is *congruous **to*** (=***with***) his character. この仕事は彼の性質に適している. ‖ It is *congruous **with*** reason. それは道理に合っている.

conjectural, *a*. 推測の.

M It is ***merely*** *conjectural*. それは推測に過ぎない.

conjecture, *n*. 推測, おく測.

V ***confirming*** the *conjecture* 果せるかな. ¶***form*** a *conjecture* 推測する. ¶This *conjecture* is not well ***founded***. この推測には大した根拠がない. ¶***give*** a plausible *conjecture* もっともらしいおく測を下す. ¶I ***have*** no other *conjecture* to offer on the subject. その問題に関してほかに推測のしようがない. ¶He made no attempt to ***hazard*** *conjecture*. 彼はあえて推測をしようともしなかった.

Q Those *conjectures* are ***correct***. それらの推量は当っている. ¶***erroneous*** *conjectures* respecting ... ...に関する誤まった推測. ¶there have been so ***many*** *conjectures* of ... ...については色々のおく測がある. ¶a ***mere*** *conjecture* 単なるおく測. ¶There is ***much*** *conjecture* as to why he has resorted to such a measure. なぜ彼がそんな手段を取ったかについてかれこれうわさがある. ¶a matter of ***pure*** *conjecture* 全くの推量. ¶make a ***suspicious*** *conjecture* 気を回す. ¶make an ***unjust*** *conjecture* 邪推をする. ¶***vague*** *conjecture* ばく然たる推測. ¶***vain*** *conjecture* つまらぬおく測. ¶***various*** *conjectures* were formed as to whether ... ...か否かについて種々のおく測が行われた. ¶***wicked*** *conjecture* 邪推.

P The rumour raised a storm ***of*** *conjectures*. そのうわさで盛んにおく測が下されている.

P² *conjectures* ***as to*** (=***respecting***) ... vary between ... and ... ...に関する推測は...と...と二色になっている.

conjecture, *v*. 推測する.

P *conjecture* the fact ***from*** ... その事実を...から推測する.

conjoin, *v*. 結合する.

P be *conjoined **in*** wedlock 夫婦になる. ¶several elements *conjoined **in*** one 一つに結合された色々な要素. ¶when *conjoined **with*** the other force 他の力に結び付けば.

conjugation, *n*. 〖文法〗動詞の変化.

Q *strong* (*weak*) *conjugation* 〖文法〗 動詞強(弱)変化.

conjunction, *n.* 連合；共同.

P work ***in*** *conjunction* with ... ...と協力する ‖ open a store ***in*** *conjunction* with ... ...と共同で店を開く. ‖ be studied ***in*** *conjunction* with ... (関連科目など)...と共同研究される. 【類】 be used ***in*** *conjunction* with ...

conjure, *v.* 迷わす；魔法で...する；手品をつかう.

M *conjure* ***up*** an awesome picture of ... [じゅ文を使いなどして] ...の恐ろしい姿を呼び出す ‖ *conjure* ***up*** the visions of one's childhood その子供のころの姿が目に浮ぶ. 【類】 *conjure* ***up*** the memories of ... / names that *conjure* ***up*** reminiscences of the past ‖ It is the business of a novelist to *conjure* ***up*** into existence the world of imagination. 想像の世界を作り出すのが小説家の仕事である.

P *conjure* him ***into*** ... 魔法で彼に...させる. ¶*conjuring* ***with*** silver coins 銀貨の手品 ‖ His is a name to *conjure* ***with.*** 彼は飛ぶ鳥も落すような勢である.

connect, *v.* 結び付ける, 関連させる.

M It is ***closely*** *connected* with this affair. それはこの事件に密接な関係がある. ¶it is *connected* ***directly*** with ... それは...と直接関係がある. ¶be only ***distantly*** *connected* with the family その家族とは遠縁にしか当らない. ¶These two words are ***etymologically*** *connected.* この二語は語原的に関連している. ¶***indissolubly*** *connected* with ... ...と離れられぬ(深い)関係がある. ¶but ***remotely*** *connected* with ... ...とほんのわずか関連して. ¶He is by marriage ***respectably*** *connected.* 彼は妻の方の縁続きにりっぱな人がいる. ¶*connected* ***telegraphically*** with ... ...と電信の連絡がついて.

P Northbound and eastbound trains *connect* ***at*** New York. 北部行と東部行の列車がニューヨークで連絡する. ¶These islands are *connected* ***by*** telegraph. これらの島には電信の連絡がある. ‖ The island is *connected* ***by*** a steamer service ***with*** (=***to***) the mainland. その島は本土と汽船の連絡がある. ¶It is *connected* ***with*** ... by a motor-bus service. ここと...間に乗合自動車の便がある. 【類】 The train *connects* here ***with*** a steamboat for Aomori. ‖ The parlour *connects* ***with*** the study. 客間と書斎は間続きになっている. ‖ He is *connected* ***with*** the iron industry. 彼は製鉄業に関係している. 【類】 There are many superstitions *connected* ***with*** this. / be *connected* ***with*** the name of Dickens / I am not *connected* ***with*** the company. ‖ Mathematics is *connected* ***with*** astronomy. ‖ He is *connected* ***with*** the family (party). 彼はその家族(など)と縁故がある. ‖ *connecting* himself by the strongest ties ***with*** ... ...とは切っても切れぬ仲となっている ‖ What religious denomination are you *connected* ***with***? あなたの宗派は何ですか. ‖ He is *connected* ***with*** our firm. 彼は当店と取引している. ‖ a night school *connected* ***with*** the Presbyterian Church 長老教会付属の夜学校.

O The Tokaido is the great road *connecting* Kyoto and Tokyo. 東海道は京都・東京を結ぶ大道路である.

connection, *n.* 連結；連絡；[しばしば *pl.*] 関係.

V ***break off*** (=***cut***) *connection* 関係を絶つ. ¶***build up*** a *connection* mutually advantageous たがいに有利な関係を造り上げる. ¶***carry on*** (=***continue***) *connection* with ... ...と関係を続ける. ¶He has ***completed*** his 21 years' *connection* with the company. 彼はその会社にすでに二十一年奉職した. ¶He steadily ***declined*** all *connection* with officialdom. 彼は一切官界との関係を辞退した. ¶The married couple ***dissolved*** the *connection.* その夫婦は離別した. ¶***establish*** [a] *connection* with ... ...と関係(連絡)をつける. ¶hurry to the telephone, ***get*** the *connection,* and ask the question, "...?" 電話にかけつけ番号を呼び...と尋ねる. ¶***have*** *connections* with a woman 女と関係を持つ(情交を結ぶ). 【類】 I have never ***had*** [a] *connection* with any female. ‖ He ***had*** *connection* with the college. 彼はその大学に関係した. ‖ ***have*** no *connection* whatever 縁もゆかりもない. ¶***make*** this *connection* ***clear*** この関係を明りょうにする ‖ *Connection* will be ***made*** at ... with the train. [汽船が] ...で汽車に連絡する. ¶I ***missed*** my *connection.* [乗換えの場合など]連絡をとりそこなった. ¶However hard I try I cannot ***obtain*** a *connection.* どうしても電話がかからない. ¶***possess*** railway *connections* 鉄道の連絡がある. ¶He ***resigned*** his *connection* with the company. 彼はその会社を辞職した. ¶***retain*** his *connection* with ... ...との彼の関係を保留する. ¶***seek*** business *connection* with ... ...との商取引を求める. ¶***sever*** one's *connection* with a party 党派との関係を絶つ. 【類】 He has ***severed*** his *connection* with our company to accept service with another concern. / ***sever*** all the *connections* with the earth. ¶an attempt to ***unravel*** its causal *connection* with ... ...との因果関係を明かにしようとする試み. ¶Trade *connections* ***existed*** between the two countries. その二国は通商をしていた.

Q whoever had any ***academic*** *connection* with the University 同大学と授業上の関係のあった人はだれでも. ¶without ***apparent causal*** *connection* 一見因果関係なしに. ¶have a ***bad*** *connection* 連絡が悪い. ¶there is a ***causal*** *connection* between ... and ... と...の間に因果関係がある. ‖ The ***causal*** *connection* cannot be regarded as yet fully established. その原因が確定したとは見なされない. ¶They have a ***close*** *connection* with each other. 両者は緊密に結ばれている. ‖ ***Close*** *connections* are made there with trains to those points. その方面へはその所で汽車との密接な連絡がある. 【類】 ***close*** *connections* between steamers and trains. ¶***criminal*** *connection* (=conversation) 〖法〗 かん通罪. ¶have a ***dark*** *connection* with ... ...と秘密の関係(やみ取引)がある. ¶with ***direct*** *connections* to Atlantic seaboard points 大西洋の沿岸方面へ直接に連絡して. ¶a ***distant*** *connection* of my wife's 私の妻の遠縁に当るもの. ¶form a ***fancied*** *connection* with ... ...と関係があるものと想像する. ¶***grammatical*** *connection* 文法的関連. ¶***hidden*** *connections* 表面に現われない関係. ¶form ***illicit*** *connections* with ... ...と不義の関係がある. ¶have an ***immediate*** *connection* with ... ...と直接に関係している. ¶it has an ***important*** *connection* with (=bearing on) ... それは...と大切な関係がある. ¶have ***improper*** *connection* with ... ...と不義(密通)をする. ¶an ***indirect*** *connection* 間接の関係. ¶there is an ***indissoluble*** *connection* between の間には切っても切れない関係がある. ¶a business with a ***large*** *connection* 顧客の多い商売. ¶***indetachable*** *connection* 不可分の関係. ¶***organizational*** *connections* 組織上の関係. ¶he has a ***remote*** *connection* with ... 彼は...の遠縁に当る. ¶***sexual*** *connection* [男女の]性関係. ¶a ***slight*** *connection* ちょっとした関係. ¶girls who have ***social*** *connections* in New York ニューヨークに社交関係を有する少女たち. ¶There is ***some*** *connection* between the two. その二つの間には何かのひっかかりがある. ¶***strict*** *connection* 密接の関係. ¶an ***unfortunate*** *connection* 腐れ縁. ¶form ***useful*** *connections* 有利なつながりを作る. ¶our ***world-wide*** *connections* 手前どもの世界的の取引関係.

Q^2 ***business*** *connections* 取引関係 ‖ establish large ***business*** *connections* 広い取引先を作る. ¶make a ***pipe*** *connection* 管でつなぐ. ¶have no ***railway*** *connections* 鉄道連絡がない. ¶there is ***steamer*** *connection* with ... と海上連絡がある. ¶***Telephone*** *connection* has been established between those places. この地区間に電話が開通した. ¶an office with ***telephone*** *connection* 電話のある事務所 ‖ there is ***telephone*** *connection* directly with ... ...との直通電話がある. ¶rapidly broadening ***trade*** *connections* 益々手広くなる取引関係. ¶make ***train*** *connections* without losing time 時間をつぶさずに乗り替えをする. ¶with ***transfer*** *connections* at ... ...で乗換え連絡のある. ¶The hotel has direct ***tunnel*** *connection* to Pennsylvania Station. そのホテルはペンシルヴァニア停車場にトンネルで直接に続いている.

P it should be stated ***in*** this *connection* that ... ちなみに記す... 【類】 ***in*** this *connection* it is of interest to note that ... / Table (表) on page 102 may be studied ***in*** this *connection.* / ***in*** *connection* with this subject, it may be mentioned that ... / Tell me all you know ***in*** *connection* with that matter. ‖ I am ***in*** *connection* with him. あの人と取引をしている. ‖ flies ***in*** *connection* 交尾中のはえ ‖ It has ***in*** *connection* a zoological garden. 付属動物園がある. ‖ a teaching hospital ***in*** *connection* with the College of Medicine その医大付属病院. 【類】 It is to be used as a teaching hospital ***in*** *connection* with the College of Medicine. ‖ taken ***in*** *connection* with the statement, this fact would seem to prove that ... その声明と照し合わして見るとこの事実は...ということを証明するように思われる. ‖ His name has been mentioned ***in*** *connection* with the Indian Viceroyship. インド総督の候補に彼の名が挙げられた.

P² The *connection* ***between*** ... and ... was severed. ...と...の間の関係が絶たれた. ‖ a *connection* ***between*** two persons (affairs) 二人(など)間の関係. ¶the *connection* ***of*** motor and coach services ***with*** railways 自動車および乗合馬車と鉄道との連絡. ¶His *connection* ***with*** the Royal Geographical Society is not merely ornamental. 王立地理学会との彼の関係は単に装飾(名誉)的のものではない. 【類】during my *connection* ***with*** the school / a man ***with*** whom I have no *connection* whatever 縁もゆかりもない人.

connivance, *n.* 黙認, 看過.

P ***through*** the *connivance* of the police 警察で黙認しているので. ¶***with*** the *connivance* of the Government 政府の黙許を得て.

P² *connivance* ***at*** his faults 彼の過失の看過 ‖ *connivance* ***at*** wrong doings (悪行). ¶*connivance* ***with*** a person ***in*** wrong doing 人の非行黙許.

connive, *v.* 看過する; 共謀する.

P *connive* ***at*** a person's doings 人の所業を見逃す. ¶*connive* (=be in collusion) ***with*** a criminal in his crime 罪人と共謀する. 【類】*connive* ***with*** another prisoner in an escape from prison.

connoisseur, *n.* [美術品の]鑑定家, 目きき.

V ***play*** the *connoisseur* くろうとらしく振舞う.

Q a ***ceramic*** *connoisseur* 陶器の鑑定家. ¶be a ***good*** *connoisseur* 鑑定眼が高い. ¶Major Sexton O'Brien, the ***well-known*** *connoisseur* of *ukiyoye* 有名な浮世絵の鑑識家セキストン・オブライエン少佐.

Q² a ***music*** *connoisseur* 音楽の専門家.

P² a *connoisseur* ***in*** pictures ‖ *Connoisseurs* ***in*** mountain scenery pronounce this outlook the most satisfying. 山景に眼識のある人はこの眺望が最もよいと言っている. ‖ *connoisseurs* ***in*** such things この方面の鑑識家. ¶a *connoisseur* ***of*** fruits=a pomologist 果樹栽培専門家 ‖ *connoisseurs* ***of*** jewellery 宝石鑑定人.

connoisseurship, *n.* 鑑識.

V He cannot be expected to ***have*** a *connoisseurship* in art. 彼に芸術の鑑識眼を期待するのは無理だ.

P He is well known ***for*** his *connoisseurship* ***in*** such matters. 彼はこの方面の鑑識で有名だ.

connotation, *n.* 内包, 含蓄.

V The word has ***acquired*** a slangy *connotation*. その語は俗語的な色彩を持つようになった. 【類】The word has ***acquired*** a bad *connotation*. ¶The term has ***gained*** a sinister *connotation*. その語は変な意味をもつようになった. ¶Current slang ***has*** a flippant *connotation*. 流行の俗語には軽薄味がある. 「宝な言葉.

Q a useful term of an ***elastic*** *connotation* 融通性のある重

connotative, *a.* [...の意を]暗示する, 内包的な.

P The word 'master' is *connotative* ***of*** 'servant.' 「主人」という語は「召使」を暗示する.

conquer, *v.* 打勝つ, 征服する.

P The country has never been *conquered* ***by*** a foreign foe. 同国はいまだかつて外敵に征服されたことがない. ‖ *conquer* ***by*** love 愛によって征服する. ¶The Prussians *conquered* the French completely ***in*** the late war. この前の戦争でプロシア軍は仏軍を完全に征服した.

conqueror, *n.* 征服者. 「*conqueror* 高峰征服者.

Q an ***aggressive*** *conqueror* 侵略的征服者. ¶a ***high peak***

P² the *conqueror* ***of*** the world's highest peak 世界最高峰

conquest, *n.* 勝利, 征服. 「の征服者.

V ***complete*** the *conquest* of the country その国を平定する. ¶he sought to ***effect*** the *conquest* of ... 彼は...を征服しようとした. ¶When the Romans ***extended*** their *conquests* to Britain (about 45 A.D.), they found there a Celtic race whom we call Britons. ローマ人が(西紀四十五年ごろ)英国に遠征したときわれわれが今ブリトン人と呼ぶケルト民族がそこに居住しているのを見た. 【類】***extend*** one's *conquests* farther on into ... / ***extended*** his *conquests* southward. ¶***make*** the *conquest* of peace by arms 武力によって平和を獲得する ‖ ***make*** *conquests* of ladies 多くの婦人をくどき落す.

Q the ignominy of a ***foreign*** *conquest* 外敵侵略の汚辱. ¶remarkable discoveries in the ***physical*** (***mental***) *conquest* of disease 病気の肉体(精神)的征服に関する顕著な発見.

Q² embark on ***world*** *conquest* 世界征服に取りかゝる.

P She came down, dressed ***for*** *conquest*. どんな男も降参するだろうと言わんばかりに装いを凝らして降りてきた.

P² the *conquest* ***of*** Persia ***by*** Alexander the Great アレキサンダー大王のペルシア征服. 【類】the *conquest* ***of*** Mount Everest / the *conquest* ***of*** the air (sea) / the *conquest* ***of*** difficulties (one's passions) ‖ *conquest* ***of*** antagonism 対立の解消 ‖ the *conquest* ***of*** liberty 自由の獲得. ¶some of man's most striking *conquests* ***over*** nature 人類の自然征服の最も顕著な数例.

conscience, *n.* 良心.

V A man cannot ***allow*** his *conscience* to be too delicate. 人はあくまでもその良心を敏感にしておくべきである. ¶I found it was not so easy to ***appease*** my *conscience* about the matter. その事に関して私の良心を満足させることはあまり容易ではなかった. ¶***arouse*** the public *conscience* to the evils of the drink traffic 酒類販売の弊害について世人を目ざめさせる. ¶***atrophy*** *conscience* 良心を麻ひさせる. ¶***consult*** one's *conscience* 自己の良心に訴える. ¶***ease*** one's *conscience* 良心を安んじる. ¶***examine*** one's *conscience* three times a day 日に三省する. ¶***feel*** a guilty *conscience* 心のやましさを感じる. ¶The wrong ***haunted*** his *conscience*. 彼はその悪い事をしたので気がとがめた. ¶I ***have*** the *conscience* to do so. 私はそうするのを本当と考える. ‖ He actually ***had*** the *conscience* to do such a thing in my house. 彼は厚かましくも私の家でこんな事をした. ‖ ***have*** no *conscience* 良心がない(どんな悪いことでもしかねない) ‖ ***have*** more *conscience* toward ...に対して一層良心的である. ¶***outrage*** one's *conscience* 良心を踏みつけにする. ¶***quicken*** our *consciences* われわれの良心を活躍させる. ¶I do not say that to persuade you, but merely to ***relieve*** my *conscience*. 君を説得するためではなく私の気休めにそのことを言うのです. ¶***rouse*** the *conscience* of the whole nation 全国民の良心を目覚めさせる. ¶I ***salved*** my *conscience* by reasoning that ... 私は気休めに...という理屈をこねた. ¶***satisfy*** one's *conscience* 良心を満足させる. ¶***smooth*** one's *conscience* 良心(のかしゃく)を慰さめる. ¶***still*** *conscience* [道徳上の問題で]妥協する. ¶***stimulate*** the *conscience* 良心を刺激する. ¶***trouble*** one's *conscience* 良心を悩ます.

V² obey what *conscience* ***dictates*** 良心の命じる所に従う. ¶but *conscience* ***intervened*** and ... ところが良心がとがめて... ¶His *conscience* ***overcame*** him. 彼は普心に立返った.

Q an ***accommodating*** *conscience* 融通のきく良心. ¶a case of ***awakened*** *conscience* on the part of ... ...が悪いと悟った一例. ¶I have a ***bad*** (=an ***evil***) *conscience* 心にやましい所がある. ¶sleep on a ***calm*** *conscience* 心にやましい所がなく眠る. ¶go with a ***clear*** (=***clean*** or ***good***) *conscience* 潔白な心を持っている. ¶have a ***guilty*** *conscience* 寝覚めが悪い. ¶a ***linguistic*** *conscience* 語学的良心. ¶develop a ***literary*** *conscience* 文学的良心を育成する. ¶The ***modern*** *conscience* is becoming sensitive respecting it. 近代人の良心はそのことについては敏感になった. ¶the ***public*** *conscience* 世人の良心. ¶I can recommend this book to anybody with a ***safe*** *conscience*. 本書は何人にも安心しておすすめができる. ¶a ***scared*** *conscience* おびやかされた良心. ¶a ***social*** *conscience* 社会的良心. ¶My *conscience* is more ***tender*** than yours. 僕の良心は君の良心より感じやすい(君ほどすれていない). ¶an ***uneasy*** *conscience* 不安な良心. ¶International law is a sort of ***universal*** *conscience*. 国際法は全世界の良心とでも言うべきものだ.

Q² ***art*** *conscience* 芸術的良心. ¶outrage a ***community*** *conscience* 社会的良心をじゅうりんする. ¶an ***umbrella*** *conscience* 借りた雨がさを返さなくても平気という鈍い良心.

P act ***according to*** *conscience* 良心に従って行動する. ¶He is stung ***by*** *conscience*. 彼は良心の苛責を受けている. ¶I cannot ***in*** *conscience* do anything to injure him. 心がとがめて彼の害になるような事はできない. ¶leave him ***to*** his own *conscience* [他から干渉しないで]彼の良心のままにさせておく. ¶***upon*** one's *conscience* 良心にかけて ‖ Every man has a stain ***upon*** his *conscience*. 何人もその良心に汚点がある. ¶***with*** a good *conscience* やましい所がなくて(明鏡止水の心境で).

conscious, *a.* 意識している, 自覚している.

M I am ***deeply*** *conscious* of my responsibility as ... 私は...としての自分の責任を痛感している. ¶I am ***profoundly*** *conscious* that ... ...を深く意識している. ¶Although dying, he was ***quite*** *conscious*. 死際でも彼は十分に意識があった.

P I was not *conscious* ***of*** having offended him. 私は彼の気にさわることをした覚えがなかった. ‖ Was he *conscious* ***of*** what he was saying at the time? その時彼が言っていたことを自分で意識していましたか. ‖ *conscious* ***of*** one's own situation 自己の立場を意識して. 【類】 *conscious* ***of*** her superiority to the rest of the world / I am quite *conscious* ***of*** his innocence. / be *conscious* ***of*** one's guilt / be *conscious* ***of*** the distinction between good and evil.

consciousness, *n.* 意識, 自覚.

V It will ***breed*** a class *consciousness* which is alien to American ideals. そうすると米国人の理想と一致しない階級意識を生じるだろう. ¶The idea (image) ***entered*** *consciousness*. その考え(など)が起った. ¶***lose*** *consciousness* 気絶する. ¶Through it all he ***preserved*** his *consciousness*. 彼はその間ずっと気を確かに持ち通した. ¶***recover*** *consciousness*=come to [one's senses] 意識を回復する ‖ ***recover*** (=***regain***) national *consciousness* 国民的意識を取戻す. 【類】 He never ***recovered*** *consciousness*. ¶He died without ***regaining*** *consciousness* (= recovering his senses). 彼は気絶したまま死んだ.

Q a ***deep*** *consciousness* of injustice 不正たることの深い意識. ¶a ***dim*** *consciousness* of ... ...のばく然たる意識. ¶I have a ***hidden*** *consciousness* that ... ...ということに心ひそかに気付いている. ¶***Impersonal*** *consciousness* is a mark of the true artist. 自己を意識しないことは真の芸術家たるゆえんである. ¶***intense*** *consciousness* 強い意識. ¶a ***national*** *consciousness* 国民意識. ¶a ***universal*** *consciousness* 世界意識.

Q² the development of ***air*** *consciousness* 航空意識の高揚. ¶***class*** *consciousness* 階級意識. ¶arrive at (=acquire) a ***race*** *consciousness* 民族意識ができる. ¶maintain (intensify) ***wartime*** *consciousness* 戦時意識を保持する(強める). ¶***world*** *consciousness* 世界意識.

P he is happy ***in*** the *consciousness* that ... ...と言うことを知って喜んでいる. ¶restore her ***to*** *consciousness* 彼女を正気づかせる.

conscription, *n.* 徴兵.

V He ***escaped*** *conscription* because he was too short. 彼は背が足りないので徴兵を免除された. ¶***evade*** *conscripion* 徴兵を忌避する. ¶*Conscription* is not ***practised*** in Great Britain. 英国では徴兵制度が行われていない.

Q the system of ***universal*** *conscription* [国民]皆兵制度.

Q² At the ***army*** *conscription* he was considered unfit for the service on account of ... 徴兵の際...の理由で軍務不適当とみなされた.

P He was called up ***for*** the *conscription*. 彼は徴兵に召集された. ¶temporary exemption of students ***from*** *conscription* 学生の徴兵猶予 ‖ the privilege of exemption ***from*** *conscription* 徴兵免除の特典.

consecrate, *v.* 神事に供する; 捧げる.

P *consecrate* a king ***by*** applying oil 油を塗って王を神聖にする. ¶the evening is *consecrated* ***to*** the memory of the late ... その晩(の宴会)は故...の記念に挙行するものである ‖ *consecrate* a church ***to*** divine service 会堂を神事に捧げる ‖ He *consecrated* his life ***to*** art. 彼は一身を美術に捧げた. ‖ edifices *consecrated* ***to*** worship 礼拝のための建物.

consensus, *n.* 一致; 世論.

V ***represent*** the *consensus* of thoughtful opinion throughout the country 思慮ある国民の総意を示す. ¶It ***voices*** the *consensus* of medical opinion. それは医学上の意見の総合を示す.

Q a sort of ***tacit*** *consensus* 一種の無言の総意.

P ***by*** a *consensus* of expert opinion 専門家の総意によって.

P² the *consensus* ***of*** usage 用法の一致 ‖ the *consensus* ***of*** opinion was that ... 一致した意見は...であった.

consent, *n.* 同意, 承諾.

V ***express*** one's *consent* 承諾の意を表示する. ¶***give*** one's *consent* to ... ...に同意する. ¶***Have*** I your *consent?* 御異存はありませんか ‖ must ***have*** the *consent* of ... ...の承認を得ていなければならない. ¶***obtain*** his *consent* 彼の同意を得る. ¶***receive*** a written *consent* from ... ...から書面で同意を受ける. ¶He ***refused*** his *consent* 彼は同意しなかった. ¶***wheedle*** *consent* from ... 説きつけて...を承諾させる. ¶***withhold*** one's *consent* 承諾をさしひかえる.

Q separate by ***common*** *consent* 話合で別居する[夫婦など] ‖ The Encyclopædia Britannica is by ***common*** *consent* the first work of its kind in the world. 大英百科辞典は一般に世界におけるその種の白眉と認められている. 【類】 By the ***common*** *consent* of critics, Shakespeare is the prince of character delineators. / He was by ***common*** *consent* the foremost man (第一者) in India. / admitted (=granted) by ***common*** *consent*. ¶by his ***express*** *consent* 特に彼の承諾を得て. ¶by ***general*** *consent* 一般の賛同を得て. 【類】 gain ***general*** *consent* ‖ He is held by ***general*** *consent* to be the most learned of our living painters. 彼はわが国の現代画家中で最も学識ある者と一般に認められている. ¶obtain his ***informal*** *consent* 内諾を得る. ¶with their ***joint*** *consent* 彼ら一同の同意を得て. ¶by ***mutual*** *consent* 合意の上で. ¶a ***qualified*** *consent* 条件づきの承諾. ¶a ***reluctant*** *consent* 渋々の承諾. ¶give a ***silent*** *consent* to it それを默認する. ¶we wrung from him a ***slow*** *consent* that ... われわれはやっとのことで彼から...と言う承諾を得た. ¶***tacit*** *consent* 默認. ¶except by ***unanimous*** *consent* 満場一致によるの外は. ¶by ***universal*** *consent* 一般に認められて. ¶give an ***unprepared*** *consent* 安受合をする. ¶a ***written*** *consent* 承諾書.

P ***at*** the mutual *consent* of ... ...が話合で. ¶***by*** *consent* of Congress 議会の承諾を経て ‖ ***by*** (=with) one *consent* 衆議一決して; 満場一致で ‖ ***by*** the *consent* and permission of ... ...の承諾と許可を得て. ¶***with*** (=by) your *consent* 貴下の御承認を受けて. 【類】 ***with*** *consent* of the author / ***with*** *consent* of the contracting parties ‖ The Emperor exercises the legislative power ***with*** the *consent* of the Imperial Diet. [旧憲法]天皇は帝国議会の協賛を経て立法権を行使し給う. ¶***with*** or ***without*** *consent* 承諾を得ようが得まいが. ¶cannot move hand or foot ***without*** the *consent* of ... ...の許可を得なければ手も足も出ない.

P² the *consent* ***of*** the will ***to*** the act 行為に対する意志の承認.

consent, *v.* 同意する, 承諾する.

M ***Finally*** he *consented*. 結局彼は承諾した. ¶***gladly*** *consent* to the extension of ... 喜んで...の延期に応じる. ¶He ***reluctantly*** *consented* to it. 彼はいやいやそれに同意した. ¶***willingly*** *consent* 快く承諾する.

P *consent* ***to*** a request 申出を承諾する. 【類】 I cannot *consent* ***to*** what you ask. / *consent* ***to*** a scheme (proposal, marriage). ¶They *consented* ***with*** one voice. 彼らは異議なく承諾した. ‖ He *consented* ***with*** a ready answer. 二つ返事で承諾した.

consequence, *n.* 結果, 成行; 重大.

V ***accept*** the *consequence* of (=abide by) ... ...の結果に甘んじる. ¶***avert*** the *consequence* of ... ...の結果を避ける. ¶***bear*** the *consequences* of one's sins 己が罪悪の結果を忍ぶ. ¶He does not ***consider*** the *consequences*. 彼は結果を考慮しない. ¶It would be only too likely to ***entail*** serious national *consequences*. それが国家に重大な結果をもたらすことはあまりに明白と思われる. ¶***foresee*** the *consequences* of one's actions 人の行動の結果を予知する. ¶It may ***have*** serious *consequences*. それは重大な結果を生むだろう. ¶***infer*** its *consequences* その結果を推測する. ¶This step ***involved*** many fateful *consequences*. この手段を取ると必然的に幾多の恐るべき結果を生ずるのであった. ¶It might ***leave*** serious *consequences*. それは重大な結果を生じるかも知れない. ¶The company now ***suffers*** the *consequences* of his mismanagement. 会社は彼の経営宜しきを得なかった余波を受けている. ¶***take*** the *consequences* [よかれあしかれ]その結果を甘受する.

V² It was feared that unpleasant *consequences* might ***ensue***. おもしろくない結果が生じるだろうという心配があった. ¶Serious *consequences* might ***follow***. そのため重大な結果を生じないとも限らない. ¶Serious *consequences* will ***result***. 由々しい結果になるだろう.

Q ***alarming*** *consequences* 不穩の結果. ¶It was not without ***baleful*** *consequences*. 悪結果を生じなかった訳ではない. ¶***baneful*** *consequences* 有害な結果. ¶The cold weather had most ***deleterious*** *consequences* among the chrysanthemums. 寒い天候が菊花にきわめて有害な結果を及ぼした. ¶entail ***destructive*** *consequences* 破壊的結果を伴う. ¶the ***evil*** *consequences* which flow from ... ...から生じる悪結果. ¶This step involves many ***fateful*** *consequences*. このやり方では多くの致命的な結果を招来する. ¶anticipation of ***future possible*** *consequences* 将来に及ぼす結果の予想. ¶bring ***grave*** *consequences* 容易ならぬ結果を招来する.

¶If your life is at stake, that is of ***great*** *consequences.* 君の命が危ないならそれは重大事だ. ‖ be nothing of very ***great*** *consequence* 何ら重大なことじゃない. ¶pregnant with ***immeasurable*** *consequences* 測り知れぬ結果を産み出しそうな. ¶as an ***indirect*** *consequence* of this この事の間接結果として. ¶Age has its ***inevitable*** *consequences.* 年は争えない. ¶be of ***little*** (***no***) *consequence* 余り(全く)重きをおくに足らぬ. ¶***momentary*** *consequences* 一時的結果. ¶It would be only too likely to entail serious ***national*** *consequences.* 国家にとって重大な結果を招くことはほとんど確定的であろう. ‖ it produces, as a ***natural*** *consequence* ... それは自然の結果として...を生じる ‖ as a ***natural*** *consequence* it followed that ... 当然の結果として...ということになった. ¶as a ***necessary*** *consequences* 必然的結果として. ¶involve ***pernicious*** *consequences* 由々しき結果をもたらすことになる. ¶***Serious*** *consequences* may arise. 重大な問題が起るかも知れない. ¶It's not a matter of very ***slight*** *consequence.* それは決して簡単な問題じゃない. ¶***terrible*** *consequences* 恐ろしい結果. ¶the temptation and its ***tragic*** *consequences* 誘惑とその悲劇的結果. ¶to be exempt from any ***unpleasant*** *consequence* おもしろくない結果を免れるために. ¶without any ***untoward*** *consequences* 事故なく. ¶a matter of ***vast*** and ***far-reaching*** *consequence* 重大で及ぼす所の広い事件. ¶avoid ***worse*** *consequence* もっと悪い結果にならないようにする.

P Do not be uneasy in mind ***about*** the *consequence.* 結果を心配するな. ¶***as*** a *consequence* of the foregoing 上述の結果として, 従って ‖ ***as*** the last *consequence* あげくの果に. ¶***by*** natural *consequence* 自然の成行で. ¶He suffered much ***in*** *consequence.* その結果随分苦しんだ. ‖ ***in*** *consequence* of foreign competition 海外競争の結果 ‖ ***in*** *consequence* of contrary winds 逆風のために ‖ Commerce is paralysed ***in*** *consequence* of a severe earthquake. 強震のため市場はまひ状態になっている. ‖ ***in*** *consequence* of holidays today and tomorrow 今明日と休日が続くので. 【類】***in*** *consequence* of the heavy rainfall (ill health) / ***in*** *consequence* of the warlike news / ***in*** *consequence* of this / ***in*** *consequence* of the frost (冷害) / ***in*** *consequence* of a gale coming on (暴風来襲) / ***in*** *consequence* of the acceptance of the Potsdam Declaration (ポツダム宣言受諾に伴い). ¶It is ***of*** *consequence* to do well what we have to do. われわれの為さねばならないことをりっぱに為すことは大切なことである. ‖ It is ***of*** *consequence* to me that you should come. 僕には君の来ることが肝心なのだ. ‖ A man is already ***of*** *consequence* in the world when it is known that he can be relied on.—Smiles. 人はその者が当てになる男だとなるとそれだけですでにこの世に大切な人間である. ‖ a man ***of*** *consequence* 重要な人 ‖ a matter ***of*** *consequence* 重要な件. 【類】It is ***of*** much *consequence.* / It is ***of*** small (=little) *consequence.* / With country people time is ***of*** no *consequence.* / whether ... or not is ***of*** no *consequence.* ¶***with*** unpleasant *consequence* おもしろくない結果になって.

P² give all one's concern to reflections on what would be the *consequence* ***of*** ... がどうなるかとそれを苦に病む.

O The *consequence* was that he lost his post. あげ句の果て彼は失業した. ¶Whatever may be the *consequence,* I will ... 結果はどうあろうと僕は...する.

consequent, *a.* 従って来る, 因って起る.

P *consequent* ***on*** the increasing vogue of motor traction 動力牽引の使用増加に伴って ‖ relieve the distress of the people *consequent* ***on*** the rise in the cost of living 生活費の高まるに伴う人民の苦しみを救う. 【類】There was severe trade depression *consequent* ***upon*** a number of serious strikes. ¶physical deterioration *consequent* ***upon*** the rush to city life 都会生活をめ求める者の激増に伴う体格の悪化.

conservation, *n.* 保存; 保護.

Q ***sane*** *conservation* [森林河川などの]当然の管理(保護). ¶***undue*** *conservation* [森林河川など]不当な管理(保護).

Q² ***forest*** and ***river*** *conservation* 森林河川の保護. ¶***soil*** *conservation* 土壌の保護. ¶***youth*** *conservation* 若さを保つこと.

P² *conservation* ***of*** energy エネルギーの不滅 ‖ *conservation* ***of*** electricity 電気の節約.

conservatism, *n.* 保守主義.

Q with a ***narrow-minded*** *conservatism* 狭量な保守主義で. ¶with ***old-fashioned French*** *conservatism* 旧式なフランス人の保守主義で. ¶***stupid*** or ***obdurate*** *conservatism* 愚かなまたはがん迷な保守主義.

conservative, *n.* 保守主義者; [C-] 保守党員.

Q a ***fanatical*** *conservative* 熱狂的保守主義者. ¶a ***staunch*** *conservative* 凝り固まった保守主義者.

P a candidate ***for*** the *Conservatives*=a Conservative candidate 保守党候補.

conservative, *a.* 保守的な.

M They are ***more*** or ***less*** *conservative* in opinion. 彼らの意見は多かれ少かれ保守的だ. ¶English people are ***naturally*** *conservative.* 英国民は生来保守的だ. ¶it is ***rather*** *conservative* to say that ... ...と言ってもあえて過言じゃあるまい.

P be *conservative* ***in*** the estimate 過少に見積る ‖ be *conservative* ***in*** one's habits 習慣を変えない ‖ Gladstone was *Conservative* ***in*** sentiment but Liberal in opinion. グラッドストーンは感情は保守党だが理論は自由党だった.

conservator, *n.* 管理人.

P² the *conservator* ***of*** a museum 博物館の管理者.

consider, *v.* 考える, 考察する; 尊敬する.

M *Consider* ***a moment.*** ちょっと考えて見給え. ¶*consider* ***away*** the opinion 熟考の上その意見をしりぞける. ¶Hold or sell as you [may] *consider* ***best.*** 持ってるなり売るなり君の考えに任せる. ¶let us now *consider* ***briefly*** ... こゝでちょっと...を考えてみよう. ¶***carefully*** *consider* the subject その問題を篤と考究する. ¶***closely*** *consider* 綿密に考える. ¶*consider* ***coolly*** 冷静に考える. ¶***etymologically*** *considered* 語原学的に考えると. ¶The more ***fully*** the proposal is *considered,* the worse it appears. その提案を考えれば考えるほど益々感心できないように思われて来る. ¶is ***fully*** and ***respectfully*** *considered* 十分敬意を払って考慮する. ¶***generally*** *considered* 一般的に考察すると. ¶***gravely*** *consider* まじめに考える. ¶He is ***greatly*** *considered* by his townsmen. 彼は町民から大いに重んぜられている. ¶***historically*** *considered* 歴史的に考慮すれば. ¶In old days a foreign language was *considered* ***largely*** as a key to the classical literature of the country. 往時外国語は一般にその国の古文学研究に対する手引と見なされていた. ¶***rationally*** *considered* 一体(そもそも). ¶***retrospectively*** *considered* it will be seen that ... 過去にさかのぼって考えてみると...ということが分る. ¶***scientifically*** *considered* 科学的に考えると. ¶*considered* ***solely*** from an ethical standpoint 純然たる倫理的見地から考えると. ¶***strictly*** *considered* 一体. ¶*Consider* the matter ***well*** before deciding. その事をよく考えた上で決定せよ. ¶*consider* ***well*** over a matter 問題を十分研究する.

P *consider* the matter ***from*** different standpoints その事を種々異なる見地から考えて見る.

O I *considered* him to be a gentleman. 僕は彼を紳士と思った. 【類】I *considered* him to be wise. ¶I *consider* him [to be] worthy of confidence. 私は彼を信用ができる男と思う. ¶He *considered* the report to be false. 彼はその報告を無根だと思った.

considerable, *a.* 考慮すべき; 重大な.

M be ***not very*** *considerable* 大したものでない.

considerate, *a.* 思慮深い; 思いやりのある.

M be *considerate* ***enough*** to ... 殊勝にも...である.

P *considerate* ***in*** (=***about***) ... ...に注意深い. ¶He is *considerate* ***of*** others. 彼は他人に思いやりがある. 【類】He is *considerate* ***of*** other people's wishes (feelings). / We should be *considerate* ***of*** the comfort of old people.

consideration, *n.* 考慮; 思いやり; 重要; 報酬.

V ***arouse*** many *considerations* 幾多の考慮を喚起する. ¶These measures ***await*** the *consideration* of the authorities. それらの方策が当局の考慮を待っている. ¶I ***bespeak*** your lenient *consideration* with respect to ... ...に関して貴下の寛大なご考慮をこう. ¶***bestow*** some *consideration* on the subject その問題を一考する. ¶***cast*** all moral and social *considerations* ***aside*** あらゆる道徳的並に社会的考慮を放棄する. ¶This naturally ***claims*** first *consideration.* 当然何よりも真先にこのことに考慮を払うべきだ. ¶I ***commend*** the most respectful *consideration* of their opinions. 彼らの意見に対し最も丁重な考慮を払われんことを望みます. ¶***confine*** its *consideration* to ... この考えを...に限定する. ¶The problem ***demands*** the most serious *consideration* of the Japanese people. これは日本人が最も真剣

に考慮すべき問題だ.【類】This may *demand* a brief *consideration.* ‖ Coming from such a distinguished statesman as ..., this opinion *demands* corresponding *consideration.* その意見は...のような有名な政治家の口から出たのであるからそれ相応の敬意を払わねばならぬ. ¶it *deserves* the earnest *consideration* of ... それは...が真剣に考慮する価値がある ‖ *deserve* little enough *consideration* at his hand 彼がしんしゃくしてやる必要は全然ない.【類】There are one or two points that *deserve* special *consideration.* ¶*disregard* personal *considerations* 個人的な考えを無視する. ¶*eliminate* personal *considerations* 個人的な考えを除く. ¶*Consideration* will be *given* severally to the style or quality of expression and the importance of the subject matter. 文体すなわち表現様式と内容の価値とに対して別々に考慮を払うことになっている.【類】*give* the matter careful *consideration* / I will *give* it further *consideration.* / *consideration* should, perhaps, first be *given* to ... ¶It will *have* our first *consideration.* それを第一に考慮します. ‖ We should *have consideration* for the rights of others. 他人の権利を尊重すべきだ. ‖ this matter is *having* the careful *consideration* of ... このことは...が慎重な考慮を払っている. ¶*ignore considerations* of profit and loss 損益関係を離れる. ¶*invite consideration* 考慮を要する.【類】The matter *invites* deep *consideration.* ¶it *involves* many *considerations*, namely:... それには色々の点を考慮する必要がある, すなわち... ¶*leaving considerations* of finance *aside* 財政の点はしばらくおいて. ¶*merit* (=deserve) the fullest *consideration* 十二分に考慮の価値がある.【類】The matter does not *merit* one's serious *consideration.* ¶It *outweighs* any other *consideration.* それは何より重要なことだ. ¶*override* the *consideration* その考えを無視する. ¶*postpone* a *consideration* as to ... ...についての考慮を後日のことにする. ¶*receive* proper *consideration* 適当な考慮を受ける.【類】The question has never yet *received* the *consideration* it has deserved. ¶*require* careful *consideration* 注意深い考慮を要する. ¶*show consideration* for one's age (position) 年齢(地位)を考えてやる.【類】*show* more *consideration* for ... than for ... ¶*solicit* your special *consideration* 貴下の特別の御考察をお願いします. ¶*take consideration* of this fact (=this fact into consideration) in punishing the criminal 犯人を罰するに当ってこの事実を参酌する ‖ *taking* all these *considerations* into account すべてこれらのことを考慮して.

v² Other *considerations prevailed.* 他の考慮が勝を制した. ¶as a very little *consideration* will *show* ちょっと考えればわかるように.

Q *adequate consideration* 十分の考慮. ¶*aesthetic consideration* 審美的配慮. ¶from *all* these *considerations,* it would seem that ... これらを総合して考えるに...であるように思われる. ¶commend it to the *attentive consideration* of ... それを...の周到な考慮にゆだねる.【類】worthy of *attentive consideration.* ¶a *basic consideration* 要点. ¶a *broad consideration* of the phenomena among civilized and uncivilized peoples 文明人及び未開人に見られる諸現象の広汎にわたる考察. ¶give *careful consideration* to the following rules 次の諸規則を十分検討する ‖ after *careful consideration* 十分検討してから ‖ I recommend it hereby to your *careful consideration.* この点を貴下に十分考慮いただければ幸いです. ¶the *dominant consideration* 主として考慮すべき点. ¶one point which has not received *due consideration* しかるべき考慮を払われなかった一つの点.【類】give the matter *due consideration* ‖ set one's seal without *due consideration* めくら判を押す. ¶The question is receiving the *earnest consideration* of some of the ablest men. その問題は最も眼識の高い二三の人によってまじめに研究されている. ¶*ethereal considerations* 超現世的考慮. ¶give *extended consideration* to a subject ある問題を広汎に考究する. ¶in the event of your *favorable consideration* 貴下の御賛成を得ました場合には ‖ in order to have a *favorable consideration* よく思われようと思って ‖【類】give *favorable consideration* to ... ¶come before the conference for *final consideration* 会議の最終審議に付せられる. ¶apart from *financial considerations* 金銭上の考えを離れて. ¶It should be the *first consideration.* それを第一に考慮すべきだ ‖ insist on low price as the *first consideration* 何よりも安価ということを主張する. ¶Please give it *further consideration.* なお御考慮願いたい. ¶*general considerations* 概論. ¶The subject is worthy of *grave consideration.* その問題はまじめに考える価値がある. ¶a *guiding consideration* 基調となる考慮. ¶on *humanitarian considerations* 人道上から. ¶a *humiliating consideration* 屈辱的な考え方. ¶upon an *impartial consideration* of the subject, it seems impossible to resist the conclusion that ... その問題については公平に考えてみて...という決論に達せざるを得ないように思われる ‖ if expense is an *important consideration* 費用が重要なことなら ‖ a further *important consideration* is ... さらに大切なことは...と言うことである. ‖ Tipping is an *important consideration* with the travelling public. 旅行者にとって心付は重要な問題である. ¶This theme has received so far in this country totally *inadequate consideration.* この問題はこれまでこの国では一向に考慮されていない. ¶*intelligent considerations* 理解ある同情. ¶*interested consideration* 我田引水の考え. ¶*kind considerations* 数々の心尽し ‖ I was never treated by him with the least degree of *kind consideration.* 私は彼からは少しも好意的には遇されなかった. ¶take *kindly consideration* of ... ...に目をかける. ¶It will be of interest to give a *little consideration* to it. 少しくそれを考察するも興味あることであろう. ¶the *main consideration* should be ... ...を要点とすべきである.【類】This should be the *main consideration* that should be before us when we are going on a journey. ¶a *material consideration* 物質的考慮(金品の報酬). ¶It is a question which still awaits our *mature consideration.* それは軽々に片付け得べき問題ではない ‖ in *mature consideration* とくと考えて. ¶The decision was not the sudden inspiration of the moment, but the result of *matured consideration.* この決意は一時の感激に励まされてできたのではなく熟考の末になったのである. ¶a very *minor consideration* ほんの第二義的な点. ¶It will be apparent on a *moment's consideration.* それはちょっと考えれば明かになる. ¶not *much consideration* has been given to ... ...には十分の考慮が払われていない. ¶*mundane considerations* 現世的な考慮. ¶*mutual consideration* 相互の思いやり. ¶a *necessary consideration* 必要な考慮. ¶where expense is *no consideration* at all 費用おかまいなしなら. ¶of *paramount consideration* 最大の考慮を要する. ¶The subject deserves more than *passing consideration.* その問題は通り一遍の考慮以上の価値がある. ¶No *personal consideration* must enter into this public affair. この公事に対しては私的な考えを許さない. ¶*practical considerations* 実際的考慮. ¶*preliminary considerations* 予備的考察. ¶a matter of *primary consideration* 最も考慮を要する事項. ¶His welfare is a *prime consideration.* 彼の幸福が第一に考慮すべき点である. ¶Health is of *prime consideration* with him. 健康は彼にとって最も考慮すべき点である. ¶That is the *principal* (=*chief or main*) *consideration.* それが主要の点である. ¶a matter of *private consideration* 情実. ¶get *prompter consideration* 一層迅速に考慮してもらう. ¶give *proper consideration* to ... ...にしかるべき考慮を払う. ¶Money is a *secondary consideration* with him. 金は彼に取っては第二の問題である. ‖ a thing of *secondary consideration* 第二義的な問題. ¶without the least *selfish consideration* 少しも利己的な考えなしに. ¶*sentimental considerations* 感傷的な考え. ¶give a matter *serious consideration* 真剣に考慮する.【類】require no *serious consideration* / deserve (=be worth) more *serious consideration.* ¶give it *slight consideration* in ... ...に重きをおかない. ¶give *special consideration* to ... ...に特別な考慮を払う ‖ solicit one's *special consideration* その特別の配慮を願う. ¶On *superficial consideration* one may think so. ちょっと考えるとそう思うでしょう. ¶The plan will receive *sympathetic consideration.* その考案は賛成されるでしょう. ¶on more *thorough consideration* one finds that... さらに深く考えて見ると...ということがわかる. ¶The suggestion deserves *thoughtful consideration.* その心添は慎重に考える価値がある. ¶treat them with the *utmost consideration* 精々注意して彼らを取扱う. ¶*Various considerations* have been taken into account. 色々な点を考慮に入れた. ¶a *weighty consideration* 重要な点.

Q² get a bill out of committee for *floor consideration* 議案を委員会から本会議に移す.

P *after* more mature *consideration* さらに熟考の上 ‖ *after* due *consideration* 十分考慮した上. ¶Intelligence and integrity stand *before* all other *considerations*. 理知と公正とは他の何物にも増して尊重すべきものである. ¶It is *beneath* the *consideration* of literature. それは文学と見なすには足らぬ. ¶I am restrained, *by consideration* of space, from ... スペースの関係で私は…に触れることは止めよう. ¶*for consideration* of time requirement 時間の都合もあって ‖ *For* your *consideration*, I enclose a clipping from the Japan Advertiser. 御参考までにジャパン・アドヴァータイザー紙の切抜を封入致します. ‖ That is a matter *for* your own *consideration*. それは君自身が考えるべき問題だ.【類】It is a matter *for consideration*. ‖ I persuaded him, *for* a *consideration*, to ... 金を出して彼に…させるように説き伏せた ‖ He might do so *for* a *consideration*. 彼は金を取ってならそうするかも知れない. ‖ *for* no *consideration* at all, in the case of poor ones 貧乏人の場合は全然無報酬で ‖ I will not do such a thing *for* any *consideration*. 僕は決してそんなことはしない. 【類】The manufacturers will not allow the option *for* any *consideration*. ‖ I spared him *from considerations* of mercy. かわいそうだから彼を許してやった. ‖ *from* a *consideration* of such ... as these, it is natural that ... …というような点から考えて, …は当然である. ¶*in consideration* of the money paid 払った金額から見ると ‖ He was pardoned *in consideration* of his youth. 彼は若いのに免じて許された. ¶This is not a heavy stone, its size being taken *into consideration*. この石は大きさの割に重くない. ¶To some passengers time is *of* more *consideration* than money. 乗客(船客)によっては金よりも時間の方が大事だ. ‖ It is *of* no *consideration*. それは重要でない. ¶*Out of consideration* for him I kept silence. 彼に免じて僕は黙っていた. ‖ leave the matter *out of consideration* そのことを問題にしない. ¶in the year now *under consideration* (=review) この調査の対象になっている年に ‖ This side of the question, however, is not *under consideration* here. しかし問題のこの点はここではふれていない. ‖ never, *under* any *consideration*, ... どうあっても…(してはいけ)ない ‖ have ... *under consideration* …は考慮中 ‖ the position for which one is *under consideration* 就こうとする地位. ¶*upon* better *consideration* 今になって考えると ‖ will not allow ... *upon* any *consideration* どうあっても…は許されない ‖ allow the option *upon consideration* of ... …を考慮して自由に選択させる. ¶*with consideration* for others 他人のことを頭に入れて ‖ *with* due *consideration* for ... …を適当に考慮して. ¶*without* due *consideration* 詮議もせずに ‖ He took the measure *without* the slightest *consideration* for the feelings of other people. 彼は他人の感情を少しも顧慮せずにその手段を取った.

P² He has no *consideration for* the age. 彼は老人に対する思いやりがない. ¶I commend it to the *consideration of* all anxious for the interests of Japan. この点日本の利益を念頭に持っているあらゆる人々の考察を促す. ‖ for *considerations of* space 余白が十分ないので ‖ *consideration of* a question 問題の討議.

consign, *v*. ゆだねる, 委託する.

P *consign* a letter *to* the wastepaper-basket 手紙を紙くずかごに棄てる ‖ It has been *consigned to* oblivion (=the limbo of forgotten things). それはもう忘れられてしまった. ‖ *consign* ... *to* the shelf=shelve ... …をたなに上げる ‖ *consign* a child *to* the care of ... 子供を…に預ける ‖ It was *consigned to* the flames. それは燃した. ‖ *consign* it *to* writing それを文書にする ‖ *consign* the body *to* the grave 死体を葬る ‖ *consign* a body *to* the flames (the water) 火(水)葬にする ‖ be *consigned to* prison 投獄される ‖ The vessel is to be *consigned to* our agents. 同船は当店の代理店に引渡すことになっている. 【類】He *consigned* his business to his brother's care. ‖ He wishes me to *consign to* your firm. 彼は小生が貴社に商品委託することを希望している.

consignment, *n*. 交付, 委託; 託送品.

V endeavor to *get* me the *consignment* その委託貨物を私の方で引受けるように努力する. ¶*receive* a new *consignment* 新規の託送品を受取る ‖ *secure* a *consignment* 出荷を確保する. ¶*send* one's *consignment* 託送貨物を送る. ¶*ship* a large *consignment* of electric apparatus for ... …に向けて電気機械の大口託送品を発送する. ¶*transfer* a *consignment* from ... to ... …から…へ出荷先を変更する.

P goods shipped *on consignment* 委託で発送した貨物 ‖ send goods *on consignment* 委託で荷を送る ‖ has ... on board *on* your *consignment* 貴下委託の…を積んでいる.

consist, *v*. …から成る; …に存する.

M *consist most* (*entirely*) of ... 大半(全部)…からなる. ¶Leadership *consists largely* in knowing people. 統率の要は主として人を知るにある. ¶Learning and personality do not always *consist together*. 学問と人格は常に両立するとは限らない.

P The true wealth does not *consist in* what we have, but *in* what we are.—Lord Avebury. 真の富は財産にあらずして人格にあり. ‖ *In* what does happiness *consist?* 幸福とは何ぞや. 【類】Snobbishness *consists in* attaching more importance to the social standing and financial competency of a person than to his character and personality. ‖ "Ebumi" *consisted in* making a person to trample under foot a portrait of Christ. 「絵踏」は人にキリストの肖像を足で踏ませることであった. ¶a farm *consisting of* ... acres …エーカーの農園 ‖ a club *consisting of* nearly 2,500 members 約二千五百人の会員を有するクラブ ‖ a cargo *consisting* chiefly *of* sundry goods 雑貨が主な船荷 ‖ the exhibits *consist of* ... 展覧物は…である. 【類】The family *consisted of* Henry, his wife, and three children. / the members of the advisory board *consist of* ... / The committee *consists of* five members. / The band *consisted of* violins and harps. / The menagerie (動物園) *consists of* elephants, lions, tigers, bears, leopards, hyenas, zebras, baboons, monkeys, etc. / The paper *consists of* eight pages. / The prizes in the games *consist of* medals and diplomas. / Lunch *consists of* hot tea or coffee, a nourishing soup, and some vegetable or meat. / a correspondence course *consisting of* twenty lessons / a lottery *consisting of* 125,000 tickets at £5 each / How many volumes does it *consist of*? ¶*consist with* principle その主義に一致する. ¶Prosperity *consists with* prudence. 繁栄は節約と両立する. 【類】Health *consists with* temperance (禁酒).

consistency, *n*. 一致, 首尾一貫.

V He is logical and *demands consistency*. 彼は物の考え方が論理的で首尾一貫を主張する.

Q a matter of *logical consistency* 理論的に筋の通っていること. ¶That would be *pushing consistency* too far. それでは余り徹底的過ぎるように思われる.

consistent, *a*. 両立する, 首尾一貫する.

P it is not *consistent for* him to ... …するのは彼にふさわしくない. ¶to be *consistent in* this plan to ... …しようというこの案を徹底させるためには ‖ He is not *consistent in* his action (statements). 彼の行動(など)は首尾一貫していない. 【類】He is not *consistent in* his statements. ¶*consistent with* national safety 国の安全に支障のない ‖ as briefly as is *consistent with* clearness 明りょうを欠かない限り簡単に ‖ infirmities *consistent with* senility 老年に付きものの病弱. 【類】It is not *consistent with* what you told me before. / You are not *consistent with* yourself.

consistently, *ad*. 両立して.

P War is always to be avoided, when it can be avoided *consistently with* duty and honor. 戦争は避けうる場合にはいつも避くべきであって決して義務と名誉はむじゅんしない.

consolation, *n*. 慰安, 慰め.

V *bring consolation* to ... …に慰安をもたらす. ¶can *derive* some *consolation* from ... …によっていく分慰められる. ¶*find consolation* in hard work 勤労に慰安を見出す ‖ You may *find* some *consolation* in the thought. そう思ったら幾分君の慰めになるかも知れない. ¶I *have* the *consolation* of knowing that ... …と言うことを知ってみずから慰めている. ¶*seek consolation* and encouragement in the thought that ... …と言う考えの中に慰安と激励を求める ‖ He *sought consolation* for his bereavement in traveling. 彼は近親を失った心のいた手を旅行で慰めようとした. ‖ They *sought* in morphine a *consolation* for their sorrows and disappointments. 彼らは悲嘆と失望に対する慰安をモルヒネに求めた.

Q It is but a *cold consolation*. それは心細い慰めにしかならない. ¶a *futile consolation* あだな慰め. ¶the one *mournful consolation* to be drawn from this unspeakable calamity is to be found in the belief that ... この言語に絶した災難から得られる唯一の痛ましい慰安は…と言う信念にこれを求めるほかはない. ¶It is a *poor consolation* to be told that others suffer as much as we do. 他の人もわれわ

れ同様やはり難儀するのだと聞かされても大した慰めにはならない. ¶a ***solitary*** (=***only***) *consolation* せめてもの心やり. ¶***spiritual*** *consolation* 精神的慰安.

P ***for*** one's *consolation* 慰めのために. ¶it is a great source ***of*** *consolation* to think that ......と考えることは非常な慰安の種である.

console, *v.* 慰める; 励ます.

M The news *consoled* them ***a great deal***. その便りで彼らは大いに元気づいた.

P The widow was *consoled* ***by*** her music. その未亡人は彼女の音楽で慰められた. ¶That *consoled* me ***for*** the loss. それでいくらか損害の埋合せになった.

consolidate, *v.* まとめる.

P the company is planning to *consolidate* its terminals ***in*** a huge block-square structure at ... その鉄道会社は…に四方街路に面した巨大な建物を造って数個所の終駅をこれにまとめようという計画を立てている. ¶be *consolidated* ***into*** one 合併して一つになる. ¶*consolidate* one's position ***with*** reinforcements 増援隊で陣地を堅める.

consonance, *n.* 調和, 一致.

P act ***in*** *consonance* with the requirements of the occasion 時宜に応じて取計らう. ¶an anachronism sadly ***out of*** *consonance* with the world's current of thought 世界の思潮と全然一致しない時代錯誤.

consonant, *n.* 〖発音〗子音.

Q ***guttural*** *consonants* [k, g などの]子音の喉(こう)頭音.

consonant, *a.* 調和する, 一致する.

M it is ***hardly*** *consonant* with ... それは…と調和し難い.

P This rule is quite *consonant* ***to*** reason. この規則は全く合理的だ. ¶travel at the most reasonable rates *consonant* ***with*** comfort and convenience 安楽と便利を犠牲にしないでしかも至極かっこうな料金で旅行する ‖ It is *consonant* ***with*** modern theories of individuality. それは近代個人主義と合致している.

consort, *n.* 配遇者.

Q^2 a ***prince*** (=king) *consort* 女王の夫君. ¶a ***queen*** *consort* 国王の皇配, 王妃.

consort, *v.* 調和する, 交わる.

M *consort* ***well*** with ... …とよく調和する.

P *consort* ***with*** each other 仲よく交わる ‖ a good-for-nothing brother who *consorts* ***with*** grooms and stablemen 馬丁や別当と仲間になっているやくざな兄(弟) ‖ *consort* (=associate) ***with*** criminals 犯罪者と交わる ‖ *consort* ***with*** medically inspected prostitutes 検ばいした売春婦を買う.

consortium, *n.* 資本合同.

P^2 a *consortium* ***of*** factories 工場財団.

conspectus, *n.* 概説.

Q give a ***good*** *conspectus* of ... の概略を知らせる.

conspicuous, *a.* 目立つ, 著しい.

P He was *conspicuous* ***among*** his comrades. 彼は同輩間で目立っていた. ¶Election enthusiasm is *conspicuous* ***by*** its absence. 選挙がばかに静かなのでかえって激戦ぶりが目立つ. 【類】In language-making, consistency is often *conspicuous* ***by*** its absence. ¶He was *conspicuous* ***for*** his honesty (gallantry). 彼は正直(など)できわ立っていた. ¶men *conspicuous* ***in*** public life 公人として著名な人. 【類】He stood *conspicuous* ***in*** every battle ***by*** his brilliant merits. ¶a fact *conspicuous* ***to*** British eyes 英人がすぐ気付く事実.

conspiracy, *n.* 共謀, 陰謀.

V ***form*** a *conspiracy* (=conspire) against his life 彼を殺害しようという陰謀を企てる. ¶***unmask*** a *conspiracy* 陰謀を暴露する.

Q a ***close-mouthed*** *conspiracy* 密謀.

P ***in*** *conspiracy* with ... …とぐるになって(共謀して).

P^2 a case of a sinister *conspiracy* ***against*** ... …を倒そうとする陰険な共謀事件. ¶*conspiracy* ***of*** silence 默殺の申合わせ.

conspirator, *n.* 共謀者, 陰謀者.

Q a ***dangerous*** *conspirator* 危険な陰謀者. ¶***vile*** *conspirators* 卑劣な陰謀者.

P a gang ***of*** *conspirators* 陰謀団.

conspire, *v.* 謀反を企てる, たくらむ.

P *conspire* ***against*** his life 彼を殺そうと計る ‖ *conspire* ***against*** the government (king) 政府(など)を倒そうと計る. ¶Many other causes *conspired* ***towards*** the result. その他色々の原因が一しょになってその結果を生んだ. ¶*conspire* ***with*** him 彼とたくらむ ‖ other causes *conspired* ***with*** the failure of ... …の失敗については他の原因も手伝った ‖ They *conspired* ***with*** him ***against*** us. 彼らは彼と共謀してわれわれに反抗した.

O All things *conspired* to make him prosperous. 色々のことが原因になって彼は成功した.

constable, *n.* 警官.

V ***fool*** the *constable* 警官をだます.

Q enroll about 200,000 ***special*** *constables* 特務警官を二十万召集する ‖ Every entrance to the park is guarded by police and ***special*** *constables*. 公園の入口にはどこも警官や特務巡査が張り番をしている.

Q^2 a ***plain clothes*** *constable* 平服の警官(捜査係). ¶a ***police*** *constable* =a policeman ‖ a judicial ***police*** *constable* 司法警察官.

constancy, *n.* 貞操, 節操.

V She ***has*** no *constancy* in love. 彼女には実(節操)がない. ¶***show*** *constancy* of love 操を立てる.

Q ***eternal*** *constancy* 久遠の貞節. ¶the ***heroic*** *constancy* of Christians キリスト教徒の勇敢な節義. ¶his ***unshaken*** *constancy* to her 彼の彼女に対する堅い操.

P^2 *constancy* ***in*** love 愛の誠. ¶The secret of success is *constancy* ***to*** purpose. 成功の秘訣は志望を変えぬことである.

constant, *a.* 変らない, 忠実な.

M ***as*** *constant* as the northern star 北極星のように不変な.

P *constant* ***in*** friendship 友情の変ることなく. ¶*constant* ***to*** tradition 伝統に忠実な ‖ *constant* ***to*** one's purpose 目的を一貫して. 【類】He is *constant* ***to*** his friends. / be *constant* ***to*** one's occupation (仕事).

constellation, *n.* 星座.

P^2 a *constellation* ***in*** the northern hemisphere 北半球の星座. ¶a *constellation* ***of*** beauties 一団の麗人.

consternation, *n.* 驚がく.

V ***feel*** *consternation* びっくり仰天する. ¶***occasion*** a *consternation* 人騒がせをする. ¶***raise*** a *consternation* in the hearts of ... の胸中に恐慌を来す. ¶The catastrophe ***spread*** a *consternation* throughout the city. その大災禍は全市を震がいさせた.

Q in ***great*** *consternation* 大恐慌を来して.

P ***in*** *consternation* 大いに驚いて. ¶***to*** one's *consternation* 驚いたことには. ¶***with*** *consternation* きもをつぶして.

P^2 *consternation* ***in*** diplomatic circles 外交界における驚がく.

constipation, *n.* 便秘.

V ***relieve*** the *constipation* by ounce doses of castor-oil ひまし油を一オンスずつ数回服用して便秘をなおす. ¶*constipation* ***alternating*** diarrhea 下痢と交互に起る便秘.

Q ***alternate*** *constipation* and diarrhea 交互に起る便秘と下痢. ¶***obstinate*** (=***stubborn***) *constipation* しつこい便秘.

P I suffer ***from*** *constipation*. 私は通じがない.

constituency, *n.* 選挙区, 地盤; 選挙区民.

V ***establish*** a *constituency* 地盤を造る. ¶***mend*** (=***patch up***) one's *constituency* [選挙で荒された]地盤を復元させる. ¶***nurse*** a *constituency* 地盤を育成する. ¶Party leaders "***stumped***" the *constituencies*. 党の幹部連が選挙区を遊説した.

Q^2 a ***three-member*** *constituency* 議員三名の選挙区.

P carry out the wishes of one's *constituency* 選挙区の要望を実現する.

constituent, *n.* 要素, 成分.

V It ***has*** three *constituents*. それには三要素がある.

Q Casein is the ***basal*** *constituent* of cow's milk. 乾酪素は牛乳の主成分である. ¶essential ***dietary*** *constituents* 食事の主要成分. ¶the ***ethnological*** *constituents* of the population 同国民の人種から見た成分. ¶three ***great*** *constituents* of modern education—the classics, modern history and literature, and science 現代教育の三主要学科すなわち古典・近代史と近代文学・及び科学. ¶Sugar is the ***main*** *constituent* of candy. キャンデーの主成分は砂糖である. ¶the ***predominant*** *constituent* 主成分. ¶the ***principal*** *constituent* 主成分.

Q^2 ***percentage*** *constituents* 百分比で示した成分.

constitution, *n.* (**1**) 体格, 体質.

V ***build up*** a strong *constitution* 体を丈夫にする. ¶***debilitate*** (=***weaken***) the *constitution* 体格を低下させる. ¶He ***has*** (=***possesses***) an iron *constitution* (=a constitution of iron). 彼は鉄のような体格をしている. ¶***rebuild*** a *constitution* 体格を改造する. ¶***shatter*** one's *constitution* 身体を台なしにする. ¶It does not ***suit*** my *constitution*. それは私の体質に合わない. ¶It may ***undermine*** a strong *constitution*. それでは丈夫な人でも健康を害するかも知れない.

Q have a ***cold*** *constitution* 冷え性だ. ¶a man of ***delicate*** *constitution* 蒲柳の質. ¶***feeble*** *constitution* 弱い体格. ¶He was of a ***fragile*** and ***delicate*** *constitution*. 彼は虚弱できゃしゃな体であった. ¶a ***frail*** *constitution* 虚弱な体格. ¶has a very ***healthy*** *constitution* いたって健康である. ¶receive from nature a *constitution* perfectly ***healthy*** すこぶる健康な体格を授かる. ¶a strong (weak) ***physical*** *constitution* 強(弱)い体質. ¶a ***poor*** *constitution* 貧弱な体格. ¶a ***robust*** *constitution* がん丈な体格. ¶a man of ***strong*** *constitution* がん丈な体格の人. ¶a ***tough*** *constitution* がん丈な体格. ¶He naturally possessed a ***vigorous*** *constitution*. 彼は天性丈夫な体格の持主であった. ‖ Despite his ***vigorous*** *constitution* his health began to fail under the multiplicity of duties. すこぶるエネルギッシュだが色々な仕事の重荷で健康が弱り出した. ¶a ***weak*** *constitution* 虚弱な体質. ¶I was born with a ***wiry*** *constitution*. 私は細くて丈夫な体に生れついている. ¶a tough ***wiry*** *constitution* 筋金入りの体躯.

Q^2 He wore out prematurely his ***cast-iron*** *constitution*. 彼は鋳鉄のような体を若い時に使い過ぎて弱くした. ¶He has ***iron*** *constitution*. 鉄のような(がん丈な)身体をしている.

(**2**) 憲法; 規約.

V ***confer*** a *constitution* to a country 国に憲法を布く. ¶***consolidate*** the *constitution* 組織を強固にする. ¶***draft*** a *constitution* 憲法を起草する. ¶***establish*** a *constitution* 憲法を制定する. ¶***grant*** a *constitution* 憲法を布かせる. ¶***promulgate*** a *constitution* 憲法を発布する. ¶***reform*** a *constitution* in a democratic direction 憲法を民主的な方向に改める. ¶***support*** and ***defend*** the *Constitution* 憲法を擁護する.

Q the ***Imperial*** *Constitution* 帝国憲法. ¶a "***made in America***" *constitution*「アメリカ製」の憲法. ¶an ***unwritten*** *constitution* 不文憲法. ¶a ***written*** *constitution* 成文憲法.

Q^2 a ***draft*** *constitution* 憲法草案.

P the movement for a revision ***of*** the *constitution* 憲法改正運動. ¶live ***under*** a *constitution* 憲政下に生活する. 【類】The New York Tammany Society was organized ***under*** a *constitution* in 1789.

P^2 The *Constitution* ***of*** Japan 日本国憲法. ¶the articles of the *Constitution* ***of*** the Club そのクラブの規約条項.

constitutional, *n.* 保養の散歩.

V ***take*** a *constitutional* 保養の散歩をする.

constitutionality, *n.* 立憲性.

V ***examine*** the *constitutionality* of legislative and administrative acts 立法・行政案の立憲性を審査する.

construct, *v.* 組立てる, 構成する.

M a well told and ***cleverly*** *constructed* story 話し方も巧いし筋もよくできている物語. ¶The story is ***skilfully*** *constructed*. その話は筋がよくできている.

P *construct* ***from*** it a smaller work それを土台にもっと小さな著作を編集する ‖ it was *constructed* ***from*** designs prepared by ... それは…の作製した設計によって建てられた. ¶*construct* a thing ***of*** some material ある材料で物を作り上げる. ¶it is *constructed* ***on*** the same principle as ... それは…と同一原則でできている. ¶*construct* a whole unit ***out of*** parts＝assemble parts into a whole unit 部分品を完成品に組立てる.

construction, *n.* 建設; 建築物; 構成, 構造; 解釈.

V ***defer*** non-essential *construction* 不急の建設を延ばす. ¶***employ*** bizarre *constructions* 奇異な作り方をする. ¶the ceremony of ***inaugurating*** the *construction* of a monument 記念碑建設の起工式. ¶***put*** a good *construction* on a man's action 人の行動を善意に解釈する. 【類】***put*** the best *construction* on the words and actions of others. ¶***superintend*** *construction* 建設工事を監督する. ¶***supervise*** the *construction* of houses and other buildings 家屋・建物の建築を監督する.

Q ***civil*** engineering and *construction* 土木建築. ¶a ***commercial*** *construction* 商売上(会社)の建物. ¶a ***defective*** *construction* 構文の不備. ¶the ***false*** *construction* of a sentence 構文の誤り. ¶place a ***favorable*** *construction* on ... …を先方の有利に解釈する. ¶a ***flimsy*** *construction* きゃしゃな建築物. ¶put a ***good*** (***bad***) *construction* upon his refusal 彼の拒絶を善(悪)意に解釈する. ¶showing ***inside*** *construction* 内部の構造を示して. ¶the projected ***naval*** *construction* 企画された海軍建設. ¶The new building is a very ***solid*** *construction*. 新建築はすこぶるがん丈な建物だ. ¶***speedy*** *construction* 突貫工事. ¶The text will admit of ***some other*** *construction*. この文はそれと違った解釈もできる. ¶wilfully put a ***wrong*** *construction* on ... …を故意に曲解する.

Q^2 ***aeroplane*** *construction* 飛行機の組立て. ¶project a plan of ***air base*** *construction* 空軍基地建設案を立てる. ¶materials for ***building*** *construction* 建築材料. ¶***concrete-building*** *construction* コンクリート・ビルの建築. ¶the major theories of ***curriculum*** *construction* カリキュラム(課程)構成の主なる理論. ¶the technique of ***film*** *construction* 映画製作の技術. ¶a ***masonry*** *construction* 石造の建物. ¶new ***public works*** *construction*＝new construction for public works 新しい公共建設事業. ¶***railroad*** *construction* 鉄道建設. ¶steam-rollers for ***road*** *construction* 道路建設用のスチームローラー. ¶a ***steel*** *construction* 鋼鉄の建物.

P It has been four years ***in*** *construction*. 建設に取りかかってから四年になる. ‖ It is of foreign style ***in*** *construction*. それは西洋式建築だ. ¶a bridge ***of*** recent *construction* 近ごろ掛けた橋. ¶railway lines ***under*** *construction* 目下敷設中の鉄道. 【類】Germany has now ***under*** *construction* four battleships of the Dreadnaught type at Stettin, Bremerhaven, Wilhelmshaven and Kiel respectively. / It has been ***under*** *construction* since last year.

constructor, *n.* 〘海軍〙造船技官.

Q a ***chief*** *constructor* 海軍作業監督官, 《米》海軍作業局長.

constructive, *a.* 建設的な.

P There is nothing *constructive* ***in*** his opinion. 彼の意見には何ら建設的なものがない.

construe, *v.* 解釈する, 翻訳する; 連用する; 〘文法〙文を組立てる.

M terms ***judicially*** *construed* and interpreted by the courts 裁判所で法的に解釈されている語. ¶In America the verb 'aim' is ***often*** *construed* with an infinitive. アメリカでは動詞 aim はしばしば不定詞とともに用いられる. ¶His remarks were ***wrongly*** *construed*. 彼の言は悪く解釈された.

P be *construed* ***as*** meaning ... …を意味するものと解する. ¶*construe* good English ***into*** bad Japanese りっぱな英語をへたな日本語に翻訳する ‖ It can be *construed* ***into*** having this meaning. それはこういう意味に解される. 【類】He *construed* this ***into*** an insult. ¶The verb 'abide' is *construed* ***with*** the preposition 'by.' abide なる動詞は by なる前置詞と連用される.

consult, *v.* 相談する; 参考する.

M They *consulted* ***long***, but could not decide. 彼らは長時間相談したがまとまらなかった. ¶the reader may ***profitably*** *consult* ... 読者は…を参考すれば得る所があろう.

P he has *consulted* us ***about*** ... 彼は…についてわれわれに相談した. 【類】He has *consulted* his physician ***about*** his health. ¶We *consulted* ***as to*** what should be done. われわれは善後策を講じた. ¶*Consult* me ***before*** acting. 行動に移る前に僕に相談し給え. ¶*Consult* your own convenience ***in*** the matter. そのことは都合のいいようになさい. ¶I wish to *consult* you ***on*** an important matter. 重要な件で貴下に御相談したい. ¶*Consult* me ***upon*** any matters connected with it. そのことは何でも私に相談なさい. ¶*consult* ***with*** one's pillow 寝て考える. 【類】*consult* ***with*** him ***about*** the matter / *consult* ***with*** a lawyer (attorney).

consultant, *n.* 顧問, 参与.

Q a ***political*** *consultant* 政治顧問.

Q^2 an ***artist*** *consultant* 芸術顧問. ¶a personal ***beauty*** *consultant* to the late Queen Marie of Rumania ルーマニアの故マリー女王付きの美容御用係. ¶an ***engineering*** *consultant* 技術顧問. ¶a ***laboratory*** *consultant* 研究所顧問. ¶Elmer Adler, former ***typography*** *consultant* for the New York Times. ニューヨーク・タイムス紙の前印刷技術顧問のエルマー・アドラー.

P^2 *consultants* ***of*** the volume 本書使用者.

consultation, *n.* 相談; 参考.

V *Consultations* can be ***arranged*** at other times by appointment. 相談は追って日をきめて協定することができます. ¶***facilitate*** *consultation* 楽に引けるようにする(辞書など). ¶***hold*** a *consultation* with him about ... …について彼と相談する.

Q through the ***arduous*** *consultation* of a dictionary 字引と首っ引きで. ¶after a ***brief*** *consultation* ちょっと診察して. ¶books for ***constant*** *consultation* 絶えず参考する書籍. ¶with ***constant*** *consultation* of the dictionary 字引と首っ

引きで. ¶The book is arranged alphabetically so that its contents are available for ***immediate*** *consultation.* 同書はABC順に排列してあるからその内容は即座に検索できる. ¶after a ***mutual*** *consultation* 互に相談の上. ¶a ***personal*** *consultation* 直談. ¶retire to another apartment for ***private*** *consultation* 内密の相談をしに別室に引込む.

Q² a ***family*** *consultation* 家庭相談.

P ***after*** much *consultation* with ... …と色々相談を重ねて. 【類】***after*** some *consultation.* ¶it can easily be learned ***by*** *consultation* with ... それは…に聞くとすぐわかる. ¶The rate of interest may be arranged ***by consultation.*** 利率は相談の上決められる. ¶Dr. Y. was called in ***for*** *consultation.* Y先生を呼んで診てもらった. ‖ How much do you charge ***for*** a *consultation?* 診察料は一回いくらですか. 【類】A specialist (専門医) was called in ***for*** *consultation.* ¶we are now ***in*** *consultation* with ... 目下…と交渉中.

P² *consultation* ***about*** one's personal affairs 身上相談.

consume, *v.* 焼き尽す; 消費する, 食べる.

M ***liberally*** *consume* green vegetables and raw and cooked fruits 野菜やなままたは料理した果物を十分食べる.

P The building was *consumed* ***by*** fire. 建物が焼失した. ¶She had *consumed* the best years of her life ***in*** custody. 彼女は女盛りを監禁のうちに過してしまっていた. ¶He is *consumed* ***with*** age. 彼は老齢でやせ衰えてしまった. ‖ *consumed* ***with*** love (envy, grief) 恋(など)で身をこがし. 【類】She looks *consumed* ***with*** jealousy.

consumer, *n.* 消費者.

Q ***immoderate*** *consumers* of tobacco たばこをのみ過ぎる人. ¶a ***mere*** *consumer* 生産をしない消費者.

Q² ***home*** *consumers* 国内消費者たち.

consummation, *n.* 成就, 完成.

Q ***practical*** *consummation* ほとんど完成.

consumption, *n.* (**1**) 消費, 消費額.

Q a ***daily*** *consumption* per head 一人一日の消費高. ¶Motion-picture production in Japan is solely for ***domestic*** *consumption.* 日本における映画製作は全く国内向けに過ぎない. ¶***industrial*** *consumption* of coal 石炭の工業における消費. ¶The work is not intended for ***popular*** *consumption.* この作品は大衆を目標としたものではない. ¶***small*** (***large***) *consumption* 小(大)消費. ¶Japan's ***total annual*** *consumption* of ... 日本の…年間消費高.

Q² cut ***coal*** *consumption* of power plants 発電所の石炭消費量を減らす. ¶for ***export*** *consumption* 輸出向けの. ¶per capita ***food*** *consumption* 一人当り消費食糧. ¶a ***fuel*** *consumption* of ... …の燃料消費高. ¶Goods for ***home*** *consumption* 国内消費物資. ¶goods for ***household*** *consumption* 家庭用消費物資. ¶for ***overseas*** *consumption* 国外向けの.

P² the *consumption* ***of*** alcohol in industry (drink) 工業用(など)としてのアルコールの消費.

(**2**) 肺病.

V There is the risk of ***catching*** *consumption.* 肺病がうつる危険がある. ¶***develop*** *consumption* 肺病になる. ¶He ***has*** *consumption.* 彼は肺病だ.

Q He had an illness which developed to ***galloping*** *consumption.* 彼は奔馬性肺結核になった. ¶the advance of ***inherited*** *consumption* 遺伝による肺病の進行.

P a remedy ***for*** *consumption.* 肺病の薬. ¶He worried (overworked) himself ***into*** *consumption.* 彼は気を使い過ぎて(過労で)肺病になった.

consumptive, *n.* 肺病患者.

Q a ***hereditary*** *consumptive* 遺伝性肺病患者.

contact, *n.* 接触.

V ***create*** understanding *contacts* between the races 各民族をして互に理解接触させる. ¶***establish*** *contact* with ... …と接触を保つ. 【類】The explorations enabled him to ***establish*** cultural *contacts* between China and the Near East, as far as Sicily and Egypt, as early as 5,000 years ago. ¶***have*** many *contacts* in the country 同国には多くの知己がある. 【類】He ***has*** some *contacts* in that company. ¶***make*** *contact* at ... …[という場所]で接触する. 【類】The Chinese first ***made*** *contact* with the Western peoples about the beginning of the Han dynasty (漢). ‖ A club is a place to ***make*** good *contacts.* クラブはよい交際を結ぶには好都合だ. ¶Japan ***needed*** stimulating *contacts* with the West. 日本は西洋と接触して刺激を受ける必要があった. ¶***regain*** *contact* with ... 以前のように…と接触する. ¶***retain*** one's *contact* with London ロンドンとの接触を続ける. ¶***strengthen*** cultural *contacts* between the two nations 二国民間の文化的接触を強固にする.

Q ***active*** *contact* with the world 世界との積極的接触. ¶be in ***close*** *contacts* with ... …と密接な関係にある. ¶people whose business take them into ***constant*** *contact* with the general public 接客業者. ¶be in ***continual*** *contact* with death 生死の間を往来する. ¶in ***daily*** *contact* with ... …と日々接触して. ¶by ***direct*** *contact* with events 種々の事件に直接接触して. ¶***English*** *contacts* with India 英国のインドとの接触. ¶The international tourist traffic helps to establish ***first-hand*** *contacts* with places and peoples. 国際観光は土地や国民との直接接触を助ける. ¶come into ***frequent*** *contact* with ... …としばしば接触する. ¶be in ***immediate*** *contact* with ... …と直接接触している. ¶They are in ***intimate*** *contact* with modern ideas. 彼らは現代思想に親しんでいる. ¶a salesman of ***many*** *contacts* 顔の広いセールスマン. ¶have ***numerous*** *contacts* with undergraduates 学生と接触が多い. ¶***Personal*** *contact* of the peoples of various countries is a safeguard for world peace. 諸国民の個人的接触は世界平和の保障となる. 【類】come in ***personal*** *contact* with ... ‖ I well remember a few days of my ***personal*** *contact* and exchange of ideas with him. 私は親しく彼に接して意見を交換した二三日をはっきり記憶している. 【類】His greatness is only fully felt by direct ***personal*** *contact.* ¶students' ***social*** *contacts* 学生の社会との接触. ¶maintain certain ***useful*** *contacts* with the underworld [警察官などが]ギャング仲間と顔をつないでおく.

Q² ***culture*** *contacts* between the two nations 両国間の文化交流. ¶be out of ***radio*** *contact* with ... …とのラジオ(無線)の連絡ができない所にある. ¶***sales*** *contacts* 販売方面(買手筋). ¶make more than ***surface*** *contact* with ... …と上っつらだけでなくもっと深い接触をする. ¶***wire*** *contact* [電話の]混線.

P ***by*** *contact* with .... …との接触により ‖ a disease communicated ***by*** *contact* 接触伝染性の病気. ¶keep ***in*** *contact* with the enemy 敵と内通している ‖ Children instinctively like to be ***in*** *contact* with mother earth. 子供らは本能的に大地に触れることを好む. ‖ come ***in*** (=into) *contact* with ... …と接触する. ¶bring the learner ***into*** direct *contact* with it 学習者を直接それに接触させる ‖ he was thrown ***into*** *contact* with ... 彼は…と接触させられた. ¶severance ***of*** all *contacts* with it それとの一切の接触絶縁. ¶Radium is a silver-white metal, which tarnishes rapidly ***on*** *contact* with air. ラジウムは銀白色の金属で空気にふれると直ちに曇る. ‖ The fluid secretion discharged by the silkworm in its larval stage solidifies ***on*** *contact* with air and forms the silk of its cocoon. 蚕が幼虫時代に出す分泌液は空気にふれると凝固してその繭の絹糸になる.

P² have no *contact* ***among*** foreign residents 在留外人とは何らの交渉がない. ¶*contact* ***between*** two 二者(物)の接触. ¶*contact* ***of*** one thing ***with*** another 一物と他物の接触. 【類】the beginning of *contact* ***with*** Western civilization (西欧文明) / *contact* ***with*** life (nature).

contagion, *n.* 伝染, 感染.

V ***spread*** *contagion* 伝染を拡大する. ¶***stop*** the *contagion* 伝染を防止する. ¶You will ***take*** the *contagion.* その病気がうつりますぞ.

P It was spread as if ***by*** *contagion.* それはまるで伝染するように広まった.

contagious, *a.* 伝染する.

M It is ***highly*** *contagious.* それには非常に伝染性がある. ¶Yawning is ***so*** *contagious,* isn't it? あくびはほんとにうつりやすいわね.

contagiousness, *n.* 伝染性.

P It spread ***by*** the *contagiousness* of example. それは模倣的に広まった.

contain, *v.* 入れる; [感情を]抑える.

P I couldn't *contain* myself ***for*** joy. よろこびを抑えることができなかった. ¶*contained* ***in*** the report 報告書に記載の ‖ 3 is *contained* ***in*** 9 three times 九の中に三が三つある.

container, *n.* 容器.

Q² an empty ***beer*** *container* 空っぽのビールの容器(びんやかんなど). ¶a ***film*** *container* フイルム容器. ¶a ***food*** *container* 食料品容器. ¶an ***incense*** *container* 香入れ. ¶a ***liquor*** *container* 酒類の入れもの. ¶a ***plant*** *container* 植木ばち. ¶icecream in a ***thermos*** *container* (=bottle, flask *or* vessel) 魔法びんに入れたアイスクリーム. ¶a ***tinplate** container* ブリキ容器.

contamination, *n.* 汚れ; 悪影響.

V be kept clean to ***avoid** contamination* 汚れがつかないように清潔にしておく.

P² the *contamination* ***of*** European civilization 欧州文明の悪影響.

contemplation, *n.* 観察; 沈思; 企図.

Q an ***aesthetic** contemplation* 審美的観照. ¶In ***legal** contemplation* "he" sometimes means "she," and sometimes they embrace each other. 法律上の解釈では「彼」は時に「彼女」を意味しまた一方が他方の意味を含めて用いられることもある.

P I have a new work ***in** contemplation.* 私は新事業を目論んでいる. ‖ He was lost ***in** contemplation.* 彼は夢中になって考え込んでいた. 【類】He was absorbed ***in** contemplation.* ‖ ***in*** the *contemplation* of ... ...を十分考慮して. ¶a new school-building now ***under** contemplation* 目下計画中の新校舎.

contemporaneous, *a.* 同時の.

P The discovery of America was *contemporaneous* ***with*** the fall of Granada. 米国発見はグラナダの陥落と同時代であった.

contemporary, *n.* 同時代の人; 同業者.

V² our *contemporaries* ***say*** that ... 同業紙いわく.

Q our ***enterprising** contemporary* わが進取的の同業紙. ¶our ***esteemed*** and ***excellent** contemporary* 貴紙(同業紙にあてた手紙などで). ¶***literary** contemporaries* 文学上の同業者たち.

Q² a ***home** contemporary* 本国の新聞(同業者).

P² *contemporaries* ***at*** school 同期生. ¶his *contemporaries* ***in*** the profession 彼の同業者. ¶a *contemporary* ***of*** ... ...と同時代の人.

contemporary, *a.* [新聞]同年代の.

P he was *contemporary* ***with*** ... 彼は...と同時代であった.

contempt, *n.* 侮辱, 軽べつ; 恥辱.

V Familiarity ***breeds** contempt.* なれると軽べつ心が起る. ¶***bring** contempt* upon the family name 家名に泥を塗る. ¶***conceal*** one's *contempt* 軽べつを表に出さない. ¶***deserve*** the *contempt* of ... ...に軽べつされるのも無理はない. ¶***disguise*** a *contempt* 軽べつを色に出さない. ¶***experience*** the *contempt* of others 他人に見くだされる. ¶***express*** a *contempt* for ... ...に対して軽べつの意を示す. ¶***feel** contempt* for ... ...を軽べつする. ¶***have*** a *contempt* of death 死を物ともしない. ¶he ***has*** a fine *contempt* for ... 彼は...をひどく軽べつしている ‖ I ***have*** a great *contempt* for him. 私は彼を大いに卑しんでいる. ¶***pour** contempt* on ... 盛んに...をくさす. ¶He tossed his head to ***show** contempt.* 彼は頭を振って軽べつの意を示した. ‖ You dare to ***show*** your *contempt* of this court! お前はこの法廷を侮辱するのか. ¶***throw** contempt* on ... ...を侮辱する.

Q ***criminal** contempt* of court 法廷侮辱罪. ¶He treated them with ***disguised** contempt.* 彼は軽べつをあらわには出さずに彼らを取扱った. ¶smile with ***indulgent** contempt* 少し軽べつの意味を含めて微笑する. ¶a ***mild** contempt* 軽い侮べつ. ¶He had a ***profound** contempt* for death. 彼は死を何とも思っていなかった. ¶***social** contempt* 社会の軽べつ. ¶a ***studied** contempt* 故意の侮辱. ¶He looked at me with ***undisguised,*** though ***mild,*** *contempt.* 彼は軽いながらもむきだしの軽べつを目に浮べて私を眺めた. ¶has a ***supreme** contempt* for ... ...に対し絶大の侮べつを持つ. ¶the ***utmost** contempt* 思い切った軽べつ. ¶a thinly ***veiled** contempt* しいて隠そうともしない軽べつ.

P His attitude is certainly ***above** contempt.* 彼の態度はたしかに軽べつできぬ. ¶His conduct is ***beneath** contempt.* 彼の行動は卑しむにも足らない. ¶***for** contempt* of its authority その権威をべっ視して ‖ ***for** contempt* of court 法廷侮辱の故をもって. ¶hold a person ***in** contempt* 人をべっ視する ‖ He was held ***in*** universal *contempt.* 彼はだれからも軽べつされた. ‖ He refused to answer ***in** contempt* of the rules of court. 彼は法廷の規則を無視して返答を拒んだ. ‖ call him a fool ***in** contempt* 彼をあなどってばかと呼ぶ ‖ gaze ***in** contempt* upon ... ...を軽べつの目で眺める. ¶It will bring him ***into** contempt.* 彼はそんなことをすると軽べつを受けるだろう. ‖ fall ***into** contempt* 恥辱をこうむる. ¶a gesture (smile) ***of** contempt* 軽べつの身振(など). ¶reject it ***with** contempt* それを軽べつしてしりぞける.

P² *contempt* ***for*** conventionality (grammar, the world's praises) 因襲(など)に対する軽べつ.

contemptible, *a.* 卑しむべき.

P He is *contemptible* ***for*** his meanness. 彼の卑劣は卑しむべきだ.

contend, *v.* 争う, 闘う; 主張する.

M he ***rightly** contends* that ... 彼が...と主張するのは当然だ. ¶***steadfastly** contend* against ... 断固として...と争う.

P *contend* ***about*** trifles ちっぽけなことを争う. ¶*contend* ***against*** an obstacle (opponent, misfortune², one's fate²) 障害(など)と闘う. 【類】No hero can *contend* ***against*** disease. ¶*contend* ***for*** its possession それを得ようと争う ‖ *contend* ***for*** a prize (principle, truth, an object) 賞品(など)のために努力する. 【類】*contend* ***for*** the faith (信仰). ¶*contend* ***in*** words 言葉で争う. ¶The frost is the greatest enemy the fruit-growers have to *contend* ***with.*** 霜は果樹栽培家に取って最大の敵である. ‖ I had to *contend* ***with*** difficulties 困難と闘う. 【類】*contend* ***with*** fogs and contrary winds (霧や逆風と闘う) / *contend* ***with*** fate / *contend* ***with*** an antagonist ‖ They *contended* ***with*** each other ***for*** the prize. 彼らは互に賞品を競った. 【類】the difficulties ***with*** which a film director (映画監督) has to *contend* ‖ *contend* ***with*** others ***for*** a prize 賞を目当てに競う.

O I will *contend* that ... 私は...と主張したい.

contender, *n.* 競争相手.

Q a 1948 ***Presidential** contender* 一九四八年度指名大統領立候補者. ☞ 政党の国民大会で大統領候補の指名を受けた者を Presidential candidate という.

content, *n.* **(1)** 満足.

V ***express** content* 満足の意を表する.

Q a ***fatuous** content* with existing conditions 現状に対するたわいない(無反省な)満足. ¶I will give you your ***full*** *centent.* 十分御満足になるように致しましょう. ¶in ***perfect*** *content* 全く満足して.

P Amuse yourself ***to*** your heart's *content,* after having worked so well. そんなによく勉強したのだから思う存分楽しみなさい. ‖ I ate ***to*** my heart's *content.* 私は思う存分食べた.

(2) 内容.

V I am not at liberty to ***divulge*** the *contents* of the message. その通信の内容は漏らしかねる. ¶***enrich*** the *content* of education 教育の内容を豊富にする. ¶I ***find*** the *contents* very useful to me. その[本の]内容は非常に役に立つ. ¶***note*** the *contents* of a letter 手紙の内容に目を通す. ¶***sell*** by auction the *contents* of the residence of the late ... 故...邸の家財を競売する.

Q the ***abdominal** contents* 内臓. ¶the ***high** content* of iron 高率の鉄の含有量. 【類】nickel ores, with ***high** content* in copper and in minerals of the platinum group. ¶***net*** *contents* 8 oz. 正味八オンス入り. ¶A bag with its ***precious*** *contents* was missing. 貴重品のはいっている袋が紛失していた. ¶The percentage of the ***total thermal** content* of coal which can be utilized is yet very low. 利用しうる石炭の全熱量の百分比率はまだ至って低い.

Q² ***alcohol** content* アルコール分. ¶maintain a satisfactory ***calory** content* in food 食物の十分なカロリーを確保する. ¶the ***carbonic acid gas** content* in the air 空気の炭酸ガス含有量. ¶the ***corn flour** content* of bread パンのコンスターチ含有量. ¶increase the ***humus** content* of the soil 腐植土の含有量をふやす. ¶goods with a high ***labor*** *content* 生産に多大の労力を要した商品. ¶The ***moisture*** *content* of the soil is high (low). 土壌の湿度は多(少)い. ¶make studies of ***newspaper** content* 新聞の記事を研究する. ¶***thought** content* 思想内容. ¶the ***vitamin D** content* of the milk 牛乳のビタミンDの含有量. ¶***water** content* 水分.

P The French newspaper is always six pages ***in** content.* フランスの新聞は通例内容が六ページある.

P² What are the *contents* ***of*** this trunk? このトランクには何がはいっていますか ‖ the *contents* ***of*** a telegram 電報の内容 ‖ The *content* ***of*** this can is enough to prepare 15 to 40 "after dinner" cups. このかん一個で食後のココア(など)が十五杯から四十杯できます. ‖ The *contents* ***of*** your letter of ... are very satisfactory. ...日付のお手紙拝見誠に満足に存じます.

content, *a.* 満足して.

M He is ***quite** content.* 彼はすっかり満足している. ¶Let us be ***well** content* to have been pioneers. 先駆者であったというだけで十分満足していようじゃないか.

P be *content* ***with*** one's present fortune 現在の境遇に甘んじる ‖ be *content* ***with*** honest poverty 清貧に安んじる ‖ I am *content* ***with*** a little. 私はわずかなもので満足している. ‖ There should be no resting *content* ***with*** such a small success. こんな小成に安んじていてはいけない.

content, *v.* 満足する, 満足させる.

P *content* oneself (=be *contented*) ***with*** one's lot 自分の運命に満足する ‖ be *contented* ***with*** a low salary 薄給に甘んじる ‖ be *contented* ***with*** small success 小成に安んじる. 【類】I must *content* myself ***with*** stating that ...

contention, *n.* 争い, 論争, 論点.

V My *contention* was ***disallowed.*** [競技などで]私の苦情は通らなかった. ¶in order to ***establish*** my *contention,* it will, I think, be sufficient to ... 私の論点をはっきりさせるには...いうだけで十分だろうと思う. ¶even if we ***grant*** his *contention* that ... よし彼の...という論旨を認めるとしても... ¶His article is foreign to *contentions* ***raised*** by myself in your columns. 彼の寄稿は私自ら貴紙に持ち出した論争に関係がない. ¶***refute*** the *contention* that ... ...という議論を反ばくする. ¶***strengthen*** one's *contention* by ... ...によってその論拠を強固にする. ¶he ***supports*** his *contention* by allusion to the fact that ... 彼は...という事実に言及して自説の支えにしている. 【類】***support*** his *contention* by a document.

Q ***bold*** *contention* 大胆な議論. ¶There were ***fierce*** *contentions* on the subject. その問題について激論が戦わされた.

P I admit, ***without*** *contentions,* that ... 私は異議なく...といいうことを認める.

P² a *contention* ***about*** ... ...についての争い. ¶a *contention* ***in*** words 論争. ¶a *contention* ***with*** a person 人との争い.

contentment, *n.* 満足.

V ***find*** *contentment* in ... ...に満足する. ¶His smiling face ***radiates*** *contentment.* 彼はいかにも満足そうににこにこしている.

Q ***manifest*** *contentment* 明白な満足. ¶in ***perfect*** *contentment* 大満足で.

contest, *n.* 競争, 競技(コンクール), 論争.

V The signal to ***begin*** or to ***end*** a *contest* was a pistol-shot. 競技の始めと終りの合図はピストルであった. ¶***decide*** a *contest* between ... ...間の論争を解決する. ¶***enter*** the *contest* その競技に加わる. ¶***hold*** a *contest* to decide who gets it だれがそれを獲得するか勝負をやる. ¶***inaugurate*** a prize essay *contest* 懸賞論文の募集を開始する. ¶the *contest* will be ***judged*** by ... その競技は...が審判をやる. ¶The newspaper is now ***running*** an enormous scenario *contest.* 同新聞社は目下大掛りな映画脚本募集をやっている. ¶The *contest* was ***staged*** on the Waseda University athletic field. その競技は早稲田大学の運動場で行われた. ¶He ***won*** the international *contest* for jumping. 彼はそのジャンプの国際競技に勝った.

V² The *contest* ***closes*** on December 15, 1926. その懸賞は一九二六年十二月十五日に締切る.

Q an ***athletic*** *contest* 運動競技. ¶a ***bitter*** *contest* over ... ...についてのはげしい競争. ¶a ***close*** *contest* 互角の競争. ¶a ***decisive*** *contest* 決戦. ¶a ***great aquatic*** *contest* (短艇競争などの)水上大競技. ¶a ***hard*** *contest* 激しい競争. ¶the ***international*** *contest* for commercial supremacy 商業覇(は)権の世界的競争. ¶a ***nation-wide*** *contest* for articles on social work 社会事業に関する論文の全国的懸賞. ¶an ***oratorical*** *contest* 雄弁競技会. ¶a ***parliamentary*** *contest* 議員選挙の競争. ¶***pedestrian*** *contest* 競歩. ¶a ***sharp*** *contest* 激烈な競争. ¶a ***spirited*** *contest* 活気ある競争. ¶The *contest* was too ***unequal*** to last long. その競争は双方の力が不釣合であったので長く続かなかった. ¶after a ***vigorous*** *contest* 猛烈な競争の揚句.

Q² a ***beauty*** *contest* 美人コンクール. ¶a ***bird-calling*** *contest* 鳥の吹き寄せ競技. ¶a ***career*** *contest* 就職試験. ¶a ***composition prize*** *contest* 懸賞作文募集. ¶a ***dueling*** *contest* 決闘. ¶an ***eating*** *contest* 食いくらべ. ¶an ***essay*** *contest* 論文募集. ¶a ***hair-dressing*** *contest* 女の結髪コンクール. ¶***inter-class*** *contests* クラス間のコンクール. ¶an ***intra-plant*** *contest* 工場内の競技. ¶a ***javelin-throwing*** *contest* やり投げ競技. ¶a ***judging*** *contest* 品評会. ¶a ***leg-beauty*** *contest* 脚線美コンクール. ¶a ***model plane*** *contest* 模型飛行機競技会. ¶***path*** *contests* at various distances 色色距離の違った競歩. ¶a ***pingpong*** *contest* (=tournament) ピンポン試合(大会). ¶a ***poster*** *contest* ポスターコンクール. ¶a ***prize*** *contest* for ... ...の懸賞コンクール. 【類】a ***prize medal*** *contest.* ¶a ***prize speaking*** *contest* 懸賞演説大会. ¶a ***quiz*** [***show***] *contest* 《ラジオ》クイズコンテスト. ¶an impromptu ***speaking*** *contest* 即席弁論大会. ¶a ***sports*** (=***sporting***) *contest* 運動競技大会. ¶a ***tug-of-war*** *contest* 綱引競争. ¶a ***water*** *contest* 水上競技. ¶a ***will*** *contest* 遺言状の争い. ¶the 1955 "***World's Most Beautiful Legs***" *contest* 一九五五年度の世界脚線美大会.

P ***in*** the *contest* in the House of Commons upon the question of ... 下院における...の問題に関する論戦で ‖ the participants ***in*** the *contest* その競技参加者 ‖ engage (=take part) ***in*** a *contest* 競技に参加する.

P² a *contest* ***against*** an opponent 相手との競争. ¶a *contest* ***at*** boxing 拳闘試合. ¶a *contest* ***between*** the two その両者間の競争 ‖ a *contest* ***between*** opposing armies 敵味方の対戦. ¶a *contest* ***for*** prizes 懸賞コンクール. ¶a *contest* ***of*** wits 知恵競べ ‖ a *contest* ***of*** words 舌(筆)戦 ‖ the *contest* ***of*** power between Russia and America 米・ソ間の勢力争い. ¶enter singly into a *contest* ***with*** ... ...との戦に単身乗出す.

contest, *v.* 競争する.

M The prize was ***hotly*** *contested.* その懸賞は激しく競争が行われた. ¶be ***successfully*** *contested* ... [国会議員など]首尾よく...から選出される.

P *contest* a seat ***for*** Parliament 《英》議員選挙をやる.

contestant, *n.* 競争者; [コンクールの]出場者.

Q a ***formidable*** *contestant* 恐るべき相手. ¶a ***successful*** *contestant* in a competition 競争の勝利者.

Q² a ***leg-beauty*** *contestant* 脚線美コンクールの出場者. ¶America's ***marathon*** *contestants* アメリカのマラソン選手たち.

P The judges vote on the designs without knowing the names ***of*** the *contestants.* 審査員たちは参加者の名も知らずにそのデザインに投票する.

context, *n.* 文脈.

P learn their meanings ***from*** the *context* 文の前後から意味をとる.

contiguous, *a.* 隣接した.

P houses *contiguous* ***to*** cemeteries 墓地に隣接する家屋 ‖ The houses are *contiguous* ***to*** each other. その両家は隣接している.

continence, *n.* 禁欲.

V ***practice*** *continence* 禁欲を実行する.

continent, *n.* 大陸.

Q the two greatest cities of the two ***American continents*** 米二大陸における最大の二都. ¶the ***European Continent*** 欧州本土.

P travellers ***on*** the *continent* 大陸の旅行者 ‖ There is really very little use of the motor-car for pleasure purposes ***on*** the *Continent* by the natives.—The Sphere. [ヨーロッパ]大陸では本国人は遊覧のために滅多に自動車を用いない.

P² the *continent* ***of*** Europe 欧州大陸.

contingency, *n.* 偶然のこと, 不慮のこと.

V ***meet*** accidental *contingencies* 不慮のできごとに会う.

V² if such a *contingency* ***arises*** そんな事故が起きれば.

Q The "air age" was a ***remote*** *contingency* no longer. 空中時代は最早遠い未来の夢ではなかった.

contingent, *n.* 不慮のできごと.

Q² a ***future*** *contingent* 未来に起るべき不慮のでき事.

contingent, *a.* 偶然の, 不慮の; ...次第の.

P It is *contingent* ***on*** success. それは成否いかんによって決まる. ¶Such risks are *contingent* ***to*** the travel. この種の危険は旅行の際に起らぬとも限らない. ¶The method is always *contingent* ***upon*** aims and details. 方法は常に目的や細目次第で決まる.

continuance, *n.* 継続, 持続.

V We have ***had*** a *continuance* of bad harvests. 不作続きであった. ¶I shall be most happy to ***receive*** a *continuance* of your favors. 引続き御愛顧にあずかりますれば幸甚の至りであります. ¶***solicit*** a *continuance* of your custom (=patronage) 相変らずお引立を願います.

continuation, *n.* 継続.

P² the *continuation* ***of*** a story 話の続き ‖ a *continuation* ***of*** good (bad) harvests 豊(不)作の連続.

continue, *v.* 続く, 続ける.

M It *continued* ***an hour*** 一時間続いた. 【類】The rain *continued* [for] ***three days.*** ¶I hope it will *continue* ***fine.*** 天気が続けばよいが. ¶The market-price of rice *continues* ***firm.*** 米の相場は引続き堅調である. ¶The fog ***still*** *continues.* まだ霧が晴れない. ‖ ***still*** *continue* in demand まだ需要がある. ¶*continue* ***upward*** 上向きを続ける. ¶He *continues* ***well.*** 相変らず丈夫です.

M² *continue* ***down*** to these days 今に続いている. 【類】This custom *continues* ***down*** to the present time. ¶Business will *continue* ***on*** as usual. 商売は相変らず行われる

だろう。

P I *continued at* the work of translation. 翻訳の仕事を継続した. ‖ *continue at* work far into the night 夜おそくまで仕事を続ける. ¶The earthquake *continued for* about ten minutes. 地震は十分ほど続いた. ¶*Continued from* yesterday. きのうの続き(新聞記事などの断り書き). ‖ *continued from* [the] previous page (preceding column) 前ページ(など)の続き. ¶The market *continues in* a very depressed state. 市場は相変らず不況だ. ¶*continue in* the government of the empire 同帝国の支配は継続している ‖ *Continued in* next column. [新聞の記事など]次の欄へ続く. ‖ He *continues in* his bad behaviour. 彼は相変らず不品行だ. *continue in* power 引続き政権の座にいる. 【類】 *continue in* command. ¶The habit *continued into* adult life. その癖は大人になっても直らなかった. ‖ This hostility has *continued into* our own day. この敵対は今日も継続している. ¶*continue on* one's course (=way) 自己の方針を続ける ‖ *Continued on* page 15 (next page). 十五ページ(など)へ続く. ¶The publication *continued through* twenty years. その刊行物は二十年間発行を続けた. ¶This practice has *continued to* the present. この慣習は現在まで継続してきた. ‖ allow a pregnancy to *continue to* its term 胎児を十分生長させる. ¶The Exhibition will *continue until* August. 博覧会は八月まで続く. 【類】 It *continues until* the present day. ¶Bacteriology *continues* today *with* its patient, useful work. 細菌学は今日もその忍耐強い有益な仕事を継続している. ‖ *continue* (=go ahead) *with* one's work (study, meal, luncheon) 仕事(など)を続ける.

continuity, *n.* 連続, 継続.

V *break* the *continuity* of ... ...を中断する. ¶It can be cut out without *harming* the *continuity* of the story. それは削除しても話の筋の続きには障りはない.

Q the *stable* and *wonderful continuity* of the Imperial Line 皇統の盤石にしてかつ驚嘆すべき万世一系.

P² a *continuity of* application 絶え間ない勤勉.

contort, *v.* ゆがめる; 曲解する.

P *contort* a passage *out of* its proper meaning 一節の本来の意味を故意に曲解する. ¶a face *contorted with* pain 苦痛でゆがんだ顔.

contortion, *n.* ゆがみ, 曲解.

V *make contortions* of the face 顔をゆがめる.

contour, *n.* 輪郭, 概略.

V *follow* the *contour* of ... ...の外郭をたどる. ¶*sketch* (=*draw*) the *contours* of ... ...の輪郭を描く.

P² the *contour of* a face 顔の輪郭 ‖ the *contours* of things 情勢 ‖ The *contour* (=outline) *of* the Atlantic coast is very irregular. 大西洋岸の外郭線はすこぶる出入りが多い.

contraband, *n.* [戦時]禁制品.

V *seize* (=*capture*) *contraband* 禁制品をだ捕する.

P² *contraband of* war 〖国際法〗戦時禁制品.

contract, *n.* 契約; 婚約.

V *accept* a *contract* 契約を承諾する. ¶*annul* a *contract* 契約を破談にする. ¶*break* his *contract* with ... ...との彼の契約を破棄する. ¶*cancel* a *contract* 契約を解除する. ¶*close* a *contract* 契約を結ぶ. ¶No *contract* has yet been *concluded.* まだ何ら契約が成立していない. ¶*dissolve* a marriage *contract* 婚約を破談にする. ¶*draw up* a *contract* 契約書を作製する. ¶*effect* a *contract* with ... ...と協定を遂げる. ¶*enforce* one's *contract* 約束を実行する. ¶*execute* (=*carry out*) one's *contract* 契約を実行する. ¶*fill* a *contract* according to a specification 明細書によって契約条件をみたす. ¶*fulfil* one's *contract* to ... ...との契約事項を実行する. ¶*get off* (=obtain a release from) a *contract* 契約を取消す. ¶*give* a *contract* to a shipbuilding yard to build a steamer 汽船建造を造船所に請負わせる. 【類】 Almost immediately afterward Paramount *gave* me a *contract.* ¶*give out* a *contract* for the construction of a large quay 大波止場の建築を請負仕事に出す. ¶*let out* a *contract* 契約を破棄する. ¶*make* a *contract* for ... with ... ...に対する契約を...との間にする. 【類】 *make* a *contract* for a supply of ... / He *made* a *contract* to supply coal at 1,500 yen a ton. ¶*make* a fresh *contract* あらたに契約を結ぶ. ¶faithfully *observe* a *contract* 協約を忠実に守る. ¶*perform* a *contract* 契約を履行する. ¶*place* a *contract* with English firms for the supply of ... ...の供給に対して英国商会と契約を結ぶ. ¶*receive* a *contract* from ... ...から請負う. ¶*renew* the *contract* we had with ... われわれが...と結んだ契約を更新する. ¶*repeal* a *contract* 契約を取消す. ¶*rescind* a *contract* 契約を解除する. ¶*secure* the *contract* for ... ...の請負仕事を手に入れる. ¶*settle* a *contract* with ... ...と契約を取りきめる. ¶*sign* a *contract* with ... ...との契約書に署名する ‖ *sign* a *contract* agreeing to the conditions その条件に同意して契約書に署名する. 【類】 the film actor *signed* a new *contract* with ... ‖ upon *signing* the *contract* その契約を結ぶに当って. 【類】 after *signing* the *contract* / the *contract signed* by the Government with ... for ... ¶This contract shall *supersede* all previous *contracts* and agreements. 本契約の発効により従来の契約および協定はすべて無効とする. ¶*contracts taken* for ... ...のためにやった請負. ¶*throw up* his *contract* with ... ...との彼の契約を棄てる. ¶*undertake* a *contract* 仕事を請負う. ¶*vitiate* a *contract* 契約を無効にする.

V² drop all advertising as the *contracts expire* 契約の期限が切れると同時に広告を一切やめる. ¶The *contract holds* good. 契約は有効である. ¶The *contract* is to *run.* その契約は継続することになっている. ¶The *contract* will not *stand.* 契約が有効でない.

Q a *definite contract* will be closed within ... 契約が...以内に確立するでしょう. ¶a *fat contract* 益になる契約. ¶a *formal contract* 形式上の約束. ¶a *hard* and *fast contract* 確実な契約. ¶The prices become lower under *large contracts.* 大量契約では値段が安くなる. ¶a *legally binding contract* 法律上有効の約束. ¶a *preliminary contract* has been signed by ... on the one hand, and ... on the other 予備契約書が一方...により他方...によって署名された. ¶by *private contract* or arrangement 個人契約もしくは協定により. ¶by a *public contract* 公の契約により. ¶The *contract* is *ready* for signature. 契約書は署名するばかりになっている. ¶The aviator is under a *seven months' contract* for £40,000. 同飛行士は四万ポンドで七カ月の契約を結んでいる. ¶a *temporary contract* 仮契約. ¶make a *verbal contract* with ... ...と口頭で契約をする. ¶a *written contract* under seal 捺印した契約証書.

Q² a *back-door contract* 裏口契約. ¶a *building contract* 建築契約. ¶emigrants and persons arriving in a country with *employment contracts* 雇傭契約によって来る移民および入国者. ¶on a *four-year contract* 四カ年契約で. ¶be employed on a *government* (*State*) *contract* 政府(国)の契約によって雇われている. ¶under an *insurance contract* 保険契約により. ¶under *London contract* ロンドン条約により. ¶by a *long-term contract* 長期契約で. ¶be under a two-year *MGM contract* 二カ年の MGM と出演契約をしている. ¶a *magazine space contract* 雑誌の(広告)スペースの契約. ¶confirmation of the existence of a *marriage contract* 婚約成立の確認. ¶sign a *movie contract* with ... ...と映画出演契約を結ぶ. ¶a *union contract* 労組協約. ¶a *union security contract* 組合保障契約. ¶a *yellow-dog contract* 〖労〗のら犬契約(労働組合に入らない雇用条件の).

P stipulate *by contract* not to ... 契約に...しないと明記する ‖ have the work done *by contract* 工事を請負でやらせる. ¶specified *in* the *contract* 契約書に明記した. ¶enter *into* a special *contract* with ... ...と特別協約を結ぶ. ¶You must pay me 100 yen for breach *of contract.* 貴下は契約破棄のかどで私に百円支払う義務がある. ‖ insist upon the fulfilment *of* a *contract* 契約の履行を主張する ‖ after the completion *of* the *contract* その契約完了の後 ‖ during the execution *of* a *contract* 契約履行中 ‖ before the commencement *of* a *contract* 契約を開始する前に ‖ Terms *of contract* appear suitable. 契約の条件が好都合のようだ. ‖ conditions *of* a *contract* 契約の条件. ¶He was engaged at a monthly salary of $175 *on* a *contract* of five years. 彼は五カ年の契約で月給百七十五ドルで雇われた. 【類】 lose a large amount *on* a *contract* with ... ¶live up *to* one's *contract* 契約を果す ‖ the parties *to* a *contract* 契約の当事者. ¶Marie Dressler is *under contract* to Metro-Goldwyn-Mayer. マリー・ドレスラーはメトロ・ゴールドウィン・メーヤー社と契約を結んでいる. 【類】 a big star *under contract* to the RKO / I am *under contract* to serve as English teacher. ¶*upon* a *contract* 契約で.

P² under a *contract between* ... and ..., dated ..., it is provided, in effect, that ... ...間の契約で...の日付の下に...

という意味の条項が規定されている. ¶a *contract* ***for*** repairs 修理契約. ¶the *contract* ***for*** the construction of ... ...の建築請負 ‖ a *contract* ***for*** a supply of ... ...を供給する契約 ‖ a *contract* ***for*** labor 労働契約 ‖ get me a *contract* ***for*** ... ...に対する私との契約が成立するように尽力して下さい. ¶*contract* ***with*** the party there 先方の相手方と契約を結ぶ ‖ under *contract* ***with*** a person 人との契約で.

contract, *v.* 請負う.

P He has *contracted* ***for*** the building of the house ***at*** 30,000 yen. 彼は三万円でその家の建築を請負った.

contracting, *n.* 契約を結ぶこと.

Q² ***labor*** *contracting* 労働契約締結.

contraction, *n.* 収縮, 収れん.

Q a sudden violent ***involuntary*** *contraction* of the muscles 筋肉の急激な不随意的収れん.

P² the *contraction* ***of*** iron by cold 寒気による鉄の収縮. 【類】 cold causes the *contraction* ***of*** liquids (gases, metals) ‖ the *contraction* ***of*** the eyebrows まゆをひそめること.

contractor *n.* 請負人.

Q² an ***advertisement*** *contractor* 広告一手引受人. ¶an ***army*** *contractor* 陸軍御用商人. ¶a ***building*** *contractor* 建築請負業者. ¶a ***coal*** *contractor* 石炭請負業者. ¶a ***Government*** *contractor* 政府事業請負業者. ¶a ***labor*** *contractor* 人夫請負業者. ¶a ***timber*** *contractor* 木材請負業者.

contradict, *v.* 反ばくする, 反対する.

M ***authoritatively*** *contradict* a statement 厳然として声明を反ばくする. ¶He *contradicted* me ***flat*** (=***flatly***). 彼は正面から私に反対した. ¶*contradict* ***point-blank*** まともに反対する.

contradiction, *n.* 反ばく, 反対; 矛盾.

V we ***give*** a flat *contradiction* to those who maintain that ... われわれは...と主張する人々に断固として反対する. ¶***incur*** a *contradiction* in terms 言葉の上に矛盾をきたす. ¶The report ***received*** the following *contradiction*. その報道は次の反ばくを受けた. ¶He can ***stand*** (=***withstand***) *contradiction* with difficulty. 彼には反対されても平気でいることはむずかしい. ¶He will not ***tolerate*** *contradiction*. 彼は反ばくされたら黙っていないだろう.

Q a ***direct*** *contradiction* むきだしの反ばく. ¶an ***emphatic*** *contradiction* of its veracity その真実性に対する断固たる否定. ¶in ***flagrant*** *contradiction* to public opinion 無謀にも世論に反対して. ¶a ***flat*** *contradiction* (=opposition) はっきりした反対.

P it has been proved ***beyond*** *contradiction* that ... ...ということは反ばくの余地なのないまでに立証された. ¶***without*** *contradiction* 矛盾なしに.

P² a *contradiction* ***between*** two ideas 二思想間の矛盾.

contradictory, *a.* 反対の.

P be *contradictory* ***of*** the rule, "......" ...という規定に反する. ¶*contradictory* ***to*** existing facts 現在の事実と反対の ‖ schemes *contradictory* ***to*** common sense 常識では受取れない計画.

contradistinction, *n.* 対比, 相反.

P ***in*** *contradistinction* to (from) ... ...に対立して.

contrariness *n.* 反対性.

Q the ***general*** *contrariness* of men and women 男女間の一般的な反対性.

contrary, *n.* 反対.

V An examination of the facts ***proves*** the *contrary*. 事実を調査して見るとその反対だということが分る.

Q the *contrary* is ***true*** of ... ...に就てはその反対が真相である. ¶The ***very*** *contrary* is the case. 実際は全くその反対だ.

P interpret ***by*** *contraries* 正反対に解釈する ‖ Dreams go ***by*** *contraries*. 夢はさか夢. ¶as long as a treaty does not provide ***for*** the *contrary* 条約にそれと反対の規定がない限り. ¶We thought it would be bad weather, but ***on*** the *contrary* we had fine sunshine. 天気が悪いと思ったが反対に晴天だった. 【類】 ***On*** the *contrary*, it is I who am in your debt. / I do not admire that man: ***on*** the *contrary* I have a great contempt for him. ¶unless instructions are given ***to*** the *contrary* それと反対の指図が出なければ ‖ until I give notice ***to*** the *contrary* 私がそれと反対の通告を発しないうちは. 【類】 if you do not hear from me ***to*** the *contrary* / express a wish ***to*** the *contrary* ‖ I have nothing to say ***to*** the *contrary*. 私に異議はありません. ‖ He may be rich for anything I know ***to*** the *contrary*. 私はそうとは思っていないがあの人は金持かも知れない. 【類】 I hear of nothing ***to*** the *contrary*. / I know nothing ***to*** the *contrary*.

contrary, *a.* 反対の.

M ***directly*** *contrary* to ... ...と正反対の.

P run *contrary* ***to*** one's interests 利益に反する ‖ *contrary* ***to*** a belief once widely prevalent かつて広く世に行われた信仰に反して. 【類】 *contrary* ***to*** the actual facts of life / He acted *contrary* ***to*** my wishes. / *contrary* ***to*** the will of the gods of the country / It is *contrary* ***to*** etiquette. / be too *contrary* ***to*** human nature / *contrary* ***to*** custom ‖ It is *contrary* ***to*** reason. それは理屈に合わない. ‖ it is *contrary* ***to*** nature to ... ...することは自然に反している ‖ It was *contrary* ***to*** the laws of the country for any foreigner to land. 外人の入国はその国のおきてに反していた. ‖ It was *contrary* ***to*** rules (=regulations). それは規則違犯であった. 【類】 *contrary* ***to*** orders (all expectation).

contrast, *n.* 対照; 相違.

V *contrast* is ***afforded*** by it against ... それが...との著しい相違を示している. ¶***bring*** the *contrast* between them into such clear relief それらの対照をこのようにはっきりきわ立たせる. ¶***bring out*** the *contrast* between ... and ... ...と...を対照する. ¶it ***exhibits*** a striking *contrast* to ... それは...に対して顕著な相違を示す. ¶it ***forms*** (=***offers***) a striking *contrast* with ... それは...と著しく相違している. ¶***give*** *contrast* to ... ...と対照させる. ¶it ***lends*** *contrast* to ... それは...と対照をなす. ¶All people ***love*** *contrasts*. 人は皆対照を好む. ¶***make*** a beautiful *contrast* with ... ...と美しい対照をなす. ¶***present*** a great *contrast* to ... ...と非常な相違を示す. ¶***supply*** a *contrast* to ... ...に対して著しい相違を示す.

Q a ***complete*** *contrast* 完全な対照. ¶a ***curious*** *contrast* 好奇心をそそる対照. ¶make a ***decided*** *contrast* with ... ...とはっきりした対照をなしている. ¶a ***delightful*** *contrast* 愉快な対照. ¶a ***flagrant*** *contrast* ひどい相違. ¶bring out ***forceful*** *contrast* 無理に対照させる. ¶a ***glaring*** *contrast* 大変な違い方. ¶in ***happy*** *contrast* to ... ...とうまく対照して. ¶an ***impressive*** *contrast* 印象的な対照. ¶an almost ***incredible*** *contrast* ほとんど信じられないほどの相違. ¶in ***marked*** *contrast* to ... ...と大いに異なり. ¶in ***odd*** *contrast* to ... ...と妙な対照をなして. ¶a ***piquant*** *contrast* 目立つ対照. ¶a ***pleasing*** *contrast* 気持のよい対照. ¶the *contrast* is not so ***pronounced*** between ... and ... ...間の相違はさほど顕著ではない. ¶a ***remarkable*** *contrast* 著しい相違. ¶make a ***sharp*** *contrast* with ... ...と鋭い対照をなす. 【類】 a ***sharp*** *contrast* between wealth and poverty (富者と貧者) ‖ stand in the ***sharpest*** *contrast* もっとも著しい対照を示している. ¶an almost ***shocking*** *contrast* はっとするような対照. ¶a ***singular*** *contrast* 格段の相違. ¶a ***social*** *contrast* [貧富などの]社会的懸隔. ¶in ***startling*** *contrast* to ... ...とびっくりするほど違って ‖ The columns of a London and a New York newspaper of equal prominence often exhibit such striking if not ***startling*** *contrasts*. どちらも有名でありながらロンドンとニューヨークの新聞はしばしばびっくりするほどでないまでも非常に顕著な相違を示すことがある. ¶bring out in ***striking*** *contrast* the difference between Occidental and Oriental ideas 東西両洋思想の相違をはっきり対照的に示す ‖ present a ***striking*** *contrast* to ... 著しい対照を示す ‖ There is a ***striking*** *contrast* as seen between snow and coal. 雪と石炭ぐらいのひどい違いがある. ¶***violent*** *contrasts* はげしい相違. ¶in ***vivid*** *contrast* to ... ...とはっきり異って. ¶a ***wide*** *contrast* 大きな相違.

P seem, ***by*** *contrast*, ... 対照して見ると...らしく見える. ¶***in*** *contrast* to the preceding period 前時代と相違して. ¶This appears small ***in*** *contrast* with that. これはそれに比べれば小さく見える.

P² some *contrasts* ***between*** Japanese and American university education 日米大学教育における二三の相違点. 【類】 a striking *contrast* ***between*** the old and the new / a *contrast* ***between*** wealth and want / a *contrast* ***between*** two civilizations / a *contrast* ***between*** London and Paris. ¶Black is a *contrast* ***to*** white. 黒は白の反対である. ¶make a strong *contrast* ***with*** ... ...と著しい相違を示す.

contrast, *v.* 対照する; 相反する, 際立って違う.

M The white sails were seen off the shore ***beautifully*** *contrasted* with the blue sky. 沖の白帆は青空に美しくきわ立って見えた. ¶*contrast* ***favorably*** with ... ...に比して劣らない. ¶The white peak *contrasts* ***finely*** with the blue sky. 白雪の峰は青空と美しい対照をなしている. ¶His Indian robes *contrasted* ***oddly*** with his fluent English. 彼のインド服は彼の流ちょうな英語と妙な対照をなしていた. ¶*contrast* ***pleasingly*** with ... ...との対照が気持よく感じられる. ¶in present-day society with the rich and the poor ***sharply*** *contrasted* 貧富の懸隔の大きい現代社会では. ¶*contrast* ***startlingly*** with ... ...とびっくりするほど相違している. ¶it *contrasts* ***strangely*** with ... それは...と妙な対照をなしている. ¶*contrast* ***strikingly*** with ... ...と顕著な対照をなす. ¶*contrast* ***strongly*** with ... ...と著しく相違している. ¶This color *contrasts* ***well*** with green. この色と緑とは対照がよい.

P *contrast* this ***with*** ... これを...と対照する ‖ as *contrasted* ***with*** ... ...と比べて. ¶*contrast* in a striking way ***with*** ... ...と著しく異る ‖ it *contrasts* ***with*** this in not ... それは...でない点がこれとは全く相違している.

contravention, *n*. 違反, 違背.

P ***in*** *contravention* of the then existing law 当時の法律に違反して. 【類】be ***in*** *contravention* of the stipulations (法律の条項) / act ***in*** *contravention* of the regulations.

contribute, *v*. (**1**) 寄付する; 貢献する.

M *contribute* ***effectively*** towards the solution of ... ...の解決にあずかって力がある. ¶***gladly*** *contribute* 喜んで寄付する. ¶It has ***greatly*** *contributed* to this result. それはこの成績に大いに貢献するところがあった. ‖ *contribute* ***greatly*** to the preservation of health 健康維持に大いに益がある. ¶Their knowledge and experience *contributed* ***immensely*** to the progress of the work. 彼らの知識経験はその仕事の進行に大いに役立った. ¶This ***largely*** *contributed* to the popularity of this route. これがこの経路の好評を得るに大にあずかって力があった. 【類】*contribute* ***largely*** to the commercial growth of the country. ¶*contribute* ***liberally*** 惜気なく寄付する. ¶*contribute* ***little*** to the solution of the problem その問題解決にはあまり役に立たない. ¶*contribute* ***much*** to the irregularities of the atmospheric conditions 気象の異変に大いに影響する. ¶hundreds of thousands of ***patriotically*** *contributed* dollars 報国の精神から献金した幾十万ドルという金. ¶*contribute* ***powerfully*** to ... ...に大いに貢献する. ¶He *contributed* ***regally*** to countless charities. 彼は王者にふさわしく無数の慈善団に寄付した. ¶He has *contributed* ***richly*** to these fields of thought. 彼はこれらの思想方面に大いに貢献した.

P *contribute* money ***for*** some work ある事業に金を寄付する. ¶*contribute* ***to*** a better understanding between ... and ... ...間の親善を助長する ‖ *contribute* ***to*** civilization (peace, happiness) 文明(など)に寄与する. 【類】*contribute* in some way ***to*** the pleasure of their trip / It is not the only cause, but I think it has certainly *contributed* ***to*** the result. / the quality that *contributed* most ***to*** his success / It *contributed* ***to*** the attractiveness of the scene. / Proper rest and good sleep *contribute* ***to*** longevity. / *contribute* ***to*** the good of the society in which he lives ‖ Each *contributed* ***to*** the general table. めいめいが持寄りで食事をした. ‖ cheerfully and liberally *contribute* ***to*** a fund 喜んでかつ惜しみなく資金に寄付する ‖ *contribute* ***to*** company needs 会社の役に立つ ‖ *contribute* ***to*** the understandability of the sentence 文の意味を明りょうにする ‖ intelligent analyses of the relative relation of the factor elements *contributing* ***to*** traffic congestion 交通混雑の諸要因に対する比較関係の筋の通った分析. ¶He *contributed* ***towards*** the achievement of these results. 彼はこれらの成果をおさめるにあずかって力があった. ‖ *contribute* ***toward*** a better understanding of the two peoples 二国民の親善を深める ‖ He *contributed* a large amount ***towards*** its production. 彼はその製作費に大金を寄付した. ‖ *contribute* one's share ***towards*** the pacification of the world 世界平和のためにその分を尽す ‖ I *contributed* my share ***towards*** the expense. 僕もその入費の幾分を負担した.

(**2**) 寄稿する.

M *contribute* ***widely*** to publications in many countries 諸国の出版物に広く寄稿する.

P articles *contributed* ***for*** publication 出版の目的で寄稿した記事. ¶*contribute* ***to*** the pages (=columns) of ... ...新聞(雑誌)に寄稿する. 【類】*contribute* ***to*** a magazine (newspaper) / *contribute* an article ***to*** a magazine (newspaper).

contribution, *n*. (**1**) 寄与; 寄附.

V ***add*** valuable *contributions* to the sum of human knowledge 人類の既成知識に貴重な寄与をする. ¶send a hat round of ***collecting*** *contributions* 寄金募集に帽子を回す. ¶It ***constitutes*** a valuable *contribution* to the study of the question. それはその問題を研究するものに取って有力な参考となる. ¶I ***enclose*** my humble *contribution* towards the fund of your society. 貴会基金の内へ軽少ながら寄付を同封してお送り致します. ¶It ***forms*** a substantial *contribution* of permanent value to our knowledge of the world in which we live. それはわれわれが生活する世界を知る上で永久的価値のあるりっぱな貢献である. ¶***levy*** *contribution* on ... ...から寄付を募る. ¶***make*** a *contribution* of ¥3,000 towards a fund (expenses) 基金(など)へ三千円寄付する ‖ ***make*** an important *contribution* to medical science 医学に対して重要なる貢献をする ‖ Every word ***makes*** its *contribution* to the general effect. 一言一言が文全体の効果に役立っている. ‖ Let us be prompt in ***making*** *contributions*. 奮って醵金しましょう. 【類】***make*** a $50,000 *contribution*. ¶***receive*** a *contribution* 寄付金を受ける. ¶***solicit*** *contributions* from the general public 一般からの寄付を仰ぐ.

Q ***benevolent*** *contributions* 慈善寄付金. ¶The book is a ***brilliant*** *contribution*. その本はすばらしい業績である. ¶***charitable*** *contributions* on behalf of the sufferers by the famine in India. インドの飢饉罹災者のための慈善寄付金. ¶These were his ***chief*** *contribution* to literature. これらは文学に対する彼の主なる貢献であった. ¶a ***deep*** *contribution* to psychological thought 心理学の研究に対する深遠なる貢献. ¶a ***definite*** *contribution* to English lexicography 確かに出色の一英辞典. ¶an ***enduring*** *contribution* to English literature 英文学に対する恒久的寄与. ¶Marconi's ***epoch-making*** *contribution* to the art of wireless telegraphy 無線電信術に対するマルコニーの画期的貢献. ¶an ***erudite*** and ***scholarly*** *contribution* 深い学術的な貢献. ¶a ***great*** *contribution* to civilization 文明に対する一大貢献. 【類】the ***great*** *contribution* made by the Greeks to world civilization. ¶the book is an ***important*** *contribution* to the present knowledge of ... その著作は...に関する既成知識への重要な貢献である ‖ an ***important*** *contribution* to the subject of acoustics 音響学の諸問題に対する重要な貢献. 【類】an ***important*** *contribution* to history / the most ***important*** *contribution* to socialist thought / be likely to prove an ***important*** *contribution* to ... ¶a most ***interesting*** and ***valuable*** *contribution* to ... ...にとってもっとも興味ありかつ貴重な文献. ¶***literary*** or ***pictorial*** *contributions* 文章又は絵画の寄稿. ¶a ***major*** *contribution* to world peace 世界平和への一大貢献. 【類】his ***major*** *contribution* to scholarship (学界). ¶***monetary*** *contributions* 金の寄付. ¶a ***new*** *contribution* to thought 思想への新しい貢献. ¶The article is a ***notable*** *contribution* to foreign journalism in the Far East. その論文は極東における外字新聞への出色な寄稿である. ¶an ***original*** and ***important*** *contribution* to Shakespearian literature シェクスピア文献への独創的にして重要なる貢献. ¶In recognition of your ***outstanding*** *contribution* to literature, we have pleasure in offering you an honorary vice-presidency in this Society. 貴下の文学に対する卓絶せる貢献を認め貴下に当会名誉副会長の職を捧呈致したいと存じます. ¶a ***profound*** *contribution* to the study of ... ...の研究に対する深遠なる貢献. ¶a ***scholarly***, ***painstaking***, and ***interesting*** *contribution* to Dante literature ダンテ文献にとっての学究的な, 骨の折れる, そして興味ある貢献. ¶In so doing you will make a ***substantial*** *contribution* to your college. そうすることによって諸君は大学に対し実質的な貢献をすることになる. ¶a ***timely*** *contribution* to the subject その問題に対する時宜に適した貢献. ¶No ***unused*** *contribution* will be returned. 没書は一切返送しません. ¶Sir Thomas Brown's "antediluvian" was a ***useful*** *contribution* to speech. トーマス・ブラウン卿の antediluvian (大洪水前の生物) なる新造語は言語に対する有益な貢献であった. ¶It is a ***valuable*** *contribution* to the study of Renaissance art. それは文芸復興期の芸術研究に対する貴重な貢献である. ‖ a ***valuable*** *contribution* to the march of civilization 文明の進歩に対する貴重なる貢献. 【類】a ***valuable*** *contribution* to folklore (民族学) / a ***valuable*** *contribution* to the stock of human ideas (思想界) / a most ***valuable*** *contribution* to electronics (電子工学). ¶He enriched English literature with ***valuable*** and ***permanent*** *contributions.* 彼は貴重で恒久的な貢献によって英文学を豊かにした. ¶the most ***valuable recent contribution*** to the literature of the subject その問題の文献に対する近来最も貴重な貢献. ¶one's ***voluntary contribution*** 自発的寄付, おぼしめし. 【類】The hospital is supported by ***voluntary*** *contributions* (有志の寄付で).

Q^2 ***charity campaign contributions*** 慈善運動によって集める寄付. ¶***cash*** (＝***money***) ***contributions*** 現金寄付.

P^2 his *contribution* ***to*** the advancement of physiology 生理学の進歩に対する彼の貢献 ‖ a *contribution* ***to*** the cause of peace through education 教育による平和への貢献. 【類】his *contributions* ***to*** the horticultural literature of the day (現代の園芸文献) / his *contributions* ***to*** the literature of his country / Lord Avebury's " A *Contribution* ***to*** our Knowledge of Seedlings ". / a *contribution* ***to*** social welfare / a *contribution* ***to*** religious thought ‖ some *contributions* ***to*** signboard curiosities 珍看板の見本二三. ¶his *contribution* ***towards*** the funds of ... 基金への彼の寄附.
 (2) 投書, 寄稿.

V The magaizne ***includes*** many interesting *contributions.* その雑誌には多くの興味ある寄稿が載っている. ¶***send*** a *contribution* to a journal or a periodical 新聞雑誌に投書する. ‖ He still ***sends contributions*** to the column of that paper. 彼は今でもその新聞に寄稿している.

contributive, *a.* 寄与して, 役立って.

P be *contributive* ***to*** common interests 共通の利益に役立つ.

contributor, *n.* 貢献者; 寄付者; 寄稿家.

Q ***celebrated contributors*** to the historical record of achievement 成功の歴史への有名な貢献者(有名な成功者たち). ¶an ***important contributor*** to the sum of human knowledge 人知の増進に対する有力な貢献者. ¶the ***largest*** *contributor* of exhibits among foreign nations in the fair 諸外国中最も多数その博覧会へ出品した国. ¶an ***outside*** *contributor* 社外の寄稿家. ¶the most ***popular*** and ***valued*** *contributor* to that paper 同新聞寄稿家中最も人気ありかつ最も重きをなしている者. ¶one of the most ***prolific*** *contributors* to the magazines and newspapers 新聞雑誌へ最も多く寄稿する文士の一人. ¶a ***regular*** *contributor* to ... ...の常連の寄稿家. ¶a ***well-rewarded*** *contributor* 手厚い報酬を受けている寄稿家.

Q^2 " ***Atlantic*** " ***contributors*** アトランチック誌への寄稿家. ¶a ***magazine*** *contributor* 雑誌寄稿家.

P He is ***amongst*** the *contributors.* 氏は寄稿家の一人である.

P^2 a *contributor* ***in*** a London paper writes : ロンドンの一新聞の寄稿家がこう書いている. ¶a *contributor* ***to*** public opinion 世論の構成に貢献する人 ‖ a *contributor* ***to*** the Red Cross Society 赤十字社への寄付者.

contributory, *a.* 貢献する, 寄与する.

P The private automobile is one of the greatest evils *contributory* ***to*** traffic congestion. 私有自動車は交通の混雑という悪結果をきたす最大原因の一つである. ‖ The measure is to be recommended as most *contributory* ***to*** the end in view. その案は当面の目的達成に最も有効のものとして推薦すべきである.

contrition, *n.* 悔悟.

V ***express*** *contrition* for one's wrong doing おのれの非行を悔悟する.

contrivance, *n.* 工夫, 発明; 装置, 考案物.

Q an ***automatic*** *contrivance* 自動的装置. ¶a ***home-made*** *contrivance* 手製のしかけ(道具など). ¶the most ***ingenious*** *contrivance* of the invention その発明の最も巧妙な点. ¶a ***mechanical*** *contrivance* 機械的装置. ¶It is a ***novel*** *contrivance.* それは新工夫だ. ¶***time*** (***labor***)***-saving*** *contrivances* 時間(など)節約の考案物. ¶a large ***umbrella-shaped*** *contrivance* 大きなかさ型の装置.

P^2 a *contrivance* ***for*** suspending ... ...をつるす装置. ¶a *contrivance* ***in*** an automobile 自動車につける装置.

contrive, *v.* 工夫する.

M a piece of mechanism ***ingeniously*** *contrived* 巧妙に工夫した一仕掛.

P *contrive* a mask ***against*** poison gas 防毒マスクを考案する. ¶*contrive* a means of escape ***from*** prison 脱獄の手段を考える.

control, *n.* 支配; 抑制.

V ***assume*** complete *control* of ... ...を完全に支配する. ¶***establish*** their *control* over ... 彼らが...を効果的に支配する. ¶the manager ***exercises control*** over ... 支配人が...を監督する. ¶It is an incident over which one ***has*** no *control.* それはだれにもどうすることもできない事件だ. ¶***gain*** perfect *control* 完全に支配する. ¶He ***has*** no *control* over himself. 彼には自制がない. ‖ Those ***having*** *control* of the skies have control of the world. 空を制する者は世界を制する. ¶***hold*** the *control* of political power 政治の支配権を握る. ¶***lose control*** of one's temper 我慢がしきれなくなる ‖ ***lose control*** of one's machine その機械の操縦がきかなくなる. 【類】***lose control*** of the legs ‖ He was seized with a paroxysm of fury and ***lost control*** of himself. 彼はかっと怒って自制ができなくなった. 【類】He ***lost*** all *control* over himself. ‖ He ***lost*** *control* of his horse. 馬が彼のいうことをきかなくなった. ¶***maintain*** one's *control* over ... よく...を抑制する. ¶***regain*** *control* of oneself [ぼうぜんとしていたものなど]われに帰る. ¶***remove control*** on ... ...の統制をはずす. ¶***resist*** Government *control* 政府の統制に反抗する. ¶***secure*** *control* of ... ...を統制する. ¶***take*** *control* 操縦を開始する. ¶***tighten*** the *control* of aliens 外人の取締を厳重にする.

Q exercise ***absolute*** *control* over ... ...に対し断固たる統制を布く. ¶exercise ***administrative*** *control* over ... ...に対して行政上の取締をやる. ¶remove ***Allied controls*** 連合軍の支配を除去する. ¶has ***complete*** *control* of ... ...を完全に統制している ‖ bring him under ***complete control*** 彼を十分に抑制する. ¶obtain ***diplomatic*** *control* over the country その国を外交的に支配する. ¶under the ***direct*** *control* of ... ...直轄の. ¶a ***divine*** *control* of human things 人事を支配する神の摂理. ¶The airplane had ***dual*** *controls,* one set for each pilot. [昔は]飛行機には二個の操縦装置があり, 二人の航空士が各々その一つを受持っていた. ¶***effective*** *control* is impracticable 取締りがつかない. ¶establish a more ***efficient*** *control* over ... ...に対しさらに有力な統制が行えるようにする. ¶Ugly as he was, that man had an ***extraodinary*** *control* over women. あの男は不(ぶ)男ではあったが婦人の操縦にかけては非凡の腕前があった. ¶A teacher ought to have ***good*** *control* over his or her class. 先生は自分のクラスの運営をうまくやって行けるべきだ. ¶a catastrophe beyond ***human*** *control* 人力でいかんともすることのできない災禍. ¶***mental*** *control* of the body 精神による肉体の制御. ¶in the absence of ***parental*** *control* 両親が監督していないので(家庭から離れなどして) ‖ Children who lack ***parental*** *control* often grow up badly behaved. 両親のしつけの悪い子供は大きくなって不品行になることがよくある. ¶exercise ***rigid*** *control* over ... ...を厳重に取締る. ¶***social*** *control* 社会的制裁. ¶exercise a ***strict*** *control* 厳重な統制を行う. ¶***wise*** *control* 賢明な統制.

Q^2 ***birth control*** 産児制限. ¶***boss control*** ボス管理. ¶***contraband control*** 密輸入品の統制. ¶***finger-tip control*** [機械など]指先であしらうこと. ¶***foreign-exchange control*** 外国為替管理. ¶***government*** *control* over prices 物価に対する政府の統制 ‖ ***government*** *control* of the economic order 経済状態に対する政府の統制. 【類】place it under ***government*** *control* ‖ military ***government*** *control* of press and curfew regulations 出版統制令および外出禁止令の軍政管理. ¶***inflation*** *control* インフレ[抑止の]統制. ¶a ***labor*** *control* over production 生産管理. ¶***light control*** 燈火管制. ¶relax ***occupation*** *controls* 占領統制を緩和する. ¶***paper*** *control* 紙統制. ¶abolish ***price*** *controls* 価格統制を廃止する. 【類】end (＝drop) ***price*** *controls* for meat / remove ***price*** *control* over rice / cry for removal of ***price*** *control* / scrap (廃棄する) ***price*** *controls* for ... / abolish consumer ***price*** (消費者価格) *controls.* ¶***production*** *control* by labor 生産管理. ¶***propaganda*** and ***press*** and ***radio*** *control* 宣伝, 新聞及びラジオの統制. ¶lift (＝eliminate *or* remove) ***rent*** *controls* [家賃など]料金価格統制を撤廃する. ¶***scent*** *control* in industry 商工業品の悪臭を除いて芳香を付加すること. ¶radio channels under ***Soviet*** *control* ソ連統制下の無線通信チャネル. ¶***state*** *control* 国家管理. ¶***State coal-mine*** *control* 石炭の国家管理. ¶" ***thought*** *control* " in Japan 日本のいわゆる思想統制. ¶***vocabulary*** *control* 語彙の統制(用語数など). ¶the termination of all ***wartime*** *controls* 戦時統制の全廃 ‖ ***wartime*** *control* of industry 産業の戦時管理. ¶emphasize the necessity of ***world*** *control* of atomic energy 原子力の世界管理の必要性を力説する. 【類】***world*** atomic *control.*

P arise from a cause ***beyond*** one's *control* 不可抗力から生じる ‖ attribute their distress to circumstances ***beyond*** their *control* 彼らの困難を止むを得ざる事情に帰する. 【類】

He lost his position through circumstances ***beyond*** his *control*. / circumstances ***beyond*** the *control* of ... ‖ The horse got ***beyond control***. 馬が御しきれなくなった. ¶he is ***in control*** of ... 彼は…を管理している. ¶The plane is ***out of control***. その飛行機は操縦の自由を失った. ¶Such a thing lies ***outside*** human *control*. こういうことは人力のいかんともするあたわざるところだ. ¶keep it ***under control*** with difficulty やっとのことでそれを抑制する ‖ The Batan Islands came ***under*** American *control* in 1900. バタン群島は一九〇〇年米国の統治に属した. ‖ ...come ***under*** Russian *control* ...はソ連支配下に入る. 【類】 the Mandatory States (委任統治国) placed ***under*** British *control* ‖ The student body is well ***under*** *control*. 学生団はよく統制がとれている. ‖ schools ***under*** the direct *control* of the Education Department 文部省直轄学校 ‖ The fire was soon got ***under*** *control*. 火事は間もなく鎮火した. ‖ keep down one's passion ***under*** due *control* 自分の感情を適当に抑える. ¶an event not ***within*** the *control* of human power 人力では何ともしがたい事件. ¶***without*** *control* 取締らずに.

P² the *control* ***of*** the thought 思想取締 ‖ the prevention and *control* ***of*** disease 疾病の予防および撲滅. ¶I have no *control* ***over*** the matter. その件では私に監督権はありません. ‖ arising from causes ***over*** which they have no *control* 彼らのいかんともなし得ない原因から発生して.

control, *v.* 取締る; 抑える.

M He *controls* his temper ***admirably***. 彼はよく怒りを抑える. ¶***effectively*** *control* 効果的に統制する. ¶***rigidly*** *control* ... ...を厳重に取締る.

controversialist, *n.* 論争者, 議論家.

Q a ***clever*** *controversialist* 巧妙な議論家. ¶a ***doughty*** *controversialist* 剛勇な論争家.

controversy, *n.* 論争, 論弁.

V ***arouse*** *controversy* 論争を引き起す. ¶***conduct*** a *controversy* with ... ...と論争をやる. ¶It ***evoked*** so much *controversy*. それは非常な論争を喚起した. ¶a question which ***excited*** much *controversy* 大論争を引き起した問題. ¶They ***had*** a bitter *controversy*. 彼らは激論をやった. ¶***make*** a better *controversy* of it その議論をより有利に進める. ¶This *controversy* was ***noised*** throughout the scientific world. この論争は科学界に波紋を起した. ¶***occasion*** some *controversy* 何らかの論争を招来する. ¶***provoke*** *controversy* 論争を引き起す. ¶***re-open*** (=***revive***) an old *controversy* 論争の蒸し返しをする. ¶It ***roused*** a great deal of *controversy*. それが非常な論争を引き起した. ¶***start*** a *controversy* by declaring that ... 論争の皮切りに...と明言する. ¶***stir*** [***up***] a *controversy* 紛争をあおる. ¶***terminate*** a *controversy* 論争にけりをつける.

V² A *controversy* ***arose***. 論争が起った.

Q It has been the subject of ***animated*** *controversy*. それは盛んな論争の題目になった. ¶a ***barren*** *controversy* 水かけ論. ¶***considerable*** *controversy* has arisen as to ... ...に関して相当猛烈な論争が起っている. ¶an ***endless*** *controversy* over ... ...に関する果しない論争. ¶this led to a ***heated*** *controversy* as to whether ... そのために果して...であるかについて猛烈な議論が起った. ¶a ***furious*** *controversy* 猛烈な論争. ¶a ***hot*** *controversy* raged on the question of ... ...の問題に関して激烈な議論が起った. ¶settlement of ***international*** *controversies* by the arbitration of judicial proceedings rather than by the waste and sufferings of war 戦争の浪費と惨禍によらずして仲裁裁判による国際紛争の解決. ¶He permitted himself to be drawn into the ***journalistic*** *controversy*. 彼はその新聞の論争の渦中に巻込まれた. ¶prove a ***lively*** *controversy* 活発な論争となる. ¶It has been the subject of ***much*** *controversy*. それは大問題となっている. ¶provoke or revive a ***never-to-be-ended*** *controversy* 果しのない論争を引き起したりむし返えす. ¶thresh out once more this very ***old*** *controversy* 以前からあるこの論争を再燃させる. ¶a ***profitless*** *controversy* 無益の論争. ¶topics that provoked ***public*** *controversy* 世間の論議を引き起した話題. ¶a ***Sino-Japanese*** *controversy* 日支紛争.

Q² a ***coal*** *controversy* (=dispute) 石炭争議. ¶a ***labor*** *controversy* 労働争議 ‖ a ***labor-management*** *controversy* 労使間の闘争. ¶It gave rise to much ***newspaper*** *controversy*. その問題は大分新聞でやかましく論ぜられた.

P That is the fact ***beyond*** *controversy*. それは議論の余地のない事実である. ¶The problem is still ***in*** *controversy*. その問題はいまだに論議されている. ‖ be skilled ***in*** *controversy* 討論が巧みだ ‖ the *controversy* ***in*** which ... engaged with ... ...が...を向うにまわして戦った論争. ¶enter ***into*** *controversy* with him on ... ...について彼と論争する. ¶the crux ***of*** *controversy* 論争の難点.

P² a *controversy* ***about*** it それに関する論争. ¶The *controversy* ***as to*** ... grew bigger and bigger ...についての論争はますます拡大した. ¶a *controversy* ***between*** two parties 二党派間の論争. ¶a *controversy* ***on*** Buddhism 仏教に関する論争. 【類】 a *controversy* ***on*** the morality (道徳性) of duelling. ¶a *controversy* ***upon*** the subject of ... ...の問題に関する論争. ¶have a *controversy* ***with*** a person on (=about) some subject ある問題に関し人と論争する.

contumely, *n.* 侮辱(的言辞).

V ***pour*** *contumely* upon them 彼らに悪口雑言を浴びせかける.

convalesce, *v.* 快方に向う, 元気づく.

M The patient is *convalescing* ***nicely***. 患者は順調に快方に進んでいる.

P He is still *convalescing* ***at*** his home ***from*** an attack of pneumonia. 彼はいまだに自宅で肺炎の病後を静養している. ¶The patient is *convalescing* ***from*** a severe illness. 患者は重病の後を静養している.

convalescence, *n.* 快方, 肥立ち, 回復期.

V since ***approaching*** *convalescence* 快方に近づいてから.

P His physicians advised him to go there ***for*** his *convalescence*. 医者は彼に病後保養のためそこへ行くように勧めた. ¶Europe ***in*** *convalescence* [戦後]回復期の欧州.

convenience, *n.* 便益; 都合; 便利な物.

V I cannot be ***awaiting*** his *convenience* in this dilatory way. 私はこんなにべんべんと彼の都合を待ってはいられない. ¶***consult*** the *convenience* of ... ...の都合を計る ‖ ***Consult*** your own *convenience*. ご都合のよいようになさい. ¶When will it ***fit*** (=suit) your *convenience*? いつ御都合がよろしいでしょうか. ¶***follow*** one's own *convenience* 自分に都合のよいようにする. ¶***make*** a *convenience* of a person 人を道具に使う. ¶make various arrangements to ***meet*** the *convenience* of passengers 乗客の便宜を図ろうとして色々な手はずをする. ¶***offer*** *convenience* to passengers 乗客に便宜を与える. ¶***promote*** one's *convenience* 便宜を計る. ¶***provide*** every *convenience* for the comfort of passengers 旅客の慰安のためあらゆる便宜を計る. ¶***respect*** the public *convenience* 公衆の便宜を尊重する. ¶***sacrifice*** *convenience* to economy 便利を犠牲にして節約する. ¶***serve*** the *convenience* of ... ...の便利を図る. ¶at any time that ***suits*** your *convenience* 御都合のよい時いつでも. 【類】 if it ***suits*** your *convenience* / so as to ***suit*** the *convenience* of ... / Two o'clock will ***suit*** my own *convenience* better. ‖ He resigned "to ***suit*** his own *convenience*." 彼は「都合により」辞職した. ‖ All right, sir. ***Suit*** your own *convenience*. よろしい. では君の勝手にしたまえ.

V² No *convenience* ***exists*** for transportation by railway or steamer. 鉄道の便も船の便もない.

Q at your ***earliest*** *convenience* ご都合つき次第. ¶***ever-increasing modern*** *convenience* 絶えず増加して行く現代の便利. ¶It would be a ***great*** *convenience* if you could answer as soon as possible. できるだけ早く御返事いただければ大変好都合でございます. ‖ The office is a ***great*** *convenience*. その事務所はしごく便利です. ¶up-to-date hotels equipped (=fitted up) with every ***modern*** *convenience* 現代のあらゆる便利な設備を整えている新式の旅館 ‖ Can you imagine life without gas, electricity, radio and other ***modern*** *conveniences*? ガス, 電気, ラジオその他の文明の利器のない人生って考えられますか. ¶for their ***mutual*** *convenience* 相互の便宜上. ¶I am dismissing you for ***my own*** *convenience*. こっちの都合でお前にやめてもらおう. ¶as a matter of ***practical*** *convenience* 実際の便宜上. ¶***various*** *conveniences* of life 生活上いろいろ便利なもの.

Q² modern ***household*** *conveniences* [電気冷蔵庫, 洗たく器など]近代的家庭道具 ‖ one of the most useful of the ***household*** *conveniences* 家庭道具で最も役立つものの一つ. ¶There are ***toilet*** and ***lavatory*** *conveniences* on each floor. 各階に化粧室と便所がある.

P ***according to*** *convenience* 都合で. ¶Arrange the matter ***at*** your own *convenience*. この件はご都合のよろしいようにお取計らい下さい. 【類】 You can repay me ***at*** your *con-*

venience. / We trust that we will hear from you ***at*** your *convenience.* / It was delayed ***at*** his *convenience.* ¶a designation ***for convenience*** 便宜上の称呼. 【類】it may be called, ***for convenience***, ... / ***for convenience*** of illustration, let us suppose that ... / ***for convenience*** of ready reference / ***for*** the *convenience* of climbers / ***for*** the *convenience* of public ‖ ***for*** the special *convenience* of holiday public 遊山客に特に便利なように. ¶it is not ***to*** his *convenience* to ... ...することは彼には都合がよくない. ¶***with*** great *convenience* to himself 彼自身にとって非常に都合よく.

convenient, *a.* 便利な, 都合のよい.

P When would it be *convenient* ***for*** you to go? おいでになるのはいつが御都合よろしいでしょうか. ‖ It is not *convenient* ***for*** me to pay just now. 今すぐ払うのは都合が悪い. ‖ a utility knife *convenient* ***for*** general purposes 何にでも使える七徳ナイフ. 【類】*convenient* ***for*** transportation. ¶hotels *convenient* ***of*** access 出入に便利なホテル. ¶This place is *convenient* ***to*** the street-car. ここは電車に便利がよい. ‖ You can have breakfast whenever *convenient* ***to*** yourself. いつでもご都合のよいときに朝のお食事を召上れます.

convention, *n.* 会議; 規約; 慣例, 因襲; 《米》政党大会.

V ***abandon*** the formal *conventions* of the past 過去の形式的な慣例を棄てる. ¶***break*** established *conventions* 旧慣を打破する. ¶the *convention* was ***brought*** to a close with an address by ... 会議は...の式辞で閉会を告げた. ¶***conclude*** a military *convention* 軍事協定を締結する. ¶***join*** the *convention* on wireless telegraphy その無線通信会議に参加する. ¶***sign*** a *convention* of peace with ... ...との平和協約に署名する. ¶the chairman ***wound up*** a *convention* with an eloquent appeal to all present to ... 議長は満堂の聴者に向って...するようにという熱弁を振って会議を終結した.

V² *Convention* now ***allows*** women to smoke in public. 今では婦人の喫煙は世間の習慣となっている.

Q an ***annual*** *convention* 年会. ¶a ***curious*** *convention* of the Tosa painters in their historical subjects was to leave out the roof of a house in order to expose the interior to view. 歴史的な画題を扱う土佐絵の画家の珍らしい手法は家の屋根を描かないで内部を見せることであった. ¶prepare a draft for international *conventions* 国際会議への草案を作る. ¶the ***National*** *Convention* 《米》[政党の]全国大会. ¶a ***political*** *convention* [政党のやる]政治大会. ¶their first ***postwar*** *convention* 彼らの戦後最初の大会. ¶***social*** *convention* 社会の伝統.

Q² have a ***mutual-admiration*** *convention* 仲間ぼめの会合をやる. ¶a ***lonely-hearts*** *convention* 集団見合い. ¶The party will hold its ***nominating*** *convention.* 党は指名大会を開くだろう. ¶a ***party*** *convention* 《米》政党大会. ¶***stage*** *conventions* 舞台のしきたり.

P Governors ***in*** *convention* 会議中の知事 ‖ the American Library Association ***in*** *convention* at Asbury Park アスベリ公園で会議中の米国図書館協会 ‖ The Esperantists meet every year ***in*** *convention.* エスペランティストたちは毎年会議を開く. ¶a slave ***to*** *convention* 因襲のどれい. ¶Russia ***under*** the Manchurian *Convention* of 1902 pledged herself to completely evacuate the whole of Manchuria by April 8th, 1903. 一九〇二年の満州協約の下にロシアは一九〇三年四月八日までに満州全体から完全に撤兵することを誓った.

convent, *n.* 尼僧院.

P go ***into*** a *convent* 尼僧になる.

conventionality, *n.* 因襲.

V ***break through*** (***observe***) the *conventionalities* of official life 役人生活の因襲を打破する(まもる).

conversant, *a.* 通じている; 関係する.

M He is ***fairly*** *conversant* with English. 英語がかなりよくできる. ¶***sufficiently*** *conversant* with the language as to be able to ... ...することができるほどにその国語に熟達している. ¶He is ***thoroughly*** *conversant* with French. フランス語に十分通暁している.

P *conversant* ***about*** some matter あることに関係する. ¶*conversant* ***in*** something あることに精通している. ¶He is *conversant* ***with*** the matter. そのことをよく知っている. 【類】those *conversant* ***with*** the business / those *conversant* ***with*** the intricacies of Japan's domestic politics and social make-up.

conversation, *n.* 会話, 談話.

V ***avoid*** frivolous *conversation* 浮薄な談話を避ける. ¶***begin*** a *conversation* with ... ...と談話を始める. ¶***brighten*** *conversation* 話に花を咲かせる. ¶This ***brought*** *conversation* to a close. これで会話を打切った. ¶***carry on*** a *conversation* with ... ...と会談する. ¶None of them can ***carry out*** even the simplest *conversation* in the language they have been learning. その内だれ一人自分の習っている外国語でごく簡単な話を続けて行くことができない. ¶***draw out*** *conversation* agreeable to the party 集った人らが喜ぶような会話を引き出す(するように持掛ける). ¶***change*** *conversation* 話をかえる. ¶go to ***enjoy*** *conversation* 話しこみに出かける ‖ I ***enjoyed*** a delightful *conversation* with him about ... ...について彼と愉快に語った. ¶*conversation* is ***enlivened*** by ... ...で話に花が咲く. ¶***enter*** (=***get***) ***into*** *conversation* with ... ...と会話を始める. ¶***exchange*** *conversation* with ... ...と談話をまじえる. ¶***extinguish*** *conversation* 話をとぎらす. ¶I ***followed*** his *conversation* with difficulty. 私はやっとのことで彼の話を聞き取った. ¶The timely topic ***got up*** a lively *conversation.* 時節柄の話題で話に花が咲いた. ¶***guide*** a *conversation* into other subjects 他の話題に話を仕向ける. ¶***have*** a little *conversation* with ... ...とちょっと話をする ‖ I ***had*** two *conversations* with him. 彼と二回話をした. ¶***hold*** a *conversation* with ... ...と会談する ‖ ***hold*** *conversations* by telephone 電話で話をする. ¶A long, polite *conversation* was ***indulged in.*** 長い丁重な談話にふけった. ¶***interrupt*** (=***break off***) a *conversation* 話をさえぎる. ¶***join*** *conversation* with him on ... ...のことで彼と話をまじえる. ¶***keep*** the *conversation* off that matter そのことを話さないようにする. ¶***keep up*** a *conversation* 談話を続ける. ¶try to ***make*** *conversation* 話をしようとする ‖ ***make*** *conversation* to ... about ... ...について...と対談する. ¶***monopolize*** a *conversation* 談話を独占する. ¶***open*** a *conversation* 話を始める. ¶Once I ***overheard*** a *conversation* in an omnibus between two elderly matrons. かつて乗合自動車の中で二人の年増女の話を漏れ聞いたことがある. ¶The practice of serving a cup of tea and a biscuit ***promoted*** the *conversation* and friendliness of those present. 一杯の茶と一個のビスケットを出すということが列座の話をはずませ親しみを増した. ¶***shift*** the *conversation* to other channels 別の方に話をそらす. ¶***start*** (=***commence***) a *conversation* 談話を始める. ¶***sustain*** (=***maintain*** or ***continue***) a *conversation* 談話を続ける. ¶***switch*** the *conversation* into another line 話を他の方面にかえる. ¶***turn*** the *conversation* to other matters 話を他のことに転じる.

V² *conversation* ***drifted*** to ... 話が...に移った. ¶the *conversation* ***drifted back*** to ... 話が...に舞戻った. ¶somehow the *conversation* ***fell upon*** ... どういうはずみだったか会話が...の話になった. ¶a *conversation* that has ***passed*** between them 彼らの間に交わされた話. ¶the following *conversation* once ***took place*** (=passed) between ... かつて...の間に次の話があった. ¶the *conversation* ***turned*** upon ... 話が...に転じた.

Q be engaged in an ***absorbing*** *conversation* with ... ...との話に夢中になっている. ¶make ***agreeable*** *conversation* 楽しい会話をする. ¶an ***animated*** *conversation* 活気のある会話. ¶a ***blundering*** and ***stupid*** and ***indolent*** *conversation* 間違いだらけでばからしいのらくら話. ¶after a ***brief*** *conversation* with ... ...とちょっと話してから. ¶a ***brisk*** *conversation* 快活な談話. ¶a ***confidential*** *conversation* 密談. ¶his ***convincing*** *conversation* 彼の説得力ある話. ¶a ***damp*** *conversation* しめっぽい話. ¶in ***deep*** *conversation* with ... ...との話に油がのって. ¶have ***desultory*** *conversation* with ... about ... ...について...と雑談を試みる. ¶in ***educated*** *conversation* 教養ある人の会話では. ¶pass the evening in ***entertaining*** *conversation* with ... ...とおもしろい話をしてその晩をすごす. ¶an ***epigrammatical*** *conversation* 警句に富んだ会話. ¶enjoy ***friendly*** *conversation* 懇談する. ¶He was addressed by ... and something like the ***following*** *conversation* took place. 彼は...から話しかけられ次のような談話が交わされた. ¶a ***free*** and ***easy*** *conversation* 自由で気楽な話. ¶At dinners of more than ten guests, ***general*** *conversation* is impossible. 十人以上の客の食卓では全体にわたる話は不可能である. ¶a ***gossipy*** *conversation* うわさ話. ¶a ***humorous*** *conversation* ひょうきんな話. ¶an ***intellectual*** *conversation* 学問上の話. ¶a ***light*** *conversation* 軽い話. ¶after a ***little*** *conversation* with him 彼とちょっと話した後で. ¶carry on a ***lively*** *conversation* にぎやかな話を続ける. ¶We walked on in ***merry*** *conversation.* 愉快に話しながら歩いた. ¶There was a lull in the ***one-sided*** *conversation.* その片方だけの話がちょっととぎれた. ¶a ***pleasant*** *conversation* 愉快な談話. ¶the ***polite*** *conversation* of cultured people 教養ある人々の上品な会話. ¶banish those slang expressions from all ***polite*** *conversations* あらゆる上品な会話からそういう俗語を閉め出す. ¶a ***private*** *conversation* 内証の話. ¶a ***profitable*** *conversation* ためになる会話. ¶a very ***rapid*** *conversation* 非常に早口の話. ¶a ***short*** *conversation* 短い会話. ¶their ***staple*** *conversation* 彼らの間にお定まりの会話. ¶a ***stimulating*** *conversation* 刺激に富んだ会話. ¶a ***sustained*** *conversation* 長ばなし. ¶a ***trivial*** *conversation* つまらない会話. ¶The weather furnishes a topic of ***universal*** *conversation.* 天気はだれにでも一つの話題を提供する. ¶a ***witty*** and ***wise*** *conversation* 機知に富み思慮深い会話.

Q ***dinner*** (***table***) *conversation* 食事中の会話. ¶a ***round-table*** *conversation* 円卓会談. ¶a ***street-corner*** *conversation* 街頭の立話. ¶in a ***telephone*** *conversation* 電話での話しで. ¶a ***tête-à-tête*** *conversation* 二人きりの秘密の会話(恋人同士の会話など).

P ***from*** *conversation* held on the road I learned that ... 路上の立話から私は...ということを知った. ¶***in*** *conversation* 口頭で ‖ deep ***in*** *conversation* with ... ...との話に身が入って ‖ he once observed to me ***in*** *conversation* that ... 彼はかつて私に...と言った. 【類】 he is ***in*** *conversation* with ... / hear an unfamiliar word or phrase ***in*** *conversation* ‖ ***in*** a *conversation* I had with him 彼との会話で. ¶scraps ***of*** *conversation* 話のはしばし ‖ his flow ***of*** *conversation* 彼の後から後へと続く話 ‖ the buzz ***of*** *conversation* 話声.

P² a *conversation* ***about*** the matter そのことに関する談話. ¶a *conversation* ***among*** the guests 来客間の話. ¶*Conversations* ***on*** Botany [書名]植物問答 ‖ *conversations* ***on*** the problems of the day 時事問題についての会話. ¶a *conversation* ***with*** friends 友だちとの談話.

conversationalist, *n.* 談話家, 座談家.

Q a ***brilliant*** *conversationalist* 座談の名手. ¶an ***engaging*** *conversationalist* 座談の名人. ¶an ***entertaining*** and ***effective*** *conversationalist* 話術の巧みな座談の大家. ¶a ***fluent*** *conversationalist* in English 流ちょうな英語の談話家. ¶a ***winning*** *conversationalist* なかなか聞かせる座談家.

converse, *n.* 〖雅〗対話, 談話. 「話する.

V ***hold*** *converse* (=carry on conversation) with ... ...と対

Q in ***friendly*** *converse* with ... ...との打解け話で ‖ There men of varied types and many social classes mingle in ***friendly*** *converse.* そこでは種々なタイプといろいろな階級の人々がまじって親しく談話する. ¶To hold ***silent*** *converse* with the great minds of the past is counted one of the real pleasures of life. 過去の偉人と無言の対話をすることは人生における真の一快事と考えられている.

converse, *v.* 話す, 談話する.

M can *converse* ***fluently*** in English 英語が流ちょうに話せる. ¶*converse* ***freely*** with ... ...と心おきなく話す. ¶*converse* ***winningly*** 人を引付けるように話す.

P We *conversed* ***at*** the dinner-table. われわれは宴会の食卓で話し合った. ¶I am trying to learn to *converse* ***in*** Spanish. 私はスペイン語の会話を習っている. ¶The old friends lounged and *conversed* ***for*** a while ***in*** a desultory way ***over*** the cigars. 旧友たちはしばらくの間横になって葉巻をくゆらしながら雑談した. ¶*converse* ***with*** him ***on*** (=***upon*** *or* ***about***) it そのことについて彼と話す.

converse, *n.* 逆.

Q The ***exact*** *converse* is true. 実際はその正反対だ. ‖ As a matter of fact, the ***exact*** *converse* is the case. 事実はそれと正反対だ.

conversion, *n.* 変更; 改宗, 転換.

V ***carry out*** the *conversion* of the railways to a standard gauge 鉄道を標準軌間に変更する. 【類】 ***carry out*** the *conversion* from horse to electric traction. ¶He ***made*** many *conversions.* 彼は多数の外教者を改宗させた. ¶Every means was used to ***obtain*** his *conversion.* 彼を改宗させようとして百方手を尽した.

P² *conversion* ***into*** Christian Church キリスト教への改宗. ¶*conversion* ***of*** notes ***into*** gold 紙幣の金貨への兌換. ¶the *conversion* ***of*** the heathens ***to*** Christianity 異教徒のキリスト教への改宗 ‖ the *conversion* ***of*** Paul ***from*** a prosecutor ***to*** a disciple 告発者の立場から弟子へと変ったパウロの転向 ‖ the *conversion* ***of*** factories ***from*** war industry ***to*** peace industry 戦時産業から平和産業への工場の転換. ¶*conversion* ***to*** Buddhism (Catholicism) 仏教(カトリック教)への改宗.

convert, *n.* 改宗者, 改心者.

V ***gain*** many *converts* 多数の改宗者を得る. ¶That ***made*** him a *convert* from communism. それが原因で彼は共産主義から転向した. ¶labor unceasingly to ***win*** *converts* to the doctrines of Auguste Comte オーギュスト・コントの説へ転向する者を得ようと不断の努力をなす.

Q a ***complete*** *convert* to cremation 完全に火葬に賛成するに至った人. ¶a ***firm*** *convert* to the belief that ... ...という信念への固い転向者. ¶This has made me a ***perfect*** *convert* to your plan. これでぜひ貴下のやり口を学ぼうという気になりました. ¶a ***zealous*** *convert* 熱心な改宗者.

P² a *convert* ***from*** a religion (principle) ある宗教(など)からの転向者. ¶He is a *convert* ***to*** Buddhism. 彼は仏教への改宗者である. 【類】 a *convert* ***to*** Catholicism.

convert, *v.* 変える; 変る; 改宗させる. 「する.

M ***ostensibly*** *convert* to orthodoxy 表向きは正統派へ転向

P *converting* the franc ***as*** 25f=£1 二十五フランーポンドと換算して. ¶*convert* milk ***from*** a food ***into*** a poison 牛乳を食物から毒に変える. ¶be *converted* ***from*** Protestantism ***to*** Catholicism 新教からカトリック教へ転向させられる. ¶*convert* property ***into*** money 財産を金にかえる ‖ *convert* it ***into*** cash それを金にかえる ‖ *convert* a newspaper ***into*** a weekly magazine 新聞を週刊雑誌に変更する ‖ the Buddha *converted* ***into*** a man 人間に化身した仏 ‖ land purchased and *converted* ***into*** a public park as a memorial 記念として敷地を買いとり公園にした土地. 【類】 slaughterhouses (畜殺場) *converted* ***into*** hospitals. ¶You will not *convert* us ***to*** your way of thinking. われわれは貴下の考え方に転向はできません. ‖ *convert* them ***to*** the practice of virtue 彼らを道徳の実践に転向せしめる ‖ *convert* them ***to*** Christianity=evangelize them 彼らをキリスト教に帰依させる ‖ *convert* him ***to*** reason [わからずやの]彼に筋の立った考え方をさせる.

convey, *v.* 運ぶ, 伝える, 伝達する.

P *convey* goods ***by*** express (truck) 速達(など)で品を運搬する. ¶*convey* luggage ***from*** his house ***to*** the station 手荷物を彼の家から停車場へ運搬する ‖ *convey* property (an estate) ***from*** father ***to*** son 財産を父から子に譲る. ¶*convey* it ***in*** a boat (carriage, cart, sledge) それを舟(など)で運ぶ ‖ I owe him more than I can *convey* ***in*** words. 私は口には言えないほどあの人に恩になっている. ¶*convey* it ***on*** a camel それをらくだで運ぶ. ¶Please *convey* ***to*** Madam the assurance of my esteem. 奥様にどうぞよろしく. 【類】 The book will *convey* ***to*** the readers the rough idea of modern mechanization of industry.

conveyance, *n.* 運搬; 乗物.

V Fares do not ***include*** *conveyance* between railway stations and steamer piers. 賃金には停車場波止場間の運賃がこめてない. ¶***prefer*** a private *conveyance* [人力車・自転車など]専用の乗物を選ぶ. ¶I ***want*** a *conveyance* to take me to the hotel. ホテルまでの乗物が欲しい.

Q a ***public*** *conveyance* 公衆の乗物(バス・電車など). ¶a ***slow*** *conveyance* おそい乗物.

Q² a ***land*** *conveyance* 乗り物.

P require nearly eight hours ***for*** *conveyance* 運搬にほとんど八時間を要する.

P² *conveyance* ***by*** land (water) 陸(水)上輸送. ¶*conveyance* ***of*** goods (passengers) 貨物(旅客)の輸送.

conveyer, *n.* 〖機〗コンベーヤー.

Q² a ***belt*** *conveyer* 〖機〗ベルト・コンベーヤー.

convict, *n.* 囚人.

Q² an ***ex-convict*** 前科者. ¶a ***long-term*** *convict* 長期服役者.

convict, *v.* 有罪とする.

M a man ***once*** *convicted* of theft 窃盗の前科ある人. ¶***unjustly*** *convicted* of a forgery charge 偽造罪のぬれ衣を被せられて.

P He was *convicted* ***by*** the jury. 彼は陪審官によって有罪と宣告された. ‖ *convicted* ***by*** their own conscience 彼ら自らの良心に責められて. ¶You are *convicted* ***in*** your own court. 君は自分の良心によって罪のあかしを立てられている. ¶He was *convicted **of*** fraud (theft, incendiarism). 彼は詐欺罪(など)に問われた. ¶He was *convicted **upon*** the evidence. 彼はその証拠にもとづいて有罪と宣告された.

conviction, *n.* 確信, 自信; 断罪.

V ***affirm*** (=confirm) a *conviction* 有罪の判決を確認する. ¶***base*** one's *conviction* on ... ...にもとづいて確信を立てる. ¶To the arm-chair critic it is often impossible to ***bring*** *conviction* by mere argument. 議論だけで机上の論者を説きふせることの不可能の場合は往々ある. ‖ His argument has ***brought*** *conviction* to many waverers. 彼の議論は幾多の浮腰の者に自信を持たせた. ¶What he says ***carries*** little *conviction*. 彼の話は人を首肯させるに足りない. 【類】This ***carries*** *conviction* with it. / To my mind it ***carries*** *conviction*. ‖ Well-balanced minds ***carry*** *conviction* to the minds of all unprejudiced readers. 公平な論者はあらゆる偏見なき読者の心に確信を持たせる. ‖ secure a delivery which will ***carry*** *conviction* to the listener 聴者に確信を抱かしめるような話振りを修得する. ¶The argument ***carries*** little *conviction* to Western readers. その議論では西欧人には割切れない. ¶The arguments are founded on facts and ***compel*** *conviction*. その議論は事実にもとづいているので信ぜざるを得ない. ¶observations ***concreted*** their *convictions* that ... 観察の結果...という彼らの確信をういよいよ深めた. ¶***confirm*** the *conviction* that ... ...とい確信を固める. 【類】***confirm*** my former *convictions* that ... ¶***declare*** his firm *conviction* that ... ...という彼の確信を言明する. ¶***deepen*** one's *conviction* その確信を深める. ¶We cannot ***escape*** the *conviction* that ... われわれは...と確信せざるを得ない. ¶***express*** one's firm *conviction* その確信を表明する. ¶a *conviction* ***formed*** during considerable intercourse with French people フランス人との長い交際から得た確信 ‖ we have ***formed*** the unshakable *conviction* that ... われわれは...という確固たる自信を持つに至った. ¶***hold*** the *conviction* that ... ...という確信をいだく. ¶***reach*** a *conviction* 心証を得る. ¶***shake*** a *conviction* 確信を動揺させる. ¶It is difficult to ***share*** his *convictions*. 彼のような確信を持つことは困難である. ¶this has ***started*** a growing *conviction* among thinking people that ... このために...ということを心ある人々にますます深く確信せしめるに至った. ¶***strengthen*** *conviction* 確信を強固にする. ¶***unsettle*** *conviction* 確信を動揺させる. ¶resulted in a decision to ***upholding*** the *conviction* 心証を裏づける判決となった. ¶***voice*** one's *conviction* that ... ...という確信を言明する.

V^2 the *conviction* has not yet ***penetrated*** that ... ...という確信がまだ徹底しない. ¶the *conviction* that ... largely ***prevails*** in this country ...という信念がこの国では圧倒的である.

Q an ***assured*** *conviction* ゆるぎない確信. ¶a man with a ***burning*** *conviction* 燃えるような確信を持った人. ¶a ***deep-seated*** (=***deep-rooted***) *conviction* 抜き難い確信. ¶a ***fervent*** *conviction* 熱烈な確信. ¶it is my ***firm*** *conviction* that ... ...ということは私の確信する所である ‖ I have the ***firmest*** *conviction* that ... 私は...というきわめて強固な確信を持っている. ¶in recent years there has been a ***growing*** *conviction* that ... 近年は...という信念が深くなっている. ¶the ***just, sure,*** and ***speedy*** *conviction* of those who break the law 法を破ったものに対する正しく確実にしかも迅速な確定判決. ¶their ***innermost*** *convictions* on the problem of life 人生問題に関する彼らの心からの確信. ¶His words carry ***irresistible*** *conviction* to all open-minded persons. 彼の言葉にはすべて虚心坦懐の人々は共鳴せざるを得ない力がある. ¶Such at least is my ***present*** *conviction*. 少くとも以上が私現在の確信である. ¶my own ***private*** *conviction* is that ... 私個人としては...と確信している. ¶his ***profound*** *conviction* 彼の深い確信. ¶the ***rooted*** (=deep-seated) *conviction* that ... という根深い確信. ¶a ***second*** *conviction* 再犯. ¶It has long been my ***settled*** *conviction* that ... ...ということは私がとうから確信しているところであった. ¶perfectly (=absolutely) ***sincere*** *convictions* 心底からの確信 ‖ my ***sincerest*** and ***deepest*** *conviction* 私の最も真剣でかつ最も深い確信. ¶with the ***solid*** *conviction* that ... ...ということを堅く信じて. ¶I have a ***strong*** *conviction* that ... 私は...ということを堅く信じている. ¶he has no ***sure*** *convictions* about ... 彼は...については確固たる自信がない. ¶an ***unjust*** *conviction* 不当な有罪判決. ¶I maintain with ***unshaken*** *conviction* that ... 断固...と主張する. ¶with the ***vague*** *conviction* that ... ...とばく然信じて. ¶there is a ***widespread*** *conviction* that ... ...ということが一般に信ぜられている.

P ***from*** a *conviction* that ... ...という信念から ‖ speak straight ***from*** one's *conviction* 所信によって率直に話す. ¶***in*** the *conviction* that ... ...と確信して. ¶I say not flatteringly but ***with*** sincere *conviction*. 私はお世辞ではなく本当のところを言うのです.

P^2 a previous *conviction* ***against*** a person ある人に対する以前の有罪判決. ¶*conviction* ***of*** guilt 服罪.

convince, *v.* 信服させる, 納得させる.

M I am ***absolutely*** *convinced* that ... 私はあくまで...と信じている.

P be *convinced* ***beyond*** a reasonable doubt どう疑ってみてもやはり信じている. ¶I am *convinced* ***by*** your arguments. 貴下の議論に得心が行きました. ¶I am *convinced* ***of*** its truth (fact). それは本当だと(その事実を)信じる. ‖ *convince* a person ***of*** his error 彼の非を悟らせる. 【類】*convince* them ***of*** the futility of such a hope.

convincing, *a.* 信服させる.

P He is not very *convincing* ***on*** this point. 彼はこの点についてはあまり徹底していない.

convoy, *n.* 護衛.

V ***have*** a *convoy* of ships of war 軍艦に護衛される.

P sail ***under*** *convoy* 援護の下に航行する.

convulse, *v.* けいれんさせる, 腹の皮をよらす.

P The elements were *convulsed* ***over*** the passing away of the great man. 偉人の長逝で天地も感動した. ¶we were *convulsed* ***with*** laughter ***at*** ... われわれは...を見て笑いこけた ‖ The audience was *convulsed* ***with*** mirth. 聴衆は腹の皮のよれるほど打興じた. ‖ He was *convulsed* ***with*** agony. 彼はもだえ苦しんだ.

cook, *n.* 料理人(コック).

V I cannot ***spare*** my *cook* just now. 今のところ料理人を手離すことはできない. ¶***train*** green *cooks* 新米の料理人を仕込む. ¶I have ***turned*** (=***sent***) my *cook* out of the house. 私は料理人を追出した. ¶A *cook* is ***wanted***: for further particulars apply at the following address. 料理人入用; 詳細は左記に照会あれ.

Q She is our ***new*** *cook*. あれが今度来たコックです. ¶a ***white-capped*** *cook* 白帽の料理人.

Q^2 a ***hotel*** *cook* ホテルのコック. ¶a ***pastry*** *cook* パン菓子の製造人.

cook, *v.* 料理する; 料理ができる.

M be *cooked* ***nicely*** よく料理してある. ¶Meat *cooks* more ***quickly*** than vegetables. 肉は野菜よりも料理が早くできる. ¶be ***thoroughly*** *cooked* 十分煮(焼い)てある. ¶*cook* ***up*** (=falsify) a story (report *or* account) 話(など)をでっち上げる. ¶These pears do not *cook* ***well***. このなしはうまく料理ができない.

P *cook* ***by*** boiling (heat) 煮て(火にかけて)料理する. ¶*cook* ***on*** a gridiron 焼網の上で料理する. ¶*cook* ***over*** hot charcoal (stove) 炭火(など)で料理する. ¶He *cooks* ***to*** perfection. 彼の料理は申分がない.

cooker *n.* 炊事用具, 料理材料.

Q a ***fireless*** *cooker* 火なしこんろ. ¶a ***good*** (***bad***) *cooker* 料理しやすい(しにくい)材料.

Q^2 a ***gas*** *cooker* 料理用ガスストーブ. ¶a high ***pressure*** *cooker* 高圧がま(など). ¶a ***steam*** *cooker* 蒸しかまど.

cookery, *n.* 料理法.

V ***understand*** *cookery* 料理を心得ている.

Q ***invalid*** *cookery* 病人向料理[法].

P a recipe ***in*** *cookery* 料理の一法.

cooking, *n.* 料理.

V ***appreciate*** good *cooking* 上手な料理がわかる. ¶***do*** the *cooking* 料理をやる ‖ ***do*** *cooking* oneself 自分で料理する. 【類】Who ***does*** the *cooking* in your house? ¶***time*** the *cooking* by sandglass in boiling eggs 卵をゆでるのに砂時計で時を計る.

Q The *cooking* is ***bad***. 料理はまずい. ¶*Cooking* is ***deplorable***. 料理がてんでなっていない. ¶***excellent*** *cooking* すばらしい料理. ¶The food is to be of pure ***Japanese*** *cooking*. その食事は純粋の日本料理が出ることになっています. ¶***Western*** (***Chinese***) *cooking* 西洋(中華)料理.

Q^2 ***home*** *cooking* 家庭料理. 【類】He looked forward to having his own home and ***home*** *cooking*.

P a formula *in cooking* 料理法の一.
P² *cooking by* gas (electricity) ガス(など)使用の料理.
¶*cooking on* visit 出張料理.

cooky, *n.* クッキー(菓子パン).
Q *home-made cookies* 手製のクッキー.
Q² bake some *raisin cookies* ほしぶどう入りのクッキーを作る.

cool, *n.* 冷気.
V *enjoy* the *cool* of the evening 夕涼みをする.
Q² the *evening* (*morning*) *cool* 夕(朝)の涼気.
P *in* the *cool* of summer evenings 夏の夕涼みに.

cool, *v.* 冷やす, 冷える.
M His affection for her gradually *cooled down.* 彼女に対する彼の愛情は次第にさめた.【類】His excitement somewhat *cooled down.* ¶Let's go and have icecream to *cool off*. アイスクリームを食べに行こう, すっとするから. ‖ *cool off* the effect ほとぼりをさます. 【類】*cool off* one's passion (情熱).
P boiled water *cooled to* proper temperature 適度の温度にさました湯. ¶*cool with* ice 氷で冷やす.

cool, *a.* 冷やかな; 涼しい.
M He is *as cool* as a cucumber. 彼は落付き払っている. ¶The evenings are *delightfully cool*. 晩は気持よく涼しい. ¶It is *pleasantly cool*. 涼しくてよい気持だ.

cooler, *n.* 冷却器.
Q² an *air cooler* 空気冷却器. ¶a *wine* (*water or butter*) *cooler* ぶどう酒(など)さまし器.

coolie, *n.* 苦力(クーリー).
V *recruit coolies* for the Transvaal mines トランスヴァール鉱山行のクーリーを募集する.
Q² an *earth coolie* 土方.

cooling, *n.* 冷却.
V *accelerate* the *cooling* of friendship for ... …に対する友情の冷却を早める.

coolness, *n.* 冷たさ; 冷静.
V *enjoy* the *coolness* (＝cool air) of the evening 納涼をやる.
Q his *imperturbable coolness* 彼の落着払った態度. ¶treat him with *marked coolness* 目に見えて彼を冷遇する.
P² There is a *coolness between* the two friends. 二人の友の間が冷たい. ¶*coolness in* danger 危険に際しての冷静.

co-op, *n.* 《口語》消費組合 (co-operative society).
Q² the *Cornell Co-op* コーネル大学の学生消費組合.

coop, *v.* 閉込める.
M Owing to beastly weather we were *cooped up* in our homes. ひどい天気で僕たちは家に閉込められた.【類】The children were *cooped* (＝shut) *up* indoors by the rain.

co-operate, *v.* 協力する, 協同する.
M *co-operate harmoniously* with ... …と心を合せて働く.
P *co-operate in* a movement ある運動に協力する ‖ *co-operate in* harmony 仲よく協力する. ¶*co-operate towards* that end その目的達成のために協力する. ¶*co-operate with* him in the work その仕事で彼と協力する. 【類】France *co-operated with* England in attacking Germany. / inability to *co-operate with* numbers of the department and the organization.

co-operation, *n.* 協力, 協同.
V He is ready to *give* his *co-operation.* 彼はいつも進んで協力する. ¶they *lent* their active *co-operation* to ... 彼らは…に大いに力を貸した. 【類】They have kindly *lent* us their *co-operation.* ¶*obtain co-operation* from ... …の協力を得る. ¶I *pledge* you in advance my willing *co-operation.* 貴下のために喜んで力添えをすることを前もってお誓いします. ¶*promote co-operation* amongst all interested in ... …に関心を持つすべての人々の間に協同の精神をふるい立たす. ¶*receive* most hearty *co-operation* from ... …から非常に熱心な協力を受ける. ¶*secure* the *co-operation* of ... …の協力を得る. ¶we *won* the hearty *co-operation* of ... われわれは…の熱心な協力を得た.
Q *cheerful co-operation* and assistance 心からの協力と援助. ¶work in *close co-operation* with ... …と密接な連絡を取って働く ‖ the necessity of *closer co-operation* between ... …の間に一層密接な協力の必要. ¶the *closest* and most *friendly co-operation* between ... …間の最も緊密かつ友好的な協力. ¶give *energetic co-operation* in attaining the object 目的達成のために大いに協力する. ¶by *friendly co-operation* 友好的な協力によって. ¶a *generous co-operation* 骨身を惜しまぬ協力. ¶*harmonious co-operation* 美しい協力. ¶the *hearty co-operation* of interested workers 興味を持った働き手の熱心な協力. ¶*helpful co-operation* 助けになる協力. ¶*international co-operation* 国際協力. ¶*mutual co-operation* 相互扶助. ¶*peaceful co-operation* with all nations in the world 世界中の国々との平和的な協力. ¶Soviet-Chinese *political* and *economic co-operation* 中ソ政治・経済提携. ¶*systematized co-operation* 組織立った協力. ¶*technical co-operation* 技術提携. ¶*thorough* (＝*perfect*) *co-operation* 十分な協力. ¶*whole-hearted* (＝*all-out*) *co-operation* 全面的協力. ¶You may count upon my *willing co-operation.* 喜んで力添をします.
Q² *air-ground* tactical *co-operation* 空陸戦術協同作戦. ¶*labor-management co-operation* 労使協調. ¶*world co-operation* 世界[国家間の]協力.
P All must succeed together *by* intelligent *co-operation.* すべての者が賢明な協力によって共に成功を期せねばならぬ. ¶*in co-operation* with ... …と協力して. ¶*with* the *co-operation* of all interests involved 関係者一同の協力をもって.
P² a *co-operation between* the State and people 官民の協力. ¶the *co-operation from* abroad 海外からの協力. ¶*co-operation of* American and Japanese capital *in* the industrial development of South Asia 南アジアの産業開発に対する日米協同投資 ‖ *co-operation of* several *in* an offense 数名の共犯.

co-operative, *n.* 消費(協同)組合.
Q² a *farm co-operative* 農業協同組合.

co-ordinate, *a.* 同等の.
P an officer *co-ordinate in* rank *with* ... …と同じ階級の将校.

co-ordinate, *v.* 同等にさせる.
P *co-ordinated with* ... …と同等の.

co-ordination, *n.* 共同作用; 対等関係.
V *secure* the closest *co-ordination* of effort できるだけ仕事の共同一致を計る.
Q the *perfect co-ordination* of the executive, legislative and judicial authorities 行政・立法・司法三権の完全分立.

co-originator, *n.* 創始者の一人.
P Alfred Russel Wallace, the naturalist, *co-originator with* Darwin of the theory of natural selection ダーウィン同様自然淘汰説を創始した博物学者のアルフレッド・ラッセル・ウォーレス.

cop, *n.* 《米口》警官.
Q² a *motorcycle* (＝*bike*) *cop* 白バイ警官. ¶a *speed cop* 速度違犯取締警官. ¶a smart-looking *traffic cop* スマートな服装の交通巡査.

co-part, *v.* 協力する.
P² *co-part with* ... …の相手役を勤める.

cope, *v.* 争う, 競う, 対抗する.
M *cope effectively* with ... りっぱに…と対抗する. ¶*successfully cope* with the situation 時局に善処する.
P *cope*, single-handed, *with* ... 独力で…と競う ‖ cannot *cope with* all the orders it is receiving 全部の注文には応じ切れない ‖ *cope with* a task (difficulty) 仕事(など)をうまく処理する ‖ The present staff cannot *cope with* the growing activity in trade. 商売がますます盛況に向うので現在の社員だけで手不足を感じる. 【類】*cope with* each other *for* a prize.

copiousness, *n.* 豊富.
P² *copiousness of* material (source material) 資材(資料)の豊富 ‖ *copiousness of* English vocabulary (water power supply) 英語語彙(〃)(水力)の豊富.

copper, *n.* 銅; 銅貨.
V *ask for* a few *coppers* [こじきなどが]二三の銅銭をこう. 【類】*ask for* the *coppers* of the charitable (慈善家). ¶His mother goes round with his cap and *collects coppers* from an admiring crowd. 彼の母は彼の帽子を持ちまわって感心して見ている群集から銅銭のもらいを集める. ¶*shower coppers* upon ... …に銅銭をばらまく. ¶*toss* (＝*cast*) a *copper* to a beggar こじきに銅銭を投げてやる.
Q He smells of *greasy coppers*. 彼には銅臭がある(金にがつがつしている).
P four pence *in coppers* 銅貨で四ペンス. ¶fine work *on copper* 銅に施したりっぱな細工.

copy, *n.* (**1**) 原稿; 謄本; 本; [同じ書物の]一部.
V The difficulty is to *get* enough good *copy* to fill the magazine. 雑誌を満たすだけのよい原稿を得るのがむずかしいところだ. ¶*install* a *copy* of the Standard Dictionary in his office 彼の事務所にスタンダード辞典を一部備え付ける. ¶*issue* 500 *copies* of the book 同書五百部を発行する. ¶*keep* a *copy* of a manuscript before sending it out to a

magazine office 原稿を雑誌社に発送する前にその写しをとっておく. ¶***make*** (=***take***) a ***copy*** of the letter 手紙の写しを取る ‖ ***make*** the second ***copy*** 清書する ‖ Contributions to this contest cannot be returned, so ***make*** a ***copy*** of your contest letter if you want to preserve. 当懸賞への応募原稿は返送致しかねますのでその保存を望まれる向は写しを作っておいて下さい. ¶***make*** (=write) ***out*** a fair ***copy*** 清書する. ¶***pick up*** from the table a ***copy*** of a New York paper ニューヨークの新聞を卓上から取上げる. ¶***prepare*** the first ***copy*** 下書をする. ¶***reproduce copies*** of the book その本を複製する. ¶***strike off*** only 100 ***copies*** of the book 同書をわずか百部だけ印刷する. ¶if you desire to ***take*** one or more ***copies*** 一部以上御希望なら. ¶***write up*** one's "***copy***" 原稿を書く.

Q a ***certified copy*** 謄本. ¶a ***cheap copy*** of a rhyming dictionary 安本の脚韻辞典. ¶a ***clean copy*** 浄書 ‖ type ***clean copies*** of rough drafts 雑な下書きをきれいにタイプで打つ. ¶a ***complete copy*** 完本. ¶***complimentary copies*** 贈呈本. ¶a ***correct*** (=***true***) ***copy*** 正確な写し. 【類】make a ***correct copy*** of a paper. ¶a ***current copy*** of the Weekly Times 週刊タイムスの最近号. ¶a ***dog-eared copy*** ページのすみの折れた本. ¶***duplicate copies*** 同文の謄本. ¶I want an ***extra copy*** of the magazine for clipping purposes. 切抜用に別にその雑誌を一部ほしい. ¶prepare the ***first*** (***second***) ***copy*** 下書をする(清書する). ¶a ***fair*** (***foul***) ***copy*** きれいな(きたない)原稿. ¶Thirty years ago a ***good copy*** of the first edition of Walton could be easily obtained for $100. 三十年前にはウォルトンの初版の美本が一部百ドルで容易に手に入ったものだ. ‖ It makes ***good copy***. それはいい新聞記事になる. ¶a ***hand-written copy*** 手写本. ¶an ***inscribed copy*** of one's book 著者署名入の本. ¶How ***many copies*** of the book have you published? その本は何部出しましたか. ¶a ***marked copy*** of a magazine (newspaper) [鉛筆などで]印をつけた雑誌(など). ¶a ***new copy*** of the book その本の新本一冊. ¶Just 200 ***numbered copies*** have been struck off. ちょうど二百部の限定版が出た. ¶a ***paper-covered copies*** 紙表紙の本. ¶a ***photostatic copy*** 直接複写写真機で写した本. ¶***returned copies*** [雑誌などの]返品. ¶first make a ***rough copy*** of ... …のまず下書をする. ¶a ***second-hand copy*** 古本. ¶a ***signed copy*** 署名入りの本. ¶a ***specially-bound copy*** 特装本. ¶a ***type-written copy*** タイプした原稿. ¶a ***weak*** (=***poor***) ***copy*** of an original story その話のへたなまね. ¶a ***week-old copy*** of the Times 一週間前のタイムス紙一部.

Q^2 distribute ***advance copies*** among an audience 講演の先刷りを聴衆に配付する. ¶an ***association copy*** 著者の署名入りの本(贈呈本など). ¶an ***autograph copy*** 自筆本. ¶***back copies*** (=numbers) of popular magazines 大衆雑誌の月後れ. ¶make a ***carbon copy*** カーボンの写しをとる. 【類】If more than four ***carbon copies*** are to be made, a typewriter with a hard platen (ローラー) should be used. ¶a ***miniature copy*** 縮図(縮刷版). ¶a ***MS. copy*** of ... …の稿本. ¶a ***photostat copy*** 写真複写本. ¶a ***presentation copy*** [出版社などからの]贈呈本. 【類】a ***presentation copy*** from Dickens to Thackeray. ¶***press copy*** 新聞原稿. ¶a ***sample copy*** 見本刷り.

P was printed ***in*** one hundred ***copies*** 百部印刷した.

P^2 a ***copy in*** choice binding 美装本 ‖ a ***copy of*** an advertisement 広告文の原稿.

(**2**) 模倣, 模写.

Q ***clumsy copies*** of American hotels できそこないのアメリカ風旅館. ¶***inferior Oriental copies*** of Western models 西洋物を模倣した劣悪な東洋もの. ¶a ***servile copy*** of ... …の下劣な模倣. ¶Assyrian architecture was a ***slavish copy*** of that of Babylonia. アッシリアの建築はバビロニアの建築をそっくりそのまま模倣したものであった.

P This picture is a ***copy from*** Raphael. これはラファエルの模写だ.

copy, *v.* 写す; ならう, まねをする.

M ***copy*** letters ***carefully*** and ***accurately*** 手紙を入念かつ正確に写す. ¶***copy closely*** 綿密に模写する. ¶***copy fair*** 清書する. ¶***copy out*** a picture (map) 絵(など)を写しとる. ¶***copy slavishly*** そっくり模倣する.

M^2 ***copy down*** 写しとる.

P ***copy after*** him (a model, an example) 彼(など)にならう ‖ ***copy after*** bad practices 悪いことを見習う. 【類】***copy after*** a movie star. ¶pictures ***copied from*** old masters 昔の大家を模写した絵 ‖ The garden has a lake ***copied from*** a noted one in China, called Seiko. その庭園には中国の有名な西湖という湖水を写した池がある. ‖ ***copy from*** [the] life 写生する ‖ ***copy from*** the original 原本(画)から模写する. ¶***copy in*** full 全部写す. ¶***copy into*** a notebook ノートブックに写し取る. ¶***copy out of*** a book 本から写す.

copyright, *n.* 版権, 著作権.

V ***hold*** the ***copyright*** of ... …の版権を所有する. ¶***infringe*** the ***copyright*** その著作権を侵害する. ¶***retain*** the ***copyright*** その著作権を保留する.

Q a ***perpetual copyright*** 永久の著作権.

P books published ***under copyright*** 版権によって出版した書物.

P^2 The ***copyright in*** the whole of Balzac's works expired on January 18, 1900. バルザックの作品の版権はすべて一九〇〇年の一月十八日で消滅した. ¶the ***copyright on*** a book 一著作に対する版権.

copywriter, *n.* 下書する人.

Q^2 an ***advertising copywriter*** 広告案文書き.

coquet, *v.* こびを呈する; もてあそぶ.

P She ***coquets with*** every fellow she sees. 彼女は会う人ごとにこびを呈する. ‖ a beauty ***coquetting with*** a fan (ball) 扇(など)をもてあそぶ美人.

cord, *n.* 綱, ひも(コード).

V ***awaken*** (=strike) in him a responsive ***cord*** 彼の心の琴線に触れる. ¶***cut through*** a ***cord*** ひもを切放す. ¶***jerk*** the bell ***cord*** wildly ベルのひもを盛んに引っぱる. ¶***slip*** a ***cord*** around one's neck 首にひもをそっと巻きつける. ¶***stretch*** a ***cord*** across ... …にひもを張る. ¶he ***struck*** a correct ***cord*** when he said that ... 彼が…と言ったのは急所をついていた. ¶***untie*** the ***cord*** ひもをほどく.

Q strike the ***right cord*** in the heart of ... …の心に共鳴させる. ¶strike a ***sympathetic cord*** in the heart of ... …の心に触れて同情心を起させる. ¶a ***tasseled cord*** of straw しめなわ. ¶the ***umbilical cord*** へその緒.

Q^2 give a pull to a ***bell cord*** 鐘のひもを引っぱる. ¶a ***communication cord*** 非常報知コード. ¶a ***release cord*** [水など出る]引きひも.

P^2 the ***cords of*** love 愛のきずな.

cordage, *n.* [集合的] 綱具類.

Q ***stout cordage*** 丈夫な綱具.

cordial, *a.* 懇篤な.

P ***cordial to*** any one だれにでも懇篤な.

cordiality, *n.* 懇切.

Q At the conclusion of his remarks the cheers given by the large body of those present were of ***unusual cordiality***. 彼の演説が終ったとき多数列座の人々によって送られたかっさいは非常に熱心なものであった.

cordon, *n.* 非常線, 警戒線.

V ***draw*** a ***cordon*** of police about the house その家の周囲に非常線を張る. ¶***form*** a ***cordon*** [警官などが]非常線を張る. ¶***pass*** (=***break through***) a ***cordon*** of police 非常線を突破する. ¶***post*** (=***place***) a ***cordon*** 非常線を張る. ¶***throw*** a ***cordon*** around a building 建物の周囲に非常線を張る. ¶***throw out*** a ***cordon*** of police 非常線を張る.

Q a ***sanitary cordon*** 防疫線.

cordon, *v.* 非常線を張る.

P Police ***cordoned off*** the area. 警官がその地域に非常線を張った.

core, *n.* 果心, 中心, 心髄.

V It ***forms*** the ***core*** of all the questions pending between Japan and the U.S. それは日米間のあらゆる未決問題の中核を成している. ¶The proposition ***has*** its ***core*** of truth. その命題には真理がこもっている. ¶The words ***touched*** the very ***core*** of her heart. その言葉が彼女の身にしみた.

Q the ***very core*** of a subject 問題の核心.

P The apple is rotten ***at*** the ***core***. そのりんごは心(しん)が腐っている. ‖ The disease lies ***at*** the ***core*** of British society. この病気は英国社会の根底に潜んでいる. ‖ a cancer ***at*** the ***core*** of the Japanese character 日本人の性格の根底に潜んでいる癌(がん)とも称すべきもの. ¶He is Catholic ***to*** the ***core***. 彼はこちこちのカトリック信者だ. 【類】He is a stanch loyalist, true ***to*** the ***core***. / He proved Yankee ***to*** the ***core***. (きっすいの米人). ‖ The pear is rotten ***to*** the ***core***. そのなしは心まで腐っている.

cork, *n.* キルク, 木せん.

V ***draw*** the ***cork*** of a bottle びんのせんを抜く. ¶***stick*** the ***cork back*** into a bottle 元通りにびんにキルクのせんをする.

V^2 ***Corks popped*** at the dinner. その晩さんでは盛んにキルクが抜かれた.

Q amid the pounding of ***champagne corks*** シャンパンの

コルクがポンポン抜かれて(宴会で).

corn, *n.* 穀粒;穀類;《英》小麦,《米》とうもろこし.

V ***grind corn*** 穀粒をひく. ¶***grow corn*** 小麦を作る. ¶***husk*** the *corn* 穀類の殻をむく. ¶***raise corn*** 《米》とうもろこしを作る. ¶***shuck*** the *corn* とうもろこしの皮をむく. ¶***winnow corn*** 穀物を唐箕(とうみ)にかける.

V² The *corn* is ***coming up***. 小麦の芽が出てきた.

Q ***cracked corn*** はじけたとうもろこし. ¶fertile plains covered with ***waving corn*** 波打つ穀物が一面にはえている肥沃(ひよく)な平野. ¶the ***whole corn*** そのままの(加工してない)とうもろこし. ¶***sweet corn*** さとうもろこし.

Q² ***field corn*** [飼馬料の]とうもろこし. ¶***Pop corn*** will not pop until it is dry. はじけとうもろこしは乾きが悪いとはぜない.

corn, *n.* [足うらの]まめ.

V You will ***have*** (=***get***) *corns* if you continue to wear such tight shoes. そんな窮屈なくつをはき続けているとまめができますよ.

V² The *corn* ***came back***. たこが一ぺん直ってまたできた.

corner, *n.* すみ,かど;窮境;買占め.

V The cyclist ***cut corners*** with lightning speed. その自転車乗は電光の速度で角を曲った. ¶***explore*** the hidden *corners* of knowledge. 知識の未開地を探検する. ¶The charitable ladies of the neighbourhood ***have*** always a *corner* in their hearts for the poor. その界隈(かいわい)のなさけ深い淑女たちはいつも貧民のことが念頭にある. ¶***make*** a *corner* in wheat (land) 小麦(など)を買占める. ¶The motor-car ***negotiated*** the *corner*. 《俗》自動車がその角を手際よく曲った. ¶***open*** a regular Esperanto *Corner* in its pages その雑誌(または新聞)の一隅にエスペラントの欄を設ける. ¶***round*** the *corner* 角を曲る. ¶***round off*** the *corners* 角を取る(人間を丸くする). ¶***turn*** the *corner* 角を曲る ‖ the third house after ***turning*** that *corner* あの角を曲って三軒目. ¶***turn down*** one *corner* of a card 名刺のすみを折る(るす宅を訪問したしるしに).

Q She keeps the secret in the most ***concealed corner*** of her heart. 彼女は心の一番奥底にその秘密を仕舞込んでいる. ¶in a ***cosy corner*** 居心地の好い片すみに. ¶in the ***far corners*** of the British Empire 英帝国のへき地(植民地)に ‖ the ***farthest corner*** of the field 野原の一番遠いすみっこ. ¶from the ***four corners*** of the globe 世界中から. ¶turn the ***mossy corner*** of three score years and ten 七十の坂を越える. ¶It is situated in an ***out-of-the-way corner*** of the country. それはその国の人里遠い片いなかにある. ‖ ***out-of-the-way corners*** of the world 世界の片すみ. ¶remove it from its ***present neglected corner*** of medical study その医学の一分科を現在のように閑却しないでもっと研究する. ¶***remote corners*** 遠く都を離れた片いなか. ¶Contact with people gradually wore off some of the ***rougher corners*** in his personality. 人と交際しているうちに彼の人格が段々円満になってきた. ¶in the ***secret corner*** of her heart=in her heart of hearts 彼女の心の奥底で. ¶turn a ***sharp corner*** 急な角を曲る. ¶a ***snug corner*** 居心地のよい片すみ. ¶The Family Club is on the ***southwest corner*** of Bush Street. 家庭クラブはブッシュ街の西南隅にある. ¶He has been in a ***tight corner***. 彼は苦しい立場におかれている. ¶take one's seat in an ***unobserved corner*** of the street-car 電車の人目につかない片すみに座席を占める.

Q² At the ***chimney corner*** sat a man in the early prime life. 暖炉のすみにまだ若盛りの男がすわっていた. ¶at a ***street corner*** 街角で ‖ windy ***street corners*** 風の吹く街角. 【類】It was the subject of conversation on every ***street corner***. ¶put stamps on the ***top left-hand corner*** of the envelope 封筒の左上すみに切手をはる. ¶Senders of registered articles are requested to put their names and addresses in the ***upper left-hand corner*** of the cover. 書留郵便物の差出人はその住所姓名を包みの左方上すみに記していただきたい[カナダの郵便規則]. 【類】The name and address of the sender of a letter is sometimes written or printed in the ***upper left-hand corner*** of the envelope to be returned in case of the letter not reaching the person addressed to. ¶Number each page of your composition (if there be more than one) in the ***upper righthand corner***. (作文が二ページ以上にわたるときは)各ページの右上のすみにページ数をつけること.

P X'mas is just ***around*** the *corner*. クリスマスはもうすぐだ. ‖ be pictured in the newspapers as just ***around*** the *corner* 新聞ではほどなく実現されるように書いている. ¶It is situated ***at*** the *corner* of A and B streets. それは A 街と B 街の角の所にある. ‖ Every road in Shanghai has a name, which is conspicuously posted ***at*** almost every *corner*. 上海ではどの街路にも名称があってそれがほとんどすべての街角にはっきりと掲げてある. ‖ Do not let books get torn or curled ***at*** the *corners*. 書物を破ったりすみをまくらしたりしてはいけない. ‖ wrinkles ***at*** the outer *corners* of the eyes 目じりのしわ. ¶***from*** all *corners* of the earth (=globe) 世界のすみずみから. ¶sit ***in*** the *corner* 部屋の片すみにすわる ‖ over there ***in*** the *corner* あそこのすみっこに. ¶They waited ***on*** the street *corner* for their car. 彼らは町角に立って電車の来るのを待った. ‖ the grocery store ***on*** the *corner* 角の所の食料品店 ‖ The house stands ***on*** the *corner*. その家は角の所だ. ¶look at it ***out of*** the *corner* of one's eyes 横目でそれを見る. ¶go ***round*** a *corner* 角を曲って行く.

P² The *corners* ***of*** his lips twitched a little. 彼のくちびるのすみの所がぴくぴく動いた.

corner, *v.* やりこめる;〖商〗買占める.

P *corner* an opponent ***in*** argument 相手を言いまくる(やりこめる) ‖ *corner* ***in*** commodities (rice, wheat) 品物(など)を買占める. ¶*corner* ***off*** one's work 自分の仕事をちゃんと仕上げる.

corner-stone, *n.* すみ石.

V ***laying*** the *corner-stone* 定礎式 ‖ He ***laid*** a very *corner-stone* in the foundations of physical chemistry. 彼は物理化学の基礎をりっぱに築き上げた一人である.

corollary, *n.* 推論;(必然の)結果.

V ***tack on*** to it some such *corollary* as ... それに...という ような推論を付加する.

Q an ***inevitable corollary*** 必然の結果. ¶the ***natural corollary*** of ... ...の当然の結果. ¶as a ***necessary corollary*** 必然の結果として.

corporal, *n.* 〖陸軍〗伍長.

Q² a ***lance corporal*** 伍長勤務上等兵.

corporation, *n.* 《英》自治団体,公団;《米》会社.

Q the president of a ***big corporation*** 大会社の社長. ¶a ***municipal corporation*** 市自治体. ¶a ***nationally known*** *corporation* 国内で有名な会社. ¶a ***special corporation*** 特別法人.

Q² the staff employed by the ***City Corporation*** 市自治体に属する職員. ¶a ***food corporation*** 食糧営団. ¶a ***Government corporation*** 政府公団. ¶the ***Japan Monopoly Corporation*** 日本専売公社. ¶a ***joint-stock corporation***《米》= a stock company 《英》株式会社. ¶It is a ***not-for-profit*** *corporation*. それは非営利公団である. ¶a ***public-service*** *corporation* [鉄道・ガス・水道などの]公共事業会社(公団). ¶a ***trade corporation*** 《米》商事会社.

P² the *Corporation* ***of*** Dublin ダブリン市の自治体.

corps, *n.* 団,部隊.

Q members of the ***diplomatic corps*** 外交団員=*corps diplomatique* 外交団. ¶a ***distinguished corps*** of experts 著名専門家の一団. ¶an ***editorial corps*** invited from America 米国から招待した記者団. ¶landing of ***French*** and ***English*** *corps* at Shanghai 仏英軍の上海上陸.

Q² an ***air corps*** 〖米空〗航空隊 ‖ an ***air training*** *corps* 航空訓練部隊. ¶an ***army corps*** 軍団. ¶the ***Manhood Corps*** of the Imperial Rule Assistance Association 翼賛壮年団. ¶a ***national*** service *corps* 報国隊. ¶a ***press*** corps 新聞記者団. ¶a ***peace preservation*** *corps* 保安隊. ¶a ***suicide*** *corps* [米軍から見た日本軍の]自殺部隊(決死隊).

P² a *corps* ***of*** teachers 教師団.

corpse, *n.* 死体,しかばね.

V ***exhume*** (=***dig up***) a *corpse* 死体を発掘する. ¶***follow*** the *corpse* to the grave 死体を墓地に送る. ¶***lay out*** a *corpse* 死体に経かたびらを着せて入棺の用意をする.

Q He is a ***living*** *corpse*. 彼は生けるしかばねである. ¶a ***mangled*** *corpse* ばらばらの死体. ¶a ***mummified*** *corpse* ミイラ化した死体. ¶a ***recent*** *corpse* 死んで間もない死体.

correct, *a.* 正しい,正確な.

M ***absolutely*** *correct* 全く正確な. ¶be only ***approximately*** *correct* 大体正確というに過ぎない. ¶***indisputably*** *correct* 無論正しい. ¶The news is ***quite*** *correct*. そのニュースは全く正確だ. ‖ be ***quite*** *correct* and all in order 全く正しく少しも変な所がない. ¶***scientifically*** *correct* 科学的に正しい. ¶***strictly*** *correct* 厳密に正しい. ¶***substantially*** *correct* 大体正確な.

P Mr. X is *correct* ***in*** his observation that ... X 氏が...

といったのは正しい.【類】Am I *correct* ***in*** thinking this? / he is *correct* ***in*** saying that ... / *correct* ***in*** a statement ‖ The account is *correct* ***in*** every particular. 彼の話は何から何まで正しい.

correct, *v.* 改正する, 修正する.

P *correct* the sheets ***for*** the press その校正をする. ¶The publication is *corrected* ***to*** May 10, 1924. この出版物は一九二四年五月十日現在を示すものである.【類】The subscription list (醵金報告) is *corrected* ***to*** December 27, 1901.

O I want to have this *corrected.* これを直して下さい. ¶*Correct* errors if any. 誤りあらば正せ.

correction, *n.* 修正, 正誤; 矯正.

V ***address*** a *correction* to the newspaper その新聞に正誤を申込む. ¶Readers are particularly requested to ***make*** the *corrections* pointed out in the table of errata. 読者各位は正誤表により御訂正下さい. ¶***require*** material *correction* 大分訂正の必要がある.

Q a home of ***juvenile*** *correction* 少年院. ¶The book has recently been published with additions and ***up-to-date*** *corrections.* その本は増補と改訂を加えて最近発行された.

Q² He made a few ***stylistic*** *corrections* in my article. 彼は私の文章に一二個所修正を加えた.

P He is bad ***beyond*** *correction.* 手のつけられない不良だ.

P² *correction* or reduction ***of*** sentence 刑の訂正または減刑. ¶*correction* ***on*** a proof-sheet 校(正刷の訂)正. ¶he writes, in *correction* ***of*** his previous statement, that ... 彼は前言を修正して...と書いている. ¶*corrections* ***to*** previous articles 前掲の諸文に対する訂正.

corrective, *n.* 矯正するもの.

P Penalties are *correctives* ***of*** faults. 罰則があるので失行が匡正される.

correctness, *n.* 正確.

V ***check*** the *correctness* of ... 引合せて確かめる. ¶He has taken much trouble to ***ensure*** *correctness.* 彼は正確を期するため非常に骨を折った. ¶***verify*** the *correctness* of ... ...の正否を確かめる.

Q with ***absolute*** *correctness* in every detail どの点も絶対正確であって. ¶with ***tolerable*** *correctness* かなり正確に.

corrector *n.* 校正係.

P² a *corrector* ***of*** the press 新聞の校正係.

correlation, *n.* 相互関係.

V ***have*** no *correlation* with ... ...と何らの関連もない.

Q bring ... into ***proper*** *correlation* ...を正しい相互関係におく.

P it should be considered ***in*** *correlation* with ... それは...との関連において考慮さるべきである.【類】be used ***in*** *correlation* with ...

P² There is little *correlation* ***between*** them. 両者間にはほとんど何ら関係がない. ¶the *correlation* ***of*** geography ***with*** other studies 地理学と他学科との関係.

correspond, *v.* 相応じる; 一致する; 文通する, 通信する.

M ***accurately*** *correspond* to ... ...と正しく符合する. ¶*correspond* ***closely*** with ... ...とぴったり合う. ¶***frequently*** *correspond* with ... ...としばしば文通する. ¶I ***regularly*** *correspond* with him. 私は規則正しく彼と通信している. ¶Appearance and reality ***seldom*** *correspond.* 外観と現実は滅多に一致しない.

P *correspond* ***for*** amusement only 全く道楽で通信する ‖ He *corresponds* ***for*** a newspaper. 彼はある新聞に通信している. ¶in the year 1694, on a day which would *correspond* in our modern calendar ***to*** November 14 一六九四年, 今日の暦で言うと十一月十四に相当する日に.【類】Our National Diet *corresponds* ***to*** the British Parliament. ‖ *correspond* ***to*** the reality 現実と符合する ‖ *correspond* actions ***to*** words 言行を一致させる.【類】His answer *corresponds* ***to*** my expectation. ¶*correspond* ***with*** (=to) facts 事実と一致する ‖ The promise and the performance do not always *correspond* ***with*** each other. 約束と行動は必ずしも一致するものでない.【類】The copy (写し) does not *correspond* ***with*** the original (原物). ‖ We have *corresponded* ***with*** each other for several years. われわれは数年来互に通信をしている.【類】*correspond* ***with*** a friend absenting himself from school.

correspondence, *n.* 通信, 文通; 符合.

V ***address*** *correspondence* to ... ...にあてゝ通信する. ¶***answer*** *correspondence* 通信に答える. ¶***await*** further *correspondence* 今後の通信を待つ. ¶***begin*** a *correspondence* with ... ...と文通を始める. ¶This pair of lovers are ***carrying on*** an ardent *correspondence.* これら恋人同志は情熱的な手紙のやりとりをしている. ¶***conduct*** *correspondence* 通信を行う ‖ The correspondence secretary ***conducts*** the *correspondence* of the Society. 協会の通信は通信係が取扱う. ¶We must ***decline*** further *correspondence* on the subject. この問題に関してはこれ限り通信をお断りする. ¶***do*** *correspondence* in Esperanto エスペラントで通信する. ¶***exchange*** *correspondence* in English 英語で通信を取交わす.【類】the *correspondence* ***exchanged*** between them. ¶This subject still ***excites*** *correspondence.* この問題について新聞社にまだ投書が来る. ¶I closely ***follow*** the *correspondence* in your columns relating to ... 私は...に関する貴紙の通信を欠かさず読んでいる. ¶I have ***had*** some *correspondence* with him. 私はあの人といくらか手紙をやり取りしたことがある. ¶***hold*** *correspondence* with ... ...と通信を取交わす. ¶*correspondence* is ***invited*** from persons, anywhere in the world, interested in ... ...に関心ある世界中どこの人からでも通信を歓迎する.【類】We ***invite*** your *correspondence.* / We wish to ***invite*** *correspondence* from the readers on ... ¶***keep up*** a *correspondence* with ... ...通信を続ける. ¶***open*** a *correspondence* 手紙のやりとりをする. ¶***open*** and ***answer*** one's private *correspondence* 私信を開封して返事を出す. ¶***open up*** *correspondence* with ... ...と文通を開始する. ¶***renew*** *correspondence* with ... 再び...と通信を開始する. ¶A business transaction may ***require*** much *correspondence* before its details are settled. 商取引はその細目が定まるまでには大分通信を重ねる必要があることがある. ¶***solicit*** *correspondence* 通信を求める. ¶***transact*** one's *correspondence* 手紙を書く. ¶***welcome*** *correspondence* from all concering it それに関する一般からの通信を歓迎する.

V² a *correspondence* has been ***going on*** with regard to ... [先ごろから]...に関する文通が取交わされている. ¶The following *correspondence* has ***passed*** between them. 次のような手紙のやりとりが彼らの間にあった.

Q ***commercial*** *correspondence* 商業通信. ¶***Considerable*** *correspondence* took place between them. 数回文書の往復があった. ¶be in ***constant*** *correspondence* with ...と絶えず文通している. ¶***diplomatic*** *correspondence* between the United States and Germany 米独間の外交文書の往復. ¶carry on an ***enormous*** (=a ***heavy***) *correspondence* 非常に沢山の通信をする. ¶***epistolary*** *correspondence* 手紙の通信. ¶do ***foreign*** *correspondence* 外国と手紙のやりとりをする.【類】conduct ***foreign*** *correspondence* in Esperanto. ¶await ***further*** *correspondence* 今後の通信を待つ. ¶***governmental*** *correspondence* 政府の通信. ¶When I came home, I found a ***huge*** *correspondence* waiting for me. 家に帰って見ると手紙が沢山きていた. ¶I had a very ***interesting*** *correspondence* with him about it. 私はそれについて彼と非常に愉快な文通をやった. ‖ An ***interesting*** *correspondence* is proceeding in the Author on the subject of ... ...の問題についてオーサー誌に興味深い文通が交わされている. ¶There has been a ***lengthened*** *correspondence* in the papers on the subject. この問題に関して新聞紙上に長い間投書が続いた. ¶***one-sided*** "*correspondence*" 一方からだけの通信(片だより). ¶***personal*** *correspondence* 私信. ¶She conducted all her husband's ***private*** *correspondence* with foreigners. 彼女は夫に代って外国人と私信のやり取りをした. ¶keep a ***regular*** *correspondence* with ... ...と絶えず文通する. ¶a ***romantic*** *correspondence* 小説的な手紙のやり取り. ¶***special*** *correspondence* 特別通信. ¶He had ***sufficient*** *correspondence* to require the services of an amanuensis. 彼は書記を要するほどに文通があった. ¶***urgent*** *correspondence* 緊急な通信.

Q² ***business*** *correspondence* 商業通信. ¶***one-way*** (***two-way***) *correspondence* 一方的(双互)通信.

P ***by*** *correspondence* directly with ... ...と直接通信して ‖ a chess match ***by*** *correspondence* 通信による将棋の勝負. ¶***from*** *correspondence* with him, it appears that ... 彼との文通から察すると...らしい. ¶put some firm ***in*** *correspondence* with us ある商会をしてわれわれと取引を開かせる.【類】I was ***in*** *correspondence* with him for years. / stand ***in*** *correspondence* with ... ...と取引する ‖ a boat running *correspondence* with a train 汽車と連絡を取っている汽船. ¶enter (=get) ***into*** *correspondence* with ... ...と文通を始める. ¶A good deal ***of*** *correspondence* has been necessary. 随分手紙のやり取りが必要であった. ¶make arrangements ***through*** *correspondence* 手紙で手筈を整える.

P[2] There has been some *correspondence* ***about*** that affair between them. その事件について文書の往復がその間に行われた. ¶*correspondence* ***between*** separated friends 離れている友だち同士の通信. ¶*correspondence* ***in*** English 英語での通信. ¶the *correspondence* ***of*** an event ***to*** a prediction あるできごとと予言との符合. ¶*correspondence* ***on*** a subject ある問題についての通信. ¶*correspondence* ***with*** a foreign friend ***about*** ... ...について外人の友人と手紙の交換. ¶*Correspondence* ***with*** the writer is invited. 筆者への御照会を歓迎します.

correspondent, *n.* 通信者, [新聞の]特派員.

Q an ***anonymous*** *correspondent* 匿名の通信者. ¶a ***bad*** (***good***) *correspondent* 筆無精(まめ)の人. ¶impose a press censorship on ***foreign*** *correspondents* 外人記者の通信を検閲する. ¶an ***indignant*** *correspondent* writes to the paper protesting against ... ある投書家が憤慨して...に対する抗議文をその新聞に寄せている. ¶an ***international roving*** *correspondent* of the New York Post ニューヨークポスト紙の国際移動通信記者. ¶a ***naval*** *correspondent* 海軍通信員. ¶a ***poor*** *correspondent* 筆無精の人. ¶a ***special*** *correspondent* of the Chicago Examiner with the Roosevelt party ルーズヴェルトの一行に加わっているシカゴ・エギザミナー紙の特派員.

Q[2] a ***business*** *correspondent* 商業文を書く人. ¶a traveling ***lady*** *correspondent* 旅行中の婦人通信記者. ¶according to our ***London*** *correspondent* 本紙のロンドン特派員によれば. ¶a ***news*** *correspondent* 新聞通信記者. ¶***Paris*** *correspondents* in Japanese newspapers 日本紙のパリー特派員. ¶a ***resident*** *correspondent* of the New York Times in Germany ニューヨークタイムス紙のドイツ常駐通信記者. ¶a ***war*** *correspondent* 従軍記者. 【類】a veteran ***war*** *correspondent.*

P ***according to*** the Times *correspondent* at Berlin ベルリン駐在タイムス特派員の報道によると. ¶***as*** the special *correspondent* to the Morning Post モーニング・ポストの特派員として.

P[2] a *correspondent* ***for*** the Sydney Daily Telegraph シドニー・デイリー・テレグラフ専属の通信員. ¶in the capacity of *correspondent* ***to*** the New York Herald ニューヨーク・ヘラルド紙の特派員の資格で. ¶a *correspondent* ***with*** an army=a war correspondent 従軍記者.

corridor, *n.* 廊下, 回廊.

Q the ***Polish*** *Corridor* ポーランド回廊.

Q[2] try to cut a ***supply*** *corridor* 供給路を断とうとする.

corroborate, *v.* 立証する.

P be *corroborated* ***by*** ... ...によって立証される.

corroborative, *a.* 確かにする, 強固にする.

P testimony *corroborative* ***of*** our claims for ... ...に対するわれわれの要求を確立させる証拠 ‖ All are *corroborative* ***of*** such an opinion. すべての人がそうした意見の確実性を証明している.

corrode, *v.* 腐蝕する.

P An iron tool, if never used, will *corrode* ***with*** rust. 鉄の道具は使わないで置くとさびる.

corrupt, *v.* 悪化する; なまる.

P You are *corrupted* ***at*** heart. お前は根性がくさっている. ¶the word has *corrupted* ***into*** ... その言葉がなまって...となった.

corruption, *n.* 腐敗, 収賄; [語の]転化.

Q ***municipal*** (=***city***) *corruption* 市政の乱れ. ¶***official*** *corruption* 官界の腐敗. ¶***pecuniary*** *corruption* 金銭の贈収賄. ¶***political*** *corruption* 政界の腐敗. ¶a ***recent*** *corruption* [語義の]新しい転化. ¶a ***vulgar*** *corruption* of a word 言葉の俗化.

corruptive *a.* 腐敗した.

P act in a way *corruptive* ***of*** public morals 風紀を乱す.

corset, *n.* コルセット.

Q[2] a ***maternity*** *corset* 妊婦用コルセット.

cortege, *n. F.* 行列, 供ぞろい.

Q a ***bridal*** *cortege* 新婦とその付添人の一団. ¶a ***melancholy*** *cortege* 憂愁の一群(葬儀の行列など).

cosmetic, *n.* 化粧品.

Q a ***white*** *cosmetic* おしろい.

Q[2] ***Coty*** *cosmetics* コテーの[高級]化粧品. ¶***eye*** *cosmetic* (目のふちを黒くくまどる)目のお化粧品.

cosmopolitan, *n.* 世界人.

P[2] a *cosmopolitan* ***by*** training and ***in*** temperament 教養上からも気質上からも世界主義の人.

cost, *n.* 費用; 値段, 原価(コスト); 犠牲.

V ***accept*** any *cost* to ... 万難を排して...する. ¶***assess*** the *cost* against ... その費用を...に割当てる. ¶***bear*** the *cost* of a suit 訴訟の費用を負担する ‖ The *cost* of upkeep is ***borne*** by the State. 維持費は国家が負担する. ¶***bring*** the *cost* within the required limit 費用を必要な範囲以内に切詰める. ¶we frequently fail to ***bring back*** the *cost.* しばしばもとがとれないことがある. ¶***bring*** the *cost* ***down*** to ... 原価を...に引下げる. ¶***cheapen*** the *cost* of production 生産費を低廉にする. ¶***collect*** the *cost* of shipment at destination 船積の費用を到着地で取立てる. ¶***compute*** probable *costs* 原価を概算する. ¶***count*** the *cost* of ... ...の原価計算をする. ¶will ***cover*** the *cost* コストは割らないだろう ‖ I enclose ls., ld., to ***cover*** *cost* and postage. 郵税込の値段支払のため一シリング一ペンスを封入致します. ‖ The prices do not ***cover*** *cost* of delivery. この代価には配達料金を含まない. ‖ barely ***cover*** the *cost* 原価かつかつだ. 【類】The present price of raw silk would hardly ***cover*** *costs.* / ***cover*** *cost* of repairs / The charge is small, ***covering*** only the actual *cost* of labor and material (手間と材料費). / Scholarships ***covering*** *cost* of tuition, room, and board are available for accepted candidates. / A remittance sufficient to ***cover*** the *cost* of purchase and postage is inclosed. ‖ ***cut*** *costs* 費用を切詰める ‖ ***cut*** operating *costs* 経常費を節減する. 【類】***cut*** (=reduce) cleaning *costs* with a new appliance (機械). ¶***defray*** the *cost* その費用を払う. ¶I expect it to ***earn*** its *cost* in less than three years. それは三年以内に元が取れると思う. ¶It ***entails*** enormous *cost.* それは巨額の費用を要する. ¶***fight*** the high *cost* of living 高い生活費で苦しむ. ¶The estimates ***give*** the total *cost* at one million yen. 費用は総額百万円の見積. ¶The show ***has*** a *cost* of 162 persons そのショーでは一六二名出場する. ¶It ***involves*** the additional *cost* of fifty yen. その上五十円の費用がかゝる. ¶It tends to ***keep down*** the *cost.* 入費を軽減せしめる傾向がある. ¶who can in some way ***meet*** the *costs* of university attendance 何とか大学授業料が払える ‖ to ***meet*** the increased *cost* of charges, the price is temporarily raised from ... to ... 諸掛り騰貴のため価格は臨時に...から...に値上した. ¶The business will not ***pay*** the *cost.* その商売は引きあうまい. ‖ Each party has to ***pay*** their own *cost* of the appeal. 双方共それぞれの上訴費用を支払わねばならぬ. 【類】will ***pay*** the *cost* of production. ¶the *cost* is ***put*** at something like ... 費用は約...の見積りである. ¶***raise*** the *cost* of production 生産費を膨張させる. ¶***reduce*** the *cost* of labor 労賃を減じる. ¶***reduce*** overhead *costs* 間接費を削る. ¶I will ***refund*** you all your *costs.* 貴下の費用は全部払戻します. ¶All *costs* will be readily ***returned.*** 費用は全部すぐお返しします. ¶The machine ***saves*** its *cost* many times over. その機械を使用すると代金の幾倍に当る節約ができる. ¶***split*** the *cost* of ... between them 割勘で行く.

Q sell at ***actual*** *cost* 実費で販売する. ¶at no ***additional*** *cost* それ以上の代金を申受けないで. ¶***advanced*** *cost* of material 原料の騰貴. ¶work together at ***all*** *costs* to evade revolution and preserve constitutional methods 革命を避け立憲的手段を維持するため万難を排して協力する. ¶the museum is supported by the university at an ***annual*** *cost* of ... その博物館は年...の費用で同大学によって維持されている. ¶hold it at ***any*** *cost* それを死守する. ¶at the ***average*** *cost* of ... 平均...の費用で. ¶at ***considerable*** *cost* 巨額の費用で. ¶at a ***disproportionate*** *cost* 不相応な費用で. ¶really ***economical final*** *cost* 結局経済になる出費. ¶at an ***enormous*** *cost* ばく大な費用で. ¶meet the ***entire*** *cost* 費用は全部出す ‖ the ***entire*** *cost* will not involve more than ...費用は全額で...を越えないであろう. ¶at ***equal*** *cost*=at the same price 同じ値で. ¶at the ***estimated*** *cost* of 12 million yen 見積り費用一千二百万円で. ¶***ever-increasing*** *cost* of living 上る一方の生活費. ¶at an ***extra*** *cost* of ... 別に...の費用を掛けて ‖ at no ***extra*** *cost* それ以外の費用をかけないで. 【類】Members receive The Bulletin without ***extra*** *cost* (送料など一切無料で). ‖ at a ***fair*** *cost* 相応の費用で. ¶We shall be simply handing it over to you at ***first*** *cost.* それではほんの元値で差上げることになります. ¶It was gained at ***great*** *cost.* それは多大な費用を掛けて手に入れた物だ. 【類】It was erected at ***great*** *cost.* / buy at

great** cost* the right to film (映画化する) stories. / gems of ***great** cost*. ¶at a ***heavy** cost* 高価で. ¶the ***human** costs* of the war その戦争における人命の犠牲. ¶at ***immense** cost* 巨費を投じて. ¶increased** costs* of newspaper materials 新聞材料の値上り ‖ to meet the ***increased** cost* of living かさなる生活費をまかなうため. ¶at an ***infinitesimal** cost* きわめて僅少の費用で. ¶install a plant at an ***initial** cost* of … …の工費を掛けて諸機械をすえ付ける. ¶at a substantially ***less** cost* それよりずっと少い費用で. ¶at [a] ***low** cost* わずかの費用で. ¶maximum production at ***minimum** cost* 最低の工費で最高の生産. ¶at a ***moderate** cost* 安い値で. ¶at ***no matter what** cost* どんなに費用が掛っても. ¶at a mere[ly] ***nominal** cost* ほんの僅少の費用で. ¶the ***probable** cost* will be about … 費用は多分…位になるだろう. ¶except at a ***prohibitive** cost* of time and money とても問題にならないほどの時と金を費さないと. ¶Beyond the London postal district, carriage will be at ***purchaser's** cost*. ロンドンの郵便配達区外は運搬費はお客様持ちです. ¶at ***reasonable** cost* 相当の代価で. ¶at a ***reduced** cost* 割引値段で. ¶a ***slight** cost* 僅少の費用. ¶at ***small** cost* 僅少の費用で ‖ at no ***small** cost* of time and labor 少なからぬ時間と労力を費して. ¶for a ***smaller** cost* もっと安値で. ¶the ***total** cost* of the scheme その計画の総費用 ‖ the work would entail a ***total** cost* of … 同工事は総額…を要するだろう. ¶at a ***trifling** cost* 僅少の費用で. ¶without charge, or at ***trivial** cost* 無料または僅少の費用で. ¶keep the ***whole** cost* under one dollar 全体を一ドル以内であげるようにする.

Q² residential ***building** costs* 住宅建築費. ¶the ***buying** cost* 仕入れ原価. ¶inflated ***construction** costs* of small homes 小住宅建設の膨張した費用. ¶***court** costs* 訴訟入費. ¶***factor** cost* 〘経済〙総合資本(土地, 建物, 金, 労働力など). ¶clear them at ***factory** cost* 工場値で売払う. ¶skyrocketing ***food** costs* 天井知らずの食料価格. ¶retail ***food** costs* 食料の小売値. 【類】raise the basic ***food** costs*. ¶***freightage** costs* 運送費(船賃). ¶original ***invoice** cost* 元の仕切り値. ¶high ***labor** cost* 高い労働費. 【類】rising (=increasing) ***labor** costs*. ¶combine ***low-unit** cost* of production with high individual earnings 生産コストの切りさげと個人賃金の高率とを両立させる. ¶current ***living** costs* 現在の生計費 ‖ high ***living** costs* 高い生活費. 【類】***Living** costs* are several times higher than they were then. / ***Living** costs* continue to rise. / ***Living** costs* soared (暴騰した). / the steady rise (漸昇) in ***living** costs* / an increase in wages to meet higher ***living** costs*. ¶***maintenance** costs* 維持(保存)費. ¶***manufacturing** costs* 製造費. ¶***material** cost* 原料のコスト. ¶the ***money** cost* of a disaster 被害の見積り金額. ¶The bill was added to ***occupation** costs*. その費用は占領(軍)費に加算された. ¶***operating** costs*= working expenses 経常費 ‖ Its ***operating** costs* overrun its revenue. 経営費が収入を上回る. ¶be faced with rising ***operation*** and ***construction** costs* 運転費および建設費の値上りに直面している. ¶***production** costs* 生産費. ¶***reparations*** and ***occupation** costs* 賠償額および占領軍費. ¶the ***running** costs* of the various airlines 航空会社の経営費 ‖ low ***running** cost* 少ない運転資金. 【類】The cooker has very low ***running** costs* (経費). ¶***school** cost* (学校だけの)教育費. ¶***telegraph*** (***telephone***) *cost* 電報(電話)費. ¶***upkeep** costs* 維持費, 保存費.

P sell ***at** cost* 原価で売る. 【類】their sale ***at** cost* / furnish (=offer) ***at** cost* ‖ The vessel was completed last year ***at*** a *cost* of one and a half millions sterling. その船は英貨百五十万ポンドを費して昨年完成した. ‖ a building constructed ***at*** the *cost* of … …の費用で建築した建物 ‖ it was built ***at*** a *cost* of … それは…の費用で建築された. 【類】The monument was erected ***at*** the *cost* of 5,000 yen. / The Panama Canal was constructed in 1915 ***at*** a *cost* of three hundred fifty million dollars. ‖ ***at*** a *cost* of five dollars a day 毎日五ドルの費用で ‖ ***at*** the *cost* of the Government 政府の金で ‖ ***at*** a *cost* of nothing ただで. 【類】Board and lodging (まかない付下宿) will be available ***at*** a *cost* of about two pounds a week. ‖ Fame, ***at*** the *cost* of character, is dearly bought. 人格を犠牲にしての名声は多大の損失である. 【類】***at*** the *cost* of her own life / ***at*** the *cost* of much blood and suffering ‖ exalt the inefficient ***at*** the *cost* of the efficient 有能者を犠牲にして無能者を励ます ‖ ***at*** his *cost* 彼に迷惑をかけて. ¶sell ***below** cost* 原価以下(コストを割って)で売る. ¶irrespective ***of** cost* 費用にかかわらず ‖ regardless ***of** cost* 費用にとん着せず ‖ bear a portion ***of*** the *cost* 費用の一部を負担する ‖ free ***of** cost* ただで. ¶for less ***than** cost* 実費以下で. ¶It is very difficult to get honest servants, as I know ***to*** my *cost*. 僕のにがい経験によると正直な召使は容易に見付からないものだ. ‖ He was loved ***to*** his *cost*. 彼は愛されたのが身のためにならなかった. ‖ I know it ***to*** my *cost*. 僕はそれには懲りている. ¶if the price is not ***under*** first *cost* 値段が原価以下でないなら. ¶it will be sent ***without** cost* on request to … それは…へ御請求になれば無代で送ります. 【類】Please send me, ***without** cost*, a booklet outlining how the Book-of-the-Month Club operates.

P² with *cost[s]* ***against*** the defendant 訴訟費は被告負担で. ¶the *cost* ***in*** human lives [戦争などにおける]人命の犠牲. ¶the *cost* ***of*** a bath 一回の入浴費 ‖ The *cost* ***of*** fittings is to be divided. 造作費は分担することになっている. ‖ the *cost* ***of*** lighterage はしけの費用. 【類】The *cost* ***of*** living has increased of late to such an extent that … / *cost* ***of*** production / *cost* ***of*** repairs ‖ the *cost* ***of*** the site 敷地の代金 ‖ the *costs* ***of*** a suit 訴訟費用 ‖ estimate the *cost* ***of*** production 原価計算をする. ¶at practically no *cost* ***to*** yourself 事実上君自身少しも損をせずに.

cost, *v.* 値する, かゝる; 失わせる.

M It will *cost* him ***dearly***. それは彼に取って大変な損失になるだろう. ‖ a method which *costs* ***dearly*** in time 結局非常な損失になる方法. ¶***How much*** does it *cost* for cleaning? みがき代はいくらか. 【類】Does it *cost* ***much***? ¶*cost* ***more*** in the long run than … 結局…より多く費用がかかる.

O It *cost* him two shillings. 彼はそれに二シリング出した. 【類】It *cost* him infinite labor. / His dissipation (放とう) *cost* him his fortune.

co-star, *v.* 〘映〙主役を共演する.

P *co-star **with*** … …と主役を共演する.

coster, *n.* 呼売商人.

Q a ***bred-and-born** coster* はえ抜きの街頭商人.

costume, *n.* 服装, 仮装服; 〘劇〙衣裳(コスチューム).

M Jesuits in China ***assumed*** the *costumes* of the literates. 中国のヤソ会士は学者風の服装をした. ¶***colorful** costumes* 色彩の豊かな服. ¶This will ***complete*** the *costume*. これで服装が整う. ¶***don*** the Japanese *costume* 和服を着る. ¶***freshen up*** the *costume* 衣裳を新しくする. ¶***hire*** a *costume* for a fancy ball 舞踏会の仮装服を賃借りする. ¶***wear*** a special *costume* 特別の服を着る.

Q in full ***academic** costume* 学校の式服を着て. ¶a ***black** costume* 黒装束. ¶a ***bright** costume* はでな服装. ¶a ***ceremonial** costume* 礼服. ¶in ***Dutch** costume* オランダの服装をして. ¶in ***elaborate** costume* 念入りな服装をして. ¶a ***fetching** costume* 人目を引く服装. ¶in ***gala** costume* 晴着で. ¶Japanese girls in ***national** costume* 和装の日本の少女たち. 【類】in her ***national** costume*. ¶They look better in their ***native** costumes* than in European or American suits. 彼らは欧州人の服や米国服を着ているよりも自国の服を着ている方がうつりがいい. 【類】a beautiful doll dressed in her ***native** costume*. ¶dressed in their ***official** costume* 彼らの官服を着て. ¶a peasant girl in ***picturesque** costume* 絵のようなきものを着た百姓娘. ¶in a ***quaint** costumes* 変った服装をして.

Q² Here we see Mrs. S in ***ball** costume*. S夫人の夜会服姿. ¶a girl in ***bathing*** (=***swimming***) *costume* 海水着をつけた少女. ¶appear in the ***circus** costume* he is wearing at the studio 工房で着ているサーカス服で出る. ¶in ***court** costume* and knickerbockers 宮廷服と半ズボンを着けて. ¶in ***cycling*** (***motoring***) *costume* 自転車(自動車)服で. ¶***drilling** costume*, according to school pattern (女子の)運動制服. ¶a group of gentlemen in ***eighteenth century** costumes* 十八世紀の服装をした紳士の一団. ¶an ***ensemble** costume* 〘服装〙アンサンブルの衣服. ¶Mrs. … in a ***garden** costume* 庭園服姿の…夫人. ¶in full ***Highland** costume* スコットランド高地地方の服装をして. ¶dressed in ***old-world** costumes* 古風な服を着て. ¶in ***peasant** costumes* 野良着で. ¶put on one's ***sports** costume* 運動服(スポーツ着)をつける. ¶in ***stage** costume* 舞台姿で. ¶She went out in ***street** costume*. 彼女は外出着で出かけた. ¶in ***walking** costume* 散歩姿(軽装)で. ¶a ***winter*** (***summer***) *costume* 冬(夏)服.

P an actor *in costume* 衣裳を着けた俳優 ‖ Danjuro ***in*** the *costume* of Benkei 弁慶の衣裳を着けた団十郎. 【類】Miss … ***in costume*** of a Red Cross nurse / ***in costumes*** of various colors and patterns ‖ appear ***in*** the *costume* of the last century 前世紀の服を着て出る ‖ dressed ***in*** the *costume* of the period その時代の服装をして ‖ a foreigner ***in*** Japanese *costume* きもの姿の外人.

P^2 The *costumes* ***of*** the figures are those of the sixteenth century. その人たちの服装は十六世紀のである.

cot, *n.* [台にズックを張った]簡易寝台; 《英》小児用寝台.

V *cots* ***vacated*** by deaths or recoveries [患者が]死んだり退院したりして空いた病院の軽便寝台.

Q^2 a ***baby*** *cot* 幼児用寝台. 「寝台のある病院.

P a hospital ***with*** more than a thousand *cots* 千以上も小

cottage, *n.* 小屋, 別荘.

V ***take*** a *cottage* at the place そこに別荘を借りる.

Q ***cosy*** *cottages* 住み心地のよいいなか家. ¶from the ***modest*** *cottage* to the most splendid mansion 粗末な家から最もりっぱな邸宅に至るまで. ¶a ***sequestered*** *cottage* いおり. ¶a ***straggling*** *cottage* or so 一二軒ぽつりぽつりと散在するいなか家. ¶an old tumble-down ***thatched*** *cottage* 古い倒れかかった草ぶきのあばら家.

Q^2 a ***country*** *cottage* いなかの小屋; 《米》いなかの別荘. ¶a ***summer*** *cottage* あずまや; 《米》避暑地にある別荘(=summer house). ¶a ***week-end*** *cottage* 《米》週末用小別荘.

P^2 a *cottage* ***by*** the sea なぎさに近い小家.

cotton, *n.* 綿, 木綿. 「*cotton* 綿をつむ.

V ***grow*** (=***cultivate or raise***) *cotton* 綿を栽培する. ¶***pick***

Q ***sanitary*** (=***absorbent***) *cotton* 脱脂綿. ¶***waste*** *cotton* くず綿. 「*cotton* 綿火薬.

Q^2 ***diamond*** *cotton* ダイヤモンド木綿(上製の綿布). ¶***gun***

couch, *n.* 寝所; 寝いす.

Q rise from a ***grassy*** *couch* 草のふしどから立ちあがる. ¶the ***nuptial*** *couch* 新婚のふしど. 「*couch* 寝所に退く.

P lie down ***on*** a *couch* 寝いすに横になる. ¶retire ***to*** one's

couch, *v.* 言表わす; 身を横たえる.

P an essay *couched* ***in*** classical language 古[典]語で書かれた漫筆 ‖ a letter *couched* ***in*** improper terms 乱暴な言葉で書かれた手紙. 【類】a poem *couched* ***in*** beautiful language / a letter *couched* ***in*** local terms (いなか言葉) ‖ The bill of health is still *couched* ***in*** the quaint, official language of earlier days. 健康証明書は今も昔のままの変った公用文で書いてある. ¶*couch* ***on*** a seat 席に横になる ‖ be *couched* ***on*** a bed of flowers 花のベッドに身を横たえて

cough, *n.* せき. └いる.

V ***emit*** short dry *coughs* = hack 短いからせきを出す. ¶***keep under*** a *cough* せきを止める.

V^2 The *cough* will ***pass away*** without medicine. そのせきは薬を飲まないでも止まる.

Q have a ***bad*** *cough* ひどくせきをする. ¶a ***choking*** *cough* 息の詰まるせき. ¶a ***convulsive*** *cough* ひきつけるようなせき. ¶a ***dry*** *cough* that may be mistaken for tuberculosis 肺結核と間違えそうなからせき. ¶a ***hacking*** *cough* ごほんごほんというせき. ¶a ***hard*** and ***dry*** *cough* 苦しいからせき. ¶a ***hoarse*** (=***husky***) *cough* しわがれたせき. ¶a ***racking*** *cough* 苦しいせき. ¶a violent ***spasmodic*** *cough* 時々せきこむひどいせき. ¶a ***suspicious*** *cough* 怪しいせき. ¶I have at last got rid of my ***troublesome*** *cough.* しつこいせきがようよう治った.

Q^2 a ***churchyard*** *cough* 死際のせき. ¶A ***staccato*** *cough* interrupted the flow of his speech. 時々出るせきで彼の話はとぎれた. ¶the ***whooping*** *cough* 百日ぜき.

P a new remedy ***for*** *cough* せきの新薬. ¶I suffer ***from*** a slight *cough.* 少しせきが出る. ¶The child ***with*** the *cough* ought to be in bed. せきの出る子供は寝かして置かないと

cough, *v.* せきをする. └いけない.

M *cough* very ***hard*** ひどくせきをする. ¶He has nearly *coughed* ***out*** his own heart. あまりひどくせき込んで心臓まで吐き出しそうだった.

M^2 be *coughed* ***down*** [話など]せき払いで邪魔される ‖ The audience *coughed* ***down*** the tedious speaker. 聴衆はせき払いをしてくどい弁士をやめさせてしまった. ¶*cough* ***up*** (=***out***) sputum (=phlegm) せきをしてたんを吐き出す.

P She *coughed* herself ***into*** fits. 彼女はせきこんで止らな

council, *n.* 会議, 評議; 参事会. └かった.

V they ***assembled*** a *council* in which it was resolved to … 彼らは会議を開いて…ということを決議した. ¶***call*** a *council* to consider what should be done to … 会議を開いて…のため何を為すべきかを審議する ‖ He ***called*** a *council* of his chief adherents (主な同志). ¶***call together*** a *council* 会議を召集する. ¶***hold*** a *council* 会議を開く ‖ ***hold*** a long *council* ***together*** 長時間にわたる会議を開く. ¶They ***took council*** and agreed that they would surrender. 彼らは会議を開いて降服することにきめた. ¶***taking council together*** 相談をして.

V^2 The *council* ***meets*** in the town-hall. 参事会が市会館で開かれる. ¶The *council* has ***risen.*** 参事会は散会した.

Q an ***advisory*** *council* 評議員会. ¶a ***deliberative*** *council* 審議会. ¶the Supreme *Council* 最高会議; 大政官.

Q^2 the ***Agricultural*** and ***Forestry Liaison*** *Council* 農林連絡協議会. ¶co-chairmen of the ***American Zionist Emergency*** *Council* アメリカ・シオン主義者緊急会議の正副議長. ¶a ***city*** (***town***) *council* 市(町)会. ¶a ***district*** *council* 《英》郡会. ¶a ***family*** *council* 親族会議. ¶the ***Far East*** *Council* 極東会議. ¶the ***four-power Allied*** *Council* for Japan 連合国側四カ国の対日会議. ¶the ***Mine Safety*** *Council* 鉱山保安審議会. ¶a ***seven-member*** *council* 七人協議会. ¶the ***Sepreme War*** *Council* 最高軍事会議. ¶a ***student*** *council* 《米》学生自治委員会. ¶the ***Wage Deliberative*** *Council* 賃金審議会. ¶a ***works*** *council* 職場会議. ¶a ***world*** *council* 世界会議. ¶the ***World Security*** *Council* 世界安全保障会議. ¶form a ***23-member*** *council* 二十三名協議会を設ける.

P ***at*** the *council* of … …の会議で. ¶questions ***before*** the *council* will concern … 評議会に上程される問題は…に関係のものであろう. ¶***in*** *council* 会議中 ‖ Readers ***in*** *Council* 紙上議会(新聞紙などの投書欄). ¶He was for nearly twenty years our associate ***on*** the *Council.* 彼は約二十年間われわれと同僚の議員であった. ‖ a man ***on*** (=member of) the *council* 評議員.

P^2 The *council* ***of*** three gave good counsel. 三人寄って良い知恵が出た. ¶the American *Council* ***on*** Education 米

councilman, *n.* 《米》市・町・村会議員. └国教育会議.

Q^2 a ***city*** (***town***) *councilman* 市(町)会議員.

council[l]or, *n.* 評議員, 顧問官.

Q an ***advisory*** *councillor* 顧問官. ¶a ***Parliamentary*** *councillor* 参与官. ¶a ***privy*** *councilor* 枢密顧問官.

Q^2 a ***town*** *councillor* 《英》市会議員. ☞米は a city coun-

P the House ***of*** *Councillors* [日本]参議院. └cilman.

P^2 a *councillor* ***in*** the Imperial Household 宮中顧問官. ¶a *councilor* ***of*** the Imperial Palace 宮中顧問官 ‖ a *councilor* ***of*** (=to) the Legislative Bureau 法制局参事官. ¶a *councilor* ***to*** the Foreign Office 外務省参事官.

counsel, *n.* 相談; 助言; 熟慮; 弁護人.

V ***ask*** *counsel* 助言を求める. ¶***buy off*** *counsel* 弁護士を買収す. ¶***despise*** his cautious *counsel* 彼の注意深い助言をべっ視する. ¶***exchange*** *counsel* 相談し合う. ¶***follow*** the *counsel* of Aristotle アリストテレスの忠告に従う. ¶***get*** one's *counsel* from … …からの助言を受ける. ¶***give*** *counsel* 助言を与える. ¶the right to ***have*** *counsel* 弁護人の援助を受ける権利. ¶They ***held*** *counsel* as to what measures they should take. 一同善後策について相談をした. ¶***keep*** one's own *counsel* 秘密を守る ‖ He is too talkative to ***keep*** his own *counsel.* あの男はおしゃべりだから人に腹を見られてしまう. ¶***name*** his own *counsel* 自己の弁護人を指定する. ¶***offer*** *counsel* to (=advise) him 彼に忠告を与える. 【類】***offer*** friendly *counsel.* ¶***seek*** *counsel* in him 彼の助言を求める ‖ ***seek*** *counsel* of God 神のみ旨を求める. ¶***take*** *counsel* of … …に相談する ‖ ***take*** *counsel* of one's pillow 寝てゆっくり考える ‖ He ***takes*** *counsel* of his heart, but not of his head. 彼は自分の胸(感情)と相談して頭(理性)と相談しない. ‖ ***take*** *counsel* with a very old friend ずっと昔からの友人と相談する ‖ ***take*** *counsel* with oneself とくと考えて見る. 【類】***take*** *counsel* together as to which course should be adopted. ¶***use*** *counsel* 熟慮する.

Q The dependant has an ***able*** *counsel.* 被告側にはりっぱな弁護人がついている. ¶a ***competent*** *counsel* 有能な弁護士. ¶the ***defendant's*** *counsel* 被告の弁護人. ¶a ***friendly*** *counsel* 親切な助言. ¶***Good*** *counsel* never comes amiss. 忠言はいつもありがたい. ¶an ***ill-weighed*** and ***injudicious*** *counsel* 無思慮・無分別な助言. ¶***practical*** *counsel* 直ぐ役に立つ助言. ¶***sagacious*** *counsels* 賢い助言. ¶a ***valuable*** *counsel* 貴重な助言. ¶***weak-kneed*** *counsels* 力のない助言.

¶a *wise counsel* 賢明な助言.

Q[2] a *death-bed counsel* to … …に与える遺訓. ¶a *defense counsel* for … …の弁護人 ‖ the chief *defense counsel* 弁護団の主席. ¶a *prosecution counsel* 原告側弁護士. ¶the Bureau of Student *Counsel* 学生相談部.

P be deliberate *in counsel* 忠告に慎重だ ‖ He is wise *in counsel*. 彼は賢明な助言を与える.

P[2] much sound *counsel concerning* … …に関する非常にしっかりした助言. ¶the *counsel for* the defendant (plaintiff) 被(原)告側の弁護人 ‖ the *Counsel for* the Crown 《英》政府側の弁護士. ¶a *counsel of* perfection 〖神学〗[神の道に入る者に対する]完全を期する勧告 ‖ it is the *counsel of* prudence to … …するのが安全だ. ¶*counsel upon* the reading of books 読書訓.

counsel, *v*. 相談する, 助言する.

M *counsel softly* おだやかに勧める.

counsel[l]ing, *n*. 相談, 助言.

Q *vocational counseling* (=guidance) 職業相談.

Q[2] *family counseling* 家庭相談. ¶*union counseling* 労組の指導(助言).

counsel[l]or, *n*. 助言者; 顧問.

Q one of the most *helpful counselors* of young men on the American platform today 今日米国の演壇における最も有力な青年指導者の一人. ¶He is a *juridical counsellor* in the Gaimusho. 彼は外務省の法律顧問だ. ¶a *straight-tongued counsel(l)or* (歯に衣をきせぬ)率直な忠告者. ¶a *trusted counselor* 信用のある助言者. ¶*vocational counselors* 職業指導者. ¶a *wise counselor* in financial matters 財政上賢明な助言者.

Q[2] a *beauty counselor* 美容顧問. ¶a *student counselor* 学生主事.

P[2] a *counselor of* insight and wisdom 識見高く賢明な助言者.

count, *n*. 計算; 点, 廉(かど).

V His indictment *contains* two *counts*. 彼の起訴されたのは二つの理由がある. ¶*keep count* of numbers 数を取る. ¶On a vacation, we pay no attention to the passage of the days and often *lose count*. 休暇だと日のたつのに注意しないから何日だかわからなくなることが往々ある. ‖ I have *lost count* of time. 今何時になるのか分らなくなった. ¶*make* an actual *count* 実数を数える. ¶must *take count* of the fact that … …という事実を考慮に入れねばならない.

Q according to an *accurate count* 精算によると. ¶eight, by *actual count* たしかに(実地当った勘定で)八つ. 【類】by *actual* (=exact) *count* a quarter of a million people. ¶be wrong on *every count* あらゆる点においてよくない. ¶ascertain it by *exact count* その実数を当って見る. ¶the *last count* made under the auspices of the city 市の手で最近取った数[通行人の数など]. ¶His case covered four *separate counts*. 彼の事件は四つの独立した罪状があった. ¶be indicted on *seven counts* 七つの罪状で起訴される.

Q[2] hold a *census count* 人口調査を行う. ¶a *nose count* 頭(あたま)数.

P *beyond* (=*out of*) *count* 数えきれないほど. ¶There were, *by count*, 72 people in the room. 数えて見るとその部屋には七十二人いた. ¶I may have missed one or two *in* the *count*. 一つや二つは数えそこねたかも知れない. ‖ include … *in* the *count* …を勘定に入れる. ¶fail *on* both *counts* どちらも失敗に終る ‖ He was sentenced to 12 months' imprisonment *on* this *count*. 彼はこのかどを以て十二カ月の禁固に処せられた. ‖ *on* the third *count*—one, two, three! 一二三と三度数えた時に.

P[2] one of the *counts against* her is that … 彼女の欠点の一つは…ということである.

count, *v*. 計算する; …と思う; 重きをなす; 数に入る; 当にする.

M In this list, children do not *count at all*. この表では子供たちは数に入っていない. ¶*count little* or *nothing* ほとんど問題にならない. ¶It may not *count much* today, but it will tomorrow. それはきょうは大したことはないがあすは重きをなすであろう. ‖ *count much* on … …を大いに当にする. ¶*count* them *one by one* into a dish 一つ一つ数えてさらに盛る. ¶*Count* me *out*. [ゲームの仲間から]私は抜かしてください. ‖ *count out* money to the poor 貧民に金を与える ‖ *count out* the numbers of … …の数を取る ‖ The House was *counted out*. [定員数に満たないので]議会は休会した. ‖ The boxer was *counted out*. その拳闘家はカウント切れで負けた. ¶*count strongly* 大いに大事だ.

M[2] *count off* 番号を数えて与える; 〖陸軍〗[班別にするため]番号をとなえる ‖ *Count off*! 番号! ¶*count up* 計上する, しめる ‖ *count up* one's versatile talents その多能を数えあげる. ¶*count up to* one hundred and *backward* 百まで数えまた逆に数える ‖ The savage can *count* only *up to* five. 野蛮人は五つまでしか数えられない.

P Quality *counts above* origin. [品物など]出所よりも質が大切である. ¶it *counts against* the value of … それが邪魔になって…の価値を損じる ‖ Mere cash can not be *counted against* these things. 単に金だけではこれらのものに匹敵できない. ¶This book *counts among* the best of his works. この本は彼の傑作の中に入る. ‖ is hardly to be *counted among* the best ちょっと第一級というわけにはいかない. 【類】The college can *count among* its alumni many distinguished personages. / The society *counts among* its members many of the leading citizens of the United States. / Periander is usually *counted among* the seven wise men of Greece. / *count* him *among* the masters of our literature / The book will not *count among* his major works. / The temple bell *counts among* the largest in the world. ‖ The enlightening of war may be *counted among* the very few advantages war brings to man. 戦争の啓蒙的効果はその人間にもたらすきわめてわずかな利益の中にこれを数えることができる. ¶*count* him *as* one 彼を数の中に入れる ‖ Two children under the age of 10 years *count as* one person. 十歳以下の子供は二人を一人に数える. 【類】It is an honor for our club to *count* him *as* a member. ‖ at the rate of … per day, portions of days to *count as* such 一日…の割合で(はんぱの日も一日に数えて) ‖ *counting* 0.5 and fractions *as* units and disregarding the rest コンマ五以下は切捨て(四捨五入). ¶They are *counted by* the tens of thousands. 彼らは万をもって数えられる. ¶Proper clothes *count for* much in business. 実業界ではきちんとした服装は大切なことである. ‖ It *counts for* little. それはほとんど価値がない. ‖ It *counts for* nothing. それは役に立たぬ. 【類】Such small defects *count* indeed *for* little or nothing in the survey of his career. ‖ Sentiment *counts for* something in this matter. こうしたことには感情がものを言う. ¶They could be *counted on* the fingers of one hand. それはわずかに五指をもって数えるだけしかない. 【類】They might be *counted on* the fingers of both hands. / The number was less than could be *counted on* the fingers of both hands. ‖ *count* (=rely) *on* a person (one's assistance) 人(など)を当にする ‖ Don't *count on* others for help. 人の助けを当にするな. ‖ May we *count on* your co-operation? 貴下の御協力を願われましょうか. 【類】I am *counting on* your joining us. / can *count on* the support of … / *count on* one's promise / Mind, I *count on* your keeping the promise. ¶Can you *count to* fifteen in Chinese? 中国語で十五まで数えられるの. ‖ it must be *counted to* his credit that … …ということはたしかに彼の功績だと認めねばならぬ ‖ You must not *count upon* me. 君は僕をあてにしてはいけない. 【類】His support can be *counted upon*. / something that will have to be *counted upon* ‖ We can *count upon* having at least eighteen. 少くとも十八だけは得られる. ¶*count with* beads ビーズ(玉)で数を取る.

O *Counting* it there are four. それを入れて四つある. ¶I *count* him rich (=a rich man). 僕は彼を金持と思う. ¶I *count* it no shame to any man to be … …であることはだれにとっても恥とは思わない. ¶I *count* that friend of his my enemy. あの彼の友だちを僕は敵と思っている. ¶Every bit *counts* どんなわずかでも粗末にできない.

countenance, *n*. 顔, 容貌; 奨励, 援助.

V *change* one's *countenance* 顔色を変える. ¶He *composed* his *countenance*. 彼は泰然自若としていた. ¶*find* no *countenance* in … …の支持は得られない. ¶*forget* the *countenance* of … …を見忘れる. ¶*give* (=*lend*) one's *countenance* to … …に賛意を表する ‖ He refused to *give countenance* to the project. 彼はその計画を支持することを拒絶した. ‖ Certain external appearances seem to *give countenance* to this view. ある客観的情勢がこの見解を裏書するように思われる. ¶*have* the *countenance* of … …の援助を得る ‖ He *has* not a pleasing *countenance*. 彼は人好きのする容貌ではない. ¶*keep* one's *countenance* 平気(まじめ)でいる ‖ Though his heart fled, yet he *kept* a cheerful *countenance*. 元気を失ったがそれでも彼は愉快そうな顔

をしていた. ¶These facts ***lend*** *countenance* to his views. これらの事実が彼の意見に力を添える. 【類】I cannot ***lend*** my *countenance* to such a thing. ¶***lose*** *countenance* 面目を失う. ¶He ***possesses*** a mild and benevolent *countenance*. 彼は温和で情深い容貌をしている. ¶***put on*** a serious *countenance* 真顔になる. ¶***read*** one's *countenance* 人の顔色を読む. ¶***refuse*** all *countenance* to his scheme 彼の計画はてんで相手にしない.

Q He has a ***bad*** *countenance*. 彼はきげんが悪い. ¶with a ***beaming*** *countenance* 晴々した顔をして. ¶his ***brooding*** *countenance* 彼の思案顔. ¶a ***cheerful*** *countenance* 明朗な顔付. ¶behold a person with a ***disdainful*** *countenance* 人をしり目に見る. ¶a woman with an ***expressive*** *countenance* 表情に富んだ顔の女. ¶a ***fine*** and ***sweet*** *countenance* りっぱなやさしい容貌. ¶with a ***grave judge-like*** *countenance* 重々しい法官めいた顔をして. ¶a man with a remarkably ***handsome*** *countenance* すばらしい美男子. ¶A ***lovely*** *countenance* is the fairest of all sights. 愛きょうのある顔ほど目に美しいものはない. ¶an ***open*** *countenance* 明けっぱなしの顔. ¶a woman of an ***oval*** *countenance* うりざね顔をした女. ¶a somewhat ***priestly-looking*** *countenance* ちょっと坊さんらしい顔. ¶a ***sad*** (***gloomy***) *countenance* 悲し気(など)な顔. ¶a ***scowling*** *countenance* にがり切った顔. ¶with a ***shining*** *countenance* 晴々した顔をして. ¶a ***smiling*** *countenance* にこにこ顔. ¶with ***unaltered*** *countenance* 自若として.

P read anger ***in*** his *countenance* 顔を見て怒っているなと悟る ‖ Please keep me ***in*** *countenance*. 僕の面目の立つようにして下さい. ¶put one ***out of*** *countenance* 人の面目をつぶす. 【類】you put me greatly ***out of*** *countenance* by saying ... ‖ I looked him ***out of*** *countenance*. 僕はにらみ付けて彼をへこました.

counter, *n.* 勘定台, 帳場台, 売場(カウンター); 計算器.

V ***haunt*** the free-lunch *counters* in Chicago シカゴの無料食堂にしばしば出入する.

Q² a ***department-store*** *counter* デパートの売場. ¶The ***Geiger*** *counter* is a device which detects and counts ionizing particles. ガイガー計算器はイオン化検出・測定をする器具だ. ¶a ***lunch*** *counter* 軽食堂のカウンター. ¶goods for sale at ***notions*** *counters* 《米》雑貨売場にある商品. ¶a ***service*** *counter* [酒場などの]カウンター.

P the man ***at*** the *counter* その帳場の番頭. ¶a girl ***behind*** the *counter* 売場の女店員 ‖ women ***behind*** the store *counters* 売場受持の女店員 ‖ serve ***behind*** the *counter* 売場に勤める. ¶toss a dollar ***on*** the *counter* [その質を試験するために]勘定台に一ドル銀貨を投げる. ¶***over*** the *counter* 〖株〗[取引所を通さず]証券屋の店先で ‖ information given orally ***over*** the *counter* 応接台越しに口頭で話す事項. ¶handle business ***under*** the *counter* やみ取引をする.

counter, *a. adv.* 反対の; 反対に, 逆に.

P It is *counter* ***to*** the spirit of the Imperial Rescript on Education. それは教育勅語の御精神に反する. 【類】*counter* ***to*** the teachings of Christianity ‖ this runs *counter* ***to*** the common assertion that ... これは...という一般の主張と説を異にしている. 【類】go (=run) *counter* ***to*** the current of the world / go *counter* ***to*** the spirit of the times (時代精神) / His plans run *counter* ***to*** mine. ‖ act *counter* ***to*** one's promise 自分の約束を破る行動をする.

counter, *v.* 反対行動をとる.

P She didn't like their plan, so she *countered* it ***with*** her own. 彼女は彼らの案を好まなかったので自分で対抗案をだした.

counterattack, *n.* 反撃.

V ***launch*** a *counterattack* 反撃に出る.

counter-attraction, *n.* 反対引力.

P Baseball is an important *counter-attraction* ***to*** the public-house. 野球は酒場への出入を防止する重要な牽制力である.

counterbalance, *v.* 釣合せる; 相殺する.

M Hard working ***often*** *counterbalances* slowness at learning. 猛勉で頭のにぶさを補う例はよくある.

P be more than *counterbalanced* ***by*** ... 比較して見ると...の方が勝っている.

counterchange, *v.* 交錯させる.

P a wall *counterchanged* ***with*** several colors 色々な色彩を施した壁.

counterfeit, *n.* まね.

Q a ***crude*** *counterfeit* 粗末な模造品.

V ***make*** a *counterfeit* of ... ...を装う.

counter-measure *n.* 対策.

V ***take*** some *counter-measure* 何か対応策を講じる.

counterpart, *n.* 写し; 相対物.

V It ***has*** no *counterpart* in the world. それは天下一品である. ‖ They ***have*** few *counterparts* in our own literature. わが国の文学にはこれらに類するものはほとんどない. ‖ We ***have*** her *counterpart* in real life. (小説ばかりでなく)実社会にもそうした女がいる. ‖ The geometrically designed canals and fountain-basins of European gardens ***have*** no *counterpart* in Japan. 欧州の幾何学的に作られた水流や泉水は日本の庭園では見られない.

Q the ***exact*** *counterpart* of ... ...と全く符合したもの ‖ The American college has no ***exact*** *counterpart* in the educational system of other countries. 米国のカレッジと全く同一の教育制度は他国にはない. ¶Mr. Steevens is the ***literary*** *counterpart* of the impressional painter. スティーヴンス氏は印象派の画家を文士にした者である. ¶Mercury is the ***Roman*** *counterpart* of Greek Hermes. ローマのマーキュリはギリシアのヘルメスに相当する. ¶The two are the ***very*** *counterpart* of each other. 二人はまるでうり二つだ.

P The Royal Academy of Fine Arts exhibition is a *counterpart* ***to*** the Paris *Salon*. [英国の]王立美術協会の展覧会はパリのサロンと好一対だ.

counterpoise, *n.* 釣合, 均衡.

V ***establish*** some *counterpoise* 幾分均勢を保たせる.

counting, *n.* 計算.

Q The number has not been arrived at by the process of ***actual*** *counting*. その数は実地計算によったものではない.

Q² ***vote*** *counting* 投票計算(開票).

P I can tell the number ***without*** *counting*. 数えなくても数は分る. ¶a mere *counting* ***of*** heads 頭数だけの計算.

country, *n.* (**1**) 国.

V ***adore*** a *country* 国を崇拝する. ¶when the *country* is ***agitated*** 世が乱れている時. ¶assassinate him to ***avenge*** one's *country* 自国のあだを報いるため彼を暗殺する. ¶he ***betrayed*** his *country* to the French during the Napoleonic Wars by ... 彼はナポレオン戦争の当時...をやって自国をフランスに売った. ¶***bring*** a *country* under one rule 国を統一する ‖ ***bring*** the *country* to the brink of disaster 国を災禍のふちに立たせる. ¶***clear*** the *country* of bandits 匪賊(ひぞく)をその国から一掃する. ¶***close*** the *country* 鎖国する. ¶***conquer*** a *country* 国を征服する. ¶***consider*** one's *country* insulted 自分の国が侮辱されたと思う. ¶They ***covered*** the *country* in their tour. 彼らは旅行でその国へも回った. ‖ ***covering*** all *countries* 全世界の国々と関係のある. ¶***defend*** the *country* against the forces of ... ...軍に対抗してその国を防ぐ. ¶***exalt*** one's *country* in the sight of all 国威を宣揚する. ¶***explore*** a *country* 国を探検する. ¶***flee*** the *country* その国を出奔する. ¶They ***freed*** the *country* from Persian domination. 彼らはその国をペルシアの支配から脱せしめた. ¶***hold*** a *country* in subjection 国を服従させて置く. ¶***involve*** the *country* in disaster その国を災禍の中にまき込む. ¶These are things by which travellers ***judge*** our *country*. これらによって旅行者はわが国を批判するのである. ¶He ***left*** the *country* for London. 彼は国を立ってロンドンへ行った. 【類】He ***left*** this *country* for his country's sake. ¶***love*** one's *country* fervently 自国を熱烈に愛する. ¶***misrepresent*** the *country* in several respects 色々な点でその国を誤り伝える. ¶***open*** a *country* to trade 国を開いて貿易する. ¶***overrun*** the *countries* of the white men 白人国をじゅうりんする. ¶***plunge*** their *countries* into war 彼らの国々を戦禍におとし入れる. ¶***poison*** the *country* 国を毒する. ¶There are enough individuals to ***populate*** a *country* like Sweden. スエーデンぐらいの国を満たすだけの人口がそこにある. ¶***protect*** a *country* against foreign invasion 外国の侵略に対して国を防護する. ¶Cholera ***ravaged*** the *country* as a sweeping epidemic. コレラが猛烈な流行ぶりを見せてその国に広がった. ¶***relieve*** the *country* of ... 国を...から救う. ¶***renounce*** one's former *country* and ruler 自分の故国と君主を棄てる. ¶He successively ***represented*** his *country*, as Minister or Ambassador, at Lisbon, Madrid, and others. リスボン, マドリードなどで公使または大使として自国をりっぱに代表した. ¶***serve*** the *country* by writing English 英文記者として国に奉仕する. 【類】those who have ***served*** their *country* most conspicuously / ***serve*** one's *country* honestly and efficiently / loyally ***serve*** one's *country* / we can best ***serve*** our *country* as ... ¶the social evil which ***smirches*** the *country* [公娼など]国辱たるこの社会的悪弊. ¶***taking*** the *country* over 全国的に言って. ¶***travel*** (=***tour***) those *countries* それらの国々を旅行する.

Q the most ***advanced*** *country* in the Occident 西洋の最先進国. ¶an ***agricultural*** *country* 農業国. ¶***allied*** and ***neutral*** *countries* 同盟および中立国. ¶in the eastern part of the ***Argentine*** *country* アルゼンチンの東部で(に). ¶***backward Asiatic*** *countries* アジア後進諸国 ‖ ***backward*** *countries* 文化の遅れた国. ¶a ***bandit-ridden*** *country* 匪賊(ぞく)の横行する国. ¶a ***bleak*** and ***cheerless*** *country* 荒涼として暗たんたる国. ¶a ***capitalistic*** *country* 資本主義の国. ¶the ***Christian*** *countries* キリスト教国. ¶Siam is a fairly ***civilized*** *country*. シャムは相当文化の高い国だ. ¶when Japan was a ***closed*** *country* 日本が鎖国であったとき. ¶***Continental*** *countries* 大陸諸国. ¶an ***earthquake-ridden*** *country* like Japan 日本のような地震国. ¶an ***effete old*** *country* 老衰国. ¶for this ***entire*** *country* この国全体にとって. ¶an ***extensive*** and ***populous*** *country* 広くて人の多い国. ¶He has gone to a ***far*** *country* over the sea. 遠く海外の国に行った. ¶a ***far-away*** *country* 遠方の国. ¶a ***fertile*** *country* 産物に富む国. ¶a ***flat*** *country* 平坦な国. ¶a ***friendly*** *country* 友邦. ¶Kai is a ***good*** *country* for vines. 甲斐はぶどうに適した国だ. ¶in every ***habitable*** *country* in the Christian globe (=Christendom) 人間の住みうるすべてのキリスト教国に. ¶a ***happy*** and ***prosperous*** *country* 明るく繁栄している国. ¶a ***hilly*** *country* 山の多い国. ¶a ***hostile*** *country* 敵国. ¶an ***imaginary*** *country* (実在していない)空想の国. ¶the ***larger*** *countries* of the world 世界の諸大国. ¶a ***lawless*** *country* 無法の国. ¶a ***maritime*** *country* 海国. ¶new countries like Australia and Canada, or old countries like Germany and Britain, or ***middle-aged*** *countries* like the United States 豪州・カナダのような新進国またはドイツ・英国のような古国あるいは米国のような中年の国. ¶a ***mountainous*** *country* (高い)山の多い国. ¶***near-by*** *countries* 近隣の国々. ¶***neighboring*** *countries* 隣国. ¶There is no such architecture in ***newer*** *countries*. [歴史の]若い国々にはそのような建築物はない. ¶He said that out in Hongkong they were very proud of the ***Old*** *Country*. 国を出て香港にいる者は非常に本国の自慢をすると彼は言った. ‖ the ***old*** *country* of an immigrant 移民の故国. ¶Japan and China are two of the ***oldest*** and most densely ***populated*** *countries* in the world. 日・中は世界で最も古くかつ人口の最も多い国である. ¶the diplomatists of our ***own*** and ***other*** *countries* わが国および他国の外交官. ¶a ***populous*** *country* 人口ちゅう密な国. ¶a ***poverty-stricken*** *country* 貧乏国. ¶a ***progressive*** *country* 進取的な国. ¶a ***promising*** *country* 有望な国. ¶Belgium is the most thickly ***settled*** *country* in Europe. ベルギーは欧州で一番人口ちゅう密な国である. ¶Japan is the most ***tourist tempting*** *country* in all the world to-day. 今日日本は世界で最も観光客を引き付ける力のある国である. ¶***tropical*** *countries* 熱帯諸国. ¶***under-developed*** *countries* 未開発諸国. ¶an ***unexplored*** *country* 未開発の国々. ¶***various*** *countries* of the world 世界各国. ¶***war-devastated*** *countries* 戦禍を受けた国々. ¶the ***Western*** *countries* 西洋諸国. ¶The ***whole*** *country* was convulsed by civil war. 国中が内乱で動揺した. ¶a ***young*** *country* with plenty of time before her 春秋に富む新進国.

Q² an ***abolition*** *country* 《米》奴隷解放国. ¶an ***aggressor*** *country* 侵略国. ¶a ***beri-beri*** *country* 脚気の多い国. ¶the ***British Commonwealth*** *countries* 英連邦に属する国々. ¶the two ***brother*** *countries* in the Far East 極東における二友邦. ¶a ***buffer*** *country* 緩衝国. ¶a ***capitalist*** *country* 資本主義国. ¶a ***coast*** *country* 沿海国. ¶***Cominform*** *countries* コミンフォルム(共産党)諸国. ¶the ***Communist*** *countries* 共産主義の国々. ¶a ***creditor*** *country* 債権国. ¶the ***Danube*** *countries* ダニューブ沿岸諸国. ¶a ***debtor*** *country* 債務国. ¶an ***earthquake*** *country* 地震国. ¶propaganda in ***enemy*** *countries* 敵国における宣伝 ‖ a former ***enemy*** *country* 以前の敵国. ¶***English-speaking*** *countries* 英語を母国語とする国々. ¶occupation troops in ***ex-enemy*** *countries*旧敵国への進駐軍. ¶a ***food exporting*** *country* 食料輸出国. ¶a ***free-trade*** *country* 自由貿易国. ¶***gold*** *countries* 金本位の国々. ¶"***have***" ("***have not***") *countries* 持てる(持たざる)国. ¶a ***high tariff*** *country* 関税率の高い国. ¶a ***hill*** *country* 山国. ¶one's ***home*** *country* 故国. ¶a ***host*** *country* [国際会議の]主催国. ¶***iron-curtain*** *countries* 鉄のカーテン内の国々. ¶an ***island*** *country* 島国. ¶two ***key*** *countries* of South America—Brazil and Chile 南米の二主要国であるブラジル・チリー. ¶the ***Marshall plan*** *countries* マーシャルプラン適用諸国. ¶***Moslem*** *countries* 回教諸国. ¶the ***mother*** *country* 母国. ¶a ***manufacturing*** *country* of the first rank 第一流の工業国. ¶***non-dollar*** *countries* 非ドル国. ¶the remaining ***non-Communist*** *countries* of Europe and Asia 欧亜に残存する非共産国. ¶her ***opponent*** *country* 相手国. ¶travellers from ***overseas*** *countries* 外客. ¶the ***Pacific*** *countries* 太平洋諸国. ¶the ***Pacific coast*** *countries* 太平洋沿岸諸国. ¶a ***peasant*** *country* 零細農業の国. ¶a ***recipient*** *country* 受入国. ¶a ***regulation*** *country* 統制国家. ¶***satellite*** *countries* 衛星諸国. ¶the two ***sister*** *countries*, Norway and Denmark 二姉妹国ノールウエーとデンマーク. ¶the ***Soviet bloc*** *countries* ソヴィエット圏の諸国. ¶a ***subject*** *country* 属国. ¶the [Universal] ***Postal*** *countries* 万国郵便同盟加入の国々. ¶major ***wheat exporting*** *countries* 主要小麦輸出国.

P ***across*** the *country* 全国の. ¶Please give me six post-cards ***for*** this *country*, and three for Europe. 内国の郵便はがき六枚と欧州向けのを三枚ください. ¶Norway, which at one time was one of the most drunken ***of*** *countries*, gradually became, through education and legislation, one of the most temperate. ノルウェーは昔は世界一番の飲酒国であったが教育と法律のおかげで漸次最も節酒の国となった. ‖ go ***out of*** one's *country* 自国を去る. ¶all ***over*** (=***throughout***) the *country*=all the country over 国中に ‖ They sowed sedition ***over*** the *country*. 彼らは国中に騒動の種をまいた. ¶***through*** the *country* 国中を(に). ¶is not general ***throughout*** the *country* 全国共通のものではない.

P² Every *country* ***in*** the world is represented among its residents. その地の居住者中には世界中の国の人がいる.

(**2**) いなか; 土地, 地方.

V It ***commands*** the surrounding *country*. そこは周囲の展望がきく. ¶***stump*** the *country* 地方を遊説する.

Q a ***bleak*** *country* 荒涼たる土地. ¶a ***broken*** *country* 起伏のある地方. ¶drive across fields and ***open*** *country* 野や木立のないいなかをドライブする. ¶surrounded by ***rolling*** *country* and wooded land 起伏した土地や森林地帯に取囲まれて. ¶a ***smiling*** *country* 楽しい土地. ¶command the ***surrounding*** *country* 周囲の土地を見晴している. 【類】We went to the top of the church and viewed the ***surrounding*** *country*. ¶Siberia is certainly the only ***unexploited*** *country* in the world. シベリアはたしかに世界唯一の未開拓地方である. ¶***wild*** and ***desolate*** *country* 未開の荒れ果てた土地.

Q² drive through an ***apple*** *country* in spring 春りんごのみのるいなかをドライブする. ¶***backwoods*** *country* (=land) 《米》辺境地方. ¶a ***hot springs*** *country* 温泉郷. ¶***mountain*** *country* 山地. ¶***rugged hill*** *country* ごつごつした山地.

P I have got back ***from*** the *country*. 私は今いなかから戻った. ‖ a girl fresh ***from*** the *country* 山出しの少女. ¶I spent a day ***in*** the *country*. いなかで一日を過した. 【類】He is ***in*** the *country*. / rest ***in*** the *country*. ¶go up ***into*** the *country* 田舎へ行く. 「囲の地方.

P² the *country* ***around*** New York City ニューヨーク市周

country-folk, *n.* いなかの人々.

Q the ***kind, hospitable,*** and ***simple-minded*** *country-folk* 親切でもてなしのよい素ぼくないなかの人たち.

countryman, *n.* 同国人.

V ***benefit*** one's *countrymen* 自国人の利益になる.

Q a ***rugged old*** *countryman* 無骨ないなか者.

Q² a ***fellow*** *countryman* 同国人 ‖ his hard-pressed ***fellow*** *countryman* 金に困った彼の同国人.

P² a *countryman* ***of*** Mr. So-and-So 某氏の同国人.

countryside, *n.* 地方, 片いなか, 地方民.

Q The ***whole*** *countryside* were in a state of great excitement. 地方民は全部非常に興奮していた.

P some little village ***by*** the *countryside* 片いなかのある小村. ¶It is one of the finest ***in*** all this *countryside*. それはこの地方で一番りっぱなものです.

coup-de-grace, *n. F.* 最後の一撃, とどめ.
V *give* the *coup-de-grace* とどめを刺す.
coup-d'état, *n. F.* クデーター.
Q a ***spectacular*** *coup d'état* はでなクーデター.
Q² the Russian ***Bolshevik*** *coup d'état* ロシアボルシェビキのクーデター.
couple, *n.* 夫婦; 一対, 二つ.
V ***induce*** unmarried *couples* to marry 未婚の男女に結婚を勧める. ¶The minister ***joined together*** over 8,000 *couples*. あの牧師は八千組以上の結婚式を手掛けた. ¶They ***made*** a happy *couple*. 二人は幸福な夫婦になった. ¶Nothing but death can ***part*** the *couple*. その夫婦の仲を裂くものはただ死あるのみである.
Q a ***bridal*** *couple* 結婚式の夫婦. ¶a ***childless*** *couple* 子なしの夫婦. ¶an ***engaged*** *couple* 婚約した男女. ¶They are a ***happy*** *couple* today 彼らは今日では幸福な夫婦だ. ¶an ***ill-assorted*** (a ***well-assorted***) *couple*=an ***ill-matched*** (a ***well-matched***) *couple* 不釣合(似合)の夫婦. ¶a ***love-crossed young*** *couple* 恋の邪魔をされた二人の若い男女. ¶a ***love-matched*** *couple* なれ合いの夫婦. ¶five ***married*** *couples* 五組の夫婦. 【類】An American husband and a French wife make an excellent ***married*** *couple*. ¶a ***wedded*** *couple* 夫婦. 【類】a newly ***wedded*** *couple*. ¶They are a ***well-matched*** *couple*. 似合いの夫婦だ. ¶a ***young*** *couple* 若夫婦.
P² in a *couple* ***of*** days (months, years) 二三日(など)経って. 【類】a *couple* ***of*** years ago / for a *couple* ***of*** years to come 今後二三年間.
couple, *v.* 二つつなぎ合わせる; 配偶する.
M a pair of lovers ***duly coupled*** in wedlock 天下晴れての夫婦.
P *coupled* ***in*** lasting bonds 久遠の縁につながれて. ¶dogs *coupled* ***to*** one another 二匹つなぎ合わした犬. ¶*coupling* (=coupled) ***with*** the fact that ... ...という事実と連関して ‖ when I *coupled* it ***with*** my knowledge that ... それを私の知っている...ということと思い合わすと.
coupon, *n.* 利札; 切取切符, ...券.
V ***cash*** a *coupon* 利札を引換える. ¶***detach*** a *coupon* 札を切取る. ¶***get*** the used *coupons* ***redeemed*** 使用券に対し現金を戻してもらう. ¶***tear off*** a *coupon* クーポンをもぎる.
Q This *coupon* is not ***redeemable*** after 31st March, 1923. この券は一九二三年三月三十一日以後は現金引換ができません.
Q² a ***clothing*** *coupon* 衣料切符. ¶a ***competition*** *coupon* [新聞などの]拡張割引券. ¶Investors may obtain further information by using the ***information*** *coupons*. 投資者には問合せ券によって市況をお知らせする. ¶One free ***inquiry*** *coupon* issued with each number. 毎号無料質問券が一枚付いています. ¶a ***hotel*** *coupon* ホテル止宿のクーポン. ¶a ***food*** *coupon* 食券. ¶a ***meal*** *coupon* 外食券. ¶sell goods with ***prize*** *coupons* 懸賞付クーポンで品物を売る.
courage, *n.* 勇気, 剛勇.
V ***call up*** one's *courage* 勇気をふるい起す. ¶They could ***command*** sufficient *courage*. 彼らは十分に勇気を振うことができた. ¶***develop*** *courage* 勇気を養う. ¶***display*** *courage* 勇気を示す. 【類】***display*** the most inflexible (不屈不とうの) *courage*. ¶***draw*** fresh *courage* from ... ...によって勇気を挽回する. ¶when I ***feel*** my *courage* ebbing 私の勇気が段々衰える気がする時に. ¶I tried to ***find*** *courage* to address him. 思切って彼に話掛けて見ようとした. 【類】I ***found*** the *courage* to say "No." ¶***gain*** *courage* by very slow degrees きわめて徐々に元気づく. ¶He ***gathered*** *courage* for the daring act. 彼はその大胆な行動をやる勇気を奮い起した. 【類】***gathering*** *courage* from this success. ¶the fact ***gave*** him new *courage* その事実で彼は新しい元気が出た. ¶she ***has*** the *courage* of her opinions as regards ... 彼女は...に関して忌憚なく意見を述べる ‖ He ***has*** *courage* in his blood. 勇気は親譲り. ‖ They ***have*** the *courage* of their convictions. 彼らには所信を述べる勇気がある. 【類】He ***had*** the *courage* to refrain from pushing his demands any further. / He ***has*** the *courage* to speak up what he thinks right. ¶***infuse*** *courage* into despondent hearts 失望した人に力を付ける. ¶***keep up*** one's *courage* がん張る. ¶***lack*** *courage* and self-respect 勇気と自尊心を欠く. ¶Cheer up! Don't ***lose*** *courage*. 元気を出せ. 気を落すな. ¶This ***made*** even his *courage* waver. これでさすがの彼も勇気を落した. ¶***muster [up]*** (=***collect***) one's *courage* 勇を鼓する. ¶***pick up*** *courage* 勇気を出す. ¶***pluck up*** *courage* 勇気を奮い起す. ¶***recover*** (=***regain***) one's *courage* 勇気を回復する. ¶***regather*** *courage* 元気を回復する. ¶***screw*** one's *courage* to a sticking place. 勇気を一点に傾注する. ¶***screw*** one's *courage* ***high*** 勇気を高める. ¶***screwing up*** my *courage* 思い切って. 【類】he ***screwed up*** his *courage* to ask whether ... ¶***show*** *courage* 勇気を示す. 【類】He ***showed*** great *courage* and determination in rescuing the drowning man. ¶***summoning*** the wild *courage* of despair 死物狂いの勇気を出して. ¶***summon up*** *courage* to attack the difficulty 勇気を振い起して困難と戦う. 【類】***summon up*** sufficient *courage* to ... ¶***take*** *courage* 元気づく ‖ ***take*** *courage* to ... 思い切って...する. 【類】To hold out against the crowd ***takes*** *courage*.
V² When one has seen that ..., *courage* ***comes***, and with it success. 人は...ということがわかると勇気が出てきて同時に成功がやって来るものだ. ¶His *courage* ***failed***. 彼は気後れがした. ¶My *courage* was ***oozing*** (=***leaking***) ***away***. 私の勇気は段々失せて行った. ¶His *courage* ***weakened***. 彼の元気はぐらついた.
Q ***calm*** *courage* 沈勇. ¶***cool*** (=***quiet***) *courage* 落付いた勇気 ‖ I admire his ***cool*** *courage*. 彼はいい度胸だ. ¶***dauntless*** *courage* びくともしない勇気. ¶***Dutch*** *courage* 酒で出した勇気. ¶***fictitious*** (=***sham***) *courage* 虚勢. ¶set about work with ***fresh*** *courage* さらに元気を出して仕事に取かかった. ¶***high*** *courage* 非常な勇気. ¶***indomitable*** *courage* 不屈の勇気. ¶***intellectual*** *courage* 知的勇気. ¶an example of ***invincible*** and ***dogged*** *courage* 不屈不撓(とう)の勇気の模範. ¶***military*** *courage* 武勇. ¶a ***moral*** *courage* 精神的勇気 ‖ lack of ***moral*** *courage* 卑屈. ¶a fighter of ***no mean*** *courage* 勇気りんりんたる闘士. ¶***physical*** *courage* 肉体的勇気. ¶***reckless*** *courage* 蛮勇. ¶give him ***renewed*** *courage* 彼に元気を出させる. ¶with a ***sacred*** *courage* 神々しい勇気を出して. ¶***serene*** *courage* 落付いた勇気. ¶bear disease and misfortune with ***silent*** *courage* 苦しみを口に出さず勇気をもって病気や不幸を忍ぶ. ¶with ***unshaken*** *courage* 不動の勇気をもって. ¶***unwavering*** *courage* ゆるがぬ勇気.
Q² ***animal*** *courage* 蛮勇. ¶***iron*** *courage* 鉄の勇気. ¶with ***lion*** *courage* ししの勇気で.
P abound ***in*** *courage* 勇気に満ち満ちている. ¶defend oneself ***with*** the *courage* of despair 必死の勇をふるって身を守る.
P² a grim *courage* ***in*** the face of danger 危険に直面しての沈勇. ¶the *courage* ***of*** one's conviction (opinion) 忌憚なく所信(など)を吐露しまたは断行する勇気.
courageous, *a.* 勇ましい.
M be *courageous* ***enough*** to ... 勇敢にも...する. ¶***morally*** as well as ***physically*** *courageous* 肉体的にも道徳的にも勇ましい.
courier, *n.* 使者, 早飛脚.
V a *courier* was immediately ***despatched*** to ... ...へ直ちに使者を立てた.
P ***by*** *courier* 早飛脚で.
course, *n.* (**1**) 進行, 進路; 経過; 成行; 方針; 策; 競走場.
V ***accelerate*** the *course* of convalescence [病気の]回復を促進する. ¶***adopt*** a wise middle *course* 賢明な中道を取る ‖ They decided to ***adopt*** a different *course* of policy from what was at first pursued. 彼らは最初と違った政策を採ることに決した. ¶***advise*** a *course* 献策する ‖ What *course* do you ***advise***? どんな風にやったらいいでしょうか. ¶***advance*** the *course* of civilization 文明を進展させる. ¶***affect*** the *course* of events (world affairs) 大勢(など)に影響を及ぼす. ¶***alter*** the *course* of development 発達の方向を変える. 【類】***alter*** a *course* to the required direction. ¶The commander ***approved*** the *course* taken by his subordinates. 司令官は部下のやり口に賛成した. ¶***change*** *course* in succession 逐次針路を変える. 【類】That little book actually ***changed*** the *course* of my whole life. / a strange figure who ***changed*** the *course* of world history. ¶Prices ***continue*** the downward (upward) *course*. 値段は相変らず下(上)り坂. 【類】The caravan ***continued*** its westward *course*. ¶if occasion ***demands*** such a *course* そうした方針を採る必要が起れば. ¶***determine*** the *course* of a river 河源を探る ‖ ***determine*** the *course* of the historic stream [英雄の行動などが]歴史の流れる方向を決定する. 【類】***determine*** the *course* of her life (人生の進路). ¶The book will show you how to ***direct*** the *course* of business. その本を見ると商売のやり方が分る. ¶The boats ***finished***

the *course* in the order given below. ボートは次の順序で決勝点に着いた. ¶*follow* the *course* of nature 自然にさからわない ‖ He takes care to *follow* the *course* of events in China. 彼は中国の情勢に注意している. ‖ *follow out* a *course* of action [ある]行動を取る. ¶You *have* three *courses* open. 君の取るべき道が三つ開かれている. ‖ The law must *have* its *course*. 法律は曲げられぬ(その規定を実行せねばならぬ). ‖ The cough has *had* its *course*. 治るときがきてせきが治った. ‖ had to *have* its *course* どうしても行く所まで行かなければならなかった ‖ *having* no other *course* open to him せっぱつまって. ¶The ship continued to *hold* her *course* eastward. 船は依然東方にコースを取った. ¶The final results will abundantly *justify* our *course*. 最後の結果がわれわれの取った方針の正当性を十分に証明するだろう. ¶no other *course* was *left* to him but ... 彼には…する外に策がなかった. ¶Such was the *course prescribed*. こういった行動を取れと言われた. ¶*pursue* one's *course* 己の進むべき道を取る ‖ We cannot but *pursue* the present *course*. われわれは現在のやり口を続けるより仕方がない. ¶*recommend* a *course* to be followed 採るべき行動を勧める. ¶*retard* the *course* of civilization 文明の進歩を遅らせる. ¶In the history the author *reviews* the whole *course* of the company. その年史に著者は同社変遷の跡を漏らさず示している. ¶The river *runs* its *course* for 16 miles. その川は延長十六マイルにわたる. ‖ It was allowed to *run* its natural *course*. 自然の成行に任した. ‖ The disease *runs* a rapid *course*. その病気はぐんぐん進む. ‖ If uncomplicated, the disease *runs* its *course* in from two to five weeks. 余病併発のない限りその病気は二週間ないし五週間で全快する. ‖ The *course* of the epidemic has now been *run*. その伝染病はもう終った. ‖ They are civilizations which have already *run* their *course* and passed out of existence. それらはすでに行詰って過去のものとなってしまった文明である. 【類】The history of the Hohenzollern Dynasty *ran* its *course* on November 9th, 1918. / It was only a fashion and *ran* its *course* very quickly. / It has *run* its *course* in the popular press. / The 20th century had *run* more than half its *course*. ‖ there is another rumour *running* its *course* to the effect that ... …というもう一つのうわさが立っている ‖ let the cold *run* its *course* かぜがひとりでに抜けるまで待つ. ¶He *saw* no *course* open to him but to give up his plan. 彼は自分の計画を断念する外に取るべき策のないことを知った. ¶the steamer *set* her *course* for ... 船は…に針路を取った. ¶*shape* our *course* for reform 改革の方針を立てる ‖ those currents of public opinion which are *shaping* the *course* of events today 今日の問題の方向を決める世論の流れ. ¶The ship was obliged to *shift* her *course*. 船は針路を転ぜざるを得なかった. ¶*steer* one's *course* by it それを目当にかじを取る ‖ *steer* its straight *course* to ... …に向ってまっすぐに進む. 【類】*steer* a middle *course* along the line of prudence and common sense. ¶*take* one's own *course* 単独行動を取る. 【類】*take* the *course* recommended / We have done our duty and things must now be allowed to *take* their *course*. ‖ This *course* he *took*, galling as it was to his pride. この方針を彼は採った, 自尊心を傷つけはしたが. ‖ let nature *take* its own *course* 自然に任す ‖ let the story *take* its *course* 話の筋を進める ‖ let things *take* their own *course* ‖ let a matter *take* its own *course* 成行に任す. ¶*trace* [*out*] the *course* of a river 川の源を探る. ¶*watch* the *course* of events with jealous eyes 油断なくことの成行を見守る. 【類】*watch* the *course* of the war with vigilance (注意深く).

Q There is no *alternative course*. 他に取るべき策がない. ¶the *best course* to pursue 最善の策 ‖ A meeting of shareholders was called to consider the *best course* to pursue. 前後策を講じるため株主会が召集された. ¶I think it a *better course* to pursue. その方針を採ったらさらに妙でしょう. ¶It is not expected in the *common course* of things. あたりまえではそんなことにはならない. ¶follow a *courageous course* 勇敢な行動を取る. ¶a *dangerous course* 危険なやり口. ¶This *course* is not *desirable*. この行き方は好ましくない. ¶in [the] *due course* of time 相当の期間に, やがて ‖ pay a draft in *due course* 為替手形を期日までに支払う ‖ I will wire you in *due course*. 機を失せず打電致します. ‖ In *due course* it developed into pneumonia. やがてそれが肺炎に変じた. ‖ in *due course* of law 法律上必然の結果として. ¶take an *easterly course* [船など]東方へ進む. ¶The *first course* was served. [食卓で]最初のさらが出された. ¶the *fundamental course* of SCAP directives 総司令部指令の本旨. ¶Its *further course* is still uncertain. その成行はどうなるかまだ判らない. ¶He pursued a very *immoral course* of life. 彼は非常に不身持なことをやった. ¶the *inside course* of events leading up to ... …に発展する事件の内幕. ¶after a *long course* of study 永く勉強した後に. 【類】engage in a *long* and *arduous course* of study. ¶deviate from the *main course* of negotiation 交渉の本筋から脱線する. ¶a dinner of *many courses* 品数の多いごちそう. ¶steer a *middle course* in a controversial question 異論のある問題において諸説の中を取る ‖ take the *middle course* 中を取る. 【類】A *middle course* is best. / steer the *middle course* between optimism and pessimism. ¶This was the *natural course* to pursue. これは当然取るべき道であった. ‖ complete its *natural course* 行くところまで行く. ¶*no other course* is open to us than to ... われわれは…するより外に取るべき道がない. 【類】there is *no other course* but to ... ¶Inflationary policies will change the *normal course* of business. インフレ政策のため事業の正しい方向が変ってくる. ¶It appears to us to be the *only course possible*. それより外に僕らの取るべき道はなさそうだ. ¶I feel that there is only *one course* for me to take. 僕の取るべき道はただ一つしかないような気がする. ¶follow the *opposite course* 逆コースを取る. ¶in the *ordinary course* of business 商売の普通のやり方では ‖ what will take place in the *ordinary course* of events 自然の成行で起って来る事. ¶run a *parallel course* 並行する. ¶a *permissible middle course* 採って差支えのない中道. ¶a *planned course* of action 予定行動. ¶the *post-operative course* 手術後の経過. ¶a *prescribed course* 予定の行動. ¶It is the *proper course* to take. それは取るべき適当な道だ. 【類】the *proper course* for you to pursue is to ... ¶a *pusillanimous course* 薄氷を踏むようなやり方. ¶the only *rational course* then left for us was to adopt ... そのときわれわれの取りうる唯一の合理的な方法は…を採用することであった. ¶in *regular course* 当り前に行けば. ¶keep a ship on her *right course* 船が正しい針路を外れないようにする. ¶the *safe course* is to avoid ... …を避けるのが安全策だ. 【類】the only *safe course*. ¶the *same course* was followed for ... …をするに同一筆法によった. ¶follow a *scheduled course* 予定通り事を運ぶ. ¶The river follows a *serpentine course*. 川はうねうねと流れている. ¶a meal of *seven* or *ten courses* 七品または十品の食事. 【類】a meal consisting of *several courses*. ¶The path took a *sinuous course* up the hill. 道は曲りくねって丘の上に続いていた. ¶There may be *some other course* to be taken. 何か外に打つ手があるかも知れない. ¶follow the *stereotyped course* 型の通りに(例によって例のごとく)やる. ¶follow the *suggested course* 教えられた方法に従う. ¶There are *three courses* which can by any possibility be pursued. とに角取りうる手段は三つある. ¶the army took a *triumphant course* through ... その軍勢は…をじゅうりんした. ¶Prices continue the *upward* (*downward*) *course*. 物価は上(下)向きを続けている. ¶in *usual course* 順当に行けば. ¶Take *whatever course* you think best. 何なり君の一番いゝと思う方法を取り給え. ¶in the *whole course* of my experience 私の今までの経験で ‖ influence the *whole course* of United States-Soviet relations 米・ソ関係を全面的に左右する. ¶It is a *wise course* to take. それは賢い手の打ち方だ ‖ the only *wise course* before you is to ... 君の取るべき唯一の賢明な道は…することだ. 【類】He took the *wisest course* open to him. / the *wisest course* to follow.

Q[2] a *dinner course* [食事の]一品. ¶a *fish course* 魚肉の一品. ¶forecast the *future course* of history 歴史の進むべき将来を予言する. ¶a *golf course* ゴルフ場 ‖ an eighteen-hole *golf course* 十八ホールのゴルフ場. ¶The party arrived on the *race course*. その一行が競馬場に着いた. ¶follow a *zigzag course* ジグザグの道をたどる.

P run *after* her *course* [船などが]その針路を追うて走る. ¶be in prison *by course* of law 服罪して入所中である. ¶*during* the *course* of a year 一年間. ¶*in course* of manufacture 製造中 ‖ now *in course* (=progress) of construction 目下建造中 ‖ The problem will solve itself *in course* of time. 同問題はやがて解決する. ‖ be *in course* of adjustment 調整中である ‖ The goods ordered are now ***in*** *course* of shipment. 注文品は目下荷積み中である. ‖ has ***in*** *course* of issue ... ...は目下発行中である ‖ ***in*** [the] *course* of nature 自然に ‖ ***in*** the *course* of events (=things) 物の成行として, 自然 ‖ he happened, ***in*** *course* of conversation, to say that ... 談話中に彼はふと...と言った ‖ ***in*** [the] *course* of a night (a day or two, the next few days, many years) 一夜(など)の中に ‖ ***in*** the *course* of the past year ここ一年間に. 【類】***in*** the *course* of several years' residence in China / ***in*** the *course* of the last few years / ***in*** the *course* of our correspondence / ***in*** the *course* of ordinary use / ***in*** the *course* of a voyage / ***in*** the *course* of disease / ***in*** the *course* of these researches / now ***in*** the *course* of publication / ***in*** the *course* of the work / The path, further on ***in*** its *course*, skirted the shepherd's cottage. その小道はそれから先へ行って羊飼の小屋を回っていた. ¶That is ***of*** *course*, if your father permits you. それは言うまでもなくお父さんのお許しがあっての上のことだ. 【類】it should be said, ***of*** *course*, that ... / Why, ***of*** *course* not! ¶a ship ***on*** a western *course* 西回りの船. ¶The regatta was held ***on*** a two-mile *course* on the lake. ボート・レースは湖上二マイルのコースで催された. ¶The race was run ***over*** a 26-mile *course*. その競走は二十六マイルコースであった. 【類】The championship race was ***over*** a four and a half mile *course*. ¶The bridge is now ***under*** (=in) *course* of erection. その橋は目下建造中である. ‖ The cause is now ***under*** *course* of examination. 原因は目下調査中である. ¶***with*** the *course* of time 時の経過とともに. ¶***within*** the *course* of a few days 数日以内に. 【類】***within*** the *course* of the next few weeks.

P[2] I feel I must oppose with all my vigour such a *course* ***of*** action. 私は全力を尽してそうした行動に反対せねばならないような気がする. ‖ the *course* ***of*** prices 物価の歩み ‖ the *course* ***of*** history 歴史の歩み.

(**2**) 科, 科目, 課程.

V ***attend*** a *course* by Dr.... ...博士の講座に出る ‖ ***attend*** the preparatory *course* 予科に通学する. ¶***complete*** one's college *course* 大学の課程を終える. 【類】***complete*** one's *course* in a college / The *course* of study is to be ***completed*** within a year. ¶He ***conducts*** *courses* in international law. 国際法の講義を担当している. ¶***establish*** a *course* in Esperanto at a university 大学にエスペラント科を創設する. ¶***finish*** one's *course* 卒業する. ¶the subjects which ***form*** the *course* of studies at the school are ... 同校の学科課程は...である. ¶***give*** a *course* in etiquette 作法を教える. 【類】***give*** *courses* in both German and English. ¶***hold*** a summer *course* in ... ...に関する夏期講習を催す. ¶***inaugurate*** a pioneer *course* 学科を創設する. ¶I never ***missed*** one *course* of his lectures during the time I was at Oxford. 私はオクスフォード大学在学中彼の講義には一度も欠席しなかった. ¶The college ***offers*** a *course* of four years, leading to the degree of Bachelor of Arts. 同大学は四カ年の課程でバチェラー・オヴ・アーツの称号を授ける. ‖ the *courses* ***offered*** in the summer school are ... その夏期学校で授ける科目は...である. 【類】***offer*** a three years' *course* in law / ***offer*** *courses* for home study (通信教授) in the following subjects. ¶***pursue*** one's college *course* 大学の課程を修める ‖ ***pursue*** an advanced *course* of study 高等科を修める. 【類】***pursue*** a four-year *course* of study / ***pursue*** a *course* in medicine. ¶***pass through*** a university *course* 大学の課程を終了する. ¶he ***received*** a full *course* in ... 彼は...を規定通りに修業した. ¶***start*** one's *course* by correspondence 通信教授を受け始める. ¶***take*** a *course* in Americanization [新来の外国人が]米化教育を受ける ‖ ***take*** a *course* in beauty culture 美容術の教授を受ける ‖ ***take*** a *cousre* in a correspondence school 通信教授を受ける. 【類】***take*** a *course* in French / ***take*** a *course* in carpentry / He ***took*** the law *course* at the University of Texas in 1900–1901 / ***take*** a special *course* of scientific study at a German university ‖ ***take*** the *course* over again [落第生など]原級に留まる. ¶Every Japanese boy ***takes up*** a five-year *course* in English in the middle school. すべて日本の少年は中学校で五年間英語の教授を受ける(旧制中学校令).

V[2] The *course* of instruction ***covers*** (=***occupies***) six months. 修業期間は六カ月. ¶the *course* will ***include*** ... 学課目は...である.

Q pursue a ***complete*** *course* of study 全課程を修める. ¶a ***minimum commercial*** *course* 速成商科. ¶an ***ordinary*** *course* 普通科. ¶take the ***politic[al]*** *course* 政治科を修める. ¶***practical*** *courses* whose object is the imparting of various skills 各種技術の熟練を目的とする実習科. ¶a ***preliminary*** *course* 予科. ¶a ***prior*** or ***concurrent*** *course* in psychology 心理学を他の学科の前または同時に履修. ¶receive a ***quick*** *course* in ... ...の速成科にはいる. ¶a ***rapid*** *course* 速成科. ¶a ***regular*** *course* 本科. ¶a ***separate*** *course* 別科. ¶take a ***special*** *course* of ... ...を専修する ‖ a ***special*** *course* of training 特別養成科. ¶a ***three years'*** *course* in law leading to the degree of Bachelor of Laws 法学士の称号をとるべき三年間の法学課程. ¶the ***whole*** *course* of study 全課程.

Q[2] ***after-school*** *courses* for secretarial training 正課後にやる秘書養成科. ¶take a ***college*** *course* 大学に進学する. 【類】after completing his ***college*** *course* / Is a ***college*** *course* necessary for a business career? ¶a school with ***college level*** *courses* 大学程度の学校. ¶a ***correspondence*** *course* of instruction in English 英語通信教授. ¶an ***extension*** *course* (大学の)公開講座. ¶take a ***four-year*** *course* in history 歴史を四カ年修業する. ¶the last year of a ***high-school*** or ***college*** *course* 高校もしくは大学の最後(卒業)の学年. ¶a ***full*** or ***partial*** *course* in ... ...の課程の全部または一部(正科または専科). ¶***holiday*** *courses* at London University ロンドン大学の(夏期などの)休日講習. 【類】a ***holiday*** *course* for foreigners. ¶Columbia University ***home study*** *courses* コロンビア大学の通信課程. ¶take a ***law*** *course* at a university 大学で法律の課程をとる. ¶a ***lecture*** *course* 講座. ¶pursue a ***liberal arts*** *course* 教養学科を取る. ¶***off-campus extension*** *courses* 学外公開講座. ¶***postal training*** *course* 通信教授. ¶take a ***post-graduate*** *course* at the University of ... ...大学の研究科を修める. 【類】take the ***post-graduate*** *course* in law at the college. ¶a ***post-graduate training*** *course* in physical chemistry 物理学の専攻研究科. ¶a ***radio*** *course* in English ラジオの英語講座. ¶a ***refresher*** *course* in English 英語補習科. ¶a ***research*** *course* 研究科. ¶a ***selfteaching*** *course* 自修科. ¶a ***seminary*** *course* ゼミナール[科]. ¶a ***short-term*** *course* in library training 短期司書養成科. ¶give a ***summer*** *course* in ... ...の夏期講習をやる. ¶a ***summer vacation*** *course* in spoken English for foreigners 外国人のための英会話夏期講習会. ¶a ***three-year junior high*** *course* 三カ年の中学課程. ¶***vacation*** *courses* 夏期講習.

P[2] The school offers, besides the courses in the academic department, *courses* ***in*** engineering, ceramics, agriculture, etc. 同校は高等普通学の課程の外に工学・窯業・農業科の各課目がある. ‖ A *course* ***in*** etiquette will be given this term in the University of the Philippines. フィリピン大学において今学期作法科が設けられる. ¶a *course* [consisting] ***of*** 20 lessons 二十課からなる講座 ‖ a *course* ***of*** lectures on ... ...に関する講座 ‖ a study of the *course* ***of*** thought in recent times 最近思潮研究. 【類】a *course* ***of*** science (literature, politics, mechanical engineering).

(**3**) 雑.

V ***mend*** one's *courses* 行状を改める. ¶She ***missed*** her *courses*. 彼女は月経を見なかった.

court, *n.* (**1**) 法廷, 裁判所.

V The *court* was then ***dismissed***. それで閉廷となった. ¶***face*** a *court* 法廷に立たされる, 裁判される. ¶***leave*** *court* 法廷を引き下がる. ¶***hold*** [a] *court* 開廷する.

V[2] The *Court* now rapidly ***emptied***. そのとき法廷から皆急いで出て行った. ¶The *court* is now ***sitting***. 裁判所は今開廷中だ.

Q an ***appellate*** *court* 控訴院. ¶a ***civil*** (***criminal***) *court* 民事(刑事)裁判所. ¶a ***collegiate*** *court* 会議裁判所. ¶a ***competent*** *court* 管轄裁判所. ¶a ***Federal*** *court* 連邦裁判所. ¶The OED is the ***final*** *court* of appeal in all matters concerning English words. オックスフォード辞典は英語語句一切に関する最高権威である. ¶a ***higher*** *court* 上級裁判所. ¶a ***juvenile*** *court* 少年審判所. ¶a ***local*** *court* 区裁判所. ¶a ***regular*** *court* 通常裁判所. ¶the ***Supreme*** *Court* 《米》州または連邦最高裁判所. ☞ 連邦最高裁判所は正式には the Supreme Court of the United States という. ¶the ***ultimate*** (=***last***) *court* of appeal 最終審裁判所.

Q² an ***appeal*** *court*=a court of appeal 上訴裁判所. ¶a ***circuit*** *court* of appeals 巡回控訴裁判所. ¶a ***district*** *court* 地方裁判所. ¶a ***domestic affairs*** *court* 家庭審判所. ¶a ***domestic relations*** *court* 家事審判所. ¶a ***law*** *court*=a court of law 裁判所. ¶a ***marine*** *court* of inquiry 海員審判所. ¶the ***Military Occupation*** *Court* 進駐軍軍事裁判所. ¶a ***moot*** *court* [学生などの]模擬裁判. ¶a ***police*** *court* 警察裁判所. ¶a ***prize*** *court* 捕獲審検所. ¶a ***probate*** *court* 遺言裁判所. ¶a ***provost*** *court* 憲兵裁判所(占領地域内の一般軽犯罪を即決する). ¶a ***three-judge*** *court* 三人判事裁判所. ¶a ***trial*** *court* 予審裁判所. ¶a ***war crime*** *court* 戦犯裁判所 ‖ a ***war crimes trial*** *court* 戦犯予審裁判所.

P The case came up ***before*** the local *court*. その事件は地方裁判所に訴えられた. ‖ in the case ***before*** the *court* 裁判になっている事件において ‖ I must bring the affair ***before*** the *court*. それは裁判にかけなければならない. ¶appear ***in*** *court* 出廷する ‖ settle the matter ***in*** *court* 出る所へ出てきまりをつける ‖ ***in*** *courts* of law 裁判所で ‖ The matter is still pending ***in*** *court*. その事件はまだ法廷で係争中である. ‖ the examination of witnesses ***in*** *court* 法廷における証人の尋問 ‖ fight ***in*** the *courts* 法廷で争う ‖ Order ***in*** the *Court!* 静粛に! (判事の注意). ¶bring cases ***into*** *court* 事件を法廷に持出す. ¶He was prepared to settle the matter ***out of*** *court*. 彼はその事件を内済にする積りだった. ¶be brought ***to*** *court* for trial (被告が)出廷する.

P² a *court* ***of*** claim 要償裁判所 ‖ a *court* ***of*** complaint 抗告裁判所 ‖ a *court* ***of*** domestic affairs=a domestic affairs court ‖ a *court* ***of*** execution 執行裁判所 ‖ a *court* ***of*** a suit 受訴裁判所 ‖ a *court* ***of*** inquiry 〘軍〙査問会.

(2) 宮廷.

V ***hold*** a *Court* 拝謁を賜う ‖ There he ***held*** his royal *court*. そこに彼は朝廷を造った. ‖ the dynasty ***held*** its *court* at ... その王朝は…に都していた.

P British representatives ***at*** European *courts*. 欧州諸国駐在英国大公使. ‖ He represented Belgium ***at*** the *Court* of Japan. 彼は駐日ベルギー大使を勤めた. ‖ the representative of France ***at*** the *Court* of St. James's 駐英フランス大使. 【類】the Japanese Ambassador ***at*** the *Court* of St. James's (駐英日本大使). ¶They were entertained at dinner ***in*** the *Court*. 彼らは宮中で酒宴を賜わった. ¶go (=proceed) ***to*** *Court* 参内する ‖ ambassadors ***to*** foreign *Courts* 外国朝廷への使臣(大使).

(3) 広場; 庭球場.

Q the ***inner*** *court* of a castle 城の中庭.

Q² an ***asphalt*** *court* for tennis テニスのアスファルト・コート. ¶a ***basket-ball*** *court* バスケットボール球戯場. ¶a ***drill*** *court* 練兵場. ¶Which do you prefer for tennis, ***grass*** *courts* or ***hard*** *courts?* テニスには芝生のコートがいいかそれとも固いコートがいいか. ¶a ***lawn [tennis]*** *court* 芝生のテニスコート. ¶a ***sun*** *court* [ホテルなど]日光浴室.

P She is a young and successful player noted for her extreme grace ***on*** the *court*. 彼女はテニスコートにおける非常に優美な姿勢で有名な若いりっぱなプレヤーだ.

(4) 求愛, 言寄り; こび.

V ***pay*** (=***make***) [one's] *court* to her 彼女に言い寄る.

Q He paid her ***assiduous*** *court*. 彼は熱烈に求愛した. ¶pay ***obsequious*** *court* to ... …にやたらに追しょうする.

courteous, *a.* 丁寧な, いんぎんな.

P *courteous* ***in*** wording 言葉づかいの丁寧な ‖ Soldiers must be *courteous* ***in*** their demeanour. 軍人は態度が礼儀正しくなくてはならない. ¶*courteous* to one's guests 客に丁寧な.

courtesy, *n.* 礼儀, いんぎん; 好意; お辞儀.

V ***accord*** this *courtesy* この礼を尽す. ¶***acknowledge*** the *courtesy* その好意を謝する. ¶He ***did*** me the *courtesy* of replying. 彼は丁重にも私に回答してくれた. ¶***drop*** a *courtesy*=curtsy (婦人が)ちょっと腰を屈めてあいさつする. ¶the *courtesy* which I ***enjoyed*** during my stay 私が滞在中に受けた好意. ¶***exercise*** due *courtesy* towards ... …に対して相当な礼を払う. ¶***extend*** the *courtesy* of a special car 特別車を仕立てて優待する ‖ The steamship company ***extended*** (=accorded) me the *courtesy* of transportation. その汽船会社が私に無料乗船の優遇を与えた. ‖ a *courtesy* which has not, I believe, been previously ***extended*** to any foreigner おそらく以前には見られなかった外人に対するいんぎんさ. ¶His Excellency was kind enough to ***give*** us the *courtesy* of an inspection. 閣下の御覧の栄を賜わった[展覧会など]. ¶***make*** a *courtesy* (=curtsy) [婦人が]腰を屈めてお辞儀する. ¶***pay*** *courtesy* to ... …に敬意を払う. ¶***reciprocate*** the *courtesy* of ... …に答礼する. ¶***return*** a *courtesy* to ... …に答礼する. 【類】***return*** the *courtesies* paid by ... ¶***show*** *courtesy* 好意を示す.

V² They say that *courtesy* should ***exist*** even among intimate friends.「親しき仲にも礼儀あり」ということがある.

Q ***artificial*** *courtesy* 虚礼. ¶This may sound like mere ***complimentary*** *courtesy*, but I assure you I mean it most sincerely. こういうとほんのお世辞のように聞えるかも知れませんが私は全く本心から言ってるのですよ. ¶with a ***deep*** *courtesy* 最敬礼で. ¶a ***fine instinctive*** *courtesy* 美しい自然な礼儀. ¶with a ***graceful*** and ***sweeping*** *courtesy* しとやかに一同へあいさつをして. ¶with ***great*** *courtesy* 非常に礼儀正しく. ¶***inbred*** (=***inborn***) *courtesy* 生れついての礼儀正しさ. ¶an act of ***international*** *courtesy* 国際儀礼の一つ. ¶***invariable*** *courtesy* いつも変らぬいんぎんさ. ¶with a ***low*** *courtesy* 腰を低くして. ¶***native*** *courtesy* 生(しょう)得の腰の低さ. ¶***polished*** *courtesy* 上品な礼儀. ¶by ***professional*** *courtesy* 商売仲間の仁義によって. ¶***quiet*** *courtesy* 地味な礼儀. ¶***scant*** *courtesy* 粗略な礼儀. ¶elaborate ***sham*** *courtesy* 念の入った虚礼. ¶I have happy and vivid memories of the ***sweet*** *courtesy* of my fellow Japanese teachers. 同僚日本人教師の美しい礼儀が楽しい鮮かな記憶として私に残っている. ‖ I have not had ***too much*** *courtesy* shown from some of the government bureaus. ある役所では親切過ぎるという待遇を受けたことはない. (「ある役所では相当不親切な取扱を受けた」ということを遠回しに言ったもの). ¶his ***unfailing*** *courtesy* 彼のいつもながらの好意. 【類】the ***unfailing*** *courtesy* with which he was everywhere received.

P She is not really Mrs. Clark; she is only called Mrs. Clark ***by*** *courtesy*. 彼女は本当はクラーク夫人ではない. 人聞きのいいようにクラーク夫人と呼ばれているだけだ. ‖ Younger sons of peers in England are ***by*** *courtesy* called lord or honourable, and the daughters are lady or honourable. 英国では貴族の次男以下には慣例上 "lord" "honourable" の尊称を付し, 娘には "lady" "honourable" の尊称を付する. ‖ ***By*** the *courtesy* of ..., we were permitted to use the photographs in this book. …の好意によって写真をこの本のさし絵に使用することができた. ‖ ***by*** *courtesy* of the author 著者の好意により ‖ ***by*** *courtesy* of usage 慣例上. ¶a breach ***of*** *courtesy* 礼法違犯. ¶***out of*** *courtesy* to me 私に対する好意上. ¶***through*** the *courtesy* of ... …の好意により. ¶Books in other libraries can be borrowed ***under*** the usual *courtesies* of library exchange. 図書交換の打合わせによって他の図書館の書籍を借出すことができる. ¶***with*** a deep *courtesy* 最敬礼をもって ‖ I was treated ***with*** the utmost *courtesy*. 私は丁重をきわめた待遇を受けた.

P² For your *courtesy* ***in*** conveying this information, please accept our hearty thanks. このことをお知らせ下すった御親切に対して私共は深く感謝いたします.

courting, *n.* 求婚.

V ***do*** the *courting* 求婚する.

court-martial, *n.* 軍法会議.

P² the *court-martial* ***on*** General Staessel ステッセル将軍に対する軍法会議. 【類】there was a *court-martial* ***on*** (=***upon***) ...

court-martial, *v.* 軍法会議にかける.

P *court-martial* a soldier ***on*** a charge of ... …の疑いで兵士を軍法会議にかける.

courtship, *n.* ごきげん取り, 求婚.

Q ***quiet*** *courtship* 地味なごきげん取り. ¶repair a ***wrecked*** *courtship* 失恋の痛手をいやす.

courtyard, *n.* 中庭.

Q an ***interior*** *courtyard* 奥庭.

cousin, *n.* いとこ(従兄弟姉妹).

Q a ***distant*** *cousin* 遠縁のいとこ. ¶a ***second*** *cousin* (=a first cousin once removed) to ... …のまたいとこ.

Q² a ***country*** *cousin* 山だしの縁者(あまりいなか臭くて都会の親類を迷惑がらせる人). ¶a ***girl*** *cousin* 少女のいとこ. ¶my ***lawyer*** *cousin* 弁護士をやってるいとこ. ¶a ***Washington*** *cousin* ワシントンにいるいとこ. ¶one's ***writer*** *cousin* 作家であるいとこ. ¶a ***young man*** *cousin* 青年のいとこ.

P He is a *cousin* ***of*** mine. 彼は僕のいとこだ. ¶a first *cous-*

in (=cousin german) *to* … …の直(ちょく)のいとこ.

covenant, *n.* 契約.

Q Books of the *Old* (*New*) *Covenant* 旧(新)約聖書.

P the obligations ***under*** this *covenant* 本規約上の義務.

P² the *Covenant* ***of*** Five Articles 五カ条の御誓文.

cover, *n.* 覆い物, ふた, カバー; 表紙, 封紙; 潜伏所; 掩護(えんご); 仮託; 膳立.

V ***beat*** the *cover* 鳥獣の潜伏所を狩りたてる. ¶the *cover* of the book was ***designed*** by … 本の表紙は…の考案である. ¶The huntsmen ***drew*** the *cover.* 猟師たちは(目的とする獲物の)潜伏所に接近した. ¶Every pot ***finds*** its *cover.* われなべにとじぶた. ¶***lay*** a *cover* 覆いを掛ける; 膳立(食卓の用意)をする. ¶*Covers* were ***laid*** for four. 食卓に四人分の用意がされた. ¶***seek cover*** from the enemy's fire 敵の砲火を避けようとする. ¶***set*** four *covers* 食卓に四人分の用意をする. ¶***take off*** the *cover* 覆いを取り去る.

Q under ***another*** (=[a] separate) *cover* 別封で. ¶a dinner of ***fifty covers*** 五十人前の食事. ¶His portrait appears on the ***front cover*** to that magazine. 彼の肖像はその雑誌のおもて表紙に出ている. ¶a box with a ***hinged cover*** ちょうつがいでふたのついた箱. ¶bound in ***chaste*** and ***appropriate covers*** 簡素でいや味のない表紙のついた(本など). ¶a book in a ***light green cover*** 薄緑色表紙の本. ¶Armchairs are often fitted with ***loose covers*** made of linen. ひじかけいすにはリンネル製のゆるいカバーがかかっていることがよくある. ¶in ***sealed covers*** 封書で. ¶we take great pleasure in sending you under ***separate cover*** … 別封で…をお送り致します. ¶in a ***tight cover*** 厳封で.

Q² The ***back cover*** of a book is generally blank. 本の裏表紙は普通白である. ¶a ***bed*** cover 寝台覆い. ¶a ***chair*** *cover* いす覆い. ¶a ***dust*** *cover* カバー(本の包紙). ¶under a ***glass cover*** ガラスの覆いをして. ¶the ***inside*** (***outside***) ***book cover*** [雑誌・書籍など]裏表紙の内(外)側 ‖ See notice on ***inside back cover*** of this pamphlet. このパンフレットの表紙裏の注意を御覧下さい. ¶the ***inside front cover*** 表(おもて)表紙の内側. ¶an ***iron manhole*** *cover* マンホールの鉄ぶた. ¶a ***magazine cover*** 雑誌の表紙. ¶be bound in ***paper covers*** 紙表紙になっている. ¶all ill-conditioned black-letter volume in ***paper cover*** 紙表紙の保存の悪いゴシック活字本. ¶a ***seat*** *cover* [いす]座席のカバー.

P useful information massed ***between*** its *covers* その本の中に収録された有益な知識 ‖ A vast amount of useful information has been compressed ***between*** two *covers.* きわめて多数の有益な記事が一巻にまとめられた. 【類】His impressions will take shape ***between*** the *covers* of a book. ‖ There are at least six opinions on manuscript before it gets ***between*** the *covers* of the Magazine. 原稿が同誌に現われるまでには少くとも六人の目で批判されるのである. ‖ information that may reasonably be sought ***between*** its *covers* その本で検索されそうな事項. 【類】She will some day put the story of her life ***between*** the *covers* of a book. ¶read ***from*** *cover* ***to*** *cover* 全篇読み通す. ¶words rarely used ***outside*** the *covers* of a scientific treatise 科学上の論文を載せた本以外には滅多に用いない言葉. ¶***under*** *cover* of an umbrella 洋がさをさして ‖ The rain does not matter as we are ***under*** *cover.* 屋根があるから降っても平気だ. ‖ ***under*** *cover* of a handkerchief he made the "switch" for … 上にハンカチを掛けて彼(手品師)は…とすりかえた ‖ This letter came for me ***under*** *cover* from Mr. Tanaka. このお手紙は田中さんから同封で私の所へきたのです. ‖ be ***under*** *cover* from the weather (storm) 雨露をしのぐ, 雨宿りをする ‖ send ***under*** *cover* to Mr. … a letter of recommendation to … …への推薦状を同封にして…氏に送る ‖ In England bills are always sent and left ***under*** *cover,* either by post or hand. 英国では勘定書はいつも封筒に入れて郵便で送るかまたは直接手渡しする. ‖ collect them ***under*** one *cover* [雑誌などへ出した文などを]一冊の本にまとめる ‖ storm the fort ***under*** *cover* of a tremendous fire from the enemy 敵の猛火を浴びて要塞を襲撃する ‖ ***under*** the *cover* of a battery 砲台の掩護(えんご)を受けて ‖ ***under*** *cover* of darkness (mist, night) (やみなど)に乗じて ‖ ***under*** *cover* of friendship 友情にことよせて ‖ ***under*** [the] *cover* of humility けんそんを装って ‖ ***under*** the *cover* of altruism and democracy 愛他主義や民主主義にかこつけて. ¶lay a table ***with*** ten *covers* 食卓に十人前の膳立をする. ¶It is wonderful to find so much information ***within*** the *covers* of a volume. ただ一冊の中にかくまで多大の事項を盛ったことは驚くべきである.

P² a *cover* ***to*** a can かんのふた.

cover, *v.* 覆う, 包む; 表装する; 隠す; えん護する.

M *cover* 20 miles ***a day*** 一日二十マイルを行く. ¶can be ***amply covered*** by assets 資産で十分埋合わせがつく. ¶The price ***barely covers*** the cost. この売値では元[値]が切れそうだ. ¶*cover* the affected parts ***liberally*** with mentholatum 患部へメンソラを十分塗る. ¶be ***perpetually covered*** with snow 万年雪で覆われている. ¶be ***safely covered*** 隠れかたが安全だ.

M² *cover* it ***in*** その上部を全部覆う. ¶*cover* it ***over*** with … それを全部…で覆う. ¶*cover* ***up*** a loss 損害を埋合わす. 【類】*cover* ***up*** the shortage (faults) / *cover* ***up*** a fact ‖ The thieves *covered* ***up*** their tracks. 盗賊はその足跡をくらました.

P This will *cover* me ***against*** the loss. これで損害の埋合わせができる. ¶The top of the mountain was *covered* ***by*** a cloud. 山頂は雲に隠れていた. ‖ The house is *covered* ***by*** insurance. その家は保険が付いている. ‖ Carriage is not *covered* ***by*** the quotation. 運賃は見積値段の中に含まれていない. ‖ during the year *covered* ***by*** this report この報告の対象たる年の間. ¶It is *covered* ***from*** our sight by a forest. それは森にさえぎられて見えない. ¶The rock *covered* us ***from*** fire. その岩のおかげで焼かれずにすんだ. ¶a sofa *covered* ***in*** gold damask 金らんどんすのソファー ‖ He has *covered* the entire distance ***in*** his motor-car. 自分の車で全距離を走った. ¶be deposited or *covered* ***into*** the Treasury to the credit of … …貸方として国庫に供託されるか移管される. ¶Chicks are *covered* ***with*** feathers. ひよっこは羽根で覆われている ‖ *cover* the floor ***with*** a mat 床にマットを敷く ‖ rocks *covered* ***with*** pinetrees 松が一面に生えている岩. ‖ The mountains are *covered* ***with*** thick drifted snow. 山々は吹寄せた雪で深く覆われている. 【類】The road was *covered* ***with*** dust (mud, snow). / The field is *covered* ***with*** waving grass (波打つ草). / *cover* the body ***with*** clothes / *cover* a table ***with*** a cloth ‖ a book *covered* ***with*** silk 絹布表装の書物 ‖ The walls are *covered* ***with*** plaster. 壁にはしっくいが塗ってある. ‖ The bottle is *covered* ***with*** wicker-work. びんは柳細工のつとの中に入っている. ‖ The speaker retired *covered* ***with*** confusion. 弁士は全く面くらって引込んだ. ‖ *cover* him ***with*** shame 大いに彼を赤面させる. 【類】He *covered* himself ***with*** disgrace. ‖ The burglar *covered* him ***with*** his revolver. 盗賊は彼にピストルを向けた. ‖ in return I *covered* him ***with*** mine (my pistol) 今度は私の方からピストルを突きつけた ‖ *covered* ***with*** wounds 大分手負いをして ‖ He *covered* her ***with*** kisses. 彼は彼女をキッス攻めにした.

coverage, *n.* 補てん.

Q ***full*** *coverage* on … …の十分な補てん.

Q² ***gold*** *coverage* 正貨準備金. ¶***round-the-globe news*** *coverage* 世界通信網. ¶***world*** *coverage* of radio news ラジオ(無電)ニュースの世界網.

covering, *n.* 覆い.

Q² ***floor*** *covering* 床の敷物.

P² a *covering* ***for*** chairs and seats いすや座席の覆い. ¶a *covering* ***of*** cloth 布製の覆い.

covert, *n.* 被護物; 口実.

P ***in*** *covert* ひそかに ‖ ***in*** (=***under***) [the] *covert* of … …に隠れて; …を口実として.

covet, *v.* 欲しがる.

M It is ***eagerly*** *coveted* by collectors. 収集家は非常にそれを欲しがっている.

P *covet* ***after*** something 何かを欲しがる ‖ those who *covet* ***after*** riches 欲の深い人たち. ¶*covet* ***for*** (=after) popularity 人気を得たがる.

cow, *n.* 雌牛.

V ***raise*** (=***breed***) a *cow* 雌牛を飼う. ¶***milk*** a *cow* 牛乳をしぼる.

V² A *cow* ***gives*** us fresh milk. 雌牛は新鮮な牛乳を出す. ¶A *cow* ***moos.*** 牝牛はもうと鳴く.

coward, *n.* おく病者.

Q a ***boastful*** *coward* から威張り.

P He is too much ***of*** a *coward* to attempt it. 彼はおく病だからそんなことはやれない. ¶a great *coward* ***about*** the water 船が大きらいな者.

cowardice, *n.* おく病, 卑きょう.

V ***show*** *cowardice* びくびくする.

Q *moral cowardice* 意気地なし.
cower, *v.* 縮み上がる, すくむ.
P *cower at* the sight of something 何かを見て縮み上がる. ¶*cower before* a lion ライオンを見て縮み上がる. 【類】He *cowered before* his accuser(告発者). ¶*cower beneath* bed clothes 恐しいので夜具をかぶる. ¶*cower over* a fire 炉の前にすくむ. ¶The dog *cowered under* the table. 犬はこわがってテーブルの下にはいり込んだ.
co-worker, *n.* 協力者.
P a *co-worker with* God for the establishment of His kingdom upon earth 神の国をこの世に建設せんがため神と
coy, *a.* 恥かしがる, 内気な. ⌊ともに働く者.
P He is *coy about* his love affairs. 彼は恋愛にかけては引っ
coyness, *n.* はにかみ. ⌊込思案である.
Q with *maiden coyness* 処女らしくはにかみながら.
crab, *n.* かに.
V^{2} The *crab crawls* sideways. かには横ばいする.
Q *canned* (=*tinned*) *crab* かにかん.
Q^{2} a *robber crab* やしがに.
crack, *n.* 亀裂, すき間;〖擬声音〗ぱちっ;《俗》痛打.
V The bowl *has* a *crack* in it. そのボール(入れもの)にはひびが入っている. ¶I'll *take* the first *crack* at it. 僕がまず打って見よう. 「裂があった.
Q There was a *big crack* in the ground. 地面に大きな亀
P *at* the *crack* of dawn 夜の引きあけに. ¶look in *through* a *crack* on the wall 壁のすきからのぞき込む. ¶*with* a *crack* ぱちっと. 「むちのぴゅうという音.
P^{2} a *crack in* an egg 卵のわれ目. ¶the *crack of* a whip
crack *v.* 割れる; ぱちっと鳴る, 痛打を食わせる.
M The fireworks *cracked overhead.* 花火が頭上でぱちぱちっと鳴った.
M^{2} *crack down* on gangsters ギャングを征伐する. ¶*crack off* the neck of a bottle びんの首をかいて取る. ¶The airplane *cracked up.* その飛行機はめちゃめちゃになった.
P The nut *cracked into* two. くるみはぱちっと鳴って二つに
cracker, *n.* クラッカ(堅焼きビスケット); 花火. ⌊割れた.
Q^{2} munch an *army cracker* 軍用ビスケットをかりかりと食べる. ¶a *cannon cracker* 大砲花火. ¶a *fire cracker* 南京花火. ¶*ready-to-serve crackers* 即席ビスケット. ¶a *safe cracker* 金庫破り. ¶*saltine crackers* 塩味のクラッカ.
crackle, *n.* ぱちぱちいう音.
V *spill forth crackles* of electric flame 電気の火花をぱち
cradle, *n.* ゆりかご. ⌊ぱち散らす.
V *rock* the *cradle* ゆりかごを揺らす.
P *from* the *cradle* to the grave 一生涯(㍈). ¶a Hercules *in* the *cradle* 未来のハーキュリーズ(力持) ‖ lay a baby *in* a *cradle* 赤児をゆりかごに入れる. 【類】rock a baby *in* a *cradle* (ゆりかご) ‖ What is learned *in* the *cradle* is carried to the tomb. 〖諺〗すずめ百まで踊りを忘れぬ.
cradle, *v.* [ゆりかごに入れて]寝かしつける; 育てる.
M *cradle up* an infant child みどり児を寝かしつける.
P He was *cradled in* the lap of penury (luxury). 彼は貧乏(ぜいたく)に育った. ¶*cradle* a baby *to* sleep 赤児を寝か
cradleland, *n.* 発祥地. ⌊しつける.
P^{2} the *cradleland of* Buddhism 仏教の発祥地.
craft, *n.* 職業, 手職, わざ; [団, 個]船.
V Many of the early printers of English books *acquired* their *craft* in Holland. 英文ものの初期印刷者の中にはその術をオランダで修得したものが多かった. ¶*learn* a *craft* 職(わざ)を覚える. 【類】*learn* the *craft* of lacquerware. ¶*ply* his *craft* with unabated skill もとに劣らぬ腕前で業を励む ‖ artisans *plying* their *crafts* 仕事に励む職人たち. ¶a native blacksmith *practicing* his *craft* 現仕事をやっている土地のかじ屋. ¶He contributed a good deal towards *raising* the *craft* to such a wonderful state of importance. 彼はその技術を今の重要な位置に高めることに大いに力があった. ¶*recover* sunken *craft* 沈没船を引上げる.
Q the *gentle craft*=angling しとやかな手わざ(魚釣りの美称). ¶a *handy, useful little craft* (=vessel) 小さくって手ごろの使いよい船. ¶the *literary craft* 文学の道. ¶one of the *steadiest craft* on the ocean 外洋で最も動揺の少ない船の一つ.
Q^{2} the *teaching craft* (=profession) 教職. ¶*anti-submarine craft* 駆潜艇. ¶*artistic leather craft* 芸術的な皮舟. ¶all kinds of *bombing craft* あらゆる型の爆撃機.

¶*coasting craft* 沿岸貿易船. ¶an *escort craft* 警護船. ¶a *fishing craft* 漁船. ¶*government craft* 官庁の船. ¶a *landing craft* 《米》上陸用舟艇. ¶a *patrol craft* 警備船. ¶*pleasure craft* 遊覧船. ¶a new type of *river craft* 新型の川船.
P workmen *in* the *craft* その職業の人々 ‖ He is engaged *in* a *craft.* 職業に従事している. ‖ He is skilled *in* a *craft.* 仕事が上手だ.
P^{2} a *craft with* her dusky crew 色の黒い船員を乗せた船.
craftsman, *n.* 工芸家, 工人. 「*man* 詩を作る人.
Q a *modern craftsman* 新しい型の工人. ¶a *poetical crafts-*
Q^{2} a *master craftsman* 名工. ¶a *telephone craftsman* 電
craftsmanship, *n.* [工人の]技能. ⌊話工.
Q *artistic craftsmanship* 芸術的技巧. ¶be of *elaborate craftsmanship* 手がこんでいる. ¶the products of his *unripe craftsmanship* 彼のまだ腕のにぶい時分の作品.
crag, *n.* けわしい岩. 「る.
V *clamber up* terrible *crags* 恐ろしくけわしい岩をよじ登
cram, *v.* 詰め込む. 「している.
M He's *busily cramming* for the exam. さかんに試験勉強
M^{2} *cram up* a history book 歴史の本を棒暗記する.
P *cram* [subjects] *for* an examination 試験勉強をする. ¶*cram* information (=knowledge) *from* a book 本から知識を速成的に仕込む. ¶*cram* articles *into* a box 箱の中に品物を詰込む ‖ *cram* knowledge *into* one's head 頭に知識を詰込む. ¶The room was *crammed with* people. その部屋は人で一杯だった. 【類】The book is *crammed with* good and useful matter. ‖ *cram* one's head *with* all kinds of knowledge 色々な知識を頭に詰込む ‖ *cram* oneself *with* food たら腹食う. 【類】His pockets are *crammed with*
cramming, *n.* 詰め込み. ⌊chocolates.
Q *hasty cramming* にわかじこみ, 一夜づけ.
cramp, *n.* けいれん.
V The swimmer *developed* a *cramp.* 水泳者がけいれんを起した. ¶I *have* the *cramp* in the stomach. 腹がつっぱる.
Q get *writer's cramp* ゆびけいれんにかかる, 手がつる.
P He was seized *with cramp.* 彼はけいれんを起した.
crane, *n.* 起重機(クレーン).
Q a *gigantic* (=*huge*) *crane* 巨大な起重機.
Q^{2} a *hand crane* 手動クレーン. ¶a *mammoth crane* 大起重機 ¶a *steam* portable *crane* 移動式蒸気クレーン. ¶a *stone crane* 石運搬用クレーン.
P The vessel can load (discharge) *at crane* up to ... feet of water. 同船は起重機で排水量...フイートまで荷積(荷卸し)ができる. ¶hoist cargo *with* a *crane* 船荷を起重機で巻き
crane, *v.* 首をのばす. ⌊揚げる.
P *crane out* (*over or forward*) 首をのばす.
O He *craned* his neck to see it better. それをよく見よう
crank, *n.* 偏狂者. ⌊と首をのばした.
Q^{2} a *peace crank* 平和狂.
crape, *n.* 喪章; 縮み(布の).
V *wear* a *crape* on one's sleeve 腕に喪章をつける.
Q^{2} *bird's-eye crape* ダイア模様の縮み.
crash, *n.* がたがたいう音.
Q a *loud crash* of thunder 耳をつんざく雷鳴. ¶The *stunning crash* of the audience greeted her. 聴衆は割れんばかりの拍手で彼女を迎えた. ¶What was *that crash?* あのガチャンという音は何だったろう. ¶There was a *tremendous crash.* けたたましい物音がした.
Q^{2} a *bank crash* 銀行の破産. ¶a *car crash* 車輛(自動車)の衝突事故. ¶a *mountain crash* [飛行機の]山に墜落(激突)すること. ¶The cause of the *plane crash* was undetermined. 飛行機墜落の原因ははっきりしなかった. 【類】Three of the crew were killed in the recent *plane crash.* ¶a *traffic crash* 自動車衝突. ¶a *train crash* 列車の激突.
P fall *with* a tremendous *crash* 恐ろしい音をさせて落ちる.
crash, *v.* がたんと音がする, がちゃっと砕ける.
M A plane *crashed out* at the airport. 飛行機が空港に墜落大破した.
P an airplane *crashed in* flames 炎に包まれ墜落する. ¶*crash into* a house [飛行機・トラックなど]家屋にどしんと突っ込む. ¶The automobile was hurled into a ditch after *crashing into* a tree. 自動車は木にがしゃんと突き当てみその中に落ち込んだ. 【類】Our street car *crashed into* another ahead. ¶The sound of military music *crashed on* the early morning air. 陸軍軍楽隊の演奏が早朝の空気

に響き渡った. ¶*crash* ***through*** the roof 屋根を突き抜ける. ¶The building *crashed* ***to*** the ground. その建物が崩壊した. ¶*crash* ***with*** the teeth 歯ぎしりする.

O *crash* as a house built of a pack of cards カードで造った家のように崩れる(瓦解する).

crater, *n.* 噴火口.

P go around the rim ***of*** the *crater* 噴火口を一周する ‖ lips ***of*** a *crater* 噴火口のふち.

crave, *v.* 懇願する, 切望する.

P *craving* ***after*** novelty 斬新を求めて. ¶*crave* ***for*** immortality 永遠を慕う ‖ *Craving* ***for*** dress and adornment is a factor of prostitution. 売女になる一つの動機は衣装や身の回りのものが欲しいことである. ¶*crave* a boon ***of*** (=*from*) him 彼の恩恵を求める.

craving, *n.* 欲望, 渇望.

V ***feel*** a great *craving* for scientific knowledge 科学上の知識を渇望する. ¶They ***have*** no intellectual *cravings*. 彼らは知識欲を持たぬ. ¶They no longer ***satisfy*** the *cravings* of educated people. それらのものは教育ある人々の渇望を最早満足させない. ‖ ***satisfy*** the *cravings* of the inner man 食欲を満たす. ¶One glass ***stirred up*** a *craving* for more. 一杯飲んだらまた一杯欲しくなった.

P[2] his *craving* ***for*** luxuries ぜいたく品に対する彼の欲望.

crawl, *n.* 徐行.

Q ***hearse-like*** *crawls* 霊柩車のような徐行.

crawl, *v.* はう.

M *crawl* ***out*** under a net [障害物競走などで]網の下をはい出る. ¶*crawl* ***forward*** はい出す.

M[2] *crawl* ***about*** on all fours 四つばいではい回る. ¶The chicky *crawled* ***off*** to the outside of the pen. ひよっこが一羽養鶏場の外へはい出した.

P *crawl* ***into*** its hole 穴にはい込む. ¶*crawl* ***on*** the belly 腹ばいになる. ¶*crawl* ***out of*** ... ...からはい出る. ¶*crawl* ***under*** ... ...の下にもぐり込む.

crayon, *n.* クレオン.

Q a ***color[ed]*** *crayon* 色クレオン.

P[2] a picture ***in*** *crayon* クレオンの絵. ¶a baby artist ***in*** *crayon* クレオンの豆画家.

craze, *n.* 熱狂; 大流行.

V ***follow*** a mere *craze* 一時の流行にならう. ¶***start*** the dance *craze* ダンスを流行させる.

V[2] The physical culture *craze* ***attacked*** me at this time. このとき僕は体育に熱中し出した. ¶The *craze* for ... ***came in***. ...熱が始まった. ¶The *craze* is ***sweeping*** [over] Japan. その流行が日本を風びしている. ¶The bicycle *craze* has ***waned***. 自転車熱がさめた.

Q a ***fashionable*** *craze* such as old coin collecting 古銭収集のような流行道楽. ¶Sleep cure is the ***latest*** *craze*. 睡眠療法が最近の流行である. ‖ the ***latest*** *craze* for the new-look jazz "mambo" 最近流行の「マンボ」という新型ジャズ. ¶satisfy the ***modern*** *craze* for "research"「研究」という近代熱を満足させる. ¶a ***national*** *craze* 国民を挙げての熱狂. ¶merely a ***passing*** *craze* ほんの一時の流行 ‖ The motor-car was once termed a ***passing*** *craze* of the rich. 自動車は金持の一時の流行といわれた時代があった. ¶a ***silly*** *craze* ばかげた流行. ¶Autoing has become with him a ***veritable*** *craze*. 本式のドライブ狂になった.

Q[2] The ***automobile promotion*** *craze* was then at its height. 自動車普及熱が当時絶頂に達していた. ¶a ***bike*** (=***bicycle***) *craze* 自転車熱. ¶the ***California Gold*** *craze* カリフオルニヤの金鉱熱. ¶a ***collecting*** *craze* 収集熱. ¶an ***investment*** *craze* 投資熱. ¶the ***no-hat*** *craze* 無帽主義の流行. ¶a ***travel*** *craze* 旅行熱.

P It is ***on*** a *craze*. それは流行している.

P[2] a *craze* ***for*** unity 統一熱 ‖ the *craze* ***for*** the rare 珍品狂. 【類】the *craze* ***for*** tango dancing / a *craze* ***for*** money-making in America.

craze, *v.* 発狂させる.

P He was *crazed* ***with*** fright. 驚きの余り発狂した.

crazy, *a.* 発狂した; 気違いじみた; 熱狂した.

P He is *crazy* ***about*** the girl (jazz, etc.). 彼は女の子(など)に夢中だ. ¶*crazy* ***for*** ... ...に熱狂して. ¶He is *crazy* ***from*** some cause. 彼はある原因のために気が狂っている. ¶He is *crazy* ***with*** delight (fear). 彼はうれしさ(など)の余り気も狂わんばかりだ.

cream, *n.* クリーム; [化粧用]クリーム; 精鋭, 精髄.

V ***beat up*** *cream* クリームをかき混ぜる. ¶*Cream* is ***formed***. クリームができる. ¶***skim*** the *cream* (=select the best) of ... ...の精鋭を選抜する.

Q the ***very*** *cream* of our manhood われわれの男盛り. ¶***whiffed*** *cream* in jelly ジェリー状の泡立ったクリーム.

Q[2] ***shaving*** *cream* ひげそりクリーム ‖ an antiseptic ***shaving*** *cream* 殺菌ひげそりクリーム.

P[2] the *cream* ***of*** society 社交界の花 ‖ the *cream* ***of*** fashion 流行の粋.

crease, *n.* 折目, しわ.

P ***without*** a *crease* しわ一つなく.

create, *v.* 創造する; ...に叙する.

M a bureau ***newly*** *created* 新設の局.

P *create* a draught ***by*** heating the chimney 煙突を温めて通風をよくする. ¶He was *created* baron ***by*** the king. 彼は王から男爵を授かった.

creation, *n.* 創造(物); 創作品; 授爵.

Q a singularly ***adroit*** *creation* of modern civilization 現代文明の非常に巧みな創造物. ¶a ***hand-wrought*** *creation* of high art 芸術味の豊かな手工品. ¶the ***lower*** *creation* 下等動物(界). ¶Language is the most important ***mental*** *creation* of man. 言語は人間の最も重要な精神的産物である. ¶English is the ***noblest*** *creation* of human minds. 英語は人間の精神的産物中最もりっぱなものである.

Q[2] an ***art*** *creation* 芸術上の創作品. ¶the ***brute*** *creation* 獣類. ‖ a member of the ***brute*** *creation* 一種の畜類.

P ***since*** the *creation* of the world かいびゃく以来.

P[2] *creations* ***of*** his own imagination 彼自身の想像の作品. ‖ the *creation* ***of*** an empire 帝国の創建 ‖ the *creation* ***of*** peerage 貴族に列すること ‖ a *creation* ***of*** a great artist 大芸術家の作品.

creator, *n.* 創作者.

Q designed and carried out by ***front rank*** *creators* of clothes 一流のデザイナーの手に成る.

P[2] Washington Irving was the *creator* ***of*** Rip Van Winkle. ワシントン・アーヴィングはリップ・ヴァン・ウインクルの作者であった.

creature, *n.* 創造物, 動物; やつ; 隷属者.

Q the most ***charming little*** *creature* imaginable それはそれは小さくてとてもかわいい生きもの. ¶***divine*** *creatures* 絶妙の創造物[美人など]. ¶They did not look like any ***earthly*** *creatures*. 彼らはこの世の者とも思われなかった. ¶a ***fabulous*** *creature* [ゴジラのような]ばかばかしい動物. ¶a ***frail*** *creature* か弱い者. ¶a ***hideous*** *creature* 恐ろしい怪物. ¶any ***human*** *creature* どんな人間でも. ¶a ***kindly*** *creature* 深切者. ¶all ***living*** *creatures* 生きとし生けるもの. ¶a ***lovely*** *creature* 愛すべきもの. ¶a ***lower*** *creature* 下等動物. ¶Foxes were supposed in old Japan as ***magic*** *creatures*. 昔日本ではきつねは魔物とされていた. ¶the ***male human*** *creature* 男. ¶a ***mysterious*** *creature* 鵺(ぬえ)的存在. ¶***Poor*** *creature!* かわいそうなやつだ. ¶She's a ***pretty*** *creature*. (米口) 彼女はかわいい娘だ. ¶Man is a ***rational*** *creature*. 人間は理性のある動物である. ¶a ***second-rate*** *creature* 第二流の存在. ¶a ***trembling, vacillating*** *creature* 戦々きょうきょうとして落付のない者. ¶an ***unsexed*** *creature* 男だか女だかわからないしろ物. ¶Poets are ***untamable*** *creatures*. 詩人は御し難い手合である. ¶***What*** a *creature!* 何というやつだ. ¶a ***wild*** *creature* 野生に住む物.

Q[2] our ***fellow*** *creatures* わが同胞. ¶a ***forest*** *creature* 森林動物.

P[2] Man is the *creature* ***of*** the age. 人は時代の産物だ. ‖ become a *creature* ***of*** adjectives 盛んに形容詞を用いる人になる ‖ a *creature* ***of*** chance 機会の産物 ‖ a *creature* ***of*** circumstances 境遇に支配される者 ‖ *creatures* ***of*** habit 習慣の奴隷 ‖ the *creatures* ***of*** his imagination 彼の想像から作りあげた色々のもの. 【類】a *creature* ***of*** one's environment.

credence, *n.* 信, 信用.

V ***attach*** full *credence* to the words その言葉を十分に信じる ‖ no *credence* is now ***attached*** to the rumour that ... ...といううわさはもう人が信じていない. ¶His words ***command*** no *credence* from me. 彼の言うことは自分には信じられない. ¶***conquer*** *credence* from a skeptical and wary reader 疑深く用心深い読者に信じられる. ¶The story ***deserves*** no *credence*. その話は信用する価値がない. ¶***find*** ready *credence* 直ちに信用される. ¶These tales ***found*** *credence* with him. この話は彼の信じる所となった. ¶Those views were too extreme to ***gain*** much *credence* or attention from the practical-minded. それらの意見は

極端なので実際家からあまり信用も注意も得られなかった. 【類】That opinion is now ***gaining*** wide *credence*. ¶I cannot ***give*** any *credence* to that statement. 私はその声明は一向信用できない. 【類】He never ***gives*** *credence* to gossip. ¶I am unwilling to ***lend*** *credence* to it. 私はそれを信じたくない.

P a story almost ***beyond*** *credence* ほとんど信じられない話. ¶It is not entitled ***to*** full *credence*. それは十分信用するに足りない.

credentials, *n. pl.* 信任状, 国書.

V an envoy ***bearing*** royal *credentials* 王の国書をもたらす使節. ¶***present*** the *credentials* [to a sovereign] 国書を捧呈する.

credible, *a.* 信じられる.

M be ***hardly*** *credible* ほとんど信じられない.

credit, *n.* (**1**) 信, 信用; 名誉, 評判, 功名; 〖教育〗単位.

V ***add*** a fresh *credit* to its admirable record そのりっぱな記録にさらに花を添える. ¶It will ***affect*** the *credit* of the store.=It will inquire the good name of the house. 店の信用にかかわる. ¶must ***award*** the *credit* to ... ...にその功績を帰せねばならぬ ‖ ***award*** *credits* to employees for efficiency of service 使用人に対し能率向上を表彰する. 【類】He can be justly ***awarded*** the *credit* of having discovered it. ¶His brilliant success ***brought*** *credit* to his family. 彼は大成功を遂げて家名を揚げた. ¶The school ***claims*** the *credit* for his success. 彼の母校は彼の成功の素地を造ったのであると公言している. ¶he ***deserves*** *credit* as being the first to ... 彼は最初に...した人だという名誉を受ける資格がある. 【類】he ***deserves*** great *credit* for ... ing ... / ***deserve*** the *credit* for it. ¶***diminish*** *credit* 信用を落す. ¶***disclaim*** the *credit* その名誉を受くべきものでないと言明する. ¶Such a book ***does*** *credit* to the writer. こういう著作はその作者の名声をあげる. 【類】The book really ***does*** great *credit* to the publisher. ‖ The suggestion ***does*** you *credit*. その御注意はさすがに貴下である. ‖ The conduct of the boy was such as did not ***do*** *credit* to his bringing up. その少年の行為はたまたまそのしつけの良くないことを立証するものであった. ‖ with a wisdom that would ***do*** *credit* to people of large experience 経験に富んだ人へ持って行っても恥かしくない賢明さで ‖ with an ingenuity which ***does*** them great *credit* 彼らの信用を大いに増すような器用さで. ¶***enjoy*** *credit* with ... ...の信用を博する. ¶***gain*** *credit* 信用を得る. ¶***get*** *credit* for being stupid or idle ばか者または怠け者の評判を取る ‖ ***get*** the *credit* for the authorship of the word その語を造った人として認められる. ¶***give*** him the *credit* of ... 彼に...の花を持たせる ‖ I ***gave*** you *credit* for your sense. 君の賢明さには敬服した. ‖ ***give*** *credit* where credit is due 信用のおける点は信用する ‖ He is liberal enough to ***give*** *credit* where it properly belongs. 彼はいい点はいいとほめうるほどの腹がある. ‖ ***give*** *credit* to all authorities quoted ... すべて引用した句にはその出所を示す ‖ ***give*** *credit* to a newspaper report 新聞記事を信じる ‖ ***give*** full *credit* to the story その話を全面的に信用する. 【類】we ***give*** the fullest *credit* to him for ... / he may fairly be ***given*** *credit* for being pioneer in ... / People ***give*** him *credit* for being honest. ¶***grant*** (=give) *credit* to ... ...を信用する. ¶***impair*** *credit* 信用を傷つける. ¶Your *credit* will be ***injured*** if you do so. そんなことをしたら君は信用を失うだろう. ‖ ***inquire*** one's *credit* with one's bank その取引銀行に対する信用を調査する. ¶the chief *credit* for this must in large measure be ***laid*** to the circumstance that ... こういうことになった主なる原因はこれを...という事情に帰せねばならぬ. ¶You will ***lose*** your *credit*. 君は信用を失うだろう. ¶***lower*** *credit* 信用を落す. ¶The school ***merits*** the *credit* for having first adopted reformed methods of language teaching. 語学教授改善法を最初に採用した功績は同校に帰すべきである. ¶***obtain*** *credit* 信用される. ¶***put*** a *credit* in the swing hour 〖ラジオ〗スイングアワーに(広告の)さしプロをする. ¶Each complete answer will ***receive*** ten *credits*. 各(試験)問題に対する完全な答案は十点に採点する. ¶It ***reflects*** *credit* (discredit) upon himself and his country. それは彼自身と彼の国の面目(不面目)となる. 【類】Do they not ***reflect*** *credit* on their teachers? / The book will ***reflect*** a high *credit* upon its author's learning. ¶***ruin*** one's *credit* その信用ががた落ちする. ¶***secure*** a great personal *credit* 大いに自分の信用を博する. ¶***sustain*** the *credit* of ... ...の評判を持続する. ¶***take*** ***credit*** upon oneself for ... ...で評判を取る. 【類】***take*** *credit* for honesty (valor). ¶He ***won*** from his customers the *credit* of being an honest merchant. 彼は正直な商人という評判をお得意の間に取った.

V² To him ***belongs*** the *credit* of originating the scheme. その計画を立てたのは彼だ. 【類】To him ***belongs*** the largest *credit*. ¶Full *credit* must ***go*** to him. 大いに彼の功を多としなければならない. 【類】the *credit* will ***go*** to him for ... ¶The *credit* ***rests*** with him. それは彼の手柄である.

Q It is the Bolshevist custom to give ***collective*** *credit* and denying triumph to individuals. 個人の功績を没却し集団に功を帰するのがボルシェヴィキ流である. ¶To him is ***due*** the *credit* which should always be given to the pioneer. 開拓者に与えらるべき名誉は当然彼が受くべきである. ‖ give ***due*** *credit* to the one who has provided the idea or the facts この思想または事実を供給した人の功績を正しく認める. ¶Their *credit* is ***feeble***. 彼らの信用は薄弱である. ¶He has ***good*** (***bad***) *credit*. 彼は善い(悪い)評判を取っている. ¶a ***lasting*** *credit* to its founder その創設者に対する永久の名声. ¶*Credit* was too ***low*** to make borrowing easy. 信用があまりなかったので金を借りることが容易でなかった. ¶He has ***moderate*** *credit*. 彼の信用はまずまずだ(大したことはない). ¶give ***no*** *credit* to a story 話を信用しない. ¶His *credit* is ***reliable***. 彼の信用は確かだ.

P a course ***for*** four *credits* 四単位の課目. 【類】take a course ***for*** the *credits* required ‖ ***for*** the *credit* of Japan 日本の名誉のために. ¶Greatly ***to*** his *credit*, he came out first. 非常に名誉なことに彼は一番になった. ‖ it is ***to*** his *credit* that ... ...は彼のおかげだ ‖ ***to*** our own *credit* be it said that ... われわれの誇りとすべきは... ‖ It is not very much ***to*** your *credit* that ... そんなことは余り自慢にならない. ¶He came out of the affair ***with*** *credit*. 彼はその事件をりっぱにやりおおせた. 【類】He acquitted himself ***with*** *credit*. ¶Extracts from this book may be used ***with*** or ***without*** *credit*. この本を抜粋した場合出所を示しても示さないでもよい.

P² He has much *credit* ***at*** Court. 彼は宮中の御信任が厚い. ¶a witness of the highest *credit* ***for*** veracity もっとも信頼のおける証人. ¶to him must be given the *credit* ***of*** ... の功績は彼に帰せねばならぬ. ¶It reflects great *credit* ***on*** those who took part in it. それは参加した者の面目を大いに施すことになる. ¶Such a student is a *credit* ***to*** his class. そうした学生はクラスの誉れである. 【類】You are a *credit* ***to*** your father. / He is a boy who will not be a *credit* ***to*** his parents. / a *credit* ***to*** those who bore him, an honor to the nation he represents / He is a *credit* ***to*** the profession. / He is hardly a *credit* ***to*** his profession. ¶He has *credit* ***with*** his master. 彼は主人に信用がある.

(**2**) 〖商〗信用貸借(クレジット); 掛売; 貸方.

V ***allow*** (=***grant***) *credit* 貸売する. ¶cannot ***arrange*** a *credit* クレジット(信用取引)を取りきめることはできない. ¶***cancel*** the *credit* opened in your favor 貴下のためにつけた融通を撤回する. ¶***contract*** ***credits*** [銀行など]貸出を引締める. ¶***establish*** a *credit* for 50,000 yen in favor of ... ...のために五万円の融通をつける ‖ Unless *credit* has already been ***established***, we make all shipments C.O.D. 前もって信用取引が成立していない場合は送荷はすべて代金引換であります. ¶***extend*** *credit* to a regular customer 常客へ掛売をする. 【類】No *credit* is ***extended*** to a new customer. / ***extend*** longtime *credit* (長期貸出) to ... ‖ The bank ***extended*** him a £ 5,000 *credit* 同銀行は彼に五千ポンドの貸出をした. ¶***give*** ***credit*** 掛売をする ‖ No *credit* ***given***. [掲示] 貸売一切お断り. ¶***meet*** a maturing *credit* 期日の来た掛を支払う. ¶***open*** (=***lodge***) a *credit* with ... ...と信用取引を始める. ¶Please ***open*** a *credit* in my favor. 〖商〗私のためにクレジットを設定して下さい. 【類】***opened*** a *credit* in your name with ... / ***open*** a *credit* with bankers or agents for payment on presentation of shipping documents (船荷証券の提示で). ¶***refuse*** ***credit*** to ... ...に掛売を断る. ¶***wire*** a *credit* in your favor with ... 貴下のために...に貸出しをするように打電する.

P purchase ***for*** *credit* 掛で買う. ¶buy ***on*** (=***upon***) *credit* for six months 六カ月の掛で買う. 【類】buy goods ***on*** *credit* / articles bought ***on*** *credit* / obtain furniture ***on*** *credit* / We do not sell ***on*** *credit*. ‖ lend money ***on*** *credit* 信用で金を貸す. ¶You have still about 100 yen left ***to*** your *credit.* まだ百円お預りになっています. ‖ Pay the money into the bank ***to*** our *credit.* その金を私どもの貸方にしてその銀行に払い込んで下さい. ‖ money ***to*** *credit* of ... in a savings-bank 貯蓄銀行にある…貸方の金 ‖ Enter this ***to*** my *credit.* これを私の貸方に記帳して下さい.

credit, *v.* 信じる; …に帰する.

M Photographs not ***otherwise*** *credited* are by the author. だれだれと断わっていない写真は著者の撮影によるものである.

P *credit* it ***to*** ... その功を…に帰する. ¶*credit* a person ***with*** genius 人を天才と見なす ‖ *credit* a person ***with*** some sense 人を相当物がわかるとみる ‖ the qualities ***with*** which he *credited* them 彼の考えによる彼らの性質 ‖ *credit* him ***with*** honesty 彼は正直であるという ‖ if it is to be *credited* ***with*** ... it should at the same time be debited with ... …という良い所もあればまた…という悪い所もある ‖ A Japanese tradition *credits* the celebrated Korean monk Gyoki ***with*** the invention of the potter's wheel. 日本の伝説では朝鮮の高僧行基が陶工ろくろを発明したことになっている.【類】He is *credited* ***with*** its invention. / *credit* him ***with*** the authorship of the book / John Ray is rightly *credited* ***with*** being the father of English natural history. / hot springs *credited* ***with*** miraculous curative powers / Salt is *credited* ***with*** great cleansing properties in Japan. / He is *credited* ***with*** having perfected a style of his own (一流を起したという). ‖ rumour has constantly *credited* him ***with*** the intention of ... 彼は…しようという意向を持っているというらわさが絶えない.

creditable, *a.* りっぱな, 名誉な.

M ***highly*** *creditable* to ... …に取って非常に名誉な.

P It is *creditable* ***to*** his judgment. それは彼の判断力のたしかなことを物語る.

creditor, *n.* 債権者.

V ***pay*** one's *creditors* in full 債権者に全部払う. ¶***satisfy*** one's *creditor* 債権者に満足を与える. ¶***settle*** the most troublesome *creditor* first まず一番やっかいな債権者から片付ける. ¶***stave off*** *creditors* 債権者をなんとか撃退する.

Q an ***extortionate*** *creditor* 高利貸 ¶an ***importunate*** *creditor* うるさい借金取り. ¶an ***inexorable*** *creditor* 鬼のような債権者. 「貿易上の債権者(国).

Q² an ***execution*** *creditor* 差押え債権者. ¶a ***trade*** *creditor*

credulity, *n.* 軽信, 盲信.

V ***exploit*** one's *credulity* 人の軽信に乗じる.

P practice ***on*** (=***upon***) one's *credulity* 人の信じやすいの

credulous, *a.* 軽々しく信じる. 」に乗じる.

M He was *credulous* ***enough*** to believe it. 彼は軽率にもそ

creed, *n.* 信条; 宗旨; 主義. 」れを信じた.

V ***follow*** one's *creed* with 100 per cent consistency あくまで自分の信条を守る. ¶They ***hold*** no religious and theological *creed.* 彼らは宗教上および神学上の信条を全然持っていない. ¶A home wedding is sometimes necessitated by the fact that the bride and groom ***profess*** different religious *creeds.* 花嫁・花婿が違った宗旨を奉じているという理由で家庭で結婚式を挙げることが往々必要になる.

Q the ***ethico-political*** *creed* of the Confucianists 儒教徒の倫理と政治をつき交ぜた信条. ¶adherents to the ***monolingual*** *creed* 一国語主義の信奉者. ¶Nihilism is a ***nebulous*** *creed.* 虚無主義は雲をつかむような主義である. ¶represent no ***particular*** *creed* 何ら特別の信条を示すものでない. ¶irrespective of ***religious*** *creed* or of political opinion 宗教信条や政見のいかんにかかわらず.

Q² our ***business*** *creed* 当店の商売上の信条. ¶the ***Communist*** *creed* 共産党の信条. ¶be converted to the ***Marxist*** *creed* マルキシズムに転向している. ¶a ***10-point*** *creed*

creel, *n.* [魚の]びく. 」信条十箇条.

V ***make*** a handsome *creel* of ... …をたくさん釣る.

creep, *v.* はう; 忍び込む. 「*ly* on. 夜がしのび寄る.

M *creep* ***out*** 抜け出る, 忍び出る. ¶The night *creeps* ***slow-***

M² *creep* ***in*** by mistake (誤植など)誤ってまぎれ込む ‖ Some errors may have *crept* ***in.*** 多少間違いがあるかも知れない. ‖ Even in the best regulated newspapers, some truths may unavoidably *creep* ***in.*** 最もよく統制のとれた新聞紙でも知らず知らず事実をいくらか伝えるものだ(皮肉な言い方). ¶*creep* ***up*** はい上る ‖ *creep* ***up*** towards ... …の方へはい進む.

P *creep* ***along*** the roof 屋根伝いにはう. ¶*creep* ***into*** bed 寝床にもぐり込む ‖ He has allowed a false idea to *creep* ***into*** his mind. 彼は間違った考えを抱くに至った. ‖ A little flush *crept* ***into*** her face. 彼女の顔にほんのりと紅がさした. ¶*creep* ***on*** all fours (the belly, the ground) 四つばい(など)にはう. ¶a wearied, languorous feeling *crept* ***over*** me, as ... …の時にいつのまにか疲れただるい感じがしてきた.【類】A drowsy feeling (ねむ気) *crept* ***over*** me. / *creep* in ***over*** the fence. ¶The sunshine *creeps* ***through*** the lattice. こうし窓から日光がさし込む. ¶A lonely feeling *crept* ***upon*** my spirit. 私はさびしい気持がしてきた.

crest, *n.* 頂, 峯; 紋章; 勇気.

V ***get*** *crest* for ... …する勇気が出る. ¶***reach*** a *crest* 頂点に達する. 「雲に包まれた山頂.

Q the ***big*** *crest* of a wave 大きい波がしら. ¶a ***cloudy*** *crest*

Q² The box is marked with our ***family*** *crest.* その箱には家の紋が付いている. ‖ The black ***haori*** bore in white the ***family*** *crest.* その黒羽織には白の家紋がついていた. ¶the Imperial ***chrysanthemum*** *crest* 皇室の菊の御紋. ¶***storm*** *crests* twenty-five feet high 二十五フィートもあがったあらしの波頭.

P Charlie Chaplin was then ***at*** the *crest* of his popularity-wave. チャーリー・チャップリンは当時人気の絶頂であった. ¶***on*** the *crest* of a hill 小山の頂上に.【類】***on*** the *crest* of the wave (波がしら).

P² the *crest* ***of*** the family 家の紋章. ¶the *crest* ***on*** a cock's head おんどりのとさか.

crew, *n.* [集合的]船員または乗組員; [集合的]仲間, 連中.

V a ship ***carrying*** a *crew* of ... …の船員を乗せている船. ¶***discharge*** a *crew* 乗員を解雇する. ¶The ship ***had*** only a small *crew* on board. その船はほんの少数の船員を乗せて

V² The *crew* have ***mutinied.*** 乗員が反乱を起した. 」いた.

Q a ***dangerous*** *crew* 危険な連中. ¶torpedo-boats manned by ***daring*** *crews* 大胆な船員の乗っている水雷艇. ¶a ***disreputable*** *crew* ぐれん隊. ¶engage a ***fresh*** *crew* 乗員を新たに雇い入れる. ¶The boat has a ***full*** *crew.* そのボートは乗組員がそろっている. ¶the search for the ***missing*** *crew* 行衛不明の乗組員の探索. ¶a ***mutinous*** *crew* 反乱を企てる船員. ¶rescue the ***shipwrecked*** *crew* of ... 難破した船員を救う. ¶He is one of the ***white-livered*** *crew.* あれは弱虫だ.

Q² train ***air*** *crews* 航空班を養成する. ¶a non-commissioned member of an ***air force ground*** *crew* 〘空〙空軍地上部隊の下士官. ¶a ***bomb*** disposal *crew* 爆弾処理班. ¶the Air Corps ***ground*** *crew* 航空部隊付地上部隊. ¶a ***gun*** *crew* 砲射班. ¶a ***landing*** *crew* to lead the plane in ... …飛行機を導く地上班. ¶a ***maintenance*** *crew* 〘航空〙整備班. ¶a ***salvage*** *crew* [沈没船]引上作業員. ¶a ***skeleton*** *crew* 減員して型ばかりの係(乗員). ¶a ***stage*** *crew* 舞台掛. ¶a member of a ***tank*** *crew* 戦車隊員. ¶a ***train*** *crew* 列車乗務員. ¶a crack oarsman on the ***varsity*** *crew* 大学ボート乗組員中の第一流ボートレース選手. ¶a ***2,400-man*** *crew* 二千四百人からなる乗組員.

P He will be in (=on) one ***of*** the *crews* in the next race. 彼は次のボートレースに参加するだろう.

P² go aboard a chaser with a *crew* ***of*** three men 三人乗りの追撃機に乗込む ‖ He was one of the *crew* ***of*** a junk. 彼はジャンク船の乗組員だった.

crib, *n.* 《俗》書きこみ, とらの巻.

V Don't ***make*** *cribs* to your books. 君の書物に(訳語など)書き込みをしておいてはいけない. ¶***use*** a *crib* とらの巻を

crib, *v.* [無断で]書取る. 」使う.

P *crib* ***from*** a book 本から無断借用する.【類】He *cribbed* a passage ***from*** the author.

crick, *n.* (筋肉の)痛み.

V ***get*** a *crick* in the neck 首の筋を違える.

cricket, *n.* 〘競技〙クリケット.

V ***play*** *cricket* クリケットをやる.

cricketer, *n.* クリケット競技者.

Q² a ***gentleman*** *cricketer* 男子のクリケット競技者.

crier, *n.* 叫ぶ人; ふれ役.

Q² a ***town*** *crier* 公けの布告をどなって歩く役人.

crime, *n.* 罪, 犯罪.

V ***accomplish*** a *crime* 犯罪を遂行する. ¶***attempt*** a *crime* 犯罪をもくろむ. ¶The *crime* was ***brought home*** to him. 犯罪は彼のしわざと知れた. ¶***commit*** a *crime* 罪を犯す.【類】Most criminals ***commit*** their first *crime* between the ages of fifteen and twenty. ¶*confess* the *crime* その罪を自供する. ¶*deny* the *crime* その罪を否認する. ¶*diminish crime* 犯罪を少なくする. ¶die to *expiate* some *crime* 犯した罪を死でつぐなう. ¶a cheap newspaper that *features crimes* 犯罪を大げさにあつかうような安っぽい新聞. ¶a punishment to *fit* the *crime* 適当な刑. ¶The *crime* was *found out.* 犯罪が知れた. ¶*have crime* thrust upon one ぬれ衣を着せる. ¶*impute* one's *crimes* to others 自分の罪を他に転嫁する. ¶*Crime* is *played up* by sensational newspapers. 黄色新聞は犯罪をでかでか載せる. ¶*precipitate* a *crime* 犯罪を激増させる. ¶*punish crimes* 罪を罰する. ¶*reduce crimes* 犯罪を少くする. ¶*solve* a mysterious *crime* 不思議な犯罪のなぞを解く.

V² His *crime* will soon *come* to light. 彼の犯罪は間もなく露顕するだろう.

Q an *atrocious crime* 残忍な犯罪. ¶an *awful crime* 恐るべき犯罪. ¶one of the most *baffling crimes* ever committed かつて類例を見ないほど複雑な犯罪. ¶a *bold crime* 大胆な犯行. ¶*brutal crimes* against women 婦人に対する暴行. ¶a *capital crime* 死罪. ¶a *dastardly crime* 卑きょうな犯罪. ¶When distress prevails *crime* is *frequent.* 生活が苦しくなると犯罪が多い. ¶a *grave crime* 重大犯罪. ¶a *great crime* 大罪. ¶a *grotesque crime* 珍妙な犯行. ¶a *heinous crime* 極悪の罪. ¶a *horrible crime* 恐ろしい犯罪. ¶an *infamous crime* 破廉恥罪. ¶an *intellectual crime* 知能犯. ¶commit a *judicial crime* 司法上の罪を犯す. ¶a *lawful crime* 合法的な犯罪. ¶a *notorious crime* 大罪. ¶an *organized crime* 組織的な犯罪. ¶a *pedagogical crime* 教授上の手落ち. ¶*political crimes* 政治犯. ¶a *crime punishable* with death 死刑に処すべき罪. ¶a *reckless crime* 無謀な犯行. ¶a *revolting crime* けしからぬ犯罪. ¶check a *serious crime* 重大犯罪を防止する. ¶a *shocking crime* ぞっとする犯罪. ¶a *social crime* 社会に対する犯罪. ¶The abduction and murder of Charles Augustus Lindbergh, Jr., son of the aviator, was termed the "most *spectacular crime* of modern times." 飛行家リンドバーグの子チャールズ・オーガスタスの誘かいと殺害は近年最も天下の目を見張らせた犯罪という評判であった. ¶*Such* a *crime* should not go unpunished. こういう犯罪は罰せずに置くべきものでない. ¶an *unsavory crime* 不気味な犯罪.

Q² a *chance crime* でき心の犯行. ¶a "*Lupin*" *style crime* ルパン式犯罪. ¶a *lynching crime* リンチ(私刑)事件. ¶a *teen-age crime* 十代の犯罪. ¶an A-class *war crime* A 級の戦犯.

P punish him *for* his *crime* 彼の罪を罰する. ¶an abettor *of* the *crime* その犯罪の教唆者.

P² a *crime against* civilization (humanity, society) 文明(など)に反する罪 ‖ a *crime against* life 殺人犯 ‖ a *crime against* the sovereign power 主権に関する犯罪. 【類】 a *crime against* the Imperial Family. ¶There has been a great deal of *crime in* that city. その市は犯罪が非常に多い. ¶a *crime of* blood 流血事件.

criminal, *n.* 犯罪者, 罪人.

V *apprehend* the *criminal* 犯人を捕縛する. ¶*bring* a *criminal* to justice 犯罪者を裁判にかける. ¶*harbour* a *criminal* 犯人を隠匿する. ¶*loose criminals* on society 犯罪者を社会に放つ. ¶The *criminal* was *sentenced* to imprisonment. 犯人は禁固刑に処せられた. ¶*track down* a *criminal* 犯人を追いつめる.

Q a *born criminal* 先天的犯罪者. ¶a *brutish criminal* どう猛な犯人. ¶a *celebrated criminal* 有名な犯人. ¶*convicted criminal* 有罪と宣告された犯人. ¶a *dangerous* and *incorrigible criminal,* a perfect wild beast 全く野獣のような危険で度し難い犯人. ¶an association for the help of *discharged criminals* 免囚保護協会. ¶shelter an *escaping criminal* お尋ね者をかくまう. ¶a *habitual* and *confirmed criminal* 性(しょう)もこりもない常習犯. ¶a *hardened criminal* 常習犯 ‖ an *honest reformed criminal* 心から改心した犯罪者. ¶a *notorious criminal* 名うての犯人. ¶an *obdurate criminal* しぶとい犯人. ¶The *suspected criminal* has been allowed out on bail. その容疑者は保釈で出獄を許された.

Q² a juvenile *sex criminal* 年少性犯罪者. ¶a *chance criminal* でき心の犯人. ¶a *master criminal* 大犯罪者. ¶be more strictly watched than a *State criminal* 国事犯以上に厳しく監視されている. ¶the 13 A-class *war criminals* 十三名の A 級戦犯 ‖ a convicted *war criminal* 有罪決定の戦犯 ‖ a suspected *war criminal*=a war criminal suspect 戦犯容疑者 ‖ Japan's top *war criminals* 日本の A 級戦犯.

P inflict penalty *on* a *criminal* 罪人を罰する.

cringe, *n.* ぺこぺこ.

V *perform cringes* へいへいぺこぺこする.

cringe, *v.* へいへいする.

M *cringe submissively* to ... 下手(ぞ)に出て…にへいへいする.

P *cringe before* power 権力の前にぺこぺこする. ¶*cringe to* a person 人にへいへいする.

cripple, *v.* 不具にする.

M The traffic was *entirely crippled* for the day. 交通はその日一日完全に止まった. ¶*cripple* France *financially* 財政的にフランスを無能にさせる.

crisis, *n.* 危機; 難局.

V The conditions in ... are *approaching* a serious *crisis.* …の情勢は一大危機にひんしている. ¶*face* a commercial *crisis* with iron nerves 不退転の勇気をもって商業危機に直面する. ¶*forestall* a terrible *crisis* 一大難局の機先を制する. ¶*meet* the *crisis* 危機に即応する. ¶*pass* the *crisis* [病人など]峠を越す ‖ *pass through* many *crises* 幾多の危機を乗切る. ¶*precipitate* the present *crisis* 現在の危機を激化させる. ¶*provoke* a *crisis* 危機を激成する. ¶The situation in ... has *reached* a *crisis.* …における情勢は最早危機に達した. ‖ The disease has *reached* the *crisis.* 病気はもう峠だ. ¶*tide over* the *crisis* 難局を切抜ける.

V² when a *crisis comes* 一朝有事の際は. ¶The *crisis is over.* 峠はもう越した. ¶Has the *crisis passed?* 危機はもう去ったか.

Q an *acute crisis* 非常な難局. ¶The *financial crisis* has become more acute. 財政上のひっ迫は一層悪化した. ¶a *grave crisis* 一大危機. ¶ride out the *immediate crisis* 目前の危機を打開(突破)する. ¶A *momentous crisis* is upon us. 重大危機迫る. ¶face a *national crisis* 国難に直面する. ¶in a *political crisis* 政界の危機に際し. ¶The country is passing through a particularly *serious crisis* in her affairs. その国は今非常時だ. ¶a Cabinet meeting called together at a *supreme crisis* 一大難局に際して召集された閣議. ¶pass through a *terrible crisis* without bloodshed 流血の惨を見ることなく一大難局を切抜ける. ¶an *urgent crisis* 一大危機. ¶a *violent crisis* 一大難局.

Q² a *cabinet crisis* 内閣の危機. ¶The *food crisis* became acute. 食料危機は切迫してきた. ¶tide over the present *food crisis* 現在の食料危機を乗越える.【類】overcome the *food crisis* / face a major *food crisis* / with the deepening of the world's *food crisis.* ¶the current *foodstuff crisis* 現在の食料危機. ¶a *Government crisis* 政府の危機. ¶The *Home Rule crisis* was then acute. 当時(アイルランドの)自治問題が大分やかましかった. ¶The *housing crisis* is just as serious as ever, and threatens to become even more serious. 住宅問題は相変らず重大であるのみかさらに悪化の徴候がある. ¶face a serious *labor crisis* 重大な労働危機に直面する. ¶ease the *world crisis* 世界危機を救う.

P *at* this *crisis* この危機に際して ‖ *at* a *crisis* of one's life 一生の危機に際して ‖ Today we stand *at* the *crisis* of the world's history. 今日われわれは世界歴史の危機に際会している. ¶We are now *in* a national *crisis.* われわれは今や国難に際している.

P² a *crisis in* a country's progress 一国進歩の途上にある難局 ‖ *crises in* British history, such as wars 英国史上の危機例えば戦争など.

criterion, *n.* 規矩, 標準.

V *employ* different *criteria* for the examination of candidates 志願者の試験に異った標準を用いる. ¶*fulfil* all the *criteria* of ... …のあらゆる審査条件を満たす. ¶*lay down* a *criterion* 標準を定める. ¶*set up* some definite *criterion* ある一定の標準を立てる.

Q a *reliable criterion* upon which to test the accuracy of ... …の正確不正確を試験すべき確かな標準. ¶It has been said that the marriage rate of a country is a *safe criterion* of its material welfare. 一国の結婚率はその国の物質的福利を測る安全な尺度であると言われている. ¶it is an *unsafe criterion* for ascertaining ... それは…を決定するには不安な標準である.

Q² *design criteria* 設計標準.

P² The *criterion of* propriety varies with time and place. 適当という標準は時と場所によって変る.

critic, *n.* 批評家, 評論家.

V *criticize* one's *critic* 自分の批評家を(逆に)批判する. ¶He *silenced* all his *critics*. 彼は批評家をことごとく沈黙させた. ¶Those *critics* cannot be *taken* seriously. そういった批評家の言うことはまじめには受取れぬ.

V[2] competent *critics* have *agreed* that ... 有能な批評家たちはひとしく...と認めた. ¶as most *critics allow* 大部分の批評家が認めているように.

Q an *acute critic* 鋭い批評家.【類】the *acutest critic*. ¶his *appreciative critics* 彼にとって好意ある批評家. ¶a *capable critic* 有能な批評家. ¶the most *captious critic* 最もしんらつな批評家. ¶a *carping critic* 口やかましい批評家. ¶a *caustic critic* 皮肉な批評家. ¶They cannot be reckoned as *competent critics*. 彼らは手腕ある批評家とは考えられない. ¶a *cross-brained critic* つむじ曲りの批評家. ¶admirable as a *destructive critic* 破壊的批評家として見事な ¶a *discriminating critic* 眼識のある批評家. ¶the most *exacting critic* きわめて厳格な批評家. ¶a *fair-minded critic* 公平な批評家. ¶one of the most *formidable critics* of Darwinism 進化論の最も強敵たる批評家の一人. ¶*friendly* (*unfriendly*) *critics* 好意ある(好意なき)批評家. ¶"He was given an apple" is a form widely used, but condemned by *grammatical critics*. He was given an apple という言い方は広く用いられてはいるが文法家はこれを非難している. ¶a *harsh critic* 酷評家. ¶an *impartial critic* 公正な批評家. ¶an *incisive critic* 痛烈な批評家. ¶an *impassioned* (*unimpassioned*) *critic* 熱烈(冷静)な批評家. ¶an *intelligent critic* 聡明な批評家. ¶more or less *interested critics* 多少その事に利害関係を持っている(局外者でない)批評家. ¶a *keen critic* 鋭い批評家. ¶a *kind critic* 同情ある批評家. ¶a *learned critic* 学識ある批評家. ¶a *literary critic* 文芸批評家. ¶a *merciless critic* 酷評家. ¶a *notable critic* 著名な批評家. ¶a *penetrating* and *astute critic* of contemporary civilization 現代文明に対する鋭敏かつ洞察力に富む批評家. ¶a *philosophical critic* 哲学の批評家. ¶No *responsible critic* can deny it. いやしくも責任ある批評家ならそれを否認できまい. ¶a *scholarly critic* 学究的批評家. ¶a *severe critic* of the Foreign Office policy 外務省の政策に対するきびしい批評家 ‖ It is acknowledged by his *severest critics*. それは彼の最も痛烈な批評家によってさえ認められている. ¶*shallow critics* 浅薄な批評家. ¶a *squeamish critic* 気むずかしい(潔癖な)批評家. ¶a *subtle critic* 敏感な批評家. ¶a *trustworthy critic* 信頼するに足る批評家. ¶an *unkind critic* says that ... 批評家は...と悪口を言う. ¶a *useful critic* 有益な批評家. ¶a *verbal critic* 用語に対する批評家. ¶a *vigorous, unconventional, outspoken critic* 勇敢で慣習に囚われず腹蔵なく直言する批評家.

Q[2] an *art* (*music*) *critic* 芸術(音楽)批評家. ¶a *columnist critic* of the administration 新聞の政治評論家. ¶an *expert critic* ベテランの批評家.

P[2] a *critic of* some renown 多少名のある批評家 ‖ First one *critic of* repute, then another, then another, spoke in his favor. 著名な批評家があとからあとへと彼をほめた. ¶an authority as a *critic on* (=*upon*) the Japanese arts 日本美術の批評家としての権威.

critical, *a.* 批評の, 批評眼のある; 危急の.

M He is *extremely critical* where women are concerned. 彼は女のことは非常にやかましい. ¶be *severely critical* upon ... ...に関して手厳しい. ¶He is *skeptically critical*. 彼は懐疑的な批評をする. ¶He is *so critical* that nobody can please him. 彼の口にかかってはだれだってたまらない. ‖ the situation was *so critical* that ... 事態は非常に危急であったから... ¶*sternly critical* 厳正に批判的な.

P He is very *critical in* his choice. 彼は物の選択に非常にやかましい. ¶he is too *critical of* ... 彼は余り...に難癖をつけたがる ‖ write a book *critical of* ... ...を批判する一書を著わす.【類】He is *critical of* grammer in the speech of other persons.

criticism, *n.* 批評; 非難.

V *arouse criticism* 物議をかもす. ¶*ask* a *criticism* 批評を請う. ¶*challenge criticisms* of ... ...の批評をいどむ. ¶*combat* hostile *criticism* 反対側の非難と戦う. ¶*defy* every *criticism* どんな批判も受けつけない. ¶*disarm criticism* 非難の気持を和らげる. ¶*encounter criticism* from ... ...から批判を受ける. ¶will not *escape criticism* on the score of ... ...のことがあるからといって非難を免れることはできない. ¶*excite* considerable *criticism* amongst ... ...間に大分非難を惹起する. ¶He has always had to *face* such *criticism*. 彼はいつもこういった非難を受けねばならなかった. ¶I *had* no *criticism* to offer against ... ...を非難することはできなかった. ¶I would *hazard* the *criticism* that ... 私はあえて...という批評を試みよう ‖ if a *criticism* may be *hazarded* もしあえて批判が許されるならば. ¶rank *criticisms* are *hurled* at or printed about ... ...について毒々しい批評が口にされまた筆にされている. ¶*influence* newspaper *criticism* 新聞の批評を左右する. ¶*invite* the *criticism* of the class クラスの批判を受ける. ¶*level criticisms* at ... ...に非難を浴びせる. ¶*offer* helpful *criticism* 有益な批評を与える.【類】*offer* a few *criticisms* on ... / it is forbidden to *offer* any *criticism* of ... ‖ *offer criticism*, not in a carping spirit (難くせをつける気ではなく), but with the earnest endeavour to ... / *offer* some *criticisms* of the argument brought forward by Mr ... ¶*pass criticism* upon ... ...を評する. ¶much hostile *criticism* has been *provoked* by the action of ... ...の行動によって随分悪評が激発された. ¶He *pulverized* the *criticisms* aimed at his work. 彼は自作に向けられた非難を粉砕した. ¶*resent criticisms* and advice from others 他人の批評や忠告を憤る. ¶an effort to *suppress criticism* 非難を押えようとする努力. ¶*tolerate* adverse *criticism* 反対の批評を甘んじて受ける.

Q *adverse criticism* 非難. ¶*appreciative criticism* 好評. ¶a *carping criticism* 毒舌. ¶*clever criticism* 賢明な批評. ¶be fertile in *constructive criticism* 建設的な批評が多い ‖ *constructive* or *destructive criticism* 建設的または破壊的批評. ¶a book of *creative criticism* like Coleridge's "Biographia Literaria" コールリッジの「文学的自叙伝」のような創造的批評の書. ¶*dramatic criticism* 劇評. ¶there were *endless criticisms* on ... ...の批評がやかましかった. ¶*favorable criticism* 好評. ¶a *frank criticism* 率直な批評. ¶a *friendly criticism* 親切な批評. ¶indulge in some *fulminating criticism* on ... ...に対してがみがみ言う. ¶*harsh criticism* 酷評. ¶*helpful criticism* 有益な批評. ¶impervious to *hostile criticism* 反対の批評を受付けない ‖ the temper in which he accepted *hostile criticism* 敵意を含んだ批評を受入れた彼の気持. ¶*idle criticism* 愚にもつかぬ批評. ¶*incisive criticism* 痛烈な批判. ¶*independent criticism* 自主的な批評. ¶*inspiring* criticism 激励的批評. ¶*irresponsible criticism* from ... ...からの無責任な批評. ¶*just criticism* 公正な批判. ¶*keen* and *sensitive criticisms* 聡明にして敏感な批評. ¶*kindly criticism* 親切な批評. ¶He has a gift for *luminous* and *suggestive criticism*. 明白なしかも示唆に富んだ批評の才を持っている. ¶*old* and *worn-out criticism* 古くてかびの生えた批評. ¶*outspoken criticism* 率直な批評. ¶*penetrating criticism* 徹底的批評 ‖ *penetrating, shrewd criticism* うがった批評. ¶impervious to *public criticism* 世評に対して平気な. ¶*reasonable criticism* もっともな批評.【類】The liberty of the press in England now allows all *reasonable criticisms*, not only of Parliament, but even of the Sovereign. ¶*scathing cricitism* 酷評. ¶I am very grateful for the benefit I have derived from his *scholarly criticism*. 私は博識の彼の批評から得た利益に対して非常に感謝している. ¶*second-rate criticism* 二流どころの批評. ¶This involved himself in *severe criticism*. このために彼はひどい非難を受けた. ¶*sharp criticism* on the Navy 海軍に対する痛烈な非難. ¶*sterile criticism* 無益の批評. ¶the *superficial* and *impious criticism* of unbelieving men 不信心者の皮相的で不敬虔な批評. ¶a *sweeping criticism* 徹底的な批判, 総まくり. ¶*sympathetic criticism* 同情的批評. ¶*temperate criticism* 穏健な批評. ¶the *textual criticism* [聖書など]本文の正否に関する批評. ¶*trenchant criticism* 鋭い批評. ¶*unbiased criticism* 公平な批評. ¶*unfavorable criticism* 不利な批評. ¶*ungenerous* and *jealous criticism* 狭量で, うるさい批評. ¶an *unjust criticism* 不公平な批評. ¶*unkind criticism* 不親切な批評. ¶contribute much *valuable criticism* 多くの貴重な批評を寄せる. ¶*wild* and *destructive criticism* 乱暴で破壊的な批評. ¶the *world's criticism* is that ... 世界の批評は...だ.

Q[2] *arm-chair criticism* 空論的批判. ¶the most suggestive contribution to *Carlyle criticism* that has appeared for a long time カーライル批評として多年公にされた中でもっとも示唆に富む一篇. ¶give *expert criticism* on ... ...に専門的な批判を加える. ¶the modern school of Old

Testament criticism 旧約聖書批判の中の新派. ¶*second-hand criticism* 受売り批評. ¶*signboard criticisms* 売名的批評.

P It is ***above criticism.*** 非の打ちようがない. ¶It is ***below criticism.*** お話にならない. ¶It is ***beneath criticism.*** それは批評の価値がない. ¶The list is by no means ***beyond criticism.*** その表は決して完全とは言えない. ¶so he said, ***in criticism*** of the views expressed by ... ...の発表した意見を評して彼はそう言った. ¶it is not in a spirit ***of criticism*** that I say ... 私が...というのは非難するつもりで言うのではない ‖ This will give rise to a good deal ***of criticism.*** これは大分批評を受けることだろう. ¶in answer ***to*** the *criticisms* levelled at him on the question, he vindicated that ... その問題に関して浴びせられた非難に答えて彼は...と弁明した. ¶He is very sensitive ***under criticism.*** 彼はとかく批評を気にする. ‖ ***under*** the frank *criticism* of ... ...から率直な批評を受けて.

P² the *criticism* ***of*** The London Times ロンドン・タイムス紙の批評 ‖ the *criticism* ***of*** authors by their brother authors 同業著者から受ける著者の批評. ¶a *criticism* ***on*** (=***upon***) art 芸術に関する批評.

criticize, *v.* 批評する; 非難する.

M *criticize* ***adversely*** それに反ばくする. ¶The Board in its resolution on the subject *criticized* the report ***favourably.*** 理事会はその問題を決議して報告に好意ある批評を下した. ¶*criticize* ***freely*** 自由に批評する. ¶***helpfully*** *criticize* 有益な批評を下す. ¶Don't *criticize* him too ***harsh*** till you know all the circumstances. 事情がはっきりするまで彼をあまりひどく非難するな. ¶He ***openly*** *criticized* the plan as unworkable. 彼は公然その案は実行不可能と批評した. ¶***severely*** *criticize* 酷評する. 【類】Don't *criticize* him too ***severely.*** ¶he was rightly ***sharply*** *criticized* by ... 彼は当然...によって猛烈に非難された. ¶***unsparingly*** (=***scathingly***) *criticize* 遠慮なくこきおろす.

croak, *v.* [からす・かえるなど]がーがー鳴く.

P Frogs began to *croak* ***with*** the rainfall. 雨が降り出すと同時にかえるが鳴きだした.

croaker, *n.* 不吉の予言者, 悲観屋, 杞憂(きゆう)家.

P I do not wish to seem a *croaker* ***of*** ill tidings. 私は不吉なことを言触らす人間だと思われたくない.

crock, *n.* 瀬戸もの.

V The *crock* is ***chipped.*** その陶器はかけている.

croon, *v.* 声低く歌う.

P *croon* a baby ***to*** sleep 子守歌を歌って赤ん坊を寝かせる.

crooner, *n.* 《米》流行歌手.

Q² a ***TV*** *crooner* テレビの流行歌手.

crop, *n.* 作, 収穫; 作物; 短髪; 一団, 一群.

V The banana ***bears*** two *crops* every year. バナナは年二度の収穫がある. 【類】The apple-tree failed to ***bear*** a *crop* last year. ¶***cultivate*** rice *crop* 米を作る. ¶the *crop* has been ***damaged*** by frosts (drought, vermin) 作物は霜(など)害を受けている. ¶***garner*** a *crop* 作物の取入をする. ¶***gather*** a *crop* 作物を取入れる. ¶***harvest*** a *crop* 作物を収穫する. ¶I have ***had*** a close *crop.* 僕は髪を短く刈った. ¶***plant*** a *crop* 作物の植付をする ‖ the best time to ***plant*** certain *crops* ある種の作物の最適の植え時. 【類】suggestions for farmers as to the best time to ***plant*** certain *crops.* ¶The soil is so fertile as to ***produce*** two *crops* of rice yearly. 土が肥えているので毎年米が二度取れる. 【類】***produce*** fine *crops.* ¶They ***promise*** a rich *crop.* 豊作の見込がある. ¶Farmers ***raise*** *crops.* 百姓は作物をつくる. 【類】***raise*** a *crop* of rice / There people ***raise*** three *crops* from the same piece of ground in a year. ¶I ***reaped*** a heavy *crop* of wheat here last year. 去年ここで私は麦をうんととりました. ¶***sow*** *crops* in a field 畑に作物の種をまく. ¶***truck*** *crops* 農作物をトラックで運ぶ. ¶***win*** *crops* from every inch of soil どんな零細な土地からも作物がとれる. ¶This land ***yields*** good *crops.* この土地は作物が良くできる. 【類】***yield*** bountiful *crops* of cereals.

V² Owing to the long drought, the *crops* have ***failed.*** かんばつが続いたため不作だった. ¶How does the *crop* ***promise?*** 作物のできはいかがですか.

Q And you will have an ***abundant*** *crop* of good flowers. そうすると好い花がたくさんに咲く. ¶the ***annual academical*** *crop* of beardless youth 年々学校から出て来るひげのない青年たち. ¶The grain (rice) is expected to be an ***average*** *crop.* 穀類(など)は平年作の見込である. ¶a ***bad*** *crop* 不作. ¶a ***bountiful*** *crop* 豊作. ¶expect a ***bumper*** *crop* of wheat 小麦の豊作を見込む. ¶a ***convict's*** *crop* 囚人の五分刈頭. ¶The *crops* are ***early*** (***backward***) this year. 作物は今年はできが早い(後れている). ¶The rice *crop* looks ***excellent.*** 米作は大変良さそうだ. ¶We expect a ***fine*** *crop* of potatoes. じゃがいもは豊作の見込みだ. ¶we shall have a ***good*** *crop* of ... ...は上作だろう. ¶***graminaceous*** *crops* 牧草の収穫. ¶***green*** *crops* 青物. ¶The wind is harmful to ***growing*** *crops.* 風は作物に悪い. ¶a ***heavy*** (=***large***) *crop* 豊作. ¶***leguminous*** *crops* まめ類の作物. ¶***magnificent*** *crops* of rice 米の豊作. ¶The ***new*** *crop* is very fine (poor). 今度の作物は豊(不)作だ. ¶a ***plenteous*** *crop* 豊作. ¶bear a ***plentiful*** *crop* of seeds 豊富な種物を産する. ¶The farmers had a ***poor rice*** *crop.* 農家は米が不作だった. ¶The *crops* are ***promising.*** 作物は良さそうだ. ¶***rotating*** *crops* 輪作作物. ¶a ***scanty*** *crop* of rice 米の不作. ¶a ***short*** (=bad) *crop* 減作. ¶a ***silk*** *crop* まゆの収穫. ¶The efforts yielded but a ***sorry*** *crop.* その努力は余り収穫がなかった. ¶***standing*** *crops* 立毛. ¶Tosa is the only province in Japan where ***two*** *crops* of rice are produced yearly. 日本で米が二度取れるのは土佐だけである.

Q² ***cereal*** *crops* 穀類の作柄. ¶***companion*** *crops* 並列作. ¶***corn*** *crops* 穀類作物. ¶the nation's ***corn*** *crop* 全国のとうもろこし作. 【類】Iowa's 1947 ***corn*** *crop.* ¶***farm*** *crops* 農作物 ‖ staple ***farm*** *crops* 主要農作物. ¶a ***field*** *crop* 畑作. ¶produce a bumper ***food*** *crop* 食料農産物は豊作である. ¶***food grain*** and ***rice*** *crops* 穀類と米の作. ¶***forage*** *crops* まぐさの収穫. ¶insects destructive to ***fruit*** *crops* 果実に有害なこん虫. ¶***garden*** *crops* 青物(野菜)作. ¶Russia's 1947 ***grain*** *crop* ロシヤの一九四七年の穀類収穫. ¶***grass*** *crop* 牧草の収穫. ¶harvest an ***ice*** *crop* 製氷を得る. 【類】an annual ***ice*** *crop.* ¶***long-season*** *crops* 長期植付作物. ¶***milk*** *crops* 搾乳量. ¶***onion*** *crop* 玉ねぎ作. ¶produce ***record*** *crops* 記録的収穫を得る ‖ A ***record wheat*** *crop* was harvested last year. 昨年の小麦作は記録的豊作であった. ¶planting of a 1948 ***rice*** *crop.* 一九四八年度稲の植付. 【類】This year's ***rice*** *crop* is the smallest in years. / ***Rice*** *crops* are now being harvested. / There is at present every prospect (見込み十分) of a large ***rice*** *crop.* ‖ last fall's bumper ***rice*** *crop* of 9,000,000 metric tons 九百万米トンの昨秋の豊作米. ¶***root*** *crops* [大根などの]根菜作物. ¶***short-season*** *crops* 短期植付作物. ¶the Manchurian ***soybean*** *crop* 満洲大豆作. ¶The new ***spring pig*** *crop* comes to market. 今年度始めての豚の春子が市場に出る. ¶the ***tea*** *crop* for the current year 今年の茶作. ¶The ***timber*** *crop* 木材の収穫. ¶a failure of the ***wheat*** *crop* in Europe ヨーロッパにおける小麦の不作. ¶If the corn *crop* fell short, the bumper ***wheat*** crop more than made up for it. とうもろこしは不作でも, 小麦の豊作で十二分に埋合わせがつく. ¶raise ***winter*** and ***spring*** *crops* of lambs 羊の冬子と春子を飼養する. ¶a ***winter*** *crop* 寒冷作. ¶refined sugar from the *1946* *crop* 一九四六年度作からの精糖.

P The weather is good ***for*** (harmful ***to***) the *crops.* この天候は作物によい(悪い). ¶a field ***in*** *crop* 作物を植付けてある畑 ‖ the area of land ***in*** (=***under***) *crop* 作付の反別. ¶in consequence of failure ***of*** the *crops* 作柄不良の結果. ¶the area ***under*** *crop* 作付反別.

P² He is suffering from a *crop* ***of*** troubles. 彼は色々の難問題に悩まされている. ‖ It produced a *crop* ***of*** questions. それで色々の問題が起った. ‖ a *crop* ***of*** wheat (corn, grain) 小麦(など)の作.

crop, *v.* 刈込む, 刈取る; 植つける; 突然現われる.

M *crop* the hair (tail) ***short*** 髪(など)を短く刈る. ¶The malady *cropped* ***out*** in many parts of the country. 全国各地で悪疫が流行し出した.

M² questions likely to *crop* ***up*** in reading 読書の際起きる疑問 ‖ We have a new man *cropping* ***up*** every session. 毎議会新人が現われる. 【類】The question *cropped* ***up.*** / Numerous evils have *cropped* ***up.*** ‖ Local accent *cropped* ***up*** in rapid speech. / when troubles arise and difficulties *crop* ***up*** / There will be danger of undesirable results *cropping* ***up.*** / *crop* ***up*** into prominence 一躍有名となる.

P *crop* a field ***with*** wheat 畑に小麦を植付ける.

cropping, *n.* 作付.

Q^2 ***rotation*** (***succession***) *cropping* 循環(連)作.

cross, *n.* 十文字, 十字形; 十字架; 雑種.

V ***Mark*** a *cross* in the square against the name of the candidate for whom you desire to vote. 自分の投票しようと思う候補者の名前と向い合っている四角形の中に十字記号をつけて下さい. ¶***put*** a *cross* (×) in front of ... ...の前に×記号をつける ‖ ***put*** *crosses* against the titles of books in a catalogue 目録中の書名に×記号をつける. ¶***take up*** the *cross* 十字架を担う.

Q It was a ***daily*** and ***hourly*** *cross* to the girl. それは少女に取っては時々刻々の苦行であった. ¶a ***red*** *cross* on a white ground 白地に赤の十字形. ¶the ***Southern*** *Cross*=the Crux 南十字星.

Q^2 the ***Distinguished Flying*** *Cross* 《米・英軍》空戦殊勲十字章. ¶the ***Distinguished Service*** *Cross* (*or* Medal) 殊勲十字章. ¶***Geneva*** *cross* 赤十字. ¶an ***Iron*** *Cross* 鉄十字勲章(一八一三年制定されたプロシア武功勲章).

P Christ's agony ***on*** the *cross* 十字架上のキリストの苦しみ ‖ death ***on*** the *cross* 十字架上の死. ¶He is ***under*** his *cross.* 彼は辛苦している. ¶die ***upon*** the *cross* 十字架上で死ぬ. ¶The airship may be described as a *cross* ***between*** a balloon and a flying machine. 飛行船は気球と飛行機の中間物と言える.

cross, *v.* 横切る; 交差する; 邪魔する; 交種する.

M *cross* (=strike) ***off*** (=***out***) (=cancel *or* erase) one's name from ... ...から名前を削除する ‖ *cross* one's name ***off*** 名を消す. ¶He *crossed* ***over*** to America. 彼は渡米した.

M^2 *cross* ***out*** a wrong word 間違っている言葉を削除する.

P The river is *crossed* ***by*** many bridges. その川には多数の橋がかかっている. ¶He is *crossed* ***in*** love. 彼は失恋している. ¶*cross* the border ***into*** another territory 越境する. ¶*cross* ***over*** a river 川を越える. ¶*cross* ***to*** the east side of the street by subway 地下道で街の東側に渡る. ¶*cross* (=mate) A ***with*** B [種取りに] A を B に掛合わせる ‖ *cross* swords ***with*** a country ある国と干戈(かん)を交える, 戦争する.

cross, *a.* 不きげんの; 背反した.

M with the eyes ***a bit*** *cross* 少しやぶの目で.

P He was *cross* ***at*** something. 彼は何かしゃくに障っていた. ‖ I'm sorry I was *cross* (=sore) ***at*** you the other day. 先日は不愉快な思いをさして失礼しました. ¶an outcome (=a result) *cross* ***to*** the purpose 目的に反した結果 ‖ It was *cross* ***to*** our design. それはわれわれの計画に邪魔だった. ¶I am not *cross* ***with*** him. 私は彼に当り散らしているのではない.

cross-cut, *n.* 早道.

P a *crosss-cut* ***for*** literary wayfarers 文学に志す者にとっての早道. ¶*cross-cuts* ***to*** information 知識を得る早道.

cross-examine, *v.* 反対尋問する.

M be ***sharply*** *cross-examined* 鋭い反対尋問を受ける.

cross-examination, *n.* 反対尋問, 対審.

V ***defy*** the *cross-examination* of time 時の審問に堪える.

cross-grained, *a.* 片意地の.

M ***apparently*** *cross-grained* ひと癖ありそうな.

crossing, *n.* 踏切; 横断; 交差.

Q We had a ***good*** *crossing* from London to New York. ロンドンからニューヨークへの航海は愉快だった. ¶a ***rough*** *crossing* (=voyage *or* passage) 難渋な航海.

Q^2 a ***grade*** (=***level***) *crossing* 平面交差, 踏切り. ¶a ***railway*** *crossing* 鉄道の踏切り. ¶at a ***street*** *crossing* 街路の横断箇所で.

P He was ***at*** a *crossing* and did not know which way to turn. 彼は十字路にやってきてどっちに曲っていいのか分らなかった. ¶The child met his death ***on*** the *crossing.* その子はその踏切でひかれて死んだ.

P^2 a *crossing* ***of*** two roads 四つつじ.

cross-reference, *n.* [同一書の]前後参照.

V ***give*** *cross-reference* to ... ...を参照させる.

crossroad, *n.* 岐路, つじ.

P capitalism ***at*** the *crossroads* 岐路に立つ資本主義 ‖ Honolulu is ***at*** the *crossroads* of the Pacific. ホノルルは太平洋の分岐点にある. ‖ stand ***at*** the *crossroads* 岐路に立つ. ¶come ***to*** the *crossroads* 交差点にやって来る.

cross-sea, *n.* 逆波.

V ***stir up*** a *cross-sea* 逆波を立てる.

cross-section, *n.* 断面.

P^2 a *cross-section* ***of*** the whole of humanity 全人類の断面.

crotchet, *n.* 奇想.

Q ***crazy*** *crotchets* 気違いじみた考え.

crouch, *v.* へたばる; 横になる.

P *crouch* ***for*** shelter 身を隠そうとちぢこまる. ¶The dog *crouched* ***to*** his master. 犬は主人の前にぺったり平たくなった. 【類】They *crouch* ***to*** their oppressors. ¶They did not *crouch* ***under*** oppression. 彼らは圧制にもひるまなかった.

crow, *n.* からす.

V ***eat*** *crow* 《米俗》=eat humble-pie 屈辱を忍ぶ. ¶I ***have*** a *crow* to pluck with you. 僕は君に文句がある.

V^2 *Crows* ***caw*** (=croak). からすが鳴く. ¶as the *crow* ***flies*** 一直線に.

Q a big ***black*** *crow* 黒い大がらす.

crow, *v.* 勝ち誇る.

P *crow* ***over*** an enemy (a defeated rival) 敵(など)に勝ち誇る ‖ *crow* ***over*** one's victory 勝どきをあげる.

crowd, *n.* 群衆, 大勢.

V ***attract*** enormous *crowds* 非常な群衆を引きつける. ¶sights that invariably ***collect*** a *crowd* きまって人山を築く光景. ¶These boxing bouts ***draw*** *crowds* of 30,000 and upward at a single contest. これら拳闘の取組は一試合に三万以上の観衆を引き付ける. 【類】***draw*** large *crowds* to ... / The ball game (野球) ***drew*** the biggest *crowd* seen for years. / ***draw*** great *crowds* of spectators. ¶The police ***drove*** the *crowd* back from the entrance. 警官が群衆を入口から追い返した. ¶***face*** the *crowd* unruffled 落着いて群衆に向う. ¶***follow*** the *crowds* 付和雷同する. ¶The police were needed to ***handle*** the *crowds* anxious to see the celebrities in attendance. 臨場の名士たちを見ようとやっきになっている群衆を整理するには警官の手が必要であった. ¶Mounted troops ***kept*** the *crowd* in order. 騎馬隊が群衆を整理した. ¶***keep back*** a *crowd* 群衆を制する. ¶***push aside*** the *crowd* as one goes 群衆を押しのけて進む. ¶go to ***swell*** the little *crowd* that is gathered round ... ...の周囲に集まった小さな人だかりに自分も加わる.

V^2. *Crowds* ***bubble*** intermittently from the underground stations. 人の群が地下鉄の停車場から絶え間なくわいて出る. ¶A *crowd* ***collected*** round the man. その人に人がたかった. ¶The *crowd* gradually ***dispersed.*** 群衆が段々散った. ¶The *crowd* ***ebbed.*** 人込が減って行った. ¶The *crowd* ***fell back.*** 群衆が退(の)いた. ¶Great *crowds* ***flock*** to see them. 大変な群衆が彼らを見に集まる. ¶a *crowd* has ***gathered*** in front of ... 人が...の前に集まった. 【類】A *crowd* is ***gathering.*** ¶The *crowds* ***melted.*** 人群が消え去った. ¶The *crowd* suddenly ***scattered.*** 群衆が急に散らばった. ¶The *crowd* ***springs up*** from nowhere. 群衆がどこからともなく集まる. ¶The quayside *crowd* ***strolled*** back out of the docks. 波止場に立つ群衆はドックからぞろぞろと戻ってきた. ¶The *crowd* ***subsided.*** 群衆が退場した. ¶A *crowd* ***surged*** outside the counting room waiting for the figures. 群衆が数字の発表を待って開票場の外側に押し寄せた. ‖ The whole *crowd* ***surged forward.*** 全群衆が潮のように押し出した. ¶*Crowds* were ***swarming*** about the place. 群衆がその近くに寄ってきた. ¶The *crowd* ***swept*** past. その群集が通って行った. ¶The *crowd* began to ***thin.*** 人群が減り始めた. ¶Great *crowds* ***thronged*** every inch of the route. 非常な群衆がちょっとのすきもなく道筋に立った.

Q the clamor of an ***angry*** *crowd* 群集の怒声. ¶a ***clamorous*** *crowd* わいわい言う群衆. ¶A ***considerable*** *crowd* has collected. 大分群衆が集まった. ¶a ***cosmopolitan*** *crowd* of the boat その船に乗合わしている世界各国の人々. ¶There was a policeman keeping back the ***curious*** *crowd.* 物見高い群衆を制している一人の巡査がいた. ¶***dense*** *crowds* of people ぎっしり詰まった群衆. 【類】***dense*** *crowds* in front of ... / The *crowds* are much ***denser*** here. ¶There an ***enormous*** *crowd* of many thousand spectators was surging. 非常に大勢の見物人が押し寄せていた. ¶a ***goodly*** *crowd* of spectators かなり大勢の見物人. ¶The game thrilled the ***huge*** *crowd.* そのゲームで大観衆は沸いた. ¶an ***immense*** *crowd* 巨大な群衆. ¶the center of a ***jeering*** *crowd* 群衆嘲弄(ちょう)の的. ¶a ***jostling*** *crowd* 押合いへし合いの群衆. ¶a ***jovial, motley*** *crowd* 陽気な色とりどりの群衆. ¶attract a ***large*** *crowd* 大勢の人を引き付ける. ¶a ***meager*** *crowd* 貧弱な人群. ¶***milling*** *crowds* なぐり合っている群衆. ¶a ***motley*** *crowd* of men and boys 大人子供の入りまじった群衆. 【類】a ***motley*** *crowd* made up of the most varied elements imaginable. ¶an ***orderly*** *crowd* 秩序正しい群衆. ¶a ***passing*** *crowd* 一時的な人だかり. ¶a *quiet, orderly crowd* 静かで秩序を守る群衆. ¶A ***riotous*** *crowd* has collected before the Russian Consulate clamouring for bread. 乱暴な群衆が露国領事館前に集まり大騒ぎしてパンを求めた. ¶***surging*** *crowds* 押寄せる群衆. ¶Here the *crowd* was ***thickest*** and most ***enthusiastic***. ここが一番聴衆の数も多く, また一番熱狂した所だ. ¶a ***well-dressed*** *crowd* りっぱな服装をした人々の群. ¶***What*** a *crowd* of automobiles! 沢山の自動車だこと.

P stand at a height ***above*** the *crowd* 群を抜く. ¶***among*** the *crowd* 群集の中に. ¶thronged ***by*** *crowds* of pleasure-seekers 行楽者の群がった ‖ He was jostled ***by*** the *crowd*. 彼は群衆にもまれた. ¶He slipped away in the *crowd*. 彼は群衆の中にこっそり姿を隠してしまった. ‖ gather ***in*** *crowds* 群がる. ¶get ***through*** a *crowd* 人込の中を抜ける. ¶The speaker appealed ***to*** the *crowd* with his usual gesture. 演説者は例のゼスチュアで群衆に訴えた.

P² There is a *crowd **of*** people in the street. 往来に人がたくさん集まっている. ‖ the *crowd **of*** Englishmen and women who inundate Switzerland every year 毎年スイスにぞろぞろ押しかける英国人男女の群. 【類】*Crowds **of*** people flocked to the theater.

Q² a near ***capacity*** *crowd* of about 50,000 約五万というほとんど満員の観衆 ‖ The circus drew a ***capacity*** first night's *crowd*. サーカスの初日は大入満員だった. ¶a mere ***chance*** *crowd* 烏合(うごう)の衆. ¶a ***holiday*** *crowd* 休日の群衆. ¶the ***quayside*** *crowd* strolled back out of the docks. 波止場の群衆はドックから流れ出て帰途についた.

crowd, *v.* 押込む, 詰込む; 押寄せる, 雑踏する.

M be *crowded* too ***closely together*** あまり立て込み過ぎている. ¶be *crowded **out*** by ... ...で圧倒される(はいれない) ‖ *crowd **out*** into the street 街路に流れ出る.

M² *crowd **in*** for seats 座席を求めてどっとはいる ‖ *crowd **in*** through a gate 門から殺到する.

P *crowd **against*** one another for warmth 暖かになろうとして互に寄りつく. ¶The exhibition was *crowded **by*** visitors. 展覧会は見物人で込み合っていた. ¶*crowd **into*** a thronged place [人などが]雑踏する場所に割込む ‖ The article is too long to be *crowded **into*** our limited number of pages. その原稿は長過ぎてページ数の少ない本誌には掲載しかねる. ‖ These thoughts are *crowded **into*** one's mind in considering the subject. その問題を考えるとこれらのことが雑然と頭に浮んで来る. 【類】They were *crowded **into*** a house (hall, room). / *crowd* many people ***into*** a small room ‖ *crowd* Kyoto ***into*** one day 京都を一日で見物する. ¶Many of them were *crowded **out of*** a room. 多数の人が部屋の外にはみ出ていた. ¶We *crowded **round*** her with congratulation. われわれはお祝を言いに大勢彼女の周囲に群がった. ¶They *crowded **through*** the gate. 彼らは門から押寄せた. ¶classes *crowded **to*** capacity 生徒を一杯に詰込んだクラス ‖ The train was *crowedd **to*** the utmost (=full) capacity. 汽車はぎっしりだった. ‖ The lecture hall was *crowded **to*** the doors. 講堂は入口までぎっしりだった. ‖ *crowded **to*** excess (=overflowing) 詰められるだけ一杯に詰込んで. 【類】The room is *crowded **to*** suffocation (息苦しいほど). ¶Incidents *crowd **upon*** my mind as I write, but one will always remain as of yesterday. 私が筆を執って書こうとすると色んなできごとがむらむらと心に浮ぶがその中の一つはいつもきのうのことのようにはっきりしている. ¶The store was *crowded **with*** holiday shoppers. その店には(クリスマスなどの)休日の買物をするお客が一杯いた. ‖ Every page is *crowded **with*** facts. どのページも知識が満載されている. 【類】The streets are *crowded **with*** traffic. / The streets are *crowded **with*** spectators (visitors, passengers). / a century *crowded **with*** great (=important) events / a year *crowded **with*** changes ‖ The textbook is *crowded **with*** mistakes in spelling and phrasing. その教科書はつづり字や句法の間違いが多い. ‖ when not *crowded **with*** work 手すきの時. 【類】The place is *crowded **with*** hotels, villas, and shops.

crowing, *n.* 鶏鳴.

P I awoke ***at*** the *crowing* of the cock. 私は鶏鳴を聞いて目を覚ました.

crown, *n.* 王冠; 帝王; 頭; てっぺん, いただき; 極致; クラウン(貨幣).

V ***forfeit*** his *crown* 王位を失う. ¶***have*** a *crown* on the head 王冠をいただいている. ¶***wear*** the *crown* of England 英国の王冠をいただく.

Q a ***bald*** *crown* はげ頭. ¶an ***elective imperial*** *crown* 選立帝王. ¶a ***hereditary imperial*** *crown* 世襲帝王. ¶a ***shaven*** *crown* 坊主頭.

Q² a ***laurel*** *crown* 月桂冠.

P A treaty was negotiated ***between*** the two *crowns*. 条約が二国王の間に商議された. ¶He is ***from*** the *crown* of his masterful head to the sole of his confident foot an American. 彼は徹頭徹尾米国人である. ¶There are five shillings ***in*** a *crown*. 一クラウンは五シリングだ.

P² the *crown **of*** a hat 帽子の頂部 ‖ the *crown **of*** a hill 小山の頂 ‖ the *crown **of*** sorrow 悲嘆のきわみ ‖ the *crown **of*** womanhood 女盛り ‖ Humanity is the *crown **of*** creation. 人間は万物の霊長である. 【類】The *crown **of*** literature is poetry.

crown, *v.* 冠をいただかす; 栄誉を加える; 報いる; 結局...となる.

P The king was *crowned **at*** Paris. 王はパリで即位した. ¶Its summit is *crowned **by*** a small shrine. その頂上には小さなほこらが建っている. ‖ He was *crowned* king ***by*** them. 彼らが彼を王に擁立した. ‖ His dissipation was *crowned **by*** suicide. 放とうのあげくの果てが自殺だった. ¶*crown* him ***with*** laurel 彼に月桂冠をいただかせる ‖ *crown* the vase ***with*** roses 花びんにばらを活ける ‖ Its summit is *crowned **with*** perpetual snow. その頂上は年中雪がある. ‖ such a glory as never *crowned **with*** before かって例のないほどの光栄 ‖ His effort has been *crowned **with*** success. 彼は努力のかいあって遂に成功した.

crucible, *n.* るつぼ.

P He was tried ***in*** the *crucible* of temptation. 彼は誘惑の試練を受けた.

P² the *crucible **of*** affliction 苦しい目.

crude *a.* なまの, 未熟の.

P *crude **in*** manner (speech) 態度(など)のぎごちない ‖ a story *crude **in*** its invention 十分練れていない創作.

crudity, *n.* 未熟の物, 未成品.

V ***ripen*** these *crudities* これらの青臭さを円熟させる.

cruel, *a.* 残忍な, 残酷な.

M He is ***mercilessly*** *cruel*. 彼はあくまで残酷だ.

P He is *cruel **to*** (=***towards***) his servants. 召使に対して残酷だ.

cruelty, *n.* 残忍, 残酷; 蛮行.

V They ***committed*** most atrocious *cruelties*. 彼らはすこぶる残忍な蛮行をあえてした. ¶***have*** the *cruelty* to ... 残酷にも...する. ¶***perpetrate*** terrible *cruelties* on ... ...に対して恐るべき蛮行を犯す. 【類】***perpetrate*** *cruelties* too horrible to mention. ¶***practice*** *cruelty* to ... ...をひどく虐待する.

Q ***calm*** and ***deliberate*** *cruelty* 冷然と落着き払った残忍. ¶a ***cold*** *cruelty* 冷然たる残忍行為. ¶***heartless*** *cruelty* 冷酷. ¶a ***persistent*** *cruelty* あくまで残忍な所業. ¶***Such*** *cruelty!* 何たる残忍さだ. ¶a ***useless*** *cruelty* 無益の殺生. ¶an act of ***wanton*** *cruelty* 無法な残忍行為. 【類】from ***wanton*** *cruelty*. ¶***wolfish*** *cruelty* おおかみのような残忍さ.

P They treated him ***with*** great *cruelty*. 彼らは彼を非常に虐待した.

P² the *cruelty **of*** fate 運命の無情. ¶*cruelty **to*** animals 動物虐待.

cruise, *n.* 巡航, 巡洋.

Q The training ship was sent on a ***distant*** *cruise*. 練習船は遠洋航海にやられた. ¶The ship arrived in the port after a ***long*** *cruise* of four years. その船は四年の長い航海の後着港した.

Q² beautiful ***inter-island*** *cruises* 美しい島巡り. ¶take a ***pratice*** *cruise* on ... ...に乗って演習航海をやる. ¶a ***world*** *cruise* 世界巡航.

P leave here ***for*** a ten day's *cruise* 十日間の巡航に向って当地を出帆する. ¶the warship ***on*** a *cruise* 巡航中の軍艦.

cruise, *v.* 巡洋する, 遊よくする.

M² *cruise **around*** 巡航する; 歩きまわる.

P *cruise **about*** the Japan Sea 日本海を遊よくする. ¶*cruise **along*** the shore 海岸を遊よくする. ¶*cruise **on*** the Pacific 太平洋を巡航する.

cruiser, *n.* 巡洋艦.

Q ***armed*** (=***armoured***) *cruisers* 装甲巡洋艦. ¶a ***converted*** *cruiser* 仮装巡洋艦. ¶a ***light*** (***heavy***) *cruiser* 軽(重)巡.

Q² a ***battle*** *cruiser* 巡洋戦艦.

crumb, *n.* パンくず.

V I have ***picked up*** some *crumbs* of information. ほんのちょっぴり調べて見た. ¶He ***whisked*** the *crumbs* off his knees. 彼はひざからパンくずを払い除けた.

Q² ***biscuit*** *crumbs* 《米》パンのくず; 《英》ビスケットのくず.

¶*bread crumbs* パンくず.

crumb, *v*. 砕く.

P *crumb* bread ***into*** milk パンを砕いて牛乳の中へ入れる.

crumble, *v*. 砕ける, 崩れる.

P *crumble* ***into*** (=to) dust (=powder) 砕けて粉みじんになる. ¶Even that imposing building *crumbled* ***to*** dust (=pieces). あの堂々たる建物すらがらがら崩壊した.

crumbling, *n*. 崩解.

P^2 the *crumbling* ***of*** old faiths 旧信仰の崩解.

crumple, *v*. しわくちゃにする(なる).

M a hat that has *crumpled* ***up*** under a heavy dictionary 重い辞書の下でくしゃくしゃになった帽子.

P *crumple* paper ***into*** a ball 紙をくしゃくしゃに丸める.

crusade, *n*. 撲滅運動, 征伐.

V ***conduct*** a *crusade* against the fly はえ退治をやる. ¶***make*** a *crusade* against ... ...を攻撃する. ¶***organize*** a *crusade* for ... ...のために革命運動を起す. ¶***start*** a *crusade* against rats ねずみ退治を始める. ¶***undertake*** an active *crusade* against ... 盛んに...反対運動をやる. ¶***wage*** a bold *crusade* against ... ...反対運動を敢行する.

Q a ***humanitarian*** *crusade* against ... ...撲滅の人道的運動. ¶start a ***vigorous*** ***crusade*** against ... ...征伐の猛烈な運動を起す.

Q^2 an ***anti-illiteracy*** ***crusade*** 文盲退治運動. ¶an ***anti-opium*** ***crusade*** in China 中国におけるアヘン禁止運動. ¶start an ***anti-vice*** ***crusade*** 悪弊退治の運動を始める. ¶a ***dry*** *crusade* 《米》禁酒運動. ¶a ***general welfare*** ***crusade*** 生活改善運動. ¶a ***one-man*** *crusade* 単独の攻撃運動. ¶a ***temperance*** *crusade* 禁酒運動.

P a *crusade* ***against*** drunkenness 禁酒運動 ‖ a *crusade* ***against*** tuberculosis 結核撲滅運動 ‖ a *crusade* ***against*** intemperance (slavery) 飲酒(など)反対運動 ‖ a *crusade* ***against*** illiteracy 文盲退治 ‖ a kind of *crusade* ***against*** ... ...退治の一種の運動. ¶a *crusade* ***for*** a warless world 戦争根絶運動.

crusader, *n*. 革新運動家.

Q^2 ***anti-tobacco(-slavery, -illiteracy)*** *crusaders* タバコ(など)禁止運動家. ¶a ***crime*** *crusader* 犯罪撲滅運動者.

crush, *n*. つぶす, 粉砕する; つぶれる.

M *crush* ***out*** a rebellion 暴動をもみ消す ‖ *crush* ***out*** resistance 抵抗を突破する ‖ *crush* ***out*** juice of the grapes in a wine-press しぼり器でぶどうの汁をしぼり出す.

P He was *crushed* ***by*** the houses falling. 彼は倒壊家屋によって圧しつぶされた. 【類】He *crushed* the box ***by*** sitting on it. ‖ He feels quite *crushed* ***by*** his misfortunes. 彼は不幸のために弱りぬいている. ‖ *crush* ***in*** the ice [船が]氷を砕いて入り込む. ¶*crush* things ***into*** a box (trunk) 物を箱(など)に押込む. ¶*crush* ... ***out of*** existence ...を撲滅する. ¶*crush* one ***to*** death 人を圧殺する ‖ *crush* it ***to*** pieces それを粉々にする ‖ Truth, *crushed* ***to*** earth, will rise again. 真理はたたきのめされても再び立ち上る. ¶The worm was *crushed* ***under*** the feet. 虫は踏みつぶされた. ¶*crush* it ***with*** the hand それを手で押しつぶす ‖ He was *crushed* ***with*** grief. 悲しみに沈んでいた.

crusher, *n*. 破砕器.

Q^2 an ***ice*** *crusher* 砕氷船. ¶a ***rock*** *crusher* 岩石破砕器.

crust, *n*. 外皮.

Q the ***earth's*** *crust* 地殻(ちかく).

Q^2 ***dirt*** *crust* on the glass ガラスの上にこびりついたちり.

P^2 a *crust* ***of*** bread パンの上皮 ‖ a *crust* ***of*** ice (水面に)張った氷.

crutch, *n*. 撞木杖(しゅもくづえ), 松葉杖.

P go (=walk) ***on*** *crutches* 松葉杖で歩く ‖ support oneself ***on*** *crutches* 松葉杖にすがる ‖ patients ***on*** *crutches* 松葉杖にすがっている患者. ¶convalescents ***with*** *crutches* or armslings 撞木杖をついたりつり腕帯をかけている回復期の患者たち.

crux, *n*. 難所, 難関.

V^2 the *crux* of the whole difficulty ***lies*** in ... 最も困難な点は...にある.

P the *crux* ***of*** the situation 局面の難所.

cry, *n*. 叫び, 鳴声, 泣声, 叫声, 呼声.

V This ***called forth*** some *cry* of "Shame" and other expressions of dissent. これに対して「恥知らず」とかその他反対の叫び声が起った. ¶***emit*** *cries* of terror 驚の叫び声を発する. ¶***give*** a *cry* of approval「賛成」と叫ぶ. 【類】The lady ***gave*** a *cry*. / ***give*** a sharp *cry* of surprise. ¶She ***had*** her *cry* out. 彼女は泣きたいだけ泣いた. ¶They ***heard*** a *cry* for help. 彼らは助けを求める声を聞いた. ¶Perhaps it is a little early yet to ***raise*** a *cry* of victory. がい歌をあげるのはまだちょっと早いだろう. 【類】***raise*** a hysterical *cry* / ***raise*** a *cry* of distress (悲鳴) / ***raise*** the *cry* of warning ‖ a *cry* of protest was ***raised*** against ... ...に反対の叫びをあげられた. ¶The baby ***sent forth*** a *cry*. 赤ん坊が泣出した. ¶The drowning man ***set up*** a *cry* for help. おぼれかけた人が声をあげて助けを求めた ‖ ***set up*** a terrible *cry* けたたましい声を立てる. ¶***stifle*** a *cry* 叫び声を抑える. ¶***utter*** a *cry* of despair (terror) 絶望(など)の声を発する ‖ ***utter*** the *cry* of justice 正義の叫びをあげる. ¶I ***want*** a good *cry*. 私は心ゆくまで泣きたい. ¶Birds ***weave*** their joyous *cries* into a kind of song without words. 鳥が彼らの喜びの鳴声を無言歌に織出す.

Q give a ***despairing*** ***cry*** 絶望の叫びをあげる. ¶It is a ***far*** *cry* from the beginning of steam navigation. 蒸気船が始めてできたころとくらべると大変な違い. ‖ From ... to ... is indeed a ***far*** *cry*. ...と...では大分距離がある. 【類】it is perhaps a ***far*** *cry* from the subject of ... to the topic of ... / from West Africa to South America is a ***far*** *cry*, but ... / from ... it is something of a ***far*** *cry* to ... ¶it is a ***far-off*** *cry* from England to Japan, but ... 英国から日本に話が飛ぶが. ¶the ***first*** *cry* of a child at birth うぶ声. ¶Crows uttered ***furious*** *cries*. からすが猛烈に鳴立てた. ¶The *cries* of those imprisoned in the fallen buildings were ***heart-rending***. 倒壊家屋に閉じ込められた人々の叫び声は聞くだに断腸の思いであった. ¶the ***insistent*** *cry* of "hard times"「不景気・不景気」の叫び声. ¶The brown-legged "kurumaya" gives a ***long, wailing*** *cry* of warning. 日焼けした脚の車屋が悲しそうな長く引いた警戒の叫びを発する. ¶He continued his speech amid ***loud*** *cries* of protest from the audience. 声を張上げた反対の叫びを浴びながら彼は演説を続けた. ¶a ***piercing*** *cry* 耳をつんざく叫び声. ¶a ***plaintive*** *cry* 哀れっぽい泣声. ¶as the result of a ***popular*** *cry* 世間でやかましく言うので. ¶the ***rallying*** *cry* for the campaign その戦役に対して士気を鼓舞する雄叫び. ¶send forth a ***rapturous*** *cry* 歓呼の声をあげる. ¶the ***raucous*** *cries* of the bus conductors 乗合自動車車掌のしゃがれ声. ¶give a ***sharp*** *cry* きゃっと叫ぶ. ¶the ***shrill*** *cry* of news-boys, "Paper!, Paper!" 新聞売子の「新聞, 新聞」というけたたましい叫び. ¶A ***sudden*** *cry* came to his ear. 突然叫び声が聞えてきた. ¶utter ***troubled*** *cries* 悲鳴をあげる. ¶a ***veritable*** *cry* for justice 正義を望む切実な叫び. ¶a ***wild*** *cry* けたたましい叫び.

Q^2 sound the ***battle*** *cry* by calling attention to ... ...に注意を引くためときの声をあげる. ¶a ***rallying*** *cry*「集合!」の叫び. ¶a ***street*** *cry* 売り声. ¶a ***war*** *cry* ときの声; 標語 ‖ a regular journalistic ***war*** *cry* 新聞の宣伝標語.

P ***amid*** hostile *cries* and jeers 敵の叫び声やちょう笑のまっただ中に. ¶He came rushing ***at*** my *cry*. 私の叫びに応じて彼はかけてきた. ¶with hounds ***in*** full *cry* 猟犬が一斉に追いかけて. ¶The dog was ***out of*** *cry*. 犬は呼んでも声の届かぬ所にいた. ¶***With*** a *cry* he dashed off. 彼は一声叫んで飛び出した ‖ ***with*** a *cry* of dismay 当惑の余りあっと声をあげて. ¶***within*** *cry* of ... ...の呼声の聞える所に.

P^2 a *cry* ***against*** social evil 公娼廃止の叫び. 【類】There was a *cry* ***against*** universal suffrage (普選). ¶There is a *cry* ***by*** some ***against*** this appointment of his. 彼のこの任命に反対の声が聞える. ¶The *cry* ***for*** reform has gone up again and again. 刷新の叫びが再三あげられた. ¶There was a *cry* ***of*** fire. 火事だという声がした. 【類】a *cry* ***of*** alarm (anger, distress, impatience, joy, pain, triumph).

cry, *v*. 叫ぶ, 泣く; 請う, 求める; 呼売する.

M *cry* ***away*** one's time 泣き暮す. ¶"Post early," the Postmaster *cries* ***beseechingly*** for weeks before Christmas, and the great public obeys. クリスマスの数週間前郵便局長は「お早く差出して下さい」と頼むように訴える, そして公衆は皆これに従う. ¶*cry* ***bitterly*** おいおい泣く. ¶She *cried* herself ***blind***. 彼は目を泣きつぶした. ¶*cry* ***exaltingly*** したり顔に叫ぶ. ¶*cry* oneself ***hoarse*** 大声を出して声をつぶす. ¶*cry* ***hotly*** 熱狂して叫ぶ. ¶He *cried* ... ***irately***. 彼は憤然...と叫んだ. ¶"My!" *cried* she ***half-aloud***.「まあ」と彼女は低い叫びをあげた. ¶*cry* ***long*** and ***bitterly*** いつまでもさめざめと泣く. ¶*cry* ***lustily*** [小児など]わーわー泣く. ¶*cry* ***out*** against the evil その悪弊を大いに攻撃する ‖ They *cried* ***out*** against the decision of the court. 彼らは法廷の判決に反対して騒ぎ出した. ‖ *cry* ***out*** for anguish 悲しくて泣きだす ‖ *cry* ***out*** for death 死にたいと叫ぶ ‖ *cry* *out* for help 助けてくれと叫ぶ ‖ ***cry out*** for peace 平和を叫ぶ ‖ ***cry out*** for war 開戦せよと叫ぶ ‖ ***cry out*** for one's mother お母さんと呼びかける ‖ ***cry out*** for settlement (peace) 大声疾呼して解決(など)を求める ‖ ***cry*** one's eyes ***out*** (=blind) 目を泣きつぶす ‖ ***cry out*** in surprise 驚きの叫びをあげる. ¶***cry triumphantly*** 勝ちどきをあげる.

M^2 ***cry down*** a religion (a new theory) 宗教(など)をけなす. ¶***cry off*** from a negotiation 交渉から手を引く旨を宣言する. ¶***cry up*** 盛んにほめる ‖ ***cry up*** to the skies ほめそやす.

P ***cry after*** one departing 去り行く者を追って呼び掛ける. ¶***cry for*** (=with) joy うれしさの余り泣く ‖ ***cry for*** quarter 命を助けてくれと叫ぶ ‖ He ***cried for*** bread. 彼はパンをくれと叫んだ. ‖ ***cry*** goods ***for*** sale 物品を呼売する ‖ ***cry for*** sorrow 泣き悲しむ ‖ ***cry for*** a raise (=rise) in pay 給与値上げを叫ぶ. ¶a state of things that ***cries for*** reform 改革を要望する事態 ‖ This deed ***cries for*** vengeance. これは復しゅうしなければならぬ. ¶***cry*** (=scream) ***in*** horror 悲鳴をあげる ‖ ***cry in*** her hands 両手で顔をおおって泣く ‖ ***cry in*** indignation 怒声をあげる ‖ ***cry in*** desperation at ... 絶望の余り…に呼掛ける. ¶She was ***crying over*** her misfortune (=bad luck). 彼女は己が不運を泣き悲しんでいた. ‖ It is no use ***crying over*** spilt milk. 取返しのつかぬことを悔んでも仕方がない. ¶***cry to*** oneself 忍び泣きをする. ‖ ***cry*** oneself ***to*** sleep 泣き寝入りをする ‖ He ***cried to*** heaven for vengeance. 彼は復しゅうを天に誓った. ¶***cry with*** pain 痛いと叫ぶ ‖ ***cry with*** vexation じれて叫ぶ ‖ ***cry*** out ***with*** a loud voice 大声でどなる ‖ ***cry with*** tears in one's eyes 目に涙をためて泣く.

crying, *n.* 泣くこと.

V ***Stop crying!*** 泣くのはよせ. ¶***suppress crying*** 涙をおさ└える.

crystal, *n.* 水晶; ⦅米⦆ 時計のガラスふた

Q^2 ***rock*** (=***mountain***) ***crystal*** 水晶.

P^2 The ***crystal of*** my watch is gone. 時計のガラスが飛ん└だ.

crystal, 水晶のような.

M^2 clear ***as crystal*** 水晶のようにすき通った.

crystal-gazing, *n.* 予想.

Q ***political crystal-gazing*** 政界予想.

crystallization, *n.* 結晶.

P the ***crystallization of*** sentiment ***into*** words and deeds 言葉及び行為による感情の表現.

crystallize, *v.* 結晶させる; 結晶する.

P ***crystallize in*** small scales 小さなうろこ状に結晶する ‖ fruit ***crystallized in*** a jug びん詰の果物の砂糖づけ ‖ His sympathy ***crystallized in*** actual work. 彼の同情が具体的に実現された. ¶The suggestion (desire, idea) has been ***crystallized into*** a fact. その提案(など)が実現された.

cub, *n.* [野獣の]子.

Q^2 a ***lion*** (***fox***) ***cub*** ライオン(きつね)の子.

cuddle, *v.* 抱きしめる; うずくまる.

M ***cuddle together*** 抱き合う. ¶***cuddle up*** at a corner す└みっこにうずくまる.

cudgel, *n.* こん棒.

V ***take up*** the ***cudgels*** in the present war 今次の戦争に参加する ‖ ***take up*** the ***cudgels*** for ... …の加勢をする ‖ ***take up*** the ***cudgels*** against the time-honored plea, "I have no time for reading." 昔からお定まりの「時間がなくて読書ができない」という言訳を攻撃する.

cue, *n.* 暗示; 玉突棒(キュー); 順番並び; 弁髪; 気分.

V he ***caught*** his ***cue*** (=hint) from ... 彼は…から暗示を得た. ¶***chalk*** one's ***cue*** キューにチョークを塗る. ¶***follow*** the ***cue*** of ... …を見習う. ¶***form*** a ***cue*** (=queue) in front of ticket window 切符売場の前に列を作る. ¶He ***gave*** me the ***cue***. 彼は私にその暗示を与えた. ¶She ***had*** her ***cue*** perfect. 彼女はすっかりのみ込んだ. ¶I ***took*** my ***cue*** from him. 私は彼を見習った(彼から暗示を得た).

P I am not ***in*** the ***cue*** to dance with her. 彼女と踊る気がしない. 【類】I am not ***in*** the ***cue*** for walking. ‖ He was ***in*** excellent ***cue***. 彼は非常にきげんがよかった. ‖ wear long hair dressed ***in cues*** (***in*** a ***cue***) 長い髪を弁髪(お下げ)に結ぶ.

cuff, *n.* カフス, そで口; ⦅米⦆ ずぼんの折り返し; 平手打.

V ***put cuffs*** on the bottoms [of trousers] [ずぼんの]すそに折返しをつける. ¶***roll back*** (=***tack up***) one's ***cuffs*** [ワイシャツの]カフスをまくり上げる.

Q ***frayed cuffs*** すり切れたそで口.

P I was ***at cuffs*** with ... 僕は…と殴り合いをやった.

P^2 a ***cuff on*** the ear 耳の平手打.

cuff, *v.* げん骨を食わす.

P ***cuff*** (=strike) ***with*** the fist げんこで殴る.

cuisine, *n.* 料理.

Q The Vanderbilt kitchen is known for its ***excellent cuisine***. ヴァンダービルト(ホテルの)料理は有名なものであ└る.

cull, *v.* 択り抜く.

M ***cull out*** weaker ones できの悪いのを間引く.

P The text-book is made up of materials ***culled from*** various sources. その教科書は種々の方面の材料で編集した└ものである.

culminate, *v.* 頂点に達する.

P His fanaticism ***culminated in*** sheer madness. 狂信が本気違いになった. ‖ The whole career of Utamaro was one of dissipation, which ***culminated in*** a term of imprisonment for libelling the Shogun. 歌麿の一生は放とうざんまいで最後は将軍を誹謗(ひぼう)したかどで獄に投ぜられたので└あった.

culmination, *n.* 頂点.

V it ***reached*** its ***culmination*** in ... それは…においてその頂点に達した.

P^2 the ***culmination of*** his many years of teaching experience 多年の教壇生活の成果.

culprit, *n.* 犯人.

Q a ***detected culprit*** 見つかった犯人. ¶bring to punishment the ***real culprit*** 真犯人を処罰する.

cult, *v.* 崇拝; 教養, 教え; 崇拝物.

V ***practice*** the ***cult*** of famous old Doctor Johnson 有名なジョンソン博士を崇拝する. ┌シェクスピヤ崇拝.

Q the ***Imperial cult*** 皇室尊崇. ¶the ***Shakespearian cult***

Q^2 I am strong for the ***beauty cult***. 私は大いに美を礼賛する. ¶a Chinese ***peasant cult*** 中国農民の崇拝物. ¶the ***tea cult*** of Japan 茶道. ┌者.

P new recruits ***to*** the ***cult*** of the nude 裸体崇拝への新参

P^2 The cherry-blossom is quite a ***cult in*** Japan. 日本において桜の花は全く崇拝されるまでになっている. ¶The ***cult of*** ... is still flourishing. …熱は未だに流行している. ‖ the ***cult of*** the jumping cat 日より見主義 ‖ the ***cult of*** nature 自然崇拝. ¶Ceramics became a ***cult with*** ladies. 陶器が婦人たちに愛がんされるに至った.

cultivate, *v.* 耕す; 栽培する; 教化する; 養成する.

M be ***assiduously cultivated*** たゆみなく耕作される. ¶The land is ***richly cultivated*** with rice, cotton, tobacco, etc. その土地では米・綿・タバコなどが盛んに栽培されている.

P It is ***cultivated for*** its fruit (beautiful flowers). その実(など)のために栽培する. ¶***cultivate*** young men and women ***in*** citizenship 青年男女の公民教育をする. ¶***cultivate*** a land ***to*** the inch 陸上をくまなく耕す. ¶The land is highly ***cultivated with*** cotton, rice, and vegetables. その土地には綿・米・野菜が盛んに栽培されている. ‖ ***cultivate*** friendship ***with*** a person 人と交際を結ぶ.

O It will take time to ***cultivate*** your talent. 技能をみがくには時間がかかる.

cultivation, *n.* 耕作, 栽培, 養殖; 修養.

V It is not absolutely barren, but is not fertile enough to ***repay cultivation***. 全然不毛だというのではないが耕作のしがいのあるほどの沃土(よくど)でもない.

Q the ***artificial cultivation*** of the commercial sponges 商品としての海綿の人工養殖. ¶the ***general cultivation*** of English among the educated in Japan 教育ある日本人の間における英語の一般的学習.

Q^2 ***garden cultivation*** 花(野菜)畑の栽培. ¶***land*** (=***soil***) ***cultivation*** 耕作.

P it has been ***in cultivation*** in Japan since ... それは…年以来日本で栽培されている. ¶the land ***out of cultivation*** 未開墾地. ¶the area ***under*** banana ***cultivation*** バナナを栽培している地域. 【類】the land ***under cultivation*** of rice.

P^2 the ***cultivation of*** trout in ponds ますの池水養殖.

cultivator, *n.* 栽培家; 開拓者; 修養者.

V In those days natural science ***had*** comparatively few ***cultivators***. 当時自然科学を開拓する人は比較的少数であっ└た.

culture, *n.* 教育, 教養; 栽培.

V ***acquire culture*** 教養を得る. ¶They ***diffused*** their ***culture*** in remote lands. 彼らはその文化を遠国に普及した. ¶***foster*** scientific and literary ***culture*** 科学および文学教育└を奨励する.

V^2 as ***culture evolved*** 文化の発展につれて.

Q ***artistic culture*** 芸術の教養. ¶***Confucian culture*** 儒教. ¶men of ***considerable culture*** よほど教養の高い人. ¶***fruit*** *culture* 果樹栽培. ¶*general culture* 一般的教養. ¶*high culture* 高等教育. ¶fire as an agent in ***human culture*** 人類文化の一要素としての火. ¶conducive to ***intellectual culture*** 知的教育を促す. ¶***intensive culture*** 促成栽培. ¶devote one's surplus energy to ***literary culture*** その余力を文学の研究に捧げる. ¶peoples of ***low culture*** 教養の低い諸国民. ¶***Modern culture*** is scientific in method, rationalistic in spirit, and utilitarian in purpose. 現代教育は方法において科学的であり, 精神において合理的であり, 目的において実用的である. ¶***moral culture*** 徳育. ¶desire for ***personal culture*** 個人の教養を高めようと望む. ¶***physical culture*** 体育. ¶***prenatal culture*** (＝education) 胎教. ¶a ***pure culture*** 〖生物〗純粋培養. ¶a ***separate*** and ***indigenous culture*** 別個にしてその国土に特有な教育. ¶the ***scientific culture*** of trees 樹木の科学的栽培. ¶a person of ***some culture*** 多少教育のある人. ¶***spiritual culture*** 精神修養. ¶These aliens brought with them a ***superior culture***. これら外国人は一層優秀な文化をもたらした. ¶***true culture*** 真の教養. ¶train them in ***Western culture*** 彼らに西洋式教育を授ける.

Q² ***beauty culture*** 美容術. ¶***bird culture*** 小鳥の飼養. ¶***chrysanthemum*** (***rose***) ***culture*** 菊(ばら)栽培. ¶Concentration inmates are given lectures in ***Communist culture***. 収容所の捕虜たちは共産党理論の講議を受ける. ¶***flat culture*** [あぜ作に対して]平地耕作. ¶the ***frame culture*** of cucumbers きゅうりの温室栽培. ¶a new way in ***health culture*** 新しい健康法 ‖ a school of ***health culture*** ある健康法の流派. ¶***memory culture*** 記憶の訓練. ¶***oyster culture*** ＝the culture of oysters かきの養殖. ¶***pear culture*** なし造り. ¶***pearl culture*** 真珠養殖. ¶***poultry culture*** 養鶏. ¶***sense culture*** 良識の養成. ¶***test-tube culture*** 試験管内細菌培養. ¶***tobacco culture*** タバコの栽培.

P ***In point of culture***, he is superior. 教養では彼の方が上だ. ¶a man ***of culture*** 教養ある人.

culture, *v.* 教化する, 修業する.

M be ***well cultured*** 教養がある.

culture-ground, *n.* 栽培地.

P such a soil is a suitable *culture-ground* ***for*** the development of ... こういう下地があると...が起りやすい.

culturist, *n.* 栽培者; 教化者.

Q an ***ethical culturist*** 倫理の先生.

Q² a ***beauty culturist***＝a beautician 美容家.

cumber, *v.* 悩ます.

P He was *cumbered* ***with*** cares. 彼は心配に悩まされた.

cunning, *n.* ずるさ, こうかつ.

Q ***hypocritical cunning*** ねこをかぶったずるさ. ¶***impudent cunning*** 厚かましいずるさ.

cup, *n.* 杯; 賞杯; *pl.* 飲酒; 運命; 禍福.

V That tea *cup* is ***chipped***. その茶わんはかけている. ¶***circulate*** wine *cups* ぶどう酒の杯をまわす. ¶***drain*** the *cup* of pleasure to its dregs 放とうの限りを尽す ‖ ***drain*** the *cup* of humiliation 屈辱の限りをなめる. 【類】***drain*** the *cup* of life. ¶***drink*** (＝***take***) a *cup* of coffee コーヒーを一杯飲む ‖ ***drink*** the *cup* dry 茶わんを飲みほす. ¶He ***filled*** (＝***poured***) yet another *cup* of wine for me. 彼はもう一杯ぶどう酒を私についでくれた. ¶***have*** a *cup* of tea (coffee) 紅茶(など)を一杯飲む. ¶He ***liked*** his *cups* better than his books. 彼は書物よりも酒が好きだった. ¶***take*** a *cup* of *sake* 一杯ひっかける. ¶***tilt*** the *cup* 杯を傾ける. ¶***turn*** a *cup* bottom upward 杯を伏せる. ¶***win back*** the *cup* 賞杯を取返す. ¶I ***wish*** a *cup* of tea. 紅茶を一杯頂きたい.

Q Have ***another cup?*** もう一杯いかが. ¶a ***bitter cup*** 苦難. ¶His *cup* was ***full***. 彼の好(悪)運は絶頂に達した. ¶***half*** a *cup* 半杯. ¶***three cups*** of tea 茶三杯.

Q² a ***canteen cup*** 酒保のコップ. ¶a ***china cup*** 茶わん, さかずき. ¶a ***class cup*** 同級祝杯(米国の大学で卒業後初めて男子をもうけた者に同級生たちが送る銀杯). ¶a ***coffee cup*** コーヒー茶わん. ¶a ***drinking cup*** さかずき. ¶pass a ***loving cup*** round the assembly 愛情のさかずきをみんなにまわす. ¶an ***early morning cup*** of tea 早朝のお茶(朝茶)一杯. ¶a ***mustache cup*** (口ひげが入らないようになっている)紳士用茶わん. ¶a ***paper cup*** 紙カップ. ¶a ***parting cup*** 送別の一杯. ¶drink the ***stirrup cup*** あぶみ酒(門出の杯)を飲む. ¶a ***trophy cup*** 優勝杯.

P ***At*** the first *cup* man drinks wine, at the second wine drinks wine, at the third wine drinks man. 一杯人酒を飲み, 二杯酒酒を飲み, 三杯酒人を飲む. ¶He gets quarrelsome ***in*** his *cups*. あれは怒り上戸だ. ‖ when ***in*** his *cups* 彼が酔うと ‖ He is ***in*** his *cups* (＝drunken). 彼は酔っている. ¶have a talk ***over*** one's *cups* 酒を飲みながら話す. ¶He is addicted ***to*** the *cup*. 彼は飲酒にふけっている.

cupboard, *n.* 食器だな.

Q² a ***corner cupboard*** 三角食器だな(部屋のすみにおく).

cupidity, *n.* 貪欲(どんよく).

V ***arouse*** the *cupidity* of ... ...の食欲を目覚ます ¶Big salaries ***excite*** the *cupidity* of employees. 高い給料が使用人の欲張り根性を刺激する. ¶***satisfy*** one's *cupidity* その食欲を満足させる.

curative, *a.* 病をなおす.

P The herb is popularly believed to be *curative* ***of*** many diseases. その薬草はいろいろの病気にきくと一般に信じられている.

curb, *n.* 抑制; 辺石; 〖株〗場外市場 (＝curb market).

V ***place*** a *curb* upon ... ...に制限を加える. ¶***put*** a *curb* upon one's desires その欲望を抑制する.

Q² an ***inflation curb*** インフレ抑制. ¶the ***rising population curb*** 人口増加抑制.

P Taxis take on or discharge passengers ***at*** the *curb* (＝curbstone). タクシーが辺石のところで客を乗せたり降したりする. ¶dealings ***on*** the *curb* 〖株〗場外取引.

cure, *n.* 治癒(ゆ); 療法, 薬.

V ***bring about*** a *cure* 全快させる. ¶***effect a cure*** 直す ‖ continue this treatment until a *cure* is ***effected*** 効が現われるまでこの治療を続ける. ¶He ran all over Europe to ***find*** a *cure*. 彼は療養のためにヨーロッパ中をかけ回った. ¶***hasten*** *cure* 全快を早める. ¶***have*** a rest *cure* of several months 五六カ月静養する. ¶In three weeks a perfect *cure* was ***obtained***. 三週間で全快した. ¶***perform*** a miraculous *cure* 奇跡的に病気を全快させる. ¶The results are not sufficiently certain yet to say that it ***provides*** a *cure* for the disease. 結果が十分判らないので果してそれでその病気が治るかどうかは言えない. ¶He almost ***reached*** a *cure* in three months. 彼は三カ月でほとんど全治した. ¶He decided to ***seek*** a *cure* in another country. 彼は外国に転地して療養することに決した. ¶***take*** the *cure* in a sanatorium 療養所で療治する ‖ ***take*** the rest *cure* 静養療法をやる. ¶I had ***tried*** one so-called *cure* after another without result. それまでにいわゆる何々療法というやつを片っぱしから試みたが効果がなかった. ¶***work*** a *cure* 全治させる ‖ ***work*** its own *cure* 自然に治る ‖ ***work*** *cures* with charms まじないでなおす. 【類】The *cure* ***works*** slowly. ¶Manuchin claims to have ***worked out*** an effectual *cure* for tuberculosis, even in advanced cases. マヌチンは進んだ結核患者の場合にでも有効な治療法を発見したと言っている.

Q What is the ***best cure*** for a cough? せきの妙薬は何ですか. ¶a ***certain cure*** (＝remedy) 特効薬 ‖ He knows a ***certain cure*** for everybody's cold but his own. 彼は自分以外のかぜ引は必ず直せる療法を心得ている. 【類】a ***certain cure*** for mental depression. ¶an ***easy*** and ***sure cure*** 容易で確実な治療法. ¶no ***effective cure*** has been found to remedy ... ...を直す良薬はまだない. ¶an ***efficacious cure*** 妙薬. ¶***fashionable*** "*cure*" 流行のいわゆる「治療法」. ¶a ***good cure*** for lying うそつきを直す良法. ¶the ***hard work cure*** 勤労療法. ¶a ***heroic cure*** 荒療治. ¶a ***hydropathic cure*** 水療法. ¶an ***infallible cure*** 確実な療法. ¶There is no ***known cure*** for the disease. その病気の妙薬はまだない. ¶a ***lasting cure*** 徹底的療法. ¶work a ***miraculous cure*** 不思議なくらいよく効く. ¶***No cure*** for a fool. ばかにつける薬はない. ¶effect a ***permanent cure*** 根治させる. ¶a ***positive cure*** 確実な療法. ¶a ***radical cure*** 根治法. ¶a ***spontaneous cure*** 自然の治癒. ¶a ***sure cure*** for ... ...の妙薬. ¶a ***tongue-rest cure*** for nervous troubles of women 婦人の神経病に対する沈黙療法. ¶***true cures*** まともな(本当の)療法.

Q² a certain ***cholera cure*** コレラの必治法. ¶begin an ***obesity cure*** やせる方法を始める. ¶a ***fasting cure*** 断食療法. ¶a ***headache cure*** 頭痛薬. ¶***hot-spring cure*** 湯治. ¶a ***hot*** (***cold***)-***water cure*** 湯(冷水)治. ¶a ***quack cure*** いんちき療法. ¶a ***terrain cure*** 山地をかけめぐる戸外運動療法. ¶the ***faith cure*** 信仰療法. ¶***water cure*** 水療法.

P They come to the hot springs ***for*** a *cure*. 客はその温泉へ療養に来る. ‖ a charm ***for*** the *cure* of diseases 病気回復の護符. ¶He is ***past*** *cure* now. 彼はもう手遅れだ.

P² Mandrake is popularly believed to be a *cure* ***for*** barrenness. 曼陀羅華(まんだらげ)は子のできる妙薬だという民間信仰がある. ‖ a *cure* ***for*** burns (a cold, asthma) 火傷(など)の薬 ‖ a new *cure* ***for*** tuberculosis 結核の新薬 ‖ a *cure* ***for*** poverty 貧乏の撃退法.

cure, *v.* なおす, 矯正する; くん製にする.

M *cure* itself ***automatically*** 自然に直る. ¶Good luck to you. I hope you will be ***completely cured***. 御きげんよう. 御病気が御全快なさるように.

P I was *cured* ***by*** a German physician. 私はドイツ人の医者の手で治った. ¶a herring *cured* ***in*** smoke くん製のにしん. ¶*cure* a person ***of*** a disease …の病気を治す ‖ *cure* a patient ***of*** rheumatism 患者のリューマチスを治す ‖ be *cured* ***of*** one's bad habit 悪癖が直る ‖ Sweet-shop assistants are usually *cured* ***of*** larceny by cloying. 菓子屋の店員は通常甘い物をたらふく食わして盗み食いを直す. ‖ he would be *cured* ***of*** that illusion if he … 彼は…するならばその誤りを悟るだろう. 【類】He was *cured* ***of*** fever (a wound). / *cure* a lad ***of*** heedlessness / I must *cure* myself ***of*** this habit. / He was *cured* ***of*** the habit ¶He was *cured* ***with*** a certain medicine. 彼の病気はある薬で治った.

curfew, *n.* 晩鐘; 消灯令.

V *curfew* was ***ordered*** from … to … …時から…時まで消灯令が布かれた.

Q² ***midnight*** *curfew* 夜半の鐘. ¶A ***7 p.m.*** *curfew* was imposed on the city. 同市は午後七時消灯令がしかれた.

curio, *n.* 骨とう品.

Q a ***dainty*** *curio* 優雅な骨とう品. ¶a ***rare*** *curio* 珍しい骨とう品.

curiosity, *n.* 好奇心; 珍品.

V ***arouse*** *curiosity* 好奇心を起させる. ¶he acquired celebrity, or, at least, ***awakened*** *curiosity* of a sort, through the mere fact that … 彼は単に…という事実のために有名になったとは言い得ないまでもとにかく一種の好奇心を喚起した. ¶***excite*** the *curiosity* of the public 世人の好奇心を刺激する. ¶***gratify*** *curiosity* 好奇心を満足させる. 【類】***gratify*** one's own intellectual *curiosities*. ¶he ***had*** the *curiosity* to inquire into … 彼は好奇心から…を調査した. 【類】I ***had*** *curiosity* to open this, and found that it contained … ¶***manifest*** intense *curiosity* 深い好奇心を示す. ¶***pique*** the reader's *curiosity* 読者の好奇心を刺激する. ‖ it ***piqued*** my childish *curiosity* with … ‖ It ***piqued*** my *curiosity* to see it for myself. ¶***provoke*** some *curiosity* among them 彼らの間に幾分好奇心を喚起する. ¶***raise*** the *curiosity* of … …の好奇心を高める. ¶***satisfy*** my *curiosity* as to … …に就て私の好奇心を満足させる. ¶***show*** *curiosity* 好奇心を示す. ¶***stimulate*** public *curiosity* 一般の好奇心を刺激する. ¶***whet*** *curiosity* 好奇心をそそる.

Q ***ardent*** *curiosity* 熱烈な好奇心. ¶The crowd looked on them with ***great*** *curiosity*. 群衆は非常な好奇心をもってそれらを眺めていた. ¶he had a ***healthy*** *curiosity* about … 彼は…について健全な好奇心を持っていた. ¶***historical*** *curiosities* 歴史上の珍品. ¶have the ***hungry*** *curiosity* for … …に対して熱心な好奇心を持つ. ¶***idle*** *curiosity* 無用な好奇心. ¶***impertinent*** *curiosity* でしゃばった好奇心. ¶I have an ***insatiable*** *curiosity* regarding everything that pertains to it. 私はいやしくもそれと関係のあることならあくまで研究したいという考えを持っている. ¶the ***intellectual*** *curiosity* of the cultivated tourist 教養ある旅行家の知的好奇心. ¶a ***literary*** *curiosity* 珍稀な文学作品. ¶***lithic*** *curiosities* (庭などの)奇石. ¶have a ***lively*** *curiosity* about it それについて好奇心をわかす. ¶the banishing of ***prurient*** *curiosity* みだらな好奇心の駆逐. ¶with ***respectful*** *curiosity* 敬けんな好奇心をもって ‖ ***scientific*** *curiosity* 科学的好奇心 ‖ a ***scientific*** *curiosity* 科学上の珍品. ¶feed his ***scholarly*** *curiosity* 氏の学究的好奇心を満足させる. ¶He is full of ***wholesome*** *curiosity*. 彼は健全な好奇心に満ちている.

P prompted (=urged) ***by*** *curiosity* 好奇心にかられて. ¶merely ***for*** the *curiosity* of the thing ただそのことが珍しいというだけで. ¶***from*** a morbid *curiosity* 病的な好奇心から. ¶***in*** *curiosity* 好奇心で. ¶guided only by the blind impulse ***of*** *curiosity* 好奇心という盲目的な衝動にのみかられて. ¶I asked ***out of*** *curiosity*. 私は好奇心にかられて尋ねた. ¶***through*** *curiosity* 物好きで. ¶yield ***to*** *curiosity* 好奇心に負ける. ¶watch … ***with*** *curiosity* …を好奇心で見まもる.

curious, *a.* 物好きの; 珍しい.

M He is ***very*** *curious*. 彼はむやみに物を聞きたがる.

P be *curious* ***about*** the origin of … …の根原を知りたがる.

O I am *curious* to see if it was still there. まだそれがそこにあるかどうかを知りたい. ¶I am *curious* to know … 私は…を知りたい. ¶*curious* to relate 妙な話だが.

curl, *n.* 巻き毛(カール).

Q She has ***long*** *curls* over her shoulders. 彼女は長い巻き毛を肩に垂らしている.

P keep one's hair ***in*** *curl* カールにしておく. ¶***with*** a *curl* on the lips 口をゆがめて.

P² *curls* ***of*** smoke rising from a pipe パイプからのぼるタバコの煙の輪.

curl, *v.* 巻き毛(カール)にする.

M² *curl* one's hair ***up*** 髪をカールにする. ¶He (the snake) *curled* himself ***up*** like a reel of rope. へびが巻なわのようにとぐろを巻いていた.

currency, *n.* 通貨; 通用, 流布.

V The idea has ***acquired*** a proverbial *currency*. その考えは諺になったくらい一般に流布した. ¶The word has ***attained*** general *currency*. その言葉は一般に広まった. ¶Government has ***decreed*** a paper *currency*. 政府は紙幣の発行を法令で布告した. ¶The custom ***enjoyed*** a brief *currency*. その風俗は少しの間行われたことがあった. ¶***gain*** *currency* (語句など)広まる. 【類】it probably ***gained*** *currency* in part owing to … ¶***give*** *currency* to (=propagate) the idea (belief, new word) 思想(など)を宣伝する ‖ ***give*** *currency* to a new word 新語を流布させる. 【類】***give*** *currency* to rumor. ¶***have*** *currency* 世間に通用している(行われている) ‖ The word ***has*** no general *currency* in America. その語は米国で一般に用いられていない. ¶***inflate*** the *currency* 通貨を膨張させる. ¶The word has ***obtained*** general *currency*. その語は一般に広まった.

Q These words sound too literary to give them ***colloquial*** *currency*. これらの語は調子があまり文学的で一般口語には用いられない. 【類】These words have gained ***colloquial*** *currency*. ¶These English words have an ***extensive*** *currency* in Japan. これらの英語は日本で広く用いられている. ¶bring in ***foreign*** *currency* 外貨を導入する. ¶give ***free*** *currency* to the word その語を盛んに用いる. ¶The new word has gained a ***general*** *currency* その新語は広く一般に用いられるようになった. ¶have ***greater*** *currency* here than elsewhere どこへ行ってもこの土地ほど流行してはいない. ¶obtain ***instant*** *currency* 直ちに広まる. ¶scientific terms that have ***international*** *currency* 万国に通用する科学上の術語. 【類】Latin once gained a sort of ***international*** *currency*. ¶***metallic*** *currency* 硬貨. ¶***occupational*** *currency* 占領地通貨. ¶***verbal*** *currency* 言葉という通貨. ¶a fallacy which has ***wide*** *currency* in certain circles ある方面に広く行われている誤った考え.

Q² ***occupation*** *currency* 軍票. ¶over-issue of ***paper*** *currency* 紙幣の発行超過. ¶a charge of 25 cents, ***United States*** *currency*, will be made. 米貨で二十五セントの料金がとられる.

P ***during*** the *currency* of the policy その方策の有効期間は.

current, *n.* 潮流, すう勢; 流れ; 電流.

V ***apply*** the *current* to … …に電流を通す. ¶***break*** the main *current* of a narrative 物語の本筋を途切らす. ¶***collect*** the *current* from … …から電流を採る. ¶It ***produced*** two different *currents* of opinion amongst responsible Japanese statesmen. そのために日本の責任ある政治家の間に二派の意見を生じた. ¶***reverse*** the *current* 時代に逆行する. ¶***set up*** *currents* 電流を起す. ¶The electric *current* has been ***shut off***. 停電した. ¶***stem*** the *current* of popular sentiment 民衆の感情に逆らう. ¶***switch off*** (***on***) *current* 電流を切る(通じる). ¶***turn off*** (***on***) the *current* 電流を止める(通じる).

Q ***alternating*** *current* 〘電気〙交流. ¶an ***electric*** *current* 電流. ¶a ***furious*** *current* 激流. ¶***main*** *currents* in American history アメリカ史の本流. ¶voice a ***profound*** *current* of public sentiment 公論感情の底流を発表する. ¶a ***slow*** *current* 緩流. ¶a ***strong*** *current* 強い流れ. ¶a ***swift*** *current* 急流.

Q² waft on ***air*** *currents* 風のまにまにただよう. ¶treacherous ***air*** *currents* 悪気流. ¶a ***sea*** *current* 海流.

P slow ***in*** *current* 流れのおそい. ¶The electric fan revolves ***under*** a *current* of 100 volts. 扇風機は百ボルトの電流で回転する.

P² the *current* ***of*** events 大勢.

current, *a.* 流布している, 広まっている.

M The old belief is still ***widely*** *current*. その古い信仰が

いまだに広く行われている.

P traditions *current* ***among*** the tribes その蛮族の間に広まっている伝説. ¶All these forms of superstition are *current* ***in*** Japan. すべてこうした迷信は日本に広まっている. ¶anecdotes that have been *current* ***of*** the great hero この大英雄に関して流布している逸話. ¶The report *current* ***with*** him is true. 世間に立っている彼のうわさは本当だ.

curriculum, *n.* 〘教育〙教科課程(カリキュラム); 学課.

V ***crowd*** the *curriculum* 学課目を多くする. ¶***cut down*** the *curriculum* 学課目を少くする. ¶The *curriculum* is ***overloaded.*** 教課目が過多になっている. ¶***simplify*** the *curriculum* 学課課程を簡単にする.

Q the *curriculum* of ... is ***incomplete*** if it does not include ... ...この学課課程は...を加えないと不完全である. ¶a ***rich*** *curriculum* 科目の多い学課課程.

Q^2 a ***cast-iron*** *curriculum* 型にはまった教科課程. ¶***core*** *curriculum* 〘教育〙一つの事に中心をおいてやる教科課程. ¶"***ivory tower***" *curriculum* 象牙の塔式のアカデミックな教科課程. ¶add ... to the ***school*** *curriculum* 学校の教科課程に...を加える. 【類】 subjects in the ***school*** *curriculum.*

P The subject is not included ***in*** the *curriculum.* その学科は課程表に入っていない. ¶place Esperanto ***on*** its *curriculum* エス語をその学校の課程に入れる.

curse, *n.* のろい; 天罰, たたり.

V ***call down*** *curses* upon the head of ... ...をのろう. ¶The jewel ***carries*** the *curse* of misfortune or violent death. その宝石は不幸や横死を招くのろいを秘めている. ¶***heap*** *curses* on ... ...を激しくののしる. ¶***incur*** a *curse* 罰があたる. ¶***invoke*** a *curse* on ... ...に天罰が下るように祈る. ¶His wealth ***proved*** a *curse* to him. 富裕がかえって彼の不幸となった. ¶***utter*** *curses*＝execrate, curse のろいの言葉を吐く.

Q a ***hereditary*** *curse* 遺伝的なのろい(たたり). ¶with a ***muttered*** *curse* ぶつぶつ言って. ¶an ***unmitigated*** *curse* ろこつなののしり.

P^2 the *curse* ***of*** drink 飲酒のたたり.

curse, *v.* のろう, 悪口を言う.

M *curse* ***loudly*** 大声であくたいをつく.

P be *cursed* ***with*** a worthless son ろくでなしの息子をもっている.

curt, *a.* ぶっきら棒の.

P be *curt* ***to*** ... ...に無愛想である.

curtail, *v.* 削減する, 縮小する.

P *curtail* a man ***in*** his privileges 人の特権を縮小する. ¶We are *curtailed* ***of*** our expenses. われわれは経費を削減された.

curtain, *n.* 幕; 窓掛(カーテン).

V ***draw*** the *curtain* 幕をあける ‖ We ***drew*** the *curtain* over his failings. われわれは彼の過失を秘密にした. ¶***draw aside*** the *curtains* 幕をあける. ¶***draw back*** (＝***undraw***) the *curtain* 幕を引あける. ¶***draw down*** (＝***let down*** *or* ***lower***) a *curtain* 幕を下ろす. ¶***draw*** the *curtains* ***together*** (***apart***) 幕を引合わせる(引離す). ¶***draw up*** (***down***) a *curtain* カーテンをあげる(下げる). ¶***drop*** the *curtain* 幕を下ろす. ¶***furl*** a *curtain* 幕をまき上げる. ¶***keep*** the *curtain* ***undrawn*** 窓掛を引かないでおく. ¶***pull down*** a *curtain* 幕を引下ろす. ¶***raise*** a *curtain* 幕を上げる ‖ ***raise*** the *curtain* [芝居の]幕をあける.

V^2 The *curtain* is ***drawing up.*** [芝居などの]幕があくところだ. ¶The *curtain* of Time has ***dropped*** long since upon that scene. そのできごとは大分過去に属する. ‖ The *curtain* ***dropped*** on the last scene. これで(芝居など)はねになった. ¶The *curtain* ***falls.*** 幕になる; はねる. 【類】 With the rising of Shimabara and its sanguinary suppression by the Government, the *curtain* ***falls*** on the early history of Christianity in Japan.—J.H. Gubbins. ¶when the *curtain* ***goes up*** 幕があくと. ¶The *curtains* ***parted.*** 幕が左右にあいた. ¶The *curtain* ***rises.*** 幕があく. 【類】 The *curtain* will ***rise*** at 9 o'clock punctually. ‖ The *curtain* ***rose*** upon the second act. / The *curtain* ***rose*** on a drama. ¶The *curtain* ***waved*** in the breeze. 風でカーテンがゆれた.

Q^2 a ***bamboo*** *curtain* すだれ; 竹のカーテン. ¶a ***black-out*** *curtain* しゃへい幕. ¶a ***casement*** *curtain* 開き窓のカーテン. ¶all of Europe outside the ***iron*** *curtain* 鉄のカーテンの外の全欧州. ¶a ***lace*** *curtain* レースのカーテン. ¶a ***smoke*** *curtain* 煙幕. ¶a ***mosquito*** *curtain* 蚊帳. ¶a ***window*** *curtain* 窓掛.

P ***behind*** the *curtain* 隠れて, 黒幕の中で. ¶sleep ***under*** a mosquito *curtain* 蚊帳をつって寝る.

P^2 a *curtain* ***over*** a bed とこの上のカーテン. ¶a *curtain* ***with*** a ruffle around it へりにひだのついたカーテン.

curtain, *v.* 幕を張る.

M *curtained* ***off*** from the public gaze 世間の目から隠れて.

curtsy, courtesy, *n.* [婦人がちょっと片ひざを折ってする]あいさつ.

V ***make*** (＝***drop***) a *curtsy* [婦人が]腰をかがめておじぎをする. 【類】 ***make*** a *curtsy* to the queen.

curve, *n.* 曲線.

V ***attain*** the highest *curve* of development 発達の最高点に達する. ¶A meteor appeared and passed directly over head ***describing*** a *curve.* 流星が現われて曲線を描きながら頭の真上を過ぎ去った.

V^2 The *curve* ***culminates*** at the age of 15 and ***falls*** rapidly after 16. [図表の]曲線は十五歳で最高点に達し十六歳以後はずんずん下向する.

Q a body with ***beautiful*** *curves* 美しい曲線を持つ肉体. ¶a ***French*** (＝an ***irregular***) *curve* 雲形定規. ¶a ***sharp*** *curve* [道路などの]急な曲線. ¶rise in a ***steady*** *curve* 着々上向線をたどる.

Q^2 a ***roadbed*** *curve* 〘鉄道〙路床の曲線. ¶an ***S-shaped*** or ***corkscrew*** *curve* S字形即ちコルク抜きのような曲線.

P It determines the form of the *curve* ***of*** work. それで成績の優劣が決定する.

curve, *v.* 曲る.

M *curve* ***sharply*** to the left [道路などが]急に左へ曲る.

cushion, *n.* 座ぶとん(クッション).

Q^2 Next he raised his quills, looking like a huge ***pin*** *cushion.* 次に彼(はりねずみ)は針をもりあげ丁度針山のように見えた.

P a sofa ***with*** a *cushion* on it クッションの置いてあるソーファー.

custodian *n.* 管理人.

Q^2 a ***building*** *custodian* 建物監理人. ¶a ***building*** and ***property*** *custodian* 建物および資産監理人.

custody, *n.* 保管; 監視.

V ***take*** *custody* of ... ...を保管する.

P ***for*** safe *custody* 安全保管のため. ¶a prisoner ***in*** the *custody* of two constables 二人の警官に監視されている一人の囚徒 ‖ The offender was led away ***in*** *custody.* 犯人は監視付きで護送された. ‖ It is kept ***in*** safe *custody.* それは安全に保管されている.

custom, *n.* (**1**) 習慣, 慣例.

V They ***abandoned*** many of their original *customs.* 彼らは大分従来の習慣を棄てた. ¶***abrogate*** a *custom* 慣習を廃する. ¶***adopt*** and ***adapt*** Western *customs* 西洋風を採用してそしてこれを消化する. ¶***break*** an old *custom* 旧習を破る. ¶The invaders ***brought*** the *custom* with them. 侵略者と一緒にその習慣が渡来した. ¶***collect*** *customs* on imported goods 輸入品から関税を取立てる. ¶Europeanization has ***destroyed*** ancient *customs* and old historic landmarks. 欧化のために昔の習慣や古い歴史上の遺跡が破壊した. ¶***discard*** foolish old *customs* 昔のばかげた慣習を棄てる. ¶The *custom* is ***established.*** その習慣が確立した. ¶***follow*** a European *custom* 欧州の習慣に従う. 【類】 ***follow*** the *custom* of the Spanish / He ***followed*** his usual *custom* of spending Sunday at his villa at Zushi. / ***following*** the Japanese *custom.* ¶***force*** a *custom* 習慣を強制する. ¶he ***had*** a *custom* to ... 彼は...する癖があった. ¶***keep up*** an old *custom* 古風を守る. 【類】 This *custom* has been ***kept up*** for two thousand years. ¶The *custom* of saluting the quarter-deck is still ***maintained*** in the British navy. 後甲板に敬礼する習慣は今日なお英国海軍に行われている. ¶A traveller should train himself to ***observe*** quite impersonally the odd *customs* of exotic peoples. 旅行者は外国民の妙な習慣を全く自分を離れて観察することに慣れなければいけない. ¶This *custom* has been ***practiced*** from early times. この慣習は昔から実行されてきた. ¶***start*** the *custom* その習慣を始める. ¶Some Europeans ***stigmatize*** our *customs* and manners as barbarous. 欧州人の中にはわれわれの風俗習慣を野蛮だと決めつける人がある. ¶This tedious *custom* has been ***suppressed*** by the commonsense of modern times. このまどろっこい習慣は近代人の常識で廃止された. ¶***take up*** a *custom* of ... ...の習慣を始める. ¶It is interesting to ***trace*** this *custom* back to its origin. この習慣の起源にさかのぼって見ることは興味あることだ. 【類】 This *custom* has been ***traced*** to an ancient tradition.

V^2 That *custom* has completely ***died out.*** その習慣は全く

姿を消してしまった. ¶The *custom* still ***exsits.*** その習慣はいまだに存続している. ¶This *custom* has ***fallen*** into disuse. この習慣はすたれてしまった. ¶Some old *customs* still ***linger.*** 昔の習慣の中にはまだ残っているものもある. ¶A similar *custom* ***obtains*** in this part of the country. 同じような習慣がこの地方に行われている. ¶In Naples the *custom* ***prevails*** of eating eels on Christmas. ナポリではクリスマスの前夜にうなぎを食べるという習慣がある. ¶A new *custom* has ***sprung up.*** 新しい習慣が生れた. ¶The *custom* has ***taken root.*** その習慣が確立した.

Q according to an ***ancient*** *custom* 古い習慣で. ¶according to ***annual*** (=***yearly***) *custom* 例年の通り. ¶an ***antique*** *custom* 古風な風俗. ¶a ***civilized*** *custom* 礼儀正しい習慣. ¶a ***dangerous*** *custom* 危険な習慣. ¶It runs counter to all ***established*** *customs.* それは従来のすべての慣習に反する. ¶a ***good*** *custom* 美風. ¶an ***immemorial*** *custom* 大昔からの習慣. ¶The wearing of the green is a pretty ***Irish*** *custom.* 緑のスーツを着るのはアイルランドの美しい習慣である. ¶a ***long-established*** *custom* 昔からきまっている習慣. ¶***native*** *customs* 土地の習慣. ¶according to ***old Japanese*** *custom* 古い日本の習慣により. ¶It is the ***Persian*** *custom* that all shall rise when a person of special distinction enters a room. 知名の士がへやに入ってきたら一同起立するのがペルシャの習慣である. ¶a ***picturesque*** *custom* 見て美しい習慣. ¶a ***pretty*** *custom* ゆかしい習慣. ¶the ***prevailing*** *custom* 一般に行われる慣習. ¶it has become the ***recognized*** *custom* to ... ...ことは一般が認める慣習になった. ¶be ruled by a rather ***rigid*** *custom* かなり厳格な習慣でしばられている. ¶***rural*** *customs* いなか風. ¶a ***settled*** *custom* きまった習慣. ¶***Social*** *customs* vary in different parts of the world. 社会慣習は地方地方で異なる. ¶a ***time-honored*** *custom* 昔からの習慣. ¶the simple ***tribal*** *customs* of savages 蛮人の簡単な民族習慣. ¶an ***unheard-of*** *custom* in Japan 日本にはない習慣. ¶It has been almost the ***universal*** *custom* to scoff at the weather forecast. 天気予報をあざけることはほとんど世界中の習慣である. ¶following our ***usual*** *custom* 弊店の慣例により. ¶a ***world-wide*** *custom* 世界中に行われる慣習(喫煙など).

Q^{2} a ***cast-iron marriage*** *custom* 型にはまった結婚の風習. ¶according to ***family*** *custom* 家風で. ¶a ***folk*** *custom* 郷土の習慣. ¶Our ***language*** *customs* do not permit us to say like that. わが国の語法ではそうは言えない.

P ***according to*** *custom* established two years ago 二年前に開かれた慣習により. 【類】***according to*** Japanese *custom.* ¶It is ***against*** the *custom.* それは慣例に反する. ¶***by*** the *custom* of the time 時代の慣習によって. ¶***in accordance with*** annual *custom* on Michaelmas Day ミカエル祭の慣例に従って. 【類】***in accordance with*** ancient *custom.* ¶the revival ***of*** the *custom* 習慣の復活. ¶***through*** *custom* 習慣上. ¶conform ***to*** *custom* 習慣に従う ‖ I'm not a slave ***to*** *custom.* 私は因習にとらわれはしない.

P^{2} *customs* ***among*** the natives of East Africa 東アフリカ土人間の習慣. ¶it is the *custom* ***in*** France to ... ...することはフランスの習慣である. ¶It is the *custom* ***of*** the world. それが世の習いだ. ‖ The Chinese *custom* ***of*** wearing the queue was forced upon the Chinese by conquering Manchus in the seventeenth century. 中国人が弁髪を垂れる習慣は十七世紀に(中国を)征服した満人が中国人に強制したのである. ‖ the Eskimo *custom* ***of*** wife-exchange エスキモー人の妻を交換する習慣. ¶it used to be the *custom* ***with*** the Japanese to ... ...するのは以前日本人の習慣であった. 【類】Is it the *custom* ***with*** (=of) foreigners to do so?

O I made it a *custom* (=rule) to read that paper. 私はその新聞を読むことにしていた. ¶as was his *custom* 例によって.

(**2**) 愛顧, 得意.

V ***capture*** the *custom* of the American middleclass consumers 米国の中流消費者の得意を取る. ¶Other persons who had been customers ***discontinued*** their *custom.* 得意客であった他の人々も買物をせぬようになった. ¶***draw*** *custom* to a house 店に客を呼ぶ(引付ける) ‖ They may not care to part with one so fit to ***draw*** *custom* to the house. 彼らはお得意を取る非常な適役者を解雇しようなどとはしないだろう. ¶The store ***gets*** the most *custom.* その店が一番商売がある. ‖ to ***get*** him more *custom* もっと客をふやそうとして. ¶***increase*** *custom* 得意をふやす. ¶***lose*** *custom* 客が減る. ¶They ran in debt to the grocer till he ***refused*** their *custom.* 彼らは乾物屋に借ができて遂に取引を断られした.

Q have a ***large*** (***small***) *custom* 得意先が多い(少い).

(**3**) *pl.* 税関.

V The penalties for ***cheating*** the *customs* are very severe. 税関を欺く罪は非常に重く罰せられる. ¶on a charge of ***defrauding*** the *customs* 税関をごま化したかどで.

customary, *a.* 慣例の; 習慣になっている.

P it is *customary* ***for*** (=***with***) ... to ... ...するのは...の慣例である.

customer, *n.* 顧客; 《米俗》 やつ, 男.

V ***attract*** *customers* to a shop 顧客を店に引付ける. ¶***charge*** *customers* 顧客から代金を取る. ¶***draw*** *customers* 顧客を引付ける. ¶a store that ***has*** many *customers* はやる店. ¶***keep*** the *customers* we have 今の顧客を失わないようにする. ¶Many a *customer* has been ***lost*** through such negligence. こうした怠慢のために顧客が随分減った. ¶It is our earnest endeavor to ***please*** our *customers.* 手前どもではお得意本位です. ¶try to ***retain*** one's *customers* お得意を逃がさないようにする. ¶***treat*** the *customers* fairly 客を公平に扱う. ¶***win*** *customers* 顧客をつかむ.

V^{2} *Customers* may ***go*** elsewhere. お客を他の店に取られるだろう.

Q a ***casual*** *customer* 通り一ぺんの客. ¶"***hard*** *customers*" いわゆる「やかまし屋」. ¶a ***likely*** *customer* 買いそうな客. ¶I am an ***old*** *customer* here. 私は昔からここで買いつけている. ¶an ***out-of-town*** *customer* 市外の顧客. ¶A ***pleased*** *customer* will recommend others to the store. 満足した客は他の客をその店に連れてくる. ¶a ***prospective*** *customer* 買いそうな客. ¶a ***queer*** *customer* 変った男. ¶a ***regular*** *customer* for the dealer その商人に取っての常得意. ¶It is an axiom in the business world that a ***satisfied*** *customer* is the best advertisement. 顧客に満足を与えるのが最善の広告になることは商業社会の公理である. ¶a ***splendid*** *customer* of the goods その品のよい顧客. ¶a ***tricky*** *customer* 気の許せない奴. ¶an ***ugly*** *customer* 手に負えないやつ.

Q^{2} a ***chance*** *customer* ふいの客. ¶a ***charge*** *customer* 掛売(つけ)の客. ¶a ***credit*** *customer* 貸売(帳面)の客. ¶a ***mail order*** *customer* 郵便註文の顧客. ¶a ***slow-pay*** *customer* 支払のおそい客. ¶a ***woman*** *customer* 婦人客.

P Japan's best foreign *customer* ***for*** ... ...を一番多く日本から買ってくれる国. ¶He is a *customer* ***of*** ours. あの方は手前どものお得意です.

cut, *n.* (**1**) 切傷; 切下げ, 削減; 木版画; 裁方(たち), 型.

V ***accept*** a 20 per cent *cut* in their scale of wages 彼らの給料の二割減に応じる. ¶He ***got*** a sharp *cut* on the back. 彼は背にひどい傷を負った. ‖ ***get*** a *cut* in price from a merchant 商人に値を引かせる. ¶***inflict*** a nasty *cut* on the face 顔にひどい切傷を負わす. ¶***make*** a ***clean*** *cut* すぱりと切る ‖ ***make*** a *cut* with the pick in ... ...につるはしで傷を付ける. ¶***receive*** *cuts* in the hand and the arm 手と腕に切傷を受ける. ¶***restore*** pay *cuts* 下げた給料を元に戻す.

Q foreign clothes of the most ***fashionable*** *cut* 一番流行する型の洋服. ¶***pictorial*** *cuts,* both in color and in black and white 色彩や黒の絵のカット(図版). ¶He had a ***slight*** *cut* on his forehead. 彼は額にかすり傷を受けた.

Q^{2} a Navy ***appropriation*** *cut* of ... 海軍予算の...削減. ¶a ***budget*** *cut* 予算削減. ¶a ***beefsteak*** *cut*[let] ビフカツ. ¶protest the ***economy*** *cuts* 経済の切詰めに文句をいう. ¶an ***electric power*** *cut* 電力減給. ¶a ***fifteen per cent*** *cut* in newsprint allotments to newspaper 諸新聞に対する新聞用紙割当十五パーセント削減. ¶a style of ***hair*** *cut* 散髪の型 ‖ Your ***hair*** *cut* is frightful. 君の頭の刈り方はひどいね ‖ get a ***hair*** *cut* and shave 散髪をしてひげをそる. ¶a ***line*** *cut* 挿入する書物のページに合うように原画を写真で縮写すること. ¶a ***personnel*** *cut* 人員整理, 人減らし. ¶***price*** *cuts* of from 10 to 20 per cent 一割から二割の物価引下げ. ¶a ***ration*** *cut* 配給量引下げ. ¶a ***school budget*** *cut* 学校予算の削減. ¶***star*** *cut* 星切り(金剛石のみがき方の一種). ¶a ***tax*** *cut* 減税. ¶a ***wage*** *cut* 賃金引下げ. ¶a ***50 per cent*** *cut* in personnel 五割の人員整理. 【類】a ***10 per cent*** *cut* in the rate of interest (利率).

P books adorned ***with*** *cuts* 木版画入りの本.

P^{2} This is a *cut* ***at*** me. これは私へのあてつけだ. ¶a *cut* ***in*** salary 減給. ¶a *cut* ***in*** the price 値引. ¶a *cut* ***on*** the leg 脚の切傷.

(**2**) 近道, 早道.

V ***Taking*** a short *cut,* you will save half a mile. 近道をすると半マイル助かる ‖ ***take*** a short *cut* to ... 近道で...へ行く.

Q an ***Irish*** *cut* 近道.

P get back to ... *by* a short *cut* 近道を通って…へ帰る.

P^{2} There is a short *cut* ***across*** the field. 畑を突切る近道がある. ¶the short *cut* ***through*** the castle grounds 城の中を通っての近道. ¶a short *cut* ***to*** knowledge 知識を得る早道. 【類】There is no short *cut* ***to*** the acquisition of ability in writing.

cut, *v.* 切る, 切り離す; 切詰める; 減価する; 胸にこたえる; 切れる.

M *cut* oneself ***adrift*** from home 家庭を離れて放浪する. ¶be compelled to *cut* ***away*** the mainmast やむなくメンマストを切り倒す. ¶*cut* ***back*** production 生産を縮小する ‖ *cut* ***back*** all the shoots 若枝をすべて元まで刈り込む. ¶He ***badly*** *cut* his hand. 彼は手をひどく切った. ¶Stale bread *cuts* ***better.*** 古いパンの方がよく切れる. ¶*cut* hair ***close*** 髪を短く刈る. ¶*cut* ***deep*** 深く切込む. ¶words that *cut* ***deeply*** 胸に痛手を負わせる言葉. ¶*cut* ***crosswise*** 斜めに切る. ¶The letter was *cut* ***open.*** 手紙が開封してあった. ¶*cut* ***out*** men's shirts ワイシャツを裁断する ‖ *cut* ***out*** round bits of paper 紙を丸く切りとる ‖ *cut* ***out*** all middlemen's profit 仲介者のもうけを全部削る, ブローカーを断わる ‖ *cut* ***out*** newspaper articles and pictures 新聞の記事や写真を切抜く ‖ He *cut* ***out*** the rest of the suitors of her daughter. その他の娘の求婚者は全部断わった. ‖ *cut* it ***out*** from consideration それを審議にかけないことにする ‖ He is *cut* ***out*** for the job. 彼はその仕事におあつらえ向きだ. ‖ He is *cut* ***out*** for a detective (soldier). 彼は探偵(など)にでき(るように生れつい)ている. 【類】He is not *cut* ***out*** to fill such a position. / You are not *cut* ***out*** for the grocery business. ‖ "*Cut* that ***out!***" barked Jim. 「よせ」とジムがどなった. ¶*cut* it ***short*** [話など]短くする ‖ I will *cut* a long story ***short.*** かいつまんでお話しよう. ‖ His life was *cut* ***short*** by cholera. 彼はコレラのために短命に終った. ‖ I *cut* ***short*** here. (話など)ここでやめる. ¶*cut* ***small*** 小さく切る. ¶The meat *cuts* ***tough.*** この肉は硬(ｶﾀ)くて容易に切れない. ¶a knife which *cuts* very ***well*** 非常によく切れるナイフ.

M^{2} *cut* ***down*** a letter 手紙を短くする ‖ *cut* ***down*** to two weeks 二週間に切詰める ‖ *cut* trees ***down*** for fuel 木を切り倒してまきにする ‖ *cut* the grass ***down*** 草を刈る ‖ *cut* ***down*** imports 輸入量を減らす. 【類】*cut* ***down*** unnecessary personnel / *cut* ***down*** the cost / *cut* ***down*** the expenses / *cut* ***down*** the price / *cut* ***down*** one's diet (食) ‖ *cut* ***down*** distances between ...間の距離を縮める ‖ a crop *cut* ***down*** by frost 霜害を受けた作物 ‖ However much I *cut* ***down*** I cannot make both ends meet. どう節約しても赤字になる(帳じりが合わない). ‖ *cut* the servants ***down*** to two meals a day 召使の食事を一日二度に切詰める ‖ *cut* ***down*** to size (誇張されていたものをその)本当の姿に縮小する ‖ *cut* it ***down*** to ... feet それを…フィートに切りつめる ‖ Can you *cut* it ***down*** to five fifty? 五ドル五十セントにまかりませんか. ‖ You *cut* me ***down*** too much. それではあんまり値切り過ぎます. ¶*cut* ***in*** (=break in) on the trade of ... …の商売に割り込む. ¶*cut* (=take) a man's head ***off*** 人の首を切り落す. 【類】He had his head *cut* ***off.*** / *cut* ***off*** water 断水する ‖ *cut* ***off*** food supplies / *cut* the water (gas) ***off*** at the main line / *cut* ***off*** the gas supply / *cut* ***off*** the supply of electricity (電気を止める) / *cut* ***off*** the supply of munitions (軍需品補給) from outside / *cut* ***off*** the communications (通信) between ... ‖ *cut* ***off*** one's telephone service その加入していた電話をやめる ‖ with all means of communication *cut* ***off*** あらゆる通信機関がしゃ断されて ‖ *cut* ***off*** the decayed part of it その腐食した分を切取る ‖ have its retreat *cut* ***off*** 退路を切断する ‖ *cut* ***off*** a corner 近道する ‖ He was *cut* ***off*** from the shore by the tide. 彼は上潮で浜から切り離された. ‖ He was *cut* ***off*** in early youth. 彼は若い時分に死んだ. ‖ be *cut* ***off*** from communication with ... …との交通を切断される. 【類】*cut* them ***off*** from food supplies / be *cut* ***off*** from all intercourse with ... (一切の交渉) / The fire spread with such rapidity that those on the top floor were *cut* ***off*** from escape. / *cut* oneself ***off*** from intercourse (=the world) / They *cut* themselves ***off*** entirely from the pleasures and enjoyments of the world. / *cut* oneself ***off*** from the world / *cut* ourselves ***off*** from the traditions of the past ‖ Escape by way of land was *cut* ***off*** to the soldiers defending the fortress. 要塞防衛軍の陸路退却路が断たれた. ‖ *cut* one ***off*** with scanty money わずかの金をやっておっ払う. ¶He *cut* ***under*** all his competitors in the shoe trade. 彼はくつの安売をやって同業者を圧倒した. ¶*cut* ***up*** her belly (手術などで)お腹を切り開く ‖ *cut* ***up*** into equal pieces 同じ大きさに切る ‖ *cut* ***up*** into sheets of eight pages 八ページの紙に切る ‖ His book has been badly *cut* ***up.*** 彼の本はひどい批評をされた.

P He *cut* ***across*** the common (field). 彼は共有地(畑)を横切って行った. ‖ *cut* a canal ***across*** ... …を横断する運河を開さくする. ¶His face was *cut* ***against*** the stones. 彼は石にぶつかって顔を切った. ¶*cut* ***at*** ... …を切ろうとする. ¶*cut* the distance ***by*** 200 miles 距離を二百マイルだけ切詰める. ¶*cut* ***in*** two [half] 二つ(半分)に切る. 【類】*cut* an apple ***in*** two [halves] / The output was *cut* ***in*** two. / *cut* a thing ***into*** small pieces / *cut* ***into*** convenient lengths (都合のよい長さに). ¶*cut* timber ***into*** lumber 立木を切って木材にする ‖ I *cut* my name ***into*** the bark with my jack-knife. 私の名を海軍ナイフで木の皮に刻みつけた. ‖ *cut* ***into*** a converstation 横合いから口を出す ‖ *cut* ***into*** one's capital 資本金に食い込む ‖ *cut* ***into*** their earnings 収入にひびく ‖ Intemperate drinking *cuts* ***into*** the support of the family. 過度の飲酒は家庭の経済に食い込む. ‖ In Detroit the automobile is *cutting* widely ***into*** railroad passenger traffic. デトロイトでは自動車がどんどん鉄道の旅客運輸に食い込んでいる. ¶The north wind *cuts* ***like*** a knife. 北風が身を切るように寒い. ¶be *cut* ***of*** wood and stone 木や石に刻む ‖ such a person cannot *cut* much ***of*** a social figure. こうした人は世の中ではばがきかない. ¶The work was *cut* ***on*** blocks and published. その著作は木版にして出版された. 【類】The book was *cut* ***on*** blocks for printing. ‖ The inscription is deeply *cut* ***on*** the stone. 銘は碑に深く刻まれている. ‖ He was severely *cut* ***on*** the thigh by falling glass. 彼はガラスが落ちてきてももをひどく切った. ‖ The shirts are *cut* ***on*** our own patterns and made in our own workrooms. このシャツは手前どもの型で裁って手前どもの工場で仕立てたものです. ¶*cut* a picture ***out of*** a newspaper 新聞から絵を切り抜く. ¶*cut* him ***over*** the eye 彼の目の上を切る. ¶He *cut* ***through*** the woods to get home. 彼は森を抜けて帰宅した. 【類】*cut* ***through*** a cemetery in order to shorten the distance ‖ *cut* one's way ***through*** the enemy's ranks 敵の中を切抜ける ‖ The vessel *cut* her way ***through*** the rough waves. 船は荒波を乗切って進んだ. ¶*cut* ***to*** pieces 細々に切る ‖ His words *cut* me ***to*** the heart (=quick). 彼の言葉が胸にこたえた. ‖ "Taxi-cab" is popularly *cut* ***to*** "taxi." 「タキシー・キャブ」は一般に略して「タクシー」と言う. ¶*cut* blocks ***with*** a razor 〖比ゆ〗もったいないことをする; くだらぬことに頭や金銭を使う.

cuticle, *n.* 表皮, 外皮.

V ***indurate*** the *cuticle* 外皮を堅くする.

cutter, *n.* 切る人(もの), 裁断師(器); カッター(船).

Q a ***tailor's*** *cutter* 裁断師.

Q^{2} a ***bar*** *cutter* 鉄筋切断機. ¶a ***copy*** *cutter* 〖新聞〗急ぐ原稿を切って植字工の持分にする係の人. ¶a ***paper*** *cutter* [製紙製本用]切断器. ¶a ***revenue*** *cutter* [税関の]密貿易監視船.

cutting, *n.* 切抜; さし木.

V ***paste*** *cuttings* on paper 切抜を紙にはる ‖ ***paste*** *cuttings* in one's scrapbook 切抜をスクラップ・ブックにはり込む.

Q^{2} ***cardboard*** *cutting* ボール紙切断. ¶***mulberry*** *cuttings* くわ(の葉)を切断したもの. ¶***newspaper*** *cuttings* 新聞の切抜.

P Can this plant be grown ***from*** *cuttings?* この木はさし木でつきますか.

P^{2} a *cutting* ***from*** a newspaper (magazine) 新聞(など)の切抜.

cutting-down, *n.* 切り倒し.

Q ***reckless*** *cutting-down* of forests and woodland 森林の濫伐.

cyanide, *n.* 〖化学〗シヤン化物.

Q^{2} ***potassium*** *cyanide* 青酸カリ.

cycle, *n.* 循環; 周期; 自転車.

V ***begin*** one's *cycle* of luck うけに入る. ¶***complete*** the *cycle* of changes [こん虫など]変態を完了する. ¶Old men, who have ***finished*** a *cycle* on this earth, dress themselves up in red and hop about, becoming infants again. 本卦(ﾎﾝｹ)還りの老人たちは再び幼年に返って赤い着物を着て飛びまわる. ¶The seasons of the year—spring, summer, autumn, and winter—***make*** a *cycle.* 四季すなわち春・夏・秋・冬は循環する.

Q the ***sexagenary*** *cycle* 干支(えと).

Q^{2} ***boom*** and ***depression*** *cycles* 景気・不景気の循環. ¶a

five-minute *cycle* of open-air exercises 一回五分間で終る戸外の運動. ¶ending of the ***inflation*** *cycle* インフレ波の終結. ¶the ***life*** *cycle* 生れて死ぬまでの一期 ‖ All sorts of coal began their ***life*** *cycle* as vegetation. あらゆる種類の石炭の振り出しは植物であった. ¶a ***romance*** *cycle* of seven volumes 七部作の(長編)小説. ¶the ***sunspot*** *cycle* 太陽黒点の週期. ¶on a ***three-year*** *cycle* 三年を一週期とした.

P Booms run ***in*** *cycles*. 景気は循環する. ‖ And so on ***in*** a vicious *cycle*. それでいたちごっこということになる. ¶ride ***on*** a *cycle* 自転車に乗る ‖ from Cape Town to Japan ***on*** a *cycle* [見出し]自転車でケープタウンから日本へ ‖ Business is ***on*** the *cycle* of recovery. 景気は好転しつつある.

P^2 the *cycle* ***of*** the seasons 季節の推移.

cycle, *v.* 自転車に乗る.

M^2 *cycle* ***over*** to ... 自転車に乗って…へ行く.

cyclist, *n.* 《英》自転車乗用家.

Q an ***ardent*** (=***keen***) *cyclist* 熱心な自転車愛用者.

cyclopaedia, *n.* 百科全書. 「字引だ).

Q He is a ***walking*** *cyclopedia*. 彼は生きた百科全書だ(生き

Q^2 a ***picture*** *cyclopedia* of flowers 花卉(き)図鑑.

cylinder, *n.* 〘機械〙シリンダー.

Q^2 ***high-(low-)pressure*** *cylinder* 高(低)圧シリンダー. ¶a ***steam*** *cylinder* 蒸気シリンダー.

cymbal, *n.* シンバル(一種の打楽器).

V ***tinkle*** *cymbals* シンバルを打ち鳴らす.

Q a ***tinkling*** *cymbal* ちりんちりん鳴るシンバル.

cynical, *a.* 皮肉な, 冷笑的な.

M I hope it is not ***very*** *cynical* to say that ... …と言ってもそう皮肉じゃあるまい.

cynicism, *n.* 皮肉.

Q ***humorous*** *cynicism* [川柳などの]ユーモラスな皮肉.

cynosure, *n.* [C-]〘天文〙小ぐま座; 人の耳目を引くもの.

P The polestar is ***in*** the *Cynosure*. 北極星は小ぐま座にある.

P^2 The town will become the *cynosure* ***of*** all eyes during the next few days. この数日間その町は万人の耳目を引きつけるであろう. ‖ the "*cynosure* ***of*** neighbouring eyes"「近所合壁の注目の的」.

cypher, *n.* ゼロ.

Q He is a ***mere*** *cypher*. 彼はコンマ以下だ. ‖ a ***mere*** *cypher* in life 生きているという名ばかりの人.

czar, tsar, *n.* 独裁者; [ある方面の]権力家.

Q Rockefeller, ***financial*** and ***commercial*** *czar* of America アメリカの金融および商業王のロックフェラー.

Q^2 Henry Kaiser, wartime ***ship-building*** *czar* of America 戦時中アメリカの造船王だったヘンリー・カイザー.

D

dab, *v.* 軽くたたく; べたべたつける.

P She *dabbed* ***at*** her face with a powder puff. 彼女は顔をパッフでぱたぱたとはたいた. ¶*dab* one ***in*** the face 人の顔をべたりとたたく. ¶*dab* paint ***on*** the wall 壁にペンキを塗る. ¶*dab* butter ***over*** (=***on***) the bread パンにバタをべたべたつける. ¶*dab* ***with*** an inkpad スタンプインキを塗る ‖ *dab* one's eyes ***with*** a handkerchief ハンケチを目に当てる. 【類】She *dabbed* her forehead ***with*** a handkerchief. / *dab* a sore ***with*** a fine lint (柔かいリント布で).

dabble, *v.* 浸す; ちょっと手を出す.

P *dabble* (=meddle) ***in*** politics (antiques, speculation, stocks) 政治(など)に手を出す ‖ those who have dabbled ***in*** the fascination of the occult 神秘のだいご味をちょっと味わった人たち ‖ He is *dabbled* ***in*** blood. 彼は血だらけだ. ¶*dabble* (=tamper) ***with*** the text 原文に手を入れる.

dabbler, *n.* いたずらに手出しする人.

P^2 a *dabbler* ***in*** medicine (philosophy, politics, political economy) 医学(など)をかじる人.

daddy, *n.* 《米口》お父さん, パパ.

Q^2 a ***sugar*** *daddy* 《米俗》[女に]甘いパパさん.

dagger, *n.* 短刀.

V ***brandish*** a *dagger* 短刀を振回す. ¶***look*** *daggers* at ... …をねめつける. ¶***plunge*** a *dagger* in the heart 心臓に短刀を突刺す ‖ ***plunge*** a *dagger* into one's breast 胸に短刀を突刺す. ¶***wear*** a *dagger* in one's bosom あいくちを一本のんでいる.

P They are ***at*** *daggers* drawn. 彼らは丸でけんか腰だ. ¶***with*** a *dagger* in hand 短刀を手にして ‖ He stabbed himself ***with*** a *dagger*. 彼は短刀で自分を刺した.

P^2 The news was a *dagger* ***to*** his heart. その知らせはどきんときた.

daily, *n.* 日刊新聞.

Q He holds a position of first rank on a ***leading American*** *daily*. 彼はアメリカの一流新聞で上席を占めている. ¶a ***local*** *daily* 地方の一新聞. ¶a ***minor*** *daily* in a local town 地方の小新聞. ¶a ***pictorial*** *daily* 写真新聞.

Q^2 a large ***city*** *daily* 大都市新聞.

daintiness, *n.* 優美.

V Her feminine instincts led her to ***impart*** a *daintiness* to her performance. 女性的本能が働いて彼女の芸にやさしさがしみ出していた.

dainty, *n.* 美味.

Q an ***expensive*** *dainty* 高価な珍味. ¶a ***favorite*** *dainty* 好物.

dainty, *a.* 口やかましい.

P She is *dainty* ***about*** her food (=eating). 彼女は口がおごっている.

dairy, *n.* 酪農場.

P They sell milk and butter ***at*** the *dairy*. 酪農場の売場で牛乳とバタを売っている.

dais, *n.* さじき.

V ***erect*** a large *dais* さじきをしつらえる.

dalliance, *n.* 痴話狂い.

Q indulge in ***amorous*** *dalliance* 情痴にふける.

dally, *v.* ふざける; ぐずぐずする.

M *dally* ***away*** one's opportunities むなしく機会を逸する ‖ *dally* ***away*** one's time 時をむだにする.

P *dally* ***in*** bed 床の内で(起きようかどうしようかと)ぐずぐずしている. ¶*dally* ***over*** one's work 仕事をなまける, 油を売る. ¶*dally* ***with*** a lover 愛人とふざける ‖ *dally* ***with*** a woman's affections 女の愛情をもてあそぶ.

dam, *n.* ダム. 「*dam* せきを造る.

V The flood ***burst*** the *dam*. 出水でせきが切れた. ¶***dig***

Q^2 ***rubber*** *dam* [だ液を歯に触れないように歯科医の用いる]弾性ゴム製の薄板. ¶a ***storage*** *dam* 貯水池.

P The river was stopped ***by*** a *dam*. 川がせきで止められた. ¶a *dam* ***across*** a river 川を横切るせき. ¶a *dam* ***in*** a river 川のせき.

dam, *v.* [水を]せき止める.

M *dam* ***out*** せき止める(水などを).

M^2 A stream was *dammed* ***up***. 川がせき止められた.

damage, *n.* 損害, 損害額; *pl.* 損害賠償.

V ***assess*** *damages* at £1,000 損害額を一千ポンドと評価する. ¶***cause*** *damage* to property 財産に損害を与える ‖ The gale ***caused*** widespread *damage*. 強風の被害は広い範囲にわたった. 【類】***cause*** *damage* estimated at ... ¶***pay*** ... dollars to ***cover*** *damages* on ... …の損害賠償に…ドル支払う ‖ The *damage* is ***covered*** by insurance. その損害は保険で償われる. ¶It will ***do*** more *damage* to British prestige in India. それはインドにおける英国の威信を一層きずつけるだろう. ‖ It ***did*** *damage* to the extent of some thirty million dollars. そのために約三千万ドルの損害を生じた. 【類】do much damage to one's credit (信用) / The storm ***did*** much *damage* to growing rice. ¶The total *damage* is ***estimated*** at between £15,000 and £20,000. 総損害額は一万五千ポンド乃至二万ポンドの間と概算される. ¶***inflict*** serious *damage* on ... …に大損害をこうむらす ‖ Extensive *damage* has been ***inflicted*** on the cotton crop. [暴風雨などが]棉花の作に大損害をこうむらした. ¶***lay*** *damages* 損害額を申し立てる. ¶***make good*** the *damage* 損害を償う. ¶***obtain*** *damages* in a court against ... for a libellous description of ... …の中傷的記事に関し法廷に訴えて…から損害賠償を得る. ¶***pay*** the *damage* 損害を償う.

¶the *damage* is ***put down*** at ... 損害額は...をもって算せられる. ¶***receive*** *damage* 損害を受ける. ¶***recover*** *damages* from ... ...に因る損害を償う ‖ ***recover*** *damages* for injury to business by ... ...のために商売がこうむった損害の賠償を取る. ¶***repair*** the *damage* caused by ... ...の被害を修理する. ¶***suffer*** serious *damage* 大損害を受ける. ¶The steamer ***sustained*** *damage* to her keel. 汽船は竜骨に損害を受けた. 【類】***sustain*** *damage* by collision / ***sustain*** little (much) *damage*. ¶***work*** great *damage* 大損害を与える.

V² No *damage* ***occurred***. 何ら被害がなかった.

Q sustain ***considerable*** *damage* to ... ...に大損害をこうむる. ¶***dire*** *damage* 大損害. ¶cause ***extensive*** *damage* to ... ...に大損害をこうむらせる. ¶She has ***great*** *damage* to bottom. 船底に大破損を受けている. ¶cause ***great*** *damage* to her keel その船の竜骨に大損害を生じる. 【類】The earthquake has caused ***great*** *damage* and loss of life. ¶***heavy*** *damage* 大損害. ¶The *damage* done is ***immaterial***. その損害は問題にならない. ¶***irretrievable*** (=***irreparable***) *damage* 回復すべからざる損害. ¶suffer but ***little*** *damage* ほとんど損害を受けない. ¶***material*** and ***immaterial*** *damages* 有形無形の損害. ¶A severe hurricane has done ***much*** *damage* to property. 猛烈な台風が財産に大損害を与えた. ¶do ***serious*** *damage* to ... ...に重大な損害を与える ‖ ***Serious*** *damage* was caused by the fire. 火事で大損害をこうむった. ¶receive ***slight*** *damage* 軽微な損害をこうむる. ¶***trifling*** *damage* わずかの損害. ¶***widespread*** *damage* 広範囲の損害.

Q² ***bombing*** *damage* 爆撃の被害. ¶***flood*** (***earthquake***) *damage* 水(震)害. ¶cause ***property*** *damage* estimated at ... ...と見積られる財産上の損害を生じる. 【類】***Property*** *damage* has mounted to millions of dollars. ¶reconstruction and repair of ***war*** *damage* 戦災の再建と修理. ¶restore ***wartime*** *damage* to ... ...に対する戦災を復興する. ¶cause ***25,000 dollars*** *damage* 二万五千ドルの損害を生じる.

P £1,000 worth ***of*** *damage* was done. 一千ポンドの損害を受けた. ¶claim ***over*** *damages* against ... ...に対する賠償を要求する. ¶She arrived ***with*** *damage* to bulwarks. 上甲板船側に損害を受けて到着した. ¶get clear ***without*** *damage* つつがなく切抜ける.

P² protect a town from *damage* ***by*** air raids 市を空襲から守る. ¶*damage* ***from*** a flood (storm, frost, drought, fire) 出水(など)による損害. ¶the destruction and *damage* ***to*** means of communication 交通機関の破壊.

damage, *v.* 損害を与える.

M the crop was ***badly*** *damaged* by ... 作物は...にひどく害された. ¶is ***considerably*** *damaged* in her rigging 索具に非常な損害をこうむる. ¶was not so ***much*** *damaged* as anticipated 予期したほどの被害がなかった. ¶be ***partially*** (***totally***) *damaged* 部分的(全面的)損害をこうむる. ¶***partly*** *damaged* by ... ...で一部被害を受けて.

P The goods got *damaged* ***by*** fire. 商品が火事で損害を受けた.

damaging, *a.* 有害な.

M ***highly*** *damaging* to the interests of ... ...にきわめて不利な.

P *damaging* ***to*** the prestige of Germany ドイツの威信を傷つけて.

damask, *v.* 花模様を織りなす.

P a bank *damasked* ***with*** flowers 花で色取られた堤.

dame, *n.* 貴婦人; 《米口語》女.

Q ***high-born*** *dames* 高貴の婦人. ¶a ***nice little*** *dame* かわいい女. ¶a ***stately*** *dame* 威厳のある貴婦人. ¶a ***titled*** *dame* 有爵婦人.

Q² an opulent ***society*** *dame* 富裕な社交界の貴婦人.

damn, *n.* 《俗》[否定的に]ちっとも.

V I don't ***care*** a *damn*. ちっともかまわん.

M It is not ***worth*** a *damn*. そんなもの三文の値打もない.

damned, *a., ad.* 《俗》べら棒に, すごく.

M I'll see you *damned* ***first***. そんな事をだれがするものか(絶対的拒絶のきまり文句). ¶It's ***so*** *damned* (=very) hot. べら棒に暑い.

P He was *damned* ***for*** a sin. 彼は罪のために地獄に落ちた.

O I'll be *damned* if it comes true. そんなものが本当にあってたまるもんか(絶対ない).

damp, *n.* 湿気.

V Don't ***cast*** a *damp* upon his spirits. 彼をがっかりさせるな. ‖ The sad news ***cast*** *damp* upon the conversation. その悲報で話がしめってしまった. ¶bricks grown green ***from*** the *damp* 湿気で緑色になったれんが.

damp, *v.* 湿らせる.

M² *damp* ***down*** a fire (furnace) 火(炉)をいける ‖ *damp* ***down*** an agitation 動乱を静める. ¶*damp* ***off*** 湿けて腐る(植物にいう).

P His ardor was *damped* ***by*** his critics. 彼の熱意は批評家のためにくじかれた. 【類】His zeal was *damped* ***by*** the apathy of the public.

damper, *n.* 元気をくじくもの.

V ***cast*** a *damper* on the enthusiasm of ... ...の熱意をくじく. ¶***put*** a *damper* on their eagerness 彼らの熱意をくじく. ¶***throw*** a *damper* (=wet blanket) over ... ...にけちをつける.

damsel, *n.* 少女; 娘っ子.

Q a ***high-born*** *damsel*, whose haughty conduct belies her tender heart その高慢な挙動を見ると, とても優しい心の持主とは思われない高貴の少女. ¶a "***strong-minded***" *damsel* 気丈な娘. ¶an ***up-to-the-minute*** *damsel* 尖端的な娘.

dance, *n.* 舞踏(ダンス); 舞踏会(ダンスパーティ).

V The *dance* was cleverly ***executed***. 舞踏は巧みに演ぜられた. ‖ He ***executed*** a little *dance* of joy. 彼は小おどりして喜んだ. ¶May I ***have*** your next *dance?* ダンスのお相手をしていただけましょうか. ‖ I am afraid I ***have*** not a *dance* to give you. あなたとはダンスができないかも知れません. ¶At the hotel *dances* are ***held*** nightly. そのホテルには毎晩ダンスパーティがある. ¶***lead*** the *dance* 踊の音頭取をやる ‖ ***lead*** a person a *dance* 散々苦労をかける, つまらぬ心配をさせる. ¶***organize*** *dances* or concerts 舞踏会または音楽会を組織する. ¶***perform*** a skirt *dance* スカート・ダンスをやる ‖ a *dance* ***performed*** to music 音楽入の舞踏.

Q an ***acrobatic*** *dance* 曲芸ダンス. ¶an ***artistic*** *dance* 芸術的舞踊. ¶a Japanese ***classic*** *dance* 日本古典舞踊. ¶an ***indecent*** *dance* 卑わいなダンス. ¶a ***lascivious*** *dance* such as cancan カンカン踊りなどのみだらなダンス. ¶a ***vulgar*** *dance* such as tango, burny hug, turkey-trot タンゴ・バーニーハッグ・ターキートロットなどの野卑なダンス.

Q² an ***ensemble*** *dance* 集団ダンス. ¶a Japanese ***folk*** *dance* 日本の盆踊り ‖ join in a ***folk*** *dance* 郷土踊りに加わる. ¶a ***foot*** *dance* 足を主にする踊り. ¶a ***hobby-horse*** *dance* 木馬踊(新年元日に踊る). ¶a ***kabuki*** *dance* 歌舞伎舞踊. ¶a ***ritual*** *dance* 儀式の舞踊. ¶a ***solo*** *dance* 単独の舞踊. ¶a ***square*** *dance* スクェーアダンス. ¶a ***sword*** *dance* 剣舞. ¶a ***toe*** *dance* トーダンス.

P She and I first met ***at*** a *dance*. 彼女と私は初めてダンスパーティで会った. ¶lead one's partner ***in*** a *dance* ダンスの相手をリードする. ¶go ***to*** a *dance* ダンスパーティに行く.

dance, *v.* 踊る.

M *dance* the hours ***away*** to the music provided by jolly orchestras 素敵なオーケストラにつれて何時間も踊りまくる ‖ *dance* ***away*** one's worries 苦労をダンスでまぎらす ‖ *dance* ***away*** with a girl ダンスをしながら女の子を連れ去る. ¶*dance* ***barefoot*** 素足で踊る. ¶They *danced* ***together*** in groups. グループになって踊った.

P We *danced* ***at*** the Embassy to the music of a piano. われわれは大使館でピアノの伴奏で踊った. ¶*dance* ***for*** (=with) joy (=delight) 欣喜雀躍する. ¶*dance* ***on*** a tight rope 綱渡りをする. ¶He *danced* himself ***out of*** breath. 彼は息の切れるほどダンスをやった. ¶*dance* ***to*** music 音楽に合わせて踊る ‖ *dance* ***to*** the tune of ... ...のリズムに合わせて踊る. 【類】*dance* ***to*** (=***after***) one's pipe (whistle). ¶The sun is *dancing* ***upon*** the waves, making them sparkle with thousands of diamonds, and turning the white-caps to silver. 太陽は海面を照して金波銀波が躍っている. ¶*dance* ***with*** ... ...と踊る ‖ Japanese *dance* ***with*** their arms. 日本人は手で踊る.

dancer, *n.* 舞踊家, ダンサー.

Q a ***graceful*** *dancer* 優雅な舞踊家. ¶a ***top-notch*** *dancer* ナンバー・ワンのダンサー.

Q² a ***ballroom*** *dancer* 社交ダンスを踊る女(一般職業ダンサー). ¶a ***ballet*** *dancer* バレエのダンサー. ¶a ***circus*** *dancer* 曲馬団の踊り子. ¶a grass-skirted Hawaiian ***hula*** *dancer* 草の腰みのを付けたハワイのフラダンスの踊り子. ¶a ***rope*** *dancer* 綱渡をする芸人. ¶a ***skirt*** *dancer* スカートダンス(長いスカートを優美にひろげて踊る)の踊り子(バレエの一種). ¶a ***tap*** *dancer* タップダンサー. ¶a ***taxi*** *dancer* チケット・

ダンサー(職業ダンサー). ¶a *wire dancer* 針金渡りの芸人.

dancing, *n*. 舞踊(ダンス).

Q *indecorous dancing* 不体裁なダンス.

Q² *ballet dancing* バレエの舞踊. ¶*ballroom dancing* 社交ダンス. ¶*exhibition dancing* 公演舞踊. ¶*folk dancing* 郷土舞踊(盆踊りなど). ¶*latter-day dancing* 今様舞踊. ¶a school of Japanese *posture dancing* 日本舞踊研究所. ¶*stage dancing* 舞台舞踊. ¶*street dancing* 街頭踊り. ¶*tap dancing* タップダンス. ¶*toe dancing* トーダンス.

dander, *n*. 《米》かんしゃく, 怒り.

V *get* one's *dander up* 《米》腹を立てる, かんしゃくを起す.

dandy, *n*. めかしや; 特上品.

Q a "*high-collar*" *dandy* ハイカラ男.

P² This is the *dandy of* the kind. これが特上品です.

danger, *n*. 危険.

V much *danger* is ***apprehended*** from ... ...の危険が大いにあると考えられている. 【類】He expressed the view that no *danger* was to be ***apprehended***. ¶***avert*** a *danger* 危険を避ける. ¶***avoid*** *dangers* of ... ...の危険を避ける. 【類】the *danger* can be ***avoided*** by ... ¶***brave*** *dangers* with impunity 平気で危険を冒す(不死身だ). 【類】***brave*** the *dangers* of ... ¶It ***constitutes*** a real *danger*. それが本当に危険だ. ¶They are among the foremost in ***courting*** *danger* in battle. 彼らは戦闘で進んで危険を冒す勇士たちだ. ¶He ***dares*** all *dangers*. 彼はいかなる危険をも冒す. ¶***despise*** *danger* 危険を軽視する. ¶***emphasize*** the *danger* of the situation 形勢の不穏を強調する. ¶***endure*** *dangers* and perils 危難に堪える. ¶The first delivery is the one which ***entails*** the greatest *dangers* to the mothers. 初産は産婦に取っては一番危険なものだ. ‖ It is apt to ***entail*** serious *dangers*. それは由々しい危険を生じやすい. ¶***escape*** a *danger* 危険を免れる. ¶***face*** a mortal *danger* 恐ろしい危険に当る. 【類】***face*** the *dangers* of death. ¶***fight*** the *danger* of industrial Germany 産業ドイツの危難と闘う. ¶a change in the patient's breathing ***foreboding*** some *danger* ある危険を前兆する患者の呼吸変化. ¶***incur*** (=bring on oneself) a *danger* 危険を招く. ¶***lessen*** the *danger* of ... ...の危険を軽減する. ¶He ***made*** *danger* of the matter. 彼はそのことを危険視した. ¶***minimize*** the *danger* of ... ...の危険をできるだけ少なくする. ¶***obviate*** a *danger* 危険を一掃する. ¶***overestimate*** the *danger* その危険を買いかぶる. ¶***portend*** *danger* 危険を前兆する. ¶***prevent*** a great *danger* 一大危険を防止する. ¶***realize*** the *danger* of the situation 形勢の不穏を看取する. ¶***remove*** the *danger* of infection 伝染の危険を除く. ¶***risk*** *danger* 危険を冒す. ¶***run*** the *danger* of ... ...の危険に身をさらす. ¶***scent*** *danger* 危険に気づく. ¶***sense*** *danger* 危険に感ずく. ¶***surmount*** a *danger* 危険を切抜ける. ¶***suspect*** *danger* 危険を感づく. ¶It ***threatens*** no *danger* to the well-being of nations. それはなんら国民の安寧を脅かさない. ¶***ward off*** a *danger* 危険を防ぐ.

V² *danger* ***lurks*** in the path of ... 危険が...の途上に潜んでいる. ¶Some *danger* ***menaces***. 危険が脅かす.

Q there is a ***certain*** *danger* of conflicting with the spirit of ... ...の精神に反する恐れがある. ¶he is in ***constant*** *danger* of ... 彼には...の恐れが絶えない. 【類】be kept in (=exposed to) ***constant*** *danger*. ¶a ***deadly*** *danger* 恐ろしい危険. ¶His life is in ***dire*** *danger* from typhoid fever. 彼は腸チブスで生命危篤だ. ¶He is in ***grave*** *danger* of losing his life. 彼は生命にかゝわる由々しい危険に陥っている. ¶be fraught with the ***gravest*** *danger* to the peace of the Pacific 太平洋の平和に最大の危険をはらんでいる. ¶Skidding is one of the ***greatest*** *dangers* in motoring. 自動車操縦には滑りがもっとも危険だ. ¶There is no ***immediate*** *danger* of the patient's death. 病人は急に死ぬようなことはない. ¶in case of ***imminent*** *danger* 危急の場合に. ¶He is little alive to the ***impending*** *danger*. 彼はさし迫っている危険をほとんど知らずにいる. ¶The ship was in ***momentary*** *danger* of shipwreck. 船は今にも難破しそうであった. ¶I feel that this state of affairs constitutes a ***national*** *danger*. こういう有様では国家の前途が危ぶまれる. ‖ repel a ***national*** *danger* 国家の危険を避ける. ¶This great multitude of semi-insane cases constitutes, on account of their criminal possibilities, a ***permanent social*** *danger*. これら多数の半狂人は犯罪の恐れがあるので永久に社会の危険分子となるのである. ¶obviate the ***possible*** *danger* to ... ...に対して起り得べき危険を一掃する. ¶a source of ***potential*** *danger* 潜在的危険の源. ¶a ***public*** *danger* 公衆の危険. ¶a ***serious*** *danger* 大なる危険. ¶a ***threatening*** *danger* 今にも起りそうな危険. ¶It is attended by ***unsuspected*** *dangers*. それには思いも寄らぬ危険がある. ¶The ***worst*** *dangers* are over. 危険の峠を越した.

Q² a ***fire*** *danger* 火事の危険. ¶freedom from ***flood*** *dangers* 水害の危険絶無. ¶political and economic problems that constitute a ***world*** *danger* 世界的脅威となる政治上経済上の諸問題.

P provide ***against*** *danger* 危険に備える. ¶He was surrounded ***by*** *danger*. 彼は危険に取りまかれた. ¶I am now free ***from*** *danger*. 僕はもう安全だ. 【類】They rescued him ***from*** *danger*. ¶His life is ***in*** *danger*. 彼の生命は危い. 【類】The patient is ***in*** *danger* of death. / be ***in*** *danger* of being forgotten / These goods are ***in*** *danger* of robbery. / His ship was ***in*** *danger* of sinking. / be ***in*** *danger* of becoming flooded. ¶get ***into*** *danger* 危険に陥る. ¶He is fearless ***of*** *danger*. 彼は危険を物ともしない. ‖ He was warned ***of*** the *danger*. 彼は危険を警告された. ‖ in case (=time) ***of*** *danger* 危険の場合には ‖ He was brave in the face ***of*** *danger*. 彼は危険を恐れなかった. ¶He is now ***out of*** *danger*. 彼はもう大丈夫だ. ¶The patient is ***past*** *danger*. 病人はもう大丈夫だ. ¶He passed ***through*** many *dangers*. 彼は多くの危険を経験してきた. ¶be exposed ***to*** many *dangers* 多くの危険にさらされている. ¶***without*** *danger* of infection 伝染の恐れなく.

P² the *danger* ***from*** disease (fire, floods) 疾病(など)の危険 ‖ You are in no *danger* ***from*** that slight cold. そんな軽いかぜは少しも心配なさることはない. ‖ The way through the wilderness was full of *dangers* ***from*** wild beasts. 荒野の道は野獣の危険が多分にあった. ¶a *danger* ***to*** their happiness 彼ら幸福の妨害物 ‖ a *danger* ***to*** life (a person, safety, wealth) 生命(など)に取っての危険 ‖ a *danger* ***to*** navigation [暗礁など]航海の危険物 ‖ a permanent *danger* ***to*** the peace of the Pacific 太平洋の平和に対する永久の障害 ‖ declaim overpopulation as a *danger* ***to*** society 人口過剰を社会の危険として痛撃する.

dangerous, *a*. 危険な.

P *dangerous* ***for*** children 子供らに危険な. ¶It is *dangerous* ***to*** society. それは社会に取って危険だ. 【類】a man who is *dangerous* ***to*** his community.

dangle, *v*. つきまとう, ぶら下が(げ)る.

P *dangle* ***about*** (=***after*** *or* ***round***) a woman 女のしりを追う. ¶The temptation was *dangled* ***before*** him. その誘惑が彼の目の前にぶら下っていた. ¶*dangle* ***from*** a hook (nail) かぎ(など)につり下がっている ‖ *dangle* ***from*** one's pocket ポケットからぶら下がっている ‖ a wrecked kite *dangling* ***from*** a telephone wire 電線にぶら下っている破れだこ. 【類】a camera case *dangling* ***from*** one's shoulder. ¶Ripe apples *dangle* ***on*** the tree. 熟したりんごが樹にぶら下がっている.

dare, *v*. 敢えてする; いどむ.

M admirable I ***hardly*** *dare* to call it, but ... りっぱだとも言い切れないが... ¶***How*** *dare* you say such a thing! よくもそんなことが言えるな. ¶He will ***never*** *dare* [to] come. 彼は決して来ないだろう. 【類】I have ***never*** *dared* [to] do it again / He *dared* ***not*** speak. 「断行する).

P He *dared* me ***to*** my face. 彼は僕に面と向っていどんだ.

O He does not *dare* to do it=He *dares* not do it. あえてやる勇気がない.

daring, *n*. 勇気.

V ***temper*** *daring* with discretion 勇気に思慮を加える(熟慮をふるって.

Q ***desperate*** *daring* やけ勇気. ¶with ***reckless*** *daring* 蛮勇

dark, *n*. 暗黒; 暗夜.

Q ***early*** *dark* 薄暮.

P He arrived ***after*** *dark*. 彼は日が暮れてから着いた. ¶***at*** *dark* 夕暮に. ¶***before*** *dark* 日暮前に. ¶burrow (=stray) ***in*** the *dark* やみに迷う ‖ All cats are grey ***in*** the *dark*. ねこは皆暗黒の中では灰色に見える. 【類】The blind are destined to live forever ***in*** the *dark*. / He sprained his foot (片足をくじいた), while walking ***in*** the *dark*. ‖ I am utterly (=quite *or* absolutely) ***in*** the *dark* as to ... 私は...の事は丸で不案内だ. ‖ I was left rather ***in*** the *dark* as to ... ...についてはまるで見当がつかなかった. ‖ keep it ***in*** the *dark* それを秘しておく ‖ leave it ***in*** the *dark* それを言わずにおく ‖ a leap ***in*** the *dark* 暴挙.

dark, *a.* 黒い；暗い.

M It is ***pitch dark*** (=as dark as pitch). 真暗だ. ¶It wasn't ***quite dark*** as yet. まだほんとに暗くはならなかった.

P The building is *dark **with*** soot and smoke. 建物はばい煙で黒ずんでいる. 【類】The night was *dark **with*** clouds.

darken, *v.* 暗くする；暗くなる

P I *darkened* the room ***by*** closing the shutters. 戸を閉めて部屋を暗くした. ¶The day *darkened **into*** night. 日が暮れた. ‖ Expectancy *darkened **into*** anxiety. 期待の影が薄くなって不安に変って行った. ¶The sky is *darkened **with*** clouds. 空は雲で暗くなっている.

darkish *a.* 黒ずんだ，暗い.

M be ***a bit darkish*** in color 色彩が少し暗い.

darkness, *n.* 暗黒.

V² as *darkness* ***came on*** 暗くなったとき. ¶*Darkness* was ***gathering*** around us. 夕やみがひしひしと迫ってきていた. ¶The lamps of the streets are just lighted, and *darkness* is ***setting in.*** 丁度街燈がついて暗くなり出した. ¶The *darkness* of night has ***settled*** on London. ロンドンの街は夜陰にとざされた. 【類】Slowly the *darkness* ***settled*** over the swamp. ¶Soon *darkness* ***settled down.*** やがて真暗になった.

Q those who have issued from ***barbarian*** *darkness* 暗黒な野蛮の域を脱した人々. ¶The *darkness* became ***deeper.*** 暗黒が増してきた. ¶He sat a long time in the ***gathering*** *darkness.* しのび寄る夕やみの中に長時間すわっていた. ¶an ***impenetrable*** *darkness* of virgin forests 原始林の見通しのきかぬ暗黒. ¶in ***mysterious*** and ***invincible*** *darkness* 神秘的圧倒的暗黒の中に. ¶in ***pitch*** *darkness* 真暗やみで. ¶in the ***pre-dawn*** *darkness* 夜明前の暗黒の中で. ¶in ***somber*** *darkness* うす暗がりで. ¶in ***thick*** (=***utter*** *or* ***dead***) *darkness* 真暗やみに. 【類】It was ***utter*** *darkness.*

P This is different as light ***from*** *darkness.* それは天地の相違だ. ‖ shifting ***from*** the *darkness* of ignorance into the twilight of partial knowledge 全くの無知からいささかの知識の微光への推移. ¶***in*** the *darkness* of night 夜の暗黒の中に ‖ be plunged ***in*** *darkness* 暗黒の中に投込まれる. 【類】We walked together ***in*** the *darkness.* / The cat can see ***in*** the *darkness.* / The stars shine brilliantly ***in*** the *darkness.* ¶under cover ***of*** *darkness* 夜陰に乗じて ‖ deeds ***of*** *darkness* 腹黒い所為.

darling, *n.* 愛児.

Q my ***little ducky*** *darling* 私のかわいい子. ¶The child was the ***pampered*** *darling.* その子は家のものから甘やかされた. ¶It is a ***perfect*** *darling.* 実にかわいい子だ. ¶***somebody's*** *darlings* 人の子.

darn, *n.* 《米俗》[主に打消しに使って] 少しも，ちっとも.

V I don't ***give*** it a *darn* (=damn). へいちゃらだい.

darn, *v.* かがる，つくろう.

M² *darn* (=patch *or* repair) ***up*** つくろう.

dart, *n.* 投げ矢；突進.

V ***fit*** a *dart* in one's bow 弓に矢をつがえる. ¶***make*** a *dart* at a thing あるものに向って突進する.

dart, *v.* 突進する；発射する.

M The sun *darts* ***forth*** his (=its) beams. 太陽は光を放つ.

M² *dart* ***down*** かけ降りる. ¶He *darted* ***off*** like an arrow. 彼は矢のようにかけ去った.

P *dart* ***at*** (=***on***) a foe 敵にとび掛る. ¶*dart* ***out of*** a house (room) 家(など)から飛び出す. ¶*dart* ***through*** the air 空中を飛ぶ. ¶He *darted* ***to*** his feet. 彼は飛び起きた.

dash, *n.* 突撃；突進；鋭気；少量；外観；ダッシュ；とんざ.

V ***cut*** (=***make***) a *dash* 外観を飾る. ¶His conduct ***has*** a *dash* of impudence in it. 彼の行為には少し厚かましい所がある. ¶***lack*** *dash* 鋭気を欠く. ¶***make*** a *dash* for liberty 自由を目ざして突進する ‖ ***make*** a *dash* at the enemy 敵に向って突撃する. ¶***put*** a *dash* of brandy into the water 水に少しブランディーを入れる ‖ ***put*** a *dash* under a word 語の下にダッシュを引く. ¶His hope ***received*** a *dash.* 彼の希望はざ折した.

Q He plays with a ***great*** *dash.* 彼は非常に元気なプレーぶりだ. ¶A ***rosy*** *dash* of light adorned the cloud of the morning. 一脈の陽光が朝雲をばら色に飾った. ¶a woman with a ***strong*** *dash* of the masculine temperament 非常に男性的な婦人. ¶wire off on a ***wild*** *dash* for the scene 超スピードで現場に急ぐ(何か事件が起ったので新聞社の報道班が).

Q² make ***lightning*** *dashes* across the tumultuous road 雑踏した道を横切って脱とのごとく突進する. ¶a ***two-em*** *dash* M 二個の長さのダッシュ. ¶win the ***100-meter*** *dash* in 10.6 seconds 一〇秒六で百メートル競走に勝つ.

P ***at*** a *dash* 一気に，奮然と. ¶The regiment is noted ***for*** its *dash.* 同連隊は勇敢をもって鳴っている. ¶cut a good deal ***of*** a *dash* 大いに見栄を張る. ¶***with*** great *dash* 大いに勇を鼓して ‖ score it out ***with*** a *dash* of his pen ペンで棒を引いてそれを消す ‖ wine ***with*** a *dash* of whiskey ウイスキーを割ったぶどう酒 ‖ His temperament was gay ***with*** a *dash* of melancholy. 彼の気性は快活の中にも幾分陰うつの所もあった. ‖ His plan met ***with*** a *dash.* 彼の計画はとんざした.

P² a *dash* ***for*** a place ある所への突進. ¶the *dash* ***of*** waves 波の打つ音 ‖ a *dash* ***of*** hero worship 幾分の英雄崇拝.

dash, *v.* 突進する，ぶっつかる；ぶっつける，ぶっかける，混ぜる；打ち払う.

M *dash* ***away*** [だっとのごとく]走り去る ‖ He *dashed* his tears ***away.*** 彼は涙を打ち払った. ¶*dash* ***back*** to one's house 一目散に家に戻る. ¶They *dashed* ***forward.*** 彼らは前方に突進した. ¶*dash* ***headlong*** 向う見ずに突進する. ¶The waves *dashed* ***high.*** 波が荒れ立った. ¶The horse *dashed* ***onward.*** 馬は突進した. ¶*dash* ***out***=erase by a stroke 末殺する ‖ *dash* (=knock) ***out*** one's brains 頭をたたき割る ‖ With the shock people *dashed* ***out*** into the street. 仰天して人々は往来に飛出した. ¶The sea *dashed* ***smartly*** at times over the boat. 大浪が時々勢いよくボートの上をかすめた.

M² The train *dashed* ***by.*** 列車がばく進して行った. ¶*dash* ***in*** the color 大急ぎで絵を描く ‖ *dash* ***in*** the detail 詳細を記述する. ¶*dash* ***off*** an epigram 即興の風刺詩を書きなぐる ‖ *dash* ***off*** an article for a newspaper 大急ぎで新聞掲載の文を書く ‖ *dash* ***off*** on an errand 使に駆け出す.

P The milk-carts *dashed* ***about*** the streets. 牛乳配達車が街上を走り回った. ¶The boat was *dashed* ***against*** a rock. 舟が岩にぶつかった. ‖ He *dashed* his head ***against*** the wall. 彼は壁に頭を打っつけた. ‖ *dash* one stone ***against*** another 石と石と打ちあてる. ¶The boys *dashed* ***along*** the street. 子供は街上を走って行った. ¶He *dashed* his slate ***at*** my head. 彼は僕の頭に石盤をぶっつけた. ¶flowers *dashed* ***by*** wind and rain 風雨に打ちつぶされた花. ¶The horse *dashed* ***down*** the hill. 馬が坂を走り下った. ¶*dashing* the tears ***from*** his eyes 涙を払いながら. ¶He *dashed* water ***in*** my face. 彼は私の顔に水をかけた. ¶*dash* ***into*** a fence さくに突込む ‖ He *dashed* ***into*** the midst of his foes. 彼は敵の真中に突進した. ¶waves *dashing* ***on*** the shore 岸打つ波 ‖ *dash* color ***on*** a canvas カンバスに色を塗りたくる. ¶The master *dashed* ***out of*** the room. 主人は部屋を飛び出した. ¶The waves *dashed* ***over*** the boat. 波がボートの上をかすめた. ‖ *dash* ***over*** the snow in a sleigh そりで雪の上を疾走する. ¶The train *dashed* ***through*** the station. 列車はまっしぐらに停車場を通過した. 【類】cars *dashing* ***through*** streets. ¶The vessel was *dashed* ***to*** pieces. 船は粉砕された. 【類】be *dashed* ***to*** pieces on the rocks. ¶*dash* ***up*** a flight of stairs はしご段を駆け上る. ¶The waves *dash* ***upon*** the rock. 波が岩にぶっつかる. ¶*dash* (=mix) wine ***with*** water ぶどう酒を水と混ぜる ‖ garments *dashed* ***with*** blood 血のほとばしった衣服 ‖ The story is *dashed* ***with*** fables. その物語には作り事がまじっている.

data, *n. pl.* 資料，材料.

V the *data* ***amassed*** by him 彼の集めた資料. ¶***bring*** *data* ***together*** from scattered sources 散在する材料をまとめる. ¶***collect*** exact *data* concerning ... ...に関する正確な資料を集める. ¶he ***contributed*** valuable *data* towards ... 彼は...に貴重な資料を寄与した. ¶***furnish*** *data* 資料を供給する. ¶***gather*** *data* 資料を集める. ¶***obtain*** *data* on the subject その問題に関する資料を得る. ¶***secure*** *data* for story writing 小説創作の資料を手に入れる. ¶critically ***sift*** the *data* 批判的に資料をふるい分ける. ¶***summarize*** the *data* which have been presented 提出された資料を要約する.

Q ***Accurate*** *data* covering it are not obtainable. それに関する正確な材料が得られない. ¶***biographical*** *data* 伝記の資料. ¶***corroborative*** *data* 参考資料. ¶no ***exact*** *data* are available for ... ...に関する正確な資料は手に入らぬ. ¶***financial*** *data,* carefully compiled from authentic sources

たしかな出所から慎重に編集した財政資料. ¶*first-hand data* 直接手に入れた資料. ¶*incomplete* and *fragmentary data* 不完全で断片的な資料. ¶We have *insufficient data* concerning it. それに関する資料は不十分だ. ¶*meager data* 貧弱な資料. ¶*objective data* 客観的資料. ¶*personal data* 経歴に関する材料. ¶*questionnaire data* 質問によって集めた資料. ¶*recent statistical data* 新しい統計上の資料. ¶*reliable data* 確実な資料. ¶accurate *scientific data* 正確な科学的資料. ¶gather *sufficient data* for the article その論文を書くための十分な資料を集める. ¶on account of the absence of *sufficient statistical data* 十分の統計がないので. ¶*trustworthy data* 信頼すべき資料.

Q² specially classified *Atomic Energy data* 原子力に関す特別な秘密資料.

P *according to* the statistical *data* published by … …の発表した統計によれば. ¶*from data* furnished by numerous correspondents 多数の人から手紙で提供した資料によると.

P² *data for* the sociologist 社会学者の参考資料. ¶*data on* this point is given in … この点に関する資料は…に出ている.

date, *n.* 日付; 日時; 年代; 時代; 期間; 約束の日時; 《米》[異性と]会合の約束, その相手.

V One has a difficulty in *accepting* the *date* on it. それに記してある年号はちと信じられない. ¶*advance* the *date* of opening the meeting from … to … 開会の日取を…から…に繰り上げる. ¶The *date* 1500 B.C. has been *ascribed* to it. それは紀元前一五〇〇年代のものとされている. ¶*assess* the *date* 年代を査定する. ¶*assign* a *date* 日時を指定する ‖ It is impossible to *assign* positively an initial *date.* いつから始まったものかはっきり言えない. ¶*attach* a *date* to … …に日付をつける. ¶The *date* 200 B.C. has been *attributed* to the Shi-King. 詩経は紀元前二百年代の物とされている. ¶a letter *bearing* the *date* of the 2nd of January 一月二日付の書面. 【類】The letter *bears date* Sept. 30. / a bell *bearing* the *date* of 1679 / The monument *bore* [the] *date* 1708. ¶*call* the *date off* 会合の約束を取消す. ¶*extend* the cancelling *date* to … 失効期日を…まで延長する. ¶definitely *fix* the *date* of departure はっきりと出発の日どりをきめる. 【類】What *date* has been *fixed* for it? / I cannot *fix* a *date* at present. / *dates* have been *fixed* for … and … ‖ A document came to light, which *fixes* the *date* of his death earlier. 一文書が公にされそれによると彼の死去の年代はもっと早くなっている. ¶*forecast* the probable *date* of its completion その完成の大よその日限を予告する. ¶*get* a *date* with a girl ある少女と会合を約束する. ¶it is difficult to *give dates* with any approach to accuracy for … …について正確に近い年代を定めることは困難である ‖ Please *give date.* どうぞ日どりを決めて下さい. ¶I *have* a *date* with … tonight 今夜は…と会合の約束がある. ¶He *has* more *dates* (=engagements) than he can keep. 彼は招待されている先が多いので一々出席ができない. ¶The *date* must be punctually *kept.* 約束の日時は厳格に守らなければならぬ. ¶*make* a *date* with … …と日どりをきめる. ¶To students of the New Testament today *marks* a *date* of interest. 新約聖書研究者に取って今日は興味ある日だ. ¶You must *name* an earlier *date.* 日どりをもっと早くしてもらいたい. ¶*place* the *date* of the building at … その建物の年代を…と推定する. 【類】Some *place* the *date* two years later. ¶What *date* do you *propose* for it? その日どりを何日になさいますか. ¶*put* the *date* to a letter 書面に日付をつける. ¶*put forward* the *date* of its completion 完成の日限を早める. ¶I am not able to *recall* the exact *date.* 正確な日付は思いだせない. ¶The *date* has been *set* for October 1. その日どりは十月一日ときまった. 【類】We finally *set* the *date* for a Tuesday evening. ‖ *set* (=place) this *date* at … この年代を…とする ‖ the *date set* for the concert 音楽会を開くことにきめた日. ¶In crossing this line (International Date Line) the *date* is *set ahead* or *back* one whole day according to direction of passage. この線(万国日付変更線)を横断するときに通過の方向によりそれぞれ日付を一日早めたり遅らしたりする. ¶*shorten* the *date* 日限を短縮する. ¶*take* one's *date* along 自分の彼女(氏)を連れて行く. ¶*telegraph* the probable *date* of … …の大よその日どりを打電する. 【類】*telegraph* the *date* of departure. ¶*transpose* Japanese *dates* into Western 日本の月日を西洋の月日に直す. ¶*verify dates* 月日を確める. ¶*Write* all the *dates* you know. 知っている(歴史上重要な)年号を残らず記せ[試験問題]. ¶The *date* of his youth *expired.* 彼の青年時代は過ぎた.

Q It is of very *ancient date.* それは非常に古い年代のものである. ¶The *correct date* for this year's *Shubun-no-hi* is the 24th. 今年の秋分の日は二十四日が正しい. ¶Postponement has followed postponement and a *definite date* for starting work is yet to be set. 延期に延期を重ねたが事業着手の日どりがまだきまらない. ¶European birds were introduced into America at *different dates.* 欧州産の鳥が色々の時代にアメリカに輸入された. 【類】maps showing the extent of the Roman Empire at *different dates.* ¶books of *distant dates* 古刊書. ¶at an *early date* 遠からず. ¶at the *earliest possible date* できるだけ早く. ¶the *effective date* of the regulations 規則の施行期日. ¶The year 1776 is an *epochmaking date* in the history of liberty. 一七七六年は自由発達史上画期的の年だ. ¶ascertain the *exact date* of an event 事件の正しい月日を確かめる. ¶a *famous date* of history 歴史上有名な年号. ¶at a *fixed date* 定日に. ¶one of our *historic dates* 歴史上重要な年代の一つ. ¶an *incontrovertible date* 確定日. ¶at a *late date* この間 ‖ be rather a *late date* to … …するのは少しく遅きに失する ‖ at *later dates* その後に. 【類】until some *later date* / occurrences of a *later date* ‖ It belongs to a much *later date.* それはずっと後の時代のものだ. ‖ name a *later date* 日どりをもっとおそくする ‖ The *latest date* is fixed as July, 1898. 一番早くって一八九八年七月になっている. ‖ The book is thoroughly revised and corrected to the *latest date.* その本は最近の年代まで改訂が加えてある. ¶at *no distant date* 近日. ¶a *notable date* in the history of … …史上注目すべき時代. ¶These years are *ominous dates* so far as … is concerned. これらの年は…から言うと凶年だ. ¶on a *predetermined date* 予定の期日に. ¶*principal dates* in the history of Japan 日本史上主要な年代. ¶What is the *probable date* of her arrival in Yokohama? その船の横浜着は大よそ幾日ごろですか. 【類】the *probable date* of sailing. ¶papers of a *recent date* 新しい日付の新聞紙. ¶Thursday is the *regular date* for the meeting. 木曜日はその会の定日だ. ¶at a very *remote date* 古い時代に. ¶antiquities of *Roman date* ローマ時代の古物. ¶on the *same date* 同日に. ¶the day previous to the *scheduled date* of sailing 予定出帆日の前日. ¶the event marks a highly *significant date* in the history of … その事変は…史上きわめて有意義なる時期を画している. ¶on a *specified date* 特定の日に. ¶At a *subsequent date* I had various opportunities of discussion with him その後になって彼と色々話しあう機会を得た. ¶payable in London at *three months' date* 日付三ケ月後にロンドンで支払うべき. ¶The *date* of his return to Japan is still *uncertain.* 彼の帰朝の日はまだ分らない. 【類】at an *uncertain date.* ¶at *various dates,* scattered over a period of two hundred years. 二百年にわたる期間のさまざまの年月に. ¶Labor Day is a holiday in the Australian states on *varying date.*「労働日」は豪州諸州では休日になっているがその日は区々だ. ¶*What date* is it today? 今日は幾日か ☞ What *day* …? は口語では何曜日に使う. ¶a telegram of *yesterday's* (*Wednesday's*) *date* 昨日(水曜)日付の電報. ¶through his life's *whole date* 彼の全生涯を通じて.

Q² the probable *adjournment date* of Congress 国会の休会の大体の日どり. ¶one's *birth date* 生年月日. ¶a *closing date* [懸賞など]締切日. ¶a *deadline date* 締切日. ¶quote early *delivery dates* 早く荷渡しのできる日付を知らせる. ¶its scheduled *expiration date* of May 15 その五月十五日の予定満期. ¶at a *future date* 後日に. ¶suggest Aug. 19 as the *meeting date* 会見日として八月十九日を提議する. ¶a *moving date* 引越しの日付. ¶the *opening date* of an assembly 会議開始の日. ¶The *publication date* is announced as May 15. 発行日は五月十五日と発表されている. ¶a *sailing date* 出帆日. ¶have a prior political *speaking date* 政治演説の約束がある. ¶a *target date* 予定期限. ¶fix a *strike date* スト開始の日どりを取りきめる. ¶a *vintage date* of wine ぶどう酒の醸造年代. ¶The steamer arrives at Kobe three days later than *Yokohama date.* 汽船は横浜より三日後れて神戸に着く.

P ***at date*** 指定の日における ‖ ***at*** some *date* in the distant future 遠き将来においていつか ‖ ***at*** this *date* (Sept. 1, 1913) (一九一三年九月一日の)本日 ‖ ***At*** what *date* shall I draw? 何日の日付で振出しましょうか. ‖ ***at*** the *date* of this writing この文を書いている日に ‖ ***at*** the *date* of maturity [手形など]支払期日に. ¶***down to*** (=up to) *date* 今日まで. ¶***from date*** of contract 契約の日から ‖ ***from date*** of notice 予告の日から. 【類】 seven days ***from*** the *date* of pledging (質入) ‖ ***from*** that *date* up to the present その時から現在に至るまで ‖ commencing ***from date*** 今日以後. 【類】 ***from date*** of departure to arrival. ¶The main part of the building is original, but ... is ***of*** later *date*. 建物の主要部分は最初のものだが...はその後の建造だ. ¶***on*** a given *date* ある一定の日に. 【類】 ***on*** a certain *date* / ***on*** the same *date* as ... ‖ The Exposition will open ***on*** its schedule *date*—February 20th, 1915. 展示会は一九一五年二月二十日の予定日に開会される. ‖ I shall expect to see you in school ***on*** that *date*, so be sure to come. 当日学校でお目にかかりたいと思いますからぜひいらっしゃい. ‖ ***on*** that *date* or thereabouts その日にかその前後に ‖ the *date* ***on*** which those regulations came into force 条例の施行せられた日. ¶It is a trifle ***out of*** *date*. それは少し時勢おくれだ. ‖ Every dictionary is, strictly speaking, ***out of*** *date* within a month of its publication. 厳密に言えばどんな辞書でも発行後一カ月以内に時勢おくれになる. 【類】 The book would be ***out of*** *date* before it was printed. / The guide-book is ten years ***out of*** *date*. / Jules Verne's "Tour of the World in Eighty Days" has become ***out of*** *date* in the rapid improvement of means of transportation. / The fashion is getting ***out of*** *date*. ¶the largest ship afloat ***to*** *date* 今まで使用の船舶中最大の船 ‖ the results ***to*** *date* of ... ...の今日までの成績. 【類】 Contributions ***to*** *date* are encouraging, but far short of needs. ¶a telegram ***under*** *date* of May 2 五月二日付の電報. 【類】 in a letter to me ***under*** *date* January 8, 1908, he writes that ... / a correspondent, writing ***under*** *date* [of] March 21st, says ... / write ***under*** a recent *date* / letters written ***under*** *dates* varying from 1883 to 1902. ¶***until*** a recent *date* 最近まで. ¶The election returns ***up to*** *date* show that 12 Progressives have been elected. 最近の選挙報告書に進歩党が十二名当選したと書いてある. ‖ The dictionary is quite ***up to*** *date*. この辞典は新語がはいっている. ‖ ***up to*** a comparatively recent *date* 比較的最近まで. ¶newspapers ***with*** *dates* to July 29th 七月二十九日までの日付の新聞紙 ‖ a letter ***with*** no *date* 日付のない手紙 ‖ go to ... ***with*** one's *date* 彼女(氏)と...に行く.

P² The *date* ***for*** departure drew near. 出発の日が近づいてきた. ‖ the *date* ***for*** a wedding (examination, sailing) 婚礼(など)の日取り ‖ the *date* ***for*** sending in the prize essays 懸賞論文の締切期日 ‖ a *date* ***for*** hearing 公判期日. 【類】 The *date* ***of*** sailing is not fixed. ‖ *dates* ***of*** erection of buildings 建物建設の年代 ‖ the *date* ***of*** his birth (death) 彼の誕生日(命日) ‖ the *date* ***of*** accession to the throne 即位の期日 ‖ the *date* ***of*** enforcement 施行期日 ‖ *date* ***of*** posting 発信の日付 ‖ *date* ***of*** employment and dismissal 就職および解雇年月. 【類】 the *date* ***of*** departure (arrival) / the *date* ***of*** a meeting.

date, *v.* 日付をする; 時代を定める; 日付がある, 始まる, 起算する.

M be *dated* way ***back*** in the 16th century 十六世紀にさかのぼる ‖ The use of peas as a food *dates* ***back*** to very early times. 豆を食用にしたのは大昔からだ. 【類】 *date* ***back*** to the time of Queen Anne / *date* [***back***] to the thirteenth century / *date* ***back*** to the Ancient Rome days / boasting a history which *dates* ***back*** to ... ‖ He is a member of a distinguished British family which *dates* ***back*** to 1200. 彼は一二〇〇年から続いている英国名門の出だ. ‖ Those *dating* about a century ***back*** are comparatively easy to acquire. 百年位前のものは比較的たやすく手に入れられる. ¶It *dates* ***back*** only a few decades. それはわずか三四十年前のことだ. ¶It *dated* ***earlier*** than the 5th century. それは五世紀以前に始まった. ¶a postmark *dated* ***the first of January*** 一月一日の消印. 【類】 a telegram, *dated* ***the 17th inst.***, from Paris. ¶His death is ***variously*** *dated* 1534 and 1546. 彼の永眠の年は一五三四年とも一五四六年ともあってまちまちになっている.

P His letter accompanying the gift was *dated* ***at*** Rome, July 12, and read:—贈物に添えた氏の書翰はローマ七月十二日付で次の文言であった. 【類】 a telegram *dated* ***at*** Paris ***on*** August 2nd. ¶The beginning of all modern scientific investigation *dates* ***from*** 1543. 近代のあらゆる科学的研究の起源は一五四三年にさかのぼる. 【類】 *date* ***from*** this period (the 16th century) / *date* ***from*** a far back period / *dating* ***from*** thousands of years back / an imposing edifice (広壮な大建築), *dated* only ***from*** a few years ago / it *dates* ***from*** the days of ... / there is much mythical lore (神話) on the subject, but the beginning of the art *dates* really ***from*** ... / It is supposed to *date* ***from*** the Victorian period. / Japan possesses a literature *dating* ***from*** A.D. 712 in the Kojiki, the sacred book of Shintoism ‖ a custom *dating* ***from*** 1563 一五六三年以来の習慣 ‖ a church *dating* ***from*** the 14th century 十四世紀に建設された教会. ¶by a letter *dated* ***from*** Paris ***on*** March 11, 1875 パリ一八七五年三月十一日付の手紙によって. ¶The circular is *dated* ***in*** March, 1901. その回状は一九〇一年三月の日付である. ¶The origin of Brussels *dates* [back] ***to*** the sixth century. ブラセッルは六世紀に起ったものだ.

daub, *v.* 書きなぐる.

M *daub* ***away*** for relaxation 気晴しに絵をかきなぐる.

daughter, *n.* 娘.

V ***acknowledge*** one's *daughter* 娘を認知する. ¶I have come to ***ask*** your *daughter* in marriage. お嬢さんを妻にいただきたいと思ってうかがいました. ¶He ***brought up*** his *daughters* in great strictness. 彼は娘をすこぶる厳格に育てた. ¶***cast*** a *daughter* ***out*** into the world 娘を家から追い出す. ¶***court*** the lovely *daughter* of ... ...の美しい娘に愛を寄せる. ¶***give*** one's *daughter* in marriage 娘を片づける ‖ He ***gave*** his *daughters* ... each as a marriage portion. 彼は持参金として娘たち一人々々に...を与えた. ¶He ***had*** a *daughter* by her. その女との間に女の子があった. ‖ a *daughter* her husband had ***had*** at an early period by an actress 彼女の夫が若いころに女優との間にもうけた女の子. ¶She has ***lost*** a little *daughter* from croup. 彼女は肺炎で幼い娘をなくした. ¶he ***married*** the *daughter* of ... 彼は...の娘と結婚した ‖ He ***married*** his *daughter* to a rich man. 彼は娘を金持に片付けた. 【類】 For many centuries five foremost Kuge (ancient court) families had the privilege of ***marrying*** their *daughters* into the Imperial line. ¶***marry off*** one's *daughter* 娘を嫁にやる. ¶***purchase*** the *daughter* of ... ...の娘を身受する. ¶***sell*** a *daughter* to a life of shame 娘を苦界に売る. ¶***wed*** the *daughter* of ... ...の娘と結婚する.

V² *daughters* ***coming*** to womanhood 年ごろの娘.

Q an ***adopted*** *daughter* 養女. ¶a ***beautiful*** and ***gifted*** *daughter* 美人で利口な娘. ¶a ***blue-eyed*** *daughter* 青い目をした娘. ¶a ***bonny*** *daughter* 美貌の娘. ¶the ***debutante*** *daughter* of Mr. and Mrs. ... 初めて社交界へ出る...夫妻の娘. ¶their ***idolized*** *daughter* ちょうよ花よで育てた娘. ¶a ***marriageable*** *daughter* 結婚適齢の娘. ¶a ***natural*** *daughter* 私生児の娘. ¶an ***only*** *daughter* 独り娘. 【類】 She fancied that she saw in me a strict resemblance to an ***only*** *daughter* whom she had lost at my age. ¶his ***sunny-haired*** *daughter* 光沢のある金髪の彼の娘. ¶the ***youthful*** *daughters* of the house of Kenwigs ケンウィッグス家の若い娘たち.

Q² his ***baby*** *daughter* 彼の赤ん坊の娘. ¶a ***country*** *daughter* いなか娘.

P² Mary, *daughter* ***of*** the Georges ジョージー家の娘メリー. 【類】 Adeline, *daughter* ***of*** Mr. and Mrs. Friendbury. ¶His mother was *daughter* ***to*** a distinguished diplomatist. 彼の母は有名な外交官の娘だ.

daunt, *v.* おどす.

M ***nothing*** *daunted* おめずおくせず.

P he was *daunted* ***at*** the sight of ... 彼は...を見ておじけた. ¶be *daunted* ***by*** threats 脅かつでおどかされた.

dawn, *n.* 夜明け, れい明, あけぼの; 初期.

V it ***marks*** the *dawn* of a new era in ... それが...における新時代を画する. ¶a cock ***proclaiming*** the *dawn* 暁を告げる鶏. ¶***see*** the *dawn* of a new day 新しい日の曙光(しょこう)を見る. ¶It ***ushers in*** the *dawn* of peace. それで平和の曙光が見られる.

P ***at dawn*** of the day 夜明けに, 払暁に ‖ ***at*** *dawn* on that day その日の夜明けに ‖ ***at*** the early *dawn* 夜が明けて間も

なく ‖ We now stand ***at*** the *dawn* of the Atomic Age. われらは今や原子時代のれい明期にある. ¶***before dawn*** 夜明け前に. ¶***from dawn*** till dusk 夜明けから日暮まで ‖ ***from*** the *dawn* of letters 文学のれい明期から ‖ ***from*** the *dawn* of history to the present day 有史以来今日に至るまで. ¶The first signs ***of*** the *dawn* appear on the horizon. 暁の曙光が地平線上に現われる. ¶We rose ***with*** the *dawn*. 僕たちは夜の引明けに起きた.

dawn, *v.* 夜が明ける; 分り出す; 現出する.

M ***At last*** it *dawned* on me. とうとう分った. ¶The day *dawned* ***calmly***. 静かに夜が明けた. ¶The fact ***gradually*** *dawned* on my mind. 事実が段々私に分ってきた. ¶The day was ***just*** *dawning*. 丁度夜の明ける所だった. ¶It ***slowly*** *dawned* on him. それがそろそろ彼に分り出した. ¶The idea ***suddenly*** *dawned* upon me. その考えが突然私の頭に浮んできた.

P The era of the air has *dawned* ***on*** Japan. 日本に航空時代が出現した. ¶A new era is now *dawning* ***upon*** the world. 世界は今や新時代に入らんとしている. ‖ When the full extent of his misfortune *dawned* ***upon*** him, he burst into a violent fit of tears. 不幸の程度がはっきりと分りかけた時彼はわっと泣き出した. ‖ it is *dawning* ***upon*** us that ... ...ということが分り出した. 【類】 As the value of his work *dawned* ***upon*** Europe, the learned societies hastened to confer degrees and honors upon him. / the truth began to *dawn* ***upon*** the minds of the thinkers that ... / The terrible truth *dawned* ***upon*** (=on) her.

day, *n.* 日; 昼; 時代; 生涯, 寿命; 勝利.

V it is likely to retard rather than ***advance*** the *day* when ... それは...する時代の出現を早めるよりはむしろ遅らせることになるらしい. ¶I must ask you to ***allow*** me four or five *days*. 四五日の猶予を願わねばならない. ¶The *day* was ***arranged***. その日が取りきめられた. ¶the *day* is hardly ***born***, when ... ...のない日はほとんどない. ¶***carry*** (=***win***) the day [ゲームなどに]勝つ; 大流行する ‖ Among English writers the term "semantics" seems to have ***carried*** the *day*. 英文家の間では "semantics"「意味論」なる語が流行するようになったらしい. ¶***celebrate*** Christmas *Day* with great pomp 花々しくクリスマス祭日を祝う. ¶Speeches by the Governor and others ***closed*** the *day*. 知事その他の演説で当日の式は終った. ‖ ***close*** one's *days* 死ぬ. ¶The *days* have not yet ***commenced***. その時代がまだ始まっていない. ¶***complete*** the happy *day* by ... ...して楽しい一日を終える. ¶***commemorate*** the happy *day* 吉日を記念する. ¶the *day* is ***consecrated*** by the Roman Church to the memory of Saint ... その日はローマ教会の方では聖...の縁日となっている. ¶The voyage ***consumed*** eighteen full *days*. 航海はたっぷり十八日かかった. ¶The new service ***cuts*** four *days* from Trans-Pacific voyage. 新航路で太平洋横断航海の日数が四日切りつめられる. ¶***dream away*** a *day* 一日を夢うつつに過す. ¶He ***ended*** his *days* there. 彼はそこで死んだ. 【類】 retire to ***end*** his *days* in peace / She ***ended*** her *days* in a convent (an orphan asylum, workhouse). / He will ***end*** his *days* on the gallows trap (絞首台). ¶This was the last item on the programme, which ***finished*** a thoroughly enjoyable *day*. これがプログラムの最後で誠に楽しい一日が終りを告げた. ¶***fix*** the *day* for ... ...の日どりをきめる. 【類】 A *day* was ***fixed*** upon which it was to take place. ¶I ***foresee*** the *day* when ... ...の日あるべしと予言する. ¶***fritter away*** the whole *day* over small domestic occupation 終日こまごました家庭の仕事をしながらくだらなく過す. ¶The ship ***gained*** a *day* having run so far to the eastward. その船は東へそれだけ進んだので一日が浮いた(同じ日が二日できた). ‖ ***gain*** the *day* 戦に勝つ. ¶He ***got*** six *days*. 彼は六日の拘留を食った. 【類】 The newspaper boy ***gets*** fourteen *days* for announcing (呼売) another "great railway accident" or a "shocking murder" to the homestaying (世間知らずの) householder. ‖ I ***got*** (=had) a *day* ***off*** from the factory. 工場から一日休暇をもらった. ¶***hasten*** the *day* of disarmament 軍備縮小の時運を促進する. ¶I never ***had*** a *day* at school in my life. 僕は生れて学校というものは一日も行ったことがない. ‖ excursionists who have ***had*** a *day* in London ロンドンに一日を送った遊覧客 ‖ Every dog ***has*** his *day*. だれにも一度は運が来る ‖ He has ***had*** his *day*. 彼はもう下り坂だ. ‖ Such a conception (=an idea) has ***had*** its *day*. こうした思想はもうすたれた. ‖ Byron will once more ***have*** his *day*. バイロンが再び流行するときが来るだろう. 【類】 It is commonly believed that the "epic" as a branch of literature has ***had*** its *day*. / These novels have ***had*** their *day* of vogue. ‖ Telephone girls ***had*** a *day* ***off*** yesterday. 交換嬢は昨日一日休暇をもらった. ¶dawn ***heralding*** a *day* 一日の先ぶれをする暁. ¶He ***holds*** his *day*. 彼は会合の約束を守る. ¶***institute*** an arbour *day* in Korea 朝鮮に植樹日を設定する. ¶the *day* is ***kept*** as an anniversary festival in commemoration of ... その日には...記念の例年祭が行われる ‖ ***keep*** a holy *day* 祝祭日を守る. ¶He has ***known*** a better *day*. 彼ももとはよかった(今は落ちぶれた). ¶How many *days* are ***left***? 幾日残っているか. ¶***lengthen*** the working *day* from eight to nine hours 一日の労働時間を八時間から九時間に延長する. ¶***let*** no *day* pass without ... ...せずに一日も送らぬ. ¶He ***lost*** not a *day*, but began. 彼は一日もむだにせずに着手した. ‖ ***lose*** the *day* 負ける. ¶Twenty-four hours ***make*** a *day*. 二十四時間で一日になる. ¶***miss*** no *days* of school 授業に必ず出る. ¶You have ***mistaken*** the *day*. 君は日を取違えた. 【類】 I have ***mistaken*** my *day*. ¶***name*** a *day* for a wedding 結婚の日取りをきめる. ¶***Note*** the first *day* of October as the latest date when applications should reach the office. 申込は十月の一日までに事務所に着くように注意して下さい. ¶His *days* are ***numbered***. 彼の命も長いことはない. 【類】 His *days* as Prime Minister are ***numbered***. 【類】 It is satisfactory to think that the *days* of the life-size portrait bust are ***numbered***. ¶***observe*** (=keep) the *day* その日を祝う(または祭る). 【類】 The *day* will be ***observed*** as a general holiday. / The States of Kansas and Massachusetts do not ***observe*** New Year's *Day*. ¶There does not ***pass*** a *day* without my consulting it. 一日としてそれを参考しない日はない. ¶***put off*** the *day* 延期する. 【類】 ***put off*** the evil *day* (凶日). ¶***recall*** the *day* when ... ...した日を思い出す. ¶It ***requires*** two *days*. 二日かかる. ¶A new *day* has been ***rung in***. 鐘の音とともに新しい日を迎えた. ¶***rule*** the *day* 勝を制する. ¶***running days*** Sundays and holidays excepted 日曜と祭日を除きぶっ通し. ¶This will ***save*** the *day* for him. これで彼の顔が立つだろう. ¶he did not live to ***see*** the *day* when ... 彼は...の日に間に合わずに死んだ. ‖ an individual who has ***seen*** better *days* もとは盛んであった人. 【類】 They had evidently ***seen*** much better *days*. / The whole town bears marks of having ***seen*** better *days*. ‖ tomatoes that had ***seen*** better *days* (=are rotten) いたんだトマト ‖ a winter suit that has ***seen*** its *day* 着古した冬服. ¶A *day* has been ***set*** (=fixed) for his departure. 彼の出発の日がきめられた. ‖ commence work the *day* you ***set*** 御指定の日に仕事を始める. ¶***set aside*** a *day* for ... ...のため一日とっておく. ¶***settle*** (=***appoint***) a *day* for ... ...の日取りを定める. ¶***shorten*** one's *days* (=life) by sake drinking 酒を飲んで命を縮める. ¶He was pensioned and enabled to ***spend*** his last *days* in peace. 彼には年金があって平和に老後を送ることができた. ‖ ***spend*** a nice quiet *day* at home 一日家で静かに楽しく暮す ‖ ***spend*** *days* having little to do 所在なく日を送る. ¶***stave off*** the evil *day* 不吉の日の起らないようにする. ¶***take*** a *day* or a week ***off*** occasionally 時々一日か一週間か暇をとる. ¶***while away*** a rainy *day* 雨天の日を楽しく過す. ¶***win*** the *day* 成功する, [ゲームなどに]勝つ.

V^2 As the *day* ***advanced***, the sun came out with a brighter luster. 朝の時間がたつにつれて太陽は一段とその光を増してきた. ¶as the *days* ***begin*** to get warmer もっと陽気が暖かになりだすと. ¶The *day* ***broke***. 夜が明けた. ¶A new *day* has ***dawned*** upon the world. 新しい日がやってきた. ¶My *days* are ***drawing*** to their close. 僕は余命いくばくもない. ¶The *days* have ***expired***. 寿命が尽きた. ¶seldom does a *day* ***go by*** without ... ...しない日はめったにない ‖ in *days* ***gone by*** 昔. ¶The *day* ***opened*** cloudly. その日は朝曇っていた. ¶Scarcely a *day* ***passes*** without some terrible accident happening to the toilers. 労働者に何か恐ろしい事故の起らない日はほとんど一日もない. 【類】 hardly a *day* ***passes*** without there being articles in the newspapers mentioning his name in connection with ... ¶the *day* ***preceding*** Christmas クリスマスの前日. ¶as the *days* ***roll on*** 日がたつと. ¶The sun grew blazing as the ***day wore on.*** 日がたけると太陽がかんかん照ってきた.

We worked ***all day.*** われわれは終日働いた. 【類】I've been busy ***all day.*** / ***all day*** long ‖ ***all*** our ***days*** 一生. ¶***all one's born days*** 一生涯. ¶each ***alternate day***＝on ***alternate days*** 隔日に. ¶on ***another day*** 日を改めて. ¶an ***artificial day*** 昼のように明るくした夜(電燈照明などで). ¶in ***ancient days*** 昔. ¶an ***annual feast day*** for boys 男の子の節句. ¶***another day*** 他日. ¶You may call ***any day*** you please. いつでもお出でください. ¶on the ***appointed day*** 定めた日に. ¶an ***auspicious day*** 縁起のよい日. ¶in the ***bad old days*** we used to be taught that ... いやな昔は…と教えられたものだ. ☞ good old days を面白くもじったもの. ¶a ***balmy day*** さわやかな日. ¶She has seen her ***best days.*** 彼女は以前は鳴らしたものである. ¶***Better days*** are coming. 景気が直ってきた. ‖ the ***better day*** will dawn only when ... …の時になって初めて幸福の日が来るだろう. ¶a ***big day*** in a law court 裁判所で大事件の公判のある日 ‖ This is a ***big day*** for our school. 今日はうちの学校では大変なんだ(運動会などで). ¶There were ***black days*** ahead for them. 彼らの前途は暗たんたるものであった. ¶in all his ***born days*** 生れてから. 【類】I was never so ill-treated (＝ill-used) in my ***born days.*** ¶***Boxing Day*** クリスマス後に出入の者に贈物をする日. ¶a ***breezy day*** そよ風のある日. ¶on their ***bridal day*** 彼らの婚礼の日に. ¶a ***bright day*** 天気の好い日 ‖ a harbinger of ***bright days*** to come よいことがある前じらせ. ¶It was then ***broad day.*** そのときは真昼だった. ¶This is my ***busy day.*** Make it short. 今日は急がしいから簡単に願います(訪問者などに). ‖ I have a ***busy day*** ahead. 今日はこれから急がしくなる. 【類】at the end of a ***busy day.*** ¶a coffee shop I frequented in ***bygone days*** 昔よく行ったコーヒー店. ¶on a ***certain day*** 一定の日に. ¶on a ***clear day*** 晴れた日に ‖ We have three ***clear days*** before the meeting. 会まで丸三日ある. 【類】after the lapse of twelve ***clear days.*** ¶on a ***cloudy day*** in March 三月の曇った日に. ¶The ***coldest days*** are over. 寒があけた. ¶***consecutive days*** 連日. ¶the ***concluding day*** of a show 見せ物の千秋楽の日. ¶Succeeding payments are to be made on the ***corresponding day*** of each month thereafter. その後の払込は毎月その当日に行うこと. ¶the ***critical day*** for the rice-crop 米作の厄日. ¶the ***day*** is not far ***distant*** when ...の日は遠くない ‖ at no very ***distant day*** 遠からず. ¶The ***day*** is ***doubtful.*** 勝敗のほどは疑わしい. ¶a ***dull day*** どんよりとした日 ‖ It was a ***dull, gloomy day.*** 気の引立たぬ陰気な日だった. ¶***Dusty day,*** isn't it? 今日はほこりがひどいじゃありませんか. ¶I shall be glad and thankful to my ***dying day*** that ... …を死ぬまでうれしくありがたく思います. ¶in ***earlier days*** 以前は ‖ the motion pictures in the ***earliest days*** of their development 初期の映画 ‖ at an ***early day*** 遠からず ‖ in ***early days*** 初めの間は ‖ in his ***early days*** 若いころ. 【類】in the ***early days*** of Christianity / in the ***early days*** of railroads / in the ***early days*** of the invention / in the very ***early days*** of foreign residence (居留地) / Having known in his ***early days*** what it was to be "hard-up (貧困)," he hated waste of any kind. / from the ***earliest days*** of the medical art. ¶In the ***embryonic day*** of the industry, motion pictures were produced entirely in the east. [米国]映画事業の初期においては製作は一切東部でやった. ¶the ***enlightened day*** 開明の時代. ¶***every day*** of our lives われわれの生涯の日々, 毎日毎日 ‖ almost ***every day*** ほとんど毎日. ¶***every second*** (＝***other***) ***day*** 一日置きに. ¶***every third day*** 二日置きに. ¶on the ***exact day*** specified 正確に指定の日に. ¶those who have lately seen ***evil days*** その身に近ごろ不幸のあった人々. ¶the ***day*** is not ***far away*** (＝distant when) ... …の日は遠くない ‖ in those ***far away*** (＝***far-off***) ***days*** あの遠い昔に. ¶That ***day*** is ***far off.*** その日は前途りょう遠だ. ¶a ***fast day*** 断食日, 斉日. ¶that ***fatal day***—the day of spring cleaning その厄介な日一春の大掃除の日. ¶The ***fateful day*** had to come. その恐ろしい日は来ずには済まなかった. ¶***fete days*** 祝祭日. ¶in ***feudal days*** 封建時代に. ¶a ***few days*** later その後数日経って ‖ in a ***few days*** more もう二三日で. ¶at the ***final day*** of the athletic meet 運動会の最終日に. ¶on the first ***fine day***＝as soon as it becomes fine＝the next fine day 天気になり次第. ¶The ***day*** was ***fine, warm,*** and ***sunny.*** その日は晴れて暖く太陽が照っていた. ¶the ***first day*** of the new (＝coming) year 元日 ‖ from the ***first day*** 初日から ‖ the ***first day*** of operation of Tokyo's first subway 東京で初めての地下鉄道開通日 ‖ in his ***first days*** as a writer 彼が作家として立った初期に ‖ on her very ***first day*** on the job 彼女が就職した日に. ¶on the ***following day*** 翌日 ‖ in the ***following*** two or three ***days*** それに続く二三日中に. ¶in ***former days*** 昔. ¶***four consecutive days*** of rain 四日続いての雨天. ¶Sundays are the only ***free days*** we have. 日曜だけがあいている日だ. ¶Christmas is the ***gladdest*** (＝happiest) ***day*** of all the year. クリスマスは一年中一番うれしい日だ. ¶a ***glorious day*** in spring うららかな春の日 ‖ the gladiator in the ***glorious days*** of Rome ローマの盛んなころの闘士. ¶***Good day.*** 今日は(あいさつ). ¶think of one's ***good old days*** なつかしい昔をしのぶ. ¶a ***great religious day*** 一大宗教日 ‖ one of the ***great days*** at the Zoological Gardens 動物園における重要なる一日. ¶the ***happiest day*** of one's life 一生涯の中で一番楽しい日. ¶have a ***happy day*** together 一日を一緒に面白く遊ぶ. ¶This is my ***heavy day.*** 今日は大骨の(教師なら授業時間の多い)日だ. ¶She was lovely in ***her day.*** 彼女は若いころはかわいかった. ¶It was a ***hideous day.*** それは(僕に取っては)悪日であった. ¶a ***high day*** 大祭日, 祝日. ¶Both events happened on the ***identical day.*** 両事件が同日に起った. ¶in ***his Indian days*** 彼のインド在住時代に. ¶a very popular artist in ***his own day*** 当時非常に人気のあった美術家. ¶in ***Homer's days*** ホーマー時代に. ¶in the ***intervening days*** その間の日に. ¶Why should their ***last days*** be spent in want and suffering? なぜ彼らは老後を貧苦に送らねばならないのか. ¶during the last (next) ***few days*** この(次の)数日間に. ¶for the ***last ten days*** 過去十日間. ¶of ***late days*** 近ごろ ‖ at this ***late day*** it is impossible to determine ... 今日となっては…を確かめることは時日がたち過ぎている ‖ even at this ***late day*** おそまきながら ‖ At a ***late day,*** he recognized that he had been on the wrong track. 自分が誤まっていることに気がついた時はおそかった. 【類】often, at a ***late day,*** they recognize that ... ‖ in his ***later days*** 彼の晩年に ‖ at a ***later day*** その後のある日に. ¶in the ***lean days*** before fame and name came to him 名もなき彼の窮乏時代に. ¶this ***livelong day*** この永い日 ‖ through the ***livelong day*** 終日. ¶a ***long-wished-for day*** 待ちかねていた日. ¶a ***lovely day*** 天気のよい日. ¶***lucky days*** for marriage 婚礼によい日 ‖ This is my ***lucky day*** 今日はなんてまがいいんだろう. ¶We have spent ***many*** a ***day*** together. われわれは長く一緒にいた. ¶in ***medieval days*** 中世に. ¶a ***melancholy day*** 憂うつな日. ¶a ***memorial day*** 記念日. ¶away back in the ***misty days*** of the ninth century 九世紀のぼうばくたる時代にさかのぼって. ¶one of the foremost artists of the ***modern day*** 現代一流の画家 ‖ in ***modern days*** 現今 ‖ in these ***modern days,*** when mothers and daughters pay regular visits to hairdressers 母と娘がきまって髪結いへ行くという今日. ¶a ***momentous day*** 大事な日. ¶July 14th is the ***national fête day*** of France. 七月十四日はフランスの国祭日である. ¶on ***New Year's*** (＝***Year***) ***Day*** 元日に. ¶the ***next day*** 次の日 ‖ There will be no rain for the ***next few days.*** 数日間雨は降らないだろう. ¶This is a ***nice day.*** 今日はよい天気だ. ¶***notable days*** in the calendar 暦の旗(物)日. ¶an ***off-day***＝a day off 休日 ‖ whip a trout stream on an ***off day*** 休みの日にます釣をやる ¶in ***old days*** 以前は ‖ in the ***old(en) days*** 昔は. ¶***one day*** last week 先週のある日 ‖ ***One day*** in time is lost (gained) on crossing 180° longitude between Pango Pango and Sydney, westward (eastward). パンゴーパンゴー・シドニー間百八十度の経線を西に(東に)向って横断するときに日が一日減る(増す). ‖ ***One day*** or another it will have to come. いつか一度はこずにはいない. ¶an ***open day*** 差支えのない日, 明いている日 ‖ the ***open days*** of the museum 博物館開館日. ¶on ***other days*** of the week その週の他の日に ‖ the ***other day*** 先日 ‖ Toys of ***Other Days*** 『書名』昔のおもちゃ. ¶of ***our day*** 現今の ‖ Much is made in ***our day*** of the relation of ethics to biology. 現今では生物学に対する倫理学の関係が大いに論じられている. ¶in ***our own day*** and generation 今日現代において. ¶the ***palmy days*** of the East India Company 東インド会社の全盛時代 ‖ in the ***palmy days*** of the city その市の全盛時代に. 【類】in the ***palmy days*** of amateur cycle racing / Rome in her ***palmiest*** *days.* / Shanghai's ***palmiest** days* as a distributing centre for practically the whole of North China were before the Russo-Japanese War. ¶I came home late on that ***particular** day.* その当日私はおそく帰宅した. ¶in ***past** days* 以前は ‖ the *day* is ***past*** when ... ...の時代は過ぎた.【類】in the ***past*** few *days.* ¶one's ***post-graduate** days* 大学院時代. ¶in one's ***post(pre)-school** days* 卒業後(学齢前). ¶in postwar (prewar) *days* 戦後(前). ¶in the ***pre-automobile*** (***pre-railway***) *days* 自動車(鉄道)のなかった時分は. ¶in ***pre-Meiji** days* 明治以前. ¶on a ***pouring wet** day* どしゃ降りの雨天に. ¶[up] to the ***present** day* 今日まで ‖ In France at the ***present** day,* the average number of children per marriage is less than two. 現今フランスでは一夫婦の子供平均数は二人以下だ. ‖ the younger people of the ***present*** *day* 現今の青年. ¶some time during the ***previous** day* 前日の何時か. ¶since the ***primeval** days* of humanity 人類の原始時代この方. ¶the ***proper** day* for ... に適当の日. ¶one ***propitious** day* 運よくある日のこと. ¶a ***proud** day* for the British Empire 大英国得意の日. ¶a ***proud*** and ***happy*** *day* for ... ...にとって晴れの楽しい日. ¶a ***quiet*** *day* of rest and devotion 平穏な休息と礼拝の日. ¶shut up on a ***rainy** day* in a lonely house 雨天の日に寂しい家に閉じこもって ‖ save money against a ***rainy** day* まさかの時の用意に貯金する. ¶of ***recent** days* 近代の. ¶a ***regular** day* for payment 決った支払日. ¶Sunday is a ***religious** day.* 日曜は神聖な日だ. ¶a ***sad** day* 悲しい日. ¶it is not to be named in (=on) the ***same** day* with ... それは...とは同日に談じられない. ¶every ***second*** (***third, fourth***) *day* 隔日(二日おき, 三日おき)に. ¶the ***selfsame** day* 同じ日. ¶***Sending-in** Day* at the Royal Academy 王立美術院の搬入日. ¶it is ***several** days* since ... 数日経ってから... ¶***Shakespeare's** day* シェイクスピア記念日. ¶I have one ***short** day* for Kyoto. 京都にはわずか一日しかいられない. ¶on a ***single** day,* in September 九月のある一日に. ¶***six*** *days* of the week [日曜を除き]一週六日. ¶***some** day* in the near future 近き将来にいつか. ¶at ***some future** day* 今後いつか. ☞一般に some day は未来 one day は過去に用いる. ¶Now I come to think of it, tomorrow is Sunday; let's go ***some other** day.* そうだ, あすは日曜だ; 別の日に行こう. ¶Even in those ***spacious** days* livings were not so easy to pick up. こういうのんきな時代でも生活は楽でなかった. ¶on a ***specified** day* 指定の日に. ¶on a ***still*** *day* 静かな日に. ¶in the ***stirring** days* of the Klondike rush クロンダイクの黄金狂時代に. ¶on a ***stormy** day* 風雨の日に. ¶He passed his ***strenuous collegiate** days* in a university. 彼はある大学で奮闘的学生時代を過した. ¶on two ***successive** days* 二日続いて. ¶on ***such*** and ***such*** a *day* かくかくの日に ‖ in ***such*** a *day* as ours 今日のような時代には. ¶It is a ***sultry*** (=***scorching***) *day.* 暑い日だ. ¶on a ***summer's** day* 夏の日に. ¶one of ***these** days* 近い中に.【類】I will call on you one of ***these** days.* ‖ in ***these** days* of high price 物価騰貴の今日 ‖ in ***these** days* of rapid fortune-making この成金時代に.【類】in ***these*** *days* of specialization (専門万能) / In ***these** days* of publicity (宣伝) it becomes more and more difficult to keep a secret. / in ***these** days* of television, talkie films, and aeroplanes / in ***these** days* of vast commercial transaction between one country and another / in ***these** days* of rapid transit and communication / Journalists in ***these*** *days* are mostly young men. ‖ "The true university in ***these** days,*" says Carlyle, "is a collection of books." 「現代における真の大学は図書の集積なり」とカーライルはいっている. ¶in ***these degenerate** days* この澆季(ぎょうき)の世に. ¶in ***these hasty** days* このテンポの早い時代に. ¶in ***these modern** days* 今の世に. ¶I think of returning on the ***third** day* from today. 私は今日から三日目に帰ろうと思う. ¶within ***thirty** days* after the treaty is effective 条約発効後三十日以内に. ¶***this** day* last year 去年の今日 ‖ At ***this** day* the company has a capital of many millions. 今日では会社に数百万の資本金がある. ‖ even to ***this very*** *day* 今日が今日まで. ¶He was an idol of mine in ***those*** *days.* 彼はそのころ私の崇拝した人物であった.【類】Business was good in ***those** days.* / college students of ***those*** *days* / The people had very little to say in ***those** days.* ‖ in ***those** days* as in these 今も昔も ‖ in ***those** days* of non-telegraphy 電信のなかった時代に. ¶in ***those good*** ***old** days* なつかしいそのころは. ¶an ***unlucky** day* 縁起の悪い日. ¶on the ***very** day* that ... ...したその日に ‖ that was the ***very** day* when ... その日こそ...した日だった ‖ until this ***very** day* 今だに. ¶a ***visitors'** day* 面会日. ¶in the evening of their ***well-spent** days* りっぱに一生を送ってきた晩年に. ¶the ***wet** days* of early summer 初夏のつゆ時. ¶***What** day* is this? 今日は何曜日か. ☞What date ...? は「何日...」に当る. ¶I spent the ***whole** day* in my study. 終日書斎にいた. ¶on a ***winter's*** (=***winter***) *day* 冬のある日に. ¶in my ***young** days* 僕の若いころに.【類】in my ***younger** days.* ¶He spent his ***youthful** days* abroad. 彼は青年時代を海外で送った.

Q² ***Arbor** Day* [合衆国のある州で]春季の祭日, [他の州で]植樹日. ¶***Armed Forces** Day* 《米》三軍記念日. ¶The Two Minutes Silence was observed officially on ***Armistice*** ***Day.*** 休戦記念日には二分間の黙とうが行われた. ¶***Army*** (***Navy, Air***) *Day* 陸(海, 空)軍記念日. ¶***ascension** day*= Holy Thursday キリスト昇天節(キリスト復活祭後四十日目). ¶This is my ***at-home** day.* きょうは私の応接日です. ¶a warm, "muggy" ***August** day* 暑いむしむしする八月の日. ¶a fine ***autumn** day* 晴れた秋の日. ¶a ***baking** day* 家庭のパン焼日. ¶a ***beach** day* しお干狩. ¶a ***bill** day* 米連邦議会の議案提出日. ¶a ***boat** day* 出帆船のある日. ¶***Be-Kind-to-Animals*** *Day* 動物愛護の日. ¶in one's ***boyhood*** [*days*] 幼少のころ. ¶one broiling ***August** day* 暑い八月のある日. ¶each ***business** day* 休日を除き ‖ almost every moment of the ***business** day* 営業時間中ほとんど引切りなしに ‖ as the ***business** day* closes 営業時間が終ると. ¶pass one's ***childhood** days* in the country 幼時をいなかで送る. ¶on ***Christmas** Day* クリスマスの日に. ¶semi-annual ***clean-up** days* 年二回の大掃除. ¶the ***closing** day* of an exhibition 展覧会の終了日 ‖ in the ***closing** days* of the war 戦争の末期には. ¶when one's ***college** days* are over 大学を出ると.【類】during one's ***college** days* / his ***college*** *days* at the University of Chicago ‖ one's ***college*** and ***graduate** days* 大学在学および研究生時代. ¶***commemoration** day* オクスフォード大学記念式. ¶on ***commencement** day* 《米》卒業式に, 学位授与日に. ¶***continuation*** (=***contango***) *day* 決算繰越日. ¶on ***Derby** Day* ダービーの日(英国 Epsom で行われる競馬の開催日)に. ¶***discount** day* 銀行の割引日. ¶on ***dividend** day* 配当金支払日に. ¶the happy ***Eden** days* of the first sweethearts 初恋同志の楽しい天国時代. ¶extend the present ***eight-hour working** day* 現在の八時間労働を延長する ‖ a legal ***eight hours working*** *day* 法定八時間労働日. ¶People are urged to vote on ***Election** Day.* 人民は投票日には棄権しないようにと呼びかけられる. ¶an ***examination** day* [定期]試験日. ¶We have a ***field** day* tomorrow. あしたは運動会がある.【類】Maypole dance (五月祭踊り) at the Annual ***Field** Day* at the Remington Typewriter Works. ¶***Fire Prevention** Day* 防火デー. ¶***fish** day* 肉食禁止日; 断食日 ‖ Friday is a ***fish*** *day* in the Roman Catholic Church. カトリック教では金曜日は断食日である. ¶a ***fog*** (=***foggy***) *day* 霧のかかった日. ¶at some ***future** day* いつか. ¶in those far-off ***Genroku** days* 遠い昔の元禄時代に. ¶that bold warrior of the troublous ***Genpei** days,* Kagekiyo 源平戦乱時代のあの勇敢な武士景清. ¶California's "***gold rush***" *days* of 1849 一八四九年のカリフォルニアの黄金熱時代. ¶***graduation*** *day* 卒業式の日. ¶the ***halcyon** days* of the honeymoon みつ月のなごやかな時期. ¶the ***Harvard Tercentenary*** *Days* ハーバード大学三百年祭. ¶It's a regular ***hay** day.* [飛行日よりなど]ほんとによい日よりだ. ¶This is my ***home-coming** day.* 今日は私の帰省日だ. ¶She was fresh and lovely in her ***honeymoon** days.* 彼女は新婚当時は水々しくかわいらしかった. ¶in the ***horse-and-buggy** days* 馬車時代に. ¶relieve a ***humdrum** day* of insipidness by reading 平凡な退屈な日を読書でまぎらす. ¶the United States ***Independence** Day* 合衆国独立記念日. ¶Tuesday is ***ironing** day* in my home. 火曜日はわが家のアイロンをかける日. ¶It was a perfect ***June** day* in early spring. まだ四月だというのに六月の陽気だった. ¶***Labor** Day* 《米》労働休日 ☞九月第一月曜日, 欧州の May Day に当る. ‖ the institution of a normal ***labor** day* 正常労働時間制度. ¶***lay*** *days* 船積み停泊期間. ¶the ***leave-taking** day* of Congress 《米》議会の終了日. ¶a ***liberty** day* 『海』上陸許可日. ¶in those ***long-ago** days* 久しい以前のそのころに. ¶a ***mail*** *day* 郵便物の出発または到着日(外国郵便などの); 郵便締切日. ¶a *March day* 三月のある日. ¶a *market day* 市日. ¶a *meeting day* 会合日. ¶Decoration Day is correctly called *Memorial Day*. デコレーション・デーはメモリアル・デー(招魂祭)と呼ぶ方が正しい. ¶a *moving day* at the White House 白亜館の引越日(大統領の代交で). ¶a *moving-in day* 引越しの日. ¶a *nomination day* 任命の日; 《米》大統領候補指名日. ¶"*no power day*" 休電日. ¶on grey *November days* どんよりした十一月の日に ‖ on that unforgettable *November day* 忘れられぬその十一月の日に. ¶the *opening day* of ... ...の初日. ¶during the *opening days* of the year 年の初めに. ¶Saturday was *pay day*. 土曜日は給料日だった. ¶a *peak day* 最高度に達した日. ¶in her *petticoat days* まだ肩あげのおりない時代に. ¶in *pioneer days* 初期に. ¶the *pioneering days* of the labor movement 労働運動の初期. ¶on *publishing day* 発行日に. ¶*punctuality day* 正しい時の日. ¶one *red-hot summer day* ある暑い夏の日. ¶a *red-letter day* in the history of ... ...の歴史において記念すべき日. 【類】Yesterday was a *red-letter day* in the annals of educational progress in Hongkong. / That day was a *red-letter day* in our nation's calendar. / Their trips from home were *red-letter days*. / a *red-letter day* in one's life. ¶*Registration Day* [大学入学の]登録日. ¶on the *Sabbath day* 安息日に. ¶on *sailing day* 出帆日に. ¶*salad days* 少壮無経験の時代. ¶a *sale day* at Peter Robinson's ピーター・ロビンソン商会(衣料店)の販売日. ¶a big *sale day* 大売出しの日. ¶learned in their own *school days* 彼らの学校時代に覚えた. ¶in our *school and college days* われわれの学校時代に. ¶We had a tiring, *scrambling day*. われわれは一日山登りで疲れた. ¶*separation day* plus one 除隊翌日. ¶a *show day* [消防員などの出ぞめなど]晴れの日. ¶the *silent days* of the film 無声映画時代. ¶the *six-hour day* 六時間労働制. ¶*speech day* 《英》大学の賞品授与式日, 終業式日. ¶*sports day* 運動会の日. ¶a beautiful *spring day* うららかな春の日. ¶the end of the *Stuart days* スチュアート時代の終結. ¶one's *student days* in Florence フロレンスにおける学生時代. 【類】in my *student days* at Clark University. ¶one's *studying day* 勉強日. ¶there are surely few pleasanter sights on a *summer day* than ... 夏の日には...以上に目を喜ばす光景はほとんどあるまい ‖ a lazy *summer day* ものうい夏の日. 【類】on late *summer days* ‖ sizzling *summer days* 極暑の候. ¶a *sweeping day* 大掃除日. ¶a *tag day* [赤い羽根などを売る]資金募集日. ¶in my *undergraduate days* at Cambridge University ケンブリッジ大学在学当時に. ¶*United Nations Day* 国連記念日. ¶his *university days* 彼の大学時代. ¶*visiting day* at a children's hospital 小児科病院の面会日. ¶about sixteen hours of our *waking day* われわれが目をさましている約 16 時間. ¶patriotic air reminiscent of the *war days* 戦時を想起させる愛国的歌曲. ¶Monday is *wash day*. 月曜は洗たく日. ¶in the *wealth-worshipping day* of the late renaissance 後期文芸復興期の黄金崇拝時代に. ¶on the *wedding day* 婚礼の日に. ¶on *week days* 週日に(日曜を除いて). ¶*What day* [of the week] is it today? 今日は何曜日か. ¶a bleak *winter day* 荒涼たる冬の日 ‖ A cloudy *winter day* is somber. くもった冬の日は陰気だ. ¶*work days*=workdays 仕事日. ¶a *working day* 〘労〙一日の労働時間 ‖ weather *working days* 晴天の日の労働時間 ‖ the length of *working day* 労働時間の長さ ‖ the tendency toward the shorter *working day* 労働時間短縮の傾向. 【類】the fixation of normal *working day*= an eight hour *working day* / lengthen the *working day* from eight to nine hours / a longer (さらに長時の) *working day* / a *working day* of eight / Their *working day* is about seven hours and a half. ¶He weighs around 330 pounds in his *wrestling days*. [角力の]場所中は体重 330 ポンドを上下する.

P The ship will sail *after* five *days*. その船は五日たって出帆する. ¶The sun shines *at day* and the moon shines at night. 太陽は昼輝き月は夜輝く. ‖ draw on ... *at* sixty *days* 六十日後払で...に手形を振出す. ¶*before day* 日の出前に ‖ That was *before* the *days* of telegraphs and cables. それはまだ電信だの海外電信などなかった時分の事です. 【類】*before* the *days* of railways. ¶He is *behind* the *day*. 彼は時代遅れだ. ¶a sleeping car [arranged] *by day* 昼間寝台車 ‖ *by day* and by night 昼夜をわかたず ‖ pay for room *by* the *day* 一日いくらでへや代を払う. 【類】work *by* the *day* ‖ *by* the 30th [*day*] of March 三月三十日までに. ¶*during* three *days* 三日の間 ‖ Bats hide themselves *during* the *day*. こうもりは昼間は隠れている. ¶He comes here *for* the *day*. 彼はその日だけ(当日限り)ここに来る. ‖ When do you stop work *for* the *day*? 一日の仕事はいつに仕舞にするのか. ‖ My work is over *for* the *day*. 今日は僕の仕事は済んだ. ‖ Tomorrow my mother and I are going to the beach *for* the *day*. あした私と母と海岸に遊びに行く. ‖ *for* the last ten *days* 過去十日間 ‖ *for* many a long *day* 長らくの間 ‖ *for* many a *day* to come この先き長く ‖ *for* several *days* back (ahead) 数日前から(ここ数日は) ‖ *for* several *days* together 幾日も続いて ‖ *for* ten *days* running 引続き十日間 ‖ *for* a whole *day* 終日. 【類】*for* three whole *days*. ¶*from day* to day 日々 ‖ *from* ancient *days* 昔から ‖ *from* the *day* of its promulgation その公布の日から ‖ I take thee for my lawful wife, to have and to hold, *from* this *day* forward, for better, for worse, for richer, for poorer, in sickness and in health, until death do us part. 今日以後御身を正妻と定める, よかれ悪しかれ, 貧富にかかりなく, 病める時も健かなる時も, 死がわれらを分かつまで(結婚式の誓詞). ¶Rome was not built *in* a *day*. ローマは一日で建設されたのでない. ‖ *in* ten *days* 十日で ‖ It will decide *in* a *day* or two. それは一両日中に決定する. ‖ The nightingale sings both by night and *in* the *day*. ナイティンゲールは昼夜ともに鳴く. ‖ twice *in* the *day*=twice a day ‖ later *in* the *day* その日もっと遅れて ‖ She was really lovely *in* her *day*. 若いころはほんとにきれいだった. ‖ William Henry's Elements of Experimental Chemistry enjoyed considerable vogue *in* its *day*, going through 11 editions in 30 years. ウイリアム・ヘンリーの「実験化学の基礎」は三十年間に十一版を重ねひところ非常に人気があった. ‖ *in days* not long past 近代に. 【類】*in days* not very far from our own ‖ *in days* gone by 昔は ‖ *in days* of old 昔 ‖ *in* this *day* of scientific pedagogy この科学的教授法の時代に ‖ England *in* the *days* of the stage-coaches and highwaymen 乗合馬車が流行しおいはぎが横行したころの英国 ‖ *in* the *days* when a ship of 4,000 tons was considered enormous 四千トンの船が巨船と思われた時代に. 【類】*in* the *days* of his youth / *in* the *days* of Julius Cæsar (our fathers, his prosperity). ¶on the morning *of* 10th March 三月十日の朝に ‖ and thus concluded the ceremony *of* the *day* かくて当時の式は終った. ¶We gave a couple *of days* to it. その見物に一両日費した ‖ in the course *of* a *day* 一日の中に ‖ in the short space *of* ten *days* わずか十日で ‖ today *of* all *days* 今日に限って ‖ He made the best *of* his younger *days*. 彼は若い時代を大に楽しんだ. ‖ *of* modern *days* 近代の ‖ the greatest poet *of* the *day* 当時の最大詩人. 【類】the great social questions *of* the *day*. ¶*on day* of receipt 受取った日に ‖ available *on day* of issue only [切符など]通用期限当日限り ‖ *on* the *day* of the tragedy その悲劇のあった日に ‖ *on* a bright *day* in early summer 初夏の天気のよい日に ‖ *on* such a *day* こんな日に ‖ *on* the *day* in question 問題になっているその日に ‖ Rain falls *on* 180 *days* in the year. 一年の中百八十日は雨が降る. ‖ It is not to be mentioned *on* the same *day* (=in the same breath) それは同日の談ではない. ¶production *per day* of ten hours 日々十時間の生産高. 【類】production is ... *per day* of 24 hours. ¶*since* the *days* of antiquity 大昔から. 【類】*since* the *days* of her kittenhood (おてんば娘時代). ¶all *through* the *day* 一日中. ¶*till* about ten *days* afterwards その後十日位まで. ¶He resolved to put an end *to* his *days* by committing suicide. 彼は自殺して清算しようと決心した. ‖ It is now five years *to* a *day*. もう丁度五年になる. ‖ down (= up) *to* this *day* 今日に至るまで. ¶It can not be ready *under* ten *days*. 十日以内ではできません. ¶even *unto* this *day* いまだに. ¶*within* three *days* after date or sight 日付後または一覧後三日以内に ‖ The pawn ticket was *within* a few *days* of running out. 質札は二三日中に期限が切れる所だった. ‖ the moon, *within* one *day* of being full 十四日の月. 【類】*within* five or six *days*. ¶*without day* 期日を定めずに(無期限に).

P[2] *Day after* day passed by. 日がどんどんたった. ‖ the *day after* the fair 後の祭り ‖ on the *day after* the second interview 二回目の会見の翌日 ‖ [the] *day* ***after*** tomorrow 明後日. ☞米口語では the を省く ‖ the *day* ***after*** reaching home 帰宅した翌日. ¶some *day* ***at*** no distant date いつか近い中に. ¶[the] *day* ***before*** yesterday 一昨日. ¶*day* ***by*** day 日々. ¶a *day* ***for*** laboring work 労働日 ‖ The *day* ***for*** looking with disrespect upon trade and the man of business is long over. 商業や実業家をさげすんだ時代はとうに過ぎた. ¶a *day* ***in*** June 六月のある日. ¶a *day* ***of*** days 特に大事な日 ‖ the *days* ***of*** the week 一週の七日 ‖ In almost every quarter the *day* ***of*** air transport has dawned. ほとんどあらゆる方面に空輸の時代が開けかかった. ‖ The *day* ***of*** compulsory Greek is already over. ギリシア語を必須課目とした時代はすでに過ぎ去った. 【類】The *day* ***of*** amassing enormous private fortunes (巨大な個人の富を作る) is past. ‖ This is the *day* ***of*** the encyclopedia. 今は百科事典の時代だ. ‖ the *days* ***of*** giants 巨人続出時代 ‖ a *day* ***of*** recreation and amusement 娯楽の時代. 【類】a *day* ***of*** rejoicing and merry-making / the *days* ***of*** our fathers ‖ The *days* ***of*** a new social order are at hand. 社会組織一新の時代は近きにある. ‖ Japan in the *days* ***of*** yore 昔日の日本 ‖ in *days* ***of*** adversity (prosperity) 失意(得意)の時代に. 【類】in the *days* ***of*** grief (joy) / in the *days* ***of*** travel by stage-coaches (駅馬車) / As the forenoon hour of ten strikes the *day* ***of*** the London Police Court (ロンドン簡易裁判所) begins. ‖ the *day* ***of*** the trouble その事件の日.

O *day* about 隔日に. ¶a few *days* after (=later) その二三日後. 【類】We met again three *days* after. ¶*day* in, *day* out 毎日々々. ¶Harrah! the *day* is ours! 万歳, 勝ったぞ.

daybreak, *n.* 夜明け.

P I packed up my clothes overnight and was ready to start ***at daybreak***. よいのうちから衣類を包んで夜明けに出発の用意をしていた. 【類】Wordsworth's lines on Westminster Bridge ***at daybreak*** commencing "Earth has not anything to show more fair," are well known. ¶a little ***before daybreak*** 夜明け少し前に. ¶You must begin ***from daybreak***. 夜明けから始めねばなりません. ¶***since*** *daybreak* 夜が明けてから.

daydream, *n.* 幻想.

V ***spin*** a *daydream* 幻想にふける.

Q a ***fantastic*** *daydream* 狂想. ¶He gave himself to a ***sudden*** *daydream*. 彼は突然もう想にふけった.

daylight, *n.* 日光; 夜明け; 昼間.

V while *daylight* ***remains*** まだ日のある中に.

Q It will now be ***broad*** *daylight* at five o'clock in the morning. 今は朝の五時は真昼のように明るい. ‖ in ***broad*** *daylight* 真昼間. 【類】When I awoke, it was ***broad*** *daylight*. ¶in ***full*** *daylight* 真昼間. ¶in ***open*** *daylight* 白昼.

P ***at*** *daylight* 夜明けに. ¶***before*** *daylight* on the 7th 七日の夜明け前に. ¶see it ***by*** *daylight* 日光でそれを見る. 【類】***By*** *daylight* it looks more attractive. ¶Do it ***in*** *daylight*. 昼間それをおやり. ‖ robbery carried on (=committed) ***in*** full *daylight* 白昼の強奪. ¶***until*** *daylight* 夜明けまでに.

daytime, *n.* 昼間.

P ***at*** (=***in*** the) *daytime* 日中. ¶***during*** the *daytime* 日中は.

dazzle, *v.* まぶしくする.

P He was *dazzled* ***by*** the spangles on her costume. 彼女の舞台衣しょうのスパンゴールが彼にはまばゆかった.

dazzling, *a.* きらきらする.

P The sunlight was *dazzling* ***on*** those plains of snow. 日光がいくつかの雪原の上にキラキラ輝いていた. ‖ *dazzling* ***with*** electric lights 電燈できらきらして.

dead, *n.* 死人たち; 最中.

V ***bury*** the *dead* 死人を葬る. ¶History ***makes*** the *dead* living and the past present. 歴史は死者を生けるがごとくし過去を現在のごとくする. ¶***raise*** the *dead* [to life] 死者をよみがえらせる. 【類】The *dead* were ***raised*** to life.

Q the ***great*** *dead* 死せる偉人. ¶these ***honored*** *dead* これらの名誉ある死者. ¶the tombs of the ***Imperial*** *dead* 御陵. ¶The ***known*** *dead* are ... [惨事などで]死者の中知名の士は... ¶one of Poland's ***living*** *dead* 人間らしい生活をしていないポーランド人中の一人. ¶the ***newly*** *dead* 新仏. ¶on the soil enriched with the blood of the ***patriotic*** *dead* 愛国の血を流した土地に.

Q² the ***Cornell*** *dead* [戦地での]コーネル大学出身の死者 ¶all of its ***university*** *dead* その国の大学出身者の戦死者全部. ¶370,000 ***war*** *dead* 三十七万人の戦死者 ‖ families of ***war*** *dead* 戦死者の遺族たち ‖ honor the nation's ***war dead*** 国民の戦死者に栄誉を与える. 【類】The city honored its ***war*** *dead*. / the return of American ***war*** *dead* from abroad for burial in that country. ¶the City's ***World II*** *dead* 第二次大戦におけるその市の死者.

P ***at*** *dead* of night 深更に. ¶We mourned ***for*** the *dead*. われわれは死者に哀悼をささげた. ‖ He was given up ***for*** *dead*. 彼は死んだものとしてあきらめられた. 【類】They left him ***for*** *dead* on the battlefield. / He was taken ***for*** *dead*. ¶Her voice sounded like a voice ***from*** the *dead*. 彼女の声はあの世からの声のように響いた. ‖ He has risen ***from*** the *dead*. 彼はよみがえった. ‖ ***in*** the *dead* of night=in the dead hours of the night 真夜中に ‖ ***in*** the *dead* of winter 厳冬に. ¶Speak well ***of*** the *dead*. 故人はほめよ.

dead, *a.* 死んだ, 枯れた; 感じのない; 正確な, 完全な.

M He was ***almost*** (=***all but***) *dead*. 彼はほとんど死んでいた. ¶He is ***as good as*** dead. 彼は死人も同然だ. ¶be ***half*** *dead* with fear (hunger) こわいの(飢え)で死にそうだ. ¶He has now been *dead* ***many years***. 彼はもう余程前に死んだ. ¶be ***nearly*** *dead* from thirst のどがかわいて死にそうになる. ¶That tree is ***quite*** *dead*. あの木は枯れてしまった.

P He is *dead* ***from*** starvation. 彼は餓死した. ¶He is *dead* ***in*** love with her. 彼は彼女にぞっこんほれている. ¶He is *dead* ***of*** a disease (fever). 彼は病気(など)で死んだ. ¶He is *dead* ***on*** the bird (=a dead shot). 彼は鳥撃ちの名人だ. ¶He is *dead* ***to*** all morality. 彼は徳義心はゼロだ. ‖ He is *dead* (=indifferent) ***to*** all sense of honor. 彼は全然体面ということを構わない. 【類】He is *dead* ***to*** all sense of shame. ¶He is *dead* ***upon*** (=sure to notice) any mistake. 彼はどんな間違いにも気がつく. ¶He is *dead* (=insensible) ***with*** palsy (cold, fatigue, hunger). 彼はしびれ(など)で感覚がない. ‖ He is *dead* ***with*** sleep. 彼はぐっすり眠っている.

deadline, *n.* 死線; [新聞・雑誌の]締切時間; 最終限界.

V ***set*** the *deadline* 締切期間を定める.

Q² an ***age*** *deadline* 年齢の制限. ¶the ***April 1*** *deadline* 四月一日の締切. ¶the ***evacuation*** *deadline* 撤兵期限. ¶the ***strike*** *deadline* ストの予告期限. ¶the ***5 P.M.*** *deadline* 午後五時締切.

P ***By*** "*deadline*" on Wednesday, June 30, the total reached ... 六月卅日水曜日に締切って総額…に達した.

deadlock, *n.* 行詰り, 停とん.

V There were many attempts to ***break*** the *deadlock*. 行詰りを打開するため色々試みられた. ¶***bring*** a *deadlock* to an end 行詰った局面を打開する. ¶A *deadlock* ***resulted***. 進退ここにきわまるということになった. ¶***resolve*** the *deadlock* which persisted between ... …の間で動かない行詰りを打開する.

P bolshevism ***at*** a *deadlock* 行詰った過激主義. 【類】The employers and the strikers are ***at*** a *deadlock*. ¶come ***to*** a *deadlock* 行詰る.

deadly, *a.* 致命的な.

P The shock was *deadly* ***to*** him. その衝撃は彼にとって致命的だった.

deadweight, *n.* 重荷; 死重.

V It is the fault of most existing encyclopedias that they ***carry*** an immense *deadweight* of obsolete and antiquated matter. 現存百科辞典の欠点は大抵不用で陳腐なことを満載していることだ.

P² the *deadweight* ***of*** a goods waggon 貨車の死重.

deaf, *a.* つんぼの.

M He is ***as*** *deaf* as a post (=door, stone, door-post, *or* door-nail). 彼は全然耳が聞えない. ¶He is ***exceedingly*** (=***very***) *deaf*. 彼は非常に耳が遠い.

P He is *deaf* ***of*** (=***in***) one ear. 彼は片耳聞えない. ¶He is *deaf* ***to*** his mother's remonstrances (advice, entreaties). 彼は母の訓戒(など)を聞流しにする. ‖ He was *deaf* ***to*** all requests for money. 彼は金銭上のすべての要求に耳をかさなかった. 【類】He is *deaf* ***to*** all argument (reason, the voice of humanity). / The king was *deaf* ***to*** all appeals from his people.

deafen, *v.* つんぼにする.

P The cataract *deafened* the ear ***with*** its roar. 滝の音で耳が聞えなくなった.

deal, *n.* 取引; 随分; [カルタなど]一番.

V ***do*** a *deal* with ... …と一回取引をする. ¶***have*** a *deal* with him in sugar 彼と砂糖の取引をする. ¶***make*** a great *deal* of ... …を大事にする. ¶We ***played*** four *deals*. 僕た

ちはカルタを四番やった.

Q a ***fair deal*** 公正な取引. ☞ the Fair Deal はトルーマンの「公平政策」. ¶That speaker has come to acquire a ***good deal*** of poise. あの弁士も大分場なれてきた. ‖ attract a ***good deal*** of attention 大いに注意を引く ‖ extract a ***good deal*** of entertainment from ... ...を大層面白がる ‖ give one a ***good deal*** of trouble ...に大層迷惑をかける ‖ the book has a ***good deal*** to say about ... その本には...のことが大分書いてある. ‖ A ***good deal*** more was said than done. 実行は口ほどにいっていなかった. ‖ It rumbles a ***good deal.*** 大分雷が鳴る. ‖ This is saying a ***good*** deal. これは大いに意味のあることだ. ‖ He has had a ***good deal*** of publicity by it. それであの人の名が大分広まった. ‖ there was a ***good deal*** of argument on the subject of ... ...の問題については大分議論があった ‖ just at present there seems to be a ***good deal*** of talk about ... 目下...についてはかなり色色のうわさがあるらしい.【類】there has been a ***good deal*** of talk about ... ‖ supply a person with a ***good deal*** of new information ...に多くの新情報を提供する. ¶attract a ***great deal*** of notice 大いに注目を引く ‖ do a ***great deal*** of damage 大損害をおよぼす ‖ expect a ***great deal*** from ... 大いに...に期待する ‖ We are having a ***great deal*** of sickness. 大分病人が多い. ‖ make a ***great deal*** of fuss about ... ...について大騒ぎをする ‖ It means a ***great deal.*** それには大いに意味がある ‖ put forth a ***great deal*** of effort 大いに努力する ‖ I have travelled a ***great deal*** of Europe. 僕は欧州を随分旅行した. ‖ take a ***great deal*** of exercise 大いに運動する ‖ He has seen a ***great deal*** of the world. 彼は世なれている. ‖ It snowed (thundered) a ***great deal.*** 大層雪が降った(雷が鳴った). ‖ there is a ***great deal*** said about ... ...については大いに議論がある ‖ There was a ***great deal*** of shouting and clapping of hands. 大へんな拍手かっさいであった. ‖ I am afraid I'm putting you to a ***great deal*** of trouble. 君に大分迷惑をかけてるんじゃないですか. ‖ He has been a ***great deal*** of a poet. 彼は余ほどの詩人であった.【類】He is a ***great deal*** of a politician. ‖ the result of a ***great deal*** of examination 厳重考査の結果 ‖ There is a ***great deal*** of truth in this. この中には多くの真理が含まれている. ¶I can well imagine that the book must have cost its compiler an ***immense deal*** of trouble. この本の編集に多大の勢力を費したことは容易に想像ができる. ¶a ***new deal*** in education 教育の革新. ¶a ***shady deal*** 後ろめたい(やみ)取引. ¶in a ***single deal*** 一取引に. ¶You may save a ***vast deal*** of your trouble. 君の手数が非常に省けるだろう. ‖ expend a ***vast deal*** of ingenuity in the fruitless attempt to prove that ... ...を証明するための無益な試みにばく大の工夫をこらす.

Q² a ***barter deal*** 物々交換. ¶give one a straight ***business deal*** ...と公正な商取引をする. ¶***Government-to-Government deals*** 政府間の折衝. ¶***grain futures deals*** 穀物先物取引.

P He is cleverer than you ***by*** a great ***deal.*** 彼は君よりは余ほど利口だ.【類】It exceeded my estimate ***by*** a great ***deal.*** ¶One story is that he lost 75,000 dollars ***in*** one ***deal.*** 一説には彼は一取引に七万五千ドルの損をしたそうだ. ¶***with*** a good ***deal*** of difficulty and danger 多大の困難や危険と闘って. ¶It can not be procured ***without*** a great ***deal*** of trouble. それは多大の困難なしには得られない.

P² I have been at a great ***deal of*** trouble. 大分骨を折ってみた. ‖ a great ***deal of*** knowledge (nonsense, skill) たくさんの知識(など) ‖ a ***deal*** (《俗》=great deal) ***of*** money たくさんの金.【類】a ***deal of*** time (trouble). ‖ There's a ***deal of*** class about him. なかなかいいところがある.

deal, *v.* 取扱う；取引する；商う；たずさわる；処置する；振舞う；分配する；密議する.

M the silk-store where I ***always deal*** 私が買付の絹物店. ¶***bluntly deal*** with ... ...をそっけなくする. ¶there is only one point we should like to see more ***completely dealt*** with, and that is ... 一層完全に処理してもらいたい点が一つある, そしてそれは...だ. ¶***deal cruelly*** 残忍に振舞う. ¶***deal cursorily*** with ... かたわら...のことも説く. ¶He was ***deservedly dealt*** with. 彼が罰せられたのは当然だ. ¶The matter must be ***dealt*** with ***dispassionately.*** それは冷静に考えなくてはいけない. ¶***drastically deal*** with those who got great profits out of the war 戦争で大もうけをした人々を手きびしく取扱う. ¶***deal effectively*** with ... ...を有効に取扱う. ¶***deal especially*** with ... ...を別取扱にする. ¶***deal exhaustively*** with the subject その問題を漏れなく説く. ¶to ***deal frankly*** with you あからさまに言えば. ¶***deal fully*** with the subject その問題を十分に説く.【類】I have ***dealt*** with ... more fully than I otherwise should have done, because ... ¶***deal*** quite ***generally*** ごく概括的に取扱う. ¶***deal hardly*** with a person 人につらく当る. ¶***deal honestly*** with all men すべての人に正直にする. ¶***deal honorably*** with ... ...に対してりっぱに振舞う. ¶consider ***how best*** to ***deal*** with the situation 善後策を講じる. ¶***deal indulgently*** 甘やかす. ¶***deal justly*** with ... ...を正しく取扱う ‖ Time can be trusted to ***deal justly*** with errors. 間違っていることは時がたてば必ず矯正される. ¶Mother nature does not ***deal kindly*** with man in the desert. 大自然はさばく中の人を厚遇しない(水の欠乏などがあるので). ¶***deal leniently*** with a person 人を寛大に扱う. ¶***deal minutely*** with ... ...を細説する. ¶***deal out*** (=distribute *or* dispense) 分配する；くばる. ¶The money was ***dealt out*** fairly. 金が公平に分配された. ‖ ***deal out*** justice 法律を執行する. ¶With this question of ... we will ***deal presently.*** ...の問題はすぐ後で説くことにします. ¶***deal promptly*** and ***rapidly*** with ... 迅速に...の始末をつける. ¶***deal realistically*** with his characters (小説家などが)作中の人物を写実的に取扱う. ¶***deal rightly*** with ... ...を公正に処理する. ¶***deal severely*** (=***sternly***) with a person きびしく人を扱う. ¶***deal summarily*** どしどし処分する. ¶***deal tactfully*** with the delicate question その難問題を手ぎわよくさばく. ¶***deal tenderly*** with ... ...を優しく取扱う. ¶I was ***dealt well*** (***ill***) by him. 彼に優(冷)遇された. ¶***deal wisely*** with the situation 事態に善処する.

P ***deal in*** rice (tea, books, furniture) 米(など)を商う ‖ a firm ***dealing in*** hardware 金物を売る店 ‖ ***deal in*** cash 現金で取引をする. ¶***deal*** in some detail ***on*** this point 幾分詳細にこの点を説く. ¶He ***dealt*** a blow to his antagonist. 彼は敵を打った. ¶You should ***deal with*** him more politely. 君はもっと丁重に彼を取扱うべきだ. ‖ Society refuses to ***deal with*** him. 彼は世間から葬られている. ‖ ***deal with*** them in the spirit of justice 正義の精神で彼らに対する ‖ in order that the case may be ***dealt with*** その訴訟事件を処理するために ‖ We have to ***deal with*** no common enemy. 相手は敵として並のものではないのだ. ‖ a hard man to ***deal with*** 扱いにくい人 ‖ Readers are kindly asked to mention the ... when ***dealing with*** our advertisers. 本紙広告者と交渉のさいは...紙御覧のむねお申添下さい. ‖ ***deal with*** it as one thinks fit 善処する.【類】A special bureau ***dealing with*** the affairs of this exhibition has just been organised in the Government at Tokyo. ‖ I ask you to ***deal with*** the matter as you think fit. よろしく頼む. ‖ have a dexterity in ***dealing*** with the affairs of ordinary life 俗務の処理がうまい ‖ ***With*** ... there is no space to ***deal.*** ...をここに書く余白がない.【類】This book ***deals with*** an important subject. / We have no space (余白) to ***deal with*** such details in a book of this scope. / books ***dealing with*** China ‖ ***deal with*** politics 政治を論じる ‖ The literature ***dealing with*** the chrysanthemum is very extensive. 菊の文献は非常に多い. ‖ I had bad luck to ***deal with.*** 私は災難にあった. ‖ He had turbulent passion to ***deal with.*** 彼は激情を抑えて行かねばならなかった. ‖ We ***deal with*** Smith & Co. われわれはスミス商会と取引している.

dealer, *n.* 商人.

V ***beat*** the ***dealer*** down to ... ...に値切る.

Q a ***rapacious dealer*** 暴利をむさぼる商人. ¶a ***sole dealer*** for Japan and China 日・中一手販売人. ¶an ***unscrupulous*** (=***wily***) ***dealer*** ずるい商人.

Q² an ***amateur dealer*** しろうとの商売人. ¶an ***art*** and ***curio dealer*** 美術骨とう品商. ¶a ***fine arts dealer*** 美術商. ¶a ***fish dealer*** 魚屋. ¶a ***horse dealer*** 馬商. ¶an ***ice dealer*** 氷商. ¶a ***junk dealer*** 古道具屋. ¶the international machinations of the ***munitions dealers*** 軍需品業者の国際的陰謀. ¶giant ***picture dealers*** of Europe 欧州の大画商たち. ¶a ***real estate dealer*** 不動産売買業者. ¶a ***retail*** (***wholesale***) ***dealer*** in rice 米の小売(卸し)商. ¶a ***scrap dealer*** くず物商. ¶a ***slave dealer*** どれい商人. ¶a ***street dealer*** 露天商人.

P² a ***dealer in*** antiques (fish, fruit, fuel and charcoal, old clothes, piece-goods, provisions, second-hand books)

骨とう(など)商 ‖ a *dealer in* paper-making materials 製紙原料商. ¶a *dealer of* hot (=stolen) goods 贓品買.

dealing, *n.* 取引, 関係; 取扱い, 処置; 待遇.

V I *had* some *dealings* with him. 彼とは少し関係したことがあった. ‖ They have *had* no *dealings* with pawnbrokers. 質屋ののれんをくぐったことがない. ¶We've *stopped dealing* at that store; the prices are too high. その店で買うのをやめた; 値段が高過ぎる.

Q *commercial dealings* 商業上の取引. ¶*double dealings* 裏表のあるやり方. ¶the firm has *extensive dealings* with ... その店は…と手広く取引をしている. ¶The firm has a character for *fair dealing* towards travellers. あの店は得意回りをよく待遇するという評判がある. 【類】the sense of *fair dealing*. ¶*fictitious dealings* on a stock exchange 株式取引所の空取引. ¶*oblique dealings* 不正な処置. ¶*regular dealings* 常取引. ¶*occasional dealings* 折々の取引. ¶merchants notorious for their *slippery dealing* ずるいので有名な商人たち ‖ I gather that you mean to task me with *slippery dealing*. 私がずるい事をやったと言う訳だね. ¶practice truth and *square dealing* 誠実且つ公正にふるまう. ¶*underhand dealings* 陰険なやり方. ¶The soul of commerce is *upright dealing*. 正直な取引は商業の道である.

Q² *business dealings* 商取引. ¶condone *blackmarket dealings* やみ取引を大目に見る. ¶*day-to-day dealings* 日日の取引. ¶*hand-to-mouth dealings* 一時しのぎの取引.

P He is ruthless *in* his *dealings* with the strong. 彼の強者に対する仕打は無慈悲である. ¶*through* honest *dealing* 正直な処置によって.

P² honorable *dealing among* people 人前で正々堂々の処置. ¶There is only small *dealing in* the Chinese rice. 南京米の取引はほんのわずかだ. ‖ make a living by *dealing in* girls 女の周旋で生計を立てる. ¶*dealings with* a person 人との交渉 ‖ extensive *dealings with* all the world 世界を相手の手広い取引.

dealt, *v.* deal を見よ.

dean, *n.* 古参, 主事; 学部長.

P² the *dean* (=doyen) *of* the diplomatic corps 外交団の古参 ‖ a *dean of* students 学生主事 ‖ the *dean of* a faculty [大学の]学部長.

dear, *a., adv.* 親愛なる, 大切な; 高価な; 高価に.

M It is *absurdly dear*. それは滅法高い. ¶It is *exorbitantly dear*. ばかに高い. ¶It is *fearfully dear*. 恐ろしく高い. ¶That seems *rather dear*. 少し高いようだ. ¶It is *too dear* for my purpose. 高過ぎて都合が悪い. ‖ I bought it much *too dear*. 私は大分買いかぶった.

P I think it would be *dear at* 20 yen. 二十円では高いと思う. ¶a man *dear to* all 万人の親愛する人 ‖ Rogues have always been *dear to* romance. 無頼漢は物語によく取扱われる. ‖ April 14th is a day *dear to* every Spanish patriot. 四月十四日はスペインのすべての愛国者にとり貴重な日だ. ‖ a book *dearest to* his inner life 彼の精神生活にとって最も貴重な本 ‖ Honor is *dearer to* him than life. 彼は名誉を命より重く見る. 【類】Nothing is *dearer to* me than the remembrance of my old school days. / *dear to* the hearts of Japanese from traditions (伝統).

dearth, *n.* 欠乏, 払底.

Q a *great dearth* of bottoms 船腹の大不足. ¶there is a *lamentable dearth* of ... …が不足しているのは残念なことである. ¶There is a *sad dearth* of masculine thinkers. 男性的思想家の欠乏は嘆かわしい.

P *in* the *dearth* of ... …が欠乏しているので.

P² a *dearth of* corn 穀物の払底 ‖ the *dearth of* contemporary English poetry 現代英詩の貧困 ‖ The *dearth of* housing poses a serious social problem. 家屋の払底は重大な社会問題を提供する.

death, *n.* 死.

V *accept death* with fatalistic resignation なにごとも運命とあきらめて死ぬ. 【類】*accept death* with perfect equanimity (自若として) / Religious fanatics willingly *accept* a *death* which secures their entrance into paradise. ¶the *death* is *announced* of ... …氏の死が報ぜられた. 【類】we regret to *announce* the *death* of Mr. ... ¶*avenge* (=revenge) one's father's *death* 父のあだを取る. 【類】*avenge* the *death* of a master. ¶His aged mother was left to *bemoan* his *death*. 老母が後に残されて彼の死をなげいた. ¶It will *bring* him sure *death*. そうすると彼はきっと死ぬ. 【類】The disaster *brought* many *deaths*. ¶You must change your clothes, or you'll *catch* your *death* of cold. 服を着かえないとかぜで命を取られるぞ. ¶The earthquake *caused* the *death* of ... persons. 地震が…名の死者を出した. ‖ This *caused* his *death*. 彼はこれが原因で死んだ. 【類】The eruption has *caused* fifteen thousand *deaths*. / *cause death* and disaster to thousands of human beings. ¶*challenge death* 死をものともしない. ¶*choose death* before dishonor 生きてはずかしめを受けるよりはむしろ死んだ方がよいと思う. ¶It is a great regret to have to *chronicle* the *death* of ... …氏の死去をここに(新聞などに)報道することはまことに遺憾なことである. ¶*compass* his *death* 彼を殺そうと図る. ¶To ... is simply to *court death*. …するのは好んで死を求めることになる. ¶*cut deaths* in half 死亡数を半減する. ¶*deplore* the *death* of ... …の死をいたむ. ¶*die* the *death* of a dog みじめな死に方する ‖ Let us *die* the *death* of the righteous. 正義の士として死にたい. 【類】*die* a hero's *death*. ¶The martyr *encountered death* with joy. 殉教者は喜んで死についた. ¶It *entails* (=involves) spiritual *death*. そうすると魂が死ぬことになる. ¶barely (=narrowly) *escape death* 命拾いをする ‖ *escape death* by a miracle 奇跡的に命が助かる. ¶*face death* with a smile かんじとして死に向う ‖ directly *face death* 死に直面する. 【類】*face death* without fear / He would *face death* rather than ridicule (ばかにされるくらいなら). ¶He *feigned death*. 死んだ振りをした. ¶the fiftieth day *following* the *death* of ... …の五十日忌. ¶*greet death* with laughter 笑って死につく. ¶*hasten* one's *death* 死期を早める. ¶He *had* a *death* in his family. 彼の家族に不幸があった. ¶Churchyard cough *heralds death*. からせきは死の前兆である. ¶*inflict death* on ... …を殺すまた死刑に処する. ¶She constantly *invoked death* for her relief and deliverance. 彼女は自己救済の道として絶えず死を祈った. ‖ *invoke death* on her 彼女の死を祈る. ¶the fatal accident *involving* 200 *deaths* 二百の死者を出したあの大事件 ‖ *involve* (=mean) almost certain *death* ほとんど必ず死ぬ. ¶deeply *lament* the *death* of ... …の死を痛惜する. 【類】His *death* was universally *lamented*. / We *lament* his *death* and extend our sympathy to his bereaved family (遺族). ¶*look* the *death* in the eye 死線を越える(死に直面する) ‖ *look death* calmly in the face 落着いて死に直面する. ¶even though his action may *mean death* to himself よしんば彼はその行動のために死ぬようなことがあっても. 【類】The cell does not act, it reacts; the total absence of stimuli would *mean* physiological *death*. ¶How did he *meet* his *death*? 彼はどうして死んだのか. ‖ He *met* his *death* with serene composure. 彼は自若として死についた. 【類】He *met death* bravely. / calmly *meet death* / He *met* his *death* out hunting (猟に出て). ‖ She *met death* with her husband. 彼女は夫と死をともにした. ‖ He *met* his *death* in a tragic manner. 彼は悲惨な最後をとげた. ¶*mourn* his *death* 彼の死をいたむ. ¶*occasion death* 死を招来する. ¶*plot* the *death* of ... …を殺そうと図る. ¶*prefer death* to such an alternative そんなことをする位なら死んだ方がよいと思う. 【類】*prefer death* to the ignominy (その恥辱). ¶*quicken death* 死期を早める. ¶Happy, too happy, even to *receive death* at so dear a hand. かくも愛する人の手にかかってなら死んでも幸福, いや幸福過ぎる位だ. ¶*record* the *death* of ... …の死を記録に留める. ¶*reduce deaths* from tuberculosis 結核による死亡を減じる. ¶The novelist's *death* was much *regretted* in England. この小説家の死は英国で非常に惜しまれた. ¶he *revenged* his father's *death* upon ... 彼は…に父の復しゅうをした. ¶*seek death* at one's own hand 自殺をはかる. ¶Toads *sham death*. ひきがえるは死んだふりをする. ¶They *suffered death* for their faith. 彼らは信仰に殉じた. 【類】They *suffered death* for their religious opinions. ¶*turn death* into life よみがえらせる. ¶To do so is to *win* instant *death*. そんなことをすれば即死だ.

V² *Death* may *come* at any hour. いつ死ぬか分らない. ¶*Death ensued* on the third day. 三日目に死んだ. ‖ where *death ensues* 死亡の場合は… ¶His *death followed* at less than a year's interval on that of his father. 父が死んでから一年たたずに彼が死んだ. ¶when *death occurs* in a family 家内に不幸のあるとき ‖ in one instance *death occurred* from ... …で死んだ例も一つある. ¶when *death* soon *results* その結果間もなく死んだ場合に. ¶the *death took place* at ... of Prof. ... ...教授は(どこそこ)で死んだ.

Q an *accidental death* 変死. ¶face almost *certain death* ほとんど確実な死に面する. ¶die a *cruel death* 無残な死をとげる. ¶a *disgraceful death* 恥ずべき死. ¶die a *dishonorable* (=an *ignominious*) *death* 不名誉な死に方をする. ¶die an *early death* 早死する. ¶the horrors of *gradual death* by starvation 飢餓のために刻一刻死を待つ恐ろしさ. ¶A *great many deaths* have taken place here lately. 当地には近ごろ死ぬ人がたくさんあった. ¶hold on to it like *grim death* 気味の悪い死神のようにそれをしかとつかむ. ¶die a *hard death* 苦しんで死ぬ. ¶die a *holy death* 神聖な死に方をする. ¶the danger of *imminent death* さし迫る死の危険 ‖ be faced with *imminent death* 死に直面する. ¶an *inglorious death* 見苦しい死に方. ¶the insect bite is said to cause *instantaneous death*. その虫にかまれると即死するそうだ. ¶the *lamentable death* of... occurred just as ... 丁度...の時...の死が伝えられた. ¶He was left to a *lingering death*. 彼は長い病気で死を待つ身であった. ¶School hours are emotionally a *living death*. 授業時間は感じから殺風景きわまるものだ. ¶die a *martyr's death* 殉死する. ¶*mental death* 精神上の死. ¶a *miserable death* 惨死. ¶a *mysterious death* 得体の知れない死. ¶die a *natural death* 定命で死ぬ ‖ The opposition movement has died a *natural death*. 反対運動は自然消滅した. ¶die a *peaceful death* 大往生を遂げる. ¶*physical death* 肉体の死. ¶sadly *premature death* 悲しむべきよう折. ¶die a *shameful death* 見苦しい死に方をする. ¶a *speedy death* 急激の死. ¶his tragically *sudden death* 彼の悲惨な急死 ‖ the *sudden death* through the accidental taking of poison まちがって毒物を飲んだための急死. 【類】His *death* was awfully *sudden*. ¶his *sudden* and *early death* 彼の突然の早死. ¶plunge to *sure death* 死ぬと分っていて突込む. ¶a *suspicious death* 怪死. ¶He met a *terrible death*. 彼は恐ろしい死に方をした. 【類】suffered a *terrible death* as martyr for his acceptance of the teaching of ... ¶his *tragic death* from an overdose of prussic acid 過度の青酸服薬による彼の悲惨な死. ¶His *death* is still *unexplained*. 彼の死因はまだ不明だ. ¶a person who has died an *unnatural death* 変死者. ¶Its completion was arrested by his *untimely death*. 彼が時ならず死んだのでその仕事は完成しなかった. 【類】He met with an *untimely death*. ¶He met with a *violent death*. 彼は変死した. 【類】They met *violent death*. / He died a *violent death*.

P It is not till *after* one's *death* that one's just worth becomes assured. 棺を覆うて事定まる. ¶his age *at death* 彼が死んだときの年齢(行年) ‖ It was the nucleus of the great fortune he left *at* his *death*. それは彼が死後にのこした大財産のもとであった. ‖ He was loved in life and regretted *at* his *death*. 彼は生存中は愛され死に際しては惜しまれた. ¶She was orphaned *by* the *death* of her sole remaining parent. 残る片親が死んだので彼女は孤児の身となった. ‖ *By* the *death* of ..., the world has lost a brilliant poet. ...の死によって世界は一大詩人を失った. 【類】*By* the *death* of George Henry, the boys of England lost one of the best friends they ever had. / *By* the *death* of ... the commercial world has lost one of its prominent figures. ¶His debauchery ended *in* [his] *death*. 彼は放とう三まいの結果とうとう死んでしまった. ‖ His drunkenness resulted *in death*. 彼の酒びたりは結局死を招くことになった. ‖ *in* the *death* of ... the society loses a distinguished member. ...の死は社会から一人の名士を失うことだ. ¶She was *near* her *death*. 彼女は死期に近づいていた. ¶We found him in the agonies *of death*. われわれが行ったとき彼は死の苦もんに落入っていた. ‖ He lay upon his bed *of death*. 彼は死の床に横たわっていた. ‖ He lay at the point *of death*. 彼は丁度息を引取る所だった. ‖ He was in danger *of death* at any time. 彼は今にも命を取られそうだった. ‖ to the day *of* my *death* 私の死ぬ日まで ‖ in the hour *of* his *death* 彼の死にぎわに ‖ He was within an hour *of* his *death*. 彼の命はもう一時間はもたないと思われた. ‖ He was snatched from the jaws *of death*. 彼は死ぬ所を救われた. ‖ On March 14, 1883, the news *of* Karl Marx's *death* flashed around the world. 一八八三年三月十四日にカール・マルクスの死がは世界中にぱっと伝わった. ‖ I was shocked to hear *of* his *death*. 死んだと聞いてびっくりした. ‖ a certificate *of death* 死亡証明書. ¶John succeeded him *on* his *death* in 1866. 一八六六年彼が死ぬとやジョンがその後を継いだ. ¶mourn *over* one's *death* 人の死を哀悼する. ¶He lost his father (beloved wife) *through death*. 彼は父(など)に死別した. ¶He lived *till* the king's *death*. 彼は王の崩御されるまで生きていた. ¶from birth *to death*. 一生涯 ‖ He was faithful *to death*. 彼は死ぬまで忠実であった. ‖ He was beaten (kicked, crushed, shot, squeezed, frozen, bled, burned, trampled, tormented, frightened) *to death*. 彼は打たれて(など)死んだ. ‖ He was condemned *to death*. 彼は死刑を宣告された. ‖ He was tired (tickled, worried) *to death*. 彼は疲れて(など)死にそうであった. ‖ He drank himself *to death*. 彼は泥酔のあげく死んだ. 【類】He grieved himself *to death*. ‖ He bores me *to death*. やつとの話は実に退屈でたまらない. ‖ He was put *to death*. 彼は殺された. 【類】He was put *to* a painless *death* by a poisonous gas. ‖ They defended the fortress *to* the *death*. 彼らは命のあらん限り城を守った(死守した). 【類】He was determined to fight *to* the *death*. ‖ a war *to* the *death* 死にもの狂いの戦い. ¶She remained a widow *until death*. 彼女は死ぬまで後家を立て通した. ¶devotion even *unto death* 死も惜しまぬ傾倒. ¶a crime punishable *with death* 死刑に処すべき罪 ‖ His influence ceased *with* his *death*. 彼の勢力はその死とともに消失した.

P² He met his *death at* the hand of an assassin. 彼は刺客の手にかかって死んだ. ‖ his *death at* so young an age 彼の非常な若死 ‖ *death at* 110 百十才での死去. ¶*death by* strangulation or decapitation 絞刑または打首による死 ‖ *death by* burning 焼死 ‖ *death by* starvation (fire, drowning) 餓死(など) ‖ *death by* exposure のたれ死(に) ‖ *death by* one's own hand 自殺 ‖ *death by* hanging (guillotine) 絞刑(など)による死 ‖ his *death by* enteric fever 腸チブスによる彼の死. ¶He suffered *death for* his crimes. 彼は死刑に処せられた. ¶He met his *death from* violent blows inflicted on his head. 彼は頭をひどく打たれて死んだ. ‖ *death from* natural causes [横死に対し]自然の原因による死. 【類】*deaths from* various causes / *death from* cholera (sickness, a snake-bite, tuberculosis, cold, influenza, drowning, famine, hunger, starvation). ¶*death in* early life 早世 ‖ The soldier met his *death in* Algeria. その兵士はアルゼリアで死んだ. ‖ the *death in* the field (=action) 戦死 ‖ There has been a *death in* the family. その家に不幸があった. ¶an announcement was made of the *death of* Mr. ... ...氏の死が報ぜられた. ¶It is *death to* us. それはわれわれにとっては打撃だ. ‖ *Death to* Fascism. ファシズ

death-bed, *n*. 死の床. └ム打倒(を葬れ).

P *at* a *death-bed* 臨終に. ¶*on* his *death-bed* 彼の死にぎわ

death-blow, *n*. 致命的打撃. └に.

V *deal* a *death-blow* to ... ...に致命的打撃を加える. ¶the theory *receieved* its *death-blow* from ... その理論は...から致命的打撃をこうむった.

death-day, *n*. 忌日.

V The *death-day* of the founder is still *kept*. 創立者の忌日は今なお守られている.

death-knell, *n*. 葬いの鐘.

V it *sounds* the *death-knell* of ... それは...の滅亡を意味する. 【類】It *sounded* the *death-knell* of the old system of ... and heralded the birth of the new.

death-rate, *n*. 死亡率.

Q a *high* (*low*) *death-rate*. 高(低)い死亡率.

death-roll, *n*. 死者名簿. ┌くなる.

V It will *increase* the *death-roll*. そうすると死者の数が多

Q A *heavy death-roll* is feared. 死亡者の多数にあがる恐

debacle, *n*. [氷の]決壊; 壊滅. └れがある.

Q² the *Pearl Harbor debacle* 真珠湾軍港の壊滅.

debar, *v*. 拒む, 禁じる.

P *debar* a person *from* entering 人を入れない. 【類】He was *debarred from* doing so. / *debar* a person *from* vot-

debark, *v*. 上陸する. └ing (投票).

P *debark at* ... ...に上陸する.

debate, *n*. 討論, 議論.

V *close* (=*closure*) a *debate* 討論を終結する. ¶In the evening we *had* a *debate*, "That lies may be justifiable." 晩になって「うその正当性」という題で討論をやった. ¶*hold* a *debate* on a subject ある題目について討論する. ¶*open* a *debate* 討論を始める. ¶The topic *provoked* an interesting *debate*. その話題は討論に花を咲かせた.

V² a *debate arose* as to ... ...について議論があった.

Q an *acid debate* 辛らつな討議. ¶a *close debate* 先決討議. ¶a *dreary debate* くだくだしい議論. ¶after a *heated debate* 激論の後. ¶an *inconclusive debate* 結論に達せぬ討論. ¶a *Parliamentary debate* 議会の討論. ¶a *violent debate* arose over a proposal to ... ...の発議に対して激論が起った.

Q² begin *floor debate* on a bill 法案に関して本会議を開始する. ¶a *full-dress debate* 本会議の討議. ¶a *House of Commons debate* 衆議院の討議. ¶an *inter-university debate* 大学対抗討論会. ¶a "*warm-up*" *debate* on the question その問題に関する予備的な討論.

P It is *beyond* (=*without*) *debate*. それは論じるまでもない. ¶*during* a *debate* 討論中. ¶questions yet *in debate* 討議中の問題. ¶Its advisability is still *under debate*. その適否は今なお論議中だ.

P² in the *debate on* ... ...に関する討論で.

debate, *v*. 討論する.

M *hotly debate* 激論する. ¶*debate out* a question 問題を十分討論する. 「ある問題を討議する.

P *debate on* (=*about*) a question (=subject *or* problem)

debater, *n*. 弁論家. 「*er*) *debater* 巧妙な論客.

Q a *powerful debater* 力のある弁論家. ¶a *skilful* (=*clev-*

debauchery, *n*. 放とう.

Q *sexual debauchery* 放とう.

debenture, *n*. 社債.

Q² *savings debenture* 貯蓄社債.

P be invested *in debentures* 社債に投資している.

debilitate, *v*. 弱くする.

P He is *debilitated by* age. 彼は老衰だ. ‖ He is *debilitated by* excesses. 彼は不節制のために体をこわしている.

debility, *n*. 衰弱.

Q cause *general debility* 身体全体が衰弱する.

debit, *n*. 借方.

P £ ... *to* your *debit*; it is all in order and correct ...ポンド貴方の借方ということで少しも間違はありません ‖ What will be the amount *to* my *debit*? 私の借方勘定はいくらになりますか. ‖ This amount has been placed *to* the *debit* of your account. この金額は貴下の勘定の借方に記入しました. 【類】the amount *to* your *debit* is ... / Please pay on demand *to* my *debit*.

debit, *v*. 借方に記入する.

P pay the money, but don't *debit* it *against* ... その金を支払え但しそれを...の借方にしてはならない. ¶*To* whom is it to be *debited*? それをだれの借方に記入すべきか. ¶The bank was not entitled to *debit* the plaintiffs *with* the amount paid on the said cheques. 同銀行は上記の小切手に対する支払金額を原告の借方に記入する権利がなかった.

debouch, *v*. 進出する.

P the troops *debouched into* the fertile fields of ... 軍隊は...のよく野に進出した. 【類】The stream *debouched into* the field (the sea). ¶Kharia lies at the foot of the mountain, where the Euphrates *debouches on to* the plain. カリヤはユーフラテス川が平野に流出する山ろくに位置している.

debris, *n*. 崩壊物.

Q the *hot debris* left by an atomic explosion 原爆の爆発の後に残された高温の崩壊物. ¶*human debris* 人間のくず.

Q² clear away the *war debris* 戦災の崩壊物を片付ける.

P He was buried *beneath* the *debris*. 彼は崩壊物の下敷になった.

debt, *n*. 負債; 恩義.

V *accumulate debts* in the lowest of drinking-dens 最下等な酒場に借金をためる. ¶We must *acknowledge* the *debt* of gratitude under which he has placed us by his valuable invention. 彼の貴重な発明によってわれわれが彼の恩義をこうむったことを認めねばならない. ¶*avoid debt* 負債を避ける. ¶*call up* a *debt* 借金の催促をする. ¶*cancel* a *debt* 借金を棒引きにする. ¶*clear* a *debt* incurred できた負債を支払う. ¶*clear off debts* 借金を払う. ¶*clear up* one's *debt* 負債を清算する. ¶*collect debts* 借金を取立てる. ¶*compound* a *debt* 借金を示談にする. ¶*contract* (=get into *or* incur) *debts* 借金をこしらえる. ¶*discharge* a *debt* 借金を返す ‖ *discharge* one's *debt* of gratitude to the memory of ... ...の霊に感謝の意を表する ¶it is impossible to exaggerate the *debt* which I *owe* to ... 僕が...からこうむっている恩義はいかに誇張しても言い過ぎではない. ¶*extinguish* a *debt* 負債を償却する. ¶I *forgave* him a *debt*. 僕は彼の債務を免除した. ¶It is very humiliating to *get* (=run) *into debt*. 借金をするのは肩身がせまいことだ. ¶I *have debts*. 負債がある. 【類】*Had* he so many *debts*? ‖ He *had* a *debt* to pay. 彼は借金があった. ¶*incur* (=*fall into*) a *debt* 借金をする. ¶*leave debts* behind [one] 借金をのこして死ぬ. ¶*meet* one's *debt* 借金を払う. ¶*owe* a special *debt* of gratitude to ... ...には特別恩義がある. 【類】*owe* a deep *debt* of gratitude to ... ‖ I *owe* him a *debt* of long standing. 彼には古い借金がある. ‖ nor should we have unmentioned here the *debt* we *owe* to ... またこの場合われわれが...に負うている恩義を不言に付すべきではなかろう. ¶*pay* one's *debts* 借金を払う. ¶*pay back* the *debt* 借金を返す. ¶He managed somehow or other to *pay off* his *debts*. 彼はどうかこうか負債を返した. ¶*recover* a *debt* 貸金を返済してもらう. ¶*refund* the *debt* by means of an American loan 対米借款によって負債を償還する. ¶a *debt released* by prescription 時効によって免除された負債. ¶*relinquish* a *debt* 貸金を放棄する. ¶*repay* one's *debts* 借金を返す. ¶*repudiate* the *debts* of one's father 父親の借金を踏み倒す. ¶*run into debt* 借金をこしらえる. ¶*settle* a *debt* 負債を決済する. ¶*sink* (=*wipe out*) a *debt* 負債を消却する. ¶*wipe off* a *debt* 借金を返す. ¶*work out* one's *debt* 働いて返金する

Q an *active debt* 利息付きの借金. ¶a *bad debt* こげついた貸金. ¶*bonded* (=*bond*) *debts* 公・社債. ¶*doubtful debts* 回収の見込がおぼつかない貸金. ¶owe a *heavy debt* to ... in co-operativeness, loyalty, and information 協力, 忠誠, および知識の点で...に負う所が多い. ¶owe an *incalculable debt* to ... ...には数え切れないほどの恩義がある. ¶owe an *inestimable debt* to ... ...には大恩を受けている. ¶a *large debt* 巨額の負債. ¶a *long-standing debt* 古い借金. ¶a *national debt* 国債. ¶an *outstanding debt* ばく大な借金. ¶a *passive debt* 無利息の借金. ¶owe a *permanent debt* of gratitude to ... ...には生涯の大恩がある. ¶the *profoundest debt* of gratitude 深甚な恩義. ¶owe a *real debt* to ... ...には本当にお世話になっている. ¶a *special debt* of gratitude is due to ... ...には特別恩義がある. ¶owe a *thousand debts* of gratitude to ... ...には多大な恩義にあずかっている. ¶I owe him a *vast debt* of gratitude. あの方には大恩がある.

Q² a *judgement debt* 法律上確証ある負債. ¶the repudiation of *war debts* 戦債の支払拒絶.

P He was handicapped *by debt*. 彼は借金で弱っていた. ¶The captain will not be responsible *for* any *debts* contracted by the crew. 船長は乗組員のした借金には一切責任がない. ‖ He was imprisoned *for debt*. 彼は借金が返せないので禁固された. ‖ give security *for* a *debt* 借財に対して抵当を入れる. ¶He is deeply *in debt*. 彼は借金で首が回らない. 【類】one heavily *in debt* / He is over head and ears *in debt*. / He died greatly *in debt*. / He is a little *in debt*. / He is *in debt* to the extent of 10,000 yen. ‖ He is *in debt* to me. 彼は僕に借金がある. ‖ He was involved *in debts*. 彼は借金をこしらえた. ¶be clear *of debt* 借金が全然ない. ¶I am *out of debt*. 僕には借金はない. ‖ *Out of debt*, out of danger. 借金のないのは安全のもと. 【類】I manage to keep *out of debt*. ¶we are *under* a lasting *debt* of gratitude to ... われわれは永久に...に負う所がある. 【類】He is *under* a heavy *debt*.

P² one's *debts of* honor 無抵当(無証文)の借入金.

debtor, *n*. 債務者.

V *prod* reluctant *debtors* 怠慢な債務者を督促する.

Q *insolvent debtors* 支払能力のない債務者.

O He has thus made all the members of the profession his *debtors*. それであるからその職業に従事している人はすべて彼の恩義に浴しているわけだ.

début, *n*. 初舞台.

V She *made* her *début* at a recital in New York. 彼女はニューヨークの独奏会でデビューした. ‖ She *made* her *début* upon the stage. 彼女は初舞台を踏んだ. ‖ a play that is *making* its *début* at a Tokyo theatre 東京のある劇場で初演中の狂言 ‖ He *made* his *début* as a hypnotist. 彼は初めて催眠術で公演に出た.

Q² She made her *film début* in ... 彼女は...で映画の初出演をした. ¶make one's *radio début* 放送に始めて出演する.

¶She will make her ***screen début*** as "Mrs. Wiggs." 彼女はウイッグ夫人として映画の初演をやる. ¶She made her ***stage début*** at the ... Theatre. 彼女は…劇場でお目見えをした. 【類】He made his ***stage début*** in his father's company. ¶She made a ***successful début***. 彼女の初舞台は大当りであった.

P² She made her ***début at*** the ball. 彼女はその舞踏会で初めて社交会に出た. ¶make one's ***début in*** letters 文壇に乗り出す.

decade, *n.* 十カ年.

Q the next ***few*** *decades* 今後の数十年. ¶early in the ***fifth*** *decade* of the present century 現世紀四十年代の始めに. ¶during the ***first*** *decade* of the nineteenth century 十九世紀の最初十年間. ¶in the ***present*** *decade* 現在の十年間に. 【類】in the ***third*** *decade* of the twentieth century.

P ***for*** several *decades* 数十年の間. ¶***in*** the *decade* of the nineties (一八)九〇年より(一八)九九年に至る十年間に.

decadence, *n.* 衰微, 衰退期.

Q show signs of ***mental*** *decadence* 精神衰退の徴候を示す.

P The Latin race is ***in*** its *decadence* ラテン民族は衰退期にある. ¶fall into the extreme ***of*** *decadence* 衰微の極に達する.

P² the *decadence* ***of*** the magazine その雑誌の衰微 ‖ the *decadence* ***of*** that firm その会社の衰微.

decamp, *v.* 逃亡する.

P *decamp* ***for*** ... …へ逃亡する. ¶*decamp* ***to*** ... …へ逐電する. ¶She *decamped* ***with*** a lover. 彼女は恋人と駆落した.

decay, *n.* 衰微, 退廃; 腐敗.

Q causes of ***national*** *decay* 国家衰微の原因. ¶***premature*** *decay* 早過ぎる衰弱.

Q² Bacterial acids are factors in most ***tooth*** *decay*. 細菌の酸が大抵虫歯の原因になる.

P It was preserved ***from*** *decay* by embalming. 香油を塗って腐敗を止(と)めた. ¶The temple has grown beautiful ***in*** its *decay*. 寺は退廃の内に美を見せている. ‖ sink ***in*** *decay* 衰微する. ¶fall ***into*** *decay* 衰微する.

P² *decay* ***of*** morals 道徳の退廃 ‖ the *decay* ***of*** lying 空想力の貧弱化. 【類】a *decay* ***of*** manners.

decease, *n.* 死.

P ***on*** the *decease* of ... …が死ぬと.

decease, *v.* 死亡する.

M of whom the former is ***unhappily*** *deceased* そのうち甲は不幸にして死んだ.

deceased, *n.* 故人.

P to the memory ***of*** the *deceased* 故人をしのんで.

deceit, *n.* 詐欺, ぺてん.

V ***discover*** a *deceit* 詐欺を見破る.

deceive, *v.* だます, 欺く.

M He has ***entirely*** *deceived* us. 彼は完然にわれわれを欺いた.

P you *deceive* yourself ***as to*** ... 君は…を誤解している. ¶be careful that one is not *deceived* ***by*** ... …にだまされないよう気をつける. ¶***In*** this expectation we have been *deceived*. こう考えたのは間違いだった. 【類】How I have been *deceived* ***in*** my hopes! ‖ You are *deceived* ***in*** him. 君は彼を見そこなっている. ¶He *deceived* me ***into*** doing it. 彼は僕をだましてそれをさせた. ¶*deceive* a person ***with*** fair words (=cajole) うまく丸め込む.

decency, *n.* 礼節; 体裁.

V He ***had*** the *decency* to put on his clothes. 彼は体裁が悪いので服を着た. ¶appear in public in any manner that may ***offend*** *decency* 不体裁な姿をして人中に出る.

Q It is a requirement of ***ordinary*** *decency*. そうするのが普通の作法だ. ¶offences against ***public*** *decency* 風俗壊乱.

P ***out of*** *decency* はばかって.

O They are man and wife for *decency's* sake. 彼らは体裁だけの夫婦だ.

decennium, *n.* 十年間.

V ***complete*** the fifth *decennium* of one's life 満五十歳に達する. ¶***enter*** the ninth *decennium* 八十の坂を越す.

deception, *n.* 詐欺.

V ***detect*** the *deception* その詐欺手段を見破る. ¶It will ***heighten*** the *deception*. そうするとだましが一層きく. ¶***practice*** a *deception* on ... …に詐欺を働く. ¶***share*** the *deception* 他同様だまされる. ¶***swallow*** one's *deception* まんまと詐欺にかかる.

Q a ***big*** *deception* 一大詐欺. ¶a ***deliberate*** *deception* 計画詐欺. ¶"There is ***no*** *deception*." 「種も仕掛もありません」[奇術師などの言]. ¶a ***subtle*** *deception* 巧妙な詐欺.

P He is ***under*** a *deception*. 彼はだまされている.

decide, *v.* 決める, 決定する; 解決する; 判決する.

M It has not yet been ***definitely*** *decided*. それはまだはっきり決まらない. 【類】it has not yet been *decided* ***definitely*** whether ... ¶it was ***finally*** *decided* on ... ついに…にきまった. ¶***mentally*** *decide* to ... 心に…することを決する. ¶unless something definite is ***quickly*** *decided* 至急に何とかはっきり決めなければ. ¶before I *decide* ***one way or the other*** いずれともきめない内に. ¶The matter is ***quite*** *decided*. その件はすっかり決まった. ¶It has been ***satisfactorily*** *decided*. それは満足に解決された. ¶now that it has been ***so*** *decided* そうきめた以上は. ¶it was ***unanimously*** *decided* to ... 異議なく…することに決まった. ¶It was ***wisely*** *decided*. その件は解決よろしきを得た.

P *decide* ***about*** the matter その件について決心する. ¶*decide* ***against*** it それを否定する ‖ The court *decided* the case ***against*** the plaintiff. 裁判所は原告に不利な判決をした. 【類】the case ***was decided against*** ... ‖ *decide* ***against*** doing so そうせぬことに決定する. ¶We have not yet *decided* ***as to*** who shall be captain. たれが主将になるかまだきめない. ¶It is impossible to *decide* ***between*** them. いずれとも決し難い. 【類】They had to *decide* ***between*** surrender and starvation. ¶*decide* ***by*** oneself 自分の考えできめる ‖ *decide* ***by*** a ballot (vote, poll, majority) 投票(など)できめる. ¶*decide* ***for*** (=in favor of) doing ... …することに決定する. ¶*decide* ***in*** the affirmative 断行ときめる ‖ The tribunal has *decided* ***in*** our favor. 裁判所はわれわれに有利な判決をくだした. ¶*decide* ***in favor of*** the defendant (plaintiff) 被告(原告)の勝となる. ¶*decide* ***on*** names for the principal characters of story 小説の主要人物の名をきめる. 【類】I've *decided* ***on*** a name for the baby. ‖ *decide* ***on*** one's future course 今後の方針を決める. 【類】*decide* ***on*** the course of action ‖ if *decided* ***on*** (=upon) そう決定すれば ‖ Let us *decide* ***on*** that plan (date). その案(など)に決めよう. 【類】Don't *decide* ***on*** important matters too quickly. / They *decided* ***on*** building a college (going to France). / *decide* ***on*** art as a career (職業) / He has not yet *decided* ***on*** a definite plan. / They drew lots (くじを引いた) in order that they might *decide* ***on*** the first speaker. / cannot do better than *decide* ***on***. ¶*decide* ***upon*** a course of conduct 今後の行動を決定する ‖ The course to be taken is not yet *decided* ***upon***. 今後の方針はまだ決まらない. ‖ *decide* ***upon*** rival claims in a disputed case 係争事件における双方の要求について判定を下す. 【類】I do not like to *decide* ***upon*** hastily such an important matter, as we are not sufficiently acquainted with the facts. / until a fixed policy has been *decided* ***upon*** / The House of Representatives *decided* ***upon*** adjourning its session (会議延長) until the 20th. ‖ No name has been *decided* ***upon***. まだ名が決まらずにいる.

decimal, *n.* 〖数〗小数.

Q a ***recurring*** *decimal* 単循環小数.

decision, *n.* 決定; 決心; 決議; 判決.

V ***alter*** one's *decision* 決心をひるがえす. ¶***await*** *decision* 決定を待つ. ¶***delay*** one's final *decision* 最後の決定を延ばす. ¶And now, ladies and gentlemen, the judges are ready to ***announce*** their *decision*. さて皆さん, 審判員が決定の発表を致します. ¶Particulars are too meagre to ***form*** a *decision*. 詳細の点が不十分で決定するわけにゆかない. ¶***give*** a *decision* 裁決する ‖ I have not yet ***given*** (=***rendered***) my *decision* on that matter. その件に関しては僕はまだ決定していない. ¶He ***has*** great *decision* of character. 彼は意志がきわめて強固だ. ‖ I must ***have*** your *decision* on or before ... …日あるいはその前に君の方で決めてもらわねばならぬ ‖ Please let me ***have*** your *decision* as soon as possible. できるだけ早く君の決心を知らせて欲しい. ¶An applicant called upon the manager to ***learn*** his *decision*. 一人の志願者が採否の決定をたずねるために支配人を訪問した. ¶***make*** a *decision* 決める. ☞この collocation は米国では普通だが英国では余り用いない. ¶***make known*** one's *decision* 決心を知らせる. ¶***modify*** one's *decision* 考え直す. ¶***postpone*** one's *decision* until ... …まで決定を延ばす. 【類】The judge ***postponed*** his *decision*. ¶***ratify*** or ***reverse*** the committee's *decision* 委員会の決議を承認しまたは無効にする. ¶they ***reached*** no *decision* regarding ... 彼らは…に関して何らの決定という段に達しなかった. ¶***reconsider*** one's *decision* 再考する. ¶*ren-*

der a *decision* to the effect that ... ...と言う判決を言渡す.【類】The court ***rendered*** its *decision* in the case. ¶The *decision* of the lower court has been ***sustained.*** 下級裁判所の判決がそのまま支持された. ¶***void*** the previous *decision* 前の決定を無効にする.

V^2 The *decision* ***lies*** (=***rests***) with you. 決定は君がするのだ.

Q make an ***arbitrary*** *decision* 独断で決定する. ¶They are to select an arbtirator, whose *decision* shall be ***conclusive*** (=final). 彼らは最後の裁決者を選定することになっている. ¶come to a ***definite*** *decision* 確定する. ¶send a note requesting an ***early*** *decision* 早期決定を催促する文書を送る. ¶a ***far-seeing*** *decision* 先見の明ある決断. ¶a ***favorable*** *decision* 有利の決定. ¶a ***final*** *decision* 〖法〗終局判決 ‖ a ***final*** *decision* has been reached as to ... いよいよ...のことが決定した ‖ his *decision* is ***final.*** 彼の考えで決定する(最後の決定権は彼にある). ¶a ***hasty*** *decision* 速断. ¶an ***important*** *decision* 重要な決定. ¶his power of ***instantaneous*** *decision* 彼の果断. ¶an ***irrevocable*** *decision* 確定判定. ¶a ***judicial*** *decision* on statutes 定款に関する裁判所の決定. ¶a ***manful*** (=***masculine***) *decision* 男らしい決意. ¶***No*** *decision* was reached. 何らの決定を見なかった. ¶an ***original*** *decision* 〖法〗原判決. ¶a ***pending*** *decision* 未決問題. ¶a ***prompt*** *decision* 即決. ¶He has the gift of ***quick*** *decision.* 彼は果断に富んでいる. ¶the power of ***swift*** and ***sure*** *decision* 速く確実な決断をくだす力. ¶the discussion resulted in a ***unanimous*** *decision* to ... 討議は満場一致で...に決した.【類】The *decision* was ***unanimous.*** ¶***unfair*** *decisions* of umpires 審判者の不公平な決定. ¶You have made a ***wise*** *decision.* 君の決定は賢明だ. ¶a ***wrong*** *decision* 間違った決定.

Q^2 a ***court*** *decision* 法廷の判決. ¶overrule a ***lower court*** *decision* 下級裁判所の判決を取消す. ¶fail to reach a ***majority*** *decision* 多数決に達しなかった ‖ in a sweeping ***majority*** *decision* 圧倒的多数決で.

P We must abide ***by*** his *decision.* われわれは彼の決定に服従しなければならぬ. ¶I concur with him ***in*** the *decision.* その決定については僕はあの人に賛成だ. ¶go back ***on*** one's *decision* 意を翻す. ¶***pending*** the *decision* of the Supreme Court 最高裁判所の判決があるまで. ¶come ***to*** (=arrive at) a *decision* 決定に至る ‖ agree ***to*** a *decision* 決議に同意する.

P^2 a *decision* ***about*** (=on) a case 事件の判決. ¶a *decision* ***of*** guilty 有罪の判決 ‖ The *decision* ***of*** the committee will be final. その委員会の決定は動かすことができぬ. ‖ The *decision* ***of*** the dispute is left to me. 私はその裁決を一任された. ¶his *decision* ***on*** the case その事件に下した彼の判決. ¶please let us have your *decision* ***regarding*** ... ...に関する貴下の御決心を聞かしてもらいたい.

decisive, *a.* 決定的な.

P It is *decisive* ***of*** the fate of the question. それによってその問題の運命が決する. ¶The opinion of ... is *decisive* ***on*** the question. ...の意見はその問題については決定的である.

deck, *n.* 甲板(デッキ).

V ***clear*** the *decks* [甲板を片付けて]戦闘準備をする. ¶***scrub*** the *deck* デッキをごしごし洗う. ¶***swab*** the *deck* 甲板を雑きんなどで洗う. ¶Waves ***swept*** the *deck.* 波が甲板を洗った.

Q^2 an ***awning*** *deck* 日よけ甲板. ¶a ***bridge*** *deck* 艦橋甲板. ¶a ***light*** *deck* [航空母艦]飛行甲板. ¶an ***iron*** *deck* 鉄張り甲板. ¶on the ***main*** *deck* [軍艦の]中甲板, [商船の]本甲板で. ¶the ***promenade*** *deck* 遊歩甲板(一等船客用). ¶a ***poop*** *deck* 船尾甲板(二等船客用). ¶a ***teak*** (***oak***) *deck* チーク(オーク)材張り甲板. ¶***'tween*** *decks* 中甲板. ¶an ***upper*** (***lower***) *deck* 上(下)甲板.

P He sprang ***on*** *deck.* 彼は甲板に飛び上ってきた. ‖ have a dictionary ***on*** *deck* 《米》手許に辞書がある. ¶The wave swept ***over*** the *deck.* 波が甲板を越した.

deck, *v.* 飾る.

M *decked* ***out*** as finely as their proud mothers could manage 娘自慢の母親たちが手のおよぶ限りりっぱに着飾った.【類】*Decked* ***out*** as usual, she went to the party.

M^2 The room was *decked* ***up*** with banners and colored tape. その室は旗や色テープで装飾してあった. ‖ She *decked* herself ***up*** with jewels. 彼女は宝石でりっぱに身を飾った.

P *deck* oneself [up] ***for*** a wedding 婚礼の盛装をする. ¶*decked* ***with*** jewels (flags, buntings) 宝石(など)で飾られた.【類】The table was *decked* ***with*** flowers.

declaim, *v.* 熱弁をふるう.

P He *declaimed* ***against*** the opposition. 彼は熱弁をふるって反対党を攻撃した.

declaration, *n.* 宣言, 告白; 宣言書.

V ***draw up*** a *Declaration* of Principles 主義の宣言書を草する. ¶***hand*** a written *declaration* 宣言書を手交する. ¶***make*** an open *declaration* of one's conversion その転向を公表する ‖ He ***made*** a *declaration* of political views. 彼は政見を発表した.

Q a ***broad*** *declaration* 公然たる宣言. ¶***formal*** *declaration* of allegiance 忠誠宣言式. ¶make ***personal*** *declaration* of such desire to ... この念願を自分から...に言明する. ¶a ***plain*** *declaration* あからさまの告白. ¶under the ecstasy of the ***rhetorical*** *declaration* 弁舌に油が乗って. ¶a ***signed*** *declaration* 署名した宣言書. ¶make a ***solemn*** *declaration* おごそかに宣誓する. ¶a ***statutory*** *declaration* 定款の発表.

Q^2 make an effective provision to implement a ***paper*** *declaration* 紙の上の声明を実行に移す手段を講じる. ¶the ***Potsdam*** *Declaration* ポツダム宣言. ¶conscious of its obligations under the ***Yalta*** *declaration* ヤルタ宣言による義務を自覚して.

P ***after*** the *declaration* of peace 平和宣言後. ¶***at*** the *declaration* of war with ... ...との宣戦布告を発したとき ‖ ***At*** that *declaration* the whole-meeting applauded vehemently. その声明を聴いて一同大かっさいをした.

P^2 the first *declaration* ***of*** symptoms 徴候最初の出現 ‖ *declaration* ***of*** disappearance 失踪(しっそう)宣告 ‖ *declaration* ***of*** value 価格申告書(保険) ‖ *declaration* ***of*** war 宣戦布告 ‖ a letter containing a *declaration* ***of*** love 艶書(えんしょ).

declare, *v.* 言明する, 宣言する; 布告する.

M ***bluntly*** *declare* 露骨に言う. ¶***contemptuously*** *declare* ごう然と言明する. ¶***emphatically*** *declare* 強調する. ¶He was *declared* ***guilty.*** 彼は有罪と宣告された. ¶is ***hereby*** *declared* that ... ...ことをここに声明する ‖ *declare* ***positively*** 断固宣言する. ¶He ***solemnly*** *declared* that it is true. それは事実だと彼は厳然言切った. ¶***sternly*** *declare* 断固言明する. ¶we ***unanimously*** *declare* that ... われわれは...と言うことを一斉に声明する. ¶*declare* ***valiantly*** against ... 勇敢に...に反対であると言い放つ.

M^2 I *declare* ***off.*** 私は御免をこうむる. ‖ *declare* ***off*** one's engagement 約束を破談にする ‖ The match was *declared* ***off.*** その縁組は破談になった. ‖ *declare* a bet ***off*** かけを取消す.

P *declare* ***against*** war 非戦論を唱える ‖ *declare* war ***against*** (=on) some power 某国に対して宣戦を布告する. ¶I *declare* ***before*** gods that ... 神々も照覧あれ. ¶It was *declared* ***by*** statute in 1922. それは一九二二年に法令で布告された. ¶*declare* ***for*** a bill (the Government$^\circ$, manhood suffrage^2) 議案(など)に賛成を表する ‖ *declare* ***for*** war 主戦論を唱える. ¶*declare* oneself ***in favor of*** ... ...に賛成と言明する. ¶*declare* war ***on*** (=***upon***) ... に戦を宣する. ¶they *declared* ***with*** one accord that ... 彼らは異口同音に...と言った.

O He was *declared* king. 彼は王と宣言された. ¶They *declared* him an enemy to humankind. 彼らは彼を人類の敵と公言した. ¶He *declared* himself [to be] satisfied. 彼は満足のむねを述べた. ¶Do you have anything to *declare?* [税関で役人が]何か申告なさるものはありませんか.

decline, *n.* 衰微; 衰弱; 減退; 下落.

V ***bring about*** its *decline* その衰微をきたす. ¶***cause*** a *decline* 衰微をきたす. ¶***hasten*** the *decline* of ... ...の衰微を早める. ¶***mark*** the *decline* of ... ...の衰微を示す. ¶The customs figures ***show*** a steady *decline* in British trade. 税関の数字で見ると英国の貿易はじり下りになっている. ¶The trade ***suffered*** a severe *decline.* その商売がひどい打撃をこうむった.

V^2 *Decline* ***sets*** in. 衰えかける.

Q the ***consequential heavy*** *decline* in the shares of the interested companies その影響を受けた関係諸会社の株の暴落. ¶a ***general*** *decline* in the rate of foreign exchange 外国為替相場の総下落. ¶a ***marked*** and ***rapid*** *decline* 著しくかつ迅速の衰微. ¶The general course of the market was ***one continuous*** *decline.* 相場の大勢は低下の一方であった. ¶the ***progressive*** *decline* of the birth-rate in France フランスにおける出生率の漸次衰退. ¶with ***rapid*** *decline* in weight 目方が急に減って. ¶a ***sharp*** *decline* in eggs 鶏卵の暴落. ¶show the tendency to a ***steady*** *decline* 徐々に衰退する傾向を示す.

Q² There will be more than sufficient ***price*** *declines* to offset the few rises. 二三値上げもあろうがそれを相殺する以上に値下げがあろう. ¶***sales*** *decline* 売行減少.

P They were all ***in*** a *decline*. 彼らはみな体が衰弱していた. ¶Prices for modern pictures are woefully ***on*** the *decline*. 現代画の価はなさけないほど下がってきた. ‖ This custom is ***on*** the *decline*. この習慣はすたれてきた. 【類】 The population is ***on*** the *decline*. / His prosperity is ***on*** the *decline*.

P² a *decline* ***in*** the standard of living 生活標準の低下 ‖ a *decline* ***in*** weight from 133 to 104 pounds 百三十三ポンドから百四ポンドに体重の減少. 【類】 a *decline* ***in*** prices / a *decline* ***in*** business. ¶a *decline* ***of*** ... per cent from 1949 一九四九年に比し...パーセントの減少. 【類】 *decline* ***of*** industry / *decline* ***of*** production.

decline, *v.* 衰える, 末になる; 傾斜する; 下落する; 断る.

M His health is ***already*** *declining*. 彼の健康はすでに衰えかかっている. ¶*decline* ***courteously*** 丁寧に断る. ¶He ***flatly*** *declined* the appointment. 彼は任命をきっぱり断った. ¶The ground on each side *declines* ***gently***. 土地は両側ともなだらかに傾斜している. ¶***gradually*** and ***steadily*** *decline* 次第にじりじりと低下する. ¶His health has ***notably*** *declined*. 彼の健康は目立って衰えてきた. ¶The summer is ***now*** *declining*. 夏ももう終りだ. ¶He ***peremptorily*** *declined* the offer. 彼はぴたりと申込を謝絶した. ¶***politely*** *decline* the invitation 丁重に招待を断る. ¶***resolutely*** *decline* 思い切って断る. ¶He ***respectfully*** *declined* the invitation. 彼は丁重に招待を断った. ‖ most ***respectfully*** *decline* the appointment 礼を尽して任命を辞退する. ¶*decline* ***tactfully*** ていよく断る. ¶The sun *declined* ***westward***. 太陽は西に傾いた. ¶*decline* ***yearly*** 年々衰える.

P prices *declined* ***from*** ... ***to*** ... 値段は...から...に下落した. ¶*decline* ***in*** health (power, prosperity, price, quality, reputation, value, wealth) 健康(など)が低下する. ¶*decline* an offer ***with*** thanks 礼を述べて申入れを辞退する ‖ I *decline* it ***with*** regret. 私は遺憾ながら断る. ‖ *decline* ***with*** advancing years 年とともに衰える ‖ Hearing sensitivity *declines* ***with*** age. 年をとると耳が遠くなる.

decoction, *n.* せんじ汁.

Q a ***strong*** *decoction* of tea 濃い茶.

decode, *v.* [暗号電報など]解読する.

M ***wrongly*** *decode* a secret message 秘密通信を誤訳する.

decomposition, *n.* 腐敗.

Q The flavor comes from ***partial*** *decomposition*. その風味は一部腐敗することによって出る.

P become acid ***by*** *decomposition* 分解して酸になる.

decorate, *v.* 飾る, 勲章を授ける.

M The room was ***elaborately*** *decorated*. その室は入念に飾ってあった. ¶The table was ***florally*** *decorated*. 食卓は花で飾ってあった. ¶the city was ***gaily*** *decorated* with greenery, floral designs, and countless flags in honor of ... 同市は...を祝して緑葉や装飾花や無数の旗ではなやかに飾られた. 【類】 ***gaily*** *decorated* for the occasion (その祝賀のため). ¶The city was ***lavishly*** *decorated* with tricolor flags. 同市は三色旗で飾り立てられた. ¶***ornately*** *decorated* 美飾した. ¶***profusely*** *decorated* 盛んに飾り立てた.

P The porcelain is *decorated* ***after*** (=***in***) the *sometsuke* style (=fashion). その磁器は染付だ. ¶be *decorated* ***by*** hand 手先で装飾してある. ¶He was *decorated* ***for*** bravery in action (distinguished service). 彼は戦功(など)によって勲章を授けられた. ‖ They *decorated* the hall ***for*** the festival. その祝典のために大広間を飾った. 【類】 The room was decorated ***with*** holly ***for*** Christmas. ¶The hall was *decorated* ***with*** flags, pictures, etc. 広間は旗・絵などで飾られた. 【類】 a tree *decorated* ***with*** Xmas trimming (クリスマスの装飾品) / *decorate* the mind ***with*** virtue.

decoration, *n.* **(1)** 装飾.

Q the art of ***floral*** *decoration* 生花. ¶***inside*** *decorations* and furnishings of the house 室内装飾と家具の設備. ¶***mural*** *decoration* 壁の装飾. ¶highly ***ornate*** *decoration* けんらんたる装飾. ¶***polychromatic*** *decoration* 極彩色. ¶***street*** *decoration* 街頭装飾. ¶a ***tasteless*** *decoration* 殺風景な装飾.

Q² ***Christmas*** *decorations* クリスマスの装飾. ¶lesson one in ***home*** *decoration* 室内装飾第一課. ¶stunted shrubs for ***house*** *decorations* 室内装飾のための盆栽. ¶***stage*** *decoration* 舞台装飾. ¶***trophy*** *decoration* 戦利品(または優勝トロフィー)の陳列. ¶***watch spring*** *decoration* 時計のぜんまい形装飾.

P use flags ***for*** *decoration* 旗を装飾として用いる.

(2) 勲章.

V ***accept*** a *decoration* 勲章を拝受する. ¶He was ***awarded*** a *decoration*. 彼は勲章を授けられた. ¶He ***holds*** the fifth class of the Order of the Rising Sun. 彼は勲五等の旭日章を持っている. ¶***wear*** a *decoration* (=an order) 勲章をはい用する.

Q the Order of St. George, the ***highest military*** *decoration* of Russia ロシアの最高勲章たるセント・ジョージ章. ¶be awarded a ***periodical*** *decoration* 定期叙勲をする. ¶his ***recent*** *decoration* by France of ... with the Order of ... 最近フランスからの彼の...勲章拝受.

decorum, *n.* 礼儀.

V Drinkers sometimes ***lose*** their *decorum*. 飲酒家は時折礼を失する. ¶***throw aside*** all *decorum* 打ちくつろぐ.

Q ***outward*** *decorum* of behavior 形式的の礼儀. ¶***professional*** *decorum* 職業的礼儀. ¶the observance of ***strict*** *decorum* 礼節の厳守.

decoy, *n.* おとり; 間ちょう.

Q² a ***police*** *decoy* 警察の回し者.

P act ***as*** a *decoy* 間ちょうとなる. ¶***for*** a *decoy* おとりに.

decoy, *v.* おびよせる.

M The duck was *decoyed* ***readily***. かもは容易におびき寄せられた.

P *decoy* a person ***from*** a place 人をおびき出す. ¶*decoy* a person ***into*** a place (doing something) 人をおびき込む(など). 【類】 He *decoyed* a customer ***into*** his shop. / *decoy* ducks ***into*** a net. ¶*decoy* ducks ***within*** gunshot かもを着弾距離におびき寄せる.

decrease, *n.* 減少.

V ***show*** a *decrease* of ... tons (...%) against the tonnage of the previous month 前月のトン数に比し...トン(...%)の減少を示す. ‖ This ***shows*** a slight *decrease* on the numbers of the previous week. すなわち前週より数が少し減っている.

Q² a ***population*** *decrease* 人口減少.

P The demand for tea is ***on*** the *decrease*. 茶の需要が減ってきた. ¶Prices for coal have shown a slight *decrease* ***against*** the previous month. 石炭の値段は先月より少し下落した.

P² *decrease* ***in*** production (number, weight) 生産(など)の減少. ¶a *decrease* ***of*** ... ***from*** the preceding year 前年よりも...方の減少.

decrease, *v.* 減少する.

M *decrease* ***gradually*** (***rapidly***) 漸(急)減する. ¶*decrease* ***sharply*** 暴落する. ¶*decrease* ***slowly*** but ***steadily*** 着実に減る.

P *decrease* ***in*** population 人口が減る ‖ The cold has *decreased* ***in*** severity. 寒さがやわらいだ. ¶The members *decreased* ***to*** three hundred. 会員は三百人に減った.

decree, *n.* 命令, 法令.

V a *decree* was ***enacted*** prohibiting ... ...禁止の法令が制定された. ¶***ignore*** a *decree* 命令を無視する. ¶In 1588 Hideyoshi ***published*** a *decree* ordering the expulsion of the Jesuits. 1588 年秀吉はヤソ会派キリスト教徒追放の法令を発布した. ¶***revoke*** a *decree* 命令を取消す.

Q an ***Imperial*** *decree* 勅令. ¶a ***ministerial*** *decree* 省令. ¶a ***peremptory*** *decree* 緊急法令.

Q² by ***Court*** *decree* 勅令により. ¶by ***government*** *decree* 政令によって.

P it is forbidden ***by*** *decree* to ... ...することを法令で禁止されている. 【類】 It was fixed ***by*** *decree*.

P² The court granted her a *decree* ***of*** divorce. 裁判所が彼女に離婚の許可を申渡した.

dedicate, *v.* 捧げる.

M the shrine is *dedicated* ***jointly*** to ... その神社には...が合祀されている.

P He *dedicated* his life ***to*** the cause of education. 彼は教育に一生を捧げた. ‖ Universities ought to be *dedicated* not ***to*** education, but ***to*** research. 大学は教育よりも研究に従事すべきだ. ‖ ***To*** my uncle I *dedicate* this volume in token of affection and gratitude. 愛と感謝の記念に本書をわが伯父君に献呈する. 【類】 *dedicated* ***to*** Prof ... on (=in honor of) the twenty-fifth anniversary of his appointment at the university of ... ‖ The shrine is *dedicated* ***to*** the memory of Sugawara Michizane. その社には菅原道真がまつってある. 【類】 *dedicated* a shrine (temple) ***to***

God (a god) ‖ the deified hero *to* whom the temple is *dedicated* この霊屋にまつられている英雄 ‖ the Sacred Hall *dedicated to* the Chinese sage [儒教の]聖堂.

dedication, *n.* 奉献. 「まつったものだ.

P the shrine was built *in dedication* to ... この神社は...を

P² *dedication of* land *to* public use *by* the owner 公衆用として地主の土地寄付.

deduce, *v.* 演えきする, 推断する. 「ら演えきした結論.

M conclusions *lamely deduced* from ... 筋道が立たず...か

P *deduce* a conclusion *from* premises 前提から結論を演えきする. 【類】 *deduce* unknown truths *from* principles already known ‖ *deduce* it *from* reports (facts) 報告(など)からそれを推断する ‖ *deduce from* cause *to* effect 原因か

deduct, *v.* 引去る, 差引く. └ら結果を推断する.

P *deduct* the amount *from* salary (cost) 俸給(など)からその金額を差引く ‖ *deduct* an item *from* an account 勘定書から一項目を除く.

deduction, *n.* 推理, 推断; 差引, 割引.

V *allow* a *deduction* 推断を許す; 値引をする ‖ if no *deduction* is *allowed* 減額が認められなければ. 【類】 A small *deduction* may be *allowed.* ¶*claim* a *deduction* 割引を要求する. ¶*draw deductions* from ... ...から推理する ‖ leave him to *draw* his own *deductions* (conclusions) 彼に勝手に推断(など)させる. ¶*make deductions* therefrom それから推理する ‖ when all *deductions* have been *made* 十分酌量して見ても ‖ after we have *made* due *deduction* for ..., he remains ... ...に対して適当のしんしゃくを加えても彼は依然...だ ‖ No *deduction* in pay is *made* for absence due to illness. 病気欠勤の場合は給料は引かれない.

Q a *logical deduction* from the general law that ... ...という通則から必然の推理.

P accept ... *with* large *deduction* 大割引で引受ける. ¶*without deduction* of any kind 一切割引なしで.

P² *Deductions from* figures should be made with caution. これらの数字(統計)によって結論を下す場合は注意を要する. ‖ *deduction from* the yearly rent 毎年の地代からの

deed, *n.* (**1**) 功績; 事業; 行為; 事実. └差引.

V He *achieved* no great or brilliant *deeds.* 彼には偉いことも花々しいこともなかった. ¶*decry* one's own *deeds* and *laud* those of others 自分の功績を軽んじ他人の手柄を賞賛する. ¶Canada has *done* great *deeds* on the battlefield. カナダは戦場で大いに功績を揚げた. ‖ *do* heroic *deeds* 勇ましいことをする. ¶*herald* his *deeds* of heroism 彼の英雄的行為を吹聴する. ¶*perform* a *deed* 事業を達成する. ¶*sing* one's *deed* その功績をたたえる. ¶*undertake* a *deed* 事業を起す. 「言行が一致しなかった.

V² Their *deeds* did not *agree* with their words. 彼らは

Q a *bad deed* 悪行. ¶*brave deeds* and brilliant exploits 勇敢な行為と赫々たる功績. ¶be frustrated in one's *criminal deed* 悪事がばれる. ¶*daring deeds* of great mountaineers 偉大なる登山家の勇敢なる行為. ¶*dark deeds* done in the dead of night 深夜の凶行. ¶a *dastardly deed* ひきょうな所為. ¶a *doughty deed* 豪胆な行為. ¶an *evil deed* 悪い行為. ¶a *gallant deed* 雄々しき所為. ¶a *good deed* a day 一日一善 ‖ A man, according to Buddhism, may be reborn as a god by *good deeds.* 仏教では人間は善根を積めば仏となって再生ができると言っている. ¶do some *great deed* 何か偉いことをやる. ¶a *heroic deed* 勇壮な行為. ¶*Kind deeds* never die. 親切な行為は決して亡びない. ¶a *meritorious deed* done by accident けがの功名. ¶a *monstrous deed* 極悪非道の行為. ¶*noble* and *manly deeds* 高潔にして男らしい所為. ¶No *single* or *memorable deed* has been recorded of him. 彼には並びない功績とか記憶すべき所業とかいうものは一つも伝えられていない. ¶names that recall to you the memory of *stirring deeds* wrought for England in every quarter of the world 世界いたる所に英国のために偉業を立てたことを追憶せしめる人々. ¶a *thrilling deed* of valor 肉おどるような剛勇の所為. ¶a *worthy deed* worthily accomplished りっぱにやりとげたりっぱな事業 ‖ One *worthy deed* may be ascribed to him. 彼には一つの手柄があった.

P *in* [very] *deed* 真に ‖ *in deed* and not in name 名目上でなく実際に ‖ a chief *in deed* as well as in name 名実ともに備わった首領 ‖ He is faithful *in* word and *deed.* 彼は言行ともに誠実だ. ¶a man of words and not *of deeds* 口先きばかりで実行の伴わない人.

P² a *deed of* arms 武勲 ‖ the *deed of* gift provides that ... その寄付行為に...ということが規定してある ‖ *deeds of* heroism, courage, and unselfishness 勇壮無私の行為 ‖ a *deed of* high glory あっぱれな功績.

(**2**) 〖法〗[なつ印した]証書.

V *acknowledge* a *deed* 証書を確実であると公(承)認する. ¶*draw* a *deed* 証書を作成する. ¶*draw up* (＝*prepare* or *write out*) a *deed* 証書を作製する. ¶*hold* a *deed* as security 証書を担保に取っておく. ¶*witness* a *deed* 証人とし

Q² a *title deed* 証書. └て証書に連署する.

deed, *v.* 《米》証書で譲り渡す.

P *deed* the estate *to* the son 子に家督を譲る.

deem, *v.* 思う, 見なす.

M I *deem highly* of his honesty. 私は彼の正直を尊重する. ¶I *deem* it *right* (*advisable, prudent*) to warn you. 君に注意するのが至当(など)と思う. ¶It was *deemed sufficient.* それは十分と見なされた.

O I shall *deem* it an honor if you will join our party. 御来臨の栄を得ますれば光栄に存じます. 【類】 I shall *deem* it a great favor if you will kindly help me.

deep, *n.* 深海; 最頂点.

Q in the *fathomless deep* 底知らずの深海に. ¶the *mighty*

Q² the *ocean deep* 深い海. └*deep* 大海原.

P have a dip *in* the *deep* 海水を浴びる. ¶her predominance *on* the *deep* (＝sea) その国の海上における優勢.

P² hide it in the *deep of* his heart それを彼の心の奥底に隠す ‖ in the *deep of* night (winter) 真夜(など)中に.

deep, *a., adv.* 深い; 厚さのある; 深く.

M He is *ankle deep* in snow. 彼はくるぶしまで雪に埋まっている. ¶a case with a rim a *few inches deep* 厚さ二三インチのふちのある箱. 【類】 The well is *ten feet deep.* ¶a rank *three men deep* 三列の隊.

P It is too *deep for* him. それは彼にはむずかし過ぎる. ‖ a thought too *deep for* words 言語に尽し得ない思想. ¶*deep in* prayer 祈禱三まいに ‖ a man *deep in* thought 思案に暮れる人 ‖ *deep in* the night 夜ふけて ‖ *deep in* the mountains 山奥に ‖ with the hands *deep in* the pockets ポケットに深く手をさし込んで ‖ a ship *deep in* water 水中深く沈んだ船 ‖ He is *deep in* work. 彼は仕事に夢中だ. ‖ He was *deep in* reading the book (magazine). 彼は読書(など)に夢中であった. ‖ he is *deep in* love with ... 彼はぞっこん...にほれ込んでいる ‖ He is *deep in* debt. 彼は借金で動きがとれない. ¶He conducted me about five hundred paces *deep into* the wood. 彼は僕を森深く五百歩も連れ込んだ.

deepen, *v.* 深くなる.

P become *deepened in* the impression that ... ...の感を深くする. ¶It is feared that his depression will *deepen into* illness. 彼は憂うつの結果病気になりはしないかと気づかわれている. ‖ The dark had now *deepened into* the darkness of night. もう暗さが増して真のやみとなった. ¶The water *deepens to* 16 feet at high water. 水深は満潮で十六

deer, *n.* しか. └フィートになる.

Q a *tame deer* 人なれたしか.

defamation, *n.* 名誉棄損.

Q *written* and *oral defamation* 筆と舌による名誉棄損.

defamatory, *a.* 名誉を棄損する.

P *defamatory of* ... ...の不名誉になる.

default, *n.* 怠慢, 違背; 欠席.

V *make default* in payment of a sum of money 金額の支払を果さない ‖ If *default* is *made* in any of the above particulars, he shall incur a penalty not exceeding twenty pounds for each default. 前項のいずれかを果さぬ場合は各違約に対して二十ポンド以下の罰金に処すべきものとす.

P the clerk *at default* 間違いをやった店員. ¶judgment *by default* 欠席裁判. ¶*In default* of paying the fine he will be imprisoned for a further period of 80 days. 科料の支払を怠るにおいてはさらに八十日間の禁固に処せらるべし. ‖ *in default* of experienced hands (male heirs, the right article) 経験者(など)がないために. ¶in case *of default* 実行しない場合には. ¶This evil has happened *through* the governor's *default.* この災害は知事の怠慢から起った.

P² a *default in* an engagement 違約 ‖ a *default in* paying a note 不払手形. 【類】 in the event of a *default in* the repayment of the loan. ¶*default of* appearance (裁判所

defaulter, *n.* 不履行者. └などへの)欠席.

Q² a *tax defaulter* 租税滞納者.

defeat, *n.* 敗北；失敗.

V ***acknowledge*** one's *defeat* 敗北を認める ‖ unwillingness to ***acknowledge*** *defeat* 負惜み. ¶ frankly ***admit defeat*** in a game 勝負に敗れたことを率直に認める. ¶ ***bring defeat*** to the Germans ドイツ人に敗北をもたらす. ¶ make him ***confess*** his *defeat* 彼に負けたと言わせる. ¶ ***court defeat*** 敗北を招く. ¶ ***encounter*** a complete *defeat* 全敗する. ¶ ***inflict*** on them a crushing *defeat* 彼らを散々に破る.【類】***inflict*** a severe *defeat* upon the enemy. ¶ that determination which ***knows*** no *defeat* あの屈することを知らない決心. ¶ ***meet defeat*** 敗北する. ¶ he ***met with defeat*** at the hands of ... 彼は...に敗れた. ¶ ***risk defeat*** in ...ing ... するのに負けても構わずやる. ¶ ***stave off defeat*** 失敗を避ける. ¶ ***suffer*** (＝***sustain***) a *defeat* 敗北する ‖ ***suffer defeat*** after defeat 失敗に失敗を重ねる. ¶ ***undergo*** a humiliating *defeat* 屈辱的大敗に会う.

Q a ***crushing defeat*** 惨敗. ¶ our ***diplomatic defeats*** in the West 西洋におけるわが外交の失敗. ¶ a ***disheartening*** *defeat* 意気をそそうさせる敗北. ¶ a ***heavy defeat*** 大敗. ¶ an ***ignominious defeat*** 惨敗. ¶ an ***irretrievable defeat*** 取返しのつかない失敗. ¶ an ***overwhelming defeat*** 壊滅的敗北. ¶ a ***ruinous defeat*** 破滅的敗北. ¶ they sustained a ***severe*** (＝***serious***) *defeat* at ... 彼らは...で大敗した. ¶ He suffered ***successive defeats*** in elections. 彼は選挙に連敗した. ¶ a ***terrible defeat*** 大敗.

P^2 a *defeat* ***in*** an election (a battle, a game) 選挙(など)の不成功.

defeat, *v.* 負かす, 破る；あざむき取る.

M *defeat* an opponent ***badly*** 相手を大いに破る. ¶ He was ***handsomely*** *defeated.* 彼は見事に失敗した. ¶ he was ***signally*** *defeated* by ... 彼は...に見事に敗れた.

P the general was *defeated* ***at*** ... 同将軍は...で敗れた. ¶ He was *defeated* ***by*** 262 votes against 211. 彼は二百十一票対二百六十二票で落選した. ‖ The Ministry has been *defeated* ***by*** a large (small) majority. 内閣は大(少)多数決で倒れた. ¶ *defeat* him ***in*** a prize fight けん闘で彼を破る ‖ He was *defeated* ***in*** his purpose. 彼の計画は失敗に終った.【類】be *defeated* ***in*** one's scheme / He was *defeated* ***in*** a battle (game). ¶ *defeat* a man ***of*** an inheritance 人の財産相続を失敗に終らせる. ¶ He was *defeated* ***through*** (＝***in consequence of*** or ***because of***) having no re-enforcements. 彼は援軍がなかったので敗れた. ¶ The general was totally *defeated* ***with*** immense slaughter. 将軍は全敗して非常な死傷者を出した.

defecation, *n.* 便通.

P ***after*** *defecation* 便通後に.

defect, *n.* 欠点, 欠陥.

V ***correct*** *defects* 欠点を直す. ¶ ***cure*** an intellectual *defect* [不正確など]知的欠陥を矯正する. ¶ The ship ***developed*** structural *defects.* 船は構造の上に欠陥を生じた. ¶ ***diminish*** the *defects* of ... ...の欠点を少くする. ¶ ***inherit*** his teacher's *defects* 教師の欠陥を伝承する. ¶ This ***made up*** the *defect* to some extent. これで幾分具合がよくなった. ¶ ***obviate*** *defects* 欠点を排除する. ¶ ***point out*** *defects* 欠点を指摘する. ¶ He ***possesses*** many *defects* of character. 彼は多くの性格上の欠点を持っている. ¶ ***remedy*** a *defect* 欠点を直す. ¶ ***repair*** the *defect* その短所を矯正する.

Q a ***fatal*** *defect* 致命的欠陥. ¶ ***glaring*** *defects* of style (型, 体裁など)文体の著しい欠陥. ¶ He sees ***grave defects*** in modern schools. 彼は近代の学校なるものに由々しい欠陥があることを認めている. ¶ an ***innate*** *defect* 先天的欠陥. ¶ with all its ***minor*** *defects* ささいの欠点は大分あるが. ¶ In the French language almost all ***personal*** *defects* begin with the letter B. フランス語ではほとんど総ての身体上の欠陥は B で始まっている. ¶ ***physical*** *defects* and their relation to mental growth 肉体の欠陥と精神的発達との関係. ¶ a ***positive*** *defect* 明かな欠陥. ¶ Some say that pride is the ***principal*** *defect* of the Japanese. 自負心が日本人の主な欠点だと言う者がある. ¶ a ***serious*** *defect* in his character 彼の性格の大欠点. ¶ I got this cloth cheap because there is a ***small*** *defect* in it. 小さいきずがあるのでこの生地を安く買った. ¶ a ***social*** *defect* 社会的欠陥. ¶ a ***technical*** *defect* 専門的欠陥.

Q^2 an ***eye*** *defect* 目の欠点. ¶ a remedy for ***voice*** *defects* 声の欠陥の薬.

P He used artificial flowers ***in*** *defect* (＝default) of the real ones. 彼は本物がないので造花を使った. ¶ remedy some ***of*** the *defects* 欠点の幾分を直す. ¶ ***through*** *defect* in consideration 考え違いから.

P^2 *defects* ***in*** our educational system わが教育制度の諸欠陥.

defection, *n.* 背反, 変節；脱走.

P^2 *defection* ***from*** a person (an association, party) 人(など)との離反. ¶ *defection* ***of*** a person 変節.

Q a ***wholesale*** *defection* from the ranks 隊からの大々的脱走.

defective, *a.* 不備の, 欠点のある.

P He is *defective* ***in*** good sense (intelligence). 彼は分別(など)を欠いている. ‖ He is *defective* ***in*** manner (body). 彼は動作(体)に欠点がある.

defence, *n.* ＝defense.

defend, *v.* 防御する, 防護する.

M It can ***easily*** be *defended.* それは要害の場所だ. ¶ He *defended* himself ***stoutly.*** 彼はがん強に弁解した.

P *defend* our countrymen ***against*** ... ...からわが国民を護る.【類】*defend* Frenchmen ***against*** the reproach of levity (軽薄との非難に対して) ‖ *defend* it ***against*** an advancing army under ... ...の率いる前進軍に対してこれを守る.【類】*defend* oneself ***against*** one's enemy (an attack, a charge). ¶ be *defended* ***by*** ramparts 城壁で防いである ‖ The village was *defended* ***by*** a river. その村は川で護られていた. ¶ *defend* one ***from*** harm (danger) 傷害(など)を受けないようにする ‖ *defend* a person ***from*** the charge of ... ...の非難から人を弁護する. ¶ *defend* ***to*** the death the right to ... ...する権利を死守する. ¶ *defend* oneself ***with*** one's sword 剣をとって自分をまもる.

defendant, *n.* 被告(人).

V ***debar*** the *defendant* from ... ...から被告を除外する. ¶ ***dissolve*** the *defendant* 被告を放免する.

V^2 The *defendant* ***prevailed*** in the case. 被告の勝訴になった.

Q an ***indigent*** *defendant* 無資力被告人.

defender, *n.* 保護者, 擁護者.

V He has ***had*** few *defenders.* 彼には擁護者がほとんどなかった.

Q its rôle of ***public*** *defender* その(法務省などの)民衆擁護の機能.

defense, 《英》**defence,** *n.* 防御, 防備, 保護；弁護.

V The prisoner refused counsel, and ***conducted*** his own *defense.* 囚徒は弁護士を頼まず自分で弁護した. ¶ ***erect*** temporary *defense* 仮りの防備を設ける. ¶ they ***maintained*** their *defense* till ... 彼らは...までその防御線を維持した(退かなかった). ¶ ***make*** an eloquent *defense* 能弁に弁護する ‖ ***make*** a brave *defense* against the invaders 侵入者を勇敢に防ぐ. ¶ ***need*** no *defense* in a work which ... ...の事業には弁護の必要がない(それがよいということが明かであるから). ¶ the *defense* ***offered*** by the man charged with ... ...で告訴された人の答弁. ¶ this *defense* would probably be ***put in*** for ... 多分...のためにこの弁明を提出するだろう. ¶ The *defense* ***set up*** was ingenious. うまく言抜けた. ¶ ***strengthen*** the *defenses* 防御陣地を強化する. ¶ I shall ***undertake*** my own *defense.* 僕は(法廷で)自分で弁護する積りだ. ¶ This will ***weaken*** the *defense.* そうすると防備が弱くなるだろう.

Q a ***bold*** *defense* 大胆な防御. ¶ a ***brave*** *defense* 勇敢な防御. ¶ work together for the ***common*** *defense* 共同防衛に協力する. ¶ his ***impassioned*** *defense* of the liberty of the press 新聞の自由を唱道する彼の熱弁. ¶ ***military*** *defenses* 軍備. ¶ ***national*** *defense* 国防. ¶ a ***naval*** *defense* 海防. ¶ There was no ***real*** *defense* against attacks from the air. 空襲に対する真の防備は絶無であった. ¶ a ***spirited*** *defense* of ... ...に対するやっきとなった弁護. ¶ a ***stubborn*** (＝an ***obstinate***) *defense* がん強な防御. ¶ make a ***vigorous*** *defense* of ... ...を力強く弁護する.

P ***in*** *defense* of his own life 自己の生命を保護するために ‖ ***in*** *defence* of oneself 自己防衛のために ‖ a fight ***in*** *defense* of the capital 首都防衛戦 ‖ ***in*** his own *defense* 自己の弁護として ‖ His reasoning ***in*** *defense* of ... is irrefutable. ...を弁護するための彼の所論は弁ばくの余地がない.【類】He wrote a book ***in*** *defense* of his doctrine. / ***in*** *defense* of one's principle / ***in*** *defense* of right. ¶ a strong team ***on*** *defense* 守備では強いチーム. ¶ ***out of*** *defense* for ... ...を弁護しようとして. ¶ They were brave ***in*** *defense.* 彼らは勇敢に防いだ.

Q^2 ***air*** *defenses* 防空. ¶ ***coast*** *defense* 海防. ¶ ***hemisphere*** *defense* 西半球の防衛. ¶ "***home front***" *defense* 国土前線防衛. ¶ a thorough system of ***marine coast*** *defences* 完全なる海防組織. ¶ ***periphery*** *defense* 国土周辺防備.

P² a *defense **against*** an attack (assault, wind, rain) 攻撃(など)に備える防御. 【類】 the fortress (wall) was erected as a *defense **against*** the incursions of ... ‖ He crossed himself in *defense **against*** evil powers. 彼は魔よけに十字を切った. ¶*defense **of*** the skies 空の守り ‖ *defense **of*** property 所有権保護 ‖ the *defense **of*** territory 地域防衛. ¶a *defense **to*** an action 訴訟に対する弁護.

defensible, *a.* 弁護できる.

M be ***grammatically*** *defensible* 文法上差支えない. ¶not ***logically*** *defensible* 論理に合わない.

defensive, *n.* 守勢.

P They remained strictly ***on*** the *defensive*. 彼らはどこまでも守勢を取っていた. 【類】 France acted (=stood) ***on*** the *defensive*. / This put the unions (組合側) sharply on the *defensive* in the battle.

defer, *v.* 延ばす.

P *defer* it ***until*** a more opportune time もっと適当な時期までそれを延ばす.

defer, *v.* 服従する.

P *defer **to*** his judgement (opinion, wishes) 彼の判断(など)に従う.

deference, *n.* 服従; 敬意.

V ***pay*** *deference* to ... ...に敬意を表する. ¶***win*** the *deference* of ... ...に尊敬される.

Q It was suggested with all ***due*** *deference*. その注意は適当の敬意を以てなされた. ¶show ***great*** *deference* to ... ...に深い敬意を表わす.

P ***in*** (=out of) *deference* to the express wish of ... 特に...の希望により. 【類】 I changed my plan ***in*** *deference* to his opinion. ¶Her name—***out of*** *deference* to her family—is changed. その家族にわざわいをおよぼすことを慮って彼女は名を変えた. ¶***With*** all *deference*, I beg to disagree. 誠に失礼ですが御意見には賛成ができません.

P² *deference **for*** his judgment 彼の判断に対する敬意. ¶I contend, with all *deference **to*** contrary opinion, that ... 反対説には大いに敬意を表するが私は...ということを主張する. 【類】 with all *deference **to*** the eminent authorities who have enunciated this theory, I venture to think that ... ¶*deference **toward*** the fair sex 女性に対する敬意.

defiance, *n.* いどみ, ちょう戦.

V ***bid*** *defiance* to him to ... 彼に...をいどむ ‖ He ***bade*** *defiance* to the police. 彼は警官たちを軽視した. ‖ ***bid*** *defiance* to ridicule 人から笑われるのをかまわない. ¶The Socialists ***declared*** open *defiance* to the Government. 社会党は公然政府にちょう戦した. ¶***send*** *defiance* いどみかける. ¶The trumpets ***sounded*** a *defiance*. ちょう戦合図のらっぱが鳴り響いた.

Q ***contemptuous*** *defiance* 侮辱的ちょう戦. ¶in ***declared*** *defiance* of convention 慣例を公然無視して. ¶There was an ***unusual*** *defiance* in his tone. 彼の語気には非常にちょう戦的な所があった.

P He set his master ***at*** *defiance*. 彼は主人をなめていた. ‖ If you set the law ***at*** *defiance*, you'll be sent to prison. 法律を無視すると刑務所へ入れられるぞ. ¶***in*** *defiance* of etiquette (the law, the storm) 礼儀(など)を無視して. 【類】 He went his own way ***in*** *defiance* of public opinion. ‖ When the soldiers act ***in*** *defiance* of orders, they shall be severely punished. 兵士が命令に従わないと厳罰に処せられる. ‖ ***in*** *defiance* of the process of nature 条理にそむくと, 無理を通すと.

deficiency, *n.* 欠乏, 不足.

V ***cover*** the *deficiency* in the estimates 予算の不足額を補う. ¶***fill up*** (=***make up*** [***for***]) a *deficiency* in ... ...の欠を補う. ¶This ***leaves*** the *deficiency* of £100. これで百ポンドの不足となる. ¶***remedy*** a *deficiency* 欠を補う. ¶Supplies ***show*** a *deficiency*. 供給が不足だ. ¶***supply*** these *deficiencies* in former treatises 以前の論文におけるこれらの欠陥を補う.

Q There is a ***great*** *deficiency* of tact in him. 彼は余ほど世才が足りない. ¶***mental*** *deficiency* 低能. ¶***Mental*** and ***moral*** *deficiency* of women must be combated. 婦人の精神上および道徳上の欠陥を除くことに努力しなければならぬ. ¶make up ***natural*** *deficiency* 天然の欠乏を補う. ¶a most ***serious*** *deficiency* in ... ...におけるきわめて重大な欠陥.

Q² ***diet*** *deficiencies* in the war years 戦時の食糧不足. ¶***food*** *deficiency* 食糧不足. ¶The ***housing*** *deficiency* (=shortage) now amounts to about 200,000 units. 家屋の不足は目下約二十万戸に上る. ¶***language*** *deficiencies* [英語が不得手であるなど]語学上の弱点. ¶persons with a ***vitamine*** *deficiency* ヴィタミン欠乏症の人々. ¶remedy the ***vocabulary*** *deficiencies* of high-school and college students 高等学校および大学学生の語いの不足を補う.

P² in the season when there is a *deficiency **in*** the supply 供給不足の季節に.

deficient, *a.* 乏しい.

P He is *deficient **in*** ability (strength, courage, capital, common sense). 彼は実力(など)に乏しい. ‖ It is *deficient **in*** clearness. それは明りょうを欠いている.

deficit, *n.* 不足, 欠損, 赤字.

V This ***caused*** a *deficit* of over £2,000. このために二千ポンド以上の欠損を生じた. ¶the company ***had*** a *deficit* of ... 会社は...の欠損であった. ¶***make up*** the *deficit* 欠損を補う. ¶***meet*** the *deficit* その不足を補う. ¶***show*** a heavy *deficit* ばく大の不足を告げる. ¶***supply*** the *deficit* 不足を満たす. ¶The Minister of Finance will shortly be in the international market for a loan to ***wipe out*** the Budget *deficits*. 大蔵大臣は予算の不足清算のため近々外債を募集することになるであろう.

Q² ***government*** revenue *deficit* 政府歳入の不足. ¶reduce the country's ***trade*** *deficit* その国の貿易上の欠損を減らす. ¶***transit operating*** *deficit* 交通機関の不備.

P² a *deficit **in*** the revenue 歳入の不足. ¶There was a *defficit **of*** fifty thousand yen. 五万円赤字になった.

defile, *v.* けがす.

P *defile* a holy place ***by*** sacrilegious deeds 不敬な所為で霊地をけがす. ¶Rivers are often *defiled **by*** waste from factories. 工場からの廃物で往々川がよごされる. ¶*defile* the temple ***with*** blood 血で神殿をけがす ‖ be *defiled **with*** ink stains インクのしみでよごれる.

define, *v.* 定義を下す, 解説する.

M ***clearly*** *defined* alignment 党派の歴然たる色分け. ¶By the usage of the United Kingdom and many other countries, migrants are ***commonly*** *defined* as persons who change their residence for a year or more. 英国本土その他多数の国では慣例上移住者とは普通一年または一年以上その住所を変更する者という定義を下している. ¶I cannot *define* ***precisely*** what that "something" is. その「ある物」が果して何であるかを正確に解説することはできない. ¶***rigidly*** *defined*, it is ... 厳格な定義を下せばそれは...だ.

P the term "..." is *defined* in Webster's Dictionary ***as*** ... 「...」なる語はウェブスターの辞典には...と解説してある. ‖ a cynic might *define* it ***as*** ... 口の悪い人ならこれに...というかもしれない. ¶learn to *define* ***betwixt*** undue extravagance and rigorous economy 分に過ぎたぜいたくときびしい節約との限界を明かに知る(すなわち中庸を得る)ようになる. ¶The powers of a judge are *defined **by*** law. 裁判官の権限は法律で定められている.

definite, *a.* 明確な.

M His attitude wasn't yet ***very*** *definite* at that time. 当時彼の態度はまだはっきりしていなかった.

P *definite **in*** answer 答が明確な.

definition, *n.* 定義.

V ***formulate*** a *definition* 定義を下す. ¶***frame*** a good *definition* of ... ...に対する適当な定義を下す. 【類】 the difficulty of ***framing*** a *definition* at the same time comprehensive and distinctive. ¶***give*** a *definition* of ... ...の定義を下す ‖ A few examples may ***give*** *definition* to these general statements. 二三の例を示すとこれらの概説が一層判明するでしょう. ¶***lay down*** a *definition* 定義を下す. ¶***put*** a narrow *definition* on ... ...に狭義の定義を下す.

Q ***brief***, ***epigrammatic*** *definitions* 簡潔奇警の定義. ¶a ***clear*** *definition* 明確なる定義. ¶an ***exact*** *definition* 正確な定義. ¶an ***exhaustive*** *definition* 遺漏のない定義. ¶a ***full*** *definition* 詳細な定義. ¶a ***good working*** *definition* 実際便利な定義. ¶a ***misleading*** *definition* 誤解のおそれある定義. ¶a ***modernized*** *definition* 現代化した定義. ¶form ***satisfactory*** *definitions* 満足な定義を下す. ¶***sharp logical*** *definition* of sentence and phrase 文と句に対する厳正かつ論理的な定義. ¶the ***threadbare*** *definition* of "flirtation" as "attention without intention" "flirtation" を「誠意のない愛想」とする陳腐な定義. ¶a ***wide*** *definition* 融通のきく定義.

Q² a ***dictionary*** *definition* 辞書所載の定義.

P² *definition **by*** contrast 対照による定義. ¶the *definition **of*** a term 用語の定義 ‖ a *definition **of*** the field to be studied 研究範囲の限定.

deflation, *n.* デフレーション.

Q[2] *price deflation* 物価下落.

deflect, *v.* それる.

P *deflect from* the meridian 子午線(など)からそれる.【類】*deflect from* some purpose (a principle).

deformed, *pa.* 不具の.

P He is *deformed in* person (his limbs). 彼は身体(など)が不具だ.

deformity, *n.* 不具; 奇形; 欠陥.

Q a *congenital deformity* 先天的不具. ¶*moral deformity* 道徳的欠陥.

Q[2] *school room deformities* 教場の諸欠陥.

P[2] the *deformities of* representative system 代表制度の諸欠陥.

defraud, *v.* かたる, 詐取する.

P *defraud* him *of* his property 彼の財産を詐取する.【類】he was *defrauded of* large sums of money by ... / She accused him of having *defrauded* her *of* twenty thousand dollars. / be *defrauded of* one's earnings ‖ be *defrauded of* one's rights 詐欺手段をもってその権利を侵害する.

defray, *v.* 支払う.

P Ten thousand yen will be *defrayed for* the expense. その費用に一万円支出される.

deftness, *n.* 巧妙.

Q do it with *magical deftness* それ(手工など)を不思議なほど巧みにやる. ¶with *nimble deftness* 手早く巧みに.

defunct, *a.* 現存していない.

M a *now defunct* Scotch weekly すでに廃刊となったスコットランドの週刊誌.

degenerate, *n.* 堕落者; 変質者.

V *sterilize degenerates* by means of the Röntgen rays レントゲン線で変質者の生殖能力をなくす.

Q a *talented degenerate* 堕落した秀才.

degenerate, *v.* 退化する, 堕落する.

P Liberty often *degenerates into* lawlessness. 自由は往々放縦に堕する. ‖ once a clear and sparkling stream, *degenerated into* a foul ditch 今は不潔なほりとなったがかつてはきらきらした清流 ‖ *degenerate into* license and unmorality (a profligate) 放縦・不徳(など)に堕落する.【類】*degenerate into* a mere thing of forms (ほんの形式) / without *degenerating into* commonplace. ¶*degenerate to* destructive criticism 破壊的批評に堕する.

degeneration, *n.* 退廃; 退化.

V To have ugly utensils perpetually in view gradually *works degeneration* in one's taste. 絶えず醜悪な器具を見ていると漸次にその人の趣味が悪くなって来る.

Q *fatty degeneration* of the heart 心臓の脂肪性変質. ¶*national degeneration* 国家の堕落. ¶*physical degeneration* 肉体の退化. ¶*social degeneration* 社会の廃退.

Q[2] *race degeneration* 民族の堕落.

P the process *of degeneration* 退化作用.

degradation, *n.* 衰退; 左遷.

V *work out* the *degradation* of a language 言語の堕落を生む.

Q *moral degradation* 道義の退廃. ¶*social degradation* 社会の堕落.

P[2] *degradation of* (=*in*) rank 降位(降等) ‖ the *degradation of* an officer 官吏の左遷.

degrade, *v.* 落す, 下げる.

P *degrade ... from* a position (an office) 地位(官職)から…を落す ‖ *degrade ... from* the office of ... …の地位より…を落す ‖ He was *degraded from* the priesthood. 彼は僧職から退けられた. ¶he was *degraded into* ... 彼は…に落された. ¶*degrade* a person *to* a lower position (=rank) 人を下級におとす.

degree, *n.* (**1**) 程度; 身分; 親等.

V *acquire* a high *degree* of dexterity 非常に巧みになる. ¶The science has *attained* a high *degree* of development. その科学は非常な発達を遂げた.【類】*attain* a high *degree* of perfection. ¶The power of composition *determines* the *degree* of familiarity with a language. 作文力はある国語に対する熟達の程度を示す. ¶*endure* a *degree* of discomfort due to limited means 資力の乏しいことから生じる不愉快を忍ぶ. ¶We *had* five *degrees* of frost last night. 昨夜は氷点下五度だった. ‖ Every circle *has* 360 *degrees*. 円はすべて 360 度ある. ¶*undergo* third *degree* (《米》拷問にかけられる.

Q to an *abominable degree* 恐ろしく. ¶It has not yet affected this trade to any *alarming degree*. それはこの商売にはまださほど恐ろしい影響はなかった. ¶people of *all degrees* of wealth あらゆる富の程度の人々. ¶to an *amusing degree* ばかげた位に. ¶in *any degree* いくらでも. ¶to a *certain degree* 幾分か. ¶to a *considerable degree* 大分, 大いに. ¶to a *conspicuous* (=an *eminent*) *degree* 際立って. ¶be increased in a *corresponding degree* それ相応に増加される. ¶with a *fair degree* of precision かなり正確に. ¶murder in the *first degree* 謀犯殺人罪. ¶the *forbidden* (=*prohibited*) *degrees* 結婚禁止の親等. ¶in *full degree* 十分に. ¶in a *great* (=*large*) *degree* 非常に.【類】to a far *greater degree*. ¶a *high degree* of efficiency 高度の能率 ‖ a man of *high* (*low*) *degree* 身分の高(低)い人 ‖ it is in the *highest degree* improbable that ... …はどうしてもありそうもない ‖ secure the *highest degree* of accuracy possible 出来るだけの正確さを得る. ¶grow up by *insensible degrees* 知らず知らず成長する. ¶be in the *last degree* wretched この上もなく不幸である ‖ emaciated to the *last degree* 極度にやせて.【類】be impartial (公平無私) to the *last degree* / uncomfortable to the *last degree*. ¶not in the *least degree* 少しも…でなく. ¶in the *least possible degree* できうるだけ少く. ¶The desire to imitate shows itself to a very *marked degree* among children the world over. 模ほう欲は世界いたるところ子供らの間に著しく現われている. ¶be in no *little degree* indebted to 少なからず…の恩義にあずかっている. ¶in a *marked degree* 著しく. ¶to a *minor degree* それほどでなく. ¶in *no degree* 決して…しない. ¶The writing is *one* or *two degrees* better than the average. その文は平均よりちょっと良い. ¶secure a *reasonable degree* of uniformity. 相当な程度の均等性を確保する. ¶to a *remarkable degree* 非常に. ¶an Asiatic Power of the *second* or *third degree* アジアの二三等国. ¶only to a *slight degree* ほんのわずか. ¶in *some degree* 幾分か ‖ to *some degree* ある程度まで ‖ These new words have won *some degree* of acceptance and use これらの新語はある程度使われている. ‖ He paid his rent with *some degree* of regularity. 彼はややきちょうめんに家賃を払った. ¶in a *surprising degree* 驚くべきほどに.【類】a relation in the *third degree*=relatives within the *third degree* of relationship by blood 三等親の親族. ¶adjectives in the *three degrees* of comparison 比較の三種の級における形容詞. ¶All savages appear to possess, to an *uncommon degree*, the power of mimicry. 野蛮人は皆非常に模ほう力を持っているらしい. ¶success in *varying degrees* 大小いろいろの成功 ‖ These two views have ever since been maintained with *varying degrees* of vigor by their adherents. その後引続きこの二つの見解が各見解を抱く人々により大なり小なり支持されてきた. ‖ They speak French with *varying degrees* of accuracy. 彼らの話すフランス語は正確さが色々だ.

Q[2] at *minus 72 degrees* centigrade 摂氏零下 72 度で.

P The temperature did not rise *above* 86 *deg.* F. 気温は華氏の八十六度以上には上がらなかった. ¶The thermometer stood *at* 20 *degrees*. 寒暖計は二十度だった. ‖ Reaumur's boiling point is *at* eighty *degrees*. 列氏の沸騰点は八十度だ. ¶*By degrees* the color faded. 段々色がさめた. ‖ *by* slow *degrees*, nearly imperceptible 目につかぬ程度に ‖ *by* slow (=small) *degrees* 徐々に. ¶differ *in degree*, not in kind 相違は程度で種類ではない. ¶glass *of* a high *degree* of transparency 非常に透明なガラス. ¶*to* a *degree* 大いに; いく分 ‖ be exasperating *to* a *degree* 非常に腹立たしい ‖ His efforts are successful *to* a *degree*. 彼の努力は非常に成功した.【類】He is insolent *to* a *degree*. / *to* any *degree*. ¶*with* any great *degree* of certainty きわめて正確に.

P[2] a high *degree of* excitement 非常な興奮 ‖ the *degree of* relationship 親等 ‖ *degrees of* heat and cold 寒暖の度. ¶one *degree on* the centigrade scale 百度計の一度. ¶Its *degree of* merit is infinitely various. その価値の程度は数限りなくある.

(**2**) 学位.

V he *attained* the *degree* of Master of Arts in ... 彼は…(大学)で文学士号を得た. ¶*award degrees* in commerce 商業の学位を授ける.【類】The *degree* of doctor of philosophy is *awarded* to him. ¶a man *bearing* a *degree* 学位のある人. ¶*confer* the *degree* of LL.D. upon ... …に法学博士の学位を授与する. ¶*get* the *degree* of B.A. バチェラー・オヴ・アーツ号を得る. ¶colleges *granting degrees* in education 教育学の学位を授ける大学. ¶He *has* a *degree* from Columbia. 彼はコロムビヤ大学から学位をもらっている. ¶women *holding degrees* from colleges 大学からの学位を有する婦人.【類】He *held* the D.C.L. from Oxford, and the LL.D. from Cambridge, Dublin, and Edinburgh. ¶The university has ***inaugurated degrees*** in commerce. その大学は新たに商業の学位を授与することになった. ¶***obtain*** a Ph. D. ***degree*** 哲学博士号をうる. ¶He ***received*** his doctor's ***degree*** from a German university. 彼はドイツの大学から博士号を授けられた. 【類】He ***received*** his ***degrees*** of B. A. and M.A. at St. John's College, Cambridge, England. / ***receive*** one's ***degree*** cum laude (=with honors) / In 1870 de Vries ***received*** his doctor's ***degree*** from the University of Leiden, on a thesis entitled "The Influence of Heat on Life-phenomena in Plants." ¶***take*** one's ***degree*** 学位を取る ‖ He ***took*** his ***degree*** with first-class honors. 彼は優等で卒業した. 【類】after ***taking*** a ***degree*** in jurisprudence / ***take*** a doctor's ***degree*** in law / those who attended but did not ***take degrees***. ¶he ***won*** his ***degree*** by writing a thesis on ... 彼は…に関する論文を書いて学位を得た.

Q an ***academic*** ***degree*** 学位. ¶The ***associate degree*** is a degree offered by the junior college. 準学士は短期大学が授ける学位である. ¶hold a ***bachelor's degree*** 学士号を持っている. ¶a man with a ***doctor's degree*** 博士号を持っている人. ¶a ***doctoral degree*** 博士の称号. ¶he holds the ***honorary degree*** of LL.D. from the University of ... 氏は…大学の名誉法学博士号を持っている. ¶take a ***Master's degree*** 修士号をとる.

Q² He has a ***college degree***. 彼は学位を持っている. ¶secure the ***Master of Arts degree*** 文学修士の称号を得る. 【類】a candidate for the ***Master of Arts degree***. ¶take a ***M.Sc.*** (=Master of Science) ***degree*** 理学修士の学位をとる. ¶hold an ***Oxford M.A. degree*** オックスフォード大学修士の称号を持っている. ¶a sapper《英》with a Cambridge honors ***science degree*** ケンブリッジの優等卒業理学士の学位を持っている工兵. ¶take a ***university degree*** 学位をとる.

P he was honored ***with*** the ***degree*** of LL.D. by ... 彼は…から法学博士号を授与された. 【類】He graduated from Harvard ***with*** the A.B. (=B.A.) ***degree*** in 1912.

P² He took his ***degree as*** M.A. at Oxford. 彼はオックスフォード大学で文学修士号をとった.

deity, *n.* 神.

V ***appease*** a malevolent, destructive ***deity*** 荒神をしずめる. ¶***propitiate*** offended ***deities*** たたる神をしずめる. 【類】***propitiate*** a ***deity*** with offerings of food, drink, etc.

Q a ***masculine deity*** 男神.

P He is worshipped ***as*** a ***deity***. 彼は神にまつられている.

dejection, *n.* 落胆.

P He went away ***in*** great ***dejection***. 彼は非常に落胆して出て行った.

delay, *n.* 遅滞; 猶予.

V ***avoid*** unnecessary ***delay*** 不必要な遅滞を避ける. ¶The matter will ***bear*** no ***delay***. この件は遅らせない. ¶problems which would not ***brook delay*** 緊急の諸問題. ¶***cause*** great ***delay*** in the completion of a work 仕事の完成を非常に遅らせる ‖ without ***causing delay*** 遅らせずに ‖ It will ***cause*** too much ***delay***. そうすると余りひどく遅れることになるだろう. ¶It would necessarily ***involve*** a ***delay***. そうなると必ず遅れる. ¶***Make*** no ***delay*** in doing what is good. 善は急げ. ¶***occasion delay*** 遅延をきたす. ¶***save delay*** 遅れないようにする. 【類】it will ***save delay*** if ...

Q a ***considerable delay*** 余ほどの遅滞. ¶without ***further delay*** これ以上遅滞なく. ¶***heavy delays*** owing to the interruption of cables 海底電線の故障による大延着. ¶a ***hidden delay*** caused by cable 海外電報の原因不明の遅延. ¶involve very ***inconvenient delay*** その結果はなはだ迷惑な遅延をきたすことになる. ¶without the ***least delay*** 早速. ¶with the ***least possible delay*** できるだけ遅れないように. ¶with as ***little delay*** as possible 大至急. ¶a ***long delay*** 長い遅延. ¶without a ***moment's delay*** 寸時の猶予もなく. ¶owing to ***postal delays*** 郵便延着のため. ¶receive a visitor after ***some intentional delay*** わざと待たして置いてから客に接する. ¶without any ***unreasonable delay*** 不当な遅延をきたさずに.

Q² with a ***minimum delay*** できるだけ遅らせずに.

P ***after*** some ***delay*** 少し遅れてから. ¶carry out ***without delay*** 遅滞なく履行する ‖ enforce the regulations ***without delay*** 規則を遅滞なく実施する ‖ ***without*** the ***delay*** of a day 一日の猶予もなく ‖ see to it ***without delay*** 遅れないように注意する.

P² my ***delay in*** replying to your letter of the 18th inst. has been occasioned by ... 本月十八日付の貴かんに対し当方からの返書の遅延は…がその原因でした ‖ ***delay in*** arrival 延着.

delay, *v.* 遅らす.

M ***seriously delay*** the train service 汽車の大遅延を生じる.

P The train was ***delayed by*** snow. 汽車は雪のために延着した. 【類】The ship was ***delayed by*** adverse wind (bad weather). ¶***delay*** delivery ***until*** further instructions さらにさたがあるまで引渡を延ばす.

delectation, *n.* 歓楽.

P solely ***for*** the ***delectation*** of ... 全く…の楽しみに.

delegate, *n.* 代表者, 代議員.

V ***call*** in conference ***delegates*** from all Pacific peoples for the purpose of ... …のため太平洋沿岸諸国全部から会議に代表者を招致する. ¶***send*** a special ***delegate*** to the congress (=conference) その会議へ特別代表者を派遣する.

Q an ***alternative delegate*** 代理代議員. ¶the ***chief delegate*** of ... to a conference 会議出席の…の主席代表. ¶a ***fraternal delegate*** 友誼的代表.

Q² a ***conference delegate*** 会議に出席する委員.

P² the ***delegates from*** Japan ***to*** the Washington Conference ワシントン会議の日本代表者たち ‖ a ***delegate to*** the International Labour Congress in 1884 一八八四年の国際労働会議代表者.

delegate, *v.* 委任する; 派遣する.

P ***delegate*** power (=authority) ***to*** an envoy 使節に権限を委任する ‖ He was ***delegated to*** the convention. 彼は会議に派遣された.

delegation, *n.* [団]代表団.

V These ladies ***headed*** the ***delegation*** to the President. この婦人たちが大統領への派遣代表団を引率した. ¶***send*** a large ***delegation*** to ... …へ多数の代表を派遣する.

Q an eight-man ***Outer Mongolian delegation*** 八人から成る外蒙古代表団.

P² a ***delegation from*** the National Diet of Japan 日本国会からの代表団.

deleterious, *a.* 有害な.

P² Foul air is ***deleterious to*** health. よごれた空気は健康に有害だ.

deliberate, *v.* 審議する, 討究する.

P ***deliberate on*** (=upon) a matter (subject, problem, the affairs of state) ある問題(など)を審議する. ¶***deliberate upon*** the state of affairs 事態を討究する. ¶I ***deliberated with*** him on his future course of conduct. 彼の将来の方針について彼と相談した.

deliberate, *a.* 慎重な.

P He was ***deliberate in*** everything that he said. 彼は何事にも注意して言った. ¶***deliberate on*** one's plan to be realized ... の案を実現するために審議する.

deliberation, *n.* 熟考.

Q after ***deep deliberation***, I have decided to ... 熟考の上私は…に決した. ¶without ***due deliberation*** よくも考えずに. ¶without ***full deliberation*** 熟考せずに. ¶The step taken was by no means an improvisation, but was the result of ***ripe deliberation***. 取った手段はにわか作りのものではなく熟慮の結果であった.

Q² ***Diet deliberations*** of important bills 議会における重要法案の審議. 【類】be currently under ***Diet deliberation***.

P The matter is now ***under deliberation***. その問題は目下考慮中だ.

delicacy, *n.* (**1**) 微妙; 優美; 巧妙.

V He ***has delicacy*** of feeling. 彼は物の感じが細かい.

Q act with ***chivalrous delicacy*** of honor 細かい武士道の精神で行動する. ¶a matter of ***extreme delicacy*** 非常に微妙な問題. ¶***feminine delicacy*** 女らしいしおらしさ. ¶be in a position of ***great delicacy*** きわめて微妙な立場にある. ¶***supersensitive delicacy*** 神経過敏. ¶he had ***no delicacy*** in reminding her of ... 彼は無遠慮に…を彼女に思い出させた ‖ Hunger knows ***no delicacy***. すき腹にまずいものなし. ¶a point of ***too much delicacy*** for me to decide upon 実に微妙で, 僕にはなかなか決めにくい点.

Q² letters which ***family delicacy*** prevents from giving to the public 家庭内情にわたるため公表できぬ手紙.

P matters ***of delicacy*** むずかしい事柄. ¶***through*** a false ***delicacy*** 間違った遠慮から.

P² the ***delicacy of*** coloring 着色の妙.

(**2**) 美味.

Q an ***appetizing delicacy*** 食欲を誘う珍味. ¶Its flesh has ***exceptional delicacy***. その肉は無類の珍味である. ¶They are considered a ***great delicacy***. 非常な美味と思われている. ¶***homely delicacies*** 手製の美味. ¶a ***much-prized***

delicacy 非常に賞美される珍味.
Q[2] a *fish delicacy* 魚肉の珍味. ¶*food delicacies* うまいもの. ¶a *table delicacy* 美味の食品.
P I was entertained with all kinds *of delicacies.* 私は山海の珍味のごち走を受けた. ¶He is used *to delicacies.* 彼は口がおごっている.

delight, *n.* 歓喜, 満足; 喜ばしい物, 好物.
V *afford* the keenest *delight* to ... ...に大満足を与える. ¶*drink in* the *delights* of nature (a place) 自然(など)の美観に見とれる. ¶*experience* the *delight* of seeing them again 再び彼らと会う喜びを得る. ¶I would like to *express* my *delight* at ... ...に対する私の喜びを述べたい.【類】*express delight* in being informed of ... ¶*find delight* in the society of women 女と交際するのを楽しむ.【類】*find delight* in the torment and the blood of man and beast (人間や動物の苦悩と血). ¶*give* an intellectual *delight* 知的満足を与える. ¶I *have* (=find) the intensest *delight* in music. 私は音楽が大好きだ. ¶*raise* one's *delight* 楽しみを増す. ¶*retaste* one's old *delights* 昔の喜びをしのぶ. ¶I *take* [a] *delight* in working at arithmetical problems. 僕は算術の問題を解くのが好きだ. ‖ He *takes* much *delight* in his studies. 彼は勉強が大好きだ.【類】In most private schools there is generally a boy who *takes* a *delight* in bullying the small fry (弱い者いじめ) and making their lives unendurable. ¶*taste* the *delights* of ... ...を楽しむ.
Q *chief delights* 主なる好物. ¶take a *childish delight* in ...ing ...して子供らしく喜ぶ. ¶a source of *constant delight* 絶えざる喜びの種. ¶a *cruel delight* 残酷な喜び. ¶The region is truly a *fisherman's delight.* その所は真に釣師の極楽だ. ¶a lover of *fleshly delights* 肉体的快楽の愛好者. ¶is his *great delight* 彼の大なる喜びである. ¶He took *intense delight* in Shakespeare. 彼はシェイクスピアが大好きだった. ¶an *intoxicating delight* 人を狂喜させる物. ¶an *irresistible delight* たまらなく好きなもの. ¶the *keen delight* of ... ...をひどく喜ぶこと ‖ read it with the *keenest delight* それを非常に面白く思って読む. ¶He takes *much delight* in dancing. 彼は踊りが大好き. ¶The radio, the cinema and *other delights* kept the little ones interested. ラジオ, 映画その他の余興で子供などは喜んだ. ¶Shopping for young people is a *real delight.* 子供のものを買うのは本当に楽しみなものだ. ¶His pictures are a *sheer delight.* 彼の絵はほんとに面白い. ¶It is a *sweet delight* to see your handwriting. 貴方のご筆跡を見るのはうれしい. ¶an *unalloyed delight* 全くの喜び. ¶I take *unceasing delight* in Conan Doyle. コナン・ドイルはいつ読んでも面白い. ¶read again and again with *unfailing delight* 度々読んでもあきない ‖ a source of *unfailing delight* and wonder 尽きない歓喜と驚異の源泉. ¶*unutterable delight* 口に言えぬ楽しみ.
P dance round him *in delight* うれしさの余り彼の回りを踊り回る ‖ *in* high *delight* 非常に喜んで ‖ He was *in* the greatest *delight* with his purchase. 彼はそれを買って非常に喜んでいた. ¶The baby laughed in an ecstasy *of delight.* 赤ん坊がきゃっきゃっと言って笑った. ¶*to* my boundless *delight* とってもうれしかったことには. ¶That book I read *with delight.* その本を私は楽しく読んだ.【類】listen *with delight* / He was transported (夢中だった) *with delight.* / gaze *with delight* on ... / He stamped (=danced) *with delight.*
P[2] the *delight of* life 人生の歓喜.【類】*delights of* city life ‖ It is the *delight of* every lover of beautiful scenery. それは風景の美を愛する人はだれでも喜ぶ. ¶a *delight to* the eye 目を喜ばす物, 目の正月.

delight, *v.* 喜ばす; 喜ぶ; 好む.
M I was *hugely delighted.* 私はとてもうれしかった. ¶I was *quite delighted.* 私は非常に喜んだ. ¶I am *really delighted* to see you. 君に会って本当にうれしい. ¶I am *sincerely delighted* to hear of your ... 君の...を聞いて心からうれしい.
P He was *delighted at* the news (one's success, coming of one's friend). 彼はその話(など)を聞いて喜んだ. ¶We were *delighted by* the concert. 音楽会が楽しかった. ‖ He was *delighted by* the news. 彼はその話を喜んだ. ¶Children *delight in* fables. 子供たちがぐう話を喜ぶ. ‖ He *delighted in* Thackeray's novels. 彼はサッカレーの小説が好きだった.【類】He *delights in* travels (music, games, a book study). / The Dutch *delight in* festivals, with fine dressing and good eating. / Some women *delight in* scandal (醜聞). / *delight in* reading and in learning / He *delighted in* doing good. / books *delighted in* by the many / Altogether it is a book to be in the hands of all who *delight in* the beautiful. / *delight in* the culture of plants (植物栽培) ‖ The geese *delight in* the sweet corn stalks. がちょうはさとうもろこしの茎を好む. ¶I am *delighted with* your words of appreciation. おほめの言葉で恐れ入ります. ‖ He *delights* himself *with* his riches. 彼は自分の富を喜んでいる. ‖ I am *delighted with* this novel (my new frock). 僕はこの小説(など)が好きだ.
O I'm *delighted* to see you. お会いしてうれしい.

delightful, *a.* うれしい, 愉快な.
M be *perennially delightful* いつまでたっても楽しい.

delineation, *n.* 線描写; 輪郭.
Q *delicate delineation* of character せん細な性格描写.
Q[2] subtle *character delineation* 微妙な性格描写.

delineator, *n.* 描写する人.
Q a too *realistic delineator* of every form of base passion あらゆる種類の下劣な情欲を余りにも写実的に描写する人.

delinquency, *n.* 怠慢, 非行.
Q *juvenile delinquency* 少年犯罪.
Q[2] seizure of property because of *tax delinquency* 税金滞納による財産差押え.
P[2] *delinquency in* one's study (doing something) 研究(など)を怠ること.

delinquent, *n.* 犯罪者.
V The *delinquents* were eventually *captured* and sent to penal servitude. 犯人は結局逮捕されて懲役の身となった. ¶*prosecute* a *delinquent* 違法者を検挙する.
Q a *juvenile delinquent* 非行少年.

delinquent, *a.* 欠陥のある.
M children who are *intellectually* and *morally delinquent* 知能並に道徳に欠陥のある小児.

delirium, *n.*〖医〗譫妄(せんもう)状態(うわごとを言ったりする).
P be *in delirium* せんもう状態にある. ¶lapse *into delirium* うわごとを言い出す. ¶be never once *out of* a *delirium* [こん睡状態から]正気に戻らない.

deliver, *v.* 引渡す; 配達する; 救出す; 加える; 述べる; 分娩させる.
M goods to be *delivered f.o.b.* 甲板渡しの現品. ¶*deliver free* alongside ship in New York Harbor ニューヨーク港内船側渡しで荷渡しする. ¶*How often* are letters *delivered* here? 当地では郵便は何回配達されますか. ¶*deliver immediately* 即時引渡す. ¶goods *promptly delivered* 現品先渡し.
M[2] *deliver over* money in trust あずかっていた金を引渡す. ¶The retiring warden *delivered over* (=*up*) the keys of the prison to his successor. 退職する刑務所長が同所のかぎを後任者に引渡した. ¶The fortress was *delivered up* to the enemy. その要塞は敵にあけ渡された.
P *deliver* an attack *against* the enemy (a position) 敵(など)に攻撃を加える. ¶They were *delivered as* broadcast talks on the Overseas Service of the B.B.C. それはイギリス放送局 (British Broadcasting Corporation) 海外放送の放送談話として述べられた. ¶*deliver* a speech *at* a meeting 会で演説する ‖ He *delivered* me a letter *at* my friend's house. 彼は友人の宅で僕に手紙を渡した. ‖ *Deliver* it *at* a house (home, office, school) 家(など)へ配達して下さい. ¶*deliver* a speech *before* an audience 聴衆の前で演説する. ¶She was *delivered for* the first time. 始めてのお産をした. ¶*deliver* the press *from* the restraints with which it was encumbered [言論]統制から新聞を解放する. ‖ We *delivered* him *from* (=out of) death (captivity, sin, the enemy, some dangerous position). われわれは彼を死(など)から救った. ¶*deliver* a speech *in* a hall 会堂で演説する. ¶*deliver* it *into* his hand それを彼に引渡す ‖ He was *delivered into* the hand of the police. 彼は警察の手に引渡された. ¶She was *delivered of* (=gave birth to) a child. お産をした. ‖ He was *delivered of* a sonnet on the subject. 彼はその題で短詩を作った. ‖ He *delivered* himself *of* the opinion. 彼はその意見を発表した. ‖ We *delivered* him *of* all his fears. われわれはあらゆる恐怖から彼を救い出した. ¶*deliver* a speech *on* a platform 壇上で演説する. ¶He was *delivered out of* (=released from) prison. 彼は

出所を許された. ‖ *deliver* it ***to*** posterity それを子孫に伝える ‖ Please *deliver* ***to*** my order. 僕の指定通り引渡して下さい. ‖ *deliver* one ***to*** the authorities (police) 人を官憲(など)に引渡す. 【類】 *deliver* a robber ***to*** the officers of the law (警官).

deliverance, *n.* 救出.

Q a *miraculous deliverance* 奇跡的救出.

P^2 *deliverance from* a danger 危険からの救出.

delivered, *pa.* 引渡済みの.

P *delivered* ***to*** order 指図人渡し.

delivery, *n.* (**1**)〘商〙引渡し; 配達.

V refuse to ***accept*** *delivery* of goods 品物の引取をこばむ. ¶ terrorize a person and ***cause*** *delivery* of property おどして財産を引渡させる. ¶ ***complete*** *delivery* of ... ...の引渡しを済ませる. ¶ ***effect*** *delivery* 引渡す. ¶ When may we ***expect*** *delivery?* いつ配達してもらえますか. ¶ ***get*** *delivery* 引渡される. ¶ We can ***give*** immediate *delivery* from stock. 在庫品から直接引渡しができる. ¶ *Delivery* is ***guaranteed*** within fourteen days. 引渡しは十四日以内と保証されている. ¶ kindly ***hurry*** the *delivery* as much as possible できるだけ配達を急いで下さい. ¶ The rate does not ***include*** *delivery*. その値段には配達料は含まれていない. ¶ ***make*** *delivery* to ... ...に引渡す ‖ *Delivery* will be ***made*** in a few days. 数日中に引渡します. ¶ ***obtain*** *delivery* to registered letters 書留書状の配達を受ける. ¶ ***receive*** *delivery* of ... ...を受取る. ¶ ***refuse*** *delivery* 引渡しをこばむ. ¶ ***secure*** *delivery* of ... ...を渡してもらう. ¶ ***stop*** the *delivery* of ... ...の配達を停止する. ¶ ***take*** *delivery* of the goods その品物を受取る. 【類】 ***take*** immediate *delivery* of ... from ...

Q buy shares for ***backward*** *delivery* 延滞受渡しで株を買う. ¶ have ***difficult*** *delivery* 難産する. ¶ ***early*** *delivery* 早い引渡し. ¶ the ***first*** *delivery* 第一便 ‖ Those who pay in within this month get the ***first*** *delivery*. 今月中に代金支払の方には最初にお引渡しをする. ¶ a ***formal*** *delivery* to the present 贈呈品の正式交付. ¶ ***forward*** *delivery* 先物(きもの). ¶ ***free*** *delivery* within 100 miles 百マイル以内の無料配達. 【類】 The prices include ***free*** *delivery* in Tokyo. ¶ ***monthly*** *deliveries* 月々の引渡し. ¶ a ***pre-date*** *delivery* 早受渡し. ¶ buy for ***prompt*** *delivery* 即時配達で買う. ¶ ***quick*** *delivery* of goods 品物の速達. ¶ the ***safe*** *delivery* of the goods 品物の安全引渡し. ¶ There are ***several*** *deliveries* daily. 毎日数回配達する. ¶ ***short*** *delivery* of goods 引渡品の不足. ¶ post a letter by ***special*** *delivery* 別配達で手紙を出す. ¶ There are ***two*** *deliveries* of letters on week-days and one on Sundays. 週日には二回日曜日に一回の書状の配達がある.

P the latest date ***for*** the *delivery* of exhibits 出品物引渡しの最後の日. ¶ be collected ***on*** *delivery* 引換に代金を徴集する ‖ pay ***on*** the *delivery* of ... ...引換に払う ‖ payable ***on*** *delivery* 引換払いで ‖ The price will be paid ***on*** *delivery*. 代価は受取のさい払います. ‖ payment ***on*** *delivery* 現品引換払 ‖ Payment, 3 s. ***on*** *delivery* and twelve monthly payments of 5 s. each. 引渡しの際三シリング払残金は五シリングずつ十二カ月払.

Q^2 see that ***food quota*** *deliveries* were met [米など]食糧の割当供出がされていたかを確かめる. ¶ a ***gaol*** *delivery* 出所者引渡し. ¶ the ***house to house*** *delivery* of bread (newspapers) パン(新聞)の戸別配達. ¶ express ***motor*** *delivery* 自動車による速配. ¶ ***quota*** (***over-quota***) *delivery* of rice 米の割当(超過)供出. ¶ step up ***rice*** *deliveries* 米の配給を推進する. ¶ the ***three-o'clock*** *delivery* 三時の配達.

(**2**) 弁舌.

Q The *delivery* was ***better*** than the matter. 論旨より弁舌の方が優れていた. ¶ a ***clear*** *delivery* 明せきな弁舌. ¶ ***oral*** *delivery* 口頭の陳述. ¶ a ***telling*** *delivery* 力ある弁舌.

(**3**) 分べん.

Q a ***difficult*** *delivery* (=birth) 難産. ¶ an ***easy*** *delivery* (=birth) 軽いお産. ¶ her ***first*** *delivery* (=confinement) 初産. ¶ a ***natural*** or ***instrumental*** *delivery* 自然または人工の分べん. ¶ ***painless*** *delivery* 無痛分べん. ¶ a ***safe*** *delivery* to children 安産.

Q^2 a ***full-term*** *delivery* 満月での出産.

delude, *v.* 迷わす.

P Her beauty *deluded* him ***to*** folly. 彼は彼女の容色に迷ってばかなことをやった.

deluge, *n.* 洪水.

Q a ***military*** *deluge* 潮のごとく寄せ来る軍勢.

P^2 a *deluge* ***of*** rain (tears) 雨(など)のはんらん ‖ a *deluge* ***of*** letters 来信の洪水. 【類】 a *deluge* ***of*** questions (protests, words, etc.).

deluge, *v.* あふれる.

P be *deluged* ***in*** tears 涙の雨にぬれる. ¶ The brook was *deluged* ***with*** water. 小川は水があふれていた. ‖ The market was *deluged* ***with*** smuggled silks. 市場は密輸入の絹ものでーぱいだった. ‖ He was *deluged* ***with*** letters. 彼のもとに手紙が殺到した. ‖ Nikko was *deluged* ***with*** foreigners. 日光へ外国人が洪水のように押寄せた. ‖ families *deluged* ***with*** offspring 子だくさんの家庭 ‖ *deluge* a country ***with*** emigrants 移民で国が一杯になる.

delusion, *n.* 幻想.

V ***cherish*** *delusions* about ... ...について空想をいだく. ¶ ***dispel*** the fond *delusion* もう想を一掃する. 【類】 It is this *delusion* we are seeking to ***dispel***.

Q get out of his head these ***favorite*** *delusions* 好んで描いたこれらのもう想を彼の頭から駆逐する.

P labor ***under*** a *delusion* もう想に苦しむ ‖ You are ***under*** a *delusion* in this matter. 君はこの点をはき違えている. ‖ he is ***under*** no *delusion* about ... 彼は...については少しも迷っていない.

delve, *v.* せんさくする, 研究する.

M *delve* ***deeper*** into ... ...をさらに深くせんさくする. ¶ *delve* ***deeply*** into things Japanese 日本の物事を深く研究する.

P *delve* ***for*** treasures 宝をさがし求める. ¶ He had a considerable Elizabethan library to *delve* ***in***. 彼はエリザベス時代の参考図書をかなり所蔵していた. ¶ *delve* ***into*** a subject (literature, philosophy) 問題(など)に没頭する ‖ *delve* ***into*** the pages of her history 彼女の過去を調べる.

demand, *n.* 要求; 需要.

V ***abridge*** *demand* 需要を縮小させる. ¶ What ***causes*** the *demand?* 何がその需要の原因か. ¶ ***concede*** the *demands* of ... ...の要求をいれる. ¶ This will ***create*** a big *demand* for the product. このために大いにその品の需要をきたすであろう. ¶ ***diminish*** *demand* 需要を低下させる. ¶ Japanese goods ***enjoy*** an increasing *demand*. 日本品は需要が増して来る. ¶ The supply ***exceeds*** the *demand*. 供給が需要を超過している. ¶ ***fill*** this growing *demand* この増加する需要を満たす. ¶ ***fill*** the present *demands* 現在の需要を満たす. ¶ I ***have*** many *demands* on my time (money). 私は時間(金銭)を色々なことに使っている. ¶ ***hold*** a *demand* against a person 人に対する請求権を保持する. ¶ ***increase*** *demand* for ... ...の需要を増す. ¶ This ***makes*** a *demand* upon my time (money). 僕はこのために時(など)を使う. ‖ ***make*** a *demand* upon ... for ... as an indemnity ...に対し損害賠償として...を要求する. ¶ The supply does not ***meet*** the *demand*. 供給が需要に応じられない. ‖ ***meet*** the *demand* of the age 時代の要求に応じる. 【類】 more than enough to ***meet*** *demand*. ¶ ***obey*** *demands* of nature 大小便をする. ¶ ***outrun*** the *demand* 需要を超過する. ¶ The supply can easily ***overtake*** the *demand*. 需要通り供給が楽にできる. ¶ ***satisfy*** a *demand* 需要を満たす ‖ ***satisfy*** the higher *demands* of the human soul 人間の霊魂の一層高尚な要求を満足させる. ¶ ***supply*** home *demands* 国内の需要を供給する. ¶ ***support*** the English *demands* 英国の要求を支持する. ¶ ***whip up*** *demand* and increase consumption 需要をあおって消費高を増す.

V^2 The *demand* has considerably ***abated***. 需要は著しく減じた. ¶ The *demand* is likely to ***continue*** (***improve, decline***). 需要は継続(など)するらしい. ‖ The *demand* still ***continues***, though not quite so brisk. 需要ははかばかしくはないがまだある. ¶ The *demand* appears to be ***reviving***. 需要は回復してきたようだ. ¶ The *demand* has ***slackened*** [***off***]. 需要は小ゆるみになった.

Q an ***active*** (=a ***brisk***) *demand* for wheat 小麦の活発な需要 ‖ There is an ***active*** *demand* for money. 資金の需要が盛んだ. ¶ satisfy the ***aesthetic*** *demands* of the eye 審美眼を満足させる. ¶ ***culinary*** *demands* 料理の希望(注文). ¶ The supply is abundant and *demand* ***dull***. 供給は過多で需要は不活発だ. ¶ there is ***eager*** (***strong, moderate, limited***) *demand* for ... ...に対する需要が活発(強硬, 控え目, 緩慢)だ. ¶ The *demand* for money is slightly ***easier***. 資金の需要は少しゆるんでいる. ¶ make the most ***exacting*** *demand* upon it それに関して最も酷な要求をする. ¶ there is an ***excellent*** *demand* for ... ...は非常な売行だ. ¶ a ***factitious*** (=artificially induced) *demand* for an article あ

る物品に対する不自然な需要. ¶***foreign demand*** 外国の需要. ¶***genuine demand*** 本当の需要. ¶There is a ***good demand*** for tonnage. 船腹に対する十分な需要がある. ‖ These goods are in ***good demand***. この品はよく売れる. 【類】owing to the ***great demand*** that has arisen for ... ¶because I feared to make too ***great*** a ***demand*** on your space 貴紙(誌)の紙面を余り多く取ってはいけないと思ったから. 【類】They are in ***greater demand*** than ever. ¶***heavy demands*** on the purses of residents by war charities 戦時の慈善事業で居住者のばく大な物入り. 【類】make ***heavy demands*** upon one's pocketbook. ¶a ***hysterical demand*** for ... ...の突飛な要求. ¶an ***importunate demand*** 強談. ¶An ***improved demand*** is looked for. 需要の増加が期待される. ¶There is always a ***keen demand*** for English journals in Brussels. ブラッセルではいつも英国の雑誌類がよく売れる. ¶The *demand* for ... has been ***languid***. ...の需要は不活発であった. ¶be in ***large demand*** 多額の需要がある. ¶the workers' ***legitimate demands*** 労働者の正当な要求. ¶a ***limited demand*** わずかの需要. ¶Wheat is in ***little demand***. 小麦は売れない. ¶a ***lively demand*** 活発な需要. ¶Flour is in ***moderate demand***. 小麦粉の売行はまずまずだ. 【類】there is a ***moderate demand*** for ... ¶She looked a ***peremptory demand*** for his attention. よそ見は許さないといったまなざしで彼をじっと見た. ¶These wares are in ***permanent demand***. この品は年中売れる. ¶there is a ***poor demand*** for ... ...の売行はわるい. ¶fit boys to meet the ***practical demands*** of life 児童を実社会の要求に適応させる. ¶supply the ***pressing demand*** 緊急の需要を満たす. ¶***prospective demand*** 将来の見込み. ¶His venture seems to have met a ***real demand***. 彼の冒険は実際の要求に適ったらしい. ¶After ***repeated*** but ***fruitless demands*** for payment, he brought a suit against the debtor. 再三支払を要求してもむだだったので彼は債務者を相手取って訴訟を提起した. ¶The data so far obtained are not conclusive enough to satisfy ***scientific demand*** in regard to ... 今までに入手した資料は...に関する科学的要求を満たすほど確定的のものでない. ¶They are now in ***small demand***. それは今あまり売れない. ¶***speculative demand*** 思わく(騰貴当込)の需要. ¶a ***steady demand*** むらのない需要. ¶Foreign goods are in ***strong demand***. 舶来品の需要は活発. ‖ There is a ***strong*** and ***growing demand*** for ... ...の需要が盛んで益々ふえる. ¶A ***sudden demand*** is sprung up. にわかに需要が起ってきた. ¶a ***terrific demand*** 猛烈な需要. ¶make ***unreasonable demands*** 難題を吹っかける. ¶a ***vigorous demand*** 活発な需要.

Q² supply ***consumer demand*** 消費者の需要を満たす. ¶the slack in ***export demand*** 海外需要の不活発. ¶meet the ***market demands*** 市場の需要に応じる ‖ fill the American ***market demand*** 米国市場の希望に添う. ¶***procurement demand*** on the Japanese Government 日本政府への調達に関する要求. ¶***special procurement demands*** 特需需要. ¶the ***three-point demand*** of the workers 労働者の三項目の要求. ¶because of ***union demands*** 組合の要求で. ¶prompt new ***wage demands*** by labor 労働者の即時新賃銀要求. ¶***wage-rise*** (=《米》***wage-hike***) ***demands*** 賃上げ要求.

P ***according to demand*** 請求次第に. ¶The services of a domestic are everywhere ***in demand***. 召使の需要は至る所にある. ‖ continue ***in demand*** 依然需要がある ‖ These articles are much ***in demand***. この品は売行がよい. ‖ things always ***in demand*** by the public 絶えず世間で需要のある品. ¶show it ***on demand*** 求められてそれを見せる ‖ a note ***on demand*** 請求払の約束手形 ‖ This will be paid ***on demand***. これは請求払だ. ‖ This bill is payable ***on demand***. この手形は請求払だ. ¶***under demand*** from ... ...から要求されて.

P² a ***demand for*** goods (commodities, labor, workers) 商品(など)の需要. 【類】There is a ***demand for*** a cheaper edition (廉価版). ‖ The ***demand for*** manufacturing products fell off. 工業製品の需要が減じた. ‖ a ***demand for*** repayment of the cost 代金払戻要求. 【類】there is no ***demand for*** ... / The ***demand for*** money is slightly easier. / ***demand for*** higher wages. ¶a heavy ***demand from*** abroad 海外からの多額の需要. ¶***demand in*** market 市場での需要. ¶the ***demand of*** the times 時局の要請 ‖ In swimming contests a minimum of clothing must be combined with the ***demands of*** modesty. 水泳競技では身に着けるものをできるだけ少くしてしかも不体裁にならないようにしなければならない. ‖ the ***demand of*** timber for the Royal Navy 英国海軍用の木材の需要 ‖ the ***demands of*** the Japanese Government ***on*** (=upon) China 中国に対する日本政府の要求. ¶The ***demand on*** my time is excessive. その方に非常に時間を取られる.

demand, *v*. たずねる; 要求する.

M ***insistently demand*** あくまで追求する. ¶***demand insolently*** 横柄にたずねる. ¶***sharply demand*** 詰問する. ¶***urgently demand*** attention しきりに注意を求める.

P I shall *demand* reparation ***from*** the company. 会社から賠償を要求しよう. ¶A war would ***demand of*** us enormous sacrifices of life and property. 一度戦争となるとわれわれにばく大な生命財産の犠牲を要求することになる. ‖ He *demanded* a dollar ***of*** me. 彼は僕に一ドル要求した. 【類】He *demanded* too high a price ***of*** me.

demean, *v*. 振舞う.

M *demean* oneself ***peacefully*** (***properly***) おだやかに(適当に)振舞う.

demean, *v*. 身を落す.

P *demean* oneself ***by*** begging for food and clothing 物ごいに身を落す. ¶*demean* oneself ***to*** a common carpenter ひら大工に身を落す.

demeano[u]r, *n*. 態度.

V ***adopt*** a more tolerant *demeanor* toward Christianity キリスト教に対して一層寛容な態度をとる. ¶The prisoner ***maintained*** a stolid *demeanor*. 囚人はがん強な態度を持続した. ¶***preserve*** a calm *demeanor*=keep one's countenance 平静な態度を失わない.

Q His *demeanor* was ***calm*** and ***steady***. 彼の態度は冷静で落付いていた. ¶a ***devout demeanor*** 敬けんな態度. ¶a ***grave demeanor*** 荘重な態度. ¶a ***modest demeanor*** 控え目の態度.

demerits, *n*. 短所.

Q ***glaring demerits*** 明白な短所.

demise, *n*. 崩御; 王位の伝承.

V ***lament*** the *demise* of ... ...の崩御をいたむ.

Q the ***unexpected demise*** of King George VI. 国王ジョージ六世の思いがけない崩御.

P² the ***demise of*** the Crown 王位の伝承.

democracy, *n*. 民主制, 民主主義; 民主国.

V art and music that ***befit democracy*** (=democratic art and music) 民衆芸術および音楽.

Q ***absolute*** (***pure***) ***democracy*** 絶対(純粋)民主制. ¶establish a ***lasting democracy*** 恒久の民主主義国を確立する. ¶***representative democracy*** 代議民主制. ¶***Western democracies*** 西欧民主主義諸国.

Q² the ***bourgeois democracy*** 有産階級民主主義. ¶***English-speaking democracies*** 英語国の民主主義諸国. ¶***tory democracy*** 保守民主主義; 保守民主派. ¶***western-type democracy*** 西欧型民主主義.

democrat, *n*. 民主主義者.

Q² the ***middle-of-the-road democrats*** (左右に偏せず)中道を行く民主主義者.

democratic, *a*. 平民的な; 民主的な.

P ***democratic of*** speech and bearing 話振りと態度の平民的な.

democratize, *v*. 民主化する.

M ***thoroughly democratized*** nations (countries) 完全に民主化された国民(国家).

demon, *n*. 悪鬼, 悪魔.

V ***drive off demons*** 悪魔を追い払う. ¶Taoist priests ***exorcise*** some *demon* which is supposed to be exercising an evil influence on a family. 道教の行者は一家にたたっていると思う悪魔をはらう. ¶***keep away demons*** and all evil influences 悪魔と一切のたたりをはらう. ¶***ward off*** malignant *demons* from disturbing the dead あだする悪魔をはらって仏の安静を保つ.

Q ***malevolent demons*** あだする悪魔.

P² a ***demon at*** golf ゴルフの名手. ¶He is a ***demon for*** work. 精力絶倫だ. ¶the ***demon of*** jealousy しっとの鬼.

demonstrate, *v*. 論証する, 証明する; 示威運動をする.

M ***abundantly demonstrate*** their ability to ... 彼らが...する能力があることを十分に示す. ¶it is ***amply demonstrated*** by ... それは...によって十分証明されている. ¶***conclusively demonstrate*** the necessity for the adoption of ... 決定的に...採用の必要を論証する. 【類】it *demonstrates* ***conclusively*** that ... ¶***decisively demonstrate*** 決定的に(明確に)論証する. ¶***indisputably demonstrate*** 弁ばくの余地のないように論証する. ¶***interestingly demonstrate*** 面白く論証す

る. ¶*demonstrate* ***irrefutably*** 反ばくの余地なきまでに論証する. ¶add another piece of ***mathematically*** *demonstrated* proof to ... ...に対する数学的に立証された証拠をもう一つ加える. ¶Fallmerayer *demonstrated* ***scientifically*** that the modern Greeks are not the descendants of the old Hellenes. フォルメレーアは現代のギリシア人は古代ヘリーネ民族の子孫でないことを科学的に証明した. ¶The fallacy of this theory is pretty ***well*** *demonstrated*. この理論の誤りは相当明瞭に証明されている.

P *demonstrate* ***against*** ... ...に対して示威運動をやる.

demonstration, *n.* 示威運動(デモ); 実演; 表明; 証明.

V ***hold*** a *demonstration* 示威運動を行う. ¶***make*** a public *demonstration* of their joy 彼らの歓喜を公然と示す ‖ ***make*** a *demonstration* of an invention before experts 発明について専門家の前で実演をやる. ¶***organize*** a great public *demonstration* in opposition to ... ...反対の一大示威運動を組織する.

Q We had ***ample*** *demonstration* of the splendid stuff of which the British girl is made. その英国少女のりっぱな素質が十分われわれに証明された. ¶an ***anti-foreign*** *demonstration* 排外示威運動. ¶a ***convincing*** *demonstration* 的確な証明. ¶a ***foolish*** *demonstration* of grammatical rules 文法の規則のばかげた証明. ¶Strike is a form of ***menacing*** *demonstration*. ストは一種の威嚇デモである. ¶a ***monster*** *demonstration* of English workmen 英国労働者の大々的示威運動. ¶the ***ocular*** *demonstration* was enough to convince them of ... その眼前の実演は彼らをして...と信ぜしめるに十分であった. ¶***outdoor*** *demonstrations* 戸外示威運動. ¶a ***patriotic*** *demonstration* 愛国的示威運動. ¶a ***public*** *demonstration* 公然のデモ. ¶a ***riotous*** *demonstration* 騒々しい示威運動. ¶They made a ***threatening*** *demonstration* against the authorities. 彼らは官憲に対して示威運動を行った.

Q² an ***after-dark*** *demonstration* 夜間示威運動. ¶an ***anti-government*** *demonstration* 政府反対示威運動. ¶an ***anti-inflation*** *demonstration* インフレ反対示威運動. ¶an ***anti-war*** *demonstration* 戦争反対の示威運動. ¶a "***give-us-bread***" *demonstration* パンよこせデモ. ¶a ***labor*** *demonstration* 労働者の示威運動. ¶a ***mass*** *demonstration* by labor 労働者による集団デモ ‖ stage a ***mass*** *demonstration* against ... ...に反対集団示威運動を行う. ¶one of the great ***May-day Labor*** *Demonstrations* in Hyde Park ハイドパークにおけるメーデー大示威運動の一. ¶a ***monster*** *demonstration* of mine workers 鉱山労働者の大々的示威運動. ¶a "***Red***" *demonstration* 共産主義者の示威運動. ¶a ***street*** *demonstration* 街頭デモ. ¶The threatened ***student*** *demonstrations* failed to materialize. 脅威を感じた学生デモはものにならなかった. ¶One of the ***welcome*** *demonstrations* for ... took the form of a big lantern parade. ...に対する歓迎の催しの一は盛んなちょうちん行列であった.

P prove it ***by*** a *demonstration* 実演によってそれを証明する ‖ teach the class ***by*** *demonstration* 公開授業を行う.

P² a *demonstration* ***against*** the government (a party, a person, shortage of food) 政府(など)反対の示威運動. ¶Another *demonstration* ***of*** the capabilities of Mr. Louis Brennan's mono-rail system was given recently in the grounds of the Brennan Torpedo Factory, Gillingham, Kent. ブレナン式単軌鉄道の可能性の実演がこのごろまたケント州ギリンガムのブレナン水雷工場構内で行われた. ¶a *demonstration* ***on*** the care of babies 幼児取扱の実演.

demonstrative, *n.* 〖文法〗指示形容詞.

Q put a ***plural*** *demonstrative* before a singular noun 単数名詞の前に複数指示形容詞を付ける.

demonstrator, *n.* 示威運動者.

Q² ***student*** *demonstrators* 示威運動を行う学生たち.

demoralization, *n.* 堕落.

V It will ***entail*** *demoralization* of the martial spirit. その結果士気そそうということになるだろう.

demur, *n.* 異議.

V acquiesce without ***making*** any *demur* 異議なく従う.

P They accepted his proposal ***without*** *demur*. 彼らは異議なく彼の申込を承諾した.

demur, *v.* 苦情をいう.

P *demur* ***at*** a difficulty 難件に対して苦情をとなえる. ¶*demur* ***to*** a statement (view) 陳述(など)に異議をはさむ ‖ *demur* ***to*** evidence 証拠抗弁.

demure, *a.* まじめな.

P He looked *demure* ***for*** some time. 彼はちょっとの間まじめくさっていた.

demurrage, *n.* 超過日数割増金.

V ***pay*** the *demurrage* 滞船料(貨車留置料, 期限外割増金)を支払う.

P be ***on*** *demurrage* 滞船料が付いている.

den, *n.* 穴; 私室.

Q one's ***snug*** *den* そのこじんまりして心地よい私室.

Q² a ***gambling*** *den* ばくち場. ¶an ***opium-smoking*** (= opium) *den* アヘンくつ.

denial, *n.* 否定; 拒絶.

V ***issue*** a *denial* of the story 報道を否定する. ¶He ***got*** a *denial*. 彼は断られた. ¶***give*** a *denial* to the rumor 風説を打消す. ¶He will ***have*** (=***take***) no *denial*. 彼はいや応言わせまい. ¶***issue*** a *denial* 否定する.

Q give a ***flat*** *denial* きっぱり断る. ¶He gave the statement an ***unqualified*** *denial*. 彼はその申立を全然否定した.

P He had not a word ***in*** *denial*. 彼は否定のしようもなかった. ¶He met ***with*** a *denial*. 彼は断られた.

denominator, *n.* 〖数〗分母.

Q a ***common*** *denominator* 公分母 ‖ the least ***common*** *denominator* 最小公分母.

denomination, *n.* 宗派; 単位名目; 種類.

V missionaries ***representing*** many different *denominations* 多くの違った宗派を代表した宣教師たち.

Q clergy of ***all*** *denominations* すべての宗派の牧師たち ‖ The Russian fleet in those waters amounts to seventy-three vessels of ***all*** *denominations*. その海上にある露国艦隊は各種の艦船七十三隻に及ぶ. ¶the ***Methodist*** *denomination* メソジスト派. ¶money of ***small*** *denominations* 表記価格の小さな銭(小銭) ‖ notes of ***small*** *denominations* 小額紙幣. 【類】silver coins of ***smaller*** *denominations*.

P Stamps were issued ***in*** *denominations* of 1, 2, 4 and 5 c. 一セント・二セント・四セントおよび五セントという種目で切手が発行された. 【類】Traveller's checks (旅行者用小切手) were issued ***in*** *denominations* of $10, $20, $50, $100 and $200. ¶plants ***under*** different *denominations* 種類の色々な植物.

P² Pounds, shillings, and pence are *denominations* ***of*** English money. 英国貨幣の単位名目はポンド・シリング・ペンスだ.

denote, *v.* 表示する, 表わす.

P *denote* ***by*** a sign 信号で表示する ‖ *denote* danger ***by*** red letters 赤字で危険を表示する.

denouement, *n. F.* 終局, 大詰.

Q a ***sad*** *denouement* 悲惨な終局.

denounce, *v.* 責める, 指弾する; 告発する; おどす.

M He was severely criticised and ***bitterly*** *denounced*. 彼はきびしい批判と指弾とを受けた. ¶***hotly*** *denounce* 激しく責める. ¶***loudly*** *denounce* 盛んに責める. ¶***vigorously*** *denounce* 激しく責める.

P *denounce* ***against*** a person 人の罪を鳴らす. ¶*denounce* a person ***as*** a traitor (misleader, cheat, an upstart, demagogue) 謀反人(など)として指弾する. 【類】*denounce* the conduct of a person ***as*** base and worthy of punishment. ¶*denounce* one ***for*** neglect of duty 人の怠慢を責める. ¶*denounce* one ***to*** the authorities 人を官憲に告発する. ¶*denounce* punishment ***upon*** a person 人を罰するぞとおどす ‖ Woes were *denounced* ***upon*** them. わざわいが彼らに降りかかった.

dense, *a.* 密集した, 濃い.

P The gorge was *dense* ***with*** soldiers. 峡谷には兵士が密集していた.

density, *n.* 密度.

Q² The ***population*** *density* of Great Britain is 685 per square mile. 大英国の人口密度は一平方マイルに 685 人である. 【類】China proper (中国本部) has a ***population*** *density* of 174 to the square mile. ¶lines showing any considerable ***traffic*** *density* 著しい交通量を示す諸線. ¶a ***traffic*** *density* of only 0.83 passenger per taxi タクシー一台平均に乗客わずかに 0.83 人という交通量.

P ***in*** *density* of population 人口密度の点では.

dentist, *n.* 歯科医師.

Q a ***cosmetic*** *dentist* 美容歯科医. ¶a ***painless*** *dentist* 無痛療治歯科医. ¶a ***registered*** *dentist* 登録済の歯科医.

Q² a ***lightning*** *dentist* 仕事の素早い歯科医.

denude, *v.* はぐ, はく奪する.

P *denude* a person ***of*** clothing 人の衣類をはいで裸体にする ‖ *denude* them ***of*** political rights 彼らの参政権をはく奪

する ‖ The mountain sides are almost *denuded **of*** vegetation, due to past eruptions. これまでの噴火で山腹にはほとんど草木がない. ‖ women *denuded **of*** all decent feelings 恥を知らない女たち.

denunciation, *n.* 非難.

V ***incur*** *denunciation* as a "Jingo" 主戦論者だと言って非難される. ¶***provoke*** his fiercest *denunciation* 彼から激しく非難される. ¶***retract*** the bitter *denunciations* of ... ...に対する痛烈な非難を撤回する.

Q a ***baseless*** *denunciation* 根拠のない非難. ¶***calumnious*** *denunciation* 中傷的非難. ¶a ***fierce*** *denunciation* 猛烈な非難. ¶It is on this matter that the *denunciations* are ***strongest.*** 非難の一番高かったのはこの問題についてであった. ¶a ***sweeping*** *denunciation* だれかれの差別ない非難.

Q² ***police*** *denunciation* 警察の摘発.

deny, *v.* 拒む, 否認する; 面会を謝絶する.

M ***curtly*** *deny* そっけなく拒む. ¶we are prepared to *deny* most ***emphatically*** that ... われわれにはきっぱりと...を拒否する覚悟がある. ¶He ***flatly*** *denied* the charge. 彼は絶対そんなことはないと言った. ¶***obstinately*** *deny* がん固に拒む. ¶***persistently*** *deny* がん強に拒む. ¶He ***stoutly*** *denied* his guilt. 彼は断固として自分の罪を否認した. ¶***vehemently*** *deny* the fact やっきとなってその事実を否認する. ¶the request was ***vigorously*** *denied* by ... その要請は...によって強硬に拒絶された. ¶This was ***wholly*** *denied* to him. このことは全然彼に許されなかった.

P He *denies* himself ***for*** the good of his family. 彼は家族のためを思って辛抱している. ¶*deny* oneself ***to*** a visitor (=caller) 面会を謝絶する. 【類】I told the maid to *deny* me ***to*** visitors. / The maid *denied* her master ***to*** me.

O He *denied* himself to be a Christian. 彼はキリスト教徒でないと言った. ¶He *denied* himself many comforts. 彼は幾多の快楽から遠ざかった(禁欲した). ¶I ordered my servant to *deny* me. 私は召使に留守だと言えと命じた.

deodorant, *n.* 臭気止め.

Q an ***under-arm*** *deodorant* わきがどめ.

Q² a ***B.O.*** (=body odor) *deodorant* 体臭(わきが)止め. ¶***perspiration*** *deodorant* 汗の臭気止め.

depart, *v.* 去る, 行く, 出発する; それる.

P The train *departs* ***at*** 6.30 a.m. 汽車は午前六時三十分に発車する. ¶*depart* ***for*** a place (another country) 某所(など)へ立つ ‖ He *departed* ***for*** home. 彼は家へ帰って行った. ‖ *depart* ***for*** Heaven 天国へ行く(昇天する). ¶*depart* ***from*** this country ***to*** my own land この国を立って故国に帰る ‖ *depart* ***from*** one's usual method いつもの手を変える. 【類】*depart* ***from*** the strict order of the programme ‖ *depart* ***from*** custom (the usual practice, a purpose, an established rule, one's resolusion) 習慣(など)に反する ‖ temptation to *depart* ***from*** the right path 正道を踏みはずさせようとする誘惑. 【類】*depart* ***from*** long-established precedent (古来の先例) / He *departed* ***from*** his principles for that once (その時だけ). ¶They *departed* ***on*** their different ways. 彼らはそれぞれ違った方向へ去った. ¶*depart* ***to*** my own country 本国へ立つ.

department, *n.* 部門; [官省の]部, 局, 省; 学部.

V It ***affects*** all *departments* of life. それは人生の各方面に影響をおよぼす. ¶***institute*** an Esperantist *department* of three pages in a magazine 雑誌に三ページのエスペラント語欄を設ける. ¶***open up*** an entirely new *department* of physics 物理学に新生面を開く.

Q the *department* ***concerned*** 所轄官署. ¶Sport is my ***favorite*** *department* in newspapers. 僕は新聞ではスポーツ欄が好きだ. ¶the ***lending*** *department* of a library 図書館の図書貸出部. ¶one of the ***operative*** *departments* of a large firm of publishers 大出版社の事業部の一つ. ¶in ***other*** *departments* of endeavor 他の活動分野において. ¶Angling is one of the ***richest*** *departments* of English letters. 釣は英文学の最も豊富な部門の一つである. ¶Literature is my own ***special*** *department*. 文学は僕の専門です.

Q² the ***commissariat*** *department* 兵站(軍需)部. ¶the ***Effects*** *Department* of the BBC 英国放送局の効果(担当)部. ¶the ***furniture*** *department* on the 7th floor 七階の家具部. ¶***Government*** *departments* or agencies 政府の部局. ¶the ***groceries*** *department* 食料品部. ¶the ***Lost and Found*** *Department* 遺失物係. ¶the ***mail order*** *department* 通信販売部. ¶Ethics is a new course in the ***philosophy*** *department*. 倫理学は哲学の新分野だ. ¶shopping by ***post*** *department* 通信販売デパートによる買物. ¶a ***publication*** *department* 出版部. ¶the ***retail*** *department* 小売部. ¶the ***sales*** *department* 販売部. ¶the ***shoe*** *department* [デパートなど]靴部. ¶a ***to-be-called-for*** *department* [デパートなど]サービス部.

P every official ***in*** the *Department* 同省内の各官吏. ¶***in*** all *departments* of human endeavour 人間活動のあらゆる部門において.

P² the *Department* ***of*** the Treasury 大蔵省 ‖ the *Department* ***of*** Home (Foreign) Affairs 内(外)務省 ‖ the *department* ***of*** sociology 社会学部.

departure, *n.* 出発; 死去; 背反, 離脱.

V It ***constitutes*** a new *departure* in journalistic enterprise. それは新聞事業における新しい試みである. ¶***contemplate*** a new *departure* in one's business 事業の新発展を企画する. ¶***defer*** one's *departure* until the last moment 最後の瞬間まで出発を延ばす. ¶***delay*** the *departure* of steamers 汽船の出発を延ばす. ¶***hasten*** the *departure* of the ship 船の出帆を早くさせる. ¶There are occasions ***justifying*** *departure* from custom. 慣例と違っても差支えない場合がある. ¶***make*** a new *departure* 新方面を開拓する(新事業を始める) ‖ A *departure* was ***made*** from old methods. 新機軸を出した. ¶His dictionary ***marked*** a new *departure* in lexicography. 彼の辞書は辞典界に新機軸を出した. ‖ His action ***marks*** a new *departure* from the customary practice. 彼の行動は従来の型を破っている. ¶I had to ***postpone*** my *departure*. 止むを得ず出発を延ばした. ¶***take*** one's *departure* 出発する ‖ He ***took*** my money and his *departure*. 彼は僕の金を持って行ってしまった. ‖ ***Taking*** his *departure* from materialism, he arrived at spiritualism. 彼は唯物主義から出発して精神主義に到達した.

Q an ***abrupt*** *departure* にわかの出発. ¶the ***earlier*** *departure* of the last train (electric cars) 終電の繰り上げ. ¶a ***gratuitous*** *departure* from ... ...からのゆえなき違背. ¶take a ***new*** *departure* 新しい試みをやる. ¶a ***radical*** *departure* from longstanding customs 長の間の習慣からの根本的離脱. ¶***revolutionary*** *departures* from tradition 伝統からの革命的離脱. ¶a ***speedy*** *departure* 遅滞なき出発. ¶a ***welcome*** *departure* from the stereotyped old method 従来の古い型からの喜ばしい脱却.

Q² a ***Saturday*** *departure* [週末旅行などへ]土曜日の出発.

P He hardly concealed his joy ***at*** his *departure*. 彼は出発に際してそのうれしさをほとんど隠しきれなかった. ¶***by*** a curious *departure* from diplomatic practice 珍しくも外交の型を破って. ¶***on*** my *departure* from ... ...から出発の際 ‖ leave one's card ***on*** *departure* [訪問の]帰りしなに名刺を残しておく. ¶***since*** his *departure* 彼の出立以来.

P² on the eve of his *departure* ***for*** the front 出征に際して ‖ my *departure* ***for*** the vacation 休暇旅行への私の出発 ‖ his *departure* ***for*** home 彼の帰国(宅). ¶a *departure* ***from*** the norm 標準からの違反 ‖ a *departure* ***from*** the policy of ... ...の方針からの転向 ‖ a *departure* ***from*** custom (precedent, rules) 習慣(など)と違うこと ‖ archaic uses which are *departures* ***from*** modern usage [語など]近世の語法に反する古風な用法. ¶a new *departure* ***in*** private enterprise 民間事業における新しい試み. 【類】a new *departure* ***in*** language teaching is marked by ... / a new *departure* ***in*** French fiction. ¶his *departure* ***to*** the unseen world (=death) 彼のめい土への旅立.

O the *departure* hence ここからの出立. ¶one's *departure* homewards 自家(国)への出立. ¶the *departure* suburbwards of the last bus 最終バスの郊外への発車.

depend, *v.* 信頼する; 頼む; よる.

M A man's success *depends* ***chiefly*** on himself. 人の成功不成功は主として本人の力による. 【類】The price of commodities ***chiefly*** *depends* upon the relation between demand and supply (需要供給の関係). ¶That *depends* ***entirely*** upon circumstances. それは全く時と場合による. ¶That ***largely*** *depends* upon how you do it. それは大いに君のやり方いかんによる. ¶it *depends* ***primarily*** upon ... それは主として...いかんによる. ¶It ***solely*** (=entirely) *depends* on what move you'll take. もっぱら君の出方一つだ. 【類】That ***solely*** *depends* upon your efforts. ¶The suit is ***still*** *depending* in court. その事件はまだ裁判中だ.

P The chandelier *depends* (=suspends) *from* the ceiling. シャンデリヤが天井からつるしてある. ¶Your advancement *depends* not **on** the favor of your employer but **on** your worth—your ability. 君の昇進は雇主のひいきによるのではなく君の価値すなわち手腕いかんによるのだ. ‖ I *depend* **on** you. 僕は君に信頼する. ‖ a person to be *depended* **on** 信頼のできる人. 【類】I *depended* **on** the truth of his statement. / You may *depend* **on** (=upon) him. / *depend* **on** assistance (circumstances, friends) ‖ *depend* **on** a mere chance 行き当りばったりでやる ‖ I *depend* **on** your co-operation. ではよろしくお願い致します. ‖ I *depended* **on** his coming at four o'clock. 彼は四時に来るものと当てにしていた. ‖ all *depends* **on** [the state of] the weather すべて天候次第だ ‖ as if his life *depended* **on** it 一生懸命に ‖ *depend* **on** another **for** support (guidance, help, food, success) 扶助(など)を他人に求める. 【類】They *depend* **on** me **for** their living. ¶I cannot *depend* **upon** his word. 彼の言うことは当てにできない. ‖ *depend* **upon** one's pen for support 文筆で生活を立てる ‖ You may *depend* **upon** the accuracy of the report. その報告は正確と信じてよい. 【類】He has promised to do so, but cannot be *depended* **upon.** / Your future success *depends* **upon** yourself. ‖ We may *depend* **upon** it that ... 請合って, 必ず. ‖ We shall have war, you may *depend* **upon** it. 戦争があります, 本当ですぞ.

dependence, *n.* 信頼; 依頼; 関係.

V ***end*** one's *dependence* on ... ...から独立する. ¶I ***have*** a firm *dependence* on the will of God. 私は堅く神意に信頼する. ¶***place*** (=***put***) *dependence* upon ... ...を頼りにする.

Q a life of ***absolute*** *dependence* upon God 神に絶対的依存の生活. ¶their ***chief*** *dependence* is on ... 彼らの主なる頼りは...だ. ¶the ***economic*** *dependence* of the wife on her husband 妻の夫への経済的依存. ¶***mutual*** *dependence* 相互の信頼. ¶He is her ***sole*** *dependence*. 彼が彼女の唯一の頼りだ. ¶***unmanly*** *dependence* on others めめしく他人に頼ること. ¶***unsupported*** *dependence* そら頼み.

P ***in*** *dependence* of ... ...を頼りにして.

P[2] the *dependence* **of** children **on** their parents 子供の親がかり. ¶the *dependence* **of** one thing **upon** another 甲の乙への依存.

dependency, *n.* 領地.

Q a ***British*** *dependency* 英国の領地. ¶a ***colonial*** *dependency* 領土植民地. ¶***over-seas dependencies*** 海外の領土.

dependent, *n.* 隷属者, 食客; 扶養家族.

V I told him I was a widow and ***had*** no one *dependent* on me. 未亡人で別に係累もないと彼に告げた.

Q an ***idle*** *dependent* 遊んでいる食客. ¶a ***parasitical*** *dependent* いそうろう.

Q[2] ***Army*** *dependents* [米駐留軍などの]陸軍々人の家族. ¶***family*** *dependents* 扶養家族(員).

P a man ***with*** *dependents* 係累のある人.

P[2] the *dependents* **of** a king 国王の従者.

dependent, *a.* 隷属する; よる.

M a *samurai* ***directly*** *dependent* on the Shogun 旗本. ¶***less*** *dependent* on him than ... ...ほど彼を頼りにしない.

P The hospital is *dependent* ***for*** resources upon the contributions of the public. その病院は資金を公衆の寄付に仰いでいる. ¶He had a mother entirely *dependent* **on** him. 彼には丸がかりの母があった. 【類】They are *dependent* **on** public charity. ‖ The reward is *dependent* **on** (= upon) your success. ¶Many thoughts are so *dependent* **upon** the language in which they are clothed that they would lose half their beauty if otherwise expressed.—Ruskin. 多くの場合思想はその表現の言葉に依存しているので言回しが変ればその美の半分は失われてしまう.

depict, *v.* 描く, 写し出す.

M ***thrillingly*** *depict* ぞっとするように描写する. ¶*depict* South Sea life so ***vividly*** and ***accurately*** あざやかにかつ正確に南洋の生活状態を描く.

P *depict* things ***in*** their true colors and proportions 原物をそのままの色彩と大きさとに写し出す.

depletion, *n.* 欠乏.

V The finances of the association have ***suffered*** *depletion* during past seven years. その会は過去七年来財政困難であった.

Q He sighed deeply from a kind of ***mental*** *depletion.* 虚脱の気味で深い吐息をついた.

deplore, *v.* 悲しむ.

M ***deeply*** *deplore* 深く悲しむ.

deport, *v.* 放逐する; 振舞う.

M *deport* oneself ***bravely*** 勇ましく振舞う. ¶She *deported* herself ***gracefully.*** 彼女は物腰がしとやかであった.

P *deport* a person ***from*** the place (country) その所(など)から人を放逐する.

deportation, *n.* 追放.

V a detention place for aliens ***awaiting*** *deportation* 放逐を待つ外国人の拘置所.

deportee, *n.* 被追放者.

Q ***political*** *deportees* 政治上追放された人々.

deportment, *n.* 挙止, 振舞い.

Q The effectiveness of what you say will depend, to a considerable degree, on your ***bodily*** *deportment* while you are speaking. 諸君の話の効果は話している間の諸君の態度いかんに大いによるものだ. ¶***exemplary*** *deportment* 模範的な振舞い. ¶She has a ***graceful*** *deportment.* 彼女は起居が優美だ. ¶a ***noble*** *deportment* りっぱな振舞. ¶a ***pleasant*** *deportment* 気持のよい振舞.

depose, *v.* 免職する; 証言する.

P *depose* a person ***from*** his office 人を免職する. ¶A witness must *depose* ***to*** such facts as are within his own knowledge. 証人は自分の知っていることだけを証言しなければならない.

deposit, *n.* 預金; 保証金; 蓄積; 〖鉱〗鉱床.

V ***check out*** a *deposit* 預金を小切手で引出す. ¶***collect*** a *deposit* of ... yen from ... ...から...円の保証金を取る. ¶***demand*** a *deposit* from a borrower 借主から保証金を請求する ‖ ***demand*** a *deposit* of ... per cent on the value その価格の...パーセントの保証金を要求する. ¶***draw*** one's *deposit* 預金を引出す. ¶***forfeit*** the *deposit* 保証金を没収される. ¶A cheque is a piece of paper written by a man who has ***got*** a *deposit* at a bank. 小切手は銀行預金者の書いた一片の書付である. ¶I cannot ***give*** a cash *deposit*, but will offer a security. 保証金を現金ではやれないが担保を提供しよう. ¶He ***has*** a large *deposit* in the bank. 彼はその銀行に預金がたくさんある. ‖ I must ***have*** a cash *deposit.* 現金の保証金を出してもらわねばならぬ. ¶Well, I'll ***leave*** a *deposit* of $250. それなら手付を二百五十ドル置こう. 【類】***leave*** a *deposit* as a pledge of good (誠意を示す意味で). ¶***make*** a *deposit* in a bank 預け入れる ‖ You have to ***make*** a *deposit* of twice the amount of rent for taking the house. その借家は敷金が家賃の二カ月分だ. ¶***offer*** a *deposit* of ... ...の保証金を提供する. ¶***open up*** coal *deposits* 石炭の山を開発する. ¶***pay in*** a *deposit* 保証金を払込む. ¶The National Penny Bank ***receives*** *deposits* from a penny upward. 国立小口貯蓄銀行は一ペンスから預金を受付ける. ¶A *deposit* of at least 10% is ***required*** on goods ordered C.O.D. by parties unknown to us. 当店と取引のない方から代金引換払で御注文の品に対して最小一割の保証金を申受けます. ¶What *deposit* do you ***wish***? 敷金はいくらです.

Q ***current*** *deposit* 当座預金. ¶increase one's weight through muscle growth or ***fat*** *deposit* 筋肉の発達かまたは脂肪の蓄積によって体重が増す. ¶as ***fixed*** *deposit* for one year 一年間定期預金として. ¶the development of her untouched ***mineral*** *deposits* その国のまだ手の付けてない鉱山の開発. ¶a ***preliminary*** *deposit* of $10 is required to reserve ... ...の予約には十ドルの手付金がいる.

Q[2] make a ***bank*** *deposit* 銀行へ預金する ‖ withdraw one's ***bank*** *deposit* 銀行預金をおろす. ¶a ***fossil*** *deposit* 化石の堆積. ¶a ***demand*** *deposit* 要求払預金. ¶alluvial ***gold*** *deposits* 砂金鉱床. ¶a ***money*** *deposit* is required of ... ...に保証金が要求される. ¶a ***tartar*** *deposit* 歯塩. ¶a ***time*** *deposit* 定期預金. ¶a ***10% cash*** *deposit* 一割の現金保証金.

P ***on*** *deposit* 預金勘定で(当座勘定と区別していう) ‖ Over $12,000,000,000 is ***on*** *deposit* in New York banks at this moment. 現在ニューヨークの銀行は百二十億ドル以上預金がある. ‖ I have placed money ***on*** *deposit* in a bank. 僕は銀行に金を預けた. ‖ receive money ***on*** *deposit* [銀行などが]金を預る. ¶***upon*** a *deposit* of ... ...の手付をすれば.

P[2] *deposit* ***at*** call 通知預金. ¶the *deposit* ***of*** its ratification 批准書寄託.

deposit, *v.* 預ける; 供託する; 産みつける.

P It was *deposited* ***in*** the left luggage office. それは車内

遺留品預り所に保管されてあった. ‖ be *deposited in* a mailbox 郵便箱に入れる ‖ *deposit* money *in* a savings-bank 貯蓄銀行に金を預ける ‖ *deposit* goods *in* a warehouse 物品を倉庫に預ける ‖ *deposit* it *in* their custody それを彼らに保管してもらう ‖ A crocodile *deposits* her eggs *in* the sand. わには卵を砂の中に産む. ¶*deposit* eggs *on* beet (cattle) てん菜(など)に卵を産みつける. ¶*deposit* money *with* a bank 銀行に金を預ける ‖ The Society's Library is *deposited with* the Library of Yale University. その協会の図書はエール大学図書館に保管されてある. ¶*deposited* the notification of ratification *with* the U.S. Government 批准の通告を米国政府に寄託した. ¶*deposit* bonds *with* a creditor *as* security 担保として有価証券を債権者に預ける.

deposition, *n.* 証言.

V *take* a *deposition* 証言調書を取る.

depositor, *n.* 預金者.

Q² a *savings-bank depositor* 貯蓄銀行預金者.

P² a *depositor in* a savings-bank 貯蓄銀行の預金者. ¶a *depositor with* a bank 銀行預金者.

depot, *n.* 倉庫; 《米》駅.

Q² an *ammunition depot* 軍需品倉庫. ¶an *army depot* 陸軍倉庫. ¶an *Army Air Forces supply depot* 空軍軍需品倉庫. ¶a *displacement depot* (=camp *or* center) [軍隊の]再配置所. ¶a *freight depot* 貨物駅. ¶a naval *marine depot* 海軍海兵隊駐とん所. ¶a *union depot* (=station) 合同駅.

deprave, *v.* 堕落さす.

M be *irreclaimably depraved* もとに戻れないほど堕落する.

deprecate, *v.* 非難する.

M Such a rash measure is *much* to be *deprecated.* そのようなとっぴなやり方は大いに非難すべきだ.

depreciate, *v.* 値が下がる; 低下させる.

P *depreciate from* year to year by reason of wear and tear and obsolescence 摩損と旧式になったために年々値が下がる.

depreciation, *n.* 下落; 卑下.

Q in *courteous depreciation* 卑下して.

Q² *currency depreciation* 通貨の下落. ¶*property depreciation* 財産の価値低減.

P *in depreciation* 悪くいう意味で, けなして.

P² the recent *depreciation in* the price of securities 担保品価格の最近の下落. ¶The *depreciation of* equipment 設備の減価償却.

depressed, *pa.* うつうつとした, 不景気の.

M Business was *greatly depressed* after the war. 戦後はひどく不況になった. ¶I feel *much depressed.* 私はとても気がふさぐ. ¶Trade is *rather depressed.* 商売は不景気の方だ. ¶He was *depressed terribly.* 彼は恐ろしく意気消沈していた.

P greatly *depressed at* the news of an earthquake at ... …の地震の報で大いに気を腐らして. ¶*depressed in* mind (=spirits) 気がふさいで. ¶*depressed over* a love affair 恋愛関係で気を腐らして.

depression, *n.* 不景気, 不振; 意気そそう; 降下.

V Acute industrial *depression* invariably *follows* a war. 戦後にはいつも産業の大不況がともなう. ¶just before the present *depression set in* 現今の不景気直前に. 【類】It appears that trade *depression* is *setting in* more quickly than was anticipated.

Q *barometric depression* 低気圧. ¶*commercial depression* 商業の不振. ¶*deep depression* 深い意気消沈. ¶collapse into a *dreary* and *hysterical depression* 陰気なヒステリー的意気消沈に陥る. ¶*economical depression* 経済界の不振. ¶Trade is in *extreme depression.* 貿易はきわめて不況である. ¶in times of *financial depression* 財界不況の折に. 【類】the *financial depression* in Germany. ¶*general depression* in trade 商業における全般的不振. ¶suffer from *mental depression* 意気消沈する. ¶*nervous depression* 神経衰弱. ¶in an *utter depression* of soul 全く意気消沈して. ¶the *widespread depression* in the coal industry of Japan 日本の石炭業における全般的不振 ‖ the *world-wide economic depression,* accompanied by unemployment to a degree unprecedented in history 史上空前の失業者を出した世界的経済不況.

Q² *agriculture depression* 農業の不振. ¶*business depression* 不景気. ¶during periods of *trade depression* 商況不振の期間中. ¶For *weather depression* there is no cure. 天候不良は処置なし. ¶avoid a *world depression* 世界的不況を避ける ‖ political aspects of the *world depression* 政治面に表われた世界的不況.

P Britain *in depression* 不景気の英国 ‖ Owing to rumors of war, trade is *in* extreme *depression.* 戦争のうわさで商業は極端の不振状態にある.

P² a *depression in* trade 商売の不振 ‖ owing to the *depression in* the iron industry 鉄工業不振のために. ¶the *depression of* trade=trade depression.

deprive, *v.* 奪う, はく奪する.

P *deprive* a person *of* his right (office, command) 人の権利(など)をはく奪する ‖ *deprive* her *of* the fruits of her victory その国から戦勝の成果をはく奪する ‖ be *deprived of* one's means of living あごが干上がる. 【類】be *deprived of* one's life (fortune) / At length a treaty was made, which *deprived* the emperor *of* a large proportion of his former territory. ‖ *deprive* a person *of* his reason 理性を奪う, 気を狂わせる ‖ be *deprived of* all hope (enjoyment in life) あらゆる希望(など)を奪い去られる. 【類】be *deprived of* military power. / The king was *deprived of* his power. / *deprive* them *of* subsistence (生計の道) / *deprive* Japan *of* her war potential ‖ His death recently *deprived* Japan *of* one of its greatest authorities on Japanese Buddhism. / The failure *deprived* the physician *of* his popularity (人気). ‖ Sickness *deprived* me *of* the pleasure of seeing you. 病気でお目に掛かれなくなった. ‖ *deprive* the finger *of* its nail 指のつめを抜く ‖ women *war-deprived of* mates 戦争で夫を失った女たち ‖ He was *deprived of* his estates by confiscation. 彼は財産を没収された. ‖ An accident *deprived* him *of* sight. 彼は不図したことで失明した.

depth, *n.* 深さ, 深所; どん底; 真中; 奥行; 奥義.

V The water *attains* a *depth* at 20 ft. 水は深さ二十フィートに達する. ¶the well *has* a *depth* of ... 井戸は深さ…ある. ¶*know* the *depths* of their loss 損失の深刻さを知る ¶That *depth* is *maintained* by dredging. 浚渫(しゅんせつ)してその深さを保持する. ¶It *proves* the *depths* of the human hearts. これで人情の深さが分る. ¶*reach* a *depth* of over 200 yards 二百ヤード以上の深所に達する. ¶*sound* the *depths* of their hearts 彼らの情愛の深さを計る. ¶The story of ... *touches* the *depths* of tragedy. …の物語は悲惨のきわみである.

Q *abysmal depth* 底知れぬ深さ. ¶The bullet penetrated to a *considerable depth.* 弾丸はよほど深く通った. ¶He was plunged into the *darkest depths* of sadness. 彼は哀愁のふちに沈んだ. ¶*fathomless depth* of suffering 苦悩のどん底. ¶in the *infinite depths* of the heavens 天の無限の高所に. ¶in the *innermost depths* of Siberia シベリアの奥地で. ¶a pond of *small depth*=a shallow pond 浅い池. ¶an *unfathomable depth* 測るべからざる深底.

P *at* the *depth* of 500 to 950 feet 五百フィートないし九百五十フィートの深所に ‖ They are found in all seas and *at* various *depths.* 彼らはどこの海にも住んで深い所にも浅い所にもいる. 【類】The waters of the mountain lake were of such transparent limpidity that a ten-cent piece might be clearly seen lying on the bottom *at* a *depth* of 100 fathoms! ¶He went *beyond* (=out of) his *depth* and was drowned. 彼は背の立たぬ所まで行っておぼれた. ¶a cry *from* the *depths* of misery 悲惨のどん底からの叫び. ¶The well is thirty feet *in depth.* その井戸は深さ三十フィートある. ‖ *in* the *depth* of winter (night) 冬(など)のさなかに ‖ with gas-jets shining *in* the *depths* of it その奥の方にガスの火口が明るくついていて ‖ buried *in* the *depth* of mountains 山奥に埋って ‖ He was *in* the *depth* of despair. 彼は失望のどん底にあった. ‖ They are sunk *in* the *depths* of vice. 彼らは悪徳のどん底に沈んでいる. ¶sink *into* the *depth* of gloom 憂うつのどん底に沈む. ¶I found myself *out of* my *depth.* 僕は背の立たぬ深みにいたことに気が付いた. ‖ feel *out of* one's *depth* 覚束ない, 自信が持てない ‖ The subject is *out of* my *depth.* その問題は僕には到底分らない. ‖ But in such psychological questions I am *out of* my *depth.* こんな心理学上の問題になると僕の手にあまる. 【類】It is in dealing with this phase of the subject that the writer has felt most *out of* his *depth.* ¶The cave runs down *to* the great *depth* of 300 ft. そのほら穴は三百フィートもある深い底に通じている. ‖ Snow fell *to* a *depth* of over ten feet. 雪は十フィート以上も深く降った.

P^2 *depth from* front to rear 正面から裏までの奥行. ¶The *depth of* the snow prevented our passage. 雪が深くて通行ができなかった. ‖ the *depth of* a forest 森林の奥 ‖ the *depth of* a building 建物の奥行 ‖ the *depth* and breadth *of* his mind and heart 彼の心情の深さと幅 ‖ *depths of* degradation 堕落の底 ‖ the *depth of* a science 科学の秘奥 ‖ the *depth of* color (shade) 色(明暗)の濃度.

deputation, *n.* [団] 代表者, 代表委員.

V a *deputation* will be ***appointed*** to wait on ... and represent to him the grievances of ... …氏を訪い総代として…の苦情を陳述すべき代表委員を選定することになろう. ¶a *deputation* was ***chosen*** to wait upon ... …氏への訪問委員が選ばれた. ¶the *deputation* ***headed*** by ... …氏を首席とする派遣委員. ¶a *deputation* ***organized*** by ... …から成る代表委員. ¶***receive*** a *deputation* from the union (association) その団体(など)の代表委員に会う. 【類】***receive*** a *deputation* of villagers. ¶***send up*** a *deputation* to ... …に代表委員を派遣する. ¶the *deputation* ***consisted*** of ... 代表委員は…から成っていた. ¶a *deputation* ***representing*** ... …の代表委員.

V^2 the *deputation* ***waited*** on ... その代表委員は…を訪問した.

Q send a ***monster*** *deputation* to the Board of Trade 貿易庁へ多数の代表を派遣する.

P ***by*** (=***in***) *deputation* 代理で. ¶members ***of*** a *deputation* 代表委員.

P^2 A *deputation* ***from*** the British Esperanto Association attended at the offices of the League of Nations. 英国エスペラント協会の代表者は国際連盟事務所に出頭した. ¶a *deputation* ***to*** the premier (the conference) 首相訪問の(会議に出る)代表委員.

deputy, *n.* 代理人.

P ***as*** *deputy* 代理として. ¶***by*** *deputy* 代理で. ¶the Chamber ***of*** *Deputies* [フランスなど]国民議会.

P^2 a *deputy* ***for*** ... …の代理人.

derange, *v.* 発狂させる; 邪魔する.

M Grief has ***apparently*** *deranged* his mind. 悲嘆の余り気が狂ったようだ. ¶those who are certified to be ***mentally*** *deranged* 狂人と医師が証明した人々.

P He is *deranged* ***by*** trouble. 彼は心配で気が違っている. ‖ I am sorry to have *deranged* you ***by*** such a small matter. こんなつまらんことでおじゃまをして恐縮です.

derangement, *n.* 錯乱, ぶん乱.

Q ***financial*** *derangement* 財政ぶん乱. ¶show signs of ***mental*** *derangement* 精神錯乱の徴候を示す.

derby, Derby, *n.* 競馬, ダービー.

Q^2 the ***homerun*** *derby* 〚野球〛ホームラン競争. ¶the ***Kentucky*** *Derby* [米国の]ケンタッキーダービー. ¶a ***soapbox*** *derby* 《米》選挙の舌戦.

derelict, *n.* 廃棄物.

V ***reclaim*** the human *derelict* 不良性の人を改心させる.

derelict, *a.* 怠慢な.

P He was *derelict* ***in*** his duty (work). 彼は職務(など)を怠った.

derision, *n.* あざけり.

V ***evoke*** his *derision* [人に]笑われる. ¶***incur*** *derision* 笑われる. ¶***provoke*** the *derision* of ... …のあざけりを買う.

P stung ***by*** *derision* あざけりを受けて. ¶cry out ***in*** *derision* 大声であざける ‖ They called him an ass ***in*** *derision.* 彼をあざけってばかと呼んだ. ‖ They held him ***in*** *derision.* 彼をばかにしていた. ¶be brought ***into*** *derision* ばかにされる. ¶an object ***of*** *derision* あざけりの的. ¶They pointed their fingers at him ***with*** *derision.* 彼らは彼にうしろ指をさして笑った.

derivation, *n.* 由来, 起原; 〚言語〛語の派生.

V ***trace*** the *derivation* of English words of Greek origin ギリシア系統の英語の由来をたずねる.

Q of ***Chinese*** or ***Korean*** *derivation* 中国か朝鮮伝来の.

Q^2 words of ***Latin*** *derivation* ラテン語から出た語.

P The word "society" means ***by*** its *derivation* a union of comrades and partners. society という語はその語原によれば友だちや仲間の団結を意味する.

P^2 *derivation* ***of*** an estate from ancestors 祖先からの財産の伝来. ¶the *derivation* ***of*** words 言葉の由来.

derivative, *n.* 派生物; 〚文法〛派生語.

P *derivatives* ***from*** personal names 個人名から出た派生語. ¶"Goddess" is a *derivative* ***of*** god. goddess は god の派生語である.

Q^2 ***coal-tar*** *derivatives* コール・タールから得られる諸物質.

derivative, *a.* 派生した.

P English words *derivative* ***from*** Latin ラテン語から派生した英単語.

derive, *v.* 得る; 由来する, 伝来する; 〚文法〛派生する.

P adjectives *derived* ***from*** proper names 固有名から出た形容詞. ‖ These words were *derived* ***from*** the same root. これらの言葉は同一語根から出ている. ‖ information *derived* ***from*** old and rare manuscripts not generally known 一般に知られていない古い珍しい稿本から得た知識 ‖ *derive* knowledge ***from*** history 歴史から知識を得る ‖ the meaning *derived* ***from*** the context, or ***from*** the circumstances under which a word is used 前後関係あるいは言葉が用いられている場合から推定した意味. 【類】*derive* pleasure ***from*** reading / Ideas *derived* ***from*** conversation, observation, and experience are in general more valuable, or at least more vital, than those from books. / The revenue is *derived* ***from*** the following sources (財源).

derogate, *v.* 傷つける.

P Such a conduct *derogates* ***from*** his merit. かかる行為は彼の価値を落す. ‖ *derogate* ***from*** one's character 人の人格を傷つける. 【類】Such a fault *derogates* ***from*** your reputation. / *derogate* ***from*** the fame of one's family.

derogation, *n.* [名声・権威など]落すこと.

P ***in*** *derogation* of one's reputation 名声を落として.

P^2 It was no *derogation* ***from*** his high manhood. それは少しも彼の高尚な性格を傷つけなかった. ‖ It is *derogation* ***from*** his character. それは彼の名誉に関する. ¶*derogation* ***of*** a man 人気の失墜. ¶It is no *derogation* ***to*** Christianity. それは少しもキリスト教の名折にはならない.

derogatory, *a.* 傷つける.

P It is *derogatory* ***to*** the dignity of the American flag. それは米国の名折になる. ‖ The report was *derogatory* ***to*** his reputation (character, dignity, rank). その取りざたは彼の面目(など)を損じた. ‖ The manager considered it *derogatory* ***to*** his position to accept the terms of the trade union leaders. 労働組合の条件をのむことはその地位にとって不名誉だと支配人は考えた.

descend, *v.* [系統などから]出る; 伝わる; 降る, 下がる; いたる; 襲う.

M he is ***lineally*** *descended* from ... 彼は直系的に…の血を引いている. ¶His family was ***well*** *descended.* 彼の家族はりっぱな家系の出だ.

P *descend* ***from*** heaven 天くだる ‖ *descend* ***from*** a tree (tower, hill, horse) 木(など)から降りる. ¶He is *descended* ***from*** a noble family (=noble ancestors). 彼は名門の出だ. 【類】the theory that the different races are *descended* ***from*** Noah's sons, Shem, Ham and Japheth / *descend* ***from*** father to son (=generation to generation) ‖ on her mother's side she *descended* ***from*** the family of ... 彼女の母方は…家の出であった. 【類】He *descended* ***from*** the Stanleys (スタンレー家). / She is *descended* ***from*** a respectable family. ¶*descend* (=go) ***into*** detail 細目に入る ‖ *descend* ***into*** a drawing-room (二階などから)応接間に降りる. ¶The plague *descended* ***on*** the province. 疫病はその地方を襲った. ¶a divinity who has *descended* ***on to*** the earth 天くだりの神様. ¶It is a family heirloom which has *descended* ***through*** the eldest male branch. それは代代長男から長男に伝わった家宝である. ¶The custom has *descended* ***to*** our day. その習慣は今日に伝わっている. ‖ The crown *descended* ***to*** the heir. 王位は世子に伝わった. ‖ *descend* ***to*** mean pursuits 卑しい職業に身を落す ‖ *descend* ***to*** (=into) particulars (=details) 細目に入る ‖ He never *descends* ***to*** such meanness. そんなけちなまねはしない. ¶The fleet *descended* ***upon*** Copenhagen. 艦隊はコペンハーゲンに攻め寄せた. ‖ *descend* ***upon*** one's friend with a large party 友人のもとに大勢で押しかけて行く ‖ *descend* ***to*** brutalities of personal abuse and recrimination 野卑な人身攻撃や罪のなすり合いに堕する ‖ a divinity who has *descended* on ***to*** the earth 地上に天くだった神.

descendant, *n.* 子孫, 後裔(こうえい).

V He has ***left*** *descendants* living at this day. 彼の残した子孫は今なお存続している.

Q Italian is a ***direct*** *descendant* of Latin. イタリア語はラテン直系の言語だ. ¶a ***lineal*** *descendant* of the author その著者の直系の子孫. ¶a ***male*** *descendant* 男子の子孫. ¶a ***remote*** *descendant* 遠い子孫. ¶a ***white*** (=***fair***)-***skinned*** *descendant* of a Negro, married to a purebred white 白人と結婚して黒人にできた皮膚の白い子.

P^2 the third *descendant* ***from*** ... …から四代目. ¶a *de-*

scendant of this union この結婚で生れた子供.

descent, *n.* 子孫, 系統; 降下, 下り坂; 襲撃.

V he ***boasts*** his *descent* from ... 彼は…の子孫と誇称している. ¶***claim*** *descent* from ... by a daughter of ... …と…の娘との間にできた子の子孫だと名乗る. ¶***make*** a *descent* on Formosa 台湾を攻める. 【類】***make*** a *descent* upon (急襲する) the enemy ‖ ***make*** a *descent* upon one of the islands 群島の一をかすめる. ¶In savagery *descent* is ***reckoned*** in the female line. 野蛮人は血統を母方できめる. 【類】the practice of ***reckoning*** *descent* not on the father's side, as with us, but on the mother's side. ¶he ***traces*** his *descent* from ... 彼は自分の家は…の子孫だと言っている ‖ ***trace*** *descent* in unbroken line from ... …から血統が連綿と続いている. 【類】The family ***trace*** their *descent* back to the MacDonalds of Glencoe in the fourteenth century.

Q it is not certain whether it can trace an ***actual*** *descent* from ... 果してそれが…の直系であるかどうかは分らない. ¶a man of ***British*** *descent* イギリス系の人. ¶a ***collateral*** *descent* 傍系の子孫. ¶he traces ***direct*** *descent* from ... 彼は…の直系である. 【類】He is the thirty-fifth representative in ***direct*** *descent* from the founder of the family. ¶Our Emperor is of ***Divine*** *descent*. われらの天皇は神の子孫である. ¶Americans of ***Dutch*** *descent* オランダ系アメリカ人. ¶More than half of New York's great population are foreign born or of ***foreign*** *descent*. ニューヨークの巨大な人口の半数以上は外国生れかまたは外国人の子孫である. ¶a lineal succession of ***four*** *descents* 四代続き. ¶a man of ***German*** *descent* on father's side 父方がドイツ系の人. ¶a ***gradual*** *descent* toward the sea 海へのゆるやかな斜面. ¶The small hand is a sign of ***high*** *descent*. 手の小さいのは生れのよい証拠だ. ¶be of ***illegitimate*** *descent* 私生児である. ¶a man of ***illustrious*** *descent* 名門の士. ¶a ***lineal*** *descent* 直系卑属. ¶an American of ***Japanese*** *descent* 日系米人. ¶a man of ***noble*** *descent* 貴族の血を引く人. ¶He was of ***royal*** *descent*. 彼は国王の血統を引いていた. ¶be of ***Saxon*** *descent* サクソン系である. ¶a ***short sharp*** *descent* 短い急な坂. ¶a ***steep*** *descent* 急な坂. ¶The police made a ***sudden*** *descent* on the premises. 突然その家に警察の手がはいった. ¶a ***vertical*** *descent* 〖航空〗垂直降下. ¶a man of ***Negro*** *descent* 黒人系の人.

Q² a ***parachute*** *descent* 落下さん降下.

P he is the seventeenth ***in*** *descent* from ... 彼は…十七代の孫である. 【類】Jimmu Tenno, the first Mikado, was the 5th ***in*** *descent* from the Sun-goddess (天照大神). ¶be proud ***of*** his *descent* from ... …の子孫であることをほこりとしている.

P² a *descent* ***by*** boat ***through*** the rapids of the Hozugawa 保津川の急流下り. 【類】a *descent* ***from*** a mountain. ‖ Tubal Cain, the sixth in *descent* ***from*** Adam アダムから六代目のチューバル・ケイン ‖ a *descent* ***from*** noble ancestors 名門の出 ‖ a *descent* ***into*** the crater of Miharayama 三原山の噴火口降下. ¶the ascent and *descent* ***of*** a mountain 山の上りと下り. ¶a *descent* ***of*** temperature 温度の降下 ‖ a table of *descent* ***of*** William I ***from*** Rolf ロルフよりウィリアム一世に至るまでの系譜. ¶the *descent* ***of*** the enemy ***upon*** our coasts 敵のわが国沿海への襲来.

describe, *v.* 叙述する; 名状する; 品評する.

M ***ably*** *describe* 達者に解説する. ¶These subjects are ***accurately*** *described*. これら諸題目が正確に叙述されている. ¶Shorthand and typewriting have been most ***appropriately*** *described* as the "twin arts." 速記とタイプライター使用とを「ふた子の技術」というのはきわめて適切な評語である. ¶Bunin might be ***best*** *described* as the Russian Flaubert. ブーニンはロシアのフローベルだといったら一番適切だろう. ¶***briefly*** *described* 一口に言うと. ¶It would be more ***correctly*** *described* as ... …と書く方が一層正確だろう. ¶*describe* ***exactly*** 正確に叙述する. ¶he ***facetiously*** *described* it as ... 彼はそれをこっけいに…と説明した. ¶***faithfully*** *describe* 忠実に叙述する. ¶*describe* it more ***fully*** それを一層十分に記述する. ¶It is so ***graphically*** *described* by ... that I cannot do better than transcribe it. それは…がきわめて明りょうに叙述しているからそれをそのまま転載するのが一番よいと思う. ¶it is ***justly*** *described* as ... それを…と言ったのは当を得ている. ¶Oxford was ***libellously*** *described* by John Bright as "the home of dead languages and undying prejudices." ジョン・ブライトはオクスフォード大学をののしって「死せる国語と死せざる偏見の本家」と評した. ¶*describe* ***minutely*** 精細に叙述する. ¶***particularly*** *describe* 詳説する. ¶***precisely*** *describe* it その通り記述する. ¶be ***rightly*** *described* as ... …と記述して誤りでない. ¶***roughly*** *describe* 略述する. ¶might be ***so*** *described* そういえないこともあるまい. ¶***tersely*** *describe* 簡潔に述べる. ¶***thoroughly*** *describe* it それを十分に記述する. ¶*describe* it rather ***vaguely*** かなりあいまいにそれを述べる. ¶*describe* ***vividly*** あざやかに解説する. ¶The newspaper is ***well*** *described* as a daily history of the world. 新聞紙を世界日々の歴史と言ったのはもっともだ.

P *describe* the man ***as*** a scoundrel その人を評して悪漢という. ¶*describe* ***in*** detail (=full) 詳細に述べる ‖ It is very difficult to *describe* a machine ***in*** words. 機械を言葉で説明するのは非常にむずかしい. ‖ A kite flies *describing* a circle ***in*** the sky. とびは大空に円を描きながら飛ぶ. ¶*describe* ... ***with*** (=***in***) four-letter words ... を四字の語で記す.

O *describe* an airplane crash as one saw it 飛行機の墜落事故を見た通り記述する.

description, *n.* 叙述, 説明; 人相書描写; 種類.

V The prisoner ***answers*** this *description*. その囚人はこの人相書に符合する. ¶The beauty of the scenery ***baffles*** (=defies) all *description*. その絶景は筆舌に尽し難い. ¶The female hands at the mill were working at a speed that ***beggars*** *description*. その工場の女工たちは驚くべき手早さで働いていた. ¶***circulate*** *descriptions* 人相書を回す. ¶The beauty ***defies*** all *description*. その美しさはとても表現のしようがない. ¶It ***deserves*** a fuller *description*. それはもっと十分に叙述する価値がある. ‖ certainly ***deserve*** the *description* to "artist" photographer 真に芸術的写真師の名にそむかない. ¶***enrich*** a *description* by comparisons 種々の比較によって叙述の内容を豊富にする. ¶***give*** a complete *description* of ... …を十分に解説する. ¶The police has ***issued*** a *description* of the offender for whom they are searching. 警察では捜索中の犯人の人相書を出した. ¶A more detailed *description* is ***required***. 一層詳細な説明を要する.

Q an ***abridged*** *description* 簡略な説明. ¶***all*** *descriptions* of goods あらゆる品物. ¶There is no food of ***any*** *description*. 食物といって何もない. ¶The machine is of the most ***approved*** *description*. その機械は一番評判が好いものだ. ¶To say that it is similar to ... would be to give the ***best*** *description* possible. …に似ているというのがその説明としては一番要領を得ているだろう. ‖ Packing must be of the ***best*** *description*. 荷造はできるだけ高級のものでなくてはならない. ¶a ***brief*** *description* of ... …の手短かな説明. ¶a ***broad*** *description* 広汎な説明. ¶***clear*** *descriptions* accompanying illustrations さし絵に伴う明りょうな解説. ¶a ***concise*** *description* 簡潔な説明. ¶a ***detailed*** *description* of the merchandise その商品の詳細な説明書. ¶give an ***elaborate*** *description* of ... …を念入りに解説する. ¶an ***epitomized*** *description* 約説. ¶articles of ***every*** *description* 各種の品. 【類】crimes of ***every*** *description*. ¶an ***exact*** *description* 正確な記述. ¶***free, uninhibited*** *description* of sex 自由奔放な性の記述. ¶a photograph and ***full*** *description* 写真と細かい説明. 【類】send a ***full*** *description* (明細書). ¶historical inaccuracies of the most ***glaring*** *description* きわめて顕著な史的不精確. ¶a ***graphic*** *description* 鮮明な描写. ¶a ***high-colored*** (=vivid) *description* 生き生きした描写. ¶a ***just*** *description* 公平な記述. ¶a ***libellous*** *description* 中傷的叙述. ¶things of the ***like*** *description* as those before enumerated 前記の品と類似の物. ¶a ***lucid*** *description* 明せきな記述. ¶a ***minute*** *description* 細かい描写. ¶a ***naive*** *description* 飾りのない記述. ¶a ***personal*** *description* 人相書. ¶a ***pictorial*** *description* 絵入りの説明書. ¶of the ***same*** *description* 同種類の ‖ people who answer much the ***same*** *description* 大体同じ部類に属する人々. ¶a ***scientific*** *description* 科学的説明. ¶the ***shortest*** *description* of ... is to say that ... それを最も手短かに言えば…となる. ¶It offers a ***simpler*** *description*. それは一層簡単な説明になる. ¶It needs no ***special*** *description*. それは何ら特別の説明を要しない. ¶a detailed ***technical*** *description* 詳細な専門的説明書. ¶The articles are models of ***terse*** but ***adequate*** *description*. その論文は簡明適切な叙述の手本である. ¶a ***verbal*** *description* [犯罪人な

どの]口述書. 【類】this *verbal description* tallies with (と符号する). ¶give a *vivid description* of ... ...を生々と描写する. ¶of *whatever description* その種類を問わず. ¶an impostor of the *worst description* 最もたちの悪い詐欺漢.

Q² a *job description* 職務解説書. ¶a short *pamphlet description* of ... ...の簡単な小冊子の説明書. ¶Japan has no smokeless coal of the quality of the *South Wales description*. 日本にはサウス・ウェールス級の無煙炭はない.

P Life at Aden is melancholy *beyond description*. アデンの生活の憂うつさは筆紙に尽し難い. 【類】The scenery is beautiful *beyond* all *description*. ¶There are too many people *of* that *description*. そういう人間はあり過ぎるほどある. ¶a friend *of* this *description* この種の友人. ¶a sale *on description* [実物を見せないで]説明書だけによる販売.

P² a *description of* a man 人相書 ‖ a *description of* business 営業科目 ‖ the *description of* one's position 人の立場の説明.

descriptive, *a.* 叙述する.

M *literally* or *figuratively descriptive* 文字通りかまたは比ゆ的に叙述した.

P folders *descriptive of* Japan 日本を説明する折りたたみパンフレット ‖ literature *descriptive of* ... ...を説明する文献. 【類】a book *descriptive of* sea adventures.

desecration, *n.* 神聖冒とく.

Q² *Sabbath desecration* 安息日の神聖冒とく.

P² *desecration of* scenery 風景の汚損.

desert, *n.* さばく.

V² The *desert burned* beneath the sun. さばくは太陽に照らされて焼けるようであった. ¶The *desert stretches* far and wide. さばくがはてしなく広がっている.

Q the *arctic desert* 北極の不毛地. ¶a *bleak desert* 荒涼たるさばく. ¶a *limitless desert* はてしないさばく. ¶a *sandy desert* さばく. ¶in a *trackless desert* 人跡絶えたさばくで.

P live *in* a *desert* さばくに住む.

P² a *desert of* snow 一面の銀世界. ¶the *Desert of* Sahara サハラさばく. ¶Life is almost a *desert to* me. 人生は私にとってはほとんどさばくにひとしい.

desert, *n.* 功績; 賞罰, 報償.

V Some men fail to *get* their *desert*. 世には相当の待遇を受けない人もある. ¶*have* (=*meet with*) one's *deserts* 相当の賞罰を受ける.

P Such an honor is far *above* my *deserts*. これは過分の光栄だ. ¶reward or punish *according to* (=*after*) one's *deserts* その功に準じて賞罰を行う. ¶His reputation falls far *below* his *desert*. 彼の評判はその実績にはるかに及ばない. ¶a man *of desert* 価値ある人.

desert, *v.* 見棄てる; 脱走する.

M The road was *completely deserted* at that time of night. 夜のその時刻にはその道は人っ子一人通らなかった.

P He was *deserted by* his friends. 彼は友だちに見棄てられた. 【類】be *deserted by* her lover. ¶*desert from* a ship (barracks) 脱船(営)する. 【類】he *deserted from* the regiment on the march to ... ¶Do not *desert* me *in* my misfortune. 不幸のときに私を見棄てないでくれ. 【類】*desert* a friend *in* need. ¶*desert to* the enemy 敵にくだる ‖ *desert to* another party 他党に走る.

deserter, *n.* 脱走者.

P He was shot *as* a *deserter*. 彼は脱走者として銃殺された.

P² a *deserter from* an army (a regiment, a ship) 脱営(など)者.

desertion, *n.* 離脱.

P² *desertion of* one's post (duty) 職場離脱.

deserve, *v.* 値する, 功または罪がある.

M He *adequately deserves* praise. 彼は十分賞賛に値いする. ¶They do not *deserve any better*. 彼らにはそれ以上何ら賞すべきほどのことはない. ¶The place *eminently deserves* a visit. その地は行って見るだけの価値が大いにある. ¶The laborer *hardly deserves* his wages. その労働者はほとんど賃金だけの値打がない. ¶*deserve ill* of a person (country) 人(国)に尽したなどと言われる価値はない. ¶*justly deserve* the memorial 真にそれで記念さるべき価値がある. ¶He *richly deserved* the punishment. 彼はその位の罰は当然受けて然るべきものだった. ‖ wishing you the success you so *richly deserve* 君が当然受くべき成功を収められんことを祈って. ¶It can *scarcely deserve* to be called by such a name. それはそんな名で呼ぶ価値はほとんどない. ¶*well deserve* the rank as ... まことに...としての階級にふさわしい. ¶The soldiers *deserve well* of this country. 軍人はこの国に功労がある.

P He *deserves* credit *for* having done so. 彼がそうしたのは賞すべきだ. ‖ He *deserved* their thanks *for* it. 彼はそのために彼らから感謝されてよかった. ¶He has not *deserved* that *from* you. 彼は君からそうされるだけのことはなかった. ‖ *deserve* attention *from* ... ...から留意される価値がある. 【類】The picture *deserves* more attention *from* the public. ¶They are *deserving of* public censure. 彼らには公衆の非難を受けるだけのことがある. 【類】He is *deserving of* great credit. / It is *deserving of* respect for the motive that lies behind it. / literary productions *deserving of* the adjective "big" / problems *deserving of* study.

desideratum, *n.* 所望物, 必要物.

V *supply* a *desideratum* long felt 長い間の要求を満たす.

Q supply a *decided desideratum* 明かな欠陥を満たす. ¶a *great desideratum* 非常に必要な物. ¶an *important desideratum* 重要な必要物. ¶a *prime desideratum* 一番の必要物.

P² a *desideratum for* ... ...にとって必要なもの. ¶a *desideratum to* all Indian scholars インドの学徒全部にとって必要なもの.

design, *n.* **(1)** 計画; 設計; [しばしば *pl.*] たくらみ, 野心.

V I think it necessary to *carry out* our *design* at once. 直ちにわれわれの計画を実行することが必要だと思う. ¶Hideyoshi *cherished designs* upon China. 秀吉は中国に野心を抱いていた. ¶*complete* the entire pre-established *design* 予定の計画を全部完成する. ¶*conceive* a *design* 案を立てる. ¶*defeat designs* 計画をむだにする. ¶*develop* the original *designs* of ...のもとの計画を進展させる. ¶The *design* was *dropped* for the moment. その計画はしばらく見合わせになった. ¶*entertain designs* for ... ...に対して野心を抱く. ¶*execute* one's *design* 計画を実行する. ¶*fathom* the *designs* of Providence 神の摂理を推測する. ¶*follow out* a *design* 計画を遂行する. ¶*form* a *design* of ... ing ...しようと企てる ‖ *form* some *design* upon ... ...に野心を抱く. ¶*frustrate* a *design* 計画を妨げる. ¶*harbor* the *design* of ... ...をたくらんでいる ‖ *harbor designs* upon (=against) a person 人に対して殺意を抱く. ¶He *has designs* against our life. 彼はわれらをなきものにしようと企らんでいる. ‖ He *has designs* upon his neighbor. 彼は隣人に対して悪意を抱いている. 【類】We *have* no *designs* on the United States. ¶*make designs* for a building 建物の設計をする. ¶*penetrate* (=*see through*) the *designs* of ... ...の魂胆を見抜く. ¶*prepare* a *design* 設計する. ¶*relinquish* the *design* その計画を放棄する. ¶*work out* a *design* 設計を完了する.

Q Japan has no *aggressive* or *territorial designs* in China. 日本は中国に攻撃的または領土的野心を持っていない. ¶form the *ambitious design* of ... ...の野心を起す. ¶It is of much merit in *architectural design*. その建築は設計が優秀である. ¶a pavilion of *classic design* 古風に設計したあずまや. ¶He has no *deep designs* in doing so. 彼がそうしたのは別に深い考えがあってのことではない. ¶He has no *evil design*. 彼には悪だくみはない. ¶a *hopeless design* 望なき計画. ¶*murderous designs* 殺害計画. ¶Their *perfidious designs* were frustrated. 彼らの裏切りの企画は失敗に帰した. ¶with a *settled design* 一定の計画を立てて. ¶the *sinister designs* of the Russians ロシア人のかん計 ‖ persons with *sinister designs* 不ていの徒. ¶*ulterior designs* 奥底の野心.

Q² be like skyscrapers of *cubist design* 立体派の設計による摩天楼のようである. ¶the *saw-tooth roof design* のこぎり歯型屋根設計.

P These buildings are *after* his *designs*. これらの建物は彼の設計によったのだ. ‖ *after designs* by ... ...の設計によって. ¶*by design* わざと ‖ *by design* and not by accident 偶然ではなく故意に. ¶it was constructed *from* the *design* of ... それは...の設計で建てられた. 【類】the building was completed *from* the *designs* of ... / built *from* the *designs* of ... / a monument erected to the memory of ... *from* the *design* of ... / *from* selfish *design*. ¶be obstructive *to* one's *design* その計画の邪魔になる. ¶*with* the *design* of ... ing ...する考えで. 【類】He is acting *with* a *design*.

P² have some hostile *design against* ... ...に対して敵意を持つ. ¶a *design in* needlework (gold) 縫取(など)細工. ¶the *design of* building (monument) 建築(などの)設計.

¶the *design* ***of*** defrauding 詐取のたくらみ‖The *design* ***of*** the editors has been successfully carried out. 編集者の計画はうまく行った. ¶German *designs* ***on*** South Africa 南アに対するドイツの野心‖The anarchist has *designs* ***on*** (=***upon***) the Prime Minister. その無政府主義者は首相を殺害しようとしている. 【類】with the *designs* ***on*** the life of ... ¶He had *designs* ***upon*** the throne (王位).

O a *design* to deceive 欺こうとする考え.

(**2**) 図案(デザイン), 模様; 型, がら. 「金属に模様を彫る.

V ***draw*** a *design* 図案をする. ¶***engrave*** a *design* on metal

Q ***commercial*** *design* 商業意匠. ¶of ***elaborate*** *design* 精密な図案の. ¶of ***elegant*** and ***ornamental*** *design* 優美な装飾的意匠の. ¶***exquisite*** *design* 精巧な意匠. ¶***fantastic*** *design* 風変りな意匠. ¶***fashionable*** *designs* in shirts ワイシャツの流行の意匠. ¶***floral*** *designs* 花模様. ¶***freak*** *designs* 珍型. ¶***industrial*** *design* 工業意匠. ¶***latest*** *designs* in ... ...最近型. ¶of the most ***modern*** *design* 最も近代型の. ¶a ***neat*** *design* すっきりした意匠. ¶a ***novel*** *design* 新型(柄). ¶in ***Oriental*** *design* 東洋風に. ¶***ornamental*** *designs* 装飾図案. ¶of ***plain*** *design* さっぱりした意匠の. ¶a ***rich*** *design* りっぱな意匠. ¶a ***smart*** *design* in caps 帽子のスマートな型. 「*sign* 近代的家具意匠.

Q^2 ***costume*** *design* 衣装の意匠. ¶modern ***furniture*** *de-*

P curious ***in*** *design* 意匠の変った. 【類】ultramodern (最新式) ***in*** *design*. ¶arts ***of*** *designs* 図案の技術‖a sleeping car ***of*** the latest *design* 最新式の寝台車. ¶a book ***with*** *design* by ... ...の装ていになる本‖It is woven ***with*** a raised *design*. それは模様を浮かし織になっている.

P^2 a *design* ***on*** a sword (some work of art) 刀剣(など)に施

design, *v*. 設計する; 積りである; 当てて置く. Lした意匠.

M it was ***primarily*** *designed* to ... それは元来...するようにできていた.

P he is *designed* ***by*** nature to ... 彼は生れながらに...すべき運命の人だ‖*designed* (=intended) his son ***for*** a newsman (carpenter, tailor) 息子を新聞記者(など)にする積りだった. ¶His father *designs* him ***for*** a lawyer (business man). 彼の父は彼を法律家(など)にする積りだ.‖The plot is *designed* ***for*** a garden. その地面は庭にする積りだ. 【類】books primarily *designed* ***for*** the use of students taking examinations‖the day I *designed* ***for*** my departure 僕の出発に当てておいた日. 【類】I *design* next Sunday ***for*** his reception. ¶*designed* ***by*** Providence for ... 神が...にする積りである. ¶it is *designed* ***on*** the model of ... それは...をひな形にして設計したものだ. 【類】buildings *designed* ***on*** the American style of architecture‖*design* an attack ***on*** ... ...襲撃をくわだてる. ¶He has *designed* ***upon*** me. 彼は僕に対して陰謀を企んだ.

designate, *v*. 指定する; 称する; 任命する.

M unless ***otherwise*** *designated* 別に指定がなければ.

P They *designated* him ***as*** a tyrant. 彼らは彼を暴君と称した. ¶He was *designated* ***as*** the next chairman of the committee. 彼は委員会の次の議長に指名された. ¶be *designated* ***by*** specific name 特殊の名がつけられている. ¶it is *designated* ***by*** the name of ... それには...という名がついている. ¶*designate* a person ***for*** an office (premiership, presidency) 人をある役(など)に任命する‖be *designated* ***for*** a certain office ある職務に任命される. ¶*designate* an officer ***for*** (=***to***) the command 将校を指揮官に任命する. ¶*designate* them ***under*** the name of ... それを...と呼ぶ.

designation, *n*. 名称; 任命.

V it ***gained*** for it the *designation* of ... それは...という名称を得た. ¶***owe*** its *designation* to ... その名は...によってできたものである.

Q Laughing gas is the ***popular*** *designation* of ether. 笑気はエーテルの通俗名称である. ¶a ***professional*** *designation* 専門的な呼称. ¶The term was at first applied as a reproach, but was afterwards adopted by the party as a ***proud*** *designation*. その言葉は初めは非難の意味に用いられたが後には関係者により誇らしい名として採用された.

P ***under*** the *designation* of ... という名称で.

P^2 *designation* ***of*** an officer ***to*** the command 将校の指揮

designer, *n*. 図案家; 〔服飾〕デザイナー. L官への任命.

Q^2 an ***aircraft*** *designer* 航空機設計技師. ¶a ***clothes*** (=***dress***) *designer* 衣服デザイナー. ¶a ***color*** *designer* 配色のデザイナー. ¶a ***corset*** *designer* コルセット・デザイナー. ¶a ***costume*** *designer* コスチューム・デザイナー. ¶a ***dictionary*** *designer* 辞書立案者. ¶the ***fashion*** *designers* of Paris パリの流行意匠家たち. ¶a ***metal*** *designer* 金属品意匠家. ¶a ***pattern*** *designer* 型のデザイナー.

desirability, *n*. 望ましいこと, 遺憾な点.

V ***emphasize*** the *desirability* of ... ...の望ましいことを強調する. ¶***feel*** the *desirability* of ... ...を希望する. ¶***recognize*** its *desirability* それを希望することの妥当性を認める. ¶***represent*** to the Government the *desirability* of ...ing ... ...あってしかるべきことを政府に陳情する. ¶***suggest*** the *desirability* of ... ...したらよかろうと言出す. ¶Salesmen explain its charms and ***urge*** its *desirability*. 売子がその長所を説明してぜひ買わせようとする.

desirable, *a*. 望ましい.

M it is ***highly*** *desirable* that ... ...することは大いに望ましい. ¶***particularly*** *desirable* 特に望ましい.

desire, *n*. 望み, 欲望; 情欲.

V ***accomplish*** one's *desire* 望みを遂げる. ¶***acquire*** the *desire* to extend human knowledge through one's own research 自己の研究によって人類の知識を拡張しようという希望を持つ. ¶I ***appreciate*** your *desire* that ... 君が...しようと望むのはもっともだ. ¶***arouse*** *desire* 欲望を起させる. ¶***attain*** one's *desire* 望みを遂げる. ¶***awaken*** a deep *desire* for pure thoughts 純潔な思想への切なる欲望を呼び起す. ¶***carry out*** their *desire* 彼らの望みを遂げる. ¶***conceive*** a *desire* to ... ...しようという希望を抱く. ¶***control*** the *desires* of men 人々の欲望を抑える. ¶those who ***cross*** his *desires* 己れの欲望に逆らう人々. ¶***curb*** one's *desire* 欲望を制する. ¶***evince*** a *desire* to ... ...したいという希望を表明する. ¶***experience*** [a] sexual *desire* 性欲を感じる. ¶***express*** a *desire* to co-operate 協力したいと言い出す. 【類】***express*** a *desire* to die / ***express*** an earnest *desire* to ... / a *desire* has frequently been ***expressed*** that ... / ***express*** a strong *desire* for reputation (fame). ¶***feel*** a *desire* to know ... ...を知りたいと思う. 【類】***feel*** a great *desire* to ... ¶***gain*** one's *desire* 望みを遂げる. ¶I hope you'll ***get*** your *desire*. あなたの欲するものが手に入ることを望みます. ¶a deity endowed with the power of ***granting*** or ***withholding*** the *desire* of the devotee 信者の願いをいれまたは拒否する権能のある神. ¶***gratify*** one's *desire* 己れの欲望を満たす. ¶***harbor*** a *desire* to ... ...の念願を抱く. ¶***have*** a *desire* for more leisure もっと暇が欲しい‖He ***had*** but one *desire* in his soul. 彼はただ一つの念願を持っていた. 【類】Experienced and unprejudiced judges (経験に富み偏見のない裁判官) ***have*** only one *desire*, namely, to do justice.‖I ***have*** a strong *desire* to go to a theatre. ぜひ芝居へ行って見たい.‖I ***have*** no *desire* for orders from ... ...から注文を受けたくない. 【類】I ***have*** no *desire* to enter into a controversy with ... ¶this ***indicates*** a growing *desire* among men that ... これで人人の間に...の希望が生じていることが分る. ¶***inflame*** the *desires* of men 人々の欲望をあおる. ¶he ***intimated*** to me his *desire* to ... 彼は私に...の希望をほのめかした. ¶He ***manifested*** an eager *desire* for knowledge. 彼には熱心に知識を求めているようすが見えた. 【類】He ***manifested*** a *desire* to secure the position. ¶***meet*** the *desire* of ... ...の望みをかなえる. ¶***nurse*** a perennial *desire* to ... ...しようとの希望を間断なく抱く. ¶***oblige*** and ***humor*** his *desires* 彼の望み通りにしてやる. ¶Movies ***produce*** a strong *desire* in juveniles to emulate deeds of violence or of robbery featured therein. 映画は少年の心にその中に現われた暴行または略奪行為に対する強い競争心を起させる. ¶***promote*** their *desire* 彼らの欲望を助成する. ¶***raise*** *desires* 欲望を起す. ¶cannot ***repress*** my *desire* to ... ...したい気持を抑えられない. ¶***resist*** the *desire* その欲望を抑える. ¶***satisfy*** their jealously fostered *desires* 宿望を満足させる. 【類】It is impossible to ***satisfy*** all the *desires* of all people. ¶***share*** the *desire* of ... ...の望みをともにする. ¶they ***signified*** their *desire* to ... 彼らは...したいという欲望を示した. ¶Eggs and oysters ***stimulate*** sexual *desire*. 卵やかきは情欲を刺激する.‖***stimulate*** the *desire* of possession 所有欲を刺激する. ¶***subdue*** one's *desires* 欲望を抑える. ¶***subserve*** their lustful *desires* 彼らの性欲を満足させる助けになる. ¶***whet*** one's *desire* to ... ...しようという欲望を刺激する. ¶***wipe out*** the *desire* of ... ...の欲望を一掃する.

V^2 whenever the *desire* ***seizes*** him 彼は欲望を起すごとに.

Q I have ***all*** the *desire* in the world to assist you, but ... お助けしたいのは山々ですが... ¶actuated by an unduly ***anxious*** *desire* あまりにもあせり過ぎて. ¶feel an ***ardent*** *desire* to ... ...することを熱望する‖in his ***ardent*** *desire* to ... ...したい一心で. ¶subdue his ***bodily*** *desires* 肉欲を抑える. ¶***burning*** *desires* 燃える欲情. ¶***carnal*** *desire* 肉(性)欲. ¶one of his most ***cherished*** *desires* was to ... 彼の最も切なる希望の一つは...することであった‖his long ***cherished*** *desire* 彼の宿望. ¶my ***chief*** *desire* is to ... 僕の第一の希望は...だ. ¶a ***deep[-rooted]*** *desire* 根強い望み. ¶his ***earnest*** (=***eager***) *desire* 彼の切なる望み. ¶an ***excessive*** *desire* 過分の望み. ¶by their ***express*** *desire* 特に彼らの希望によって. ¶***feverish*** *desires* 熱烈な望み. ¶***Gargantuan*** *desires* 巨大な望み. ¶the ***general*** *desire* of the assemblage 会合者一同の希望. ¶a ***genuine*** and ***disinterested*** *desire* for ... ...に対する純真で私心のない希望. ¶the ***great*** *desire* of his heart 彼の切なる希望. ¶a ***healthy*** *desire* 健全な望み. ¶his ***heart's*** *desire* 彼の衷心からの希望. ¶an ***honest*** *desire* for a settlement 事件解決に対する誠意. ¶actuated by the very ***human*** *desire* for victory rather than by a zeal for truth 真理に対する熱誠からというよりむしろ人間の落ち入りやすい勝利欲に駆られて. ¶***inmost*** *desire* 心の底からの願望. ¶I refused to comply with his ***inordinate*** *desires*. 私は彼の法外な欲望をいれなかった. ¶an ***insatiable*** *desire* for knowledge あくことを知らぬ知識欲. ¶an ***intense*** *desire* 切なる願望. ¶an ***irresistible*** *desire* 押え切れぬ欲求. ¶a ***keen*** *desire* to help others 他人を助けようとする切なる願い. ¶Americans have a ***laudable*** *desire* to learn and to improve themselves. 米人は自力で自己を向上させようとする奇特な念願を持っている. ¶the so-called "***lower***" *desire* いわゆる劣情. ¶there is, in some quarters, a ***manifest*** *desire* to ... ある方面には...しようという欲望がはっきりと見える. ¶The ***master*** *desire* is for novelty. 主たる欲望は新奇ということにある. ¶a ***moderate*** *desire* 適度の望み. ¶a ***natural*** *desire* for ... ...に対する自然の欲望. ¶***overwhelming*** *desire* to murder ... ...を殺そうという押え切れない欲望. ¶a ***passionate*** *desire* for ... ...に対する熱烈な欲望. ¶a ***pathetic*** *desire* 悲願. ¶a ***pious*** *desire* 敬けんな望み. ¶the ***praiseworthy*** *desire* to ... ...したいという殊勝な願い. ¶a ***secret*** *desire* 人知れぬ望み. ¶a ***selfish*** *desire* 虫のよい考え. ¶placate one's ***sensual*** *desire* 肉欲を抑える. ¶excite ***sexual*** *desire* 肉欲を刺激する. ¶He was animated by a ***sincere*** *desire* for his country's good. 彼は国家のために尽そうというまじめな考えに動かされた. ¶had a ***sudden*** *desire* to ... 急に...したい気になった. ¶a ***trembling*** *desire* 切なる望み. ¶a convenient place for the gratification of ***uncontrollable*** *desire* 制し難い欲望を満たすには便利な場所. ¶there is a ***universal*** *desire* that ... ...したいという希望が一般に見える. ¶have a ***vehement*** *desire* 切望する. ¶feel a ***wanton*** *desire* 気まぐれな欲望を起す. ¶a ***warm*** *desire* to ... ...しようという熱心な望み. ¶a ***wicked*** *desire* 邪念. ¶there is a ***widespread*** *desire* to ... ...しようとする希望が広く行きわたっている. ¶a ***worthy*** *desire* 奇特な望み.

Q[2] a ***space-saving*** *desire* 場所を節約する工夫.

P ***against*** one's own *desire* 不本意ながら. ¶***at*** the *desire* of ... の頼みで‖I will do it ***at*** your *desire*. ご希望通り致しましょう. ¶***by*** [the] *desire* of ... ...の頼みで. 【類】***by*** his *desire*‖move a piece ***by*** hasty *desire* あせってこまを動かす‖He worked hard ***from*** a *desire* to please his parents. 彼は両親を喜ばせたさに一所懸命に働いた. ¶***with*** the *desire* of getting helpful suggestions 有益な示唆を得たいと思って. ¶He was filled ***with*** a *desire* to learn. 彼は知識欲で一杯だった.‖He was seized ***with*** a *desire*. 彼は一つの望を起した.‖in compliance ***with*** his *desire* 彼の希望通り. ¶***without*** any *desire* for reward 報酬を望まないで.

P[2] the *desire* ***after*** riches 富貴欲. ¶a *desire* ***for*** applause 賞賛(など)の欲望‖*desire* ***for*** the praise of others 他人からほめられたいという欲望. ¶the *desire* ***for*** novelty in expression 新奇な表現というねらい‖I have no *desire* ***for*** wealth, glory, and power. 僕は富や名誉や権力を望まない. 【類】Japan has no *desire* ***for*** war.‖I express my *desire* ***for*** your acceptance of my excuse for the delay. 遅延の段お許しあらんことを. ¶the *desire* ***of*** fame 名誉欲‖the *desire* ***of*** an heir あとつぎの欲しさ‖the *desire* ***of*** women to join in the sports of men 男子の競技に参加したいと言う女子の希望.

O a *desire* to rise in the world 出世欲. 【類】the *desire* to prove the alleged knowledge to be true / a *desire* to please (entertain) a visitor.

desire, *v.* 望む, 願う; 所望する.

M be ***ardently*** *desired* 切望されている. ¶we ***earnestly*** (=***ardently or eagerly***) *desire* to ...切に...せんことを願う. ¶***honestly*** *desire* 衷心から希望する. ¶***sincerely*** *desire* to ... まじめに...したがっている. ¶if he ***so*** *desires* それが望みなら. ¶I ***strongly*** *desire* to ... 切に...せんことを望む.

P if *desired* ***by*** a customer 客の請求があれば. ¶*desire* her ***for*** one's wife 彼女を妻に所望する‖*desire* an object ***for*** oneself (a purpose) 自分(など)のために物を所望する‖He *desires* her ***for*** his wife. 彼は彼女を妻にもらいたがっている.

desirous, *a.* 希望する.

M he is ***anxiously*** *desirous* of ... 彼は...を切望している. ¶be ***equally*** *desirous* of ... ひとしく...を希望する. ¶he is ***keenly*** *desirous* that I should ... 彼は僕が...することを熱心に望んでいる. ¶He is ***strongly*** *desirous* of fame. 彼は非常に名誉を望んでいる.

P I am *desirous* ***of*** the position. 私はその地位を望んでいる.‖I am *desirous* ***of*** success. 私は成功を望んでいる. 【類】Everybody is *desirous* ***of*** something better and higher. / He has long been *desirous* ***of*** visiting America.‖Persons *desirous* ***of*** further details are referred to Mr. ...'s work on the same subject. 詳細を知りたい人はその問題に関する...氏の著書を参考されたい.

O I am *desirous* to speak good English. 僕は正しい英語を話したい. 【類】I am *desirous* to know further details.

desist, *v.* やめる, 止める.

P *desist* ***from*** talking 話をやめる. ☞ *desist* to talk はまれ‖plead with her to *desist* ***from*** her evil ways 正道に帰るように彼女に説く. 【類】*desist* ***from*** a purpose (a scheme, an attempt, some intention) / *desist* ***from*** further action.

desk, *n.* 机.

V ***clear up*** a *desk* 机の上を片付ける. ¶***dust*** a *desk* carefully 丁寧に机のちりを払う.

Q He has a ***disorderly*** *desk*. 彼は机の上をきちんとして置かない. ¶He sits at the ***first*** *desk* as you go in. 君が室に入ると彼はしょっぱなの席にいる. ¶a ***swaying, wobbly*** *desk* ぐらぐらする机.

Q[2] the ***cash*** *desk* 現金取扱机. ¶a ***copy*** *desk* 〖新聞〗整理係のデスク(一般にデスクと呼ぶ). ¶a ***cylinder*** (=***roll-top***) *desk* かまぼこ形の自在ふた付き机. ¶a ***four-drawer*** *desk* 四引出しの机. ¶a girl at the ***information*** *desk* 案内掛の少女. ¶a ***kneehole*** *desk* 両そで机. ¶a ***loan*** *desk* [図書館の]貸出口. ¶our daily drudgery at the ***office*** *desk* われわれが事務所の机に向ってやる型にはまった日々の仕事. ¶a ***registry*** *desk* (ホテルの)帳場. ¶a ***roller-top*** *desk* かまぼこ形の自在ふたのある机. ¶the girl at the ***telephone*** *desk* 電話係の少女. ¶a ***writing*** *desk* 書きもの机.

P a man ***at*** the *desk*=a desk man, a clerk 事務員; 机に向っている人‖sit ***at*** one's *desk* 机に向う. 【類】work ***at*** one's *desk*.

desolate, *a.* 荒れた.

P It is *desolate* ***of*** all vegetation. そこには草木は少しも生えていない.

desolation, *n.* 荒廃; 荒廃地.

V ***spread*** terrific *desolation* over a fertile plain 肥えた土地を一面に荒らす.

Q the ***blackened*** *desolation* around railway stations 停車場付近の黒ずんで殺風景なながめ. ¶a ***boundless*** *desolation* 見渡す限りの荒地. ¶the ***endless*** *desolation* of the north 北方の果なき荒地. ¶a ***sad*** *desolation* 悲惨な荒涼.

despair, *n.* 失望, 落胆, 絶望.

Q ***black*** *despair* 大落胆. ¶***crushing*** *despair* 絶望. ¶in a state of ***dumb*** *despair* 失望の余りあ然として. ¶give it up in ***sheer*** *despair* 全く失望してそれをやめる. ¶I found him in ***utter*** *despair*. 行って見たら彼は大失望の体であった.

P He attempted (committed) suicide ***in*** *despair*. 彼は失望して自殺を図った(遂げた). 【類】give up ***in*** *despair*. ¶I was thrown ***into*** *despair*. 僕はがっかりした. ¶He was the picture ***of*** *despair*. 彼は失望そのものであった.‖He is in the depth ***of*** *despair*. 彼は失望のどん底にいる. ¶half ***out of*** *despair* なかばあきらめて. ¶abandon oneself ***to*** *despair* 絶望に陥る. ¶He was driven ***to*** *despair* by his misfortune. 彼は不幸のために絶望に陥った.

P[2] He is the *despair* ***of*** all his friends. 彼は友人全部から

見離されている；彼にはかなわないと皆の友人が思われてい

despair, *v.* 失望する, 断念する. ⌊る.

M He ***almost*** *despaired* to recover it. 彼はそれを回復することをほとんど断念してしまった. ¶***Never*** *despair* of success. 決して成功をあきらめるな.

P *despair* ***of*** one's future ...の将来覚つかないと思う. ¶I began to *despair* ***of*** success. 成功は覚つかないと私は思い始めた. ‖ I *despair* ***of*** attaining my object. 私には到底目的が達せられないと思う. ‖ come to *despair* ***of*** him 彼に愛想がつきる ‖ He *despaired* ***of*** his life. 彼は自分の命はもうないものと思った. 【類】He did not *despair* ***of*** victory in the end.

despatch, dispatch, *n.* 速達; 急速; 急信, 急電; 急派, 急送; 殺すこと.

V ***ensure*** a quick *despatch* 迅速な処理を保証する. ¶***facilitate*** the *despatch* of business 事務をはかどらせる. ¶***require*** *despatch* 至急を要する. ¶***secure*** quick *despatch* 迅速な処理を保証する.

Q a ***happy*** *despatch* 切腹. ¶a ***rapid*** *despatch* 迅速な処理.

Q² a ***circular*** *despatch* 回章. ¶with almost ***lightning*** *despatch* 電光石火のごとく. ¶a ***news-agency*** *despatch* from London says that ... ロンドンからの新聞通信社至急報によれば... ¶a ***newspaper*** *despatch* from Berlin ベルリンからの新聞急報.

P He shows ability ***in*** the *despatch* of business. 彼は仕事が早い. ¶He concluded the negotiation ***with*** *despatch*. 彼は迅速に談判をまとめた. ‖ ***with*** all *despatch* 大至急. 【類】***with*** all possible *despatch*.

P² the *despatch* ***of*** a fleet 艦隊の急派 ‖ the *despatch* ***of*** the mails 郵便物の急送.

despatch, dispatch, *v.* 派遣する, 急派する; 殺す.

M The children have been ***hastily*** *despatched* out to school. 学校へせきたてられた.

P *despatcch* a person ***for*** a thing 物を取りに人をやる. ¶*despatch* a fleet ***to*** a port 港へ艦隊を急派する. 【類】*despatch* a person ***to*** a conference (country, place). ¶He was *despatched* ***with*** one stroke of a dagger. 彼は短刀の

desperado, *n.* 凶漢. ⌊一突きでやっつけられた.

Q a ***reckless*** *desperado* 向う見ずの凶漢.

desperate, *a.* やけっぱらの.

M be ***somewhat*** *desperate* やけ気味である.

P grow (=become) *desperate* ***at*** ... ...に対してやけになる ‖ be *desperate* ***at*** the failure 落第したのでやけになっている. ¶be *desperate* ***for*** money 金銭のため死物狂いになっている.

desperation, *n.* やけっぱら, 捨てばち.

P say ***in*** *desperation* 捨てばちになって言う ‖ ***in*** his *desperation* やけになって ‖ At last, ***in*** *desperation*, he killed himself. とうとうせっぱ詰まって彼は自決した. ¶That drove him ***to*** *desperation*. そのため彼は捨てばちになった.

despise, *v.* 軽べつする.

P Children who cheat at the examination will be *despised* ***by*** their classmates. 試験に不正をやる子はみんな

despite, *n.* 侮べつ, 軽べつ. ⌊に軽べつされる.

V ***do*** *despite* to ... ...を侮べつする.

P ***in*** *despite* (=scorn) 傍若無人に ‖ He seized my hand ***in*** *despite* of my efforts to the contrary. そうさせまいとし

despoil, *v.* 奪う. ⌊たが彼は私の手を捕えた.

P *despoil* a person ***of*** his belongings 人の持物を奪う ‖ *despoil* a person ***of*** honors (rights) 人の栄誉(など)を奪う. 【類】be *despoiled* ***of*** all his money.

despond, *v.* 落胆する.

P *despond* ***about*** ... ...を悲観する. ¶*despond* ***at*** the first difficulty 最初の困難に落胆する.

despondency, *n.* 落胆. 「がっかり.

Q ***deep*** *despondency* 非常な落胆. ¶***light*** *despondency* 少し

despondent, *a.* 落胆している.

P He became *despondent* ***of*** success. 彼は成功をあきらめてしまった. ¶He is *despondent* ***over*** ill health (lack of employment, the future). 彼は不健康(など)を悲観している.

despotism, *n.* 暴政.

Q² ***iron*** *despotism* 無情な暴政.

dessert, *n.* デザート(食後の菓子・果物など).

V ***serve*** *dessert* デザートを出す. ☞英国では菓子 (sweets) のあとに出る生の果物.

P² as a *dessert* ***to*** this delicate repast この御馳走の後口と

destination, *n.* 目的地; 目的. ⌊して.

V ***obtain*** one's *destination* 目的を達する. ¶The ship must now be ***nearing*** her *destination*. 船は今目的地に近づいているに相違ない. ¶***reach*** one's *destination* 目的地に着く. 【類】***reach*** its *destination* (手紙など).

Q his ***final*** *destination* 彼の落付く先. ¶obtain ***military*** *destination* 武名を揚げる. ¶our ***ultimate*** *destination* for the day われわれのその日の最後の目的地 ‖ the address at the ***ultimate*** *destination* 最後の目的地の宿所. ¶***unknown*** *destination* 計るべからざる運命.

Q² the ports and ***supply*** *destinations* 港と商品供給地.

P points ***beyond*** my *destination* 私の着く駅より先の方. ¶The charge is 50 yen ***for*** all *destinations* (=irrespective of distance). 料金はどこへ行くにも五十円です. ‖ trains ***for*** *destination* or an intermediate point その方面行の列車. ¶He left ***for*** his *destination*. 彼は行先へ立った. ¶I was carried miles ***past*** my *destination*. 私は目的地より数マイル先きに持って行かれた.

P² the *destination* ***of*** one's journey 旅行の目的地. ¶tickets in *destination* ***to*** Berlin ベルリン行きの切符.

destine, *v.* 運命づける; 仕向ける; 用途を定める.

P men *destined* ***for*** business (law) 実業(など)に従事することになっている人々 ‖ He was *destined* ***for*** the army from birth. 彼は生れつき軍人になる運命だった. ‖ *destine* the room ***for*** the reception of the general そのへやを将軍接待の用に充てる ‖ Articles which are not *destined* ***for*** personal use should be declared at the frontier. 身の回りの品以外の荷物は国境で税関に申告しなければならない. 【類】prepare adequately students *destined* ***for*** commerce, journalism, and the public services / passengers *destined* ***for*** the United States / The ship is *destined* ***for*** London. ¶The prince was *destined* ***from*** birth to be a king. 皇子は王位をつぐように運命づけられていた. ¶*destine* a ship ***to*** ... ...へ船を向ける ‖ *destine* a son ***to*** the bar 息子を弁護士に仕込む. 【類】He is *destined* ***to*** failure.

O They were *destined* to meet rough weather. 彼らはどうしてもしけに会うような運命になっていた.

destiny, *n.* 運命, 命数; 宿縁.

V ***achieve*** its *destiny* その使命を果たす. ¶***affect*** the *destinies* of nations 諸国民の運命に影響する. ¶***carve out*** one's *destiny* 運命を開拓する. ¶***control*** the Empire's *destiny* 帝国の運命を支配する ‖ the medieval belief that the stars ***controlled*** our *destinies* 星がわれわれの運勢に関係があるという中世紀の信仰. 【類】those gentlemen who ***control*** the *destinies* of movies in Japan. ¶***decide*** the *destinies* of a lifetime 一生涯の運命を決する. ¶***direct*** the *destinies* of a nation 一国民の運命を左右する. ¶cannot ***escape*** one's *destiny* 命数は免れない. ¶***forge*** (=***form*** or ***mold***) the *destiny* of ... ...の運命を作る. ¶***fulfil*** a *destiny* as ... ...としての使命を果す. ¶***guide*** in the right way the *destinies* of the country 正しく国運のかじを取る. 【類】the statesmen who ***guide*** the *destinies* of their countries. ¶He ***has*** a high *destiny*. 彼には大使命がある. ¶***influence*** the national *destinies* 国家の運命を左右する. ¶***seal*** one's *destiny* 自己の運命を封じる. 【類】Her *destiny* is ***sealed***. ¶the power to ***shape*** the *destinies* of the race 民族の興廃を左右する力. 【類】***shape*** the *destinies* of the world. ¶***sway*** the *destinies* of the education in Japan 日本における教育の前途を左右する. ¶***turn*** the *destiny* this way or that 運命を左右する. ¶***work out*** one's own *destiny* 自己の運命を開拓する. 【類】***work out*** our *destiny* in harmony with the design of the Nature's God (大自然の神).

Q ***adverse*** *destiny* 非運. 【類】He fought in vain against ***adverse*** *destiny*. ¶By what ***evil*** *destiny* did they become man and wife? いかなる悪縁で彼らは夫婦になったのか. ¶her ***future*** *destiny* among the nations of the earth 全世界の国民の間に処して行くその国将来の運命. ¶confidence in the country's ***high*** *destiny* その国の大使命に対する確信. ¶work out the ***manifest*** *destiny* 天の命じる所を決行する. 「きらめている.

P He is now resigned ***to*** his *destiny*. 彼は今では運命とあ

P² "The *destiny* ***of*** our country depends upon this battle." 「皇国の興廃この一戦にあり」.

destitute, *a.* 欠けた; 貧困な.

M In a sense, the school is a refuge of the ***intellectually*** *destitute*. 考えようによってはその学校は知的欠陥者の逃げ場である. ¶He is ***utterly*** *destitute* of shame. 彼は全く恥を

知らない. 【類】become ***utterly*** *destitute* of modesty (あばずれ).

P a school ***for*** the *destitute* 貧民学校. ¶people *destitute* ***of*** money (means, clothing, religion, principle, valour) 金(など)のない人々 ‖ They were *destitute* ***of*** the necessaries of life. 彼らは生活の必需品にこと欠いていた. 【類】a country (an island) *destitute* ***of*** inhabitants.

destitution, *n.* 貧窮.

V ***suffer*** *destitution* 貧窮に悩む.

Q He died in ***complete*** *destitution.* 彼はすっかり貧乏して死んだ. ¶get into ***utter*** *destitution* どん底生活に陥る. 【類】The wife and children are in ***utter*** *destitution.*

P The war brought us nothing ***but*** desolation and *destitution.* 戦争の残したのは荒廃と貧窮だけだった. ¶people ***in*** *destitution* 困っている人々. ¶He fell ***into*** *destitution.* 彼は貧乏になった.

destroy, *v.* 破壊する.

M All trace is ***effectively*** *destroyed.* 形跡がことごとく効果的に消されている. ¶be ***partially*** (***totally***) *destroyed* 半(全)壊する.

P We have had our premises totally *destroyed* ***by*** fire. 邸宅は火事で跡形もなくなった. 【類】The building was *destroyed* ***by*** fire. / His house was *destroyed* ***by*** a flood (an earthquake). ‖ The collection was *destroyed* ***by*** the burning of a portion of Smithsonian building in 1865. その収集は一八六五年スミソニヤン・ビルディング半焼のときに焼けてしまった. ¶the house was *destroyed* ***in*** the big fire of ... その家屋は…の大火で焼けてしまった.

destroyer, *n.* 駆逐艦.

Q an ***over-age*** *destroyer* 老朽駆逐艦.

Q^2 a ***tank*** *destroyer* 対戦車砲.

destruction, *n.* 破滅, 破壊.

V ***bring*** *destruction* upon oneself 自滅する. ¶***cause*** great *destruction* of life and property 生命財産の大損失を生じる. ¶***court*** *destruction* 破滅を招くようなことをする. ¶***escape*** *destruction* 破滅を免れる. ¶***meet*** *destruction* 破滅に会う. ¶***spread*** *destruction* like a pestilence 伝染病のように破壊を拡大する. ¶it is ***working*** the *destruction* of ... それが…の破滅をきたしつつある.

Q ***atomic*** *destruction* of civilization 原子による文明の破壊. ¶There was ***great*** *destruction* of property, but no loss of life. 財産には大損害があったが死者はなかった. ¶***unnecessary*** *destruction* of beautiful natural scenery 自然美の無益な破壊.

Q^2 the atomic bomb and other weapons of ***mass*** *destruction* 原子爆弾および他の大量破壊兵器.

P^2 *destruction* ***by*** fire 焼失. ¶*destruction* ***to*** life and property 生命財産の損失.

destructive, *a.* 破壊する.

M bugs ***most*** *destructive* to beans 豆類に最も有害な虫. ¶The gales were ***very*** *destructive* to the crops. 烈風のため作物が大損害をこうむった.

P Drinking is *destructive* ***of*** health. 酒は健康に大害がある. ‖ Earthquakes are generally more *destructive* ***of*** life than volcanic eruptions. 地震の方が普通火山の破裂よりも一層人命をそこなうものだ. ¶a fly *destructive* ***to*** the fruit 果実に有害なはえ ‖ Such a habit is *destructive* ***to*** the morals of youth. かかる習慣は青年の風紀に大害がある.

destructor, *n.* 《英》廃物焼場.

Q^2 a ***dust*** *destructor* ごみ焼場.

detach, *v.* 離す.

P be *detached* ***from*** the main building 母屋(おもや)から遊離した ‖ *detach* a man ***from*** a party 仲間から人を引離す. 【類】*detach* a state ***from*** a confederation ‖ *detach* a locomotive ***from*** a train 列車から機関車をはずす. 【類】*detach* a rock ***from*** its bed (岩床).

detachment, *n.* 分離; 分遣隊.

Q^2 a ***language*** *detachment* 語学班. ¶the ***Headquarters*** *Detachment* of the Tokyo Provost Marshall Office 東京憲兵司令部分遣隊.

detail, *n.* 詳細; 細目, 細項.

V ***arrange*** *details* 詳細の手はずをきめる ‖ Every *detail* was carefully ***arranged.*** 万端手落ちなく準備ができた. ¶Let us ***cast aside*** minor *details.* 細かいことは捨置くことにしよう. ¶***exclude*** pedantic *details* げん学的な細説をしりぞける. ¶***fill in*** the *details* 委細を書込む. ¶***furnish*** *details* 詳述する. ¶***give*** full *detail* of the matter そのことの一部始終を語る. ¶***leave*** the *details* to ... 詳細は…に譲る. ¶he ***masters*** the intricate *details* of ... 彼は…の入組んだ事情に明るい. ¶We ***omitted*** all the minor *details* 細かいことは一切はぶいた. ¶***overload*** *details* 余り細事にわたり過ぎる. ¶***regulate*** the *details* of carrying into effect ... …の実施に関する細目を定める. ¶The *details* are ***represented*** in the following figures. 詳細は次の数字の通りである. ¶He ***told*** me all the *details.* 彼は私に委細を話した. ¶the thread that ***unites*** the *details* 細事をつなぐ糸. ¶***withhold*** *details* 詳細の発表を差控える. ¶***work out*** the *details* 細則を作る. 【類】Every *detail* is ***worked out.*** / The *detail* has been ***worked out*** with great faithfulness and accuracy.

Q ***chief*** *details* 主な細目. ¶in ***complete*** *detail* きわめて詳細に. ¶***concrete*** *details* 具体的な細目. ¶omit ***confusing*** *detail* まぎらわしい細目をはぶく. ¶be treated with ***considerable*** *detail* はなはだ詳細に記述される. ¶enter into the ***deeper*** *details* そのことの詳細を述べる. ¶***dry*** *detail* 無味乾燥な細目. ¶***essential*** *details* 大事な細目. ¶report ***every*** *detail* of ... …を逐一報告する. ¶I think we need not trouble too much about those ***fine*** *details.* そんな細かい点は余り心配するに及ばないと思う. ¶describe in ***full*** *detail* 細かに述べる. 【類】with ***fuller*** *details.* ¶***graphic*** *details* こく明に表現された細部. ¶He has studied this subject in ***great*** *detail.* 彼は丹念にこの問題を研究した. 【類】in ***greater*** *detail.* ¶the ***gruesome*** *details* of a great war 大戦のぞっとするようなてん末. ¶amid the ***homeliest*** *details* of daily life 日常生活の最も平凡な細目の中で. ¶the less ***important*** *details* たいして用のない細かい点. ¶weave the ***innumerable*** *details* into a homogeneous whole 無数の細項を統一あるものにする. ¶in every ***meticulous*** *detail* 細か過ぎるほど詳細に. ¶in ***microscopic*** *detail* 細微にわたって. ¶only in ***minor*** *details* 細かい事柄においてのみ. ¶He investigated the matter in ***minute*** *detail.* 彼は詳細に事件を調査した. ¶consider it in ***more*** *detail* それを一層詳細に考慮する. ¶***precise*** *details* 細かい箇条. ¶***revolting*** *details* of a crime 犯罪のいまわしい委細. ¶its most ***salient*** *details* その最も目ぼしい細項. ¶It is unnecessary to enter into ***technical*** *details.* 専門的のことにわたる必要はない. ¶an ***unimportant*** *detail* 重要でない細目. ¶avoid ***unnecessary*** *details* いりもせぬ詳細事項を避ける ‖ leave out ***unnecessary*** *details* 不必要な細目を省略する.

P describe (=comment) ***in*** *detail* 詳細に解説する ‖ enumerate ***in*** *detail* 詳細に数え上げる. 【類】explain it ***in*** *detail* / discuss the point more ***in*** *detail* / we shall come back to this ***in*** more *detail* later; suffice it for the present to say that ... / the affair ***in*** all its *details.* ¶take up too much space to go ***into*** *details* 余り紙面をふさぐので詳細にわたれない. ¶a matter (=an affair) ***of*** *detail* 細事.

P^2 the *details* ***of*** duty 職務の細目. ¶go through the small *details* ***of*** domestic drudgery 家庭の細かい仕事を一一やる ‖ *details* ***of*** the crime その犯罪のてん末. 【類】the *details* ***of*** a report.

detail, *v.* 詳述する; 選任する.

M The report is not *detailed* ***enough.*** その報道は十分詳細を尽していない.

M^2 They are *detailed* ***off*** for their various duties. 彼らはそれぞれの任務に派遣されている.

P *detail* a person ***for*** some duty (work) 人をある任務(など)に振り当てる ‖ Government officers especially *detailed* ***for*** the purpose その目的のために特派された官吏. ¶*detail* a person ***on*** a special service 特務に人を選任する. ¶He was *detailed* ***to*** some work (duty). 彼はある仕事(など)に選任された.

detain, *v.* 引留める; 留置する.

M I will not *detain* you ***long.*** 手間はとらせない.

P a person captured and *detained* ***as*** hostage in the castle その城に人質として捕われて留置されている人. ¶He is *detained* ***at*** an office (a police station). 彼は役所(など)に拘留されている. ¶I was *detained* ***by*** a friend who called. 友たちが訪問したので抜けられなかった. 【類】I was *detained* ***by*** rain. ¶be *detained* ***in*** a canal 運河の中にとめられている ‖ The vessel is *detained* ***in*** quarantine. 船は検疫でとめられている. ‖ a drunkard *detained* ***in*** the cooler ぶた箱に入れられた酔っぱらい.

detect, *v.* 見付ける, 看破する.

M an error ***happily*** *detected* in time for correction 幸い訂正が間に合うように見つかった誤り.

P *detect* it ***by*** the sense of smell それをかぎつける. ¶*detect* an imitation ***from*** a real thing 本物とにせ物を見分ける. ¶He was *detected* ***in*** a fraud. 彼は詐欺を見破られた. ¶The sensualist can be *detected* ***through*** all his disguises. 好色家はいくら隠しても分る.

detection, *n.* 露顕, 発覚.

V Methods of ***electronic detection*** of aircraft are known. 航空機の電子探知法ができている. ¶The fraud ***escaped*** *detection.* 詐欺は露顕しなかった.

Q^2 scientific ***crime detection*** 科学的犯罪捜査.

P^2 the *detection* ***of*** crime=crime detection.

detective, *n.* 探偵; [警察]捜査係.

V ***detail*** *detectives* to watch the criminals 刑事を派して犯人を見張らせる. ¶***play*** the *detective* 探偵をやる.

Q a ***private*** *detective* 私立探偵.

Q^2 an ***amateur*** *detective* しろうと探偵. ¶a ***plain clothes*** *detective* 私服刑事. ¶a ***police*** *detective* 捜査係.

detector, *n.* 発見器.

Q^2 a ***lie*** *detector* うそ発見器. ¶a ***mine*** *detector* 機雷発見器. ¶a ***radio*** *detector* (=radar) 電波探知器. ¶a ***vacuum tube*** *detector* 真空管検波器.

detention, *n.* 拘留, 留置.

Q the number of days of ***unconvicted*** *detention* 未決拘留日数.

P ***during*** his *detention* at the hospital 彼がその病院に入院中. ¶He is ***in*** *detention* in connection with the bribery affair. 彼はわいろ事件に関連して拘留されている. ¶a house ***of*** *detention* 拘留所. ¶He is ***under*** *detention.* 彼は拘留中だ.

P^2 a *detention* ***by*** quarantine at a port 港内で隔離(伝染病者の)による停船. ¶*detention* ***in*** custody 監禁 ‖ *detention* ***in*** a labor house 労役場留置.

deter, *v.* 思い止まらせる.

P *deter* a person ***from*** an attempt (doing something) 企て(など)を思い止まらせる. 【類】Nothing can *deter* him ***from*** his purpose. / He is *deterred* ***from*** crime by fear of punishment. / Failure didn't *deter* him ***from*** trying it again. / I shall never be *deterred* ***from*** doing my duty by threats.

deterioration, *n.* 悪化, 退化.

V ***suffer*** some *deterioration* 多少悪化する. ¶The food ***undergoes*** no *deterioration* in the tropics. その食物は熱帯地方でも悪くならない.

Q rapid ***moral*** *deterioration* 急速な道徳的退廃. ¶***physical*** *deterioration* 肉体的退化.

P^2 *deterioration* ***in*** health 健康の悪化.

determinant, *n.* 決定するもの.

Q a ***prime*** *determinant* of ... ...を主として決定するものの一つ.

determination, *n.* 決心, 決定; 測定.

V He ***bore*** *determination* in his face. 彼には決心の色が見えていた. ¶***declare*** one's *determination* 決心を声明する. ¶This *determination* he had ***made*** in early youth, and carried out with characteristic pertinacity. 彼は青年の初期にこのことを決心し彼独特の根気強さでこれを実行した. ¶inwardly ***register*** a *determination* not to ... ...しないことに意を決する. ¶***show*** fixed *determination* to ... ...しようという堅い決意を示す.

Q ***accurate*** *determination* 正確な測定. ¶with a ***dogged*** *determination* がん強な決意をもって. ¶make a ***fresh*** *determination* 決意を新たにする. ¶with a ***full*** *determination* to go 行こうと十分決心して. ¶her ***inflexible*** *determination* to ... ...しようとする不屈の決意. ¶***invincible*** *determination* 打ちかちがたい決心. ¶need ***more*** *determination* もっと腹をきめる必要がある. ¶with the ***secret*** *determination* to ... ...すべくひそかに決心して.

P a matter ***for*** *determination* by cases 場合場合によって決定すべき問題. ¶come ***to*** a *determination* 決心がつく. ¶carry out the plan ***with*** *determination* 断固としてその計画を遂行する ‖ I entered upon my duties ***with*** a *determination* to win professional success. 僕はその方の専門家として成功しようと決心してその職についた.

P^2 *determination* ***by*** the proper authorities その筋の決定. ¶the *determination* ***of*** the question その問題の決定 ‖ the *determination* ***of*** the tribunal 法廷の決定 ‖ the *determination* ***of*** the periods of time 期間の算定.

determine, *v.* 決定する.

M *determine* ***beforehand*** ... ...を前もってきめる. ¶What country is indicated by that name has not yet been ***definitely*** *determined.* その名称でどの国を指すかはまだはっきりしてない. ¶the one ***finally*** *determined* upon 最後に決定したこと. 【類】It ***finally*** *determined* him to do it. ¶be ***firmly*** *determined* 固く決心している. ¶I have not yet ***fully*** *determined.* 私はまだ腹がしっかりきまらない.

M^2 He *determined* ***on*** to go. 彼は行くことにきめた.

P *determine* a matter ***by*** a vote (yeas and nays) 投票(など)で問題を決定する ‖ The part of speech to which a word belongs is *determined* only ***by*** its function in the sentence. ある語の属する品詞は文の中のその語の役目によってのみ決まる. ¶He *determined* ***on*** coming. 彼は来ることに決した. ‖ *determine* (=decide) ***on*** one's course of future 将来の方針を決める. 【類】*determine* ***on*** a different course / He, out of revenge, *determined* ***on*** ...'s death. ‖ He *determined* ***on*** retaliation. 彼は復しゅうしようと決心した. 【類】*determine* ***on*** (=***upon***) the commission of a crime / *determine* ***on*** a voyage to Europe.

O This *determined* him to go immediately. このために彼は直に行くことに決心した.

deterrent, *n.* 妨害物.

P It would act ***as*** a *deterrent.* それは引とめ役をするだろう. ¶a *deterrent* ***to*** industrial progress 工業進歩の障害.

detestable, *a.* 忌むべき.

P *detestable* ***to*** ... ...にいやがられる.

detestation, *n.* いみきらい.

V ***arouse*** *detestation* けん悪感を起す.

P have (=hold) ... ***in*** *detestation* ...をいみきらう.

detonation, *n.* 爆音.

V I ***heard*** a violent *detonation* in the direction of ... 私は...の方向に激しい爆音を聞いた.

detour, *n.* 遠回り, 回路.

V ***make*** a long (=wide) *detour* 遠回りをする. 【類】He ***made*** a *detour* of many miles.

Q you can make a ***delightful*** *detour* by ... ...を行けば楽しく遠回りができる.

P^2 a *detour* ***round*** the place その所を中心にした回り道.

detract, *v.* 引去る, 損じる.

M The defect *detracts* ***greatly*** from the value of the article. そのきずで品物の価値が大いに減じる. ¶this, however, does not *detract* ***in the least*** from the fact that ... しかしこのことのため...にという事実を少しも傷つけない.

P be *detracted* ***by*** ... ...に気を取られる. ¶*detract* ***from*** its effectiveness その効果を損う. 【類】This fact does not *detract* ***from*** the greatness of her achievements. / His absence *detracted* ***from*** the interest of the occasion. / *detract* ***from*** its interest (merit) / *detract* ***from*** one's reputation (honor, fame) / *detract* something ***from*** one's influence (power, reputation) / It *detracts* nothing ***from*** the credit (信用) due to him. / The defect *detracts* little ***from*** its intrinsic value (真価).

detraction, *n.* 毀損(きそん).

V ***outlive*** *detraction* [of one's fame] 名誉を全うする.

detractor, *n.* 中傷者.

Q an ***envious*** *detractor* ねたんで悪口する人.

P So it is called ***by*** its *detractors.* 悪口にそういう名が付けられている.

detrain, *v.* [列車から]降りる.

P *detrain* ***at*** ... ...で列車から降りる.

detriment, *n.* 損害, 損失; 害物.

V ***receive*** no *detriment* 損害を受けない.

P ***to*** the *detriment* of others 他人に迷惑をかけて ‖ He sits up very late, ***to*** the *detriment* of his health. 彼は夜ふかしをするのが体に悪い. ‖ I know nothing ***to*** his *detriment.* 何も彼の悪いことは知らない. 【類】This suspicion was ***to*** his *detriment.* ‖ a *detriment* ***to*** morals 道徳を害するもの ‖ His generosity is a great *detriment* ***to*** his property. 彼の大まかなのが彼の財産には大損害だ.

detrimental, *a.* 有害な.

M This is ***decidedly*** *detrimental* to the good name of the society. これは確かにその協会の盛名を傷つけるものだ.

P It is *detrimental* ***to*** the public interest. それは公益に害がある. 【類】This is *detrimental* ***to*** the interests of the Empire. / It is *detrimental* ***to*** health (industry, one's business).

devaluation, *n.* 平価切下げ.

Q^2 ***currency*** *devaluation* 平価切下げ.

P^2 the *devaluation* ***of*** the pound ポンドの平価切下げ.

devastate, *v.* 荒廃させる.

P towns *devastated* ***by*** fire (floods, war, earthquakes).

¶The whole town was *devastated* ***in*** the war flames. 戦火で町は全部荒廃した.

devastation, *n.* 荒廃. 「旧.

Q² rehabilitation of ***war devastation*** 戦争による荒廃の復

develop, *v.* 発達する(させる), 発展する(させる); 分明になる; 現像する.

M the nucleus of what *developed* ***afterwards*** into a mighty work 後に発達して偉大な事業となったものの中核. ¶***conspicuously*** *develop* 著しく発達する. ¶Modern music was ***first*** *developed* in Italy. 近代音楽は始めてイタリアで発達した. ‖ The knowledge acquired by the mind is ***gradually*** *developed* into wisdom. 心が獲得した知識は漸次発達して知恵となる. ¶*develop* ***intellectually*** 知的発展をする. ¶***partially*** *develop* 局部的に発達する. ¶be rather ***poorly*** *developed* どちらかというと発達の程度の低い. ¶The situation *developed* ***rapidly***. 事態は急速に進んだ.

P *develop* ***by*** leaps [and bounds] とんとん拍子に発展する. ¶A blossom *develops* ***from*** a bud. 花はつぼみから発育する. ‖ Lung fever *develops* ***from*** flu. 流感がもとで肺炎を併発する. ¶I hope his eldest son may *develop* ***into*** a good man. 彼の長男が成長して善人となればよいが. 【類】An acorn *develops* ***into*** an oak. ‖ The manufacture *developed* ***into*** a large and flourishing industry. その製造業が発展して盛大な産業となった. ‖ *develop* ***into*** a fullblown university department 大学の堂々たる学部に発展する ‖ *develop* ***into*** the "real thing" 本物(一大事)になる. 【類】When nervousness gets beyond a certain stage it *develops* ***into*** a disease. / *develop* ***into*** a more serious illness ‖ Acquaintance has *developed* ***into*** friendship. 知り合い程度から親しくつきあうようになった. ¶This city *developed* ***out of*** a fishing village. この都市は漁村から発展した. ¶*develop* ***to*** a high degree of maturity 成熟の域に入る. 【類】be *developed* ***to*** a point of high excellence. ¶*develop* ***with*** practice 練習とともに成熟する.

O It *developed* that he had another wife living and his indictment for bigamy followed. 彼には別に妻がいることが分り重婚で起訴となった.

development, *n.* 発達, 発展, 発育; 開拓.

V It ***achieved*** a remarkable *development* in the nineteenth century. それは十九世紀に著しい発達を遂げた. ¶***actuate*** the *development* of closer commercial intercourse 一層密接なる通商の発達を誘致する. ¶***affect*** her commercial *development* その国の商業上の発達に影響する. ¶***aid*** the material *development* of the country その国の物質的発展を助ける. ¶***arrest*** mental *development* 知能の発達を阻害する. ¶***attain*** its full *development* その十分な発達を遂げる. 【類】***attain*** its finest and fullest *development*. ¶***await*** *development* 開拓を待つ. ¶***check*** the country's commercial and industrial *development* その国の商工業の発達を阻害する. ¶***follow*** the gradual *development* of ... ...の漸次的発展の跡をたどる. ¶it is impossible to ***forecast*** the future *development* of ... ...の将来の発展は予測しがたい. ¶***forward*** the *development* of English instruction in junior high schools 中学校の英語教授の発達を助成する. ¶***hamper*** (=***hinder***) the *development* of ... ...の発達を妨げる. ¶***improve*** one's physical *development* 身体の発達を助ける. ¶films that have ***marked*** a definite *development* in cinematography 活動写真術における画然たる発達を標示した映画. ¶it ***owes*** its *development* to ... その発展については...に負う所がある. ¶***prevent*** *development* 発達を妨げる. ¶***promote*** their physical *development* 彼らの体育上益がある. ¶Oculists find that a child's eyes do not ***reach*** full *development* until about twelve years of age. 子供の目は十二歳ごろにならないと十分に発達しないことを眼科医は認めている. ¶The art ***received*** its greatest *development* in that period. その芸術はその時期に極度に発達した. ¶***retard*** the *development* of society 社会の発達を妨げる. ¶***review*** step by step the *development* which led to ... ...とまで発達した跡を一歩一歩たどる. ¶***show*** its highest *development* その最大の発達を示す. ¶***stunt*** the spiritual *development* of ... ...の精神的発達を阻害する. ¶Today will show what *development* the war will ***take***. 戦争が今後どう発展するか今になって分るでしょう. ¶***thwart*** the *develpoment* of ... ...の発展を阻害する. ¶***undergo*** a marked *development* 著しく発展する. ¶***watch*** the *development* of the committee with the keenest interest 熱心な興味を以て委員会の行動を注視する ‖ intently ***watch*** the *development* of the infant mind 幼児の精神の発達を熱心に見守る.

V² A great *development* ***took place***. 大々的発展をした.

Q take on an ***abnormal*** *development* 異状の発達を遂げる. ¶***aesthetic*** *development* 美感の発達. ¶***after-war*** *development* 戦後の発展. ¶***alarming*** *development* 驚くべき発達. ¶Japan's ***amazing*** *development* in ship-building 造船術における日本の驚くべき発達. ¶***arrested*** *development* 阻害された発展. ¶the ***better*** *development* of the power of self-control 自制力の一層十分な発達. ¶come (=be brought) into ***brilliant*** *development* 輝かしい発展を遂げる. ¶present a ***clear, logical*** *development* of a subject ある問題の明りょうで筋の通った発達を示す. ¶***complete*** *development* of personality 人格の十分な発達 ‖ attain its ***complete*** *development* 十分に発達する. ¶***defective intra-uterine*** *development* 母胎での発育不十分. ¶It is universally admitted that English life reaches its most ***delightful*** and ***unique*** *development* in their country houses. 英人の生活は村荘において最も喜ばしい無比の発達を遂げているということは一般に認められている. ¶***disproportionate*** *developments* 不均等の発達. ¶the Powers interested in the ***economic*** *development* of China 中国の経済発展に関心を持つ列強 ‖ ***Economic*** *development* and defense are inseparable. 経済的発展と国防は分離しがたい. ¶an atmosphere favourable to its ***fruitful*** *development* その有利な発達に都合のよいふん囲気. ¶reach its ***full*** *development* 十分な発展を遂げる. ¶What are the ***future*** *developments* of atomic-power applications? 原子力応用の今後の成行はどうなるだろう. ¶advance with the ***general*** *development* of science 科学全般の発達と歩調を合わせる. ¶the ***harmonious*** *development* of all the faculties すべての機能の円満な発達. ¶It attained a ***high*** (=***great***) *development* in ancient Japan. それは古代の日本において大いに発達した. ¶***historical*** *development* of art 美術の歴史的発達. 【類】study the law in its ***historical*** *development*. ¶a phase in ***human*** *development* 人類発達の一面. ¶an ***imperfect*** *development* of the brain 脳の不完全な発達. ¶There will be many ***important*** *developments* in the industry in 1930. 一九三〇年にはその産業に幾多重要なる発展を見ることでしょう. ¶That peace will lead to a great ***industrial*** and ***commercial*** *development* in this part of Asia その平和がアジアのこの地方に商工業の大発展をきたすであろう. ¶an ***insufficient*** *development* of the force of the will and of the power of resistance 意志の力と抵抗力との不十分な発達. ¶***intellectual*** *development* 知力の発達. ¶the ***latest*** *developments* in the world of fashion 流行界における最近の傾向. 【類】the ***latest*** *developments* of atomic power industry. ¶the company's two ***major*** *developments* of 1930 一九三〇年におけるその会社の二方面への大発展. ¶***national*** *development* 国家的発展. ¶a ***new*** *development* in the social program 社会政策の新発展 ‖ a ***new*** *development* (=departure) in baby carriages 乳母車の新形 ‖ ***new*** and ***startling*** *developments* 驚くべき新発展. ¶Buddhism and its ***peculiar Japanese*** *developments* 仏教と日本におけるその特殊の発達. ¶an arrest or retardation of ***physical*** *development* 身体発達の停止または遅滞. ¶A practical joke is after all a ***poor*** *development* (=expression) of the sense of humor. 悪ふざけは結局ユーモアのセンスがつたなく表われたものである. ¶defective ***post-natal*** *development* 出生後の発育不全. ¶***precocious sexual*** *development* 早熟の性的発達. ¶***prodigious*** *development* 大発展. ¶the ***progressive*** *development* of the vocabulary 語いの漸次の増大. ¶***recent*** *developments* in European thought 欧州の思潮における近年の発達. ¶***serious*** *development* 局面の由々しい進展. ¶growing out of the new developments in the ***social, industrial, commercial,*** and ***political*** *developments* of the people 人民の社会的産業的商業的および政治的発達の新発展から生じる. ¶***striking*** *developments* 著しき発達. ¶***symmetrical*** *developments* 均斉のとれた発達. ¶the ***unfettered*** *development* of the individual mind 個々の知能ののびのびした発達. ¶experience a ***wonderful*** *development* of power 権力の驚くべき増大に気付く.

Q² all phases of ***atomic energy*** *development* 原子エネルギー発展のあらゆる方面. ¶striking ***building*** *development* 注目すべき建築上の進展. ¶***irrigation*** *developments* in the arid areas 乾燥地域におけるかんがい方法の発達. ¶*land development* in Japan 日本国土開発. ¶trace the *sense development* of a word 言葉の意味の発展経路を調べる. ¶*water power development* 水力利用の発達. ¶*world developments* of shipping industry 海運業の世界的発展.

P² these *developments in* civilization 文化方面におけるこれらの発達 ‖ regard these as a *development in* the desired (=right) direction これらを好ましい方向への進展と見なす. ¶the *development of* backward countries 後進国の開発 ‖ the *development of* Japan *from* a primitive feudal state *into* a state of representative democracy, founded on Western ideas of liberty and law 原始的な封建制度から西欧の自由と法律の思想にもとずいた民主主義国への日本の進展.

deviate, *v.* それる; 離れる.

M His statement seemed ***slightly*** to *deviate* from the truth. 彼の陳述は少し事実をゆがめていたようだ.

P *deviate from* the beaten track (a route) 普通通る道(など)から他にそれる ‖ *deviate from* the right path 正路をはずれる.【類】*deviate from* the standard (a target) ‖ *deviate from* the main theme (話が)横道にはいる ‖ *deviate from* one's purpose (principle) 目的(など)をそれる.

device, *n.* 考案; 仕掛, 装置; 計略, 方策; *pl.* 考え, 意思.

V ***adopt*** the *device* of ... ...の考案を採用する. ¶***follow*** one's own *devices* 自分の考え通りにする. ¶***invent*** all the possible *devices* to ... できるだけの工夫をこらして...する. ¶***use*** every *device* known to ... ...に知られているあらゆる手段を用いる ‖ ***use*** an ingenious *device* which allows ... ...することのできる巧妙な仕掛を用いる.

V² a *device* ***consisting*** of ... ...という仕掛.

Q a ***cheap*** *device* つまらぬ考案. ¶a ***cowardly*** *device* 卑劣な計略. ¶the ***devious*** *devices* used by burglars and sneak thieves 夜盗やこそ泥などの用いる不正な手段. ¶an ***efficacious*** *device* for ... ...に有効な方法. ¶a ***favorite*** *device* of the humorist ユーモア作者のよく使う手. ¶a ***helpful*** *device* 役に立つ考案. ¶an ***illicit*** *device* for cheating the Post Office 郵便局をあざむくための不法考案. ¶an ***ingenious*** *device* うまい思い付. ¶the ***latest*** *devices* for safety 最新式の安全装置. ¶a ***makeshift*** *device* 間に合わせの工夫. ¶a ***mechanical*** *device* 機械仕掛. ¶***mnemonic*** *devices* 記憶術. ¶the use of phonetic alphabets as a ***pedagogical*** *device* 教授上の一手段としての音標文字使用. ¶It will not be ended by ***petty*** *devices.* それは小細工では片がつくまい. ¶a ***pious*** *device* [布教上の]方便. ¶a ***protection*** *device* 保護装置. ¶a ***rhetorical*** *device* 修辞的技巧. ¶a ***shallow*** *device* 浅薄な計略. ¶a ***simple*** *device* 簡単な装置. ¶an ***unworkable*** *device* 実用的でない考案.

Q² The juice extractor is a practical ***household*** *device.* [レモンなどの]汁絞りは実用向きな家庭用具である. ¶a ***labor-saving*** *device* 労力節約手段. ¶a black threecornered hat with a ***skull*** and ***crossbones*** *device* in white sewn upon it どくろと交差した人骨の模様を白糸で縫取った黒い三角帽. ¶***teaching*** *devices* 諸種の教授法. ¶an automatic ***train-control safety*** *device* 列車自動操作安全装置. ¶an ***underwater echo ranging*** *device* 水面下音響発射装置.

P ***by*** *devices* of diplomacy 外交策で. ¶***through*** a legal *device* 合法的手段で. ¶What would you do, if left ***to*** your own *devices?* 君の考え通りにやれと言われたらどうするか.

P² a *device* ***for*** convenience (comfort) 便利(など)なやり方.

devil, *n.* 悪魔; やつ.

V I ***had*** the *devil* of a time explaining that. 僕はその弁解でひどい目にあった.

V² *Devils* ***crawled away*** to hide among the rocks. 悪魔どもははって岩の間に隠れようとした. ¶*Devils* ***scamper out;*** luck, slip in. 鬼は外福は内.

Q a ***foreign*** *devil* 毛唐. ¶a ***hideous*** *devil* いやな野郎. ¶a ***poor*** *devil* かわいそうなやつ. ¶a ***printer's*** *devil* 印刷屋の小僧. ¶a ***reckless*** *devil* 向う見ずの野郎.

Q² a ***forest*** *devil* (=a stump-extractor) 《方》木の株を抜く道具. ¶be ***'twixt*** *Devil* and the deep sea 進退きわまる.

O There will be the *devil* to pay. あとのたたりがこわい.

devilment, *n.* いたずら.

P ***out of*** mere *devilment* ほんのいたずらに.

devise, *v.* 工夫する, 考案する.

M it is ***so devised*** that ... ...という仕掛けになっている.

P *devise* a scheme ***for*** earning money 収入の道を計る.

devoid, *a.* ない, 欠けている.

P Sound waves cannot be transmitted through a space *devoid* ***of*** air. 音波は空気のない所へは通じない. ‖ The chess is said to be the only game which is entirely *devoid* ***of*** luck. 西洋将棋だけは運不運がないということになっている. 【類】The garden is *devoid* ***of*** artistic interest (殺風景だ). / The sentence looked absolutely *devoid* ***of*** sense. / He is absolutely *devoid* ***of*** musical sense (音痴). / He is *devoid* ***of*** common sense (foresight, principle, taste).

devolve, *v.* 伝わる, 回る, 帰する.

P The whole matter *devolves* ***on*** the one point. 問題全部がこの一点に帰着する. ‖ that duty *devolved* ***on*** ... ...がその役目を勤めることになった. ‖ The responsibility *devolves* ***on*** you. 責任は君にある. ¶It doesn't *devolve* ***upon*** us to settle it. それを解決するのはわれわれの任でない. 【類】The responsibility *devolves* ***upon*** him as president. / it *devolved* ***upon*** me to undertake the task of ... / ***upon*** him *devolves* the important duty of ... / The work has mainly *devolved* ***upon*** him. ‖ In case of failure of direct descendants, the throne *devolves* ***upon*** the nearest prince. 直系の子孫がない場合は一番近い皇族が王位につくことになっている.

devote, *v.* ゆだねる, 当てる, 向ける; ささげる.

M *devote* oneself ***assiduously*** and ***faithfully*** to the duties of one's profession 自分の職分に熱心かつ忠実に身をささげる. ¶*devote* oneself ***disinterestedly*** to the good of the people 人民の利益に私心なく身をささげる. ¶be ***domestically*** *devoted* 家庭的に忠実である(いい父親である) ‖ the special session will *devote* itself ***entirely*** to ... 特別議会は全く...に充てられる. 【類】*devote* oneself ***almost entirely*** to the study of science ‖ There is an opening in the world of bookselling for one who will *devote* himself ***entirely*** to musical literature. 音楽書を専門にする書店があってもよい. ¶*devote* oneself ***exclusively*** to a study of ... ...の研究に専念する ‖ The magazine *devotes* itself ***exclusively*** to the furtherance of theological learning (magazine, etc.) その雑誌はもっぱら神学(など)の発展を目標としている. ¶*devote* himself ***faithfully*** to his arduous task 自分の根仕事に忠実に没頭する. ¶*devote* ourselves ***heart and soul*** to ... 熱心に...に身をゆだねる. ¶A day may ***profitably*** be *devoted* to its inspection. それを見るために一日を当てるのが有利でしょう(観光旅行などの場合). ¶His activities were *devoted* ***solely*** to his master's interest. 彼はもっぱら主人のために活動した. 【類】*devote* one's time ***solely*** to the study of ... ¶*devote* oneself ***unreservedly*** to the cause of democracy 民主主義のために全力を注ぐ. ¶*devote* oneself ***wholly*** to literary pursuits もっぱら文筆に親しむ.

P *devote* oneself ***to*** reading (the pursuit of a pleasure) 読書(など)にふける ‖ He is *devoted* ***to*** yachting. 彼はヨットに熱中している. ‖ *devote* one's energies (time, fortune) ***to*** the work 精力(など)をその仕事に向ける ‖ *devote* one's life ***to*** the study of literature 文学の研究に一生をささげる ‖ He *devoted* ***to*** it his spare time as well as his spare money. 彼は余分の金と時間とを皆それに向けた. ‖ The problem is so fundamental that it is necessary at this point to *devote* ***to*** it a brief discussion. この問題は根本的のものであるからここに少しく論じる必要がある. 【類】*devote* a sum ***to*** some purpose / *devote* so much of his attention ***to*** ... / *devote* the whole morning ***to*** hard work ‖ periodicals *devoted* ***to*** a great variety of interests 種々な読者層に仕向けた雑誌 ‖ a newspaper *devoted* ***to*** the cause of Philippine independence フィリッピンの独立運動を唱道する新聞紙 ‖ He is *devoted* ***to*** himself alone. 彼は虫がよい. ‖ The city was *devoted* ***to*** destruction (flames). 都市は破壊された(焼かれた). 【類】A little time *devoted* ***to*** it pays for itself many times over.

devotee, *n.* 信者.

V ***number*** many *devotees* 多くの信者を有している.

Q² a ***sex life*** *devotee* 道楽者.

P² the *devotees* ***of*** this cult この宗旨の信者.

devotion, *n.* 礼拝, 勤行; 熱心, 熱誠, 奉仕, 執着; *pl.* 祈禱.

V ***pay*** one's *devotions* at a shrine 神社に参詣する. ¶resort to cemeteries to ***perform*** their *devotions* 墓参りをする. ¶***practice*** *devotions* [聖職者など]お勤めをする. ¶The lover did this just to ***prove*** his *devotion.* その愛人はただ

自分の誠意を示すためにこのことをやった. ¶***show*** single *devotion* to one's religion ひたすら自分の宗教に帰依していることを示す.

Q ***absolute unswerving*** *devotion* to ... ...に対する絶対不動の熱心. ¶his ***altruistic*** *devotion* to the cause 彼のその主義のための犠牲的奉仕. ¶***earnest*** *devotion* to duty 勤務に対する熱心. ¶***entire*** *devotion* to one's pursuit 自己の職業に対する専心. ¶an ***inflexible*** *devotion* to an ideal 理想に対する不屈の執着. ¶one's ***loyal*** *devotion* to onc's alma mater 母校に対する熱誠. ¶a ***noble*** *devotion* to one's country 国家に対する高潔な忠誠. ¶***self-forgetful*** *devotion* 自己の利害を顧みぬ熱誠. ¶to be copied, not with a ***servile*** *devotion*, but a generous emulation 単に卑屈な信奉に止まらず大らかな競争心で追随すべき. ¶the type of ***single-hearted*** *devotion* 二心なき忠誠の典型. ¶an ***unselfish*** *devotion* to the development of human welfare 人類福利増進に対する献身的奉仕. ¶***womanly*** *devotion* to her country 女の母国愛.

Q^2 the fruition of her own ***life time*** *devotion* to the study of ... ...の研究に一生をささげた結晶.

P He was ***at*** his *devotions*. 彼は祈禱していた. ¶***with*** the *devotion* of a martyr 殉教者の熱情をもって ‖ She nursed her sick child ***with devotion***. 彼女はかいがいしくその病児を看護した ‖ burn ***with devotion*** 熱誠に燃える ‖ ***with*** single *devotion* 一心不乱に.

P^2 the virtues of courage and loyalty and ***devotion to*** duty 勇気と忠義と職務に対する熱誠という美徳. ¶an enthusiast in her *devotion* ***to*** her art その芸術に打込んでいる女 ‖ *devotion* ***to*** parents (master, children) 父母(など)に対する奉仕 ‖ *devotion* ***to*** details 細事に対する忠実.

devour, *v.* むさぼる; のみ込む.

M He ***eagerly devoured*** novel after novel. 彼は熱心に次から次へと小説をたん読した. ¶He *devours* ***voraciously*** all the books he can lay his hands on. 彼は手当り次第に本をたん読する.

P I was *devoured* ***by*** fear. 恐しさで気が気でなかった. ¶She was *devoured* ***by*** consumption. 彼女は胸の病で倒れた. ¶I was *devoured* ***with*** anxiety. 私は心配で心も空であった. ‖ *devour* ... ***with*** one's eyes ...に見とれる.

devourer, *n.* むさぼる人.

Q an ***impatient*** *devourer* of fiction しきりに小説をむさぼり読む人.

dew, *n.* 露.

V^2 The dcw ***falls***. 露がおりる.

Q A ***heavy*** *dew* fell. 露がひどくおりた. ¶***Morning*** *dews* glitter in the sun. 朝つゆが朝日に輝く.

dexterity, *n.* 巧妙, 器用.

V In the practical and mechanical arts, the Japanese ***show*** great *dexterity*. 実用的と機械的の技術にかけては日本人は非常に巧妙な所がある.

Q a matter of ***digital*** *dexterity* 指先の器用でやること. ¶***manual*** *dexterity* 手先の器用. ¶He shows a ***remarkable*** *dexterity* in hotel management. 彼はホテル経営が非常に上手である.

P ***with*** wonderful *dexterity* 非常にうまく ‖ work ***with*** *dexterity* 手際よく仕事をする.

P^2 *dexterity* ***at*** handling figures 数字を扱うことが巧妙 ‖ *dexterity* ***at*** cards カルタ遊びの巧妙. ¶*dexterity* ***in*** composition 作文のうまさ. ¶*dexterity* ***of*** hand (movement, management) 手先(など)の器用 ‖ The *dexterity* ***of*** his fingers is marvelous. 彼の指先の器用は驚くべきものがある. ¶*dexterity* ***with*** the pen 運筆の妙.

dext[e]rous, *a.* 上手な.

P He is very *dextrous* ***in*** (=***at***) doing it. 彼はそれがうまい. ‖ be *dexterous* ***in*** handling men 人扱いが上手である.

diagnose, *v.* 〖医〗診断する.

P *diagnose* his case (=illness) ***as*** malaria (consumption) 彼の病症をマラリヤ(など)と診断する.

diagnosis, *n.* 〖医〗診断; 判断.

V The case ***defies*** *diagnosis*. その患者は診断しかねる. ¶***make*** a *diagnosis* 診断する. ¶This ***settled*** the *diagnosis*. これでそう診断することができた.

Q an ***economic*** *diagnosis* 経済上の打診. ¶make ***erroneous*** *diagnosis* 誤診する. ¶make ***exact*** *diagnosis* of ... ...を正しく診断する. ¶***personal*** *diagnosis* 人物考査.

P ***according to*** my *diagnosis* of the circumstances 私の状況判断によれば.

P^2 *diagnosis* ***by*** the nose 臭覚による診断.

diagram, *n.* 図, 図表(ダイヤグラム).

V ***draw*** a *diagram* 図表を作る. ¶***make*** a *diagram* to show the relation of ... ...の関係を示す図表を作る.

Q a ***comparative*** *diagram* 比較図表.

P It is shown ***by*** a *diagram*. それが図解してある.

dial, *n.* ダイヤル.

V ***turn*** a *dial* of (=dial) the radio ラジオのダイヤルを回す.

Q^2 tune in by using a ***radio*** *dial* ラジオのダイヤルを回して波長を合わせる. ¶a ***telephone*** *dial* 電話のダイヤル.

dial, *v.* ダイヤルを回す.

M *dial* ***home*** ダイヤルを回して自宅へ電話を掛ける.

P *dial* ***to*** ... ...に電話をかける.

O *dial* the number その番号を回す.

dialect, *n.* 方言; 語風; 通語.

Q a ***complimentary*** *dialect* 儀礼の言葉. ¶"A good sport" in the ***daily*** and ***athletic*** *dialect* of the Yankeeland is "one who always cheerfully and modestly does his best for the good of his side." "A good sport" という言葉は米国では運動に関する日常語で自分の仲間の利益のためにいつも快活かつ謙虚に最善を尽す人の意である. ¶one's ***rustic*** *dialect* そのいなか弁. ¶a ***social*** *dialect* 社交界の通語. ¶a ***vulgar*** *dialect* 卑俗の方言.

Q^2 a ***country*** (=provincial *or* local) *dialect* いなかの方言. ¶***London*** (=cockney) *dialect* ロンドン方言.

P ***in*** a *dialect* of Irish アイルランドの方言で.

dialogue, *n.* 問答, 問答体.

V ***hold*** a *dialogue* together 話し合う.

Q an ***amusing*** *dialogue* 一口ばなし. ¶a ***fragmentary*** *dialogue* 談片. ¶a ***natural*** and ***crisp*** *dialogue* 気取らないさわやかな対話.

P write ***in*** *dialogue* 問答体に書く.

diameter, *n.* 直径.

V it ***has*** a *diameter* of ... それは直径...ある.

Q ***internal*** *diameter* 内径.

P It measures ... ft. ***in*** *diameter*. それは直径...フィートある.

P^2 about ... in. *diameter* ***at*** the thick end 太い方の端で直径約...インチ. ¶the *diameter* ***of*** a tree trunk 樹幹の直径 ‖ What is the *diameter* ***of*** it? それは直径いくらか.

diamond, *n.* ダイヤ[モンド]; 〖野球〗内野, 野球場.

V *Diamond* ***cut*** *diamond*. 両雄がしのぎを削る. ¶No substance can ***surpass*** the *diamond* in hardness. 堅さではダイヤモンドにまさる物はない. ¶***wear*** *diamonds* ダイヤを身に着ける.

V^2 The *diamond* ***sparkles***. ダイヤはきらきら光る.

Q a ***rough cut*** *diamond* あらごしらえのダイヤ. ¶an ***uncut*** *diamond* まだみがかないダイヤモンド.

Q^2 a maneuver on the ***baseball*** *diamond* 野球場での練習 ‖ The first ***baseball*** *diamond* was laid out in 1839, at Cooperstown, N.Y., by General Abner Doubleday. 野球場は一八三九年ニューヨークのクーパーズタウンにダブルデイ将軍が始めて作ったものだ. ¶an ***imitation*** *diamond* ダイヤの模造品. ¶a ***paste*** *diamond* ねり物のダイヤ.

P a ring set ***with*** *diamond* ダイヤの指環.

diarrhea, *n.* 下痢.

V ***have*** *diarrhea* 下痢をする.

Q ***explosive*** *diarrhea* 水瀉(しゃ)下痢.

diary, *n.* 日記, 日誌.

V I ***keep*** my *diary*. 僕は日記をつけている ‖ ***keep*** a *diary* of work 仕事の日誌を作る. 【類】In all his tours he ***kept*** a careful *diary*. ¶***write*** a *diary* in English 英語で日記をつける. ¶***write up*** one's *diary* [詳細に]日記をつける.

Q a ***physician's*** *diary* 臨床日誌.

Q^2 a ***travel*** *diary* 旅行日誌.

P^2 a *diary* ***during*** the Russo-Japanese war 日露戦争中の日誌. ¶a *diary* ***for*** 1935 一九三五年の日誌.

dice, *n. pl.* → die.

dice, *v.* [さいころ]ばくちをやる.

M *dice* ***away*** one's fortune ばくちで財産を失う.

dictate, *n.* 命令, 指図.

V ***obey*** the *dictates* of conscience 良心の命じる所に従う.

P ***according to*** the *dictates* of common sense 常識の命じる所に従って.

P^2 the *dictates* ***of*** his passions or of his interest 彼の情欲または私心の命じる所.

dictate, *v.* 命令する; 書取らせる.

P It is plainly *dictated* ***by*** common sense. それは明らか

に常識の命じる所だ. 【類】 *dictated* ***by*** the spirit of vengeance (復しゅう心). ¶*dictate* [***to***] him 彼に指図する ‖ *dictate* ***to*** class [教室で]生徒に書取をさせる ‖ It is not for me to *dictate* ***to*** you. 僕から君にかれこれ指図すべきいわれはない. ‖ I will not be *dictated* ***to***. 僕は指図は受けない. ‖ *dictate* laws ***to*** the empire 法を天下にしく ‖ *dictate* letters ***to*** one's clerk (typist, secretary) 書記(など)に手紙の文句を書取らせる.

dictation, *n.* 書取(ディクテーション), 口述, 口授; 指図.

V ***give*** *dictation* to [the] class クラスに書取を課す. ¶We ***have*** *dictation* today. 今日は書取がある. ¶***take*** the *dictation* of ... ...の口授を書取る ‖ ***take*** *dictation* accurately by shorthand 口授を速記で正確に書取る.

Q take ***fast*** *dictation* 早口の口授を書取る.

P I wrote the letter ***at*** his *dictation* その手紙はあの人の口授で私が書いたものだ. ‖ ***at*** the *dictation* of ... ...の指図を受けて ‖ typewrite ***at*** boss's *dictation* マスターの指図を受けてタイプする. ¶take down ***from*** *dictation* 口述を書取る. ¶write ***to*** *dictation* 口授を受けて書く.

P^2 *dictation* ***from*** another person 他人からの指図.

dictator, *n.* 独裁者, 支配者.

Q^2 a ***labor*** *dictator* 労働運動の指導者. ¶the ***Soviet*** *dictator,* Mr. Josef Stalin ソ連の独裁者ヨーセフ・スターリン氏.

P^2 He is a "*dictator* ***of*** fashion" 彼はいわゆる流行の支配者だ.

dictatorship, *n.* 独裁(制政治).

V ***establish*** a *dictatorship* of speech 言葉の用法を独断的に決める.

Q^2 a ***Fascist*** *dictatorship* in the Iberian Peninsula イベリヤ半島における国粋党独裁政治. ¶the ***Nazi*** *dictatorship* ナチ(ドイツ国家社会党)の独裁政治.

diction, *n.* 言い方, 話し方, 語法.

V ***use*** faulty *dictions* 間違った語法を用いる.

V^2 His *diction* ***sounds*** queer. 彼のいい回しは変だ.

Q ***archaic*** *diction* 古風な語法. ¶common examples of ***faulty*** *diction* 誤った語法のありふれた例. ¶***heightened*** *diction* 誇張した言い方. ¶a theory of ***poetic*** *diction* 韻文語法の一原理. ¶***splendid*** *diction* 素晴らしい言葉使い. ¶They speak not in the ***stilted*** *diction* of the space before the footlights, but in the speech of the green room. 彼らはせりふめいた話し方は止めて楽屋内の打とけた調子で話す.

P^2 some questions of *diction* ***regarding*** verbs 動詞に関する語法上の問題.

dictionary, *n.* 辞書.

V ***consult*** the *dictionary* freely どんどん辞書を引く. 【類】 ***consult*** the *dictionary* when confronted by an unfamiliar word. ¶I always ***have*** a *dictionary* for consultation. 私は常に辞書を座右におく. ¶***look up*** the *dictionary* 辞書を引く. ¶if you ***open*** any *dictionary* you will find the word signified ... どんな辞書でも開いて見ればその言葉が...の意味である事が分る. ¶***rack*** the *dictionary* to find complimentary adjectives with which to express one's admiration of ... 言葉の限りを尽くして...に賛辞を呈する. ¶***search*** the *dictionary* for a word 辞書を引いて言葉をさがす. ¶***thumb*** a *dictionary* 辞書に指の跡を付ける(始終使う). ¶***turn up*** the *dictionary* 辞書をめくる. ¶***use*** the *dictionary* faithfully まめに辞書を引く.

Q a ***bilingual*** *dictionary* [二国語の]双解辞典. ¶Webster's ***collegiate*** *dictionary*. ウェブスター大学生用辞典. ¶a ***historical*** *dictionary* 歴史辞典. ¶study these words in a ***large*** *dictionary* これらの語を大辞典で調べる. ¶a ***live*** (=***walking***) *dictionary* 生字引. ¶an ***occupational*** *dictionary* 職業辞典. ¶I have not the purse nor the shelf-room for such a ***voluminous*** *dictionary*. 私はこんな膨大な辞書を買う金もなくまた置場もない.

Q^2 a ***college*** (***high school***) *dictionary* 大学(高校)生用辞典. ¶a big ***desk*** *dictionary* 大型の事務用辞典. ¶Webster's ***Everyday Use*** *Dictionary* ウェブスター常用辞典. ¶a ***handy-size*** (***pocket-size***) *dictionary* 手ごろの(ポケット)辞書. ¶the ***landmark*** *dictionary* of Dr. Samuel Johnson of 1765 一七六五年刊行サミュエル・ジョンソン博士の画期的辞書. ¶a ***one-language*** (=a ***monolingual***) *dictionary* [対訳に対して]一国語辞書(英英辞典など). ¶In the case of the full-size ***one-volume*** *dictionary,* the average weight is about twenty pounds. 大版一冊本の辞書では平均の重量約二十ポンドだ. ¶the ***Oxford*** *dictionaries* オックスフォード諸辞典. ¶a ***pronouncing*** *dictionary* of American English 米語発音辞典. ¶a ***standard*** *dictionary* of the language 標準辞書. ¶a ***two-language*** (=bilingual) *dictionary* 二国語(対訳)辞典.

P look up a word ***in*** a *dictionary* 辞書で言葉をさがす.

P^2 A *Dictionary* ***to*** the Plays and Novels of Bernard Shaw バーナード・ショーの劇並に小説辞書.

dictum, *n.* 格言, 金言.

V heartily ***endorse*** the *dictum* 心から金言の真理を認める. ¶Poe's ***famous*** *dictum* of a hundred lines ポーの有名な百行説(詩は百行を越えるべからず, という論).

didacticism, *n.* 勧善懲悪主義.

P The story is told ***without*** *didacticism*. その物語の筋は勧善懲悪になっていない.

die, *n.* さいころ; 鋳型.

V ***cast*** (=***throw***) a *die* さいころを振る ‖ The *die* is ***cast***. 命数すでに定まれり(またいかんともすべからず).

Q force into the ***same*** *die* 同じ型にはめる.

P He lost his fortune ***at*** *dice*. 彼はとばくで財産をなくした. ¶the spots ***on*** a *die* さいころの目. ¶The country was then ***upon*** a (=the) *die*. その国は当時危機に陥っていた. ¶play ***with*** *dice* さいころでやる.

P^2 a *die* ***of*** three spots 目の三つあるさいころ.

die, *v.* 死ぬ; 枯れる; 亡びる; なくなる, 止む.

M He *died* ***aged thirty-five***. 彼は三十五で死んだ. ¶*die* ***away automatically*** 自然消滅する. ¶The wind *died* ***away*** at sunset. 日没時に風がないだ. ‖ The day *died* ***away***, and still he was wanting. 日が暮れた, だがまだ彼の姿は見えなかった. ¶Herbaceous plants die down to the ground, tender shoots *die* ***back*** to the old wood. 草は枯れて地に伏し木の柔い芽はもとの茎に枯れ下がる. ¶He *died* a ***beggar***. 彼はこじきになって死んだ. ¶A man is born ***but*** to *die*. 人は一旦生れたら死ぬるに定っている. ¶*die* ***calmly*** 静かに往生する. ¶*die* ***courageously*** 敢然と死につく. ¶He *died* ***eventually*** of fever. 彼はとうとう熱病で死んだ. ¶He *died* ***fighting*** on the battlefield. 彼は戦死した. ¶***gladly*** *die* for one's country 国家のために喜んで死ぬ. ¶He *died* ***gloriously*** for his country. 彼は国家のために名誉の死をとげた. ‖ Better to *die* ***gloriously*** than live disgraced. 生きてはずかしめられるよりは花々しく死ぬ方がよい. 【類】 They ***gloriously*** *died* in defence of their home and country. ¶He did not *die* ***happily***. 彼は死に方が悪かった. ¶He *died* ***happy***. 彼は幸福な死に方をした. ¶Alchemy *died* ***hard***. 錬金術はなかなかその跡をたたなかった. ‖ Old superstitions *die* ***hard***. 古い迷信は中々跡をたたない. 【類】 Old prejudices *die* ***hard***. ‖ Now they will make an end of me! Anyhow, I will *die* ***hard***! 今彼らは僕を片付けようとしている. とに角僕はなかなか死なないぞ. ¶He *died* almost ***immediately*** from his injuries. 彼は数カ所のけがのためほとんど即死だった. ¶*die* ***instantly*** 即死する. ¶He *died* a ***lunatic***. 彼は気違いになって死んだ. ¶He *died* a ***martyr*** to liberty. 彼は自由のために殉死した. ¶*die* ***miserably*** みすぼらしい死に方をする. ¶He ***nearly*** *died* of laughter (hunger). 彼はもう少しで笑い(など)死にをするところだった. ¶This conviction *died* ***out*** very slowly in many quarters. この信念は諸方面において徐々に消滅した. ‖ The practice of footbinding is rapidly *dying* ***out***. [中国の]てん足の風習は急速にすたれつつある. ‖ The northern branch *died* ***out*** after a few generations. 北朝は数代の後滅びた. ‖ The movement *died* ***out*** of itself. その運動は自然に消滅した. 【類】 The custom has *died* ***out***. / Memories *die* ***out***. / The fire in the factory *died* ***out***. ¶*die* ***outright*** 即死する. ¶He *died* ***placidly*** (=***peacefully***). 彼は静かに死んだ. ¶He *died* ***poor***. 彼は窮乏のうちに死んだ. ¶I did not think that he would ***possibly*** *die*. あの人がよもや死のうとは思わなかった. ¶I had ***rather*** *die* than yield. 降参するよりはむしろ死んだ方がよい. ¶He *died* ***rich***. 彼は富んで死んだ. ¶That noble tree is now ***slowly*** *dying* of old age. あの名木も今は老樹となって段々枯れて行く. 【類】 He is *dying* ***slowly*** of consumption. ¶We shall *die* ***some day***. われわれはいつかは死ぬ. ¶He will *die* ***soon***. 彼はやがて死ぬ. ‖ I would ***sooner*** *die* than disgrace myself. 生きて恥をかくよりはむしろ死んだ方がよい. ¶He *died* ***suddenly***. 彼は急死した. ¶*die* ***together*** for love 心中する. ¶He *died* ***two months ago***. 彼は二月前に死んだ. ¶She *died* a ***virgin***. 彼女は処女で死んだ. ¶*die* ***young*** (***old***) 若(老)死にする.

M^2 curiosity *died* ***down*** 好奇心が消失した ‖ Old rancours

are *dying down*. 多年の怨が次第に薄らいで来る. ‖ The flames were allowed to *die down*. 火炎が消えるままにして置いた. ‖ after the leaves have *died down* 葉が枯れてから. 【類】The wind *died down*. / Shooting is *dying down*.

P he *died* **at** the age of ... 彼は…歳で死んだ. 【類】He *died* **at** fifty years of age. / *die* **at** [the age of] eighty ‖ He *died* **at** peace. 彼は静かに死んだ. ‖ He *died* **at** his post. 彼は職に殉じた. ‖ He *died* **at** sea. 彼は海で死んだ. ‖ He *died* **at** the stake. 彼は火刑にされた. ¶ He *died* **by** drowning himself in the Sumida. 彼は隅田川へ身を投げて死んだ. ‖ *die* **by** drowning (fire, poison) でき死(など)する ‖ He was too conscientious to *die* **by** his own hand. 彼は良心が強く自殺などはできなかった. ‖ He *died* **by** hand of another man. 彼は人手にかかって死んだ. ‖ *die* **by** hanging 首をくくって死ぬ ‖ *die* **by** the sword 切られて死ぬ ‖ *die* **by** violence 横死する ‖ was *dying* **by** (=in) inches before her face 彼女の眼前で徐々に死んで行った. ¶ *die* **for** his belief (=faith) 殉教する ‖ To him it was a religion to live for, to *die* **for** if necessary. それは彼にとってそのために生きまた必要の場合にはそのために死すべき宗教であった. ‖ *die* **for** one's country (a principle) 国(など)のために死ぬ ‖ He is determined to carry it out, even if he *die* **for** it. 彼は命にかけてそれを実行する決心である. ‖ He *died* **for** the crime he had committed. 彼はその犯した罪のために死刑になって死んだ. 【類】He *died* **for** want of food (water). / finally *die* **for** lack of air (窒息) ‖ He *died* **for** his master. 彼は主人のために死んだ. ‖ *die* **for** honor 名誉のために死ぬ ‖ a girl that young men are *dying* **for** 青年たちが死ぬほどこがれている少女. ¶ He *died* **from** acute pneumonia. 彼は急性肺炎で死んだ. ‖ He *died* **from** septicæmia following influenza. インフルエンザに敗血症を併発して死んだ. ‖ *die* **from** a stroke of apoplexy (an attack of typhoid fever) 卒中(など)で死ぬ. ‖ You may depend upon it that more *die* **from** stuffing than from starvation! 飢えで死ぬのよりも飽食で死ぬ方が多いのはたしかだ. ‖ He *died* **from** repletion (overwork, loss of blood, weakness, indigestion, cold, hunger, drowning). 彼は食べ過ぎ(など)で死んだ. 【類】*die* **from** a disease (wound, an accident, broken heart) / *die* **from** a fit of coughing (せき) / Many natives *die* every year **from** snake bites. / He *died* **from** drinking too much brandy. / He *died* **from** eating to excess. ‖ He *died* **from** the effects of pleurisy (his wound, a fall from his horse). 彼はろく膜炎(など)がもとで死んだ. ☞ 余病を発して死んだ場合に "She *died* **from** a cold" のような省略形を用いるのは正しくないと説く文法家もある. ‖ He *died* **from** some unknown cause. 彼は不明の原因で死んだ. ¶ *die* **in** agony もだえ死ぬ ‖ *die* **in** battle (action) 戦死する ‖ *die* **in** one's bed 定命で死ぬ ‖ *die* **in** office 在職中に死ぬ ‖ He *died* greatly **in** debt. 彼は借金を一杯背負って死んだ. ‖ *die* **in** a ditch のたれ死にをする. 【類】*die* **in** pain (agony, torment) / *die* **in** prison ‖ *die* **in** one's place 身代りに死ぬ ‖ *die* **in** a strange land 客死する ‖ *die* **in** water 水死する ‖ He *died* **in** 33 B.C. 彼は紀元前三十三年に死んだ. ¶ The twilight *died* **into** the dark. たそがれは過ぎて暗夜となった. ¶ *die* **of** sickness 病死する. ¶ *die* **of** grief (hunger) 悲嘆の余り死ぬ(餓死する) ‖ *die* **of** inanition 栄養失調で死ぬ ‖ *die* **of** shame 愧(き)死する. 【類】He *died* **of** consumption (cholera, cold, fever, gout, small pox, typhoid fever, heart disease, heart failure, paralysis of the heart). / He *died* **of** pneumonia following an attack of Spanish flu. / He *died* **of** a prolonged cold. / *die* **of** poison (thirst, hunger, shame, overwork, love, inaction, old age, too much whisky) / He *died* **of** a fall over a cliff. / *die* **of** the bite of a snake / The number of those who *died* **of** starvation in London during 1906 was 48.—The Socialist Annual. / Some of his children *died* **of** undernourishment (栄養不良). / he has *died* **of** wounds received at ... ‖ The Roman Empire *died* **of** excessive urbanization.—Dr. Emil Reich. ローマ帝国は過度に都会化したので亡びた. ‖ I cannot *die* **of** that! それで死ぬようなことがあるものか. ¶ He *died* **on** a Friday. 彼は金曜日に死んだ. ‖ He *died* **on** the scaffold. 彼は絞首台上の露と消えた. ‖ He *died* **on** the spot. 彼は立ち所に死んだ. ¶ He *died* **through** the bursting of a blood vessel. 彼は血管が破裂して死んだ. ‖ The baby *died* **through** his clothes being burned. 赤ん坊は着物に火がついて死んだ. ‖ *die* **through** neglect 放っておかれて死ぬ. ¶ You must *die* **to** the place. 君はその所のことは忘れなくてはいかん. ¶ *die* **under** the [surgeon's] knife 手術中に死ぬ ‖ *die* **under** peculiar circumstances 妙な事情で死ぬ. ¶ *die* **upon** his own sword 自刃する. ¶ He *died* **with** horror at the thought. 彼はそのことを考えて恐怖の余り死んだ. 【類】*die* **with** hunger (fatigue, thirst, sword) ‖ He *died* **with** joy. 彼はうれしさの余り死んだ. ☞ *die* **with** a disease は正しくない ‖ His secret *died* **with** him. 彼の秘密は彼の死とともに葬られてしまった. 【類】His fame *died* **with** him. ‖ *die* **with** (=of) laughing 抱腹絶倒する. ¶ Love (ambition, envy) *died* **within** (=in) him 彼の恋(など)は消えた.

O Never say *die*. 悲観するな. ‖ I'm *dying* to know the result. 結果が待ち遠しい.

die-hard, *n.* がんばり屋.

Q[2] ***Fascist** die-hards* こちこちの国粋主義者たち.

diet, *n.* 国会.

V The *diet* **convenes.** 国会が召集になる. ¶ The *Diet* is now **sitting.** 国会は開会中だ. ¶ The *Diet* **was** in session only two weeks. 国会はわずか二週間開会した.

Q the ***National** Diet* 国会.

Q[2] the ***post-election** Diet* 総選挙後の議会.

P It was approved **in** the *Diet*. それは議会の協賛を得た. ¶ a member **of** the *Diet*=a Diet member 国会議員.

diet, *n.* 食物.

V ***abjure*** a flesh *diet* 肉食を断つ. ¶ The lady had stomach trouble and had to ***follow*** a strict *diet*. その婦人は胃病で食物をちゃんと定めて食べなければならなかった. ¶ ***keep*** (=***take***) *diet* 食事養生をする.

Q maintain a ***balanced** diet* 常に均衡の取れた食事をする. ¶ a cleverly ***combined** diet* 巧みに取合わせた食事. ¶ a ***costly** diet* of flesh 上等の肉食. ¶ a ***farinaceous** diet* でん粉質の食物. ¶ a ***fat-reducing** diet* 脂肪を減らす(やせさせる)食物. ¶ use a ***good** diet* よい食事をする. ¶ an ***invigorating** diet* 気力を付ける食物. ¶ most ***liberal** diet* (=table) [下宿など]盛りたくさんの食事. ¶ I was put on ***low, strict** diet*. 粗食を厳命された. ¶ child nutrition on a ***low-priced** diet* 廉価食物による小児の栄養. ¶ a ***meatless** diet* 精進料理. ¶ a ***one-sided** (**varied**) diet* 一方に偏した(多様な)食事. ¶ a ***reasonable** diet* 合理的な食事. ¶ He lives upon [a] ***restricted** diet*. 彼は食物を一定している. ¶ I like a ***simple** diet* best. 淡白な食物が一番好きだ. ¶ guard one's health by ***strict** diet* 食事に注意して健康を守る. ¶ a ***strong*** and ***lavish** diet* 濃厚でぜいたくな食物. ¶ The *diet* should be ***suitable,*** being neither too rich nor too meagre. 食物は適当であるべきで滋養が多過ぎても少な過ぎてもいけない. ¶ a book advocating a ***vegetarian** diet* 菜食宣伝の本.

Q[2] the American ***home** diet* 米国の家庭食物. ¶ The physician prescribed for her a ***milk** diet*. 医師は彼女に牛乳の食事を命じた. ‖ You must go upon a purely ***milk** diet* for six days. 六日間は牛乳以外のものは何も食べてはいけない. 【類】put a patient on a ***milk** diet*. ¶ The doctor has put me upon ***starvation** diet*, that is, he allowed me only tea and milk. 医師は何も食べぬよう私に命じた. もっとも茶と牛乳だけは許したが. ¶ live on a ***subsistence** diet* ごく少量の健康維持食で命をつなぐ. ¶ put patients on a ***vegetable** diet* 患者に菜食を命じる. ¶ a ***1,800-calory** diet* per person per day 日々一人当り 1,800 カロリーの食物.

P He is luxurious **in** *diet*. 彼は食物がぜいたく. ‖ He used great moderation **in** his *diet*. 彼は食物を非常に控え目にした. ¶ He lived **on** a *diet* of bread and water. 彼はパンと水を食べていた. ¶ put a patient **upon** a *diet* of three meals a day 病人に一日三食させる ‖ **upon** a *diet* of boiled rice and beancurd 飯と豆腐を食べて.

diet *v.* 食事をとらせる.

M people who *diet* themselves ***luxuriously*** 口のおごった人々.

P *diet* oneself **on** vegetation 菜食する.

dietman, *n.* 国会人, 議員.

Q a ***former** Dietman* 前国会人, 前代議士. ¶ a ***onetime** Dietman* もと代議士.

dietwoman, *n.* 婦人代議士.

Q a ***high-hatted** (=**priggish**) Dietwoman* 高慢な婦人代議士.

differ, *v.* 違う, 異なっている; 意見を異にする.

M His opinion *differs* ***entirely*** from mine. 彼の説は僕のとまるで違う. ¶ do not *differ* ***essentially*** from ... 本質的には…と違わない. ¶ *differ* very ***markedly*** from ... …と大いに異なる. ¶ *differ* ***materially*** 重大な相違がある. ¶ Customs *differ* ***much*** in different countries. 習慣は国々で余

ほど違う. ¶be *practically differ* in use from ... 実際上...とは用法が異なる. ¶*differ profoundly* from ... ...と非常に違う. ¶*differ sharply* from ... ...とははっきり違う. ¶*differ radically* from the type その型とは根本的に違う. ¶in a form *somewhat differing* from ... ...とやや違った形式で. ¶*strongly differ* with ... ...と大いに説を異にする. ¶*differ widely* from ... ...とは天地の差である. 【類】*differ widely* in character from the predecessors in the same series.

P We *differ about* the matter (question). われわれはその事柄(など)について意見を異にする. ¶Customs *differ among* different nations. 国々によって習慣が違う. ¶opinions may *differ as to* ... ...に関して意見がまちまちだろう. ¶His age *differs by* two years *from* your own. 彼は君と年が二つ違う. ¶Iron *differs from* lead. 鉄と鉛とは違う. ¶He calls every one a fool who *differs from* his pet opinion. 彼はその持論と合わない者を一切ばか呼ばわりする. 【類】*differ from* another in one's view of life ‖ I beg to *differ from* you on that question. 失礼ながらその問題については君と考えが違う. 【類】I am sorry to *differ from* you. / it *differs from* them in being ...; it resembles them in ... / Dogs *differ from* wolves in shape. ‖ The United States *differs from* Britain in having a written Constitution. 米国は成文憲法を有する点で英国と違う. ‖ English pronunciation *differs* much more *from* American pronunciation than English spelling does from American spelling. 英人の発音と米人の発音との違いは英人のつづり字と米人のつづり字との違いより大きい. ‖ *differ from* individual *to* individual 人によってそれぞれ違う. ¶they *differ in* opinion as to ... 彼らは...に関して意見を異にしている. 【類】*differ in* degree (quality, substance, color, structure) / *differ in* detail. ¶It is a matter *on* which opinions *differ*. それは諸説が紛々たる問題だ. ¶This, however, is a matter *upon* which opinions may *differ*. しかしこれは人によって意見を異にするかもしれない. ¶I *differ with* you *on* the subject. その問題については僕は君と意見を異にしている. ‖ Customs *differ with* countries. 習慣は国によって違う. ‖ *differ with* a person *in* opinion 人と意見を異にする. 【類】*differ with* him emphatically (断じて).

difference, *n.* 差異, 相違; 異論; 不和, 争論.

V *accord* a *difference* 差異を調節する. ¶*adjust differences* 仲直りさせる. ¶*arrange* the *difference* on the best terms possible できるだけ好い条件で不和を調停する. ¶immediately *detect* the *difference* in quality 質の相違をすぐに発見する. ¶*discern* the *difference* between ... and ... ...間の相違を識別する. ¶*distinguish difference* 相違を見分ける. ¶*find differences* 相違を発見する. ¶*harmonize differences* 不和を調停する. ¶Those two friends have *had* a *difference*. その二人の友だちが口論をした. ¶*iron out* the *difference* 相違をなくする. ¶*make* a *difference* between them それらを区別する. ‖ It *makes* little *difference* to me. それは私にとっては同じようなもんだ. 【類】*make* all the *difference* in the world / Whether it is large or small *makes* little *difference*. / It *makes* no *difference* to me which side may win or lose. ‖ I will *make* you *known* the *difference* between an ordinary man and a fencing expert. 普通の人間と剣道の達人とどう違うか見せてやろう. ¶*make up* the *difference* between ... ...の差違をなくする. ¶*notice* the *difference* 相違に気がつく. ¶*perceive* the *difference* 相違に気づく. ¶*realize* the *difference* between paste and diamond 練り物と本もののダイヤの相違が分る. ¶*recognize* the *difference* 相違を認識する. ¶*reconcile differences* 相違点を調和させる. ¶I can *see* a great *difference*. 私は大きな相違があると思う. ¶*settle differences* with ... on a political basis and through negotiations 政治的にまた交渉によって(武力を用いないで)...との紛争を解決する. ¶offer to *split* the *difference* 双方から譲り合うことにしようと言い出す. ¶*submit* a *difference* to arbitration 争論を仲裁裁判に付する. ¶*tell* the *difference* between ... and ... ...の相違を識別する. ¶*thrash out* their *differences* 意見の相違を十分に検討する. ¶the unity *underlying* all outward *differences* 外見は不調和ながら根底に横たわる一致点.

V² a *difference* of opinion has *arisen* between ... ...間に意見の相違が起った. ¶Here *lies* the *difference*. 相違点はここだ.

Q There is little if *any difference*. 違いはあるにしても大したことはない. ¶a *big differnce* 大きな相違. ¶*British differences* in usage of words 英国における語の用法の相違. ¶a *characteristic difference* 特質上の相違. ¶There are *considerable differences* of opinion on this point. この点には随分意見の相違がある. 【類】There is *considerable difference* of opinion on the subject. ¶a *decided difference* 確然たる差異. ¶*dialectic differences* 方言的相違. ¶a *domestic difference* 夫婦げんか. ¶*essential differences* 本質的相違. ¶a *great difference* 大なる差異. ¶*inappreciable difference* 感じられないほどわずかな相違. ¶detect some *indescribable difference* between the two 両者の間の名状し難い相違を発見する. ¶in spite of *intellectual differences* 知能の違いはあるが. ¶make a *large difference* in ... ...について大きな差になる. ¶there is *little difference* in cost between ... and ... ...と...との値段の相違はほとんどない. 【類】with *little* or *no difference*. ¶There are *many differences*. 多くの相違点がある. ¶a *marked difference* 著しい区別. ¶Such a *marvellous difference* oiling has produced! 油を差しただけでああも違うものか. ¶*minor differences* 小さな相違. ¶There is *much difference* of opinion on the subject. その問題で大分もめる. ¶There is practically *no difference*. 実際では全く違わない. 【類】I can see *no difference* between them. ¶It is marked by *notable difference*. 著しい違いがある. ¶one of the most *noticeable differences* 最も顕著な相違の一つ. ¶the *only difference* between ... ...間の唯一の相違. ¶a *radical difference* 根本的相違. ¶a very *serious difference* はなはだ重大な相違. ¶*sharp differences* of opinion regarding ... ...に関する著しい意見の相違. ¶But this *difference* is so *slight* as to be almost negligible. しかしこの相違はきわめて微々たるものであるからほとんど顧みないでよい. ¶the *social differences* existing between ... ...間に存する社会的差別. ¶a *startling difference* 驚くべき相違. ¶a *stupendous difference* 大変な差異. ¶a *substantial difference* 本質的な相違. ¶there is a *subtle difference* between ... and ... ...と...の間には微妙な相違がある. ¶a *trifling difference* ささいの差異. ¶make a *vast difference* 大いに違う. ¶There is *wide difference* of opinion about its propriety. その当否については大いに異論がある. ¶a *world-wide difference* 非常な差異.

Q² *East-and-west differences* can be ended peacefully. 東西の相違は平和的に解決ができる. ¶a *family difference* 家庭の不和. ¶same uniforms for officers and enlisted men with *rate* and *rank differences* indicated by insignia 記章で示される等級および階級を異にする将校並に兵員の軍服. ¶*sex difference* 性の相違. ¶*surface differences* 表面上の相違.

P distinguish *by* a *difference* 差異で区別する.

P² *differences among* men 人々の異論. ¶What is the *difference between* A and B? AとBとはどこが違うか. ‖ It will settle the *differences between* the employer and the employee. それは労資の不調和を調節するだろう. 【類】the *difference between* extreme temperatures / the *difference between* ... is now satisfactorily (円満に) arranged / the *differences between* synonyms (類語) / the *difference between* cost and proceeds (原価と売上高) / the *difference between* Oriental and European ideas as regards matrimony (結婚に関する). ¶a *difference in* their social status 彼らの社会的地位における相違 ‖ a shade of *difference in* signification 意義の微妙な差. 【類】a *difference in* intelligence (age, price, principle) / the *difference in* meaning between the two words. ¶*differences of* opinion exist with regard to ... ...について意見の相違がある ‖ There is a *difference of* opinion. 意見が違っている. 【類】a *difference of* opinion *between* experts (専門家) / *differences of* viewpoint / a *difference of* one thing from another. ¶a *difference with* his partner 彼の仲間との不和. 【類】my *difference with* ...

different, *a.* 異った, 相違している.

M The case is *altogether different* with him. 彼の場合は全然話が違う. ¶is not *appreciably different* from ... ...と目立つほど違っていない. ¶This is *as different* as light from darkness. これは天地の違いである. ¶*entirely different* from ... ...と全く違う ‖ This and that are two *entirely different* cases. これとそれとはまるで話が違う. ¶*qualitatively different* from ... 本質的に...と違った.

¶ That is ***quite different*** from this. それとこれではまるで違う. ¶ be ***radically different*** 根本的に違っている. ¶ be ***slightly different*** わずかな差である. ¶ be ***strikingly different*** 目立って違う. ¶ be ***substantially different*** 本質的に差異がある. ¶ ***subtly different*** from ... わずかに...と違った. ¶ ***totally different*** まるで違う. ¶ ***utterly different*** from ... ...と全然違う. ¶ ***vastly different*** from ... ...とは大いに異る. ¶ He is ***very different*** from his brother. 彼は弟とは大分違っている. ¶ They are ***widely different*** from each other in education. 彼らの教育には大差がある. 【類】 be ***widely different*** in opinion.

P Each individual is ***different from*** every other individual. 各個人はそれぞれみんな異っている. ‖ The sample was ***different from*** the goods furnished. 持ってきた品物は見本と相違していた. ‖ Things are very ***different from*** what they used to be. 事情が今までと大いに違う. 【類】 My plan is ***different from*** yours. / It has turned out ***different from*** what I expected. ¶ be ***different in*** localities 場所によって違う. ¶ The case is ***different in*** this ***from*** that. それとこれとは話がちがう. ¶ "***Different to***" and "***different than***" are colloquialisms prevalent in England. "different to" や "different than" は英国で広く用いられる口語である. ¶ ***With*** him it is ***different***. 彼の場合は訳が違う.

differential, *n*. 差別.

Q[2] It is called "***China differential.***" それはいわゆる「中共差別」と呼ばれる.

differentiate, *v*. 区別する; 分化する.

P ***differentiate between*** two objects 二物間の異同を弁じる. ¶ ***differentiate*** man ***from*** brutes 人間と獣を区別する ‖ ***differentiate*** a species ***from*** another [生物学上の]一つの種を他の種から区別する ‖ Some scientists hold the theory that man became ***differentiated from*** the common ancestral type in the pliocene period. ある科学者の説によると人間は鮮新世において同一祖先から分派したものだとのことである.

differentiation, *n*. 区別.

V ***make*** the ***differentiation*** その区別を立てる.

difficult, *a*. 困難な, むずかしい.

M ***How difficult*** it is! おっそろしくむずかしい. ¶ become ***increasingly difficult*** ますます困難になる. ¶ be ***interestingly difficult*** むずかしいだけに面白くもある. ¶ I found English much ***more difficult*** to learn. 英語の方がずっとむずかしかった. ¶ It is ***too difficult*** to learn quickly. むずかしいので早く覚えられない.

P it is ***difficult for*** some people to do ... 人によっては...することは困難である ‖ this makes it ***difficult for*** me to ... これだから私には...することができなくなる. ¶ a man ***difficult of*** access 取っつきにくい人. 【類】 The place, being precipitous (けわしい), is very ***difficult of*** access. / be ***difficult of*** proof (証明) / It is ***difficult of*** solution (definition, explanation). / This makes the subject ***difficult of*** investigation. ¶ Nothing is ***difficult to*** a man who wills. 志の立った人には困難なものはない.

O He is ***difficult*** to please. あの人は気むずかし屋だ.

difficulty, *n*. 困難, めんどう; 難事, 難局; 窮境; 不和, 争論.

V satisfactorily ***adjust difficulties*** 争論を満足に調停する. ¶ ***aggravate*** the ***difficulty*** of ... ...の困難を増す. ¶ ***anticipate difficulty*** in carrying it out その実行に伴う困難を予想する. ¶ ***arrange*** a ***difficulty*** = compromise 不和を調停する ‖ All ***difficulty*** is now ***arranged.*** ごたごたはすっかり話がついた. ¶ ***attack*** a ***difficulty*** 難事に当る. ¶ ***avoid*** the ***difficulty*** by ... ...によってめんどうを避ける. ¶ It ***caused*** me no ***difficulty*** at all. 私は一向困らなかった. ¶ The ***difficulty*** has been ***cleared.*** 困難は除かれた. ¶ ***clear away*** all ***difficulties*** あらゆる困難を一掃する. ¶ ***clear up*** a ***difficulty*** 困難の点を除く. ¶ ***combat*** a ***difficulty*** 困難と戦う. ¶ successfully ***compass*** all ***difficulties*** あらゆる難点をりっぱに切抜ける. ¶ while things were in this situation, a new and unexpected event occurred to ***complicate*** the ***difficulties*** of ... こんな状態になっている間に新しい予期しないことが起って...の困難を悪化した. 【類】 the ***difficulty*** was further ***complicated*** by ... ¶ boldly ***confront*** a ***difficulty*** 大胆に困難に立向う. ¶ The ***difficulty*** has been ***conquered.*** その困難に打勝った. ¶ This ***constitutes*** a serious ***difficulty***. これが非常にむずかしい所だ. ¶ It will ***create*** an unnecessary ***difficulty***. そうするといたずらに困難を生ぜしめることになる. ¶ ***dodge*** a ***difficulty*** 困難をそらす. ¶ ***encounter difficulties*** 困難に出会う. ¶ ***enhance*** rather than ***diminish*** the ***difficulty*** 困難を減少せずにかえって増大する. ¶ ***experience*** great ***difficulty*** to ... ...するために大なる困難を感じる. ¶ ***explain away*** a ***difficulty*** = get rid of a difficulty by explanation 難点を説明してのける. ¶ did not ***experience*** the slightest ***difficulty*** in ... ...するに当っていささかの困難をも感じなかった. ¶ ***face out*** one's ***difficulties*** 困難を忍ぶ. ¶ ***feel*** a ***difficulty*** in ... ...に関して困難を感ずる. ¶ ***find difficulty*** in securing work 就職難を感じる ‖ ***find*** no ***difficulty*** in proving that ... ...ことを造作なく証明できる. 【類】 I ***found*** some (a, no, little) ***difficulty*** in ... ¶ ***get around*** a ***difficulty*** 困難を切抜ける. ¶ ***get over*** a ***difficulty*** 困難を乗り切る ‖ The ***difficulty*** was ***got over*** by a compromise. 問題は示談によって解決された. ¶ I ***grasped*** the ***difficulties*** of the task from the start. 私は初めからその仕事がむずかしいということを見てとった. ¶ We ***have difficulty*** in distinguishing one from the other. 一方を他方と区別することが困難である. ‖ You will ***have difficulty*** in finding accommodation. あなたは泊る所を探すのに困るでしょう. ¶ one ***has difficulty*** in accepting the date [古物など]その年号がちょっと受取れない. 【類】 He ***has*** a great ***difficulty*** in walking. / I ***have difficulty*** in going to sleep. ‖ I ***have*** great ***difficulty*** with the authorities. 当局者との交渉が非常にむずかしい. 【類】 The boy ***had*** no ***difficulty*** with arithmetic. ‖ He ***has*** many ***difficulties*** to struggle against. 彼は幾多の困難と戦わなければならない. ¶ ***increase*** the ***difficulty*** of ... ...の困難を増す. ¶ It ***involves*** no ***difficulty***. それは何ら困難を伴わない. ‖ It is simple and ***involves*** no ***difficulty***. それは簡単で一向めんどうがない. ¶ ***iron out difficulties*** 困難を除く. ¶ ***magnify difficulties*** 困難を大きくする. ¶ The Custom-House people will ***make difficulties.*** 税関がやかましいだろう. ‖ ***make*** no ***difficulty*** about ... = make nothing of ... ...をちっともおっくうがらない ‖ Never was such a man for ***making*** so many ***difficulties.*** こんなに事件を起す人ったらありやしない. ¶ ***master*** a ***difficulty*** 困難に打勝つ. ¶ ***meet*** the ***difficulty*** 難局に当る ‖ skill in ***meeting difficulties*** 難局に対処する手腕. ¶ The ***difficulties*** of ... will be greatly ***multiplied.*** ...の困難が大いに増すだろう. ¶ ***nip*** a ***difficulty*** in the bud 禍を未然に防ぐ. ¶ ***obviate*** a ***difficulty*** 困難を除く. ¶ it ***offers*** (= presents) no ***difficulty*** to ... それは...にとって一向困難にならない ‖ It ***offers*** no ***difficulty*** at all. それは一向苦にならない. ¶ ***overcome difficulties*** 困難に打勝つ. ¶ He would not ***place*** unreasonable ***difficulties*** in the way of your promotion. 彼は君の地位が高くなるのをしいてじゃまをするようなことはないだろう. ¶ ***plane away difficulties*** 困難を除き去る. ¶ ***present difficulties*** to foreigners 外国人にとって困難である ‖ It ***presented*** almost insuperable ***difficulties.*** それはほとんど打勝ちがたい困難であった. 【類】 pronunciation of English and foreign proper names that ***present*** some ***difficulty***. ¶ This ***put*** serious ***difficulties*** in the way of learning it. ためにその学習に非常な困難を生じた. 【類】 ***put*** a ***difficulty*** in the path of ... ¶ ***raise*** new ***difficulties*** さらに難題を引き起す. 【類】 He ***raised difficulties.*** / She ***raised difficulties*** when her daughter said she would marry a foreigner. ¶ ***recognize difficulties*** 困難を認める. ¶ ***relieve*** the ***difficulties*** by ... ...によって困難を緩和する. ¶ ***remove*** needless ***difficulties*** from the path of the learner 勉学者の前途から無用の困難を取除く. ¶ The ***difficulty*** was finally ***settled*** by recourse to arms. その紛争は決局武力に訴えて解決された. ¶ He is practiced in the art of ***shirking difficulties***. 彼はめんどうを回避する術に長じている. ¶ ***smooth away*** (= ***out***) the ***difficulties*** 困難を除く. ¶ ***solve*** the ***difficulty*** by ... ...によって難事件を解決する. 【類】 try to ***solve*** one's ***difficulties*** oneself. ¶ ***stem*** a ***difficulty*** 困難を抑える. ¶ ***straighten*** the ***difficulty*** 困難を調整する. ¶ ***surmount*** a ***difficulty*** 困難に打勝つ. ¶ ***sweep away*** all the ***difficulties*** in its path その行く手に横たわるあらゆる困難を一掃する. ¶ ***take difficulties*** for impossibilities 難事を不可能事とはき違える. ¶ ***throw*** some ***difficulty*** in the way of enquirers 調査者の前途に困難を投じる. ¶ ***tide over*** the ***difficulties*** of the post-war period 戦後の難局をうまく切り抜ける. ¶ ***underrate*** the ***difficulty*** of ... ...の困難を見くびる. ¶ ***vanquish*** every ***difficulty*** あらゆる困難を征服する.

V[2] A ***difficulty arises.*** 一つの困難が起る. ¶ Fresh ***diffi-***

culties ***bristled up***. さらに困難が続出した. ¶Another *difficulty* ***came up***. 更に困難がもち上った. ¶But here ***entered*** a *difficulty*. しかしここにやっかいなことが起った. ¶the *difficulty* ***lies*** in the fact that ... 困難は…ということにある. 【類】It is in these points that the *difficulty* ***lies***. ¶*Difficulty* ***rises***. 困難が起る. ¶the *difficulties* which ***surround*** a foreigner who undertakes to write on Japanese subjects 日本に関して書こうとする西洋人の遭遇する幾多の困難.

Q He is in ***acute financial*** *difficulty*. 彼は財政上非常な困難に陥っている. ¶Come to me if you are in ***any*** *difficulty*. 困ることがあったら僕の所へ来給え. ¶a release from ***besetting*** *difficulties* 難局からの脱却. ¶the ***chief*** *difficulty* is ... 一番困るのは…だ. ¶a route of ***considerable*** *difficulty* 中々困難な通路 ‖ be placed in a position of ***considerable*** *difficulty* 苦境に立つ. ¶the ***crowning*** *difficulty* 最大の困難. ¶in the face of the most ***crushing*** *difficulties* 最も激しい困難にもかかわらず. ¶An ***economic*** *difficulty* intervened. 生活難が起った. ¶It gives ***endless*** *difficulty* to the foreigner learning English. それが英語を習う外国人にとって始末におえないやっかいになるのである. ¶***enormous*** *difficulty* 大変な困難. ¶a task of ***extreme*** *difficulty* きわめてむずかしい仕事. ¶He is in some ***financial*** *difficulty*. 彼は少しく財政上の困難に陥っている. ¶***first*** (=***initial***) *difficulties* 最初の困難. ¶a ***good stiff*** *difficulty* かなりこたえる困難. ¶Insufficiency of water is a ***grand*** *difficulty* of housekeeping. 給水の不足は家政上の大困難である. ¶a ***great*** (=***grave***) *difficulty* 大困難 ‖ I am in ***great*** *difficulties*. 私は非常に困っている. ¶an ***insuperable*** *difficulty* in one's way ahead その前途に横たわる打勝ちがたい困難. 【類】It offers no ***insuperable*** *difficulties*. / it appears to be a matter of ***insuperable*** *difficulty* to ... / present almost ***insuperable*** *difficulties*. ¶He found himself in the midst of ***insurmountable*** *difficulties*. 彼は打勝ちがたい困難の真ただ中にあることに気付いた. 【類】There is no ***insurmountable*** *difficulty* in the way of ... ¶a ***like*** *difficulty* is liable to be encountered relative to ... 同じような困難が…に関して起りがちだ. ¶in spite of ***linguistic*** *difficulties* 言語上の色々な困難にもかかわらず. ¶One of the ***main*** *difficulties* in studying Russian is the accent. ロシア語を勉強する上の主な困難の一つはアクセントである. 【類】the ***main*** *difficulty* with which they had to contend was ... ¶The *difficulties* in the path of ... are ***mountainous***. …の前途に横たわる困難は累々と山なすほどである. ¶I have ***much*** *difficulty* in understanding what you say. 君の言うことを理解するのは私には中々むずかしい. ‖ With ***much*** *difficulty* the matter has been carried so far. やっとのことでここまでこぎつけた. ¶find ***no*** *difficulty* with ... …は一向むずかしくない. ¶***pecuniary*** (=***money***) *difficulties* 財政上の困難. ¶Here, another ***practical*** *difficulty* arises. ここにも一つ実際上の困難が起る. ¶the ***present*** *difficulty* in obtaining freight space 目下の船腹の不足. ¶There is a ***real*** *difficulty* here. 真の困難はここにある. ¶in spite of the ***seeming*** *difficulty* 見掛の困難にもかかわらず. ¶It presents ***serious*** *difficulties*. それに非常な困難が伴う. ¶with no ***small*** *difficulty* 相当骨を折って. ¶There is ***some*** *difficulty* ahead of you. 君の前途には困難がある. ‖ with ***some*** *difficulty* I understood that ... ちょっと考えたが…ことが分った. ¶present some ***special*** *difficulty* 特殊の困難がある. ¶tide over a ***temporary*** *difficulty* 急場をしのぐ. ¶it presents ***tremendous*** *difficulties* to ... そのために…に非常な困難が生じる. ¶an ***unavoidable*** *difficulty* 避けることのできない困難. ¶These present ***unexpected*** *difficulties*. それが思い掛けない難事である. ¶encounter ***unforeseen*** *difficulties* 予期しない困難に遭遇する. ¶combat ***various*** *difficulties* 色々な困難と戦う. ¶Pronunciation is the ***worst*** *difficulty* in acquiring a foreign language. 外国語の修得に発音が一番の困難である.

Q² encounter ***engineering*** *difficulties* in building a railway 鉄道敷設に当って技術上の困難にぶっつかる. ¶because of ***housing*** *difficulties* 住宅払底のため. ¶***labor-management*** *difficulties* 労使間のトラブル. ¶the ***language*** *difficulty* in Continental travel 大陸旅行における言語上の困難. ¶***pupil*** *difficulties* 生徒とのごたごた. ¶It means no ***teaching*** *difficulty*. それは教授上の困難を意味しない. ¶***transport*** *difficulties* 《英》輸送上の困難. ¶***transportation*** *difficulties* 《米》輸送上の困難. ¶***travel*** *difficulties* 旅行の困難. ¶a ***wages*** *difficulty* 賃金のもんちゃく.

P ***after*** much *difficulty* 非常に困難したあげくに. ¶struggle ***against*** *difficulties* 困難と戦う. ¶during the four years spent ***at*** *difficulty* 難渋して送った四年間に. ¶be beset ***by*** *difficulties* 色々な困難に悩まされている. ¶I am hindered ***by*** a *difficulty*. 私は難事に悩んでいる. ¶He was ***in*** *difficulties* for want of money. 彼は金がないので困っていた. ‖ help over a man ***in*** a *difficulty* 困っている人を救う ‖ The movement is ***in*** *difficulty*. その運動は行悩みになっている. ¶***in spite of*** the *difficulties* of the time (戦争などで)当時の窮状にもかかわらず. ¶fall (=get) ***into*** a *difficulty* 困難に陥る. ¶a work ***of*** *difficulty* 困難な仕事. ¶get ***out of*** *difficulty* 困難を脱出する ‖ He helped me ***out of*** the *difficulty*. 彼が私をその窮境から救い出してくれた. ‖ until some way ***out of*** this *difficulty* be found この困難から脱却する道が開かれるまでは. ¶get us ***over*** this *difficulty* われわれにこの難局を切抜けさせてくれる. ¶to add ***to*** my *difficulties* かてて加えて(泣面にはちで). ¶win success ***under*** *difficulty* 困難の下にあって成功する. ¶***with*** *difficulty* ようようのことで ‖ though ***with*** *difficulty* どうやら ‖ He hears ***with*** great *difficulty*. 彼は大分耳が遠い. ‖ it was only ***with*** *difficulty* that ... やっとのことで… ‖ fight (=combat) ***with*** the *difficulty* of ... …という困難と闘う. 【類】I am able to read and converse in French and German ***with*** no *difficulty*. ¶***without*** [any] *difficulty* 何の苦もなく.

P² a *difficulty* ***about*** a matter (person) ある事柄(など)についての困難. ¶*difficulty* ***between*** two persons 二人の間の不和. ¶I am in *difficulties* ***for*** money. 僕は金に困っている. ¶*difficulty* ***in*** articulation 舌もつれ ‖ *difficulty* ***in*** recalling names of persons 人の名を思い出すことの困難 ‖ pronunciation, the worst *difficulty* ***in*** a foreign language 外国語修得上最大難関たる発音. 【類】*difficulty* ***in*** obtaining supplies of raw materials. ¶The *difficulty* ***of*** the task was great. 仕事の困難は非常なものであった. ¶He had *difficulties* ***with*** the authorities and resigned his position. 彼は当局者と折合が悪くて辞職した. ‖ the *difficulty* ***with*** the theory is that ... その説の欠点は…である.

diffidence, *n.* 自信のなさ, 内気.

V This *diffidence* should be ***dismissed*** from their minds. この内気を彼らの心から取り去らねばならない.

Q the author feels a ***certain*** *diffidence* in ... 著者は…の点にしゅん巡を覚える.

P ***with*** *diffidence* はにかんで.

P² *diffidence* ***to*** women 婦人に対する内気.

diffident, *a.* 自信のない.

P He is *diffident* ***of*** success. 彼には成功の自信がない.

diffusion, *n.* 伝ぱ, 普及.

V ***check*** its *diffusion* その伝ぱを防ぐ.

dig, *n.* [俗] 突き; 諷刺.

V ***give*** a *dig* with the elbow ひじで突く ‖ ***give*** a person a *dig* in the ribs [くすっと笑って]人のあばらを突く.

P This was a *dig* ***at*** Frank. これはフランクへのあてつけであった.

dig, *v.* 掘る, 探り出す.

M *dig* ***deeper*** into the report その報告をせんさくする. ¶*dig* ***out*** a corpse 死体を掘出す ‖ *dig* ***out*** a tunnel トンネルを掘る. 【類】*dig* ***out*** a grave / *dig* ***out*** a hole ‖ *dig* ***out*** the past 発掘によって過去の歴史を明らかにする. ¶*dig* a grave ***open*** 墓をあばく.

M² *dig* ***down*** 掘り倒す, 掘り下げる, 掘り取る ‖ *dig* ***down*** a big tree 大木を掘り倒す. ¶*dig* ***in*** at one's school work 《米俗》学科をコツコツ勉強する. ¶*dig* ***up*** roots 根を掘り出す. 【類】*dig* ***up*** the weeds (雑草) ‖ *dig* ***up*** facts from papers 新聞から色々な事実をさがし出す ‖ I'll *dig* you ***up*** in New York City. ニューヨークで君を探し当てよう.

P *dig* ***for*** treasure (gold) 宝(など)を掘り探がす. ¶*dig* ... ***from*** (=out of) the earth (ground, ruins) 土中(など)から…を掘り出す. 【類】*dig* gold ***from*** a mine. ¶*dig* ***in*** the ground 土を掘る. 【類】*dig* ***in*** the sand with one's shovel. ¶*dig* a hole ***into*** the earth 地に掘り込む ‖ *dig* ***into*** the derivation (etymology) of words 語の由来(など)を調べる. ¶He *dug* himself ***out of*** prison. 彼は牢の下を掘って逃げた. ¶*dig* ***over*** the ground 土を掘り返す. ¶*dig* ***through*** a wall 壁を掘り抜く. ¶*dig* ***with*** a spade すきで掘る.

digest, *n.* 摘要, 編集, 綱領.

Q a ***comprehensive*** *digest* of information 一般にわたる知識の集成. ¶a ***concise*** *digest* 簡明な編集.

P² a *digest **of*** laws 法律綱領.

digest, *v.* 消化する; 編集する.

M ***inwardly digest*** 心で消化する.

P These materials have been *digested **into*** a handy volume. これらの材料は一冊の手ごろの本に編集された.

digestibility, *n.* 消化性.

Q a ***high digestibility*** of food 食物の高度の消化性.

digestible, *n.* 消化しやすい.

Q Few foods are ***more digestible*** [than this]. [これほど]消化のよい食物は少い.

digestion, *n.* 消化, 消化力.

V ***aid digestion*** 消化を助ける ‖ walk to ***aid digestion*** 腹ごなしに歩く. ¶***disturb*** the *digestion* 消化を妨げる. ¶***impair digestion*** 消化を害する. ¶It is good for ***promoting*** *digestion* それは消化力を増進するによい. ¶***spoil*** one's *digestion* 消化を害する. ¶***upset*** one's *digestion* おなかをこわす.

Q He has a ***good digestion.*** 彼は胃が丈夫だ. ‖ a good eater with a ***good digestion*** 消化力の盛んな大食家. ¶***impaired*** *digestion* 消化不良. ¶people with ***weak digestion*** 胃の弱いたち ‖ My *digestion* is too ***weak*** for pork. 胃が弱くて豚肉は食べられない. 【類】He has a ***weak digestion.***

P ***for digestion*** 腹ごなしに. ¶It is easy (hard) ***of** digestion.* それは消化しやす(がた)い.

digger, *n.* 掘る人, 坑夫.

Q² a ***coal digger*** 炭坑夫. ¶a ***grave digger*** 墓掘人夫.

digit, *n.* ゼロから九までのアラビア数字.

Q figures of ***four*** or ***more digits*** 四位あるいは四位以上の数字. ¶There are two systems of numeration for numbers of ***ten digits*** or more. 十位またはそれ以上の数字を数える方法は二通りある.

dignified, *pa.* 威厳のある.

P He is *dignified **in*** his bearing (manner, attitude). 彼は態度(など)に威厳がある.

dignify, *v.* 威厳をつける.

P he *dignified* it ***with*** the name of ... 彼はもったいぶってそれに…という名をつけた. 【類】a school *dignified **with*** the name of a college ‖ The cruelty, *dignified **with*** the name of punishment, long prevailed in schools. 懲罰という美名で蛮行が長いこと学校に行われていた.

dignitary, *n.* 高位者, 高官.

Q ***civic dignitaries*** 町のお歴々. ¶a ***high dignitary*** 高位の人. ¶a ***liveried dignitary*** 官服を着けた顕官. ¶the ***loftiest*** *dignitary* 最高位(官)の人.

Q² ***Government dignitaries*** 政府の高官連. ¶***Occupation*** *dignitaries* 占領軍の高官たち. ¶presidents, kings, emperors, and ***world dignitaries*** 大統領, 国王, 皇帝および世界の貴顕.

dignity, *n.* 品位; 威厳, 尊厳.

V ***assume*** the *dignity* of ... …の権威を装う. ¶The boy has ***attained*** the *dignity* of a latchkey. その少年は表戸のかぎをあずけられる一人前の年齢に達した. ‖ Dentistry has ***attained*** the *dignity* of a profession. 歯科はりっぱな高級職業になった. ¶it does not ***befit*** the *dignity* of ... それは…の品位に相応しない. ¶***degrade*** the *dignity* of man 人間の品位を落す. ¶***give dignity*** to the society by their famous names 彼らの有名な名前によってその会の品位を高める. ¶***hurt*** the *dignity* of ... …に恥をかかせる. ¶***impair*** the national *dignity* or the prestige of the country 国威や名声を傷つける. ¶***lose*** one's *dignity* by being angry 怒って自己の品位を失う. ¶***lower*** one's *dignity* 男をさげる ‖ ***lower*** the *dignity* of ... …の品位を落す. ¶properly ***maintain*** the *dignity* of their offices 彼ら官職の威厳を適当にたもつ. ¶***possess*** priestly *dignity* 聖職らしい威厳を備えている. ¶***sacrifice*** *dignity* to ... 体裁をかまわず…する.

Q ***calm dignity*** 落着いた貫録. ¶rise to a ***high dignity*** 高位にのぼる. ¶that ***highbred*** *dignity* of bearing, that ease and grace of manner あの上品な威厳のある姿, あのゆったりした気品のある態度. ¶a living worthy of ***human dignity*** 人間らしい生活. ¶unworthy of ***masculine*** *dignity* 男らしくない. ¶***mock dignity*** から威張り. ¶the sentiment of ***national dignity*** 国民としての誇り. ¶walk with ***quiet dignity*** ゆったりと重々しく歩く ‖ It has a ***quiet dignity*** of design. それは意匠が渋くて高尚だ. ¶it sounds simple and has nothing of ***verbal*** or ***phonetic dignity*** about it, yet ... それは平凡に聞えて言葉の上からも発音の上からも一向堂々たる所がないが…

P Such an act would be ***below*** my *dignity* (=beneath me=infra dig [俗]). そんなことをすると私のこけんが下がる. ¶an occupation ***beneath*** the social *dignity* of the highbred man 上品な人の社会的品位を傷つけるような職業 ‖ Slang is ***beneath*** the *dignity* of a professorial chair. 俗語などを使っては教授の威厳にかかわる. ¶depart ***from*** the *dignity* of ... …の威厳を捨てる. ¶stand (=be) ***in*** one's *dignity* 見識ぶる ‖ people high ***in** dignity* 位の高い人々. ¶put on air ***of** dignity* 威張る ‖ To his many good qualities he cannot add that ***of** dignity* in defeat. 彼は美しい性質に富んでいるが負けても悪びれないという美質に欠けている. ¶"Chanoyu" is drinking tea exalted ***to*** the *dignity* of an art. 茶の湯は茶を飲むことを一つの芸術に作り上げたものである. ‖ derogatory ***to*** the *dignity* of the Japanese flag 日本の国威にかかわる ‖ feelings raised ***to*** the *dignity* of religion 宗教となるまで高められた感情. ¶He stood ***upon*** his *dignity.* 彼は高ぶっていた. ¶I did this ***with*** as much *dignity* as I could command. 私はこれをできるだけ威厳をくずさずにやった.

P² the *dignity **of*** labor 労働の尊厳 ‖ the *dignity **of*** the chief of the police 警察署長の威厳 ‖ the *dignity **of*** self-respect 品位ある自尊.

digress, *v.* 枝葉にわたる.

P *digress **from*** the main subject 本筋から横道にはいる. ¶*digress **into*** some topic (question, subject) ある話題(などにそれる.

digression, *n.* 主題を離れること, 余談.

V to ***cut short*** this *digression* 余談はさておき. ¶***make*** a *digression* from one's subject 主題を離れる.

Q It is a ***useless digression.*** それは無用の余談だ.

dilate, *v.* 膨張させる; ふえんする, 膨張する.

P The air becomes *dilated **by*** the heat. 空気は熱のために膨張する. ¶The lungs *dilate **in*** breathing. 肺は息を吸込むと膨張する. ¶*dilate **on*** one's view (theory) 人の説(など)をふえんする ‖ He *dilated **on*** the horrors of the war. 彼は戦争の惨事を長々と述べた. ¶*dilate **upon*** the painful fact that ... …という痛ましい事実を詳しく述べる. 【類】it is needless to *dilate **upon*** ... ¶His nostrils *dilated **with*** pride. 彼は意気揚々と鼻をうごめかした. 【類】My heart *dilated **with*** unutterable happiness.

dilemma, *n.* 窮境, 板ばさみ.

V ***solve*** a *dilemma* 窮境を脱する.

Q a ***self-imposed dilemma*** 自分で招いた窮境.

P ***in*** the *dilemma* of life and death 生死の境に ‖ ***in*** this *dilemma* この窮境にあって ‖ I am ***in*** an awkward *dilemma.* 進退きわまった.

dilettantism, *n.* 「道楽半分の」享楽気分, ディレタント風.

V ***enjoy dilettantism*** 道楽半分の享楽気分を味わう. ¶***satisfy*** one's *dilettantism* 享楽気分を満足させる.

diligence, *n.* 勤勉, 精励.

V ***exercise diligence*** in ... …に精励する. ¶***use*** great *diligence* to learn the language 大いに勉強してその国語を学ぶる.

Q reward his ***patient diligence*** 彼のたゆまぬ努力にむくい

P he rose ***by** diligence* to ... 彼は勉強して…になった. ¶study ***with diligence*** 勤勉に学ぶ ‖ ***with*** remarkable *diligence* 大いに勉強して ‖ He returned to his books ***with*** tenfold *diligence.* 彼はまた前の十倍も勉強し出した.

diligent, *a.* 勤勉な, 精励する.

P He is *diligent **at*** his lessons. 彼は課業に勤勉だ. ¶He is *diligent **in*** his study (work, business). 彼は勉強に精励している.

dilly-dally, *v.* 《俗》ぐずぐずする.

P *dilly-dally **with*** a matter 物事にぐずぐずする.

dilute, *v.* 水を割る, 稀薄にする.

P *dilute* wine (milk) ***with*** water ぶどう酒(など)に水を割る ‖ *dilute* it ***with*** water to the required consistency それを適度に水で薄める.

dim, *a.* 曇った, ぼんやりした.

P The window-panes are *dim **with*** steam. 窓ガラスが湯気で曇っている. ‖ Her eyes were *dim **with*** tears. 彼女は目が涙で曇ってよく見えなかった.

dim, *v.* 薄暗くする, 曇らせる.

M ***dim out*** a light 燈火を薄暗くする ‖ The whole block was ***dimmed out*** in no time. その区域全体がまたたく間に薄暗くなった(警戒警報など).

P The sky was *dimmed **by*** clouds. 空は雲で暗くなった. ¶with their eyes *dimmed **with*** tears 目を涙で曇らして.

dimension, *n.* 大きさ, 寸法; 規模, 範囲.

V The fire rapidly ***assumed*** great *dimensions.* 火事はどん

どん大きくなった. ‖ The question is *assuming* great *dimensions.* 問題が段々大きくなって来た. 【類】In a few years obscure fishing villages along the coast began to *assume* the *dimensions* of stately watering-places (りっぱな海水浴場). / The rising *assumed* very serious *dimensions.* ¶The labor question is quickly *attaining dimensions.* 労働問題はますます大きくなって来る. ¶It is a subject that *has dimensions.* それは深みのある題目だ. ¶*take* the *dimensions* of … …の寸法を取る.

Q a house of *considerable dimension* 大きな屋敷. ¶a portly man of *enormous dimensions* 非常に大きな太った男. ¶*external dimensions* 外法(そと のり). ¶of *great* (*gigantic, huge*) *dimensions* 大き(巨大)な. ¶*internal dimensions* 内法(うち のり). ¶a work of a *large dimension* 巨大な作品. ¶grow to *menacing dimensions* 恐しく大きくなる. ¶the question shrinks to comparatively *small dimensions* when we remember that … その問題はわれわれが…を思うとき比較的小さなものになる. ¶While we are forging the new weapons of conflict in the *third dimension,* we must maintain our ground and sea forces at adequate levels. 三次元戦争の新兵器を作り出している一方陸海軍も十分に維持して行かねばならない. ¶a figure in *three dimensions* 立体の像.

Q^2 assume *mammoth dimensions* 巨象のように大きくなる.

P The card is $3\frac{1}{4}$ by $5\frac{1}{2}$ inches *in dimensions.* そのカードは横三インチ四分の一縦五インチ二分の一である. ‖ a box, 4 or 5 inches *in* each *dimension* 横たて四五インチの箱.

P^2 the *dimensions of* this room is … feet by … この室の広さは横…フィート縦…フィートだ.

diminish, *v.* 減じる.

M *gradually diminish* 漸減する. ¶*diminish progressively* with age 年とともに段々減少する.

P *diminish* something *from* an object ある物から何か減らす ‖ Nothing is *diminished from* the royal dignity. 少しも国王の威厳を損じない. ¶*diminish in* size 形が小さくなる ‖ *diminish in* population (quantity, strength) 人口(など)が減退する.

diminution, *n.* 減少.

V The figures *show* no *diminution.* その数字が少しも減少しない.

Q a *considerable diminution* 著しい減少. ¶a *steady diminution* 確実の減少.

P^2 a *diminution in* … …の減少. 【類】When prices rise, there is a *diminution in* the real value of money. ¶*diminution of* members 会員の減少 ‖ with no *diminution of* youth or vigour かくしゃくとした.

diminutive, *a.* 小形の.

P *diminutive in* size (stature) 形(背)の小さい.

dimple, *n.* えくぼ.

V She *has dimples* on her cheeks and chin. 彼女はほおやあごにえくぼがある. ¶*turn on* the *dimples* えくぼを出す.

P^2 the *dimple on* the chin あごのえくぼ ‖ There is a *dimple on* the ground. 地上に小さいくぼみがある.

din, *n.* けん騒, ごうごう.

V I *have* a perpetual *din* in my head. 頭が始終がんがん鳴っている. ¶The children were *making* so much *din* that … 小供たちががやがや騒ぐので…

Q The babel of cries increases till the *din* is *deafening.* 泣き叫ぶ声がつのって遂に騒々しさ耳をろうせんばかりである. ¶a *hideous din* ひどい騒音. ¶The *din* is *horrible.* その騒々しいこと恐ろしいばかり. ¶a *joyous din* 歓呼の声. ¶a *raucous din* しわがれた声の騒音.

P away *from* the *din* and bustle of a large city 大都会のけん騒からのがれて.

din, *v.* やかましく言う.

P His wife *dinned into* his ears morning, noon, and night that it is quite impossible for them to stay where they are any longer. 彼の妻はこんな所にはもうとてもいられないと朝も昼も晩も彼の耳にやかましくどなった.

dine, *v.* 食事する.

M *dine later* than usual いつもよりおそく食事する. ¶I *mostly dine* at six. 私は大抵六時に食事をする. ¶*dine out* 外食する. 【類】I am engaged to *dine out* Saturday and Sunday; so, you see, I could not manage to get way. / Let's *dine out* / *dine out* at one's relation's / I never heard of his *dining out,* except at his relation's, or …'s. / I think my brother is to *dine out* today. ¶*dine sumptuously* ぜいたくな食事をする. ¶*dine together* 会食する.

M^2 *dine off* (=on) rice and fish 米飯と魚で食事をする.

P *dine at* a fixed price 定食を取る ‖ *dine* at the table *of* … …の所で食事に呼ばれる ‖ *dine at* the table d'hote 定食を食う ‖ I *dined at* his hospitable board. 彼の家で御ちそうになった. 【類】after *dining at* … ¶*dine by* the bill of fare 好みの注文で食事する. ¶*dine on* fish and eggs 魚と卵で食事する. ¶*dine with* a person 人と食事をともにする.

diner, *n.* 食事をとる人; 〖鉄道〗食堂車.

Q a *late* (an *early*) *diner* 遅(早)く主食を取る人.

Q^2 a *mid-day diner* 正午に主食を取る人. ¶a *train diner* =a dining-car 食堂車.

ding, *v.* がんがん鳴る.

M Another trolley came by, *dinging noisily.* またも無軌道電車がやかましい音を立てて通って行った.

dining-car, *n.* 食堂車.

V *attach* a *dining-car* to a train 列車に食堂車を連結する.

dining-table, *n.* 食卓.

Q^2 an *extension dining-table* 伸縮自在の食卓.

dinner, *n.* 正餐(せい さん), 食事; 御ちそう.

V *abolish dinner* 一日の主食を廃する. ¶Children *bring* their *dinners* to schools. 子供たちは弁当持参で登校する. ¶*cancel* a *dinner* きょう宴を取消す. ¶*cook dinner* 御ちそうの料理をする ‖ The *dinner* was badly *cooked* and badly *served.* 御ちそうは料理がへたで給仕もよくなかった. ¶*eat* one's *dinner* 食事をする. ¶*give* a complimentary *dinner* to … …を招待してきょう応する ‖ He *gave* a *dinner* to eighteen of his closest friends last evening. 彼は昨晩十八人の親友たちに御ちそうした. 【類】A *dinner* is to be *given* in his honor. ¶We *have dinner* at six o'clock. われわれは六時に夕食を食べる. 【類】I *had dinner* in a restaurant. ¶*hold* a *dinner* きょう宴を張る. ¶The *dinner* was *laid* in the large banqueting hall of the club. きょう宴はクラブの大食堂で催された. ¶*order dinner* 食事を命じる. ¶the *dinner* was *organized* by … そのきょう宴は…によって発起された. ¶*postpone* a *dinner* 宴会を日延べする. ¶*provide* a *dinner* 食事の用意をする. ¶*put up dinner* till … …まで夕食を延ばす. ¶A *dinner* was *served* at the Grand Hotel. きょう宴がグランド・ホテルで催された. ¶*serve up dinner* 御ちそうをぜんに上ぼす. ¶*Dinner* was now *set* on the table. 食事はもう食卓に出された. ¶*snatch* a hasty *dinner* and rush to … 急いで食事をして…へあたふた出て行く. ¶A good cocktail is a capital thing to *start* the *dinner* with. 上等なカクテルは食事の始めに絶好なものだ. ¶*take dinner* with … …と食事をともにする.

Q a *big dinner* 《俗》大御ちそう. ¶a *bridal dinner* 結婚披露の宴会. ¶a *coarse dinner* 粗末なきょう宴. ¶We had a *comfortable dinner.* われわれは結構な御ちそうをいただいた. ¶I was entertained at a *complimentary dinner.* 私は宴会に招待されて御ちそうになった. ¶a *cordial dinner* 丁寧な御ちそう. ¶an *early* (*late*) *dinner* 昼(晩)さん会. ¶an *elaborate dinner* こった料理. ¶They invited me to a very *excellent dinner* of the newly formed association. 私は今度できた協会の大へんりっぱなきょう宴に招待された. ¶We gave him a *farewell dinner.* われわれは彼のために送別会を開いた. ¶a *freak dinner* 風変りな御ちそう. ¶I cooked this fowl especially for you, so you must make a *good dinner.* この鳥はあなたのために料理したのですからたくさん召上ってください. ¶a *grand dinner* りっぱな御ちそう. ¶He has eaten a *hearty dinner.* 彼は腹一杯食べた. ¶an *inaugural dinner* 就任披露のきょう宴. ¶It would be like eating *last night's dinner* or this morning's breakfast over again. それは夕べの御ちそうや今朝の朝飯をもう一度食うようなものだ. ¶a *neat* and *elegant dinner* きれいで上品な御ちそう. ¶He gave me such a *nice dinner.* 彼は私に大いに御ちそうしてくれた. ¶a *palatable dinner* 口に合う御ちそう. ¶a *plain* (=*early*) *dinner* あっさりした食事. ¶*Dinner* is *ready.* 食事の用意ができた. ¶a *regular dinner* 本格的料理. ¶a *scratch dinner* にわか作りの食事. ¶a *stylish dinner* こった食事. ¶a *sumptuous dinner* ぜいたくな食事. ¶a *swanky dinner* 豪華な宴会. ¶a *well-cooked* and *well-served dinner* 料理も給仕も結構な食事.

Q^2 an *alumni dinner* 校友晩さん会. ¶an *anniversary dinner* 例年のきょう宴. ¶a *buffet dinner* 簡易食堂の夕食. ¶a *Cambridge* and *Oxford dinner* ケンブリッジ・オックスフォード同窓会の宴会. ¶a *Christmas dinner* クリスマス・デナー. ¶one's *farewell dinner* from the University 大学卒業生送別宴会. ¶a *many-course dinner* 品数の多い食事. ¶the

Princeton-in-Peking Society dinner 北京プリンストン協会の晩さん. ¶a ***shore dinner*** いそ料理. ¶a ***stag dinner*** at the White House 白亜館における男だけの晩さん会 ‖ He told me you gave a ***stag dinner*** last week. 彼の話では君は先週男だけの宴を張ったそうだね. ¶a ***state dinner*** 国賓への晩さん会. ¶a ***table d'hote dinner*** 定食.

P ***after dinner*** 食後に. ¶in a speech ***at*** a ***dinner*** given in honor of Mr. ... ...氏のために催されたきょう宴でのあいさつに ‖ ***at dinner*** this evening 今晩の宴会で ‖ He wore full dress ***at dinner***. 彼は晩さんに礼服を着けた. ‖ A fire broke out as I was ***at*** my ***dinner***. 私の食事中に火事が起った. ‖ I found her ***at dinner***. 彼女は食事中だった. ¶road workmen ***at dinner*** 昼のお弁当を使う道路工夫たち. 【類】 The party is (=are) ***at dinner***. ¶***before dinner*** 食前に. ¶***during dinner*** 食事中. ¶Elaborate preparations ***for*** a ***dinner*** of twenty-four covers were made. 二十四人前のきょう宴に念の入った準備が整えられた. ‖ What are we going to have ***for dinner?*** 晩さんには何が出るだろう. ‖ dress ***for dinner*** 晩さんに礼服を着ける. ¶It's time ***for dinner***. 夕食の時刻だ. ¶Don't linger too long ***over*** your ***dinner***. いつまでも食べているな. ¶He asked me ***to dinner***. 彼は私を晩さんに招いた. ‖ He treated me ***to*** a good ***dinner***. 彼は結構な御ちそうをおごってくれた. 【類】 be invited ***to dinner*** / I am going ***to dinner***. / Will you not come ***to dinner*** with us some evening? / sit down ***to dinner***. ¶They are through ***with dinner***. 彼らは食事がすんでいる.

P² a ***dinner of*** six courses = a six-course dinner 六品付の御ちそう.

dinner party, 宴会.

P ***at*** a ***dinner party*** 宴会で.

dinner table, 食卓.

P Many weighty affairs of State are discussed ***over dinner tables***. 多くの重要な国務が食事をしながら議される.

dint, *n.* 力, 努力.

P He gained the first prize ***by dint*** of steady application. 彼は不断の努力で一等賞を得た. ‖ What education he possesses he had gathered without a teacher ***by dint*** of hard work and perseverance. 彼の教育はすべて彼が教師につかず勤勉忍耐の結果得たのであった. ‖ ***by dint*** of force (money, industry, earnest solicitation) 強制(など)によって.

dinner-hour, *n.* 正餐(さん)時.

Q² during the ***midday dinner-hour*** 正午の食事時間の間に.

diopter, *n.* 光線屈折率の単位.

Q myopes of ***four diopters*** or more 四度以上の近視眼の人.

dip, *n.* 一浴び; 下落.

V ***have a dip in the water*** [川などで] 浴びする. ¶***take*** a ***dip*** in the surf いそ打つ波に一浴びする. 【類】 ***take*** a ***dip*** in the sea.

Q a ***briny dip*** 海水浴.

Q² wholesale butter prices took a $3^1/_2$ cent ***per pound dip***. バターの卸値が一ポンドにつき $3^1/_2$ セント下落した. ¶take a moderate ***price dip*** 幾分値が下がる.

P ***for*** a ***dip*** in the sea 海で一浴びやりに. ¶a ***dip in*** the ground 地面の凹(くぼ)み.

dip, *v.* ちょっと浸す; くみ取る; すくい取る; ちょっとつかる; ちょっと手出しする.

M ***dip out*** soup with a ladle しゃくしでスープをすくう.

M² ***dip up*** water from a well 井戸から水をくみ上げる ‖ ***dip up*** a sample of rice 見本として米をさじですくい上げる ‖ ***dip up*** sand with a bucket バケツで砂をすくい上げる.

P ***dip*** water ***from*** a boiler 銅つぼから水をくみ取る ‖ ***dip from*** the well of truth 真理の井戸からくむ. ¶***dip*** a pen ***in*** ink ペンをインキにちょっと浸す ‖ ***dip*** a pail ***in*** a stream 川におけをちょいとつける ‖ The plane ***dipped in*** its flight. 飛行中の飛行機が急降下した. ¶***dip*** one's head ***into*** water 頭を水に突込む. 【類】 ***dip*** one's hand ***into*** a bag ‖ ***dip into*** one's savings 貯金を引出す ‖ He ***dipped into*** this thriving business. 彼はこの繁じょうする商売に手を出した. 【類】 ***dip into*** politics (speculation) ‖ ***dip into*** a book 書物をのぞく ‖ ***dipped*** more than a little ***into*** books, though deeper into the dice-box かなり本をのぞいた, さいころをふる方が多かったが. ¶***dip*** water ***out of*** a boat ボートから水をくみ出す. ¶***dip*** water ***with*** a pail おけで水をくむ.

diphthong, *n.* 〖発声〗二重母音.

Q a ***consonantal diphthong*** 複合子音 (tʃ, dʒ, など).

diploma, *n.* 免状; 卒業証書.

V ***allot diplomas*** 卒業証書を与える. ¶He ***got*** his ***diploma*** (=sheepskin) last year. 彼は去年大学を卒業した. ¶***grant diplomas*** to applicants after examination 試験後志望者に卒業証書を授ける ‖ ***grant*** a ***diploma*** in nursing after examination according to a given standard 一定の標準に従って試験後看護婦免状を授ける ‖ No ***diplomas*** will be ***granted*** for this course. この科には卒業証書を授与しない. 【類】 ***Diplomas*** will be ***granted*** to those who pass an examination. ¶After passing the required test examination, a ***diploma*** is ***issued*** by the abbot. 規定の試験に及第した後免許状が僧院長によって授与される. ¶***obtain*** a ***diploma*** 卒業証書をもらう. ¶***present diplomas*** to ... ...に卒業証書を出す. ¶He ***received*** a ***diploma*** from Harvard in 1890. 彼はハーバード大学を一八九〇年に卒業した. 【類】 His bad conduct kept him from ***receiving*** a ***diploma***. ¶She ***took*** her ***diploma*** in 1916. 彼女は一九一六年に卒業した. ¶***win*** the ***diploma*** of Tokyo University 東大を卒業する.

Q² receive a ***college diploma*** 大学卒業証書をもらう. ¶a ***high-school diploma*** 高等学校卒業証書. ¶receive a ***gold medal diploma*** 金牌(ぱい)賞を授けられる.

P² a ***diploma for*** grand prize 優等賞状. ¶a ***diploma of*** graduation 卒業証書 ‖ a ***diploma of*** merit 賞状.

diplomacy, *n.* 外交, 外交策.

V ***abandon diplomacy*** for force 外交策を捨てて武力をとる. ¶***break down*** "secret ***diplomacy***" 「秘密外交」を打破する. ¶***use diplomacy*** 外交手腕をふるう.

Q The day of ***armed diplomacy*** has passed. 武力外交の時代はもう過ぎた. ¶***doubtful diplomacy*** あいまいな外交策. ¶resort to ***evasive diplomacy*** ごまかし外交策を採る. ¶***German "psychological diplomacy"*** ドイツの「心理外交術」. ¶***spineless (=weak-kneed) diplomacy*** 腰抜け外交. ¶***uncertain diplomacy*** あやふや外交. ¶***weak-kneed diplomacy*** 軟弱外交.

Q² a form of "***dollar diplomacy***" 一種の「ドル外交」. 【類】 impose "***dollar diplomacy***" on the rest of the world. ¶***jelly-fish diplomacy*** こんにゃく外交. ¶***power diplomacy*** 武力外交. ¶***shirt-sleeve diplomacy*** 非公式の(くだけた)外交. ¶***United States diplomacy*** toward China 合衆国の対中外交.

P practice all the wiles ***of diplomacy*** あらゆる外交手段をろうする.

diplomat, *n.* 《米》外交家, 外交官.

Q an ***international diplomat*** 国際的外交家. ¶a ***sagacious diplomat*** そう明な外交家. ¶the bland, persuasive guile of a ***master diplomat*** すぐれた外交家のいんぎんな言葉巧みな手管. ¶a ***tongue-tied diplomat*** 口の重い外交官.

Q² He has spent most of his time as a ***career diplomat***. 彼は本職(生え抜き)の外交官として一生の大部分を送った. ¶a ***front-rank diplomat*** 第一流の外交家.

diplomatic, *a.* 外交にたけた, 外交的な.

P You must be more ***diplomatic with*** him. 君は彼に対してもっと外交的にやらなくてはいけない.

diplomatist, *n.* 《英》外交家, 外交官.

Q a ***polished diplomatist*** 円滑な外交官(家).

direct, *v.* 向ける, あてる; 道を教える; 指導する, 指図する.

M if ***properly (wisely) directed*** 指導よろしきを得れば.

P ***direct*** a gun ***against*** a fort とりでに大砲を向ける ‖ a satirical poem ***directed against*** the Puritans 清教徒にあてつけた風刺詩 ‖ a novel ***directed against*** yellow journalism 黄色新聞を攻撃した小説 ‖ ***direct*** effort ***against*** a person (country, movement) 人(など)を攻撃する. ¶His remarks were ***directed at*** you. 彼は君に当てて言ったのだ. ¶victims of propaganda ***directed from*** Europe ヨーロッパから働きかけた宣伝の犠牲者. ¶He asked a native to ***direct*** him ***to*** a certain church which he wished to find. 彼は見つけたいと思ったある教会に行く道を教えてくれと土地の人に頼んだ. 【類】 Can you ***direct*** me ***to*** the post-office? / ***direct*** a person ***to*** his destination (行先) ‖ ***direct*** a person ***to*** a chair 人をいすにつかせる ‖ ***direct*** one's thought ***to*** the uncertainty of life 人の考えを人生の無常に向けさせる. 【類】 ***direct*** one's attention ***to*** it / He ***directed*** his energies ***to*** the task. / ***direct*** one's eyes ***to*** the sky ‖ The letter is ***directed to*** him. 手紙は彼あてになっている. ‖ He ***directed*** his step ***toward*** home. 彼は家路についた. ‖ German ambition was ***directed toward*** political as well as commercial domination. ドイツ人の野心は商業並に政治上の優越権

を得ようという方面に向った. ‖ Everybody's eyes were *directed toward* him. 皆が彼の方に目を向けた.
O I *directed* him to buy it for me. それを買ってくれるように彼に言ってやった. 【類】I *directed* him to go at once.

direction, *n.* (**1**) 指導; [通例 *pl.*] 指図, 指令.
V I have now thoroughly ***abandoned*** to him the *direction* of all my steps. 僕は自分の身の振り方を一切彼に任してしまった. ¶***follow*** *directions* carefully (=closely) よく指図を守る ‖ ***follow*** one's *directions* to the letter 全く指図通りにする. ¶***follow out*** *directions* 指図通りに実行する. ¶***give*** *directions* to a servant 召使いに言いつける ‖ ***give*** *direction* to forces now operating 現に行動中の軍隊に指命する. ¶***Have*** you any *directions* to give me as to …? …について何かお指図がありますか. ¶***obey*** *directions* 指定通りやる. ¶faithfully ***observe*** the *directions* 命令を忠実に守る. ¶***undertake*** the *direction* of that department その部の長になる.
Q the research work is being made under the ***brilliant*** *direction* of … その研究は…の手腕ある指導の下に行われつつある. ¶under ***competent*** *direction* 有力な指導の下に. ¶under his ***distinguished*** *direction* 彼の優れた指導の下に. ¶***elaborate*** *directions* 念の入った指図. ¶***full*** *directions* 十分な指図. ¶under the ***general*** *direction* of … …が総指導者となって ‖ take the ***general*** *direction* of a magazine 雑誌の一切の切り盛りをやる. ¶***important*** *directions* 注意要項. ¶under the ***personal*** *direction* of … …の直接指導の下に.
Q² ***sailing*** *directions* 水路誌. ¶***stage*** *directions* ト書き.
P ***according to*** your *directions* 貴命に従い. ¶***by*** *direction* of … …の命により. ¶***under*** his *direction* 彼の指図を受けて ‖ a paper whose policy is ***under*** the *direction* of … …の指図で方針を決める新聞 ‖ a corps of over 60 readers and assistants working ***under*** the *direction* of the editorial staff 編集員の指揮の下に働いている 60 人以上の校正係と校正助手の一団.
P² *directions* ***about*** shipment 発送に関する指図. ¶the *directions* ***for*** making … …を作るための注意書き. 【類】*directions* ***for*** the use of medicine. ¶*direction* ***of*** an action 戦闘指揮. ¶the *directions* ***on*** the bottle びんにはってある用法 ‖ *directions* ***to*** students 学生心得.
(**2**) 方向.
V ***follow*** the *direction* of the arrow 矢の方向をたどる ‖ Every eye ***followed*** the *direction* in which his finger pointed. 皆の目が彼の指さした方向に向いた. ¶His discovery ***gave*** the science a new *direction*. 彼の発見でその科学に新生面が開拓された. ¶***point*** the *direction* 方向を指示する. ¶The average Londoner, in pointing out the way to a stranger, will ***punctuate*** his *directions* with references to well-known taverns. ロンドン人が普通道を土地不案内の人に教える場合に有名な酒場を目標にする. ¶He has ***taken*** a new *direction*. 彼は新らしい方向を取った.
Q fled in ***all*** *directions* 四方八方に逃げた. ¶in a ***contrary*** *direction* 反対の方向に. ¶in ***each*** (=***either***) *direction* (=way) 行きも帰りも. ¶in an ***easterly*** *direction* 東の方向に. ¶in ***every*** *direction* 八方に. ¶At the distance of about ten miles in a ***northerly*** *direction*, I perceived another island. 北方十マイルばかりの所にも一つの島が見えた. ¶The river takes at first a ***northwesterly*** *direction*, but afterwards flows to the westwards. その川は初めは西北の方向を取るが後に西方へ流れる. ¶step in the ***opposite*** *direction* 反対の方向に歩んで行く. 【類】move in ***opposite*** *directions*. ¶in a *direction* ***parallel*** to … …と平行して. ¶in the ***reverse*** *direction* 反対の方向に. ¶move in the ***right*** *direction* 正しい方向に進む. 【類】This is a move (=step) in the ***right*** *direction*. ‖ a trend in the ***right*** *direction* 正しい方向への傾向. 【類】a step in the ***right*** (***wrong***) *direction*. ¶in the ***same*** *direction* 同じ方向に.
Q² ***compass*** *directions* コンパスの方向.
P ***from*** the *direction* of … …の方面から ‖ I couldn't find his house ***from*** your *directions*. 君に教えられた通り行ったが彼の家が見つからなかった. ¶turn ***in*** *direction* of arrow shown on … …に示してある矢の方向に回る ‖ ***in*** the *direction* of the clock 時計の針の動く方向に(右回りに) ‖ bow ***in*** the *direction* of … …の方に向って遥拝する ‖ Excess ***in*** one *direction* cannot be remedied by excess in the opposite. ある方面への行き過ぎは反対方面への行き過ぎでは矯正されない. 【類】looking ***in*** the *direction* of … ‖ the latest move ***in*** this *direction* has been made by … この方面の最近の進展が…によってなされた. 【類】I thank you kindly for whatever assistance you may be able to give me ***in*** this *direction*. / Has he any talent ***in*** that *direction* (=line)? ‖ In a token of thanks, the ballerina waved a hand ***in*** the *direction* of the box where Secretary Marshall was seated. 感謝の印としてその踊り子はマーシャル国務長官の着席している方に向って手を振った.

directive, *n.* 指令.
Q² those affected by the ***purge directive*** 追放指令にひっかかった人々. ¶a ***SCAP directive*** 連合軍総司令官の指令. ¶the ***SCAP political purge directive*** of January 一月連合軍総司令官の政治的追放指令.
P ***upon*** the *directive* of … …の指令により.

directive, *a.* 支配する, 律する.
P rules *directive* ***of*** all our actions われわれの行動一切を律する規則.

directness, *n.* 率直.
Q there is a ***curt, epigrammatic*** *directness* 寸鉄胸を刺すような迫力がある. ¶There is ***manly*** *directness* about his manner of talk. 彼の話しぶりには男らしい率直な所がある. ¶be told with a ***simple*** *directness* むき出しに話される.
P² *directness* ***in*** manner (speech) 態度(など)の率直さ.

director, *n.* 管理者, 理事, 取締役.
Q an ***athletic*** *director* 運動部長. ¶a ***managing*** *director* 専務取締役. ¶a ***provisional*** *director* 仮理事. ¶a ***sleeping*** *director* 匿名理事.
Q² an ***admissions*** *director* 学生入学掛主事. ¶an ***art*** *director* 〖映〗技術監督. ¶a ***club*** *director* クラブ管理人. ¶a ***company*** *director* 会社の取締役. ¶a ***film*** (=***motion picture or screen***) *director* 映画監督. ¶a firm of ***funeral*** *directors* 葬儀社. ¶a ***guinea-pig*** *director* ロボット理事. ¶a ***program*** *director* 番組主任. ¶a ***personnel*** *director* 人事部長. ¶a ***placement*** *director* 大学(などの)就職係主事. ¶a ***radio program*** *director* 放送番組編成者. ¶a ***Red Cross field*** *director* 赤十字現地指導者. ¶a ***research*** *director* 研究部長. ¶a ***stage*** *director* 舞台監督.
P the *Director* ***of*** the Civil Administration 民政局長官.

directorship, *n.* 指揮. は幹部の地位.
Q ***corporate*** *directorship* or executive positions 理事または幹部の地位.
P ***under*** the *directorship* of … …の指揮の下に.

directory, *n.* 住所氏名録.
Q a ***private*** *directory* 個人用の住所録.
Q² a ***city*** *directory* 市民名簿. ¶a ***telephone*** (=***phone***) *directory* 電話帳.

dirge, *n.* 哀歌.
V Brahmin priests ***chanted*** a monotonous *dirge*. バラモン教の僧りょたちは単調な御詠歌を唱えた. ¶***wail forth*** *dirges* 哀歌を歌い出す.

dirt, *n.* 汚物, ごみ; 悪口.
V She fell down and ***got dirt*** on her dress. 彼女はころんで着物をよごした. ¶Fenders ***keep dirt*** off the car. 泥よけが自動車のよごれを防ぐ. ¶***make*** a *dirt* ふんをする. ¶***rub off*** the *dirt* よごれをこすり落す. ¶***throw*** *dirt* on political opponents 政敵に悪口を放つ. ¶***wash*** the *dirt* ***off*** from … …の泥を洗い落す.

dirtiness, *n.* 不潔.
V ***make*** the *dirtiness* of a dress conspicuous 着物の汚れを目立たせる.

dirty, *a.* よごれた.
P make one's hands *dirty* (=dirty one's hands) ***with*** mud 手を泥だらけにする.

disability, *n.* 無力, 無能.
V *disability* ***arising*** from infirmity 病身から起る仕事の不可能.
Q exemption from conscription for ***physical*** *disability* 体格虚弱のための徴兵免除. ¶he has a ***pronounced*** *disability* in … 彼が…に対して無能なことは明らかだ.
P A blind man labors ***under*** great *disability*. 盲人は仕事に骨が折れる. ¶He was conscious of his *disability* ***in*** this direction. 彼は自分がこの方面に無力なことを知っていた.

disable, *v.* 無力にする.
M be ***personally*** *disabled* 体が不具になる. ¶the ***physically*** *disabled* 身体障害者. ¶His illness ***totally*** *disabled* him from following his vocation. 彼は病気のために業務に従事することが全く不能になった.
P people *disabled* ***by*** age or sickness 老年または病気のための不能者. ¶It *disabled* him ***for*** military service. 彼は

そのため軍務が勤まらなくなった. ¶*disabled **from*** doing something 何かをすることができなくなって || I have *disabled* myself ***from*** walking by a fall. ころんだために歩けなくなった.

disablement, *n.* 無能, 無力.

P ***in the event of*** my *disablement* 私の体がきかなくなった場合には.

disabuse, *v.* さとらせる.

P *disabuse* him ***of*** his superstition (illusion, false notion) 彼に迷信(など)をさとらせる. 【類】*disabuse* one's mind ***of*** errors.

disadvantage, *n.* 不利, 不便; 不利の境遇; 損失.

V ***counterbalance*** the parallel *disadvantages* 一方の不利益をうめ合わせる. ¶***discuss*** the advantages and *disadvantages* of ... ...の利害を論じる. ¶it ***has*** the further *disadvantages* of ... それにはさらに...という不便がある || as a setback, it ***has*** this *disadvantage,* that ... その代り...という不利がある || good as it is, it ***has*** also its *disadvantages* 良いには良いがまた悪い点もある. ¶***offset*** these *disadvantages* これらの不利益を相殺する. ¶The advantages derived from them far ***outweigh*** the *disadvantages* which they entail. これらから得られる利益はそのために起る不利益を補うて余りがある. ¶***surmount*** *disadvantages* 不便に打勝つ.

Q it had a ***counterbalancing*** *disadvantage* in ... その方には... という不利が伴ていた. ¶suffering from the ***natural*** *disadvantage* of being at odds 衆寡(ᶜ)敵せず. ¶an ***obvious*** *disadvantage* 分りきった不利. ¶without involving ***offsetting*** *disadvantages* それを相殺する不利益を伴うことなく. ¶use one's strength to ***one's own*** *disadvantage* 自分の力をかえって自分の不利になるように使う. ¶The route has ***slight*** *disadvantage* in time. その経路は少し時間の上の損がある. ¶be to the ***ultimate*** *disadvantage* of ... 結局...の不利になる.

P He is ***at*** a *disadvantage* in being conversationally unacquainted with English. 彼は英語が話せないという点で不利である. || It put me ***at*** a great *disadvantage.* それが大いに私の不利になった. || I was taken ***at*** a *disadvantage.* 僕は弱身につけ込まれた. ¶It will be ***to*** our mutual *disadvantage.* それではわれわれお互の不利益になるだろう. || It is ***to*** his *disadvantage* that he lacks initiative. || sell ***to*** *disadvantage* 損をして売る. ¶***under*** great *disadvantages* 非常な不利の下に. 【類】This placed me ***under*** a heavy *disadvantage.* ¶***without*** *disadvantage* 不都合なく.

disadvantageous, *a.* 不利な, 不便な.

P *disadvantageous* ***for*** attack (defense) 攻撃(防御)に不便な. ¶It is *disadvantageous* ***to*** me. それは私にとって不利である.

disaffected, *pa.* 不満の.

P He is *disaffected* ***to*** the government. 彼は政府に不満を抱いている.

disaffection, *n.* 不平, 不満.

V *Disaffection* ***broke out*** almost from the start. ほとんど最初から不平が起った.

P excite *disaffection* ***against*** government 政府に対して反感を起させる. ¶***with*** *disaffection* 不満をもって.

disagree, *v.* 合わない, 一致しない; 意見を異にする.

M *disagree* ***sharply*** ひどく意見が合わない.

P *disagree* ***about*** a matter 問題について意見を異にする. ¶People *disagree* ***in*** opinion ***about*** the matter. そのことについて人々は意見を異にしている. ¶*disagree* ***to*** something あることに異議を唱える || The Lords' amendment was *disagreed* ***to.*** 上院の修正案には異議があった. ¶Something has *disagreed* ***with*** me. 僕は何かの中毒をした. || This dish invariably *disagrees* ***with*** me. この料理を食べると私はきまってあたる. 【類】The food *disagrees* ***with*** my taste. / *disagree* ***with*** one's stomach / Doesn't this close atmosphere (うっとうしい陽気) *disagree* ***with*** your health? || I *disagree* ***with*** those who take the stand that ... ...という論者には私は賛成できない. || He *disagrees* ***with*** his relatives. 彼は親類と折合わない. 【類】His conduct *disagrees* ***with*** his words. ¶*disagree* ***with*** each other ***over*** ... ...の件で一致を欠く || *disagree* ***with*** one's pocket book 自分には買いきれない.

disagreeable, *n.* 不愉快な経験.

P[2] the *disagreeables* ***of*** life 人生のいやなこと.

disagreeable, *a.* 不愉快な, 不相応な.

M It is not ***altogether*** *disagreeable.* 全然不愉快と言う訳ではない. ¶***somewhat*** *disagreeable* to the taste 味がいく分よくない.

P Such conduct is *disagreeable* ***to*** her natural sincerity. かかる行為は彼女の生れつきまじめな性質に合わない. || It is *disagreeable* ***to*** anyone. それはだれにとってもいやなことだ. || sound *disagreeable* ***to*** the ear 〖比ゆ〗耳が痛い.

disagreement, *n.* 不同, 不和; 争論.

V ***express*** my *disagreement* with ... ...と意見が違うと言う. ¶He ***had*** a *disagreement* with his wife. 彼は細君とけんかした.

Q following ***sharp*** *disagreements* with ... ...と大げんかをしたあげく.

P *disagreement* ***between*** two objects (persons) 二物(など)の不一致. ¶What's the *disagreement* ***with*** him? どうして彼と仲違いしたのか.

disallow, *v.* 却下する.

P It was *disallowed* ***by*** the authorities. それはその筋から却下された.

disappear, *v.* 消える, 見えなくなる.

M It *disappeared* ***mysteriously*** from a locked case. それは錠を下した箱から不思議になくなった. ¶a type which is ***rapidly*** *disappearing* どんどん消滅する型(の人). ¶***suddenly*** and ***mysteriously*** *disappeared* 不思議やぱっと消えうせた.

P The rumour had to *disappaer* ***before*** facts. そのうわさも事実が明かになって自然消えた. ¶The ship *disappeared* ***below*** the horizon. 船は水平線下に没した. || *disappear* ***from*** the public eye 世間から姿を消す. 【類】*disappear* ***from*** the face of the earth / *disappear* ***from*** view (=sight) || The street has *disappeared* ***from*** the map of London. その町はロンドンの地図から消えてしまった. ¶*disappear* ***from*** use すたれる. ¶*disappear* ***in*** the crowd 人込みの中に姿を没する. 【類】*disappear* ***in*** the bushes. ¶The island *disappeared* ***into*** the sea. その島は海の中に消え失せた. || He *disappeared* ***into*** the night. 彼はやみに吸込まれてしまった. ¶We watched him as he *disappeared* ***over*** the hill. われわれは彼の姿が丘の向うに見えなくなるまで見送っていた. ¶He *disappeared* ***to*** the Continent. 彼は大陸に逃避した. ¶The cat *disappeared* ***up*** a tree. ねこが樹上に姿を消した.

disappearance, *n.* 消失, 失そう.

Q make a ***mysterious*** *disappearance* 神隠しにあう || a case of the ***mysterious*** *disappearance* 不思議な失そう事件.

disappoint, *v.* 失望させる, 意外に感じさせる.

M I was very ***agreeably*** *disappointed.* 僕は非常に失望はしたが実にいい気持だった. ¶I was ***completely*** *disappointed.* すっかり失望した. ¶He was ***deeply*** *disappointed.* 彼は痛く失望した. ¶I was ***greatly*** *disappointed* in that affair. 私はそのことでは大いに失望した. ¶How ***much*** *disappointed* he will be! さぞ失望することだろう. 【類】I feel ***very much*** *disappointed* at (=because of) your failure to pass the examination. / I should have been very ***much*** *disappointed.* ¶hopes ***repeatedly*** *disappointed* 次々とくつがえる希望. ¶be ***sadly*** *disappointed* in ... ...にひどく当てが外れる. ¶be ***utterly*** *disappointed* あきれはてる.

P We are *disappointed* ***about*** the weather. 天気の当てが外れた. ¶I was *disappointed* ***at*** your absence. 君が不在なので失望した. || We are *disappointed* ***at*** (=in) the result of the election. 選挙の発表にはわれわれはがっかりした. ¶I am *disappointed* ***in*** him. 私は彼には失望した. 【類】I am *disappointed* ***in*** our new teacher. / He was *disappointed* ***in*** love (失恋). / be *disappointed* ***in*** one's expectations. ¶He is *disappointed* ***of*** his wages. 彼は賃金の当てがはずれてがっかりした. 【類】be *disappointed* ***of*** one's hope (purpose) || I was *disappointed* ***of*** the car. 私は待つ車が来ないのでがっかりした. || He *disappointed* me ***of*** a visit. 彼は僕に待ちぼけをくわせた. ¶Edison was *disappointed* ***over*** the intellectuality of college men. エディソンは大学出の学力には愛想をつかした. ¶I am *disappointed* ***with*** my new bicycle. 今度の自転車には失望した.

disappointing, *a.* 失望させる.

M it is ***rather*** *disappointing* to hear that ... ...と聞いてはいささかがっかりだ. ¶The result was ***very*** *disappointing.* その結果はきわめて面白くなかった.

disappointment, *n.* 失望; 失望させる物.

V to ***avoid*** *disappointment* and delays 失望や遅滞を避けるために. ¶It ***caused*** deep *disappointment.* それが非常な失望を生ぜしめた. ¶I ***had*** a great *disappointment.* 非常に失望した. ¶***lighten*** one's *disappointment* ...の失望をなぐさめる. ¶To ***prevent*** *disappointment,* copies should be secured at once. 失望のないように早速お買取りください(雑誌など). ¶Please order at once to ***save*** *disappointment.* 品切れの恐れがありますから早めに御注文下さい. ¶You could ***see*** *disappointment* written all over the guests' faces. お客の顔に失望の色が読まれた. ¶***soften*** one's *disappointment* …の失望をやわらげる. ¶He ***swallowed*** his *disappointment* as best he could. 彼は失望をできるだけ顔に出すまいとした. 【類】He philosophically (あきらめて) ***swallowed*** his *disappointment.*

Q a ***bitter*** *disappointment* 非常な失望. ¶Our *disappointment* was ***complete!*** われわれの失望は極点に達した. ¶a ***grave*** *disappointment* 大失望. ¶after many ***grievous*** *disappointments* 数々のにがにがしい失望のあげく. ¶an ***intense*** *disappointment* はげしい失望. ¶a ***terrible*** *disappointment* 非常な失望.

Q^2 ***business*** *disappointments* and reverses 商売の見込違いと失敗.

P It was somewhat ***of*** a *disappointment.* それには幾分失望した. ¶He was doomed ***to*** *disappointment* and failure. 彼は失望と失敗の非運に陥らなければならなかった. ‖ ***to*** my great *disappointment,* I found that … がっかりしたことには…であった. ‖ very much ***to*** the *disappointment* of his father 彼の父が非常に失望したことには.

P^2 *disappointment* ***at*** failure 失敗での落胆. ¶*disappointment* ***in*** love 失恋. ¶*disappointment* ***of*** hope (expectation) 希望(など)の消失. 【類】such was the *disappointment* ***of*** his over … ¶He was a *disappointment* ***to*** us. 彼にはわれわれは失望した.

disapproval, *n.* 不賛成, 否認.

V ***express*** *disapproval* of a proposal 提議に対して不賛成の意を表する ‖ ***express*** *dispproval* of (=deprecate) war 開戦に不同意をとなえる. ¶***heap*** *disapproval* on his head 盛んに彼に非難を浴びせる.

Q ***emphatic*** *disapproval* 断固たる否認. ¶fear ***social*** *disapproval* 人の口を恐れる. ¶voice their ***unanimous*** *disapproval* of … 一同…に不同意だと言明する.

P ***from*** *disapproval* of … …に不賛成である所から.

disapprove, *v.* 非とする, 非難する; 否認する.

M ***strongly*** *disapprove* of … …に対し大不賛成をとなえる. ¶I ***wholly*** *disapprove* of what you say. 君の言うことには全面的に不賛成である.

P *disapprove* carelessness ***in*** him 彼の不注意を非難する. ¶*disapprove* ***of*** a bill (plan, one's marriage) 法律案(など)を否認する ‖ Japanese ethics do not *disapprove* ***of*** suicide. 日本の道徳は自殺を否認しない.

disarm, *v.* 武装を解かせる; 融和する.

P Her smile *disarmed* me ***for*** some moments 彼女がにっこりしたのでちょっとの間気をゆるした. ¶*disarm* him ***of*** his weapons 彼の武器を取り上げる ‖ *disarm* a snake ***of*** its fangs へびから毒歯を取り除く ‖ Religion *disarms* death ***of*** its terrors. 宗教は死を恐ろしいものでなくする.

disarmament, *n.* 軍備縮小.

Q a ***general*** *disarmament* of all the civilized states 文明諸国の一斉軍縮. ¶***industrial*** *disarmament* 産業武装解除. ¶***universal*** *disarmament* 一般軍備縮小.

Q^2 ***world*** *disarmament* 世界各国の武装解除.

disaster, *n.* 災難, 災禍, 惨事.

V ***avert*** a *disaster* 災難を避ける. 【類】the only way to ***avert*** *disaster* to the company. ¶It will ***bring*** *disaster* in its wake. それに付随する災禍が起るだろう. ¶This defect in educational methods ***caused*** widespread *disaster.* この教授法の欠陥が広く害毒を流した. ¶***court*** *disaster* 自分で災難を招くようにする ‖ It may be said to have ***courted*** *disaster.* それは飛んで火に入る夏の虫とも言えよう. ¶***endure*** *disaster* after disaster 打続く災難を忍ぶ. ¶***escape*** *disaster* 避難する. ¶The cathedral has ***had*** many *disasters.* その大寺院は幾多の災害に会った. ¶***invite*** *disaster* by misconduct 不行跡のために災難を招く. ¶***meet*** *disaster* 災厄に会う. ¶***portend*** *disaster* 災害を予表する. ¶… ***spell*** *disaster* …は災禍と言って差支えない. ¶***stem off*** a *disaster* 災害を防止する. ¶***suffer*** *disaster* from earthquake, flood, or fire 地震・洪水・火事のために災害を受ける.

Q an ***approaching*** *disaster* 迫り来る災禍. ¶a ***dire*** *disaster* 恐ろしい惨事. ¶a ***double*** *disaster* in the shape of earthquake and fire 地震と火事という二重の災禍. ¶an ***irreparable*** *disaster* 償い難い災難. ¶a ***national*** *disaster* 国難. ¶a ***naval*** *disaster* 海軍の惨事. ¶The country is on the brink of a ***serious*** *disaster.* その国は今や重大な国難に面している. ¶an ***unforeseen*** *disaster* 思いがけない災難. ¶an ***unsuspected*** *disaser* 不測の災害.

Q^2 an ***air*** *disaster* 航空惨事. ¶victims of a ***mine*** *disaster* 鉱山災害の犠牲者たち. ¶a ***railroad*** *disaster* 鉄道の惨事. ¶a ***traffic*** *disaster* 交通惨事. ¶***sea*** and ***road*** *disasters* 海上・交通の惨事.

P^2 a *disaster* ***to*** one of our latest submarines わが国最新式の一潜水艦の惨事. 【類】a *disaster* ***to*** a person (country). ¶*disasters* ***upon*** one 身に降りかかる災難.

disavowal, *n.* 否認.

V ***obtain*** a *disavowal* of … …に否認される.

disbelief, *n.* 不信, 不信仰.

V ***have*** a *disbelief* in God and dislike for the Christian religion 神を信ぜずキリスト教をきらう.

P^2 *disbelief* ***in*** Christianity (ghosts) キリスト教(など)を信じないこと. ¶*disbelief* ***of*** a story 話に対する不信.

disbelieve, *v.* 信じない.

P *disbelieve* ***in*** the value of … …の貴重なことを信じない ‖ *disbelieve* ***in*** the existence of God 神の存在を信じない.

disbeliever, *n.* 信じない人.

P^2 a *disbeliever* ***in*** … …を信じない人.

disburden, *v.* 重荷をおろす; なくする.

P The river *disburdens* itself ***into*** the sea. その川は海に注ぐ. ¶*disburden* ***of*** ornament 装飾を取り去る ‖ *disburden* one ***of*** grief (care) 人の悲しみ(など)を除く ‖ I *disburdened* myself ***of*** the secret. 私はその秘密を打明けてしまった.

disbursement, *n.* 支出, 支払額.

V ***advance*** *disbursement* 支払を前払いする. ¶funds to ***meet*** the *disbursements* 支払に当てる資金. ¶***pay*** *disbursements* 勘定を払う.

Q a ***heavy*** *disbursement* 容易でない支払金. ¶a ***light*** *disbursement* 少額の支払金.

P What was the total ***of*** *disbursement* during the first half of the year? 上半期の支払総額はいくらだったか.

discard, *v.* 見捨てる.

P *discard* one ***for*** another 甲を捨てて乙を取る.

O be *discarded* as unnecessary 必要がないとして捨てられる.

discern, *v.* 識別する; 差異を弁別する.

P *discern* ***between*** two qualities (things) 二つの性質(など)の異同を弁別する. 【類】*discern* ***between*** the true and the false. ¶*discern* a thing ***from*** another 一物を他物と識別する. 【類】*discern* good ***from*** evil.

discernible, *a.* 認識できる.

M The outline of the vessel is ***hardly*** *discernible* now. 船の輪郭がもうほとんど見分けられない.

P be *discernible* ***through*** the mist 霧を通して見分けられる.

discernment, *n.* 識別.

Q ***critical*** *discernment* 批評眼.

discharge, *n.* 免除, 釈放; 発射; 解雇; 履行.

V He ***got*** his *discharge.* 彼は解雇された. ¶The prisoner ***obtained*** his *discharge.* 捕虜が釈放された. ¶He ***received*** his *discharge* from the army. 彼は除隊になった.

Q a ***constant*** *discharge* of cannon 絶え間ない砲撃. ¶a ***dishonorable*** *discharge* 不名誉な解雇. ¶a ***faithful*** *discharge* of the small duties of life 人生の小さな務めに対する忠実な履行. ¶a ***loyal*** *discharge* of one's duties 任務の忠実な履行. ¶a ***sexual*** *discharge* 射精.

Q^2 a ***mass*** *discharge* of workers 労働者の大量解雇.

P ***after*** *discharge* from the service 解職後. ¶***in*** the *discharge* of duty 任務の遂行において. ¶an allowance to a soldier ***on*** his *discharge* 除隊兵への手当.

P^2 a *discharge* ***from*** a debt (an obligation) 債務(など)の免除. ¶a *discharge* ***of*** a debt (an obligation) 返金(など)の履行 ‖ the *discharge* ***of*** one's duties その職務執行 ‖ a *discharge* ***of*** arrows 矢を放つこと ‖ a *discharge* ***of*** water ***from*** a spout 水はけ口から水の流出. 【類】a *discharge* ***of*** blood ***from*** a blood-vessel (出血).

discharge, *v.* 免職する, 解雇する; 免除する; 履行する; 荷おろしする; 放つ; 注ぐ.

M The soldier was wounded and ***honorably*** *discharged.* あの軍人は名誉の負傷で軍務を解かれた. 【類】***honorably*** *discharged* from military service.

P He was *discharged* ***for*** dishonesty (inaptitude). 彼は不正直(など)のために解雇された. ¶He was *discharged* ***from*** military service on account of disablement. 彼は廃疾のゆえをもって軍務を解除された. 【類】He was *discharged* *from* the army as unfit for military service. ‖ He was *discharged from* hospital. 彼は退院した. 【類】 be *discharged from* prison ‖ *discharge* a person *from* a debt 債務を免除する ‖ *discharge* an arrow *from* a bow 弓につがえた矢を放つ ‖ *discharge* a cargo *from* a ship 船から荷をおろす. ¶The stream *discharges* itself *into* the sea. 川は海に注ぐ. ‖ The cargo is being *discharged into* lighters. 船荷がはしけにおろされているところだ. ¶*discharge* a ship *of* her cargo 船の荷をおろす ‖ *discharge* oneself *of* one's duty = discharge one's duties 自分の任務を果す. ¶*discharge* a blow *upon* a person's head 人の頭上に一撃を加える.

disciple, *n.* 弟子, 門弟; 信徒.

Q the *ardent disciples* of ... ism, in their enthusiasm, are apt to ... ...主義を深く信奉している人たちは熱心の余りややもすれば...しがちである. ¶four of the most *brilliant disciples* of science 四人の最もすぐれた科学者. ¶a *direct disciple* of ... ...の直弟子. ¶a *favorite disciple* of ... ...の愛弟子. ¶*profound* and *enthusiastic disciples* of Karl Marx カール・マルクスの深奥にして熱心なる学徒. ¶a *prominent German disciple* of Darwin ダーウィン学説の卓越したドイツ人学徒. ¶Carlyle was a *puritan disciple* of German philosophy. カーライルはドイツ哲学の清教徒的学徒であった.

P² *disciples of* Nimrod and Izaak Walton 猟天狗や太公望連.

disciplinarian, *n.* 訓練主義者.

Q a *strict* (= *rigid*) *disciplinarian* 厳格な師.

discipline, *n.* 訓練, 修養; 規律.

V It *affords* good *discipline*. それはりっぱな訓練になる. ¶It would be *corrupting discipline* to leave him unpunished. 処分をせずに置いたのでは見せしめにならない. ¶*enforce discipline* among ... ...の間に規律を励行する. ¶*maintain discipline* and set an example 規律を固守して範をたれる.

Q The ascetic gave himself up to *austere discipline*. 行者は荒行をやった. ¶*brutal* and *unintelligent discipline* 残忍でばかげた訓練. ¶*corporate discipline* 団体訓練. ¶a *firm* but *sympathetic discipline* 確固たるしかし同情的な訓練. ¶The study of synonyms has long been regarded as a valuable *intellectual discipline*. 同意語の研究は余ほど以前から知的訓練に重要であると考えられてきた. ¶yield to *irksome discipline* 骨の折れる訓練を受ける. ¶language study as a *mental discipline* 頭脳訓練としての語学. ¶*military discipline* 軍紀 ‖ They are governed by *military discipline*. 軍隊式にやるようになっている. ¶Religion for women is in a much less degree than for men a *moral discipline*. 宗教は女子においては男子におけるよりもはるかに道徳的訓練の効力が薄い. ¶*official discipline* 官紀. ¶They are subject to *rigid discipline*. 彼らは厳重な規律に支配されている. 【類】 The *discipline* is *rigid*. ¶*rigorous discipline* 厳格な規律. ¶The learning of a dead language is a *useful mental discipline*. 死語の研究は知能訓練上有益である. ¶a *valuable mental discipline* 貴重な頭脳訓練.

Q² *home discipline* 家庭のしつけ. ¶maintain an *iron discipline* over ... ...に対して鉄の規律を堅持する. ¶*party discipline* 党の規律. ¶*school discipline* 学校の規律. ¶*Union discipline* is weak. 団結の力(または労組の規律)がゆるんでいる.

P *for discipline* みせしめに. ¶strict *in discipline* 規律の厳重な. ¶the maintenance *of discipline* 規律の維持. ¶The school is *under* good *discipline*. 学校は規律が正しい.

P² the *discipline of* adversity 逆境の訓練. ¶a *discipline with* the rod むちを用いての訓練.

disclose, *v.* 明かす.

P He *disclosed* the secret *to* me. 彼は秘密を僕に打明けた. ‖ The secret was *disclosed to* the public. その秘密が世間にばれた.

disclosure, *n.* 暴露, 露顕.

V *make* a sensational *disclosure* 世人を驚かすほどの暴露をやる.

Q a *startling disclosure* 一大暴露事件.

P² the *disclosure of* a fraud 詐欺の露顕.

discomfort, *n.* 不快, 不自由.

V *accentuate* the *discomfort* 不愉快を増す. ¶*bear* a little *discomfort* 少しの苦痛を我慢する ‖ *bear* bravely *discomforts* 男らしく不自由を忍ぶ. ¶*have* the *discomfort* of travelling in crowded trains 混みあう列車で旅行する不快さを味わう.

Q One of the *greatest discomforts* I experienced while travelling in Holland was the want of good drinking water. 私がオランダ旅行中経験した一番困ったことはよい飲料水のないことであった. ¶*personal discomfort* 自身の不自由. ¶*physical discomfort* 肉体上の不自由. ¶live in this *psychic discomfort* 不安な気持で暮す. ¶*severe personal discomfort* 非常な肉体上の不自由.

P go *at* much personal *discomfort* 多大な不自由を忍んで出かける. ¶I was *in* considerable *discomfort* from the aching eye. 私は目が痛んで大変困っていた. ¶It is a cause *of* great *discomfort*. それが大不快の原因だ. ¶*without discomfort* 不自由なく.

discomfort, *v.* 不愉快にさせる.

P be *discomforted over* trifles つまらぬことで気持を悪くする.

disconcert, *v.* まごつかせる.

P Their plans were *disconcerted by* the late arrival of one of the speakers. 彼らの計画は講演者の一人が遅刻したのでまずいことになった.

disconnect, *v.* 分離させる; スイッチを切る.

P *disconnect* an electric fan *by* pulling out the plug. 扇風器のスイッチを切る(さしこみを抜く). ¶*disconnect* oneself *from* a club (movement) クラブ(など)と縁を絶つ. ¶*disconnect* a machine *into* parts 機械をばらばらにする.

disconsolate, *a.* 憂いに沈んだ, 快々(おう)として楽しまない.

P He is *disconsolate at* the loss of his younger brother. 彼は弟が死んだので憂いに沈んでいる. ¶He is *disconsolate over* the death of his favorite concubine and weary of his life. 彼は愛妾(しょう)が死んだのでがっかりし人生がいやになった.

discontent, *n.* 不満, 不平.

V *abate discontent* 不平を和げる. ¶*diffuse discontent* 不平で当り散らす. ¶*foster discontent* among ... ...の間に不満の念を起させる. ¶the energy spent in *organizing discontent* 不平を組織化しようとする努力. ¶*promote discontent* 不平を高める. ¶it will *stir up discontent* with ... そうすると...に対して苦情を言うようになる. ¶This *voices* the general *discontent*. これは一般の不満が漏れたのである.

Q "*divine discontent*" 「義憤」. ¶*grumbling discontent* ぶつぶつ言う不平. ¶*latent discontent* 心にひそむ不平. ¶*outspoken discontent* 遠慮なく述べた不満. ¶*popular discontent* 人々の不満. ¶*discontent* is *rife* among ... ...の間に不満が多い. ¶*social discontent* 社会的不満. ¶there is *widespread discontent* at ... ...には至る処不平だらけだ.

Q² *labor discontent* 労働者の不満.

P a man *in discontent* 不満のある人. ¶murmur *with discontent* ぶつぶついう. ¶there appears to be a growing *discontent about* ... ...についてはますます不平が募っているらしい.

discontent, *v.* 不満を感じさせる.

P He is *discontented at* trifling inconveniences. 彼はちょっとした不便に不満をいだいている. ¶I am *discontented with* him. 私は彼に不満をいだいている. 【類】 He is *discontented with* his position (lot, pay).

discontinuance, *n.* 廃止.

V *order* the *discontinuance* of the magazine その雑誌の廃刊を命じる.

discord, *n.* 不和; 不調和.

V *assuage discord* 不調和を和らげる. ¶*sow discord* between ... ...の間に不和の種をまく. 【類】 *sow discord* among one's friends.

Q His home is a scene of *constant discord*. 家庭に風波が絶えない. 【類】 They were in *constant discord* (角づき合い). ¶*domestic discord* 家庭の不和. ¶*internal discord* 仲間割れ ‖ a period of great *internal discord* 戦国時代. ¶*international discord* 国際的の不和. ¶*irreconcilable discord* 調停し難い不和. ¶*perpetual discord*, veiled or overt 陰に陽に永続する不和. 【類】 A family blown up into a *perpetual discord* and aversion to each other by one of those wicked go-betweens. ¶the U.S. Soviet *political discord* 米ソ両国の政治的不和. ¶a *shocking discord* 実にいまわしいあつれき.

Q² *family discord* 家庭の不和. ¶cause a *labor discord* 労働者の不和を生ぜしめる. ¶*party discord* 党内の不和.

P be *in discord* 不和になっている.

P² *discord among* her supporters 彼女の後援者間の不和. ¶*discord between* people (members) 人々(など)の間の不和. ¶Music out of tune is an excruciating *discord to* our ears. 調子はずれの音楽は耳ざわりだ.

discordance, *n.* 不調和, 矛盾.

V *awake discordance* 不調和をきたさしめる.

P² *discordance between* one's words and action＝*discordance of* one's words *with* his action 言動の矛盾.

discount, *n.* 割引.

V *allow* 20% *discount* from list prices 定価表値段から二割の割引をする ‖ conditionally on your *allowing* the *discount* asked for 当方希望の割引をして下さるという条件付きで. 【類】We *allow* 10% *discount* off (＝on) the prices named. / Do you *allow* any *discount* for cash? ¶At some shops you *get discount*. 店によっては割引をする所もある. ¶*give* no *discount* even to the booksellers 本屋にも割引をしない. ¶We *make* (＝allow) a *discount* of ... off (＝on) the prices in the catalogue. 目録の値段から...お引き致します.

Q U.S. money is at a *considerable discount* in India today. 米国のドルは現在インドでは著しく法定価以下になっている. ¶*liberal discounts* allowed to export trade 輸出業に対しての大割引. ¶obtain a *material discount* from ... ...から大分割引をしてもらう. ¶Capitalism (Socialism) is at a *sad discount*. 資本(社会)主義は非常に受けが悪い. ¶allow a *special discount* of 15 per cent on ... ...に対して一割五分の特別割引をする.

Q² You are also entitled to a *ten per cent cash discount* if your remittance accompanies the order. 御注文と同時に御送金下さればなお一割の現金割引を致します. ¶a *trade discouut* from the prices 同業者に対する割引.

P *at* a *discount* 割引して, 額面以下で ‖ *at* 25% *discount* 二割五分引で. 【類】sell *at* a *discount* of 35 per cent / These shares (株) are *at* a *discount*. ‖ Spirits were high and discretion was *at* a *discount*. みなはしゃいで無礼講といったものであった. ‖ Just now Bushido sentiment is *at* a *discount* in Japanese commercialism. 現在日本人の商人かたぎから見て武士道的精神は影がうすい. ¶lodge a note in a bank *for discount* 手形を銀行で割引させる. ¶*Under* this *discount* the dealer is unable to make a handsome profit. こんなに割引しては商人はよいもうけができない.

P² a *discount for* quantity (cash) 多量(など)取引に対する割引. ¶a *discount to* the trade 同業者への割引.

discount, *v.* 割引する.

P Three months' bills are *discounted at* 4 per cent per annum. 三カ月払いの手形は年四分の割引になっている.

discourage, *v.* 落胆させる, 止めさせる.

P I was *discouraged against* learning English. 私は英語を習う勇気をくじかれた. ¶He is easily *discouraged by* difficulties and obstacles. 彼は困難や障害に会うとすぐと気がくじける. ¶He *discouraged* me *from* undertaking the work. 彼は私にその仕事を引受けてもだめだからよせと言った. ‖ His father's death *discouraged* him *from* his attempt. 彼は父親をなくしたのでがっかりしてその企てを中止した. 【類】Fear of war *discouraged* him *from* going abroad. / The weather *discouraged* us *from* climbing the mountain. ¶He was *discouraged in* his enterprise. 彼はその事業に失望した. ¶He was *discouraged over* the matter. 彼はそのことでがっかりした.

discouragement, *n.* 意気そそう; 落胆.

V *meet discouragement* がっかりする目にあう.

Q plunge back into the *deepest discouragement* 再び失望のふちに沈む.

P² It was a great *discouragement to* him. それは彼にとって実になさけないことであった.

discourse, *n.* 談話, 談論, 演説.

V *changing* the *discourse* 話題を変えて. ¶He *gave* us a long *discourse* on duty. 彼は義務に関して長々と弁じた.

Q an *extemporary discourse* 即席演説. ¶a *public* and *solemn discourse* 公開かつ厳粛な講話. ¶Many expressions which may be used in conversation are not suited to *written discourse*. 話には使えるが文には適しない言葉がたくさんある.

P² a *discourse on* a subject (philosophy) ある問題(など)についての談論.

discourse, *v.* 話す, 談じる, 論じる.

M *discourse at* length 長々と論じ. ¶*discourse learnedly* on this ism or that ist この主義あの主義者について学者ばりの話をする.

P² *discourse on* (＝*upon*) politics 政治を語る.

discourtesy, *n.* 失礼, 無礼.

V No international *discourtesy* can be *laid* to Japan's charge. 日本が国際礼儀を欠いたという非難をされるはずがない.

P² It is no *discourtesy with* him to do so. そうしたって彼は非礼にはならない.

discover, *v.* 発見する; あらわす.

M We *often discover* our mistakes when too late. われわれは自分の過失に気のつくのがおそ過ぎることが往々ある.

P It was *discovered among* waste paper. それはほごの中から出た. ¶*discover* it *by* the naked eye それを肉眼で見付ける ‖ The islands were *discovered by* an English Army captain. その島々は英国陸軍大尉に発見された.

O We *discovered* him to be an impostor. 彼は詐欺師だということがわれわれに分った. ¶Sooner or later truth *discovers* itself. 真理はいつか分るものだ.

discoverer, *n.* 発見者.

Q a *medical discoverer* 医学上の発見者.

discovery, *n.* 発見; 発見物.

V The Greeks *ascribe* the *discovery* of iron to themselves. ギリシア人は鉄の発見は自分らがやったものだとしている. ¶*claim* the *discovery* of ... ...を発見したと主張する. ¶he *made* the mighty *discovery* that ... 彼は...という大発見をやった ‖ Anybody may *make* this *discovery* from observation. 何人も観察によってこの発見をなすことができる. ¶*provoke discovery* 発見を促がす.

Q *brilliant discoveries* in science 科学上の大発見. ¶an *epoch-making discovery* 画期的発見. ¶a *fruitful discovery* 有益な発見. ¶make a *great discovery* 大発見をする. 【類】America was the *great discovery* of Columbus. ¶an *important discovery* 重要発見. ¶a great *moral discovery* 一つの大きな悟り. ¶be a comparatively *recent discovery* 比較的近ごろの発見だ. ¶a *scientific discovery* 科学上の発見. ¶*startling discoveries* 驚くべき発見. ¶It was a really *wonderful discovery* in astronomy. それは全く天文学上の大発見だった. ¶a *world-shaking discovery* 世界を震がいさせるような発見.

Q² *research discoveries* 研究上の諸発見.

P² the *discovery of* America アメリカ発見 ‖ a *discovery of* science 科学上の一発見 ‖ a *discovery of* great importance 一大発見.

discredit, *n.* 不信用, 不信任; 不名誉, 不評判.

V *bring discredit* on his name 彼の名誉を傷つける ‖ a proceeding that will *bring discredit* upon ... ...の信用を害するやり口. ¶*cast discredit* on ... ...を非難する. ¶You will only *gain discredit*. 君が不評判を招くだけだ. ¶it does not *reflect* any *discredit* on ... そうしたからといって何ら...の不名誉にはならない. ¶*throw discredit* on ... ...の体面を汚す ‖ *throw discredit* upon the system その制度を非難する. 【類】Such looseness and inaccuracy *throw discredit* upon the whole work.

Q² It brought him *serious* and *unmerited discredit*. それは彼にとって重大なかつ不当な不名誉になった.

P It brought the story *into discredit*. そのためにこの話は信じられないようになった. ¶things *to* his *discredit* 彼の不名誉になる色々の事柄.

P² It would be *discredit to* the Japanese name. それは日本の名折れとなるであろう. 【類】He is a *discredit to* his family. ‖ it is no *discredit to* him that ... ...ということは決して彼の名誉を傷つけるものではない.

discredit, *v.* 信用を失わせる.

P *discredit* them *with* purchasers 彼らに対する買手の信用を失わせる.

discreet, *a.* 思慮ある, つつしみ深い.

M it would be *more discreet* to ... ...する方が一層賢明だろう.

P He is *discreet in* word (deed, his bearing). 彼は言葉ず かい(など)につつしみ深い.

discrepancy, *n.* 相違, 差異, 矛盾.

Q these *glaring discrepancies* こうした顕著な相違. ¶a *marked discrepancy* はっきりした差異.

P² *discrepancy between* two things (statements, accounts) 二者(など)間の相違 ‖ *discrepancy between* two accounts (statements) 二つの計算書(声明)の間のくい違い ‖ The *discrepancy between* effort and result is appalling. 努力と成績との差が著しい. ‖ the *discrepancy between* the theories and the practice of the late William Morris 故

ウイリアム・モリスの理論と実際との間の矛盾. ¶*discrepancy* ***in*** ability (age, accounts) 力量(など)の相違.

discretion, *n.* 思慮, 分別, 慎重.

V arrive at the years that might have ***brought*** *discretion* 分別がつきそうな年配になる. ¶***exercise*** (=use) due *discretion* 適当の分別を働かせる. 【類】***exercise*** *discretion* with regard to ... ¶***forget*** one's *discretion* われを忘れる. ¶***show*** admirable (great) *discretion* りっぱ(など)な分別振りを示す. ¶***use*** one's *discretion* in ... ing ...に当って適宜の処置を取る ‖ ***Use*** your own *discretion.* 君のよいと思う通りにしなさい.

Q a man of ***great*** *discretion* 思慮の深い人. ¶at ***individual*** *discretion* めいめいの考えで. ¶exercise ***proper*** *discretion* in the choice of ... ...の選択を誤らない. ¶The instructions leave me a ***wide*** *discretion.* その指図は大体のことで, 自分の考えを実行する余地が大いにある.

P at his ***own*** *discretion* 彼一個の量見で ‖ ***at*** the *discretion* of the court 法廷の裁量で ‖ Act ***at*** (=***on***) your *discretion.* 君の量見でやれ. ‖ surrender ***at*** *discretion* 無条件で降服する. 【類】Buy ***at*** your *discretion.* ¶the court may ***in*** its *discretion* ... 法廷はその裁断の自由をもって...できる ‖ be selected by ... ***in*** its *discretion* ...その裁量によりこれを選定する. ¶age (=years) ***of*** *discretion* 分別年齢. ¶Everything was left ***to*** his own *discretion.* 万事彼の計らいに任せた. ‖ The matter is subject ***to*** your *discretion.* その件は君に一任する. ¶***with*** due *discretion* 適当に考えて ‖ if used ***with*** *discretion* 使いようによっては ‖ act ***with*** *discretion* 慎重にやる. 【類】***with*** the greatest possible *discretion.* ¶It is ***within*** your *discretion* to settle the matter. そのことの解決は君の裁量でできる. ¶I hope I may touch it ***without*** *discretion.* 私は遠慮なくその点に触れてよいと思う.

P² The editor has not used the wise *discretion* ***in*** the manipulation of materials. 編集に当った人が材料の取扱いを十分慎重にやらなかった.

discriminate, *v.* 区別する, 弁別する.

M ***carefully*** *discriminate* synonyms 細かい類語の異同を弁じる.

P *discriminate* ***against*** a country (person) 国(など)に不利な差別を立てる ‖ not *discriminating* ***against*** race or color 民族やはだ色に対して差別待遇をしない. 【類】*discriminate* ***against*** a person because he is a Jew. ¶*discriminate* ***among*** synonyms 同意語を区別する. ¶*discriminate* ***between*** degrees of guilt 罪の等級を区別する ‖ *discriminate* carefully ***between*** strangers and customers 他人と顧客を区別する. 【類】*discriminate* ***between*** what is right and what is simply expedient. ¶*discriminate* true ***from*** false modesty 真の謙そんとにせの謙そんとを弁別する.

discrimination, *n.* 区別, 弁別, 差別; 識別力.

V ***enforce*** *discrimination* against the Japanese 日本人に対して不利な差別待遇をする. ¶Strict *discrimination* is ***exercised*** for the admission of members. 会員の入会に対して厳選をする. ¶***show*** great *discrimination* in the choice of means 手段の選択に卓見を示す. ¶***train*** artistic *discrimination* 芸術眼を養う.

Q ***aesthetic*** *discrimination* 審美眼. ¶cultivate an ***exquisite*** (=***subtle***) *discrimination* 微妙な識別力を養う. ¶***instinctive*** *discrimination* 本能的識別力. ¶***invidious*** *discrimination* いやな差別立て. ¶abolition of ***racial*** *discrimination* 人種的差別の撤廃. 【類】There is no ***racial*** (=race) *discrimination* to be felt in this part.

Q² ban ***employment*** *discrimination* because of race, creed, or color 人種・信条あるいは皮膚の色による雇用差別待遇を廃止する. ¶***trade*** *discrimination* 貿易上の差別待遇.

P a man ***of*** *discrimination* 眼識のある人. ¶select ***with*** *discrimination* 識別して選ぶ.

P² end the *discrimination* ***against*** Japanese immigrants 日本移民に対する不利な差別待遇を廃する. ¶*discrimination* ***between*** right and wrong 正邪の区別. ¶*discrimination* ***in*** employment 差別的雇用. ¶the *discrimination* ***of*** A ***from*** B 甲乙の区別.

discuss, *v.* 論議する.

M No man in America is better fitted to *discuss* it ***adequately.*** 米国でこの人以上その問題を十分に論じるに適した人はない. ¶***exhaustively*** *discuss* 徹底的に論じる. ¶*discuss* ***freely*** and ***rationally*** 自由かつ合理的に論じる. ¶***fully*** *discuss* the matter 論議を尽す. ¶*discuss* ***geographically*** 地理の観点から議論をする. ¶*discuss* ***glibly*** とうとうと論じる. ¶***keenly*** *discuss* 盛んに論じる. ¶***thoroughly*** *discuss* the matter その件を十分に論じる. ¶The question was ***warmly*** *discussed.* その問題は盛んに論議された.

P *discuss* ***about*** merits and demerits 功過を論じる. ¶*discuss* a matter ***at*** a meeting (conference) 会合(など)の席である件を討議する. ¶We entered a tea-room, and *discussed* the question ***over*** tea and cakes. われわれは喫茶店に入って茶菓を喫しながらその問題を論じた. ¶*discuss* ***with*** more prejudice than reason 条理を立ててと言うよりはむしろ偏見にとらわれて論じる. ¶*discuss* the matter ***with*** him 彼とそのことを話合う. 【類】*discuss* politics (literature, business) ***with*** ...

discussion, *n.* 議論, 審議, 討論.

V ***arouse*** much *discussion* 物議をかもす ‖ The radium treatment of cancer has ***aroused*** public *discussion* only equaled in sensationalism by the popular furore over the Friedman's treatment of tuberculosis.—Scientific American. がんのラジューム治療法は世間で騒がれた点ではフリードマンの結核治療法と好一対だ. ¶to ***avoid*** further *discussion* これ以上の議論を避けるため. ¶The subject does not ***bear*** *discussion.* その問題は議論の価値がない. ¶***begin*** a *discussion* about ... ...について議論を始める. ¶Let us ***break off*** a futile *discussion.* 無益の論はやめにしよう. ¶***cause*** much *discussion* 大分議論が出る. ¶***close*** a *discussion* 討論を終る. ¶It ***created*** much *discussion.* それは随分議論を産み出した. ¶***devote*** a brief *discussion* to the subject その問題を簡単に論評する. ¶***elicit*** much *discussion* 大分異論をまき起す. ¶There is not space in this article for an ***extended*** *discussion* of ... この文では紙面の関係上...を詳説することはできない. ¶the *discussion* on ... has been ***fanned*** by ... ...に関する議論は...のために気勢を増した. ¶***follow*** a rather prolonged *discussion* かなり長い議論を続ける. ¶we ***had*** several *discussions* about ... われわれは...について度々討議した. ¶***invite*** *discussion* 是非の批評を招く. ¶the question has ***provoked*** much *discussion* among ... その問題が...の間に大分異論をよび起した ‖ an interesting class *discussion* may be ***provoked*** over the question of ... ...の問題に関して自然興味ある教場での意見交換をすることもあろう. ¶***rouse*** helpful *discussion* concerning ... ...に関して有益な議論を喚起する. ¶***start*** a *discussion* about ... ...について討議を開始する. ¶***stir up*** some *discussion* ちょっと問題になる.

V² a long *discussion* ***arose*** as to ... ...について長い意見の交換があった. ¶*Discussions* were ***going on*** among the people about ... ...に関しいろいろな議論が行われていた.

Q ***abstract*** and ***academic*** *discussion* 抽象的で学究的な論議 ¶an ***academic*** and ***otiose*** *discussion* う遠で無益な議論. ¶We had an ***adequate*** *discussion* on the subject. われわれは大分その問題を練った. ¶an ***amusing*** *discussion* 面白い議論. ¶have ***animated*** *discussion* over ... ...について活発な論を戦わす. ¶a ***barren*** *discussion* 無益な議論. ¶a ***brisk*** *discussion* 愉快な議論. ¶a ***brisk conversational*** *discussion* 四角ばらない談話. ¶a ***candid*** *discussion* of a delicate and irritating question 微妙にして扱いにくい問題についての腹蔵ない討議. ¶It created ***considerable*** *discussion.* それは大分問題になった. 【類】after ***considerable*** *discussion.* ¶***constructive*** *discussion* 建設的討議. ¶an ***earnest*** *discussion* 誠意ある議論. ¶***frank*** *discussion* of prostitution as a social problem 社会問題としての売笑問題に対する卒直な議論. ¶***frank*** and ***friendly*** *discussions* 卒直友好的な討議. ¶the right of ***free*** *discussion* 言論の自由. ¶a ***fruitful*** *discussion* 有益な議論. ¶a ***fruitless*** *discussion* 水掛論. ¶a ***full*** *discussion* 熟議 ‖ If you argue that way, no ***further*** *discussion* would be possible. そういってしまえばそれまでだ. ¶It gave rise to much ***heated*** *discussion.* そのため非常な激論になった. 【類】The *discussion* was very ***heated.*** ¶a ***hot*** *discussion* 白熱した議論. ¶an ***informal*** *discussion* 四角ばらない意見の交換. ¶an ***impersonal*** *discussion* さしさわりのない議論. ¶***lengthy*** *discussion* 長談義. ¶There was a ***lively*** *discussion* going on. 活発な議論が戦わされていた. ‖ there has been the ***liveliest*** *discussion* as to ... ...に関してきわめて活気ある議論が行われた. ¶a ***long*** *discussion* 長い議論. ¶There has been ***much*** *discussion* with regard to the subject and it is still in dispute. その問題について随分議論があったがいまだに議論がつきない. ¶after some ***noisy*** *discussion* かなりやかましい議論があった後. ¶the point under ***present*** *discussion* 今ここに論

じる点. ¶***profitable*** *discussion* 有利な議論. ¶have a ***prolonged*** (=***protracted***) *discussion* with ... respecting ... ...について...と長時間にわたり議論する. ¶a ***stormy*** *discussion* 大激論. ¶difficult ***technical*** *discussion* on currency 通貨に関するむずかしい専門的の議論. ¶***unpleasant*** *discussions* 不愉快な議論. ¶a ***vigorous*** *discussion* 盛んな議論. ¶a ***warm*** *discussion* 激論.

Q^2 ***class*** *discussion* 教室における討議. ¶***corridor*** *discussions* [議場でなく]廊下での議論. ¶a ***group*** *discussion* 集団審議. ¶carry on ***panel*** *discussions* on various topics of current interest 興味ある種々の時事問題について座談会を催す. ¶the leader of a ***round-table*** *discussion* 円卓会議の司会者.

P ***after*** careful *discussion* 周到に論議した後. ¶it is ***beyond*** *discussion* that ... ...は論をまたない. ¶a topic taken up ***for*** *discussion* とりあげた論題. ¶waste time ***in*** *discussion* 議論に時を費す. ¶enter ***into*** *discussion* 討論を始める. ¶liberty ***of*** *discussion* 討論の自由. ¶The question gave rise ***to*** much *discussion*. その問題が大分やかましくなった. ¶the subject (problem, question) ***under*** *discussion* 討議中の問題 ‖ the bill, then ***under*** *discussion* in Congress 当時米議会で審議中の法律案. 【類】the point ***under*** *discussion*.

P^2 a *discussion* ***about*** ... ...に関する討議. ¶a long *discussion* ***on*** the subject 同問題に関する長い議論.

disdain, *n.* 軽べつ, べつ視.

V ***have*** a *disdain* for an offer (another's favor) 他の申出(など)を潔しとしない.

Q He was treated with ***chilly*** *disdain*. 彼は冷やかな軽べつを受けた. ¶treat with ***lordly*** *disdain* 王侯のように横柄に扱う.

P treat ***with*** *disdain* 軽べつする.

disdain, *v.* 侮る.

O He does not *disdain* to be witty. 彼は(厳格だが)こっけいを言うだけの余裕がある.

disease, *n.* 病気; 病弊.

V *Disease* may be ***aggravated*** by anxiety. 病気は心配のために悪くなることがある. ¶***alleviate*** a *disease* 病気を軽くさせる. ¶The Amazon lowlands are hot and rainy and ***breed*** *disease*. アマゾン低地は暑気激しく雨量が多く病気を起しやすい. ¶***carry*** *disease* into one's own family 病気を外から家に持って来る. ¶***catch*** some *disease* ある病気にかかる. ¶***cause*** *disease* 病気を引き起す. 【類】*Disease* is usually ***caused*** by germs. ¶***charm off*** a *disease* 病気をまじないでなおす. ¶***combat*** the *disease* その病気と戦う. ¶Rat-fleas ***communicate*** a *disease* to man. ねずみののみは人間に病気を伝える. ¶***contract*** a *disease* 病気にかかる. 【類】He ***contracted*** the *disease* in the course of his investigation. ¶***cure*** a *disease* 病気をなおす. ¶***diagnose*** a *disease* 病気を診断する. ¶***eradicate*** (=***stamp out***) *disease* 病気を根治する. ¶***feign*** a *disease* 仮病をつかう. ¶Slums ***germinate*** *disease*. 貧民くつは病気を発生させる. ¶***neglect*** a *disease* 病気をなおざりにする. ¶***outgrow*** a *disease* 年をとって病気が出なくなる. ¶***palliate*** a *disease* 病気を和らげる. ¶***produce*** a *disease* 病気を起す ‖ tend to ***produce*** *disease* of the liver 肝臓病を起しやすい. ¶the power to ***resist*** a *disease* 病気に抵抗する力. ¶Rats ***spread*** *disease*. ねずみは病気を伝える. ¶***take*** a *disease* 病気にかかる. ¶***treat*** *disease* by ... ...によって病気を療治する. ¶***ward off*** *diseases* 病気を予防する.

V^3 The *disease* ***came on*** in 1894, when the patient was forty-eight years old. 一八九四年患者が四十八歳のときその病気にかかった. ¶Some *diseases* are ***catching***. 病気によってはうつる. ¶the *disease* ***lingered*** longest in the neighbourhood of ... その病気は...の近傍に一番長く残っていた.

Q an ***acute*** *disease* 急性病. ¶an ***airborne*** *disease* 空気伝染病. ¶a ***bad*** (=***foul***) *disease* 悪疾. ¶a ***benign*** (=***benignant***) *disease* 良性の病気. ¶***chest*** *disease* 胸の病. ¶***chronic*** *diseases* 慢性病. ¶***communicable*** *diseases* 伝染病. ¶give another a ***contagious*** *disease* 伝染病を他人にうつす. ¶a ***curable*** *disease* なおる病気. ¶a ***dangerous*** *disease* 恐ろしい病気. ¶conquer a ***deadly*** *disease* 難病に打勝つ. ¶an ***endemic*** *disease* 風土病. ¶***epidemic*** *diseases* 伝染病. ¶capable of curing almost ***every known*** *disease* ほとんど万病を直すことができる. ¶Dementia præcox is not in itself a ***fatal*** *disease*. 早発性痴ほうはそれ自体命取りの病気ではない. ¶a ***febrile*** *disease* 熱病. ¶a ***germ-produced*** *disease* 菌性病. ¶suffer from ***heart*** *disease* 心臓病にかかる. ¶a ***hereditary*** *disease* 遺伝病. ¶a ***human*** *disease* 人間の病気. ¶an ***incurable*** *disease* 不治の病. ¶an ***ineradicable*** *disease* 根治不可能の病気. ¶catch the ***infectious*** *disease* [比喩]その熱にかぶれる. ¶an ***insidious*** *disease* 内攻性の病気. ¶an ***intractable*** *disease* がん固な病気. ¶an ***inveterate*** *disease* 不治の(がん固な)病. ¶a ***lingering*** *disease* 長びく病気. ¶Leprosy is a ***loathsome*** *disease*. らい病はいやな病気だ. ¶a ***malignant*** *disease* 悪性の病気. ¶a ***medical*** *disease* 内科病. ¶produce ***mental*** *disease* 精神病を起す. ¶the most ***murderous*** *diseases* 最も死亡率の高い病気. ¶a ***nervous*** *disease* 神経病. ¶a ***neurotic*** *disease* 神経系の病気. ¶an ***obstinate*** *disease* 難治の病気. ¶an ***occupational*** *disease* 職業病. ¶a ***painful*** but not ***dangerous*** *disease* 苦しいが危険でない病気. ¶a ***physical*** *disease* 肉体の病気. ¶a *disease* very ***prevalent*** in China 中国によくある病気. ¶***preventive*** *diseases* 予防しうる病気. ¶a difficult delivery followed by ***puerperal*** *disease* 続いて産じょく熱を起した難産. ¶a ***quarantinable*** *disease* 隔離することのできる病気. ¶a ***refractory*** *disease* 手に負えない病気. ¶a ***serious*** (=***severe***) *disease* 重病. ¶be afraid of getting a ***social*** *disease* 花柳病にかかるのを恐れている ‖ Poverty is a ***social*** *disease*. 貧乏は社会病である. ¶*diseases* ***somatic*** in origin [精神に対し]肉体の病気. ¶a ***sporadic*** *disease* 偶発病. ¶a ***surgical*** *disease* 外科手術の病気. ¶the German Society for Combating ***Venereal*** *Diseases* ドイツ性病撲滅協会. ¶***verminous*** *diseases* 寄生虫(のみ, しらみなど)による諸病. ¶a ***zymotic*** *disease* 〖旧医学〗発酵病.

Q^2 an ***artery*** *disease* 動脈の病気. ¶a ***family*** *disease* 遺伝病. ¶a ***germ*** *disease* 菌性疾患. ¶He contracted ***hip*** *disease* through a fall downstairs in childhood. 子供のとき二階から落ちたので腰の関節炎にかかった. ¶Asparagus is to be avoided in ***kidney*** *diseases*. アスパラガスはじん臓病に禁物. ¶owing to indications of ***lung*** *disease* 肺病の徴候があるために. ¶***plant*** *diseases* 植物の諸病. ¶***potato*** *disease* in Wales ウェールスのじゃがいもの病気. ¶a contagious ***sex*** *disease* 伝染する性病. ¶a ***skin*** *disease* 皮膚病.

P He was attacked ***by*** the *disease*. 彼はその病にかかった. ¶a specific ***for*** a *disease* 特効薬. ¶suffer ***from*** a painful *disease* 苦しい病気をする. ¶It is used as a remedy ***in*** these *diseases*. こういう病気に使ってきく. ¶dissemination ***of*** *disease* 病気の伝ぱ ‖ the crisis ***of*** a *disease* 病の峠 ‖ I am cured ***of*** the *disease*. 私は病気がなおった. ‖ die ***of*** a *disease* 病死する. ¶He fell a victim ***to*** *disease*. 彼は病気にかかった. ¶He has gradually grown weak ***under*** his *disease*. 彼は病気のため次第に衰弱した. ¶He is affected ***with*** a *disease*. 彼は病気にかかっている.

P^2 It became a *disease* ***among*** us. それはわれわれの間の病弊となった. ¶a *disease* ***in*** the chest 胸の病 ‖ a *disease* ***in*** sheep 羊の病気. ¶a *disease* ***of*** children (the eyes) 小児(など)の病 ‖ a *disease* ***of*** long duration 長のわずらい. ¶Headache is a chronic *disease* ***with*** me. 頭痛は私の持病だ.

disembark, *v.* 上陸する.

P *disembark* ***at*** ... for ... ...に上陸して...に向う. 【類】*disembark* marines (海兵隊員) ***at*** a beachhead (上陸拠点). ¶soldiers *disembarking* ***from*** a transport 運送船から上陸する兵士.

disengage, *v.* 離す, 脱せしめる.

P *disengage* oneself ***from*** another's arm (hand) 他人の腕(など)から身をふり離す ‖ *disengage* a person ***from*** a promise 約束を解除する ‖ *disengage* a boat ***from*** the weeds 海草にひっかかっている舟を引離す ‖ *disengage* the mind ***from*** study 勉強から心を引離す. 【類】*disengage* a person ***from*** an occupation.

disengaged, *pa.* ひまな.

M Are you *disengaged* ***just now***? 今おひまですか. ¶I shall be *disengaged* ***tomorrow***. 私は明日は用がない.

disentangle, *v.* 解く.

P *disentangle* oneself ***from*** political affairs 政治と絶縁する. 【類】*disentangle* one (=oneself) ***from*** perplexity.

disfavo[u]r, *n.* 不賛成; 不人気.

P he is ***in*** *disfavor* with ... 彼は...に受けがよくない. ¶He fell ***into*** *disfavor*. 彼は人気がなくなった. ¶He looked upon the project ***with*** *disfavor*. 彼はその計画に不賛成であった.

disfigure, *v.* 醜くする.

P His face is *disfigured* ***with*** the scar. 彼の顔は傷あとで

ひどくなっている. ‖ a page *disfigured **with*** typographical errors 誤植のひどいページ.

disfigurement, *n.* 醜くすること.

Q a scenic spot with ***hideous*** *disfigurements* by billboards 広告看板のために非常に風致を害された景勝地区.

P^2 a *disfigurement **to*** … …の目ざわり.

disgrace, *n.* 恥辱, 不面目, 不名誉, 汚名.

V ***bear*** *disgrace* 恥辱を忍ぶ. ¶***bring*** *disgrace* upon one's own head わが身に不名誉を招く ‖ ***bring*** *disgrace* upon his family 家名を汚す ‖ ***bring*** *disgrace* to one's parentage 家門を汚す. ¶It ***carries*** no *disgrace* with it. それは何ら不名誉を伴わない. ¶***meet*** *disgrace* 恥をかく. ¶***remove*** the *disgrace* which has been attached to his name 彼の汚名をそそぐ. ¶***suffer*** some *disgrace* 幾分汚名をこうむる. ¶***wipe off*** a *disgrace* 汚辱をぬぐい去る.

Q a ***civic*** *disgrace* and danger 市の恥と危険. ¶a ***deep*** *disgrace* 大恥辱. ¶a ***national*** *disgrace* 国辱. ¶Honest poverty is ***no*** *disgrace*. 清貧は少しも恥辱でない. 【類】 think it ***no*** *disgrace* to …

P He is somewhat ***in*** *disgrace*. 彼はいささか首尾が悪い. ‖ He was dismissed ***in*** *disgrace*. 彼は不首尾で免職になった. ¶He fell ***into*** *disgrace* with his master. 彼は主人の不興を買った.

P^2 It is one of the *disgraces **of*** modern civilizaton. それは近代文明の恥辱だ. ¶a *disgrace **to*** the nation (city) 国辱(など). 【類】 a *disgrace **to*** the family (school) ‖ a *disgrace **to*** her sex 女のつら汚し. ¶a *disgrace **upon*** a person (family) 人(など)のつら汚し.

disgrace, *v.* はずかしめる.

P He *disgraced* himself ***by*** his conduct. 彼は品行で名声「を落した.

disguise, *n.* 変装, 仮装; 仮面.

V ***pierce*** the *disguise* 真相を見抜く. ¶pride in ***some*** *disguise* or other 何とか仮装を自慢している. ¶***throw off*** one's *disguise* 正体を現わす.

Q in ***female*** *disguise* 女に化けて. ¶a woman in ***man's*** *disguise* 男装した女. ¶Vituperation is a ***poor*** *disguise* of want of reason. 悪口はへ理屈を隠すためのまずい仮面である. ¶under the ***thin*** *disguise* of … …という見え透いた仮面をかぶって.

Q^2 a city in ***blackout*** disguise 燈火管制下の都市

P ***beneath*** its *disguise* その仮装の下に. ¶go ***in*** *disguise* to … 姿を変えて…に行く. ¶a democracy ***in*** *disguise* 仮装の民主国. ¶***in*** the *disguise* of a pilgrim 巡礼に身をやつして ‖ He is a rogue ***in*** *disguise*. 彼は実は悪漢だ. ‖ a prince ***in*** *disguise* 御微行の皇族 ‖ travel ***in*** *disguise* 微行する ‖ The thief was ***in*** *disguise*. 賊は変装していた. ‖ a fraud ***in*** *disguise* ていのよい詐欺 ‖ Victory is only defeat ***in*** *disguise*. 勝利は仮装した敗北にすぎない. ¶***under*** the *disguise* of … …にことよせて ‖ ***under*** the thinnest of *disguises* 最も薄弱な口実で.

disguise, *v.* 変装する, 仮装する; 隠す.

M ***thinly*** *disguise* his hatred of … 彼の…に対する憎悪の念をしいて隠さない.

P *disguise* oneself ***as*** a ***monk*** 僧に姿を変える. ¶*disguised **as*** a woman (farmer, man, groom) 女(など)に姿を変えて. ¶*disguised **by*** sobriety しらふの振りをして ‖ He was *disguised **by*** a false beard. 彼は付けひげで変装した. ¶*disguise* a fact ***from*** him 事実を彼に隠す. ¶*disguised **in*** (=***with***) wine (=liquor *or* drink) 酒に紛らして ‖ He was *disguised **in*** female attire. 彼は女装していた.

disgust, *n.* いや気.

V ***awaken*** (=***arouse***) *disgust* in … …にいや気を起させる. ¶***cause*** *disgust* いや気を起させる. ¶***evoke*** *disgust* いや気を起させる. ¶***feel*** *disgust* at … …にいや気がさす. ¶***return*** *disgust* for disgust 泥試合をやる. ¶He tossed his head to ***show*** his *disgust*. 彼はいやがって頭を振った. ¶***take*** a *disgust* at the sight of … …を見ると身ぶるいがする.

Q with an expression of ***indescribable*** *disgust* upon him 何ともいえないいやな顔をして. ¶The sight excited ***strong*** *disgust* in her. それを見て彼女はひどくいやな気持になった. ¶commit suicide from an ***unconquerable*** *disgust* for existence (=*taedium vitae*) 生活がどうしてもいやになって自殺する.

P He resigned ***in*** *disgust*. 彼はいやになって辞職した. 【類】 The smell was so bad that he turned away ***in*** *disgust*. ‖ put it down ***in*** *disgust* いやだと思ってやめる. ¶***to*** the great *disgust* of … …が非常にいやになったことには. ¶shrink back ***with*** *disgust* いやがってしり込みする.

disgust, *v.* いや気を起させる.

M I am ***quite*** *disgusted* at it. それは全くいやだ. ¶be ***thoroughly*** *disgusted* すっかりくさる.

P The failure *disgusted* him ***against*** further effort. ¶*disgusted **at*** his cowardice (behaviour) 彼のおく病(など)に愛想をつかして ‖ I am *disgusted **at*** (=with) him. 彼には愛想がつきた. ¶I was *disgusted **by*** his proceedings. 彼のやり口がいやになった. 【類】 I was *disgusted **by*** his fulsome flattery (へどの出そうなお世辞). ¶I was quite *disgusted **with*** it. 僕は全くそれに愛想をつかした. ‖ I became *disgusted **with*** life. 私はこの世がいやになった. ‖ He is greatly *disgusted **with*** you for not coming. 彼は君の来ないのを大層怒っている. 【類】 I was *disgusted **with*** her foppery (おしゃれ). / *disgust **with*** a person ***at*** his cowardice.

disgusting, *a.* いやな.

M His very sight is ***quite*** *disgusting*. 彼は全く見るのもい「やだ.

P It is *disgusting **to*** the smell (taste). それはいやなにおいがする(味がいやだ).

dish, *n.* さら; 料理, 御ちそう, 食品.

V ***clear*** *dishes* from a table (=clear a table of dishes) 食卓のさらを片付ける. ¶***clear away*** *dishes* さらを片付ける. ¶***consume*** every *dish* to the end 出す御ちそうを片っぱしから残らず平げる. ¶I have ***had*** the same *dishes* so often. 私は同じ料理を幾度も食べた. ¶***lick*** a *dish* さらをなめる. ¶***prepare*** *dishes* 御ちそうを調理する. ¶***put away*** *dishes* さらを片付ける. ¶***select*** the *dishes* we want われわれの好きな料理を選ぶ. ¶***serve*** Chinese *dishes* 中華料理を出す. ¶All the *dishes* were ***set*** upon the table. 御ちそうは全部食卓に出してあった. ¶***wash*** *dishes* in a dishpan (sink) 洗いおけ(流し)でさらを洗う. 「る.

V^2 This *dish **disagrees*** with me. この料理を食べるとあた

Q an ***appetizing*** *dish* 食欲をそそる料理品. ¶a ***cold*** *dish* 冷たい食物. ¶***customary*** *dishes* at Christmas クリスマスのお定まり料理. ¶***dainty*** (=***delicious***) *dishes* うまい料理. ¶a ***favorite*** *dish* 気に入った料理, 好物 ‖ Roast goose is the ***favorite*** *dish* on Michaelmas Day (Sept. 29th). 焼が鳥はミカエル祭日にはきまって出る御ちそうである. ¶a ***heavy*** *dish* しつっこい料理. ¶***homely*** (=***plain***) *dishes* そうざい料理. ¶a haggis, "great chieftain of the pudding race," the ***national*** *dish* which to the palate of the true-born Scot surpasses all that the South can offer プッディング類の王座を占めかつ正銘のスコットランド人にとって英国南部のどの料理にもまして口に合うハッギス料理. ¶a ***novel*** *dish* 目新しい料理. ¶the ***principal*** *dish* 主な料理. ¶a ***rich*** *dish* うまい物. ¶a ***standing*** *dish* いつもきまって出る料理. ¶a ***steaming*** *dish* of soup 湯気のたっているスープ. ¶a ***sweet*** *dish* うまい料理. ¶***tasty*** *dishes* made with chicken 鶏肉の美味な料理. ¶a ***toothsome*** *dish* of apple pudding おいしいりんごプッディング. ¶***vegetarian*** (=***vegetable***) *dishes* 野菜料理. ¶a ***warm*** *dish* 暖かい食物.

Q^2 ***breakfast*** *dishes* 朝食の御ちそう. ¶a ***butter*** *dish* バターを入れるさら. ¶a ***combination*** *dish* つけ合わせ(一さら盛り)の料理. ¶a ***fishmeat*** (***shellfish***) *dish* 魚(貝)の料理. ¶a savory ***meat*** *dish* おいしい肉料理.

P^2 a *dish **of*** meat and vegetables 肉と野菜のつけ合わせ.

dish, *v.* さらに盛る.

M *dish **out*** potatoes さらにいもをつけ分ける ‖ *dish **out*** to a person さらに盛って出す.

M^2 *dish **up*** a roast turkey 焼いた七面鳥をさらに盛る.

disharmony, *n.* 不調和.

V one note which ***strikes*** *disharmony* 不協和をきたす一音.

dishearten, *v.* 気を落させる.

M I was ***quite*** *disheartened* on hearing it. 私はそれを聞いてがっかりした. 「障が出て悲観した.

P He was *disheartened **by*** small obstacles. 彼はちょっと故

dishonest, *a.* 不正直な.

M ***incorrigibly*** *dishonest* 手のつけようのないほど不正直な. ¶***wilfully*** *dishonest* 故意に不正直な.

dishonesty, *n.* 不正直.

V ***discourage*** *dishonesty* in dealings with foreigners 外国人と取引するに当って不正のないようにさせる.

Q ***ingrained*** *dishonesty* 根っからの不正直. ¶***successful*** *dishonesty* うまく行った不正行為.

P They charged him ***with dishonesty***. 彼らは彼を不正直者と非難した.

dishono[u]r, *n.* 不名誉, 不評判, 恥辱.

V ***bring** dishonor* on one's country 国家の体面を汚す. ¶The actor ***did** no dishonor* to the original. その俳優は原作をはずかしめなかった(迫真的だった). ¶***keep** dishonor* alive 引続き世間から悪評を立てられる. ¶***reap** dishonor* 悪評を招く.

P choose death ***before** dishonor* 不名誉よりむしろ死を選ぶ. ¶a notice ***of** dishonor* 〖商〗不渡りの通知.

P² be a *dishonor **to*** one's family 家名の恥辱である.

disillusionment, *n.* 幻滅, 覚醒(ｶｸｾｲ).

Q a ***sad** disillusionment* 幻滅の悲哀.

disinclination, *n.* 好まぬこと, きらい.

V How can I ***conquer*** my *disinclination* to talk in company? 私が人中で話すことを好まない性分をどうしたら直すことができようか. ¶***have** disinclination* to work 仕事をする気になれない. 「the fair sex 女ぎらい.

P² *disinclination **for*** duty 仕事ぎらい. ¶*disinclination **to***

disincline, *v.* きらわせる, いやがらせる.

P I am *disinclined **for*** study (=to study). 勉強がきらいだ. ‖ Loss of sleep *disinclines* one ***for*** work. 睡眠が不足すると働くのがいやになる. ¶This *disinclined* him ***from*** the enterprise. このために彼はその事業がいやになった.

disinfect, *v.* 消毒する.

P *disinfect* a room ***with*** chemical powder (solution) 薬剤で部屋を消毒する.

disinfectant, *n.* 消毒剤.

Q a ***chemical** disinfectant* 化学的消毒剤. ¶a ***good** disinfectant* 効果的消毒剤. ¶a ***powerful** disinfectant* 強力な消毒剤.

P It is used ***as*** a *disinfectant*. それは消毒に使う.

disinfection, *n.* 消毒.

V ***carry out** disinfection* 消毒をする.

Q² ***sunshine** disinfection* 日光消毒.

disintegrate, *v.* 分解する.

P The rocks were *disintegrated **by*** frost and rain. 岩石が霜や雨のために分解されていた.

disintegration, *n.* 崩解, 分裂.

Q a ***political** disintegration* 政界の分裂.

disintegrator, *n.* 破砕器.

V ***replace*** a *disintegrator* 破砕機を新規のものと替える.

disinter, *v.* 発掘する.

P *disinter* a body ***from*** a grave (cemetery) 死体を墓(など)から掘出す ‖ *disinter* ... ***from*** the soil ...を発掘する. 【類】*disinterred **from*** a tomb at ...

disjoint, *v.* 関節をはずす; ばらばらにする.

P *disjoint* a chicken ***for*** cooking にわとりをつぶす. ¶Great Britain, *disjointed **from*** her colonies. 領土をもぎとられた英国.

disk, disc, *n.* 円盤; 音盤(レコード).

V ***put*** a *disk* on the phonograph 蓄音機にレコードをかける.

Q the ***sun's*** (the ***moon's***) *disk* 太陽(月)の表面.

Q² an ***identity** disk* [軍人などの]識別票. ¶a ***phonograph** disk* 蓄音機のレコード.

P² the *disk **of*** the moon (the sun) 月(太陽)の面.

dislike, *n.* 嫌悪(ｹﾝｵ), いや気.

V ***acquire*** a *dislike* for ... ...がいやになる. ¶***conceive*** a *dislike* to ... ...をきらう. ¶***create** dislike* among ... ...の間に嫌悪の情を起させる. ¶***develop*** strong *dislike* for ... ...がひどくいやになる. ¶***entertain*** a latent *dislike* for ... ...をひそかにきらう. ¶***feel*** a *dislike* to ... ...をきらう ‖ ¶***have*** a *dislike* for (=of) ... ...をきらう ‖ He ***has*** a great *dislike* to being lionized or mobbed. 彼はもてはやされたりやじられたりすることが大きらいだ. ¶He ***manifested*** a strong *dislike* for his father's business and determined to strike out a career for himself. 彼は父の商売を大いにきらって独立しようと決心した. ¶***profess*** a *dislike* for ... あからさまに...がきらいだと言う. ¶He ***took*** a *dislike* to me (mathematics). 彼は僕(など)をきらった.

Q have a ***deep-seated** dislike* against ... ...を根強くきらう. ¶I took a ***great*** (the ***greatest***) *dislike* for him. 僕は彼を非常に(など)きらった. ¶I feel a ***growing** dislike* for ... ...がますますいやになる. 【類】There is a ***growing** dislike* on the part of the public in Germany for American films. ¶he had a ***hearty** dislike* for ... 彼は...を心底からきらった. ¶his ***rooted** dislike* to a change 彼のあくまで変化をいとう心. ¶He had a ***strong** dislike* for things commercial. 彼は商売に関することを非常にきらった. ¶They have taken a ***violent** dislike* to him. 彼らは彼を非常にきらっていた. ¶a ***wholesome** dislike* 健全な(当然そうあるべき)嫌悪.

P² a *dislike **for*** work (study, a person, a thing, strangers) 仕事(など)に対するきらい ‖ her *dislike **for*** her partner 相手の男に対する嫌悪の情. ¶my *dislike **to*** his theory of ... 彼の...説に対する私の嫌悪.

dislocate, *v.* 脱きゅうさせる; 混乱させる.

P He had his leg *dislocated **by*** missing his footing. 彼は足をすべらして片脚が脱きゅうした. ‖ Traffic was *dislocated **by*** the snow storm. 吹雪のために交通が混乱した.

dislocation, *n.* 脱きゅう; 乱雑.

V ***reduce** dislocation* of the shoulder 肩の脱きゅうを復位させる. ¶***suffer*** a *dislocation* of the arm 腕が脱きゅうする.

Q a ***serious** dislocation* of traffic 交通の非常な混乱. ¶***uterine** dislocation* 子宮の転位.

Q² ***trade** dislocations* due to war 戦争による商売の混乱.

dislodge, *v.* 追い出す; 取除ける.

P The boulder was *dislodged **by*** the vibration of the moving train. その円石は進行する汽車の震動で脱落したものである. ¶*dislodge* the enemy ***from*** a hill (position, fort) 敵を小山(など)から追いはらう ‖ *dislodge* stones ***from*** a cliff がけから石ころを取除く.

disloyal, *a.* 不忠な, 不義の.

P *disloyal **to*** a person (one's country, lord, king, master) 人(など)に対して不忠な ‖ *disloyal **to*** her husband 夫に対して不貞な.

disloyalty, *n.* 不忠, 不義.

P² *disloyalty **in*** trusted servants 信用されている下僕の不忠.

dismals, *n. pl.* 憂うつ.

P He was always ***in*** the *dismals*. 彼は始終沈んでいた.

dismantle, *v.* 装備などを取除く.

P *dismantle* a house ***of*** its walls and roofs 家屋から壁や屋根をはぎとる ‖ The plant was *dismantled **of*** all its equipment and furniture. その工場は備品や家具の全部を撤去された.

dismast, *v.* 帆柱をもぎとる.

P be *dismasted **in*** a gale 強風の最中に帆柱を失う.

dismay, *n.* 驚がく, ろうばい.

V striving to ***conceal*** his *dismay* 彼の驚がくを隠そうと努めて. ¶***strike** dismay* into (=throughout) the army 全軍を驚がくさせる.

P ***to*** my *dismay* 驚いたことには. ¶I learn ***with** dismay* from this morning's paper, that ... 今朝の新聞で...ということを承知して驚きました. ‖ I was struck ***with** dismay*. 僕は仰天した. ¶I cannot think of such a battle ***without** dismay*. こんな戦闘は考えるだに恐ろしい.

dismay, *v.* 驚かす.

P He was *dismayed **at*** the result. 彼は結果を見て驚いた. ‖ I am *dismayed **at*** (=to hear) the news. 私はその話を聞いてびっくりしています.

dismiss, *v.* 免職する, 追い出す; 放免する.

M He was ***disgracefully** dismissed* from the room. 彼は不面目にも室から追い出された. ¶This is not a subject to be ***lightly** dismissed*, seeing how much of the well-being of the nation depends upon it. この問題は国民の福利に大関係があるのだからこれを軽々しく葬り去るべきではない. ‖ The question cannot be ***lightly** dismissed* as a fad or a dream. この問題は気まぐれだとか空想だとか言ってあっさり片付ける訳には行かない. ¶The statement may ***safely*** be *dismissed* as incorrect. その陳述は間違いとして葬り去っても大丈夫だ. ¶I ***soon** dismissed* it from my mind. 私はやがてそれを気に掛けなくなった. ¶The proposal was ***summarily** dismissed*. その提案はあっさり片付けられてしまった.

P He was *dismissed **by way of*** disciplinary punishment. 彼は懲戒免職になった. ¶He was *dismissed **for*** drunkenness. 彼は酒癖で解職された. 【類】He has been *dismissed **for*** neglect of his duty. / be *dismissed **for*** being dishonest. ¶He was *dismissed **from*** the chair of biology at the College. 彼はその大学の生物学講座を罷免された. ‖ He was *dismissed **from*** the class in geography today. 彼はきょう地理の時間に教場から出された. 【類】He was *dismissed **from*** school (退校). / He was *dismissed **from*** his service (=post *or* office). / Gen. MacArthur was *dismissed **from*** his four Far Eastern commands. ‖ *Dismiss* such thoughts ***from*** your mind. こんなことは念頭におくな. ¶It may be *dismissed **in*** a few more words. [解説な

ど]それはあと数語で終了しよう. ¶He was *dismissed with* a reprimand and a warning. 彼は懲戒と警告を与えられて放免になった.

dismissal, *n.* 解雇, 免職, 解任.

V He ***got*** disciplinary *dismissal.* 彼は懲戒免職にされた. ¶***receive*** prompt *dismissal* (雇人などが)即時解雇される.

Q a ***disciplinary*** *dismissal* 処罰的解雇. ¶letters of ***honorable*** *dismissal* 本人に欠点のない解職を証明する手紙. ¶a ***summary*** *dismissal* あっさりした終了. ¶a ***sweeping*** *dismissal* of employees 使用人の大量解雇.

Q^2 an ***employe*** *dismissal* 従業員解雇.

P^2 *dismissal* ***from*** office (=service) 免職 ‖ *dismissal* ***from*** the army 除隊. ¶*dismissal* ***in*** disgrace 懲戒免職. ¶*dismissal* ***of*** an appeal 上告棄却 ‖ *dismissal* ***of*** public prosecution 公訴棄却.

dismount, *v.* おろす; 降りる.

P *dismount* a gun ***for*** shipping 輸送のため砲を(砲座から)おろす. ¶*dismount* ***from*** one's horse 馬から降りる.

disobedience, *n.* 違反, 不服従.

P^2 *disobedience* ***from*** malice prepense 悪気あっての違反.

disobedient, *a.* 不従順な.

P *disobedient* ***to*** a person (the law) 人(など)に服従しない.

disobey, *v.* 従わない.

M ***consciously*** *disobey* 自覚して神にそむく.

disobliging, *a.* 不親切な.

P He is *disobliging* ***to*** me. 彼は私に不親切だ.

disorder, *n.* 不規律; [軽い]病気, 乱雑.

V ***check*** the *disorder* among the multitude 群衆を制する. ¶***end*** the *disorders* in the city 市中の混乱を静める. ¶***recompose*** the *disorder* of her dress 彼女の着物の乱れを直す. ¶aid in ***relieving*** *disorders* of the stomach, kidneys, and intestines 胃・じん臓および腸の病気に効がある.

Q ***dyspeptic*** *disorders* 消化不良. ¶***gastro-intestinal*** *disorders* 胃腸病. ¶Affairs in China were then in ***great*** *disorder.* 当時中国の情勢は非常に乱れていた. ¶***mental*** *disorders* 精神病. ¶a ***minor*** *disorder* 小患. ¶a ***painful*** *disorder* 苦痛をともなう病気. ¶a ***physical*** *disorder* 体の不調. ¶***Renewed*** *disorder* broke last night. 昨夜騒動が再発した. ¶The desk is in ***sad*** *disorder.* 机の上は大乱雑になっている.

Q^2 a ***heart*** *disorder* 心臓病. ¶a ***speech*** *disorder* 言語障害. ¶a ***stomach*** *disorder* 胃病.

P ***in*** *disorder* 乱雑になって. ¶The crowd fell ***into*** general *disorder.* 群集は大騒ぎになった. ‖ The country was thrown ***into*** *disorder.* その国は乱れた.

P^2 a *disorder* ***of*** (=***in***) mind (body) 心(など)の異常 ‖ a *disorder* ***of*** development 発育関係の病気.

disordered, *pa.* 乱れた.

P a man *disordered* ***in*** brain (=mind) 精神異常の人 ‖ *disordered* ***in*** stomach おなかの調子の悪い.

disorientation, *n.* 錯誤, 惑乱.

V ***produce*** *disorientation* of time 時間の見当がつかなくなる.

P^2 *disorientation* ***for*** place and persons [精神病者など]場所や人に対する認識不能.

disown, *v.* 縁を切る, 勘当する.

P He was *disowned* ***by*** his father. 彼は父に勘当された.

disparagement, *n.* 非難; 不名誉.

Q terms of ***personal*** *disparagement* 人を非難する言葉.

P say ***in*** *disparagement* of a person 人をそしっていう. ¶Poverty is no *disparagement* ***to*** greatness. 貧乏はえらさの妨げにはならない ‖ say something that will be ***to*** his *disparagement* with his new employer 新しい雇主から悪く思われるようなことを彼についていう.

disparity, *n.* 不同, 差異, 懸隔.

P^2 *disparity* ***in*** (=of) years (age, rank, number) 年齢(など)の不同 ‖ *disparity* ***in*** social standing 身分の懸隔. ¶*disparity* ***of*** tastes between husband and wife 夫婦間の趣味の相違.

dispatch, *n.* =despatch.

dispatcher, *n.* 指令する人.

Q^2 a ***train*** *dispatcher* 〖鉄道〗運転係.

dispensary, *n.* 施薬所, 施療院.

Q a ***free*** *dispensary* 無料治療所.

Q^2 an ***anti-tuberculosis*** *dispensary* 結核診療所. ¶an ***Army*** *dispensary* 陸軍診療所.

dispensation, *n.* 分配; 天命.

Q thanks to a ***benign*** *dispensation* of fate 天運で. ¶by a ***blessed*** *dispensation* of Providence 天の慈愛深き摂理によって. ¶a ***happy*** *dispensation* ***of*** nature 自然の妙. ¶by a ***merciful*** *dispensation* 御方便なもので. ¶by ***Providential*** *dispensation* 天の配剤で. ¶look upon loathsome diseases as ***special*** *dispensations* of Providence いやな病気を特別な天意によるものと見なす. ¶by the ***wise*** *dispensation* of Providence 天の配剤で, うまいぐあいに.

dispense, *v.* 分配する, 施す; 免除する.

P *dispense* a person ***from*** an obligation 人の義務(責任, 債務など)を免除する. ¶*dispense* medicine ***to*** the poor 貧民に施薬する. ¶I can *dispense* ***with*** a hat. 僕は帽子はなくとも済む ‖ *dispense* ***with*** the wearing of swords 帯刀を廃する ‖ Give us the luxuries of life and we will *dispense* ***with*** its necessaries. われわれに生活上のぜいたく品を与えてくれるならわれわれはその必需品はなしで済まそう. ‖ *dispense* ***with*** ceremony (=formalities) 儀式張らずにやる ‖ Let us *dispense* ***with*** compliments. あいさつは抜きにしよう. 【類】He knew a little Japanese so he can *dispense* ***with*** an interpreter. / *dispense* ***with*** middlemen (仲介者) / I can *dispense* ***with*** your service. / I cannot *dispense* ***with*** this dictionary. / propose that the second reading (第二読会) be *dispensed* ***with.***

dispenser, *n.* 薬剤師.

Q^2 an electronic ***soap*** *dispenser* 電子的石けん代用品.

dispersal, *n.* 疎開, 散開.

V ***sound*** the *dispersal* 散開のらっぱ(など)を吹く.

P^2 *dispersal* ***of*** population 人口の疎開.

disperse, *v.* 散らす.

M The Jews are ***widely*** *dispersed.* ユダヤ人は広く諸方に散らばっている.

M^2 The soldiers were *dispersed* ***along*** a wide front. 兵士が広い戦線に沿うて散開した.

P The clouds have *dispersed* ***from*** the sky. 雲が散った. ¶They are now *dispersed* ***throughout*** the world. 彼らは今世界中に散在している.

displace, *v.* 置き換える; 解職する.

M people ***forcibly*** *displaced* by the invaders 侵略軍のため強制的に土地を追われた人々.

P He was *displaced* ***by*** his junior clerk. 彼は年下の店員と位置を換えられた. ‖ The radio is doomed to be *displaced* ***by*** television. ラジオはテレビに取って代られる運命にある.

displacement, *n.* 排水量.

Q^2 ships of under ***10,000 tons*** *displacement* 排水量一万トン以下の船.

display, *n.* 誇示; 表示; 陳列.

V an airman ***giving*** a *display* 手並を示す飛行家 ‖ ***give*** a fireworks *display* 花火を打揚げる. ¶***make*** a *display* of one's wealth 大尽風を吹かす ‖ He ***made*** a great *display* of his learning. 彼は学問を見せびらかした.

Q an ***appetizing*** *display* at a department restaurant 百貨店食堂の食指の動く料理品陳列. ¶a ***big*** *display* of firework 花火大会. ¶exhibit in ***bold*** *display* the printed legend "No Bottles" 「空びんなし」という文字の印刷してある札を目につくように出す(くず屋がうるさいので). ¶***catastrophic*** *display* of natural forces (地震洪水など) 自然の偉力を示す災害. ¶an unnecessarily ***conspicuous*** *display* 必要以上に目立った陳列. ¶a ***gorgeous*** *display* of fireworks 花やかな花火の打揚げ. ¶celebrate the event with a ***great*** *display* of fireworks 盛んに花火を打揚げてそのお祝いをする. ¶an ***imposing*** *display* of learning 堂々たる学識の表示. ¶a ***judicious*** *display* of force 賢明な実力の誇示. ¶a ***lavish*** *display* of flags にぎにぎしい旗の掲揚. ¶a ***magnificent*** *display* of fireworks 大花火の打揚げ. ¶an ***ostentatious*** *display* of wealth これ見よがしの富の見せびらかし. ¶a ***public*** *display* of sentiment 感情のあらわな表現. ¶when the last ***pyrotechnic*** *display* exploded over the harbor 最後の花火が港の上にどんとさく裂したとき. ¶a most ***representative*** *display* of the best bicycles of the latest design 最新型最優良自転車の最も代表的な陳列. ¶a ***spectacular*** *display* of fireworks 花火の壮観.

Q^2 a ***chrysanthemum*** *display* 菊花陳列. ¶a ***fireworks*** *display* 花火大会 ‖ Nature's free ***firework*** *display,* showers of stars, Leonids and comets 流星の雨, しし座の流星群, すい星といった類の自然界の無料花火打揚げ. ¶a ***lantern*** *display* [祭典などの]ちょうちん行列. ¶A ***mass*** *display* of fireworks explodes into the sky over the river. 大花火の打揚げた玉が川の上空で開く. ¶a ***store window*** *display* 飾窓陳列. ¶an attractive ***window*** *display* 人目を引く飾窓の陳列. ¶a ***fashion*** *display* ファッション・ショー.

P It is not a thing *for* public *display*. それは公開すべき性質の物ではない. ¶They are now placed ***on display***. 品はもう陳列してある. ‖ Stores have these pictures ***on display*** in the windows. これらの絵画が店の窓に陳列してある. ¶The conduct was a ***display of*** seamanship of a very high order. その行動は非常にすぐれた航海術を示したものであった. ‖ a ***display of*** dahlia ダリアの陳列 ‖ the ***display of*** one's power 権力の表示 ‖ a ***display of*** courage and skill 勇気と技量の表示.

display, *v.* 表示する; 陳列する; 誇示する.

M The notice is ***openly*** *displayed*. 掲示は公然と出してある. ¶***proudly*** *displaying* the insignia of his order 自慢そうに勲章を見せびらかして.

P It was *displayed **at*** the Paris Exhibition of 1867. それは一八六七年のパリ博覧会に出品された. 【類】a flag *displayed **at*** the building. ¶The sun flag is *displayed **from*** the houses. 家々に日章旗を掲揚した. ¶The notice is *displayed **in*** the front window. 掲示が正面の窓にはり出してある. ¶The goods are *displayed **to*** view. 品は目立つように陳列してある.

displease, *v.* 不快に思わす, 立腹させる.

P I am *displeased **at*** (=***by***) his conduct (the thing). 彼の行為(など)が気に入らない. 【類】be *displeased **at*** the news (sight). ¶He is much *displeased **with*** me. 彼は僕に腹を立てている. ☞ be *displeased **with*** a thing はまれ.

displeasing, *a.* 不快な.

P *displeasing **to*** a person 人に取って不快な.

displeasure, *n.* 不快, 不きげん, 立腹.

V ***incur*** an Imperial *displeasure* げきりんに触れる. 【類】***incur*** the king's *displeasure* ‖ I was ill-fated enough to ***incur*** his *displeasure*. 運悪く彼の不興を買った. ¶***manifest*** one's *displeasure* at ... ...に対して不興がる. ¶The king, to ***show*** his *displeasure*, imprisoned him. 王は怒って彼を投獄した. ¶***veil*** one's *displeasure* 不快(立腹)を顔に出さない. ¶***vent*** his *displeasure* on ... ...にあたる(怒りを移す).

Q It was a ***constant*** *displeasure* to him. 彼にはそれが始終不快なのであった.

P push out the lips ***in*** *displeasure* ふくれてくちびるを突出す. ¶a man ***under*** the official *displeasure* その筋からにらまれている男.

disposal, *n.* 処理, 処分.

Q He has a good library at his ***immediate*** *disposal*. 彼は蔵書がたくさんあるので即座に使える. ¶defective arrangements for ***sewage*** *disposal* 汚水処理に不完全な設備.

Q[2] ***garbage*** (=kitchen waste) *disposal* 台所汚物の処理. ¶***refuse*** *disposal* ごみ処理. ¶***waste*** *disposal* 廃物処理.

P He has courteously placed ***at*** my *disposal* his large collection of photographs. 彼は多数収集した写真を好意で私の随意に使わしてくれた. ‖ He has time (material, money) ***at*** his own *disposal*. 彼は時間(など)を勝手に使える. ‖ He has only a limited period ***at*** his *disposal*. 彼には自由にできる時間がほんの少ししかない. ‖ My services are quite ***at*** your *disposal*. 御用は何でも致します. ¶*disposal **of*** rubbish (property) ごみ(など)の処理 ‖ the *disposal **of*** business affairs 事務の処理.

dispose, *v.* 心を向けさす; 処理する.

M He is not ***athletically*** *disposed*. 彼は運動競技に気が向いていない. ¶a property ***freely*** *disposed* of without duress 強迫によらず自由に処分した財産. ¶I don't know ***how*** to *dispose* myself today. きょうはどうして暮らそうかと迷っている. ¶*dispose **lightly*** あっさりと片付ける. ¶I am *disposed **rather*** to agree with ... どっちかというと...に同意したい. ¶a ***religiously*** *disposed* man 求道(ぐどう)心のある人. ¶The labor difficulty has been ***satisfactorily*** *disposed* of. 労働争議は満足に片付いた. ¶***sympathetically*** *disposed* toward ... ...に対し同情を寄せている. ¶He is not very ***well*** *disposed* toward you. 彼は余り君に好意を持っていない.

P Do you feel *disposed **for*** a walk? 散歩に出ませんか. ¶*dispose* one's fortune ***in*** charity 財産を慈善事業に使用する ‖ *dispose* a fleet ***in*** the form of crescent 艦隊を新月形に排列する. ¶*dispose **of*** articles (property, rubbish, waste) 品物(など)を処分する ‖ *dispose **of*** one's time 時間を利用する. 【類】*dispose **of*** it for a small amount (安く) ‖ A driving rain brought the water in faster than the drain could *dispose **of*** it. 大雨でみぞがはき切れないほど水量が押寄せてきた. ¶This painting belongs to a private collector who finds it necessary to *dispose **of*** it. この絵は手放す必要のあるさる収集家の所蔵品である. ‖ He *disposed **of*** his daughter in marriage. 彼は娘を片付けた. ‖ *dispose **of*** work more expeditiously もっと早く仕事を片付ける ‖ *dispose **of*** it with a sneer 一笑に付してしまう ‖ He *disposed **of*** 10 dishes and 5 bottles of beer in a short time. ちょっとの間に十さらの料理とビール五本を平らげた. 【類】It is to be *disposed **of*** as he may think fit. / These accusations and demands so boldly made are not to be *disposed **of*** by mere mockery. ¶Suspicions *dispose* husbands ***to*** jealousy. 疑惑は夫をしっと深くする. ‖ He is *disposed **to*** reform (=innovation). 彼は革新する気になっている. ‖ a critic *disposed **to*** paradox might say that ... 逆説好きの批評家は...というかも知れない.

O I'm *disposed* to think that way either. 私もそうも考えたい.

disposition, *n.* (**1**) 性質, 気質; 気分, 傾向.

V ***embitter*** one's *disposition* 気分をそこねる. ¶This ***encouraged*** her pessimistic *dissposition*. このために彼女は一層悲観的な人間になった. ¶***exhibit*** a *disposition* to fight to the last extremity 最後まで戦うという意気を示す. ¶***feel*** a *disposition* to ... ...したい気がする. ¶He ***has*** a good *disposition*. 彼は気立てがよい. ‖ He ***has*** an unruffled *disposition*. 彼は落着いた性質を持っている. ‖ He ***has*** no *disposition* to do so. 彼はそうする気がない. ¶They have ***shown*** no *disposition* to follow the advice given. 彼らは与えられた忠告に従う気にならなかった. ‖ ***show*** a *disposition* to ... ...しようという色を表わす.

Q an ***affectionate*** *disposition* 優しい性質. ¶a man of a ***bright*** and ***cheerful*** *disposition* 快活な性質の人. ¶a young man of ***buoyant*** *disposition* 浮々した気質の青年. ¶a ***calm*** *disposition* 穏かな気質. ¶a man of a ***curious*** *disposition* 好奇心の強い性質の人. ¶a man of a ***dissolute*** and ***wasteful*** *disposition* 放らつでむだ使いをする癖の人. ¶He is of an ***easy-going*** *disposition*. 彼はのんきな性質だ. ¶a person of ***frivolous*** *disposition* 軽薄な気質の人. ¶***genial*** *disposition* 温和な性質. ¶He is of a ***gentle*** *disposition*. 彼は性質が優しい. ¶a ***gloomly*** *disposition* 陰うつな気質. ¶of ***good*** *disposition* 気立てのいゝ. ¶a ***grasping*** *disposition* 欲深な性質. ¶be of an ***impetuous*** *disposition* 過激な性質だ. ¶his ***innate*** *disposition* 彼の本性. ¶of a ***lively*** *disposition* 活発なはだ合の. ¶a ***melancholy*** *disposition* 陰気な性質 ‖ a girl of a very ***melancholy*** *disposition* 非常に憂うつな気質の少女. ¶of a ***merciful*** *disposition* 慈悲深い性質の. ¶a ***mild*** *disposition* 穏かな性質. ¶have a ***nervous*** *disposition* 神経質だ. ¶an ***obliging*** *disposition* 親切な性質. ¶an ***optimistic*** *disposition* のんきな気質. ¶a ***pleasant*** *disposition* 快活な性質. ¶a lady of ***pliant*** *disposition* 従順な性質の婦人. ¶a woman of ***quiet*** and ***sweet*** *disposition* 静かな愛きょうのある女. ¶of a ***reserved*** *disposition* 遠慮勝な気質の. ¶***restless*** *disposition* 落付かない性質. ¶a gentleman of a ***retiring*** *disposition* 内気な紳士. ¶The boy was of a ***roving*** *disposition*. その少年には放浪性があった. ¶a ***roving adventurous*** *disposition* 放浪・冒険を好む気質. ¶have a ***selfish*** *disposition* 利己的な性質だ. ¶be of ***slovenly*** *disposition* だらしないたちである. ¶a ***strong*** *disposition* 強い気質. ¶a ***sweet*** *disposition* やさしい気質. ¶a ***sympathetic*** *disposition* 同情的性質. ¶a ***time-serving*** *disposition* 日より見的な性質. ¶a ***timid*** and ***gentle*** *disposition* おく病でやさしい性質. ¶the ***uncommunicative*** *disposition* of the people towards strangers その国民の外人に対するむっつりした性質. ¶be of a ***wandering*** *disposition* 放浪癖がある. ¶a ***yielding*** *disposition* すなおな性質.

P He is rather retiring ***in*** *disposition*. 彼は非常に内気な性質だ. ‖ mild ***in*** *disposition* 気質のおだやかな.

P[2] a *disposition **in*** flowers to turn toward the sun 花の向日性. ¶a *disposition **in*** bodies ***to*** putrefaction 死体の腐敗しやすい傾向.

O a *disposition* to drink 酒好き. 【類】a *disposition* to do gambling.

(**2**) 配置, 手配; 処分.

V ***make*** *dispositions* for defense 防御の手配をする ‖ He had ***made*** a good *disposition* of his property. 彼はうまく財産を処分した.

Q the ***eventual*** *disposition* of ... ...の最後的処分. ¶***provisional*** *disposition* for the purpose of provisionally settling the state of affairs 事態収拾のための暫定処置.

¶*summary disposition* 略式処分. ¶a *tentative disposition* (=measure) 暫定措置. ¶*unjust disposition* 不公平な処分.

P² the *disposition of* property for public sale 財産公売による処分 ‖ the *disposition of* the infantry and cavalry 歩兵と騎兵の配置. 【類】the *disposition of* soldiers in battle.

dispossess, *v.* …の所有物を奪う; 追い出す.

P He was *dispossessed by* a lawful owner. 彼は持物を正当の所有者に取られた. ¶He was *dispossessed from* his home (=house). 彼は家を追い出された. ¶*dispossess* a person *of* anything 人からその所有物を奪う ‖ The king was *dispossessed of* his crown. 王はその王位を奪われた. ‖ He was *dispossessed of* his estate. 彼は財産を奪われた. ‖ I must have *dispossessed* you *of* your seat. 私はあなたの席を占領してしまったようですね.

dispraise, *n.* 非難, そしり.

P The word "zeiroku" like "Yankee" is used *in dispraise.*「ぜい六」という語は「ヤンキー」と同様軽べつに用いられる. ‖ He said so *in dispraise* of you. 彼は君をそしってそう言った.

disproof, *n.* 反証.

P adduce facts *in disproof* 反証を示す ‖ offer evidence *in disproof* of … …の反証を挙げる.

disproportion, *n.* 不つり合, 不均衡.

Q the *gross disproportion* between … and … …間におけるはなはだしい不つり合.

P² the *disproportion between* A and B 甲乙間の不均衡. ¶ *disproportion in* age 年齢的に不つり合. ¶the *disproportion to* the man's arms *to* his body その人の腕と胴体との不つり合.

disproportion, *v.* 不つり合にする.

P Its length was rather *disproportioned to* its breadth. その長さはその幅にやゝ不つり合であった.

disproportionate, *a.* 不つり合な, 均衡を失した.

M *altogether disproportionate* to … …と全く不つり合な. ¶it is *strikingly disproportionate* to … それは…と目立って均衡を失している.

P The limbs were *disproportionate to* the body. 手足の大きさが胴体に不つり合であった. 【類】live *disproportionate to* one's means.

disprove, *v.* 論ばくする.

M be *abundantly disproved* by … …からさんざん論ばくされる.

disputation, *n.* 論争.

Q a *theological disputation* 神学上の論争.

dispute, *n.* 議論; 争議, けんか; 異論, 異議.

V They were able to *accommodate* their *dispute.* 彼らは争議を円満に解決することができた. ¶*adjust* a *dispute* between parties at variance 反目する両者間の紛議を調停する ‖ *adjust disputes* among … …間の紛争をまとめる. ¶*avoid* a *dispute* if possible なろうことなら論争を避ける. ¶*carry* a *dispute* into court 争議を裁判ざたにする. ¶*court dispute* やぶへびになる, けんかを買う. ¶with a tone to *cut off* all *dispute* 否応言わせないという(断固たる)調子で. ¶*decide* a *dispute* fairly. 争議を公平に解決する. ¶*foment* a *dispute* けんかをそそのかす. ¶We have *had* a *dispute.* われわれはけんかをした. ¶*hear* and *determine* any *dispute* 一切の紛争を裁判する. ¶*refer* (=*shift*) a *dispute* to a legal trouble-shooter 紛争を法定仲裁人(調停委員)に移す. ¶*settle* the *dispute* among themselves 争議を示談で解決する. 【類】*settle* a *dispute* out of court / *settle disputes* peacefully (=amicably) / as a means of *settling* a *dispute.* ¶war as an instrument for *solving* international *disputes* 国際紛争の解決手段としての戦争. ¶*submit* a *dispute* to arbitration 紛争を仲裁裁判に付する. 【類】*submit* a *dispute* to a referee for arbitration.

V² a *dispute* once *arose* among … as to which of them was … …の中いずれが…であるかの論争がかつて…の間に起った.

Q a *bitter dispute* 大論争. ¶I had *frequent disputes* with him. 僕は彼としばしば争った. ¶a *hot dispute* 激論. ¶*incessant* (=*unceasing*) *disputes* 不断の争い. ¶a complicated *industrial dispute* 複雑な産業争議. ¶an *interminable dispute* 間断ない争い. ¶war (arbitration) as a method of settling *international disputes* 国際的紛争を解決する方法としての戦争(など) ‖ settle an *international dispute* by diplomacy 国際争議を外交によって解決する. ¶settle *labor dispute* 労働争議を解決する. ¶a *legal dispute* 合法的争議. ¶a *long-standing dispute* between … …間の長年の争議. ¶a *public dispute* 公開討論. ¶we had *several disputes* concerning … われわれは…をたびたび論じた. ¶Some *trivial dispute* is said to be the cause. つまらない争いがその原因だそうだ. ¶a *warm dispute* 激烈な論争.

Q² a *border* (=*boundary*) *dispute* 国境の論争. ¶an *employer-employee dispute* 労使間の争議. ¶a *frontier dispute* 国境の論争. ¶an *interpretation dispute* 解釈上の紛議. ¶a *jurisdiction dispute* 管轄権争い. ¶settle a *labor dispute* 労働争議を解決する. 【類】a month-old *labor dispute* / The *labor dispute* continues unabated (緊張したまゝ続く) / a *labor dispute* involving the Government. ¶the *language dispute* in Belgium ベルギーにおける言語上の異論. ¶a *party dispute* 党派争い. ¶working days lost through *trade disputes* 労働争議で失われた勤労日数. ¶a *trade union dispute* 労働組合争議. ¶arbitrate a *wage dispute* 賃金争議を仲裁する. 【類】adjust a wage *dispute.*

P It has been settled *beyond dispute.* それはすっかり解決された. ‖ It is quite *beyond dispute.* 少しも疑いがない. ‖ This is, *beyond dispute,* the best English dictionary. これはたしかに最良の英語辞典だ. ¶an invention the authorship of which is *in dispute* between them 彼らの間で本家争いをしている発明 ‖ the matter *in dispute* 係争問題 ‖ the point *in dispute* 争点. ¶It admits *of* no *dispute.* それは疑いを入れない. ‖ a subject *of dispute* among … …間の係争問題. ¶a *dispute on* a subject (matter) 一問題(事)に関する物議. ¶*out of dispute* 無論. ¶It is now *past* [all] *dispute* that the ancient records are untrustworthy. 昔の記録の当にならないことは今や疑いを入れない. ¶the subject *under dispute* 論議中の問題. ¶*without dispute* 異論なく.

P² the *dispute about* … …についての議論 ‖ there is now a *dispute about* … between … 目下…間に…について論争がある. ¶a *dispute among* people (members) 人々(など)の間の論争. ¶*disputes as to* the existence of any fact 事実の存否に関する紛争. ¶a *dispute between* two persons (countries) 二人(など)間の論争. ¶a *dispute concerning* irrigation rights かんがい権に関する争議(用水論). ¶a *dispute on* a subject (matter) 問題(など)についての争い. ¶a *dispute over* a commission 手数料についての争い. ¶a *dispute with* a person *over* … …に関してある人との論争.

dispute, *v.* 論争する, けんかする; 論破する; [勝敗などを]争う.

M it can *hardly* be *disputed* that … …はほとんど疑いを入れない. ¶*warmly dispute* 激論する.

P *dispute about* a matter ある事件について論争する. ¶There is no *disputing about* tastes. 趣味は思案の外. ¶*dispute as to* who is the greatest English poet 英詩人ではだれが一番かを論じる. ¶*dispute* (=strive) *for* the prize 賞品を得ようと争う. ¶*dispute* one *into* compliance 人を議論でまるめこむ. ¶*dispute* one *out of* the truth 無理を通す. ¶There is nothing to be gained by *disputing with* him. 彼と争っても何の益もない. ¶*dispute with* him *on* (=*about or over*) … …について彼と争う.

disqualification, *n.* 失格, 無能力.

V *cause* the *disqualification* 失格させる. ¶He cannot *overcome* this *disqualification.* 彼はこの失格を防ぐことはできない. ¶It might *prove* a *disqualification.* その結果失敗となるかも知れない.

Q² *sex disqualification* 性による失格.

P² *disqualification for* labor (study, office) 労働(など)に対する無能力.

disqualify, *v.* 無資格にする.

P He was *disqualified by* his age *for* the office. 彼は年齢の関係上その職には資格がなかった. 【類】He is *disqualified for* the post (work, position) ‖ *disqualify* a person *for* a public employment 人の公職につく資格を奪う. ¶He was *disqualified from* serving Government in any capacity. 彼はどんな資格ででも官庁に務めることができなくなった. 【類】He has been *disqualified* for 10 years *from* competing in any race which may be held in that country.

disquisition, *n.* 研究; 論文.

Q a *learned disquisition* on … …に関する学問的な論文. ¶*philological* and *grammatical disquisitions* 言語学的および文法的研究.

disregard, *n.* 軽べつ, 無視.

V *have* an absolute *disregard* for … …に一向とん着しな

い.【類】He *has* the greatest *disregard* for all formality (形式). ¶*show disregard* of one's own life 自分の命を顧みない.

Q *contemptuous disregard* 軽べつ的無視. ¶his *entire disregard* of money 彼の金銭に対する徹底的無とん着. ¶pursue knowledge merely for knowledge's sake with a *lofty disregard* for utilitarian considerations 功利的な考えはさらりと捨てて全く知識のために知識を求める. ¶a *royal disregard* of the cost 費用などを顧みない大名風. ¶in *utter disregard* of ... 全然...を顧みないで.

P treat a friend *with disregard* 友をおろそかに取扱う.

P² the spirit of *disregard for* law 法律無視の精神. ¶*disregard of* law 法律の無視. 【類】*disregard of* the laws of health (健康法).

disregard, *v.* 顧みない, 無視する.

M *disregard alike* the yea and nay of the world 世の中の是非を意としない. ¶It is not to be *lightly disregarded.* そのことは等閑に付すべきではない. ¶*openly disregard* the principle その主義を公然と無視する.

O *disregarding* our will われわれの意志を無視して.

disrepair, *n.* 破損, 荒廃.

Q The house is in *considerable disrepair.* 家屋はひどく破損している.

P be *in* [a state of] *disrepair* [修繕もきかない位に]荒れ果てている. ¶The house got (=fell *or* went) *into disrepair.* 家屋はあばら屋になった.

disrepute, *n.* 不評判.

P they are held *in* great *disrepute* among ..., and specially by ... 彼らは...間, 殊に...によってよく思われていない ‖ Remedies formerly used are now *in disrepute.* 以前用いられた療法も今はすたれている. ¶It brought him *into disrepute.* それで彼は評判が悪くなった. ‖ He got (=fell) *into disrepute.* 彼は評判を落した.

disrespect, *n.* 不敬, 軽侮.

V Such a proceeding will *bring disrespect* upon one's fellows. そんなことをすると自分の仲間が人から軽べつされるようになる. ¶No *disrespect* is *intended.* 別に非礼の積りはない(列記名の順序不同など). ¶*show disrespect* to the Sabbath 安息日を守らない. 「敬にわたるまい.

P I may *without disrespect* say that ... 私は...と言っても不

P² *disrespect for* tradition 伝統に対する軽視 ‖ *disrespect for* government 政府に対するべっ視. ¶one's *disrespect to* one's parents 両親に対する非礼.

disrespectful, *a.* 不敬な, 無礼な.

P *disrespectful to* a person 人に礼を失する. ¶He is *disrespectful to* the gods. 彼は神々を尊信しない.

disrobe, *v.* 衣を脱がせる.

P Autumn *disrobes* the field *of* verdure. 秋になると野原の緑がなくなる. 【類】In winter most trees are *disrobed of* their leaves.

disrupt, *v.* 分裂させる, 崩壊させる.

M seem *likely* to *disrupt* the union 結合を分裂に導くよう

disruption, *n.* 分裂. 」に思われる.

Q the *utter disruption* of the family (state) 一家(など)の破滅. 「分裂が...に始まった.

P² the *disruption of* their realm began in ... 彼らの国の

dissatisfaction, *n.* 不満, 不平.

V *betray* one's *dissatisfaction* 不満を顔に表わす. ¶*cause* much *dissatisfaction* on the part of ... ...に大不満をきたす. ¶the announcement *created* a considerable *dissatisfaction* among the friends of ... この発表は...の友人間に非常な不満をひき起した. ¶*excite* general *dissatisfaction* 一般の不満を買う. ¶*express* one's *dissatisfaction* at ... ...に対してその不満を表明する ‖ *express dissatisfaction* with ... ...に対して不平を鳴らす. ¶*produce* much *dissatisfaction* in ... ...に対する大不満を引き起す. ¶*signify* one's *dissatisfaction* at ... ...に対してその不満の意を表わす. ¶*voice* one's *dissatisfaction* 自分の不満をもらす.

Q *deep dissatisfaction* 大不満. ¶there is a *general dissatisfaction* with ... 一般に...に対し不満がある. ¶There has been for many years *growing dissatisfaction* with results obtained in English teaching in the middle school. 中学校における英語教授の成績に対して数年この方不満の声が高まってきた. ¶*profound dissatisfaction* 大不満. ¶cause *serious dissatisfaction* 大不平の種となる. ¶There is *widespread dissatisfaction* with existing conditions. 現状に対する不満の声が至る所に聞かれる.

P without demur or any sign *of dissatisfaction* 異議あるいは不満の形跡もなく.

P² *dissatisfaction with* the present conditions of home life 家庭生活の現状に対する不満 ‖ *dissatisfaction with* one's lot 自分の運命に対する不満.

dissatisfactory, *a.* 不満な, 不平な.

P The measure was *dissatisfactory to* any one. その処置はだれにも不満であった.

dissatisfy, *v.* 不満ならしめる.

P What cause have you to be *dissatisfied with* her? どういう訳で君は彼女が気に入らないのか. 【類】I am *dissatisfied with* his conduct (my life). / *dissatisfied with* the status quo (現状) / I am *dissatisfied with* my salary.

dissection, *n.* 解剖.

P *on dissection* 解剖して見たら.

P² the *dissection of* a dog (human body) 犬(人体)の解剖.

dissembler, *n.* とぼける人.

Q I am a very *bad dissembler* and cannot appear what I am not. 僕は空とぼけるのがはなはだへたでねこをかぶるこ

dissemination, *n.* 伝ぱ, 流布. 」とができない.

Q the *gradual dissemination* of the potter's wheel over Europe 陶工ろくろの漸次欧州全般への伝ぱ. ¶urge a *wider dissemination* of facts on health 保健思想普及の必要を説く. 「る普及.

Q² the *press* and *radio dissemination* 新聞および放送によ

P² the *dissemination of* information concerning ... ...に

dissension, *n.* あつれき, 不和. 」関する知識の普及.

V *sow dissension* among friends 友人間にあつれきの種子をまく ‖ the German propaganda to *sow dissension* 紛争の種子をまこうとするドイツの宣伝.

Q *domestic* (=*family*) *dissention* 内輪もめ. ¶She has for years past been torn by *internal dissensions.* 同国は数年来国内の不和で分裂している.

Q² *world dissension* 世界的紛争.

P² *dissension among* men (members) 人々(など)の間の不和 ‖ It is obvious that Volapuk died of the *dissensions among* its adherents. 世界語ヴォラピュックがその一派の人人の間における意見の不一致のために失敗に終ったことは明かなことである. ¶*dissension between* two persons 二人間の紛争. ¶*dissension in* a party 仲間もめ.

dissent, *n.* 不同意, 異議.

V emphatically *express dissent* 極力異議を唱える. ¶*show* (=*signify*) *dissent* 不同意を表示する. ¶*voice* one's *dissent* 異議を表明する.

P² there can be no *dissent from* the conclusion that ... ...という結論に対して異議のあるはずがない.

dissent, *v.* 意見を異にする, 異議を唱える.

P *dissent* (=differ) *from* the view taken by ... ...と見解を異にする ‖ *dissent from* his opinion (judgment) 彼と意見(など)を異にする.【類】I *dissent from* that decision. / He and I *dissented from* each other. / I am sorry that I have to *dissent from* you. ‖ *dissent from* the Church of England 英国々教に従わない ‖ *dissent from* one's order (laws) その命令(など)にそむく. ¶I *dissent in* opinion. 僕は意見

dissenter, *n.* 反対者. 」が違う.

P² *dissenters from* the Greek Church ギリシア教会に反対

dissentient, *n.* 不同意者. 」する人々.

P The resolution was carried *with* only two or three *dissentients.* 決議案はわずか二三名の不賛成者があっただけで通過した. ‖ *with* no (=*without*) *dissentient* 異議なく.

dissertation, *n.* 論文.

V a *dissertation submitted* to the faculty of the University in partial fulfilment of the requirements for the Degree of Doctor of Philosophy 哲学博士号請求の為に同大学教授会に提出した一論文. ¶*write* a *dissertation* for a degree 博士論文を書く.

Q a *comprehensive dissertation* upon ... ...に関する大論文. ¶a *doctoral dissertation* 博士論文. ¶a *learned dissertation* 学問的な論文. ¶*Master's* and *Doctor's dissertations* 修士および博士論文. ¶a *philosophical dissertation* 哲学上の論文.

P² a *dissertation on* the subject その問題に関する論文. ¶a *dissertation upon* this exceedingly interesting subject このきわめて興味ある題目に関する論文.

dissever, *v.* 裂く.

P *dissever* a branch ***from*** the stem 幹から枝を裂く.

dissimilar, *a.* 異なっている.

M ***widely dissimilar*** in … …の点で大いに異なっている.

P *dissimilar* ***in*** character 性質の異なる. ¶*dissimilar* ***to*** each other たがいに似ていない ‖ A is *dissimilar* ***to*** B ***in*** … …の点で甲は乙と異なる.

dissipate, *v.* 散らす; 皆無にする.

M All doubts have ***now*** been *dissipated.* 疑いがすっかり晴れた.

P Whole harvests were *dissipated* ***by*** violent hurricanes. 作物は台風で全滅した. ‖ all the fortune *dissipated* ***by*** an extravagant son 放とう息子によってつぶされた財産.

dissipation, *n.* 放とう.

V ***sleep off*** the *dissipation* of the previous night 前夜の放とう三まいの疲労を寝て回復する.

dissociate, *v.* 分ける, 離す.

P *dissociate* oneself ***from*** a person (an association) 人(など)との関係を断つ.

dissolute, *a.* 放らつな, 放とうな.

P *dissolute* ***in*** thought 考えがしっかりしていない ‖ *dissolute* ***in*** conduct 身持のおさまらない.

dissolution, *n.* 分解, 解消.

V ***obtain*** the *dissolution* of one's marriage with … …との結婚を解消する.

P^2 *dissolution* ***of*** partnership 組合の解体.

dissolve, *v.* とかす; とける; 分解する.

P He is *dissolved* ***by*** pleasure. 彼は遊とうにふけっている. ¶*dissolve* sugar ***in*** water 砂糖を水に入れてとかす ‖ She was *dissolved* ***in*** tears. 彼女はさめざめと泣いた. 【類】 The medicine *dissolves* ***in*** water. ‖ *dissolve* ***in*** (***out***) 〘映〙 画面が次第に明るくなる(暗くなる). ¶*dissolve* ***into*** space 空中に消えてなくなる ‖ *dissolve* water ***into*** hydrogen and oxygen 水を分解して酸素と水素にする.

dissuade, *v.* 思い止まらせる.

P *dissuade* his countrymen ***against*** coming to Japan 彼の同国人に日本へ来ることを思い止まらせる. ¶*dissuade* a man ***from*** his purpose 人にその目的を思い切らせる. 【類】 *dissuade* women ***from*** the pursuit of a vicious life / *dissuade* him ***from*** leaving school (going on the stage).

distance, *n.* 距離; 遠方; 敬遠, 疎遠.

V The *distance* was ***accomplished*** by the winning boat in 7.8 minutes. 優勝ボートは 7.8 分でコースをこぎ終った. ‖ The aeroplane ***accomplished*** the *distance* from … to … in … hours. 飛行機は…から…までを…時間で飛んだ. ¶We are making astonishing progress in "***annihilating*** *distance.*" われわれはいわゆる「距離の絶滅」において驚くべき進歩を遂げつゝある. ¶The *distance* ***compassed*** during the excursion was … miles. この遠足行程は…マイルであった. ¶***conquer*** *distance* 距離を征服する. ¶***considering*** the *distance* away from town 町からの距離を考えると. ¶The train will ***cover*** the *distance* between … and … in less than one hour. 汽車は…から…まで一時間足らずで達する. ¶***diminish*** *distance* and time 距離と時間を短縮する. ¶***go*** the *distance* on foot = walked the distance 徒歩で行く. ¶***increase*** (***reduce***) the *distance* [船など]距離を増す(減じる). ¶***keep*** a certain *distance* between cars 電車と電車の間に一定の距離をおく. 【類】 ***keep*** a safe *distance.* ¶***measure*** a *distance* 距離を測る. ¶***take*** the *distance* 距離を測る. ¶These one-hump camels ***travel*** enormous *distances* over the desert regions at a high rate of speed. これらの単こぶらくだはさばく地方を非常な速力で随分遠距離まで旅行する. ¶The stage coaches ***traverse*** the *distance* between … and …daily. 馬車は…間を毎日通る. 【類】 Automobiles ***traverse*** (= cover) this *distance* in one hour. ¶***trudge*** the remaining *distance* into … 残りの道程をとぼとぼ歩いて…にはいって行く.

Q members within ***attending*** *distance* 出席のできる距離以内の会員. ¶mountains visible in the ***blue*** *distance* 青く遠方に見える山々. ¶within a ***calling*** *distance* 呼べば聞える所に. ¶at a ***certain*** *distance* 一定の距離に. ¶at a ***considerable*** *distance* かなり遠くに. ¶within ***convenient walking*** *distance* to important business centres 繁華な商業街へぶらりと歩いて行ける所に. ¶in the ***dim*** *distance* 遠くかすんだかなたに. ¶an ***easy*** *distance* 楽に行ける距離. 【類】 within ***easy*** *distance* of … ¶in the ***far*** *distance* = far in the distance はるかかなたに. ¶at a ***few steps'*** *distance* farther on そこからさらに数歩行った所に. ¶My house is at ***four miles*** *distance* (= four miles distant) from the sea. 私の家は海から四マイル離れている. ¶a ***good*** *distance* off かなり離れて. ¶at a ***great*** *distance* 遠く離れて. ¶in the ***grey*** *distance* of the plain 平原の灰色にくすんだかなた. ¶within ***hailing*** *distance* of … …から声を掛けてとどく所に. ¶in the ***hazy*** *distance* かすみたな引くかなたに. ¶at a ***long*** *distance* 遠くに ‖ swim (walk) a ***long*** *distance* 長距離を泳ぐ(歩く) ‖ a ***long*** *distance* (= way) off 遠く離れて. ¶call (= phone) … by ***long*** *distance* 長距離電話を…にかける. ¶We are within ***measurable*** *distance* of the termination of the war. 戦争の終局も近きにある. 【類】 He is within ***measurable*** *distance* of death. / get within ***measurable*** *distance* of success. ¶in the ***middle*** *distance* 前景と背景との間に. 【類】 in the ***middle*** *distance* between … and … ¶at a ***moderate*** *distance* 余り遠くない所に. ¶It lies at a ***month's*** *distance* from here. それはここから一カ月で行ける距離にある. ¶at ***no great*** *distance* of time あまり遠からぬ時に. ¶Keep him at a ***respectable*** *distance.* 彼には余り接近するな. ¶stay at a ***respectful*** *distance* from … …を敬遠している. ¶from a ***safe*** *distance* 安全距離から. ¶at a ***short*** *distance* [to the] southward 南方へ少し離れて. ¶it is within ***six minutes'*** *distance* of … それは…から六分で行ける所にある. ¶***some*** *distance* ahead 少し先きに ‖ ***some*** *distance* away 少し離れて. ¶extend to an ***unknown*** *distance* 際限のない遠方まで延びている. ¶the stars an ***unthinkable*** *distance* off from the earth 地球から考えられないほどの遠距離にある恒星.

Q^2 within easy ***boating*** *distance* of … …からボートで楽に行けるところに. ¶within a ***gun-shot*** *distance* 弾丸の届くほどの距離内. ¶be within ***reaching*** *distance* 手の届く距離にある. ¶within a ***short-walking*** *distance* of … …から歩いて遠くないところに. ¶within a ***stone's throw*** *distance* of … …から石を投げて届く範囲内に. ¶venture within ***striking*** *distance* 思い切って打込めるところまで進む. ¶be within ***twenty-four hours mailing*** *distance* of … …から廿四時間以内に郵便の届く距離にある. ¶The school was within ***walking*** *distance.* その学校は歩いて行かれる所にあった.

P ***at*** some *distance* 少し離れた所に ‖ those who live ***at*** a *distance* 離れている人たち ‖ answer questions put to it by correspondents ***at*** a *distance* 遠方の通信者からそれにかけられた質問に答える ‖ ***at*** *distances* of eight or ten yards = eight or ten yards apart 八ヤードあるいは十ヤードずつ離れて ‖ a farm ***at*** a *distance* from the city 都市から離れている農園 ‖ A two-masted schooner lay ***at*** some *distance* from the coast. 二本マストの帆船が岸から少し離れて停泊していた. ‖ I write ***at*** a *distance* from my works of reference. 私は参考書から離れて見られない所で書いている. 【類】 it stands ***at*** about half a mile *distance* from … / keep it ***at*** a *distance* from fire / The temple of Sinai is situated in the desert ***at*** a *distance* of five days' camel journey from Suez. ‖ It is difficult to say ***at*** this *distance* to what extent the public in the United States desired war. 遠く今日となっては米国の一般民衆がどの程度まで戦争を希望していたかは言い難い. ‖ The chief exports are raw silk, then ***at*** some *distance,* tea and next, rice and coal. 主要輸出品は生糸少し下って茶それから米・石炭の順になる. ¶reckon (hire) ***by*** *distance* 距離で勘定する(など). ¶***for*** a *distance* of … miles …マイルの間. ¶view … ***from*** a *distance* 少し離れた所から…を見る. 【類】 guests coming ***from*** a *distance* ‖ ***from*** this *distance* これだけ離れた所(時)から. ¶I saw some one ***in*** the *distance.* だれやらが遠方に見えた. 【類】 The light was seen ***in*** the *distance.* ¶extend ***over*** a *distance* of 20 miles 二十マイルにわたって拡がる ‖ look back ***over*** a *distance* of fifty years 五十年の昔をふり返る. ¶***to*** any *distance* どこまでも. ¶***to*** some *distance* 少し離れて. ¶The holiday resort is ***within*** easy *distance* of the capital. その遊覧地は首都から容易に行ける所にある.

P^2 the *distance* ***between*** Tokyo and Osaka 東京大阪間の距離. ¶a *distance* ***of*** 25 days ***from*** any railway どの鉄道からも二十五日かゝる所. ¶What is the *distance* ***to*** Nagoya? 名古屋までどれほど道のりがありますか.

distant, *a.* 遠い, 遠方の, へだたっている; 懸隔がある; 疎遠な.

M the day (time) is ***far distant*** when … …となるまでには前途りょう遠だ. ¶The town is ***four miles distant.*** 町へは四マイルある. ¶We have always been ***rather distant.***

お互いにいつも疎遠勝ちであった. ¶The town is ***three miles*** *distant*. その町まで三マイルある. ¶It is ***very*** *distant* from the truth. それは大いに事実に反している. ¶a practice ***widely*** *distant* from Christianity 大いにキリスト教に反している慣例.

P Canada and the United States are no more than a nine or ten days' voyage *distant* ***from*** Japan. カナダや米国は日本から九日か十日の航海にすぎない. 【類】 Yokohama is *distant* about eighteen miles ***from*** the capital, with which it is connected by a line of railway. / It is ten days *distant* ***from*** here. ¶They are *distant* ***towards*** us. 彼らはわれわれに対して隔意がある.

distaste, *n.* きらい, 嫌悪(けんお).

V ***create*** a *distaste* for ... ...をきらうようにさせる. ¶***express*** one's *distaste* for ... ...に対する嫌悪を表明する. ¶he ***got*** a *distaste* for ... 彼は...がきらいになった. ¶This ***gave*** me a *distaste* for sea-bathing. こんな訳で海水浴というものがきらいになった. ¶I ***have*** a *distaste* for society. 私は人中に出るのがきらいだ. 【類】 I ***have*** a *distaste* for meat. / ***have*** a *distaste* for intoxicating drink of any kind whatever.

Q He has a ***great*** *distaste* for ostentation. 彼は虚飾が大きらいだ. ¶I have a ***strong*** *distaste* for mathematics. 私は数学が大きらいだ.

P² *distaste* ***for*** intellectual employment 知的労作に対する嫌悪.

distasteful, *a.* 気に入らない.

P those *distasteful* ***to*** the authorities その筋の覚えめでたからぬ人々 ‖ work *distasteful* ***to*** him 彼の気に入らない仕事.

distil[l], *v.* 蒸留する, 蒸留して取る; 抽出する.

M The dew is *distilled* more ***abundantly*** upon the grass than upon the gravel. 露は砂利の上よりも草の上の方にたくさん降りる. ¶***doubly*** *distilled* 二重に蒸留した.

P *distil* brandy ***from*** wine ぶどう酒を蒸留してブランデーを取る. 【類】 *distil* fresh water ***from*** sea water ‖ Whisky is *distilled* ***from*** grain. ウイスキーは穀物から留造する. ‖ a liquor *distilled* ***from*** sweet potatoes いも焼ちゅう. 【類】 Gasoline is *distilled* ***from*** crude oil. ¶be *distilled* ***into*** perfume (抽出して)香水にする.

distillation, *n.* 蒸留.

P Shochu is obtained from potatoes ***by*** *distillation*. 焼ちゅうはいもを蒸留して造る.

distinct, *a.* 異なった; 別個の.

M They are ***quite*** *distinct* from each other. それは全く別々のものだ. ¶be ***radically*** *distinct* from ... ...とは根本的に違う.

distinction, *n.* (**1**) 抜群, 優秀; 高貴, 高名; 栄誉, 殊遇; 特徴.

V ***achieve*** *distinction* 群を抜く ‖ ***achieve*** the *distinction* その栄誉を獲る ‖ ***achieve*** literary *distinction* 文名をとどろかす. ¶***acquire*** military *distinction* 抜群の武名をかがやかす. ¶They ***attained*** *distinction* and eminence of their respective walks of life. 彼らはそれぞれの職業に卓越せる地歩を占めた. ¶***attain*** much *distinction* in scholarship 学者として大いに名声を揚げる. ¶***award*** the *distinction* of ... to ... ...の名誉を...に帰する. ¶***claim*** the *distinction* of never having had a cold 一度もかぜを引いたことがないということを誇りとする. ¶it would ***confer*** *distinction* upon ... そうすると...が有名になる. ¶***earn*** international *distinction* 国際的に卓越する ‖ ***earn*** some *distinction* at school 学校で幾分優良の成績を収める. ¶***enjoy*** the unique *distinction* of being ... ...たるの独特な栄誉を得る. ¶***establish*** a *distinction* as a writer 作家として名を成す. ¶***gain*** the *distinction* その名誉を得る ‖ He ***gained*** *distinction* as a writer of fiction. 彼は小説家として名を成した. ‖ They ***gained*** great *distinction* in various fields of scholarly activity. 彼らは種々な学問の分野において卓越した成果を収めた. ¶The book is sufficient to ***give*** *distinction* to his library. この本は彼の蔵書を貴重なものとするに足りる. ¶He ***has*** the *distinction* of being an honorary member of the club. 彼は名誉会員たるの名誉を有する. ‖ ***have*** the *distinction* of pioneering 先べんを着ける ‖ It ***has*** marked *distinction*. それは一際目立っている. ¶Captain Horace B. Wild ***holds*** the *distinction* of being the first navigator of a dirigible in America. H.B. ワイルド大尉は米国で初めて飛行船を操縦したという名誉をになった人である. ¶His style ***lacks*** *distinction*. 彼の文体には特徴がない. ¶***maintain*** the *distinction* 名声を維持する. ¶he ***obtained*** *distinction* at the battle of ... 彼は...の役で武名を揚げた. ¶***owes*** its *distinction* to ... その栄誉は...のおかげである. ¶a person who has ***received*** a *distinction* of rank from the Emperor 陛下から位を賜わった人. ¶***seek*** *distinction* 栄達を求める. ¶Babylon, the ancient Chaldea, ***shares*** with Egypt the *distinction* of being one of the two chief fountains of culture. 古代カルディヤ人の国バビロンはエジプトとともに文化の二大源泉の一たる栄誉をになうものである. ¶*Distinctions* were ***showered*** upon him. 彼は数々の栄誉に浴した. ¶He ***won*** *distinction* as a critic. 彼は批評家として名声を博した. ‖ He ***won*** *distinction* in public life. 彼は公生活において名を成した. ¶*Distinction* of that kind did not ***appeal*** to him. そうした名誉は彼の心を引きつけなかった.

Q the Pushkin prize, the highest ***academic*** *distinction* in Russia ロシアにおける学界の最高名誉たるプーシキン賞. ¶the ***chief*** *distinction* of Russian literature ロシア文学の主なる特徴. ¶universities enjoying the ***doubtful*** *distinction* of bigness 大きいだけで内容のあやしい大学. ¶a man of ***great*** *distinction* 高名の人. ¶achieve the ***highest*** *distinction* as an artist 芸術家として最高の名誉を博する. ¶attain ***intellectual*** *distinction* 学問で名を成す. ¶He is ambitious of ***literary*** *distinction*. 彼は文名をあげようとの野心を抱いている. ¶honor ... with ***marked*** *distinction* ... に殊遇を賜う. ¶a ***much-coveted*** *distinction* 世人の渇望する栄誉. ¶a man of ***no*** *distinction* 無名の人. ¶the splendid possibilities of ***personal*** *distinction* 一身の栄達を遂げうるりっぱな可能性. ¶attain high ***political*** *distinction* 政界に高名をはせる. ¶the ***proud*** *distinction* of being ... belongs to ... ...たるの栄誉は...のものである. ¶a man of much ***social*** and some ***literary*** *distinction* 社交界で非常に有名で文学上にも多少秀でた人. ¶win ***special*** *distinction* 特別の栄誉を得る. ¶he has the ***unenviable*** *distinction* of ... 彼に対しては...という望ましからぬ評判がある. ¶it may claim the ***unique*** *distinction* of being ... それは...であるという独特の名声をわがものと主張して差支えない.

P a journalist ***of*** *distinction* 有名な新聞記者 ‖ receive him with marks ***of*** *distinction* 彼に格別の礼遇を与える. 【類】 a specialist ***of*** *distinction*. ¶He served ***with*** *distinction* under Wellington in Spain. 彼はスペインにおいてウェリントン将軍の配下にあって功を立てた. 【類】 He served ***with*** *distinction* in the Great War. ‖ He passed the examination ***with*** *distinction*. 彼はりっぱな成績でその試験に及第した.

P² Lady Purkes achieved the *distinction* ***of*** being the first woman actually to climb the top of Fuji. パークス夫人は事実最初に富士山の頂上に登った婦人たるの名誉を得た.

(**2**) 区別, 差別, 分け隔て.

V ***clarify*** the *distinctions* between synonyms 同意語の相違を明らかにする. ¶***create*** an invidious class *distinction* 不快な階級差別を立てる. ¶***draw*** a *distinction* between ... ...の間に区別をつける ‖ ***draw*** no *distinctions* 区別を立てない ‖ ***draw*** invidious *distinctions* between ... ...間に不快な区別を立てる. ¶The *distinction* between ... and ... is rigidly ***maintained***. ...間の差別は厳重に立てられている. ¶***make*** *distinctions* 分け隔てをする ‖ He ***made*** no *distinctions* of them. 彼は彼らの分け隔てをしなかった. ‖ ***make*** a clear *distinction* between ... ...の間にはっきりした区別を立てる ‖ I ***make*** this *distinction* between the two cases. 僕はこの二つの場合をこう区別する. ‖ ***make*** a *distinction* without a difference 相違がないのに区別を立てる ‖ what *distinction* can you ***make*** between ... and ... ...と...との間にはどんな違いがあるか. ¶***obliterate*** race *distinctions* 人種的差別を撤廃する. ¶***observe*** the *distinction* between ... ...間の区別を認める ‖ The *distinction* is not always ***observed***. その区別は必ずしも守られない(言葉の慣用など). ¶***set up*** a *distinction* between ... and ... ...と...とを区別する.

Q draw the ***clear*** *distinction* between ... ...間にこの明白な区別を立てる. 【類】 there is a ***clear*** *distinction* between ... ¶***clear cut*** *distinctions* はっきりした区別. ¶a ***convenient*** *distinction* 便利な区別. ¶***delicate*** *distinctions* 微妙な相違. ¶draw very ***fine*** *distinctions* 非常に細かい区別を立てる. ¶***hair-splitting*** *distinctions* やたらに細かい区別. ¶attempt any ***hard-and-fast*** *distinction* between ... ...の間に厳密な区別を試みる. ¶***grammatical*** *distinctions*

文法的区別. ¶***impalpable*** *distinctions* 微細な区別. ¶an ***important*** *distinction* 大切な区別. ¶avoid ***invidious*** *distinctions* 不快な区別を避ける ‖ make a somewhat ***invidious*** *distinction* 少しく不快な区別を立てる. ¶a ***nice*** *distinction* 細かい区別. ¶***obscure*** *distinctions* あいまいな区別. ¶In Japanese words the *distinctions* between surd and sonant consonants are often ***optional***. 日本語には清音と濁音の区別は立てゝも立てなくてもよい場合が往々ある. ¶a ***racial*** *distinction* 人種的差別. ¶a ***sharp*** *distinction* はっきりした区別. ¶at a period when ***social*** *distinctions* between the greater and the lesser territorial magnates were far marked than it is now 大地主とそれ以下の地主との社会的区別が現今より一層顕著だった時代では. ¶there may be some ***subtle*** *distinction* between … …の間には微妙な区別があるかも知れない.【類】***subtle*** *distinctions* in synonyms (同意語).

Q^2 ***ancestry*** *distinction* 栄誉ある祖先. ¶an abolition of ***class*** *distinctions* 階級差別の撤廃. ¶there is no ***dress*** *distinction* between … …の間に服装の差別はない. ¶a ***hairline*** *distinction* きわめてわずかの区別.

P ***for*** *distinction* 区別するために. ¶***in*** *distinction* from … …と区別して. ¶write ***with*** *distinction* りっぱに文を書く ‖ ***with*** no *distinction* 差別なく. ¶***without*** *distinction* of sex (race, class, creed, nationality, birth, station) 性(など)の差別なく ‖ old and young, ***without*** *distinction* 老幼の差別なく.【類】all ***without*** *distinction*＝all alike.

P^2 without *distinction* ***as to*** party affiliations どこの党に所属していようと. ¶The *distinction* ***between*** … and … is subtle. …と…との差は微妙である ‖ *distinctions* ***between*** the rich and the poor 貧富の別. ¶There is no *distinction* ***in*** meaning. 全く意味の差がない. ¶*distinction* ***without*** a difference 差異のない区別(無用の区別立て).

distinctiveness, *n.* 特殊性; 区別.

V ***give*** it *distinctiveness* それを特徴あるものとする, 特徴づける.

P^2 a *distinctiveness* ***of*** significance 意義の相違.

distinguish, *v.* 区別する; 見分ける, 認める; 著名にする; 分類する.

M *distinguish* ***carefully*** between fact and legend 事実と伝説を念入りに区別する. ¶***clearly*** *distinguish* しゅん別する. ¶To say the truth, my liking for him was so extreme that it was *distinguishing* very ***nicely*** to deny that I love him. 実を言うと私は極端に彼が好きだったので私が彼を愛してんじゃないというと言葉に微妙な区別を立てるおそれがある. ¶can be ***readily*** *distinguished* as … …と容易に見分けがつく. ¶***sharply*** *distinguished* from … …とはっきり区別して.

P The dog is *distinguished* ***above*** all other animals for its faithfulness. 犬は忠実という点で他のすべての獣類にまさるものとされている. ¶This *distinguishes* a person ***as*** a born aristocrat. これで生れながらの貴族として見わけがつく. ‖ He is *distinguished* ***as*** a poet. 彼は詩人として有名だ. ¶*distinguish* a bird ***at*** a distance 遠方にいる鳥を何鳥と見分ける. ¶through failure to *distinguish* ***between*** two things that greatly differ 大いに異なる二物の見分けがつかなかったので ‖ *distinguish* ***between*** innocent and guilty (the good and the bad) 無罪と有罪(など)とを見分ける.【類】the ability to *distinguish* ***between*** words that resemble each other in meaning (意味の類似する語). ¶*distinguish* oneself ***by*** scholarship (bravery, good shooting) 学識(など)をもって有名になる ‖ They are *distinguished* ***by*** an asterisk. それらは*印で区別してある.【類】*distinguish* oneself ***by*** winning a prize ‖ His presents are *distinguished* ***by*** the thought and care bestowed on the choice. 彼の進物には品物の選択に十分考慮と注意を払っている所が見える. ‖ It is written in a style which is *distinguished* ***by*** refinement and charm. それは洗練と魅力とを有する文体で書かれている. ‖ *distinguished* ***by*** a small head (red nose) 頭の小さい(など)特徴のある ‖ *distinguished* ***by*** novelty of view or originality of utterance 独創的な言論で名のある. ¶men *distinguished* ***for*** their mental gifts その才能のすぐれた人々 ‖ He is *distinguished* ***for*** cleanliness, politeness, and courage. 彼はきれい好きで丁寧でかつ勇気があるので有名だ.【類】America is a country *distinguished* ***for*** "big things." / He is *distinguished* ***for*** his crimes. ‖ plants *distinguished* ***for*** hardiness in winter 冬の寒さに強い植物.【類】a family *distinguished* ***for*** its public service. ¶literature as *distinguished* ***from*** mere prose composition 単なる散文の作文と区別しての文学 ‖ *distinguish* friend ***from*** foe (right from wrong) 友と敵(など)を見分ける.【類】*distinguish* true poetry ***from*** sham poetry ‖ It is almost impossible to *distinguish* some forgeries (にせもの) ***from*** genuine antiquities. ‖ *distinguish* the imitations ***from*** the originals 本物と模造品を見分ける.【類】Ability to talk *distinguishes* human beings ***from*** animals. ¶a man *distinguished* ***in*** science (literature) 科学(など)に長じた人. ¶*distinguish* a lesser ***from*** a greater evil 小弊害と大弊害を区別する. ¶*distinguish* oneself ***in*** literature 文学で名を成す ‖ *distinguish* one ***in*** the crowd 人ごみの中の人を見分ける ‖ be *distinguished* ***in*** an accomplishment 一芸にひいでている. ¶*distinguish* things ***into*** classes (groups, kinds) 物を種類(など)別にする.

distinguishable, *a.* 区別しうる, 見分けのつく.

M ***plainly*** *distinguishable* 容易に見分けのつく. ¶***readily*** *distinguishable* by … …によってすぐ見分けのつく.

P *distinguishable* ***from*** … …と区別しうる. ¶A simple idea is not *distinguishable* ***into*** different ideas. 簡単な観念は種々の観念に分け得ない.

distinguished, *a.* 著名な.

M the ***most*** *distinguished* among the guests 来客の中でも最も著名な人々.

distort, *v.* ゆがめる.

P His features were *distorted* ***with*** pain. 彼は痛いので顔がゆがんでいた.

distortion, *n.* 曲解; ゆがみ.

Q ***deliberate*** *distortion* of facts 故意に行う事実のわい曲. ¶Japan often suffers from ***repeated*** *distortions* of national life. 日本はその国民生活がしばしばゆがめられて伝えられるので困る. ¶a ***wilful*** *distortion* of facts 故意に行う事実のわい曲.

distract, *v.* 気をそらす; 迷わす; 取乱させる.

P He was *distracted* ***at*** some occurrence. 彼はあるできごとのために心を取乱した. ¶He was *distracted* ***between*** two objects. 彼は二つの物に気を配った. ¶Her mind is *distracted* ***by*** fear (grief) 彼女は恐怖(など)のため気が狂いそうだ. ‖ My ears are *distracted* ***by*** noises. 私はやかましくて耳ががんがんする. ¶*distract* one's mind ***from*** a task 人の心を仕事から他に転ぜしめる.【類】His attentions were *distracted* ***from*** his study. / Noise *distracts* my attention ***from*** reading. ¶*distract* the mind ***with*** cares 心配で心を取乱す ‖ *distract* a person ***with*** talk (＝conversation) 話しかけて人の気を散らす.

distraction, *n.* 気晴らし; 騒じょう; 狂乱, 乱心.

Q ***political*** *distractions* 政治上の紛争. ¶***worldly*** *distractions* 俗事.

P She scarcely knew what she was doing ***in*** her *distraction*. 彼女は気が転倒して自分が何をしてるのかも分らないほどだった. ¶***through*** *distraction* うっかりして. ¶The headache drives me ***to*** *distraction*. 私は頭が痛くてたまらない. ‖ love … ***to*** *distraction* 気が狂うほど…にほれる.

P^2 a *distraction* ***from*** grief 気晴らし.【類】Labor is often a *distraction* ***from*** gloomy thoughts. ¶*distractions* ***in*** a state 国内の騒じょう.

distrain, *v.* 差押える, 強制執行する.

P *distrain* property ***from*** a person 人の財産を差押える.

distraint, *n.* 動産差押え.

P His property was placed ***under*** *distraint*. 彼の財産は差押えられた.

distress, *n.* 苦痛; 苦難; 傷心; 動産差押え.

V ***alleviate*** Germany's economic *distress* ドイツの経済的困難を緩和する. ¶***feel*** excessive *distress* 非常に悲しい. ¶***mitigate*** (＝alleviate) the *distress* occasioned by … …のため起った困難を軽減する. ¶***levy*** *distress* on (＝distrain) … …を差押える. ¶***occasion*** mental *distress* はんもんを起す. ¶***relieve*** *distress* 困難を救う. ¶***suffer*** *distress* from loss of friends 友をなくして傷心する.

Q the current ***economic*** *distress* 目下の不況. ¶He is in ***deep*** *distress*. 彼は非常に難渋している. ‖ in the hours of his ***deepest*** *distress* 彼がどん底生活をしていた時に. ¶a ***dire*** (＝***terrible***) *distress* 大難. ¶Few professors are freed from ***economic*** *distress*. 生活難で苦しまない大学教授は少ない. ¶General ***financial*** *distress* pervaded the country. 全般的な財政難が国中に拡まった. ¶secret proprietary cures for stomach trouble or ***intestinal*** *distress* 胃腸病の家伝秘薬. ¶***triple*** *distress* 三重苦.

Q^2 ease ***stomach*** *distress* 胃病を楽にする. ¶***unemploy-***

ment distress 就職難. 「友.
P ships *in distress* 難船 ‖ a friend *in distress* 難渋している
P² *distress by* bereavement 死に別れた心の悩み. ¶ *distress for* rent 家賃の悩み. ¶ *distress from* thirst 苦しいのどのかわき. ¶ He is a great *distress* ***to*** the family. 彼は家族に
distress, *v.* 苦しめる, 悩ます. ∟とって悩みの種だ.
M His family is ***deeply*** *distressed.* 彼の家族は非常に困っている. ¶ The news *distressed* me ***greatly.*** その知らせには実に困っている. ¶ I am ***much*** *distressed* to hear it. そのことを聞いて非常に心を痛めている. ¶ He is ***sorely*** *distressed.* 彼はひどく困っている.
P He *distressed* himself ***about*** the matter. 彼はそのことで悩んだ. ¶ He is *distressed* ***at*** his loss of property. 彼は財産を失ったことを悩んでいる. ‖ be *distressed* ***at*** the sight (news) その光景(など)に失望している.【類】I am *distressed* ***at*** your failure. ¶ I am *distressed* ***by*** thirst. 私はのどがかわいたのに苦しんでいる.【類】He is *distressed* ***by*** misfortune. ¶ I am *distressed* ***for*** him. 彼のことが心配だ. ‖ He is *distressed* ***for*** money. 彼は金に困っている. ¶ He is *distressed* ***in*** feelings (mind). 彼は胸(など)に悩みをいだいている. ¶ *distress* a city ***into*** surrender 都市を攻めて降参させる. ¶ He is *distressed* ***over*** the action of the City Assembly. 彼は市会の行動に心を痛めている. ¶ He is *distressed* ***with*** pain. 彼は痛みで弱っている. ‖ He is *distressed* ***with*** debts. 彼は借金で困っている.
M ***greatly*** *distressed* 大いに失望落胆して. ¶ She was ***more*** *distressed* in his attitude than at the failure of business 仕事の失敗そのものよりも彼の態度により失望した.
distribute, *v.* 分配する, 配布する; 分類する; 散布する.
M more ***equally*** *distributed* もっと同じように配分されて. ¶ *distribute* the paint ***evenly*** over the wall ペンキを壁に均等に塗る ‖ be ***evenly*** *distributed* among … …に平等に分配される. ¶ *distribute* ***far*** and ***wide*** 広く配布する. ¶ *distribute* ***free*** (=***gratis***) 無料で配る. ¶ ***widely*** *distribute* 広く配布する.
P *distribute* books in a library ***according to*** their subjects 図書室の書籍を科目別に分ける. ¶ *distribute* books ***among*** students 書物を学生の間に配る.【類】*distribute* alms ***among*** the poor ‖ the sexes are evenly *distributed* ***among*** … …では男女の数が平均している. ¶ The fund will be wisely *distributed* ***in*** the best interests of those in need of relief. その資金は救助を必要とする者にとって最も有利に配布するのが賢明であろう. ¶ *distribute* plants ***into*** orders 植物を分類する. ¶ *distribute* ink ***on*** printing rollers 印刷機のローラーにインキを塗る. ¶ *distribute* manure ***over*** a field 肥料を畑一面にまく ‖ The army *distributed* itself ***over*** the country. 軍隊を国内至る所に配備した. ¶ *distribute* gas ***through*** the house 家中各所にガスを引く. ¶ *distribute* ***throughout*** a country 国内一般に配布する ‖ *distribute* broadcast ***throughout*** the globe 世界中に放送網をしく. ¶ *distribute* prizes ***to*** the victors 優勝者に賞品を授与する ‖ *distribute* folders ***to*** passengers 旅客に折本を配布する ‖ Christ *distributed* the loaves ***to*** his disciples. キリストは弟子たちにパンを分け与えた. ¶ *distribute* mail matters ***within*** the delivery zone 配達区域内に郵
distribution, *n.* 分配, 配布, 分布; 配達. ∟便物を配る.
Q a more ***equitable*** *distribution* of wealth より公平な富の分配. ¶ an ***erratic*** *distribution* of letters by post office 郵便局の手紙の誤配. ¶ not for ***gratuitous*** *distribution* 無料配布ではない. ¶ They have a very ***limited*** *distribution.* その流布の範囲がきわめて狭い. ¶ a ***nation-wide*** *distribution* of an article 品物の国内一般の流布. ¶ the ***seasonal*** *distribution* of moral offenses 性犯罪の季節的な配分(夏は多く秋は少いといったような). ¶ ***uneven*** *distribution* of materials 原料の不均衡の配給. ¶ an ***unfair*** *distribution* of lights and shades 不公平な重点のおき方(歴史家など). ¶ be microfilmed for ***world-wide*** *distribution* 広く世界に配布するためにマイクロフィルムに取る.
Q² collect food from farmers for ***city*** *distribution* 都市に配給するため農民から食糧を集める. ¶ make ***food*** *distribution* uniform throughout the country 全国の食糧配給を一様にする. ¶ ***ration*** *distribution* 食糧配給. ¶ ***rice*** *distribution* 米穀配給.
P ***for*** private *distribution* 個人的な配布を目的として.
P² *distribution* ***of*** vessels (freight wagons) 配船(配車). ¶ *distribution* ***of*** an estate ***among*** children 子供たちへの財産分配.
distributor, *n.* 分配者.
Q ***sole*** *distributor* for America 米国一手販売店.
district, *n.* 地方, 区域.
V ***stump*** a *district* 《米》ある地方を遊説する.
Q an ***agricultural*** *district* 農業地方 ‖ a purely ***agricultural*** *district* 純農業地方. ¶ a ***distant*** *district* 遠隔裁判区. ¶ an ***electoral*** *district* 選挙区. ¶ a ***far-famed*** *district* 音に響いた土地. ¶ a ***favored*** *district* 天恵の地. ¶ a ***flat*** *district* 平地(山国に対し). ¶ a ***germ-infected*** *district* 伝染病流行地方. ¶ a ***judicial*** *district* 裁判区. ¶ a ***military*** *district* 軍区. ¶ a ***mountainous*** *district* 山国地方. ¶ a thickly ***populated*** *district* in South London 南ロンドンの人口密集区域. ¶ a ***postal*** *district* 郵便区. ¶ travel in ***remote*** *districts* 辺ぴな土地を旅行する. ¶ live in a ***neighboring*** (=***nearby***) *district* 隣り(近く)の区域に住む. ¶ live in a ***rural*** *district* of North Carolina 北カロライナのいなかに住む. ¶ the ***smallest administrative*** *district* 最小行政区域. ¶ the ***stricken*** *district* [洪水などの]罹災地. ¶ ***suburban*** *districts* 郊外区域. ¶ the ***theatrical*** *district* 劇場街. ¶ ***urban*** and ***rural*** *districts* 都会および田園地方. ¶ ***wooded*** *districts* 森林地帯.
Q² the ***business*** *district* of a city 都市の商業地区 ‖ Chicago's hoop ***business*** *district* シカゴ市のたる製造地区. ¶ one of the quieter ***city*** *districts* 静かな都会区域の一つ. ¶ the ***coal*** *district* 石炭地方. ¶ the supervisor of a ***correction*** and ***rehabilitation*** *district* 矯正保護管区長. ¶ Superstition is still rife in ***country*** *districts.* いなかでは今なお迷信が盛んに行われている. ¶ a ***farming*** *district* 農業地. ¶ his ***home*** *district* 彼の郷里. ¶ the ***lake*** *district* 湖水地. ¶ the ***low-lying sea-front*** *districts* of Tokyo 東京の下町海岸区域. ¶ a ***manufacture*** *district* 工業地. ¶ a ***manufacturing*** *district* 工業地. ¶ a ***midtown*** *district* 都心地区. ¶ in ***mountain*** *districts* 山岳地方では. ¶ a ***poor*** *district* 細民地区.【類】the ***poorest*** *district* of London. ¶ a ***red-light*** *district* 紅灯区域. ¶ a ***remote country*** *district* 僻地. ¶ a newly developed ***residence*** *district* 新開住宅地.【類】the finest ***residence*** *district.* ¶ the heart of the ***retail*** *district* 小売店街区. ¶ the busiest ***shopping*** *district* of the city その市で一番にぎやかな商店街. ¶ a ***silk-growing*** *district* 養蚕地. ¶ a ***slum*** *district* 貧民くつ. ¶ a ***stock-raising*** *district* 牧畜地. ¶ the celebrated ***tea*** *district* of Uji 有名な宇治の茶所. ¶ three blocks off from the heart of the ***theater*** *district* 劇場街の中心から三丁ほど.
P² the *district* ***of*** Hongo=Hongo Ward 本郷区 ‖ a *district* ***of*** campaign=a sector 戦区. ¶ the *district* ***under*** juris-
distrust, *n.* 不信, 疑念, 疑惑. ∟diction 管轄区域.
V ***breed*** *distrust* 不信をかもす. ¶ ***create*** *distrust* between … …の仲をさく. ¶ ***harbor*** *distrust* 疑念を抱く. ¶ He ***has*** a *distrust* of dictatorship. 彼は執政権に対して疑惑を抱いている. ¶ ***sow*** a *distrust* in … …に対する疑惑をいだかせる. 「を保持した.
Q He preserved a ***wise*** *distrust.* 彼は不信という賢い態度
P listen ***with*** *distrust* 疑いをもって聴く.
P² *distrust* ***of*** a person (thing) 人(など)に対する不信.
distrustful, *a.* 疑をいだいている, 疑い深い; 自信のない.
P I am *distrustful* ***of*** his motive (ability). 私は彼の動機(など)に対して疑いをいだいている. ‖ He is *distrustful* ***of*** others. 彼は人を信じない.【類】He is *distrustful* ***of*** him-
disturb, *v.* 妨げる, 騒がす, 不安にする. ∟self.
M All Europe was ***deeply*** *disturbed* by the French Revolution. フランス革命のためにヨーロッパ全土が非常に動揺した. ¶ I am sorry that the dog *disturbed* you ***last night.*** 犬が昨晩あなたの安眠のおじゃまをしてすみませんでした. ¶ be ***mentally*** *disturbed* 精神に異状がある. ¶ *disturb* a person ***unnecessarily*** 不必要に人のじゃまをする.
P I was *disturbed* ***by*** unpleasant dreams. 私は悪夢に安眠を妨げられた. ‖ I was *disturbed* ***by*** callers. 私は客にじゃまをされた. ¶ *disturb* a person ***in*** his sleep (study) 睡眠(など)のじゃまをする ‖ he is much *disturbed* ***in*** mind about … 彼は…を非常に心配している. ¶ He was *disturbed* ***with*** fear. 彼は恐怖で不安にされた. ‖ *disturb* the surface of a pond ***with*** a stick 棒で池の水面をかき回す.
disturbance, *n.* 騒じょう, 騒動, 動揺; 妨害.
V ***cause*** a *disturbance* 動揺をきたす. ¶ ***create*** (=***raise***) a *disturbance* before the house of … …の家の前で騒動を起

す. ¶*foment disturbances* 騒じょうをかもす. ¶*make a disturbance* 騒ぎをやる. 【類】*make* a great *disturbance* about a trifle. ¶call in the police to *quell* a *disturbance* 騒ぎを静めるため警官を呼び入れる. ¶The *disturbances* have been *quieted*. 騒動が静まった. ¶*repress* a *disturbance* 騒ぎを鎮圧する. ¶*suppress* a *disturbance* 騒ぎを静める.

Q an *atmospheric disturbance*〘無電〙空中障害. ¶a *digestive disturbance* 消化不良. ¶Drunken fellows make *frequent disturbances* on the street. 酔っぱらいが往々往来で騒ぎを起す. ¶a *passing disturbance* 一時の騒ぎ. ¶a *political disturbance* 政事上の騒動. ¶suffer from a *psychic disturbance* 精神病にかかる. ¶This led to a *regrettable disturbance* of Austro-Russian relations. これでオーストリア・ロシア国交の悲しむべき破たんとなった. ¶a *seismic disturbance* 地震. ¶a *slight disturbance* ちょっとした妨害.

Q[2] a *labor disturbance* 労働争議. ¶a *school disturbance* 学校騒動.

P *without disturbance* 故障もなく.

disturber, *n.* 妨害者.

Q[2] a *peace disturber* 平和を乱すもの. ¶a *program disturber* 番狂わせ.

disunion, *n.* 分裂, 不和.

Q suppress all *internal disunion* 内輪もめを静める.

disuse, *n.* 不用; 廃止.

Q The word has passed into *complete disuse*. その言葉は全くすたれてしまった.

P rust *from disuse* 使わないのでさびる. ¶come (=fall) *into disuse* すたれる. ¶be rusty *through* (=*by*) *disuse* 使用しないのでさびている.

disuse, *v.* 用いない.

P *disused to* toils 労働に慣れてない.

ditch, *n.* みぞ, ごう.

V *jump* a small *ditch* 小さなみぞをとび越す.

Q die in the *last ditch* 最後まで奮戦して死ぬ ‖ support him to the *last ditch* 最後まで彼を援助する ‖ be driven to the *last ditch* 最後のどんづまりまで追いつめられる.

ditch, *v.* みぞを掘る;〘航空〙不時着させる.

M *ditch out* ごうで防ぎ止める(内へ入れないように).

M[2] The fortress was *ditched in* all around. その城さいは周囲にごうをめぐらしてあった. ¶*ditch up* みぞを掘る.

P The train was *ditched at* ... 列車は…で脱線した. ¶The plane was *ditched off* the shore. 同機は沖合いで不時着した.

ditty, *n.* 歌.

Q a *doleful ditty* 悲しげな歌. ¶a *nursery ditty* 童謡.

divan, *n.* 長いす; サロン.

V There was a *divan placed* near the fireplace. 暖炉のそばに長いすがおいてあった.

Q[2] a *cigar divan* 喫煙室.

dive, *n.* 潜水, 飛込み; 没頭;〘航空〙急降下.

V *make* a *dive* from a spring-board 飛板から水に飛込む ‖ He *made* a *dive* into the nearest restaurant. 彼はもよりの料理店へ飛込んだ. ¶*take* a *dive* into the subject その問題の研究を試みる.

Q What a *beautiful dive!* 実にあざやかな飛込みだ. ¶venture a *high dive* into shallow water 危険を冒して浅い水中に高飛込みをする.

Q[2] go into a *nose dive* 急降下する. ¶a *swallow dive*《米》つばめ型飛込み(両腕を拡げまっさかさまに飛込むこと). ¶a *swan dive*〘水泳〙スワン・ダイヴ.

dive, *v.* 水にもぐる; 没頭する, 専心する.

M *dive deep* into the records of ... …の記録をせんさくする ‖ *dive deep* into the study of ... …の研究に没頭する.

P if you *dive below* the surface you will see that ... 少し突っこんで研究すると…ということが分る. ¶*dive beneath* (=*under*) the water 水底にもぐる. ¶*dive for* pearls 真珠を取りにもぐる. ¶*dive in* the water 水にもぐる. ¶*dive into* the pocket ポケットに手を突込む ‖ *dive into* the sea 海中にもぐる ‖ *dive into* politics 政治に没頭する ‖ *dive into* the depths of science 科学を深く研究する ‖ *dive into* the secrets of ... …の奥義をきわめる. ¶*dive to* the bottom of a subject 問題の根底まできわめる.

diver, *n.* 潜水夫.

V *employ* a *diver* to have the ship examined 船を検査させるために潜水夫を雇う.

Q[2] an *oyster diver* かき(貝)とり(女など). ¶a *pearl diver* 真珠採取夫.

diverge, *v.* 分れる, それる, 分岐する.

P *diverge from* the main road (a track, a person's view) 本道(など)をそれる ‖ *diverge from* the center 中心を離れる ‖ *diverge from* the proper ends of procreation 生殖の本来の目的からそれる. ¶*diverge into* some subject (=topic *or* question) ある問題にそれて行く.

divergence, *n.* 分岐; 相違.

Q there is *considerable divergence* of opinion as to ... …については相当意見がまちまちになっている. ¶a *wide divergence* of opinion 大きな意見の相違. 【類】On this very point the *widest divergence* of view prevails.

P be familiar *with* every *divergence* of opinion 意見の相違をことごとく熟知している.

divergent, *a.* 相違した.

P be *divergent in* opinion 意見がまちまちだ.

diversify, *v.* 様々にする, 不同にする.

P happily *diversified by* ... …のために幸にも単調が破られて. ¶The surface is *diversified with* high mountains and fertile valleys and plains. その土地は高山や肥えたる流域や平原やで変化に富んでいる.

diversion, *n.* 転換; 気晴し, なぐさみ, 娯楽.

Q a drive through the Finger Lakes section of New York is a *delightful diversion* at any time during the summer. ニューヨークのフィンガー湖方面を自動車で乗り回すのは夏期いずれのときにでも愉快な気晴しである. ¶Watching the clouds is a *fascinating diversion*. 雲を見るのは楽しい気晴らしだ. ¶Chess is a *favorite diversion* of mine. 将棋は私の好きな遊びだ. ¶afford a *mental diversion* to ... …に精神的娯楽になる. ¶Golf is a *popular diversion*. ゴルフは人気のある娯楽だ. ¶a *social diversion* 社会的娯楽.

P[2] the *diversion of* the mind *from* study 心を勉強から他に転じること(気ばらし). ¶the *diversion of* the purpose *to* another object 目的を他のことに転じること.

diversity, *n.* 相違, 不同.

V great *diversity* of opinion *obtains* as to ... …については大いに意見の不一致がある.

Q Concerning ... there is *great diversity* of opinion. …に関しては大いに意見の相違がある. ‖ *Great diversity* of opinion exists as to the origin of the word "shilling." シリングという語の起源に関しては意見がなかなか一致しない. ¶there is *wide diversity* of opinion regarding ... …に関して非常な意見の相違がある.

P[2] a *diversity in* unity [団体などの]不統一 ‖ *diversity in* disposition 性質の相違. ¶*diversity of* language 言葉の相違 ‖ there has been some *diversity of* opinion as to ... …については幾分異論がある.

divert, *v.* 他にそらす; 転用する; 気を転じさせる.

M He is *easily diverted*. 彼はつまらない事を喜ぶ.

P *divert* one's interest (attention) *from* something あるものから興味(など)を他に転じさせる ‖ He was *diverted from* his purpose. 彼は目的を変えた. ¶*divert* money *from* military *into* civil channels 資金を軍事方面から民間の事業に向ける ‖ *divert* the subject *into* another channel (=a side issue) 話題を他の方面に転じる ‖ *divert* a stream *into* a new channel 川の流れを別の方向へ転じる ‖ She *diverts* herself *in* singing. 彼女は気晴しに歌を歌う. ¶The money was *diverted to* some other purposes. その金は他の目的に転用された. ¶The boys were *diverted with* sports. 子供らは遊びに気を取られていた.

divest, *v.* はぐ, 奪う.

P *divest* a person *of* his rank (title, right) 人の位階(など)を奪う ‖ I have endeavored to *divest* this book as much as possible *of* technicalities. この本にはできるだけ術語を使わないように努力した. ‖ He *divested* himself *of* his clothes. 彼は着物を脱いだ. ‖ I cannot *divest* myself *of* the idea. 私はその考えから脱することができない. ‖ be *divested of* the disguise ばけの皮がはげる. 【類】*divest* the subject *of* all sentimental considerations / *divest* one's mind *of* fear.

divide, *n.* 分割; 分水れい.

Q the *Great Divide* 大分水れい(米国ロッキー山脈をいう) ‖ Four years have drifted by since he crossed the *Great Divide*. 彼が幽明境をことにしてからすでに四年たった.

divide, *v.* 分ける, 割る; 隔離する; 区分する; 分配する; 分裂させる; 分裂する.

M Garden crops may be *conveniently divided* into fruits, flowers and vegetables. 園芸作物は便宜上果物・花き・野菜に区分される. ¶We may hope that happiness is more *equally divided* than wealth. 幸福が富よりも一層平等に配分されているものと見てよかろう. ‖ The meeting was attended by 2,000 men and women, about ***equally divided***. その会にはほぼ半々の男女が二千名出席した. ¶profits ***properly divided*** according to the efforts made by the partners. ¶*divide* ***right*** in two 真二つに割る. ¶***sharply divided*** 画然と区分して.

P a city *divided* ***against*** itself 内輪もめをやっている都市.【類】The party was *divided* ***against*** itself. ¶*divide* the student body ***along*** sex lines 学生団体を性別に取扱う(これでは共学の意味がない). ¶He *divided* his property ***among*** the children. 彼は財産を子供らに分けてやった.【類】*divide* profits ***among*** shareholders (株主) / He *divided* the cake ***among*** six boys. ¶*divide* it ***between*** two persons それを二人に分配する.【類】*divide* profits ***between*** partners / Expenses are to be *divided* ***between*** us. ‖ the Nobel prize was *divided* ***between*** ... and ... そのノーベル賞は…と…と二人で受けることになった. ¶Twelve can be *divided* ***by*** three. 十二は三で割れる. ‖ *Divide* 8 ***by*** 2, and you get 4 (8÷2=4). 八を二で割ると四になる. ‖ *divide* ***by*** lot くじで分ける. ¶may fairly be *divided* ***for*** literary purposes with two periods of almost equal length, from ... to and from ... to ... 文学上の目的にはほゞ同じ長さの二つの時期すなわち…から…まで及び…から…までに分けられる. ¶A wall *divides* the room ***from*** the parlour. このへやと客間は壁で仕切ってある. ‖ *divide* the sick ***from*** the others 病人を隔離する ‖ *divided* ***from*** the main land by a strait 一衣帯水の. ¶Doctors are *divided* ***in*** opinion as to the hygienic value of indoor skating. 屋内スケートの衛生的価値については医者の意見がまちまちである.【類】The meeting was greatly *divided* ***in*** opinion. ‖ *divide* an apple ***in*** two りんごを二つに割る. ¶*divide* it ***into*** two halves それを二等分する.【類】be *divided* ***into*** equal proportions / may be *divided* ***into*** three sections (三節に) / the subject may be *divided* ***into*** the two following groups (次の二部に): / *divide* the cases (その事件を) ***into*** three groups / The river *divides* the city ***into*** two parts. / *divide* the earth ***into*** two hemispheres (両半球に) ‖ Here the river *divides* ***into*** two branches. ここで川が二つに分岐する. ‖ a trade *divided* ***into*** several branches 数部門に分れている商売.【類】*divided* ***into*** two grades designated B and C class / *divided* ***into*** five categories (=divisions) / They can be *divided* ***into*** four headings. / They may be *divided* ***into*** two general classes. / may be *divided* ***into*** three subgroups / They are *divided* ***into*** many camps (幾派にも). / They *divided* ***into*** two bands. ‖ France is *divided* ***into*** 87 departments. フランスは八十七県に区画されている. ‖ The country was *divided* ***into*** twenty-eight feudal lordships or principalities. 国家は廿八の藩すなわち大名の領地に分れていた. ‖ *divide* chemistry ***into*** inorganic and organic 化学を無機と有機とに分ける ‖ The land was *divided* ***into*** house lots. その土地は譲地になった. ‖ how a word is *divided* ***into*** syllables 語のつづりによる分け方. ¶The advocates of direct taxation are further *divided* ***into*** two schools. 直接税の賛成者はさらに二派に分れている. ‖ The school year is *divided* ***into*** three terms. 学年は三学期に分れる. ¶*divide* the House ***on*** a question ある問題に関し(賛否の数を確かめるために)議員を二組に分ける ‖ They are going to *divide* ***on*** this matter. この問題では彼らの意見が分れそうだ.【類】Opinion is *divided* ***on*** the point. ¶The journey occupied some ten months of almost continuous travel, *divided* ***over*** two summers. それは二夏にわたる十カ月間の旅行でほとんどひっきりなしに旅から旅を続けた. ¶Critics have *divided* (=differed) ***upon*** this matter. 批評家たちはこの問題に関して説をことにした. ¶*divide* profits ***with*** workmen 利益を職工と分ける ‖ Since the Revolution of 1868, the *samurai* of Choshu have *divided* ***with*** those of Satsuma the chief direction of public affairs. 一八六八年の維新後は長州の武士と薩摩の武士とが主として国務に参与した.

dividend, *n.* 利益配当, 配当金.

V The shares ***brought*** no *dividend* last term. 株は前期に配当がなかった. ¶The Hamburg-American line, for the first time for fifteen years, failed to ***declare*** a *dividend*. ハンブルグ・アメリカ汽船会社はこの十五年間に初めて配当金の支払ができなかった. ‖ ***declare*** *dividends* of 25 per cent per annum 年二割五分の配当をする ‖ ***declare*** no *dividend* 配当据置とする.【類】The company is expected to ***declare*** a larger (smaller) *dividend* than last. ‖ A *dividend* at the rate of 20 per cent per annum was ***declared*** for the half-year ending 30th June. 年二割の利益配当が六月三十日をもって終る半期分として告知された. ¶***distribute*** a *dividend* at the rate of 14 per cent 一割四分の割で配当をする. ¶***draw*** *dividends* on half-a-million pounds' worth of stock 五十万ポンドの株券に対して利益配当を受ける. ¶***earn*** a handsome *dividend* 結構な利益配当を受ける. ¶***equalize*** *dividends* 配当金を平等にする. ¶***maintain*** its *dividend* at 12 per cent 一割二分の配当を維持する. ¶***make*** a *dividend* from ... …から配当金を受ける. ¶The company was forced to ***pass*** its *dividend*. その会社は無配当のやむなきに至った. ¶***pay*** good *dividends* よい配当をする ‖ ***pay*** a *dividend* at the rate of ... per cent …パーセントの利益配当をする.【類】The company is in a position to ***pay*** a *dividend* of 40% in comparison with 10% for 1908-9. ¶The company had to ***suspend*** *dividends*. 会社は無配当のやむなきに至った.

Q pay a ***big*** *dividend* 大分の配当金を払う. ¶pay ***fair*** *dividends* upon the capital 資本金に対してかなりの配当をする. ¶a ***fat*** *dividend* 好配当. ¶declare a ***heavy*** *dividend* 巨額の利益配当を告知する. ¶The directors have resolved to pay an ***interim*** *dividend* of ... per cent. 重役は…パーセントの中間配当を払うことに決定した. ¶***last annual*** *dividend* 昨年度の配当金 ‖ The shares yielded ... % p. a. on ***last annual*** *didend*. その株は前年度の配当で年…パーセントの利回りになった. ¶The company pays a ***regular, reasonable*** *dividend* which it has not missed paying since its corporation. 同会社はいつもきまって相当な配当金を払ってきたのである. ¶a ***special*** *dividend* 特別利益配当.

Q² pay a 50 per cent dividend plus a 100 per cent ***stock*** *dividend* as a bonus 十割の株式配当の外に五割の特別配当をする.

P² a *dividend* ***of*** ten per cent 一割の配当金. ¶a *dividend* ***on*** shares 持株に対する配当. ¶*dividends* ***to*** shareholders 株主配当金. ¶*dividends* ***upon*** investments 投資に対する配当.

dividing-line, *n.* 分界線.

V it is difficult to ***draw*** a sharp *dividing-line* between ... and ... …間に画然たる分界線を設けることは困難である.

Q a ***precise*** *dividing-line* between ... …間の正確な分界線.

divination, *n.* 占い.

V ***practice*** *divination* 占いを業とする.

diving, *n.* 飛込み(ダイビング).

Q² ***fancy*** *diving* 曲飛込み. ¶***somersault*** *diving* 宙返り飛込み.

divinity, *n.* 神格; 神.

Q Is Kompira a ***Buddhist*** or a ***Shinto*** *divinity?* 金比羅様はお寺ですか神社ですか. ¶a ***false*** *divinity* 偽りの神. ¶Mercury was the ***presiding*** *divinity* over commerce. マーキュリーは商業の守り神であった.

P² Doctor ***of*** *Divinity* 神学博士 (D.D. と略す).

divisible, *a.* 分けられる.

M they are ***broadly*** *divisible* into ... それは…に大別することができる.

P² be *divisible* ***by*** 2 二で割れる. ¶It is naturally *divisible* ***into*** four distinct periods. それは自然四つのはっきりした時代に区画することができる.

division, *n.* 分割, 区分; 分配; 部, 組; 採決; 異論.

V ***base*** a *division* solely on ... 全然…に基いて区分する. ¶The *division* of the property was fairly ***made***. 財産の分配が公平になされた. ‖ ***make*** a threefold *division* of the period into ... その時代を三分して…とする. ¶The *division* was ***taken***. 決をとった. ¶*division* ***arose*** over the interpretation of ... …の解釈に対して異論が起った.

Q the largest ***administrative*** *division* of the country その国の最大の行政区画. ¶a ***broad*** *division* is made between ... and ... …に大別されている. ¶There is ***considerable*** *division* of authority on the subject. この問題に関して典拠が著しく異なっている. ¶leaders in all the ***different*** *divisions* of life 各方面の指導者たち. ¶upon an ***equal*** *division* 平等に分配すると. ¶Professor James E. Lough, Dean of the ***Extramural*** *Division* of New York University ニューヨーク大学校外教育部部長ジェームズ・イー・ラウ教授. ¶***factious*** *divisions* 党派の区分. ¶the ***girls'*** *division* of the Aoyama-gakuin 青山学院女子部. ¶a ***judicious*** *division* of labor 賢明な労力の分配. ¶three ***main*** *divisions* 三大別. ¶the existing ***political*** *divisions* of the earth 現在の世界の政治的分野. ¶a ***twofold*** *division* 二分

法(二種に分類すること).

Q^{2} the *Accommodation Division* 調達部. ¶an ***administration division*** 行政部. ¶a ***branch division*** 支部. ¶a ***mail-sales division*** 通信販売部.

P The Opposition has therefore lost one seat, counting two votes ***on*** a *division*. それ故反対党は一座席を失って採決の結果二票を算した. ¶bring ... ***under*** this *division* ... をこの部門に入れる. ¶get all the benefits ***without division*** 一手に利益を占める ‖ carry, ***without division***, a motion that ... …という動議を全会一致で可決する.

P^{2} the *division* ***of*** opinion on the bill 該案に対する意見の相違 ‖ a *division* ***of*** spoils 分捕品の分配. 【類】a *division* ***of*** opinion among ...

divorce, *n.* 離婚; 分離.

V ***get*** a *divorce* 離縁ができる ‖ ***get*** a *divorce* and get clear 離別して結婚生活を清算する. ¶***justify*** *divorce* 離婚を正当と認める. ¶He ***procured*** a *divorce* from her, after fifteen years of wedded life. 結婚生活十五年の後彼は妻と離婚した. ¶refuse to ***recognize*** a *divorce* 離婚の承認を拒否する. ¶***secure*** (=***obtain or get***) a *divorce* from her husband 彼女の夫と縁を切る. ¶***seek*** *divorce* 離縁を求める. ¶***win*** a *divorce* from ... …から離婚することができる.

Q ***collusive*** *divorce* なれ合いの離婚. ¶***complete*** *divorce* (別居でない)本式の離婚. ¶A *divorce* is ***impending.*** 離婚が差迫っている. ¶***limited*** *divorce* 夫婦別居.

P^{2} I am not in favor of the *divorce* ***between*** English composition and English grammar. 私は英作文と英文法との分離教授には賛成しない. ‖ a *divorce* ***between*** husband and wife 夫婦別れ. ¶Who ever heard of a man getting a *divorce* ***from*** a woman who was a good cook? 料理のうまい細君と離婚した男が一体あったろうか. ¶*divorce* ***of*** sense ***from*** sound in verse 韻文における音と意味の不調和.

divorce, *v.* 離婚する; 関係を絶つ.

M be married and not ***legally*** *divorced* 結婚していてまだ法律上離婚の手続をしていない.

P He was *divorced* ***from*** his wife. 彼は妻と離婚した. ‖ *divorced* ***from*** commercialism 商人気質を離れて ‖ He *divorced* himself ***from*** the party. 彼は党と関係を絶った. ‖ education *divorced* ***from*** religion 宗教から分離した教育 ‖ become *divorced* ***from*** real life 実生活から退く.

divorcee, *n.* 被離婚者.

Q a ***32-year-old*** *divorcee* 三十二歳の被離婚者.

do, *v.* なす, 行う; 見物する; 翻訳する; 起居する.

M The novel would *do* ***admirably*** for the stage. その小説は舞台に掛けたら(上場したら)すばらしいだろう. ‖ He *did* the host ***admirably.*** 彼は主人役をりっぱにやった. ¶*do* ***again*** やり直す. ¶Everything cannot be *done* ***at once.*** 何でもとっさにできるとは限らない. ¶*do* ***away*** with the evils of ... …の弊害を除く ‖ Let's *do* ***away*** with all ceremonies. ざっくばらんにやろうじゃないか. ‖ *do* ***away*** with the last hope of ... …の最後の希望を失わせる. 【類】*do* ***away*** with superstitions (an evil practice, a custom) / *do* ***away*** with the necessity of ... ‖ The Shogun Yoshimune *did* ***away*** with the proscription of European books. 将軍吉宗はヨーロッパの書籍閲読の禁止を解いた. ‖ The ordinance was straightway *done* ***away*** with. この法令は直ちに廃された. ¶He *did* ***badly*** at trying to suppress a smile. 彼はこみあげる微笑を押え切れなかった. ¶upon this head I cannot *do* ***better*** than quote some remarks by ... この項目に関して…の言説を引用するのが最もよいと思う. 【類】One who wishes to know the English language cannot *do* ***better*** than give his days and his nights to the study of the New English Dictionary.—G. H. Krapp, Modern English. ‖ Do not buy if you think you can *do* ***better*** by waiting. 待っている方がよいと思うなら買うな. ‖ resolve to *do* ***better*** next time この次にもっとよくやろうと決心する ‖ You can *do* no ***better*** than that. そうするに越したことはない. ‖ Nothing that one art can *do* ***better*** should be attempted by the other. 一つのやり方でよりよくやれることは別のやり方でやってはいけない. 【類】These are things they *do* ***better*** abroad than we do them at home. ¶Most ***certainly*** I *do*. 確かにそうです (Do you like (etc.)... 型の疑問文の答えとして). ¶I want to *do* the Rhine and Switzerland ***comfortably*** in 3 weeks; please say how you would advise to divide the time. 私はライン地方とスイスを三週間で楽に見物したいと思います. どう時間を割当てたらよいものでしょう. ¶Perhaps you can persuade him to *do* it ***differently.*** 多分君ならそれを別なやり方でやるように彼に忠告できるでしょう. ¶Oh, that is ***easily*** *done.* えー, それは容易にできます. ¶be ***easily*** *done* for やすやすやられる. ¶*do* that ***effectively*** 有効にそれをする. ¶It *does* most ***excellently.*** りっぱに役に立つ. ¶Well begun is ***half*** *done.* 物事は始めが大事. ¶He *did* (=treated) us ***handsomely.*** 彼はわれわれを手厚くもてなした. ¶They asked ***how*** he was *doing.* 彼らは彼がどうしているかたずねた. ¶***How beautifully*** the landscape is *done!* 風景画が実に美事にできている. ¶I ***just*** can't *do* it. 私にはそれはどうしてもできない. ¶*do* ***little*** toward ... …のためにほとんど尽さない. ¶He lives longest who *does* ***most.*** 最も多く仕事をした人が最も長生きをした人だ. ¶*do* so ***much*** to ... …するのにあずかって大いに力がある. ¶*do* ***much*** to humanity 大いに人道のために尽す ‖ It will *do* ***much*** to accelerate its realization. それはその実現を早める上に大いに効果があるだろう. 【類】I will *do* as ***much*** as I can. ¶It will ***never*** *do.* そりやだめだ. ¶That will *do* very ***nicely.*** それで結構です. ¶a firm which is *doing* ***none too well*** 一向振わない商店. ¶What are you *doing* ***out here***? (子供に)こんなとこで何してるの. ¶Everything had to be *done* ***over again.*** すっかり新規まき直しにしなければならなかった. ¶A little thing *done* ***perfectly*** is better than a big thing done badly. 小事も完全にやれば大事を不完全になすにまさる. ¶Can such a thing be ***possibly*** *done?* 一体そんなことができるだろうか. ¶What is worth doing is worth *doing* ***promptly.*** 善は急げ. ¶*do* it ***reluctantly*** いやいややる. ¶***resolutely*** *do* it 断固としてそれを行う. ¶you will *do* ***right*** to ... 君は…するがよい ‖ frighten the young to *do* ***right*** 若い人をおどかして正しいことをやらせる ‖ fail to *do* ***right*** by ... …に対して処置を誤まる. ¶be ***simply*** *done* 造作ない. ¶by ***so*** *doing* そうすれば ‖ I should have *done* ***so.*** そうすべきであった. ¶Those fruit trees are *doing* ***splendidly.*** その果樹は成績がよい. ¶*do* one's work ***thoroughly*** 仕事を十分にやる. ¶***unwillingly*** *do* one's work 不承無承仕事をする. ¶*do* ***unwisely*** in ... …についてまずいことをする. ¶carefully *done* ***up*** in paper 丁寧に紙包にした. ¶It cannot be *done* ***vicariously.*** それは代理ではできない. ¶*do* ***well*** in his college work 大学の勉強をりっぱにやる ‖ ***Well*** *done,* son! [息子に]よくやった. 【類】The task has been ***well*** *done.* / All the boys except one have *done* ***well.*** / The great geniuses of the world have rarely *done* ***well*** in their schools. / He *did* ***well*** in English but badly in mathematics. ‖ You have *done* ***well.*** 君はでかした(えらい). ‖ It would *do* ***well*** to follow the intelligent German example. この賢明なドイツの例にならうがよかろう. ‖ You'll *do* ***well*** to go home. うちへ帰る方がよい. ‖ You may *do* ***well*** in keeping it secret. 黙っていた方がいい. ‖ He is *doing* ***well,*** thank you. 無事でいる. 有難う. ‖ Wounded soldiers are *doing* fairly ***well.*** 負傷者は経過がよい. ‖ it will *do* ***well*** to ... すべからく…すべし ‖ The publisher *did* so ***well*** with the book that a cheaper edition of it will be issued shortly. その本がよく売れたので出版者は間もなく普及版を出すだろう. ‖ I *did* ***well*** not to have done so. そうしなくってよかった. ‖ That will *do* just as ***well.*** それでもよい. ‖ It would *do* us ***well.*** それもわれわれの薬になる. ¶you will *do* ***wisely*** to ... 君は…するのが賢明だ. ¶*do* ***wrong*** やり損う ‖ The children *did* very ***wrong*** to laugh at you. 子供たちが君をちょう笑するなんて飛んでもないことだ.

M^{2} Excuse my left hand; my right hand was *done* ***in*** in Canada. 左手で失礼します; 右手をカナダで使いすぎましたから[英国皇太子が歓迎攻めにあった後での言葉]. ¶I *did* my work ***over.*** 仕事をやり直した. ‖ The house needs to be *done* ***up.*** その家は改装を要する. ‖ a house neatly *done* ***up*** きれいに片づいた家 ‖ *do* ***up*** (=put into order) one's room へやを片づける ‖ *do* ***up*** a bundle (parcel) 包みを作る ‖ *Do* this ***up*** in paper for me. これを紙に包んで下さい ‖ *do* ***up*** things in bundles 品物を束ねる. 【類】*do* ***up*** books in a package 本を包みにする ‖ *do* ***up*** one's hair 髪を結う ‖ her hair *done* ***up*** in a fashionable way 当世風に結い上げた髪 ‖ We were completely *done* ***up*** after walking many miles. 何マイルも歩いたのでへとへとになった.

P What shall be *done* ***about*** it? それはどうすればよいか. ‖ I want something *done* ***about*** it. [言葉でなく]実行しても

らいたい. ¶He is *doing* very well ***at*** his business. 彼は商売でもうけている. ‖ *do* well ***at*** games 競技をうまくやる. ¶there is nothing to *do* ***beyond*** just to ... しさえすればよい. ¶Do to others as you would be *done* ***by***. 人にやってもらいたいように人にせよ. ¶*do* something ***by*** the surroundings (a person) 周囲の事情(など)によってことをなす ‖ *do* ***by*** halves 中途半ばにやる. ¶What have they *done* ***for*** humanity? 彼らは人道のために何を為したか. ‖ I'm afraid he is *done* ***for***. 彼はしてやられはしなかったかと心配している. ‖ You must not throw that away; it will *do* ***for*** something. それを捨ててはいけない, 何かの役に立つだろう. ‖ Please *do* what you can ***for*** me. 君にできることをして下さい. ‖ You won't *do* ***for*** a teacher (=school). 教師には向かない. ‖ He is fond of talking and anyone *did* ***for*** a listener. あの人は相手かまわずしゃべるのが好きだ. ¶"*do*" her ***in*** water-colors 彼女の姿を水彩画にする ‖ *Do* it ***in*** spare time. それを暇のときにしなさい. ¶*do* (=render *or* translate) literally ***into*** English 英語に逐語訳する. ¶My goodness! What's the receiver *doing* ***off*** the hook? おやまあ! 受話機が外れて, どうしたんでしょう. ¶They've *done* me ***out of*** my money. あれらは私の金をせしめた. ¶He was *done* ***to*** death (=killed). 彼は殺された. ‖ These things have been *done* ***to*** death in print. これらのことはすでに論じつくされた. ‖ *do* one's duty ***to*** others 他人に対する自己の務めを果す ‖ fish *done* ***to*** a beautiful brown きつね色によく焼けたさかな. ¶*do* something ***toward*** the happiness (=good) of others 他人の幸福のために何かを為す ‖ *do* much ***toward*** ... 大いに...のために尽す. ¶We must *do* ***unto*** others as we would have them do unto us were our relations reversed. わが身をつねって人の身の痛さを知るようにせねばならない. ¶One does not know how to *do* ***with*** a fellow like you. 君のような男にはどうして良いか分りやしない. ‖ What is to be *done* ***with*** it? それをどう処置したらよいか. ‖ but what's that got to *do* ***with*** ...? しかし...と何の関係があるか ‖ I will return it to you as soon as *done* ***with***. 用が済んだらすぐ返します. ‖ those who have almost *done* ***with*** life and those who are just beginning it 年寄りと赤ん坊 ‖ What do you intend to *do* ***with*** your future? 君は将来どうする積りか. ‖ This is an object lesson teaching how much can be *done* ***with*** little. これは小をもって為しうる所いかに大なるかの実物教訓である. ‖ He has *done* London ***with*** his red guide-book under arm. 彼は赤い案内書を小わきに抱えてロンドンを見物した. ‖ this *done* ***with***, I shall next ... それから... ‖ Let's have *done* ***with*** it. もうそんなことはよそう. ‖ I don't know what to do ***with*** him. 彼をもてあましている. ‖ I don't know what to *do* ***with*** myself. 自分自身をどうしてよいか分らない. ‖ Be a man, and have *done* ***with*** her. 男だ, 思い切ってしまえ. ‖ I wished he had the courage to have *done* ***with*** life. 彼が命を捨てるだけの勇気があればよいと思った. ‖ I have nothing to *do* ***with*** the matter. 僕はそのことと全く無関係だ. ‖ That won't *do* ***with*** me. それは始末におえない(だめだ). ‖ It could only be *done* ***with*** difficulty. それはなかなか骨が折れるだろう. 【類】 Nothing can be *done* ***with*** the matter yet. / But what has that to *do* ***with*** this? ‖ I am *done* up ***with*** writing all day. 《俗》終日書き物をしたのでひどく疲れた. ¶Before buying anything it is well to ask whether one could not *do* ***without*** it. 何でも買う前にそれなしに済まされないかどうかを考えて見るがよい.

docility, *n.* 温順.

Q with the ***greatest*** *docility* いかにも温順に.

dock, *n.* 船渠(ドック); 被告席.

V ***dry*** *dock* ドックの水を干す. ¶***enter*** a *dock* ドックに入る.

Q² a ***dry*** *dock* 乾渠(普通のドック). ¶a ***floating*** *dock* 浮ドック. ¶a ***ship-building*** *dock* 造船ドック.

P ships at sea or ***at*** *dock* 海上または船渠にある船. ¶stand ***in*** the *dock* 法廷で調べられる, 審問される ‖ The ship is said to be ***in*** *dock*, her repairs not having been yet completed. 船は入渠中でまだ修繕が終らないということだ. ¶come ***into*** *dock* 入渠する ‖ tack a ship ***into*** *dock* 船をドックに入れる ‖ The Leviathan went ***into*** No. 1 dry *dock* at Rowloon on Saturday morning. レヴァイアサン号は土曜日の朝ロールーンの一号乾船渠に入った. ¶come ***out of*** *dock* 出渠する

dock, *v.* 入渠する.

P *dock* ***at*** a port ある港で入渠する. ¶The ship will have to *dock* ***for*** repairs. 修理のためドックに入れなければならないだろう.

docket, *n.* 《英》訴訟事件一覧表; 《米》事務予定表.

Q² the ***trial*** *docket* 訴訟事件一覧表.

P be placed ***on*** the *docket* 予定表にのっている.

docketing, *n.* 訴訟事件表記.

P² *docketing* ***of*** appeal 上訴事件の事件表記.

doctor, *n.* 医者; 博士; 《俗》修繕師.

V ***call in*** a *doctor* 医者を呼ぶ. ¶***consult*** a *doctor* 医者にかゝる ‖ I have ***consulted*** a *doctor* on this point. この点について医者と相談した. ‖ I suggest [that] you ***consult*** the *doctor* at once. 直ぐに医者にかかり給え. ¶***get*** a *doctor* 医者に来てもらう. ¶Go and ***fetch*** a *doctor*. 医者を呼んで来い. ¶***see*** a *doctor* 医者にみてもらう.

V² *Doctors* ***differ***. 医者の意見が違う. ¶You should not ... until the *doctor* ***sanctions*** it. 医者の許しがないうちは...をしてはいけない.

Q a ***fashionable*** *doctor* 良い患家のある医者. ¶a ***medical*** *doctor* 医師. ¶***Chinese*** *doctors* 漢方医. ¶***our*** *doctor* かかりつけの医者. ¶a ***practicing*** *doctor* 開業医.

Q² an ***army*** *doctor* 軍医. ¶a ***beauty*** *doctor* 美容術師. ¶an ***eye*** *doctor* 目医者. ¶a ***chair*** *doctor* いす修繕屋. ¶the ***family*** *doctor* かかりつけの医者. ¶a ***herb*** *doctor* 漢法医. ¶an ***intern*** *doctor* 病院居住の医師. ¶a ***lady*** *doctor* 女医. ¶an ***old-school*** *doctor* 旧式の医者. ¶a ***panel*** *doctor* [地方医師簿所載の]健康保険医. ¶a ***port*** *doctor* 港務所付属医. ¶a ***quack*** *doctor* やぶ医者. ¶***women*** *doctors* 女医たち.

P He set up ***as*** a *doctor*. 彼は医者を開業した. ‖ He is registered ***as*** a *doctor*. 彼は医者の登録が済んでいる. ¶He is attended ***by*** a good *doctor*. 彼は良い医者にかかっている. ¶go ***for*** a *doctor*医者を呼びに行く. 【類】 send ***for*** a *doctor*.

P² He is a *doctor* ***by*** profession. 彼の職業は医者. ¶He is a *doctor* ***in*** name only. 彼は名ばかりの医者だ. ¶*Doctor* ***of*** Divinity (Literature, Medicine, Laws, Philosophy) 神(文, 医, 法, 哲)学博士.

doctor, *v.* 治療する.

M try to *doctor* him ***back*** to health 彼の健康を回復させようと試みる.

doctorate, *n.* 博士号.

V Since 1876, at least 85 *doctorates* were ***granted*** to colored persons by outstanding universities in America. 一八七六年以来米国著名の大学によって少くとも八十五名の黒人に博士号が授けられた. ¶He has ***had*** a *doctorate* ***conferred*** upon him. 彼は博士号を授けられた. ¶He ***obtained*** his *doctorate*. 彼は博士号を得た. ¶He ***received*** a *doctorate* of philosophy in political science at Columbia University. 彼はコロンビヤ大学で政治学の博士号を受けた.

doctrine, *n.* 教義, 主義, 学説.

V ***accept*** Christian *doctrine* キリスト教の教義を信奉する. ¶***advocate*** the *doctrine* of ... ...の説を唱道する. ¶***enunciate*** the *doctrine* 主義を言明する. ¶***outrage*** the *doctrine* of collective responsibility 連帯責任の主義を無視する. ¶***practice*** the *doctrine* that "time is money" いわゆる「時は金なり」の主義を実践する ‖ ***practice*** the *doctrine* of Neo-Malthusianism 新マルサス主義の学説を実践する. ¶***practice*** as well as ***preach*** one's *doctrine* その教義を説くと同時に実践する ‖ ***preach*** Buddhist *doctrine* 仏教の教義を説く. ¶***propound*** the non-recognition *doctrine* for Outer Mongolia 外蒙に対する非承認主義を提起する. ¶He ***raised*** his *doctrine* to the dignity of a national religion. 彼は自己の教義を国家の宗教にまで高めた. ¶***repudiate*** a *doctrine* 主義を排斥する. ¶***set forth*** a *doctrine* 教義を立てる. ¶It ***supports*** no *doctrine* or party or creed. それはいかなる教義も党派も信条も支持しない. ¶***uphold*** the *doctrine* that ... ...という説を唱える. ¶The *doctrine* ***exploded*** long since. その説はとうにすたれてしまった.

Q the ***Celtic*** *doctrine* of rebirth ケルト民族の再生説. ¶the ***Christian*** *doctrine* that self-slaughter is a sin 自殺は罪悪なりというキリスト教の教理. ¶A History of ***Economic*** *Doctrines* 経済学説史(書名). ¶an ***effete*** *doctrine* 無力な教義. ¶a ***false*** and ***feeble*** *doctrine* 虚偽・薄弱な教義. ¶a ***generally accepted*** *doctrine* 広く信奉されている教義. ¶an ***obsolete*** *doctrine* すたれた説. ¶a ***political*** *doctrine* 政治上の主義. ¶a ***profound*** *doctrine* 深奥なる学説. ¶the ***proscribed*** *doctrine* 禁止された教. ¶a ***religious*** *doctrine* 宗教の教義. ¶***social*** *doctrines* 社会の教義. ¶***strange*** and *false doctrines* 異説・邪教. ¶ the ***three doctrines*** 三教.

Q² according to the ***Buddhist doctrine*** 仏典によれば. ¶ accept the ***Communist** doctrine* 共産主義を信奉する. ¶ the United States ***Monroe Doctrine*** of 1823 1823 年の合衆国モンロー主義. ¶ a new and broadened ***Monroe Doctrine*** 拡大された新モンロー主義. ¶ the suppression of any criticism of the ***Nazi** doctrine* ナチ(ドイツ国粋社会党)の主義に対する批評の抑圧. ¶ the "field tests" of the "***Truman Doctrine***"「トルーマン主義」の実地検討.

P sound ***in** doctrine* 教義の正しい.

P² the *doctrine **of*** duality 二元論. ¶ preach the *doctrine **of*** small families 小家族(産児制限)主義を説く.

document, *n.* 文書, 書類, 証書.

V ***attach** documents* to one's draft その草稿に書類を添える. ¶ ***capture** documents* 書類を押収する. ¶ ***classify*** official *documents* 公文書を分類する(重要性に応じて). ¶ ***deliver*** the *documents* against the payment of ... ...の支払に備えて書類を渡す. ¶ ***draw up*** (=***prepare or write out***) a *document* 書類を作成する. ¶ ***fill up*** a *document* 書類の空白に書込む. ¶ ***forge*** an official *document* 公文書を偽造する. ¶ ***forward** documents* by air mail 書類を航空便で送る. ¶ ***seal*** a *document* with one's thumb 書類に母印を押す. ¶ They ***signed*** the *document* with their blood. 書類に血判した. ¶ ***witness*** a *document* 証人として証書に記名する.

Q *documents **attached*** 添付書類. ¶ a ***blank** document* 書込み用紙. ¶ armed with ***bulky** documents* 分厚な書類をそばにおいて. ¶ ***classified** documents* 〚軍〛[重要度に応じて]分類してある機密文書. ¶ It is the ***earliest literary** documents* of that language. それがその語で書いた最古の文献である. ¶ invaluable as a ***historical** document* 歴史上の文献としてきわめて貴重な. ¶ a ***history-making** document* 歴史上重要な文書. ¶ Every face is a ***human** document*, a mirror of emotions. すべて顔は人生の記録, 感情の鏡である. ‖ a very interesting "***human** document*" in the shape of the diary of a wounded German prisoner 負傷したドイツ兵捕虜が日記体で記した興味深いいわゆる人生記録. 【類】The book is a ***human** document* of great interest and significance. / a ***human** document* of exceptional interest and worth. ¶ an ***innocent-looking** document* 一見平凡な書類. ¶ preparation of ***legal** documents* 法律関係の文書調製. ¶ severely ***legal-looking** document* いかめしく法律文めいた書類. ¶ study London from the ***living human** documents* of the present, not from the yellow parchments of the past 過去の黄色になった書類からではなく現在の生きた人間を材料としてロンドンを研究する. ¶ important ***national** documents* 国家の重要書類. ¶ It was compiled from ***official** documents*. それは公文書から編集したものだ. ¶ based on ***official*** and other ***authentic** documents* 公文書その他の確実な文書に基いて. ¶ the ***oldest historical** document* 最も古い歴史上の記録. ¶ ***original** documents* and monuments in Japanese history 日本歴史の根本資料. ¶ a ***political** document* 政治上の文書(独立宣言など). ¶ a ***preliminary** document* 準備書面. ¶ ***primary** documents* 根本資料. ¶ a ***printed** document* 印刷にした記録. ¶ a ***private** document* 私文書. ¶ a ***public** document* 公文書. ¶ a ***spurious** document* 偽造文書. ¶ a ***valuable** document* for permanent reference 永久保存の貴重(参考)書類. ¶ Shakespeare's plays, particularly the great tragedies, are the most ***vital human** documents* in literature. シェークスピア劇特にその偉大な悲劇は文学上最も重要な人間記録である.

Q² ***business** documents* 商業書類. ¶ ***campaign** documents* 選挙運動用書類. ¶ a ***family** document* 家系に関する書類. ¶ ***microfilm** documents* マイクロフィルムにした諸文書. ¶ ***shipping** documents* 積荷書類. ¶ a ***three-hundred-page** document* 三百ページの文書. ¶ read in English a ***1,500-word** document* 1,500 語の英文文書を読む.

P leave property ***by*** a *document* 証書にして財産を残す. ¶ in the body ***of*** a *document* 文書の本文中に. ¶ ***with** document* attached certifying its authenticity その確実であることを証する書類を添付して.

P² a *document **of*** a judgment 判決書. ¶ a *document **on*** leather 皮革に書いた記録.

document, *v.* 文書で立証する.

M be ***fully** documented* 博引旁証がある. ¶ It is ***richly** documented* with quotations from standard authors. それは権威ある著作から多数文献を引用して立証してある.

documentation, *n.* 旁証.

V too plain to ***need** documentation* 旁証する必要のないほど明らかな.

Q ***microphotographic** documentation* 書類縮写.

dodge, *n.* 回避; 奇計.

V There! We've caught him! He is trying to ***work*** that *dodge* on us. うん, そうだ. やっこさん僕たちを例のぺてんにかけようとしているんだ.

Q an ***artful** dodge*=a clever trick うまいおとし穴.

Q² a ***confidence** dodge* 信用させてぺてんに掛けること.

P He saved himself ***by*** a *dodge* to the left. 危く左によけて命が助かった.

dodge, *v.* 巧みに身をかわす.

M *dodge* blows ***right and left*** 右左にパンチを避ける.

M² *dodge **about*** ひらりひらりと飛びかわす.

dodger, *n.* 巧みに免れる人.

Q He has the reputation of being a ***deft** dodger*. 彼は(借金などの)逃口上がうまいという評判だ.

Q² a ***tax** dodger* 脱税者.

dodging, *n.* ごま化し.

Q² ***tax** dodging* 税金のがれ.

doer, *n.* 行動する人, 生育する植物.

Q an ***evil** doer* 不正をする人. ¶ a ***good*** (***bad***) *doer* 〚生物〛生育のよい(悪い)植物.

dog, *n.* 犬.

V No *dogs* are ***allowed*** in the buildings. 屋内に犬を入れることお断り. ¶ ***break** dogs* 犬をならす. ¶ ***breed*** (=***raise***) *dogs* 犬を育てる. ¶ ***bring*** the *dog* with us 犬も一所に連れて行く. ¶ ***call*** one's *dog* 犬を呼ぶ. ¶ ***chain*** a *dog **up*** 犬をつないでおく. ¶ ***feed*** a *dog* 犬に食物を与える. ¶ ***hit*** a *dog* 犬をなぐる. ¶ ***keep*** a *dog* without a license 無鑑札で犬を飼う. ¶ ***leash** dogs* 犬を皮ひもでつなぐ. ¶ Do not ***let*** the *dog* into the house. 犬を内に入れるな. ‖ ***Let*** the *dog **loose.*** 犬を放してやれ. ¶ Do not ***let*** the *dog **out.*** 犬を出すな. ¶ Love me, ***love*** my *dog*. 〚諺〛坊主憎けりゃけさまで憎い. ¶ ***molest*** a *dog* 犬をいじめる. ¶ ***muzzle*** a *dog* 犬に口輪をはめる. ¶ have to ***punish*** a *dog* 犬をこらさなければいけない. ¶ ***Put out*** the noisy *dog*. あのやかましい犬を追出せ. ¶ ***send*** one's *dog* out of doors 犬を戸外へ出す. ¶ He ***set*** his *dogs* upon me. 彼は僕に犬をけしかけた. ¶ ***slip** dogs* 犬を放す. ¶ ***train** dogs* 犬をならす. ¶ ***spell*** the word *dog* dog という語をつづる. ¶ ***test*** the *dog* for rabies その犬が狂犬かどうか検査してもらう. ¶ ***tie*** a *dog* to a tree 木に犬をつなぐ. ¶ ***whip*** a *dog* on the head 犬の頭をむち打つ. ¶ ***whip*** a *dog **hard*** 犬をひどくむち打つ. ¶ ***whip off*** a *dog* 犬をむちで追いのける.

V² The *dog **barks*** at a stranger. 犬が見慣れない人にほえる. ¶ *Dogs **slink about*** at night. 犬は夜中こそこそ歩き回る. ¶ The *dog **whined.*** 犬がくんくん鼻を鳴らした.

Q a ***faithful*** (=***devoted***) *dog* 忠犬. ¶ a ***frisky** dog* よくふざける犬. ¶ a ***fierce** dog* 猛犬. ¶ a ***mad** dog* 狂犬. ¶ a ***homeless** dog* 野犬. ¶ the ***native** dog* of Tosa 土佐犬. ¶ To keep a ***noisy** dog* is a nuisance. よくほえる犬を飼うのはうるさいことだ. ¶ an ***ownerless** dog* 野犬. ¶ Beware of ***Savage** Dogs!* 〚掲示〛猛犬に注意. ‖ He keeps "***savage***" *dogs* to frighten away beggars. 彼は物もらいがはいらないようにいわゆる「猛犬」を飼っている. ¶ Let ***sleeping** dogs* lie. 〚諺〛寝ている犬はそーっとして置け(やぶへびをするな). ¶ ***unmuzzled** dogs* 口輪をはめていない犬. ¶ a ***vagabond** dog* 野良犬. ¶ a ***vicious** dog* 癖の悪い犬. ¶ a ***vigilant** dog* 番犬.

Q² a good ***bird** dog* よい鳥猟犬. ¶ a ***collie** dog* 羊犬. ¶ a ***family** dog* 飼犬. ¶ a ***hunting** dog* 猟犬. ¶ a ***police** dog* 警察犬. ¶ a ***pug** dog* [ブルドックににた]ちん ‖ a thoroughbred ***pug** dog* 純血種のちん. ¶ a ***sheep** dog* 羊犬. ¶ a ***sporting** dog* 猟犬. ¶ a ***stray** dog* 迷い犬. ¶ a ***toy** dog* 愛がん用の犬. ¶ be protected by a lone watchman and a ***watch** dog* 一人の番人と一匹の番犬に保護されている.

P accompanied ***by*** his *dog* 犬を連れて. ¶ Keep away ***from*** the *dog*. 犬に構うな. ¶ ***with*** the *dog* at his heels 犬をつれて.

P² a *dog **in*** the neighboring house 隣りの犬.

doggerel, *n.* まずい詩.

Q ***monotonous** doggerel* 単調なへぼ歌.

dogma, *n.* 定説, 教理; 独断説.

Q the ***old** dogma:* it is good for a boy to learn what he does not like.「少年がいやなことを学ぶことはよいことだ」という昔の教え. ¶ a ***scientific** dogma* 科学的定説.

dogmatism, *n.* 独断.
Q a *hasty* *dogmatism* 気ばやな独断.
dogmatize, *v.* 独断を下す.
P *dogmatize* **about** pronunciations 発音について独断を下す. ¶*dogmatize* **on** (=**upon**) controverted points 論点に対して独断的意見をはく.
dogtime, *n.* 正午.
P At 12 o'clock **in** the *dogtime* it is noon. 昼の十二時は正午だ.
doing, *n.* 行為, 所業, 仕事; なすこと.
Q an **adventurous** *doing* 冒険的行為. ¶**daily** *doings* 毎日の仕事. ¶the **day's** *doings* その日の仕事. ¶some **evil** *doing* ある不正行為. ¶There is **little** *doing* in grain from your place. 御地からの穀類の取引はあまりありません. ¶those who are acquainted with his **recent** *doings* 彼の消息をご存じの方は. ¶**scandalous** *doings* 醜行. ¶**treacherous** *doings* 二心ある行為.
P **by** so *doing* こうすることによって. ¶**in** so *doing* こうやって. ¶news **of** their *doings* 彼らの動静.
P² *doings* **for** the month 当月の行事. ¶the *doings* **of** the Kobe Walking Society 神戸歩行会の事業 ‖ this is said to be the *doing* **of** ... ...の仕わざだということだ.
doldrum, *n.* 無風状態, ふさぎ込み.
Q pull Britain out of her **economic** *doldrums* 英国を経済的沈滞から救い出す. ¶emerge from **post-war** *doldrums* 戦後の虚脱状態を脱する.
P be **in** the *doldrums* ふさぎ込んでいる.
dole, *n.* 施し; 失業手当.
V **draw** the *dole* 失業手当を受ける.
Q² a **relief** *dole* 義えん金.
P a person **on** the *dole* 失業手当をもらっている人.
dole, *v.* 少しずつ分け与える.
M Fruit is usually *doled* **out** to children in small quantities. 果実は通例少しずつ子供たちに与える.
doll, *n.* 人形; 《口語》人形のような美しい女.
V **play** *dolls* 人形遊びをする. ¶**nurse** a *doll* 人形の守りをする.
Q She is nothing but a **pretty** *doll*. 彼女は美しいだけで頭がない. ¶a **wire-pulled** *doll* あやつり人形.
Q² a **baby** *doll* 赤ん坊人形; 赤ん坊のような女. ¶a **clay** *doll* 泥人形. ¶a Japanese **Kabuki** *doll* 歌舞伎人形. ¶a **life-size** *doll* 等身大の人形.
P play **with** *dolls* 人形をもてあそぶ.
dollar, *n.* ドル; 金.
V I'll **bet** *dollars* to doughnuts it is ... 私は...だとしてドルとドーナッツでかけをしてよい. ¶**earn** an honest *dollar* 正直に金をもうける. ¶He never **had** a *dollar* ahead in his life. 一生よい越しの金を持たなかった. ¶**scrape together** some fifty *dollars* 五十ドルほど才覚する. ¶Ten *dollars* was **spent**. 十ドル使った. ¶**take off** one *dollar* from ... ...から一ドル引く. ¶**turn out** (=earn) the honest *dollar* 正直に金をもうける.
Q the **almighty** *dollar* 万能の金力. ¶It has been said that the **American** *dollar* is the American God. アメリカでは黄金万能だと言われている. ¶a **cool million** *dollars* 大枚百万ドル. ¶Oh, that nice, hot bath made me feel like a **million** *dollars*. あの暖かな風呂にはいると百万ドルもらったようないい気持だ.
Q² **C.R.B.** *dollars* 中央準備銀行ドル (C.R.B.=Central Reserve Banks).
P **at** a *dollar* a yard 一ヤール一ドルで. ¶I cannot go **beyond** a *dollar*. 一ドル以上は出せない. ¶I sold it **for** a *dollar*. 私はそれを一ドルで売った.
domain, *n.* 領域, 領地; 勢力範囲, 活動範囲.
V The Shogun deposed the daimyo and **confiscated** his *domains*. 将軍はその大名をしりぞけて彼の領地を没収した.
Q violate Japanese **aerial** *domains* 日本の領空を侵犯する. ¶a **feudal** *domain* 藩. ¶a **public** domain 公有財産(著作権の喪失した書籍など). ¶the **human** *domain* 人間の活動範囲. ¶He has chosen chemistry as his **special** *domain*. 彼は化学を専攻することにした.
P **in** the *domain* of applied science 応用科学界において ‖ **in** the *domain* of letters 文学界で. ¶It is **out of** my *domain*. それは私の畑違いだ.
P² the *domain* **of** science 科学の領域.
dome, *n.* 丸屋根, 頂閣.
Q a **polygonal** *dome* surmounted by a cupola 丸屋根のある多角形の頂閣.
domestic, *n.* 召使; *pl.* 家庭用品.
Q a **female** *domestic* 下女.
Q² **basement** *domestics* 地下室用家庭用品.
domestic, *a.* 家庭向きの.
M She is *domestic* **rather** than literary. 彼女は文学型というよりはむしろ家庭向きだ.
domesticate, *v.* 親しくする.
P The stranger *domesticated* himself quickly **among** us. 客はすぐにわれわれの家族に親しんだ.
domicile, *n.* 居所.
Q a **permanent** *domicile* 本籍. ¶They have a **regular** *domicile*. 彼らには一定の居所がある.
domicile, *v.* 定住させる; 定住する.
M persons **permanently** *domiciled* in Germany ドイツに永住する人々.
P It is necessary to ascertain whether she is really *domiciled* **at** the address given by her. 彼女が言っている住所に果して住まっているかどうか確める必要がある. ¶He is *domiciled* **in** a city (district). 彼は市(郡)に本籍を持っている. ¶I temporarily *domiciled* **with** him. 私は一時彼の家に同居していた.
dominance, *n.* 統治.
Q² American **air** *dominance* 米国航空の優越.
P come **under** *dominance* of ... ...の統治下に属する.
P² the *dominance* **of** the novel in our current literature. わが国の現代文学における小説の優勢.
dominant, *a.* 抜きんでている.
P a peak *dominant* **over** all other hills 群峯を抜く高峰 ‖ The idea is *dominant* **over** all the others. その考えが支配的である.
dominate, *v.* 支配する; 優勢な位置を占める.
M *dominate* China **commercially** 商業上中国を統御する.
P *dominate* **over** other nations 他国民より優位を占める.
domination, *n.* 支配; 優勢, 優位.
V The Jesuits made an attempt to **obtain** civil *domination* through religious propaganda. ジエズイト教徒は宗教宣伝によって政治的優勢を占めようと企てた. ¶**enter upon** war to **win** a world *domination* 世界を支配しようとして戦争をやる.
Q the **American** *domination* of the cinema アメリカの映画界に対する優位.
Q² an abolition of **class** *domination* 階級的優越の廃止. ¶free the Japanese motion picture industry from **government** *domination* 日本映画製作を政府の支配から解放する. ¶fall under **Red** *domination* 共産陣営に加わる. ¶resist **Soviet** *domination* ソ連の支配に反抗する. ¶attain **world** *domination* 世界制覇を(〃)遂げる. 【類】 prevent "**world** *domination* by American imperialism."
P It is **under** the *domination* of China. それは中国の支配に属する. ‖ He was so much **under** the *domination* of these emotions that they interfered with his reasoning powers. 彼はこうした感情に支配されたためその理性が曇るようになった.
domineer, *v.* 支配する; 権を振う; 威張る.
P He is *domineered* **by** his mistress. 彼は細君のしりに敷かれている. ¶He *domineers* **over** his inferiors. 彼は目下の者にいばる.
dominion, *n.* 領土; 主権, 支配.
V **establish** its *dominion* over ... ...にその主権を確立する. ¶**have** (=**hold**) *dominion* over ... ...を支配する.
Q **world-wide** *dominions* 世界中に散在する領土.
Q² Japan and her **overseas** *dominions* 日本とその海外領土. ‖ the chief **overseas** *dominions* 主要海外領土.
P Russia **under** Bolshevist *dominion*=Soviet Russia 過激主義者の支配下にあるロシア ‖ bring it **under** *dominion* それを服従させる.
P² *dominion* **over** sea and land 海陸の支配権 ‖ Man has *dominion* **over** the lower animals. 人間は下等動物に君臨する.
donate, *v.* 寄付する.
P *donate* ... yen **for** church expenses 教会費に...円寄付する. ¶*donate* a certain sum of money **from** one's private purse 私財の中からある金額を寄付する. ¶*donate* ... yen **to** a school (hospital) ...円を学校(など)へ寄付する. 【類】 *donate* funds **to** a public library. ¶*donate* ... yen **towards** the funds その資金中へ...円を寄付する.
donation, *n.* 寄付, 寄付金, 義えん金.
V he has **given** a *donation* of ... towards the fund for ... 彼は...の基金に...を寄付した. ¶Their Majesties have **made** large *donations* to aid sufferers. 両陛下には罹災者救済の思召から多額の金員を賜わった. ¶A *donation* of ... has been **presented** to the society by a wealthy lady. あ

る金持の婦人がその会へ…の寄付をした. ¶*promise* a *donation* of £100 to the fund 基金に対し百ポンドの寄付を約束する. ¶the society *received* a *donation* of 20,000 yen from … 協会は…から二万円の寄付を受けた. ¶*donations* should be *sent* to … 寄付金は…に送ること.

Q a *generous donation* 多額の寄付. ¶make some *handsome donations* かなり多額の寄付をする. ¶send in one's *promised donation* 約束した寄付金を送付する. ¶The hospital is supported by *public donations*. その病院は一般の義えん金で維持している.

Q^{2} a *cash donation* 現金の寄付.

P^{2} a *donation of* … was made by him towards the building fund for … …の建築資金に彼は…寄付した. ¶as a *donation to* the funds of … …の基金に対する寄付金として.

donkey, *n.* ろば;《口語》がんこ者.

V *drive* a *donkey* ろばを追う. ¶*ride* a *donkey* ろばに乗る.

O be [as] stubborn as a *donkey* がんこ一徹だ.

donkey-pump, *n.* 補助ポンプ.

Q an *independent donkey-pump* 単用の補助ポンプ.

donkey-ride, *n.* ろば乗り.

V Children *enjoy* a *donkey-ride*. 小供たちはろば乗りを喜ぶ.

donor, *n.* 寄贈者.

Q an *anonymous donor* 匿名の寄贈者.

Q^{2} a *blood donor* 血液寄贈者. ¶a *part donor* 共同寄贈者の一人.

don't, *n.* 不可.

P^{2} *Don'ts for* business women. [書名]職業婦人べからず帳.

doom, *n.* 運命, 非運, 死; 裁決.

V *meet* one's *doom* 死ぬ. ¶*pronounce doom* upon a culprit 罪人に判決を宣告する. ¶The *doom* of the company is *sealed*. その会社はもう先が見えた.

P fall *by doom* of battle 武運つたなく戦死する.

doom, *v.* 運命を定める, 罪を宣告する.

M *eternally doomed* 永久に浮ぶ瀬もなく.

P These attempts are *doomed to* failure in the future. これらの企ては将来失敗するにきまっている. 【類】The plan appears to me *doomed* in advance *to* failure. ‖ I think I am *doomed to* poverty. 私は貧乏するように生れついてる. 【類】His hope is *doomed to* disappointment.

doomsday, *n.* 世の終り.

P from now *till doomsday* 今日以後永久に.

door, *n.* 戸(ドア); 出入口, 玄関.

V The maid *answered* the *door*. 女中が玄関で取次いだ. ¶He *banged* the *door* after him. 彼は出がけに戸をばたんとしめた. ‖ He *banged* the *door shut*. 彼はドアをばたんとしめた. ¶*bar* the *door* 戸にかんぬきをかける. ¶*barricade* one's *doors* 入口にバリケードを作る. ¶The *doors* and windows were *blockaded* with ice and snow. 戸口が雪と氷で閉されていた. ¶Will you *bolt* the *door* when you come in this evening? 君今晩帰ったら戸締りをして下さらんか. ¶The burglar *broke in* the *doors* of a bathroom. 賊は風呂場の戸を押入った. ¶*Close* the *door* after you. 出たら戸をおしめ. ‖ The school has *closed* its *doors*. それは廃校になった. 【類】The school was forced to *close* its *doors* temporarily. ‖ A Furniture and Fittings Show has just *closed* its *doors*. 家具建具の展覧会はちょうどおしまいになった所だ. ‖ *Close* the *door* behind you. [掲示]ドアはあけ放しにせぬこと. ¶Don't *darken* my *doors* again. 二度と私の所のしきいをまたがないでくれ. ¶The *door* was *denied* [to] me. 私は入れてもらえなかった. ¶every student who *entered* the *doors* … その校門をくぐった学生という学生は … ¶He *fastened* his *door* against the whole world. その門戸をとざして世人と交りを絶った. 【類】He *fastened* the *door* upon us. ¶*force open* the *door* 戸を無理にこじあける. ¶*keep* a *door* open (shut) 入口を明け(しめ)っぱなしにする, しまら(明かない)ないようにしておく. ¶*kick open* a *door*=*kick* a *door open* 戸をけ明ける. ¶*knock* the *door* 戸をたたく. ¶The *door* was *knocked in*. 戸をたたき明けた. ¶*leave* the *door ajar* とびらを少しあけておく. ¶The *door* was *left open*. 入口を明け放しにして置いた. ¶*lock* one's *door* with a key 入口にかぎを掛ける ‖ That film was so bad that it nearly *locked* the *door* of my screen future. その映画は不出来であったので僕の映画俳優としての前途がほとんどとざされてしまった. ‖ *lock* the *door* behind one はいってから戸締りをする. ¶The exhibition *opened* its *doors* yesterday. 博覧会は昨日開場した. ‖ The school *opened* its *doors* to students last year. 同校は去年開校した. 【類】The school has already *opened* its *doors*. / The new store *opened* its *doors* to the public on November 8. / *open* their *doors* to customers ‖ These clubs *open* their *doors* to ladies—not as members, but as guests. これらのクラブは婦人に対して会員ではなく客としてその門戸を開放する. 【類】Commodore Perry *opened* the *doors* of Japan to the West. ¶*pass* one's *door* 人の門前を通る. ¶*push back doors* that are ajar 少し開いている戸を押して締める. ¶*reclose* the *door* 戸をしめ直す. ¶I *showed* him the *door*. 彼を追出した. ¶*shut* a *door* without slamming ばたんと音のしないように戸をしめる ‖ Society *shut* its *door* in his face. 世間は彼を排斥した. ¶The indignant housewife *slammed* the *door* in his face. 主婦は怒って彼の面前で戸をぴしゃんと締めた. ‖ His answer was to *slam* the *door*. 返事もしないで戸をぴしゃんと締めた. ‖ *slam* a *door shut* ばたんとドアをしめる. ¶*throw open* its *doors* to … …にその門戸を開放する. ¶*unbolt* the *doors* 戸のかんぬきをはずす. ¶*unlock* a *door* with a key かぎで戸をあける ‖ They wouldn't *unlock* the *door* for me. 戸をあけてくれなかった. ¶Do not *use* this *door*. こゝからの出入を禁ず. ¶*watch* the *door* of our lips お互いの口を慎む.

V^{2} The *door clicked shut*. 入口がかちっとしまった. ¶The *door sticks*. ドアがつかえてあかない. ¶The *doors* slowly *swang open*. ドアは静かにゆれて開いた.

Q The *door* was *ajar*. ドアが少し開いていた. ¶slip out at the *back door* 後の戸からこっそり出て行く ‖ Wall Street by the *back door* ウオール・ストリートの内幕. ¶*banging doors* ばたんばたんとあおる戸. ¶a *creaking door* きしむ戸. ¶He is at *death's door*. 彼は死にかかっている. ¶a *double door* 観音開き. ¶a *few doors* away 二三軒先 ‖ a *few doors* west of Fifth Avenue 第五大通りの西へ数軒. ¶Wait a moment at the *front door*. 表でちょっと待って下さい. ¶those who have passed through his *hospitable doors* 彼のもてなしのよい家を訪れた人々. ¶Japan is *next door* to China. 日本は中国の隣国である. ‖ the very *next door* to her own house 彼女の家のすぐ隣り. 【類】The house is *next door* to the school. ‖ Who lives *next door* to you? あなたの隣りに住んでいるのはだれですか. ‖ The house *next door* but one to us was taken by a foreigner this morning. 一軒おいて隣りの家は今朝外国人が借りました. maintain an *open door* for trade 商業上門戸解放主義を維持する ‖ The *door* was wide *open*. 戸は一杯に開いていた. ¶escape through a *secret door* 隠れ口からのがれる.

Q^{2} a *carriage door* 乗りもののドア. ¶with a *communicating door* between the two houses 二軒の間を通じる戸口のある. ¶a *cottage door* 小屋の入口. ¶the lobby of the *entrance door* 入口の控室 ‖ the main *entrance door* 表玄関 ‖ The *entrance door* was of lattice. 入口はこうし造りだった. ¶a stoutly-built *oak door* がん丈なオーク作りの戸. ¶She opened my *room door* softly. 彼女は私の室の戸をそっとあけた. ¶a *side door* 横の入口. ¶a *sliding paper door* 障子. ¶a *street door* 通りに面した入口. ¶a *swing door* ゆれ戸. 【類】heavy *swing doors*.

P He is *at* the *door*. 彼は戸の所にいる. 【類】I have a taxi waiting for you *at* the *door*. ‖ go out (come in) *at* the back *door* 後の戸から出て行く(入ってくる) ‖ There came a rap (=knock) *at* the *door*. 戸をたたく音がした. ‖ The guilt is *at* your *door*. 君のせいだ. ‖ lay the blame *at* the *door* of … その罪を…にぬりつける ‖ Now who's that *at* the *door*? そら玄関にだれかきた. 【類】*at* every *door*. ¶They met *behind* closed *doors*. 彼らは秘密に会を開いた. ¶enter *by* (=at) the front *door* 表玄関から入る. ¶He went begging *from door to* door. 戸毎に物ごいして歩いた. ¶bore a hole *in* the *door* 戸に穴を明ける. ¶a name-plate (name) *on* (=*upon*) the *door* 戸口の表札 ‖ There was a knock (=rap) *on* the *door*. 戸をノックする音がした. ¶*out of doors* 戸外で. 【類】It is very cold *out of doors*. ¶a signboard *over* a *door* 戸口の上の看板 ‖ the room *over* the front *door* 表口の上のへや. ¶I saw him *to* the *door*. 彼を戸口まで送って出た. ¶*with* closed (open) *doors* 戸をとざして, 秘密に(戸を開け放して, 公然と). ¶remain *within doors* 屋内にとどまる. ¶*without doors*=out of doors, outdoors 屋外では.

P^{2} a few *doors beyond* our house うちから二三軒先. ¶a few *doors from* … …から数軒離れて ‖ He lives two *doors from* my house. 彼は僕の家から二軒目に住んでいる.

¶The *door* ***into*** his room was closed. 彼の部屋の戸は締まっていた. ¶a country which had most to do with the opening of its *doors* ***to*** Western influence その国の門戸を開いて西洋文明と接触せしめるにあずかって最も力のあった国. 【類】open (shut) the *door* ***to*** a visitoor.

O There is the *door* [for you]! Please go, and quick! このドアから早く出て行って下さい.

door-bell, *n*. 玄関の呼びりん.

V ***answer*** the *door-bell* 玄関の呼びりんに答える. ¶***ring*** the *door-bell* 玄関の呼びりんを鳴らす.

doorknob, *n*. [ドアの]とっ手(ハンドル).

V^2 This *doorknob* doesn't ***work***. このドアのとっ手(ハンドル)がきかない.

doorman, *n*. 玄関番(ドアマン).

Q^2 an ***appartment-house*** (a ***hotel***) *doorman* アパート(ホテル)のドアマン.

doorway, *n*. 戸口, 出入口.

Q a ***curtained*** *doorway* 幕のたれている出入口.

P appear ***in*** the *doorway* 戸口に現われる.

dormant, *a*. 眠っている.

P He is lying *dormant* ***in*** the sun. 彼は日なたに眠っている.

dormitory, *n*. 寄宿舎, 寮.

Q a ***neat*** and ***comfortable*** *dormitory* きれいで住心地のよい寄宿舎.

dose, *n*. 薬の一服, 服量, 用量.

V ***administer*** a *dose* 投薬する. ¶***take*** three *doses* a day, one after each meal 食後に一服ずつ一日三服のむ.

Q drink alcohol in ***injurious*** *doses* 害になるほど酒を飲む. ¶when taken in ***large*** *doses* 多量に飲むと. ¶in ***medicinal*** *doses* 適量に. ¶in ***poisonous*** *doses* 過量に. ¶a ***strong*** *dose* of poison 過量の毒.

P I got rid of my cold ***with*** a *dose* of medicine. 一服の薬で私のかぜが抜けた.

P^2 three *doses* ***of*** medicine 薬三服. ¶give a person a *dose* ***of*** flattery. 人におべっかを言う.

dose, *v*. 投薬する.

P I *dosed* him ***with*** advice. 彼に苦言を呈した.

dot, *n*. 点; ちびっこ.

V ***put*** the *dots* on (=dot) the i's アイ (i) の字に点を打つ.

Q groups of ***raised*** *dots* as in Braille alphabet 点字の字母におけるごとき浮上った点の群. ¶since I was a very ***small*** *dot* 私がほんのちびっこであったころから.

P leave ***on*** the *dot* of 5.30 五時三十分きっちりに立つ. ¶The dealers know his taste ***to*** a *dot*. 商人たちは彼の好みを十分のみ込んでいる.

dot, *v*. 点を打つ; 点てつする.

M be *dotted* ***cheerfully*** with lights 陽気に点々と明りが見えている.

P a place *dotted* ***with*** ruins 廃きょが点在している場所 ‖ a mountain range *dotted* ***with*** peaks 幾つもの峰がそびえている山脈 ‖ the foreground is *dotted* ***with*** flowers 前景には点々と花が咲いている. 【類】The sea is *dotted* ***with*** islands. / a landscape *dotted* ***with*** cottages (summer houses).

dotage, *n*. おいぼれ, もうろく.

Q elderly men and women with ***incipient*** *dotage* もうろくしかかった老人の男女.

P an old man ***in*** *dotage* もうろくした老人. ¶be ***on*** one's *dotage* 老い込んでいる.

dote, *v*. でき愛する.

P *dote* (=doat) ***on*** the idea of ... ...の思想に恋々とする ‖ *dote* ***on*** (=***upon***) a woman (child) 女(など)の愛におぼれる.

double, *n*. 相似物, 生写し; 〖映〗代役.

Q Movie actors sometimes ***employ*** their *doubles* 映画俳優はときに代役を使う. ¶***literary*** *doubles* [小説などにある]性格の似た人物.

P This is the portrait ***of*** the Kaiser's *double*, Herr Max Nitschke, Silesia. これはカイゼル生き写しのマックス・ニッチケ君の肖像画だ.

double, *v*. あと戻りする, 引き返す; 重ねる, 二つに折る.

M I *doubled* ***back*** without loss of time. 私はときを移さず引き返した.

M^2 *double* ***up*** one's body 体を二重に折る ‖ *double* ***up*** one's fists in anger 怒ってげんこを固める ‖ *double* ***up*** with relatives or friends 親類あるいは友人と同居する ‖ *double* (=curl) ***up*** one's hair 髪を縮らす. ¶*double* ***over*** a leaf to mark the page 印をつけるためにページを折る.

P *double* [up] ***with*** laughter 抱腹絶倒する.

doubt, *n*. 疑い, 疑念; 疑問.

V It is rather calculated to ***arouse*** *doubts* than cause convictions. それでは確信をいだかしめずむしろ疑念を生ぜしめることになる. ¶in order to ***avoid*** any *doubt* 少しでも疑いをかけられないように. ¶***cast*** *doubts* on the value of ... ...の真価を疑う ‖ ***cast*** a *doubt* upon the soundness of a system ある制度の堅実さを疑う. 【類】A *doubt* was ***cast*** upon its authenticity. ¶***clear up*** *doubts* 疑いを晴らす. ¶may ***create*** grave *doubt* as to ... ...について大なる疑惑を生じないとも限らない. ¶***destroy*** *doubts* 疑点を一掃する. ¶***dismiss*** *doubts* 疑惑を晴らす. ¶How can I ***dispel*** her *doubts* and fears? 彼女の疑惑と恐怖をいかにしたら払い去れるだろう. ¶All *doubts* have now been ***dissipated***. 疑いがすっかりはれた. ‖ It has sufficed to ***dissipate*** my last *doubts*. それは私の最後の疑念を晴らすに十分であった. ¶***entertain*** a *doubt* upon this subject この問題に関して疑念をいだく ‖ we can hardly refrain from ***entertaining*** serious *doubts* as to (=about) ... われらは...について大なる疑念をいだかざるを得ない. ¶***express*** some *doubt* as to whether ... ...かどうかについて疑惑を表明する. ¶I have ***felt*** some *doubt* as to ... 私は...について幾分疑いを持っていた. ¶we ***have*** grave *doubts* as to whether ... われわれは...なるかについて大なる疑念をいだいている ‖ I ***have*** no *doubt* whatever of this. 私はこれについて何らの疑念をもいだいていない. ¶***induce*** *doubts* as to the sincerity of ... ...の誠実を疑わせる. ¶an examination of it ***leaves*** no *doubt* that ... それを調べて見ると...ということを疑う余地がない. 【類】His researches ***leave*** absolutely no *doubt* on this point. / it ***leaves*** little *doubt* with regard to ... ¶I ***make*** no *doubt* of it. 私はそれを疑わない. 【類】I ***make*** no *doubt* of your succeeding. / I ***make*** no *doubt* that ... ¶***raise*** a *doubt* as to ... ...について疑いを起させる ‖ It ***raised*** many *doubts* in their minds. そのために彼らの心に色々疑念が起った. 【類】a *doubt* has been ***raised*** about the probability of ... ¶***remove*** all *doubts* すっかり疑いを晴らす. ¶***resolve*** one's *doubts* 疑いを晴らす. ¶I am inclined to ***share*** your *doubt* as to ... 私も君と同様に...を疑いたくなって来た. ¶***throw*** *doubt* on its safety それが果して安全かどうかについて疑いをはさむ ‖ ***throw*** *doubt* on his story 彼の話を疑う. 【類】***throw*** some *doubt* upon ...

V^2 All *doubt* has ***disappeared*** (=***vanished***). 疑いがすっかり晴れた. ¶grave *doubt* ***exists*** as to ... ...については深い疑いがある. ¶a *doubt* ***arose*** in my mind 心中に疑いが起った.

Q There is a ***considerable*** *doubt* about it. 大いに疑わしい. ¶a ***gloomy*** *doubt* 疑心暗鬼. ¶cast ***grave*** *doubt* on ... ...に対して大いに疑問を持つ ‖ I have ***grave*** *doubts* in regard to ... 私は...について深い疑いを持っている. ¶There is ***great*** *doubt* whether he did so or not. あの人がそうしたかどうか大いに疑わしい. ¶an epoch of ***heart-searching*** *doubt* and spiritual struggle 心底から疑惑を起し精神のはんもんする時代. ¶***historic*** *doubts* relative to ... ...に関する歴史上の疑問. ¶I haven't the ***least*** *doubt* about ... ...については私は少しも疑わない. ¶there is very ***little*** *doubt* that ... ...ということはほとんど疑を容れる余地がない. ¶His heart was filled with the most ***maddening*** *doubts* and fears. 彼はいとも心狂わしい疑念と恐怖で胸がふさがった. ¶This is true, ***no*** *doubt*. これはたしかに本当だ. ‖ There is ***no*** *doubt* that he did so. 彼はきっとそうしたのだ. ‖ ***No*** *doubt* he is a Texan. たしかに彼はテキサス生れだ. ¶a ***paralysing*** *doubt* 心苦しい疑惑. ¶indulge a ***passing*** *doubt* whether ... ...かどうかと一時疑って見る. ¶a ***philosophic*** *doubt* 哲学上の疑問. ¶there could be no ***possible*** *doubt* as to ... ...については決して疑いがあろうはずがなかった. ¶a most ***presumptuous*** *doubt* in ... ...に対するきわめて無礼な疑惑. ¶a ***reasonable*** *doubt* もっともな疑い. ¶***serious*** *doubts* were at one time entertained as to ... ...について一時大いに疑いがいだかれていた. ¶there is very ***slight*** *doubt* that ... ...ということはほとんど疑いがない. 【類】It is a question concerning which very ***slight*** *doubt* can arise. ¶express ***strong*** *doubts* 強い疑いを表明する.

P I believe ***beyond*** all *doubt* that ... 僕は...と確信する. ‖ It has been proved ***beyond*** *doubt* in many ways. それは色々と証明されたので疑われなくなった. ¶be tortured ***by*** *doubt* 疑惑に苦しめられる. ¶there is no room ***for*** *doubt* that ... ...は疑いを容れる余地がない. 【類】there is no room left ***for*** *doubt* as to ... ¶he is ***in*** *doubt* as to (=about) ... 彼は...について疑っている ‖ He is ***in*** *doubt* what to do. 彼はどうしようかと迷っている. 【類】I am ***in*** *doubt* what I should do. / I am ***in*** *doubt* whether to go or stay.

‖When *in doubt* leave out. どうかなと思ったら抜かすこと(取捨選択の場合). ¶in case ***of*** *doubt* 疑わしい場合には ‖ show beyond shadow ***of*** *doubt* that ... …ということについては疑いの余地はみじんもない. ¶It is not open ***to*** *doubt*.=It admits of no doubt. それは疑いを容れない. ¶***with*** grave *doubt* as to ... …について大いに疑いをいだいて. ¶***Without*** *doubt* this is the best. 確かにこれが一番よい. ‖***without*** any *doubt* 疑いなく.

P² There is no *doubt* ***about*** the soundness of this observation. この言説の確実なことについては疑いがない. ‖I have no *doubt* ***about*** it. 私はそれを少しも疑わない. ‖I have some *doubts* ***about*** his succeeding. 私は彼の成功については幾分の疑いを持っている. ¶I am in *doubt* ***as to*** what to do. どうしようかと迷っている. ¶I have *doubts* ***of*** the wisdom of the method adopted. 採用された方法が果して賢明かどうか僕は疑問に思う. ¶throw *doubt* ***on*** the value of ... …の真価を疑う. ¶The book is usually ascribed to him, but the discovery of this MS. throws *doubt* ***upon*** the authorship. この本は通常彼が書いたものとされているがこの原稿の発見によって彼が作者であったかどうか疑われている.

doubt, *v.* 疑う.

M I *doubt* ***greatly*** whether ... …かどうかと非常に迷う. ¶it can ***hardly*** be *doubted* that ... …ということはほとんど疑いない. ¶You are *doubting* me ***unjustly***. 君は僕を疑っているがそれは不当だ. ¶it may well be *doubted* if ... …という疑問が当然起りうるのである.

P I *doubt* ***of*** my success. 私の成功はおぼつかない. ‖I *doubt* ***of*** his ability. 私は彼の手腕を疑う.

O I do not *doubt* [but] that he ... 彼が…なることを私は疑わない. ¶I *doubt* if he will come. 彼は来るかどうか疑わしい. ¶I *doubt* whether it is true or not. 私はその真偽を疑う. 【類】I *doubt* whether he will be at home. / it has been *doubted* whether ...

doubtful, *a.* 疑わしい.

M That's ***rather*** *doubtful*. それはちと疑わしい.

P I am *doubtful* ***as to*** his success. 彼の成功はおぼつかないと私は思う. ¶We are *doubtful* ***of*** the patient's recovery. その患者の全快はおぼつかないと僕たちは思う. ‖We are *doubtful* ***of*** the fact. われわれはそれが事実であるか疑をいだいている.

O It is *doubtful* whether it is true or not. 真偽のほどは疑わしい.

douche, *n.* [治療の]注水浴.

V ***take*** a cold *douche* 冷水を浴びる.

dough, *n.* 練り粉; 《米俗》金銭.

V I ***have*** no *dough* about me. 私はお金をもっていない. ¶***knead*** *dough* ねり粉をこねる.

Q a chance to make some ***easy*** *dough* 楽に金を作る機会.

P This I've done, not ***for*** *dough*. それは金のためにやったんじゃないよ.

doughnut, *n.* ドーナッツ.

V ***take*** some *doughnuts* for the family 家のものにドーナッツを買ってやる.

Q ***American*** *doughnuts* [穴のあいた] アメリカ式のドーナッツ.

dove, *n.* はと.

V² A *dove* ***coos***. はとはぽっぽっと鳴く.

P² a *dove* ***of*** peace 平和ばと.

dovecot, *n.* はと小屋.

V ***flutter*** (=cause a flutter in) the *dovecot* 平和な里に動揺を起こす.

dovetail, *v.* ぴったり合う.

M Everything *dovetails* ***beautifully***. 万事そつがなくうまくゆく. ¶The various bits of evidence *dovetailed* so ***completely*** that the mystery was worked out. 色々な証拠がうまくそろってその秘密が解けた.

P *dovetail* ***with*** others 他人とうまく合う.

down, *n.* 降下; 非運.

P go ***through*** the ups and *downs* of life 人生の浮き沈みを経験する.

down, *v.* 倒す, 打落す.

P He is not to be *downed* ***by*** censure. 非難されて参るような男ではない. ‖The enemy plane was *downed* ***by*** an A.A. gun. 敵機は対空砲によって撃墜された. ¶The workers *downed* tools ***in*** each of their working shops. 労働者たちはそれぞれの職場でストに入った. ¶***Down with*** Hitler! ヒットラー打倒. 【類】***Down with*** the Y Administration (Government).

downed, *a.* 倒れて.

P He is *downed* ***with*** flu. 流感で寝ている.

downfall, *n.* 没落.

V It finally ***brought about*** his *downfall*. それが結局彼の没落ということになった. ¶***meet*** a speedy *downfall* たちまち没落する.

Q² a ***Cabinet*** *downfall* 内閣の崩壊.

P the *downfall* ***of*** the early Christian Mission in Japan 日本における初期キリスト教伝道の没落.

downpour, *n.* どしゃ降り, 豪雨.

V We are ***having*** a *downpour*. こりゃどしゃ降りだ.

Q a ***drenching*** *downpour* びしょぬれになるような豪雨. ¶a ***heavy*** *downpour* どしゃ降り. ¶There is a ***regular*** (=***steady***) *downpour*. 本降りだ. ¶in a ***torrential*** *downpour* 車軸を流すようなどしゃ降りに.

P ***in*** a *downpour* [of rain] どしゃ降りに.

dowry, *n.* 嫁入持参金.

V ***Has*** she a large *dowry?* 彼女の持参金はたくさんかい. ¶***provide*** a *dowry* for girls 娘の嫁入持参金を用意する.

P give a farm ***for*** a *dowry* 持参金として農地をやる. ¶He married a woman ***with*** a *dowry*. 彼は持参金のある婦人と結婚した.

doyen, *n.* 《仏》古参者, 首席, 筆頭.

P² the *doyen* ***of*** all South Sea mariners and explorers 南洋航海者や探検家中での元老 ‖the *doyen* ***of*** the diplomatic corps 外交団の最長老 ‖the *doyen* ***of*** the European monarchs ヨーロッパ諸元首中の筆頭 ‖Mr. William Winter, the *doyen* ***of*** American critics 米国批評家中の長老ウイリアム・ウィンター氏. ‖Mr. Henty was the *doyen* ***of*** writers of stories for boys. ヘンティー氏は少年物語作家中の第一人者であった.

doze, *n.* 微睡.

P He fell ***into*** a *doze*. 彼はうとうと眠った.

doze, *v.* 仮睡する, まどろむ.

M *doze* ***away*** one's time うかうか過ごす. ¶try to *doze* ***off*** again 又うとうと眠ろうとする ‖*doze* ***off*** to sleep うとうとして眠ってしまう ‖be *dozing* ***off*** in one's seat 腰掛けたまゝうとうと眠っている.

P *doze* ***over*** one's work (a book) 仕事(読書)をしながらうとうと眠る.

dozen, *n.* 一ダース; *pl.* 数十.

Q ***many*** *dozens* of cattle たくさんの牛. ¶a ***round*** *dozen* 正味一ダース.

P sold ***by*** the *dozen* 一ダース単位で売る ‖pay for them ***by*** the *dozen* 一ダース単位でその価を払う. ¶His tongue went nineteen ***to*** the *dozen*. とうとうとまくしたてた.

P² a *dozen* ***of*** eggs 一ダースの卵 ‖*dozens* ***of*** times 何十ぺんとなく ‖*dozens* ***of*** people (apples, eggs, etc.) 何十人という人々(など) ‖six *dozen*[s] ***of*** pencils=six dozen pencils 六ダースの鉛筆. 【類】*dozens* ***of*** British explorers / *dozens* ***of*** FBI agents (G メン).

drab, *n.* 淡かっ色.

Q² ***olive*** *drab* かんらんのような淡かっ色.

draft, draught, *n.* (1) 一飲み, 一杯; すきま風; 喫水; けん引; [薬の]一回分; 《米》徴兵.

V ***escape*** the *draft* 徴兵をのがれる. ¶***feel*** a *draught* from ... …から入るすき間風に当る. ¶***have*** a *draft* of beer (ale) ビールをぐっとやる. ¶If you shut the door, it will ***lessen*** the *draught*. 戸をしめればすき間風が少くなる.

Q I do not like him and his kindness to me is a ***bitter*** *draught* to drain. あの人はきらいだ, であの人から親切にされるのは心苦しい. ¶sit in ***constant*** *draft* 絶え間なく吹通す風に当ってすわる. ¶a cart of ***easy*** *draft* 引きやすい荷車. ¶have a ***good*** *draught* of water 水を一杯たっぷり飲む. ¶***light-water*** *draught* 浅喫水(積荷のない船の喫水). ¶***load-water*** *draught* 積載喫水. ¶a ***long*** *draught* of beer ビールのぐっと一飲み. ☞米語用法では have a *draft* of beer (=《英》draught). ¶***mechanical*** *draft* 機械通風. ¶***natural*** *draft* 自然通風. ¶drink in ***ox-like*** *draughts* 牛飲する. ¶a ***sleeping*** *draught* 睡眠剤. ¶a ***soothing*** and ***sedative*** *draught* 鎮静剤.

Q² a ***cooling*** *draft* 一杯の清涼飲料. ¶a compulsory ***man-power*** *draft* 強制徴用.

P drink ***at*** one (=a) *draught* 一息に飲みほす. ¶a vessel ***of*** large *draught* 喫水の大きい船 ‖a beast ***of*** *draft* けん引用牛馬 ‖a ship ***of*** 18 feet *draught* 十八フィート喫水の船. ¶beer ***on*** *draught* (=[drawn] from the wood) 生ビール.

P² the *draft* ***from*** the windows 窓から吹込む風. ¶the *draft* ***of*** cold, night air 吹通す寒い夜風 ‖her *draft* ***of*** water when laden (light) is ... 荷物を積んだ(荷物のない)場合の喫水は…フィートだ.

(2) 為替; 草稿.

V cannot ***accept*** *draft* without documents attached 添付文書がなければ手形を引受けられない. 【類】***accepted*** the *draft* for honor of the drawer (振出人の信用を重んじて) / Please ***accept*** the *draft* when presented (呈示したら). ¶***buy*** a *draft* on London ロンドンあてに振り出した

為替手形を買う. ¶*discount* a *draft* 手形を割引く. ¶*dishonor* a *draft* 手形の支払を拒絶する. ¶*get* a *draft* on America for 100 dollars 米国向け百ドルの為替を組む‖*get* a *draft* cashed 手形を現金に替える. ¶*honor* a *draft* against shipment 船積に対する手形を引受ける. 【類】*honor* one's *draft* by the debit of (の借方として). ¶*issue drafts* on the principal cities of the country 同国の重要都市あて為替手形を振出す. ¶*make* a *draft* on a firm (person) for $... through a bank 銀行を通して商会(人)へ...ドルの為替を組む. ¶*negotiate* a *draft* 手形を売渡す. ¶*prepare* (=make out) a *draft* of ... 原案を作成する. ¶*protect* a *draft* 手形を払う. ¶*secure* from a bank a *draft* in my favor for $... on their N.Y. Branch そのニューヨーク支店に振出し私を受取人として...ドルの為替手形を受取る. ¶*take up* a *draft* 手形を引受ける.

Q pass a *bad draft* for $... ...ドルの不渡手形を出す. ¶remittances by *banker's draft* on New York City ニューヨーク市あての銀行為替手形による送金. ¶a *clean draft* 普通為替. ¶a *commercial* (=*trade*) *draft* 貿易手形(貿手). ¶a *dishonored draft* 不渡手形. ¶a *documentary draft* 荷為替. ¶write the *first draft* of a story 物語の最初の草案を書く. ¶a *preliminary draft* 草案. ¶frame a *rough draft* of one's message その使命の草案を作る.

Q² a *bank draft* 銀行手形. ¶a *discount draft* 割引手形. ¶the original *manuscript draft* of the book is the author's own handwriting 著者自筆のその本の原稿. ¶an *original draft* 最初の草稿. ¶make a good copy from a *rough draft* 下書を清書する. ¶a *sight draft* 一覧払手形. ¶a *time draft* 支払日指定手形.

P pay by check or *by draft* 小切手か手形で支払う.

P² a *draft for* $50 五十ドルの為替手形. ¶the *draft of* a peace treaty 平和条約の草案. ¶a *draft on* a government bank 国立銀行あて振出した為替手形‖a couple of *drafts on* you, and indorsed to my order 貴下に振出した私の指図人渡しに裏書した二枚の為替手形. ¶a *draft upon* ... for ... ¥($)...円(ドル)の...あて振出しの手形. ¶a *draft with* documents attached 荷為替.

draft, *v.* 選抜する, 徴兵する; 分遣する; 起草する.

M *draft out* an address 演説の草稿を作る.

P He has been *drafted as* a soldier. 彼は兵役に取られた. ¶*draft* stout young men *for* war 戦争でがん丈な青年を兵に取る. ¶*draft* men *from* the navy 海軍から兵を分遣する. ¶He was *drafted into* the Army. 彼は陸軍に召集された.

draftsman, *n.* 画家; 起草者, 立案者.

Q a *parliamentary draftsman* 議会の議案起草者.

P a *draftsman in* pen and ink ペン画を書く人.

drag, *n.* 引きずること; 歯止め; 邪魔物; 《俗》ひいき.

V *have* a *drag* with one's employer 主人に気に入られる. ¶A coach *requires* a *drag* when going down hill. 馬車は下り坂のときは歯止めをかけねばならない.

Q a *heavy drag* up hill 上り坂の遅々たる足取り.

P walk *with* a *drag* 足を引きずって歩く. ¶a *drag on* (=*upon*) another 人の足手まとい‖He was a *drag on* my career. 彼は僕の出世のじゃま物だった.‖Old ideas are a *drag on* progress. 旧思想は進歩の妨げをする. ¶She was a *drag to* him. 彼女は彼の重荷だった.

drag, *v.* 引きずる; 引き網で探す; ぐずぐず進む.

M *forcibly drag* in (out) むりやりに引きずり込む(引っぱり出す). ¶*drag out* a miserable existence 見すぼらしい生活を続ける. 【類】*drag out* one's lecture (speech). ¶He *dragged* the feet *slowly along.* 彼は足を引きずってのろのろ歩いた.

M² *drag along* のろのろ歩く. ¶The day *dragged by.* 日のたつのがおそかった. ¶*drag down* the whole family into the abyss of consequences 因果のふちへ家族全体を引きずり込む‖be *dragged down* into defeat 敗北に引きずり込まれる‖*drag down* to earth 地面に引き倒す. 【類】*drag* man *down* lower than the beasts of the field. ¶*drag in* (=into) by the head and shoulders (=neck and crop) 頭や肩をつかまえて引きずり込む. ¶*drag* him *off* to the police station 彼を警察署に引張って行く. ¶The war *dragged on.* 戦争が長引いた.‖Time *drags on* when you have nothing to do. 何もすることがないときは時間のたつのがおそい. 【類】The work of reconstruction has been *dragging on* for a long time.

P *drag* one foot *after* the other 一足一足引きずる. ¶*drag* it *along* the ground 地面を引きずって行く‖*drag along* the skirt すそをずるずる引きずる. ¶*drag at* his collar (arm) 彼のえり首(など)をひっぱろうとする‖*drag at* anchors いかりを引き上げようとする. ¶*drag for* a drowned body 引網で水死人を探す. ¶*drag* her down *from* her high position 彼女をその高い地位から引きずり降ろす. 【類】*drag* archaic words (古語) *from* their graves. ¶*drag* a country *into* war ある国を戦争にひっぱり込む‖*drag* a person *into* an affair (a place, a quarrel) 人を事件(など)にひっぱり込む. ¶*drag on* charity 慈善にすがる‖*drag on* a miserable existence till the tomb closes over one 死ぬまでみすぼらしい生存を続ける. ¶*drag* a person *out of* a room 人をへやからひっぱり出す. ¶*drag* a person *to* the dust 人を没落させる.

drain, *n.* 排水; 下水のみぞ; [財貨などの]流出.

V *block* the *drain* 排水管を詰まらす. ¶The *drains* have been all *disinfected.* 下水のみぞをことごとく消毒した. ¶*fix* the *drain* under the sink 流しの下の管を直す. ¶It *imposes* a heavy *drain* upon the pocket. それは大分ふところ(財政)に響く. ¶*scour* a *drain* みぞをさらう.

Q the *continued drain* of the Shakespeare folio from England シェイクスピアの二つ折版の英国から海外への絶えざる流失. ¶an *enormous drain* on the internal economy of the country その国内の経済におけるはなはだしい負担. ¶The war is a *heavy drain* upon her financial resources. 今の戦争はその国の財政上の一大負担だ.

Q² stop *dollar drain* ドルの流出を止める.

P² the *drain of* specie *from* a country 正金の流出. ¶a *drain on* one's strength その労力の消費‖the *drain of* the war *on* the population of the European countries その戦争がもたらしたヨーロッパ諸国の人口の減少‖I find my motor-car a great *drain on* my purse. 僕は自動車で大分経費がかさむ. ¶It is a *drain upon* the nation and a burden upon the taxpayers. それは国民の富を枯渇させるものであり納税者の重荷である.

drain, *v.* 排水する; 中味をなくする.

M *drain away* manpower 人力を消耗する‖His life was *draining away.* 彼は命まじかに迫っていた. ¶This land does not *drain well.* この土地は排水がよくない.

M² *drain off* liquids 液体をはかせる(からからにする)‖*drain* the land *off* その土地の排水をする‖The water of low ground slowly *drains off.* 低地の水は徐々にはける.‖The boiler *drained off.* ボイラーの水がなくなった.

P The country is *drained by* two rivers. その地方には二つの川が流れている. ¶*drain* the field well *for* crops 作付のために畑の排水をよくする. ¶*drain* water *from* land 排水する. ¶The river *drains into* the sea. その川は海に注ぐ‖The field is *drained into* the river. その野原の水は川にはける. ¶*drain* a vessel *of* its contents 器の中味を空にする. 【類】The war *drained* the country *of* its resources. ¶I am resolved to *drain to* the dregs. 私はあくまでやり通す決心だ.

drainage, *n.* 排水, 放流.

V The ocean *receives* the *drainage* of rivers. 海は河水の放流を受ける.

drama, *n.* 劇, 芝居; 劇的事件.

V *act* a *drama* 芝居をやる. ¶*enact* a little *drama* ちょっと芝居をやる. ¶one of the greatest *dramas* ever *staged* in this country この国でこれまで上演した最も偉大な演劇の一つ. ¶Many an unpleasant family *drama* was *unfolded.* 幾多のいまわしい家庭の不和が起った.

Q an *allegorical drama* 寓意劇. ¶The massacre of Hara concluding the insurrection of Shimabara was a *bloody drama.* 島原の乱の終幕となった原の殺りくは血なまぐさい悲劇であった. ¶a *clearly-constructed drama* 筋の明らかな劇. ¶a classical *French drama* フランス古典劇. ¶Japan must play her part worthily in the *great drama* unfolding [itself] in the Far East. 日本は極東において開幕する大演劇にその役目をりっぱに演じなければならない. ¶life's *little drama* 人生の寸劇. ¶a *poetic drama* 詩劇. ¶a *religious drama* 宗教劇. ¶a *serious drama* 堅い劇. ¶a *silent drama* 無言劇.

Q² a *church drama* 宗教劇. ¶a *Kabuki drama* 歌舞伎. ¶children's *picture drama* 子供の見る紙芝居. ¶a good *motion picture drama* すぐれた劇映画. ¶a four-cornered *problem drama* 四角関係を取扱った劇. ¶a *real-life drama* 社会劇.

P the characters represented *in* a *drama* 劇中の人物.

¶ form a novel *into* a *drama* 小説を劇に仕組む.
P² the *drama of* yesterday and today 過去および現在の劇.

dramalogue, *n.* せりふ.
Q² a *radio dramalogue* 放送劇の台詞(せりふ).

dramatic, *a.* 劇的な.
M be *quite dramatic* in performance やり方が全く芝居がかっている.

dramatics, *n.* 劇.
Q² *radio dramatics* 放送劇. ¶ *school dramatics* 学校劇.

dramatist, *n.* 劇作家.
Q Eugene O'Neill, *American dramatist* No. 1., ... アメリカ劇作家第一人者のユージン・オニールは... ¶ Mr. Pinero was enthusiastically hailed as the *premier dramatist* of Great Britain. ピネロ氏は英国劇作の第一人者であるとまで言われた.

dramatization, *n.* 脚色, 劇化.
V *make* a *dramatization* of "Vanity Fair" 「虚栄の市」を劇化する.

drape, *v.* [布で]飾る, (布で)おおう.
P *draped in* white 白布で飾った ‖ regimental standards *draped in* mourning 喪布でおおった連隊旗. ¶ His box in the theatre was *draped with* American and British flags. 劇場の彼の特別席は英米の国旗で飾られていた.

drapery, *n.* かけ衣; きもの.
Q *loose Oriental drapery* ゆったりした東洋のきもの. ¶ mountains in their *snowy drapery* 雪白のきものをまとった山々.
P² a *drapery for* the couch 長いす用のカバー.

draw, *n.* 人を引付ける物, 呼び物; 引分け.
V *take* a *draw* in a lottery 富くじを買う.
Q Mr. T is a *good draw* at political meetings. T 氏は政治的会合における人気者だ. ¶ The new play is a *great draw*. その新作の劇は非常な人気だ. ¶ A free sight in a street is a *never-failing draw*. 街で何かろはで見物のできるものがあるときっと人がたかる. ¶ a "*safe draw*" 大入請合の興行.
Q² a *lottery draw* 抽せん.
P The match ended *in* a *draw*. 試合は引分けになった.
P² a *draw in* a game 引分け. ¶ He's quick (slow) *on* the *draw*. [ピストルなどを]抜く手が早い(のろい).

draw, *v.* (1) 引く; 引出す; 引抜く; 寄せ集める; 描く; [水を]くむ; くじ引きで選ぶ; 近寄る; 進む; 人を集める(ひきつける); 引きのびる; 抜ける; 頼りにする; 風が通る; 喫水する.
M The speaker *always draws*. その弁士はいつも聴衆を引付ける. ¶ *draw* a boat *ashore* 舟を海岸に引上げる. ¶ *draw* a person *aside* 人を脇に引張って来る. ¶ *draw* attention *away* from ... ...から注意をそらす. ¶ *draw away* from other boats 他のボートから段々離れて行く. ¶ *draw back* a window curtain カーテンをあける ‖ *draw back* the first proposal 最初の提案を撤回する ‖ Snails *draw back* into their shells when danger comes near. かたつむりは危険が近づくと殻の中へ引込む. ‖ *draw back* from a contract (an agreement) 契約(協定)から手を引く. ¶ He *draws cleverly*. 彼は絵がうまい. ¶ Spring *draws closer* to summer. 春が段々夏の方に近寄る. ‖ the task of *drawing* the American and British peoples *closer* together 英米人をますます接近させようとする企図. ¶ The boat *draws deep*. その船は喫水が深い. ¶ *draw* a well *dry* 井戸をくみほす. ¶ The cart *draws easily*. その車は引きよい. ‖ The tooth *drew easily*. その歯はわけなく抜けた. ¶ The jury was *drawn* very *fairly*. 陪審員はきわめて公平に選ばれた. ¶ *draw forth* applause かっさいを博する ‖ *draw forth* productive energies 生産力を振い起す ‖ The urgent needs of the time *drew forth* their latent capabilities. 必要に迫られて彼らの隠れた才能が現われてきた. ¶ The chimney *draws freely*. その煙突は通りがよい. ‖ *freely drawing* on his deep learning そのうんちくを傾けて. ¶ with a face *grimly drawn* 物すごいしかめ面をして. ¶ *draw largely* on ... ...をしきりに利用する. ¶ *draw* it *mild* 穏やかに言う. ¶ *mostly drawn* from the highest nobility of France 主としてフランスの最高位の貴族から抜てきした. ¶ The examination is drawing near. 試験が近づきつつある. ¶ Christmas is *drawing nearer* to us. クリスマスが近づく. ¶ *draw out* one's revolver 拳銃を取出す ‖ *draw out* a cigarette from the pack 箱から巻タバコを一本引出す ‖ *draw out* one's watch 懐中時計を(ポケットから)取出す ‖ The engagement was long *drawn out*. その婚約は延び延びになった. ‖ *draw* it *out* into wire それを引延して針金にする ‖ *draw out* one's prayers to a great length 長々と祈る ‖ A little flattery *drew* him *out*. 少しおべっかを言ったら彼はしゃべり出した. ‖ The king ordered the regiment to be *drawn out*. 王は連隊に整列を命じた. ¶ He is hard to "*draw out*." 彼から話を引き出すのはむずかしい(秘密など). ¶ *draw it strong* 大げさに言う. ¶ *draw* it *tighter* もっとしっかり引きしめる. ¶ I *drew* myself *together* for another effort. 私はもう一息と身を引き締めた. ¶ An army of about 1,000 men was *drawn together*. 約千名の軍隊が召集された. ‖ The two ships gradually *drew together*. 両船が次第に接近した. ¶ The play *draws well*. その芝居は大入りだ. ‖ The tax *draws well*. 租税がよく集まる. ‖ Rubber *draws well*. ゴムはよくのびる. ‖ This pipe doesn't *draw well*. このパイプは通りがわるい.
M² They all *drew around* at the table. 一同食卓の回りに集った. ¶ The day *drew by*. 日が暮れた. ¶ *draw* a curtain *by* カーテンを引く. ¶ *draw down* beef 牛肉を煮詰める ‖ *draw down* blessings upon ... ...の上に祝福を祈る ‖ *draw down* the vengeance of Heaven *on* ... ...に天罰の下るのを祈る ‖ *draw down* a window (curtain) 窓(など)をおろす. ¶ *draw in* one's breath 息を吸い込む ‖ be *drawn in* behind ... ...の後ろに引っぱり込まれる ‖ a bait which has *drawn in* many to their ruin 多くの人々を破滅に落し入れた誘惑物 ‖ The days are *drawing in*. 日がつまりつゝある. ‖ He was *drawn in* to buy it. だまされて買わされた. ‖ *drew in* one's breath sharply 激しく息を引く ‖ *draw in* but lightly a gown under the arms 寛衣の腕の下をほんの少しつめる. ¶ *draw off* stockings くつ下を脱ぐ ‖ *draw off* water from rice-fields 田の水を落とす ‖ *draw off* excess currency 余剰通貨を回収する ‖ *draw off* one's gloves 手袋を取る ‖ *draw off* the urine by the catheter カテーテルで尿を取る ‖ *draw off* troops 軍隊を引上げる ‖ *draw off* one's attention to その注意を...の方に向ける. ¶ *draw on*＝draw near to death *or* be in a dying state 死になんなんとしている ‖ as evening *draws on* 夕暮近くなると. 【類】 Christmas is *drawing on* (＝near). ‖ draw one *on* to speak of ... 人に...の話をするように持ちかける ‖ Most great pianists find that as the years *draw on* their fingers grow stiff. 大抵の大ピアニストは年をとると指がこわばることに気付く. ¶ be *drawn over* by fear おどして(A 党所属者を B 党に)くらがえさせる. ¶ *draw up* a report 報告を作成する ‖ *draw up* the blind 日よけをあげる ‖ *draw up* a contract 契約書を作成する. 【類】 *draw up* a city plan (都市計画) / *draw up* a program (番組) / *draw up* tactics accordingly (これに応じる戦術) / *draw up* a document (文書) / *draw up* rules for ... / *draw up* a table (表) / *draw up* a list of ... / *draw up* a summons (呼出状) / *draw up* a new law / *draw up* a code (法典) / A report (報告書) is now being *drawn up*. / *draw up* a petition (請願書) / *draw up* a classification (分類) / *draw up* an outline / *draw up* an argument (論旨) / *draw up* a memorandum (覚書) / *draw up* an official report (公報) on ... / *draw up* the text of a final draft (最後の草稿の本文) / *draw up* a naval program (海軍計画) / *draw up* business company articles (商事会社の定款) / The balance sheet (貸借対照表) is properly *drawn up*. / *draw up* a balance sheet of Europe's economic resources and need (欧州の経済資源と欠乏) ‖ They are *drawn up* in rows. 幾列にも整列させられる. ‖ The automobile *drew up* at our doors. 自動車がわが家の入口で止った. 【類】 The carriage *drew up* at the door. / *drew up* at the school gates to discharge its cargo (荷をおろすために) / The train *drew up* to the station. ‖ She *drew* her horse *up* short. 彼女は乗馬をぴったり止めた. ‖ *draw* oneself *up* proudly そり身になる. 【類】 *draw* oneself *up* in dignity ‖ He *drew* himself *up* for the fight. 格闘しようと身構えた. ‖ The Oxford began slowly but steadily *drawing up* with the Cambridge crew. オックスフォード・クルーはゆっくりと始めたが着々ケンブリッジ・クルーに追いついた. ¶ The public funds in deposit were *drawn upon* for illegal purposes. 預金してあった公共の基金が違法の目的に引出された.
P *draw* one's sword *against* ... 剣を抜いて...に立向う. ¶ *draw after* his father 彼の父に似ている. ¶ *draw along* the ground 地を引きずる. ¶ *draw by* force 無理やり引きずる ‖ a cart *drawn by* hand 手で引く車. 【類】 The wagon was *drawn by* horses. / I *drew* my sled *by* a rope. ¶ the moral *drawn from* the event そのできごとから得た教訓. ¶ young men *drawn for* the army 陸軍に引っ張られ

た青年. ¶*draw* a thing *from* a pocket (drawer) 物をポケット(など)からひっぱり出す ‖ *draw* a salary *from* a firm 会社から月給を取る ‖ animals *drawn from* life (=nature) 動物の写生 ‖ The character was *drawn from* life, ... being the model. その人物は実在の人間をもとにして描かれ, ...がそのモデルだ. 【類】 pictures *drawn from* models ‖ *Draw* what money you require *from* the bank. 君の必要なだけいくらでも銀行から出し給え. ‖ *draw* exhibitors *from* Europe and America 欧米から出品者を誘致する ‖ *draw* one's sword *from* the scabbard 剣のさやを払う ‖ *draw* tears *from* a person 人に涙を催させる ‖ *draw* a conclusion (=an inference) *from* ... ...から結論を得る ‖ the conclusion to be *drawn from* the views presented here is that ... ここにあげた意見から帰納さるべき結論は...ということである ‖ *draw* water *from* a well 井戸から水をくむ. ‖ *draw from* university graduates for appointments in the foreign service 大学出身者の内から外交官を採用する. 【類】 Its members are *drawn from* all ranks of society and scattered over the whole of the country. ‖ boat crews *drawn from* members of the engineering department ‖ an elaborate picture of Far Eastern life *drawn from* observation and experience 観察と経験に基いた極東の生活の精巧な描写. ¶*draw* air *into* the lungs 肺に空気を吸込む. ¶*drawn in* water-color 水彩で描いた ‖ *draw* a prize *in* a lottery 当りくじを引く. ¶to be *drawn into* the vortex (=maelstrom) その渦潮に巻き込まれる ‖ if this country ever is *drawn into* war この国が戦争に巻き込まれるようなことがあれば. ¶reluctant to be *drawn into* a conflict 闘争に巻き込まれることをいやがって. ¶*draw on* reserves 予備(準備)金を引出す ‖ *draw on* one's credit 信用借をする ‖ *draw on* the strength of ... ...の力に頼る ‖ *draw on* another's income 人の収入を当てにする. 【類】 *draw on* a friend's sympathy ‖ *On* whom shall I *draw* for the advance? だれからその前借りができようか. ‖ She has behind it large financial resources *on* which to *draw* for propaganda purposes. その国は宣伝に使用しうる大きな財源を背後に持っている. ‖ "*draw*" him *on* the question of ... ...の問題について彼の意見を引出す ‖ He *drew* largely *on* the works of his predecessors in the field. 彼はその方面の既刊著作を大いに参考にした. ‖ a map *drawn on* a scale of one to a hundred 百分の一地図 ‖ *draw* examples *on* this collection 例をこの収集から取って来る ‖ *draw on* one's big imagination その大きな想像力をたくましくする ‖ *draw* one's sword *on* (=*against*) one's foe 敵に刀を抜いて切りつける. ¶*draw* a person *out of* the mire 困っている者を助ける. ¶*draw over* the stones 石の上を引く ‖ Horses *draw* sleighs *over* the ice and snow. 馬は氷雪の上でそりを引く. ¶*draw* a boat *through* the water *to* the shore 水中を岸までボートを引張って来る. ¶This *drew* a lecture *to* a close (=an end *or* its close). 講演はこれで終了した. ‖ The day *draws to* a close. 日が暮れる. 【類】 The year is *drawing to* a close. ‖ He *drew* my attention (=notice) *to* the fact. 彼はその事実に私の注意を引いた. ‖ The portrait is *drawn to* the life. その肖像画はまるで生写しだ. 【類】 His figures are real flesh and blood (血の通った), *drawn to* the life. ‖ maps *drawn to* the same scale 同一縮尺の地図 ‖ The map is *drawn to* (=on) the scale of one inch for each 100 miles. その地図は百マイルを一インチで表わす縮尺で描いてある. ¶It *drew towards* night. 夜がふけてきた. ‖ The book *draws towards* the end. その本が終りに近づく. ¶You are *drawing upon* yourself unmerited abuse. 君は言われる訳のない悪口を自分で招いている. ‖ *draw upon* a document 荷為替を組む ‖ *draw upon* foreign sources for a narrative 物語を書くに種を外国の資料に採る ‖ *draw upon* one's experience 自分の経験を利用する ‖ *draw upon* one's imagination 想像に訴える ‖ his writings have been freely *drawn upon* ... 彼の著述は大いに...を参考にして書かれたものである. 【類】 He has *drawn upon* his own early experience for his new enterprise. / The author has *drawn upon* the materials collected during his several visits to Russia and on personal notes made in European libraries and galleries. ¶pictures *drawn with* pen and pencil ペンと鉛筆で描いた絵 ‖ *draw with* a pen ペンで描く ‖ *draw with* a team (person) 団(人)と引分けになる.

(**2**) 手形を振出す.

M *draw* money *out* at a bank 銀行から金を引出す ‖ I cannot allow you to *draw out*. 手形を振出すことは許せない.

P bills *drawn against* securities or produce 有価証券または生産物を担保に振出した手形. ¶*draw at* seven days' date 七日払の手形を振出す ‖ *draw at* sight 一覧払の手形を振出す ‖ *draw at* thirty days' sight 三十日後一覧払の手形を振出す. ¶*draw on* him for $200 彼あてに二百ドル振出す ‖ for payment *draw on* us *through* A Bank 代金支払はA銀行を通じ手形振出しをこう ‖ *draw* a bill *on* (=upon) a firm 会社あて手形を振出す ‖ a check *drawn on* a bank 銀行あて振出しの小切手 ‖ drafts for a large amount *drawn on* all parts of the commercial world 商業界のすべての方面に振出した巨額の為替手形. ¶a check *drawn to* the order of ... ...指図人あて振出しの小切手 ‖ *draw* a check *to* one's order 指図式に手形を振出す.

drawback, *n.* 障害物, 故障; 払戻金, 払戻税.

V *allow* a *drawback* 税を払戻す. ¶Everything *has* its *drawback*. 何事も一得一失は免かれない. ‖ Old age *has* its *drawbacks*. 老令にはそれ相応の弱味がある. ¶*mitigate drawbacks* and difficulties 障害や困難を軽減する. ¶*possess* the far more serious *drawback* of being ... ...になるというさらに大なる障害がある. ¶*remedy* a *drawback* to ... ...の障害を除く. ¶*remove* a *drawback* from ... ...から故障を除く.

Q a *positive drawback* in any walk of life どんな方面の仕事においても一つの明かな不利. ¶without any *serious drawback* さしたる障りもなく.

P² a *drawback to* success 成功を妨げるもの. 【類】 Envy is a *drawback to* friendship.

drawbridge, *n.* つるべ橋.

V *lower* (=*let down*) a *drawbridge* つるべ橋を降ろす. ¶*raise* (=*draw up*) a *drawbridge* つるべ橋を上げる.

drawer, *n.* 引出し.

V *lock* a *drawer* 引出しに錠をかける. ¶*open* (*shut*) a *drawer* 引出しを開ける(締める).

Q the *second drawer* from the top 上から二番目の引出し. ¶a *secret drawer* of his old-fashioned desk 彼の古風な机の秘密引出し.

Q² You will find it in the *bottom drawer*. それは一番下の引出しにある. ¶a *bureau drawer* たんすの引出し. ¶a *cabinet drawer* たんすの引出し. ¶put it away in a *desk drawer* それを机の引出しに仕舞う.

P a chest *of drawers* たんす一さお.

drawers, *n. pl.* ずぼん下, ズロース, さるまた.

Q² *half-length drawers* 半長のずぼん下, すててこ. ¶*knit drawers* メリヤスのずぼん下. ¶*bathing drawers* 水泳パンツ.

drawing, *n.* 図画; 製図.

V A famous artist *did* the *drawing*. 有名な画家がその絵を描いた. ¶*make* a *drawing* 絵を描く; 図面を引く ‖ *make drawings* of specimens ひな形の図面を引く. ¶*produce drawings* デッサンを描く. ¶We *reproduce* here a *drawing* of the cottage. その小屋の図面がここに出してある. ¶*submit drawings* for a prize contest コンクールに絵を出品する.

Q The bonds are redeemable by *annual drawings* at par. その公債は年々額面値段で回収ができる. ¶a *finished drawing* 完成した製図. ¶a minutely *executed drawing* 密画. ¶*mechanical* (=*instrumental*) *drawing* 用器画.

Q² *black-and-white drawings* 墨絵. ¶a *chalk drawing* 白墨画. ¶*character drawing* 人物描写. ¶*charcoal drawing* 木炭画法. ¶a *detail drawing* 明細図. ¶*freehand drawing* 自在画法. ¶a *frontispiece drawing* 口絵. ¶an *Indian-ink drawing* 墨絵. ¶a *line* (=*lineal*) *drawing* 線画. ¶*model drawing* 実物描写. ¶a *pen and ink drawing* ペン画. ¶a *scale drawing* 比例尺の図. ¶a *water-color drawing* 水彩画. ¶a *whole-page* (*half-page*) *drawing* 一ページ大(半ページ大)の絵. ¶a *working drawing* 施工図.

P a satire *in drawing* 風刺画.

P² sepia *drawings by* Kano Tannyu 狩野探幽の描いた墨絵. ¶a *drawing from* the brush of a painter 画家の筆になった絵 ‖ Japanese art is distinguished by directness, facility, and strength of line, a sort of bold dash due probably to the habit of writing and *drawing from* the elbow, not from the wrist.—Chamberlain. 日本画は線の卒直・軽妙・強さすなわち大胆な筆力の点で卓越している, これは恐らく手首で描かずにひじで描く習慣によること

であろう. ‖ [a] *drawing from* the round 立体模型写生画法(画). ¶a *drawing in* pen [and ink] ペン画 ‖ a *drawing in* water-color 水彩画. ¶a *drawing on* the block (=wood) 木版画.

drawing-card, *n.* 切札.

Q He is a *big drawing-card* in the troupe. 彼はその一座の大立物である.

drawing-room, *n.* 応接間.

Q a *finely-tapestried drawing-room* りっぱな壁掛けのある応接間.

dread, *n.* 恐怖.

V *allay* one's *dread* 恐怖を静める. ¶grow to *have* a *dread* of ... ...を恐れるようになる ‖ He *has dread* of speaking in public. 彼は人前で話すことを恐れる.

Q have an *awful dread* of ... ...を非常にこわがっている. ¶Her heart was relieved of its *blackest dread*. 彼女は深い心配がなくなって安どの胸をなで下したのであった(戦死したといううわさの息子が無事帰宅したときなど). ¶live in *constant dread* of ... ...を絶えず恐れている. ¶an *excessive dread* of foreign customs 外国の習慣に対する過度の恐怖. ¶He has an *instinctive dread* of dogs. 彼は生来犬をこわがる. ¶He is in *perpetual dread* of exposure. 彼は始終露顕を恐れている. ¶an *unnatural dread* of water 不自然な水ぎらい(恐水病など). ¶the *vague dread* of ... ...に対するばく然たる恐怖. ¶a *wholesome dread* of the law 法律に対する健全な恐怖心.

P shrink *in dread* 恐れてちぢこまる ‖ be *in dread* of ... ...に絶えずおびえている. ¶*with* a strange *dread* of evil 薄気味悪く. ¶a *dread of* snakes へびぎらい.

dreadful, *n.* 《俗》ぞっとするような物語.

Q a *penny dreadful*=blood-and-thunder story [新聞など連載の]せん情的小説, スリラーもの.

dreadnaught, *n.* ド級戦艦.

Q² a *giant dreadnaught* 巨大なド級戦艦. ¶a fleet of *motor dreadnaughts* from the Fujiya garage 富士屋(ホテル)の車庫から出て来る大型車の群.

dream, *n.* 夢; 夢想.

V It was supposed to *bring* pleasant *dreams*. そうすると愉快な夢を見ると言われている. ¶he *cherished* throughout his active life the *dream* of ... 彼はその活動的生涯を通じて...の夢想をいだいていた. ¶*convert* their *dreams* into reality 彼らの夢想を実現させる. ¶*dream* beautiful and happy *dreams* 美しい愉快な夢を見る. ¶*exceed* his wildest *dreams* 彼のとてつもない夢ですらかなわない. ¶get a diviner to *expound* one's *dream* 易者に夢を判断してもらう. ¶My *dream* has been *fulfilled*. 私が夢に見たことが本当になった. ¶I have *had* a curious *dream*. 私は妙な夢を見た. ‖ The boy *had dreams* of being a hero. その子は英雄を夢みていた. 【類】I *had* a *dream* about you last night. ゆうべ君の夢を見た. ‖ Of course, I *have* a *dream* of travelling in Europe and studying in Paris, but I am afraid that time will be long in coming. もちろん私は欧州を旅行しパリで勉強する夢を描いているんだがその時は急には来そうもない. ¶*interpret* a *dream* 夢判断をする. ¶in order to *obtain* oracular *dreams* 夢に神託を受けるために. ¶*realize* one's *dream* of ... ...という夢想を実現する. ¶*relate* one's *dream* 夢を語る. ¶*seek* oracular *dreams* at a shrine 神社で夢に神意を授かるようにと祈願する. ¶*translate* a *dream* into action 夢想を実行に移す. ¶Boy-Satyrs *whispered dreams* in his ear. 少年サチロス神たちが彼の耳に夢をささやいた.

V² My *dream* has *come* true. 夢が本当になった. ¶The *dream melts away*. 夢は消え去る. ¶A *dream vanishes*. 夢は消える.

Q I had *awful dreams*. 私は恐ろしい夢を見た. ¶have a *bad dream* 夢見が悪い. ¶a *cheerful dream* 愉快な夢. ¶it has for many years been a *cherished dream* of his to ... ...することは彼が多年の宿望であった. ¶a *dreadful dream* 恐ろしい夢. ¶an *erotic dream* 性欲的な夢. ¶an *evil dream* 悪夢. ¶a *fantastic dream* ばかげた夢. ¶a *favorite dream* of ... ...の気に入りの夢想. ¶a *fearful dream* 恐ろしい夢. ¶realize one's *fondest dreams* about ... ...に関する宿願を実現する. ¶It is an impossible if not a *foolish dream*. ばかげていないまでもあり得ない夢想だ. ¶a *funny dream* おかしな夢. ¶vague remembrances of a *ghastly dream* 薄気味の悪い夢のばく然たる記憶. ¶a *good* and *prosperous dream* 吉夢. ¶a *hideous dream* 悪夢. ¶a *horrible dream* 恐ろしい夢. ¶Such a hope is not an *idle dream*. こうした希望は空想でない. ‖ it is scarcely an *idle dream* to look forward to the time when ... ...の時代を期待することはあだな夢ではない. ¶the collapse of Yuan Shihkai's *imperial dream* in 1916 一九一六年における袁世凱の大野心が失敗に帰したこと. ¶an *insubstantial dream* あだな夢. ¶seminal loss following a *lascivious dream* 好色な夢に伴う遺失精. ¶an *ominous dream* 凶夢. ¶The land is a *perfect dream*. それは全く夢の国だ. ¶Good night and *pleasant dreams*! お休みなさいそしてよい夢を御覧なさい. ¶a *prophetic dream* 夢の知らせ. ¶*rash dreams* of youth 青年時代の途方もない夢. ¶a *shadowy dream* ぼんやりした夢. ¶I wish you all a very *sweet dream*. 皆さんよい夢を御覧なさい. ¶a *terrible dream* 恐ろしい夢. ¶disturbed by *tormenting dreams* 悪夢に悩まされて. ¶an *ugly dream* いやな夢. ¶an *unfinished dream* 見果てぬ夢. ¶an *unreliable dream* 当にならない夢. ¶This *Utopian dream* is far beyond the range of possibility. こんな夢みたいな話はとうていあり得ない. ¶a *vain dream* 空想. ¶a *vivid dream* ありありとした夢. ¶a *waking dream* 空想. ¶a *wet dream* 遺精. ¶His *wild dream* came to life. 彼の途方もない夢が実現した. 【類】In my *wildest dreams* I never thought I would become a professional waiter.

Q² a *day dream* 白日夢.

P *during* a *dream* 夢を見ている間に. ¶awake *from* a *dream* 夢がさめる. ¶appear to a person *in* a *dream* その夢まくらに立つ ‖ I often return *in dreams* to the country of my birth. 僕は度々夢の中で故国に帰る. 【類】I saw him *in* a *dream*. / I saw a beautiful girl *in* a *dream*. ‖ live *in* a *dream* 夢うつゝで暮す ‖ as *in* a *dream* まるで夢のような. ¶the land *of dreams* 夢の国.

P² the realization of Bellamy's *dreams in* "Looking Backwards"「回顧」の中にあるベラミーの夢想の実現. ¶the *dream of* one's youth その青年時代の夢 ‖ She knew that this *dream of* her heart would come true. 彼女はこの思いこがれる夢が実現することを知っていた. ‖ a *dream of* past 過去の夢 ‖ make reading in school a *dream of* pleasure 学校の読方を愉快な夢のような仕事にする.

dream, *v.* 夢見る; 夢想する.

M *ardently dream* 熱心に夢想する. ¶*dream away* one's life うかうかと一生を過す ‖ The foolish young man is *dreaming away* (=*out* or *through*) his time. その愚かな青年は時をむだに使っている. ¶*dream forward* to an event (a day) できごと(など)を夢に待つ. ¶*little dreaming* that he was leaving the place for the last time 彼はその土地を去るのはこれが最後となろうとは夢にも知らずに. 【類】*Little* did I *dream* of succeeding so well. ¶he *never dreamed* that ... would ... 彼は...なるだろうとは夢想だにしなかった. 【類】I *never dreamed* of meeting you here. ‖ such wealth as he had *never even dreamed* of 彼が夢想だにしなかった富.

P *dream about* a person (matter) 人(など)のことを夢に見る ‖ I *dreamed about* home. うちのことを夢に見た. ¶*dream of* one's future 将来を夢想する ‖ *dream of* honors 栄達を夢見る. ‖ One cannot even *dream of* the possibility of such a thing. そんなことができるなんて思いも寄らない. 【類】I *dreamed of* my friend in the Navy. / To *dream of* money in bags or boxes denotes misfortune of some kind.

dreamer, *n.* 夢想家.

Q a *mere dreamer* ほんの夢想家. ¶a mere *theoretical dreamer*, totally lacking in social efficiency 社会的能力を全然欠いているほんの学理的夢想家. ¶a *Utopian dreamer* 理想郷を夢見る人.

P² a *dreamer of* innovation 革新を夢みる人.

dredger *n.* しゅんせつ機.

Q² a *self-propelling dredger* 自動推進しゅんせつ機. ¶a *steam dredger* 蒸気しゅんせつ機.

dregs, *n. pl.* くず, かす.

P² the *dregs of* mankind 人間のくず ‖ It is surely the *dregs of* bitterness in his cup of woe. それはたしかに彼の悲しみ中の最も心を苦しめる所である.

drench, *v.* びしょぬれにする.

M *thoroughly drenched* ぬれねずみになって. ¶He is *drenched through* and *through*. 彼はびしょぬれだ.

P garments *drenched in* blood 血だらけの着物 ‖ He was *drenched in* dew. 彼は露でびしょぬれになっていた. ¶He was *drenched to* the skin. 彼はびしょぬれであった. ¶Napoleon *drenched* Europe *with* war. ナポレオンはヨーロッパを戦じんのちまたと化した. ‖a garment *drenched with* water (blood) 水(など)がしみ込んだ着物. 【類】He is *drenched with* rain. ‖voice *drenched with* love 恋にうるんだ声.

dress, *n*. 衣服, 服装.

v *adjust* one's *dress* 服の乱れを直す. ¶*cast aside* her *dress* 彼女の着物を脱ぎ捨てる. ¶She went upstairs to *change* her *dress*. 彼女は着替えに二階に上った. ‖The sexes are forbidden to *change dress*. 異性の服装は禁じられている. ¶*do up* a *dress* 着物をつくろう. ¶The *dress* of the people has been largely *Europeanized*. 国民の服装が大に欧化した. ¶*forsake* the national *dress* 国民伝来の服装を捨てる. ¶*get* a new *dress* 新しい服を求める. ¶*iron* the *dress* to make it smooth しわをのばすために着物にアイロンをかける. ¶*lace up* a *dress* 着物にレースを付ける. ¶My *dress* must be *let out*. 私の着物はのばさなければならない. ¶*loosen* one's *dress* 着物をゆるくする. ¶*make* a *dress* for her doll 彼女の人形の着物を作る. ¶*pin up* a *dress* 着物をピンで止める ‖*put on* the *dress* of a sailor 水兵服を着る. ¶The British Isles will then *put on* gala *dress*. 英本国ではそのときは盛装することであろう(祝典の飾りつけなど). ¶She managed to *scramble on* her *dress*. 彼女は大急ぎでどうにかこうにか着物を身に着けた. ¶A passing vehicle *splashed* her *dress* with mud. 通りかかった乗物が彼女の着物に泥をはねかした. ¶*spoil* a *dress* 着物をよごす. ¶*tidy* [*up*] *dress*＝tidy oneself 服装をきちんとする. ¶*trim* a *dress* with ribbons (lace) 着物にリボン(など)をつける. ¶*try on* a *dress* 着物を着て見る. ¶*undo* a *dress* 着物をぬぐ. ¶*wear* full *dress* 正装する ‖*wear* light, pretty *dresses* [婦人など]軽いきれいな着物を着る. 【類】a child *wearing* a beautiful *dress*. ¶This *dress becomes* (＝*suits*) you. この着物は君に似合う.

Q *ancient classical dress* 昔の古典的な服装. ¶put on one's *blue* (*pink*) *dress* 青い(桃色の)服を着る. ¶a *brown dress* 茶色の服. ¶in *ceremonial dress* 式服で. ¶soldiers in *civilian dress* 平服を着た軍人. ¶people in plain *civic dresses* 質素な普通の服装をした人々. ¶*Costly dresses* are inappropriate in the office. 高価な服装は事務所用には不適当だ. ¶in a badly *creased dress* 折目がくしゃくしゃになった服を着て. ¶It is requested that *easy dress* be worn on account of the heat. 暑気のことですから簡易な服装をせられるようにお願します[招待などの場合]. ¶in its *English dress* その英訳本で ‖He deemed the book worthy of an *English dress*. 彼はその本が英訳する価値があると思った. 【類】give it an *English dress*. ¶wear *fancy dress* 仮装舞踏服を着る. ¶in *fashionable dress* 社交界のドレスを着て(夜会服など). ¶wear *female dress* 女の服を着る. ¶a girl in *festive dress* 晴着姿の少女. ¶a *formal dress* 礼服. ¶in *full dress* 礼服を着て. ¶in *full Japanese dress* 日本の礼服を着て. ¶a *fussy dress* 手数のかかった着物. ¶a lady in *gala dress* 晴着を着た婦人. ¶an *ill-fitting dress* 身につかない着物. ¶He was clothed in *incombustible dress*. 彼は耐火服を着ていた. ¶in *Japanese dress* 和服で. ¶a *lady's dress* 婦人服. ¶a *loud dress* けばけばしい着物. ¶a *low dress* ローネックの婦人礼服. ¶Hamlet in *modern dress* 今様ハムレット. ¶the *national dress* 自国の服. ¶All Japan appears in a *new dress* at New Year. 正月に全日本は新装する. ¶in their *official dress* それぞれ官服を着て. ¶She had an *open dress*. 彼はゆっくりした着物を着ていた. ¶a *patched dress* つぎはぎの着物. ¶a *plain dress* 質素な着物. ¶a *poky dress* 《英》みすぼらしい着物. ¶He was clad in his *poor cotton dress*. 彼は粗末な綿服を着ていた. ¶a *presentable dress* 人に見られてはずかしくない服装. ¶in *private dress* 平常服で. ¶in their own *religious dress* 彼らの宗派の服を着て. ¶a *rustic dress* いなかびた着物. ¶a *scanty dress* わずかしか身につけていない着物. ¶a *shabby dress* 見すぼらしい服装. ¶a *simple dress* 質素な着物. ¶a young lady in a *white dress* 白い服装した若い婦人.

Q² *battle dress* 戦闘服. ¶a marine in *combat dress* 戦闘服をつけた海兵. ¶a man in *country dress* いなかの服装をした人. ¶resplendent in *court dress* きらびやかな参内服を着て. ¶wear *dinner* and *evening dress* 正餐兼夜会服(タキシード)を着る. ¶crush-hatted men in *evening dress* 夜会服を着てオペラ帽をかぶっている人. 【類】ladies and gentlemen in *evening dress*. ¶wear *fancy dress* 仮装服を着る. ¶women in *farm dress* 労農服を着ている女たち. ¶the fashionable *head dress* [紳士淑女の]夜会用の帽子. ¶put on a *holiday dress* 外出着を着る ‖streets and shops in *holidays dress* 休日の飾りつけをした街路と商店(クリスマスなど). ¶in *gymnasium dress* 体操服で. ¶*Morning dress* will be worn both at dinner and at the theatre. モーニングは正餐にも芝居へ行くにも着る. ¶a *party dress* パーティ(園遊会, 夜会など)用の服. ¶a lady in *riding dress* 乗馬服の婦人. ¶a *service dress* 職務服. ¶a *sports dress* (女の)スポーツ着. ¶We wear *street dress* for our daily activities. われわれは日々の勤務に外出着を着る. ¶in regular *student dress* 学生服で. ¶a *visiting dress* 訪問着. ¶wear a dark *walking dress* 黒っぽい散歩服を着ている. ¶*wear-to-office dress* 婦人通勤服. ¶in one's *working dress* 仕事着姿で.

P *in dress* of yore 昔の服装で ‖He is extravagant *in dress*. 彼は着道楽だ. ‖She is slovenly *in* her *dress*. 彼女は身なりがだらしない. ‖She looks stylish *in* this *dress*. 彼女はこれを着るといきだ. ¶a man *of dress* 衣装好みの男. ¶spend a good deal of money *on dress* 着物にたくさんの金をかける. ¶We had to wade *with* our *dresses* tucked up. われわれは着物をまくって川をわたらなければならなかった.

P² the *dress of* ceremony 礼服.

dress, *v*. 衣服を着せる; 装う, 飾る; 調理する; 服装する.

M be *absurdly dressed* ばかげた服装をしている. ¶They were *dressed alike*. 彼らは同じような服装をしていた. ¶make them feel *cheaply dressed* by comparison 他と比べて安物を着ていると思わせる. ¶She was *colorfully dressed*. 彼女は美々しく装うていた. ¶be *decently dressed* 上品ななりをしている. ¶*dress effeminately* にやけた服装をする. ¶a stylish gentleman *elegantly dressed* in the latest fashion 最新流行の上品な服装したハイカラ紳士. ¶*expensively dressed* 金のかかったなりをして. ¶*expressively dressed* 深い印象を与える服装をして. ¶*exquisitely dressed* in the very height of fashion 流行の先端を行くりっぱな服装をして. ¶You are *finely dressed* today. 今日はおめかしですね. ¶*dress flashily* けばけばしい服装をする. ¶He is *fully dressed*. 彼は正装している. ‖All the warships in port were *fully dressed*. 停泊中の軍艦は皆満艦飾を施していた. ¶She *dressed* herself *hastily*. 彼女は急いで身支度をした. ¶She is *ill dressed*. 彼女は身なりが悪い. ¶*immaculately dressed*. すっきりとした服装をして. ¶He was *inexpensively*, but *neatly*, *dressed*. 彼は金はかゝらないがさっぱりしたなりをしていた. ¶*dress lightly* (*heavily*) 薄(厚)着をする. ¶*nicely dressed* きれいな身支度をして. ¶go *plainly dressed* 質素な服装をしている. ¶*plainly* but *neatly dressed* 質素ではあるがさっぱりしたなりをして. ¶be *poorly dressed* みすぼらしい服装をしている. ¶be *dressed properly* for school 通学にふさわしい服装をしている. ¶He is *quaintly dressed*. 彼はおかしななりをしている. ¶He was so *quietly dressed* that only with difficulty could I recall that he wore a white waistcoat. 彼は非常に地味ななりをしていたので私はやっとのことで彼が白いチョッキを着ていたことに気がついた. ¶She is *respectably dressed*. 彼女ははずかしくない服装をしている. ¶She was *richly dressed*. 彼女はりっぱに着飾っていた. ¶*shabbily dressed* みすぼらしい服装をして. ¶*smartly dressed* スマートな格好で. ¶a clerk *sprucely dressed* きちんとしたなりをした店員. ¶*stylishly dressed* しゃれた服装をして. ¶*suitably dressed* それ相応な服装をして. ¶*dress out* (＝*up*) [船などを]飾り立てる; めかす. ¶be *thickly dressed* うんと着込んでいる. ¶*dress* oneself more *warmly* もっと暖かい服装をする. ¶*dress well* on £20 a year 一年二十ポンドでりっぱななりをする. ¶To be *well dressed* needn't mean *luxuriously dressed*. 服装がよいということは必ずしもぜいたくななりをすることではない.

M² I'll *dress* him *down*. 《口語》うんと油をしぼってやろう. ¶*dress* [*up*] ship 船飾を施す ‖women *dressed up* in men's clothes 男装の女たち. 【類】a doll *dressed up* in *kimono* ‖go out, fully *dressed up* 正装して出かける.

P *dress above* one's circumstances 身分不相応の服装をする. ¶She was *dressed after* the English fashion. 彼女は英国風に装った. ¶*dressed as* a man (woman, working-man) 男(など)の風をして. ¶*dress for* dinner 正餐用の服装をする ‖*dress for* a ball 舞踏会の衣装をつける ‖*dress* a fowl or a salad *for* dinner 晩餐に鳥またはサラダを調理す

る‖He *dressed* himself ***for*** a ride. 彼は乗馬服を着けた.‖She *dressed* herself ***for*** an outing. 彼女は外出の服装をした.‖*dress* ***for*** the day 当日の飾りをする. ¶*dressed* entirely in black 全く黒装束で‖He is *dressed* ***in*** white (blue). 彼は白(など)服を着ている.‖*dressed* ***in*** a uniform (silk) 制服(など)を着て‖be *dressed* ***in*** l'européenne 洋服を着ている. 【類】be *dressed* ***in*** livery (使用人などの制服) / be *dressed* ***in*** morning (モーニング) / be *dressed* ***in*** white (白衣) / *dressed* ***in*** lounge suits and informal clothes (散歩服や略服) / *dressed* ***in*** full uniform (正装)‖*dressed* ***in*** elegant attire 上品ななりをして‖*dress* ***in*** the cheapest and meanest clothes 一番安くて一番粗末な着物を着る‖*dressed* ***in*** *hakama* はかまをはいて. ¶The ship was *dressed* ***with*** flags. 船は旗で飾ってあった.‖She *dresses* her hair ***with*** taste. 彼女はいきに髪を結う.

dresser, *n.* 着付けをする人. 「《俗》めかし屋.
Q a ***careful*** *dresser* 服装に注意する人. ¶a ***swell*** *dresser*
Q^2 a ***vine*** *dresser* ぶどう園の園丁.

dressing, *n.* 着つけ, 衣服; 包帯; サラダソース; 肥料.
Q ***sterile*** *dressing* 消毒した包帯. ¶give a ***thin*** *dressing* of ... 薄い施肥をする.
Q^2 ***oyster*** *dressing* かきにかける白ソース. ¶***salad*** *dressing* サラダ用ソース. ¶a ***top*** *dressing* 敷肥. ¶***window*** *dressing* 陳列窓飾り.

dressing-down, *n.* きびしい小言.
Q give a person a ***good*** *dressing-down* 人をうんとしかる.

dressing-gown, *n.* [パジャマの上に着る]一種のどてら.
Q a ***quilted*** *dressing-gown* どてら.

dress-pattern, *n.* 〖装飾〗裁断の型.
Q^2 ***cutting*** *dress-patterns* 服地の裁断型.

dribble, *v.* したたる, たれる; ちびちび与える; よだれをたらす.
M Infants ***generally*** *dribble* when they are teething. 幼児は大抵歯が生えるころになるとよだれをたらす. ¶*dribble* ***out*** one's secret aid to ... ...にちょいちょい秘密の援助を与える.
P Rain water *dribbles* ***from*** the eaves. 雨水が軒からしたたる. ¶streams of men *dribbling* ***through*** the streets between six and seven 六時と七時の間に町をぞろぞろ通る人 ⌊々の群.

driblet, *n.* 少量, 少額.
P ***by*** *driblets* ちびちび, 少しづつ. ¶He paid the money ***in*** *driblet*. 彼はその金をちびちび払った.

drift, *n.* すう勢, 傾向; 漂流物, 吹きだまり; 趣旨; 推移; 駆力.
V ***discern*** a *drift* toward ... ...への傾向を識別する. ¶***follow*** the *drift* of one's thoughts 思想の筋をたどる... ¶***remove*** snow *drifts* 雪の吹きだまりを取除ける. ¶***understand*** (=***see, get*** or ***catch***) the *drift* of the talk (=words) 話の大意を理解する.
Q ***cultural*** *drift* 文化のすう勢. ¶a ***floating*** *drift* of logs 漂流する丸太. ¶the ***general*** *drift* of a discourse 講話の大意‖the ***general*** *drift* of affairs on the Continent [英国から見ての]欧州大陸の大勢. ¶The whole town was practically buried under a ***heavy*** *drift* of snow. 町全体が雪のひどい吹きだまりの下にまったく埋ってしまった. ¶the ***westward*** *drift* of the Huns フン族の西移.
Q^2 ***road*** *drift* 道ぶしんで道路からかき取った土砂.
P ***under*** the *drift* of passions 情にかられて.
P^2 a *drift* ***of*** bullets 雨あられと飛ぶ弾丸‖the *drift* ***of*** a current 漂流‖a *drift* ***of*** ice resulting from the wind 風のための浮氷の移動. ¶a *drift* ***of*** cloud ***across*** the sky 空を横切る浮雲. ¶a *drift* ***toward*** nationalism 国家主義への ⌊傾向.

drift, *v.* 漂う, 流れる; 放浪する; 吹きたまる.
M *drift* ***aimlessly*** through life 一生をぶらぶら送る. ¶The boat *drifted* ***ashore*** on an island. ボートが島の岸に漂着した. ¶the conversation *drifted* ***away*** to ... 話が...の方へ移って行った. ¶The ship *drifted* ***out*** to sea. 船は沖の方へただよった. ¶The boat *drifted* ***seaward*** helplessly. ボートはどうすることもできずに海の方へ流れて行った.
M^2 *drift* ***about*** in the sea 海中をあちらこちら漂う‖The ship *drifted* ***about*** at the mercy of the wind. 船は風のまにまにただよった. ¶*drift* ***on*** to the street (売春婦が)街路をうろつく‖*drift* ***on*** to the shore 岸辺に漂流する.
P He *drifted* ***about*** the Continent for a while. 彼はしばしの間大陸を放浪した. ¶The ship *drifted* ***before*** the wind. 船は風に追われてただよった. ¶*drift* ***down*** a stream (=downstream) 川を流れ下る. ¶a foolish girl who has *drifted* ***from*** home 家出をしたばかな少女. ¶*drift* ***from*** one country ***to*** another 甲の国から乙の国へと漂泊する. ¶He *drifted* ***into*** literature. 彼は文学の方に転向した.‖We *drifted* ***into*** such a melancholy conversation. われわれはそんな憂うつな話に転じた. 【類】He began in English, but soon *drifted* (=switched) ***into*** Japanese.‖*drift* ***into*** immoral habits 知らず識らず不道徳な習性に陥る‖he *drifted* ***into*** the city of ... 彼は...市へ流れて行った‖The collection *drifted* ***into*** the hands of wealthy families. その収集は金持の手にはいった. ¶The bottle containing the message was found, after *drifting* ***on*** the ocean for 35 years. その通信文を入れたびんが大洋を三十五年間漂流した後に発見された. ¶We two set out to *drift* ***through*** London. われわれ二人はロンドン市中をぶらつきに出かけた. ¶snow *drifted* ***to*** the depth of ... 雪が...の深さに吹きだまった‖The conversation *drifted* ***to*** some subject (person). 談話がある問題(など)に移って行った. ¶the iron-bound, sailless lighters, that *drift* ***with*** the tide like logs 丸太のように潮のまにまにただよう帆のない装甲伝馬船.

drill, *n.* (**1**) けい古, 訓練, 教練, 練習.
V ***carry out*** lifeboat *drill* 救命艇操縦の練習をやる. ¶***perform*** a *drill* 教練を行う. ¶***receive*** a daily *drill* 毎日訓練を ⌊受ける.
Q ***individual*** *drill* 各個教練.
Q^2 ***battalion, company,*** and ***squad*** *drill* and exercise 大隊・中隊および小隊教練と演習. ¶***class*** *drill* in ... ...における課業. ¶a ***field martial*** *drill* 野戦演習. ¶a ***fire*** *drill* 消防演習. ¶a squad of recruits at ***rifle*** *drill* 拳銃教練中の補充兵分隊.
P ***at*** *drill* 訓練中. ¶*drill* ***on*** pronunciation 発音の練習.
(**2**) きり; 〖機〗穴あけ器具(ドリル).
V ***use*** a *drill* to bore a hole in ... ...に穴をあけるにきりを使う. 「ドリル.
Q an ***automatic*** *drill* 自動式ドリル. ¶a ***dental*** *drill* 歯科用
Q^2 a ***diamond*** *drill* ダイヤモンドぎり. ¶a ***jump*** *drill* 舞ぎり. ¶a steam-power (handpower) ***rock*** *drill* 蒸気(手動)せん岩ドリル. ¶a ***twist*** *drill* トウィスト・ドリル.
P pierce ***with*** a *drill* きりで穴をあける. ¶*drills* ***in*** the use of ... ...に使用するきり.

drill, *v.* 訓練する, しつける.
P Chinese soldiers *drilled* ***by*** foreign officers 外国武官に訓練された中国兵. ¶*drill* students ***in*** these exercises これらの練習題で学生を鍛える‖He is thoroughly *drilled* ***in*** English grammar. 彼は英文法に通じている.‖*drilled* ***in*** the art of courtesy 礼儀を心得ている‖*drill* a girl ***in*** all that she should do 女のなすべきことを厳重にしつける. ¶*drill* it ***into*** his mind insistently しいてそれを彼の心の中に植え付ける. ¶He is *drilled* ***to*** the factories. 彼は工場で働くように仕込んである.

drilling-machine, *n.* 〖機〗ボール盤.
Q a ***portable*** *drilling-machine* 卓上ボール盤.

drink, *n.* 飲物; 酒; 飲酒.
V He ***carries*** his *drink* like a gentleman. 彼は自分の酒酔を人に見せない. ¶It ***forms*** (=is) a pleasant and refreshing *drink*. それは気持が良く気の引立つ飲料である. ¶***Give*** me a *drink* of water. 水を一杯下さい. ¶We ***had*** a *drink* last night in a saloon. 昨夜ある酒場で一杯やった.‖***have*** a *drink* of brandy straight 《米》ブランデーをストレートで(割らないで)一杯やる. ¶***sip*** fountain *drinks* at a drug store 《米》ドラグ・ストアでソーダ水をちびちび飲む. ¶***sleep off*** the *drink* 眠って酔をさます. ¶***take*** a *drink* from a fountain 泉の水を一杯飲む‖***take*** a *drink* of brandy neat き一本のブランデーを一杯やる. ¶***taste*** strong *drink* 強い酒を飲む. ¶The cow ***wanted*** a *drink*. 雌牛が水を飲みたがった.
Q ***alcoholic*** *drinks* 酒精飲料. ¶an ***all year round*** *drink* 四季共通の飲物. ¶a ***cooling*** *drink* 清涼飲料. ¶***fancy*** *drinks* 変った酒. ¶a ***heating*** *drink* like coffee コーヒーのような暖かい飲料. ¶***hot*** *drinks* like tea or coffee 茶やコーヒーのような暖かい飲物. ¶***iced*** *drinks* 氷で冷した飲料. ¶never touch ***intoxicating*** *drink* 決して酒類を口にしない. ¶Let's have a ***little*** *drink*. 一杯やろう. ¶have a ***long*** *drink* of ... ...をぐっと飲む. ¶***mixed*** or ***adulterated*** *drink* 混ぜもののある酒. ¶Tea is the ***national*** *drink* of Japan. 茶は日本の国民的飲物である. 【類】beer, our ***national*** *drink*. ¶Coffee was a ***new*** *drink* in England then. コーヒーは当時英国

では目新しい飲物であった. ¶a ***popular drink*** 一般の飲物. ¶***restorative drinks*** 元気を回復させる飲物. ¶have ***several drinks*** 数回飲む. ¶***soft drinks***《米俚》アルコール分のない飲料. 【類】confine the satisfying of their thirsts to ***soft drinks***. ¶***stimulating drinks*** 刺激性飲料. ¶***strong drink*** 強い酒. ¶***table drinks*** such as lemonade, iced tea, etc. レモネード・冷し紅茶などの食卓の飲料. ¶***drinks vinous*** and ***spirituous*** 醸造酒や蒸留酒. ¶a ***tonic drink*** 強壮飲料. ¶Water is a ***wholesome drink***. 水は健康によい飲料である.

Q² a ***cooling drink*** 清涼飲料. ¶***temperance drinks*** アルコール分のない飲料. 【類】The standard ***temperance*** "***drinks***" of London are lemonade, ginger beer, and ginger ale. ¶***winter*** (***summer***) ***drinks*** 冬(夏)の飲みもの.

P a craving ***for drink*** 飲酒欲. ¶***in drink*** 酔っぱらって. 【類】He becomes pugnacious when ***in drink***. ‖ He is temperate ***in drink***. 彼は酒を節している. ¶his love ***of drink*** 彼の酒好き. ¶spend much money ***on drink*** 酒に大金を費す ‖ ***on*** the ***drink*** 酒にひたって. ¶He is a slave ***to drink***. 彼は酒におぼれている. ‖ He is given ***to drink***. 彼は酒におぼれている. ‖ take ***to drink*** 酒が好きになる.

P² I gave him a ***drink of*** warm tea. 私は彼に暖かいお茶を一杯飲ませた.

drink, *v*. 飲む; 乾杯する; 飲める.

M ***drink away*** 酒のために…を失う ‖ ***drink away*** one's reason or one's property 酒のためにその理性もしくは財産を失う ‖ He ***drank*** his estates ***away*** and senses, too. 彼は酒のために不動産を失い, さらに本性までも失った. ¶***drink deeply*** 大いに(酒などを)飲む. ¶***drink*** oneself ***drunk*** 飲んでへゞれけになる ‖ He ***drank*** his companions ***drunk***. 彼は仲間を酔いつぶした. ¶***drink*** the cup ***dry*** 杯を飲みほす. ¶***drink*** a bowl ***empty*** 大杯を飲みほす. ¶"***drink fair***" out of a ginger beer bottle 一本のジンジャービアーを「らっぱのみ」する. ¶This wine ***drinks flat***. このぶどう酒は気が抜けている. ¶***drink freely*** of … …を大いに飲む. ¶He ***drinks hard***. 彼はのんだくれだ. ¶***drink heavily*** したゝか飲む. ¶***drink moderately*** 適度に飲む. ¶***drink*** whisky ***straight***《米》ウイスキーを割らないで飲む. ☞英語は neat. ¶This wine ***drinks*** very ***well***. このぶどう酒は中々飲める.

M² He ***drank*** himself ***down***. 彼は酔いつぶれた. ‖ ***drink down*** sorrow 悲しみを酒にまぎらす. ¶The thirsty ears ***drank in*** the music. こうこつとして音楽を聞いた. ‖ A plant ***drinks in*** oxygen from the atmosphere. 植物は空気から酸素を吸収する. ‖ I stopped for a while to ***drink in*** the beauty of the scene. 私はしばらく足を止めて美しい景色に見とれた. ‖ ***drink in*** all that one says …の言うことを一言一句残さず聞きとる. 【類】***drink in*** knowledge. ¶***drink off*** a cup of cordial リキュールを一杯飲みほす ‖ ***drink off*** a deadly poison by mistake 誤って猛毒薬を飲みほす. ¶***drink up*** a glass of wine ぶどう酒のコップを飲みほす ‖ The heated air ***drinks up*** the moisture of the earth. 熱した空気が地面の湿気を吸い上げる.

P ***drink at*** a spring 泉の水を飲む ‖ The horse ***drank at*** the stream. 馬は川の水を飲んだ. ¶***drink by*** the lips すする. ¶***drink from*** a bubbling spring ぶくぶくわき出している泉を飲む ‖ ***drink from*** a faucet じゃ口から飲む. 【類】***drink from*** a tumbler (大コップ) ‖ I want something to ***drink*** water ***from***. 何か水を飲む物がいる. 【類】The tea is ***drunk from*** cups without handles. / ***drink*** milk ***from*** a glass (cup). ¶***drink in*** large draughts がぶがぶ飲む. ¶***drink*** oneself ***into*** unconsciousness 飲んで正体を失う. 【類】***drink*** oneself ***into*** an illness. ¶***drink like*** a fish 鯨飲する. ¶***drink*** plentifully ***of*** hot water 湯をがぶがぶ飲む. ¶***drink wine out of*** (=from) a glass ぶどう酒をコップから飲む ‖ ***drink*** oneself ***out of*** a situation 酒を飲んで免職になる. ¶***drink to*** the health of … …の健康を祝して杯をあげる. 【類】***drink to*** elevation (昇進) / ***drink to*** the success of some one / ***drink*** health (success) ***to*** a person / Let us ***drink to*** the prosperity of the cause (主義). ‖ ***drink to*** the King in milk 王の戴冠式に牛乳で祝杯をあげる ‖ One proposed to ***drink to*** France out of compliment to three Frenchmen present. 列席していた三人のフランス人に対するお世辞の意味で一人がフランス国万歳の祝杯をあげることを提議した. ‖ ***drink to*** the dregs 飲みほす. 【類】He has ***drunk*** both the cups of pleasure and pain ***to*** the dregs. ‖ ***drink to*** excess 飲み過ごす ‖ ***drink to*** one's heart's content 思う存分飲む ‖ ***drink to*** death 飲み過ぎて死ぬ.

drinker, *n*. 飲酒家.

Q a ***confirmed*** sake ***drinker*** 大酒飲み. ¶a ***habitual drinker*** 常習酒飲み. ¶a ***maudlin drinker*** 泣き上戸. ¶a ***moderate drinker*** ほどのよい上戸. ¶a ***hard*** (=***heavy***) ***drinker*** 大酒家. ¶a ***slavish drinker*** of rum 大のラム酒飲み. ¶a ***social drinker*** 社交的飲酒家. ¶a ***solitary drinker*** 独酌を好む人.

Q² an ***alcohol drinker*** 上戸. ¶an ***ask-for-more drinker*** 「後引き上戸.

drinking, *n*. 飲むこと, 飲酒.

V He has ***given up*** (=***left off***) ***drinking***. 彼は酒をやめた. ¶***stop*** (=***quit***) ***drinking*** 禁酒する. ¶***swear off drinking*** 誓って禁酒する. ¶***toss drinking off*** at a gulp ぐーっと一息に飲みほす.

Q ***excessive drinking*** 飲過ぎ. ¶***heavy drinking*** 鯨飲. ¶***moderate drinking*** 適度の飲酒. ¶Too ***much drinking*** is harmful. 大酒はからだに毒だ.

Q² stick to ***coffee drinking*** コーヒーをやめずにいる. ¶ceremonial ***sake drinking*** at wedding 三々九度.

P abstain ***from drinking*** 禁酒する. ¶He is abstemious ***in drinking***. 彼は節酒をしている. ¶be temperate (moderate) ***in drinking*** 酒を節している(適度にやっている). ¶He took ***to drinking***. 彼は飲酒にふけった.

drinking-shop, *n*. 飲酒店.

Q a ***low-class drinking-shop***=《米》a joint 下等の飲酒店.

drip, *n*. したたり.

V ***fix*** the ***drip*** in the faucet 飲み口のしたたりを止める.

Q a ***dreary drip*** of dilatory declamation—as Lord Salisbury once phrased it ソールズベリー卿がかつていったようにボツリボツリ述べる退屈千万で長たらしい演説.

drip, *v*. たれる.

M The rain is ***dripping down***. 雨がぽつりぽつり降っている.

P The water ***drips from*** the eaves. のきから水がしたたり落ちる. ¶The rain-water is ***dripping through*** a crack on the ceiling. 天井のすき間から雨だれがしている. ¶***dripping with*** perspiration 汗びっしょりになって.

drive, *n*. 馬車・自動車を駆ること; 運動.

V ***conduct*** (=***carry on***) a ***drive*** (=campaign) for the Junior Red Cross 少年赤十字運動をやる. ¶We have ***enjoyed*** the ***drive*** very much. 僕たちは自動車でかけ回って大変愉快だった. ¶***have*** a ***drive*** to raise money for charity 慈善募金運動をやる. ¶***launch*** a ***drive*** to … 運動を起す. ¶***make*** a ***drive*** for funds 資金募集運動をする. ¶The road ***provides*** a pleasant ***drive***. 道路が良いのでドライブが愉快にできる. ¶***take*** (=***have***) a ***drive*** in the open air 戸外でドライブする.

Q an ***all-out drive*** 総出の運動. ¶an ***energetic drive*** to induce tourist traffic 観光客誘致の猛運動. ¶make an ***extensive drive*** to raise a charity fund 慈善基金募集のため広範囲の運動をする. ¶it can be reached after ***five minutes' drive*** from … そこへは…から自動車で五分で行ける. ¶the ***foreign drive*** against American goods 米国商品防止の外国の運動. ¶take a ***long drive*** 遠乗り(自動車の)をする. ¶a ***menacing drive*** against … 反対の威かく的運動. ¶a prime mover in the union's ***organizational drive*** 労組組織運動の主唱者.

Q² an ***advertising drive*** against accidents 事故防止宣伝運動. ¶the United States ***anti-Communist propaganda drive*** 米国の反共宣伝運動. ¶an ***anti-Red drive*** 反共運動. ¶an ***auto drive*** for recreation 気晴しのドライブ. ¶a ***buy-home-made-goods drive*** 国産品使用運動. ¶open a ***charity drive*** 慈善資金募集運動を開始する. ¶a ***Community Chest drive*** 共同募金運動. ¶go for a ***cross-country drive*** 野外遠乗りに出掛ける. ¶a ***fund-raising drive*** 基金募集運動. ¶a ***law enforcement drive*** 遵法運動. ¶a new ***morality drive*** 新道徳運動. ¶a ***motor***[***-car***] ***drive*** ドライブ. ¶an ***owner drive*** 自家用車の持主運転. ¶run ***production drives*** 生産運動を挙行する. ¶a big ***recruiting drive*** for 100,000 nurses for the Civil Nursing Reserve 民間看護婦予備隊のため十万人大募集運動. ¶launch a ***safety drive*** 安全運動を始める. ¶a public ***savings encouragement drive*** 一般貯蓄奨励運動. ¶a ***stop-Communism drive*** 共産主義抑圧運動. ¶launch a seven day ***traffic safety drive*** 七日間にわたる交通安全運動を始める. ¶open a ***$100,000 fund drive*** 十万ドル資金募集運動を開始する.

P He took me out ***for*** a ***drive***. 彼は僕をドライブに連れ出した. 【類】Let me take you down ***for*** a ***drive***.

drive, *v.* かる；駆逐する；追払う；推進する；馬車で運搬する；射出する；打込む；ねらう；勉励する；激しく当る.

M He *drives about* on a bicycle. 彼は自転車を乗り回す. ¶be *driven ashore* in a storm しけで岸に吹き寄せられる. ¶They *drove away* in a car. 彼等は自動車で去った. ‖ *drive away* an enemy 敵を駆逐する ‖ *drive away* flies はえを追う ‖ He is *driving away* at the work night and day. 彼は日夜その仕事に励んでいる. ¶*drive* them *back* 彼らを追返す ‖ *drive back* in a car 自動車で戻る. 【類】*drive back* the powers of darkness (やみの威力). ¶This reflection *drove* him *back* into despair. このことを反省して彼は再び絶望に陥った. ‖ They were *driven back* with great loss. 彼らは大損害を受けて撃退された. 【類】The police *drove* the crowd *back* from the entrance. ¶*drive cross-country* [自動車で]野外遠乗をする. ¶*drive* a machine *electrically* 機械を電気で運転する. ¶*drive fast* 自動車を疾走させる. ¶*drive four in hand* (＝a coach and four) 四頭立馬車を駆る. ¶The rain was *driving hard* in our face. 顔に雨がひどく当っていた. ¶*drive* a nail *home* くぎをしっかり打込む ‖ the point we wish to *drive home* to you is that ... われわれが君によく分ってもらいたいと思う点は ... ということである. ¶It nearly *drove* me *mad*. そのことで私はほとんど気違いになった. ¶*drive out* the enemy (invaders) 敵(など)を追出す ‖ The automobile has *driven out* the horse. 自動車が馬車を駆逐してしまった. ‖ *drive out* on one's holiday tour 自動車で休日の旅行に出る. 【類】*drive out* into the country ‖ *drive out* a bullet 弾丸を抜き取る. ¶*drive slow* 自動車を徐行させる. 【類】*Drive slower*. ¶*drive well* うまく自動車を運転する.

M[2] A crowd was *driven off*. 群集が追払われた. ¶*drive in* a nail くぎを打込む.

P We *drove across* the field. われわれは畑を横切って馬車を駆った. 【類】The clouds *drove across* the sky. ¶*drive against* the enemy 軍用車を駆って敵軍にあたる ‖ They *drove* the vessel *against* the rock. 彼らは岩に乗上げた. ‖ The wind *drives against* the sails. 風が激しく帆に当る. ¶*drive along* the beach 海岸に沿うて自動車を走らせる. ¶*drive* a stone *at* a dog 犬をねらって石を投げつける ‖ what I am *driving at* is that ... 私の言おうと思う所は...ということである ‖ What are you *driving at*? そりゃ何の話だ. ‖ They had an end that they *drove at* and labored to accomplish. 彼らにはねらいを定めて達成しようと努力している目的があった. ¶The ship *drove before* the wind. 船は追風を受けて疾走した. ¶The ship was *driven by* a gale *from* its course. 船は暴風に吹きあおられてその針路をはずれた. ‖ *driven by* necessity 必要に迫られて ‖ *Driven by* jealousy he killed his wife. しっとにかられて彼は妻を殺した. 【類】He is *driven by* his work. ‖ He was *driven by* the rain into a cottage. 彼は雨に追われていなか家にかけ込んだ. ‖ a pair of horses *driven by* a coachman 一人の御者に御される二頭の馬 ‖ It is *driven by* a motor. それはモーターで動く. ‖ *drive by* the lash むちでかる ‖ *drive by* ... ...の側を自動車をかる. 【類】A mill is *driven by* water. / *driven by* water-wheel (水車). ¶*drive down* a highway 公道をドライブする. ¶*driven from* (＝out of) one's pleasure (楽しみから) ‖ The smoke *drove* the firemen *from* the building. 消防夫は煙にまかれやむなく建物を出た. ‖ Michizane was *driven from* a position of power by his enemies. 道真は敵のために権勢の地位から追い出された. ¶*drive in* a carriage 馬車を駆る ‖ He *drove* the horse *in* his carrige. 彼はその馬を馬車に使った. 【類】His Highness *drove in* a court carriage (宮廷馬車). ¶*drive into* the city 市中に乗込む ‖ *drive* him *into* exile 彼を島流しにする ‖ *drive* him *into* a corner (＝to the corner) 彼を窮地に落し入れる ‖ *drive* a nail *into* wood 木にくぎを打込む ‖ *drive* him *into* doing it 彼をかり立てゝそれをやらせる ‖ *drive* one *into* a passion 人を怒らせる ‖ *drive* a lesson *into* one's head 教訓を頭へたたき込む. ¶*drive* a ship *on* the ocean 大洋上で船を進める ‖ The ship was *driven on* the rocks. 船は坐礁した. ¶*drive* a person *out of* a city (country, politics, business) 人を町(など)から追い出す ‖ *drive* him nearly *out of* his mind 彼を半狂乱にする ‖ be *driven out of* employment 解雇される ‖ *drive* foreign goods *out of* the market 外国品を市場から駆逐する ‖ He was *driven out of* existence. 彼は生活ができなくされた. ‖ The ship was *driven out of* its course by a storm. 船は暴風のためにその針路からはずれた. ¶The cab *drove over* his leg. 馬車(タクシー)が彼の脚をひいた. ‖ *drive over* a road (route) 道路(など)をかる. ¶*drive through* a park 自動車で公園を通り抜ける ‖ *drive* a tunnel *through* a hill 丘にトンネルを通す ‖ The captain *drove* his ship *through* the hostile fleet. 艦長は船を進めて敵艦隊の間を突き抜けた. ¶when at last *driven to* confession he made this statement as to ... せっぱ詰って彼は...についてこういう陳述をした ‖ *drive* him *to* the wall 彼を追い詰める ‖ *drive* all animosity *to* the winds えん恨を全く捨ててしまう ‖ *driven to* desperation 捨てばちになって. 【類】*drive* a person *to* ruin (poverty, despair) / Repeated failures *drove* him *to* despair. / Despair *drove* him *to* suicide. ‖ be *driven to* frenzy 気が狂う ‖ be *driven to* his wits' end 途方に暮れる. 【類】*drive* him *to* the end of his wits ‖ questioned and *driven to* her last retreat せっぱ詰って ‖ *drive to* the door 戸口に馬車を着ける ‖ I advise you not to *drive* him *to* extremities. あくまで彼を追求することはよしたがよい. ‖ It *drove* him *to* extreme measures. それが彼をして非常手段を取るに至らしめた. 【類】*drive* men *to* drink ‖ He *drove* me *to* the hotel. 彼は僕の馬車を宿屋に着けた. ‖ *drive to* market 市場へ馬車をかる. 【類】You can have the luggage *driven to* the station. ¶be *driven under* the speed limit 速力制限以下で運転される.

drivel, *n.* たわごと.

V It is certainly surprising that such a highly reputable magazine should *print* such childish *drivel*. かゝる有名の雑誌がそんな子供臭いたわごとを載せるとは実に驚くの外はない. ¶*write drivel* for magazines 雑誌掲載の雑文を書く.

driver, *n.* 運転手; 〔機〕ドライバー.

Q[2] an *auto driver* 自動車運転手. ¶a *back-seat driver* 《米俗》運転手に世話を焼く自動車客. ¶a *bus driver* 乗合自動車の運転手. ¶a victim of a *hit-and-run driver* ひき逃げ運転の犠牲者. ¶an *owner driver* 自家用を自分で運転する人. ¶coolies operating a *pile driver* くい打機を操作する労働者たち. ¶a *screw driver* スクルー・ドライバ (ねじ回し). ¶a *stage driver* 乗合馬車の御者. ¶a *steam[-power]* (*hand*) *pile driver* 蒸気(手動)くい打機. ¶a *taxi driver* タクシー運転手. ¶a *truck driver* 貨物自動車運転手.

driveway, *n.* 自動車専用道路.

Q A chain of parks connected with *splendid driveway* is desirable. りっぱな自動車道路で連絡された一連の公園が望ましい.

driving, *n.* 操縦, 運転.

Q *drunk driving* 酔いどれ運転. ¶*reckless driving* 無鉄砲な運転.

drop, *n.* 点滴; 微量; 降下, 墜落; [菓子]ドロップ.

V He had not *drunk* a *drop*. 彼は一滴も飲まなかった. ¶*give* a person the *drop* 人をだし抜く. ¶I *had* a *drop* too much. 僕は飲み過した. ‖ He *has* not a *drop* of pity. 彼には哀れみの心などはみじんもない. ‖ He *had* a *drop* of about twenty feet. 彼は二十フィートばかりの所から墜落した. ‖ The Falls *have* a *drop* of 302 feet. その滝は直下三百二フィートある. ‖ He *has* a *drop* in his eye. 一杯飲んでいる目付きだ. ¶Foreign features imported into America during 1929 *showed* a *drop* of almost 25 per cent from 1928. 一九二九年中に米国に輸入された外国の長尺映画は一九二八年に比較して二割五分方減少した. ¶*Take* ten *drops* every four hours. 四時間毎に十滴ずつ飲みなさい. ‖ *take* a *drop* 一杯やる ‖ He used often to *take* a *drop* too much. 彼はよく(酒を)飲み過した. ¶*Drops* of perspiration *stood out* on my forehead. 玉の汗が私の額に出た.

Q swear by all that is holy that he will not take *another drop* of liquor もう酒は一滴も飲まないと八百万の神々にかけて誓う. ¶*big drops* of rain 大粒の雨. ¶There came a *decided drop*. がた落ちとなった. ¶at the *first drop* of rain 雨が降り出すとすぐに. ¶The rain is falling in *large drops*. 大粒の雨が降っている. ¶He sweated *large drops*. 彼は玉の汗であった. ¶a *mere drop* in the ocean 大海の一滴. ¶*peppermint drops* 薄荷ドロップ. ¶cause a *sharp drop* in prices 物価の急落をきたす. ¶a *severe drop* どか落ち. ¶a *sudden drop* in the temperature 温度の突然の降下. ¶it is a *tiny drop* compared with ... それは...に比べるとほんのけし粒だ.

Q[2] *birth rate drop* 出生率低下. ¶medicated *cough drops* せき止めドロップ. ¶*dew drops* 玉の露. ¶a mass *parachute drop* 集団落下さん降下. ¶*tear drops* 涙滴. ¶show a *62 per cent drop* in the crime rate 犯罪率が六十二パーセント

の低下を示す.

P fall *in drops* ぱらぱら降る ‖ rain *in* small *drops* 雨がぽつぽつ降る ‖ shed tears *in drops* 涙をぽろぽろ落す ‖ The sweat rolled off *in* great *drops*. 玉の汗が流れた.

P² *drop by* drop 一滴ずつ. ¶a *drop from* a limitless ocean 大海の一滴 ‖ it seemed a *drop from* the clouds to the earth when he said, "..." 彼が「...」と言ったのはあたかも積雲から地上に降った一滴の雨のごとき感があった. ¶It is but a *drop in* the bucket. それは大海の一滴に過ぎない. ‖ my "*drop in* the bucket" 私の寸志(寄付金など). 【類】It is a *drop in* the ocean certainly. ‖ a *drop in* price 値段の下落 ‖ There has been a great *drop in* the temperature since yesterday. きのうから気温が非常に下がった. ¶a *drop of* water 一滴の水.

drop, *v.* 落す, 降ろす; 削除する; 落ちる, 下落する; 下流へ流される; 知らない間に...になる.

M *drop asleep* すぐ眠りにつく. ¶The company *dropped away* (=*off*). 来客がぽつぽつ帰って行った. ¶*drop back* into one's seat 席に戻る ‖ *drop back* into the old habit いつしかもとの癖に戻る. ¶*drop dead* 急死する. ¶He suddenly "*dropped out*" (=disappeared). 彼は突然行方不明になった. ‖ *drop out* 脱会する, 退去する. ¶The sides of the crater *drop* almost ***perpendicularly*** for hundreds of feet. その噴火口内の四壁は数百フィートにわたってほとんど垂直になっている. ¶The temperature has ***suddenly dropped*** to 40 degrees F. 気温が突然華氏四十度に下った.

M² The hill *drops* sharply *down* into the water. 山が急こう配で水際にせまる. ‖ The boat began to *drop down* with the tide. 舟は潮で下流へ流されだした. ¶*drop in* to call 立寄る ‖ I will *drop in* at ten tomorrow. 私は明日十時にお寄りします. ‖ *drop in* at the library 図書館に立寄る ‖ The dean asked me to *drop in* at his office. 学監は事務所にちょっと来るように私に言った. ‖ just *drop in* for a little social call 別に用がないがちょっと立寄る ‖ *drop in* with (=on) a friend 不意に友人に出会う ‖ *drop in* with some occurrence あるできごとに偶然出くわす ‖ A lot of land *dropped in*. 地所が偶然手にはいった. 【類】*drop in* at a cigar store (たばこ屋) / A friend *dropped in* just as I was about to start. / He *dropped in* on us last Monday. / Please *drop in* [on us] when you come this way. / *drop in* for a last drink, which is a preliminary to so many drinks after the last / a party he accidentally *dropped in* with. ¶He *dropped off* into a peaceful slumber. 彼はすやすやと寝付いた. ‖ *drop off* to sleep 寝入る ‖ The vaccination scab has *dropped off*. 種痘のかさぶたが取れた. ‖ Whenever he saw me *dropping off*, he woke me up. 彼が私の眠り込むのを見るといつも起してくれた. ‖ The flowers *drop off*. 花がぽとぽと落ちる. ‖ The membership of the society began *dropping off*. 会員はぽつぽつ脱会し始めた. ‖ While he was yet speaking his hearers began to *drop off*. 彼がまだ演説中に聴衆はぽつぽつ帰り始めた. ‖ *drop* me *off* at ... ...で私を降ろして下さい.

P *drop* me *at* ... ...で降ろして下さい(バスなどで). 【類】*drop* passengers *at* ... ‖ *drop* a parcel *at* one's door [配達人など]小包を戸口におく. ¶*drop behind* others 人後に落ちる. ¶*drop* him [out] *from* the list of members of the Society 同協会の会員名簿から彼を削除する. 【類】His name is now *dropped from* the list. / Those who do not pay the club fee will be *dropped from* the membership. ‖ *drop* a letter *from* a word 語のつゞりを一字書き落す ‖ *drop* it *from* his grasp それをつかみそこなう. ¶*drop* a nickel *in* a slot 自動器の中に白銅貨を入れる ‖ *drop in* a faint 失神して倒れる. ¶*drop* a letter *into* the post-box (=mail-box) 手紙を投かんする. 【類】*drop* a letter *into* the mail ‖ A boy *dropped into* the sea. 子供が海に落ちた. ‖ *drop into* a shop (room) 店(など)に立寄る ‖ *drop into* a chair (seat) いす(など)にどっかと腰掛ける ‖ *drop into* the ranks of the second or third-rate merchants 二流または三流の商人に落ちる ‖ I soon *dropt into* a profound sleep. 私は間もなくぐっすり寝入った. ‖ *drop* suddenly *into* the grave とん死する ‖ *drop into* perdition 地獄に落ちる ‖ He now begins to *drop into* years. 彼はそろそろ年を取り出した. ‖ *drop into* vulgar slang 野卑な言葉を使う ‖ *drop into* reveries 夢うつゝの状態になる. ¶*drop off* the train 汽車から降りる ‖ a purse *dropped off* one's hand 手から抜け落ちた財布. 【類】The ball *dropped out of* his hand. ¶More quickly than it takes to tell it, he *dropped on* his knees, and begged my pardon. なんと形容してよいか分らないほど手早に彼はひざまずいて私にあやまった. ¶A pitying angel *dropped out of* the clouds. なさけ深い天使が天降った. ‖ The song *dropped* altogether *out of* public favor. その歌は全くすたれてしまった. ‖ *drop out of* a race レースで落伍する. 【類】*drop out of* the rank ‖ be *dropped out of* use after a temporary vogue 一時はやった後すたれる. ¶*drop to* the rear 落後する ‖ My look *dropped to* the floor. 私の視線が床の上に落ちた. ‖ we *dropped to* ... 僕たちの乗っている船は...に停泊した. ¶They were about to *drop with* fatigue. 疲れて今にも倒れそうだった.

droppings, *n.* ふん.

Q² *day* (*night*) *droppings* of fowls 昼(夜)の鳥のふん.

P² The *droppings from* the fowls make the ground rich in nitrogen. 鳥のふんは地中の窒素を増す.

drought, *n.* ひでり, かんばつ; 欠乏.

Q in periods of ***financial drought*** 財政窮乏の際に.

P ***during*** the *droughts* of summer 夏の日照続きに.

drove, *n.* 《米》群.

P² a *drove of* cattle 牛の一群.

drown, *v.* おぼれさす; 忘れさす, まぎらす.

M They were *drowned out* by the recent flood. 彼らは最近の洪水で水死した.

P He was *drowned at* sea. 彼は海でおぼれた. ¶His voice was *drowned by* (=in) the noise. 彼の声はその音響で聞えなかった. ¶*drown* one's troubles *in* drink 自分の苦労を酒にまぎらす. 【類】*drown* one's cares *in sake* / She tried to *drown* her sorrows *in* excitement. ‖ *drown* oneself *in* a river (waterfall) 川(など)に投身する. 【類】He was *drowned in* that shipwreck. ‖ He is *drowned in* wine. 彼は酒びたりになっている. ‖ He is *drowned in* sleep. 彼は熟睡している. ‖ She was (=Her eyes were) *drowned in* tears. 彼女は涙にくれていた. ‖ He is *drowned in* love. 彼は愛におぼれている.

drowning, *n.* 水死.

V He narrowly ***escaped drowning***. 彼はあぶなくおぼれる所であった.

Q The result may be ***two drownings***. 二人とも水死することになるかも知れない.

P He was saved ***from drowning***. 彼は水死する所を助けられた.

drudge, *v.* あくせく働く.

M *drudge away* a day いやな仕事に一日を送る. ¶*drudge out* one's routine work その日課にあくせくする.

P *drudge at* a tedious work いやな仕事をあくせくとやる. 【類】*drudge at* dictionary-making ***for*** a poor pay. ¶*drudge from* dawn ***till*** dark 朝から晩まであくせく働く.

drudgery, *n.* 骨折仕事, 苦役.

V ***do*** domestic *drudgery* 家庭の骨折仕事をやる. ¶***undergo*** *drudgery* つまらない仕事をやってのける.

Q There is no more ***disagreeable*** *drudgery* than to attempt to make men learn who are unfitted or unwilling to learn. 学問に適しない者や学問のきらいな者に勉学させようとするくらいくだらないむだ骨はない. ¶***distasteful*** *drudgery* 好ましくない仕事. ¶He is in the hurrying pressure of life's ***dull*** *drudgery*. 彼は人生のつまらない仕事をせっせといそがしくやっている. ¶a mere ***formal*** *drudgery* ほんのきまりきったつまらない仕事. ¶do cheap ***literary*** *drudgery* 安い文筆の下っぱ仕事をする. ¶***painful*** and ***unrewarded*** *drudgery* えんの下の力持.

Q² ***household*** *drudgery* 家庭の雑用. ¶eliminate ***teaching*** *drudgery* 教授上の雑務を除く.

drug, *n.* 薬品, 売薬; はけない品.

V ***compound*** a *drug* 薬を調合する. ¶***dispense*** Russian *drugs* ロシアの薬を売る. ¶***prescribe*** suitable *drugs* 適薬を処方する. ¶***sell*** (=***vend***) his *drugs* 薬を販売する.

V² The *drug* ***acts*** upon the nerves. この薬は神経にきく.

Q a very ***active*** *drug* 劇薬. ¶a ***dangerous*** *drug* 有害薬物. ¶the ***dreggiest*** *drug* on a surfeited market 品が多過ぎてよくよくはけの悪い品. ¶an ***effective*** *drug* 妙薬. ¶***habit-forming*** *drugs* 癖になる薬. ¶Opium is a ***narcotic*** *drug*. アヘンは麻酔薬だ. ¶a ***poisonous*** *drug* 毒薬. ¶try all sorts of ***vile*** (=***nasty***) *drugs* いやな薬をあれこれとのんでみる.

Q² a ***mineral*** *drug* 鉱物質薬品. ¶a ***miracle*** *drug* 妙薬. ¶a ***package*** *drug* 容器に入れた薬品. ¶a ***vegetable*** *drug* 植物性薬品. ¶a ***sleeping*** *drug* 催眠剤. ¶a ***stimulating*** *drug*

興奮剤. ¶a ***wonder drug*** 神薬.

P² a *drug* ***for*** stimulating nerves 興奮剤. ¶a *drug* ***in*** the market 売残り品 ‖ all the *drugs* ***in*** the pharmacopoeia 薬局方に出ているありとあらゆる薬. ¶It became a *drug* ***on*** the market. それは売口の遠い品になった.

drum, *n.* 太鼓.

V ***beat*** a *drum* 太鼓を打つ. ¶***play*** a *drum*=drum 太鼓をたたく. ¶***thump*** a *drum* 太鼓をどんと打つ.

V² A *drum* began to ***beat.*** 太鼓が鳴り出した. ‖ The *drums* are ***beating.*** 太鼓が鳴っている. ‖ with *drums* ***beating*** and colors flying 太鼓を打ち軍旗を翻して. ¶A *drum* ***boomed out.*** 太鼓がどんどんと鳴りひびいた. 「から聞える太鼓.

Q a ***bodeful*** *drum* 不吉な太鼓の音. ¶a ***distant*** *drum* 遠く

P the tapping (=beating) ***of*** the *drum* 太鼓を打ち鳴らすこと ‖ the roll ***of*** *drums* 太鼓の音. ¶beat a march ***on*** one's *drum* 行進曲に合わせて打つ ‖ three taps ***on*** a *drum* 太鼓の三打. ¶a signal ***with*** a *drum* 太鼓の合図.

drum, *v.* 太鼓を打つ; やかましく繰返して言う; 《米》ドラムをたたいて宣伝する(客を集める).

M He was ***drummed out.*** 彼は太鼓で追立てられた.

M² ***drum up*** children for a show 太鼓をたたいて見世物に子供を集める ‖ ***drum up*** trade by extravagant advertising and absurd claims 大々的広告や法外の効能書きで商売に景気をつける.

P *drum* something ***into*** one's head (ears) あることを繰返して教え込む(聞かせる) ‖ *drum* a lesson ***into*** a person 一つの教訓を人にたたきこむ. 【類】 *drum* Latin ***into*** a boy's head / His lessons had to be *drummed* ***into*** him because he disliked school. / They were *drummed* so often ***into*** my ear that I could recite them backward while asleep. ‖ *drum* ***into*** unheeding ears 馬の耳に念仏を唱える. ¶*drum* ***on*** the table テーブルをどんどんたゝく. ¶They ought to be *drummed* ***out of*** society. 彼らはよろしく社会から放逐すべきだ. ¶*drum* ***with*** one's fingers 指でつづみ

drunk, *n.* 酔っぱらい. 　 ⌊を打つ.

Q They robbed the ***heavy*** *drunk* of all the money he then possessed. 彼らはへべれけの酔漢から所持金を全部

drunk, *pa.* 酔っている. 　 ⌊奪った.

M be ***beastly*** *drunk* へべれけに酔っている. ¶He was ***blind*** (*sl.*=very) *drunk*. 彼はずぶ六になっていた. ¶He is ***dead*** (=***thoroughly***) ***drunk.*** 泥酔している.

P be *drunk* ***like*** a fish 泥酔している. ¶make oneself *drunk* ***on*** beer ビールに酔う ‖ I am *drunk* ***on*** green tea. 僕は緑茶に酔った. ¶be *drunk* ***with*** wine 酒に酔っている ‖ I am *drunk* ***with*** delight. 僕はうれしくてたまらない. 【類】 He is *drunk* ***with*** flattery.

drunkard, *n.* 大酒家, よっぱらい.

V ***play*** the *drunkard* 酔払いのまねをする. ¶***reclaim*** *drunkards* のんべいに酒をやめさせる.

Q a ***besotted*** *drunkard* たわいのない酔いどれ. ¶a ***chronic*** *drunkard* 常習飲酒家. ¶a ***confirmed*** *drunkard* のんべい.

dry, *v.* かわかす, 干す; かわく.

M Don't be so ***drying up,*** my boy! そんなに黙り込むなよ. ‖ The road has now ***dried up.*** 路はもうかわいた. ¶***dry up*** the springs of ... …の源泉を枯渇させる ‖ The sources of force are ***dried up.*** 力の源が干上ってしまった. ‖ ***dry*** [***up***] a cow 雌牛の乳を止める ‖ ***Dry up***?—No, I won't ***dry up.*** 黙れと? なに, 黙るもんか. 【類】 The sun will soon ***dry up*** the roads. / The clothes will soon ***dry up*** in the wind. / Their source of inspiration ***dried up.***

P *dry* one's steaming handkerchief ***at*** the fire 湯気の立つハンカチを火でかわかす. ¶*dry* it ***by*** heat それを熱してかわかす ‖ *dry* it ***by*** exposure to the sun それを日に当ててかわかす. ¶*dry* it ***for*** food それをかわかして食用にする. ¶*dry* it ***in*** smoke それをいぶしてかわかす ‖ *dry* it ***in*** the sun それを日にかわかす. ¶*dry* it ***on*** the napkin それをふきんでふく. 【類】 *dry* one's hands ***on*** one's apron. ¶His perspiration had *dried* ***upon*** him. 彼の汗はひとりでにかわいていた. ¶*dry* it ***with*** blotting-paper それを吸取紙で取る ‖ The glass broke while she was *drying* it ***with*** a cloth. 彼女が布でガラスをふいていたときそれがこわれた. ‖ *dry* oneself ***with*** (=on) a bathtowel. 【類】 *dry* dishes ***with*** a cloth.

dry, *a.* かわいた; 乳の出ない.

P It is very *dry* ***for*** this season of the year. この季節にしては非常に雨が少ない. ¶I am very *dry* ***with*** singing. 歌を歌ったので大変のどがかわく. ‖ The cow has been *dry* ***for*** a week. 牛は一週間乳が出ない.

dry-dock, *v.* 乾ドック(日本語のドック)に入れる.

P be *dry-docked* ***for*** survey 検査のためドックに入れられる.

dryer, drier, *n.* 乾燥器(ドライヤー).

Q a ***centrifugal*** *drier* 回転式乾燥器.

Q² a ***towel*** *dryer* タオル乾燥器.

duality, *n.* 二重.

Q² the ***Jekyll-Hyde*** *duality* ジェキル・ハイド式二重人格.

P strange *duality* ***of*** character 珍しい二重人格の例.

duarchy, *n.* 二人政治.

Q the ***Japanese*** *duarchy* [朝廷と幕府の]公武政治.

dub, *v.* …と名付ける.

O He *dubbed* me "shorty." 彼は私に「ちび」とあだ名をつけた.

dubious, *a.* 疑わしい.

P I am very *dubious* ***about*** it. 私はそれが非常に疑わしい. ¶be *dubious* ***of*** success 成功が疑わしい.

duck, *n.* あひる.

V ***make*** (=play at) *ducks* and drakes (石などで)水切をする.

V² The *duck* ***quacks*** (=***cackles***). あひるががあがあ鳴く. ¶The *duck* ***waddles.*** あひるがよちよち歩く.

Q a ***domestic*** *duck* あひる. ¶She walks like a ***waddling*** *duck*. 彼女はあひるのようによちよち歩く. ¶a ***wild*** *duck* のがも. ¶a fine day for ***young*** *ducks* あひるの好天(雨天のこと).

Q² a ***decoy*** *duck* おとりのかも; ぺてん師. ¶a ***mandarin*** *duck* おしどり.

duck, *v.* ひょいと水に突込む; 水にくぐる.

P *duck* a person ***in*** a pond 池にひょいと突き入れる. ¶*duck* ***out of*** town 町からちょっと姿を消す. ¶*duck* ***under*** water 水にもぐる.

ducking, *n.* 水中に突込むこと.

V ***give*** a person a *ducking* 人を水中に突込む.

Q get a ***good*** *ducking* ずぶぬれになる. ¶The rain came down in sheets and gave us a ***regular*** *ducking*. 雨がざあざあ降って例のごとくずぶぬれになった.

dudgeon, *n.* 立腹.

Q in ***high*** (=***deep***) *dudgeon* 非常に立腹して.

due, *n.* 当然払うべき物; 負債; 会費; 税; 当然受くべき物.

V To ***give*** him his *due*, he is honest. 公平に言えば彼は正直者だ(他に欠点はあるかも知れないが). ¶***have*** one's *dues* 相当の報いを受ける. ¶***pay*** one's *dues* 借金を返す. ¶***receive*** its *due* その手数料(使用料, 謝礼など)を受取る.

Q The ***annual*** *dues* are ten dollars. 会費は年額十ドル. ¶his ***exact*** *due* 彼が当然受くべきもの. ¶***customary*** *dues* 慣例の料金. ¶accept, as his ***just*** *due*, the adoring glances of ... …の敬慕のべっ見を当然のものとして受ける.

Q² ***canal*** *dues* 運河通航税. ¶***club*** *dues* クラブの会費. ¶***dock*** *dues* ドック使用料. ¶***Membership*** *dues* are two dollars a year. 会費は年額二ドル. ¶***tonnage*** *due* トン税.

P ***according to*** one's *due* 分相応に. 「金.

P² *dues* ***on*** the vessel, cargo, etc. 船・船荷などに対する税

due, *a.* 当然払うべき; …に帰すべき; …する筈; [方向]真…

M The wind is ***due east*** 風は真東だ. ¶His failure is ***entirely*** *due* to his carelessness. 彼の失敗は全く不注意のせいだ. ‖ *due* ***entirely*** to want of caution 全く不注意のため. ¶The ship is *due* ***here*** at 3 p.m. その船は午後三時当地着のはず. ¶his success is ***largely*** *due* to ... 彼の成功は…がその大原因を成している. ¶a bill *due* ***next month*** 来月払の手形. ¶it is ***partly*** *due* to ... それは幾分…に因る. ¶be *due* ***primarily*** to ... 第一に…のためで. ¶it is *due* ***solely,*** or at any rate ***mainly,*** to ... それは全くあるいは少くとも主として…に基因する. ¶The park is *due* ***south*** from the city. その公園は同市から真南に当る. ¶sail *due* ***west*** 真西に向って航行する.

P The steamer is *due* ***at*** Yokohama tomorrow. その汽船は明日横浜着港のはず. 【類】 I am *due* ***at*** Mr. A's at six o'clock. / The train is *due* ***at*** 7.30 p.m. ‖ It is *due* ***at*** the end of the month. それは月末に払うのだ. ¶Surely the moon is *due* ***by*** this time. もう月が出るはずだ. ¶*due* ***for*** payment (redemption) 当然支払う(弁償す)べき ‖ the tax *due* ***for*** the number of months still to run 残余の月に対する税金 ‖ repayment of sums *due* ***for*** the maintenance of prisoners of war 捕虜収容に対するる費用の償還. 【類】 the amount *due* ***for*** the maintenance of extracurricular activities (課外活動). ¶debts *due* ***from*** customers 取引先から当然払ってもらうべき負債 ‖ The steamer was *due* ***from*** San Francisco about the middle of December. 汽船は十

二月半ばごろサンフランシスコから到着することになっていた. ‖ the honor which is *due **from*** the pupil ***to*** the teacher 生徒から先生に払うべき尊敬. ¶He is *due **in*** London to-morrow. 彼はあすロンドンに着くはずになっている. ‖ He is *due **in*** thirty minutes. 彼はあと三十分で着く. ‖ a bill *due **in*** three months 三カ月払の手形. ¶pressure *due **to*** head of water 水源に基く水圧 ‖ That is *due **to*** carelessness on your part. それは君の方の不注意のせいだ. ‖ His downfall was *due **to*** drink. 彼の没落は酒が原因であった. ‖ this is probably in part *due **to*** ... and in part ***to*** ... これは多分一つは…により一つは…による事であろう ‖ It is *due **to*** a combination of circumstances (=owing to various circumstances). それは色々の事情にもとずく. ‖ neologisms *due **to*** the Great War 大戦でできた新語 ‖ The question is being asked in some quarters as to the possibility of the floods *due* indirectly ***to*** the new comet. あの洪水は今度のすい星が果して間接の原因をなしているかどうかの問題が目下ある方面で疑問とされている. ‖ It was *due **to*** the weather (carelessness, illness). それは天気(など)が原因であった. ‖ Do what is *due **to*** you. 君の当然なすべきことをせよ. ‖ His failure, *due **to*** poor preparation, mortified him greatly. 準備不足のために失敗したので彼は非常に残念に思った. ‖ honor is *due **to*** ... …に尊敬を払うが当然だ ‖ with all the honor *due **to*** his rank 彼の身分相当の尊敬を払って ‖ To him undoubtedly belongs the honor *due **to*** the pioneer. 開拓者に当然帰すべき名誉は疑いもなく彼のものである. ‖ acknowledgment is *due **to*** ... …に謝意を表す ‖ ***to*** him is *due* the credit of ... …の名誉は当然彼に帰すべきである ‖ These are charges *due **to*** him. これは彼に渡すべき料金である. ‖ About 100 yen is *due **to*** you. 君におよそ百円上げる分がある. ‖ I consider that a payment of 2,000 yen is *due **to*** the man. その男に二千円払うのが当然だと僕は思う. 【類】His death was *due **to*** heart disease. / The abundance of the harvest is *due **to*** rain. / It is *due **to*** some cause (chance, negligence). / His dotage (もうろく) is *due **to*** old age. / My success is *due **to*** him. / injury *due **to*** unexpected causes / for this thanks are *due **to*** ... / the credit is justly *due **to*** ...

O He was *due* to arrive at Kobe last Tuesday. 彼は前の火曜日に神戸に着くことになっていた. ‖ The steamer is *due* to sail for New York tomorrow. 汽船はあすニューヨークに向け出帆のはず. ‖ He was *due* to leave London that evening. 彼はその晩ロンドンを立つことになっていた.

duel, *n.* 決闘, 果し合い.

V be challenged to ***fight*** a *duel* 決闘をいどまれる. ¶A *duel **took place***. 決闘があった.

Q a ***principal*** (***second***) *duel* 介添人のない(ある)決闘. ¶a ***rough*** and ***ready*** *duel* 荒っぽくて型破りの決闘.

Q^2 a ***gun*** *duel* 拳銃の決闘.

dull, *a.* つまらない; にぶい.

M ***deadly*** *dull* ごくつまらない. ¶Business is ***deplorably*** *dull*. 商売は上ったりだ.

P *dull **in*** appearance 外観上つまらない. ¶He is *dull **of*** apprehension (=comprehension *or* understanding). 彼はのみ込みが悪い. ‖ The ear grew *dull **of*** hearing from old age. 年のせいで耳が遠くなった.

dullard, *n.* 鈍物.

V try to ***bring up*** the *dullards* to an efficiency standard 鈍物を有能者の基準まで引上げようと努める.

dullness, *n.* 不活発, 不景気.

V ***enliven*** the *dullness* 不景気を活気付ける.

Q the ***deadly*** *dullness* of the place その土地の非常な不振.

P the depth ***of*** *dullness* 不景気の深刻さ. ¶the *dullness **of*** trade (briskness) 不(好)景気.

dumb, *n.* おし.

V ***Keep*** *dumb* and no talk about it, see? 口をきかずにいるんだ, いゝか. ¶***play*** *dumb* about ... …について黙っている.

dumb, *a.* おしの, 口のきけない.

P be *dumb **from*** birth 生れつきのおしである. ¶He is *dumb **on*** the subject. 彼はその問題に関しては黙っている. ¶He was *dumb **with*** astonishment. 彼は驚がくのあまりあ然としていた.

dumbfound, *v.* あ然たらしめる.

P He was *dumbfounded **by*** the shock. 彼は驚いて開いた口がふさがらなかった.

dummy, *n.* 人形; 手先.

V ***hire*** a *dummy* for one's part その役にかえ玉(吹き替え)を使う.

Q a ***tailor's*** *dummy* 洋服屋の店頭飾り人形.

P shoot ***at*** a *dummy* 人形を標的に射つ.

dump, *n.* ごみ捨て場; 置場.

Q^2 an ***ammunition*** *dump* 軍需品積置場. ¶a ***lumber*** *dump* 材木置場. ¶a ***rubbish*** *dump* 共同ちり捨場.

dump, *v.* 一時に投げ出す; 外国へ送って廉売する.

P *dump* goods ***into*** the country 品物をその国へ送ってダンピングを行う. ¶*dump* goods ***upon*** the market 品を一時に市場に投げ出す.

dumping, *n.* 投売(ダンピング).

V ***conduct*** (=***practice***) heavy *dumping* 非常な投売をやる. ¶They are ***trying*** *dumping* on overseas markets. 彼らは海外の市場で投売をやっている.

Q^2 ***exchange*** *dumping* 為替ダンピング(為替相場を下げ不当な廉価で輸出すること). ¶***social*** *dumping* 海外ダンピング(労働条件を他国より低くして生産費を下げ外国に安売りすること).

dumping-place, *n.* ごみ捨て場.

P^2 a *dumping-place **for*** rubbish ごみ捨て場.

dumps, *n. pl.* 憂うつ.

P He is ***in*** the *dumps*. 彼はきげんが悪い, ゆううつだ.

dun, *v.* やかましく催促する; 無心する.

P *dun **for*** payment of debt 借金を催促する. 【類】*dun **for*** money before it is due (まだ支払期日の来ない中に) ‖ *dun* him ***for*** ... 彼に…の無心をする.

dunce, *n.* 鈍物.

Q a ***dense*** *dunce* 大のろま.

dung, *n.* ふん.

Q^2 ***horse*** (***cow***) *dung* 馬(牛)ふん.

dungeon, *n.* 土ろう.

P be locked up ***in*** a *dungeon* 土ろうに監禁されている.

dupe, *n.* だまされやすい人.

Q an ***ignorant*** *dupe* 無知でだまされやすい人.

dupe, *v.* あざむく, だます.

P *dupe* a person ***into*** playing a trick 人をだましていたずらをやらせる.

duplicate, *n.* 複写, 謄本.

P send messages ***in*** *duplicate* 通信を正副二通送る. 【類】We have made out the invoice ***in*** *duplicate*. / documents (文書) ***in*** *duplicate*.

duplicate, *v.* 複写する, 複製する.

M a feature which would be difficult if not impossible to *duplicate **elsewhere*** よそでまねすることがよしんば不可能でないまでもむずかしい一つの特色.

P this feat was *duplicated **by*** ... この妙技を…もやった ‖ Some of these may be *duplicated **by*** any handy man. この中には器用な人ならまねできるのもあるかも知れない.

duplication, *n.* 重複.

Q avoid ***unnecessary*** (=***needless***) *duplication* 不必要な重複を避ける.

durability, *n.* 耐久力, 持久力.

V ***destroy*** its *durability* その耐久性を破壊する. ¶***secure*** *durability* 耐久力を確保する.

durable, *n.* 耐久品.

Q^2 Such "***consumer*** *durables*" as automobiles, refrigerators and washing machines 自動車・冷蔵庫・洗たく機のような半消耗品.

duration, *n.* 耐久, 持続; 期間.

Q Thus ended a journey of ***fifty days'*** *duration*. こうして五十日にわたる旅行が終った. ¶an obstacle of an ***indefinite*** *duration* 不定期間の障害. ¶a disease of ***long*** *duration* ながの病気. ¶the ***natural*** *duration* of life 寿命. ¶after a struggle of ***six years'*** *duration* 六年間奮闘の後. ¶***some months'*** *duration* 数カ月の期間. ¶holidays of ***three weeks'*** *duration* 三週間にわたる休暇. 【類】His absence from the capital is expected to be of ***three weeks'*** *duration*.

P ***for*** the *duration* of (=during) the war 戦争中.

dusk, *n.* 薄暮, たそがれ.

V as the *dusk **deepened*** 夕暮が迫ると. ¶As *dusk **falls*** sweethearts crowd the shady alleys of the Park. たそがれ時になると恋人たちは公園の木かげ深き小道に集まって来る.

P ***after*** *dusk* 日が暮れてから. ¶just ***at*** *dusk* 丁度日暮時に. ¶from dawn ***till*** *dusk* 朝から晩まで. ¶thick ***with*** *dusk* 夕やみがせまって.

dust, *n.* ちり, ほこり, ごみ.

V problems which lie neglected and are ***accumulating*** *dust* upon the shelves of the Department その省で閑却してたなに上げてある懸案の諸問題. ¶***allay*** the *dust* ほこりをしずめる. ¶Two of the reconnoitring party ***bit*** (=***licked***) the *dust*. 偵察隊の中の二人は戦死した. ¶***drive*** the *dust* in our eyes われわれの目にごみを入れる. ¶***flick off*** *dust* ちりをつめではじき落す. ¶they should be reposing in the attic quietly ***gathering dust*** with ... それらは...と一緒に静かにほこりをかぶって屋根裏の物置に仕舞いこんであるべきだ. ¶***kick up*** (=***raise***) a *dust* 砂煙を立てる, 騒ぎを起す. ¶***lay*** the *dust* ちりをしずめる. ¶***remove dust***, smuts, and grease from the face with *papier poudre* 紙おしろいで顔のちりや汚れやあぶらを取る. ¶He has ***shaken*** the *dust* of Scotland from (=off) his feet (=boots) to give his life to literature in London. 彼は憤然としてスコットランドを去り一生を文学にささげようとロンドンに出た. ¶Grey does not ***show*** the *dust*. ねずみ色はちりが目立たない. ¶***sweep up dust*** ごみを掃く. ¶***throw dust*** in the eyes of the public 一般民衆の目をくらます. ¶the *dust* ***settles*** on ... ほこりが...の上につもる.

Q ***fine dust*** こまかいちり. ¶***gritty dust*** 砂ごみ. ¶remains reduced to "two handfuls of ***white dust***" 「二つかみの白骨」と化した遺がい.

Q² ***tobacco dust*** 粉たばこ.

P be crumbled ***into dust*** みじんに砕ける. ¶fall back ***to*** *dust* (死んで)土に帰る.

dust, *v.* ちりを払う, 掃除する.

M Please *dust* more ***carefully***. もっと注意して掃除して下さい. ¶*dust* oneself ***up*** 自分のほこりを落す.

dust-bin, *n.* ごみ箱.

Q a ***literary*** *dust-bin* 文芸かき寄せ文.

duster, *n.* 上っぱり(ダスター).

V ***wear*** a *duster* in the office オフィスで事務服を着る.

Q² a ***sleeve*** *duster* そでにつけるダスター. ¶a light ***spring*** *duster* for women's wear 《米》婦人用の軽い春着用のダスター・コート.

Dutch, *n.* オランダ人, オランダ語; 《俗》ドイツ人, ドイツ語.

V ***go*** *Dutch* 《口語》わりかんで行く.

Q It is ***double*** *Dutch* to me.=It is incomprehensible to me. 私にはちんぷんかんぷんだ. ¶***Low*** *Dutch* 北部ドイツ人またはその言語.

Q² He speaks ***Pennsylvania*** *Dutch*. 《米》彼はペンシルバニヤのドイツ方言を使う.

duty, *n.* (**1**) 義務, 本分; 任務, 勤務; 敬意.

V ***accomplish*** one's *duty* 自己の任務を果す. ¶***assume*** *duty* as ... ...に就任する. 【類】The newly appointed official has ***assumed*** the *duties* of office. ‖ ***assume*** the *duties* of an officer of the day 当直将校の勤務に当る. ¶The committee ***carried out*** the *duties* entrusted to it in an exemplary manner. 委員会はこれに付託された任務をりっぱに実行した. ¶The Government Office ***commenced*** *duty*. その役所は事務を開始した. ¶***conduct*** one's *duties* 自己の職務を行う. ¶***delegate*** *duties* 任務をゆだねる. ¶He ***deserted*** his *duty* from infatuation for a girl. 彼は恋のためにその職を捨てた. ¶***discharge*** one's *duty* successfully その本務をりっぱに尽す. 【類】***discharge*** one's *duty* to society / faithfully ***discharge*** the *duties* of / ***discharge*** its *duties* with scrupulous conscientiousness (非常に入念に) ‖ He ***discharged*** his arduous *duties* with conspicuous ability. 彼は困難な職務をすぐれた手腕をもってなし遂げた. ¶***divide*** *duties* 仕事を分担する. ¶***do*** *duty* for ... ...の代りを務める; ...として役立つ ‖ ***Do*** your *duty*, come what may! どうあっても君の任務を果せ. ‖ The watch ***does*** its full *duty* as a good timepiece. 懐中時計がりっぱに用を足す. ‖ When your wages are ten shillings a week you have to make one pair of shoes ***do*** *duty* for a very long time indeed. 一週十シリングの給金では一足のくつを随分長いこともたせねばならない. 【類】***do*** our *duty* to (=by [*archaic*]) our fellow-men / ***do*** their *duty* to the country / He ***does*** his *duty* loyally to the country. / ***do*** *duty* as an executive (幹部として) / He has merely ***done*** his *duty*. / manfully ***do*** one's *duty* / learn the joy of ***doing*** one's *duty*. ¶***escape*** the *duty* 義務を回避する. ¶never ***forget*** one's *duty* to ... ...に対する義務をいつも忘れない. ¶this ***forms*** the first *duty* of ... これが...の第一の務めとなっている. ¶For all that, I must ***fulfil*** my *duty*. それだってするだけのことはしなければならない. ‖ he is worthy to ***fulfil*** the high *duty* of ... 彼には...のりっぱな任務を果すだけの貫禄がある ‖ Has society really ***fufilled*** its *duty* in this direction? 社会はこの方面において本当によくその任務を果しているか. ‖ ***fulfil*** one's *duty* toward the race 人類に対する義務を果す(産児など) ‖ ***fulfil*** the *duties* of ... in his absence 彼が不在だから代って...役を務める. 【類】incapable of ***fulfilling*** the *duties* of matrimony. ¶***impose*** a *duty* on ... ...に義務を課する. ¶***keep on duty*** 務めを続けてやって行く. ¶***lay aside*** one's *duties* その職を辞する. ¶carefully ***maintain*** *duty* to parents 両親に対し変らず心を入れてつとめる(親孝行をする). ¶however grossly the landlord may ***neglect*** his *duty* 家主がどんなにその義務を怠ろうとも ‖ ***neglect*** one's marital *duties* 夫としての務めを怠る. ¶***pay*** (=***send***) one's *duty* to ... 謹んで...に敬意を表する. ¶He ***performed*** his *duty* with great skill. 彼は非常に巧みに仕事を成し遂げた. ‖ ***perform*** the *duties* of the office with infinite credit and distinction 無限の信用と高評とを博してその職務を果す ‖ ***perform*** *duties* in a perfunctory and absent-minded way よいかげんにそして上の空で仕事をやる. 【類】their fitness (適性) to ***perform*** the *duties* for which they are appointed / My mind is full of distress at my inability to ***perform*** my *duties* at the office. / while ***performing*** *duty*. ¶***place*** a *duty* on ... ...に任務を課す. ¶Closing of his safe was a *duty* which he had never ***relegated*** to a subordinate. 金庫をしめることは部下のだれにも決して任せたことのない仕事であった. ¶Her deafness ***rendered*** social *duties* arduous to her. 彼女はつんぼだったために社会的義務を尽すのに骨が折れた. ¶***resume*** one's *duties* 仕事を再び始める. ¶He ***sends*** his *duty* to you. 彼はあなたによろしくと申しました. ¶***shift*** a *duty* 任務を譲る. ¶***shirk*** one's *duty* as a soldier 軍人としての義務を逃げる. ¶***shuffle off*** a *duty* on someone else 義務をごまかして他人に負わせる. ¶***specialize*** the *duties* of employees 雇人の仕事を分担させる. ¶***take over*** one's *duties* その役を引受ける 【類】***take over*** the *duties* of a sick fellow-official. ¶***take up*** one's *duties* 就任する ‖ He arrived at ... to ***take up*** his new *duties*. 彼は...の新任地に着いた. ¶***undertake*** the arduous *duties* of the Vice-Chancellorship 副大法官という骨の折れる任務を引受ける.

V² When *duty* ***calls***, one must obey. 義務の命令にはいつでも従わねばならない. ¶This *duty* ***devolves*** on him. 彼の肩にこの任務がかかる. ¶There his *duty* ***ends***. それで彼の義務は解除される(これ以上する必要はない). ¶this *duty* ***falls*** on the shoulders of ... この義務が...の双肩に掛る.

Q servicemen on ***active*** *duty* 現役の軍人. 【類】soldiers and sailors on ***active*** *duty*. ¶an ***agreeable*** *duty* 愉快な仕事. ¶quite an ***arduous*** *duty* 全く骨の折れる仕事. ¶it is my ***bounden*** *duty* to ... ...するのは私の責務だ. ¶do one's ***Christian*** *duty* キリスト教徒としての務めを尽す. ¶perform ***difficult*** *duties* 困難な役目を果す. ¶have various ***distracting*** *duties* 様々な気の散る仕事がある. ¶do ***double*** *duty* 二重の務めを尽す. ¶It is a woman's ***essential*** *duty* to have charms. 魅力を有することは女がぜひ心掛くべきことである. ¶it is a ***father's*** *duty* to ... ...することは父たる者の務めである. ¶the ***first*** *duty* of educators 教育者第一の務め ‖ Stimulating teaching is the ***first*** *duty* of a college. 刺激を与える教授をすることが大学の最も肝要なことである. 【類】The ***first*** *duty* of a soldier is obedience. ¶do one's ***full*** *duty* to the community 社会に対する自己の全任務を尽す. ¶regard it as a ***glorious*** *duty* and privilege to ... ...することを光栄な義務および特権と見なす. ¶it is our ***imperative*** *duty* to ... ...することはわれわれのぜひつくすべき義務である. ¶perform ***important*** *duties* 大切な務めを果す. ¶his ***inalienable*** *duty* 彼がどうしても自分でしなければならない務め. ¶one of the most ***irksome*** *duties* connected with Royal life 王者たる身にかかる最も退屈な任務の一つ. ¶on ***land*** (***sea***) *duty* 陸(海)上勤務の. ¶a ***legal*** *duty* 法律上の義務. ¶its ***main*** *duty* is to ... その主なる務めは...することである. ¶***manifold*** *duties* 多方面の務め. ¶fulfill her true ***maternal*** *duties* admirably 母たるの本務をりっぱに尽す. ¶***military*** *duties* 軍務. ¶***minor*** *duties* of life 人生の微々たる務め. ¶a ***moral*** *duty* 道徳上の義務. ¶***multifarious*** *duties* 多様な任務. ¶***multiform*** *duties* 多種多様な仕事. ¶women's ***natural*** *duties* as wives and mothers 妻たり母たる女の当然の務め. ¶take over ***new*** *duties* 新職につく. ¶in spite of ***numerous*** and ***urgent*** *duties* 数多い緊急な仕事にもかかわらず. ¶perform ***official*** *duty* 公務を遂行する. ¶He resumed his ***official*** *duties*. 彼は帰任した. ¶***onerous*** *duties* わずらわしい任務. ¶one's ***painful*** *duty* to ... ...する苦しい役目. 【類】I have never performed this ***painful*** *duty* before. ¶a ***patriotic*** *duty* 愛国者としての一つの義務. ¶I feel it a ***pleasant*** *duty* to gratefully acknowledge that ... 私は...ということ

に対して感謝するのは愉快に存じます.【類】there remains to me the ***pleasant*** *duty* of expressing my thanks to … ¶a ***pressing*** *duty* 緊急な任務. ¶It is the ***primary*** *duty* of medicine to save life. 人命救助が医術の本務である. ¶overburdened with ***professional*** *duties* 本業の方に追われて. ¶the performance of ***public*** *duties* 公務の遂行. ¶***routine*** *duties* 日常の務. ¶a ***sacred*** *duty* 一つの神聖な義務. ¶It is a ***serious*** *duty* of … to do this. これをなすことは…の重大な義務である. ¶He was driven to the most ***servile*** and ***degrading*** *duties*. 彼はいやしい不名誉な仕事をやるような破目になった. ¶***social*** *duties* 世間の義理(交際).【類】perform the ***social*** *duty* of rearing a family / fail to perform one's ***social*** *duties*. ¶on ***special*** *duty* 特別任務で. ¶***spiritual*** and ***secular*** *duties* 精神界および俗界の務め. ¶the ***stern*** *duties* he is called upon to discharge 彼が果すべく要求されたきびしい任務. ¶in the intervals of ***strenuous*** *duties* 骨の折れる任務のあい間に. ¶an ***unavoidable*** *duty* 免れ難い義務. ¶fulfill ***unliterary*** *duties* 文筆に縁のない現業に従事する(大学の文科を出てタクシーの運転手になるなど). ¶an ***unpleasant*** *duty* 迷惑な役. ¶discharge an ***unwelcome*** *duty* ありがたくない任務を果す.

Q² on ***air*** (***ground***) *duty* 〔航空〕空中(地上)勤務の. ¶Most of the men had been on ***combat*** *duty* abroad それらの兵の大多数は海外で実戦を経験した. ¶***day*** (***night***) *duty* 昼(夜)間勤務. ¶perform their ***everyday*** *duties* 日常の職務を果す. ¶***fatigue*** *duty* [軍隊などの]雑役. ¶***field*** *duties* [赤十字などの]戦地勤務. ¶on ***guard*** *duty* 歩しょう勤務で. ¶***home*** *duties* 家庭の務め. ¶return to ***household*** *duties* [女工などが]家庭の務めに戻る ‖ attend to ***household*** *duties* 家事を見る ‖ go about her ***household*** *duties* 家事に取りかかる. ¶remain on ***night*** *duty* 夜勤で居残る. ¶carry out the ***occupation*** *duties* 占領任務を遂行する.【類】as long as ***occupation*** *duties* continue / be on ***occupation*** *duty* / varied ***occupation*** *duties* / the transition from combat to ***occupation*** *duties*. ¶leave for ***overseas*** *duty* 外地勤務に赴任する.【類】with 25 per cent additional pay (加俸) for ***overseas*** *duty*. ¶***patrol*** *duty* 巡回勤務. ¶men on ***picket*** *duty* ピケラインを張っている人たち. ¶a policeman on ***point*** *duty* 交通整理の立番警官. ¶***sea*** *duty* 海上勤務. ¶be on ***sentry*** *duty* 歩しょう任務についている. ¶be assigned to ***shipboard*** *duty* 海上勤務を命ぜられて. ¶***shore*** (***sea***) *duty* 陸(海)上勤務. ¶return to their ***teaching*** *duties* 教職に戻る. ¶as their men came back from ***war*** *duty* 彼らの部下が戦争任務から帰還したので.

P impelled ***by*** *duty* 責任感から. ¶He was discharged ***from*** his *duties*. 彼は職を免ぜられた. ¶***in*** *duty* bound to … 義務として…すべき ‖ I am bound ***in*** *duty* to … 私には…する義務がある. ‖ fail ***in*** one's *duty* to the state 国家に対する義務を怠る. ¶neglect ***of*** *duty* 職務怠慢 ‖ as a matter ***of*** *duty* 義務として ‖ from a sense ***of*** *duty* 義務観念から ‖ honest performance ***of*** *duty* 義務のまじめな遂行. ¶I am ***off*** *duty* today. 僕は今日は非番だ.【類】a waiter ***off*** *duty* / when ***off*** *duty* ‖ I could not get ***off*** *duty*. (いそがしくて)職務の方が抜けられなかった. ¶when ***on*** *duty* 当番の時 ‖ an operator ***on*** *duty* 担当者.【類】the policeman who was ***on*** *duty* for the night / a constable ***on*** *duty* ‖ go ***on*** *duty* 出勤する ‖ remain ***on*** *duty* until … …まで勤務を続ける ‖ be ***on*** *duty* for crime prevention 防犯当番である. ¶I charge you ***with*** this *duty*. 君にこの任務を命じる.

P² do *duty* ***as*** … …として役立つ. ¶persuade the neglectful parent to do his or her *duty* ***by*** the child 不注意な親にその子供に対する義務を尽すようによく話す. ¶do *duty* ***for*** … …の名代をする. ¶the *duties* ***of*** a secretary 秘書の任務. ¶The vote is a *duty* ***of*** citizenship. 投票は国民の一つの義務である. ‖ *duties* ***of*** the employee ***to*** his employer 雇主に対する雇人の義務. ¶our *duty* ***to*** our parents 親に対するわれらの義務 ‖ our *duty* ***to*** God and ***to*** men 神と人間に対するわれわれの務め. ¶our *duty* ***with*** conscription 兵役.

O he thought it his *duty* to … …するのが彼の義務と考えした.

(2) 税, 関税.

V ***abolish*** the *duty* on … …の税を廃止する. ¶The *duty* on … will be ***abolished*** …税は廃止になるだろう. ¶***bear*** a heavy *duty* 重税がかゝる. ¶***impose*** a *duty* on the exports of iron ore 鉄鉱の輸出に対して課税する. ¶***lay*** a *duty* on … …に税金を課する. ¶***levy*** a *duty* upon an article 品物に課税する ‖ ***levy*** a *duty* on an article or a transaction 品物または取引に対して税を課する ‖ ***levy*** *duties* at certain fixed rates upon … …に一定の率で課税する. ¶***lower*** (***raise***) the *duty* 税を下げる(上げる).

Q Owing to the imposition of ***heavy*** *duty*, beans are not imported to America to a great extent. 重税を課せられるので豆類はあまり米国に輸入されない. ¶goods *duty* ***paid*** 関税済の貨物. ¶***preferential*** *duty* 特恵関税. ¶impose ***prohibitive*** import *duties* on foreign goods 外国品に禁止的輸入税を課する. ¶***specific*** *duties* 従量税. ¶impose pretty ***stiff*** *duties* on imported goods 輸入品にかなりの重税を課する.

Q² an ***advalorem*** *duty* of 15% will be assessed against … 一割五分の従価税が…に対して課せられる. ¶***customs*** *duties* 関税. ¶***death*** *duties* 遺産相続税. ¶***entertainment*** *duty* 遊興税. ¶***export*** (***import***) *duty* 輸出(輸入)税. ¶assess ***import*** *duty* upon … …に輸入税を課す. ¶***legacy*** *duty* 遺産税. ¶***probate*** *duty* 遺産相続税. ¶***stamp*** *duty* 印紙税. ¶***tariff*** *duties* on … …の関税. ¶***transit*** *duty* 通過関税; 通行税.

P an article free ***of*** *duties* 無税の品物. ¶the article which is subject ***to*** a custom *duty* (=customs duties) 関税を課せられるべき品物. 「輸入品に対する税金.

P² *duty* ***on*** (=***upon***) foreign goods (=imported goods)

dwarf, *v*. 少さくする.

P a building *dwarfed* ***by*** the surrounding hills 丘に囲まれているので小さく見える建物.

dwell, *v*. 住む, 居住する; 詳説する; 気にかける.

M I will not *dwell* ***any longer*** upon this subject. 私はこの上この問題は論じない. ¶*dwell* ***at length*** on … …に関して詳説する. ¶his mind ***constantly*** *dwelled* on … 彼は始終…に心を留めた. ¶*dwell* ***freely*** on … …を存分詳説する. ¶***strongly*** *dwell* on … …を力説する. ¶*dwell* ***together*** in amity and concord 親密に和合して同せいする. ¶*dwell* ***too much*** on … …について詳しく述べ過ぎる.

P *dwell* ***at*** (=in) a place ある場所に住む ‖ *dwell* in generality ***at*** … 大がい…に住む. ¶His mind *dwells* ***in*** a world of stars. 彼の心は星の世界に住んでいる. ¶*dwell* ***on*** the earth 地球上に住む ‖ Don't *dwell* ***on*** thoughts that annoy you or cause you trouble. 心配や苦労はあまり考えてはいけない. ‖ *dwell* ***on*** a thought あることを苦にする ‖ this is not the place in which to *dwell* ***on*** … ここは…を詳述すべき場所がらでない ‖ *dwell* ***on*** one's indebtedness to him 彼に負う恩義をあつく謝する ‖ It is needless to *dwell* ***on*** familiar spectacles. 人のよく知っている景色を詳しく述べるのはやぼだ.【類】the important point to *dwell* ***on*** in teaching is that … / The subject is too unpleasant to *dwell* ***on***. / *dwell* unduly ***on*** a truism (分り切ったこと) ‖ *dwell* ***on*** grievances 愚痴をこぼす ‖ Don't allow your mind to *dwell* ***on*** your past failure. 過去の失敗を思い出さないようにしたまえ. ‖ *dwell* for a time ***on*** one subject しばらく一問題について細説する. ¶I shall not *dwell* ***upon*** your misbehavior towards me. 君の私に対する失行についてはくどくど言いますまい. ‖ Her thoughts *dwell* ***upon*** it. 彼女はそれを忘れない. ‖ That story *dwells* still ***upon*** my mind. あの話はいまだに私の心に残っている. ‖ *dwell* ***upon*** this phase of the question 問題のこの方面を細かく論じる.

dweller, *n*. 住む人, 居住者.

Q² a ***cave*** *dweller* 穴居者. ¶Few ***city*** *dwellers* are priviledged to enjoy it. 都市居住者でその楽しみを得られる者はほとんどない. ¶the jaded palate of the European ***city*** *dweller* 美食になれている欧州の都市居住者の味覚. ¶a ***town*** *dweller* 都市住民.

P² *dwellers* ***in*** towns (large cities) 町(など)に住む人.

dwelling, *n*. 住宅, 住所.

V ***build*** a *dwelling* 住宅を建てる. ¶You have ***changed*** your *dwelling*, haven't you? あなたは御移転なさったのでしょう. ¶He ***had*** his *dwelling* there. 彼はそこに住んでいた. ‖ ***have*** no *dwelling* and no trade 家もなく職もない.

Q a ***foul*** and ***insanitary*** *dwelling* きたなくて非衛生的な住宅. ¶***human*** *dwellings* 人間の住宅. ¶a ***model*** *dwelling* モデル住宅. ¶a ***modern*** *dwelling* 文化住宅. ¶***palatial*** *dwelling* りっぱな邸宅. ¶a ***rental*** *dwelling* 借家.

Q² one's ***home-town*** *dwelling* その生れた町の自宅. ¶a ***slum*** *dwelling* 貧民住宅.

dwelling-ground, *n.* 住宅地.
Q a *noted dwelling-ground* 有名な住宅地.

dwindle, *v.* 減少する; 衰える.
M *dwindle away* to nothing (=the point of extinction) なくなってしまう.
P *dwindle from* 100 *to* 20 百から二十に減少する. ¶*dwindle in* size (numbers) 大きさ(など)が減る. ¶*dwindle into* a small thing 小さなものになってしまう ‖ *dwindle into* nothing when compared with ... ...と比べると物の数でない. ¶*dwindle to* insignificance 無価値なものになってしまう. 【類】*dwindle to* nothing ‖ *dwindle to* a dot 一個の点に縮まる.

dye, *n.* 染料.
V *fix* a *dye* 色を定着させる. ¶This cloth *holds dye* well. この布は色が落ちない. ¶The stuff *takes dye* well. その生地はよく染まる. ‖ will not *take dye* 染まらない. ¶The *dye comes* out of the silk. 色が絹地から落ちる.
Q *aniline dyes* アニリン染料. ¶a crime of the *blackest dye* 凶悪犯罪. ¶villains (criminals) of the *deepest dye* 極悪人の悪漢(など) ‖ a crime of the *deepest dye* 極悪の罪 ‖ outwardly a Confucianist, but inwardly a Taoist of the *deepest dye* 外観は儒教徒であるが内心は徹底的な道教信徒. ¶flowers of *every dye* 千紫万紅.
P It is used *as* a *dye*. それは染料に使う.

dye, *v.* 染める; 染まる.
M get it *dyed black* それを黒に染めさせる. ¶*dye blue* with ... ...で青に染める. ¶This cloth *dyes well*. この織物はよく染まる.
P *dye in* blue (gray, yellow, red) 青色(など)に染める ‖ yarn *dyed in* the wool (=grain) トップ染の毛糸. ¶*dye with* blood 血で染める.

dying, *n.* 臨終, 死.
P just enough to prevent them *from dying* of starvation やっと餓死を防ぐ程度に. 【類】keep a light *from dying*.

dynamite, *n.* ダイナマイト.
V *set* (=*touch*) *off* the *dynamite* ダイナマイトを爆発させる.
P charge *with dynamite* ダイナマイトを仕掛ける ‖ blew it up *with dynamite* ダイナマイトでそれを爆発させた.

dynamo, *n.* 発電機(ダイナモ).
Q[2] a *hand dynamo* 手動発電機. ¶a *motor dynamo* 電動発電機.

dynasty, *n.* 代, 王朝.
V *change* a *dynasty* 王朝を変える. ¶*establish* (=*found*) a *dynasty* 一王朝を建設する. 【類】*founded* the *dynasty* of ... / *found* a new *dynasty*. ¶*overthrow* a *dynasty* 一王朝を倒す.
V[2] The present *dynasty stretches back* in unbroken line to the Emperor Jimmu. 現在の皇朝は神武天皇以来連綿として伝わる.
Q The Imperial family of Japan is (=represents) the *oldest dynasty* in the world. 日本の皇室は世界最古の皇朝である. ¶an *unbroken dynasty* 連綿たる王朝.
Q[2] under the *Mongol Dynasty* 元朝の下に. ¶the fall of the Mongols and the rise of the *Ming*, or *native Chinese dynasty* 元の衰亡と中国に生え抜きの王朝たる明の興起. ¶struggles of *rival dynasties* 二王朝の紛争. ¶the *Tokugawa dynasty* of Shoguns 徳川将軍家.
P *Under* the Ming *dynasty* China was in a prosperous condition. 明朝時代のシナは隆盛であった. ‖ Japan was then *under* two *dynasties*—the southern and the northern. 日本はその当時二つの朝廷—南朝と北朝のもとにあった.
P[2] a *dynasty of* gods 神代.

E

each, *n.* 各自, それぞれ.
V They sat *facing each other* with a table between. テーブルをはさんで二人は相対してすわった. ¶The cars *struck each other*. 車は衝突した.
P[2] They gave two apples to *each of* the children. 彼らは子供たち一人一人にりんごを二つずつ与えた. ¶The sides of the two triangles are equal *each to* each. 〖数〗二つの三角形の各辺はそれぞれひとしい.

eager, *a.* 熱心な, 切望して.
M be *too eager* for success 功をあせる.
P a pretty daughter *eager for* amusement 遊び好きのかわいらしい娘 ‖ Every recruit was *eager for* action. 新兵はいずれも実戦を切望していた. 【類】be *eager for* one's favor (honor, reputation) ‖ He is *eager for* martyrdom for the cause. 彼は主義に殉じる意気込みでいる. ¶He is very *eager in* his studies. 彼は勉学にはなはだ熱心だ. 【類】The opponents do not appear very *eager in* competing.
O I am not *eager* to defend them. 私はしいて彼らを弁護しようとは思わない. ¶He is very *eager* to become rich. 彼は金もうけにあくせくしている. 【類】He is *eager* to learn how to ride a bicycle.

eagerness, *n.* 熱心.
V *show* an *eagerness* to ... ぜひ...したいという意向を示す.
Q She was *all eagerness* to go to the theatre, 彼女はとても芝居に行きたがっていた. ¶watch it with *intense eagerness* 熱意をこめてそれを見まもる.
P *in* his *eagerness* to ... 彼は...したさのあまり. ¶*with eagerness* 熱心に.
P[2] his great *eagerness for* wealth 富に対する非常な欲望.

eagle. *n.* わし.
Q a *bald eagle* 白頭わし. ¶"*daring eagles*"「荒わし」部隊.

ear, *n.* 耳; 穂.
V *accustom* the *ear* to English sounds 英語の音声に耳をならす. ¶It painfully *affects* my English *ear*. それは英人の私には非常に耳ざわりだ. ¶he *applied* his *ear* to ... 彼は...に耳を当てた. ¶*assail* one's *ear* 耳を襲う. ¶I can't *believe* my *ears*. 自分で自分の耳を疑う(信じられない). 【類】Am I to *believe* my *ears?* ¶*box* his *ear* 彼の片耳にパンチを食わせる. ¶*catch* the *ear* of the people 世人の注意を引く. ¶*charm* one's *ears* [音楽など]耳を喜ばせる. ¶*close* one's *ears* 聞こうとしない. ¶The dog *cocked* the *ears*. 犬が耳を立てた. ¶*command* the world's *ear* 世界の耳目をそばだたせる. ¶The cataract *deafened* the *ear* with its roar. 滝の音で耳もろうせんばかりであった. ¶His words *defeated* my English *ears*. 彼の言ったことは英人の私には聞き取りかねた. ¶*delight* the *ears* of his listeners 聴取者の耳を喜ばせる. ¶Our *ears* are *dinned* with a constant cry of discontent in India. われわれの耳はインドにおける騒がしい不満の声を絶えず聞いている. ¶The request *found* the readiest *ear* from him. その願いを彼は快く聞いてくれた. ¶*gain* (=*win*) the *ear* of the public 世人の注意を引く. ¶Children sometimes *get* (=have) their *ears pulled* when they misbehave. 子供は行儀が悪いとときどき耳を引っ張られる. ¶He *gave ear* to this prudent advice. 彼はこの思慮ある忠告に耳を傾けた. 【類】You must *give ear* to what the teacher tells you. / *give* no *ear* to ... ¶unfamiliar sounds that *greet* one's *ears* 耳にはいる聞き慣れない音. ¶Walls *have ears*. 壁に耳あり. ‖ I *have* no *ear* for music. 私には音楽が分らない. ‖ I don't think you can *have* his *ears*. 君のいうことがあの人に聞いてもらえるとは思わない. ¶He *had* his *ear boxed*. 彼は耳をげんこつでなぐられた. ¶*hold* one's *ears* 耳を押える. ¶*lend* one's *ear* to ...に耳を貸す ‖ *lend* an open *ear* to the theories of socialism 社会主義の学説に卒直に耳をかたむける. 【類】He *lent* an attentive *ear* to the words of wisdom. / *lend* a willing *ear*. ¶*meet* the *ear* of ... ...の耳にはいる ‖ It has a deeper meaning than that which *meets* the *ear*. それは耳に響くよりももっと深い意義がある. ¶Golden words *offend* the *ears*. 忠言耳にさからう. ‖ The pronunciation *offends* English *ears*. その発音は英人の耳ざわりになる. 【類】The music *offended* their *ears*. ¶*open* one's *ears* 傾聴する. ¶*perk* one's *ears* 耳を澄ます. ¶*pick* [*up*] the *ears* 耳をぴんとあげる; 傾聴する ‖ I wonder whether a new work from his pen would make the critics *prick* [*up*] their *ears*. 彼の新著が批評家連の一顧に価するかどうか怪しい. ¶*pinch* one's *ear* tight ひどく耳をつねる. ¶*please* sensitive *ears* 感じの早い耳を喜ばせる. ¶Ru-

mours *reached* his *ears*. 風説が彼の耳にはいった. 【類】 The distant roll of thunder (遠雷) *reached* our *ears*. ¶Slang *shocks* the refined *ear*. 俗語は高雅な耳を驚かせる. ¶*shut* their *ears* entirely to ... 全然...に耳を貸さない. ¶The word *smites* one's *ear* as unfamiliar. その語は聞き慣れない感じがする. ¶*stop* one's *ears* 耳をおゝう, 聞かない. ¶*strain* one's *ears* to catch words 聞き取ろうとして耳をそばだてる. ¶The noise *struck* the *ear*. その物音が聞えた. 【類】 Does not such dialogue as this frequently *strike* the *ear*? ¶*stuff* one's *ears* with cotton-wool 耳に生綿(きわた)をつめる. ¶*syringe* the *ear* 耳を洗じょうする. ¶*take* one's *ears* 耳を傾けさせる. ¶*tear out* the *ears* 耳をむしり取る. ¶*train* the *ear* of young students 若い学生の耳をならす. ¶He *turned* a deaf *ear* to my entreaties. 彼は僕が折入って頼むのに知らん振りをしていた. 【類】 *turn* a deaf *ear* to their cries for protection / He was a compassionate man who never *turned* a deaf *ear* to a cry of distress. / These are considerations to which man cannot always *turn* a deaf *ear*. ¶*twitch* one's *ears* 耳をぴくぴくさせる.

V² My *ears itch* for information. そのことをぜひ聞きたい. ¶*Ears ring*. 耳鳴りがする. ¶My *ears* are *tingling* (=*humming*). 私は耳鳴りがしている.

Q During his speech I was *all ears*. 氏の演説中僕は一心不乱に傾聴していた. ¶refreshing to *American ears* 米人の耳には清々する. ¶listen with the very *attentive ear* 謹聴する. ¶I have a *bad ear*. 私は耳が悪い. ¶It sounds very strangely to *British ears*. それは英人の耳には変に聞える. ¶a *correct ear* 音楽を聞きわける力. ¶a person with a *cultivated ear* 耳の修養の積んだ人. ¶a *deaf ear* そら耳 ‖ This would have been addressed thirty years ago to *deaf ears*. 三十年前にはこれに耳をかす者はなかったろう. ‖ The protest fell on *deaf ears*. その抗議はぬかにくぎであった. ¶have a *delicate ear* for music せん細な音楽[鑑賞]の耳を持っている. ¶The physician listened with a *distracted ear* to the troubles of his patient. 医者は患者の悩みをうわの空で聞いていた. ¶his *fine ear* for rhythm リズムに対する彼の敏感な耳. ¶He has not a *fine* enough *ear* to learn music. 彼には音楽を習うだけの良い耳がない. ¶He has a *good ear*. 彼は耳が良い. ¶have *itching ears* for=have a longing to hear (news, or some novelty) 聞きたくてたまらない. ¶the *listening ear* きき耳. ¶hear in one's *mind's ear* ... 心の耳で...を聞く. ¶those who have a *musical ear* 音楽の耳がある(聞きわける力のある)人人 ‖ Those false notes caused agonies to the *musical ear*. その調子っぱずれの音が音楽を聞きわける耳には大なる苦痛であった. ¶have a *natural ear* [音をゆがめずに取入れる]くせのない耳を持つ. ¶I heard him say so with my *own ears*. 私はこの耳で(確かに)彼がそう言ったのを聞いた. ¶lend a *patient ear* and give a courteous answer to any question どんな質問でも辛抱強く聞き, 丁寧に答える. ¶The *practiced ear* may recognize a classic flavor. 肥えた耳には古典的風韻があると気付くだろう. ¶to my *provincial* but *travelled ear* いなか者だが諸方を旅した私の耳には. ¶He has a *quick ear*. 彼は耳が早い. ¶give the *ready ear* to wise counsel 喜んで忠言を容れる. ¶Vulgarized, corrupted words offend the *scholarly ear*. なまった下品な言葉は学者には耳ざわりになる. ¶He has a *sharp ear*. 彼は耳が鋭敏だ(地獄耳). ¶He has a *true ear* for melody. 彼はメロディーを正確につかむ. ¶His advice fell on *unheeding ears* 彼の助言は顧みられなかった. ¶The appeal fell on *unsympathetic ears*. その願いは聞かれなかった. ¶lofty thoughts unfit for *vulgar ears* 俗耳に入らない高尚な思想. ¶His name has become familiar to *Western ears*. 彼の名は西洋人も知るようになった. ¶hear ... with *willing ears* ...を喜んで聞く.

Q² an *asylum ear* 精神病患者通有の耳疾. ¶a *button ear* [犬などの]たれ耳. ¶a *tangerine ear* みかん色の耳.

P perceive *by* the *ear* 聞きわける. ¶The greater part of the speech came in *at* one *ear* and went out at the other. 話の大半は耳から耳へ抜けた. ¶I pulled him *by* the *ears*. 私は彼の耳を引っ張った. ‖ He plays [on] the piano *by ear* only. 彼は譜を見ずにピアノをひく. ¶Just a few words *in* your ear! ちょっとお耳拝借. ¶shout *in* one's *ear* 耳の所でどなる. 【類】 scream it *in* his *ear*. ‖ ringing *in* the *ears* 耳鳴り ‖ It may sound strange *in* the American *ear*. 米国人の耳には変に聞えるかも知れない ‖ rice plants *in* the *ear* 穂が出た稲 ‖ with pen *in ear* 耳にペンをはさんで. ¶he whispered *into* (=in) my *ear* that ... 彼は...と僕に耳打した. 【類】 He whispered a word or two *into* her *ear*. ¶A harsh voice grates *on* my *ears*. だみ声は耳ざわりだ. ‖ I gave him a box *on* the *ear*. 彼の横っつらに一撃をくらわした. 【類】 He got a box *on* the *ear*. ‖ hold a pencil *on* the *ear* 耳に鉛筆をはさむ. ¶come *through* the *ear* 耳からはいる. ¶This came *to* the *ears* of the Emperor. このことが陛下のお耳に達した. ‖ it has since come *to* my *ears* that ... ...がその後僕の耳にはいった ‖ pleasant *to* the *ear* 耳にこころよい ‖ be up *to* the *ears* in debt 借金で首が回らない. ¶We listened to him *with* all our *ears*. われわれは熱心に彼の話を聞いた. 【類】 I lay listening *with* all my *ears*.

early, *a.*, *ad.* 早い; 早く, 初期に.

P It is too *early for* getting up. 起きるには早すぎる. ¶*early in* the morning (evening) 朝(など)早く ‖ *early in* life 若いときに ‖ *early in* 1932 一九三二年の初めに ‖ She is *early in* her twenties. 彼女は二十歳ちょっと過ぎだ. ‖ I shouldn't be sorry to be *early in* bed on such a cold evening. こんな寒い晩には早く寝た方がましだ.

earmark, *n.* 耳じるし(所有主を表わすために牛などの耳に施した印).

V The whole book *bears* the *earmarks* of the scholar who is enamoured with his subject. 書物全体の上にそのテーマに愛著を持つ学者の面影が浮んでいる.

P² a film with all the *earmarks of* Chaplin チャプリン一流の特徴を十分に備えた映画.

earmark, *v.* 別勘定に(イヤマーク)する.

P *earmark* $... *for* reparations 賠償用として...ドルを別勘定にする ‖ *earmarked for* credit クレジットとして保管された(金貨など).

earn, *v.* もうける, 得る.

M He has *richly earned* his title. 彼にはその爵位に相当するだけの功績は十分にある.

P money *earned by* hard labor 刻苦してもうけた金 ‖ *earn* distinction *by* service (toil) 功(など)によって名を得る. ¶His services *earned for* him the gratitude, the respect, and the admiration of his fellow-citizens. 彼は功労によって同市民の感謝・尊敬および感嘆を獲得した.

earner, *n.* 利得者.

Q² an *income earner* 個人(収入)所得者. ¶a *salary earner* 給料生活者. ¶a *small-income earner* 小額所得者. ¶a manufacturing *wage earner* 生産会社の賃金労務者(職工). ¶*wage* and *salary earners* 賃金および俸給生活者. 【類】 large cities with their populations of *wage* and *salary earners*.

earnest, *n.* 手付, 保証; 前兆.

V The sun was rising over the peak, *giving* an *earnest* of a considerably hot day. 太陽は峰の上に昇り, その日の非常に暑くなる前兆を示した.

P Take this *as* an *earnest* of what we have agreed upon. 契約の手金にとっておきたまえ.

P² an *earnest of* the good faith with which he has approached the question 彼がその問題を忠実に取扱ったことの証左 ‖ It was an *earnest* (=foretaste) *of* what was to follow. それは後から出るものの前菜(あじみ)であった.

earnest, *n.* 本気, まじめ, 真剣.

Q he is in *deadly earnest* about ... 彼は...にばかに真剣だ. ‖ fight for ... in *dead earnest* 死にもの狂いになる ‖ a matter of *deadly earnest* 真剣なこと. ¶commence the campaign in *downright earnest* 真剣にその運動を始める. 【類】 The rain is now pouring down in *good earnest*. ‖ Are you in *good* (=*serious, sober, very or real*) *earnest*? 君は本気か. ‖ The battle began in *real earnest*. 戦いが本式に始まった. ¶in *terrible earnest* 恐ろしく真剣に.

P Evening set in *in earnest*. 日もとっぷりとくれた. ‖ be terribly *in earnest* with the study of ... ...の研究に本腰である. ‖ He was only half *in earnest*. 彼は余り真剣でなかった. 【類】 set to work *in earnest* / Are you *in earnest* in saying that? / Are you *in earnest* about resignation?

earnest, *a.* 熱心な.

P He is *earnest for* success. 彼は成功を収めることに躍起となっている. ¶He is *earnest in* his endeavors (=efforts). 彼は熱心に努力している. ¶He is so *earnest over* it. 彼はそれに非常に熱心だ.

earnestness, *n.* 熱心.

Q *fiery earnestness* 火のような熱誠さ.

P say ... *with* all *earnestness* 熱意を込めて言う ‖ *with*

great *earnestness* 非常に熱心に.

earning, *n.* かせぎ; *pl.* 所得, もうけ.

V *spend* their *earnings* in excessive drinking and noisy revelries 大酒やばか騒ぎに収入を使い果たす. ¶ *waste* one's *earnings* in ... ...にもうけを乱費する.

Q *average earnings* 平均収入. ¶ the *average weekly earning* of a worker 労働者の一週間の平均収入(所得). ¶ This resulted naturally in *diminished earnings*. これで自然減収という結果になった. ¶ *gross earnings* 総収入. ¶ *guaranteed earnings* to piece workers 請負工の保障稼ぎ高. ¶ *hard earnings* 骨を折って得た収入. ¶ one's *honest earning* 正直な利得. ¶ *illicit* (=*clandestine*) *earnings* 不正をして得たもうけ(あぶく銭). ¶ *net earnings* 正味利得. ¶ guaranteed *minimum earning* 最低保障所得. ¶ *pecuniary earnings* 金銭上の利得. ¶ *scanty earnings* わずかな利得. ¶ *surplus earnings* 余分の収入.

Q² add a little to the *family earnings* 家計の足しにする. *wartime earnings* 戦時収入.

P an increase *of earnings* 収入の増加. ¶ He lives *on* his *earnings*. 彼は自分の働きで暮している.

P² *earnings from* prostitution 売春による収入.

earshot, *n.* 聴力範囲.

P *beyond* (=*out of*) *earshot* of the siren サイレンの聞えない所に. ¶ people *within earshot* 言葉の聞える所にいる人々 ‖ He was born *within earshot* of Bow bells. [ロンドンの中央にある] Bow Church の鐘の聞える所で生れた(きっ粋のロンドン子).

earth, *n.* 地球; 土地; 地, 大地, 陸地; 土; 世界; 現世, しゃば.

V *bank up earth* 土を堤状に築く. ¶ The fog *envelops* the *earth*. 霧が大地をこめる. ¶ The strong shall *inherit* the *earth*. 強き者全世界を継承せん(予言). ¶ *kiss* the *earth* and thank God 大地にひれ伏して神に謝する. ¶ *throw in* the *earth* [埋葬のとき]土を(墓穴に)投入れる. ¶ *till* the *earth* 土地を耕す. ¶ the greatest man that ever *walked* the *earth* およそこの世に生れた人間の中で一番の偉人. ¶ where the *earth ends* and the sea begins 陸地が尽きて海の始まる所に. ¶ The *earth turns round* from west to east. 地球は西から東に回転する.

Q the *bared earth* [雪がとけて]むき出しの地表 ‖ lie on one's belly on the *big earth* 大地に腹ばいになる. ¶ *close earth* かたく塊った土地. ¶ this *English earth* この英国の土地. ¶ the *fertile earth* 肥えた土. ¶ on this *imperfect earth* この不完全なしゃばに. ¶ *loose earth* 土がゆるんだ土地. ¶ *solid earth* 堅い地面. ¶ a *smiling earth* ほほえむ大地.

Q² *Mother Earth* 母なる大地.

P Pearls are not found *in* the *earth*. 真珠は陸にはない. ‖ a wooden post planted *in* the *earth* 地に立てた木の柱 ‖ bury ... *in* the *earth* ...を地中に埋める. ¶ a slip *of earth* 地すべり ‖ the two greatest empires on the face *of* the *earth* 地球上の二大帝国 ‖ to the ends *of* the *earth* 世界の果てまで. ¶ establish the kingdom of God *on* the *earth* 地上に神の国を建設する ‖ all the cities *on* the *earth* 地球上の全都市 ‖ There are not, *on earth* at least, eternal griefs. 少くとも現世には永遠の悲痛というものはない. ‖ the room where he spent the last two weeks *on earth* 彼がこの世で最後の二週間を送った室 ‖ while he was *on earth* 氏の在世中 ‖ a paradise (hell) *on earth* 地上の楽園(など) ‖ beyond comparison the greatest industrial country *on earth* 地球上に比類なき最大工業国 ‖ the absurdest spectacle *on earth* 地球上最もばかげた光景. 【類】 pedagogues, perhaps the stupidest class of literate men *on earth*—Mencken ‖ What *on earth* was I to do? 一体僕はどうすればよかったのか. 【類】 What *on earth* is the matter here? / How *on earth* did you know it? / Where *on earth* did you get them? ¶ He fell *to* the *earth*. 彼は地べたに倒れた. ¶ The diamond is the costliest precious stone *upon earth*. ダイヤモンドは世界で最も高価な宝石だ.

earthquake, *n.* 地震, 動揺.

V *feel* an *earthquake* 地震を感じる. 【類】 A slight *earthquake* was *felt*. ‖ Did you *feel* the *earthquake* this morning (a few hours ago)? 君けさ(など)の地震を知っているか. ¶ *predict earthquakes* 地震を予報する. ¶ buildings to *withstand earthquakes*=earthquake-proof buildings 耐震建築.

V² If an *earthquake comes*, this roof will fall. 地震があればこの屋根は落ちる. ¶ The *earthquake died away* with a low rumbling sound. 地震は低いごう音とともにやんだ. ¶ when an *earthquake happens* 地震が起ると.

Q *after earthquakes* 余震. ¶ the *Great Earthquakes* of 1923 一九二三年の大震災. ¶ the *Japanese earthquake* of 1891 一八九一年の日本の地震. ¶ The *earthquake* last night was *long*. 昨夜の地震は長かった. ¶ There is a sort of *permanent earthquake* at a busy street-car junction. 交通ひん繁な電車の交差点ではひっきりなしに地震が揺れているようなものだ. ¶ Indeed, it was the *sharpest earthquake* we have experienced for some years past. 確かにその地震は近年にない大きなものだった. ¶ There was a *slight earthquake*, the vibration lasting a few seconds. 微震があって数秒間揺れた.

P *Apropos of earthquakes*, I felt one last night. 地震と言えばゆうべもあった. ¶ The building was destroyed *by* an *earthquake*. その建物は地震でこわれた. ¶ At about a quarter to six o'clock on Friday morning a shock *of earthquake* was felt in Yokohama. 金曜日の朝五時四十五分ごろ横浜に地震があった.

ease, *n.* 安楽, 気楽, 安心; 容易, 自在.

V *acquire ease* in translating from a foreign language 楽に外国語を翻訳できるようになる. ¶ *afford ease* くつろがせる, 気を楽にさせる. ¶ *desire ease* 安楽を願う. ¶ *gain ease* 安楽を得る. ¶ so that one may *have ease* in old age 年を取って楽ができるように. ¶ *love* one's *ease* 安楽を愛する. ¶ *take* one's *ease* 身を楽にする ‖ *take* one's *ease* in one's inn (=at an inn) 宿屋に落付く ‖ Here we will *take* our *ease*. こゝで一休みしよう. ‖ sit and *take* one's *ease* while enjoying a cup of coffee 腰を掛け気を楽にして一杯のコーヒーを気持よく飲む.

Q with *comparative ease* 比較的楽に. ¶ a retired high official reposing in *dignified ease* りっぱに隠退生活をしている退職したもと高官. ¶ He took his *lettered ease*. 彼は閑居して風雅を楽しんだ. ¶ The last fifteen years of the life of Marx were years of general recognition, fame, and *material ease*. マルクスの生涯の最後の十五年は一般からも認められ名声もあがり物質的にも余裕があった. ¶ with *perfect ease* 全く楽々と. ¶ *slothful ease* ものぐさ, のんき. ¶ This will give one *social ease*. こうすると社交場裡で動じないようになる. ¶ talk (write) with *undress ease* ゆかた気分で語る(など).

P feel *at ease* 安心する ‖ set one's mind *at ease* 安心させる ‖ he is *at ease* about ... 彼は...のことを安心している ‖ sit (live) *at ease* くつろぐ(住み心地がよい) ‖ He was agitated and ill *at ease*. 彼はいらいらして落着かなかった. 【類】 he seemed ill *at ease* with the presence of ... ‖ I was quite *at* my *ease*. 私はのんきだった. 【類】 He is now quite *at* his *ease*. / He is living *at* his *ease*. ‖ be *at* his *ease* on the job 仕事に慣れる. ¶ *for ease* of consultation (reference, conveyance) 使用(など)上の便宜のため. ¶ *ease from* pain (care) 苦痛(心配)が薄らぐ. ¶ It can be done *with* great *ease*. それは楽にできる. ‖ The *ease with* which he did it quite surprised us. 彼は楽々とそれをやってのけるのにはわれわれも驚いた.

P² *ease from* pain 苦痛がなくなること. ¶ *ease of* mind 安心 ‖ *ease of* body and mind 心身のくつろぎ ‖ *ease of* manner しゃ脱な態度 ‖ *ease of* reference [参考書など]使用上の便利.

ease, *v.* 軽くする; 免れさせる.

M *Ease away* (=*off*)! ゆるく(綱具をゆるめるときの号令).

M² It was an object with them to *ease off* the market. 市況を緩慢にするというのが彼らのねらいだった. ‖ The rates will soon *ease off*. [料金など]率がじきに下るでしょう.

P *ease* a person *of* pain 人の苦痛を軽くする ‖ *ease* a porter *of* his load 人足に荷物をおろさせる ‖ I'll *ease* you *of* that care. 君にその心配のないようにしてあげよう.

easiness, *n.* たやすさ; 気軽さ.

P² *easiness of* acquisition ぬれ手であわのつかみどり.

east, *n.* 東; 東方, 東国; [the E-] 東洋; 《米》 [the E-] 東部.

Q the *Christian East* (=Orient) キリスト教の行われる東洋. ¶ the *Extreme East* 極東. ¶ He was proud to have trained the greatest Admiral of the *Far East*. 彼は極東最大の提督を養成したことを光栄としていた. ¶ in the *immediate east* lies ... すぐ東に...がある. ¶ the oil country of the strategic *Middle East* 戦略的要衝である中東の石油国. ¶ the *Near East* 近東(トルコ・イランなど).

P The region of the Terrestrial Paradise was placed by

the mediæval maps *at* the extreme *east* of the Old World. 中世の地図によると地上の楽園の位置は旧世界の東端にあった. ¶*from east* to west and from north to south throughout Europe 欧州を通じて東から西へ北から南へ. ¶The sun rises *in* the *east* and sets in the west. 太陽は東から出て西に没する. ‖ The wind is *in* the *east*. 風は東風だ. ‖ Japan is *in* the *east* of Asia. 日本はアジアの東にある. ‖ the largest city *in* the *East* 東洋第一の都会. ¶Japan faces the Pacific *on* the *east*. 日本は東は太平洋に面する. ¶it lies *to* the *east* of ... それは…の東方に位している. 【類】Barking is seven miles *to* the *east* of London.

P² *east by* north (south) 北(南)微東. ¶Yosemite Valley is due *east of* San Francisco ヨセミテ溪谷はサンフランシスコの真東に当る.

O down *East* [米国の] New England (に), 特に Maine 州(に). 【類】He lives down *East*.

eastward, *n.* 東方.

P A is distant from this place some 17 miles *to* the *eastward*. A はここから東方約十七マイルの所にある. 【類】The coast extends far *to* the *eastward*.

easy, *a.* 容易な; 安楽な; 痛みのない; くつろいだ; ゆう揚たる; ゆるい.

M He is *comparatively easy* of access. 彼は比較的近づきやすい人だ. ¶He has become *fairly easy* in his circumstances. 彼は生活がかなり楽になった. ¶be *less easier* to learn than ... …より覚えにくい. ¶I am *much easier* since my wound was dressed. 傷に手当をしてから大層楽になった. ¶English is *not easy* to learn. 英語はむずかしい. ¶The nut of the screw is a little *too easy*. らせんのナットが少しゆる過ぎる. ¶it is *very easy* to see that ... …はきわめてわかりやすいことだ.

P Make yourself *easy about* the matter. その件については安心なさい. ¶It is *easy for* me to do so. そうするのは僕には楽だ. ¶He is *easy in* conversation and graceful in manner. 彼の談話は堅くならずその態度も優雅だ. 【類】He is *easy in* his behavior. ‖ He went away *easy in* mind. 彼は心残りなく行かれた. ‖ I feel *easy in* mind. 心配がない. 【類】they were by no means *easy in* their minds as to ... ¶He is *easy of* access, patient of hearing, and courteous and affable in discourse. 彼は近づきやすくてよく人の話も聞きその談話は丁重で愛想がいい. ‖ Originality in philosophy is not *easy of* attainment. 哲学の方面の独創は容易でない. ‖ He is *easy of* belief. 彼は物事を信じやすい人だ. ‖ a book *easy of* reference 参考に便利な書物. 【類】be *easy of* success / be *easy of* handling / rearrange material to make it *easier of* consultation. ¶I feel *easy on* this point. 私はこの点は安心だ. ‖ I made him *easy on* the subject. 私はその件について彼を安心させた. ¶Writing is *easy to* me. 書くのは僕には楽(ﾗｸ)だ. ¶O, pray be *easy with* me. どうぞお楽に. ‖ He was very *easy with* me on that debt. 彼は私にその負債を少しも催促しなかった. ‖ Life is less *easier with* old people. 人生は年をとった者の方がつらい.

O *easy* to find 見つけやすい. ¶*easy* to understand 分りやすい. ¶Take it *easy!* のんきにやれ; [別れの際]ごきげんよう.

eat, *v.* 食べる, 味がする.

M I have *eaten a great deal*. 十分食べた. ¶be *eaten away* with rust さびで腐食している ‖ *eat* her life *away* 彼女の人生を自分でめちゃめちゃにする. ¶It is *eaten cooked* like cabbage. それはキャベツのように料理して食べる. ¶*eat freely* of various fruits 色々の果物を盛んに食べる. ¶*eat* it *greedily* がつがつ食う. ¶how to *eat healthfully* 健康食の取り方. ¶*eat heavily* of ... …をうんと食べる. ¶It is *eaten hot* with butter. バタを付けて暖かい中に食べる. ‖ Potatoes *eat* better *hot* than *cold*. じゃがいもは冷たいのより暖かい方がうまく食える. ¶*eat hungrily* 腹がへってがつがつ食う. ¶*eat largely* 大いに食う. ¶*eat leisurely* ゆっくり食べる. ¶*eat liberally* of ... たくさん…を食べる. ¶*eat* one's heart *out* with ... …で心を悩ます ‖ A handsome room was on the ground floor, *eating out* a backyard. 裏庭の方にでっ張っているりっぱな一室が一階にあった. ¶*eat outdoors* 戸外で食事する. ¶It is *eaten raw*. それはなまで食べる. ¶This cake *eats short* and *crisp*. この菓子はたべるとぱりぱりする. ¶*eat sparingly* 少な目に食べる. ¶*eat spasmodically* むら食をする. ¶*eat voraciously* がつがつ食う. ¶This fish *eats well*. この魚は中々おいしい.

M² *eat off* the silver plates 銀ざらに盛った物を食べる ‖ The rats have *eaten off* the old ropes. ねずみどもが古ロープをかみ切った. ‖ I'd rather *eat* my tongue *off* than say it in words. そんなことを口にする位ならいっそ舌をかみ切ってしまいたい. ¶The puppy *ate up* the hems of mats. 小犬はたたみのへりをかじりとってしまった. 【類】He has *eaten up* the whole cake. ‖ On they went *eating up* all the neighboring countries. 彼ら(軍隊)は進撃して付近一帯の国国を蚕食した. ‖ those who are *eaten up* with debts and taxes 借金と税金に苦しめられている手合 ‖ He *ate* her *up* with eye-devouring. 彼は彼女を穴のあくほど見つめて困らせた. ‖ The flame *ate up* the forest. 火炎が森林をなめ尽した. ‖ He is *eaten up* with pride. 彼はうぬぼれきっている.

P *eat against* time かっ込む. ¶These roomers *eat at* the restaurant. これら間借をしている人たちは飲食店で食事をする ‖ *eat at* the same table 食卓をともにする. ¶To *eat between* meals is injurious to health. 間食は体によくない. ¶What have you *eaten for* luncheon? 昼食に何を食べたか. ¶*eat from* a bowl どんぶりで食べる. ¶Japanese *eat* meals *from* tables about a foot high. 日本人は高さ一フィート位の台で食事する. ‖ *eat* pie *from* a plate パイをさらから食べる ‖ Olives are *eaten from* the fingers. オリーブは手で食べる. 【類】Celery and asparagus, when served whole, can be *eaten from* the fingers. / A giraffe can *eat from* tall trees. / The bird is so tame that it will *eat from* my hand. ¶*eat in* moderation ほどよく食べる. ¶*eat into* the heart of ... …のしんに食込む ‖ Acid *eats into* metals. 酸は金属を腐食する. 【類】The insects have *eaten into* the wood. / The rust has *eaten into* the iron. ‖ These two sicknesses have *eaten* deeply *into* his savings. この二度の病気で大分貯金に食込んだ. ¶*eat of* an apple りんごを食べる. ¶*eat to* repletion 十二分に食べる ‖ *eat to* excess 食べ過ぎる ‖ *eat to* fullness たらふく食べる ‖ He has *eaten to* his heart's content. 彼は思う存分食べた. ¶*eat* a thing *with* salt (sugar) 塩(など)をつけて物を食べる. 【類】We *eat* ice cream *with* a teaspoon. / Melons should be *eaten with* a spoon or a fork. ‖ *eat* it *with* relish それをおいしく食べる ‖ *eat* it *with* lunch それを弁当と一しょに食べる.

eatable, *n. pl.* 食物.

V Let's *have* some *eatables*. 何か食べよう.

eater, *n.* 食う人.

Q a *big eater* 大食家. ¶The Russians are *hearty eaters* and use great quantities of bread. ロシア人は健たん家で多量のパンを用いる. ¶*Large eaters* are never constipated. 大食家に便秘はない. ‖ a *light* (=*small or poor*) *eater* 小食家. ¶a *spare eater* 節食家.

Q² a *non-meat eater*=a vegetarian 菜食家.

eating, *n.* 食うこと; 食料.

Q The swan is said to be *excellent eating* when young. 白鳥はひなの時分は結構な食料だそうだ. ‖ It is *good* (*poor*) *eating*. それはおいしい(まずい). 【類】Squirrels are not very *good eating*. ¶*prudent eating* ほどよく食べること.

P He is abstemious *in eating* and drinking. 彼は飲食を節している. ‖ The proof of the pudding is *in* the *eating*. プディングは食べて見て始めてそのよしあしがわかる.

P² *eating for* fun 食道楽. ¶*eating to* excess 食い過ぎ.

eating-house, *n.* 食堂.

Q a *cheap eating-house* 簡易食堂, なわのれん. ¶a *public eating-house* 大衆食堂.

ebb, *n.* 干潮.

V *reach* its lowest *ebb* その最衰期(どん底)に達する.

Q reach a *low ebb* 不振に陥る ‖ His fortune is at a *low ebb*. 彼の身代は傾いてきた. 【類】Painting was then at its *lowest ebb*. / From three of the morning until four is the hour when the city's heartbeats are at its *lowest ebb* of the twenty-four. / The religious feeling was at a *low ebb* then.

P be *on* the *ebb* 退潮を示している ‖ Crime is *on* the *ebb*. 犯罪は減少している. ¶recede *to* a low *ebb* 衰える.

ebb, *v.* 潮が引く.

M Time *ebbs away* fast. 時は早く過ぎて行く.

ebbing, *n.* 退潮.

P² *ebbing of* morals 道義の退廃.

ebullition, *n.* ぼっ発.

Q College spirit should be something more than the *noisy ebullition* of boyishness set free from restraint 大学精神は解放された子供のばか騒ぎ以上のものであるべきだ.

P^2 the *ebullition* ***against*** the government 政府反対熱の爆発.

eccentric, *a.* 風変りな.

P He is a bit *eccentric* ***in*** some of his ways. 彼のやり方にはいささか風変りな所がある.

eccentricity, *n.* 風変り.

V He ***has*** many *eccentricities.* 彼には色々な風変りな所がある.

Q We must be well prepared for ***meteorological*** *eccentricities.* われわれは天候に色々気まぐれがあるものと十分覚悟せねばならない.

echelon, *n.* 〖軍〗 梯(ﾃｲ)形陣; 部隊.

Q the ***forward*** *echelon* of the air base 空軍基地の前衛空隊. ¶ the "***top*** *echelon*" of the American Communist Party 米共産党の首脳部.

Q^2 an ***assault*** *echelon* 攻撃部隊.

P fighters ***in*** *echelon* 梯形編隊の戦闘機.

echo, *n.* 反響; 反映.

V ***arouse*** an *echo* 反響を起す. ¶ ***find*** an *echo* in every man's heart 各人の心に響く. 【類】 This opinion ***found*** no *echo* in responsible quarters in Japan. ¶ have ***had*** few *echoes* in ... ...から余り反響がない. ¶ The translation only succeeded to ***preserve*** some *echo* of the beauty of the original. その翻訳は原文の美を幾分反映するに過ぎなかった. ¶ This ***returned*** no *echo.* これは何らの反響もなかった. ¶ The pedlar ***woke*** the *echoes* of quiet streets with his trade announcement. その行商人は売声で街の静けさを破った.

Q the ***last*** *echoes* of church bells for the night 教会の最終の夜の鐘. ¶ find a ***responsible*** *echo* in the breasts of the majority of ... 大多数の...の胸に響く. ¶ His opinion does not awaken any ***sympathetic*** *echo* in our sentiments. 彼の説にはわれわれは共鳴しかねる.

P applaud ***to*** the *echo* 拍手で反響する.

P^2 an *echo* ***among*** the hills 山彦. ¶ an *echo* ***from*** Greek philosophy ギリシア哲学の投影 ‖ *echoes* ***from*** the study 書斎からの反響(研究の発表) ‖ *echoes* ***from*** examination papers 試験答案の批判. ¶ The *echoes* ***of*** thunders rattle. 雷のごろごろという響き.

echo, *v.* 反響する, とどろく.

M *echo* ***back*** a noise 音を反響させる.

M^2 The sound of the cannon *echoed* ***around.*** 大砲の音が四面にとどろいた.

P *echo* one's teacher ***in*** reading あとについて読む. ¶ The sonorous voice of ... *echoed* ***round*** the room. ...の朗々たる声がへや中に響いた. ¶ The reverberations of the report of a cannon fired at ... *echoed* ***through*** the hills. ...で発射した大砲の砲声が山々に響き渡った. 【類】 The applaud *echoed* through the hall. ¶ The very heaven *echoed* ***with*** the noise. 天までこの音でとどろいた. 【類】 Railway stations *echoed* ***with*** the shouts of these youngsters. / The hills *echoed* ***with*** the roll of thunder. / The valley *echoed* ***with*** their cries.

eclat, *n.* 大景気.

Q celebrate the occasion with ***much*** (=***great***) *eclat* その祝典をはなばなしく挙行する.

eclecticism, *n.* 折衷主義.

Q He adopted this policy by a ***wise*** *eclecticism.* 彼は賢明な折衷主義を取ってその政策を採用した. ‖ show a ***wise*** *eclecticism* 折衷よろしきを得たことを示す.

eclipse, *n.* 〖天文〗 食.

V His reason ***suffered*** an *eclipse.* 彼の理性は光を失った(理性を失った).

Q a ***lunar*** *eclipse* 月食. ¶ a ***partial*** *eclipse* 部分食. ¶ a ***solar*** *eclipse* 日食. ¶ His glory suffered a ***temporary*** *eclipse.* 彼の名誉は一時光を失った(失墜した). 【類】 the ***temporary*** *eclipse* of Germany as a world power. ¶ a ***total*** *eclipse* 皆既食. ¶ the *eclipse* was ***visible*** at ... 食は...で見えた.

P His power is ***in*** *eclipse.* 彼の権勢も下火になった. ¶ He is ***under*** an *eclipse.* 彼は逆境に立っている.

P^2 There will be an *eclipse* ***of*** the moon next month. 来月月食がある.

eclipse, *v.* 食する, ...にまさる.

P the place was *eclipsed* ***by*** ... その土地の繁栄を...に奪われた.

economical, *a.* 倹約な.

M The engine is ***fairly*** *economical* of fuel. そのエンジンでは燃料が相当節約できる.

P He is *economical* ***of*** his time. 彼は時間を経済的に使う. ‖ She is *economical* ***of*** her smiles. 彼女はめったに笑顔を見せない.

economics, *n.* 経済学.

Q^2 ***farm*** *economics* 農業経済. ¶ ***home*** *economics* 家政. ¶ ***wartime*** *economics* 戦時経済. ¶ the structure of ***world*** *economics* 世界経済の機構.

P take up a course ***in*** *economics* 経済学を学ぶ.

economist, *n.* 経済学者.

Q a ***bourgeois*** *economist* [共産主義者の言う]ブルジョア経済学者.

Q^2 according to most ***Government*** *economists* 多くの政府側経済専門家によれば. ¶ a ***labor*** *economist* 労働経済学者.

economize, *v.* 倹約する.

P The government urged people to *economize* ***in*** sugar. 政府は人民に砂糖の節約を力説した. ‖ *economize* ***in*** food (time) 食物(など)を節約する. 【類】 The government urged people to *economize* ***in*** iron.

economizer, *n.* 節約家(器具).

Q^2 be a ***fuel*** *economizer* 燃料の節約になる.

economy, *n.* 倹約, 節約; 経済.

V This will ***accomplish*** an *economy* of time and effort. これは時間と勤労の節約になる. ¶ ***achieve*** the utmost *economy* in construction 建築上できうるだけ節約する. ¶ Greater *economy* of space has been ***attained.*** ずっと場所の経済になった. ¶ ***develop*** a stable *economy* 経済の安定を助長する. ¶ ***effect*** considerable *economies* 非常な節約を行う. 【類】 Great *economy* can often be ***effected*** in this way. ¶ ***encourage*** *economy* 倹約を奨励する. ¶ ***exercise*** *economy* 節約をする. 【類】 It is therefore essential that the utmost *economy* should be ***exercised*** in the use of sugar. ¶ ***practice*** *economy* 節約を実行する. 【類】 Strict *economy* is ***practiced*** in every department. / ***Practice*** *economy* by using the best. ¶ It ***proves*** better *economy* in the end. それは結局かえって経済になる. ¶ ***revitalize*** the nation's *economy* 国民経済を復活させる. ¶ where *economy* has to be ***studied*** 金を掛けずにやろうという場合には. ¶ ***use*** *economy* 倹約する. 【類】 if greater *economy* is not ***used.***

Q it would be ***bad*** *economy* to spend much effort in ... ...に多くの労力を費すのは不経済だろう. ¶ ***domestic*** *economy* 家庭経済. ¶ effect an ***enormous*** *economy* in time 非常に時間の経済になる. ¶ practise ***every conceivable*** *economy* ありとあらゆる節約を断行する. ¶ it is ***false*** *economy* to ... ...してはかえって不経済だ ‖ "Penny-wise and pound-foolish" is called ***false*** *economy.* 「一文惜しみの百知らず」は誤れる経済とされている. ¶ practise a ***little*** *economy* 少しく倹約する. ¶ There will be ***many*** *economies* in this wholesale production. こんな風に大量生産をやれば色々経費の節減ができるだろう. ¶ stabilize the ***national*** *economy* 国民経済を安定させる ‖ Her ***national*** *economy* has been completely drained. 国民経済は全く疲弊している. ¶ It is ***poor*** *economy.* それは大した経済にならない. ¶ ***political*** *economy* 経済学 ‖ applied (pure) ***political*** *economy* 実践(理論)経済学 ‖ bourgeois ***political*** *economy* ブルジョア経済学. ¶ It is ***poor*** *economy* to use it in that way. それをそんな具合に使うのは不経済だ. 【類】 The use of coal is ***poor*** *economy* as compared with that of oil. ¶ exercise every ***possible*** *economy* できるだけ経済的にやる. ¶ Japan's ***postwar*** *economy.* 日本の戦後経済. ¶ a ***questionable*** *economy* いかがわしい経済. ¶ There is no ***real*** *economy* in buying old ones, even if they are cheap. 安いにしても古いのを買うのは実際経済にならない. ¶ practise ***rigid*** *economy* ごく倹約にする. ¶ ***rural*** *economy* 農村経済. ¶ have to practice ***sharp*** *economy* 抜目なく倹約せねばならない. ¶ ***short-sighted*** *economy* 短見的な経済. ¶ establish a ***stable*** *economy* 経済を安定させる. ¶ practice ***strict*** *economy* 厳重な節約を断行する. 【類】 with ***strict*** *economy.* ¶ it is ***true*** *economy* to ... ...するのが本当の倹約だ. ¶ practice ***undue*** *economy* 過度の倹約をする. ¶ ***unwise*** *economy* 愚かな倹約. ¶ secure the ***utmost*** *economy* in labor できるだけ労働力を節約する. ¶ ***vast*** *economy* 巨額の節約. ¶ a ***viable*** *economy* 存立可能な経済. ¶ It is ***wise*** *economy* to use only the best. 一等品だけ使うのが得だ.

Q^2 ***animal*** *economy* 動物界の経済. ¶ the ***barter*** *economy* バーター制の経済. ¶ a combination of ***mass production*** *economy* and ***low wage*** *economy* 大量生産経済と低賃金経済の組合わせ. ¶ the ***money*** *economy* 金融経済. ¶ equipment not needed for ***peacetime*** (=***wartime***) *economy* 平(戦)時経済に不必要な施設 ‖ The normal requirements of the country's ***peacetime*** *economy.* その国の平時経済にお

ける正常の必要条件. ¶*penny economy* 一文惜しみの百失い的やり方. ¶rebuild *Philippines economy* 比島経済を再建する. ¶*state economy* 国家経済. ¶transition from *war economy* to *peace economy* 戦争経済から平和経済への移行.

P *for economy* of space 紙面節約のために. ¶*in* the *economy* of life 人生の経済において. ¶a man *of economy* 倹約家. ¶*with economy* 経済的に ‖ *with economy* of time 時間の節約によって. ¶*with a view to economy* 経済を目的として.

P² *economy in* dress 衣服の倹約 ‖ *economy in* expenditure 経費節約. ¶*economy of* words 言葉の節約.

ecstasy, *n.* 有頂天, 無我夢中.

P He is *in* an *ecstasy* of joy. 彼は狂喜している. ¶He was thrown *into ecstasies.* 彼は有頂天になった. ¶*with ecstasy* 夢中になって. ¶He is in *ecstasies over* the new work. 彼は新作に夢中になっている.

edge, *n.* 刃; 鋭鋒, 鋭利; 縁(ふち), 端; 間際.

V *blunt* the *edge* of a sword 刀の刃をにぶらす. ¶*give* a sharp and keen *edge* to ... ...に鋭利な刃をつける ‖ *give* an *edge* to the appetite 食欲をそゝる. ¶This razor *has* a keen *edge.* このかみそりはよく切れる. ‖ This knife *has* no *edge* at all. このナイフは全然切れない. ‖ *have* an *edge* over ... ...よりも有利だ. ¶*polish off* the rough *edges* of a writing 文章を推敲(すい)する. ¶*put* an *edge* on a knife ナイフに刃をつける. ¶*set* a keen *edge* on appetite 食欲を増進させる. ¶*sharpen* the *edge* of disagreement between ... ...間の不和をせん鋭化する. ¶*soften down* the *edges* 角を丸くする. ¶*take* the *edge* off one's appetite 食欲を減退させる. ¶*test* the *edge* of a sword 刀の切れ味をためす. ¶This hard wood *turns* the *edge* of the saw. この木は堅いからのこぎりの歯が曲る. ‖ The *edge* of the knife is *turned.* ナイフの刃がめくれた. ¶*turn down* the *edge* of a page ページの端を折る.

V² The *edge bends* (=turns). 刃がまくれる.

Q The remark has a *biting edge* to it. その評はてきびしくて人を刺すようである. ¶hold a *decided edge* in ... ...においては断然有利である. ¶the *fine edge* of a razor かみそりの薄刃. ¶*gilt edges* [書物の]金ぶち. ¶The assailant fell under the *keen edge* of a Japanese blade. 襲撃者は鋭利な日本刀のさびとなった. ‖ The *keen edge* of desire 痛切な欲望 ‖ The *keen edge* of his sorrow grew more blunt. 痛切な悲しみも一層薄らいだ. ¶a silver coin with a *milled edge* ぎざぎざのついた銀貨. ¶a *razor's edge* かみそりの刃. ¶a bread-knife with *serrated edge* のこぎり歯のあるパン切りナイフ. ¶The sword has a *sharp edge.* その剣は切れ味がよい. ¶*sweetly-cutting edge* [かみそりなどの]すらすらと切れる刃. ¶This small service to him may be the *thin edge* of the wedge. 彼にこのたやすい用をしてやることが彼との関係の深まる縁になるかも知れない. ¶The *trenchant edge* of the Japanese sword is notorious. 日本刀の鋭利なのは定評がある. ¶The ship caught fire and burned to the *water's edge.* 船から火事を出して水ぎわまで焼けた.

Q² walk the *knife* (*sword*) *edge* 刀(剣)の刃渡りをする.

P *at* the *edge* of the Libyan Desert リビアのさばく地帯のはずれで ‖ "Shrouds have no pockets," says the grim old proverb; and all property must be laid down *at* the *edge* of the grave. 「経かたびらにポケットなし」という無気味な古いことわざがあるが総ての財宝は死ぬときは置いていかなければならない. ¶sit *on* the *edge* of a chair いすのはしに腰を掛ける ‖ *on* the *edge* of a precipice がけのふちに ‖ He is *on* the *edge* of death. 彼は死にひんしている. ‖ Sei-yoken *on* the *edge* of Uyeno Park. 上野公園の端にある精養軒. ‖ stand the book *on edge* 本を立てる ‖ His nerves were *on edge.* 彼はいらいらしていた. ‖ set one's teeth *on edge* 歯の浮く思いをさせる(不快にさせる) ‖ They were all *on edge* to go to war. 戦争したくてうずうずしていた. ‖ stand *on* the *edge* of self-sufficiency, agriculturally 農業から言ってもう一息で自給自足だ ‖ dance *on* the *edge* of a crater 噴火口の上で踊る(危い芸当をする). ¶cut it *to* an *edge* 切ってそれをとがらせる ‖ *to* the *edge* 《俗》この上もなく. ¶a book *with* a rough *edge* (切りそろえないで)小口のざらざらしている書物 ‖ a sword *with* two *edges* 両刃(もろは)の剣 ‖ an appetite *with* an *edge* to it それに対する激しい食欲. ¶the *edge of* daylight 夜の明けぎわ ‖ the *edge of* starvation 餓死するかせぬかの境.

edge, *v.* 刃をつける; へりをつける; じりじり進む.

M *edge away* from ... ...から横ばいして退く ‖ Christianity has been seen constantly *edging away* from oppressions. キリスト教は絶えず圧制から逃れてきている. ¶*edge* a knife *sharp* ナイフに鋭い刃をつける(とぐ).

M² The dog was *edging down* upon his rival for a fight. その犬はけんかしようと敵の方にじりじりと(斜めに)つめよって行った. ¶*edge in* a word or two 一言二言口をはさむ ‖ *edge in* with the mainland 次第に本土に接近する.

P *edge along* a cliff がけに添うて進む. ¶*edge* one's way *through* a crowd 群集の中に割り込んで行く. ¶*edge* a handkerchief *with* lace ハンカチにレースのふちをつける ‖ The road was *edged with* grass. 道路の両側に草が生えていた.

edict, *n.* 勅令, 布告.

V *evoke* an *edict* 勅令を発する. ¶*issue* an *edict* against ... ...禁止の勅令を発布する. 【類】an *edict* was *issued* against wearing the queue (ちょんまげ). 【類】*issue* an *edict* forbidding ... ...禁止の勅令を公布する. ¶*rescind* an *edict* 布告を撤廃する.

Q an *anti-Christian edict* キリスト教禁止令. ¶the *Imperial edict* 勅令. ¶issue a *prohibitory edict* 禁止令を発布する. ¶The King abolished it by a *royal edict.* 国王は勅令によってそれを廃した. ¶obey the *unwritten edict* 不文律に従う.

Q² a *deportation edict* 追放令.

P *under* Imperial *edict* 勅令により. ¶the revocation of the *edict against* Christianity キリスト教禁止令の廃止. ¶the Imperial *Edict on* Education 教育勅語.

edification, *n.* 教導, 啓発.

V *derive* much *edification* or instruction from ... ...から啓発され教えられる所が多い.

P *for* your *edification* ご参考までに. 【類】*for* the *edification* of visitors.

edifice, *n.* 殿堂, 堂宇.

V *build* a new *edifice* on a new foundation 新規に堂宇を築く. ¶*rear* an *edifice* 殿堂を建立する.

Q a *historic edifice* 歴史上著名な殿堂. ¶a *holy edifice* 大寺院.

edit, *v.* 編集する, 発行する.

M an *ably edited* magazine 編集の行き届いている雑誌.

P The School Review, *edited by* the Department of Philosophy and Education of the University of Chicago. シカゴ大学の哲学教育部で発行した「学校評論」. ¶It was *edited from* the original text. それは原文によって編集したものだ. 【類】*edit* data *from* various sources. ¶a book *edited with* notes 註釈付きの本.

edition, *n.* 版, 刊行; 刊本.

V *bring out* a third *edition* of a book 書籍の第三版を発行する. 【類】*bring out* an entirely new *edition.* ¶It has just *entered* the seventh *edition.* それは第七版を出したところだ. ¶The first *edition* was soon *exhausted.* 初版はすぐなくなった. ¶*get out* an extra *edition* announcing that ... ...の号外を出す. ¶*issue* a fresh *edition* 新刊を出す. ¶The *edition* is *limited* to 225 copies, numbered and signed by the author. この版は番号および著者署名入りの二百二十五部の限定版だ. ¶*pirate* the copyright *edition* 版権のある本からひょう窃(偽版)する. ¶*print* (*publish*) a second *edition* 第二版を印刷(出版)する. ¶The book *reached* its fourth *edition.* 同書は第四版に達した. ¶A third *edition* was *required.* 第三版が必要だった. ¶*stereotype* an *edition* 版を鉛版に取る. ¶Seventeen *editions* of the book have already *appeared.* その本はすでに十七版を重ねた. ¶The *edition consisted* of 300 copies. その版は発行部数三百だった.

Q an *abridged edition* of a larger work 抄本. ¶an *edition artistique* 豪華版. ¶bring out a *cheap edition* 廉価版を出す ‖ Shandygaff is a *cheap edition* of champagne. シャンディギャフ(ビールにレモネードを混ぜたもの)はシャンペン酒の安代用品だ. ‖ a *cheap edition* 廉価版 ‖ this *cheaper* and more *convenient edition* この一層低廉で便利な版. ¶a *classical edition* 最良版. ¶there is no *complete edition* of the works of ... ...の全集はできていない. ¶The book went through *countless editions.* その本はおびただしく版を重ねた. ¶*cumbrous edition* [かさ張って]扱いにくい版. ¶the *current edition* of the year book その年鑑の現行版. ¶an *edition de amateurs* 私行版. ¶the *definite edition* of Wilde's works ワイルド物の限定版. ¶a *definitive edition* 決定版. 【類】the *definitive* and the *best edition* of the novel. ¶an *edition de luxe*=

《米》a ***de lux edition*** 豪華版. ¶collate the latter with the ***earlier edition*** あとに出た版と古い版を校合する. ¶an ***enlarged edition*** 増補版. ¶an ***evening edition*** 夕刊. ¶an ***expurgated edition*** 削除版. ¶an ***extra edition*** 臨時増刊, 特別号(雑誌の), 号外(新聞の). ¶***extra-special editions*** 最終版(夕刊新聞の). ¶the ***first edition*** 初版. ¶***Four editions*** were issued in the first seven months. 最初の七カ月に四版を重ねた. ¶a ***fresh edition*** of the works of ... ...の作品の新版. ¶a ***garbled edition*** [原作の]改ざん本. ¶a ***gem edition*** 袖(ｿﾃﾞ)珍版. ¶a ***handy edition*** ポケット版. ¶The regular ***hard-bound edition*** is on sale at book stores for $3.00. 普通の堅表紙版は本屋に行くと三ドルで売っている. ¶an ***improved edition*** of the airship destroyed at ... ...で破壊した飛行船を改良したような物.【類】She is an ***improved edition*** of her mother. ¶He's an ***inferior edition*** of his father. 彼はおやじよりできが悪い. ¶It has passed through ***innumerable editions***. それは数多く版を重ねてきた. ¶The ***last edition*** has been exhausted. 最新版は売切れになった. ¶A special ***limited edition*** of the catalogue has been printed. そのカタログの特製限定版が印刷されている. ¶printed in a ***limited, numbered edition*** 限定版で番号付出版した(本など). ¶an ***edition magnifique*** 豪華版. ¶the ***metropolitan (local) edition*** [新聞]都内(地方)版. ¶a ***miniature edition*** 縮刷版. ¶a ***modern edition*** of ... ...の近代版, 今様... ¶a ***new, enlarged,*** and ***improved edition*** 増補改訂の新版. ¶the ***next previous edition*** 直前の版. ¶a ***pirated*** (=***spurious***) ***edition*** 偽版. ¶a ***popular edition*** 普及版. ¶issue a ***revised edition*** 改訂版を出す. ¶a ***revised*** and ***enlarged edition*** 訂正増補版. ¶a completely ***revised*** and ***reset edition*** 全ページ改訂組み直し版. ¶a ***second edition*** 再版. ¶***Several editions*** were issued. 数版を重ねた. ¶Only a ***small edition*** is issued of it. それは小型版だけ出ている. ¶bring out a ***special edition*** 特別号を発行する. ¶a ***subsequent edition*** 後版. ¶the ***suburban edition*** of the telephone book 電話帳の市外版. ¶be now in its ***third edition*** 目下三版になっている.【類】reach a ***third edition*** in three years / There have been no less than ***thirty-four editions*** of the book. ¶***unexpurgated editions*** [初版そのまま]無削除版. ¶a ***variorum edition*** of Shakespeare シェークスピアの集註版.

Q² an ***airmail edition*** 航空郵便用の小型版. ¶the ***country editions*** of newspapers 新聞の地方版. ¶a ***diamond edition*** 縮刷版(ダイアモンド活字で印刷したもの). ¶the ***English language edition*** of the *Moscow News*「モスコーニューズ」の英語版. ¶a ***library edition*** 図書館版. ¶a ***London edition*** ロンドン版. ¶a ***miniature edition*** 縮刷版. ¶his ***one-volume edition*** その(著者の)一巻もの. ¶an ***overseas edition*** 海外版. ¶a ***pocket edition*** ポケット版. ¶the ***school edition*** of a book ある本の学生版. ¶the "***six o'clock edition***" of newspapers 夕刊の「午後六時」版. ¶***spring*** and ***fall editions*** of a catalogue 目録の春秋二期版. ¶a ***souvenir edition*** 記念版. ¶the ***student edition*** of ... ...の学生版. ¶a ***subscription edition*** 予約(限定)版. ¶a new ***twenty-volume edition*** of his works 氏の著作の新刊二十巻もの. ¶a popular ***two-volume edition*** 二巻ものの普及版. ¶issue an "***under ground***" ***edition*** 秘密出版物を出す.

P ***in*** future ***editions*** 将来版を重ねるに当って ‖ ***in*** the present ***edition*** この版に ‖ to be issued ***in*** an ***edition*** limited to 100 copies 百部限定版で出す. ¶The book went ***through*** a hundred ***editions***. その本は百版を重ねた.

P² an American ***edition of*** modern Venice 近代ヴェニスを米国に移したもの ‖ an ***edition of*** 500 copies 一版五百部 ‖ the ***edition of*** 1933 千九百三十三年版.

editor, *n*. 編集人.

Q an ***advisory editor*** 編集顧問. ¶his ***associate editor*** is Prof. ... 彼と共著をやった人は...教授である. ¶a ***chief editor*** 編集長. ¶a ***financial editor***=《英》city ***editor***〘新聞〙経済部長. ¶He was employed as ***full-time editor*** of the dictionary. 彼はその辞書の専任者として勤めることになった. ¶a ***general editor*** 編集長(主幹). ¶the ***philological (phonological) editor*** of a dictionary 辞書の言語(発音)学担当者.

Q² a ***city editor***〘新聞〙《英》経済部長;《米》社会部長(市内版および地方版の責任者).【類】A ***city editor*** is in charge of city news, having direct control of local reporters. ¶a ***copydesk editor***〘新聞〙整理副部長(俗にデスク). ¶a ***corresponding editor*** for The Studio, London ロンドンのスタディオ誌特別寄稿家. ¶an ***emergency editor*** 非常事件編集部長. ¶the ***fiction editor*** of Collier's コリヤーズ誌の小説部長. ¶a ***managing editor*** 編集局長.【類】Under the ***managing editor*** are the city editor, the telegraph or news editor and various department ***editors***. ¶a brilliant and successful ***newspaper editor*** 花々しい成功した新聞記者. ¶The ***revising editor*** of "The Historian's History of the World."「世界歴史家の歴史」の改訂編集部長.

editorial, *n*.《米》社説, 論説.

Q a highly ***explosive editorial*** きわめて激越な論調の社説. ¶a ***scarifying editorial*** 酷評にわたる社説. ¶a ***strong editorial*** in the Boston Herald ボストン・ヘラルド紙の強硬な社説.

Q² a ***full-page editorial***〘新聞〙全ページにわたる論説. ¶the ***lead editorial*** in today's New York Times 今日のニューヨークタイムス紙の社説.

P there is an ***editorial on*** this subject in ... ...に該問題に関する社説が載っている.

editorialize, *v*. 社説で論じる.

P be ***editorialized on*** a subject その問題を社説で論じる.

editorship, *n*. 主筆の職; 編集, 監修.

V ***accept*** the ***editorship*** of a magazine 雑誌の編集を引受ける. ¶***assume*** the ***editorship*** of ... ...の主筆に就任する. ¶***undertake*** the ***editorship*** of ... ...の主筆を引受ける.

Q The book was issued under his ***general editorship***. その本は氏の監修で発行された. ‖ under the ***general editorship*** of ... ...監修の下に. ¶under the ***joint editorship*** of ... ...と共編で.

P ***during*** his ***editorship*** 彼の編集長時代に. ¶the newspaper is ***under*** the ***editorship*** of ... その新聞は...が編集を主宰している.【類】that book was translated ***under*** the ***editorship*** (監修) of ... / ***Under*** its new ***editorship*** the magazine has been very much improved.

educate, *v*. 教育する.

M ***brilliantly educated*** りっぱに教育された. ¶a youth ***expensively educated*** 金を惜しまず教育された青年. ¶the ***hastily educated*** 速成科出身者. ¶***highly educated*** 高等教育を受けた. ¶a man ***liberally educated*** 紳士教育を受けた人. ¶***patiently educate*** themselves in this subject このテーマについて営々として独学する. ¶He ***virtually educated*** himself. 彼は独学でやったも同然だ.

P He was ***educated at*** Harrow and Oxford University. 彼はハロー校とオクスフォード大学で教育された. ¶He was ***educated for*** the law (army). 彼は法律家(など)になるように教育された.【類】***educate*** a person ***for*** a profession (trade). ¶***educate*** the public ***on*** the subject of ... ...問題に関して公衆を教育する. ¶***educate*** a person ***out of*** prejudice (a false idea) 人を教育して偏見(など)を持たないようにさせる. ¶be ***educated to*** (=***in***) literature (fine arts) 文学(など)の教育を受けている ‖ ***educate*** one's ear ***to*** music 耳を音楽に慣らす.

education, *n*. 教育.

V ***acquire*** an ***education*** 教育を受ける. ¶***Education*** is ***carried on*** with mutual esteem and respect between faculty and students. [大学の]教授団と学生とが互いに尊敬しあって教育が行われる. ¶***complete*** one's ***education*** abroad 外国で学問の仕上げをする. ¶***conduct*** the ***education*** of ... ...の教育をやる. ¶Training in these subjects ***constitutes*** a complete ***education***. これらの課目を訓練するのは完全な教育になる. ¶***continue*** one's ***education*** at the university 大学で教育を継続する. ¶the ***education*** which men and women ***derive*** from life and the world 男女が人生と社会から受ける教育. ¶***despise education*** 教育を軽視する. ¶***dispense*** higher ***education*** to American youth 米国の青年に高等教育を授ける. ¶He has ***enjoyed*** a splendid ***education***. 彼はりっぱな教育を受けた. ¶***extend*** and ***deepen*** one's ***education*** 自分の学業を広めかつ深める. ¶His father had no funds with which to ***finance*** his ***education***. 彼の父は彼を教育する資金がなかった. ¶***finish*** one's ***education*** at [a] college 大学教育を終える.【類】***finish*** their college ***education*** in America. ¶***gain*** (=***get***) a broader ***education*** 一層広い教育を受ける ‖ He ***got*** his ***education*** without any schooling. 彼は学校教育を受けないでその教養を得た. ¶He deprived himself of many pleasures in order to ***give*** his children a good *education*. 彼は子供にりっぱな教育を受けさせようとして自分では多くの快楽をしりぞけた. ¶***have education*** 学がある. ¶He has ***had*** a higher *education*. 彼は高等教育を受けた. ¶***impart*** commercial *education* 商業教育を授ける. ¶***internationalize*** Japanese *education* 日本の教育を国際化する. ¶***key*** *education* to utility 実利を教育の基調とする. ¶No country can afford to ***neglect*** *education*. どこの国でも教育は軽視できない. ¶***obtain*** *education* in public schools [米国]公立学校の教育を受ける. 【類】 the youth of promise who have not the means of ***obtaining*** higher *education* for themselves / ***obtain*** high (college) *education*. ¶He ***oriented*** (=***orientated***) *education* in Japan toward the West. 彼は日本における教育の範を西欧に採った. ¶go abroad for the purpose of ***perfecting*** their *education* 彼らの学問の仕上げに洋行する. ¶He ***picked up*** an *education* from self-study. 彼は独学でどうにか教育ができた. ¶He ***possesses*** an ordinarily good *education*. 彼には一通りの教育がある. ¶***promote*** higher commercial *education* 高等の商業教育を奨励する. ¶boys and girls who desire to ***pursue*** *education* further さらに学問を続けたいと思う少年少女. ¶He ***received*** his *education* at the college. 彼はその大学で教育を受けた. 【類】 he ***received*** his first *education* at ... / ***receive*** a learned *education* (学問). ¶Her musical *education* was ***secured*** at the Academy of Music in the capital. 彼女は首府の音楽学校で音楽教育を受けた. ¶***seek*** higher *education* 高等教育をこころざす. ¶***spread*** *education* 教育を普及させる. ¶***superintend*** the *education* of one's children 子供などの教育を監督する. ¶schools ***supplying*** secondary *education* 中等学校(高校を含む).

V² as *education* ***grows*** (=***spreads***) 教育が普及するに従って. ¶*Education* ***pays***. 教育は受けて損はない.

Q a young man of ***academic*** *education* 学校教育を受けた青年. ¶obtain ***advanced*** *education* 高等教育を受ける. ¶***art*** (=***aesthetic***) *education* 趣味教育. ¶***average*** *education* 世間並の教育 ‖ persons of ***average*** or ***limited*** *education* 普通もしくはわずかな教育しか受けていない人々. ¶a ***catholic*** *education* 全般的な教育. ¶receive a ***classical*** *education* 古典(文学)の教育を受ける. 【類】 secure an excellent ***classical*** *education*. ¶receive a ***collegiate*** *education* 大学教育を受ける. ¶***commercial*** *education* 商業教育 ‖ an all-round ***commercial*** *education* 全般の商業教育. ¶no *education* is ***complete*** without ... …を除いては完全な教育と言い難い. ¶***compulsory*** *education* 義務教育. ¶***cultural*** *education* 人格教育. 【類】 the importance of ***cultural*** as distinguished from ***vocational*** *education* (職業教育). ¶he received his ***early*** *education* in ... 彼は…で幼時の教育を受けた. ¶***elementary, secondary*** and ***specialized*** *education* 初等・中等・専門教育. ¶***enlightened*** and ***humane*** *education* 進んだ文雅な教育. ¶receive a ***fair*** *education* 相当の教育を受ける. 【類】 give a person a ***fair*** *education*. ¶the ***fireside*** *education* of the masses 庶民の家庭教育. ¶He has had very little ***formal*** *education*. 彼は正式の教育はほとんど受けていない. ¶*Education* is ***free*** and ***compulsory*** up to the age of fourteen. 教育は十四歳までは無料で義務である. ¶***further*** *education* 補習教育. ¶A ***general*** *education* is essential in every case as foundation for any superstructure of technical knowledge. 普通教育はいかなる場合にも専門教育の基礎として肝要である. ¶He is provided with a ***good*** *education*. 彼はりっぱな教育を受けている. ¶institutions of ***higher*** *education* 高等教育機関 ‖ People pay too great a price for a ***higher*** *education*. 世人は高等教育のために金を使い過ぎる. 【類】 a man of the ***highest*** *education*. ¶***industrial*** *education* 実業教育. ¶an essential part of a ***liberal*** *education* 人格教育の主要部. 【類】 The goal of the pilgrims was usually some splendid church, the sight of which was a ***liberal*** *education*. ¶women of ***limited*** *education* 教養の十分ない婦人たち. ¶the disadvantages of a ***meagre*** *education* 不十分な教育の不利. ¶He received a ***medical*** *education*. 彼は医学の教育を受けた. ¶They have had the advantage of a ***modern*** *education*. 彼らには現代教育を受けたという強味がある. ¶each branch of ***national*** *education* 国民教育の各科. ¶secure an ***Occidental*** *education* 泰西の教育を受ける. ¶***ocular*** *education* 見学. ¶***official*** *education* 正式な教育. ¶a man of ***ordinary*** *education* 普通の教育ある人. ¶***parental*** *education* 親の教育. ¶***patriotic*** *education* 愛国的教育. ¶the ***political*** *education* of England's public men 英国公人の政治教育. ¶***popular*** *education* 通俗教育. ¶the partisans of a ***practical*** *education* 実用教育の主唱者. ¶He has not received a ***scholastic*** *education*. 彼は学校教育を受けなかった. ¶***scientific*** *education* 科学教育. ¶He gave his son a very ***slender*** *education*. 彼はその息子を余り教育しなかった. ¶give a ***sound commercial*** *education* しっかりした商業教育を授ける. ¶persons of ***superior*** *education* 高い教育を受けた人人. ¶***technical*** and ***professional*** *education* 技術および職業教育. ¶the end of all ***true*** and ***worth-while*** *education* 真実にして価値あるすべての教育の目的. ¶***universal*** *education* 普通教育. ¶***visual*** *education* 視覚教育. ¶***vocational*** *education* 職業教育. ¶***vocational*** and ***technical*** *education* 職業および技術教育.

Q² ***adult*** *education* by means of public lectures 公開講座による成人教育 ‖ the museum as an institution of ***adult*** *education* 成人教育の機関としての博物館. ¶***bread-and-butter*** *education* 職業教育. ¶***character*** *education* through service 奉仕を通じての人格教育. ¶***citizenship*** *education* 公民教育. ¶He had a ***college*** *education*. 彼は大学教育を受けた. ‖ those who are fortunate enough to receive a ***college*** *education* 幸にして大学教育を受けられる人々 ‖ a young man with a technical ***college*** *education* 技術方面の大学教育を受けた青年. ¶must have at least a ***common school*** *education* 少くとも小学校の学力は必要だ. ¶***formal school*** *education* 正式の学校教育. ¶He has only a ***grade-school*** *education*. 彼は小学校しか出ていない. ¶receive a ***high-school*** *education* 中等教育を受ける. ¶***home*** *education* 家庭教育. ¶***immigrant*** *education* [米国などの]移民教育. ¶***mass*** *education* 大衆教育. ¶***mass-production*** *education* 大量生産式教育. ¶***middle-class*** *education* 中等教育. ¶***parent*** *education* 両親教育. ¶***post-high-school*** *education* 中等学校補習科. ¶***pre-school, primary***, and ***secondary*** *education* 幼稚園・小学・中等教育. ¶***school*** and ***adult*** *educations* 学校および成人教育. ¶***sex*** *education* 性教育. ¶***teacher*** *education* 師範教育. ¶the opening of ***university*** *education* to women 女子への大学教育開放 ‖ A ***university*** *education* was once the hall-mark of a gentleman. 大学教育はかつては紳士の極印であった. ¶***youth*** *education* 青年教育.

P ***By*** *education* he is a jurist. 彼の専攻は法学だ. ¶I paid ***for*** his *education*. 彼の学資を出してやった. ¶She is beneath him ***in*** *education*. 彼女は教育の点では彼に劣っている. ¶a man ***of*** *education* 教育ある人 ‖ the progress (spread) ***of*** *education* 教育の進歩(普及).

P² *education* ***for*** citizenship 公民教育 ‖ *education* ***for*** leadership 指導者教育 ‖ *education* ***for*** life 人生のための教育. ¶an *education* ***in*** disillusionment 幻滅によって得る教育(悟り) ‖ His *education* ***in*** youth was not much attended to. 彼は若いころあまり教育されていなかった. ¶the higher *education* ***of*** women (females) 女子(女性)の高等教育. ¶*education* ***through*** play 遊戯による教育 ‖ *education* ***through*** travel in Europe 欧州旅行から受ける教育 ‖ *education* ***through*** visual aids 幻灯や絵などを利用した教育.

educative, *a.* 教育となる.

P *educative* ***to*** ... …の薬になる.

educator, *n.* 教育者.

Q a ***broad-minded*** *educator* 雅量のある教育者.

efface, *v.* 削除する; 除去する.

M As a politician, he has ***completely*** *effaced* himself by this imprudent act. 彼はこんなまずいことをやって政治家として完全に自滅した.

P *Terrae incognitae* have been *effaced* ***from*** the map of the world. 人跡未踏の地はもはや地球の表面から消えてしまった. ‖ *efface* some lines ***from*** a book 書籍から数行を削除する ‖ *efface* a false notion ***from*** one's mind 人の誤った考えを除く.

effect, *n.* 結果; 効力, 実施; 影響, 感化; *pl.* 家財, 動産; 趣旨; 意味.

V some *effect* might be ***achieved*** by ... …で幾分の効果をあげることができよう. ¶***add*** a striking *effect* to ... …に顕著な効果を添える. ¶***arrest*** the damaging *effect* その有害な影響を防止する. ¶***avert*** the disastrous *effects* of war

戦争の悲惨な結果を避ける. ¶It failed to ***bring about*** the desired *effect.* それは希望通りの結果をもたらし得なかった. ¶***cool off*** the *effect* ほとぼりをさます. ¶***counteract*** the *effects* of ... ...の影響を消す(中和する). ¶Newspapers sometimes tamper with the realities to ***enhance*** the *effect* of news. 新聞紙は記事の効果を増すために現実を曲げることがある. ¶***exercise*** a great moral *effect* 大なる精神的感化を及ぼす. 【類】 ***exercise*** a profound *effect* on the popular mind. ¶He began to ***experience*** the evil *effects* of drinking. 飲酒の中毒にかかり始めた. ¶begin to ***feel*** the *effect* of ... [薬・酒など]だんだん身体にきいてくる. ‖ I am still ***feeling*** the *effects* of my seasickness. まだ船酔が残っている. ‖ a calamity the *effects* of which would be ***felt*** all over the world その影響を世界中が感じるような災禍. ¶***gain*** (=***get***) some *effect* いく分効果がある. ¶***get together*** my few *effects* 私のわずかばかりの家財を寄せ集める. ¶***give effect*** to the regulations その規則を施行(実施)する. ‖ ***give*** practical *effect* to an idea 一つの考えを実行する ‖ to ***give effect*** thereto その履行を期するため. ¶***have*** an *effect* on ... ...に影響を及ぼす ‖ it will in time ***have*** the *effect* of ... それはやがて...の結果に至るであろう ‖ may ***have*** some *effect* いくらかは効果があるだろう ‖ in so far as it ***had*** any *effect* at all とに角その結果としては ‖ The reproof ***had*** the desired *effect.* 戒めは所期の効を奏した. ‖ it ***had*** more *effect* than anything else in ... それは...の点において他の何物よりも一層大なる効を奏した. 【類】 ‖ A word from one of his teachers will ***have*** a great *effect* on my son. / Our efforts are beginning to ***have*** an *effect.* ‖ The medicine has ***had*** no *effect,* either good or bad, on his symptoms. その薬をのんでも一向ききめがなくよくも悪くもならなかった. ‖ ***have*** the *effect* of priming the pump 呼び水となる. 【類】 ***have*** no *effect* upon their imagination. ¶***heighten*** the *effect* by contrast 対照によって効果を増す ‖ ***heighten*** a dramatic *effect* 劇的効果を増す. ¶In printing titles of distinction, such as LL.D., F.R.S., etc., even small capitals often ***improve*** general *effects.* LL.D. とか F.R.S. とかの称号を印刷するにはよし小形でも頭文字を用いると体裁がよい. ¶***lessen*** the *effect* of ... ...効力を低める. ¶***lose*** its *effect* その効力を失う. ¶***make*** or ***mar*** the artistic *effect* of ... ...の芸術的効果を強めまたは弱める. ¶***manifest*** its good *effects* in the form of improvement in ... ...の改善という形でその善い効果を現わす. ¶***mar*** the *effect* of ... ...の効果を弱める. ¶***minimize*** the *effects* of ... ...の影響をできるだけ軽減する. ¶Here again the danger exists of ***mistaking*** the *effect* for the cause. ここにもまた結果を原因と取違える危険がある. ¶***mitigate*** the disastrous *effects* of ... ...の悲惨な影響を軽減する. ¶It ***produced*** an *effect* opposite to what was designed (=intended). それは企図したとは反対の結果を生じた. ‖ These events ***produced*** *effects* little short of miraculous. これらのできごとは奇跡に近い結果を生じた. ‖ in the hope of ***producing*** an *effect* on their imagination 彼らの想像に深い印象を与えようとして. ¶***relate*** an *effect* to its cause 結果をその原因に関連させる. ¶***reflex*** *effect* 効果を反映させる. ¶completely ***ruined*** the *effect* なにもかも打ちこわしになった. ¶***secure*** the *effect* desired 希望通りの結果を得る. ¶The liquor began to ***show*** its *effect.* 酔がまわってきた. ‖ ruins in Antwerp ***showing*** the *effect* of the German bombardment ドイツ軍砲撃のあとを示すアントワープの残がい. ¶***sleep off*** the *effects* of the wine 寝て酒の酔をさます. ¶Unskillful work ***spoiled*** the *effect.* 不手ぎわでそれをぶちこわしてしまった. ¶The medicine ***took*** *effect.* その薬の効験があらわれた. 【類】 Poison ***takes*** *effect.* / It ***took*** *effect* instantly. ‖ The law ***took*** *effect* on July 1, 1912. その法律は一九一二年七月一日に実施された. 【類】 This tariff (税率) ***took*** *effect* September 21, 1922. / This increase in price will ***take*** *effect* on and after the 1st July. ¶***weaken*** the *effect* of ... ...の効果を弱める.

Q have an ***adverse*** *effect* on ... ...に逆効果を及ぼす. ¶so as to produce the most ***aesthetic*** *effect* 最も美的な効果を生じるように. ¶***after*** *effects* 余波 ‖ ***after*** *effects* (=aftereffects) of medicine taken 薬の副作用 ‖ a volcanic outburst and its ***after*** *effects* 火山爆発とその後の影響. 【類】 suffer from the ***after*** *effects* of the war. ¶***analogous*** *effects* are produced by ... ...によって類似の効果が現われる. ¶it will have a ***bad moral*** *effect* upon ... それは...に対して道徳上悪影響を及ぼすであろう. ¶exercise a ***baneful*** *effect* upon ... ...に対して有害な影響を及ぼす. ¶It cannot fail to have a ***beneficial*** *effect.* それは必ず有益な効果を奏するに違いない. 【類】 ***beneficial*** *effect* on trade of ... ¶produce a ***certain*** *effect* ある結果を生じる. ¶Flowers arranged in a vase give a ***charming*** *effect* to a room. 花びんにいけた花は室を美しくする. ¶enjoy the ***cheerful*** *effects* of a temperate life 節制による明るい生活を楽しむ. ¶have a ***civilizing, ennobling,*** and ***elevating*** *effect* 文明化し, 高尚化し, 向上化する効果がある. ¶heighten the ***comical*** *effect* of the situation その場合のこっけい味を増す. ¶might have ***considerable*** *effect* in ... ...にかなりの効果があるかもしれない. ¶produce exactly the ***contrary*** *effect* 全く正反対の結果を生じる ‖ Self-interestedness, if ill directed, will have a quite ***contrary*** *effect* from what is intended. 自己中心もよろしきを得ないと思ったとは全く反対の結果を生じることになる. ¶the ***corrupting*** *effects* of money 金銭の人を腐敗せしめる力. ¶Hot springs have ***curative*** *effects.* 温泉は病気にきく. ¶produce a ***dark*** and ***gloomy*** *effect* 暗くて陰うつな結果を作り出す. ¶It had no ***decisive*** *effect.* それは何ら決定的効果を奏しなかった. ¶provide a genuinely ***decorative*** *effect* 著しい色彩を織出している. ¶a ***deep*** *effect* 深甚(じん)の結果. ¶Alcohol has a specially ***deleterious*** *effect* upon fertility. アルコールは多産に対して特に有害な結果を及ぼす. ¶the ***demoralizing*** *effect* of prison life 刑務所生活の道徳に及ぼす悪影響. ¶have a ***depressing*** *effect* 憂うつな結果になる. ¶get a ***desired*** *effect* 所期の効果を得る ‖ This resolute language produced its ***desired*** *effect* upon him. この強硬な言葉は彼に対してこちらで希望したきき目があった. 【類】 fail to produce the ***desired*** *effect.* ¶this will have an extremely ***detrimental*** *effect* on ... これは...に対して全く有害な結果を及ぼすであろう. ¶have no ***direct*** *effect* on ... ...には何ら直接の影響はない. ¶a very ***disastrous*** *effect* はなはだ悲惨な結果. ¶It will have bad ***disciplinary*** *effect* on others if it is left unpunished. そのまゝにして置いたのでは他の人への示しにならない. ¶Its *effect* was ***dramatic*** in the extreme. その結果はきわめて劇的の(目覚ましい)ものであった ‖ lack ***dramatic*** *effect* 劇的効果を欠いている. ¶in order to obtain a ***droll*** *effect* 道化式(茶番狂言的)の効果を出すため. ¶This has had a ***dual*** *effect.* これは二つの結果を生じた. ¶produce ***evil*** *effects* 悪結果を生じる ‖ Wealth, luxury, and enervation are the ***evil*** *effects* of a long peace. 富・ぜいたく・文弱は永く続いた平和の悪弊である. ¶It has a sexually ***exciting*** *effect* on its drinker. それを飲むと性的興奮が起る. ¶It will have ***far-reaching*** *effects.* それによる影響は遠大であろう. ¶have a ***fatal*** *effect* upon the purchasing power of the laboring classes 労働階級の購買力に致命的結果を及ぼす. ¶The camera has a ***fattening*** *effect.* そのカメラで写すと(やせた人を)肥って見せる. ¶a ***fine*** *effect* is produced by ... ...によってよい結果が生れる. ¶a decision to the ***following*** *effect* 次の意味合いの決定. ¶enhance the ***general*** *effect* 全般の効果を増す. 【類】 The ***general*** *effect* is distinctly foreign. / The ***general*** *effect* of this picture appeals to me. ¶produce a ***good*** *effect* よい結果を産む. 【類】 without ***good*** *effect.* ¶have a ***hampering*** *effect* on ... ...に対しては障害になる. ¶It has had the ***happiest*** *effect* both mentally and physically. それは精神的にも肉体的にも最もよい結果を収めた. ¶It has little, if any, ***harmful*** *effect.* それはほとんど弊害がない. ¶have a ***healthy*** *effect* on ... ...に健全な効果をもたらす. ¶the study of geographic causes and their ***human*** *effects* 地理的原因とその人事に及ぼす影響の研究. ¶the ***humanizing*** *effect* of music 音楽の人心をやわらげる力. ¶The medicine produces no ***ill*** *effect.* その薬は何ら副作用を起さない. ‖ without ***ill*** *effect* 悪影響なしに. ¶with little ***immediate*** *effect* てきめんにきくというわけには行かないが. ¶have an ***important*** *effect* upon ... ...に重大な影響を及ぼす. ¶have an ***indirect*** *effect* on ... ...に間接的に影響を及ぼす. ¶produce ***injurious*** *effects* 有害な結果を生じる. ¶The magic touch took ***instant*** *effect.* その魔力ある接触は効能てき面であった. 【類】 It produced an ***instant*** *effect.* ¶Milk rarely produces a ***laxative*** *effect.* 牛乳を飲むとまれに下痢することがある. ¶have the same ***legal*** *effect* as regards ... ...に関しては同

様の法的効力がある. ¶The Greco-marionettes move their limbs in a natural way and even roll their eyes with ***life-like*** *effect*. そのギリシア操り人形は手足を自然に動かして生きた人間のように目をくるくるさせる. ¶The physician had a ***like*** *effect* with another patient. その医者はもう一人の病人においても同様の結果を得た. ‖ The news has produced very ***little*** *effect* on the mind of the public. その知らせは一般公衆の心にほとんど影響を与えなかった. ¶The *effect* was ***magical***. その効果はすばらしいものであった. ‖ produce a ***magical*** *effect* upon ... ...に不思議とよくきく. ¶have a ***marked*** *effect* 顕著な効果を収める. ¶it must have had a ***material*** *effect* upon ... それは...に対して重大な影響を与えたに相違ない. ¶***movable*** *effects* 動産. ¶Punishment does not seem to have ***much*** *effect* on him. 罰を課しても彼にはあまり効果がないらしい. ¶it comes in ***net*** *effect* to ... それは結局...ということになる. ¶He found that the treatment produced ***no*** *effect* at all. 彼はその療法が一向効験がないことを知った. ¶the ***pernicious*** *effect* of an intemperate use of alcohol アルコール過用から生じる有害な結果(酒害). ¶***personal*** *effects* 私有品. 【類】***personal*** *effects* of the dead man. ¶These combined to produce a very ***picturesque*** *effect*. これらが結合して非常に美しい効果を産んだ. ¶the ***poisonous*** *effect* of bacteria バクテリヤの毒性. ¶produce a ***powerful*** *effect* on the mind of ... ...の心に強い感化を及ぼす ‖ have a ***powerful*** *effect* on the system 身体に強力に効く. ¶put aspirations into ***practical*** *effect* 理想を実行に移す. ¶produce a very ***pretty*** *effect* 非常に美しい結果を生じる. ¶have a ***refreshing*** and ***stimulating*** *effect* 元気を回復し興奮する効果を有する. ¶experience a ***rejuvenating*** *effect* in the company of young people 青年たちと交わって気持が若返る. ¶have a ***reverse*** *effect* 逆効果をもたらす. ¶for ***rhetorical*** *effect* 言葉をかざる目的で. ¶to produce ***rustic*** *effects* 田園趣味を出すために. ¶The reprimand had its ***salutary*** *effects*. そのけん責はためになった. ¶has ***soothing*** *effect* 鎮痛の効果がある. ¶Such a lecture will produce on the hearer only a ***soporific*** *effect*. そんな講演はたまたま聴者に眠気を催させるにすぎない. ¶have good ***spectacular*** *effects* for the stage 目覚しい舞台効果がある. ¶in order to produce ***striking*** *effect* 異彩を放たせるため. ¶He said "...," or words to ***that*** *effect*. 彼は...とかなんとか言った. ¶get a ***three-dimensioned*** *effect* 立体的効果をあげる. ¶have ***thrilling*** *effects* ぞっとする(ぞくぞくする). ¶The piano is celebrated for its ***tonal*** *effects*. そのピアノは音色の効果的なので有名である. ¶have a ***tranquilizing*** *effect* 興奮をしずめる効果がある. ¶this had the ***unexpected*** *effect* of ...ing これが...という意外の結果を生じた. ¶produce a very ***ungainly*** *effect* はなはだ見苦しい結果を生じる. ¶this had a ***wholesome*** *effect* on ... これは...に対して有益な結果を及ぼした.

Q[2] wonderful ***cloud*** (***sunset***) *effects* [絵など]すばらしい雲(など)の効果. ¶***color*** *effects* 配色効果. ¶***long-range*** *effects* 遠大な影響.

P ***by*** the *effect* of years 年のせいで. ¶merely ***for*** *effect* ほんの体裁に ‖ He acted only ***for*** *effect*. 彼は表面的の効果だけをねらった. ¶trace ***from*** *effect* to cause 結果から原因へさかのぼる ‖ suffer ***from*** the *effect* of the heat 暑気当りで苦しむ. 【類】He received injuries ***from*** the *effect* of which he died a few hours later. ¶continue ***in*** *effect* [規定など]引続き効力を有する. ¶***In*** *effect* the situation is this. つまり形勢はこうである. ‖ this is ***in*** *effect* equivalent to ... これは結局...と同様である. ‖ ***in*** *effect* if not in name 名目はともかく実際において. 【類】it means, ***in*** *effect*, that ... / his conclusion was, ***in*** *effect*, that ... / His poetry was, ***in*** *effect*, his life. / The nation that cannot even exist without the commodity of another nation, is ***in*** *effect* the slave of that other nation.—Coleridge. / The characteristic material problem of the nineteenth century, ***in*** *effect*, was rapid transit (交通の迅速). ¶carry it ***into*** *effect* それを実行する ‖ come ***into*** *effect* 実施される. ¶The searching has been ***of*** no *effect*. その捜索は無効に終った. ¶The letter is ***to*** the *effect* (=purport) that he will soon arrive. その手紙は彼が間もなく到着するという意味のものだ. ‖ I received a telegram ***to*** the *effect* that ... 私は...という意味の電報を受取った. ‖ an edict ***to*** this *effect* has been issued by ... この意味の勅令が...によって発布された. 【類】There were early traditions ***to*** this *effect*. / An Imperial edict ***to*** this *effect* has been issued. / Some one has said that a man's history begins one hundred and fifty years before his birth, or words ***to*** that *effect* (そんな意味の言葉). ‖ It was all ***to*** no *effect*. それはまるでだめだった. ¶***with*** little or no *effect* ほとんどもしくは全く効果なく. ¶He always speaks ***with*** *effect*. あの人の言うことにはむだがない. ¶***without*** *effect* 効験なく. 【類】***without*** any injurious (=harmful) *effect*.

P[2] This will contribute to the *effect* ***of*** repose sought by the designer. そうすると設計者の求めた落付きが一層効果的になる. ‖ recover from the *effects* ***of*** a foreign journey 外国旅行から受けた刺激から落付く ‖ the *effect* ***of*** comparison with other firms 他店とのふり合い. 【類】the *effects* ***of*** a storm / the *effect* ***of*** ... upon British politics ‖ the *effect* ***of*** morphia ***on*** the human system 人体に及ぼすモルヒネの影響. ¶the war and its *effect* ***on*** trade 戦争及びその貿易への影響. 【類】The speech did not fail to have its *effect* ***on*** the audience. / Some one has said that a succession of little worries (小さな心配が重なること) has a worse *effect* ***on*** the nervous system (神経系統) than one great big worry. ¶the *effect* of physical environment ***upon*** man's life 人間の生活に及ぼす環境の影響 ‖ the *effects* of changes in the barometer ***upon*** our spirits 気候の変化のわれわれの精神に及ぼす影響.

effective, *n.* 実兵力.

Q[2] the ***war*** *effective* of 100,000 十万の戦時兵力.

P an army ***of*** 200,000 *effectives* 二十万の実兵力を有する陸軍.

effective, *a.* 効力のある, 効験のある.

P be *effective* ***against*** cancer がんにきく. ¶*effective* ***for*** a person 人に効験のある. ¶be *effective* ***from*** ... ***to*** ... ...から...まで有効である. ¶*effective* ***in*** fighting 戦争に有効な ‖ be *effective* ***in*** publicity 宣伝効果がある. ¶Summer fares to Yellowstone National Park will be *effective* ***on*** and ***after*** June 1. イェローストーン国立公園への夏期割引賃金は六月一日から実施になる.

effectiveness, *n.* 効果.

Q ***dramatic*** *effectiveness* 劇的効果.

Q[2] ***teaching*** *effectiveness* 教授効果.

effectuate, *v.* 達成する.

M try to *effectuate* one's desire ***somehow or other*** 自分の欲望を何とかして達成しようとする.

effectuation, *n.* 発効.

P ***with*** the *effectuation* of the peace treaty 平和条約の発効と同時に.

effervescence, *n.* あわ立ち, 沸騰.

V flat beer which has ***lost*** its *effervescence* あわが立たなくなった気の抜けたビール.

efficacious, *a.* 効力のある, きき目のある.

P a medicine *efficacious* ***against*** fever = a febrifuge 解熱剤. ¶resorts *efficacious* ***for*** every variety of bodily ill あらゆる病気に効験ある保養地. ¶The hot springs are said to be *efficacious* ***in*** rheumatism. その温泉はリューマチに効験があると言われている.

O You will find that medicine *efficacious*. その薬の効験あることが分るでしょう.

efficacy, *n.* 効力, 効験.

V ***doubt*** the *efficacy* of the treatment その療法の効験を疑う. ¶This medicine ***has*** no *efficacy* in that disease. この薬はその病気にはきき目がない. ¶This medicine has ***lost*** its *efficacy*. この薬はばかになった.

Q of ***miraculous*** *efficacy* 不思議によくきく. ¶In Europe a ***superstitious*** *efficacy* is attributed to the silver bullet. ヨーロッパでは製銀の弾丸はよく的中するという迷信がある.

P[2] Camphor-wood has *efficacy* ***against*** the attacks of insects. くすのき材は虫が食わない. ¶it will have some *efficacy* ***in*** preventing ... それは...を予防するに幾分効果があるだろう. ¶the *efficacy* ***of*** a drug 売薬のきき目.

efficiency, *n.* 能率; 能力.

V ***achieve*** *efficiency* 能率を増す. ¶***add*** *efficiency* to the kitchen end of the home 家庭の台所の方に能率があがる. ¶***cut down*** one's *efficiency* 人の能率をそぐ. ¶***decrease*** the fighting *efficiency* of ... ...の戦闘能率を減じる. ¶Webster ***defines*** *efficiency* as "the quality of producing effects." ウエブスター辞典には efficiency を「効果を生じる性質」と定義してある. ¶***develop*** *efficiency* 能率を増進する. ¶***hurt*** one's *efficiency* 人の能率を害する. ¶***im-***

pair the *efficiency* of the work 仕事の能率をそこなう. ¶*improve* the *efficiency* of ... …の能率を増す. ¶He has done much to *increase* the *efficiency* of French teaching in this country. 彼はこの国におけるフランス語教授の能率増進に貢献する所が多かった. ‖ *increase efficiency* and diminish cost of output 生産能率を増進しその費用を減少する. ¶*make good* an *efficiency* 能率を増進する. ¶*promote efficiency* in ... …における能率を増進する. ¶*raise* the *efficiency* from ... to ... から…へ能率を高める. 【類】*raise* the *efficiency* of ...

Q *comparative efficiency* 比較的能力. ¶give it a *greater efficiency* それを一層有効にする. ¶The machine is not working at its *highest efficiency*. その機械は最大能力を発揮していない. ¶*instructional efficiency* 教授上の能率. ¶*low efficiency* 能率の低さ. ¶*military efficiency* 軍の能率(戦闘力). ¶*Physical* and *mental efficiency* is greatest in a climate where the temperature is moderate and variable. 身心の能率は気温が適度で変化に富んだ地方において最も多く発揮される. ¶*reduced efficiency* 能率低下. ¶*technical efficiency* 技術的能率. ¶*vocational efficiency* 職業的能率.

Q² be up to the peak of *combat efficiency* 最高の戦闘力に達している. ¶*fighting efficiency* 戦闘力. ¶reach *second degree efficiency* [柔道など]二段になる. ¶*teaching efficiency* 授業能率. ¶*work efficiency* 作業能率.

P a study *in efficiency* 能率研究 ‖ Our Navy is second to none *in efficiency*. わが海軍は能力の点で他に譲らない.

P² for more *efficiency in* the home 家政の能率をあげるために. ¶the *efficiency of* the work of ... …事務の成績.

efficient, *n.* 動因.

V The machine *gives* an *efficient* of ... per cent. その機械は…%の能率を出す.

efficient, *a.* 効果がある.

M to be *fully efficient* 十分に効果を出すには.

effigy, *n.* 立像.

Q² a *marble effigy* of ... …の大理石の立像.

efflorescence, *n.* 開花; 隆盛.

Q the *extraordinary efflorescence* of new verse during the war period and immediately afterwards 戦争中及びその直後における新しい詩の大流行.

efflux, *n.* 流出.

P² an *efflux of* gold coin *from* the country その国からの金貨の流出.

effort, *n.* 努力, 尽力, 骨折; 努力的作品.

V *abandon efforts* 努力をやめる. ¶He will *appreciate* your *effort* in his favor. あなたのあの人のためにして下さるお骨折を彼は有難いと思うでしょう. ¶*attempt* serious *efforts* to ... …しようとまじめに努力する. ¶try to *belittle* his *efforts* in behalf of ... 彼が…のために尽した努力を軽んじようとする. ¶*bend* every *effort* to attain the goal 目的達成にあらゆる努力を傾ける. ¶they will not *cease* their *effort* until ... 彼らは…するまでその努力をやめないでしょう. ¶*clog* their *efforts* 努力をにぶらす. ¶*combine* their *efforts* to ... 彼らの力を合わせて…する. ¶*concentrate* our *efforts* in this direction この方面にわれらの努力を集中する. ¶He *continued* his *efforts* in this direction for several years. 彼は数年間この方面に努力を続けた. ¶it *cost* her an *effort* to ... 彼女にとって…することは一骨だった. ¶They *crowned* his *efforts* of many years with the erection of a monument. 彼らは彼の数年間の努力に対し記念碑を建造してこれに報いた. ‖ Their *efforts* were *crowned* with success. 彼らの努力は成功した. ¶*dedicate* one's best *efforts* to the cause of ... …のために最善を尽す. ¶Its authorship has hitherto *defied* all *efforts* at identification. その作者の何人であるかを知らんとする今日までのあらゆる努力は水泡に帰した. ¶*devote* considerable *efforts* to ... …に多大の努力をささげる. ¶*direct* one's *efforts* to ... …に努力を向ける. ¶*discourage* further *efforts* それ以上の努力をはばむ. ¶*economize effort* 努力を節する. ¶The original *eludes* the *efforts* of the translator to convey its delicate beauties. 原文のせん細な妙味を伝えんとしても翻訳者の力が及ばない. ¶*enlist* the best *efforts* of able men 有能な人の最善の協力を得る. ¶*exert* all possible *efforts* あらゆる努力を払う. 【類】considerable *effort* has been *exerted* to ... ¶*expend effort* 努力する. ¶*focus* one's *effort* on the endeavour to ... …せんとの骨折に力を集中する. ¶*frustrate* the *efforts* of ... …の努力を水泡に帰せしめる. ¶*give* an organized *effort* to ... …に対して組織立った努力を払う. ¶*hamper effort* 努力の邪魔をする. ¶The *efforts* have been *inaugurated*. その努力が開始された. ¶*join effort* with ... …と協力する. ¶*lend* one's *effort* to ... …のためにひとはだ脱ぐ. ¶We shall gladly *lend* every *effort* in our power toward its realization. その実現に対して私どもの及ぶ限り喜んで尽力致します. ¶He *made* an *effort* to do well. 彼はりっぱにやろうと努力した. 【類】more *effort* has yet to be *made* to ... / The railroad and steamer companies *make* every *effort* to contribute to comfort and safety of their lady passengers. / He was *making* an *effort* to appear as democratic as possible (平民的に見せかけようと). / *make effort* to preserve one's employment (解雇されないように) / No *effort* has been *made* at literary refinement (文章の推こうに). ¶*neutralize* the *efforts* 努力を無効にする. ¶*put forth efforts* 努力する. 【類】*put forth* more *effort* ‖ a spur to *put forth* his *efforts* 彼を発奮させる刺激. ¶No man can cultivate himself mentally or physically to the highest point except by *putting in* his best *effort*. 何人も全力を傾注するのでなければ精神的にも肉体的にも最高の修養は期し得ない. ¶*redouble* one's *efforts* 努力を倍加する. ¶*relax* one's *efforts* 気をゆるめる. 【類】It is an *effort* that must never for a moment be *relaxed*. ¶*renew* the *effort* その努力を新たにする. ¶It *repays* the *effort* spent in learning it. それを学ぶに費した努力は報いられる. ¶work *requiring* muscular *effort* 筋肉の力を要する仕事. ¶Organized *efforts* are being *set* on foot for it. 組織立った努力がそれに対してなされている. ¶*slack* (=*slacken*) one's *efforts* 気をゆるす. ¶*spare* no *effort* to secure ... …を得んとの労力を惜しまない. ¶The patient on whom the physician *spent* much *effort* has recovered. その医者が骨を折った病人は回復した. ¶*stimulate* one's *efforts* to ... …せんとする努力を刺激する. ¶*strain* one's utmost *efforts* towards ... …に対して最善の努力を払う ‖ They *strained* their futile *efforts* against the stream of the times. 彼らは時代の潮流に抗しようとしたが徒労に帰した. ¶*summon up efforts* 努力を奮い起す. ¶The physician *took* all *efforts* with him. その医者は彼のためにできるだけのことをした. ‖ It is hard work, and *takes* much time and patient *effort*. それは困難な仕事であり多くの時間とねばり強い努力が必要である. ¶We all joined in the tug of war *timing* our *efforts* by appropriate exclamations. 僕らも一緒になって綱引をし掛声で調子をとって引張った. ¶*turn* their *efforts* in that direction 彼らの努力をその方面に向ける. ¶*unite efforts* for a purpose 力をあわせてある目的に当る. ¶*use* every *effort* 及ぶ限りを尽す. ¶... or our *efforts* will be *wasted* …でなければわれわれの努力も水のあわであろう.

V² no *efforts* will be *lacking* to ... …するためあらゆる努力を尽すであろう.

Q an *additional effort* その上の努力. ¶make *all-out effort* 全力を尽す. ¶*ancillary efforts* 補助的努力. ¶years of *assiduous effort* and study 多年のたゆまない努力と勉学. ¶in an *avowed effort* to ... 誓って…せんとして. ¶a *belated effort* おそまき. ¶*benevolent effort* 慈善事業への尽力. ¶They are using their *best efforts* to further the usefulness of the association. 彼らは同協会をして一層有益な存在たらしめるため全力を尽している. ¶The drunken man was making *boozy efforts* to stand very straight. その酔いどれは直立しようとしてひょろひょろしていた. ¶a *Brobdingnagian effort* 巨大な努力. ¶under his *ceaseless effort* and fostering care 彼が絶え間ない努力と情のこもった心使いの下にあって. ¶*clumsy efforts* つたない努力. ¶by *collective effort* 共同的努力によって. ¶the *colossal effort* of workers in medicine 医学研究家たちの巨大な努力. ¶with *concerted effort* 協力して. ¶If a *concerted effort* were made, it would surely bring good results. 協心協力するならばたしかに好結果をもたらすであろうが. ‖ make *concerted efforts* to ... 共同して…しようと努力する. ¶His compositions bear traces of *conscious effort*. 彼の文章には苦心のあと歴然たるものがある. ‖ without *conscious effort* 別に骨を折らないで ‖ promote the improvement of language by *conscious effort* 自覚した努力によって言葉の改善を図る ‖ traces of *conscious effort* 努力の跡. ¶put forth *considerable effort* 大いに努力する. ¶*consistent efforts* to ... …しようとする一貫した努

力. ¶*constant efforts* 不断の努力. ¶a *convulsive effort* 必死の力. ¶*co-operative effort* toward that end その目的のための協力. 【類】the necessity of *co-operated efforts.* ¶a *courageous effort* 奮起. ¶the fun of *creative literary effort* 文芸の創作に努力する面白さ. ¶*crude efforts* 悪あがき. ¶by *daily effort* 日々の努力によって. ¶make a more *deliberate effort* 一層慎重な努力を払う. ¶*diligent efforts* 勤勉. ¶make *desperate efforts* 決死の努力をする. ¶make a *determined effort* to ... 断固として...しようと努力する ‖ *determined* and *painstaking efforts* have been made to ... ...するため堅い決意の苦心が払われている. ¶make an *earnest effort* 誠意をもって努力する. 【類】make *earnest effort* to ... ¶*eccentric effort* 風変りな努力. ¶*educational efforts* 教育上の努力. ¶*efficient efforts* 有効な努力. ¶an *energetic effort* 猛烈な努力. ¶exert *every effort* in ... ...に全力を尽す. ¶make *every possible effort* to ... ...するようできるだけ尽力する. ¶*extravagant efforts* 過度の努力. ¶*fanatic[al] efforts* 死にもの狂い. ¶The weak combined and united their individually *feeble efforts.* 弱者たちは共同して彼らの薄弱な力を合わせた. ¶our *first efforts* should be to ... われわれはまずもって...することに努力せねばならない. ¶*forced* and *unnatural effort* 無理なそして不自然な努力. ¶The Conference of Paris was the first *formal effort* to liquidate World War II. パリ会議は第二大戦を清算するための始めての正式な努力の現われであった. ¶with *frantic effort* 死に物狂いになって. 【類】make a *frantic effort* to ... ¶make *fresh efforts* to ... ...すべく努力をあらたにする. ¶make *frowning efforts* through the glare to read from a blackboard ぎらぎらする光を透して黒板の字を読もうとしてまゆを寄せる. ¶*fruitless effort* かいのない努力. ¶satisfaction after *full honest effort* 正直に全力を尽した後の満足. ¶make *furious efforts* to ... ...するよう死力を出す. ¶inspire a person to *further efforts* 人に元気をつけて一層の努力をさせる. ¶make a *genuine effort* to ... ...のために真の努力をする. ¶*Great efforts* are being made to ... ...するに大努力を払っている. ¶make a *Herculean effort* 非常に大きな努力をする. ¶make a *heroic effort* to ... ...しようと雄々しい努力をする. ¶*human effort,* whether of brain or hand 頭脳を用いるものであれ手を用いるものであれ人間の努力. ¶put forward *impressive effort* 人を感動させるような努力をする. ¶*independent efforts* それぞれ単独の努力. ¶*individual* and *collective efforts* 個々及び全体の努力. ¶*ineffectual efforts* むだな努力. ¶commercially *inspired efforts* 商業上刺激された努力. ¶recently much *intelligent effort* has been directed to ... 最近学者は...に多大の努力を費した. ¶*interpretative efforts* 解釈上の努力. ¶*isolated efforts* 孤立的努力. ¶The book was one of the novelist's *juvenile efforts.* この本はその小説家の少年時代の著作の一つであった. ¶*laudable efforts* 称賛すべき努力. ¶the "law of *least effort*" in English habits of speech 英語の言語習慣における「最小努力の法則」. ¶*legislative efforts* to enforce ... ...を実施しようとする立法上の努力. ¶his *lifelong efforts* 彼の一生の努力. ¶a fine *literary effort* りっぱな文芸作品. ¶*loyal* and *unselfish efforts* 忠実にして利己心をはさまない努力. ¶his *maiden effort* 彼の処女作. ¶without the expenditure of some *mental effort* on the part of the readers 読者に何ら頭の骨を折らせないで. ¶*misdirected efforts* 見当違いの努力. ¶*mistaken effort* 誤った努力. ¶with *much effort* やっこらさっと. ¶put forth the *necessary effort* 必要な努力をする. ¶their *noble efforts* 彼らの気高い努力. ¶Just *one more effort* and the work will be done. あともう一息きというところだ. ¶Such was his *opening effort* at conversation. こういって彼は話の皮切りをした. ¶a great *oratorial effort* 一大雄弁の試み. ¶an *organized effort* was begun to ... ...すべく組織的努力を開始した ‖ through *organized effort* 組織だった努力によって. ¶*painstaking efforts* have been made to ... ...しようと非常に骨を折った. ¶*past efforts* of my life 私の今までの努力. ¶make *patient efforts* 辛抱強く努力する. ¶*perpetual effort* 不断の努力. ¶the *persistent efforts* of a few private philanthropic bodies 二三私設慈善団体のたゆまざる努力. ¶make *plucky efforts* [競技などで]勇敢に戦う. ¶a *praiseworthy effort* 称賛に値する努力. ¶The article was his last *printed effort.* その文は彼の絶筆であった. ¶*Recent efforts* at a simplification of spelling have, in spite of much ridicule, made noteworthy progress. つづり字を簡単にしようという近ごろの努力は随分世間のちょう笑を受けたにもかかわらず著しい進歩をとげた. ¶make *redoubled efforts* to ... ...しようと努力を倍加する. ¶*renewed efforts* were made to ... ...しようとさらに努力を新にした. ¶make a *serious effort* to ... ...しようと真剣になる ‖ We all agreed that, though a big undertaking, it was well worth a *serious effort.* それは大きな事業ではあるがまじめに努力する価値のある仕事であるとわれわれは意見一致した. ¶a *simple effort* of memory will recall ... ちょっと考えれば...が思い出されよう. ¶a *sincere effort* to produce a useful book 有益な著作をしようというまじめな努力. ¶a thoroughly *sincere* and *unaffected effort* 全く真剣でしかもてらわない努力. ¶he succeeded by a *single effort* in producing ... 彼は一挙にして...を造り出すことができた. ¶a *slight effort* ちょっとした努力. ¶*Spasmodic efforts* are useless. 間欠的努力は役に立たない. ¶put forth a *special effort* to ... ...しようと特に努力する. ¶by *sporadic effort* とぎれとぎれの努力によって. ¶*steady efforts* 堅実な努力. ¶by *strenuous effort* 心をこめて. ¶spare no *strenuous efforts* 献身的努力を惜しまない. ¶put forth *strenuous* and *unremitting efforts* in order to accomplish one's aim その目的を達するため粉骨砕身する. ¶a *strong effort* will be made to ... ...しようと大いに努力する所があるであろう. ¶*successive efforts* 連続的努力. ¶It was only with an almost *superhuman effort* that I broke myself free from the habit. ほとんど超人的努力をもって初めて私はその悪習を脱却したのであった. 【類】He exerted almost *superhuman effort* in this direction. ¶*sustained effort* in the acquisition of knowledge 知識の獲得における不断の努力. ¶it will take *tremendous efforts* by ... ...にとって大努力を要する. ¶*unabated efforts* ゆるみない努力. ¶by his own *unaided efforts* 自分一個の力で. ¶His *efforts* were *unavailing.* 彼の努力は効を奏しなかった. ¶lack *united effort* 気がそろわない ‖ a *united effort* of all the civilized nations あらゆる文明国の協力. 【類】thanks largely to the lack of *united effort.* ¶by *united* and *resourceful efforts* 気を合わせ色々手を尽して. ¶make *unnumbered efforts* to ... ...しようと色々様々の努力をする. ¶through the *untiring effort* of ... ...のたゆまぬ努力によって. 【類】expend *untiring effort.* ¶*unwearied efforts* 疲れを知らない努力. ¶making the *utmost efforts* 死力を尽して. ¶make *vain effort* to free himself 逃げようとして不成功に終る. ¶make a *valiant effort* to ... ...しようと勇敢に努力する. ¶with a *vigorous effort* 腕によりをかけて. ¶Miss Rockett felt a warmth ascending to her ears, and made a *violent effort* to look unconcerned. ロケット嬢は両耳がぽうっと熱くなるのを感じた, そして一所懸命平静をよそおうと努めた. ¶*way-breaking* (=*pioneering*) *efforts* 道を切り開こうとする(開拓者の)努力. ¶*well-considered efforts* 考慮よろしきを得た努力. ¶*well-meaning* but *wrongly conceived efforts* 意志はよいが考えを誤まった努力. ¶be worth *whole-hearted effort* 全面的な努力を払う価値がある. ¶by *wisely-directed effort* 賢明な努力によって.

Q² the *brain effort* 頭脳の(知的)努力. ¶an *exclamation aiding effort* 力を添える掛声. ¶a *large-scale effort* to ... ...しようとする大規模の努力. ¶feverish *last-minute efforts* to ... ...しようとする熱烈な最後の努力. ¶the Anglo-American *merger efforts* 英・米の協力. ¶China's *reconstruction efforts* 中国再建の努力. ¶a *peace effort* 平和への努力. ¶*propaganda efforts* 宣伝の努力. ¶*self-help efforts* 自助の力. ¶obstruct the *war effort* 戦争努力を妨げる ‖ contributed towards Japan's *war efforts* 日本の戦争努力に貢献した. 【類】direct the *war effort* / an important contribution to the national *war effort* / be too weak to support satisfactorily a large-scale protracted *war effort* / They threw everything they had into the *war effort.* / as part of the *war effort.* ¶*world efforts* toward peace 平和への世界の努力.

P *after all* his *effort* 精々努力したにもかかわらず. ¶produce ... *at* one *effort* 一奮発で...を造り出す. ¶be attained *by effort* 努力で得られる ‖ *by* continued *effort* 継続的努力によって ‖ win independence *by* his own *efforts* 彼自身の努力によって独立する. ¶league *in* an *effort* to ... ...しようとして連盟する ‖ be done *in* an *effort* 一気にやる ‖

waste more time ***in*** useless *effort* 無益の努力により多くの時間を費す. ¶We failed ***in spite of*** our *efforts.* われわれは骨折損をした. ¶***notwithstanding*** many *efforts* 色々と努力したにもかかわらず. ¶largely ***through*** the *efforts* of ... 主として...の尽力で ‖ Everything that she had was hers ***through*** her own *efforts.* 彼女のものはすべて彼女自身の努力で得たものだった. ¶***with*** little *effort* ほとんど努力せずに ‖ ***with*** much *effort* 大いに骨を折って. 【類】***with*** some *effort.* ¶Nothing can be obtained ***without*** *effort.* 努力せずには何物も得られない. ‖ acquire, ***without*** conscious *effort,* the correct pronunciation of a foreign language 自分の意識した努力なしに外国語の正しい発音を修得する.

P² a relaxation of *efforts* ***at*** improvement 改善しようとの努力のゆるみ ‖ a student's *efforts* ***at*** self-support 自活しようとの学生の努力. ¶There must be some organized *effort* ***behind*** the rumours. うわさの裏面には何か組織的な計画があるに相違ない. ¶*effort* ***without*** effect 徒労.

O It may be worth our *effort* to investigate the matter analytically. そのことを細かに調査して見る価値があるだろう.

effrontery, *n.* 厚かましさ, 鉄面皮.

Q ***presumptuous*** *effrontery* さしでがましいずうずうしさ. ¶with ***unblushing*** *effrontery* 鉄面皮にも.

P. apologize ***with*** calm *effrontery* 厚かましくも平気で申開きをする.

effulgence, *n.* 光輝.

Q² the ***spring*** *effulgence* of myriad cherry blossoms 春らんまんの幾万の桜花.

effusion, *n.* 流出, 表現, 吐露.

Q a ***lengthy*** *effusion* [詩文などの]長たらしい表現. ¶***poetical*** *effusions* わき出る感情を歌った詩. ¶a ***political*** *effusion* 政見の発表. ¶***wild*** *effusions* of an angry politician 激した政治家の思い切たっ言葉.

P. talk ***with*** an *effusion* of heart 胸きんを開いて語る.

egg, *n.* 卵, 鶏卵.

V ***beat*** (=***whip***) *eggs* into a froth 卵をかきまぜてあわ立たせる. ¶***beat up*** *eggs* 卵をかきまぜてあわにする. ¶***blow*** an *egg* by pricking a hole in each end with a pin ピンで上下に穴をあけて卵を吸う. ¶***boil*** an *egg* hard (soft) 卵をかたく(半熟に)ゆでる. ¶Don't ***boil*** the *eggs* hard. 卵を固くゆでるな. ¶***break*** an *egg* on one's forehead 額に当てて卵を割る. ¶***brood*** her *eggs* [雌鳥が]卵を抱く. ¶We ***color*** *eggs* for Easter. イースター祭には卵に彩色する. ¶recipes for ***cooking*** *eggs* in twelve different ways 卵の料理法十二種. ¶***fertilize*** the *eggs* of the female 卵子に受精させる. ¶***hatch*** *eggs* 卵をふ化する. ¶***incubate*** *eggs* 卵を抱く. ¶***lay*** *eggs* 卵を産む. 【類】How many *eggs* a day do your hens ***lay***? ¶I ***like*** the *eggs* ***soft boiled.*** 私は卵を柔かくゆでたの(半熟)が好きだ. ¶***place*** *eggs* under incubation 卵を抱かせる. ¶***poach*** an *egg* 卵を割って半熟にする. ¶All the pigeon tribe generally ***produce*** two *eggs.* すべてはと類は通常卵を二つずつ産む. ¶***put*** (=***have***) all one's *eggs* in one basket 一事業に全資本を投じる. ¶***set*** *eggs* 卵を抱かせる. ¶***suck*** *eggs* 卵をすゝる. ¶***test*** an *egg* 検卵する. ¶***turn*** the *eggs* over to the pure food officers for whatever action they take in the matter 卵を専門の食料係官に引渡して適当に処分をしてもらう.

Q an ***addle*** (=***addled***) *egg* 腐れ卵. ¶a ***bad*** *egg* 《俗》不良少年. ¶a ***black rotten*** *egg* 黒い腐れ卵. ¶a ***boiled*** *egg* ゆで卵. ¶a ***brown*** *egg* (殼が)とび色の卵. ¶a ***coddled*** *egg* とろ火で煮た卵. ¶a ***dirty*** or ***stained*** *egg* よごれたりしみのついた卵. ¶a ***double-yolked*** *egg* 黄味の二つある卵. ¶***even-sized*** *eggs* 粒のそろった卵. ¶a "***fertile***" *egg* 受精した卵. ¶a ***fresh*** *egg* 新鮮な卵. ¶***fried*** *eggs* 卵フライ. ¶***golden*** *eggs* 大きい利益, 大もうけ. ¶***hard***[***-boiled***] *eggs* ゆで卵. ¶a ***hatching*** *egg* ひなになる卵. ¶***home*** *eggs* 地卵. ¶an ***ill*** (=a ***badly***)***-shaped*** *egg* 格好の悪い卵. ¶The ***new-laid*** *egg* is one of the most delicious morsels to the human palate. 産みたて卵は食べてもっともおいしいものだ. ¶an ***over-sized*** *egg* 大き過ぎる卵. ¶a ***poached*** *egg* 落し卵. ¶a ***raw*** *egg* なま卵. ¶a ***rotten*** *egg* 腐った卵. ¶***scrambled*** *eggs* いり卵. ¶***soft-boiled*** *eggs* 半熟卵. ¶a ***soft-shelled*** *egg* 殼の柔かい卵. ¶a ***speckled*** *egg* 斑点のついた卵. ¶a ***stale*** *egg* 古い卵. ¶a ***thin, brittle*** *egg* [殼が]薄くてこわれやすい卵. ¶an ***uncooked*** *egg* なま卵. ¶an ***undersized*** *egg* 小粒の卵.

Q² a ***dummy*** *egg* [せとなどで作った]おとり卵. ¶***Easter*** *eggs* 復活祭の進物に用いる色どり卵または模造卵. ¶a ***second-grade*** *egg* 二級品の卵. ¶a ***nest*** *egg* 巣ごもり卵(一つだけ残しておくもの, 人工のものもある). ¶a ***shell*** *egg* [粉でない]普通の卵. ¶a ***table*** *egg* 食用卵. ¶a ***three-minute*** *egg* 三分ゆでの卵. ¶a ***wind*** *egg* 無精卵.

P check it ***in*** the *egg* それを卵のうちに(未発に)阻止する. ¶till the age ***of*** an *egg* 卵の時代まで. ¶A hen sits ***on*** *eggs.* 雌鶏は卵を抱く.

egg, *v.* 鼓舞する, 扇動する.

M² *egg* (=urge) ***on***...to... ...を鼓舞して...をさせる ‖ *egg* a person ***on*** to fight with another つかみ合いをけしかける ‖ Hachiro tried to *egg* ***on*** the *samurai* of the Satsuma. 八郎はさつまの武士を扇動しようとした.

ego, *n.* 自我, 自己.

V ***develop*** our *ego* われわれの自我をのばす. ¶***perfect*** the moral *ego* 道徳心を造り上げる.

egotist, *n.* 利己主義の人.

Q an ***arrogant*** *egotist* ごう慢な利己主義者. ¶a ***dogged*** *egotist* がん固なうぬぼれ者.

egress, *n.* 外へ出ること, 出口.

Q The theatre affords the audience ample means of ***safe*** *egress.* その劇場には観客に非常口の設備が十分にある.

ejaculation, *n.* 叫び.

P² an *ejaculation* ***of*** welcome 歓迎の叫び.

eject, *v.* 追い出す.

P *eject* a person ***from*** a house (place) 人を家(など)から追い出す ‖ They have lately been *ejected* ***from*** the place. 彼らは最近そこから追立てられた.

eke, *v.* 補う, 延ばす; やりくりする.

M ***eke out*** a living on a tiny income わずかな収入で細々と暮しを立てる ‖ ***eke out*** a meager living as ... ...としてかろうじて生計をたてる. 【類】***eke out*** one's income with odd jobs.

elaborate, *v.* 苦心して仕上げる.

P *elaborate* ***on*** a theory 理論を大成する ‖ *elaborate* ***on*** a plan 計画を練る. ¶a theory *elaborated* ***upon*** this view この見解にもとずいたある一つの説.

elaboration, *n.* 骨折り, 推敲(すい).

V ***forgo*** further *elaboration* here ここでこれ以上の推敲は控えて置く. ¶***reach*** great *elaboration* [技術が]大分発達する.

elastic, *a.* 弾力のある; 伸縮自在な.

M be not *elastic* ***enough*** 融通がきかない. ¶The word is ***so*** *elastic* that it means nothing. それは非常に融通のきく語で結局何のことかわからなくなる.

elasticity, *n.* 弾力.

V A rubber band ***has*** *elasticity.* ゴムひもは伸縮する. ¶***lose*** its *elasticity* その弾力を失う ‖ The mind ***loses*** its *elasticity* and its receptivity. 心がその融通性と包容性を失う.

elate, *v.* 得意がらせる.

M He was ***highly*** *elated* about it. それで彼は大いに得意がっていた.

P cannot be very *elated* ***about***......に対してあまりうれしくない. ¶not *elated* ***by*** success nor disturbed by failure 成功のために得意がりもせずまた失敗のために落胆もせず. ¶*elated* ***in*** spirits 意気揚々. ¶He was much *elated* ***over*** this. 彼はこれを大いに得意がっていた. ¶He is *elated* ***with*** joy. 彼は得々然としている. 【類】He is *elated* ***with*** results (success).

elbow, *n.* ひじ.

V ***lean*** an *elbow* on the table テーブルに片ひじを突く. ¶***rest*** one's *elbows* on the table テーブルに両ひじをつく. ¶***rub*** the *elbow* with ... ...と親密(懇意)にする. ¶***spread out*** one's *elbows* ひじを張る. ¶***square*** the *elbows* ひじを張る. ¶***Take*** your *elbows* off the desk! 机にひじを突くな.

P keep the volume ***at*** one's *elbow* 座右にその本を備える. 【類】have the book always ***at*** one's *elbow* / It is a handbook which should stand ***at*** the *elbow* of every student of English. ‖ The book ought to be ***at*** the *elbow* of every one who wishes to write accurately. その本はだれでも正確な文を書こうとする者の座右に備えて置くべきものである. ‖ assistants ***at*** his *elbow* 彼の手近の助手 ‖ He is out ***at*** *elbows.* 彼は見すぼらしい身なりをしている. ¶lean ***on*** both *elbows* 両ひじを突く. 【類】lean ***on*** one's *elbow* (片ひじ). ¶raise oneself ***upon*** an *elbow* 片ひじで身を起す. ¶push ... ***with*** the *elbows* ...をひじで押す.

elbow, *v.* ひじで押す, ひじで突く.

M *elbow* people ***aside*** 人々をひじで押しのける.

M² *elbow* ***up*** to counters 人を押分けてカウンターに進み寄る.

P *elbow* people *off* the way 人を押しのけて行く. ¶The small farming class have been gradually *elbowed out of* their holdings. 小自作農たちは次第にその土地を手離すことになってきた. ¶We *elbowed* our way *through* the crowd. われわれは人込みの中をひじで押し分けて行った.

elder, *n.* 年上の人, 先輩.

V *Respect* your *elders.* 先輩をうやまえ. ¶*ape* their *elders* 彼らの年長者をまねる.

Q He is *my elder.* 彼は僕より年上だ.

P² He is the *elder of* the two. 二人の内彼の方が年上だ.

O He is about five years the *elder.* 彼の方が五つばかり年上だ(二人の兄弟の中で).

elect, *v.* 選挙する, 選ぶ.

M he was *unanimously elected* to be ... 彼は...に満場一致で選ばれた.

P He was *elected by* ballot. 彼は投票で選ばれた. ‖ *elected by* a plurality of votes 多数決によって選挙された. ¶He was *elected for* Cork City in 1895. 彼は一八九五年にコルク市から選挙された. ‖ The President of France is *elected for* seven years. フランスの大統領は七年の任期である. ¶*elect* a chairman *from* the members 議員中から議長を選ぶ. ¶He was *elected into* the committee. 彼は委員に選挙された. ¶be *elected to* office 選出されて就任する ‖ He was *elected to* Parliament (Congress). 彼は英国(米国)国会議員に選ばれた. 【類】the first woman *elected to* Congress / be *elected to* Congress from a district in Tennessee / he was *elected to* the Sixty-eighth Congress, defeating Hon. ... / In 1858 he was *elected to* a Fellowship (特待研究生) at Trinity College. / He was *elected to* the Supreme Court Bench (最高裁判事). / he has been *elected to* the Principalship of St. Edmund Hall, vacated by the resignation of ... / He was *elected to* membership in the Society. ‖ Professor Otto Kinkeldey was *elected to* the chair of muscology in Cornell University. オットー・キンケルデー教授はコーネル大学の蘚苔(せんたい)学講座担任に選ばれた. 【類】He was *elected to* the vacancy.

Q He was *elected* President＝They elected him President. 彼は大統領に当選した.

elect, *a.* 選ばれた.

P my darling, *elect from* the face of the whole earth 世界にただ一人の私の愛人.

election, *n.* 選挙; 選択.

V we wish to *announce* the *election* of Mr. B as president of ... B氏が...会長に選挙されましたので御披露致します. ¶*carry* an *election* 選挙に勝つ, 当選する. ¶*conduct* an *election* of members 会員の選挙を行う. ¶The *election* to membership shall be *effected* by the General Committee by ballot—two objections to exclude. 会員選挙は委員総会の席上投票によって行われるただし二人の反対投票があった場合には落選のこと. ¶*seek election* to an office ある官職に就職運動をやる. ¶*win* the *election* 当選する.

V² The *election* will *take place* in March. 選挙は三月に行われる.

Q a *contested election* 《英》定員以上の候補者のせり合う選挙; 《米》[無効だという]異議のある選挙. ¶the last *general election* to the National Diet この前の国会議員総選挙. ¶a *gubernatorial election* 知事選挙. ¶in the coming *presidential election* 次の大統領選挙に. ¶a *special election* 《米》補欠選挙. ¶The *election* is *void.* その選挙は無効だ.

Q² the London Borough *Council elections* ロンドンの自治区の市会選挙. ¶go to the polls for a *Mayoralty election* 市長選挙の投票に行く ‖ the Chicago *mayoralty election* シカゴ市長選挙. ¶a *mid-term election* 中間選挙. ¶a *mock election* 擬国会. ¶the *off-year elections* of 1946 《米》一九四六年の中間選挙. ¶a *run-off election* 決戦投票. ¶*Upper House election* 上院選挙.

P vote *at* an *election* 選挙で投票する ‖ the votes he polled *at* the last *election* numbered ... この前の選挙で獲得した投票数は...であった. ¶He was chosen *by election.* 彼は選挙によって選ばれた. ¶stand *for election* 候補に立つ. ¶become a member *on election* 選挙されて会員になる.

P² in the *election for* the Austrian Parliament オーストリア国会議員の選挙で. ¶the *election to* membership of ... ...の会員として選挙されたこと ‖ He is seeking *election to* the House of Representatives. 彼は衆議院議員に当選を希望している.

elective, *n.* 選択科目.

P These subjects are all required, while the rest are *among electives.* これらの学科はみな必修だが, その他は選択だ.

elective, *a.* 選挙の; 選択自由の.

M *popularly elective* 民選の.

elector, *n.* 選挙人.

Q² a *prince elector* 選挙侯(ドイツの).

electric-car, *n.* 電車.

Q a *trackless electric-car* 無軌条電車, トローリー.

electrician, *n.* 電気工夫.

Q² a *head electrician* 電工長.

electricity, *n.* 電気.

V *carry electricity* to ... 電気を...に通じる. ¶Franklin *discovered electricity* by flying a kite in a thunderstorm. フランクリンは雷雨にたこをあげて電気を発見した. ¶*generate electricity* 電気を起す ‖ *electricity generated* at waterfalls 水力電気. ¶*turn on* (*off*) *electricity* 電流を通じる(切る).

Q *mountain-born electricity* 水力電気. ¶[There is] *no electricity* for today. 今日は休電.

P It is worked *by electricity.* それは電力で動くようになっている. ‖ be lighted *by electricity* 電灯がついている ‖ The engine is driven *by electricity.* その機関には電力を用いている. 【類】Telegrams are news sent *by electricity.* ¶It is charged *with electricity.* それには電気が通じている.

electroplate, *v.* 電気メッキする.

P *electroplated with* gold 電気金メッキがしてある.

elegance, *n.* 優美, 優雅.

Q her *aristocratic elegance* 彼女の貴族的な上品さ. ¶*lofty elegance* 高雅. ¶with a tone of *quiet elegance* 物静かで上品な調子で.

P² *elegance of* manner 優美な物腰.

elegant, *a.* 優美な.

P She tried best to make herself look *elegant in* his presence. 彼女は彼の前では出来るだけ優美にと心掛けた. 【類】*elegant in* taste (speech, dress, manner).

elegy, *n.* 哀歌, 悲歌.

Q² a *funeral elegy* 哀悼歌.

P² an *elegy on* his friend 彼の友をいたむ歌. 【類】*elegies on* the fall of the Roman Empire.

element, *n.* (1) 要素, 成分, 分子; 活動範囲, 本領; 元素; *pl.* 初歩.

V a further *element* of romance was *added* to the case by ... ...のためにこの事件の小説的色彩が一段と増した. ¶*contain* the *element* of the universal 〖哲学〗一般概念の要素を含む. ¶*eliminate* the personal *element* (＝equation) 個人的な考えを取り除く, 平等にやる. ¶*feel* the ludicrous *element* こっけいな面があるのを感得する. ¶The Chinese *form* (＝*represent*) the greatest foreign *element* in Japan. 日本における外人の中で中国人が一番多い. ¶capable of *fusing* the discordant *elements* 調和しない分子を融合させることができる.

Q an *appositional element* 〖文法〗同格的要素. ¶They form a *bellicose element.* 彼らがけんか好きな分子を成している. ¶age, one of the *chief elements* in rank 社会階級上主なる要素の一たる年齢. ¶There are some *discontented elements* in the party. 党中には不平分子も多少いる. ¶There is just one *discouraging element* in the situation. 時局にただ一つ思わしくない点がある. ¶Those boys represented a *disturbing element* in the class. それらの生徒がクラスの不穏分子であった. ¶Oxygen and hydrogen are the *essential elements* to constitute water. 酸素と水素は水の構成に必須の成分である. ¶*fat-forming elements* 脂肪成分. ¶the *foreign elements* in the language その語の外来的要素 ‖ the introduction of a *foreign element* into Japanese art 日本の芸術への外国の要素の取り入れ. ¶*heterogeneous elements* 異分子. ¶*homogeneous elements* 同類分子. ¶an *important element* 重要な成分. ¶*incongruous elements* [水に油など]不調和な分子. ¶the *intellectual element* in the country 同国の知識階級. ¶terrorize the more peaceful and *law-abiding element* 平和を愛し法律を守る念の強い人々を威す. ¶The open air was his *natural element.* 戸外は彼の性に合っていた. ¶remove "*old elements*" 古顔を除く. ¶*pacific elements* in the country その国民中の平和な分子. ¶Current slang must be regarded as the very *real element* of colloquial speech. 現代俗語は口語の中でもすこぶる現実的な要素と見なすべきである. ¶the *rowdy element* in the audience 観

(聴)衆の中の騒々しい連中. ¶There may be ***some element*** of truth in this view. この見解には幾分の真理があるかも知れない. ¶a ***subversive element*** 破壊分子. ¶***undesirable elements*** among the employees 雇人中の好ましからぬ分子. ¶the ***vicious element*** in society 社会の邪悪な分子. ¶a leader of the ***younger element*** in national politics 国の政治におけるいわゆる「年少分子」の一首領.

Q² ***extremist elements*** on both the right and the left 左右両派の極端分子. ¶extract the most valuable ***food elements*** from beef 牛肉から食料の最も貴重なエキスをとる. ¶There is just the ***gipsy element*** in it. ちょっと野趣味がある. ¶the ***left(right)-wing elements*** 左(右)翼分子. ¶the ***man element*** in commerce 商業における人的方面(物的方面に対して).

P he was more ***in*** his *element* later at the ... School kept by ... 彼はその後...の経営する...学校に入って一層その所を得たのであった ‖ He is ***in*** his *element* when talking politics. 彼は政治の話はお手のものだ. ‖ is thoroughly ***in*** his *element* with ... ...では全く板についている ‖ He is ***in*** his own (=proper) *element*. 彼はその所を得ている. ‖ He is ***in*** his *element* when he takes part in a debate. 議論となると彼は水を得た魚だ. ¶It was resolved ***into*** its *elements*. その元素に分解された. ¶He is ***out of*** his *element*. 彼は水を離れた魚も同然だ. 【類】He is ***out of*** his *element* when filling an educational post as he is now.

P² *elements* ***of*** civilization 文明の要素 ‖ It has in it something of the *elements* ***of*** tragedy. その中に幾分悲劇的な要素を含んでいる. ‖ the *elements* ***of*** arithmetic 算術の初歩 ‖ Water is the *element* ***of*** fishes. 水は魚類の生息区域だ. ‖ The book has in it all the *elements* ***of*** popularity. 同書は売れそうな要素を皆備えている.

(**2**) [地・水・火・風の]四行.

V ***brave*** the *elements* (=inclement weather *or* rain) 風雨を冒す. ¶a ship in storm ***fighting*** the *elements* しけに会って風雨と戦う船. ¶***resist*** the *elements* better than ... ...よりも一層雨露にたえる.

V² The *elements* were ***howling*** around her. 風波(風雨)があたりにうなりを立てていた.

elemental, *a.* 自然力の.

M There is something so ***nakedly elemental*** about a bull fight. 闘牛には何となくいかにもむきだしの野蛮な点がある.

elephant, *n.* 象; やっかいな物. 「長物.

Q a ***trick elephant*** 芸をする象. ¶a ***white elephant*** 無用の

P He is seated ***on*** an *elephant*. 彼は象に乗っている.

P² The mill was almost an *elephant* ***on*** his hands, what with being out of repair and needing new machinery. その工場は修繕もしなければならず新しい機械も入れなければならずほとんど彼の手に負えないしろ物であった.

elevate, *v.* 高める, 揚げる; 向上させる.

M be ***noisily elevated*** はしゃいでいる.

P *elevate* oneself ***above*** others 自分を他の人々以上に高める ‖ *elevate* us ***above*** our neighbours 群を抜く. ¶*elevate* a bucket ***by*** a rope ロープでバケツをつり上げる ‖ *elevate* our souls ***by*** religion われわれの心を宗教によって向上させる. ¶The word has been *elevated* ***from*** the status of slang ***to*** colloquialism. その語は俗語の域から口語の域にまで高められた. ¶*elevated* ***in*** rank 位の高い. ¶He was *elevated* ***to*** the peerage. 彼は華族に列せられた. 【類】*elevated* ***to*** knighthood ***for*** bravery.

elevation, *n.* 上昇; 高地, 高度, 高さ.

V ***attain*** an *elevation* of about 15,000 feet 約一万五千フィートの高さに達する. ¶It ***has*** an *elevation* of 4,000 feet. その高さは四千フィートある. ¶***reach*** an *elevation* of 7,020 feet 七千二十フィートの高度に達する.

Q a ***slight*** *elevation* 小高い所.

P ***at*** an *elevation* of about 2,000 feet above the sea 海抜約二千フィートの高さで. ¶The mountain is about 1,300 feet ***in*** *elevation*. その山は高さ約千三百フィートである. ¶the angle ***of*** *elevation* 〘測量〙仰角. ¶mountain ranges ***with*** an *elevation* of over 5,000 feet above sea level 海抜五千フィート以上の高さのある山脈.

P² the *elevation* ***of*** mind (thought) 精神(思想)の向上. ¶his *elevation* ***to*** the peerage 彼の貴族に列せられたこと.

elevator, *n.* 昇降機(エレベーター).

V ***operate*** an *elevator* 《米》エレベーターを運転する ☞ 英語用法は run a lift.

V² The *elevator* doesn't ***stop*** at floors 1, 2 and 3. エレベーターは一, 二, 三階は止りません.

Q a ***hydraulic*** *elevator* 水力エレベーター.

Q² a ***hotel*** *elevator* ホテルのエレベーター.

P go up (down) ***in*** an *elevator* エレベーターで上(下)る.

elicit, *v.* 引出す, 誘出する.

P *elicit* information ***by*** inquiring 尋問して聞き出す. ¶*elicit* surprise ***from*** people 人々を驚かせる ‖ *elicit* sparks ***from*** flints 火打石で火を切る.

eligible, *a.* 選ばるべき, 被選挙資格のある.

P Women are not *eligible* ***as*** members of Parliament. 女は(英国)国会議員に選ばれる資格がない. ¶They are *eligible* ***for*** membership. 彼らは会員に選ばれる資格がある. ‖ He is *eligible* ***for*** (=***to***) re-election. 彼には再選される資格がある. 【類】be *eligible* ***for*** re-employment by ... / be *eligible* ***for*** the situation.

elimination, *n.* 除去, 削除.

V when an *elimination* is ***made*** 削除を行った時は.

P examine applicants ***for*** *elimination* 志願者を試験選衡

eliminate, *v.* 除去する. 「する.

P *eliminate* politics ***from*** the conference その会議から政治問題を除外する ‖ *eliminate* waste matter ***from*** the system 老廃物を体外に排出する.

elite, *n. F.* 精華, 精鋭.

V They ***represent*** the intellectual *elite* of China. 彼らは中国学界の代表である.

ellipsis, *n.* 〘文法〙省略法.

V ***supplement*** the *ellipsis* 省略部分を補う. ¶***use ellipsis*** wherever it is possible 省略法を用いうる所にはこれを用いる.

elocution, *n.* 雄弁術, 弁舌.

P an Athenian celebrated ***for*** his *elocution* その弁舌をもって有名なアテネ人.

elope, *v.* 駆落ちする; 逐電する.

P *elope* (=run away) ***with*** a lover 恋人と駆落ちする ‖ I know a man who once ***eloped with*** a married woman. 私は人妻と駆落ちしたことのある男を知っている. ‖ The treasurer of that company has ***eloped with*** the funds. あの会社の出納係が社の金を持ち逃げした.

elopement, *n.* 駆落ち.

V ***make*** one's *elopement* 駆落ちする.

Q ***a scandalous elopement*** 人聞きの悪い駆落ち事件.

P² the *elopement* ***of*** ... ***with*** ... ...と...との駆落ち.

eloquence, *n.* 能弁, 雄弁.

V By her many kindnesses she ***achieves*** *eloquence* without wasting words. 彼女は幾多の親切な行為によっていたずらに言葉を費さずに雄弁の目的を遂げている. ¶A fallen general should not ***spend*** his *eloquence* over his failure. 敗軍の将は兵を談ぜず. ¶***use*** all the *eloquence* at his command 力一杯弁舌を振う.

Q The hall rang with his ***fiery*** *eloquence*. 会場は彼の熱弁でとどろいた. ¶the ***flowery*** and ***persuasive*** *eloquence* of the auctioneer of fruit 果物せり売り屋の面白く人を説き付ける弁舌. ¶He is endowed with a ***graceful*** and ***spirit-stirring*** *eloquence*. 彼は上品で人を感奮させる弁舌の才を持っている. ¶with ***growing*** *eloquence* 演説に油が乗ってきて. ¶***impassioned*** *eloquence* 熱弁. ¶expressed in ***lucid*** *eloquence* あざやかな弁舌で述べられた. ¶***overwhelming*** *eloquence* あたるべからざる気炎. ¶***polished*** *eloquence* 洗練された弁舌. ¶He is gifted with ***rare*** *eloquence*. 彼はまれに見る雄弁家だ. ¶his counsel's ***scathing*** *eloquence* 彼の弁護士のきびしい弁舌. ¶***torrential*** *eloquence* 懸河の弁. ¶***vehement*** *eloquence* 熱弁.

P He is unrivaled ***in*** *eloquence*. 彼は弁才にかけては比類がない. ¶The regimental colors tell ***with*** silent *eloquence* a story of valour and patriotism. その連隊旗は無言の雄弁をもって勇敢と愛国心とを物語っている. ‖ a speech burning ***with*** *eloquence* 燃えるような弁舌.

eloquent, *a.* 雄弁な, 能弁な. 「う.

M Eyes are ***more eloquent*** than lips. 目は口ほどに物をい

P The record is *eloquent* ***of*** national prosperity. この記録は国家の繁栄を雄弁に物語っている. ‖ squalid alleys, *eloquent* ***of*** poverty most abject 貧乏のどん底を雄弁に物語っている小ぎたない裏町通り ‖ whose very name is *eloquent* ***of*** ... その名を聞くだに...を思い浮べる... ¶wax *eloquent* ***on*** (=***over***) ... 油が乗ってきて...をちょうちょうと弁じ立てる. ¶he is *eloquent* ***upon*** the necessity of ... 彼は...の必要性をとうとうと論じる.

elucidation, *n.* 説明, 弁明.
Q *a disappointing elucidation* 不徹底な説明.
P he said, *in elucidation* of his statement, that ... 彼はその言説の釈明として...と言った.
elucidator, *n.* 説明者.
Q a *great elucidator* of ... ...の偉大なる解説者.
elude, *v.* 逃げる, まく.
M be *nimbly eluded* すばやく逃げる.
P *elude* one's pursuers *by* a trick 追手をうまくまく.
emanate, *v.* 出る, 発出する.
M the order has *presumably emanated* from ... その命令はおそらく...から出たものだ.
P The intelligence is believed to have *emanated from* an enemy source. その報道は敵側から出たと信ぜられている.
emanation, *n.* 流出; 発散気.
P² Fragrance is an *emanation from* flowers. 芳香は花からの発散気である.
emancipate, *v.* 解放する; げ脱させる.
M *emancipate* oneself *altogether* from ... ...から完全に自由になる.
P *emancipated from* the thraldom (=bondage *or* shackles) of ... ...の束縛から解放された ‖ *emancipate* people *from* some evil (slavery) ある害悪(など)から人々をのがれさせる. 【類】 *emancipate* a person *from* errors or prejudices (偏見) / *emancipate* oneself *from* the habit of gambling (smoking, drinking) / be *emancipated from* the control of the government.
emancipation, *n.* 解放.
Q *intellectual emancipation* through philosophy 哲学による知的解放(びゅう見からの解脱).
P² *emancipation of* women *from* discriminative treatment 差別待遇からの婦人の解放.
emasculate, *v.* 骨抜きにする.
M The bill, *heavily emasculated,* became law. その議案は骨抜きになって法律化した.
embankment, *n.* 堤防.
V An *embankment* has been *thrown up.* 堤防が急速に築かれた.
V² The *embankment collapsed.* 堤防がくずれた.
Q the *sodded embankment* of a railway 鉄道線路の芝のはえた堤防. ¶ drive [a car] along a *U-curved embankment* U字型曲線堤防をドライブする.
embargo, *n.* 出港停止; 禁制; 輸出禁止.
V *lay* an *embargo* on (=upon) a ship 船に出港停止を命じる ‖ *lay* an *embargo* on foreign commerce 海外貿易を禁止する ‖ *lay* an *embargo* on free speech 言論の自由を抑圧する. ¶ *lift* (=*remove or take off*) the *embargo* on (=upon) the export of coal to ... ...への石炭輸出を解禁する ‖ The *embargo* on private codes has been *lifted.* 私用暗号電信の禁止が解かれた. ¶ an *embargo* has been *placed* upon the export of ... ...の輸出は禁止になった. 【類】 *place embargo* on a ship.
Q *American embargo* on Japanese hosiery 米国側の日本のくつ下(メリヤス)類輸入禁止.
Q² Before the *gold embargo* the dollar-yen parity was 49 7/8. 金禁止前のドル円のレートは四九・八分の七だった.
P removal (=lifting) *of* the *embargo* 解禁. ¶ Gold is *under* an *embargo.* 金は輸出禁止になっている. ‖ lay a trade (ship) *under* an *embargo* 貿易(船の出港)を禁止する.
P² *embargo of* gold 金の輸出禁止. ¶ a removal of the *embargo on* gold shipments 金輸出の解禁 ‖ There is an *embargo on* (=*upon*) the export of rice. 米の輸出は禁止されている.
embark, *v.* (資金などを)投じる, おろす; 乗船する, 乗込む; 乗出す.
P *embark at* Kobe 神戸から乗込む. ¶ We *embarked for* home by the steamer on which we came. われわれは乗って来た汽船で帰国した. ‖ *embark for* a country (port) ある国(など)に向って乗船する. ¶ *embark in* a steamer 汽船に乗込む ‖ *embark in* matrimony 結婚生活にはいる ‖ individuals *embarking in* enterprises beyond their own means 自分の資力の及ばない事業に手を出す人々 ‖ *embark* one's capital *in* trade or speculation 商売または投機に投資する. 【類】 *embark in* the poulty business (養鶏業). ¶ *embark on* a vessel called ... ...という船に乗込む. 【類】 *embark on* the Asama-Maru at Yokohama / He *embarked on* the steamer Florida for America. / *embark on* an uncharted sea (海図にない海) ‖ They were afraid to *embark on* the novel scheme. 彼らはその目新しい事業に手を出すのを恐れていた. 【類】 when once *embarked on* an enterprise (a business, adventure) / *embark on* a great undertaking ‖ Having *embarked on* this course, they had to stick to it. やりだしたものだからどこまでもそれをやり通さなければならなかった. ‖ *embark on* the policy of economic development ‖ *embark on* life 人生に船出する ‖ the young man *embarking on* a commercial career 商売に乗出す青年 ‖ *embark on* matrimony 結婚生活にはいる ‖ The Daily Herald is *embarking on* a nation-wide campaign for increased circulation. デイリー・ヘラルド紙は購読者拡張運動を全国的にやっている. ¶ *embark upon* winter cruises 冬期海上巡航に向って船出する ‖ *embark upon* an enterprise ある事業に乗出す ‖ *embark upon* the publication of ... ...の出版に乗り出す. 【類】 He left that business to *embark upon* a career more to his liking (もっと自分の気に向く商売). ‖ The lure of the stage proved stronger than the urge to *embark upon* a business career. 舞台の魅力は商売に乗出す気持よりも結局強かった. ‖ The student of English literature has indeed *embarked upon* a limitless ocean. 英文学の学生は限りない大洋に向って乗り出したも同然だ. ¶ *embark with* them *in* the same boat 彼らと同船する.
embarrass, *v.* 困らせる, 悩ます.
M That *embarrassed* me *a great deal.* それで大いに困った. ¶ He is *embarrassed financially.* 彼は財政難に陥っている.
P The firm is *embarrassed by* debts. 同商会は借金で困っている. ¶ He is greatly *embarrassed in* his domestic economy. 彼は一家の経済に非常に困っている. ¶ I am greatly *embarrassed with* this work. 私はこの仕事を大いにもて余している.
embarrassment, *n.* 困難; 当惑.
V to *ease* his *embarrassment* 彼の迷惑をやわらげるために. ¶ *feel* great *embarrassment* at this delay この遅延で大いに迷惑する. ¶ I *find* no *embarrassment* in ...ing ... 私は...しても迷惑を感じない. ¶ *Imagine* my *embarrassment* upon being left alone in the room. そのへやに一人残された時の私の当惑といったら御推察下さい.
Q Her *financial embarrassment* was so crippling that she had no other means left but to conceal her whereabouts. 彼女の財政困難は手に余るものであったので所在をくらますより他に手段がなかった. ¶ a *friendly embarrassment* ありがた迷惑.
P *to* my great *embarassment* 大へん当惑したことには. ¶ *without embarrassment* どぎまぎせずに, 平然と.
embassy, *n.* 使節; 大使館.
Q allow *standing embassies* to be established *in* ... 大使館を...に常置することを許す.
Q² the *U.S. Embassy* in Tokyo 在東京アメリカ大使館.
P Morrison was sent *on* an *embassy* to Peking with Lord Amherst. モリソンはアムハースト卿に随行して北京に派遣された. ¶ He was attached to the Japanese *Embassy at* Washington, D.C. 彼は在ワシントン府日本大使館付であった.
embellish, *v.* 飾る, 装飾する.
P be *embellished with* many capital drawings by ... ...の手になるすばらしい絵で飾りたててある ‖ *embellish* a story *with* details 話に尾びれをつける(面白くする). 【類】 *embellish* a dress *with* lace and ribbons.
embellishment, *n.* 装飾, 修飾.
Q indulge in *rhetorical embellishments* あまりに修辞をろうする.
ember, *n.* もえさし, 余燼(じん).
V *fan* dying *embers* into new life 余燼をあおって新生面を開かせる. ¶ *rekindle* the dying *embers* of feudalism 封建制度の消えなんとする余燼を再び燃やす.
embezzle, *v.* 私消する, 使い込む.
P *embezzle* money *from* a person (bank) 人(など)から金を横領する. 【類】 The cashier *embezzled* $50,000 *from* the bank.
embezzlement, *n.* 横領, 委託金費消罪.
V *commit embezzlement* 公金を私消する.
P on a charge *of embezzlement* 委託金費消の罪科で.
emblazon, *v.* 紋章で飾る.
P The escutcheon was *emblazoned with* an emblem. その紋章には寓(ぐう)意画が付いていた.
emblem, *n.* 象徴, 標章, 紋章; 〖紋〗寓意画.
V The chrysanthemum *constitutes* an Imperial *emblem.* 菊花は御紋章になっている. ¶ *lay off* the *emblems* of sov-

ereignty 主権者の位を去る.

Q the ***Imperial emblem*** 皇室のご紋章. ¶The shamrock is the ***national emblem*** of the Irish. つめくさはアイルランド国民の象徴である. 【類】The crescent (三日月) is the ***national emblem*** of Turkey. 【類】the proper ***national emblem*** of America. ¶The dress is the ***outward emblem*** of the inner man. 衣装は内的人間の外的標章である. ¶the three ***sacred emblems*** of sovereign rule 三種の神器.

P[2] The sheep is the *emblem* ***of*** the coming year. 来年はひつじの年である. ‖ the *emblems* ***of*** conjugal felicity 夫婦和合の象徴 ‖ The crane is an *emblem* ***of*** longevity. つるは長命の象徴である. 【類】an *emblem* ***of*** good fortune / The dove is the *emblem* ***of*** peace. / The plum-blossom (梅) is the *emblem* ***of*** spring time, youth and health.

emblematic[al], *a.* 象徴する, 標章たる.

P The forget-me-not is *emblematic* ***of*** friendship or fidelity. 忘れな草は友情や忠実を象徴する. ‖ A crown is *emblematic* ***of*** royalty. 冠は王位を象徴する. 【類】The first postage stamp issued by France, on New Year's Day of 1849, bore the head of Ceres, *emblematic* ***of*** Liberty. / a lamb *emblematic* ***of*** Christ / Kan'non, the goddess *emblematical* ***of*** mercy ‖ engraved with figures *emblematic* ***of*** Faith, Hope, and Charity 信仰・希望・及び慈善の象徴たる人物が彫刻してある.

embodiment, *n.* 具体, 体現. 「ながらに具現するもの.

Q a ***living embodiment*** of the spirit of ... ...の精神を生き

P[2] He is an *embodiment* ***of*** perfect health. 彼は健康その

embody, *v.* 具体化する. 」ものである.

P *embody* one's idea ***in*** a speech その考えを言葉で表わす ‖ The project is now being *embodied* ***in*** a bill for presentation to the Diet next session. この計画は目下作成中の議案として来るべき国会に提出の予定である. ¶*embody* a theoretical opinion ***into*** a definite scheme 学説を体系

embolden, *v.* 大胆にさせる. 」づける.

P *emboldened* ***by*** this これで気が大きくなって. 【類】*emboldened* ***by*** the success of ...

embosom, *v.* 囲む, 包む, 取巻く.

P *embosomed* ***among*** a family of lofty mountains. 高い連峰に抱かれて. ¶The temple is *embosomed* ***in*** a grove. 神殿は森に取囲まれている. ¶a house *embosomed* ***with*** woods 森に囲まれている家.

embrace, *n.* 抱擁. 「る.

V ***seek*** the *embraces* of their wives 彼らの妻の抱擁を求め

Q softly disengaging himself from her ***fond embrace*** 彼女の愛の抱擁から静かに身を離して. ¶He held her to him in a ***warm embrace***. 愛人を自分の方にぐっと抱きよせた.

P welcome him ***with*** rapturous *embraces* 歓喜の抱擁をもっ

embrace, *v.* 抱きつく. 」て彼を迎える.

M a boy ***closely*** *embraced* by his mother 母親に抱きしめられた男の児. ¶***tightly*** *embrace* each other しっかと抱き

P *embrace* ***round*** the neck くびに抱きつく. 」合う.

embroglio, imbroglio, *n.* 紛糾.

Q the ***Far Eastern*** *embroglio* 極東の紛糾.

embroider, *v.* 縫取りする, 刺しゅうする.

P *embroidered* ***in*** gold thread 金糸で刺しゅうした. ¶a silken neckerchief *embroidered* ***in*** the corner ***with*** the initials of the actress 女優の頭字をすみに縫取りした絹のネッカチーフ. ¶*embroider* figures ***on*** velvet びろうどに模様を刺しゅうする ‖ *embroidered* ***on*** fabrics 織物に縫取りした. ¶*embroidered* ***with*** figures 模様を縫取りした.

embroidery, *n.* 縫取り, 刺しゅう.

V ***do*** (=***make***) some *embroidery* 刺しゅうをする.

Q covered with ***gold*** or ***silk*** *embroidery* 金糸または絹糸の刺しゅうが施してある. ¶***gorgeous*** *embroidery* 豪華な刺しゅう. 「る.

P[2] do *embroidery* ***on*** rich grounds りっぱな地に刺しゅうす

embroil, *v.* 混雑させる, 渦中に投じる.

P All Europe is now *embroiled* ***in*** war. 欧州全土は今戦争の渦中に投ぜられている. ‖ *embroil* a kingdom ***in*** civil war 王国を内乱の渦中に投じる ‖ *embroil* oneself ***in*** dispute 自己をけんかの渦中に投じる. ¶*embroil* it ***with*** ... それを...と

embryo, *n.* 胚(はい); 胚胎, ほう芽. 」混同する.

P At that time the plan, now complete, was barely ***in embryo***. 今は完成しているその計画も当時はようやく立案されたばかりであった. ‖ a little dancer ***in embryo*** ダンサーの卵 ‖ The plan is still ***in embryo***. その計画はいまだに実現されずにある.

emerge, *v.* 出現する; 脱出する.

M No new idea ***emerged during*** his speech. 彼の演説からは何ら新しい意見も出なかった. ¶***distinctly*** *emerge* from the ruck of khaki books カーキ色の本(安本)の中では出色だ.

P He *emerged* ***from*** the ordeal triumphant[ly]. 彼はその試練をりっぱにやりおおせた. ‖ He *emerged* ***from*** the difficulty. 彼はその困難から脱出した. ‖ *emerge* ***from*** a place ある場所から出現する ‖ The moon *emerged* ***from behind*** the clouds. 月は雲のかげから顔を出した. ‖ *emerge* ***from*** barbarism ***into*** civilization 野蛮時代を脱して文明に入る. ¶*emerge* ***into*** a street 街上に現われる ‖ *emerge* ***into*** full membership in the group of Great Powers 堂々と列強の間に伍(ご)する ‖ Laborers have *emerged* ***into*** self-consciousness. 労働者は自分を意識するに至った. ¶a writer who has barely *emerged* ***out of*** obscurity 名を売り出した

emergency, *n.* 偶然のこと, 事変, 急変. 」ばかりの文士.

V a man called upon to ***face*** an *emergency* 難局に当らせられた人. ¶***meet*** some sudden *emergency* 突発事故にあう ‖ I have made every arrangement to ***meet*** any *emergency*. あらゆる事態に対応できるようにしてある. ¶***use*** this *emergency* as an occasion for ... この危機を...に逆用する.

V[2] when a sudden *emergency* ***arises*** 危急な事変が起ると. ¶when the *emergency* ***occurs*** その急変が起ると.

Q in ***extraordinary*** *emergencies* 非常の事変に. ¶training for ***fire*** *emergency* at schools 学校での消防演習. ¶during a ***national*** *emergency* 国家有事の時. 【類】in case of ***national*** *emergency*. ¶on ***pressing*** *emergencies* 危急な事変に際して. ¶a ***sudden*** *emergency* 緊急事態. ¶in the time of ***unforeseen*** *emergencies* 予想しない事変突発の時に.

Q[2] except in cases of ***life-and-death*** *emergency* 命にかかわる(危急な)場合は除いて.

P bear a brunt of state affairs ***at*** a dire *emergency* like this このような恐ろしい事変に際して国務の衝に当る. ¶***in*** an *emergency* 非常の際に ‖ ***in*** [case of] *emergency* 一朝事あった場合に ‖ for use ***in*** [an] *emergency*=for emergency use 非常用の(に). 【類】teach them how to act ***in*** *emergencies*. ¶This signal is only used ***on*** an *emergency*. この信号は急場の時だけに用いる.

emigrant, *n.* 移住民, 出稼ぎ人.

V ***ship out*** *emigrants* 移住民を船で送り出す.

Q[2] a ***bounty*** *emigrant* 保護移民(奨励金で招致される移民).

P[2] Japanese *emigrants* ***for*** Brazil ブラジル行の日本移民. ¶*emigrants* ***from*** Italy イタリアからの移民. ¶an *emigrant* ***to*** America アメリカへの移民.

emigrate, *v.* 他国に移住する.

P *emigrate* ***from*** Europe ***to*** the United States ヨーロッパから合衆国へ移住する.

eminence, *n.* 高位; 卓越, 抜群; 丘.

V ***achieve*** *eminence* 傑出する. ¶***attain*** *eminence* in mathematics 数学が抜群だ ‖ ***attain*** *eminence* amongst their own people 彼ら自国民の間に傑出する. ¶***reach*** *eminence* as a doctor (statesman, writer) 医師(など)として有名になる.

Q names of ***first-class*** *eminence* 第一級の人々. ¶***intellectual*** *eminence* 知能優秀. ¶men of ***international*** *eminence* 国際的名声のある人々. ¶men of ***literary*** *eminence* 文名のある人々. ¶a ***lofty*** *eminence* 非常な卓越. ¶the ***lonely*** *eminence* of Cromwell's last days クロムウェルの晩年における超然たる孤立. ¶Dr. Eames, of international ***musical*** *eminence* 世界的音楽家イームズ博士. ¶a ***national*** *eminence* 全国的の尊重. ¶a man of great ***scientific*** *eminence* 科学に傑出した人. ¶***social*** *eminence* 社会的に高い地位. ¶a ***vernal*** *eminence* みどりが丘. ¶a ***woody*** *eminence* 森の丘.

P a poet ***of*** *eminence* 傑出した詩人. ¶***on*** an *eminence* overlooking ... ...を見下ろしている丘の上に. ¶rise ***to*** *eminence* in one's profession その道に傑出する.

P[2] on an *eminence* ***above*** the lake 湖水の上の小高い所に. ¶those artists who are noted for *eminence* ***in*** painting

eminent, *a.* 卓越した; 名のある. 」傑出した画家.

P *eminent* ***among*** his contemporaries 当時の人の中では傑出した ‖ The bishop is *eminent* ***for*** his piety and good works. その僧正は信仰とりっぱな著作で有名だ. ‖ be *emi-*

nent for valor 勇敢な点で有名である. ¶men *eminent in* science, learning, and art 科学･学問･芸術に傑出した人々.

emissary, *n.* 使者.

Q² a *peace emissary* 平和使節の特使.

emission, *n.* 放射; 放射物.

Q *seminal emission* 射精.

P² the *emission of* heat *from* a fireplace. 【類】the *emission of* light *from* a desk lamp (スタンド).

emit, *v.* 発する, 出す, 放つ.

P heat and smoke ***emitted by*** fire 火が発散する熱と煙 ‖ feel the refreshing fragrance ***emitted by*** perfumes 香水が発散するさわやかな香を感じる. ¶The moon is *emitting* cool light ***through*** clouds. 月は冷い光を雲間から投げている.

emolument, *n.* 報酬, 役得.

V continue to ***draw*** the *emoluments* of his office without doing the work 仕事はしないが引続き俸給を受ける.

P² *emolument of* authors 著作家の収入.

emotion, *n.* 情緒; 感情, 激情.

V ***arouse*** religious (sexual) *emotions* 宗教的(などの)情緒を喚起する. 【類】***arouse*** the poetic *emotion* of the sightseer. ¶***awaken*** our *emotions* われらを感動させる. ¶***betray*** one's *emotions* 感情を顔に表わす. ¶The book ***calls up*** fresh *emotions* every time he reads it. その本は読むたびに読者に新しい感興を喚起させる. ¶***control*** one's *emotion* 自己の激情を抑える. ¶It did not ***evince*** the slightest *emotion*. それは少しも感動させなかった. ¶words which ***evoke*** aesthetic *emotion* 審美的感情を呼び起す言葉. ¶***excite*** the most patriotic and pleasurable *emotions* 最も愛国的にして愉快な感情を喚起する. ¶***feel*** no *emotion* but that of boredom 退屈な感じ以外の何物をも感じない ‖ The *emotion* has been genuinely ***felt***. その感情は実感したものであった. ¶***hide*** one's *emotion* 自己の激情を表わさない. ¶***kindle*** one's *emotion* 人を感激させる. ¶***lull*** the *emotion* of modesty あまりはにかまないようにさせる. ¶***repress*** *emotions* 情緒を抑える. ¶***stifle*** one's *emotions* 自己の感情を顔に見せまいとする. ¶***stimulate*** the sexual *emotions* 性的感情を刺激する. ¶***stir*** one's *emotions* 人の感情を激発する. 【類】***stir*** the *emotions* of the masses. ¶***stir up*** the deepest *emotions* of pride and satisfaction 最も深い自尊心と満足感とを喚起する. ¶***suppress*** one's *emotions* 自己の感情を抑える. ¶***sway*** the *emotion* 感情を左右する. ¶***thrill*** one's *emotions* 大いに感動させる. ¶***touch*** the *emotions* 情緒に触れる.

Q He is apt to be carried away by ***blind*** *emotion*. 彼は盲目的感情に走りやすい. ¶***conflicting*** *emotions* 矛盾する感情 ‖ He was giddy with ***contending*** *emotion*. 彼は矛盾する感情に迷って頭がふらふらした. ¶***crude*** *emotions* 自然のままの情緒. ¶To watch such a scene is an ***inspiring*** *emotion*. こうした光景を眺めると霊感を覚える. ¶excite a ***mild*** *emotion* おだやかな感情を起させる. ¶***mixed*** *emotions* 複雑な感情. ¶***primitive*** *emotions* such as fear and anger 恐怖とか憤怒とかいう原始的感情. ¶***sentimental*** *emotion* 涙もろい感情. ¶a man of ***strong*** *emotions* 感情の強い人. ¶***subtle*** *emotion* 微妙な感情. ¶express ***sudden*** *emotion* 激情を示す. ¶a whirlpool of ***various*** *emotions* 色々様々な感情の渦巻. ¶She lost her reason in consequence of a ***violent*** *emotion* caused by a fire. 彼女はひどく火事に驚いて気が狂った.

P weep ***with*** *emotion* 感泣する ‖ My breast was filled ***with*** *emotion*. 胸が一杯になった. ¶I can never hear those chimes ***without*** *emotion*. 私はあの鐘の音を聞いて平気でいることができない.

emperor, *n.* 皇帝, 天皇.

V ***force*** the *emperor* to abdicate 皇帝に迫って退位させる. ¶***restore*** the *emperor* to his ancient authority 王政を復古する. ¶***reverence*** the *emperor* 天皇を敬う.

Q Ashikaga Takauji set up a ***rival*** *emperor*. 足利尊氏は対抗上別に天皇を擁立した. ¶Perry took the Shogun to be the "***secular*** *emperor*" of Japan. ペリーは将軍を日本の実質的帝王と思った. ¶the Mikado or ***spiritual*** *emperor* みかど即ち精神的な方面での帝王. ¶the Shogun or ***temporal*** *emperor* 将軍即ち俗事的の帝王.

Q² China's ***boy*** *emperor* 中国の幼君主. ¶China was never more illustrious or powerful than under the ***Mongol*** *emperor*, Kublai. 中国はモンゴル帝忽必烈の時が最盛最強であった. ¶Pu-yi, Japanese sponsored ***puppet*** *Emperor* of Manchuria 日本のかいらい満州帝国皇帝溥儀(ふ).

P ***for*** the *Emperor* and expulsion of barbarians 尊王攘夷(じょうい).

Q He was created (=declared) *Emperor*. 彼は皇帝の位についた.

emphasis, *n.* 語勢, 文勢; 強調.

V Higher tribute cannot be paid; no words of mine can ***add*** *emphasis* to this eulogium. これ以上の賛辞は呈し得ない. 私の言葉ではどうしてもこの讃辞に蛇足(だそく)を添えるだけのことしか出来ない. ¶***cast*** *emphasis* upon ... …を強調する. ¶This is so important that it ***deserves*** special *emphasis*. これは非常に重要であるので特に強調する価値がある. ¶***distort*** *emphasis* 軽重を誤る. ¶***give*** a false *emphasis* 余計な所に力を入れる. ¶***improve*** the *emphasis* 強勢の点の配置を改める. ¶***lay*** *emphasis* on ...=give weight to ... …を強調する ‖ ***lay*** less *emphasis* on ... …をもっと控目に言う ‖ the *emphasis* is ***laid*** on ... …に力点を置く. ¶This last point is one that will ***merit*** a little *emphasis*. この最後の点は少しく強調する価値がある. ¶It is too well known to ***need*** *emphasis*. それは非常によく知れているのでことさら言い立てる必要がない. ¶***place*** special *emphasis* upon ... …を特に強調する. ¶***put*** (=place) *emphasis* on ... …を強調する. 【類】***put*** forcible *emphasis* on home discipline (しつけ). ¶That point should ***receive*** *emphasis*. その点は強調さるべきである. ¶That... ***requires*** no *emphasis*. …ということは改めて言うまでもない. ¶***throw*** the whole *emphasis* upon ... …に全力を注ぐ.

Q give ***considerable*** *emphasis* to ... …を大いに力説する. ¶lay ***disproportionate*** *emphasis* on ... …を偏重する. ¶Two considerations deserve ***explicit*** *emphasis*. 二つの点を特に強調する価値がある. ¶all that has been said on this question applies with even ***greater*** *emphasis* to ... この問題に関して述べたことはすべてこれを一層強調して…についても同様に述べられる. ¶He threw a ***hard*** *emphasis* on the words. 彼はその言葉を強めて言った. ¶throw the ***main*** *emphasis* upon ... 主として…を強調する. ¶place ***major*** *emphasis* on ... …に重点をおく. ¶lay ***special*** *emphasis* on ... …をことさらに強調する. 【類】give ***special*** *emphasis* to the study of grammar / ***special*** *emphasis* is to be laid on the fact that ... ¶too ***strong*** *emphasis* cannot be put upon the fact that ... …という事実はいかに強調してもし過ぎるということはない. ¶lay ***undue*** *emphasis* upon ... …を過度に強調する.

P We wish this to say ***with*** all the *emphasis* at command. われわれは あらん限りの力をこめてこう申し上げたいうこと.

P² *emphasis* ***on*** a matter (word) ある事柄(など)を強めてい

emphasize, *v.* 力を入れて言う.

M it cannot be *emphasized* ***enough*** that ... …はいくら強調してもし過ぎることはない. ¶*emphasize* it more ***fully*** 更にそれを強調する. ¶I need ***hardly*** *emphasize* the point. その点を私が特に力説するの必要はほとんどない. ¶***pointedly*** *emphasize* 特に力説する.

emphasizing, *n.* 力説すること.

V an advantage which ***needs*** no *emphasizing* 力説するを要しない利益.

emphatic, *a.* 力を入れた; 力説する.

P he was *emphatic* ***in*** his assertion that ... 彼は断固として…ということを主張した.

empire, *n.* 帝国; 領域; 統治権.

V ***build up*** an *empire* 帝国を建設する. ¶The *empire* which he had ***established*** would be in danger of dissolution. 彼の建設した帝国は壊滅の危険にひんするものと思われた. ¶They attempted to ***overthrow*** the *empire* and transform it into a socialist State. 彼らは帝国を倒して社会主義の国家に改造しようと企てた. ¶Their services have ***raised*** the *empire* to a leading place among the world's great Powers. 彼らの力で帝国の地位が高まって世界強国の間に伍(ご)するようになった. ¶He ravished Asia to ***win*** a great *empire*. 彼はアジヤを攻略して大帝国を建設した.

Q the dismembered ***Celestial*** *Empire* ばらばらになった中国. ¶a ***colossal*** *empire* 巨大な帝国. ¶The British was a ***colonial*** *empire*. 英国は植民地を多く持った帝国であった. ¶a ***dual*** *empire* 二元君主国. ¶England is the mistress of a ***far-flung*** *empire*. 英国は広く世界に版図を有する国である. ¶the Krupp ***industrial*** *empire* クラップ工業王国. ¶one of the world's ***mightiest*** *empires* 世界最大帝国の一. ¶a ***moribund*** *empire* 滅亡にひんする帝国. ¶a ***sea-locked*** *empire* 海に囲まれた帝国. ¶Japan, with China to draw upon, is undoubtedly becoming more and more a ***self-supporting empire***. シナから物資を得られる日本はたしかにますます自給の帝国になりつゝある. ¶a ***vast empire*** 広大な帝国. ¶united the ***whole empire*** under his scepter 彼の旗下に全帝国を結合した. ¶a ***world-wide empire*** その領土が世界にわたる帝国.

Q² renunciation by Italy of all her ***overseas empire*** イタリアの海外領土完全放棄.

P all ***over*** the *empire* 帝国中に. ¶simultaneously ***throughout*** the *empire* 全国一斉に.

P² the *empire* ***of*** man over things 人間の万物に対する支配権 ‖ the *Empire* ***of*** Japan 日本帝国 ‖ the *Empire* ***of*** the Sun 日の本 ‖ the *empire* ***of*** reason 理性の領域.

emplacement, *n.* 陣地.

Q² an ***anti-aircraft*** *emplacement* 高射砲陣地.

emplane, *v.* 《口語》飛行機に乗る.

P *emplane* ***at*** Honolulu ホノルルで機上の人となる. ¶*emplane* ***for*** ... 空路...に向け出発する.

employ, *n.* 雇用, 奉公, 使用; 仕事, 職業.

V He ***entered*** the *employ* (=service) of the company in the electrical department. 彼はその会社の電気部にはいった. ¶***make*** practical *employ* of what one learns 自分の学ぶ所を実地に応用する.

Q a chauffeur in ***regular*** *employ* 専属の運転手.

Q² be in the ***Government*** *employ* 公務員である.

P men ***in*** their *employ* 彼らに雇われている人々 ‖ a physician ***in*** the company's *employ* 会社専属の医者. 【類】He has been ***in*** the company's *employ* for nearly 60 years. / a clerk ***in*** the *employ* of the ... Company / He is ***in*** the *employ* of the Government. / He was formerly ***in*** my *employ*. / As a clerk he was in the *employ* of a small firm over twenty years. / He remained ***in*** his *employ* (the employ of the Government) for over thirty years. ¶Electric traction ***in*** Tokyo has thrown a great number of jinrikisha coolies ***out of*** *employ*. 東京における交通の電化は多数の人力車夫を失業させた.

employ, *v.* 従事させる, 使う, 使役する.

M She is very ***demurely*** *employed* on sewing. 彼女は黙然として縫物をやっている. ¶be ***extensively*** *employed* 広く用いられている. ¶My master keeps me so ***fully*** *employed* that I never have any opportunity to study. 私の所の主人はしょっちゅう仕事を言付けるので勉強する暇がちっともありません. ¶the number of women ***gainfully*** *employed* 職業婦人の数. ¶workers ***happily*** *employed* 満足している労務者. ¶be ***manually*** *employed* in industry and agriculture 生産方面及び農園で働いている. ¶His genius was ***nobly*** *employed*. 彼はその天才をりっぱに伸ばした. ¶Your time can be more ***profitably*** *employed*. 君は時間をもっと有効に使える. ¶in some way *employ* oneself ***usefully*** 何か有用な仕事をする.

P It is a pity that such an ability as his should be *employed* ***about*** such trifle matters. 彼のような手腕のある人がこんなつまらない事に使われているのは惜しい. ¶*employ* English ***as*** official language 公用語として英語を使う ‖ *employ* alcohol ***as*** a solvent アルコールを溶剤として使う ‖ He is *employed* ***as*** one of the editorial staff ***at*** a salary of 20,000 yen. 彼は二万円の月給で編集部員として雇われている. ¶How many workmen do you *employ* ***at*** your factory? 貴下の工場に職工を何人使っていますか. ¶he is *employed* ***by*** ... 彼は...に使われている. ¶*employ* one's time ***in*** reading 読書に時間を使う. 【類】*employ* the holidays ***in*** shooting ‖ She is *employed* ***in*** sedentary work. 彼女は座業に従業している. ‖ He was *employed* ***in*** a bank (firm). 彼は銀行(など)に勤めていた. ‖ British vessels *employed* ***in*** trading to the Far East. 極東の貿易に従事する英国船. 【類】be *employed* ***in*** the coasting trade (沿岸貿易). ¶the labor and staff *employed* ***on*** the bridge その橋の架設に従事した労働者と係員 ‖ Today there are 2,000,000 men *employed* ***on*** the railways. 今日鉄道従業員は二百万人いる. ‖ He was *employed* ***on*** the N.Y. Times. 彼はニューヨーク・タイムス紙に勤めていた. ¶I am at present *employed* ***with*** Messrs. So-and-So. 私は目下...商会に勤めている.

employe, employee, *n.* 雇人, 使用人.

V ***discharge*** (=***cast, discard or dismiss***) *employees* 使用人を解雇する. ¶***hire*** and ***dismiss*** *employees* 従業員を雇入れたり解雇したりする. ¶***orient*** new *employees* 新任者に仕事の手ほどきをする. ¶***sweat*** one's *employes* 従業員を搾取する. ¶***throw*** out of jobs many *employees* 多数使用人を解雇する.

Q an ***auxiliary*** *employee* 雇員. ¶***civilian*** *employees* of the Army 陸軍の軍属たち. ¶a ***junior*** *employee* 雇人. ¶a ***minor*** *employee* of the government 小役人. ¶a ***postal*** *employee* 郵便局員. ¶a ***professional*** *employee* 専門的従業員. ¶a ***prospective*** *employee* 就職希望者. ¶a ***public*** *employee* 公務員. ¶a ***salaried*** *employee* 月給取り(サラリーマン). ¶a ***subordinate*** *employee* 下級職員. ¶the elimination of ***surplus*** *employes* 過剰人員の整理.

P² an *employee* ***in*** that intrigue その陰謀に使われた人.

Q² a ***bakery*** *employe* パン屋の雇人. ¶a ***city*** *employe* 都市職員. ¶a ***concessionaire*** *employe* 《米》公園の使用人. ¶a ***Federal*** *employe* 《米》連邦政府の官吏. ¶the unionization of ***Government*** *employes* 官公職員の組合組織化 ‖ a military ***government*** *employee* 軍政府の役人. ¶a ***hotel*** *employee* ホテルの従業員. ¶***industry*** *employes* 生産事業労務者たち. ¶***motor-vehicle*** *employes* 自動車工場労務者たち. ¶an ***office*** *employee* 事務職員. ¶a ***part-time*** *employee*=a part-timer 嘱託, パートタイム(の勤務者). ¶***public utility*** and ***public service*** *employes* 公団職員及び公務員. ¶***rank and file*** *employees* 平社員(役付に対し). ¶***State*** *employes* 《米》州の職員. ¶a ***store*** *employe* 商店員. ¶a ***white collar*** *employe* (=workers) サラリーマン, 勤め人.

employer, *n.* 雇主.

V ***threaten*** the *employer* with strike unless ... ...しなければストライキをやると言って雇主をおどす.

Q an ***unappreciative*** *employer* 目のない主人.

employment, *n.* 仕事, 職; 雇用; 使用.

V ***afford*** *employment* to a large number of men 多数の人に職を与える. ¶The industry ***creates*** *employment* for hundreds of thousands of workers. その産業によって何十万という人が職業にありつくことが出来る. ¶***desire*** *employment* as ... ...に雇われたいと志願する. ¶He ***entered*** the *employment* of Messrs. ... as a shop-lad. 彼は小店員として...商会に雇われた. ¶***exercise*** one's *employment* 自分の商売をやる. ¶It ***finds*** *employment* for a good many deserving people who would otherwise have been thrown out of work かなり多数の役に立つ人たちがこのために失業しないで職業にありついている. ‖ They ***find*** *employment* for camels. らくだを有効に使用している. ‖ Shipping, the principal index of international trade, is ***finding*** more *employment*. 海外貿易の主なる指針たる船舶業はますます仕事がふえつつある. ¶***follow*** one's *employment* 仕事につく ‖ The wounded worker was unable to ***follow*** his *employment* for many weeks. けがをした職工は幾週間も彼の仕事につくことが出来なかった. ¶The factory ***furnishes*** *employment* to more than one thousand skilled hands. 同工場は一千人以上の熟練工を使用している. ¶***get*** *employment* on a newspaper 新聞社で就職する. ¶***get*** and ***retain*** *employment* 口にありついてその仕事を続ける. ¶The Government will undertake great public works which ***give*** *employment* to large numbers of people. 政府は多数の人に職を授けるような大公共事業を起すであろう. ‖ The company ***gives*** *employment*, direct and indirect, to more than one thousand people. その会社は直接間接に一千名以上の者に職を与えている. ‖ The factory ***gives*** *employment* to 500 hands. その工場は五百人の職工を使っている. ‖ ***give*** *employment* to vessels lying idle 休んでいる船に仕事を与える. ¶What *employment* ***has*** he? 彼は何商売か. ¶***hunt*** *employment* 職を探す. ¶***increase*** *employment* 職業を増す(失業者を少くする). ¶He has ***left*** his *employment*. 彼は辞職した. ¶Many officials ***lost*** their *employment*. 多数の官吏がその職を失った. ‖ the fear of ***losing*** *employment* 失業の恐怖. ¶He ***obtained*** *employment* at the works. 彼はその工場で口を見付けた. ‖ assist them to ***obtain*** *employment*=aid (=help) them in ***obtaining*** *employment* 彼らの就職を世話する ‖ There is but little possibility of ***obtaining*** *employment*. とても職につけそうもない. ¶Can you ***offer*** any *employment* for him? 彼を何かに使って頂けませんか. ¶He made efforts to ***preserve*** his *employment*. 彼は解雇されないように努力した. ¶The making of books ***provides*** *employment* for a large section of the community. 書籍の出版は社会の多数人に職を与える. ¶***secure*** remunerative *employment* もうかる仕

事にありつく.【類】There is much difficulty for them in *securing employment* after education. / *secure employment* in ... ¶*seek employment* as ... ...の職につこうとする‖*seek employment* at insignificant salaries 薄給の職を探す.【類】He came to London to *seek employment.* ¶*take employment* elsewhere よそで職につく.【類】*take employment* in a newspaper office.

Q He has ***another employment.*** 彼はもうつ一仕事を持っている. ¶*Employment* is ***brisk*** in the trade. その方面の事業では新たに人を大分入れている. ¶***congenial*** *employment*, light work, and short hours はだに合う職業, 軽い仕事, そして短い時間.【類】We must have ***congenial*** *employment* in order to be enthusiastic. ¶in ***constant*** *employment* 絶えず仕事をして. ¶spurious cigar shops, manicure establishments, and other ***counterfeit*** *employments* 怪しげなタバコ屋・マニキュア屋・その他のいんちき商売. ¶engaged in some ***decent*** *employment* 何か正業についている‖girls in ***decent*** *employment* かたぎの商売の娘たち(女店員など). ¶a ***desirable*** *employment* 願わしい仕事. ¶***full*** *employment* 完全雇用. ¶a ***genteel*** *employment* 上品な仕事. ¶***hazardous*** *employment* 一か八かの仕事. ¶an ***honorable*** *employment* 正業. ¶A large proportion of the population is engaged in ***industrial*** *employment*. その大部分の人は産業に従事している. ¶seek other more ***lucrative*** *employments* 他のもっともうかる仕事を探す. ¶To him teaching was a "***mean*** *employment*". 彼の考えでは教師はつまらない仕事だった. ¶spend five years in ***official*** *employment* 公務員として五年勤める. ¶***over-full*** *employment* 超完全雇用. ¶He has no ***permanent*** *employment*. 彼は定職がない. ¶***precarious*** *employment* 不安定な職業. ¶the ***profitable*** *employment* of spare funds 遊金の有利な運用. ¶a ***public*** *employment* 公職. ¶Universal City gives ***regular*** *employment* to one thousand workers. ユ社映画製作市は常に一千人の人を使っている. ¶a ***remunerative*** *employment* 有利な仕事. ¶***reputable*** *employment* りっぱな職業. ¶***secondary*** *employments* [重要さから言って]第二次的の仕事. ¶be assured of ***steady*** *employment* 失業の心配がない. ¶secure ***well-paid*** *employment* 待遇の良い仕事につく.

P persons ***in*** their *employment* 職についている人々‖place ... ***in*** *employment* ...を就職させる.【類】persons ***in*** the *employment* of the government. ¶those ***in*** and ***out of*** *employment* 有職無職の人々. ¶take ... ***into*** *employment* ...を雇入れる. ¶reside at a walking distance ***of*** their [places of] *employment* 勤務先から徒歩で通える距離に居住する. ¶a person ***out of*** *employment* 失業者‖throw them ***out of*** *employment* 彼らを失職させる. ¶be ***without*** *employment* 徒食する.

P[2] He obtained *employment* ***as*** chemist. 彼は薬剤師として仕事を得た. ¶He took *employment* ***in*** a newspaper office. 彼は新聞社で職についた. ¶*employment* ***of*** children 児童使用‖*employment* ***of*** modern machinery 現代的機械の使用.【類】*employment* ***of*** one's time / the *employment* ***of*** the convicts at productive labor. ¶take *employment* ***with*** (=serve) a foreigner 外国人に使われる.

Q[2] ***full-time*** *employment* 常勤. ¶***long-term*** *employment* 長期雇用. ¶***part-time*** *employment* パートタイム, 非常勤. ¶***summer*** *employment* of undergraduates 大学生の夏期アルバイト.

emporium, *n.* 大市場, 商業中心地.

Q a ***natural*** *emporium* of trade 天然の商業中心地.

Q[2] a ***mammoth*** *emporium* 大商店, 大百貨店.

P[2] become the *emporium* ***of*** trade for ... ...(商品)の集散地になる.

empty, *a.* 空虚の, あいている, 空しい.

P The room was nearly *empty* ***of*** furniture. その室にはほとんど家具がなかった.‖a bottle *empty* ***of*** wine ぶどう酒のあきびん‖a spacious garden almost *empty* ***of*** plants ほとんど草木の生えていない広い庭.

empty, *v.* からにする; 明ける; からになる; 注ぐ.

M At the variety theatres the stalls for some reason ***empty first.*** よせではどういう訳か平土間が最先きに(客が出て)空になる. ¶***empty out*** the water from a pail おけの水を明ける. ¶The classroom *emptied* ***rapidly*** after the lecture. 講義がすむと教室は間もなくからになった.

P The river *empties* ***into*** the harbor. その川がその港に注ぐ.‖Here the river *empties* [itself] ***into*** the sea. この所でその川は海に注ぐ.‖*empty* water ***into*** a vessel 水を器物に明ける. ¶He *emptied* his pockets ***of*** their contents. 彼は自分のポケットの物を皆取り出した.【類】The closet had been *emptied* ***of*** all its things. / The huge baggage vans (手荷物車) were *emptied* ***of*** their contents. ¶*empty* a bag ***on*** the tray 袋の中の物を盆の上にあける.

empty-headedness, *n.* 頭の空白.

V ***disguise*** one's *empty-headedness* by playing the parrot 人まねで頭のからっぽをカムフラージュする.

emulation, *n.* 競い, 競争心.

V ***arouse*** *emulation* 競争心を起させる. ¶*emulation* is ***fostered*** by ... 競争心が...によって養われる. ¶***stimulate*** *emulation* and effort 競争心と奮発心を刺激する.

P incited ***by*** *emulation* 競争心に駆られて. ¶***in*** *emulation* of his example 彼のお手本にならって.

P[2] an *emulation* ***among*** the boys who wish to be foremost 少年たちが自分こそ一番にと意気ごむ競争. ¶*emulation* ***for*** the first place 第一位を得ようと競うこと. ¶*emulation* ***in*** scholarship 学力競争.

enable, *v.* 得させる, 出来るようにする.

O His friends will *enable* him to pay his debts. 彼の友人たちは彼が借金を支払うことが出来るようにしてやるだろう. ¶Endurance *enabled* him to win the race. 彼は忍耐のお陰で競走に勝てたのだ.【類】His recovery of health *enabled* him to pursue his study.

enact, *v.* [法律などを]制定する; 上演する, 演じる.

P a play *enacted* ***by*** the ... troupe ...一座によって上演された劇. ¶*enact* a part ***in*** life 人生で一役演じる. ¶The bills were *enacted* ***into*** private law. それらの法案は私法として制定された.

enactment, *n.* 法令, 条例.

Q by ***Government*** *enactment* 法令で. ¶a ***tyrannical*** and ***unpopular*** *enactment* 専制的で不評判な法令.

enamel, *v.* エナメルを塗る; 飾り立てる.

P shoes *enameled* ***at*** the point 先にエナメルをつけたくつ. ¶a field *enameled* ***with*** wild flowers 野草の咲きしげる野.

enamor, *v.* ほれ込ませる, 恋着させる, 心を奪う.

M became ***deeply*** *enamored* of ... ...にぞっこんほれ込むようになった.

P be *enamored* ***of*** a man or woman 男あるいは女にほれている‖The poet is *enamored* ***of*** beauty. あの詩人は美に心を奪われている.‖He is *enamored* ***of*** study (science, books). 彼は勉学(など)に心を奪われている.【類】In his youth he was *enamored* ***of*** romantic poetry. ¶He is *enamored* ***with*** a book. 彼はある書物を読みふけっている.【類】He is *enamored* ***with*** scientific researches.‖he became *enamored* ***with*** ... 彼は...の恋のとりことなった.

encamp, *v.* 陣取る, 野営する.

P the soldiers *encamped* ***at*** ... 兵士たちは...に陣取った. ¶they *encamped* overnight ***in*** ... 彼らは...に野営した.

encase, *v.* 包む, かぶせる.

P a bullet *encased* ***in*** steel 鋼鉄をかぶせた銃弾.

enchant, *v.* 魅する, うっとりさせる.

P I was *enchanted* ***by*** her singing. 私は彼女の歌に聞きほれた. ¶He is *enchanted* ***with*** her manners. 彼は彼女の物腰に魅せられた.【類】I was *enchanted* ***with*** the music.

enchantment, *n.* 魔法; 魅惑.

V It is distance that ***lends*** *enchantment* to the view. 遠方で見るとよく見えるものだ「遠くの芝は青く見える」. ¶She ***set*** her *enchantments* at work. 彼女は魔術を使った.

P as if ***by*** *enchantment* 魔法でも使ったように.

encircle, *v.* 囲む, 取巻く; 抱擁する.

M The Mediterranean Sea is ***almost*** *encircled* by the lands of Europe, Asia, and Africa. 地中海は欧州, アジアおよびアフリカによってほとんど全く囲まれている.

P The country is *encircled* ***by*** the sea. その国は海に囲まれている.【類】a pond *encircled* ***by*** trees. ¶*encircle* a person ***in*** the arms 人を抱擁する. ¶an ancient city *encircled* ***with*** walls and castles とりでで囲まれた古い都市‖*encircle* the waist ***with*** a girdle 帯で腰を巻く.

enclose, *v.* 囲う, 取巻く; 封入する; 閉じこめる.

M I *enclose* ***herewith*** a check for $200.=Enclosed please find a check for $200. 二百ドルの小切手を封入致します.

P *enclose* the words ***by*** brackets その語を括弧でくくる. ¶He is *enclosed* ***in*** a monastery. 彼は僧院に閉じこもっている.‖*enclose* the word ***in*** quotation marks その語に引用符を付ける‖I herewith return [you] his letter which was *enclosed* ***in*** yours. 貴下のお手紙に封入してあった彼の手紙を同封してお返し致します.【類】*enclose* money ***in*** a letter.

¶ *enclose* a word ***with*** a circle 語を丸で囲む ‖ *enclose* ***with*** parentheses 括弧で包む ‖ The house is *enclosed* ***with*** a high brick wall. その家には高いれんがべいがめぐらしてある. 【類】 a respectable house *enclosed* ***with*** hawthorn hedges (さんざしの生けがき).

enclosure, *n.* 封入物; 構内, 囲い.

V ***clip*** an *enclosure* to the covering letter 添付物を手紙に付ける.

Q The ***intended*** *enclosure* is missing. あるべき添付物が同封してない. ¶ a ***royal*** *enclosure* 貴賓(皇族)席. ¶ the ***third*** *enclosure* 三の丸. ¶ within a ***walled*** *enclosure* へい囲いの構内に.

Q² a ***barbed-wire*** *enclosure* 有刺線の囲い.

P money ***for*** *enclosure* to ... ...あての手紙に同封すべき金. ¶ ***within*** the *enclosure* of ... ...の境(構)内に.

encomium, *n.* 賛辞.

Q a ***written*** *encomium* 賞状.

encore, *n.* 再演の所望(アンコール).

V ***call for*** a spontaneous *encore* 自然に再演を求めさせることになる. ¶ Her performance ***evoked*** an enthusiastic *encore*. 彼女の演技は熱心にアンコールを求められた. ¶ The audience ***insisted on*** many *encores*. 聴衆は何度もアンコールを求めてやまなかった. ¶ ***receive*** an *encore* アンコールの所望を受ける.

P she gave us an *encore* ***to*** her song "..." 彼女はアンコールを所望されて「...」を歌った.

encounter, *v.* 遭遇する; 敵対する.

M *encounter* ***stubbornly*** がん強に敵対する.

P *encounter* ***with*** difficulties (the enemy) 困難(など)に遭遇する.

encounter, *n.* 遭遇.

Q an ***accidental*** *encounter* 遇然の会合. ¶ ***unsuccessful*** *encounters* with the facts of life 不遇の一生.

encourage, *v.* 奨励する, 激励する, 鼓舞する.

M get ***greatly*** *encouraged* 大いに力を得る. ¶ if ***rightly*** *encouraged* 奨励の方法を誤らないならば. ¶ ***warmly*** *encourage* ... 熱心に...を奨励する.

P be *encouraged* ***at*** favorable indications 有望な気配に元気づく. ¶ *encouraged* ***by*** his example 彼のお手本に力を得て ‖ *encouraged* ***by*** our pusillanimity われわれが小胆であるのをよいことにして. 【類】 *encouraged* ***by*** those words (this good record). ¶ *encourage* one ***in*** doing something 人を激励して何かをやらせる. ¶ *encourage* the people ***to*** hostility 人々を鼓舞して反抗させる. ¶ *encourage* a person ***with*** promise (aid) 約束(など)で人を鼓舞する. 【類】 *encouraged* ***with*** the promise of ...

O *encourage* a person to do something 人を激励して何かやらせる.

encouragement, *n.* 奨励, 激励, 鼓舞.

V ***derive*** *encouragement* 激励を得る. ¶ It ***deserves*** far greater *encouragement* in Japan than it actually receives. それは日本で実際受けているよりも一層大なる奨励を受ける価値がある. ¶ These people ***find*** *encouragement* enough in any lucrative employment. これらの連中はもうかる仕事とさえ言えばなんでもやって見ようという気になる. ¶ ***give*** him *encouragement* to ... 彼が...をするように鼓舞する. ¶ We ***received*** no *encouragement* from that quarter. われわれはその方面から何らの激励をも受けなかった. 【類】 ***receive*** much *encouragement*, especially from ... ¶ ***take*** *encouragement* from ... ...から刺激を受ける.

Q it is desirable that ***every*** *encouragement* should be given to ... ...のためにあらゆる声援を送ることが望ましい. ¶ ***sincere*** *encouragement* 衷心からの奨励. ¶ There is ***some*** (***no***) *encouragement* in doing it. それをやるに少しは張合がある(少しも張合がない).

encroach, *v.* 侵入する, 侵害する, 蚕食する.

P *encroach* ***on*** the domain of ... ...のなわ張りに足を入れる ‖ *encroach* ***on*** functions that do not belong to one 自分に関係のない(人の)職分を侵害する ‖ *encroach* ***on*** the scope (=province) of ... ...の領域に侵入する. 【類】 *encroach* ***on*** (=upon) one's rights (liberties, territory). ¶ *encroach* ***upon*** the realm of ... ...の領土に侵入する. 【類】 *encroach* ***upon*** the domain of psychiatry (精神病学) / *encroach* ***upon*** the functions of an encyclopaedia (百科全書の領分) / *encroach* ***upon*** the province of the sterner sex (男性の領分) ‖ persistently attempted to *encroach* ***upon*** the English sphere of influence 英国の勢力範囲にあくまで食い入ろうと試みた ‖ *encroach* ***upon*** the time of ... ...の時間に食込む.

encroachment, *n.* 侵入, 侵害.

P² *encroachments* ***on*** our territory わが領土への侵入 ‖ an *encroachment* ***on*** (=upon) his rights 彼の権利の侵害. 【類】 *encroachment* ***on*** personal privacy (私生活). ¶ *encroachment* ***upon*** their own domain (one's personal liberty) 彼らの領土(など)への侵入.

encumber, *v.* 邪魔する, わずらわす, 負債を負わす.

P His movements were *encumbered* ***by*** his mantle. 彼はマントで行動を妨げられた. ¶ *encumber* one's mind ***with*** cares 心配でくよくよする ‖ *encumber* trade ***with*** heavy duties 重税で商業の発展を妨げる. 【類】 *encumbered* ***with*** debts / He is *encumbered* ***with*** a large family. ‖ Far from being single, he is now *encumbered* ***with*** a wife and children. 独身どころかあの男にはもう妻子という足手まといがある.

encumbrance, *n.* 厄介物; 係累.

V it ***constitutes*** a serious *encumbrance* to ... それは...の由由しい障害になる. ¶ a man ***without*** *encumbrance* 係累のない人.

encyclop(a)edia, *n.* 百科全書.

Q a ***human*** *encyclopaedia* 生字引. ¶ a ***moving*** (=walking) *encyclopaedia* of baseball data 野球の生字引. ¶ a ***veritable*** *encyclopaedia* of football lore フットボールの生字引. ¶ He is a sort of "***walking*** *encyclopaedia*" on movie topics. 彼は映画の話と来たらまず生字引という所だ.

encyclopaedist, *n.* 百科辞典編集者.

Q² the ***eighteenth century*** French *encyclopaedists* 十八世紀のフランス百科全書派の人々(ダランベールなど).

end, *n.* (1) 目的, 成果.

V ***accomplish*** its *end* その目的を達する ‖ ***accomplish*** the *end* desired 所期の目的を達する. ¶ ***achieve*** chosen *ends* 選択した目的を達成する. 【類】 to ***achieve*** these *ends*. ¶ It is more calculated to ***answer*** the *end* proposed. それは計画した目的に一層よくかなうと考えられている. 【類】 sufficient to ***answer*** the *end* in view. ¶ fully ***attain*** one's *end* その目的を十分に達成する. 【類】 How you ***attain*** this *end*? We can tell you in four words. ¶ sparing no expense to ***compass*** his *ends* 彼の目的を遂げるためには費用を惜しまずに. ¶ ***defeat*** its own *ends* その本来の目的を失わせる. ¶ to ***ensure*** this *end* この目的達成のために. ¶ ***follow*** the *end* of the war 戦争目的を追求する ‖ ***follow*** the same *ends* 同じ目的を追求する. ¶ ***gain*** the *end* sought 所期の目的を達する ‖ You have much to do, ere you can ***gain*** your *end*. 君が目的を達するにいたるまでにまだいろいろやることがある. ¶ the *end* I ***have*** in view 私の抱く目的. ¶ He should force himself to go into company, and whether he blushes or not, he should "***hold up*** his *end*." 彼は無理に人中に割込んで行って赤面すると否とにかかわらず自分の目的をあくまで通さなければいけない. ¶ ***keep*** one's *end* ***up*** 自己の目的を持続する. ¶ choose the best means of ***obtaining*** the *end* 目的を達する最善の方法を選ぶ. ¶ ***promote*** an *end* 目的の達成を促す. ¶ ***pursue*** one's own *ends* 自分の目的を追求する. ¶ They believe that fair *ends* may be ***reached*** by foul means. 彼らは不正手段によって正しい結果が得られると信じている. 【類】 in order to ***reach*** this *end*. ¶ ***secure*** the desired *end* 望み通りの結果を得る. ¶ ***serve*** its *end* 目的にかなう. 【類】 It ***serves*** the *end* in view. / It ***serves*** the *ends* of culture (修養). ¶ ***suit*** one's own *ends* 自身の目的に適する. ¶ ***work out*** an *end* 目的を達成する.

Q Leisure is the ***chief*** *end* of life. 閑暇は人生の主要目的である. ¶ work together for a ***common*** *end* 同じ目的のために共に働く. ¶ achieve this ***difficult*** *end* この困難な目的を達成する. ¶ To do so would serve no ***good*** *ends*. そうしても何の役にも立たないだろう. ¶ have ***higher*** *ends* もっと高い目的を持つ. ¶ for ***partisan*** *ends* 党利のために. ¶ gain a ***political*** *end* 政治上の目的を達する. ¶ solely to suit (=serve) their own ***personal*** *ends* 全く彼らめいめいの目的に適合するように. ¶ Men seldom flatter without some ***private*** *end* in view. 人がおもねる時は大がい下心がある. ¶ labor for ***public*** *ends* 公共のために働く. ¶ achieve the ***same*** *end* 同一目的を達する. ¶ serve one's own ***selfish*** *end* 自分だけのためになることをやる. ¶ The theatre serves a ***social*** *end*. 演劇は社会のために奉仕する. ¶ This will serve a ***useful*** *end*. これで有益な成果があがる. ¶ use some field of knowledge for profitable ***utilitarian*** *ends* 有益な目的のためにある種の知識を使用する. ¶ It serves a ***valuable*** *end*. これは一面から見て効果がある. ¶ aid him to the utmost of their power in the movement for such ***worthy*** *ends* そうしたりっぱな目的のための運動に彼らが力

の及ぶ限り彼を助ける.【類】serve two *worthy ends.*

P They are *after* the same *end.* 彼らは同一目的を追求している. ¶*for* selfish *ends* 利己的な目的で ‖ *For* what *end?* 何の目的で. ¶means *to* an *end* 目的を達するための手段 ‖ *to* that *end* その目的を達するために ‖ *to* this *end* recourse has been had to ... この目的を達するために...の手段が取られた.【類】utilize it *to* one's own *ends.* ¶*with* this *end* in view この目的を掲げて.

(2) 端, 末, 終り, 最後; 死.

V *approach* an *end* 終りに近づく. ¶He *deserves* no *end* of praise for his noble deed. 彼はそのりっぱな行為に対して限りない称賛に値する. ¶It *does* no *end* of mischief. それはどこまでも害になる. ¶Reading *furnishes* no *end* of pleasure. 読書によって無限の愉快が得られる. ¶*give* an *end* to it その始末をつける ‖ He *gave* us no *end* of a spread.《口語》彼は私に山海の珍味を出した. ¶*hold* one (the other) *end* of the rope ロープの(今一つの)端を握る. ¶*have* an *end* 終了する. ¶*join end* to end 端と端とをつなぐ. ¶*knell* the *end* of ... ...の終末をつげる. ¶*make* an *end* of ... ...を終える.【類】I know that he is as widely hated as feared, and I wonder why some earnest young patriot does not *make* an *end* of him through assassination. ‖ *make* his *end* easy 彼の死に際をよくする. ¶fail to *make* [both] *ends* meet 収支をあわせられない, やりくりがつかない.【類】He has much difficulty to *make* both *ends* meet. / struggle to *make* both *ends* meet / They have great difficulties in *making* both *ends* meet. / He is trying to *make* both *ends* meet on a small salary. ¶He *met* his *end* (=died). 彼は最期を遂げた. ‖ *meet* an untimely *end* 悲業の死を遂げる. ¶*pack up* one's *ends* and awls 家財道具を荷造してさっさと出て行く. ¶*put* an *end* to one's existence 命を捨てる ‖ *put* an *end* to his career 彼の一生を終る. ‖ He resolved to *put* an *end* to his days (=life) by committing suicide. 彼は自殺をしてこの世を去ろうと決心した. ‖ try to *put* an *end* to one's mental suffering by hanging 首つりして精神の苦痛を脱しようとする.【類】Death *put* an *end* to his views and prospects. / An urge *put* an *end* to reason. / The Government is determined to *put* an *end* to this intolerable situation. (忍ぶべからざる局面) / *put* an *end* to a trouble / *put* an *end* to an argument / *put* an *end* to war. ¶*reach* the *end* of a railway journey 汽車旅行の終点に着く. ¶*see* the *end* of it 最後を見届ける. ¶*take* no *end* of pleasure in ... ...に無限の喜びを感じる ‖ *take* no *end* of trouble to ... ...のため骨身を惜しまない.

Q attract tourists from *all ends* of the earth 世界中から観光客を引きつける. ¶at the *back end* of the year 年末に. ¶get the *better end* of ... ...に勝つ(まさる). ¶a contest to the *bitter end* あくまでやる闘争. ¶the *blunt end* of a chopper 包丁のまくれ刃先. ¶The *end* is still *far* to see. なお前途ほど遠い. ¶come to a *happy end* めでたしめでたしで終る. ¶These expenses left him with scarcely a shilling in his pocket at the *journey's end.* かく物入りが多かったので旅行を終えた時彼の財布には一シリング足らずの金しか残らなかった. ‖ come to (=reach) one's *journey's end* in life 人生の終点に着く(死ぬ). ¶at the *latter end* of a hard week 苦しい一週間の終りに.【類】at the *latter end* of the summer. ¶follow it to its *logical end* それを徹底的に追求する. ¶cause a person *no end* of trouble 人に限りなく迷惑をかける ‖ There is *no end* to it. きりがない. ‖ He was *no end* disappointed at the news. そのニュースを聞いてひどく失望した. ¶a person on (=at) the *other end* of the line 電話の相手方. ¶the *proper end* of art 芸術の本領. ¶a *small end* of a candle ろうそくの燃え残り. ¶at the *southern end* of the road 道の南の端に. ¶bring it to a *successful end* それを首尾よく終らせる. ¶the *thin end* of a wedge くさびの刃 ‖ get (=drive) in the *thin end* of a wedge 見かけは小さいようで実は重大なことをやり始める. ¶the *top end* of a pole 棒の先(うら). ¶come to a *tragic end* 悲劇に終る. ¶He met (=came to) an *untimely end.* 彼は若死をした. ¶from the *uttermost ends* of the earth 世界のすみずみから. ¶he met with a *violent end* at the hands of ... 彼は...の手にかかって非業の最期を遂げた. ¶The physician seemed to be at his *wit's* (=*wits'*) *end.* 医者は途方に暮れていたようだった. ¶approach a subject from the *wrong end* 問題をあべこべの方から着手する. ¶Please investigate the matter at *your end.* そちらで取調べてください. ‖ the railway station at *this* (*your*) *end* 当方の(あなたの)発駅.

Q[2] on her *beam ends* [船が]真横に傾いて ‖ go on one's *beam ends* 万策つきる. ¶at the *broadcasting* (*listening*) *end* 放送(聴衆)側で. ¶the *business end* of a knife ナイフの刃の方. ¶a *butt end* [巻きタバコの]燃えさし. ¶*cigarette end* 巻きタバコの燃えさし. ¶the *fag end* of a cigar《英》葉巻のもえさし. ¶the *manufacturing end* of the wool business 羊毛事業の生産側. ¶at the *tail end* of August 八月の末に.

P *about* the *end* of the present month 今月の末ごろ. ¶The strike is *at* an *end.* 罷業は終りを告げた. ‖ My horizon seemed black and all things *at* an *end.* 私の前途は暗たんとして万事休したように思われた. ‖ appear to be *at* an *end* もう終りらしい.【類】The day's work was almost *at* an *end.* / *at* the *end* of 25 days / *at* the *end* of the accounting period / *at* the *end* of the working day / *at* the *end* of seven years ‖ if left unredeemed *at* the *end* of ... [質物など]...の末に受出さないと ‖ apparently *at* the *end* of his resources 明らかに万策尽きて ‖ a silver watch *at* the *end* of a chain 鎖の端につけた銀時計 ‖ have it *at* one's fingers' *ends* それを熟知している ‖ *At* the *end* of his solo, another started one of his own. 彼の独奏が終ったのでもう一人が独奏を始めた. ¶*by* the *end* of the third quarter of 1931 一九三一年の九月末までに. ¶*from* one *end* of the country to the other 国内を通じて ‖ The information has been scattered *from* an *end* of the earth to the other. その報道は世界中に吹聴された. ‖ *from end* to end 端から端まで ‖ *from* year's *end* to year's end 年がら年中 ‖ advices *from* your *end* ご通知. ¶*in* the *end* of the 16th century and the early part of the seventeenth 十六世紀の末葉から十七世紀の初期にわたって. ‖ All will come right *in* the *end.* 結局万事都合よく行くだろう. ‖ He found it cheaper *in* the *end* to marry her. 彼は彼女と結婚するのが結局安上りに行くと悟った. ¶He is *near* his *end.* 彼は死にかかっている. ¶My hair stood *on end* with fright (=horror). 私はおそろしさに身の毛がよだった. ‖ for hours *on end* (=at a stretch *or* together) 数時間ぶっ通しに.【類】sleep hours *on end* / for as many as forty-eight hours or more *on end.* ¶*since* the *end* of the war (=war's end) 終戦以来. ¶look *through* the wrong *end* of a telescope 望遠鏡を逆にのぞく. ¶hope *to* the *end* いつまでも望んでやまぬ ‖ These things are mysteries, and mysteries they remain *to* the *end* of the chapter. これらの事は神秘である, そしてその神秘は終りまで解けないのである. ‖ The event will not be forgotten *to* the *end* of his days by any one who witnessed it. それを目撃した者は一生忘れないだろう. ‖ That will remain a secret *to* the *end* of time. それは永久に秘密となっていることだろう. ‖ resist up *to* the *end* 最後まで抵抗する ‖ thrilling down *to* the very *end* [小説など]最後の一ページまで興味しんしんたる ‖ Go *to* the *end* of this alley and turn right there. この通りをつき当ったら右へ曲りなさい. ¶*towards* the *end* of 1898 一八九八年の末つ方.【類】*towards* the *end* of the present month. ¶*until* the *end* of time 時の終りまで. ¶*with* no *end* of practical uses 無限の実用性のある. ¶*without end* 限りなく ‖ a story *without* an *end* 終りのない話.

P[2] the *end of* a book 巻末 ‖ the *end of* a controversy 議論の結末 ‖ the *ends of* the earth 地球の果 ‖ the *end of* the year 年末 ‖ This cough will be the *end of* me. 僕はこのせきに命を取られるだろう. ‖ That would be the *end of* the chapter. それで万事休すだ. ‖ You'll be the *end of* me. お前は私の命とりとなるだろう. ‖ if ..., there is an *end of* scientific anthropology もし...すると科学的人類学なるものの存在がなくなって仕舞う ‖ That's the *end* [*of* it]. それまでだ. ‖ he took no *end of* trouble to ... 彼はまごころこめて...した. ¶It means an *end to* poverty. そうすれば貧乏は根絶する. ‖ there is really no *end to* the list of ... ...は実際枚挙にいとまあらずだ.

end, *v.* 終る, 完結する.

M The hero of this novel *ended badly.* この小説の主人公は悲劇に終った. ¶It *ended disastrously.* それは悲惨な結末をつげた. ¶Two cases of cholera, one of which has *ended fatally,* have occurred here. 当地にコレラ患者が二人出てその一人は命を取られた. ¶It *finally ended* in a failure. それは結局失敗に終った. ¶The story *ended* ***happily***. その物語はめでたしめでたしで終った. 【類】all *ends* ***happily*** in her restoration to her parents and her marriage with ... / Everything *ended* ***happily***. ¶I forgot ***how*** the story *ended*. その話のおしまいがどうなっているか忘れた. ¶*end* ***quite unexpectedly*** 突然終了する. ¶The poll *ended* ***unsuccessfully***. 投票の結果は失敗だった. ¶The war is ***virtually*** *ended* 戦争は事実上終っている. ¶All is well that *ends* ***well***. 終りがよいのがよい.

M[2] If you continue to steal, you'll *end* ***up*** in prison. 盗みを続けるなら, 末は刑務所行きだ. ‖ *end* ***up*** before a minister 結婚の式をあげるということでけりがつく. ‖ He set the box there, *end* ***up***. 彼は箱をさかさに据えた.

P He will *end* ***by*** marrying her. 彼はしまいには彼女と結婚することになるだろう. ‖ he *ended* ***by*** remarking that ... 彼は最後に...と述べた ‖ he will *end* ***by*** falling in love with ... 彼はしまいに...と恋に落ちることになるだろう. ¶That affair will *end* ***in*** his dismissal. あの事件は彼の解雇でけりがつくだろう. ‖ He will *end* ***in*** being punished. 彼は罰せられることになるだろう. ‖ a protracted debate, finally *ending* ***in*** nothing being done 結局徒労に帰す長談議(小田原評定) ‖ This softening of the brain would *end* ***in*** madness. この精神機能の低下が結局狂気ということになるだろう. 【類】It *ended* ***in*** a complete cure. / Such an effort is almost sure to *end* in disaster. / *end* ***in*** total failure / *end* ***in*** fiasco (failure, smoke, sobs, nothing) ‖ iniquitous pleasures, which often *end* ***in*** death しばしば死に終る不義の快楽 ‖ The negotiation *ended* ***in*** a rupture. 交渉は不調に終った. 【類】The titanic struggle (大戦闘) has *ended* ***in*** a victory so glorious for our army. ‖ The incident *ended* ***in*** a hearty laugh. その出来事は大笑に終った. ‖ The match between ... and ... *ended* ***in*** a draw. ...対...の仕合は無勝負に終った. ‖ The enterprise *ended* ***in*** smoke. 計画は煙と消えた. ¶The book *ends* ***with*** a summary and its conclusion. その本は要約とその結論で終っている. ‖ The story *ends* ***with*** the familiar "all lived happy ever after." その小説は例の「めでたしめでたし」で結んである. ‖ We started with soup and had ice-cream to *end* ***up with***. [晩さんが]スープで始まり, 終りがアイスクリームであった.

endanger, *v.* 危険にさらす.

M ***How much*** his life was then *endangered*, nobody knew. 彼がどんなに危険な状態であったかはだれも知らなかった.

P His health is *endangered* ***by*** overwork. 彼は過労で健康を害している.

endear, *v.* かわいがる.

P He *endeared* himself ***to*** all his friends. 彼は友だちみんなにかわいがられた. ‖ His inexpressibly charming smiles *endeared* him ***to*** all who knew him. 彼の微笑には何とも言えない愛きょうがあったので彼を知っている人にはだれにでもかわいがられた.

endearment, *n.* ちょう愛.

P The young mother lavished kisses ***of*** *endearment* upon her baby. その若いお母さんはかわいさのあまり赤ちゃんにやたらとキスした.

endeavo[u]r, *n.* 骨折, 努力, 尽力.

V ***do*** one's *endeavor* 努力する. ¶***exert*** all the *endeavors* in one's power 力の限りを尽す. ¶***invoke*** their *endeavors* for the realization of the object 目的実現のために彼らの努力を喚起する. ¶an *endeavor* is being ***made*** to ... ...しようと努力している ‖ every *endeavor* has been ***made*** to ... ...しようとあらゆる努力をした. 【類】an *endeavor* should be ***made*** to ... ¶***paralyse*** *endeavor* 努力を無力化する. ¶***put forth*** his best *endeavors* to ... ...しようと彼の最善を尽す. ¶***redouble*** their *endeavors* to ... ...しようと彼らの努力を倍加する. ¶***stimulate*** healthy *endeavor* 健全なる努力を刺激する. ¶***use*** every *endeavor* できるだけ手を尽す.

Q ***active*** *endeavor* 進んでやる努力. ¶***altruistic*** *endeavors* 私心のない尽力. ¶"The fate of the Empire hangs solely on this battle, and all must use their ***best*** *endeavors*."「皇国の興廃この一戦にあり, 各員一層奮励努力せよ」. ¶a ***conscientious*** *endeavor* has been made to ... ...しようとまじめな努力が払われた. ¶It shall be our ***constant*** *endeavor* to relieve our neighbours of their cares and anxieties. われわれは隣人の苦労心配を取除くことに絶えず尽力しよう. ¶he made a ***desperate*** *endeavor* to ... 彼は...しようと必死に努力した ‖ be among the society's ***first*** *endeavors* 同協会の主な努力の一つである. ¶after some months spent in ***fruitless*** *endeavors* to ... ...しようと数カ月むだな努力したあげく. ¶***futile*** (= ***lost***) *endeavor* むだな骨折. ¶after ***heroic*** *endeavors* 勇敢な努力の後で. ¶in an ***honest*** *endeavor* to ... ...しようと正直に努力して. ¶every field of ***human*** *endeavor* 人間活動のあらゆる方面 ‖ these branches of ***human*** *endeavor*—hunting and fishing 人間活動のこれらの方面—狩猟と漁業. ¶my ***humble*** *endeavor* is to show ... 私が微力をいたしているのは...ということを示したいためである. ¶my ***main*** *endeavor* will be to show that ... 私は主として...ということを示すことに努めましょう. ¶a ***meretricious*** *endeavor* まやかし的な努力. ¶it has been ***our*** *endeavor* to ... われわれは...することに努力してきた. ¶the ***pioneering*** *endeavors* 先駆者的努力. ¶use all ***possible*** *endeavors* できるだけ尽力する. ¶a ***serious*** *endeavor* has been made to ... ...するためにまじめに尽力した. ¶make a ***strong*** *endeavor* to ... ...するために大いに努力する. ¶the embodiment of half a century's ***unremitting*** *endeavor* 半世紀にわたるたゆみない努力の結晶. ¶***unselfish*** *endeavor* 私心のない努力. ¶use one's ***utmost*** *endeavors* to ... ...しようとできるだけ努力する. ¶in the ***vain*** *endeavor* to ... ...しようとのむだな骨折に.

Q[2] ***group*** *endeavor* 集団的努力.

P ***in*** my *endeavors* to ... ...しようとする私の努力において.

P[2] an *endeavor* ***at*** improvement 改善(進歩)しようとの努力. ☞今では an *endeavor* to improve または an *endeavor* to make improvement を多く用いる. ¶*endeavor* ***by*** word or deed 言葉または行為による努力. ¶my *endeavors* ***towards*** facilitating the study of the English language in Japan 日本における英語研究を容易ならしめようとする私の努力.

endeav[u]or, *v.* 努力する.

M ***energetically*** *endeavor* to attain its object その目的を達成するため大いに努力する. ¶*endeavor* ***honestly*** to ... ...しようと正直に努力する. ¶***steadfastly*** *endeavor* to avoid it それを避けようと不断の努力をする.

P *endeavor* ***after*** wealth (happiness, eminence) 富(など)を得ようと骨を折る. ☞*endeavor* ***at*** または *endeavor* ***for*** は古体.

endemic, *a.* 特有の; 風土性の.

P a disease *endemic* ***in*** ... ...に特有の病気.

ending, *n.* 終了, 結末.

Q A ***good*** *ending* is better than a good beginning. 始めよきより終りよきがよし. ¶The novel has a ***happy*** *ending*. その小説はめでたしめでたしで終っている. 【類】come to a ***happy*** *ending*. ¶an ***inflectional*** *ending* 屈折語尾. 【類】***Inflectional*** *endings* are still found in abundance in German nouns or French verbs. ¶a ***sad*** *ending* 悲しい最後.

Q[2] ***chess*** *endings* 色々な将棋の詰め方.

endorse, indorse, *v.* 裏書する; 保証する.

M his advocacy of ... was ***heartily*** *endorsed* 彼の...の唱道は心から賛同された. ¶The book is ***highly*** *endorsed* by prominent people. その本は有名な人々によって推奨されている.

P It is *endorsed* ***by*** the public opinion. それは世論によって裏書されている. ¶*endorse* one's name ***on*** a note 手形の裏書をする. ¶*indorse* a document ***with*** a signature = indorse one's name on a document 署名して文書に裏書する.

endorsement, *n.* 裏書; 是認.

V ***give*** an unofficial *endorsement* 非公式に是認する. ¶The theory has ***received*** the *endorsement* of excellent scholars. その説はりっぱな学者たちの承認を得た. ¶***sign*** an *endorsement* 裏書署名する.

P[2] *endorsement* ***to*** a plan ある案への賛成.

endow, *v.* 寄付する, 補助金を与える; 賦与する.

M he is ***especially*** *endowed* by nature for ... 彼は生れながらにして特に...の才能を賦与されている. ¶This country is ***favorably*** *endowed* climatically. この国は気候の点で恵まれている. ¶He is ***highly*** (= ***richly***) *endowed*. 彼は天分豊かに授かっている. ‖ ***highly*** *endowed* by nature with literary talent 大いに文才に恵まれた. ¶Her beauty made her the envy of many less ***lavishly*** *endowed*. 彼女は美人なのでそれほど美しさに恵まれていない多くの人たちのうらやみの的となった. ¶***plentifully*** *endowed* with strong common sense しっかりした常識を豊かに恵まれて. ¶a man ***richly*** *endowed* by nature 天分豊かな人. ¶a man ***singularly*** *endowed* with original ideas 珍しく独創的な人.

P be *endowed* ***by*** nature ***with*** genius 生来天分に恵まれている. 【類】a man *endowed* ***by*** nature ***with*** the inventive mind (発明心). ¶He was *endowed* ***with*** the power of acute observation. 彼は鋭敏な観察力を賦与されていた. 【類】a mind which was *endowed* ***with*** powers of no common order / *be endowed* ***with*** sound common sense / Man is *endowed* ***with*** reason. / their only daughter, aged twenty-one, *endowed* ***with*** remarkable beauty and grace / *endowed* ***with*** wit and beauty ‖ *endow* a hospital ***with*** a fund 病院に基金を寄付する ‖ was *endowed* ***with*** a fief of ... *koku* of rice ...石の領土に封ぜられていた.

endowment, *n.* 寄付金, 補助金; 天賦の才.

V ***establish*** *endowments* 基本金を設ける. ¶a munificent *endowment* was ***given*** by ... 多額の寄付が...によってなされた.

Q his ***extraordinary intellectual*** *endowments* 彼の非凡な知的才能. ¶possess ***natural*** *endowments* 天才を有する. ¶supported by ***philanthropic*** *endowment* 慈善寄付金によって維持されて. ¶The colleges have ***various*** *endowments.* それらの大学には色々な基金がある.

P The hospital is ***under*** an *endowment.* その病院は寄付金で維持されている.

P² The Smithsonian Institution was founded by an *endowment* ***from*** James Smithson, an Englishman. スミスソニアン協会(米国国立博物館)は英国人のゼームス・スミスソン氏の寄付金をもって設立された. ¶the gift of an *endowment* ***of*** a professorship of German to the University of Cambridge ケンブリッジ大学におけるドイツ語講座基金の寄付.

endurance, *n.* 忍耐, 我慢; 持続.

Q ***exhaustless*** *endurance* 無尽蔵な忍耐力. ¶a burden of ***fifty years'*** *endurance* 五十年間の苦痛. ¶His life was one of ***heroic*** *endurance.* 彼の一生は雄々しい忍苦の一生であった. ¶***muscular*** *endurance* 肉体上の耐久力.

P It is almost ***beyond*** (=***past***) *endurance.* それはほとんど忍び難い.

P² the *endurance* ***of*** the weak やせ我慢.

endure, *v.* 忍ぶ, 我慢する.

M *endure* ***patiently*** 我慢強く忍ぶ. ¶He will no longer *endure* it ***quietly.*** 彼はもうそれをじっとして堪えていないだろう. ¶*endure* ***ungrudgingly*** the pangs of labor 甘んじてお産の苦しみに耐える.

P Few of the runners *endured* ***to*** the finish. 最後までがん張った走者はほとんどなかった.

enema, *n.* かん腸剤.

V ***give*** (=***administer***) an *enema* to ... ...にかん腸を施す. ¶***take*** an *enema* かん腸剤を用いる. ¶***use*** an *enema* every day 毎日かん腸剤を用いる.

enemy, *n.* 敵, 敵軍.

V ***attack*** an *enemy* 敵を攻撃する. ¶***check*** the *enemy* 敵を食止める. ¶***circumvent*** the *enemy* 敵を出し抜く. ¶***conciliate*** *enemies* 敵をなだめる. ¶***conquer*** an *enemy* 敵に勝つ. ¶***defeat*** an *enemy* 敵を破る. ¶***dislodge*** the *enemy* from his position 敵兵をその陣地から駆逐する. ¶***disperse*** the *enemy* 敵軍を四散させる. ¶The army ***drove*** the *enemy* before it. その軍は敵を排して前進した. ¶***drive away*** an *enemy* 敵を駆逐する. ¶***drive out*** the *enemy* 敵を追出す. ¶***engage*** an *enemy* 敵と戦う. ¶The soldiers ***faced*** the *enemy* bravely. 兵士は勇敢に敵軍に向った. ¶***Know*** thy *enemy.* 敵を知れ. ¶If you say that, you will ***make*** an *enemy* of my wife. 君がそれを言うと僕の妻を敵にするようなことになる. ‖ He denounced it with such boldness as ***made*** him many *enemies.* 彼は大胆にそれを非難したので多くの敵を作った. ¶We ***pressed*** the *enemy* for the evacuation of the fort. 敵を圧迫して要さいを撤退させた. ¶***punish*** an *enemy* 敵をやっつける. ¶***put*** the *enemy* to flight 敵を壊乱させる. 【類】The *enemy* was ***put*** to rout. ¶***rout*** the *enemy* 敵を敗走させる. ¶***scent*** an *enemy* 敵のありかをかぎつける. ¶***spoil*** an *enemy* 敵の物を略奪する. ¶***strike*** (=***take***) the *enemy* in the rear 敵の背後を突く ‖ ***strike*** the *enemy* to the quick 敵に痛撃を加える. ¶The *enemy* was ***surprised.*** 敵は不意打を食った. ¶***take*** the *enemy* by surprise 敵の不意を襲う. ¶***turn*** an *enemy* into an ally 敵を味方につける.

V² An *enemy* is ***coming on.*** 敵が近づきつつある.

Q ***alien*** *enemies* 敵国人. ¶Fire is an ***arch*** *enemy* of man. 火事は人間の大敵である. ‖ his ***arch*** *enemy* and detractor 彼の大敵であり誹謗(ひぼう)者たるもの. ¶his ***avowed*** *enemies* 彼の公然の敵. ¶He is a good friend and a ***bad*** *enemy.* 彼は味方としてはたのもしく敵としては恐ろしい. ¶a ***bitter*** *enemy* うらみ重なる敵. ¶our most ***deadly*** *enemies* われわれの不倶戴(たい)天のあだ. 【類】the ***deadliest*** *enemy.* ¶Smallpox is a ***formidable*** *enemy.* 痘そうは恐るべき敵である. ¶The barroom is the ***great*** *enemy* of the home. 酒場は家庭の大敵. ¶a ***hereditary*** *enemy* of the family 家代々の敵. ¶an ***implacable*** *enemy* 執念深い敵. ¶***indefatigable*** *enemies* 根気強い敵. ¶an ***inexorable*** *enemy* がん迷な敵. ¶an ***invisible*** *enemy* 見えない敵(心の敵). ¶a ***long-time*** *enemy* of communism 共産主義という長期にわたる敵. ¶***main*** *enemies* 主な敵. ¶one's ***mortal*** *enemy* 不倶戴天の敵. ¶a ***mortal*** and ***bloody*** *enemy* 残虐な敵. ¶a ***mysterious*** *enemy* なぞの敵. ¶a ***national*** *enemy* 国民の敵. ¶a ***natural*** *enemy* 天敵. ¶an ***open*** *enemy* to Christianity キリスト教の公然の敵. ¶a ***parasitic*** *enemy* しし身中の虫. ¶a ***personal*** *enemy* 一身の敵. ¶a ***powerful*** *enemy* 強力な敵 ‖ condemn a ***public*** *enemy* to death 公敵を死刑に処する. ¶Kiyomasa was a ***relentless*** *enemy* of Christianity. 清正はキリスト教の大敵であった. ¶a ***secret*** *enemy* 秘められた敵. ¶he is a ***severe*** *enemy* of ... 彼は...には大反対である. ¶a ***sworn*** *enemy* 宿敵. ¶the machinations of an ***unscrupulous*** *enemy* 不法きわまる敵の謀略. ¶A ***wise*** *enemy* runs for his life. 利口な敵は三十六計の手を使う. ¶The advocates of a cause are often its ***worst*** *enemies.* ある主義の擁護者は往々その主義の最悪の敵たることがある.

Q² ***insect*** *enemies* こん虫という敵.

P defend ***against*** the *enemy* 敵を防ぐ ‖ took up arms ***against*** the *enemy* 敵に対抗してほこを取った. ¶fire ***at*** the *enemy* 敵に発砲する. ¶fly ***before*** an *enemy* 敵に後を見せる. ¶make a dashing attack ***on*** the *enemy* 敵を襲撃する ‖ make war ***on*** an *enemy* 敵を攻める. ¶He has gone over ***to*** the *enemy.* 彼は敵に合流した. ‖ desert ***to*** the *enemy* 敵側に走る. ¶fight ***with*** an *enemy* 敵と戦う.

P² the *enemy* ***from*** within (without) 内(外)からの敵. ¶an *enemy* ***of*** that very cause 主義そのものの敵 ‖ an *enemy* ***of*** (=to) a person ある人の敵. ¶an *enemy* ***to*** success (peace) 成功(など)の敵. 【類】an *enemy* ***to*** society (mankind) ‖ an *enemy* ***to*** tyranny, either in church or state 教権または政権における暴虐の敵 ‖ He is an *enemy* ***to*** work. 彼は仕事がきらいだ. 【類】He is no *enemy* ***to*** wine.

energetic, *a.* 元気おう盛の.

M He is ***constitutionally*** *energetic.* 彼は生来元気盛んだ. ¶be *energetic* ***enough*** to ... ...するほど張切っている.

P be *energetic* ***to*** the uttermost 極度に張切っている.

energy, *n.* 精力, 元気.

V This ***absorbs*** his *energy.* 彼はこの仕事に没頭している. ¶Such possibilities ***await*** our *energies.* われわれの活動にはかゝる将来性がある. ¶***bend*** its *energies* to the support of ... ...の維持にその精力を傾注する ‖ ***bend*** every *energy* to securing money 金策にあくせくする ‖ ***bend*** one's *energy* on (=upon) ... ...に精力を集中する. ¶***blight*** the *energies* of the nation 国民の元気をくじく. ¶***concentrate*** one's *energies* on ... ...に精力を集中する. ¶***consolidate*** its *energies* in ... その精力を...に集中する. ¶***damp*** one's *energy* 元気をくじく. ¶***dedicate*** immense *energy* to ... ...に多大の精力をささげる. ¶***devote*** one's chief *energies* to the task of ... 主として...の仕事に身をゆだねる. ¶***direct*** one's *energies* to ... ...に精力を向ける ‖ Let your *energies* be ***directed*** into the channels of constructiveness. 君の精力を建設の方面に向け給え. ¶***display*** indomitable and unremitting *energy* うまずたゆまぬ精力を示す. ¶***dissipate*** *energy* in worry 気に病んで精力を消耗する. 【類】***dissipate*** our *energies* upon ... ¶***divert*** one's *energy* to more useful channels その精力をより有益な方面に振り向ける. ¶***employ*** one's *energies* in study 学問に精力を使う. ¶***exert*** one's *energies* 精力をふるう. ¶***expend*** one's surplus *energies* upon ... ...に余力を費す ‖ ***expend*** (=***use up***) *energy* without restoring it by rest=burn the candle at both ends 精力を使い果す. ¶***exhibit*** *energy* 元気を見せる. ¶***gather*** reserve *energy* 振いたつ. ¶the work to which he has ***given*** his best *energies* 彼が最大の精力を傾けた事業. ¶***harness*** the sun's *energy* for industrial purposes 太陽エネルギーを工業に利用する. ¶he ***has*** not *energy* enough to ... ...彼には...するだけの元気がない. ¶a movement ***lacking*** *energy* 活気を欠いている運動. ¶***reestablish*** (=***restore***) *energy* to the tired body 疲れた体の元気を回復する. ¶***relax*** one's *energies* when at leisure 骨

休めをする. ¶***rouse*** all one's *energies* 元気を振い起す. ¶The work has ***sapped*** his *energy*. その仕事で彼は精力を使い果した. ¶***show*** one's *energy* in ... ...で元気を示す. ¶***stimulate*** the *energies* 元気を鼓舞する. ¶***summon energy*** to its aid その加勢のために元気を出す. ¶***tax*** the *energies* of ... ...の精力をしぼらせる. ¶He ***throws*** *energy* into everything that he does. 彼は何んでも自分のやることに精力を傾注する. ¶***waste*** our *energies* upon ... ...にわれわれの精力を浪費する.

Q ***atomic*** *energy* 原子エネルギー. ¶production of ... horse-power of ***electric*** *energies* ...馬力の電力発動 ‖ various applications of ***electrical*** *energy* 種々の電力応用. ¶the ***feeble procreative*** *energy* of the parents その両親の虚弱な生殖力. ¶carry on with ***feverish*** *energy* 熱狂的元気でやる. ¶***fiery*** *energy* 盛んな元気. ¶***high*** *energy* 高度のエネルギー. ¶show ***indefatigable*** *energy* in ... ...に不屈の精力を示す. ¶a man of most ***indomitable*** *energy* and imperious will 不屈の精力と覇気(はき)とを有する人. ¶***mental*** and ***physical*** *energy* 心身の精力. ¶Call it ***misdirected*** *energy* if you will. それが血気にはやるものと言わば言え. ¶***misspent youthful*** *energies* むだな青年の血気. ¶***initial*** *energy* 初勢. ¶appliances of ***nuclear*** *energy* 種々の核エネルギー応用器具 ‖ the peacetime possibilities of ***nuclear*** *energy* 核エネルギー平時利用の使い道. ¶the ***potential*** *energy* of uranium 235 ウラン二三五の想定エネルギー. ¶***resilient*** *energy* 屈しない元気. ¶a man of ***restless*** *energy* うむことを知らない活動家. ¶***spiritual*** *energy* 気力. ¶His *energy* is ***unbounded***. 彼は精力絶倫だ. ¶***unflagging*** *energy* 衰えを知らざる元気. ¶with ***unremitting*** *energy* たゆまぬ精力で. ¶The successful carrying out of the scheme is largely due to his ***untiring*** *energy*. その計画の成功は彼のうむことを知らない精力に負う所が多い. ¶***vivid*** *energy* はつらつたる元気. ¶***wasted*** *energy* むだ骨. ¶at a trifling expense of ***well-directed*** *energy* 統制よろしきを得て大した骨も折らずに.

Q^2 ***nerve*** *energy* 精根. ¶***Transportation*** *energy* by rail and steamship has been increasing three times as rapidly as production proper. 汽車・汽船の輸送力は生産力その物の三倍に増加している.

P He has succeeded ***by dint of*** *energy*. 彼は精力によって成功した. ¶full ***of*** *energy* 元気一杯, 張切って ‖ He devoted much ***of*** his *energy* to the propagation of the principles. 彼はその主義の普及に多大の精力を用いた. ¶***through*** their own *energy* and enterprise 彼ら自身の精力と進取的気性とで. ¶He worked ***with*** *energy*. 彼は元気に働いた. ‖ return to one's studies ***with*** redoubled *energy* 更に旧に倍する元気で再び勉強を始める.

P^2 Thanks to the *energy* ***of*** its originator, the scheme of founding the club has at last been realized. その発起人が精を出したお陰でクラブ新設の計画が実現された.

enervate, *v.* 弱くする.

P become *enervated* ***by*** the luxury of palace life 豪華な宮殿生活で無気力になる. ¶He is *enervated* ***with*** (=***from***) dissipation. 彼は放とうで体をこわした.

enfeeble, *v.* 弱くする.

P a mind *enfeebled* ***by*** old age 年で弱くなった気力.

enfeeblement, *n.* 衰弱.

Q ***intellectual*** *enfeeblement* 知力衰退.

enforce, *v.* 実施する.

M ***rigidly*** (=***strictly***) *enforce* a rule 規則を励行する ‖ Discipline was ***rigidly*** *enforced*. 規律は励行されていた. ¶***rigorously*** *enforce* laws 法を厳正に施行する. ¶have the laws ***rigorously*** and ***impartially*** *enforced* 法を厳正公平に実施させる.

P The law was *enforced* ***to*** the letter. その法律は文字通りに実施された.

enforcement, *n.* 実施, 励行.

Q California is one of the few States that have a sterilization law in ***actual*** *enforcement*. カリフォルニア州は不妊法を実施している少数の州の一だ. ¶The station received ***considerable*** *enforcement*. そのとん所は相当兵員増強があった. ¶a ***rigid*** *enforcement* 励行. ¶a ***strict*** *enforcement* of the law 法律の励行. ¶the ***vigorous*** *enforcement* of the law 法律の励行 ‖ ordered the ***vigorous*** *enforcement* of laws against the Christians キリスト教徒弾圧の法令の強力な施行を命じた.

Q^2 ***law*** *enforcement* 法律執行.

enfranchisement, *n.* 特権授与.

Q women's ***political*** *enfranchisement*=the political enfranchisement of women 婦人への参政権授与.

engage, *v.* 約束する; 婚約する; 雇う; たずさわらせる; たずさわる, 保証する; 戦う.

M be ***actively*** *engaged* in the teaching of English 英語教師として活躍している. 【類】He was ***actively engaged*** as a social reformer (社会改良家). ¶He is ***busily engaged*** upon a book. 彼はある本の著作で忙しい. 【類】I have been ***busily*** *engaged* all this month. ‖ be ***busily engaged*** in phoning 忙しそうに電話をかけている. ¶My time is ***fully engaged***. 私は暇が全然ない. ¶he is ***hotly engaged*** in ... 彼はひたむきに...をやっている. ¶I am very ***much*** *engaged*. 私は非常に忙しい. ¶thousands of hands are ***ordinarily*** *engaged* on ... 常に数千人が...に従事している. ¶Here and there in the Russian provinces I met Englishmen ***successfully engaged*** in trade. 私はロシアのいなかで折々りっぱに商売をしている英人に会った. ¶I am *engaged* ***today*** at five o'clock. 今日五時に約束がある.

P *engage* ... ***as*** a guide (clerk, teacher, an engineer) ...を案内者(など)に雇う. ¶while *engaged* ***at*** this occupation この仕事に従事している間に ‖ He is *engaged* ***at*** a shop (bank, hotel). 彼は商店(など)に雇われている. ‖ I have *engaged* rooms ***at*** the hotel. そのホテルに室を取っておいた. ‖ He was *engaged* ***at*** a salary of 10,000 yen. 彼は一万円で就職した. ¶*engage* a carriage ***by*** the hour (distance) 馬車を時間(など)で雇う. ¶I *engaged* her ***for*** the position. 僕はその仕事に彼女を雇った. ‖ I am *engaged* ***for*** everything—my programme is quite full. 私は何のかのと約束があって予定は一杯になっている. ‖ That's more than I can *engage* ***for***. それは私としてはお約束しかねる. ‖ he has been *engaged* ***for*** several years ***upon*** a memoir of ... 彼は数年間...の回顧録について執筆中だ. 【類】I am *engaged* ***for*** tomorrow. ‖ *engage* ***for*** his honesty 彼の正直なことを保証する. ¶He was *engaged* ***from*** abroad. 彼は外国から招待したのだ. ¶He was *engaged* ***in*** the Government service for fourteen years. 彼は十四年間官吏生活をしていた. ‖ an investigator *engaged* ***in*** serious research 重大な調査に従事している研究家. ‖ he was *engaged* ***in*** a controversy on the subject with ... 彼は...とその問題について論戦した ‖ he was *engaged* ***in*** animated conversation with ... 彼は...と元気に話をしていた ‖ *engage* ***in*** contest 勝負をする ‖ *engage* ***in*** warfare with ... ...と戦争する ‖ an incident occurred which threatened to *engage* us ***in*** hostilities with ... 今にもわれわれを...との戦争の渦中に巻き込みそうな事件が起った. 【類】He is *engaged* ***in*** business. / be *engaged* ***in*** conversation / He is *engaged* ***in*** official duties (公務). / a gentleman *engaged* ***in*** business / *engage* ***in*** other employment / *engage* ***in*** mercantile pursuits (商業) / The English Government does not allow its officials to *engage* ***in*** trade. / Owing to the high cost of living more women will *engage* ***in*** industry than in the past. / *engage* ***in*** labor / *engage* ***in*** politics (art) / be *engaged* ***in*** charitable work (慈善事業) / he was *engaged* ***in*** the work of ... / *engage* ***in*** a fruitless effort (むだ骨) / I am *engaging* ***in*** writing an article. / The rest of the world was *engaged* ***in*** a life-and-death struggle (命がけの戦い). ‖ *engage* ***in*** the cause その目的に奔走する ‖ I do not *engage* myself ***in*** such affairs. 僕はそんなことに関係しない. ¶He is at present *engaged* ***on*** a work. 彼は目下著述に従事している. 【類】He has been long *engaged* ***on*** that book. / he is *engaged* ***on*** a volume, the subject of which is ... / He is at present *engaged* ***on*** a new edition (改訂) of his dictionary. / a subject ***on*** which I have been *engaged* for some years / The architect, Mr. ..., has been *engaged* ten years ***on*** the work. / One task ***on*** which he is *engaged* is of the greatest interest to classical scholars. / be *engaged* ***on*** an undertaking of this kind ‖ he was until lately *engaged* ***on*** the staff of the ... 彼は近ごろまで...紙の編集に関係していた ‖ a housewife *engaged* ***on*** the family wash うちのものを洗たくしている細君 ‖ ***On*** what terms are you *engaged?* どんな条件で雇われているか. ¶*engage* a man-servant ***through*** an employment agency 職業安定所の手をへて下男を雇う. ¶He is *engaged* ***to*** a girl. 彼はある少女と婚約ができている. ‖ *engage* himself ***to*** her to be married 彼女と婚約をする ‖

He *engaged* himself ***to*** a merchant. 彼は商人に雇われる約束をした. ‖ I am *engaged* ***to*** dinner (party). 晩さん(会)の約束がある. ¶*engage* ***upon*** a work [著述家などが]著述に従事する. 【類】complete the various literary ventures ***upon*** which he is *engaged* / persons *engaged* ***upon*** the dictionary ‖ He was *engaged* ***upon*** the construction of the railway lines. 彼はその鉄道の敷設工事に従事していた. ¶be *engaged* ***with*** Mr. T T氏に雇われる ‖ At present I am *engaged* ***with*** the revision of that book. 目下僕はその本の改訂に従事している. 【類】he is busily *engaged* ***with*** preparations for ... ‖ the enemy I had to *engage* [***with***] 私が戦うことになった敵 ‖ He has been *engaged* ***with*** the company. 彼はその会社に雇われた. ‖ I *engaged* ***with*** him that ... 私は彼と...のことを約束した. ‖ The teeth in one wheel *engage* ***with*** those of another. 一の歯車の歯がも一つの歯車の歯とかみ合う.

engagement, *n.* 約束, 約定; 婚約; 用務; 交戦.

V I am open to ***accept*** *engagements.* 私は約束に応じることができる. ¶Their *engagement* was ***announced*** in the newspapers. 両人の婚約は新聞紙上で発表された. ¶The artiste ***booked*** an *engagement* with the syndicate. その芸人はその企業組合と契約を結んだ. ¶***break*** a tennis *engagement* for a meeting 会があるのでテニスの約束を取消す ‖ ***break*** [***off***] one's *engagement* 婚約を破棄する. 【類】He ***broke off*** his *engagement* to her. ¶***call off*** (=break) an *engagement* [結婚]を破約する. 【類】I know you will understand that only imperative and unexpected business would have made me ***call off*** our *engagement.* ¶All *engagements* will be faithfully ***carried out.*** 約束はことごとく忠実に履行します. 【類】be quite capable of ***carrying out*** all *engagements.* ¶The singer ***completed*** her *engagements* in London. 歌手はロンドンでの契約を取りきめた. ¶***declare*** an *engagement* ***off*** 契約を取り消す. ¶***fulfil*** one's *engagement* 約束を履行する. ¶***have*** another *engagement* 外に約束がある ‖ I ***have*** an *engagement* to fulfil. 僕は約束がある. 【類】I ***have*** an *engagement* today at five o'clock. ‖ We ***had*** an *engagement* with the enemy yesterday. きのう我軍は敵軍と会戦した. ¶***keep*** one's *engagement* to ... ...との約束を守る. 【類】return to ... by train to ***keep*** an *engagement*. ¶He ***met*** his *engagement*. 彼は約束を履行した. ¶The manager ***offered*** her an *engagement* of one performance. 興行者が彼女に一興行の相談を持出した. 【類】He has been ***offered*** *engagements* at the most famous halls in London and New York. ¶The theatrical company will ***open*** an *engagement* at the Imperial Theatre on January 15. その劇団は一月十五日から帝劇で興行をやる. ¶The opera company ***played*** an *engagement*. 同歌劇団は契約ができて一興行やった. ¶***secure*** an *engagement* with a company 会社に職を得る. ¶The screen actor has ***taken*** an *engagement* with the ... company. その映画俳優は...会社と契約ができた. ¶The *engagement* of the managing director has been ***terminated.*** 専務理事の任期が満ちた.

Q enter into a ***binding*** *engagement* 契約を結ぶ. ¶a ***broken*** dinner *engagement* すっぽかした晩さん会出席の約束. ¶a ***definite*** *engagement* 確固たる約束. ¶had a ***fierce*** *engagement* with ... ...と激戦を交えた. ¶be open to no ***further*** *engagements* これ以上雇用契約には応じられない(芸能人など). ¶I have an ***important*** *engagement* at four o'clock. 私は四時に大事な約束がある. ¶an ***international*** *engagement* 国際協定. ¶a ***naval*** *engagement* off Salamis サラミス沖の海戦 ‖ a decisive ***naval*** *engagement* 運命を決する海戦. ¶They announced that their *engagement* was ***off***. 彼らは婚約取消しの発表をした. ¶Owing to ***pressing*** *engagement*, I am unable to attend. 差迫った用事があるので私は来られません. ¶A ***previous*** *engagement* prevents my attendance. 先約があるので参られません. ¶He discovered afterwards that he had a ***prior*** *engagement* on the same date. 彼は後になって同日先約があったのに気が付いた. ¶a ***sanguinary*** *engagement* 血戦. ¶I have many ***social*** *engagements* to fill. たくさん社交上の約束がある.

Q² a ***dinner*** *engagement* 正さんの約束 ¶a ***land*** and ***sea*** *engagement* 陸海戦. ¶I have a ***luncheon*** *engagement* with ... ...と昼食を一しょにする約束がある. ¶his ***speaking*** *engagements* in Tokyo 東京における氏の演説予約 ‖ He cancelled all the ***speaking*** *engagement* ***for*** the next week. 彼は翌週の演説の約束を全部取消した. 【類】hurry to a ***speaking*** *engagement* (演説の約束の場所).

P ***after*** a naval *engagement* 海戦後に. ¶I was prevented ***by*** a previous *engagement*. 私は先約に妨げられた. ¶withdraw ***from*** an *engagement* 約束を取消す. ¶***on account of*** a previous *engagement* 先約のため. ¶keep ***to*** one's *engagement* 約束を守る.

P² an *engagement* ***for*** meeting with ... ...と会見の約束. ¶*engagement* ***in*** business 商売に従事すること. ¶the *engagement* ***of*** Miss. ... ***to*** Mr. ... ...氏と...嬢との婚約. ¶be ***under*** an *engagement* with ... to ... ...することは...と約束済みである. ¶a theater's *engagement* ***with*** actors 劇場と俳優との契約 ‖ Keep your *engagement* ***with*** me. 僕との約束を守って下さい. ¶an *engagement* ***with*** a firm (company, an office) 会社(など)の職.

engine, *n.* 機関, 機械; 機関車.

V The *engine* is ***driven*** by steam. その機関は蒸気で動く. ¶***pull out*** an *engine* 機関車を引き出す. ¶The *engine* can be ***regulated*** at pleasure. その機械は自由に調節ができる. ¶***reverse*** an *engine* 機械を逆転させる. ¶***run*** an *engine*=《米》operate a locomotive 機関車を運転する. ¶***set*** the *engine* at work 機関を運転させる. ¶***start*** the *engine* [車の]エンジンをかける.

V² The *engine* has ***broken down***. 発動機が破損した. ¶The *engine* ***came*** to a standstill. 機械が止まった. ¶The *engine* ***goes*** by gas. その発動機はガスで動く. ¶The *engine* ***plowed*** [its way] through the streets. 消防のポンプが街上の群集をのけながら進んだ. ¶The *engine* ***runs*** day and night. 機械は昼夜運転する. ¶The *engine* ***wheeled*** to the scene of fire. 蒸気ポンプが火事場へ出動した.

Q an ***air-cooled*** *engine* 〘航空〙空冷式エンジン. ¶an ***automotive*** *engine* 自動推進機. ¶an ***economical*** *engine* 経済的なエンジン. ¶Shinto was often used as a ***political*** *engine*. 神道はよく政治的道具に使われたものだ. ‖ The atomic bomb is an extremely ***powerful*** *engine* of destruction perfected in 1945. 原爆は一九四五年に完成した超強力な破壊器具である. ¶a ***rotary*** *engine* 回転式エンジン. ¶a ***semi-portable*** *engine* 半移動式エンジン. ¶a ***stationary*** *engine* 固定式エンジン.

Q² an ***air*** *engine* 〘空〙航空発動機. ¶a ***blowing*** *engine* 送風エンジン. ¶a ***condensing*** *engine* 復水機関. ¶a ***fire*** *engine* 蒸気ポンプ. ¶a chemical ***fire*** *engine* 化学消火ポンプ. ¶an "Otto" ***gas*** *engine* オットー式ガスエンジン. ¶***gas***, ***petrol***, and ***oil*** *engines* ガス, ガソリン石油及び重油によるエンジン. ¶a ***gasoline*** *engine* ガソリン機関車. ¶a ***high-pressure*** *engine* 高圧エンジン. ¶a ***hoisting*** *engine* 巻き上げエンジン. ¶a "Buckett" ***hot-air*** *engine* バケット式熱風エンジン. ¶a ***jet*** *engine* 噴射(ジェット式)エンジン. ¶a ***jet-condensing*** *engine* 噴射式復水機関. ¶a ***locomotive*** *engine* 機関車. ☞英は主に engine, 米は locomotive を多く使っている. ¶a ***man*** *engine* 鉱山用人員昇降機. ¶a condensing ***marine*** *engine* 復水船舶機関. ¶a ***pumping*** *engine* 大型往復ポンプ. ¶a ***reversing*** *engine* 逆転エンジン. ¶a ***right-hand*** (***left-hand***) *engine* 右(左)ねじ機関. ¶a horizontal ***screw*** *engine* 水平ねじ切りエンジン. ¶***self-regulating wind*** *engine* 自動調節式風力エンジン. ¶***single-cylinder*** horizontal *engine* 単一シリンダー水平エンジン. ¶a ***steam*** *engine* 蒸気機関; 蒸気機関車 (=a steam locomotive). ¶a ***steam fire*** *engine* 蒸気ポンプ. ¶a ***traction*** *engine* トラクター. ¶a ***three-cylinder*** *engine* 三気筒エンジン. ¶a ***vertical*** *engine* 垂直エンジン. ¶a ***water-pressure*** *engine* 水圧エンジン. ¶a ***wildcat*** (=a runaway) *engine* 暴走機関車. ¶a ***winding*** *engine* 巻き上げ機.

engineer, *n.* 技師, 技手; 《米》機関士.

Q an ***assistant*** *engineer* 技手. ¶a ***chief*** *engineer* 技師長; 〘船〙機関長. ¶a ***civil*** *engineer* 土木技師. ¶a ***consulting*** *engineer* 顧問技師. ¶an ***electrical*** *engineer* 電気技師. ¶an ***inspecting*** *engineer* 監督技師. ¶a ***marine*** *engineer* 造船技師. ¶a ***mechanical*** *engineer* 機械技師. ¶a ***sanitary*** *engineer* 衛生技師.

Q² an ***air*** *engineer* 航空技師. ¶an ***Army Construction Engineer*** 陸軍土木建築技師. ¶a ***city*** *engineer* 都市土木技師. ¶a bogus ***efficiency*** *engineer* いんちき能率技師. ¶a ***forest*** *engineer* 森林技師. ¶an ***irrigation*** *engineer* かんがい技師. ¶a ***locomotive*** *engineer* 《米》=an engine driver 《英》機関士. ¶a ***mining*** *engineer* 鉱山技師. ¶a ***production*** *engineer* 生産技師. ¶a *research enginner* 研究技師. ¶a *sales engineer* 販売部技師. ¶a *water engineer* 水道技師. ¶a *water-works engineer* 水道技師.

P² an *engineer to* the docks その造船所の技師 ‖ an *engineer to* the corporation 同会社専属の技師.

engineering, *n.* 工学; 工業; 管理.

Q *agricultural engineering* 農業土木. ¶*architectural engineering* 建築工学. ¶*civil engineering* 土木工学. ¶*electrical engineering* 電気工学. ¶*human engineering* 人物経済. ¶*industrial engineering* 産業管理. ¶*mechanical engineering* 機械工学. ¶*military engineering* 軍事工学(工兵学). ¶*practical engineering* 応用工学. ¶*rural engineering* 農耕学. ¶*textile engineering* 紡績学.

Q² *construction engineering* 建設工学. ¶*mining engineering* 採鉱工学. ¶*railroad engineering* 鉄道工学. ¶*road engineering* 道路工学.

England, *n.* 英国.

Q "*Merrie England*" すばらしい英国. ☞ merrie は古くは mere といった Anglo-Saxon 語の形容詞で excellent, illustrious, famous, *or* renowned の意. ¶*young England* 若い者の英国.

English, *n.* 英語, 英文.

V *brush up* [on] one's *English* 英語をやり直す(みがきをかける). ¶*correct* one's *English* その英語を直す. ¶*dish up* students' *English* 学生の英語を添削する. ¶*improve* one's *English* 英語の力を伸ばす. ¶I *know* a little *English.* 私は英語を少し知っている. ¶*learn English* under a foreign teacher 外人教師から英語を習う. ¶*mishandle* (=*murder*) the King's *English* 間違った英語を使う. ¶*perfect* one's *English* 英語の力を完成する. ¶*possess English* as speech 英語の活用ができる. ¶He *speaks English* well. 彼は英語を達者に話す. ¶the power of *speaking* and *writing English* accurately 正確に英語を話し英文をつづる力. ¶*study English* for one's own interest (for one's profession) 趣味で(商売上)英語を学習する. ¶*try* one's *English* on (=upon) a foreigner 外人相手に英語を使って見る.

Q *American* (*British*) *English* 米(英)国英語. ¶in *bad broken English* 悪い間違った英語で. ¶speak most *beautiful English* beautifully 実に見事な英語を見事に話す. ¶It has a flavour of *Biblical* or *Shakespearian English.* それは聖書またはシェークスピアの使った英語の風韻を備えている. ¶speak *broken English* めちゃくちゃな英語を話す. ¶in *ceremonious English* 四角張った英語で. ¶be written in *clear concise English* 簡潔な英語で書いてある. ¶*colloquial English* 口語体の英語. ¶*conversational English* 会話体の英語. ¶write *correct* and *winsome English* 正確で感じのよい英文を書く. ¶*dead* (*living*) *English* すたれた(現代)英語. ¶speak *excellent English* 見事な英語を話す. ¶*false English* 間違っている英語. ¶in *faulty English* 間違った英語で. ¶in *fluent* and *polished English* 流ちょうな洗練された英語で. ¶write *forceful* and *lucid English* 力強く明白な英文を書く. ¶in *foreign* (=*foreigners'*) *English* 他国なまりの英語で. ¶in *formal* (*informal*) *English* 正しい(くだけた)英語で. ¶The story is told in *good English.* その物語はりっぱな英語で書いてある. ¶in *graceful English* 優雅な英語で. ¶*grammatical English* 文法にかなった英語. ¶*idiomatic English* 語法にかなった英語. ¶it is *incorrect English* to say "..." ...と言うのは正しい英語でない. ¶"the *King's English*" and "the *President's English*" いわゆる国王の英語(英国語)と大統領の英語(米国語). ¶*literary English* 文語体の英語. ¶write and speak *masterly English* 達者に英語を話し英文をつづる. ¶speak *nice, stiff, correct English* りっぱで堅苦しい正確な英語を話す. ¶*Old* (*Middle, Modern*) *English* 古代(中世, 近世)英語. ¶It is *normal English* to say: I *will* ... "I will ..." というのは正しい英語だ. ¶in *plain English* this means that ... 分りやすい英語で言えば...ということになる. ¶write in *plain, grammatical, forcible English* 分りやすい, 文法に合った力強い英文で書く. ¶learn *practical English* 実用英語を学ぶ. ¶*printable English* 出版しても恥かしくない英文. ¶*printed English* 印刷した英文. ¶*proper English* 正しい英語. ¶*pure English* 純正英語. ¶expressed in quite *readable English* すらすらと読める英語で表現して. ¶*slipshod* (=*slovenly*) *English* ぞんざいな英語 ‖ the *slovenly English* of so many modern writers 多くの近代作家が書く整わない英語. ¶*spoken English* 口語の英語. ¶works written in *standard English* 標準英語で書かれた作品. ¶*terse* and *vigorous English* 簡潔で力のある英文. ¶*unconventional English* 型破りの英語. ¶speak *ungrammatical English* 文法に合わない英語を使う. ¶*unliterary English* くだけた英語. ¶*up-to-date English* 現代英語. ¶*vigorous* and *arresting English* 力強い魅力のある英語. ¶*vulgar English* 下品な英語. ¶reply in *well-rounded English* 巧みな英語で答える. ¶*World Standard English* 世界の標準英語. ¶*written English* 文語の英語.

Q² the writer of *everyday English* 日常英語を書く人. ¶professors of *graduate* and *undergraduate English* 大学及び大学院の英語教授たち. ¶*pidgin English* ピジョンイングリシュ(中国・メラネシヤなどの). ¶in *present-day English* we do not normally say, "..." 現代英語では「...」というのは普通使わない. ¶*schoolbook English* 教科書の英語. ¶*World English* "Britannic" 世界英語ブリタニック.

P The earliest newspapers *in English* were printed in Amsterdam in 1620. 一番古い英字新聞は一六二〇年にアムステルダムで刊行された. ‖ What is this called *in English?* これは英語で何といいますか. ‖ He is quite at home *in English.* 彼は英語はお手のものだ. ‖ We make it a rule to converse *in English* with each other. われわれは英語で話し合うことにしている. 【類】excellence *in English* / He improved much *in English.* / I can make myself understood *in English.* ¶I turned this *into English.* 僕がここを英訳した. ¶He has a good command *of English.* 彼は英語が自由だ. ¶get on *with English* 英語が進歩する.

P² What is the *English for* "..."?「...」の英語は何ですか. ¶"John" is the *English* [equivalent] *of* the French "Jean." フランス語の "Jean" は英語では "John" に当る.

Englishman, *n.* 英国人.

Q a *John-bullying Englishman* ジョンブル気取りの(英国人らしい)英国人. ¶He became a *naturalized Englishman* in 1907. 彼は一九〇七年に英国に帰化した. ¶a *true-hearted Englishman* きっすいの英国人.

engraft, ingraft, *v.* 接木する, 移植する.

P *engraft* an idea *in* the mind 思想を心に植えつける. 【類】Honesty and thrift are *engrafted in* his character. ¶Peach trees can be *engrafted upon* plum trees. 桃の木はすももの木につぎ木ができる.

engrave, *v.* 彫る, 彫刻する.

M It is *indelibly engraved* on the memory. それは(消えないように)深く心に銘している.

P It is *engraved from* a photograph. それは写真から彫刻したのだ. ¶*engrave in* mezzotinto メゾティント版にする. ¶*engrave* designs *on* copper (wood, stone) 意匠を銅(など)に彫る ‖ classical texts *engraved on* stone 石に刻んだ古文. 【類】his posthumous name (戒名) *engraved on* the tomb ‖ It is *engraved on* my memory. 私はそれをよく覚えている. ¶*engrave* a stone *with* designs 模様を石に彫る ‖ The stone wall is *engraved with* dates ranging from 1571 to 1586. 石がきには一五七七年より一五八六年に至る年号が彫ってある. 【類】It is *engraved with* letters (figures).

engraver, *n.* 彫版師.

Q² a *steel engraver* 鋼版彫版師.

engraving, 彫刻, 彫刻版, 鋼版彫刻術.

Q² *copperplate engraving* 鋼版彫刻術. ¶*steel engraving*

P² from an *engraving after* a painting by ... ...の描いた絵の彫刻版から. ¶the art of *engraving in* (=*on*) wood for the purpose of impression 木版術.

engross, *v.* 独占する; 夢中にする.

M He is *deeply engrossed* in the development of the invention which has made his name famous. 彼は自分の名をあげた発明の改良に夢中になっている. ¶He is *thoroughly engrossed* in his studies. 彼は勉強に夢中だ. ¶She appeared *totally engrossed* in the subject before her. 彼女は当面の問題にすっかり夢中になっているようだった.

P My morning was *engrossed by* the garden. 僕は庭いじりで朝が丸つぶれになった. ¶He is *engrossed in* his work (business, game). 彼は仕事(など)に夢中だ. 【類】be *engrossed in* political work / while *engrossed in* conversation. ¶get *engrossed with* one's work 仕事に熱中する.

engulf, *v.* 巻き込む.

P *engulf* a person *in* much misfortune 人を大きな不幸の中に巻き込む.

enigma, *n.* なぞ.

Q an *insoluble* (=*a puzzling*) *enigma* 難解のなぞ.

P[2] It is an *enigma to* foreigners. それは外国人には不可解なことだ.

enjoin, *v.* 命じる; 禁じる.

P *enjoin* him *from* infringing others' rights 彼に他の権利を侵害せぬように言付ける. ¶*enjoin* diligence (honesty) *on* pupils 生徒に勉強(正直に)するように命じる ‖ *enjoin* a duty *on* a person 人に義務を課する ‖ *enjoin on* (=*upon*) children the duty of obedience to parents 子供らに孝順の義務をさとす.

enjoy, *v.* 楽しむ, 享楽する.

M The show was over before we could *fully enjoy* it. ショーはもっと見たいというところで幕になった. ¶We *heartily enjoyed* the feast. われわれはごちそうを十分頂だいた. ‖ *enjoy* oneself *heartily* with... ...で心から楽しむ. 【類】We *enjoyed* the game *heartily.* ¶*How* did you *enjoy* the concert? 音楽会はどうでした. ¶*enjoy* works of art *intuitively* and *instinctively,* not *critically* 芸術品を批判的でなく直覚的・本能的に賞美する. ¶I *quite enjoyed* myself. 私は全く面白かった. ¶I can *rather enjoy* Japanese music. 私はどっちかというと和楽が好きだ. ¶I *enjoyed* myself *thoroughly* (=*very much or to the full*). 私はとても面白かった.

P *enjoy* oneself *over* one's wine 楽しく酒を飲む.

O *enjoy* good health (music, longevity) 健康(など)を楽しむ.

enjoyment, *n.* 快楽, 娯楽, 享楽.

V *afford* the highest intellectual *enjoyment* 最も高尚な知的快楽を与える. ¶*block* one's *enjoyment* of ... ...の喜びのじゃまをする. ¶The parents appear to *derive* quite as much *enjoyment* as the children. 両親も子供ら同様に面白がっているようだ. ¶*enhance enjoyment* 楽しさを増す. 【類】*enhance* the *enjoyment* of a journey. ¶*find* no *enjoyment* in ... ...を面白く思わない. ¶*furnish enjoyment* to ... ...に楽しみを与える. ¶*get enjoyment* out of life 人生を楽しむ. ¶The play has *given* me great *enjoyment.* その芝居は大層面白かった. ¶*heighten* the *enjoyment* of ... ...の感興を高める. ¶*provide enjoyment* 娯楽を供する.

Q read and re-read with *ever-growing enjoyment* 度の重なるにつれ興を増していくども読み返す. ¶The old man is in the *full enjoyment* of his mental faculties. その老人は少しももうろくしていない. ‖ whilst in *full enjoyment* of ... 楽しみの最中, 歓楽たけなわの時. 【類】wild animals in the *full enjoyment* of their native freedom (生来の自由). ¶derive *immense enjoyment* and stimulus from ... ...から多大な喜びと刺激を得る. ¶*intellectual enjoyment* of the highest order きわめて高級な知的快楽. ¶with an *intense enjoyment* 熱烈な喜びをもって. ¶give *keen enjoyment* 非常な快楽を与える. ¶very *lively enjoyment* きわめて活発な娯楽. ¶Some say that there is not *much enjoyment* in a game of cards with a man unless one gambles. かけなくてはトランプ遊びは大して面白くないという人がある. ¶Here I settled down to the *placid enjoyment* of watching their floats. ここで落着いて私は静かにうきを見つめていた. ¶for their own *selfish enjoyment* 彼らの自分勝手の快楽のために. ¶He pronounced all *sublunary enjoyments* to be "vanity." 彼は現世の快楽はことごとく「空」であると言った. ¶He has been in the *uninterrupted enjoyment* of the best health. 彼は引続いて壮健であった. ¶*vulgar enjoyments* 卑俗な快楽. ¶He is fond of *worldly enjoyments.* 彼は現世の快楽に恋々としている.

Q[2] *teaching enjoyment* 教えることの喜び.

P I hope you are *in* the *enjoyment* of good health. 御壮健を祈る. ‖ *in* the *enjoyment* of luxuries undreamed of in their own homes 自分の家では夢にも見ないぜいたくをして. ¶I can read a novel in French *with enjoyment* and a fair understanding. 私はフランス語の小説を面白くまた相当の理解をもって読める.

enlarge, *v.* 増大する; 拡張する; 〖写真〗引伸ばす; 詳説する.

M it is not necessary to *enlarge further* to show that ... ...を説明するにはこれ以上詳述の要はない. ¶photographs *twice* enlarged from the most satisfactory of the pictures 一番できのよいのを二倍大に引延ばした写真.

P a photograph *enlarged from* the original 原撮りを引伸した写真. ¶The magazine will be greatly *enlarged in* number of pages. その雑誌は大いにページ数を増すことになる. ¶He followed up and *enlarged on* the work his father had so nobly begun. 彼はその父があんなにりっぱに創始した事業を引継いでこれを拡張した. ‖ it is not necessary to *enlarge on* the importance of ... ...の重要性は今さら説く必要はない. 【類】*enlarge on* one's favorite subject / *enlarge on* this by saying that ... ¶The dictionary has been *enlarged to* 1,500 pages. その辞書はページ数が増して千五百ページになった. ‖ Ten years ago the house was *enlarged to* the present size. この家屋は十年前に現在の大きさに増築した. ¶I had no need to *enlarge upon* it. それをくどくどしく私が言う必要はなかった.

enlargement, *n.* 〖写真〗引伸ばし; 拡張.

V *give enlargement* and sobriety to the ideas of the age その時代の精神を拡大しかつ合理化する. ¶*make* an *enlargement* of a building 建物の増築をする.

Q a *life-size enlargement* of a photograph 写真の実物大引伸ばし. ¶a plant capable of *subsequent enlargement* 拡張可能な工場.

P[2] *enlargement of* a site (premises) 敷地(建物)の拡張.

enlighten, *v.* 啓発する.

M if any one wishes to be *thoroughly enlightened,* let him read up ... 完全に真実を知ろうとする者は...を読み給え.

P this information was sufficient to *enlighten* me *as to* ... この報道は...に関して僕を啓発するに十分であった. ¶*enlighten* the ignorant *on* ... ...の点で無知の人々を啓発する.

enlightenment, *n.* 啓発, 啓もう, 光明.

V *attain* supreme *enlightenment* 大悟徹底する ‖ *attain* a philosophical *enlightenment* 悟りを開く. ¶I *gained* a good deal of *enlightenment* from ... 私は...から大いに悟る所があった. ¶This will *give* some *enlightenment.* これで幾分その間の消息がわかる. ¶*need enlightenment* with regard to some word ある語の真の意味を知ろうと欲する. ¶*seek* further *enlightenment* さらに研究を進める. ¶the wave of *enlightenment radiating* from the film 映画から発射する啓発の波.

Q *complete enlightenment* 大悟. ¶possess *perfect enlightenment* 大悟徹底している.

P work *for* the *enlightenment* of mankind 人類の啓もうのため働く ‖ The information is useful *for* the *enlightenment* of Americans landing in England. その事は英国に上陸する米人が知っていて参考になる.

enlist, *v.* [兵士などを]募集する; 招請する; 応募する; 味方に加わる(加える).

P *enlist for* a soldier (volunteer) 一兵士(など)として応募する ‖ He *enlisted for* active service in the war. 彼はその戦争に出征した. ‖ *enlist for* military service 兵役に服する. ¶*enlist in* the army (navy) 入隊する. 【類】be *enlisted in* military service / *enlist in* the United States Army / *enlist in* (=join) the regular forces (常備軍) / The vessel has been *enlisted in* the Standing Squadron (常備艦隊) ‖ *enlist in* a faction 徒党に加わる ‖ *enlist* one *in* an enterprise (a cause) 事業(など)に人を加入させる ‖ *enlist in* the cause of justice 正義のために尽そうとする ‖ *enlist* one's sympathies *in* the cause of charity 慈善事業に人の同情を得る. ¶*enlist* him *into* the service of the company 彼を会社に雇入れ(社員にす)る. ¶he *enlisted* himself *under* the banners of ... 彼は...の旗下に付いた. ¶He saw service in Cuba and then *enlisted with* the 30th infantry of regulars. 彼はキューバで実戦を経験してから第三十歩兵常備隊に加わった.

enlistment, *n.* 兵籍編入.

V *nullify enlistment* 籍を取消す.

Q *extended enlistment* 再服役.

P *since* his *enlistment* last January 去る一月入営以来.

enliven, *v.* 活気をつける, 景気をつける, 勢づける.

P *enlivened by* the spirit of competition 競争心に駆られて. ¶The journey was *enlivened with* songs. 旅行が歌で勢づいた. ‖ a scene *enlivened with* singing, dancing, and music 歌や舞踊や音楽でにぎやかな場面 ‖ The conversation was *enlivened with* jokes. 話は冗談で活気がついた. 【類】The text (文本) is *enlivened with* comic sketches.

enmesh, *v.* 網にかける.

P be *enmeshed in* the web of ... ...のわなにかかる.

enmity, *n.* 恨み, 反目, 不和.

V *breed* life-long *enmity* 終生の恨みをかもす. ¶*fear* the *enmity* of newspapers 新聞紙の反目を恐れる. ¶*harbor enmity* against ... ...に恨みをいだく. ¶I *have* no *enmity* against ... 私は...には何の恨みもない. ¶*incur* the *enmity* of ... ...の恨みを買う. ¶*stir up enmity* 不和を起す.

Q incur his *bitter enmity* 彼の痛烈な恨みを買う. ¶his *in-*

veterate and *inappeasable enmity* to ... ...に対する彼の根深く, なだめようのない敵意.

P be *at enmity* with ... ...とは犬猿(えん)の仲である. 【類】The Jews were *at* (=*in*) *enmity* with the Samaritans.

P² *enmity against* ... ...への反感. ¶the *enmity between* the two persons 両人の反目.

ennui, *n. F.* けん怠, 無聊(ぶりょう).

V *cause ennui* 惰気を催す. ¶*chase away* one's *ennui* けん怠を払う. ¶*dispel* one's *ennui* ねむけを覚ます. ¶*relieve* the *ennui* of a traveler 旅情を慰める.

P I was relieved *from ennui* by reading. 僕は読書で退屈をしのいだ.

P² the *ennui of* a wealthy and unemployed class 仕事のない富豪階級の無聊.

enough, *n.* 十分.

V He never *has enough*. 彼は足ることを知らない. ‖ I have *had* quite *enough*. 十分頂戴しました. ‖ He *had enough* to do. 彼は結構仕事があった. ¶I feel that I have *had enough* of ... ...が鼻につく. 【類】I've had *enough* to *say* about it. / They *have* not *enough* of food. ¶*Enough* has been *said*. 十分言うだけの事は言った.

enough, *a., ad.* 十分な, 十分に.

M *curiously enough* 妙なことには. ¶It isn't *far enough* to be worth hiring a motor-car. 自動車を雇うほど遠くはない. ¶The salary is *just enough* to live. 給料はわずかに生活ができるだけだ. ¶*often enough* 相当ひんぱんに.

P provisions *enough for* ten days 十日分の糧食. 【類】It is *enough for* five days. ‖ *enough for* some purpose ある目的を果すに十分な. 【類】Have you money *enough for* the journey?

O They are not fools *enough* to think so. 彼らはそう考える程のばかでもない. ¶Be good *enough* to shut the door. 戸をしめて下さい.

enquire, *v.* =inquire.

enquiry, *n.* =inquiry.

enrage, *v.* 怒らせる.

M I was *terribly enraged* with him. 僕は彼に対して大いに立腹した.

P He was *enraged against* his opponent (enemy). 彼は敵対者(など)に対して立腹していた. ¶He was *enraged at* the insult (remark). 彼はその侮辱(など)を立腹していた. ¶He is *enraged with* me. 彼は私に対して立腹している.

enrapture, *v.* うっとりさせる.

P He is *enraptured with* this stroke of good fortune. 彼はこの思いがけない幸運に有頂天になっている.

enrich, *v.* 富ます.

P *enrich* one's vocabulary *by* careful reading 注意深く読書して語彙を増す. ¶*enrich* one's experiences *with* foreign travel 外国旅行で見聞を広める ‖ be *enriched with* three hundred illustrations 三百枚のさし絵で引立っている ‖ *enriched with* vitamine B complex ビタミンB複合体で強化された(栄養剤など). 【類】*enrich* food *with* milk or butter.

enrichment, *n.* 豊富にすること.

Q *unjust enrichment* 不当利得.

Q² *soil enrichment* 土壌改良.

enrol[l], *v.* 登録する; 学籍(会員名)簿にのせる.

P *enroll* ... *among* the saints ...を聖徒に列する. ‖ He was *enrolled among* the ranks of the immortals. 彼は青史に不朽の名を留めた. 【類】be *enrolled among* leading businessmen. ¶*enroll* ... *as* a member ...を会員として登録する. 【類】Gentlemen desiring to be *enrolled as* members should send their names to the Secretary. / Please *enroll* me *as* an entrant (参加者) in the contest. ‖ All contestants must *enroll by* October 15, 1953. 競技参加者は1953年の十月十五日までにその名を登録しなければいけない. ¶*Enroll* me *for* associate membership in the American Asiatic Association for one year. 私を一カ年間米アジア協会の準会員として登録して下さい. ¶*enroll* ... *in* the army ...を兵籍に登録する ‖ *enroll* students *in* a school 学生を学籍に登録する ‖ students *enrolled in* a college 大学に入学した学生. 【類】students *enrolled in* ... classes / He *enrolled in* the correspondence course offered by the institution. / Barthelmess prepped at the now defunct Manor School, in Connecticut, and upon graduation *enrolled in* Trinity College, of the same state. ¶the names newly *enrolled on* the scroll of fame 新しく栄典にあずかった人々. ¶*enroll* him *on* their staff 彼を社員として採用する ‖ *enroll* him *on* the list of ... 彼を...の名簿に載せる. ¶*enroll* him *upon* the eligible register 彼を被選挙人名簿に登録する. ¶*enroll with* an employment agency 職業安定所に登録する.

enrol[l]ment, *n.* 名簿記入.

V Advance *enrollments* in the summer course in English are being *filed* in unusual volume. 英語夏期講習会への開期前申込は平常よりも多数に上っている. ¶The school *has* a total *enrollment* of 300. その学校の生徒総数は三百人. 【類】The college *had* an *enrollment* of 22,710 in 1928.

Q The school has a 15 per cent *larger enrollment* than last year. その学校の入学は昨年よりも一割五分も多い.

Q² The present *class enrollment* is 30. 現在クラス名簿に載っているのは三十名だ. ¶a *record enrollment* of students 最高記録の在籍学生数. ¶The *student enrollment* of Harvard was about 7,500 last year. ハーバード大学の昨年度学生総数は約七千五百人だった. 【類】a university with a *student enrollment* of 180,000.

P² The *enrollment at* the school this year is larger than it has ever been. その学校の入学者が本年はいつもになく多い. ¶a continuous increase *in enrollment* いよいよふくれる入学数. 【類】*Enrollments in* engineering, teaching, journalism, and architecture have fallen off, but *enrollments in* law, medicine, and dentistry are slightly up. ¶The fee should be paid *on enrollment*. 会費は入会の際納付して下さい.

en route, *F.* 途次.

P Sir William Young and Lady left London on Saturday for Liverpool, *en route for* Canada. ウイリアム・ヤング卿と同夫人はカナダへ渡航の途次去る土曜日リヴァプールへ向けロンドンを出発した. ¶*en route from* ... *to* ... ...から...への途次. ¶The letter was dated "*En route to* Honolulu." その手紙には日付の所に「ホノルルへの途次」と書いてあった.

ensconce, *v.* 落着かせる.

P They were soon *ensconced at* a hotel. 彼らは直にホテルに落着いた.

ensemble, *n. F.* 総体; 集団効果; 合唱, 合奏.

Q in *pleasing ensemble* 全体として気味よく感じられて. ¶They made a *splendid* and *harmonious ensemble*. それらが全体的にりっぱな調和のある効果を出した.

P lending life and beauty *to* the *ensemble* 全体に活気と美を添えて.

enshrine, *v.* 安置する.

P *enshrine* the divinity *in* a temple 神殿に御神体を安置する ‖ a memory *enshrined in* the heart 心に秘められた思い出.

ensign, *n.* 軍艦旗; 記章.

V the *ensign dropped* half-mast high 半旗点に下した軍艦旗. ¶*haul down* the *ensign* 軍艦旗をおろす. ¶*hoist* the *ensign* 軍艦旗を掲げる.

Q an *armorial ensign* of the Order その勲章の紋章.

Q² a *revenue ensign* [米国の]税関監視船旗.

enslave, *v.* 奴隷にする.

P He was *enslaved by* drink (the passions). 彼は酒(など)の奴隷となった. ‖ be *enslaved by* convention 因習にとらわれる. ¶He became *enslaved to* his own convention. 彼は自分の型にとらわれてしまった. ‖ He *enslaved* himself *to* avarice. 彼は貪欲の奴隷となった. ‖ *enslave* music *to* philosophy 音楽を哲学に隷属させる.

enslavement, *n.* 奴隷化.

Q² *mass enslavement* 大衆の奴隷化.

enslaver, *n.* 奴隷にする人.

Q a *fair enslaver* 男泣かせ.

ensue, *v.* 結果する.

P What will *ensue from* (=*on*) this? これはどんなことになるか.

ensure, *v.* 安全にする; 請合う, 保証する.

P The goods are *ensured against* (=*from*) risks. 商品には保険が付けてある. ¶His ability will *ensure* success *to* (=*for*) him. 彼は腕があるからきっと成功する.

entail, *v.* 残す, 伝える; 引起す, 及ぼす.

P *entail* inconvenience *on* a person 人に迷惑を掛ける ‖ *entail* disease *on* posterity 子孫に疾病を遺伝する. 【類】His intemperance (酒癖) will *entail* the curse of insanity *on* his innocent children.

entangle, *v.* からめる, 引っかける; もつれさせる.

M He is *inextricably entangled* with the affair. 彼はその事件と切っても切れない関係がある.

P be *entangled by* the charms and flattery of a bad woman 悪い女の魅惑と甘い言葉にひっかかる. ¶get *entangled in* the machinery その機械に引っかゝる ‖ *entangle* one's feet *in* briers いばらに足を引っかける. 【類】*entangle* a *person in* a labyrinth (迷宮) ‖ He was *entangled in* a plot. 彼は陰謀に巻込まれた. 【類】*entangle* fish *in* the meshes of a net (網の目). ¶ She was *entangled **with*** a man. 彼女はある男に引っかかった. ‖ The question is *entangled **with*** many others. その問題は多くの外の問題とからみ合っている.

entanglement, *n.* 紛糾.

Q It is independent of ***political** entanglements.* それは政治的紛糾とは無関係だ.

Q^2 ***barbed wire entanglements*** 鉄条網.

entente, *n. F.* 協約, 協商.

V ***cement*** the *entente* between them その間の親善を強固にする. ¶ ***form*** a military *entente* 軍事協約を締結する. ¶ ***further*** a still closer *entente* between the British Empire and France さらに英仏の親善を増す. ¶ ***promote*** an intellectual *entente* between ... and ... …間の知的協力(提携)を助成する ¶ ***strengthen*** the *entente cordiale* 親善を強固にする. ¶ ***upbuild*** *entente cordiale* 親善を図る.

Q a ***commercial*** *entente* 通商協約. ¶ It will go a long way towards the establishment of a ***real*** *entente cordiale* between Japan and the West. それは日本と西洋の真の親善を樹立する上に大いに貢献することとなろう. ¶ an ***unwritten*** *entente* 不文の同盟.

enter, *v.* 入る; 加入する, 参加する; 開始する; 入れる, 加入させる; 記入する; 差し込む; 提起する.

M the power of *entering* ***absolutely*** into the feelings of others 他人の感情を完全に会得しうる力. ¶ The sword *entered* ***deep***. 剣が深くささった. ¶ He *entered* ***deeply*** into the affair. あの人はその事件に深い関係があった. ¶ ***forcibly*** *enter* a private dwelling 個人の私宅に押入る. ¶ *enter* ***freely*** into society さかんに交際場裡(ᵓ)に入る. ¶ *enter* ***fully*** into the spirit of the book 本の精神にまで入り込む, 眼光紙背に徹する ‖ Into that subject it is impossible to *enter* ***fully*** here. その問題についてはここに詳説することはできない. ¶ *enter* ***further*** into particulars さらに委細をつくす. ¶ We *entered* ***heartily*** into the convivialities of the occasion. われわれは十分の祝賀気分が持てた. ¶ Barley *enters* ***largely*** into the peasants' diet. 大麦が主として百姓の常食になる. ‖ The chrysanthemum *entered* ***largely*** into all the ceremonies of the day. その日の儀式には大いに菊を用いた. 【類】 Music *enters* ***largely*** into the catalogue of London's worries. ¶ negotiations were ***officially*** *entered* into with ... …との交渉は正式に開始された. ¶ *enter* ***rudely*** into a room へやにずかずかはいって来る. ¶ *enter* a house ***unlawfully*** 家に押入る.

M^2 *enter* ***up*** 記入する.

P *enter* an action ***against*** ... …を相手取って訴訟を起す ‖ *enter* it ***against*** one's account それをだれだれの勘定につける. ¶ He was *entered* ***among*** the members. 彼は会員に加えられた. ¶ I will *enter* myself ***as*** a clerk. 私は自分を書記と記入しましょう. ¶ In 1501 Martin Luther was *entered* ***at*** the University of Erfurt, in Thuringia. 一五〇一年にマルチン・ルーテルはツーリンギァのエルフルト大学に入学した. ‖ We are unable to ascertain ***at*** what college he *entered*. 彼が何大学に入校したかははっきり分らない. ‖ *enter* ***at*** the principal doorway 表玄関からはいる. 【類】 *enter* [a house] ***at*** the gate (front door) ‖ Large quantities of cotton are *entered* ***at*** the port. その港で多量の棉花の入税手続がされた. ¶ *enter* ***by*** a window 窓からはいる ‖ *enter* ***by*** the back door (side gate) 裏口(など)からはいる ‖ He *entered* the room ***by*** stealth. 彼はそっとへやにはいった. ¶ *enter* ***for*** the examination その受験を申込む ‖ those who propose *entering* ***for*** the the examinations of ... 受験志望者 ‖ Six boats *entered* ***for*** the second race. 六隻のボートが二回目のレースに参加した. 【類】 *enter* ***for*** a competition (=contest) / Many competitors have *entered* ***for*** the prize (games, race). ¶ *enter* the house ***from*** the rear 裏から家にはいる. ¶ *enter* ***in*** the race 競走に加入する ‖ *enter* a name ***in*** the list 名を名簿に記入する ‖ *enter* the account ***in*** the journal 勘定を日記に記入する ‖ *enter* the item ***in*** the records of the office その事項を事務所の記録に載せる ‖ *enter* an item ***in*** a book (register) 事項を帳簿(など)に記入する. ¶ I am anxious to *enter* ***into*** correspondence with a Frenchman for mutual improvement in languages. 私はお互の語学上達の目的でフランス人と通信を開始したいと熱望している. ‖ *enter* ***into*** conversation with ... …と会話を始める ‖ She did not *enter* ***into*** my mood. 彼女は私の気分に乗って来なかった. ‖ The iron of war had *entered* ***into*** their souls. 戦争の苦しさが彼らの心にしみ込んだ. ‖ *enter* ***into*** commercial (public) life 商業界(など)に入る ‖ *enter* ***into*** an elaborate investigation 細密な調査を開始する. 【類】 *enter* ***into*** calculations of great nicety / The company *entered* ***into*** motion picture production in 1897. / *enter* ***into*** an enterprise / *enter* ***into*** the manufacturing business in competition with ... ‖ *enter* ***into*** a careful and patient investigation of ... …の念入りで根気のよい調査を始める ‖ *enter* ***into*** a state of war 戦闘状態に入る ‖ *enter* ***into*** business (politics) 実業界(など)に入る, 商売を始める ‖ *enter* ***into*** a war with ... …と戦争を始める ‖ *enter* ***into*** the comity of nations 列国と国際友好を結ぶ ‖ *enter* ***into*** partnership with ... …と共同事業を起す ‖ *enter* ***into*** a transaction on behalf of the company その会社を代表して取引をする ‖ *enter* ***into*** a treaty with ... …と条約を結ぶ. 【類】 *enter* ***into*** a contract with ... / *enter* ***into*** further controversy (更に議論) with ... / *enter* ***into*** negotiations with ... / *enter* ***into*** agreement for their mutual interests ‖ *enter* ***into*** an alliance with ... against ... …に対抗して…と同盟を結ぶ ‖ *enter* ***into*** relations with ... …とわたりをつける ‖ *enter* ***into*** amorous relations with ... …と情交関係を結ぶ ‖ *enter* ***into*** further details さらに詳細に説く ‖ This cannot be *entered* ***into*** in detail here. これはここには詳説することはできない. 【類】 *enter* ***into*** particulars ‖ *enter* ***into*** military service 軍務に服する ‖ He *entered* ***into*** the service of Nobunaga. 彼は信長に仕えた. ‖ *enter* ***into*** the bonds of matrimony 結婚生活に入る ‖ *enter* ***into*** this category この部類に入る ‖ *enter* ***into*** the bliss of Heaven 極楽往生をとげる ‖ The book has now *entered* ***into*** its fourth edition. その本は今度第四版が出た. ‖ The question does not *enter* ***into*** his calculation. 彼はその問題を眼中に置かない. ‖ He *entered* plump ***into*** the plan. 彼はすっかりその計画に乗気になった. ‖ We *entered* ***into*** the sport with zest. われわれは熱心にその競技に参加した. ‖ *enter* ***into*** the making of ... …製造の材料になる. 【類】 it *enters* ***into*** the manufacture of ... ‖ *enter* again ***into*** possession of ... 再び…の所有に帰す ‖ it *enters* ***into*** the composition of ... それは…の成分をなす ‖ *enter* ***into*** the presence of ... …と対面する ‖ *enter* ***into*** the spirit of a poem 詩の精神をつかむ. 【類】 The illustrator *enters* ***into*** the spirit of the text. ‖ Reason does not *enter* ***into*** the problem of spelling. つづりの問題は理屈ではない. ‖ *enter* ***into*** general use 一般化する ‖ The arrow *entered* ***into*** his head. 矢が彼の頭にささった. ¶ He has just *entered* ***on*** a business career. 彼は商業に身を投じたばかりである. ‖ *enter* ***on*** a diplomatic career 外交界に入る ‖ *enter* ***on*** a new existence 新生面を開く. 【類】 *enter* ***on*** a new stage of life / *enter* ***on*** a fresh stage ‖ *enter* ***on*** the duties その職につく ‖ *enter* ***on*** the duties (=a career) of office 役人の生活に入る. 【類】 He *entered* ***on*** his second year of office as Premier on October 1. ‖ He is *entering* ***on*** his 30th year. 彼は三十歳になるところだ. ‖ *enter* the name ***on*** the notice-board その名を掲示板に載せる ‖ The magazine *entered* ***on*** its third volume. その雑誌は第三巻に入った. ¶ Every care vanishes the moment I *enter* ***under*** my own roof!—Burke. 私がわが家に入るなり一切の心配は消えてしまう. ¶ and here we *enter* ***upon*** an extremely important chapter in the history of ... そしてここから…の歴史のきわめて重要な章にはいる ‖ *enter* ***upon*** negotiation[s] on the subject その問題で交渉を開始する ‖ I am desirous of *entering* ***upon*** a course of Advanced Study or Research 私は専攻科に入学を志望している. 【類】 *enter* ***upon*** the freedom of university life in strange towns ‖ Japan is *entering* ***upon*** a new era. 日本は新時代に入りつゝある. ‖ He had already dissipated the greater part of his virile power before *entering* ***upon*** marriage. 彼は結婚生活に入らない内にその性能力を大部分消耗してしまっていた. 【類】 We have *entered* ***upon*** the "atomic age." ‖ *enter* ***upon*** a religious career 信仰生活に入る. 【類】 *enter* ***upon*** another era (新時代) / *enter* ***upon*** a bread-winning life (独立の生活) / *enter* ***upon*** barrack life (兵営生活) / *enter* ***upon*** wifehood / *enter* ***upon*** one's new duties / *enter* ***upon*** the position of ... / The method of writing history *entered* ***upon*** a new phase. / with ... *enter* ***upon*** a fresh phase (新局面) ‖ He *entered* ***upon*** his eightieth year. 彼は八十歳になった. ‖ *enter* ***upon*** the change of life 人生の転換期に入る ‖ *enter* ***upon*** a period of permanent decay 永久的没落の時代に入る ‖ women who are too old to *enter upon* a life of vice 今更夜の女もできぬうば桜 ‖ *enter upon* a partnership with ... ...と組合を組織する ‖ *enter upon* one's duties at an office 社で事務を始める ‖ *enter upon* the task with an insufficient preparation 不十分な準備で仕事に取りかゝる ‖ *enter upon* and dispute the field with ... [競争に]参加して...と首位を争う ‖ before *entering upon* the consideration of ... it is fitting to note the fact that ... ...の考察に取りかゝる前に...という事実に注目することは当を得たことである.【類】*enter upon* one's work with enthusiasm / *enter* with zeal *upon* one's labor.

enterprise, *n.* 事業, 企業, 計画; 企業心, 進取的気性.

V *advertise* an *enterprise* 事業を宣伝する. ¶The *enterprise* was *attended* with difficulty. その事業には困難が伴った. ¶*build* an *enterprise* 事業を起す. ¶*carry* the *enterprise* to a successful conclusion その事業を物にする. ¶*carry forward* an *enterprise* 事業を進める. ¶*conduct* an *enterprise* to a successful issue 事業に成功する. ¶So much heroic *enterprise* has been *displayed* over geographical discovery. 地理上の発見には非常に勇敢な冒険心が発露された. ¶*exploit* an *enterprise* 事業を起す. ¶*finance* an *enterprise* 事業に出資する. ¶*float* a commercial *enterprise* 事業を起す. ¶He *has* no *enterprise*. 彼には進取の気性がない. ¶*inaugurate* an *enterprise* 事業を創始する. ¶*invite* the *enterprise* of the merchant 商人の奮起を促す. ¶the capacity to *manage* their own *enterprises* 彼ら自身の事業を経営して行く手腕. ¶*paralyse enterprises* 諸種の事業をまひさせる. ¶*push forward* an *enterprise* 事業を進めて行く. ¶the merchants *showed* their *enterprise* by ... その商人らは...によってその活動ぶりを示した. ¶*start* some industrial *enterprise* 何か工業を始める. ¶*steer* the *enterprise* technically その事業の技術方面を指導する. ¶*succeed* an *enterprise* 事業を成功させる. ¶*temper enterprise* with discretion 分別をもって企業心を善導する. ¶*undertake* an *enterprise* 事業を企てる.

V² The *enterprise* *ended* in failure. 事業は失敗した. ¶The *enterprise* has *resulted* in a loss. その事業は損失に終った.

Q an *altruistic enterprise* 博愛事業. ¶a somewhat *audacious enterprise* 少しく大胆な事業. ¶a *British enterprise* 英国の企業. ¶in the history of *charitable enterprises* 慈善事業の歴史において. ¶The dictionary is a *colossal literary enterprise*. その辞書は文学上の偉業である. ¶He showed a *commendable enterprise* in managing the business. 彼はその店の経営において推奨するに足る活動振りを見せた. ¶a merely *commercial enterprise* 純然たる営利的事業. ¶finance *commercial* and *industrial enterprises* 商工業に出資する. ¶a *dangerous enterprise* 危険な事業. ¶a privately *financed enterprise* 個人出資の事業. ¶a *fresh enterprise* 新事業. ¶embark on a *hazardous enterprise* 危険な事業に乗出す. ¶be carried out by *individual enterprise* 個人営業でやっている. ¶one of the greatest *literary enterprises* ever undertaken これまで企てられた最も大なる文芸上の事業の一つ. ¶the *maritime enterprise* of the Spanish and Portuguese スペインおよびポルトガルの海上事業. ¶*medium* and *small-sized enterprises* 中小企業. ¶for the purpose of *missionary enterprise* 伝道事業のために. ¶a *money-making enterprise* 営利事業. ¶a *municipal enterprise* 市の事業. ¶a *patriotic* and *disinterested enterprise* 愛国的で私心のない事業. ¶a *philanthropic enterprise* 慈善事業. ¶*postwar enterprise* 戦後の経営. ¶by *private enterprise* 民間企業によって ‖ It is the outcome of *private enterprise* and the handiwork of private citizens. それは民間の事業及び個人手工業の結果である. 【類】The United States has developed very largely through *private enterprise*. ‖ The steamer service is conducted by *private enterprise*. ¶*productive enterprise* 生産事業. ¶a *rash enterprise* 無謀な事業.

Q² stimulate *business enterprise* 企業心をあおる ‖ As a *business enterprise* university extension can hardly be called a success as the term is known in the business world. 企業としては大学課外講座は実業界におけるいわゆる成功と言うべきものではない. ¶*civil engineering enterprises* 土建業. ¶*gift enterprise* 贈答品の商売. ¶*government* and *non-government enterprises* 官業及び民間事業. ¶*mushroom enterprises* 雨後のたけのこのような新興事業. ¶promoters of a wildcat *oil enterprise* 無謀な石油事業の発起人ら. ¶*pioneer steamship enterprise* of Japan 日本草創の汽船業. ¶*public utility enterprises*=public utilities 公共事業. ¶a *small-scale enterprise* 小企業. ¶a *State enterprise* 国営事業.

P He lost property *by* the *enterprise*. 彼はその事業で財産をなくした. ¶He is concerned *in* the *enterprise*. 彼はその事業に関係している. ‖ take part *in* an *enterprise* 事業にあずかる. ¶The plan has been materialized *through* his *enterprise*. その計画は彼の起した事業で実現された.

P² the *enterprise of* the publishers 出版事業.

entertain, *v.* もてなす, 供応する; 楽しませる.

M *entertain extensively* and *expensively* 多数の人を招いて盛宴を張る. ¶He *entertains* his guests *handsomely* (*badly*). 彼は客を手厚く(粗末に)もてなす. ¶*entertain highly* 厚くもてなす. ¶he was received and *hospitably entertained* by ... 彼は...によって歓迎され手厚くもてなされた. ¶He *entertains* his guests very *poorly*. 彼は客の接待がへただ. ¶*entertain royally* 王侯のように豪華なもてなしをする. ¶The show *entertained* us *very much*. そのショーはとても面白かった.

P *entertain* his friends *at* his own table 家庭の食卓で友人を供応する ‖ *entertain* him *at* dinner at a club 彼にクラブで晩さんを供応する.【類】*entertain* him *at* a banquet / They were *entertained at* a garden party. ¶People go to theatre to be *entertained by* a show. 人々は見て楽しむために劇場へ行く. ‖ I was *entertained by* him. 私は彼に供応された. ¶People *entertained* great expectations *of* him. 世人は彼に大なる期待をかけていた. ¶*entertain* 160 people *to* breakfast 朝食に百六十人を招く ‖ The prince was *entertained to* luncheon on board the ship. 王子は船内で御昼食をお取りになった.【類】I was *entertained to* tea by ... ¶*entertain* them *with* auto rides 彼らを自動車に乗せてもてなす ‖ I was *entertained with* all kinds of delicacies. 私は山海の珍味を供応された. 【類】We were *entertained with* refreshments (茶菓) in another room. / They *entertained* us *with* music.

entertainer, *n.* 接待人; 芸人.

Q *first-rate* (*second-rate*) *entertainers* 一(二)流芸能人. ¶He is a most *hospitable entertainer*. 彼は非常にもてなしのよい人だ.

Q² an *amateur entertainer* しろうとの芸能人. ¶the gramophone as a *home entertainer* 家庭娯楽用としての蓄音器. ¶a *music-hall entertainer*=a vaudevillian バラエテ・ショー出演者たち(ボードビリアン). ¶a *radio* (*video*) *entertainer* ラジオ(テレビ)出演者.

P geisha girls and acrobats were *among* the *entertainers* 余興には芸者や曲芸師もいた.

entertaining, *a.* 面白い.

M *vastly entertaining* 限りなく興味のある.

entertainment, *n.* ちそう, 歓待; 娯楽, 催物, 余興.

V Books *afford* excellent *entertainment* for idle hours. 本はつれづれの折この上もない娯楽になる. ¶*arrange* a large number of *entertainments* for ... ...にいろいろな娯楽を供する. ¶The *entertainment* was *enlivened* by band music. 余興は楽隊のために活気が付いた. ¶*find entertainment* in reading 読書を楽しむ. ¶Biography *furnishes entertainments* to the reader. 伝記を読むといろいろ面白い事がある. ¶They *got up* a variety *entertainment* among themselves. 自分たちで諸芸大寄せを組織した. ¶*give* a dramatic *entertainment* 演劇を催す ‖ *give* a big *entertainment* at the hotel そのホテルで大宴会を張る. ¶London *offers* many *entertainments*. ロンドンには娯楽物がたくさんある. ¶*postpone* the *entertainment* to Saturday 催し物を土曜日に日延べする. ¶*provide* no *entertainment* 何の風情もない ‖ *entertainments* to be *provided* 出しもの. ¶*spread* a handsome *entertainment* for a guest お客にりっぱな御ちそうを出す. ¶The *entertainment consisted* of comic songs, dances, acrobatic performances, and wound up with a screamingly funny farce. 余興には喜劇や舞踏や軽わざがあり, しまいに腹の皮がよれるほどこっけいな道化芝居があった.

Q the *best entertainment* この上もないごちそう.【類】No *better entertainment* could be expected. ¶an hour or two's *bright* and ever *changing entertainment* 一二

時間の明朗で変化の多い娯楽. ¶a *charitable entertainment* 慈善の催物. ¶Biography has always been the most *delightful entertainment* of my life. 伝記は私の平生最も楽しむ所のものであった. ¶a *dramatic entertainment* at Waseda University 早稲田大学における演劇. ¶provide an *enjoyable entertainment* 面白い余興を出す. ¶a *farewell entertainment* 送別会. ¶the movie as a *genteel intellectual entertainment* 上品な知的娯楽としての映画. ¶a *grand entertainment* was given by … …が盛宴を張った. ¶a *musical entertainment* 音楽の演奏. ¶give an *original entertainment* 目新しい芸をお目にかける. ¶give a *parting entertainment* to … …のために別宴を張る. ¶a *pleasant entertainment* to the dilettante 芸術愛好者にとってうれしいみもの(ききもの). ¶Visiting the falls was a *popular entertainment*. 滝を見ることが一般民衆の楽しみであった. ¶a place (=house) of *public entertainments* 公衆演芸場. ¶*questionable entertainments* いかゞわしい娯楽. ¶*simian entertainments* さるの芸当. ¶a *sincere entertainment* 心からのもてなし. ¶*social entertainment* 社交上の娯楽(ゲームやダンスなど). ¶a *splendid entertainment* 盛宴. ¶a *theatrical entertainment* 演劇. ¶*varied* and *attractive entertainments* 各種の面白い演芸.

Q[2] an *after-dark entertainment* 夜の娯楽. ¶*benefit entertainment* 慈善興行. ¶creature comforts for *Christmas entertainment* クリスマスのもてなしに必要な飲食物. ¶a *drawing-room* (=*parlor*) *entertainment* 室内遊戯. ¶*film* (=*motion-picture* or *screen*) *entertainment* 映画の娯楽. 【類】The school offers its students *motion-picture entertainment* at a small charge. ¶a *magic lantern entertainment* 幻灯. ¶*mass entertainment* 大衆娯楽. ¶certain types of *radio entertainment* ラジオのある種の娯楽番組. ¶*society entertainment* クラブなどの余興. ¶On Thursday nights high-grade *vaudeville entertainment* is offered. 木曜日の夜は高級の寄せ演芸がある.

P *at* a public *entertainment* 公開の演芸で. ¶*for* the *entertainment* of convalescent soldiers in hospitals 病院で静養中の兵士たちを慰めるために.

P[2] a house of *entertainment* *for* travellers 旅行者の娯楽機関. ¶a source of much *entertainment* *to* men 大いに人を楽しますもの.

enthuse, *v.* 《米口》熱心である.

P *enthuse about* autoing (cycling, dancing) 自動車(自転車, ダンス)に熱中する.

enthusiasm, *n.* 熱心, 熱情; 発奮.

V *arouse* the *enthusiasm* of … …の発奮を促す. ¶*awake* lifelong *enthusiasm* 一生続く奮発心を起させる. 【類】*awake* great *enthusiasm* / *awake* a new *enthusiasm* for … ¶*check enthusiasm* 熱意に水をかける. ¶*chill* (=*damp*, or *dampen*) one's *enthusiasm* for … …に対する人の熱をさます. ¶*create enthusiasm* 熱意を起させる. ¶*diminish* one's *enthusiasm* その熱意をそぐ. ¶*display* much *enthusiasm* 大なる熱意を示す. ¶*evince* enormous and unprecedented *enthusiasm* かつてないほどの熱意を示す. ¶*excite* general *enthusiasm* 人々の熱をあおる. ¶*inspire enthusiasm* 奮起させる. ¶*kindle* their *enthusiasm* 彼らの熱情を動かす. ¶*revive* the *enthusiasm* for Napoleon ナポレオン熱を復活する. ¶*rouse enthusiasm* 奮発心を喚起する. ¶*stir up enthusiasm* for mountaineering in Young Japan 日本の青年に登山熱を吹込む. ¶*weaken* one's *enthusiasm* その熱心を弱める.

V[2] The wild *enthusiasm* with which the game was first greeted *cooled* after a time. その競技は初め盛んな熱心をもって迎えられたがほどへてそれが薄らいだ. ¶His *enthusiasm* for collecting antiquities rapidly *developed*. 彼の古物収集熱がますますつのった. ¶The *enthusiasm died down*. その熱がさめた. ¶*Enthusiasm wanes*. 熱意がさめる.

Q full of *all* the *enthusiasm* of new converts 新しく改宗した者らしい熱情にあふれて. ¶*boundless enthusiasm* 無限の熱情. ¶the *characteristic enthusiasm* of youth 青春特有の熱情. ¶With *common enthusiasm* all ages and classes rushed for health or pleasure to the sea. 老幼上下を問わず一様に熱狂して保養とか娯楽のために海へと押しかけた. ¶*contageous enthusiasm* 伝染する熱狂. ¶*ebullient enthusiasm* あふれる熱情. ¶He was welcomed with *great enthusiasm*. 彼は熱心に迎えられた. 【類】be received with *great enthusiasm* / exclaim with *great enthusiasm*. ¶damp the *growing enthusiasm* だんだんたかまって行く熱情を鈍らす. ¶The occasion was celebrated with *much enthusiasm*. その式典は盛大に行われた. ¶The *national enthusiasm* knew no bounds. 国民の感激は限りがなかった. ¶an outburst of *patriotic enthusiasm* 愛国的情熱の発露. ¶*pertinacious enthusiasm* 不屈の熱意. ¶arouse *popular enthusiasm* 民衆の熱狂を喚起する. ¶the *professional enthusiasm* of the teacher 教師の職業的熱心. ¶kindle a *real enthusiasm* 真の熱情をかきたてる. ¶with *renewed enthusiasm* 熱意を新たにして. ¶*spontaneous enthusiasm* 自発的熱心. ¶The Royal party was welcomed with *subduced*, but evidently *genuine enthusiasm*. 皇族のご一行はひかえ目ではあるが明かに純真な熱情をもって迎えられた. ¶amid *tremendous enthusiasm* 熱狂のうちに. ¶an *unquenchable enthusiasm* 抑えがたい熱情. ¶with a *whole-souled enthusiasm* 満こうの熱情をもって. ¶a scene of *wild enthusiasm* 熱狂的な場面.

P The A team defeated the B *amid* wildest *enthusiasm*. A チームは興奮しきった観衆の熱狂のうちに B チームを破った. ¶He was carried away *by* his own *enthusiasm*. 彼は自分の熱意に陶酔した. ¶He played tennis whenever and wherever it was possible to play and what he lacked in skill he made up *in enthusiasm*. 彼はテニスをやれる機会さえあれば時と所にお構いなくやった, そして熟練を欠いていてもそれは熱心で埋合わせた. ¶*with* the *enthusiasm* of youth 若さの熱情を傾けて ‖ The proposal was received *with* the greatest *enthusiasm*. その提案はこの上もない熱心さで迎えられた. 【類】*with* some *enthusiasm* / He inspired me *with enthusiam* for art.

P[2] There was no *enthusiasm among* the populace. 民衆はやっきとなっていなかった. 【類】great *enthusiasm among* the students. ¶an *enthusiasm for* research (sport, war, work) 研究(など)熱. ¶intense as has been the *enthusiasm over* his novels 彼の小説は大いに歓迎されたが.

enthusiast, *n.* 熱心家(フアン).

Q an *ardent enthusiast* for the combination of travel and study 旅行と研学とを結び付けることを盛んに唱道する人. ¶a *fiery enthusiast* 烈火のような熱心家. ¶a *sanguine-souled enthusiast* 猛烈な熱心家.

Q[2] an *amateur enthusiast* しろうとの熱心家. ¶a *brother enthusiast* 同志. ¶a *dance* (*movie, ball, judo, music*) *enthusiast* ダンス(など)フアン. ¶Mr. Cecil J. Sharp, the well-known *folklore enthusiast* 民俗学に熱心で有名なセシル・ジェー・シャープ氏. ¶a *keep fit enthusiast* 体位向上熱心家. ¶the *Montessori enthusiast* [イタリアの]モンテソーリ女史崇拝者. ¶an ardent *radio enthusiast* ラジオ狂. ¶a *research enthusiast* 研究家. ¶a *sports enthusiast* スポーツ・フアン.

P[2] an *enthusiast about* politics 政治狂. ¶an *enthusiast for* international peace 国際平和の支持者 ‖ an *enthusiast for* Japan 日本びいきの人 ‖ an *enthusiast for* clocks and bells 時計や鐘の研究家. 【類】an *enthusiast for* the cold plunge / an *enthusiast for* music (sports, art). ¶an *enthusiast in* education 教育の熱心家. ¶an *enthusiast of* pure science 純粋科学の熱心家. ¶an *enthusiast on* the subject of … …の問題に熱心な人.

enthusiastic, *a.* 熱中している, 熱心な.

P They are not *enthusiastic about* the war. 彼らは戦争に熱中していない. ¶*enthusiastic for* a scheme 計画に対して熱心な. ¶he is *enthusiastic in* his praise of … 彼は盛んに…を称揚している ‖ He is *enthusiastic in* his manner of speech. 彼の話し振りに熱がある. 【類】be *enthusiastic in* work. ¶be *enthusiastic over* one's favorite actress ひいきの女優に熱をあげている.

entice, *v.* 誘惑する, 釣り込む.

M *entice* a girl *away* from home 少女を家から誘かいする.

P *entice* a person *into* a place 人をある場所に誘い込む ‖ *entice* him *into* the general talk 彼を皆の話の中に釣り込む.

O *entice* a person to do something wrong 人を誘惑して悪いことをやらせる.

enticing, *a.* 心を引付ける.

M What could be *more enticing* on a hot July or August day than to loll on the sand between dips in the surf? 暑い七八月の日に寄せ波に浸っては砂土にころげまた浸ってはころげるほど愉快なことがあろうか.

entire, *n.* 全部.

P[2] the *entire of* the night 夜通し ‖ the *entire of* his property 彼の全財産.

entire, *a.* 完全な, 無きずの.

P *entire from* any fault 全然きずのない.

entirety, *n.* 完全, 十全; 全体, 総体.

P have the land ***by*** *entireties* その地所全部を占有している. ¶***in*** *entirety* そのまゝそっくり ‖ "Hamlet" ***in*** its *entirety* 「ハムレット」の通し狂言 ‖ viewed ***in*** its *entirety* 全般から見て ‖ see the picture ***in*** its *entirety* その映画を終りまで見る. 【類】quote it ***in*** its *entirety* / The letter is given ***in*** its *entirety*. / It was reprinted ***in*** its *entirety*.

entitle, *v.* 権利を与える, 資格を与える; 称号を与える.

M be *fully entitled* to ... ...する資格が十分ある.

P An admiral is *entitled* ***to*** a salute of 17 guns. 海軍大将は十七発の礼砲を受ける. ‖ be *entitled* ***to*** all respect あらゆる尊敬に値いする. 【類】many persons, whose opinions are *entitled* ***to*** respect, have maintained that ... ‖ This *entitles* him ***to*** unreserved praise. これあるがために彼は十分称賛を受ける資格がある. 【類】A fine collection of antiques today *entitles* the possessor of it ***to*** a place in Sunday supplement society (新聞の日曜付録に載せられるもの). / the coupons *entitle* the holder ***to*** the services of (のサービス) ... / This ticket *entitles* you ***to*** a free lunch. ‖ *entitle* him ***to*** rights (privileges) 彼に権利(など)を与える ‖ The proposal is not *entitled* ***to*** consideration. その提案は考慮の余地がない. ‖ I am *entitled* ***to*** the money. その金は当然私がもらってよいわけだ. ‖ information *entitled* ***to*** credit 信頼できる情報 ‖ become *entitled* ***to*** a pension 恩給がもらえる.

Q They *entitled* him to do it. 彼らは彼にそれをする資格を付与した. ¶An ambassador is *entitled* 'Your Excellency.' 大使は閣下の称号を与えられる. ¶The new book is *entitled* '...' その新著の題名は「...」だ.

entity, *n.* 実体.

Q a ***political entity*** 一国家(独立国). ¶a ***public entity*** 公共団体.

entomb, *v.* 埋葬する.

P Iyeyasu was *entombed* ***among*** the forests and mountains of Nikko. 家康は日光の森や山々の間に埋葬された. ¶girls who were *entombed* ***in*** the ruins of the school house つぶれた校舎の中に埋没した少女たち.

entrain, *v.* 汽車に乗る.

M ***hastily*** *entrained* for ... 急いで汽車に乗り...に向った.

P *entrain* ***at*** a station 停車場で乗車する.

entrance, *n.* 入場, 入学; 着手; 入口.

V ***block*** the *entrance* to the harbour 港の入口を封鎖する. ¶***effect*** an *entrance* into ... ...にはいる. ¶The word ***found*** an *entrance* into good society. その言葉は上流社会に用いられるようになった. ¶try to ***force*** an *entrance* into ... ...へ無理にはいろうとする. ¶***gain*** *entrance* はいる. ¶His *entrance* was ***greeted*** with applause. 彼の入場は拍手をもって迎えられた. ¶***make*** one's *entrance* 入り込む. ¶***obtain*** *entrance* by bribing the porter 門番にわいろを使ってはいる ‖ ***obtain*** *entrance* into ... ...にはいる. ¶***secure*** *entrance* through a gate 門からはいる.

Q have ***free*** *entrance* to ... ...に自由に出入りが許されている. ¶at the ***front*** *entrance* of a school 学校正面入口に. ¶Visitors use the ***front entrance*** but tradesmen and delivery boys use the ***back entrance***. 来客は玄関から商人や御用聞は裏口から出入りする. ¶the ***main*** *entrance* 正門. ¶***No*** *entrance*. [掲示]出入禁止. ¶a ***tradesmen's*** *entrance* 商人通用門.

Q² blockade the ***harbor*** *entrance* 港口を閉鎖する. ¶a ***service*** *entrance* 通用口.

P They gathered ***about*** the *entrance*. 彼らは入口のあたりに集まった. ¶***at*** the *entrance* of the river into the sea その川が海に流れ込む所に ‖ ***at*** the *entrance* to a station (port) 停車場(港)の入口で. 【類】park one's car ***at*** the *entrance*. ¶take examinations ***for*** *entrance* to a university 大学の入学試験を受ける. ¶not far ***from*** the *entrance* to Yokohama harbor 横浜港口にほど遠からぬ所に. ¶He stood ***in*** the *entrance*. 彼は入口に立った. ¶***On*** (=***Upon***) my *entrance* he started back and stared at me for some moments. 僕がここへはいると彼はびっくりあとじさりして数分間僕をじろじろ見つめた. ¶The telephone number was proudly displayed ***over*** his *entrance*. 電話番号が彼の玄関の上に誇り顔に掲げてあった.

P² since my *entrance* ***at*** college 僕が大学に入って以来. ¶*entrance* ***by*** (=***through***) the door 戸口よりの入場. ¶the age of students at the time of *entrance* ***in*** college 学生が大学入学当時の年齢. ¶The time of his *entrance* ***into*** public life marked his first step to success. 彼の公生活にはいった時が成功への第一歩であった. ‖ *entrance* ***into*** a port 入港 ‖ *entrance* ***into*** school 入学 ‖ *entrance* ***into*** office 任官, 就職 ‖ two years before our *entrance* ***into*** the war その戦争にわが国が参加する二年前 ‖ His own abilities gained him an *entrance* ***into*** learned society. 彼は自分の力で学者仲間と交際を結ぶことができるようになった. ‖ *entrance* ***into*** Nirvana ねはんに入ること. ¶the *entrance* ***of*** an heir ***into*** his estate 嗣子の財産相続. ¶the *entrance* ***of*** Japan ***upon*** the stage of the world's history 世界歴史の舞台への日本の進出. 【類】the *entrance* ***of*** an actor ***upon*** the stage. ¶the *entrance* ***to*** the tunnel そのトンネルの入口 ‖ an *entrance* ***to*** a country 入国 ‖ The *entrance* ***to*** the hall is a winding, leafy lane. その会堂へはうねりくねった緑葉深い小道を通って行く. 【類】The *entrance* ***to*** the cave had been blocked up. ‖ *entrance* ***to*** the throne 即位. ¶*entrance* ***upon*** study 研究開始 ‖ one's *entrance* ***upon*** his twentieth year 二十歳になること. ¶*entrance* ***within*** the gates 門内に入ること.

entrance, *v.* 有頂天にする.

P I was *entranced* ***at*** his brilliant talk. 彼の快談に完全に魅せられた. ¶He was *entranced* ***in*** thought. 彼は考え込んでいた. ¶He was *entranced* ***with*** joy. 彼は無我夢中に喜んだ.

entrant, *n.* 新入者, 新参者.

V Many firms appear to ***expect*** their *entrants* to come from school with a complete commercial knowledge of the language desired. 多数の会社は新しく雇入れる学校の卒業生が執務に必要な商用外国語を完全に修得していることを期待しているらしい.

Q an ***illegal*** *entrant* 不法入国者.

P² *entrants* ***to*** a universiy 大学の新入生.

entrap, *v.* おとしいれる.

P *entrap* a person ***by*** a trick into confession うまくだまして白状させる.

entreat, *v.* 懇願する, 嘆願する.

P *entreat* a person ***for*** mercy 人に慈悲を哀願する. ¶*entreat* mercy (assistance) ***of*** another 他人に慈悲(など)をこう ‖ May I *entreat* a little favor ***of*** you? 少々お願いがありますが. ‖ I *entreated* [***of***] him to do it. 私はそれをしてくれと彼に頼んだ.

entreaty, *n.* 懇願, 嘆願.

V ***grant*** *entreaties* 嘆願をいれる ¶***make*** an *entreaty* 折入って頼む. ¶***reject*** their *entreaties* 彼らの哀願をしりぞける.

Q a ***piteous*** *entreaty* 哀願.

P listen ***to*** his *entreaties* 彼の嘆願を聞入れる ‖ turn a deaf ear ***to*** one's *entreaties* 人の哀願をいれない.

entree, entrée, *n. F.* 入場; 入場許可.

V ***have*** the *entree* of a house 家に出入を許されている. ¶***obtain*** *entree* for ... ...の入場許可を得る.

P² It was nothing but an *entree* ***to*** a series of misfortunes. それが全く引続く不幸の皮切りであった.

entrust, *v.* 任せる, ゆだねる, 委託する.

M ***quietly*** *entrust* soul and body to the care of the Savior 全身全霊を安らかに救世主の手にお任せする. ¶can be ***safely*** *entrusted* to ... ...に任せて安全である.

P The task could not well have been *entrusted* ***to*** a more competent hand. その仕事はそれ以上手腕のある人にゆだねることができなかった(適任者を得たのであった). ‖ *entrust* the matter ***to*** him (his care, his charge) その事を彼に一任する. 【類】*entrust* children ***to*** the care of ... ¶I *entrusted* him ***with*** the task of ... 私は...の仕事を彼に一任した ‖ be *entrusted* ***with*** powers 権力を委譲される. 【類】be *entrusted* ***with*** great power of influencing others / *entrust* the teacher ***with*** the education of his children / I *entrust* you ***with*** the care of my property. / I *entrusted* him ***with*** a large sum of money.

entry, *n.* 入場; 入口; [帳簿の]記入; [辞書の]記入事項.

V ***block*** the *entry* 入口を封鎖する. ¶The latest edition of the glossary ***contains*** 5,000 *entries*. その用語集の最近版は五千語を収録している. ¶This *entry* should be ***deleted***. この記入事項は削除すべきである. ¶***force*** one's *entry* into a run 家畜の囲いの中に押入る. ¶***gain*** *entry* 入場する. ¶Outsiders ***have*** free *entry* to these lobbies. 会員外の者もこれらの控室には自由に出入が出来る. ¶He has consented to ***judge*** *entries* for the prize competition. 彼はその懸賞の審判者となることを承諾した. ¶He ***made*** an *entry* of the memorial event in his diary. 彼はその記念すべき出来事を日誌に記入した. 【類】***make*** an *entry* of an item in the account book (会計簿) ‖ The country *made* her *entry* in the war in 1915. その国は一九一五年にその戦争に参加した. ‖ *make* her first *entry* upon the stage 初舞台を踏む(デビューする). ¶An outsider can *obtain entry* to the performances at the No Club. 会員外の者でも能楽クラブの演奏会に出席することができる. ‖ There were no signs at all to show where the burglars had *obtained* an *entry*. 賊がどこからはいったものか全然見当がつかなかった. ¶It is very difficult to *secure entry* into many New York clubs. ニューヨークのクラブには入会のむずかしいものが多数ある. ¶knock at the door and *seek entry* 戸をたゝいて案内をこう. ¶*sign* and *seal* an *entry* 記載事項に署名押印する.

Q disappear "down the *back entry* of Time" 時の裏口から消える(忘れられて行く). ¶*China's entry* into war 中国の参戦. ¶make a *correct entry* 正しく記帳する. ¶*double* (*single*) *entry* 複式(単式)[簿記]. ¶make *false entries* in the company's books 会社の帳簿に不正の記入をする. ¶They have the right of *free entry* to the exhibition. 彼らはその展覧会に自由に出入する権利がある. ¶The *last entry* in his journal runs as follows: 彼が日誌に残した最後の記事はこうである. ¶The General made his formal *public entry* into Tokyo. 将軍は正式の入京をした. ¶make a *solemn entry* into the town 堂々とその町に入る. ¶a *triumphal entry* into a city がいせん入市. ¶*Unauthorized entry* prohibited. [掲示]無許可入場お断り.

Q² a *docket entry* 事件表記載事項.

P 500 applicants *for entry* to the school 同校五百の入学志望者 ‖ an *entry for* a game (contest, competition) 競技(など)への参加. ¶The *entries from* one school are limited to five players. 一校からの参加選手数は五名以内となっている.

P² He made the following *entry in* his diary. 彼は日誌に次のように記した. ‖ an *entry in* a register (ledger, book) 帳簿(など)への記入 ‖ There were about 200 *entries in* the show. その展覧会には約二百の出品があった. ¶the first anniversary of the *entry into* the great war of the United States of America 米国の大戦参加第一周年記念日. ‖ Formal education is a preparation for *entry into* life. 学校教育は実生活に入る準備である. 【類】The chief treasure of the temple is a gigantic *kakemono* of Buddha's *Entry into* Nirvana (仏陀入定の図), by Kano Yasunobu, which is shown only during the month of April. ¶the *entry of* the Mikado *into* Yedo 明治大帝の江戸御入城 ‖ the *entry of* America *into* the world struggle 米国の世界戦争への参加 ‖ the *entry of* women *into* professions, commerce, and industry 婦人の高等職業・商業・工業への進出. ¶an *entry on* the debtor side of an account 借方への記入.

entwine, *v.* まとう, からませる.

P *entwine* it *about*... ...の周囲にそれをからませる. ¶Their arms *entwined* one another's waist 彼らの腕は互の腰を抱き合った. ¶*entwine* it *with*... それに...を巻付ける ‖ The two rocks, large and small, are *entwined with* sacred ropes and paper. 大小二個の岩にはしめなわをめぐらしてある.

enunciate, *v.* 発音する.

M *enunciate distinctly* はっきり発音する.

enunciation, *n.* 声明; 発音.

Q *good enunciation* よい発音.

P² an *enunciation of* particulars 詳説.

envelop, *v.* 包む, おおう.

P He is *enveloped in* a mantle. 彼はマントをまとっている. ‖ The house was *enveloped in* mist (smoke, flames). 家屋は霧(など)に包まれていた. ‖ mountain-tops *enveloped in* (=*with*) clouds 雲に包まれた山頂 ‖ be *enveloped in* the gathering gloom 夕やみに包まれる.

envelope, *n.* 封筒, 状袋.

V *address* an *envelope* 封筒にあて名を書く. ¶*close up* an *envelope* 封筒を閉じる. ¶fold once to *fit* its *envelope* その状袋にはいるように一度折り畳む. ¶*inclose* a self-addressed and stamped *envelope* 自己のあて名を記して切手をはった封筒を封入する. ¶*mark* their *envelopes* "..." 彼らの封筒に「...」と記す. ¶*open* an *envelope* 封を切る. ¶*seal* [*up*] an *envelope* [手紙の入った]封筒の封をする. ¶*secure* (=*fasten*) and *seal* an *envelope* 封筒を封ろうで固く封をする. ¶*send* a stamped directed *envelope* to ... 切手をはってあて名を書いた封筒を...に送る. ¶*tilt up* an *envelope* 封筒を傾けて中味を出す.

Q in the *accompanying envelope* 別封で. ¶use the *enclosed return envelope* for a reply 返信に封入の返信用封筒を用いる. ¶an *end-opening envelope* 端開き封筒. ¶a *moisture-proof envelope* [ビニール製の]湿気止め封筒. ¶post in *open envelope* 開封で郵便に出す. ¶a *self-addressed* (=*self-directed*) *envelope* 自分で住所氏名を記入した封筒. ¶a *side-opening envelope* 横開き封筒. ¶a *stamped* [and] *addressed envelope* 切手をはってあて名を記した封筒. ¶a *wax-sealed envelope* 封ろうで厳封した封筒.

Q² a workers' *pay envelope* 勤労者の俸給封筒. ¶a meagre *pay envelope* 中味の少ない月給袋. ¶a *window envelope* 窓付封筒.

P the postmark *on* the *envelope* 封筒上の消印. 【類】write the address *on* the *envelope*.

envious, *a.* ねたむ, うらやましがる.

P He is *envious of* my good fortune (wealth, success). 彼は僕の幸運(など)をねたんでいる. ¶He is never *envious of* others *for* their wealth. 彼は決して他人の富をうらやまない.

environment, *n.* 環境, 周囲.

V *beautify* the *environment* 環境を美しくする. ¶*create* a new *environment* 新しい環境を作り出す. ¶*enter* a person's *environment* そのけいがいに接する. ¶look about and *inspect* one's new *environment* あたりを見回してその新しい環境を見る.

Q *adverse economic environment* 不利な経済的環境(貧困). ¶*bad domestic environment* 悪い家庭の環境. ¶put one under a *favorable environment* 人を有利の環境におく. ¶*languorous environment* 元気のない(引締っていない)周囲. ¶explore the *literary environment* of a work 作品の文学的背景を探る. ¶*moral environment* 道徳的環境. ¶the *physical environment* of man 人間の物質的環境. ¶He was born in the country and brought up in a *picturesque environment*. 彼は田園に生れ美しい自然の中に育った. ¶Schools should be surrounded by a *pure* and *healthy environment*. 学校は純潔にして健全な環境に置くべきである. ¶a *quiet*, *cordial* and *homelike environment* 静かで親切でかつ家庭的な環境. ¶Nikko is one of the most *scenic environments* in Japan. 日光は日本で最も風景美に富んだ地域の一つである. ¶a *solitary environment* さびしい環境. ¶an *unfavorable environment* 恵まれない環境. ¶These pine-trees on rocks wrest an existence from the most *unpropitious environment*. これらの岩に生えた松はその恵まれない境地でわずかに露命をつないでいる. ¶live in an *unsympathetic environment* 同情のない環境に生活する.

Q² a *home environment* 家庭環境. ¶a decent *home* and *living environment* 相当の家庭及び生活環境. ¶a *work environment* 作業環境.

P live *in* a depraved *environment* 腐敗した環境に生活する. ¶Man is not the product *of* his *environment*. 人はその環境の産物ではない.

environs, *n., pl.* 付近; 郊外.

Q an evening walk in the *green* and *umbrageous environs* 緑の木陰の多い付近における夕方の散歩. ¶London and *its environs*. ロンドンとその郊外.

P² the *environs of* the city 同市の郊外.

envisage, *v.* 心に描く.

P programs *envisaged by* the Government 政府の企画.

envoy, *n.* 使節, 使臣.

V *despatch* an *envoy* 使節を派遣する. ¶be *made* the *envoy* among one's friends.

Q a *cultural envoy* 文化使節. ¶an *Envoy Extraordinary* 全権使節. ¶a Prime Minister's *personal envoy* 首相の個人使節. ¶a *Presidential envoy* 大統領使節. ¶a *special envoy* 特使.

Q² America's *goodwill envoys* 米国の親善使節. ¶a *peace envoy* from... ...からの平和使節 ‖ a roving *peace envoy* of Japan 日本の移動平和使節.

P² an *envoy to* another country 他国への使節.

envy, *n.* しっと, せん望, さい疑心.

V *arouse envy* しっとを起させる. ¶*dart* (=*emit*) *envy* from her eyes 彼女の目からしっとの光をひらめかす. ¶*excite envy* さいぎ心を刺激する. ¶*feel* no *envy* at ... ...を一向うらやましく思わない. ¶*have* a great *envy* of one's success 人の成功を大いにうらやむ. ¶*raise envy* しっと心を起させる.

Q It fills us with ***admiring envy.*** われわれはそれに対してせん望にたえない. ¶***competitive envy*** 競争から来るねたみ.

P That was all done ***out of envy.*** そうしたのは全くさいぎ心からのことであった. ¶All this was done ***through envy.*** これらのことは全くしっとざただ. ¶His eyes were green with ***envy at*** his enemy's success. 彼は敵の成功を見てしっと深い目をむき出していた. ¶look on ... ***with envy*** うらやましそうに...を眺める ‖ ***with*** keen ***envy*** 垂ぜんおくあたわずといったように.

P² he has become the ***envy of*** others because of ... 彼は...のために世人のせん望の的となった ‖ My mother had a wardrobe which was the ***envy of*** all the neighbourhood. 私の母は近所中のせん望の的になったほどの衣装持であった.

envy, *v.* うらやむ, ねたむ.

M The poor ***generally envy*** the rich. 概して貧者は富者をねたむ. ¶***How*** I ***envy*** you! まあおうらやましい. ¶I ***quite envy*** these happy fishermen. 私はこうした幸福な漁師たちがうらやましい. ‖ I ***quite envy*** you your good fortune (health). 貴下の幸運(など)は全くうらやましいです.

P ***envy at*** one's success 人の成功をうらやむ. ¶***envy*** others ***for*** (=on account of) their success 他人の成功をうらやむ.

epaulet[te], *n.* [士官の]肩章.

V ***win*** one's ***epaulet*** [下士官が]士官に昇進する.

epicure, *n.* 美食家.

V It will ***delight*** even the most blasé ***epicure.*** それは珍味にあきた美食家でも喜ぶだろう.

epidemic, *n.* 流行病; 流行.

V ***stamp out*** an ***epidemic*** 流行病を撲滅する.

V² An ***epidemic*** has ***broken out.*** 流行病が始まった. ¶Since the murder of the Czar Alexander II in 1882 a sort of ***epidemic*** of political assassination has ***prevailed*** in Europe. 一八八二年露帝アレキサンダー二世の殺害以来一種の暗殺病が欧州の政界に流行した.

Q a ***severe epidemic*** 激しい流行病.

Q² the death-rate in the last ***cholera epidemic*** この前コレラの流行したときの死亡率. ¶the ***flu*** (=influenza) ***epidemic*** 流行性感冒. ¶a ***typhus epidemic*** 流行しているチフス.

P² There was an ***epidemic of*** cholera in the city last summer. 昨年夏その市にコレラが流行した. 【類】All the schools in the city were closed because of an ***epidemic of*** scarlet fever (しょう紅熱). ‖ an ***epidemic of*** railway accidents ひんぴんと起る鉄道事故 ‖ the ***epidemic of*** burglary 夜盗のひん発. ¶He was attacked with the ***epidemic of*** cholera. 彼はコレラにかかった.

epigram, *n.* 警句.

V ***discharge epigrams*** 警句を吐く. ¶***make*** an ***epigram*** 警句を作る.

Q a ***metaphysical epigram*** 奥妙の警句. ¶a very ***significant epigram*** 大いに意義ある警句.

P The paradox is a special type ***of epigram.*** 逆説は警句の特種な型である.

epigrammatist, *n.* 警句家.

Q a ***conversational epigrammatist*** 話の合間に警句を吐く人.

epilepsy, *n.* てんかん.

P He often falls a victim to a fit ***of epilepsy.*** 彼はよくてんかんを起す.

episode, *n.* そう話; できごと; 〖映画〗篇.

V a ***half-humorous, half-tragic episode*** of life ユーモアと悲劇が織りまじった人生のそう話. ¶These facts ***illustrate episodes*** in its early history. これらの事実によってその初期の歴史の一端がうかがわれる.

Q a ***dramatic episode*** 劇的そう話. ¶a ***farcical episode*** of the "follow-your-leader" variety やじうま騒ぎという種類の(映画)こっけい場面. ¶a ***humorous episode*** こっけいなそう話. ¶a minor ***international episode*** in the shape of the presentation of an ancient Japanese sword to the town of Fair Haven フェア・ヘィヴンの市に日本古刀を贈呈するという一つの小さな国際的できごと. ¶some ***ludicrous episode*** of domestic life 家庭生活のあるばかげたそう話. ¶a ***pathetic episode*** in the war 戦争中の悲そうなそう話. ¶a ***romantic episode*** 小説的なそう話. ¶one of the ***strangest episodes*** in the history of crime 犯罪史上最も珍奇な一そう話. ¶a ***thrilling episode*** スリルに富んだ事件. ¶a ***touching episode*** 人を感銘させる(悲しい)そう話. ¶an ***unpleasant episode*** 不愉快なできごと[の話].

Q² a ***shooting episode*** 狩猟の一そう話.

P² an ***episode in*** history (one's life) 歴史(人生)の一そう話.

epitaph, *n.* 碑銘, 碑文.

P² "Failed for lack of an education" would be a fit ***epitaph for*** many an unfortunate.「無教育のために失敗せり」という文句は多数の薄幸者によく当てはまる碑銘になるだろう. ¶an ***epitaph on*** a tombstone 墓碑銘.

epithet, *n.* 性質形容詞; あだ名.

V ***apply*** a harsh ***epithet*** to ... ...にひどい形容詞を適用する(こきおろす). ¶***heap up epithets*** concerning their stupidity, cruelty, and lawlessness 彼らの愚劣・残忍・無法に対して形容詞(悪口)を並べたてる.

Q an ***abusive epithet*** alluding to ... ...にちなんだ口ぎたない形容語. ¶this does not seem to be a very ***appropriate epithet*** to apply to ... これは...に適用するきわめて適当な形容詞とは思われない. ¶a ***controversial epithet*** 物議をかもした形容語. ¶a ***contumelious epithet*** 無礼なあだ名. ¶a ***hackneyed epithet*** 陳腐な形容詞. ¶repeat the ***offensive epithets*** 腹のたつような形容詞をくり返す. ¶an ***otiose epithet*** 無用の形容詞. ¶***spiteful*** and ***opprobrious epithets*** 口ぎたない下劣な文句. 【類】Many ***opprobrious epithets*** have been thrown at him.

P² "Cool" is often used as an ***epithet of*** reproach. cool という語は往々非難の意味の形容詞に用いられる.

epitome, *n.* 大意; 縮図.

Q man, the ***world's epitome*** 世界の縮図たる人間.

P the world ***in epitome*** 世界の縮図 ‖ He is a vast library ***in epitome.*** 彼は大図書館の縮図ともいうべきものだ(博学だ).

P² Brussels is an ***epitome*** [in little] ***of*** Paris. ブラッセルはパリの縮図. ‖ an ***epitome of*** religion 宗教大意.

epitomize, *v.* 要点を述べる, 摘要する.

P it may be ***epitomized by*** saying that ... ...という言葉でこれを要説することができよう. ¶***epitomize in*** the single word "..."「...」の一語でこれをおおう ‖ a brief history of the ancient City ***epitomized in*** pageantry 戸外劇の中に収めたその古都の沿革.

epoch, *n.* 時代, 紀元.

V American labor-saving inventions ***form*** an ***epoch*** in the history of the race. 米国における労働節減の諸発明はその民族史上に一新紀元を画するものだ. ¶***mark*** (=***make***) an ***epoch*** in education 教育史上一新紀元を画する ‖ About this time I had one of those salutary turns that have ***marked epochs*** in my life. このころ私は私の一生の一新時期を画する健全な心機一転を経験した. 【類】***mark*** an ***epoch*** in Egyptological studies (エジプト学研究) in this country / The invention of dynamite ***marks*** an ***epoch*** in the history of civilization. / ***mark*** an ***epoch*** in the history of the science. ¶***usher in*** a new ***epoch*** in the history of ... ...史上に一新紀元を開く.

Q mark ***another epoch*** in the advancement of ... ...の進歩において更に一進境を示す. ¶a ***glorious epoch*** 光栄ある時代. ¶an ***important epoch*** in the history of Japan 日本史上重要な一紀元. ¶It marked a ***new epoch*** in the boy's career. それがその少年の生涯に新時代を画した. ¶***remote epochs*** 遠い時代. ¶a ***rough, warfaring epoch*** 殺伐な戦闘時代.

P ***at*** a very ancient (=remote) ***epoch*** 上古において. ¶***in epochs*** beyond historical reach 有史以前において.

P² an ***epoch in*** the life of ... ...の生涯における新時期. ¶this ***epoch of*** ours 我らのこの時代 ‖ the ***epoch of*** the three Kingdoms 三国時代.

epoch-maker, *n.* 新時代を開く人.

Q the ***world's epoch-makers*** 世界の新時代を樹立する人々.

equal, *n.* 匹敵するもの; 同等の人.

V He ***has*** no ***equal*** in eloquence. 雄弁にかけては彼に匹敵するものはない. 【類】He ***has*** no ***equal*** for running. / not ***having*** its ***equal*** in the world. ¶I never ***saw*** its ***equal.*** それに匹敵するものを見たことがない(景色など).

Q Some advocate the idea that woman must be man's ***economic*** and ***political equal.*** 経済的に政治的に女は男と平等たるべしという意見を唱えている者がある. ¶In ... he has had ***few equals*** and probably no superior. ...にかけては彼に匹敵するものが少なくまた恐らく彼にまさるものはなかろう. 【類】He has ***few equals*** among living authors (現存作家). ¶the stimulating conversation of one's ***intellectual equals*** or superiors 知力的に自分と同等又は同等以上の人の啓発的談話. ¶a ***social equal*** 社会的に同等の人. ¶***our equals*** われらの同輩.

P mix *with* one's *equals* 同等の人と交る. ¶It is *without equal* in the history of journalism. それは新聞業史上にその比を見ない.

equal, *a.* 等しい; 平等の, 対等の; 耐える, …する能力のある.

M *identically equal* 全く同様の.

P *equal in* number (weight, proportion) 数(など)の等しい ‖ All men are *equal in* the eye of the law. 法律の目から見ればすべての人は平等だ. ‖ The two are *equal in* ability. 二人の手腕は同等だ. ‖ be *equal in* scholarship to ... 学力で…に負けない. 【類】be *equal in* strength (knowledge, talent) *to* ... ¶One *ri* is *equal to* 2.44 English statute miles, or, roughly speaking, to a distance a trifle under two and a half miles. 一里は英国の 2.44 法定マイル即ち大ざっぱに言って二マイル二分の一ちょっとかける. ‖ It is worth an amount *equal to* ... of our money. それはわが国の貨幣で…の価値がある. ‖ I cannot accept the articles as they are not *equal to* samples. 見本と品物が違うから受取れない. ‖ He was *equal to* the situation. 彼は時局に善処した. ‖ Always *equal to* the emergency situation! いつも非常時を乗切る, あざやかなものだ. ‖ *equal to* the occasion とん知をきかして. 【類】His ability proved *equal to* the task. ‖ None of us feels *equal to* the delicate task of enlightening him. 彼を啓発するなんてむずづかしい仕事はわれわれの中でだれ一人できると思っているものはない. 【類】think oneself *equal to* the task ‖ The quality is not *equal to* the sample submitted. その品質は渡した見本ほどはよくない. ‖ officers whose intelligence is *equal to* their courage 知勇兼備の士官たち ‖ He was so knocked out that he did not feel *equal to* the exertion of writing. 彼は非常にがっかりしたので物を書いて見るという努力に耐えないと思った. ‖ Her sight is *equal to* threading a needle without glasses. 彼女は視力がたしかで眼鏡をかけずに針に糸を通すことができる. ‖ His health is not *equal to* the voyage. 彼の健康ではその航海には耐えられない. ‖ I am *equal to* nothing this morning. 僕は今朝はなにもやれない. ‖ He is *equal to* anything. 彼はなんでもやってのける. 【類】those who are not *equal to* much in the way of mathematics. ¶All of the people are *equal under* the law. [憲法]すべての国民は法の下に平等である.

equal, *v.* 匹敵する.

P *equal* an elephant *in* size 大きさが象に匹敵する. 【類】No man *equals* him *in* strength.

equality, *n.* 平等, 対等, 同権.

V can *claim equality* to ... …と同等たることを主張しうる. ¶*establish* the political *equality* of races, irrespective of geography, creed, or color 地理的関係や信教のいかんを問わず有色・白色の別なく人種の政治的平等を確立する.

Q claim *racial equality* 人種の平等を要求する. ¶*vicious equality* 悪平等.

Q[2] Some women workers protest their right to *sex equality* in employment. 雇用における男女同権を主張する勤労婦人もある.

P He is *on* an *equality* with you. 彼は君と対等だ.

P[2] *equality between* the sexes 男女同権.

equalization, *n.* 均一化.

P[2] *equalization of* income 収入の均一化.

equalize, *v.* 対等にする.

P *equalize* ... *to* (=*with*) ... …を…と対等にする.

equanimity, *n.* 平静, 安静, 平気.

V This did not *disturb* his *equanimity*. このために彼が動じるということはなかった. ¶*recover equanimity* 平静を回復する. ¶*shake* one's *equanimity* 驚かす, 腹を立てさせる. ¶This *upset* his *equanimity*. これで彼はかんしゃくを起した.

Q said, with *complete equanimity* 冷静そのものといった調子で言った.

P bear one's misfortune *with equanimity* 不幸に平気で耐える ‖ look on ... *with equanimity* 落着いて…を見る.

equation, *n.* 均分; 誤差; 〖数〗方程式.

V It is always wise to *eliminate* the personal *equation* from our judgments of literature as of other things that nearly concern us.—James Russel Lowell. われわれに密接の関係ある他物の批判と同様に文学にたいする批判からもわれわれの個人的誤差を除去するのは常に賢明なやり方である. ¶Every self observer *has* his personal *equation* which he is bound to eliminate cautiously. 自己の観察者はたれにもつとめて除去しなければならない個人的誤差があるものだ. ¶*solve* an *equation* 方程式を解く.

Q a *chemical equation* 化学方程式. ¶a *differential equation* 〖数〗微分方程式. ¶The *personal equation* is always the dominating factor. 当事者のいかんということがいかなる場合にも主たる要素となる. ¶a *simple* (*quadratic, cubic*) *equation* 一(二, 三)次方程式.

equator, *n.* 赤道.

P be more than four times around the earth *at* the *equator* 地球の赤道を四回以上回る距離である.

equidistant, *a.* 等距離の.

P Tsingtao is *equidistant from* Port Arthur and Shanghai, about 300 miles. 青島は旅順港からも上海からも約三百マイルの同距離にある.

equilibrium, *n.* 均衡, 均勢, 釣合.

V *disturb* the psychic *equilibrium* 精神の均衡をかき乱す. ¶*establish* the *equilibrium* in East Asia 東亜の均勢を確立する. ¶*lose* one's *equilibrium* その均勢を失う(よろめく). ¶*menace* the *equilibrium* of Europe 欧州の均勢をおびやかす. ¶*re-establish* the *equilibrium* 均勢を再び確立する. ¶*restore* the disturbed *equilibrium* 破れた均勢を取戻す. 【類】*restore* the *equilibrium* and normal life of continental nations shattered by the struggle of 1914–1918. ¶Such a proceeding will *upset* the foreigner's *equilibrium*. こんなことをすると外国人は面くらうだろう. 【類】The danger *upset* his *equilibrium*.

Q a *perfect equilibrium* of forces 諸力の完全な均勢. ¶a *political equilibrium* 政治上の均勢. ¶*unstable equilibrium* 不安定な均衡.

P bodies *in equilibrium* つり合の取れた物体.

P[2] the *equilibrium of* demand and supply 需要と供給の均衡.

equinox, *n.* 春(秋)分.

Q the *autumnal equinox* 秋の彼岸. ¶the *vernal equinox* 春の彼岸.

Q[2] at the *spring equinox* 春の彼岸に.

equip, *v.* 艤(ぎ)装する; 武装させる; 供給する; 装わす; 準備させる.

M He is so *admirably equipped* for his task. 彼はりっぱにその仕事に当る実力ができている. ¶He is *fully equipped* for the battle of life. 彼にはすっかり生活戦線に立つ準備ができている. ¶he *equipped* himself most *thoroughly* for ... 彼は徹底的に…の準備をした. ¶He is *well equipped* for it. 彼はりっぱにその仕事に当れる.

P He is *equipped by* considerable experience of it. 彼はそれについてはかなりの経験を積んでいる. ¶*equip* a person *for* an occupation ある職業のために養成する ‖ *equip* a ship *for* a voyage 船を艤装する. 【類】*equip* young men *for* the struggle of life ‖ She came out of her room *equipped for* the ball. 彼女は舞踏会へ行く身支度をしてへやから出てきた. ¶She is *equipped in* good style. 彼女は体裁よく着飾っている. ¶a factory *equipped with* the new type of machinery 新式機械を設置した工場 ‖ a bicycle *equipped with* a reflector of prescribed powers 指定性能の反射鏡を備え付けた自転車. 【類】The building is *equipped with* a gymnasium, swimming pool, etc. / The ship is *equipped with* wireless apparatus. / soldiers *equipped with* arms ‖ *equip* him *with* ... pounds for an undertaking 事業を起すについて彼に…ポンドの金を供給する ‖ He is *equipped with* full dress. 彼は礼服を着けている. ‖ He was *equipped with* knowledge for the vocation. 彼はその職業に必要な知識をそなえていた. 【類】be *equipped with* enough knowledge and experience for ...

equipage, *n.* 装備, 道具一式.

Q[2] *camp equipage* 野営(キャンプ)の装備. ¶*tea equipage* 茶道具一式. ¶with a bundle tied to the end of a stick, his *travelling equipage* 彼の旅装であるステッキの先に結びつけた包みを携えて.

equipment, *n.* 支度, 準備, 設備, 装置.

V These *completed* their *equipment*. これらでその道具がそろう. ¶*improve equipment* 施設を改善する. ¶*install* the *equipment* suggested 注意されたように施設をする.

Q *complete equipment* 完全な設備. ¶*electric[al] equipment* 電気装置. ¶*intellectual equipment* 知的能力. ¶*linguistic equipment* 語学の素養. ¶*mental equipment* for a tour 漫遊に対する予備知識. ¶*military equipments* 軍備. ¶hostelries with *modern equipments* 現代式に設備した旅館. ¶a *necessary equipment* of correspondence clerks 商業通信係として必要な知識. ¶the *new equipment* necessary for a comeback 復興に必要な新しい施設. ¶perfect

professional** equipment* 職業的素養を完成する. ¶gain a ***proper** equipment* for one's task 仕事に役に立つ適当の施設を得る. ¶This will generally be a ***sufficient** equipment* for a foreign journey. 海外旅行の支度としては普通これで十分だ. ¶usual** equipment* いつもの支度.

Q² ***arms** equipment* 武装. ¶modernize her ***army** equipment* 同国の陸軍施設を近代化する. ¶***delivery** equipment* 荷物輸送設備 (trucks, horses, wagons, harness, etc.). ¶***electric utility** equipment* 電気器具類. ¶***farm** equipment* 農園施設. ¶***fire protection** equipment* 防火施設. ¶grain and its ***flour** equipment* 穀類とその製粉設備. ¶The mother tongue cannot be satisfactorily mastered by students without some ***foreign language** equipment*. 外国語の知識がいくらかなくては学徒は自国語を満足に修得できない. ¶***harbour** equipment* 港湾施設. ¶***heating** equipment* 暖房設備. ¶***household** equipment* 家具調度品. ¶proper ***housing** equipment* 適切な収容施設. ¶removal of ***industry** equipment* from ... ...からの工業用設備の撤去. ¶***laboratory** equipment* 実験所の設備. ¶***life-saving** equipment* 人命救助用具. ¶The value of the ***material** equipment* of Columbia University, including a library of 450,000 volumes, is about $37,000,000. コロンビア大学の物質的設備は四十五万冊の図書を含めてその価格約三千七百万ドルである. ¶***motion-picture sound** equipment* 映画音響装置. ¶install ***motor** equipment* 電動機を据えつける. ¶***office** equipment* オフィス用品. ¶***plant** equipment* 工場施設. ¶change-over of ***railroad** equipment* from coal to fuel oil 石炭から重油への鉄道施設の切換え. ¶the latest ***research** equipment* 最近の研究施設. ¶***stand-by** equipment* 非常使用装置. ¶***store** equipment* 商店施設 (counters, shelving, scales, measures, etc.). ¶***traffic** equipment* 交通施設. ¶manufacturers of ***transportation** (**communication**) equipment* 輸送(通信)用機械製造業者.

P² *equipment **for*** a factory (gymnasium) 工場(など)の設備. ¶*equipment **of*** water-supply 水道工事.

equity, *n*. 公正.

V This is not what *equity **requires**.* これでは公正とは言えない.

equivalent, *n*. 同等物, 等価物; 同意語.

V It ***has*** no satisfactory English *equivalent*. 的確にそれに当る英語はない. ¶graduate students ***holding*** the *equivalent* of a bachelor's degree 学士と同等の学位を有する卒業生. ¶The phrase ***lacks*** a satisfactory colloquial *equivalent*. 的確にこの句に当る俗語はない. ¶***pay*** an *equivalent* for ... ...に対して同等の価格を払う. ¶He managed to ***receive***, through the medium of correspondence magazines, the *equivalent* of a college education. 彼は講義録でどうにか大学程度の教育を収めた.

Q 'The term "stalwart" is perhaps the nearest ***English** equivalent* we have to the Japanese *otokodate*.' 英語の "stalwart" が恐らく日本語の「男達」に一番よく当っているだろう. ‖ for lack of proper ***English** equivalents* 英語には適当な同意語がないので. ¶an ***exact** equivalent* 全く同等のもの. ¶not ***exact***, but ***partial** equivalents* 正確ではないが幾分同意の語. ¶a ***fair** equivalent* for ... ...の正当の価値. ¶You expect to receive the ***full** equivalent* of your money. 君は君のお金に全く相当するものをもらう積りだね. ¶the ***Japanese** equivalent* of the English "..." 英語の...に該当する日本語. ¶There is no ***literal** equivalent* for it in Japanese. それと正確に同意義の語は日本語にない. ¶a ***near** equivalent* 同等に近いもの. ¶***popular** equivalents* of Latin botanical names ラテン植物名の通称. ¶a ***precise*** *equivalent* for ... 的確に...と同意義の語.

Q² The uncertain state of the rate of exchange prevents the accurate showing of ***dollar** equivalents*. 為替レートが不安定のためドル価による正確な評価はできない. ¶***rice** equivalents* 米代用食料.

P ***as*** an *equivalent* for a supply of beer ビール代として. ¶It was purchased ***for*** the *equivalent* of $45. それは米貨の四十五ドルで買った.

P² five dollars or its *equivalent **in*** kind 五ドルもしくは同価値の物資. ¶We cannot find a precise Japanese *equivalent **for*** the word. その語と全く同意義の日本語が見当らない. ¶receive in pay the *equivalent **of*** ... in American money 支払として米貨...に相当する金額を受取る. 【類】 an *equivalent **of*** 500 German marks.

equivalent, *a*. 同等の.

P How many miles is a Japanese *ri equivalent **to***? 日本の一里は何マイルに当るか. ‖ Silence is sometimes *equivalent **to*** a lie. 沈黙は時としてはうそに当ることがある. 【類】 His remark is *equivalent **to*** an insult. ‖ What is $10 *equivalent **to*** in French money? 十ドルはフランスの何フランになるか.

equivocation, *n*. あいまいな言葉, ごまかし.

P prove this ***beyond*** all *equivocation* はっきりとこれを証明する. ¶Answer ***without** equivocation*. はっきり返事をして下さい.

era, *n*. 時代; 紀元.

V ***bring in*** a new *era* 新時代を招来する. ¶***create*** a new *era* 新時代を作る. ¶We are ***entering*** a new *era* of prosperity. われわれは繁栄の新時代に入ろうとしている. ¶***inaugurate*** the *era* of ... ...の時代を開始する. ¶***initiate*** a new *era* 新時代を樹立する. ¶***introduce*** a new *era* in the advancement of man 人類の発達に新紀元を画する. ¶***mark*** a new *era* in the company's operations 会社の経営に新時代を画する. 【類】 The appearance of the book has ***marked*** a new *era* in the history of the question. ¶***open*** [***up***] a new *era* of navigation 航海史上に新時代を開く. 【類】 We do not hesitate to say that the publication of this dictionary ***opens*** a new *era* in Japanese speaking by foreigners. ¶***usher in*** a new *era* in the history of Japan 日本の歴史に新時代を招来する.

V² A new *era* has ***dawned***. 新時代の初光が見えた. ¶The *era* of machinery ***opened***. 機械の時代が始まった.

Q the ***billowy** era* at the turn of the century 世紀更新期の巨浪ほうはいたる時代. ¶the first seven hundred years of the ***Christian** era* キリスト紀元の最初七百年. ¶a ***chronological** era* 年号. ¶in this ***economical** era* この緊縮時代に. ¶During the ***iconoclastic** era* which followed the Restoration, some of the finest gardens in the Empire were destroyed by vandals. 王政復古直後の因襲打破の時代には国内の名園で蛮行者のために破壊されたものも多少あった. ¶The book marks a ***new** era* in literature germane to the subject. その書はその問題に関する文献に一新紀元を画する. ¶the ***pre-Christian** era* キリスト前の時代. ¶the ***pre-Meiji** era* 明治維新前. ¶inaugurate a ***revolutionary** era* 革命時代を現出する. ¶***transitional** eras* in thought 思想の過渡時代. ¶the early ***Victorian** era* ヴィクトリア時代の初期.

Q² the passing of the "***drink cheap***" *era* 安酒時代の終了. ¶in this ***high-cost-of-living** era* この生活費の高い時代に. ¶the ***laissez faire** era* 自由放任時代. ¶the ***new yen** era* 新円時代. ¶the ***railroad** era* of American history アメリカ史上の鉄道時代. ¶the ***Roosevelt** era* ルーズベルト時代. ¶We are entering a ***world** era* that is more or less socialistic. 今や世界は多少とも社会主義化した時代になりつつある.

P ***in*** the Meiji *era* 明治時代に. ¶It is not known what *era* this poet was ***in***. この詩人はいつごろの人か分らない. ¶***since*** the Meiji *era* dawned 明治以降.

P² A new *era **in*** education is dawning. 教育における新時代が出現しようとしている. ¶An *era **of*** scientific study may be fairly said to have set in. 科学的研究の時代がきたと言って差支えない. ‖ the *era **of*** universal disarmament (world peace) 世界軍縮(など)の時代. 【類】 the *era **of*** Alexander.

erase, *v*. 削除する.

M memories that will not ***easily*** be *erased* 容易に払しょくできない記憶.

P *erase* it ***from*** a list それを表から削除する ‖ wish to *erase **from*** the agreement the following 協定書から次の事項を削除したいと思っている.

erasure, *n*. まっ殺.

V ***make*** an *erasure* of ... ...をまっ殺する.

erect, *v*. 建てる; 昇格させる.

P be *erected **from*** designs by ... ...の意匠によって建てられる. ¶The monument was *erected **in*** his honor. その記念碑は彼のために建てられたのだ. ¶*erect* a territory ***into*** a state 《米》 準州を州に昇格させる. 【類】 *erect* a church ***into*** a cathedral. ¶the land ***on*** which the building was *erected* 建物の敷地. ¶The monument was *erected **over*** their remains. 記念碑が彼らの遺がいの上に建てられた. ¶the auditorium was *erected **to*** the memory of ... その公会堂は...の記念に建てられたものだ. 【類】 The temple was *erected **to*** the memory of ...

erection, *n.* 建立；建築物.

V The *erection* of the school was *begun* early this year. その学校の建築は今年の初めに着手された. ¶send a man to *superintend* the *erection* of machinery 人を派して機械の組立てを監督させる.

Q There are many *ancient erections* of unknown use. 往古の建築物には何に用いたのか分らないものが沢山ある.

P The building is in course *of erection*. その建物は建築中である.

P² *erection of* frameworks 建前(たてまえ).

erethism, *n.* 〖生理〗神経過敏.

Q a greater *nervous erethism* among Westerns 西欧人に強く見られる神経過敏.

erosion, *n.* 〖地質〗浸食.

Q² *coast erosion* 海岸の浸食. ¶*soil erosion* 土壌の浸食.

err, *v.* 誤る；それる.

M *err egregiously* = blunder はなはだしい間違いをする. ¶We shall not *greatly err* if we assume that ... ...と仮定して大差なかろう.

P *err from* the right path 正道をふみはずす ‖ *err from* the truth 真理からはずれる. ¶unless we have *erred in* observation われらの観察に誤りなければ. 【類】*err in* one's judgement. ¶Preferring to *err on* the side of copiousness, I will give further illustrations. むしろ豊富に失する方がよいと思うのでなお進んで例証をあげることにする. ‖ He *errs on* the side of mercy. 彼は寛大に失する. 【類】It is best to *err on* the safer side. ¶*Err* rather *upon* the side of brevity than of length in a table speech. テーブル・スピーチは長過ぎるより短か過ぎる方がよい. ¶he *erred with* us in ... 彼もわれわれ同様で...で誤った.

errand, *n.* 使い；使いの用向；使命.

V *do* the *errand* quickly その使いを早くやる. ¶He *has* an *errand* to do. 彼は使いの用がある. ‖ He *had* another *errand* to do in town. 彼は別に町へ行く用事があった. ¶*make* an *errand* 用たしに出る. ¶*run* (=go on) an *errand* 使いに行く ‖ *run errands* for pay 報酬をもらって使いをする ‖ *Errands* are *run* by messenger boys. 走り使いはメッセンジャー・ボーイがする. 【類】one who earns livelihood by *running errands*. ¶He *told* his *errand*. 彼は使いの用向を告げた.

Q on a *diplomatic errand* 外交上の使命を帯びて. ¶on an *official errand* for ... ...のため出張を命ぜられて. ¶his *ostensible errand* was to ... 彼の表向きの使命は...であった. ¶he was sent on a *political errand* to ... 彼は政治上の使命を帯びて...へ派遣された. ¶go abroad on a *public errand* 公用で外国へ行く.

Q² on a *business errand* 商用で. ¶on a *mercy errand* 慈善の仕事で.

P go *on* an *errand* 使いに行く ‖ run *on errands* 走り使いをする. 【類】How much should I give the boy for sending to Yokohama *on* an *errand?*

erratic, *a.* 放逸な.

P He was most *erratic in* his life. 彼は実に自堕落な生活をした.

erroneous, *a.* 誤った.

M This is *completely erroneous*. これは大間違いだ. ¶It is *glaringly erroneous*. それはとんでもない間違いだ.

error, *n.* 錯誤, 誤びゅう；びゅう見；過失.

V *acknowledge* an *error* 過失を認める. ¶*admit* an *error* 過失を自認する. ¶*amend errors* 誤びゅうを改める. ¶*avoid* an *error* 過失を避ける. ¶*commit* a gross *error* 大間違いをする ‖ *commit* an *error* in diet 悪いものを食べる ‖ *commit* a manifest *error* of taste どう見ても悪趣味としか思えないことをする. ¶*correct* the *error* その誤りを正す. ¶*detect* (=*locate*) an *error* in speech 話し方の誤りを見つける. ¶*dispel* (=*dissipate*) *errors* 誤りを一掃する. ¶*eliminate errors* 誤りを除く. ¶*Errors* and omissions *excepted*. 誤記脱落はこの限りにあらず. ¶*make* an *error* in calculation 計算違いをする. ¶*note* an *error* 間違いに気付く. ¶So the *error* was *perpetuated*. かくして過失がそのまま続いた. ¶*point out* an *error* 誤りを指摘する. ¶*produce* curious *errors* 変な間違いを生じる. ¶*recognize errors* 間違いだと認める. ¶*rectify* an *error* 誤りを正す. ¶in order that we may not *repeat* the *errors* of the past 過去の誤りを繰り返さないように. ¶Later on he *saw* his *error*. 後で彼は自分の間違いが分った. ‖ I have brought him to *see* his *error*. 私は彼に間違いを悟らせた. ¶I *showed* him his *errors*. 私は彼の心得違いをさとした. ¶*weed out errors* 間違いを除く.

V² I trust that any *errors* which may have *crept* into this book will be looked upon with a lenient eye. 書中あるいは誤りあらんもこの点は読者の寛恕せられることと信ずる. ¶*Errors crept in*. いつの間にか間違いができた.

Q an *annoying error* 困った[自分の]誤り. ¶a *bad error* まずい誤り. ¶a *cardinal error* 基本的な誤り. ¶a *clerical error* 書き損じ. ¶uncover *current errors* as to ... ...に関する現在の誤りをさらけ出す. ¶*dietetic errors* 食物の不注意. ¶*downright* and *inexcusable errors* in translation ゆるすべからざる大きな誤訳. ¶however *excusable* his *error* may be 彼の過失がいかにむりのないものであっても. ¶a *fatal error* 致命的な誤り. ¶a *fortunate error* かえってよかった間違い. ¶a *flagrant error* 目ざわりになる誤り. ¶a *fundamental error* 根本的の誤り. ¶a *gigantic error* 大々的の間違い. ¶a *glaring error* 顕著な間違い. ¶a very *grave scientific error* きわめて重大な科学上の誤り. ¶a *gross error* はなはだしい間違い. ¶a *heinous* and *common error* 悪質で, しかもよくある誤り. ¶a *harmless error* 害にならない誤り. ¶a *hideous error* 恐ろしい過失. ¶an *irrecoverable error* 訂正のできない誤り. ¶an *irreparable error* 取返しのつかない間違い. ¶a *national error* 国策上の誤り. ¶an *original error* 原差. ¶a *painted error* 粉飾した誤り. ¶a *plain error* まぎれもない誤り. ¶This book contains many *printers' errors*. この本には誤植が多い. ¶a persistently *recurrent error* しつようsaid繰返される誤り. ¶It would be a *serious error*. それは大きな誤りである. ¶a *slight error* さ細な間違い. ¶a *social error* 社交界での禁物. ¶a *technical error* in the construction of the ship 船舶建造に関する技術上の手おち. ¶a *textual error* (註釈などに対する)本文の誤り. ¶a *trifling error* ささいな間違い. ¶The Editor cannot hope that the book is free from *typographical errors*. 編者はこの本に誤植がないということは申上げられない. ¶an *error* not *uncommon* ありがちの間違い. ¶a *vital error* 根本の誤り. ¶The *error* is *widespread* and *deep-rooted*. そのびゅう見は至る所にまんえんして根深いものがある.

Q² an *azimuth error* 〖天文〗方位誤差. ¶a small *drafting error* 起草上の小さな誤り. ¶a *speech error* 言葉の上の誤り.

P I cautioned him *against error*. 彼に過失を犯さないように注意した. ‖ guard *against error* 過失のないように用心する. ¶It was reported *by* an *error*. それは誤報であった. ¶He made amends *for* his *error*. 彼は自分の過失をつぐなった. ‖ make a liberal allowance *for errors* 過失を寛大に取扱う. ¶a dictionary not quite free *from* printers' *errors* 誤植が全然ないとは言えない辞典. ¶*in error* = by mistake 間違って ‖ you are *in error* in supposing that ... 君が...と思うのは間違いだ ‖ The letter was addressed *in error*. その手紙はあて名が違っていた. ‖ Our perspicacious reader will doubtless have observed that "Berlin Government" was printed *in error* for "British Government." わが賢明な読者は "British Government" は "Berlin Government" の誤植であったことに無論気づかれたことでしょう. ‖ stand *in error* 誤信している. ¶He fell *into* a serious *error*. 彼は重大なびゅう見に陥った. 【類】He was led *into error*. ¶*owing to errors* in diet (= faulty food) 悪いものを食べたので. ¶*through* some *error* or oversight 何かの間違いか見落しで. ¶Every man is liable *to error*. 間違いはだれもする.

P² an *error by* oversight 見落し. ¶... is an *error for* ... ...は...の間違い. ¶*errors in* (=of) commission and omission 間違いや脱落 ‖ an *error in* grammar = a grammatical error 文法の誤り ‖ an *error in* opinion びゅう見. 【類】There is an *error in* his opinion (=view). ‖ It is an *error in* taste to be always "talking like a book." いつも本を読むような(堅くるしい)言葉使いをするのは悪趣味である. ‖ an *error in* writing (printing) 筆記(など)の誤り. ¶an *error in regard to* time 時間の誤り. ¶an *error of* spelling (judgment) つづり字(など)の誤り ‖ *errors of* taste in dress 服装における悪趣味. 【類】an *error of* judgment ‖ an *error of* jurisdiction 管轄違い. ¶an *error on* your part 君の方の過失 ‖ an *error on* the side of modesty 度を過ぎた謙そん.

ersatz, *n.* 代用品.

P serve *as* an *ersatz* for ... ...の代用として役立つ.

erudition, *n.* 博学, 博識.

V it *needs* no great *erudition* to tell that ... ...博学の人でなくても(三歳の童子も)...は知っている. ¶He *wears* his *erudition* lightly. 彼は余り博識を鼻にかけない.

Q his *deep* and *well digested erudition* 彼の深くてよく消化した学識. ¶a man of *great erudition* 大学者. ¶the *profound erudition* of the writer その筆者の博識. ¶his *vast* and *curious erudition* 彼のひろく興味深い知識.

P he is better qualified *by erudition* for ... 彼は博学なので一層...に適している. ¶His range *of erudition* is wide. 彼の学識は広い.

eruption, *n.* 破裂, 噴火; 吹出物.

Q a *nation-wide eruption* of leftist-inspired violence 国中に広がった極左扇動の暴動ぼっ発. ¶The volcano went into *violent eruption*. その火山が猛烈に噴火した. ¶*volcanic eruption* 火山の噴火.

P The town was buried *by* the *eruption* of Vesuvius. その町はヴィシューヴィアス山の噴火で埋まってしまった. ¶Mt. Aso *in eruption* 阿蘇山の噴火.

P² an *eruption on* (=*of*) the skin (face) 皮膚(など)の吹出物.

escapade, *n.* 悪戯.

Q a *dangerous escapade* of boys such as putting a stone on the rail 鉄道線路に石を載せるような少年の危険ないたずら. 「のどんちゃん騒ぎ.

Q² *Christmas escapade* in Japan 日本におけるクリスマス

escape, *n.* 免れること; 逃走, 脱走.

V He *effected* his *escape* in disguise. 彼は変装して逃走した. ¶We can *find* no *escape* from this dilemma. われわれはこの板ばさみをのがれることはできない. ¶*have* a narrow *escape* 九死に一生を得る. ¶He *had* his *escape cut off*. 彼は逃げ路を断たれた. ¶*make* one's *escape* 逃走する ‖ They *made good* their *escape*. 彼らはうまく脱出した. ¶*seek escape* (=refuge) from the heat of the metropolis 首都の炎熱を避ける.

Q He had a *hair breadth escape* from a wild boar. 彼はいのししに出会って九死に一生を得た. ¶one of the most *hazardous* and *thrilling escapes* 全く命がけのぞっとするような命拾いの一例. ¶an *ineluctable escape* よんどころない逃走. ¶He has had a *marvellous escape* from death. 彼は不思議に命拾いをした. ¶He had most absolutely *miraculous escape*. 彼は全く不思議に助かった. ¶Several firemen had *narrow escapes* from death at this fire. 数名の消防夫はこの火事で全く命拾いをした. ‖ He grew quite sentimental at thinking what a *narrow escape* he had had. 彼は何と危い所を助かったかということを考えて全く感傷的になった. ¶a *near escape* 命拾い. ¶There is *no escape* from it. 逃げ道はない. ¶a *providential escape* 天助. ¶There were not many *successful escapes* from the prison. 脱獄者は多くはなかった. ¶a *thrilling escape* from jail ぞっとするような脱獄事件.

Q² a *fire escape* 火災避難装置. ¶have a *hairbreadth escape* 間一髪で助かる. ¶a *mass escape* of prisoners 囚人の集団脱獄.

P a turret *for* the *escape* of smoke 煙出し用の小塔.

P² make one's *escape by* a backdoor 裏口から逃走する. ¶an *escape from* captivity 監禁からの脱出 ‖ an *escape from* detection 発覚を免れること ‖ an *escape from* reality 現実からの逃避. ¶*escape of* blood *from* ... ...からの出血 ‖ *escape of* prisoners *from* ... ...からの囚人脱獄.

escape, *v.* 免れる, 逃れる, 漏れる.

M He *barely escaped*. 彼はかろうじて免れた. ¶His name *just escaped* me. 彼の名前はちょっと忘れてしまった. ¶He *miraculously escaped* being punished. 彼は不思議にも罰を免れた. ¶He *narrowly escaped* being left behind. 彼はあぶなく置いて行かれる所だった. 【類】He *narrowly escaped* death. / I *narrowly escaped* being run over by a car. ¶He *escaped unhurt*. 彼は無事に逃げた.

P *escape by* artifice 計略で逃げる ‖ *escape by* the backdoor 裏口から逃げる. ¶try to *escape from* justice 法網をくぐろうとする ‖ *escape from* the world *to* his ink-bottle 世を捨てて文筆に親しむ ‖ The prisoner *escaped from* his escort. その囚人は護送中に脱走した. ‖ *escape from* imprisonment 脱獄する ‖ The matter *escaped from* my mind. 私はそのことは忘れた. ‖ Gas *escapes from* the pipe. ガスが管から漏れる ‖ *escape* [*from*] death (starvation, an epidemic) 死(など)を免れる ‖ the desire to *escape from* ordinary surroundings 平凡な環境からのがれたいという気持. ¶*escape through* the cordon of soldiers 哨(しょう)兵線を突破する ‖ *escape through* the wide meshes of a net 網の広い目から逃げる. ¶He *escaped to* a foreign land. 彼は外国へ逃げた. ¶He *escaped with* difficulty. 彼はやっと逃げた. ‖ He hardly *escaped with* bare life. 彼は命からがら逃げた. 【類】He *escaped with* bare life. ¶He *escaped without* harm. 彼は無事に逃げた.

escapism, *n.* 逃避主義.

Q a life of *aloof escapism* 象牙の塔的生活.

escort, *n.* 護衛, 保護.

Q We had the pleasure of admiring his collection under the *personal escort* of the envied owner. われわれは人もうらやむ所有者自身の案内でその収集品を鑑賞することができた. 「*escort* 警官に護衛されて.

Q² a *motor-cycle escort* オートバイの護衛. ¶under *police*

P merchant ships *under escort* 護衛されている商船 ‖ ladies *under* the *escort* of gentlemen 紳士付添いの婦人たち. ¶travel *without* male *escort* 男子の付添いなしに旅行する.

escort, *v.* 護衛する, 護送する.

M *escort* her *home* 彼女を家まで送る.

M² *escort* them *round* the sights of the city 市内の見物に彼らの案内をする.

P *escort* the guests *to* the table 賓客を食卓に案内する. 【類】*escort* a lady *to* ...

escutcheon, *n.* 紋章.

P a taint (=blot) *on* one's *escutcheon* 名折れ.

especial, *n.* 特別.

P *in especial* 特に, とりわけ.

esplanade, *n.* 散策地; 広場.

P² a fine *esplanade for* motoring and walking 自動車操縦と散策に適したりっぱな広場.

espouse, *v.* 嫁にやる.

P He *espoused* his sister *to* a friend. 彼は妹を友人の嫁にやった.

esprit de corps, *n. F.* 団結心.

V *develop* an *esprit de corps* 団結心を発揮する. ¶*promote esprit de corps* 団結心を助長する.

essay, *n.* 論文, 随筆; 試み, 企て.

V *exchange essays* for criticism 相互批評のため作文を交換する(生徒間などで). ¶*make* an *essay* to benefit a friend 友人のためになるようなことをしようと企てる. ¶*read* an *essay* on ... at the club そのクラブで...に関する論文を朗読する ‖ *read* an *essay* to a meeting of the Society その協会の会合で論文を朗読する. ¶*write* an *essay* on the subject その問題に関する論文を書く.

Q a *bold essay* in the field of prophecy 予言界における大胆な試み. ¶a *critical essay* 批評論文 ‖ *critical* and *biographical essays* 批評及び伝記文. ¶a *deep essay* 深奥な論説. ¶a *dignified essay* 堂々たる論文. ¶a *hightoned essay* 調子の高い随筆. ¶a *little essay* 小論. ¶*occasional* and *desultory essays* 随筆. ¶*outspoken essays* on social subjects 社会問題に関する忌たんない評論. ¶a *thoughtful essay* 深みのある論文.

Q² a *contest essay* 懸賞論文. ¶the *graduate essay* of a college student 大学生の卒業論文. ¶a *manuscript essay* まだ作文にならない文. ¶a *prize* (=*prize-winning*) *essay* 入選論文. ¶a *three-part essay* 三段論文 (introduction, development, conclusion).

P *in* a short *essay* of this nature one cannot find space for a detailed account of ... この種の短かい論説では...の詳細な説明を試みる余地がない. ¶the subject *of* an *essay* 論文の題目.

P² an *essay at* reform 刷新の企て. ¶*Essays in* Applied Economics 応用経済学論文集 ‖ an *essay in* English 英語で書いた論文. ¶*Essays on* Modern Dramatists 近代劇作家に関する論文集. ‖ His *essays on* Russian literature are among the classics of criticism. 彼のロシア文学論は古典的評論になっている.

essayist, *n.* 随筆家, 評論家.

Q an *economic essayist* 経済評論家. ¶a *literary essayist* 文芸評論家. ¶a *religious essayist* 宗教評論家.

essence, *n.* 実質, 本体; 要素, 粋, 精; 香水.

V *absorb* the *essence* of ... ...の粋を吸収する. ¶He has at command the phrase which *condenses* the *essence* of a paragraph or a page. 彼は一項又は一ページの大要を約言し得べき語句を自由に考え出せる. ¶*extract* the *essence* of journals 諸新聞の粋を抜く. ¶*lose* its *essence* 骨抜きになる, ばかになる. ¶*use* loud *essence* 香の高い香水を使う.

Q in its *ultimate essence* せんじ詰めれば. ¶Even more than beauty, daintiness is the *very essence* of feminine charm. 優雅こそ女性魅力の本質であって美貌すら及ばない. 【類】The *very essence* of happiness is self-forgetfulness.

Q² ***Meat** essences* are made by extracting the most valuable food elements from beef. 食肉エキスは牛肉の最も貴重な食要素を抽出したものである.

P ***in** its essence* 要するに ‖ the same ***in** essence* 実質において同じ物 ‖ unlike ***in** essence* 本質の異った ‖ it means, ***in** essence*, that ... それは結局...ということになる.

P² the *essence **of*** religion 宗教の真髄 ‖ *essence **of*** beef 牛肉精 ‖ The *essence **of*** Christianity is the sublimation of love. キリスト教の本質は愛の昇華である. ‖ Time is to be considered the *essence **of*** the agreement. 時がこの協約の根本をなしていると考えられる.

essential, *n.* 要素, 要義.

V ***grasp** the essential* 要領を得る. ¶He was wise enough to ***keep*** that *essential* in view. 賢明な彼はその要領を忘れなかった. ¶it ***lacks*** the first *essentials* of ... それは...の根本において欠ける所がある.

Q an ***absolute** essential* 絶対的緊要事項. ¶get down to ***bare** essentials* ほとんど丸裸同様になる (strip show で). ¶***basic** essentials* 根本要義. ¶the ***first** essential* 第一要義. ¶one of the ***prime** essentials* for success 成功の根本要素の一つ. ¶*essentials **unclogged*** by superfluities 無用の長物にわずらわされない要綱.

Q² ***food** essentials* 食成分 (vitamine (B_1), niacin, iron). ¶Husky boots and a knapsack are ***hiking** essentials.* 登山ぐつとルックサックはハイキングの必要品だ. ¶basic ***living** essentials* 基本的生活必需品.

P² *essentials **in*** civil government 民政の要義 ‖ *essentials **in*** religion 宗教の要素. ¶*essentials **to*** beauty (success, health) 美(など)に欠くべからざるもの.

essential, *a.* 須要の, 不可欠の.

M Impartiality is ***absolutely** essential* to a judge. 裁判官にとって公平無私が絶対必要である. ¶In a country like Japan a navy is still ***more** essential* than an army. 日本のような国では海軍の方が陸軍よりもなお一そう必要だ. ¶***structurally** essential* 構成上必要な.

P it is *essential **for*** a right understanding of ... ...を正しく理解するにはそれが必要だ. ¶Punctuality is *essential **in*** the business world. 実業界では時間の正確が重要である. ¶French was once considered *essential **to*** the equipment of any diplomat. フランス語は外交家が知らなくてはならないものと考えられていた時代があった. 【類】It is *essential **to*** health (happiness, beauty, life).

establish, *v.* 確定する; 確証する, 確立する; 設立する; 制定する; [職などに]つかせる.

M The patient *established* herself ***bravely.*** その患者は気丈に我慢した. ¶it has been very ***clearly** established* that ... ...という事実が確認された. ¶It cannot be regarded as ***definitely** established.* それははっきり確定したものとは見なされない. ¶The scheme is now ***firmly** established.* 考案は既に確定している. ‖ *establish* oneself ***firmly*** in ... ...におけるその地位を確立する. 【類】The usage is now ***firmly** established.* ¶***legally** establish* a claim 権利を法的に確立する. ¶The theory is not yet ***scientifically** established.* その理論はまだ科学的に確立していない. 【類】It cannot be regarded as ***scientifically** established.* ¶His belief is too ***well** established* to be overthrown. 彼の信念は強固だからくつがえされるようなことはない. ¶*established **100 years*** 創立百年の(会社など). ¶*established **1890*** 一八九〇年創立の(学校など).

P It is *established **as*** a fact. それはりっぱに事実とされている. ‖ He is *established **as*** a tailor. 彼は仕立屋を営んでいる. ‖ *establish* mechanics ***as*** a science 機械学を科学として確立する. ¶it is *established **beyond*** controversy that ... ...ということはりっぱに確証されているから議論の余地がない. ¶The proof was *established **beyond*** question. その証拠は動かし難いものとなった. ¶a barrier *established **for*** the surveillance of travelers 関所. ¶*establish **by*** law 法律で制定する. ¶*establish* a person ***in*** business (an office) 人を実業(など)につかせる ‖ He *established* himself ***in*** business. 彼は実業に腰を落付けた. ¶the Lectureship is *established **on*** an ample foundation by the bequest of ... その講座は...の遺贈に係る多額の基金をもって設けられた. 【類】It was *established **on*** no solid basis.

establishment, *n.* 設立; 確立, 制定; 設立物, 会社, 店舗; 建物, 居宅; 世帯, 生計; 定員.

V ***break up*** the *establishment* at ... ...の店をたたむ. ¶He has ***founded*** an *establishment* for the maintenance of orphans. 彼は孤児院を立てた. ¶He ***keeps*** a large *establishment.* 彼は大きな暮しをしている. ¶***keep up*** a large *establishment* 大きな世帯を張っている. ¶***maintain*** an *establishment* in London ロンドンに店を持っている. ¶***reduce*** an *establishment* 定員を減らす. ¶The Government has ***sanctioned*** the *establishment* of the school. 政府は同校開設を認可した. ¶***seek** establishment* in that business その商売で身を立てようとする.

Q operate ***another** establishment* for education 学校をもう一つ経営する. ¶a ***bacteriological** establishment* 細菌研究所. ¶goods manufactured by that ***celebrated** establishment* あの有名な店が製造した商品. ¶The restaurant is the most ***elegant*** and ***best appointed** establishment* of the kind in London. その飲食店はロンドンの同業中一番上品で設備もいい. ¶***higher educational** establishments* 高等教育の機関. ¶an ***industrial** establishment* 工場. ¶a clerk in a ***mercantile** establishment* 商館の事務員. ¶***old** establishment* 老舗(しにせ). ¶the ***photographer's** establishment* 写真店. ¶a ***prosperous** establishment* 繁じょうしている店. ¶a ***public** establishment* 公共の建物(市民会館など). ¶companies of more ***recent** establishment* もっと新しい会社. ¶erect a red-brick ***hydro-electric** establishment* 赤れんがの水力電気会社を建てる. ¶It is among the most ***renowned*** and ***fruitful educational** establishments* in the world. それは世界中で最も有名で効果的な教育機関の一つだ. ¶a ***separate** establishment* 別館. ¶a ***subsidiary** establishment* 付属(補助)の建物. ¶a ***teetotal** establishment* 酒を一切出さない(飲食)店.

Q² an ***amusement** establishment* 娯楽場(劇場など). ¶a ***banking** establishment* 銀行. ¶a ***bathing** establishment* 水泳場(プールなど). ¶a ***branch** establishment* 支店, 出張所. ¶a ***business** establishment* 商会. ¶a ***convict** establishment* 囚人授護会. ¶an ***eating** establishment* owned and operated by third power nationals 第三国人の所有であり経営されている食堂. ¶an ***eating*** and ***drinking** establishment* 飲食店. ¶an ***interior decorating** establishment* 室内装飾業の店. ¶a ***liquor** establishment* 酒屋. ¶***peace (war)** establishment* 平(戦)時編成. ¶a large and well-equipped ***printing** establishment* 大規模な設備の整った印刷工場. ¶***shore** establishments* 陸上施設. ¶a ***welfare** establishment* for mothers and children 母子寮. ¶***wholesale*** and ***retail** establishments* おろし小売店.

P ***at*** the *establishment* of Messrs. Chappell and Co. チャペル会社の店で.

P² an *establishment **for*** the training of nurses 看護婦養成所. ¶the secure *establishment **of*** a doctrine 学説の確立 ‖ an *establishment **of*** fortification 築城 ‖ *establishment **of*** righteousness and security of the country 立正安国. ¶the *establishment **of*** Delhi ***as*** the capital of the Indian Empire in 1912 一九一二年に印度の首府としてデリーを制定したこと.

estate, *n.* (**1**) 財産; 地所, 不動産.

V ***administer*** a deceased's *estate* 死者の財産を管理する. ¶***bank*** an *estate* 財産を抵当にして銀行から金を借りる. ¶He ***bought*** an *estate* in the suburbs, where he settled down to a life of study. 彼は郊外に屋敷を買って書斎生活にはいった. ¶His former *estate* is being ***divided*** into lots and sold. 彼の以前の邸宅地は今分譲されつつある. ¶The *estate* is heavily ***engaged*** (=***encumbered***). 地所は高い抵当に入っている. ¶He ***has*** some house and *estate.* 彼は土地・家屋を持っている. ¶These soldiers ***held*** their *estates* as fiefs from the Shogun. これらの武士は将軍から封土として土地を所有していた. ¶***inherit*** a valuable *estate* 高価な財産を相続する. ¶he ***left*** an *estate* of \$... 彼は...ドルの財産を残した ‖ he ***left** estate* of the value of ..., with net personalty of £ ... 彼は正味...ポンドの動産と...の価格の不動産を残した. ¶The *estate* is ***mortgaged.*** その地所は抵当に入っている. ¶***own*** a landed *estate* 地所を所有する. ¶He ***purchased*** a little *estate* and built a house. 彼は小さな地所を買って家を建てた. ¶***sell*** one's ancestral *estate* 先祖の家屋敷を売る. ¶The father ***willed*** his *estate* to his son. 父はその財産をその子に譲るように遺言した. ¶***wrest** estate* from ... ...から財産を奪いとる.

V² The *estate **came down*** to him. その財産は彼に伝わった. ¶A large *estate* has ***fallen*** to him. 大資産が彼の手にはいった. ¶Real *estate* has ***sagged*** (***recovered***). 不動産の値が下った(回復した).

Q He lives on a ***beautiful*** *estate*. 彼はりっぱな屋敷に住んでいる.【類】a ***beautiful*** *estate* with a country house (別荘) and a swimming pool. ¶He left behind him a ***considerable*** *estate* which was dissipated by a gentleman of the family. 彼はかなりの財産を残して死んだが遺族中の放とう息子が滅茶々々にしてしまった. ¶his ***former*** *estate*. 以前彼の所有であった土地. ¶***landed*** and ***residential*** *estates* 地所及び宅地. ¶***personal*** *estate* 動産. ¶hold ***real*** *estate* 土地家屋を所有している.【類】In New York and in many other States Japanese can hold ***real*** *estate* and transmit it to their heirs. / He owns considerable ***real*** *estate*.

Q² The rich have gone on vacations to their ***country*** *estates*. 金持ちは休暇中いなかの屋敷へ出かけた. ¶Hendon airfield would make an excellent ***housing*** *estate*. ヘンドン飛行場はおそらくすばらしい宅地になるだろう. ¶a ***rubber*** *estate* ゴム園. ¶a ***tea*** *estate* 茶園.

P a successor ***in*** one's *estate* その財産相続人 ‖ He has succeeded his father ***in*** the *estate*. 彼は父の財産を継いだ. ¶the main building ***on*** the Masujima *estate* 増島邸の主な建物 ‖ They reside ***on*** an *estate* a short distance outside of London. 彼らはロンドンに近い郊外に住んでいる.【類】live in retirement (隠居する) ***on*** his *estate* at ... ‖ Pure water is supplied in abundance by an artesian well (掘抜き井戸) specially sunk ***on*** the *estate*. ¶He is heir ***to*** a large *estate*. 彼は大資産の相続人だ.

P² They have *estates* ***across*** the Channel. 彼らはイギリス海峡の向う側に地所を持っている. ¶an *estate* ***in*** land 不動産.

(2) 身分, 地位; 階級.

V ***reach*** man's *estate* 成年に達する.

Q Radio has grown in a single decade from a fascinating toy to occupy the position of a ***fifth*** *estate*. ラジオはわずか十カ年の中に非常な発達を遂げて始めは面白いおもちゃ位に見られていたのが今では一躍(社会の第四階級たる新聞紙に次いで)第五階級の地位を占めるようになった. ¶arrive at ***man's*** *estate* 成年に達する.【類】A boy attains ***man's*** *estate* at 20. / grow to ***man's*** *estate*. ¶the long procession of events which have led the British Empire to its ***present high*** *estate* among the nations of the world 英帝国が世界列国間において今日の堂々たる地位を作るまでに至った長いいきさつ.

P² descend to the *estate* ***of*** a rag-picker くず拾いに落ちぶれる.

esteem, *n.* 尊敬, 尊重.

V ***command*** other's *esteem* 他人の尊敬を博する. ¶***earn*** the *esteem* of one's fellow countrymen 同胞の尊敬を得る. ¶***enjoy*** the *esteem* of ... ...の尊敬を得る. ¶***feel*** no *esteem* for ... ...に対して尊敬の念が起らない. ¶***forfeit*** people's *esteem* 人に尊敬されなくなる. ¶***gain*** high *esteem* 非常に尊重される. ¶I ***have*** a great *esteem* for his ability. 私は彼の手腕には大いに敬服している. ¶***lessen*** the *esteem* of his followers 彼の部下の尊敬心を薄くする. ¶***lose*** the *esteem* of the public 一般から尊重されなくなる.【類】He has ***lost*** my *esteem*. ¶We will strive in every way to ***merit*** the *esteem* of our friendly readers. われわれは好意ある読者諸君の敬意にそむかぬよう全力を尽すつもりである. ¶***win*** *esteem* in the world 世の中で尊重される.

Q He is held in ***high*** *esteem*. 彼は非常に尊敬されている. ¶their place in ***public*** *esteem* 公衆の目から見た彼らの地位 ‖ He stands high in ***public*** *esteem*. 彼は大いに公衆の尊敬を受けている.【類】It will lower him in ***public*** *esteem*. ¶Art was held in ***slight*** *esteem*. 芸術は軽視されていた. ¶His character won for him ***universal*** *esteem*. 彼の性格は彼のために広く世の尊敬をかちえた.

P This raised Japan ***in*** the *esteem* of the world. このために世界における日本の評価を高めた. ‖ he was held ***in*** great *esteem* for ... 彼は...で大いに重視された. ¶a man ***of*** *esteem* 尊重すべき人.

esteem, *v.* 尊重する; 評価する; 思う.

M be ***highly*** *esteemed* among ... ...間では大いに尊敬を受けている ‖ I *esteem* your advice ***highly***. 御忠告を大いに尊重する.【類】Asparagus is ***highly*** *esteemed* for the table. ¶*esteem* money ***lightly*** 金銭を軽く見る.

P It is *esteemed* much ***above*** the others. それは他のものよりははるかに重んじられている. ¶I shall *esteem* it [*as*] a favor. かたじけなく存じます. ¶His poems were highly *esteemed* ***by*** (=***among***) his contemporaries. 彼の詩は同時代の人々に大いに重んじられていた.

O *esteem* him to be happy 彼を幸福と思う. ¶I *esteem* it a great favor to be remembered so kindly. かくも御親切に御記憶下さることはまことにありがたく存じます.

estimate, *n.* 見積り, 評価; 予算, 概算, 見積り額.

V ***base*** one's *estimates* on the fact that ... ...という事実に基いて評価する.【類】***base*** an *estimate* upon reliable data. ¶***form*** *estimates* 見積りをする.【類】We can ***form*** some *estimate* of the difficulty of the task. / It is too early to ***form*** an *estimate* of the crops. / ***form*** a true *estimate* of ... ‖ some *estimate* may be ***formed*** of the labor bestowed on ... from the fact that ... ...に対してどれだけの努力が払われたかは...という事実からして幾分これを測定することができよう. ¶an *estimate* of ... may be ***got*** from the fact that ... ...という事実によって...という推定ができよう. ¶***give*** an *estimate* for repairing a roof 屋根の修繕費の見積りを出す. ¶We ***have*** an accurate *estimate* of cost of our living. 私たちは生活費の見積りをきちんと立てている. ¶***heighten*** one's *estimate* of another's ability 人の能力を高く評価する. ¶***make*** an *estimate* 見積る. ¶***make out*** an approximate *estimate* 大体の見積書を作製する. ¶***make up*** an *estimate* 見積書を作成する. ¶***present*** the *estimate* for the Budget to the Diet 議会に予算案を提出する. ¶***raise*** the public *estimate* of ... ...について世人の評価を高める. ¶I shall be pleased to ***submit*** *estimates* and drawings against specifications of requirement. 明細書に添えて見積書と図面をお送り致しましょう.

Q form an ***accurate*** *estimate* of ... ...を正確に見積る. ¶make out an ***approximate*** *estimate* of ... ...の大体の見積りを立てる. ¶A ***conservative*** *estimate* of the value of this property is about $2,000,000 この財産は内輪に見積って約二百万ドルである.【類】at a very ***conservative*** *estimate* / It is certainly a very ***conservative*** *estimate*. / a table (表) compiled from ***conservative*** *estimates*. ¶form a ***correct*** *estimate* of Japan 日本を正しく評価する. ¶a ***critical*** *estimate* of Mr. Kipling's literary position キップリング氏に対する文学的評価. ¶a ***depreciative*** *estimate* of the masses 大衆の軽べつ的批評. ¶A hundred million dollars is not an ***exaggerated*** *estimate*. 一億ドルは大げさな見積りではない. ¶I can form a ***fair*** *estimate* of ... 私は...について公正な評価を下しうる. ¶The ***general*** *estimate* of the crop is good. 作物の概況は良である. ¶A ***higher*** *estimate* has been made. もっと高く見積る人もある. ¶***itemized*** *estimates* of the cost of ... ...費の項目別見積. ¶a ***just*** *estimate* of Ruskin ラスキンの正しい評価. ¶a ***low*** *estimate* of their numbers would be ... 内輪に見積ってその数は...となるだろう.【類】at a ***low*** (=moderate) *estimate* ‖ The ***lowest*** *estimate* would put the worth of the jewel at 50,000 yen. その宝石はどう安く見積っても五万円の価値があるだろう. ¶It would be a ***moderate*** *estimate* to place the property at $30,000. その財産は三万ドルに見積るなら内輪の方だろう. ¶Five thousand yen is probably as ***near*** an *estimate* as can be made. 五千円という見積りがまず動かない所だろう. ¶The above *estimate* seems to us to be very ***optimistic***. 上記の見積りははなはだ楽観的なもののように思われる. ¶***preliminary*** *estimates* 予算. ¶according to a ***recent*** *estimate* 最近の見積りによると. ¶A ***rough*** *estimate* of the value of the building is given at £300,000. その建物の価格は概略三十万ポンドと見積られている. ¶exceed the most ***sanguine*** *estimates* 非常に楽観的な予想を上回る.

Q² the Finance Ministry's ***draft budget*** *estimates* 予算の大蔵省案.

P He mentioned two years ***as*** a rough *estimate* of time for the completion of the work. 同氏はその工事の完成には大体二カ年を要すると言った. ¶***below*** the original *estimate* 最初の見積り以下で. ¶***In*** the *estimate* of the world, perhaps, he did not accomplish anything of note. 世人の目から見ると恐らく彼は注目に値することを何一つやらなかったことになるだろう. ¶***on*** (=***at***) a conservative *estimate* 内輪に見積って.

P² an *estimate* ***for*** a building (bridge, budget, crops) 建物(など)の見積り. ¶What is your *estimate* ***of*** the crop? 作柄の具合はどの位とお考えですか.

estimate, *v.* 見積る, 評価する.

M the expense is ***conservatively*** *estimated* at ... その費用は内輪に見積って...だ. ¶be ***highly*** *estimated* among ... ...仲間では高く評価されている. ¶cannot be too ***highly*** *es-*

timated その任務はどんなに重く見積っても重く見過ぎることはない. ¶*estimate **justly*** 正しく評価する. ¶it is ***roughly*** *estimated* at ... それは概略...と見積られる. ¶the population of the country is ***variously*** *estimated* at from ... to ... その国の人口は...から...の間でまちまちに計上されている.

P The time for its construction was *estimated **at*** eight years. その建築に要する期間は八カ年と見積られた. ‖ The age of the Buddhist image is *estimated **at*** three hundred years. その仏像は三百年前の作と見られている. 【類】a crowd *estimated **at*** ten thousand. ¶Ask the contractor to *estimate **for*** the repair of the building. 修繕がどの位かかるか請負師に聞いてくれ. ¶The value of the work is not to be *estimated **in*** pounds, shillings, and pence. その本の価値は金高に見積るわけにはゆかない. ‖ His fortune is *estimated **in*** seven figures. 彼の財産は百万台と見積られている.

O It is *estimated* to be about ... tons. それは約...トンと計算される.

estimation, *n.* 評価; 尊重.

Q a ***high*** *estimation* 重視 ‖ He is always held in ***high*** *estimation.* 彼はいつも大いに尊敬されている. ¶He is a savant in his ***own*** *estimation.* 彼は自分では大学者のつもりでいる. ¶He stood high in ***public*** *estimation.* 彼は大いに世人に尊重された. ¶form a ***true*** *estimation* of ... ...を正しく評価する.

P Who, ***in*** your *estimation,* is the greatest living composer? 貴下の考えで現代の最も偉大な作曲家はだれです. ‖ He comes first ***in*** my *estimation.* 僕の目では彼が一番だ. ‖ be low ***in*** *estimation* 見積りは低い ‖ rise (fall) ***in*** the *estimation* of the public 世人の評判が良く(悪く)なる.

P² *estimation **of*** ground (=land) 地所の評価.

estrange, *v.* うとんじる, 疎遠にする.

P *estrange* one's friends ***by*** behaving foolishly ばかなまねをして友人を失う. ¶She became *estranged **from*** her family by marrying a gardener. 彼女は園丁と結婚したので家庭の人たちにうとまれるようになった. 【類】He was *estranged **from*** his friends. ‖ Public opinion is *estranged **from*** the cabinet. 世論は内閣から離反している. ‖ What has *estranged* the two friends ***from*** each other? 何でその二人は仲たがいしたのか. ‖ *estrange* oneself ***from*** ... ...から遠ざかる.

estrangement, *n.* 疎隔.

V ***cause*** *estrangement* between old friends 旧友間にみぞを作る.

P² *estrangement **of*** one friend ***from*** another 友人間の疎隔.

etceteras, *n.* 付加物.

P 10,000 yen ***without*** *etceteras* 一万円かっきり.

etch, *v.* 〘画〙腐食する.

P *etch* designs (figures) ***on*** a copper-plate 銅板に模様(など)を腐食する.

etching, *n.* 〘画〙腐食画法(エッチング).

P² *etching **on*** copper sheets 銅板の腐食画(エッチング).

eternity, *n.* 永遠, 無窮.

Q A ***little*** *eternity* in love! [恋人同志の惜別など]一日千秋の思いだ. ¶Every minute seemed to me a ***little*** *eternity.* 一分一分が私にはちょっと永遠のように思われた.

P ***through*** all *eternity* 永遠に.

P² live an *eternity **in*** a minute 一日千秋の思いで暮す.

ethic[s], *n.* 倫理, 道徳; 倫理学.

V ***set up*** an *ethic* which encourages monogamy 一夫一婦を奨励するような道徳を打ち立てる.

Q ***commercial*** *ethics* 商業道徳. ¶***journalistic*** *ethics* 新聞道徳. ¶***practical*** *ethics* 実践倫理学. ¶***theatrical*** *ethics* 俳優道徳.

Q² ***press*** *ethics* 新聞倫理.

ethnographer, *n.* 民俗学者.

Q² a ***field*** *ethnographer* 実地調査の民俗学者.

ethnology, *n.* 人種学.

P an authority ***on*** *ethnology* 人種学の大家.

etiology, *n.* 原因論.

V ***determine*** its *etiology* その原因を決定する.

Q have the same ***common*** *etiology* 同病原である. ¶The *etiology* is ***obscure.*** その原因は不明である.

etiquette, *n.* 礼儀, 作法(エチケット).

Q transgress the limits of ***diplomatic*** *etiquette* 外交上の儀礼にそむく. ¶***formal*** *etiquette* かた苦しい礼式. ¶***international*** *etiquette* 国際儀礼. ¶***Strict*** *etiquette* and formality are now relaxed. かた苦しい礼式や作法は今ではゆるやかになっている. ‖ ***strict*** *etiquette* requires that ... 本式にやると...となる.

P It is ***against*** *etiquette.* それはエチケットに反する. ‖ In golf it is ***against*** the *etiquette* of the game to talk. ゴルフでは話をすることは競技の作法に反している. ¶He is brought up ***in*** strict *etiquette.* 彼は厳格な礼儀にしつけられた. ¶The Chinese code ***of*** *etiquette* is an elaborated one. 中国の礼式はやかましいものだ. ‖ a breach ***of*** *etiquette* 不作法. ¶The ceremony was conducted ***with*** grave *etiquette.* その式は厳粛に行われた.

P² *etiquette **among*** neighbours 隣人間の礼儀. ¶*etiquette **in*** the home (church) 家庭(など)の礼儀作法. ¶*etiquette **of*** visiting 訪問の作法. ¶*etiquette **with*** royalty 王者に対する礼儀.

etymology, *n.* 語原学; 語原.

V ***hazard*** an *etymology* 語原を当てずっぽうに言ってみる.

Q a ***false*** *etymology* 誤った語原説. ¶***popular*** (=***folk***) *etymology* 通俗語原説.

P² the *etymology **of*** a word ある言葉の語原.

eugenics, *n.* 優生学.

P from the viewpoint ***of*** *eugenics* 優生学の見地から.

eulogium, *n.* =eulogy.

V ***bestow*** the highest *eulogiums* on ... ...を絶賛する.

Q pass a ***high*** *eulogium* on ... ...を大いに称賛する.

eulogy, *n.* 賛辞.

V ***pronounce*** a fitting *eulogy* upon ... ...に対して適切な賛辞を述べる.

Q launch forth into an ***eloquent*** *eulogy* of ... ...をとうとうとほめ立てる. ¶***indiscriminate*** *eulogies* べたぼめ. ¶Mr. Asquith's ***noble*** *eulogy* to King Edward エドワード王に対するアスキス氏の美しい賛仰の辞. ¶it may be said without ***undue*** *eulogy* to him that ... 彼に対して...と言っても溢美(いつ)の言とはなるまい. ¶***win*** the *eulogy* of ... ...の賛辞を受ける.

P addresses ***in*** *eulogy* of the eminent naturalist were made by ... and ... この有名な博物学者に対する称賛の辞が...及び...によって述べられた.

P² a *eulogy **on*** a person (thing) 人(など)に対する賛辞 ‖ an *eulogy **on*** the late ... 故...の頌(しょう).

euphemism, *n.* えん曲の語句.

V ***employ*** a *euphemism* えん曲の語句を用いる.

Q We find in the Old Testament that by a ***curious*** *euphemism* the sexual organs are sometimes referred to as "the feet." 旧約全書には不思議にも生殖器をえん曲に「足」としてある所がある. ¶Work in some universities is often a ***mere*** *euphemism* for pleasure or pastime. ある大学では課業が体裁よく言い換えた娯楽や余興にすぎないことがある.

P express ***by*** a *euphemism* えん曲に言い表わす.

P² "Queer" is a *euphemism **for*** "mad." 「変だ」というのは「気狂だ」というのをえん曲に言ったものだ. 【類】"Passing away" is a *eupemism **for*** "dying."

euphony, *n.* 語呂(ごろ), よい口調.

V The word is heavy and ***lacks*** *euphony.* その言葉はかた苦しくて語呂が悪い.

Europe, *n.* ヨーロッパ, 欧州.

V ***startle*** *Europe* 欧州を震がいさせる. ¶***tour*** *Europe* ヨーロッパを漫遊する.

Q an ***astonished*** *Europe* 震がいの欧州. ¶the principal countries of ***Continental*** *Europe* 欧州大陸の主要諸国. ¶***German*** *Europe* ドイツ系ヨーロッパ. ¶***middle*** *Europe* 中欧. ¶***non-Russian*** *Europe* ソ連領を除いた欧州. ¶***Northern*** (***Southern***) *Europe* 北(南)欧. ¶***Western*** (***Eastern***) *Europe* 西(東)欧.

European, *n.* ヨーロッパ人, 欧州人.

Q ***Continental*** *Europeans* 大陸の欧州人. ¶a ***newly-landed*** *European* 新たに入国した欧州人.

evacuant, *n.* 下剤.

V ***use*** an *evacuant* 下剤をかける.

evacuate, *v.* 撤兵する, 明け渡す.

P those districts *evacuated **by*** Russia ソ連が撤兵したそれらの地方. ¶*evacuate* non-combatants ***from*** ... 非戦闘員を...から疎開させる.

evacuation, *n.* 明渡し, 撤兵; 疎開; 排せつ.

Q ***nocturnal*** *evacuation* 夜の小便. ¶I have ***regular*** *evacuations.* 私は通じがきまってある. ¶a ***regular daily*** *evacuation* of the bowels 毎日の規則正しい通じ. ¶a ***speedy*** *evacuation* of troops 兵の迅速な撤退.

Q² ***emergency*** *evacuation* because of war 戦争による非常疎開. ¶a ***mass*** *evacuation* 大量疎開. ¶***rice-water*** *evacuation* コレラ患者のはき出すかゆのような排せつ物.

P We pressed the enemy ***for*** the *evacuation* of the fort. われわれは敵にとりでの明渡しを迫った.

P² the *evacuation of* children from London ロンドンからの児童疎開.

evacuee, *n.* 疎開者.

P² *evacuees from* Paris パリからの疎開者たち.

evade, *v.* 避ける, 回避する.

M He ***cunningly evaded*** any definite answer. 彼は巧みに一切の確答を避けた. ¶He ***knowingly evaded*** his duties. 彼は故意に自分の任務を回避した.

evader, *n.* 忌避者, 脱税者.

Q² an ***income tax evader*** 所得税回避者.

evaluate, *v.* 評価する.

M fail to ***properly evaluate*** importance 本末を誤る.

evaluation, *n.* 評価.

Q the ***critical evaluation*** of the student's academic work 学生の成績に関する批判的評価.

Q² ***job evaluation*** 職務評価.

evanescence, *n.* 消失, 消散.

Q ***vaporous evanescence*** 雲散霧消.

P² ***evanescence of*** human life つかの間の人生.

evangelist, *n.* 伝道者.

Q² an ***open-air evangelist*** 戸外伝道者.

evangelization, *n.* 福音伝道.

Q the work of ***Christian evangelization*** キリスト教福音伝道事業.

evaporate, *v.* 蒸発させる.

M² ***evaporate down*** to a proper consistency 適度の密度に達するまで蒸発させる.

P ***evaporate into*** a firm consistence 蒸発させて固結させる. ¶Absolutely pure water when ***evaporated to*** dryness in a platinum vessel leaves no residue. プラチナ器物で百パーセント純良な水を蒸発させると全然かすが残らない.

evaporation, *n.* 蒸発, 発散, 消散.

P It is obtained ***by evaporation.*** それは蒸発させて取る. ‖ It is condensed ***by evaporation.*** 蒸発によって凝結させる.

evasion, *n.* 回避, 逃避; 言い抜け.

Q a ***mean evasion*** 卑劣な逃避.

P He took shelter ***in evasions.*** 彼は言い抜けた.

P² ***evasion of*** duties 義務の回避.

eve, *n.* 晩; 祝祭日の前夜; まぎわ.

V ***celebrate*** Christmas ***Eve*** クリスマスの前夜祭を祝う.

Q In theatrical circles, ***New Year's Eve*** is considered the worst in the whole twelve months. 劇界では大みそかの晩は一年中で一番入りが悪いことになっている.

Q² on ***Christmas Eve*** クリスマスの前夜祭に. ¶***New Year Eve*** 大みそか. ¶***Saturdays*** and ***holiday eves*** 日曜及び休日の前の晩. ¶***spring eves*** 春宵(しゅん).

P ***on*** New Year's ***Eve*** 大みそかの晩に ‖ It is ***on*** the ***eve*** of completion. それはまさに完成されんとしている. ‖ You are ***on*** the ***eve*** of complete recovery. 君はもうすぐ全快する. ‖ ***on*** the ***eve*** of success 成功の瀬戸際に ‖ ***on*** the ***eve*** of death 死にひんして. 【類】 be ***on*** the ***eve*** of a panic (revolution) / Unfortunately he died young, and quite suddenly, ***on*** the ***eve*** of taking over a large business. / We were ***on*** the ***eve*** of an important election. ‖ the ship was ***on*** the ***eve*** of her departure for ... 船は...に向けて出発する所であった. 【類】 ***on*** the ***eve*** of sailing.

even, *a., ad.* 同等の, 互角の; 同平面の; さえ, すら, だに.

M I ***never even*** opened the book. その本を開けてもみなかった. ¶***even so,*** still I can show that ... よしそうだとしても私は...を示しうる.

P ***Even for*** an aeroplane it seems almost impossible to cover the distance so quickly. 飛行機にしてもそれだけの距離をそんなに早く飛ぶことはほとんど不可能と思われる. ¶***even in*** that case その場合にでも. ¶intelligible ***even to*** a child 子供にさえ分る. ¶***Even with*** the appointed hour he departed. ちょうど指定の時刻に彼は出掛けた. ‖ get (= be) ***even with*** an antagonist 敵に復しゅうする. 【類】 resolve to be ***even with*** ... ‖ ***even with*** the ground 土地と同平面の.

O ***even*** though I were in his place 私が彼の地位に在ったとしても. 【類】 ***even*** if you don't like it. ¶I haven't ***even*** so much as thought of you. 私は君のことを考えることさえしなかった.

even, *v.* 平均させる.

M² ***even up*** accounts with ... ...との勘定を清算する.

evening, *n.* 晩, 夕刻; 晩年; 衰微期.

V ***devote*** one's ***evenings*** to the study of ... 晩年を...の研究に使う. ¶I have ***enjoyed*** the ***evening*** very much. [帰りがけに]今晩はまことにありがとうございました. ‖ ***enjoy*** a sociable ***evening*** 楽しく一晩語り合う. ¶I will ***keep*** the ***evening clear.*** [会合ができるように]その晩はあけて置きましょう. ¶***pass*** a merry ***evening*** with his friends 彼の友だちと一晩楽しく過す. ¶***set apart*** an ***evening*** for a friendly talk 一夜をさいて親しく語る. ¶I ***spent*** my ***evening*** there till dark. 私はそこで暗くなるまで夕を過した. 【類】 a pleasant ***evening*** was ***spent*** at the home of ...

V² as soon as the ***evening began*** 晩になるや否や. ¶when the ***evening closed in*** 夕やみ迫るころ. ¶as the ***evening deepened*** 夜のふけるにつれて. 【類】 The ***evening deepens*** in the streets outside. ¶as the ***evening drew on*** 晩が近づくにつれて. ¶***Evening*** was just ***falling.*** 丁度晩になりかかっていた. ¶as the ***evening wore on*** 夜がふけるにつれ.

Q the ***evening*** was so far ***advanced*** that ... 夜もいたくふけていって... ¶I hope you have had an ***amusing evening.*** 今晩は面白かったでしょう. ¶a ***balmy evening*** in spring かぐわしい春のひと夜. ¶on the ***bridal evening*** 新婚の夕に. ¶a ***cheerful evening*** 楽しい一夜. ¶a ***cool evening*** 涼しい晩. ¶altogether a ***delightful evening*** 全く愉快な晩. ¶during the ***early evening*** よいの内. ¶A popular programme of music completed a most ***enjoyable evening.*** 大衆音楽のプログラムでいかにも楽しい夕が幕になった. ¶an ***eventful evening*** 多事なりし一夜. ¶***Good evening!*** 今晩は. ¶spend a ***jolly evening*** at ... ...で一晩愉快に過ごす. ¶It was ***late evening.*** 晩もおそかった. ¶a ***merry evening*** 楽しい一夜. ¶have a ***musical envening*** 音楽の夕を催す. ¶the ***other evening*** 先だっての晩. ¶This has been a very ***pleasant evening.*** [帰る時]今晩は十分楽しませていただきました. ¶the ***same evening*** その同じ晩. ¶on a ***wet evening*** 雨の降る晩に. ¶On ***what evening*** shall I attend you? 何日の晩にお伺いしたらよろしいでしょうか.

Q² an ***autumn evening*** 秋の夕. ¶the gloom of ***blackout evenings*** 停電の夜の陰うつさ. ¶organize a ***charity evening*** 慈善興行の夕を計画準備する. ¶on a ***moonlight evening*** 月夜に. ¶on a ***summer evening*** 夏の夕に. ¶Will ***tomorrow evening*** suit you? 明晩は御都合いかがでしょうか.

P ***After*** the ***evening*** it is night. 夕方に続いて夜となる. ¶Many thousands of people who work in the City pour in with the morning and stream out ***at evening.*** 市内で働く大勢の人が朝なだれこんで来て晩には流れて出て行く. ‖ the forest ***at evening*** 夕の森林. 【類】 A rainbow ***at evening*** means that the next will be fair. ‖ ***at*** the ***evening*** of his life (=days) 彼の晩年に. ¶***by*** tomorrow ***evening*** 明晩までには. ¶***from evening*** to midnight 晩から夜中まで ‖ ***from*** this ***evening*** on to tomorrow evening 今晩から明晩にかけて. ¶early ***in*** the ***evening*** of the next day 翌日の晩早く ‖ All lights are out by 10 o'clock ***in*** the ***evening.*** 灯火は皆夜の十時までには消される. ‖ a great novel that can be read with enjoyment ***in*** an ***evening*** or two 一晩か二晩で楽しんで読むことのできる有名な小説 ‖ ***in*** the ***evening*** of their well-spent days このりっぱな生涯(がい)の晩年に. ¶at about six o'clock ***of*** an ***evening*** ある晩六時ごろに. 【類】 He often comes to see me ***of*** an ***evening.*** / A jolly soldier boy offered the teashop girl to take her out ***of*** an ***evening.*** ¶***on*** an ***evening*** when a play by Dumas was being produced ある晩デューマの劇がかかっていた時 ‖ ***on*** the ***evening*** of the 5th of May 五月五日の晩に. ¶from noon ***to evening*** 正午から晩まで. ¶***toward*** the ***evening*** 晩方. 【類】 ***towards evening*** the next day.

P² in the ***evening of*** his power 彼の権力の衰微期に.

event, *n.* できごと, 事件; 大事; 結果, 成行; 番組, 勝負.

V an ***event*** specially ***arranged*** to honor Mr. ... ...氏のために特に設けた催し. ¶***await events*** (=developments) 成行を待つ. ¶***celebrate*** the ***event*** by ... そのできごとを...によって祝賀する ‖ The ***event*** was ***celebrated*** in the customary manner. 式は常例によって行われた. ¶***commemorate*** an ***event*** of singular importance in British railway history 英国鉄道史上特に重要なできごとを記念する. ¶***describe events*** できごと(ことの経過)を説明する. ¶***hasten*** (=***advance***) an ***event*** ある事件の発生を早める. ¶***make*** this ***event*** a great world affair このできごとをして世界的大事件たらしめる. ¶to ***mark*** the ***event*** このできごとを記念するために. ¶***narrate events*** of the past 過去のできごとを語る. ¶***trace*** an ***event back*** to its logical causes and to look forward to its logical effects ある事件を論理的にその原因にさかのぼりかつ論理的にその結果を観測する.

¶*outline* the *event* その事件の概略を示す. ¶*present* the *events* of the century in correct historic perspective その世紀の事件を正しい歴史的背景によって述べる.

V² the chain of *events* that ***led up*** to it それを誘致した事件の連鎖. ¶***Events marched*** swiftly. 局面がずんずん進展して行った. ¶Three *events* will always ***stand out*** in the history of Cornell University. コーネル大学の歴史において三つの事件が何時も際立っている. ¶*Events* are ***taking place***. 色々なできごとが起りつつある. ¶the *events* ***transpiring*** in different parts of the world 世界の各方面に起りつつある事件.

Q an ***annual*** *event* 一つの年中行事. 【類】 regular ***annual*** *events*. ¶in ***any*** *events* ともあれ. ¶one of the greatest ***athletic*** *events* of the year 一年中で最も大きな運動界のできごと ‖ treasured trophies, won in ***athletic*** *events* 競技会で獲得した貴いトロフィー. ¶an ***awful*** *event* 恐ろしいできごと. ¶a ***brilliant*** *event* 輝かしいできごと. ¶a ***calamitous*** *event* 災禍. ¶a ***cardinal*** *event* in the history of mankind 人類の歴史における主要なできごと. ¶The festival is now considered the ***central*** *event* in the Irish musical year in London. この祭は今やロンドンにおけるアイルランド人の音楽年中行事の中で最も重視されている. ¶the ***chief*** *events* of his administrations 彼の執政中の主なるできごと(首相・大統領など). ¶a ***contingent*** *event* 不慮の事件. ¶the ***crowning*** *event* of the day's celebration その日の祝典で一番際立ったできごと. ¶***current*** *events* 時事. ¶His settling in England was a ***decisive*** *event* in the life of Marx. マルクスが英国に定住したのは彼の一生の運命を決するできごとであった. ¶a ***dolorous*** *event* 悲しい一事件. ¶the ***epoch-making*** *events* of history 歴史の画期的事件. ¶an ***evil*** *event* 凶事. ¶a ***fatal*** *event* 致命的な事件. ¶***forthcoming*** *events* まさにきたらんとするできごと. ¶a ***fortunate*** *event* 吉事. ¶New Year's Day is a ***great*** *event* in Japan. 元旦は日本においては一大行事である. 【類】 ten ***great*** *events* of the year / a ***great*** *event* in the history of ... ¶It is a ***happy*** *event* for him. 彼にとってはうれしいできごとである. ¶a ***historical*** *event* of no small import かなり重要な歴史上の事件. 【類】 days (時代) of important ***historical*** *events* / a great ***historical*** *event*. ¶a ***horrifying*** *event* 恐ろしい一事件. ¶an ***important public*** *event* 重要な公の一事件. ¶We often look upon death as an ***inevitable*** but ***remote*** *event*. われわれはとかく死を避けることができないが遠い未来のことのように思う. ¶an ***international*** *event* 国際的事件. ¶Like a torrent ***last year's*** *events* in our theatrical world rush through my memory. わが劇界における昨年のできごとは私の記憶に奔流のようにわいてくる. ¶such ***like*** *events* そのような類似した諸事件. ¶a great ***literary*** *event* of this month 今月の文学上の重大なできごと. ¶***main*** *events* for the day 〖スポーツ〗当日の主要種目. ¶***major*** *events* of the month 今月の主な事件. ¶***major social*** *events* of the capital 首都の主な社会的できごと(社界面のニュースなど). ¶a ***melancholy*** *event* 憂うつなできごと. ¶the ***memorable*** *events* which were then transpiring in the East その当時東洋に発生しつつあった記憶すべきできごと. ¶a ***miraculous*** *event* 不可思議な一事件. ¶the most ***momentous*** *event* in the world's history 世界史上最も重要な事件. ¶a ***much-heralded*** *event* あらかじめ大いに吹聴された事件. ¶His illness was regarded as a ***national*** *event* of the first moment. 彼の病気は最も重大な国家的できごとと思われた. ¶an ***ordinary*** *event* ありふれたできごと. ¶an ***outstanding*** *event* in the history of ... ...史上顕著のできごと. ¶a record of ***past*** *events* 過去の事件の記録. ¶***present*** (=current) *events* 時事. ¶***principal*** *events* 主なできごと. ¶***prominent*** *events* in the history of Japan 日本史上著名な事件. ¶***public*** *events* at home and abroad 国内及び国外の公的事件. ¶It is still a ***recent*** *event*. それは至って最近のできごとである. ¶***salient*** *events* of Japanese history 日本歴史の顕著なできごと. ¶a ***sensational*** *event* 人の血をわかせるできごと. ¶a ***social*** *event* 社会的事件. ¶The pageant is one of the most ***spectacular*** *events* of the Exposition. その野外劇は博覧会の最も壮観なものの一つである. ¶The bicycle race was a ***spirited*** *event*. 自転車競走は勇ましい催しであった. ¶a ***stirring*** *event* 心をおどらせるできごと. ¶a ***trifling*** *event* つまらぬできごと. ¶in the ***unlikely*** *event* of ... 万一...の場合には. ¶His violent and inappropriate statement was an ***untoward*** *event* of the evening. 彼の過激な脱線的な言明はその晩の見苦しいできごとであった. ¶the march of the ***world's*** *events* 世界の動き. ¶a ***yearly*** *event* 一つの年中行事.

Q² ***amateur sporting*** *events* ノン・プロの運動競技会. ¶a ***field*** *event* 陸上(フィールド)競技. ¶***July*** *events* in Europe 欧州における七月の行事. ¶a prominent ***news*** *event* 重大ニュース. ¶a notable ***publishing*** *event* 注目すべき出版界のニュース(大著作など). ¶***sporting*** (=***sport***) *events* 運動競技(スポーツ) ‖ the premier ***sporting*** *event* of the year 一年中で一番重要な競技会. 【類】 a review (回顧) of the important ***sports*** *events* of 1936 / baseball and other ***sports*** *events*. ¶an international ***student sport*** *event* 国際学生運動競技. ¶***track and field*** *events* 陸上競技. ¶swiftly moving ***world*** *events* 刻々変る世界の動き. ¶keep them informed of important ***world*** *events* 彼らに重要な世界のできごとを絶えず知らせる.

P ***At*** all *events* you had better do it. ともかく君はそれをやった方がよい. 【類】 ***At*** all *events* I am told so. ¶***in*** any *event*=in any case いずれにしても, どんなことがあっても. 【類】 But, ***in*** any *event*, I cannot give you my consent. ¶***in*** either *event* どっちみち ‖ ***in*** no *event* どうあっても(...しない) ‖ his participation ***in*** the *events* of 1817 彼の一八一七年事件参加 ‖ ***in*** that *event* その場合には ‖ ***in*** [the] *event* 結局 ‖ ***in*** the *event* of war 戦争が起ったあかつきには. 【類】 ***in*** the *event* of dispute (討論) / ***in*** the *event* of need / ***in*** the *event* of liquidation (清算) / ***in*** the *event* of this becoming known / A small stock of medicines was put in my saddle-bags ***in*** the *event* of my illness on the road. / defend the country ***in*** the *event* of invasion / ***In*** the *event* of our father's death, we shall be left poor. / ***In*** the *event* of his absence, leave the letter with his servant. ¶a train ***of*** *events* 事件の連鎖(引続き) ‖ the course ***of*** the *events* ことの成行き. 【類】 in the [natural] course ***of*** *events*. ¶leave the rest ***to*** the *events* それから先は天運(成行き)に任せる.

P² consider it as an *event* ***of*** deep significance それを非常に重要なことと思う ‖ The *events* ***of*** the day were a bicycle race, foot race, high jumps, etc. 当日の番組は自転車競走・徒歩競走・高とびなどであった. ‖ the *event* ***of*** an enterprise 事業の成績.

eventuate, *v.* 終る, 帰着する; 起る.

M The point at issue *eventuated* so ***well***. 係争中の問題は非常に好結果に終った.

P The fighting *eventuated* ***from*** a dispute. その闘争は口論から起った. ¶*eventuate* (=end) ***in*** a failure 失敗に終る ‖ The discussion *eventuated* ***in*** a compromise. 議論は結局折合がついた.

ever, *ad.* いつも, 始終; かつて, いつか.

M *ever* ***afterward***=ever since それからずっと. ¶He ***hardly*** *ever* comes now. 彼はこのごろはめったに来ない. ‖ I have ***hardly*** *ever* seen any such. かつてそんなものを見たことがない. ¶Thank you *ever* ***so much***. 本当にありがとうございます(多く女性が言う).

P He left his home ***for*** *ever*. 彼は家出をしそれきり帰らなかった. ‖ He would go on talking ***for*** *ever* (=forever). ‖ ***for*** *ever* and *ever* 永久不変に ‖ ***for*** *ever* and a day 常に, いつまでも. ¶The plan has worked perfectly *ever* ***since*** its introduction. その計画は実施以来ずっと具合よく進行してきた.

O He seldom, if *ever*, goes there. 彼はめったにそこへ行かない.

everlasting, *n.* 永遠, 無窮.

P ***from*** *everlasting* ***to*** everlasting 永遠から永遠へ.

everybody, *pron.* たれもが.

V² as *everybody* ***knows*** だれもが承知のごとく. ¶*Everybody* ***likes*** the new principal. だれもが今度の校長が好きだ.

everything, *pron.* 万事, 万物; 最も大切なもの.

V That ***beats*** *everything* I ever heard. こんな驚くべきことを聞いたことがない. ¶He thought he could ***carry*** *everything* before him. 彼は万難を排して進みうると思った. ‖ The craze is ***carrying*** *everything* before it for the moment. その流行は今の所向う所敵なしという勢だ. ¶***do*** *everything* in one's power 精一杯やる ‖ The book ***did*** *everything* but sell. その書物は一向売れなかった. ‖ ***do*** *everything* on (=upon) the square 何でもきちょうめんにやる. ¶He ***has*** *everything* to lose and nothing to gain. 彼には失う所多くして得る所少ない. ¶He always has to ***overdo***

everything. 彼は何でもやり過ぎるくせがある. ¶*take everything* for Gospel 何でも本当と思う.
Q *Everything good* comes from France. なんでも良い物はフランスから来る. ¶*everything possible* ありとあらゆるもの.
P You ought to correct that habit *above everything*. まず第一にその癖を直すことだ. ¶Health is valuable *before everything* else. 健康は外のなに物よりも貴い. ¶manufacturers of *everything in* nets 網類一切の製造者. ¶Money is *everything to* him. 彼にとっては金ほど大事なものはない. ‖His wife is *everything to* him. 彼は細君でなければ夜も日も明けぬ.

everywhere, *ad.* 至る所.
P *everywhere about* here この辺至る所. ¶*everywhere in* the city 市中至る所. ¶*everywhere through* the country 国中至る所.

evict, *v.* 立ちのかせる, 追払う; 受戻す.
M The police *forcibly evicted* the students from the premises. 警官は学生たちを構内から無理に追い出した.
P The tenant was *evicted by* the sheriff for not paying his rent. 借家人は執政官の命により家賃延滞のかどで立ちのかされた. ¶He *evicted* the property *from* its unlawful possessor. 彼は財産をその不法な所有者から取戻した. ¶*evict* him *out of* his present post 彼を現職から追い出す.

eviction, *n.* 追立て, 立ちのき.
V *seek eviction* 借家人に出てもらう.

evidence, *n.* 証拠, 証言; 形跡.
V *adduce evidence* to show that ... ...を示す証拠を提示する ‖ *adduce evidence* in support of ... 証拠をあげて...を援助する. 【類】in view of the whole of the *evidence adduced.* ¶*afford* abundant *evidence* of ... ...の十分な証拠を提供する. ¶*balance evidence* with a calm and impartial head 冷静にして公平な頭で証拠を検討する. ¶It *bears evidence* of very serious labor. それは非常に骨の折れた仕事であったように見受けられる. ‖ *bear evidence* of remarkable skill 著しい熟練の証跡を示す. ¶*belittle* the *evidence* as purely circumstantial その証拠をほんの情況証拠として軽んじる. ¶*collect evidence* for a trial 公判のために証拠を集める ‖ *collect* and *preserve evidence* 証拠を収集して保管する. ¶*compare* and *weigh* the *evidence* collected 収集した証拠を比較検討する. ¶This documentary *evidence* is *corroborated* by archaeological facts. この文書の示す証拠は考古学上の事実がその正確を証明している. ¶*destroy evidence* 証拠をいん滅する. ¶a spectacle which makes one *disbelieve* the *evidence* of one's own eyes 自分の目を疑わしめるような光景. ¶*disclose evidence* of ... ...の証拠を明かにする. ¶She tries to *disguise* the *evidence* of her advancing age. 彼女は寄る年波の証跡を隠そうとする. ¶without *examining* the *evidence* 証拠調べもせずに. ¶*examine* and *weigh* the *evidence* その証拠を調査し考量する. ¶*furnish evidence* 証拠を提供する. ¶*gather* fresh *evidence* upon ... ...に関する新しい証拠を収集する ‖ *gather evidence* against ... ...の反証を集める. ¶Ruskin's writings everywhere *give evidence* that "The style is the man." ラスキンの作はその至る所に「文体は人なり」の言を立証している. ‖ There are two men who can *give evidence* on the matter. この事柄を立証しうる人が二人いる. 【類】At both school and college he *gave evidence* of his literary tastes (文学趣味) by editing school and college papers. ¶*hear* the *evidence* of witness 一目擊者の証言を聞く. ¶The *evidence* cannot be *impugned*. その証言は反ばくすることができない. ¶*multiply evidence* 証拠をふやす. ¶*obliterate evidence* 証拠をまっ殺する. ¶*obtain* full *evidence* 十分な証拠を得る. 【類】It is difficult to *obtain* reliable *evidence.* ¶*pile up evidence* 証拠をたくさん集める. ¶*present evidence* to indicate that ... ...ということを示すために証拠を提出する. ¶*produce evidence* in favor of ... ...に有利な証拠を提出する. 【類】He has not yet *produced* indubitable *evidence* (確かな証拠). ¶*rebut evidence* 証拠を論ばくする. ¶The building *shows evidences* of neglect and decay. その建物は腐朽するがままに放任されていた形跡が歴然と見えている. 【類】it *shows all* the *evidences* of ... ¶*sift* the *evidence* carefully 証拠を精査する. ¶*take evidence* from interested bodies 関係筋から資料を収集する(国立公園設定などの場合).
V² all the *evidence points* to ... 証拠はすべて...であることを示している. ¶the *evidence tells* against ... 証拠は...の不利なことを物語っている.
Q give *abundant evidence* in support of ... ...を支持して十分な証拠を示す. 【類】there is *abundant evidence* that ... ¶*after-discovered evidence* 事後発見の証拠. ¶afford an *answerable evidence* that ... ...という責任ある証拠を提供する. ¶all *available evidence* goes to show that ... これという証拠はすべて...であることを示している. ¶be confirmed on the very *best evidence* 最善の証拠に基づいて確認される. ¶*buried evidences* of ancient life 古代生活の埋没している証跡. ¶*certain evidence* of genuineness 純真なことを明示する証拠. ¶pass judgment on ... on *circumstantial evidence* 情況証拠で...に判決を言い渡す. 【類】He was convicted (有罪と判決された) on *circumstantial evidence.* / *circumstantial evidence*, or facts indicating that something is probably, but not certainly, true. ¶*collateral evidence* 傍証. ¶afford *conclusive evidence* that ... ...という確証を与える ‖ *conclusive evidence* of the merit of ... ...が価値あることの確かな証拠. 【類】I do not think the *evidence* is *conclusive.* ¶*conflicting evidences* 矛盾する証拠. ¶there is *considerable evidence* to show that ... ...ということを示す幾多の証拠がある. 【類】there is *considerable evidence* to justify a presumption of ... (...という仮定を正当化する). ¶Thank you *ever so* much. [主に婦人]本当にありがとう. ‖ If I were *ever so* rich. 私があんな金持なら. ¶*contemporary evidence* 同時代の証拠. ¶*corroborative evidence* of a fact ある事実の立証に役立つ証拠. ¶*criminating evidence* 罪を負わせる証拠. ¶It is the *direct evidence* that connects the prisoner with the deed. それは犯人とその行為との関係を示す直接の証拠である. ¶*documentary evidence* 証拠書類. ¶*encouraging evidence* 意を強くする証拠. ¶there is *every evidence* that ... ...はどう見ても間違いはない. ¶give *false evidence* 偽証する. ¶*firsthand evidence* from eye-witnesses 目撃者からの直接の証拠. ¶no *evidence* has yet been *forthcoming* to show that ... ...ということを示す証拠はいまだ現われて来ない. ¶gather *fresh evidence* upon ... ...に関する新証拠を集める. ¶there is *good evidence* to show that ... ...ということを示すりっぱな証拠がある. ¶*hearsay evidence* 伝聞証拠. ¶seek, by *historical evidence*, to show ... 歴史的に...を示そうとする. ¶it is shown, upon *indisputable evidence*, that ... それは論破することのできない証拠で...だということを明かにしている. ¶He was declared innocent on the ground of *insufficient evidence*. 彼は証拠不十分のかどをもって無罪を宣告された. ¶an *irrefutable evidence* of antiquity 古いということの歴然とした証拠. ¶He has very *little evidence* to produce. 彼には持ち出すべき証拠がほとんどない. ¶there is *little* or *no evidence* of ... ほとんど...の形跡がない. ¶there are *many evidences* that ... ...という証拠がたくさんある ‖ reveal *many evidences* that ... ...という色々な徵候が現われている. 【類】there are *many evidences* of this in ... ¶*negative evidence* 消極的な証拠. ¶There was *no evidence* to show the cause of his death. 彼の死因は調べようがなかった. ¶*outward evidence* 外部の証拠. ¶This is a *pleasing evidence* in New York's amateur musical circles. これはニューヨークのしろうと音楽界における愉快な事実である. ¶give *prima-facie evidence* of the reason 〖法〗疏明する. ¶by *proper evidence* 然るべき証拠によって. ¶there exists no *rational evidence* for ... ...の合理的な証拠はない. ¶*reliable evidence* 確かな証拠. ¶on such *slight evidence* こうしたつまらない証拠に基づいて. 【類】He was imprisoned on the *slightest evidence.* ¶*statistical evidence* 統計上の証拠. ¶*striking evidence* of ... ...の注目すべき証拠. ¶show with *strong evidence* that ... 強力な証拠によって...を明かにする. ¶give *strong prima facie evidence* to a theory ある説に対して有力な顕証を示す. ¶be supported by *substantial evidence* 有力な証拠にささえられている. ¶it is *sufficient evidence* for the fact that ... それは...という事実に対して十分な証拠である ‖ there is not *sufficient evidence* to warrant the conclusion that ... ...という結論を裏づけるだけの十分な証拠がない. ¶*tangible evidences* of ... ...のたしかな証拠. ¶These works bear *unmistakable evidences* of a falling off in artistic excellence. これらの作品には芸術的優秀性の低下して行く証跡が明りょうに現われている. ¶furnish *valuable evidence* of ... ...という貴重な証拠を提供する. ¶it is *welcome evidence* of an increasing interest in ... それは...に

対する興味が増進して行くという喜ばしい証拠である.

P I enclose my card *as evidence* of good faith. (新聞への投稿などに)誠意の証左として私の名刺を封入する. ‖ *as evidence* it is pointed out that ... 証拠として…ということが指摘されている. ¶produce *in evidence* 証拠として提出する ‖ He took the following examples *in evidence.* 彼は証拠に次の例をあげた. ‖ Foreigners were not much *in evidence.* 外国人はあまり目につかなかった. ¶a mass *of evidence* 一まとめの証拠 ‖ There is a conflict *of evidence.* 証拠が矛盾している. ¶*on* the *evidence* of ... …の証拠として ‖ we have it *on* trustworthy *evidence* that ... われわれは確実な証拠に基づいて…ということを言明しうる. ‖ *on* internal *evidence* 内部の証拠で ‖ infer *on* slight *evidence* わずかな証拠で推断する. ¶*without* any *evidence* 別に証拠もなく.

P² an *evidence against* a fact (person) 反証 ‖ So far there is no *evidence against* him. 今までの所彼に不利な証拠はない. 【類】that there might be no *evidence against* themselves afterwards. ¶give statistical *evidence as to* ... …について統計上の証拠をあげる. ¶There is no *evidence for* his guiltiness. 彼が有罪だという証拠は少しもない. ¶*evidence from* (=of) facts 事実に基づく証拠. ¶We have historical *evidence in favor of* the theory. その説を可とする歴史上の証拠がある. ¶The antique bears unmistakable *evidence of* age. その古物はたしかに時代ものだという証跡がある. ¶*evidence to* the contrary 反証.

O there is *evidence* to show that ... …なることを示す証拠がある, たしかに…らしい.

evidence, *v.* 証明する.

P it is *evidenced by* ... それは…によって証明されている. 【類】His pleasure was *evidenced by* his smile.

evident, *a.* 明白な, 明りょうな.

M it is *abundantly evident* that ... …ということはたしかに明りょうである. ¶it is *indisputably evident* that ... …ということは疑いもなく明りょうである. ¶it is *quite evident* that ... …は極めて明りょうだ. ¶It is *too evident* to require proof. それは証明するまでもなく明りょうである.

P it is *evident to* any one that ... …はだれの目にも明りょうである.

evil, *n.* 弊害, 害悪; 禍; 悪疾.

V *aggravate* the *evil* 弊害を募らせる. ¶*avert evil* from ... …の魔よけをする. ¶*bode evil* 凶兆を示す. ¶*breed evils* 害悪をかもす. ¶War *brings* many *evils* in its train. 戦争はこれに付随する幾多の禍害をもたらす. ¶*check* an *evil* 悪弊を阻止する. ¶Something can surely be done to *combat* the *evil.* たしかにその弊害を除去する手段が講じられる. ¶*correct evils* in current practices 現今の慣習上における弊害を矯正する. ¶*crush* the *evil* その弊害を打破する. ¶*cure* an *evil* ある悪弊を改める. ¶*do evil* 悪事をする. ¶*eliminate evils* 弊害を除去する. ¶*emphasize* the *evils* of ... …の弊害を力説する. ¶*exaggerate evil* 害悪を誇張する. ¶*extirpate* an *evil* 弊害を根絶する. ¶*forebode* the *evil* to come 凶事の来ることを予知する. ¶*foresee* the *evil* 凶事を予想する. ¶*foreshadow* an *evil* 凶事の徴候を示す. ¶*invoke evil* upon ... …の上に禍のきたらんことを祈る(…をのろう). ¶*mitigate* an *evil* 悪弊を軽減する. ¶the way to *oppose* the social *evil* is to ... 売春を阻止する方法は…することにある. ¶The good *overbalance* the *evil.* 功は罪をつぐなって余りがある. ¶*overcome* an *evil* 禍に打勝つ. ¶*plot* no *evil* against ... …に対して害悪をたくらまない. ¶It *portends evil.* それは悪い前兆だ. ¶It is held to *presage* deadly *evils.* それは恐ろしい禍害を予示すると信じられている. ¶*prevent* an *evil* 禍を防ぐ. ¶*rectify* an *evil* 弊害を矯正する. ¶*redress evils* 弊害を矯正する. ¶*remedy evils* 悪弊を改める. ¶*remove evils* 弊害を除く. ¶*repress* the social *evil* 売春を防止する. ¶*requite evil* with good 善をもって悪のつぐないをする. ¶To *resist evil* by evil is evil. 悪をもって悪に抗するのは悪である. ¶*return evil* for good 恩をあだで返す. ¶*stamp out* the *evil* その害悪を根絶する. ¶*strike* the *evil* at its source その悪弊を根こそぎにする. ¶*supervise* the social *evil* 売春を取締る. ¶*turn evils* into blessings 禍を転じて福となす. ¶an amulet to *ward off evil* 災難よけの護符. ¶This *wrought* much *evil.* これが非常な害毒を流した.

V² *evils* have *developed* as a result of ... …の結果として弊害が現われた.

Q *attendant evils* それに伴う弊害. ¶a *crying evil* そのままにして置けない弊害. ¶an *economic evil* 経済の弊害. ¶They can only lead to intensification of *existing evils.* 彼らは今の弊害を一層はげしくするにすぎない. ¶Everyone knows how alcoholism may be a *grave social evil* (=scourge). アルコール中毒はいかに由々しき社会悪であるかはだれでも知っている. ¶fear of *impending evil* 降りかかる災禍に対する恐怖心. ¶*king's evils* るいれき. ¶a *lesser evil* それより小さな害悪. ¶a *long-standing evil* 宿弊. ¶a *modern evil* 文明病. ☞ 例えば soft food のため gum が十分の massage を得ないので歯が浮き気味になるのもその一例. ¶a source of *multitudinous evils* 情弊百出の因. ¶They call the social evil a *necessary evil.* 彼らは売春を必要悪と称している. ¶remedy this *pernicious evil* この有害なる悪弊を矯正する. ¶correct *public evils* 社会の悪弊を改める. ¶a *serious evil* 一大害悪. ¶extirpate the *social evil* 社会悪(売春)などを根絶する. ¶War, famine and flood are *terrible evils.* 戦争, 飢餓, 洪水は恐ろしい災害である. ¶the *twin evils* of poverty and corruption 貧乏と背徳という密接な関係にある二つの害悪. ¶poverty with all its *ugly attendant evils* 貧乏とこれに伴うあらゆる見苦しい弊害. ¶an *unmitigated evil* はなはだしい悪弊. ¶a source of *untold evils* in after life 晩年における非常な害悪の根源. ¶*various attending evils* これに伴う各種の弊害. ¶a *vast evil* 一大害悪.

Q² the *drink evil* 酒の害. ¶the *examination evil* 試験地獄. ¶a *present-day evil* 今日の弊害. ¶the *sweatshop evil* 『労』搾取制度の弊害. ¶the *tipping evil* チップ制度の弊害.

P the return *of evil* for good 恩をあだで返すこと ‖ the root *of* much *evil* 非常な弊害の根源.

P² an *evil of* long standing 宿弊 ‖ *evils* of *misgovernment* 失政の弊害.

evil, *a.* 有害の.

P *evil in* principle 根本義において有害な.

evil-doer, *n.* 犯罪者.

V *abet* an *evil-doer* 犯罪者を扇動する.

evolution, *n.* 発展, 発達, 進化.

V *follow* the *evolution* of events 事件の展開を見守る.

Q the *historical evolution* of Buddhism in China 中国仏教の歴史的沿革. ¶a *social* and *economic evolution* 社会的及び経済的発展.

P the theory *of evolution* 進化論. ¶*with* the *evolution* of factory industry 工場工業の発達とともに.

P² a collection of ..., showing *evolution from* the oldest *to* the most modern type 最古型より最新型に至るまでの進展のあとを示す…の収集. ¶the *evolution of* man 人間の進化 ‖ the *evolution of* a tragedy 悲劇の展開.

exact, *a.* 正確な.

M *minutely exact* きわめて正確な. ¶to be *more exact* より正確に言うなら.

P He is *exact in* his statement (account, words). 彼はその叙説(など)において正確である. ‖ a man *exact in* keeping appointments 約束を守ることの堅い人.

exact, *v.* 強要する, 強制する.

P *exact* money or a thing *from* a person 人から金品を強請する ‖ *exact* obedience *from* (=of) the students 学生に服従をしいる. ¶His gray hair *exacts of* us a particular respect. 彼の白髪はわれわれに特別の尊敬を払わせる. ‖ a sum of money *exacted of* a person guilty of a crime 不正行為をした人から取上げた金額.

exacting, *a.* きびしい.

M Don't be *so exacting,* and let him go. そうやかましく言わないで許してやり給え. ¶a *very exacting* piece of work 非常に骨の折れる仕事.

P be *exacting about* cleanliness 清潔にかけては口やかましい.

exaction, *n.* 強制取立て.

P² *exaction of* an indemnity of ... …の賠償金の取立て.

exactitude, *n.* 正確, 厳正.

Q reproduce the extreme niceties of *phonological exactitude* 音声学的に正確な細かいニューアンスを再生する. ¶with *scientific exactitude* 科学的正確さをもって.

P ascertain *with exactitude* 厳正に確かめる.

exactness, *n.* 正確.

P *with* sufficient *exactness* 十分正確に.

exaggerate, *v.* 大げさに言う.

M *grossly exaggerated* はなはだしく誇張された(針小棒大にした). ¶The fact is *incredibly exaggerated.* その事実はあまりにも信じ得ないほど誇張されている. ¶The thing is *much exaggerated.* 話が大きい. ¶*exaggerated purpose-*

ly 故意に誇張された. ¶The matter is ***somewhat*** *exaggerated.* 話が少し大き過ぎる.

exaggeration, *n.* 誇張, 誇大の言.

Q ***farcical*** *exaggeration* 茶番じみた誇張. ¶This turned out to have been a prophecy, though at the time of its utterance a ***gross*** ***exaggeration.*** それを言ったときには大ぼらであったが後になってそれが予言であったということが明らかになった. 【類】a very ***gross exaggeration*** of the truth. ¶if I may be allowed a ***little*** *exaggeration* すこし大げさに言えば. ¶***ludicrous*** *exaggeration* ばかげた誇張. ¶a ***morbid*** *exaggeration* of the normal condition 常態の病的誇張. ¶it may be said without ***much*** *exaggeration* that ... ...と言うもあまり過言ではなかろう. ¶it is ***no*** *exaggeration* to say that ... ...というも過言ではない.

P ***without*** *exaggeration,* it may be said, that ... 誇張でなしに...と言えよう. 【類】I speak ***without*** *exaggeration* when I say that I have constructed three thousand different theories in connection with the electric light.—⌊Edison.

exalt, *v.* 高める, 上げる.

P He was *exalted* ***to*** the most eminent station. 彼は最高の地位まで出世した. ‖ *exalt* (=extol) a person ***to*** the skies 人を激賞する.

exaltation, *n.* 狂喜; 発揚.

Q with ***great*** *exaltation* 狂喜して. ¶***spiritual*** *exaltation* ⌊精神の発揚.

examination, *n.* 検査, 調査; 試験, 考査.

V ***allow*** an annual *examination* of their books of account by a competent official appointed by ... 彼らの帳簿を毎年...によって任命された専門家である役員に検査してもらう. ¶***attend*** an *examination* 試験に出席する. ¶This theory will not ***bear*** ***examination.*** この説は論拠が薄弱だ. ‖ It will not ***bear*** a moment's *examination.* ちょっと調べればすぐ悪い点が分る. ¶***carry out*** a medical *examination* 身体検査を行う. ¶***conduct*** *examinations* for positions in clerical service 書記任用の試験を行う. 【類】the persons ***conducting*** the *examinations* (=examiners). ¶They learned the trick of ***defeating*** the *examination.* 彼らは試験をごま化す法を覚えた. ¶This *examination* is ***divided*** into two parts, a preliminary and final, and covers the following subjects. この試験は予備試験と本試験の二部に分たれ次の諸学科をふくむ. ¶***enter*** an *examination* 受験する. ¶***give*** an *examination* to a group of students 一団の学生に試験を課する. 【類】The teacher ***gave*** us an *examination* in English. ¶We ***have*** an *examination* in mathematics today. きょう数学の試験がある. ¶***hold*** *examinations* and grant certificates 試験の上免状を授与する. 【類】an *examination* will be ***held*** on ... ¶*Examinations* were ***instituted*** to test the fitness of the teachers to do their work in English. 英語教師の適否を試みる試験が開始された. ¶***make*** critical *examination* of ... ...を批判的に調べる(吟味する). ¶***pass*** an *examination* successfully 試験に首尾よく及第する. 【類】***pass*** one's *examination* with honors (優等で) / ***pass*** *examinations* in physical, moral, and intellectual powers (身体・道徳および知力) / ***pass*** an *examination* on paper (筆記試験) / those whose sole aim is to ***pass*** *examination* / fail to ***pass*** an *examination* / ***pass*** a satisfactory *examination* / an applicant is required to ***pass*** an *examination* on ... / The result was a failure to ***pass*** his *examinations.* / prepare students to ***pass*** *examinations* in the works of Mr. Rudyard Kipling. ¶no *examination* will be ***required*** for admission to ... ...にはいるには何ら試験を要しない. ¶***set*** an *examination* 試験を課する. 【類】pass *examinations* ***set*** on the subject. ¶It cannot ***stand*** critical *examination.* それは精密な吟味にたえ得ない. ¶***take*** *examinations* in specified subjects 指定した学科目の試験を受ける. 【類】girls ***taking*** *examination* for service in a department store. ¶***undergo*** an *examination* in English 英語の試験を受ける. 【類】***undergo*** stiff *examinations* (むずかしい試験) before being promoted to ... / you will be required to ***undergo*** a medical *examination* (健康診断) at ...

V² The *examination* ***came off*** yesterday. その試験はきのうすんだ. ¶The *examination* of the third term ***extends*** over the work of the whole year. 第三学期の試験は全学年の授業にわたる. ¶an *examination* ***lasting*** four days 四日間にわたる試験. ¶When does your *examination* ***take place?*** 君の試験はいつありますか.

Q make a very ***careful*** *examination* 非常に綿密な検査をやる ‖ after ***careful*** *examination* of these papers I venture to say that ... これらの書類を精密に調査した上で私はあえて...と言う. ¶on ***closer*** *examination* of the evidence その証拠をさらに調査の上. 【類】on ***closer*** *examination* it proved that ... ¶at the ***coming*** *examination* 次の試験に. ¶by ***competitive*** *examination* 競争試験によって. ¶a ***critical*** *examination* of socialism 社会主義に対する厳密な批判. ¶an ***easy*** *examination* 平易な試験. ¶He passed ***excellent*** *examinations.* 彼の試験は成績優良であった. ¶it was found at the ***first*** *examination* to be ... 最初の検査で...と分った. ¶be seen on ***further*** *examination* to be ... 再審査の結果...が分る. ¶a ***medical*** *examination* 健康診断. ¶undergo ***mental*** *examination* 精神状態検査を受ける. ¶a ***microscopic*** *examination* 検鏡 ‖ ***microscopic*** *examination* shows that ... 検鏡の結果...ということが分った. ¶The argument will not bear a ***moment's*** *examination.* その議論の不当さはちょっと考えれば分る. ¶an ***oral*** *examination* 口頭試問. ¶pass a ***periodical*** *examination* 定期試験に合格する. ¶a ***personal local*** *examination* 局部身体検査. ¶***physical and mental*** *examinations* 身体および精神検査. ¶***practical*** (***theoretical***) *examination* 実地(学理)試験. ¶a ***preliminary*** (***final***) *examination* 予備(本)試験 ‖ a judge of ***preliminary*** *examination*=an examining judge 予審判事. ¶take the ***prescribed*** *examination* from the state board of examiners 国家試験を受ける. ¶a ***professional*** *examination* 職能試験 ‖ coaching for the ***professional*** *examinations* of the civil service 文官試験の準備教授. ¶a ***qualifying*** *examination* 資格試験. ¶a ***quiet*** *examination* of realities 地味な実状調査. ¶candidates selected after ***rigid competitive*** *examination* 厳重な競争試験によって選ばれた志望者. ¶make a ***rigorous*** *examination* of ... ...を厳密に調査する. 【類】He was subjected to a ***rigorous*** *examination.* ¶***scathing*** *examination* of a criminal 厳しい審問(取調べ). ¶give it a very ***searching*** *examination* それを綿密に検査する ‖ make a ***searching*** *examination* of ... ...を穴のあくほどよく見る ‖ pass a ***searching*** *examination* in English literature 英文学の厳密な試験に及第する. ¶***selective*** *examination* 選抜試験. ¶pass a ***severe*** *examination* 厳重な試験に及第する. ¶a ***sham*** *examination* 模擬試験. ¶a ***stiff*** *examination* むずかしい試験. ¶after a ***successful*** *examination* 試験に及第してから. ¶on a ***superficial*** *examination* 表面的に観察すると. ¶The bacteriologists conducted a ***systematic*** *examination* of mosquitoes. その細菌学者たちは蚊の組織的な調査を行った. ¶a ***tentative*** *examination* 仮試験. ¶make a ***thorough*** *examination* 十分に調査する. ¶a ***thoroughgoing*** *examination* 徹底的な調査.

Q² an ***admission*** *examination* 入学(会)試験. ¶take the ***bar*** *examination* 弁護士試験を受ける. ¶a ***certificate*** *examination* 検定試験. ¶a teachers' ***certificate*** *examination* 教員検定試験. ¶a ***cross*** *examination* 証人反問. ¶a ***degree*** *examination* 学位試験. ¶an ***English*** (a ***history***) *examination* 英語(など)の試験. ¶an ***entrance*** *examination* 入学試験. ¶make an ***expert*** *examination* and report on ... ...に関して専門的な調査を遂げて報告する. ¶a ***health*** *examination* 健康診断. ¶a ***history*** *examination* 歴史の試験. ¶an ***index-finger*** *examination* of the anus 肛門の人さし指診察. ¶a ***licensing*** *examination* 免許状下付の試験. ¶a ***matriculation*** *examination* 入学試験. ¶a ***medical licensing*** *examination* 開業医試験. ¶a ***mid-term*** *examination* 中間試験. ¶a ***page-to-page*** *examination* 一ページ一ページ調べること. ¶enter for ***state*** *examinations* 国家試験受験の申込みをする. ¶a ***talent*** *examination* 技能試験. ¶a ***term*** *examination* 学期試験. ¶an ***X-ray*** *examination* エックス線による検査.

P students successful ***at*** the *examination* 試験に及第した学生 ‖ get nervous ***at*** an *examination* 試験のときに神経過敏になる. ¶a chemist ***by*** *examination* 《英》国家試験合格の薬剤師. ¶go up (=come up *or* go in) ***for*** one's *examination* 試験を受ける ‖ sit ***for*** an *examination* 受験する ‖ enter ***for*** an *examination* 受験する ‖ present themselves ***for*** *examination* 試験に出頭する ‖ offer oneself ***for*** *examination* 試験を志願する ‖ cramming ***for*** an *examination* 試験のための詰め込み. ¶withdraw ***from*** an *examination* 受験をやめる. ¶appear ***in*** *examination* 試験に出る ‖

cheating *in* an *examination* カンニング ‖ fail *in* the *examination* 落第する ‖ He got plucked *in* his *examination.* 《英口》 彼は落第した. ☞ 米語用法は He flunked [*in*] the *examination.* ‖ obtain a good result *in* an *examination* 試験に好成績をあげる ‖ He won high ratings (=marks) in all his *examinations.* 試験は全優をとった. ‖ He headed the list *in* the last *examination.* 彼はこの前の試験で首席を占めた. 【類】 He scored high marks *in* his *examinations.* ¶it proved *on examination* to be ... それは調べて見ると...と分った. 【類】 be found *on examination* that ... ‖ recognize ... *on* the briefest *examination* ちょっと調べて...と認識する ‖ Licenses and certificates are issued *on* (*without*) *examination.* 試験の上(無試験で)許可証・証明書を下付する. ‖ I was careful to cram the obvious facts which I knew would be asked *on* the *examination.* 私はその試験で私がきっと尋ねられるだろうと思った明白な事実を詰め込もうとした. ¶I have got *through* my *examination.* 私は試験に及第した. ¶subject the theory *to* a critical *examination* その学説を厳密な批判にかける. ¶His conduct is *under examination.* 彼の行為は審議中である. ‖ a criminal *under examination* 審問中の罪人 ‖ a candidate *under examination* 受験中の志願者. ¶appoint ... *upon examination* ...を試験の上採用する. 【類】 Students are admitted only *upon examination.* / *upon* closer *examination* it turned out that ... / be given a job *upon examination.* ¶He was admitted *without examination* into the school. 彼は無試験でその学校へ入学を許可された. 【類】 be entitled to admission to the school *without examination* / approval *without examination.*

P² he was put through a searching *examination as to* ... 彼は...について厳密な審問にかけられた. ¶an *examination by* questioning 問答法による試験. ¶*examinations for* teachers' certificates 教員検定試験 ‖ *examinations for* the diplomatic and consular services 外交官及び領事試験 ‖ *examinations for* admission to college 大学入学試験 ‖ an *examination for* entering service 入社試験. ¶an *examination in* English (botany, chemistry) 英語(など)の試験. ¶an *examination into* the matter (=affair) その事件の調査 ‖ an *examination into* the authorship of the book 同書の著作者に関する調査. ¶an *examination of* candidates for ... guides licences ...ガイドの免許状下付試験 ‖ the *examination of* the London Chamber of Commerce ロンドン商業会議所の試験 ‖ an *examination of* accounts 会計検査. ¶An applicant must pass an *examination on* the subject. 志望者はその科目の試験に通過せねばならない. ¶*examination through* a binocular 双眼鏡での検査.

P² pass an entrance *examination to* West Point 米国陸軍士官学校の入学試験に及第する.

examine, *v.* 調べる; 診察する; 試験する.

M *examine carefully* 綿密に調べる ‖ Have yourself *carefully examined.* よく診察してもらえ. ¶*clinically examine* 臨床診察をする. ¶*examine* it more *closely* それをもっと細かに調べる. ¶*examine critically* じろじろ見る. ¶*examine microscopically* 顕微鏡で調べる. ¶*examine minutely* 綿密に検査する. ¶all candidates are first of all *orally examined* in their knowledge of ... 候補者はすべて真先に...の知識を口頭で考査される. ¶*examine* a person *viva voce* 口頭尋問をする.

P *examine by* touch 手でさわって調べる ‖ *examine by* tasting whether a food is poisonous or not 毒味をする. ¶*examine for* proficiency in ... ...の能力を試験する. ¶*examine* students (candidates) *in* ... 学生(など)を...のテストをする. 【類】 *examine* pupils *in* grammar / I was *examined in* Macaulay's Lord Clive. ¶*examine into* the conditions of ... ...の情況を調査する ‖ I will *examine into* the question (=affair). この問題を調査しよう. ‖ *examine into* details 詳細を調査する. ¶*examine through* the glasses 双眼鏡で見る. ¶*examine* them *upon* their knowledge of the laws 彼らに法律の試験を課する. ¶*examine with* the eye (nose) 目(など)で検査する ‖ *examine* it *with* a magnifying glass それを拡大鏡で調べる.

examinee, *n.* 受験者.

V *cast* (=*reject*) *examinees* 受験者をはねる.

Q *Chinese examinees* in English 英語の中国人受験者.

examiner, *n.* 試験官.

V the subjects of examination in which candidates have failed to *satisfy* the *examiners* 受験者が不成績であった試験科目 ‖ after duly *satisfying* the *examiners* 適当な受験成績を得た上で.

Q² *national-bank examiners* 国営銀行監査官.

P² *examiners in* shorthand to the London Chamber of Commerce ロンドン商業会議所付速記術試験官.

examining, *n.* 審査.

Q² *patent examining* 特許審査.

example, *n.* 見本, 標本, 手本, 鑑, 模範; 例.

V *adduce examples* 例をあげる ‖ *adduce* another *example* もう一つ例をあげる. ¶*afford* an *example* to other nations 他国民に範をたれる ‖ it *affords* another *example* of ... それは...のもう一つの例になる. ¶He even *bettered* his *example.* 彼はそのお手本以上になり(出藍(らん)の誉を)得た. ¶it would be an endless task to *cite examples* which ... ...の例は枚挙にいとまあらずである ‖ to *cite* one *example* 一例を挙げれば. ¶*copy* their *example* 彼らを見ならう. ¶*examples drawn* from history 歴史から引用した実例. ¶*emulate* its *example* それをお手本にする. ¶The *example* will be *followed* by others. 人がそのまねをするだろう. ‖ New York has *followed* the *example* of Paris in establishing a brigade of police-dogs. ニューヨークはパリの例にならって一隊の警察犬を設けることにした. 【類】 *follow* the bad *example* set by ... / I will *follow* his *example.* / You may well *follow* her *example.* / *following* the *example* of ... ¶*furnish* an *example* 模範を示す. ¶*give* an *example* 範をたれる ‖ as the *examples given* below 下にあげた例にならって. ¶*imitate* the high *examples* of virtue 道徳のりっぱな模範にならう. 【類】 *imitate* his *example.* ¶*instance examples* 例をあげる. ¶*keep* these *examples* of intellectual giants before one これら偉人の亀鑑を座右から離さない. ¶Commander Hirose was always a model officer, and he *leaves* a meritorious *example* and memory which will be everlasting. 広瀬中佐は常に模範的将校であって永久に消えないあっぱれな亀鑑と遺烈とを残している. ¶*make* an *example* of him 他の見せしめに彼をこらす. 【類】 He insisted upon the necessity of *making* an *example.* ¶to *mention* a single *example* 一例をあげれば. ¶It would be needless to *multiply examples.* 例を多くあげることは不必要であろう. 【類】 It is not necessary to *multiply examples.* / *Examples* might be *multiplied* indefinitely. / we might go on *multiplying examples* until ... ¶this *offers* another *example* of ... これもまた...の例になる. ¶*point out* a few *examples* 二三の例を指摘する. ¶the museum *possesses* a few *examples* of ... 同博物館は...の標本を二三収蔵している. ¶it *presents* an admirable *example* of ... それは...のりっぱな例になる. ¶It *provides* the best *example.* それは適例になる. ¶*Examples* of this sort might be *quoted* in hundreds. この種の例は何百と引用し得よう. ¶*set* an *example* to others 人に範をたれる ‖ *set* an *example* of virtue to ... 美徳の範を...に示す ‖ he himself *setting* the *example* 彼はみずから範をたれて ‖ *set* a bad *example* to ... ...に示しがつかない. 【類】 America has already *set* us an *example* in this way. ¶*show* a typical *example* 好適例を示す. ¶*shun* their *example* こういう連中の手本をまねないようにする. ¶*simulate* England's profitable *examples* 英国の有利な例をまねる. ¶to *take* an *example* 例えば. ¶*take example* by ... ...の例(故知)にならう ‖ *take* an *example* from him 彼の例にならう.

V² *Examples abound.* 例は幾らもある. ¶The *examples follow.* その例を次に示す. ¶as the *example shows* 例にあるごとく. ¶a few *examples* will *suffice* to show the utter absurdity of ... ...の全くばかげていることを示すには二三の例でことたりる.

Q an *actual example* 実例. ¶an *apt example* 適例. ¶a *beautiful example* of his power of description 彼の筆力を示すすばらしい例. ¶Mr. Lubitsch is the *bright* and *shining example* of the German film directors. ルビッチ氏はドイツ映画監督のりっぱな代表者である. ¶a *brilliant example* of patriots 愛国者のりっぱな亀鑑. ¶*ceramic examples* 陶磁器の標本数種. ¶a *classical example* of an intellectual criminal 知能犯罪者としてよくあげられる例. ¶to give a *common example* 早い話が. ¶to take a *concrete example*, let us imagine A to be ... 具体的な例を採って A が...であると想像して見よう ‖ Let us take a *concrete example* to serve as an illustration. 説明の助けに具体的な

一例を取って見よう. ¶a ***conspicuous*** *example* 顕著な例. ¶***copious*** *examples* たくさんの例. ¶He set me a ***dangerous*** *example*. 彼は僕に悪いお手本を示した. ¶the influence of ***evil*** *example* 悪いお手本の影響. ¶an ***excellent*** *example* of the modern application of scientific method to ... ...に最新の科学的方法を適用した絶好の例 ‖ an ***excellent*** *example* of straining at a gnat and swallowing a camel 末節に拘泥して大事をゆるがせにする好適例. 【類】an ***excellent*** *example* of brevity (簡潔の文). ¶***extreme*** *examples* 極端な例. ¶a ***fair*** *example* of this class この種の好例. ¶to cite (=take) a ***familiar*** *example* 早い話が. ¶a ***fine*** *example* of intellectual vitality in advanced age 老年に及んで知力の衰えないりっぱな一例 ‖ a ***fine*** *example* of the 17th-century Japanese art 十七世紀日本芸術のりっぱな標本. ¶as illustrations of ..., we may take the ***following*** *examples*:— ...の説明としてわれわれは次の例をあげてよかろう. ¶set a ***generous*** *example* 太っ腹な一例を示す. ¶a ***glaring*** *example* of mental inefficiency 精神的無能の顕著な一例. ¶follow a ***good*** *example* よい例を見習う. ¶set a ***heroic*** *example* 勇敢な手本を示す. ¶an ***ideal*** *example* 理想的な例. ¶***illustrative*** *examples* from books and newspapers 書籍や新聞からの引例. ¶an ***impressive historical*** *example* 感銘的な史上の例. ¶***Innumerable*** *examples* of this kind might be adduced. この種の例は幾らでも引用し得よう. ¶an ***inspiring*** *example* 感激させるお手本. ¶These are not ***isolated*** and ***unique*** *examples*. これらは単独で唯一の例ではない. ¶to give the ***latest*** *example* 最近の例をあげれば. ¶Ptolemy Philadelphus was perhaps the most ***marked*** *example* of the love of learning. トレミー・フィラデルファス(エジプト王)は恐らく篤学の最も著しい例であったろう. ¶a ***model*** *example*=a pattern 範例. ¶The book affords a ***monumental*** *example* of industry. その書は労作の不朽の模範を示す. ¶***noble*** *examples* of men who have mastered their circumstances 自分の境遇に打勝った人々のりっぱな例. ¶a ***notable*** *example* 著しい例. ¶give ***numerous*** *examples* 多数の例を示す. ¶by ***personal*** *example* 身をもって範を示して. ¶to cite a ***plain*** *example* 早い話が. ¶a ***remarkable*** *example* 著しい例. ¶He is a ***shining*** *example* of "plain living and high thinking." 彼は「簡素生活と高潔な思考」のりっぱな見本である. ¶to take a ***single*** *example* 一例をあげれば. ¶Japanese swords are ***splendid*** *examples* of the work of the smith. 日本刀はかじ工のさえた腕を例証したものである. ¶a ***stock*** *example* 古くさい例. ¶a ***striking*** *example* of the success of these efforts is seen in ... これらの努力が成功した顕著な例が...に見られる. 【類】in the case of ... we have a ***striking*** *example* of ... ¶a ***telling*** *example* 有力な一例. ¶a ***typical*** *example* of early Tudor architecture チュードル王朝初期建築の好標本. ¶a very ***unedifying*** *example* of an extremely unhappy marriage, originally contracted as a pure love match もともと純然たる恋愛結婚であったものがきわめて不幸な結婚に終ったという教育上きわめて面白からぬ例.

P ***after*** the *example* of ... ...の範にならって. ¶***as*** an *example* of ... may be cited the fact that ... ...の例として...という事実を引用してよかろう ‖ Take, ***as*** an *example*, Spain of today. 例えば今日のスペインを見よ. ¶***beyond*** (=***without***) *example* 前例のない, 空前の. ¶teach this reason ***by*** *example* この理を例によって教える ‖ illustrate ***by*** *example* 例示する. ¶***by way of*** *example*=as an example 一例として. ¶victims, ***for*** *example*, of a railway accident 例えば鉄道事故の犠牲者. 【類】Great men have often risen from poverty—Lincoln and Edison, ***for*** *example*. / if the question were asked, ***for*** *example*, why ..., (例えば「何故...か」) ... / ***for*** *example*, to take but one instance. ¶it can be seen ***from*** the *example* that ... その例からして...ということが分る.

P² an *example* ***for*** us ***in*** ... われわれの...の上において学ぶべきお手本. ¶an *example* ***in*** arithmetic 算術上の一例 ‖ an *example* ***in*** point 適切な一例. ¶an *example* ***of*** misdirected energy 入れ所を誤った力こぶの一例 ‖ *examples* ***of*** the early American glass blower's skill アメリカ初期時代におけるガラス工の熟練を示す標本. ¶as an *example* ***to*** other people 他人への見せしめに. 【類】set a good *example* ***to*** others.

exasperate, *v*. 怒らす; じらす.

P He was *exasperated* ***against*** the informer. 彼は密告者のことを怒っていた. ¶They were *exasperated* ***at*** the failure of their first efforts. 彼らは最初の努力が失敗したのでいら立っていた. 【類】I was *exasperated* ***at*** his conduct. ¶I was *exasperated* ***by*** his proceeding. 彼の仕打に腹が立った. 【類】the pain *exasperated* ***by*** rough treatment. ¶I am *exasperated* ***with*** him. 私は彼に対して怒っている.

exasperating, *a*. 腹の立つ, しゃくにさわる.

P There are many things in Japan which are *exasperating* ***to*** a Westerner. 西洋人にとって腹の立つようなことが日本にたくさんある.

exasperation, *n*. かんしゃく.

P ***in*** *exasperation* かんしゃくを起して.

excavation, *n*. 発掘.

V during *excavations* ***conducted*** by ... ...がやった発掘中に. ¶***make*** (=***undertake***) *excavations* at ... ...を発掘する.

exceed, *v*. 越える, 超過する; まさる.

P Export *exceeds* import ***by*** six million dollars. 輸出超過六百万ドルに及ぶ. ‖ It *exceeded* my estimate ***by*** a great deal. 大層見積りを超過した. ¶*exceed* ***in*** number (weight, size) 数(など)においてまさる. 【類】London *exceeds* New York ***in*** size. / Platinum *exceeds* gold ***in*** value.

excel, *v*. まさる, すぐれる, ひいでる.

M He ***pre-eminently*** *excels* in English. 彼は群を抜いて英語にすぐれている.

P *excel* ***as*** an orator 雄弁家としてすぐれている. ¶He *excelled* ***at*** historical romance. 彼は歴史的小説にすぐれていた. ‖ how to *excel* ***at*** the game その競技の上達法. ¶how to *excel* ***in*** study 勉強ができるようになる方法 ‖ He *excels* ***in*** speaking English (mathematics). 彼は英語を話すこと(など)が得意だ. 【類】*excel* ***in*** scholarship (学問) / He *excels* ***in*** virtue. / He *excelled* the others ***in*** handwriting. / Solomon *excelled* ***in*** wisdom. / None can *excel* him ***in*** workmanship (細工).

excellence, *n*. 卓越, 優秀, 優越.

V ***attest*** its *excellence* その優秀さを証明する. ¶His composition can ***claim*** first *excellence*. 彼の作文は最優等だと言われる. ¶Few women can ***dispute*** *excellence* with her in the beauty of form. 曲線美において彼女と肩をならべ得る女は少ない. ¶***emulate*** the *excellences* 優秀さを競う. ¶None can ***gainsay*** the *excellence* of his work. 何人も彼の作の優秀を否定できない. ¶***inherit*** or ***acquire*** great *excellence* in one direction 一方面において非常な卓越を先天的または後天的に得る.

Q its ***artistic*** *excellence* それの芸術的優秀. ¶reach ***high*** *excellence* 優秀の域に達する. ¶***literary*** *excellence* 文学的優秀. ¶the ***wellknown*** *excellence* of British workmanship 広く知られている英国職工の技術の高さ.

P He received a prize ***for*** *excellence* in mathematics. 彼は数学で優等を取った. ¶New Jersey, that home for the trusts ***par*** *excellence* 本格的トラストの本場たるニュージャージー ‖ Liquid ammonia is, ***par*** *excellence*, the best antidote for snake-bites. アンモニア液はへびにかまれた時に特別よくきく解毒剤である.

P² ***for*** *excellence* ***in*** scholarship 学術優秀で. ¶by the *excellence* ***of*** their scholastic work 彼らの学業優秀のために. ¶his ever-present self-consciousness and sense of *excellence* ***over*** others 彼の不断の自意識と他人に対する優越感.

excellent, *a*. 優秀な, 結構な.

P Pickles are *excellent* ***for*** the promotion of appetite. つけ物は食欲増進にもってこいだ. ¶students *excellent* ***in*** English and other foreign languages 英語及び他の外国語に優秀な学生.

except, *v*. 除外する; 異議を唱える.

P *except* him ***from*** blame 彼をとがめずに置く ‖ *except* one ***from*** (=***out of***) the whole company 一座の中から一人を除外する ‖ ***From*** his statement this must be *excepted*. 彼の言明からこれを除外しなければならない. 【類】Those who passed the first test were *excepted* ***from*** the second. ¶*except* ***to*** a statement (view) 申立(など)に対して異議を唱える.

O *Excepting* this child, all were rescued. この子の他はみんな救助された.

except, *prep*. ...を除いて.

P The house is deserted, *except* ***for*** the keeper. 家は番人がいるだけで空家も同然だ. ‖ He is naked *except* ***for*** a loin-cloth. 彼はふんどしだけの丸はだかだ. ‖ Achilles was invulnerable *except* ***for*** his heels. アキレスはかかとを除いては不死身だった.

O The account is correct, *except* that the carriage is omitted. 運賃が落ちいてるだけで勘定に間違いはない. ‖ every day *except* [on] Sunday 日曜を除いて毎日.

exception, *n*. 例外, 除外, 除外例; 不服.

V constitute no exception to ... …に除外を設けない. ¶exceptions excepted 例外は別として. ¶This forms the exception, not the rule. これは例外であって通則でない. ‖ It forms an exception to the general rule. それは概則に対して例外をなしている. 【類】form exceptions to this rule / form no exception to the rule. ¶grant exceptions 例外を認める. ¶make an exception for ... …を除外する ‖ make an exception in favor of ... …のために特別扱いをする ‖ exceptions are made as when ... …というような場合は別である. 【類】an exception, however, has been made in the case of ... / exception might be made in favor of ... / an exception must be made of ... ¶take exception 不服を唱える ‖ take exception at ... …に気を悪くする ‖ take exception to (=against) ... …に反対する ‖ take exception to one of the twelve jurymen 十二人の陪審官の内一人を忌避する.

V^2 Exceptions occur, but it is nowhere believed that they are frequent or serious. 例外はあるが決してひん繁でもなくまた大したこともないとだれも信じている.

Q an apparent exception 外観上の例外. ¶a conspicuous exception 明々白々の例外. ¶with few exceptions あまり例外というものもなく. 【類】There are a few exceptions to this rule. / with a few brilliant exceptions. ¶the one great exception I know to this is ... 私の知る限りではこの一つの著しい例外は…である. ¶with a few honorable exceptions 二三のりっぱな例外はあるが. ¶an important exception 重要な例外. ¶It is the inevitable exception that proves the soundness of the rule. それは避くべからざる例外であってかえって規則の確実さを証することになる. ¶But this is not an isolated exception. しかしこれは唯一の例外ではない. ¶though to this rule there are many exceptions この規則には多数の例外があることはあるが. 【類】A rule with many exceptions is of little use. ¶a marked exception 著しい例外. ¶He was no exception to this rule. 彼も御多聞に漏れなかった. ¶with the notable exceptions of ... …という顕著な例外はあるが. ¶There are occasional exceptions to the rule. その規則には折々例外がある. ¶permissible exceptions 許しうる例外. ¶with rare exceptions まれに例外はあるが. ¶take sharp exception to ... …に強硬に反抗する. ¶shining exceptions りっぱな例外. ¶with perhaps the single exception of ... 恐らく…という唯一つの例外だけで. 【類】with the single exception of ... / with a single conspicuous exception. ¶Tolstoi's novels and stories, with the solitary exception of the Kreutzer Sonata, have been very well received. 「クロイツァー・ソナタ」だけは別だがトルトスイの小説類は非常に歓迎された. ¶take strong exception to ... …に強硬に反対する. ¶an unavoidable exception 避くべからざる例外.

Q^2 a wartime exception 戦時特例.

P with the exception of ... …は別として. 【類】with some exceptions / with this exception ‖ They passed with the exception of three. 三人の外は及第した. ¶A language without exceptions is like a human being without faults. 例外のない言語は欠点のない人間のようなものだ. ‖ without [an] exception 残らず ‖ taking up one by one without exception しらみつぶしに. 【類】without any exceptions.

P^2 There is no exception to the rule. その規則には例外がない. 【類】There are some exceptions to every rule. / There are, of course, exceptions to this rule.

O It is the exception rather than the rule. それは規則よりはむしろ例外だ.

exceptional, *a*. 異数の.

M very exceptional 極めて異数の.

excerpt, *n*. 抜粋.

P^2 excerpts from literature 文献からの抜粋数種.

excess, *n*. 過剰; 過度, 過分; 不節制, 放縦.

V pay excess of first over third class fare 三等から一等への変更増徴を支払う. ¶shun excess 極端を避ける.

Q to a ludicrous excess ばかばかしく度を過して. ¶rhetorical excesses 修飾に失する言葉. ¶Her husband has been exhausted by earlier sexual excesses, so that he retains no more than remnants of virility. 彼女の夫は若いころ性の快楽にふけりすぎて精根を消耗したので精力のかすが残っているに過ぎない. ¶a victim of solitary excesses 過度の自慰の犠牲者. ¶youthful excesses 青年時代の放とう.

P You must pay for the excess. 貴下は制限超過に対して金を払わねばなりません. ‖ for the excess of one's passion …を思う(愛する)の余り. ¶drink in (=to) excess 過度に酒を飲む ‖ be greatly in excess of my wants 私の必要とする数量をはるかに越えている ‖ Usury is the interest in excess of a legal rate. 高利とは法律上の率よりも高い利息である. ‖ be one in excess of ... …より一つだけ余計である. ‖ in an excess of nervous agitation 神経興奮の極に達して ‖ in his excess of mirth (=delight) うれしさの余り. 【類】100 in excess of last year / slightly in excess of ... ¶become speechless through excess of joy うれしさのあまり言葉がでなくなる. ¶He is generous to excess. 彼は寛大に過ぎる. ‖ pleasures carried to excess 過度の快楽.

P^2 an excess in eating or drinking 過度の飲食 ‖ Any excess in payment will be refunded. お支払い金額が超過の場合はお返し致します. ¶the excess of births over deaths 死亡数に対する出産数の超過 ‖ an excess of imports over exports 輸入超過 ‖ an excess of blood 多血 ‖ excess of rain 過多の雨 ‖ Excess of sorrow laughs, excess of joy weeps. 悲しみが度を越すと笑いうれしさが度を越すと泣く. ‖ the excesses of the Right and the Left 右翼と左翼の行き過ぎ. 【類】the excess of my expenditure over my income.

exchange, *n*. (1) 交換, 交易; 取引所; 電話交換所.

V gain (lose) the exchange [将棋など]交換して得(損)をする. ¶We had an exchange of views among ourselves. われわれは互に意見を交換した. ¶I made an exchange with him. あの人と取換えっこをした. ¶operate telephone exchanges 電話の交換をやる.

Q a brief exchange of views ちょっとした意見の交換. ¶a cultural exchange 文化の交換. ¶a frank and candid exchange of views with ... …とのざっくばらんな意見の交換. ¶a hurried exchange of good nights あわただしい「お休み」のあいさつの交換. ¶international exchange in educational thought and practice 教育思想と実際の国際的交換 ‖ international exchange of merchandise 国際貿易. 【類】international exchange of opinion / an international exchange of informed and intelligent criticism applied to ... ¶a mutual exchange of thoughts (=ideas) 相互の思想交換. ¶underneath the pleasant exchange of compliments and courtesy lurked ... 愉快に取交わすあいさつと礼儀の下に…がひそんでいた.

Q^2 a dummy exchange 練習用交換局. ¶an employment exchange 職業安定所. 【類】a women's employment exchange. ¶a fee-charging employment exchange 有料職業紹介所. ¶a labor exchange 職業紹介所. ¶transactions on the New York Exchange ニューヨーク株式取引所の取引き. ¶a post exchange=PX《米》酒保. ¶a busy morning on the stock exchange 株式取引所の多忙な朝 ‖ a speculation on the Stock Exchange 株の投機. ¶student and professor exchanges among nations 国家間の学生及び教授交換. ¶a telephone exchange [office] 電話交換局. ¶Quotations for December delivery on the Tokyo Rice Exchange yesterday ruled at ¥21,000 東京米穀取引所十二月渡しの相場はきのう二万一千円で取引された. ¶a two-way exchange 双方からの交流. ¶the favorable yen exchange 有利な円交換.

P after an exchange of greetings あいさつを取交わしてから. ¶meet socially for the exchange of ideas and opinions 思想や意見を交換するために親しく会合する. ¶The goods are not delivered except in exchange for money. 品物は現金と引換えでなければ渡しません. ‖ payable in exchange for the bill of lading (=B/L) 船荷証券(貨物引換証)引換払い ‖ deliver goods in exchange for a receipt 受取書と引替えに品を渡す. 【類】I gave him old magazines and received a dictionary in exchange (代りに).

P^2 an exchange for another thing 別のと引替え. ¶an exchange of healths 祝杯の交換 ‖ exchange of confidences between ... …間の打明け話 ‖ exchange of the revenues of daimyos for pensions 大名の封禄の年金への切り換え ‖ an exchange of war prisoners 捕虜の交換. 【類】exchange of letters.

(2) 為替; 為替相場.

V can buy (sell) exchange on New York (London) 対米(英)買(売)為替で買う(売る). ¶stabilize exchange 為替相場を安定させる.

Q at current exchange of $49^5/_8$ 四十九ドル八分の五の現在為替相場で. ¶direct exchange 直接為替. ¶a long exchange 長期為替手形.

P at the exchange of 1s. 4d. for the rupee 一ルピーに対し

一シリング四ペンスの為替相場で ‖ ***at*** the *exchange* of 52 pence to the dollar 一ドル対五十二ペンスの為替相場で.【類】***at*** an *exchange* of 2d. to the mark. ¶What is the present rate ***of*** *exchange* on London? 対ロンドンの現在為替レートはいくらですか. ‖ Prices are liable to alteration in accordance with the fluctuation ***of*** *exchange*. 価格は為替相場で上がり下りがある. ¶***owing to*** low *exchange* 為替相場が低いために.

P² steady *exchange* ***between*** London and New York ロンドン対ニューヨーク間の変動のない為替相場. ¶the rate of *exchange* ***for*** dollars ドルの為替相場.

exchange, *v.* 交換する; 両替する.

P Will you *exchange* this ***for*** that? これとそれと換えてくれませんか. ‖ *exchange* old yen ***for*** new 旧円を新円と換える. ¶*exchange* American money ***into*** English 米貨を英貨に両替する. ¶Let me *exchange* seats ***with*** you. あなたと席を交換しましょう.【類】*exchange* letters ***with*** a foreign friend / *exchange* views (confidences, things) ***with*** another person.

exchequer, *n.* 国庫; 財源, 財政.

Q the poverty of the ***Imperial Exchequer*** 国庫の窮乏. ¶a ***lean*** *exchequer* 貧弱な財源. ¶My *exchequer* is ***low***. 僕の財政は豊かでない.

Q² my ***family*** *exchequer* 僕の家計.

excise, *n.* 国産税.

V ***levy*** an *excise* 国産税を課する.

P *excise* [tax] ***on*** a home product (sugar, tabacco) 国産品(など)の物品税.

excision, *n.* 削除.

V The censor ***made*** *excisions* and changes in the film. 検閲官はその映画の削除変更を施した.

excite, *v.* 興奮させる, 激こうさせる; 扇動する.

M He gets ***easily*** *excited* to anger. 彼はすぐに腹を立てる. ¶It ***especially*** *excited* their inquisitiveness. 彼らは殊にそのことを聞きたがっていた. ¶be ***greatly*** *excited* 大騒ぎをやる. ¶be ***much*** *excited* 大騒ぎをする. ¶He was ***wildly*** *excited*. 彼は大いに激こうした.

P get *excited* ***about*** something あることに腹を立てる. ¶He was *excited* ***at*** discovery (=exposure *or* disclosure). 彼は露顕したので興奮していた. ‖ She is *excited* ***at*** the prospect of a journey. 彼女は旅を控えて興奮している. ¶I was *excited* ***by*** him. 僕は彼に対して腹をたてた. ‖ He was *excited* ***by*** some act (fact). 彼はある行動(など)によって鼓舞された.【類】The whole country was *excited* ***by*** the news of victory. ¶be *excited* ***over*** the news そのニュースを聞いて興奮する.【類】Don't get *excited* ***over*** such a little matter. ¶I *excited* him ***to*** anger. 私は彼を怒らせてしまった. ‖ *excite* the people ***to*** rebellion 人民を扇動してむほんを起させる. ¶He was *excited* ***with*** joy at the success. 彼は成功したうれしさで興奮していた.【類】we were *excited* ***with*** boundless joy (歓喜おくあたわざるものがあった) at the news of the fall of ...

excitement, *n.* 刺激, 興奮; 激こう; 激励, 鼓舞.

V ***allay*** popular *excitement* 民衆の激こうを静める ‖ ***allay*** nervous *excitement* 神経の興奮を静める. ¶It is going to ***cause*** great *excitement* in many quarters. それは各方面に非常な興奮を引き起そうとしている. ¶***calm*** *excitement* 興奮を静める. ¶***combat*** *excitement* 激こうを抑制する. ¶I think I successfully ***concealed*** my inner *excitement*. 私は私の胸さわぎをうまく隠し得たと思う. ¶It ***created*** no little *excitement* in the world of science. それは科学界に少なからぬ反響を起した. ¶***experience*** a strong sexual *excitement* 強い性の刺激を経験する. ¶***feel*** no *excitement* over ... …に対して騒がない. ¶in order to ***induce*** (=***provoke***) sexual *excitement* 性的刺激を誘起するために. ¶it ***produced*** much *excitement*, if not alarm, among ... それは…間に驚がくほどではなかったが非常な興奮を引き起した.

V² *excitement* ***grew***, and ... 興奮がたかまって… ¶Very great *excitement* ***prevails***. 大興奮が渦を巻いている. ¶the *excitement* ***waxed*** strongest when ... …のとき激こうが頂点に達した.

Q act under ***alcoholic*** *excitement* 酒の上でやる. ¶***confused*** *excitement* 取乱した興奮. ¶***considerable*** *excitement* was felt as to ... …については大いに感激した. ¶***emotional*** *excitement* 感情の興奮. ¶***feverish*** *excitement* 熱烈な興奮. ¶The crowd was in a state of ***hysterical*** *excitement*. 群集はヒステリー的な興奮状態であった. ¶***Immense*** *excitement* prevailed. 非常な興奮が起っていた. ¶a ***political*** *excitement* 政変. ¶a ***stirring*** *excitement* 血わき肉おどる感激. ¶in ***unabated*** *excitement* 興奮のままに. ¶a ***wild*** *excitement* すさまじい興奮.

P cry ***in*** *excitement* 興奮して叫ぶ ‖ ***in*** his *excitement* 興奮して. ¶explosiveness of speech ***under*** *excitement* 興奮しているときの「べらんめえ」口調 ‖ laws passed ***under*** strong but transient emotional *excitement* 強烈なしかし一時的興奮に支配されて通過した法律案. ¶flushed ***with*** *excitement* 興奮のため顔を赤くして.

P² *excitement* ***of*** hope 希望に満ちた興奮.

exclaim, *v.* 叫ぶ, 絶叫する.

M ***breathlessly*** *exclaim* 息をもつかず絶叫する. ¶***loudly*** *exclaim* against it 声を高くしてそれに反対する. ¶***ruefully*** *exclaim* 残念がって叫ぶ.

P *exclaim* ***against*** oppressions 圧迫に対しその非を鳴らす. ¶*exclaim* ***in*** despair 悲鳴をあげる. ¶*exclaim* ***with*** one voice 一せいに叫ぶ ‖ *exclaim* ***with*** delight 喜んで叫ぶ.

exclamation, *n.* 絶叫, 感嘆.

V ***give*** an *exclamation* of joy 歓喜の声をあげる. ¶They ***made*** very loud *exclamations* of grief. 彼らははなはだ高い悲しみの叫び声を発した. ¶***utter*** an *exclamation* 感嘆の声を発する.

Q an ***indignant*** *exclamation* 憤怒の叫び. ¶though an ***unpremeditated*** *exclamation* 不用意の叫びだったが.

P "Oh" is used ***as*** an *exclamation* of surprise. "Oh" は驚がくの叫びとして用いられる.

P² an *exclamation* ***of*** surprise (joy, sorrow, amazement) 驚き(など)の叫び.

exclude, *v.* 拒絶する; 除く.

P be *excluded* ***from*** membership 入会を拒まれる ‖ *exclude* the item ***from*** the agenda of the conference 会議の日程からその事項を取除く ‖ *exclude* one nation ***from*** the ports of another 一国の港にある他国民の入港を許さない.【類】He was *excluded* ***from*** honorary membership in the Royal Geographical Society (王立地理学協会の名誉会員). ‖ may be *excluded* ***from*** repatriation (送還).

exclusion, *n.* 排斥, 除外; 放逐.

P the movement ***for*** the *exclusion* of ... …の排斥運動. ¶***to*** the *exclusion* of (=excluding) other nationals 他国人を除外して ‖ in conjunction with, not ***to*** the *exclusion* of, ... …を除外せずこれと共同で. ¶an *exclusion* ***from*** a country (village, an association) 国(など)からの放逐.

exclusive, *a.* 除いて.

P *exclusive* ***of*** (=excluding) hotel expenses 旅館の費用は勘定に入れずに ‖ *exclusive* ***of*** the regular holidays 定休日を除いて. ¶this is a feature that is *exclusive* ***with***... これは…にしかないのが特色である.

exclusiveness, *n.* 除外.

Q ***social*** *exclusiveness* 社会的排他.

excommunicate *v.* 破門する.

P be *excommunicated* ***from*** the church 教会から破門される.

excreta, *n. pl.* 排せつ物.

V ***void*** *excreta* 脱ぷんする.

Q ***human*** *excreta* 人間の排せつ物.

excursion, *n.* 遠足, 遊覧.

V ***arrange*** *excursions* to places of interest 名所遊覧の手はずを取きめる. ¶***conduct*** a school *excursion* 学校の遠足を行う. ¶How did you ***enjoy*** your *excursion*? 遠足はどうでした. ¶***make*** an *excursion* of a few weeks 数週間の遠足をやる ‖ ***make*** an *excursion* into the country いなかへ遠足をする ‖ ***make*** *excursions* twice a year 年二回遊覧旅行をする. ¶The *excursion* has been ***postponed***. 遠足は延期になった. ¶***run*** cheap *excursions* 割引遊覧列車を運転する.【類】the railway [company] ***runs*** *excursions* to ... ¶We ***took*** a nice *excursion*. われわれは愉快な遠足をやった.

Q special ***cheap*** *excursions* [鉄道の]臨時割引回遊旅行. ¶a ***cross-country*** *excursion* 断郊旅行. ¶What a ***lovely*** *excursion* we have had! 僕らの遠足はとても面白かった. ¶a ***rural*** *excursion* いなかの旅行.

Q² an ***angling*** *excursion* 釣の出遊. ¶a ***boating*** (=***boat***) *excursion* ボートでの遠出 ‖ We are just going out on ***boat*** *excursion* 僕たちは今舟遊びに出かけるところだ. ¶go on a ***country*** *excursion* 近郊遠足に出かける. ¶run ***express*** *excursions* to ... 急行回遊列車を…に運転する. ¶a ***fishing*** *excursion* 釣遊び. ¶a ***hunting*** *excursion* 狩猟遠足. ¶an ocean *excursion* 外洋巡航. ¶an ***owner-driver*** *excursion* 自家用車によるドライブ (自分の車を自分で運転する). ¶a *pedestrian excursion* 徒歩旅行. ¶ a ***pleasure excursion*** 遊覧旅行. ¶ a ***riding excursion*** 遠乗り. ¶ have a pleasant ***sea excursion*** 海上遊覧旅行をする ¶ plan a ***shopping*** *excursion* [どの店からどの店と]買物の道筋を計画する. ¶ ***shore*** *excursions* of cruises 巡洋の沿海航行. ¶ a ***summer*** *excursion* 夏の遠足. ¶ a ***water*** *excursion* 水上行遊. ¶ a ***walking*** *excursion* ハイキング. ¶ a ***weekend*** *excursion* 週末旅行.

P take part ***in*** an *excursion* 遠足に参加する. ¶ He set out ***on*** his business *excursion*. 彼は商用で旅行にでかけた. ‖ kiddies ***on*** their *excursion* 遠足途上の子供たち ‖ We had capital fun ***on*** our *excursion*. 僕たちは遠足で素敵に面白かった.

P² an *excursion* ***by*** steamer (rail) 船(など)の行楽. ¶ an *excursion* ***in*** an automobile 自動車遊覧旅行. ¶ an *excursion* ***into*** the country いなかへの旅行. ¶ *excursions* ***off*** so-called "beaten track" いわゆる「おきまりの場所」でない所への遠足. ¶ an *excursion* ***to*** Atami 熱海への慰安旅行.

excursionist, *n.* [回遊]旅行者.

Q² ***Sunday*** *excursionists* 日曜旅行者たち. ¶ ***weekend*** *excursionists*=weekenders 週末旅行者たち.

excuse, *n.* 言わけ, 弁解, 断り, わび; 口実, 言抜け.

V it ***affords*** ample *excuse* for ... それは...に対して十分に申訳になる. ¶ ***cook up*** (=***concoct***) an *excuse* 言抜けを考える. ¶ ***find*** an *excuse* for ... ...に対して言わけを見つける. ¶ ***give*** (=make) some *excuse* ある口実をもうける ‖ Please ***give*** them my *excuses* for being late. 私がおそくなったのをみんなに言わけをしておいて下さい. ‖ ***give*** his audience an *excuse* for yawning 聴衆にあくびをさせるようなことをする. ¶ I ***have*** an *excuse* from my guardian. 私は保証人の届書を持っています[学校欠席のときなど]. ‖ You ***have*** no *excuse* for being idle. 君はなまけていてはすまない. ‖ He ***has*** lots of *excuses* for neglecting his duties. 彼はその職務怠慢についてはいくらでも口実がある. ¶ ***invent*** *excuse* for ... ...の申訳をこしらえる. ¶ he ***made*** some *excuse* for ... 彼はなにかにこと寄せて...した ‖ You are wrong, ***make*** what *excuse* you may. どう言わけしても君が悪い. ‖ I will ***make*** your *excuses*. 君のことは私から言わけをしよう. 【類】 He is good at ***making*** *excuses*. ‖ ***make*** one *excuse* or another 言を左右に託す ‖ ***make*** it an *excuse* to ... それを...する口実にする ‖ be ***made*** the *excuse* for ... ...のだしに使われる ‖ ***make*** it an *excuse* for rowdyism 不礼講の言わけにする. ¶ ***manufacture*** *excuses* 口実を作る. ¶ ***manipulate*** some *excuse* for ... 巧みに...の申訳を作る. ¶ he ***offered*** the *excuse* that ... 彼は...と弁解した. 【類】 ***offer*** no *excuse*. ¶ Certainly I ***owe*** you every *excuse* for it. それに対して私は貴下に重々申訳がありません. ¶ *Excuse* must be ***rendered*** for all absences from required exercises. 必須学課を欠課する場合は必ず届を出すこと. ¶ it ***requires*** no *excuses* to ... ...しても差支えない. ¶ He has ***sent in*** an *excuse*. あの人は断って来た. ¶ the same *excuse* cannot be ***urged*** for ... ...に対してはこれと同様の弁解は立たない.

Q an ***adequate*** *excuse* 十分な申訳. ¶ make ***appropriate*** *excuses* しかるべき弁解をやる. ¶ an ***awkward*** *excuse* へたな申しわけ. ¶ a ***blind*** *excuse* でたらめの言わけ. ¶ regard ... as a ***brilliant*** *excuse* for spending a day or two in town ...を一両日都会で暮す絶好の口実と見る. ¶ a ***clumsy*** *excuse* まずい申訳. ¶ a tissue of ***dull*** *excuses* へたな言分けの連続. ¶ You can find an ***easy*** *excuse* for it. それはなんとでも申訳が立つ. ¶ a ***flimsy*** *excuse* 薄弱な申訳. ¶ make a ***glib*** *excuse* 口先だけの言わけをする. ¶ a ***groundless*** *excuse* 筋の立たない弁解. ¶ an ***insufficient*** *excuse* 不十分な申し開き. ¶ make ***lame*** *excuses* つじつまの合わない弁解をやる. ¶ a ***legitimate*** *excuse* 合理的な言わけ. ¶ with the ***like*** *excuses* そういったような言わけをして. ¶ have ***little*** *excuse* for ... ...に対してまず弁解のしようがない. ¶ a ***mere*** *excuse* for ... ...に対するほんの申訳. ¶ There is not now so ***much*** *excuse* for it. それに対し以前ほど弁解が立たなくなっている. ¶ Ignorance of the law is ***no*** *excuse*. 法律を知らないことが弁解にはならない. ‖ allowing ***no*** *excuse* (=willy-nilly) 有無を言わせず ‖ You didn't know is ***no*** *excuse* for it. 知りませんでしたじゃ済まない. ¶ ***No better*** *excuse!* うまく言抜けたものだ. ‖ Have you got ***no better*** *excuse* [to give]? もっとうまい言わけはないのか. ¶ with ***one*** *excuse* or another 言を左右にして. ¶ my ***only*** *excuse* is that ... 私の言わけは...ということだけです. ¶ a ***pitiful*** *excuse* あわれな申訳. ¶ a ***plausible*** *excuse* もっともらしい言わけ. ¶ a very ***poor*** *excuse* はなはだまずい申訳 ‖ That's a ***poor*** *excuse*. そんなの言わけになっちゃいない. ¶ make a ***reasonable*** *excuse* 筋の通った弁解をする. ¶ a ***rotten*** *excuse* つまらない言分け. ¶ The ***same old*** *excuse!* その言わけは古い. ¶ give a ***satisfactory*** *excuse* 満足の行く言わけをする. ¶ a ***slight*** *excuse* ちょっとした言わけ. ¶ on ***some*** *excuse* or other なんらかの口実で. ¶ see through his ***specious*** *excuse* 彼の言わけはもっともらしいが怪しいとにらむ. ¶ a ***strained*** *excuse* 苦しい弁解. ¶ a ***subtle*** *excuse* 巧妙な申訳. ¶ it is not a ***sufficient*** *excuse* for ... それは...に対して十分な申訳にならない. 【類】 there can be no ***sufficient*** *excuse* for ... ¶ a ***thin*** *excuse* 薄弱な弁解. ¶ a ***transparent*** *excuse* 見えすいた口実. ¶ it is no longer a ***valid*** *excuse* for ... もはや...に対して筋の立った言わけにはならない. 【類】 it is no ***valid*** *excuse* for you to say that ...

P I have not a word to say ***in*** *excuse*. 私は一言の申訳もありません. ‖ plead ignorance ***in*** *excuse* 知らなかったと言って弁解する ‖ I have no word to say ***in*** *excuse*. 一言もない. ‖ take shelter ***in*** vague *excuse* ばく然たる申訳をして逃げる. ¶ ***on*** one *excuse* or another 種々と口実を設けて. ¶ ***under*** various *excuses* 色々な口実の下に.

P² I make no *excuse* ***for*** having published it. それの出版理由については説明を加えない(だれにも想像のつくことだから).

excuse, *v.* 申訳する, 弁疏する; 許す; 免除する.

M You ***really*** must *excuse* me. 本当にゆるして下さいよ(酒などもう一杯といわれて).

P *excuse* me ***for*** insisting しつっこいようですが... ‖ *Excuse* ***for*** my gloves (overcoat). 手袋(など)をはめたままで失礼します. ‖ *Excuse* me ***for*** my abrupt question. つかんことをうかがいますが. 【類】 *Excuse* me ***for*** asking the queston. / Please *excuse* him ***for*** staying home. / You will *excuse* me ***for*** not recognizing you at once. / He *excused* himself ***for*** coming late. ‖ *Excuse* me ***for*** interrupting you. お話中ですが. ‖ Ignorance of a law does not *excuse* a man ***for*** violating it. 法律を知らないということは人が法律を犯した申訳にはならない. ‖ Please *excuse* him ***for*** being away those two days. その二日間欠席致しますから御承知下さい[子供の学校欠席などの場合]. ¶ He had been *excused* ***from*** military service on account of short-sightedness. 彼は近眼で兵役を免除された. 【類】 *excuse* one ***from*** responsibility for ... ‖ He is *excused* ***from*** attendance at these studies. ‖ *Excuse* me ***from*** work on Friday. 金曜は休ませて頂きます(雇人が主人に言う言葉). ‖ I'd rather be *excused* ***from*** it. 御免をこうむりたいものだ. 【類】 I want to *excuse* myself ***from*** the work. ‖ *excuse* one ***from*** attendance. ¶ *Excuse* me ***to*** him today. きょうは失礼すると彼に伝えて下さい. ¶ He *excused* himself ***with*** humble words. 彼は辞を低くしてわびた.

Q I cannot come this evening, so I ask (=beg) you to *excuse* me. 今晩はあがれませんからご勘弁願います.

execute, 履行する; 死刑に処する.

M be ***exquisitely*** *executed* (細工ものなど)巧妙に作られている. ¶ All orders ***promptly*** *executed*. 御注文はすべて迅速に調達致します. ¶ ***rigorously*** *execute*=strictly carry out 厳密に履行する. ¶ were ***specially*** *executed* for ... 特に...の御用のため調達されたのであった. ¶ Your order will be *executed* as ***speedily*** as possible. 御注文はできるだけ迅速に調達致します. ¶ The order has been very ***well*** (***badly***) *executed*. その注文は申分なく(まずく)調達された.

P He was *executed* ***with*** fire (the sword). 彼は火刑(など)に処せられた.

execution, *n.* 実行; 執行; 死刑, 処刑; 演奏; 効果, 威力.

V The hangman ***carried out*** 250 *executions*. その絞刑吏は二百五十件の死刑を執行した. ¶ Every shot ***did*** *execution*. どの弾丸も命中した. ‖ The speech ***did*** good *execution* for our side. その演説はわが党のために大いに気勢を揚げた. ‖ He ***did*** great *execution* among the dishes. 彼は料理をさんざんに食いあらした. ¶ ***suspend*** *execution* of a dishonorable discharge 執行を中止する.

Q ***bad*** (=***poor***) *execution* 不でき. ¶ ***compulsory*** *execution* 強制執行. ¶ ***florid*** *execution* 派手やかな演奏振り. ¶ ***forcible*** *execution* 強制執行. ¶ The degradation of an officer is a ***moral*** *execution*. 将校の左遷は精神的死刑である. ¶ ***provisional*** *execution* 仮執行. ¶ a ***public*** *execution* 公刑

の面前での死刑執行. ¶***strict*** *execution* of an edict (a law) 布告(など)の励行.

P ***during*** the *execution* of a contract 契約実行の期間中. ¶***in*** the *execution* of official duty 公務の執行に当って. ¶carry ***into execution*** 実行する.【類】we have decided to put (=carry) ***into execution*** the project of ...

P^2 *execution **of*** construction work 建設工事の施行 ‖ *execution **of*** a judgment 判決の執行.【類】*execution **of*** obligations (義務). ¶an *execution **without*** trial 審問を経ないない処刑.

executive, *n.* 執行者, 実行者; 幹部, 理事.

Q a ***big*** *executive* 重役. ¶***chief*** *executives* 経営の首脳者(重役) ‖ the *Chief Executive* 《米》最高行政官(大統領のこと). ¶a ***high*** *executive* of a company 会社幹部の一人 ‖ their ***higher*** *executives* 上役 ‖ the ***highest*** *executive* in the country 政府最高責任者(首相). ¶***major*** *executives* 会社の重役連. ¶***minor*** *executives* 下級の幹部.

P^2 an ***advertising*** *executive* 宣伝部長. ¶a ***bank*** *executive* 銀行重役. ¶***business*** *executives* 経営者側. ¶***company*** *executives* 会社の上役(普通部長級以上). ¶***newspaper*** *executives* 新聞社の経営担当者ら. ¶***party*** *executives* 政党幹部. ¶a ***plant*** *executive* 工場経営者(工場長など). ¶the ***production*** *executives* of Hollywood ハリウッドの映画製作首脳連. ¶a ***$12,000 a year*** *executive* 年俸一万二千ドルの幹部社員.

executor, *n.* 遺産管理人.

Q a ***literary*** *executor* 遺稿管理人.

exemplification, *n.* 好例; 例証.

Q an ***executory*** *exemplification* 執行力ある正本. ¶He is the ***very*** *exemplification* of piety. 彼は信者のよいお手本だ.

P ***in*** *exemplification* of ... ...を例証するために.

exemplify, *v.* 例証する.

P it is strongly *exemplified **in*** ... それは...の中に有力な例証が示されている.

exempt, *a.* 免除された.

P Tickets costing $10 or less are *exempt **from*** taxation. 十ドルまたはそれ以下の切符は免税になっている. ‖ They are *exempt **from*** customs duty. それらの品は関税がかからない.

exempt, *v.* 免除する.

P ... may be *exempted **from customs*** examination ...は税関の検査を免除される ‖ *exempt* them ***from*** taxes (a fine, military service) 彼らに課税(など)を免除する.

exemption, *n.* 免除.

V grant subsidies or ***allow*** *exemptions* from taxation 助成金を下付するか課税を免除する.

Q ***partial*** *exemption* from ... ...の一部免除. ¶***total*** *exemption* from ... ...の全部免除.

Q^2 claim ***dependency*** *exemptions* 扶養家族の申告をする. ¶be entitled to ***tax*** *exemption* 免税の資格がある.

P^2 temporary *exemption **from*** conscription 徴兵猶予 ‖ *exemption **from*** military service 兵役免除.

exercise, *n.* 運用, 行使; 練習, 演習, 鍛練, 修養; 課業, 練習問題; 運動, 体操; 式, 次第.

V how to ***attack*** an *exercise* in geometry 幾何学課題の解き方. ¶***do*** an *exercise* in English composition 英作文の練習課題をやる ‖ ***do*** one's *exercise* well 課題をよく練習する. ¶***facilitate*** the *exercise* of political power 政権行使を容易にする. ¶you may ***find*** profitable *exercise* in ...ing ...すると有利な練習になるであろう. ¶***Getting*** some *exercise*. 少し運動をやっているとこさ. ¶***have*** *exercise* in the open air 戸外で運動する. ¶***make*** *exercise* in composition 作文の筆ならしをする. ¶***need*** some *exercise* 少し運動させなくちゃいけない. ¶***practice*** a few *exercises* with dumb-bells あれいで二三回体操をやる.【類】***practice*** this *exercise* morning and evening each day. ¶***pursue*** one's athletic *exercises* with zest 熱心に競技運動をやる. ¶In 1825 Queen's College was enabled to ***resume*** its *exercises* by a gift from Henry Rutgers, whose name it adopted. 一八二五年にクイーンズ・カレジはヘンリー・ラットガーズの寄付によって復活することができ校名も寄付者の名を襲用することになった. ¶***take*** light *exercises* 軽い運動をする ‖ ***take*** much *exercise* in the open air 大いに戸外運動をする ‖ *Exercise **taken*** with pleasure is doubly beneficial. 愉快にやる運動は二倍の利益がある. ¶***translate*** one's *exercises* 翻訳の練習問題をやる. ¶***work*** *exercises* 練習問題をやる. ¶***write out*** *exercises* on paper 練習を紙に書く.

Q ***abundant*** *exercise* 十分な運動. ¶the ***closing*** *exercises* to the school その学校の終業式. ¶analysis as a ***disciplinary*** *exercise*「訓練」としての文の解剖. ¶with them it is a ***favorite*** *exercise* to ... 彼らにとって...するのはよくやる運動である. ¶Construction of difficult passages in English is a ***fine*** *exercise* in clear thinking. 英文難句の解釈は明りょうな思考に資する適当な訓練である. ¶***free*** *exercise* of religion=freedom of worship 信仰の自由. ¶a ***fruitful*** *exercise* 有益な練習. ¶a ***gentle*** *exercise* 軽い運動. ¶Swimming is a ***good*** *exercise*. 水泳はよい運動だ.【類】Running is a ***good*** *exercise*. ¶at the ***graduating*** *exercises* of a college 大学の卒業式に. ¶deadly dull ***grammatical*** *exercise* きわめて興味のない文法練習. ¶***gymnastic*** *exercises* 体操. ¶It is much patronized by those in search of ***healthful*** (=healthy) *exercise*. それは健康増進の運動を求めている人々に大層受けている. ¶***mental*** *exercise* 知的訓練. ¶***military*** *exercises* 軍事教練. ¶***moderate*** *exercise* 適度の運動. ¶***open-air*** *exercises* 戸外運動. ¶take ***outdoor*** *exercise* 戸外運動をやる. ¶***physical*** *exercise* 肉体的な運動. ¶as a ***preparatory*** *exercise* 予行練習として. ¶take ***regular*** *exercise* きまって運動する. ¶***religious*** *exercise* 勤行. ¶with ***restricted*** *exercise* 十分に運動ができないで. ¶***spiritual*** *exercise* 精神修養. ¶a ***valuable*** *exercise* 大切な練習. ¶take some ***vigorous*** *exercise* in the open air 戸外でなにか活発な運動をやる. ¶***violent*** *exercise* 過激な運動.

Q^2 ***bedside*** *exercises* 寝台の前での運動(就寝起床時の). ¶***closing*** (***opening***) *exercises* 閉(開)会式. ¶***commencement*** *exercises* 《米》=graduation exercises 大学の卒業式. ¶***dedication*** *exercises* 献納式. ¶***drill*** *exercises* 訓練, 教練. ¶***field*** *exercises* 野外演習. ¶***five-finger*** *exercises* on the piano 五本指を使うピアノの練習. ¶***health*** *exercises* 健康増進の運動. ¶***horse*** *exercise* 乗馬(運動のためなど). ¶take a good deal of ***outdoor*** *exercise* 盛んに戸外運動をやる. ¶***school*** *exercises* 学校の課業. ¶***sword*** *exercise* 剣道のけいこ. ¶***terrain*** *exercises* 地形利用の演習.

P work ***at*** *exercises* 練習問題をやる. ¶develop it ***by*** *exercise* 運動によってそれを発達させる ‖ ***by*** the *exercise* of (=by dint of) industry 勤勉の力で ‖ ***by*** the *exercise* of one's own free will and discretion 自分の意志と裁量によって.【類】It is easily discriminated ***by*** the *exercise* of ordinary judgment (普通の判断力). / ***by*** the *exercise* of the prerogative of the Crown (王権). ¶walk ***for*** *exercise* 運動のために散歩する ‖ ***for*** *exercise* in composition 作文の練習に. ¶***in*** the *exercise* of one's duties 職権をもって.【類】***in*** *exercise* of the authority vested in him (与えられた権能). ¶take plenty ***of*** *exercise* 大いに運動する. ¶***through*** deficient *exercises* 練習不足のために.

P^2 Of all *exercises **in*** composition, original verse affords the best training. 作文のあらゆる練習の中で韻文の創作が一番よい練習になる.【類】an *exercise **in*** debate (討論) / an *exercise **in*** horsemanship (馬術). ¶the *exercise **of*** hospitality 客に親切に尽すこと ‖ the *exercise **of*** one's office 職務の実行 ‖ the *exercise **of*** a trade 商売の経営. ¶*exercise **on*** the irregular and defective Greek verbs ギリシア語の不規則及び不完全動詞の練習. ¶*exercises **with*** diverse gymnastic apparatus 色々な体操の道具を使ってする運動.

exercise, *v.* 運用する, 行使する; 練習する; 苦心させる; 及ぼす.

P He is much *exercised **about*** his health. 彼は大いに健康を気にしている. ¶*exercise* oneself ***in*** music 音楽を練習する. ¶too much care cannot be *exercised **in*** ... ...にはくれぐれも注意が肝要だ. ¶*exercise* a salutary influence ***over*** ... ...に有益な影響を及ぼす ‖ He was much *exercised **over*** the affair. 彼はそのことに大層苦心していた. ‖ *exercise* oneself ***over*** the question of ... ...の問題で頭を悩ます.

exerciser, *n.* 体操用具.

Q ***modern*** *exercisers* for body-building (=bodybuilders) ボディビルの新型体操具.

Q^2 Sando's ***patent*** *exercisers* サンドウ専売特許の体操用具.

exertion, *n.* 努力, 尽力.

V ***bear*** mental *exertion* 精神的努力に耐える. ¶***continue*** one's unremitting *exertions* 不断の努力を続ける. ¶He finds tennis and cricket ***demanding*** too much *exertion*. 彼はテニスやクリケットは過大な努力を要するものだと知った. ¶***diminish*** one's *exertion* 努力をゆるめる. ¶He ***made*** his best *exertions*. 彼は最大の努力を尽した. ¶***put forth*** exertion 力をふるう. ¶redouble one's exertions 一倍努力する. ¶It requires enormous exertion. それはばく大の努力を要する.【類】It requires no exertion. ¶use every exertion 百方力を尽す.

Q make another exertion 更に一奮発する. ¶by the continued and persevering exertions of human intellect 人知の間断ない不屈の努力によって. ¶desperate exertions 必死の努力. ¶earnest and conscientious exertions for the moral and social improvement of ... ...の道徳及び社会改良のための熱心で忠実な努力. ¶by his indefatigable exertion 彼の根強い努力で. ¶mental and physical exertion 精神的及び肉体的努力. ¶his personal exertions 彼の個人としての努力. ¶fatigue on slight exertion ささいな努力での疲労. ¶strenuous exertion at games 運動競技への熱烈な精進. ¶undue exertion 過労. ¶untiring exertions うまずたゆまぬ努力. ¶He made unwonted exertions. 彼はいつにもなく骨を折った.

P by his own exertions 自力で ‖ The fire was soon extinguished by the exertions of the soldiers. 火事は軍人の努力で間もなくおさまった. ¶through the exertions of ... ...の骨折で. ¶without any exertion 少しも骨を折らずに.

P^2 an exertion of mind 精神的努力 ‖ an exertion of physical strength 体力による努力(労力).

exhaust, *v.* 疲れはてさせる; 尽す, からす.

M He is much exhausted. 彼は大分疲れている. ¶Our stock is nearly exhausted. うちのストックはもう切れかかっている. ¶They felt quite exhausted when they got to ... ...に着いたときはひどく疲れを感じた. ¶be totally exhausted くたくたに疲れている. ¶He lay down utterly exhausted. 彼はぐったり横になった.

P exhausted by labor 労働でくたくたになって ‖ a man exhausted by disease 病気で疲れ切った人 ‖ The moisture of the earth is exhausted by evaporation. 土地の水分は蒸発で取られてしまう. ¶exhaust the air from an air-pump 空気ポンプから空気を抜いてしまう ‖ much exhausted from excessive excitement (work) 過度の興奮(など)で大分疲れて. ¶I am exhasted with toil. 僕は骨折仕事で疲れた.

O exhaust oneself working (walking) 働き(歩き)疲れる.

exhauster, 排気弁.

Q^2 a pump exhauster ポンプの排気弁.

exhaustion, *n.* 疲労.

P from exhaustion 疲れ切って. ¶He died of exhaustion. 彼は衰弱して死んだ. ¶He fell down with exhaustion. 彼は力尽きて倒れた.

exhaustive, *a.* 徹底的な.

M The list is practically exhaustive. その表はほとんど(遺漏のない)完全なものであった.

exhaustiveness, *n.* 徹底.

P have no desire to put forth a claim to exhaustiveness. あくまで要求を出そうという考えはない.

exhibit, *n.* 展覧物, 陳列品.

V display the entire Hawaiian exhibit 全ハワイの出品を陳列する. ¶forward exhibits 出品を送る(博覧会などに). ¶hold an exhibit of ... ...の展覧会を催す. ¶make an exhibit 出品する. ¶This winter the Metropolitan Museum organized three exhibits, one of arms and armour, one of Egyptian art, and one of Far Eastern art. この冬メトロポリタン・ミュージアムは三種の陳列を催した. その三種というのは武器・具足とエジプト芸術と極東芸術である. ¶rotate exhibits 陳列を順次に替えて行く. ¶exhibits shown in ... ...に出品した陳列物.

Q The 1940 volume contained descriptive exhibits for 494 accredited junior colleges. 一九四〇年版には四百九十四の認定短期大学について列記してあった. ¶There were many other exhibits of interest. 他にも色々興味ある出品があった. ¶a series of brilliantly planned and equally well-timed exhibits 考案の面白いしかも時宜に適した陳列の続行. ¶a spectacular exhibit 花々しい見物[出初式など]. ¶a tabular exhibit 表. ¶unsold exhibits 売れ残りの陳列品.

Q^2 an art exhibit 図画・工作・手芸などの出品. ¶telephone exhibits at the World's Fair 世界博覧会に出品の電話機. ¶a travelling exhibit 旅行展覧会.

exhibit, *v.* 出品する, 縦覧に供する.

P a picture exhibited at the Royal Academy, 1905 一九〇五年王立美術館に出品の絵画 ‖ It was exhibited at a World Fair. それはある世界博覧会に出品された. ¶exhibit before the public 公衆の縦覧に供する.

exhibition, *n.* 展覧, 陳列; 公演, 興行; 博覧会, 展覧会; 陳列品.

V The museum is arranging a special exhibition. その博物館は特別陳列を催す準備中である. ¶The school will give an exhibition for the entertainment of the parents and other relatives of the pupils. その学校は生徒の父兄のために展覧会を開く. ‖ give exhibitions of dancing 舞踊を公演する. ¶She will have (=hold or give) an exhibition of her pictures. 同女史は個展を開く. ¶hold a little exhibition and sell their own productions 小展覧会を催し自分らの作品を即売する. ¶make an exhibition of oneself 人の笑い物になる ‖ make a public exhibition of ... ...を公衆の展覧に供する. ¶an exhibition was opened and will remain until ... 展覧会が開かれ...まで継続する. ¶The exhibition is organized by the Y Shimbun. その展覧会はY新聞主催である. ¶run an exhibition 展覧会をやる. ¶stop the exhibition of a certain film ある映画の公開を停止する.

Q a big exhibition of fireworks 花火大会. ¶a competitive exhibition 共進会. ¶She gave the first exhibition of her aerial feats in Japan over the reclaimed land at Susaki. 彼女は洲崎埋立地の上空でその日本における最初の飛行技術公演を行った. ¶Japan is one great exhibition in the art, mistakes, or want of clothes.—Marie C. Stopes. 日本は服装の芸術・失敗・または簡略の一大展示場である. ¶an industrial exhibition 勧業博覧会. ¶an international exhibition 万国博覧会. ¶a memorial exhibition of the works of Thomas Allen (1849-1924) トーマス・アレンの遺作をしのぶ展覧会. ¶hold passing (continuous) exhibitions [博物館などが]臨時(継続的)展覧会を開く. ¶a pitiful exhibition of incompetence 無能の恥さらし. ¶give public exhibitions 公衆の展覧に供する.

Q^2 the art exhibitions at Uyeno 上野の美術展覧会. ¶a boxing exhibition けん闘の公開試合(エキシビジョンゲーム). ¶the "Britain Can Make It" Exhibition「英国製作品」展示会(英国内の). ¶give a cinematograph (=movie) exhibition 映画会を催す. ¶the Efficiency Exhibition organized by the London Daily Mail at Olympia, Kensington ロンドンデイリー・メール社がケンジントンのオリンピヤ市に催した能率展覧会. ¶a fireworks exhibition 花火大会. ¶a floating exhibition of British industries 英国産業の海上展覧会. ¶give a flying exhibition 飛行技術を公演する. ¶the Fuel Economy Exhibition 燃料節約展示会. ¶a home exhibition 内国博覧会. ¶a loan exhibition through the courtesy of the Louvre ルーブル博物館の厚意による借用品展覧会. ¶He held a one-man exhibition of his works covering a period of twenty years. 彼は二十年間の作品を陳列して個展を開いた. ¶a photo exhibition 写真展示会.

P as an exhibition of the depravity of a brute. そこが畜生の浅ましさで. ¶We request the pleasure of your attendance at the Exhibition. 展覧会になにとぞ御来場の栄を得たいと存じます. ‖ an article at an exhibition 展覧会の陳列品. ¶during its exhibition その陳列期間中. ¶now on exhibition (=show or view) at the museum 目下その博物館に陳列中の ‖ articles on exhibition 出品物.【類】the pictures which are on exhibition ‖ place (=put) ... on exhibition ... を展覧に供する.

P^2 an exhibition of the pupils' work 生徒作品展覧会 ‖ The wrestlers will give a series of exhibitions of their skill. その力士たちは色々とその妙技をふるうことであろう. ‖ an exhibition of Japanese fencing and *judo* 剣道柔道の公開試合.

exhibitor, *n.* 出品者.

Q England is the largest exhibitor. 英国が一番大口の出品者だ.

P^2 an exhibitor at the St. Louis Exposition セント・ルイス博覧会の出品者.

exhort, *v.* 勧める.

P exhort a person to diligence (=be diligent) 人に勉強を勧める.【類】exhort one's pupils to good deeds (りっぱな行為).

exhortation, *n.* 勧告.

Q earnest exhortations 熱心な勧告.

exigency, *n.* 危機; 切迫; 急務.

V meet the exigencies of the moment 焦眉(ビ)の急をしのぐ. ¶I am prepared to suit the exigencies of ... 自分には...の急場に応じるだけの用意がある.

Q pecuniary exigencies 金銭上のひっ迫. ¶an unforeseen exigency 意外の危機.

P in this exigency この急場に. ¶Their country was reduced *to* great *exigency*. 彼らの国は非常な危機に陥った.

exile, *n*. 追放, 流刑; 追放人; 亡命者.

V *recall* an *exile* 流人を召還する.

Q He was condemned to *life-long exile*. 彼は終身流刑に処せられた. ¶a *political exile* 政治上の流刑者. ¶a *religious exile* 宗教上の流刑者.

P The political refugee lived *in exile* in England. その政治家は英国に亡命していた. ‖ He was sent *in exile* on a remote island. 彼は遠島に流された. ¶go *into exile* 流刑につく. ¶condemn ... *to exile* ... を流刑に処する.

P² an *exile from* the homeland 母国からの亡命者. ¶*exile of* political prisoners *to* Siberia 政治犯人のシベリア追放.

exile, *v*. 追放する.

P He was *exiled from* his country. 彼は自国を追われた. ¶He was *exiled to* a distant land. 彼は遠国に追放された.

exist, *v*. 存在する; 生存する; 存続する.

M *exist happily* with incomes which are but a small part of those required by the rich 裕福な人の必要とする収入のほんの一部分で幸福に暮す.

P the friendship that *existed between* them 彼らの間に続いた友情. ¶it *exists for* the purpose of ... その使命は…である. 【類】This society *exists for* the purpose of promoting friendly relations between the United States and Japan. ¶Barbers *existed from* very early ages. 髪床は大昔からあった. ¶a plan of the city as it *existed in* 1650 一六五〇年現在の状態を示す同市地図 ‖ No comprehensive history of it *exists in* the English lauguage. 英語にはその全般的の歴史は存在していない. ‖ Salt *exists in* solution *in* the sea. 塩は溶解して海水中に存在する. ¶*exist on* food (an income, a salary) 食物(など)で命をつなぐ ‖ He is able to *exist on* very little and eager for work at any pay. 彼はわずかあれば暮して行けるので給料はどうでもよいから職を得たがっている. ¶We cannot *exist under* such a government. われわれはかかる政府の下に生を送ることはできない. ¶Crime often *exists with* poverty. 犯罪はしばしば貧と共存する. ¶We cannot *exist without* air. 空気がなくては生きていられない.

existence, *n*. 存在, 存立, 存続; 生存, 生活.

V The United States *began* their *existence* as a nation in 1492. 合衆国の国民としての存在は一四九二年に始まった. ¶They are deprived of all that *brightens* and *beautifies existence*. 彼らは生活を豊かにしかつ美化するすべての物を奪われている. ¶threaten the *continued existence* of the prevailing form of government 現在の政治形体の存続をおびやかす. ¶*deny* the objective *existence* of ... …の客観的存在を否定する. ¶*doubt* the *existence* of ... …の存在を疑う. ¶All they can do is to *drag on* a miserable *existence* till the tomb closes over them. 彼らの力では死ぬまでだらだらとみじめな生活を送るのが関の山だ. ¶a weak-bodied man *dragging out* a miserable *existence* みじめな生活を送って行く虚弱な人. 【類】There is no object in my *dragging out existence* under such circumstances. ¶*earn* one's own *existence* 自活する. ¶*eke out* a miserable *existence* やりくり算段でみじめな生活を送る. ¶He *ended* his troubled *existence* by committing suicide. 彼は自殺してその多難な一生を終えた. ¶These are fictitious characters that *have* no *existence* in history. これらは仮想人物で歴史的存在はない. 【類】The Gregorian calendar (太陽暦) *had* no *existence* until the year 1582. ¶*ignore* its *existence* その存在を無視する. ¶It does not *justify* its *existence*. それだけではその存在の名分が立たない. ¶*lead* a nomad *existence* 遊牧生活を送る. ¶*lose* her national *existence* その国家的存在を失う. ¶*maintain* one's *existence* 生存を続ける. ¶*menace* the national *existence* 国家的存立をおびやかす. ¶the library *owes* its *existence* to the bequest of ... その図書館ができたのは…の遺贈資金のおかげである ‖ the publisher to which we *owe* its *existence* その本を刊行した出版者. ¶His *existence* was *recognized*. 彼の存在が認められた. ¶These plants manage to *support* their *existence* on rocks. これらの植物はどうにかして岩の上にその生存を続けて行く. ¶*suspect* the *existence* 存在を疑う. ¶*threaten* her very *existence* as a nation その国家としての存立その物をおびやかす.

Q The company is still in *active existence*. その会社は今日でも隆盛なものである. ¶the termination of his *authorial existence* 彼の著者生活の終了. ¶eke out a *bare existence* かろうじて露命をつなぐ. ¶after only a *brief existence* つかの間の一生を終えて. ¶a *carefree happy existence* 苦労のないな幸福生活. ¶The building has had a *checkered existence*. その建物は波らんある過去を持っている. ¶The society has had a *continuous* and *useful existence* to the present day. その協会は今日まで引続き有用な存在を続けてきた. ¶the scenes of one's *daily existence* 日常生活の情景. ¶lead a *drab existence* 単調な生活を送る. ¶a *dual existence* 二重生活. ¶his *earthly existence* 彼の現世生活. ¶of *ephemeral existence* 露の命の. ¶May not this earth of ours be hell, and we all here to expiate crimes committed by us in a *former existence*?—G. B. Shaw. 現世は地獄でわれわれは皆前世で犯した罪をつぐなうためにここにいるのではないか. ¶*geographic existence* 地理的存在. ¶*inanimate existence* 活気のない生活. ¶It has no longer an *independent national existence* それはもはや独立国としての存在を失った. ¶It has a *long* and *useful existence* ahead of (=before) it. その前途は長く有用である. ¶the soul of *national existence* 国家的存在の魂(根本義). 【類】a great threat to *national existence*. ¶the struggle of *postwar existence* 戦後の生存競争. ¶The professional model has a somewhat *precarious existence*. モデルを商売にしているものの生活には幾分不安がともなう. 【類】maintain a *precarious existence*. ¶in a *previous existence* 前生で. ¶The magazine has had a *prosperous existence*. その雑誌は好況を続けてきた. ¶have a *real existence* 実在している. ¶lead a *savage existence* 野蛮な生活を送る. ¶eke out a *scanty existence* 細々暮しを立てる. ¶His *existence* has become *shadowy*. 彼の存在は目立たなくなった. ¶The newspaper had a very *short-lived existence*. その新聞は永続しなかった. ¶drag on a *weary existence* 疲れ切った生活をだらだら続ける. ¶a *wretched existence* みじめな生活.

Q² our *busy*, *bustling*, *everyday existence* われらの忙しいどさくさした日常生活. ¶*future existence* 死後の存在, 来世. ¶live a *hand-to-mouth existence* その日暮しの生活をする. ¶the *one-time existence* of reptiles かつて存在していた爬(は)虫類.

P *after* an *existence* of three and a half centuries 三百五十年間存続の後. 【類】The magazine ceased to appear *after* an *existence* of five years. ¶*during* the *existence* of the war 戦争中. ¶a struggle *for existence* 生存競争. ¶be still *in existence* まだ生存している ‖ the only copy known to be *in existence* [本など]現存している唯一のもの. 【類】There are, it is said, over 10,000 biographies of Napoleon Bonaparte (ナポレオンの伝記) *in existence*. / She doubted whether there was a newspaper *in existence* that had not women on its staff. / It is still *in existence*. ¶call (=bring) *into existence* 成立させる ‖ come (=start) *into existence* 成立する. ¶snuff it *out of existence* それを消滅させる.

exit, *n*. 出口; 退出, 退場.

V *find* an *exit* in ... …にはけ口を見出す. ¶*give exit* to ... …を退出させる. ¶*make* one's *exit* 退出する, (俳優など)退場する ‖ The bird *made* its *exit* through an open window. 鳥はあいてる窓からとび出た.

Q² an *emergency exit* 非常口. ¶a *fire exit* 火災用非常口.

P wait *at* the *exit* of ... …の出口で待つ.

P² an *exit from* a railway station 停車場の出口. ¶an *exit to* ... St. …街への出口.

exodus, *n*. 退去, 外出.

Q Vacation came, with its *annual exodus* from the city. 休暇が来たので例年通り人が都市からどんどん出て行った.

Q² a *mass exodus* (休日などで都市からの)大量外出.

P² a large *exodus from* London ロンドン市民の大量流出(休日などに). ¶an *exodus of* specie 正貨の流出.

exonerate, *v*. [罪などの]明しを立てる; [義務などを]免除する.

P *exonerate* him *from* responsibility (a task, duty, payment) 彼の責任(など)を免除する ‖ *exonerate* one *from* an accusation of crime 告訴を免れさせる ‖ He is *exonerated from* blame (=reproach). 彼はけん責を免れた. ¶*exonerate* oneself *of* a crime 自分の罪のあかしを立てる ‖ *exonerate* him *of* his money 彼の金銭の負担を解除する.

exotic, *n*. 『植物』外国種.

Q² a *hothouse exotic* 温室育ちの外国種植物.

expand, *v*. 膨張する; 広げる; ふえんする.

M He did not *expand greatly* on his statement 彼は自分

の所言をあまりふえんしなかった. ¶The shipbuilding industry of the south is ***rapidly expanding*** to great proportions. 南部の造船事業は敏速に大発展を示しつつある.

P Metals *expand* ***by*** heat. 金属は熱で膨張する. ‖ *expand* the chest ***by*** inspiration 息を吸い込んで胸をふくらませる. ¶*expand* a phrase ***into*** a sentence 句をふえんして文にする. ¶*expand* ***upon*** one's notes 控えを種にしてこれをふえんする.

expanse, *n.* 広がり, びょうぼうたる場所.

V The ship ***traversed*** the vast *expanse* of the Pacific. 船はびょうぼうたる太平洋を横断した.

Q the ***blue*** *expanse* 青空. ¶a ***broad*** *expanse* of water びょうぼうたる一面の水 ‖ with a ***broad*** *expanse* of brow 広い額の. 【類】To the east is a charming bay stretching out to meet the ***broad*** *expanse* of the Pacific. ¶a ***large*** *expanse* of pasture-land 広ばくたる牧場地. ¶a ***vast*** *expanse* of water びょうぼうたる水の広がり. 【類】a ***vast*** *expanse* of Manchurian plains. ¶a ***vast rolling*** *expanse* of houses 見渡す限り起伏した一面の家屋.

expansion, *n.* 膨張, 拡張, 拡大, 発展.

Q the cause of the ***British Imperial*** *expansion* 英国帝国(領土拡大)主義. ¶The subject is one capable of almost ***indefinite*** *expansion.* その問題はほとんど無限に拡大の可能性がある. ¶***national*** *expansion* 国家的膨張. ¶***naval*** *expansion* 海軍拡張. ¶a ***rapid*** *expansion* of trade 貿易の敏速な発展. ¶***symmetrical*** *expansion* 均勢的膨張. ¶Japan's steady ***territorial*** *expansion* 日本の着実な領土拡張. ¶***transoceanic*** *expansion* 海外発展. ¶the ***worldwide*** *expansion* of the English race イギリス民族の全世界にわたる発展.

Q² block ***Communist*** *expansion* 共産主義拡大をはばむ. ¶Japan's ***overseas*** *expansion* 日本の海外発展. ¶a ***plant*** *expansion* 工場の拡張. ¶***trade*** (***business***) *expansion* 貿易(業務)の拡張 ‖ ***trade*** *expansion* with China 対中貿易の拡大.

P² an *expansion* ***of*** a monograph on ... ...に関する専門論文のふえん ‖ the *expansion* ***of*** currency 通貨の膨張 ‖ *expansion* ***of*** food production 食料増産.

expansionism, *n.* 拡張論.

V ***advocate*** *expansionism* 拡張論を推進する.

Q² ***Soviet*** *expansionism* ソ連膨張(帝国)主義.

expansionist, *n.* 拡張論者.

Q an ***American*** *expansionist* 米国拡張論者(帝国主義者). ¶***Red*** *expansionists* 赤色帝国主義者たち.

expatiate, *v.* ふえんして説く.

P *expatiate* ***on*** (=***upon***) his favorite subject 彼の得意の問題を詳述する. 【類】I need not *expatiate* ***on*** the question any further.

expect, *v.* 予期する, 期待する, 当てにする.

M be ***anxiously*** *expecting* a letter from a person ある人からの手紙を首を長くして待っている. ¶He is *expected* ***back*** early in December. 彼は十二月の初めに戻って来るはずだ. ¶it is ***confidently*** *expected* that ... ...ということは堅く期待されている. ¶I *expect* him ***every moment.*** あの方は今にも見えるでしょう. ¶The work is making as much progress as can ***fairly*** be *expected.* 工事は大体予定通り進行している. ¶***fully*** *expect* to ... ...しようと大いに期待する. ¶He is *expected* ***here*** about the middle of next month. 彼は来月半ばごろ当地に来るはずだ. ¶A great battle is ***hourly*** *expected.* 大会戦が時々刻々迫っている. ¶He came up when we ***least*** *expected* him. 全く思いがけない時に彼がやってきた. ‖ I had ***least*** *expected* that the things would come to such a pass. まさかこんなことになろうとは思わなかった. ¶The king's condition is hopeless and the end is ***momentarily*** *expected.* 国王の御容体は絶望で崩御も今か今かと思われる. ¶*expect* so ***much*** for so little えびでたいを釣ろうとする ‖ That's *expecting* too ***much.*** そうは問屋でおろさない. ¶as is ***naturally*** *expected* 当然そうと思われるように ‖ That's ***naturally*** to be *expected.* それはそのはずだ. ‖ as might ***naturally*** be *expected* of a creature of low intelligence そこが畜生の浅ましさで. ¶There they are assured of as much comfort as they could ***reasonably*** *expect.* 彼らが正当に予期しうるだけの安楽はそこで必ず得られる. ¶That's what can ***reasonably*** be *expected.* それが理の当然だ. 【類】can ***reasonably*** be *expected* under the circumstances. ¶Will he be back late?—I *expect* ***so.*** 彼はおそくなりますか—おそくなるでしょう. ¶You are *expected* ***tomorrow.*** 明日お待ちしています. ¶Do not *expect* ***too much*** of him. 余り彼に期待するな.

P He is *expected* here ***at*** any moment. 彼は今にも来るかと思う. ¶you can hardly *expect* such kindness ***from*** ... ...にそんな親切は先ず望めない. 【類】I cannot *expect* aid ***from*** him. ‖ short addresses are *expected* ***from*** ... ...に簡単な演説をやってもらうはずだ ‖ more might have been *expected* ***from*** ... ...からはそれ以上期待できたかもしれない. 【類】What can you *expect* ***from*** (=***of***) him? ‖ Men do *expect* purity and goodness ***from*** women. 男性が女性に望むものは純潔と善良さである 【類】The French *expect* ***from*** their daily journals (日刊新聞), not information, but entertainment. ¶as might be *expected* ***of*** him あの人のことだから. ¶It is not to be *expected* ***in*** him. そんなことは彼の柄(ガラ)にない. ¶I didn't *expect* such a thing ***of*** (=from) you. 君にそんなことをしてもらおうとは思わなかった. 【類】People *expected* great things ***of*** him. ¶He is *expected* here ***on*** the tenth of next month. 彼は来月の十日に当地に来るはずだ. ¶We *expect* guests ***to*** dinner. 晩さんに客が来るはずだ.

O Little did I *expect* to meet him again. 彼に再び会おうとは思わなかった. ¶We cannot *expect* him to do such a thing. 彼にそんなことを期待するわけにはいかない. ¶Guests are not *expected* to tip. お客様は心付には及びません.

expectancy, *n.* 期待.

V ***give*** the patient the *expectancy* of cure 病人に病気がなおるものと思わせる.

Q wait in ***breathless*** *expectancy* 息を殺して待ち設ける. ¶all were looking with ***dull*** *expectancy* in the direction of ... 一同が...の方向をおぼつかなげに見やっていた.

Q² ***life*** *expectancy*=the expectation of life 〖生命保険〗平均余命.

expectant, *a.* 期待して.

P *expectant* ***of*** (=expecting) something bright and hopeful 何か明るい希望に満ちたものを期待して.

expectation, *n.* 予期, 予想, 期待; 見込み.

V He did not ***answer*** the *expectations* of his friends. 彼は彼の友の期待に添わなかった. ¶***awaken*** *expectation* of ... ...の期待を起させる. ¶It ***belied*** (=fell short of) my *expectation.* それは僕の期待にそむいた. ¶***defeat*** an *expectation* 失望させる. ¶***entertain*** great *expectations* of his ability 彼の手腕に大きな望みをかける. ¶The results ***exceeded*** *expectation.* 結果は予期以上であった. ‖ The realization ***exceeded*** the *expectations.* 実際は予想以上だった. ¶***fulfil*** the *expectations* of ... ...の期待を満足させる. 【類】The *expectation* is abundantly ***fulfilled.*** ‖ ***fulfil*** God's *expectation* for us われわれに対する神の期待に添う. ¶He ***has*** great *expectations* from his rich uncle. 彼には金持ちの伯父から遺産をもらう見込みが大いにある. ‖ I ***have*** every reasonable *expectation* of being able to ... 私には...することができるという十分な見込みがある. ¶Great *expectations* were ***held*** by his parents for his college career. 両親は彼の大学生活には多大の望みをかけていた. ¶***invite*** *expectation* 気を持たせる. ¶The result ***met*** my *expectations.* 結果は私の予期通りであった. ‖ fail to ***meet*** *expectations* 期待にそむく. ¶***put*** one's *expectations* too high 望みを余り大きく持つ. ¶***raise*** unrealizable *expectations* 実現のできない望みを起す. ¶***realize*** great *expectations* 大なる期待を実現する. 【類】My *expectations* were fully ***realized.*** ¶***resign*** (=***renounce***) one's *expectations* of ... ...の期待を放棄する. ¶***surpass*** my *expectations* 私の予期以上に出る. 【類】It ***surpassed*** all *expectations* (番狂わせ). ¶***upset*** his *expectation* 彼の期待をくつがえす. ¶do not ***warrant*** any sanguine *expectations* regarding ... ...に関してはなんら楽観的期待を許さない.

V² These *expectations* did not ***materialize.*** これらの期待は実現するに至らなかった.

Q according to ***common*** *expectation* 一般の見込みによれば. ¶the ***confident*** *expectation* that ... ...という自信ある見込み. ¶with ***large*** *expectations* of fortune from ... ...から巨万の財産を譲られる見込みのある. ¶It greatly surpassed my ***utmost*** *expectation.* それは僕の最大限度の見込みよりもはるか以上に出た. ¶a ***Utopian*** *expectation* 空想的な期待. ¶a ***vain*** *expectation* of success 成功の空頼み. ¶surpass one's ***wildest*** *expectations* どんなとっぴな予想も及ばない. 【類】quite in excess of our ***wildest*** *expectations.*

P The results were ***below*** *expectations.* 結果は予期に満た

なかった. ¶succeed ***beyond*** all *expectations* 思ったよりもずっとうまくゆく. 【類】The result was ***beyond*** my *expectation*. ¶watch ***in*** breathless *expectation* 息を殺して今か今かと見張る ‖ linger ***in expectation*** もしやと思ってぐずぐずする ‖ I was baulked ***in*** my *expectation*. 私の当てがはずれた ‖ ***in*** *expectation* of war 開戦を見越して. 【類】I did it ***in*** *expectation* of a reward. / unwillingness to sell (売惜しみ) ***in*** *expectation* of better prices ‖ ***in*** the *expectation* that ... ...の積りで. ¶I was on the tiptoe ***of*** *expectation*. 僕は待ちこがれていた. ¶contrary ***to*** *expectation* 見込みに反して ‖ turn out goods ***to*** our *expectations* 商品を見込み通り製造する ‖ The sale did not come up ***to*** his *expectations*. 売上は彼が思ったほどには行かなかった. ‖ measure up ***to*** one's *expectations* 期待に添う. ¶***with*** the *expectation* that ... ...の見込みで ‖ burn ***with*** *expectation* for ... ...を待ちこがれる. 【類】All looked forward to his return ***with*** much *expectation*. ¶either ***with*** or ***without*** *expectation* of gain 代償を受けると受けないとにかかわらず.

expectorate, *v.* たんを吐く.

P Don't *expectorate* ***on*** the sidewalks. 歩道にたんを吐くな. ¶*expectorate* ***outside*** the car 車外にたんを吐く.

expediency, *n.* 便法.

Q a ***social*** *expediency* 社会の便法.

expedient, *n.* 方策, 便法, 方法.

V ***adopt*** the *expedient* of ... ...の便法を取る. ¶***exhaust*** every *expedient* for ... ...に百方手を尽す. ¶***try*** various *expedients* 種々の方策を試みる.

Q resort to the ***old-fashioned*** *expedient* 旧式な方法を取る. ¶by ***questionable*** *expedients* いかがわしい方法で. ¶a ***simple*** *expedient* 簡単な方法. ¶adopt it as a ***temporary*** *expedient* 一時の便法としてそれを採用する.

expedient, *a.* 適宜の, 得策の.

O I deemed it *expedient* to ... ...するにしかずと私は考えた. ‖ you will find it *expedient* to ... ...するが得策と君は思い当るだろう.

expedite, *v.* 早める.

P *expedite* negotiation ***between*** ... ...間の交渉を促進させる.

O *expedite* the growth of plants 植物の成長を早める.

expedition, *n.* (**1**) 遠征, 探検; 遠征隊, 探検隊.

V he ***commanded*** the *expedition* to ... 彼が...遠征隊を率いた. ¶***conduct*** an *expedition* into a warm country 旅行団体を暖国に案内する ‖ ***conduct*** a successful *expedition* against ... ...攻撃の遠征軍を引率して勝利にみちびく. ¶***dispatch*** an *expedition* 探検隊を派遣する. 【類】an *expedition* was ***despatched*** from ... to ... ¶***finance*** an *expedition* 遠征隊の資金をまかなう. ¶***fit out*** an *expedition* consisting of several vessels 数隻の船からなる遠征隊をぎ装する. ¶They volunteered to ***join*** the *expedition*. 彼らは進んで遠征隊に参加した. ¶He was appointed to ***lead*** an *expedition*. 彼が遠征隊の引率を命じられた. 【類】***lead*** an *expedition* to ... / ***lead*** an *expedition* against a rebel (逆徒討伐). ¶***make*** an *expedition* to gather flowers 隊を組んで花摘みに出掛ける ‖ ***make*** *expeditions* into the country いなかへ遠征する. ¶***organize*** a mighty *expedition* against ... ...攻撃の大遠征隊を組織する. ¶***send*** a punitive *expedition* against ... ...へ討伐隊を派遣する. ¶an *expedition* was ***sent out*** by the Society to make an extensive study of ... 広く...を研究するために同協会は探検隊を派遣した.

Q an ***Antarctic*** (***Arctic***) *expedition* 南(北)極探検隊. ¶start on a ***dangerous*** *expedition* 危険な探検に出掛ける. ¶***punitive*** *expeditions* against the revolutionaries 革命軍討伐隊. 【類】a short ***punitive*** *expedition* to Formosa in reprisal for local piracy (土地の海賊に対する報復として). ¶a ***retaliatory*** *expedition* under Drake and Norris ドレーク・ノリス両提督の率いる報復遠征艦隊. ¶***successive*** *expeditions* into South Africa 南アフリカへ相ついでの探検旅行. ¶a ***triumphal*** *expedition* to ... ...へのがい旋出征軍. ¶make a ***warlike*** *expedition* into ... ...へ出征する.

Q² He is leaving Seoul for America on one of his ***flying*** *expeditions* for more funds in support of his work. 彼はその事業の資金をさらに募集するため京城を立って米国に向おうとしている. ¶a ***holiday*** *expedition* 休日遠足. ¶despatch a ***relief*** *expedition* 救援遠征隊を急派する. ¶a ***shopping*** *expedition* 買物のための外出. ¶a ***whaling*** *expedition* 捕鯨隊.

P the leader ***of*** the *expedition* その遠征隊の引率者 ‖ members ***of*** the *expedition* 探検隊員. ¶They started ***on*** an *expedition*. 彼らは遠征の途についた. 【類】They were sent ***on*** an *expedition* to the North Pole. / go ***on*** an *expedition*.

P² his *expedition* ***against*** Jerusalem 彼のエルサレム遠征 ‖ an *expedition* ***against*** barbarians 蛮人征伐. ¶an *expedition* ***into*** Thibet チベット探検. 【類】the Italian *expedition* ***into*** Ethiopia. ¶an *expedition* ***to*** Egypt エジプトへの遠征. ¶the British Antarctic *expedition* ***under*** Captain Scott スコット大佐の率いる英国の南極探検隊.

(**2**) 急速, 敏速.

V ***use*** *expedition* てきぱきやる.

Q send a letter with all ***possible*** *expedition* なるたけ早く手紙を出す.

P The work was done ***with*** *expedition*. その仕事は迅速に行われた.

expel, *v.* 追出す.

P *expel* a person ***from*** a country 人を国外に追放する. 【類】He was *expelled* ***from*** the school. / He was *expelled* ***from*** the society.

expend, *v.* 消費する, 散財する.

M *expend* ***judiciously*** ほどよく散財する. ¶*expend* money ***wisely*** and ***honestly*** 金銭をうまく正直に使う.

P *expend* money ***in*** the purchase of ... ...の買入に金を使う ‖ It is computed that 70 per cent of the cost of coal getting is *expended* ***in*** labor. 石炭産出費の七割は労銀ということになる. ‖ *expend* money (time, energy) ***in*** doing something. ¶He *expended* all his capital ***on*** his new scheme. 彼は新計画にありたけの資金をかけた. 【類】*expend* £48 a year ***on*** clubs and club-life / Large sums were *expended* ***on*** model farms (模範農場).

expenditure, *n.* 消費; 費用, 経費.

V It ***costs*** a large *expenditure* of money. それは大変入費がかかる. ¶***curtail*** *expenditure* for ... ...の費用を節約する. ¶***economize*** the *expenditure* of ammunition 弾薬の消費を節約する. ¶***entail*** an annual *expenditure* of ... 年に...の出費を必要とする. ¶No publisher was prepared to ***face*** the *expenditure* that would be required. 必要な入費を負担しようという出版者は一人もなかった. ¶***increase*** *expenditure* on armaments 軍備費を増す. ¶this, at a minimum, ***involves*** an *expenditure* of ... これは最低額...の入費を要する. 【類】A war ***involves*** a great *expenditure* of money. ¶***lavish*** *expenditure* on ... ...に金を惜しまない. ¶in order to ***meet*** this heavy *expenditure* この巨費を負担するために. ¶***pinch*** their other *expenditure* in order to send their sons to good schools 息子たちをよい学校に入れるために他の費用を切り詰める. ¶***practice*** wasteful *expenditure* 経費の濫費をする. ¶***reduce*** (=***cut***) *expenditure* 経費を減らす. ¶***require*** very heavy *expenditure* 多額の費用を要する. ¶***retrench*** the *expenditure* その経費を削減する. ¶***restrict*** one's *expenditures* その支出を制限する. ¶***slash*** *expenditure* 経費を大削減する. ¶ask the Diet to ***vote*** the *expenditure* required for ... ...に必要な経費の可決を国会に求める.

Q ***actual*** *expenditure* 実費. ¶by a ***colossal*** *expenditure* of money 巨額の出費によって. ¶***decreased*** *expenditure* on ... ...に関する出費の減少. ¶an ***enormous*** *expenditure* 多額な費用. ¶the ***estimated*** *expenditure* for ... ...に関する予算額. ¶***extraordinary military*** *expenditure* on national defence 国防に関する臨時軍事費. ¶an ***extravagant*** *expenditure* 法外な入費. ¶a ***foolish*** *expenditure* ばかげた出費. ¶the ***heavy*** *expenditure* involved in the publication of that voluminous work その多大な本の刊行に必要な多額の出版費. ¶require a ***high*** *expenditure* of energy 大いなる精力を必要とする. ¶his ***household*** and ***personal*** *expenditure* 彼の家族及び自分の費用. ¶an ***immense*** *expenditure* 多額な入費. ¶recommend a more ***lavish*** *expenditure* on ... ...にもっとじゃんじゃん金を出すように勧める. ¶with the ***least*** *expenditure* of time and energy 時間と精力の最小消費をもって. ¶By using the method, a rapid proficiency is acquired with the ***minimum*** *expenditure* of time and effort. その方法によると最小限度の時間と努力で速く上達することができる. ¶Quite as much pleasure can be purchased by a ***modest*** *expenditure* as by the most extravagant outlay. 法外な出費によると全く同様の快楽が適度の出費であがなわれる. ¶one's own ***personal*** *expenditures* その個人的費用. ¶avoid ***unnecessary*** and ***wasteful*** *expenditure* of money 不要でむだな支出を避ける.

Q² ***American tourist*** *expenditure* in the United Kingdom

英本土における米国漫遊者の消費額. ¶*consumer expenditures* 消費者の出す費用. ¶*per capita expenditure* 一人当りの経費. ¶*Tourist expenditure* is the livelihood of whole districts in many countries. 多くの国では旅行者の落す金がその全地域の生活費になる. ¶*war expenditures* 軍事費. ¶*working expenditure* 経常(運営)費.

P ***at*** a mininum *expenditure* of effort 最小限度の努力で. ¶He is profuse ***in*** his *expenditure*. 彼は金使いが荒い. ¶***with*** a large *expenditure* of money 多大の金を費して. ¶***without*** a great *expenditure* of energy 大して骨も折らずに.

P² an *expenditure* ***for*** ... ...費. ¶*expenditure* ***of*** a wasteful character むだな費用. ¶the total *expenditure* ***on*** army and navy amounted to ... 陸海軍の総経費は...に達した ‖ *expenditure* ***on*** armaments 軍備費.

expense, *n*. 費用, 入費; 散財; 損害, 犠牲.

V can ***afford*** the *expense* of education 教育費を払う資力がある ‖ I can ill ***afford*** the *expense*. 私はその金を出すのは苦しい. ¶No *expenses* will be ***allowed*** in that case. その場合は費用は支給しない. ¶***assume*** (=***stand***) all the *expense* 入費全部を引受ける. ¶in order to ***avoid*** *expense* 費用のかからないように. ¶***bear*** the whole *expense* of ... ...の費用全部を負担する. ¶The receipts were enough to ***clear*** all the *expenses*. 収入で一切の費用が支払われた. ¶It ***cost*** us much *expense*. そのためにわれわれは大いにふところを痛めた. ¶***count up*** all one's *expenses* 諸入費を計上する. ¶***cover*** the *expense* of ... ...の費用に当てる. 【類】The amount will ***cover*** all *expenses*. / My fee barely ***covers*** my *expenses*. / The receipts do not ***cover*** the *expenses*. ¶***curtail*** (=***cut*** [***down***]) *expenses* 費用を切り詰める. ¶***defray*** the *expense* of a lawsuit 訴訟入費を支弁する. 【類】grant them ... yen to ***defray*** their *expenses* / ***defray*** all the *expenses* needed for traveling. ¶the *expenses* are to be equally ***divided*** between ... and ... 入費は...間に平等に割り当てるはず. ¶***eliminate*** the *expense* for ... ...の入費を削除する. ¶This will ***entail*** some considerable *expense*. これにはかなりの費用を要するだろう. ¶***figure out*** *expense* 費用を計算する. ¶***Hang*** the *expense*, let's stay at the best places and see all there is to be seen. 入費が何だ, 一番良い所に滞在して見るものは残らず見物しよう. ¶All *expenses* are ***included*** in the price quoted. 費用はすべて書き出した価格に含まれている. ¶It is likely to ***increase*** *expense*. そうすると入費が増しそうだ. ¶You will ***incur*** great *expense* by this. こうすると費用がたくさん掛かる. 【類】no *expense* is to be ***incurred*** in the matter of ... ¶***involve*** *expense* 費用がかかる. ¶The business will not ***justify*** the *expense*. その仕事にそんな費用をかけるということはない. ¶***Keep*** *expenses* as low as possible. できるだけ費用を切り詰めなさい. ¶A prudent man ***limits*** his *expenses* by his income (=lives within his means=cuts his coat according to his cloth). 慎重派は収入内で暮しを立てる. ¶It ***means*** considerable *expense*. それは相当高いものになる. ¶find it hard to ***meet*** one's *expenses* なかなか収支のバランスがとれない. 【類】I had the greatest difficulties in ***meeting*** current *expenses* (経常費). / A part of the *expense* is ***met*** by the city or the state. ¶It ***occasions*** great *expense*. それには非常な入費がかかる ‖ *expenses* ***occasioned*** by ... ...による費用. ¶It did not ***pay*** our *expenses*. それでは入費もまかなえなかった. 【類】He offers to ***pay*** my *expenses* through the university. ‖ The machine will soon amply ***pay*** its own *expenses*. その機械はすぐ購入費ぐらいらくに浮かしてしまう. ‖ ***pay*** the *expenses* incurred かかった費用を払う. ¶***proportion*** one's *expenses* to one's means 資力相当の金使いをする. ¶***recoup*** *expenses* 費用を回収する. ¶We did not ***recover*** our *expenses*. われわれは出費が取り返せなかった. ¶***reduce*** *expenses* 費用を節減する. ¶***save*** *expenses* 費用をはぶく. ¶I will ***share*** the *expenses* with you. 君とその費用を分担しよう. ¶***spare*** no *expense* in ... ...に入費を惜しまない. 【類】You must not ***spare*** *expense*. / no *expense* has been ***spared*** to ... / no *expense* was ***spared*** for ... ¶I cannot ***support*** the *expense*. 私には費用が出し切れない. 【類】He is not able to ***support*** the *expense* of an appeal (控訴). ¶***take*** on oneself all the *expenses* 入費全部を引受ける. ¶***whittle down*** *expenses* 出費を削減する.

V² *expenses* already incurred ***amounts*** to ... これまで掛けた費用は...に達する. ¶provided that *expenses* do not ***exceed*** ... 入費が...を超過しなければ. ¶My *expenses* have ***run up*** considerably. 私の出費が大分かさんだ. ¶*Expense* ***was*** of little object. ほとんど金に糸目をつけなかった.

Q an ***additional*** *expense* 追加の費用. ¶an ***annual*** *expense* 歳費. ¶at ***considerable*** *expense* かなりの入費をかけて. ¶***current*** *expenses* 経常費. ¶***domestic*** *expenses* 家計. ¶In spite of the new breakwater, constructed at ***enormous*** *expense*, the harbour is a desert. ばく大な金をかけて防波堤を新設したのだが港は依然荒野のようだ(船影を認めない). ¶***extra*** *expenses* 臨時費. ¶***funeral*** *expenses* 葬儀費. ¶at ***great*** *expense* ばく大な費用で. ¶He has ***heavy*** *expenses* to meet. 彼は多大な費用を負担しなければならない. ¶at ***immense*** *expense* ばく大の費用で. ¶***incidental*** *expenses* 臨時諸費. ¶at the ***joint*** *expense* of ... and ... ...と...の出し合いで. ¶at ***large*** *expense* 多額の費用で. ¶at ***little*** (***less***) *expense* あまり(もっと)費用をかけずに. ¶***light*** *expenses* 軽少な費用. ¶***miscellaneous*** (=***sundry or incidental***) *expenses* 雑費. ¶***multifarious*** *expenses* 多方面の入費. ¶supply all ***necessary*** *expenses* 必要な費用は全部支弁する. ¶at a ***nominal*** *expense* ほんの名目だけの費用で. ¶***outside*** *expenses* 臨時費. ¶***overhead*** *expenses* 間接諸費. ¶He had his book printed at his ***own*** *expense*. 彼は自費でその本を出版した. ¶***petty*** *expenses* 雑費. ¶at the least ***possible*** *expense* できるだけ費用をかけないで. ¶The *expense* is ***prohibitive***. そんな費用はとても出せない. ¶a school maintained at ***public*** *expense* 公費経営の学校. 【類】a pauper school at ***public*** *expense*. ¶The book will not pay its ***publishing*** *expenses*. その本は出版費用が出まい. ¶at ***reasonable*** *expenses* むりのない費用で. ¶***running*** *expenses* 経常費. ¶***school*** *expenses* 学資. ¶***side*** *expenses* 余分の費用. ¶at a very ***slight*** *expense* きわめてささいな費用で. ¶at no ***slight*** (=small) *expense* 少なからざる費用で. ¶at very ***small*** *expense* ごく少しの費用で. ¶***social*** *expenses* 交際費. ¶enrichment at ***somebody else's*** *expense* 他人に迷惑をかけて自分の懐を肥やすこと. ¶at ***trifling*** *expense* ささいな費用で. ¶incur an ***unexpected*** *expense* とんだ散財をする.

Q² go to ***advertising*** *expenses* 広告の方にとられる. ¶***business*** *expenses* 事務(営業)諸費. ¶***construction*** *expenses* 建設諸費. ¶***detection*** *expenses* 捜査諸費. ¶***development*** *expenses* [事業の]拡張諸費. ¶***entertainment*** *expenses* [会社の]接待諸費. ¶initial ***equipment*** *expenses* 初回設備諸費. ¶***food*** *expense* 食費. ¶be sent abroad to study at ***Government*** *expense* 官費で留学させられる. ¶***homekeeping*** (=***household***) *expenses* 家計費. ¶cut down ***labor*** *expense* 労務費を削る. ¶earn enough to pay one's ***living*** *expenses* 生活費が十分支弁できるくらいもうける. ¶***lump sum*** *expenses* [一切引っくるめた]渡し切り諸経費. ¶***office*** *expenses* 事務諸費. ¶***operating*** *expenses* 運営諸費. ¶***running*** (=***working***) *expenses*=《米》operating costs 経常費, 運転資金. ¶***schooling*** *expenses* [学校]教育費. ¶***society*** *expenses* 社交費. ¶a school maintained at ***State*** *expense* 国立の学校. ¶***Transit*** *expenses* can in no way be negligible. 交通費は決してばかにできない. ¶cover the ***traveling*** *expenses* of ... の旅費に当てる ‖ Traveling *expenses* will be allowed. 旅費は支給される.

P ***at*** the *expense* of ... ...の費用で; ...の犠牲において. ¶The carriage both ways will be ***at*** our *expense*. 運賃は往復ともわれわれの負担になるだろう. ‖ ***at*** any *expense* どんなに費用がかかっても. 【類】publish a book ***at*** one's own *expense* (自費で) / He was educated ***at*** an uncle's *expense*. / He lives ***at*** his father's *expense*. / He returned to Japan after three years' study in Russia ***at*** the *expense* of the Government. / the cost of the railway trip is to be ***at*** the *expense* of ... / a building completed ***at*** an *expense* of ... / ***at*** very little *expense* / ***At*** an *expense* of over $50,000 the National Geographic Society sent a notable series of expeditions into Peru to investigate the traces (遺跡) of the Inca race. ‖ ***at*** the *expense* of extra labor at first 初めは余分に働いて ‖ They were laughing ***at*** my *expense*. 彼らは僕をばかにして笑っていた. ‖ benefit oneself ***at*** the *expense* of others 他人に迷惑をかけ自分の利益を計る ‖ ***at*** the *expense* of grace 優美を犠牲にして. 【類】clear oneself ***at*** another's *expense* ‖ I am not by any means one of those who like to praise the past ***at*** the *expense*

of the present.—Miss Ellen Terry. / learn a language ***at*** the *expense* of one's own / He did it ***at*** the *expense* of his character. / If all your study is silent, then you train your eye ***at*** the *expense* of your ear. ‖ ***at*** the *expense* of her discretion うっかりと ‖ You must not adhere too much to form ***at*** the *expense* of spirit. 精神を忘れて形式にとらわれ過ぎてはいけない. ¶ regardless ***of expense*** 金にあかして. ¶ put a person ***to expense*** 人に金を使わせる ‖ go ***to*** the *expense* of hiring a foreign teacher 奮発して外人教師を雇う ‖ I am inclined to learn Japanese, but not disposed to go ***to*** the *expense* of engaging a teacher. 僕は日本語を習いたいが金を出して教師に来てもらおうとまでは考えていない. 【類】 go ***to expense*** to accomplish a purpose. ¶ supply ... yen ***towards*** their *expenses* 彼の入費の足しに…円を給与する ‖ contributors ***towards*** the building *expenses* 建築費寄付者. ¶ ***with*** great *expense* 大金をかけて. 【類】 ***with*** little *expense*. ¶ ***without expense*** to you 君のふところを痛めずに.

P² *Expense* ***for*** books is small. 本代はわずかだ. ‖ the *expense* ***for*** removal 移転料 ‖ The *expense* ***for*** the examination is ¥3,000 per student. 受験料は一名につき金三千円とす. ¶ the *expense* ***of*** a war 戦費 ‖ the *expense* ***of*** ... has been exceedingly heavy ...の費用は非常にかさんでいる. ¶ His sons have been a great *expense* ***to*** him. 彼の子供らには大層金がかかった.

O *Expense* no object. 費用は一切お構いなし. ¶ The business is not worth the *expense*. この仕事はそれだけの金をかける値打がない.

expensive, *a.* 費用のかかる, 値の高い.

M It was *less expensive* than was expected. 思ったより安くあがった. 【類】 Living in the country is *less expensive* than in the city. ¶ is not *so expensive* as you might expect 君の思うほどは高くない. ¶ be ***too*** *expensive* for one's pocketbook あまり高価で自分には出しかねる. 【類】 Meat was scarce during the war and *too expensive* for ordinary people. ¶ a ***very*** *expensive* mode of living ぜいたくな生活様式 ‖ It will come ***very*** *expensive*. それはとても高いものにつく.

experience, *n.* 経験, 見聞, 体験.

V ***accumulate*** *experience* 場数を踏む. ¶ ***acquire*** *experience* 場を踏む. ¶ ***add to*** (=***enlarge***) his *experience* 彼の経験を増す. ¶ ***bear*** this *experience* in mind この経験を心に留める. ¶ In all collecting one must ***buy*** *experience*. すべて収集では月謝を払って(にせ物をつかまされて)経験を積まねばならない. ¶ He ***detailed*** his *experiences* at the Olympic Games. 彼はオリンピック大会での経験談を細かに述べた. ¶ ***enrich*** one's *experience* in ... …で経験を豊かにする. ¶ ***face*** an unaccustomed *experience* なれない経験をする. ¶ ***gain*** *experience* 場を踏む. 【類】 ***gain*** new *experience* / ***gain*** one's *experience* at first hand (体験する). ¶ ***get*** practical *experience* to supplement theoretical training 学理的訓練を補足するため実地の経験を得る. ¶ ***have*** a novel *experience* 珍しい経験をする ‖ He ***has*** no *experience* in such an affair. 彼はこんなことには経験がない. 【類】 I have ***had*** enough *experience* to lead me to think I know something. ‖ That foreigner ***has*** *experience* with Japanese students. その外人は日本の学生を扱いなれている. ¶ ***improve*** one's *experience* 経験を利用する. ¶ a mere bookworm ***lacking*** human *experience* 世間の事情にうといほんの紙魚(しみ)同様の人間. ¶ He ***narrated*** his own personal *experience* of the Russian bath. 彼はロシヤ風呂の実験談をした. ¶ There are not many who can afford to ***neglect*** the accumulated *experience* of man. [文学という] 人類経験の蓄積を等閑に付すことは多数の人の為し得ざる愚策である. ¶ ***pool*** *experiences* [相互の]経験を持ち寄る. ¶ ***purchase*** *experience* at a high price 高い代金を払って経験を買う(ひどい目に会って利口になる). ¶ ***recount*** one's *experiences* 経験談をやる. ¶ I will ***relate*** my own *experiences*. 私は自分の経験談を致しましょう. ¶ ***state*** *experiences* 経験を述べる. ¶ ***undergo*** *experience* 経験をする. ¶ ***widen*** one's *experience* 経験を広める.

V² as my *experience* ***enlarged*** 私の経験が増して行くにつれて. ¶ as far as my *experience* with men ***goes*** 人々に対し私が経験した所では. ¶ *experience* ***leads*** me to think that ... 経験によって私は…と考えるに至った. ¶ my *experience* ***tells*** that ... 私の経験では… ¶ as our *experience* ***widens*** われわれの経験が広まるにつれて.

Q with ***accumulated*** *experience* 経験を積んでいるので. ¶ a ***bitter*** *experience* にがい経験. ¶ a man of ***broad*** *experience* 経験の広い人. ¶ the ***capitalized*** *experience* of the past 資本化した(金もうけに利用した)過去の経験. ¶ It is a ***common*** *experience* in life. 世間によくあることだ. 【類】 Proverbs are the result of the ***common*** *experience* of the world. ¶ I have ***considerable*** *experience* of it. 私はそれにはかなりの経験がある. ¶ ***constant*** *experience* has shown me that ... 不断の経験で…が明かとなっている. ¶ a ***cruel*** *experience* 残酷な経験. ¶ in our ***daily*** *experience*, we know that ... われわれは日常の経験で…ということが分る. ¶ a ***dearly bought*** *experience* 高価な経験. ¶ ***deep*** *experiences* 深い経験. ¶ a ***delicious*** *experience* 会心の経験. ¶ ***direct*** *experience* 直接経験. ¶ after many ***discouraging*** *experiences* 色々悲観させる経験のあげく. ¶ a ***disheartening*** *experience* がっかりする経験. ¶ have a ***dull*** *experience* 退屈なときを過す. ¶ ***educative*** *experiences* of life 教育的効果ある人生の経験. ¶ ***emotional*** *experience* 感情上の経験. ¶ gain some ***expensive*** *experience* 金のかかる経験をする. ¶ understand life from ***firsthand*** *experience* [書籍からでなく] 直接の経験から人生を理解する. 【類】 ***firsthand*** *experience* of English life. ¶ The failure was a ***good*** *experience* to me. その失敗は私の薬になった. ¶ ***hard*** *experiences* つらい経験. ¶ a ***hair-raising*** *experience* 身の毛がよだつ経験. ¶ a person of ***industrial*** *experience* 産業上の経験ある者. ¶ an ***idyllic*** *experience* 田園の詩的経験. ¶ ***inherited*** *experience* 継承した経験. ¶ ***intensive*** *experience* 熱烈な経験. ¶ It is an ***interesting*** *experience*. それは興味ある経験だ. ¶ This is no ***isolated*** *experience* of mine. こういう経験をしたのは僕一人ではない. ¶ He has had ***journalistic*** *experience*. 彼には新聞記者の経験がある. 【類】 his early (若いころの) ***journalistic*** *experience*. ¶ men of ability and ***large*** *experience* 才能あり経験の豊かな人. 【類】 a lesson learned by (=from) ***large*** *experience*. ¶ May the writer be permitted here to record a ***little*** *experience* of his own? 記者はここで少しく彼自身の経験を記すことを許していただきたい. ¶ a housekeeper of ***long*** *experience* 長い経験のある女中頭. ¶ It is a ***melancholy*** *experience* to be invited to hear a class sing a French song when all the vowel sounds are hopelessly mispronounced. クラスがフランスの歌を歌う所へ招かれ生徒が母音をどれもこれも思い切って間違って発音しているのを聞かされたときは憂うつな気持になる. ¶ a very ***nasty*** *experience* 非常にいやな経験. ¶ meet with a ***new*** *experience* 新しい経験に遭遇する. ¶ an ***odd*** *experience* 変った経験. ¶ bring in one's ***own*** *experience* 自分の経験を生かす ‖ lay before you my ***own*** *experiences* as an author 私の作家としての経験を申上げる. ¶ a ***painful*** *experience* 苦しい経験. 【類】 I found from ***painful*** *experience* that ... / they know only too well from ***painful*** *experience* that ... ¶ have some ***peculiar*** *experiences* ある特異な経験をなめる. ¶ have a ***personal*** *experience* of ... …を実地に経験する ‖ from my ***personal*** *experience* 私個人の経験からは ‖ be the growth of an extensive ***personal*** *experience* 個人の手広い経験の結晶である. ¶ ***personal*** or ***vicarious*** *experience* 自身のまたは身代りの経験. ¶ have a ***pleasing*** *experience* 楽しい経験をする. ¶ He has ***practical*** *experience* of a fire. 彼は実際火事にあっている. ‖ teachers of ***practical*** *experience* 実地経験のある教師. ¶ by ***protracted*** *experience* and exceptional ability as a writer 作家としての長い経験と異常な才能とによって. ¶ a record of her ***recent*** *experience* of life in Japan 彼女の最近日本訪問中の経験の記録. ¶ my ***repeated*** *experiences* convince me that ... 私の度重なる経験で…ということがはっきり言える. ¶ ***rich*** *experience* 豊富な経験. ¶ the results of a ***ripe*** *experience* 円熟した経験の結果. ¶ he has had ***sad*** *experience* of ... 彼は…という悲しい経験をした. ¶ It may be only twenty years' ***sea-going*** *experience* that one will become a chief purser. 主席事務長になるにはどうしても海上生活二十年の経験が必要だ. ¶ have a ***severe*** *experience* つらい経験を持つ. ¶ I found from a ***small*** *experience* that ... 私はあるちょっとした経験から…ということがわかった. ‖ of ***small*** *experience* 経験に乏しい. ¶ he has had ***some*** *experience* of ... 彼は…について少し経験がある. ¶ ***sordid*** *experience* 人聞きの悪い経験. ¶ He has ***sound*** *experience* in commercial correspondence. 彼は商業通信文の確実な経験を持っている.

¶have a ***stormy*** *experience* 悲惨な経験をなめる. ¶***sunshiny*** *experience* 楽しい経験. ¶***30 years'*** *experience* 三十年の経験. ¶He has ***three years'*** *experience* of the profession. 彼には三年間その職業の経験がある. 【類】a married man of ***three years'*** *experience.* ¶a ***thrilling*** *experience* ぞっとするような経験. ¶have some ***trying*** *experiences* あるつらい経験をなめる. ¶the ***unanimous*** *experience* has been that ... みんなが一様に経験したことは...である. ¶***unexperienced*** *experiences* 知ったかぶり. ¶an ***unforgettable*** *experience* 忘れられない経験. ¶his ***unfortunate*** *experiences* with the press 彼の新聞関係の不幸な経験. ¶a most ***unpleasant*** *experience* in life 一生の中で非常に不愉快なできごとの一つ. ¶an ***unwelcome*** *experience* ありがたくない経験. ¶That was a ***valuable*** *experience* for me. それは私にとって貴重な経験であった. ¶a journalist of ***varied*** *experience* 多方面の経験を積んだ新聞記者. ¶***vicarious*** *experience* [伝聞・読書などによる]間接経験. ¶has had ***wide*** *experience* in business 手広い商売上の経験がある. ¶He is little more than a boy in ***worldly*** *experience.* 彼は世間の経験にかけては子供にすぎない. ‖ a man of vast ***worldly*** *experience* すいもあまいもかみわけた人.

Q^{2} a gentleman of wide ***banking*** *experience* 銀行業に広い経験のある紳士. ¶***battle*** *experience* 戦闘経験. ¶have ***broadcasting*** *experience* 放送の経験がある. ¶previous ***business*** *experience* 昔とったきねづか. ¶the ship's first ***combat*** *experience* 同艦の最初の戦闘経験. ¶a universal ***everyday*** *experience* 一般的に毎日受ける経験. ¶She has already had ***library*** *experience* to burn. 《米》彼女は図書館についてはすでに十分経験がある. ¶knowledge acquired through study and ***life*** *experience* 勉学と人生の経験から得た知識. ¶He had some ***newspaper*** *experience* as a youth. 彼は若いころ新聞社にいたことがあった. ¶***soul*** *experience*—joy, sorrow, pleasure, pain, love, hope, aspiration 心の経験—喜び, 悲しみ, 楽しみ, 苦しみ, 愛, 希望, 抱負. ¶in my ***teaching*** *experience* 私の教師としての経験で ‖ have no ***teaching*** *experience* 先生をやったことがない. ¶***work*** *experience* 仕事の経験.

P ***according to*** my *experience* 私の経験によると. ¶***after*** ten years' *experience* of ... ...についての十年の経験を積んでから. ¶I know this ***by*** *experience.* 私は経験でこれが分る. 【類】I know ***by*** (=from) *experience* that ... / People learn ***by*** *experience.* / You may profit ***by*** the *experience.* ¶***from*** our own *experience* we know that ... われわれ自身の経験からして...ということが分る ‖ speaking ***from*** large *experience* 広い経験から言うと. ¶He lacks ***in*** *experience.* 彼は経験が乏しい. ‖ ***in*** our *experience* われわれの経験上. ¶The belief is founded on the dictates ***of*** *experience.* その信念は経験の教える所に基ずいている. ‖ lessons ***of*** *experience* 経験から得る種々の教訓. ¶It is based ***on*** *experience.* それは経験に基ずいている. ¶write ***out of*** *experience* 経験によって書く. ¶***through*** a varied *experience* 色々な経験を経て. ¶I learned (=found) ***through*** dear *experience* that ... 私は高価な経験をもって...ということを知った. ¶It is based ***upon*** my personal *experience.* それは私の体験に基ずいている. ¶a skipper ***with*** an *experience* of fifty years at sea 海上五十年の経験ある船長.

P^{2} his *experience* ***among*** the insane 彼の精神病者から得た経験. ¶gain a wide *experience* ***as*** a mining engineer 鉱山技師として広い経験を得る ‖ with this *experience* ***as*** a guide この経験を頼りにして. ¶it has been the *experience* ***at*** the station that ... ...ということが駅頭の経験である. ¶have enough *experience* ***for*** ... ...に十分な経験がある. ¶Have you had any *experience* ***in*** teaching? 君は教壇に立ったことがあるか. 【類】He has had wide *experience* ***in*** financial affairs. / He has got much *experience* in salesmanship. / have many years' *experience* ***in*** selling ... ¶the *experience* ***of*** a lifetime 一生にわたる経験 ‖ her *experiences* ***of*** Indian life 彼女の在印当時の経験. ¶I have had *experience* ***of*** his kindness. 私は彼の親切を受けたことがある. ¶my *experiences* ***with*** them 彼らとつき合った私の経験. 【類】his *experiences* ***with*** Chinese bandits / my own *experience* ***with*** servants.

O an *experience* not easily to be forgotten 容易に忘れることのできない経験.

experience, *v.* 経験する, 体験する.

M ***less*** *experienced* in writing than in teaching 書くより教える方に経験の深い. ¶***little*** (***much***) *experienced* in business work 商売にはあまり経験がない(大いに経験のある). ¶***richly*** (***poorly***) *experienced* 経験の豊かな(乏しい). ¶they are ***thoroughly*** *experienced* in ... 彼らは...に十分経験がある. ¶***well*** *experienced* in industrial management 産業経営に経験豊かな. ¶He is not ***yet*** *experienced* in teaching. 彼はまだ教えることは慣れていない.

P the cordial reception I *experienced* ***from*** him 私が彼から受けた丁重な接待. ¶She is *experienced* ***in*** love affairs. 彼女は恋愛に経験がある.

O It has to be *experienced* in order to be understood. それがわかるには実地経験をしなければならない.

experiment, *n.* 試験, 実験.

V ***attempt*** the *experiment* of ... ...の実験を試みる. ¶He ***began*** a series of *experiments* in high explosives. 彼は高性能爆薬の実験を連続的に始めた. ¶***carry on*** *experiments* on ... ...の実験を行う. ¶certain *experiments* have just been ***carried out*** with submarines in order to test ... ...試験を目的とした潜水艦に関するある実験がちょうど行われた所だ. ¶***conduct*** *experiments* with ... ...の実験を行う. 【類】*experiments* have been ***conducted*** by ... ¶***hazard*** an *experiment* 冒険的に実験をやる. ¶***make*** careful *experiments* 細心に実験をやる ‖ I ***made*** an *experiment* on him. 私は彼に当って見た. 【類】***make*** *experiments* in electricity. ¶***perform*** *experiment* 実験を行う. ¶***substitute*** *experiment* and observation for speculative theories 純理論に替えて実験と観測を行う. ¶He ***tried*** his *experiment* with success. 彼は実験をやって成功した. 【類】***try*** an *experiment* of ... ‖ ***try*** *experiments* upon oneself 自己に対して実験して見る. ¶***try out*** an *experiment* あくまで実験をやって見る.

V^{2} The *experiment* ***worked*** well. その実験は成績が良かった.

Q a long series of ***careful*** *experiments* 長期にわたる注意深い実験. ¶a series of ***curious*** *experiments* were made on the subject by ... 永く続いた珍らしい実験が...によりその題目に関して行われた. ¶***extravagant*** *experiments* とっぴな実験. ¶a ***hazardous*** *experiment* 冒険的な実験. ¶an ***interesting*** *experiment* is being tried in ... 面白い実験が...に関して行われている. ¶after ***long*** and ***exhaustive*** *experiments* 長いかつ周到な実験の後. ¶***new*** *experiments* with Lippmann's color photography リプマンの色彩写真に対する新しい実験. ¶an entirely ***original*** and ***unprecedented*** *experiment* 全く風変りで, 前例のない実験. ¶model villages or ***other idealistic social*** *experiments* 模範村その他理想的社会に関する実験. ¶a statement of the results of their ***own*** *experiment* 彼らの自己実験の結果の発表. ¶a ***practical*** *experiment* 実験. ¶a ***rash*** *experiment* 無謀な実験. ¶a ***scholarly*** *experiment* in play acting 演劇に関する学的実験. ¶conduct ***scientific*** *experiments* 科学上の実験を行う. ¶a ***valuable educational*** *experiment* 貴重な教育上の実験. ¶try ***various*** *experiments* on animals 動物に対して色々な実験を試みる.

Q^{2} ***animal*** *experiments* 動物による諸実験. ¶try the ***two-meals-a-day*** *experiment* 一日二食主義の実験をする.

P ***as*** an *experiment* 一つの実験として. ¶I employed him ***by way of*** *experiment.* 私は彼を試みに採用した. ¶***during*** *experiments* in wireless telegraph 無線電信の実験中. ¶***for*** *experiment* 実験のために. ¶publish ... ***on*** *experiment* 試験的に...を出版する.

P^{2} make *experiment* ***in*** electricity 電気の実験をやる ‖ *experiments* ***in*** sound 音の実験. ¶*experiments* ***on*** living animals 生きてる動物による諸実験 ‖ make some special *experiments* ***on*** the growth of sponges 海綿の生長に関してある特殊の実験を行う. ¶an *experiment* ***with*** words (the memorydrugs, wireless telegraph) 言葉(など)の実験.

experiment, *v.* 試験する, 実験する.

P *experiment* ***in*** (=on) chemistry 化学の実験をやる. ¶*experiment* ***on*** electricity 電気の実験をやる. 【類】the subject ***on*** whom he is *experimenting.* ¶*experiment* ***with*** various methods 色々な方法で実験する. 【類】*experiment* ***with*** new methods of teaching / Several medicines, even narcotics (麻酔薬), were *experimented* ***with.*** / *experiment* ***with*** radium / *experiment* ***with*** a new device for communication by means of wireless telephony (無線電話) between vessels.

expert, *n.* 熟練家, 老練家; 専門家.

Q an ***accomplished expert*** 練達の専門家. ¶an ***acknowledged expert*** 定評ある熟練家. ¶a ***chemical expert*** 化学専門家. ¶***Columbia-trained experts*** in education コロンビヤ大学仕込みの教育専門家. ¶a ***culinary expert*** 料理の名人. ¶a ***financial expert*** 金融専門家. ¶a ***linguistic expert*** 語学の専門家. ¶***naval experts*** 海軍の専門家. ¶a ***philological expert*** 言語学者. ¶a ***professional expert*** 職業上の専門家. ¶Mr. R.L. Hobson, the ***prominent expert*** in pottery of the British Museum 英国博物館の有名な陶器専門家たるR.L. ホブソン氏. ¶a ***scientific expert*** 科学的専門家. ¶a ***statistical expert*** 統計専門家. ¶a ***technical expert*** 技術専門家; [国会などの]専門委員. ¶a ***well-known expert*** in these matters この方面で有名な専門家.

Q² an ***administration expert*** 政治委員. ¶a ***balloon expert*** 気球技術者. ¶a ***beauty expert***=a beautician 美容師. ¶a ***bowling expert***〘競技〙ボーリングの名手. ¶a ***crop expert*** 篤農家. ¶an ***efficiency expert*** 能率増進の専門家. ¶an ***engineering expert*** 技術家. ¶an ***explosive expert*** 熟練した爆発係(鉱山などの). ¶a ***farm expert*** 農業技術専門家. ¶a ***fashion expert*** 流行服飾専門家. ¶a ***finger-print expert*** 指紋専門家. ¶a ***foreign affairs expert*** 外交専門家. ¶a ***government expert*** 技術官. ¶a ***grain expert*** 穀類専門家. ¶an ***intelligence expert*** 知能考査専門家. ¶a ***language expert*** 語学専門家(郵便物検閲などの). ¶a ***merchandise expert*** 商品鑑定人. ¶bankers and ***money experts*** 銀行家及び金融専門家たち. ¶an energetic ***newspaper expert*** 精力的な老練新聞記者. ¶a ***nutrition expert*** 栄養専門家. ¶a ***pottery expert*** 熟練した陶器製作者. ¶a ***publicity expert*** 宣伝のエキスパート. ¶a ***radio speech expert*** 放送演説専門家. ¶a ***rose expert*** ばらの専門家. ¶a ***trade expert*** 貿易方面の練達者. ¶a ***water expert*** 水道技術者. ¶a ***weather expert*** 測候所技師.

P Dr. Luther Halsey Gulick, well known ***as*** an ***expert*** in physical exercise 体育の専門家として有名なルーサー・ハルセー・ギュリック博士.

P² employ a well-paid foreign ***expert as*** adviser 高給外人専門家を顧問として招く. ¶***experts at*** their work その仕事に熟練した人たち. ¶an ***expert in*** English speech 英語演説の達者な人 ‖ all ***experts in*** their respective subjects (=special fields) それぞれの専門家 ‖ an ***expert in*** questions of international law 国際法の問題に明るい人 ‖ an ***expert in*** whist〘トランプ〙ホイストの達人 ‖ an ***expert in*** money-making 金もうけのじようずな人. ¶***experts of*** (=in) finance (mathematics) 財政(など)の専門家. ¶an ***expert on*** chess=a chess expert 専門棋士 ‖ an ***expert on*** mining 鉱山技師. ¶owned and managed by those who are ***experts on*** international trade 国際貿易に明るい人々が所有しかつ管理している. ¶an ***expert with*** the sword (needle, gun) 刀剣(など)使用の熟練家.

expert, *a.* 熟練した, じようずな.

P become ***expert at*** figures 計算に熟達する ‖ a man ***expert at*** his trade 自分の商売に明るい人. ¶The Egyptians were especially ***expert in*** the working of stone. エジプト人は石工において特に熟練していた.

expiate, *v.* あがなう, つぐなう.

P they ***expiated with*** their lives the misdeeds of ... 彼らは身をもって...の非行をあがなった.

expiation, *n.* しょく罪, 罪滅ぼし.

V Indeed these two worthy gentlemen seemed to be convenient mediums through which their superiors might ***render*** a vicarious ***expiation*** for their offences. 全くこれら二人のりっぱな紳士は彼らの長上たちが自分の罪悪の身代りに立てるには都合のよい人たちのように思われた.

P ***in expiation*** of sin 罪滅ぼしに.

expiration, *n.* 終了, 満了; 絶息, 死.

P ***at*** its ***expiration*** それの満了したとき ‖ ***at*** the ***expiration*** of the term 期間切れ(満了)の際 ‖ ***at*** his ***expiration*** he said ... 彼は臨終に...と言った ‖ The business was transferred to the present address ***at*** the ***expiration*** of the lease of its former premises. 同商事会社はその以前の敷地の借用期限が切れたときに今の番地に移った. 【類】***at*** the ***expiration*** of the agreement ‖ ***at*** the ***expiration*** of a notice (予告期間) given by ... / He voluntarily retired ***at*** the ***expiration*** of the term of service (office). / ***at*** the ***expiration*** of the period / ***at*** the ***expiration*** of the twelve months and seven days' grace (猶予). ¶***before*** the ***expiration*** of the present vacation この休暇が終らない内に.

P² ***expiration of*** the validity term 有効期間の満期終了 ‖ The copyright will run until the ***expiration of*** fifty years after the author's death. 版権は著者の死後五十年間継続する.

expire, *v.* 絶息する, 死ぬ; 満期になる, 終了する.

M ***expire calmly*** 静かに息を引取る. ¶***expire peacefully*** 平安に息を引取る.

P He ***expired at*** midnight. 彼は真夜中に息を引取った. ¶***expire in*** agony 苦しんで息を引取る. ¶The month ***expired on*** Saturday. その月の終りは土曜日だった. ¶The subscription ***expires with*** the current number. 購読料は本号で尽きます. 【類】Your subscription to the magazine ***expires with*** the number now issuing from the press.

expiry, *n.* 終了, 満了.

P ***at*** the ***expiry*** of the lease (this time) 借地期限(など)満了に当って. ¶apply for extension ***before expiry*** [切符など]期間満了前に使用延長を申込む. ¶***on*** the ***expiry*** of ten years from the date of ... ...の日付から十年の期間満了の際に. 【類】He leaves for home on the 19th of next month, ***on*** the ***expiry*** of his five years' term office.

explain, *v.* 説明する, 解釈する.

M ***explain apologetically*** 弁解して言う. ¶It is difficult to ***explain*** it ***away***. それをうまく弁護するのは困難だ.【類】***explain away*** one's error / ***explain away*** the circumstances. ¶***briefly explain*** 簡単に説明する. ¶This is ***easily explained***. その説明は簡単にできる. ¶I cannot ***explain*** it ***exactly***, but it seems to me that ... 私はそれを正確に説明はできないが...らしく思われる. ¶***fully explain*** 十分に説明する. ¶***lucidly explain*** あざやかに解説する. ¶I want to ***explain, parenthetically***, that ... 私は注釈的に(付け加えて)...と言っておきたい. ¶***roughly explain*** one's idea 考えを大体話す. ¶This phenomenon has not as yet been ***satisfactorily explained***. この現象はこれまで満足に説明されていない.

P ***explain by*** analogy 類推によって説明する. ¶this may be ***explained from*** the fact that ... このことは...という事実からして説明ができるだろう. ¶It is not easily ***explained in*** words. それは言葉に言い表わすのはむずかしい. 【類】***explain*** a foreign passage ***in*** one's own language. ¶it cannot be ***explained on*** the theory of ... それは...説では説明はできない. ¶***explain to*** one's full satisfaction これならば満足だと思うように説明する ‖ ***explain*** the matter ***to*** him そのことを彼に説明する.

explanation, *n.* 説明, 解釈, 弁明; 和解.

V ***add*** a supplementary ***explanation*** 補足的な説明を加える. ¶***await explanation*** 説明を待つ. ¶***demand*** (=call for) ***explanation*** from ... ...から弁明を求める. ¶No satisfactory ***explanation*** has yet been ***discovered***. 何ら満足のゆく解説がまだ見出されていない. ¶***facilitate explanation*** 説明を容易にする. ¶in this we ***find*** the ***explanation*** of ... この中に...の説明が見出される ‖ That will help ***find*** an ***explanation*** of the mystery. それによってその神秘を解くかぎも見出されよう. ¶You will be able to ***furnish*** an ***explanation***. 君にその説明がしてもらえるでしょう. ¶I cannot ***get*** a satisfactory ***explanation***. 私は満足な説明が得られない. ¶***give*** full ***explanation*** to ... ...に十分な説明を与える. 【類】***give*** a satisfactory ***explanation*** / he can ***give*** no ***explanation*** of ... ¶I should like to ***have explanation***. どういう訳だか聞かしてもらいたい. ‖ Few of the exhibits ***have explanations*** in English attached. 出品物の中には英語の説明が付いているものは少ない. ¶the ***explanation*** has been ***hazarded*** that ... ...という説明が試みられた. ¶***make*** an ***explanation*** 説明をする. ¶The subject may ***merit*** a brief ***explanation***. その問題は簡単に説明を加える価値があろう. ¶It ***needs*** no ***explanation***. それは説明の要なし. ‖ be too familiar to ***need explanation*** 周知のことであえて説明を要しない. ¶I could not ***obtain*** any satisfactory ***explanation*** from him. 私は彼から何ら満足な釈明を得ることができなかった. ¶He ***offered*** no ***explanation*** for it. 彼はそのことに対して何ら説明をしようとはしなかった. 【類】no ***explanation*** is ***offered*** as to the origin of ... / Of this he ***offers*** four ***explanations***. / Allow me to ***offer*** an ***explanation***. / if I were to ***offer*** an ***explanation***, I should say that ... / Various ***explanations*** have been ***offered***. ¶Thanking you for ***publishing*** this ***explanation***. [手紙の終り]この

説明の御公表に対し感謝しつつ. ¶It seems to ***require*** ***explanation***. それは説明を要するようである. 【類】It ***requires*** no ***explanation***. ¶An ***explanation*** must be ***sought*** in an entirely different direction. 説明は全然異った方面にこれを求めなければならない. ¶***think out*** an ***explanation*** 説明を考え出す. ¶***try*** an ***explanation*** 説明を試みる. ¶I don't ***understand*** the ***explanation***. 私にはその説明がふに落ちない.

V² the same ***explanation*** ***applies*** to ... 同じ説明が...にも当てはまる. ¶The ***explanation*** ***shows*** nothing but an evasion. その説明は逃口上にすぎない.

Q the most ***acceptable*** ***explanation*** 一番もっともな説明. ¶I cannot accept it as an ***adequate*** ***explanation***. 私にはそれは適当な説明とは受取れない. ¶an ***additional*** ***explanation*** 付加的説明. ¶a dictionary with ***bilingual*** ***explanations*** 双解辞書. ¶a ***clarifying*** ***explanation*** 明解. ¶a ***clear*** and ***lucid*** ***explanation*** 明りょうであざやかな説明. ¶This ***explanation*** is not ***convincing***. この説明は納得ができない. ¶a ***deeper*** ***explanation*** 一層深い説明. ¶a ***detailed*** ***explanation*** 詳細な説明. ¶with ***due*** ***explanations*** その訳を言って. ¶an ***elaborate*** and ***labored*** ***explanation*** 入念にこしらえ上げた説明. ¶an ***excellent*** ***explanation*** りっぱな説明. ¶***flimsy*** ***explanation*** 薄っぺらな説明. ¶a ***foolproof*** ***explanation*** ばかでも分る説明. ¶it is not yet a ***full*** ***explanation*** of ... それではまだ...の十分な説明にはならない. ¶an ***illuminating*** ***explanation*** よく分る解説 ‖ more ***illuminating*** is the ***explanation*** of ... ...の説明の方が一層明白である. ¶I must have an ***immediate*** ***explanation***. さっそくその理由をぜひ説明して欲しい. ¶an ***improbable*** ***explanation*** ありそうもない説明. ¶an ***intelligible*** ***explanation*** わかりのいい説明. ¶give a ***lucid*** ***explanation*** はっきりした説明をする. ¶a ***mutual*** ***explanation*** 双方からの説明. ¶I will call on you and make a ***personal*** ***explanation***. 私が貴下を訪問して親しく説明致します. ¶a very ***plausible*** and ***reasonable*** ***explanation*** 至極もっともらしい筋の通った説明. ¶offer a ***possible*** ***explanation*** of ... ...の可能な説明をする. 【類】this is a ***possible*** ***explanation*** of the fact that ... ¶a ***printed*** ***explanation*** 印刷した説明書. ¶the ***probable*** ***explanation*** is that ... ...というのが恐らく真に近い説明である. ¶a ***rational*** ***explanation*** 理屈の通った説明. ¶give it a ***satisfactory*** ***explanation*** それを十分に説明する. ¶It is incapable of ***scientific*** ***explanation***. それは科学的に説明はできない. ¶the ***stock*** ***explanation*** of this is ... これに対する紋切り型の説明は...である. ¶That is a quite ***sufficient*** ***explanation***, I think. それで結構説明されたものと思います. ¶a ***superficial*** ***explanation*** 皮相的な説明. ¶proposed ***tentative*** ***explanations*** 暫定的に提供した説明. ¶the ***true*** ***explanation*** is to be found in ... 真の説明は...に求めなければならない. ¶a ***verbal*** (=***viva-voce***) ***explanation*** 口頭での説明. 「よる説明.

Q² ***news*** ***explanation*** 時事解説. ¶a ***word*** ***explanation*** 語に

P urge ***as*** an ***explanation*** that ... 弁明として...と言張る. ¶***by way of*** ***explanation*** 説明として. ¶I asked ***for*** an ***explanation***, which was frankly given. 私が釈明を求めたら率直に言ってくれた. ¶***from*** this ***explanation*** you will see that ... この説明で貴下は...ということが分るでしょう. ¶***in*** ***explanation*** I would say that ... その説明に私は...と言いたい ‖ notes ***in*** ***explanation*** 注解 ‖ add some few words ***in*** ***explanation*** 説明のために二三語を付け足す. ¶***to*** my ***explanation*** that I wished to see ... 私が...を見たいということを説明したのに対して. ¶as it might be understood ***without*** ***explanation*** 読んで字のごとく ‖ It is almost unintelligible ***without*** ***explanation***. それは説明がないとほとんど分らない.

P² an ***explanation*** ***for*** his action 彼の行動に対する一つの説明. ¶An ***explanation*** ***of*** their delay was demanded. 彼らの遅刻に対する弁明が求められた. 【類】***explanation*** ***of*** signs (記号). ¶an ***explanation*** ***on*** current events 時事解説.

O the ***explanation*** is that ... その説明は...である.

explanatory, *a.* 解釈上の.

P the notes ***explanatory*** ***of*** ... ...を解説する注釈.

explication, *n.* [意義の]解明.

Q need very ***little*** ***explication*** あまり多くの説明を要しない. ¶subjoin a ***short*** ***explication*** to ... ...に小注をつけ加える.

explicit, *a.* 明白な, あからさまの.

M be ***quite*** ***explicit*** about political affairs 政治問題についてはきわめて率直である.

P be ***explicit*** ***in*** one's statement 腹蔵なく話す.

explode, *v.* 破裂する, 爆発する.

P The player was universally hissed and ***exploded*** ***off*** the stage. その俳優は大向うからやじられ舞台から追い出された. ¶***explode*** ***with*** anger (=wrath) どなる ‖ ***explode*** ***with*** laughter どっと笑い出す.

exploit, *n.* 偉業, 手柄, 勲功.

V ***perform*** ***exploits*** 勲功をたてる. ¶***sing*** his ***exploits*** 彼の手柄をほめたてる.

Q ***astounding*** ***exploits*** of their enemies 敵側の驚嘆すべき戦勲. ¶***dare-devil*** ***exploits*** 大胆な離れわざ. ¶***fine*** ***exploits*** of arms 武勲. ¶***heroic*** ***exploits*** 勇敢な手柄. ¶an account of one's ***military*** ***exploits*** 手柄話. ¶***naval*** ***exploits*** 海軍の武勲. ¶***successful*** ***exploits*** りっぱな成功. ¶***valiant*** ***exploits*** 雄々しい手柄. 「山家としての偉業.

Q² ***flying*** ***exploits*** 空の手柄. ¶***mountaineering*** ***exploits*** 登

P He won the medal ***for*** his ***exploit*** in Korea. 彼は朝鮮での戦功で勲章を授けられた.

exploit, *v.* 利用する; 搾取する.

P General Tom Thumb, the world-famous midget, ***exploited*** ***by*** Barnum バーナム(興行師)が売物にした世界的名声のある一寸法師トム・サム大将 ‖ colonies ***exploited*** ***by*** their sovereign nation その主権国に搾取された植民地.

exploitation, *n.* 開拓, 利用; 搾取.

V ***repay*** ***exploitation*** 開拓して引合う.

Q electric lighting and its ***commercial*** ***exploitation*** 電気照明とその商業上の利用.

Q² ***capitalist*** ***exploitation*** 資本家の搾取.

exploiter, *n.* 開拓者.

P² ***exploiter*** ***of*** South Africa 南アフリカの開拓者.

exploration, *n.* 探検; 調査.

V ***make*** ***explorations*** 探検をやる.

Q ***aerial*** ***exploration*** 飛行機による探検. ¶***Arctic*** ***exploration*** under Nansen ナンゼン指揮下の北極探検. ¶give long hours of toil to the ***patient*** ***exploration*** of written records 長時間丹念に文献調査に骨を折る.

Q² ***mountain*** ***exploration*** 山岳探検.

P The answer to this question is now ***under*** ***exploration***. この質問に対する解答は目下調査中である.

P² the ***exploration*** ***of*** the sea depths 海底探検.

explorer, *n.* 探検者.

Q an ***intrepid*** ***explorer*** 大胆な探検家.

Q² a ***submarine*** ***explorer*** 潜水者.

explosion, *n.* 破裂, 爆発; ぼっ発.

V² At last the ***explosion*** ***came***. やがて事がばれた.

Q a ***loud*** ***explosion*** of gas ごう然たるガスの爆発. ¶a ***premature*** ***explosion*** 予定時前の爆発. ¶a ***tremendous*** ***explosion*** of public opinion 世論のすさまじい爆発.

Q² a ***bomb*** ***explosion*** 爆弾破裂. ¶be wrecked by a ***gas*** ***explosion*** ガス爆発で破壊される. ¶a ***gunpowder*** ***explosion*** 火薬爆発.

P The ship was sunk ***by*** an ***explosion***. 船が爆沈した. ¶blow up ***with*** a terrific ***explosion*** ごう音を立てて爆発す

P² an ***explosion*** ***of*** a boiler ボイラーの破裂. しる.

explosive, *n.* 爆薬.

Q a shell filled with ***high*** ***explosive*** 高性能爆薬の詰めてあ

exponent, *n.* 代表者; 解説者. しる薬きょう.

Q an ***able*** ***exponent*** of ... ...の有力な解説者. ¶an ***accomplished*** and ***encyclopedic*** ***exponent*** of things Japanese 日本事情のたん能にして百科辞典的な解説者. ¶those ***fearless*** ***exponents*** of educational reform who do not shrink from iterating the truth whenever opportunity offers 機会のあるごとに真理を進んで詳説するかの勇敢な教育改革者たち. ¶T.H. Green was perhaps the ***foremost*** ***exponent*** of Hegel. T.H. グリーンは恐らくヘーゲルの哲学を最もよく解釈していた人であろう. ¶a ***leading*** ***exponent*** of ... ...の大家 ‖ one of our ***leading*** ***exponents*** わが一流解説者の一人. 【類】one of the world's ***leading*** ***exponents*** of psychoanalysis (精神分析). ¶the greatest ***living*** ***exponent*** of *judo* 柔道の現存の最高権威. ¶a ***noted*** ***exponent*** of Mendelism メンデル派の有名な学者. ¶his ability as a ***popular*** ***exponent*** of science 科学の通俗解説者としての彼の手腕. ¶according to its ***recognized*** ***exponents*** 専門大家の説によれば. ¶a ***reliable*** ***exponent*** of ... ...の信頼できる解説者.

¶the ***topnotch*** *exponents* of the new dances《米》新舞踊の一流大家連.

Q² an ***expert*** *exponent* of modern dancing 近代舞踏のすぐれた代表者.

P² an *exponent* ***of*** the age その時代の批判家. ¶Lincoln is an *exponent* ***of*** self-education. リンカーンは独学の代表的人物である.

export, *n*. 輸出；輸出品.

V ***ban*** the *export* of … …の輸出を禁止する. ¶***cut off*** our *exports* わが国の輸出を減退させる. ¶Our imports now ***exceed*** our *exports*. わが国の輸入は今や輸出を超過している. ¶***prohibit*** (=***stop***) the *export* of … …の輸出を禁止する. ¶*Exports* ***go down*** (=***decline***). 輸出が減退する.

Q impose a quota system in the Colonies to limit the flood of Japanese ***cheap*** *exports* 日本の廉価輸出品のはんらんを制限するために(英領)植民地において割当制度を課する. ¶Beet sugar is one of the ***chief*** *exports* of Germany. 甜菜(てんさい)糖はドイツの重要輸出品の一つである. 【類】Next to wine, cork is the ***chief*** *export* of Portugal. ¶These are among the more ***important*** *exports*. これらは他に比して一そう重要な輸出品に属している. ¶***invisible*** *export* 無形輸出(観光事業など). ¶the ***principal*** *exports* 主要輸出品.

Q² ***cotton textile*** *exports* 輸出用綿製品.

P sundry goods ***for*** *export* 輸出用雑貨 ‖ they are manufactured ***for*** *export* to … その品は…へ輸出のために製造される. ¶the volume ***of*** American *exports* and imports at Canton 広東における対米輸出入品の数量.

P² foreign *exports* ***from*** the port of Yokohama 横浜港から外国への輸出品. ¶the *exports* ***of*** Japan ***to*** China 日本から中国への輸出品.

export, *v*. 輸出する.

P be *exported* ***on*** a commercial basis 商品として輸出されている. ¶*export* goods ***to*** a foreign country 外国へ輸出する.

exportation, *n*. 輸出.

P an embargo ***on*** the *exportation* of food stuffs 食料品の輸出禁止.

P² They are extensively made for *exportation* ***to*** the West. その品は西洋への輸出向に広く製造されている.

expose, *v*. さらす，露出する；あばく；店に陳列する.

M He was *exposed* ***incessantly*** to the charge of insincerity. 彼は始終ふまじめであると非難されていた. ¶***mercilessly*** *expose* a secret 容しゃなく秘密をあばく. ¶*expose* troops ***needlessly*** 軍隊を不必要に危地に置く.

P Their jobs were all *exposed* ***by*** the press. 彼らの「内職」は全部新聞ですっぱ抜かれた. ¶*expose* goods ***for*** sale 商品を陳列して売る. ¶*expose* goods ***in*** a shop 品を店に陳列する. ¶*expose* him ***of*** ridicule 彼を人の笑い物にする ‖ He is *exposed* ***to*** the ridicule of the public. 彼は世人の笑い物にされている. 【類】be *exposed* ***to*** the public eye ‖ see … *exposed* ***to*** the light of day … …を明るみへ出す ‖ Do not *expose* it ***to*** the sun (light, weather, air, rain). それを太陽(など)にさらすな. 【類】be *exposed* ***to*** the sea-breeze / be *exposed* ***to*** cold winds / be *exposed* ***to*** wintry storms (吹雪) ‖ *expose* an orchard ***to*** the southerly sun 果樹園を南向きにする.

exposition, *n*. 説明，解釈；《主に米》博覧会.

V an *exposition* to be ***designated*** … …と命名さるべき博覧会. ¶he ***gives*** an *exposition* of his views as to … …について彼の意見を説明する. ¶The *exposition* was ***held*** February 5 to 28. 博覧会は二月五日から二十八日まで開かれた.

Q a very ***able*** *exposition* and defense of the company's attitude 会社の態度に関する非常にりっぱな説明と弁護. ¶The book is the only ***adequate*** *exposition* of the subject in English. その本はその問題の英語の唯一の適当な解説書である. ¶an ***authoritative*** *exposition* of … …についての権威ある解説. ¶a ***clear*** *exposition* 明りょうな説明. ¶a ***complete, accurate,*** and ***authoritative*** *exposition* of … …についての完全にして正確，かつ権威ある解釈. ¶a ***critical*** *exposition* 批判的説明. ¶an ***industrial*** *exposition* 産業博覧会. ¶possess the power of ***lucid*** *exposition* あざやかな解説力を有する. ¶a ***lucid*** and ***touching*** *exposition* 明快で感動的な説明. ¶by far the best ***popular*** *exposition* of … …のはるかに通俗的な解説. ¶a ***practical*** *exposition* 実際的説明. ¶a ***scientific*** *exposition* 科学的解説. ¶He has the gift of ***simple*** *exposition*. 彼は簡明に説明しうる腕を持っている. ¶a ***startling*** *exposition* 一驚を喫する説明. ¶a ***systematic*** *exposition* of … …の組織的説明. ¶It is written with notable clarity and with a minimum of ***technical*** *exposition*. それは著しく明快にかつできるだけ専門的な解説を避けて書いてある. ¶a ***valuable*** *exposition* of a fascinating subject 魅力ある題目についての貴重な解説.

Q² the ***Paris*** *Exposition* of 1889 一八八九年のパリ大博覧会.

P² an *exposition* ***of*** … …の説明.

expostulate, *v*. 忠告する.

P *expostulate* ***with*** him ***on*** (=***upon***) … …について彼に忠告する.

exposure, *n*. 露出，暴露，摘発.

Q the ***indecent*** *exposure* of the body in public 人前での不体裁なはだの露出. ¶a ***lurid*** *exposure* of Italian politics 赤裸々なイタリア政治の内幕. ¶a ***moral*** *exposure* 道徳上の摘発. ¶a ***public*** *exposure* 公然のすっぱぬき. ¶a ***sensational*** *exposure* 扇情的な暴露. ¶It is certainly a case of ***shameful*** *exposure*. それは全くいい恥さらしだ. ¶a house with a ***southern*** *exposure* 南向きの家.

P It was dried ***by*** *exposure* to the sun. それを日に当てて乾した. ‖ a rock weathered ***by*** *exposure* 雨ざらしになって風化した岩. ¶He committed suicide ***on*** *exposure*. 彼はことがばれて自殺した. ¶The destruction of the building is attributed to *exposure* ***to*** a fire which originated elsewhere. その建物は類焼だということだ.

P² *exposure* ***to*** danger 危険状態におくこと. ¶*Exposure* ***to*** the rain has spoiled this machine. 雨ざらしにしておいたのでこの機械は使いものにならない. 【類】*exposure* ***to*** the sun (wheather).

expound, *v*. 解釈する.

M ***adequately*** *expound* 十分に解釈する.

expounder, *n*. 解説者.

Q a ***scientific*** *expounder* of socialism 社会主義の科学的解説者.

express, *n*. 急行列車；速達便；《米》[客車便などで]急送.

Q a ***limited*** *express* 特急.

Q² on the ***four-twenty*** *express* 四時二十分の急行で.

P twelve hours ***by*** *express* 急行で十二時間 ‖ I am going to travel ***by*** *express*. 私は急行で行こうと思う. ‖ send a package ***by*** *express*《米》小荷物を急行便で送る；《英》小包を速達便で送る. ¶The next day I left for Kyoto, second class, ***on*** the *express*. その翌日私は急行の二等で京都に向って立った.

express, *v*. 言表わす，述べる；しぼる；《米》急送する.

M I cannot ***adequately*** *express* my sentiment. 私は自分の感情を適切に言表わすことができない. ¶be *expressed* ***admirably*** on this subject この問題については実にりっぱに言表わされている. ¶*express* oneself ***bitterly*** opposed to … …に対する大反対を表明する. ¶*express* oneself ***calmly*** and ***judicially*** 落着いて思慮深く考えを述べる. ¶He *expressed* himself ***carefully***. 彼は自分の意見を注意深く述べた. ¶*express* oneself ***clearly*** 明白に所思を述べる. 【類】his inability to *express* himself ***clearly***. ¶*express* oneself ***clearly*** and ***forcibly*** はっきり力強く意見を述べる. ¶It is very ***clumsily*** *expressed*. それは表現が非常にへただ. ¶*express* oneself ***coherently*** in intelligible simple English つじつまが合うように分りやすい英語で述べる. ¶*express* oneself ***correctly*** in English 考えを英語で正確に述べる. ¶*express* oneself ***crudely*** むき出しな表現をする. ¶He ***delicately*** *expressed* his refusal. 彼はうまく断った. ¶*express* oneself ***effectively*** 効果的に意見を述べる. ¶select the words which will most ***felicitously*** *express* one's mind 自分の考えをきわめて適切に表現する語を選ぶ. ¶*express* ***frankly*** 卒直に述べる. ¶***freely*** *express* oneself as to … …について所存を遠慮なく述べる. ¶be apt to *express* himself ***freely*** and ***forcibly*** とかく思い切ったことを言いがちである. ¶I cannot ***fully*** *express* the debt I owe to … …に対する御恩は口では言いつくせない. ¶for years it has been an opinion very ***generally*** *expressed* among … それは何年間も…の間ではだれもが言ってる意見である. ¶The author *expresses* ***happily*** many ideas that have lain unnamed in my mind. 著者は私の胸に言葉なく秘められていた幾多の思想を巧妙に表現している. ¶***How*** do you *express* that in English. それは英語でどう言いますか. ¶*express* oneself in English ***intelligibly*** 思う所を英語で分るように言表わす. ¶have not *expressed* themselves ***officially*** on the matter その件はまだ公式に述べていない. ¶as he ***paradoxically*** *expressed* it 彼がそれを逆説的に述べたように. ¶he *expressed* himself very ***positively*** on the subject of … 彼は…の問題に関してきわめて断固とした考えを述べた. ¶*express* it ***publicly*** 公然とそれを口にする. ¶As it has been ***punningly*** *expressed*, a print may be "rare because not well done." 版画はしゃれた言葉にもあるように「できが悪いので珍らしい」(もう一つの意味は「よ

く煮えていないからなま」な)こともあろう. ¶as he ***quaintly*** *expressed* it 彼がそれを変った言葉で言ったように. ¶*express* oneself ***readily, accurately,*** and ***clearly*** in one's own language 自国語で直ちに, 正確に明白に述べる. ¶cannot *express* oneself ***satisfactorily*** in English 英語で考えを満足に述べられない. ¶*express* himself ***sincerely*** in his address to the graduating class of the university その大学の卒業クラスに卒直な心持で話しをする. ¶*express* oneself very ***strongly*** on ... ...に関し力説する. 【類】*express* oneself ***strongly*** in favor of peace settlement. ¶I cannot ***sufficiently*** *express* my appreciation of the kindness of ... ...の御親切に対しては感謝の言葉もないほどです. ¶***tersely*** *express* 簡潔に言表わす. ¶*express* oneself very ***vaguely*** すこぶるあいまいに述べる. ¶be too complicated to *express* ***verbally*** 口頭で説明するにはあまり複雑過ぎている. ¶more ***vigorously*** *expressed* 一層力強く言表わせば.

P *express* his deep regret ***at*** the untimely death of ... ...の夭(ﾖｳ)折に対し彼の深い哀悼の意を表わす. ¶*express* it ***by*** euphemism それをえん曲に言表わす ‖ It cannot be *expressed* ***by*** words. それは言葉には言表わせない. ¶*express* apples ***for*** cider りんご酒を造るためにりんごの汁をしぼる. ¶*express* juice ***from*** grapes ぶどうから液をしぼる. ¶The general effect of the exhibition may be *expressed* ***in*** the word respectable. 同展覧会の概評は「相当なもの」という言葉で言表わし得よう. ‖ *expressed* ***in*** a few words its main result was ... 要するにその大体の結果は...であった. 【類】His purpose was *expressed* ***in*** good English. / Ideas must be *expressed* ***in*** the medium of words. / He will *express* it ***in*** his own tongue. ¶*express* a package ***to*** ... 《米》 ...に小包を急送する(郵送でなく). 【類】*express* merchandise ***to*** ... ¶*express* sympathy ***with*** the relatives of the deceased 死者の親戚に対して弔意を表する.

expressage, *n.* 《米》運賃.

V These prices all include *expressage.* この価格はすべて運賃(送料)も含まれている.

expressible, *a.* 表現しうる.

M easily felt but not ***readily*** *expressible* それと容易に感じられるがちょっと表現し難い.

P They are *expressible* ***by*** signs. それらは記号で表わすことができる. ¶It is *expressible* ***in*** simple formulae. それは簡単な式で表わすことができる.

expression, *n.* 表現, 表示; [顔の]表情; 語句, 言回し; ようす, 顔付.

V Kindly ***accept*** this *expression* of my thanks. 私のこの感謝の意をお受け下さい. ¶***acknowledge*** the numerous *expressions* of sympathy and congratulation 同情と祝賀の数多いあいさつを感謝して受ける. ¶***avoid*** clumsy *expressions* 拙劣な表現を避ける. ¶to ***borrow*** a favourite *expression* of the Japanese poets 日本詩人の慣用句を借りて言えば. ¶an *expression* ***coined*** by Carlyle カーライルが初めて使った表現. ¶His speech ***contained*** rash *expressions.* 彼の演説中には軽卒な言葉使いがあった. ¶if you will ***excuse*** me the *expression* こう申してはなんですが. ¶This desire for freedom ***found*** *expression* in the French Revolution. この自由への切願がフランス革命となって現われた. ‖ It ***found*** *expressions* in various public prints. それが色々な刊行物中に現われた. 【類】This interest (この興味) ***found*** *expression* in the organization of scientific societies (科学協会). ¶***fix*** the *expression* in mind その言葉を心に留める. ¶***give*** *expression* to one's gratitude (sentiment) 感謝の意(感情)を表する. 【類】***give*** *expression* to one's real conviction (確信) / He has the enviable gift of being able to ***give*** *expression* to his thoughts in an admirably lucid style. ¶He ***has*** a singularly sweet *expression.* 彼は際立って美しい表現力を持っている. ¶***make*** a public *expression* of our gratitude to ... われわれの...に対する感謝を公式に言表わす. ¶***offer*** an *expression* of regret 遺憾の意を表する. ¶horse manure, if you ***pardon*** the *expression* ... ...尾ろうなことを申して失礼ですが馬ふん肥料は. ¶if such an *expression* may in any way be ***permitted*** こういう言葉を使うのもなんだが(はばかりがあるが). ¶I ***read*** a pleased *expression* on her face. 私は彼女の顔にうれしさが浮んでいるのを見て取った. ¶***soften*** *expressions* by using "please," "kindly," or "thank you" 「どうぞ」とか「すみませんが」とか「ありがとう」とか言って語気を和げる. ¶Buildings on a rainy day ***take on*** a sleepy *expression.* 雨の日の建物は眠ったような光景を呈する. ¶to ***use*** a very modern *expression* ごく先端的な言葉を用いると ‖ to ***use*** a somewhat trite *expression* 少し古い言草ではあるが ‖ if one may ***use*** this *expression* こう言ってよいなら. ¶***utter*** some felicitating *expression* 祝詞を述べる. ¶***vary*** an *expression* 言替える. ¶***watch*** one's *expression* 人の顔色を見まもる. ¶his face ***wore*** an *expression* of ... 彼は...の顔付をした.

V² The whole *expression* of her face ***changed, softened,*** and ***brightened.*** 彼女の顔色が全く変って柔かい朗かなものになった. ¶An *expression* of rage ***came*** into his face. 怒りの色が彼の顔に現われた.

Q an ***alternative*** *expression* 代りになる(今一つの)表現. ¶the sentiments of the nation have found a most ***appropriate*** *expression* in ... 国民の感情は...にきわめて適切に現われた. ¶an ***apt*** *expression* 適切な表現. ¶an ***archaic*** *expression* 古めかしい表現. ¶men with a gift for ***artistic*** *expression* 芸術的表現の才ある人々. ¶an ***awkward*** *expression* 拙劣な言回し. ¶with a ***benevolent*** *expression* of face 情深い顔付をして. ¶***broken*** *expressions* とぎれとぎれの言葉. ¶***clear, forceful*** *expression* はっきりした力強い表現. ¶***clumsy*** *expression* つたない表現. ¶sound thinking and ***clear, intelligible*** *expression* 健全な思考と明白でよく分る言葉. ¶***colloquial*** *expression* くだけた言回し. ¶a ***common*** *expression* among doctors 医師間での通用語. ¶give ***concrete*** *expression* to an abstract idea 抽象的な思想を具体的に述べる. ¶***correct*** *expression* in English 英語での正しい表現. 【類】A, not B, is the ***correct*** *expression* in English. ¶***courteous*** *expression* 丁重な言葉. ¶***descriptive*** *expressions* for intoxication 酔態を形容した色々な文句. ¶receive from them ***distinguished*** *expressions* of regard 彼らからはっきりと敬意を表わす意味の言葉を受取る. ¶***double-meaning*** *expressions* 二義ある(あいまいな)言葉. ¶***duplicate*** *expressions* 意味の同じ言葉. ¶the study of ***effective*** *expression* 効果的な表現の研究. ¶an ***elegant*** *expression* 優雅な表現. 【類】"Frutta di mare" is the ***elegant*** Italian *expression* for the miscellaneous products of the sea. ¶an ***elliptical*** *expression* for ... ...に対する省略した言い方. ¶An ***emphatic*** *expression* of thanks is due for the industry of the editor. 編者の努力に対しては当然大いに感謝の意を表すべきだ. ¶***facial*** and ***mouth*** *expression* 顔の表情と言語の表現. ¶a ***faulty*** *expression* 誤った言回し. ¶a ***favorite*** *expression* of the day 現時好んで使われる文句. ¶a ***figured*** *expression* しゃれた表現. ¶the gift of ***fluent*** *expression* 流ちょうな表現の才. ¶***forcible*** *expressions* 力のある言回し. ¶This has found ***frequent*** *expression* in recent literature. このことは最近の文学によく出ている. ¶find ***full*** and ***adequate*** *expression* in ... ...の中に十分かつ適切に現われる ‖ the ***fullest*** *expression* of public feeling 民意の十分な表明 ‖ come to its ***fullest*** *expression* in ... ...で本領を現わす. ¶it is the ***general*** *expression* that ... ...は世間一般に言うことだ. ¶only a ***geographical*** *expression* (政治上でない)地理的な言葉. ¶his power of ***graphic*** *expression* 絵のように明りょうな彼の表現力. ¶a ***grave*** and rather ***saturnine*** *expression* of face きまじめで幾分むっつりした顔付. ¶a ***great*** *expression* of the American soul アメリカ魂の偉大な表現. ¶a ***grim*** *expression* すご文句. ¶***gross, rank*** and ***vulgar*** *expressions* 野卑で下品で俗悪な言葉. ¶***grotesque*** *expressions* used by immigrants 移住民の使う変てこな言葉. ¶a ***hackneyed*** *expression* 常とうの文句. ¶a ***happy*** *expression* うまい言回し. ¶a ***hearty*** *expression* of welcome 心からの歓迎. ¶***heavy*** *expressions* 重々しい言葉使い. ¶the ***highest*** *expression* of his genius 彼の天才の最もすぐれた表現. ¶***homely*** *expressions* 平凡な言回し. ¶***honest*** *expression* いつわりない表現. ¶These are English ***idiomatic*** *expressions* different from our way of framing the thought. これらは英国の慣用的な語法でわれわれの思想表現法とは違っている. ¶suggest an ***improved*** *expression* こう書き直してはどうかと提言する. ¶His face wore a somewhat ***infantile*** *expression.* 彼は少しく子供っぽい顔付きをしていた. ¶an ***insincere*** and ***meaningless*** *expression* 出まかせな無意義な言葉. ¶an ***insulting*** *expression* in English 英語の侮辱的な言葉. ¶He has a very ***intelligent*** *expression.* 彼は中々理知的な顔付きをしている. ¶He has a ***languishing*** *expression.* 彼は思い

悩んだ顔付きをしている. ¶a ***lifelong*** *expression* of affection and good wishes 命のあらん限りの愛情と好意の表示. ¶other forms of ***literary*** *expression* 他の色々な文学的表現形式. ¶his genius found its ***loftiest*** *expression* in ... 彼の天才は...に最も気高く現われた. ¶***low*** *expressions* 野卑な言葉. ¶to use a ***mild*** *expression* おだやかに(良く)言えば. ¶a ***nautical*** *expression* 海上語. ¶a ***nicer*** *expression* than ... ...よりも一層良い言い方. ¶a ***nonsense*** *expression* 無意義な言葉. ¶receive ***numerous*** *expressions* of concern from ... ...から色々関心を示した言葉を頂だいする. ¶a ***newly coined*** *expression* 新語的表現. ¶***original*** *expressions* ざん新な言い方. ¶have ***parallel*** *expressions* 並行した(同じような言回しの)言葉がある(二つの国語などに). ¶a ***parenthetical*** *expression* そう入句. ¶a ***pet*** *expression* with the writer その作家の常用句. ¶the exchange of ***platitudinous*** *expressions* of mutual good will 相互の好意を表わす常とう語の交換. ¶***polite*** *expressions* of friendly feeling 友情を示す丁重な言葉. ¶a ***proper*** *expression* 適当な言葉. ¶a ***proverbial*** *expression* ことわざ(風の表現). ¶***public*** *expression* of the results of one's study and reflection 自己の研究考察の結果発表. ¶gaze with a ***puzzled*** *expression* 途方に暮れた顔をして凝視する. ¶a ***questionable*** *expression* きわどい文句. ¶the ***racy*** *expression* of plain people 一般大衆の使うきびきびした言葉. ¶a ***rhetorical*** *expression* 美辞麗句. ¶***roundabout*** *expressions*＝periphrases 遠回しの言葉. ¶a ***rueful*** *expression* 浮かぬ顔. ¶This finds ***sentimental*** *expression* in popular songs. これが歌謡曲に感傷的な言葉となって現われている. ¶have a persistently ***sour*** *expression* ...にはしつようなまでひねくれた表現がある. ¶a ***stereotyped*** *expression* 定りきった文句. ¶a ***suggestive*** *expression* 思わせぶりな表現. ¶His face wore a very ***surprised*** (***annoyed*** *or* ***concerned***) *expression*. 彼は非常に驚いた(困った, 心配そうな)顔付きをしている. ¶***tame*** *expressions* 平凡な言葉. ¶a ***tangible*** *expression* of sympathy [口先だけでなく物質的な]同情の実質的表現 ‖ This present is a ***tangible*** *expression* of their esteem. この贈物は彼らの敬意を端的に表わしたものである. ¶***technical*** *expressions* for ... ...の専門語. ¶***tender*** *expression* of condolence 心からの弔意. ¶his ***terrified*** *expression* 彼のびっくりした顔付き. ¶Tennyson's gift of ***terse*** and ***vivid*** *expression* テニスンの簡明で生々した表現をなしうる才能. ¶these ***three*** *expressions* of opinion これら三つの見解. ¶a ***trite*** and ***hackneyed*** *expression* きまり文句. ¶a ***turgid*** *expression* 誇張した表現. ¶the literary value of a fresh ***unhackneyed*** *expression* 使い古しでない新しい言葉の文学的価値. ¶an ***unseemly*** *expression* 不体裁な言葉. ¶the ***verbal*** or ***written*** *expression* of one's thoughts 口頭または書面による所感. ¶He has a ***vivacious*** *expression*. 彼の表情は発らつとしている. ¶a ***weary*** *expression* 退屈そうなようす. ¶***widespread*** *expressions* of discontent with the present state of things 社会の現状に対する広く耳にする不満の声. ¶indulge in ***wild*** *expressions* of emotion 奔放な言回しを盛んに使って感情をさらけ出す. ¶a ***wistful*** *expression* もの欲しげな表情. ¶with a ***woebegone*** *expression* on his face なさけない顔付きをして. ¶He had a ***worn, weary*** *expression*. 彼はやつれて疲れた顔をしていた.

Q² ***everyday*** *expression* 日常語. ¶Some ***slang*** *expressions* are vigorous, expressive, and picturesque. 俗語的表現の中には力強い, 表現の豊かなかつ生々したものがある. ¶***underworld*** *expressions* 下層社会(ギャング)の言葉.

P I feel a sense of satisfaction and gratitude ***beyond*** *expression*. 私は言い知れない満足と感謝の念をいだいている. ‖ ***beyond*** the *expression* of words 言葉で言表わし得ない. ¶I thank you ***for*** your *expression* of appreciation. あなたのほめ言葉に対し感謝します. ¶concise ***in*** *expression* 表現の簡潔な. ¶be petulant ***in*** *expression* 言方がつっけんどんである. ¶***notwithstanding*** effusive *expressions* of international "amity" and of "cooperation" 国際的「親善」とか「協力」とかいう語をあきるほど聞くにもかかわらず. ¶the lucidity ***of*** *expression* 表現の明快 ‖ turns ***of*** *expressions* 言回し ‖ his way ***of*** *expression* 彼の表現法. ¶be included ***under*** the *expression* "..."「...」の句の下に包括してある. ¶***with*** an *expression* of his cast-iron phiz 鋳鉄のような顔付きをして ‖ ***with*** a puzzled *expression* 困った顔をして ‖ ***with*** an *expression* of appreciation for ... ...に感謝の意を表して ‖ speak (play) ***with*** *expression* 表情豊かに話す(奏する).

P² An *expression* ***of*** shame crossed his face. はじらいの色が彼の顔に現われた ‖ *expression* ***of*** the eyes 目つき ‖ an *expression* ***of*** opinion 意見の表示.

expressive, *a.* 言表わす, 表現する. 「十分に表現する.

M ***really*** and ***adequately*** *expressive* of ... ...を本当にかつ

P a face *expressive* ***of*** satisfaction (joy, sorrow) 満足(など)の面持. 【類】a look *expressive* ***of*** hope (despair).

expropriate, *v.* (土地を)収用する.

P *expropriate* a person ***from*** an estate 人から地所を取り上げる.

expropriation, *n.* [土地の]収用.

P² *expropriation* ***of*** land 土地収用.

expulsion, *n.* 放逐, 除名.

V ***demand*** his *expulsion* from the country 彼の国外放逐を要求する.

Q ***private*** *expulsion* 村八分.

Q² the ***mass*** *expulsion* of Greeks from Asia Minor in 1922 一九二二年の小アジアからのギリシア人の大量放逐.

P² *expulsion* [***of*** a boy] ***from*** a school 放校 ‖ *expulsion* ***from*** a club クラブからの除名. 【類】*expulsion* ***of*** air ***from*** the lungs.

expurgate, *v.* [不当の文句など]削除する.

P *expurgate* one's mss. ***for*** publication 出版のため原稿からぐあいの悪い語句を削る.

expurgatory, *n.* 〖カトリック〗禁書目録.

Q² ***Index*** *Expurgatorius*＝Expurgatory Index [カトリック教の]一部禁書目録.

extend, *v.* 延長する; 伸ばす, 及ぼす; 拡張する; 張る; 伸びる.

M *extending* ***back*** many generations 過去数代にわたって. ¶By this time the fire had ***greatly*** *extended* itself. このときまでに火は大分燃え広がっていた. ¶The Aryans *extended* ***westward***. アリアン民族は西方に伸びて行った. ¶The plains *extend* [***far*** and] ***wide***. その平野は広々とひろがっている.

P *extend* a rope ***across*** the street 往来を横切ってなわを張る. ¶his knowledge of Russian does not *extend* ***beyond*** ... 彼のロシア語の知識は...の程度を越えない ‖ His power *extends* ***beyond*** the seas. 彼の勢力は海外に及んでいる. ¶The exhibition will *extend* (＝remain open) ***for*** a fortnight. 展覧会は二週間にわたる. ¶*extend* ***for*** miles around 数マイルにわたる. ¶*extending* ***from*** Monday ***to*** the early hours of Thursday morning 月曜から木曜の早朝にかけて ‖ his visit will *extend* ***from*** ... ***to*** ... 彼の訪問(期間)は...より...に及ぶだろう. 【類】*extend* the railway ***from*** A ***to*** B / Its commerce *extended* ***from*** China ***to*** Europe. ¶in cases where a stay *extends* ***into*** months 滞在数カ月にわたる場合には ‖ His knowledge *extends* ***into*** many corners of Mohammedan history. 彼の知識はマホメット教史のすみずみにまで及んでいる. ¶His researches *extended* ***over*** ten years. 彼の研究は十カ年にわたった. 【類】The festival *extends* ***over*** three days. / The strike *extended* ***over*** ten weeks. / His peculation (公金私消) *extended* ***over*** [a period of] several years. / preliminary study (準備的研究) *extending* ***over*** two years / *extend* ***over*** a period of fifty years. ¶This river *extends* ***through*** several countries. この川は流域数カ国にわたっている. ¶The chapter *extends* ***to*** a hundred pages. その章は百ページにわたっている. 【類】The first volume *extends* ***to*** 362 pages. / The passage (渡航) *extends* ***to*** 12 days and two hours. / *extend* the book ***to*** three volumes / the railway line *extends* ***to*** the length of ... miles ‖ *extend* an invitation (a congratulation) ***to*** ... ...を招待(慶賀)する ‖ *extend* a call ***to*** the Rev. Dr. ... to the pastorate of the church ...師を同教会の牧師に招く ‖ *extend* a helping hand ***to*** (＝***towards***) the poor 貧者に救いの手を伸ばす ‖ *extend* the benefits ***to*** the outsiders 局外者にも利益を及ぼす ‖ Endeavour to get the time *extended* ***until*** the end of next month. 来月の末まで延期してもらうように尽力して下さい.

extension, *n.* 拡張; 増築; 延長; 延期; 科外講座.

V ***enjoy*** a greater *extension* of liberty 一層大きな自由を享受する. ¶***get*** (＝have) an *extension* [支払などを]延期してもらう. ¶***give*** an *extension* [支払などを]延期する ‖ I cannot ***give*** [an] *extension* of time. 延期はできない. ¶***grant*** a further *extension* of ... ...をさらに延期する. ¶I must ***have*** an *extension* of time. 猶予してもらわなければならない. ¶A further *extension* is ***required***. もっと延期してもら

う必要がある. ¶in order to *secure* an *extension* 延期してもらうために. ¶I *want* an *extension* until ... ...まで延期してもらいたい.

Q *colonial extension* 植民地の膨張. ¶*considerable extensions* of a work 工場の著しい拡張. ¶*figurative extension* of the meaning of words 語義のひゆ的拡大. ¶a *new extension* built on the old school 古い校舎に接する新しい増築. ¶the *phenomenal extension* of the merchant fleet was chiefly achieved through ... 商船の驚くべき拡張は主に...によって遂げられた.

Q² *business extensions* 支店, 営業所など. ¶*library extension* 図書館拡張. ¶*railway extension* 鉄道の延長. ¶allow a *six-month extension* of his permitted stay 氏の認可された滞在期間六カ月の延長を許す. ¶*time extension* 日延べ. ¶*university extension* 大学公開(科外)講座.

P originally it meant "..."; *by extension* it has come to mean "..." もとは「...」の意味であったが段々転じて今では「...」を意味するようになった.

P² *extension of* enlistment 服役延期 ‖ the *extension of* education *among* the working classes 労働階級における教育の普及.

extent, *n.* 範囲; 程度, 限度; びょうぼうたる所.

V *ascertain* the *extent* of ... ...の範囲を確定する. ¶*reach* an almost morbid *extent* ほとんど病的の程度に達する ‖ *reach* the *extent* of one's intended pilgrimage 予定の巡礼の最終点に達する. ¶*reduce* the *extent* of the law's application 法の適用範囲を制限する. ¶in order to *view* the *extent* of the stock 在庫品の範囲を知るために.

Q to an almost *alarming extent* ほとんど驚くべき程度に. ¶to an *appalling extent* 驚くべき程度に. ¶to an *appreciable extent* 目立つ位に. 【類】to any *appreciable extent*. ¶The sky is of *boundless extent*. 天空は際限なく広い. ¶to a *certain extent* ある程度まで. ¶to a *considerable extent* 著しく. ¶to a *dreadful extent* 恐ろしい程度に. ¶The matter was carried to a *foolish extent*. その件はばかばかしいことになった. ¶utilize to the *fullest extent* 十分に利用する. ¶to a *good extent* 相当に. ¶The adult is to a *great extent* a bundle of habits. 大人は癖の固まりみたいなものである. 【類】It was to a *great extent* his own fault. / to a *greater extent* than heretofore. ¶to an *important extent* 余ほど. ¶The results of his investigations are to a *large extent* accepted to this day. 彼の研究の結果は今日においても大分是認されている. ¶to the *least extent* 最小限度に. ¶to a *lesser extent* よりわずかに. ¶to a *limited extent* 幾分. ¶to a *not inconsiderable extent* かなりの程度に. ¶to a *ridiculous extent* おかしいほど. ¶to the *same extent* as ... ...と同一程度に. ¶to a very *slight extent* ごくささいな程度に. ¶to a *small extent* 少しばかり. ¶To *some extent* you are right. ある程度までは君の言う通りだ. ‖ to *such* an *extent* as to ... ...するほどに. 【類】it has developed to *such* an *extent* that ... ¶to *that extent* それほど. ¶to an *undue extent* 過度に. ¶to the very *utmost extent* 極度に. ¶a *vast extent* of a fertile plain びょうぼうとした沃野(よくや). ¶in the *whole extent* of Japanese territory 日本全土にわたって.

P They were cheering *at* the full *extent* of their lungs. 彼らは声を限りに歓呼していた. ¶*in* its full *extent* 十分に, 一杯に ‖ make long marches, days *in extent* 数日にわたる長行軍をやる. ¶co-operate *to* the *extent* of ... ...の程度まで協力する ‖ You may go *to* the *extent* that ... ...という点まではやってもよろしい. ‖ May I bother you *to* the *extent* of outing your opinion on this matter? この件に関してせめて御意見だけでもうかがわれましょうか. ‖ *To* what *extent* are you concerned? どの程度ご関係がおありですか. ‖ Sellers refuse to sell *to* any *extent* at present low prices. 業者は今の安値では販売は一切断わっている. 【類】he may be trusted *to* the *extent* of ...

P² What is the *extent of* damage? 損害はどの程度ですか. ‖ the *extent of* his travels 彼の旅行の全行程.

extenuation, *n.* 軽減, しゃく量.

P He pleaded circumstances *in extenuation* of his guilt. 情状しゃく量による減刑を申立てた.

exterior, *n.* 外面, 外ぼう.

V manage to *keep* the *exterior* どうにかこうにか外面をつくろって行く.

Q a man of *fine exterior* りっぱな容姿の人. ¶a man of *prepossessing exterior* 人好きのする容ぼうの人. ¶Under his *stupid exterior* there may lie a heart of gold. あんな間抜け面をしているが心の中は黄金なのかも知れない. ¶an old maid who on account of a somewhat *unattractive exterior* had failed to obtain a husband 面が少しまずいので夫を持ちそこねた老嬢.

P The portable house for fowls is covered *on* the *exterior* with tar paper. 移動鶏舎は外側にコールターを塗った紙が張ってある.

exterminate, *v.* 絶やす.

M It was *exterminated root and branch*. それは根こそぎ絶やされた.

O *exterminate* vermin (rats, fleas, lice, bedbugs, mice) 害虫(など)を絶やす.

extermination, *n.* 根絶.

P² the *extermination of* the H. family H家の家系中絶 ‖ the *extermination of* Christianity キリスト教の撲滅.

externals, *n. pl.* 外形, 儀礼.

V He is better at *observing externals* than at reading hearts. あの男は奥底を見すかさないで上っ面を見る癖がある.

Q *mere externals* [真髄にふれない]ほんの外面的のこと.

extinct, *a.* 死滅した.

M become *automatically extinct* 自然消滅になる. ¶It is now *practically extinct*. それは今では絶滅しているも同然だ.

extinction, *n.* 絶滅.

Q² *fire extinction* 消火.

P² on the *extinction of* heirs male 男系の相続人が絶えたので.

extinguish, *v.* [光などを]消す; 光を失わせる.

M Even the last gleam of his hope was *sadly extinguished*. 彼の最後の望みの光すらあわれにも消滅した. ¶he seems *utterly extinguished* by his brother in ... ...の点では彼は全然兄(弟)に歯が立たないようだ.

extinguisher, *n.* 消火器.

Q a *chemical extinguisher* 化学消火器.

Q² a *fire extinguisher* 消火器.

extol, *v.* 賞揚する.

P He was *extolled as* the founder of their Florentine school. 彼はフロレンス派の創始者として賞揚された. ¶*extol* a person *to* the skies 人を激賞する. ¶*extol* him *with* ecstatic enthusiasm 無我夢中に彼をほめ立てる.

extort, *v.* 無理に取る.

P *extort* money *from* a person 人から金をしぼる ‖ *extort* a confession (promise) *from* a person 無理に白状(など)させる ‖ *extort* a meaning *from* a word 無理な解釈をする. 【類】My agonies *extorted* tears *from* me.

extortion, *n.* ゆすり.

V *practice extortions* ゆする.

extra, *n.* 余分の物, 別勘定; 号外.

V The bill *contains* a good many *extras*. 付けには別勘定のものがかなり付いている. ¶The London papers *issued extras* for every bulletin. ロンドンの諸新聞は公報の出るごとに号外を出した. ¶*pay* a little *extra* to a chauffeur 運転手に少し酒手をやる.

P² You must pay *extra for* a larger room. 大きいへやの方は割増を取られる. ¶an *extra to* the Asahi 朝日新聞の号外.

extract, *n.* 抜粋, 抜書.

V *make extracts* 抜粋する. ¶*read extracts* from ... ...の抜書を読む. ¶*reproduce extracts* from ...の抜書を複写する.

Q *choice extracts* from the writings of ... ...の著作物からの抜粋. ¶*copious extracts* 豊富な抜書. ¶*garbled extracts* [勝手に手を入れた]改ざん抜すい本. ¶make very *liberal extracts* どしどし抜書する.

P² *extracts from* Shakespeare シェクスピア抄本 ‖ an *extract from* a letter (book) 手紙(本)からの抜粋.

extract, *v.* 抜取る; しぼり取る.

P *extract* examples *from* ... ...から見本(実例)を抜く ‖ The bullet was *extracted from* a wound in his body. 彼の体のきず口からその弾丸を抜取った. ‖ *extract* essential oil *from* flowers 花から精油をしぼり取る. 【類】*extract* pleasure *from* daily toil / *from* which I *extract* the following:—

extraction, *n.* 抽取; 家系, 血統, 出所.

Q a family of *ancient extraction* 旧家. ¶words of *French extraction* in English 英語中のフランス語系の語. ¶He was of *humble extraction* 彼は微賤(びせん)から身を起した. ¶Americans of *Japanese extraction* 日系米人. ¶He was born of *low extraction*. 彼はいやしい家柄だ. ¶a lady of *Portuguese extraction* ポルトガル系の婦人. ¶with a population of only 2,000 souls, mostly of ***Scotch*** and ***Irish*** *extraction* 人口わずかに二千を有しその大部分はスコットランド系とアイルランド系だ. ¶a Chinese of ***Southern*** *extraction* 南方系(出身)の中国人.

Q² the cyanide process of ***gold extraction*** 金抽出のための「シアン化法.

P a Welshman ***by extraction*** 血統はウェールス人.

P² the *extraction* ***of*** iron ***from*** its ores 鉱石からの製鉄 ‖ *extraction* or rendition ***of*** fugitives 逃亡犯罪人の引渡し.

extravagance, *n.* 無茶, 濫行; 濫費.

V ***check*** Government *extravagance* 政府の濫費を抑制する. ¶***commit*** *extravagances* とっぴなことをする. ¶***cut out*** all his *extravagances* 彼の濫費を一切節約する. ¶It necessarily ***involves*** a needless *extravagance* of expenditure. それには必然的に無用の濫費が伴う.

Q ***heedless*** *extravagance* 不注意な濫費. ¶on ***unjustified*** *extravagance* 不正の濫費をして.

P He has run through all his fortune ***through*** *extravagance.* 彼は財産をことごとくらん費してしまった.

extravagant, *a.* 放縦な, ぜいたくな.

P *extravagant* ***in*** expenditure 金使いが荒い ‖ *extravagant* ***in*** one's way of living 暮し向きのぜいたくな ‖ *extravagant* ***in*** dress 着道楽の ‖ *extravagant* ***in*** conduct 行の放縦な ‖ be *extravagant* ***in*** his admiration of ... ...を盛んにほめる, ...を激賞する. ¶He is too *extravagant* ***with*** his clothes. 彼は着物におごり過ぎる.

extreme, *n.* 極端, 極度.

V Extremes ***breed*** *extreme.* 極端は極端を生む. ¶*Extremes* ***meet.*** 〖諺〗両極端は一致する. ¶***represent*** two *extremes* of opinion 両極端の見解を示す.

Q It was carried to an ***absurd*** *extreme.* それをばかげて極端までやった. ¶push it to a ***dangerous*** *extreme* それを危険な極端まで押通す. ¶carry it to the ***full*** *extreme* それをやれる所までやる. ¶carry it to the ***furthest*** *extreme* それを行詰まる所までやる. ¶run into an ***opposite*** *extreme* 反対の極端に走る. ¶go to the ***other*** *extreme* その正反対の極端に走る. ¶in the ***perilous*** *extreme* 危険をともなうほど極度に. ¶push it to a ***ridiculous*** *extreme* それをばかばかしいほど極端にやる.

P the golden means ***between*** the two *extremes* 両極端の中庸. ¶It would be foolish ***in*** the *extreme.* それは愚の極だ. 【類】ridiculous ***in*** the *extreme* / be wearisome ***in*** the *extreme* / be disappointing ***in*** the *extreme.* ¶run ***to*** an *extreme*＝go ***to*** *extremes* 極端に走る ‖ go ***to*** the *extreme* of ... ...という極端な手段をとる ‖ exposed ***to*** *extremes* of cold 極寒にさらされて.

P² *extremes* ***of*** fortune 浮沈, 栄枯盛衰. ¶the two *extremes* ***of*** the social scale 社会階級の両極端.

extremism, *n.* 極端(過激)主義.

Q ***political*** *extremism* 政治的過激主義(左派・右派とも).

extremist, *n.* 過激論者(主義者).

Q² a ***leftist*** *extremist* 極左派の人.

extremity, *n.* 極端; 窮境, 危地.

V ***expect*** the *extremity* 決死の覚悟をきめる.

Q be driven to the ***last*** *extremity* 最後のどたん場に追い込まれる. ¶the ***lower*** *extremities* 脚部.

P ***at*** its northern *extremity* その北端に. 【類】***at*** the southern *extremity* of a peninsula. ¶He is ***in*** *extremity.* 彼は窮境にある. ‖ What shall I do ***in*** this *extremity?* こう行詰まってはどうしたらよいものか. ¶The city is reduced ***to*** *extremity.* 市は危地に陥った. ‖ drive him ***to*** *extremity* 彼を窮地に陥れる ‖ go (＝proceed) ***to*** *extremities* 断固たる非常手段に訴える.

extricate, *v.* 救い出す, 脱せしめる.

M *extricate* oneself ***gracefully*** りっぱに身を引く.

P *extricate* oneself ***from*** (＝***out of***) a crisis (difficulty, ruin) 難局(など)を脱する ‖ *extricate* a friend ***from*** debt 友の負債を片付けてやる.

exuberance, *n.* 繁茂; 豊富.

P² *exuberance* ***of*** foliage 茂った枝葉 ‖ *exuberance* ***of*** joy (delight, mirth) あふれる喜び.

exuberant, *a.* おい繁った, 豊かな.

P be *exuberant* ***in*** the growth of vegetables 野菜の生長が著しい ‖ *exuberant* ***in*** zeal (energy, spirit) 熱意(など)あふ⌊れて.

exult, *v.* 勝ち誇る, こおどりする.

M ***Inwardly*** she *exulted.* 彼女は心ひそかに得意であった.

P He *exulted* ***at*** the happy change. 彼はこの好転に対してこおどりした. ¶He *exulted* ***in*** his success. 彼は成功にこおどりした. 【類】*exult* ***in*** one's victory. ¶He *exulted* ***over*** his fallen enemy. 彼は敗れた敵に勝ち誇った.

O he *exulted* to find that ... 彼は...と分って大いに喜んだ.

exultant, *a.* 大喜びの.

M be ***naturally*** *exultant* over ... 当然...に対して胸をおど「らしている.

exultation, *n.* 大喜び, 狂喜.

Q The multitude shouted with ***savage*** *exultation.* 群集は熱狂的に歓呼した.

P ***with*** *exultations* in our souls 衷心大いに喜んで.

P² There was *exultation* ***over*** the naval victory.

eye, *n.* 目; 眼識, 見地; 注目, 注意; 目付, ようす; 望み, 意向; 眼目.

V ***abase*** (＝cast down) the *eye* 目を伏せる. ¶***affront*** the *eye* 目ざわりになる. ¶There is much to ***arrest*** the *eye* of the traveller. 大いに旅客の目を引くものがある. ¶***avert*** (＝turn away) one's *eyes* from ... ...から目を転じる. ¶***avoiding*** the *eyes* of others 人目をしのんで. ¶***bandage*** one's *eyes* 目を包帯する. ¶I cannot ***believe*** my *eyes.* これ(今見ていること)が本当かと驚く. ‖ He could scarcely ***believe*** his *eyes.* 彼は自分の目を疑った. ¶***bend*** one's *eyes* on ... ...に目を向ける. ¶***blear*** one's *eyes* 人の目をくらます, あざむく. ¶***blind*** the *eyes* of ... ...の目をくらます. ¶His *eyes* were ***blindfolded.*** 彼の目には目隠しが当てられていた. ¶***blink*** one's *eyes* またたきする. ¶***blur*** the *eyes* with tears 涙で目をくもらせる. 【類】My *eyes* are ***blurred*** today. ¶To see the scenes of the past one must ***borrow*** the *eyes* of the past. 過去の情景を見るには過去の身になって見なければならない. ¶***carry*** the *eye* from one to the other 一物より他物に目を移す. ¶***cast*** one's *eyes* upon (＝on) ... ...の方に目を投げる ‖ ***cast*** an *eye* at ... ...に目をやる ‖ trusting that whenever Mr. ... happens to ***cast*** his *eyes* on these lines, he will remember his lessons from ... ...氏がたまたまこの数行の文句を見た時は...から習ったことがあると思い出して下さるでしょう[教師から生徒に贈った本に記した文句]. ¶***cast*** one's *eyes* stealthily ***about*** こっそりあたりに目をくれる. ¶***cast down*** one's *eyes* 目を伏せる. ¶***cast up*** one's *eyes* 見上げる. ¶readily ***catch*** the *eye* すぐ目に付く. 【類】the first object which ***catches*** our *eye* as we go into the room is ... / if this should ***catch*** his *eye* / try to ***catch*** the *eye* of ... / I underlined the idiomatic parts of the sentence (文章の慣用語の下に線を引いた) to ***catch*** your *eye.* / At that moment something ***caught*** my *eye* that I desired to photograph. ¶when the *eyes* of the world are ***centred*** on the Far East 世界の耳目が極東に集中されているときに. ¶He has never ***clapped*** *eyes* on her again. 彼は二度と彼女に会わなかった. ¶***close*** one's *eye* on ... ...を見ながら(眠ってまたは死んで)目をつぶる. ‖ These are facts to which we cannot ***close*** (＝shut) our *eyes.* これらはわれわれの看過し得ない事実だ. 【類】we cannot ***close*** our *eyes* to the evidence that ... ‖ ***close*** the *eyes* of one's father 父の死目にあう. ¶***cock*** an *eye* at ... ...の方に目くばせする. ¶One ***comforts*** the *eye* as one gazes across the harbor. 港のかなたのながめは見て美しい. ¶***completing*** the *eyes* of a painted dragon 画竜点睛(せい). ¶***cover*** one's *eyes* with one's hand 片手で両目をおおう. ¶She ***cried*** her *eyes* ***out.*** 彼女は目を泣きはらした. ¶***dazzle*** one's *eyes* [光で]人目をくらます. ¶The beautiful scenery ***delighted*** my *eye.* その美しい風景が私の目を喜ばせた. 【類】the *eye* is constantly ***delighted*** by .... ¶The *eyes* of all Europe and America are now ***directed*** towards China. 欧米人の注意は今や中国に向けられている. 【類】All *eyes* were ***directed*** toward the door. ¶***drop*** one's *eyes* 伏目になる. ¶***dry*** one's wet *eyes* with (＝on) a handkerchief ぬれた目をハンカチでふく. ¶***dull*** the *eye* 目を曇らせる. ¶***educate*** the *eye* 目を肥やす. ¶There is something chic about her which ***engages*** the *eye.* 彼女には人目を引きつけるいきな所がある. ¶No topic of the hour ***escapes*** the eagle *eyes* of Mr. Punch. 時事問題は何一つパンチ誌の鋭い目から漏れるものはない. ¶***fasten*** one's *eyes* upon ... ...を見詰める. ¶***feast*** one's *eyes* with (＝on) everchanging scenery of rare beauty 変化きわまりない絶景に見とれる. ¶I ***felt*** his *eyes* narrowly upon me, but could not look at him. 彼にじっと見られているなと感じたが彼をまともに見ることはできなかった. ¶***fill*** the *eye* with pleasure 目を十分に喜ばせる. ¶***fix*** one's *eyes* full upon

… …をまともに見る ‖ the *eyes* of the world are at the present moment ***fixed*** upon … 世界の注意は今や…に向けられている. ¶***give*** an *eye* to … …に幾分注意する ‖ ***give*** one a black *eye* 鉄拳をくらわして目の縁にあざをこしらえさせる. ¶His head would have ***gladdened*** the *eyes* and heart of an artist. 彼の頭は芸術家が喜ぶようなものであった. ‖ ***gladden*** his mother's *eyes* with … …で母の目を喜ばせる. ¶***goggle*** one's *eyes* 目をぎょろつかせる. ¶***gouge out*** the *eyes* of … with thumbs 親指で…の目玉をえぐりとる. ¶the first thing that ***greets*** the *eye* まず目に入る物 ‖ our *eyes* are ***greeted*** with … …がわれわれの目に入った ‖ should these lines ***greet*** the *eye* of … この手紙が…の目にふれるようなことがあれば. ¶He ***has*** an *eye* for the fair and the beautiful. 彼には審美眼がある. ‖ one who ***has*** an *eye* for beauty and a heart for associations 自然の美と史趣を解する人 ‖ ***have*** an *eye* to the property 財産に目をつける ‖ I ***had*** my *eye* on this house long before I bought it. 私は買う余ほど以前からこの家に目をつけていた. ‖ ***have*** an *eye* to the future 将来に目を向ける. ¶minor celebrities who have in some form or other ***held*** the public *eye* あれやこれやで公衆の目を引いた二流所の名士たち. ¶***hold down*** one's *eyes* 下を見る. ¶***hurt*** the *eyes* by small print 小さい字で目を痛める. ¶***injure*** one's *eyes* 目を痛める. ¶***intrigue*** the *eye* 目の正月をさせる. ¶***Keep*** your *eyes* upon him. 彼に目をつけろ. ‖ I asked my neighbour to ***keep*** an *eye* on my house. 私は家を気を付けて下さいと隣りの人に頼んだ. ‖ She ***kept*** her *eyes* on the ground for some time. 彼女はしばらくうつむいていた. ‖ a man that I cannot ***keep*** my *eyes* ***off*** 目が離されない人 ‖ ***keep*** one's *eye* open 用心する. ¶I have not ***laid*** eyes ***on*** him for a week. 私は一週間も彼に会わない. ¶***leer*** the *eye* しり目に見る. ¶***let*** your *eye* ***travel*** to … お目を…にお留め下さい. ¶***lift*** [***up***] one's *eyes* 目を上げる. 【類】***lift up*** our *eyes* unto the hills. ¶A smile ***lighted up*** the keen *eyes*. にっこり笑って鋭い目を光らせた. ¶***lose*** an *eye* 一眼を失う. ¶***lower*** one's *eyes* 目を落す. ¶She ***made*** *eyes* at me. 彼女は僕にウインクを送った. ‖ ***make*** sheep's *eyes* at … …にウインクを送る ‖ ***make*** the *eye* ***keener*** to see the beauties of nature 自然の美に対して目をもっと敏感にする ‖ ***make*** the *eye* ***smart*** 目がぴりつく ‖ The smoke from the logs burning in the fireplace ***made*** our *eyes* ***water***. 炉に燃える丸太の煙で私たちは涙が出た. ¶***meet*** one's *eye* 目に付く ‖ She could not ***meet*** my *eye*. 彼女は[心にやましいことがあるので]私の方を見ることができなかった. ¶His *eyes* are seldom ***moistened*** by a tear or his features relaxed by a smile. 彼はめったに涙をこぼしたりにっこり笑って相好をくずしたりしない. ¶***offend*** the *eye* 目ざわりになる ‖ He drew the blinds so that the light should not ***offend*** his *eyes*. 光が目にさわらないように彼は日よけを下げた. ¶The remark ***opened*** my *eyes*. その言葉に私は目を見張った. 【類】***open*** one's *eyes* questioningly / make a person ***open*** his *eyes* ‖ ***open*** the *eyes* of the people to … 国民を…に目ざめさせる. 【類】***open*** the public's *eyes* to the importance of … / The exhibition ***opened*** Japanese *eyes* to what Europe and America were doing. / ***open*** their *eyes* to the absolutely vital nature of scientific research in its bearing on industrial prosperity (産業の発展に関係ある) / Two years in France had ***opened*** his *eyes* to the beauty of his own countryside (郷里). ¶to stimulate the intellect as well as to ***please*** the *eye* 目を楽しませると同時に知能を啓発するために. ¶***pluck out*** an *eye* 眼球を抜取る. ¶wear sunglasses to ***protect*** the *eye* from the glare of the sun 強い日光から目をまもるためにサングラスをかける. ¶***put out*** his own *eyes* in order not to see … …を見ないように自分の目をつぶした. ¶***raise*** one's *eyes* to heaven 天を仰ぐ. ¶He ***rolled*** his *eyes*. 彼は目をくりくりさせた. ¶***rub*** one's *eyes* in surprise (間違いではないかと)驚いて目をこする. 【類】***rub*** one's *eyes* and stare at … / that makes us ***rub*** our *eyes*, wondering whether … ¶***run*** one's *eye* over a map on the wall 壁にかけた地図に目を走らす ‖ He ***ran*** (=***swept***) his *eyes* over us. 彼はわれわれを見回した. ¶It is the most awful out-of-the-world ledge of a place you'll ever ***set*** *eyes* on if you live to a hundred. それは君が百まで生きればいつか一度見ることができるような恐ろしく辺びな所だ. ‖ ***set*** one's *eye* dancing with delight 喜んで目をきょときょとさせる. ¶***shading*** his *eyes* with his hand 目に手をかざして. ¶***shock*** our *eyes* われわれの目を驚かす. ¶***shun*** the public *eye* 人目を忍ぶ. ¶***shut*** one's *eyes* to the defects その欠点を看過する ‖ we do not of course ***shut*** our *eyes* to the fact that … われわれはもちろん…の事実を不問に付しはしない. 【類】deliberately ***shut*** one's *eyes* to the truth / ***shut*** one's *eyes* to a disagreeable fact (いやなこと) / ***shut*** their *eyes* to the true situation. ¶***strain*** one's *eyes* 目を見張る. ¶The building ***strikes*** (=catches) the *eye* at once. その建物はすぐに目につく. 【類】immediately ***strikes*** the *eyes*. ¶Her *eyes* were ***suffused*** with tears. 彼女の目は涙で一杯だった. ¶he never ***took*** his *eyes* from … 彼は決して…から目を離さなかった. ¶She seemed hardly able to ***take*** her *eyes* ***off*** the thing. 彼女は殆どその物から目を離すことができなかったらしい. ¶He ran mad and ***tore off*** (=***out***) his own *eyes*. 彼は気が狂って自分の目の玉をえぐりとった. ¶***throw*** one's *eyes* to … …に目を向ける. ¶***turn*** his *eyes* longingly to … …にあこがれの目を向ける ‖ He ***turned*** his *eyes* another way (=aside). 彼は目を他へそらした. 【類】all the *eyes* were ***turned*** toward … / the goal towards which all workers in artistic London ***turn*** their *eyes*. ¶***turn away*** our *eyes* from … …からわれわれの目を転じる. ¶He ***turned up*** his *eyes*. 彼は目を上に向けた. ¶***twinkle*** one's *eyes* 目をきらめかす. ¶He evidently ***used*** his *eyes*. 確かに彼は目を使った(上の空ではいなかった). ¶***wear out*** our *eyes* with looking at … …を熟視して目を疲らせる. ¶***weary*** the *eye* 目を疲らす. ¶***wink*** one's *eye* まばたきをする. ¶***wipe*** one's *eyes* 目をぬぐう.

V² Her *eyes* were ***blazing*** as she heard how cruelly the children were treated. 子供たちがいかにひどい取扱いを受けたかを聞いた時彼女の目はきらめいた. ¶Her *eyes* ***danced*** with malice. 彼女の目は意地悪げにくるくると回った. ¶the *eye* ***dwells*** with delight upon … …に目を奪われる. ¶Her *eyes* ***fell***. 彼女は伏目になった. ‖ My *eye* ***fell*** on this: 一次のことが私の目にふれた. ¶My *eyes* ***filled***. 私は目に涙が一杯になった. ¶Her *eyes* ***filmed*** with tears. 彼女の目は涙でくもった. ¶His *eyes* ***flashed*** like lightning. 彼の目は電光のように光った. ¶Her *eyes* ***glistened*** with tears. 彼女の目は涙で光った. ¶His *eyes* ***grew blood-shot***. 彼の目は血走った. ¶Our *eyes* almost ***leaped*** from their sockets in awestruck astonishment. びっくり仰天目の玉が飛びだすばかりであった. ¶Her *eyes* ***lighted*** on me. 私は彼女の目にふれた. ‖ My *eye* ***lighted*** on a curious sign. 妙な看板が僕の目にとまった. ¶Their *eyes* ***met***. 二人の視線が合った. ¶as far as the *eye* can ***reach*** 目の届く限り. ¶the *eye* ***rests*** with pleasure on … …が目を喜ばせる. 【類】My *eyes* ***rested*** upon a terrible sight. ¶My *eyes* ***smart*** intolerably. (タバコなどで)目がひどく痛む. ¶Her *eyes* ***squinted*** when she took off her glasses. 彼女は目がねをはずしたら目が細くなった(近眼のため). ¶I felt as if my *eyes* ***started*** [***out***] from my head. [恐怖・憤怒などの結果]目の玉が飛びだしたかと思った. ¶toward the east, the *eye* ***travels*** over … 東の方…の上に目が走る. 【類】his *eyes* ***traveling*** eagerly over the floor, noted a spot where … ¶His *eyes* ***twinkled*** with joy. 彼の目は喜びできらめいた. ¶His *eye* ***wandered*** round the room. 彼はへやをぐるっと見まわした.

Q ***alert eyes*** 鋭い目. ¶an ***angry eye*** 怒った目付(ようす). ¶see with an ***artist's eye*** 芸術家の目で見る. ¶***asymmetrical eyes*** 不ぞろいの目. ¶***azure-blue eyes*** そら色の目. ¶***beautiful*** *eyes* 美しい目. ¶a ***black*** (=***blackened***) *eye* なぐられてあざのできた目. 【類】He got a ***black eye***. ‖ a child with ***black eyes*** 目の黒い子 ‖ He is a ***black eye*** to our family. あいつはうちの恥さらしだ. ¶***black, sparkling eyes*** 黒いきらきら光る目. ¶***blear eyes*** かすんだ目. ¶turn a ***blind eye*** 見て見ないふりをする. ¶***blindfolded*** *eyes* 目隠しされた目. 【類】the goddess with ***blindfolded eyes***. ¶have ***bloodshot*** *eyes* 血まなこになる. ¶***blue eyes*** 青目. ¶with ***bound eyes*** 目を包帯して. ¶***bright eyes*** ぱっちりした目. ¶watch … with ***bulging eyes*** and open mouth [驚いて]目を見張り口あんぐりで…を見る. ¶look with ***calm, scrutinizing eyes*** 冷静に穴のあくほど見る. ¶***clear eyes*** 澄んだ目. ¶Many a good picture does not appeal to the ***commercial eyes***. 良い絵でも商売人が手を出さないのがいくらもある. ¶My inward eye suspected a forgery before my ***corporeal eye*** beheld the object. 実物を見ない前にこれはにせ物だなと腹で感じた. ¶cast (=

set) one's ***covetous eyes*** upon (=on) ... …のどから手が出る. ¶coldly ***critical eyes*** あくまで批判的な目 ‖ cast a ***critical eye*** upon ... …に批判的な目を向ける. 【類】 keep a ***critical eye*** on ... ¶***cunning eyes*** こうかつな目付. ¶become an object of ***curious eyes*** 人から好奇の目で見られる. ¶Hide it where ***curious eyes*** won't see it. それを物見高い人の目につかない所に隠しておきなさい. ¶***deep eyes*** くぼんだ目 ‖ His *eyes*were ***deep*** in his head. 彼の目はくぼんでいた. ¶have ***deep blue eyes*** こん青色の目をしている. ¶***deeply-placed*** (=***deep-set***) ***eyes*** くぼんでいる目. ¶***deep staring eyes*** かなつぼまなこ. ¶He cast a ***disapproving eye*** on our proceedings. 彼は非難の目でわれわれの処置を見やっていた. ¶He has a ***discerning eye.*** 彼には眼識がある. ‖ to the ***discerning eye*** 具眼者には. ¶***downcast eyes*** 下目(しため). ¶***dreamy eyes*** ぼんやりした目. ¶***drunken eyes*** 酔眼. ¶There was not a ***dry eye*** in the whole assemblage. 満座皆泣いた. ¶***dull eyes*** どんよりした目. ¶they gazed upon me with such ***eager eyes*** that ... 彼らはじろじろ私を見詰めたので… ‖ His ***eager eyes*** devoured her. 彼は彼女に見とれた. ¶***emmetropic eyes*** 正視眼. ¶The costume gave them the appearance of waiters in ***English eyes.*** 彼らの服装が服装なので英国人には給仕と見えた. ¶cast ***envious eyes*** upon ... …をうらやましそうに見る. ¶It was seen for the first time by ***European eyes.*** それを西洋人が見たのはこれが始めてだ. ¶a witch with a very ***evil eye*** 邪悪な目をした魔女. ¶***far-away eyes*** うっとりした目. ¶***farsighted eyes*** 老眼. ¶***fine eyes*** 美しい目. ¶***fishy*** (=***dull or vacant-looking***) ***eyes*** どんよりした目. ¶Their ideas of enjoyment are rather strange in ***foreign eyes.*** 彼らの快楽の観念は外人にはむしろ不思議に思われる. ¶see with a ***friendly eye*** ひいき目に見る. ¶watch with a ***furtive eye*** 盗み目で見守る. ¶***glistening, longing eye*** きらきら光るなつかしそうな目付. ¶***goggling eyes*** ぎょろぎょろする目. ¶He has ***good eyes.*** 彼は目が良い ‖ have a ***good eye*** for coloring 色彩感覚が鋭い. ¶***grey eyes*** 灰色の目. ¶with ***haggard eyes*** 物すごい目で. ¶her ***hazed eyes*** 彼女のかすんだ色の目. ¶***hazel eyes*** 薄茶色の目. ¶***heavy eyes*** 眠そうな目. ¶***hollow eyes*** くぼんだ目. ¶with an ***impartial eye*** 公平な目で. ¶He has an ***inflamed eye.*** 彼の目は炎症を起している. ¶The stage has always looked upon its hybrid offshoot, the movies, with a ***jaundiced eye.*** 劇の方では始めからその混血の分派たる映画をしっとの目で見て来たのである. ¶with a ***jealous eye*** ねたんで. ¶with ***keen eyes*** のみ取りまなこで ‖ have a ***keen eye*** for beauty 審美眼がある ‖ a man with a ***keen eye*** to his own interests 自分の利害には抜目がない人. ¶his ***keen observant eyes*** 彼の観察の鋭い目. ¶***kind*** but ***penetrating eyes*** 柔和だが鋭敏な目. ¶a ***lacklustre eye*** つやのない目. ¶***lambent eyes*** 柔和にかがやく目付. ¶***large eyes*** 大きな目. ¶look upon ... with a ***lenient eye*** 柔和な目で…を見る. ¶***lewd*** (=***lustful***) ***eyes*** みだらな目. ¶***lidless eyes*** [へびなどの]まぶたのない目. ¶cast a ***longing eye*** on ... …にあこがれの目を投げる. ¶***long*** (***near***)***-sighted eyes*** 遠(近)視眼. ¶call up in one's ***mind's eye*** ... 心の目に…を想起する. 【類】 bring ... before our ***mind's eye*** / we can see with our ***mind's eye*** ... ¶It can be seen with the ***naked eye.*** それは肉眼で見える. 【類】 scarcely distinguishable by the ***naked eye.*** ¶with ***oblique eyes*** 横目で. ¶an ***observant eye*** will perceive that ... 注意する人には…が分る. ¶Each musician in a band plays with ***one eye*** on his music and the other on the conductor. バンドの楽士は片目で楽符を片目で指揮者を見ながら演奏する. ¶the ***outward*** and ***inward eyes*** 肉眼と心眼. ¶I saw with my ***own eyes.*** 自分はこの目で見た. ¶***partial eyes*** 公平でない目. ¶consider (=watch) with a ***philosophic***[***al***] ***eye*** 冷静に考える. ¶ not visible to the ***physical eye*** 肉眼には見えない. ¶***pink eyes*** 赤目(眼炎). ¶it needs, perhaps, a ***poet's eye*** to recognize ... …を認めるには恐らく詩人の眼識が必要だ. ¶***projecting eyes*** 出目. ¶***prominent*** (=***protruding***) ***eyes*** 出目. ¶***prying eyes*** 偵察眼. ¶unabashed in the ***public eye*** 人前で平気な ‖ He is now "a man in the ***public eye.***" 彼は今問題の人となっている. ‖ men prominent in the ***public eye*** 名士. ¶a ***quick eye*** けい眼. ¶***radiant eyes*** 輝く目. ¶Every scene invited the ***ravished eye.*** どの場面も見る者の目を奪うものであった. ¶***red-shot eyes*** 血走った目. ¶***red-rimmed eyes*** 目ぶちの赤い目. ¶be blind in the ***right eye*** 右の目が見えない. ¶We watched her constantly with a ***scheming eye.*** われわれは絶えず彼女を計画的に見張った. ¶He has the ***seeing eye*** rather than the analytic brain. 彼は分析的頭脳よりも物を見る目を持っている. ¶keep a ***sharp eye*** on ... 油断なく…に注意する ‖ Mariners have ***sharp eyes*** (=are sharp sighted). 水夫は目が早い. ‖ with ***sharp eyes*** うの目たかの目で. ¶his ***sharp, observing eyes*** 彼の鋭い観察眼. ¶make ***sheep's eyes*** at a woman 女にウインクする. ¶he has a remarkably ***shrewd eye*** for detecting ... 彼は…を探知する非常に鋭い目を持っている. ¶It is like looking in the mirror to try to see how you look with your ***eyes shut.*** それは目をつぶったらどんな顔になるかと鏡を見るようなものだ. ¶***sightless eyes*** 盲目. ¶a ***skilful eye*** 老練な目. ¶***slanting eyes*** しり下り(上り)の目. ¶rub one's ***sleepy eyes*** 眠い目をこする. ¶***smiling eyes*** にこやかな目. ¶the advice is given in all sincerity with a ***sole eye*** to ... この忠告は全く…のことを考えて誠心誠意をもって申上げたものである. ¶***sore eyes*** ただれ目. ¶***sparkling black eyes*** きらきら光る黒い目. ¶The country is casting a ***speculative eye*** upon China. 同国は中国に対して思わくありげな目を向けている. ¶***steel-blue eyes*** 灰青色の目. ¶***straight-forward eyes*** 直視する目. ¶His ***eyes*** are ***sunk*** deep in his head. 彼の目はくぼんでいる. ¶cast a ***supercilious eye*** upon ... …を高慢げに見る. ¶with a ***suspicious eye*** いぶかしげに. ¶***swimming eyes*** 目まい. ¶to a ***sympathetic eye*** ひいき目には. ¶***sympathetic female eyes*** grew moist over ... 思いやりのある婦人連は…を見て涙ぐんだ. ¶with ***talking eyes*** 目に物を言わせて(目で知らせて). ¶***tear-bleared eyes*** 涙でかすんだ目. ¶***tearful eyes*** 涙をためた目. ¶a long-drawn face and ***tear-laden eyes*** しおれた顔と涙を流している目. ¶cannot talk about ... with ***tearless eyes*** 涙なくして…を語ることはできない. ¶***terror-stricken eyes*** おびえた目. ¶Her ***timid, gentle eyes*** beamed winsomely. 彼女の気の弱そうな優しいまなざしに愛きょうの光が見られた. ¶***tiny eyes*** ちっちゃい目. ¶cast a ***tolerant eye*** over ... …を大目に見る. ¶The picture, even to his ***trained eye,*** seemed priceless. その絵は彼の(その道に明るい)くろうと目にも貴重に見えた. ¶***twinkling eyes*** きらきらする目. ¶her ***ultramarine eyes*** 彼女の群青色の目. ¶to ***unaccustomed eyes*** 慣れない目には. ¶The defect can be detected by the ***unaided eye.*** そのきずは肉眼でも分る. ¶with the ***unassisted eye*** 肉眼で. ¶examine the matter with an ***unbiased eye*** 公平な目でそれをがん味する. ¶look with ***unfavorable eye*** upon ... 冷たい目で…を見る. ¶have an ***unlucky eye*** for color in the selection of his clothes 着物を選ぶ際色合の見立がまずい. ¶in the glare of hundreds of ***unsympathetic eyes*** 数百の同情のない人に監視されて. ¶to the ***untutored*** (=***uninitiated***) ***eye*** しろうと目には. ¶keep a ***wary eye*** on ... …を監視する. ¶keep a ***watchful eye*** over ... 油断なく…を見張る. ¶***watery eyes*** 涙にうるむ目. ¶***wearied eyes*** 疲れた目. ¶Her ***eyes*** were ***wet*** with tears. 彼女の目は涙でぬれていた. ¶look at ... with ***wide open eyes*** of astonishment …に驚きの目を見張る. 【類】 [with] one's ***eyes wide open.*** ¶a ***wistful eye*** 物ほしげな目. ¶have ***wonderful eyes*** to observe 驚くべき観察力を持っている.

Q² His ***quick*** and ***expert eye*** at once detected the deception. 彼の目ざとい熟練した目はすぐに詐欺だとわかった. ¶cast a ***weather eye*** in the direction of ... 天候いかんと…の方向を見る.

P be directly ***before*** one's ***eye*** すぐ目前にある ‖ ***before*** our admiring ***eyes*** われわれが感心して見ている前で ‖ have ... ***before*** their mind's ***eye*** …を心の目に浮べる. ¶estimate ***by*** [the] ***eye*** 目分量で見積る. ¶hide oneself ***from*** the ***eyes*** of the public 人目を避ける. ¶***in*** my ***eyes*** 私に言わせれば ‖ Is there anything ***in*** my ***eye?*** 私の目に何かはいっていますか. ‖ with tears ***in*** her ***eyes*** 目に涙を浮べて. 【類】 The tears were ***in*** her ***eyes*** when she shook hands with me. / Alas, tears bead ***in*** my ***eyes*** as I write. ‖ Is there any green ***in*** my ***eye?*** 僕はそんな甘ちゃんじゃないぞ. ‖ ***In*** the ***eyes*** of her family she could pass as cured. 家族のものから見て彼女の病気は治ったものと認められた. ‖ She is old ***in*** the ***eyes*** of a young country. その国は新進国から見れば古い. ‖ see ***in*** the mind's ***eye*** 心の目に映じる ‖ a sensual look ***in*** one's ***eyes*** そのみだらな目つき ‖ He may look a fool ***in*** the ***eyes*** of sensible men. 彼は利口な人の目にはばか者と見えるかも知れない. ‖ Such an attitude will belittle us *in* the *eyes* of other nations. こんな態度に出ると列国から安っぽく見られるだろう. ‖ Beauty lies *in* the *eye* of the beholder. 美は見る人の目に存する(古いことわざ). 【類】*in* the *eyes* of all the world, he seems ... / *in* the *eyes* of common sense / *in* the *eyes* of the law / The constitution renders all equal (万民平等) *in* the *eye* of the law. ¶ see with a sweep *of* the *eye* さっと見渡す ‖ in the twinkling *of* an *eye* またたく間に. ¶ He could not see at all *out of* one *eye*. 彼の片方の目は全く盲であった. ¶ education *through* the *eye*=ocular education 視覚教育. ¶ a feast *to* the *eye* 目の保養(正月) ‖ entirely new *to* the *eyes* of the Western world 西洋人の目には全然新しい ‖ be invisible *to* the naked *eye* 肉眼では見えない. 【類】He was a pretty boy *to* any *eye*. ¶ *under* the *eye* of ... ...の注目の下に ‖ He has fallen *under* the *eye* of the government. 彼は政府に目をつけられた. ‖ be *under* your very *eyes* 鼻の下にぶら下っている. ¶ He is *up to* his *eyes* in work. 彼は仕事に没頭している. ‖ He is *up to* his *eyes* in debt. 彼は借金で首が回らない. ‖ A neighbour's estate, mortgaged *up to* the *eyes*, was sold under the hammer. 全部抵当にはいっていた隣人の財産が競売に付せられた. ¶ *with* all one's *eyes* 熱心に見詰めて ‖ *with* an *eye* to one's future その将来を考慮して ‖ ascertain *with* one's own *eyes* 自分の目でしかと見届ける ‖ see *with* another *eye* 観点を変える ‖ *with* half an *eye* 一見して, 容易に ‖ *with* one's *eyes* open (shut) 目を開いて(閉じて) ‖ *with eyes* upcast and hands uplifted piously 敬けんに天を仰ぎ両手をあげて ‖ see *with* the *eye* of the seer 予言者の目をもって見る. 【類】look about one *with* the *eyes* of an observer and a student (研究家).

P^2 It is really a delightful place for one who has an *eye for* beauty and a heart for associations. 自然の美と史趣を解する人にとってはそれは実に結構な所です. 【類】That cannot fail to appeal to those who have an *eye for* the beautiful. / The Japanese have an *eye for* the picturesque. ¶ The *eye of* the public was upon him. 世間は彼に注目していた. ‖ Athens, the *eye of* Greece ギリシアの眼目たるアテネ. ‖ the *eye of* a needle 針の目; 囲いに付した弓形の小門 ‖ the *eyes of* the storm (typhoon) あらし(台風)の目. ¶ have one's *eyes on* the future 将来に目を着ける. ¶ run one's *eye over* a list 急いで表に目を通す. ¶ have an *eye to* the future 将来に目を着ける. ¶ We should work with our *eyes towards* it. われわれはその方に目を付けて働くべきだ.

eye, *v*. 見る.

M *eye askance* at a person 人をしり目にかける. ¶ *eye* a person *closely* 人をつくづく見る. ¶ *eye* a person (thing) *curiously* 珍らし気に見る. ¶ He *eyed* me *doubtfully*. 彼は疑わしい目付で私を見た. ¶ I *eyed* him *narrowly*. 私はじろじろ彼を見た. ¶ *eyeing* him *sternly* きびしい目で彼を見て.

P He *eyed* me *from* top *to* toe (=from head to foot) 彼は私を頭からつま先まで見た. ¶ *eye* a stranger *with* suspicion 知らない人を疑わし気に見る. 【類】*eye* anything new *with* curiosity.

eyebrow, *n*. まゆ.

V Formerly married women in Japan blackened their teeth and *extirpated* the *eyebrows* 以前日本では既婚の女は歯を黒くしまゆを落した. ¶ *pencil* the *eyebrows* まゆを引く.

Q finely *arched eyebrows* 弓なりの美しいまゆ. ¶ *beetling eyebrows* 突出たまゆ. ¶ *heavy* (=*thick*) *eyebrows* 太い(濃い)まゆ. ¶ *shaggy* (=*rough or bushy*) *eyebrows* むしゃむしゃしたまゆ. ¶ *shapely eyebrows* 格好のよいまゆ. ¶ *slanted eyebrows* 八の字まゆ. ¶ *smooth eyebrows* 毛の寝たまゆ. ¶ *strong eyebrows* 太いまゆ.

P look at one *with* raised *eyebrows* まゆをあげて人を見る.

eyeful, *n*. 《米俗》美貌の女.

Q an *exciting eyeful* すばらしい美人.

eyelash, *n*. まつげ.

Q blue eyes with *long wet eyelashes* 長いぬれたまつげのある青い目.

eyelid *n*. まぶた.

Q a *double-edged* (*single-edged*) *eyelid* 二重(一重)まぶた. ¶ a *drooped eyelid* たれ下ったまぶた.

eye-opener, *n*. 《米俗》奇談, 珍事.

Q There are changing views from the summit—a *real eye-opener* to the climbers. 頂上からのながめが刻々に変る, これは登山者にとっては本当に驚異である. ¶ a *woeful eye-opener* 悲壮な珍事.

eyeshot *n*. 視界.

P *beyond* (*within*) *eyeshot* of ... ...から目の届かない(見える)ところに.

eyesight, *n*. 視力.

V *injure* one's *eyesight* 視力を害する. ¶ He has *lost* his *eyesight* through disease. 彼は病気で失明した.

V^2 My *eyesight* is beginning to *fail*. 私の視力はだんだん弱くなりだした.

Q He has *bad eyesight*. 彼は目が悪い. ¶ a person with *good* (*poor*) *eyesight* 視力のよい(弱い)人. ¶ on account of *impaired eyesight* 視力を損じたので. ¶ *weak* (*strong*) *eyesight* 弱(強)い視力.

P a trouble *in* one's *eyesight* 視力の障害.

eyesore, *n*. 目ざわり.

P^2 Posters and bills in the park are *eyesores to* the visitors. 公園のポスターや張り紙は観光客にとって目ざわりである.

eye-strain, *n*. つかれ目.

V *relieve eye-strain* 目の疲労を除く.

F

fable, *n*. ぐう話; 作り話, うそ.

Q *Aesop's Fables* イソップ物語. ¶ a *mere fable* ほんの作り話. ¶ *old wives' fables* 愚にもつかない話. ¶ he regards as *pure fable* the belief that ... 彼は...という信仰をほんの作りごとと考えている. ¶ a *shrewd Eastern fable* うがった東洋の作り話. ¶ a *wild fable* 荒唐無けいな作り話.

P^2 a *fable about* a fox きつねのたとえ話. ¶ a *fable of* Aesop=an Aesop fable イソップ物語の一つ.

fabric, *n*. 織物, 布地; 組織.

V *iron fabrics* while slightly damp 少し湿っている中に布地にアイロンを掛ける.

Q rubber or other *air-tight fabrics* ゴムその他防水生地. ¶ *durable fabrics* 丈夫な布地. ¶ the *economic fabric* of the country その国の経済組織. ¶ real *hand-loomed* (=home-spun) *fabrics* 本当の手織物. ¶ *home-spun fabrics* 手織. ¶ issues that concern the *inmost fabric* of life and society 人生と社会の最も深い組織に関する問題. ¶ The whole *social fabric* was threatened with disintegration. 社会的組織をくつがえす恐れがあった. ¶ *textile fabrics* 織物. ¶ *woolen fabrics* 羊毛織物.

Q^2 *clothing fabrics* 服地. ¶ *cotton fabrics* 木綿もの. ¶ *dress fabrics* 服地. ¶ *paper-making fabrics* [巻タバコ用紙など] 製紙用布地.

P^2 a *fabric for* ladies' dresses 婦人服地.

fabrication, *n*. 虚構, うそ.

Q an *out-and-out fabrication* 真赤なうそ. ¶ a *pure fabrication* 全くのうそ.

façade, *n*. 建物の正面.

V^2 Its *façade covers* one city block. その正面は市の一かくを占めている.

face, *n*. 顔, 顔付; 面; 表面; 局面, 形勢; 面目; 面前.

V *accept* his *face* 彼の顔を立てる. ¶ *avert* the *face* 顔をそむける. ¶ *bear* a cheerful *face* 愉快な顔をしている. ¶ *burn* one's *face* 赤面する. ¶ a revolution that would radically *change* the *face* of the earth 世界の形勢を根本的に変えるような革命. 【類】Free education had *changed* the *face* of the globe. ¶ *cover* one's *face* with black veil 黒いベールで顔を包む. ¶ *disfigure* one's *face* 顔を醜くする. ¶ This consideration *gives* some *face* to the proceedings. こう考察するとそのやり方が幾分面目が立つ. ¶ He *has* a pimpled *face*. 彼はにきびだらけの顔をしている. ‖ He *had* the *face* to do it. 彼はそれを平気でやれるだけつらの皮が厚かった. ‖ How can you *have* the *face* to tell me this? なんの面目あって君はこのことを僕に話すのか. ¶ I have *no face* to turn to. 合わせる顔がない. ¶She ***has*** two *faces*. 彼女は裏表がある. ¶Mohammedans never ***have*** their *faces* ***photographed***. マホメット教徒は決して顔を写真にとらせない. ¶***hide*** her *face* in her hands 彼女の顔を手で隠す. ¶It was hard to ***keep*** my *face* straight. 真顔でいることはむずかしかった. ¶***lather*** one's *face* before shaving そる前に顔に石けんあわを塗る. ¶***lift*** one's *face* to the east knowing surely that the dawn will come 夜明けの近いことを察して東方を仰ぐ. ¶***lift up*** the *face* [祈願のときのように]仰ぐ. ¶Her little *face* is already ***lined*** with the cares of domestic life. 彼女のまだ若い顔には既に家庭生活の苦労でしわが寄っている. ¶***lose face*** 面目を失う. ¶***make faces*** in the mirror 鏡に向って色々な顔をする ‖ ***make faces*** at ... ...にしかめ面をする ‖ ***make*** (=***pull*** *or* ***draw***) a long *face* いやな顔をする; 悲しそうな顔をする ‖ children ***make*** rude *faces* at ... 子供らは...に憎たらしい顔をする ‖ ***make*** ugly *faces*=contort the features 顔をゆがめる ‖ ***make*** a wry *face* 顔をしかめる. ¶***muffle up*** the *face* 覆面する. ¶***paint*** [her *face*] thickly 厚化粧をする. ¶His *face* is ***peppered*** with freckles. 彼の顔はそばかすだらけだ. ¶***powder*** the *face* 顔におしろいをつける. ¶***press*** one's *face* against the windowpane 窓ガラスに顔を押しつける. ¶***pucker*** her pretty *face* into a frown 彼女のきれいな顔をしかめる. ¶***pull*** a wry *face* しかめ面をする. ¶***put*** a bold *face* on the matter その事柄に対して虚勢を張る ‖ ***put*** a good *face* on the affair その件をうまく取りつくろう. ¶***put on*** a grave *face* まじめな顔をする. ¶He did not ***relax*** his *face*. 彼は顔の緊張をゆるめなかった. ¶I ***remember*** his *face*, but do not know his name. 私は彼の顔は覚えているが名前は知らない. ‖ I ***remember*** two *faces*. 私は二人だけ顔を見知っている. ¶Her *face* will have been ***restored*** by then. それまでにはその国の面目が回復されているだろう. ¶***rub*** one's *face* with a towel タオルで顔をふく. ¶***save*** one's *face* 面目を全うする ‖ ***save*** the *face* of ... ...の顔を立てる. ¶***scan*** one's *face* narrowly その顔をじろじろながめる. ¶***set*** one's *face* toward home 帰路につく ‖ I ***set*** my *face* against such practices (proposals) かかる慣習(提案)に対して私は大反対である. ‖ resolutely ***set*** our *face* and raise our voice against ... ...には断固として反対しその非を鳴らす ‖ ***set*** the best *face* on it それは最もよく見せかける. 【類】The Government has ***set*** its *face* strongly against any profiteering (暴利). ¶***shave*** one's *face* with a razor かみそりで顔をそる. 【類】Two generations ago, every self-respecting Englishman ***shaved*** all his *face* except the cheeks (ほお以外). ¶How dare you ***show*** your *face* here again? よくも二度とここにやって来られたものだ. ‖ He will not dare to ***show*** his *face*. 彼はまさか顔を出そうとはしまい. ‖ Never ***show*** your *face* again here! 二度とここへ顔を出すな. ¶***sink*** one's *face* into one's hands 顔を手に埋める. ¶***slap*** (=***smack***) one's *face* 顔をぴしゃりと打つ. ¶The north-east wind and December sleet ***sting*** your *face*. 東北風と十二月のみぞれが顔を刺す. ¶***straighten*** one's *face* 真顔になる. ¶***survey*** (=***study***) one's *face* その顔をじろじろ見る. ¶***turn*** a smiling *face* on ... ...ににこにこした顔を向ける ‖ She did not even ***turn*** her *face* toward me. 私の方に見向きもしなかった. 【類】The crowd ***turned*** their *faces* upwards. ¶***turn face about*** 反対の方へ向き直る. ¶***turn away*** one's *face* 顔をそむける. ¶***twitch*** the *face* 顔をぴくぴくさせる. ¶***watch*** men's *faces* 人々の顔を見まもる. ¶A true friend will not ***wear*** a false *face*. 真の友は仮面をかぶらない. ‖ Film stars ***wear*** their "natural *faces*" when off work. 映画の俳優は仕事の時以外では素顔をしている. ¶***wipe*** his perspiring *face* 彼の汗の流れる顔をぬぐう.

v² His *face* ***beams*** with smile. 彼の顔は微笑で輝く. ‖ He listened to my story, his *face* ***beaming*** with compassion. 彼は満面に同情の色を浮べて私の話を傾聴していた. ¶His *face* ***blanched*** 彼は青くなった. ¶her *face* ***blushed*** when ... ...したとき彼女は顔を赤らめた. ¶his *face* ***brightened*** when ... ...したとき彼は晴々した顔をした. ¶his *face* ***burning*** with shame and rage 彼の顔は屈辱と怒りに燃えて. ¶His *face* ***clouded***. 彼は顔を曇らした. ¶His *face* ***fell*** when I told him that. それを彼に話したらがっかりした. ¶Their *faces* ***glistened*** with perspiration. 彼らの顔に汗の玉が光っていた. ¶His *face* ***gloomed over***. 彼はすっかり顔を曇らせてしまった. ¶His *face* ***lighted up*** with pleasure. 彼の顔は喜びで晴れやかになった. 【類】His *face* ***lighted up*** with a smile of relief. / His *face* ***lighted up*** or ***clouded over*** as he passed from one mood to another. ¶the prisoner's *face* ***relaxed*** into a grim smile when ... ...したとき捕虜の苦い顔に微笑が浮んだ. ¶His *face* fairly ***shone*** with joy. 彼の顔は喜びであざやかに輝いた.

Q a ***beaming*** *face* 朗かな顔. ¶put a ***bold*** *face* on it それに対して平気を装う. ¶a ***bony*** *face* 骨張った顔. ¶a ***brazen*** *face* 厚顔. ¶a ***broad*** *face* 広い顔. ¶a ***care-worn*** *face* 心配にやつれた顔. ¶a ***comely*** *face* みめよい顔. ¶a ***crimson*** *face* 真赤な顔. ¶a ***crying*** *face* 泣顔. ¶He makes a a ***disagreeable*** *face* when told to do something. 彼は何かやれと言われるといやな顔をする. ¶a *face* ***drawn*** with pain 苦痛でゆがんだ顔. ¶an ***elongated*** *face* 細長い顔. ¶Though the children's lips remain silent, their *faces* are ***eloquent***. 子供らは口をつぐんでいても顔が盛んに物を言う. ¶an ***emaciated*** *face* やせ衰えた顔. ¶a ***fair*** *face* 美貌. ¶a ***fair, finely cut*** *face* 色の白い格好のよい顔. ¶On Halloween we wear ***fake*** *faces* (=masks) 万聖節の前夜にはわれわれは面をかぶる. ¶There will be many ***feminine*** *faces* in the new Diet. 新国会には婦人の議員が多いだろう. ¶a ***fine*** *face* りっぱな顔. ¶with ***flushed, eager*** *faces* 紅潮しやっきとなった顔をして. ¶Her profile is better than her ***full*** *face*. 彼女は正面から見るより横顔の方がよい. ¶a ***ghastly*** *face* 青白い顔. ¶a ***glum*** *face* 陰気な顔. ¶wait with a ***grave*** *face* and a dread foreboding of his heart 沈痛な顔をして心に恐ろしい予感をいだきながら待つ. ¶a ***haggard*** *face* やつれた顔. ¶a ***handsome*** *face* 美しい顔. ¶a crowd of ***happy*** *faces* 楽しそうな顔をした群集. ¶a ***hatchet*** *face* 細おもて. ¶a ***haughty*** *face* ごう慢な顔付. ¶an ***ill-made*** *face* 造作のよくない顔. ¶The jury listened attentively, and with ***impassive*** *faces*. 陪審官は平然たる顔をしてじっと耳を傾けた. ¶an ***impressive*** *face* 強い印象を与える顔. ¶a ***kindly*** *face* 温顔. ¶a tall girl whose *face* was ***lean*** and ***bony*** やせて骨っぽい顔をしたせいの高い少女. ¶He has a ***long*** *face*. 彼は長い顔をしている. ‖ pull a ***long*** *face* 憂うつな顔をする. ¶a ***lovely*** *face* 愛らしい顔. ¶her satisfactorily ***made-up*** *face* うまくおつくりをした顔. ¶a ***narrow*** *face* 細おもて. ¶a ***new*** *face* 新顔, 新参者 ‖ a ***new*** *face* of affairs 新局面 ‖ an old friend with a ***new*** *face* 新装した古物 ‖ spring a ***new*** *face* 新しい女ができ上る. 【類】among the ***new*** *faces* that were seen there. ¶an ***oval*** *face* うりざね顔. ¶a ***pale*** *face* 青白い顔. ¶a ***pallid*** *face* surmounted by an ice-cap 頭に氷のうを載せた青白い顔. ¶with a ***pensive*** *face* 思案顔で. ¶She has a ***plain*** *face*. 彼女はきりょうがよくない. ¶Her *face* is ***pleasing***. 彼女は気持のよい顔をしている. ¶a ***pouting*** *face* ふくれっつら. ¶a ***pox-pitted*** *face* あばた面. ¶a ***pretty*** *face* 美しい顔. ¶a ***proud*** *face* ごう慢な顔. ¶a ***puffy*** *face* ふっくりした顔. ¶a girl with a ***rosy, clear-cut, animated*** *face* ばら色のくっきりした活気のある顔をした少女. ¶the ***rough*** (***smooth***) *face* of ... ...のあらい(なめらかな)表面. ¶have a very ***round*** *face* 丸顔だ. ¶a ***roundish oval*** *face* 丸みを帯びたうりざね顔. ¶***ruddy*** *faces* 赤ら顔. ¶We can read in the ***sad, dejected*** *face* the sorrowful thoughts that are passing through the sufferer's mind. 打ちしおれて元気のない顔にその悩める者の心の中に起る悲哀に満ちた思いが読まれる. ¶a ***sallow, clean-shaven*** *face* 薄黄色いきれいにそった顔. ¶***scratched*** *faces* つめでひっかいた顔. ¶with a ***serious*** *face* 真顔で. ¶a woman with a ***severe classical*** *face* きりっとした上品な顔の女. ¶an old woman with a ***shriveled*** *face* 梅干ばばあ. ¶a ***shy*** *face* 恥ずかしげな顔. ¶his ***silent, abstracted*** *face* 静かなポカンとした顔. ¶A cube has ***six*** *faces*. 立方体は六面を有する. ¶a ***sleek*** *face* すべすべした顔. ¶a ***smiling*** *face* and a happy heart にこにこした顔と楽しい心. ¶a ***sober*** *face* まじめな顔. ¶a ***sour*** *face* 渋い顔. ¶He has a ***squarish, irregular, weather-beaten*** *face*. 彼は角ばった不格好な潮風にさらされた顔をしている. ¶people with ***sunny*** *faces* 晴々した顔の人々. ¶a ***sweet*** *face* かわいい顔. ¶have a ***sympathetic*** *face* 思いやりのある顔をしている. ¶a ***thin*** *face* やせた顔. ¶with ***troubled*** *face* 心配そうな顔をして. ¶an ***unclouded*** *face* 晴々した顔. ¶in her ***unpainted*** *face* 彼女の素顔で. ¶an ***unshaven*** *face* そってない顔. ¶the sea of ***upturned*** *faces* 仰向いた人の顔の海(高い所でだれかが演説をするので). ¶with hunger and privation depicted on their ***wan*** and ***thin*** *faces* 彼らの青白いやせた顔に飢と窮乏

とを表わして. ¶Her *face* is ***visible*** in profile. 彼女の横顔が見える. ¶a ***wasted*** *face* 衰えた顔. ¶his ***weather*** (= ***sun)-tanned*** *face* 彼の日にやけた顔. ¶gracious words and ***welcoming*** *faces* 心尽しの言葉と喜び迎える顔. ¶a ***well-fleshed*** *face* 肉付のよい顔. ¶make a ***worse*** *face* at ... ...に対して一層いやな顔をする. ¶a ***wrinkled*** *face* しわのよった顔. ¶with a ***wry*** *face* しかめ面をして.

Q² a ***brandy*** *face* 《俗》飲酒家. ¶a ***quarter*** *face* [四分の一だけ見える]横顔. ¶But you have a ***tell-tale*** *face*. しかしお前の顔に書いてある. ¶a ***three-quarter*** *face* 写真の横顔.

P An expression of doubt flitted ***across*** his *face*. 疑惑の色が彼の顔にちらりと表われた. ‖ He struck me ***across*** the *face*. 彼は僕の顔をぴしゃと打った. ¶***before*** one's *face* その面前で. ¶sweep ... ***from*** the *face* of the earth ...を地球の表面から一掃する. ¶laugh ***in*** one's *face* 面と向って笑う ‖ ***in*** the *face* of an enemy 敵の面前で ‖ ***in*** the *face* of the whole congregation 全会衆の前で. ¶***in*** [the] *face* of the difficult problem 困難な問題に面と向って ‖ It is blessed to be wise in truth ***in*** *face* of opinion. 反対の意見を向うに回して真実のために健闘することは幸福である. ‖ ***in*** the *face* of the surrounding disapproval はたのものが不賛成をとなえる中に立って ‖ wrinkles ***in*** the *face* 顔のしわ ‖ He looked me ***in*** the *face*. 彼は僕を真ともに見た. ‖ strike him ***in*** the *face* 彼の顔をなぐる ‖ ***in*** the *face* of these facts これらの事実を考えるに ‖ He persevered ***in*** the *face* of all obstacles. 彼はあらゆる困難を忍んだ.【類】***in*** the *face* of these figures / ***in*** *face* of these facts it is idle to ... / ***in*** the *face* of such circumstances it became impossible for him to ... / ***in*** the *face* of such a disaster / He was always brave ***in*** the *face* of danger. / A publisher must have courage to publish a good book ***in*** the *face* of a known financial loss. / ***in*** the *face* of heavy fire from the enemy. ¶***on*** the *face* of the globe 地球の表面に ‖ there never was a man ***on*** the *face* of the earth who ... 地球上に...ような人は一人もなかった ‖ The following statement shall be made ***on*** the *face* of the invoice. 送状の表面には次の文言を認むべし. ‖ Where is my nose?—Your nose is ***on*** your *face*. 私の鼻はどこにあるか—顔の上にあります. ‖ fall down ***on*** his *face* うつぶせに倒れる ‖ He fell ***on*** his *face* like a dead man. 彼は死人のようにうつ伏した.【類】the look ***on*** the *face* of a girl / red pimples (ふき出もの) ***on*** the *face* / She was very hairy ***on*** the *face*. / with a smile ***on*** his *face* / with an unusual expression ***on*** his *face* ‖ There was a smile, almost seraphic in its beauty, ***on*** his *face*. 彼の顔には天使のようにけだかく美しい微笑があった. ‖ lie ***on*** one's *face* うつ伏せになる ‖ give a severe blow ***on*** the *face* 顔をひどく打つ ‖ ***On*** the *face* of it, the proportion seems high. それだけから見ると割合が高いようであるが. ¶smiling all ***over*** her *face* 満面に微笑をたたえて ‖ A flicker of emotion ran ***over*** his *face*. 感動のひらめきが彼の顔に現われた. ¶You are telling me lies ***to*** my very *face*. 君は僕に面と向ってうそをついている. ‖ flatter a man ***to*** his *face* and revile him behind his back 面と向ってはほめ陰ではくさす.【類】speak ill of people ***to*** their *faces* ‖ be *face* ***to*** face with ... ...と差し向かいになっている ‖ bring a person face ***to*** *face* with ... ...を...と対面させる. ¶He died with a smile ***upon*** his *face*. 彼は顔に微笑を浮べて死んだ. ‖ every nation ***upon*** the *face* of the earth 地球上のあらゆる国民. ¶***with*** her *face* buried in her hands 彼女の顔を両手で押し隠して ‖ ***with*** a serious *face* まじめな顔をして.

P² a *face* ***in*** profile 横顔. ¶the *face* ***of*** a clock 時計の面 ‖ the *face* ***of*** a country 地勢 ‖ the *face* ***of*** a crystal 結晶体の面 ‖ the *face* ***of*** the earth (a type) 地球(など)の表面 ‖ the *face* ***of*** the note 手形の額面.

face, *v.* 面する, 向う; 対抗する; 上張(ばり)する; 見ばをよくする.

M ***boldly*** *face* a task 大胆に仕事に向う. ¶He tried to *face* it ***out***. 彼はそれを平気で押し通そうとした. ‖ She had the nerve to *face* it ***out***. 彼女はそれを平気で押し通すほどの強い心臓の持主だった. ¶a large window *facing* ***south*** 南向きの大きな窓.【類】a room *facing* ***south***. ¶*face* it ***squarely*** それに直面する. ¶*face* an obstacle ***unflinchingly*** ひるまず障害物に対抗する.

M² *face* ***down*** 威圧する. ¶*face* ***round*** くるりと向き直る. ¶*face* ***up*** to a great problem with courage and foresight 勇気と深慮とをもって一大問題に立向う.

P He is *faced* ***by*** the dilemma of ... ing or ... ing. 彼は...するか...するかの羽目に直面している. ¶The house *faces* ***on*** the sea (river, street). 家は海(など)に臨んでいる. ¶The building *faces* ***to*** the south. 建物は南向きだ. ¶The house *faces* ***towards*** the south. 家は南に向いている. ¶The bathroom is *faced* ***with*** tile. 浴場内はタイル張りになっている. ‖ *face* tea ***with*** coloring matter 茶に色を着けて見ばをよくする ‖ be *faced* ***with*** the necessity of ... ...の必要に迫られている ‖ be *faced* ***with*** two alternatives 二者いずれを採るかという羽目になっている.

face-about, *n.* 転換.

Q make a ***complete*** *face-about* (=about-face) 百八十度の転換をする.

face powder, おしろい.

V ***wear*** *face powder* おしろいをつけている.

facile, *a.* 巧妙な.

P He is *facile* ***in*** expedients. 彼は臨機応変だ.

facility, *n.* 容易; 便利; 機関; 設備.

V ***acquire*** *facility* of speech in the language その国語を楽に話すようになる. ¶***afford*** every *facility* for ... ...に対してあらゆる便宜を与える. ¶***extend*** traveling *facility* to ... ...に旅行の便を与える. ¶***give*** *facility* in correct expression 容易に正しく発表できるようにさせる. ¶***grant*** proper *facilities* for ... ...に対して適当な便宜を与える. ¶He ***has*** an unfortunate *facility* for saying the wrong thing when he happens to speak. 彼はたまたま口を開くととかく間違ったことをいう欠点がある. ¶***improve*** transport *facilities* 運輸機関を改善する. ¶Having ***increased*** our manufacturing *facilities*, we are advertising to obtain more users. 私どもは工場の設備を拡張したので売広めのため宣伝をやっています. ¶Our city ***needs*** more *facilities* for recreation. 本市はもっと娯楽機関が必要だ. ¶***offer*** every *facility* for ... ...にあらゆる便宜を与える. ¶***provide*** *facilities* for ... ...に対する便宜を与える.【類】***provide*** improved educational *facilities* / Ample *facilities* are ***provided*** for breaking the journey (途中下車) at various points of interest. ¶They ***put*** every *facility* in my way. 彼らは私のために便宜を与えてくれた.

Q there are ***abundant*** (=ample) *facilities* for ... ...に対して十分の便利がある. ¶give ***ample*** *facilities* for ... ...に非常な便利を与える ‖ ***ample*** hotel *facilities* 十分な宿泊上の便宜. ¶***athletic*** *facilities* 体育上の設備. ¶***capital*** *facilities* for ... ...に対する最上の設備. ¶***conversational*** *facility* 話の熟達. ¶it has ***every*** *facility* for ... に対してあらゆる便利がある. ¶give him ***every available*** *facility* 彼にあらゆる便利を提供する. ¶It has ***excellent street*** *facilities*. そこにはりっぱな街上設備がある. ¶have ***exceptional*** *facilities* for ... 特に...に対しての便がある. ¶give ***full*** *facilities* with regard to ... ...について十分な便宜を与える. ¶afford ***great*** *facility* for ... ...に大なる便利を与える. ¶with ***increased*** *facilities* for reaching ... ...に行くことが便利になったので. ¶be equipped with the most ***modern*** *facilities* 最も近代的な設備を有している. ¶***monetary*** *facilities* 金融機関. ¶There are but ***poor*** *facilities* for ... ...に対しては貧弱な設備しかない. ¶provide every ***possible*** *facility* for ... ...に対するありとあらゆる便宜を与える. ¶***recreational*** *facilities* 娯楽設備. ¶there is ***scant*** *facility* for ... ...の便が乏しい. ¶***self-supporting*** *facilities* at the school 同校における苦学生のための便宜. ¶***social*** *facilities* 社交上の機関. ¶afford ***special*** *facilities* to ... 特に...の便を図る.【類】has ***special*** *facilities* for ... ¶***terminal*** *facilities* 終点駅における(輸送上等の)設備.

Q² ***after-care*** *facilities* 結核患者の病後保護施設. ¶***amusement*** *facilities* 娯楽機関. ¶***Banking*** *facilities* are limited. 金融機関が不十分であ. ¶***communication*** *facilities* 通信の便. ¶various ***carrying*** *facilities*, both rail and water 鉄道及び船舶による各種の輸送機関. ¶expand ***college*** *facilities* 大学の設備を拡張する. ¶have electric ***cooking*** and ***heating*** *facilities* 電気による調理及び暖房設備. ¶***docking*** *facilities* ドックの設備. ¶higher ***education*** *facilities* 高等教育機関. ¶public ***health*** *facilities* 公衆保健設備. ¶public ***health*** and ***welfare*** *facilities* 公衆保健厚生施設. ¶***hospital bed*** *facilities* 病院の寝台設備. ¶There are no ***hotel*** *facilities*. 旅館の設備がない. ¶lack of ***housing*** *facilities* 住宅設備の不足. ¶towns where ***library*** *facilities* are wanting or deficient 図書館の設備がないかあるいは不完全な町. ¶improvise ***lodge*** and ***eating*** *facilities* 宿泊及び食事の施設を応急的にする. ¶hospitalization and

nursing facilities 病院及び看護設備. ¶***emergency*** medical ***facilities*** 応急医療施設. ¶adequate ***off-street parking facilities*** 十分な道路外駐車設備. ¶***parking facilities*** 自動車駐車の便. ¶owing to the lack of ***printing facilities*** 印刷設備がないために. ¶***power production facilities*** 発電設備. ¶***production facilities*** 生産施設. ¶About one half of the schools in New York have ***projection facilities***. ニューヨークの学校の約半数は映写施設を持っている. ¶***rail*** and ***water facilities*** at the port その港における鉄道及び船舶の便. ¶***rail-shipping facilities*** 船車連絡設備. ¶***recreation facilities*** 娯楽施設. ¶***refrigeration facilities*** 冷凍設備. ¶***research facilities*** 研究設備. ¶better ***safety facilities*** 安全施設の改善. ¶reactivation of ***shop facilities*** at the Yokosuka Navy Yard 横須賀海軍工しょうにおける工場設備の復旧. ¶***shopping*** and ***amusement facilities*** 買物及び娯楽施設. ¶***street-lighting facilities*** 街路照明設備. ¶***telephone facilities*** 電話の設備. ¶the development of ***tourist facilities*** 観光施設の発達. ¶the extension of ***traffic facilities*** 交通上の設備拡張. ¶***transit facilities*** 交通の利便 ‖ rapid ***transit facilities*** 高速度交通の施設. ¶minor ***transport facilities*** 小運送. 【類】the lack of ***transport facilities*** / improve ***transport facilities*** ¶***transportation facilities*** 《米》輸送施設. 【類】railroad ***transportation facilities*** / paralyze (麻ひさせる) ***transportation facilities*** / routes where ***transportation facilities*** are crowded ‖ ***transportation*** and ***storage facilities*** 輸送及び倉庫保管設備. ¶extend ***traveling facilities*** 旅行施設を拡張する.

P read it ***with facility*** それを楽に読む.

P² ***facilities for*** locomotion 交通機関 ‖ as the ***facilities for*** travel increase 旅行が便利になるにつれて ‖ ***facilities for*** carriage 運搬の便 ‖ ***Facilities for*** communication and transportation have been much improved. 通信・運輸の機関が大いに改善された. ¶***Facility of*** intercommunication between the nations has made us all citizens of the world. 各国間の交通が便利になったのでわれらはすべて世界の公民となった. ‖ The ***facilities of*** approach there have been multiplied. そこへ行く便利が大いによくなった.

O She has ***facility*** to blush. 彼女はじきに顔を赤くする.

facsimile, *n.* 複写, 生写し.

P reproduced ***in facsimile*** 複写した(書類・絵画など). 【類】a map ***in facsimile***.

P² ***facsimiles from*** early printed books in the British Museum 大英博物館の古版本からの複写. ¶a ***facsimile of*** a rubbing taken from a stone tablet 石文拓本の複写.

fact, *n.* 事実; 実際, 実状; 事実の申立て; 犯罪行為.

V he ***accentuated*** the ***fact*** that ... 彼は...という事実を強調した. ¶The ***fact*** is ***accepted*** as established. それは事実と認められている. ¶***adduce facts*** to show that ... ...ということを示すために事実をあげる. ¶it does not ***alter*** the ***fact*** that ... ...しても事実に変更をきたさない. ¶***admit*** a ***fact*** ある事実を認める. ¶***ascertain facts*** 事実を確かめる. ¶history (experience) ***attests*** the ***fact*** that ... 歴史(など)が...という事実を証明する. ¶***authenticate facts*** 事実を確かめる. ¶***belie*** (=***misrepresent***) ***facts*** 事実を誤り伝える. ¶I do not ***blink*** the ***fact*** that ... ...という事実を私は見て見ない振りはしない. ¶without being questioned, he ***blurted out*** the ***fact*** that ... 問われもしないのに彼はうっかり...という事実を口走った. ¶***bring*** into relief a certain ***fact*** ある事実をくっきりと目立たせる ‖ ***bring*** to light new ***facts*** about ... ...に関する新事実を発表する. 【類】***bring*** to light the ***fact***, hitherto kept secret, that ... ¶***bring forward*** a large body of ***facts*** to support a view ある説を支持するために色々と事実をあげる. ¶this table ***brings out*** the important ***fact*** that ... この表は...という大切な事実を明らかにする. ¶***bring*** related ***facts together*** 関係事項を総合する. ¶***camouflage*** the ***fact*** that ... ...の事実をごまかす. ¶***carry home*** the ***fact*** that ... ...という事実をさとらせる. ¶***check facts*** in reference books 参考書で事実を調べて見る. ¶in support of this deduction, the ***fact*** was ***cited*** that ... この推論を支持するために...という事実を引用した. ¶***facts collected, classified,*** and ***tabulated*** 収集され分類されそして表に作られた事実. ¶a tablet ***commemorating*** the ***fact*** has just been placed on the front of ... その事実を記念する扁額が...の表面にちょうど掲げられた所だ. ¶***conceal*** the bitter ***fact*** that ... ...という苦々しい事実を隠す. ¶***confess*** the ***fact*** その事実を白状する. ¶***conjecture*** a ***fact*** from ... ...によって推察する. ¶a ***fact*** thoroughly ***corroborated*** by archaeological evidence 考古学的立証によって十分確認された事実. ¶no one can ***deny*** the ***fact*** that ... ...という事実をだれも否定できない. ¶enquiries ***developed*** the ***fact*** that ... 色々調べて見たら...という事実が判明した. ¶a recent investigation ***disclosed*** the ***fact*** that ... 最近の調査によって...という事が判明した. 【類】without ***disclosing*** the ***fact*** that ... ¶***disguise*** a ***fact*** from a person ある事実をある人に包み隠しておく. ¶no one will ***dispute*** the ***fact*** that ... ...という事実に対しては何人も疑わないだろう. ¶***distinguish fact*** from fiction 事実と虚構との見分けをつける. ¶***distort*** the actual ***facts*** 事実を曲げる. 【類】***distort*** the ***facts*** of the situation. ¶examination of the matter ***divulged*** the ***fact*** that ... その事件を調べて見たら...という事実が暴露した. ¶The ***fact*** that ... cannot reasonably be ***doubted***. ...という事実を疑うのは無理だ. ¶***drag facts*** out of him by questioning 尋問によって彼に泥を吐かせる. ¶enquiry ***elicited*** the ***fact*** that ... 調べて見たら...という事実が分った. ¶***emphasize*** the ***fact*** that ... ...という事実を力説する. ¶***establish*** the ***fact*** that ... ...という事実を証明する. 【類】abundantly ***establish*** the ***fact*** that ... ¶***express*** a simple ***fact*** 簡単な事実を言表わす. ¶***face*** the ***fact*** frankly 卒直に事実に直面する ‖ squarely ***facing*** the ***fact*** that ... ...という事実を直視して. 【類】fear to ***face*** the ***facts*** / We must have the courage and honesty to ***face facts*** as we find them. / but the ***fact*** must be ***faced*** that ... ¶deliberately ***falsify facts*** 故意に事実を曲げる. ¶***find*** the astonishing ***fact*** that ... ...という驚くべき事実を見出す. ¶***gainsay*** a ***fact*** 事実を反ばくする. ¶***facts gleaned*** from the experience of ... ...の経験から割出した事実. ¶he has wisely ***grasped*** the ***fact*** that ... 彼は賢明にも...という事実をつかんだ. 【類】completely ***grasp*** these ***facts***. ¶The ***fact*** was ***guessed,*** but never creditably ***demonstrated***. この事実を推量はしたが決してりっぱに証明はしなかった. ¶***hide*** this ***fact*** from the world この事実を世人に秘する. ¶***ignore*** the ***fact*** that ... ...という事実無視する. ¶***impress*** this ***fact*** forcibly on the consciousness of ... ...に意識させるようにこのことを強く印象づける. ¶***interpret facts*** 事実を解釈する. ¶***intimate*** the ***fact*** to ... ...にその事実を知らせる. ¶***keep*** in mind the ***fact*** that ... ...という事実を心に留める. ¶We cannot decide until we ***know*** all the ***facts***. 事実を全部分るまでは決定し難い. ‖ the ***facts***, as far as ***known,*** are ... 今までに分っている事実は...である. ¶***look*** the ***facts*** in the face 事実を事実とする. 【類】***look*** the ***facts*** of life in the face. ¶***marshall facts*** 事実を排列(整とん)する. ¶***marshall*** and ***present facts*** in such manner as to be effective 事実を効果的であるように整とんして提示する. ¶***mention*** a personal ***fact*** 一身上のことを述べる. ¶***note*** the ***fact*** that ... ...という事実に注意する. ¶The paper tends to ***obscure*** unfavorable ***facts*** under a cloud of controversy. その新聞は自分らに不利な事実を議論の雲でぼかす傾向がある. 【類】nothing can ***obscure*** the ***fact*** that ... ¶one must not ***overlook*** the ***fact*** that ... ...という事実を見のがしてはならない. ¶***overstate facts*** 事実を誇張する. ¶***pervert facts*** 事実を曲げる. ¶***place*** the real ***facts*** before the world 本当の事実を世人に示す. ¶***point out*** the indisputable ***fact*** that ... ...という否定し得ない事実を指摘する. ¶***possess facts*** 事実を知っている. ¶the ability to ***present facts*** convincingly 事実を有効に提示する力. 【類】the art of ***presenting facts*** with accuracy and attraction. ¶***provide*** some interesting ***facts*** 二三の興味ある事実を供給する. ¶***publish*** the ***fact*** to the world 天下に向ってその事実を公表する. ¶***facts put forward*** in this paper 本紙に述べた事実. ¶duly ***realize*** the ***fact*** that ... ...という事実をよく認識する. ¶***recognize*** the ***fact*** liberally わだかまりなくその事実を認める. ¶frankly ***recognize*** the fact. ¶***record*** the ***facts*** rather than lay down arbitrary rules 勝手な規則を定めるよりもむしろ事実を記録する. 【類】***record*** the ***facts*** of English usage in pronunciation. ¶It has to be examined how far accurately this report ***represents*** the ***facts***. どの点まで正確にこの報告が事実を伝えているか考査の必要がある. ¶minute examination ***revealed*** the startling ***fact*** that ... しさいに調査して見たら...という驚くべき事実が現われた. ¶***seeking*** more ***facts*** I questioned ... それ以上の事実を知ろうとして私は...と質問した. ¶I ***sensed*** the ***fact*** that ...

…という事実を感知した. ¶***separate fact*** from fiction 事実と虚構とを分離する. ¶***set forth*** the essential *facts* of … …という根本的事実を示す ‖ the *facts* ***set forth*** in this volume 本書に記した事実. ¶***sift facts*** 様々な事実をふるい分ける. ¶***state*** the bare *facts* 事実を赤裸々に述べる. 【類】***state*** a *fact* attractively / ***state facts*** without prejudice / ***state*** a positive *fact* / His book hardly ***states*** the *fact* fairly. ¶***stress*** the *fact* that … …という事実を力説する. ¶He sarcastically remarked that the newspaper ***strikes*** a *fact* once in a while. その新聞はどうかすると本当のことも書くというのが彼の皮肉な評である. ¶***suppress facts*** 事実を隠ぺいする. ¶Let us ***take facts*** as we find them. 事実をありのままに受け入れよう. ‖ ***taking*** all these *facts* into consideration, I am induced to believe that … これらの事実をことごとく考慮した結果…を信じるようになった. ¶***Tell*** me the *facts* of the case just as they are. この事件の実状をそのまま話して下さい. ¶I have no desire to ***understate*** the *facts*. 私にはこれらの事実を内輪に述べようとする考えはない. ¶he ***unearthed*** several *facts* which threw light on … 彼は…に光明を投げる五六の事実を発見した. ¶***verify*** the *fact* that … …という事実を確かめる. ¶***weigh facts*** for themselves 彼ら自ら事実を検討する. ¶***write fact*** like fiction 事実を小説のように書く.

V² The *fact* ***blazed*** abroad, so marvellous it seemed. その事実はぱっと世間に広まったほど変り種のように思われた. ¶the *fact* ***came*** to my knowledge when … …の時に私はその事実を知った. ¶But the *facts* ***lie*** far otherwise. 所が事実はこれと大いに異っている. ¶But the real *fact* ***remains*** yet to be known. しかし真相はまだ分っていない. ‖ the *fact* ***remains*** that … …という事実には依然変る所がない.

Q an ***absolute*** *fact* 絶対的な事実. ¶an ***accomplished*** (=established) *fact* 既成事実 ‖ Woman suffrage will soon be an ***accomplished*** *fact*. 婦人参政権は間もなく実現されるであろう. 【類】In the near future it will be an ***accomplished*** *fact*. / It is an idea not likely to become an ***accomplished*** *fact* in the lifetime of the present generation. ¶It represents the ***actual*** *fact*. それは事実に合致している. ‖ in ***actual*** *fact* 実際. ¶These are ***admitted*** *facts*, not baseless assertions. これらは認められた事実であって根拠のない言明とは異っている. ¶An ***amazing*** *fact* was discovered that … …という驚くべき事実が見きわめられた. ¶I find the ***astonishing*** *fact* that … …という驚くべき事実を発見する. ¶***bald*** *facts* むきだしの事実. ¶the ***bare*** *fact* that … …というありのままの事実 ‖ ***bare unadorned*** *facts* むきだしの飾りのない事実. ¶the ***basic*** (=***key***) *facts* concerning … …に関する基礎的事実. ¶Sex is the ***central*** *fact* of life. 性は人生の中心を成す. ¶***clear*** *facts* 明白な事実. ¶when boiled down to ***cold*** *facts* 事実だけにせんじ詰めると. ‖ As a matter of ***cold*** *fact*, no human being wholly understands himself or herself.—George Trumbell Ladd. これは全くの事実であるが人間はだれも自分を十分理解しているとは遺憾ながら言い得ない. ¶a ***common*** *fact* in writing 作文に共通な事実. ¶***concrete*** *facts* 具体的な事実. ¶the ***deplorable*** *fact* that … …という悲しむべき事実. ¶a ***disquieting*** *fact* 不穏な事実. ¶***distorted*** *facts* 曲げられた事実. ¶a very ***encouraging*** *fact* to … …に取って非常に奨励になる事実. ¶an ***essential*** *fact* 根本的の事実. ¶an ***established historical*** *fact* 確立した歴史上の事実. ¶His *facts* are ***false***. 彼の事実の申立てはうそだ. ¶a ***familiar*** *fact* 有りふれた事実. ¶the ***further*** *fact* that … 更に…の事実. ¶the ***grievous*** *fact* remains that … …という悲しむべき事実は依然として残っている. ¶let the people know the ***hard*** *facts* of the situation 事態の冷厳な事実を国民に知らせる. ¶a quite ***incontestable*** *fact* 全く疑いを容れ得ない事実. ¶it is an ***incontrovertible*** *fact* that … …ということは争われない事実である. ¶prove by ***indisputable*** *facts* 明々白々な事実によって証明する. 【類】point out the ***indisputable*** *fact* that … ¶These ***interesting*** *facts* were brought home to the reader. これら興味ある事実を読者はしみじみ感じた. ¶a perfect mine of ***interesting*** *facts* 興味ある事実の完全な集成. ¶bring out some very ***interesting*** and ***enlightening*** *facts* 二三の非常に興味ある且つ啓蒙的な事実を紹介する. ¶***interesting*** and ***valuable*** facts 興味と価値のある諸事実. ¶***intractable*** *facts* 扱いにくい事実. ¶it is a ***lamentable*** *fact* that … …ということは嘆かわしい事実である. ¶among the ***likeliest*** *facts* of the near future is the assumption that … 近い将来に最も起りそうな事実の中に…という仮定がある. ¶a grasp of the ***main*** *facts* 要点の把握(はあく) ‖ carping such as this leaves untouched the great ***main*** *fact* that … このように理屈をこねると…という重要事実に触れないでしまう. ¶a reluctance to face ***manifest*** *facts* 明白な事実を認めることのいやさ. ¶***meagre*** *facts* 不十分な事実. ¶A cable brought him the first tidings of the ***melancholy*** *fact*. 海外電報が彼にその悲しい事実の最初の消息をもたらした. ¶Internationalism has recently become the most ***momentous*** *fact* in human affairs. 国際主義は最近人事における最も重要な事実となった. ¶a ***memorable*** *fact* 記憶すべき事実. ¶***mere bald*** *facts* 少しも飾らない事実. ¶it is a ***noteworthy*** *fact* that … …ということは注目すべき事実である. ¶a ***numerical*** *fact* 数で示された事実. ¶***obvious*** and ***wellworn*** *facts* 明白にして陳腐な事実. ¶The *facts* are too ***offensive*** to be proclaimed from a public platform. この事実はあまりにも耳障りであるから公会の壇上から述べるべきではない. ¶an ***outstanding*** *fact* 顕著な事実. ¶a ***paradoxical*** *fact* 逆だと思われる事実. ¶a ***patent*** *fact* 明白な事実. ¶a ***physical*** *fact* 物理学的事実. ¶a ***plain*** *fact* on sex hygiene 性衛生に関する卒直な事実. ¶a ***profound*** *fact* 深遠な事実. ¶it is now a ***proven*** *fact* that … …ということは今や証明ずみの事実である. ¶knowing the ***real*** *fact* of the case その事件の真相を知っているので. ¶it is a ***recognized*** *fact* that … …ということは世に認められた事実である. ¶it is a ***sad*** *fact* that … …ということは痛ましい事実だ. ¶***salient*** *facts* 顕著な事実. ¶a ***self-evident*** *fact* 自明の事実. ¶it is a ***sheer*** *fact* that … …ということは全くの事実である. ¶it is a ***significant*** *fact* that … …ということは意義のあることである. ¶it was a ***singular*** *fact* that … …ということは奇異なことであった. ¶tales of woe which make up in picturesque detail what may be lacking in ***solid*** *fact* 動かせない事実に欠けている所を美しい描写で埋合わした悲哀物語. ¶***sound*** *facts* about … …に関するりっぱな事実. ¶***statistical*** *facts* 統計上の事実. ¶a ***straight*** *fact* 飾りのない事実. ¶a ***strange*** *fact* 奇妙な事実. ¶It is a ***terrible*** *fact* that 20,000 families, nearly a third part of the population of Dublin, live in one-room tenements. ダブリンの人口の約三分の一たる二万の家族が一へやの棟割長屋に住んでいるとは聞くも恐ろしい事実である. 【類】Some ***terrible*** *facts* are set forth in his report on the public health of the city. ¶an ***unchallengeable*** *fact* 論ばくし得ない事実. ¶an ***undebatable*** *fact* 議論の余地のない事実. ¶an ***undeniable*** *fact* 否定し難い事実. ¶it is an ***undisguised*** *fact* that … …というのはありのままの事実である. ¶an ***undisputed*** *fact* 争われない事実. ¶it is an ***undoubted*** *fact* that … …ということは疑いを容れない事実である. ¶an ***unflattering*** *fact* 芳しくない(面白からぬ)事実. ¶hitherto ***unknown*** *facts* concerning … …に関してこれまで世に知れていない事実. ¶that painful sifting of tedious authorities for the proof of ***unnecessary*** *facts* in which historians delight 歴史家の道楽にやるいらないことの博引旁証的検討. ¶it is an ***unquestionable*** *fact* that … …ということは疑いのない事実である ‖ in the face of these ***unquestionable*** *facts* これらの疑いのない事実があるにもかかわらず. ¶This we know for an ***unshakable*** *fact*. このことは動かすべからざる事実としてわれわれは承知している. ¶This picture is the more significant from the ***very*** *fact* that the subject-matter is common. この絵は画題の平凡な所にかえって味がある. ¶a ***well-ascertained*** *fact* 十分確かめた事実. ¶a ***well-attested*** *fact* 十分証明された事実. ¶a ***well-known*** *fact* 周知の事実.

Q² ***by-way*** *facts* 枝葉にわたる事実. ¶find out ***food*** *facts* the world over 全世界の食糧に関する事実を調査する. ¶***number*** *facts* (=statistics) 統計. ¶***root*** *facts* of life 人生に関する根本的諸事実.

P the truth ***behind*** the *facts* ことの裏面にひそむ真相. ¶***despite*** the *fact* that … …と言う事実にもかかわらず. ¶That I know ***for*** a *fact*. そのことは私は事実として知っている. 【類】I know ***for*** a *fact* that … ¶***from*** the *fact* that …, it would appear that … …という事実から推して…が分るだろう ‖ I inferred it ***from*** the *fact* that … …の事実から私は推論した. ‖ apart ***from*** the *fact* that … …の事実は別として. ¶***in fact***=in point of fact 実際 ‖ It is …

in fact, but not in name. 名目はそうでなくても事実は…である. ‖ Great Britain is a republic *in fact*, but not in form. 大英国は事実上共和国であるが形の上ではそうでない. ‖ Many persons—*in fact*, most women—have never made an effort to understand themselves. 多くの人々—事実大概の女—は決して自己を了解しようと努力しなかった. ‖ Things apparently one are often *in fact* two. 一見一つに見えるものが実は二つであることはよくあることだ. ‖ the difficulty lies *in* the *fact* that ... 困難は...の事実に存する ‖ He was caught *in* the *fact*. 彼は現行犯でつかまった. ¶ Let us look *into* the *facts* of the case. 事件の真相を調べよう. ¶ as a matter *of fact* 事実上 ‖ his skill in marshalling a multitude *of facts* into good order 非常に多くの事実をりっぱに整とんする彼の手腕 ‖ I am aware (ignorant) *of* the *fact*. 私はその事実を知っている(知らない). ‖ I am not quite sure *of* the *facts*. 私は事実であるかどうか確かなことは知らない. ¶ He laid a stress *on* the *fact*. 彼はその事実を力説した. ‖ is based *on facts* 事実に立脚している ‖ This novel is founded *on fact*. この小説は事実に基ずいている. ‖ light *on* a *fact* attractive to any one who ... ...する者にとって興味ある事実に出会う ‖ I take my stand *on facts*. 私は事実を根拠としている. ¶ shut one's eyes *to* the *fact* 事実を見て見ぬ振りする ‖ this is to be traced *to* the *fact* that ... これは...という事実に帰すべきものだ. ¶ the first *fact* we hit *upon* was ... 第一に直面したことは...であった. ¶ *with* that *fact* in view その積りで.

P² a *fact of* daily observation 日常目につくこと ‖ This is a *fact of* human nature. このことは人間性に関する一つの事実だ. ‖ the *fact of* the matter is that ... その真相は...だ ‖ The *fact of* its being a translation is not indicated on the title-page. それが翻訳であるということがその本のとびらに示してない. ¶ *facts on* fire prevention 火災予防に関する事実. 【類】*facts on* women workers.

O the *fact* is that ... 事実は...である.

fact-finding, *n*. 実情探索.

Q *above-board fact-finding* 公明正大な事実探索.

faction, *n*. 徒党, 党派.

Q *contending factions* いがみ合う党派. ¶ *political factions* 政党.

Q² keep *extremist factions* under control 過激派を抑圧しておく. ¶ the *left-wing factions* of the Socialist Party 社会党左派. ¶ *opposition factions* 反対党. ¶ a *party faction* 政党内の党派. ¶ a *splinter faction* of a party 政党内の脱離派.

factor, *n*. 要素, 要因, 《英》代理人; 〔数〕因数.

V It *constitutes* a very important *factor* in the world's progress. それは世界の進歩にはなはだ重要な原動力となっている. ¶ The English-speaking peoples together *form* the dominant *factor* in the world affair. 英語国民というものが世界の主役を演じている. ¶ a dietary *lacking* the essential food *factors* 肝要な栄養分を欠いている規定飲食. ¶ *reduce* the chance *factor* to a minimum 偶然性を最小限度まで除く.

V² *factors affecting* the birth and marriage rates 出生及び結婚率に影響する要因. ¶ various *factors* that have *combined* to produce the result 相よってその結果を生じるに至った色々な要因. ¶ many *factors contributed* to ... 幾多の原因が重なって...した. ¶ analysis of the *factors creating* traffic congestion 交通の混雑を生じる原因の分析.

Q a *basic factor* 基礎的原因. ¶ There is no greater *binding factor* than a language. [人心の]総括力において国語にまさるものはない. ¶ a great complexity of *causal factors* 原因となる要素の非常な複雑性. ¶ a predominantly *causative factor* 特に原因となる要素. ¶ the *chief factor* in ... ...の主要素. ¶ a *common* (the *prime*) *factor* 〔数〕公(素)因数. ¶ The company has been the *controlling factor* in the American film industry. 同会社はアメリカ映画製作業界の支配者であった. ¶ *co-operative factors* 共同要因. ¶ a *deciding factor* in picking out a man for the position その地位に人を選抜するに当っての決定的要素. ¶ Air power is the *decisive factor* in modern war. 空軍力は近代戦の決定的要素だ. ¶ some *deep factors* 二三の深い要因. ¶ In the conference his voice was a *determining factor*. その会議において彼の発言は決定的な力を持っていた. 【類】He upheld the doctrine that climate, soil, food, and the aspects of nature are the *determining factors* in intellectual progress. / Merit (真価) is the only *determining factor* in life. ¶ a *domestic* (*foreign*) *factor* 国内(外国)代理業者. ¶ it has been one of the most *potent factors* in ... ¶ the *emotional factor* 感情的要素. ¶ *environmental factors* 環境的諸要因. ¶ an *essential factor* 必須な要素. ¶ *etiological factors* 病因的要素. ¶ one of the most *forceful factors* 最も有力な要因の一つ. ¶ the *governing factor* 主因. ¶ a *great factor* 偉大な原動力. ¶ Japanese coal is an *important factor* in the coal markets of the Far East. 日本の石炭は東洋の石炭市場における重要な位置を占めている. 【類】Time is a most *important factor* in this matter. ¶ one of the *important contributing factors* to ... ...に対して重要な原因をなすものの一つ. ¶ The tourist business is an *important economic factor*. 観光事業は経済上大切な要素である. ¶ The country is now an *industrial factor* of the first importance. その国は今日世界一流の工業国である. ¶ New York City is a *key factor* in national politics. ニューヨーク市は国政における重要都市である. ¶ a *leading factor* 主なる要素. ¶ a *mediating factor* of great influence 有力な仲裁的勢力. ¶ a *moral factor* 道徳的要素. ¶ has been a *powerful factor* in ... ...にあずかって大いに力がある. ¶ a *predisposing factor* それを起しやすい要因. ¶ the *predominating* (=*predominant*) *factor* in ... ...において勢力を占めている要素. ¶ The specialist is a *recognized factor* in the book-collecting world of today. ある部門を専門とすることは今日収集書界において認められている事実である. ¶ the newspaper as a *social factor* 社会の一要素としての新聞. ¶ Sentiment is not a *strong factor* in business. 感情は商売上の有力な要素ではない. ¶ *transitional factors* in the development 発展における一時的現象. ¶ a *valuable factor* in education 教育上貴重な要素. ¶ It is a *vanishing factor* in contemporary thought. それは現代思想には影が薄い. ¶ the *vital factor* in ... ...における重大要素.

Q² *long-term factors* making toward war 戦争に導く長期にわたる諸原因. ¶ *short-term factors* against war 戦争を防止する短期間の原動力. ¶ the shrinkage of the *time-space factor* 時間的空間的要因の短縮.

P food *as* a *factor* in living 生活の一要素としての食物 ‖ *as* a *factor* in the causation of disease 病気の発生の一原因として.

P² a *factor in* its extinction それが絶滅するに至った一原因. ¶ They are sold on terms so easy that the price need not be a *factor in* the mind of anyone. これらは非常に安く売っているので値段などはだれにも心配の種にならない. 【類】Energy and perseverance were *factors in* his success. / Amoy will altogether cease to be a *factor in* the tea trade of Formosa.

factory, *n*. 工場.

V *direct* a *factory* 工場を管理する. ¶ *dismantle* a *factory* 工場の設備を撤去する. ¶ *erect* (=*set up or build*) a *factory* on his own ground 自分の地所に工場を建てる. ¶ *start* a *factory* 工場を創設する.

Q a *complete factory* for making ... ...を製造する完備した工場. ¶ A big whaling ship is really a *floating factory*. 大型の捕鯨船は実際水上の工場だ. ¶ a *model up-to-date factory* 模範的で最新式設備のある工場. ¶ *stifling factories* むっと息詰まるような工場.

Q² an *aircraft* [*production*] *factory* 航空機工場. ¶ an *armament factory* 兵器工場. ¶ an *auto*[*mobile*] *factory* 自動車工場. ¶ The saloon has been sometimes said to be "a *convict factory*." 酒場は往々「罪人製造所」といわれてきた. ¶ a *clothing factory* 衣料工場. ¶ Japan is the world's *earthquake factory*. 日本は世界の地震工場だ. ¶ an *explosives* and *armaments factory* 爆発物および兵器工場. ¶ a *glass* (*soap*) *factory* ガラス(石けん)工場. ¶ a *munitions factory* 軍需品工場. ¶ an *ordnance factory* 兵器工場. ¶ a *salmon factory* さけかん製造所. ¶ a packer in a *sweet* [*stuff*] *factory* 製菓工場の包装員. ¶ a *textile factory* 織物工場. ¶ a *war clothing factory* 被服廠(しょう). ¶ a *washing factory* 洗たく工場.

P the waste *from* a *factory* 工場から出るくず. ¶ These articles are made *in factories*. これらの品物は工場で造られる. ¶ the owner *of* a *factory* 工場主.

faculty, *n*. (**1**) 才能, 能力, 力.

V *acquire* the merman's *faculty* of living under water 人魚のように水中に住む力を得る. ¶ Travel *brightens* the *faculties* and expands the ideas. 旅行は能力をみがき思想

を拡大する. ¶I ***collected*** my scattered *faculties* as best I could. 私は乱れた心をできるだけ取り直した. ¶… ***constitute*** the *faculty* of … …が…教授団を構成する. ¶***cultivate*** a *faculty* for saying things with propriety 正しいものの言方をする能力を養う. ¶***develop*** one's critical *faculty* その批判力を発達させる. 【類】Mathematics ***develops*** the reasoning *faculties*. ¶***elicit*** latent *faculties* 潜在する諸能力を引出す. ¶***excite*** and ***educate*** the æsthetic *faculties* 審美力を刺激しこれを養成する. ¶***exercise*** one's own *faculties* 自分の力を働かせる. ¶***handicap*** the soaring *faculty* of genius 縦横無尽に働く天才の力を制約する. ¶She ***has*** a *faculty* of housekeeping. 彼女は家政の手腕がある. ¶***lessen*** intellectual *faculties* 知能を低下させる. ¶He ***maintained*** his *faculties* to the last almost undiminished. 彼はほとんど最後(死ぬ)まで彼の知能を低下させることなく持続した. ¶***offend*** (***satisfy***) the æsthetic *faculty* 審美眼に不満を与える(を満足させる). ¶he ***possesses*** a rare *faculty* of … 彼は…というまれな力を持っている ‖ ***possess*** the *faculty* of foresight 先見の明がある. 【類】He ***possesses*** the happy *faculty* (長所) of choosing suitable lieutenants (適当な補佐役) to carry out his policies and to manage the industries he has created. ¶***preserve*** her mental *faculties* 彼女の知能を保持する. ¶***quicken*** the pupils' *faculties* of auditive perception 生徒の聴取力を発達させる. ¶***sharpen*** one's mental *faculty* その知能を鋭敏にする. ¶The New World has often ***shown*** a happy *faculty* for coining new words when needed, and forcing them into currency. 新大陸(米国)は必要なときに新語を作って無理にこれを通用させるという長所をしばしば示している.

V^2 His *faculties* ***returned***. 正気づいた.

Q education of the ***artistic*** *faculty* 趣味教育. ¶by a constant exercise of the ***best*** *faculties* 最善能力を絶えず練磨することによって. ¶Sympathy is a ***deeper*** *faculty* than curiosity. 同情は好奇心よりも一層深い力である. ¶***dormant*** *faculties* 眠っている能力. ¶excite and educate the ***aesthetic*** *faculties* 審美力を起させかつ養成する. ¶have a ***great*** *faculty* of reception 受容力にひいでている. ¶the limitations of ***human*** *faculty* 人間能力の限界 ‖ The faculty of intuition, a great ***human*** *faculty*, was obvious enough to the Asiatics and the ancients. 人間の偉大な能力である直感力はアジア人および古代人にはきわめて明白だった. ¶***intellectual*** *faculties* 知力. ¶***inventive*** *faculties* 発明力. ¶draw out the ***latent*** *faculties* of the mind 心の中の潜在能力を抽き出す. ¶Her ***mental*** *faculties* became deranged. 彼女は乱心した. ¶a man of ***notable*** *faculty* 敏腕家. ¶The ***organizing*** *faculty* is a rare gift. 組織力はまれに見る才能だ. ¶***rare critical*** *faculty* まれな批判力. ¶the ***rational*** *faculty* in man 人に備わっている理性. ¶develop one's ***reasoning*** *faculties* 推理力を発達させる. ¶a ***selective*** *faculty* 選択能力. ¶handicap the ***soaring*** *faculty* of genius 天才の天馬空を行く能力を妨げる. ¶Her *faculties* are still ***unimpaired***. 彼女の能力はいまだに衰えない.

Q^2 with some ***business*** *faculty* 幾分の事業の才を持って. ¶the ***teaching*** *faculty* 教授能力.

P He was ***on*** the *faculty* there for 33 years. 彼は三十三年間その学部に勤務した. ¶I found wine soothing ***to*** my excited *faculties*. ぶどう酒を飲んだら私の興奮した心が静まった.

P^2 a *faculty* ***for*** doing two things at once 一時に二事をなす能力. 【類】a great *faculty* ***for*** arithmetic. ¶the *faculty* ***of*** speech 言語の力.

(**2**) 専門家の団体; 教授団, 教授会; 学部, 分科.

V He ***joined*** the *faculty* of the university in 1898. 彼は一八九八年その大学の教授になった.

Q the ***whole*** *faculty* of professors その全教授団.

Q^2 the ***Harvard*** *faculty* ハーヴァード大学教授団. ¶members of the ***university*** *faculty* 大学学部の教職員.

P be ***on*** the *faculty* of Oxford オックスフォード大学の教職にある. ¶the total registration ***under*** the *faculties* of … was … …の(大学)諸分科における在籍学生総数は…であった.

P^2 the *faculty* ***of*** engineering 工学部 ‖ The University of Lille dates from the day of Charles V., and its *faculties* ***of*** law, letters, medicine, and science are luxuriously housed. リール大学はシャルル五世の時代に始まりその法律・文学・医学及び理学の諸分科はぜいたくな建物をもっている.

fad, *n.* 気まぐれ, 道楽; 気まぐれ流行.

V I ***have*** the *fad* of collecting books. 私には集書の道楽がある. ¶***start*** a *fad* ある道楽を始める.

Q Collecting stamps is a ***good*** *fad*. 切手収集はよい道楽だ. ¶"Deep breathing" is a ***great*** *fad* just now among the educated class in this country. 深呼吸はこの国の教養ある階級の間に目下大流行である. ¶a ***passing*** *fad* 一時の流行. ¶He has a ***queer*** *fad*. 彼には妙な道楽がある. ¶Red neckties are a ***recent*** *fad*. 赤ネクタイは最近の流行だ.

Q^2 yo-yo, the latest ***college*** *fad* 最近の大学生間に流行しているヨーヨー. ¶the ***pen-collecting*** *fad* ペン収集道楽.

P^2 a *fad* ***among*** youngsters 若い者の間の流行. ¶the *fad* ***for*** no hats 無帽の流行. ¶The *fad* ***of*** queer dance music is sweeping the whole country. 妙なダンス音楽が全国に流行している.

faddist, *n.* 物ずき.

Q^2 a ***diet*** *faddist* 食物により好みのある人.

fade, *v.* [色が]あせる; 衰える; 消える.

M *fade* ***away*** into the mists of the past 過去の霧中に消える ‖ *fade* ***away*** little by little 次第に消える. ¶This color *fades* ***fast***. この色はすぐさめる. ‖ The plane was *fading* ***fast*** on the horizon. 飛行機は見る見る水平線上に消えて行った. ¶*fade* ***out*** 〘映画〙 溶暗する ‖ Stars *faded* ***out*** from the sky. 星が空から消えた. ¶She got ill and ***slowly*** *faded* away. 彼女は病気にかかって次第に衰えて行った.

M^2 *fade* ***in*** 〘映画〙 溶明する.

P His name will never *fade* ***from*** the memory of the world. 彼の名は世人の記憶から決して消え去らないであろう. 【類】All the memory of her past days had *faded* ***from*** her mind. / The remembrance (思い出) of your kindness will never *fade* ***from*** my memory. ¶*fade* (=sink) ***into*** insignificance beside (=when compared with) … …と比較すると顔色なしである. ¶The bustle and din gradually *faded* ***to*** silence as night advanced. 夜のふけるにつれて騒々しさが段々沈静に落ちて行った.

fag, *n.* 苦役, 骨折仕事.

Q ***What*** a *fag!* いやな仕事だ.

Q^2 a remedy for ***brain*** *fag* 頭の仕事に対する薬.

fag, *v.* せっせと働く; 疲れ果てさせる.

M *fag* ***away*** at making a dictionary 辞書編集に非常な努力をする. ¶*fag* oneself ***ill*** 過労で病気になる. ¶be *fagged* ***out*** and tired 疲労困ぱいする. 【類】be *fagged* ***out*** by exhausting heat / He was almost *fagged* ***out***. ‖ This sort of work *fags* me ***out***. こういう仕事は疲れる. 【類】When I came home I was so *fagged* ***out*** and tired that I couldn't go to sleep for a long time.

P *fag* oneself ***to*** death 過労で死ぬ.

fag-end, *n.* 切れっぱし.

P^2 a *fag-end* ***of*** nobility 華族のはしくれ.

fag[g]ot, *n.* まきの束.

P^2 a *fagot* ***of*** firewood まきの一束.

fail, *n.* 失敗, 仕損じ.

P I will call on you ***without*** *fail*. 間違いなくお伺いします. 【類】It must be ready in three days ***without*** *fail*.

fail, *v.* 仕損じる, 失敗する, しくじる; [健康・視力が]衰える; 絶える; 失望させる.

M *Failed* ***again!*** また失敗. ¶*fail* ***completely*** すっかり仕損じる. ¶*fail* ***dismally*** ひどく失敗する. ¶Words *fail* me ***here***. この感じを何と言ってよいか分らない(演説などの場合). ¶The attempt *failed* ***ignominiously***. その企ては不面目な失敗に帰した. ¶The plan *failed* ***miserably***. その計画は惨たんたる失敗に終った. ¶he ***never*** *fails* to … 彼は必ず…する. ¶How ***rapidly*** he *fails!* 彼の衰弱の早いこと. 【類】Her health (sight) is *failing* ***rapidly***. ¶***sadly*** *fail* 惨敗する. ¶*fail* ***signally*** 著しい失敗となる. ¶Our food and water will ***soon*** *fail* [us]. われわれの飲食物はすぐ尽きてしまうだろう. ¶He will ***undoubtedly*** *fail*. 彼はきっとしくじるだろう. ¶They *fail* ***utterly*** to understand their own obligation. 彼らは自分らの義務を全く理解しない.

P He *failed* ***after*** all his labors. 彼は八方手を尽したが結局失敗した. ¶*fail* ***for*** want of help 援助が無いので失敗する. ¶He *failed* ***in*** his examination (scheme). 彼は試験(など)に失敗した. ‖ *fail* ***in*** business 商売に失敗する ‖ He *failed* ***in*** an action at law. 彼は敗訴した ‖ *fail* ***in*** one's duty 役目が立たない. 【類】A citizen *fails* ***in*** his duty to his community as well as to himself if he does not endeavour to preserve his health. ‖ *fail **in*** its objects その目的を果しそこねる ‖ *fail **in*** getting job 仕事にあぶれる ‖ having *failed **in*** the object of his visit 彼の訪問の使命を果さずに. 【類】*fail **in*** one's promise to ... / *fail **in*** one's efforts to ... ¶ It is likely to *fail **of*** its purpose. その目的を達し得ないであろう. ‖ it *fails **of*** its purpose if ... もし...ならその目的は達し得られない. 【類】*Failing **of*** its purpose, it was abandoned. / The policy is bound to *fail **of*** its object (=defeat its own purpose). ‖ The Bill *failed **of*** passage in the last Congress. その議案は前議会で通過しなかった. ‖ These endeavours have *failed **of*** their effect. これらの努力はその効を奏しなかった. ‖ He *failed **of*** promotion. 彼は昇進しそこねた. 【類】He *failed **of*** success. ¶ He *failed **through*** carelessness. 彼は不注意のために失敗した. ¶ The business *failed **with*** him. 彼の商売は失敗だった.

O He *failed* half the students he taught. 彼は彼の教えている生徒の半数を落第させた. ¶ The expected results *failed* to come. 期待した結果が現われなかった. ¶ on your *failing* to do so 君がそうしない場合には.

failing, *n.* 欠点, 短所; 仕損じ.

V The best men in art and letters are known to ***have*** *failings.* 芸術文学に最もすぐれた人にも短所があるものだ.

Q a ***feminine*** *failing* 女の弱点. ¶ a ***human*** *failing* 人間の弱味. ¶ his ***many*** *failings* 彼の幾多の短所.

P We must love our friends ***with*** all their *failings.* 友だちには色々短所があってもこれを愛さねばならない.

failure, *n.* 失敗; 欠乏; 不履行; 失敗者, 失敗ごと; 破産; 減退.

V ***attribute*** the *failure* of the company to the want of working capital 会社の破産を運転資金欠乏に帰する. ¶ ***confess*** *failure* 失敗を自白する. ¶ ***deserve*** *failure* 失敗するだけのことはある. ¶ ***dread*** *failure* 失敗を恐れる. ¶ To ... is to ***invite*** (=***court***) *failure.* ...することは失敗のもとである. ¶ If you fail, ***make*** *failure* a stepping stone to success. 失敗したらこれを成功に達する飛石とせよ. ‖ ***make*** a *failure* of it へまをやる. ¶ ***outlive*** a *failure* 失敗を回復する. ¶ ***prevent*** a *failure* 失敗を防ぐ. ¶ ***Regard*** each *failure* as a stimulus to further effort. 失敗する度にそれを今後の努力への刺激と考えよ. ¶ I have had to ***register*** two *failures* in my treatment. 私の治療で治らなかったものが二人あった. ¶ ***repeat*** a *failure* 失敗をくり返す. ¶ ***score*** a *failure* 失敗をする. ¶ I can't ***survive*** such *failure.* こんな失策をやっては私は生きておれない.

Q the most ***abject*** *failure* 最も悲惨な失敗. ¶ ***Certain*** *failure* is assured in advance. 必ず失敗することが始めから分っている. 【類】It will result in ***certain*** *failure.* ¶ It turned out a ***comparative*** *failure.* それは比較的失敗だということが判明した. ¶ a ***complete*** *failure* 大失敗. ¶ a ***conspicuous*** *failure* 目立った失敗. ¶ It was all a ***dead*** *failure.* それは全く大失敗であった. ¶ a ***decided*** *failure* 明らかな失敗. ¶ a ***disheartening*** *failure* 意気をそそうさせる失敗. ¶ a ***disastrous*** *failure* 悲惨な失敗. ¶ a ***dismal*** *failure* 惨敗. ¶ an ***entire*** *failure* 全然の失敗. ¶ a ***fiasco*** *failure* 大失敗. ¶ a ***financial*** *failure* 財政上の失敗(破産など). ¶ almost a ***flat*** *failure* ほとんど全くの失敗. ¶ a ***general*** *failure* in water-supply 広範囲の給水不能. ¶ a ***glaring*** *failure* in ... ...における大失敗. ¶ a ***glorious*** *failure* 名誉ある失敗. ¶ a ***heavy*** *failure* 大失敗. ¶ It proved a ***hopeless*** *failure.* それは望みなき失敗となった. ¶ an ***ignominious*** *failure* 不面目な失敗. ¶ a ***lamentable*** *failure* 悲しむべき失敗. ¶ a ***ludicrous*** *failure* こっけいな失敗. ¶ a ***partial*** *failure* 部分的失敗. ¶ a ***perfect*** *failure* 全然の失敗. ¶ a ***sudden*** *failure* of memory どう忘れ. ¶ owing to a ***temporary*** *failure* of health 一時健康がすぐれないので ‖ ***temporary*** *failure* of memory どう忘れ. ¶ class him among ***total*** *failures* 彼を全くの失敗者中に入れる. 【類】***total*** *failure* was the result of ... ¶ prove an ***unequivocal*** *failure* 明白な失敗となる. ¶ an ***utter*** *failure* 大失敗.

Q^2 a ***bank*** *failure* 銀行の破産. ¶ in [the] case of a ***crop*** *failure* 不作の場合に. ¶ The plane accident was ascribed to ***engine*** *failure.* 飛行機事故は発動機故障のためとされた. ¶ an ***investment*** *failure* 投資の失敗. ¶ a ***petrol*** *failure* [自動車の]ガソリン欠乏. ¶ ***power*** *failure* 動力不給, 停電 ‖ The thunderstorm caused ***power*** *failures* in many places. 雷雨であちこちに停電を生じた. ¶ an out-and-out ***school*** *failure* [学校で]全然ものにならなかった一例. ¶ a ***100 percent*** *failure* 百パーセントの失敗, 完敗.

P be disappointed ***at*** one's *failure* その失敗のために落胆する. ¶ undaunted ***by*** *failure* 失敗してもひるまずに ‖ learn ***by*** many *failures* and some successes, that ... 幾多の失敗と多少の成功によって...ということを悟る ‖ ***by*** the *failure* of the rice crop 米作不作のため. ¶ The attack ended ***in*** *failure.* その攻撃は失敗に終った. ‖ ***In*** *failure* of your compliance herewith, legal measures will be adopted to ... あなたがこれを承諾されぬ場合は...するように法律上の手続をふむことにします. ¶ He died ***of*** heart *failure.* 彼は心臓病で死んだ. ¶ ***On*** the *failure* of the health, he went back to Europe. 彼は健康を害して欧州に帰国した. ‖ ***on*** the *failure* of heirs in the direct line of the family その家に直系の嗣子のないときは. ¶ ***on account of*** the *failure* of the rain 雨が降らないので. ¶ ***owing to*** the sudden *failure* of electric power supply 配電が突然止ったので. 【類】***owing to*** the *failure* of the machinery (crop). ¶ ***through*** his business *failure* 彼の商売の失敗で. ¶ The scheme is foredoomed ***to*** *failure.* その計画は失敗に終る運命になっている.

P^2 a *failure* ***from*** the first 最初からの失敗. ¶ a *failure* ***in*** attendance 欠席 ‖ a *failure* ***in*** business 事業の失敗 ‖ a *failure* ***in*** the crop 不作 ‖ a *failure* ***in*** duty 勤務の怠慢 ‖ a *failure* ***in*** love 失恋 ‖ a *failure* ***in*** machinery 機械の故障 ‖ *failure* ***in*** studies 学業の不成績 ‖ The student was a flat *failure* ***in*** his study. その学生は勉強が全然できなかった. ¶ the *failure* ***of*** memory (sight) 記憶力(など)の減退 ‖ the *failure* ***of*** a promise 約束不履行 ‖ the *failure* ***of*** rain かんばつ ‖ the *failure* ***of*** stream 河水の枯渇. 【類】a *failure* ***of*** the potato crop ‖ *failures* ***of*** the medical profession 医者の手で治らなかった病人たち ‖ a *failure* ***of*** justice [裁判上]誤判の一例.

faint, *n.* 気絶, 人事不省.

Q He fell into a ***dead*** *faint.* 彼は人事不省に陥った. 【類】a patient in a ***dead*** *faint.*

P He recovered ***from*** a *faint.* 彼は生気づいた. ¶ fall (=drop) ***in*** a *faint* 気絶する.

faint, *a.* 青ざめている, 弱っている; 小胆な; 気の遠くなりそうな.

M ***How*** *faint* he looks! あの人の血色の悪いこと.

P *faint* ***in*** color 色が青ざめて ‖ He is *faint* ***in*** well-doing. 彼は善を為すに小胆だ. ¶ He is *faint* ***with*** fatigue (hunger). 彼は疲労(など)で弱っている. 【類】get *faint* ***with*** joy.

O feel *faint* 気が遠くなる. ¶ grow *faint* 失神状態になる.

faint, *v.* 気絶する, 目をまわす.

M He *fainted* ***away.*** 彼は気絶した.

P He *fainted* ***from*** the heat. 彼は暑気のために目をまわした.

fair, *n.* 市(いち), 定期市; 《米》博覧会.

V ***hold*** a *fair* 市を開く.

Q an ***agricultural*** *fair* 農産博覧会. ¶ a ***world's*** *fair* 万国博覧会.

Q^2 a ***book*** *fair* 書籍市. ¶ the ***British Industries*** *Fair* 大英勧業博覧会. ¶ a ***fancy*** *fair* 《英》慈善小間物市. ¶ a ***horse*** *fair* 馬市. ¶ a ***monster*** *fair* 大博覧会. ¶ In connection with various temple festivals, ***night*** *fairs* are held in many Japanese towns once or twice a month at fixed dates. 各種の祭礼に関連して日本の多くの都市では月一二回定期に夜の市が開かれる. ¶ a ***pumpkin-and-prize-pig country*** *fair* 《米》かぼちゃ優秀豚共進会. ¶ a ***rag*** *fair* ぼろ市. ¶ a ***statute*** *fair* 公設市. ¶ a ***trade*** *fair* 見本市. ¶ Chicago's ***1934*** *Fair* = the ***Chicago*** *Fair* of 1934 千九百三十四年のシカゴ博覧会.

P a day [too late] ***after*** the *fair* あとの祭(六日のあやめ, 十日の菊). ¶ a second-hand bookstall ***at*** a *fair* 縁日に出る古本露店. ¶ go ***to*** the *fair* 市に行く.

fair, *a.* 美麗な; 公明正大な.

M it is ***only*** *fair* to ... 当然...すべきである. ¶ Her eyes were ***very*** *fair.* 彼女の目は非常に美しかった.

P He is *fair* ***in*** his dealings. 彼はその行為において公明正大である. ¶ It is *fair* ***to*** both victor and vanquished. そうすると征服者被征服者双方に公平だ. ‖ She is not very *fair* ***to*** us. 彼女(先生)はわれわれにあまり公平じゃない. ¶ It is important that we should be *fair* ***with*** one another. われわれは互いに公明正大であることが肝要だ.

fairness, *n.* 公正, 正直.

V No one will ***question*** the *fairness* of the above statement of the case. その事件について上に述べた説の正しいことをだれも疑う者はあるまい. ¶ ***take*** *fairness* of dealing

into consideration 振り合いを考える.
Q it may in ***common fairness*** be said that ... ...と言って少しも差支えないと思う. ¶ ***dispassionate fairness*** 公平無私. ¶ however, in ***due fairness***, I must say that ... しかし公平に見て私は...と言わねばならない.
P it should ***in fairness*** be stated that ... 公平に見て...と言わねばならない. 【類】 ***in fairness*** to him let me say that...

fairy, *n.* 精.
Q² a ***snow fairy***=a snow woman 雪女郎.

fairyland, *n.* 仙(せん)境.
Q This is a ***veritable fairyland*** in a desert of mortar and brick. これはしっくいやれんがの建物ばかりの中でさながら仙境のようなものだ.
P² a ***fairyland of*** epicureanism 食道の極楽.

faith, *n.* 信仰, 信念, 信条; 信用; 信義; 誓約; 宗教.
V They were compelled to ***abjure*** their *faith*. 彼らは信仰を棄てなければならなかった. ¶ ***attach*** much *faith* to ... ...を大いに信用する. ¶ ***avow*** one's *faith* in face of persecution 迫害を恐れず自己の信仰を公言する. 【類】 he ***avows*** his absolute *faith* in ... ¶ he has ***broken*** *faith* with ... 彼は...に背信行為をした. ¶ ***corrupt*** the *faith* 信仰を壊乱する. ¶ ***crush*** the forbidden *faith* 禁教を撲滅する. ¶ ***deepen*** *faith* in Christ キリストに対する信仰を深める. ¶ ***defend*** one's *faith* 自己の信仰を護る. ¶ ***destroy*** one's *faith* 信用を裏切る. ¶ ***embrace*** the *faith* of Mohammed マホメットを信仰する. ¶ ***engage faith*** 約束する. ¶ They succeeded in ***eradicating*** the new *faith* from Japan. 日本からこの新教を一掃することができた. ¶ ***extend*** the Buddhist *faith* 仏教をひろめる. ¶ All Europe, with the exception of Turkey, ***follows*** the Christian *faith*. トルコ以外の全欧州はキリスト教を信奉している. ¶ ***forsake*** a *faith* 信仰を棄てる. ¶ We ***have*** great *faith* in his judgment. われわれは彼の判断を確信している. ‖ ***have*** *faith* in reason 理性を信じる ‖ I ***have*** a *faith* in the infinite possibilities for good in the cinema. 私は映画の利用には無限の将来性があることを信じている. 【類】 ***have faith*** in the future of our English race / They ***have faith*** in a silly superstition. / I ***have*** no *faith* in whatever he tells me. / I ***have*** little *faith* in grammatical studies as a preparation for writing good English. ¶ This does not ***increase*** one's *faith* in human nature. これを見ると人間の心のきたないのにあきれる. ¶ ***inspire*** in his countrymen a *faith* in their ability to win 勝利の信念を国民に鼓吹する. ¶ keep one's *faith* 信仰を棄てない ‖ ***keep faith*** with the public 世人の信望に添う. ¶ ***kindle*** this *faith* この信頼を起させる. ¶ ***lack*** *faith* in ... ...に対する信念を欠く. ¶ ***let*** not our *faith* and sympathy waver for ... ...に対するわれわれの信念と同情を薄めないようにしよう. ¶ ***lose*** *faith* in one's fellow creatures 同胞に対する信頼の念を失う. 【類】 He ***lost*** *faith* in Christianity. / He ***lost*** *faith* in old traditions. ‖ He ***lost*** the old *faith* (古い信仰). ¶ ***pin*** one's *faith* to (=on) a theory ある学説を固く信じる ‖ Don't ***pin*** your *faith* to quack remedies for nervousness. 神経病のいかさま療法を信じてはいけない. ¶ ***place*** little *faith* in ... ...をあまり信じない. ¶ ***pledge*** *faith* 忠実を誓う. ¶ ***profess*** the Buddhist *faith* 仏教を公然信仰する. 【類】 persons ***professing*** the Roman Catholic *faith*. ¶ ***promulgate*** a *faith* 教えを広める. ¶ ***propagate*** the *faith* その宗教を宣伝する. ¶ ***put*** *faith* in him 彼を信頼する ‖ He was one of those generous, true-hearted men who ***put*** their *faith* in a light woman. 彼は浮気女を信じるような寛大で信実な男の一人であった. 【類】 Let me advise you not to ***put*** your *faith* in such a remedy (療法). ¶ He ***received*** *faith* and was converted. 彼は信仰を起してその教えに入った. ¶ fully ***reinstate*** the Shinto *faith* 神道の信仰を完全に旧に復する. ¶ ***renounce*** the Catholic *faith* 旧教を棄てる. ¶ ***repose*** *faith* in ... ...を信じる. ¶ ***retain*** *faith* 信仰を失わない. ¶ ***shake*** one's *faith* in him as a teacher 教師としての彼に対するわれわれの信用をぐらつかせる. 【類】 His *faith* in the existence of Santa Claus has been ***shaken***. ¶ to ***show*** his good *faith* 彼の好意を示すために. ¶ ***spread*** one's *faith* 自分の信じる宗教を広める. ¶ ***strengthen*** one's religious *faith* その信仰を堅固にする. ¶ ***violate*** one's *faith* 約束を破る.
Q toleration of ***all faiths*** あらゆる信仰への寛容. ¶ ***bad faith*** 不信. ¶ ***blind faith*** 盲目的信仰. ¶ by ***blind emotional faith*** 盲目的で感情的な信仰で. ¶ the spread of the ***Christian faith*** キリスト教の普及. ¶ have the ***deep-seated faith*** in ... ...を根強く信じている. ¶ followers of ***different faiths*** それぞれ異る宗教の信奉者. ¶ the ***firm faith*** in the possibility of a world made better through complete mutual understanding 完全な相互理解を通じて世界をもっとよいものにすることができるという確信. ¶ the ***four faiths*** [神仏道耶の]四教. ¶ He acted in ***good faith*** and with reasonable care. 彼は誠意をもってかつ相当の注意を払って行動した. 【類】 written in ***good faith*** / believe in the ***good faith*** of ... / These promises have been made in ***good faith***. ‖ a third peron acting in ***good faith*** 〘法〙善意の第三者. ¶ He has ***implicit faith*** in her. 彼は一ずに彼女を信じている. ¶ Japan's ***indigenous faith*** 日本固有の宗教. ¶ I have ***infinite faith*** in ... 私は...を無限に信じている. ¶ of ***lukewarm faith*** なまぬるい信仰の. 【類】 a ***lukewarm faith***. ¶ a ***monotheistic faith*** 一神教的信仰. ¶ the ***mutual faith*** of brothers 兄弟の信義. ¶ the ***primal faiths*** 主要な信条. ¶ with ***profound faith*** in ... ...を深く信じて. ¶ ***rational faith*** 合理的信仰. ¶ a ***reasoning faith*** 筋道の立った信仰. ¶ adherents of various ***religious faiths*** 各種宗教の信者. ¶ a ***renewed faith*** in his country's future 彼の国の将来についての更新された信念. ¶ a ***rival faith*** [仏教に対するキリスト教のごとき]対立の宗教. ¶ the ***sacred faith*** of man in man 人間に対する人間の神聖な信用. ¶ heroes and heroines of ***steadfast faith*** and will 信仰と意志の強固な男女の勇者. ¶ a ***sturdy faith*** in his own powers 彼自身の力に対する堅固な信念. ¶ They have an ***unquestioning faith*** in God. 神を絶対に信じている. ¶ his ***unwavering faith*** and devotion 彼のゆるぎない信仰と帰依.
Q² embrace the ***Buddhist faith*** 仏門に帰依する.
P He is a Presbyterian ***by faith***. 彼は長老派の信者である. ‖ ***by*** my *faith* 誓って. ¶ fight ***for faith*** その信じる宗教のために戦う. ¶ He is weak ***in faith***. 彼は信仰が弱い. ‖ He was brought up ***in*** the Christian *faith*. 彼はキリスト教の中に育った. ¶ the articles ***of faith*** 信仰個条. ¶ accept a principle ***on faith*** 誓ってある主義を奉じる ‖ I take it all ***on faith***. 私は信用して(証拠を見ないで)それを全部引取る. ¶ ***through faith*** we understand that ... 信仰を通してわれわれは...ということが分る. ¶ ***upon*** my *faith* 誓って. ¶ ***with*** unshaken *faith* ゆるぎない信念をもって ‖ ***with*** firm *faith* that it will ... それが...するという確信を持って.
P² *faith* ***in*** medicine (God) 薬の効能(など)の信仰. 【類】 His *faith* ***in*** the ultimate success of ... was unshaken.

faithful, *n.* 忠実な人.
Q² a ***party faithful*** 忠実な党員.

faithful, *a.* 忠実な, 信実な, 誠実な.
M His servant was ***nobly faithful*** and honest. 彼の召使は気高いほど忠実でかつ正直であった.
P ***faithful from*** first to last 誠実で一貫した. ¶ ***faithful in*** word and deed 言行の信実な. ¶ ***faithful in*** service 勤務に忠実な. ¶ ***faithful to*** duties (one's word, a person) 義務(など)に忠実な. ¶ ***faithful to*** the end 忠実で終始一貫する(有終の美をなす) ‖ ***faithful to*** death 死ぬまで忠実な ‖ ***faithful to*** a fault 極端に忠実な. 【類】 ***faithful to*** her husband (his wife) / be ***faithful to*** reality.

faithfulness, *n.* 忠実.
P² ***faithfulness in*** little things 小事に忠なること. ¶ his ***faithfulness to*** his duties 彼の義務に対する忠実.

fake, *n.* 偽造品, にせもの; いかさま師.
Q His illness was a ***perfect fake***. 彼の病気は全く仮病だ.
Q² a ***ginseng fake*** 朝鮮にんじんのにせ物. ¶ a ***real estate fake*** 不動産詐欺. ¶ a ***rich widow fake*** 金持未亡人詐欺.

faithless, *a.* 不忠実な.
P prove ***faithless to*** one's master 主に不忠になる.

fake, *v.* でっちあげる; 偽造する.
M² ***fake up*** a business report 事業報告をでっちあげる. 【類】 The whole story had been ***faked up***.

falcon, *n.* はやぶさ.
Q² a ***hunting falcon*** 狩用のはやぶさ.

fall, *n.* 落下, 降下; 墜落; 転倒; 低下; 下落; 没落; 衰退, 衰退期; [相撲の]投げ, 一勝負.
V ***anticipate*** a *fall* in the market 市場における下落を予想する. ¶ If you have to jump from a window, throw out mattress and bedding to ***break*** your *fall*. 窓から飛降りなければならないときは落ちてもふうわりするように床敷やふとんを投げ出しなさい. ¶ It does not ***constitute*** a *fall*. [相

撲で]それは負けにはならない. ¶It will ***endanger*** a *fall*. そうすると倒れる危険がある. ¶***frequent*** *falls* in market prices たびたびの市価の下落. ¶***gain*** a *fall* [相撲などに]勝つ. ¶***get*** a bad *fall* ひどくころぶ ‖ I am sorry to see you ***get*** such a *fall*. そんなにころんでお気の毒です. ¶***have*** a *fall* from a bicycle 自転車から落ちる ‖ He ***had*** a *fall* which injured the scalp. 彼はころんで頭をけがした. ‖ ***have*** a great *fall* ひどく倒れる; 〖商〗大低落を見る. ¶***lose*** a *fall* [相撲など]負ける. ¶He ***won*** two *falls* out of three. 彼は三番の中で二番勝った.

Q This is rather a ***big*** *fall* of snow for Tokyo. これは東京としてはかなりの大雪だ. ‖ There was a ***big*** *fall* in Bank of Ireland stock. アイルランド銀行株が暴落した. ¶a ***disastrous*** *fall* in the price of ... ...の価の惨落. ¶the ***first*** *fall* of prostitutes 売春生活への始めての堕落. ¶I had a ***hard*** (=***severe***) *fall*. 私はひどくころんだ. ¶have a ***heavy*** *fall* of rain (snow) 大雨(など)が降る. ¶a ***sharp*** *fall* in the temperature 温度の激しい低下. ¶a ***steady*** *fall* of rain 降りしきる雨. ¶There was a ***sudden*** *fall* in prices. 物価が急に下落した. ¶a ***thin drizzling*** *fall* しとしと降る細雨. ¶the ***twilight's*** *fall* 夕暮.

Q² the ***birth-rate*** *falls* 出生率低下. ¶a ***two-inch*** *fall* of snow 二インチの降雪.

P The sale is complete ***at*** the *fall* of the hammer. [競売で]つちをぽんと打つと取引がきまる. ¶The rent is ***on*** the *fall*. 家賃が下り気味だ. ‖ ***on*** the *fall* of the Shogunate and the restoration to power of the Mikado 幕府が倒れて王政復古になったとき. ¶a waterfall ***with*** a *fall* of 500 yards 五百ヤードの落差のある滝.

P² a *fall* ***from*** a horse 落馬. ¶a *fall* ***in*** prices (stocks) 価格(など)の下落 ‖ a *fall* ***in*** one's income 収入の減少. ¶the *fall* ***of*** leaves 落葉 ‖ a *fall* ***of*** temperature 温度の降下. 【類】a *fall* ***of*** mercury in a thermometer / the *fall* ***of*** prices (rents) ‖ the *fall* ***of*** an Empire 帝国の滅亡 ‖ after the *fall* ***of*** the Shogunate 将軍家の没落後 ‖ the *fall* ***of*** Port Arthur 旅順の陥落 ‖ the *fall* ***of*** life 晩年 ‖ the *fall* of wind なぎ ‖ the *fall* ***of*** a day (year) 日(など)の暮. ¶a *fall* ***on*** the (=one's) back 仰向けの転倒.

fall, *v.* 落ちる, 沈む; 下がる; 減退する; 下落する, 堕落する; 零落する; ...になる; 降りかかる; 当る; 取りかかる; 付く; 漏れる.

M After a brief season of useful labor there, she *fell* ***asleep*** in Jesus, lamented by all who knew her. そこでしばらく有益な働きをしてから彼女はすべての知人に悼まれながら天国の眠りについた. ‖ He *fell* ***asleep*** over it. 彼はそれを読みながら眠った. 【類】I cannot *fall* ***asleep***. ¶*fall* ***away*** from faith 信仰を棄てる. 【類】*fall* ***away*** from duty (allegiance) ‖ *fall* ***away*** in flesh 肉が落ちる. 【類】I *fall* ***away*** in summer. ‖ *fall* ***away*** allegiance to ... ...に寝返りを打つ ‖ The population has *fallen* ***away***. 人口が減じた. ‖ It has certainly *fallen* ***away*** in public interest. それは確かに一般世人の興味から離れてしまった. ¶*fall* ***back*** into silence もと通りの静寂に復する ‖ *fall* ***back*** into a chair 再びいすに腰を下ろす ‖ *fall* ***back*** into the power of ... 再び...の権力を握る ‖ *fall* ***back*** on the teachings of the Master キリストの教えに慰安を求める ‖ *fall* ***back*** on the second front 退いて第二線による ‖ be forced to *fall* ***back*** upon the other alternative 第二の策に頼らざるを得ない ‖ They have no private means to *fall* ***back*** upon. 彼らは失敗したとき頼るべき私産がない. ‖ *fall* ***back*** to their final defense lines 退いて最後の防御線に拠る. ¶he *fell* ***deeply*** in love with ... 彼は...と深い恋仲に落ちた. ¶With a scream, she *fell* ***down*** senseless on the ground. きやっと叫んで彼女は人事不省になって地上に倒れた. ¶The bill *falls* (=becomes) ***due*** next month. 手形は来月支払わなくてはならない. ¶These problems *fall* ***easily*** into three groups which may be called problems of ..., ..., and ... これらの問題は容易に三部類に分けて...の問題, ...の問題, 及び...の問題とすることができる. ‖ The word "..." *falls* so ***easily*** from our lips. 一にも...二にも...である. ¶The practice is ***fast*** *falling* into disuse. この習慣はどんどんすたれて行く. ‖ Snow *falls* ***fast*** on our lawn. 雪が芝生にどんどん降る. ‖ Her tears *fell* ***fast***. 彼女は涙がとめどもなく流れた. ¶*fall* ***flat*** on one's back 仰向けざまにばったり倒れる ‖ *fall* ***flat*** to the ground 地上にばったり倒れる. ¶*fall* ***foul*** of ... [船など]...と衝突する ‖ *fall* ***foul*** with ... ...とけんかする. ¶*fall* ***frequently*** into this error しばしばこの誤りに陥る. ¶The army *fell* ***furiously*** upon the city. 軍隊は猛烈にその市を攻撃した. ¶it *falls* more ***gently*** on the ears to say ... ...と言った方が感じがよい ‖ The rain was ***gently*** *falling* 雨がしとしと降っていた. 【類】Snowflakes *falling* ***gently*** down on the ground. ¶*fall* ***gradually*** into disuse だんだんすたれる ‖ The land *falls* ***gradually*** to the sea. 土地が次第に海の方に下っている. ¶*fall* ***headlong*** down the flight of stairs 階段から真さかさまに落ちる. ¶Prices *fall* ***heavily***. 値段がどんと下落する. ‖ Rain now began to *fall* ***heavily***. 雨が今ひどく降り出した. ¶*fall* ***ill*** 病気になる. ¶*fall* ***lower*** and ***lower*** in one's class クラスで段々席次が下がる. ¶They ***naturally*** *fall* into three classes. 当然三種類に分れる. 【類】***naturally*** *fall* into two main divisions. ¶*fall* ***nearly*** over the cliff がけから落ちそうになる. ¶***Occasionally*** he *falls* into strange errors. 折々彼は妙な誤りに陥る. ¶A feather *fell* ***out***. 羽根が抜けた. 【類】Sometimes hair *falls* ***out*** after illness. ‖ Seeds *fall* ***out*** on the ground. 種子が地上にこぼれる. ‖ The bottom of the box *fell* ***out***. 箱の底が抜けた. ‖ They never *fall* ***out*** when they are at play. 彼らは遊び事をしていると決してけんかをしない. ‖ it *fell* ***out*** (=happened) one day that ... ある日...ということが起った ‖ *fall* ***out*** among themselves 内輪争いをする ‖ Two friends of old standing do not *fall* ***out*** for such a trifle. 古なじみの二人の友人はこんなつまらぬことでけんかはしない. 【類】Some of the soldiers *fell* ***out*** from fatigue. ‖ *fall* ***out*** with one another about trifles つまらないことで互いにけんかをする. ¶He *fell* ***overboard*** and drowned. 舷側(げんそく)から落ちて水死した. ¶*fall* ***passionately*** in love with ... 熱烈に...を恋する. ¶His well-chosen words *fell* ***pleasantly*** on our ears. 彼の洗練された言葉はわれわれの耳に気持よく響いた. ¶*fall* ***plop*** into the water 水中にぽちゃんと落ちる. ¶*fall* ***prostrate*** 平伏する. ¶Such a bubble of a name will ***quickly*** *fall* into the oblivion which it deserves. こんな泡沫(ほうまつ)にひとしい名はたちまち忘れられてしまうであろうがそれも当然のことである. ¶Geographically this region *falls* ***roughly*** into four great divisions. この地方は地理的に言うと大体四大区になる. ‖ *fall* ***roughly*** into the following classes 大体次の種類に分れる. ¶*fall* ***senseless*** 卒倒する. ¶The rope *fell* ***short***. 綱が短くって届かなかった. ‖ the quantity *fell* ***short*** of ... 数量が...に達しなかった ‖ sales *falling* ***short*** of output 産出額に及ばない売上. 【類】Our exports *fall* ***short*** of our imports. ‖ *fall* far ***short*** of £7,000 per annum 年に七千ポンドをぐっと下る. 【類】*fall* ***short*** of provisions. ‖ The scenes depicted by poets *fall* ***short*** of the reality. 詩人の描写する光景は現実に及ばない. ‖ *fall* ***short*** of our expectation われわれの期待に添わない. ¶He *fell* ***sick*** with a fever. 彼は熱病にかかった. ¶The rain is *falling* ***softly***. 雨がしとしと降っている. ¶Prices have ***steeply*** *fallen*. 値段が急に下落した. ¶but it ***unluckily*** *fell* out that ... ところが運悪く...となった. ¶she *fell* ***wildly*** in love with ... 彼女は...を熱烈に恋した.

M² *fall* ***behind*** in work (payment) 仕事(支払)が遅れる. ¶Japan *falls* far ***behind*** of Europe in ... 日本は...においてヨーロッパより余ほど後れている. 【類】*fall* ***behind*** in one's school work (学業) / *fall* ***behind*** in a race. ¶*Fall* ***in***! =Rally! 集まれ ‖ The roof *fell* ***in***. 屋根が落ち込んだ. 【類】Part after part of the roof continued to *fall* ***in***. ‖ *fall* ***in*** for his share 彼の分前になる ‖ if it *falls* ***in*** with your view 御同意なら ‖ I presume you will *fall* ***in*** with his wish. 君は彼の希望に同意するだろうと思う. 【類】He *fell* ***in*** with my proposal (提案). ‖ *fall* ***in*** with one's own taste 趣味に合う(うまが合う) ‖ On the road I *fell* ***in*** with an old friend. 道路上でひょっくり旧友に会った. ‖ The ship *fell* ***in*** with the steamer derelict and towed her in here. その船が遺棄された汽船を偶然見つけてここへ引いてきた. ¶They *fall* ***in*** and ***out*** many times a day. 彼らは一日何度もけんかする. ¶I almost *fell* ***off***. すんでのことに落ちる所だった. ‖ *fall* ***off*** badly 下火になる, すたれてくる. 【類】Supplies are *falling* ***off*** rapidly. / Its circulation (発行部数) *fell* ***off*** sharply. / Demand *fell* ***off***. / Most members *fell* ***off*** one by one. / Export trade *fell* ***off***. / The output (産出高) gradually *fell* ***off***. / His appetite (食欲) *fell* ***off***. / Business has *fallen* ***off*** considerably. / Employment (就職) is *falling* ***off***. ‖ His hair is gradually *falling* ***off***. 彼の

毛髪はだんだん薄くなる. ‖ Enrollment in teachers' colleges has *fallen off*. 師範大学の入学者が減った. ‖ Words *fall off* by disuse. 言葉は使わないとすたれる. ‖ A dish *fell off* of the table. 《米》さらが食卓から落ちた. ‖ He *fell off* of the cliff. 《米》彼はがけから落ちた. ¶ *Fall on*! 攻撃開始! ¶ The rain is *falling on* and *off*. 雨が降ったりやんだりしている. ¶ The meeting *fell through*. 会がお流れになった. ¶ You may consider the business *fallen through*. その取引はだめだったとお考え下さい. ‖ The charter has *fallen through*. 雇船契約が失敗に終った. 【類】 Our plan *fell through* (お流れとなった). / Negotiations for peace have *fallen through*. / There is a probability of the negotiations *falling through*.

P The shadow *fell across* the street. それが影を街に投じた. ¶ *fall against* ... …に倒れかかる. ¶ *fall among* enemies 敵の手中に落ちる. ¶ *fall at* one's feet 人の足下にひれ伏す ‖ His spirits *fell at* the sad news. 悲報に接して彼は気を落した. ¶ His eyes *fell before* her gaze. 彼女がじーっと見たので彼は目をうつむけた. ‖ Once at least he *fell before* temptation. 少くとも一度彼は誘惑に負けた. ¶ *fall behind* foreign competitors 外国の競争者に負ける ‖ a man who has *fallen behind* his age 時代に取残された人. 【類】 Dutch commerce was now *falling behind* that of England. ¶ He *fell below* his master in skill. 彼は熟練の点で師匠に及ばなかった. ¶ *fall beneath* the dominion of Japan 日本の領土となる. ¶ *fall between* two stools あぶはち取らずになる. ¶ *fall down* the embankment 土手から落ちる. ¶ I'll not *fall for* any more of his tricks. もうこの上彼の術策に引っかからない. ‖ He *fell for* her at first sight. 《米》彼は一目見て彼女にほれ込んだ. ¶ Hangings *fell from* the walls around. 周囲の壁に掛物がかけてあった. ‖ The minister *fell from* favor at Court. その大臣は朝廷の信任が薄らいだ. ‖ though *fallen from* grace 恩ちょうを失ったが ‖ It *fell from* my pocket when I was taking a walk a few days ago. それは私が数日前散歩していたときポケットから落ちた. ‖ *fall from* the back of a horse 落馬する. 【類】 *fall from* a bridge (tree, height, boat) ‖ He *fell from* Christianity and turned pagan. 彼はキリスト教を捨てて異教徒になった. ‖ These words *fall* often *from* people's lips. これらの言葉はしばしば人の口からもれる. ¶ The rain *fell in* torrents. 土砂降りであった. ¶ It is one of the most interesting books which have *fallen in* my way. それは私の手に入った最も興味ある本の一つである. ‖ It has been my custom for many years to examine them as they *fell in* my way (=came under my observation[4]). それが目にふれると注意して見るのがここ数年来私の習慣であった. ‖ By the old calendar, the seventh day of the seventh month would *fall in* the autumn season. 旧暦では七月七日は秋の季節になる. ‖ He has *fallen in* the public estimation. 彼は世間の評判が悪くなった. ‖ do not *fall in* line with ... …の線に沿わない ‖ *fall in* step with ... …と歩調をそろえる ‖ *fall in* love with words 言葉に深い興味を持つ ‖ men who *fell* (=were killed) *in* the war (=action, active service *or* war service) 戦死者 ‖ *fall in* one's circumstances 零落する. ¶ *fall into* another's arms 人の腕に抱きこまれる ‖ The work of translating it has *fallen into* competent hands. その翻訳仕事はしっかりした人が引受けた. ‖ prisoners who *fell into* our hands われわれの手にかかった捕虜. 【類】 Some of the greatest treasures in book collecting have *fallen into* the hands of men of moderate incomes. / The Zeppelin was the first German giant aeroplane to *fall into* the hands of the Allies. ‖ Rather would I render myself to God than *fall into* the hands of those men. それらの者どもの手にかかるよりはむしろこの身を神様の御手にお任せした方がよい. ‖ *fall into* a well 井戸に落ちる. 【類】 *fall into* the water / *fall into* the hold (船艙) of a ship / *fall into* the bottom of Hell (地獄のどん底) / *fall into* the slough (泥沼) / *fall into* a hole which one has dug for others / The river *falls* (=empties) *into* a sea after a long journey. / Here the river *falls into* a bay. ‖ *fall into* trick (snare) わなにかかる. 【類】 He himself *fell into* snares spread for her. ‖ *fall into* danger あぶない目に会う ‖ *fall into* one's fangs その毒手にかかる ‖ A pretty trap we have *fallen into!* えらいわなにかかったものだ. 【類】 *fall into* the power of the Anglo-Saxon ‖ *fall into* three main classes 大きく三種に分かれる ‖ It does not *fall into* either class. それはどの部類にも属さない. 【類】 they will naturally *fall into* these two classes: / *fall into* two general (distinct) classes / Ancient history, treated ethnographically (民俗学的に), *falls* (=can be divided) *into* two great divisions—Eastern and Western peoples. / The book *falls into* three sections. / The story *falls into* three parts. / The subject *falls into* the following divisions: / *fall into* three chief categories / not *falling into* the above category / *fall into* four (two main) groups ‖ The period naturally *falls into* two phases. その期間は自然二つの局面に分かれる. ‖ The history naturally *falls into* three periods. その歴史は当然三期に分かたれる. ‖ *fall into* two periods, viz. that ..., and that ... 二つの時期すなわち…と…に分かたれる ‖ The industry *fell into* decay. その工業は衰亡した. ‖ Pancake Day has *fallen into* desuetude as a festival. ざんげ節は祭日としてはすたれてしまった. 【類】 The treasury *fell into* extreme difficulties. / The firm will *fall into* financial difficulties. ‖ It has *fallen into* disfavor. それははやらなくなった. 【類】 *fall into* deep disfavor / He *fell into* disfavor at the Court of Alexander III. / The practice (custom) *fell into* total disrepute. / The practice has *fallen into* almost complete disuse. / The rite has *fallen into* general (total) disuse. / words that have *fallen into* disfavor (=disuse) / The cheaper sorts have *fallen into* disfavor (不人気). / The doctrine has *fallen into* discredit. / He is *fallen into* disgrace (不評判). ‖ *fall into* the good graces of ... …の気に入る ‖ *fall into* disorder (=confusion) 混乱に陥る ‖ *fall into* a faint 失神状態になる ‖ *fall into* dissolute habits 身を持ちくずす ‖ *fall into* a habit of smoking 喫煙のくせがつく ‖ *fall into* ill health 健康をそこのう ‖ Tortured by unsatisfied longing, he *fell into* a sheer love-sickness. 思いこがれて彼は恋わずらいになった. ‖ *fall into* a truculent mood 殺気をおびる ‖ girls who have *fallen into* shame 泥水にはまった少女たち ‖ *fall into* neglect 無視されるようになる ‖ The name has *fallen into* oblivion. その名は世に忘れられてしまった. 【類】 allow it to *fall into* oblivion / *fall into* obsolescence / *fall into* a passion of delight (喜悦の情) / He *fell into* rages over nothing. ‖ a samurai who had *fallen into* poverty 貧乏になった武士. 【類】 *fall into* dire poverty ‖ The temple has *fallen into* very bad repair. そのお寺は大層荒れている. 【類】 decay and *fall into* ruin ‖ It *fell into* that sweet, soft, gentle repose so characteristic of healthy, happy childhood. その子は丈夫で幸福な幼年時代に特有なあの美わしいやさしい眠りに落ちた. ‖ *fall into* a deep (=sound) sleep 深い眠りに落ちる. 【類】 *fall* at once *into* profound sleep undisturbed by dreams ‖ *fall into* a stupor (=comatose condition) こん睡状態に陥る ‖ *fall into* a state of somnolence し眠状態に陥る ‖ *fall into* sentimentality 感傷的になる ‖ He *fell into* a state of penury bordering on misery. 彼は悲惨ともいうほどの貧困状態に陥った. ‖ The company *fell into* dire straits financially. 会社は財政上苦境に陥った. ‖ *fall into* the extraordinary blunder of ... …という飛んでもない間違いに陥る ‖ *fall into* an error (=a mistake) 間違いをする ‖ *fall into* the error of thinking 思考上の誤りに陥る. 【類】 *fall into* the same error / *fall into* many errors / *fall into* a fallacy (誤り) / *fall into* the mistake of thinking that ... ‖ *fall into* pieces 崩壊する ‖ *fall into* a quarrel with ... …とけんかをする ‖ *fall into* the way of ...ing …するようになる ‖ *fall into* anecdotage [老人の]話がくどくなる ‖ Something *fell into* my eye. なにか僕の目にはいった. ‖ It *fell into* the garden below. それは下の庭に落ちた. ‖ *fall into* a chat with ... …と雑談に入る ‖ happen to *fall into* conversation with ... 偶然…と話をするようになる. 【類】 on the train I happened to *fall into* conversation with ... ‖ The Irish have *fallen into* line with the Liberals since the time of Gladstone's Home Rule. アイルランドはグラッドストーン主唱の自治政策当時以来自由党に加わった. ‖ unconsciously *fall into* step 思わず(音楽に合わして)足踏みをする(踊り出す). ¶ Banks were *falling like* ninepins. 銀行は(恐慌で)将棋倒しの状態であった. ‖ *fall like* a thunderbolt from the blue 晴天のへきれきのごとく落ちる. ¶ He *fell off* the chair (motor-car, horse). 彼はいす(など)から落ち

た. ‖ Leaves *fall off* the trees in the autumn. 秋になると葉が木から落ちる. ‖ allow the ship to *fall off* her course 船が針路を転じるままにして置く. ¶ Business then *fell on* bad days. 当時事業は不振の状態にあった. ‖ The meetings *fall* (=occur) *on* the same day. 両方の会が同日にぶつかる. ‖ in view of the 7th anniversary of the birth of ..., which *falls on* ..., ...の第七回誕生日が...とかさなるので. 【類】 owing to the Emperor's Birthday *falling on* that day / The time fixed *falling on* Sunday, a postponement was found necessary. / Christmas Day *falls on* Sunday this year. / In 1912 Hallowe'en (万聖節の宵祭) *fell on* a Thursday. ‖ A shadow *fell on* the paper sliding-door. 影が障子に映った. ‖ words that *fall on* the ear 耳に入る言葉 ‖ The demand *fell on* deaf ears. その要求は馬耳東風であった. ‖ His warnings *fell on* indifferent ears. 彼の警告は馬の耳に念仏であった. ‖ *fall on* one's hands ころんで両手をつく ‖ *fall on* one's knees ひざまずく ‖ *fall on* one's buttocks しりもちをつく ‖ *fall on* one's hips quite neatly 見事にしりもちをつく ‖ The responsibility *falls* entirely *on* their shoulders. その責任は全く彼らの双肩にふりかかる. ‖ The suspicion *fell on* a neighbor. けん疑は隣人にかかった. ‖ his eyes *fell on* ... 彼はたまたま...が目に付いた ‖ the choice *fell on* ... ...が選ばれた ‖ The rain *falls on* the earth. 雨は地上に降る. ‖ The seed *fell on* a favorable soil. 種子はたまたま良い地に落ちた. ‖ The highwaymen *fell on* a party of travelling merchants. 追いはぎは旅商人たちを襲った. ‖ They *fell on* their own swords to escape the disgrace of capture. 彼らは捕虜の汚名を避けるため自刃した. ‖ The accent *falls on* the first syllable. アクセントは第一音節に付く. ‖ *fall on* fighting 戦闘を始める. ¶ *fall out of* use (=into disuse) 廃止になる ‖ *fall out of* the saddle くらからころげ落ちる ‖ *fall out of* employment 失業する. ¶ *fall over* head and heels 真逆様に落ちる ‖ The cascade *falls over* a tall cliff. その滝は高いがけを落下する. ‖ *fall over* a precipice (an embankment) がけ(など)からころげ落ちる ‖ The ball *fell over* (=beyond) the line. ボールが線の外に落ちた. ‖ Then the public "*fell over* one another" in their eagerness to invest in the new enterprise. それから大衆はこの新事業に投資しようと「お互いどうし重なり合う」ほどの熱心さだった. ‖ A hush *fell over* the onlookers. 傍観している人々は声をひそめた. ‖ *fall through* temptation 誘惑に負ける. ¶ the honors *fall to* ... その名誉は...に帰する ‖ The bidding *fell to* ... at ... yen. 競売は...円で...に落ちた. ‖ *to* ... *fell* the task of welcoming ... ...が...を歓迎する役目になった ‖ The lot *fell to* me. くじは私に当った. ‖ the lot *falls to* me (=it falls to my lot *or* it falls to me as my lot) to ... ...するのが私の運命だ ‖ The successor *fell to* the lot of ... 後任は...に札が落らた ‖ it rarely *falls to* the lot of ... それは滅多に...の運命とはならない ‖ He has had the same educational advantages that *fall to* the lot of most city boys. 大概の都会の少年が持っていると同じ教育を受ける機会を彼も持っていた. ‖ A display of Oriental magnificence as rarely *falls to* the lot of Western eyes to witness. これほどの東洋の壮麗美観は滅多に西洋人の目撃する所とはならない. ‖ the veteran financier who *fell to* an assassin's bullet 刺客の弾丸にたおれた老財政家 ‖ Her look *fell to* the carpet. (へやで)彼女は下を向いた. ‖ The word has now *fallen to* vulgar use. その語は今では下等な言葉になった. ‖ *fall* a victim *to* her charms 彼女の美容に迷う ‖ *fall* victim *to* the Spanish influenza スペインかぜにかかる ‖ *fall* heavily *to* the floor with a bang どしんと重く床の上に落ちる ‖ *fall* head over heels *to* the ground 真逆様に地上に落ちる ‖ The aeroplane capsized and *fell to* the ground. 飛行機は転覆して地上に落ちた. ‖ The theory *falls to* the ground. その理論は成り立たない. ‖ The scheme *fell to* the ground. その計画は画べいに帰した. ‖ *fall to* the earth 地に落ちる ‖ *fall to* pieces 崩壊する ‖ The house is *falling* to pieces. その家はくずれかかっている. ‖ The empire was rapidly *falling to* pieces. その帝国は崩壊しつつあった. ‖ *fall to* ruin 破滅に帰する ‖ *fall to* one's share その手に入る ‖ *fall to* sleep 眠る ‖ His voice *fell to* a whisper. 彼は声を落してささやいた. ‖ The sun *falls to* the west. 太陽が西に沈む. ‖ *fall to* thinking ... ...と考え始める ‖ *fall to* work 仕事に取りかかる ‖ *fall to* blows (argument) なぐり合い(議論)になる ‖ *fall to* smart fisticuffs 激しいなぐり合いになる ‖ While there were 446 American students in German universities in 1891, their number *fell* gradually *to* 252 in 1908. 一八九一年にはドイツの大学に四四六人の米国学生がいたが一九〇八年には漸次二五二人に減じた. ‖ The winter there is very severe, the thermometer frequently *falling to* 26° below zero. そこの冬は非常な厳寒で寒暖計がしばしば零下二十五度に降る. ¶ The aeroplane *fell towards* the earth. 飛行機が地上に向って落下した. ‖ All material bodies tend to *fall towards* the earth. すべての物体は地球の方に落ちる傾向がある. ¶ Her parents dying while she was an infant, she *fell under* the care of a widow and childless aunt. 彼女の両親は彼女の幼少のころ死んだので彼女は寡婦で子のないおばさんの世話になった. ‖ He *fell under* the wheels of (=was run over by) an automobile. 彼は自動車にひかれた. ‖ She beat the child with an umbrella, which was the first thing that *fell under* her hand. 一番先に目についたかさでその子を打った. ‖ *fall under* his displeasure 彼ににらまれる(不興を買う) ‖ *fall under* the description of ... ...の部に入る ‖ *fall under* the ivory hammer 競売に付される ‖ That *falls under* this head. それはこの項目にはいる. 【類】 What I have to say will *fall under* three general heads (=headings). ‖ Species *fall under* genera. 〘理〙 種は属の中に入る. ¶ The business *fell under* his management. その店は彼が経営することになった. ‖ It *fell under* Spanish rule. それはスペインの支配下に属した. ‖ *fall under* the influence of ... ...の影響を受ける ‖ *fall under* one's observation (=notice) その目にとまる ‖ I *fell under* his spell instantly. 私はすぐ彼の魔力で魅せられた. ‖ those who have *fallen under* the spell of Japanese *netsuke* 日本の根付けに興味を持ちだした人々. 【類】 *fall under* the spell of the delightful book. ¶ A log *fell upon* his foot. 丸太が彼の足の上に倒れた. ‖ The accent *falls upon* the first syllable. アクセントは第一音節にある. ‖ The industry has *fallen upon* evil days. その産業は衰運に向いた. ‖ ...when there *fell upon* my ears a most startling scream その時私の耳にけたたましい叫声が聞えた ‖ She *fell upon* his neck.=She threw her arms round his neck.=She embraced his neck. 彼女は彼の首にだきついた. ‖ *fall upon* the retina 目にふれる ‖ The lot of ... *fell upon* me. ...と同じな運命が私の身に降りかかった. ‖ this work *falls upon* the shoulders of ... この仕事を...が負担することになった ‖ Fear *fell upon* (=on) them. 彼らは恐怖に襲われた. ‖ A great awe *fell upon* the people. 人々は非常な畏怖(い)の念にかられた. ‖ The choice has *fallen upon* him. 彼が選に当った. ‖ *fall upon* an enemy 敵を襲撃する. ¶ Feudalism in Japan *fell with* the Tokugawa. 日本の封建制度は徳川幕府とともに亡びた. ¶ This does not *fall within* the province of the present paper. これは本論文の範囲外である. ‖ They hardly *fall within* the scope of this chapter. それらは本章において論ずべき性質のものでない. ‖ *fall within* this category この部類に属する.

fallacy, *n.* あやまり, 間違い; びゅう見.

v *demonstrate* the *fallacy* of ... ...の誤りを証明する. ¶ *cherish* a *fallacy* びゅう見を抱く. ¶ *dispel* the *fallacy* that ... ...というびゅう見を打破する. ¶ *explode* a *fallacy* びゅう見を打破する. ¶ *expose* the *fallacy* of ... のびゅう見を暴露する.

v² *fallacies* that *masquerade* as truisms 本当らしく見せかけている間違い. ¶ The *fallacy rests* in the premises. 誤びゅうはその前提にある.

Q an utterly *absurd fallacy* 全くばからしい間違い. ¶ a *great economic fallacy* 経済上の大錯誤. ¶ a *logical fallacy* 論理上の誤びゅう. ¶ the *popular fallacy* that ... ...という一般人のびゅう見. ¶ a *transparent fallacy* 明白な誤り. ¶ a *widespread popular fallacy* 広く一般の誤り.

fallibility, *n.* 誤りやすいこと.

Q *human fallibility* 人間の誤りやすいこと.

falling, *n.* 下降.

Q We expect a *temporary falling* of supplies in consequence of decline in prices. 物価下落のため供給が一時減るだろう.

falling-off, *n.* 減少.

v The decline in prices will *cause* a *falling-off* in supplies. 物価の下落が供給の減少をきたすだろう. ¶ the sales *show* a *falling-off* of ... 販売高は...の減少を示している.

Q There will be a very *decided falling-off* in the tourist

business in the Orient. 東洋における観光業は確実に衰微するだろう. ¶a ***great falling-off*** in sugar exports 砂糖輸出の大減少. ¶a ***slight falling-off*** in numbers 数におけるわずかの減少.

P² the *falling-off* ***in*** the demand for ... …に対する需要の減退. ¶the general *falling-off* ***of*** ... …の一般的減少.

falling-out, *n.* けんか, 口論.

V We ***had*** a *falling-out*. われわれはけんかした.

fallout, *n.* 落下物, 原子灰.

P exposed ***to*** [atomic] *fallout* on the Pacific 太平洋上で「原子灰にさらされて.

false, *a.* 誤った; 不実の, 不忠実の.

M ***substantially*** *false* 実質的に誤った[論法・観念・見解など]. ¶The report is ***utterly*** *false*. その報告は全く間違っている.

P He is *false* ***of*** heart. 彼には誠意がない. ¶He is *false* ***to*** his promise. 彼は約束を守らない. ‖ be *false* ***to*** a trust 信用を裏切る. 【類】He is *false* ***to*** his country (friends).

falsehood, *n.* 虚偽; 虚言, うそ.

V ***act*** a *falsehood* 虚偽の行動をする. ¶widely ***disseminate*** *falsehoods* うそを言いふらす. ¶***publish*** all kinds of *falsehoods* あらゆるうそを発表する. ¶***speak*** (=***utter***) a *falsehood* うそをつく. ¶He is quite above ***telling*** a *falsehood*. 彼はうそをつくような男でない.

Q an ***absolute*** (=a ***downright***) *falsehood* 真赤なうそ. ¶a ***palpable*** *falsehood* 分りきったうそ. ¶a ***pure*** (=an ***utter***) *falsehood* 全くのうそ. ¶a ***transparent*** *falsehood* 見えすいたうそ. ¶by means of ***unblushing*** *falsehood* ずうずうしいうそをついて. ¶an ***unscrupulous*** *falsehood* おく面もないうそ. ¶a ***vicious*** *falsehood* たちの悪いうそ.

P He tried to take shelter ***in*** *falsehood*. 彼はうそをついて逃れようとした.

falsetto, *n.* 作り声.

Q He replied in a ***long-drawn, high*** *falsetto*. 彼は永く引いたかん高の作り声で答えた.

falsification, *n.* 偽造.

P² *falsification* ***of*** accounts 帳面づらのいんちき; つけかけ.

falter, *v.* どもる; ためらう.

M *falter* ***out*** a reply (an excuse) どもりながら答(など)をする ‖ He *faltered* ***out*** that he meant no harm. 彼は何も危害を加える積りではないとどもりながら言った.

P Never *falter* ***in*** noble resolution. りっぱなことを決心するにちゅうちょするな. ‖ He *faltered* ***in*** his speech. 彼の演説にはよどみがあった.

fame, *n.* 評判, 名声; 盛名, 有名; 風説.

V he ***achieved*** world-wide *fame* by ... 彼は…によって世界的名声を博した. 【類】the ghosts of heroes who have ***achieved*** the *fame* of which poets in all ages delight to sing. ¶***acquire*** *fame* in a war 戦争で名をあげる. 【類】***acquire*** great *fame* by ... ¶His new discovery ***adds*** *fame* to science (=scholarship) at Yale. 彼の新発見はエール大学の学府としての名声に一段の光彩を添えるものである. ¶***attain*** *fame* 名を成す. ¶***bear*** a world-wide *fame* for ... …で世界中に知れ渡っている. ¶It ***brought*** him *fame* and fortune. そのために彼は名誉と財産を得た. 【類】Columbus's discoveries of other worlds ***brought*** Spain more *fame* than any of her most famous battles. ¶***care*** or ***follow*** *fame* 名誉を追求する. ¶***earn*** enduring *fame* on account of ... …によって不朽の名声を博する. ¶***enhance*** the *fame* of Japanese hospitality 日本人がよく外来の客を厚遇するという評判を高める. ¶This work ***established*** his *fame* as a great novelist. この著作で彼は大小説家としての名声をあげた. 【類】he ***established*** his *fame* by a novel called "...". ¶***extend*** one's *fame* 更に名をあげる. ¶He first ***gained*** *fame* by his "Treasure Island." 彼は「宝島」で初めて名を揚げた. 【類】He ***gained*** *fame* throughout the world. ¶He ***has*** *fame* among foreigners. 彼は外人間に評判が好い. ¶***make*** his *fame* in ... …で名をなす. 【類】***make*** *fame* and money. ¶***outdo*** the *fame* of ... …の名声をしのぐ. ¶His *fame* was ***overshadowed*** by that of his great predecessor. 先代が偉かったので彼の名は一向に揚らなかった. ¶In the earlier years Fitz-Gerald had ***predicted*** Tennyson's *fame*. フィッツジェラルドはつとにテニスンの盛名を予言した. ¶***protect*** the fair *fame* of our nation against shame and scandal 恥辱と汚名をこうむらないようにわが国の名誉を擁護する. ¶***purchase*** literary *fame* 文名を博する. ¶***pursue*** *fame* on an empty stomach 食うものも食わずに名誉を求める. ¶***reach*** *fame* 名声を獲得する. ¶***secure*** his works a *fame* 彼の著書を名高くする. ¶***stake*** one's *fame* upon a cast 名誉を賭(か)ける. ¶***transmit*** a lustrous *fame* to posterity かくかくたる名声を後世に伝える. ¶He ***won*** *fame* as a novelist. 彼は小説家として名を揚げた. ‖ ***win*** *fame* on the battlefield 戦場で名を成す ‖ He ***won*** for himself a *fame* that spread through the civilized world. 彼は文明諸国に名をとどろかした. ¶***win*** and ***maintain*** a *fame* 名声を博しそれを持続する.

V² before *fame* ***came*** to him 彼がまだ有名でなかった時分. ¶a *fame* that will never ***die*** 不朽の名. ¶people whose *fame* has ***endured*** even unto our day 今日までも名声を持続した人々. ¶The *fame* of his eloquence had ***preceded*** him there. 彼が行かない先に彼の雄弁家としての名声はその地に伝わっていた. 【類】His *fame* ***preceded*** him to Japan. ¶His *fame* ***spread*** throughout the country. 彼の名は国中に広まった. 【類】His *fame* ***spread*** to the United States.

Q the ***after*** *fame* of one's work …の著作の後年の名声. ¶women of ***bad*** *fame* 評判のよくない(春を売る)女. ¶search for ***cheap*** *fame* 安っぽい美名を求める. ¶the ***culinary*** *fame* of Vienna ウィンナの料理の評判. ¶acquire ***durable*** *fame* 不朽の名を得る. ¶the Savoy, with its abundance of ***fair*** *fame* 盛名さくさくたるサボイホテル. ¶gain ***far-flung*** *fame* 広く名声を博する. ¶***fickle*** *fame* 永続きのしない名声. ¶***good*** *fame* 好評判. ¶scholars of ***high*** *fame* 評判の高い学者. ¶He was at the height of ***human*** *fame*. 彼は人としての名誉の絶頂にあった. ¶***ill*** *fame* 醜聞, 不名誉 ‖ a house of ***ill*** *fame* 娼家. ¶poems of ***immortal*** *fame* 永久に伝わる詩. ¶***imperishable*** *fame* 不朽の誉. ¶a scholar of ***international*** *fame* 世界的名声のある学者. 【類】win ***international*** *fame*. ¶he achieved ***lasting*** *fame* for ... 彼は…のために不朽の名を成した. ¶the fickleness of ***literary*** *fame* 文名のはかなさ. ¶a wrestler of ***local*** *fame* 地元で有名な力士. ¶***posthumous*** *fame* 死後の誉. ¶a novelist of ***rising*** *fame* 日の出の人気小説家. ¶***secular*** (=enduring) *fame* 不朽の名声. ¶The Hope diamond has a ***sinister*** *fame* as the unluckiest diamond in the world. ホープ・ダイヤモンドは世界で一番不吉なダイヤだという面白くない評判を取った. ¶win ***undying*** *fame* 名を後世に残す. ¶She has earned for her a ***well-deserved*** *fame*. 彼女は実力通りの名声を博した. ¶a poet of ***wide*** *fame* 広く知られている詩人. ¶Its *fame* is ***world-wide***. その名は世界に知れ渡っている. 【類】pictures (a firm) of ***world-wide*** *fame* / a physicist (物理学者) of ***world-wide*** *fame*.

Q² rise to ***film*** *fame* 映画界で有名になる. ¶Sir James Ross, of ***magnetic pole*** *fame*. 磁極発見の名誉を担うサー・ジェームス・ロッス. ¶achieve ***nation-wide*** *fame* 国中に名声を博する. ¶though their names may not be known to ***newspaper*** *fame* 彼らの名は新聞に載らないにしても. ¶at the height of her ***stage*** *fame* 彼女の舞台人気の絶頂に達したとき. ¶made steady progress up the ladder of ***tennis*** *fame* until she reached the top 最高位に上るまで彼女は庭球選手としての名声を着々高めて行った. ¶gain (=win) ***world*** *fame* for ... …で世界的名声を博する. 【類】men of ***world*** *fame* / that brilliant young novelist who has reached ***world*** *fame* before he was thirty.

P ***At*** the *fame* of his approach the enemy retreated northward. 彼が近くまで来たといううわさを聞いて敵軍は北方に退却した. ¶dazzled ***by*** *fame* 名声にまどわされて. ¶work for money, not ***for*** *fame* 働くのは金のためで, 名のためじゃない. ¶It has had the good fortune to be lifted ***into*** *fame* by two of the "Lake poets." それは幸にも二人の湖畔詩人の筆によって名高くなった. ¶old Dr. Hepburn ***of*** dictionary *fame* 辞書で有名な老ヘボン博士 ‖ Dr. Jenner, ***of*** vaccination *fame* 種痘で有名なジェンナ博士. ‖ reach the zenith ***of*** one's *fame* 名誉の頂点に達する. 【類】the Noguchi ***of*** American *fame*. ¶cast a stain ***on*** one's *fame* 名誉を汚す. ¶come (=rise) ***to*** *fame* 有名になる ‖ the road ***to*** *fame* 名声への道 ‖ He is unknown ***to*** *fame*. 彼は無名だ.

P² achieve *fame* ***as*** an artist 芸術家として名を揚げる. ¶the *fame* ***of*** Lincoln リンカンの名声.

famed, *pa.* 有名な.

P. He is *famed* ***as*** (=to be) cruel. 彼は残忍だとの評判だ. ‖ He is *famed* ***as*** a poet. 彼は詩人だと評判されている. ¶Detroit is *famed* ***for*** the beauty of its environs. デトロ

イトは近郊の美景で有名だ. ‖ He is *famed* ***for*** his learning. 彼は学問で名高い. 【類】the Benedictines, an order (宗派) justly *famed* ***for*** its pursuit of learning.

familiar, *a*. 熟知している, 精通している; 懇意な; 隔てのない; 平易な; かねて承知の.

M we are already ***fairly familiar*** with ... われわれはもう…をかなりよく知っている. ¶I am not *familiar* ***enough*** with the subject to ... 私は…するだけその問題がよく分っていない. ¶He is ***thoroughly familiar*** with the business. 彼はその仕事に精通している. ¶It is ***too familiar*** for comment. それは余りに平易で説明を要しない. ‖ Her ***too familiar*** ways make people say things about her. 彼女のやり口が心安だて過ぎるので人が色々なことをいう.

P Your name is *familiar* ***to*** me. 御高名はかねて承知しております. ‖ There were faces not *familiar* ***to*** me. 見慣れない人たちがいた. 【類】things *familiar* ***to*** us. ¶I have been *familiar* ***with*** him for years. 私は彼と年来懇意にしてきた. ‖ He is *familiar* ***with*** English. 彼は英語に明るい. ‖ not being *familiar* ***with*** Osaka 大阪は不案内なので. 【類】He is *familiar* ***with*** customs (conditions, affairs). / I am *familiar* ***with*** his character. / a statement that no one *familiar* ***with*** the facts will be inclined to question.

familiarity, *n*. 習熟, 通暁; 懇意; なれなれしいこと.

V ***acquire*** some *familiarity* with ... …に多少習熟する. ¶***attempt*** *familiarity* 習熟しようと努める. ¶There is always something inexpressible in her which would ***check*** *familiarity* and annihilate impertinence. 彼女にはいつも何とも言いようのない一種の威容がそなわっていて親しみ難く無礼なことなど絶対にできないのである. ¶***have*** personal *familiarity* with ... と直接親しい関係にある.

V^2 No *familiarities* ***took place*** between them. 彼ら二人の間には少しも慣れ慣れしいことなどなかった.

Q with an ***easy*** *familiarity* 四角ばらずに. ¶You should not treat the young lady with so ***much*** *familiarity;* you've only known her for a week! あの若い婦人にそんなに慣れ慣れしくしてはいけない, 近づきになってほんの一週間だから. ¶***offensive*** *familiarity* しゃくにさわる慣れ慣れしさ. ¶a ***thorough*** *familiarity* with the language その国語に通暁していること. ¶an ***undue*** *familiarity* between them 彼ら(男女)のあやしい親密さ.

familiarize, *v*. 慣らす; 通暁させる, 習熟させる.

M he is ***sufficiently*** *familiarized* with ... 彼は十分…に通暁している.

P Christian theology has *familiarized* us ***with*** the idea that ... キリスト教神学はわれわれに…の思想を普及した. ‖ *familiarize* a person ***with*** the Bible 聖書に通暁させる ‖ *familiarize* them ***with*** the business その商売に習熟させる. 【類】*familiarize* students of English literature ***with*** ... / he *familiarized* his countrymen ***with*** a knowledge of ... / *familiarize* the ready public ***with*** the idea of ... / *familiarize* oneself ***with*** the situation (condition) / *Familiarize* yourself ***with*** the spoken tongue. 「科.

family, *n*. 家族; 家門, 家系; 名門; 子女, 子供; 民族; 語族;

V ***abandon*** one's *family* 家族を見棄てる. ¶I don't think New York is a good place to live and ***bring up*** a *family*. ニューヨークは住んで家族を育て上げるには良い所と私は思わない. ¶***disgrace*** one's *family* 家名を汚す. ¶***exterminate*** a *family* 一家皆殺しにする. ¶***feed*** and ***clothe*** their *families* 家族たちに衣食を与える. ¶***found*** a *family* 家を起す. ¶He ***has*** a *family* of four sons and two daughters. 彼は息子四人娘二人の家族を抱えている. ‖ The couple ***have*** a *family* of eight. 夫婦には八人の子供がある. ‖ He is married and ***has*** a large *family*. 彼は結婚して家族が多い. ‖ be ready to start ***having*** a *family* 世帯を持つ準備ができている ‖ ***have*** no *family* to care for 面倒をみる家族もない. ¶***join*** an English *family* as a paying guest 下宿人として英人の家族に同居する. ¶***keep*** one's *family* from want 家族が困らないようにする. ¶He ***left*** his wife and *family* behind. 彼は妻子を残して死んだ. ¶***limit*** one's *family* 産児を制限する. ¶He successfully ***maintains*** the *family* of eight. 八人の家族をりっぱに養っている. ¶***raise*** a *family* on milk 牛乳で子供たちを育てる. ‖ She ***raised*** a large *family*. 彼女はたくさんの子供を育てた. ¶***reduce*** his *family* to poverty 家族を貧困に陥らせる. ¶***reunite*** broken *families* ばらばらになった家族を一堂に集める. ¶***support*** a *family* in comfort 安楽に家族を扶養する ‖ ***support*** a *family* on ... yen a month 月…円で家族を支える.

V^2 Our *family* ***consists*** of eight. 家族は八人だ.

Q ***alcoholic*** *families* 酒飲の家族. ¶He belongs to an ***ancient, aristocratic,*** and highly ***respectable*** *family*. 彼は古い堂々たる貴族の家の出だ. ¶Have they ***any*** *family?* あの人たちには子供がありますか. ¶the (=one's) ***bereaved*** *family* その遺族. ¶bring up a ***big*** *family* in a small cottage 小さな小屋で大勢の家族を育て上げる. ¶the requisition of German homes by ***British*** and ***Allied*** *families* 英国及び連合軍の家族によるドイツ家庭の接収. ¶an English girl of ***good*** *family* 良家の英国少女. ¶the ruling clique of ***great*** *families* 財閥. ¶a man with a wife and a ***growing*** *family* 妻と, 成長期にある子供らを抱えた人. 【類】people with ***growing*** *families*. ¶All the world as a family—a ***happy*** *family* 八紘(こう)一宇. ¶***historic*** *families* of Europe 歴史に名高いヨーロッパの家族. ¶The nations are members of one great ***human*** *family*. 諸国民は人類という一大家族に属するのである. ¶a scion of the ***illustrious*** *family* 名門の子孫. ¶members of the ***Imperial*** *family* 皇族の方々. ¶a chart of the ***Indo-European*** *family* of *languages* インドヨーロッパ語系の言語の表. 【類】English, French and German are the ***Indo-European*** *family*. ¶a married man with a ***large*** *family* 大家族を抱えている人. ¶He has a ***large*** *family* to support. 彼は扶養家族が多い. ¶a ***little*** (=small) *family* 小家族. ¶She comes of a ***long-lived*** *family*, her father, mother, and sister all having lived to be nearly 100. 彼女は長命の血統で父も母も姉(妹)も皆百歳位まで生きた. ¶huge ***monopolistic*** *families* 財閥. ¶He came of a ***musical*** *family*. 彼は音楽好きの家族の出だ. ¶a ***needy*** *family* 貧困家族. ¶a ***noble*** *family* 貴族. ¶She is herself the mother of a ***numerous*** *family*. 彼女は彼女自身大勢の子供の母だ. ¶an ***old*** and ***illustrious*** *family* 古い有名な一族. ¶a ***poor*** *family* 貧家. ¶Some of them represent the ***proudest*** *families* of England. その中には英国で最高の名門の出のものもある. ¶a ***reputable*** *family* 名門. ¶boys in ***respectable*** *families* ちゃんとした家庭の少年. ¶The family which is slowly accumulating a little library is always a ***rising*** *family*. 徐々に蔵書をふやしつつある家庭はきまって向上する家庭である. ¶the ***royal*** and ***princely*** *families* of Europe ヨーロッパの王族及び諸侯. ¶a ***servantless*** *family* 召使なしの家庭. ¶His *family* is ***short-lived***. 彼の血統は短命だ. ¶late marriages and ***small*** *families* 晩婚と小人数の家族 ‖ a naturally (artificially) ***small*** *family* 自然に(産児制限をして)子供の少ない家族. ¶They are of a ***tuberculous*** *family*. その家族は肺病の血統である. ¶the head of a household with an ***uprising*** *family* ずんずん大きくなる子供らを控えた家族の戸主. ¶a ***wealthy*** *family* 富豪の家. ¶a ***well-to-do*** *family* 裕福な家庭. ¶Of ***what*** *family* is he sprung? 彼はどういう家柄の人か. ¶The ***whole*** *family* are in tears. 家族中泣いている. ‖ The ***whole*** *family* are pests. あの家族はみんな大変なしろものだ. ¶a ***young*** *family* 年のゆかない子供ら.

Q^2 ***army dependent*** *families* 陸軍軍人の家族. ¶a ***banking*** *family* 銀行家の家族. ‖ Rothschild, head of the English branch of the great ***banking*** *family* 大銀行一家の英国系の親分ロスチャイルド. ¶members of the ***deer*** *family* しか科の動物. ¶fresh-water ***fishes*** of the ***carp*** *family* こい科の淡水魚. ¶a real ***farm*** *family* 生っ粋の農家. ¶The mental state underlying blushing belongs to the ***fear*** *family*. 赤面の精神状態は恐怖の種類に属する. ¶the ***head*** *family* 宗(本)家. ¶the ***Krupp*** *family* クルップ家. ¶a ***landowning*** *family* 地主. ¶a well-known ***Louisiana creole*** *family* 有名なルイジアナ地方の黒人種. ¶the men and women of the great ***Macy*** *family* [百貨王として]有名なメーシー家の家族. ¶belong to a ***middle-class*** *family* 中流家庭の出だ. ¶a ***millionaire*** *family* 百万長者の一家. ¶***Occupation*** *families* 占領軍の家族たち. ¶the ***Percy*** *family*= the House of Percy ペレー家. ¶metals of the ***platinum*** *family* 白金族の金属. ¶a ***relief*** *family* 救済を受けている家族. ¶The ***rose*** and ***bean*** *families* belong to the same order. ばら科とまめ科は同じ目(もく)に属する. ¶the ***string*** *family* 弦楽器類. ¶an ***upper-income*** (middle-income, lower-income) *family* 収入の多い(中位の, 少い)家族. ¶the ***Ural-Altai*** *family* of nations ウラル・アルタイ系民族. ¶The doublebass is the giant of the ***viol*** *family*. ダブルベースは弦楽器中の巨大なものである. ¶the ***world*** *family* of nations making up the United Nations 国際連合を構成する世界国民.

P work *for* a *family* 家族のために働く. ¶He was the youngest of three sons *in* a *family* of laborers. 彼は労働者の家族で三人息子の中の最年少者であった. 【類】Now they are five *in family*, and they have three servants. ‖ There was insanity *in* the *family*. あの家族は気違いの系統を引いていた. ‖ It runs *in* the *family*. それは親ゆずり(遺伝)である. ¶a man *of family* 名門の人. ¶Give my kind regards *to* all your *family*. 御家族御一同へよろしく. ¶He left a widow *with* a large *family*. 彼は妻と大勢の子供を残して死んだ. ¶*with* a *family* of seven on his hands 七人の家族を抱えて.

P^2 We are a *family of* six in all. 家族は皆で六人だ. 【類】*family of* children ‖ as a member of the *family of* nations 列国の一員として ‖ the *family of* free nations 自由主義国家群 ‖ daughters of a *family of* culture 良家の子女 ‖ The *family of* Hōjō was overthrown. 北条の一族は倒された. ‖ a *family of* languages 同系の国語. ¶a *family with* four children 子供四人の家族.

famine, *n*. ききん, 凶荒; 飢餓; 不足, 払底.

V A *famine* was *feared*. ききんの恐れがあった. ¶*threaten famine* ききんの恐れがある.

V^2 A *famine broke forth*. ききんになった. ¶*Famine stared* us in the face. われわれに飢餓が迫った. ¶A big *famine visited* that part of the country. 大ききんがその地方を襲った. 「ききん.

Q a *grievous famine* 悲惨な凶荒. ¶a *severe famine* ひどい

Q^2 a *bread famine* パンの欠乏. ¶a *coal* (*water*, *small change*) *famine* 石炭(など)の払底. ¶a *paper* (*cotton*) *famine* 用紙(綿)ききん. ¶a *timber famine* 材木ききん. ¶a threat of *world famine* 世界的ききんの脅威.

P die *of famine* 餓死する. ¶He perished *with* (=*by*) *famine*. 彼はききんで死んだ.

P^2 *famine in* petrol (musicians) ガソリン(など)の払底. ¶a *famine of* ideas 思想の貧困.

famish, *v*. 餓死する.

P *famish to* death 餓死する.

famous, *a*. 有名な, 名高い; ⦅俗⦆ ひいでた, すてきな.

M a place *famous historically* or *scenically* 歴史的にまたは風景の点で有名な場所. ¶*infamously famous*=notorious 悪名天下に聞えた[人物など]. ¶become *internationally famous* 国際的に有名になる. ¶a *once famous* doctrine かつて有名だった説. ¶He is *rather famous* as a speechmaker. 彼はむしろ演説家として有名だ.

P a restaurant *famous among* epicures 美食家の間に有名な料理店. ¶Everett, *famous as* "The City of Smokestacks"「煙突の市」として有名なエヴァレット. ¶He is *famous at* fencing. 彼はフェンシングで有名だ. ¶a place *famous for* picturesqueness 美景で有名な所. ‖ What's he *famous for?* 彼は何で有名なのか. 【類】Manchuria has become *famous for* the bean (大豆) trade. ‖ He is *famous for* his learning. 彼は学問で名高い. 【類】He is *famous for* [his] skill as a marksman. ¶places *famous in* history 史跡. ¶places which Kipling has made *famous through* his stories キップリングがその小説で有名にした場所. ¶a statesman *famous throughout* the world = a statesman of world-wide fame 世界に聞えた政治家.

fan, *n*. 扇, 扇風機.

V *flirt* a *fan* 扇をせわしく使う. ¶*furl* (*unfurl*) a *fan* 扇をたたむ(ひろげる) ‖ The peacock *unfurled* his magnificent *fan*. くじゃくがりっぱな羽根を広げた.

Q be cooled by *electric fans* 扇風機で冷してある ‖ The [*electric*] *fan* is working busily. 扇風機がさかんに回っている. ¶a *folding fan* 扇子. ¶a *ventilating fan* 換気用扇風機.

Q^2 a *blowing fan* 送風機. ¶a *ceiling fan* 天井扇風機. ¶a *desk-set fan* 卓上扇風機. ¶a *palm-leaf fan* しゅろ葉のうちわ. 「熱をあおった.

P^2 His jealousy was a *fan to* his passion. しっとは彼の情

fan, *v*. あおぐ; 扇動する.

M *fan away* flies あおいではえを追払う. ¶*fan* oneself *busily* せわしく扇を使う.

P The flame was *fanned by* the west wind. 火は西風にあおられた. ¶*fan* the coals *into* a blaze 石炭の火をあおいで燃やす ‖ He *fanned* the Lower House *into* a blaze of resentment. 彼は下院を扇動して烈火のごとく憤激させた. ¶*fan* his rage *to* a blaze 彼をかんかんに怒らせる. 【類】*fan* national pride *to* passionate heat. ¶*fan* oneself *with* a handkerchief ハンカチで自分をあおぐ.

fan, *n*. ⦅口語⦆ 熱狂者(ファン).

Q an *ardent fan* 大ファン. ¶a *confirmed* skiing "*fan*" 猛烈なスキー狂. ¶*vociferous fan* 大のファン.

Q^2 *broadcast* (=*radio*) *fan* ラジオ狂. ¶a *Conrad* (*Disney*, *Chaplin*) *fan* コンラッド(など)のファン. ¶a *film* (=*movie or screen*) *fan* 映画ファン.

fanatic, *n*. 狂信家, 熱狂家.

Q There are some people who are *perfect fanatics* about having the window open at night. どうあっても夜間窓を明けておくようにしている人もある. ¶a *religious fanatic* 狂的な信者. ¶*violent fanatics* like Bakunin バクーニンのような猛烈な熱狂家.

Q^2 a great *morality fanatic* 道徳一点張りの人. ¶an *ultranationalist fanatic* 極端な国家主義の狂信者.

fanatic, *a*. 狂信している.

P The Turks are *fanatic in* their devotion to Islam. トルコ人は回教の熱狂的信徒である.

fanaticism, *n*. 熱狂.

Q *Bolshevistic fanaticism* ロシア共産党の熱狂. ¶*religious fanaticism* 狂的な信仰. ¶an act of *revolutionary fanaticism* 革命的な熱狂の行動.

fancier, *n*. 愛好者. 「好者.

Q^2 a *poultry fancier* 養鶏家. ¶a *seafood fancier* 海産物愛

fancy, *n*. 想像力, 想像, 空想; 考案, 気分; 愛好心, 恋.

V *attract* the *fancy* of ... ...の愛好心をそそる. ¶This house has *captured* my *fancy*. 私はこの家が気に入った. ‖ 【類】The idea *captured* the students' *fancy*. / *capture* the *fancy* of American motion picture audiences. ¶His book *caught* (=*took or attracted*) the *fancy* of the public at once. 彼の本は直ちに世間の好みに投じた. ¶The fact that she was a woman *caught* the public *fancy*. ‖ Once a new word *catches* the popular *fancy*, it "sticks." 新語が人気に投じると「根がはえる」. 【類】*catch* the *fancy* of (=please^4) the public. ¶*check* her *fancy* for a lover 愛人に対する恋を抑える. ¶*fancies conjured up* in later days 後日になって思い浮べた空想. ¶free to *follow* their *fancies* 思うままにやってよい. ¶She *has* a *fancy* for dressing well. 彼女は着飾ることが好きだ. ‖ *have* a *fancy* for the woman その女に気がある ‖ I *have* a great *fancy* for travelling (golf). 私は旅行(など)が大好きだ. ‖ *have* no *fancy* for ... ...を好かない ‖ He *has* curious *fancies*. 彼には妙な好みがある. ‖ *having* a *fancy* to drink a cup of tea 茶を一杯飲みたかったので. ¶Her person happened to *hit* his *fancy*. 彼女の姿がたまたま彼の気に入った. ‖ it *hit* the European *fancy* as a good substitute for ... (それはりっぱに)...の代用品として欧州人の好みに投じた. ¶Then you think he'll *marry* his present *fancy?* で君は彼が今の愛人と結婚すると思うのだね. ¶*please* the *fancy* of ... ...の気に入る. ¶a man she *sets* her *fancy* on 彼女が思いを寄せている男. ¶*stir* one's *fancy* その愛好心を呼び起す. ¶*strike* the popular *fancy* 人気に投じる. 【類】*strike* the *fancy* of the public. ¶*suit* his *fancy* 彼の気に入る ‖ Each selected those which *suited* his *fancy*. 銘々が思い思いに選んだ. ¶if it *takes* your *fancy* お気に召せば ‖ *take* a *fancy* to ... ...が好きになる. 【類】That picture has *taken* my *fancy*. / I have *taken* quite a *fancy* to her. / I *took* a special (=great) *fancy* to him. ¶*want* (=*lack*) *fancy* 想像力を欠く.

V^2 as *fancy dictates* 気が向くままに.

Q a *grotesque fancy* 奇怪な空想. ¶That's *half fancy*. それは半分想像だ. ¶an *idle fancy* 愚にもつかぬ考え. ¶He has a *lively fancy*. 彼は活溌な想像力を持っている. ¶according to *individual fancy* 思い思いに. ¶a highly *ingenious* and *vigorous fancy* はなはだ巧妙な力強い空想. ¶That is a *mere fancy*. それは単なる空想に過ぎない. ¶The love was a *passing fancy*. その恋はでき心であった. ¶a *pleasing fancy* 面白い思い付き. ¶a *poetic fancy* 詩的な想像. ¶It does not take the *popular fancy*. 一般の受けがよくない. ¶take the *public fancy* 人気を取る. ¶*fancy unbridled* by experience 経験に拘束されない空想.

Q^2 the *cat fancy* ねこ好き.

P each *according to* his *fancy* 各人が思い思いに. ¶a thing *after* one's *fancy* 自分の気に入った物. ¶luxuriant

***in** fancy* 想像力が豊富. ¶a flight ***of** fancy* 奔放な想像. ‖ He is full ***of** fancy*. 彼は色々空想を描いている.

P² the *fancy **of*** youth 青年の空想.

fancy, *v.* 想像する, 想う ; 好む.

M *fancy* oneself [to be] ***beautiful*** 美しいとうぬぼれる. ¶*fancy* oneself ***dead*** 自分を死んだものと想像する. ¶***Just*** *fancy!* ちょっと考えて御覧なさい. ¶It is not an article that I *fancy* ***much***. それは私が大して欲しいと思う品ではない. ¶***Only*** *fancy!* 思っても見給え. ¶She *fancies* herself still ***young***. 彼女はまだ若いとうぬぼれている.

fang, *n.* きば.

V The wolf ***buried*** his *fangs* in his flesh. おおかみは彼の肉にきばを立てた.

Q² a ***poison*** *fang* 毒牙.

far, *a.* & *adv.* 遠く, はるかに ; 遠くへ ; 大いに, はなはだ.

M look *far* [***ahead***] into the future 遠く将来を見通す. ¶live *far* ***away*** 遠くに住んでいる. ¶***How*** *far* did they go? どの位遠くまでみんなは行ったか. 【類】***How*** *far* is it from here to Osaka? ‖ ***How*** *far* are you going, soldier? 兵隊さん, どちらまで(列車などで). ‖ I cannot say ***how*** *far* his story is true. 彼の話はどこまでが本当なのか分らない. ¶***So*** *far*, it is only talk. 今日までの所それは話題たるに過ぎない. ‖ There has ***so*** *far* been no relapse. 今の所ぶり返しはない(病気などの). ‖ ***so*** *far* as I know 僕の知っている所では ‖ I went ***so*** *far* as to call him a coward. 私は思い切って彼をおく病者といってやった. ‖ He is ***so*** *far* from doing it. 彼は中々そんなことをする人ではない. ‖ the story ***so*** *far* あら筋(続き物の今までの概略) ‖ geographically ***so*** *far* from ... ...から距離が遠い. 【類】***so*** *far* as my knowledge is concerned. ¶Are we ***still*** *far* from the town? まだ町まで余ほどありますか. ¶The end is ***still*** *far* to see. 前途りょう遠である. ¶***thus*** *far* これまでのところ. ¶He is ***too*** *far* in years (=old) to be a pupil now. 彼はもう生徒となるには年をとり過ぎている.

M² ***as*** *far* as I can できるだけ ‖ I will go with you ***as*** *far* as London. ロンドンまでお供しましょう. ¶It's not *far* ***off*** the mark. 当らずといえども遠からずである. ‖ It is *far* [***off***] from home. ここから遠い.

P it is better fitted ***by*** *far* for ... その方が...にははるかによく適している ‖ Psychologists incline to the belief that ***by*** *far* the greater number of cases of stammering are due to mental causes. 心理学者間にはどもりの大多数は精神的原因によると信じる傾向がある. ‖ He is ***by*** *far* the best boy in the class. 彼は級で図抜けて優秀だ. ‖ Diabetes is ***by*** *far* most frequent among overweight persons. 体重の多すぎる人には糖尿病が非常に多い. 【類】***By*** *far* the largest part of the tourist traffic to and from Italy is by rail. / ***By*** *far* the shortest way to learn to read a language is to begin by speaking it. ¶*Far* ***from*** it! とんでもない. ‖ ***from*** *far* 遠くから ‖ come ***from*** *far* and near 遠近から来る ‖ when ships are *far* ***from*** land 船が陸から遠く離れている時 ‖ His work is very *far* ***from*** the average. 彼の成績は断然平均以上だ. ‖ Their demands are *far* ***from*** just. 彼らの要求ははなはだ公正を欠く. ‖ His friends would be *far* ***from*** approving it. 彼の友人たちは決してそれに賛成しまい. ‖ In good writing elliptical expressions are *far* ***from*** uncommon. りっぱな文章には省略形を用いることが決して少くない. ‖ it is *far* ***from*** unlikely that ... ...は随分ありそうなことだ ‖ The class numbers not *far* ***from*** one hundred students. その級の生徒数は百名を多く出ない. ‖ *Far* be it ***from*** me to hurt his feeling. あの人の感情を害するなんてでんで私の心にもないことだ. 【類】*far* ***from*** home / He was *far* ***from*** the attainment of his object. / It really isn't *far* ***from*** the truth. / be *far* ***from*** ideal / be *far* ***from*** satisfactory / *far* ***from*** being disappointed / be *far* ***from*** being a failure / *Far* ***from*** being honest, he is a big crook (くせもの). / He is very *far* indeed ***from*** being above reproach. / He is *far* ***from*** prudent. / *Far* ***from*** despising, I greatly respect him. / *Far* ***from*** being rich, I am over head and heels in debt. ¶go *far* ***into*** the forest 遠く林の中へはいる ‖ The cape extends *far* ***into*** the ocean. みさきは遠く大洋に突出している. ‖ We sat talking *far* ***into*** the night. われわれは夜ふけまで語り続けた. 【類】It went on raining *far* ***into*** the night. ‖ He pushed his researches *far* ***into*** antiquity. 彼は遠く古代にさかのぼってその研究を進めた. ¶*far* ***to*** the northward 遠く北の方に. 【類】*Far* ***to*** the south of the Philippines is Australia. ¶*far* ***up*** the hill 遠く丘の上に.

farce, *n.* 茶番, こっけい芝居.

V ***act*** a *farce* 茶番をやる.

Q a ***ludicrous*** *farce* 面白い茶番.

fare, *n.* (**1**) [汽船・乗物の]賃金.

V I ***borrowed*** the *fare* and went to her. 旅費を借りて彼女の所に行った. ¶***charge*** a *fare* 賃金を課する. ¶The conductor proceeded to ***collect*** (=receive) *fares*. 車掌が賃金を集め始めた. ¶***demand*** an unreasonable *fare* 不法な賃金を請求する. ¶attempt to ***extort*** exorbitant *fares* from newcomers 新来者(土地不案内のもの)から法外な賃金をゆすろうとする. ¶***give*** reduced *fare* to working men 労働者のために賃金の割引をする. ¶***levy*** *fare* of 1 d. per mile 一マイル一ペニーの賃金を課する. ¶***lower*** the *fares* 賃金を下げる. ¶European railroads have ***pared*** *fares* 30% and hotels in most countries have lowered their tariffs 36%. ヨーロッパの鉄道は三割の割引をし大抵の国のホテルは料金を三割六分下げた. ¶***pay*** separate *fares* 別々に賃金を払う ‖ ***pay*** *fare* in proportion to distance 距離に応じて乗車賃を払う. ¶***raise*** *fares* 賃金の値上げをする. ¶***receive*** the legal *fare* 法定の賃金を受取る. ¶The *fares* are ***reckoned*** by distance (=the journey) or by time (=the hour). 賃金は距離または時間で計算する.

Q without any ***additional*** *fare* 追加料金を徴収しないで. ¶pay ***another*** *fare* 賃金を二度払う. ¶give just the ***bare*** *fare* ちょうど賃金だけ与える. ¶***double*** *fare* 倍額の賃金. ¶pay ***full*** *fare* 全額賃金を払う. ¶at ***half*** *fare* 半額(の賃金)で. ¶***legal*** *fares* (自動車などの)法定乗車賃. ¶The *fares* are ***low***. 乗車賃は安い. ¶what is the ***rail*** [***way***] *fare* to ...? ...までの汽車賃はいくらですか. ¶at a ***reduced*** *fare* 割引(賃金)で. 【類】at greatly ***reduced*** *fares* / give ***reduced*** *fare* to working men / specially ***reduced*** *fares* for parties of more than ...(以上の団体). ¶carry passengers at ***separate*** *fares* 別々の料金で旅客を運ぶ. ¶***single*** (***return***) *fare* 片道(往復)乗車賃 ‖ ***single*** *fare* 片道賃金. ¶for a ***slight extra*** *fare* 少額の追加賃金で. ¶The Tube charges are a ***uniform*** *fare* of 2d. for any distance. [ロンドン]地下鉄の乗車賃は二ペンス均一である. ¶***usual*** *fares* 並の賃金.

Q² ***boat*** *fare* 船賃. ¶***bus*** (***train***) *fare* バス(など)賃. ¶save ***car*** *fare* 車代を節約する. ¶***commute*** *fare* 《米》定期乗車券代金. ¶***excess*** *fare* 〖鉄道〗乗越賃, 優等車乗換不足賃. ¶***half-price*** *fare* 半額の賃金. ¶cheap ***holiday*** *fares* 安い休日の乗車賃. ¶pay a ***railway*** *fare* 汽車賃を払う. ¶***spring*** *fare* 〖スコットランド〗春漁 (たら, いわしなど). ¶***steamer*** *fare*=passage money 船賃. ¶A universal ***5-cent*** *fare* is charged for street-cars in New York. ニューヨークの電車の乗車賃は五セント均一だ.

P ***at*** a *fare* of ... ...の賃金で ‖ special trips ***at*** *fares* lower than the ordinary 平常より賃金の安い特別列車 ‖ Return tickets are issued ***at*** a single *fare* for the double journey. 片道の賃金で往復切符を売る. ¶Any small change ***for*** the *fare?* 電車(バス)賃にこまかいのがあるか.

P² *fare* ***for*** distance (time) 距離(など)きめの賃金 ‖ *fare* ***for*** returning home 帰郷運賃. ¶the first-class *fare* ***from*** the Metropolis ***to*** ... is ... 首都から...への一等乗車賃は...だ. ¶*fares* ***on*** the railway=railway fares. ¶What is the *fare* ***to*** London and back? ロンドンまでの往復賃金はいくらか.

(**2**) 乗客.

V The cabman ***carried*** his *fare* to a wrong address. 運転手は乗客の行先を違えた. 【類】The driver ***carried*** his *fare* to an inn (a hatter's shop).

Q ***All*** *fares*, please! みなさんお乗りください. ¶his ***beautiful*** *fare* [タキシーなどの]美人のお客.

P The chauffeur refused to take me ***as*** a *fare*. 運転手は僕の乗車をこばんだ.

(**3**) 食物, 料理.

V ***eat*** native *fare* その国の食物を食べる.

Q a ***coarse*** *fare* 粗食. ¶live on ***dainty*** *fare* 不断うまい物を食べる. ¶a ***good*** (***bad***) *fare* うまい(まずい)物. 【類】The *fare* is ***good*** at that hotel. ¶***invalid*** *fare* 病人の食物. ¶***luxurious*** *fare* ぜいたくな食物. ¶a ***plain*** *fare* 粗食. ¶live on ***slender*** *fare* 粗末な食物でやって行く. ¶a ***tolerable*** *fare* かなりの食物. ¶***unappetizing*** *fare* まずい食事.

Q² rude ***mountain*** *fare* 粗末な山の食事.

fare, *v.* 成り行く ; やって行く ; 飲食する.

M We *fared* ***badly*** at the hotel. ホテルではひどい目にあった. ‖ He *fared* ***badly*** in the transaction. 彼の交渉はうまく

行かなかった. ‖ The stuff *fares badly* in the laundry. その布地は洗たくがききかない. 【類】 It sometimes happens that a company *fares* so *badly* that it cannot pay the dividends on its preference shares (優先株の配当). ¶*fare* no *better* この上よくはならない. ¶Before sunrise he was *faring* gallantly. 日の出前に彼はさっそうと旅立った. ¶It will *fare hard* with them if they don't alter their scheme. もしプランを一部変更しなければ彼らはひどい目に会うだろう. ¶*How fares* it with you? どうです(うまく行きますか). 【類】 *How* did the enterprise *fare*? / *How* did you *fare* in your journey? ¶It *fares ill* with him. 彼はどうもうまくゆかない. ¶The traveler *fared slowly* on his way. その旅行者はゆっくり旅をした. ¶*fare sumptuously* in restaurants 飲食店でぜいたくな食事をする. ¶*fare well* うまくやって行く. ¶*fare worse* もっと悪くなる.

P It is not clearly known how things have *fared with* him. 彼はその後どうなったかはっきり分らない.

farewell, *n.* 別れのあいさつ; 告別.

V I must *bid* you *farewell*. おいとまします. ‖ I *bade farewell* to him (=*bade* him *farewell*) with relief. [長居の客などに] やれやれと思って別れを告げた. ‖ There remains but to *bid farewell* to this phase of Living London. 今のロンドンのこの方面はこれで筆をおくことにする. ‖ *bid farewell* to one's paternal roof 親のひざもとを辞する. ¶They *bowed farewell* to their native land. 彼らは故国に別れを告げた. ¶*exchange farewells* with ... ...と別れのあいさつを交わす. ¶He *kissed* her *farewell*. 彼は彼女に別れのキスをした. ¶*make* one's *farewells* 別れをつげる. ¶His Highness *received* a cordial *farewell* from royalty. 殿下は王族たちから懇篤な告別のあいさつをお受けになった. ¶*say farewell* 告別のあいさつをする. ¶*take* one's *farewell* 別れる ‖ *take farewell* of ... ...と別れる. ¶*wave* a *farewell* at ... ...に手(など)を振って告別する. 【類】 they *waved farewells* to ...

Q He bade her an *affectionate farewell*. 彼は彼女に心づくしの別れを告げた. ¶bid an *eternal farewell* to ... ...に永遠の別れを告げる. ¶We waited to wave a *final farewell* as we steamed away. 汽車が停車場を出て行ったときわれわれは手を振って最後の別れを告げるために立っていた. ¶extend ¶bid a *fond farewell* 名ごり惜しそうに告別する. ¶extend a *hearty farewell* to ... ...に心から別れを告げる. ¶They waved with their hats, shawls, and handkerchiefs a *last farewell* to their friends and the native land. 彼らは帽子やショールやハンケチを振って友だちと故国に最後の別れを告げた. ¶a *lingering farewell* 低回去りやらぬ別れ. ¶bid her son a *loving farewell* 息子にいとしい別れを告げる. ¶As the last sip is swallowed, Burgundy leaves on the palate a most *pleasing* "*farewell*." ブルガンディーのぶどう酒は最後の一すすりを飲み干すと何ともいえないあと味が舌に残る. ¶bid him a *sorrowing farewell* 彼に悲しい別れを告げる. ¶*tender farewells* いとしい別れ. ¶They bade one another a *touching farewell* by letter. 彼らは手紙で心をこめた別れの言葉を取交わした.

P² this proved to be his *farewell to* ... これが...との彼の別れであった ‖ *Farewell to* happiness! 幸福よさらば! (この世の幸福ももうこれ限りだ). ‖ a *farewell to* the earth 地球へのさよなら ‖ *Farewell to* arms! 武器(戦争)よさらば.

farm, *n.* 農場; 飼養場.

V *hire* (=*rent*) a *farm* from ... ...から農場を借入れる. ¶*lay out* a *farm* 農場を開く. ¶*run* a *farm* 農場を経営する. ¶*take* a *farm* on a lease of five years 五年契約で農場を借受ける. ¶*work* a *farm* on shares 利益分与の約束ぶわけで農場で働く.

Q an *experimental farm* 試験農場. ¶a *fertile farm* 土地の肥えた農場. ¶a *horse-breeding farm* 馬匹飼養場.

Q² a *bee farm* 養蜂(ﾎｳ)園. ¶He has a small *chicken farm*. 彼は小さい養鶏場を持っている. ¶a *dairy farm* 酪農場. ¶The *egg farm* has accommodation for 100,000 birds. その卵用種養鶏場は十万羽の収容力がある. ¶a *goose farm* が鳥飼育場. ¶a *milk farm* 酪農場. ¶an *opium farm* [香港・シンガポール・サイゴン・ジャバなど東洋植民地の]アヘン販売権または専売権. ¶a *pearl* (an *oyster*) *farm* 真珠貝(かき)養殖場. ¶Inmates of a *poor farm* 老人(など)保護所の入所者. ¶a *poultry farm* 養鶏場. ¶a *salt farm* 塩田. ¶live on a *six-acre farm* 六エーカーの農地に住む. ¶the *spirit farm* in Singapore シンガポールのアルコール専売権. ¶a *stock farm* 牧畜場. ¶a good *tillage farm* 良好な耕地. ¶a *three hundred acre farm* 三百エーカーの農場.

P many animals *in* the *farm* その牧場にいる多数の動物. ¶the yield *of* a *farm* 農場の産額. ¶a cottage *on* the *farm* 農場の小屋. ¶work *on* a *farm* at ... ...の農場で働く.

farm, *v.* 農耕する; 賃貸する; 《米》小リーグに預ける.

M To raise money, the bishop planned to *farm out* his land. 金の才覚に僧正は自分の地所を賃貸する計画を立てた. ‖ The player was *farmed out*. 〚野〛その選手は小リーグのチームに預けられた.

P *farm on* one's own land 自作農をやる.

farmer, *n.* 農夫, 栽培者.

Q an *easy farmer* 有福な農場主. ¶*farmer* 相当な農場主. ¶a *sizable* (=*biggish*) *farmer* 相当な農場主.

Q² an *absentee farmer* 不在地主. ¶a *baby farmer* えい児養育者. ¶a *blackmarketeering farmer* やみ売り農家. ¶a *dairy farmer* 酪農. ¶an *egg farmer* 養鶏業者. ¶a *fox farmer* 養狐(ｺ)業者. ¶*fruit farmers* (=growers) in California カリホルニア州の果実栽培者. ¶a *gentleman farmer* 大百姓(農場主で自分は労働しない). ¶a *livestock farmer* 畜農. ¶a *pearl* (an *oyster*) *farmer* 真珠貝(など)の養殖業者. ¶a *poultry farmer* 養鶏業者. ¶a *small-hold farmer* 零細農. ¶a *stock farmer* 牧畜業者. ¶a large (small) *tenant farmer* 大(小)小作農. ¶a *tobacco farmer* タバコ栽培家. ¶a *truck farmer* (=gardener) 《米》蔬(ｿ)菜栽培者.

farming, *n.* 農業, 農耕.

Q *diversified farming* 多角農業. ¶*scientific modern farming* 科学的近代化農業.

Q² *baby farming* えい児保育. ¶*chicken farming* 養鶏業. ¶*dairy farming* 酪農. ¶*egg farming* 養鶏業. ¶*fruit farming* 果樹栽培. ¶*fur farming* 毛皮獣飼養. ¶*garden farming* [野菜の]畠作. ¶*ostrich farming* だ鳥飼育. ¶*oyster farming* かき養殖. ¶do *part-time farming* 片手間に百姓をする. ¶*poultry farming* 養鶏. ¶*sheep farming* 牧羊. ¶*truck farming* 蔬(ｿ)菜栽培.

farm-land, *n.* 農地.

V *lease farm-land* 農地を賃借(貸)する.

farm-life, *n.* 農園生活.

Q² the *prairie farm-life* of Kansas カンサス州の大草原農場生活.

farm-yard, *n.* 農家の庭.

Q a *large farm-yard* 広い農家の庭.

farther, *a., adv.* さらに遠い; 一層遠く.

M *How much farther* have we to go? このさきまだどの位あるか. ¶*No farther*. もうよい, 分った. 【類】 can walk *no farther*.

M² He lives *farther on*. 彼の家はもっと先です.

P Nothing could be *farther from* the truth. それはとんでもない間違いだ. ‖ Nothing is *farther from* my mind (=intention) than such an idea. こんなことは私は夢にも考えていない.

farthest, *a., adv.* 最も遠い; 最も遠く.

P He counted on staying away from me no more than a week *at* [the] *farthest*. 彼は私と離れているのは精々一週間位のものだと思い込んでいた. ‖ within one, two, or *at farthest* three miles of London ロンドンから一二マイルか遠くて三マイル以内に. ¶*farthest from* the schoolhouse 校舎から最も遠い.

farthing, *n.* 英国の小銅貨; 極小量.

V I do not *care* a *farthing* whether you go or not. 君が行こうと行くまいと一向構わない. ¶I will not *give* a *farthing* to such an ungrateful fellow any more. こんな恩知らずにはもう一銭だってやらない.

P I have paid him *to* the utmost *farthing*. 僕はありったけ彼に払った. ¶*without* a *farthing* 一文なしで.

fascinate, *v.* 迷わす.

P be *fascinated by* her charms 女の色香に迷う. ¶He was *fascinated with* her beauty (=charm). 彼は彼女の容色に迷った.

fascination, *n.* 魅力, 魅惑.

V When a movement is forbidden and branded as dangerous, it *acquires* a *fascination* for young men. 何か運動が禁止されて危険のらく印を押されるとそれがかえって青年を魅惑するものだ. ¶The detective story *exercises* a certain *fascination* over the "general reader." 探偵小説は一般読者にとってある魅力を持っている. ¶The subject has always *had* a *fascination* for me. 私はその題目に対していつも興味を持っていた. ‖ Being Red *has* the *fascination* which children feel for fire. 赤であることは子供が火に感じるような魅力がある. ¶It *possesses* a positive *fascina-*

tion for her audience. それは彼女の聴衆に対して実際魅力を持っている.

Q It exercised an ***irresistible fascination*** on the working classes. それは労働階級を圧倒的に魅惑した. ¶it has an ***overwhelming fascination*** for ... それは...に対して圧倒的魅力を有する.

fashion, *n.* 流行, 時流; 流行物; [集合的に]上流の人士; 様式, やり方, 風.

V ***create*** a *fashion* 流行を生む. ¶***design fashions*** 流行を案出する. ¶***dictate*** the *fashions* of women 婦人界の流行を左右する. ¶***follow*** the *fashion* 流行を追う ‖ ***follow*** a *fashion* too late 流行に遅れる. ¶It ***formed*** the *fashion* of the day. それが当時の流行となった. ¶he ***has*** a *fashion* of ... 彼には...の癖がある. ¶***inaugurate*** a new *fashion* 新流行を起す. ¶***lead*** the *fashion* 流行のさきがけをする. ¶Marie Antoinette is said to have ***set*** the *fashion* in using the perfumes of violet and rose. マリ・アントワネットがすみれとばらの香水をはやらせたのだそうだ. ‖ The actors ***set*** the *fashion* in Japan. 日本では役者が流行のさきがけをする. ‖ the car that has ***set*** the *fashion* to the motoring world 自動車界流行のさきがけをした自動車. ¶*Fashions* in 1935 will be ***swayed*** by "stream lines." 一九三五年の流行は「流線型」で支配されるであろう. ¶***take up*** the *fashion* of ... ...の流行になろう.

V^2 *Fashions* ***change*** quickly. 流行はすぐに変る. 【類】 The *fashions* are constantly ***changing.*** ¶The *fashion* has ***come*** to stay. その流行は一時的のものでなくなった. ¶A new *fashion* is ***coming in.*** 新しい流行が目についてきた. ¶The *fashion* has ***passed.*** その流行はすたれた. ¶The *fashion* ***spread*** rapidly. その流行は迅速に広まった. ¶The *fashion* has ***sprung*** into being. それがはやり出した. ¶This *fashion* does not ***take.*** この流行は永続きがしない. ¶The *fashion* began to ***wane.*** その流行はすたれかけた.

Q live in a ***beggarly*** *fashion* こじきのような生活をする. ¶in the ***conventional fashion*** ありきたりの方法で. ¶in a ***curious fashion*** 変な風に. ¶discourse in ***entertaining*** *fashion* on ... ...を面白く語る. ¶pronounce after the ***English*** *fashion* 英国風に発音する. ¶She was dressed after the ***European*** (=***Western***) *fashion.* 彼女は洋装していた. ¶an ***exotic*** *fashion* 異国風. ¶***fantastic*** *fashion* in dress 服装の風変りな流行. ¶The *fashion* never became ***general.*** その様式は一般化せずに終った. ¶in a ***half-playful*** *fashion* 半ばこっけい的に. ¶select in a ***haphazard*** *fashion* 慢然と選ぶ. ¶seat, ***Japanese*** *fashion,* on mats 日本流の畳の上にすわる. ¶It is the ***latest*** (=***newest***) *fashion* それは最新流行です. ¶in a ***mechanical*** *fashion* 機械的に. ¶inspect in ***military*** *fashion* 軍隊式に検閲する. ¶The ***old*** *fashion* of ... is reviving now. 昔風の...が復興しかかっている. 【類】 He wears a queue (ちょんまげ) in the ***old*** *fashion.* / a garment of the ***old*** *fashion.* ¶their knees closely bent against their stomachs in ***Oriental*** *fashion* 彼らは東洋風にしゃがんで. ¶in the ***orthodox*** *fashion* 従来の型通りに. ¶in a ***perfunctory, half-sleep*** *fashion* うわのそらで半ば眠って(祈禱するときなど). ¶explain it in a ***plausible*** *fashion* もっともらしくそれを説明する. ¶according to the ***present*** *fashion* 目下の流行に従って. ¶the ***prevailing*** *fashion* 流行している様式. ¶in a ***primitive*** *fashion* 原始式なやり方で. ¶a building in a ***Romanesque*** *fashion* ロマネスク様式の建物. ¶in a ***routine*** *fashion* 型の通り. ¶in much the ***same*** *fashion* as ... 大体...と同様に. ¶in a ***silly*** *fashion* ぼやぼやして. ¶accept this idea in a ***skeptical*** *fashion* 半信半疑でこの考えを聞く. ¶in ***Stateside*** *fashion* アメリカ(本国)風に. ¶in a ***superfluous*** *fashion* 冗語的に. ¶in the most ***systematic*** *fashion* きわめて組織的に. ¶in ***true Italian*** *fashion* 本当のイタリア式に. ¶in the most ***unceremonious*** *fashion* ごく手軽(略式)に.

Q^2 this year's ***beach*** *fashion* 今年の海水着の新型. ¶in ***butterfly*** *fashion* うわついた調子で. ¶***dress*** *fashions* 色々の衣服の流行型. ¶the ***fall*** *fashion* 秋の流行. ¶***hairdressing*** *fashions* いろいろの調髪の流行型. ¶***man-of-war*** *fashion* 海軍風(秩序整然として規律ある). ¶a patchwork enterprise of meeting emergencies in ***piecemeal*** *fashion* 急場しのぎの間に合せ企業. ¶the ***resort*** *fashion* 海水着などの新型. ¶The prices shot up in ***skyrocket*** *fashion.* 物価がものすごく高騰した.

P ***after*** a *fashion* とも角も; 幾分か; どうにかこうにか. 【類】 He can speak and write French—***after*** a *fashion.* ‖ ***after*** the *fashion* of France フランス風に ‖ ***after*** the *fashion* of the time 時流にならって ‖ He was dressed ***after*** the *fashion* of a sailor. 彼は水夫の風をしていた. ‖ a man who runs ***after*** the *fashion* 流行を追う人 ‖ He did it ***after*** his own *fashion.* 彼は自己流にやった. ¶fall ***behind*** the *fasion* 流行に後れる. ¶The beach is frequented ***by*** *fashion.* その海岸は流行界の人々がよく行く所だ. ¶***in*** a *fashion*=after a fashion 幾分 ‖ pieces much ***in*** *fashion* at that time 当時大いにはやった狂言 ‖ Mahjong is now ***in*** *fashion.* マージャンは今はやっている. ‖ Her gowns are always ***in*** [the] *fashion.* 彼女のガウンはいつも流行風になっている. ‖ go to a university to amuse themselves or to be ***in*** *fashion* 楽しみにかまたは世間並に大学へ行く ‖ pronounce French words ***in*** English *fashion* フランス語を英語風に発音する ‖ ***in*** a *fashion* quite different from ... ...とはまるで違った風に ‖ ***in*** a like *fashion*=in like manner 同様に. 【類】 ***in*** the Elizabethan *fashion.* ¶come ***into*** *fashion* はやり出す ‖ bring it ***into*** *fashion* それをはやらせる ‖ grow ***into*** *fashion* 流行してくる. ¶a man ***of*** *fashion* 上流の人 ‖ All the *fashion* ***of*** the town were present. その町の上流の人々は皆列席した. ‖ those who would be in the van ***of*** *fashion* 流行のさきがけたらんとする人々. ¶These hats are now ***out of*** *fashion.* こういう帽子はもう流行遅れだ. ‖ go (=get) ***out of*** *fashion* すたれる. 【類】 That hat of yours is little ***out of*** *fashion.*

P^2 it is the *fashion* ***for*** gentlemen to ... ...するのは紳士の習いだ. ¶it is not the *fashion* ***in*** their country to ... ...するのはその国でははやらない ‖ *fashion* ***in*** clothes 着物の流行. ¶it became the *fashion* ***of*** the day to ... ...するのが当時の流行となった ‖ the *fashion* ***of*** the hour 目下の流行 ‖ be the *fashion* ***of*** the moment 現在流行している. 【類】 The novel is the *fashion* ***of*** the day.

O it used to be the *fashion* to ... 以前は...することが流行したものだ.

fashion, *v.* 形造る; 適合させる.

P *fashion* them ***into*** various shapes それを種々の形に造る ‖ *fashion* clay ***into*** a pipe ねん土をパイプの形に造る ‖ *fashioned* ***into*** the form of ... ...の形に造った ‖ *fashion* the lecture ***to*** the audience's understanding 講演を聴衆の理解力に合わせる. 【類】 Law ought to be *fashioned* ***to*** the manners and conditions of the people.

fashionable, *n.* 上流の人.

Q There a party of ***London*** *fashionables* repair for fishing, flirtation, and holidaymaking in general. そこへロンドンの上流社会の連中が釣や桃色遊びや行楽に出かける.

fashionable, *a.* 流行を追う.

P Automobiles were becoming *fashionable* ***among*** the wealthy people in Japan. 自動車は日本の富豪の間にはやり出していた.

O It was then *fashionable* to be a Francophile. 当時フランスびいきははやりものであった.

fast, *n.* 断食.

V ***break*** one's *fast* on ... ...を朝食に食べる ‖ ***break*** a long *fast* 長い断食を止める. ¶***perform*** a *fast* of twenty one days' duration 二十一日間の断食を行う.

P^2 a *fast* ***in*** memory of ... ...の記念に行う断食.

fast, *v.* 断食する, 節食する.

P *fast* ***from*** ... ...を断つ. ¶*fast* ***on*** bread and water パンと水だけで食事する.

fast, *a.* 固着している; 動けない.

M a ship *fast* ***aground*** かく座して動かない船.

P a stake *fast* ***in*** the ground 地にしっかり立っているくい. ¶He is *fast* ***with*** the gout. 彼は痛風で動けない.

O stick (stand, sit) *fast* ぴったりくっつく(など).

fast, *a., ad.* 早い; 早く.

M Please don't speak ***so*** *fast.* そんなに早口に話さないで下さい. ¶The clock is ***three minutes*** *fast.* その時計は三分進んでいる. ¶The watch is half an hour ***too*** *fast.* その時計は三十分進んでいる. 【類】 My watch is three minutes ***too*** *fast.*

fasten, *v.* しっかり締める(つける); くっつく, 付きまとう.

M *fastened* ***tight*** to ... ...にしっかり結びつけた. ¶We use pins to *fasten* things ***together.*** われわれは物を留めるのにピンを使う.

M^2 The bag was *fastened* ***down*** with leather tape. その袋は革ひもでしばってあった. ‖ The lid of the box is *fastened* ***down.*** 箱のふたは打ちつけてある. ‖ To *fasten* ***down*** its sense, the affix "Evangelical" may suffice.「福音の」という語が前に付けてあるからその意味がはっきりするだろう. ¶fasten off a thread 糸を留める(結び目・返し針などで).

P the transmission of the disease through fleas which fasten on rats ねずみについているのみを通じての病気伝染. ‖ fasten the guilt on another 人に罪をきせる ‖ fasten a flag on a pole さおに旗をつける ‖ fasten one's hope on a promise 約束に望みをかける ‖ fasten one's eyes on ... ...に目を留める ‖ Such habits fasten on natures that are already enfeebled. すでに弱っている性質の者にはこうした癖がつく. ¶fasten a rope to a post なわを柱にくくりつける. 【類】 The telephone wires are fastened to the poles. / The gate is fastened to a post. / The shelf is fastened to the wall. / Hotel keys are fastened to a big brass star or rosette. (真ちゅうの星かばらむすび). ¶fasten up a box 箱をくぎづけにする ‖ fasten (=zip) up one's coat 上着にチャックをかける. ¶The beggars fastened upon me. こじきが僕に付きまとった. ‖ Sickness has fastened upon him. 病気が彼に取りついた. ‖ fasten a nickname upon one 人にあだ名をつける. ‖ fasten a quarrel upon another 人にけんかをふっかける. ¶fasten ... with buttons (nails) ボタン(くぎ)で...を留める ‖ fasten ... with nails to ... ...をくぎ付けにする. 【類】 fasten a badge with a pin / fasten ... with a lock / fasten an envelope with a seal.

fastener, *n.* 留めるもの; チャック.

Q^2 a paper fastener 書類とじ. ¶a slide fastener チャック. ¶a snap fastener スナップ止め. ¶a zip fastener=a zipper チャック.

fastening, *n.* 締めること; 囲い.

V The baboons busted the fastenings of their cage. ひひがおりを破った. ¶The hat has no fastenings. その帽子には留めひもがついていない.

Q^2 a trunk with leather (steel) fastenings 皮(鉄)の締め具のついたトランク.

fastidious, *a.* 気むずかしい.

P fastidious in the choice of ... ...の選択に小むずかしい ‖ fastidious in dress (taste) 服装(など)に小むずかしい.

fat, *n.* 脂肪.

V lay on fat 脂肪を増す. 【類】 If a man does put (=lay) on fat, he may know that he is eating more than he needs. ¶wear off the fat 運動して脂肪をとる.

fat, *a.* 肥った.

P be fat (=thick) in head=be stupid のろまである.

fatal, *a.* 致命的な; 有害な.

M an accident terribly fatal きわめて不幸なできごと.

P It is fatal to life. それは生命にかかわる. 【類】 It is fatal to one's hope (success, interest). ‖ Such a scandal is fatal to the reputation of a minister. かかる醜聞は牧師の名声には致命傷だ.

fatalism, *n.* 運命[論].

P by a fatalism beyond their own wills 自己の意志を超越した運命により.

fatality, *n.* 死亡; 運命; 死傷事故.

V^2 Fatalities number two hundred. (流行病などで)死亡者二百を算する. ¶if a fatality occurs 死者を出したときは.

Q^2 airline fatalities 航空死傷事故[件数]. ¶coal mine fatalities 数件の炭坑死傷事故. ¶highway fatalities 街頭の諸死傷事故. ¶motor vehicle fatalities 数件の自動車死傷事故. ¶summer drowning fatalities 夏季の水死事故[数件]. ¶traffic fatalities 交通諸死傷事故.

P by a (=some) strange fatality 不思議な運命で.

P^2 fatalities from mountain climbing 登山死傷事故.

fate, *n.* 運命, 成行; 悪運, 悲運.

V accept one's fate 往生する, あきらめる. ¶affect the fate of a nation 国民の運命を左右する. ¶avoid one fate only to find another 一つの厄を逃れたかと思うとまた一つの厄に会う. ¶He went home in despair to await his fate. 彼は天命を待つべく失望の体で帰宅した(失策をした官吏など). ¶bewail the fate of his child 彼の子の不運を嘆く. ¶challenge the fate 運命を物ともしない. ¶curse one's hard fate 身の不運をのろう. 【類】 More than once Marx cursed his fate for having undertaken the burden of a family (妻帯). ¶decide (=fix) the fate of the whole campaign 全戦の運命を決する. ¶piteously deplore one's fate 身の不運を嘆く ‖ deplore the fate that has befallen 身に降り掛った運命を嘆く. ¶He deserves his fate. 彼はああ成るのが当然だ. ‖ Most of them deserve no better fate than to swell the ocean of oblivion. 彼らの多数は忘却の海に葬られるのが当然だ. ¶determine the fate of ... ...の運命を決する. ¶He barely escaped a like fate. 彼はかろうじて同じような運命に陥るのを免れた. 【類】 He narrowly escaped a similar fate. ¶He had a like fate. 彼も同じような運命を持っていた. ¶lament one's hard fate 身の不運を嘆く. ¶meet a worse fate もっとひどい目にあう. 【類】 meet (=suffer) the same fate ‖ He met his fate like a brave man. 彼はりっぱな往生を遂げた. ‖ The Titanic met her fate by crashing into a huge iceberg. 汽船タイタニック号は氷山と衝突して沈没した. ¶mourn their tragic fate 彼らの悲惨な運命をいたむ. ¶predict the same fate 同じような運命になると予言する. ¶propitiate the fates 運命の女神の機げんを取る. ¶rule one's fate その運命を支配する. ¶Today is to seal the prisoner's fate. きょう囚人の運命が決定する. 【類】 This event sealed his own fate. / the fate of ... was sealed when ... ¶settle fate 運命を定める. ¶share the fate with ... ...運命をともにする. 【類】 share a like fate with ... / They may have shared the same fate. ¶He suffered the same fate. 彼も同じ運命に会った. 【類】 suffer the fate common to ...

V^2 The fates befriended her when she had gone out into the world. 世の中に出てから彼女は万事都合よく行った. ¶as fate would have it 運命で.

Q a bitter fate 悲惨な運命. ¶This painting had a curious fate. この絵には不思議な運命がつきまとっていた. ¶Evil fate in the shape of ... stepped between them. 運悪く何の某という悪人がその間に現われてきた. ¶had fate been kinder=had his lot been otherwise これほど不運でなかったなら. ¶a hapless fate 不運. ¶it was his luckless fate to ... ...したのはその人の不運であった. ¶The Japanese nation took a great resolve to stake their national fate upon the issue. 日本国民はその勝敗に国家の運命をかける一大決意を固めた. ¶by a relentless fate 冷酷な運命により. ¶weep one's sad fate 悲運に泣く. ¶What a strange fate! いかにも不思議な運命だ. ¶an untoward fate 不運. ¶He cannot expect to escape the usual fate of the spendthrift. 彼は道楽者のおきまりの運命を免れることは望めない. ¶the worst fate that can befall mankind 人間に降りかかる最悪の非運.

P sorrow at one's hard fate 身の不運を嘆く. ¶resign oneself to fate 成行に任せる ‖ submit to fate 運命に甘んじる.

P^2 The fate of the crew and passengers is unknown. 船員と船客の運命は不明である.

fated, *pa.* 運命づけられた.

P His life was fated to a violent death. 彼は横死すべき運命の人であった.

O He seems fated to meet with accidents. 彼は災難に会う運命と見える. ¶His life was fated to be of short duration. 彼は若死すべき運命の人であった. 【類】 The temple was so often fated to be destroyed by fire.

father, *n.* 父; 祖先; 建設者; *pl.* 長老.

V He lost his father when he was a baby. 彼は赤ん坊のとき父を失った. ¶revere a father 父を敬う. ¶in order to rejoin her father in Paris パリにいる彼女の父と一緒になるために.

V^2 The father gradually came into his heart. 彼はだんだん父性愛に目覚めてきた. 【類】 All the father rose in my heart.

Q a son of an alcoholic father 酒飲みの父の息子. ¶a bereaved father 子に先立たれた父. ¶an earthly father この世の父(在天の父に対し). ¶since our Lord God created Adam, our first father 主なる神がわれわれの最初の祖先たるアダムを造ってからこの方. ¶America's Founding Fathers アメリカ建設者たち. 【類】 The Founding Fathers of our democracy. ¶a heartless father 無情な父親. ¶our Heavenly Father 天にましますわれらの父. ¶Be a kind father to the motherless children. 母亡き後の子供たちに親切な父となって下さい(死にひんする妻の夫に対する言葉). ¶an honest father 律義な父. ¶her natural father 彼女(私生児)の父. ¶the putative father of a child 子供の推定上の父. ¶her tyrannous father 彼女の暴虐な父. ¶unmarried fathers and mothers 結婚しないで子を持つ父母たち. ¶a well-meaning but misguided father 子供のためを思ってはいるが方法を誤っている父.

Q^2 the City Fathers of New York ニューヨークの市当局者. ¶a conscript father 古ローマの元老院議員, 父老; 兵役に徴集された者. ¶a Jesuit father 伴天連(ばてれん). ¶He had a millionaire father. 彼は百万長者を父に持っていた. ¶her *multimillionaire father* 彼女の億万長者の父.

P take *after* one's *father* 父親に似る. ¶handed down *from father* to son 父から子へと伝わった.

P² He is the *father of* a family of four children. 彼には四人の子供がある. ‖ the *father of* English advertising 英国における広告の元祖 ‖ Brontë, *father of* the authoresses 女流作家ブロンテ姉妹の父 ‖ a *father of* his country 国父. 【類】George Washington is the *father of* his country. / the *father of* modern Russia, Peter the Great / Homer is the *father of* epic poetry (叙事詩). / He is called the *father* of English musicians. / *father of* the fleet ‖ *fathers of* a town (city) 町(市)の長老たち ‖ Procrastination is the *father of* failure. 遅滞は失敗の本. ‖ Prince Ito, *father of* New Japan 新日本の父の伊藤公. ¶The King is *father to* his people. 国王は民の父である. ‖ He was a *father to* those poor children. 彼はそれらの貧しい子供たちに対して慈父のようであった. ‖ The wish is *father to* the thought. 念願は思想を生む(欲が判断を手伝う).

father, *v.* …の作であるという; …の父たるの責を負わす.

M the book is *falsely fathered* on … by … その著作は…によって誤って…の作であると言われる. ¶"Language was given to men to conceal their thoughts," is by Montreux, but is *generally fathered* on Talleyrand. 「言葉は思想を隠すために人間に与えられた」とはモントルーの言であるが一般にはタレーランの言だとされている.

P *father* the child *on* him 彼をその子の父だとする ‖ They *fathered* his riots *on* his youth. 彼らは彼の放らつは若さのためとした. ¶He had asked her to *father* it *upon* the gardener. 彼はそれを園丁がやったものとするように彼女に頼んだ.

O get some *hakase* to *father* it [出版などの際に]だれか博士に名を借りる.

fatherhood, *n.* 父たるの資格.

Q *illegitimate fatherhood* 正統でない父の資格(庶出子に対してなどの場合).

fatherland, *n.* 祖国.

P do one's level best *for* one's *fatherland* 祖国のために全力を尽す.

fathom, *n.* 尋(ひろ); 深度, 深さ; 知力.

Q *twenty fathom[s]* 二十尋(ひろ).

P a subject *beyond* one's *fathom* その知力で達し得ない問題. ¶go *out of* one's *fathom* (=depth) 背の立たない所まで行く.

fatigue, *n.* 疲労, 疲れ.

V *banish fatigue* of travel 旅の疲れをいやす. ¶The sick lady cannot *bear* the *fatigue* of a long journey. あの病気の婦人は長旅の疲労に耐え得ない. 【類】I am afraid I shall not be able to *bear* the *fatigue* of a long journey. ¶*break* the *fatigue* of a long journey by spending a night at a hotel 一夜を旅館に過して長旅の疲れをいやす. ¶*dissipate* one's *fatigue* 疲労を除く. ¶*endure fatigue* 疲労を我慢する. ¶*hasten fatigue* 疲労を早める. ¶*lessen fatigue* 疲労を減じる. ¶A few hours of sleep were sufficient to *relieve* his *fatigue*. 数時間の睡眠は彼の疲労をいやすに十分であった. ¶*sleep away* (=*off*) the *fatigue* of a long day's journey 長い一日の旅の疲れを眠っていやす. 【類】I *slept off fatigue*.

Q tired with a *dull listless fatigue* 物うい気のりのしない労苦に疲れて. ¶*intellectual fatigue* 頭の疲労. ¶*mental fatigue* 気づかれ. ¶*occupational fatigue* 職業からの疲労. ¶*physical fatigue* 肉体の疲労. ¶without *undue fatigue* あまり疲れないで. ¶without *unnecessary fatigue* 不必要な疲労なしに.

Q² *brain fatigue* 頭の疲れ. ¶*combat* (=*war*) *fatigue* 《米》「戦争ぼけ」.

P *after* the *fatigues* of one's journey 旅の疲れの後 ‖ *after* much *fatigue* 非常に疲れてから. ¶overcome *by fatigue* 疲労でぐったりして. ¶suffer *from fatigue* 疲労で苦しむ. 【類】His health was running down (からだが弱ってきた) *from fatigue*.

fatigue, *v.* 疲らせる.

M be *entirely* (=*utterly*) *fatigued* 疲れはてている. ¶He is *too much fatigued* to eat. 彼は疲れて物が食べられない.

P I was *fatigued with* (=*from*) work (travelling, sitting up all night). 私は仕事(など)で疲れていた.

fatten, *v.* 肥える; ふとらせる.

M² hogs well *fattened up* 丸々とふとった豚.

P *fatten on* the calamities of their country 彼らの国の災難で腹を肥やす ‖ He was *fattened on* the fire. 彼はその火事で金もうけをした. ‖ The fowls are *fattened on* rice. 鶏は米を食わせてふとらせる.

faucet, *n.* 《米》水せん.

V² The *faucet turned* loose and water kept running. せんがゆるんでいて水が出通しだった. 「水道のじゃ口.

Q² a *wash-basin faucet* 洗面台の水せん. ¶a *water faucet*

fault, *n.* 過失; 欠点, 短所; 所為(せい).

V I *acknowledge* my *fault*. 私は自分の欠点を認める. ¶*admit* a *fault* あやまちを認める. ¶*amend* one's *fault* 自分のあやまちを改める. ¶*commit* a *fault* 過失を犯す. ¶He was reluctant to *confess* his *fault*. 彼は過失を自白することをいやがった. ¶*correct* the *fault* そのあやまちを改める. ¶*cover up faults* 落度を隠す. ¶quick in *discerning* the *faults* of others よく他人の欠点を見つける. ¶*discern* the *faults* of men 人々の欠点を見つける. ¶*excuse* his *faults* or his failings 彼の過失あるいは欠点をゆるす ‖ *find* a *fault* or two in everything one does はしのあげおろしにあらを見つける. ¶He *finds faults* with everything I do. 彼はなんでも僕のすることに文句をつける. ‖ *find fault* with one's tools 道具に難くせをつける ‖ if there is any *fault* to be *found* 欠点をあげれば. 【類】She *finds fault* with everything and everybody. / He is always ready to *find fault* with other people. ¶I *have* no *fault* to find with him. 彼には非の打ち所がない. ¶*lay* one's *fault* on … …に罪をかぶせる. ¶*mend* its *fault* その短所を直す. ¶*overcome* a *fault* 欠点に打勝つ. ¶*overlook* (=*pass over*) one's fault その誤りを見のがす ‖ I will *overlook* your *fault* this time. こんどは見逃してやる. 【類】*overlook* little *faults* and seek out greater virtues (大なる美点). ¶*own* one's *faults* and feel sorry for them その過失を自白してこれを犯したことを悔いる. ¶*pick* (=find) *fault* あらを捜す. ¶*punish* the *fault* 罪を罰する. ¶*remedy faults* あやまちを改める. ¶*repair* a *fault* あやまちを償う. ¶He demands perfection in others, but cannot *see faults* in himself. 彼は他人には完全を求めるが自分の欠点が見えない. ¶*suppress* the *fault* of hastiness 急速から来る欠点が出てこないようにする. ¶*thrust* the *fault* on another 罪を人になすりつける.

V² The *fault lies* (=*is*) with me, not with you. それは君が悪いのではない, 僕が悪いのだ.

Q a *common fault* 普通の欠点. ¶a *glaring fault* 大欠点. ¶a *grave fault* 重大な過失. ¶A *great fault* is found with the captain. 船長が大いに非難されている. ¶a *grievous fault* 悲しむべき短所. ¶a *gross fault* 大過失. ¶a man of *many faults* 欠点の多い人. ¶a few *minor faults* 二三の小過失. ¶The teacher found *much fault* with him for idleness. 教師が彼の怠惰を手厳しく責めた. ¶That's *no fault* of yours. それは君のせいではない. ¶It was probably my *own fault*. 多分私自身の落度だろう. ¶The *fault* is not very *serious*. そう大した失態ではない. ¶a *twofold fault* 二重の過失. ¶a not *uncommon fault* ありがちの過失. ¶It has its *undoubted faults*. それには色々欠点があることは明らかだ. ¶a *venial* (=*excusable*) *fault* ゆるすべき過失. 「ようにする.

Q² overcome one's *spelling faults* つづり字の誤りのない

P The guide was *at fault*. 案内者が悪かった. ‖ I find I am *at fault*. 私が間違っていることに気付いている. ‖ I am quite *at fault*. 私は全く当惑している. ‖ He blushed *at* his own *faults*. 彼は自分の落度に赤面した. ‖ wink *at* a *fault* 過失を見逃す. 【類】My memory is *at fault*. / I was *at fault*, I'm sorry. Please forgive me. ¶He was dismissed *by* (=through) no *fault* of his own. 彼は自分になんらの落度なく職を解かれた. ‖ injury occasioned not *by* the *fault* of … …の過失で生じたのではない損害. ¶He is free *from fault*. 彼には落度はない. ¶I think you are very much *in fault*. 君が大いに悪いと僕は思う. ¶a *fault into* which young people naturally fall 青年の陥りやすい過失. ¶This mistake was made entirely *through* your *fault*. この間違いは全く君のせいであった. ‖ *through* no *fault* of his own (mine) 彼(私)には落度がなくて. ¶He is hospitable *to* a *fault*. 彼は客を優遇し過ぎる. ‖ He is generous (lenient, faithful, honest) *to* a *fault*. 彼は寛大(など)すぎる. ¶*with* all his *faults*, he is still … 彼には随分欠点があるがそれでも… ‖ charge him *with* a *fault* 過失を彼のせいにする.

P² I find a *fault in* … 私は…に欠点を認める. ‖ Tautology is a *fault in* rhetoric 同義の反覆は修辞上いけない. ¶He is liable for the *fault of* his servant. 彼は召使の過失に対して責任がある. ‖ It must be the *fault of* the weather. そ

れは天気のせいに違いない. ‖ the *fault* ***of*** our emphasis 誇張の欠点 ‖ *faults* ***of*** commission and omission 誤記及び脱漏の欠点. 【類】 *faults* ***of*** construction and grammar. ¶There is no *fault* ***on*** my part. 僕の方にはなんら落度はない.

faulty, *a.* 誤りの多い.

P *faulty* ***in*** arithmetic そろばんにうとい.

fauna, *n.* 〖動物〗動物区系.

P² the *fauna* ***of*** tropical America 熱帯アメリカの動物区系.

favo[u]r, *n.* 恩恵, 恩ちょう, ひいき; 許可; 書簡.

V ***accept*** a *favor* from ... ...の世話になる ‖ Do not expect to ***accept*** any *favor* from any person. だれにも一切世話になろうと思ってはならない. ¶***acknowledge*** a *favor* 好意を感謝する. ¶The new remedy has ***acquired*** an extraordinary *favor*. この新治療法は非常な人気だ. ¶The *favor* of an early reply will be ***appreciated***. 至急御返事下さらば幸い. ¶May I ***ask*** a *favor* of you? お願いがありますが聞いて頂けましょうか. ‖ I wish to ***ask*** a *favor* of you. 一つお願いがあります. ‖ I came to ***ask*** you a big *favor*. 御厄介なお願いがあって参りました. 【類】 May I ***ask*** you a little *favor* (ちょっとお願い)? ¶***Awaiting*** the *favor* of your prompt attention. 至急御回答を願いつつ. ¶I ***beg*** a *favor* of you. 一つお願い致したい. ¶***beg*** the *favor* of co-operation from ... ...から協力をお願いする. ¶***bestow*** a *favor* on ... ...に好意を寄せる. ¶***catch*** popular *favor* 一般の人気を取る. ¶it will be ***conferring*** a great *favor* on me if you will ... ...して下されば御厚意ありがたく存じます ‖ Readers of ... will ***confer*** a *favor* on the publisher by mentioning the name of the paper when communicating with advertisers. ...の読者は広告主と通信の際は新聞名を御記載下さるよう出版者からお願い致します. 【類】 by so doing you would be ***conferring*** a *favor* on ... ¶***court*** his *favor* 彼の愛顧を求める. ¶***curry*** *favor* meanly=truckle おひげのちりを払う ‖ ***curry*** *favor* with influential people 有力者にこびる. ¶***Do*** me the *favor* to come. どうぞお出で下さい. ‖ I can ***do*** the *favor* requested. 御依頼に応じられます. 【類】 will you ***do*** me the *favor* to ...? / May I ask to ***do*** me a *favor?* ¶***emphasize*** the *favor* done to one 恩にきせる. ¶***enjoy*** the *favor* of ... ...のお覚えめでたい ‖ I have ***enjoyed*** many *favors* at your hands. あなたには色々お世話になりました. ¶One naturally ***expects*** such a *favor* from a friend. 友だちであって見ればそれ位のことはしてもよさそうなものだ. ¶***extend*** a special *favor* to ... 特に...を優遇する. ¶The system is gradually ***finding*** *favor* in Japan. その制度は日本で次第に歓迎されている. ‖ The proposal ***found*** little *favor*. その提案は余り賛成されなかった. ‖ He ***found*** *favor* with the Emperor. 彼は天皇の恩ちょうを受けた. 【類】 He ***found*** *favor* with the aristocratic class. / the excellence of his work at once ***found*** him *favor* with ... / The book ***found*** *favor* with the American public. / His teaching ***found*** *favor* alike with painters and sculptors. / The good ***found*** great *favor* with the Orientals. ‖ It is rapidly ***finding*** *favor* in the eyes of the discriminating buyers. それは目のある買手からますます歓迎されている. ¶slowly ***gain*** *favor* 徐々に取り入る. 【類】 he managed to ***gain*** the *favor* of ... ‖ The opinion has ***gained*** much *favor* in authoritative quarters. その説は権威ある方面に大いに受けた. ¶***give*** *favors* to ... ...をひいきにする. ¶***grant*** a *favor* 恩恵を垂れる ‖ liberally ***grant*** *favor* to ... ...に対して十分好意を示す. ¶I ***have*** a *favor* to ask of you. 一つあなたにお願いしたいことがあります. ¶***invoke*** the *favor* of God 神に願いをかける. ¶***lose*** *favor* 行われなくなる ‖ he ***lost*** *favor* with ... 彼は...のお覚えがめでたくなくなった. ¶***make*** a great *favor* of ... ...を大層恩にきせる. ¶when a man seeks to ***obtain*** a *favor* from one of the Shinto or Buddhist divinities, he makes a present of ... to ... 神仏の加護を受けようとするときには...に...の供物をする. ‖ The book ***obtained*** wide *favor*. その本は広く世間から歓迎された. ¶worshippers desirous of ***receiving*** divine *favor* 御利益を受けようとする参けい人 ‖ I have ***received*** your *favor*. 貴書落手致しました. ¶***refuse*** one a *favor* 人の頼み事を断る. ¶I called upon him to ***request*** a *favor*. 私は頼み事をしに彼を訪問した. ¶***retain*** an undiminished *favor* 元通りの人気を博している. ¶***return*** *favor* for favor 恩に報ゆるに恩をもってする ‖ ***return*** his *favor* by ... ...によって彼の好意に報いる. ¶***seek*** *favor* 恩恵を求める. ¶***sell*** *favors* 金銭で不公平な取扱いをする. ¶I ***showed*** him great *favor*. 私は大いに彼に目をかけた. ¶***solicit*** a *favor* 世話を頼む. ¶***win*** *favor* 評判を取る, 人気がある ‖ ***win*** the *favor* of ... ...の歓心を得る. 【類】 ***win*** the popular *favor* (人気) / it is ***winning*** a quick *favor* among ... ¶***woo*** the *favor* of the Muses ミューズの神の恩ちょうを求める.

Q a ***Divine*** *favor* 天助. ¶it found no ***great*** *favor* with ... それは...にあまり気に入られなかった. ¶The minister is in ***high*** *favor* at Court. 同大臣は宮中でのお覚えが誠にめでたい. ‖ in ***high*** *favor* with ... ...間に高評のある. ¶***impartial*** *favor* 不偏の愛顧. ¶bask in the ***Imperial*** *favor* 聖恩に浴する. ¶find ***increasing*** *favor* with the general public 一般社会にますます高評を博する. ¶every ***material*** *favor* that wealth can offer あらゆる物質的の恩恵. ¶find ***much*** *favor* with the public 一般の評判がよい. ¶the ***partial*** *favor* of his father 彼の父の偏した愛. ¶It is doubtful whether he will survive in ***popular*** *favor*. 彼が世間の人気を受け続けるかどうかは疑問である. 【類】 In course of time, ***popular*** *favor* will swing to one of the two pronunciations, which will then become the only "correct" one. ¶advance rapidly in ***public*** *favor* 世間の評判がますますよくなる. 【類】 The week-end trip is most in ***public*** *favor*. ¶find ***ready*** *favor* たちまち好評を博する. ¶receive marks of ***royal*** *favor* 皇室の恩ちょうの印を頂だいする. ¶In response to your request of July 19, we have placed your paper on our exchange list, and trust that you will do us a ***similar*** *favor*. 七月十九日付の貴需に応じて貴紙を当社の交換名簿に登録致しました, つきましては貴方においても同様の御好意を当社に対してお示し下さることを是非お願い致します. ¶pass an examination by ***special*** *favor* おなさけで及第する. ¶The *favor* was ***unasked*** and ***unpromised***. その世話は頼まれたものでも約束したものでもなかった. ¶It has good qualities to recommend it to ***universal*** *favor*. それは広く世間から歓迎されるだけの価値がある. ¶***unmerited*** *favor* 受ける資格のない好意. ¶The party system is in ***waning*** *favor* with the people. 政党内閣制は世間の人気を失いつつある. ¶The invention found ***wide-spread*** *favor*. その発明は一般に好評を博した.

Q² ***marriage*** *favors* 婚礼の際に用いる花束またはリボンの花結び. ¶regain ***Soviet*** *favor* ソ連の好意を回復する.

P ***as*** a *favor* 好意上. ¶***By*** *favor* of Mr.... ...氏に託して(封筒の添え書) ‖ ***by*** your *favor* お陰で. ¶ask ***for*** *favor* 引立を求める ‖ Please accept my thanks in advance ***for*** the *favor* of reply. どうぞ御返事にあずかりたく存じます. ¶The present rate of exchange is strongly ***in*** our *favor*. 為替の現相場は大いにわが国に有利である. ‖ the balance of probability is ***in*** *favor* of ... ...の方が可能性がある ‖ the balance of evidence seems ***in*** *favor* of ... 証拠を比較して見ると...が正しいようだ ‖ The authority of good writers is ***in*** *favor* of that expression. 権威あるりっぱな作家たちはその言い方を可としている. ‖ I have heard much ***in*** *favor* of the place. 私はそこが好いということを随分聞かされている. ‖ abandon poetry ***in*** *favor* of prose 作詩から散文に転向する ‖ speak ***in*** *favor* of the motion 動議に賛成の意を表する ‖ All ***in*** *favor* of this proposition will please say "Aye." この提議に御賛成の方は皆「賛成」と言って下さい. ‖ The odds are ***in*** his *favor* (against him). 彼の方に勝目がある(ない). ¶refreshments most ***in*** *favor* with ... ...が一番好きな茶菓 ‖ his arguments ***in*** its *favor* were so convincing that ... それを可とする彼の議論は非常に有力であったから... ‖ a society ***in*** *favor* of constructing playgrounds for children 児童運動場設置期成会. 【類】 So far, everything is ***in*** our *favor*. / Its trade with us is lopsidedly ***in*** our "*favor*." / The judgment given was ***in*** your *favor* (against you). / Prices are ***in*** buyers' *favor*. / The evidence (証拠) is ***in*** *favor* of the defendant. / Verdict (判決) is given ***in*** *favor* of (against) me. / with these remarkably fine results ***in*** their *favor* / a point ***in*** one's *favor* / the chances are ***in*** *favor* of ... / the popular feeling was strongly ***in*** *favor* of ... / decide ***in*** *favor* of ... / I am not at all ***in*** *favor* of them. / ***in*** *favor* of this view, it may be mentioned that ... ¶he is ***out of*** *favor* with ... 彼は...にきらわれている. ¶an escape (attack) ***under*** [the] *favor* (=cover *or* aid) of night (=darkness) 夜に乗じた逃亡(など). ¶look ***with*** *favor* on ... ...をひいき目に見

る ‖ treat a person ***with favor*** 好意をもって人を遇する ‖ He was received ***with*** the utmost *favor*. 彼はこの上もなく好遇された.

P² The practice has never found *favor* ***among*** people of good breeding. この慣習は教養ある人々の間には全然受けなかった. ‖ It is in high *favor* ***among*** those who choose the finest. それは最優等品を求める人々の間に好評を博している. ‖ The *favor* ***of*** your attendance is requested. 御出席をお願い致します. ‖ Your *favor* ***of*** yesterday is to hand. 昨日付のお手紙受取りました. ¶He is high in *favor* ***with*** his Sovereign. 彼は王のお覚えがめでたい.

favo[u]r, *v.* 恵む; 恩恵的に与える.

M Can you ***kindly*** *favor* me with your influence? 貴下のお力添えを願われますまいか. ¶They have so ***liberally*** *favored* us with their patronage in the past. あの人たちはこれまで格別私どもをひいきにして下さった. ¶The song is ***most*** *favored* among young women. その歌は若い女性に一番人気がある. ¶countries ***particularly*** *favored* by nature, such as Italy, Switzerland, France, Austria, etc. 特に自然に恵まれたイタリア・スイス・フランス・オーストリアなどの国々.

P *favored* ***by*** a series of similar good luck 続けざまに同じような幸運に恵まれて ‖ Please *favor* us ***by*** answering the following questions. どうか私どもの次の質問にお答え下さい. ¶Will you *favor* me ***with*** your company? どうか御出席下さい. ‖ get him to *favor* me ***with*** his influence 彼に力添えをしてもらう. ‖ I was *favored* ***with*** an invitation. 私は招待を受けた. ‖ We beg to be *favored* ***with*** your orders. どうぞ御用命のほどお願い致します. ‖ *Favor* us ***with*** a song. 歌を一つ聞かして下さい. 【類】We trust to be *favored* ***with*** an interview. / Please *favor* me ***with*** an answer.

favo[u]rable, *a.* 都合のよい, 有利な.

M Circumstances were ***entirely*** *favorable* to us. 万事われわれに好都合であった. ¶conditions ***most*** *favorable* for the execution of the plan その計画の実行に最も好都合な事情.

P Conditions are *favorable* ***for*** him to carry out the plan. 情勢は彼がその計画を実行するに有利である. 【類】A rich, warm, mellow soil is most *favorable* ***for*** the growth of cabbage. ¶The position of his premises, facing as they do the eastern wing of the British Museum, has proved to be *favorable* ***to*** business. 彼の店は大英博物館のちょうど東翼に向いているので場所は商売に有利であった. 【類】The weather was *favorable* ***to*** the gathering of a large crowd.

favo[u]rite, *n.* ちょう児, 人気者; 好きな物.

Q the most ***cherished*** *favorite* 最も大事にされているお気に入り. ¶a ***fortune's*** *favorite* 好運児. ¶She's a ***general*** *favorite* as a jazz singer. 彼女はジャズ歌手として一般に人気がある. ¶a subject which was so ***great*** a *favorite* with Italian masters イタリアの画家たちが非常に好んだ題目 ‖ the book was a ***great*** *favorite* with … それは…の愛読書であった. ¶a ***household*** *favorite* 家庭の人気者. ¶an ***immense*** *favorite* 非常なお気に入り. ¶be ***no*** *favorite* with the reading public 読書界に人気がない. ¶The actor is a ***popular*** *favorite*. その俳優は人気がある. 【類】the ***popular*** *favorite* of the day. ¶a ***prime*** *favorite* with the public 世間一番の流行児. ¶a ***universal*** *favorite* だれにも好かれるもの(人).

Q² a ***film*** *favorite* 映画の人気俳優. ¶a ***footlight*** *favorite* ひいきの役者. ¶some ***movie fan*** *favorites* 映画ファンに人気のある俳優たち. ¶a ***stage*** *favorite* 人気役者.

P² my *favorite* ***among*** his novels 彼の小説中僕の好きなもの. 【類】Venice is my *favorite* ***among*** the Italian towns. ¶The ship became a *favorite* ***for*** excursionists. 同船は遊覧旅行者間に評判がよくなった. ¶a *favorite* ***of*** fate 運命のちょう児. ¶a great *favorite* ***with*** the ladies 婦人たちに大もてのする男 ‖ The shipping company has become a *favorite* ***with*** the travelling public. その汽船会社は一般旅行者間に評判がよくなった. 【類】The autumn moon has always been a *favorite* ***with*** poets and lovers of nature. / It is a *favorite* ***with*** the author himself. / He is a great *favorite* ***with*** married women.

favo[u]ritism, *n.* えこひいき, 不公平, 私情.

V ***show*** no *favoritism* to … …に対して一切えこひいきをしない.

Q from ***political*** *favoritism* 政治上の情実から. ¶show ***unfair*** *favoritism* 不正なえこひいきをする.

P promotion ***by*** *favoritism* 情実による昇進. ¶***through*** (=by the aid of) *favoritism* えこひいきで. ¶***without*** *favoritism* for any one だれをもえこひいきすることなく. 【類】***without*** *favoritism* toward those who have money.

fawn, *v.* こびる, おもねる; じゃれつく.

P *fawn* ***on*** the rich (one's superior) 金持(など)におもねる. ¶*fawn* ***upon*** … [犬などが]…にじゃれつく.

fealty, *n.* 忠義, 忠節.

V ***acknowledge*** *fealty* to … …に恭順を示す. ¶***give*** one's *fealty* to the nation 国に忠義を尽す. ¶***make*** (=***do***) *fealty* 忠義を尽す. ¶***profess*** *fealty* to … …に臣従することを言明する.

P² *fealty* ***to*** their lords 彼らの主君に対する忠義.

fear, *n.* 恐怖; 不安, 心配, 懸念.

V What traces I did find of her were not calculated to ***allay*** my anxious *fears*. 彼女の足跡について確かめ得た所では私の不安を鎮めるに足るものはなかった. ¶He is unable to ***analyse*** his *fear*. 彼には自分の心配の理由が判り兼ねる. ¶The news ***aroused*** much *fear* in Germany. その報道はドイツにおいて不安の念を起した. ¶***banish*** *fear* 心配を駆逐する. ¶***confirm*** one's *fear* …の心配した通りであることが確かめられる. ¶No advancement in life is possible until the *fear* of failure is ***conquered***. 失敗をこわがるようでは出世は不可能だ. ¶***dissipate*** (=***dismiss***) one's *fear* (their fears) その(彼らの)心配を吹飛ばす. 【類】***dissipate*** the *fears* of the patient. ¶You need ***entertain*** no *fear*. 君なにも心配することはない. ‖ *fears* are ***entertained*** as to … …について懸念がいだかれている. 【類】*Fears* are ***entertained*** that the railway will be blocked by snow. ¶***express*** the *fear* that … …という懸念を口にする. ¶I ***feel*** no *fear* for her future. 彼女の今後については私はなにも心配していない. ‖ *Fears* were ***felt*** for the safety of the missing 行方不明者の安否が気づかわれている. ¶My *fear* was ***fulfilled***. 私の懸念が実際となって現われた. ¶He ***has*** such a *fear* of death that one can hardly say the dread word in his presence. 彼は死をこわがっているので彼の面前でその恐ろしい言葉を口にすることがちょっとできない位である. 【類】I ***have*** no *fear* of it. ¶He ***knows*** no *fear* of death. 彼には死の恐ろしさが分らない. ¶Galapagos hawks have never ***learned*** the *fear* of man. ガラパゴスのたかは人間のこわいことを知らない. ¶***look*** the *fear* squarely in the face 恐怖をものともしない. ¶He did not ***manifest*** the slightest *fear* of death. 彼は少しも死を恐れる気色がなかった. ¶***quiet*** the *fears* of … …の心配を静める. ¶***still*** one's *fears* その心配を静める. ¶***throwing*** all *fears* aside 何物も恐れないという腹をすえて. ¶***whet*** a *fear* 心配を高める.

V² The *fear* will ***abate***. 不安が薄らぐだろう. ¶*Fear* ***came*** over him. 恐怖の念が彼に迫って来た. ¶A *fear* ***came down*** upon him with crushing effect. 恐怖の念が押しつぶすような勢いで彼を襲った.

Q an ***acute*** *fear* 激しい心配. ¶There is not ***any*** *fear* of catching cold. かぜを引く心配はない. ¶a ***baseless*** *fear* 根拠のない心配. ¶he is in ***constant*** *fear* of … 彼は…を絶えず恐れている. 【類】tremble in ***constant*** *fear*. ¶***cowardly*** *fear* おく病な恐怖. ¶we lived in ***daily*** *fear* of … われわれは毎日…を恐れながら暮した. ¶There is an ***ever-lurking*** *fear* in the heart of every actress that she may be slipping from her place as a star. どの女優も自分がスターとしての立場を失いはせぬかと絶えずひそかに心配をしている. ¶an ***ever-present*** *fear* 絶えず付きまとう不安. ¶***Great*** *fears* were entertained for his safety. 彼の安否が非常に気使われた. ¶a ***groundless*** *fear* as to … …についての根拠のない心配. ¶the ***haunting*** *fear* that … …という始終付きまとう心配. ¶that this is not an ***idle*** *fear* may be realized when it is remembered that … これが無用の心配でないのは…ということを思い起すとよく分るだろう. ¶He seems to feel an ***intense*** *fear* and dislike of speaking in public. 彼は人前で話すことをひどく恐れ, またいやがるようだ. ¶He had a ***lurking*** *fear* of discovery of his wrongdoing. 彼はその悪事がばれやしないかとひそかに心配していた. ¶be in ***mortal*** (=***dire***) *fear* ひどく恐れている. ¶feel some ***nameless*** *fear* なにかしら不安を感じる. ¶There is ***no*** *fear* of that. その心配はない. ¶***panic*** *fear* (=terror) ろうばい. ¶a ***popular*** *fear* 世間一般の不安. ¶***profound*** *fear* 非常な恐怖. ¶a ***reasonable*** *fear* 無理もない心配. ¶did not show the slightest *fear* 少しも恐怖の色を表わさなかった. ¶a ***strong*** *fear* 大いなる懸念. ¶a ***su-***

perstitious fear 迷信的恐怖. ¶a ***wholesome*** *fear* of ... ...に対する(病的でない)健全な恐怖.

P tremble ***for*** *fear* おそろしさに震える ‖ ***for*** *fear* of losing it それをなくしはせぬかとの心配から ‖ I have omitted calling on you ***for*** *fear* of disturbing you. 私はお邪魔になりはしないかと心配してお伺いしませんでした. 【類】 for fear of being stolen / ***For*** *fear* of accidents, please drive slowly. / ***for*** *fear* of failure / She cried out ***for*** *fear*. ¶refrain from women ***from*** *fear* of venereal infection 性病感染が恐ろしいので女との関係を避ける ‖ I obeyed ***from*** *fear*. 私はこわいので服従した. ¶***in*** his *fear* 心配のあまり ‖ hide ***in*** *fear* of assassins 刺客がこわいので隠れる ‖ ***in*** *fear* of discovery 露顕を恐れて ‖ She brought up her children ***in*** the *fear* of God. 彼女は神を恐れるように(正しく)その子供を育て上げた. ‖ They kept dumb ***in*** *fear* and trembling. 皆恐れおののいて黙りこくっていた. 【類】 Being very ill, and ***in*** *fear* of death, he made his will (遺言書). ‖ ***in*** *fear* of one's life 命を気使って ‖ ***in*** the *fear* of ... ...を恐れて ‖ stand ***in*** great *fear* and awe of ... ...を大いに畏怖(ふ)する. ¶***through*** *fear* of his creditors 彼の債権者がこわいので ‖ They retreated ***through*** *fear* of an ambush. 彼らは伏兵を恐れて退却した. ¶labor ***under*** a baseless *fear* 理由のない恐怖心で悩む. ¶***with*** *fear* and trembling こわくってふるえながら ‖ all palpitating ***with*** *fear* 一同がびくびくしながら ‖ white (pale) ***with*** *fear* 恐ろしさで真青になって. ¶***without*** *fear* or reservation 心配や遠慮なしに.

P² He was kept at home by *fear* ***for*** his money. 彼は金が心配なので常に家にいた ¶There is little *fear* ***from*** rivalry in this line. この方面では競争者の心配がない.

fear, *v.* 心配する, 気使う.

P Some of the students were so diligent that I *feared* ***for*** their health. 学生の中には非常に勉強する者がいたので私は彼らの健康を気使った. ¶he has nothing to *fear* ***from*** ... 彼は...については少しも心配がない.

fearful, *a.* 恐れて, 心配して.

M ***nervously*** *fearful* of ... ...にびくびくして.

P He was *fearful* ***of*** the consequences. 彼は結果を心配していた.

fearless, *a.* 恐れない.

P *fearless* ***of*** danger 危険を恐れないで.

feasibility, *n.* 実行できること; 成否.

V ***consider*** the *feasibility* of a plan 計画の成否を考える. ¶***demonstrate*** the *feasibility* of ... ...の実行性を証明する.

feast, *n.* きょう宴, 御ちそう; 祝祭.

V This *feast* of the god is ***kept*** twice a year. その祭典は一年に二度執行する. ¶***provide*** a *feast* of ever-changing scenic beauty 絶えず目先の変る風景美を見せる.

Q a ***delectable*** *feast* うまい御ちそう. ¶a ***fixed*** *feast* [クリスマスのように]期日の確定した祭日. ¶a ***high*** *feast* 大きょう宴. ¶Easter is a ***movable*** *feast*. 復活祭は期日不定の祭日である. ¶a ***noisy*** *feast* 騒がしいきょう宴. ¶a ***riotous*** *feast* どんちゃん騒ぎのきょう宴. ¶***rustic*** *feast* いなかの御ちそう. ¶We partook of a ***sumptuous*** *feast*. われわれはぜいたくなちそうを頂だいした. ¶that ***uncloying*** *feast*, the sight of her adored youth あのあくことなき目の御ちそうである彼女の気高い青春の姿. ¶a ***veritable*** *feast* for our eyes 本当に目を 喜ばすもの.

Q² share their ***marriage*** *feast* 結婚の宴につらなる. ¶a ***noon*** *feast* 昼のきょう宴. ¶at a ***wedding*** *feast* 結婚の披露宴で.

P a Japanese ***at*** a *feast* 宴会席上の日本人. ¶***on*** the *Feast* of the Epiphany 主出現節の折に.

P² the *Feast* ***of*** Dolls ひな祭 ‖ There was a *feast* ***of*** reason in his speech. 彼の演説は理路整然としていた. ¶a *feast* ***to*** the eye (ear) 目(など)の正月.

feast, *v.* 御ちそうになる; 楽しませる.

M Then we returned home, hungry and tired, to *feast* ***away*** the night. それからわれわれは一晩飲み明かすために腹をへらし疲れて家に帰った.

P *feast* one's eyes ***on*** flowers 花を見て楽しむ ‖ those big fires which *feast* ***on*** cities 都市をなめる大火災. ¶my eyes were *feasted* ***with*** the sight of ... 私は...の光景を眺めて目を楽しませた. 【類】 *feast* one's eyes ***on*** (=***upon***) noted pictures

feat, *n.* 妙技, 芸当; 偉業.

V ***accomplish*** a *feat* 妙技を演じる ‖ He ***accomplished*** one of the most remarkable *feats* on record. 彼は史上最も顕著な偉業の一つを成し遂げた. ¶***achieve*** a *feat* 偉業を成し遂げる. ¶He ***did*** a marvellous *feat*. 彼は驚くべき離れ業をやった. ¶see the wrestlers ***exhibit*** their professional *feats* 相撲取の妙技を見る. ¶He ***had*** two *feats* that he challenged any mortal to duplicate. 彼はだれにもまねができないと自慢している二つの芸当を持っていた. ¶***perform*** the remarkable *feat* of ... ...というめざましい妙技を演じる. 【類】 ***perform*** *feats* of heroism (勇ましい働き). ¶***undertake*** a *feat* 離れ業をやる.

Q do (=perform) ***acrobatic*** *feats* 軽業を演じる. ¶a really ***astounding*** *feat* ほんとにどぎもを抜くような芸当. ¶a ***brilliant*** *feat* of arms 花々しい武勲. ¶a ***common*** *feat* 平凡な芸当. ¶a ***dangerous*** *feat* 危い芸当. ¶a ***daring*** *feat* 離れわざ. ¶It involved some remarkable ***engineering*** *feats*. その工事にはある顕著な工業上の妙技が必要であった. ¶achieve ***famous*** *feats* 有名な偉業を成し遂げる. ¶do ***impossible*** *feats* 不可能と見える離れわざを演じる. 【類】 These are days when apparently ***impossible*** *feats* are accomplished by science. ¶a ***remarkable*** *feats* of pilotage 水先案内の顕著な偉業. ¶He was called upon to perform some ***risky*** *feats*. 彼はある冒険的な離れわざを演じることを求められた. ¶a most ***successful*** *feat* of condensation 巧みな要約の一例. ¶the ***superhuman*** *feats* of the hero その勇士の超人的偉勲. ¶The juggler performed some ***surprising*** *feats* of skill and agility. その手品師は熟練と敏速との驚くべき離れわざを演じた. ¶***ticklish*** *feats* きわどい早わざ. ¶an almost ***unattainable*** *feat* ほとんど他の追随を許さない妙技. ¶a ***wonderful*** *feat* 驚くべき妙技.

Q² a stupendous ***engineering*** *feat* 驚くべき難工事. ¶a ***record*** *feat* 記録的偉業. ¶a ***tight rope*** *feat* [曲馬の]綱渡り.

P² a *feat* ***in*** indexing 巧みな索引作成の一例. ¶*feats* ***of*** agility 早わざ ‖ *feats* ***of*** horsemanship [曲馬などの]馬乗り芸当 ‖ *feats* ***of*** strength 力わざ.

feather, *n.* 鳥の羽根.

V ***pluck*** *feathers* from a fowl 鶏の羽毛をむしる. ¶***preen*** (=***trim***) *feathers* with beak くちばしで羽根を整える. ¶***ruffle*** *feathers* 羽毛を逆立てる. ¶These women go to a theatre merely for the sake of ***showing*** fine *feathers*. これらの女はただ美しい衣装を見せるために劇場に行く.

Q When I last saw him, he was in ***fine*** (=***good or high***) *feather*. この前彼に会ったときは元気だった. ¶She was in ***full*** *feather*. 彼女は着飾っていた. ¶He was in ***high*** *feather*. 彼は大元気であった. ¶***resplendent*** *feathers* ぴかぴかした羽毛. ¶show the (=a) ***white*** *feather* in battle 戦でおく病風を吹かせる.

Q² ***tail*** *feathers* 尾の羽根.

P Birds ***of*** a *feather* flock together. 類は友を呼ぶ.

P² It is a *feather* ***in*** his cap. それは彼の手柄である.

O as light as a *feather* 羽根のように軽く.

feather, *v.* 羽根がはえる; [羽根のように]ふわふわする.

M a chick not ***fully*** *feathered* 羽のはえそろっていないひな. ¶The chickies will soon *feather* ***out***. 間もなくひなに羽がはえるだろう. ¶The willows are beginning to *feather* ***out***. 柳のわたが出始めた.

M² The snow came *feathering* ***down***. 綿雪がふわふわ落ちてきた.

feature, *n.* (1) 特徴, 特色, 要点; 呼び物; 〖映〗特作映画.

V ***combine*** *features* of ... with ... ...の特徴と...とを併有する. 【類】 ***combine*** the best *features* of the old and the new. ¶It ***constitutes*** the central *feature*. それが最も重要な特色を成している. ¶The building ***contains*** many novel *features* of construction. その建物は構造上幾多の新奇な特徴を持っている. ‖ The dictionary is the first in the English language which ***contains*** this *feature*. こういった編集をした英語辞典はこれが最初である. ¶It is ***deemed*** an essential *feature*. それは基本的特質とされている. ¶***embody*** all the good *features* of ... ...のあらゆる長所を備える. ¶It ***formed*** a striking *feature* in the procession. それが行列中特に目立っていた. ¶it ***has*** several *features* which sharply define it from ... それは...と画然類を異にする幾多の特徴を備えている ‖ The exhibition ***has*** many *features* of interest. その博覧会は幾多の興味ある特色を持っている. ¶***introduce*** a new *feature* 新らしい特徴を作る. ¶***make*** a special *feature* of ... ...を特色とする ‖ ***make*** a great *feature* of ... ...を一大特徴とする. ¶***outline*** the essential *features* of a plan 計画の骨子を概述する. ¶The tunnel ***possesses*** some novel *features*. そのトンネルにはざん新な点がある. ¶It does not ***present*** any marked *features*. そ

れには著しい特色はない. ‖ It *presents* no *features* of interest. それは平々凡々である. ¶ *Features* ***selected*** from the Gothic and Romanesque styles are combined in its architecture. ゴシック及びローマン様式から採った特色がその建築に応用されている. ¶ ***sketch out*** the general *features* 一般を略述する.

Q be without noticeable ***American*** *features* in vocabulary and idiom 語彙(ごい)と慣用法には取立てていうほどの米語法はない. ¶ the most ***amusing*** *feature* of the day 当日第一の見もの(聞きもの). ¶ the ***arresting*** *feature* about it is that ... それが注意を引く点は... ¶ an ***astounding*** *feature* 驚くべき特質. ¶ the most ***attractive*** *feature* of the day その日の呼びもの. ¶ Her eyes are her ***best*** *feature*. 彼女は目が一番美しい. ¶ ***bodily*** *features* からだの格好. ¶ a ***central*** *feature* 主要点. ¶ a ***characteristic*** *feature* 特色. ¶ its ***chief*** *features* その特徴. ¶ a ***civic*** *feature* 都市の特色. ¶ a ***commendable*** *feature* in the book その本の取るべき点. ¶ They have one ***common*** *feature*. それらには一つの共通点がある. ¶ a ***concomitant*** *feature* 一共通点. ¶ a ***conspicuous*** *feature* 目立つ点. ¶ The picture formed one of the ***crowning*** *features* of the art section of the exhibition. その絵は博覧会の美術部中呼びものの一をなしていた. ¶ the ***decorative*** *features* of a park 公園の装飾. ¶ One of the most ***delightful*** *features* of German academic life is its "migratory possibilities." ドイツ大学の最も喜ぶべき特色の一つはいわゆる (registration book と写真付 student card さえあればどの大学でも聴講ができるという)「移動の便宜」である. ¶ The meeting was not free from some ***disagreeable*** *features*. その会には面白くない点が多少あった. ¶ a very ***disappointing*** *feature* 大いに失望するような点. ¶ one of the ***disgraceful*** *features* 不体裁な点の一つ. ¶ a ***disquieting*** *feature* of the disturbances is the fact that ... この騒ぎの心配になる点は...ということである. ¶ one of its ***distinctive*** *features* その目立った特色の一つ. ¶ ***distinguishing*** *features* 顕著な特色. ¶ a ***dominant*** *feature* of the landscape その景色の中で特にすぐれている点. ¶ Mt. Fuji forms the ***dominating*** *feature* in the landscape. 富士山がその風景中で断然群を抜いている. ¶ ***dramatic*** *features* 演劇上の特色. ¶ an ***especial*** *feature* 特色. ¶ its ***essential*** *feature* その必須な点. ¶ this is an ***exclusive*** *feature* with ... これは...に特有な点である. ¶ ***facial*** *features* 目鼻立ち. ¶ ***frequent*** *features* in the careers of Occidental nations 西洋国民の経歴によく見る点. ¶ the ***geographical*** *features* of the land その土地の地形. ¶ an ***important*** *feature* of Karuizawa summer life 夏期軽井沢生活の重要な点. ¶ a ***leading*** *feature* of Britishers 英国人の主な特徴. ¶ the ***main*** *features* of the program 主要番組 ‖ one of the ***main*** *features* of the markets last week 先週の市場の主要取引の一つ. ¶ a ***marked*** *feature* 著しい特色. ¶ It has many ***meritorious*** *features*. それは幾多の価値ある特色を備えている. ¶ the ***natural*** *features* of the regions その土地の地勢. ¶ possess one ***new*** *feature* in that it ... ...という点に一つの新しさがある. ¶ the most ***notable*** *feature* in the history of ... ...の歴史中最も著しい点. ¶ a ***noteworthy*** *feature* in ... ...の注目すべき特徴. ¶ a ***novel*** *feature* 目新しい点 ¶ the most ***original*** *feature* of the machine その機械の最も新しい点. ¶ the ***outstanding*** *feature* of the company's operations for the past year 過去一年間における会社の事業の顕著な点. ¶ a ***painful*** and ***conspicuous*** *feature* of our business world to-day 今日わが事業界の目立って悲惨な状態. ¶ ***peculiar*** *features* of the epoch その時代の特異な状態. ¶ ***physical*** *features* 地勢 ‖ the ***physical*** *features* of an old farm 古くからある農場の外観. ¶ The ***predominant*** *feature* of his character was pride. 彼の性格の目立った特色は自尊心だった. ¶ a ***preponderant*** *feature* 主な点. ¶ a very ***pretty*** *feature* 非常に美しい点. ¶ a ***prominent*** *feature* in the Yezo landscape 北海道の風景中著しい点. ¶ there were some ***redeeming*** *features* connected with ... ...に関連して二三の埋合せになる特色があった. ¶ The fish hawker is a ***regular*** *feature* of street life. 魚の呼売人は都会生活にきまってよく見る情景である. ¶ a ***salient*** *feature* 特に目立った点. ¶ one of the most inspiring ***scenic*** *features* of ... ...中で最も人の感興をそそる風景美の一つ. ¶ The ball is a ***social*** *feature* of the season. 舞踏会はその季節の社交的行事の一つである. ¶ a ***special*** *feature* of the work その仕事の特色. ¶ a ***strange*** *feature* of the case is that ... その事件の変った所は...ということである. ¶ ***striking*** *features* 顕著な特徴. ¶ a ***striking architectural*** *feature* of a building 建物の顕著な建築上の特色. ¶ a ***strong*** *feature* in his character 彼の性格の中で一つの著しい特徴. ¶ a very ***timely*** *feature* 非常に時宜にかなった点. ¶ This system has many ***undesirable*** *features*. このやり方には幾多の面白くない点がある. ¶ It has a ***unique*** *feature* in this. これがその特色である. ¶ a ***useful*** *feature*. 有益な点. ¶ A complete index is another ***valuable*** *feature* of the book. 完全な索引もその本の一つの貴重な特色である.

Q² many ***amusement*** *features* 幾多の余興. ¶ ***entertainment*** *features* 余興. ¶ ***magazine*** *features* 雑誌の呼びもの記事. ¶ ***radio*** *features* ラジオの呼び物. ¶ the ***Sunday*** *features* of the Chicago Tribune シカゴ・トリビューン紙の日曜特集. ¶ a ***surprise*** *feature* in a trial 裁判の異例.

P This must be accepted ***as*** an inevitable *feature* of Siberian touring. これはシベリア旅行の避け難い点として忍ばなければならない. ¶ different ***in*** its essential *features* from ... その枢要な点において...と異って. ¶ The film has been suppressed ***on account of*** certain *features* which were considered to be objectionable. その映画はある不都合な点があるので禁止された.

P² its attractive *features* ***as*** a holiday resort 休日の遊覧地としてのその人気を呼ぶ点. ¶ the leading *features* ***in*** his character 彼の品性中の主な特色 ‖ a *feature* ***in*** a movie program 〖映〗特作映画. ¶ Easy accessibility is a *feature* ***of*** the Austrian Alps. 容易に登山のできることがオーストリア・アルプスの特徴である. ‖ Athletics form a great *feature* ***of*** school life there. 運動競技はそこの学校生活の一大特色をなしている. 【類】the *features* of American college life. ¶ two (three) *features* ***on*** one bill 〖映画〗二(三)本立のプロ.

(2) 目鼻だち; *pl.* 相.

V ***beautify*** the *features* by the Arabian process アラビア式の美顔術を用いる. ¶ ***contort*** the *features* = make ugly faces 顔をゆがめる. ¶ I could not ***distinguish*** their *features* because of the poor light. 照明が十分でなかったので彼らの顔がはっきりしなかった. ¶ ***distort*** the *features* 顔をしかめる. ¶ He ***mutilated*** the *features* of his enemy. 彼はその敵の顔を傷つけた. ¶ There was not light enough to ***recognize*** *features*. 暗くって顔が分らなかった.

Q ***agreeable*** *features* 気持のよい顔. ¶ Her mouth is her ***best*** *feature*. 彼女は口元が一番よい. ¶ ***charming*** *features* 人を魅するような顔. ¶ her ***delicate*** *features* 彼女のきゃしゃな顔立ち. ¶ ***forbidding*** *features* すごい形相. ¶ a man of ***handsome*** *features* 美男子. ¶ ***imperturbable*** *features* 物に動じない顔 ¶ ***melancholy*** *features* 憂うつな顔. ¶ the ***pallid*** *features* of the consumptive 肺病患者の青白い顔. ¶ She has ***plain*** *features*. 彼女は平凡な顔をしている. ¶ a splendidly built young man of ***pleasing*** *features*, perfect health, brisk alertness, and the happiest disposition 容ぼうの気持のよいきわめて健康体なてきぱきしていて気だてのごくよいりっぱな体格の持主である一青年. ¶ ***sharp*** *features* 鋭い目鼻立ち. ¶ a man of ***strong*** *features* きつい顔の人.

feature, *v.* 特筆大書する.

P The success of the flight to Australia was *featured* ***in*** all the papers in editorial and special articles. 豪州への飛行の成功はあらゆる新聞の社説や特別記事に大書された. 【類】a story *featured* ***in*** a magazine = a magazine feature.

febrifuge, *n.* 解熱剤.

P valuable ***as*** a *febrifuge* 解熱剤として貴重な.

feces, *n. pl.* 大便.

P evacuation ***of*** the *feces* 便通.

fecundation, *n.* 姙娠.

V ***practice*** artificial *fecundation* in man 人間に人工姙娠法を施す.

fecundity, *n.* 生殖力.

Q ***great*** (= ***prodigious***) *fecundity* 非常な多産. ¶ ***high*** *fecundity* 高率の生殖力.

federate, *v.* 連合させる.

P In 1910 the four states, Cape of Good Hope, Natal, Transvaal, and the Orange River, were *federated* ***into*** the Union of South Africa. 一九一〇年ケイプオヴグッドホープ・ナタール・トランスヴァールおよびオレンジリヴァの四州は連合して南ア連邦となった.

federation, *n.* 連盟.

Q the ***American*** *Federation* of Labor (略 AFL) 米国労働

総同盟. ¶the ***National Federation*** of Labor 全国総同盟. ¶the ***regional federation*** of musicians 地方音楽家連盟.

Q² the ***All-Japan Federation*** of Organizations for ... ... 全日本連盟. ¶the ideal of ***world federation*** 万国連合の理想. 【類】The United Nations Organization (国連機構) is perhaps the best developed organ of the embryonic (未完成の) ***world federation***.

fee, *n.* 謝礼, 報酬, 手数料, 入場料.

V ***advance*** tuition ***fees*** 授業料を前納する. ¶He ***asks*** no *fee* for his cures. 彼はその治療に対して謝礼金を求めない. ¶***charge*** a small (=nominal) *fee* わずかの入場料を取る ‖ No *fee* will be ***charged*** to listeners. 聴取者から料金を取らない. ¶***pay*** a *fee* of two guineas 二ギニーの礼金を払う ‖ You must ***pay*** the *fee* in postal stamps. 郵便切手で料金を払わねばならない. 【類】***pay*** one's *fee* by two halves or three instalments (分割払で). ¶Of course this *fee* is ***waived*** if the patient is not able to pay. もちろん患者に資力がなければこの謝礼金は免除する.

Q The ***annual fee*** on such a permit is $5.00. この許可に対する年会費は五ドルである. ¶the ***doctor's fee*** for a visit 往診料. ¶The guide is said to have asked an ***excessive fee***. そのガイドは過分の謝礼金を求めたそうだ. ¶charge an ***extra fee*** 余分の料金を取る. ¶at a ***high fee*** 高い礼金で. ¶***inclusive fees*** 手数料を込めて. ¶The *fees* charged are very ***low***. 料金は非常に安い. ¶at ***moderate fees*** 相当の料金で. ¶a ***monthly (weekly) fee*** 一月(週)の料金. ¶at ***nominal fees*** 名ばかりの料金で. ¶***fee paid*** 料金支払いずみ. ¶for a ***small nominal fee*** ほんのわずかな謝礼で. ¶It is thrown open to the public for a ***trifling fee*** それはわずかな入場料を取って公開している.

Q² charge an ***admission fee*** of ... 入場料...をとる. ¶***club fee*** クラブの会費. 【類】***club membership fees***. ¶pay one's ***college fee*** (大学学費). ¶***consultation fee*** 診察料. ¶***dinner fee*** 晩さんの代金. ¶pay an ***entrance fee*** of ... yen ...円の入場料を払う ‖ be charged an ***entrance fee*** of ... ...の入場料を払わされる. 【類】A film-goer pays his ***entrance fee*** at a cinema. ¶pay the ***initiation fee*** at a school 学校で入学金を払う ‖ a reasonable ***initiation fee*** 適当な入会金. ¶a ***license fee*** 免許料. ¶***membership fee*** 会費. ¶for a ***postage fee*** of 10 yen 十円の郵税で. ¶a ***record fee*** とび切り高い料金. ¶a ***registration fee*** 入会金. ¶***reinstatement fee*** 復職手数料. ¶***schooling fee*** 授業料. ¶***service fee*** サービス料. ¶***student fees*** 授業料. ¶monthly ***tuition fee*** 月謝. 【類】low ***tuition fee*** / pay a very stiff ***tuition fee*** (高い月謝) in exchange for the information that ...

P teach ***at*** a *fee* of 1,000 yen 千円の謝礼金で教える. ¶***for*** a *fee* 手数料を徴収して ‖ ***for*** a *fee* of ... ...の謝礼金で.

P² the annual *fee* ***for*** membership 会費年額 ‖ *fees* ***for*** ski lessons スキーの講習料. ¶*fee* ***of*** membership 会費. ¶The *fee* ***on*** P.O.D. mail includes insurance or registration. 代金取出郵便の料金は保険または書留手数料を含む.

feed, *n.* 食物; 飼料.

V We stopped to let our horses ***have*** a *feed*. われわれは馬に飼料をやるために止った.

Q There was ***enough*** *feed* for a few more weeks' living. もう二三週間分の食物が十分あった. ¶give a ***full feed*** of cracked grain just before dark 日のあるうちに割麦を十分食わせる. ¶have a ***good feed*** 御ちそうを食べる. ¶***granulated feed*** 粒にした食物. ¶furnish ***green feed*** [餌など] 青味をやる. ¶There was ***little feed*** left for the horses. 馬の飼料がほとんど残っていなかった. ¶***soft feed*** 軟い飼料.

Q² the use of grain as ***livestock feed*** 家畜の飼料としての穀物の用途. ¶***paste feed*** (for pet birds) [飼鳥にやる]すり餌. ¶a high protein ***poultry feed*** たんぱく質の高い飼鳥のえさ.

P Eels have been ***on*** the *feed* in the Lower Thames. 今テームズ川の下流でうなぎが食立っている.

P² as a *feed* ***for*** cattle 牛の飼料として.

feed, *v.* 食物を給する, 養う; [必要物を]給する; 食う, 食って生きている.

M ***badly fed*** and badly clothed 乏しい衣食を給されて. ¶*feed* ***chiefly*** on ... 主として...を食わせる. ¶*feed* ***heavily*** on ... ...を多食する. ¶*feed* ***voraciously*** on ... がつがつ...を食う.

M² *feed* cattle ***off*** for sale 売るために牛を肥やす. ¶There are thousands of children who need ***feeding up***. 十分給食を要する子供が何千人もいる. ‖ I'm ***fed up*** with that sort of junk. Take it away. そんながらくたはいやになった. そっちへ持って行け.

P the fountain ***fed from*** the adjacent hills 付近の山から流れ出る泉. ¶Vultures ***feed on*** corpses はげたかは死体を食とする. ¶The tiger ***feeds on*** flesh. とらは肉を食とする. ‖ *feed* a baby ***on*** cow's milk=《米》*feed* cow's milk to a baby 赤ん坊に牛乳をやる. 【類】The seals ***feed on*** living fish. / The silkworm ***feeds on*** the mulberry. / ***feed on*** vegetable diet / What does this bird ***feed on***? / cattle ***feeding on*** grass / He ***feeds*** oats (からす麦) ***to*** his cattle. =He ***feeds*** his cattle ***on*** oats. ‖ ***feed on*** hope 希望に生きる ‖ ***feed on*** a promise 約束を頼みにする. ¶The cat was ***fed out of*** his hand. 彼の手からねこに餌を食わせた. ¶*feed* mulberry leaves ***to*** silkworms 蚕にくわの葉を食わせる ‖ *feed* a moist mash ***to*** fowls 鶏に麦粉に水を混ぜた餌を与える ‖ *feed* grain ***to*** a mill ひきうすに穀物を入れる ‖ *feed* paper ***to*** a printing press 印刷機に紙を差す. 【類】*feed* rice-gruel ***to*** a child with a spoon / *feed* cow's milk ***to*** a cub (きつねの子など). ¶Silkworms ***feed upon*** the leaves of mulberry trees. 蚕はくわの葉を食って育つ ‖ a parasite ***feeding upon*** human weakness 人間の弱点につけこんで飯を食っている寄生虫のような人間 ‖ the public which ***feeds upon*** periodicals 定期刊行物の読者. ¶The Donetz region ***feeds*** the greater part of Russian industry ***with*** fuel. ドウネツ地方は露国工業の大部分に燃料を供給している. ‖ ***feed*** a person ***with*** hopes 希望をもって人を喜ばせる.

feeder, *n.* 食う人.

Q a ***large feeder*** 大食者. ¶a ***quick feeder*** 早めしの人.

Q² an ***oil feeder*** 注油器. ¶a ***livestock feeder*** 家畜飼養者.

P² As a general rule these middle schools are ***feeders for*** the higher schools. 概してこれらの中学校は上級学校の予備校である.

feeding, *n.* 給食, 給養.

Q the ***artificial feeding*** of infants 幼児の人工保育. ¶***ill-balanced feeding*** 偏食. ¶***natural maternal feeding*** 自然的な母乳保育. ¶***poor feeding*** 給食の不足. ¶the ***public feeding*** of school children 学校児童の公費給食.

Q² ***breast feeding*** 母乳保育. ¶oil cake for ***cattle feeding*** 牛の餌にする油かす. ¶for ***infant feeding*** 幼児保育用の. ¶***mass feeding*** 集団給食. ¶***school feeding*** 学校給食.

feel, *n.* 手ざわり, 感触.

V ***hate*** the *feel* of the blanket against her skin 彼女は毛布のはだざわりをきらう.

Q This handle has a ***sticky feel***. この取っ手はにちゃにちゃする.

P I know this is silk ***by*** the *feel*. 手ざわりで絹だということが分る.

feel, *v.* 感じる, 感知する, 思う; 感じがする; 手ざわりがする; さわって見る; 手探りする; 同情する.

M this makes me ***feel abashed*** to ... それで私は...することを恥ずかしく思う. ¶***feel acutely*** the difficulty of ... ...の困難を痛感する. ¶***feel affectionately*** なつかしく思う. ¶***feel anxious*** 心配になる. ¶***feel awkward*** きまりが悪い. ¶I hope that you are ***feeling better***. 段々およろしいことと存じます(病人に向って). ¶I ***feel bound*** in honor to ... 私は面目にかけても...せねばならぬと思っています. ¶From his youth he had ***felt called*** to great tasks. 彼は少年のころから自分の天職の重きを感じていた. ¶I ***feel certain*** that ... 私は...は確かだと思う. ¶***feel cold*** 寒く感じる. ¶An easy-chair ***feels comfortable***. 安楽いすはかけ心地がよい. ¶I ***feel confident*** that ... 私は...と確信している. ¶***feel convinced*** 確信している. ¶it will be ***deeply felt*** by ... それは...によって深く感じられるであろう. ‖ I ***feel deeply*** for you. ほんとにお気の毒です. ¶should one ***feel disposed*** to ... ...したいと思えば. ¶I hope you will be successful, but I ***feel doubtful***. 君が成功してくれればよいと思っているがどうやらあやしい. ¶I ***felt*** a good deal ***embarrased***. 私は随分困った. ¶***feel envious*** うらやましく思う. ¶How are you today?—***Feeling fine***, thanks. 《口語》きょうはどうだね.—お陰で元気です. ¶***feel*** one's way ***forward*** 手さぐりで進む. ¶make one ***feel happy*** 人をうれしがらせる. ¶***feel helpless*** 頼りなく思う. ¶***feel hurt*** 感情を害する. ¶***feel ill*** 加減が悪い(病気で) ‖ ***feel ill*** at ease 間が悪い. ¶if you ***feel inclined*** to ... ...したい気持になったら. ¶I ***feel indebted*** to you. 感謝しています. ¶***feel*** nothing ***intensely*** 一向強くは感じない. ¶it is at once ***felt intuitively*** that ... ...と

直覚的に感じる. ¶*feel **keenly*** for ... ...に切に同情する ‖ he ***keenly felt*** that ... 彼は...ということを痛切に感じた.【類】*feel **keenly*** the necessity of ... / The scarcity of public libraries is ***keenly felt***. ¶*feel **kindly*** towards the poor 貧民に同情する. ¶The house is so large that one *feels **lost*** within it. 家が広いので戸惑いする. ¶*feel **pessimistic*** 悲観する. ¶*feel* most ***poignantly*** the death of mother 母の死を最も痛切に感じる. ¶*feel **proud*** of ... ...を自慢する. ¶*feel **relieved*** 安心する, ほっとする. ¶*feel **rough*** on the surface 表面がざらざらしている. ¶The storm was *felt **severely*** on the coast. 沿海は暴風がことの外ひどかった. ¶*feel* oneself ***slighted*** ばかにされたような気がする. ¶Silk *feels **smooth***. 絹は手ざわりがなめらかだ. ¶*feel **softly*** about ... ...について強く感じない. ¶I *feel **sorry***. 私はお気の毒に思う. ¶*feel **strongly*** that ... ...ことを痛切に感じる.【類】it is ***strongly*** *felt* that he should ... ¶I *feel **sure*** that ... ...と確信する. ¶I am beginning to *feel **tipsy***. 私は少し酔ってきた. ¶*feel **uneasy*** about ... ...を不安に思う. ¶*feel **weary*** 疲れを覚える. ¶I am not *feeling* very ***well***. 私は少し身体の調子がよくない.

M² *feel **about*** with the hands 手で探り回る ‖ *feel **about*** (=***around***) in the dark for ... 暗やみを手さぐりで...を求める.

P *feel* oneself ***above*** one's position 自分はこんな地位に満足できないと思う. ¶*feel* (=grope) ***after*** the handle とっ手を手さぐりで捜す. ¶We began to *feel **at*** ease. 僕たちは互にくつろぎだした. ‖ *feel **at*** home 気楽に感じる ‖ *feel **at*** leisure のんびりした気持がする ‖ I do not *feel **at*** liberty to mention his name. その人の名前を申上げることは遠慮しなければならない. ¶*feel **for*** the enemy 敵のありかをさぐる ‖ I *felt **for*** my purse and found it gone. 僕の財布をさぐって見たらなくなっていた. ‖ I *feel **for*** you. 僕は君に同情する. ¶*feel **in*** her hand-bag 彼女の手さげ袋の中をさぐる. ¶*feel **in*** the pocket ***for*** a purse ポケットの中の財布をさぐる. ¶*feel **like*** a cad きまりが悪い ‖ I don't *feel **like*** it. やりたくない. ‖ I *feel **like*** catching cold. かぜを引いたような気がする. ‖ It *feels **like*** velvet. それはびろうどのような手ざわりだ. ¶He *felt **of*** his ears. They were stiff and cold. 彼は耳をさわって見た. すると固くつめたくなっていた. ¶He never *feels **out of*** spirits. 彼はいつも元気だ. ¶I know how you *feel **toward*** him. 君が彼に対してどう感じているか僕には分る. ¶I *feel **with*** him. 僕はあの人に同情する. ‖ Much sympathy will be *felt **with*** the bereaved father and mother in the loss of one of their sons. あの両親が息子を一人亡くしたその不幸に対して多大の同情が寄せられるであろう.

O He is *felt* to be a little stiff. 彼には少しぎごちない所がある. ¶*feel* the earth shake 地震を感じる.

feeler, *n.* 触角.

V ***put*** (=throw) ***out*** a ***feeler*** 触手を伸ばす; さぐりを入れる. ¶A *feeler* might be dexterously ***thrown out*** before hazarding it. その冒険をやる前に手際よくさぐりを入れて見ることができよう.

feeling, *n.* 感情, 気持, 感じ, 気受け; 同情.

V ***affect*** the *feeling* 感情を害する. ¶***alarm*** and ***inflame*** American *feeling* 米国人の感情を興奮させ激させる. ¶***alienate*** the good *feelings* of friendly foreigners 好感を持っている外人の同情を失う ‖ ***alienate*** the kindly *feelings* of ... ...の好意を失う. ¶***allay*** one's troubled *feelings* 悩める心を静める. ¶I fully ***appreciate*** his *feelings* when he wrote ... 私には彼が...と書いた気持が十分に分る. ¶***arouse*** patriotic *feeling* 愛国心を喚起する. ¶women in whom erotic *feeling* is totally ***atrophied*** 色情が全然衰えた女. ¶***awaken*** *feelings* of regret at ... ...に対する遺憾の念を喚起させる. ¶***banish*** the *feeling* of languor 疲労感を駆逐する. ¶It tends to ***blunt*** the finer *feelings* of our nature. それはわれわれが生れながらにして持っている一層高尚な感情を鈍らす傾向がある. ¶***bring about*** a better *feeling* and understanding 一段の好感と理解とをもたらす. ¶***build up*** a *feeling* of cordiality 温情を増す. ¶***cast aside*** any *feelings* of trade rivalry 商業上の競争という感情を全然棄てる. ¶***cause*** intense anti-British *feeling* among the natives 土人の間に激しい反英感情を喚起する. ¶***check*** this *feeling* instantly 即座にこの考えを抑制する. ¶***cherish*** a hostile *feeling* towards ... ...に対して敵意を懐く. ¶***command*** one's *feelings* 自分の感情を抑制する. ¶***conceal*** one's *feelings* 自分の感情を隠す. ¶I could not ***contain*** my *feeling*. 腹にしまっておけなかった. ¶By a masterful effort she ***controlled*** her *feelings*. あっぱれな努力によって彼女は自分の感情を抑制した. ¶***create*** a *feeling* which can only be described as one of bewilderment 当惑というのが最も当っている感情を生じさせる ‖ ***create*** ill *feeling* 悪感情を起させる.【類】for the purpose of ***creating*** good *feeling* (好感) between ... and ... ¶***cultivate*** a friendly *feeling* with ... ...との友情を温める.【類】***cultivate*** all the *feelings* of an independent nation. ¶***deepen*** the *feeling* on each side 双方にその感を深からしめる. ¶***depict*** one's *feeling* 自己の感情を叙述する. ¶it is impossible to ***describe*** the *feelings* of solemnity and awe which overwhelm the beholder upon his first entrance into ... 見物人が初めて...にはいるときになんとも名状し難い尊厳と畏(い)敬の念に打たれる. ¶***develop*** a *feeling* of national unity 国民の一致団結心を養う.【類】It was not calculated to ***develop*** national *feeling*. ¶***dispel*** sad *feelings* 悲しい感情を一掃する. ¶***dominate*** *feelings* 感情を支配する. ¶I quickly ***drove*** that *feeling* ***away***. 私はすぐその感情をおいのけた. ¶***embitter*** *feeling* 感情を悪化する. ¶***emphasize*** the good *feeling* which exists between ... ...間にある好感を強める. ¶Secrecy is apt to ***engender*** a *feeling* that justice has not been done. 秘密はなにか後暗い感情を生じやすい. ¶***entertain*** a friendly *feeling* towards the United States 合衆国に対して好感を持つ. ¶That *feeling* must be ***eradicated***. その感情は根絶しなければならない. ¶***establish*** the *feeling* that ... ...という感情を確立する. ¶***evince*** the most exultant *feelings* of delight at the sight of ... ...を見てこの上もない歓喜の情を示す. ¶***excite*** the *feeling* of wonder 驚異の念を起させる.【類】***excite*** a *feeling* of loathing (けんおの念) / ***excite*** rather bitter *feeling*. ¶***experience*** a *feeling* of deep gratitude for ... ...に対して深い感謝の念を持つ.【類】***experience*** a *feeling* of relief / ***experience*** a *feeling* of satisfaction (as.of intoxication) / ***experience*** a *feeling* of calm intellectual content (知的満足感). ¶***express*** a *feeling* 感情を言表わす.【類】***express*** the *feeling* that ... / they ***expressed*** their kind *feelings* towards ... ¶***feel*** a sickening *feeling* 胸が悪くなる. ¶***fight*** the *feeling* [そう思ってはいかぬと]気を取直す. ¶***foment*** the *feeling* 感情を激成させる. ¶***foster*** a *feeling* of friendship among the people of different nations living in the Pacific area 太平洋地域に住む諸国民の間に友誼の念をつちかう. ¶***generate*** a *feeling* of ... ...の感を生じさせる. ¶***get*** the *feeling* that ... ...という感じがする. ¶A high ceiling ***gives*** a *feeling* of airiness and spaciousness. 高い天井は風通しがよくて広々した感じを与える. ¶***gratify*** one's own *feelings* 自分自身の感情を満足させる. ¶***harass*** the *feelings* of ... ...の感情を悩ます. ¶***have*** a *feeling* of impatience じれったく思う ‖ They ***have*** no *feelings* of humanity. 彼らには人情がない ‖ ***have*** a *feeling* of being in the Occident 西洋にいるという感じがする.【類】We ***had*** a *feeling* that something dreadful was nearing with the storm. ‖ anyone who ***has*** a *feeling* for grammar. ¶***heat*** the *feelings* 感情を興奮させる. ¶could not ***help*** a *feeling* of awe 畏(い)敬の念を禁じ得なかった. ¶***hide*** one's own *feelings* 自分の感情を隠す. ¶London Punch ***hits off*** the popular *feeling* in the matter in a cartoon representing ... ロンドンのパンチ誌は...の漫画によってその事件に対する世人の感情をうがっている. ¶***hold back*** an emotional *feeling* 感情を抑える. ¶Never needlessly ***hurt*** the *feelings* of anybody. 訳もなく人の感情を決して害してはならない.【類】for fear of ***hurting*** her *feelings* / without ***hurting*** *feelings* / The best way to avoid ***hurting*** people's *feelings* is to put yourself in their place / He has the knack of being witty (しゃれのこつ) without ***hurting*** people's *feelings*. ¶***impair*** the good *feeling* existing between them 彼らの間にある好感を害する. ¶***improve*** (=***increase***) the friendly *feeling* among them 彼らの間の友情をますます固める. ¶***indicate*** a *feeling* of amity towards ... ...に対して好意を示す. ¶***insult*** his *feelings* 彼の感情を無視する. ¶***intensify*** the anti-foreign *feeling* 排外的感情をたかめる. ¶***keep*** their *feelings* to themselves 彼らの感情を胸にたたんでおく. ¶***lacerate*** the *feelings* of others 他人の感情を傷つける. ¶He had ***lost*** all *feeling* in his left arm. 彼は左腕の感じがまるでな

くなった. ‖ He ***lost*** all *feeling* of affection for children. 彼は子供たちに対する愛情を全く失った. ¶develop the power to ***make*** one's *feelings* articulate 自分の感情を表現する力を養う. ¶He did not for a moment ***manifest*** in his force or movement any *feeling* of emotion. 彼は力や行動にちっとも感情を表わさなかった. ¶***numb*** the *feelings* of fatigue by alcohol 飲酒で疲労を忘れる. ¶***offend*** the public *feelings* 世人の感情を害する. ¶***pacify*** popular *feelings* 人心をやわらげる. ¶***pen up*** passionate *feelings* 激情を抑止する. ¶***pour forth*** one's *feelings* in a torrent of speech 思う所をとうとうとひれきする. ¶***preserve*** good *feelings* and harmony 好感と親和を失わないようにする. ¶The peaceful settlement of the question has ***produced*** a *feeling* of general satisfaction here. その問題の平和的解決は当地一般の人々に満足を与えた. ¶***promote*** good *feeling* between ... ...間の好感を増進させる. 【類】***promote*** the *feeling* of community (団体精神). ¶***provoke*** evil *feelings* 悪感を起させる. ¶***put feeling*** into words spoken 述べる言葉の中に感情を打込む. ¶He, on his part, ***reciprocated*** this *feeling*. 彼はこれに同情した. ¶***renew*** the *feeling* of hostility to ... ...に対する敵意を新たにする. ¶***respect*** the social *feeling* surrounding him 彼の周囲の社会的感情を尊重する. ¶***rouse*** a pleasant *feeling* of ... ...という愉快な感情を起させる. ¶***satisfy*** a *feeling* of ill will one bears another 他人に対して抱いている悪感情を満足させる. ¶I ***share*** his *feeling* of deep regret at ... 私は彼とともに...対して深く遺憾に思う. ¶***show*** a *feeling* of sympathy 同情の念を表わす. 【類】No one had ever seen him ***show*** sympathetic *feeling*. ¶***stimulate*** sexual *feeling* 性欲を刺激する. ¶***stir*** his *feelings* to their depths 彼の感情を真底まで動かす. ¶***stir up*** religious *feeling* 宗教的感情を起させる. 【類】***stir up*** ill *feeling* between America and Japan. ¶***suppress*** the *feeling* of shame 恥を忍ぶ ‖ completely ***suppress*** or ***subdue*** one's *feelings* 自分の感情を全く抑えまたはやわらげる. ¶***swallow*** one's *feelings* 感情を抑える. ¶***throw off*** all *feelings* of constraint 十分くつろぐ. ¶Of course I ***understand*** your *feeling*. お気持は分ります. ¶His utterances ***voiced*** the general *feeling*. 彼の言葉は一同の気分を言表わした. ¶***waken*** moral *feelings* 道念を呼び起す. ¶***work up*** one's *feelings* 人の感情を激興させる. ¶***wound*** another's *feelings* 他人の感情を傷つける.

v² much ill *feeling* ***exists*** among ... ...の間に非常な悪感情がある. ¶The class *feeling* ***fell off*** from her. 彼女は身分の差など忘れてしまった. ¶the *feeling* ***got abroad*** that ... ...という感じが一般に広まった. ¶A *feeling* of alarm ***prevails***. 驚がくの念が広まっている. ¶Political *feeling* ***runs high***. 政治上の感情が激烈になる. ¶The *feeling* of alarm has ***subsided***. 驚がくの念が薄らいだ.

Q a total absence of ***altruistic*** *feelings* 利他的観念の全的欠乏. ¶an ***antagonistic*** *feeling* 反感. ¶At that period, ***anti-foreign*** *feeling* still ran high. 当時なお排外的感情が激烈であった. ¶a ***bad*** *feeling* 悪感. ¶The Y.M.C.A. is doing much to promote a ***better*** *feeling* between the East and the West. キリスト教青年会は東西両洋間の親善に大いに努力している. ‖ Now there is a much ***better*** *feeling* among them. 今では彼らの感情がずっとよくなった. ¶***commercial*** *feeling* 金銭上の考え, 商売気. ¶have a ***deep*** *feeling* for beauty in nature 自然の美に対する深い感受性を持っている. ¶The ***deepest*** *feelings* of satisfaction are created by the announcement. その発表によって最も深い満足が示された. ¶a ***deep-seated*** (=***deep-rooted***) *feeling* of hostility 根深い敵意. ¶destroy all my ***devotional*** and ***pious*** *feelings* 私の献身的な敬けんの念を全くぶちこわす. ¶a ***dull, sinking*** *feeling* にぶい沈んだ感じ. ¶produce ***erotic*** *feeling* 色情を起す ‖ In her ***erotic*** *feeling* is totally atrophied. 彼女は色情が全くなくなった. ¶***esthetic*** *feelings* 美的感情. ¶This *feeling* was ***evanescent***. この感情はつかの間のものであった. ¶cause an ***excited*** *feeling* 興奮させる. ¶An ***extraordinary*** *feeling* crept over him then. 突飛な感情がその時彼の胸をかすめた. ¶A ***firm*** *feeling* prevails on the Bourse. 株式市場は強含みである. ¶Loyalty to the Emperor is the ***first*** *feeling* in every Japanese heart. 天皇に忠なることはすべての日本人の心に一番重きをなしている. ¶the ***first*** *feeling* of the beholder is ...; his ***next*** *feeling* is ... 目撃者の第一印象は...である; 次は...である. ¶the ***fraternal*** *feeling* of union 共同という友情. ¶have a ***freezing*** *feeling* 冷い感じがする, ぞっとする. ¶there is a ***general*** *feeling* among ... that ... ...の間に...という感情が一般に懐かれている. ¶The ***general*** *feeling* was against it. それは一般の気受けがよくなかった. 【類】There is a ***general*** *feeling* of unrest owing to the economic disorder. ¶A very ***gloomy*** *feeling* prevails on the Bourse. 株式市場には悲観論がみなぎっている. 【類】A ***gloomy*** *feeling* of desperate, eternal solitude and estrangement, surged up and overwhelmed his soul. ¶There is a very ***good*** *feeling*. 非常な好感を持たれている. ¶There is a ***growing*** *feeling* against this practice on the part of the more intelligent of the public. 社会の一層理解ある方面にこうした慣習をきらう心が段々高まりつつある. 【類】there is a ***growing*** *feeling* in favor of ... ¶with a ***happy*** *feeling* 快く感じて. ¶produce a ***healthier*** *feeling* throughout the trade 貿易を通じて一層健全な感情を起させる. ¶a perfect ***heavenly*** *feeling* 全く天へでも昇った感じ. ¶It gives one a ***homely*** *feeling*. それは家庭的な感じを与える. ¶the ***hostile*** *feeling* of the public towards ... 世人の...に対する反感. ¶entertain ***ill*** *feelings* against ... ...対して悪感を懐く. ¶an ***indifferent*** *feeling* 冷淡な気分. ¶***innate*** *feeling* 生来の感情. ¶an ***intense*** *feeling* 熱烈な感情. ¶***kindly*** *feeling* which exists between ... ...の間に存する好感. 【類】create a ***kindlier*** *feeling* toward ... ¶***local*** *feeling* 地方的な感情. ¶express their ***loyal*** *feelings* on the great day [戴冠式など]その晴れの日に彼らの忠誠を言い表わす. ¶***maternal*** *feelings* 母の情. ¶with ***mingled*** *feelings* 色々な感情が混って. ¶the growth of a truly ***national*** *feeling* 真に国家的な感情の発達. 【類】in cosequence of the strengthening of ***national*** *feeling*. ¶The people have no real ***national political*** *feeling*. その国民は本当の国家的な政治上の感情を持っていない. ¶a ***natural*** *feeling* in one who ... ...の人が当然抱く感情. ¶maintain good relations and ***neighborly*** *feeling* 親善関係と友邦的感情を持続する. ¶not dictated by any ***paltry*** *feelings* of jealousy or pride しっとあるいはごう慢といったつまらない感情からでなく. ¶The ***patriotic*** *feelings* of the masses were abnormally excited. 大衆の愛国心が異常な刺激を受けた. ¶I have no ***personal*** *feeling* against him. 私は個人として彼に反感を懐いていない. 【類】from my ***personal*** *feeling*. ¶This gives it a ***pleasant*** *feeling* of privacy and security. このために人目を避け安全という感じがする. ¶***poetical*** *feelings* aroused by ... ...のために起された詩的感情 ‖ the state of ***political*** *feeling* between ... and ... ...間における政治的感情状態. ¶the ***popular*** *feeling* of the day 今日の大衆の感情 ‖ speeches that inflame ***popular*** *feeling* 民衆の感情を扇動する演説. 【類】the ***popular*** *feeling* was strong in favor of ... ¶That is my ***present*** *feeling*. それは私の現在の感じである. ¶one who has any ***proper*** *feeling* 正しい感情を有する人. ¶***public*** *feeling* was excited over ... ...に対して人心が興奮していた. ¶cause a ***quieter*** *feeling* 感情を静める. ¶full of holiday rather than ***religious*** *feelings* 宗教的気分よりも休日気分が一杯で. 【類】stimulate one's ***religious*** *feeling*. ¶with a ***sick*** *feeling* at her heart 彼女の心を痛めて. ¶a ***social*** *feeling* 社会的感情. ¶the ***strained*** *feeling* that has resulted その結果として起った緊張した気分(気まずさ). ¶***Strong*** *feelings* of indignation were aroused. 強い憤りの念が呼び起された. ¶the ***subconscious*** *feeling* 潜在的感情. ¶***tender*** *feeling* やさしい感情. ¶I was seized with an ***uncanny*** *feeling* that there are ghosts in the chamber. 私はその室に幽霊がいるという薄気味の悪い気持に襲われた. ¶an ***undefinable*** *feeling* of melancholy 言うに言われない憂うつな感じ. ¶the ***underlying*** *feeling* that ... ...という奥底の感じ. ¶An ***uneasy*** *feeling* begins to crawl up the spinal cords. 不安な気分が背筋からしみ出した. ¶I trust I shall not be suspected of ***unpatriotic*** *feeling* in suggesting that ... ...ということをほのめかしても非愛国的感情を抱くと疑われることはあるまいと信じる. ¶a tumult of ***vehement*** *feeling* 猛烈な感情の激動. ¶awaken a very ***widespread*** *feeling* of resentment 広く世人一般に憤慨の念を起させる. ¶soothe ***wounded*** *feelings* 傷ついた感情を和らげる.

Q² The ***anti-Communist*** *feeling* here is deep and growing. 当地では反共感情が深刻でかつ深まりつつある. ¶"***at*** *home*" *feeling* くつろいだ気持. ¶the *fellow feeling* 同情. ¶*fraternity feeling* 友情. ¶Londoners have always the *home feeling* strongly upon them on Christmas Eve. ロンドン人はクリスマス前夜にはいつも家庭的気分にひたるのである. ¶promote ***friendship*** *feelings* between ... and ... ...間の親善関係を助成する. ¶The ***party*** *feeling* was strong. 党派的感情が強かった.

P ***according to*** the *feelings* of the moment その場のせつな的な感じで. ¶***by*** a *feeling* of compassion 同情して‖swayed ***by*** *feelings* of jealousy しっとの念に駆られて. ¶unbiassed ***by*** personal *feeling* 私情にとらわれないで. ¶***from*** the *feeling* that ... ...という感じから‖***from*** a *feeling* of affection (duty, gratitude) 愛(など)の心から. ¶I live happily ***in*** the *feeling* of duty accomplished. 私は本分を尽したという感じで愉快に暮している. 【類】***in*** the *feeling* that ... ¶enter ***into*** another's *feeling* 人の身になって見る. ¶collision ***of*** *feeling* 感情の衝突‖a man ***of*** *feeling* 多情多感の人‖acquire control ***of*** their *feelings* and desires 彼らの感情・欲望を制御する‖a score ***of*** other *feelings* connected with sentiment, duty or interest 情操・義務または興味に関連したその他色々の感情. ¶be lost ***to*** all *feelings* of humanity 人間的な情が少しもない. ¶speak ***with*** *feeling* 感情をこめて語る‖I cannot help regarding it ***with*** a *feeling* of satisfaction. 私はそれを満足に感ぜざるを得ない‖***with*** *feelings* of relief ほっとして‖view ***with*** *feelings* of pride ... ...を誇らしげに見る. 【類】***with*** a *feeling* of profound content / ***with*** every *feeling* of respect (うやうやしく) / I continued to regard her ***with*** *feelings* of affection. / ***with*** a *feeling* of stupefaction (気が遠くなって) / ***with*** a *feeling* of uncertainty (ひやひやして)‖Anyone ***with*** a *feeling* for grammar will not make such a mistake. 少しでも文法のわかる人ならだれでもこんな間違いはやらない. ¶engage in a talk with one ***without*** any *feeling* to timidity 臆(おく)することなく人と会話を交える‖not ***without*** a *feeling* of ... ...の感なしとしない.

P^2 stir up *feeling* ***against*** evils 破邪の心を起させる‖*Feeling* ***against*** it was running very high. それを排斥する気分が大いに高まっていた. 【類】there is a strong *feeling* throughout the land ***against*** ... ¶It aroused an uneasy *feeling* ***among*** the Japanese. それが日本人の間に不安の念を呼び起した. ¶promote good *feeling* ***between*** ... and ... ...の間の親善を図る. ¶a *feeling* ***for*** idiom 語の慣用に対する感覚‖It is impossible to expect that absolutely correct *feeling* ***for*** the language in one of Japanese birth. 日本に生れた者にその外国語に対するかく絶対的に正しい感じを起させようとしてもそれは不可能なことだ.‖They have little *feeling* ***for*** good use of language. 彼らは言葉の正しい使用に対する感じが乏しい. ¶The general *feelings* ***in*** business circles approach a panic. 実業界における一般の情勢は恐慌に近いものがある. ¶there seems to be a *feeling* ***of*** national pride in the fact that ... ...は国の誇りだという感じでいるらしい‖I had a little *feeling* ***of*** envy. 私は少しうらやましかった.‖They are ever alive to the *feeling* ***of*** honor. 彼らはいつも名誉ということを考えている.‖the *feeling* ***of*** national honor 国家的名誉心‖a *feeling* ***of*** duty 責任観念‖a *feeling* ***of*** security 安全感‖a *feeling* ***of*** tension in the head 緊張感‖persons whose deepest *feelings* ***of*** love and friendship go out only to persons of their own sex その最も深い愛と友ぎの情が彼らと同性の人だけに限られている人々. 【類】Now I have a *feeling* ***of*** safety. ¶their *feeling* ***towards*** Russia 彼らのロシアに対する感情. ¶the *feeling* ***of*** the people ***towards*** foreigners 外人に対する国民感情. 【類】The *feeling* ***of*** the population ***toward*** the stranger is exceedingly friendly. / entertain good *feeling* ***toward*** ...

feign, *v.* 風をする.

M *feign* oneself [to be] ***mad*** (***sick, ill***) 気違い(病)の風をする.

feint, *n.* 見せかけ, 風.

V ***make*** a *feint* of attacking 攻撃するように見せかける.

P ***in*** *feint* いつわって. ¶by way ***of*** *feint* [敵をあざむくためのけん制として.

felicitate, *v.* 祝う.

P *felicitate* a person ***on*** his success (good fortune) 人の成功(など)を祝する.

felicitation, *n.* 祝賀.

V ***offer*** one's *felicitation* 祝意を述べる. ¶***send*** *felicitations* to him on the occasion of ... ...に際し彼に祝意を述べる.

felicity, *n.* 幸福; 巧妙.

V ***trouble*** the domestic *felicity* 家庭の幸福を乱す.

Q have ***considerable*** *felicity* in the versifiers' art 作詩の技巧がきわめて巧みである.

P ***with*** *felicity* 手際よく.

P^2 *felicities* ***of*** phrasing 言い回しの巧妙.

fellow, *n.* 仲間, 同志; やつ; 相手; 片方; 大学の特待校友.

V I cannot ***abide*** that fellow. 私はあいつには我慢がならない. ¶He shall never ***find*** his *fellow*. 彼に相手になる者があるまい. ¶I have ***lost*** the *fellow* to this glove. この手袋の片方を失くした. ¶***pass*** all one's *fellows* 仲間を抜く. ¶a chance to ***render*** our *fellows* a service 同胞(社会)に奉仕する機会.

Q an ***annoying*** *fellow* 厄介な男. ¶an ***argumentative*** *fellow* 議論好きな男. ¶an ***awkward*** *fellow* 武骨者. ¶a ***burly*** *fellow* 荒くれ男. ¶a ***capital*** *fellow* すばらしい男. ¶a ***chubby*** *fellow* 丸々太った男. ¶a ***clever*** *fellow* 利口な男. ¶***cut-throat*** *fellows* 命知らずの猛者連. ¶a ***facetious*** *fellow* こっけいな男. ¶a ***foolish*** *fellow* ばかなやつ. ¶a ***good*** *fellow* 気のよい人. ¶a ***good-for-nothing*** *fellow* ぐうたら. ¶a ***good-natured*** *fellow* お人よし. ¶a ***good, honest*** *fellow* 人のいい正直もの. ¶an ***irresolute*** *fellow* 優柔不断な男. ¶a ***jobless*** *fellow* 失業者. ¶a ***joking, old*** *fellow* 冗談を言う元気な爺さん. ¶a ***jolly square*** *fellow* 快活な一本気の男. ¶***Knowing*** *fellow*, isn't he! 知ったかぶりをする奴ですね. ¶A ***lucky*** *fellow*! うまくやりやがったな. ¶a ***mean*** *fellow* 下劣な男. ¶I never saw a more ***obstinate*** *fellow*. あんながん固な奴は見たことがない. ¶a ***pert*** *fellow* 無遠慮な男. ¶***Poor*** *fellow!* かわいそうに! ¶a ***regular*** *fellow* 《米》好漢. ¶a ***robust young*** *fellow* たくましい青年. ¶a ***saucy*** *fellow* 生意気なやつ. ¶a ***rustic*** *fellow* いなかっ平. ¶I gave him credit for being a more ***sensible*** *fellow*. 彼はもっと物分りのよい人間だと思っていた. ¶a ***sensitive*** *fellow* 敏感な男. ¶a ***sinister-looking*** *fellow* 悪相な男. ¶a ***stalwart*** *fellow* がん丈な男. ¶a ***strong, handsome*** *fellow* 強い好男子. ¶a ***stupid*** *fellow* のろま. ¶"He is the ***sweetest*** *fellow* in the whole world," said she.「あの人は世界一のいい人です」と彼女が言った. ¶a ***waggish*** *fellow* ひょうきんな男. ¶***What*** a *fellow!* 何たるやつだろう. ¶a ***wicked*** *fellow* 太い野郎. ¶an ***X-legged*** *fellow* がに又の男. ¶a ***young*** *fellow* 若者.

Q^2 a ***country*** *fellow* いなか者.

P separated ***from*** his *fellows* 仲間から離れて.

P^2 a *fellow* ***of*** a college 大学の特待校友.

fellow-enthusiast, *n.* 同好者.

P^2 a *fellow-enthusiast* ***in*** things Byzantine ビザンティンの事物に関する同好者.

fellowship, *n.* 親交, 交際; 共同団体.

Q promote ***good*** *fellowship* 親ぼくをはかる‖A feeling of ***good*** *fellowship* prevailed at the social gathering. その懇親会には和気がみなぎっていた. 【類】Great cordiality (くつろぎ) and ***good*** *fellowship* prevailed at the gathering. ¶an ***intellectual*** *fellowship* 知的な親交. ¶prayer as ***intimate personal*** *fellowship* with the unseen Friend 目に見えない友たる神と親しく語り合う祈禱. ¶***social good*** *fellowship* 社会的交誼(ぎ).

Q^2 ***world*** *fellowship* 国際的親ぼく. 【類】a ***world*** *fellowship* of business and professional men.

P ***by*** *fellowship* with bad companions 悪友との交際で. ¶a mortal ***in*** *fellowship* ***with*** angels [昔の聖者のごとき]天使と親交ある人間. ¶go abroad ***on*** a *fellowship* 奨学金をもらって洋行する.

felon, *n.* 重罪人.

Q^2 a ***war*** *felon* 戦争犯罪人.

felt, *n.* フエルト.

P^2 *felt* ***for*** roofing (carpeting) 屋根(など)用のフェルト.

female, *n.* 女子.

Q the ***adult*** *female* of man 成熟した女子. ¶a ***faithless*** *female* 不実な女. ¶a ***slatternly*** (=***slovenly***) *female* だらしのない女. ¶an ***unseductive*** *female* かさかさした女.

feminine, *n.* 女性.

Q the ***eternal*** *feminine* 永遠の女性(女性の本質).

femininity, *n.* 女らしさ; 《集団》女性.

V ***keep*** her *femininity* 女らしさをもっている.

Q^2 ***London*** *femininity* ロンドンの女性.

feminization, *n.* 女性化.

P^2 Women teachers mean the *feminization* ***of*** education. 女教員は教育の女性化を意味する.

fence, *n.* かき[ね], さく.

V ***break down*** a *fence* かきを撤去する. ¶***clear*** a *fence* へいを飛越える. ¶***erect*** a *fence* かきねを作る. ¶This *fence* should be ***propped up***. このへいには支柱を施さねばならない. ¶***put*** a *fence* around ... ...の周囲にかきを作る. ¶***ride*** the *fence* 《米》[馬に乗って牧場の]柵を見回り修理する.

V² The *fence* ***gave way***. へいが倒れた.

Q surrounded by an ***unclimbable*** *fence* 登り越すことのできないへいに囲まれて.

Q² a ***bamboo*** *fence* 竹がき. ¶enclose a bit of land within ***barbed-wire*** *fences* 狭い土地を有刺線で囲む. ¶a ***board*** *fence* 板べい. ¶a ***picket*** *fence* さく. ¶build a ***rail*** *fence* 横棒のさくを造る. ¶a ***steel*** *fence* 鉄がき. ¶a ***wire*** *fence* 針金の柵.

P throw stones ***across*** the *fence* へい越しに石を投げる. ¶lean ***against*** the *fence* へいによりかかる. ¶He is ***on*** the *fence*. 《米》彼はほらがとうげをきめこんでいる. 【類】sit (=stand) ***on*** the *fence*. ¶jump ***over*** the *fence* さくを飛び越える. ¶enclose ... ***with*** a *fence* ...さくで囲む.

fence, *v*. へいで囲む; 防衛する; 言い抜ける.

M² *fence* ***about*** (=***round***) a place 場所を囲う. ¶*fence* ***in*** a lot 地所をさくで囲む. 【類】The land is *fenced* ***in***. ¶*fence* ***off*** an area from the public その区域に人が入らぬようにさくでさえぎる. 【類】*fence* [***off***] a place from the wind. ¶*fence* ***up*** a place 場所をかきで仕切ってしまう.

P *fence* oneself ***against*** the enemy 敵を防ぐ. ¶*fence* the house ***from*** the north wind 北風から家を防ぐ. ¶The garden was *fenced* ***with*** stones on two sides. 庭は二方石がきになっている. ‖ He cleverly *fenced* ***with*** a question. 彼は質問を巧みに受け流した.

fencer, *n*. 剣士.

Q² a ***master*** *fencer* 剣豪.

fencing, *n*. 剣道; かき囲い.

V ***practice*** *fencing* 剣道をやる.

Q a bit of ***verbal*** *fencing* 一席の問答.

Q² ***barbed-wire*** *fencing* 有刺針金の囲いがき. ¶***iron-hurdle*** *fencing* 鉄さくの囲い. ¶***tournament*** *fencing* 剣道の試合. ¶***wire*** *fencing* 針金の囲い. ¶***woven-wire*** *fencing* 網囲いがき. ¶ornamental ***wrought-iron*** *fencing* 鍛鉄の飾りさく.

fend, *v*. [攻撃質問を]受け流す.

M² *fend* ***off*** an attack 攻撃を受け流す. 【類】*fend* ***off*** a blow ‖ *fend* ***off*** inflation インフレを防止する ‖ *fend* ***off*** questions 質問を受け流す.

P Now that his father is dead, he has to *fend* ***for*** himself. 父が亡くなったので彼は自立しなければならない.

ferment, *n*. 騒乱, ごたごた.

Q there is ***considerable*** *ferment* concerning ... ...に関し随分ごたごたがある. ¶Rumors of war caused ***national*** *ferment*. 戦争のうわさで国内が騒然となった. ¶***social*** *ferment* 社会の動揺.

P The country is ***in*** a *ferment*. その国は人心沸騰している. ‖ the ideas were ***in*** *ferment* in the mind of ... その考えは...の胸中に醸成されつつあった.

ferment, *v*. 発酵する.

M ***actively*** *ferment* 盛んに発酵する.

fermentation, *n*. 発酵; 動乱, 騒ぎ.

Q ***acetic*** *fermentation* 醋酸発酵. ¶***putrefactive*** *fermentation* 腐敗発酵.

P ***during*** *fermentation* 発酵中 ‖ ***during*** the *fermentation* その動乱中.

fern, *n*. しだ.

Q the ***royal*** *fern* ぜんまい.

Q² a ***maiden-hair*** *fern* はこねぐさ.

ferocity, *n*. どう猛, 残忍.

Q The attack will be resumed with ***redoubled*** *ferocity*. その攻撃は一層のものすごさを加えて再開されるだろう. ¶spring with ***tiger-like*** *ferocity* on its opponent その敵に向ってとらのようなどう猛さで食ってかかる.

ferret, *v*. 狩り出す; 捜索する.

M *ferret* ***out*** a criminal 犯人を捜し出す. 【類】Detectives are employed to *ferret* ***out*** secrets. / *ferret* ***out*** publishers and importers of immoral publications (わい本) / *ferret* ***out*** particulars about ... ‖ The teacher is trying to *ferret* ***out*** (=up) the perpetrator of the mischief. 教師はいたずらの犯人を探り出そうと骨を折っている.

M² *ferret* ***about*** 狩りまくる.

P *ferret* rabbits ***out of*** their bush うさぎをやぶから狩り出す.

ferro-concrete, *n*. 鉄筋コンクリート.

P The new building is ***of*** *ferro-concrete* (=reinforced concrete). 今度の建物は鉄筋コンクリートである.

ferry, *n*. 渡し船; 渡船場.

V ***board*** the *ferry* for Shimonoseki 連絡船に乗って下関に向う. ¶***cross*** a *ferry* in a boat 小舟で渡船場を渡る.

Q² ***air*** *ferry* 飛行機連絡. ¶Hokkaido is joined to the main land by a ***steam*** *ferry*. 北海道は本州と汽船で連絡している. ¶a ***train*** *ferry* 列車連絡船.

P the river is crossed ***by*** *ferry* to ... 渡船で川を渡って...に行く ‖ We got across the river ***by*** *ferry*. われわれは渡船で川を越えた.

ferry, *v*. 船で渡す, 船で渡る.

M² *ferry* them ***over*** 舟で彼らを渡してやる.

P *ferry* a person ***across*** a river 渡船で川向うに人を渡す ‖ We *ferried* ***across*** the river. 渡船で川向うに渡った. ¶He *ferried* them ***over*** the river. 彼は彼らを渡船で川向うに渡した.

fertile, *a*. 多産の, 豊じょうな.

P He is possessed of a mind *fertile* ***in*** expedients. 彼は知謀に富んでいる. ¶The district is *fertile* ***of*** wheat. その地方は小麦を多く産する. ‖ be *fertile* ***of*** invention (imagination) 工夫(想像)力が豊富である.

fertility, *n*. 豊じょう, 肥沃(ょく).

Q soil of ***surpassing*** *fertility* 非常に肥えた土壌. ¶The soil is characterized by its ***virgin*** *fertility*. その土壌は処女地としての豊じょうさを持っている.

P² *fertility* ***of*** fancy (invention) 空想(独創)力の豊富さ.

fertilization, *n*. 施肥; 〖生物〗受精.

V ***accomplish*** *fertilization* 土地を肥沃(よく)化する.

fertilize, *v*. 施肥する; 受精させる.

M ***artificially*** *fertilize* flowers (eggs) 人工的に花(卵子)に受精させる.

fertilizer, *n*. 肥料; 受精媒介物.

Q Flies and bees are ***good*** *fertilizers*. はえやみつばちはよく受精媒介をする.

Q² a ***nitrogen*** *fertilizer* 窒素肥料.

fervo[u]r, *n*. 熱心, 熱情.

V The orator skilfully ***worked up*** the mental *fervor* of his listeners. 弁士は巧みに聴衆の血をわかした.

Q a period of ***patriotic*** *fervor* 愛国心の高潮期. ¶aglow with a ***poetic*** *fervor* 詩的熱情に燃えて. ¶in a surge of ***religious*** *fervor* 宗教的熱情がほとばしって. 【類】***Religious*** *fervor* was the background of the Greek stage. ¶***savage*** *fervor* 猛烈な熱情. ¶the ***Tolstoyan*** *fervor* トルストイ流の熱情.

P preach ***with*** *fervor* 熱心に説教する ‖ ***with*** the *fervor* of a first love 初恋の熱心さで.

P² The *fervor* ***of*** my passion died. 僕の熱はさめた.

fester, *v*. [怒りが]胸にうずく.

P The insult *festered* ***in*** his mind. その侮辱は彼の胸にぐっとこたえた.

festival, *n*. 祝典, 祭礼; 祝祭日の宴会.

V ***celebrate*** a *festival* 祝典をあげる. ¶***hold*** a *festival* 祭典を行う. ¶***keep*** a *festival* 祭典を祝う. ¶***observe*** a *festival* 祝祭を行う. ¶Signalizing the 50th anniversary of the passing of Wagner, innumerable cities will ***present*** special *festivals* and expositions. ワグネルの死去五十年祭記念として多くの都市が特別の祭典や展覧会を催すであろう.

V² Some *festival* was ***going on*** (=***proceeding***) there when I passed last night. 私が昨夜そこを通ったとき何かのお祭りだった.

Q the ***Five*** *Festivals* 五節句. ¶They hold a ***high*** *festival* at Christmas. クリスマスには盛んな祝典を催す. ¶an ***immovable*** (a ***movable***) *festival* 一定している(一定していない)祭日. ¶the ***New Year's*** *festival* 正月の祝い. ¶on ***special*** *festivals* 臨時祭礼のときに.

Q² a ***Church*** *festival* 教会の祭典. ¶the ***Court*** *Festival* on New Year's Day 四方拝. ¶a ***harvest*** *festival* 収穫感謝祭, 収納祭, 田祭. ¶the ***Lantern*** *Festival* うら盆. ¶a ***music*** *festival* 音楽祭. ¶an ***open-air*** *festival* 野外祝典. ¶the ***silver jubilee*** *festival* 二十五年記念祝典. ¶a ***spring*** (an ***autumn***) *festival* 春(秋)祭り. ¶a ***strawberry*** *festival* in the summer 夏のいちご祭り.

P on the occasion ***of*** the *festival* その祭礼の折.

P² the *festival* ***at*** the Hachiman Shrine 八幡神社の祭典.

festivity, *n*. 祝祭; お祭り騒ぎ.

V ***keep*** the *festivities* ***alive*** お祭り騒ぎを続ける.

Q ***social*** *festivities* 社交的お祭り騒ぎ.

Q² ***Christmas*** *festivities* クリスマス祝典. ¶***pre-Coronation*** *festivities* 戴冠式の前景気. ¶***wedding*** *festivities* 婚礼の祝典.

P² the *festivities* ***on*** July 4 including a parade and fireworks 行列や花火大会のある七月四日(独立祭).

festoon, *n.* [装飾用の]花づなやリボン・色テープなど.

V ***stretch*** straw *festoons* しめなわを張る.

P adorn a hall ***with*** (=*by*) *festoons* 花づなでホールを飾る.

P² *festoons* ***of*** streamers テープの五色糸(出港のときの).

fetch, *v.* 生返らせる.

M *fetch* ***away*** [揺れて台の物が]おどり出す. ¶This won't *fetch* ***much,*** I'm afraid. これは高く売れまい. ¶*fetch* ***out*** the colors of marble 大理石の色つやを出す.

M² *fetch* ***down*** the price of ... ...の値を下げる ‖ This vast number of shot were not sufficient to *fetch* the elephant ***down.*** 無数の弾をうったが象を倒すことはできなかった. ¶*fetch* ***up*** a memory [to mind] 記憶を呼び起す ‖ *fetch* ***up*** a child 子供を育てる.

P *fetch* a person ***from*** a faint 正気づける ‖ *Fetch* me the papers ***from*** Mr. Johnson's office. ジョンスンさんのへやからその書類を持って来てくれ.

fete, fête, *n.* 祝宴, きょう宴.

Q² ***Bank Holiday*** *fetes* 銀行休日の祝宴.

fetish, *n.* 崇拝物体, 霊物.

V ***make*** a *fetish* of ... ...を崇拝する.

Q Curiosities such as peculiar stones and bits of wood become ***powerful*** *fetishes* to African sorcerer. 特殊な石や木片のような妙な物がアフリカの魔術者には有力な霊物になる.

fetter, *n.* 足かせ; 拘束物, きずな.

V ***break*** the *fetters* of ... ...のきはんを脱する. ¶It is in ignorance rather than by vice that many ***forge*** *fetters* for their own bondage. 自じょう自縛の多いのは悪徳によるよりもむしろ無知に基因する. ¶He ***has*** *fetters* ***on.*** 彼は足かせを掛けられている. ¶***shake off*** *fetters* きはんを脱する.

P He is ***in*** *fetters.* 彼はとらわれの身となっている.

P² *fetters* ***for*** the foot 足かせ ‖ be bound up in *fetters* ***of*** conventionalism 因襲のきずなにしばられて.

fetter, *v.* 拘束する.

P *fettered* ***by*** tradition 因襲にとらわれて.

feud, *n.* 不和, 確執, 反目.

V he ***has*** a personal *feud* with ... 彼は...と個人的に反目している.

Q a ***long-standing*** *feud* 年来の闘争. ¶an ***unending*** *feud* between the two clans 両氏族間の果てしない闘争.

Q² a ***family*** *feud* 家庭の不和. ¶a ***gambling*** *feud* 賭博(とばく)からのけんか. ¶be drawn into a ***name-calling*** *feud* 悪口雑言のけんかに巻き込まれる.

P The couple are ***at*** deadly *feud* with each other. その夫婦は犬猿(けんえん)もただならぬ仲である. 【類】The two families had been ***at*** *feud* with each other for generations. ¶he is ***in*** *feud* with ... 彼は...と不和になっている.

P² a *feud* ***among*** brothers 兄弟間の不和. ¶a *feud* ***between*** two persons 二人間の不和. ¶his *feud* ***with*** Christianity 彼のキリスト教に対する敵視.

feudalism, *n.* 封建制度.

V *Feudalism* was not ***abolished*** in England until 1660, and it lasted in Scotland until 1747. 封建制度はイングランドでは一六六〇年に至って初めて廃止されスコットランドでは一七四七年まで続いた.

feudatory, *n.* 封土; 封臣.

V The duke ***summoned*** his *feudatories* to aid him in the war. 公は交戦のため重臣を召集した.

Q² ***Tokugawa*** *feudatories* 徳川幕下.

fever, *n.* 発熱, 熱, 熱病; 熱狂.

V ***abort*** a *fever* ひどく高まらない内に熱を下げる. ¶***allay*** *fever* 解熱する. ¶***banish*** yellow *fever* from ... ...から黄熱病を駆逐する. ¶***bring*** the *fever* ***under*** 熱を下げる. ¶He ***caught*** the racing *fever* at last. 彼はとうとう競馬に熱中し出した. 【類】Take care not to ***catch*** a *fever.* ¶***chart*** *fever* 熱のグラフを作る. ¶***develop*** a *fever* 発熱する. ¶***have*** a *fever* 熱がある ‖ ***have*** a little *fever* 少し熱がある. ***shake off*** one's *fever* 熱を下げる.

V² The *fever* is ***abating.*** 熱が下りつつある. ¶A *fever* has ***raged*** in the town. その市に熱病が流行をきわめた. ¶The ... *fever* ***took hold*** of him. 彼は...熱(流行)にとりつかれた.

Q an ***anti-foreign*** *fever* 排外熱. ¶a ***continual*** *fever* 続く熱. ¶***gastric*** *fever* 腸チフス. ¶a ***hectic*** *fever* [結核性]消耗熱. ¶a ***high*** *fever* 高熱. ¶an ***inflammatory*** *fever* 炎症熱. ¶an ***intermittent*** *fever* 間欠熱. ¶an ***inward*** *fever* 真熱. ¶a ***lingering*** *fever* 長びく熱. ¶a ***malarial*** *fever* マラリア熱. ¶a ***malignant*** *fever* 悪性の熱. ¶a ***prevalent*** *fever* 流行性の熱病. ¶a ***puerperal*** *fever* 産じょく熱. ¶a ***putrid*** *fever* 発しんチフス.

Q² The ***election*** *fever* is at its highest during the General Election. 選挙熱は総選挙の間が最高潮である. ¶***fishing*** *fever* 釣魚熱. ¶***gold*** *fever* 金鉱熱. ¶***hay*** *fever* 《米》かれ草熱. ¶***scarlet*** *fever* しょう紅熱. ¶***spring*** *fever* 春の熱病. ¶She caught ***typhoid*** *fever* from visiting in the parish. 彼女は貧民区を訪問してチフスにかかった. ¶***typhus*** *fever* 発しんチフス. ¶***war*** *fever* 戦争熱. ¶***yellow*** *fever* 黄熱病.

P He is suffering ***from*** a low *fever.* 彼は微熱に悩んでいる. ¶be ***in*** a *fever* of anxiety 大層心配している. 【類】The whole city is ***in*** a *fever* of excitement. ¶He is confined to bed by an attack ***of*** *fever.* 彼は熱病で寝ている. ‖ He is ill ***of*** a *fever.* 彼は熱病にかかった. ¶He is down ***with*** *fever.* 熱病で寝ている. ¶He was attacked ***with*** *fever* every other day. 彼は隔日に熱が出た. 【類】He is sick in bed ***with*** *fever.*

P² a *fever* ***of*** enthusiasm 熱狂. ¶He was in a *fever* ***of*** impatience. 彼はじれ込んでいた.

few, *n.* 少数の人または物.

V There is space here to ***mention*** only a *few.* ここにほんの二三の例を述べるだけの余白しかない.

Q the ***chosen*** *few* 選ばれた少数の者. 【類】They are the so-called ***chosen*** *few.* ¶the ***cultured*** *few* 教養ある少数の人. ¶the ***erudite*** *few* 少数の博学者. ¶the ***favored*** *few* with fat pocket-books 金に困らない少数の恵まれた者. ¶the ***fortunate*** *few* 幸運な少数の者. ¶a ***good*** *few* [of them] 相当の数. ¶To the ***idle*** *few* dress is a business; to the busy many it is a hobby. 少数の有閑者にとっては服装は仕事であり大勢の忙しい者にとっては道楽である. ¶It appeals to the ***initiated*** *few* only. それは少数の通人にだけ喜ばれる. ¶a ***passionate*** *few* 少数の熱情家. ¶the ***privileged*** *few* その特権を得た少数のもの. ¶***quite*** a *few* of them 《米》相当の数. ¶a ***select*** *few* of old friends 旧友中よりぬきの二三人.

P² *Few* ***of*** them were there. 彼らの中そこにいたものは多くなかった. ‖ A *few* ***of*** his friends were there. 彼の友だちは少しはそこにいた.

few, *a.* 少数の.

M contain ***comparatively*** *few,* but long, entries 比較的項目が少くて説明が長い(旧式の百科事典など).

P They are very *few* ***in*** number. その数ははなはだ少ない.

fiasco, *n.* [演奏などの]大失敗.

V The concert ***turned out*** a *fiasco.* 音楽会は大失敗であった.

Q a ***virtual*** *fiasco* 実際上の大失敗.

P The entertainment ended ***in*** a *fiasco.* 演芸は大失敗に終った.

fib, *n.* 《俗》罪のないうそ.

V ***tell*** one a *fib* 人に罪のないうそを言う.

fiber, fibre, *n.* 繊維; 筋力, 力; 品性, 素質.

V ***loosen*** the moral *fiber* 道徳力を弱くする.

Q a man of ***coarse*** *fiber* 品性粗野な人. ¶a weakening of the ***moral*** *fibers* 道徳力の弱化. ¶a man of the ***poetical*** (***political***) *fiber* 詩人(など)の素質ある人. ¶a man of ***real*** *fiber* 実力のある人. ¶a boy of ***solid*** *fiber* 屈強な男児. ¶men of ***stupendous*** *fiber* 恐ろしい腕力のある人. ¶***synthetic*** *fiber* 合成繊維.

Q² synthetic ***glass*** *fiber* 合成ガラス繊維. ¶pull the ***silk*** *fibers* off the cocoons on to a spindle 繭から絹の繊維を引き出して紡錘に巻きつける. ¶***wood*** *fiber* 木繊維.

fickleness, *n.* うわ気, むら気.

P² *fickleness* ***in*** love うわ気. ¶*fickleness* ***of*** fortune 変転きわまりない運命.

fiction, *n.* 虚構; 作り事, 作り話, 小説.

V ***circulate*** *fiction* 作り話を言い触らす. ¶***start*** the *fiction* that ... ...という根も葉もないことを言い触らす.

Q a writer of ***American*** *fiction* 米国の小説家. ¶***detective*** *fiction* 探偵小説. ¶a ***downright*** *fiction* 明白な作り事. ¶Sergeant Cuff in Wilkie Collins's The Moonstone is the first detective in ***English*** *fiction.* ウイルキー・コリンズのムーンストーン中にある「カフ軍曹」は英国小説に現われた最初の探偵である. ¶a ***libelous*** *fiction* 非難的な作り事. ¶***machine-made*** *fiction* 型にはまった創作. ¶the lightest and most ephemeral of ***modern*** *fiction* 近代小説中最も低級でかつ最も短命なもの. ¶modern ***psychological*** *fiction* 近代心理小説. ¶This story of ... is ***pure*** *fiction.* この...の話は全く虚構である. ¶***putrescent*** *fiction* 退廃小説. ¶***realistic*** *fiction* 写実小説. ¶***recent*** *fiction* 最近の小説.

¶*reputable* fiction 評判のよい小説. ¶*romantic fiction* ロマン派小説. ¶*supernatural fiction* 超自然的小説. ¶*tenth-rate fiction* 三文小説.

Q² "*pass the time*" *fiction* ひまつぶしの小説.

P a figure *in fiction* to be remembered 記憶すべき小説中の人物. ¶a writer *of fiction*=a fiction writer 小説家. ¶Such a thing is by no means new *to fiction*. こうしたことは小説には決して新しいものではない.

fiddle, *n.* 提琴.

V *play* the *fiddle* バイオリンをひく ‖ *play* first (second) *fiddle* 第一(第二)バイオリンを勤める; 上(下風)に立つ.

fiddle, *v.* いじくる, ぶらぶらする.

M *fiddle away* one's time ぶらぶら時間を過す.

M² *fiddle about* with a piece of string 一本のひもをもてあそぶ ‖ *fiddle about* doing nothing 何一つしないでなまけている.

fiddler, *n.* 提琴家.

Q the *first* (*second*) *fiddler* 第一(二)バイオリニスト.

fidelity, *n.* 忠実, 貞節.

V *pledge* mutual *fidelity* 相互に契りを結ぶ. ¶*show fidelity* towards ... ...に誠実を尽す.

Q the *conjugal fidelity* of the husband to his wife 夫の妻に対する信実. ¶*literal fidelity* to the original 原文に対する文字通りの忠実. ¶breaches of *marital fidelity* 操を破ること. ¶show with *photographic fidelity* how it is made その製法を写真のように忠実に示す. ¶The camera has registered the sheer beauty of this lovely spot with *rare fidelity*. 写真にこの美しい風景がまれに見る如実さで写されている. ¶*unwavering fidelity* to the Crown 君主に対する確固不動の忠節.

P the oath *of fidelity* 忠実の誓い. ¶*with* the *fidelity* of a diary 日記のような克明さで ‖ reproduce ... *with* complete *fidelity* 本物そっくりに...を複製する.

P² *fidelity to* detail 細部にわたる忠実 ‖ *fidelity to* one's lord 君に対する忠実 ‖ *fidelity to* fact 事実に対する忠実. 【類】*fidelity to* one's principles ‖ his *fidelity to* his master's interests 彼の主人を思う忠実さ.

fidget, *n.* せかせか, そわそわ.

V *have* the *fidgets* そわそわする.

P He is always *in* a *fidget*. 彼は始終そわそわしている.

fidget, *v.* せかせかする.

P He is always *fidgeting about* something. 彼は始終なにかせかせかしている.

field, *n.* 野, 原, 畑; 戦場, 戦地; 戦争; 活動範囲; 競争場裡(ʳ); 界, 分野; 地.

V *afford* a splendid *field* for ... ...に対しすばらしい活動範囲を与える. ¶*beat* the *field* 原野を踏み歩く. ¶*clear* the *field* of imported goods 競争場裡から外国品を一掃する. ¶*conquer* the *field* 目的を遂げる. ¶His inventions *cover* a wide *field*. 彼の発明は広範囲にわたる. 【類】In these days authorship *covers* a very large *field*. / The book *covers* a new *field*. ¶*develop* unexplored *fields* of industries 新産業を開拓する. ¶*discover* a new *field* of enterprise 新しい方面の事業を発見する. ¶*dispute* the *field* with ... ...と競争する. ¶*enlarge* the *field* of knowledge 知識の領域を拡大する. ¶New rivals *entered* the *field*. 新手の競争者が現われた. ‖ *enter* the *field* with cheap goods 廉価の商品をひっさげて競争場裡に入る ‖ *enter* the *field* as a colonizing power in Africa アフリカにおける植民国として現われる ‖ *enter* the *field* of international politics 国際政治に参与する. 【類】*enter* the *field* of international competition / *enter* the *field* of journalism (新聞界). ¶*explore* with the pen an entirely new *field* ペンをもって全然新しい方面を開拓する. ¶*fertilize* corn *fields* 麦畑 ((米)とうもろこし畑)に施肥する ‖ a country that debonairly *fertilizes* its *fields* with sewage 下水をもって平気でその田野をかんがいする国. ¶*fill* a *field* of its own 自己独特の地位を占める. ¶*find* a wider *field* for publications 出版物を一層売り広める. ¶*keep* (=*maintain*) the *field* 地歩を維持する. ¶English goods *held* the *field* until it was superseded by imports from Japan. 日本品が取って代るまで英国品がその市場を独占していた. ¶*lose* (*win*) the *field* 戦いに敗れる(勝つ). ¶The *fields* must be *manured*. 畑に施肥をしなければならない. ¶*monopolize* the *field* 活動の舞台を独占する. ¶*mow* a *field* 野の草または穀物を刈り取る. ¶It *offers* a tempting *field* of operations. それは是非手を出したくなる活動方面である. ¶*open* a *field* for trade 商業の新市場を開拓する. 【類】The book *opened* a new *field* in fiction. ¶*open up* a new *field* for research 研究の新生面を開く ‖ *open up* a big *field* for discussion 議論を戦わす一大問題を提供する. ¶*pitch* (=*set*) a *field* 陣営を張る. ¶*plow up* a *field* 畑を耕す. ¶*prepare* the *field* for ... ...を作るために畑を耕す. 【類】They found the ox plow method of *preparing fields* for planting more economical than the use of machinery. ¶The magazine *seeks* a *field* in three nations. その雑誌は三カ国に購読者を求める. ‖ *seek* a new *field* for one's labors 新規に働き先を捜す. ¶The farmers are *sowing* their *fields*. 百姓たちは畑に種をまいている. ¶*survey* comprehensively this extensive *field* 概括的にこの広はんな題目を論じる. ¶*take* the *field* as a private 一兵卒として出征する ‖ The Kokura and Sendai Divisions will be the first to *take* the *field*. 小倉と仙台の師団が真先に出征する. ‖ *take* the *field* against ... ...に対抗する. ¶*take up* the *field* of literature 文学を職業とする. ¶*till* one's *field* 自分の畑を耕す. ¶*widen* its *field* of operations 行動範囲を広げる. ¶farmers who were *working* the *fields* 野良の仕事をしていた百姓.

Q an *athletic field* 運動場. ¶She made herself a prominent figure in her *chosen field*. 彼女はその選んだ職業方面で名を成した. ‖ one's *chosen field* of study その専門研究の分野. ¶make a *clear field* for oneself 競争者を倒して舞台を独占する. ¶an *enclosed athletic field* 囲いのある運動場. ¶look over the *entire field* 全体を観測する. 【類】survey the *entire field* of English law (イギリス法). ¶*fair field* 均等の機会. ¶he found an especially *fertile field* in ... 彼は...が特に収獲の多い方面だということを知った. ¶a cultivated and well *fertilized field* 耕して十分肥料を施した畑. ¶There is a *fine field* for botanists in the Philippines. フィリッピンでは植物学者はりっぱな職が得られる. ¶a *florid field* 花咲く野. ¶a *fruitful field* 収穫の多い方面. ¶this *great field* of human endeavour 人間努力のこの偉大なる方面. ¶a *hardfought field* 悪戦苦闘の分野. ¶an *important field* of research 重要な研究方面. ¶an *industrial field* 工業方面. ¶in the *intellectual field* 知的方面で. ¶an *interesting field* of psychology 心理学の興味ある方面. 【類】an *interesting field* of research may be found in ... ¶an *inviting field* of scientific research 科学研究の面白い方面. 【類】it is an *inviting field for* ... ¶cover a *large field* 広範囲にわたる. ¶This is too *large* a *field* for us to plough in the short time at our disposal. わずかの時間しか使えないわれわれにはこの題目は手にあまって扱い兼ねる. ¶a *lean field* やせた畑. ¶afford a more *lucrative field* もっと有利な活動方面を供給する. ¶the *magnetic field* 磁界. ¶a *moral field* 道徳方面. ¶their *new field* of labor この新しい努力の方面. ¶a *new* and *stimulating field* of research 新しい興味のある研究方面. ¶an *open field* 樹木などのないあき地. ¶point out a few of the *outstanding fields* of efforts 活動方面の顕著なもの二三を示す. ¶Each is supreme in his *own field*. めいめいその方面の第一人者だ. ‖ That happens to be my *own field*. それはたまたま僕の専門だ. ¶a scientist who is an authority in his own *particular field* その専門では権威者である科学者. ¶in the *periodical field* 雑誌界で. ¶*playing fields* 運動場. ¶a *plowed field* 耕した畑. ¶the *potter's field* 窯業場. ¶a *profitable field* of inquiry 有益な研究部面. ¶His *proper field* was not in politics, but in learning. 彼の本領は政治ではなくて学問であった. ¶The signs appear in white on a *red field*. 記号は赤地に白で出ている. ¶They are each specialists in their *respective fields*. それぞれその道の専門家である. ¶a *safer* and more *attractive field* of investment 投資の一層安全で人気を呼ぶ方面. ¶laborers in the *same field* 同じ方面に活動する人々 ‖ the achievement of ... in the *same field* 同一方面における...の業績. ¶the *scientific field* 学術界. ¶*smiling fields* of grain 穀物の豊かに実る畑. ¶His *special field* is thyroid gland. 彼の専門は甲状腺である. ‖ his own *special field* of study 彼の専門研究. 【類】It is his *special field*. ¶a *field tempting* to historians 歴史家にとってきわめて興味深い方面. ¶It has *three main fields* of effort. それには三つの主要な努力の方面がある. ¶an almost *unexplored field* of educational research 教育研究のほとんど未踏の方面. ¶it offers a *unique field* of activity for ... それは...にとって独特な活動方面である. ¶an *untilled field* 未耕地 ‖ Lesbos still remains an *untilled field* for the archaeologist. レスボス島は今なお考古学者の手をつけぬ畑である. ¶an untrodden field 未踏の地. ¶various fields of thought 思想の各方面 ‖ from various fields of endeavor 諸方面の研究から. ¶a virgin field of endeavor 研究の処女地 ‖ The field is a virgin one needing cultivation. その方面は処女地であって開拓を要する. ¶the visual field 視野. ¶The book covers a wide field. その本は広い方面にわたっている. 【類】He has a wide field of activity (活動範囲).

Q² On the baseball field, the umpire's word is final. 野球場では審判の言は動かすことはできない. ¶in the book field (=world) 出版界で. ¶a camp field 陣地. ¶coal (oil) fields 炭(油)田. ¶a corn field 麦畑《英》; とうもろこし畑《米》. ¶in the export field 輸出方面で. ¶a flying field 飛行場. ¶a home field 農家宅地. ¶an ice field 氷原. ¶a labor field 職場. ¶a landing field 着陸場 ‖ an emergency landing field 非常着陸場. ¶a mission field 宣教の対象地. ¶enter the "movie" field 映画入りをする. ¶in the newspaper field 新聞界で. ¶paddy and upland fields 田畑. ¶the peacetime field of atomic energy 原子力の平和的利用範囲. ¶their eminence on the playing (=sporting) fields 運動界における彼らの高名 ‖ a public playing field 公衆運動場. ¶a potato field じゃがいも畑. ¶a practice field [競技の]練習場. ¶a rice field 水田. ¶a rice paddy field 水田. ¶a riverside field 川沿いの畑. ¶a root field 根菜畑. ¶a salt field 塩田. ¶a school playing field 学校の運動場. ¶a seed field 播種畑. ¶a snow field 雪原. ¶a strawberry field いちご畑. ¶in the student personnel field 学生監督の方面で. ¶a turnip field かぶ畑. ¶a university field 大学運動場. ¶a wheat field 小麦畑.

P A baseball game is to be held at the field. その球場で野球試合がある. ¶the labors of my predecessors in the field この方面における先輩の努力 ‖ other predecessors in the same field 同じ方面の他の先輩 ‖ These are not in my field (=line). これは私の専門でない ‖ workers in the field of production 生産方面に活動する人々 ‖ in any field of endeavor いかなる活動方面においても. ‖ Last year Fortune "broke the tape" in the field of travel advertising among all general monthly publications. 昨年度においてあらゆる一般月刊雑誌の中でフォーチューンは旅行広告の多いことにおいて首座を占めた. ¶in the fields where law and medicine meet 法律と医学の交渉する方面で. 【類】work in the field of sociological speculation (社会学的思索) / the completest and the most scholarly work (学究的な作品) in its own field / well known in the field of literature as "..." / The artist did not appear in the field until several years later. / almost alone in the field without a rival (独舞台) / But it soon transpired that profits of 200 and even 300 per cent were being realised by those who had been early in the field in the rubber planting movement. ¶one of the leading magazines of the field その方面の主要雑誌. ¶the beasts (plants) of the field 野生の獣(など). ¶for valor on the field of battle 戦場における勇気に対して ‖ Training alone wins the world's greatest victories, whether on the field of battle or in the battle of life. 戦場においても人生の戦においても独り訓練によってのみ世界の最大勝利が得られるのである. ‖ The Salvationist is taught to obey as is the soldier on the field of battle.—W. Booth. 救世軍軍人は戦場の軍人も同様服従することを教えられる. 【類】killed on the field of battle ‖ the Society for the Relief of the Families of Soldiers on the Field 出征軍人家族救済会 ‖ He died on the field of honor. 彼は名誉の戦死を遂げた. ¶take to the field 〖野球〗守備につく. ¶This is outside my field. これは私の専門外だ.

P² seek a fresh field for one's activities その活動に対する新生面を求める. ¶a field of corn 麦畑 ‖ a field of cultivated land 耕地. 【類】the field of English literature / in that interesting field of investigation which deals with ... ‖ the field of ocean 海洋 ‖ fields of knowledge 知識の分野.

field, v. 〖野球〗守備をする, 球をさばく.

M field a ball smartly 〖野球〗ボールを巧みにさばく.

fielding, n. 〖野球〗守備, 球さばき.

Q clean fielding 見事な守備. ¶poor (clever) fielding 〖野球〗へたな(うまい)球さばき(守備).

field marshal, n. 〖陸軍〗元帥.

Q Every private in the British army is a potential field marshal. 英軍の兵卒はみな元帥まで上進しうるのである.

fieldwork, n. 〖軍〗野堡(ほう).

V throw up fieldworks 野堡を築く(土のうなどを積みあげる).

fiend, n. 悪魔, 鬼, ...狂.

Q² the tragedy of a drink fiend and his innocent victims 飲ん平とその罪のない犠牲者の悲劇. ¶a high blood pressure fiend 血圧の高いのを苦にやむ人. ¶a morphine fiend モヒ中毒患者. ¶the organ (baseball, movie) fiend オルガン(など)狂. ¶an opium fiend 麻薬中毒者.

P² a fiend from Tartarus 地獄から出てきた鬼. ¶a fiend of mathematics 数学狂.

fierce, a. 恐ろしい, 猛烈な.

M Though very fierce outwardly, the dog was well tamed. 見たところすごいがその犬はよく人になれていた.

fiercest, n. 最も猛烈なこと.

P a debate at its fiercest その猛烈の絶頂に達した論争.

fight, n. 戦, 戦闘.

V carry a fight through 戦争をやり通す. ¶have a severe (=hard) fight 激しく戦う. ¶lead the fight for ... ...運動を指揮する. ¶lose a fight 戦に負ける. ¶make a good fight for ... ...のために善戦する. ¶put up a stubborn fight with the police 警察官とがん強に戦う. ¶The man immediately showed fight. その男は直ちに戦う気勢を示した. ¶start a fight on a trifle つまらないことでけんかを始める. ¶wage a losing fight 負け戦をやる. ¶win one's fight 戦に勝つ.

Q an all-out fight against ... ...に対する全力をあげての戦い. ¶there ensued the most awful fight between ... それから...間に恐ろしいけんかがあった. ¶a bloody fight 残忍な血戦. ¶covert fights 暗闘. ¶make a decisive fight for hegemony 雌雄を決する. ¶a defensive fight 防御戦. ¶after a desperate fight 死物狂いの戦をやったあげく. ¶a drunken fight 酔いどれのけんか. ¶after a fierce fight against ... ...との激しい戦の後. ¶a furious fight 猛烈な戦い. ¶have a hard fight 苦闘する. ¶The team won praise for its plucky fight. そのチームは勇敢な戦いで賞賛を博した. ¶They have no serious fights to fight. 彼らは別に本物の戦争をやる要はない. ¶a sham fight 擬戦. ¶a sharp fight 激戦. ¶a single fight 一騎打. ¶the game promises to be a snappy fight between ... その勝負は...間の小気味よい戦になりそうだ. ¶after putting up a strong fight to ... ...と激しく戦った後. ¶He fell in an unequal fight. 衆寡敵せずして彼は倒れた.

Q² a land (sea) fight 陸(海)戦. ¶make a last-ditch fight 背水の陣をしく. ¶a prize fight 〖拳闘〗懸賞試合. ¶a pillow fight "まくら合戦" (船上でやる遊戯). ¶a running fight 追撃戦. ¶a stand-up fight 〖拳闘・レスリング〗堂々たる勝負. ¶the hero of a hundred street fights 市街戦の勇士. ¶a bayonet fight 銃剣戦(白兵戦). ¶start a fist fight なぐり合いを始める. ¶The losing team put up a game fight. 負けかけていたチームがファイトをかき立てた(勇敢に戦った). ¶a gun fight 砲戦. ¶a hand-to-hand fight 白兵戦. ¶a knock-down-and-drag-out fight against ... ...とのなぐり倒し引きずり回す戦い.

P go for a fight けんかをやる.

P² a fight against crime 犯罪防止運動. ¶Sickness is just a fight between life and death. 病気は全く生と死の戦いである. ¶a fight for superiority (first place) 争覇(は)戦 ‖ an effective weapon in the fight for success 成功を収めるに有効な手段 ‖ a brave fight for right against wrong 破邪顕正のための勇敢な戦. ¶We had quite a fight on the subject. われらはその問題に関して随分戦った. ¶The religious fight over the use of chloroform is a thing of the past. クロロホルム使用に関する宗教上の論争は既に解決されている. ¶a fight to death 果し合い ‖ a fight to a finish in which either the one or the other dies どちらかが死ぬ果し合い. ¶have a fight with ... ...と戦う.

fight, v. 戦う, 争う.

M fight away 戦い続ける. ¶fight back 抵抗する, 食い止める, 口答えする. ¶fight bravely with ... ...と勇敢に戦う. ¶The race was very closely fought. その競走は非常な接戦であった. ¶fight desperately 死にもの狂いで戦う. ¶fight down 圧服する. ¶fight gallantly 勇敢に戦う. ¶fight hand-to-hand 接戦する. ¶fight heroically 勇敢に戦う. ¶fight magnificently 善戦する. ¶fight manfully against instead of weakly succumbing to ... ...にめめしく屈服す

ることなく男らしく戦う. ¶*fight **out*** to the better end あくまで戦って勝つ. ¶*fight* it ***out*** without fear おくせずあくまで戦う. ¶*fight **out*** a battle (quarrel) あくまで戦う(けんかする). ¶*fight **resolutely*** 奮闘する. ¶*fight **shy*** of eatables one is not used to 食べ慣れない食物に手を出さない. ¶***stoutly*** *fight* a disease 闘病する. ¶*fight **stubbornly*** against ... …とがん強に戦う. 【類】*fight **stubbornly*** for survival. ¶*fight* vermin ***successfully*** 害虫, 鳥, 獣など)を駆逐する. ¶They were *fighting **together*** for the prize. 彼らは賞を目指してともに戦った. ¶*fight **tooth and nail*** 極力戦う. ¶They fell *fighting **valiantly.*** 彼らは勇敢に戦って倒された.

M² *fight **off*** from a labor dispute 争議(スト)から手を引こうと努める. ¶*fight **on*** to the end 徹底的に戦い抜く ‖ *fight **on*** until we defeat the enemy 敵を撃破するまで戦い続ける. ¶prepare to *fight* the court conviction ***through*** to the Supreme Court 有罪判決に対して最高裁判所まで戦い抜く準備をする. ¶*fight **up*** against ... …と力戦奮闘する.

P *fight **against*** fearful odds 恐ろしい大敵と戦う ‖ *fight **against*** nature 横車を押す ‖ He has many temptations to *fight **against.*** 彼は抗戦すべき色々な誘惑を持っている. ‖ reformers *fighting **against*** an evil 悪弊と戦う改革者. 【類】*fight **against*** difficulties (the enemy, the country). ¶*fight **among*** themselves 同志打ちをする. ¶go to *fight **for*** one's country (the king) 祖国(など)のために戦う ‖ We are *fighting **for*** the cause of world civilization. われわれは世界文明のために戦っている. ‖ *fight **for*** liberty (peace) 自由(平和)のために戦う. ‖ For six years she *fought **for*** health. 六年間彼女は病と戦った. 【類】*fight **for*** existence / *fight **for*** fame / Some men *fight **for*** glory; some *fight **for*** wages. / *fight **for*** higher wages and better conditions of labor ‖ *fight **for*** the tram-car 電車に乗ろうと先を争う ‖ *fight **for*** one's life 必死に戦う. ¶*fight **for*** justice ***against*** force 正義のために暴力と戦う. 【類】*fight **for*** the weak ***against*** the strong. ¶He *fought **in*** fifty-seven battles. 彼は五十七回戦に参加した. ‖ He *fought **in*** several engagements. 彼は数回実戦に参加した. 【類】He *fought **in*** the Franco-Prussian War. / he *fought **in*** the battle of ... ‖ *fight **in*** a duel 決闘する ‖ He is *fighting **in*** its defence. 彼はその擁護のために戦っている. ‖ *fight* one's way ***in*** life (=***in*** the world) 奮闘して人生の進路を開拓する. ¶*fight **like*** a lion ししのごとく戦う. ¶The birds are *fighting **over*** an insect. 鳥が虫の奪い合いをやっている. ¶*fight* one's way ***through*** the enemy's country 敵国を切り抜ける. ¶*fight **to*** the death to regain liberty 自由を取戻すために死ぬまで戦う ‖ *fight **to*** the finish (=end) 最後まで戦う ‖ *fight **to*** the last [extremity] 最後まで戦う. 【類】I am quite determined that the lawsuit shall be *fought **to*** the last. 私は最後までその訴訟のために戦う覚悟である. ¶he *fought **under*** General ... 彼は…将軍の部下として戦った. 【類】In the battle of Anegawa (1570) Iyeyasu *fought **under*** Nobunaga. ¶*fight **with*** (=against) an enemy 敵と戦う ‖ He is now *fighting **with*** death in a hospital. 彼は今病院で死と戦っている. ‖ *fight **with*** a force twice their numbers 二倍の軍勢と戦う ‖ He *fought **with*** the robber for life. 彼は殺されまいとして賊と戦った. ‖ *fight **with*** swords (the fists) 刀(など)で戦う ‖ *fight **with*** great bravery 非常に勇敢に戦う ‖ *fight **with*** each other ***for*** ... …のために互いに争う ‖ *fight **with*** success against ... …と戦って勝つ ‖ Words and facts are the weapons ***with*** which business battles are *fought*. 言葉と事実は商売上の戦の武器だ.

fighter, *n.* 闘士; 戦闘機.

V The province has ***bred*** the best *fighters* and the best thinkers. その国から一番りっぱな軍人や一番りっぱな思想家が出た.

Q a ***two-fisted*** *fighter* 両こぶしで戦う人.

Q² an ***air*** *fighter* 飛行戦士. ¶a ***fire*** *fighter* 消防士. ¶an amateur ***fire*** *fighter* しろうと消防士. ¶a ***first-line*** *fighter* 第一線の軍人. ¶an ***inflation*** *fighter* インフレ抑制者. ¶a ***jet*** *fighter* ジェット戦闘機. ¶a ***Lightning*** *fighter* ライトニング戦闘機. ¶a ***long-range*** *fighter* 長距離戦闘機. ¶an ***underground*** *fighter* 潜行闘士.

P² *fighters **in*** the election 選挙の闘士.

fighting, *n.* 戦闘, 闘争.

V We had not ammunition enough to ***hold out*** a single day's *fighting*. こっちにはたった一日の戦争を継続するほどの弾薬もなかった. ¶***shirk*** *fighting* 戦闘を回避する.

Q ***bitter*** *fighting* 激戦. ¶***fierce*** *fighting* 激戦. ¶after ***heavy*** *fighting* 激戦の後. ¶a ***severe*** *fighting* 一回の激戦. 【類】It was the ***severest*** *fighting* ever staged during the war period. ¶***sharp*** *fighting* 烈しい戦闘. ¶they did such ***splendid*** *fighting* at ... 彼らは…で非常にりっぱな戦闘振りを見せた. ¶***stubborn*** *fighting* がん強な戦闘.

Q² old-fashioned ***fire*** *fighting* 旧式の消防. ¶***full-scale*** *fighting* 本格の戦闘. ¶desperate ***hand-to-hand*** *fighting* 必死の白兵戦. 【類】ugly ***hand-to-hand*** *fighting* (なぐり合いのけんか) between ... ¶a ***large-scale*** *fighting* 大規模の戦闘. ¶There was a great deal of ***street*** *fighting* staged during the revolution. 革命の間にはしばしば市街戦が行われた.

P The garrison of 2,000 surrendered ***without*** *fighting*. 二千の守備隊は戦わずして降参した.

P² bitter *fighting **at*** close quarters 激烈な近接戦.

fighting-man, *n.* 戦士.

Q The Turkish soldier has been known as an ***excellent*** *fighting-man*. トルコの兵士は由来りっぱな戦士として知られている.

figurative, *a.* 比ゆ的な.

M ***highly*** *figurative* 非常に比ゆ的な.

figure, *n.* (**1**) 数字; 価, 値段.

V They will be willing to ***accept*** lower *figures*. 先方ではもっと安い値でも承知するでしょう. ¶***add up*** *figures* 数字を計算する. ¶***change*** a *figure* 数字を変更する. ¶***cite*** *figures* (統計の)数字を引用する. ¶His work now ***commands*** huge *figures*. 彼の作は当今巨額の値がする. ¶*figures* ***compiled*** by the Home Department show that ... 内務省編集の統計によると…となる. ¶***erase*** a *figure* 数字を消す. ¶***give*** *figures* 数字を示す. 【類】No *figure* was ***given.*** ¶***Name*** the lowest *figure* you can take. いくらまで引けるか言って御覧なさい. ¶Reducing the results of his investigations to the ratios per 10,000, he ***obtained*** the following *figures*: 彼の調査の結果を一万の比率に引直して見て彼は次の数字を得た. ¶He was not ***offered*** a round *figure*. 彼はまとまった金は提供されなかった. ¶***pay*** a tall *figure* for his services 彼に対して多額の俸給を払う. ¶Some ***place*** the *figure* at 10,000. この数字を一万とする者もある. ‖ some more sanguine and optimistic ***place*** the *figures* as high as ... もっと希望的観測をする連中はこの数字を…位にまで高く見積る. ¶***publish*** some alarming *figures* showing ... 驚くべき数字を発表しているがそれによると… 【類】He ***published*** the following *figures* as a result of his investigations. ¶***put*** the *figure* at 50,000 この数字を五万とする. ¶*Figures* ***quoted*** are approximate only. あげた数字は概略にすぎない. ¶This will ***raise*** the *figure* considerably. そうすると余ほど数字が大きくなる. ¶The *figure* of 10,000 has been ***reached.*** 一万台に達した. ¶Nowadays people ***regard*** such a *figure* as small! 今日から見るとこうした数字は大したものとはみられない. ¶***run*** the *figure* ***up*** 数を増大する. ¶***show*** a record *figure* 記録的な数字を示す. ¶the *figures* ***tabulated*** in this publication この刊行物に表示された数字.

V² The *figures* ***show*** that ... その統計によると…となる. The *figures* do not ***tally*** with ours. その数字はわれわれの方と合わない.

Q an ***actual*** *figure* 実数. ¶The number of Western books brought into Japan, or translated into Japanese, more or less fully, reaches ***amazing*** *figures*. 日本に輸入されたまたは多少とも日本語に翻訳された西洋の本は驚くべき数字に達する. ¶an ***approximate*** *figure* 近似値. ¶an ***astonishing*** *figure* 驚くべき数字. ¶as a cap upon all these ***astounding*** *figures* こうした巨大な数字があるその上に. ¶run into ***astronomical*** *figures* 天文学的(億とか兆とかいう)数字に達する. ¶result in ***big*** *figures* 大きい数字になる. ¶By November this organization showed ***black*** *figures*. 十一月にはこの会社の赤字がなくなった. ¶sell at a ***close*** *figure* 原価に近い値段で売る. ¶show in ***cold*** *figures* 赤裸々な統計で示す. ¶***conservative*** *figures* 内輪に見積った数字. ¶run up to a ***considerable*** *figure* 相当の数に上る. ¶a ***decimal*** *figure* 小数. ¶before his age had got into ***double*** *figures* 十代前に. ¶***delusive*** *figures* 人を誤らせる数字. ¶The ***exact*** *figures* with regard to ... are difficult to obtain. …に関する正確な数字は得難い. ¶reach (count) ***four*** *figures* 四けたの数字に達する(なる). ¶at a ***high*** *figure* 高価で ‖ the ***higher*** *figures* [二つの数の内]大きな方の数.

¶*important figures* on glassware production just given out by the Government 政府が発表したばかりのガラス器生産高に関する重要な数字. ¶an *inferior figure* 下添小文字(H_2 などのような). ¶the *larger figure* [二つの中]大きい方の数字. 【類】Last year's foreign trade shows the *largest figures* ever recorded. ¶according to the *latest available figures* 手に入れられる最近の数字によると. ¶fall to extremely *low figures* 極めて小さい数字になる ‖ offer at *low figures* 安い値段で提供する. 【類】supply at an exceedingly *low figure* ‖ a *low figure* for the population その人口に対する内輪の数. ¶at the *lowest possible figure* できるだけ内輪に見積って. ¶rent houses at *moderate figures* 安い家賃で家を貸す. ¶according to the *official figures* of the Chamber of Shipping 海運会議所の公表した数字によると. 【類】though there are no *official figures*. ¶The articles are marked in *plain figures*. その品は正札付である. ¶*Precise figures* are not obtainable. 正確な数字は得られない. ¶*prewar figures* 戦前の数字(値段など). ¶a *provisional figure* 暫定数字. ¶at a *reasonable figure* 相当の値段で. ¶*reliable figures* 確かな数字. ¶in *rough figures* 概算で. ¶in *round figures* 端数を棄てて, 大づかみで. ¶reach the rather *staggering figure* of $376,000 三十七万六千ドルという驚異的数字に達する. ¶verify *statistic figures* 統計の数字を確かめる. ¶sell at a *stiff figure* 高い価で売る. ¶a *stupendous figure* in that day 当時としては巨大な数字. ¶*superior figures* (A^2 のごとき)肩書数字. ¶*tabulated figures* 表にした数字. ¶The *total figures* are the biggest for the last five years. その総数はこの五年間で最も大きい. ¶The foreign trade has risen to an *unprecedented figure*. 外国貿易が未曽有の数字に上った.

Q² the *bedrock* (=*bottom*) *figure* 最低値段. ¶be first in *circulation figures* 発行部数において首位を占める. 【類】the *circulation figures* of the various newspapers. ¶*December figures* 十二月に対する数字. ¶according to *Government figures* 政府発表の数字によると. ¶*population figures* 人口統計. ¶reach *record figures* 記録的の数に達する. ¶a *red ink figure* 赤字. ¶The President told them his $37.5 billion budget was a "*rock bottom*" *figure*. 大統領は 375 億ドル予算は最小の数字だと彼らに語った. ‖ We buy publishers' "remainders" at a price that enables us to sell them at *rock bottom figures*. われわれは出版者の残品を最底値段で売っても引合うほどの値で買う. ¶a *subscript figure* [O_2 などのような] 数字の下に添えた小数字. ¶the *unemployment figure* reached almost 90,000 as a result of ... …の結果失業者の数はほとんど九万に達した. ¶a *10-digit figure* 十億. ¶enter into the *2,000,000 figure* 二百万台になる.

P remain *above* the 300,000 *figure* 三十万台に留まる. ¶He is good *at figures*. 彼は計算がうまい. ‖ I will supply *at* the *figures* named. 仰せの値段で差上げましょう. ‖ *at* a good *figure* 良い価で. ¶His fortune is counted *by* the six *figures*. 彼の財産は十万位をもって数えられる. ¶the world *in figures* 統計で示した世界 ‖ estimate ... *in figures* …数字で評価する. ¶a man *of figures* 数学家, 統計家 ‖ a sum (number) *of* four *figures* 四けたの金額(数字). ¶check up *on* the *figures* 数字をチェック(照合)する. ¶attain *to* the enormous *figure* of ... …というばく大な数字に達する ‖ mount up *to* a *figure* somewhere in the neighborhood of ... …近くの数字に達する. ¶juggle *with figures* in order to disguise the fact that ... …という事実を隠すために数字をごまかす.

P² a *figure* somewhere *around* $18,000 一万八千ドルがらみの代価. ¶*figures in* tons トンで示した諸数字.

(**2**) 格好, 姿, 形状; 像, 肖像; 模様; 図; 人物, 立物; 顕著, 異彩; 羽振り.

V *adopt* the *figure* of a lion as their trademark ライオンの模様を店の商標として採用する. ¶a coin that *bears* the *figure* of an angel 天使の像のついている貨幣. ¶*cut* a miserable *figure* みじめなことになる ‖ *cut* a brilliant *figure* りっぱな風に見える, 目立つ, 異彩を放つ ‖ The salaries of the junior teachers would *cut* but little *figure*. 下級の教師の俸給は大した金高にはならない. ¶He *cuts* no *figure* (=counts for nothing). 《米》彼はとるに足らない(ものにならない). ‖ *cut figures* from paper 紙から型を切る ‖ a *figure cut* in marble 大理石に彫刻した像. ¶*embroider figures* on velvet びろうどに模様の縫取りをする. ¶*erect* one's *figure* 姿勢を正す. ¶The peak *forms* a conspicuous *figure* in the landscape. その峰がそこの景色の中で目に立つ. ‖ Cat's cradle is a game played by *forming figures* from string. あや取りは糸であやを造る遊戯である. ¶She *has* the *figure* of a sylph. 彼女はすらりとした姿をしている. ¶*improve* the *figure* 姿をよくする. ¶*make* a *figure* in the eye of the public 人目に立つ ‖ *make* (=cut) a sorry *figure* みすぼらしい ‖ What can have induced you to *make* such a *figure* of yourself? なんだって君はこんな変なことをする気になったのか. ‖ *make* a *figure* of a cross 十字形を成す. ¶The corset *molds* the *figure*. コルセットは姿をよくする. ¶*play* quite a social *figure* among ... …間に大いに幅をきかす. ¶She *possesses* a good *figure*. 彼女は姿が良い. ¶His death *removes* a *figure* long familiar in the club. 彼が死んでクラブで長い間見慣れた姿が見られなくなった. ¶a *figure sculptured* in relief 浮彫にした像. ¶I could *see* a dark *figure* in the moonlight. 月光に暗い物影がうかがわれた. ¶His *figure* was *swallowed up* in the gloom. 彼の姿は暗の中に吸込まれてしまった.

「春期にむっちりしてくる.

V² The *figure* of a girl *fills out* at puberty. 少女の姿は青

Q cut an *abject figure* before the eyes of the nations 世界国民の目前であさましい格好をする. ¶He is of *athletic figure* and tendencies. 彼は運動家の体と好みを持っている. ¶George Washington is the *best known figure* in American history. ジョージ・ワシントンは米国史上最も著名の人物だ. ¶a *bronze figure* 銅像. ¶the *central figure* of a story 話の主人公 ‖ the *central figure* of the group その一団の中心人物. 【類】Plato, the *central figure* in Greek philosophy / the *central figure* of his epoch (時代) / the *central figure* in the British welcome extended to ... ¶the *chief figure* in the celebration 祝賀の中心人物. ¶a *colossal figure* 巨大な人物. ¶cut a *conspicuous figure* 頭角を現わす. 【類】a *conspicuous figure* in the political world. ¶cut a *dashing figure* 羽振りがよい. ¶cut a most *disreputable figure* はなはだ人聞きの悪いことをやる. ¶*distinguished figures* in the faculty 教職員中有力な人物. ¶a *distinguished public figure* 知名の公人. ¶a *dominant figure* in the moving picture world 映画界の巨頭. ¶Goethe is the *dominating figure* of German literature. ゲーテはドイツ文学の驍(ぎょう)将である. ¶an *eminent figure* in the history of England's industrial supremacy 英国の産業発達史中卓越した人物. ¶a *familiar figure* in unfamiliar garb—General ... in civilian's dress 見慣れない服装の見慣れた人物—平服の…将軍. ¶He cut a *fine figure* in that matter. 彼はその事件で男をあげた. ¶a *five-sided figure* 五角形. ¶She has a *frail figure*. 彼女はかよわい(なよなよしている). ¶a *geometrical figure* 幾何学的図形. ¶a *gigantic figure* of Buddha hewn out of the living rock 自然岩に刻んだ巨大な仏像. ¶The girl has a *good figure*. その少女の姿がよい. ¶make a *great figure* in the world 世界の大立物になる. 【類】a *great figure* in South African politics / a *great figure* in a great cause (大義を唱うる) / Count Mirabeau, one of the *great figures* of the French Revolution. ¶a *grotesque figure* 奇怪な像. ¶a *historic figure* 歴史的人物. ¶make an *imposing figure* 押し出しが堂々としている. ¶an *international figure* 世界的人物. ¶his *lanky figure* 彼のやせぎすな姿. ¶the *leading figure* in English politics 英国政界の巨頭. 【類】the *leading figures* in art, screen, stage, and radio. ¶a *life-sized nude figure* 等身大の裸像. ¶a *long, slim figure* 高くてほっそりした姿. ¶a *long, skinny figure* のっぽでやせっぽ. ¶the *main figure* in the picture その映画の主役. ¶a *miserable figure* みすぼらしい格好. ¶a *mystic figure* 神秘的人物. ¶become a *national figure* 国家的な人物になる. ¶The price cuts *no figure*. It is a case of "shut your eyes and buy." 《米》値段は問題にならない. それは目をふさいで買えるようなものだ. ¶a *notable figure* in the pantheon of contemporary letters 現代文士中の著名な人物. ¶one of the most *odious figures* 最も忌まわしい人物. ¶the *outstanding figure* in the electrical world 電気界に傑出した人物. 【類】an *outstanding figure* in Japanese politics. ¶The sick child was a *pathetic* little *figure*. その病児は哀れな小さな姿をしていた. ¶cut a *peculiar figure* in the English eye 英国人の目に異様に見える. ¶a most *picturesque figure* 見てきわめて美しい人物. ¶he cut a *pitiable figure* in the eyes of ... 彼は...から見て特に可哀相であった. ¶He makes but a ***poor figure*** in the House. 彼は議院では一向目立たない. ‖ cut a ***poor figure*** in the last performance この前の演技でへまをやった. ¶a ***popular figure*** in nightclub life 夜間クラブ生活の人気者. ¶The muslin is of a ***pretty figure***. このモスリンの模様は美しい. ¶one of the ***principal figures*** in the organization その団体で重要な人物の一人. ¶a ***prominent figure*** in Japanese journalism 日本新聞界で傑出した人物. 【類】a ***prominent figure*** is early submarine telegraphy / a ***prominent figure*** in the public library world. ¶a ***queenly figure*** 女王のような姿. ¶a ***recumbent figure*** 横になった姿. ¶a ***ridiculous figure*** おかしな人物. ¶He has got up to a very ***respectable figure*** now. 彼は今は非常にりっぱな人物になっている. ¶Dr. Eliot was one of the most ***revered figures*** in the world of learning. エリオット博士は学界で最も尊重されている一人であった. ¶a ***romantic figure*** 小説的な人物. ¶the ***shapely figure*** of Mt. Fuji 富士山の格好のよい姿. ¶He was a ***slender figure***, rather below than above the medium height. 彼は中背以上といいたいが寧ろ以下のやせぎすな男であった. ¶a ***slender*** and ***graceful figure*** やせぎすでしとやかな姿. ¶His ***figure*** is ***small***. 彼は小作りだ. ¶cut a ***sorry figure*** みそをつける. ¶a ***spare figure*** 痩せぎす. ¶make a ***splendid figure*** 異彩を放つ. ¶a ***stalwart figure*** がん丈な骨格. ¶a ***stooping figure*** こごんでいる姿. ¶a ***striking figure*** in our national life 日本人中異彩を放っている人物. ¶his ***tall, bent, spare figure*** 彼の背の高い前こごみのやせたからだ. ¶see a ***thick set figure*** in the distance 遠くに肥ってずんぐりした人の姿が見える. ¶a ***unique figure*** 独特の人物. ¶a ***venerable figure*** 気高い高齢の人物. ¶have a ***well-developed figure*** 発育のよいからだをしている. ¶a ***well-known*** and ***respected figure*** 有名な尊敬されている人物. ¶a ***white-robed figure*** 白衣の人物. ¶a popular soprano with a voice of fine timbre, a ***willowy figure***, cherry lips, chestnut hair, and hazel eyes 音色の美しい声, 柳のような姿, 桜色のくちびる, くり色の毛髪, はしばみ色の目の人気あるソプラノ歌手. ¶Such people always make a ***figure wretched***. こういう人間はへまをやる.

Q^2 an ***academy figure*** けいこ画(人物特に裸体の); 落着または釣り合のとれていない人物画. ¶the ***key figures*** in Japan's public life 日本の政界における要人. ¶a ***movieland figure*** 映画人. ¶***plane figures*** 平面図形. ¶Chinese ***tomb figures*** 中国墳墓の模様. ¶a ***world figure*** 世界的人物.

P live ***in figure*** はでに生活する. ¶a man ***of*** some ***figure*** 多少世に知られた人.

P^2 great ***figures in*** literature 文豪 ‖ a ***figure in*** wood (stone, bronze) 木(など)像. ¶the ***figure of*** the earth 地球の形状. ¶***figure of*** distress 苦痛の姿.

(3) 詞藻(しそう), 文彩.

V to ***change*** the ***figure*** 比ゆをかえて言うと. ¶This ***figure*** may be ***taken*** literally. この比ゆは文字通りに解釈してよい.

Q It is no ***mere figure*** of speech to call business a profession. 商売を高等職業と呼ぶのは単なる言葉のあやではない(実際知力が必要だから). ¶"Only a cold," is a ***static figure*** of speech.「ほんのかぜです」というのはきまり文句である.

P ***without*** a ***figure*** 全く形容を抜きにして.

P^2 a ***figure of*** speech 言葉のあや ‖ a ***figure of*** rhetoric 文章のあや.

figure, *v.* 計算する, 数字で記す, 目立つ, 異彩を放つ; 表示する; 《米口》考える, 察する.

M ***figure accurately*** and ***quickly*** 正確にかつ敏速に計算する. ¶***approximately figure*** 概算する. ¶The Franco-Austrian War of 1859 was a war in which France ***figured chivalrously***. 一八五九年の仏墺戦争はフランスが勇名をとどろかした戦争であった. ¶***figure conspicuously*** 著しく目立つ. ¶***figure foremost*** in the listその表で真先に目立つ. ¶***figured gallantly*** in the days of ... ...の時代に異彩を放った. ¶The topic ***figured largely*** in the conversation. その話題が会話で幅をきかした. ‖ Commerce ***figures largely*** in the prosperity of the city. 商業が同市繁栄の主因を成している. 【類】The diseases ***figure*** most ***largely*** in the death-rate (死亡率) of the nation. ¶These commodities ***figure little*** in foreign trade. これらの商品は外国貿易で重きをなさない. ¶Just ***figure*** it ***out*** yourself. 《米》まあ自分で考えて見給え. ‖ This is the way the report ***figures*** it ***out***. 報告ではこういう説明をしている. ‖ ***figure out*** a sum 総計を出す. 【類】***figure out*** the tax rate (税率) ‖ be ***figured out*** at ... 合計...と算出される ‖ try to ***figure out*** what is behind the utterances 言葉の裏を察しようと試みる ‖ How can you ***figure*** that ***out***? どうしてそれがわかりますか. ¶the persons who ***figure in*** the novel その小説に出て来る人物. ¶***figure prominently*** before the world 世界で異彩を放つ ‖ Shiraz ***figures prominently*** in the history of Persian literature. シラーズはペルシア文学史上異彩を放つ都市である. 【類】The place ***figured prominently*** in the late war. ¶men whose names probably ***rarely figure*** in the newspapers except when ... ...以外には滅多に新聞紙上に名前を書き立てられることのない人々.

M^2 ***figure off*** (=***away***)=show off てらう, 見せびらかす. ¶***figure up*** 計算する, 合計する ‖ ***figure*** them all ***up*** それらを全部計算する ‖ I can't ***figure up*** what he meant to say. 私は彼が何を言おうとするのか一向分らない.

P He ***figured in*** the war. 彼は戦争で名を揚げた. ‖ Those names ***figure in*** the story of human progress. これらの名前が人類発達史上著しいものだ. 【類】He has already ***figured in*** this story. ‖ ***figured in*** pounds ポンドで示せば ‖ No less than a thousand persons ***figured in*** the funeral procession. 千人を下らない人が葬列に加わった. ‖ The exploit was ***figured in*** bronze. その功績は青銅に刻して表彰された. ‖ He scorns to ***figure in*** anything less than ten thousand. 彼は何につけても数万以下の取引をばかにする. ¶***figure on*** (=look to *or* depend on) a person for success (help) 《米》成功(など)で人を当てにする ‖ She ***figured*** (=counted) ***on*** marrying him. 彼女は彼と結婚することを当てにした. ¶***figure to*** oneself 心に描く, 想像する. ¶Plymouth ***figures*** in Anglo-Saxon times ***under*** the name of Tamarworth. プリマスはアングロ・サクソン時代にはタマーワースであった. ¶***figure upon*** the nation's finances 国家の財政を計算する.

O I ***figured*** him to be about thirty years of age. 私は彼を「三十歳位と推定した.

figurine, *n.* 小像.

Q^2 an ***ivory figurine*** 象牙の小像. ¶a ***pottery figurine*** 陶器「の小像.

filament, *n.* 繊維; 〖電気〗[電球の]フィラメント.

V The ***filament*** is ***wound off*** on a reel. [繭の]糸は糸巻に巻き取る.

V^2 The ***filament*** has ***snapped***. 繊維(電球の繊条など)がプッ「ツリ切れた.

Q a ***tenuous filament*** 細いフィラメント.

file, *n.* とじ込(ファイル); 列.

V ***keep*** a ***file*** of the magazine for reference 参考用にその雑誌のつづり込みを保存して置く.

Q wait in a ***long file*** 長い縦列になって待つ. ¶a ***permanent file*** 保存書類つづり込み. ¶march in a ***single file*** 一列縦隊になって行進する.

Q^2 Your name will be removed from our ***mailing file***. 郵送簿から貴名を削除します. ¶There are some breaks in the ***newspaper file***. 新聞とじ込みに欠号がある. ¶be recorded on the ***police file*** 警察の書類に記録される(前科者など).

P This card should be kept ***on file*** for reference. このカードは参考用にファイルしておかねばならない. ‖ We have principal Tokyo dailies ***on file***. 主な東京の日刊新聞はファイルしてあります. 【類】These are ***on file*** at the office. / place the documents ***on file***.

file, *v.* とじ込む; [願書などを]提出する; 列をなして進む.

M ***file away*** letters 手紙をとじ込む. ¶The spectators ***filed out*** into the street. 見物人は街上へ縦列をなして出て行った.

M^2 The guests ***filed in*** through rows of waiting footmen. 客は待ち受けている給仕人の間を列を作ってくり込んで行った.

P ***file*** a petition ***against*** a person 人を相手取って告訴する. ¶***file*** an application ***for*** admittance to a school 入学願書を提出する. 【類】An application was ***filed for*** permission (許可請願書). ¶The jury ***filed into*** the jury room to make their decision. 陪審員が採決のために陪審員室へ入って行った. ¶***file past*** ... 列を成して...の前を通過する. ¶***file*** an application (a petition) ***with*** the authorities 当局に願書(など)を出す. 【類】A large number of applications have been ***filed with*** the local government. ‖ accusations ***filed with*** the police 警察に持出した告訴.

file, *n.* やすり.

V It ***need*** the *file*. まだ仕上げがいる(未完成だ).
Q a ***finger nail*** *file* 指のつめやすり.

file, *v*. やすりをかける.

M *file* ***away*** (=***off***) rust さびをやすりで削り落す. 【類】*file* ***away*** (=***off***) the rough surface of ... ¶*file* it ***smooth*** やすりをかけてなめらかにする.

filial, *a*. 孝順な.

P *filial* ***to*** one's parents 親に孝行な.

filings, *n. pl.* [やすりをかけた]削りくず.

Q^2 be flecked with ***brass*** *filings* 真ちゅうの削りくずではん点がついている. ¶***iron*** (***steel***) *filings* 鉄(鋼鉄)の削りくず.

fill, *n*. 十分, 一杯.

V She ***cried*** her *fill*. 彼女は思う存分泣いた. ¶***Eat*** and ***drink*** your *fill*. There is plenty for all of us. 腹一杯飲み食いし給え. 十分行き渡るほどあるんだから. ¶Let her ***fret*** her *fill*. じれるだけじらして置け. ¶***get*** one's *fill* 腹一杯食う(飲む). ¶***have*** one's *fill* of pure air 新鮮な空気を胸一杯に吸う. ¶***take*** one's *fill* of refreshments 腹一杯茶菓を平げる. ¶***weep*** one's *fill* 思う存分泣く.

P^2 a *fill* ***of*** tobacco 一服のタバコ.

fill, *v*. 満たす, 一杯にする.

M *fill* a position ***capably*** 職務をりっぱに果す. ¶*fill* ***out*** the attached blank 添付した白紙に書き入れる ‖ *fill* ***out*** an order form 注文用紙に書入れる ‖ *fill* ***out*** (=***in***) a questionnaire 質問書に事項を書入れる ‖ ***properly*** *fill* ***out*** a blank 空白に適当な書入れをする ‖ The tea was *filled* ***out***. 茶がなみなみ注がれた. 【類】You are requested to *fill* ***out*** the blank (=*fill* ***up*** the form). / Please *fill* ***out*** the answers to the following quetions. ¶The hall was ***pretty much*** *filled*. ホールはかなり一杯だった. ¶The theatre was *filling* ***rapidly***. 劇場はたちまち込んできた.

M^2 *fill* ***in*** a moat 堀を埋め立てる ‖ *fill* [***in***] the blanks 空所を埋める ‖ *fill* ***in*** the detail 細目を書込む ‖ *fill* ***in*** a page 一ページ埋める ‖ *fill* ***in*** particulars into a form 事項を用紙に書込む ‖ *fill* ***in*** ellipses 文の省略した部分を書入れる ‖ *Fill* ***in*** when applicable and when information is available. 事項が該当するかまたは適当ならそれを書入れて下さい. 【類】The article is long enough to *fill* ***in*** two pages and some more columns. / *fill* ***in*** the gap. ¶*Fill* ***up*** the rat's hole right away. ねずみの穴をすぐにふさぎなさい. ‖ *fill* ***up*** a form=《米》*fill* ***out*** a blank 用紙に書入れる ‖ Please *fill* ***up*** the blanks in the order sheet. 注文用紙に書き入れて下さい. ‖ A report of the accident *fills* ***up*** a column of that paper. その事件の報道はその新聞の一段を埋めている. ‖ The old lady *filled* ***up*** the time between supper and retiring with knitting. その老婦人は夕食と就寝の間の時間を編物に使った. ‖ *fill* ***up*** a deficiency 不足を補う ‖ *fill* ***up*** a lacuna in one's knowledge その知識の欠陥を補う ‖ a metal foil for *filling* ***up*** a decayed tooth 虫歯を埋める箔 ‖ I have no duty to *fill* ***up*** for the moment. 当面の用事がない. ‖ a river *filled* ***up*** with sand and mud 砂と泥でふさがった川. 【類】*fill* ***up*** an application form and hand it back to the secretary / *fill* ***up*** documents in detail / *fill* ***up*** a vacancy (空席) / a room *filled* ***up*** with various articles of furniture.

P The auditorium was *filled* ***to*** the doors. 講堂は立すいの余地もなかった. ¶The hall was *filled* ***to*** overflowing. その会館は満員であった. ‖ It was *filled* ***to*** capacity. 満員であった. ‖ cars *filled* ***to*** their utmost limits 最大限度に満載した車 ‖ a basin *filled* ***to*** the brim with water なみなみと水をたたえた水ばち. 【類】The building was *filled* ***to*** its utmost capacity. ‖ The hotels of the capital are *filled* ***to*** repletion (満員) overnight with visitors from all parts of the country. ¶I was *filled* ***with*** envy of his digestive powers. 私は大いに彼の消化力の偉大さをうらやんだ. ‖ It *fills* us ***with*** admiring envy. ただもう感心するやらうらやましいやら. ‖ His kindness *filled* my heart ***with*** gratitude. 彼の親切に対する感謝の念で私の胸が一杯だった. ‖ Their eyes were *filled* ***with*** tears. 彼らは目に一杯涙をたたえていた. ‖ a letter *filled* ***with*** compliments お世辞たっぷりの手紙 ‖ *filled* ***with*** pride 自負心に燃えて ‖ *fill* a person ***with*** surprise 人をびっくりさせる. 【類】*filled* ***with*** delight / be *filled* ***with*** anxiety as to the future / This plot (陰謀) *filled* us all ***with*** terror. / And now buses and trams begin to *fill* ***with*** laughing, chattering myriads returning from the theatres, and with shop assistants just emancipated. / *fill* the purse ***with*** money / a theatre *filled* ***with*** people / The vessel was *filled* ***with*** water.

filling, *n*. 詰め物; 記入.

Q ***blank*** *filling* 様式記入.

Q^2 ***gold*** *fillings* in teeth 歯に金の充てん.

P^2 *filling* ***for*** a tooth 歯の充てん物.

fillip, *n*. 刺激物.

V ***give*** them a real *fillip* 彼らに本当の刺激を与える. ¶The business has ***received*** a *fillip*. その商売は刺激を受けた.

P^2 That acted as a *fillip* ***to*** my spirits. それが刺激となって私は元気が出た.

film, *n*. フィルム, 映画; 薄膜; 目のかすみ.

V The Board of Reviews has the power of ***banning*** a *film*. 検閲局が映画上映禁止の権能を有している. ¶***censor*** *films* 映画を検閲する. ¶***develop*** *films* フィルムを現像する. ¶***display*** *films* 映画を見せる. ¶the *film* being ***exhibited*** when we entered showed ... われわれがはいったときやっていた映画は…の場面であった. ¶*Films* have been ***founded*** on these novels. これらの小説は映画化された. ¶the *film* is now being ***produced*** at a studio at ... その映画は今…の撮影所で製作している. ¶The *film* is to be ***released*** through the ... circuit. 同映画は…系を通じて封切される. ¶The distributors ***route*** each *film* from one end of the country to the other. 配給者が各映画を国の端から端へと順次配給する. ¶***show*** a *film* 映画を上映する.

Q a ***banned*** *film* 禁止になった映画. ¶American ***comic*** and other ***dramatic*** *films* 米国喜劇及びその他の劇映画. ¶a ***documentary*** *film* 記録映画. ¶an ***educational*** and ***cultural*** *film* 教育び文化映画. ¶***entertainment*** *films* 娯楽映画. ¶an ***imported*** *film* 輸入映画. ¶a ***non-commercial*** *film* 文化映画. ¶a ***superimposed*** [*film*]〖映〗スーパーの入った映画. ¶when *films* were ***young*** 映画の初期に.

Q^2 an ***action*** *film*〖映〗活劇もの. ¶an ***advertising*** *film* 広告映画. ¶a ***box-office*** *film*=a BO film 入りのいい映画. ¶a ***Chaplin*** (***Disney***) *film* チャップリン(ディズニー)映画. ¶a ***feature*** [*film*] 特作映画. ¶a ***full-length*** *film*〖映〗長尺もの. ¶a ***gangster*** *film* ギャング映画. ¶a ***Hollywood*** *film* ハリーウッド製作映画. ¶an ***instruction*** *film* 教育映画. ¶a ***million-dollar*** *film* 百万ドル映画. ¶a ***motion-picture*** *film* 映画. ¶a ***natural color*** *film* 天然色映画. ¶a ***news-reel*** *film* 時事映画. ¶a ***propaganda*** *film* 宣伝映画. ¶a ***super-color*** *film* 超彩色映画. ¶a ***three-dimension***[***ed***] (=***3 D***) *film* 立体映画. ¶a ***technicolor*** [*film*]《米》天然色映画. ¶a ***travel*** *film* 旅行映画. ¶a ***wartime propaganda*** *film* 戦時宣伝映画.

P her career ***in*** *films* 彼女の銀幕経歴. ¶She will stay ***in*** *films*. 彼女は映画に落ちつくだろう. ¶go ***on*** the *films* 映画界に入る ‖ world history ***on*** the *film* 映画による世界歴史 ‖ David Copperfield ***on*** the *films* 映画化したデーヴィッド・カッパーフィールド.

P^2 a spool (=roll) ***of*** *film* フィルム一巻. ¶a *film* ***on*** a liquid 液体の薄い表皮. ¶a *film* ***over*** the eye 目のかすみ.

filmdom, *n*. 映画界. 「米国の影響を除く.

V ***de-Americanize*** Italian *filmdom* イタリアの映画界から

Q famous stars in ***American*** *filmdom* アメリカ映画界の一

film-land, *n*. 映画中心地. L流スター.

Q^2 ***Hollywood*** *film-land* ハリーウッド(映画製作地).

filter, *n*. ろ過器.

Q a ***domestic*** *filter* 家庭用ろ過器.

Q^2 an ***army regulation*** *filter* 陸軍規定のろ過器. ¶an ***electrostatic dust*** *filter* (静)電気フィルター. ¶a ***feedwater*** *filter* 給水ろ過器. ¶a ***reservoir*** or ***waterworks station*** *filter* 貯水池あるいは水道給水場ろ過器.

P purify water ***by*** a *filter* ろ過器で水を清浄にする. ¶pass it ***through*** a *filter* それをろ過器にかける.

filter, *v*. こす; 浸透する.

P European influence soon began to *filter* ***into*** Japan. やがて欧州の影響が日本にしみ込み始めた. ¶*filter* water ***through*** ... …で水をこす. 【類】*filtered* ***through*** the sand.

filth, *n*. 不潔; ごみ.

V Many of the most eminent of the early saints deliberately ***cultivated*** personal *filth*. 最も有名な昔の聖人中には努めて身体を不潔にした者が多かった.

P The ***alley*** was littered with garbage and other *filth*. 路次には台所のごみやその他いろいろのごみが散乱してい

fin, *n*. ひれ;〖空〗垂直安定板. Lた.

Q fish of ***every fin*** あらゆる魚類.
Q² a ***tail fin*** 尾翼の垂直安定板.

final, *n.* [しばしば *pl.*] 決勝戦, 最後の試合.
V ***play*** (***run***) ***in*** the *finals* 決勝に残る. ¶***take*** one's *finals* 最終試験を受ける.
Q the ***tennis*** (***baseball***) *finals* テニス(野球)決勝戦.

final, *a.* 最後の.
M My decision is ***quite*** *final.* 僕の決断は全く最後的のもLのだ.

finale, *n.* 終曲.
Q a ***fitting*** *finale* 適切な終局. ¶the ***grand*** *finale* came when ... …で大団円となった.

finality, *n.* 終局.
Q There appears to be ***no*** *finality* in the making of new kind of golf ball or club. 新型のゴルフ球や棒は続出して果しがないようだ.
P speak ***with*** *finality* 断固として言う(決定など).

finance, *n.* 財政; 財源.
V ***adjust*** the *finances* 財政を整理する. ¶***cripple*** the *finances* of the company 同会社の財政を乱す. ¶Great Britain no longer ***dominates*** international *finance* as she did. 大英帝国はもはや昔のように世界の金融界を支配していない. ¶***improve*** the *finances* of the country その国の財政を改善する. ¶***order*** *finances* 財政を整理する. ¶***readjust*** the *finances* 財政を再整理する. ¶Those officials do not ***understand*** *finance* at all. あの役人たちは一向財政のことが分っていない.
Q discuss ***high*** *finance* with a great banker 大銀行家と高等財政を論じる. ¶He made a speech on ***national*** *finance,* which is his favorite subject. 彼は得意の題目である国家財政について演説した. ¶***public*** *finance* 財政. ¶provide ***sufficient*** *finances* to ... …に十分な財源を供給する. ¶a ***wasteful*** and ***unskilful*** *finance* むだが多くて拙劣な財政.
Q² ***household*** *finance* 一家の財政. ¶***student*** *finance* 学生の経済.

finance, *v.* 財政をつかさどる; 資金をまかなう.
M ***adequately*** *finance* ... …に十分の資金を注ぎ込む. ¶*finance* ***wisely*** 財政をうまくやる.
P universities *financed* ***by*** the Government 官立大学. ¶*finance* students ***through*** schools and colleges 学生たちの学費をまかなってやる.

financier, *n.* 財政家.
Q an ***able*** *financier* 有能な財政家. ¶My wife is not a ***good*** *financier.* 僕の妻は家庭の経済がへただ. ¶Viscount Shibusawa, one of the most ***prominent*** *financiers* 最も有名な財政家の一人たる渋沢子爵. ¶***shady*** *financiers* うしろL暗い財政家.

financing, *n.* 財政をつかさどること.
Q ***central*** *financing* 財政の集中.
Q² ***deficit*** *financing* 赤字財政. ¶***occupation*** *financing* 占L領財政.

find, *n.* 見つけ物, 掘出し物.
V ***make*** a great *find* 大見つけ物をする‖It takes me to ***make*** a *find* like this. こういう掘出しは僕でないとできない(新スター発見など). ¶That anything still remains to be unearthed concerning Napoleon seems incredible; yet new *finds* are ***made*** every year. ナポレオンに関係のある遺物がまだ掘り出されるとは信じられないようだがしかも毎年新しい掘出し物がある.‖an interesting *find* was ***made*** by archæologists among the ruins of ... 考古学者が…の廃虚で興味ある発見をした.
P places of important ***archæological*** *finds* 考古学上重要な出土品のあった場所. ¶a ***big*** (=***great***) *find* in a second-hand bookstore 古本屋での大した掘出し物. ¶a ***lucky*** *find* うまい掘出し物. ¶a ***rare*** *find* 掘出しもの. ¶a sensational new ***screen*** *find* すばらしい映画の新人.

find, *v.* 見出す; 知る, さとる; 認定する; 支給する; 事件を決定して宣告する.
M *finding* myself ***alone,*** I began to think how ... 独りきりだったので…と考え始めた.‖She was *found* ***alone.*** 行って見たら彼女は一人でいた. ¶I *found* it very ***annoying,*** at first. 初めはうるさかった. ¶He was *found* ***dead.*** 彼は死んでいた. ¶Westerners *find* it ***difficult*** to enter into the spirit of Japanese art. 西洋人は日本の芸術の精神に透徹することがむずかしい. ¶There you'll *find* your way ***easily.*** そこから道は分りやすい. ¶I *found* him [to be] ***foolish.*** 彼はばかだと私に分った. ¶I *found* it ***gone.*** 私はそれがなくなっているのに気が付いた. ¶He was *found* ***guilty.*** 彼は有罪と認定された. ¶Such men are ***hardly*** to be *found.* こんな人たちはほとんどいない. ¶***How*** do you *find* yourself today? 今日は気分はどうですか.‖***How*** could you *find* your way there? どうしてそこで道が分りましたか. ¶I *found* it ***impossible.*** 不可能であるということが分った. ¶The jury *found* him ***innocent.*** 陪審官は彼を無罪と認定した. ¶it has been *found* ***invaluable*** for the cure of a long list of diseases and ailments, among which may be mentioned. ... それは色々な病気の治療に極めて有効であることが分った, そしてその中に…をあげることができる. ¶These qualities are not ***often*** *found* together. これらの性質を兼備する場合は余りない. ¶He *found* ***out*** the riddle. 彼はなぞを解いた.‖*find* ***out*** a thief (spy) 盗人(など)を見つける‖I couldn't *find* my way ***out.*** 出口が見つからなかった.‖science *found* ***out*** the law which regulates ... 科学は…を支配する法則を明らかにした‖endeavor to *find* ***out*** who are likely to tender their services 奉仕を申出そうな人間を見つけ出そうと努める‖I *found* him ***out.*** 出かけたが留守だった.‖cannot *find* ***out*** a proper answer 適当な答えが見つからない. 【類】*find* ***out*** a secret / *find* ***out*** a mistake (an error) / *find* ***out*** the cause of death (死因). ¶We *found* them most ***unequivocally*** in the Russian camp. 彼らがまぎれもなくソ連側であることを確かめた. ¶It will be *found* ***useful.*** それは有益だと分るだろう. ¶It has been *found* ***wanting.*** それが欠けていることが分った.
M² *find* ***up*** a money lender 金貸しを探し出す.
P I *found* him ***at*** home. 行って見たら彼は家にいた. ¶I *found* ***by*** long experience to ... 私は…することを長い経験によって知った. ¶The jury *found* ***for*** the plaintiff. 陪審員は原告に有利な認定をした. ¶I *found* an enthusiastic coadjutor ***in*** the person of a young fellow named ... 私は…という名の熱心な青年助手を得た.‖Dostoievski *finds* brothers ***in*** thieves and murderers. ドストイエフスキーは盗賊や人殺しを兄弟のように思う.‖***In*** him I *found* a true friend. 彼こそ真の友であった.‖We *found* victory ***in*** defeat. われわれは負けるが勝だと知った. ¶It will be *found* ***of*** interest. それはやって見ると面白いだろう.‖I *found* it ***of*** great use. それは大層私の役に立った. ¶A dagger was *found* ***on*** him when he was searched. 彼の体をしらべたら短刀がでた. ¶That is the only fault to be *found* ***with*** him. それは彼の唯一の欠点だ.
O if you add these all you will *find* that they total ... これら全部を寄せると皆で…になることが分るだろう.

finder, *n.* 探知機.
Q² a ***radio direction*** *finder* 無線方向探知機. ¶a ***range*** *finder* 測遠器.

finding, *n.* 決議, 評決.
V ***draw up*** *findings* 決議を起草する.
Q² ***cost*** *finding* 工費算定. ¶***fact*** *finding* 事実認定. ¶a ***United Nations*** *finding* 国際連合加盟国の評決.
P² *finding* ***of*** guilty 有罪認定.

fine, *n.* 罰金, 科料; 結末.
V ***assess*** a *fine* of ... against a person for ... …のかどにより その人に…の罰金を課する. ¶***impose*** a *fine* upon ... …に科料を課する. 【類】***impose*** a *fine* of 20 s. for each offence (違犯) / A *fine* will be ***imposed*** should this rule not be complied with. ¶***incur*** a *fine* of five shillings 五シリングの科料に処せられる. ¶***inflict*** a *fine* of ... on ... …を…の科料に処する. ¶a matter ***involving*** a *fine* 科料を免れない事件. ¶I have had to ***pay*** a *fine* on this letter. 私はこの手紙に不足税を払わされた. ¶***remit*** a *fine* 罰金を免除する.
Q a ***corrective*** *fine* 科料. ¶a ***heavy*** (***light***) *fine* 重い(軽い)科料. ¶a ***major*** *fine* 罰金. ¶impose the ***maximum*** *fine* of ... …という一番重い科料を課する. ¶a ***severe*** *fine* 重い科料. ¶pay a ***small*** *fine* 少額の科料を払う.
Q² ***freedom*** *fine* 同業組合加入金. ¶***police*** *fine* 科料. ¶a ***traffic violation*** *fine* 交通違犯科料.
P any violation of the provisions of the act is to be punished ***by*** a *fine* not to exceed ... この法律に触れた者は…を越えない額の罰金に処せられる. ¶***in*** *fine* 結局‖His demeanour, ***in*** *fine,* was truly that of a great king. 彼の態度は結局真に大王のそれであった.
P² a *fine* ***for*** an offence 違犯に対する科料‖sentence one to a *fine* ***for*** trespass 侵害に対し科料に処する. ¶a *fine* ***of*** ... yen …円の科料.

fine, *v.* 細かくする(なる).
M He endeavored ***to*** *fine* ***away*** the objections of his op-

ponents. 彼は反対者の抗議を次第に緩和するよう努めた. ‖ His coarse habits have gradually *fined away*. 彼の粗野な習癖が次第に洗練されてきた.

fine, *v*. 科料に処する.

M He was *fined* ***heavily*** for a breach of the police regulations. 彼は規則違犯で重い科料に処せられた.

P He was *fined* $... ***for*** participating in the assault. 彼はその襲撃に加わったかどで...ドルの科料に処せられた.

fine, *a*. 精巧な, こまかい; 純粋な.

M an ***exceptionally*** *fine* number of a magazine 雑誌の特別豪華版. ¶gold ***22 carats*** *fine* 二十二金.

P *fine* ***in*** texture (織物の)地はだのこまかい.

finery, *n*. 美装.

Q ***cheap*** *finery* 安物の装身具. ¶***female*** *finery* 婦人美装品. ¶***second-hand*** *finery* 古着の美装品.

Q² ***birthday*** *finery* 誕生日の美服. ¶hills in their ***fall*** *finery* 秋色美しい山々. ¶boys and girls in their ***Sunday*** *finery* 晴着を着た少年少女.

finesse, *n*. *F*. 手腕, 術策.

Q parts of the ***natural*** *finesse* of the game 予定行動の段階. ¶a ***paltry*** *finesse* 拙策.

finger, *n*. 指; 弾奏.

V Here you are rather apt to ***burn*** your *fingers*. ここんとこへ来ると皆がよく手を焼く. ¶My *fingers* are so ***contracted*** that I cannot hold my pen. 指がかじかんでペンが持てない. ¶I ***cut*** my *finger* with the knife. 僕はナイフで指を切った. ¶***flex*** one's *fingers* 指を曲げる. ¶He ***had*** his *finger* in the pie. 彼はいらぬことに干渉した. ¶***hold up*** a warning *finger* at ... ...に向って警告の指を示す. ¶***ink*** their *fingers* over their Latin exercises 彼らはラテン語の宿題で指をインキだらけにする. ¶***jam*** a *finger* in a door ドアで指をつぶす. ¶***kiss*** one's *fingers* to ... 自分の指にキスして遠くにいる...とのキスに替える. ¶***lay*** a *finger* on ... ...に責任を負わせる. 【類】No historian can ***lay*** his *finger* on any individual man and say he is the founder of the system of Bushido. ¶***lock*** one's *fingers* ***together*** 指を組合わせる. ¶She has been engaged before, and ***needs*** all her *fingers* to count how often. 彼女はこれまで婚約をしたことがある, でその数は指を皆使わなければ数えきれない. ¶***point*** one's *finger* at ... ...を指し示す ‖ ***point*** the *finger* of scorn at ... ...に軽べつの指を向ける. ¶***prick*** her *finger* with a thorn ばらで指を刺す. ¶***put*** one's *finger* in painting 絵に指を染める ‖ ***put*** one's *finger* on the trigger 引金に指を当てる ‖ ***put*** one's *finger* on a fault 欠点を指し示す ‖ ***put*** their *finger* upon the weak spots in its armor [会社の財政など] 武装の弱点を明示する. 【類】***put*** our *finger* accurately upon ... / ***put*** one's *finger* on the right thing from the first / he will have no difficulty in ***putting*** his *finger* on the root cause of (根本原因). ¶***raise*** a *finger* of protest against ... ...に反抗の指をあげる. ¶***run*** one's *fingers* through hair 髪の毛に指をつっ込む. ¶The master ***shook*** his *finger* at the idle boy. 先生は訓戒の指を振って怠け者の少年を戒めた. ¶***snap*** one's *fingers* at ... ...を指弾(軽べつ)する. ¶***twist*** one's *fingers* 指をねじる.

Q a ***burnt*** *finger* やけどした指. ¶the products of their ***deft*** *fingers* 彼らの器用な指で造った物. ¶point a ***denunciatory*** *finger* at ... ...に指をさして非難する. ¶the ***first*** *finger* of the hand 手の第一(人さし)指 ‖ as thick as one's ***first*** *finger* 人さし指位の太さの. ¶***flexible*** *fingers* しなやかな指. ¶She has a ***good*** *finger*. 彼女は楽器をうまく弾く. ¶***nimble*** *fingers* 指先の早業. ¶***slender*** *fingers* 細い指. ¶He has a very ***small little*** *finger*. 彼の小指は非常に小さい. ¶the ***third*** *finger* 第三(薬)指. ¶with a ***wet*** *finger* ぬれ手で, やすやすと.

Q² an ***index*** *finger* 《主に米》ひとさし指. ¶***taper*** *fingers* with rosy nails 桜色のつめのある先のほっそりした指. ¶***lily*** *fingers* ゆりのような白い指. ¶a ***ring*** *finger* くすり指. ¶hold up a ***warning*** *finger* at ... 指をあげて...を警戒する ‖ shake a ***warning*** *finger* at ... ...に向って警戒の指をふる.

P rub it ***between*** the *finger* and the thumb 指と親指との間でそれをこする ‖ a hair held ***between*** *finger* and thumb 親指と指の間に持った一本の毛髪. ¶The wedding ring should never be drawn ***off*** the *finger* after it has been placed there on the wedding day. 結婚の指輪は結婚の日に一たんはめたら決して指から抜くべきものでない. ¶wear a ring ***on*** a *finger* 指輪を指にはめる ‖ hair ***on*** the *finger* 指毛 ‖ They are so few in number that you may count them ***on*** your *fingers*. 非常に少いので指で数えることができる. ‖ count them off ***on*** one's *fingers* それを指で数える. 【類】place a ring ***on*** her *finger* / The engagement ring is to be worn ***on*** the third *finger* of the left hand. / I put my thimble ***on*** my *finger*. / I can count ***on*** my *fingers* ... / They could be numbered ***on*** the *fingers* of a single hand. / you can count ***on*** the *fingers* of one hand (五本の指で) the men in the country who ... / They might be counted ***on*** the *fingers* of one hand. ¶blow the nose ***with*** the *fingers* 手ばなをかむ ‖ ***with*** one's *finger* in one's mouth 指をくわえて, なす所なく.

finger, *v*. 指でさわる, 指でいじくる.

M *finger* ***out*** a tune on ... ...[楽器]で一節を指でかなでる.

M² Between peninsulas the misty ocean seemed ***to*** *finger* ***up*** like the fiords of Norway. その両半島間に霧深い大洋がノルウェーの峡湾のように指型に拡がっているらしかった.

P *finger* ***with*** a cat's tail ねこのしっぽをいじくる.

fingerprint, *n*. 指紋.

V Each word ***bears*** the *fingerprint* of a personality. 言葉はそれぞれそれを使う者の人格を示す. ¶***register*** (***take***) their *fingerprints* 彼らの指紋を取る.

finger-tip, *n*. 指先.

P a man of the world ***to*** his *finger-tips* あくまで世間なれのした人.

finical, *a*. 小やかましい.

P he is extremely *finical* ***upon*** matters of ... 彼は...にかけては実にやかましい.

finish, *n*. 終了, 完結; 仕上げ.

V ***add*** a *finish* to a view ある光景に点睛する. ¶His speech ***made*** a tame *finish*. 彼の演説は終りが振わなかった.

Q an ***artistic*** *finish* 芸術的仕上げ. ¶a ***close*** *finish* [競馬など] きわどい決勝. ¶a ***hot*** *finish* 手に汗を握らせる決勝. ¶***literary*** *finish* 文学的仕上げ.

P The prisoner behaved creditably ***at*** the *finish*. 犯人の最後の態度は見上げたものであった(死の宣告を下されたときなど). ¶resist this ***to*** the *finish* 最後までこれに抵抗する ‖ fight ***to*** a *finish* 勝負のつくまで戦う ‖ The rat is an enemy to be feared and fought ***to*** the *finish*. ねずみは恐るべき敵でとことんまで戦わねばならない ‖ a fight ***to*** the *finish* 決戦 ‖ The work has come ***to*** the *finish*. その仕事は終った.

P² the *finish* ***of*** a person's manners 行儀作法の仕上げ.

finish, *v*. 終える, 仕上げる; 尽す; 終る; 死ぬ.

M The war is ***evidently*** *finished*. 戦争はたしかに終った. ¶be ***nearly*** *finished* あらかたでき上っている. ¶be ***partly*** *finished* 一部でき上っている. ¶be not yet ***quite*** *finished* まだでき上らない. ¶His speech was *finished* a little too ***soon***. 彼の演説は切上げが少々早過ぎた.

M² *finish* it ***off*** それを完成する ‖ He *finishes* ***off*** the story in his usual manner. 彼はその物語の終りをいつものようにまとめている. ‖ A final is the ornament *finishing* ***off*** the apex of a roof, pediment, gable, canopy, and so on. 最後は屋根のせん頂, 破風, 切妻, 天がいその他の完成による装飾である. ‖ *finish* ***off*** with one's work その仕事を仕上げる. ¶He'll soon *finish* it ***up***. 彼は間もなく仕上げるだろう. ‖ If I can *finish* ***up*** my business soon enough, I shall be back. 仕事が早く済んだら直ぐに戻ります.

P We *finished* a bottle of wine ***between*** us. われわれは二人でぶどう酒一びん平げた. ¶The ground-work will be *finished* ***by*** that time. 基礎工事はその時までには完成するだろう. ‖ *finish* this ***by*** tomorrow あすまでにこれを仕上げる. ¶I am *finished* ***for*** the day. 私は今日(の仕事)はもうこれでお仕舞い. ¶*finished* ***in*** pure gold leaf 純金ぱくで仕上げを施した. ¶I have *finished* with China and is going to India. 私はもう中国の見物は終えたから印度へ出かける所だ. ‖ I have now *finished* ***with*** her. = I'm now through with her. 私はもう彼女とは絶縁した. ‖ Please return it to me when you have *finished* ***with*** it. 御用済みになったら返して下さい. ‖ They have *finished* ***with*** each other. 彼らは刺し違えて死んだ. ‖ The young fellow has *finished* ***with*** school. その青年は学校を卒業した.

finishing up, *n*. 最後の仕上げ.

P² the *finishing up* ***of*** one's studies ***in*** child psychology 児童心理学研究の仕上げ. 【類】the *finishing up* ***of*** one's work ***in*** art (sculpture).

fire, *n*. 火, 火事, 火災; 射撃, 発射, 砲火; 情火, 熱情.

V ***answer*** the *fire* of the enemy 敵の砲火に応じる. ¶It

aroused my *fire*. それが私の熱情を喚起した. ¶***bank*** [***up***] a *fire* 火を埋(い)ける. ¶it only ***blew*** the *fires* of ... それはかえって...の熱情をあおるにすぎなかった. ¶She ***breathes*** the *fires* of the very same inferno. 彼女はその苦界に身を沈めている. ¶***build*** a *fire* in a barn 納屋で火を起す.【類】***build*** a large *fire*. ¶***build up*** a *fire* たき火をする. ¶***call*** *fire* by its proper name 火を(蛮人のように red flower など言わずに)普通の名で言う. ¶The school ***caught*** *fire* the other night and is now a heap of charred timbers and ashes. 先だっての晩学校から火事を出して今では焼け残った木材や灰のかたまりになっている.【類】Suppose your school ***caught*** *fire*, what should be done first? / ***catch*** *fire* from another burning house / a *fire* ***caught*** from next door. ¶a *fire* ***caused*** by (=which started as the result of) carelessness in throwing away a lighted cigarette 火のついている巻タバコをうっかり棄てたために起った火事. ¶,'***Cease*** *fire!*'' [大砲など]打方止め! ¶Hydrants were set to work with such effect that the *fire* was speedily ***checked***. 消火せんを開いたものだから火事がすぐに鎮まってしまった. ¶***concentrate*** the *fire* 砲火を集中する. ¶***direct*** a hot *fire* 猛烈な砲火を向ける. ¶A burnt child ***dreads*** the *fire*.〖諺〗やけどした子は火をこわがる. ¶with eyes ***emitting*** *fire*, he exclaimed—"...!" 目から火をだして(かっと怒って)彼は...と叫んだ. ¶***escape*** the *fire* 火災を免れる. ¶***exchange*** *fire* with the enemy 敵と砲火を交える. ¶The *fire* was quickly ***extinguished***. 火事はすぐ鎮まった. ‖walk upon ashes under which the *fire* is not ***extinguished*** まだ下に火が燃えている灰の上を歩く. ¶***feed*** the *fire* with fuel 火に燃料を加える. ¶***fend*** (=***cherish***) the *fire* 火を消えないようにする. ¶The *fire* was ***fought*** by more than 100 firemen. 百人以上の消防夫がその火事で働いた. ¶The *fire* has been ***got under***. 火事は鎮火した. ¶***hang*** *fire* (銃砲が)急に発火しない. ¶***hold*** their *fire* 彼らの熱情を抑える ‖Sheridan, as all know, "***hung*** *fire*" in his first speech. シェリダンはだれも知るように初めての演説ではとちった. ‖Thus is settled forever the question which has for a long time ***hung*** *fire*. 長らく未決であった問題がかくして永久に解決した. ¶a question which is ***hanging*** *fire* 未決の問題.【類】The transaction ***hangs*** *fire*. ¶***ignite*** *fire* 発火させる. ¶***keep in*** (=burning *or* ignited) a *fire* 火を燃やして置く. ¶***keep off*** gun *fire* 砲火を防ぐ. ¶***keep up*** a running *fire* of the most brilliant witticism 最も花やかなとん知に富む弁舌を続ける. ¶***kindle*** a *fire* in a fireplace 暖炉に火をたきつける. ¶***lay*** a *fire* 火をたく支度をする. ¶***let*** *fire* ***break out*** in one's own house 自家から火を出す. ¶***light*** a *fire* 火をたきつける. ¶***Make*** a *fire* in my room (the stove). 私のへや(など)に火を起しなさい. ‖***make*** *fire* by friction-sticks 摩擦棒で火を起す.【類】gather twigs to ***make*** a *fire*. ¶***mend*** the *fire* 消えそうな火をかきたてて燃やす. ¶***miss*** *fire* [銃など]発火しない. ¶the *fire* was ***occasioned*** by ... その火事は...から出た. ¶***open*** *fire* 砲火を開く. ¶The *fire* was completely ***overcome*** by daybreak. 夜明けまでに全く鎮火した. ¶***poke*** a *fire* 火をかきたてる. ¶take special precautions to ***prevent*** *fire* 特に火の元に注意する. ¶***produce*** *fire* by the friction of ... ...の摩擦によって火を起す ‖***produce*** *fire* by striking sparks from steel with a flint stone 鋼鉄と火打石で火花を出して火を起す. ¶***put out*** (=extinguish) all the *fires* before one retires 寝る前に全部火を消す ‖It is like ***putting out*** a *fire* with kerosene. それは石油で火を消す(火に油をそそぐ)ようなものだ. ‖The *fire* was ***put under*** [control]. 火事が消し止められた. ¶***quell*** a *fire* 火を消す. ¶***quench*** a *fire* by water 水で火を消す. ¶***rain*** *fire* 砲火を雨のごとく浴びせる. ¶***rake*** the *fire* with a poker 火かき棒で火をかき立てる. ¶***replenish*** a *fire* 火をつぐ. ¶***return*** a *fire* 応砲する. ¶***set*** *fire* to a house (jungle) 家(など)に火をつける ‖***set*** grass or timber *fires* 草あるいは木材に火をつける.【類】The man was caught in the act of ***setting*** *fire* to the house. ¶***stand*** the *fire* 敵の砲火にたえる. ¶We use matches to ***start*** a *fire*. われわれは火を起すのにマッチを使う.【類】***start*** the *fire* in the stove / Overheating (過熱) is supposed to have ***started*** the *fire*. ¶***stifle*** a *fire* 火事をもみ消す. ¶***stir*** the *fire* 火をあおる ‖***stir*** the intellectual *fire* of students 学生の研究心を盛んにする. ¶A flint ***strikes*** *fire* with steel. 火打石は鋼鉄とぶつかって火を出す ‖***strike*** *fire* with a flint (match) 火打石(など)で火をすりだす. ¶The *fire* was ***subdued*** before considerable damage had been done. 大したことにならないうちに火事を消し止めた. ¶At about 300° it ***takes*** *fire*. 約三百度でそれは発火する. ‖Shavings soon ***take*** *fire*. かんなくずは火がつきやすい.【類】It is reported that the post-office ***took*** *fire* last night. / Light the match. Turn on a little gas. Put the match near the burner. When the gas ***takes*** *fire*, put out the match. ¶***urge*** the *fire* by a pair of bellows ふいごで火をあおる.

V² a *fire* ***broke out*** last night at ... ゆうべ...に火事があった. ¶The *fire* is still ***burning***. 火がまだ燃えている. ‖The *fire* is ***burning low***. 火がとろ火になっている. ¶The *fire* has ***gone out***. 火が消えてしまった.【類】The *fire* will ***go out***, if not attended to. ¶The *fire* which started in the cellar, ***mushroomed*** upstairs. 地下室から出た火がたちまち二階に燃え広がった. ¶A *fire* ***occurred*** in his house. 火事が彼の家から出た. ¶The *fire* is ***smouldering***. 火がくすぶっている. ¶A *fire* ***spreads***. 火が燃え広がる. ¶the house in which the *fire* ***started*** 火元の家. ¶A *fire* ***took place*** in that street. あの街に火事があった.

Q an ***abortive*** *fire* 早く消し止めた火事. ¶an ***accidental*** *fire* 失火. ¶a ***big*** *fire* さかんな火, 大火. ¶a ***blazing*** *fire* さかんな火. ¶beside ***bright*** *fires* of a winter night 冬の夜の赤々と燃える炉辺で. ¶under the ***concentrated*** *fire* of all the guns 全砲門の集中砲火を浴びて. ¶a ***dead*** (=***dull***) *fire* 消えかかった火. ¶pour out a ***deadly*** *fire* 猛火を噴出する. ¶a ***destructive*** *fire* 大火事. ¶a ***devastating*** *fire* 荒れ狂う火事. ¶a ***disastrous*** *fire* 惨たんたる火事, 大火. ¶a ***dying*** *fire* 消えかかった火. ¶an ***extensive*** *fire* 大火. ¶a ***fatal*** *fire* 恐ろしい火事. ¶A ***fearful*** *fire* is raging in the mountain forests near here. この近くの山の森が恐ろしく燃えている. ¶a ***fierce*** *fire* from the enemy 敵の猛射. ¶We have ***frequent*** *fires* in Tokyo. 東京は火事が多い. ¶a ***good*** *fire* いい火. ¶a ***great*** *fire* 大火. ¶a ***great flaming*** *fire* 盛んに燃える火. ¶I smoked many a pipe before his ***hospitable*** *fire*. 彼の家に呼ばれてその炉辺で幾度パイプをくゆらしたか知れない. ¶an ***incendiary*** *fire* 放火. ¶Thirty per cent of ***industrial*** *fires* result in business failure. 工場が焼けると三割までは破産になる. ¶a ***joyous wood*** *fire* 気持のよいたき火. ¶a ***lambent*** *fire* なめるように燃え進む火. ¶a ***large*** *fire* 大火. ¶in the ***late*** *fire* 先だっての火事で. ¶a ***mysterious*** *fire* 怪火. ¶an ***open*** *fire* おおいのない(裸の)火. ¶keep up a ***perpetual*** *fire* against ... ...に連射する. ¶breathe the true ***poetic*** *fire* 真の詩的熱情を漏らす. ¶the ***recent*** *fire* at Kanda この間の神田の火事. ¶A ***roaring*** *fire* raged through the buildings. 盛んに燃える火が建物中を荒れ狂った. ¶a ***running*** *fire* of questions 矢継ぎ早の質問. ¶a ***sham*** *fire* [消防隊などの]模擬火災. ¶There was a ***slight*** *fire* at the house some time ago. この間その家にぼやがあった. ¶place it over a ***slow*** *fire* それをとろ火にかける. ¶a ***small*** *fire* ぼや. ¶keep up a ***steady*** *fire* 砲火を続け様に浴びせかける. ¶***subterranean*** *fire* 地下の火. ¶A ***terrible*** *fire* is now raging. 今恐ろしい火事がたけり狂っている. ¶***unquenchable*** *fire* 消し難い火. ¶a ***warm*** and ***blazing*** *fire* 暖かいよく燃える火.

Q² an ***air-raid*** *fire* 空襲火災. ¶***anti-aircraft*** *fire* 対空砲火. ¶open ***artillery*** *fire* upon ... ...に対して砲火を開く ‖heavy ***artillery*** *fire* 激しい砲火. ¶a ***camp*** *fire* キャンプファイヤを作る. ¶a ***daytime*** *fire* 昼火事. ¶a ***death*** *fire* 人だま. ¶an ***elf*** *fire* 鬼火. ¶a ***forest*** *fire* 山火事. ¶a ***home*** *fire* 家庭の炉火. ¶a ***hell*** *fire* 地獄の火, 業火. ¶a ***hotel*** *fire* 旅館の炉火. ¶The plane was forced down by ***ground*** *fire*. 飛行機が地上砲火で撃墜された. ¶cover landing beaches by ***gun*** and ***machine gun*** *fire* 砲火及び機関銃火で上陸する海浜をえん護する. ¶the great ***London*** *fire* in 1799. 一七九九年のロンドンの大火. ¶sit by a ***peat*** *fire* 泥炭塊の火のそばに腰掛ける. ¶the ***post-earthquake*** *fires* of September, 1923 大正十二年九月の地震後の火災. ¶a ***prairie*** *fire* 野火. ¶He was killed by ***shell*** *fire* in France. 彼はフランスで砲火のために死んだ. ¶***wood*** (***coal***) *fire* まき(石炭)の火. ¶an ***18-hour*** *fire* 十八時間燃え続けた火事.

P a visit of condolence ***after*** a *fire* 火事見舞. ¶insure a building ***against*** *fire* 建物に火災保険を付ける ‖I'm insured ***against*** *fire*. 僕は火災保険をつけている. ‖proof ***against*** *fire*=fireproof 耐火の. ¶We sat ***around*** the *fire*. われわれは炉を囲んですわった. ¶dry wet clothes ***at*** the fire ぬれた着物を炉の火で乾かす ‖ Warm yourself ***at*** the *fire*. おあたりなさい. ‖ He gave assistance ***at*** the *fire*. 彼はその火事のときに手伝ってくれた. ¶stand ***before*** a hot *fire* さかんに燃えている火の前に立つ ‖ bake ... ***before*** a *fire* 火で…をあぶる. ¶sit ***beside*** the *fire* 炉辺にすわる. ¶***between*** two *fires* 腹背に敵を受けて, 二進も三進も行ないで. ¶doze ***by*** the *fire* 炉辺で居眠りする ‖ The building was destroyed ***by*** [a] *fire*. 建物は火事で焼けた. ¶Bring coal[s] ***for*** the *fire*. 火をたく石炭を持ってこい. ¶Keep away ***from*** the *fire*. 火から離れていろ. ¶The house was burnt ***in*** the late *fire*. その家は先だっての火事で焼けた. 【類】burn it ***in*** the *fire* / He perished ***in*** the *fire*. / a sort of cloth that will not burn ***in*** *fire* but be cleansed by it. ¶It was thrown ***into*** the *fire*. それは火に投げ込まれた. ¶a blaze (=flame) ***of*** *fire* 火炎 ‖ The cause ***of*** the *fire* is spontaneous combustion. その火事は自然発火が原因だ. ‖ an outbreak ***of*** *fire* 一件の火事. ¶Take it ***off*** the *fire*. それを火から取り出せ. ¶His clothes were ***on*** *fire*. 彼の着物に火が付いていた. ‖ The house is ***on*** *fire*. その家は燃えている. ‖ set the river (=Thames) ***on*** *fire* どえらいことをやる ‖ My soul was ***on*** *fire* to teach. 私は教師たらんとの熱情に燃えていた. ‖ put some coal ***on*** a *fire* 火に石炭をつぐ ‖ The ship was abandoned ***on*** *fire*. その船は火災を起して放棄された. 【類】We have had our premises ***on*** *fire*, but damage is not serious. / a house ***on*** *fire* / set a house ***on*** *fire*=set fire to a house. ¶The pan is hung ***over*** a *fire*. なべが火の上につるしてある. ‖ warming his hands ***over*** a tiny *fire* ほたるのような火に手をかざして暖めながら. ¶go ***through*** *fire* and water for another 人のために水火の難を冒す. ¶advance ***under*** the enemy's *fire* 敵の砲火を冒して進む ‖ We were ***under*** *fire*. われわれは射撃されていた. ‖ be driven back ***under*** *fire* 砲火を浴びて撃退される ‖ They swam a river ***under*** *fire*. 砲火を浴びながら川を泳いだ. 【類】Japanese infantry crossed the river ***under*** *fire*. ¶burn it ***with*** *fire* それを火で焼く ‖ The enemy opposed the advance of our army ***with*** *fire* of small arms and cannon. 敵は小銃・大砲を発射してわが軍の前進に抵抗した. ‖ fight fire ***with*** *fire* 砲火を交える. ¶There is no smoke ***without*** *fire*. 火のない所に煙は立たぬ.

P² a *fire* ***in*** a Japanese town 日本町の火事 ‖ There was a *fire* ***in*** the neighbourhood of Asakusa last night. 昨夜浅草辺に火事があった.

fire, *v*. 発射する, 発砲する, 射撃する; 燃える; 興奮する; 《米》追い出す.

M *fire* ***at random*** 乱射する. ¶*Fire* ***away*** then. [話など]それなら始め給え. ‖ *fire* ***away*** all one's shot[s] その持っている弾丸を全部使い尽す ‖ *fire* ***away*** at the enemy 敵を目がけて撃ちまくる. ¶*fire* ***back*** at the enemy 敵に撃ち返す. ¶*fire* ***kneeing*** ひざ射ちする. ¶*fire* ***lying*** 伏射する. ¶Boss *fired* him ***out*** in no time. 《口語》社長は立ち所に彼を首にした. 【類】He had been *fired* ***out*** from his office. ¶*fire* a pistol ***point-blank*** at ... 拳銃で…をまともにねらい打つ. ¶*fire* ***standing*** 立射する. ¶be ***summarily*** *fired* 容赦なくやめさせられる.

M² *fire* ***off*** a kiln かまどの火を止める. ¶be *fired* ***on*** (=***upon***) 砲撃される. ¶He *fired* ***up***. かんかんに怒った. ‖ A big flare *fired* ***up***. 大きなせん光が起った.

P *fire* a shot (revolver, torpedo) ***at*** ... …に弾丸(など)を放つ ‖ Shots were *fired* ***at*** the enemy (target). 敵(など)をねらってぽんぽん射撃した. ‖ I *fired* my imperfect Dutch ***at*** him, making inquiry as to ... 私は不完全なオランダ語を彼に浴びせて…を尋ねた. ¶*fired* ***by*** our example われわれの例に刺激されて. 【類】His imagination was *fired* ***by*** what he had read. ¶He was *fired* ***from*** his job. 《口語》彼はお払い箱になった. ‖ He was *fired* ***from*** Stanford University for ... 彼はスタンフォード大学を…で出された. ¶The fort *fired* ***upon*** (=***on***) the man-of-war. 要塞がその軍艦に発砲した. ¶The old locomotive is *fired* ***with*** wood. その旧式機関車はまきをたく. ‖ *fired* ***with*** the desire to ... …の念に燃えて.

fire-alarm, *n*. 半鐘; [火事の]警報.

V ***ring*** the *fire-alarm* 半鐘を鳴らす.

firearm, *n*. [通例 *pl*.] 火器, 銃砲.

V ***discharge*** *firearms* 銃砲を発射する.

Q ***silent*** *firearms* 無声銃.

fire-bell, *n*. 半鐘, 警鐘.

V ***sound*** (=***ring***) the *fire-bell* 半鐘を鳴らす.

fire-brigade, *n*. 消防隊.

V² The *fire-brigade* ***turned out*** promptly. 消防隊が迅速に出動した.

firecracker, *n*. 南京花火, 爆竹.

V ***shoot*** a *firecracker* 南京花火を打ちあげる.

V² The *firecracker* just ***fizzled***. 南京花火が今しゅしゅと音を立てた. ¶*Firecrackers* ***pop***. 南京花火がぱんと破裂する.

firefly, *n*. ほたる.

P The place is noted for the brilliancy ***of*** the *fireflies*. そこはほたるがよく光るので有名だ. ‖ the gleam (=glimmer or glow) ***of*** *fireflies* ほたるの光り.

firelight, *n*. 炉辺の火.

P sit ***by*** the *firelight* 炉辺に腰を掛ける. ¶sit talking ***in*** the *firelight* 炉辺の火かげで座談をする.

fireman, *n*. 消防夫; 火夫.

Q² a ***railway*** *fireman* 鉄道の火夫.

fireplace, *n*. 暖炉.

P a shelf ***over*** a *fireplace* 炉架.

fire-power, *n*. 火(砲)力.

V The enemy ***has*** greater *fire-power*. 敵の火力は味方のより優勢だ.

fireside, *n*. 炉辺.

Q the ***warm*** *fireside* of the home 家庭の暖かい炉辺.

P a good book ***by*** a warm *fireside* 暖かい炉辺で読むに良い本. ¶travels ***by*** the *fireside* 炉辺旅行(旅行記を読むこと).

firewood, *n*. まき.

V ***cut*** *firewood* まきを切る.

fireworks, *n. pl*. 花火.

V *Fireworks* were ***displayed*** both day and night. 夜昼花火があった. ¶***let off*** (=***fire off or discharge***) *fireworks* 花火を打上げる. ¶***set off*** *fireworks* 花火を打上げる. ¶***shoot off*** *fireworks* 花火を打上げる.

V² *Fireworks* ***sparkle***. 花火がきらめく.

Q a display of ***conversational*** *fireworks* 座談のにぎわい.

Q² ***Day*** *fireworks* were set off. 昼花火を打上げた.

P a piece ***of*** *fireworks* 一本の花火 ‖ A magnificent display ***of*** *fireworks* took place to celebrate the occasion. 当日を祝賀するための花火大会があった.

firing, *n*. 射撃.

V ***practice*** *firing* 射撃の練習をやる.

Q ***hot*** *firing* 猛烈な射撃. ¶***simultaneous*** *firing* 一斉射撃.

firm, *n*. 商会, 商館.

V He ***entered*** the prosperous *firm*. 彼はその繁盛している店にはいった. ¶***join*** the *firm* of ... …に入社する. ¶We have authorized Mr. ... to ***sign*** our *firm* per procuration from this date. 弊社は今日以後…氏をもって弊社を代表して署名することに致しました. ¶He is thinking of ***starting*** another *firm* in Paris. 彼はパリにも一つ店を出そうともくろんでいる.

Q a ***big*** *firm* 大商会. ¶a ***commercial*** *firm* 商店. ¶a ***defunct*** *firm* 閉鎖した商会. ¶Messrs. I. & P. Higson of Manchester, the ***eminent*** *firm* of mining engineers 有名な鉱業商たるマンチェスターのアイ・アンド・ピー・ヒグソン商会. ¶a ***financial*** *firm* 金融会社. ¶a ***four centuries old*** *firm* 四百年のしにせ. ¶the ***leading*** *firm* of publishers in New York ニューヨークの第一流出版会社. ¶a ***mercantile*** *firm* 商事会社. ¶an ***old-established*** and ***well-known*** *firm* of the highest repute 最も評判のよい古い有名な商会. 【類】an ***old-established*** *firm* of printers. ¶a ***private*** *firm* 個人経営の商会. ¶a more ***progressive*** *firm* 一層進歩的な商会. ¶Meijiya, a ***prominent*** *firm* of purveyors in Japan 日本の有名な食料品店の明治屋. 【類】Short Bros., a ***prominent*** *firm* of English shipbuilders in Sanderland. ¶a very ***reliable*** *firm* 非常に信用のできる商会. ¶a ***reputable*** *firm* 評判のよい商会. ¶a ***rival*** *firm* 競争店. ¶a ***trustworthy*** *firm* 信用のできる商会. ¶a ***well known*** *firm* established over 100 years 創業百年を越えた有名な店.

Q² a canvasser for an ***advertising*** *firm* 広告会社の勧誘員. ¶a big ***business*** *firm* 大商店. 【類】a British ***business*** *firm*. ¶a great ***chainstore*** *firm* 大連鎖店商社. ¶a ***drapery*** *firm* 呉服商店. ¶an ***engineering*** *firm* 土建会社. ¶an ***export[ing]*** *firm* 輸出商社. ¶a ***horse-breeding*** *firm* 産馬会社. ¶a ***large retail*** *firm* 大きな小売商店. ¶a ***law*** *firm* 法律事務所. ¶a ***London*** *firm* of razor makers ロンドンのかみそり製造会社. ¶a machinery ***import*** *firm* 機械輸入会社. ¶a ***manufacturing*** *firm* 製造会社. ¶a young ***New York publishing*** *firm* ニューヨークの新進出版会社. ¶a ***shipping*** *firm* 海運会社. ¶a ***stockbroking*** *firm* 株式仲買

店. ¶a tailoring firm 洋服店.

P^{2} leading firms in the cotton trade 綿糸貿易の一流商会. ¶the firm of Longmans ロングマン商会 ‖ a firm of long standing しにせ ‖ a firm of nursery gardeners and florist, Messrs. Cull and Rook 温室栽培並に花屋のカル・アンド・ルック商会 ‖ a French firm of perfumers フランス人の香水店. 【類】The Firm of Thos. Cook & Son (トマス・クック父子商会) was established in England in 1841.

firm, a. 堅い. 堅固な.

M as firm as a rock (stone) 岩(石)のように堅固な. ¶Prices keep comparatively firm. 物価が割合に落付いている.

P he is firm in the belief that … 彼は…と固く信じている ‖ he is quite firm in the view that … 彼は…という非常にしっかりした考えを持っている. 【類】a man firm in his resolutions / be firm in one's decision. ¶I am afraid you are not firm enough with your son. どうも君は子供に少し甘いようだ.

firmament, n. 大空.

Q the starry firmament 星空.

firmness, n. 堅固.

Q with dogged firmness あくまで手強く. ¶with gentle firmness やさしいがしっかりと.

first, n. 最初(のもの); 一等, 一流; 一等賞.

V I experienced my first. 私は初めて経験をした. ¶the country keeps her first among … その国は…の中で引続き首位を占めている.

Q famous firsts 有名な最良品(一流メーカー品). ¶from the very first そもそもの始めから.

P Young women are always among the first to take up new slang. 若い女はいつも新しい俗語流行のさきがけをやる. 【類】He was among the first to recognize a writer of merit (有能な作家) in the author. ¶I found English difficult at first. 私は初め英語がむずかしかった. ‖ Damage is greater (less) than was at first anticipated. 被害は最初に予期されたより大き(小さ)かった. ¶He had so changed that I could not recognize him at first. 彼は見違えるほど変っていた. ¶from first to last 初めから終りまで ‖ I liked that preacher from the very first; he is so free from affectation. 私は最初からあの説教者が好きだった. 気取るなんてことが全くないから. 【類】I know from the first that …

P^{2} the first among scholars 学者間の第一人者. ¶a long way the first in point of … …の点は図抜けて第一人者 ‖ They were the first in the field. 彼らはその方面の先駆者だ. ‖ the first in fifty years 五十年振り. ¶the first of the New Year 元日 ‖ the first of cheese チーズの一等品 ‖ the first of the new crop 作物の走り ‖ Paul Verlaine, the first of modern French poets 近代フランス詩人の第一人者ポール・ヴェルレーヌ. ‖ The first of a series 双書の第一巻. ‖ the first of the English Rothschilds 英国ロスチャイルド家の初代. ¶the first on earth 天下一品.

O He was the first to round the Cape of Good Hope. 彼は喜望峰を回航した初めての人であった.

first, a., ad. 第一に.

M easily first 優に一番.

P He stands first in his class. 彼は級では一番. ¶be first (last) in the line その方面で一流(しんがり)だ ‖ first in importance 最も重要な. ¶You will be judged by your speech first of all. 君は第一に君の言葉づかいで判断される. ‖ He came in first of the two. 二人の中で彼の方が先きに来た. ¶The dog ran here and there, first on this side, then on that. 犬はあちこち, 始めにこっちへそれからあっちへと走った.

first-born, n. 初児.

Q her first-born 彼女の初児.

fish, n. 魚, 魚肉.

V catch fish 魚を捕る. 【類】catch a big fish. ¶cook fish 魚を料理する. ¶cure fish 魚を保蔵する. ¶dress fish 魚を料理する. ¶eat fish 魚を食う ‖ eat a fish skin and bone (=bone and all) 魚を皮と骨ぐるみ食う. 【類】eat fish raw (なまで) / eat a fish whole (まるごと). ¶They ate the fish for supper. 彼らは夕食にその魚を食べた. ¶feed the fishes =be drowned; be seasick 魚腹を肥やす; 船酔する. ¶fillet fish 魚肉を切身に切る. ¶fry fish in oil 魚を天ぷらにする. ¶gut a fish 魚の腸を抜く. ¶hook a fish 魚を釣り針にひっかける. ¶pack fish 魚をかん詰にする. ¶scale a fish 魚のうろこを取る. ¶prepare fish for supper 魚を晩食に料理する. ¶take fish in a net 網で魚を捕る. ¶take a fish off the hook 魚を針からはずす.

V^{2} This fish does not agree with me. 僕はこの魚を食べるとあたる. ¶A fish nibbles at the bait. 魚が餌に食いつく.

Q baked fish 焼き魚. ¶boiled fish 煮ざかな. ¶a bony fish 骨の多い魚. ¶a common fish on American coasts 米国の海岸に多い魚. ¶dried fish 乾魚(ひもの). ¶an edible fish 食用魚. ¶freshwater fish 淡水魚. ¶fried fish 魚フライ. ¶a game fish 釣る魚. ¶muddy-flavored fish 泥くさい魚. ¶Old fish stink. 日ましの魚は臭い. ¶pickled fish つけ魚. ¶a queer fish 変人. ¶raw fish 鮮魚. ¶Rotten fish are smelling. 腐った魚が臭い. ¶salted fish 塩魚. ¶a slippery fish ぬるぬるした魚. ¶smoked fish くん製魚. ¶The fish is sound (unsound). その魚はいきがよい(悪い).

Q^{2} a bank fish 砂場魚(ニューファンドランドの浅瀬で取れる魚をいう). ¶a deep-sea fish 深海魚. ¶a food fish 食用魚. ¶a fresh (salt) water fish 淡(かん)水魚. 【類】The rivers are well stocked with many varieties of freshwater fishes. ¶mid-water fish 中層生息魚族(水の中層に住む魚族の総称). ¶quality canned fish 魚の優良かん詰. ¶a sea (river, lake) fish 海(川, 湖)魚. ¶table fish 食用魚.

P I feel the bait nibbled by some fish. 何か魚が餌をつっついている(のが自分にわかる). ¶a dealer in fish 魚屋. ¶drink like a fish 大酒を飲む. ¶a good string of fish どっさり釣って糸などに刺した魚 ‖ a shoal of fish 魚の群. ¶There are many fish in the lake. その湖には魚が沢山いる.

fish, v. 魚を取る, 漁する; 探り出す.

M He fished out the shoes which he thought he had lost. 彼はなくしたと思ったくつを探し出した.

M^{2} fish up a thing missing 失なった品を探し出す.

P fish by night 夜釣りをする. ¶fish for trout ますを釣る. ¶fish for a living 生計のために漁する ‖ The visitor fished for a card, wrote his name upon it and placed it on the tray. 訪問者はカードを探り出してそれに名前を書き盆の上に置いた. ‖ fish for complements お世辞を言わせるように仕向ける ‖ fish for information by a letter of inquiry 照会状で報道を求める ‖ Oh! oh! I see what he's driving at. He's fishing for a loan. ああ分った. あいつ金を借りようとしているんだな. 【類】fish for a missing watch. ¶fish from a boat 小舟に乗って魚を取る ‖ fish a secret (fact) from (=out of) a person 人から秘密(など)を探り出す ‖ He fished a map from the back of one of his desk drawers. 彼は机の一つの引出しの後ろから一枚の地図を探し出した. 【類】fish from the shore or the boat. ¶fish in the river その川で釣りをする ‖ fish in the air 木によって魚を求める. ¶fish on a pond or a stream 池や小川で漁する. ¶fish through the ice 氷を割って魚を捕る. ¶fish with an angle (a rod and line) はり(釣りざお)で魚を釣る.

fisherman, n. 漁夫.

Q^{2} an amateur fisherman 釣り好き, 太公望. ¶a trout fisherman ますを釣る人.

fishery, n. 漁業.

Q^{2} vessels engaged in deep-sea fisheries 深海漁業に従事する船. ¶in-shore fisheries 近海漁業. ¶lake and river fishery 淡水漁業. ¶ocean fisheries 大洋漁業. ¶off-shore fisheries 沖合漁業. ¶the salmon fisheries of Alaska アラスカのさけ漁.

fishing, n. 魚捕り, 魚釣り; 漁場.

V The river affords good fishing. その川は釣りによい. ¶I did some fishing that day. その日私は少し魚釣りをやった. ¶Fishing can be had (=indulged in) there. そこでは魚釣りがやれる. ¶Good fishing may be obtained in this neighborhood. この辺は釣りに好い.

Q^{2} go black bass fishing in the lake 湖水にバス(すずきの類)釣りに出かける. ¶deep-sea fishing 深海漁業. ¶The lake affords good perch and pike fishing. その湖はすずきとかますがよく釣れる. ¶It affords excellent trout fishing. そこはます釣りにはもってこいだ.

P divert oneself in fishing 気晴らしに魚釣りをやる.

P^{2} go fishing for turtles (trout) かめ(など)釣りに出かける. ¶trout fishing on a Highland stream スコットランド高地方の川でのます釣り ‖ fishing on a lake 湖上の魚釣り. ¶fishing with cormorants 鵜飼(うかい).

fission, n. 分裂.

Q Nuclear fission releases tremendous amounts of energy 核分裂は驚くべき多量のエネルギーを放出する.

fissure, *n.* 割れ目.

Q a *yawning fissure* 大きく開いた割れ目.

P[2] a *fissure in* the ground 地面の割れ目.

fist, *n.* 拳(こぶし), 拳固; (俗) 筆跡, 手跡.

V *clench* his *fists* in a threatening manner おどかすように拳を固める. 【類】 *clench* the left *fist* desperately (死物狂いに) / *clench* your *fists* tightly (しっかりと). ¶ *double* one's *fist* at … …に拳を固めて突きつける. ¶ *Give* us your *fist*. 握手しましょう. ¶ I *know* his *fist*. 私は彼の筆跡を知っている. ¶ *make* a good (poor) *fist* at … …をうまく(まずく)やる. ¶ *shake* one's *fist* at … …に向って拳固を振回す. ¶ *strike* one's *fist* recklessly on the table 拳固でむやみにテーブルをたたく. ¶ *write* a good *fist* 筆跡がうまい. 【類】 He *writes* a tolerable *fist*.

Q a *clenched fist* 握りしめたこぶし. ¶ the Kaiser's "*mailed fist*" カイゼルの「武装したげん固」(武力). ¶ fight with *naked fists* なぐり合う.

P I struck him *with* my *fist*. 僕のげん固で彼を打った.

fist, *v.* こぶしで打つ, 握る.

M *fist* an oar *firmly* かいを固く握る.

M[2] be *fisted about* among … …の間に次々に渡される.

fist-fight, *n.* なぐり合い.

V[2] *fist-fights broke out* between … …の間になぐり合いが始まった.

fistful, *n.* (俗) 一握り, 一つかみ.

P monopolized by a *fistful of* exclusive syndicates 少数の排他的な企業組合によって独占されて.

fisticuff, *n.* 殴打.

Q a *smart fisticuff* こっぴどい殴打.

fit, *n.* 発作, ひきつけ; 一時の情熱.

V *have* a *fit* 発作を起す ‖ *have* a fainting *fit* 気絶する ‖ He *had* a *fit* of coughing. 彼はせき込んだ. 【類】 *have* a *fit* of epilepsy (てんかん) ‖ *have* a *fit* of work and laziness 気まぐれに働いたりなまけたりする. ¶ They are sincere, while the *fit lasts*. 彼らは気の向いている間は誠意がある.

Q die from an *apoplectic fit* 卒中で死ぬ. ¶ He is subject to *dangerous fits*. 彼は危険なさしこみを起しやすい. ¶ in a *drunken fit* 一杯きげんで. ¶ have an *epileptic fit* てんかんを起す. ¶ He fell in a *fainting fit*. 彼は気絶した. ¶ a *shivering fit*＝a fit of ague おこりの発作. ¶ If any stranger happened to be present, the baby was taken with a *shy fit*. 見ず知らずの人がたまたま居合わせるとその赤ん坊は人見知りして泣いた.

P He did everything *by fits* and starts, but stuck to nothing long. 彼は何でも発作的にやるが何をやっても長続きしなかった. ¶ startle a person *from* his *fit* of brown-study ぼんやり考え込んでいる人をびっくりさせる. ¶ She fell down *in* a *fit*. 彼女はさしこみで倒れた. ‖ *in* a *fit* of despair (madness) 急に失望(など)して. ¶ *in* a *fit* of anger かっとなって ‖ *in* a *fit* of jealousy (passion, rage) かっとしっと心(など)を起して ‖ be *in* a *fit* of the blues ふさぎ込んでいる ‖ *in* a *fit* of desperation やぶれかぶれになって. ¶ burst *into* a *fit* of laughter 吹出して笑う.

P[2] a *fit of* laughter 突然わっと笑うこと. ¶ a *fit of* sickness (weeping) 病気(など)の発作.

fit, *n.* 適合; きちんと合う衣服.

Q a *bad fit* of clothes 着物のきちんと合わないこと. ¶ The coat is an *exact fit*. その上衣はきっちり合う. ¶ Be sure to make me a *good fit*. [服など]必ずよく合うように作ってくれ. ¶ a *perfect fit* 工合よく合う衣服. ¶ The coat is a *poor fit*. この上衣はよく合わない. ¶ This coat is a *right fit* but the vest is a bad one. この上着はぴったり合うがチョッキが合わない. ¶ a *tight fit* きちんと合う衣服 ‖ The *basha* was reputed to hold eight, but we four found it a *tight fit*. 馬車は八人乗りということであったが僕たち四人でぎっしりであった. ¶ The shoes are just *your fit*. そのくつは君の足にぴったりだ.

fit, *a.* 適当な, 相当な.

M Can't you make it *fit better*? もっと体に合うようにしてくれないか. ¶ be *more fit* for preaching than printing 印刷より説教に一層適している. ¶ he is *physically fit* to be … 彼は肉体的に…に適している. ¶ be *scarcely fit* for the work その仕事にほとんど向かない.

P Such a boat is *fit* only *for* a calm sea. こうした船は平穏な海にだけ適する. ‖ I think it an occupation *fit for* a gentleman. それは紳士に適する職業だと思う. ‖ a subject *fit for* poetry 詩にふさわしい題材 ‖ The horse is *fit* only *for* the knacker's yard. その馬はつぶすより外に仕方がない. ‖ be *fit for* sale (food) 売りものになる(食べられる). 【類】 He is *fit for* that position. / not fit *for* my purpose / This stuff is not *fit for* food. / food *fit for* a dog.

O I am not *fit* to be seen. この体たらくでは人様にお目にかかれない. ‖ the news that is *fit* to print 印刷してよい新聞記事 ‖ The water is not *fit* to drink. その水は飲めない. 【類】 This fish is not *fit* to eat.

fit, *v.* 合わす, 適合させる; 準備させる; 備え付ける; 合う, 適合する.

M That *fits* you *all right*. それは君にしっくりする. ¶ *best fitted* for the work その仕事に最も適した. ¶ The coat *fits closely*. 上衣がきっちり合う. ¶ he is *eminently fitted* for … 彼はとりわけ…に適している. ¶ The coat *exactly fits* me. この上衣はきちんと私に合う. ¶ He is *ideally fitted* for the task. 彼はその仕事に打ってつけの人物だ. ¶ be *ill fitted* for … …には不向である ‖ he is *ill fitted* to play the part of … 彼は…の役目を演じるには不適当だ. ¶ be *fitted out* for an expedition 遠征のために準備される ‖ *fit out* a place for an airport 空港にする目的である場所を整理する ‖ *fit out* a steamer 汽船を出帆準備する. ¶ The peculiar connotation of the word makes it *fit* so *neatly*. その言葉には独特の含蓄があるのでぴったりと当てはまる. ¶ This hat (coat) *fits* me *perfectly*. この帽子(など)は私にぴったり合う. ¶ be *physically fit* to be … 肉体的に…に適している. ¶ a vessel *plainly fitted* 簡単な装備の船. ¶ *temperamentally fitted* to work well with … …とそりが合う. ¶ They don't *fit together*. ぴったり合わない(切った図形など). ¶ his experience *uniquely fits* him for … 彼はその経歴から言って…に極めてよく適している. ¶ he is peculiarly *well fitted* for … 彼は特に…に適している ‖ *fit* in *well* with the times 時代とよく調和する.

M[2] do not *fit in* with … …とそぐわない ‖ *fit in* with the facts 事実に合う. 【類】 That does not *fit in* with my experience. ‖ *fit in* a new glass of one's watch 時計に新しいガラスを入れる. ¶ *fit up* a refrigerator 冷蔵庫を備える ‖ *fit up* a room for guests 来客用にへやを飾り立てる(調度品などで) ‖ *fit up* a home in foreign style 家を外国風にする ‖ be *fitted up* with the latest improvements 最新式の改良を取入れてある. 【類】 The entire building is *fitted up* with (で設備する) electric lights, gas and steam heaters.

P *fit* pupils *for* admission to colleges 生徒の大学入学準備をする ‖ *fit* boys *for* their life-work 少年たちに一生の仕事の準備をさせる ‖ Different individuals are innately *fitted for* different kinds of employment. 人は生来それぞれ異った仕事に適する. ‖ *fit* oneself *for* a journey 旅行の準備をする. 【類】 *fit* a ship *for* sea (＝voyage) / *fit* oneself *for* a job / She is in every way *fitted for* the intended voyage. / *fit* them *for* a career abroad or at home. 【類】 a subject *fitting for* the philosopher and student of sociology. ¶ a book *fitted in* a case 箱入りの本. ¶ A button-hole is a hole *into* which a button *fits*. ボタン穴はボタンのはまる穴である. ‖ They *fit into* three categories. これを三種に分ける. ‖ *fit* one *into* social circles 人を社会に出られるように仕立てる. ¶ A square thing does not *fit into* a round hole. 『比喩』 四角なものは丸い穴に合わない. 【類】 Square men when choosing a profession are apt to be *fitted into* round holes. ¶ words that *fit* close *to* the thoughts 概念にぴったり合う言葉 ‖ *fit* a fact *to* one's theory (view) 事実を理論(など)に合わせる ‖ *fit* a hat *to* the head 帽子を頭に合わせる ‖ wire fencing *fitted to* wood posts 木柱に取付けた鉄線かき根. ¶ The Japanese parasol is *fitted with* wires which act as the aerials. 日本の日傘には針金が付いていて空中線の働きをやる. ‖ The steamers are *fitted with* wireless [telegraphy]. 汽船には無電装置がある. ‖ *fit* a customer *with* a coat (hat) お得意の上衣(など)を調製する. 【類】 These vessels are *fitted with* firstclass accommodation for passengers. / The room is *fitted with* easy chairs. / The building is not *fitted with* the necessary machinery. / old machinery *fitted with* modern improvements / The house is *fitted with* a fireplace. / The room is *fitted with* electric lights. / Each drawer is *fitted with* a strong lock (丈夫な錠前).

Q About that I know little and I am not *fitted* to write of it. そのことは余り知らないから私が書くのは適当でない.

fitness, *n.* 適当, 適格.

Q He believes in the ***innate*** *fitness* of a man for some special vocation. 彼は人が生れながらにして何か特殊の職業に適していることを信じている. ¶***physical*** *fitness* 体質の適性.

P It is ***in*** the *fitness* of things that the early biographies of Æsop, the great fabulist, should be entirely fabulous. あの偉大なぐう話作家たるイソップの古い伝記類が全くぐう話のような作りものであったとは似つかわしいことである. ¶***in accordance with*** the *fitness* of things そうするのがふさわしいことであるから. ¶No one doubts his *fitness* ***for*** the position. 彼がその地位に適していることはだれも疑わない.【類】He was selected solely ***for*** his *fitness* for the post.

fittings, *n. pl.* 装具, 取付け.

Q ***electric*** *fittings* 電装部品. ¶***interior*** *fittings* 屋内取付け. ¶***office*** *fittings* オフィスの調度品(机・いすなど). ¶***sanitary*** *fittings* 衛生用品.

Q² ***gas*** and ***electric light*** *fittings* ガス及び電燈器具. ¶***Japanese sword*** *fittings* 日本刀付属品.

five, *n.* 五, 五個.

Q the ***Big*** *Five* 五大国. ¶One man in ***every*** *five* was killed or wounded. 五人に一人は死ぬかけがをするかした.

Q² in ***sentence*** *five* 五番目の文において.【類】Continued on ***page*** *five* 五ページに続く.

fix, *n.* 《俗》苦境, 難関.

Q be in a ***bad*** *fix* にっちもさっちも行かない. ¶I am really in a ***nice*** *fix*. 私は本当ににっちもさっちも行かない.

P be ***in*** a *fix* 動きが取れない. ¶run him ***into*** a *fix* 彼を苦境に陥らせる.

fix, *v.* 据える; 定める, きめる; かぶせる, 負わせる; 固定する; [心などに]留める; 書き留める; 《俗》整える.

M I'll *fix* it up ***alright.*** 《口語》私がうまく片をつけます. ¶it was ***definitely*** *fixed* that ... ...とはっきりきまった. ¶*fix* it ***firmly*** in mind (=the memory) それをしっかりと記憶に留める. ¶The boat-race has been ***officially*** *fixed* for Thursday, April 2. ボートレースは四月二日の木曜日と正式に決定された. ¶The date has been ***provisionally*** *fixed* for Thursday, May 4th. 日はかりに五月四日の木曜日にきめられた. ¶trunks of trees *fixed* ***upright*** in the ground 地面から直立している立木の幹. ¶*fix* it ***well*** in one's mind それをよく頭に入れる.

M² *fix* ***up*** a quarrel けんかをまとめる ‖ I'll *fix* you ***up*** later on. 後で君とその話をきめよう.【類】The doorknob doesn't work. Can you *fix* it ***up*** (直す) for us?

P Many authorities *fix* this date ***as*** 1722. その年号を一七二二年としている著者が多い.【類】The date of departure is *fixed* ***as*** ... ¶The fee for full membership of the Congress is *fixed* ***at*** £1. 同会議の正会員の会費は一ポンドとなっている. ‖ *fix* one's residence ***at*** Edinburgh エジンバラに住居を定める.【類】The passage money (船賃) has been *fixed* ***at*** £5 per head. / the minimum price is *fixed* ***at*** ... / *fix* one's salary ***at*** ... ¶a custom *fixed* ***by*** tradition 因襲によって固められた習慣 ‖ *fix* a tent ***by*** means of pegs 木くぎで天幕を止める. ¶The date of my departure is *fixed* ***for*** March 20. 私の出発の日取は三月二十日にきまっている.【類】The concert (Next meeting) is *fixed* ***for*** tomorrow evening. / The date of the next session was *fixed* ***for*** Saturday. / The execution (死刑執行) is *fixed* ***for*** tomorrow. ‖ *fix* oneself ***for*** going out 外出の支度をする. ¶I'll *fix* tea (lunch) ***for*** you. お茶(など)をあげましょう. ¶*fix* the expression ***in*** mind その言葉を心にしっかり留める.【類】The effort of copying it will serve to *fix* it ***in*** the memory. ¶His eyes are *fixed* ***on*** the ground as he strides along. 彼は大またで歩きながら目を地上に据えている. ‖ *fix* a value ***on*** ... ...を相当価値あるものとする ‖ *fix* one's thought ***on*** paper 考えを紙上に書留める ‖ The crime was *fixed* ***on*** him. その罪は彼にきせられた. ‖ We can *fix* only ***on*** the following terms. 次の条件ならば決めてよい.【類】with his eyes *fixed* ***on*** the sky / with their eyes steadily *fixed* ***on*** the future. ¶*fix* a mirror ***to*** a wall 鏡を壁に取りつける. ¶*fix* ***upon*** a plan 方法をきめる ‖ They *fixed* ***upon*** me to do this work. 彼らはこの仕事を僕にさせることにきめた. ‖ My mother *fixed* ***upon*** him for my husband. 母は彼を私の夫にきめた ‖ The place was *fixed* ***upon*** as the exhibition grounds. その場所は博覧会の敷地に決定した

fixer, *n.* [色の]定着剤.

Q² a ***color*** *fixer* 色どめ.

fixing, *n.* 決定, 確定.

Q a ***suitable*** *fixing* of the proportions of the ingredients 成分割合の適正な決定.

Q² ***cosumer price*** *fixing* 消費者価格の確定. ¶basic ***food price*** *fixing* 基本食糧価格の確定.

P² *fixing* ***of*** the amount of costs of a suit 訴訟費用の確定 ‖ *fixing* ***of*** date=dating 日取の取決め.

fixture, *n.* 競技, 種目または番組; 造作.

V ***play*** the *fixture* [予定の]競技を行う.

Q² ***electric-light*** *fixtures* 電灯装置. ¶a room with leaky ***gas*** *fixtures* ガスのもれるへや. ¶***lighting*** *fixtures* 照明装置. ¶***plumbing*** *fixtures* 鉛管取付(ガス・水道など). ¶***sport*** *fixtures* スポーツ用具. ¶***store*** and ***office*** *fixtures* 商店及び事務所の造作.

fizzle, *v.* しくじる; 落第する.

M I *fizzle* ***out*** completely when it comes to the task of ... 私は...の仕事となると完然にしくじる.【類】His business had a good start, but *fizzled* ***out*** like a firecracker (竜頭だ尾).

P Nearly the whole class *fizzled* ***in*** algebra. ほとんど全級の生徒が代数で落第した.

flag, *n.* 旗; 司令旗.

V ***attach*** a *flag* to the pole 旗をさおにつける. ¶The wind is ***blowing*** the *flag*. 風が旗に吹付けている. ¶The general rule is that *flags* should always be ***broken*** after hoisting, with the important exception that the ensign is never sent aloft to be broken. 旗は揚げてから広げるのが一般の規則であるが特に例外として国旗は揚げてから広げるということは絶対にない. ¶children ***carrying*** Allied *flags* 同盟国の旗を持つ子供たち ‖ vessels ***carrying*** the American *flag* 米国国旗を掲揚している船舶. ¶***cheer*** the *flag*, crying Hurrah! Hurrah! 万歳! 万歳! と旗に歓呼する. ¶***cross*** national *flags* 国旗を交差する. ¶***crisscross*** two national *flags* 国旗を交差する. ¶***dip*** the *flag* [敬意を表するため]旗をちょっと下げてからもとへ戻す. ¶***dishonor*** (=insult *or* disgrace) a national *flag* 国旗を侮辱する. ¶***display*** a *flag* at half mast 半旗を掲げる.【類】***display*** the Japanese *flag* over the entrance of the school. ¶***erect*** the red *flag* of "danger ahead!" on ... ...の上に「この先きに危険あり」の赤旗を立てる. ¶***exhibit*** *flags* on their roofs 彼らの屋根に旗を掲げる. ¶***float*** the *flag* over the British Consulate 英国領事館の屋上に国旗を翻す. ¶***fly*** *flags* in honor of the day 当日を祝して国旗を掲げる.【類】***fly*** the *flag* of the Stars and Stripes (星条旗) / *flags* ***flown*** by vessels. ¶***furl*** *flags* 旗を巻き収める. ¶*flags* ***hung*** at half mast 半旗. ¶***hang out*** a *flag* from a window 窓から旗を掲げる. ¶***haul down*** a *flag* 旗をたぐり降ろす. ¶***haul up*** a *flag* 旗を掲揚する. ¶*Flags* are being ***hoisted*** over buildings. 建物の屋上に旗が掲揚されている. ¶The *flags* of the two countries were ***intertwined.*** 両国の国旗が交差されていた. ¶the glory with which Nelson and his men ***invested*** the British *flag* ネルソンとその部下が英国国旗に与えた光栄. ¶***lift*** a *flag* 旗を掲げる. ¶***lower*** the *flag* 旗を降ろす. ¶***plant*** a national *flag* on the island 国旗をその島に立てる. ¶***protect*** her own *flag* from insult 自国の体面を全うする. ¶The national *flags* were ***put up*** in the streets. 町には国旗が掲揚してあった. ¶***raise*** *flags* of the United Nations 国際連合の旗をあげる ‖ A *flag* was ***raised.*** 旗が揚げてあった. ¶***respect*** the *flag* of one's home country 故国の国旗を敬う. ¶The Japanese *flag* was ***run up*** at the fore. 前マストに日本国旗が掲げてあった. ¶***salute*** the *flag* 旗に敬礼する. ¶*Flags* were ***set up*** (=***put up, erected, or displayed***) at every door. 戸毎に旗が立ててあった. ‖ ***set up*** their own *flags* 自分の旗(派)を立てる. ¶***stone*** a *flag* 旗に石を投げつける. ¶***show*** a *flag* 旗を掲げる. ¶***strike*** one's *flag* [敬意・降服などを示すために]旗を降ろす. ¶***toast*** the *flag* 国旗に対して乾杯する. ¶the Admiral ***transferred*** his *flag* to ... 提督はその指揮を...に譲った. ¶***turn*** the *flags* ***down*** 旗をたたむ. ¶The Japanese *flag* is ***unfurled.*** 日本の国旗が翻っている. ¶***wave*** *flags* and cheer ... 旗を振って...を歓呼する.

V² A *flag* ***floats*** from the bow. 旗が船首からなびいている. ‖ The British *flag* ***floats*** in every quarter of the globe. 英国国旗は地球上至る所に翻っている. ¶A *flag* ***flutters*** in the breeze. 旗が微風で揺れる. ‖ The commodore's *flag* ***fluttered*** slowly to half-mast. 提督旗はしずしずと翻って半

旗の位置を取った.【類】*Flags* ***flutter*** over the buildings. ¶The Japanese *flag* ***flies*** over the railway station at that point. その鉄道の停車場には日本の国旗が屋上に翻っている.【類】An American *flag* was ***flying*** over the tent occupied by Roosevelt. / in those ports over which ***flies*** the British *flag*. ¶The *flag* is ***streaming*** in the wind. 旗が風に翻っている. ¶*Flags* ***wave*** high and low. 旗が高く低くはためく. 【類】the *flag* ***waved*** from the top of ... / *Flags* were ***waving*** in the wind.

Q *Flags* were ***half-masted*** at all the embassies and legations in Tokyo as a token of mourning. 東京の大公使館が全部弔意を表して半旗を掲げていた. ¶The ***national*** *flags* are flown from every building. どの建物からも国旗がひらめいている. ¶fly the Russian ***naval*** *flag* ソ連の海軍旗を翻す.

Q^2 tattered ***battle*** *flags* ボロボロにした軍旗. ¶***Communist*** *flags*—Red banners of defiance 共産党の旗―挑戦の赤旗. ¶hoist a ***fighting*** *flag* 戦闘旗を掲げる. ¶a ***palmetto*** *flag* しゅろ旗(南カロライナ州旗). ¶colored "***paper carp***" *flags* 着色したこいのぼり. ¶a ***quarantine*** *flag* 検疫船旗, 伝染病信号旗. ¶hang out a ***war*** *flag* 戦旗を掲げる.

P fight ***for*** one's *Flag* (=country's flag) 国のために戦う. ¶loyalty ***to*** the *Flag* 国家に対する忠義. ¶serve ***under*** the *flag* 軍隊に勤める.【類】The steamer inaugurated a new river service ***under*** the British *flag* on the Karun river in Persia. ‖ He distinguished himself at Plevna ***under*** the *flag* of the Czar Alexander II. 彼は露国皇帝アレキサンダー二世の幕下に属しプレヴナにおいて名声をとどろかした. ‖ ***under*** a *flag* of truce 休戦中. ¶The ship was dressed ***with*** *flags*. 船は旗で飾られた. ‖ The town is gay ***with*** *flags*. 市中は旗で飾りたててある.

P^2 a *flag* ***at*** half-mast 半旗 ‖ The ship showed the Japanese *flag* ***at*** the fore. 船は前マストに日本の国旗を掲げていた. ¶a *flag* ***of*** truce 休戦(白)旗 ‖ For a time the *flag* ***of*** Holland floated nowhere else in the world but on that distant spot. しばらくの間オランダの国旗はその遠隔の地(出島)を除いては世界中どこにも翻っている所はなかった.

O *Flags* were out to welcome the general and his troops. 将軍とその軍隊を歓迎するため旗が出された.

flagrant, *a.* 名うての.

M ***outrageously*** *flagrant* すさまじいほど悪らつな.

flagstaff, *n.* 旗ざお.

P hoist a blue flag ***on*** a *flagstaff* 旗ざおの上に青色旗を立てる.

flail, *v.* むちで打つ.

M^2 *flail* a pony ***along*** with a stick 棒で小馬をなぐって進める.

flair, *n.* 眼識, 勘.

V ***develop*** the collector's *flair*, that mysterious sixth sense that comes by handling and practice 扱い慣れることから来るあの不思議な第六感たる収集家の勘を養う. ¶He ***has*** the *flair* for research. 彼は研究に対して勘がいい. ‖ The merchant ***has*** a *flair* for bargains. あの商人は取引がうまい.

Q his ***extraordinary*** *flair* for making friends with great souls 大人物を友人にする彼の非凡な才能.

flake, *n.* 薄片, 片(ぺ).

Q The snow is falling in ***large*** *flakes*. ぼたん雪が降っている. ¶Snow has ***pretty-shaped*** *flakes*. 雪片は美しい形をしている.

Q^2 canned ***salmon*** *flakes* さけの薄切りのかん詰. ¶***Snow*** *flakes* are dancing in the air. 雪が空中に舞っている.

P separate ***in*** *flakes* 薄片になって離れた.

P^2 *flakes* ***of*** fish (salmon, bonito) 魚(など)のフレーク. 【類】*flakes* ***of*** ice floating on the lake.

flake, *v.* はがす, はぐ.

M The surface of the granite pedestal was *flaked* ***off*** in spots by the heat of the conflagration that raged through this quarter of the city. 花こう岩の台石の表面は市のこの方面をなめた大火の熱でところどころはげていた.

flame, *n.* 炎, 火炎; 火; 情熱; 光輝; 《俗》情人.

V bags of sand to ***blanket*** *flame* 炎を消すための砂袋. ¶try to ***combat*** *flames* set by high explosives 強い爆薬で立てられた火炎を消そうと試みる. ¶***extinguish*** the *flames* 火を消す. ¶***fan*** the *flames* of racial hostility 人種的敵意に拍車をかける ‖ The *flame* was ***fanned*** by a strong wind. 火炎は強風にあおられた. ¶***feed*** the *flame* of her lover's heart 彼女の愛人の情火をたきつける. ¶***ignite*** and ***spread*** the *flames* 火をつけて広げる. ¶He lost his life while ***fighting*** the *flame*. 彼は猛火と戦って生命を失った. ¶the spark that ***kindled*** the *flame* 火炎を起した火花 ‖ ***kindle*** the *flame* of discord among ... ...の間に不和の火をたきつける. ¶***occasion*** so great a *flame* in burning that ... 燃えるとき非常な火炎を出す... ¶***overcome*** the *flames* 火を消し止める. ¶***put out*** the *flames* 火を消す. ¶They succeeded in ***quenching*** the *flames*. うまく火を消し止めた. ¶***shoot out*** the *flames* out of ... ...から火炎を吹き出す. ¶***subdue*** *flames* 鎮火させる. ¶The volcano ***vomited*** *flames* and hurled cinders for many leagues. その火山は炎を吐いて幾リーグにも渡って火山灰を飛ばした.

V^2 A *flame* ***came*** into her cheeks. 彼女はさっとほおを赤らめた. ¶*Flames* ***flicker*** in the wind. 炎が風に揺らぐ. ¶*flame* ***spurted*** from ... 火炎が...から噴出した.

Q a ***green*** *flame* 緑色の火炎. ¶a ***lambent*** *flame* なめるように広がって行く火炎. ¶an ***old*** *flame* of mine 私の昔の情人. ¶an ***open*** *flame* 裸火. ¶burn with ***purple*** *flames* 紫色の炎を立てて燃える. ¶a ***quenchless*** *flame* 消し難い炎. ¶a ***sooty*** *flame* すすを吐く火炎.

Q^2 A ***candle*** *flame* flickers. ろうそくの火が揺らぐ ‖ the old gas jets with their "***fish-tail***" *flames* 魚尾状の炎を立てるガス. ¶a ***gas-light*** *flame* ガス灯の炎. ¶Houses burned up in ***war*** *flames*. 多数の家屋が戦火で焼失した.

P the area swept ***by*** the *flames* 焼け跡. ¶Very soon the whole house was ***in*** *flames*. たちまち家中が火炎に包まれた.【類】Houses in the villages were ***in*** *flames*. ‖ The sun went down ***in*** *flame* on the far horizon. 太陽が遠方の地平線にあかあかと輝いて没した. ‖ He perished ***in*** the *flames*. 彼は焼け死んだ. ‖ People were ***in*** a *flame* on account of the war news. 民衆は戦争のニュースで興奮していた. ¶burst ***into*** *flame* ぱっと燃え上がる. ¶on the approach ***of*** a *flame* 火が近づくときに. ¶commit it ***to*** the *flames* それを火にくべる. ¶burn ***with*** a bright *flame* あざやかな炎を立てて燃える ‖ burn ***with*** scarcely any *flame* ほとんど炎を立てずに燃える.

P^2 the *flame* ***from*** the fire 火事の炎. ¶A *flame* ***of*** scarlet crept across her cheeks. 彼女はさっとほおを赤らめた.

flame, *v.* 火炎をあげる, 燃え立つ; [情熱・怒りが]燃え上る.

M The light *flamed* ***out*** from the lantern. ちょうちんの火がぱっと燃え上った. ‖ His anger *flamed* ***out*** (=***up*** *or* ***forth***) 彼はかっとなった. ¶Her cheeks *flamed* ***suddenly***. 彼女はさっとほおを染めた.

M^2 *flame* ***up*** furiously 恐ろしく立腹する.

flank, *n.* 側面.

V ***cover*** one's *flank* 側面を守る. ¶***turn*** the enemy's *flank* 敵の側面を回って背後をつく.

P ***in*** *flank* 側面に ‖ attack the enemy ***in*** the *flank* 敵の側面をつく. ¶attack the enemy ***on*** the right *flank* 右側面から敵を攻撃する.

flank, *v.* ...の側面に立つ.

P *flank* ***on*** the sea 海を横に控えている. ¶The town is *flanked* ***with*** (=***by***) the sea. その町は海をわきに控えている.

flannel, *n.* ネル; [洋服布地の]フラノ地.

V ***wear*** *flannels* フラノの洋服を着る(ずぼんをはく).

Q^2 ***Canton*** (=***cotton***) *flannel* 綿ネル.

flap, *n.* 羽撃ち; [ポケットの]たれ.

V ***paste*** the *flap* of the envelope 封筒の折り返しをのりづけする.

Q the ***front*** (***back***) *flap* of a book 本のとびら(見返し). ¶***tide*** *flap* 汐留下水のとびら.

P^2 the *flap* ***of*** an eagle's wings わしの羽ばたき.

flap, *v.* はたく; ひらひらさせる.

M *flap* flies ***away*** (=***off***) はえをぱたぱた打払う. ¶*flap* ***out*** [灯火などを]ぷっと吹き消す.

M^2 *flap* ***up*** (***down***) ひらひら舞上る(降りる).

flare, *n.* 炎; 〖服装〗フレア.

Q a ***sudden*** *flare* of trumpet 突然鳴るトランペットの音.

P^2 the *flare* ***of*** a match マッチの炎. ¶the *flare* ***of*** a skirt スカートのぱっと開くこと; 〖服飾〗スカートのフレア.

flare, *v.* ぱっと燃え上る; 〖服装〗フレアにする.

M^2 *flare* ***over*** 朝顔形に開く(器にいう). ¶*flare* ***up*** (=***out***) ぱっと燃え上る; かっとなる. ¶*flare* ***up*** into flames ぱっと燃え上る ‖ Flames *flared* ***up*** against the blackness. 真暗な空に火炎がぱっと燃え上った. ‖ The question *flared* ***up*** again. その問題が再燃した. ‖ He *flared* ***up*** in anger. 彼はかっとなった. ‖ The bull *flared* ***up*** at the sight of a red cloak. 雄牛は赤い外とうを見るといきり立った. ‖ We *flared* ***up*** again last night and hailed the New Year with the usual ceremonies. われわれはゆうべも飲み騒ぎ例のやり方で新年を祝した.

flash, *n.* せん光, ひらめき.

V ***emit*** *flashes* of brilliant flame ぴかっとせん光を発する.

Q a ***blinding blue*** *flash* 目もくらむ青いせん光. ¶After a ***few fitful*** *flashes* it went out. 二三度ぴかりぴかりと光ってから消えた. ¶a ***single*** *flash* of light 一回のきらめき(ぴかり). ¶a ***sudden*** *flash* into consciousness of the solution 突然解決を得たという自覚のひらめき.

Q^2 a ***lightning*** *flash* 電光のひらめき.

P ***at*** the first *flash* (=glance) 一見して. ¶He was killed ***by*** a *flash* of lightning. 彼は落雷で死んだ. ¶***in*** a *flash* 即座に, 即刻. ¶He drew his sword ***with*** a *flash.* 彼はきらりと剣を抜いた.

P^2 a *flash* ***in*** the pan ぱっと燃えてすぐ消えること(線香花火式). ¶a *flash* ***of*** hope 一るの望み ‖ a *flash* ***of*** wit 機知のひらめき ‖ like a *flash* ***of*** light (=lightning) 電光一せん.

flash, *v.* ひらめく, ぴかりとする, ぱっと心に浮ぶ.

P The lightning *flashed* ***across*** the sky. 電光がサッとひらめいた. ‖ A sudden thought *flashed* ***across*** his brain (=mind). 突然考えが彼の頭にひらめいた. ‖ A quick suspicion *flashed* ***across*** me. 急に疑念が胸に浮んだ. ‖ *flash* news ***across*** the world ニュースを世界中に伝送する. ¶*flash* ***back*** the sunshine 日光を照し返す. ¶A good idea *flashes* ***before*** my mind. 私に好い考えが浮んだ. ¶scarlet *flashing* ***in*** the sun 日光にきらめくあざやかな紅色. ¶*flash* (=suddenly burst) ***into*** consciousness like lightning from a clear sky 晴天の稲妻のようにハッと気づく ‖ He *flashed* (=leaped) ***into*** fame. 彼は一朝にして名を成した. ¶His eyes *flashed* ***like*** lightning. 彼の目は稲光のように光った. ‖ programs *flashed* ***into*** the ether 番組が電波に乗せられる(放送される). ¶*flash* a message ***on*** the air 通信を無電で送る. ¶it *flashed* ***through*** my mind that ... …という考えが急に頭に浮んだ. 【類】A thought (=An idea) *flashed* ***through*** his mind. / "Who is he?" was the question which immediately *flashed* ***through*** my mind. / There *flashed* ***through*** my mind one desperate possibility of escape, and I acted on it without a moment's hesitation. ‖ The divine power had *flashed* ***through*** the humanity of Christ. キリストの人間性に神の力が通ったのであった. ¶it *flashed* ***upon*** me that ... …という考えが胸に浮んだ ‖ The scene *flashed* ***upon*** his sight. その光景がちらりと彼の目に映った. ¶His eyes *flashed* ***with*** rage. 彼の目は怒りに燃えていた.

flask, *n.* フラスコ(びん).

Q^2 a ***thermos*** *flask* 魔法びん. ¶a ***vacuum*** *flask* 魔法びん.

flat, *n.* 平面; 刀の平(ひら).

Q^2 a ***river*** *flat* 河床.

P ***on*** the same *flat* 同一平面に. ¶strike ... ***with*** the *flat* of one's sword 刀の平(ひら)で…を打つ.

P^2 the *flat* ***of*** one's hand 手の平.

flat, *n.* 《英》家屋の床, アパート式共同住宅の一つ.

Q^2 a ***ground-floor*** *flat* 一階のフラット. ¶a block of ***service*** *flats* 軍用共同住宅. ¶a ***three-room*** *flat* 三室の割貸家.

flat, *a.* 平たんな, ぺったりくっついた; 味のない.

M The Bourse is ***decidedly*** *flat* 株式取引所は断然低調である. ¶Sale is ***very*** *flat.* 売行がはなはだ悪い.

P lie *flat* ***on*** the ground 地上にばったり倒れている ‖ spread a map *flat* ***on*** the ground 地図を地面に広げる. ¶This beer drinks *flat* ***to*** the taste. このビールは気が抜けている. ‖ Life seems *flat* ***to*** him. 人生は彼にとって味気ないものらしい.

flatness, *n.* 平たん.

P I came to feel that, naturally thin, I was rapidly becoming reduced ***to*** the *flatness* of a sardine. 本来やせている私であるから見る見る干物のようにぺしゃんこになって行くような感じがした.

flatten, *v.* 平にする, ぺちゃんこにする.

M *flatten* ***out*** a piece of metal by hammering it 一片の金属をたたき延ばす.

P crops *flattened* ***by*** a storm あらしにやられた作物.

flatter, *v.* へつらう, こびる; 喜ばせる.

M You *flatter* me ***immensely***! そう言われると恐縮します(とんでもない). ¶You are ***merely*** *flattering* me. おじょうずをおっしゃって. ¶I felt very ***much*** *flattered* by the honor which had been done me. 私は敬意を表されて大いにくすぐったい感じがした. ¶be too ***obviously*** *flattering* へつらいが見え透いている.

P I felt greatly *flattered* ***at*** the request that I should make a speech on the occasion. 私にその折演説をせよということで大いに得意だった. ¶She was *flattered* ***by*** his attentions. 彼女は彼にちやほやされてうれしがった. ‖ I felt *flattered* ***by*** his approval. 私は彼に結構だと言われたのでうれしく思った.

O I'm *flattered!* [ほめられて]とんでもないことです.

flattering, *a.* うれしい.

P It was very *flattering* ***to*** me to be taken for such a distinguished man. 私はそんな有名な人と間違われて非常にうれしかった. ‖ It's not very *flattering* ***to*** our pride. 余り名誉にならない.

flattery, *n.* へつらい, おべっか.

V ***swallow*** *flattery* おべっかを真(ま)に受ける.

Q ***coarse*** *flattery* 見えすいたおべっか. ¶***delicate*** *flattery* 言葉巧みなへつらい. ¶***insincere*** *flattery* 心にもないへつらい.

P He is ***above*** *flattery.* 彼はおべっかに乗らない. ¶He is proof ***against*** *flattery.* 彼にはおべっかはきかない. ¶He obtained my consent ***by*** *flattery.* 彼はおだてて僕に同意させた. ¶gain one's object ***by means of*** *flattery* おべっかで目的を遂げる. ¶He is much exposed ***to*** *flattery.* 彼は人から大いにへつらわれるような立場にある.

flattop, *n.* 《軍俗》航空母艦.

P planes taking off ***from*** or landing ***on*** the *flattop* as guided by signals 信号に従って航空母艦に離着する飛行機.

flavo[u]r, *n.* 風味; 香, 香気; 趣味, 風致.

V ***absorb*** the *flavor* of ... …の香を吸う. ¶***acquire*** the *flavor* of ... …の風味を持つに至る. ¶***bring out*** the full *flavors* of the other ingredients その他の成分の味を十分に出す. ¶***contract*** the *flavor* of ... …の香が移る. ¶***enhance*** the *flavor* of ... …の風味を高める. ¶***give*** a *flavor* to ... …に風味を添える. ¶***have*** a *flavor* of ... …の香気がある. 【類】The flower ***has*** very little *flavor.* / Tea ***has*** a good *flavor.* ¶***impart*** a delicate *flavor* to the beverage その飲料に微妙な風味を添える. ¶***keep*** its *flavor* その香を失わないようにする. ¶Sweet corn should be used as soon as possible after the ears are removed from the stalks as it ***loses*** its *flavor* very quickly. とうもろこしは風味を失いやすいから茎から取ったらできるだけ早く食べるがよい. ¶***possess*** a pleasant *flavor* 良い風味がある. Standing a day ***ripens*** the *flavor.* 一日置くと味がよくなる. ¶The full *flavor* of foreign letters cannot be ***translated.*** 外国文学の味は翻訳では十分移し得ない. ¶***try*** the *flavor* 味をみる.

Q This water has an extremely ***acid*** *flavor.* この水は非常に酸味がある. ¶an ***agreeable*** *flavor* 気持のよい風味. ¶give a ***bitter*** *flavor* to ... …に苦味(にがみ)をつける. ¶ice-cream with a ***chocolate*** *flavor* チョコレートの味をつけたアイスクリーム. ¶***colloquial*** *flavor* 口語調. ¶sweets with ***different*** *flavors* 様々の味をつけた菓子. ¶a ***fine*** *flavor* よい味. ¶the ***foreign*** *flavor* in phraseology 表現における外国調. ¶an old-fashioned phrase with a ***literary*** *flavor* 文学的風味のある古風な句. ¶a ***meaty*** *flavor* 肉の味. ¶a ***mellow*** *flavor* ほんのりした風味. ¶a ***native*** *flavor* 固有の香. ¶***natural*** *flavor* 自然の風味. ¶It suffices to give the buildings a distinctly ***nautical*** *flavor.* それはその建物にはっきりと海上趣味を添えるに十分だ. ¶a ***pleasant*** *flavor* 気持のよい味. ¶a ***racy*** *flavor* 風味. ¶The sentence so reconstructed takes on ***rhetorical*** *flavor.* その文をそう作り直すと美辞的な趣が出る. ¶a ***sharp*** *flavor* ぴりっとした風味. ¶It has a ***strong*** *flavor* of the Orient. それは大いに東洋風を帯びている. ¶a ***subtle*** *flavor* all its own 全く独特の風味. ¶***tasty*** *flavor* よい味. ¶an ***undesirable*** *flavor* 感心しない風味.

Q^2 a leisurely ***old-world*** *flavor* ゆったりした昔風.

P^2 the *flavor* ***of*** America アメリカの風味 ‖ the *flavor* ***of*** the sixteenth century 第十六世紀の風味. 【類】It has a *flavor* ***of*** old times about it.

flavo[u]r, *v.* 味を付ける.

M be ***deliciously*** *flavored* 味がいい. ¶be ***richly*** *flavored* よくだしが出ている. ¶be ***strongly*** *flavored* with salt 塩がよくきいている.

P It is *flavored* ***with*** ginger. それはしょうがの味がつけてある. ‖ ice-cream *flavored* ***with*** lemon レモンで味をつけ

たアイスクリーム ‖ a story *with* a *flavor* of romance ロマンスの香りのする物語.

flaw, *n.* 欠点, 欠陥, きず.

V I was unable to *find* a *flaw* in his argument. 私には彼の議論に弱点を見出すことができなかった. ¶*pick flaws* in … …のあら探しをする.

Q the *fatal flaw* in this argument is that … この議論の大欠点は…ということだ. ¶goods which contain *hidden flaws* 目につかないきずのある品物. ¶But these are trifles. A far more *serious flaw* is this. しかしこれらはささいなことで, はるかに重大な欠点はこれだ. ¶a *trivial flaw* わずかなきず.

P[2] a *flaw in* one's character 性格上の欠陥 ‖ a *flaw in* a jewel 玉にきず 【類】 These are *flaws in* the crystal.

flea, *n.* のみ.

V *Fleas bite.* のみがさす.

P *with* a *flea* in one's ear 耳の痛いことを言われて.

flea-bite, *n.* のみ食いのあと.

Q The wound was a *mere flea-bite.* それはほんのちょっとしたきずであった. ‖ The cost is a *mere fleabite.* その位の費用は何でもない.

fleck, *n.* そばかす; はん点.

V You *got flecks.* 君はそばかすがある.

P[2] a *fleck of* snow (dust, cloud) 一片(点)の雪(ごみ, 雲) ‖ *flecks of* color on a bird's breast 鳥の胸にある着色はん点.

fleck, *v.* はん点をつける.

P the shadow *flecked through* the branches of trees. ¶a sky *flecked with* clouds 雲の点在している空.

fledge, *v.* 羽が生えそろう.

M *fledge out* 羽が生えそろう.

fledged, *a.* 羽の生えた.

M a *fully fledged* newsman=a full-fledged newsman 一人前の新聞記者.

flee, *v.* 逃げる; 消散する.

M He *fled away* at the first sign of danger. 彼は危険と見るや逃げてしまった. ¶He *fled precipitately.* 彼はあわてて逃げた.

P They *fled before* the dreadful enemy. 彼らは敵の勢いに恐れて逃げた. ‖ The clouds are *fleeing before* the wind. 雲が風に吹払われている. ¶He *fled by* night. 彼は夜逃げをした. ¶He *fled for* his life. 彼は命からがら逃げた. ‖ *flee for* refuge (=shelter *or* safety) 避難する. ¶*flee from* reality 現実を離れる ‖ *flee from* responsibility (duty) 責任(など)を回避する ‖ *flee from* justice 逮捕を避ける ‖ *flee from* a country (city) 国(など)から逃亡する ‖ The color *fled from* his face. 彼は色を失った. 【類】 The smile *fled from* her cheeks. / They *fled* defeated *from* the field of battle. / *flee from* one's own crime. ¶They *fled in* disorder. 彼らは算を乱して逃げた. ¶He *fled into* a forest. 彼は森に逃げ込んだ. ‖ *flee into* a passion 熱情に走る. ¶He *fled through* fear. 彼はこわいので逃げた. ¶He will soon *flee to* Manchuria. 彼は間もなく満州へ逃げるだろう. ¶She *fled with* her two children. 彼女は二人の子供を連れて逃げた.

O They had to *flee* the country. 彼らは国から逃げ出さなければならなかった.

fleece, *v.* 羊毛; けば.

P[2] have a *fleece of* hair 羊毛のような頭髪だ. ¶the *fleeces of* descending snow ぼたん(綿)雪.

fleece, *v.* [羊毛などで]一面におおう; 詐取する.

M a knit shirt *thickly fleeced* inside 裏毛のメリヤスシャツ.

M[2] The trees are *fleeced over* with snow. 樹木は一面に雪でおおわれている.

P *fleece* one *of* all one possesses 所有物を全部巻き上げる. ¶*fleece* him *out of* every cent he had 一銭残らず彼から巻き上げる. ¶The sky was *fleeced with* white clouds. 空には白雲が浮んでいた.

fleet, *n.* 艦隊, 船隊.

V *annihilate* a *fleet* 艦隊を撃滅する. ¶*cripple* the Russian *fleet* ソ連艦隊を立つ能わざらしめる. ¶*despatch* a *fleet* to a port 港に艦隊を派遣する. ¶*fit out* a *fleet* of seven vessels 七隻の船隊を装備する. ¶The United States *maintains* a very powerful *fleet* in Oriental waters. 米国は東洋に極めて有力な艦隊を保持している. ¶*winter* her *fleet* at … その艦隊を…で越冬させる.

Q an *American fleet* under Commodore Perry ペルリ提督旗下の米国艦隊. ¶The *blockading fleet* is insufficient. その封鎖艦隊は手薄だ. ¶a *combined fleet* 連合艦隊. ¶a *hostile fleet* 敵艦隊. ¶Germany's *magnificent naval* and *commercial fleets* ドイツの堂々たる艦隊及び商船隊.

Q[2] the repulse of the *Mongol fleet* sent by Kublai Khan フビライ派遣の元(げん)艦隊を撃退. ¶a *mosquito fleet* 小型艦隊. ¶a *U.S. fleet* under Admiral Halsey ホールシー提督旗下の米海軍.

P[2] a *fleet in* being 現存艦隊. ¶a *fleet of* ships 船隊 ‖ a *fleet of* cabs (=taxis) 一会社所属の全タクシー群.

fleet, *a.* はやい.

P He is *fleet of* foot. 彼は足がはやい.

flesh, *n.* 肉; 肉体; 肉付, 肥満; 人間; 肉欲.

M *gain* (=*get*) *flesh*=get stout 太る, 肉づく. ¶*lose flesh* =become thin 肉が落ちる, やせる. ¶situations that *make* the *flesh* creep きもを冷すような事態. ¶*mortify* the *flesh* for the sake of saving the soul 霊魂を救うために肉欲を制する. ¶*put on* (=*pick up*) *flesh* 肉づく. ¶*reduce* one's *flesh* やせる. ¶*sear* the *flesh* 体をしなびさす.

V[2] His *flesh fell* rapidly *away.* 彼はどんどんやせた.

Q *all flesh* 一切衆生(しゅじょう); 人間. ¶*flaccid flesh* しまりのない肉. ¶He lost one of *his* [*own*] *flesh* [and blood]. 彼は骨肉の一人を失った. ¶*plump flesh* 体を太らせる. ¶*putrefying flesh* 腐敗しかけた肉. ¶*raw flesh* すりむいた赤はだ.

Q[2] *fruit flesh* 果物の肉. ¶the roll of *waistline flesh* でぶ女.

P *after* the *flesh* 人間的に. ¶a bruise *in* the *flesh* はだの打傷 ‖ *in* the *flesh* うつし身となって; 生きて ‖ *in flesh* and blood 生き身の(人間として). 【類】 long, long, long ago in the days when Gautama Buddha (しゃかむに) himself walked *in* the *flesh* in distant India … ‖ whom I have never seen *in* the *flesh* その人には(手紙のやりとりだけで)直接会ったことがない.

flesh, *v.* 肉をつける.

M be *well fleshed* 肉づきがいい.

fleshiness, *n.* 肉づき.

Q *hard fleshiness* かた太り.

fleshy, *a.* 太った.

M be *too fleshy* 太り過ぎている.

flexibility, *n.* 融通性.

V He *lacks* the *flexibility* of a Parliamentary politician. 彼には議会政治家の変通性が無い(融通がきかない).

Q A man devoid of *imaginative flexibility* could not be a successful actor. 変通自在の想像力がなければりっぱな俳優にはなれない.

flexible, *a.* しなやかな.

M[2] *as flexible* as a reed あしのようにしなやかな.

flick, *n.* ぱちっという音,

P *by* the *flick* of a switch スイッチをぱちっとひねって.

flick, *v.* [むちで]ぴしと打つ; 払い落す.

M *flick away* (=*off*) mosquitoes from … …から蚊をたたいて払う. ¶*flick* dust *off* … …からほこりをはたき落す. 【類】 *flick* the ash *off* into the ash-tray.

flicker, *n.* 揺れる光.

Q an *uncertain flicker* of light 消えそうな光のゆらめき.

P[2] the *flicker of* a candle ろうそくの灯のゆらぎ.

flicker, *v.* [炎が]揺れる, 明滅する.

M The light *flickered out* in the wind. 灯火が風でちらちらして消えた.

M[2] The last faint hope *flickered up* and died. 最後の望みの光もちらと見えたが消え失せた.

P The light *flickered in* the wind. 灯りが風でちらちらゆれた.

flier, *n.* 飛行士.

Q[2] an *army flier* 陸軍飛行士 ‖ a *stunt flier* 高等(曲乗)飛行士. ¶a *woman flier*=an aviatrix 女流飛行家.

flight, *n.* 飛行; 急過; 逃走, 逃亡; 飛程; 飛躍; 飛群; 連発; 階段.

V *attempt* a *flight* around the world in an airplane 飛行機で世界一周飛行を試みる. ¶*carry out* trial *flight* 試験飛行を行う. ¶He *completed* the *flight* in 25 hours and 50 minutes. 彼はその飛行を二十五時間と五十分で終えた. ¶three aeroplanes *conducted* a *flight* in the direction of … 三機が…の方向に飛行した. ¶The wild goose *has* a *flight* of 100 miles per hour.=The flight of the wild goose is 100 miles an hour.=The wild goose flies at the rate of 100 miles per hour. がんは一時間に百マイル飛ぶ. ¶*make* a *flight* of … miles …マイルの飛行をする ‖ He *made* a *flight* from … to … 彼は…から…へ飛行した. ¶he *took flight* on hearing the sound of … 彼は…の音を聞いて逃げた. ¶the bird *winged* its *flight* to … その鳥は…へ飛んで行った.

Q go up *another flight* [of stairs] もう一つ階段を登る. ¶a staircase of *easy* (steep) *flights* こう配のゆるい(急な)階

段. ¶an *extended flight* 長距離飛行. ¶*hair-raising flights* 身の毛もよだつ飛行の離れ業. ¶Look! There is a *large flight* (=flock) of wild geese. 見給え, がんが群をなして飛んで行く. ¶the *loftiest flights* of oratory 最高級の雄弁. ¶a *metaphorical flight* [白髪三千丈式の]思い切った想像. ¶*oratorical flights* 気炎. ¶a *precipitous flight* of stairs 急こう配の階段. ¶a *steep flight* of stone-steps 急こう配の石段. ¶The plane made a *successful flight* over 16,000 km. その飛行機は首尾よく 16,000 キロをしょう破した. ¶attain a height by *sudden flight* 一挙に高所に達っする. ¶If you met them in the street, you would not think in your *wildest flights* of fancy that their address is Rowton House, Hammersmith Road. 往来で彼らに会ったのではどう考えても彼らの宿所がハマースミス街のラウトン・ハウス(安宿の名)だとは思うまい.

Q^2 an *air-mail flight* 郵便飛行. ¶an *airplane flight* 飛行. ¶a *continent-to-continent flight* 大陸間飛行. ¶make a *coast-to-coast flight* 《米》大陸横断飛行をやる. ¶a *courier flight* 急行飛行. ¶a *dare-devil flight* 無鉄砲な飛行. ¶an *endurance flight* 耐空飛行. ¶an *exercise flight* 練習飛行. ¶an *exploration flight* 探検飛行. ¶the spring and *fall flights* of birds 春秋の鳥の移動. ¶*high altitude flight* 高空飛行. ¶make a *long-distance flight* [犯人が]高飛びをする. ¶a *night flight* 夜間飛行. ¶a *patrol flight* 巡回飛行. ¶He made the first *non-stop air flight* across the Atlantic. 彼は最初の大西洋横断無着陸飛行を行った. ¶a *pioneer flight* 草分け飛行. ¶a *radio flight* 無線連絡飛行. ¶on his *return flight* 帰りの飛行のとき. ¶a *round-the-world flight* 世界一周飛行. ¶a *shuttle flight* 往復飛行. ¶Lindbergh's *solo flight* over the Atlantic リンドバーグの単独大西洋横断飛行. ¶*stratosphere flights* of balloons (airplanes) 気球(飛行機)の成層圏飛行. ¶a *surveillance flight* 巡戒飛行. ¶have its first *test flight* 最初の試験飛行を行う. 【類】a successful *test flight*. ¶on a *training flight* 練習飛行のとき.

P His room is approached *by* a *flight* of steps. 彼のへやへは階段を一つ上がって行くのだ. ¶foretell events *from* the *flights* of birds 鳥の飛び方で占う. ¶seek safety *in flight* 逃げて安全を図る. ¶a flock of birds *in flight* 飛んでいる一群の鳥. 【類】The swallow is swift *in flight*. ‖ Mr. Mars *in flight* on Baldwin biplane ボールドウィン機で飛行中のマース氏. ‖ her companion *in flight* 彼女の逃亡の道連れ ‖ The thief *in flight* waived (=threw away) the goods stolen. 逃走中に賊は盗んだ品を投げ出した. ¶study the art *of flight* 航空術を研究する. ¶a new commercial liner *on* a test *flight* over ... …上空に試験飛行の新旅客機. ¶put the enemy *to flight* 敵を敗走させる ‖ He took *to flight*. 彼は逃げ出した. ¶*with* the *flight* of time 時の経過につれて.

P^2 *flight from* prison (danger) 脱獄(避難). ¶a *flight of* cranes roaring high overhead 空高く鳴く一群のつる ‖ the *flight of* time 早くたつ月日 ‖ the *flight of* an airship 飛行船の飛程 ‖ a *flight of* arrows 矢の連発 ‖ a *flight of* ambition 天をつく大望 ‖ a *flight of* ideas [しり取文句に見るような]思想の飛躍. ¶a *flight on* the beam 〖空〗無線連絡飛行.

flinch, *v*. しり込する, ひるむ.

P *flinch at* pain 痛みでひるむ. ¶He never *flinches from* doing what is right. 彼は決して正しいことにしりごみしない. 【類】The brave man does not *flinch from* danger.

flinching, *n*. ひるむこと.

P He did the duty *without flinching*. 彼はひるまず本分を尽した.

fling, *n*. 投げ; 悪口; わがまま.

V He *gave* the stone a *fling*. 彼はその石を投げた. ¶*have* a *fling* at ... =make an attempt at ... … を試みる. 【類】*have* a *fling* at an enterprise ‖ Let him *have* his *fling*! 彼は思う存分やらしておけ.

P He has done his work *at* one *fling*. 彼は一気にその仕事をやっつけた. ¶He has done such a thing *in* a *fling*. 彼はわがままからこんなことをした.

fling, *v*. 投げる; 投げ込む; 打振る; 放つ.

M *fling away* (=*aside*) one's ambition 野心を捨てる. ¶*fling back* one's head 頭を後ろに振る. ¶*fling* the door *open* (shut) 戸を押し開ける(ばたんと閉じる). ¶The spring *flings out* about ten tons of water in a minute. その泉は一分間に約十トンの水を噴出する. ‖ *fling out* one's arms 両腕をぐっと伸ばす ‖ *fling out* hard words against another 他人に対して暴言をはく ‖ *fling out* a ball 球を力強く投げる.

M^2 *fling* oneself *about* のたくり回る. ¶*fling* it *in* his face それを彼の顔に投げ付ける ‖ In settling accounts, I *flung in* a small sum. 勘定を払うとき私は小額の金を余分に渡した. ¶*fling* one's coat *off* 上衣をかなぐり捨てる. ¶He *flung* his coat *on*. 彼は手早く上着を着た. ¶The girl will *fling* him *over*. 《俗》その娘は彼を見捨てるだろう. ¶The horse *flung up* his heels. 馬が後脚でけ上げた.

P *fling* a penny *at* the beggar こじきに一ペニー投げてやる ‖ *fling* herself *at* a man's head 男に夢中になる. ¶*fling* oneself *from* one's horse (carriage) 馬(など)から飛び降りる. ¶*fling* one's arms *in* air 両手を高く振り上げる. ¶*fling* a copper *into* the box 箱に銅貨を一つ投込む ‖ *fling* a person *into* prison 人を投獄する ‖ She *flung* herself *into* his arms. 彼女は彼の両腕にすがった. ¶*fling* a ship *on* the rocks 船を岩と衝突させる ‖ They *flung* themselves *on* the enemy. 彼らは敵に攻め寄った. ‖ the seaweed *flung on* the shore by the waves 波で海岸に打上げられた海草. ¶The tree *flung* shade *over* the grass. その木は芝生に陰を投げた. ¶He *flung* himself *upon* me. 彼は僕に飛びかかった.

flint, *n*. 火打石; [ライターの]石.

V *chip flint* 火打石をちびらす. ¶He would *skin* a *flint* [if he could]. =He is very miserly. あの男は火打石の皮もはぎ兼ねない(ほどのしみったれ). ¶*use flints* for striking fire 火を起すに火打石を使う.

P He has a heart *of flint*. 彼は石のように冷酷だ.

P^2 a *flint for* the lighter ライターの石.

O His heart is as hard as a *flint*. 心は石のように冷い.

flip, *v*. ぽんとはじく, ぴしっと打つ.

M The twig *flipped back* and scratched his face. 小枝がはね返って彼の顔を引っかいた.

M^2 *flip* a speck of dust *off* 一点のちりをはじき落す ‖ *flip* ash *off* one's cigarette シガレットから灰をおとす ‖ *flip* a mosquito *off* from one's leg 脚をたたいて蚊を追い払う.

P The driver *flipped at* a fly *with* his whip. 御者がむちではえをたたいた.

flirt, *n*. はすっぱ女.

Q a *clever flirt* 利口なはすっぱ女. ¶an *incorrigible flirt* 度しがたい浮気女.

flirt, *v*. ひらりと飛ぶ; ふざける.

P *flirt at* the idea of ... …をうぬぼれる. ¶The flag *flirts in* the breeze. その旗が微風に翻る. ¶The paper must have *flirted into* the fire. 紙は吹飛んで火の中へはいったに違いない. ¶*flirt with* a woman (husband) 女にふざける(夫に甘たれる).

flit, *v*. ひらひら(すいすい)飛ぶ.

P The idea *flitted across* (=*through*) my brain. その考えがふと浮んだ. ¶bees that *flit from* flower *to* flower 花から花へと飛ぶみつばち.

flitting, *n*. 逃避.

Q^2 a *moonlight flitting* [借金取を避けるためなどの]夜逃げ.

float, *v*. 浮ぶ, ただよう; 浮べる, ただよわせる.

M *float downstream* 川を流れ下る. ¶Now and again the old tunes *float out* on the silence of the night. ときどきなつかしい曲が夜の静けさに流れる. 【類】The aroma (におい) of boiling cabbage *floats out* through the kitchen windows. / Dreamy waltz music was heard *floating out* upon the quiet night from the colossal Cecil (セシルの大ホテル). ¶The boat *floated rapidly* in mid-stream. 舟が川の真中をどんどん流れて行った. ¶The ship was grounded, but *successfully floated* after lightening. その船は座礁したが(積荷を減らして)軽くしてから首尾よく浮上った.

M^2 White fleecy clouds are *floating above*. 羊毛のような白雲が頭上に浮いている. ¶Leaves *float on* the top of the water. 木の葉が水の表面に浮ぶ. ¶The English flag now *floats over* ... 英国の旗が今…に掲げられている. ¶The stranded vessel *floated off*. 座礁船が浮き上った.

P *Above* the building the Stars and Stripes are *floating*. その建物の上に星条旗が翻っている. ¶*float down* a stream 川を流れ下る ‖ *float* timber *down* a river 材木を川下に流す. ¶flags *float from* ... 旗が…に翻る. ¶*float in* the water (air) 水中(など)に浮ぶ. ¶The tide *floated* the ship *into* the harbour. 船は潮流にただよって港に入った. ¶*float on* the sea 海上にただよう ‖ *float on* one's back 仰向けになって浮く. 【類】What is that *floating on* the water? / *float on* the surface / Through the open windows snatches of melody *float on* the night air (夜風に乗って), announcing to all that a dance is in progress. ¶a colony *over* which the Union Jack now *floats* supreme 大英国国旗が今堂々と翻っている植民地. 【類】in every land that the stars and stripes (星条旗) ***float over*** ‖ The balloon was *floated* ***over*** the city. 気球を市の上空に揚げた. ¶The field was *floated* ***with*** blood. 戦場は流血にまみれた.

floating, *n.* 漂流.

P^2 the *floating* ***of*** icebergs 氷山の漂流.

O a *floating* up into a high sphere 高空への上昇.

flock, *n.* 群; 会衆; 信徒.

V A *flock* of birds ***hovers*** around the farm. 一群の鳥が畑のあたりを飛びまわる. ¶raise one's ***first*** *flock* 初めての羊群を飼育する.

Q a ***large*** *flock* of pigeons はとの大群. ¶***numerous*** *flocks* of wild geese 無数のがんの群.

P gather (come, live) ***in*** a *flock* 群をなして集まる(など). ¶The shepherd watches ***over*** his *flock*. 羊飼が羊たちの番をする. 【類】The pastor watches ***over*** his *flock* (会衆).

P^2 a *flock* ***of*** sheep without a shepherd 烏合(うごう)の衆 ‖ a *flock* ***of*** sea-gulls かもめの群 ‖ a *flock* ***of*** young girls (geese, goats, pigeons, sparrows) 少女(など)の群.

flock, *v.* 群がる, 群集する.

M *flock* ***in*** 群をなして入込む. ¶*flock* ***out*** 群をなして出る. ¶Birds *flocked* ***to*** the tree in numbers to feast on it. 木の実を食べるためにおびただしくその樹に鳥が集った. ¶*flock* ***together*** 群がる.

P *flock* ***about*** a person 人の回りに集まる. ¶*flock* ***in*** a room 室内に集まる. ¶*flock* ***to*** his standard 彼の旗下に集まる ‖ Crowds of people *flock* ***to*** the seaside. 群衆が海辺に集まる.

flog, *v.* むち打つ.

P *flog* ... ***with*** a scourge ...をむち打つ.

flogging, *n.* むち打ち.

Q give a boy ***repeated*** *floggings* 少年を何べんもむち打つ.

flood, *n.* 洪水, はん濫; 上げ潮, 満潮.

V I ***have*** a *flood* of callers. 私の所へはひっきりなしに来客がある. ¶He ***produced*** a *flood* of literature on the subject. 彼はその問題に関して沢山の著作を出した. ¶She ***shed*** a *flood* of tears. 彼女は万こくの涙を流した. ¶Is there any hope of ***stemming*** the *flood?* この大勢を食止めることができようか. ¶This discovery ***throws*** a *flood* of light on the mystery. この発見はそのなぞに多大の光明を投じる.

V^2 The *flood* is ***decreasing***. 水が退(ひ)いている. ¶*Floods* ***fell*** upon the city. 洪水がその市を襲った. ¶The *flood* is ***rising***. はんらんが増水している. ¶The *flood* has ***subsided***. 水が引いた. ¶The *flood* ***swelled*** in volume. [はんらんの]水かさが増した.

Q a ***great*** *flood* of books 本の大はんらん. ¶love at its ***highest*** *flood* その最高潮に達した恋愛. 【類】He is at his ***highest*** *flood* of material prosperity. ¶***Immense*** *floods* prevail. 大洪水がしばしば起る. ¶***main*** *flood* 満潮; 大洋. ¶***What*** a *flood* of rain! なんというひどい雨でしょう.

P an angry river ***at*** *flood* はんらんした奔流. 【類】a stream ***at*** its *flood* ‖ when the tourist tide is ***at*** *flood* 観光客が殺到するとき. ¶The building was destroyed (carried away) ***by*** a *flood*. 建物は洪水でつぶ(流)された. ¶a river ***in*** *flood* はんらんの川. ‖ She burst ***into*** a *flood* of tears. 彼女はわっと泣きだした. ¶The fish enter with the tide ***of*** *flood*. 魚は上げ潮につれてはいって来る.

P^2 *floods* ***of*** fire 猛火の海 ‖ *floods* ***of*** rain 盆をくつがえす雨 ‖ the *flood* ***of*** joy in one's breast 胸にあふれる喜び ‖ A *flood* ***of*** pride rose in him. 得意満面であった. ‖ a *flood* ***of*** words とうとうと口をついて出る言葉.

flood, *v.* あふらせる; 殺到する.

M The houses were *flooded* ***roof-deep*** (***floordeep***) 家の屋根(床)まで浸水した.

P rivers *flooded* ***by*** heavy rain-storms 豪雨のためはんらんした河川. ¶Japanese goods were literally *flooding* ***into*** the Australian market. 日本品は豪州の市場へ文字通りに殺到しつつあった. ¶The room is *flooded* ***with*** light (sunlight). へやは光(など)がみなぎっている. ‖ the eyes *flooded* ***with*** tears 涙で一杯の目 ‖ be *flooded* ***with*** pamphlets 小冊子がはんらんしている ‖ I am *flooded* ***with*** orders (letters). 注文(書面)が殺到して来ている. 【類】The market is now *flooded* ***with*** sales (売方).

flood-tide, *n.* 上げ潮.

P ***in*** *flood-tide* [川など]上げ潮のとき.

floor, *n.* 床; [家屋の]階, 層; 議員席, 発言権.

V ***clear*** the *floor* for dancing 舞踊のために床のものを取片づける. ¶***have*** (=***get or obtain***) the *floor* in debate 《米》討論で発言権を得る. ¶***lay down*** a *floor* 床を張る. ¶***mop*** a *floor* 床にぞうきんをかける. ¶***pace*** the *floor* 床の上をゆっくり歩く. ¶***scour*** the *floor* 床をみがく. ¶***scrub*** the *floor* 床をこすり洗う. ¶***sweep*** the *floor* clean きれいに床を掃く. ¶***take*** the *floor* 《米》討論に加わる; 舞踏に加わる ‖ At the conclusion of the paper Mr. Sexton ***took*** the *floor*. その朗読が終るとセクストン氏が登壇した. ¶***wax*** a *floor* 床にろうを塗る. ¶I can ***wipe*** the *floor* with you. 君を倒すことができる.

V^2 The *floor* is ***giving***. 床が落ちかかっている.

Q the basement, ***first, second***, and ***third*** *floors* 地階・一階・二階・三階 ☞ the first floor は米国では一階を指し英国では二階を指す. ¶***linoleum-covered*** *floor* リノリウムを敷詰めた床. ¶The hall has a ***tiled*** *floor*. 廊下はタイル張りだ. ¶a ***waxed*** *floor* ろうを引いた床. ¶On ***what*** *floor* is he? 彼は何階にいるか.

Q^2 on the ***convention*** *floor* 会議の議員席で. ¶a ***dance*** *floor* ダンスホールの床. ¶a ***dirt*** *floor* 《米》土間. ¶an ***earth*** *floor* 土間. ¶the ***ground*** *floor* 一階 ☞ 米国では first floor と同義. ¶The bill reached the ***Senate*** *floor*. その法案は審議に付せられた. ¶lift the ***wage*** *floor* (40 cents an hour) set in the Wages and Hours Act 賃銀及び時間法で定めてある最低賃銀(一時間 40 セント)を上げる.

P This elevator stops ***at*** every *floor*. この昇降機は各階に止まります. 【類】elevators waiting ***at*** the ground *floor*. ¶The carpet lies ***on*** the *floor*. 床にはじゅうたんが敷いてある. ‖ Give me a room ***on*** the second *floor*. 《英》三階のへやにして下さい. ‖ These hotels have passenger lifts, bath rooms ***on*** every *floor*. 《英》これらのホテルは各階に客専用の昇降機と浴室とがある. ‖ sit ***on*** the *floor* of Congress 《米国》議会に席を持つ ‖ ***on*** the *floor* of the conference 会議の席上で. 【類】Toilet and lavatory conveniences ***on*** each *floor*. / It is not important what *floor* the room is ***on***. / There are consulting room and office ***on*** the first *floor*. ¶He fell ***to*** the *floor*. 彼は床に倒れた. ¶The bill was approved by the Committee and sent ***to*** the *floor* of the House. その法案は委員会の承認を得たので本会議に回付された.

floor, *v.* 床を張る; [床上に]打ち倒す.

P get *floored* ***by*** a knotty problem 難問に参る. ¶be *floored* ***with*** boards 板で床を張ってある ‖ *floor* a person ***with*** a fist げんこでのす.

flop, *n.* どしん, どかっ.

P sit down ***with*** a *flop* どかっと腰をおろす.

flop, *v.* ばたりと腰を下ろす; 突然に変る.

M^2 The fish we had caught were *flopping* ***about*** in the bottom of our boat. われわれの捕った魚はボートの底でばたばたはねた. ¶*flop* oneself ***down*** どかっと腰を下ろす ‖ He *flopped* ***down*** on his knees and begged for money. 彼はペタリとひざまずいて銭をくれといった. ¶The shark had to *flop* ***over*** to catch at his prey. そのふかは反転してえじきを捕えねばならなかった.

P *flop* ***on*** one's knees ひざまずく. ¶He *flopped* ***to*** the other party. 彼は突然他党に走った.

flora, *n.* [一地方]植物群.

V The *flora* of Europe ***embraces*** about 10,000 species. 欧州産の植物は約一万種ある.

Q an ***alpine*** *flora* 高山植物. ¶a ***tropical*** *flora* 熱帯植物.

Q^2 a ***valley*** *flora* 渓谷植物.

P This place is remarkable ***for*** its *flora*. ここは植物で名高い.

florescence, *n.* 開花期, 繁栄期.

Q in its ***greatest*** *florescence* 最も花やかだった時代において.

florescent, *a.* 花盛りの.

P Dahlias are *florescent* ***from*** June. ダリアは六月から花が咲く.

florist, *n.* 花き栽培者.

Q ***Japanese*** *florists* in Los Angeles ロスの日本人花屋.

Q^2 the ***open-air*** and the ***hot-house*** *florist* 戸外及び温室花き栽培者.

flotilla, *n.* 艇隊.

Q a ***patrolling*** *flotilla* 巡ら艇隊.

Q^2 a ***torpedo-boat*** *flotilla* 水雷艇隊.

flounce, *v.* 身をもがく; 飛び出す.

M *flounce* ***out*** in a rage 憤然として飛出す.

M^2 *flounce* ***down*** on a sofa 長いすにどかっとすわる.

P He *flounced* ***from*** the water. 彼は水から飛出した. ¶He *flounced* ***out of*** the room with an angry expression on his face. 彼は怒色を顔に見せてへやを飛出した.

flounder, *v.* 深みへはまる；まごつく.
P *flounder* ***in*** the mud (sand) 泥(など)の中でころがる ‖ He *floundered* ***in*** an argument. 彼は議論でまごついた. ‖ *flounder* ***in*** a morass of contradictions 矛盾だらけでしどろもどろだ. ¶*flounder* ***through*** a song しどろもどろに歌う.

flour, *n.* 粉.
V ***make*** *flour* into dough 麦粉で生パンを作る.
Q² ***bean*** *flour* 豆粉. ¶***bread*** *flour* パン粉. ¶***rice*** *flour* しん粉. ¶***wheat*** *flour* 麦粉.

flourish, *n.* 振ること；麗句；飾り書き；花やかな吹奏.
Q Dicky flung the doors open with a ***dramatic*** *flourish* and let them in. デッキーは芝居がかりに戸を押し開いて彼らを迎え入れた.
P rattle in the ear ***like*** a *flourish* of trumpets らっぱの吹奏のように耳に響く. ¶His speech is full ***of*** *flourishes.* 彼の演説は美辞麗句が多い. ¶***with*** a *flourish* of trumpets ラッパを吹き立てて ‖ ***with*** *flourishes* on a bugle ラッパを花やかに吹き立てて ‖ announce the name ***with*** a *flourish* 名にふしをつけて呼ぶ.
P² the *flourishes* ***about*** an initial letter 頭文字の飾り書き. ¶a *flourish* ***of*** a whip (sword) むち(など)の一振り.

flourish, *v.* 栄える，繁茂する；全盛をきわめる；ひらめく.
M Alchemy *flourished* ***vigorously*** during the Middle Ages. 錬金術は中世紀において盛んに行われた. ¶Evil *flourishes* ***unrebuked.*** 悪が大びらに行われている.
P The plant *flourishes* ***in*** Japanese soil. その植物には日本の地味がよく合っている. ‖ Spenser *flourished* ***in*** the reign of Queen Elizabeth. スペンサーはエリザベス時代に時めいた人である. ¶The sword *flourished* ***over*** his head. 刀は彼の頭上にひらめいた. ¶England *flourished* ***under*** the Tudors. 英国はチューダ家の時代に栄えた. ¶Feudalism in Japan *flourished* ***with*** the Tokugawa. 日本の封建制度は徳川時代に全盛をきわめた.

flout, *v.* 愚ろうする.
M *flout* him ***pitilessly*** 容赦なく彼を愚弄する.

flow, *n.* 流水；流出量；流れるように続き進む物；上げ潮.
V ***excite*** the *flow* of urine 尿の出をよくする. ¶***facilitate*** the *flow* of blood 血のよく出るようにする. ¶***increase*** the *flow* of goods 品の出回りを増す. ¶The spring ***has*** a *flow* of 300,000 gallons a minute. その泉は一分間に三十万ガロンの水を噴出する. ¶***interrupt*** the *flow* of thought 思想の流出を中断する. ¶***obstruct*** the *flow* of the water 水の流れを妨げる. ¶***regulate*** the *flow* of credit 信用貸の継続を調整する. ¶***retard*** the *flow* of the water 水の流れをゆるめる(止める). ¶***stop*** the *flow* of blood 血液の循環を妨げる. ‖ A comma here ***stops*** the *flow* of the sentence. ここにコンマを打つと文の流れが止まる.
Q a ***constant*** *flow* of water from a spring 泉の水の不断の流れ. 【類】the ***constant*** *flow* of population from the country into the towns. ¶The river joins ... after an ***easterly*** *flow* of about ... miles その川は約…マイル東に流れて…に合する. ¶have a ***good*** *flow* of water 水の出がいい. 【類】a ***good*** *flow* of oil from a well (油井). ¶There is a ***great*** *flow* of ***milk.*** [母など]乳が十分出る. ¶an arrest of the ***menstrual*** *flow* 月経閉止. ¶the ***monthly*** *flow* (＝menses) 月経. ¶a ***pleasant*** *flow* of speech 流ちょうな言葉. ¶a rapid *flow* of speech 早口. ¶his ***ready*** *flow* of words 即座に口をついて出る言葉 ¶***rhythmic*** *flow* of a sentence 韻律の整った流ちょうな文. ¶stymie (＝hinder) the ***smooth*** *flow* of trade 貿易の順調さを妨げる. ¶pour out words in a ***steady*** *flow* 少しも途切れず口をきく ‖ a ***steady*** *flow* of materials to the job その仕事の材料の絶えない出回り.
Q² A ***tourist*** *flow* to Germany is increasing. ドイツへ行く観光者の流れは増している.
P The tide is ***on*** the *flow.* 潮がさしている.
P² a *flow* ***of*** eloquence 懸河の弁 ‖ a *flow* ***of*** joy あふれるばかりの喜び ‖ the *flow* ***of*** migration from Japan 日本からの移民の流れ ‖ a vast *flow* ***of*** water 広大な水の流れ.

flow, *v.* 流水させる；流す；流れる；出る；あふれる；[潮が]さす.
M The low-grounds along the river are ***annually*** *flowed.* 川辺の低地は年々浸水する. ¶So fast the years *flow* ***away.*** 歳月はかくも速かに流れ出る. ¶*flow* ***downward*** (***upward***) 下(上)方に流れる. ¶Words *flow* ***easily*** and ***naturally*** from the lips. 言葉がすらすらと自然に口をついて出る. ¶This river *flows* ***eastward*** to the North Sea. この川は東に流れて北海に注ぐ. ¶The water all *flowed* ***out*** little by little. 水は少しずつ流れ出た. ¶Deep rivers *flow* ***silently.*** 深い川は静かに流れる. ¶Sentences *flow* ***smoothly*** and ***effortlessly.*** 文がすらすらと流れ出る. ¶The tide ebbs and *flows* ***twice*** in twenty-four hours. 潮は二十四時間に二度満干がある.
M² Rivers *flow* ***down*** into the sea. 川は海に流入する. ¶His beard *flows* ***down*** upon his breast. 彼のひげは胸の上に垂れている. ¶Orders for the new kind of ware *flowed* ***in*** upon him. 新製品の注文が殺到した. ¶*flow* ***over*** with honey みつであふれる.
P *flow* ***from*** a fountain 泉から流れ出る ‖ Beautiful thoughts *flow* ***from*** his fountain-pen. 美しい思想が彼の万年筆からわいて出る. ‖ the injury which would *flow* ***from*** ... …から生じる損害 ‖ The river *flows* ***from*** north ***to*** south. その川は北から南へ流れる. ‖ See the consequences that *flow* ***from*** this fact. この事実から生じる結果を見給え. ‖ Wealth *flows* ***from*** industry and economy. 富は勤勉と節倹とから生じる. 【類】The blood was *flowing* ***from*** her mouth. / Tears *flow* ***from*** the eyes. ¶*flow* ***in*** drops ぽたぽたと垂れる. ¶where the river *flows* ***into*** the sea その川が海にはいる所に. ¶the river *flows* ***through*** the city of ... その川は…の市中を流れる. ¶The river *flows* north ***to*** the sea. 川は北流して海へ入る. ¶A good deal of water has *flowed* ***under*** the bridge since then. それから幾多の歳月が過ぎた. ¶Hot air *flows* ***up*** the chimney. 熱い空気は煙突を上って行く. ¶The river *flows* ***with*** a lively current. その川は勢いよく流れる. ‖ The streets *flowed* ***with*** men. 街々は人であふれた. ‖ a land *flowing* ***with*** milk and honey 乳とみつとが有り余る国，豊沃(ﾖｸ)の地 ‖ *flow* a plate ***with*** varnish 板にニスを塗る.

flower, *n.* 花；精英，精華；若盛り；詞藻(ｿｳ)；《化》華.
V ***arrange*** (＝***set***) *flowers* in a vase 花びんに花を生ける. ¶That plant ***bears*** very beautiful *flowers.* その木は非常に美しい花が咲く. ¶These *flowers* are ***forced*** [***open***]. この花は温室で咲かせたのだ. ¶***gather*** *flowers* 花を摘む. ¶Some *flowers* were ***grown*** in the garden. 庭園で栽培した草花もある. ¶***fertilize*** *flowers* 花きに肥料を施す. ¶*Flowers* were ***littered*** all along. 道にずっと花がまいてあった. ¶Frost ***nips*** *flowers.* 霜が花をいためる. ¶***offer up*** *flowers* and water before the tomb 墓前に花と水をたむける. ¶The cherry-tree has ***opened*** its *flowers.* その桜に花が咲いた. ¶***pick*** (＝***pluck***) wild *flowers* 野の花を摘む. ¶***plant*** *flowers* 草花を植える. ¶***pluck*** *flowers* from a garden 庭から花を折り取る. ¶***pot*** *flowers* 草花をはちに植える. ¶***produce*** *flowers* 花を持つ. ¶***put*** the *flowers* ***out*** on the veranda 草花を縁側に出す ‖ ***put out*** (＝***forth***) *flowers* [草木が]花を持つ. ¶***raise*** *flowers* 花を作る. ¶***scatter*** *flowers* across their path 彼らの通路を横ぎって花をまく. ¶live to ***see*** the *flowers* of the grave on one's head 頭に墓の花が咲く(白髪が生える)まで生きる. ¶***smell*** *flowers* 花をかぐ. ¶***strew*** *flowers* in his way 彼の通路に花を振りまく. ¶***transplant*** *flowers* 草花を移植する. 【類】one of those *flowers* which cannot be ***transplanted.*** ¶She always forgets to ***water*** these *flowers.* 彼女はいつもこの花に水をやるのを忘れる. ¶***wear*** a *flower* in one's coat 上衣に花を着ける.
V² *flowers* ***appearing*** in early spring 初春の花. ¶The *flowers* ***are*** out. 花が咲いた. ¶*Flowers* ***bloom*** luxuriantly. 花がらんまんと咲く. ¶*Flowers* ***blossom*** (＝***bloom***). 花が咲く. ¶*Flowers* ***blow.*** 花が咲く. ¶The *flowers* are ***coming on.*** 花が段々咲く. ¶The *flowers* ***come out*** before the leaves. その花は葉の出る前に咲く. ¶*Flowers* ***fall*** [***off***]. 花が散る. ¶The *flowers* are ***shrivelled up.*** 花がしおれた. ¶The *flowers* ***withered up*** (＝***away***). 花がしおれてしまった.
Q Whether pink or white, the long-stemmed Calanthe is an ***admirable*** *flower* for cutting. 桃色でも白でもくきの長いカランテは切花にはもってこいの花だ. ¶***artificial*** *flowers* 造花. ¶come into ***brilliant*** *flower* 見事な花をつける. ¶like plants which bear ***double*** *flowers,* but no fruit 八重の花を持つが実を結ばない草木のように. ¶***dried*** *flowers* and other mementos of his journey 押花その他の旅行記念品. ¶***early*** (***late***) *flowers* 早(おそ)咲きの花. ¶a ***faded*** *flower* しぼんだ花. ¶Orchids have ***fantastic*** and ***brilliant*** *flowers.* らんには変った見事な花が咲く. ¶***fragrant*** *flowers*

芳しい花. ¶in *full flower* 満開で. ¶a *full-blown flower* 満開の花. ¶bear ***great, flaunting red*** *flowers* 大きな見だてのある赤い花を持つ. ¶***many-tinted*** *flowers* 色様々の花. ¶The rose is the ***national*** *flower* of England. ばらは英国の国花だ. ¶***No*** *flowers*. 御贈花の儀はお断りします(死亡広告など). ¶***odorous*** *flowers* 芳しい花. ¶a ***pressed*** *flower* 押花. ¶***regular*** *flowers* 整斉花. ¶a ***scentless*** *flower* 香りのない花. ¶***sear[ed]*** (=***withered***) *flowers* しおれた花. ¶a ***social*** *flower* 社交界の花. ¶a ***stale*** *flower* 古い切花. ¶***sweet-smelling*** *flowers* 香気ふくいくたる花. ¶the ***very*** *flower* of our art 実にわが国芸術の精華. ¶***wild*** *flowers* 野の花. ¶in ***youth's*** *flowers*=in the flower of youth 血気盛りで.

Q² one's ***birth-month*** *flower* その誕生月の花. ¶***cut*** *flowers* 切り花. ¶English ***garden*** *flowers* blooming gaily in Italy イタリアできれいに咲いている英国の庭花. 【類】I don't care much for ***garden*** *flowers*. ¶a ***hothouse*** *flower* 温室の花. ¶a ***pot*** *flower* はち植の花. ¶***summer*** *flowers* 夏の花々. ¶***table*** *flowers* 卓上のさし花.

P a butterfly flying ***from*** *flower* to flower 花から花へ遊ぶちょう. ¶***in*** the *flower* of one's age その若盛りに ‖ The plums were still ***in*** blossom, although getting a little rusty. 色は少しあせたがすももはまだ咲いていた. ‖ when knighthood was ***in*** *flower* 騎士道花やかなりしころ. 【類】He was a handsome man, ***in*** the *flower* of his age. ‖ He died ***in*** the *flower* and promise of youth. ¶The plant is coming ***into*** *flower*. その木は花が咲きかけている. ¶a handsome banquet ***of*** *flowers* 百花りょうらん. ¶The road was covered ***with*** *flowers*. 道路は花で覆われていた. ‖ The table was decorated ***with*** *flowers*. 食卓は花で飾られていた. ‖ a garden planted ***with*** *flowers* 草花を植えた庭園. ‖ Say it ***with*** *flowers*. その心を花で(花屋の宣伝標語). ¶***without*** *flowers* of description 形容は抜きにして.

P² a bunch of *flowers* ***in*** a vase 花びんにさした一束の花. ¶the *flower* ***of*** an army 軍の精鋭 ‖ the *flower* ***of*** life=youth 若盛り ‖ the *flower* ***of*** womanhood 女盛り ‖ *flowers* ***of*** speech 詞の花 ‖ the *flower* ***of*** the mind 心の花 ‖ *flowers* ***of*** sulfur いおう華.

flower, *v.* 花咲く.

M This plant *flowers* ***freely***. この木はよく花を持つ.

P Most fruit trees *flower* (=blossom) ***in*** the spring. 果樹は大抵春に花を持つ.

flowing, *n.* 流れ.

P² *flowing* ***in*** of the tide 潮の差し込み.

fluctuate, *v.* ぐらつく; 変動する.

P *fluctuate* ***between*** two opinions これかあれかと意見がぐらつく. ¶*fluctuate* ***in*** price (opinion) 値段(など)が変動する.

fluctuation, *n.* 変動, 動揺, 高下.

Q a ***constant*** *fluctuation* in ministerial policy 内閣の政策の絶えざる変動. ¶a ***continued*** *fluctuation* 〘相場〙引続いての変動. ¶a ***great*** *fluctuation* 〘相場〙乱高下. ¶We do not expect ***heavy*** *fluctuations*. ひどい変動がないと思う. ¶a ***sharp*** *fluctuation* in exchange 為替相場の激変. ¶a ***violent*** (=***wild***) *fluctuation* in prices 物価の激変.

Q² All quotations are subject to ***market*** *fluctuation*. 相場はすべて市場の変動で変る.

P² *fluctuations* ***in*** temperature (market price) 温度(など)の上下. ¶the *fluctuation* ***of*** public opinion 世論の動揺 ‖ the *fluctuation* ***of*** tide 潮の干満.

flue, *n.* 送気管.

Q² a ***hot-air*** *flue* 熱気伝導管. ¶a ***ventilating*** *flue* 通風孔.

fluency, *n.* 流ちょう.

V ***acquire*** conversational *fluency* in a foreign language 外国語で流ちょうに話ができるようになる. ¶***gain*** *fluency* 流ちょうになる.

Q ***colloquial*** *fluency* 談話の流ちょう. ¶speak English with ***reasonable*** *fluency* 相当流ちょうに英語を話す. ¶***ungrammatical*** *fluency* 文法はでたらめな流ちょうさ.

P ***with*** *fluency* 流ちょうに. 【類】speak two or three languages ***with*** some *fluency*.

fluff, *v.* 毛をふくらませる.

M The bird *fluffed* ***out*** its feathers. 鳥が羽根を立てた. ‖ the puss *fluffed* itself ***out*** against ... 小ねこは…に向って毛を逆立てた.

fluid, *n.* 流動体, 液体.

V² *Fluid* ***includes*** both liquids and gasses. 流動体は液体とガス体を含む.

Q² a ***disinfecting*** *fluid* 消毒液. ¶***tear*** *fluid* 涙液. ¶black ***writing*** *fluid* 墨汁.

flurry, *n.* 混乱, ろうばい; 一陣の烈風; 《米》突然の降雪(雨).

V ***have*** a *flurry* of snow 突然雪がちらちら降る. ¶***raise*** a *flurry* in an assembly 集会にひと波らんを起す.

Q The boat was overset by a ***sudden*** *flurry* from the north. ボートは北方からの突風で転覆した.

P They are all ***in*** a *flurry*. 彼らはあわてふためいている.

P² the *flurry* ***of*** city life あわただしい都会生活 ‖ a *flurry* ***of*** wind 一陣の烈風.

flush, *n.* 赤面; 赤らみ; 感奮; 優勢; 激増.

V On cheeks ***blossomed*** the *flush* of dawning womanhood. 彼女のほおに成熟近い赤らみが現われていた. ¶It ***brought*** the faint *flush* to her cheeks. それで彼女はほんのり顔を赤くした. ¶***feel*** a *flush* of joy やれうれしやと思う. ¶She ***showed*** a faint pink *flush*. 女はこころもち顔を赤らめた. ¶The *flush* ***deepened*** in her cheeks. 彼女はほおを真赤にした.

Q after the ***first*** *flush* of joy was over やれうれしやと思っていると. ¶The young shoots are now in ***full*** *flush* after a heavy shower. 大雨があってから新芽が今を盛りとも え出ている. ‖ in the ***full*** *flush* of his popularity 彼の人気盛りに. 【類】in the ***full*** *flush* of hope. ¶The street had a ***sudden*** *flush* of people. 街上は突然人が激増して来た. ¶After much thought there was ***sudden*** *flush* of the truth. 色々と考えているうちに真相がふと頭に浮んだ. ¶It was the ***very*** *flush* of summer. 盛夏のころであった. ‖ in the ***very*** *flush* of life ほんとの若盛りに.

P It impressed me ***at*** the first *flush* as rather singular. それは初めはむしろ不思議に思われた. ¶He is ***in*** the *flush* of youth. 彼は若盛りだ. ¶***with*** a *flush* of triumph on his face 彼は顔に喜色を浮べて.

P² the *flush* ***on*** the clouds at sunset 夕焼の雲.

flush, *v.* 赤らむ; 襲来する; 得意にさせる; [水で]洗い流す.

M *flush* the street ***all along*** その通りをずっと洗い流す. ¶Her cheeks *flushed* ***brightly*** in the sun. 彼女のほおは日に当ってぱっと紅潮した. ¶Her face *flushed* ***hotly***. 彼女の顔はほてった. ¶His face *flushed* ***red*** as flame. 彼の顔は火のように真赤になった.

M² She *flushed* ***up***. 彼女の顔は紅潮した.

P A happy inspiration *flushed* ***into*** his head. うまい考えが彼の頭に浮んだ. ‖ Blood *flushed* ***into*** his face. 彼はぱっと顔を赤くした. ‖ He *flushed* ***into*** rage. 彼は真赤になって怒った. ¶*flush* ***to*** scarlet at hearing ... …と聞いて真赤になる. ‖ He *flushed* ***to*** the roots of his dark hair. 彼はその黒い髪の根まで赤くなった. ¶He was *flushed* ***with*** anger (shame, wine, shyness). 彼は怒って(など)赤くなった. ‖ a meadow *flushed* ***with*** primroses 桜草で真紅ににおう牧場. ¶The team was *flushed* ***with*** victory over ... そのチームは…に勝ってわいていた. ‖ He is *flushed* [up] ***with*** success. 彼は成功して得意になっている. ‖ His face was *flushed* ***with*** *sake*. 彼の顔は酒を飲んで赤くなっていた. 【類】*flush* ***with*** the exercise of gymnastics (体操).

flush, *a.* 裕福な; 同一平面上の.

P He is *flush* ***of*** money. 彼は金に困らない. ¶In block style, each line is *flush* ***on*** the left with the lines above and below. ブロック式(でタイプした)手紙では左方の各行は上下の行と一直線をなしている. ¶be *flush* ***with*** money [お金の]気前がよい.

flushing, *n.* 赤らむこと; 洗い流すこと.

Q² ***street*** *flushing* 街路の水洗.

P ***without*** a *flushing* of the cheeks ほおを赤らめもせずに.

flute, *n.* 笛(フルート).

V ***play*** [on] the *flute* フルートを吹く. ¶***put*** the *flute* to one's lips 笛をくちびるに当てる.

Q² a ***bamboo*** *flute* 尺八. ¶a ***five-hole*** *flute* 五つ穴の笛(尺八など).

P I played him a tune ***on*** the *flute*. 私は彼に笛を一曲吹いて聞かせた.

fluting, *n.* たてみぞ(ひだ).

Q a crest formed by ***sixteen*** *flutings* of the chrysanthemum [十六弁の]菊の紋.

flutter, *n.* 混乱, 動揺.

V the news ***caused*** quite a *flutter* among ... その知らせは…間に動揺を与えた. ¶She ***experienced*** quite a *flutter* of heart when told of his coming. 彼女は彼が来ると聞いて胸騒ぎがした. ¶***make*** a *flutter* among the ladies [俳優のうわさなどが]婦人社会を色めかせる.

P She is ***in*** a *flutter* of excitement. 彼女はどぎまぎしている. ‖ put one ***in*** a *flutter* 気をもませる. ¶fall ***into*** a *flutter* どぎまぎする.

flutter, *v.* ひらひらする；まごつく.

M² The blossoms *fluttered* ***about*** in the wind. 花は風にひらひら飛んだ. ¶Leaves *flutter* ***down.*** 木の葉がひらひら落ちる.

P *flutter* ***about*** the room 室内をうろうろする. ¶Here and there were seen butterflies *fluttering* ***among*** the garden flowers. 庭花の中をちょうがあちこちとび回っていた. ¶A butterfly was *fluttering* ***in*** the sunshine. ちょうが日なたをひらひら飛んでいた. ‖ A sail *flutters* ***in*** the wind. 帆が風にはためく.

flux, *n.* 流れ；変遷.

Q After a ***stately*** *flux* of five hundred miles, the river flows into the sea. その川は洋々として五百マイルも流れて海に注ぐ.

Q² ***soldering*** *flux* ろう着剤.

P The market is in a constant state ***of*** *flux.* 市場は絶えず動揺している. ‖ All things are in a state ***of*** *flux.* 万物は流転する.

fly, *n.* はえ；蚊ばり.

V Sugar ***attracts*** *flies.* 砂糖ははえが寄る. ¶***cast*** the *fly* 蚊ばりで釣りをする. ¶***catch*** *flies* はえを捕える. ¶***fan*** the *flies* ***away*** あおいではえを追う. ¶Screens in the window ***keep out*** *flies* and mosquitoes. 窓の網戸がはえと蚊を防ぐ. ¶***kill*** a *fly* with a spear 鶏を割くに牛刀を用いる. ¶***swat*** a *fly* はえをぴしゃっとたたく.

V² A *fly* ***bites.*** はえは刺す. ¶*Flies* ***buzz.*** はえはぶんぶんいう.

Q The *flies* are very ***annoying.*** はえが実にうるさい.

Q² a ***fruit*** *fly*=《学名》Drosophila しょうじょうばえ. ¶a big ***house*** *fly* 大形の家ばえ. ¶the ***tsetse*** *fly* ツェツェばえ (眠り病の病菌を伝ばする).

P a cloud ***of*** *flies* たくさんのはえ ‖ We are suffering from a plague ***of*** *flies.* はえがうるさいので困っている.

fly, *n.* 飛ぶこと.

P board the street-car ***on*** the *fly* 市内電車に飛乗りをする.

fly, *v.* 飛ばす；飛ぶ；[飛行機が]飛ぶ, [飛行機を]飛ばす；空輸する；跳ぶ；飛び去る；爆発する.

M They *flew* ***away*** into their hiding places. 彼らは隠れがに飛び去った. ‖ as the minutes *flew* ***away*** その数分が経過したときに. ¶The door *flew* ***back.*** 戸が急に開いた. ‖ He *flew* ***back*** to Japan after a short stay in Korea. 彼は朝鮮に短期間滞在した後空路日本に帰還した. ‖ be *flown* ***back*** to ... ...へ空路送り返される. ¶birds *flying* ***high*** 高く飛ぶ鳥 ‖ *fly* ***high*** into the sky 空中高く飛ぶ. ¶Pigeons *fly* ***home*** from a distance. はとは遠方から飛び帰る. ¶***How*** time *flies!* 時のたつのが早いこと! ¶The time ***just*** *flies.* ほんとうに時間がたつのは速い. ¶The birds *flew* ***low.*** 鳥が低空を飛んだ. ‖ The plane *flew* ***low,*** nearly skimming the sea. その飛行機は海面とすれすれに低空飛行を行った. ¶*fly* ***nonstop*** from New York to Berlin ニューヨークからベルリンへ無着陸で飛行する. ¶The lid of my watch *flies* ***open,*** when I touch the spring. 私の時計のふたはばねにふれるとぱっと開く.【類】The door *flew* ***open.*** ¶His fortune will ***soon*** *fly.* 彼の財産はすぐにふっ飛んでしまうだろう. ¶The bird *flew* ***out*** again. 鳥が再び飛び立った. ‖ *fly* ***out*** against one's master 主人に食って掛かる. ¶*fly* ***swiftly*** toward ... ...の方に急速に飛ぶ.

M² A bird *flew* ***in*** by the window. 鳥が窓から飛込んだ. ¶*fly* ***off*** at the handle 〖比ゆ〗脱線する ‖ *fly* ***off*** with public money 公金を持逃げする(高飛びする). ¶*fly* them ***over*** to the Western front 西部戦線に彼らを空輸する. ¶The crow *flew* ***up*** into a high tree with it からすがそれをくわえて高い木に飛んで行った.

P A bee *flew* ***about*** the room. はちが室内を飛回った. ¶The airman *flies* ***above*** Tokyo today. その飛行家がきょう東京の上空を飛ぶ. ¶*fly* ***at*** an altitude of ... meters ...メートルの高度を飛ぶ. ¶The bulldogs *flew* ***at*** each other's throat. ブルドッグが互いにのどを目がけて飛びかかった. ‖ The dog *flew* ***at*** the stranger (robber). 犬が見知らぬ人(など)に飛び付いた. ‖ *fly* ***at*** his approach 彼が近づいてきたので逃げる. ¶*fly* ***before*** an enemy 敵に後ろを見せる ‖ The ship *flies* ***before*** the wind. その船は追風に疾走する. ¶It is to be *flown* ***by*** BOAC. それは BOAC で空輸されるはず. ¶*Fly* ***for*** your life. 一生懸命に逃げろ. ¶*fly* a flag ***from*** a building (mast) 建物(など)から旗を翻す ‖ She *flew* ***from*** her home. 彼女は家出をした ‖ *fly* ***from*** the heat of the plains 平地の暑さを避ける ‖ *fly* ***from*** coast ***to*** coast 《米》東西岸を横断飛行する. ¶*fly* ***in*** the air 空を飛ぶ ‖ *fly* ***in*** a monoplane from ... to ... 単葉機で...から...へ飛ぶ ‖ a practice which *flew* ***in*** the face of all the Japanese precedent 日本人の習わしと全く逆なやり方. ¶He *flew* ***into*** a great passion (=rage *or* anger). 彼はかっとなった(かんしゃくを起した). ‖ *fly* ***into*** raptures 有頂天になる. ¶*fly* ***like*** lightning 電光石火のように飛ぶ. ¶*fly* ***on*** wings 翼で飛ぶ. ¶The Airlines *fly* five Clippers ***on*** its Pacific route. その航空会社は太平洋航空路に五機のクリッパーを就航させている. ¶*fly* ***out of*** the room へやから飛び出す ‖ Fire *flew* ***out of*** my eyes. [物に頭をぶっつけて]目から火が出た. ¶Eight aeroplanes *flew* ***over*** the city of Osaka this morning. 飛行機が八機けさ大阪市の上空を飛んだ. ‖ the writer of novels which *fly* ***over*** the whole world 全世界に読者を持つ小説の作者.【類】Birds *fly* ***over*** the sea. / The party came to Japan *flying* ***over*** the Pacific. / *fly* ***over*** hills and fields. ¶*fly* ***past*** a small town 小都市を飛び過ぎる. ¶*fly* ***through*** the air 空を突切って飛ぶ. ¶Insects *fly* ***to*** the flame. 虫が飛んで火に入る. ‖ The child *flew* ***to*** his mother. 子供が母に飛びついた. ‖ I *fly* ***to*** your aid. 至急御助力をこう. ‖ The glass *flew* ***to*** pieces. そのコップがみじんになった. ¶*fly* ***with*** great swiftness 非常に速く飛ぶ ‖ A bat *flies* ***with*** his wings. こうもりは翼で飛ぶ.

O *fly* the beam 〖空〗無線信号通り飛ぶ.

flying, *n.* 飛行.

Q all *flying,* ***civil, military, naval, private*** 民間・陸軍・海軍・私人など一切の飛行. ¶***trans-continental*** (=***coast-to-coast***) *flying* 大陸横断飛行. ¶***trans-oceanic*** *flying* 海洋横断飛行.

Q² a ***high altitude*** *flying* 高空飛行. ¶***non-stop*** *flying* 無着陸飛行. ¶***squadron*** *flying* 編隊飛行. ¶***stratosphere*** *flying* 成層圏飛行. ¶***stunt*** (=***trick***) *flying* 曲乗飛行. ¶***formation*** *flying* 編隊飛行.

fly-leaf, *n.* 〖製本〗見返し.

Q a ***browned*** *fly-leaf* of the old book その古本の茶色になった巻頭の白紙.

P with the author's autograph ***on*** the *fly-leaf* 見返しページに著者の自署のある(本など).

foam, *n.* あわ.

P The horse is all ***in*** *foam.* 馬は口一杯あわを吹いている. ¶The surface of the water is full ***of*** (=covered ***with***) *foam.* 水面はあわだらけだ.

P² the *foam* ***of*** breaking waves 砕け波のあわ ‖ the *foam* ***of*** the mouth [馬などの]口のあわ. ¶the *foam* ***on*** liquids caused by boiling 沸騰によって生じた液体面のあわ.

foam, *v.* あわを吹く, あわ立つ.

M *foam* itself ***away***=foam off あわとなって消える.

P the insurance man, *foaming* ***at*** the mouth, was telling ... その保険勧誘員は口角あわを飛ばして...と言っていた.

fob, *v.* ごまかす, [にせものを]つかませる.

M² *fob* ***off*** a worthless article upon a customer 顧客に役に立たない物を押し付ける ‖ *fob* ***off*** phoney (=imitation) pearls on ... 偽の真珠を...につかませる ‖ *fob* ***off*** the right of the people 人民の権利をごまかす.

focus, *n.* 焦点, 中心点.

V ***get*** a principal *focus* 焦点を得る. ¶***take*** the *focus* ピントを合わせる.

Q The trend is not yet in ***clear*** *focus.* 形勢がまだはっきりしていない.

P The image is ***in*** (***out of***) *focus.* この映像はピントが合っている(いない). ‖ Rays meet ***in*** a *focus.* 光線は焦点に集まる. ¶an object brought ***into*** *focus* ピントを合わせた物体.

P² the *focus* ***of*** the world's attention (=public attention) 世人の注意の的. ¶a *focus* ***of*** trouble between nations 国家間の紛争の焦点.

focus, *v.* 焦点に集める.

P *focus* the sun's rays ***on*** ... with a burning glass 天日取で...の上に太陽光線を集める. ¶The eyes of the world are *focus[s]ed* ***on*** him. 世人の注意は彼に集まっている.【類】His effort were *focused* ***on*** the matter. / The country *focused* her attention ***on*** the Chinese situation. ¶the rays are brought to *focus* ***upon*** ... 光線を...に集める.

fodder, *n.* かいば.

Q² ***gun*** (=***cannon***) *fodder* 大砲に射たれて死ぬ人(兵隊など).【類】Such people were regarded as ***cannon*** *fodder* in case of war.

foe, *n.* 敵, 敵兵.

V ***bear*** (=***face***) a *foe* 敵に手向う. ¶***honor*** brave and effective *foes* 勇ましい腕のある敵を尊重する. ¶he ***met*** a deadly *foe* in ... 彼は...という恐ろしい敵に出会わした. ¶They steadily ***pushed*** their *foes* before them. 着々彼らの敵を追まくった.

Q the ***common*** *foe* of man 人間の公敵. ¶a ***dangerous*** *foe* 危険な敵. ¶the most ***deadly*** *foe* of democracy 民主主義の大敵. ¶a ***fallen*** (=***vanquished***) *foe* 敗戦の敵. ¶a ***formidable*** *foe* 強敵. ¶a ***gallant*** *foe* 勇敢な敵. ¶an ***implacable*** *foe* 執念深い敵. ¶an ***inveterate*** *foe* 不倶戴天の敵. ¶a ***national*** *foe* 国民の敵. ¶a ***political*** *foe* 政敵. ¶a ***sworn*** *foe* 不倶戴天のあだ. ¶an ***unwary*** *foe* 油断している敵.

Q^2 the ***legion*** *foe* 多勢の敵. ¶***fruit*** *foes* 果実の敵. ¶a ***longtime*** *foe* of communism 共産主義という宿敵.

P^2 Cleanliness is a *foe* ***to*** disease. 清潔は病気の敵だ‖Nobunaga was a bitter *foe* ***to*** Buddhism. 信長は仏教の強敵であった.

fog, *n.* 霧.

V The steamer ***experienced*** a thick *fog* on her voyage. 汽船は航海中濃霧にあった.

V^2 The *fog* ***is breaking away.*** 霧が晴れてきた. ¶A thick ***fog came on.*** 濃霧が襲来した. ¶The *fog* ***cleared*** [***off***]. 霧が晴れた. ¶The *fog* ***dispersed.*** 霧が散った. ¶The *fog* has ***lifted.*** 霧が晴れた. ¶Thickening *fogs* ***prevailed*** at the time. そのときいや増す濃霧が一面にかかっていた. ¶The *fog* ***thickened.*** 霧が深くなった.

Q London has a very ***bad*** *fog* in winter. ロンドンの冬は霧がひどい. ¶A ***dark*** *fog* swept the sea. 暗黒な霧が海上に広がった. ¶The steamer is enveloped in a ***dense*** *fog*. 汽船は濃霧に包まれている. ¶The mind of the objector is in a ***hazy*** *fog*. 反対者の頭は五里霧中の状態. ¶a ***heavy*** *fog* 濃霧. ¶The steamer ran on a sunken rock in a ***thick*** *fog*. 汽船は濃霧のために暗礁に乗り上げた. 【類】A ***thick*** *fog* hung low over the town.

Q^2 ***smoke-laden London fogs*** ばい煙を込めたロンドンの霧.

P The valley is shrouded ***by*** *fog*. 谷は霧に覆われている. ¶***during*** a *fog* 霧のかかっている間. ¶be ***in*** a *fog* 途方にくれる. ¶The boat was soon lost sight of ***in*** the *fog*. 舟が間もなく霧の中に見えなくなった. 【類】The vessel went ashore ***in*** a thick *fog*. / a town enveloped ***in*** a dense *fog*. ¶a ship which is moving ***through*** a dense *fog* 濃霧中を進行している船.

fog, *v.* 霧がかかる; 枯れる.

M *fog* (=dump) ***off*** 湿気のために枯れる; 腐ってしまう‖The cuttings have all *fogged* ***off***. さし木が湿気のために枯れた.

fogbank, *n.* 霧の峰.

Q ***heavy*** *fogbanks* 濃霧の峰.

foible, *n.* [性格の]弱点, 欠点.

V ***hit off*** the *foibles* of fashionable frivolity 浮薄な上流階級の人々の弱点を突く.

Q reveal ***human*** *foibles* 人間の弱点をうがつ.

P^2 *foibles* ***of*** the Japanese race 日本人の欠点.

foil, *n.* 箔(ﾊｸ); 引立役をなすもの.

V Trees ***make*** an effective *foil* to architectural work. 樹木が建築物を有効に引立てる. ¶***play*** the *foil* to the chief actor 主演俳優の引立役を勤める.

Q act as an ***excellent*** *foil* to ... ...の素晴らしい引立役となる. ¶beat out silver into ***thin*** *foil* 銀を薄い箔に打延ばす.

Q^2 ***gold*** (***silver, tin, lead***) *foil* 金(など)箔.

P^2 An ugly woman serves as a *foil* ***to*** a pretty girl. 醜婦は美人の引立役になる.

foil, *v.* 敗る, くじく.

P He was *foiled* ***in*** an attempt. 彼は仕事に失敗した.

foist, *v.* こっそりはめ込む; 押付ける, かぶせる.

M^2 *foist* (=palm) ***off*** bad money on someone 悪貨をだれかに押し付ける.

P *foist* an unfit person ***into*** a position 不適任者を職にはめ込む. ¶*foist* worthless goods ***on*** a customer 顧客につまらない物を押し付ける. ¶The University *foists* them ***upon*** the world as bachelors of art. 大学は彼らを文学士として世間に押しつける. 【類】A spurious document (偽証文) was *foisted* ***upon*** me.

fold, *n.* ひだ; [へびなど]とぐろ巻き; 折り.

Q ***Another*** *fold* gives 32 mo. もう一度折ると三十二折になる.

P A cascade lies ***in*** a *fold* of the hills. 小滝が山あいにある.‖The python crushed its prey ***in*** its *folds*. うわばみが餌食をぎゅうぎゅう締めつぶした. ¶gather ***into folds*** ひだをとる.

P^2 a *fold* ***in*** a garment 着物のひだ. ¶the *fold* ***of*** a mountain 山のふところ.

fold, *v.* たたむ, 折り重ねる; 抱く; 包む.

M *fold* a thing ***back*** (=***down***) 物を折り重ねる‖sit with the leg *folded* ***back*** from the knee [日本式に]すわる. ¶***neatly*** *fold* paper きちんと紙を折る.

M^2 paper *folded* ***down*** the middle 真中で折った紙. ¶*fold* ***off*** clover クローバを羊の飼料にする. ¶*fold* ***up*** our tents われわれの天幕を畳む. 【類】*fold* ***up*** a letter‖*fold* ***up*** in compact form 固くたたむ.

P *fold* her arms ***about*** (=***round***) his neck 彼の首に抱き付く. ¶A kimono is *folded* ***from*** left ***to*** right. 着物は左から右へ重ねる. ¶*fold* a child ***in*** one's arms 子供を抱きかかえる‖*fold* a thing ***in*** paper 物を紙に包む‖hills *folded* ***in*** a mist 霧に包まれた小山. ¶*fold* a piece of paper ***into*** three 一枚の紙を三つ折にする. ¶*fold* a child ***to*** one's breast 子供を抱きしめる.

folder, *n.* 折本(フォルダー).

Q^2 an ***advertising*** *folder* 広告用フォルダー. ¶a ***timetable*** *folder* 時刻表.

P^2 a *folder* ***on*** Japan 折本式の日本案内.

folding, *n.* 折ること.

Q^2 ***paper*** *folding* 折紙.

foliage, *n.* [団]葉.

V trees which ***produce*** much *foliage* and little fruit 葉ばかり茂って実がほとんどならない木.

Q ***Dark*** *foliage* clothes the hills. 黒ずんだ木の葉が小山を覆うている. ¶***darkening*** *foliage* こんもりとした葉. ¶***luxuriant*** *foliage* うっそうたる葉. ¶***thick*** *foliage* 茂っている葉.

Q^2 amid ***autumn*** *foliage* 秋の木の葉の中に.

P a cedar tree thickly covered ***with*** *foliage* こんもりと葉の茂った杉の木.

folio, *n.* 大版本(二つ折本).

Q^2 a ***registry*** *folio* 登記用紙.

P read Milton ***in*** *folio* 大版本のミルトンを読む.

folk, *n.* 人々, 人民; *pl.* 家族, 一族.

V *folk* ***say*** that ... 人のうわさによると...

Q Birmingham is a great centre of ***bookloving*** *folk*. バーミンガムは愛書家の一大中心地である. ¶***decent*** *folk* 堅気の人々. ¶the ***elder*** *folk* 年長の人々. ¶we ***English*** *folk* われわれ英国民. ¶***funny*** *folks* 面白い人々. ¶***good*** (=***gentle***) *folk* 善良な人々. ¶promote the independence of ***literary*** *folk* 文士の独立を促進する. ¶***little*** *folks* in many lands 諸国の子供たち. ¶our austere ***northern*** *folk*, the product of a severe climate and a severe creed 酷烈な気候としゅん厳な信条とが産んだ冷厳な北方民族. ¶***middle-class*** *folk* 中流社会の人々. ¶the ***old*** *folks* at home うちの年寄たち. ¶***old-fashioned*** *folk* 昔風の人たち. ¶This is beyond the comprehension of ***ordinary*** *folk*. これは普通の人には分らない. ¶***poor*** *folk* 貧しい人々. ¶***smart*** *folk* of every sort 一切の気のきいた人々. ¶***thoughtless*** *folk* 思慮の欠けた人々. ¶***workaday*** *folk* あくせく働く人々. ¶***young*** *folk* 若い人々.

Q^2 ***actor*** *folks* 芝居もの. ¶***business*** *folk* 実業家たち. ¶***country*** *folk* いなか者たち. ¶How are you and your [***family***] *folks*? 皆さんお元気? ¶***farming*** *folk* 百姓. ¶***home*** *folks*=family people うちの連中. ¶They were ***sea-faring*** *folk*, those early residents of Nantucket. 彼らすなわちナンタケットの初期の居住者は船乗であった. ¶***stage*** *folk* 芝居者(俳優)‖the legitimate ***theatre*** *folk* [映画に対し]正統の芝居者. ¶***twentieth century*** *folk* 二十世紀人. ¶little ***village*** *folk* 村の子供たち‖the local ***village*** *folk* 村の衆. ¶Where are ***women*** *folks*, I wonder? 女たちはどこにいるのか.

folk-lore, *n.* 俗説.

P ***In*** Japanese *folk-lore* the cat is regarded as a mysterious animal. 日本の俗説ではねこは魔物ということになっている.

folk-tale, *n.* 伝説物語.

Q ***uncanny*** *folk-tales* of China 中国の不思議な伝説物語.

follow, *v.* したがう, 同伴する; 続く, 次ぐ; あとをつける; 得ようとする; 随喜する; ならう, のっとる; 目送する; 了解する; 次いで起る.

M *follow* one's advice ***blindly*** 盲目的にその忠告に従う. ¶That conclusion ***by no means*** *follows*. そんな結論は決して出て来ない. ¶One thing *follows* ***close*** on another. 一物が他物に密接に続く.‖His death *followed* ***close*** on his failure. 彼は失敗して間もなく死んだ. ¶*follow* ***closely*** the American line 緊密にアメリカの線に添う. 【類】*follow* ***closely*** nature's way (自然のやり口) / *follow* ***closely*** (よく目を通す) the news of the day. ¶She *followed* him ***dumbly***. 彼女は黙って彼について行った. ¶***faithfully*** *follow* the instructions 正直に言付けを守る. ¶a practice ***frequently*** *followed* よくやる手. ¶be ***immedi-***

ately followed by… 直後に…が続く. ¶The dog *followed* his master ***home***. その犬は主人について帰った. ‖ *follow* ***home*** 追い詰める. ¶***implicitly*** *follow* one's advice 一も二もなくその忠告に従う. ¶***invariably*** and ***conscientiously*** *follow* the same rule 相変らず実直に同じ規則を遵奉する. ¶it *follows* ***justly*** that… 当然…ということになる. ¶If one writes poetry, it ***naturally*** *follows* that he must understand poetry. 詩を作れば自然詩が分ってくる訳だ. ¶it doesn't ***necessarily*** *follow* that… 必ずしも…という結論にはならない. ¶*follow* ***out*** directions 指図通りやる ‖ *follow* ***out*** a suggestion 注意に従う ‖ *follow* ***out*** the scheme of work outlined below 次に略記する仕事を計画通り実行する ‖ *follow* ***out*** the provisions of a will 遺言書の規定通り遂行する ‖ *follow* it ***out*** to its local logical conclusion それを徹底させる. ¶I do not ***quite*** *follow* you. 君の話は僕には合点が行かない. ¶***scrupulously*** *follow* another's example 後生大事に他人の例にならう. ¶The formal negotiations will *follow* ***shortly***. やがて正式交渉の段取となるだろう.

M² the trouble and misery that are sure to *follow* ***on***… …に続いて起るに相違ない紛争と難儀 ‖ *Follow* your ball ***on*** after you hits it. ボールを打ったらそのゆくえを確かめよ. ¶*follow* it ***through*** それをやり通す. ¶*follow* ***up*** a clue どこまでも手掛りをたどる ‖ *follow* ***up*** hints 暗示をたどる. 【類】*follow* ***up*** (=pursue) one's study / *follow* ***up*** one's linguistic studies ‖ *follow* ***up*** a victory 戦果を拡大する ‖ *follow* ***up*** with another question 別の質問でたたみかける.

P I *followed* [***after***] him. 彼のあとについて行った. ‖ *follow* ***after*** peace 平和を追求する. ¶*follow*… ***at*** a distance …を遠く離れて追う. ¶be *followed* ***by*** a complement あとに補足語がつく. 【類】A typhoon hit the island only *followed* ***by*** a still more violent one. / The lecture will be *followed* ***by*** questions and discussion as usual. ‖ The clause is *followed* ***by*** a dash. その句の後にダッシュが来る. 【類】According to Proctor, if from a single pair, for 5,000 years, each husband and wife had married at 21 years of age and there had been no death, the population of the earth would be 2,199,915 *followed* ***by*** 144 ciphers (百四十四けた). ¶it *follows* ***from*** it that… それから勢い…ということになる ‖ it does not *follow* ***from***… that… …するからといって必ずしも…であるとは言えない ‖ ***from*** this it *follows* that… …してみれば. ¶He entered and I *followed* him ***in***. 私は彼のあとに続いて入った. ¶*follow* ***in*** the footsteps of foreign practice 外国の慣例にならう. 【類】*following* ***in*** the footsteps of his father and grandfather ‖ *follow* ***in*** his steps (=path *or* track) 彼にならう. 【類】The father was a chemist, and it was intended that the lad should *follow* ***in*** his father's footsteps. ‖ *follow* ***in*** old and beaten tracks 旧慣に則る ‖ Don't *follow* ***in*** the wake of such men. こんな人たちのてつを踏むな. ¶*follow* him ***into*** the house (church) 彼について家(など)にはいる. ¶Acquaintance, intimacy, friendship, fast *followed* ***on*** each other. 面識から懇意へ懇意から親交へとぐんぐん進んだ. ¶*following* ***on*** hard work 辛苦の結果たる. 【類】*following* ***on*** the difficulties attending…, there are others attending… ¶I have no space to *follow* him ***through*** it in detail. 明細に彼のやり口について述べる余地がない. ¶*follow* a person ***to*** the door 戸口まで人を見送る ‖ *follow* him ***to*** the grave 彼の後を追って死ぬ. ¶*follow* close ***upon*** the heels of… …のすぐ後について行く. ¶*follow* a departing vessel ***with*** one's eyes 出て行く船を目送する ‖ be *followed* ***with*** intense interest 熱心な興味をもって追求される.

O Just before the battle the general addressed his army as *follows:* 開戦の直前に将軍は部下に次の訓示を下した. ¶Wait and see what *follows*. どんなことになるか見ていたまえ.

follower, *n.* 随員, 崇拝者, 教徒, 学徒.

Q a ***blind*** *follower* めくら滅法の随喜者. ¶an ***enthusiastic*** *follower* 熱心な崇拝者. ¶a ***faithful*** *follower* 忠実な追従者. ¶a ***servile*** *follower* of the crowd 俗におもねるもの. ¶a ***spiritual*** *follower* 精神的崇拝者. ¶a ***zealous*** *follower* of truth 熱心な真理の追求者.

Q² a ***camp*** *follower* [戦闘員でない]軍隊随行者. ¶a ***Christ*** *follower* キリスト教徒. ¶***Ibsen*** *followers* イブセンの崇拝者.

P² a *follower* ***of*** tradition 伝統崇拝者 ‖ He is not a *follower* ***of*** any particular school. 彼は一流を立てた人だ. ‖ *followers* ***of*** Christianity キリスト教徒.

following, *n.* 配下, 部下; 次の事物.

V ***contribute*** the *following* to the discussion その討議に次の事項を寄与する. ¶***gain*** a large *following* 沢山の配下を得る. ¶I ***had*** the *following* to say on the subject. その問題に関して次のことを言わねばならなかった. ‖ They ***have*** a *following* of their own. 彼らには彼ら自身の配下がある.

Q a magazine of long standing with a ***devoted*** *following* 熱心な愛読者を有し長く継続してきた雑誌. ¶The novelist has an ***immense*** *following*. あの小説家はすばらしく愛読者が多い. 【類】His gospel now has an ***immense*** *following*. ¶a political leader with a ***large*** *following* 多くの部下を有する政界の指導者. ¶Emile Zola has never had a ***large*** *following* in America. エミール・ゾラは初めから米国には余り愛読者がなかった. ¶a columnist with a ***wide*** *following* 多数の愛読者を有する雑誌の特殊欄担当記者.

P it is as ***in*** the *following* それは次の通り.

follow-up, *n.* 追かけ.

Q² ***job order*** *follow-up* 求職口追及調査.

folly, *n.* 愚行, 不品行.

V ***commit*** a *folly* ばかなことをする. ¶***counterfeit*** *folly* ばかを装う. ¶***denounce*** one's *folly* そのばかさを非難する. ¶We have ***seen*** the *folly* of such a course. われわれはこうした仕打の愚かさを知っている.

Q I count it ***absolute*** *folly* to… 私は…することを絶対に愚かしいことと思う. ¶could there be ***deeper*** *folly* than to…? …するなんてばかなことがあるか. ¶To say that… is most ***egregious*** *folly*. …というのはばかの骨頂だ. ¶***mad*** *folly* 狂気じみた愚行. ¶do ***ruinous*** *follies* 破滅的なばか気たことをする. ¶He has given up ***youthful*** *follies*. 彼は若気の放とう生活を切上げた. 【類】a thoughtless expression of ***youthful*** *folly*.

P He is ***above*** such *folly*. 彼はそんなばかなことはしない. ¶hint ***at*** one's *folly* その愚行を暗に指す. ¶seduce a person ***into*** *folly* 人をそそのかしてばかをさせる. ¶a mere act ***of*** *folly* 一片の愚行 ‖ a life ***of*** *follies* ばかげた生活 ‖ What a piece ***of*** *folly!* なんというばかなことだ. ¶***through*** his *folly* 彼の不品行から. ¶Her beauty deluded him ***to*** *folly*. 彼は彼女の容色に迷ってばかをやった. ‖ He is generous ***to*** a *folly*. 彼はむやみに人に金をやる.

folly, *a.* 愚かな.

M it is ***utterly*** *folly* to… …することは全くばからしい.

fond, *a.* 好む, 好く.

M He is ***awfully*** *fond* of jesting. 彼は恐ろしく冗談が好きだ. ¶He is ***enthusiastically*** *fond* of angling. 彼は釣りにこっている. ¶he is ***exceedingly*** *fond* of… 彼は…が非常に好きだ. ¶She is ***passionately*** *fond* of poetry. 彼女は熱烈に詩が好きだ. 【類】The Swiss are ***passionately*** *fond* of their mountains. ¶he is ***very*** *fond* of… 彼は…が大好きだ.

P Some writers are *fond* ***of*** superlatives. 最上級の語句を好んで使う文士もある. 【類】She is very *fond* ***of*** salt things (塩からいもの). / a lazy fellow, never *fond* ***of*** school / He is *fond* ***of*** quoting these lines (詩句). / women *fond* ***of*** pretty clothing. / He is *fond* ***of*** society (company, traveling).

fondness, *n.* でき愛; 好み.

V ***cultivate*** a *fondness* for good literature 高尚な文学趣味を養成する. ¶***develop*** a *fondness* for playing "hooky" 学校を無断欠席してなまけ遊ぶ癖がつく. ¶***exercise*** *fondness* for… …の趣味を養成する. ¶I ***have*** a *fondness* for (=am fond of) sake. 私は酒が好きだ. 【類】I ***have*** no *fondness* for games. ¶He ***possesses*** some *fondness* for science. 彼は多少科学が好きだ.

Q She has for him a kind of ***grateful*** *fondness*, something like love. 彼女は彼に対して一種の感謝の念からきた愛情を持っているが, ちょっと恋愛に似たものだ. ¶He has a ***great*** *fondness* for reading. 彼は読書が非常に好きだ. ¶with an ***intense*** *fondness* for… …が非常に好きで. ¶Cats have a ***peculiar*** *fondness* for the catnip. ねこは妙にいぬはっかが好きだ. ¶his ***private*** *fondness* for money 彼が心ひそかに持つ金銭の愛着. ¶he has a ***special*** *fondness* for… 彼は特別…が好きだ. ¶The Americans have a ***traditional*** *fondness* for big things. 米国民は伝統的に大きな物を好む. 「the use of… …の愛用.

P² a *fondness* ***for*** reading 読書趣味. ¶one's *fondness* ***for***

font, *n.* 洗礼盤.
Q a ***baptismal*** *font* 洗礼盤.
P He is so well known by that name that many people suppose him to have been so named ***at*** the *font*. 彼はその名でよく通っているので多数の人はそれを彼の本名だと思っている.

food, *n.* 食物, 食料; 食品; 営養物; 資料, かて.
V ***afford*** (=give) *food* for reflection 思想のかてを与える. ¶***avoid*** animal *food* 動物性の食物を避ける. ¶Young children are apt to ***bolt*** their *food*. 子供らは食物をうのみにする癖がある. ¶***bring up*** one's *food* 自分の食物を持ってくる. ¶establish a base at which sufficient *food* is ***cached*** 十分な食料を貯蔵して置く根拠地を設ける. ¶***Chew*** your *food* thoroughly. 食物は十分にかめ. ¶***cook*** one's own *food* 自炊する. ¶***eat*** nourishing *food* 滋養物を食べる. ¶***flavor*** *food* 食物に味をつける. ¶it ***forms*** the chief *food* of ... それは...の主要食物になっている. ¶***give*** *food* to the hungry 飢えたる者に与える. ¶***gobble*** one's *food* 食物をうのみにする. ¶***grow*** *food* for one's family 家族のために食糧になる物を作る. ¶***grudge*** a person his *food* 食う物も食わせたがらない. ¶***gulp down*** one's *food* 食物をうのみにする. ¶We must ***have*** *food* to eat. われわれは食物が要る. ¶Its flesh ***makes*** but poor *food*. その肉は決してよい食料ではない. ¶Learn to thoroughly ***masticate*** your *food*. 食物は十分かむようにしなさい. ¶***offer*** *food* for reflection 思想の糧を提供する. 【類】***offer*** no *food*. ¶***prepare*** *food* over a spirit lamp アルコール・ランプにかけて食物を煮る. ¶***provide*** *food* for ... ...をまかなう. ¶***put out*** *food* for the birds 鳥に食物を出しておいてやる. ¶He ***refuses*** *food*. 彼は出した食物を食べない. ¶***serve*** *food* 食物を出す. 【類】***serve*** fish and other sea *foods*. ¶***share*** *food* with him 彼のお相伴をする. 【類】The dog ***shared*** its *food* with the cat. ¶***supply*** foreign *food* 洋食を食べさせる. ¶He ***takes*** neither *food* nor sleep. 彼は食も取らず睡眠もしない. ‖ ***take*** one's *food* with appetite and relish 食物をどっさりおいしく食べる ‖ The bird will ***take*** *food* from his hand. その鳥は彼の手から餌を取って食う. ¶a starveling who has not ***tasted*** *food* for twenty-four hours まる一日なにも食わず飢え衰えた人. 【類】pass two days, and as many nights, without ***tasting*** *food*. ¶***throw up*** one's *food* 食べた物を吐く. ¶I have not ***touched*** *food* today. 私は今日はまだ何も食べない. ¶You ought to ***try*** *food* a little. 君なにか少し食べて見たらよかろう.
P² This *food* ***disagrees*** with me. 私はこれを食べるとあたる. ¶There ***remains*** only *food* for three. 三人分の食物しか残っていない. ¶Our *food* is ***running short***. 私どもの食料はなくなりかけている.
Q give ***abundant*** *food* for speculation 思索の十分な資料を供する. ¶an ***agreeable*** and ***beautiful*** *food* 口にあう見事な食物. ¶Onions are the most ***antiscorbutic*** *food* known. 玉ねぎは壊血病予防に最もきく食物だ. ¶***appetizing*** *food* 食欲をそそる食物. ¶***aquatic*** *foods* 水産食料品. ¶***calorific*** *food* カロリー価の高い食物. ¶***coarse*** *food* 粗食. ¶***cooked*** *food* 調理した食物. ¶***delectable*** *food* うまい食物. ¶***farinaceou*** *foods* でん粉質の食物. ¶***fat-producing*** *food* 脂肪を生じる食物. ¶Do you like ***foreign*** *food?* 君洋食が好きですか. ¶***fresh*** *food* for thought 新しい思想のかて. ¶Water is a very ***good*** *food*. 水は非常によい食物である. ‖ rest and ***good*** *food* 静養と滋養物. 【類】Bread and milk are ***good*** *foods*. ¶***green*** *food* for farm animals 農耕用家畜に与える青もの. ¶***heat-producing*** *foods* 熱を生じる食物. ¶***high-priced*** *foods* 高価な食物. ¶***human*** *food* 人間の食物. ¶***hunger-deferring*** *food* 腹持ちのいい食物. ¶***Indigestible*** *food* oppresses the stomach. 不消化な食物は胃にもたれる. ¶the ***intellectual*** *food* of thousands 幾千人の知識のかて. ¶one of the cheapest and most ordinary articles of ***Japanese*** *food* 日本食料品の最も安価にして最も普通なるものの一つ. ¶***light*** *food* 軽い食物. ¶***liquid*** *food* 流動物. ¶***mental*** *food* 精神のかて. ¶***multi-purpose*** *food* 万能食. ¶***nourishing digestible*** *food* 滋養になる消化の良い食物. ¶***nutritious*** *food* 滋養物. ¶***palatable*** *food* うまい食物. ¶***perishable*** *food* 腐敗しやすい食物. ¶***plain*** *food* 簡素な食物. ¶He lives on ***poor*** *food*. 彼は粗食している. ¶***preserved*** *foods* 貯蔵食物類. ¶a ***principal*** *food* (=article of food) 主要食物. ¶*foods* ***proper*** for preserving health 健康保全に適当な食品. ¶***rich*** *food* 濃厚な食物. ¶***rotten*** *food* 腐敗した食物. ¶The cause of weak gums is ***soft*** *food*. 歯根の弱いのは柔かい食物を食べるためである. ¶***standard*** *foods* 規格食事. ¶Rice is the ***staple*** *food* in the Orient. 米は東洋の主要食物である. ¶***starchy*** *food* でん粉質食物. ¶***substantial*** *food* こくのある食物. ¶***succulent*** *food* 汁気の多い食物. ¶have ***sufficient*** *food* 食物が十分ある. ¶***sustaining*** *food* 腹もちのよい食物. ¶***tasty*** *food* うまい食物. ¶The *food* is ***uninviting***. この食物はまずそうだ. ¶***vegetable*** *foods* 菜食. ¶***wholesome*** *foods* 健康食.
Q² ***animal*** *food* 動物性食物. ¶***body repair*** *food* 体の補いになる食物. ¶Oatmeal is a ***breakfast*** *food*. オートミールは朝食の食物だ. 【類】Bran (ふすま) is a good ***breakfast*** *food*. ¶***dog*** *food* 犬の餌. ¶an ***egg*** *food* (鶏などの)催卵飼料. ¶***fish*** *food* 魚肉. ¶***grain*** *foods* 穀物の食糧. ¶***invalid*** *foods* 病人向きの食物. ¶***left-over*** [*food*] 食事の残り; 残飯. ¶a ***plant*** *food*=food for plant 植物に与える肥料. 【類】the iron (鉄分) as a ***plant*** *food* / Manures (肥料) are sources of ***plant*** *foods*. ¶***protein*** *foods* たん白素を含む食物. ¶***process*** *food* 加工食物. ¶***sea*** *foods* 海産食料品. 【類】We have many fascinating ways (うまい調理法) of preparing *sea foods*.
P ***as*** *food* for dogs 犬の餌として. ¶He is temperate ***in*** *food* and drink. 彼は飲食物を節する. ¶use bananas ***for*** *food* バナナを食料とする ‖ It is good ***for*** *food*. それは食べられる. ¶lay in a supply ***of*** *food* 食料品を買入れる ‖ I have not had a morsel ***of*** *food* since the morning. 私は朝から一口も食べていない. ‖ Rice is the principal article ***of*** *food* in Japan. 米は日本の主要食物である. ¶live ***on*** foreign *food* 洋食を常食にする. ¶provide him ***with*** *food* 彼に食物を与える. ¶You must not go ***without*** *food*. 君なにも食わずにいてはいけない.
P² become *food* ***for*** fishes (worms) 魚(など)の餌食となる ‖ *food* ***for*** laughter 笑いのたね ‖ It gives us *food* ***for*** thought. それは参考になる.

food-cost, *n.* 食物の代価.
Q ***low*** *food-costs* 低廉な食料品値段.

food-fish, *n.* 食用魚.
Q one of the most ***important*** *food-fishes* in Japan 日本における最も重要な食用魚の一つ.

foodstuff, *n.* 食料品.
V ***prepare*** *foodstuff* 食料品を準備する.
Q ***staple*** *foodstuffs* 主食物. ¶***substitute*** *foodstuffs* 代用食.

fool, *n.* ばか者; 愚ろうされる人.
V ***act*** (=***play***) the *fool* ばかなまねをする. ¶***make*** a *fool* of oneself 不体裁を演じる ‖ Most men ***make*** *fools* of themselves over women. 大抵の男は女にかけてはばかなまねをする ‖ Don't ***make*** a *fool* of me. 人をばかにするな. 【類】You are ***making*** a *fool* of me. / be ***made*** a *fool* of by ...
Q a ***big*** *fool* 大ばか者. ¶a ***blind*** *fool* who fails to recognize it それが分らないようなあきめくら. ¶You ***bloody*** *fool!* べらんめえ. ¶a ***born*** *fool* (=idiot) 天性の白痴(今は主にからかう言葉として用いられる). ¶a ***downright*** *fool* 全くのばか者. ¶an ***empty-pated*** *fool* 頭が空っぽのばか. ¶No fool like an ***old*** *fool*. 年寄のばかほど手におえないものはない. ¶***silly*** *fools* 薄のろ. ¶He is not ***such*** a *fool* as to do it. 彼はそれをやるほどにばかではない. ¶a ***thick-headed*** *fool* 低能. ¶an ***utter*** (=a ***perfect***) *fool* 全くばか者. ¶***What*** a *fool!* 間抜けめが.
Q² be made an ***April*** *fool*. 四月ばかにさせられる(だまされる).
P He is next door ***to*** a *fool*. 彼はばかの一歩手前だ.
P² a *fool* ***for*** believing that one shilling is less than twelve pence 一シリングは十二ペンスより少いと信じるほどのばか者. ¶a *fool* ***of*** circumstances (fortune) 境遇(など)のなぶり者.

fool, *v.* だます; 愚ろうする; ばかなことをする.
M *fool* ***away*** one's time (money) ばかなことをして時間(など)を浪費する ‖ I ***had*** *fooled* all my money ***away***. 私はばかなまねをして持金全部を使ってしまっていた.
M² *fool* ***about*** (=***on***) ばかなまねをする, 怠け暮らす. ¶Where have you been *fooling* ***around***? どこでのらくらしていたのだ. ‖ *fool* ***around*** with ... ...をばかにする.
P He was *fooled* ***by*** a woman. 彼は女にだまされた. ¶*fool* a person ***into*** doing something 人をだましてなにかをやらせる ‖ *fool* a person ***into*** a belief 人をだまして信じさせる. ¶*fool* one ***out of*** one's money 人をだまして金をしぼる.

¶ You shouldn't *fool with* a dog when he is eating. 犬が食べているときにからかってはいけない.

foolish, *a.* 愚かな, ばかな.

M No one is *foolish enough* to endorse it. そんなことに賛成するばかはない. ¶ *how foolish* of him to ... ...するなんて何てばかだろう.

P It was *foolish for* (=*of*) him to take that expensive house. あの高い家を借りるなんてあの男もばかなことをしたもんだ. ‖ It was very *foolish of* me. 自分は実にばかだった. 【類】It was *foolish of* him to waste his money on such trifles.

foot, *n.* 足; フィート; 歩, 歩調; 末席, 末尾; ふもと; 歩兵.

V ***chap*** one's *feet* 足にひびを切らす. ¶ ***contest*** every *foot* of advance 一歩一歩前進を競う. ¶ ***direct*** one's weary *feet* toward ... ...の方へ疲れた足を向ける. ¶ ***drag*** one's weary *feet* 疲れた足を引きずる. ¶ ***draw*** the *feet* of ... ...フィート喫水がある ‖ This ship ***draws*** 28 *feet* of water. この船は喫水二十八フィートである. ¶ He ***gained*** his *feet*, only to be knocked down. 彼は立ち上るなりたたきのめされた. ¶ They are waiting to ***get*** the *foot* on the first rung of Fame's ladder. 彼らは名声というはしごの第一段に足を踏掛けようと待ち構えている. ‖ ***get*** wet *feet* by wading 徒渉で足をぬらす. ¶ He ***has*** one *foot* in the grave. 彼は棺おけへ片足突込んでいる. ¶ ***keep*** one's *feet* 足を踏みしめ倒れずにいる ‖ ***keep*** one's *foot* ***extended*** in the passageway 片足を通路に延ばして(電車などの座席に)すわる. ¶ ***measure*** another's *foot* by one's own last おのれをもって人を測る. ¶ ***miss*** one's *foot* 失脚する, 足を踏外ずす. ¶ ***place*** one's *foot* upon the soil of ... ...に上陸する. ¶ The wrestler ***planted*** the *feet*. その力士が四股(ᴱ)を踏んだ. ¶ from the moment I ***put*** my *foot* on shore 私が上陸した瞬間から. 【類】when one ***puts*** (=sets) his *foot* on French soil ‖ ***put*** one's *foot* inside a cottage 小屋の内に足を踏み入れる ‖ ***put*** *foot* in it それを始める ‖ ***put*** one's *foot* in it [足を突っ込むから]まずい破目になる ‖ ***put*** (=set) one's *foot* ***down*** しかと踏みしめる, 度胸をすえてかかる ‖ ***put down*** their *foot* once for all on ... ...を断然決行する. ¶ ***rest*** one's *feet* 足を休める. ¶ ***scrape*** one's *feet* (=shoes) on the scraper くつふきの上でくつをふく. ¶ ***set*** *foot* in Japan (the streets of Paris, the new world) 日本(など)に上陸する. ‖ ***set foot*** into an airplane 飛行機に乗る ‖ ***set foot*** on British soil 英国に足を踏入れる. 【類】They first ***set foot*** on their soil as adventurers. / from the day we first ***set foot*** on your shores / ***set foot*** on the platform / He has never ***set foot*** upon French soil. / They ***set foot*** upon the first foreign soil they had ever trod. / since the white man ***set*** *foot* in America. ¶ ***shuffle*** one's *feet* ***along*** 足を引きずって歩く. ¶ ***slip*** one's *feet* into Japanese straw sandals (one's slippers) ぞうり(など)をつっかける. ¶ ***sprain*** one's *foot* 足をくじく. ¶ That child ***stamps*** her *foot* when she is in a passion. あの子は怒ると足を踏み鳴らす. ‖ ***stamp*** their *feet* on the pavement to keep them warm 足を暖めるために歩道で足踏をやる ‖ He may ***stamp*** his *foot* at my saying such a thing. こんなことを言ってはあの人にしかられるかも知れない. ¶ ***tickle*** one's *feet* 人の足をくすぐる. ¶ my *foot* was ***trodden on*** by ... 私は...に足を踏みつけられた. ¶ ***warm*** one's *feet* at a fire 火で足を暖める. ¶ ***wipe*** one's *feet* (=boots or shoes) upon the doormat before entering a house 家にはいる前にくつふきでくつをふく.

V² The director's *foot* ***comes*** stamping down upon the boards. 舞台監督が(じりじりして)どたばた舞台にやって来る. ¶ All at once his *foot* ***slipped***. 思わず彼は足をすべらした. ¶ I loved these countries before my *feet* ***trod*** them. 私はこれらの国に足を踏入れないうちから好きだった.

Q ***chapped*** hands and *feet* ひびの切れた手足. ¶ ***cubic*** *foot* 一立方フィート. ¶ These are spots where ***foreign*** *feet* have seldom trod. そこへは外人が滅多に行ったことがない. ¶ the ***4th*** *foot* (=regiment of foot) 歩兵第四連隊. ¶ I went with ***lagging*** *feet* and a heavy heart. 私は進まない足と重い気分で行った. ¶ He has a ***light*** *foot*. 彼は足が軽い. ¶ a ***long*** *foot* 大足. ¶ with ***naked*** *feet*=barefoot はだしで. ¶ a ***square*** *foot* 一平方フィート ‖ Not a ***square*** *foot* was unoccupied. 立すいの余地もなかった. ¶ ***weary*** *feet* 疲れた足. ¶ ***Webbed*** *feet* help geese to swim. 足に膜があるのでが鳥は水を楽に泳げる. ¶ jump about on his ***well*** *foot* 何ともない方の足で飛び回る.

Q² a ***club*** *foot* えび足. ¶ in his ***stocking*** (=***socks***) *feet* くつを脱いで ‖ The stature was measured in ***stocking*** *feet*. その身長は(くつを脱ぎ)くつ下になって測ったものであった. 【類】She was in her ***stocking*** *feet*.

P ***at*** the *foot* of the hill 丘のふもとに ‖ Then merchants stood ***at*** the *foot* of the social ladder. 当時商人は社会の最下位にあった. ‖ He took his place ***at*** the *foot* (head) of the table. 彼はテーブルの末(上)席に着いた. ‖ See explanatory notes ***at*** *foot* of this page. このページの脚註を見よ. ‖ He is ***at*** the *foot* of a class (the procession). 彼は級(など)のびりだ. ‖ ***at*** the south *foot* of the mountain その山の南ろくに ‖ I sat ***at*** his *feet* for many years. 私は多年あの方に師事した. ¶ the room (ground) ***beneath*** our *feet* われわれのいるすぐ下のへや(など). ¶ ***beyond*** a few *feet* 数フィート先きに. ¶ the pain ***in*** his blistered *foot* 彼の水まめを踏みだした足の痛み. ¶ He is swift ***of*** *foot*. 彼は足が速い. ‖ a company ***of*** *foot* 歩兵一個中隊. ¶ ***off*** one's *feet* 足をさらわれて ‖ carry a person ***off*** his *feet* [風・波など]人の足をさらう; 夢中にさせる ‖ His speech swept the members of the House ***off*** their *feet*. 彼の演説は下議院員をあっと言わせた. ‖ shock the spectators ***off*** their *feet* 見物人のどぎもを抜く. ¶ It takes about thirty minutes ***on*** *foot*, or fifteen by jinrikisha. 徒歩で約三十分車で十五分かかる. 【類】I came ***on*** *foot*. / The infantry march ***on*** *foot*. / I walk (run) ***on*** my *feet*. ‖ trudge along ***on*** *foot* towards ... ...の方へとぼとぼと歩いて行く ‖ I wear shoes ***on*** my *feet*. 私は足にくつをはいている. 【類】with silk stockings ***on*** her *feet* ‖ Every man should be able to say something ***on*** his *feet*. だれでも立ってなにかしゃべれなくてはいけない. ‖ He was ***on*** his *feet* in a moment. 彼はいきなり立上った. ‖ He popped up ***on*** his *feet* like a jack-in-a-box. 彼はびっくり箱のようにぬっと立ちあがった. ‖ Working as a shop girl, standing ***on*** your *feet* all day, is no bed of roses. 一日立通しで女店員のように働くのは楽じゃない. 【類】He is ***on*** his *feet* for sixteen hours a day. ‖ In three days you will be ***on*** your *feet!* 三日たつとあなたは立って歩けます. ‖ hop ***on*** one *foot* 片足で飛ぶ ‖ A toe is ***on*** one's *foot*. 足指は足にある. ‖ He is not yet old enough to stand ***on*** his *feet* (=legs). 彼はまだ独り立ちできる年じゃない. ‖ as soon as his business could stand ***on*** its own *feet* 商売が一本立になるや否や ‖ schemes are ***on*** *foot* for ... ...の計画が着手中である. 【類】a movement is now ***on*** *foot* to ... / there is a move ***on*** *foot* to ... ‖ set ***on*** *foot* a movement to ... ...しようという運動を起す ‖ Inquiries were set ***on*** *foot* which led to his trial. 色々調査をやって見た結果彼を裁判にかけることになった. ‖ He is quick ***on*** his *feet* as a rabbit. 彼はうさぎのように足が早い. ¶ ***over*** six *feet* tall 背丈が六フィート以上. ¶ scrutinize him from head ***to*** *foot* 彼を頭からつま先まで し細に見る ‖ He started ***to*** his *feet*. 彼は飛び上った. ‖ He took ***to*** his *feet*. 彼は歩きだした. ‖ Get ***to*** your *feet*, young man! 立て, 若いの! ‖ The earth quaked ***under*** his *feet*. 足下の地面が揺れた. ¶ trample it ***under*** *foot* それを足下に踏みにじる ‖ People were trodden ***under*** *foot* by the tyrant. 人民はその暴君にじゅうりんされた. ¶ stand (walk) ***upon*** one's own *feet* 一本立になる(独立独行する). ¶ ***with*** stealthy *foot* 抜足で ‖ ***with*** one's *feet* on the earth 地に足をつけて ‖ an old man ***with*** one *foot* in the grave 片足をかんおけにつっ込んだ老人.

P² set *foot* ***in*** a craft (=ship) 船に乗り込む ‖ set *foot* ***in*** this country この国に足を踏入れる. 【類】He never sets *foot* ***inside*** a theatre. ¶ a *foot* ***of*** snow 一フィートの雪 ‖ the *foot* ***of*** a bed 寝台の脚部の方.

foot, *v.* 《俗》合計...となる.

M ***foot up*** all items 全部しめる; 費目を合計する ‖ The loss will *foot* ***up*** to enormous totals. その損失は驚くべき総計となるだろう. 【類】his debts (these figures) *foot* ***up*** to ... / The foreign trade of the United States for this calendar year 1900 will *foot* ***up*** into these magnificent figures. / Aggregate investments *foot* ***up*** to more than three thousand millions.

football, *n.* しゅう球.

P play a match ***at*** *football* 蹴球の試合をやる.

footfall, *n.* 足音.

Q ***ghostly*** *footfalls* overhead 頭上に怪しい足音.

foot-hill, *n.* 山ろくの小丘.

P Buddha was born about 567 B.C. at Kapilavastu,

north-east of Benares, ***in*** the *foot-hills* of the Himalayas. 仏陀は紀元前約五百六十七年ごろヒマラヤ山脈中の小丘に在るベナレスの東北に当るカピラヴァスチュに生れた.

foothold, *n.* 足場; 地盤.

V ***afford*** no *foothold* 足場がない. ¶***establish*** a *foothold* 足場を作る. ¶***gain*** a *foothold* in Manchuria 満州に地盤を得る ‖ Those newly coined words have ***gained*** *foothold* (=come to stay). それらの新語は(一時的流行でなく)常用されるようになった. 【類】 The idea (thought, notion) ***gained*** *foothold.* ¶***get*** *foothold* in Japan (キリスト教など)日本に地盤を得る. ¶The market didn't seem to ***give*** any *foothold* for Japanese goods. ¶***obtain*** a *foothold* in the Far East 極東に地盤を得る ‖ The word has ***obtained*** a firm *foothold* in the language. その語はりっぱにその国語に取入れられた. ¶***secure*** a *foothold* in China 中国に地盤を得る. 【類】 ***secure*** one's *foothold* in the communities.

Q gain a ***firm*** (=***solid or strong***) *foothold* 堅固な地盤を得る. ¶a ***sure*** (=***secure***) *foothold* 確実な地盤.

P^2 Mt. Robson, monarch of the Canadian Rockies, is solid rock from top to bottom with hardly any *foothold* ***for*** vegetation. カナダ・ロッキー山脈中の王者たるロブソン山はいただきからふもとまで全山岩石から成り植物のはえる場所がほとんどない.

footing, *n.* 立場, 地歩, 足場, 地盤; 間柄.

V In the commencement of the seventh century Buddhism had ***attained*** a sure *footing* in the Japanese Islands. 第七世紀の初めに仏教が日本において確固たる地盤を作っていた. ¶***establish*** a *footing* in a country [キリスト教などが]ある国において確立した地歩を占める. ¶***find*** safe *footing* 安全な足場を見出す. ¶***furnish*** a good *footing* for horses 馬匹に対してよい足場を供する. ¶He has ***gained*** a *footing* in the commercial world. 彼は商業界に地歩を占めた. 【類】 Fascism has ***gained*** a *footing* (=taken root). ¶***get*** a secure *footing* on the island 同島で安全な足場を得る. ¶***have*** a firm *footing* 確固たる地盤がある. ¶***keep*** one's *footing* 自己の立場を守る. ¶***lose*** one's *footing* 倒れる; 立場を失う ‖ He ***lost*** his *footing* and precipitated to the ground. 足をふみはずし真さかさまに地上に落ちた. ¶He ***missed*** his *footing.* 彼は足を踏みはずした. ¶He has ***obtained*** a *footing* at court. 彼は宮廷において勢力を得た. ¶***pay*** one's *footing* 入会金を払う, 渡りをつける. ¶***recover*** one's *footing* 足場を回復する. ¶***secure*** a *footing* in society 社会的地歩を確保する. 【類】 ***secure*** a *footing* (=foothold) in political circles (the publishing world).

Q trade on the most ***advantageous*** *footing* 最も有利な立場での取引. ¶They met on a ***common*** *footing.* 彼らは上下抜きの会(無礼講)をやった. ¶He is on a ***different*** *footing.* 彼は異った立場にある. ¶stand on an ***equal*** *footing* with ... ...と同等な立場に立つ. 【類】 put them all on an ***equal*** *footing.* ¶I am on a ***familiar*** *footing* with him. 私は彼と親しくしている. ¶a ***firm*** *footing* 強固な地盤. ¶We live on a ***friendly*** *footing* with them. われわれは彼らと親密にしている. ¶There was ***no*** (***not much***) *footing* on the steep cliff. その懸がいには足がかりが(あまり)なかった. ¶on the ***same*** *footing* as men 男子と同じ立場で. ¶place the trade on a ***satisfactory*** *footing* 商業を満足な立場に置く. ¶They are on the same [***social***] *footing.* 彼らは同じ[社会的]地位にある. ¶The venture is established on a ***solid*** and ***durable*** *footing.* その冒険事業は堅固にして永続的な立場におかれている. ¶The trade has been placed upon a reasonably ***sound*** *footing.* その商業は相当安定な立場におかれてあった. ¶place the company on a ***stable*** and ***prosperous*** *footing* 同会社を安定で繁栄する立場に置く. ¶a ***treacherous*** *footing* あぶなっかしい立場. ¶The business rests on an ***uncertain*** *footing.* その仕事は基礎がぐらついている.

Q^2 the strength of its army on a ***peace*** (***war***) *footing* 平時(戦時)編成における戦力. ¶the rehabilitation of industry to a ***peace-time*** *footing* 産業の平時編成への復旧. ¶remain on (=retain) a ***war*** *footing* 戦時体制を続ける ‖ be put on a ***war*** *footing* 戦時体制に置かれる.

P struggle ***for*** a *footing* in society 社会的地位を得ようと努力する. ¶treat them ***on*** a *footing* of equality 彼らに均等の待遇を与える ‖ I advise you ***on*** a *footing* of a friend. 友人の立場で君に忠告する. ‖ You see ***on*** what *footing* we are. われわれがどんな間柄にあるかはお分りでしょう.

footlights, *n. pl.* 脚光; 舞台.

P address the audience ***across*** the *footlights* 《米》観客に呼びかける. ¶She made her first appearance ***before*** the *footlights* last evening. 彼女はゆうべ初舞台を踏んだ. ¶***behind*** the *footlights* 観覧席に. ¶His air smells ***of*** the *footlights.* 彼の挙動には役者らしい所がある.

footmark, *n.* 足跡.

V We ***found*** certain *footmarks* in a field. われわれはその原っぱにある足跡を見付けた. ¶The burglar ***left*** *footmarks* all over the garden. 泥棒が庭一面に足跡を残した. ¶*footmarks* ***retained*** in history 史上の足跡.

footnote, *n.* 脚註.

Q ***copious*** *footnotes* 豊富な脚註. ¶by an ***occasional*** *footnote* 所々そう入した脚註によって.

footprint, *n.* 足跡.

V Neither fingerprint nor *footprints* have been ***found*** so far. 今までのところ指紋も足跡も見つかっていない. 【類】 They ***found*** her *footprints* in the snow. ¶***leave*** our *footprints* on the sands of time 時の砂上にわれわれの足跡を印する. 「つける.

Q follow the trail of ***muddy*** *footprints* 泥まみれの足跡を

P^2 *footprints* ***in*** the snow (sand) 雪(など)上の足跡. ¶*footprints* ***of*** a man 人の足跡.

foot-race, *n.* 徒歩競走.

P take part ***in*** the *foot-race* その徒歩競走に加わる.

footstep, *n.* 足跡; 足音; 足取り.

V ***dog*** one's *footsteps* in the streets 街頭でそのあとをつける. ¶***follow*** the *footsteps* of William Morris ウイリアム・モリスをまねする. ¶***follow in*** one's *footslep* 人をお手本にする. ¶The child ***heard*** his father's *footsteps* on the stairs. その子は階段を上ってくる父の足音を聞いた. 【類】 He ***heard*** the hurried *footsteps* of his sister at the door. / ***hear*** *footsteps* nearing to ...

Q I heard ***hurried*** *footsteps* behind me. 私は背後にあわただしい足音を聞いた. ¶***light*** and ***heavy*** *footsteps* 軽快な足取りと重い足取り. ¶***quiet*** *footsteps* 静かな足音. ¶follow [in] the ***fatal*** *footsteps* of one's predecessors 恐るべき先人の覆てつを踏む. ¶***tottering*** *footsteps* よろめく足取り.

Q^2 Father wants him to follow in his ***banking*** *footsteps.* 父は彼が銀行の経営を継承することを望んでいる.

P I trod ***in*** his *footsteps.* 私は彼の後について行った; 彼の志を継いだ. ¶***with*** the *footsteps* of a phantom 幽霊のよ

footwalk, *n.* 歩道. うな足どりで.

P passengers ***on*** the *footwalk* going to and fro あちこち

forage, *n.* まぐさ; 食料. へ行き交う歩道の通行人.

P be ***on*** the *forage* 馬料徴発, 食料あさり.

forage, *v.* 食料をさがす.

M^2 *forage* ***about*** in the kitchen for something to eat 台所でなにか食物をさがし回る.

P *forage* ***among*** old papers ***for*** ... ...を求めて古新聞をあ

forbear, *v.* 忍ぶ, 差控える. さる.

P *forbear* ***from*** evil 悪事を差控える. 【類】 *forbear* ***from*** doing wrong=forbear to do wrong / *forbear* ***from*** asking for a loan of money (借金) ‖ I cannot *forbear* ***from*** expressing my thanks to him for ... 私は...に対し彼に感謝せざるを得ない. ¶*forbear* ***with*** it それを忍ぶ.

forbearance, *n.* 我慢, 差控え; 寛容.

V ***have*** a little *forbearance* with each other お互いに少し我慢し合う. ¶***show*** *forbearance* for ... ...を堪忍する. 【類】 ***show*** *forbearance* to him. ¶*Forbearance* ***consists*** in bearing what is unbearable. ならぬ堪忍するが堪忍.

Q ***mutual*** *forbearance* お互いの我慢.

P be ***beyond*** *forbearance* 目に余る. ¶He pardoned my fault ***with*** his usual *forbearance.* 彼は例の雅量で僕の過失を許してくれた.

P^2 *forbearance* ***from*** the use of tobacco (alcoholic liquors) 禁煙(酒). ¶*forbearance* ***toward*** the weak 弱者に対

forbid, *v.* 禁じる, 禁制する. する寛容.

M It is ***expressly*** *forbidden.* それは明かに禁じられている. ¶***imperatively*** *forbid* the use of ... 断然...の使用を禁じる. ¶*forbid* it ***outright*** 即時それを禁止する. ¶it is ***rigidly*** *forbidden* to ... ...することは厳禁である. ¶It is ***sternly*** *forbidden.* それは厳重に禁止されている. ¶Smoking is ***strictly*** *forbidden.* 喫煙厳禁.

P the authorities *forbade* minors ***from*** entering ... 当局は未成年者の...に入ることを禁じた. ¶Entrance to China was then *forbidden to* all foreigners. 当時外人が中国へ入国することは全く禁ぜられていた. ¶This is *forbidden under* pain of death. これを犯す者は死刑に処せられる.

force, *n.* (**1**) 力; 腕力, 暴力; 威力, 勢力; 実施, 効力; 真意.
v ***abate*** the *force* of an opposition 反対党の勢力をそぐ. ¶***acquire*** legal *force* 法律上の効力を生じる. ¶***admit*** the *force* of an argument 議論が正しいと認める. ¶***apprehend*** the *force* of an argument (import of a statement) ある議論の筋(など)を理解する. ¶***break*** the *force* of wind 風の勢をくじく ‖ ***break*** the *force* of objection 反対のほこ先を鈍らす. 【類】 ***break*** the *force* of one's fall from a great height by parachute. ¶Only by ***concentrating*** all psychic *forces* on the desired aim can only be assured of perfect success. 目標に精神力を傾倒して始めて十分の成功が期せられるのである. ¶***gain force*** 力を増す. ¶***gather force*** from habit 惰性で力を増す. 【類】 The movement is slowly but surely ***gathering force***. ¶***give force*** to what we say われわれが言うことに重みをつける. 【類】 ***give force*** to reason. ¶***harness*** natural *forces* to do the work 自然の力を利用してその仕事をやる. ¶Her tears ***have force*** to move you. 彼女の涙には君を動かす力がある. ‖ The word ***has*** the *force* of a preposition. その語は前置詞同様の力を持っている. ‖ These collocations ***have*** in use the *force* of single words. これらの連語には一語と同様の力がある. ¶***increase*** the working *force* (=personnel) 人員をふやす. ¶***join forces*** with ... ...と力を合わせる ‖ ***join forces*** with the association at its Golden Jubilee Convention 協会の輝く創立五十年会議に参加する ‖ these two companies ***joined forces*** and became one known as ... この二会社は合併して...という名義になった. ¶These phrases ***lack*** idiomatic *force*. これらの句は慣用語的の力を欠いている. ‖ He ***lacks force*** and determination. 彼は優柔不断である. ¶The fact ***lends force*** to my supposition. その事実が私の想像に力を添える. ¶***meet force*** with force 暴に報ゆるに暴をもってする. ¶***mold*** the *forces* of nature to man's use and comfort 自然の力を利用して人間の使用と慰安に供する. ¶***muster*** their *forces* for a struggle 彼らの力を集めて一戦に当る. ¶***outstand*** the *force* of waves 浪の力に耐える. ¶***prepare*** and ***gather force*** for ... ...に対する準備と力を養う. ¶***recognize*** the *force* of one's remarks その説をもっともだと思う. ¶***reconcile*** the warring *forces* of labor and capital 資本家と労働者の闘争を調停する. ¶***resist*** the *force* of ... ...の力に抵抗する. ¶***revive*** one's spent *force* 元気をかい復する. ¶***scatter*** one's *forces* 精力を消耗する. ¶He ***saw*** the *force* (=point *or* truth) of my argument. 彼は私の言分はもっともだと思った. 【類】 I ***see*** the *force* of your remarks. ¶The storm has ***spent*** its *force*. あらしはもう静まってきた. ¶***stir*** the latent or dormant *forces* of a people 国民の潜在しまたは眠っている力を目覚ませる. ¶***summoning up*** all his *forces* 彼の全力を振い起して. ¶***use force*** 腕力に訴える, 強制的にやらせる. 【類】 ***use*** no *force*. 【類】 *Force* must be ***used*** to educate them to a wholesomer frame of mind (健全な精神教育). ¶the *force* of this criticism has been ***weakened*** by the fact that ... この批評の効力は...のために弱くなった.

Q ***aesthetic*** *forces* which have guided the nation in their path of progress その国民が進歩の道程をたどるに当ってこれを指導した審美力. ¶an ***ameliorative*** *force* of much importance 重要な改善力. ¶employ ***brutal*** *force* 暴力を行使する ‖ by mere ***brute*** *force* 暴力一点張りで. 【類】 Man is doomed to struggle against the ***brute*** *force* of nature (自然の暴力). ¶a ***central organized*** *force* 組織された中心勢力. ¶the ***civilizing*** *force* of steam and electricity 蒸気と電気の文化力. ¶Advertising is the greatest ***commercial*** *force* of the 20th century. 広告は二十世紀における商業上最大の力だ. ¶The spirit of inquiry is a ***compelling*** *force* in the university and the wider world. 研究心は大学及び更に広い世間において強大な力となっている. ¶the Opposition as a ***constitutional*** *force* 立憲政治の一勢力としての反対党. ¶with ***crushing*** *force* 破竹の勢で. ¶gather a ***cumulative*** *force* as it goes 破竹の勢を示す. ¶a ***demoralizing*** *force* 風紀を乱す力. ¶Words with "be" prefixed have a ***disparaging*** *force*. 「be」の接頭語を有する語にはけなす意味がある. ¶a ***divine*** *force* working behind the events 事件の背後に働いている神の力. ¶Great men are the ***dominating*** *forces* of the world. 偉人は世界を支配する力だ. ¶regulate the subject by positive law instead of leaving it to the uncontrolled play of ***economic*** *forces* その問題を無統制な経済力の支配に委ねずに積極的法律によって取締る. ¶***elastic*** *force* 弾力. ¶the argument applies with ***equal*** *force* to ... その議論は...に適用しても同じく力がある. ¶appeal to one with ***exceptional*** *force* 異常な力で人に訴える. ¶The law is in ***full*** *force*. その法律は完全に実施されている. ‖ He is, in the ***full*** *force* of the words, a good man. 彼は本当の善人である. ¶bring to one's aid the ***gigantic*** *forces* of nature 力を偉大なる自然に借りる. ¶a preacher of ***great*** *force* 非常に力のある説教家 ‖ Language is a ***great*** *force*. 言語は偉大な力である. 【類】 Work, play, love, and worship are ***great*** *forces* of life. / Zola is a ***great*** *force* in fiction (小説界の大立物). ‖ It applies to this with even ***greater*** *force*. それは更に一層適切にこの場合に当てはまる. ‖ He is an ***inspiring*** *force*. 彼は(人に霊感を与える)大人物である. 【類】 have more ***inspiring*** *force*. ¶It has binding ***legal*** *force*. それには拘束する法律上の効果がある. ¶***intellectual*** *force* 知力. ¶her eloquence and ***magnetic*** *force* were so pronounced that ... 彼女の雄弁と魅力とは非常にすぐれたものであったので... ¶by ***main*** *force* 力づくで ‖ These are three ***main*** *forces* that have been at work during this period. これがこの期間に活動していた三大勢力である. ¶by the ***mere*** *force* of habit 全く惰性で. ¶Buddhism as a ***moral*** *force* 道徳の力としての仏教. ¶Religion is a ***motive*** *force* of thought and action. 宗教は思想と行動との原動力だ. ¶laws governing the great ***natural*** *forces* 偉大なる自然力を支配する法則 ‖ Many Greek deities or legendary figures were originally personifications of ***natural*** *forces*. ギリシアの神や伝説的人物は本来多くは自然力を人格化したものであった. ¶The worship of the ***obscure*** *forces* of fate is not yet entirely extinct even with us. 運命の持つ神秘の力は今日においてもこれを崇拝することが絶滅していない. ¶with an ***overwhelming*** *force* 圧倒的な力で. ¶He was a ***personal*** *force* of the period. 彼はその時代の一勢力(人物)であった. ¶His ***physical*** *force* was weak, but his ***mental*** and ***moral*** *forces* were very great. 彼は体力こそ弱かったが知力と道徳力はきわめて偉大であった. ¶the novel as a ***political*** *force* 政治上の力としての小説. ¶Sentiment is, after all, one of the most ***potent*** *forces* in the world. 結局感情はこの世で最も権威ある勢力の一つである. ¶the ***powerful*** *force* of public opinion 世論の強い力. ¶the ***probative*** *force* of evidence 証明力. ¶Sex and the belief in the unseen—love and faith—are the two greatest ***ruling*** *forces* of mankind. 性と霊界に対する信念一恋愛と信仰一が人類を支配する二大勢力である. 【類】 Some cynic has said that the two great ***ruling*** *forces* of mankind are Obscenity (わいせつ) and Superstition. ¶The liberals are a ***secondary*** *force* in Chinese affairs. 自由党は中国の政治においては第二位の権力者である. ¶by ***sheer*** *force* of volition (character and perseverance) 全く意志(など)の力で. ¶Newspapers guide and influence public opinion more than any other ***single*** *force*. 新聞は他のいかなる一個の勢力よりも強く世論を指導しかつそれに影響を及ぼすものである. ¶preach with ***singular*** *force* and persuasion the necessity of ... ...の必要を特異な力と説得力とで述べる. ¶the power of music as a ***social*** *force* 社会の一勢力としての音楽の力. ¶use the drama as a ***sociological*** *force* in getting people together and acquainted with one another 人々を集めて互に知り合うという社会学的一勢力として劇を用いる. ¶the importance of aiding Japan to rise so that she become a ***stable*** *force* for peace in the Far East 日本が極東の平和を維持する安定勢力となるように日本を援助し復興させることの重要性. ¶with ***tremendous*** *force* すさまじい勢で. ¶The ***twin*** *forces* of capital and labor are warring against each other. 資本と労働の二勢力は互に闘争している. ¶the importance of the Pope and the clergy as ***unifying*** *forces* in medieval civilization 中世文化における統一的勢力としてのローマ法王と僧の重要性 ‖ The Chinese ideographs are a ***unifying*** *force* in China. 中国では漢字が一つの統一力になっている. ¶an unlawful ***physical*** *force* applied or threatened 行使されるかまたは脅かされた不当の体力. ¶***vital*** *force* 活力.
Q² abounding in ***nerve*** *force* 気力旺盛(おう)で.

P the League of Nations *as* a *force* for peace 平和を致す力としての国際連盟. ¶I obtained his consent *by force*. 私は強いて彼に承諾させた. ¶seize her *by force* 彼女を腕ずくで捉える. 【類】take one's money *by force* / collect the money *by force* / suppress a riot *by force* of arms (武力) ‖ *by force* of contrast 対照上 ‖ *by force* of use 用法上 ‖ *by force* of numbers 数の力で ‖ The boy was precocious *by force* of circumstances. その少年は境遇のせいで早熟であった. ¶*by dint of force* 力ずくで. ¶do *from force* of habit 習慣でやる ‖ *from* the *force* of circumstances 事情止むなく. ¶equal *in force* 力のひとしい ‖ These countries were all represented *in force* in the exhibition. これらの国は全部その博覧会において有力に代表されていた. ‖ the system *in force* 現行制度 ‖ the rules *in force* at ... ...で行われている規則 ‖ The new import tariff was put *in force* today. 新輸入税率は今日から実施になった. ‖ the quarantine now *in force* will be abolished on ... 現在実施している隔離は...日に廃止される. 【類】The Gregorian calendar (新暦) has been *in force* ever since the 1st January, 1873. / laws relating to ... *in force* in 1917 in the United States. ¶The new law goes *into force* from the day of its promulgation. 今度の法律は発布の日から効力を生じる. ‖ The new tariff came *into force* with the New Year. 新関税法は新年から実施になった. ‖ carry the law *into force* その法律を実施する. ¶to be *of force* as such, must ... その力を持つには...しなければならない ‖ A promise made under compulsion is *of* no *force*. 強制されて結んだ約束は無効だ. ¶go *out of force* 廃止になる. ¶resort *to force* 腕力に訴える. ¶attack *with* bitter and crushing *force* 猛烈な力で攻撃する ‖ The last syllable is pronounced *with force*. 最後の音節は強く発音する. ¶*with* all my *force* 力一杯に ‖ *with* all the *force* he could summon 力任せに ‖ *with* great *force* もろに. 【類】throw a stone *with* great *force*. ¶*with* or *without force* 腕力を用いてまたは用いずに.

P² a *force for* good 善い方への力. ¶*force in* execution 実行力 ‖ That's the *force of* habit. それは習慣の力だ. 「力.

(**2**) [しばしば *pl.*] 兵力, 軍備力; 軍隊; 団体, 警察隊, 警察

V *concentrate* a strong *force* in ... ...に主力を集める. ¶The Allies *combined* their *forces*. 連合国はその兵力を合した. ¶They *constitute* a fighting *force* of no mean order. 彼らはりっぱな戦闘隊をなしている. ¶*cut* their *forces* in Germany ドイツ占領軍を縮少する. ¶*despatch* a *force* to ... ...に軍隊を派遣する. ¶*direct forces* against ... 兵を...に向ける. ¶*double* or *treble* the *force* of clerks 書記の人員を二倍または三倍にする. ¶*draft* a *force* of policemen to the scene 警官を選抜して現場に派遣する. ¶*employ* a large *force* 大勢の人を使う. ¶young policemen *entering* the *Force* 警務につく若い巡査たち. ¶*land* a *force* of marines and bluejackets 一隊の水平を上陸させる. ¶It was he that *led* the *force* which relieved Kumamoto. 熊本を救った軍隊を率いたのは彼であった. ¶*maintain* a powerful military *force* 強力な陸軍を維持する. ¶*move* their *forces* 彼らの軍隊を動員する. ¶Italy *put* her *forces* in motion. イタリーは兵を出動させた. ¶*raise up forces* in defence of right 義師を起す. ¶The party *rallied* its *force* for the election. 政党は選挙のために党員を召集した. ¶*send* an armed *force* against ... ...討伐軍を派遣する. ¶*strafe* ground *forces* 地上軍を空襲する. ¶*withdraw forces* from ... ...から軍隊を撤退する.

Q the U.S. *Armed Forces* 米軍(陸·海·空三軍を含めて). ¶use the *armed forces* of coercion against ... 武力を用いて...強制する. 【類】send *armed forces* across national frontiers / place *armed forces* on a war footing. ¶a *British expeditionary force* abroad 英国の海外派遣隊. ¶lead an *expeditionary force* 遠征軍を率いる. ¶taxation necessary for the maintenance of *huge military* and *naval forces* 巨大な陸海軍を維持するに必要な課税. ¶His *Majesty's forces* 陛下の軍隊. ¶raise the needed *military force* of 2,100,000 二百十万の必要な兵員を募る ‖ He has been rejected as unfit for the *military* and *naval forces* of the Crown. 彼は英国陸海軍には適しないという理由で罷免された. ¶*rival forces* 敵対軍. ¶The police were present in *strong force* to prevent a breach of peace. 治安維持のために警官が大勢臨場していた. ¶an "ever *victorious force*" 常勝軍.

Q² an *air force* 空軍. ¶a nation having strong *air* and *sea forces* 強力な空軍と海軍を持つ国. ¶*air, sea* and *ground forces* 空軍海軍及び地上軍. ¶the native *anti-Communist forces* in French Indo-China 仏印の土人反共軍. ¶the chief of the *Army Air Forces* 陸軍航空司令官. ¶*army ground forces* 陸軍地上部隊. ¶*Armies, navies* and *air forces* "eat up" major parts of the national budgets. 陸海空軍が国家予算の大部分を食っている. ¶the *Army Service Forces* 陸軍部隊. ¶He is the dominant *business force* in the country. 彼はその国の実業界の威力である. ¶a *carpenter force* 木工部隊. ¶a *combat air force* 戦闘機部隊. ¶the *Communist forces* 共産軍. ¶an *elevator force* エレベーター係(総称して). ¶*enemy forces* 敵軍. ¶an *exploration force* 探検隊. ¶order *ground forces* into action 地上部隊に行動を命じる. ¶a *guerrilla force* ゲリラ部隊. ¶sell one's *labor force* 労働力を売る. 【類】the percentage of women in the *labor force* / the acquisition of *labor force* / The *labor force* of the country is estimated at 500,000. ¶a *land force* 陸軍. ¶*non-Communist forces* 非共産軍. ¶the Allied *Occupation Forces* 連合国占領軍. 【類】a soldier of the *occupation force* / withdraw *occupation forces*. ¶an *office force* = a staff 係員たち ‖ keep only a reduced *office force* to transact emergency business 緊急事務処理のため事務所要員の数を減じる. ¶a *police force* 警察隊 ‖ serve on the *police force* 警察に奉職する ‖ set Japan's *police force* in order 日本の警察力を整備する ‖ an undermanned *police force* 手不足の警察力 ‖ acceleration of the establishment of an international *police force* 国際警察隊組織の促進. 【類】Local youth run their own *police force*. / place women on the *police force* to meet the growing need of the service / a woman member of the *police force* — a policewoman. ¶a *non-selling force* 非販売員(エレベーター係り, 出納係など). ¶the *Red forces* 赤軍. ¶a *reserve force* 予備軍. ¶a *scout force* 偵察隊. ¶an armed *sea force* 海軍. ¶a *security force* 保安隊. ¶a *task force* 〖陸〗特務部隊; 〖海〗機動艦隊. ¶winds of *typhoon force* 台風級の風. ¶*watchmen force* 監視力. ¶the *working* (= labor) *force* 労働力 ‖ reduce a *working force* 要員を減らす. ¶the nation's non-agricultural *working forces* 国の非農業労働者.

P The town was occupied *by* the German *forces*. その町はドイツ軍に占領された. ¶He came *with* so great a *force*. 彼は非常な大軍を率いて来た.

P² a *force of* seven thousand men 七千の軍勢 ‖ a great *force of* ants ありの大軍 ‖ a *force of* workmen 工員団. ¶the *force of* arms 武威.

force, *v*. しいる, 無理にさせる; 無理に押付ける.

M *force* it *away* それを力ずくで奪う. ¶The police *forced* the crowd *back*. 警官が群衆を押戻した. 【類】He was *forced back* by the flames. ‖ try to *force back* prices 物価を下げようと試みる. ¶be *forced out* as vice premier 副首相の職を追われる ‖ *force out* [a runner] 〖野球〗封殺する.

M² The plane was *forced down*. 飛行機が不時着陸をした. ‖ The plane was *forced down* on a beach. その飛行機は海浜に不時着した. ¶*force* a bill *through* 法案を無理に通過させる.

P he was *forced by* circumstances to ... 彼は事情止むなく...した. ¶His narrative *forced* tears *from* our eyes. 彼の話はわれわれを泣かせた. ¶*force* it *into* one's mouth それを口に押込む ‖ He was *forced into* crime by circumstances. 彼は境遇に迫られて罪を犯すに至った. ‖ She was *forced into* prostitution. 彼女は止むなく色を売ることになった. ‖ *force* them *into* vassalage 彼らを従属させる ‖ *force* ... *into* the glare of publicity あかるみへ...を出す ‖ They have *forced* an entrance *into* my dwelling. 彼らは私の住宅に押入った. 【類】The fellow *forced* his way *into* my home. ¶I am sorry to *force* business *on* you. 君に仕事をしいて気の毒です. ‖ *force* one's opinion *on* another 意見を人にしいる. ¶*force* (= break) *through* the line 戦線を破る ‖ He *forced* his way *through* the crowd. 彼は群衆を押分けて進んだ. ¶*force* slaves *to* labor どれいを無理に労働させる. ¶War is *forced upon* us. われわれは戦争をしいられている. ‖ It is *forced upon* our attention. それはわれわれの注意を促している. ‖ The truth *forces* itself *upon* the attention of all who have the welfare of their country at heart. いやしくも国を憂える人はこの事実に注目せざるを得ない. ‖ *force* goods *upon* a person 人に押売りする ‖ sedulously *force* counterfeits *upon* the market まやかし物をしいて市場に持ち出す. 【類】*force* a quarrel *upon* a person / The necessity of a decision was *forced upon* him.

forcefulness, *n.* 力強さ.

P^2 *forcefulness* **on** the stage 舞台上の迫力.

forcer, *n.* 促成器.

Q^2 an *egg forcer* 孵(ふ)卵促成器.

Ford, *n.* フォード自動車.

V ***buy*** a '55 *Ford* (一九)五五年型フォードを買う.

Q^2 a 1921 ***Model T Ford*** 千九百二十一年T型フォード自動車.

ford, *n.* 浅瀬.

P^2 a *ford* **in** a river 川の浅瀬.

fore, *n.* 前部, 前面.

P The question is again **to** the *fore*. この問題がまた持上った. 【類】The question is at present so much **to** the *fore*. / Thus it came **to** the *fore*. ‖ Among Welsh resorts Llandudno is well **to** the *fore*. ウェールスの保養地中でランディドノは第一位を占めている. ‖ The author is still **to** the *fore*. その著者はまだ盛んである.

forebode, *v.* 予想する.

P *forebode* disaster **for** the future 将来災害が予想される.

foreboding, *n.* 予覚, 前兆.

V It ***carries*** an ominous *foreboding* of evil times. それは不吉の前兆である. ¶ ***dispel*** their gloomy *forebodings* 陰気な予感を追払う. ¶ I ***have*** a *foreboding* that ... ...と私に虫が知らせる. ‖ ***had*** no *foreboding* of the catastrophe あの災難の予感はなかった.

Q The ploblem is laden with ***anxious*** *forebodings*. この問題には色々前途の不安がまつわっている.

forecast, *n.* 予測; 予想; 予報.

V ***attempt*** a *forecast* 予測を試みる. ¶ ***give*** a fairly accurate *forecast* of what may be expected to happen at ... ...で起りそうなことをかなり正確に予想する. ¶ ***hazard*** a *forecast* 冒険的に予測して見る.

Q^2 ***business*** statistics and *forecasts* 市況の統計と予想. ¶ ***production*** *forecast* 生産予想. ¶ furnish ***weather*** *forecasts* 天気予報を出す. 【類】The official ***weather*** *forecast* for today predicts north-easterly wind; fair, partly cloudy. ‖ ***Weather*** *forecast:* Rain or hail. Bright intervals. N.E. wind. Cold. 天気予報: 雨あるいはあられ, 晴間もある, 北東風, 寒い.

P^2 the *forecast* **for** the rice crop 米作予想.

forecaster, *n.* 予報者(器).

Q^2 a ***business*** *forecaster* 市況予測者. ¶ an ***earthquake*** *forecaster* 地震予報者. ¶ a ***weather*** *forcaster* 天気予報者.

forecasting, *n.* 予報, 予測.

Q^2 the new science of "***business*** *forecasting*"「市況予報」という新科学. ¶ ***weather*** *forecasting* 天気予報. ¶ ***world*** *forecasting* 世界の動静予想.

foredoom, *v.* あらかじめ運命を定める.

M The attempt is ***necessarily*** *foredoomed* to failure. その企は始めからきっと失敗するにきまっている.

P Such a contribution is *foredoomed* **to** the waste-paper basket. こんな投書は初めから紙くずかごに棄てられる運命を持っている. 【類】The experiment was *foredoomed* **to** failure.

forefront, *n.* 最前部, 真先.

P the great nations which stand **in** the *forefront* of modern civilization 現代文明の最前線に立っている大国民. 【類】He has been **in** the *forefront* of the movement. / place them **in** the *forefront* of the nations of the world / This places England **in** the *forefront* **of** world aviation.

foregather, *v.* 出合う; 親しむ.

P *foregather* **with** a person 人と親しむ ‖ we arranged to *foregather* again **with** ... **at** ... われわれは...で...とまた出合うように手はずをした.

foregoing, *n.* 前述の事項.

P **from** the *foregoing* it will be seen that ... このことから...ということが分る.

O The *foregoing* are only a few of the examples. 以上はほんの少数の例に過ぎない.

foreground, *n.* 前景, 最も目に立つ位置.

P The subject has been kept **in** the *foreground* of public attention. その問題は大いに世人の注意をひいた. ‖ with rippling waves **in** the *foreground* 前景には小波が寄せて.

forehead, *n.* 前額部, 額.

V ***knit*** one's *forehead* 額に八の字を寄せる. ¶ ***mop*** (=***wipe***) one's *forehead* 額をぬぐう. ¶ ***tap*** one's *forehead* 額をたたく. ¶ ***wrinkle*** [***up***] one's *forehead* 額にしわを寄せる.

Q His *forehead* is ***ample***. 彼は額が広い. ¶ a ***broad*** *forehead*. 広い額. ¶ a ***furrowed*** *forehead* しわの寄った額. ¶ with an abnormally ***high*** (***low***) *forehead* ばかに広い(狭い)額をした. ¶ a ***large*** *forehead* 大きな額. ¶ a ***prominent*** *forehead* おでこ. ¶ a ***receding*** (=***retreating***) *forehead* くぼんだ額. ¶ a ***round*** *forehead* 丸い額. ¶ a ***smooth*** *forehead* つるつるした額. ¶ a ***wrinkled*** *forehead* しわの寄っている額.

P spectacles **on** *forehead* 額に眼鏡を当てて ‖ a scar **on** the *forehead* 額の古傷. ¶ pressing his hand **to** his *forehead* 額に手を当てて.

foreign, *a.* 縁遠い, 関係のない, 合わない.

M words which are still ***sufficiently*** "*foreign*" to be usually printed in italics 通例イタリックで印刷されるまだ国語化していない言葉. ¶ The Marxian spirit is ***utterly*** *foreign* to Asiatic people. マルクス精神はアジア人には全然合わない.

P It is a purpose *foreign* **from** his pursuits. それは彼の研究とは縁のない目的である. ¶ points *foreign* **to** utility 実用にならない諸点 ‖ matters *foreign* **to** the cause 訴訟に関係のないことがら. ¶ Aggressiveness and imperialism are *foreign* **to** Japan's national psychology. 侵略主義や帝国主義は日本国民の心理と相容れない. ‖ one who is *foreign* **to** this sentiment この感情を解しない人. 【類】Statecraft is *foreign* **to** his nature. / *foreign* **to** the spirit of our institutions / The cart is *foreign* **to** Tibetan culture. / What you say is *foreign* **to** (=from) our present purpose. / matters *foreign* **to** one's own experience and stretching beyond one's personal horizon.

foreigner, *n.* 外国人, 他国人.

Q an ***English-speaking*** *foreigner* 英語を話す他国人. ¶ a ***European*** *foreigner* [米国人などに対し]欧州の外人. ¶ an ***ignorant*** *foreigner* 無知の外人. ¶ a "***red-haired*** *foreigner*" 紅毛人. ¶ a ***blue-eyed*** *foreigner* 碧眼の外国人 ¶ a ***Western*** *foreigners* 西洋人.

forelock, *n.* 前髪.

P take an opportunity **by** the *forelock* 機会に乗じる. 【類】seize a chance (=an occasion) **by** the *forelock*.

foreman, *n.* 職長; 陪審長.

Q a ***printers'*** *foreman* 印刷職長.

Q^2 a ***deputy*** *foreman* [of a jury] 副陪審長.

foremost, *a.* 真先の.

P He is *foremost* **in** adopting a novel method. 彼は率先して新規な方法を採る. ¶ Dr. W.E. Du Bois, *foremost* **of** Negro intellectuals 黒人インテリの第一人者W.E.ジュボア博士. 【類】the *foremost* **of** our poets.

forenoon, *n.* 午前.

P It is nine o'clock **in** the *forenoon*. 午前九時だ. ¶ **on** Sunday *forenoon* 日曜の午前に ‖ **on** the *forenoon* of the 5th of May 五月五日の午前に.

forerunner, *n.* 先ぶれ, 前兆.

Q It will prove a ***sure*** *forerunner* of disappointment. そんなことをしたらきっと失望する.

P^2 Moral corruption is the *forerunner* **of** national decline. 道徳の退敗は国民衰亡の前兆である. 【類】*forerunners* **of** the Japanese Navy—the Fuso, the Kongo, the Hiyei, etc. ‖ Anglo-Saxon was the *forerunner* **of** English. アングロ・サクソン語は英語の先駆だった. ‖ the *forerunner* **of** the present abstractionism 現在の抽象画の前身.

foresee, *v.* 予知する.

M ***dimly*** *foresee* うすうす予知する.

foreshore, *n.* 前浜, なぎさ.

V ***reclaim*** the *foreshore* 海面を埋立てる. ¶ ***travel*** the *foreshore* for fish 浜で引網をする.

foresight, *n.* 先見.

V ***lack*** *foresight* 目先がきかない. ¶ ***show*** very little *foresight* as to ... ...についてほとんど目先がきかない.

Q ***statesmanlike*** *foresight* 政治家らしい先見.

P He is a Daniel **in** *foresight*. 彼は先見の明がある. ¶ The failure is the result of our own stupidity and lack **of** *foresight*. この失敗はわれわれ自身愚かであったためと先見の明を欠いていたためである. 【類】a man **of** *foresight* / He is destitute **of** (=without) *foresight*.

forest, *n.* 森林.

Q a *deep forest* 深い森林. ¶a *dense forest* 密林. ¶*impenetrable forests* and swamps 通過しにくい森林と沼沢. ¶*primeval forests* 原始林. ¶a *public forest* 公有林. ¶a *trackless forests* 人跡未踏の森林. ¶a *virgin* (=primeval) *forest* 処女林.

Q² a *deer forest* しか狩を行う森林. ¶a *hardwood forest* 硬木林. ¶a *rubber forest* ゴム林. ¶a California *Sequoia forest* カリフォルニア州のセコイア樹林.

P He got lost *in* the *forest*. 彼は林の中で迷った. ¶We walked *through* the *forest*. われわれは林の中を通って歩いた. ¶the total area of the Empire *under forest* 帝国の森林総面積. 【類】About 26,000 square miles of the country are *under forest*.

P² a *forest of* masts 林立するマスト ‖ a *forest of* factory chimneys 林立する工場の煙突 ‖ a *forest of* stacks 煙突の林立. 【類】*forests of* masts in a harbor.

forest, *v.* 植林する.

M be *heavily forested* 密に植林されている.

foretaste, *n.* 試食, 毒味.

V I feel as if already *enjoying* the *foretaste* of the country. 私はその国に行かない先からまるでその試食をしているかのように感じる. ¶*get* (=*obtain*) a *foretaste* of ... ...の試食をする.

P² a *foretaste of* heaven この世における天国の感じ.

foretell, *v.* 予言する. 「て事件を予言する.

P *foretell* events *from* the flights of birds 鳥の飛び方を見

forethought, *n.* 先慮, あらかじめの深慮.

V *exercise forethought* 予め考慮する.

P *by* (=*with*) wise *forethought* 賢明に前もって考慮して. ¶*without* much *forethought* 余り考えずに.

forewarn, *v.* あらかじめ警告する, 前もって警戒する.

P he is *forewarned against* ... 彼は...に陥らないよう前もって警戒されている. ¶*forewarn* a person *of* death 人にあら

forfeit, *n.* 科料, 罰金. Lかじめ死を警告する.

V He shall *pay* the *forfeit* with his head. そのとがによって彼を手打にする. ‖ *pay* the *forfeit* of one's life for murdering a man 人を殺した罰に命を取られる ‖ Life is a *forfeit* we must *pay* shortly. 人生は短かい. ¶*take* [the] *forfeit* of ... 科料として...を取上げる. 「で.

P under penalty *of* a *forfeit* [違犯者は]科料に処する条件

P² His life was the *forfeit of* his crime. 彼はその罰として命を取られた.

forfeit, *v.* [権利などを]喪失する; 没収される.

P He had *forfeited* his property *by* his crime. 彼は犯罪のために財産を没収された. ‖ He *forfeited* his life *by* careless driving. 運転を誤って生命を失った. ¶His property shall be *forfeited to* the Government. 彼の財産は政府に没収さ

forfeiture, *n.* [権利などの]喪失. Lれるべきである.

V *work forfeiture* of their privileges 彼らの特権を失う.

P the falling of land to the State *by forfeiture* 権利喪失による土地の国有化.

forge, *n.* ふいご.

Q a *portable forge* 携帯用ふいご.

Q² a *jobbing forge* 端物仕事をする鍛冶屋の店.

forge, *v.* 鍛えて造る.

P A bayonet blade is *forged from* the finest steel. 銃剣の刃は最良質の鋼鉄を鍛えて造る.

forgery, *n.* 偽造; 偽造物.

V *commit forgery* 偽造する.

Q a *modern forgery* of a sixteenth-century Swiss panel 後に偽造した十六世紀スイス羽目板. ¶a *rank forgery* 真赤

P² the *forgery of* official papers 公文書偽造. Lなにせ物.

forget, *v.* 忘れる; 言い落す.

M the name *long forgotten* in literary circles 長く忘れられていた文名. ¶She *nearly forgot* to give him a tip for his service. ¶You should *never forget* to ... ...することをゆめ忘れてはならない. ¶I *quite forgot* to ... ...することをコロッと忘れた. ¶be *utterly forgotten* すっかり忘れられている.

P I had *forgotten* all *about* it. 私はそのことはすっかり忘れていた. ¶*forget for* the moment 胴忘れをする. ¶*forget* oneself *in* one's subject 研究に熱中してわれを忘れる ‖ I *forgot* it *in* the train. 私は汽車の中にそれを忘れた. ¶Pray don't *forget* me *to* your uncle. 忘れないでおじさんによろ

forgetful, *a.* 忘れがちな; 不注意な. Lしく言って下さい.

P They meet in social intercourse, *forgetful of* the strife of politics. 彼らは政治上の闘争を忘れて互に社交的交際をやる. ‖ The hotel is *forgetful of* the comfort of its guests. 同ホテルは客へのサービスが足りない. ‖ He is reading, *forgetful of* all cares. 彼はすべての苦労を忘れて読書して

forgetfulness, *n.* 忘れがち, 健忘; そこつ. Lいる.

V Such a great man will *survive* the *forgetfulness* of the centuries. こうした偉人は幾百年も人から忘れられずにいるだろう.

Q live in *blissful forgetfulness* of the outer world 外界のことを一切忘れて幸福に生活する. ¶*temporary forgetfulness* of proper names 固有名詞の胴忘れ.

P *through* his *forgetfulness* 彼のそこつで.

P² one's *forgetfulness of* promise 約束を忘れがちなこと.

forgiveness, *n.* 容赦, 勘弁.

V I *ask* your *forgiveness* for ... ...に対して御勘弁をこう. 【類】I *asked* his *forgiveness*. ¶*beg forgiveness* 勘弁をこう. ¶I *crave* your *forgiveness*. ひとえに御勘弁を願います. ¶*exercise forgiveness* 容赦する. ¶I gladly *give* him my *forgiveness*. 私は喜んで彼を許してやる. ¶He could not but *presume* his *forgiveness* was at no desperate distance. 彼はどうにかわびがかないそうになったと推察せざるを得なかった. ¶*seek* the *forgiveness* of ... ...に容赦を求める.

Q the idea of *mutual forgiveness* 互に許し合うという考え.

fork, *n.* フォーク; [道の]分れ.

Q² a *hay fork* 乾草かき. ¶a *table fork* 食卓用フォーク.

P a set *of forks* 一組のフォーク.

P² come to the *fork of* a road 道路の分岐点にさしかかる.

fork, *v.* 分岐する; 《口語》手渡しする. 「へ分岐する.

P here the railway *forks to* ... and ... ここで鉄道は...と...

M He *forked* (=paid *or* handed) *out* (=*over*) the money to me. 彼は僕にその金を払った. 「気.

form, *n.* 形; 形体; 容姿; 形式, 様式; 礼式; 書式, 用紙; 元

V He *adopted* the prose (metrical) *form* in writing it. 彼はそれを書くに散文(韻文)の形式を取った. ¶*assume* her own *form* 彼女の正体を現わす ‖ *assume* the *form* of a lovely woman 美しい女に化ける ‖ They *assume* the most varied *forms*. 彼らは千差万別の形となって現われる. ¶*change form* 形を変える. ¶*copy* the *forms* ひな形を写す. ¶*employ* a correct and proper *form* of letter writing 書簡に正しい適当な形式を用いる. ¶*establish* a rudimentary *form* of constitutional government 幼稚な立憲政治を樹立する. ¶*fill in* the *form* and file the same with the secretary 用紙に書き込んでそれを秘書官に提出する. ¶*fill out* (=*up*) a *form* 用紙に書き込む. ¶*give form* to ... ...の形を造る. ¶It *has* the *form* of gelatine. それはゼラチン状をなしている. ¶falsely *interpret* the outer *forms* 外形によって判断を誤る. ¶*observe* the *form* but neglect the spirit of ... ...の形式に拘泥してその精神を等閑に付する. ¶*prefer* one *form* to the other 甲の形より乙の形の方がよい. ¶an account of the various changes the work has gone through before *reaching* its present *form* その仕事が現状に達するまでの色々な変遷の物語. ¶*recover* one's usual *form* 平生の元気を回復する. ¶It still *retains* its ancient *form*. それはいまだに昔の状態になっている. ¶*set up* a *form* of government ある政体を打立てる. ¶She *showed* excellent *form* in high diving. 彼女は高飛込であざやかな型を見せた. ¶It *took form* in the so-called "Folk Laws." それはいわゆる「民衆律」として具体化した. ‖ patriotism, when it *takes* this *form*, is apt to be embarrassing to ... 愛国心もこうなると...にとってとかく厄介なものになりやすい ‖ the disease *took* the *form* of ... その病気は...という形で現われた. 【類】The memorial is to *take* the *form* of a speech-room. / Mania (マニヤ) *takes* many *forms*. ‖ The meeting *took* the *form* of a dinner in my honor. その会合は私のための晩さん会になった. 【類】The gathering *took* the *form* of a dinner. ‖ Some honeymoons *take* the *form* of a journey round the world. / The book inspired him with an enthusiasm that *took* the *form* of a letter of admiration to the author. ‖ *take* the *form* of a man 人に化ける. ¶*take on* (=assume) a concrete *form* 具体化する ‖ *take on* morbid *forms* 病的になる.

Q in an *abridged form* 省略した形で. ¶put this knowledge into *accessible form* この知識を一般に行き渡るようにする. ¶fill in the *accompanying form* 同封の用紙に書

き込む. ¶assume an ***active form*** 積極的態度を取る. ¶in an ***acute form*** 急性の. ¶a disease in its ***advanced forms*** 症状の進行した病気. ¶in an ***aggravated form*** 一層はなはだしい形の. ¶alcohol in ***all forms*** あらゆる形の酒精飲料. ¶the law in its ***amended form*** 修正した形の法律 ‖ the ***ancient forms*** observed at the Coronation of a British king 英国王の戴冠式に行われる古い形式. ¶Stiegel glass is the most ***aristocratic form*** of American antique collecting. スティーゲルガラス器はアメリカ人の古器物収集中で一番貴族的なものである. ¶extraordinary susceptibility of ***artistic form*** and the music of words 芸術的形式と音楽的用語に対する非凡な敏感さ. ¶present ... in an ***attractive form*** ...を人の目を引く形で表わす. ¶a play presented in either ***auditory*** or ***visual form*** 耳に訴えるかまたは目に訴える形にした劇. ¶a novel written in ***autobiographical form*** 自叙伝体の小説. ¶It is considered ***bad form.*** それは非礼だとされている.【類】It's ***bad form*** to remark upon a person's dress. ¶books in ***bound form*** とじ本(巻物などに対して). ¶in the ***briefest form*** 最も簡単に. ¶He has a ***burly form.*** あの人はたくましい体をしている. ¶classics reprinted in a ***cheap form*** 廉価版にした古典. ¶a ***cheap*** and ***wholesome form*** of recreation 廉価で健康に適する娯楽. ¶alter it to a ***circular form*** それを円形に変える. ¶"Ægis" is the ***classic form*** of "egis." aegis は egis の古形である. ¶his contributions to newspapers and magazines were subsequently republished, in a ***collected form,*** under the title of ... 彼が新聞雑誌に送った寄稿は後になって本にまとめて...の表題の下に刊行された.【類】publish them in a ***collective form.*** ¶a ***combining form*** (Anglo- などの)合成に用いられる形. ¶The book presents useful information in a ***compact form.*** その本は参考になる事項を簡潔につづってある. ¶His works have now been first published in ***complete form.*** 氏の作品は今度初めて全集になって出版された. ¶in an easily ***comprehensive form*** わかりやすいように. ¶edit it in a ***concise form*** それを圧縮編集する. ¶our present essay is an attempt to furnish, in a ***concise form,*** the information on ... この論文は簡潔な形で...に関する知識を提供しようという試みである.【類】condensed in ***concise form.*** ¶in ***concise, handy form*** 簡潔で軽便な形で. ¶in a ***concise*** and ***intelligible form*** 簡潔で分りやすいように. ¶in a ***concrete form*** 具体的に. ¶in a ***condensed form*** 簡約した形で. ¶the ***continuous form*** 〚文法〛[動詞の]継続を示す(進行)形の. ¶bring together in a ***convenient from*** 便宜の形式にまとめる.【類】in a ***convenient form*** for quick consultation (手早く参照). ¶***conventional forms*** from nature [雪はいつも六花のごとき]図案化した自然物. ¶***conversational form*** of English 会話体の英語. ¶"Ten minutes of six" is a ***correct form.*** 六時十分前を "ten minutes of six" という言い方は正しい. ¶a ***corrupt form*** of ... ...のなまり. ¶in ***crescent form*** 新月形をした. ¶a ***dangerous form*** [病気などの]危険性. ¶***dead forms*** 虚礼. ¶The plan has not yet taken ***definite form.*** その計画はまだ具体化していない.【類】The plan is taking ***definite form.*** ¶presented in ***diagrammatic form*** 図式で示した. ¶be expressed in a ***different form*** 別の形で表わされる. ¶in a very ***dilute form*** 十分希釈して. ¶in ***dramatic form*** 劇に仕組んで. ¶the ***dramatic form*** of writing 劇めいた文体. ¶make a written application in ***due form*** in the Japanese language 日本語で正式に願書を認める. ¶an ***empty form*** 有名無実. ¶express in ***epigrammatic form*** 警句で言い表わす. ¶in an ***epitomized form*** 要点をつまんで. ¶the most ***equitable form*** of remuneration 最も公正な報償. ¶adopt the ***epistolary form*** in novels 小説に書簡文体を採用する. ¶stated in an ***exaggerated form*** 誇張して述べた. ¶Wagering often takes ***fantastic*** and ***amusing forms.*** かけは往々変ったこっけいな形になって現われる. ¶reincarnated in ***female form*** 女に生れ変った.【類】the beauty of the ***female form.*** ‖ The outline of a ***female form*** became visible. [反魂香をたくと]女の姿がぼんやりと現われてきた. ¶in the ***full form*** of a sentence 完全な文の形で. ¶in ***general form*** 一般的な形で. ¶It is not [considered] ***good form*** to smoke in the presence of a lady. 婦人の面前で喫煙するのは失礼だ. ‖ it is ***good form*** to ... ...するのが礼だ.【類】Is it ***good form*** to rise and stand up when a lady comes into a room? ‖ for several years it has been "***good form***" to despise ... この五六年...を軽べつすることはいわゆる「お上品」であった ‖ Marquis Okuma in ***good*** (=***great***) ***form*** 大元気の大隈侯. ¶be found in ***good*** and ***due form*** 良好妥当なるを認める. ¶a ***graceful form*** 優美な姿. ¶show in a ***graphic form*** 図解式で示す.【類】put the results in a ***graphic form.*** ¶offer a great fund of information in a ***graphic*** and ***fascinating form*** 豊富な事項を図解式で面白く見られるようにして提供する. ¶a ***grave*** or ***slight form*** of a disease 重いまたは軽い病. ¶summarize in ***handy form*** the information which ... ...の見聞を手ごろの形で約説する.【類】in the ***handiest*** possible ***form.*** ¶his ***huge ungainly form,*** clad in badly fitting garments 体に合わない着物を着た彼の大きい不格好な姿. ¶the ***human form*** in art 芸術上の人間の姿. ¶Foxes were believed to have the power to assume the ***human form*** at will. きつねは人間に化けようと思えば化けられる力を持っていると信じられていた. ‖ a vampire in ***human form*** 人間の格好した吸血鬼. ¶an ***improved form*** of the instrument その道具を改良したもの. ¶the word is an ***incorrect form*** of ... その語は...の間違った形である. ¶The text is now easily accessible in ***inexpensive form.*** その本文は今では廉価版で容易に手に入る. ¶an ***insensible form*** 知覚のない体. ¶disloyalty in its most ***insidious form*** 最も陰険な不忠. ¶in an ***intensified form*** 強調した. ¶present it in an ***interesting form*** それを面白い形で提供する. ¶Confucius is the ***Latinized form*** of Kong-fu-tse. Confucius は孔夫子のラテン語形だ. ¶***legal forms*** 法令諸様式. ¶***lighter forms*** of hypochondria and melancholia ヒポコンデリーや憂うつ症の軽症. ¶in the ***lower forms*** of plant and animal life 下等の動植物では. ¶a ***luxurious form*** of mental entertainment ぜいたくな種類の精神的娯楽. ¶in a ***magnified form*** 拡大した形で. ¶Marriage is often a ***mere form.*** 結婚はほんの形式の場合が往々ある. ¶a ***mild form*** of madness 軽い精神病.【類】Neurasthenia (神経衰弱) is the ***mildest form*** of psychoneurosis. ¶in a ***mitigated form*** 軽減した形の. ¶in a somewhat ***modified form*** 少し く修正した形で. ¶in ***myriad forms*** 千姿万態で. ¶in its ***new form*** その新形の ‖ ***New forms*** of life are created by the forces of evolution. 新しい形の生物は進化の力で創造される. ¶Written in ***numerical form,*** it would look like this:... 数字で書くとこのように見えるだろう. ¶an ***obsolete form*** of the word その語のすたれた形. ¶in ***one form*** or another あれやこれやの. ¶highly ***organized forms*** of life 高度に組織された生物. ¶assume its ***original form*** 正体を現わす ‖ in its ***original form*** その原形の. ¶in essence as well as in ***outward form*** 実質外形ともに. ¶put it in a less ***paradoxical form*** それをもっと平たく言う. ¶I kept it in ***perfect form.*** 私はそれを完全に保存した. ¶It is important to have some of the results of the investigation in more ***permanent form.*** その研究の結果の中にはもっと永久的な形のものにして保存する必要のあるものがある. ¶The word has two ***plural forms.*** その語の複数形は二つある. ¶in a ***portable form*** 携帯用の型の. ¶his sympathy took a ***practical form*** in the shape of ... 彼の同情は実際に...の形となって現われた. ¶the ***preferred form*** 可とせられる形. ¶the poem in its ***present form*** 現在の形式の詩. ¶a very ***primitive form*** of ... きわめて原始的形式の... ¶He wrote his message in the ***printed form.*** 彼はその式辞を印刷に付した.【類】submit a dissertation in ***printed form*** / The ***printed form*** of many words is identical or very similar in English and French. ¶in a very ***pronounced form*** きわめて顕著な. ¶registered in ***proper form*** 正式の登記を終った. ¶be published in a ***revised*** and ***abridged form*** 改訂簡約して出版されている. ¶a book in its ***revised*** and ***corrected form*** 改訂本. ¶books in ***rolled form*** 巻物式の本. ¶one of the ***safest forms*** of wealth 富の最も安全な形の一つ. ¶The bow-and-arrow in the ancient ***Scythian*** or ***Tartar form*** has to be bent inside out to string it. 昔のスキチア人やダッタン人の用いた弓矢は弦を張るに内側を外に曲げなければならない. ¶appear in a ***separate form*** 単行本で出る. ¶publish in ***serial form*** 続きものとして出す.【類】The novel will appear in ***serial form*** in Pearson's Weekly and on its completion will be issued in volume form. / write a novel for publication in ***serial form.*** ¶The ***set form*** of congratulating a friend upon his birthday is this: Many happy returns of the day. 友人

の誕生日を祝賀するきまり文句は「御誕生日おめでとう」である. ¶of ***short form*** 短躯の. ¶"Olympics" is a ***shortened form*** of "Olympic games."「オリンピックス」は「オリンピック・ゲームズ」の略形. ¶***social forms*** 社交の礼法. ¶his ***stalwart forms*** 彼のがん丈な体. ¶a ***standard form*** to be filled in and signed 書入れて署名する標準書式. ¶a ***stereotyped form*** of excuse 紋切型の申訳. ¶order upon the ***subjoined form*** 添付の用紙で注文する. ¶in as ***succinct*** and ***handy*** a ***form*** as possible できるだけ簡明で軽便な形で. ¶in ***such form*** as prescribed by ... ...によって規定されている形式で. ¶in a ***suitable form***=in a proper manner 適当な方法で. ¶present the main facts of ... in a ***systematic form*** ...の主要事項を組織立った形式で提示する. ¶state the classification in [the] ***tabular form*** 分類を表にして示す. 【類】 a report in ***tabular form.*** ¶in ***tabulated forms*** 表にして. ¶one's admiration (affection) in a ***tangible form*** [物を贈るなどして]具体的に表現された嘆賞(など)の気持. ¶put it in ***terse form*** それを簡潔な形で示す. ¶in a ***translated form*** 翻訳して. ¶a ***triangular form*** 三角形. ¶The memorial will take the ***twofold form*** of a monument and of a stained-glass window. その記念事業は記念碑と着色ガラス窓という二様の形式を取ることになるだろう. ¶All copy should be in ***typewritten form.*** 原稿はすべてタイプライターで打ったものでなければいけない. ¶present it in easily ***understandable form*** それを容易に理解できる形で提示する. ¶in ***up-to-date form*** 最新の形式で. ¶assume ***varied forms*** 様々な形をとる ‖ diarrhoea in its ***varied forms*** 色々な種類の下痢. ¶a rugged country of ***varied topographic form*** 起伏の多い地形の国. ¶***various forms*** of transport—railways, navigation, aviation, motor transport 各種の運輸—鉄道・船舶・航空・自動車. 【類】 Patriotism manifests itself in ***various forms.*** / exist under ***various forms.*** ¶a statement quoted in ***verbatim form*** 原文のままの陳述. ¶in a more ***virulent form*** 一層激しい形で. ¶a ***weak*** or ***mild form*** of a disease 弱いあるいは軽い病気. ¶a fetishism in a ***well-marked form*** 本格的な拝物. ¶He has a ***well-proportioned form.*** 彼は均整のとれた姿をしている. ¶a ***written form*** of oath 誓文.

Q[2] an ***application form*** 申込書式 ‖ fill out a detailed ***application form*** 申込用式に細かく書入れる. ¶be published in ***book form*** 本の形で出版されている. 【類】 be brought out (=published) in ***book form*** / magazine articles in ***book form*** / bring papers together (論文をまとめる) in ***book form*** / its publication in ***book form*** / The lectures were collected in ***book form.*** ‖ a reproduction in ***book form*** 本の形での復刻(雑誌などに連載されたものの). ¶***business forms*** 商業諸書式. ¶Bon Ami is made in both ***cake*** and ***powder forms.*** ボナミは固形と粉末とある. ¶in ***chart form*** 図式で. ¶standard ***contract forms*** 標準契約書式. ¶in ***dialogue form*** 対話体で. ¶be arranged in ***dictionary form*** 辞書体に排列されている. ¶in ***draft form*** [薬など]水薬にした; 草案の形にして. 【類】 medicine in ***draft form;*** a book in ***draft form.*** ¶a ***dress form*** 〘服飾〙人台(ﾀﾞﾐｰ). ¶proofs in ***galley form*** 棒組の校正刷. ¶a lecture in ***handbook form*** 小形本にした講義. ¶reduction of aluminum scrap to ***ingot form*** アルミニウムくずの鉱塊への変形. ¶a printed ***invoice form*** 印刷した送り状用紙. ¶the ***joint-stock form*** of business organization 合資形態の商業組織. ¶a book in ***manuscript form*** 稿本. ¶The gratitude did not take a ***material form.*** 感謝の贈りものは物質ではなかった. ¶a ***measurement form*** [洋服屋の]寸法書用紙. ¶These lectures were put into ***mimeograph form.*** これらの講演は謄写印刷にした. ¶a ***negligé form*** of speech 四角ばらない演説. ¶fill in an ***order form*** 注文用紙に書込む. ¶The type is set and made into ***page forms.*** 活字はページ組になっている. ¶proofs in ***page form*** ページ組の校正刷. ¶reprint in ***pamphlet form*** パンフレットにして復刻する. 【類】 issue the articles in ***pamphlet form*** / The address was later published in ***pamphlet form.*** ¶***penitence form*** of the Salvation Army 救世軍の悔い改めの座. ¶bind the issues of the magazine in ***permanent form*** 雑誌を合本にする. ¶medicines in ***powder form*** or tablets 粉末または錠剤の薬. ¶read a book in ***proof form*** 本の校正刷を読む. ¶in easy ***reference form*** 容易に参照しうる形で. 【類】 in a convenient ***reference form.*** ¶a ***registration form*** 登録用紙. ¶a brief statement in mere ***skeleton form*** 骨子だけの簡単な叙述. ¶collect material in ***slip form*** 紙片の形で材料を集める. ¶a piece of music in ***sonata form*** ソナタ形式の曲. ¶fill out the attached ***subscription form*** 添付の購読用紙に書込む. ¶be grouped in ***table forms*** under ... ...という見出しのもとに表の形にまとめられてある. ¶a ***telegram form*** 頼信紙. ¶in the ***verse form*** of an elegy 哀歌の詩形で. ¶publish a work in ***volume*** (=***book***) ***form*** 著作を本として出版する. 【類】 be republished in ***volume form*** / The novel was published originally in ***three-volume form*** (三巻もの). ¶***word forms*** 語形.

P The dialogue is, of course, not new ***as*** a literary *form.* もちろん対話は文学の形式としては新しくはない. ¶write a message ***in*** a telegram *form* 用紙に電文を書く ‖ a bill complete ***in*** *form* 形式の完備した手形 ‖ representing ***in*** its *form* ... ...の形をした ‖ abjure all partisanship ***in*** all its *forms* 一切の党派心を棄てる ‖ disease ***in*** all its *forms* その種の一切の病気 ‖ the entire eradication of selfishness ***in*** all *forms* 一切の利己主義の絶滅 ‖ He likes everything ***in*** the *form* of a dog. 犬なら何でも好き. ‖ ***in*** the *form* of a tortoise かめの格好をした ‖ gold ***in*** the *form* of bar 棒地金になっている金 ‖ reproduce Japanese poetry ***in*** an English *form* 日本の詩歌を英訳する ‖ He abstains from the use of tobacoo ***in*** any *form.* 彼は一切タバコはのまない. 【類】 detest a lie ***in*** any *form* / Their memories, honored by this monument shaped ***in*** the *form* of a beautiful building, will remain enshrined in the history of the University, the Alma Mater which they so honored. / Some of the material incorporated in the book has appeared in various magazines ***in*** the *form* of articles. / a report issued by a newspaper ***in*** the *form* of a "gogai" / communicate the result of his researches to the members of the society ***in*** the *form* of a lecture / The Association set forth its object and rules ***in*** the *form* of a prospectus ***in*** 1907. ‖ rewards ***in*** the *form* of praise or marks 賛辞または点数で表わした表彰 ‖ a work ***in*** a *form* so handy and inexpensive 手ごろで廉価な作品. 【類】 a story told ***in*** the *form* of letters / The book is given ***in*** the *form* of plain lectures. / a book written ***in*** the *form* of letters to her sister / ***in*** the *form* of fiction / arranged ***in*** the *form* of tables / bring money to the state ***in*** the *form* of taxes / set aside a large sum ***in*** the *form* of savings ‖ a memorial tablet, ***in*** the *form* of a bas-relief 半肉彫の記念牌 ‖ the edition is similar ***in*** *form* to ... [本の]その版は形が...と同じだ. ¶change it ***into*** a *form* of ... それを...の形に変える. ¶a tray ***of*** rectangular *form* 長方形の盆. ¶will be recorded ***on*** this *form* この用紙に記録される. ¶it is rather ***out of*** *form* that ... ...することはむしろ無作法だ. ¶***under*** another *form*=in disguise 形を変えて ‖ ***under*** varying *forms* 色々な形で ‖ the Holy Ghost ***under*** the visible *form* of a dove はとの姿となって現われた聖霊. ¶really and in essence one thing ***with*** diverse *forms* of manifestation 色々な表現形式をなしているが実は本質上唯一個のもの.

P[2] a *form* ***for*** a deed 証書の書式. ¶a *form* ***of*** words used in conjuring, such as "hocus-pocus" ホーカス・ポーカスのような魔法に使う語の形式 ‖ The tempter took the *form* ***of*** an angel. その悪魔は天使の姿に化けていた. ‖ a *form* ***of*** government 政体. ¶*forms* ***of*** worship 崇拝の諸形式. ¶Wood, coal, and oil are *forms* ***of*** fuel. まき・石炭・石油は燃料の種類だ. 【類】 all *forms* ***of*** disease (insanity) 一切の病気(など) ‖ the establishment of some *form* ***of*** tribunal (裁判所) where international controversies like private disputes may be settled by principles of law and justice rather than by brutality and bloodshed ‖ a *form* ***of*** application for enrolment 入学(など)申請書式 ‖ *forms* ***of*** animal life 動物の生態.

form, *v.* 形づくる; 形成される; 整列する.

M The ice *formed* ***early*** and stayed late. 早く結氷しておそくまで溶けなかった. ¶Clouds are *forming* ***quickly*** in the sky. 空には雲が急速にわき出している. ¶we ***readily*** *form* a habit of ... われわれはとかく...の癖がつきやすい.

P *form* ... ***after*** the model of ... ...を...の見本にならって作る. ¶Ice *forms* ***at*** a temperature of 32° F. 氷は華氏三十二度の温度で張る. ¶It is *formed* ***by*** decomposition. それは分解によってできる. ¶a word *formed* ***from*** the initial letters of … …の頭文字を取って造った語.【類】*form* nouns *from* adjectives. ¶*form* a schedule *for* one's journey 旅行の予定表を作る. ¶*form in* line 整列する‖*form in* ranks 整列する‖The troops *formed in* cloumn. 軍隊は縦隊に整列した. ¶*form* it *into* a very good imitation of a butterfly それをちょうそっくりのものに造る‖*form* … *into* a ball …を球に作る‖*form* … *into* line …を並べる‖*form into* ridges (=ridge) うねを成す. ¶Japan is *formed of* four large islands. 日本は四大島から成る.‖God *formed* man *of* the dust of the ground. 神は地のちりをもって人を造れり. ¶Frost *forms on* the ground. 霜が地上に結ぶ. ¶the pattern *upon* which we must *form* ours われわれがのっとるべき手本. ¶The design is *formed with* triangle. その模様は三角でできている.

formal, *a.* 形式的な.

M become ***merely*** *formal* 形式に流れる. ¶be ***strictly*** *formal* 形式がやかましい.

formality, *n.* 形式厳守; 虚礼; *pl.* 手続.

V ***casting aside*** the *formalities* of politeness 遠慮は抜きにして. ¶***complete*** the *formality* of taking out their citizenship 彼らの帰化手続を済ます. ¶This ***entails*** complicated *formalities*. これには込入った手続が必要である. ¶***omit*** the *formality* of reading the reports 報告朗読の形式を略する. ¶***perform*** *formalities* 手続きをふむ. ¶Let's ***quit*** all *formalities*. 無礼講でいこう.

Q ***factitious*** *formality* 不自然な形式厳守. ¶the wearisome slowness of ***legal*** *formality* 法律上の繁文じょく礼. ¶dispense with ***rigid*** *formality* いかめしい形式を略する. ¶***stiff*** *formality* いかめしい形式. ¶the abolition of several ***useless*** and ***vexatious*** *formalities* 種々な無用でめんどうな手続の廃止.

Q² attend to the necessary ***passport*** *formalities* prior to leaving for … …への出発に先立って必要な旅券下付の手続をする. ¶after going through all the ***police*** *formalities* あらゆる警察関係の手続を済ませた後.

P a contact stripped ***of*** *formalities* ざっくばらんの交際. ¶go ***through*** the *formalities* of asking for a leave of absence 賜暇願の手続をする. ¶***without*** *formality* 儀式張らずに, 手軽に.

format, *n.* *F.* [菊判四六判などの]判(はん), 体裁.

Q ***attractive*** *format* of the book 人目を引くその本の装てい. ¶cheap books in a ***dainty*** *format* 優美に仕立てた廉価本. ¶be issued in ***pleasing*** *format* きれいな装ていで出ている. ¶The typography and *format* generally are very ***tasteful***. 印刷も装ていも概してはなはだ上品である.

P² the *format* ***of*** the book その本の体裁.

formation, *n.* 構造; 隊(陣)形; 編隊; 岩層, 層.

V ***change*** the *formation* from order of cruising to order of battle 航走序列を戦闘序列に変える. ¶***preserve*** the *formation* (軍艦など)陣形を保持する.

Q The U.S. planes were seen flying in ***beautiful*** *formation*. 米機が美事な編隊を組んで飛んでいるのが見えた. ¶a ***Cretaceous*** *formation* 白亜紀層. ¶in ***curved*** *formation* わん曲して. ¶***picturesque*** and ***grotesque*** ***geologic*** *formations* 絵のような奇怪な岩層の姿.

Q² ***eccentric rock*** *formations* 奇妙な岩層. ¶***habit*** *formation* 習慣の形成. ¶a view of rugged ***mountain*** *formations* ががたる山岳地方の眺め. ¶a peculiar ***rock*** *formation* 特異な岩層. ¶has a ***web*** *formation* 網状構造を示している.

P fly ***in*** *formation* of 20 to 25 planes 二十機ないし廿五機の編隊を組んで.

former, *n.* 前者.

P² They keep horses and cattle: the *former* ***for*** riding, the latter for food. 彼らは馬と牛を飼っている. 前者は乗用で後者は食用である.

formidable, *a.* 恐ろしい, あなどり難い.

M a ***very*** *formidable* fellow 仲々のくせ者.

P an enemy *formidable* ***by*** (=***in***) strength (numbers) あなどり難い力(など)の敵. ¶*formidable* ***to*** the enemy 敵にとって恐ろしい.

forming-up, *n.* 勢ぞろい.

Q² a demonstration *forming-up*=the forming up of a demonstration 示威運動の勢ぞろい.

formula, *n.* 法式; 信条; 〖数・化〗式.

V ***follow*** careful religious *formula* どこまでも宗教上の儀式による. ¶the *formula* ***used*** in Baptism 洗礼に用いられる法式.

Q a ***chemical*** (***molecular***) *formula* 化学(分子)式. ¶a ***conjuring*** *formula* じゅ文. ¶a ***conversational*** *formulas* 会話体. ¶a ***legal*** *formula* 法律常用の文句. ¶a ***mathematical*** *formula* 数式. ¶a sauce made by our ***secret*** *formula* 弊家の秘伝で造ったソース. ¶a ***set*** *formula* きまり文句.

Q² this ***business*** *formula* 商売のやり方. ¶the ***Mohawk-Valley*** *formula* モーホーク・ヴァレー方式. ¶an ***over-all peace*** *formula* 全面的平和方式.

P² a *formula* ***for*** the manufacture of diamonds 金剛石製造の一法.【類】*formulas* ***for*** making soap / The *formula* ***for*** water is H_2O. ¶after an exchange of a few brief *formula* ***of*** politeness 二三簡単なおきまりのあいさつを交した後.

forsake, *v.* 見放す.

P *forsake* literature ***for*** politics 文学から政治に転向する.

fort, *n.* 保塁, とりで.

V ***bombard*** the *forts* of … …の保塁を砲撃する. ¶He ***founded*** the *fort* named after himself. 彼は保塁を築いてそれに自分の名を付けた. ¶***hold*** a solitary *fort* against the enemy 孤塁を守って敵に対する. ¶***raise*** a *fort* 要さいを築造する. ¶The army ***took*** the *fort* on the first onslaught. その軍は最初の猛襲で保塁を占領した.

forte, *n.* 長所, 得手.

V He ***has*** a *forte* for horse racing. 彼は競馬が得意だ.

Q That is ***his*** *forte*. それが彼の得手だ.

fortification, *n.* 保塁.

Q ***improvised*** *fortification* 臨時築城. ¶***strong*** *fortifications* 堅固な保塁.

Q² ***land*** and ***coast*** *fortifications* 陸上及び海岸保塁. ¶a ***seacoast*** *fortification* 海岸保塁. ¶the ***vitamin*** *fortification* of rice ビタミン補強米.

fortify, *v.* 築城する, 保塁で固める.

P *fortify* oneself ***against*** such attacks (temptations) このような攻撃(など)に対して心をしっかり持つ.【類】*fortify* a town ***against*** the enemy. ¶there is a general impression, *fortified* ***by*** experience, that … 経験によって確証された…という印象が一般にある‖*fortified* ***by*** a good lunch 昼飯でしっかり腹をこしらえて. ¶*fortify* a city ***with*** works 都市に保塁を築く‖*fortify* a young man ***with*** right ideals 一青年に正しい理想を持たせる‖a drink *fortified* ***with*** alcohol アルコールで飲料を強める‖*fortified* ***with*** a drink of brandy ブランデーを一杯やって元気をつけて.

fortitude, *n.* 堅忍, 剛毅(き).

V ***display*** heroic *fortitude* 男らしい剛毅さを示す. ¶He ***showed*** *fortitude* in spite of his misfortunes. 彼は不幸に会っても気強い所を見せた.

Q ***invincible*** *fortitude* 堅忍不抜. ¶A ***sudden*** *fortitude* came to him. たちまち勇気づいた. ¶the ***superhuman*** *fortitude* displayed by the martyr その殉教者の示した超人的堅忍.

fortnight, *n.* 二週間, 十四日.

V ***take*** a *fortnight* over the job その仕事に二週間かかる.

P ***for*** a *fortnight* 二週間. ¶***in*** a *fortnight* 二週間たって.

fortress, *n.* 要さい, 城さい.

V ***abandon*** impregnable *fortresses* 難攻不落の要さいを放棄する. ¶***besiege*** an enemy's *fortress* 敵要さいを包囲する. ¶***dismantle*** all the *fortresses* 要さい全部の防備を解く. ¶***evacuate*** a *fortress* 要さいを明渡す. ¶***surrender*** a *fortress* to the enemy 要さいを敵に渡す. ¶***reduce*** a *fortress* 要さいを降(くだ)す. ¶***storm*** a *fortress* 要さいを襲撃する.

O a ***floating*** *fortress* 海上の要さい(軍艦). ¶a "***flying*** *fortress*"「空の要さい」. ¶a ***maiden*** *fortress* まだ落ちたことのない城さい. ¶a ***ruined*** *fortress* 廃墟となった要さい. ¶B-50 ***Super-Flying*** *Fortresses* 超「空の要さい」B-50. ¶The *fortress* is ***untenable***. その要さいは守りきれない.

P The town is under the shelter ***of*** a *fortress*. 同市は要さいで守られている.

fortunate, *a.* 幸運な, 仕合わせな.

M *fortunate* ***enough*** 幸運なことに. ¶The year has been an ***especially*** *fortunate* one for me. その年は私にとって特に幸運の年であった. ¶He is ***peculiarly*** *fortunate* in his wife. 彼は細君には実に運がよい. ¶It was ***really*** *fortunate* of me. 本当によかった. ¶I feel myself ***singularly*** *fortunate* in living to such an advanced age. 私は自分でこんなに長生ができたのを不思議なほど仕合せだと思っている. ¶This is ***very*** *fortunate* for our country. これはわが国のために実に仕合わせなことだ.

P We are *fortunate* ***in*** having fine day. 晴天で仕合わせ

だ. 【類】he was *fortunate* ***in*** having the sevices of ... ¶it is *fortunate* ***for*** me that ... ...ということは私にとって仕合わせなことだ.

fortune, *n.* (**1**) 財産, 身代.

V ***accumulate*** (=make) a *fortune* in commercial (=business) pursuit 商売で財産をこしらえる ‖ ***accumulate*** colossal *fortunes* ばく大な財産を作る. ¶***acquire*** a large *fortune* 大きな財産を作る. ¶***amass*** a *fortune* 一財産作る. 【類】***amass*** a *fortune* of many millions of dollars. ¶He ***bequeathed*** me a *fortune*. 彼は私に財産を残した. ¶***build up*** *fortune* out of nothing はだか一貫で身代をこしらえる. 【類】***build up*** a large *fortune*. ¶***desire*** a *fortune* 財産が欲しい. ¶***dissipate*** a *fortune* 財産をとう尽する. ¶He has ***enhanced*** *fortunes* during the war. 彼は戦時中身代を太らした. ¶He ***has*** a large *fortune*. 彼には大きな身代がある. 【類】He has ***had*** a *fortune* left to him. ¶He ***inherited*** an ample *fortune* at the death of his father. 彼は父の死と同時に巨万の財産を受け継いだ. 【類】He ***inherited*** a great *fortune* from his father. ¶***lay by*** a snug little *fortune* 小金を貯える. ¶He ***left*** a very large *fortune* to his widow and children. 彼は妻子に沢山の遺産を残した. 【類】he ***left*** a *fortune* of ¥... / He was ***left*** a *fortune*. ¶He went to Australia to ***make*** his *fortune* by sheep-farming. 彼は牧羊で財産を作ろうとしてオーストラリアに行った. 【類】He has ***made*** a *fortune* by means of industry. / he ***made*** a *fortune* out of ... / endeavour to ***make*** a *fortune* ‖ He ***made*** two *fortunes* and lost them, dying a poor man. 彼は二度金持になったがなくしてしまい貧乏で死んだ. ¶He has ***married*** a *fortune*. 彼は金持の女と結婚した. ¶***muddle away*** one's *fortune* その財産を浪費する. ¶a man ***needs*** a large *fortune* to ... ...するに大きな財産が必要である. ¶***pile up*** (=amass) a *fortune* 財産を作る. ¶***possess*** an ample *fortune* 大財産を所有する. ¶***reap*** *fortune* at one swoop 一かくに千金を得る. ¶***ruin*** one's *fortune* by reckless speculation 無鉄砲な投機をやって財産をとう尽する. ¶He ***ran through*** his *fortune*. 彼は財産をとう尽した. ¶It is possible nowadays to ***secure*** a *fortune* from the proceeds of a single book. 今日ではただ一つの著作の売上から身代を作ることができる. ¶The machine is ***spinning*** the inventor a huge *fortune*. その機械の発明者は巨大な財産を作りつつある. ¶Imprudent investment has ***swept away*** his *fortune*. 彼は無茶な投資で財産をとう尽した.

Q a hardly ***acquired*** *fortune* 骨折ってもうけた財産. ¶retire with an ***ample*** *fortune* しこたまため込んで引退する. ¶He made a ***big*** *fortune* out of the industry. 彼はその事業で大きな財産をこしらえた. ¶a ***comfortable*** *fortune* 相当の財産. ¶acquire a ***competent*** *fortune* 相応の財産を造る. ¶build up a ***colossal*** *fortune* 巨大な財産をこしらえる. ¶a ***considerable*** *fortune* かなりな財産. ¶build up a ***fabulous*** *fortune* ばく大な財産をこしらえる. ¶I had the ***good*** *fortune* to succeed. 私には相続するかなりの財産があった. ¶a ***handsome*** *fortune* 豊かな財産. ¶He made a ***huge*** *fortune*. 彼は大きな財産をこしらえた. ¶a ***humble*** *fortune* わずかな財産. ¶amass a ***large*** *fortune* 多大の財産を作る. ¶people of ***moderate*** *fortunes* 相当の暮しをしている人々. ¶His father had left him a very ***pretty*** *fortune*. 彼の父は彼に相当の財産を残した. ¶He left a ***princely*** *fortune* to his descendants. 彼は子孫に王侯ほどの財産を残した. ¶spend a ***small*** *fortune*. わずかな資産を費消する ‖ sell for a ***snug*** *fortune* 相当の金で売る. ¶a ***vast*** *fortune* 巨大の財産. ¶***war-made*** *fortunes* 戦争でもうけた金.

Q^2 He founded the ***Morgan*** *fortune*. 彼がモルガン家の財産を築き上げた.

P sell it ***for*** a *fortune* それを売ってひともうけする. ¶He came ***into*** a *fortune*. 彼は財産を受けついだ. ‖ step ***into*** a *fortune* 身代を継ぐ. ¶a man ***of*** *fortune* 財産家 ‖ a gentleman formerly ***of*** great *fortune* もとは大きな財産家. ¶He was born ***to*** a large *fortune*. 彼は財産家に生れた. ‖ succeed ***to*** a *fortune* 財産を継ぐ. ¶***without*** a *fortune* 財産なしに.

(**2**) 運; 幸運; 運命.

V ***affect*** one's *fortune* その身の運命にかかわる. ¶It will ***bring*** good *fortune*. それは好い前兆だ. ¶It is believed to ***bring about*** ill *fortune*. それは運が悪いという前兆となっている. ¶***cast in*** one's *fortunes* with ... ...と運命をともにする. ¶***cultivate*** one's *fortune* 運を開く. ¶***follow*** the *fortunes* of a high-born lady 高貴の身分の女性のもつ運命をたどる. ¶***hew out*** one's *fortune* その運命を開拓する. ¶he ***had*** the good *fortune* to obtain the services of ... 彼は...を頼むことができて好都合であった. ¶***have*** one's *fortune* ***told*** 運勢を占ってもらう. ¶They agreed to ***join*** *fortunes*. 彼らは運命をともにすることにした. ‖ ***join*** *fortunes* with ... ...と運命をともにする. ¶***leave*** one's *fortune* with Heaven 運を天に任せる. ¶***mend*** one's *fortune* その運命を開拓する. ¶***push*** one's *fortunes* 運命を開拓する. ¶***read*** one's own *fortune* 運勢を占って見る. ¶These repeated losses ***reduced*** the *fortunes* of the firm to a very low depth. かく重ね重ねの損失で会社の事業が極めて振わなくなった. ¶He thought of some way of ***repairing*** his shattered *fortunes*. 彼は左前になった家運をばん回する方法を考えた. ¶He did so much to ***restore*** the fallen *fortunes* of his country. 彼は自国の非運回復に大いに尽す所があった. ¶He came up to London to ***seek*** his *fortune* in 1812. 彼は一八一二年に運命を開拓すべくロンドンにやってきた. 【類】***seek*** one's *fortune* elsewhere / In early youth he went to ***seek*** his *fortune* in a foreign country. / ***seek*** *fortune* by sea as well as on land / ***seek*** one's *fortune* in a new land. ¶The two friends ***shared*** each other's *fortunes*. 二人の友は互に運命をともにした. ¶***share*** their *fortunes*, good and bad 幸運も不運もともにする. ¶***tell*** one's *fortune* 身の上を判断する. 【類】***tell*** *fortunes* with the cards (トランプで). ¶***try*** their *fortunes* amongst ... ...の間で彼らの運だめしをやる ‖ to ***try*** his *fortune* in Hollywood ハリウッドで運だめしをやるために. 【類】***try*** their *fortune* in the world's Metropolis. ¶those with whom they propose to ***unite*** their *fortunes* 彼らが結婚を申込もうと思う相手の人たち.

V^2 if *fortune* ***favors*** 運が向けば ‖ *Fortune* ***favors*** the brave. 幸運の女神は勇者に味方する. ¶One's *fortune* ***swells***. 運が向いてくる. ¶The *fortunes* of ..., ***waned***. ...の運勢が衰えた.

Q He will survive the storm of ***adverse*** *fortune*. 彼は逆境の荒波を乗り切るだろう. ¶Let us live in hopes of ***better*** *fortune*. 運の向くのを当てにしていよう. ¶a piece of ***colossal good*** *fortune* もっけの幸. ¶face ***fickle*** *fortune* 有為転変を体験する. ¶He was loved by anyone who has had the ***good*** *fortune* to know him. 彼を知った人はだれでも彼に好意を持った. ‖ it has been my ***good*** *fortune* to come into contact with ... ...と接触するに至ったのは私の仕合わせであった. ¶He never had the ***good*** or ***ill*** *fortune* to meet the ghost of the man. 幸か不幸かその男の幽霊に出会わなかった. ¶the ***later*** *fortunes* of ... ...のその後の運命. ¶the betterment of ***personal*** *fortune* 出世. ¶***singular*** *fortune* 不思議な運命. ¶***unexpected*** *fortune* 思いがけない幸運.

P be favored ***by*** *fortune* 運が向いてきている ‖ ***by*** rare good *fortune* まれに見る幸運で. ¶a child ***of*** *fortune* 運命のちょ児 ‖ a ticket with a forecast ***of*** one's *fortune* おみくじ札.

P^2 Buddhism and its *fortunes* ***in*** Japan 仏教とその日本における運命. ¶The *fortunes* ***of*** the British transport system are largely dependent upon tourists. 英国運輸事業の運命は主として漫遊者に係る. 【類】the *fortunes* ***of*** the company during the century of its existence / the *fortunes* ***of*** war (戦局) were favoring ...

fortune-maker, *n.* 金をこしらえる人.

Q a ***simple*** *fortune-maker* 金作りというだけの人.

fortune-teller, *n.* 易者.

V ***consult*** a *fortune-teller* 易者に身の上判断をしてもらう.

forty, *n.* 四十.

P Life begins ***at*** *forty*. 人生は四十から.

forum, *n.* 論壇, 座談会.

Q an ***open*** *forum* for responsible representatives of ... ...の責任ある代表者の座談会. ¶a ***radio*** *forum* ラジオ座談会. ¶The University *Forum* of the Air 〘ラジオ〙大学教授の放送座談会.

P ***during*** the *forum* which followed I was asked simple questions about ... [講演後の]座談会で...について簡単な質問を受けた.

forward, *a.* 早熟の, 進歩している; 進んでやる, 出過ぎた.

M It is ***rather*** *forward* of you to say such things. 君がそんなことをいうのは少し生意気だ.

P Germany is *forward* ***among*** the nations in electrical, chemical, and manufacturing industries. ドイツは電気・

化学及び製造工業では世界の先進国である. ¶The boy is *forward for* his years. あの少年は年の割にませている. ¶He is *forward in* English, but backward in mathematics. 彼は英語は進んでいるが数学は後れている. ‖ He is *forward in* good works. 彼は善いことは進んでやる.

forward, *v.* 送る, 送達する.

M be *forwarded immediately* by passenger train 客車便で直ちに発送される. 【類】 have goods *forwarded immediately.*

P *forward* it *by* sailing vessel (steamer) それを帆船(など)で送る ‖ We have *forwarded* you *by* rail the book you wrote for. お申越の書物列車便にて発送致しました. ¶Applications should be *forwarded through* the prefectural authorities. 願書は県当局を通じて送達すること. ¶The letter has been *forwarded to* him. その手紙は先方に転送した. 【類】 *forward* a letter *to* a new address. ¶*forward* it *with* a letter 手紙と一しょにそれを送る.

forwarder, *n.* 運送業者.

Q a *freight forwarder*=《米》 a shipping agent 貨物運搬業者.

forwarding, *n.* 輸送.

Q² *express forwarding* 至急便発送.

fossick, *v.* 《方言》 さがし回る, あさる.

M² *fossick about* among the street curio sellers 町の骨とう屋をあさる.

P *fossick for* old books 古本をあさる.

foul, *a., adv.* よごれている; 引っかかった; 衝突した.

P a gun *foul from* firing 使用したのでよごれている鉄砲. ¶The boat is *foul of* a rock. 舟が岩に引っかかっている. ‖ The ship fell *foul of* a junk. その船はジャンク船と衝突した. ¶wheels *foul with* mud 泥だらけの車輪 ‖ be *foul with* impurities. 不純物でよごれている.

found, *v.* 基礎を据える, 基づかせる; 創立する.

M *founded more or less* on the principle of ... 多かれ少かれ...の原理に基づいている. ¶This conjecture is not *well founded.* この推量には十分の根拠がない. 【類】 The complaint is in my opinion *well founded.* / The prognositcation (予断) is *well* (*ill*) *founded.*

P The college was *founded by* him in 1888. その大学は一八八八年彼によって創立された. ¶The tradition is probably *founded in* fact. その伝説は多分事実であろう. ‖ a belief *founded in* experience 経験からきた信念 ‖ His claim is *founded in* justice. 彼の主張は正当である. 【類】 The Society was *founded in* 1804. ¶It is *founded on* mere conjecture. それはほんの推量だ. ‖ American humor is largely *founded on* hyperbole. 米国のこっけいは大体誇張が土台になっている. 【類】 a country *founded on* democracy / his hopes are *founded on* ... / be *founded on* principles / The hospital was *founded on* an endowment fund provided by subscription (寄付による基本財産). / This novel is believed to be *founded on* incidents in real life. / His conclusion is *founded on* very superficial knowledge (皮相な知識). ‖ an architecture *founded on* European models ヨーロッパ風の建築 ‖ A Chinese philosophy is *founded on* the heavenly and earthly, or male or female, principles of nature. あらゆる中国の哲学は自然の乾坤(けんこん)または陰陽の原理に基づいている. ¶Future generations will be able to say whether or not our choice was *founded upon* wisdom. われわれの選択が果して賢明であるか否かは後世の人が判断するであろう.

foundation, *n.* 建立, 創建; 基礎, 土台; 根拠; 奨学資金; 財団.

V it *affords* a good *foundation* on which might be built ... それは...を建設しうるようなりっぱな土台を提供する. ¶*build up* a sound *foundation* in English 英語のしっかりした基礎を築く ‖ *build up* the *foundations* of a fortune 財産の基礎をすえる. ¶the journal *denies* all *foundation* for the rumour that ... 同紙は...という風評を根本から否定している. ¶*establish* a *foundation* for a perpetual lectureship in ... ...の永久講座を設けるための土台を据える. ¶*form* the *foundation* of ... ...の基礎になっている. ¶The charge *has* some *foundation* in fact. その非難には幾分事実上の根拠がある. 【類】 It *has* some *foundation* in truth. / This report *has* no *foundation.* ‖ The doctrine *has* little *foundation* to rest upon. その説は一向より所がない. ¶*lay* the *foundations* of a building 建物の土台を据える ‖ *lay* the *foundations* of his fame 彼の名声の土台を据える. 【類】 *lay* the *foundations* of a new Japan / He was then *laying* the *foundation* for his subsequent successes. / He *laid* the *foundation* for Western engineering in Japan. He *laid* the *foundations* of the science of bacteriology. ‖ A *foundation* has been *laid* upon which a superstructure of ... can be effectively erected. 上部工事を有効に建築しうべき土台が据えられた. 【類】 Frederick the Great of Prussia *laid* the *foundations* of the greatness of modern Germany. / The *foundation* of the Castle of Yedo was *laid* in the year 1455 A.D., during the reign of the 103rd Emperor of Japan, Go-Hanazono (1429-1464). ¶drive in piles to *make* a firm *foundation* 堅固な土台を作るためにくいを打ち込む. ¶*re-lay* the *foundations* of the country その国を再興する. ¶*solidify* the *foundation* of ... ...の基礎を固める. ¶The *foundations* of national glory are *set* in the homes of the people. 国家の光栄はその基礎が国民個々の家庭に据えられてある. ¶*undermine* the *foundations* on which the whole national fabric has been built up 国家全体の組織を載せてある土台をくつがえす.

Q without *adequate foundation* 十分な根拠なしに. ¶Athens and Corinth are examples of national greatness built up on a *commercial foundation.* アテネとコリントは商業の土台の上に築かれた国家的偉大性の範例である. ¶the *common foundation* underlying them all それら全部にわたる共通の基礎. ¶lay a *firm foundation* for a superstructure of ... ...の上部建築をやるための堅固な土台を据える. ¶built on *flimsy foundations* 薄弱な土台の上に築かれた. ¶a *good foundation* りっぱな基礎. ¶Is there any *historical foundation* for Thackeray's character of "Henry Esmond"? サッカレーの書いた人物ヘンリ・エズモンドには歴史的根拠があるか. ¶Japanese history prior to the Nara Epoch rests upon an *insecure foundation.* 奈良朝時代以前の日本歴史はその根拠が不確実である. ¶There is *no foundation* for his charges. 彼の非難には根拠がない. ¶a *safe foundation* 安全な土台. ¶a colony established on a very *secure foundation* はなはだ安定な基礎の上に樹立された植民地. ¶built on a *shaky* (*solid*) *foundation* ぐらぐらの(堅固な)土台に建って. ¶place international arbitration on *solid foundations* 国際仲裁裁判を堅固な土台の上に置く. ¶a *sound foundation* 確固たる基礎. ¶a *thorough foundation* 十分な土台. ¶an *unstable foundation* 不安定な基礎.

Q² deliver lectures on the *Hibbert Foundation* at Manchester College マンチェスター大学でヒッバート奨学基金に基づいて講義する. ¶a *national research foundation* 国民研究財団. ¶a *non-profit foundation* 公益法人. ¶a *one-piece foundation* 一続きになった土台. ¶a *rock foundation* 岩磐. ¶a *stone foundation* 石の土台.

P the laws that lie *at* the *foundation* of all the sciences あらゆる科学の根底に横たわるところの法則 ‖ *at* the *foundation* lies the fact that ... その根底に...という事実が横たわる ‖ scientific *at* its *foundation* その根底において科学的な. ¶the upheaval of society *from* its very *foundation* 社会のそもそもの根底からの転覆. ¶Agriculture is the *foundation on* which the Philippine Islands rest. 農業は比島の基礎である. 【類】 a *foundation on* which to build / This lecture was originally delivered at the University of California *on* the Weinstock *Foundation.* / *on* this *foundation* was established an annual course of lectures on ... ¶*since* the *foundation* of the paper 同紙創刊以来. ¶shake the earth *to* the *foundation* 大地を土台までもゆすぶる. ¶He laid the *foundation upon* which the superstructure rose by rapid steps. 彼が据えた土台の上に上部建築をどんどん進めて行った. ¶a statement which is *without foundation* in fact 事実に根拠を置いていない説 ‖ The story is utterly *without foundation.* そのうわさは事実無根だ.

P² There is no *foundation for* rumors of war. 戦争の風説には根拠がない. ¶This has no *foundation in* fact. これには事実上の根拠がない. ¶It has no *foundation of* truth. それは根のない説だ.

foundation-stone, *n.* 土台石, 礎石.

V He *laid* the *foundation-stone* of Japan's enlightenment and international equality. 彼は日本の文化及び国際的平等の礎石を据えた. 【類】 The founding of Batavia *laid* the *foundation-stone* for Dutch supremacy in the East Indies.

founder, *n.* 元祖, 開祖.
Q John Wesley, the ***great** founder* of the sect of Methodism メソジスト派の偉大な開祖たるジョン・ウェスレー. ¶the ***immortal** founder* of ... 千古に名を成す…の創立者. ¶Turan, ***mythical** founder* of the Turkish race トルコ人種の神話的な開祖たるチューラン.
P² the *founder **of*** a line 一家の先祖.【類】the *founder **of*** the Tokugawa family / the *founder **of*** a religious sect (開祖).

foundry, *n.* 鋳物工場.
Q² an ***iron** (**glass, type**) foundry* 鉄製品(ガラス・活字)工場.

fount, *n.* 《雅》源泉.
Q He is a practically ***inexhaustible** fount* of knowledge on the subject. 彼はその問題に関する知識においてこんこんとして尽きない源泉である.
Q² a ***drinking** fount* 飲料泉水.

fountain, *n.* 泉, 噴泉.
V a *fountain **fed*** from the adjacent hill 近くの山から出てくる泉.
V² A *fountain **gurgles**.* 泉がゴボゴボわき出す. ¶There *fountains **plash*** and ***dimple***. そこには泉がこんこんとわいている. ¶The *fountain **played*** beneath the sun, casting its diamond bright waters to the sky. 泉はそのダイヤモンドのように光る水を吹き上げながら日光の下に戯れていた. ‖ The *fountain* is not ***playing*** today. 噴水はきょうはとまっている.
Q a ***live** fountain* こんこんとわきだす泉. ¶a ***playing** fountains* 噴水.
Q² a ***drinking** fountain* 飲料泉水.【類】a public ***drinking** fountain*. ¶a drug-store with ***soda** fountains* 薬屋を兼ねたソーダ水店. ¶a ***soda-water** fountain* ソーダ水やジュースの容器; 《米》ソーダ水の屋台及びその店 (drug store など).
P The blood streamed out ***like** a fountain*. 血が泉のように流れた.
P² the *fountain **of*** youth 青春の泉. ¶a *fountain **of*** pleasure 快楽の泉.【類】the *fountain **of*** truth (beauty) 真理(美)の泉 ‖ The university is a *fountain **of*** scholarship. その大学は学問の源泉である. ‖ Almighty God, the *fountain **of*** all goodness すべての善の源泉たる万能の神.

fountain-head, *n.* 源泉.
P study English ***at** the fountain-head* 本家本元へ行って英語を勉強する.

fountain-pen, *n.* 万年筆.
V² The *fountain-pen **scratches***. その万年筆はペンがひっかかる. ¶This *fountain-pen **writes*** smoothly. この万年筆はすべりがいい.

four, *n.* 四.
P He believes that novel-writing and the green-growing business are ***on** all fours*. 彼は小説を書くことと野菜を栽培することはぴったりそりが合ってると信じている. ‖ crawl (creep, walk) ***on** all fours* 四つんばいになってはう(など).

fourth, *n.* 第四, 第四日.
Q the "***Glorious** Fourth*" 光栄ある七月四日の米国独立記念日(一般には July fourth と呼ぶ).

fowl, *n.* 鶏, 家禽(きん); [集合的に] 鳥.
V ***breed** fowls* 家禽を飼養する. ¶***keep** fowls* 家禽を飼う. ¶I ***overfeed** fowls*. 私は鳥に餌をやり過ぎる. ¶***pluck** fowls* 鳥の毛をむしる. ¶***underfeed** fowls* 鳥に餌を十分に与えない.
Q ***domestic** fowls* 家禽. ¶***drawn** (**undrawn**) fowls* 腸を抜いた(抜かない)鳥. ¶a ***grown** fowl* 生長した鳥. ¶a ***matured** fowl* 成熟した鶏. ¶The cock is a ***proud** fowl*. おんどりは高慢な鳥だ. ¶prepare ***undrawn** fowl* for the table 腸を抜いてない鳥を食卓に出すように調理する. ¶***wild** fowl* 野鳥.
Q² a ***guinea** fowl* ほろほろ鳥. ¶as a ***market** fowl* 市場に出す鳥として. ¶have a ***roast** fowl* for dinner 正さんに鳥のむし焼きを食う. ¶***sea** (**game**) fowl* 海(猟)鳥. ¶as a ***table** fowl* 食用鳥として.【類】one of the best ***table** fowls*. ¶a ***utility** fowl* 色々利用しうる肉用の鳥. ¶raise ***water** fowl* 水鳥を飼う. ¶***yard** fowls* 放し飼にする鳥.
P² the *fowls **of*** the air 空飛ぶ鳥. ¶*fowls **on*** range 放し飼いの鳥.

fox, *n.* きつね; こうかつ漢.
V ***play*** [the] *fox* ずるをきめる, ねこをかぶる.
V² A *fox **yelps***. きつねがキャンキャン鳴く.
Q He is an ***old*** (=a ***sly***) *fox*. 彼はとてもこうかつだ. ¶a ***white** fox* 白ぎつね.
Q² a ***fresh-water** fox* 淡水ぎつね(英国でこいの異名, こうかつだという俗説から). ¶a ***silver** fox* 銀ぎつね.
P He was bewitched ***by** a fox*. きつねに化かされた. ‖ He is possessed ***by*** (=***with***) a *fox*. 彼はきつねつきだ.

foyer, *n.* [ホテルなどの]ロビー.
Q² a ***smoking** foyer* 喫煙室.

fraction, *n.* 部分; 端数, 少し; 〖数〗分数.
V It does not ***contain*** a *fraction* of truth. それにはみじんも本当のことを含んでいない. ¶***pocket*** a *fraction* of the change [女中などが買物で]釣銭をごま化す.
Q a ***decimal** fraction* 小数. ¶a ***proper** (**improper**) fraction* 真(仮)分数. ¶a ***small** fraction* of the number 一小部分.【類】of the hundreds who are ..., I wonder what ***small** fraction* are aware that ... ‖ reckoned to the ***smallest** fraction* ごくわずかな端数まで計上して. ¶but a ***tiny** fraction* of the figure その数字のほんの一小部分.
P ***at** a fraction* of the usual cost いつもの値段の何分の一かで. ¶***for** the fraction* of a second 一秒の何分の一の間. ¶They are all ***in** fraction*. それが皆ばらばらになっている.

fragment, *n.* 断片, 破片; 零細.
V Historians ***combine** fragments* into a harmonious whole. 歴史家は断片を集めて調和ある完全体にする. ¶***save*** the *fragments* of time 零細の時間を節約する.
Q ***literary** fragments* 断章. ¶a ***mere** fragment* of its former self 残党. ¶The explosion shattered the store into a ***thousand** fragments*. 爆発で店が粉みじんになった.
Q² a ***rock** fragment* 岩片. ¶***thought** fragments* 断想.
P break ***into** fragments* みじんに砕ける ‖ burst ***into** fragments* 破裂してみじんに砕ける. ¶The vessel was dashed ***to** fragments*. その船はぶつかってみじんに砕けた.
P² *fragments **from*** my diary 私の日記の断片. ¶a *fragment **of*** an ancient writing 古文書の断片 ‖ He has not a *fragment **of*** chivalry. 彼はみじんだに義侠心がない.

fragrance, *n.* 香気, 芳香.
V ***carry*** a pleasant *fragrance* about one's person その身の周囲に芳香を放つ. ¶***exude*** delightful *fragrance* 芳香を発散する. ¶These proverbs thus rendered ***lose*** all their spicy *fragrance*. これらの格言もかように訳すとその高い香気を失ってしまう. ¶Flowers ***send forth** fragrance*. 花は芳香を発する. ¶***spread*** its *fragrance* far and wide その芳香を遠く広く発散する.
Q The soap has a ***delicate, flower-like** fragrance*. その石けんは微妙な花のような香りがする. ¶***faint** fragrance* かすかな香気. ¶***flower-born** fragrance* [香水など]花から取った香. ¶a pine forest with its ***resinous** fragrance* 樹脂のかおり高い松林. ¶***sweet** fragrance* 芳香.
P² the *fragrance **of*** roses (lilies) ばら(など)の香り.

fragrant, *a.* 芳ばしい, ふくいくたる.
P *fragrant **with*** that indescribable incense あのなんとも言いようのないふくいくたる芳香の.【類】Her name is *fragrant **with*** good deeds (りっぱな行為) as the woods at this season are *fragrant **with*** the delicate scents of spring.

frailty, *n.* ぜい弱, 繊弱; 弱点.
V ***exploit*** her *frailty* 女の弱身につけこむ. ¶***pass over*** all the petty *frailties* すべての小さな弱点を見のがす.
Q ***female** frailty* 女[心]のかよわさ. ¶***human** frailty* 人間の弱さ.
P² *frailties **of*** mankind 人間の弱点.

frame, *n.* 組織; 体格, 身体; 気分, 心持; わく, 額ぶち.
V ***adopt*** a cheerful *frame* of mind 気を引き立てる. ¶The old man ***carried*** his *frame* upright. その老人は腰が曲らなかった.
Q in an ***anxious** frame* of mind as to ... …について不安な気分で. ¶Do not attempt to deal with a criticism when under the sway of emotion; have it until you can deal with it in a ***calm, collected** frame* of mind. 感情に駆られているときは批評の応答を試みようとしてはならない, 冷静な気分でやれるまで待つがよい. ¶in a ***complacent** frame* of mind 満足した気分で. ¶a ***curious** frame* of mind 不思議な気分. ¶He is a man of ***delicate** frame*. 彼は虚弱な体質である. ¶in a ***devout** frame* of mind 敬けんの念を持って. ¶a man of ***gigantic** frame* 体格巨大な人. ¶a ***good** frame* of mind すぐれた気分. ¶in a ***happy** (**sad**) frame* of mind 幸福な(憂うつな)気分で ‖ cultivate a ***happy** frame* of mind 楽観的な気分を養う. ¶a ***melancholy** frame* of mind 憂うつな気分. ¶man's ***mortal** frame* 現身(うつしみ). ¶a man with an ***overstrung** frame* 緊張し過ぎた身体の人. ¶a ***portly, commanding** frame* 太った堂々たる体格. ¶a ***sceptical** frame* of mind 懐疑的な気分. ¶a ***silvergilt** frame* 銀ぶちの額. ¶a girl of ***slender** frame* きゃしゃな少女. ¶in a more ***submissive** frame* of mind 一層折れて. ¶a man of ***weak** frame* 弱い体格の人. ¶***wellknit***

frames がっしりした体格. ¶a more ***wholesome international*** *frame* of mind 一層健全な国際的態度.

Q^2 a slate roof on ***iron*** (***steel***) *frames* (鋼)鉄製の骨組みで支えたスレートぶきの屋根. ¶a ***picture frame*** 額縁. ¶a ***wicker*** *frame* 枝編細工.

P advertisements ***in frames*** わく縁に入れた広告 ‖ the portrait of a girl, set ***in*** a *frame* 額縁に入れた少女の肖像 ‖ place it ***in*** a *frame* manufactured of wood taken from … それを…の材木で作った額縁に入れる. ¶put … ***into*** a *frame* …を額縁に入れる. ¶He is naturally ***of*** a feeble *frame*. 彼は天性弱い体である.

P^2 a *frame* ***for*** a picture 絵を入れる額縁. ¶a *frame* ***for*** embroidery 刺しゅう台. ¶one's *frame* ***of*** mind 気の持ちよう(気分) ‖ the *frame* ***of*** society 社会組織 ‖ The picture shows part of the *frame* ***of*** a house. この絵は木造家屋の柱建ての一部である.

frame, *v.* 組立てる.

M ***lavishly framed*** in silver ぜいたくな銀ぶちに入れて. ¶He *frames* ***well*** in speaking. 演説家として物になりそうだ.

M^2 *frame* ***up*** one's life after the pattern of … …のやり方をまねた生き方をする ‖ *frame* ***up*** a plan for the purpose of … …の目的で計画を立てる.

P *frame* one's thoughts ***into*** words 思想を言葉に表わす. ¶a bank *framed* ***upon*** the model of … …にのっとって組織した銀行.

framework, *n.* 骨組, 結構.

Q ***grammatical*** *framework* 文法上の構造.

Q^2 a ***skeleton*** *framework* 骨組. ¶a bridge with a ***steel*** *framework* 鋼鉄の骨組を有する橋.

framing, *n.* 額縁に入れること.

Q The picture is ***worth*** *framing*. その絵は額縁に入れる価値がある.

franchise, *n.* 選挙権, 参政権; 経営権.

V ***give*** (=***extend***) the Parliamentary *franchise* to women 国会議員の選挙権を女子に与える. ¶This paper ***has*** an AP *franchise*. 〘新聞〙この新聞は AP と特約を結んでいる.

Q the ***elective*** *franchise* 選挙権. ¶fully utilize one's ***voting*** *franchise* 選挙権を十分利用する.

P^2 a *franchise* ***for*** bus service バスの営業権.

franchisement, *n.* 選挙権, 参政権付与.

P^2 the *franchisement* ***of*** women (working classes) 女子(など)への選挙権付与.

frank, *a.* 淡白な, 包み隠しのない, あからさまな.

M to be ***brutally*** *frank* 酷評すれば, 露骨に言えば. ¶***indelicately*** *frank* 無作法なほどに率直な. ¶to be ***perfectly*** *frank* 実は. ¶I will be ***quite*** *frank* with you. すっかり打明けて申上げましょう. ¶***rudely*** *frank* 極めてぶしつけな.

P He was *frank* ***about*** the matter. 彼はそのことについて包み隠しをしなかった. ¶He is *frank* ***by*** nature. 彼は天性淡白だ. ¶*frank* ***in*** manner 態度が率直な ‖ Children are *frank* ***in*** speech. 子供は正直だ. ¶if we are *frank* ***with*** ourselves, we shall admit that … 僕たちは自らを欺かないと…ということを認めるだろう ‖ to be *frank* ***with*** you 打明けて言うと.

frankness, *n.* 率直, 淡白.

Q ***brutal*** *frankness* ばか正直. ¶with ***engaging*** *frankness* 気持のいい率直さで. ¶a ***disarming*** *frankness* 相手の気持をやわらげる率直さ. ¶***wholesome*** *frankness* 健全な率直さ.

P speak ***with*** great *frankness* 腹蔵なく語る ‖ ***with*** the *frankness* of long acquaintance 永年知合いのざっくばらんさで. 【類】discuss their weakness ***with*** *frankness*. ¶There are probably a good many people in the world who are with him ***without*** his *frankness*. それほど露骨に言い切らないが彼と同感のものは世間に大分あるだろう.

frantic, *a.* 狂気の.

P He was almost *frantic* ***with*** grief (joy). 彼は悲しみ(など)のあまりほとんど狂気のようであった. ‖ *frantic* ***with*** anxiety (pain) 心配(など)で気が狂いそうに.

fraternity, *n.* 団体; 仲間.

Q a ***Greek-letter*** *fraternity* 《米》男子大学生の友愛会(クラブには Phi-Beta-Kappa などのようにギリシア文字を冠した名前がついている). ¶one of the ***light-fingered*** *fraternity* すり仲間の一人. ¶a ***religious*** *fraternity* 宗教の団体.

Q^2 the ***stage*** *fraternity* 芸能人仲間.

fraternize, *v.* 兄弟のように交わる.

M *fraternize* too ***eagerly*** with strangers 見知らない者と懇意にし過ぎる.

P *fraternize* ***with*** one another 互に兄弟の交わりを結ぶ.

fraud, *n.* 詐欺, ぺてん.

V ***commit*** a *fraud* upon the public 公衆を欺く. ¶***compound*** a *fraud* for £1,000 一千ポンドで詐欺行為を内済にする. ¶***condone*** a *fraud* on … …に対する詐欺を大目に見る. ¶***discover*** (=***find out***) a *fraud* 詐欺を発見する. ¶***expose*** a *fraud* 詐欺を暴露させる. ¶He ***played off*** a *fraud* upon me. 彼は僕をぺてんにかけた. ¶***practice*** (=***perpetrate***) a *fraud* on (=upon) … …を欺く ‖ ***practise*** *fraud* in the sale of their wares 彼らの商品販売にごま化しをやる. 【類】*fraud* either consciously or unconsciously ***practiced***. ¶I ***saw through*** the *fraud*. 私はその詐欺を見抜いた.

Q a very ***clever*** *fraud* 巧妙な詐欺. ¶a ***camouflaged*** *fraud* 体(てい)のよい詐欺. ¶a ***deliberate*** *fraud* たくらんだ詐欺. ¶a ***downright*** *fraud* 明白な詐欺. ¶a ***gigantic*** *fraud* 大がかりな詐欺. ¶a ***mail*** *fraud* 郵便による詐欺. ¶***palpable*** *fraud* 見えすいた詐欺. ¶a ***pious*** *fraud* [宗教的な]方便のうそ. ¶an ***undoubted*** *fraud* まぎれもない詐欺. ¶a ***well-organized*** *fraud* うまくたくらんだ詐欺.

Q^2 an ***election*** *fraud* 選挙詐欺. ¶a ***passport*** *fraud* 旅券詐欺. ¶a ***vote*** *fraud* 投票詐欺.

P money obtained ***by*** *fraud* 詐欺で得た金. ¶He is to be tried ***for*** *fraud*. 彼は詐欺で調べられることになっている. ¶He was committed for trial on a charge ***of*** *fraud*. 彼は詐欺のかどで裁判に付された. ‖ He is accused ***of*** *fraud*. 彼は詐欺で訴えられた. ¶I will not be a party ***to*** a *fraud*. 私は決して詐欺の仲間には入らない.

fraught, *a.* 満載している, 伴っている, はらんでいる.

M He returned to Japan ***full*** *fraught* with new learning. 彼は新知識を十分詰込んで帰朝した. ¶The ship is ***richly*** *fraught* with goods. 船は荷物を一杯積んでいる.

P events *fraught* ***with*** important consequences 重要な結果をはらんでいるできごと. 【類】a heart *fraught* ***with*** sorrow / The news is *fraught* ***with*** joy. / This scheme is *fraught* ***with*** danger to society. / Liberty is *fraught* ***with*** blessings. / a task *fraught* ***with*** hideous (恐ろしい) danger ‖ a social phenomenon *fraught* ***with*** significance 意義のある社会事象 ‖ *fraught* as they are ***with*** far-reaching consequences それは遠大な重要性を持っているので.

fray, *v.* ほぐす, ばらばらにする.

M sleeve edges ***pretty much*** *frayed* and soiled. 相当いたんでよごれているワイシャツのそで口.

P be *frayed* ***into*** a fringe 端がばらばらになる.

freak, *n.* 気まぐれ; たわむれ, いたずら; 奇形.

Q an ***architectural*** *freak* 建築上の珍品. ¶a ***childish*** *freak* 子供っぽい気まぐれ. ¶The scenic spot is one of nature's ***curious*** *freaks*. その名勝地(耶馬溪など)は造化の妙をきわめたものの一つである. ¶a ***human*** *freak* かたわな人間(因果者). ¶***odd*** *freaks* of nature 造化の不思議なたわむれ(奇形児など). ¶a ***queer*** *freak* 不思議な気まぐれ.

P ***by*** a *freak* of nature 造化のいたずらで. ¶Boys are fond ***of*** *freak*. 子供は気まぐれが好きだ. ¶***out of*** mere *freak* ほんのでき心で.

P^2 a *freak* ***of*** nature 造化のたわむれ(奇形児など).

free, *n.* 無料.

P all ***for*** *free* ただで.

free, *a.* 自由の, 自主の; ひまな; ない; 免れている; 打解けた; 大まかな; 無料の.

M And these are ***all*** *free*. そしてこれらはみなただだ. ¶I am ***comparatively*** *free* from work today. 今日は比較的仕事がない. ¶His conversations are ***delightfully*** *free* from bookishness and priggishness and cant. 彼の話はぎごちない文句や気取りや隠語などがなくて気持がよい. ¶Three-in-One is a clear sweet-smelling oil, ***positively*** *free* of grease, acid or any harmful ingredient. 三徳油は脂肪・酸その他いかなる有害な成分をも絶対に含んでいない透明で香のよい油である. ¶He is not ***quite*** *free* from blame. 彼は過失が全然ない訳ではない.

P *Free* ***for*** all [comers]. 飛入勝手. ‖ It is *free* ***for*** (=to) you to do so. そうするのは君の勝手だ. ¶*free* ***from*** blame 無難 ‖ *free* ***from*** interference 干渉を受けずに ‖ He is *free* ***from*** pecuniary anxieties. 彼には金銭上の心配がない. 【類】*free* ***from*** worldly cares (浮世の心配) / be *free* ***from*** danger (fear) / be *free* ***from*** partisanship (党派的偏見) / be *free* ***from*** pedantry (学者気取り) / *free* ***from*** worry / We are *free* ***from*** pain (care, danger, errors, defects) / *free* ***from*** slavery (どれい制度) ‖ I am *free* ***from*** work (business, duty). 私は仕事(など)がない. ‖ This city is *free* ***from*** (=of) thieves. この町には盗賊がいない. ‖ a woman *free from* disease 病気のない女 ‖ wish to be *free from* the mother country 母国の干渉を受けまいと念願する ‖ be warranted *free from* mortgage 担保になっていないという保証がある ‖ be *free from* tuition charges 月謝を免除されている ‖ be *free from* being amateurish しろうとばなれがしている ‖ *free from* alien influence 他国からの影響を受けない ‖ The class-rooms are *free from* outside sound. 教室は雑音防止になっている. ¶We are ***free in*** action. われわれは行動の自由を有している. ¶be ***free of*** debts 借金がない ‖ ***free of*** charge and post free 無料の上郵送料も要らない ‖ ***free of*** cost 無料で ‖ official houses ***free of*** rent 家賃なしの官舎. ‖ The fairway here is ***free of*** ice. その航路は結氷していない. ‖ He is ***free of*** money. 彼は金銭に大まかだ ‖ be ***free of*** speech 勝手なことをしゃべる. 【類】air ***free of*** dust / be not ***free of*** fault (欠点) / ***free of*** all restrictions / ***free of*** all expense / Education is entirely ***free of*** expense in that school. ¶The hospital is ***free to*** the poor on their own application. その病院は自分で申込めば貧民は無料である. ‖ ***free to*** all 入場随意 ‖ The library is opened ***free to*** the public. 図書館は無料で一般に公開されている. ‖ be ***free to*** the touch 手をふれてもよい. ¶He is ***free with*** me. 彼は私にはあけっぱなしだ. ‖ She is afraid of being too ***free with*** him. 彼女は彼とあまりなれなれしすぎることを恐れている. ‖ you are warned against being ***free with*** your credit to ... ...に多額の信用貸をするのは警戒した方がよい ‖ He is ***free with*** his money. 彼は金ばなれがいい. ¶He is ***free with*** his tongue. 彼は何でもずけずけ言う.

free, *v.* 自由にする; 免れさせる.

P *free* oneself ***from*** financial anxiety 財政上の心配を脱する ‖ *freed* ***from*** the bondage of a formula 形式の拘泥から脱して ‖ feet *freed* ***from*** the leathery prison of their shoes 彼らのくつの窮屈さを免れた足 ‖ Travel *frees* us ***from*** provinciality. 旅行はわれわれの眼界を広くする. 【類】*free* a person ***from*** responsibility (restrictions, bonds, cares, debts) ‖ *free* police departments ***from*** politics 警察部を政治から分離する ‖ The subject cannot be ***freed from*** technicalities. その題目は術語を使わずには論じられない. ¶Eva *frees* you ***of*** superfluous hair. [広告] エバを使うとむだ毛が取れます. ‖ *free* a person ***of*** fetters (debts, responsibility) 人を束縛(など)から免れさせる. ¶birds *freed* ***out of*** a cage かごから放たれた小鳥.

freedom, *n.* 自由; 自主; 免除; 容易; 無遠慮.

V ***abridge*** religious *freedom* 宗教の自由を制限する. ¶***abuse*** such *freedom* こうした自由を濫用する. ¶Cripples are ***allowed*** *freedom* from conscription. 足の悪い者は徴兵を免除される. ¶***celebrate*** one's *freedom* with old "pals" 昔友だちとくつろぐ. ¶***confer*** the *freedom* of the city (borough) on a distinguished visitor 都市(など)の特権を著名な訪問者に与える. ¶***extend*** human *freedom* 人間の自由を拡張する. ¶***gain*** one's *freedom* (どれいなど)解放される. ¶***give*** legitimate *freedom* 正当な自由を与える. ¶seriously ***hamper*** his *freedom* of action 大いに彼の自由行動を妨げる. ¶fowls ***having*** the *freedom* of the field 放し飼いした鶏. ¶seriously ***imperil*** the *freedom* of the will 大いに意思の自由を危くする. ¶A university should ***permit*** perfect *freedom* of teaching to professors. およそ大学は教授の講義に完全な自由を許すべきだ. ¶***receive*** the *freedom* of the city 都市の特権を授与される. ¶***regain*** their *freedom* 彼らの自由を取戻す. ¶***restore*** *freedom* to ... ...の自由を回復する. ¶***retain*** complete *freedom* of action 完全な行動の自由を保留する. ¶***suppress*** *freedom* of opinion 言論の自由を圧迫する. ¶***use*** the *freedom* wisely 自由を賢明に行使する. ¶***violate*** religious *freedom* 宗教の自由に違反する. ¶***win back*** one's *freedom* 自由を取戻す.

Q ***academic*** *freedom* 学問の自由. ¶***academic*** and ***educational*** *freedom* 学問と教育の自由. ¶***careless*** *freedom* 気楽. ¶***constitutional*** *freedoms* 憲政の自由. ¶with an ***honorable*** *freedom* from national jealousy 国民的しっと心をりっぱに超越して. ¶Japan's history of ***human*** *freedom* 日本の人間解放史. ¶those authors who combine correctness with ***idiomatic*** *freedom* of speech 正確でしかも自由にその国語特有な語法を使いこなす作家. ¶annihilate ***individual*** *freedom* 個人の自由を滅却する. ¶***intellectual*** *freedom* 研究の自由. ¶Nudists fully appreciate their ***new-found*** *freedom* from the chains of clothing. 裸体主義者は彼らが新たに発見した衣服の束縛を脱却したことを非常に喜んでいる. ¶their ***newly won*** *freedoms* 彼らの新たに得た自由. ¶one's ***personal*** *freedom* 個人的自由. ¶He laughed with the ***utmost*** *freedom*. 彼は遠慮会釈なく笑った. ¶This will afford me a ***wide*** *freedom* of action. これで私は十分行動の自由が得られる.

Q² infringement of the principle of ***press*** *freedom* 出版の自由という原則の侵害. ¶***student*** *freedm* 学徒の自由.

P ***in*** *freedom* 自由に. ¶a martyr ***to*** *freedom* of speech and teaching 言論と教授の自由に対する殉難者. ¶speak ***with*** *freedom* 自由自在に話す.

P² a *freedom* ***for*** investigation 研究の自由. ¶*freedom* ***from*** bias 偏見のないこと ‖ *freedom* ***from*** charge 無料 ‖ *freedom* ***from*** disease 免疫 ‖ assert *urbi et orbi* their *freedom* ***from*** party ties 彼らが全く党派に関係のないことを内外に宣言する ‖ *freedom* ***from*** fear 恐怖からの自由(ルーズベルトの宣言). 【類】*freedom* ***from*** responsibility / *freedom* ***from*** cares (risk, error) / *freedom* ***from*** tradition (prejudices) / *freedom* ***from*** laws of extra-territoriality (治外法権) / take advantage of his *freedom* ***from*** official duties to continue his study of .. ¶*freedom* ***in*** teaching 教授の自由. ¶*freedom* ***of*** speech (thought, religion) 言論(など)の自由 ‖ *freedom* ***of*** the press 出版の自由 ‖ *freedom* ***of*** information 報道の自由 ‖ *freedom* ***of*** conscience and religion 良心及び信教の自由 ‖ the *freedom* ***of*** a library 図書館に自由に出入する権利 ‖ *freedom* ***of*** the people from the bondage of ... ...の束縛からの人民解放.

free-for-all, *n.* 飛入り勝手の競技(試合).

Q a ***grand*** *free-for-all* 無礼講, 上下なしの会.

freeze, *v.* 凍らせる; 凍えさせる; 凍る.

M It *freezes* ***hard***. ひどい氷だ. ¶*freeze* three inches ***thick*** 厚さ三センチの氷が張る.

M² Six vessels lay *frozen* ***in***, at a considerable distance from the town. 六隻の船がその町から遠く離れた所で氷にとざされた. ¶a moat *frozen* ***over*** all winter 冬中凍結している堀 ‖ wait till the lake is *frozen* ***over*** 湖水が凍結するまで待つ. ¶*freeze* ***up***=become formal and cold in demeanor 態度がよそよそしくなる ‖ All the hot dishes cooled and finally *frozen* ***up***. さめてとうとう凍ってしまったあったかい食物 ‖ *freeze* ***up*** the *tongue* 舌を封じる.

P Water *freezes* ***at*** 32° F. 水は華氏の三十二度で凍る. ¶*frozen* ***into*** ice 氷結した. ¶He was *frozen* ***to*** death. 彼は凍死した. ¶He is *frozen* ***with*** cold. 彼は寒さでこごえている. ‖ This *froze* me ***with*** fright. これを聞いて恐ろしさでぞっとした.

freezing, *n.* 凍結.

Q² ***bank deposits*** *freezing* 銀行預金凍結.

freight, *n.* 運送貨物; 運賃; 《米》貨物列車.

V ***carry*** *freight* 貨物を運送する. ☞ 英国は主に水上運送に, 米国は空・陸・水運共使う. ¶The steamer is ***disgorging*** her *freight*. 汽船は荷をおろしている. ¶***quote*** *freight* by direct steamer 直航汽船での運賃を示す. ¶***reduce*** *freight* for tea to ... 茶の運賃を...に下げる. ¶try to ***secure*** a return *freight* 返り荷を得ようと努める.

V² *Freight* is ***declining***. 運賃が下りつつある. ¶*Freight* will ***slacken off*** shortly. じき荷動きが緩慢になるだろう.

Q the ***current*** *freights* are ... 現行の運賃は...だ. ¶*Freights* are ***firm*** and will probably advance. 運賃は手堅く多分今後上るであろう. ¶*freight* ***free*** 運賃無料で. ¶***Homeward*** *freights* are well maintained with an upward tendency. 本国への積荷は引続き上向きを示している. ¶***perishable*** *freight* 腐敗性の荷物. ¶*Freights* are ***weak*** and will probably decline. 運賃は弱気味で今後大方下るだろう.

Q² a ***coal*** *freight* 石炭積荷.

P send goods ***by*** *freight* 貨物便で品を送る. ¶travel ***on*** a *freight* 貨物列車で旅行する.

P² the *freight* ***on*** ... ...の運賃.

freight, *v.* 貨物を積込む.

P² a ship *freighted* ***with*** various sorts of merchandise 各種の商品を積んだ船. ¶*freight* goods ***to*** ... ...に貨物を送る.

freightage, *n.* 運賃.

P² *freightage* ***on*** luggage sent to ... ...へ送った手荷物の運賃.

freighter, *n.* 《米》貨物船.

V ***board*** a *freighter* 貨物船に乗る.

P go to America ***on*** a *freighter* 貨物船で米国に行く.

French, *n.* フランス語.

V He ***has*** *French*. 彼はフランス語ができる. ¶***speak*** good *French* 上品なフランス語を話す.

P He knows much of English, but little *of French.* 英語はくわしいがフランス語はまずい.

P² "Maison" is the *French for* the English "house." フランス語の"maison"は英語の「家」である.

frenzy, *n.* 乱心, 狂暴.

Q in a sort of ***drunken*** *frenzy* 酔って気が狂ったような様子で. ¶abandon oneself to a ***fine*** *frenzy* 全く狂暴に身をゆだねる.

P ***in*** a *frenzy* of the moment 一時の逆上で ‖ ***in*** a *frenzy* of grief 悲しみのあまり気を取乱して.

frequency, *n.* ひん度; 〘理〙周波数.

Q ***alarming*** *frequency* びっくりするほどの頻繁さ. ¶in order of ***decreasing*** *frequency*, they are ... これをひん度漸減の順序にすると...となる. ¶with ***disgusting*** *frequency* いやになるほどひん繁に. ¶***high*** (***low***) *frequency* 高い(低い)ひん度; 〘理〙高(低)周波. ¶The pulse is of ***normal*** *frequency.* 脈はくが普通である. ¶***painful*** *frequency* 痛ましいひん繁さ.

Q² ***radio*** (***video***) *frequency* ラジオ(テレビ)の周波数. ¶***word*** *frequency* 語の使用ひん度.

P ***with*** extraordinary *frequency* 非常にひん繁に.

P² *frequency* ***of*** accident 災害ひん度率. ¶*frequency* ***of*** use 使用ひん度. ¶The magazine diminished in size and *frequency* ***of*** issue. その雑誌は大きさも発行回数も減った.

frequent, *a.* ひん繁な.

M Railway accidents are ***alarmingly*** *frequent* of late. 鉄道事故は近来驚くほどひん繁だ. ¶***distressingly*** *frequent* 心配になるほどひん繁な.

frequent, *v.* しばしば訪れる.

M The resort is ***most*** *frequented* by visitors. その行楽地は遊覧客の出入がひん繁だ. ¶He *frequented* the house ***night and day.*** 昼夜を問わずひん繁にその家を訪れた.

P The cinema is *frequented* ***by*** about 99 per cent of the population. 映画見物人の数は人口の約九十パーセントになる. ¶Kamakura is much *frequented* ***for*** sea-bathing. 鎌倉は海水浴で大いに繁盛する.

frequenter, *n.* 常連.

Q² ***concert*** *frequenters* 演奏会の常連.

fresco, *n.* 壁画.

Q It is the fashion nowadays to decorate public buildings with ***allegorical*** *frescoes.* 公共の建物を風喩(ゆ)的な壁画で飾ることは当今の流行だ. ¶***tempera*** *fresco* テンペラ壁画.

P Buddhist *frescoes* ***on*** its walls その壁に描いてある仏教「壁画.

fresh, *n.* 初め, 初期.

P ***in*** the *fresh* of the morning 早朝に ‖ ***in*** the *fresh* of the「year 年の初めに.

fresh, *a.* 新来の, ...したての; 元気のよい; ありありとした; 《米俗》でしゃばりの, 生意気な.

M Though nearly seventy years of age, he is still ***as*** *fresh* as paint (=a rose, a daisy *or* an oyster). 七十近いのだが彼はまだみずみずしい. ¶be ***still*** *fresh* in living memory 今なお生きている人々の記憶に新たである.

P The troops were *fresh* now ***for*** action. 軍隊は今や元気いっぱいに戦を望んでいた. ¶with as handsome features as if *fresh* ***from*** the chisel of Phidias フィデアスののみででき上ったばかりのような美しい目鼻立をした ‖ a maid *fresh* ***from*** the country 山だしの女中. ‖ coins *fresh* ***from*** mint 造幣局を出たばかりの貨幣. 【類】*fresh* ***from*** Europe / young men *fresh* ***from*** the universities / London dailies *fresh* ***from*** the press. ¶events *fresh* ***in*** the memory 記憶になお新たな事件 ‖ You feel *fresh* ***in*** the morning. 朝は気持のよいものだ. ¶get *fresh* ***with*** a woman 《米俗》女にふざける.

O Don't be *fresh!* 生意気言うな.

freshet, *n.* 出水.

Q² a ***midwinter*** *freshet* 真冬の出水. ¶a ***spring*** *freshet* 春の出水.

freshman, *n.* 大学新入生.

Q an ***unsophisticated*** *freshman* うぶな新入生.

P² a *freshman* ***at*** college 大学新入生.

freshness, *n.* 新鮮, 涼味.

V I rose early to ***catch*** the *freshness* of the morning. 僕は早朝の新鮮味を味わおうとして早起をした. ¶His complexion ***has*** a rosy *freshness.* 彼の顔色はばらのようにつやつやしている. ¶She manages to ***preserve*** the beauty and youthful *freshness* of the complexion. 彼女は顔色の美しさと青春のはつらつさを失わないようにしている.

Q a ***breezy*** *freshness* さばさばした感じ. ¶the morning all in the ***dewy*** *freshness* すがすがしい露にぬれた朝. ¶cut flowers of ***doubtful*** *freshness* 疲れた切花.

fret, *n.* 気をもむこと.

P² be ***in*** a *fret* about ... ...についてじりじりしている.

fret, *v.* 怒る, じれる; すり減らす.

M *fret* ***away*** (=***out***) one's life やきもきして暮す. ¶*fret* oneself ***ill*** (=***sick***) 気をもんで病気になる.

P *fret* ***about*** trifles ちょっとしたことにふくれる. ¶*fret* ***at*** a person's idleness (=inactivity) 人の怠惰を怒る. ¶The garment was *fretted* ***by*** moths. 蛾(が)で上衣がいたんでいた. ¶Baby *frets* ***in*** hot weather. 赤ん坊は暑い日にはむずかる. ‖ *fret* ***in*** one's ill luck 自己の不運に悩む. ¶*fret* ***over*** one's mistake 間違いを苦にする. 【類】He *fretted* ***over*** this for a long time. ¶*fret* ***with*** ... ...を苦にする.

friar, *n.* 修道士.

Q a ***mendicant*** *friar* たくはつ僧.

friction, *n.* 摩擦; あつれき, 不和.

V ***avoid*** *friction* あつれきを避ける. ¶***cause*** a little *friction* 少し摩擦を生じさせる. ¶this ***constitutes*** the *friction* in our relations with ... このためわれわれと...との関係においてあつれきを生じている. ¶***foment*** international *friction* 国際間の不和を醸成する. ¶***minimize*** *friction* でき得る限りあつれきを軽減する. ¶It ***produces*** some *friction* in the household. それで家庭に少し風波が起った.

V² *Friction* has ***arisen*** among the men employed. 雇人の間にあつれきが生じた.

Q massage and ***dry*** *friction* マッサージと乾燥摩擦. ¶***international*** *friction* 国際的不和.

Q² ***East-West*** *friction* 東西両洋間のあつれき. ¶***family*** *friction* 家庭の不和. ¶***rolling*** *friction* 回転摩擦.

P Heat is produced ***by*** *friction.* 熱は摩擦によって起る. ¶get on together ***without*** *friction* 円滑にやって行く.

P² *friction* ***among*** people 人々の間の不和. ¶there has been a *friction* ***at*** the university for ... 同大学に...のためあつれきがあった. ¶*friction* ***between*** two parties 二党間のあつれき. ¶*friction* ***with*** ... ...でのごたごた.

friend, *n.* 友人, 味方, 同情者.

V He ***adjured*** his *friend* to be more careful. 彼はその友人にもっと注意するよう真剣に言った. ¶***alienate*** (=***estrange***) a *friend* from another 二人の友情に水を差す. ¶***assist*** a *friend* 友を助ける. ¶***authorize*** a *friend* to act in his absence 自分の留守中友人に代理を務める権限を与える. ¶***back up*** one's *friend* 友人を後援する. ¶He ***bored*** his *friends* for weeks talking about this bargain. この掘出し物のことを幾週も話すので友人たちはあてられた. ¶***Bring*** your *friend* with you. 君のお友だちを連れて来給え. ***choose*** one's *friend* 友を選ぶ. ¶***desert*** (=***forsake***) a *friend* 友人を棄てる. ¶***entertain*** a *friend* 友人をもてなす. ¶I ***expect*** *friends* to tea. 友だちがお茶に来ることになっている. ¶I ***found*** a true *friend* in him. 彼は全く忠実な友であった. ‖ You will always ***find*** a *friend* in me. どこまでも貴下の力になりましょう. ¶***gain*** *friends* 味方を得る. ¶***get*** *friends* 友を得る. ¶"It's great to ***have*** *friends* like Don and Mary" said Chaplin. 「ドンとメリーのような友だちがあるのは素敵だ」とチャップリンは言った. ‖ ***have*** no *friend* to talk to 話しかける友もない. ¶Missiles sometimes ***hit*** *friends* as well as foes. 飛道具はときどき敵と同様味方にも当る; ひいきの引倒しということもある. ¶***introduce*** a *friend* to the meeting 友だちを一同に紹介する. ¶***keep*** *friends* with ... ...と仲よくする ‖ ***keep*** old *friends* 古い友人を失わないようにする. ¶I have ***made*** many *friends* in that country. その国に友だちが沢山できた. ‖ Better not be too quick to ***make*** *friends.* 友を作るには急がないがよい. ‖ ***make*** *friends* again 仲直りする ‖ You should not ***make*** a *friend* of any one who is not fit to be your friend. 友人として不適当な人を友人とすべきではない. ‖ ***make*** *friends* with another (others) 人と親しくする. 【類】***make*** new *friends* (友人, 顧客) / He has not ***made*** a single *friend* there. / soldiers ***making*** *friends* with children. ¶go to the railway station to ***meet*** a *friend* 友を迎えに停車場へ行く. ¶I ***miss*** my *friend* very much. 友人がいなくなって非常にさびしい. ¶He ***needs*** a *friend* badly. 彼は話相手がなくって困っている. ¶***pester*** one's *friend* for money 金のことで友だちをわずらわす. ¶***receive*** a *friend* 友を迎える. ¶***retain*** old *friends* 旧友と交りを続ける. ¶I have been to Ueno to ***see*** a *friend* of mine off. 友人の一人を見送りに上野へ行って来た. ¶I had just ***seen*** a *friend* ***off*** on a midnight train at Umeda. そのとき私はちょうど梅田駅で友だちが夜汽車で立つのを見送った所であった. ¶He tried to ***seek out*** a *friend* in the city. 彼はその町で友だちを探し出そうとした. ¶***sell*** one's *friend* 友を売る. ¶***sunder*** *friends* 友だちを離間する. ¶***win*** new *friends* 新しい味方を得る.

Q a ***Basic*** *friend* ベーシック英語に賛成している人. ¶a ***bosom*** *friend* 腹心の友. 【類】the circle of his ***bosom*** *friends.* ¶a ***breast*** *friend* 親友. ¶a ***candid*** *friend* 無遠慮に物を言う友人.【類】a ***candid*** *friend* of Japan. ¶a ***close*** (=intimate) *friend* 親友. 【類】one of his ***closest*** *friends.* ¶a ***close personal*** *friend* 親密な友. ¶my ***closest, staunchest,*** and most ***loyal personal*** *friend* 私の最も親密で堅固でそして最も忠実な盟友. ¶a ***common*** *friend* 双方の友人. ¶a ***competent*** *friend* 実力のある友. ¶a ***congenial*** *friend* 気の合った友人. ¶a ***cordial*** *friend* 心からの友. ¶a ***devoted*** *friend* 忠実な友. ¶Be kind to your ***dumb*** *friends.* 物が言えない(馬, 犬, 小鳥)に親切にせよ. ¶a ***false*** *friend* 偽友. ¶a ***far-away*** *friend* 遠く離れている友. ¶a ***fast*** (=***steady***) *friend* 変らぬ友, 断金の友. 【類】They had been ***fast*** *friends* for years. ¶a ***firm*** *friend* 盟友. ¶a ***flattering*** *friend* こびへつらう友. ¶one's ***foreign*** *friend* 外国人の友人. ¶a ***genuine*** *friend* 真の友. ¶They are ***good*** *friends.* 彼らは仲がよい. ¶a ***good*** and ***constant*** *friend* 善良で忠実な友. ¶He became a ***great*** *friend* of mine. 彼は私の大の親友となった. ¶His social position won for him many ***influential*** *friends.* 彼の社会的地位が彼に多くの有力な友を得させた. ¶I received him into the number of my most ***intimate*** and ***confidential*** *friends.* 私は彼を最も親密な腹心の友の仲間に加えた. ¶his ***journalistic*** *friends* 彼の新聞記者である友人. ¶The ***kindest*** *friend* I have is my dear mother. 僕の最も親切な友だちはお母さんだ. ¶one's ***life-long*** *friend* 一生の友. ¶a ***literary*** *friend* 文学上の友. ¶a ***loving*** *friend* 愛する友. ¶a ***musical*** *friends* 音楽好きの友. ¶He is our ***mutual*** *friend.* 彼はわれわれお互の友人だ. ‖ I met him at the house of a ***mutual*** *friend.* 私が彼に会ったのはお互の友だちの家であった. ¶a ***near*** *friend* 親しい友. ¶old foes as ***new*** *friends* きのうは敵今は友. ¶a ***new-found*** *friend* 新に得た友. ¶an ***old*** *friend* of mine 私の旧友. ¶an ***old*** and ***tried*** *friend* 気心の解っている旧友. ¶***older*** *friends* 先輩の友人たち. ¶an ***open*** and ***avowed*** *friend* 打明けた親友. ¶a ***personal*** *friend* of mine 私自身の友 ‖ the private language of ***personal*** *friends* 友だち同志のうちとけた言葉使い. ¶his ***political*** *friend* or foe 彼の政治上の友または敵. ¶their ***private*** *friends* 彼らの私交上の友. ¶a ***professed*** *friend* 自称友人. ¶a ***short-sighted*** *friend* of the common people 先見の明のない民衆の友. ¶my ***sick*** *friend* 病気の友人. ¶my ***sometime*** *friend* かつて友人であった人. ¶a ***staunch*** *friend* of Japan 大の日本の味方 ‖ He was one of the ***staunchest*** *friends* the working women of the country ever had. 彼はこの国の女子労働者に取って最も強健な擁護者の一人であった. ¶a ***staunch*** and ***loyal*** *friend* しっかりした忠実な友. ¶a ***steadfast*** *friend* 確かな友. ¶a ***steadfast*** and ***trusted*** *friend* 腹心の友. ¶a ***strong*** *friend* among weaker friends 弱い友だち中の強い友. ¶a ***sympathetic*** *friend* 同情のある友. ¶an always ***tardy*** *friend* いつも時刻を遅らす友人. ¶a ***tried*** *friend* 確かな友. ¶a ***true*** *friend* 信実の友. ¶an ***unfailing*** *friend* 確かな友. ¶one of the ***unknown*** *friends* whom the book has made for him その書物のためにできた彼の見知らぬ友の一人. ¶an ***unseen*** *friend* 未見の友. ¶a ***valued*** (=***esteemed***) *friend* of mine 私の畏(い)友. ¶a ***warm*** *friend* of Japan 日本の熱心な同情者. ¶a ***warm personal*** *friend* じっ懇な友人.

Q² ***angling*** *friends* つり仲間. ¶a young ***artist*** *friend* of his 彼の若い芸術家の友. ¶our ***banker*** *friends* われわれの銀行家の友. ¶She has several ***boy*** *friends.* 彼女には数人の男性の友がある. ¶***business*** *friends* 商売仲間. ¶a ***childday*** *friend* おさな友だち. ¶a ***childhood*** *friend* 竹馬の友. ¶***family*** *friends* 家族一同の友だち. ¶a ***fair-weather*** *friend* 都合のよい時だけの友. ¶her ***gentleman*** *friends* 彼女のだんな(パトロン)たち. ¶a ***girl*** *friend* 女の友ちだ. ¶a ***high-brow*** (***low-brow***) *friend* インテリの(でない)友人. ¶***insect*** *friends* こん虫である友だち. ¶a ***lady*** *friend* 女友だち. ¶a ***lawyer*** *friend* of mine 弁護士をしている友人. ¶I have some ***men*** *friends* over here, playing cards. 私の男の人の友だちが家へ来ているのよ, トランプをやりに. ¶his ***millionaire*** *friend* 彼の百万長者の友. ¶A letter came from my ***New York*** *friend.* ニューヨークの友人から手紙が来た. ¶his ***one-time*** *friends* 彼の以前の友人たち. ¶a New Year ***post-card*** *friend* 年賀状を出す程度の友. ¶***women*** *friends* 女友だち. ¶I took off for Morocco with my ***writer*** *friend.* 作家の一友人と空路モロッコに飛んだ.

P I was now ***among*** *friends.* 私は(敵から逃れて)もう味方と一しょになっていた. ¶Tell me, ***as*** a *friend,* what shall I do. どうしたら良いか友人として言ってくれたまえ. ‖ He acted ***as*** a *friend* to me. 彼は私に友人のように親切にしてくれた. ‖ I advise [with] you ***as*** a *friend* not to meddle with it. それに干渉しないよう友人として忠告する. ¶He was admired both ***by*** *friend* and foe. 敵も味方も彼を賛美した. ¶We know him ***for*** a *friend.* われわれは彼を仲間と思っている. ‖ stand up ***for*** one's *friends* 友の後援に立つ. ¶a letter ***from*** a *friend* in ... ...にいる友からの手紙. ¶the most kind-hearted ***of*** *friends* 友として最も親切な者. ¶I gained admission ***through*** a *friend.* 友だちに頼んで入場させてもらった. ‖ I made his acquaintance ***through*** a mutual *friend.* お互の友を通じて彼と知合になった. ¶He is staying ***with*** a *friend* (at a friend's). 彼は友人の所に泊っている.

P² a *friend* ***in*** town 都の友 ‖ A *friend* ***in*** need is a friend indeed. 困ったときこそ友は真の友である. ¶a *friend* ***of*** his schoolboy days 彼の学校時代の友. 【類】a *friend* ***of*** mine / a *friend* ***of*** my own ‖ a *friend* ***of*** English education 英語教育の尽力者. ¶a *friend* ***to*** truth 真理の味方 ‖ he is no *friend* ***to*** ... 彼は...の味方ではない. ¶I am *friends* ***with*** him. 私は彼と仲好しだ.

friendly, *a.* 親しい; 親切な; 好都合の.

M ***outwardly*** *friendly* 表面上好意のある.

P rain *friendly* ***to*** ripening fruits 果実の熟するに好都合の雨 ‖ be known as *friendly* ***to*** their enemy 敵と親しいと言われている. ¶He is *friendly* ***towards*** (=to) me. 彼は私に対して親切だ. ¶I should like to be very *friendly* ***with*** him. 私は彼と親しくしたい.

friendship, *n.* 友情, 友誼(ぎ), 好意; 親交.

V ***acquire*** the *friendship* of ... ...の好意を得る. ¶Explosive epistles ***blast*** *friendships.* 過激な手紙は友情を破壊する. ¶***break*** *friendship* with ... ...と友だちの縁を切る. ¶***break off*** a *friendship* of twenty years' standing 二十年来の親交を断つ. ¶We have ***built up*** quite a *friendship.* 私たちは随分親密な間柄になった. ¶***cement*** the *friendship* between the two peoples 二国民間の友誼を固める. ¶***command*** the *friendship* and respect of the world 広く世界の友情と尊敬を集める. ¶It was then that he ***commenced*** his romantic *friendship* with her. 彼が彼女と小説的な親交を始めたのはその時であった. ¶***contract*** a real *friendship* with ... ...と真の友誼を結ぶ. ¶***cultivate*** our *friendship*[*s*] with one another お互の友誼を厚くする. 【類】***cultivate*** *friendship* with ... ¶I earnestly ***desire*** your *friendship.* あなたとの親交を切望します. ¶***dissolve*** old *friendships* 旧交を棄てる. ¶A close *friendship* was ***established*** between the two. この両者間に親交が結ばれた. ¶***form*** a *friendship* with ... ...と交りを結ぶ. 【類】an intimate *friendship* was thus ***formed*** between ... and ... ¶***gain*** their *friendship* 彼らの友誼を得る. ¶I ***have*** a *friendship* with him. 私は彼と交際している. ¶***impair*** our *friendship* with ... ...とのわれわれの交誼をそこのう ‖ ***impair*** the *friendship* of the two 両者間の交誼を傷つける. ¶***improve*** the *friendship* already begun すでに結んだ交誼を深くする. ¶***keep*** old *friendships* in repair 昔からの友誼が薄らがないようにする. ¶***lose*** a precious *friendship* 大事な友人を失う. ¶Japan and America should endeavour to ***maintain*** their historic *friendship* unbroken. 日米はその歴史的の友誼を維持することに努力すべきである. ¶***make*** *friendships* 交誼を結ぶ. ¶***mark*** *friendship* by a gift 贈り物を友情の印とする. ¶He ***needed*** *friendship.* 彼は友人が欲しかった. ¶Women who ***offer*** *friendship* to a man usually find that he responds with an offer of love. 男に友人としての交際を申出る女はその男が愛の申出をもってこれに応じるということをよく経験する. ¶***promote*** international *friendship* and good will 国際の親善と好誼を増進する. ¶***renew*** *friendship* and talk over old school days 旧交を

温めて昔の学生時代を語る. 【類】 ***renew*** the *friendship* that formerly existed between us. / ***renew*** old *friendships* and make some new ones. ¶***renounce*** *friendship* 絶交する. ¶I ***respect*** your *friendship* very highly. 私は君を友人に持つことを非常に有難く思う. ¶***return*** *friendship* 友情に報いる. ¶***revive*** old *friendship* 旧交を復活する. ¶keenly ***seek*** the *friendship* of ... 熱心に…の交誼を求める. ¶***show*** one's *friendship* for ... …に対してその友情を示す. ¶***strike [up]*** *friendship* with ... …と懇親を結ぶ. ¶He ***swore*** eternal *friendship*. 彼は永久変らない交誼を誓った. ¶***treasure*** another's *friendship* 人の友情を非常に有難く思う. ¶***violate*** *friendship* 友情を破棄する. ¶***weaken*** the *friendship* 友情を弱める. ¶try to ***win*** his *friendship* 彼と交誼を結ぼうと努める. 【類】 work to ***win*** the *friendship* and trust of other nations.

Q ***another*** *friendship* formed at this period was with ... この時期に得たもう一人の友人は…であった. ¶Nietzsche formed a ***close*** *friendship* with a young scientist Dr. Paul Rée. ニイチェは若き科学者のパウル・レー博士と親交を結んだ. ¶***durable*** *friendship* 永続きする交誼. ¶form an ***enduring*** *friendship* with ... …と末永い友誼を結ぶ. ¶Before long the two formed a ***fast*** *friendship*. 間もなく二人は親交を結んだ. ¶a ***firm*** *friendship* 固い友誼. ¶the ***growing*** *friendship* between Japan and China 日華間に深まり行く親交. ¶an ***honorable*** *friendship* りっぱな友人関係. ¶form an ***intimate*** *friendship* with ... …と親交を結ぶ. ¶An ***intimate*** and ***lasting*** *friendship* sprang up between them. 親密な永続する友情が彼らの間に生じた. ¶a ***lasting*** *friendship* 永く変らない交誼. ¶***loving*** *friendship* 親交. ¶***neighbourly*** *friendship* 善隣のよしみ. ¶form ***new*** *friendship* 新たに交りを結ぶ. ¶never to forget ***old*** *friendships* 古い友情を決して忘れないように. ¶cultivate ***personal*** *friendship* 親交を結ぶ. ¶strictly ***Platonic*** *friendship* [男女間の]全く清い交際. ¶I need not say that I shall always hold in grateful remembrance your ***proven*** *friendship* in this hour of need. 私はこの窮乏のときに際してあなたのいつも変らぬ御同情を永久に感謝して忘れないことは申上げるまでもありません. ¶contract a ***strong*** *friendship* for ... …と大の親友になる. ¶forty years of ***unbroken*** *friendship* 四十年続いた友人関係. ¶***unfailing*** *friendship* 確実な友情. ¶A very ***warm*** *friendship* sprang up between them. はなはだ温い交情が彼らの間に生じた.

Q^2 renew ***school*** *friendship* between them おたがいに同窓時代の旧交を温める. ¶***world*** *friendship* 世界各国の親交.

P He was endeared to me ***by*** a warm *friendships* of 33 years. 彼は三十三年の親交で私には大事な男であった. ¶shake hands ***in*** *friendship* 親しく握手する. ¶under the mask ***of*** *friendship* 深切ごかしに. ¶***out of*** *friendship* for ... …に対する友人としての好意から. ¶Do not presume ***upon*** my *friendship*. 友人だと言って余りつけあがるな. ‖ Relying ***upon*** (=on the strength of) our *friendship*, I asked a favor of him. 私は懇意にしているので彼に頼んだ.

P^2 the promotion of *friendship* ***among*** ... …間の交情の増進. ¶promote *friendship* ***between*** Japan and England 日英間の交誼(ぎ)を増進する. ¶His *friendship* ***for*** Byron began in the same year. 彼のバイロンとの交情は同じ年に始まった. ‖ I have a *friendship* ***for*** him. 私は彼に好意を持っている. ¶a *friendship* ***with*** a person (country) 人(など)との交情. ¶*friendship* ***without*** intimacy 親しいとまでは行かない友人関係.

fright, *n.* 驚がく, 恐怖; 恐ろしいもの.

V *fright* ***caused*** by a fire 火災による恐怖. ¶I ***got*** (=had) a great *fright*. 私はこわい目にあった. ¶You ***gave*** me a *fright*. そりゃ驚いた. ¶What a *fright* I have ***had!*** ほんとにこわかった. ¶***take*** *fright* at the sight of ... …を見てびっくりする ‖ the horse ***took*** *fright* at ... 馬が…に驚いた.

Q live in a ***constant*** *fright* on account of ... …のために始終びくびくして暮す. ¶He seemed to be in a ***great*** *fright*. 彼は非常に驚いている様子であった. ¶She is a ***perfect*** *fright*. 彼女は丸でおばけだ.

Q^2 suffer from "***mike*** *fright*" マイクロフォンを前にするとあがってしまう. ¶have (=get) a ***stage*** *fright* 舞台(場所)負けする. 【類】 does not suffer from ***stage*** *fright*.

P die ***from*** (=***of***) *fright* びっくりして死ぬ. ¶***in*** his *fright* 驚いて ‖ put a person ***in*** a *fright* 人をこわがらせる ‖ he was ***in*** a *fright* lest ... …かと思ってこわがっていた. ¶She is ill ***of*** *fright*. 彼女はこわがって病気になった. ¶She got faint ***through*** (=***with***) *fright*. 彼女は驚きの余り気を失った. ‖ He started ***with*** *fright*. 彼ははっとした. ‖ She shivered ***with*** *fright*. 彼女はこわくて震えた. ‖ overcome ***with*** *fright* びっくり仰天して. ¶He was near dead ***with*** *fright*. 彼は驚いて死なんばかりだった.

frighten, *v.* 驚かす, びっくりさせる.

M *frighten* ***away*** children out of door びっくりさせて外へ逃出させる ‖ The onionseed bed was planted with waving peacock feathers to *frighten* ***away*** the birds. 小鳥おどしに玉ねぎの種床にひらひらするくじゃくの羽を立てた. ¶I was ***badly*** *frightened*. 私はひどくびっくりした. ¶I was ***terribly*** *frightened*. 私は恐ろしくびっくりした.

P You needn't be *frightened* ***at*** the dog. その犬はこわがることはない. ‖ be *frightened* ***at*** the sight (noise, sound) それを見て(など)驚く. ¶I was *frightened* ***at*** (=***of***) a wolf. 私はおおかみを見てびっくりした. ¶be *frightened* ***by*** the audience 聴衆を見てあがる. ¶The rioters were *frightened* ***into*** submission. 乱暴を働いた人たちはおどかされて服従した. ‖ He was *frightened* ***into*** fits. 彼はびっくりしてけいれんを起した. ¶I was *frightened* ***out of*** doing it. 私はびっくりしてそうすることができなかった. ‖ I was nearly *frightened* ***out of*** my wits by ... 私は…のためにびっくりして周章ろうばいせんばかりであった. 【類】 Although she was *frightened* ***out of*** her wits, she managed to stammer. ‖ *frighten* a person ***out of*** his plan おどして彼の計画をやめさせる. ¶He was *frightened* ***to*** death. 彼は死ぬくらいびっくりした. ¶*frighten* children ***with*** a story 子供たちがこわがるような話をする.

fringe, *n.* はし, 縁; [婦人の]切りさげ前髪.

V I have only ***touched*** the *fringe* of this great subject. 私はこの大問題の一端に触れただけだ. ¶***wear*** a *fringe* 髪を額にたらしておく.

Q the ***radical*** *fringe* of the labor movement 労働運動の左翼.

P Hampstead Heath is ***on*** the northern *fringe* of London. ハムプステッド・ヒースはロンドンの北郊にある. ‖ It is only ***on*** the *fringe* of a subject teeming with interest. それは興味に満ちた問題のほんの入口の所に過ぎない. ‖ Maid servants usually live ***on*** the *fringe* of luxury. 女中たちは普通ぜいたくを見せ付けられて生活している.

P^2 a *fringe* ***of*** hair hung over one's forehead 額に垂れ下っている髪 ‖ have a *fringe* ***of*** curls on the forehead 額に巻毛の前髪がある.

fringe, *v.* ふち取りする.

P It is *fringed* ***with*** gold (gem). それには金(など)のふち取がしてある. ‖ a track *fringed* ***with*** grass 両側に芝生のある道路.

frisk, *v.* ふざける.

M^2 *frisk* ***about*** ふざけまわる.

fritter, *v.* くだらなく費す.

M *fritter* ***away*** (=***down***) money (time, energy) 金(など)をむだに費す. 【類】 *fritter* ***away*** one's mental strength by talking.

frock-coat, *n.* フロックコート.

V ***wear*** an imposing *frock-coat* いかめしいフロックコートを着る.

Q a ***wrinkled*** *frock-coat* しわだらけなフロックコート.

P men ***in*** *frock-coats* フロックコートを着た人々.

frog, *n.* かえる.

V^2 *Frogs* ***croak***. かえるが鳴く.

Q^2 ***table*** *frogs* 食用がえる.

P^2 a *frog* ***in*** the throat しゃがれ声.

frolic, *n.* ふざけ.

Q a ***drunken*** *frolic* 酔余の悪ふざけ.

P be ***in*** *frolic* ふざけている.

frond, *n.* [しだなどの]葉.

Q^2 a ***bamboo*** *frond* ささ.

front, *n.* 前面,正面; 戦線, 戦場; 対抗, 反抗; 厚顔.

V ***extend*** the *front* 正面(間に)を拡大する. ¶***form*** a united *front* against ... …に対して一致的行動を取る. ¶***pledge*** a united *front* against ... …に対して共同戦線を張ることを誓う. ¶***present*** a united *front* against (=to) the enemy 共同して敵に対抗する. ¶***Putting on*** a bold *front*, I informed the robber that he could take all the money I had. 大胆に構えて私は泥棒にあり金を皆持って行けと言った. ¶***show*** a bold *front* いきまく, 大胆に構える.

Q a ***brazen*** *front* 鉄面皮. ¶present a ***common*** *front* to ...

協力して…に対抗する. ¶a ***hardened** front* 厚顔. ¶the ***industrial** front* 生産面. ¶the ***popular** front* 人民戦線. ¶a ***smiling** front* 笑顔. ¶a ***united** front* 統一戦線 ‖ present a ***united*** (=***unbroken***) *front* to … 気をそろえて…に当る.

Q^{2} the ***action** front* 戦線. ¶widen the ***battle** front* 戦線を拡げる. ¶on the ideological ***battle** front* 思想戦線で. ¶the ***beach** front* on the Pacific 太平洋の海岸. ¶the ***cold** front* 〘気象〙寒冷前線. ¶the ***fighting** front* 戦線. ¶the ***harbor** front* 港の前面. ¶the ***high street** front* of the Town Hall 市役所の街路に面した正面. ¶on the ***home** fronts* 銃後で. ¶the country's wartime ***home** front* その国の戦時国内戦線. ¶unification of all ***labor** fronts* 全労働戦線の統一 ‖ a call for a united ***labor** front* 統一労働戦線の必要. ¶Thus the ***research** front* against influenza is truly international and world-wide. このように流行性感冒に対する研究戦線は真に国際的世界的だ. ¶belligerent moves on the ***wage** front* 賃銀戦線における交戦的な動き. ¶the China ***war** fronts* 中国戦線. ¶the ***water** front* 海(湖水)に面する部分; 海岸通り, 港湾地区 ‖ reclaim the ***water** front* from the bay 湾の前面を埋立てる.

P a son ***at*** the *front* 出征中の息子 ‖ our soldiers ***at*** the *front* 戦線における我軍の兵 ‖ The question, "Who will be the next President?" is ***at*** the *front* again. 今度の大統領はだれかという問題が再び世評に上っている. 【類】 the noble son fighting for England ***at*** the *front* / as a memorial to a son killed ***at*** the *front* / those who are already ***at*** the *front*. ¶start ***for*** the *front* 戦場に向って出発する. ¶the news ***from*** the *fronts* 戦地からの報知. ¶Please go ***in*** *front*. どうぞお先きにお出下さい. 【類】 Say "Excuse me," when you walk ***in*** *front*. / ***in*** *front* of a house / From my study window, you can see Fuji just ***in*** *front* of you. / The auto was parked ***in*** *front* of the house. ‖ New York stands ***in*** the *front* of the world's seaports. ニューヨークは世界の海港中首位に位する. ¶apply a blister ***on*** *front* of the chest, over the seat of the heart 胸部の正面心臓の上に吸出しこう薬を張りつける ‖ this glorious British victory ***on*** the celluloid *front* 映画における英国の勝利 ‖ the battle-line (air fighting) ***on*** the western *front* 西部戦線(など). ¶***over*** the *front* of the building is a large sign bearing the words, "…" 建物の正面上部に「…」と記した大看板がある. ¶It is very much ***to*** the *front* of people's minds. それは大分一般の人の頭に浮んでいる. ‖ come ***to*** the *front* 頭角を現わす, 出世する ‖ go ***to*** the *front* 従軍する. ¶write the name and address ***upon*** the *front* of an envelope 封筒の表面に住所氏名を書く. ¶He met the accusation ***with*** a bold *front*. 彼は敢然その非難に当った.

front, *v.* 面する, 向う; 前を飾る.

P The house *fronts* ***on*** the main street. その家は大通りに向いている. 【類】 *front* ***on*** large lake / The moor is *fronting* ***on*** a pretty garden. ¶The house *fronts* ***toward*** the south. 家は南向きになっている. ¶His house is *fronted* ***with*** marble. 彼の家は正面が大理石で飾ってある. ‖ The shop is *fronted* ***with*** glass. 店の正面はガラス張りになっている.

frontage, *n.* 正面; 向き.

V The house ***has*** a fine *frontage* of marble. 家は大理石のりっぱな正面がついている.

Q The room has no ***wide** frontage* to the sun. そのへやは日当りがよくない.

P^{2} *frontage* ***to*** northerly wind 北風を受ける向き.

frontier, *n.* 国境, 辺境.

V ***advance*** the *frontier* of human knowledge 人知を発達させる. 【類】 ***advance*** the *frontiers* of civilization. ¶***cross*** a *frontier* 国境を越える. ¶***harass*** the *frontiers* 辺境を荒す. ¶***pacify*** the north-western *frontier* 西北境を平定する. ¶They struggled valiantly to ***push back*** the *frontiers* of knowledge. 彼らは知識の領域を拡大するために勇敢に戦った. ¶***set up*** *frontiers* 国境を設定する.

Q an ***ethnographic[al]** frontier* 民族的境界. ¶the ***Russo-Chinese** frontier* 露支国境. ¶on the ***Sino-Mongolian** frontier* 中国と蒙古の国境に.

P forts ***on*** the *frontier* 国境の要さい. 【類】 The garrisoning of the Alps ***on*** the Franco-Italian *frontier* is extremely difficult in winter. ¶Since 1914 she has never had a peace ***within*** her *frontires*. 一九一四年以来その国は国内平穏なことが絶えてなかった.

P^{2} The *frontier* ***between*** erotic love and friendship is vague. 恋愛と友情の境目はばく然としている.

frontispiece, *n.* 口絵.

V A picture ***forms*** a beautiful *frontispiece* to the book. 一つの絵がその本の美しい口絵になっている.

P^{2} a *frontispiece* ***to*** a magazine (book) 雑誌(など)の口絵.

frost, *n.* 霜; 氷点以下の温度.

V We ***had*** a severe *frost*. ひどく霜が降った. ¶***melt*** the *frost* from the heart of the world 世界の心にある氷を溶かす(四海同胞の温情を呼び起す).

V^{2} Flowers perish when *frost* ***comes.*** 霜が降りると花が枯れる. ¶*Frost* ***falls.*** 霜が降る. ¶*Frost* ***forms*** on the ground. 地上に霜が降る. ¶*Frost* ***occurred.*** 霜が降った. ¶Killing *frost* ***prevailed*** last night over the crop. 昨夜作物に霜害があった. ¶when the *frost* ***sets in*** 霜が降ると.

Q ***biting** frosts* 身を切るような霜. ¶an ***early** frost* 初霜. ¶a ***hard** frost* ひどい霜. ¶a ***heavy** frost* 大霜. ¶a ***hoar*** (=***hoary** or **white***) *frost*=rime 白霜. ¶a ***light** frost* 小霜. ¶We are having a ***severe** frost*. このごろはひどい霜だ. ¶a ***sharp** frost* はげしい霜 ‖ ***Sharp** frost* has set in here. ここではひどく霜が降りた. ¶A ***slight** frost* occurred. 小霜が降った. ¶There was a ***smart** frost* during the night, and the rime lay white on the grass. 夜中ひどい霜が下りて草が真白になっていた. ¶a ***strong** frost* ひどい霜.

Q^{2} tackle with ***Jack** Frost* 「冬将軍」と取組む.

P protect fingers and toes ***against*** the *frost* 指と足指の霜焼を防ぐ. ¶flowers nipped ***by*** the *frost* 霜でいためられた花. ¶damage ***from** frost* 霜害. ¶an iron handle covered ***with** frost* 霜で覆われた鉄のハンドル. ¶5 degrees ***of** frost* (=below zero) 《英》氷点下五度. ¶*frost* ***on*** the grass (window) 草(など)においた霜.

frost, *v.* 霜枯れさせる; 糖衣をきせる.

M^{2} All the leaves *frosted* ***off*** by the recent cold snap. 最近の急な寒気で葉が皆な霜げて落ちた.

P *frost* a cake ***with*** a mixture of sugar and whites of eggs ケーキに砂糖と卵の白味の衣をかける.

froth, *n.* あわ.

P^{2} a *froth* ***on*** beer ビールのあわ.

froth, *v.* あわを吹く.

P *froth* (=foam) ***at*** the mouth when talking 話すとき口からあわをふく.

frown, *n.* 渋面, 不興顔.

Q an ***angry** frown* 怒った渋面. ¶There was a ***deep** frown* on his face. 彼はひどいしかめっつらをしていた. ¶with a ***puzzled** frown* 途方に暮れまゆをひそめて. ¶a ***suspicious** frown* けげんな顔付.

P He silenced me ***with*** a *frown*. 彼は不興顔をして私の口を封じた.

frown, *v.* まゆをひそめる, にがい顔をする; 厳然と構える.

M ***severely** frown* upon a suggestion 提案を手ひどくやっつける.

M^{2} The company *frowned* him ***down.*** 仲間たちはにがい顔をして彼の申出をしりぞけた. ‖ *frown* ***down*** a proposition にがい顔をして申出をしりぞける.

P She *frowned* ***at*** her child. 彼女は子供ににがい顔をした. 【類】 He *frowned* ***at*** me for laughing at him. ‖ He *frowned* ***at*** her want of judgment. 彼は彼女の不見識にまゆをひそめた. ¶*frown* a person ***into*** silence にがい顔をして人をだまらせる. ¶*frown* ***on*** one's doing そのやることにまゆをひそめる ‖ The temple *frowns* ***on*** the plains. 寺院は平野に厳然と立っている. ¶She *frowned* ***to*** me. 彼女は私ににがい顔をした. ¶*frown* ***upon*** commoners 平民どもに対して厳然と構える. ¶He *frowns* ***upon*** gambling. 彼はとばくを排斥する.

frozen, →freeze.

fructify, *v.* 実を結ぶ.

P his efforts *fructified* ***in*** … 彼の努力は…となって実を結んだ.

frugal, *a.* 倹約な.

P He is *frugal* ***of*** money (=his expenses). 彼はつましい.

frugality, *n.* 節倹, 倹約.

V ***practice** frugality* 倹約する.

Q with ***patient** frugality* 倹約を守って. ¶live with the ***utmost** frugality* できるだけ倹約して暮す.

P ***with** frugality* 倹約して.

P^{2} *Frugality* ***of*** praise is not one of his weaknesses. あの人は賞賛を惜しむような人ではない.

fruit, *n.* [単数及び集合的に] 果物, 果実; 産出物; 結果.

V refuse to ***abandon*** the *fruits* of their victories 勝利の成果を放棄することを拒む. ¶The ***kaki bears*** a *fruit* about the size of an apple. 柿はりんごほどの実を結ぶ. ‖ ***bear*** no *fruit* 実を結ばない ‖ ***bear*** rich *fruit* りっぱな成績を示す ‖

bear fruit in after life 後年に至って実を結ぶ.【類】I hope your study will bear good fruit in time. / These efforts seemed to bear little fruit. / None of these schemes have borne fruit. / The temporary discomforts he may experience will bear fruits that will far outweigh their disadvantages (不利益を償って余りある効果). ¶bring forth good fruit りっぱな結果をもたらす. ¶collect (=gather) fruit 果実を取収める. ¶We now enjoy the fruits of the collective achievements of our ancestors. われらは今やわれらの先祖たちの綜合的成果を享楽する. ¶foresee the fruits of a course of action 一連の行動に対してその結果を予知する. ¶grow fruit for market 果実を作って市場へ出す. ¶I will have some of this fruit preserved. この果実を少し貯蔵させよう. ¶How do you like this fruit? この果実はいかがです. ¶pare a fruit 果実(なしなど)の皮をむく. ¶peel a fruit 果実(バナナなど)の皮をむく. ¶pick wild fruit 野生の果実を摘む. ¶pluck a fruit from a tree 木から果実をもぎ取る. ¶preserve fruit in a pot 果実をつぼに入れて砂糖づけにする. ¶produce (=bear) fruit 実を結ぶ; 結果を産む ‖ to produce the fruit to the best advantage it is necessary to ... 最も効力ある結果を生じるためには…する必要がある. ¶reap the fruit of one's labor 労働の結果を収める.【類】reap the first fruits of her own deeds / reap the fruits of the long struggle of the past century / Russia, France, and Germany interfered to prevent Japan from reaping the fruits of her victory over China. ¶He did not live to see the fruits of his labor. 彼はその努力の成果を見ずに死んで行った. ¶We stored up some fruit for the winter. われわれは冬の用意に果実を少し貯蔵した. ¶strip fruits from trees 木から果実をもぐ. ¶The lawyer touched the first small fruits of success in his profession. その弁護士は自分の職業で得た最初のわずかな金を手にした. ¶yield fruit 実を結ぶ.

V^{2} This fruit does not agree with me. この果実は私の性に合わない(食べるとあたる). ¶The fruit is coming on. 果実がなり始めた. ¶The fruit is getting ripe. 果実が熟してきた. ¶This fruit is going (=turning) fade. この果実は味が落ちてきた. ¶This fruit will spoil if kept too long. この果実は長く置くといたむ.

Q yield more abundant fruit もっと沢山の実を結ぶ ‖ this will no doubt bear abundant fruit in strengthening friendship between ... and ... これは…と…間の交情を固める上において確かに十分の効果を収めることだろう. ¶Bruised fruit will soon decay. きずのついた果実はじきに腐る. ¶choice fruits 選り抜きの果実. ¶crystallized fruits 砂糖づけの果実. ¶delicious fruits 美味な果実. ¶dried fruits 干した果実. ¶early fruits 早い果実, はしり ‖ The fruit is early this year. 今年は実のなりようが早い. ¶This fruit is forced. この果実は温室作り. ¶Olives bear their first fruit when two years old. かんらんの木は二年たって始めて実がなる. ‖ the first fruit of his research 彼の研究の最初のみのり. ¶fresh fruit 新鮮な果実. ¶bear good fruit よい結果を産む.【類】Fruit is good for the health. / This fruit is good to eat. ¶juicy fruit 汁気の多い果実. ¶These efforts seem to have borne little fruit. これらの努力は大した結果を生まなかったようだ. ¶a luscious fruit うまい果実. ¶bear much fruit たくさん実がなる. ¶mural (=wall) fruits 墻(しょう)果. ¶preserved fruits 貯蔵果実. ¶raw fruits なまな実果. ¶That institution has already borne rich fruits. その団体はすでにりっぱな成績を収めている. ¶This fruit is not ripe. この果実は熟していない. ¶a ripe juicy fruit 熟した水々しい果実. ¶sleepy fruits 腐りかけた果実(りんご・なしなど). ¶sound (unsound) fruits 腐りのはいらない(はいった)果実. ¶spoiled fruit 腐った果実. ¶stewed fruit とろ火で煮た果実. ¶succulent fruits 汁の多い果実. ¶sun-ripened fruits 日光で熟した果実. ¶the tangible fruits of their labors 彼らの努力の確実な結果. ¶a tasteless fruit 味のない果実. ¶tropical and subtropical fruits 熱帯及び亜熱帯の果実. ¶Unripe fruit is not wholesome. 未熟の果実は体によくない.

Q^{2} a California fruit 加州産の果実. ¶citrus fruit かんきつ類. ¶a dessert fruit デザートに出る果実. ¶foothill fruit 山ろく丘りょうでできる果実. ¶luxury fruit ぜいたくな果実. ¶a stone fruit たねのある果実. ¶a waxwork fruit ろう細工の果実.

P a dealer in fruit 果実商人 ‖ a cherry tree in fruit 実のなったみざくら(実桜). ¶a cluster of fruit 一ふさの果実 ‖ Lessons so conducted will bear the maximum of fruit. 学課をこういう風に教えると最大効果を産む. ¶The animal lives on fruit. その動物は果実を常食とする. ¶trees heavy with fruit 枝もたわわになっている木.【類】The branches bent low with ripened fruit.

P^{2} fruits from the tropics 熱帯産の果実. ¶fruit in (out of) season しゅん(しゅんはずれ)の果実 ‖ fruits in sugar 砂糖づけの果実. ¶fruits of the earth (=ground) 地の作物 ‖ fruit of prime quality 上等の果実 ‖ the fruits of industry (labor) 勤勉(など)の結果 ‖ fruit of a misdirected zeal 指導宜しきを得ない熱心の結果 ‖ the fruit of his father's amours before his marriage 父が結婚前にできた子 ‖ The boy is the fruit of this union. その男の子がこの結婚における愛の結晶である. ¶the fruit on the tree 木になっている実.

fruitage, *n.* 結実; [団] 果実.

V bear richest fruitage 非常に豊富に実を結ぶ.

fruit-cake, *n.* フルーツケーキ.

V^{2} The fruit-cake contains dried currants and raisins. そのフルーツ・ケーキにはほしぶどうが入っている.

fruitful, *a.* 実の多い; 豊かな, 豊富な.

P The years spent there were fruitful in friendships. そこで送った年月に多くの友を得た. ‖ China is fruitful in material (=natural) resources. 中国は天然資源に富んでいる.【類】a session fruitful in great measures (重大法案). ¶He is fruitful of expedients (=devices). 彼は策略に富んでいる.【類】an enterprise fruitful of the best results ‖ an assembly fruitful of controversy, and barren of effect 議論沢山で成績のあがらない会合.

fruitfulness, *n.* 多数, みのりの多いこと.

V Machinery increases the fruitfulness of human industry. 機械は人間努力の効果を増す.

fruiting, *n.* 収穫.

P barren orchards which grow for twenty years without fruiting 二十年間無収穫の不生産的な果樹園.

fruition, *n.* 成果.

P hopes brought to fruition 成果を生じた希望.

P^{2} the fruition of one's studies 研究の成果.

fruitless, *a.* 効果のない.

P an enterprise fruitless of profit (results) 利益(など)のない事業.

fruit-tree, *n.* 果樹.

V grow fruit-trees 果樹を栽培する.

frustrate, *v.* 失敗させる, ざせつさせる.

P frustrate a person in his designs (scheme) その意図(計画)をざせつさせる ‖ He was frustrated in his first attempt. 彼の最初の試みは失敗に終った.

fry, *n.* 揚げ物, フライ.

Q^{2} an oyster fry かきのフライ.

fry, *n.* [団] 小魚, ちび.

Q small fry 小魚; 《米》小物, 雑輩 ‖ catch small fry 小魚をとる ‖ give small fry a lesson in ... ちび共に…のけいこをつけてやる.

fry, *v.* 油で揚げる, フライにする.

P fish fried in oil (butter) 油(など)で揚げた魚. ¶fry it to a crisp, golden brown それをかりかり黄金色になるまで油で揚げる.

frying-pan, *n.* あげなべ(フライパン).

P get out of the frying-pan into the fire.〖諺〗あげなべから火の中へ, 小難を脱しようとして大難にかかる.

fuel, *n.* 燃料, 薪炭.

V add fuel to the fire たき付ける ‖ add fuel to the flame たき付ける; ことを荒立てる. ¶administer fuel to lust 欲望を増長させる. ¶heap fuel on the fire of fleshly lust 肉欲をあおる. ¶put on fresh fuel 燃料を足す.

Q add fresh fuel to a controversy 議論に拍車をかける. ¶gaseous fuel 気体燃料. ¶liquid fuel 液体燃料. ¶There was no fuel left for the stove. 暖炉にたく燃料が残っていなかった.

Q^{2} high octane fuel オクタン価の高い燃料. ¶substitute oil for coal as a marine fuel 石油を石炭の代りに船の燃料とする. ¶motor fuel 発動機の燃料. ¶oil fuel 石油燃料. ¶patent fuel 特許燃料. ¶steam fuels [石炭など]蒸気用燃料. ¶wood fuel 薪.

P Coal is used as (=for) fuel. 石炭は燃料に用いる. ¶owing to [the] lack of fuel 燃料欠乏のため ‖ a cart-load of fuel 車一台の燃料. ¶feed fire with fuel 火に燃料をたす.

fugitive, *n.* 逃亡者.

V track down a "fugitive from justice"「正義の逃避者」「(犯罪人)を追跡する.

Q collar a ***long-missing*** *fugitive* 長いことゆくえ不明だった罪人をつかまえる.

Q^2 hunt a ***jail*** *fugitive* 刑務所から逃亡した罪人を捜索する.

P^2 *fugitives* ***from*** bombed areas 被爆地からの避難者.

fulfil, *v.* 果たす, 履行する.

M *fulfil* duties ***admirably*** 義務をりっぱに果たす. ¶*fulfil* a promise ***to the letter*** りっぱに約束を履行する.

fulfilment, *n.* 履行.

V ***await*** the *fulfilment* of time 他日完成されるはずである.

Q in ***partial*** *fulfilment* of the requirements for a doctor's degree 学位請求の必要事項の一部履行として. ¶the ***punctual*** *fulfilment* of a contract 契約の期限通りの履行.

P ***in*** *fulfilment* of his promise 彼の約束を守って ‖ He married her ***in*** *fulfilment* of an early betrothal. 彼は幼いときの婚約を履行して彼女と結婚した.

full, *n.* 十分, 完全.

V I ***ate*** my *full*. 僕は腹いっぱい食った. ¶I have no time to ***tell*** you the *full* (=particulars) of it. 私は時間がないのでくわしいお話はできない.

P The moon is ***at*** the *full*. 満月だ. ‖ ***at*** the *full* of the moon 満月に ‖ The tide of business was ***at*** the *full*. [市場などの]取引の盛り時であった. ¶I paid him ***in*** *full*. 彼に全部支払った. 【類】payment ***in*** *full*. / The money was returned ***in*** *full*. ‖ It does not explain ***in*** *full*. その説明では十分でない. ‖ The programme could not be carried out ***in*** *full*, owing to the illness of some students who were to have taken part. プログラムは参加するはずであった学生の一部が病気のためにやることができなかった. ‖ The abbreviation "Rev." is always pronounced ***in*** *full*. 略語の "Rev." はいつも "Reverend" と[略さずに]発音する. ‖ What is your name ***in*** *full?* 君の姓名は略さないでなんと言いますか. 【類】write one's name ***in*** *full*. ¶The bloom is ***past*** the *full*. 花は盛りをすぎた. ¶I appreciate your kindness ***to*** the *full*. 御親切は重々感謝します. ‖ carry out ***to*** the *full* the ideas of ... ...の思想を徹底的に実行する. 【類】enjoy ***to*** the *full* all that money and society give a man / He should be punished ***to*** the *full*. / realize ***to*** the *full*.

full, *a.* 充満した, 十分な, 胸一杯の.

M This bottle is only ***half*** *full*. このびんには半分しかはいっていない. 【類】find a bottle ***half*** *full* of whisky. ¶The spacious hall was ***quite*** *full*. 広いホールは全く一杯であった. ¶His heart was ***so*** *full*. 彼は胸が一杯だった.

P The future seems to be *full* ***of*** promise. 将来は希望に満ちているように見える. ‖ The future is full ***of*** hope. 将来は多望だ. ‖ He is *full* ***of*** mischiefs. 彼はいたずらばかりしている. ‖ He is *full* ***of*** fun. 彼はふざけてばかりいる. ‖ be *full* ***of*** anxiety 気が気でない ‖ be *full* ***of*** pep (=energy)《米俗》元気盛んで ‖ He is *full* ***of*** life (=spirit *or* vitality). 彼は元気盛んだ. ‖ He is *full* ***of*** wit (compassion). 彼は機知(など)に富む. ‖ He is *full* ***of*** self-help 彼はあくまで自力で行く. 【類】He is *full* ***of*** pride. / be *full* ***of*** gratitude to ... / be *full* ***of*** juice / a jug *full* ***of*** grape juice / The remark is *full* ***of*** suggestion (示唆に富む). ‖ I have my hands *full* ***of*** business. 僕は仕事で手一杯だ. ‖ young men *full* ***of*** years 春秋に富んだ青年 ‖ He died *full* ***of*** years and honors. 彼は天寿も名誉も十分に享有して死んだ. ‖ Her calendar is *full* ***of*** engagements. 彼女の日常はお約束が多い. ‖ *full* ***of*** errors (blunders, contradictions) 間違い(など)だらけの. ¶The sky is *full* ***of*** stars. 星が降るようだ. 【類】The river is *full* ***of*** ice. / *full* ***of*** meaning / The air was *full* ***of*** the fragrance of a thousand flowers. / a world *full* ***of*** enjoyment / a mind *full* ***of*** doubts / be *full* ***of*** self-confidence ‖ a boy *full* ***of*** dreams and hopes 空想と希望にふけっている少年 ‖ a life *full* ***of*** vicissitudes (=ups and downs) 変転の多い一生 ‖ a cloth *full* ***of*** wrinkles しわだらけの布 ‖ be *full* ***of*** help for ... ...に対して大いに役立つ ‖ be *full* ***of*** guts《俗》きもがすわっている, 腹ができている ‖ be *full* ***of*** go《口語》精力盛んである ‖ volumes *full* ***of*** emptiness つまらないことで埋めた数巻の本 ‖ Those who are *full* ***of*** themselves are generally the emptiest fellows. 自分のことばかりいう人間は大概頭脳の最も空っぽの人間だ. ¶The book is *full* ***to*** overflowing ***with*** information. その本はあふれるばかりに記事が盛られている. 【類】The makers of these machines have their order-books *full* ***to*** overflowing (註文があふれるほど). ‖ The hotel is *full* ***to*** the roof. そのホテルは満員だ. ‖ The theatre was *full* ***to*** suffocation. その劇場は息苦しいほど一杯であった. ‖ a glass *full* ***to*** the brim あふれんばかりについだコップ.

full, *adv.* 満員で.

M Bus after bus comes up *full* ***inside*** and ***out***. 来るバスも来るバスも大入り満員だ(二階のあるバスなど).

full-fashioned, *a.* [くつ下]フルファッションの.

M Ladies' hose are ***mostly*** *full-fashioned*. 婦人くつ下は大ていフルファッションだ.

fullness, *a.* 完全, 十分な.

V all the necessities and luxuries that go to ***make up*** the *fullness* of modern living 現代生活を充実させるあらゆる必要品やぜいたく品.

Q discuss with ***elaborate*** *fullness* of detail 微を尽し細を極めて論じる. ¶be recorded with ***great*** *fullness* 極めて詳細に記録される. ¶He stated the facts with ***some*** *fullness*. 彼はやや詳細にわたって事実を述べた. ¶The matter is covered in a ***well-rounded*** *fullness* in his article. そのことが彼の文に余す所なく記されている.

P ***in*** its *fullness* 十分に ‖ ***in*** some *fullness* of detail かなり詳細に ‖ ***in*** the *fullness* of one's sorrow (joy) 悲しみ(など)のあまり ‖ ***in*** the *fullness* of time 機熟して. ¶cry ***with*** *fullness* of joy at ... ...を狂喜して大声をあげる.

fulminate, *v.* 大かつする.

P *fulminate* ***against*** a person 人をどなりつける.

fumble, *v.* 手探りする; いじくり回す.

P He *fumbled* ***about*** his waist. 彼はしきりに腰のあたりをさがした. ¶They rushed in *fumbling* ***for*** seats. 彼らは座席を得ようとしてどっとはいった. ¶I *fumbled* ***in*** my pocket ***for*** money. 銭が無いかとポケットを探した. ‖ *fumble* ***in*** the darkness ***for*** ... 真暗がりで...手探りする. ¶*fumble* ***through*** the leaves of a huge volume 大きな書物のページをあちこちくる. ¶He *fumbled* ***with*** a soft cap in one hand. 彼は片手でやわらかい帽子をいじくり回した.

fume, *n.* 煙, 臭気; 怒気.

Q ***exhale*** *fumes* 臭気を発散する. ¶the ***bad-smelling*** *fumes* from the crater 火口から発する悪臭の噴気. ¶***deadly*** *fumes* 命取りの噴気. ¶***sulphureous*** *fumes* arising from hot springs 温泉から立つ硫黄のにおい.

Q^2 ***cigar*** *fumes* 葉巻の煙. ¶vents to take away ***cooking*** *fumes* 調理の香を出す通気穴. ¶a Buddhist image blackened with ***incense*** *fumes* 線香の煙で黒ずんだ仏像.

P He is ***in*** a *fume*. 彼はぷんぷん怒っている. ‖ Something has put him ***in*** a *fume* against his wife. 彼はなにか細君に腹を立てた. ¶The air was thick ***with*** the *fumes* of cigar and cigarettes. 空気はタバコの煙りでむんむんしていた.

P^2 *fumes* ***of*** hay ほし草のむっとする臭気. 【類】*fumes* ***of*** heat.

fume, *v.* いぶす.

M *fume* ***away*** [煙・香が]発散する ‖ The chagrin *fumed* ***away***. その無念は晴れた. ‖ The madness of joy will *fume* ***away***. 狂喜が静まるだろう.

P fret and *fume* ***over*** (=***about***) trifles ささいなことでやきもきする. ¶*fume* straw ***with*** sulfur 硫黄で麦わらをいぶす.

P *fumigate* a room ***with*** smoke (sulfur) へやを煙(など)でいぶす.

fumigate, *v.* いぶす.

fun, *n.* 戯れ, 冗談; 面白いこと, 面白味.

V He ***enjoyed*** the *fun* very much. 彼はその冗談を非常に喜んだ. ¶***have*** much *fun* 愉快に思う. ¶We ***had*** lots of *fun* at the picnic. ピクニックは非常に面白かった. ¶Let's ***have*** some *fun*. なにか面白いことをやろう. 【類】***have*** some *fun* with the kids ‖ I have simply been ***having*** a little *fun* with you. 僕はただちょっと君に冗談を言っただけのことだ. ‖ We shall ***have*** no *fun* unless you go with us. 君が同行してくれなければ面白くない. ¶***make*** *fun* of a person in a poem 詩で...をひやかす ‖ ***make*** an enormous *fun* of an event その事件を大騒ぎをやって興じる. 【類】We must not ***make*** *fun* of the ideas others have about God, even though we think that their ideas are false. / You're ***making*** *fun* of me. ‖ ***make*** *fun* with a cat ねことじゃれる. ¶***poke*** *fun* at ... ...を冷かす ‖ ***poke*** kindly *fun* at ... ...に軽く冗談を言う. ¶Publicity ***spoiled*** the *fun*. [微行が見つかったので]興をそがれた.

Q have ***capital*** *fun* at ... ...を素敵に面白がる. ¶It is ***fine*** *fun*. そりゃ本当に面白い. ‖ Fishing is a ***fine*** *fun* when there is a good take. よく釣れると釣りは面白い遊びだ. 【類】We had ***fine*** *fun* with it. ¶it is ***great*** *fun* to ... ...するのは大そう面白い ‖ He is ***great*** (=***good***) *fun*.《俗》彼は非常に面白い人だ. ¶a time for games and ***harmless*** *fun* 競技と無害の娯楽をするとき. ¶a ***huge fun*** 素敵に面白いこと. ¶an ***innocent*** and ***wholesome fun*** 無邪気で健全な遊び. ¶There is not ***much fun*** in that. それはあまり感心しない(面白くない). ¶for the ***pure fun*** of it ほんのなぐさみに. ¶He had ***some fun*** at my expense. あの男は僕が迷惑するような冗談を言った. ¶***What fun!*** こりゃ面白い.

P It is ***for fun*** that they did it. 彼らは冗談にそれをやったのだ. ‖ I thought he was doing it ***for fun.*** 彼は冗談にそれをやっているのだと僕は思った. ‖ just (＝merely) ***for*** the *fun* of doing so そうするのが面白さに. ¶***in fun*** ふざけて ‖ half ***in fun*** 冗談半分に. ¶It is a fine piece ***of fun.*** それはうまいしゃれだ.

function, *n.* (**1**) 機能, 官能; 任務, 役目.

V ***abuse*** one's *functions* 自己の職務を悪用する. ¶one man ***combines*** the *functions* of ... and of ... 一人で…と…の任務を兼ねる. ¶***discharge*** a *function* 職分を尽す. 【類】***discharge*** two *functions.* / ***discharge*** the high *functions* of the university / adequately ***discharge*** their proper *functions.* ¶***dishonor*** one's spiritual *functions* with shameful passions and crimes 恥ずべき欲情や罪悪をもって自分の精神的任務を汚す. ¶You must not ***exceed*** your *functions.* 権限を越えてはいけない. ¶***exercise*** a *function* 役目を実行する ‖ ***exercise*** governmental *functions* 政府の職責を行う. ¶properly ***fulfil*** its *function* as educator 教育機関としての任務を適当に果す. 【類】A university should ***fulfil*** its social *function.* / She is wholly unfit to ***fulfil*** her *function* in society. ¶It ***has*** no useful *function.* それは一向役に立たない. ¶***imperil*** this *function* この職能を危くする. ¶One's nose ***loses*** its *function* through taking cold. かぜを引いて鼻がばかになる. ¶***perform*** an important *function* in ... …という大切な役目を果す ‖ respectively ***perform*** these *functions* これらの機能を分担する. 【類】***perform*** the *functions* of ... / failure to ***perform*** its proper *function* / The *function* was ***performed*** amidst the acclamations (かっさい) of men in every grade of life and holding every shade of opinion. ¶Jealousy, however antisocial it may be, ***retains*** a *function* in zoological economy: viz., to conserve the individual as against the group. さい疑は非社交的なものではあるが動物経済上の役目すなわち群に対抗して個々を保存するという役目を持っている. ¶The appendix ***serves*** no known *function.* 盲腸は今までの研究ではなんらこれという役に立たないものとなっている. ¶***stimulate*** the organic *functions* 身体機能の働きを刺激する. ¶***unify*** the *function* of production with that of distribution 生産の機能と分配機能を統一する.

Q exercise the ***administrative*** *functions* 政治を行う. ¶***bodily*** *functions* 肉体の機能. ¶The capacity to exercise ***civic*** *functions* 公民の任務を遂行する能力. ¶the ***clerical*** *functions* 僧職. ¶Its *function* is mainly ***decorative.*** その役目は主として装飾的である. ¶He has a ***double function*** to perform. 彼は二役勤めなければならない. ¶perform a remarkable ***educational*** *function* in disseminating exact knowledge 正確な知識を伝えるという教育上顕著な仕事をやる. ¶point out ***grammatical*** *functions* 文法上の役目を指摘する. ¶the regularity of one's ***intestinal*** *functions* 腸の機能の順調. ¶***investigative*** *functions* 調査機能. ¶the ***leading*** *function* 主な働き. ¶an organ of ***no known*** (＝***unknown***) *function* 機能の明かでない器官. ¶Their *functions* are ***passive*** rather than ***active.*** 彼らの機能は能動的というよりは受動的である. ¶***organic*** *functions* 器官の機能. ¶the ***primary*** *function* of art 芸術の主なる任務. ¶the ***primary*** and ***indispensable*** *functions* of banking 銀行の主にしてかつ欠くことのできない任務. ¶the ***proper*** *function* of literature 文学の本領 ‖ It is necessary for the ***proper*** *functions* of the bodily organs. それは肉体諸器官の正常な機能に必要だ. ¶a failure of a ***psychic*** *function* 精神機能の衰退. ¶exercise a ***public*** *function* 公務を行う. ¶the most ***sacred*** of all *functions* given to woman 女に授けられたあらゆる任務の中で最も神聖なもの. ¶a ***secondary*** *function* 第二義的な任務. ¶dishonor one's ***spiritual*** *functions* その聖職を汚す. ¶the ***supreme*** *function* of training the rising generation 青年を教育するという至高な任務. ¶Women's ***supreme social*** *function* is bearing and rearing children. 子供を産みかつ育てることが女の最高の社会的任務である. ¶the organization's ***threefold*** *function* この組織の三重の任務. 【類】for the exercise of the ***threefold*** *function* of ..., ..., and ... ¶perform an ***unnatural*** *function* 無理をする. ¶It has another ***vital*** *function* to perform. それには遂行すべきもう一つの重要な任務がある.

Q[2] ***word*** *function* 言葉の役目.

P Punctuation has ***for*** its primary *function* the displaying of grammatical structure. 句読法の主な任務は文法上の構造を示すにある.

P[2] The first *function* ***of*** conscience is to warn. 良心の第一任務は警告するにある. ‖ the *function* ***of*** the heart 心臓の機能.

(**2**) 祭典; 祝宴; 行事.

V ***attend*** a *function* 会に出席する.

Q a great ***annual*** *function* 重要な年中行事. ¶a ***great*** *function* in some great house ある大家の大祝宴. ¶a ***nonpolitical*** *function* 政治的でない会. ¶It was one of the most ***notable*** *functions* of the season. それは季節の最も顕著な会の一つであった. ¶the Society's ***public*** *functions* 同協会の公の会合. ¶attend a ***social*** *function* 社交的祝宴に出席する. 【類】a pleasant ***social*** *function.*

Q[2] ***charity*** *functions* 慈善会. ¶make European dress compulsory at the ***court*** *functions* あらゆる宮廷の儀式には必ず洋服を着用することにする. ¶***evening*** *functions* 晩の会. ¶a ***society*** *function* 協会の行事.

P speak ***at*** a *function* 会で話す. ¶The American people are fond ***of*** *functions.* アメリカ人はお祭りが好きだ.

function, *v.* 役目を果す.

M The telephone does not *function* ***properly.*** 電話の具合が悪い. ‖ make sure that every organ in his body is *functioning* ***properly*** 彼の体の諸器官が正しい働きをやっているかをたしかめる.

P Make yourself familiar with that part of English grammar which *functions* ***in*** correct written and oral speech. 文語や口語の正確さに関係のある英文法の事項をよく覚えるようにせよ.

functionary, *n.* 官吏, 役人.

Q ***blue-coated*** and ***brass-buttoned*** *functionaries* 青い上衣を着た真ちゅうボタンの役人. ¶***civil*** and ***military*** *functionaries* 文武官. ¶***high*** *functionaries* 高官. ¶***petty*** *functionaries* 小役人. ¶***public*** *functionaries,* civil and military 文武の官吏.

functioning, *n.* 作用.

Q Pure air is necessary for the ***proper*** *functioning* of our organs. われわれの諸器官が順調に働くには純良な空気が必要である. ¶the ***smooth*** *functioning* of the executive 行政部の円滑な運営. ¶be essential to the ***successful*** *functioning* of ... …がうまく運用されるために必要である. ¶***swift*** and ***efficient*** *functioning* 敏速有効な機関活動.

fund, *n.* 資金, 基金; 資料, うん蓄; *pl.* 公債.

V ***accumulate*** a *fund* sufficient to ... …するに十分な資金を積む. ¶properly ***administer*** a *fund* 資金を適当に管理する. ¶The banks are beginning to be more cautious in ***advancing*** *funds* for such undertakings. 銀行はそんな企業に資金を貸すことは一層警戒しかけている. ¶***appropriate*** *funds* from a budget 予算から資金を支出する. 【類】***appropriate*** *funds* to finance the event. ¶***arrange*** the reserve *fund* 準備金を整理する. ¶an endeavour to ***benefit*** a *fund* for ... …の資金を支援しようという努力. ¶***build up*** a reserve *fund* 予備金をこしらえる. ¶***commit*** a *fund* to the care (＝charge) of trustees 基金を管理人の手に託する. ¶***contribute*** a *fund* towards ... …に資金を寄付する. ¶***create*** a *fund* 基金を設ける. ¶The traveller's *funds* were ***depleted.*** その旅行者の資金が尽きた. ¶***divert*** *funds* to ... …に基金を流用する. ¶***donate*** to the University a *fund* to be known as "the ... Memorial Foundation" 「…記念基本金」として同大学に基金を寄付する. ¶The Museum ***draws*** no *funds* from the university. 博物館は財政上大学の補助を受けていない. ¶***establish*** a relief *fund* for needy people 貧困者のために救済基金を設定する. 【類】***establish*** a *fund* for the relief of sick and distressed members. ¶***found*** a *fund* 基本金を設ける. ¶I can ***furnish*** the necessary *funds.* 私は必要な資金が出せる. 【類】***furnish*** *funds* for carrying it out. ¶Do the American Communists ***get*** *funds* from Russia? 米国の共産党員はソ連から資金を得るのか. ¶We ***have*** no *funds* in our hands. われわれは持合わせの金がない. ¶***hold*** *funds* amounting to ... …の資金を保有している. ¶Students are eager to ***increase*** their *fund* of knowledge and experience. 学生はその知識や経験を増すことに熱中している. ¶He gave money to ***institute*** a prize *fund.* 彼は賞与基金を設けるために金を寄付した. ¶I have ***kept*** a reserve *fund* in case of accidents. 私は不慮に備える予備金を作って置いた. ¶***open*** a *fund* for the relief of ... ...救済資金の募集を開始する ‖ he has sent us the money to be added to the *fund* recently ***opened*** in our columns for the benefit of ... 彼は本紙で最近募集を開始した...救済資金への寄付としてその金額を送ってきた. ¶Do not ***permit*** *fund* to become exhausted. 資金を切らさないようにして置きなさい. ¶***raise*** *funds* for relief work among the poor of the city 同市貧困者の救済事業に充てる資金を募る. 【類】***raise*** *funds* for the relief of the sufferers (罹災者) by ... / ***raise*** a big *fund* to aid ... / ***raise*** a *fund* in support of this good cause (正しい運動) / *funds* were ***raised*** for the purpose of ... ‖ She tried to ***raise funds*** to finish her college course by acting as book-agents in rural districts. 彼女はいなかで本屋の取次をやって大学課程を修了する資金を調達しようとした. ¶***start*** a *fund* for a new natural science building 新しい博物会館の基金募集を始める. 【類】***start*** a relief *fund.* ¶***subscribe*** *funds* for the support of the new undertaking 新事業の後援に資金応募の予約をする. ¶***swell*** the war relief *fund* 戦時救助基金を増額する. ¶***telegraph*** necessary *funds* 必要な資金を電報で取寄せる. ¶Many bank depositors ***withdrew*** their *funds.* 払戻しする銀行預金者が多かった.

V² Our *funds* are ***running low.*** われらの資金は尽きかけている. ¶His *funds* were ***sinking lower*** and ***lower.*** 彼の持金が益々少くなって来た.

Q He has at present no *fund* ***adequate*** to the undertaking. 彼は今の所この事業に対して十分な資金がない. ¶shortage of ***available*** *funds* 運転資金の欠乏 ‖ after all ***available*** *funds* are exhausted. ¶a ***benevolent*** *fund* 慈善基金. ¶a ***charitable*** *fund* for the benefit of ... ...のための慈善基金. ¶a ***commercial*** *fund* 貿易基金. ¶a ***common*** *fund* 共有資金. ¶a ***contingent*** *fund* 臨時資金. ¶***frozen*** *funds* こげつき資金. ¶The sailor had an ***inexhaustible*** *fund* of stories. その船乗は話の種が尽きなかった. ¶***limited*** *funds* 豊かでない資金. ¶*Funds* are ***low*** in the treasury. 資金が乏しい. ¶apply for ***necessary*** *funds* to ... ...へ必要な資金を請求する. ¶a ***provident*** *fund* 準備金. ¶***public*** *funds* 公金. ¶need ***ready*** *funds* 現金が必要だ. ¶raise ***sufficient*** *funds* for ... ...に対し十分な資金を作る ‖ The check came back marked "Not ***sufficient*** *funds.*" その小切手は「積立金不足」の印がついて戻ってきた. ¶We have such ***trumpery*** *funds* at our disposal to back our ambitions. われわれの希望を実行する資本がいかにも貧弱である. ¶The book has an ***unfailing*** *fund* of information. その本は無尽蔵の知識の庫である.

Q² require a ***building*** *fund* 建築基金を要する. ¶oil money given to ... for ***campaign*** *funds* 運動費として...に支給したガソリン代. ¶***capital*** *funds* including ***building*** *funds* [学校の]建築基金を含む資金. ¶a drive for ***charity*** *funds* 慈善募金運動. ¶the Children's ***Country Holiday*** *Fund* 小児国祭日基金. ¶a ***defense*** *fund* 防衛資金. ¶an ***emergency*** *fund* for the relief of ... ...救済のための非常予備金. ¶an ***endowment*** *fund* 寄付による基金. ¶an ***enterprising*** *fund* 事業資金. ¶an ***equalization*** *fund* 平衡資金. ¶a ***health*** and ***welfare*** *fund* 厚生基金. ¶a ***maintenance*** *fund* 維持資金. ¶***mission*** *funds* 伝道用基金. ¶establish a ***mutual relief*** *fund* 相互扶助基金を設定する. ¶an ***operating*** *fund* 運営資金. ¶a ***prize*** *fund* for literary achievements 文学賞基金. ¶a ***relief*** *fund* 救済資金. ¶a ***research*** *fund* 研究資金. ¶a ***reserve*** *fund* 積立金 ‖ capitalize a portion of ***reserve*** *fund* 積立金の一部を資本化する. ¶a ***retirement*** *fund* 退職基金. ¶The temple has started a ***restoration*** *fund.* その寺は復興資金の募集を始めた. ¶a ***scholarship*** *fund* 奨学資金. ¶a ***sinking*** *fund* 償却資金. ¶***stop-gap*** *funds* 一時しのぎの資金. ¶a ***strike*** *fund* 同盟罷業基金. ¶a ***student aid*** *fund* 学生援助資金. ¶raise a ***sustenance*** *fund* 維持費を調達する. ¶a ***thrift*** *fund* 積立基金. ¶establish ***trust*** *funds* 信託資金を設ける. ¶***war*** *funds* 軍資金. ¶the union's ***welfare*** and ***retirement*** *fund* 組合厚生及び退職基金.

P He is ***in*** *funds.* 彼はふところが暖かい. 【類】I shall not be ***in*** *funds* until the end of this month. ‖ He has £10,000 ***in*** the *funds.* 彼は公債で一万ポンド持っている. ‖ My money is invested ***in*** the *funds.* 私は金は公債にして置く. ‖ put a person ***in*** *funds* 人に金を持たせる. ¶for want ***of*** *fund* 資金難で. ¶He is carrying on his work at Cleveland Western Reserve University ***on*** *funds* granted by the Rockefeller Foundation. 彼はロックフェラー奨学基金から出ている金でクリーヴランド・ウェスターン・リザーヴ大学で研究をやっている. ¶He is ***out of*** *funds* at present. 彼は今の所金がない. ‖ He paid me ***out of*** his own *funds.* 彼は自分のふところから私に払った. ¶the scientists who have worked ***under*** the Abel *Fund* アベル基金の下に働いた科学者たち.

P² Donations of books, or *funds* ***for*** their purchase are welcome. 書物またはその購入費の寄付を歓迎します. ¶He has a *fund* ***of*** humor (common sense, wit, tenderness). 彼はかいぎゃく(など)に富んでいる.

fundamental, *a.* 根本の, 肝要な.

P *fundamental* ***to*** a true comprehension of ... ...を本当に理解するに肝要な. 【類】The ideas of law and order were *fundamental* ***to*** all his political teaching (政治論).

funeral, *n.* 葬儀; 葬列.

V A military *funeral* was ***accorded*** to the old soldier. この老軍人は陸軍葬をもって遇された. ¶***announce*** the *funeral* (=sound the deathknell) of the old internationalism 古い考えの国際主義を葬る. ¶***attend*** (=take part in) his *funeral* 彼の葬儀に参列する. ¶*funerals* economically ***conducted*** 経済的に行われた葬儀. ¶He ***had*** a pauper's *funeral.* 彼は貧民扱いの葬式で埋葬された. ¶The *funeral* will be ***held*** on Monday. 葬式は月曜日に行われる.

Q a ***beautiful*** *funeral* りっぱな葬式. ¶a ***decent*** *funeral* 見苦しくない葬式. ¶an ***elaborate*** *funeral* 盛んな葬儀. ¶a ***large*** *funeral* 参列者多数の葬列. ¶a ***naval*** *funeral* 海軍葬 ¶be their ***own*** *funeral* 自分で自分の墓穴を掘ることになる. ¶a ***showy*** *funeral* 派手な葬式.

Q² a ***State*** *funeral* 国葬.

P scenes ***at*** the *funeral* of ... ...の葬儀光景 ‖ I was ***at*** the *funeral.* 私は葬儀に列した. ‖ I have to be present ***at*** the *funeral.* 私は葬式に行かねばならない. ¶The *funeral* will ***be*** in Shinto rites. 葬儀は神式で行われる.

funnel, *n.* 煙とつ.

Q² a ***dummy*** *funnel* にせの煙とつ(カモフラージのためなど).

funnies, *n. pl.* 《米》漫画, 漫文.

Q² ***Sunday*** *funnies* [新聞の]日曜漫画.

funny, *a.* おかしい.

M be ***irresistibly*** *funny* たまらないほどおかしい. ¶It was ***screamingly*** *funny.* それはきゃっきゃっと言うほどおかしかった.

fur, *n.* 毛皮; *pl.* 毛皮製外とう.

V ***put*** the *fur* of a fox on coats 上着にきつねの毛皮をつける.

Q wear ***expensive*** *furs* 高価な毛皮のオーバーを身につける. ¶a ***glassy*** *fur* ガラスのように光る毛皮.

P He was wrapped ***in*** *furs.* 彼は毛皮のオーバーをまとっていた. 【類】an old lady ***in*** *furs.* ¶The clothes are lined ***with*** *fur.* その服は毛皮の裏が付いている.

furious, *a.* 怒り狂う.

P She was *furious* ***with*** him. 彼女は彼に対してひどく怒っていた. 【類】He was *furious* ***with*** anger.

furlough, *n.* 休暇; 賜暇.

V ***employ*** his *furlough* in ... 彼の休暇を...して暮す. ¶He ***got*** a *furlough.* 彼は休暇を取った. ¶I ***had*** a week's *furlough.* 私は一週間の休暇をもらった.

Q leave for home on a ***short*** *furlough* 短期賜暇で帰国する. ¶their ***stateside*** *furloughs* [国外在住者などの]米本国での賜暇. ¶on ***twelve months'*** *furlough* 一年の賜暇で. 【類】leave for the U.S. for a ***30-day*** *furlough.*

P He returned ***on*** *furlough.* 彼は賜暇で帰った. 【類】foreign missionaries ***on*** *furlough.*

P² his *furlough* ***in*** Europe 彼の賜暇欧州帰国.

furnace, *n.* 炉; 試錬.

Q² a ***blast*** *furnace* 溶鉱炉.

P refine a metal ***in*** the *furnace* 炉火で金属を精錬する ‖ He was tried ***in*** the *furnace.* 彼はきびしい試錬を受けた.

furnish, *v.* 着ける; 給与する; 飾りつける; 造作を付ける.

M No part of England is ***better furnished*** with good hotels and inns than the Thames above bridge. イギリス中でロンドン橋から上手のテムズ川付近ほどりっぱなホテルや旅館のある所はない. ‖ I must *furnish* this room ***better.*** 私

はこのへやをもっとよく飾りつけをしなければならない. ¶a room ***cheerfully*** and ***tastefully furnished*** 明朗に優美に装飾したへや. ¶a room ***comfortably furnished*** 居心地よく装飾したへや. ¶***elegantly furnish*** a room へやを上品に装飾する. ¶a room very ***genteelly furnished*** はなはだ上品な家具の付いているへや. ¶***gladly furnish*** information 喜んで報道する. ¶***furnish*** information ***gratuitously*** 無報酬で照会に応じる. ¶a ***handsomely furnished*** room 美しく装飾したへや. ¶***luxuriously furnish*** ... ...をぜいたくに装飾する. ¶***furnish out*** a dinner table 正さんの食卓を用意する. ¶a house ***partly furnished*** 一部造作付きの家. ☞一般に furnished というと, 家具・造作一切ついた意. ¶a modest room, ***plainly furnished*** 家具の質素な地味なへや. ¶a ***sparsely furnished*** room 家具の少いへや. ¶an office room ***thoroughly furnished*** for all purposes 机・電話など一切完備した何にでも向くオフィス. ¶a composition book ***well furnished*** with examples for practice 練習用の例がたくさん付いている作文書. ‖ I got myself ***well furnished*** as a defense against the sun. 私は日射を防ぐため十分身支度をした.

P a room *furnished* ***in*** luxurious fashion ぜいたくに装飾したへや. ¶*furnish* food ***to*** the hungry 飢えた者に食を与える. 【類】*furnish* tools ***to*** workmen / The company *furnishes* electric power and light ***to*** every town and city in the district. ‖ Meals are *furnished* ***to*** order 命じれば食事ができる. ¶Each car is ***furnished with*** lavatory accommodation. 各車に洗面所を設けてある. ‖ The objects exhibited are ***furnished with*** explanatory labels. 出品には説明札が付いている. ‖ *furnish* the body ***with*** raiment 衣服を体に着ける ‖ *furnish* a person ***with*** materials (money, clothes) 人に材料(など)を供給する ‖ He *furnished* me ***with*** the necessary information. 彼は私に必要な情報を与えてくれた. 【類】*furnish* us ***with*** assistance / The room is ***furnished with*** books and periodicals. / be ***furnished with*** apparatus for ...

furnisher, *n.* 装飾者.

Q^2 an artistic ***house furnisher*** 芸術的な室内装飾家.

furnishings, *n. pl.* 造作, 設備品.

V the *furnishings* of the building were ***supplied*** by ... その建物の造作は...がやった.

Q ***elaborate furnishings*** 凝った造作. ¶***men's furnishings*** 男子装身具. ¶***rich furnishings*** that give elegance to a room 室に優雅の趣を添えるりっぱな設備品. ¶***soft furnishings*** [幕など]柔かい装飾品.

Q^2 ***household furnishings*** 住宅の造作. ¶***mill furnishings*** 「工場の設備.

furniture, *n.* [団]家具, 装具; 内容; 中味.

V ***buy*** some *furniture* for the new house 新築家屋の家具を買う. ¶A plain table and a few plain chairs ***comprise*** all the *furniture* of the room. 質素なテーブルと二三質素ないすがそのへやの家具全部である. ¶***dust*** the *furniture* 家具のちりを払う. ¶***move*** the *furniture* into ... 家具を...に移す. ¶I have ***ordered*** new *furniture*. 私は新しい家具を注文した. ¶***pawn*** all one's *furniture* 家具を全部質に入れる. ¶***remove*** *furniture* [引越などで]家具を運ぶ.

Q particles of dust on ***choice furniture*** 結構な家具の上のじんあい. ¶***collapsible furniture*** 畳込式の家具. ¶***costly furniture*** 高価な家具. ¶I would like ***elegant, solid furniture***. 私は上品でがん丈な家具がいい. ¶***modern and antique furniture*** 近代及び古代式家具. ¶He has not the ***necessary mental furniture***. 彼はそれに必要な知識を持合わしていない. ¶a room with ***poor furniture*** 貧弱な家具のあるへや. ¶***rickety furniture*** ぐらぐらの家具. ¶***trumpery furniture*** 見かけ倒しの家具. ¶***used*** (=***second-hand***) ***furniture*** 古手家具. ¶***worn-out furniture*** 使い古した家具.

Q^2 ***camp furniture*** キャンプ装具. ¶***church furniture*** 教会用備品. ¶***garden furniture*** 庭園備付品. ¶***kitchen furniture*** 台所用具. ¶heavy ***oak furniture*** がっしりしたかしの木の家具. ¶***office furniture*** (desks, safes, letter files, etc.) 事務室用具. ¶representative specimens of ***period furniture*** 時代家具の代表的標本. ¶***school furniture*** 学校備品. ¶***table furniture*** 食卓備品. ¶"***utility***" ***furniture*** 用途が広い重宝な家具.

P several articles ***of furniture*** 五六点の家具 ‖ a set ***of furniture*** 一そろいの家具 ‖ I want this piece ***of furniture*** moved to another part of the room. この建具をあっちに持ってってもらいたい.

P^2 ***furniture of*** one's pocket 懐中の所持金 ‖ ***furniture of*** one's shelves たなの中味(蔵書など) ‖ ***furniture of*** one's mind 心の中味(知識など).

furor, *n.* 熱狂.

Q^2 the ***motion-picture furor*** 映画熱.

furrow, *n.* あぜ. 「land あぜを作る.

V ***break*** a new *furrow* 新天地を開拓する. ¶***cut*** *furrows* in

Q ***newly turned furrows*** 新しく掘り返したあぜ. ¶***upturned furrows*** of a ploughed field すいた畑のひっくり返

further, *adv.* 更に遠く. 」したあぜ.

M A ***mile further***, and we shall be at our journey's end. あと一マイルで目的地に着く.

P get no ***further than*** a step 一歩以上先へ出ない.

furtherance, *n.* 促進, 助長; 贊助.

P ***for*** the *furtherance* of this country's good この国家の利益を増進するために. 【類】***for*** the *furtherance* of medical science and the benefit of mankind / ***for*** the *furtherance* of trade. ¶***in furtherance*** of this idea (these objects) この趣意(目的)で. 【類】Any assistance given ***in furtherance*** of the idea above suggested (上記の案) would be greatly appreciated. / ***in furtherance*** of his master's will / ***in furtherance*** of the principle of ...

P^2 ***furtherance of*** one's interest (talent) 興味(など)の増進.

furthest, *a.* 最も遠い.

P I hope to return in a week ***at furthest***. 私はおそくも一

fury, *n.* 激怒; 狂暴, 激烈. 」週間後には帰れると思う.

V at length unable to ***restrain*** his *fury* 遂に彼の激怒を抑えきれなくなって. ¶***show*** the *fury* of desperation 必死の猛烈さを見せる. ¶***vent*** one's *fury* on ... ...にうっぷんを漏らす.

Q He worked with ***characteristic fury***. 彼は彼一流の猛烈さで働いた. ¶***maniacal fury*** 狂人めいた猛烈さ. ¶She had an air of ***restrained fury***. 彼女は憤怒を抑えているようすだった. ¶***unbridled fury*** 手のつけられない憤激. ¶It excited him to ***ungovernable fury***. それを彼は始末のつかないほど怒った.

P increase ***in fury*** 怒りを増す ‖ He was ***in*** a ***fury***. 彼は立腹していた. ‖ He turned upon me ***in*** a ***fury***. 彼は怒って僕に食ってかかった. ‖ The epidemic (rebellion) raged ***in*** all its *fury*. 伝染病(など)が猛烈を極めた. ‖ ***in*** the ***fury*** of his passion 激怒のあまり. 【類】He destroyed everything ***in*** a *fury*. ¶The typhoon lashed the sea ***into fury***. 台風は怒とうを立たせた. ¶He was stung ***to fury***. 彼はかっと怒った. ¶the storm raged ***with*** such *fury* that ... 暴風雨が非常に猛威をたくましくしたので... ‖ He was beside himself ***with fury***. 彼はわれを忘れて怒った. ‖ His face was livid ***with fury***. 彼は青くなって怒った.

P^2 the *fury* ***of*** war 戦争の猛威.

fuse, *n.* 導火線; ヒューズ.

V ***blow*** a *fuse* ヒューズを飛ばす.

Q^2 a ***detonating fuse*** 爆発導火線. ¶a ***safety fuse*** 安全ヒュ

O The *fuse* is gone. ヒューズが飛んだ. 」ーズ.

fuse, *v.* ヒューズをつける; 《米》合併する.

M *fuse* (=fuze) ***off*** ヒューズが飛ぶ.

P *fuse* minor parties ***into*** a big powerful one 小党を結合

fusion, *n.* 融合, 合併. 」して大政党を作る.

Q the ***recent fusion*** of the two great railways 二大鉄道の最近の合併. 「融点.

P metals ***in fusion*** 溶解した金属. ¶the point ***of fusion***

P^2 a *fusion* ***of*** ... ***into*** one (=a whole) ... を融合して一つ

fuss, *n.* 空騒ぎ, 騒動. 」にすること.

V I don't ***have*** a ***fuss made*** about such nonsense. 私はそんなばかげたことに空騒ぎはさせない. ¶***make*** such a *fuss* about it 大騒ぎをする ‖ ***make*** a *fuss* about nothing なんでもないことに空騒ぎをやる. 【類】***make*** much *fuss* about trifles.

P a great deal ***of fuss*** was made over ... ...について大騒ぎがあった. ¶He asked himself why he had made all that ***fuss about*** so simple a matter. 彼はなぜそんな簡単なことに大騒ぎをやったものかと自分に問うてみた.

fuss, *v.* 騒ぎ立てる.

M^2 Don't ***fuss up*** about trifles. つまらぬことに大騒ぎをするな. 【類】He was all ***fussed up*** about nothing.

P Don't ***fuss about*** me. 私のことはかまわないで下さい.

fussy, *a.* 大騒ぎの.

P be very ***fussy about*** food 食物にこうるさい. ‖ They

were *fussy* ***about*** her new clothes.

futility, *n.* 無効.

Q a *tragic futility* 悲惨な徒労. ¶the ***utter futility*** of ... ...の全然無効なこと.

P[2] the *futility* ***of*** such a hope あだ.

future, *n.* 未来, 将来.

V ***anticipate*** a prosperous *future* 栄える将来を予想する. ¶This ***assures*** it a *future* of importance. 将来それが重要なものになることはこれで明らかだ. ¶***augur*** a better *future* よりよい未来を約束する. ¶Your *future* is ***bound up*** with the fate of your fatherland. 君らの運命は祖国の運命と関連している. ¶***brighten*** the *future* of ... ...の将来を明朗にする. ¶***carve out*** one's own *future* 自己の運命を開拓する. ¶***face*** a bright *future* 明るい将来に向う. ‖ I can't let you ***face*** the *future* alone. 今後お前を一人で浮世の荒浪にあてるに忍びない. ¶***forecast*** the *future* of the opera on the screen 映画歌劇の将来を予想する. ¶No sane man imagines that he can foretell the *future* with accuracy. 狂人でもなければ未来を正確に予言しうるなどと思わない. ¶a business that ***has*** a *future* 将来性のある事業. ¶He ***has*** a big *future* ahead of him. 彼は前途に大きな未来を持っている. ‖ ***have*** a long *future* before one 春秋に富む. ¶***imperil*** the *future* of ... ...の将来を危くする. ¶***leave*** the *future* to providence 将来を天に任せる. ¶***map out*** one's *future* 将来の計画を立てる. ¶help ***mold*** the *future* of our country わが国の将来をりっぱに築き上げる助けになる. ¶***place*** the *future* of the institution beyond fear of financial collapse 同協会の将来をして財政上破たんの憂のないようにする. ¶***plan*** the *future* hopefully 希望を持って将来の計画を立てる. ¶***predict*** the *futures* of boys 少年たちの将来を予言する. ¶***prospect*** the *future* by the light of the past 過去によって未来を判断する. ¶***ruin*** one's *future* 一生を棒に振る. ¶No man ever ***saw*** the *future*. 未来を見た者はない. ¶help to ***shape*** the political *future* of the country その国の政治的将来を建設する助けとなる. 【類】These are important factors in ***shaping*** the *future* of our country. / It plays an important part in ***shaping*** Japan's *future*. ¶it ***suggests*** a great *future* for ... それは...に対して偉大な将来を暗示する. ¶***view*** the *future* optimistically 将来を楽観する.

V[2] predict what the *future* ***holds*** in reserve for us われわれの将来(の運命)を予言する.

Q help towards the ***better*** *future* of his country 彼の国の将来を一層よくすることに助力する. ¶He has a ***bright*** *future*. 彼には輝やかしい将来がある. ‖ with a ***bright*** *future* ahead 前途洋々として. ¶A ***brilliant*** *future* lay before her. 彼女には輝やかしい前途があった. ¶He has a ***dark*** *future* before him. 彼の前途は暗たんとしている. ¶in the ***dim*** *future* ぱんやりした未来に. ¶in some ***distant*** (=***far-off***) *future* ある遠い未来において ‖ in no ***distant*** *future* 遠からざる未来において. 【類】the more ***distant*** *future* of the market. ¶predict a ***fine*** *future* for ...のために幸(さち)ある未来を予言する. ¶in the ***foreseeable*** *future* 見越しうる将来において. ¶a ***glorious*** *future* 光輝ある未来. ¶a ***good*** *future* 楽しい未来. ¶there is a ***great commercial*** *future* for ... ...には商業(財政)上大きな将来性がある. ¶May the *future* of the Netherlands be even ***greater*** than her past! オランダ国万々歳! ¶a ***hopeful*** *future* 有望な将来. ¶in the ***immediate*** *future* 最も近い将来において. ¶in the ***near*** *future* 近い将来において. ¶There is ***no*** *future* to it. それには発展性がない. ¶A great ***political*** *future* lay before him. 彼の前途には偉大な政治的将来があった. ¶in the (not) ***remote*** *future* 遠(くな)い未来において ‖ in some more or less ***remote*** *future* 多少遠い未来において. ¶The *future* of our industries and foreign trade is by no means ***rosy***. わが国の産業ならびに外国貿易の将来は決して楽観を許さない.

P He is building castles in the air ***about*** his *future*. 彼はその将来について空中楼閣を描いている. ¶***at*** the not very distant *future* あまり遠くない将来に. ¶The infant born yesterday will be a very old man ***before*** a distant *future*. きのう生れた赤ん坊でも遠からず老翁となるであろう. ¶mechanical civilization ***for*** the *future* 未来の機械文明. ¶I ordered him to be more careful ***for*** the *future*. 私は将来一層気を付けるように彼をいましめた. ‖ Such a bad practice must be discontinued (=abandoned) ***for*** the *future*. そういう悪習は今後は廃さなければならない. ‖ I have done with you ***for*** the future. これで君とは絶交だ. 【類】A married man ought to provide ***for*** the *future* of his family. / You know how anxious she was ***for*** your *future*? ¶I hope I shall be more prompt ***in*** the *future*. 今後は一層敏速にやりたいものです. ‖ That day is dim ***in*** the *future*. その時代は遠い将来に属する. ¶glance ***into*** the *future* 将来を見通す ‖ look far ahead ***into*** the *future* 遠い将来に思いをはせる. ¶Aluminium is the metal ***of*** the *future*. アルミニウムは将来性のある金属である. ‖ judge ***of*** the *future* 未来を判断する ‖ This is the problem ***of*** your own *future*. これは君自身の将来に関する問題だ. ‖ those who are ***of*** the *future* (past) 未来有望の(過去に属する)人々 ‖ look forwerd ***to*** the *future* in the light of the past 過去の光で将来を照して見る. ¶look upon it as a cloud ***upon*** *future* それを未来にかかる一片の雲のごとくに見なす. ¶a country (youngster) ***with*** a *future* 将来のある国(など) ‖ an industry ***with*** *futures* 発展性をもつ産業.

P[2] She has a great *future* ***as*** a singer. 彼女には歌手としての大きな将来がある. ¶We see a bright *future* ***before*** him. われわれは彼に輝やかしい将来のあることを知る. ¶What will be the *future* ***of*** Japan? これからの日本はどうなるか.

futurity, *n.* 〖文法〗未来.

Q *simple futurity* 単純未来.

G

gab, *n.* むだ口.

V ***flow*** the *gab*=tip off one's secret 秘密を漏らす. ¶***Stop*** your *gab*! おしゃべりは止せ.

gabble, *v.* おしゃべりをする.

M You *gabble* me ***crazy***. そうぎゃーぎゃーいうと頭が変になるよ. ¶People *gabbled* ***outside***, no word clearly heard. 表でみんながやがや話していたが一言もはっきり聞取れなかった.

gaberdine, *n.* 〖服飾〗ギャバ[ジン].

Q ***fashion-tailored*** *gaberdines* 新型仕立てのギャバずぼん.

Q[2] 100% ***virgin-wool*** *gaberdines* 百パーセント純毛のギャバずぼん.

gad, *v.* ぶらつく.

M *gad* ***about*** for pleasure every night 毎晩夜遊びに出かける. ¶*gad* ***abroad*** ぶらぶら出歩く. ¶*gad* ***out*** 遊び歩く.

gadget, *n.* 仕掛け.

Q A lighter is a ***simple*** *gadget*. ライターは簡単な器具だ.

Q[2] a ***kitchen*** *gadget* 台所道具.

gaff, *n.* 見世物.

Q[2] a ***penny*** *gaff* 見世物 (安っぽいショーなど).

gag, *n.* さるぐつわ; 冗談.

V ***place*** a *gag* upon freedom of speech 言論の自由を束縛する.

P just ***for*** a *gag* ほんの冗談に.

O What's the *gag*, huh? それどういう意味だい.

gaiety, *n.* 陽気; *pl.* 浮れ騒ぎ.

Q[2] In the seventies the Strand was the center of ***London*** *gaiety*. 一八七〇年にはストランド街はロンドンの盛り場であった. ¶Her sorrow is masked beneath a bright ***surface*** *gaiety*. 彼女の悲しみは明るいうわべだけの陽気さに包まれている.

gain, *n.* 利益, 利得; 増加.

V ***consolidate*** the *gains* already made in war 戦果を確保する. ¶He ***got*** a clear *gain* ***of*** 300 yen. 彼は三百円丸もうけをした. ¶***have*** a double *gain* 両得をする. ¶***make*** quick *gains* どんどんもうける ‖ ***make*** a *gain* of a pound in weight 体重が一ポンド増す. ¶The *gain* is ***outweighed*** by the loss. 失う所多く得る所が少い. ¶***seek*** *gain* by immoral practices 色を売ろうとする. ¶***show*** a ***gain*** (loss) 黒(赤)字を出す ‖ ***show*** a ***gain*** in numbers 数において増加している.

Q a ***clear gain*** 手取り, 純収益. ¶He exploited a mine purely for ***commercial gain.*** 彼は全く商売を目的として鉱山を開いた. ¶a ***considerable gain*** 非常なもうけ. ¶a ***counterbalancing gain*** うめ合わせの利益. ¶a ***distinct gain*** 確かな利益. ¶a ***double gain*** 二重の利益. ¶a ***doubtful gain*** おぼつかない利益. ¶***fraudulent gains*** 不正なもうけ. ¶it would be a ***great gain*** to ... それは...にとって大きな利益となるだろう. ¶A priest's ***gross gains*** are net profits. 坊主丸もうけ. ¶***ill-gotten gains*** 不正な利益. ¶an ***illicit gain*** 不正の利得. ¶***important gains*** have been made in ... ...に大きな進歩が見られた. ¶***material gains*** 物質的利益. ¶***moral gains*** 無形の利益. ¶have a ***net gain*** of ... ...の純益がある. ¶***No gains*** without pains. 骨折なくして利得なし. ¶***work*** for better pay and ***other gains*** for wage-earners 労働者の賃金値上げその他の利得のため運動する. ¶Their motive is not ***pecuniary gain.*** 彼らの動機は金銭上の利益ではない. ¶prefer the public welfare to ***personal gain*** 個人的利益よりも公衆の福利を念願とする. ¶Taken all in all, the loss of inflections in English is a ***positive gain.*** 大体から見て英語に語尾の変化がなくなったことは明白な利益である. ¶a privately owned enterprise, prosecuted for ***private gain*** and profit 個人の利益と収得を目的に実行した個人の事業. ¶a ***prodigious gain*** ぼろいもうけ. ¶His ***gains*** are ***small.*** 彼の利得は少額だ. ¶get very ***substantial gain*** from ... ...から多大の利益を得る. ¶make ***sufficient gain*** in weight 体量が十分増す.

Q² a ***Communist gain*** 共産党の利得. ¶***10 per cent gain*** on investment 投資額に対する一割のもうけ.

P ***for gain*** 欲得で.

P² a ***gain in*** flesh (weight) 肉(など)が付くこと. ¶love ***of gain*** 利欲 ‖ a ***gain*** (=an increase) ***of*** 10 per cent over 1911 一九一一年に比し一割の増加 ‖ the ***gain of*** business 商売のもうけ. ¶the ***gain over*** the cost of ... ...のコストを上回る利益. ¶a ***gain to*** the cause of morality 道徳上喜ぶべきこと.

gain, *v.* 利益する, 得る; 増す; 勝つ; 侵食する.

M The sick man ***gains daily.*** 病人が日増しによくなる.

M² ***gain*** him ***over*** 彼を引入れる(ろう絡する).

P ***gain by*** losing 損をして得を取る ‖ It ***gains by*** comparison. 比較するとかえって得になる. 【類】But this can only be ***gained by*** practice. / He has nothing to ***gain by*** telling a lie. ¶the book ***gained for*** its author the patronage of ... その本で著者は...からの支援を得た. ¶***gain*** something ***from*** an experience (a conference) 経験(など)から何物かを得る. ¶Fashion ***gains in*** brilliancy every year. 流行は年々はなやかになる. ‖ ***gain in*** favor [商品など]受けがよくなる. 【類】***gain in*** health (beauty, weight, strength) / The holiday resort is ***gaining in*** popularity with travel-loving people. / ***gain*** ten pounds ***in*** weight / ***gain in*** respect and reverence. ¶***gain on*** him in a race 競走で彼に追いつく ‖ The sea is ***gaining on*** the land along the coast. 海は海岸一帯の陸地を侵食している. ‖ The days are ***gaining on*** the nights. 日が長くなりつつある. ‖ Pumps are now ***gaining on*** the water. ポンプは今水を吸い上げている. 【類】Faster! He's ***gaining on*** you. ¶***gain ... over*** to one's side ...に自分の方の肩を持たせる. ¶He is ***gaining upon*** his master's heart by degrees. 段々主人に気に入られるようになっている. ¶Nothing can be ***gained without*** an effort. 骨を折らなくては何も得られない.

O I've ***gained*** 10 pounds since over here. [外人など]こちらへ来てから十ポンド目方がふえた.

gait, *n.* 歩きぶり, 足どり.

V He ***has*** an unsteady ***gait.*** 彼の足取りはあぶなっかしい.

Q an ***affected gait*** 気取った歩きぶり. ¶at an ***awkward gait*** 足どりも危なかしく. ¶This horse has an ***even gait.*** この馬は歩きつきが整っている. ¶The horse went off at a ***fast gait*** down the road. 馬は道を早足で行った. ¶a ***heavy, awkward gait*** 重々しいぎこちない足取. ¶a ***mincing gait*** (小刻みの)気取った歩き振り. ¶walk in a ***jerky gait*** ぎこちない足取で歩く. ¶walk with a ***shuffling gait*** 足を引きずって歩く. ¶a ***slovenly gait*** だらしない歩き方. ¶He was riding at a ***slow gait.*** 彼は騎馬でゆっくりやって行った. ¶His ***gait*** was ***ungainly.*** 彼の歩きぶりは無様だった. ¶with an ***unsteady gait*** おぼつかない足どりで.

gaiters, *n. pl.* ゲートル.

Q² a pair of ***leather gaiters*** 皮ゲートル一足.

galaxy, *n.* きら星のような一群.

P² a ***galaxy of*** beauties 美人の群 ‖ a ***galaxy of*** candles ずらりと列んだろうそく.

gale, *n.* 強風, 疾風.

V It came on to ***blow*** a ***gale.*** 大風になった. ‖ It is ***blowing*** a ***gale.*** 大風だ. ¶The vessel ***encountered*** a heavy ***gale*** in the vicinity of the Japanese coast. 同船は日本沿岸で大強風に会った.

V² The ***gale increases.*** 強風が強まる. ¶The ***gale subsides.*** 強風が吹き止む.

Q a ***brisk gale*** 強風. ¶an ***equinoctial gale*** 彼岸のころの強風. ¶a ***fresh gale*** 疾強風. ¶It is blowing a ***full gale.*** 本式の強風が吹いている. ¶a ***gentle gale*** 軟風. ¶a ***heavy gale*** 烈風. ¶a ***high gale*** 強風. ¶a ***moderate gale*** 中位の強風. ¶encounter a ***severe gale*** and heavy seas 烈風と荒浪に出会う. ¶The boat foundered in a ***stiff gale.*** その小舟は強い風で沈んだ. ¶a ***strong gale*** 大強風. ¶She was totally wrecked during a ***terrific gale.*** 船は烈風で完全に破壊された. ¶a ***tremendous gale*** 猛烈な強風. ¶a ***violent gale*** 烈風. ¶a ***whole*** (=***hard***) ***gale*** 全強風.

Q² a ***fifty-five-mile-an-hour gale*** 時速五十五マイルの疾風.

P The ship was driven on the rock ***in*** a ***gale.*** その船は烈風で暗礁に乗り上げた.

P² a ***gale from*** the north (the sea) 北(など)から吹く強風.

gall, *n.* 《米俗》ずうずうしさ.

V ***have*** the ***gall*** to ... ずうずうしくも...する.

P I'm astonished ***at*** his ***gall*** (=cheek). あいつの図々しいのには驚く.

gallant, *n.* 当世男, やさ男.

V ***play*** the ***gallant*** (=cavalier) to a lady 婦人に優しくする.

gallant, *a.* 女にやさしい.

P ***gallant to*** ladies 婦人にやさしい.

gallantry, *n.* 勇敢, 豪気; [婦人に対する]いんぎんさ.

V He ***displayed*** great ***gallantry*** in trying to save a lady from drowning. 彼は婦人のでき死を救おうとして非常に勇敢な働きをした.

Q ***dare-devil gallantry*** 命知らずの蛮勇.

P ***for gallantry*** in action 勇敢な行動のゆえをもって. ¶He was seen escorting her ***with*** great ***gallantry.*** 彼は丁重いんぎんに彼女を送って行った.

gallery, *n.* 聴衆席; 向うさじき; 美術品陳列場.

V ***fascinate*** the ***gallery*** 大向うをうならせる. ¶The photographer ***has*** his own ***gallery*** in ... street. その写真師は...町に陳列場を持っている.

Q the ***reporter's gallery*** [国会などの]記者席. ¶***sky-lighted galleries*** 天窓のある美術品陳列場.

Q² an ***art gallery*** 美術品陳列所. ¶a ***picture gallery*** 画廊. ¶the ***press gallery*** in the House [of Representatives] 下院の新聞記者席. ¶a ***shooting gallery*** 射的場.

P go ***to*** the ***gallery*** [芝居の]立見に行く ‖ play ***to*** (=***for***) the ***gallery*** [俳優など]大向うに受けるようにやる.

P² a ***gallery of*** paintings 絵画館.

galley, *n.* ゲラ刷り(印刷).

P set type ***in galley*** 棒組にする ‖ read proofs ***in galley*** ゲラ刷で校正を読む.

gallon, *n.* ガロン.

P sell ***by*** the ***gallon*** 一ガロンいくらで売る.

gallop, *n.* [馬の]かけ; かけ足.

V We ***had*** a ***gallop*** through the field. われわれは馬を飛ばして原を通り抜けた.

Q at ***full gallop*** かけ足で. ¶make progress at a ***snail's gallop*** 牛歩のあゆみを続ける.

P The horse, feeling the whip, started ***at*** a ***gallop.*** むちをあてられて馬はかけ出した.

gallop, *v.* [馬が]かける; 全速力でかける; ざっと読む.

M ***gallop away*** まくし立てる.

M² ***gallop down*** two flights of steps 階段二つをかけ降りる. ¶***gallop off*** at top speed 全速力でかけ去る.

P The horse ***galloped at*** full speed. 馬は全速力でかけた. ¶***gallop over*** (=***through***) a book ざっと本に目を通す.

gallows, *n.* 絞首台.

V He ***has*** the ***gallows*** in his face. あの人相では絞首台行きだ.

P The criminal was hanged ***on*** the ***gallows.*** 罪人は絞首刑に処せられた. ¶He came ***to*** the ***gallows.*** 彼は絞首台の露と消えた.

galvernize, *v*. [電気をかけたように]急に活気づかせる.
P be *galvernized* ***into*** action (life) 急に活発に動き出す(生き返る).

gamble, *v*. とばくでなくす; かけ事をする.
M He *gambled* ***away*** £80,000 (all his fortune). 彼は八万ポンド(など)をとばくでなくしてしまった.
P *gamble* ***at*** cards 花札(トランプ)でばくちをやる. ¶*gamble* ***in*** stocks (wheat) 株(など)の投機をやる. 【類】*gamble* ***in*** oil shares (石油株). ¶*gamble* ***on*** horse-races (exchange) 競馬(など)でかけ事をやる. ¶He *gambled* himself ***out of*** house and home. 彼はばくちで身上をつぶした. ¶*gamble* ***with*** others ***on*** ... ...について人とかけをやる.

gambler, *n*. とばく者, ばくち打ち.
Q an ***inveterate*** *gamblers* 常習的ばくち打ち. ¶an ***out-and-out*** *gambler* 全くのばくち打ち.
Q[2] a ***boss*** *gambler* ばくち打ちの親分. ¶a ***stock*** *gambler* 株投機師.

gambling, *n*. とばく, ばくち.
V ***give up*** (=***quit***) *gambling* ばくちをやめる.
Q ***organized*** *gambling* 組織化したばくち.
P He has a passion ***for*** *gambling*. 彼はばくちが大好きだ. ¶He lost a lot of money ***in*** *gambling*. 彼はばくちで金をうんとなくした. ‖ indulge ***in*** *gambling* ばくちにふける. ¶a form ***of*** *gambling* 一種のばくち. ¶He ran through all his money ***through*** *gambling* and drink. 彼は打つ飲むで金を皆なくしてしまった. ¶He is given up ***to*** *gambling*. 彼はばくちにふけっている.

game, *n*. (**1**) 勝負事, 競技(ゲーム), 遊戯; [比ゆ的に] 作戦, 手; 冗談.
V ***attend*** a *game* 試合を見に行く. ¶The *game* will be ***called*** at 3 sharp. 競技は正三時に始まる. ¶***cancel*** a *game* 競技を取消す. ¶We ***carried off*** the *game*. われわれは競技に勝った. ¶Never ***enjoyed*** a *game* so much in my life. こんな面白い勝負は今までにない. ¶Will you ***have*** a *game?* 一勝負やりませんか. ‖ ***have*** a *game* at cards (billiards, baseball) カルタ(など)を一勝負やる. ¶The Olympic *Games* were ***held*** in Australia in 1956. オリンピックは一九五六年に豪州で開かれた. ¶They ***lost*** their *game*. 彼らは負けた. ¶***make*** *game* of a person 人をからかう ‖ You are ***making*** *game* of my calamities. 君は僕の災難をひやかしている. ¶players "facing" in ***opening*** a *game* of ... ...の競技開始に当って顔合わせの選手. ¶***play*** *games* with ... ...と勝負をやる ‖ ***play*** a *game* with marbles ビーズ(玉の遊戯)をやる ‖ ***play*** a fair *game* at chess 将棋で正々堂々と戦う. 【類】***play*** a *game* of football / ***play*** the *game* of hide-and-seek / ***play*** *games* of pure hazard (一か八か) / Let us ***play*** the *game* fairly. ‖ ***play*** the Kaiser's (=German) *game* カイゼルの手先になる. ¶The ball *game* is ***scheduled*** for 9.30 in the morning. 球戯は午前九時半の開始予定になっている. ¶***spoil*** the *game* しくじる, みそをつける. ¶***start*** a *game* of chess 将棋の勝負を始める. ¶***throw up*** the *game* in despair 絶望してその勝負を投げ出す. ¶Who[m] shall we get to ***umpire*** the *game?* だれに競技の審判をやってもらおうか. ¶***watch*** a baseball *game* 野球を見る. ¶***win*** a *game* at chess 将棋に勝つ. 【類】***win*** two *games* out of three.
V[2] Tell me how the ball *game* ***came out***. 野球はどんな結果になったか.
Q an ***admirable*** *game* りっぱな勝負. ¶Golf is rather an ***aristocratic*** *game*. ゴルフはどちらかというと貴族的な遊戯だ. ¶She was the victim of a ***clever swindling*** *game*. 彼女は巧妙な詐欺的計画の犠牲であった. ¶a ***close*** *game* 手に汗を握らせる勝負. ¶a hotly ***contested*** *game* 熱烈な競技. ¶a ***dangerous*** *game* 危険なゲーム. ¶fight out a ***desperate*** *game* at their master's orders 主命で決死的な勝負をやりとげる. ¶a politician playing a ***difficult*** *game* with a mastery hand さえた腕前で難問を突破する政治家. ¶play a ***double*** (=***deep***) *game* たくらみ事をやる. ¶a ***drawn*** *game* 引分け. ¶an ***educational*** *game* 教育遊戯. ¶He plays an ***excellent*** *game* of tennis. あの人はテニスがなかなかうまい. ¶an ***exciting*** *game* はらはらするゲーム. ¶a ***fascinating*** *game* 心を引き付ける競技. ¶His ***favorite*** *game* is golf. 彼の好きな競戯はゴルフだ. ¶Our team won the ***first three*** *games*. 味方が最初に三番勝った. ¶He plays a ***good*** (poor) *game* of billiards. 彼は玉突がじょうず(へた)だ. ¶***indoor*** (***outdoor***) *games* 室内(戸外)遊技. ¶croquet, "the most intellectual of ***outdoor*** *games*"「もっとも知的な戸外遊戯である」クローケー. ¶I saw through his ***little*** *game* in no time. 私は彼のけちなトリックをすぐ見破った. ¶To act rashly is a ***losing*** *game*. 無鉄砲なことをやっては負けになる. ¶His talk is a ***mere*** *game*. 彼の話はほんの冗談だ. ¶Cricket is the English ***national*** *game*. クリケットは英国の国技である. ‖ Baseball, borrowed from America, is now Japan's ***national*** *game*. 米国伝来の野球は今や日本の国民的ゲームである. ¶a ***one-sided*** *game* [相手に点を取らせない]一方的なゲーム. ¶***open-air*** *games* 戸外競技. ¶The most ***popular*** *game* on board is tennis. 船中の最も人気のある競技はテニスだ. ¶a ***prearranged*** *game* 八百長. ¶The ***same old*** *game!* また例の手だな. ¶a ***sold*** *game* 八百長. ¶Football is a ***students'*** *game*. しゅう球は学生の競技だ. ¶a ***two*** (***four***)***-handed*** *game* 二(四)人でやる勝負ごと. ¶play a ***waiting*** *game* 時機を待つ, 潮待をする. ¶Angling is quite a ***waiting*** *game*. 釣は相当気の長い遊びだ. ¶So that is ***your*** *game*, is it? I thought so. 人を乗せようというのだな, そうだろうと思った. ‖ None of ***your*** *games!* その手は食わぬ. ¶That's ***your*** little *game!* そんな幼稚な手は食わんよ.
Q[2] in their ***ball*** (=baseball) *game* against ... 対...の野球試合で. ¶watch a ***baseball*** *game* 野球を見る. ¶a ***card*** *game* トランプ遊び. ¶a ***championship*** *game* 選手権(優勝)試合. ¶Potter was arrested on a charge of operating a ***confidence*** *game*. ポッターは取込み詐欺をやったけん疑で逮捕された. ¶a "***dream*** *game*"〘野球〙[オールスターの]ドリーム・ゲーム. ¶hold ***dice*** *games* ばくちを開帳する, さいころ遊びをやる. ¶an ***exhibition*** *game* 模範試合 (勝負に重きを置かず技術を示すのが目的の競技). ¶***field*** *games* 野外(フィールド)競技. ¶Card-playing is one of the most common of ***family*** *games*. トランプは最も普通な家庭遊戯の一つである. ¶a numbers ***gambling*** *game* 数を当てる勝負ごと. ¶a ***guessing*** *game* あてっこ遊び. ¶play a ***hide-and-seek*** *game* with ... ...とかくれんぼをやる. ¶a ***love*** *game* 零敗のゲーム ☞ a love match は「自由結婚」. ¶a ***National League*** *Game* [米野球の]ナショナル・リーグ側のゲーム. ¶an ***open*** *game*〘競〙オープンゲーム(公式選手権試合に対し, 自由組合わせ試合). ¶a ***parlor*** *game* 室内遊戯. ¶a ***pit*** *game* 闘鶏. ¶a ***practice*** *game* 練習試合. ¶a ***proball*** *game* 職業野球試合. ¶a ***regulation*** *game*〘野球〙公式試合. ¶a ***seesaw*** *game* シーソー・ゲーム. ¶the ***spring*** *games* at a college 大学の春の競技. ¶a ***string*** *game* 糸取り遊び. ¶a ***team*** *game* チームに別れてやる試合. ¶the honor roll of the Fourth Olympic ***Winter*** *Game*, 1936 一九三六年の第四回冬期オリンピック競技参加選手の優勝者名簿.
P spend an evening ***at*** a *game* of cards トランプをやって晩を過ごす ‖ have fun ***at*** a *game* 一ゲームをやって楽しむ ‖ good ***at*** *games* 勝負事がうまい ‖ That's a *game* ***at*** which two can play. その手で来ればこっちもその手で行くまでだ(負けているものか). ¶***in*** the *game* of life 人生という競技において ‖ loss ***in*** a *game* of patience 根気まけ.
P[2] a *game* ***at*** dominoes (dice, chess) ドミノ札(など)遊び. ¶*games* ***for*** money=gambling とばく. ¶a *game* ***of*** skill 手練のいる勝負ごと ‖ a *game* ***of*** chance 一六勝負 ‖ the *game* ***of*** diplomacy 外交上のかけ引き. ¶*games* ***with*** cards トランプ遊び ‖ *games* ***with*** other schools 他校との試合 ‖ We had such a *game* ***with*** him. われわれは彼と非常に面白いことをした.
(**2**) [団]狩猟; 鳥獣.
V ***bag*** *game* 獲物を手に入れる. ¶***bring down*** the *game* 猟鳥を射落とす. ¶***chase*** (=***pursue***) the *game* 獲物を追う. ¶He did not ***get*** any *game*. 彼は猟の獲物はなかった. ¶***hunt*** big *game* [ライオンなど]大物狩りをする. ¶***shoot*** *game* 猟鳥獣を射る. ¶***start*** (=***rouse***) the *game* 猟鳥獣を狩り出す. ¶The hounds ***trace*** the *game* by the scent. 猟犬は臭気で獲物を追跡する.
Q He was looked upon as ***fair*** *game*. 彼はいいむくどりと見られた. 【類】a ***fair*** *game* for the crook (悪漢). ¶***forbidden*** *game* 禁猟の鳥獣. ¶***winged*** *game*=game fowl 猟鳥.

gamester, *n*. ばくち打ち.
Q a ***notorious*** *gamester* 名うてのばくち打ち.

gamin, *n*. *F*. 浮浪児, 不良少年.
Q from Royalty to the ***street*** *gamin* 上は皇族から下はちまたの浮浪児に至るまで.

gamut, *n*. 全範囲.
V ***feel*** the whole *gamut* of emotional experience 感情上

のあらゆる経験を味う. ¶***run*** the *gamut* of dissipation 放とうの限りを尽す ‖ ***run*** the *gamut* of emotions あらゆる感情を経験する ‖ He ***ran*** the *gamut* of Russian-American relations. 彼は米ソ関係の全体にわたって論じた. 【類】He has ***run*** the *gamut* of disease. / Old Chinese gowns ***run*** the *gamut* of gorgeous hues.

Q the ***entire*** *gamut* of theology 神学の全範囲 ‖ run the ***entire*** *gamut* of ... ...の全般にわたる. ¶the ***whole*** *gamut* of literary production 文筆業の全貌.

P The stocks were running up and down the *gamut* ***from*** $10 ***to*** $100 a share. その株式は一株十ドルから百ドルの間を上下していた.

P^2 a *gamut* ***of*** moods—philosophic, poetic, mystic and analytic 哲学的・詩的・神秘的・分析的 というようなあらゆる気分.

gang *n.* 一群, 党類.

Q a ***tough*** *gang* 暴力団.

Q^2 a ***chain*** *gang* じゅずつなぎで服役する囚徒. ¶a ***dress*** *gang* 分業で魚料理をする人など. ¶a ***kidnap*** *gang* 誘かい団. ¶a "***knock-out***" *gang* [競売で]なれ合いせりおとし団. ¶a railway ***repair*** *gang* 鉄道修理班. ¶wipe out "***terrorist*** *gangs*" テロ団を一掃する.

P burglars ***of*** a *gang* 一つ穴の賊.

P^2 a *gang* ***of*** bandits (robbers, conspirators) 盗賊(など)の群 ‖ a *gang* ***of*** laborers 一団の労働者. ¶a *gang* ***of*** children《米》子供の一群.

gang-boss, *n.* 親方.

Q a ***shirt-sleeved*** *gang-boss* シャツ姿になった(土方などの)親方.

gangster, *n.* ギャング.

Q^2 ***underworld*** *gangsters* ギャング仲間.

gaol, =jail.

gap, *n.* 間げき; 峡谷; 切れ目, 空所, 欠陥.

V ***bridge*** the cultural *gaps* of East and West 東西の文化を融合する. ¶to ***fill*** the *gap* その欠陥を補うために. 【類】The work ***fills*** a *gap* which has hitherto existed in our archaeological literature (考古学の文献). ¶advertisers, ***filling up*** *gaps* with ten-year-old snippets from home magazines 本国の雑誌から取った十年前の切抜でお茶をにごす広告機関. ¶His going ***leaves*** a sad *gap* in our circle. 彼が去るのでわれわれ仲間は非常にさびしくなる. ¶***lessen*** the *gaps* which now seem impassable 今は越えそうに思われない間げきを狭くする(天地の懸隔を融和する). ¶His death ***makes*** a *gap* in Scotch writers. 彼の死去はスコットランドの文壇の一損失である. ¶***stop*** a *gap* 間げきをふさぐ.

Q There was an ***awkward*** *gap* in the conversation. 対話が途切れてばつが悪かった. ¶fill a ***definite*** *gap* はっきりしたギャップを埋める. ¶fill a ***distinct*** *gap* in literatuer 顕著な文献上の欠陥を補充する. ¶There is ***no*** great *gap* separating the psychoneurosis from insanities. 神経病と精神病には大した差はない. ¶There is a very ***large*** *gap* to be bridged over. 埋めねばならない一大間げきがある. ¶a ***wide*** *gap* 広い間げき.

Q^2 ***air*** *gap*〖電〗空げき.

P It has been used only ***for*** a stop *gap*. それは埋め草に使われたに過ぎない. ¶see ***through*** a *gap* in the wall 壁のすき間からのぞく. ¶History bridges the *gap* ***between*** the past and present. 歴史は過去と現在の橋渡しをする. ¶*gaps* ***in*** his knowledge of the subject そのことに関する彼の知識中の欠陥. ¶the *gap* ***on*** the wall caused by removal of the portraits 肖像画を取除けたためにできた壁上の空所.

gape, *n.* あくび.

V ***give*** one the *gapes* あくびをさせる. 【類】There was another hour of music which ***gave*** us the *gapes* instead of delight. ¶***have*** the *gapes* しきりにあくびをする.

gape, *v.* あくびする; ぼんやりながめる.

M *gape* ***away*** one's time あくびして時を過ごす. ¶*gape* ***foolishly*** at ... ...をぽかんとして見ている.

P *gape* ***after*** (=***for***) ... ...を欲しがる. ¶stand *gaping* ***at*** ... ...をぼんやり口をあけてながめる.

garage, *n.* 自動車車庫.

Q a ***lock-up*** *garage* 錠が下りる自動車車庫.

Q^2 an ***auto*** *garage* 自動車車庫.

garb, *n.* 服装.

V ***adopt*** the *garb* of women 女装する. ¶***assume*** the *garb* of a navvy (beggar) 土方(など)の服装をする. ¶***take on*** a new *garb* 新しい服を着る. ¶The newspaper ***wears*** an English *garb*. その新聞紙は英国風をまねている.

Q a man in ***clerical*** *garb* 聖服の人. ¶a mountaineer in ***exploring*** *garb* 探検服を着た登山者. ¶in ***foreign*** *garb* 外国の服装をして. ¶in a ***peasant's*** *garb* 野良姿をして.

Q^2 in her ***everyday*** *garb* ふだん着で. ¶a mountain in its ***summer*** *garb* 夏の装いをした山. 【類】the garden in its ***winter*** *garb* (雪原). ¶a ***working*** *garb* 作業服.

P live ***in*** the *garb* of Adam アダムのように裸で生活する ‖ The book has appeared ***in*** English *garb* (=translation). その本は英訳が出た. ‖ Faust ***in*** Japanese *garb* 和訳のファウスト. ¶***under*** the *garb* of a nun 尼に扮して.

P^2 the *garb* ***of*** a priest 僧服.

garb, *v.* 装う.

M a ***comically*** *garbed* man こっけいな服装をした人.

P He is *garbed* ***in*** a foreign dress. 彼は洋装している.

garden, *n.* 庭, 庭園; 畑.

V The *garden* was ***broken up.*** その畑をすき返えした. ¶***build*** a *garden* 庭を造る. ¶***lay out*** a *garden* 庭を設計する. ¶***plant*** a *garden* 庭に木や花を植える. ¶***rake*** a *garden* [with a rake] くまででで庭(花壇, 菜園など)を作る. ¶***trim up*** a *garden* 庭の手入をする. ¶***water*** a *garden* 庭に水をまく. ¶***weed*** a *garden* 庭草をむしる.

Q a tastefully ***arranged*** *garden* 風雅に造った庭. ¶a ***botanical*** *garden* 植物園. ¶a ***noble*** *garden* 高雅な庭園. ¶a ***public*** *garden* 公園. ¶a ***spacious*** *garden* 広い庭. ¶a ***symbolic*** *garden* 象徴的な庭(日本庭園のような). ¶a ***well-shaded*** *garden* 日かげの多い庭. ¶a ***zoological*** *garden* 動物園.

Q^2 an ***allotment*** *garden* 分割してある庭. ¶slake the summer thirst in a ***beer*** *garden* ビーヤガーデンで夏の渇をいやす. ¶a ***concert*** *garden* 野外音楽場. ¶a ***flower*** *garden* 花畑. ¶a ***home*** *garden* 家庭菜園. ¶the ***Kensington*** *Gardens* [英国の]ケンシントン公園. ¶a Japanese ***landscape*** *garden* 日本の山水式庭園. ¶a ***kitchen*** *garden* 菜園. ¶a ***pleasure*** *garden* 子供の遊び場になっている庭園. ¶a ***plum*** *garden* 梅園. ¶a ***rock*** *garden* 岩景園. ¶a ***roof*** *garden* 屋上庭園. ¶a ***truck*** *garden*《米》市場向け野菜を栽培する農園. ¶a ***vegetable*** *garden* 野菜畑 ‖ a flower-bordered ***vegetable*** *garden* まわりに花を植えてある菜園. ¶a ***verandah*** *garden* ベランダ庭園(船などの).

P lay out ***as*** a *garden* 庭に仕上げる. ¶the roses ***in*** the *garden* 庭のばら. ¶The room looks out ***into*** the *garden*. そのへやは庭に面している. ¶Let us take a turn ***round*** the *garden*. 庭を回って見ましょう.

P^2 a *garden* ***of*** rare, beautiful flowers 珍奇で美しい花のある庭園. ¶the *garden* ***of*** the Emperor's Palace 御えん. ¶The house has a *garden* ***to*** it. その家には庭がついている. ¶a *garden* ***with*** pine trees 松の木のある庭.

gardener, *n.* 庭師.

Q^2 a ***landscape*** *gardener* 庭師(日本式庭園の). ¶a ***truck*** (=market) *gardener*《米》野菜栽培家.

gardening, *n.* 庭造り; 園芸.

Q^2 ***vegetable*** *gardening* 野菜作り.

garish, *a.* けばけばしい.

P Her dress is *garish* ***in*** taste and color. 彼女の服装は好みも色もけばけばしい.

garland, *n.* 花環, 花冠; 栄冠.

V ***carry away*** (=***gain, get or win***) the *garland* (競技などで)勝利を得る.

P deck a grave ***with*** a *garland* 墓を花環で飾る.

P^2 a *garland* ***for*** the head 頭にいただく花冠.

garment, *n.* 衣服.

V The nudist ***discards*** a *garment*. 裸体主義者は衣服を用いない. ¶He ***hired*** the *garment* for the day. 彼は当日借着をした. ¶***knit*** *garments* 毛糸で衣服を編む. ¶a *garment* ***lined*** with fur 毛皮裏の上衣. ¶***mend*** a *garment* 着物の繕いをやる. ¶***pick*** a *garment* to pieces 衣服をほどく. ¶***sew*** *garments* 衣服を縫う. ¶***stain*** *garments* 着物をよごす. ¶Suppose you ***take off*** your upper *garments*. 上衣をお脱ぎになったらいかがです. ¶***turn*** *garments* 着物の裏返しをやる. ¶***wear*** a loose *garment* ゆるやかな上衣を着る.

Q clad in ***cast-off*** *garments* 古着を着て. ¶a ***ceremonial*** *garment* 式服. ¶eschew the *kimono* for the more ***liberty-according*** *garments* of the West 日本服をさけて一層体の自由を与える洋服を着る. ¶***man-tailored*** *garments* 男仕立ての女物. ¶***outdoor*** *garments* 外出用の着物. ¶an ***outer*** *garment* 外衣. ¶a ***rented*** *garment* 賃借した着物. ¶***sec-***

ond-hand garments (=clothes) 古着. ¶*seedy garments* 見すぼらしい着物. ¶*sumptuous garments* ぜいたくな着物. ¶a woman's *upper garment* 女の上衣. ¶*worn garments* 着古した着物.

Q² *basement* (=foundation) *garments* 〘服飾〙 フアンデーション(コルセット, ガードルなど). ¶*fashion garments* 流行服. ¶"*ready-to-fit*" *garments* でき合い服. ¶a *sports garment* スポーツ着. ¶a *working garment* worn over our clothes 上張りの作業服.

P a fold *in* a *garment* 上衣のひだ. ¶a change *of garments* 着替え.

P² *garments for* males 男子服. 【類】 *garments for* outing.

garner, *v.* 貯蔵する.

M *garner away* 貯蔵する.

M² wheat *garnered up* for the winter 冬囲いした小麦.

garnish, *v.* 飾る; つけ合わせる.

P an oration *garnished with* metaphors 隠喩(ゆ)で潤飾した演説. ¶*garnish* a dish *with* vegetable 御ち走に野菜をつけ合わせる. 【類】 a room *garnished with* flowers.

garret, *n.* 屋根裏.

P search *from garret to* kitchen (=cellar *to garret*) 家中残らず探す.

garrison, *n.* 守備隊.

V *command* a *garrison* 守備隊を司令する. ¶*place* a *garrison* of 400 men 兵四百の守備隊をおく. ¶*starve* a *garrison* into surrender 守備隊を兵糧攻めにする. 【類】 *starve out* a *garrison*. ¶A *garrison* is *stationed* there. そこには守備隊が駐とんしている. ¶*strengthen* the *garrison* 守備隊を増員する. ¶*surprise* a *garrison* 守備隊の不意打ちをする. ¶The *garrison* had to *surrender*. 守備隊はやむなく降参した.

Q a *standing garrison* 常駐守備隊.

Q² the towns where there are *Army garrisons* 陸軍守備隊の駐とんしている町々. ¶a *token garrison* 名目だけの守備隊.

garrison, *v.* 守備する.

P The city is *garrisoned with* no less than 3,000 soldiers. 同市は三千を下らない兵士で守備されている.

garrulity, *n.* 多弁.

Q the *proverbial garrulity* of age 世話にも言う老人の多弁.

garrulous, *a.* 多弁な.

P a woman *garrulous about* nothing 愚にもつかないことをおしゃべりする女.

gas, *n.* ガス.

V *blow out* the *gas* ガスを爆発させる. ¶*give off gas* ガスを発散する. ¶*lay on gas* ガスを取付ける ‖ Water and *gas* are *laid on*. 水道ガスつき. ¶*leave* the *gas* full *on* for ten minutes ガスを十分間いっぱいに出しておく. ¶*light* the *gas* in the stove ガスストーブに火をつける. 【類】 after the *gas* is *lighted*. ¶*Gas* is *obtained* from coal. ガスは石炭から採る. ¶*put out* the *gas* ガスを消す. ¶*reduce* the *gas* to half full on ガスの出を半分に低める. ¶*shut off* the *gas* ガスをしゃ断する. ¶*smell gas* ガスのにおいに気付く. ¶*turn* the *gas down* ガスの火を細くする ‖ *turn down* the *gas* quite low ガスの火を十分に落す. ¶*turn* the *gas off*=turn off the *gas* ガスを消す. ¶*turn* the *gas on* ガスをつける ‖ boil it up over the *gas turned* threequarter full *on* 四分の三だけ出したガス火にかけてそれを煮る. ¶*turn* the *gas out* ガスを消す. ¶*turn up* the *gas* ガスの火を大きくする.

Q *asphyxiating gas* 窒息ガス. ¶*heating gas* 熱用ガス. ¶*illuminating gas* 灯用ガス. ¶emission of *internal gas* 体内ガスの放出. ¶*noxious gases* 有毒ガス. ¶exhale a *poisonous gas* 有毒ガスを発散する. ¶*toxic gases* 有毒ガス.

Q² carbonic *acid gas* 炭酸ガス. ¶an explosion of *coal gas* 石炭ガスの爆発. ¶*fuel gas* 燃料用ガス. ¶*marsh gas* 沼気. ¶*methane gas* メタンガス. ¶*poison* (=poisonous) *gas* 有毒ガス. ¶*power gas* 動力ガス. ¶*tear gas* 催涙ガス. ¶*waste gas* 廃気ガス.

P The engine is driven *by gas*. その機関はガスで運転する. ¶the amount of moisture *in* a *gas* ガス中の湿気の量. ¶convert it *into gas* それをガス化する.

O The *gas* is on if you blow out the fire. 火を吹消してもガスは出ている. ¶The *gas* is *half* up. ガスが半分出してある.

gas, *n.* 《米口》 ガソリン.

P step *on* the *gas* 《米俗》 スピードを出す, 急ぐ(自動車の加速器を踏む意から. step on it ともいう). ¶We're getting *out of gas*, ma'am. 奥様ガソリンが切れかかってきましたよ.

gas-fitter, *n.* ガス取付け人.

V *call in* a *gas-fitter* ガス屋を呼ぶ.

gash, *n.* 切傷.

Q² a *10-inch gash* 十インチの深手.

gas-jet, *n.* ガス灯の炎.

Q lighted by a *flaring gas-jet* swung from the roof 屋根から下ったぎらぎらするガス灯で照明した.

gasoline, *n.* ガソリン.

V *use gasoline* for its fuel 燃料にガソリンを使う.

Q² high *octane gasoline* 高オクタン価のガソリン.

gasp, *n.* あえぎ.

P He was conscious to the *last gasp*. 彼は息を引取るまで意識があった.

P He is *at* his last *gasp*. 彼はもう息を引取る.

gasp, *v.* あえぐ.

M *gasp* one's life *away* (=*out*) 息を引取る ‖ *gasp out* a few words 二三語あえぎながら話す.

M² *gasp up* 絶息する.

P *gasp for* breath あえぐ. ¶He *gasped with* rage. 彼は怒りにせきこんだ.

gate, *n.* 門, 出入口.

V *bar* the *gate* [かんぬきをかけて]門を閉じる. ¶*crash* the *gate* 《口語》 入場料を払わないではいる. ¶*enter* its *gates* その門内にはいる. ¶*gain* the *gate* of the city 市街の門をはいる. ¶*get* the *gate* 《米口》 首になる. ¶*give* a person the *gate* 《米口》 追い出す; 首にする. ¶*keep* the *gate* 門を守衛する. ¶*keep* a *gate shut* 門を閉じておく. ¶*leave* a *gate open* 門を開け放しておく. ¶*open* the *gates* to dictatorships 独裁主義侵入のすきを与える. ¶*pass* one's *gate* その門前を通る. ¶*put up* a *gate* 門を設ける. ¶*throw open* the *gate* 門を明け放す. ¶Perry *unbarred* the *gate* of the island empire. ペルリが島帝国の門戸を開いた. ¶*unlock* the *gate* 門の錠をあける.

V² The *gate closes* at 10 p.m. 門限は午後十時.

Q the *back gate* of the school 学校の裏門. ¶a *five-barred gate* 横木の五本ある門. ¶strangers who are temporarily within the *hospitable gates* of the Metropolis 首都にしばらく滞在している外来者たち. ¶a *postern gate* of a palace 御殿の裏門. ¶The *gate* is *unsteady*. 門が堅固でない.

Q² the Deva kings guarding the *Buddhist temple gates* 寺院の門を守る仁王. ¶a *flood* (=tide) *gate* 水門, 閘(こう)門. ¶bring a *record gate* of $3,000,000 未曽有の入場料三百万ドルをもたらす. ¶with $2,000,000 "*gate*" 二百万ドルの入場売上げがあって.

P a notice *at* the entrance *gate* 入口の掲示. 【類】 Who is the man *at* the *gate?* / He is out *at* the *gate*. ‖ He is *at* the *gate* of death. 彼は死にひんしている. ‖ He entered *at* the *gate*. 彼は門からはいった. ¶There is no nameplate *on* the *gate*. 門に表札がない. ¶go (=pass) *through* a *gate* 門内に通る. ¶The horse is tied *to* the *gate*. 馬は門につないである. ¶The dog got in creeping *under* the *gate*. 犬は門の下をくぐり込んだ. ¶*within* (*outside*) the *gate* 門内(外)に. ¶He stood *without* the *gate*. 彼は門外に立った.

P² a *gate of* approach from the north 北門. ¶There was a *gate of* thousands. 何人という入場者があった.

gateman, *n.* 門番.

Q² a *railway crossing gateman* 踏切り番.

gateway, *n.* 門口, 出入口.

P² the *gateway for* trade with the Orient 東洋との貿易上の門戸. ¶a *gateway to* a temple 山門. 【類】 Shanghai is the *gateway to* China. / Kobe is the *gateway to* the Osaka region (京阪地方) / The book is the *gateway to* a thousand joys. / The church is no longer a *gateway to* Heaven. / a *gateway to* success (victory, knowledge).

gather, *v.* 寄せ集める, 推測する; 集まる; 〘服飾〙 ギャザーをとる.

M material *painstakingly gathered* 骨折って集めた材料. ¶may be *roughly gathered* from … …によっておおよそ知られる. ¶a blouse *slightly gathered* at the waist ウエストでちょっとギャザをとったブラウス. ¶The children *gathered together*. 子供らが寄り集まった.

M² *gather in* treasure (farm crops) 宝物を集める(作物を取入れる). 【類】 *gather in* the first harvest of the great victory. ¶*gather up* her skirt at the waist スカートのウエストにギャザーを寄せる ‖ *gather up* one's scattered wits 気を静める. 【類】 *gather up* the rubbish (shavings).

P A crowd *gathered about* the entrance. 入口の辺に人がたかった. ¶He *gathered around* him so many staunch friends. 彼の周囲に非常に大勢の忠実な味方が集まった. ¶*gather* data *from* all sources available 入手できるあら

ゆる方面から材料を集める ‖ I *gather* ***from*** what he said that ... 彼の 言葉から 私は…と推測する. 【類】***from*** your remark (言葉) ‖ I *gather* that ... ‖ so far as can be *gathered* ***from*** ... …から推測しうるところでは. ¶*gather* ***in*** a block 一群となって集まる. 【類】*gather* ***in*** crowds (群をなして) / *gather* ***in*** groups ‖ tears *gathering* ***in*** the eye 目にたまる涙. ¶*gather* grapes ***into*** a basket ぶどうをとってかごに入れる. ¶*gather* hay ***into*** a heap かれ草を一所に積み重ねる. 【類】*gather* string ***into*** a ball / *gather* together ***into*** a crowd / These essays have been published before, but, in *gathering* them ***into*** one volume, they have been more or less enlarged and retouched (増補・訂正がしてある). ¶Dust *gathered* ***on*** it. ちりがその上にたまった. ¶Children *gathered* ***round*** the paper-theatre man. 子供らが 紙芝居の 小父さんの周囲に集まった. ¶The chickens *gathered* ***under*** the hen. ひよこはめん鶏の下に集まった.

gatherer, *n.* 集める人.

Q² a *news gatherer* [新聞記事の]種取り. ¶a *tax gatherer* 徴税員.

gathering, *n.* 収集; 集会, 会合.

M ***address*** a *gathering* of distinguished persons 知名なお歴々の集会に向って話す. ¶***commence*** the *gathering* of the new crop 新作物の取入れを始める. ¶*gatherings* ***drawn*** from all quarters of the world 世界中から参集した会合. ¶orators ***haranguing*** the *gathering* from extempore platforms にわか作りの演壇から集会に向って大声疾呼する弁士たち. ¶***organize*** a *gathering* 会を組織する.

Q He addressed a ***crowded*** *gathering* under the auspices of the Canadian Club. 彼はカナダ・クラブ主催の会の大勢の聴衆に向って 演説をした. ¶A ***distinguished*** *gathering* was present 知名の士が集まっていた. ¶at a ***festive*** *gathering* お祝いの席で. ¶a ***homely*** *gathering* 質素な集会. ¶a ***huge*** *gathering* 大会合. ¶an ***informal*** *gathering* 儀式張らない会合. ¶The funeral was attended by a ***large*** *gathering* of mourners. その葬式には大勢の会葬者があった. ¶an "***old school***" *gathering* 同窓会. ¶an ***out-of-door*** *gathering* 戸外の集会. ¶a ***public*** *gathering* 公けの会. ¶a ***quiet*** *gathering* of friends free from ceremony 遠慮抜きの友だち同志の落付いた集会. ¶a ***social*** *gathering* 懇親会.

Q² ***fall*** *gathering* of crops 作物の秋の取入れ. ¶a "***good-will***" *gathering* 懇親会. ¶a ***luncheon*** *gathering* 昼食の会. ¶***mushroom*** *gathering* きのこ狩り. ¶***news*** *gathering* [新聞の]取材. ¶a ***party*** *gathering* パーティの集まり. ¶a ***representative*** *gathering* 代表者の集会. ¶a ***society*** *gathering* 社交会.

P ***at*** a *gathering* 集会の席で. ¶***In*** the *gathering* was Mr. Hori. 会には堀君も見えた.

P² a *gathering* ***of*** friends 友だちの会合.

gathers, *n. pl.* 〖服飾〗 ギャザー.

P ***with*** *gathers* around the waist ウエストでギャザーをとって.

gauge, gage, *n.* 尺度, 計器; 軌間.

Q a ***narrow*** (***broad***) *gauge* 〖鉄道〗 狭(広)軌.

Q² a ***marking*** *gauge* けい引き. ¶a ***pressure*** *gauge* 圧力計. ¶a ***rain*** (***wind***) *gauge* 雨量(風速)計. ¶***standard*** *gauge* 〖鉄道〗 標準軌間(四フィート八インチ). ¶a ***steam*** *gauge* 蒸気圧力計. ¶a ***wire*** *gauge* 針金の太さを計る器具.

P measure men and manners ***by*** the *gauge* he sets up for himself 手前勝手の尺度で他人やその態度を律する. ¶4 ft. 8½ in. *gauge* 四フィート八インチ半の軌間. ¶a *gauge* ***for*** measuring the amount of rainfall 降雨量を測定する機械. ¶The railway has a *gauge* ***of*** 3 ft. 8½ in. 鉄道の軌間は三フィート八インチ半ある.

gauntlet, *n.* こて.

V ***fling*** (=***throw***) ***down*** the *gauntlet* to ... …に挑戦する. ¶***run*** the *gauntlet* of their attacks 攻撃の矢面に立つ. ¶***take up*** the *gauntlet* 挑戦に応じる.

Q have a ***harder*** *gauntlet* to run 余計苦しい思いをしなければならない.

gauze, *n.* ガーゼ.

Q ***sterilized*** *gauze* 消毒ガーゼ.

Q² ***bandage*** *gauze* ほうたい用のガーゼ.

gay, *a.* 派手に飾った; 陽気な.

M ***as*** *gay* as a lark ひばりのように陽気な.

P the town was *gay* ***with*** flags in honor of the visit of ... その町は…の訪問に敬意を表して旗を立ててにぎわっていた. 【類】The city was *gay* ***with*** all colors of bunting (万国旗).

gayety, gaiety, *n.* 愉快, 陽気.

V ***heighten*** the *gayety* 座興を深める.

gaze, *n.* 凝視, 注視.

V ***attract*** the *gaze*=catch the eye 人目を引く. ¶***bring*** the *gaze* of the public to a degree on ... …に対して大いに社会の注目を引く. ¶***escape*** public *gaze* 人目を避ける. ¶***fix*** one's *gaze* upon the horizon 地平線上を見つめる ‖ The investigator should ***fix*** his *gaze* solely on the search for truth. ¶***lower*** one's *gaze* when meeting people 人に会うと下を向く. ¶***maintain*** a fixed *gaze* on an object ある物から目を離さずにいる. ¶***meet*** another's *gaze* fearlessly 他人の凝視を恐れず見返す ‖ the nearest inn which first ***met*** my *gaze* 最初に私の目についた一番近い宿屋. 【類】the sight that dimly ***met*** his *gaze* through the frosted pane (窓の曇りガラス). ¶***turn*** their *gaze* upon ... …の方に視線を向ける. ¶***turn*** one's *gaze* ***off*** ... to ... …から目を転じて…を見つめる. ¶then her *gaze* ***shifted*** to ... それから彼女の目は…に転じた. ¶his *gaze* ***traveled up*** to ... 彼の目は…の方を見上げた. 「に転じる.

V² the world's *gaze* ***turns*** towards ... 世界の注目は…の方

Q an ***admiring*** *gaze* 賞賛の目. ¶look with a ***fearless*** *gaze* at ... ひるまずに…を見る. ¶fix my ***parting*** *gaze* on ... 別れにのぞんで…をじっと見る. ¶lie hidden from ***public*** *gaze* 人目のつかない所にある.

P They stood ***at*** *gaze*. 彼らはじっとながめて立っていた ‖ set him ***at*** *gaze* 彼の目を引く. ¶The trophy was placed ***before*** the public *gaze*. 戦利品は一般の観覧に供せられた. ¶Her cheeks grew hot ***beneath*** the *gaze* of so many curious eyes. そんなに大勢の物珍らし気な目で見つめられて彼女のほおは熱くなった. ¶***under*** the critical *gaze* of ... …の批評眼でにらまれて.

gaze, *v.* 凝視する, 見つめる.

M *gaze* ***absorbedly*** at ... ぽかんと…をながめる. ¶*gaze* ***disconsolately*** at ... がっかりして…を見つめる. ¶*gaze* ***dreamily*** out over a river 夢心地で川面をながめる. ¶*gaze* ***earnestly*** at ... 熱心に…をながめる. ¶***fearfully*** *gaze* upon ... 恐る恐る…を見つめる. ¶*gaze* ***fixedly*** at ... じっと…を見つめる. ¶*gaze* ***intently*** 余念なく見つめる. ¶He *gazed* ***out*** across the sea. 彼は海の彼方をつくづくながめた. ¶*gaze* ***skyward*** 天の一方をながめる. ¶*gaze* almost ***vacantly*** into the fire ほとんどぼんやりと炉火に見入る. ¶*gaze* ***wonderingly*** at ... いぶかし気に…をながめる. ¶*gaze* ***wordless***[***ly***] at ... 無言で…を見つめる.

M² Sometimes I go out into the garden and *gaze* ***up*** at the stars. 私は庭に出て星を見つめることがある.

P She *gazed* sadly ***after*** him until he was out of sight. 彼女は彼が見えなくなるまで悲し気に彼を見送った. ¶*gaze* ***at*** ... vacantly ぽかんと…を見つめる. 【類】What are you *gazing* ***at***? ‖ *gaze* back ***at*** a person intently じっと人を見返す. ¶*gaze* ***in*** one's face=gaze one in the face 人の顔をじっと見入る. ¶*gaze* ***into*** the stranger's face その見知らぬ人の顔をじっとながめる. ¶He *gazed* ***on*** her with rapture. 彼は彼女に見とれていた. 【類】He rested absorbed in *gazing* ***on*** her. ¶*gaze* ***upon*** the moon (starry heavens) 月(など)をながめる.

gazette, *n.* 官報, 公報.

Q an extra of the ***Official*** *Gazette* 官報の号外.

P His appointment has been announced ***by*** the Official *Gazette*. 彼の任命は官報に出た. ¶appear ***in*** the Official *Gazette* 官報にのる.

gazette, *v.* 官報にのせる; 任命する.

M it was ***officially*** *gazetted* that ... …のむね官報で公布された. ¶He has been *gazetted* ***out***. 彼の免官は官報に発表された.

P he was *gazetted* ***to*** ... 彼は…に任命された.

gear, *n.* 〖機〗 連動装置; 工合のよいこと.

Q ***loose*** *gears* ゆるんだ歯車. ¶Since the war the Ruhr production has been running in ***low*** (***high***) *gear*. 戦後のルールの生産はずっと振わない(高調子だ).

Q² ***fishing*** *gear* 釣道具. ¶***horse and cattle*** *gear* 馬や牛の引き具. ¶***sporting*** *gear* スポーツ用具. ¶***steam starting*** *gear* 蒸気始動ギヤ. ¶***steering*** *gear* 操舵(だ)器. ¶***war*** *gear* =weapons 兵器.

P ***in*** (***out of***) *gear* [機械が]連動している(していない); 調子が合っている(いない) ‖ The machinery is ***in*** (***out of***) *gear*. その機械は運転している(いない). ¶get ***into*** one's *gears* 仕事にかかる. ¶The whole system is ***out of*** *gear*. 全体の調子が狂っている.

gear, *v.*〘機〙連動装置にする.
M The cogs *gear* ***smoothly***. 歯がよくかみ合っている.
M² *gear* ***up*** production 生産を高める ‖ *gear* ***up*** (***down***) a motor-car 自動車の速度を上(下)げる.
P The steel industry was *geared* up ***to*** the need of the war. 鉄鋼業は軍需産業に切り換えられた.

gearing, *n.*〘機〙連動装置.
Q² ***chain*** (***rope***) *gearing* チェーン(ロープ)ベルト装置.
P ***in*** (***out of***) *gearing* 連動装置になっている(なっていない).

gem, *n.* 宝石; 珠玉, 宝.
V ***extract*** a few *gems* of eloquence from the speech of … …の演説から二三珠玉の言を抜粋する.
Q an ***antique*** *gem* 古代の宝石. ¶ the ***architectural*** *gem* (= glory) of the Exposition 博覧会建築物中の白び. ¶ ***beautiful*** and ***exquisite*** *gems* of bird life 羽毛の美しい鳥. ¶ a ***literary*** *gem* 文学上の逸品. ¶ This poem is a ***perfect*** *gem*. この詩は完ぺきだ. ¶ a ***rare*** *gem* まれな宝石. ¶ ***scenic*** *gems* within the park その公園内で特に風景のよい場所.
P engrave figures ***on*** *gems* 宝石に人物花鳥などを彫刻する. ¶ adorn a person ***with*** *gems* 宝石で身を飾る.
P² a *gem* ***from*** a Khotan weaver's loom [中央アジア]コータンのにしき織. ¶ a *gem* ***of*** a boy 玉のような男の子 ‖ the *gem* ***of*** the whole collection 全収集中の白び. 【類】the *gem* ***of*** the library collection.

gender, *n.*〘文法〙性.
Q For convenience in writing, the ***masculine*** *gender* is used throughout in this book. 便宜上この本には一貫して(主語は)男性を用いてある.

general, *n.* 将, 将軍; 一般, 総体.
V the *general* ***placed*** over the whole army 全軍指揮の将軍.
Q a ***full*** *general* 陸軍大将. ¶ a ***good*** *general* 良将. ¶ a ***great*** *general* 名将. ¶ He is ***no*** *general*. 彼は将軍たるの器でない. ¶ the ***shrewdest, keenest***, most ***expert*** and ***experienced*** business *generals* 最もそう明な, 最も鋭利な, 最も練達な, そして最も経験に富んだ実業界の巨頭連. ¶ a ***visiting*** *general* 目下滞在中の将軍.
Q² an ***adjutant*** *general*〘軍〙高級副官(大佐, 中佐級). ¶ a ***brigadier*** *general* 代将. ¶ a ***commissary*** *general* 弁務長官. ¶ a ***five-star*** *general* = a General of the Army《米》五ツ星の将軍(元帥).
P deduce ***from*** *generals* to particulars 総説から細説に及ぶ. ¶ ***in*** *general* it may be said that … 一般的には…と言ってよかろう ‖ people ***in*** *general* 一般民衆 ‖ ***in*** the *general* 一般に; ばく然と; 大体において. ¶ a caviare ***to*** the *general* 高尚過ぎて一般に受けないもの.
P² the *general* ***in*** command = the commanding general 司令官. ¶ a *general* ***under*** … …部下の将.

generality, *n.* 概説; 大体; 大部分.
V ***leave*** *generality* unsaid 一般的なことを言わずに置く.
P proceed ***from*** *generalities* to particulars 一般より詳細へ進む ‖ which distinguishes him ***from*** the *generality* of men そのことで彼は一般人と違っている. ¶ deal ***in*** *generality* 大体を論じる ‖ ***in*** the *generality* of cases 一般の場合において.
P² the *generality* ***of*** his hearers (readers) 彼の聴衆(読者)の大部分 ‖ the *generality* ***of*** mankind 一般人類.

generalization, *n.* 概括, 総合.
V ***deduce*** a *generalization* from facts collected 収集した事実から推論する. 【類】***deduce*** *generalization* from facts. ¶ ***draw*** the most sweeping *generalizations* on the basis of scanty data at one's disposal 持合わせている貧弱な論拠を土台としてきわめて概括的な議論をする. ¶ ***found*** one's *generalizations* upon data 材料に基づいて概論する. ¶ ***make*** a *generalization* of … …を概括する.
Q a ***half-baked*** *generalization* 論拠不十分の概括. ¶ ***hasty*** *generalizations* 速断. ¶ ***sweeping*** *generalizations* of this kind この種の十ぱ一からげの概括. 【類】It cannot be dispatched in ***sweeping*** *generalizations*.
P It would be unwise to be hasty ***in*** *generalization*. 速断してはまずいだろう.

generalize, *v.* 概括する.
M It will mislead others into *generalizing* too ***hastily***. そうすると人に早のみ込みをさせる恐れがある.
P When we use "he" we *generalize* ***for*** both sexes. われわれが「彼」と言うときは男女両性を意味する.

generalship, *n.* 将たる器, 統率の才.
V He ***showed*** bad *generalship*. 彼は統率宜しきを得なかった.
Q a ***true*** *generalship* 真に将たる器.

generate, *v.* 生じる, 発生する.
P a sensation *generated* ***by*** his speech 彼の演説によって起った波紋 ‖ an epidemic *generated* ***by*** ill drainage 不完全な排水から発生した流行病. 【類】hatred *generated* ***by*** racial discrimination.

generation, *n.* (**1**) 時代, 世, 代; 時代の人々.
V ***build up*** a new *generation* 新時代の人物を育成する. ¶ ***educate*** and ***improve*** the present *generation* of young Englishmen 現代の若い英国人を教育し改善する. ¶ He left those thoughts which still ***influence*** our *generation*. 彼の残した思想は今日なおわれわれに感化を与えている. ¶ You secondary-school teachers are laying the foundation of the careers of the men who are to ***lead*** the next *generation*. 中等学校の教師として諸君は次の時代を率いるべき人々の基礎教育をしているのである. ¶ It ***takes*** three *generations* to make a gentleman. 一人の紳士を作るには三代かかる.
V² as the *generation* ***went by*** 代(時)をへるにつれて.
Q the ***coming*** *generation* 青年. ¶ through the ***countless*** *generations* yet to come 今後数知れない世代を通じて. ¶ By the death of Mrs. Lynn Linton the ***elder*** *generation* of English women of letters has been brought almost, not quite, to a close. リン・リントン夫人の死によって英国のすぐれた女流作家の時代は全くではなくもほとんど終末を告げるに至った. ¶ a ***future*** *generation* 未来の世代. 【類】***future British*** *generations*. ¶ the ***growing*** *generation* 少国民. ¶ the ***new*** *generation* in the United States have … 米国の新時代の人々は… ¶ people of the ***older*** *generations* 老人たち. ¶ the [***on***]***coming*** *generation* まさに来るべき時代の人々. ¶ the karma of three *generations*, ***past, present*** and ***future*** 過去・現在・未来三世の因果. ¶ ***remote*** *generations* 遠い将来の世代. ¶ the ***rising*** *generation* of Americans アメリカの青年子弟. 【類】the ***rising*** *generation* of citizens / Here ***several*** *generations* of the family are buried. ¶ a ***second*** *generation* of French residents in London ロンドン住居の二世フランス人. ¶ for a ***single*** *generation* 一代の間. ¶ the ***subsequent*** (= ***succeeding or following***) *generation* その後の時代. ¶ through ***successive*** *generations* 代々. ¶ Danjuro of the ***tenth*** *generation* 十代目団十郎. ¶ It is said that all Negro characteristics disappear after the ***third*** *generation* from the original black-and-white mating. 黒人と白人が結婚した場合三代たつと黒人の特質が消失するそうだ. ¶ ***three*** *generations* of American readers 三代にわたる米国の読者. ¶ ***twelve*** *generations* of ancestors 十二代にわたる祖先. ¶ ***unborn*** *generations* これから世に生れ出る世代. ¶ for ***untold*** *generations* 幾代となく. ¶ a ***young*** *generation* 青年たち. 【類】some of the ***younger*** *generation* of Japanese mountaineers / among the ***young*** *generation*.
P ***above*** a *generation* 一時代以上. ¶ The line breaks ***on*** the fifth *generation*. 五代目で血統が絶えている. ¶ ***for*** *generations* ahead 今後数代にわたって. 【類】even ***for*** a *generation* or two. ¶ one of the heirlooms which were handed down ***from*** *generation* to generation 代々伝わった家宝の一つ. ¶ his ancestor ***in*** the ninth *generation* 彼の九代目の先祖. ¶ in the course ***of*** a *generation* 一代の中に ‖ we ***of*** this *generation* われわれ現代人. ¶ It has come down ***through*** five *generations*. それは五代にわたって(その家に)伝わった.
P² three *generations* ***of*** the family その家族の三代.
(**2**) 発生.
Q ***spontaneous*** *generation* 自然発生.
P² the *generation* ***of*** gas (electricity) ガス(電気)発生.

generator, *n.* 発電機.
Q a ***thermo-nuclear*** *generator* 熱核発電機.
Q² a ***fuel*** *generator* 火力発電機.

generosity, *n.* 寛大, 寛仁, 大度, 大まか.
V He ***has*** the *generosity* of a prince. 彼には王侯のような大ようさがある.
Q ***beautiful*** *generosity* 美しい雅量. ¶ of ***easy*** *generosity* 物をやることの好きな, 大風(おうふう)な. ¶ ***public-spirited*** (= ***community-minded***) *generosity* 公共事業に寄付をおしまない気持ち. ¶ ***undiscriminating*** *generosity* 盲目的寄付. ¶ ***wise*** *generosity* 賢明な気前のよさ.

P *by* the *generosity* of a donor ある寄付者の義侠によって. ¶***through*** the *generosity* of ... ...の義侠的出資によって.

P^{2} *generosity **toward*** the enemy 敵に対する寛大. ¶*generosity **with*** discernment 識別力のともなった気前のよさ.

generous, *a.* 寛大な; 気前のよい, 鷹揚(おう)な.

P He was very *generous **in*** his treatment of the captives. 彼は捕虜を遇するに寛大であった. ¶It was most *generous **of*** you to forgive me. 私をお許し下さいました大きなお心を感謝致します. 【類】It was indeed *generous **of*** him to admit that. ¶He is *generous **towards*** (=*to*) his friends (subordinates). 彼は友人(など)に対して寛大だ. ¶He is *generous **with*** his money. 彼は金銭に大まかだ.

genesis, *n.* 起原, 発生.

P^{2} the *genesis **of*** the British Empire イギリス帝国の創建.

geniality, *n.* 親切.

V ***show*** *geniality* and tact 親切と気転を見せる. 「護神.

genius, *n.* 天才家, 天才; [時代・文明などの]精神; 神霊, 守

V ***discover*** *genius* 天才を発見する. ¶***display*** one's *genius* 天才を示す. ¶He ***has*** a *genius* for music (languages, invention) 彼には音楽(など)の天才がある. ¶He has ***shown*** a really wonderful creative *genius*. 彼は真に驚くべき創造の天才を示した. ¶the nursery of ***suckling*** histrionic *geniuses* のびゆく演劇の天才家養成所. ¶England has never ***supplied*** a great musical *genius* to the world. 英国は偉大な音楽の天才を世界に送り出していない.

Q in ***administrative*** *genius* 行政上の天分において. ¶an ***artistic*** *genius* 天才画家. ¶a ***budding*** *genius* 天才児. ¶the greatest ***commercial*** *genius* of the age その時代の最も偉大な商業上の天才. ¶a Swedish ***culinary*** *genius* スエーデンの料理の天才. ¶Maurice Maeterlinck is the most original ***dramatic*** *genius* that Belgium has produced. モーリス・メーテルリンクはベルギーの最も独創的な天才的劇作家である. ¶an ***electrical*** *genius* 電気の天才家. ¶one's ***evil*** *genius* その悪霊 ‖ his ***evil*** *genius* suggested that ... ...というのは魔がさしたのだ. ¶Germany's ***farfamed*** *genius* for organization ドイツの, 世に隠れない組織の天才. ¶one's ***good*** *genius* その守護神. ¶the ***guiding*** *genius* of the organization その機構の首脳者. ¶a ***heavendescended*** *genius* 天来の鬼才. ¶the ***inventive*** *genius* of the United States 米国の発明的天才. ¶***latent*** *genius* 潜在する天才. ¶a ***lexicographical*** *genius* 辞書編集の天才. ¶the greatest ***mathematical*** *genius* of his generation その時代の最も偉大な数学の天才家. ¶a ***mechanical*** *genius* 機械の天才家. ¶Napoleon made his brilliant success by sheer force of ***military*** *genius*. ナポレオンは全く軍事的天才によって大成功をした. ¶He seems to have a ***positive*** *genius* for doing the wrong thing. あの男はどうもへまをやる方の天才があるらしい. ¶a ***rare*** *genius* まれにみる天才. ¶he has a ***real*** *genius* for ... 彼は実際...の天才がある. ¶a ***sphinx-like*** *genius* スフィンクスのような(不可解な)天才. ¶an ***unappreciated*** *genius* 世に認められない天才家. ¶a man of ***undoubted*** *genius* まぎれのない天才. ¶He has been called a "***universal*** *genius*," for he was noted as a scholar, an inventor, a scientist, and an author. 彼は「万能天才」と称せられた, というのは彼は学者としても発明家としても科学者としても, また著述家としても有名であったからである. ¶a ***versatile*** *genius* 多能多芸の人. ¶Shaw is "the most ***versatile*** and ***cosmopolitan*** *genius* in the drama of ideas that Great Britain has yet produced." ショーは「大英国がこれまで輩出した中での最も多能なかつ世界的な思想劇界の鬼才」である. 「才.

Q^{2} the ***colonizing*** *genius* of France フランス人の植民的天

P regard him ***as*** a *genius* 彼を天才と見なす. ¶a man famous ***for*** *genius* 天才をもって名ある人. ¶a man ***of*** no *genius* 凡才. ¶The phonograph has been given to the world ***through*** the *genius* of Edison. 蓄音機はエジソンの天才によって世に出たものである. ¶***with*** a *genius* for ... ...の天才をもって. ¶a man ***without*** *genius* 天才のない人.

P^{2} Paul Muni, a *genius **at*** characterization and make-up 性格表現と扮装の天才パウル・ムニ. ¶He has a *genius **for*** business (making money, disguise). 彼は実務(など)の天才である. ¶J.P. Morgan was a *genius **in*** finance. J.P. モルガンは財政の鬼才であった. ¶the *genius **of*** our language (the age) わが国語(など)の精神 ‖ the *genius **of*** the twentieth century civilization 二十世紀文明の本質.

gentility, *n.* 紳士気どり.

Q ***shabby*** *gentility* [金もないのに]さもしい紳士気どり.

gentle, *a.* 優しい.

P He was a man *gentle **in*** manner but firm in action. 彼は態度は優しいが行動は断固とした男であった. ‖ *gentle **in*** voice 声のやさしい. ¶He is kind and *gentle **to*** (=***toward***) the weak. 彼は弱いものに親切で優しい.

gentleman, *n.* 紳士.

Q an old *gentleman*, ***affable*** and ***courteous*** あいそのよいいんぎんな老紳士. ¶a true ***Christian*** *gentleman* to be reverenced and admired 尊敬と称賛に値する真のクリスチャン紳士. ¶a ***clean-shaven young*** *gentleman* ひげをきれいにそった若紳士. ¶a ***clerical*** *gentleman* 聖職にある紳士. ¶a ***cultured*** *gentleman* 教養ある紳士. ¶the ***deceased*** *gentleman* 物故した紳士. ¶an ***elderly*** *gentleman* 初老の紳士. ¶a ***ferocious-looking military*** *gentleman* こわい顔をした軍人. ¶a ***fine old*** *gentleman* with grey hair 白髪の上品な老紳士. ¶the "***Grand Old*** *Gentleman*" in the architectural world 建築界の元老. ¶a ***hale old*** *gentleman* かくしゃくとした老紳士. ¶a ***jovial*** *gentleman* 上きげんの紳士. ¶the ***leading*** *gentleman* of the town 同町の重立った紳士. ¶a ***light-fingered*** *gentleman* 手先の早い紳士(すりの別称). ¶a ***middle-aged*** *gentleman* 中年の紳士. ¶a ***polished, educated*** *gentleman* 上品な教育のある紳士. ¶a ***portly*** *gentleman* でっぷりした紳士. ¶a ***quiet, respectable, well-behaved*** *gentleman* 静かで上品でりっぱな態度の紳士. ¶a ***Scotch-American*** *gentleman* スコットランド系の米国紳士. ¶a ***short*** (***tall***) *gentleman* せいの低(高)い紳士. ¶a ***stout*** *gentleman* でっぷり太った紳士. ¶a ***thorough*** (=***perfect***) *gentleman* 非の打ちようのないりっぱな紳士. ¶a ***wealthy*** *gentleman* 金持ちの紳士.

Q^{2} a ***country*** *gentleman* いなか紳士.

P ***In*** a *gentleman* bad manners are rare. 紳士に不行儀は滅多にない. ¶It was not the act ***of*** a *gentleman*. それは紳士にあるまじき仕業である. ‖ an amiable and ornamental set ***of*** *gentlemen* 愛きょうのよい盛装した紳士の一組.

P^{2} He is a *gentleman **by*** birth. 彼は身分のある人だ. ¶a *gentleman **from*** Kyoto 京都出身の方. ¶the *gentleman **in*** question 問題の紳士. ¶a *gentleman **of*** literary taste and culture 文学趣味のある修養を積んだ紳士 ‖ a *gentleman **of*** wealth and position 富と地位のある紳士 ‖ a *gentleman **of*** leisure 暇のある紳士.

gentleness, *n.* 温雅.

P He is a case of *gentleness **without*** weakness. 彼は温雅にして犯すべからずといった人柄である.

gentry, *n.* [団]《口語》手合, 連中.

Q the ***light fingered*** *gentry* 手先の早い連中(すりの別称). ¶the ***racketeering*** *gentry* ゆすり連(会社ごろなど).

genuine, *a.* 本物の.

P The article is *genuine **in*** its quality. その品は本物だ.

genuineness, *n.* 本物なること, 真正.

V ***doubt*** the *genuineness* of ... ...を偽物ではないかと思う. ¶***examine*** the *genuineness* of ... ...の真偽を調べる.

genus, *n.* 種類, 属.

Q^{2} animal of the ***rat*** *genus* ねずみ族の動物.

P^{2} a *genus **of*** trees (reptiles) 樹(など)の一種.

geography, *n.* 地理学; 地勢. 「調べる.

V ***study*** the *geography* of the Antarctic 南極大陸の地勢を

Q ***commercial*** (***historical, political***) *geography* 商業(歴史・政治)地理学. ¶Man and his Work—an Introduction to ***Human*** *Geography* [書名]人間とその仕事—人文地理の入門書. ¶***physical*** *geography* 地文学.

P^{2} a *geography **of*** Africa アフリカ地理書.

geometry, *n.* 幾何図.

Q ***projective*** *geometry* [用器画の]投射図.

germ, *n.* 病原菌; 起原; 芽.

V objects ***carrying*** the *germs* of the disease 病菌を伝達するもの. ¶***destroy*** any *germs* that might lurk in ... ...に潜んでいるあらゆる病原菌を撲滅する. ¶***discover*** the *germ* of ... ...の病原菌を発見する. ¶***isolate*** the *germ* of rabies 狂犬病の病原菌を分離させる.

Q ***air-borne*** *germs* 空気伝染する病原菌. ¶***disease***[***-bearing***] *germs* 病原菌. 【類】the rapid growth of ***disease***

P ***in*** *germ* まだ芽ばえの. ⌊*germs*.

P^{2} the *germ **of*** life 生の芽ばえ ‖ the *germ **of*** war 戦争の禍根. 【類】In this attempt was the *germ **of*** the United States Steel Corporation.

German, *n.* ドイツ語；ドイツ人.
V those who do not *read German* ドイツ語の読めない人人.
Q *High German* 高地ドイツ語(今はドイツの標準語). ¶*Low German* 低地ドイツ語(オランダに接する地方で用いられる).
「下のドイツ人の教化.
Q² the indoctrination of *Soviet-zone Germans* ソ連支配

germane, *a.* 密接の関係のある.
P A brief outline of ... is *germane* ***to*** the subject. ...の大要を概説するのも無用のことではなかろう.【類】But such questions are not *germane* ***to*** my central theme, and so I pass them over lightly.

Germany, *n.* ドイツ.
Q ***de-Nazified*** *Germany* ナチ色一掃のドイツ. ¶***renascent*** *Germany* 復興ドイツ. ¶***Western*** (***Eastern***) *Germany* 西(東)ドイツ (West (East) Germany ともいう).

germination, *n.* 発芽.
V² when *germination* ***begins*** 発芽する時.

gesticulation, *n.* 身振り.
Q with some ***angry*** *gesticulation* 少し怒った身振りで.

gesture, *n.* 手まね, 身振り(ゼスチュア).
V ***make*** a *gesture* of despair (astonishment, apology) 絶望(など)の身振りをする.【類】***make*** *gestures* with hands and arms. ¶When one has no knoweldge of language, *gesture* ***helps*** one out in such cases. 言葉を知らないとこういった場合に手まねが役に立つ. ¶***use*** *gesture* 手まねをやる.
Q ***antic*** *gestures* 色々な変てこな身振り. ¶***enthusiastic*** *gestures* 種々の熱情をこめた身振り. ¶too ***expansive*** *gestures* 誇張し過ぎた身振り. ¶make a ***friendly*** *gesture* 友情的態度を示す. ¶"Go right away!" he barked with an ***imperative*** *gesture*.「すぐ出かけろ」と彼は命令するような身振りでどなった. ¶an ***imperious*** *gesture* ごう慢な態度. ¶a ***responsive*** *gesture* [相手に]共鳴する身振り. ¶an ***insulting*** *gesture* consisting in ... ...といった軽べつの身振り. ¶***manual*** *gesture* 手振り. ¶with a ***menacing*** *gesture* すごんで. ¶Her refusal was a ***mere*** *gesture*. 同国の拒否はゼスチュアにすぎなかった. ¶a ***political*** (***displomatic***) *gesture* 政治(外交)的ゼスチュア. ¶with a ***pretty, appealing*** *gesture* 美しい哀願するような身振りをして. ¶a ***significant*** *gesture* 意味あり気な身振り ‖ The union was a ***significant*** *gesture* towards breaking down the barriers of race prejudice. その結婚は人種的偏見のかきを破る意味では重要な働き掛けであった. ¶***spontaneous*** *gestures* 自然に出る身振り. ¶with many a ***tragi-comic*** *gesture* and ejaculation 悲喜こもごもの身振りや叫び声と共に.
P ***at*** a *gesture* from the master 主人の動作に応じて. ¶speak ***by*** word or *gesture* 言葉または手まねで話す(外人などに).【類】speak ***by*** *gesture*. ¶***in*** *gesture* of supplication 哀願するような身振りで. ¶***with*** a *gesture* of impatience 我慢しきれないという身振りで ‖ ***with*** a *gesture* of distaste いやだという身振りで.
P² a *gesture* ***of*** contempt 軽べつの身振り.

gesture, *v.* 身振りする.
M *gesture* ***vehemently*** 激しく身振りをする. ¶The orator *gestured* ***vigorously***. 弁士は盛んに身振りをした.

get, *v.* 得る, 獲る, 手に入れる；[人に]...してもらう, [物を]...させる；来たす；[ある状態]になる, 達する；利益を得る.
M The rumor has *got* ***abroad***. そのうわさが世間にぱっと立った. ¶The patient is now sufficiently strong to *get* ***afoot***. 病人はもう歩けるだけの力がついた. ¶*get* it ***again*** それを再び手に入れる. ¶*get* ***aground*** 浅瀬に乗上げる；行詰まる, 行悩む. ¶*get* ***ahead*** in the world 出世する ‖ *get* ***ahead*** with one's work 仕事がはかどる ‖ He soon *got* ***ahead*** of the other boys. 彼は間もなく他の生徒を追越した.【類】He *gets* ***ahead*** of me in mathematics. ¶All work and no play does not *get* you ***anywhere***. 勉強ばかりやって遊ばなくちゃ好いことはありゃしない. ‖ He tries hard and he tries his best, but he never *gets* ***anywhere***. 彼は骨も折るしできるだけの事もするがどうにもならない. ¶*get* ***ashore*** on a shoal 浅瀬に乗り上げる. ¶*get* ***asleep*** 寝入る. ¶*get* ***astray*** from a companion 連れとはぐれる. ¶*get* ***astride*** of ... ...に馬乗りになる. ¶I was too busy to *get* ***away***. 私は忙しくて出られませんでした.【類】If I can *get* ***away***, I will go to join you there next week. / I have managed to *get* ***away*** from my work. / The ship is ready for sea but cannot get ***away*** owing to bad weather. ‖ There is no *getting* ***away*** from the true facts. 本当のことはどこまでも本当だ. ‖ *get* ***away*** from civilization 文明から離脱する(開けない所へ旅行する) ‖ many people are unable to *get* ***away*** from the notion that ... ...という考えを脱し得ない人が多い ‖ *Get* ***away*** with you! 出て行け. ‖ The thief *got* ***away*** with the jewels. その盗人は宝石を持って逃げた.【類】The robbers *got* clear ***away*** with their booty. ¶*get* ***back*** a right 権利を取戻す.【類】*get* ***back*** the invested money / I want to *get* it ***back*** right soon. / She has *gotten* ***back*** her dearest Teddy Bear (小ぐまのおもちゃ). ‖ Austria *got* ***back*** (＝recovered) its hold on Italy. オーストリアはイタリーに対する支配権を回復した. ‖ *get* ***back*** into business [休日の後など]また仕事を始める ‖ *get* a plant ***back*** into operation 工場を復興させる ‖ *Get* ***back*** into your box.《口語》黙って引込め. ‖ The soldier *got* ***back*** into civilian clothes for the evening. 軍人はその晩平服に着替えた. ‖ *get* ***back*** to one's former office 原職に戻る ‖ *get* ***back*** to nature 自然に帰る ‖ *get* ***back*** to normalcy (＝normal conditions) 平常に戻る.【類】His only one desire is to be cured and to *get* ***back*** to work. / *get* ***back*** to prewar production of silk ‖ the determination of the British to *get* ***back*** on their feet 英国の一人立ちしようとする決意 ‖ *get* himself ***back*** in Mrs. ...'s good graces ...のおかげでもとへもどる(健康になるなど) ‖ *get* ***back*** at ... ...に仕返しをする ‖ He was trying to *get* ***back*** at his critics. 彼に反対する批評家にさかねじを食わせようとした.【類】I ought to *get* ***back*** at him by some means or other (何かの方法で). ¶*get* ***behind*** 落後する. ¶Things are *getting* ***better***. 万事思わく以上だ. ¶You are *getting* ***big***, dear. [子供に]大きくなったね. ¶*get* ***bitten*** with the autograph hunting craze サイン収集に夢中になる. ¶*get* ***caught*** in the rush 人ごみの中に巻きこまれる. ¶*get* ***clear*** of ... ...を脱する. ¶*get* ***closer*** to the heart of things [研究で]物事の根底をつく. ¶It's *getting* ***cool*** (***chilly***) mornings and evenings. 朝夕は涼しく(寒く)なってきた. ¶You had better go home before it *gets* ***dark***. 暗くならない中にお宅へお帰りになる方がよございます. ¶let us *get* it ***deep*** into the consciousness that ... ...ということはお互に強く意識しようじゃないか. ¶I will *get* the work ***done*** in a week. 一週間の内に仕事を仕上げさせます. ¶I'll *get* ***even*** with you some day. その内かたきをとってやる(覚えていろ). ¶I think they haven't *gotten* very ***far*** as yet. 彼らはまだあまり遠くは行っていまい. ‖ This did not *get* him very ***far*** on the road to fame or towards the big money. これは彼が名声や財産を得るのにはあまり役に立たなかった. ¶*get* ***farther*** with one's work 仕事が一層はかどる ‖ He could *get* no ***further*** with his speech. 彼の話の先が出なかった. ¶*get* ***forward*** 進む；栄える. ¶*get* a person ***free*** 人を自由にしてやる. ¶*Get* you ***gone!*** 去れ. ¶*get* ***home*** 帰宅する；目的を達する ‖ *get* a person ***home*** 人をその家に送り届ける. ¶*get* ***hot*** 熱くなる；激する. ¶***How early*** did you *get* there? そこに着いたのはいつごろだったか. ¶I ***immediately*** *got* into communication with ... 私は直ちに...と通信を始めた. ¶He doesn't want his school to *get* ***large***. 彼はその学校の大きくなることを欲しない(大きくなると学校は悪くなるから). ¶It is *getting* ***late***. もう(時刻が)おそくなる. ¶*get* him ***loose*** 彼を自由の身とする. ¶Van Cortland Park is so immense that one can easily "*get* ***lost***." [ニューヨーク市の]ヴァン・コートランド公園はばかに大きいので全く戸惑いをする.【類】They *got* ***lost*** in the forest. ¶The fire is *getting* ***low***. 火が消えかかっている. ¶He *got* ***mad*** at the message.《米》その伝言に腹をたてた. ¶They *got* (＝were) ***married*** over thirty years ago. 彼らは三十年以上前に結婚した. ¶He *got* ***mixed up*** with dishonest men. 彼は不正直な人々と交わった. ¶It is *getting* ***near*** to Christmas. クリスマスが近い.【類】The boat *got* ***nearer*** to the shore. ¶You'll soon *get* ***next*** to the situation.《米口》じき事情がお分りになります. ¶will *get* him ***nowhere*** 何ら彼を益するところがない ‖ result in *getting* ***nowhere*** あぶはち取らずになる. ¶*get* them ***obeyed*** 彼らを服従させる. ¶*Get* ***out***! そこのけ；出て行け ‖ *Get* me ***out***, please! 僕を出してくれ.【類】The door was locked and we couldn't *get* ***out***. ‖ *get* a nail ***out*** くぎを抜く ‖ I have *got* ***out*** some facts. 私はある事実を聞き出した. ‖ *get* ***out*** a scheme 案を立てる ‖ *get* ***out*** (＝publish) a book 本を発行する ‖ *get* a prisoner ***out*** on bail 囚人を保釈で出所させる ‖ He managed to *get* ***out*** a few

words. 彼は辛うじて二三語口に出しただけだった. ‖ The secret will soon *get* ***out.*** その秘密はじきばれる. ‖ After cross-examinations we had *gotten* ***out*** some facts from him. 厳しい反対尋問の後われわれは彼から若干事実を吐かせた. ‖ The morning *got* ***out*** very fine. 朝は上天気になった. ‖ The lark could scarcely *get* ***out*** his usual note. ひばりはいつもの鳴声が仲々出なかった. ¶*get* it ***overboard*** それを船外に出す. ¶*get* ***paid*** for this これで金がもらえる. ¶*get* rich ***quick*** 手取り早く金持になる. ¶I must *get* ***ready*** to start. 私は出発の用意をしなければならない. 【類】*Get* the dinner ***ready.*** ¶*get* ***red*** in the face 赤面する. ¶*get* the shoes ***repaired*** くつを修繕してもらう. ¶I try to *get* ***rid*** of my cold. 私はどうにかしてかぜを治そうとしている. ¶We must have *got* ***right*** among the longest days. きっともう日の長い頂上です. ¶*get* him ***round*** 彼に用意させる. ¶I *got* it ***secondhand.*** 私はそれを古(ふる)で買った. ¶I *got* ***shaved.*** 私はひげをそらせた. ¶*get* ***sick*** 《米》=become ill 病気になる. ¶*get* ***straight*** into bed 直ちに床に入る. ¶He'll soon *get* ***there.*** すぐそこへ着くだろう. ‖ I can't *get* you ***there.*** そこんとこが分らない. ¶The appropriation bill *got* ***through*** at last. 支出予算案が遂に通過した. ‖ An effort will be made to *get* it ***through*** as a war measure. 戦時手段としてそれをやり通すことに努力するだろう. ‖ I don't know how to *get* ***through*** with my work. 私はどうして仕事を片付けてよいか分らない. ¶*get* ***tired*** 疲れる. ¶The teachers and parents *got* ***together*** on Saturday afternoon. 先生とピーテーエー会員は土曜日の午後集まった. ¶Things are *getting* ***tough*** with us. 世間はますます住みにくくなる. ¶*get* ***underweight*** 目方が不足である. ¶*get* ***unerringly*** at the central thought of a passage [文の]一節の中心思想を正しくつかむ. ¶Now that we have *got* ***used*** to it, it doesn't seem so bad, after all. 慣れて見るとやっぱりそんなに悪くないようだ. 【類】I hope you'll soon *get* ***used*** to the customs and manners over here. ¶He has *gotten* ***vastly.*** 彼は大変金をもうけた. ¶*get* ***well,*** again 平ゆする ‖ If she *gets* ***well,*** I will give this as a reward. あれ(女)が治ったらこれをお礼に差上げます. ¶Don't let him *get* his clothes ***wet.*** 彼に自分の着物をぬらさないように気を付けさせなさい. ¶The telephone service, like everything else, was *getting* ***worse*** all the time. 電話交換も他の例にもれずだんだん悪くなって来た. ‖ I hope you'll soon *get* ***wise*** to our way of living. じきわれわれの生活に慣れますよ. ¶*get* ***worse and worse*** 段々悪くなる.

M[2] when it *gets* ***about*** それが知れたら ‖ can speak English sufficiently to *get* ***about*** 何とかやって行ける位英語が話せる. ¶Nowadays we cannot *get* ***along*** on 10,000 yen a month. 今日では月一万円ではやって行けない. ‖ I am *getting* ***along*** very well. 私は(病気が治って後)何ともありません. ‖ *get* ***along*** well with one's work 仕事がうまく行く ‖ *get* ***along*** amazingly well すばらしく調子がよい ‖ *get* ***along*** with few comforts 切詰めてやって行く. ‖ be hard to *get* ***along*** with ... ...とはつき合いにくい. 【類】She does not *get* ***along*** with her mother. / He could not *get* ***along*** well with the others. ‖ How is he *getting* ***along*** with his school work? あの人は勉強の方はどうです. ¶Nobody can *get* ***along*** in the city without money. 都会じゃ金がなくちゃやって行けない. ‖ You are wanted there, and we can *get* ***along*** without you. 君はそこでは必要な人間なんだがここでは君がいなくてもやって行ける. ¶*get* ***around*** (=over) difficulties 困難を切抜ける ‖ word *got* ***around*** about ... ...についてのうわさが立った ‖ *get* ***around*** to read those books そういう本も読むようになる. ¶*get* ***behind*** in trade competition 商売の競争で遅れをとる. ¶I'll *get* ***down*** at the next stop. 次の駅(駐車場)で降ります. ‖ *get* ***down*** from a ladder はしごから降りる ‖ The temperature *got* ***down*** to zero. 温度は零度に下がった. ‖ really *get* ***down*** to the business 本腰になってかかる ‖ *Get* ***down*** to work, boys! 皆な仕事にかかれ. ‖ *get* ***down*** to bedrock 根底を極める ‖ Both sides *got* ***down*** to plain talking. 両者とも卒直に話し合った. ‖ I won't *get* (=let) you ***down*** any longer. これからは君に苦労はかけないよ(落胆させないよ). ‖ *get* ***down*** at the bottom of ... ...を徹底的に調べる. 【類】*get* ***down*** to fundamental causes (根本原因). ¶*Get* me ***in,*** please. 中へ入れて下さい. ‖ *get* ***in*** one's harvest 収獲を取り入れる. 【類】Farmers are busily *getting* ***in*** the crops. / We had to *get* ***in*** all the hay left outside. ‖ The dog *got* ***in*** creeping under the gate. 犬は門の下をくぐってはって入って来た. ‖ I can't *get* ***in*** with him at all. 彼とはどうも親しくなれない. ‖ *get* ***in*** for ... at the coming election 次の選挙に...から打って出る. ¶Take a train for ... and *get* ***off*** at ... ...行の列車に乗り...で降りなさい. 【類】We must *get* ***off*** now, we are at the end of our journey. ‖ You *get* ***off*** (out of) there! = Beat it! どけろ! 出て行け! ‖ *Get* ***off*** the grass. 芝生に入らないで下さい. ‖ The tug failed to *get* the vessel ***off.*** 引舟は同船を(陸地から)引き出すことができなかった. 【類】Tugs were engaged to *get* her ***off.*** ‖ She is stranded, but will probably be *got* ***off*** after lightening. 座礁したがおそらく軽荷になったら離礁するだろう. ‖ *got* ***off*** on the rising tide あげ潮で岸を離れた. 【類】Hopes are entertained that she will *get* ***off*** next tide. / Chances of *getting* her ***off*** are extremely small. ‖ She *got* her baby ***off*** to sleep. 彼女は赤ん坊を寝かしつけた. ‖ She doesn't have her breakfast until after she's *got* her children ***off*** to school. 彼女は子供たちを学校に出してから朝食をとる. ‖ *get* ***off*** scotfree 無事に済む ‖ *get* ***off*** with a whole skin 傷一つ受けないで逃げる. 【類】He *got* ***off*** with a scratch or two. ‖ I *got* ***off*** cheaply. 私は高価(高い犠牲)を払わずに済んだ. ‖ He was very fortunate to *get* ***off*** with only a fine. 罰金刑位ですんだのは運がよかった. ¶*get* ***on*** [to] the train 汽車に乗込む ‖ *Get* ***on*** or get out. 乗るなら乗れ乗らないならどけ. 【類】*get* ***on*** at Tokyo Station ‖ How are you *getting* ***on***?—Oh, so, so, nothing to complain of. どうです景気は?—まあまあ申し分ありませんな. ‖ I am now slowly *getting* ***on*** better with my schoolmates. 私は生徒仲間と段々親しくなって行く. 【類】He did not *get* ***on*** well with his father. / I *get* ***on*** exceedingly well with the other sex (女にもてる), although not a good-looking man. / You would *get* ***on*** very well with him, I am sure. / We do not *get* ***on*** well together. / He is a hard man to *get* ***on*** with (つき合いにくい). ‖ The work is *getting* ***on*** in good shape. 仕事はすこぶる順調だ. ‖ She is *getting* ***on*** to middle age 彼女はもうそろそろ中年だ. ‖ Shall we *get* ***on*** to the high road soon? もうすぐ街道に出るでしょうか. ‖ She's *getting* ***on*** to it, see? 彼女はだんだん気がついて来たぞ. ‖ These shoes are so small that I can not *get* them ***on.*** このくつは小さくて私の足が入らない. ‖ We soon lit a good fire and *got* the kettle ***on*** for supper. われわれはじき火をおこし, 夕飯の仕度にやかんをかけた. ‖ One gets weak as one *gets* ***on*** in years. 年を取ると体が弱る. ‖ You can't *get* ***on*** at all with a low pay of ¥8,000 or so. 八千円やそこらの安月給ではてんでどうにもならない. ‖ *get* ***on*** with repairs immediately すぐ修繕にとりかかる. 【類】One can scarcely *get* ***on*** without some knowledge of English. ‖ We have *got* ***on*** with the erection as far as ... その建設は...の程度まで進んだ. ‖ a man *getting* ***on*** for forty 四十がらみの男 ‖ She *got* far ***on*** in the family way. お腹が大きくなってきた. 【類】How's your kid *getting* ***on*** in school (学校の成績)? / I am *getting* ***on*** well in my business. / How are you *getting* ***on*** with the work? ‖ I have *got* ***on*** with the translation as far as the third chapter. その翻訳は三章までこぎつけた. ‖ Very soon we *got* ***on*** to very deep horticultural topics. たちまち話が園芸のことに深入りした. ‖ *get* ***on*** socially 社交界で成功する ‖ We are *getting* ***on*** famously. われわれは絶好の成績をあげている. ‖ *get* ***on*** [well] in the world 出世する ‖ *get* ***on*** swimmingly とんとん拍子にうまく行く. ¶*get* ***over*** a gate 門を乗り越える ‖ *get* ***over*** a difficulty 困難を乗り越える. 【類】*get* ***over*** one's ailment (病気) / *get* ***over*** an impediment (故障) ‖ *get* ***over*** evidence 証拠を消そうと努める ‖ She never quite *got* ***over*** her disappointment. 彼女はまだ完全には失望から回復していなかった. ‖ *get* ***over*** (=cover) a hundred miles a day 一日百マイル進む ‖ The sooner you *get* the interview ***over,*** the better. 会見するなら早いほどいい. ‖ I can't *get* ***over*** this peculiar smell. この妙な臭気には我慢がならない. ‖ No explanation could *get* ***over*** the fact that he was dead. 彼が死んだという事実は何と説明しても消すことはできなかった(どうにもならなかった). ¶I'll *get* it ***through*** in a couple of minutes. 私は二三分間にそれをやってしまう. 【類】I'll *get* this ***through*** right away (直ちに). ‖ if the bill *gets* ***through*** その議案が通れば. ¶The fire was *got* ***under.*** 火がおさまった. ‖ The fight was not *got* ***under*** till policemen came up. け

んかは警官がやって来て始めておさまった. ¶*get up* at dawn (=daybreak, sunrise) 暁(など)に起きる. ¶*Get up* when awake. 目を覚したら起きなさい. ‖ Late to retire and late to *get up*. よいっぱりの朝寝坊. ‖ *get up* to recite a poem [クラスで]詩を暗誦するため立上る ‖ He started to *get up*. 彼ははっとして立ち上った. ‖ *get up* on one's feet=rise 立ち上る ‖ *get up* into a tree 木にのぼる ‖ This tumbler doesn't *get up* soon. このだるまはすぐ起きない. ‖ The wind *got up* with the sun. 風は太陽ののぼるに連れて勢を増した. ‖ Smoke (Vapor) is *getting up*. 煙(水蒸気)が立っている. ‖ The afternoon was spent in *getting up* arrears of correspondence. たまっている手紙の返事を片付けるのに午後を使った. ‖ *get up* one's health 健康を進める ‖ I never *get up* the gumption to ask her to marry me. 彼女に結婚申込みをするほどの心臓ではない. ‖ *get up* a slander 悪口の種をまく ‖ He devoted studious hours to *getting up* the subject to be discussed. 彼は論議さるべき問題の特別研究に数時間を当てた. ‖ You are *getting up* another book, aren't you? 新しい著作におかかりですね. ‖ The actor was well *got up*. その俳優は衣装がよくできていた. ‖ She was *got up* (=dressed) to kill us. ほれぼれするような身なりをしていた. ‖ We *got up* to page 16, line 10, last lesson, didn't we? この前は十六ページの十行目まで進みましたね. ‖ The fire looked larger as our ship was *getting up*. 船が近づくにつれ火がいよいよ大きく見えてきた. ‖ The book is beautifully *got up*. 本(の装てい)が美しくできた. ‖ We'll soon *get up* to the others. 僕らはじきみんなに追いつくよ. ‖ *get up* a service of boats 船の乗客施設を整える ‖ Suppose we *get up* some sort of entertainment to pass the time? 時間つぶしに何か余興でもやろうか. ‖ *get up* (=ahead) with one's work 仕事を進める.

P *get aboard* (=board) a ship 船に乗り込む. ¶He *got above* [others] in English. 彼は英語では抜群だった. ¶*get across* a river (street, lake) 川(など)を渡る. ¶*Get among* the people as much as you can; this in itself is a liberal education. できるだけ世人と交われ, それが取りも直さず高等教育になる. ¶Here lies a man who knew how to *get around* him cleverer men than himself. 自分より賢い人を周囲に集めることを知っていた人がここに永眠している. ¶We finally *got at* a ledge of rock near the summit. われわれはとうとう頂上近くのたな岩に着いた. ¶It is not easy to *get at* (=see) him. あの人に面会するのは骨が折れる. ‖ *get at* the heart of things 事物の真髄に触れる ‖ *get at* the keynote of their trouble 彼らの悩む根本原因を会得する ‖ *get at* the sore spots and heal them 痛みの個所をつき止めてそれを治す(弱点を直す) ‖ *get at* the exact meaning of a sentence 文の正確な意味をつかむ ‖ The soul of a people can be *got at* fully only through a knowledge of its language. 国民の精神はその国語を知ることによってのみ十分にこれをつかむことができる. 【類】*get at* the sense (=meaning) of a passage / *get at* the truth (facts, root of things) / *get at* the kernel (核心) of the subject / *get at* the secret (奥儀) of fencing (chess, bowling) / There are no means of *getting at* the thoughts of men (人の心) / *get at* the reason why … ¶*get before* one 人の前へ出る. ¶He *got between* them, and prevented a fight. 彼が彼らの間にはいってけんかをさせずに済ました. ‖ *get between* the sheets 床にはいる ‖ *get* in *between* the rivals 競争者の中に割って入る. ¶Her grief *got beyond* words. 彼女の悲しみは言語に絶した. ‖ *get beyond* one's depth 背の立たない所へ行く; 深間へはいる ‖ It does not *get* much *beyond* the region of conjecture. それではおく測の範囲をあまり出ない. 【類】His anger has *got beyond* control. ¶I *got* him *by* the throat. 私は彼ののどをつかまえた. ‖ *get* it *by* heart それを暗記する ‖ *get* it *by* rote それを機械的に覚える. 【類】*get* a person *by* the hand (wrist, hair). ¶I *got* it *for* 2,000 yen. 私はそれを二千円で求めた. ‖ I *got* 5,000 yen *for* my pains. 私は骨折に五千円もらった. ‖ That's what you *get for* … …するからそんなことになるんだ. 【類】I'll *get* another dictionary *for* you. / This is a new wrist watch I *got for* my birthday. ¶*get* machinery [out] *from* Europe 機械をヨーロッパから取寄せる ‖ *get* it *from* a person それを人からもらう ‖ We *get* ham *from* pigs. ハムは豚肉で作る. ¶*get in* touch with … …と接触する, 連絡を取る ‖ *get* her *in* tow その船を引船で引く ‖ The movie star *got* a number of her admirers *in* tow. その映画スターのあとからファンがぞろぞろついて行った. ‖ *get in* the way of … …の邪魔になる ‖ They *got in* line. [出札口などで]皆が列を作った. ¶Something has *got into* my eye. 何か僕の目にはいった. ‖ *get into* conversation with … …と談話を始める. 【類】he *got into* correspondence with … ‖ He *got into* (=lay on) bed. 彼は床についた. ‖ *get into* general circulation 一般に行き渡る ‖ The train *gets into* the city at half past three. 汽車は三時半にその町に着く. ‖ The regiment has *got into* action. その連隊が出征した. ‖ They *got into* quite a little argument about it. 彼らはそれについてちょっぴり議論をやった. ‖ *get into* a fight 戦(けんか)を始める. 【類】You must not *get into* any fights with the neighbour's children. ‖ *get into* a panic 恐慌をきたす ‖ *get into* the habit of … …の習慣がつく ‖ We didn't *get into* the new house until September. われわれは新築の家には九月になってはいった. ‖ In 1910 the film business was *getting into* its strides. 一九一〇年になって映画事業が躍進し出した. ‖ a system that has *got into* evil odour 評判の悪くなった方法 ‖ *get into* dock [船が]ドック入りをする ‖ *get into* one's trousers (boots) ズボン(など)をはく ‖ *get into* better ways 品行をよくする ‖ *get into* a rage 怒る ‖ Owing to his various reverses, he *got into* low water. 彼は失敗を重ねて悲境に陥った. ‖ *get into* a perspiration 汗をかく ‖ *get into* the red《米》赤字になる ‖ *get into* debt 負債を作る ‖ *get into* the blackbooks of … …のブラックリストに載る ‖ *get into* the saddle くらに収まる; 緒につく ‖ *get into* disgrace 恥をかく ‖ *get into* a dispute with… ‖ fall out with … …と仲違いをする ‖ He managed to *get* his manliness *into* everything that he wrote. 彼は何を書いてもその男らしい精神を打込むようにした. 【類】*get into* the hands of the police / *get into* mischief ‖ He is *getting into* his chief's favor (お気に入りになる). ‖ *get into* politics 政界に入る, 政治を論じる ‖ *get into* Parliament [英国で]代議士になる ‖ *get into* the movies 映画人になる ‖ This story *got into* the newspapers. この話が新聞にのった. 【類】He begged them not to let any word of it *get into* the papers. ‖ *get into* shape 具体化する ‖ *get* it *into* print それを印刷に付する ‖ Some drunken coolies *got into* a row last night, down on Water Street. 酒に酔った人夫数名が昨夜下町のウォータ街で乱暴を働いた. ‖ Government employees are more liable than others to *get into* a rut. 役人は一般の人よりも型にはまりやすい. ‖ *get into* trouble (difficulty) やっかい(など)なことになる ‖ *get into* a horrible scrape 恐しい困難に陥る ‖ The second day out, the liner *got into* a swell. 出帆二日目にその定期船は大波に出合った. ‖ *get into* trade in a small way 小規模で商売を始める ‖ The airplane *got into* trouble and crashed on the take-off. 飛行機は故障を起し, 離陸の際墜落した. 【類】I *got into* serious trouble with the authorities, which came near resulting in my expulsion (放校). ‖ Physicians *get into* the way of looking at patients as so many "cases" of this or that disease. 医者は患者を皆それぞれ病気の標本扱いにする癖がつく. ‖ *get into* general use 一般に使用されるようになる. 【類】People gradually *got into* using the word. ‖ *get into* a frightful passion 猛烈に怒り出す ‖ He *got* it *into* his head that everybody was persecuting him. 彼はみんなが自分をいじめると信じ込んだ. ‖ Trade grew much more active after he *got into* office. 彼が就任してから商売が大分活発になった. ¶*get off* the back of a horse 馬の背から降りる ‖ somewhat *get off* the track 少し脱線する ‖ I cannot *get off* duty today. 僕きょうは抜けられない. ‖ *get off* [the train] at … …で[汽車を]降りる ‖ I endeavored to *get* as much as I could *into* the new policy of the government. 政府の新政策をできるだけよく知ろうと努力した. ‖ My mind is *getting into* a sort of a whirl, though you do not seem disturbed. 私の心はきりきり舞をしている, あなたは落着いてるようだけれど. ¶*get off* the rocks [船が]離礁する ‖ I cannot *get* this thing *off* (=out of) my mind. このことが私の頭を離れない. ¶*get on* a car (train) 電車(など)に乗る ‖ *get on* (=*to*) one's feet 起立する ‖ *get* it *on* the gramophone それを蓄音機に吹込む ‖ *get on* the roof 暗礁に乗りあげる ‖ Call the office and *get* Mr. A *on* the phone. 会社に電話して A さんを電話口に出してくれ. ‖ You've *got on* my nerves. 君ってしゃくにさわる男だ. 【類】Why, I'm so sick and tired of insurance men that the sight of one *gets on* my nerves. ‖ *get on* heat 交尾期にはいる. ¶*get*

out of a carriage (=horse, bed) 馬車(など)から出る.【類】The bird has *got out of* the cage. ‖ She has attempted too much and has *got out of* her depth. 彼女はあまり大きくやり過ぎて手に余るようなことになった. ‖ *get out of* one's debt 借金が抜ける ‖ *get* ***out of*** difficulty 困難を脱する ‖ *get* ***out of*** order (turn) 秩序(調子)が乱れる ‖ *get* ***out of*** repair 修繕がきかなくなる ‖ *get* ***out of*** rut 気を転じる ‖ When women *get* once ***out of*** compass, there are no length of licentiousness that they are not capable of running. 女の脱線ときたら止め度がなくなる. ‖ *get* ***out of*** practice すたれる ‖ *get* ***out of*** shape 形がくずれる ‖ *get* ***out of*** the way of a car 車をよける. 【類】*Get* ***out of*** my way, please. ‖ You *get* ***out of*** this house this instant! たった今出て行ってくれ. ‖ *get* ***out of*** position 失職する ‖ I *got* nothing ***out of*** him. 彼からは何も聞くことができなかった. ¶*get* ***over*** a bridge 橋を渡る ‖ *get* ***over*** one's dislike (prejudice) 嫌い(など)がとれる ‖ help a person to *get* ***over*** the difficulties 力を貸して困難を切抜けさせる ‖ *get* ***over*** a loss 損失を回復する ‖ *get* a person ***over*** a ferry 向側へ船で人を渡す ‖ have to lighten to *get* ***over*** the bar [船が]その砂洲(す)を越えるには目方を軽くしなければならない ‖ He *got* ***round*** the corner out of sight. 角をまがって見えなくなった. ¶*get* it ***through*** the customhouse その通関手続をすませる ‖ *get* a bill ***through*** the Diet 法律案を議会で通過させる ‖ He *got* ***through*** a dangerous illness. 彼は大病で命拾いをした. ‖ when you *get* it ***through*** それが済んだら.【類】‖ He has *got* ***through*** an immense amount of correspondence at his house before breakfast. / *get* ***through*** one's task with great speed / *get* ***through*** a college with a *cum laude* in English. ¶Every effort ought to be made to *get* him ***to*** a hospital. どうしても彼を入院させるべきだ. ‖ *get* ***to*** the core of the matter 肯綮(こう)に当る ‖ *get* ***to*** the other side of a street 町の向側に行く. 【類】*get* ***to*** New York ‖ *get* ***to*** the phone. 【類】How can I *get* ***to*** the city police? ‖ to *get* ***to*** the theme of my story 話の本筋に返して(閑話休題) ‖ "Shut up, everybody, and *get* ***to*** work." —Shaw's motto.「みんなおしゃべり抜きで仕事にかかれ」. ‖ *get* ***to*** sleep with difficulty ようやく眠る.【類】I'll never *get* ***to*** sleep till this pain leaves me. / *Get* you ***to*** bed quickly. ‖ *get* ***to*** the head of one's class クラスで一番になる ‖ *get* ***to*** the heart (=core) of the issue その問題の中心を突く ‖ *get* closer ***to*** each other お互いに接近する.【類】Professors have but little opportunity to *get* ***to*** close quarters with their students. ‖ those who have already *got* ***to*** the end of their restricted literary tether [小説家など]すでにその貧弱な創作力に行きづまりを来たしている人々. ‖ *get* a ship ***under*** way 船を出す ‖ as the conference *got* ***under*** way 会議が始まったから ‖ *get* ***under*** water 侵水する ‖ *get* ***under*** a motor-car 自動車にひかれる ‖ The fire has been *got* ***under*** control. 火事は消し止めた. ‖ *get* ***under*** sail 出帆する ‖ *get* ***under*** arms 武装して立つ. ¶*get* ***upon*** (=***on***) one's feet 立ち上る ‖ *get* ***upon*** a horse 馬に乗る ‖ *get* him ***upon*** the subject 彼にそのことを話させる ‖ The giddy wildness of young girls often *get* ***upon*** the loose. はすっぱ娘はよく軌道を踏みはずす.

O *get* to feel comfortable 気が楽になる. ¶Please *get* me a towel. タオルを取(持)ってきて下さい. 【類】I'll *get* you another dictionary. ¶Can you *get* me? 分るか. 【類】He said he *got* it (=the idea).

getting, *n.* 入手.

Q² the technique of ***job getting*** 就職のこつ.

getup, *n.* 《口語》[本などの]装てい, 体裁.

Q an ***elaborate getup*** こった装てい(体裁).

ghost, *n.* 幽霊; 霊魂; 代作文士.

V ***employ*** a "*ghost*" 代作家を使う. ¶***give up*** (=***yield***) the *ghost* 息が絶える. ¶I ***have*** not the *ghost* of a chance to ... 私は少しも...する機会がない. ¶***lay*** a *ghost* (=spirit) 幽霊を退散させる ‖ this ***laid*** the *ghosts* of ... それで迷夢も破れた. ¶***play ghost*** 幽霊のまねをする; 代作をする. 【類】I ***played*** "*ghost*" to him in the production of ... ¶***raise*** a *ghost* 幽霊を出させる. ¶***summon*** the *ghost* of a dead person 死霊を呼び出す.

V² The *Ghost Goes West*. [映画の題名] 幽霊西へ行く. ¶***Ghosts haunt***. 幽霊が出る. ¶The *ghost* ***walked*** (=showed itself). そのおばけが出た.

Q the ***haggard*** *ghost* of an omnibus 乗合馬車のおばけ(骨組だけ残った). ¶the ***Holy Ghost*** 聖霊. ¶a ***pale ghost*** 青ざめた人. ¶an ***unquiet*** *ghost* haunting the scenes of its by-gone hopes and endeavors その昔の希望と努力の場所に出没する浮かばれない魂.

P a house haunted ***by*** a *ghost* 幽霊の出る家. ¶look ***like*** a *ghost* [やせて]幽霊みたいだ.

giant, *n.* 巨人.

Q a ***four-motored giant*** 四発の巨人機. ¶the ***literary giants*** of the Victorian Age ヴィクトリア朝の文豪たち.

Q² a ***forest giant*** 森の巨人.

P² ***giants in*** the business world 実業界の巨頭連. ¶a ***giant of*** letters 文豪.

gibber, *v.* しゃべる.

M The monkeys *gibbered* ***angrily*** at each other. さるどもはお互いに怒り声でしゃべっていた.

gibberish, *n.* たわ言.

Q a ***barbaric gibberish*** 野卑なたわ言. ¶a ***meaningless*** *gibberish* 意味のないたわ言.

gibbet, *n.* 絞首台.

P hang a criminal ***on*** *gibbet* 罪人を絞首台にかける.【類】perish (=die) ***on*** the *gibbet*.

gibe, *n.* あざけり.

Q it is a ***familiar gibe*** at socialism that ... ...とは社会主義に対してよくやる痛論である.

gibe, *v.* あざける.

P *gibe* ***at*** ... ...をあざける.

gift, *n.* たまもの, 贈物; 天賦, 天賦の才.

V I beg you to ***accept*** this *gift* as a trifling mark of my esteem. ほんの私の志ですからこの品をお納め下さい. ‖ corruptly ***accept*** a *gift* of £100 as an inducement for showing favor to ... ...に有利な取扱をしてもらうために贈った百ポンドの収賄をする. ¶a letter ***accompanying*** a *gift* 贈物の添状. ¶***acknowledge*** a *gift* with a cordial note of thanks 丁重な感謝状で進物に対するあいさつをする. ¶***bestow*** a *gift* of ... towards ... ...に対し...を寄贈する. ¶***discriminate*** *gifts* [適不適を考え]贈物をそれぞれ区別する. ¶***envy*** his wonderful and superior *gifts* 彼の驚くべきすぐれた天賦の才をうらやむ. ¶***have*** the *gift* of cajoling speech 生れつき口がうまい. ‖ He ***has*** the *gift* of a vivid and passionate eloquence. 彼には活気があって熱情のこもった弁舌の才がある. ‖ be specially blessed in ***having*** the *gift* of improvisation [歌や詩など]即席に作る才能にたけている. 【類】He ***has*** the *gift* of oratory (雄弁). / ***have*** the *gift* of tongues (語学の才能) / He ***has*** the *gift* of overpowering the most intractable (最も御し難い者). / He ***has*** the *gift* of making friends. / He ***has*** the *gift* of persuasion (説得). ¶he ***made*** a *gift* of one million dollars to ... 彼は...に百万ドルを贈呈した. ¶One ***needs*** a very strong *gift* of optimism to expect it of him. 余ほど楽観的でなくては彼にそれを期待することはできない. ¶***offer*** *gifts* to ... ...に進物をする. ¶He ***possessed*** a *gift* of eloquent and magnetic speech. 彼は流ちょうで人を引きつける弁舌の才を持っていた.【類】It has sometimes been said that the British people do not ***possess*** the "*gift* of tongues" (語学の才). ¶***present*** a *gift* 贈物をする. ¶he ***received*** a *gift* of $150,000 from ... 彼は...から十五万ドルを贈呈された. ¶***refuse*** a *gift* 進物を断わる. ¶***send*** a *gift* to ... ...に進物を贈る.【類】An uncle of mine ***sent*** me a *gift* over from New York. ¶***utilize*** the *gifts* of science 科学の才を利用する. ¶gladly ***welcome*** *gifts* for the upkeep of the work その事業の支持に対する贈物を歓迎する. ¶***withhold*** a *gift* 贈物を差控える.

Q an ***acceptable*** *gift* ありがたい贈物. ¶The farm is an ***ancestral*** *gift*. その農場は先祖伝来のものである. ¶an ***anonymous*** *gift* 匿名の寄贈. ¶a most ***appreciated*** *gift* 実にありがたい頂き物. ¶They make very ***appropriate*** *gifts* for a wedding. それは誠に適切な結婚の贈物になる.【類】a most ***appropriate*** *gift* for the season. ¶a ***bridal*** *gift* 花嫁への贈物. ¶a ***charming*** *gift* in a woman 女の持つ美しい天資. ¶I've brought you a little ***congratulatory*** *gift*. わずかばかりのお祝を持参致しました. ¶a ***courteous*** *gift* 丁重な贈物. ¶He has a ***distinct*** *gift* for drawing. 彼には明らかに図画の才がある. ¶an ***embarrassing*** *gift* もらって迷惑する贈物. ¶an ***enduring*** *gift*, always appreciated and always useful いつもありがたがられいつも重宝がられて長持ちのする進物. ¶an ***exceptional*** *gift* 特別の贈物. ¶great ***forensic*** *gifts* 偉大な法廷弁論の才. ¶He offered his discovery as a ***free gift*** to the world. 彼はその発見を無償の贈物として世人に提供した. ¶a ***generous gift*** of money from the alumni commemoration of … …の記念に当って卒業生から多分の贈金. ¶a ***happy gift*** うれしい贈物. ¶a ***heaven-sent gift*** 天与の賜物. ¶an ***Imperial gift*** 御下賜品. ¶an ***inborn gift*** 生れついた才能. ¶bring out young writers of ***intellectual gifts*** or originality 知的才能または独創力に富んだ青年作家を世に出す. ¶a writer of keen instinct and ***literary gift*** 鋭敏な直感と文学的才能のある作家. ¶This was the most ***magnificent single gift*** ever received by the institution. これは同協会がそれまで受けた中で最も多額な一口の寄付であった. ¶a ***moderate*** and ***small-sized gift*** 小額の寄付金. ¶a ***natural gift*** 生得の才能. ¶a ***New-Year's gift*** お年玉. ¶the ***noble gift*** of Mr. Andrew Carnegie アンドルー・カーネギー氏のりっぱな志から出た贈物. ¶a ***philanthropic gift*** 慈善的寄贈. ¶a ***pious gift*** to a temple お寺への信心深い寄進. ¶a ***poor gift*** 貧弱な贈物. ¶one of the ***potent gifts*** of civilization 文明の有力な賜物の一つ. ¶a ***precious gift*** 貴重な贈物. ¶a singer of ***rare gifts*** まれな天分の歌手. ¶has a ***real gift*** for … 真に…の才能がある. ¶a ***gift serviceable*** as well as ***attractive*** 見て美しく同時に役に立つ贈物. ¶a ***trifling gift*** 軽少な贈物. ¶an ***unrestricted gift***, offered without limiting conditions 別に条件をつけずに提供した自由な寄付. ¶an ***unsurpassed gift*** of … …という類のない贈物. ¶a ***voluntary gift*** 任意の寄付. ¶a ***welcome gift*** もらってうれしい贈物.

Q² a ***birthday gift*** 誕生日の贈物. ¶an admirable ***Christmas gift*** すばらしいクリスマスの贈物. ¶a ***farewell gift*** in money はなむけの金. ¶a ***graduation gift*** 卒業祝いの贈物. ¶a ***parting gift*** 送別の贈物.

P It is given ***as*** a ***gift***. それは贈呈したのです. ‖ having got it ***as*** a ***gift*** or something それをもらいか何かして. ¶None will take it ***at*** a ***gift***. そんな物やろうとしたってもらい手がありゃしない. 【類】I wouldn't take (=have) it ***at*** a ***gift***. ¶They presented him ***with*** a ***gift*** of money. 彼らは彼に金を贈った. ‖ a man ***with*** the ***gift*** of [the] gab 口舌の雄. 【類】be conferred ***with*** a ***gift*** of poetry (art, language).

P² a ***gift for*** my sister 私の姉(妹)への贈物 ‖ I have no ***gift for*** languages. 私には外国語を学ぶ才能がない. 【類】have a ***gift for*** organization (組織). ¶a ***gift from*** … …からの贈物. ¶He has the ***gift of*** the gab. 彼は弁が立つ. ‖ help the Institute in other ways than ***gifts of*** money 金銭以外の点でその協会を援助する ‖ a ***gift of*** nature 天賦の才 ‖ a ***gift of*** repartee 当意即妙の返事をする才 ‖ a ***gift of*** the people 人民の贈物 ‖ Dr. George H. Clapp recently made a ***gift of*** $15,000 to the endowment fund of the Carnegie Institute, Pittsburgh. ジョージ・エッチ・クラップ博士が先ごろピッツバーグにあるカーネギー研究所の奨学基金に一万五千ドルを寄付した. ‖ this statue, the ***gift of*** tens of thousands of his admirers 何万という彼の崇拝者の贈物であるこの像. ¶The Lincoln Birthplace was recently presented as a ***gift to*** the nation by the Lincoln Farm Association. リンカーンの誕生地は先般リンカーン農場組合によって国家へ寄贈された. ‖ his ***gift to*** the nation of his famous museum 彼の有名な博物館を国へ寄付したこと. 【類】a ***gift to*** schools (the town).

gift, *v*. 才能を賦与する.

M He seems ***gifted physically, intellectually***, and ***morally***. 彼は肉体的にも知的にもまた道徳的にも十分に恵まれているらしい. ¶She is very pretty and ***socially gifted***. 彼女は非常に美しくまた社交の才がある. ¶He is ***richly gifted*** by nature. 彼には生れながらに豊かな才能がある.

P a man ***gifted*** far ***beyond*** the intelligence of his age 彼の時代よりも知識(の)はるかにすぐれている人. ¶a man ***gifted by*** nature ***with*** powers of observation. ¶a man ***gifted with*** a strong memory 記憶力のよい人 ‖ a man ***gifted with*** talents (a keen intellect) 才(など)のある人. 【類】He is ***gifted with*** rare eloquence. / a large and cultured class ***gifted with*** leisure / be ***gifted with*** the faculty of using common sense (常識が豊か) / be ***gifted with*** a great power of speech.

gigantic, *a*. 巨大な.

P be ***gigantic in*** intellect 偉大な知能を有している.

giggle, *v*. くすくす笑う.

M ***giggle away*** one's idea 人の考えを笑殺する. ¶***giggle away*** (=***out***) one's time 時間を笑いつぶす.

gimlet, *n*. 手ぎり.

V ***work*** a ***gimlet*** 手ぎりをもむ.

gin, *n*. ジン酒.

V ***drink gin*** from a black bottle 黒いびんのジン酒を飲む.

ginger, *v*. 刺激する.

M² ***ginger*** him ***up*** for … …のために彼を刺激する.

gipsy, *n*. ジプシー.

Q a ***vagabond gipsy*** 放浪のジプシー.

gird, *v*. 帯びる, 着ける; 囲う, めぐらす.

M² ***gird on*** one's sword 剣をはい用する. ¶He ***girded up*** his loins. 彼は緊褌(え)一番した.

P ***gird*** it ***with*** a fence それにへいをめぐらす.

girder, *n*. 〚鉄道〛ガード.

Q² a ***wrought-iron girder*** 錬鉄製のガード.

girdle, *n*. 帯.

V ***tie*** the ***girdle*** 帯を締める. ¶***unfasten*** one's ***girdle*** 帯をほどく.

P carry it ***at*** the ***girdle*** それを腰に帯びる. ¶bind it ***with*** a ***girdle*** それを帯で縛る.

P² a ***girdle of*** trees around the pond 池をとりまく立木.

girdle, *v*. とりまく.

P a city ***girdled by*** wide roads (high walls) 広い道路(など)で囲まれた都市.

girl, *n*. 少女, 小娘.

V ***date*** a ***girl*** 女の子と外出の約束をする. ¶***educate girls*** to independence 少女を独立のできるように教育する. ¶***fit girls*** for the practical business and duties of life 人生の実務と本務に適するよう少女たちを仕込む. ¶***have*** a ***girl serve*** a customer 少女に客の応待をさせる. ¶***jilt*** a ***girl*** 少女をだまして後になって振捨てる. ¶The brilliance of the stage life ***lures*** young ***girls*** to the footlights. 舞台生活の花々しさが少女に脚光を浴びることをあこがれさせる. ¶***marry off*** a ***girl*** 少女を嫁にやる.

Q an ***adolescent girl*** 妙齢の少女. ¶an ***attractive girl*** 人好きのする娘. ¶a ***beautiful, fair-headed girl*** 美しい金髪の少女. ¶my ***best girl*** 《米》私の情婦. ¶a ***bobbed girl*** 断髪の娘. ¶a ***bouncing girl*** お転婆娘. ¶a ***bright-eyed girl*** 目のぱっちりした少女. ¶a ***charming girl*** 魅力のある娘. ¶a ***cute little girl*** 《米》かわいい娘っ子. ¶a ***dancing girl*** on the stage 舞台でダンスをやる少女. ¶a ***decent girl*** 良家の娘. ¶a ***delicate-natured girl*** 情緒の細やかな女の子. ¶a ***dirty, slovenly girl*** 不潔でだらしのない少女. ¶a ***little Dutch girl*** 《米俗》ドイツ人の娘っ子. ¶an ***engaging girl*** 愛きょうのある少女. ¶an ***erring girl*** 身を誤る少女. ¶a ***finished flirt girl*** すご腕のいちゃつき娘. ¶a ***flipperty-flopperty girl*** しまりのない少女. ¶a ***gently-bred girl*** しつけの上品な少女. ¶***gossiping girls*** 人のうわさをする少女. ¶a ***homely girl*** 顔のぱっとしない少女. ¶an ***incorrigible girl*** 手に負えない娘. ¶a ***marriageable girl*** 年ごろの少女. ¶***my girl*** 私の愛人. ¶a ***modern girl*** モダン・ガール. ¶a ***nubile girl*** 年ごろの娘. ¶a ***personable girl*** 器量の悪くない女の子. ¶a rather ***plain girl*** あまり器量のよくない娘. ¶***Poor girl!*** かわいそうな娘だ. ¶a ***poor, unlettered*** country ***girl*** 気の毒な無学のいなか娘. ¶a ***precocious girl*** おませな娘. ¶a ***pretty girl*** きれいな少女. ¶a ***pure girl*** 純な少女. ¶a ***religious-minded girl*** 信仰心のある少女. ¶***salary-earning girls*** 月給取りの少女. ¶a ***saucy girl*** ずうずうしい娘. ¶a ***serious-looking girl*** in a ***pince-nez*** 鼻眼鏡をかけたまじめそうな少女. ¶an aggresively ***sexy girl*** いやに性的な娘. ¶a ***shy, self-conscious girl*** 内気な, きまりの悪そうな少女. ¶a ***shy, tremulous girl*** of nineteen 花もはじらう十九歳の乙女. ¶a ***slim girl*** すらりとしたお嬢さん. ¶a ***slim, undernourished girl*** 栄養不良でやせている娘. ¶a ***sophisticated girl*** すれた娘. ¶a ***sporty girl*** いやに派手な少女. ¶a ***stony-hearted girl*** 薄情な少女. ¶a ***tall girl*** with dignity of carriage 背が高くって体のこなしの上品な少女. ¶a ***tall slender girl*** 背が高くてすらっとした少女. ¶a ***tempestuous girl*** じゃじゃ馬娘. ¶an ***uneducated girl*** 教育のない娘. ¶an ***unsophisticated girl*** うぶな娘. ¶***venturesome young girls*** from the country いなか出の向う見ずの娘たち. ¶a ***wayward young girl*** 無軌道娘. ¶***young*** and ***blooming girls*** 妙齢の花と咲きにおう乙女たち.

Q² an ***adult girl*** 成育した娘. ¶a ***bachelor girl*** 独身女. ¶a ***business girl*** 女店員, 女事務員. ¶a ***cash girl*** キャシャー係の娘. ¶***chorus girls*** who are wild, reckless and even "sporty" 無鉄砲で浮気なコーラスガール. ¶***cigarette girls*** タバコ売娘たち(劇場などでタバコを売り歩く). ¶a *circus girl* サーカスの女. ¶a ***college girl*** 《米》女子大学生. ¶the ***Connors girls*** コナー家のお嬢さんたち. ¶a raw ***country girl*** ぽっと出のいなか娘. ¶an ***elevator girl*** 女子のエレベーター係. ¶an ***ex-service girl*** もと軍籍にあった女. ¶a ***factory girl*** 女工員. ¶a ***fisher girl*** 漁師の女. ¶a ***floor-show girl*** キャバレーの客席の踊り子. ¶a ***flower girl*** 花売娘. ¶a ***glamor girl*** 《米》[性的魅力のある]女優. ¶a ***hat-check girl*** 帽子係の女. ¶an ***idiot girl*** うすのろの女の子. ¶a ***junior high girl*** 《米》女子中学生. ¶a ***magazine cover girl*** 雑誌の表紙にでも出る美人娘. ¶an ***office girl*** 女事務員. ¶an "***open-air girl***" 出歩きの好きな娘. ¶an ***orphan girl*** [両親または片親のない]みなし児. ¶a ***San Francisco*** (=***Frisco***) ***girl*** シスコの娘. ¶one's favorite ***pin-up girl*** 好きな美人(写真または本もの). ¶a ***room girl*** [ホテルの]客室係の女の子. ¶a rosy ***school girl*** ばら色のほおの女学生. ¶a ***servant girl*** 女中. ¶a ***service girl*** 接客係. ¶a ***shop girl***=a salesgirl 女店員. ¶a ***show girl*** ショーの踊子; 看板娘. ¶a ***slave girl*** どれい女. ¶a ***society girl*** 社交界の令嬢. ¶a ***street girl*** 夜の女. ¶a ***summer girl*** 避暑地で会う女. ¶a ***teen-age girl*** 十代の娘. ¶a ***teashop girl*** 喫茶ガール. ¶a [***tele***]***phone girl***=《米》a hello girl 電話交換手. ¶a ***theme girl*** 映画の中心になる娘. ¶a ***white collar girl*** 《米》女子事務員. ¶a pretty ***waiter girl*** きれいな女給仕. ¶a ***working girl*** 職業婦人 ‖ a decent ***working girl*** 地道な職業の娘.

P ***in*** a *girl* twenty years of age 二十歳の少女において. ¶***with*** the *girl* of his heart 彼の意中の少女と一しょに ‖ He is quite smitten ***with*** the *girl*. 彼はその少女にうつつをぬかしている.

P² a *girl* ***in*** her late teens (twenties) 十八九(二十代)の娘 ‖ a *girl* ***in*** her early twenties 二十一二の女 ‖ the girl ***of*** the people 平民の女 ‖ the *girl* ***of*** his affections 彼の愛情を捧げた女.

girlhood, *n.* 娘時代.

V Her *girlhood* was ***spent*** in the country. その娘時代をいなかで送った.

girth, *n.* 胴まわり.

V The "Grizzly Giant," Mariposa Grove, near Yosemite National Park, ***has*** a *girth* of 91 feet at the level of the ground. ヨセミテ国立公園の近傍マリポサ・グローヴのグリズリー・ジャイアント(大木)は根もとの周囲が九十一フィートある. ¶***measure*** the *girth* of one's chest 胸囲を計る.

P ... feet ***in*** *girth* 胴まわり…フィート.

gist, *n.* 要領, 要点.

V ***get*** the *gist* of a book 書物の要領をつかむ. ¶***grasp*** the *gist* of ... その要領を得る. 【類】The boy was exceedingly keen and quick in ***grasping*** the *gist* of a situation.

Q The ***main*** *gist* of the long story is as follows: この長物語の主要点は次のようになる.

P² a *gist* ***of*** the proceedings 議事録の要領 ‖ the *gist* ***of*** a question (story, speech) 問題などの要点 ‖ the *gist* ***of*** a claim クレームの趣旨 ‖ "...," was the *gist* ***of*** my thought 私の考えたことは大体…であった.

give, *v.* 与える; 渡す, 託する; 伝える; 起させる; 捧げる, ゆだねる; 演じる.

M² The opera is to be *given* ***again*** next month. その歌劇は来月再演のことになっている. ¶He *gave* ***away*** most of his income to his mother. 彼は収入の大部分を母にやった. 【類】He *gave* ***away*** most of his income to support the poor family. ‖ *give* ***away*** the prizes 賞品を授与する ‖ I am here incognito, so you must not *give* me ***away***. おれはここへは微行なのだから本当のことを言ってはいかん. ‖ *give* ***away*** (=tip off) a secret 秘密を漏らす. 【類】General Sherman wouldn't be told a secret. He said he would *give* it ***away*** to the first person he met. ‖ His accents *gave* him ***away***. 言葉のなまりで彼のお里がわかった. ‖ The old bridge *gave* ***away*** by the recent flood. 古橋は最近の洪水で落ちた. ¶*Give* it ***back*** to me when you're through. 終ったら返してくれ. ‖ *give* ***back*** insult for insult 悪口の言合いをする ‖ So they *gave* ***back*** and came no farther. というわけで奴らは引っ込み二度と来なかった. ‖ He *gave* ***back*** my reproaches. 彼は私の非難に抗弁した. ‖ *give* ***back*** at the first repulse 最初の排撃で退却する ‖ *Give* me ***back*** the days of my youth. 青春時代にもう一度返してくれ. ¶The fields *give* ***forth*** an odour of spring. 野辺は春のにおいを発散する. ‖ *give* ***forth*** a deep, lingering sound 低く響く音を発する ‖ *give* ***forth*** the same view 同じ見解を発表する. 【類】He *gave* ***forth*** a series of works in rapid succession. ¶She ***freely*** *gave* her assistance. 彼女は進んで援助を与えた. ¶to him is ***generally*** *given* the credit of introducing ... to ... …を…に紹介した功績は一般に彼に帰すべきものとされている. ¶the subtitle to ... is *given* rather ***grandiloquently*** as "..." 副題目は少し大げさに…としてある. ¶information and advice *given* ***gratuitously*** 無料の情報や助言 ‖ Our services are *given* ***gratuitously***. 私どもは無料奉仕です. ¶***grudgingly*** *give* 出し惜しみをする. ¶He *gave* ***liberally*** to the academy. 彼はその学校に多大の寄付をした. ¶He *gave* ***liberally***, but ***unostentatiously***, to many charities. 彼は多くの慈善団体に惜気なくまた目立たないように寄付をした. ¶He *gave* ***out*** that he had seen heavenly visions. 彼は天使の姿を見たと言いふらした. 【類】The "Kojiki," or "Records of Ancient Matters," was *given* ***out*** in the year 712 A.D. / It was *given* ***out*** that he was bankrupt. ¶*give* ***out*** questions 質問を発する ‖ *give* it ***out*** into custody それを保管させる ‖ *give* ***out*** rations 食糧を配付する ‖ *give* ***out*** a bad odor 悪臭を放つ ‖ He has *given* ***out***. 彼は根気がつきた. 【類】The power has *given* ***out***. / The water *gave* ***out***. / Before spring their finances (金ぐり) may *give* ***out***. ‖ *give* ***out*** (=allocate rations 配給量を割当てる ‖ give out money until it *gives* ***out*** 続く限り金を出す ‖ The engine *gave* ***out*** for a time. そのエンジンはちょっと(故障で)動かなかった. ¶The prices must be *given* ***separately***. 価格は品別につけなければならない. ¶Invitations were *given* ***verbally***. 招待は口頭でされた. ¶***willingly*** *give* aid 喜んで援助を与える.

M² *give* ***about*** prints (writings) 印刷物(など)を配布する ‖ *give* ***about*** a rumor of war 開戦のデマを飛ばす. ¶as *given* ***below*** (***above***) 下(上)記の通り. 【類】It is *given* ***below*** (=***under, underneath***). ¶*give* ***in*** one's adherence to ... …に加盟する, 参加する ‖ *given* ***in*** one's allegiance to ... …に忠誠を誓う ‖ The strikers *gave* ***in***. 争議側が折れた. 【類】The employers have *given* ***in*** and re-opened their works. ‖ *give* ***in*** to a demand (desire, wishes) 要求(など)に応じる ‖ The plants *gave* ***in*** to the cold weather. 植物は寒気でだめになった(霜枯れした). ‖ According to the boxing phrase, he showed "the white feather" and *gave* ***in***. 拳闘用語でいうと彼はいわゆる「白い羽根」を見せてのびた. ‖ *give* ***in*** one's papers 書類を提出する. 【類】Names of contestants (競技者の姓名) shall be *given* ***in*** before the end of the month. ¶*give* ***off*** (=cool) the effect ほとぼりを冷ます ‖ *give* ***off*** heat (light) 熱(光)を発する. 【類】*give* ***off*** heavy smoke / The chimney was *giving* ***off*** volumes of black smoke (黒煙もうもう). / Every piece of open water is constantly *giving* ***off*** vapor. 外にある水の一滴々々からは絶えず水蒸気を発散している. / *give* ***off*** a very strong smell (強烈な臭気) / *give* ***off*** tremendous clouds of steam and black smoke ‖ *give* ***off*** a note [楽器が]音を出す ‖ Arteries *give* ***off*** many branches. 大動脈から多くの支脈がでる. ¶*give* him ***over*** to law 彼を法律の手に引渡す ‖ *give* ***over*** a package to his keeping 包みの保管を彼に託す ‖ *give* ***over*** an attempt (a habit, a mode of life) 企図(など)を放棄する ‖ It's time she *gave* ***over*** that sort of pride. 彼女はもうあんな見栄は捨てていい時分だ. ‖ *give* ***over*** the fight for lost 負けとあきらめて戦闘から手を引く. 【類】be *given* ***over*** for dead / His friend had *given* him ***over*** for lost. ‖ The rest of the evening was *given* ***over*** to sports and games. その晩はそれから競技や遊戯をやって過した. ‖ ask to be *given* ***over*** to the police [自分を]警察に引渡してもらいたいと頼む ‖ a package which he *gave* ***over*** to my keeping 彼から預かった小包 ‖ She *gave* ***over*** to despair and fell down. 彼女は失望のあまり気を失った. ‖ be *given* ***over*** to a press section and spectators 新聞記者席と傍聴席に当ててある. 【類】pages of the book are *given* ***over*** (=devoted) to ... / The fifth floor is *given* ***over*** to the administrative offices (お役所). ‖ *give* oneself ***over*** to ideals 理想にふける ‖ *give* herself ***over*** to the life of prostitution 売春を業とする. 【類】*give* oneself ***over*** to drinking (smoking, gambling). ¶Visitors are not required to *give* ***up*** their sticks, umbrellas or parasols before entering the galleries. 参観人は入館に先立ちステッキ・かさ・日がさなどを預けなくともよいことになっています. ‖ *give* oneself ***up*** to pleasure (wine, woman) 快楽(など)にふける ‖ The upper floors are *given* ***up*** to sleeping rooms, and a special "den" for Mr. E. 二階から上は寝

室やE君の特別私室に当ててある. ‖ *give* ***up*** an account (a petition) 報告(など)を提出する ‖ We do not *give* ***up*** the names of our contributors. わが社は寄稿者の姓名を公表しない. ‖ *give* ***up*** hope of living to see the dictionary published 辞書の完成まで生きていようという望みを捨てる. 【類】*give* ***up*** the atomic secrets (原子秘密) ‖ I *give* ***up***.=I lose. まいった. ‖ *give* ***up*** (=quit) smoking (drinking, gambling) タバコ(など)をやめる. 【類】He finally *gave* ***up*** the attempt. / *give* ***up*** a discussion (an argument, a negotiation) / *give* ***up*** all hope / *give* ***up*** one's travel plan (旅行計画) / *give* ***up*** the plan of a professional career (知的職業) / *give* ***up*** one's faith (信仰) / *give* ***up*** a fight / *give* ***up*** one's hobby (よい道楽) / *give* ***up*** the pursuit (追求) / *give* ***up*** the study of ... / *give* ***up*** one's political life (政治生活) / *give* ***up*** a tenancy (借地(家)権) / *give* ***up*** her mandate (委任統治権) / *give* ***up*** a quest (追及) / *give* ***up*** one's American citizenship (アメリカの国籍) / *give* ***up*** the idea of going abroad / *give* ***up*** one's position as a teacher (教職) / *give* it ***up*** as hopeless / *give* ***up*** a lucrative post (役得のある地位) / *give* ***up*** the right of ... ...の権利を放棄する / *give* it ***up*** as unattainable (手に入らないものと) / The picnic was *given* ***up***. / *gave* it ***up*** in despair (がっかりして) ‖ *give* ***up*** possession of ... ...を手離す ‖ *give* ***up*** one's seat to ... ...に座を譲る ‖ Nature is slowly *giving* ***up*** some of her secrets to scientific research. 自然は次第に科学研究の前にその秘密の一部を現わし始めた. ‖ *give* ***up*** an old car for a new one 古い車を売って新車を買う ‖ *give* ***up*** one's life ***for*** it それに一生を捧げる ‖ *give* ***up*** patriotism for internationalism 愛国主義を国際主義にくらがえする ‖ reluctance to *give* it (a person) ***up*** 未練 ‖ The rebels *gave* ***up*** arms and surrendered. 反乱軍は武器を投じて降服した. ‖ *give* ***up*** membership in a political party 脱党する ‖ The film actress *gave* ***up*** her career and married ... その映画女優は映画から足を洗って...と結婚した. 【類】*give* themselves ***up*** to a full day of bright and innocent enjoyment ‖ *give* oneself ***up*** to thought (meditation) 思いに悩む ‖ *give* oneself ***up*** to justice 自首して出る. 【類】*give* oneself ***up*** to the police confessing that ... ‖ *give* himself ***up*** to her wholly 彼女に心から打込む ‖ *give* oneself ***up*** to one's emotions 哀楽の思いにふける. 【類】Those men seemed to *give* themselves ***up*** to debauchery (酒色). / Young and old have *given* themselves ***up*** to the joy of living. / She *gave* herself ***up*** to him body and soul (心身とも). ‖ The ascetic *gave* himself ***up*** to austere discipline. 行者は難行苦行で身を鍛えた.

P The judge *gave* the case ***against*** him. 裁判官はその事件に対し彼に不利な判決を下した. ¶*give* a person ... ***as*** a present 人に...を進物としてやる. ¶The number of the enemy is *given* ***at*** 10,000. 敵の軍勢は一万と号している. 【類】Its weight is *given* ***at*** 13 tons. / The latest census (最近の国勢調査) *gives* the population of Japan ***at*** 90 millions. ¶be *given* good word ***by*** ... ...にほめられる. ¶*give* one's life ***for*** [the sake of] the country 国家のために生命を捨てる ‖ He has *given* £700 ***for*** Red Cross work. 彼は七百ポンドを赤十字に寄付した ‖ I *gave* five shillings ***for*** it. 私はそれに五シリング払った. ‖ what would I not *give* ***for*** ...? ...を手に入れることができたら何でもやるんだが ‖ *give* ***for*** the relief of the families of the victims of a disaster 罹災者の家族救助に...を寄付する ‖ *give* a cup ***for*** competition 競技に賞杯を授与する. 【類】How much (=what) did you *give* ***for*** that? / Premiums (賞) *given* ***for*** exhibits may consist of merchandise, cash, ribbons, certificates or merit cards and flags. ¶They are *given*, *passim*, ***in*** the book. それはその本の中の所々に載せてある. ‖ *give* one's answers ***in*** English 英語で答える ‖ Such words ought not to be *given* ***in*** a dictionary. こんな言葉は辞書に載せるべきものでない. ‖ be *given* ***in*** marriage 嫁にやる ‖ *give* an extract ***in*** ***extenso*** (=at length) 文を省略せずに引用する. ¶*give* a prisoner ***into*** proper custody 囚人を然るべく看守させる ‖ *give* it ***into*** custody of ... ...それを...に預ける ‖ *give* it ***into*** his charge to deliver to ... それを...に渡してもらうために彼にあずける. ¶No leave can be *given* ***on*** a telegram except in cases of emergency. 緊急の場合の外電報で賜暇願を出してはならない ‖ a walled enclosure with a gate that *gives* ***on*** the side street 横町に出られる門があって垣をめぐらした地所. ¶*give* money ***to*** a beggar こじきに銭をやる. 【類】He *gives* good wages ***to*** his servants. / Old clothing and furniture should be *given* ***to*** charity (慈善事業) instead of being burned or thrown away. ‖ He is *given* ***to*** hypercriticism. あの男はよく人の揚足を取る. ‖ *give* it ***to*** the world それを公にする(本など). 【類】In the year 1653 Walton *gave* ***to*** the world his Compleat Angler (釣魚大全). / he is going to *give* ***to*** the public another volume of ... / of all the books that have been *given* ***to*** the public on the problem of ... / *give* ***to*** the world the result of one's studies ‖ they all *gave* three hearty cheers ***to*** ... ...に対し一同熱心に万歳を三唱した ‖ *give* a disease ***to*** another 病気を他人に移す ‖ Please *give* my compliments ***to*** your family. どうぞお宅の皆様へよろしく御伝え下さい. ‖ *give* motion ***to*** something ある物を動かす ‖ *give* a turn ***to*** a key in the lock かぎを錠前に入れてねじる ‖ *give* currency ***to*** a rumor 風説を流布させる ‖ *give* the sails ***to*** the wind 帆を風に任せる ‖ *give* one's time (life, energy) ***to*** one's duty (work) 自分の務(など)に時(など)を捧げる ‖ *give* one's service ***to*** God 神に奉仕する ‖ *give* oneself [up] ***to*** study 勉強に熱中する ‖ be *given* ***to*** stealing 手癖が悪い ‖ The soldiers *gave* themselves ***to*** plunder (略奪). / He is *given* ***to*** drinking (idleness, pleasures). ‖ Americans are usually *given* ***to*** over-generosity in tipping. アメリカ人は通常チップをやりすぎる. ‖ *give* way ***to*** despair とうとう失望する. ¶He *gave* nothing ***towards*** that object. 彼はその目的に何物をも貢献しなかった. ¶a document *given* ***under*** my hand and seal 私が自筆署名して作成した証書. ‖ The earth *gave* ***under*** the feet. 足もとの地面がめりこんだ.

O he *gave* his friends to understand that in future they must ... 彼は友人たちに今後...しなくてはいけないと言含めた. ¶*Give* him an inch, and he will take an ell. あの男はああしてやればこうしてくれと増長する.

give-and-take, *n.* やり取り.

Q She is inured to the ***rapid*** ***give-and-take*** of conversation on any topic, human and divine. 彼女は人間のことでも神のことでもどんな問題に対しても応対に慣れている.

P on the principle (policy) ***of*** ***give-and-take*** 互譲の原則(方針)にのっとって.

giver, *n.* 贈与者.

Q one of the most ***discriminating*** and ***broad-minded*** *givers* in the world 世界中で一番分別がありまた寛大な贈与者の一人. ¶a ***generous*** *giver* だし惜しみしない寄贈者. ¶***large*** (***small***) *givers* 大(小)口の寄付者. ¶a ***quick*** and ***ready*** *giver* いつでもおいそれと金を出してくれる人.

P To the *Giver* ***of*** all blessings a mother's thanks are offered for this great gift. すべての祝福を与え給う神に向ってこの大なる賜物に対し母としての感謝を捧げる.

giving, *n.* 贈与.

Q ***unselfish*** *giving* 博愛的な贈与. ¶***wise*** *giving* 賢明な贈与.

Q[2] ***party*** *giving* 会を開くこと. ¶annual ***prize*** *giving* 毎年の賞金(品)贈与.

glad, *a.* 喜んでいる, うれしがっている.

M I am ***heartily*** *glad*. 私は衷心から喜んでいる. ¶I am ***very*** *glad* to see you. お目にかかって実にうれしい. 【類】I should be ***very*** *glad* to go.

P He was *glad* ***at*** the report of your success. 彼は君の成功を聞いて喜んでいた. 【類】I am *glad* ***at*** the news (sight). / I am *glad* ***at*** hearing of ... ¶I am *glad* ***for*** his sake. 私は彼のために喜んでいる. ¶I am very *glad* ***of*** it. 私はそれを大層うれしく思っている. 【類】I should be *glad* ***of*** any information respecting ... / He is *glad* ***of*** my success. ‖ I am *glad* ***of*** its being over. 私はそれが済んでうれしい.

M You will be *glad* to hear that I was successful. 私が成功したと聞いたらあなたは喜んで下さるでしょう.

glade, *n.* 空地.

Q a ***woody*** *glade* 樹間の空地.

gladness, *n.* 喜び, 喜悦.

P Mother kissed the boy ***in*** her *gladness*. 母は喜びのあまり少年にキッスした. ¶***with*** *gladness* 喜んで ‖ leave it ***with*** the *gladness* of a convict escaping prison 囚人が牢獄を脱走するときのような喜びでそれを去る.

glamo[u]r, *n.* 魔力, 魅力.

V ***cast*** a *glamor* over ... ...に魅力を与える. ¶***destroy*** the *glamor* of ... ...の魅力を破る. ¶Flights across the Atlantic and Pacific have ***lost*** much of the *glamor* which surrounded them a few years ago. 五・六年前までとは違って大西洋・太平洋横断飛行も今ではその魅力が大分薄らいだ. ¶ ***throw*** the *glamor* of poetry over ... ...に雅趣を添える.

Q sweetly interprets the ***Celtic*** *glamor* ケルトの固有の魅力を美しい言葉で言い表わす. ¶ acquire a ***new*** *glamor* 新しい魅力が加わる.

P ***under*** the *glamor* of the moment 一時の迷いで.

glance, *n.* 一見, 一べつ.

V ***bestow*** a rapid *glance* on ... ...をちらっと見る. ¶ ***cast*** a *glance* at it それを一べつする. 【類】***cast*** a *glance* of surprise at the scene / ***cast*** a *glance* back over the period dealt with by ... ¶ ***dart*** a fierce *glance* at ... ぎょろっと...をにらむ. ¶ ***exchange*** *glances* 目くばせする. ¶ ***give*** a *glance* at ... ...をちらりと見る ‖ ***give*** a person a piercing *glance* 人に鋭い一べつを与える. ¶ it ***requires*** only a *glance* at this table to reveal the fact that ... ...という事実を明かにするにはこの表を一目見れば足りる. ¶ He ***shot*** me one *glance* I shall never forget. 彼は私が到底忘れることのできない一べつを私に投げた. ¶ ***steal*** *glances* at a person 人をぬすみ見をする. ¶ ***take*** a *glance* at ... ...をべっ見する ‖ ***take*** a *glance* into the future 将来をべっ見する. ¶ ***throw*** a furtive *glance* at ... ...をぬすみ見る.

V² her *glance* ***fell*** upon ... 彼女は...をちらっと見た.

Q He cast ***admiring*** *glances* at her. 彼は見とれたという風情で彼女をちょいちょい見た. ¶ cast ***amorous*** *glances* at ... ...にウインクを送る. ¶ exchange ***amused*** *glances* 愉快だという目付をかわす. ¶ a ***backward*** *glance* 過去への一べつ. ¶ cast a ***brief*** *glance* over the centuries 過去数世紀を一べつする. ¶ at a ***casual*** *glance* ちょっと見て ‖ even a ***casual*** *glance* at ... shows that ... ...を一べつしさえすれば明白だ. ¶ They gave me a ***chilly*** *glance*. 彼らは冷やかな目付で僕を見た. ¶ exchange ***consulting*** *glances* 相談するように顔を見合わす. ¶ with a ***contemptuous*** *glance* 軽べつした目付で. ¶ a ***coquettish*** *glance* あだっぽい目, 色目. ¶ steal a ***covert*** *glance* at her face 彼女の顔をこっそりと見やる. ¶ You could not tell by a ***cursory*** *glance*. ちょっと見ただけでは分らないだろう ‖ a ***cursory*** *glance* at the list will show that ... 表を一見しただけで...ということが分る. ¶ cast a ***disapproving*** *glance* on ... ...をたしなめる目でちらりと見る. ¶ cast a ***dubious*** *glance* at ... ...を疑わしい目でちょっと見る. ¶ cast many an ***envious*** *glance* at ... ...を幾度もうらやましそうな目付で見る. ¶ though it is less apparent at ***first*** *glance* 最初見たときはそれとははっきり分らないが ‖ The phenomenon of fatigue is more complex than it seems at ***first*** *glance*. 疲労の現象は最初見たより一層複雑である. 【類】at ***first*** *glance* it would seem that ... / At the ***first*** *glance* it may have an appearance of plausibility. ¶ We cast ***frequent*** and ***expectant*** *glances* toward the gate. われわれは門の方をちょいちょい今か今かと眺めた. ¶ cast a ***hasty*** *glance* behind 急いで後をふりむいて見る. ¶ cast a ***hostile*** *glance* on ... ...を反抗的態度でにらむ. ¶ turn toward her with an ***indignant*** *glance* むっとした目付で彼女の方を振向く. ¶ by a ***mere*** *glance* ほんの一目で. ¶ with a ***melting*** *glance* うっとりした目付で. ¶ ***One*** *glance* was enough. 一目りょう然であった. ¶ give her a ***pitying*** *glance* 哀れむような目付で彼女を見る. ¶ he shot a ***quick*** *glance* at ... 彼は...をちょっと一べつした. ¶ He gave me one ***quick, searching*** *glance*. 彼はちょっと鋭い一べつを私に向けた. ¶ a ***roguish*** *glance* いたずらっぽい目付. ¶ a ***scrutinizing*** *glance* せんさくするような目付. ¶ throw (=cast) a ***side*** *glance* at ... ...をちょいと横目で見る. ¶ cast ***sidelong*** *glances* of admiration at ... ...を感心したという風に横目で見る. ¶ fix one's ***sidewise*** *glance* on ... じろっと...を横目で見る. ¶ exchange ***significant*** *glances* 意味あり気に互に見交わす. ¶ short paragraphs that can be read at a ***single*** *glance* ただ一目で読める短い一節. ¶ a ***surreptitious*** *glance* こすい目付. ¶ a ***suspicious*** *glance* 疑い深い目付. ¶ a ***sweeping*** *glance* 広く見渡すこと. ¶ an ***upward*** *glance* 上目使い. ¶ dwell upon one's face with a ***wistful*** and ***yearning*** *glance* 慕わしげなあこがれの目付でその横顔をじいっと見入る.

P take it in ***at*** a *glance* 一目で合点する ‖ show ***at*** a *glance* that ... 一目で...と分る. 【類】I could tell ***at*** a *glance*. / In the following tabular view these may be seen ***at*** a *glance*. ‖ Telephone numbers ***at*** a *glance*. 電話早見表. 【類】It is manifest ***at*** a *glance*. ¶ ***by*** a *glance* at the map it will be seen that ... 地図を一見すれば...ということが分ろう. ¶ see a group of words ***in*** one *glance* 一目で一語群を見る. ¶ ***under*** the *glance* of the sun 白昼. ¶ ***with*** side *glances* 横目で.

P² a *glance* ***at*** the past 過去の一べつ. 【類】a *glance* ***at*** English history will afford a pretty fair clue to the reason for. ... ¶ a *glance* ***into*** the history of ... shows that ... ...の歴史を一べつすると...ということが分る. ¶ as a *glance* ***on*** the map will show 地図を一目見れば分るように. ¶ take a retrospective *glance* ***over*** Chinese history 回顧的に中国史を一べつする. ¶ a *glance* ***through*** the pages of ... ...のページを繰って一回目を通すこと.

glance, *v.* 一見する, 一べつする; それる; 暗示する; ちらと向ける.

M *glance* ***anxiously*** at ... 心配気に...をちらと見る. ¶ *glance* (=flash) ***back*** 反射する, 照り返す ‖ *glancing* ***back*** over the path one has come たどってきた道を顧みると. ¶ *glance* ***covertly*** at ... ...をこっそりと見る.

M² *glance* ***down*** a list 表を一べつする ‖ *glance* ***down*** into the clear water きれいな水をのぞき込む. ¶ The bullet *glanced* ***off*** (=***aside***). 弾丸はそれた.

P *glance* ***about*** one あたりを見回す. ¶ *glance* ***at*** one's watch 時計をちらっと見る. 【類】I have only *glanced* ***at*** it. ¶ *glance* ***into*** Japanese interiors 日本内地をべっ見する. ¶ *glance* ***over*** a bill (letter, papers) 勘定書(など)にざっと目を通す ‖ *glance* ***over*** a landscape 景色を見渡す. ¶ *glance* ***through*** a magazine (a book) 雑誌(など)に目を通す. ¶ *glance* ***towards*** a person (place) 人(など)の方をちらっと見る. ¶ *glance* one's eye ***upon*** an object ある物に目をちらと向ける.

glare, *n.* きらめき, せん光; にらみ.

V It is highly unpleasant ***to have*** the *glare* of publicity thrown upon one's private business and family life. 私ごとや家庭生活を(新聞などに)さらけだされるのは実に不愉快だ.

Q with an ***angry*** *glare* 怒ってぎょろっと目をむいて. ¶ He was in the ***full*** *glare* of the sun. 彼はぎらぎらした太陽の直射を受けていた. ¶ a ***raucous*** *glare* of shop lights 店の灯のいやにぎらぎらする光.

P ***in*** the *glare* of the footlights 脚光の強い光の中に. ¶ ***under*** the *glare* of the sun 白昼日の照る中を.

P² the *glare* ***of*** torches たいまつのきらめき.

glare, *v.* ねめつける.

M *glare* ***back*** にらみかえす. ¶ He *glared* ***fiercely*** as he spoke. 彼は話しながら恐ろしい目付をした.

M² The tropical sun *glared* ***down*** on us. 熱帯の太陽が頭上にぎらぎら照った.

P They stood *glaring* ***at*** each other. 彼らはにらみ合って立っていた. ¶ *glare* ***on*** one's foe 敵をにらみつける.

glass, *n.* ガラス; 洋杯(グラス), コップ; 双眼鏡, 鏡; 晴雨計; *pl.* 眼鏡.

V ***apply*** one's *glasses* to one's eye 眼鏡をかける. ¶ ***Chinking*** *glasses* strikes an Englishman as a foreign habit. グラスをかちんと打合せることは英国にはない習慣であって英国人は異様に感じる. ¶ Hot water has ***cracked*** a *glass*. 湯でコップにひびが入った. ¶ He ***drained*** the *glass* to the bottom. 彼はグラスを飲み干した. ¶ ***drink*** a *glass* to the memory of ... ...を記念して祝杯をあげる. ¶ ***empty*** a *glass* at a draught コップを一口に飲み干す. 【類】***empty*** four *glasses* of champagne. ¶ ***Fill*** your *glass*. グラスにおつぎ下さい. 【類】***fill*** the *glass* up to the brim (一杯に). ¶ ***fill up*** a *glass* グラスに一杯つぐ. ¶ ***level*** one's *glasses* at ... 双眼鏡を...に向ける. ¶ ***lift*** one's *glass* 杯をあげる. ¶ Please ***pour*** me ***out*** a *glass* of beer. ビールを一杯ついで下さい. ¶ quaff a *glass* ***of*** beer ビールを一杯ぐいとあおる. ¶ ***raise*** one's *glass* to one's lips グラスを口に持って来る ‖ ***raise*** one's *glass* to propose (=drink) the health of ... ...のために祝杯をあげる. ¶ I was called on to ***take*** a "social" *glass*. つきあいに一杯やれと言われた. 【類】***Take*** one more *glass*. / I have ***taken*** a *glass* too much. ¶ ***turn*** one's *glass* ***down*** 杯を伏せる. ¶ I must ***wear*** dark *glasses* to screen my eyes from the glare. 私は目に日光を当てないように黒眼鏡をかけねばならない.

V² The *glass* is ***rising*** (***falling***). 晴雨計は上昇(下降)している.

Q a pair of ***binocular*** *glasses* 一個の双眼鏡. ¶ early ***excavated*** *glass* 出土の古代ガラス. ¶ ***frosted*** *glass* つや消しガラス. ¶ ***heavy*** *glass* 厚ガラス. ¶ ***heavy, horn-rimmed*** *glasses* がん丈な角ぶち眼鏡. ¶when put under a powerful ***magnifying*** *glass* 強力な拡大鏡で検査して見ると. ¶a small pocket ***magnifying*** *glass* 小型拡大鏡. ¶***organic*** *glass* 有機ガラス. ¶***plastic*** *glass* プラスチック製ガラス. ¶a ***restorative*** *glass* of wine 元気をつけるぶどう酒一杯. ¶***rimless*** *glasses* 縁なし眼鏡. ¶In viewing Japan he evidently wears his ***rosecolored*** *glasses*. 彼の日本観察は明かに楽観的だ. ¶wear ***strong*** (***weak***) *glasses* 強度の(度の弱い)眼鏡をかける.

Q[2] a ***beverage*** *glass* 飲料水用コップ. ¶a ***burning*** *glass* 天日取鏡. ¶"***one-way***" *glass* 片面ガラス(内側からしか見えない). ¶***safety*** *glass* 安全ガラス(合成ガラス). ¶***sheet*** *glass* 板ガラス. ¶a ***spy*** *glass* [携帯用]望遠鏡. ¶***table*** *glass* 食卓用ガラス器類. ¶a ***vanity*** *glass* 化粧袋に入れる小鏡.

P look at oneself ***in*** the *glass* 鏡に写った自分の姿をながめる. ¶a bit ***of*** *glass* 一片のガラス ‖ two panes ***of*** *glass* 二枚のガラス. ¶pictures ***on*** *glass* ガラス絵. ¶drink wine ***out of*** (=*from*) a *glass* コップでぶどう酒を飲む. ¶He is a jolly fellow ***over*** his *glass*. 彼は酒を飲むと愉快なやつだ. ¶look at things ***through*** *glasses* colored by one's own inclinations 色めがねで物事を見る. ¶flowers grown ***under*** *glass* 温室で育った草花. ¶The hysterical person looks at everything ***with*** a magnifying *glass*. ヒステリ性の人はなんでも物を拡大鏡で(大げさに)見る. ¶I can't see ***without*** my *glasses*. 私は目がねをかけなくては物が見えない.

P[2] *glasses* ***in*** gold frame 金縁めがね. ¶a *glass* ***of*** wine 一杯のぶどう酒.

glassful, *n.* コップ一杯.

P[2] a *glassful* ***of*** water コップ一杯の水.

glassware, *n.* ガラス器.

Q ***ornamental*** *glassware* 装飾ガラス器. ¶***useful*** *glassware* 重宝なガラス器. ¶***utilitarian*** *glassware* 実用向ガラス器.

gleam, *n.* せん光, 微光.

V They ***caught*** the *gleam* of the distant sea. 彼は遠い海をちらりと見た. ‖ ***catch*** the first *gleam* of its rising sun. しょ光を見る; 先覚者となる. ¶***feel*** a *gleam* of mad joy 有頂天になる. ¶She ***had*** a deadly *gleam* in her eye. 彼女は目に怒気を浮べていた. ¶It ***shed*** a feeble *gleam* of light upon the dark subject. それはその不可解な問題に一微光を投げた(ちょっと分りかけた).

Q a ***faint*** *gleam* of hope かすかな希望の光. ¶a ***sudden*** *gleam* of light 突然のせん光.

P[2] a *gleam* ***of*** hope 希望のひらめき ‖ the *gleam* ***of*** a distant lighthouse 遠くの灯台からのかすかなせん光.

gleam, *v.* きらめく, 光る, 輝く.

M Wit *gleamed* ***out*** in his talk. 彼の話には機知のひらめきがあった.

P A cottage *gleamed* ***through*** the trees. 一軒のいなか家が樹間から光って見えた. ¶The moon *gleamed* ***upon*** the lake. 月が湖上に輝いた.

glean, *v.* あちこちから拾い集める.

M The plague *gleaned* ***away*** thousands of people. ペストで何人という人が死んだ.

P material *gleaned* and carded ***from*** my own reading 私の読書中に集めてカードをとった材料. 【類】a knowledge of the latest result laboriously *gleaned* ***from*** a variety of sources ‖ facts *gleaned* ***from*** books (newspapers) 書物(など)から拾い集めた事実. 【類】These facts are *gleaned* chiefly ***from*** oral narration.

gleaning, *n.* 収集; 収集物.

V ***make*** a systematic *gleaning* of words and phrases through current literature 現代文献の中から語句を組織的に収集する.

glee, *n.* 喜び, 歓喜.

Q with ***complacent*** *glee* 満足した喜びで. ¶I am in ***high*** *glee* this moring. 私はけさは大元気だ.

P I advanced ***with*** great *glee*. 私は喜び勇んで前進した.

glib, *a.* 口達者な.

P He is *glib* ***of*** tongue. =He has a glib tongue. 彼は口が達者だ.

glide, *n.* 滑走.

P The skater is moving ***with*** a *glide*. スケートをする人がなめらかにすべっている.

P[2] a *glide* ***of*** ... meters ...メートルの滑走.

glide, *v.* 滑走する, すべるように進む.

M *glide* ***away*** to some other topic 他の問題に話をそらす. ¶*glide* ***out*** すっと出る.

M[2] And the train *glided* ***by***. そして汽車はすべるように出て行った. ¶Time *glided* ***on***. 知らない間に時がたった. ‖ The first sound *glides* ***on*** to the next. 発音のとき第一の音は第二の音と連続する. ¶The boat *glided* ***up*** to the pier. 船は桟橋の方に徐行した.

P *glide* ***in*** the air ***like*** a kite とびのように大空を滑走する. ¶He *glided* ***into*** telling me the secret. 彼はうっかり秘密を僕にもらした. ¶*glide* ***off*** our own right. いつか自分の権限を越える. ¶A swan is *gliding* gracefully ***on*** the pond. 一羽の白鳥が池の上を優美に泳いでいる. ¶*glide* ***out of*** a room へやからそっと出る. ¶*glide* ***over*** the ice 氷上を滑走する. 【類】*glide* ***over*** the smooth lake. ¶The stream *glides* ***through*** the meadow. 川が静かに草原を流れる. 【類】A small brook *glides* ***through*** the valley with a murmur (さらさらと).

glider, *n.* 滑空機(グライダー).

V ***maneuver*** a *glider* グライダーを操縦する.

glimmer, *n.* 微光.

V I ***have*** no *glimmer* of hope in the future. 私には将来に希望の微光すらない.

Q a ***pale*** *glimmer* of hope かすかな希望の光.

P[2] the *glimmer* ***of*** distant lamps through the mist 霧を通してはるかに見えるランプの光. 【類】There wasn't a *glimmer* ***of*** light to be seen.

glimmering, *n.* 微光.

V I ***get*** a *glimmering* who they are. 彼らがだれだかうすうす分かる.

glimpse, *n.* 一見, 一べつ; せん光.

V it ***affords*** pretty *glimpses* of ... そこから...の美しい風景がながめられる. ¶***cast*** some *glimpse* at ... ...をちらりとながめる. ¶***catch*** a *glimpse*, in passing, of ... 通りがかりに...をちらりと見る. 【類】***catch*** (=***get***) a *glimpse* of ... / ***catch*** the first *glimpse* of ... ¶***gain*** a *glimpse* of ... ...をちらりと見る. ¶***get*** a *glimpse* of China on the way 途中ちょっと中国をのぞく. ¶***have*** a *glimpse* of ... ...を一目見る. ¶***obtain*** dim *glimpses* of ... ...をぼんやり見る ‖ The pamphlet will enable one to ***obtain*** *glimpses* into the subject. そのパンフレットでその問題がいくらか分かる. ¶***snatch*** some vivid *glimpse* of his character 彼の品性をややはっきりとつかむ. ¶***take*** a *glimpse* at ... ...をちょっとのぞく.

Q take ***brief*** *glimpses* at ... ちょっと...をべっ見する. ¶get the ***first*** *glimpse* of Oriental life 東洋人の生活を初めて一べつする. 【類】obtain the ***first*** *glimpses* of the Pacific. / Yokohama is the port where so many of the tourists get their ***first*** as well as their ***last*** *glimpse* of the Land of the Rising Sun. ¶catch a ***hurried*** *glimpse* of ... ...をちらと見る. ¶catch ***passing*** *glimpses* of ... ついでにちょっと...をのぞいて見る. 【類】obtain a ***passing*** *glimpse* of the many attractive features of the town. ¶This affords a ***strange*** *glimpse* into the working of the British mind. これで英国人の心理の奇妙な方面がうかがわれる.

Q[2] ***behind-the-scenes*** *glimpses* as to ... ...に関する楽屋話.

P ***by*** the *glimpse* I took of him I could easily perceive that he ... 彼をちらりと見て私は容易に彼が...であることを察し得た.

P[2] a *glimpse* ***at*** the art of Japan 日本美術のべっ見. 【類】a *glimpse* ***at*** Guatemala (the theatres, the park). ¶*glimpses* ***into*** plant life 植物界のべっ見. ¶*glimpses* ***of*** the past 過去のべっ見 ‖ Progress that was being made is afforded by his article.

glimpse, *v.* ちらと見える.

P the town *glimpsed* ***from*** the air 空中から見たその市.

glint, *v.* 照り返す; ひらめく.

M *glint* ***back*** light 光を反射する.

P *glint* ***in*** the sunshine (darkness) 日光(など)にひらめく.

glisten, *v.* きらめく, 輝く.

P The gilded statue on the tower *glistened* ***in*** the sun. 金ぱくの像や塔が日を受けてきらきら輝いた. ¶*glisten* ***like*** diamonds ダイヤのようにきらめく. ¶Her eyes *glistened* ***with*** joy (tears). 彼女の目は喜び(涙)で輝いた.

glitter, *n.* 輝き.

P The child was attracted ***by*** the *glitter* of Christmas decoration. その子はぴかぴか光るクリスマス装飾に引きつけられた.

glitter, *v.* ぴかぴか光る, 輝く.

P *glitter* ***in*** the sunlight 日光に輝く. 【類】stars *glittering* ***in*** the frosty sky. ¶*glitter* ***with*** precious stones 宝石でぴかぴか光る. 【類】The green boughs *glittered* ***with*** all their pearls of dew (真珠のような露).

gloat, *v.* うれしそうにながめる; 気持よげにながめる.

M She ***fairly*** *gloated* over the recital of her troubles. 彼女は全く楽しそうにその病気の悩みを語った.

P *gloat on* (=*upon*) a heap of treasure 山と積んだ宝をうれし気にながめる. ¶The miser *gloated over* his gold. けちんぼは自分の黄金を見てほくそえんだ. ‖ I *gloated over* the book, rapt clean out of myself. 私は全く没我の境地でその書物をむさぼり読んだ. 【類】*gloat over* another's embarrassment / *gloat over* another's misfortune / *gloat over* the corpse of an enemy.

globe, *n.* 地球; 球; 地球儀.

V You may *circle* the *globe* on President Liners in no more than 110 days. プレジデント・ラインの船で行くとわずか百十日で世界一周ができる. ¶The language of England *girdles* the *globe*. 英語が地球を取り巻く(世界に行き渡っている).

Q a *clear globe* 透明球. ¶the *English-speaking globe* 英語を話す世界(国々). ¶a [*terrestrial*] *globe* 地球儀.

Q² an electric *light globe* (=bulb) 電球.

P form it *into* a *globe* それを球に作る. ¶one of the greatest commercial nations *of* the *globe* 世界第一流の商業国 ‖ the largest empire on the face *of* the *globe* 世界最大の帝国. ¶all the land *on* the *globe* 地球上の全土. 【類】There is no place *on* the *globe* where the pressure of Western civilization does not now make itself felt. ¶a ramble *round* the *globe* 世界漫遊.

gloom, *n.* 暗黒; 憂うつ; 暗たん.

V His death *casts* a *gloom* over the country. 同氏の死去に対し国民こぞって悲しんでいる. ¶*dispel* the *gloom* うつを晴らす. ¶*lighten* the *gloom* of … …の憂うつを軽減する. ¶*throw* a *gloom* over the festivities of … …の盛典を憂うつにする.

Q in the *deepening gloom* of a winter's evening 冬の夕やみ迫る中で. ¶*ebony gloom* 黒たんのような(真の)やみ. ¶the *gathering gloom* せまる宵やみ. ¶the *ominous gloom* 不吉な暗所. ¶Over the question there is a *settled gloom*. その問題の上には密雲がかかっている. ¶a

P² the *gloom of* a forest (midnight) 森(など)のくらがり ‖ the *gloom of* warfare 戦争の憂うつさ. ¶He was then in the *gloom of* despair. 当時彼は絶望のやみに迷っていた.

glorification, *n.* 賛美.

P² the *glorification of* a guilty passion 罪の情熱賛仰.

glory, *n.* 光栄, 栄誉; 光輝; 壮観.

V *add* new *glory* to the University 同大学に新しい光栄を添える. ¶*bequeath* one's *glory* to … その栄誉を…に伝える. ¶*bring glory* on themselves 彼ら自身に光栄をもたらす. ¶*covet* a *glory* 栄誉を欲しがる. ¶*diminish* his *glory* 彼の栄誉を傷つける. ¶the heroes who have *given glory* to the pages of Russian history ロシアの歴史を飾る勇士. ¶*reflect glory* on one's ancestors 先祖の名をあげる. ¶*retrieve* the *glory* of one's ancestors その先祖の名誉を回復する. ¶*seek* the *glory* of martyrdom 殉教の光栄を求める. ¶*share* the *glory* of doing the world's work 世界の事業に参加するの光栄をになう.

V² to him *belongs* the *glory* of having first … 初めて…した名誉はすなわち彼が受けるべきものである. ¶The *glory* of the London coffee-shops has considerably *departed*. ロンドンのコーヒー店も大分盛りの時代が過ぎた. ¶Its *glory paled* sensibly. その名声が著しく衰えた.

Q its *ancient glories* as … …としてのその昔の隆盛. ¶The cathedral forms one of the *architectural glories* of the British Empire. その大寺院は英帝国における建築上の壮観の一つをなしている. ¶Grass is the *chief glory* of English gardens. 芝生は英国の庭園の主な誇りである. ¶the *crowning glory* of a great career 偉人の一生におけるとう尾の光栄. ¶in a *flashing glory* of sunset 輝く夕陽の壮観に. ¶The flowers will then be in their *full glory*. 花はそのころ盛りでしょう. ¶No *greater glory* could be gained. それにまさる栄誉は他にない. ¶The *industrial glory* of England is departing. 英国は産業の偉大さを失いつつある. ¶a lust for *military glory* and territorial aggrandizement 軍の栄誉と領土拡大の欲望. ¶Some reminders of its *old-time* (=*former*) *glory* are still in evidence. 昔の繁栄の名残がまだ見られる. ¶the *past glories* of the house 同家の過去の名誉. ¶obtain *posthumous glory* 死に花を咲かせる. ¶He is distinguished from a *reflected glory* from the achievements of his followers. 彼は部下の功績のお陰で名高いのだ. ¶*undying glory* 不朽の光栄.

P *for* the *glory* of … …の栄誉のために. ¶womanhood *in* all its *glory* 女の盛り. 【類】The boy and girl sweethearts of these London streets are *in* their *glory* on Bank Holiday. ¶The city was then at the pinnacle *of glory*. 当時その市は隆盛の頂点に達していた.

P² the *glory of* arms 武のほまれ ‖ the *glories of* ancient Rome 古ローマの壮観. 【類】the *glory of* the trees in autumns. ¶*Glory to* God! 栄光神にあれ.

glory, *v.* 誇る, 自慢する; 喜ぶ.

P Japan *glories in* the beauties of nature. 日本は自然の美を誇る. 【類】The statesman *glories in* his honorable poverty. ‖ Ascetics *glory in* hardships. 苦行者は難渋を喜ぶ. ‖ a confirmed thief *glorying in* his smartness 自分の腕を自慢する常習犯の盗賊. 【類】He of all things *gloried* (=delighted) *in* his physical strength. / *glory in* success (a victory) / *glory in* the profession of war (軍人) / *glory in* the fact (theory) that … / Behave so that your parents may *glory in* having such a son. / Leyden (ライデン市) *glories in* its university, and considers itself the brain of the nation. / *glory in* one's work / *glory in* the home-spun white linen frills and ruffles (白麻のふち飾り) / He used to *glory in* his wickedness (不行跡). ‖ They would *glory in* my defeat. 彼らは私が失敗するのを見て喜ぶのが常であった. 【類】He seems to *glory in* his poverty.

gloss, *n.* 光沢.

V he *got* his final *gloss* under … …彼は…について最後の仕上げをやった. ¶It *has* a beautiful *gloss*. それは光沢が美しい.

Q silk cloth with a *good gloss* つやのよい絹布.

gloss, *v.* 光沢を付ける.

M² *gloss over* one's fault (mistake) 失錯をごまかす.

gloss, *n.* 注釈, 注解.

V² A *gloss explains* 油 as 紬. 注には油者紬也とある.

Q The classics have been spoiled by the *critical glosses* of generations of commentators. それらの古典は長い間に注釈家が加えた評注のために悪くなった. ¶the Divina Commedia of Dante with *interlinear glosses* 行間に注釈の付いたダンテの神曲.

P² a *gloss on* a word (phrase) 語(句)の注.

glossary, *n.* 字解, 用語解.

P² an *index glossary* 索引用語表.

P² a *glossary to* Shakespeare シェイクスピア用語解.

glove, *n.* 手袋; 〔野球〕グローブ; 〔拳闘〕グラブ.

V *draw on* (*off*) *gloves* 手袋をはめる(ぬぐ). ¶*Excuse* my *glove*. 手袋のままで失礼いたします(握手のとき). ¶*get on* (*off*) *gloves* 手袋をはめる(脱ぐ). ¶He *has gloves on*. 彼は手袋をはめている. ¶*pull off* one's *gloves* 手袋を脱ぐ. ¶*put on* one's *gloves* 手袋をはめる. ¶My *gloves* must be *stretched*. 手袋を伸ばさねばならない. ¶*take off* one's *gloves* 手袋を脱ぐ. ¶*wear* one's *gloves* 手袋をはめている.

V² The *gloves* will *stretch* with use. 手袋ははめている内に伸びる.

Q an *odd* (=a *single*) *glove* 一方だけの手袋. ¶a great variety of ladies's *superior gloves* 色々の種類の婦人用高級手袋. ¶*tight* (*loose*) *gloves* きつい(ゆるい)手袋.

Q² a *boxing glove* 拳闘用グラブ. ¶a *catcher glove* 捕手グローブ. ¶a *five-finger glove* 指の分れた手袋. ¶a *kid glove* やぎ皮の手袋. ¶a *leather glove* 皮手袋. ¶*mousquetaire gloves* 婦人用長手袋. ¶*work gloves* 軍手.

P fit *like* a *glove* きちんと合う. ¶a pair *of gloves* 手袋一対. ¶I have lost the mate *to* this *glove*. この手袋の片方をなくした.

glow, *n.* 白熱, 光; 紅色; 熱烈.

V I *felt* a pleasant *glow* in all my veins from the wine. 私は酒を飲んでとう然とした. ¶*get* quite a *glow* of enthusiasm 非常に熱中する.

Q Now I see a *bright glow* in the sky. 私は今空が明るく輝くのを見る. ¶the *fiery glow* of the contest 競技の白熱的な激しさ. ¶a *great red glow* in the western sky 西の空の大きい真赤な輝き. ¶The exercise gives a *healthy glow* to the faces of skaters. 運動のためにスケートをやる人たちの顔に元気そうな赤味がさす. ¶the *pale glow* of a firefly ほたるの青白い光. ¶the *rosy glow* of dawn 暁のばら色.

Q² in the *amber glow* of the wintry day どんよりした鉛色の冬の日に. ¶the *evening* (=*sunset*) *glow* 夕焼け.

P Rub with the finger-tips until the skin is *in* a *glow*. 指先で皮膚が真赤になるまで十分にこすれ. ‖ He is all *in* a *glow* with hard riding. 彼は激しく馬で乗回したので真赤になっている. ¶*Under* the *glow* of thousands of electric lamps the great building makes a brilliant and entrancing picture. 幾千という電灯の光でその大きな建物はさんらんとして見るからにうっとりさせる絵のようである. ¶The setting sun shone *with* a red *glow*. 夕日が真赤に輝いた.

P² She has the *glow* ***of*** health in the cheeks 彼女のほおは健康そうにつやつやしている. 【類】Their faces have the *glow* ***of*** health instead of the hectic flush of disease (結核性の赤らみ). ‖ the *glow* ***of*** sunset 真赤な夕焼 ‖ feel a *glow* ***of*** pleasure 熱烈な喜びを感じる. ¶a red *glow* ***on*** the face 顔の赤びかり.

glow, *v.* しゃく熱する; 光る, 輝く; [情など]熱する, 燃える; 真赤になる.

P patriotism *glowing* ***in*** his breast 彼の胸中に燃える愛国心 ‖ The sunset *glows* ***in*** the west. 夕焼けで西の空は真赤に輝く. ¶*glow* ***into*** enthusiasm 熱意が燃えている. ¶*glow* ***like*** fire 火のように光る. ¶The coals *glow* ***on*** the hearth. 石炭が炉でかっかと燃える. ¶his cheeks *glowing* ***with*** a florid red 花のように赤く輝く彼のほお ‖ His face *glows* ***with*** exercise. 彼は運動したので顔が真赤だ. ‖ The oven *glows* ***with*** heat. かまは熱で赤くなっている. ‖ *glow* ***with*** indignation (enthusiasm, ambition, delight) 憤り(など)で真赤になる ‖ His heart *glows* ***with*** patriotism. 彼の心は愛国心に燃えている. ‖ Woods and forests *glow* ***with*** autumn tints. 森も林も紅葉で燃えている.

glue, *n.* にかわ.

V² This *glue* ***sticks*** fast. このにかわはしっかり着く.

P fasten it ***with*** *glue* それをにかわ付けにする.

glue, *v.* にかわ付けにする; ぴったり着ける.

M *glue* two things ***together*** 二物をにかわ付けにする.

M² *glue* ***up*** for binding 製本ののりづけをする.

P She sat there with her eyes *glued* ***on*** the stage. 彼は舞台から目を離さずにそこにすわっていた. ¶his eyes were *glued* ***to*** ... 彼は目を...にすえていた. 【類】His lips were *glued* ***to*** hers for some time.

glut, *n.* 供給過剰.

P² a *glut* ***in*** the market 市場の在荷過多. ¶There is a *glut* ***of*** goods in the market. 市場には品が余っている.

glut, *v.* 過多に供給する; あかす.

P Two years of war *glutted* his appetite ***for*** more adventures. 二年間の戦争で彼の冒険欲は満ち足りた. ¶The market is *glutted* ***with*** products. 市場には品が有り余っている. ‖ *glut* oneself ***with*** pleasures (dainties) 楽しみ(美食)にあきる.

glutton, *n.* 大食家, 健たん家.

Q a *literary glutton* 文学にふける人.

P² a *glutton* ***for*** books 書物ずき ‖ a *glutton* ***for*** work 仕事ずき.

gnashing, *n.* 歯ぎしり.

V ***cause*** some *gnashing* of molars 切歯させる.

P² the *gnashing* ***of*** the teeth [無念の]歯ぎしり, 切歯.

gnat, *n.* 蚊, ぶよ.

V² *Gnats* ***buzz***. 蚊がぶんぶんいう.

gnaw, *v.* かむ, かじる.

M *gnaw* ***away*** at the bark and the wood. 立木の皮や森を蚕食する.

P fear and anxiety *gnawing* ***at*** the heart 心をむしばむ恐怖や心配. ¶He *gnawed* his lip ***in*** rage. 彼は怒ってくちびるをかんだ. ¶Rats *gnaw* ***into*** a wall. ねずみは壁をかじって穴を作る. ¶*gnaw* the meat ***off*** a bone 骨の肉をかじり取る. ¶Rats *gnawed* a hole ***through*** the wall. ねずみが壁をかじって穴を明けた. ¶*gnaw* ***upon*** food (bone) 食物(など)をかじる.

go, *v.* 行く, 往く; 歩く, 通る; 動く, 回る; [うまくまたはまずく]いく, 運ぶ; 成行く, 成る; やって行く; 通じる, 至る; のっとる, 拠る; 定まる.

M *go* ***aboard*** 乗船する. ¶*go* ***abroad*** 洋行する. ¶*go* ***adrift***=deviate 漂流する, 脱線する. ¶*go* ***ahead*** to ... 進んで...する ‖ *Go* ***ahead*** all you can. できるだけがん張れ. ‖ *Go* straight ***ahead***. 真っすぐにおい出なさい. ¶My brother quickly passing him, *went* ***ahead***. 僕の兄(弟)は早くも彼を追抜いた. ‖ *go* ***ahead*** and fill a better job 昇進していい位置につく ‖ The work is *going* ***ahead*** in good style. 仕事は順調に発展している. ‖ *Go* ***ahead*** in your own way. 君我流でやり給え. ‖ *go* ***ahead*** with one's work (study, investigation) 仕事(など)を進める. 【類】He is far *gone* ***ahead*** of us in English. ¶We should *go* ***all out*** to help him. われわれは全力をあげて彼を援助しなければならない. ‖ He hasn't *gone* ***all-out*** on this thing. 彼は本当に乗気になってやっていない. ¶Did it *go* ***all right***? うまく行きましたか. ¶*go* ***aloft*** マストに登る. ¶*go* it ***alone*** それを独力でやる. ¶This will *go* ***a long way*** toward world peace. これは世界平和に大いに役立つだろう. ¶*go* ***amiss*** うまく行かない, しくじる. ¶the ship *went* ***ashore*** off the coast of ... その船は...海岸沖で座礁した. ¶The arrow *went* ***aside*** and pierced his heart. 矢がわきへそれて彼の心臓を貫いた. ¶*go* ***asleep*** 眠りにつく. ¶*go* ***astern*** [船が]後進する. ¶The letter has *gone* ***astray*** in the post. その郵便に出した手紙はゆくえ不明になった. ¶*go* ***at length*** into the history of ... ...の歴史を詳細に述べる. ¶*Go* ***away***, *go* ***away***. どけどけ. ‖ *Go* right ***away***! すぐ出かけろ. ‖ *go* ***away*** from home to get a change 気分転換のため旅に出る ‖ *Go* ***away*** from me. そっちへ行け. ‖ Oh, *go* ***away*** and learn your job. おい出直してこい. ‖ *go* ***away*** for a rest 休息のため立ち去る ‖ *go* ***away*** for the weekend 週末旅行に出かける. 【類】*go* ***away*** for holidays (=a vacation) ‖ He has *gone* ***away***, the destination unknown. 彼は去って行先不明である. 【類】He has *gone* ***away*** nobody (=God) knows where. / *go* ***away*** into the country for a short time / *go* ***away*** with a feeling that ... ¶He *went* ***back*** home absorbed in thought. 彼は考え込んで家に帰って行った. 【類】*go* ***back*** home to one's family (boarding-house) ‖ *go* ***back*** whence they came (=where they came from) もと来た道に引き返す ‖ *go* ***back*** to private life 野に下る ‖ *go* ***back*** into retirement 隠退する ‖ *Go* ***back*** as you please. どうぞご自由にお引取り下さい. ‖ The strikers have *gone* ***back*** to (=resumed) work. 罷業者は仕事に復帰した. ‖ I will never *go* ***back*** from my work. 私は決して仕事から手を引かない. ‖ Nothing will induce me to *go* ***back*** to it. どんなことがあっても立戻るものか. ‖ *go* ***back*** at him また彼を攻撃する ‖ *go* ***back*** on one's word 約束を守らない ‖ Some member has *gone* ***back*** on his comrades だれかが仲間を裏切った ‖ *go* ***back*** in price 価格が低下する ‖ *go* ***back*** to the first century 第一世紀にさかのぼる ‖ *go* ***back*** into newspaper work as a cartoonist 漫画家として新聞にカムバックする ‖ *go* ***back*** to one's old ways (=practice) 従来のやり方に戻る. 【類】Its origin *goes* ***back*** into medieval times (中世紀). / The history of this Day *goes* ***back*** to 1916. / *go* ***back*** into the country. ¶*go* ***backstage*** after the show 演芸が済んで楽屋へはいり込む(ファンなどが). ¶*go* ***backward*** 退歩する; 具合がわるくなる, 左前になる. ¶fruit and vegetables which are beginning to *go* ***bad*** 腐りかかっている果実や野菜. 【類】These oranges are beginning to *go* ***bad***. ¶*go* ***bald-headed*** into a thing がむしゃらにぶつかって行く. ¶Things *go* ***badly*** with him. 万事彼はうまく行かない. ¶The ship *went* ***bang*** up into the dock. 船はドックにどかんとぶつかって入った. ‖ ***Bang*** *went* the gun! どんと鉄砲が発射した. ¶He *went* ***bankrupt*** for £1,890. 彼は一千八百九十ポンドの負債で破産した. ¶*go* ***bareheaded*** under the sun 日に照らされて帽子なしで行く. ¶*go* ***behind*** and look for it 裏面に立入ってそれを捜す. ¶*go* ***blind*** 盲になる. ¶*go* ***bluntly*** to the point without finesse or beating about the bush 術策をろうしたり探りを入れたりせず単刀直入問題に触れる. ¶*go* ***boldly*** into battle 大胆に戦闘を始める. 【類】*go* ***boldly*** up to a front seat. ¶*go* ***broke*** 《米口語》文なしになる. ¶*go* ***carefully*** into the matter 周到にその事件を調べる. 【類】*go* ***carefully*** through the exposition of one's methods. ¶Everything *went* ***cheap*** at the auction. 競売でなにもかも安かった. ¶*goes* ***counter*** to the current of the world 時の流れに逆行する. ¶the language *goes* ***current*** among ... その国語は...間に一般に通用する. ¶*go* ***deep[ly]*** into details 細部にわたって深く調べる ‖ The sales of the book *went* ***deeply*** into the millions. その本の売高は数百万部に上った ‖ *go* ***deeply*** into the enterprise その事業に深入りする. 【類】He doesn't *go* ***deep*** into any subject. ¶*go* ***downhill*** (***uphill***) 坂を下(上)る. 【類】they *went* ***downhill*** to ... ¶*go* ***downstairs*** (***upstairs***) 階下に降りる(階上に行く). ¶*go* ***downstream*** (***upstream***) 川を下る(さか上る). ¶*go* ***downtown*** shopping 下町へ買物に行く. ¶The well *goes* ***dry*** in summer. この井戸は夏はひ上がる. ¶*go* ***early*** from work 早退する. ¶*Go* ***easy***! ゆっくりやれ, せくな. ¶*go* ***elaborately*** into an examination of ... ...の調査を念入りにやる. ¶it will *go* ***far*** to show ... ...を明らかにする上において大いに役に立つことであろう ‖ I have *gone* too ***far*** to turn back. 深みにはまり込んで引込みがつかない. ‖ he was not *going* too ***far*** when he said ... 彼が…と言ったのは行き過ぎ(無理)じゃなかった ‖ You are too ***far*** *gone* to play tonight. 君は酔っているからおやめなさい. ‖ Thus ***far*** they shall *go* and no further. ここまで行かせようから先はだめだ. ‖ That's *going* too ***far***! そりゃあんまりだ. ‖ I was too ***far*** *gone* to reason then. そのときは私は夢中でなにがなんだか分らなかった. ‖ *go* ***far*** toward ... …に大いに効がある. ‖ I don't *go* quite so ***far*** as that. まさかそうとも思いません. ‖ There are people who *go* so ***far*** as to say that ... …とさえ言う人がある. ‖ His pleading *went* ***far*** with the judge. 彼の弁護は大いに裁判官を動かした. ‖ He is ***far*** *gone* in a consumption of the lungs. 彼は肺病が大いに進んでいる. ‖ ***far*** *gone* in intoxication 大分めいていして ‖ he had to *go* ***far*** out of his way to see his friend, Mr. T. 友人T氏を訪問するのでずっと回り道をしなければならなかった. 【類】 Indeed it is perhaps hardly *going* too ***far*** to say that it is very little use trying to convince any one by argument. / £4 a year in those days would *go* as ***far*** as forty will go now. ¶His death *goes* no ***farther*** than twenty years. 彼の死んだのは二十年前以上にはならない. ‖ *go* ***farther*** than the facts warrant 事実が証明する以上の取扱をする ‖ *Go* ***farther*** and fare worse. 先へ進めば進むほど具合が悪くなる. ¶as ***fast*** as they can *go* できるだけ手早に. ¶At first things *went* ***favorably***. 最初は万事好都合に行った. ¶*go* ***fishing*** for trout ます釣りに出かける. ‖ Won't you come and *go* ***fishing*** with me? どうだ僕と釣りに行かないか. ¶It is *gone* ***forever***. それは永遠に去ってしまった. ¶*go* ***forth*** from one's home 自宅から出かける ‖ The decree has *gone* ***forth***. その命令が布告された. ‖ He *went* ***forth*** to battle and was heard of no more. 彼は出征しそれっきり音さたがなかった. ¶If he thinks he is right, he *goes* straight ***forward***. 彼は正しいと考えると直言直行する. ‖ *go* bravely ***forward*** 勇往まい進する ‖ "What's *going* ***forward***?"—"Ball, sir," said the waiter.「なにをやってるのか」「野球です」と給仕が言った. ‖ *go* ***forward*** by railway 汽車で出かける. 【類】 He will *go* ***forward*** by the 2 p.m. train. ¶He is *going* ***fourteen***. 彼は十四になる所だ. ¶I'll let you *go* ***free***. 君を自由にしてやる. ¶*go* no ***further*** than ... …で止る, …に終る ‖ *go* even a little ***further*** and ... 一歩進んで… ‖ It is unnecessary to *go* ***further*** into details. これ以上詳細にわたる必要はない. 【類】 the story will *go* ***further*** to make Russia known to English readers than ... ¶I would ***gladly*** *go* to my death for you. 私はあなたのためなら喜んで死んで行く. ¶Criminality ***habitually*** *goes* with dirtiness. 犯罪は不潔につきものだ. ¶*go* ***half-way*** up the hill (pole) 丘(など)を半分ほど登る. ¶Constancy and humbug, you know, can't *go* ***hand in hand***. 実直とごまかしとは両立しませんからね. 【類】 The industrial progress of the country *went* ***hand in hand*** with its military advance. ¶It will *go* ***hard*** with you. 君ひどい目に会うぞ. 【類】 It might have *gone* ***hard*** with him, had the mistake been discovered. ‖ Things are *going* ***hard*** with us. 世間はだんだん暮しにくくなる. ¶He has ***hardly*** *gone* to the root of the matter. 彼がその事件の根底までつきとめたとはちょっと言えない. ¶The sea *went* ***high***. 海は荒れた. ‖ Prices will have to *go* ***higher*** yet. 値段がもっと高くなるだろう. ¶*go* ***hiking*** [***skating***, ***skiing***, ***shopping***, ***biking***, ***autoing***] ハイキング(など)に出かける. ¶when I am *going* ***home*** from work 仕事から帰りがけに. ‖ The argument *went* ***home***. その議論は相手の胸にこたえた. 【類】 *go* ***home*** to dinner / *go* ***home*** to America for higher education / *go* straight ***home***. ¶I wonder ***how*** it will *go*. それはどうなるだろう. ‖ ***How*** was the money *going*?. 金はどうなっている. ‖ ***How*** *goes* the world with you? 景気はどうです. ‖ ***How*** do you *go* about it? それはどうしてするの. ‖ ***How*** *go* turnips? かぶらのできはどうです. ¶The water *goes* ***hot*** and ***cold*** at intervals. 水がときどき熱くなったり冷たくなったりする. ¶*go* ***hunting*** and ***shooting*** 狩にでかける. ¶Pride is a luxury that *goes* ***ill*** with poverty. 自尊心は貧乏とは調和しないぜい沢である. ¶***immediately*** *go* to work すぐ仕事に着手する. ¶It has ***just*** *gone* (=struck) six. 丁度六時になったとこだ. ¶*go* ***largely*** into a discussion 十分に論議をつくす. ¶*go* ***leisurely*** ゆっくりやる(行く). ¶I won't be *gone* ***long***. あまりおそくならないつもりだ. 【類】 He's been *gone* ***long***. What's wrong, I wonder? ¶Prices will have to *go* ***lower***. 物価は下るはずだ. ‖ unless you *go* much ***lower*** もっとずっと(値段を)まけなければ. ¶*go* ***mad*** 気が狂う. 【類】 He nearly *went* ***mad*** with vexation. ¶Are you *going* ***modern***? 君モダン主義になったのか. ¶You have (=There are) three ***more*** to *go*. [クイズゲームなどで]あと三問. ¶*go* ***much*** into society 盛んに交際をする. ¶*go* stark ***naked*** まる裸になる. ¶*go* ***out*** shooting (hiking, skiing, fishing) 狩猟(など)にでかける ‖ My heart *went* ***out*** to the orphan. 私はその孤児に同情した. 【類】 The sympathy of the public will *go* ***out*** to the bereaved family (遺族). ‖ *go* ***out*** for air 出て外気に当る ‖ *go* ***out*** for pleasure (recreation) 遊び(など)にでかける. 【類】 *go* ***out*** for a trip abroad / *go* ***out*** for a row (sail, drive, trip) / *go* ***out*** for a stroll (=walk) in the park / *go* ***out*** for a visit ‖ The shipment will *go* ***out*** from Yokohama. 船荷は横浜から出る. ‖ His feet *went* ***out*** from under him and fell down. 足がぐらぐらして倒れた. ‖ *go* ***out*** into the open air 戸外に出る. 【類】 *go* ***out*** into the countryside ‖ *go* ***out*** into the world at tender age 年端も行かないで世間へ出る ‖ *go* ***out*** into nothing 失敗に終る ‖ *go* ***out*** on raids 急襲する. 【類】 *go* ***out*** on a holiday trip / *go* ***out*** on a boat excursion ‖ The workers *went* ***out*** on a strike, crying for a wage hike. 労働者は賃金値上げを叫んでストに突入した. ‖ *go* ***out*** to battle 出征する. 【類】 *go* ***out*** to work (one's office) ‖ He *went* ***out*** unobserved. 彼はいつのまにか出て行った. ‖ The candle-light *went* ***out*** of itself. ろうそくの光が独りでに消えた. 【類】 The lamp suddenly *went* ***out***. / Be sure not to let the fire *go* ***out***. ‖ *go* ***out*** dancing unchaperoned [令嬢が]つき添いなしでダンスに出かける ‖ the alarm *went* ***out*** that ... …という警報が発せられた ‖ The Government will *go* ***out*** before long. 内閣は間もなく辞職するだろう. ‖ His source of joke will not *go* ***out***. 彼の冗談の種は仲々尽きない. ‖ The year *goes* ***out***. 年が暮れる. 【類】 The year 1955 is *going* ***out*** in a few weeks. ‖ wait till the tide *goes* ***out*** 潮の引きを待つ ‖ The practice of the duel in England has utterly *gone* ***out***. 決闘の習慣は英国では全然廃れた. ‖ His heart *went* ***out*** more and more to the beautiful girl. 彼の心はだんだんあの美しい少女の方に引き付けられた. 【類】 He is a philanthropist (博愛家), and his heart *goes* ***out*** to anyone who seems at all oppressed. ‖ Since the bridge *went* ***out***, the traffic has stopped. その橋がこわれて以来交通が止っている. ¶*go* ***overboard*** on ... …を思い切ってやる. ¶Her heart was *going* ***pit-a-pat*** with expectation. 今か今かと彼女の胸はどきどきしていた. ¶It is not necessary to *go* ***purposely***. わざわざ行く必要はない. ¶*go* ***quick*** 急いで行く. ¶His pulse *goes* very ***rapidly***. 彼の脈はくは非常に速い. ¶*go* ***right*** to the point 直ちに要点に入る ‖ *go* ***right*** to bed すぐ床につく. ¶*go* ***roundly*** to work 勇んで仕事に取りかかる. ¶His remarks *went* ***sadly*** against the grain with us. 彼の言い分はひどく僕らのしゃくにさわった. ¶*go* ***short distances*** (***three miles***) 近距離(など)を行く. ¶*go* ***sight-seeing*** 観光に行く. ¶All items entering into their production have *gone* ***skyward***. その製作材料は総て暴騰した. ¶The car *went* ***slow*** till it stopped at the end of a bridge. 車は徐行して橋のたもとで止った. ‖ You'd better *go* ***slow*** in reaching a conclusion. 結論は急がない方がよい. ¶Matters *went* on very ***smoothly***. ことはすこぶる順調に運んだ. 【類】 But, after this, things never *went* quite so ***smoothly*** as before. ¶*go* ***somewhere*** for a tour どこかへ旅行に出る. ¶*go* ***southward*** 南方へ行く. ¶That old mill is ***still*** *going* as it was ten years ago. あの古い工場は今も十年前と同様に動いている. ¶see that everything *goes* ***straight*** 万事不都合のないように注意する ‖ girls who *go* ***straight*** (are falling) 堅気の(堕落する)少女 ‖ *go* ***straight*** home 真っすぐ家へ帰る. ¶everything *went* [on] ***swimmingly*** till ... …までは万事都合よく運んだ. ¶*go* at it ***systematically*** 組織的にそれにとりかかる. ¶You'd lose a good deal by *going* ***the road***. 君その道を行くとうんと損するよ. ¶Now's the chance. ***There*** you *go*! 今がチャンスだ. それ行け. ¶The author has *gone* somewhat ***thoroughly*** into the subject with which he deals. この作者はその取扱う主題をほとんど徹底的に調べている. ¶A fine appearance and comfort do not usually *go* ***together*** 体裁と快適とは普通両立しない. 【類】 Vanity and virtue do not *go* ***together***. ¶I was allowed to *go* ***unmolested***. 私のやることにはだれも手出しはしなかった. ¶If evildoers *go **unpunished**,* moral standards will decline. 悪事を働いても罰せられないと道徳がすたれる. ¶Faithful service must not *go **unrewarded**.* 忠勤は表彰しなくてはいけない. ¶*go **upstairs*** 階上に行く. ¶I'm determined to *go* my ***way***. 私は自分の道を歩もうと決心している. ‖ Are you *going* that ***way**?* I'm *going* this [***way***]. So long! 君そっちへ行くのか. 僕はこっちだ. 失礼. ¶it will *go* some (a long) ***way*** towards ... それは...に幾分(大分)助けになるだろう. ¶His work is *going **well***. 彼の仕事はうまく行っている. 【類】 Everthing *goes **well*** with him. / So far everything had *gone **well***. / I expect to be back by the end of November if all *goes **well*** (万事好都合にゆけば). ‖ The old furniture *goes* very ***well*** with the house. 古い家具が家によくうつる. ¶"*Where* is Civilization *Going?*" [書名]文明よどこに行く. ¶*Whither Goes* Capitalism? 資本主義の運命如何. ¶*Go* at it ***wholeheartedly***. 本腰を据えてかかる. ¶*go **wild*** with fear and vexation 恐怖と心痛で気が狂いそうになる. ¶The Dutch are fond of flowers, and at one time they *went* almost ***wild*** over tulips. オランダ人は花が好きで一時はチューリップ熱に浮かされたものだ. ¶She told me how she first *went **wrong***. 彼女はつまずきの第一歩を私に話した. ‖ Everything has *gone **wrong*** (=***amiss. awry***) with us so far. 今までは万事うまく行かない. 【類】 if things *go **wrong***.

M^2 *go **about*** with one's eyes wide 目を見張って警戒する ‖ be guilty of *going **about*** in a circle in ... ...について悪循環的なやりかたをしていると言われても仕方がない ‖ *go **about*** a shirt sleeves 上衣をぬいで活動する ‖ A rumor *went **about*** that he had murdered them. 彼が彼らを殺したというデマがとんだ. ¶Let's *go **along***. 一緒について行こうよ(二人での相談). ‖ Things *went **along*** smoothly. 万事好都合に行った. ‖ *go **along*** to the movies with the children 子供連れで映画に行く ‖ I'd like to have you *go **along*** with me. 御同行下さると有難いんですが. 【類】 He asked me to *go **along*** with him. ¶*go **around*** to the post office 郵便局へ回る. ¶as the years *go **by*** 年のたつにつれて. 【類】 hardly a week *goes **by*** in which ... ‖ let it *go **by*** 成行きにまかせる. ¶The market value has *gone **down***. 市価が下った. ‖ Prices are *going **down*** in the market. 相場が下っている. ‖ I'll *go **down*** to that price. その値で折り合いましょう. ‖ They *went **down*** with the ship. 船と運命をともにした. 【類】 The captain was standing on the bridge when his ship *went **down***. / There ran such a sea (波がひどく荒れたので) that we expected every moment the boat would *go **down***. ‖ Five of the cigaret packs *went **down*** before his shooting. [射的で]シガレット五個を射落した. ‖ The wind had altogether *gone **down***. 風はすっかり止んだ. ‖ ***Down*** it *went* floating on the stream. それは浮いて流され行った. ‖ His name will *go **down*** in history as one of the few ... 彼の名は小数の...として歴史に伝わるだろう. 【類】 The conference will *go **down*** the history as ... / The year that will *go **down*** in economic history (経済史) as that of ... / *go **down*** to posterity as ... / It is as a novelist that he will *go **down*** to fame. / The wedding will *go **down*** in Washington tradition (ワシントンの伝統に) as the most remarkable ever held at the White House. ‖ *go **down*** on one's knees (=narrowbones) ひざまずく ‖ *go **down*** into (=to) the country いなかに行く ‖ The road *goes **down***. 道路は下り坂になる ‖ *go **down*** into a mine 鉱坑におりて行く. 【類】 One day he *went **down*** to the stream for water. ‖ *go **down*** into degradation 墜落する ‖ The sun never *goes **down*** on the English flag. 英国の領土には決して太陽が没しない. 【類】 The sun was *going **down***. ‖ *go **down*** to one's office 事務所へ出向く ‖ *go **down*** to breakfast (dinner) 朝食(など)に降りて行く ‖ *go **down*** to defeat 戦い(ゲーム)に破れる ‖ This chapter *goes **down*** to the death of James II. この章にはジェームス二世の崩御まで載せてある. ‖ *go **down*** before the conqueror 勝利者の前に屈服する ‖ The story won't *go **down*** with anyone. その話はだれにも相手にされないだろう. ‖ Let not the sun *go **down*** upon your wrath. 君の怒りを次の日に持ち越すな. ‖ Such a story does not *go **down*** with me. そんな話は私のふに落ちない. ‖ The wind has altogether *gone **down***. 風は全くやんだ. ‖ His hunger makes his stale bread *go **down***. 彼は飢えているので古パンでものどを通る. ‖ He would not *go **down*** among readers of the present day. 彼は現代の読者には歓迎されないだろう. ¶*go **in*** bathing 水浴する ‖ The thread will not *go **in***. 糸が(針に)通らない. ‖ Please *go **in*** first. どうぞお先に(お入り下さい). ‖ *Go* right ***in***! ずっと中へ. ‖ He *went **in*** deep with his studies. 彼は自分の研究に深くはいった. ‖ *go **in*** at the front door 玄関から入って行く ‖ Let it *go **in*** at one ear and out at the other; never report it again. そのことは聞き流しておけ, 人に話してはならない. ‖ *go **in*** for the examination その試験を受ける. ‖ *go **in*** for the stage 俳優に志す ‖ *go **in*** for duckshooting かも打ちを始める ‖ *go **in*** for motoring (gambling, politics) ドライブ(など)にふける ‖ *go **in*** too eagerly for gaiety あまりに華美に走る ‖ He *goes **in*** for whatever thing he finds new. 彼はなんでも新しいものに飛付く. ‖ *go **in*** for spelling reform つづり字改善に賛成する ‖ The firm *goes **in*** exclusively for this class of goods. 同商会はこの種の品を専門に扱っている. ‖ *go **in*** with drinking pals 飲んべ友だちと仲よくする. 【類】 *go **in*** for an examination before a jury (陪審) appointed by ... / Prof. Weekley is a well known etymologist (語原学者) who has "*gone **in***" for the popularization of linguistic knowledge (語学の民衆化). ¶*go **off*** (=***out***) shopping 買物に出かける ‖ Tugs have *gone **off*** to assist. タグボートは(座礁の船などを)引き出すために出かけた. ‖ *go **off*** for their honeymoon 彼らの新婚旅行に出かける. 【類】 *go **off*** on one's world tour / I don't see why people would not *go **off*** to summer resorts if they can afford it. ‖ The function *went **off*** without a slip (=hitch). その会は無事に済んだ. ‖ That is *going **off*** from the subject. それでは問題から脱線する. ‖ Everything will *go **off*** smoothly. 万事好都合に運ぶだろう. 【類】 All has *gone **off*** well. ‖ The feeling gradually *went **off***. この感情は次第に薄らいだ. ‖ The pain will *go **off***. 痛みが取れるだろう. ‖ The dyeing will not *go **off***. その染めはさめません. ‖ They *went **off*** into the praises of her beauty. 彼らはにわかに彼女の美ぼうをほめだした. ‖ *go **off*** to sleep 寝つく ‖ *go **off*** into a faint こん睡する ‖ The bargain *went* (=broke) ***off***. 約束は不履行となった. 【類】 The marriage may *go **off*** (破談). / As you did not telegraph, the business has *gone **off***. ‖ The wedding *went **off*** beautifully. 結婚式は首尾よく終った. ‖ He *went **off*** pretty easy. 彼はかなり楽に死んだ. 【類】 She was better a few hours before her death, and then *went **off*** suddenly. ‖ The gunpowder *went **off*** unexpectedly. 火薬が不意に爆発した. ‖ fail to *go **off*** 不発に終る. 【類】 The gun would not *go **off***. / The balloon (風船) *went **off*** with a crack (ぱちん). / The fire-cracker did not *go **off*** with a bang. ‖ Tickets *went **off*** (=sold out) with a rush. チケットは忽ち売切れとなった. ‖ This style of hair-do has *gone **off***. この髪型はすたれた. ‖ *go **off*** into a fit of laughter どっと笑いだす ‖ *go **off*** into fits of merriment over ... ...に対して急に陽気になる ‖ *go **off*** to business 商売にとりかかる ‖ *go **off*** with public money 公金を持って逃げる. ¶the ship *went **on*** to ... その船は...へ継航した ‖ *go **on*** bombarding ... ...砲撃を続ける ‖ *go **on*** with one's journey (reading) その旅行(など)を進める. 【類】 *go **on*** with one's work / *go **on*** with the loading (荷積) / *go **on*** with the sale / He sipped tea and *went **on*** with the story. / She *went **on*** with her reading after supper. ‖ the principle they *go **on*** with is ... 彼らの取っている主義は...である. ‖ He is gone, but his work *goes **on***. 彼は死んだが彼の事業は継続する. ¶I'm told there's a war *going **on*** between ... and ... ...間に戦争が起っているということだ. ‖ As time *went **on***, he grew impatient. 時の移るにつれて彼はこらえきれなくなった. ‖ Negotiations are *going **on*** satisfactorily. 交渉は満足に進んでいる. ¶Work is *going **on*** very slowly. 仕事はあまりはかどらない. ‖ Everything is *going **on*** well (badly). 万事好調(調子が悪い). 【類】 The harvest is *going **on*** splendidly. / Business is *going **on*** as usual. ‖ There is nothing strange to speak of *going **on*** in town. 市には別にこれといって変ったこともない. ‖ be satisfied with the way things are *going **on*** now 現状に満足している ‖ A little more and things will *go **on*** smoothly. もう少しの辛抱です. ‖ We *went **on*** very sociably together. われわれはお互いとても仲よくつき合った. ‖ He *went **on*** to his chief's desk for orders. 彼は用をききに課長のデスクに行った. ‖ Prices *go **on*** upward. 物価は上ぼる. ‖ *go **on*** complaining 不平だらだらだ ‖ *go **on*** to the platform 登壇

する ‖ He *went* ***on*** to quote two passages from the Bible. 彼は聖書から二個所引用した. 【類】If you *go* ***on*** to learn at this rate, you'll soon become competent. ‖ He *went* ***on*** to say that ... 彼は更に...と言った. ¶*go* ***over*** to America 渡米する. 【類】*go* ***over*** to Germany in one of the wagon tracks (大型トラック). ‖ *go* ***over*** to the opposition party 反対党に走る. 【類】*go* ***over*** to communism / Some of the soldiers *went* ***over*** to the rebels (寝返りを打った). / Morillo has *gone* ***over*** to the French side with part of his force. ‖ *go* ***over*** a list 表に目を通す. 【類】The teacher was busily *going* ***over*** examination papers. / *go* ***over*** the papers twice or three times / He and me (=I) have been *going* ***over*** the old letters. / Let's *go* ***over*** the lesson again (復習). / It has been carefully *gone* ***over*** in all its details. それは微に入り細にわたって調べられた. / The buyer had *gone* ***over*** the house (下見分) before taking it ‖ *go* ***over*** with a person about a matter その件について人と話し合う ‖ The film is *going* ***over*** big with audiences. その映画は観衆に大いに受けている. ¶The earth (wheel) *goes* ***round.*** ‖ He *went* ***round*** with his hat for the collection of money. 彼は寄付を求めて帽子を持回った. ‖ *go* ***round*** to one's office 自分の事務所に回って行く ‖ a story is *going* ***round*** in fashionable circles that ... ...といううわさが上流社会に流れている ‖ *go* clear ***round*** ぐるっと回る(百八十度の転回) ‖ *go* ***round*** by the valley 谷間に添うて曲って行く ‖ I fear the meat wouldn't *go* ***round.*** 食肉はみんなに行渡ればいいが. ‖ *go* ***round*** and ***round*** ぐるぐる回る. ¶*go* ***through*** without stopping anywhere どこにも止まらずに直行する. ‖ The proposition did not *go* ***through.*** 建議は可決されなかった. ‖ He only *went* ***through*** with it. 彼だけがそれをやってのけた. ‖ I had to *go* ***through*** with it as my duty. 私は自分の職務としてそれをやり通さねばならなかった. ¶*go* ***under*** in a struggle《口語》戦闘中に倒れる. ‖ He deserves to *go* ***under.***《口語》彼は零落するのが当り前だ. ¶*go* ***up*** by leaps and bounds とんとん拍子に出世する ‖ *go* [***up***] to town 上京する;《米口》成功する ‖ *go* ***up*** [into] an apple tree りんごの木に登る ‖ If other costs *go* ***up,*** rents will be affected. もし他の費用があがれば, 賃貸料もその影響を受けるだろう. ‖ *go* ***up*** for examination 受験する ‖ A roar of laughter *went* ***up.*** どっと笑声があがった. ‖ *go* ***up*** into one's bedroom [階上の]寝室に入る ‖ Against the pale blue of the sky the smoke *went* ***up*** straight. 青色の大空を背景に煙りはまっすぐに立ち登った. ‖ The balloon was *going* ***up and up*** till it disappeared. 風船はどんどん上って行きとうとう見えなくなった. ‖ The corporation was then in danger of *going* ***up.***《米口》会社は当時破産にひんしていた. ‖ *go* ***up*** into the country いなかに行く ‖ the curtain has *gone* ***up*** on the last act of ... ...の最後の場で幕が上った ‖ His hands *went* ***up*** in horror. 彼は恐怖のあまり両手をあげた. ‖ *go* ***up*** well to one's bridle 縦横その圧迫にへき辟易しない ‖ *go* ***up*** and ***down*** in a lift エレベーターで上り降りする. 【類】Market prices have *gone* ***up*** considerably of late. / A shout *went* ***up*** from the crowd at the brave deed (勇敢な行為). / A loud laugh *went* ***up*** on all sides (四方から). / there *went* ***up*** a cry of "Miss ... for ever (万歳)!" / *go* ***up*** in the elevator / *go* ***up*** in a balloon.

P She *went* ***about*** her work in a cold way. 彼女は冷静に仕事に取掛った. ‖ This is certainly the most stupid way to *go* ***about*** it. このやり方は全然なっていない. ‖ This creature called "man" is very easily handled if you *go* ***about*** it in the right way. 人間というものは持って行き方さえ間違わなければ取扱いやすいものだ. 【類】How do you *go* ***about*** it? / *go* ***about*** one's work with one's eye open (油断なく) / The man who is content to *go* ***about*** his daily task in a beaten track, year in and year out, becomes a mere automaton (自動人形). / It is high time that they *went* ***about*** their own business. ¶*go* ***above*** the world's level 世界の水準を抜く ‖ I cannot *go* ***above*** 5 yen. 五円以上は出せない(物を買う場合). ¶*go* ***across*** a bridge (sea, hill) 橋(など)を越す. ¶We are *going* ***after*** a fine stag. われわれは見事な雄じかを追っている所だ. ‖ *go* ***after*** a beautiful woman 美人のあとをつける. ¶*go* ***against*** nature 自然に逆う, 無理をする. ‖ This *goes* ***againt*** my grains. これは私の性に合わない. ‖ Ill luck *goes* ***against*** the grain. 不運はいやなものだ. ‖ Everything *goes* ***against*** me. 私は八方ふさがりだ. ‖ It *goes* ***against*** the stomach. それはへどを催させる. ‖ That'll *go* ***against*** the rule (law) それは規則(法)に反する. 【類】dare to *go* ***against*** medical counsel (医者の注意). ¶He has never *gone* ***against*** my wishes. / He never *goes* ***against*** the dictates of his own conscience (良心の命じる所). / The case had *gone* dead (まるきり) ***against*** them from the beginning. ¶*go* ***along*** the bank of the river 川岸に沿うて行く ‖ *go* right ***along*** this road for another mile この道に沿うてもう一マイル行く. ¶*go* ***among*** the savage people 蛮人の間を出入する. ¶It takes only forty days to *go* ***around*** the world. 世界を一周するに四十日しかかからない. ¶*go* ***at*** it systematically 組織的にそれに取掛る ‖ Let it *go* ***at*** that. それでいいことにしよう. ‖ *go* at once ***at*** the business in hand 早速用談に取掛る. ¶He *went* ***before*** a court. 彼は裁判所に訴えた. ¶*go* ***behind*** a previous decision (agreement) 以前の判決(など)を再審する ‖ You'd better *go* ***behind*** the plan and make sure. その計画の内幕を調べて大事を取る方がよい. ¶*go* ***below*** deck 甲板から下に行く. ¶*go* ***beneath*** the surface 表面下にはいる. ¶You must not *go* ***beyond*** the rate quoted. 見積り価格を上回っちゃいけない. ‖ The day seems to have *gone* ***beyond*** recall. その時期はもう過ぎ去ったらしい(取りかえしがつかない). ‖ do I *go* far ***beyond*** the facts in asserting that ...? 私が...と断言しても果してそれは余ほど事実に合わないだろうか ‖ *go* ***beyond*** him 彼にまさる; 彼を欺く ‖ *go* ***beyond*** oneself 夢中になる. ¶*go* ***by*** steamer (boat, carriage, train, car) 汽船(など)で行く. 【類】*go* ***by*** sea (land) ‖ as days *go* ***by*** 日が立つにつれ. 【類】Days and weeks *went* ***by*** uneventfully (事もなく). ‖ If so, all these fine theories *go* ***by*** the board (=overboard). もしそうだとこれらのりっぱな説は皆だめになってしまう. ‖ *go* ***by*** chance 運で定める ‖ *go* ***by*** one's decisions その裁断通りにやる ‖ Gipsies *go* ***by*** the hand in telling your future. ジプシーは運勢を見るのに手相でやる. ‖ Promotion *goes* solely ***by*** length of service. 昇進は全く勤務年限で定まる. ‖ The shop *went* ***by*** the name of Aburaya. その店は「油屋」の名で通っていた. 【類】The street still *goes* ***by*** that name. / usually *go* ***by*** curious name of ... / From that time this class of vessels (この型の船) has *gone* ***by*** that name. / What name does he *go* ***by***? ‖ *Gone* ***by*** the board! [船から]人が落ちた! ‖ *go* ***by*** default 欠席裁判になる ‖ The information you ask for *goes* ***by*** first post. 御照会の件は折返しお答え致します. ‖ Everything does not *go* ***by*** rule. 万事が規則で行くとは限らない. ¶*go* ***down*** a hill 小山を下る ‖ let things *go* ***down*** the wind 万事運に任せる. ¶*go* ***for*** a drive (row, walk, stroll) ドライブ(など)に出掛ける. 【類】*go* ***for*** a good walk / *go* ***for*** a short tour in China / *go* ***for*** a holiday in the country / where are you *going* ***for*** your vacation? ‖ *go* ***for*** the police (doctor) 警官(など)を呼びに行く ‖ How much will you *go* ***for***? いくらで行くかね. ‖ *go* ***for*** little あまり役に立たない ‖ But these precautions *went* ***for*** nothing. しかしこれらの用心もむだになった. ‖ The dog *went* ***for*** (=attacked) him as soon as he opened the gate. その犬は門を開くと同時に彼にとびかかった. ‖ A couple of novelists have *gone* ***for*** the critics. 二三の小説家がその批評家に立向った. ‖ She was pretty, and that *went* ***for*** something. 彼女が美しかったのが相当物を言った. ‖ be *gone* ***for*** good and all (=forever) 永久に去る ‖ *go* ***for*** guidance to Ruskin ラスキンの著作を読んで参考にする. ¶He has *gone* away ***from*** home. 彼は家出した. ‖ *go* ***from*** place ***to*** place 旅から旅へ行く ‖ Matters *went* ***from*** bad ***to*** worse. 事態は益々悪化していった. ‖ *go* ***from*** home ***to*** work 自宅から通勤する ‖ She has *gone* ***from*** Mayfair ***to*** the movies. 彼女は上流社会から映画に転出した. ¶*go* ***in*** evening clothes 夜会服で行く ‖ *go* ***in*** mufti (=plain clothes) 平服で行く ‖ He is *going* ***in*** (=***on***) fifteen. 彼は十五歳になる所だ. ‖ The money *went* ***in*** tram fares. その金は電車賃に使った. ‖ *go* ***in*** profit to ... ...の利益になる ‖ *go* ***in*** boats on a river ボートで川を行く ‖ Mother, may I *go* ***in*** the films? ママ私映画に行ってもいい? ‖ a story *went* ***in*** the family that ... ...というのがその家の言伝えだった. ¶Studying *went* ***into*** the background. 勉強はそっちのけになってしまった. ‖ *go* ***into*** conference with oneself 自分で考える ‖ *go* ***into*** exile 流刑に処せられる ‖ He *went* ***into*** enforced exile on account of the revolutionary troubles. 彼は革命の紛争で国外に放逐された. ‖ The study of German, in France, *goes* ***into*** the shade when compared with English. フランスにおけるドイツ語の研究は英語に比べると言うにたらないほどだ. ‖ The incident is not worth *going* ***into*** greater detail. その事件は詳記する価値がない. 【類】There is no need to *go* ***into*** details. / *go* ***into*** all the details. / *go* ***into*** more detail / *go* ***into*** particulars (=details) ‖ The institution will *go* ***into*** operation beginning on April 1. その学校は四月一日から授業を始める. ‖ The new train "Asia" *goes* ***into*** service. 新設列車「アジア」は運転を開始する. 【類】The railway will *go* ***into*** service on the 1st of next month. ‖ *go* ***into*** society 交際場裡にはいる ‖ *go* ***into*** bankruptcy=go bankrupt 破産する ‖ *go* ***into*** battle 出征する ‖ *go* ***into*** action 行動に移る ‖ *go* ***into*** business (politics) 実業(政)界にはいる ‖ *go* ***into*** the cabinet 入閣する. 【類】*go* ***into*** business for oneself (独立して) ‖ The money will *go* ***into*** the bank. その金は銀行に預ける. ‖ *go* ***into*** camp 野営をする ‖ *go* ***into*** the darkness 暗がりに出て行く ‖ *go* ***into*** a barber's shop and ask for a shave 床屋に行ってひげをそってもらう ‖ I have not found time to *go* carefully ***into*** the book. 私はその本を熟読する暇がなかった. ‖ *go* ***into*** the Church 聖職につく ‖ The audience almost *went* ***into*** convulsions of merriment. 聴衆はほとんど抱腹絶倒の有様だった. 【類】She *went* ***into*** convulsions at a mouse put into her bosom by another girl. ‖ They feared that she was *going* ***into*** a consumption. 彼らは彼女が肺病になりはしないかと心配した. ‖ *go* ***into*** rehearsal 試演をやる段になる ‖ *go* ***into*** the streets 夜の女になる ‖ *go* ***into*** open opposition to the Government 政府に公然反対の立場を取る ‖ men who *went* ***into*** uniform ***from*** farm jobs 農業出身の軍人 ‖ his soul *went* ***into*** the body of ... 彼の魂が...の肉体に宿った ‖ *go* ***into*** debt as madly as possible むちゃくちゃに借金する ‖ The new regulations *go* ***into*** effect today. 新条例はきょうから実施になる. 【類】The contract is to *go* ***into*** effect at once. ‖ *go* ***into*** history 歴史に残る ‖ *go* ***into*** (=lodge in) a furnished apartment 家具つきのアパート(のへや)にはいる ‖ The lodger has *gone* ***into*** housekeeping. あの下宿人は所帯を持った. ‖ The old woman *went* ***into*** hysterics. その婆さんはヒステリーを起した. ‖ *go* ***into*** life 独立する, 自活する ‖ Brains and heart and good red corpuscles *go* ***into*** the making of a magazine. 頭脳と心と健全な赤血球とが合して雑誌をつくり出す. ‖ The whole country *went* ***into*** mourning. 国をあげて喪に服した. ‖ She shocked Mrs. Grundies by refusing to *go* ***into*** full mourning. 彼女は正式の喪服を着けたくないと言って口やかまし屋の奥さん方を驚かした. ‖ Pattie *went* ***into*** deep mourning (近親の喪服) and all the household heard that her sister was dead. ‖ *go* ***into*** partnership with ... under the firm name of "... Company"「...会社」と言う名で...と協力する ‖ Her father did not approve of Sally's *going* ***into*** pictures. 彼女の父はサリーが映画女優になることには賛成しなかった. ‖ without *going* ***into*** the question whether ... or ... ...かまたは...かの問題には立入らずに. 【類】those who wish to *go* ***into*** the question in detail must consult the works of ... ‖ *go* ***into*** office 就任する ‖ *go* ***into*** a rage かっとなる ‖ *go* ***into*** a panic 恐慌を来たす ‖ The Diet *went* ***into*** recess after two-month sitting. 国会は二カ月の開期後休会に入った. ‖ *go* ***into*** retirement 隠退する ‖ *go* ***into*** seclusion for the rest of his life on a little farm彼の余生を小農場で隠居してくらす ‖ *go* ***into*** discipline as soldiers 兵士として教練を受ける ‖ *go* ***into*** one's study 研究を始める ‖ The book *went* ***into*** an immense number of reprints in America and this country. その本は米国とこの国での複刻がばく大な数に及んだ. ‖ The book *went* ***into*** a second edition of 3,000 copies. その本は三千部の第二版になった. ‖ Why did you *go* ***into*** teaching? なぜ君は教師になったか. ‖ The days *went* ***into*** weeks and the weeks into months. 日が週となり週が月となって行った. ‖ *go* out ***into*** the firing-line 戦線に立つ ‖ *go* out ***into*** the world 世の中に出る ‖ *go* ***into*** conference with ... ...と相談する ‖ Many factors *go* ***into*** the making of a great nation. 大国民は多数の要素から成っている. ‖ *go* ***into*** poultry as a money-making opening 金もうけ仕事として養鶏をやる ‖ There is an old proverb which declares that a person who cannot smile should not *go* ***into*** retailing. にっこり笑えない人は小売商人になるべきでないという古い諺がある. ‖ A writer, be he poet or writer of prose, must be able to *go* ***into*** the feelings of the creatures of his imagination. 詩人にせよ作家にせよその創作した人物の感情を体得する必要がある. ¶The door *goes* ***into*** the garden. ドアを開けると庭になる. ¶*go* ***like*** the wind (=swiftly) 風のように(速かに)行く. 【類】This horse *goes* ***like*** the wind (千里の馬). ‖ *go* ***like*** blazes 死物狂いに走る. ¶let *go* ***of*** her hair 彼女の髪をつかんだ手を離す ‖ He is *going* ***of*** (=***on***) fifty. 彼は五十歳になろうとしている. ¶*go* ***off*** duty 務めを避ける(怠る) ‖ *go* "***off*** the handle" やけを起す. ¶*go* ***on*** the ice 氷上を行く ‖ *go* ***on*** a journey (trip, hike, picnic, an excursion) 旅(など)に立つ. 【類】*go* ***on*** a day's trip (一日の旅) / *go* ***on*** an American tour ‖ *go* ***on*** a pilgrimage 遍歴する. 【類】*go* ***on*** a long voyage / *go* ***on*** a cruise in the South Pacific / *go* ***on*** sale 売出す ‖ *go* ***on*** a strike ストに突入する ‖ *go* ***on*** *dates* ランデブーをやる ‖ *go* ***on*** an errand 使いに行く ‖ *go* ***on*** foot (bicycle, scooter, horseback) 徒歩(など)で行く ‖ *go* ***on*** the stump《米》遊説旅行に立つ ‖ They will *go* ***on*** board the steamer this evening. 彼らは今晩その船に乗込む. ‖ The House of Commons *goes* ***on*** a committee on a bill. 下院はある法律案に関して委員会を開く. ‖ *go* ***on*** (=***into***) the streets 夜の女になる ‖ He is *going* ***on*** 17. 彼は十七になるところだ. 【類】He is four years old—*going* ***on*** five. 【類】*go* ***on*** the 5.30 a.m. express ‖ *go* ***on*** one's knees つまずく ‖ *go* ***on*** a lonely road さびしい路を行く ‖ *go* ***on*** shore 上陸する ‖ I wanted to give up college and *go* ***on*** the stage. 私は大学をやめて俳優になろうとした. ‖ *go* ***on*** the table to undergo a surgical operation 外科手術を受けるため手術台に乗る ‖ *go* there ***on*** their way to ... ...への途次そこへ行く. ¶He is dead *gone* ***on*** the girl. 彼はその女の子にうつつを抜かしている. ‖ We didn't *go* much ***on*** that kind of cattle here. この辺ではそんな種類の牛はあまり飼わなかった. ¶*go* ***out of*** a harbor [船が]港から出て行く ‖ He was compelled to *go* ***out of*** business. 彼は廃業のやむなきに至った. ‖ *go* ***out of*** a country 国外に出る ‖ Much of the land has *gone* ***out of*** cultivation. 大部分の土地が耕作されなくなった. ‖ It has now *gone* ***out of*** date. それはもう時代後れになった. 【類】Prostitution is *going* ***out of*** fashion and out of credit. / The society has *gone* ***out of*** existence. ‖ The practice is *going* ***out of*** use. この慣習はすたれかかっている. ‖ Her military machinery had rusted and *gone* ***out of*** gear. その国の軍事機関はさびついて乱雑になっていた. ‖ suddenly *go* ***out of*** his mind (=senses) 急に気が狂う ‖ *go* ***out of*** print [書籍が]絶版になる ‖ *go* ***out of*** the way to ... 回り道して...に行く ‖ *go* ***out of*** one's way to help a friend 犠牲を払って友人を助ける ‖ Pray, *go* ***out of*** my way. 後生だどいてくれ. ‖ *go* ***out of*** sight 見えなくなる ‖ *go* ***out of*** one's possession 人手に渡る ‖ *go* ***out of*** debt 借金が抜ける ‖ *go* ***out of*** the yard at recess 休み時間に学校から脱け出す. ¶*go* ***over*** a mountain (precipice) 山(など)を越す. 【類】We were thoroughly spent and had no power left to *go* ***over*** the pass (峠). ‖ *go* ***over*** the hill《軍俗》脱営する ‖ I will not *go* ***over*** the ground afresh. そのことは再論しない. ‖ It is a pleasure to *go* ***over*** a good road in an automobile. 自動車で良い道路を飛ばすのは愉快だ. ‖ *go* ***over*** a building (an estate) 家屋(など)を一通り検分する ‖ *go* ***over*** the morning's papers 朝の新聞に目を通す. 【類】*go* ***over*** a printed matter very carefully / *go* ***over*** the accounts (計算書) / busily *going* ***over*** examination papers / *go* ***over*** it very carefully after writing / The school-boy *goes* ***over*** his lesson (復習する) early in the morning. ‖ *go* ***over*** the explanation two or three times 二三度説明をくり返す ‖ *go* nuts ***over*** a girl《俗》女の子に首ったけ. ¶*go* ***through*** a course of instruction in ... ...の課程を終了する ‖ *go* ***through*** the Diet (Congress, Parliament) 国会を通過する ‖ It is dangerous to *go* ***through*** life without either religion or philosophy. 宗教か哲学かを持たなくては世渡りは危険だ. ‖ *go* ***through*** due formalities 正規の手続を踏む ‖ *go* ***through*** the ceremony of ... ...の儀式を済ませる. 【類】All the required formalities have been *gone* ***through***. / *go* ***through*** the formality of asking for a leave of absence (賜暇) / smartly *go* ***throuh*** the necessary formalities ‖ *go* ***through*** many changes 幾多の変遷を経る. 【類】*go* ***through*** extraordinary vicissitudes (並大抵でない波らん) ‖ *go* ***through*** the final examination 学期末試験を受ける. 【類】*go* ***through*** a course of gymnastic exercise (体育) ‖ *go* ***through*** several editions 五六版を重ねる. 【類】*go* ***through*** many editions and revisions ‖ The thread *goes* ***through*** the eye of the needle. 糸が針の目を通る. ‖ *go* ***through*** fire and water for another ある人のために水火の中をも辞さない ‖ *go* ***through*** sad troubles 辛苦を経験する ‖ *go* ***through*** a series of hardships 幾多の困難を切抜ける ‖ *go* ***through*** pages of Homer and Horace and Vergil for the pure glory of their sound [意味が分らないでも]調子が面白いのでホーマーやらホレースやヴァージルやらを読み通す ‖ *go* ***through*** a similar performance 同じようなことを繰返す ‖ The book is now *going* ***through*** the press. その本は今印刷中だ. ‖ *go* ***through*** the process of ... ...の手続を終える. 【類】*go* ***through*** the procedure of entering (=enrolment at) a school / *go* ***through*** with one's work ‖ That's a second pair of socks I've *gone* ***through*** inside of a week. それが一週間もたたない中にきらした二足目のくつ下なんだ. ‖ The cold seems to *go* right ***through*** me. この寒さは骨身に徹するようだ. ¶ the prizes will *go* ***to*** ... その賞品は...に授与される ‖ *go* ***to*** ... and back ...へ往復する ‖ immediately before *going* ***to*** bed 床につく直前に. 【類】He slipped out of the house after the rest of the household had *gone* ***to*** bed. / *go* ***to*** bed late and rise early ‖ *go* ***to*** business 出勤する, 仕事に出かける ‖ *go* ***to*** Congress 代議士に選出される ‖ *go* ***to*** her assistance [船が]その船の救助に行く ‖ *go* ***to*** the bad 不良化する ‖ *go* ***to*** a better world あの世へ往く ‖ *go* ***to*** one's death 死んで行く ‖ The blossoms are *going* ***to*** seed. 花はもうあがりだ. ‖ The stage *goes* ***to*** seed year by year. 劇は年々衰微する. ‖ *go* ***to*** a shop for supplies 店に用品を買いに行く ‖ *go* ***to*** college (school) 大学(など)へ行く ‖ Japan *went* ***to*** school, as it were, with Europe. 日本はいわばヨーロッパという学校にはいったようなものであった. ‖ the whole thing *goes* ***to*** pieces if ... もし...すれば一切だめになる ‖ The most ingenious method will *go* ***to*** pieces in the hands of a mechanical teacher. 最も巧妙な方法も機械的な教師の手にかかると台なしになってしまう. ‖ The arrow *went* ***to*** the mark. 矢は的に当った. ‖ The company is *going* ***to*** smash. その会社はつぶれる. ‖ *go* ***to*** rust さびつく; 役に立たなくなる ‖ The house had *gone* ***to*** ruin from neglect. 手入れを怠ったので家はすっかりいたんでいた. ‖ The Empire is *going* ***to*** the dogs. その帝国はもうだめだ(末路だ). ‖ *go* ***to*** naught (=nothing) 水泡に帰する ‖ The project *went* ***to*** the ground. その計画は失敗に終った. ‖ The company *went* ***to*** the present home last October. その会社は去る十月に今の建物に移った. ‖ *go* ***to*** great (=considerable) trouble to ... わざわざ...する ‖ *go* ***to*** the trouble and expense of ... 骨折って金を使って...する ‖ the great trouble you *went* ***to*** in arranging ... ...整理について君が取った非常な労力 ‖ If you can hire, do not *go* ***to*** the expense of buying. 借りられるものならわざわざ買う必要はない ‖ He *went* ***to*** great expense to complete it. ‖ *go* ***to*** the pains of gathering detailed statistics on the matter 骨折ってそのことに関するくわしい統計を収集する ‖ Ignorant of the danger, the girl *goes* ***to*** her doom. 危険を知らずに少女は破滅の途をたどる. ‖ It has long since *gone* ***to*** ruin. それはとうの昔に崩壊してしまった. ‖ *go* ***to*** the expense of legal assistance 弁護士を頼むことにする. 【類】You may *go* ***to*** any expense which you think necessary. ‖ You may *go* ***to*** the fullest extent. [買入れなど]徹底的にやってよろしい. ‖ He has *gone* ***to*** considerable expense in the matter. 彼はそのことで多額の金を使った. ‖ *Sake goes* ***to*** my head. 私は酒をやると頭へ来る. ‖ His kind acts *went* ***to*** the heart of people. 彼の親切な行為が人々の胸にこたえた. 【類】His counsel (忠告) *went* ***to*** the heart. ‖ He is *going* ***to*** law about the matter. 彼はその事件に関して訴訟しようとしている. ‖ *go* ***to*** the bar 弁護士になる ‖ He *went* ***to*** all lengths to compass his purpose. 彼は目的を果すためにあらゆる手段を採った. ‖ They are extreme in the lengths ***to*** which they will *go*. 彼らは思いきったことをやる. ‖ he *went* ***to*** the length of believing that ... 彼は...と信じる所まで行った. 【類】there are people who *go* ***to*** the length of saying that ... / the lengths ***to*** which he is willing to *go* ... ‖ events and experiences which *went* ***to*** the making of the man その人の人物を作り上げるに役立った事件や経験. 【類】He has the qualities (素質) which *go* ***to*** the making of a good teacher. / the various ingredients (色々の要求) that *go* ***to*** the making of a good novel ‖ He was disinclined to copy the works of "old masters"; he *went* ***to*** nature for all his patterns. 彼はいわゆる「老大家」の作品を模することはきらいであった; 彼はその模範をすべて自然に求めた. ‖ One evening we *went* ***to*** the play at Drury Lane. ある晩われわれはドルーリー・レーン劇場(ロンドン)へ行った. ‖ *go* ***to*** the movie[-house] (=cinema) 映画を見に行く ‖ *go* ***to*** the poll 投票しに行く ‖ The chickens *went* ***to*** their roost. ひな鳥はねぐらについた. ‖ Twenty-five francs *go* ***to*** the pound. 二十五フランは一ポンドに当る. ‖ at the time this book *goes* ***to*** press この本が印刷にかかるとき. 【類】as this volume *goes* ***to*** press / shortly before this publication *went* ***to*** print ‖ The proceeds of the concert will *go* ***to*** the Red Cross Funds. 音楽会の収入は赤十字に寄付する. ‖ *go* ***to*** the root of a matter ある事柄を徹底的に調べる ‖ *go* ***to*** the heart of the problem その問題の根底を突く ‖ The ship is now fit to *go* ***to*** sea. 同船は今や航海に使える. 【類】Captain Turner first *went* ***to*** sea in 1864, and spent nearly forty years in the service of the Cunard Company. ‖ Make it a rule to *go* ***to*** stool at a regular hour, even when this seems unnecessary. 便通の必要を感じないときでも時間をきめて便所に行くようになさい. 【類】Often four or five days would pass without my being able to *go* ***to*** the toilet. ‖ *go* ***to*** the game with ... ...とゲームをやる ‖ The victory *went* ***to*** the visiting team. 勝利は遠征軍に帰した. ‖ The weakest *goes* ***to*** the wall. 一番弱い者が負ける. ‖ Japan does not want to *go* ***to*** war with ... 日本は...と戦争する気がない. ‖ To *go* ***to*** the combat without these weapons means defeat. これらの武器なくして戦に臨めば敗北するにきまっている. ‖ *go* ***to*** work 仕事に取掛る ‖ *go* ***to*** confession ざんげをする ‖ *go* ***to*** extremes 極端に走る ‖ *go* ***to*** the other extreme 逆の方向に走り過ぎる ‖ *go* ***to*** law with ... ...を相手取って訴訟を起す ‖ *go* ***to*** one side 片側へ寄る ‖ I'll *go* ***to*** his side. 私は彼に賛成だ. ‖ It *goes* ***to*** the old lady's support. それは老婦人の生活費になる. ‖ The money won't *go* ***to*** him. これは彼にやる金じゃない. ‖ The ship *went* ***to*** the bottom. その船は沈没した. ‖ All our sympathy *went* ***to*** him. 彼にわれわれの同情が集まった. ‖ The game began, Waseda *going* ***to*** bat first. 〖野球〗試合開始, 早稲田先攻. ‖ This song *goes* ***to*** the old air. この歌は古い曲に合う. ‖ *go* ***to*** the Jews 《俗》高利貸の所に金を借りに行く ‖ The thermometer *went* up ***to*** 20 degrees. 寒暖計は二十度に上った. ¶ *go* ***to*** him ***for*** advice (help) 相談(など)に行く. 【類】*go* ***to*** him ***for*** a loan of money ‖ *go* ***to*** a dictionary ***for*** a word 単語を引くため辞書を見る ‖ *go* ***to*** law ***for*** remedy 訴訟によって解決しようとする. 【類】*go* ***to*** law ***for*** damage. ¶ *go* ***toward*** ... ...方面へ行く ‖ this may *go* some way ***towards*** ... これは...に少し役立つだろう. 【類】A foreign language properly taught will *go* far ***towards*** widening our mental horizon. / the fundamental features which *go* ***towards*** the making of modern Christmas ‖ *go* only a short way ***toward*** remedying the evil 弊害を除去する上に大して役に立たない. ¶ The firm has *gone* ***under***. 会社は衰微した. 【類】The fire (flame) is *going* ***under***. ‖ That play *goes* ***under*** his name. その劇は彼の作とされている. ‖ usually *go* ***under*** the name of ... 通例...の名で通る ‖ He will *go* ***under*** knife tomorrow. 彼はあす手術を受ける. ‖ *go* ***under*** the ether 麻薬をかけられる. ¶ *go* ***up*** a hill (stairs) 山(など)を登る ‖ *go* ***up*** a river 川をさか上る. 【類】I found it hard to *go* ***up*** the slope. ‖ You may *go* ***up*** head. 君は(クラスで)トップになれるかも知れんよ. ¶ Let us *go* ***upon*** this rule. [競技で]このルールで行こう. ‖ All this scandalous talk *goes* ***upon*** a mere supposition. この醜聞は単なる想像によっている. ‖ have no data to *go* ***upon*** 根拠になる資料がない ‖ *go* ***upon*** another track 別な線路にはいる; 方面を変える ‖ *go* ***upon*** a milk diet 牛乳食をとる. ¶ *go* ***with*** the stream 流れに従って下る ‖ *go* ***with*** the wind 風の吹き回しで飛んで行く. ☞ "*Gone* with the Wind"「風とともに去りぬ」‖ Any hat *goes* ***with*** tuxedo except a tall one. シルクハット以外のものならどんな帽子でもタキシードに用いられる. 【類】Big companies are to be found almost everywhere throughout the country; and ***with*** big companies *go* big salaries. ‖ It has been said that the gift of tongues *goes* ***with*** general stupidity. 数カ国の言葉ができるものは知力が全体に足りないということだ. 【類】An adverb is a word that *goes with* a verb. / A healthy mind *goes with* a healthy body. / I should like to *go with* you. / welcome new ideas and *go with* the time / He is dead, and there *goes with* him one of the most original personalities (独創的な人物) of our time. ‖ That tie doesn't *go with* this suit. あのネクタイはこの背広とよく合わない. 【類】Salad *goes with* ham and cheese. ‖ Tranship expenses are to *go with* the goods. 積換料はその貨物に付随します. ‖ Five acres of land *go with* the house for rent. その貸家は五エーカーの土地付である. ‖ His parents never allow him to *go with* boys that will teach him those things. 彼の両親はこんなことを教えるような男の子とは決して遊ばせなかった. ¶*go without* food＝fast 食事をせずにいる. 【類】*go without* one's dinner. ‖ it *goes without* saying that ... ...は言うまでもない. 【類】That correct spelling is just as important as correct pronunciation should *go without* saying.

O It is *going* to be a very fine day. きょうは天気がよくなりそうだ. ¶There isn't *going* to be any war! 戦争なんかありそうもない. ¶He said I was *going* to be late, but here I am right on time. 彼は僕が遅れると言ったがこの通り時間きっちりだ. ‖ The weather is *going* to stay fine, I hope. 天気は続きそうだ. ¶The typewriter has *gone* (＝been sent) to be mended. タイプライターは修繕にやってある. ¶What good is it *going* to do me? これがなんの役に立つのかしら(つまらない). ¶all the qualities of mind and person that *go* "to grace a gentleman" 紳士の体面を飾るに役立つ身心のあらゆる資格. ¶inquiries *go* to prove that ... 調べて見ると...ということが分かる. ¶those things which *go* to make a home 家庭を作るに要(い)るもの. ¶I *went* to visit the grave today. きょうは墓参に行った. ¶Anything *goes* (＝will do). なんでも差支ない(間に合う). ¶later investigations *go* to show that ... その後の調査によると...ということだ.

go, *n.* 元気; 大ばやり.

V *have* a *go* at ... ...をやってみる.

Q This type of hair-do is *all* the *go* in New York. この髪型はニューヨークで大流行である. ¶an old, old horse with *no go* in him 老朽馬 ‖ It is *no go* (＝"n.g."). だめだ. ¶Here's a *pretty go!* 弱ったな.

P be full *of go* 元気一杯 ‖ Old as he is, he still has plenty *of go* in him. 年はとってもまだまだ元気だ. ¶He is always *on* the *go* about it. 彼はいつもその件で忙しく活躍している.

O It's sure to be a *go*. そりゃきっと大当りだ.

goad, *v.* 刺激する.

P *goad* a person *into* (＝to) fury (rebellion) 人を刺激して激怒(など)させる. 【類】I *goaded* him *into* doing it. ¶*goaded to* frenzy by the approach of midnight 夜もふけるので気が気でなく(バナナ屋など縁日商人).

goading, *n.* かしゃく.

Q *moral goadings* 良心のかしゃく.

goal, *n.* 決勝標, 決勝点; 目的.

V *achieve* a *goal* 目的を達成する. ¶*attain* one's *goal* 目的を達する. ¶*carry out* the *goal* of conspiracy 陰謀の目的を実現する. ¶*get* (＝*kick, take or win*) a *goal* 〔蹴球〕球をゴールに入れる. 【類】*get* the *goal* first (一番). ¶*make* (＝*score*) a *goal* 一点を得る. ¶The loan *passed* the $... *goal*. その公債の募集は...ドルの定額を突破した. ¶*reach* the *goal* with one bound 一躍して決勝点に達する ‖ They *reached* the *goal* of their journey. 彼らは旅行の目的地についた. 【類】*reach* the *goal* of one's ambition / *reach* the *goal* to production as scheduled. ¶This will *supply* a fitting *goal* to our activity. これでわれわれの活動に対する適当な目標ができた.

Q a *distant* and *shadowy goal* 遠くってばく然とした目標. ¶this *long-sought goal* of complete self-government 宿願たる完全自治制. ¶the attainment of the *much-sought goal* 非常にあこがれた目的の達成. ¶An ever *progressing goal* must be continually kept in view. 日進月歩の目標を絶えず眼前に置かねばならない. ¶achieve its *true goal* 本来の目的を達成する. ¶the *ultimate goal* 窮極の目的.

Q² a *holiday goal* 土曜(など)の終業の合図(十二時の汽笛など). ¶a *long-range goal* 長期計画の目標. ¶set a specific *production goal* for ... ...に対し特別の生産目的を設定する. 【類】in order to achieve the ***36 million ton 1948 production goal.***

goat, *n.* やぎ.

V Such a fellow *gets* my *goats*. ああいう男には全く腹が立つ.

V² *Goats bleat*. やぎが鳴く. ‖ *Goats flock* together. やぎは群生する.

go-between, *n.* 仲人.

P act *as go-between* 仲人役を勤める.

goblet, *n.* 大コップ.

Q a *water goblet* 水飲み大コップ.

god, *n.* [G-] 天帝; 神; 〔劇〕高桟敷, 大向う.

V *adore god* 神を崇拝する. ¶*Blessed* be *God!* ありがたい! ¶*call Gods* to witness 神々の御照覧を祈る. ¶*glorify God* 神の栄光を賛美する. ¶may it *please God*, that ... ...が神のみ心にかなわんことを. ¶*God* be *praised*, I am myself. ありがたい, 私は本心に立帰った. ¶figures intended to *represent* this *god* この神を現わす偶像. ¶*Thank God.*＝God be thanked. やれやれ. ¶*worship gods* 神々を敬う. ¶*serve* a *god* 神につかえる. ¶the *god worshipped* here is ... ここの祭神は...である. ¶*God deigned* to reward him with ... 神が彼に...をたまわった. ¶*worship* false *gods* 偽りの神を崇拝する.

V² The *god appeared* to him. 神様が彼に姿をお現しになった. ¶*God bless* you! あなたの身に幸あれ. ‖ *God bless* me! おやおや, あらまあ. ¶*God forbid* that ... どうか...でありませんように. ¶*God grant* that he may succeed! 神よ願わくば彼をして成功せしめたまえ. ¶Do you understand me? *God knows* (＝assuredly), I should think it highly improbable.—R.L. Stevenson. あなたは私の言うことが分かりますか. どうもお分かりにならないらしい. ¶*God speed* you! ごきげんよう.

Q *Almighty God*＝God Almighty 全能の神. ¶an *anthropomorphic god* 人間化した神. ¶a *benevolent god* 慈悲深い神. ¶a worshipper of a *foreign* and *new God* 外国の新しい神を敬う人. ¶He was heroized as a *guardian god* of constitutionalism. 彼は立憲制度の守護神としてあがめられた. ¶a *malevolent god* 悪の神. ¶The *old gods* have been cast down, but no new ones fill the empty niches. 従来信仰して来た神々は放棄されその空座に新しい神様が安置されていない. ¶He proved a *perfect god* sent to us in the journey. 彼は旅行中全く天の助けともいうべき人であることが分かった.

Q² *gallery gods* 天井桟敷, つんぼ桟敷の観客. ¶*household gods* 家庭に祭ってある神. ¶a *river god* 川の神.

P I was *among* the *gods*. 僕はつんぼ桟敷で見物した. ¶*In God* we live and move. われわれは生きるのも動くのも神様の御心で. ‖ believe *in God* 神を信じる. ¶Glory *to God*. 栄光神にあれ. ‖ swear *to God* 神に誓う. ¶Our enterprise, *under God*, will some day be crowned with success. われわれの事業は神様のお力によっていつか成功の光栄に浴することであろう. ¶Old Henry, now *with God* 今は故人となったヘンリー翁.

P² the *God in* man 人間の持っている神性. ¶the *god of* love＝Cupid 恋の神 ‖ the *god of* war＝Mars 軍神 ‖ *gods of* heaven 天の神々. ¶a *god upon* earth 現世の神.

go-down, *n.* 倉庫.

Q an *explosive go-down* 火薬庫.

god-speed, *n.* 道中の安全または成功の祈願.

V *bid* him *God-speed* 彼の門出を祝う. ¶*wish* us *god-speed* on our journey われわれの旅立つに当って道中の安全を祈ってくれる. 【類】There were many people at the station to *wish* him *God-speed*.

P wish *god-speed to* Japan's departing soldiers 日本の出征兵士の道中を祈る.

goer, *n.* [劇・映画の]愛好者.

Q² a *movie(theater) goer* 映画(劇)ファン. ¶*play* and *concert goers* 劇と音楽会の常連.

goings-on, *n.* 行為.

Q *scandalous goings-on* 醜行為. ¶His mother would rise in horror from her grave could she know of *these goings-on*. 彼の母がこれらのていたらくを知ったら驚いて墓場から抜け出て来るだろう.

gold, *n.* 金; 金貨; 純良物.

V rock *carrying gold* 金を含む岩石. ¶*extract gold* from the sea 海水から金を採る. 【類】*extract gold* from quartz by the amalgamating process (アマルガム操作によって石英から). ¶autographs that the collector would *give gold* for 収集家が手に入れるためには金を惜しまない自筆. ¶*mine gold* 金を採掘する.

V² All is not *gold* that *glitters*. 〔諺〕輝くものすべてが金ではない(人はみかけによらぬもの).

Q *alluvial gold* 砂金. ¶*bright gold* 輝く金. ¶*glittering*

gold ぴかぴかする金. ¶The rising sun danced in water like ***molten*** *gold*. 朝日が溶けた金のように水に躍った. ¶It is of ***pure*** *gold*. それは純金でできている. ¶***rolled*** *gold* きせ金. ¶gain ***untold*** *gold* by his genius as an actor 好演技によって巨額の報酬を得る.

P search ***for*** *gold* 金をさがす. ¶a statue ***in*** *gold* 黄金の像 ‖ a book-cover printed ***in*** *gold* 金文字入りの本の表紙 ‖ set a diamond ***in*** *gold* 金にダイヤをちりばめる ‖ freight payable ***in*** *gold* 金貨支払の運賃. ¶an ounce (a lump) ***of*** *gold* 一オンス(など)の金 ‖ a small nugget ***of*** *gold* 小さな金塊 ‖ a heart ***of*** *gold* 高潔の士 ‖ a voice ***of*** *gold* 美声. ¶overlay it ***with*** *gold* それに金をきせる ‖ fringe it ***with*** *gold* それを金でふち取る.

goldfish, *n.* 金魚.

Q an ***iridescent*** *goldfish* [見る位置で]色の変る金魚.

gold-mine, *n.* 金山; 金穴, 財源.

Q it is a ***veritable*** *gold-mine* for ... それは...にとってさながら金穴(ドル箱)である.

P² a *gold-mine* ***for*** ... ...のドル箱.

golf, *n.* ゴルフ.

P play ***at*** *golf* ゴルフをやる. ¶a club used ***in*** *golf* ゴルフの打球棒.

gong, *n.* どら, ゴング.

Q² a ***dinner*** *gong* 食事のゴング.

good, *n.* 善, 善事; 幸福, 利益; よい部分.

V He was able to ***accomplish*** so much *good* in such a litte while. 彼はそんなに短い間にそんなに多くの善事をなし遂げた. ¶***achieve*** a *good* 善事をなし遂げる. ¶I do not ***augur*** much *good* to the firm from the new policy. 私には新方針によって会社が大してよくなるとは思われない. ¶There's good in everybody; ***bring out*** the *good*. だれにでもよいところがある, そのよいところを発揮せよ. 【類】 ***bring out*** the *good* that is in the heart (心の美徳) of ... ¶***develop*** the *good* that is in him 彼の持っている長所を伸ばす. ¶The change will ***do*** you *good*. 転地は君のためによかろう. ‖ The rain has ***done*** some (much) *good* to the crops. その雨は作物にいくらか(大分)よかった. ‖ be active in ***doing*** *good* to others 人のために奔走する ‖ ***do*** one's heart *good* 心を楽しくする ‖ the practice of ***doing*** *good* 善をなす習慣 ‖ the *good* that has been ***done*** by the use of ... ...の使用によって得られた有益 ‖ It has ***done*** little *good* and much harm. それは益少く害が多い. 【類】 It will ***do*** much *good* to your health. / Did your trip to the seaside ***do*** you any *good?* / The hot spring is found to ***do*** *good* in certain cases. / It has ***done*** some *good* in directing public attention to the matter. ¶Education ***draws out*** the *good* that is in one. 教育は人の持っている良い所を引き出す. ¶He ***effected*** much *good* with his small means. 彼は少ない資力で大きな効果をあげた. ¶I am persuaded that there are few books so bad that one may not ***gather*** a little *good* from them. 私は少しもためにならないほど悪い本というものはほとんどないと信じている. ¶***have*** the *good* of mankind closely at heart 大いに人類の幸福を心がける. ¶He has learned somehow to ***know*** *good* from bad, true from false. 彼はどうやら善悪・真偽を弁別することを知った. ¶***promote*** the general *good* of the community 社会全般の利益を促進する. ¶***regard*** the *good* of the whole country 国全体の利益を尊重する. ¶***return*** *good* for evil 悪に報いるに善をもってする. ¶***sacrifice*** future *good* for present gain 現在の利得のために未来の幸福を犠牲にする. ¶***see*** (=***recognize***) the *good* in others 他人の長所を知る. ¶***seek*** the *good* of ... ...のためを図る. ¶***undo*** the *good* done by ... ...のやった善事を無効にする. ¶***work*** *good* to the community 社会のためになる.

V² Much *good* will ***come*** from learning English. 英語の学習によって多大の利益が得られるだろう.

Q Is this ***any*** *good* for you? これは何かの役に立ちますか. ¶work for the ***best*** *good* of society 社会の一番ためになるように働く. ¶the ***chief*** *good* おもな利益. ¶work for the ***common*** *good* 一般の利益のために働く. ¶for the ***general*** *good* of human society 一般人間社会のために. ¶do them ***lasting*** *good* 永久に彼らのためになる. ¶It is for the ***national*** *good*. それは国のためになる. ¶He's ***no*** *good* for the work. 彼はその仕事にはだめだ. 【類】 He was branded as ***no*** *good* (無用のレッテルをはられて) and fired. / To cry out would have done ***no*** *good*. ‖ It would be ***no*** *good* to do so. そうしても何の役にも立たないだろう. ‖ He is up to ***no*** *good*. あいつは何の役にも立たない. ¶for ***our own*** *good* われわれ自身のために. ¶for the ***public*** *good* 公益のために ‖ make for the ***public*** *good* 公益になる. 【類】 be devoted to the ***public*** *good* / be against the ***public*** *good*. ¶It will do ***untold*** *good* to ... ...すると非常な利益になるだろう. ¶***What*** *good* is it?=What's the use of it? それが何の役に立つのか.

P ***for*** the *good* of the public (world) 世(界)のために ‖ I say this ***for*** your *good*. 君のためを思ってこう言うんだ. ‖ ***for*** the *good* (=benefit) of my health 私の健康のために. 【類】 ***for*** the *good* of one's country ‖ the precious sentiment of working in a purely disinterested way ***for*** the *good* of humanity / work ***for*** the *good* of all (the world) / ***for*** the *good* of a great cause (大義) / use life ***for*** the *good* of one's fellows ‖ He is going away ***for*** *good*. あの人は行ったきりもう帰ってはこないのです. 【類】 the problem of ending war ***for*** *good* / He always told me that he had done with the mother country ***for*** *good* and all. ¶It does me a world ***of*** *good*. それは僕に非常に役に立つ. ‖ It is ***of*** no *good*. それは一向役に立たない. ¶What's the *good* ***of*** complaining about what cannot be avoided? 仕方がない事をくよくよ言ってみた所で何の役に立つ.

good, *a.* 良い, 優美な; 親切な; 有効な, ためになる; 食べられる, 美味の.

M just ***as*** *good* 丁度同じ位よい ‖ He is ***as*** *good* as gold. 彼は本当にりっぱな人だ. ‖ He was ***as*** *good* as his word. 彼は約束を守った. 【類】 No answer to this question, or a delayed negative answer, is ***as*** *good* as a confession. ‖ He is ***as*** *good* as dead. 彼は死人同然だ. ‖ ***as*** *good* as new 新品同様 ‖ not ***as*** *good* as one wish it to be 思わしくない. ¶***astonishingly*** *good* 驚くほどよい. ¶***distinctly*** *good* 際立ってよい. ¶One foreign language is *good* ***enough*** for me. 私は外国語一つ知っていれば沢山だ. ‖ He was *good* ***enough*** to show us the way. 彼は親切にも道を教えてくれた. ‖ This is *good* ***enough*** for me. 私はこれで結構です. ‖ be *good* ***enough*** for all practical purposes 何に使っても実用には申分ない ‖ Be *good* ***enough*** to hold your tongue. そうしゃべらないで. ‖ The bidding was not *good* ***enough***. 入札は低過ぎた. ‖ Your offer is not *good* ***enough***. あなたのおっしゃる条件では十分じゃない. 【類】 The security (担保) offered is not *good* ***enough***. ¶***How*** *good* (=kind) of you to come [and] see me? わざわざお出で下すってまあ御親切に. ¶***just*** *good* for drinking (eating, a short stay, rest) 丁度具合がよい. ¶***Mighty*** *good!* 《米口》 すばらしい, 大いに結構. ¶be ***particularly*** *good* at the invention of stories うそをつくのが特にうまい. ¶be ***radically*** *good* 根本的によい. ¶You're ***really*** *good* at thinking up excuses. 君は言い抜けが本当にうまい. ¶so far so *good*, but ... そこまではよかったが ‖ It's ***so*** *good* to have a nice house to come to after a hard day's work. 一日苦労した後にいい家庭に帰れるとは本当にありがたい. ‖ Will you be ***so*** *good* as to lend me that knife? そのナイフを貸して下さいませんか. 【類】 Be ***so*** *good* as to shut the door. ¶My hearing is ***still*** *good*. 私の耳はまだ確かだ. ¶***studiously*** *good* いかにも親切な. ¶***tolerably*** *good* かなりよい. ¶Such a gift is ***too*** *good* for him. こんな贈物は彼にはよ過ぎる ‖ The news is ***too*** *good* to be true. その話はあまりよ過ぎて本当とは思えない. ¶be ***vastly*** *good* 非常にいい.

P The flesh of the frog is *good* ***as*** food (=to eat). かえるの肉は食物になる. ¶He's very *good* ***at*** figures. あの人は計算が達者だ. 【類】 He is *good* ***at*** outdoor games and sports. / This cat is *good* ***at*** catching rats (=a good mouser). / be *good* ***at*** swimming / I am not all *good* ***at*** remembering faces and names. ¶Exercise is *good* ***for*** health. 運動は健康に良い. ‖ It is *good* ***for*** food. それは食べられる. ‖ a salve *good* ***for*** burns やけどにきくこう薬 ‖ It is not *good* ***for*** a man to be alone. 男は独身でいることはよくない. ‖ Every man is *good* ***for*** something. 人はだれでも何かの役に立つ. ‖ a man *good* ***for*** nothing 何にも役に立たない男 ‖ This medicine is *good* ***for*** a cold (toothache, fever). この薬はかぜ(など)にきく ‖ His credit is *good* ***for*** a hundred thousand yen. 彼の信用では十万円の融通ができる. ‖ The tickets are *good* ***for*** two years. その切符は二ケ年有効だ. ¶He is *good* ***in*** arithmetic. 彼は算術ができる. ¶It is *good* ***of*** you to come down and see me (see us off.) お出で(など)下されてありがとう. ¶This ticket is not *good* ***on*** this line. この切符はこの線では通用しない. ¶Beef is *good **to*** the taste. 牛肉はうまい. ‖ A father should be *good **to*** his children. 父は子供によくすべきものだ. ‖ *good **to*** animals 動物に親切な. 【類】 He is *good **to*** everybody. ‖ be *good **to*** the palate (=taste) 味がよい. ¶He is *good **with*** the rifle (fishing tackle). 彼は猟(釣り)がうまい.

O The flesh of the rhinoceros is *good* to eat. 犀(さい)の肉は食べられる. ¶water *good* (=fit) to drink 飲める水.

good-bye, *n.* 別れのあいさつ, 告別の辞.

V ***bid** good-bye* to ... ...に別れを告げる. ¶***call** good-bye* to ... ...に告別の言葉を呼び掛ける. ¶***kiss** good-bye* to ... ...に別れの接ぷんをする. ¶***nod** good-bye* to ... 頭をちょっと下げて...に別れのあいさつをする. ¶***say** good-bye* to ... ...にさよならをいう. 【類】 I must ***say** good-bye.* ‖ To all this he ***said** good-bye.* 彼はこれらと一切縁を切った. 【類】 Probably she will ***say** good-bye* to the screen (映画界). ¶***wave*** a person *good-bye* 手(など)を振って別れを告げる. ¶I have called to ***wish** good-bye.* 私はお暇ごいに上りました.

Q This would be the ***last** good-bye* I can say to you all. これがお別れだ.

P² *Good-bye **for*** today! きょうはこれで失礼. ¶*Good-bye **till*** tomorrow. あすまでさよなら. ¶If you do not work hard, it would be *good-bye **to*** any chance of passing the examination. もし君が一所懸命に勉強しなければ及第の見込はとうていなくなるだろう.

good-nature, *n.* お人よし.

P take advantage ***of*** one's *good-nature* 人の好いのにつけこむ. ¶He acted so ***out of** good-nature.* 彼は人が好いのでそうした.

goodness, *n.* 善良; 親切.

V ***Have*** the *goodness* to lend me your pencil. どうぞ鉛筆をお貸しください. ‖ Will you ***have*** the *goodness* to show me the way? 道を教えて下さいませんか. ¶***Thank** goodness* (=God), I have recovered from my illness. ありがたいことに病気が全快した. ‖ ***Thank** goodness,* you'll be away from him for some time! へえ, じゃ君は当分彼とは会わないんだね.

V² *Goodness* (=God) ***knows.*** どうだか分かるもんか.

Q ***goody-goody** goodness* いやに善人振った善. ¶***My** goodness!* おやまあ.

P ***out of*** the *goodness* of his heart 彼の親切から. ¶I wish ***to** goodness* that the worst will not come. そんないやなことにならないようにしたいものだ.

P² *goodness **of*** man 人間の善性.

goods, *n. pl.* 商品, 品物; 貨物; 動産.

V I beg you to ***accept*** the *goods* (my services) gratis in this case. 今回はこの財物(御用など)をどうぞお収め下さい. ¶***advertise** goods* for sale 品物販売の広告を出す. ¶***boycott*** German *goods* ドイツ商品の不買同盟をする. ¶***bring*** the *goods* into market 品物を市場に持込む. ¶***buy*** British *goods* 英国商品を買う. ¶***carry** goods* to a storehouse 貨物を倉庫へ運ぶ. ¶***consign** goods* to ... 貨物を...へ託送する. ¶***deliver** goods* 品物を引渡す. ¶***display** goods* 商品を陳列する. ¶***give up** goods* to ... 動産を...に譲る. ¶Please come in and ***inspect*** my *goods.* どうぞおはいり下すって品を御覧下さい. ‖ ***inspect** goods* without intention of buying 品物をひやかす. ¶do not ***keep*** the *goods* beyond next month その品は来月に持越すな. ¶***land** goods* 貨物の陸上げをする. ¶***load** (**unload**) goods* 貨物を積込む(おろす). ¶***mark down** goods* 商品の値札を引下げる. ¶***pack** goods* 貨物を荷造する. ¶***pledge** goods* 品を抵当に入れる. ¶***push*** their *goods* in China 彼らの商品を中国に売り広める. ¶***reject*** inferior *goods* 劣等な品物を拒絶する. ¶***renounce*** all one's worldly *goods* 現世の財貨をことごとく放棄する. ¶***sell** goods* to ... on credit 品物を...に掛で売る ‖ ***sell** goods* cheap for cash 品を現金で安く売る. ¶***send*** him the *goods* on trial 試験的にその商品を彼に送る. ¶***ship** goods* 商品を発送する. ¶***stamp** goods* 商品に刻印を押す. ¶***store*** the *goods* for account of the owners 持主の責任でその品を預る. ¶***supply** goods* to ... ...に商品を供給する. ¶***throw** goods* overboard 貨物を海中に投捨てる. ¶The *goods* cannot be ***traced*** at this end. 当方で品のゆくえを調べることはできない. ¶***tranship** goods* 貨物を他船に積換える. ¶***transport** goods* from ... to ... 品物を...から...に輸送する.

V² The *goods **arrived*** in good order. 品物は無事に着いた. ¶The *goods* do not ***come*** up to the mark (my expectation, usual standard). 品物は標準(など)に達しない.

Q ***canned** goods* かん詰類. ¶***coarse** goods* あらもの. ¶***customable** goods* 関税のかかる品目. ¶***dangerous** goods* 危険品. ¶***dry** goods* 乾物類(英); 呉服類(米). ¶***economic** goods* 物財. ¶***essential** goods* 必需品. ¶***famous-named** goods* 有名品. ¶***finished** (**unfinished**) goods* 完(未)製品. ¶The *goods* are ***first-rate.*** 品物は上等だ. ¶***fragile** goods* 損じやすい品. ¶***half-finished** goods* 半製品. ¶***heavy** (**light**) goods* 重(軽)い貨物. ¶***honest** goods* 出の確かな品(不正品に対し). ¶***house-furnishing** goods* 室内装飾品. ¶***industrial** goods* 生産物資. ¶***inflammable** goods* 可燃性物品. ¶***Japan-made** goods* 日本製品. ¶***knit** goods* メリヤス製品. ¶***manufactured** goods* 製品. ¶***perishable** goods* =perishables 変質性貨物(野菜・鮮魚など). ¶***printed** goods* プリントのもの(さらさなど). ¶***processed** goods* 加工品. ¶replace the ***rejected** goods* 返品を取り換える. ¶***released** goods* 放出品. ¶***seasonal** goods* 季節品. ¶***standard** goods* 規格品; 本場もの. ¶***strategic** goods* 戦略物資. ¶***substandard** goods* 場違いもの. ¶***substitute** goods* 代用品. ¶receivers of ***stolen** goods* けいず買. ¶***unsold** goods* 売残り品. ¶***wet** goods* 酒類 (dry goods に対しかいぎゃく的に). ¶He has very little of this ***world's** goods.* 彼は浮世の財産をほとんど持っていない. ¶measure success by the possession of ***worldly** goods* 財産の額によって成功不成功を測定する. ¶foist ***worthless** goods* on a customer いんちきものを客に押しつける.

Q² ***bargain** goods* おつとめ品. ¶***black-market** goods* やみ物資. ¶***clearance** goods* 処分品. ¶an assortment of ***Christmas fancy** goods* クリスマス用小間物の取合わせ. ¶***consumer** goods* 消費物資. ¶essential ***consumer** goods* 主要消費材 ‖ ***consumer*** durable *goods* 消費備品(自動車, 冷蔵庫など). ¶***contraband** goods* 輸出入禁制品. ¶***cotton*** and ***wool piece** goods* 綿及び毛製品. ¶***dress** goods* 衣類. ¶***earthenware** goods* 陶器. ¶***high-quality** goods* 高級品. ¶Many of the ***household** goods* had to be sold to pay bills. 勘定支払いのため家財を払いに出す. ¶***india-rubber** goods* ゴム製品. ¶***luxury** goods* ぜいたく品. ¶***measurement** goods* 〘鉄道〙容積貨物. ¶industries of ***peace-time** goods* 平和物資生産の諸産業. ¶***quality** goods* 上等品 ‖ poor ***quality** goods* 下級品. ¶a sale of ***salvage** goods* 救難(引揚げ)作業用品の販売. ¶***sporting** goods* スポーツ用品. ¶***spring dress** goods* 春向呉服もの. ¶***war** goods* 戦争物資 ‖ special demand ***war** goods* 特需品.

P a lot ***of** goods* 沢山の品物.

P² fancy *goods **for*** presents 贈答用(美術)小間物. ¶the *goods **from*** the sunken ship 沈没船から引揚げた貨物.

goodselves, *n. pl.* 貴社.

P if this proposition should prove acceptable ***to*** your *goodselves* もしこの話が貴社の御好意を得られますれば.

goodwill, good will, *n.* 好意; [商店などの]株, のれん.

V he ***bears*** no *goodwill* toward ... 彼は...に対して好意を持っていない. ¶***bring** goodwill* to ... ...に好意をもたらす. ¶***build** goodwill* 得意をつくる. 【類】 ***build** [**up**]* international *goodwill* ‖ ***build up*** the *goodwill* of a firm 会社の株(のれん)をこしらえる. ¶***create*** and ***strengthen** goodwill* お得意を作ってその基礎を強固にする. ¶***embody** goods* 好意を具体化する. ¶***feel** goodwill* toward ... ...に対して好意を持つ. ¶***lose*** the *goodwill* of ... ...の好意を失う. ¶***obtain*** their *goodwill* 彼らの好意を得る. ¶***promote** goodwill* 好意を増進する. ¶***sell*** the *goodwill* of one's business 商売の株(のれん)を売る. ¶***win*** the *goodwill* of ... ...の好意を得る. ¶***win back*** the *goodwill* of ... ...の好意を取り戻す.

Q build up a ***great** goodwill* 大なる好意を築き上げる. ¶a champion of ***international** goodwill* 国際的親善の擁護者.

P an expression ***of** goodwill* 好意の表現.

P² the *goodwill* of the Russian people ソ連国民の好意. ¶*goodwill **to*** (=***toward***) ... ...に対する好意.

goose, *n.* がちょう; ばか者.

V It is a case of "***killing*** the *goose* that lays the golden eggs." それが「大欲は無欲」ということだ. ¶***make*** a *goose* of ... ...をだます. ¶The old woman is ***picking*** her *geese.* 雪が降っている. ¶He ***regards*** all his *geese* as swans. 彼はいつも買いかぶる, うぬぼれている.

V² *Geese **cackle.*** がちょうががあがあ鳴く. ¶The *goose* ***hangs high.*** 《米口》万事が好都合だ.

Q a ***green** goose* がちょうの若鳥. ¶He is ***such*** a *goose.* 彼は実にばかだ. ¶a ***tailor's** goose* 裁縫用大型火のし. ¶***What*** a *goose* he is! 彼はなんというばか者だろう.

P a flock *of geese* がちょうの一群.【類】a drove *of geese*.
O All his *geese* are swans. 彼はいつもうぬぼれている.

goose-flesh, *n*. 鳥はだ, 総毛だち.
V ***get*** (=***have***) *goose-flesh* 総毛立つ. ¶***make*** *goose-flesh* ***rise*** 総毛立たせる.

goose-step, *n*. 歩調教練.
Q It is a ***mere*** *goose-step*, all action and no progress. それはほんの歩調教練のようなもので手足ばかり動かして一向進まない.

gorge, *n*. 谷間, 峡谷; のみ下す物.
V a novel suspension bridge in Formosa ***spanning*** a deep *gorge* 台湾の深い峡谷に渡した目新しいつり橋. ¶***vomit*** (=***cast or heave***) one's *gorge* へどを吐く.
P² a *gorge* ***between*** precipices 断がい間の峡谷.

gorge, *v*. 飽食する.
P *gorge* oneself ***with*** meat 肉を腹一杯食う.

gorgeous, *a*. 華麗な, きらびやかな.
P The dinner table was *gorgeous* ***with*** silver, rare china, and flowers. テーブルは銀器・珍らしい磁器・花などで花やかであった.

gorilla, *n*. ゴリラ;《俗》[ゴリラのように]みにくい男, 悪漢.
Q a ***human*** *gorilla* 色魔; 乱暴者(など).

gospel, *n*. 福音; 説教; 真理.
V ***believe*** in the *gospel* of soap and water 清潔の効用を信じる. ¶***enunciate*** the *gospel* of health 健康の福音を説く. ¶***preach*** the *gospel* 伝道する. ¶***spread*** the *gospel* of unity and love throughout the world 世界中に和合と愛の福音を伝える. ¶***talk*** *gospel* まっこう臭い話をする.
Q a ***political*** *gospel* 政治の信条. ¶the ***simple*** *gospel* of repentance, forgiveness, and redemption くい改めと寛容としょく罪の単純な福音.
Q² the ***Leninist*** *gospel* レーニン主義者の信条.
P They took his words ***for*** *gospel*. 彼らは彼の言を真実と思った. ¶the truths taught ***in*** the *Gospels* 福音書中に教えてある真理. ¶a minister ***of*** the *gospel* 福音伝道者.
P² the *gospel* ***of*** efficiency 能率主義 ‖ the *gospel* ***of*** laissez-faire 放任主義. ¶preach the *gospel* ***to*** ...=evangelize ... ...に福音を伝える.

gossip, *n*. [人の]うわさ, 雑談.
V ***exchange*** the latest *gossip* in business circles お互に実業界最近の世間話をする. ¶***retail*** *gossip* 人のうわさを言いふらす. ¶***talk*** *gossip*=gossip 雑談する. ¶***write*** *gossip*=gossip 漫録する.
V² *Gossip* ***travels*** fast. うわさ千里.
Q ***endless*** *gossips* はてしない空談. ¶***entertaining*** *gossip* 面白いうわさ話. ¶the mere ***fashionable*** *gossip* of the hour ほんの一時の話題. ¶have a ***good*** *gossip* with a neighbor over the garden fence. 庭のかき根越しに隣人と色々うわさ話をする. ¶a ***harmless*** *gossip* 罪のない雑談. ¶talks which are only hearsay or ***idle*** *gossips* うわさやつまらない空談にすぎない話. ¶some particularly ***interesting*** *gossip* ある特に面白い世間話. ¶an ***old*** *gossip* おしゃべりのばあさん.
Q² ***studio*** *gossip* [映画の]スタジオすずめの話.
P The rumour has been traced ***to*** idle *gossip*. そのうわさは空談から起ったことが分かった.
P² the *gossip* ***among*** ... for several years past has been to the effect that ... この五六年間...の間に立ったうわさは...という意味合いのものであった. ¶there has been much *gossip* ***in*** political circles as to ... ...について政界に随分うわさがあった. ¶It has become the *gossip* ***of*** the town. それが町のうわさに上った.

gossip, *v*. 世間話する, むだ話する.
M *gossip* ***garrulously*** with a neighbor of ... 隣人と...のことをぺちゃくちゃ話す.
P *gossip* ***about*** a person (thing) 人(など)のうわさ話をする. ¶*gossip* ***on*** trivial matters つまらないことをおしゃべりする. ¶*gossip* ***over*** coffee and wine and cigarettes コーヒーやぶどう酒やタバコをのみながら雑談する. ¶Do not *gossip* ***with*** the servants. 召使とむだ話するな.

gouge, *v*. えぐる.
M *gouge* ***out*** the eyes with one's thumb 親指で両眼をえぐりだす.

gout, *n*. 痛風.
P a sovereign remedy ***for*** *gout* 痛風の妙薬. ¶He has an attack ***of*** *gout*. 彼は痛風にかかっている. ¶He is a martyr ***to*** *gout*. 彼は痛風に悩んでいる. ¶He is afflicted ***with*** *gout*. 彼は痛風を病んでいる.
P² *gout* ***in*** the hip 腰骨痛風.

govern, *v*. 支配する.
P Tradition and habit *governed* ***with*** an iron hand. 伝統と習慣が偉力を揮っていた.

governess, *n*. 女家庭教師.
Q² a ***nursery*** *governess* 幼児の家庭教師.
P² a *governess* ***to*** children 子供たちの女家庭教師.

government, *n*. 政治; 政府, 政庁; 内閣; 管理.
V ***aid*** the *Government* in its efforts to ... ...しようとする政府の努力を助ける. ¶***attack*** a *government* 政府を攻撃する. ¶***blame*** the *government* for its foreign policy 政府の対外政策を非難する. ¶The *government* was finally ***downed*** by the rebellious forces. 政府は反乱軍によって遂に打倒された. ¶***establish*** a *government* 政府を樹立する. ¶***form*** a *government* (=ministry) 内閣を組織する. ¶The party ***has*** a weak *government*. その政党の組織した政府は力が薄弱だ. ¶***overturn*** (=***overthrow***) the *government* 政府を倒す. ¶***petition*** the *government* for ... 政府に...を請願する. ¶his ability to ***run*** a *government* 経世の才. ¶***set up*** a strong *government* 強力な政府を樹立する. ¶***subvert*** the *government* 政府を転覆する. ¶***support*** the *government* 政府を援助する. ¶***undermine*** a *government* by ... ...によって政府を転覆する.
V² A new *government* has ***come*** in office. 新内閣ができた. ¶Mr. Balfour's *Government* ***went out***. バルフォーア内閣は崩解した.
Q the ***Allied*** *government* 連合国政府. ¶***bureaucratic*** *government* 官僚政治. ¶petition the ***central*** *government* 中央政府に陳情する. ¶countries which have ***conservative*** *governments* 保守政府をもつ国々. ¶a ***de facto*** *government* 事実上の政府. ¶a ***de jure*** *government* 法律上の政府. ¶The ***dual*** *government* by Mikado and Shogun was ended in 1868. 天皇と将軍による二重政治は一八六八年に終を告げた. ¶They had no ***established*** *government* at that time. 当時は確立した政府というものがなかった. ¶the ***Federal*** *Government* 《米》連邦政府. ¶the ***Imperial*** *Government* 《英》[植民地政庁に対し]帝国政府. ¶set an ***interim*** *government* 臨時政府を設ける. ¶a ***legitimate*** *government* 正統政府. ¶old ***local*** *governments* 各藩. ¶the ***military*** *government* 軍政府.【類】the Eighth Army's ***Military*** *Government*. ¶a ***municipal*** *government* 市役所 ‖ ***municipal*** *government* 市政. ¶He has served in an engineering capacity in the ***prefectural***, ***municipal***, and ***central*** *governments*. 彼は技師の資格で府県, 市, 及び中央官庁に勤めた. ¶***parliamentary*** *government* 議会政治. ¶the ***previous*** *government* 前内閣. ¶a ***provisional*** *government* 仮政府. ¶the ***Republican*** *Government* 共和党政府. ¶a ***settled*** (=stable) *government* 安定した政府. ¶a ***sovereign*** *government* 主権を有する政府. ¶a ***strong*** and ***enduring*** *government* 強力で長続きのする政府. ¶***tyrannic*** *government* 暴政.
Q² ***boss*** *government* ボス政治. ¶overthrow the ***bourgeois*** *government* ブルジョア政府を打倒する. ¶***business*** *government* 実業家の政治参与. ¶a "***caretaker***" *government* without real authority 実権のない管理政府. ¶set up a ***caretaker interim*** *government* pending the holding of free elections 自由選挙終了までの臨時の管理内閣を樹立する. ¶an officer of the ***city*** *government* 市庁の役人. ¶***clan*** *government* 藩閥政治. ¶form a ***coalition*** *government* with ... ...と連合内閣を作る ‖ join the ***coalition*** *government* 連合内閣に入る. ¶the ***non-Communist*** Chinese *Government* 中国の反共政府. ¶Berlin with its ***four-power*** *Government* 四国共同政府をもつベルリン. ¶consult with the ***home*** *government* 本国政府と相談する. ¶the ***Labour*** *Government* in Britain=the British Labour *Government* 英労働党政府. ¶Rumania's ***leftist*** *government* ルーマニアの左翼政府. ¶the ***London*** *Government* said that ... 英国政府の発表によれば... ¶the ***mandate*** *government* 委任統治政府. ¶a ***military clan*** *government* 幕政. ¶a ***multi-party*** *government* 政党諸派連合政府. ¶a ***one-party*** *government* 一党の単一政府. ¶In ***party*** *government* the majority party forms the cabinet. 政党政治では多数党が内閣をつくる. ¶the ***Peiping*** *Government* 北京政府. ¶***petticoat*** *government* 《口語》かかあ天下. ¶install a ***puppet*** *government* かいらい政権を打立てる. ¶Chungking, seat of the ***refugee Nationalist*** *government* 亡命国民政府の所在地重慶. ¶a ***shadow*** *government* 《英》影の政府(在野党の作る). ¶the ***Stalin*** *Government* スターリン政府. ¶a ***State*** *Government* 《米》州政府. ¶a ***student*** *government* 学生自

治会. ¶a *strong-arm government* 強力政府. ¶the *Tsarist* (*Fascist*) *government* [ロシアの]帝政(ファッショ政府). ¶a *world government* 世界政府.

P. He plotted *against* the *government*. 彼は倒閣をたくらんだ. ¶live *beneath* a *government* ある政府の下に生活する. ¶a good form *of government* 善良な政体 ‖ the system *of government* 政体 ‖ the reins *of government* 政権. ¶He was given an office *under Government*. 彼はある官職を与えられた. ‖ be *under* parliamentary *government* 議会政治の下にある ‖ He occupied a post of some kind *under* the *Government* of the Bombay Presidency. 彼はボンベイ総督府である地位を占めた. ‖ institutions *under* the *Government* 直轄学校(など) ‖ India *under* British *government* (=rule) 英国統治の下にある印度.

P² the *Government at* Tokyo 東京の政府. ¶*government by* consent 人民の同意による政治 ‖ *government by* law 法治 ‖ *government by* party 政党政治. ¶The *government of* the University is committed to a board of twenty-one trustees. 同大学の管理は二十一人からなる委員会に委任してある. ‖ the *Government of* Japan 日本政府.

governor, *n.* 知事, 長官; 先生.

Q the *civil governor* 民政長官(奉行). ¶the *military governor* 軍政長官.

Q² a *deputy governor* 副知事. ¶a *lieutenant governor* 《米》[州の]副知事; 《英》[植民地の]副総督. ¶《米》a *State Governor*=the Governor of a State 州知事. ☞実際の用法は Mr. Thomas Dewey, *Governor* of New York となる.

P² the *governors of* Bolton Grammar School ボルトン予備校の監理者 ‖ *governors of* provinces 県知事 ‖ the *Governors of* the University その大学の幹部.

gown, *n.* 長上衣.

V *wear* doctor's *gown* 博士の式服を着る.

Q a *furred gown* 毛皮のついたガウン.

Q² a *bath gown* 浴衣. ¶None of the ladies wore *décolleté gowns*. 婦人たちの中一人もデコルテ上衣を着ている人はいなかった. ¶a *dressing gown* 化粧着. ¶an *evening gown* [婦人の]夜会服(イーブニング). ¶a *night gown* 寝室着.

P students *in* caps and *gowns* [卒業式参列の]式帽式服姿の学生.

grab, *v.* ひっつかむ.

M *grab off* a few dreams ちょいちょいまどろむ.

P *grab* a cat *around* the neck ねこの首玉をつかむ. ¶*grab at* a thing 物をひっつかむ. ¶He *grabbed* me *by* the arm. 彼は僕の腕を捕えた.

grace, *n.* 恩恵, 恩ちょう; 優美; 猶予; 食事前後の祈禱.

V *gain grace* 恩ちょうを得る. ¶I will *give* you a day's *grace*. 君に一日猶予してやろう. ‖ *give* an added *grace* to what is already beautiful 錦上花を添える. ¶He *had* the *grace* to acknowledge my superiority. 私の優位を認めるだけの雅量が彼にあった. ¶*observe grace* before meals 食前に祈をする. ¶*say grace* aloud before or after a meal 食事前後に声を出して祈禱をする. ¶*win* the good *graces* of ... ...の恩ちょうを得る. 【類】*win* the *graces* of a lady.

V² I hope the *grace* of God would *descend* on me. 私は神の恩ちょうに与かるようにと思っている.

Q yield with a *bad grace* しぶしぶ譲歩する. 【類】He lent me the book with a very *bad grace*. ¶submit to these restrictions with a *good grace* 快くこれらの制限を守る. 【類】He admitted his mistake with a *good grace*. ¶*hospitable graces* あいそのよいもてなし. ¶accept with *ill grace* いやいや応じる. ¶I agreed to it with as *much grace* as I could [command]. 私はできるだけきげんよくそれに同意した. ¶the *saving grace* of culture 修養という取柄 ‖ She has the *saving grace* of modesty. 彼女には謙虚という取柄がある. 【類】His writing is imbued with the *saving grace* of humour. ¶*scholarly grace* of phrases 学者的な気品のある文句. ¶with a *smiling grace* 愛想よく. ¶a *tender grace* やさしさ. ¶Self-abasement and avoidance of offense to others are *twin graces* of old culture. 謙そんと人の気にさからわないことは古い文化の二つの美徳である.

P *by* special *grace* 特別のおなさけで ‖ *by* the *Grace* of God 神の恵みによって. ¶*in* (=*with*) a good *grace* 快く ‖ He is *in* his master's good *graces*. 彼は主人の気に入っている. ¶He got *into* her good *grace*. 彼は彼女に取入った. ¶serve wine *with* a *grace* しとやかにおしゃくする. 【類】work for others *with* a good *grace* (気持よく) ‖ She danced *with* a *grace* that surprised us all. 彼女の優雅なダンス振りにはわれわれもびっくりした. ‖ *with* the *grace* of three years 三年の猶予で ‖ We cannot *with* any *grace* ask him. 面目がなくて彼には頼めない.

P² a *grace at* meals 食事のときの祈禱.

grace, *v.* 飾る, 光栄を加える.

P The meeting was *graced by* the presence of ladies. その会合に婦人たちが花々しく出席した. 【類】The function was *graced by* the presence as guests of noted literary personalities. / He *graced* the meeting *with* his presence.

graceful, *a.* 優美な.

P She is *graceful in* manner (speech, movement). 彼女は態度(など)が優美だ.

gracious, *a.* 慈悲深い, 情のある.

P He is *gracious to* his inferiors. 彼は目下の者によくする.

gradation, *n.* 漸次に進むこと.

Q by a process of *easy gradation* 徐々に. ¶emerge from one into another by *imperceptible gradations* [状態などが]目立たないよう徐々に移って行く.

P make a change *by* easy *gradations* 徐々に変化する.

grade, *n.* 等級, 階級; 学級; 位階; 傾斜, こう配.

V *ascend* a *grade* 坂を登る. ¶*award* high *grades* 良い点をやる. ¶The teacher was notorious for *giving grades*. その先生は採点について悪い評判があった. ¶The school *has* eight *grades*. 同校は八学年級になっている. ¶*make* the *grade* 急な坂を上る; 困難に打勝つ. ¶He *received* a "*grade*" of 80 on this examination. 彼はこの試験に八十点取った. ¶*representing* all the various *grades* of well-being 多様な生活程度を示して. ¶Students *securing* satisfactory *grade* will be awarded a certificate of proficiency. 成績佳良の学生には修業証を授与する.

Q attain an *average grade* of more than 75% (on a scale of 100) 平均百分の七十五の高さに達する. ¶*common grades* 普通品. ¶be on the *down grade* 《米》下りこう配になっている. ¶the railway ascends by *easy grades* to ... 《米》鉄道は...へ緩こう配で上る. ¶of *fair grade* 相当の. ¶the *first grade* 一等. ¶He has a *high grade* of intelligence. 彼は高い知性をもっている. ¶of *inferior grade* 劣等の, 劣悪の. ¶a *low grade* of intelligence 低級の知力. ¶men of *low intellectual grade* 低能な人間. ¶a class of Europeans of a *lower social grade* 下層階級のヨーロッパ人. ¶the *second grade* 二等. ¶the *senior* (*junior*) *grade* of the first rank 正(従)一位. ¶*slow grade* 《米》緩いこう配. ¶women of different *social grades* 社会的地位の異なる女. ¶It is constructed on the rack-rail system on a *steep grade* of 1 in 15. それは十五分の一急こう配に歯車式の軌条を用いて造ってある. ¶*up grade* 《米》上りこう配.

Q² *pay grade* 俸給率. ¶an institution of *university grade* 大学程度の学校.

P Milk is sold *in grades*. 牛乳は品質別に(等級をつけて)売られる. ¶*of* all *grades* あらゆる階層の. ¶It is *on* the down *grade*. それは下り坂になっている. ¶*up to grade* (=the mark) [品質が]規格に達して. ¶*through* the *grades* 《米》小学校を終えて.

P² students of Daigaku and Semmongakko *grade in* Japanese schools 日本の大学及び専門学校程度の学生 ‖ His school *grade in* English was good. 彼は学校で英語の成績は良かった.

grade, *v.* 等級をつける.

M eggs *fully graded* to size, shape, and color 大きさ, 形, 色ではっきり等級をつけた鶏卵.

P be *graded* A *in* mathematics.

gradient, *n.* 傾向, こう配.

V In the Abt system a railway train *ascends* a very steep *gradient* by means of a rack or toothed line, in which cogged wheels on the locomotive engage. アプト式では汽車が非常に急な坂路を歯車式の軌条と機関車の歯車とでかみ合わせて登って行く. ¶The hill *has* a *gradient* of 35°. その山は三十五度のこう配だ.

Q It rises to the height of 1600 feet by an *easy gradient*. それは千六百フィートの高さまで緩こう配になっている. ¶there is *no gradient* between ... ...間にはこう配はない. ¶a *steep gradient* 急な坂.

P the angle *of gradient* 傾斜の角度. ¶*with* a slight *gradient* 少しの傾斜で.

graduate, *n.* 卒業生.

V *turn out graduates* [学校が]卒業生を出す.

Q Taft, the most ***brilliant graduate*** of his year at Yale 彼と同年にエール大学を卒業した者の中で最も光っているタフト. ¶"***Europe-returned***" *graduates* of Oxford and Cambridge ヨーロッパに遊学したことのあるオックスフォード及びケンブリッジ大学卒業生. ¶a ***fresh graduate*** 新卒業生. ¶a ***medical graduate*** of Edinburgh University エジンバラ大学医科卒業生. ¶a twenty-two-year-old, ***newly-gowned graduate*** 二十二歳の大学新卒業生. ¶a ***recent graduate*** of the College 同大学最近の卒業生. ¶The job hunt faces ***young graduates***. 若い卒業生は就職問題に直面する.

Q² a ***business-college graduate*** 実業大学の出身者. ¶a ***college*** (***high school***) ***graduate*** 大学(高校)出身者. ¶a ***law graduate*** of a university 大学法科出身. ¶a recent ***Michigan graduate*** 最近のミシガン大学出身者. ¶a ***medical school graduate*** 医学校出. ¶a ***middle school graduate*** 中(学)卒(業者). ¶***University of California graduates*** カリフォルニア大学出身者.

P² *graduates* ***from*** the course in ... ...科の卒業生. ¶a *graduate* ***in*** the famous class of 1853 at Yale University エール大学一八五三年の有名な組の一卒業生 ‖ a *graduate* ***in*** law of the Imperial University of Tokyo 東京大学法科出身. 【類】a *graduate* ***in*** English of the University of Leeds. ¶a *graduate* ***of*** the Universities of Nebraska and Chicago ネブラスカ・シカゴ両大学卒業生.

graduate, *v.* 卒業させる, 学位を授ける; 目盛りする; 卒業する; 漸次推移する.

M He was *graduated* ***A.B.***, and afterward ***A.M.*** 彼は学士の学位を授与されそれから修士になった. ¶Focusing scales are ***generally*** *graduated* in yards, feet, or meters. 焦点距離尺は通常ヤード・フィートまたはメートルの目盛りになっている. ¶Alice Joice ***gracefully*** *graduated* from silent pictures into articulate ones. アリス・ジョイスは無声映画から発声映画へとりっぱに転向した. ¶He *graduated* ***second*** in his class. 彼は級で二番で卒業した. ¶... ***where*** he was *graduated* 彼が卒業した...

P He *graduated* ***as*** M.D. ***at*** Edinburgh in 1807. 《英》彼は一八〇七年にエジンバラ大学を医学ドクターとして卒業した. ¶He *graduated* ***at*** ... ***as*** valedictorian of his class. 彼はその級の卒業生総代として...を卒業した. ‖ He was *graduated* ***at*** Yale in 1920. 《米》彼は一九二〇年にエール大学を卒業した. ¶An income tax was *graduated* ***for*** a higher rate. 所得税はさらに高率に引上げられた. ¶He was *graduated* ***from*** grammar school in 1956. 《米》彼は一九五六年初等中学校を卒業した. ☞《英》He completed his grammar school course ... ¶He *graduated* ***from*** Yale at sixteen. 彼は十六歳でエール大学を卒業した. 【類】He was twenty-three when he *graduated* ***from*** Harvard. / *Graduating* ***from*** Harvard with the degree of M.D., he became an instructor in physiology in that college. / he was *graduated* ***from*** ... in 1900 with the degree of M.A. / As to education, Mr. [J.P.] Morgan *graduated* ***from*** the English High School of Boston and then entered the University of Göttingen, Germany. ☞米国では *be graduated from ...* は formal でいく分 archaic だという. 現在は graduate from ... が通例: He *graduated* ***from*** Cornell in 1956. ‖ He *graduated* ***from*** grammar into language. 彼は文法から言語学にはいった. ‖ Early advertisement writers *graduated* ***from*** newspaper editorial rooms. 昔の広告文案者は新聞の編集室から出たものだ. 【類】He has *graduated* ***from*** the bookshop to the library. ¶He *graduated* ***in*** mathematics ***from*** Trinity College, Dublin. 彼はダブリンのトリニティ大学数学科を卒業した. 【類】He was *graduated* ***in*** medicine at Edinburgh. / They both *graduated* ***in*** the same class. / He was *graduated* ***in*** the law school of Washington. ¶Year by year a few of these slang terms prove so useful that they *graduate* ***into*** respectable society, so to speak. 年々これらの卑語中の少数のものは非常に重宝なので言わば上流の仲間入りをするようになる. ‖ The dawn *graduated* ***into*** day. 夜も段々明け放れ朝となった. ¶when these students *graduate* ***out of*** boardinghouses これらの学生が下宿生活を卒業する時. ¶Helen Keller *graduated* ***with*** honors ***at*** Radcliffe College. ヘレン・ケラー女史はラッドクリフ大学の優等卒業者である. 【類】He was *graduated* ***with*** honors and a Phi Beta Kappa key (P.B.K. クラブの会員). ‖ He *graduated* ***with*** reputation in 1778. 彼は一七七八年りっぱな成績で卒業した.

O Wesleyan University, Connecticut, *graduated* its last co-educational class last month. コネティカット州のウェスレーアン大学は先月その最後の男女共学のクラスを卒業させた(これでそのクラスは廃止になった).

graduating, *n.* 卒業すること.

P soon ***after*** *graduating* 卒業して間もなく. ¶***on*** (=***upon***) *graduating* from ... ...を卒業するやいなや. ¶The student withdrew ***without*** *graduating*. その学生は中途退学をした.

graduation, *n.* 卒業.

P ***after*** his *graduation* as an engineer ***from*** Cooper Union クーパー・ユニオンの工科を卒業して後 ‖ ***after*** his *graduation* ***from*** the university of ... ...大学を卒業して後. ¶***At*** *graduation* those students have to work off their conditions. 卒業の際はこれらの学生は追試験をパスしなければならない. ¶leave high school ***before*** *graduation* 卒業前にハイスクールを去る. ¶***On*** [his] *graduation* from college, he entered the government service. 大学を卒業するや彼は官途についた.

P² the *graduation* ***of*** its first class 同校第一期生の卒業.

graft, *v.* つぎ木する.

P *graft* the pear ***on*** (=upon) the plum 西洋すももになしをつぎ木する ‖ The new building has been *grafted* ***on*** the old. 新しい建物を古い建物につぎ足した. ¶Japan *grafted* Western civilization ***upon*** (=on) the stock of their ancient civilization. 日本は古来の文化を土台としてこれに欧米の新文化を融合した.

grain, *n.* 穀粒, 穀物; 微量; 木目; 本性, 性質.

V The native Japanese papers print the wildest rumours as facts, and it requires much sifting to ***get*** a few *grains* of truth from a large measure of chaff. 土地の日本新聞はとんでもないでたらめなうわさを事実として書くのでもみ殻だらけの記事の中からわずか数粒の真実をつかむには大分えりわけをする必要がある. ¶***grind*** *grain* to flour 穀物を製粉する. ¶***grow*** *grain* and keep cattle 穀物を栽培し牛を飼う.

Q ***brewer's*** *grains* ビールの醸造かす. ¶eat up ***every*** *grain* of rice in one's bowl 茶わんの飯粒を一つ残さずきれいに食べる. ¶Mahogany has a ***fine*** *grain*. マホガニー材は目がつんでいる. ‖ timber of ***fine*** (***coarse***) *grain* 目のつんだ(あらい)材木. ¶***ground*** *grains* 粉にひいた穀物. ¶the ***incalculable*** *grains* of sand on the seashore 浜の数限りない真さご.

Q² ***bread*** *grains* パン用穀類(小麦やライ麦). ¶***cereal*** *grain* 穀物. ¶***food*** *grains* 食料になる穀類.

P I have done it ***against*** the *grain*. 私はいやいやながらそれをやった. ‖ It goes ***against*** the *grain*. それはしゃくにさわる. ¶He trades (=deals) ***in*** *grain*. 彼は穀物を商っている. ¶be dyed ***in*** the *grain* しんまで染めた; 生粋の. ¶He feeds the horse ***on*** *grain*. 彼は馬に穀物を食わして置く. ¶take a report ***with*** a *grain* of salt 報告をまゆにつばをつけて聞く ‖ Nobody ***with*** a *grain* of sense underestimate the great importance of good cookery. 多少でも良識のある人ならだれでもうまい調理の大切なことは分かる. 【類】What he says must be taken ***with*** some *grains* of allowance.

P² There is not a *grain* (=an ounce) ***of*** truth in it. それにはみじんも本当のことはない. ‖ the *grain* ***of*** wood 木目. ¶a boy ***without*** a *grain* of sense 全然聞き分けのない少年.

grain, *v.* しみこむ.

P This vice is *grained* ***into*** him. この悪が彼にしみこんでいる.

grammar, *n.* 文法; 文法書.

V He has never ***opened*** a French *grammar*. 彼はフランス語の文法書を見たことはない. ¶***use*** good (bad) *grammar* 文法に合った(合わない)言葉を使う. ¶***violate*** *grammar* 文法にそむく.

P some common errors ***in*** *grammar* 普通に見る文法上の間違い. ¶fall ***into*** bad *grammar* 文法の誤りをする. ¶refer ***to*** the *grammar* 文法を参照する.

grammarian, *n.* 文法家.

Q a ***conservative*** *grammarian* 保守的な文法学者.

gramophone, *n.* 蓄音機.

P sing a popular song ***into*** the *gramophone* 流行歌を蓄音機に吹き込む.

granary, *n.* 穀倉.

Q an ***inexhaustible*** *granary* of wealth 無尽蔵の富の倉.

grand, *n.* グランド・ピアノ; 《俗》偉い人.

V *do* the *grand* 《俗》気取る.

Q² a *baby grand* 家庭用平型ピアノ.

grand, *a.* 堂々たる, りっぱな.

P the type of humanity ***at*** its *grandest* 最も高まいな典型的人間.

grandeur, *n.* 壮大, 偉大, 荘厳.

V ***appreciate*** the full *grandeur* of Togo's achievement 東郷元帥の偉業を十分に認識する. ¶These ruins sufficiently ***attest*** the former *grandeur* of the place. これらの廃虚がその地のありし昔の壮観を十分しのばせる. ¶This ***gives*** a moral *grandeur* to his achievements. これあるがために彼の功績が道徳的偉大性を持つようになる.

Q the ***amazing*** *grandeur* of the Niagara Falls ナイアガラばく布の驚くべき壮観. ¶I was fascinated at the ***awful*** *grandeur* of Niagara. 私はナイアガラの荘厳な偉大さに打たれた. ¶its ***moral*** *grandeur*, its spiritual beauty その道徳的な偉大さ, その精神的な美しさ. ¶the ***rugged*** *grandeur* of the Rockies ロッキー山脈のががたる荘厳さ. ¶The towering peak of Fuji-san rises in ***solitary*** *grandeur*. 富士の峰はひとり毅(き)然として雲表にそびえる.

P ***in*** the *grandeur* of the mountain solitudes 山奥の荘厳な閑寂さの中に. ¶I was much struck ***with*** the *grandeur* of ... 私は...の壮大さに大いに打たれた.

P² the *grandeur* ***of*** the scenery その風景の壮観.

grand-master, *n.* 大家.

Q a ***past*** *grand-master* of the subject その道の大家.

grandmother, *n.* 祖母.

Q a ***doting*** *grandmother* 孫に目のない祖母.

grandson, *n.* 孫.

Q a ***great-great-great*** *grandson* of ... ...の四代目の孫.

Q² three ***teen-age*** *grandsons* 三人の十代の孫息子.

grandstand, *n.* 観覧台.

Q an ***arboreal*** *grandstand* used by unpaid spectators 入場料を出さない見物人の樹木観覧台(野球試合などで人のなった大木).

grant, *n.* 補助金; 許可.

V ***make*** a *grant* towards the expenses incurred by ... ...に要する費用に対して助成金を与える. 【類】I will ***make*** you a *grant* of £100 a year. ¶he applied for and ***obtained*** a *grant* of money from ... 彼は...に補助金を願い出てこれを得た. 【類】***obtain*** a Government *grant* of £10,000 annually for the aid ***of*** ...

Q an ***ample*** *grant* of money 巨額の補助金. ¶The Society has an ***annual*** *grant* of £5,000 同協会は年五千ポンドの補助金を受けている. ¶make a ***special*** *grant* of £1,000 toward the erection of ... ...の建設に対して一千ポンドの特別補助金を与える.

Q² a ***cash*** *grant* 現金の補助. ¶***death*** *grant* and injury allowance for prisoners 収容者死傷手当. ¶give an ***eight-year*** *grant* totaling $1,000,000 八年間に総計百万ドルに達する奨学金を与える. ¶***foundation*** *grants* 基金補助. ¶a ***Government*** *grant* to ... ...に対する政府の補助金. ¶the local ***finance equalization*** *grants* 地方平衡補正金. ¶Each year a certain number of ***money*** *grants* have been made. 毎年一定数の補助金が与えられる. 【類】give small ***money*** *grants* towards the cost of ... ¶give special ***research*** *grants* to universities 大学に特別研究費を下付する. ¶a ***retirement*** *grant* of 100,000 yen 十万円の退職手当. ¶universities receiving annual ***State*** *grants* 国庫からの補助をもらう諸大学.

P work ***on*** a *grant* from a foundation 基金からの補助金で研究する. ¶***under*** a *grant* from ... ...から補助を受けて.

P² a *grant* ***from*** the crown to ... 皇室から...への補助金 ‖ a $700,000 *grant* ***from*** the Carnegie Foundation カーネギー財団からの七十万ドルの補助金. ¶a *grant* ***in*** aid of ... ...の助成金. ¶make a *grant* ***in*** money or in kind 金品で補助を与える. ¶a *grant* ***of*** the exclusive right of ... ...の独占権の許可.

grant, *v.* 許す; 与える.

M Licences are *granted* ***easily***. 許可証はすぐおりる.

P *grant* ... ***towards*** the expenses (cost of repair) その費用(など)に対し...補助する. ¶The King *grants* an annuity ***unto*** the work. 王がその事業に年々助成金を下賜されている.

O *granting* that ... 仮りに...としても.

granting, *n.* 許可.

P² the *granting* ***of*** divorce 離婚許可.

grape, *n.* ぶどう.

V ***gather*** *grapes* of thorns or figs of thistles いばらからぶどうまたはあざみからいちじくを取る(木によって魚を求める).

Q ***luscious*** *grapes* 甘美なぶどう. ¶***over-ripe*** (***unripe***) *grapes* 熟し過ぎた(熟さない)ぶどう. ¶***sweet*** *grapes* 甘いぶどう.

P a bunch ***of*** *grapes* 一房のぶどう ‖ the juice ***of*** the *grape* ぶどう液.

graph, *n.* グラフ.

V² *graphs* ***showing*** ... ...のグラフ.

grapple, *v.* つかむ, 取組む, つかみ合う.

M ***effectively*** *grapple* with a problem 問題をりっぱに取りさばく. ¶***pluckily*** *grappling* with difficulties 困難と勇敢に戦って. ¶*grapple* ***successfully*** with the problem of ... (this difficult task) ...の問題(など)を手際よく始末する.

P *grapple* ***at*** each other 互につかみ合う. ¶*grapple* a boat ***to*** a wharf ***with*** a steel hook 舟を鋼鉄のかぎで岸壁に引寄せる. ¶*grapple* ***with*** a task 仕事を成し遂げようと努力する ‖ *grapple* ***with*** adverse circumstances (difficulties, antagonists) 逆境(など)と戦う ‖ *grapple* ***with*** a stranger 見知らぬ者と取組む ‖ *grapple* ***with*** examiners 試験官の試験を受ける. 【類】have neither time nor patience to *grapple* ***with*** the enormous literature (ぼう大な文献) treating of ... / have neither time nor patience to *grapple* ***with*** the subject.

grasp, *n.* つかみ; にぎり; 会得, 理解力.

V ***acquire*** a general *grasp* of the existing knowledge on the subject その題目に関する現存知識を大体つかむ. ¶***elude*** our *grasp* われわれの手をのがる. ¶***get*** a good *grasp* of ... ...をしっかりつかむ. ¶***give*** young pupils a clear *grasp* of ... 幼い児童たちに...をはっきり会得させる. ¶They ***have*** a great *grasp* of intellect. 彼らは知力に富む. ¶***let loose*** one's *grasp* にぎりをゆるめる. ¶***loosen*** one's *grasp* にぎりをゆるめる. ¶it ***owes*** frail *grasp* on existence to ... そのかよわい生存を持続しうるのは...のお陰である. ¶***relax*** one's *grasp* 手をゆるめる. ¶He ***shows*** so thorough a *grasp* of the question. 彼はその問題を完全に会得していることを示している. ¶***tighten*** one's *grasp* on the English language. 英語の理解を強める.

Q The author has a ***complete*** *grasp* of his subject 著者は自己のテーマを完全に把握している. ¶He has ***firm*** *grasp* of the law. 彼にはしっかりした法律の知識がある. ¶have a ***good*** *grasp* of ... ...をよく会得している. ¶He has no ***real*** *grasp* of the subject. 彼にはその問題が本当に分かっていない. ¶with a ***rudimentary*** *grasp* of the responsibilities of his position 彼の地位の責任感を十分会得しないで. ¶his ***splendid*** *grasp* of living questions in every walk of life あらゆる方面における刻下の問題に対する彼のりっぱな理解. ¶have a ***thorough*** *grasp* on all the problems of ... ...のあらゆる問題に対して十分の理解を持つ.

P ***beyond*** one's *grasp* その力に及ばない ‖ one of those things that are ***beyond*** the *grasp* of the foreign intellect 外国人に理解しかねることの一つ. ¶The point is ***in*** the *grasp* of the enemy. その地点は敵の掌中にある. ¶the power ***of*** *grasp* 把握力. ¶He has a good opportunity ***within*** his *grasp*. 彼にはつかみうる良い機会がある. ‖ Now success is ***within*** my *grasp*. もうこうなりゃしめたものだ. ¶He has a very firm *grasp* ***on*** the subject. 彼はその問題をよく理解している.

grasp, *v.* つかむ, 握る; 会得する.

M *grasp* ***easily*** 容易に会得する. ¶I *grasped* his right hand ***firmly*** in mine. 私は私の手に彼の右手をしっかりと握った.

P *grasp* ***at*** the air 空気をつかもうとする ‖ A drowning man will *grasp* ***at*** a straw. おぼれんとする者はわらをもつかむ. ‖ In *grasping* ***at*** the shadow she has lost the substance. 彼女は影をつかもうとして実物を失ってしまった(家庭を捨てた女など). ¶*grasp* a person ***by*** the wrist (arm, hand, collar) 人の手首を握る. ¶*grasp* it ***in*** (=***with***) one's hand それを手に握る.

grasping, *a.* むさぼる, よく深い.

M ***less*** *grasping* than ... ...ほど欲ばらない. ¶Don't be ***so*** *grasping*; he gave you one yen; that is something. そんなによく張るな, その人が一円くれたじゃないか, それで結構じゃないか.

P *grasping* ***as regards*** money 金銭にかけてはがっちりしている.

grass, *n.* 草, 牧草; 芝生.

V The horse was ***cropping*** the *grass*. 馬が草をちぎりちぎり食べていた. ¶***cut*** (=***mow***) the *grass* on a lawn 芝生の草を刈る. ¶Green *grass* ***grows*** in the yard. 庭に緑の草がはえる.

v² The *grass* is ***coming up.*** 草がもえ出ている. ¶*grass* ***grows*** on … …の上に草がはえる.

Q a ***common*** *grass* ありふれた草. ¶walk through the ***dewy*** *grass* 露にぬれた草の中を歩く. ¶***flowering*** *grasses* 草花. ¶***rank*** *grass* はびこる草. 【類】tall ***rank*** *grass.* ¶***various*** *grasses* 各種の草. ¶the ***verdant*** *grass* 緑の芝生.

P a snake sleeping ***in*** the *grass* 草の中に眠っているへび. ¶a blade ***of*** *grass* 草一本. ¶Keep ***off*** the *grass.* 芝生に入るべからず. ¶cattle feeding ***on*** *grass* 草を食べている牛 ‖ play ***on*** the *grass* 芝生の上で遊ぶ ‖ throw oneself ***on*** the *grass* 草の上に横になる. ¶spread a blanket ***over*** (=on) the *grass* 草の上に毛布を敷く. ¶crawl ***through*** the *grass* 草の中をはう. ¶The yard is covered ***with*** *grass.* 庭は草だらけだ. ‖ fields green ***with*** *grass* 草で青い野原.

P² a *grass* ***of*** the same genus with millet きびと同種類の草.

grasshopper, *v.* きりぎりす.

v² The *grasshopper* ***hops.*** きりぎりすがはねる.

grate, *v.* こすれる, きしる; [耳などに]さわる.

P *grate* ***against*** … …にこすれる. ¶Harsh voice *grates* ***on*** one's ear. しわがれ声は耳ざわりだ. ‖ "None was at home," though a strictly correct form, seems to *grate* ***on*** the ear a little. "None was at home" という言い方は決して間違っている言い方ではないがちょっと耳ざわりのようだ. ¶His talk *grated* ***upon*** all present. 彼の話はそこにいるすべての人の耳ざわりであった.

grateful, *a.* 恩に感じる, ありがたく思う.

M he was ***deeply*** *grateful* to know that … 彼は…と知って深く感謝していた. ¶I am ***heartily*** *grateful* [to you] for what you've done to me. 私は衷心から御親切をありがたく思っています. ¶we are ***particularly*** *grateful* to him for … われわれは…に対し特に彼に感謝している. ¶I shall be ***profoundly*** (=***very***) *grateful* if you will … …して下されば感謝にたえません.

P I am *grateful* ***for*** your kindness. 御親切ありがとう存じます. 【類】I feel *grateful* ***for*** your help. ‖ I'm very *grateful* ***for*** the benefit I have derived from his scholarly criticism. 氏の学者的批評から受けた私の利益に対し大いに感謝している. ¶a doctrine *grateful* ***to*** scientific men 科学者に取ってありがたい説 ‖ Your kindness is *grateful* ***to*** me. 御親切はありがたい. ‖ I am *grateful* ***to*** you for your sympathy. 御同情に対し感謝しています.

grater, *n.* おろし金.

Q² a ***horse radish*** *grater* わさびおろし.

gratification, *n.* 満足.

V ***express*** *gratification* over the success 成功に対して満足の意を表する. ¶***find*** one's *gratification* (=satisfaction) in … …を喜ぶ. ¶***provide*** *gratification* for the lust of others 人の欲望に満足を与える. ¶***seek*** sexual *gratification* with prostitutes 売春に接して性的満足を求める.

Q marry for ***mutual*** *gratification* 相互満足のために結婚する. ¶***physical*** *gratification* 肉体的満足. ¶it is with ***sincere*** *gratification* and no little pride that … …ということに対し衷心よりの満足と少なからざる誇りを感じる.

P² express one's *gratification* ***at*** … …に対して満足の意を表わす.

gratify, *v.* 満足させる, 喜ばす.

P You'll be *gratified* ***by*** joining us to work together. われわれと協力なさることによって御満足なさるでしょう. ¶I am *gratified* ***with*** the result. 私は結果に満足している.

O It *gratifies* me to observe that things are making a change for the better. 事態が好転しつつあるのは喜ばしい. ¶I am *gratified* to hear of the result. 私は結果を聞いて満足している.

gratifying, *a.* 満足な, うれしい.

M The news is ***most*** *gratifying.* その話は極めて痛快だ.

P The result is *gratifying* ***to*** me. 成績が良好でうれしい. ‖ dishes more *gratifying* ***to*** the eye than to the palate 食べておいしいよりも見て美しい料理.

gratitude, *n.* 感謝, 報恩.

P Pray ***accept*** my deep *gratitude.* ありがたく感謝します. ¶His action ***deserves*** our warmest *gratitude.* 彼の行動はわれわれの最も熱心な感謝に値する. ¶adequately ***display*** one's *gratitude* その感謝を適切に表わす. ¶he ***earned*** the *gratitude* of all men by … 彼は…によって万人の感謝を受けた ‖ the authorities would assuredly ***earn*** the *gratitude* of the public if they improved … 当局者がもし…を改善すれば必ず一般公衆から感謝されるだろう. ¶especially must I ***express*** my *gratitude* to … 特に私は…に対し感謝の意を表わさねばならない. 【類】he ***expressed*** his *gratitude* and delight at the hospitality shown him by … / I wish to ***express*** my *gratitude* for the abundant assistance received from … ¶***lose*** one's *gratitude* to … …に対する感謝の念を失う. ¶***mark*** *gratitude* for … by … …に対し…から感謝の意を示す. ¶he well ***merits*** the *gratitude* of … 彼は十分…の感謝を受ける価値がある. ¶we ***owe*** endless *gratitude* to … われわれは…から限りない恩義をこうむっている ‖ mankind ***owes*** its *gratitude* to the memory of … for … 人類は…に対し…の霊に感謝しなければならない. ¶***preserve*** sincere *gratitude* for … …に対し相変らず心から感謝している. ¶let us here and now ***record*** our deep *gratitude* to … 今ここに…に対するわれわれの深い感謝を記すことにする. ¶***show*** their *gratitude* for … …に対して彼らの感謝を示す. ¶***tender*** his sincere *gratitude* to … …に対して心からの感謝を捧げる.

Q acknowledge it with ***deep*** *gratitude* それに対して深い感謝を表する ‖ we consider ourselves under a debt of ***deep*** *gratitude* to … われわれは…に対して深く感謝せねばならない義理があると思う. ¶we owe the ***highest*** *gratitude* to … …に対し最大の感謝をしなければならない. ¶the ***national*** *gratitude* is shown in a bronze statue by … 全国民の感謝が…製作の銅像によって表明されている. ¶the ***truest, warmest,*** and ***heartfelt*** *gratitude* 最も真実にして熱心な衷心からの感謝. ¶show ***unbounded*** *gratitude* for … …に対して限りない感謝を示す.

P ***from*** one's *gratitude* to one's benefactor 恩人に対する感謝の念から. ¶he contributed a large sum to the fund ***in*** *gratitude* for … 彼は…に対する感謝の念を表するため基金の中へ多額の寄付をした. ¶in token ***of*** my *gratitude* 私の感謝の印として ‖ I owe you a debt ***of*** *gratitude* which I shall never be able to repay. 私はとても返せないほどあなたに恩になっている. ¶***out of*** *gratitude* for … …に対する報恩のために. 【類】***out of*** *gratitude* to God. ¶***with*** deep *gratitude* I look back upon the kindness and consideration shown by … …によって示された親切と同情を思い出して非常にありがたく感謝する.

P² *gratitude* ***for*** one's generosity その寛大に対する感謝.

gratuity, *n.* 施し物; 祝儀, 心付.

V ***accept*** a *gratuity* 心付を受ける. ¶***allow*** a *gratuity* 心付をやる. ¶***distribute*** *gratuities* 心付を分配する. ¶She ***expects*** a *gratuity.* 彼女は心付をもらう気でいる. ¶***give*** a small *gratuity* わずかの心付をやる.

Q the ***customary*** *gratuity* おきまりの心付. ¶***No*** *gratuities* accepted. お心付けは一切お断り致します.

P² a *gratuity* ***to*** a waiter (cabman) 給仕(など)への心付.

grave, *n.* 墓; 墓穴.

V ***desecrate*** the *graves* of their ancestors 彼らの先祖の墓をけがす. ¶***dig*** one's own *grave* 自分の死ぬのを待つ ‖ How true is the saying that "many people ***dig*** *graves* with their teeth!" 「自分の墓を自分の歯で掘る者が多い」ということがあるがこれはいかにも本当のことだ(歯を大事にしないで命を縮める意). ¶***escape*** a watery *grave* でき死を免れる. ¶***find*** one's *grave* in a far-off foreign land 遠い異国の土になる. ¶***mark*** one's *grave* 墓標を立てる. ¶This burning of the candle at both ends ***means*** an untimely *grave.* かく多岐にわたって精力を消耗するのは結局若死を招くことになる. ¶Hyenas are said to ***rob*** *graves.* ハイエナは墓をあばいて死体を食うそうだ. ¶***visit*** a *grave* 墓参をする.

Q This ended in epilepsy and an ***early*** *grave.* 結局てんかんになって早死した. 【類】Such a bad habit leads man to an ***early*** *grave.* / sink into an ***early*** *grave.* ¶a ***green*** *grave* 新しい墓. ¶the remains of … rest in a ***nameless*** *grave* …のなきがらは無名の墓に眠っている. ¶visit an ***unknown*** *grave* 無名の墓にもうでる. ¶find (=meet with) a ***watery*** *grave* おぼれ死ぬ. 【類】Every summer a number of boys terminate their youthful career in a ***watery*** *grave.*

Q² ***mass*** *graves* 戦死者などの会葬墓地. ¶***war*** *graves* 戦没者たちの墓.

P There will be a service ***at*** the *grave* and the placing of a wreath. 墓場で式があって花輪が手向けられます. ‖ worship ***at*** the *grave* その墓にもうでる. ¶the land ***beyond*** the *grave* めい土. ¶pull a person ***from*** a watery *grave* 身投げした人を引上げる. ¶long after they are ***in*** their *graves* 彼らが死んでから余ほど後に ‖ an old man with one foot *in* the *grave* 墓(棺おけ)に片足突込んでいる老人. ¶the stone *over* the *grave* of ... …の墓石 ‖ a monument *over* a *grave* 墓上に立てた記念碑. ‖ He wept *over* the *grave* of his child. 彼はその子供の墓で泣いた. ¶from the cradle *to* the *grave* 生れてから死ぬまで. ¶the grass is not yet green *upon* the *graves* of ... …の墓にはまだ草が青々とはえてない(埋めてから日がたっていない). 【類】place a wreath *upon* the *grave* of ...

P² The sea is the *grave of* thousands. 板子一枚下は地獄. ¶a *grave under* a willow tree 柳の下の墓.

grave, *v.* 銘記する; 彫刻する.

P His words are *graven on* my heart. 彼の言葉は私の心に銘じている. ¶*grave* the stone *with* letters 文字を石に彫刻する.

grave, *a.* まじめな; 重々しい.

M He looks *terribly grave*. とっても深刻な顔をしていた.

P He is *grave in* manner. 彼は動作が重々しい.

gravel, *n.* 砂利.

Q² *river gravel* 川砂利.

P The road is covered *with gravel*. 道路には砂利が敷いてある.

gravestone, *n.* 墓石.

Q a *moss-grown gravestone*＝a gravestone covered with lichens こけむした墓石.

P an epitaph *on* a *gravestone* 墓石の碑銘.

gravitate, *v.* [引力で]引きつけられる, 向かう.

P *gravitate into* one congenial sub-group 自然同類の一小分科を成す. ¶*gravitate to* the bottom 底に沈下する ‖ public opinion *gravitated to* ... 世論が…に落付いた. ¶Isaac Newton *gravitated* in his school days always *towards* the bottom of his class. アイザック・ニュートンは学校時代いつも級の末席の方にい勝ちだった. ‖ Industry *gravitates towards* towns. 工業は都会へ集まる傾向がある.

gravitation, *n.* 引力.

Q The center of *international gravitation* has been shifted to the Pacific. 国際関係の中心は太平洋に移った.

P² the *gravitation of* population *to* big cities 人口の大都会への集中.

gravity, *n.* 厳粛; 重大; 重力.

V It will *intensify* the *gravity* of the situation そうすると時局がますます悪化する. ¶*keep* one's *gravity* 重々しい態度を持する ‖ I could hardly *keep* my *gravity*. 私は笑わずにはいられないほどだった. ¶*realize* the *gravity* of the position and act accordingly 事態の重大性を感知してそれ相応の行動を取る. ¶It *upset* my *gravity*. それで私は思わず吹き出した. ¶*weigh* the *gravity* of a crime 罪の軽重をはかる.

Q All the Embassies regard the position as one of *increasing gravity*. 何れの大使館でも形勢いよいよ非と見ている. ¶with *mock gravity* まじめを装うて. ¶with a *solemn gravity* 謹厳に. ¶*specific gravity* 比重.

P The stone rolled down the mountain *by gravity*. その石は重さで山から転がり落ちた. ¶a question *of* little *gravity* 重大でない問題 ‖ the center *of gravity* 重心. ¶He spoke *with* the utmost *gravity*. 彼はきわめて重々しく話した.

gray, *n.* 灰色; 灰色の衣服; 白髪.

Q *light* (*dark*) *gray* うす(濃い)ねずみ色. ¶The sky was turning to the *pearly gray* of dawn. 空は夜明けの真珠のような灰色に変りつつあった. ¶*premature gray* 若白髪.

Q² *Oxford gray* 濃灰色. ¶a *slate gray* 黒ずんだねずみ色.

P *in* the *gray* of the morning 夜明けに, 朝まだきに ‖ a man (woman) dressed *in gray* 灰色の衣服をつけた人.

graze, *v.* 皮膚をむく.

M a bullet or two *nearly grazing* his scalp 彼の頭をかすめた一二発の弾丸.

M² make the skin *graze off* 皮膚(上皮)をすりむく.

graze, *v.* 草を食う.

P a herd of cattle *grazing in* the pasture 牧場で草を食っている一群の家畜(牛). ¶send one's cows and horses to *graze upon* (＝*on*) the common fields 牛馬を共有地の原っぱにやって草を食わせる.

grease, *n.* あぶら, 脂肪.

V *avoid grease* of all kinds to hair 一切油を頭髪につけないようにする. ¶*remove grease* from one's coat 上衣から油を抜く.

P a spot *of grease* 油の斑点. ¶It is smeared *with grease*. それは油だらけになっている.

grease, *v.* 油のしみをつける.

M get one's coat *greased all over* 上衣を油のしみだらけにする.

grease-mark, *n.* 油のしみ.

P² *grease-marks on* one's shirt そのシャツの油しみ.

great, *n.* 偉大な人.

Q our *dead* (＝*departed*) *great* 故人となったわが国の偉人.

great, *a.* 偉大な; うまい; 姙娠している.

M The crop produced will be *much greater* (far short of) the estimate made. 作物の実収高は予想よりはるかに上回る(ずっと少ない)だろう. ¶be *vastly greater* ずっと偉い. ¶a *substantially greater* percentage is devoted to ... それより余ほど大きなパーセンテージが…の方に向けられている.

P He is *great at* checkers. 彼はチエッカーズ(将棋の一種)がうまい. ¶a nation *great in* arts 芸術上偉大な一国民. ¶*great of* heart 心の偉大な(人). ¶Chinese are *great on* decorum. 中国人は礼節において傑出している. ¶She is *great with* child. 彼女は姙娠している. 【類】The sow (雌豚) is *great with* young.

O I'll get you a new one.—It's *great*. 新しいのを買ってやる. そりゃあすてきだ.

great-coat, *n.* オーバー.

Q a *fur-lined great-coat* 裏に毛皮のついたオーバー. ¶a *natty great-coat* スマートなオーバー.

greatness, *n.* 偉大.

V *achieve greatness* 偉業を成しとげる. ¶*establish* commercial *greatness* 商業上の偉業を成就する. ¶*gauge* the *greatness* of a man by his achievements 人のえらさをその業績によってはかる. ¶she *owes* her present *greatness* to ... 彼女の今日のりっぱな地位は…のお陰である. ¶*predict* future *greatness* for him 彼は将来えらくなると予言する. ¶*Greatness* has been suddenly *thrust* on them without preliminary leisure to grow up to it. 彼らは徐々にえらくなったのでなく急に偉くさせられてしまった.

Q *American greatness*. アメリカの偉大さ. ¶*military greatness* 軍事上の偉大性. ¶the dream of *national grseatness* 国家隆盛の夢. ¶when the youngster gets into the company of great men, and has a *reflected greatness* thrust upon him 若者が偉人の仲間に入りそのお陰で人から偉人扱いにされるとき.

greed, *n.* どん欲, どんらん.

Q *commercial greed* 商人根性. ¶*grasping greed* どん欲. ¶a policy of aggression and *territorial greed* 侵略及び領土欲の政策. ¶those with *unbounded greed* for profit 利欲に目のない手合.

P² *greed for* gold (money, gain) 金(など)の欲.

greediness, *n.* どん欲.

Q with *wolfish greediness* [おおかみのように]がつがつして.

greedy, *a.* 欲張りの, どん欲の.

P He is *greedy for* (＝*after*) fame (praise, honor). 彼は名声(など)をむさぼり求める. ¶a man *greedy of* money (wealth) 金(など)に欲の深い人 ‖ be *greedy of* gain 欲が深い ‖ be *greedy of* something new 新しいものには目がない.

Greek, *n.* ギリシア語.

Q It is *all Greek* to me. それは私にはちんぷんかんぷんだ. ¶*modern* (*Ancient*) *Greek* 現代(古代)ギリシア語.

green, *n.* 緑色; 芝地.

Q the *fluffy green* of the forest 森の若葉.

Q² a *bowling green* 球技場. ¶*Christmas greens* クリスマス用の常緑樹. ¶a *croquet green* クロケー球技場. ¶a *village green* 村の緑地(共有地).

P play *on* the *green* 芝生の上で遊ぶ. ¶Victory was *with* the *green*. 緑組が優勝した.

green, *a.* 新らしい, 世慣れない; そう白な(顔色など).

P a young man *green* (＝fresh) *from* America 米国から来たての青年. ¶*green in* experience 経験の浅い. ¶youngsters *green to* the ways of the world 世故に慣れない若者. ¶he was *green with* envy at ... 彼は…に対するしっとで顔がそう白になっていた.

greenery, *n.* 〖集〗緑地; 緑樹.

Q unsullied *greenery* 新緑.

Q² *summer greenery* 夏の緑.

greengrocer, *n.* 《英》八百屋.

Q a *sanctimonious greengrocer* ずるい青物屋.

greenroom, *n.* (昔の劇場の)楽屋.

V *talk greenroom* 楽屋話をする.

greet, *v.* あいさつする, 会釈する, 迎える.

M "Good afternoon!" he *greeted affably*. 「今日は」と彼

は愛想よく会釈した. ¶greet warmly 丁寧にあいさつする.
P be greeted at a station on one's arrival from ... 駅で出迎えを受ける. ¶He is so short-sighted that he usually fails to greet us in the street. 彼は近眼で町で会っても大抵あいさつをしない. ¶greet a person with a smile 微笑をもって人を迎える ‖ be greeted with a storm of derision あざけりの声のあらしで迎えられる. 【類】greet the visitor with a "Good morning" or "Good afternoon", as the case may be ‖ He greeted me with a nod. 彼はうなずいて私にあいさつした. 【類】He was greeted with the most enthusiastic banzai. ‖ He was greeted with roars of laughter. 一同が彼に爆笑を浴せた. 【類】He was greeted with a rousing cheer (ringing cheers). / He was greeted with a chilly silence. / The lecturer was greeted with a packed house (立すいの余地のない盛況).

greeting, *n.* あいさつ, 会釈, 祝賀, 敬礼.
V The King acknowledged a loyal greeting from the crowds. 王は群集からの熱誠な敬礼に会釈された. ‖ acknowledge the greeting with a friendly smile 愛想よく微笑して敬礼にあいさつする. ¶exchange greetings あいさつを交わす. ¶extend Xmas greetings to ... ...にクリスマスのあいさつをする. ¶offer greetings to ... ...に敬意を表する. ¶receive greetings from ... ...からあいさつを受ける. ¶She returned his greeting as cordially as she could. 彼女はできるだけ丁重に彼のあいさつに答えた. ¶send greetings on the occasion of the gold wedding of ... ...の金婚式に際し祝辞を寄せる. ¶I beg to tender you the greeting of the New Year. 新年おめでとう存じます.
Q cheery greeting 気持ちのよいあいさつ. ¶after formal greeting 正式のあいさつを交わした後. ¶with fraternal greetings to our Allies in the Far East 極東におけるわれらの同盟国に親しく敬意を表して. ¶friendly greetings 友情のこもったあいさつ. ¶She received me with a gentle, half-shy greeting. 彼女はやさしい半ばはにかんだあいさつをして私を迎えた. ¶the usual elaborate Oriental greetings 例の念の入った東洋風のあいさつ. ¶with a polite greeting, he said ... 丁寧にあいさつして彼は...と言った. ¶I wish you the season's greetings. 時候のあいさつを申述べます. ¶the gift was presented with seasonable greetings from ... その贈物は...から時候のあいさつを添えて贈られた. ¶sympathetic greetings were sent from ... [「盛会を祝す」などいう]同情的なあいさつが...から送られた.
Q² pictorial Christmas greetings クリスマスの絵入カード. ¶wedding greetings 結婚の祝詞. ¶send Xmas and New Year greetings to ... クリスマス及び年賀のあいさつを送る.
P with Xmas greetings クリスマスのあいさつを申添えて. ¶without greeting あいさつなしに.
P² greetings from ... ...からのあいさつ, 祝詞. ¶Mrs. Asquith's greeting to her husband on his return from Biarritz アスキス氏がビアリッツから帰った時夫人の夫君に対するあいさつ ‖ My best greetings to your father. 御尊父によろしく.

grenade, *n.* 手りゅう弾.
V throw a grenade at ... ...をめがけて手りゅう弾を投げる.
Q² a hand grenade 手りゅう弾. ¶a bottle grenade＝a Molotov cocktail 火炎びん.

grey, ＝gray.

greyhound, *n.* 《米》快速艇.
Q² an ocean greyhound 大洋航行の快速汽船.

grief, *n.* 悲哀, 憂うつ; 苦痛の種.
V assuage her grief 彼女の悲哀を和らげる. ¶drown grief in dissipation 放とうに悲哀を紛らす. ¶My poor friend had the great grief of losing his only son. 私の友は不幸にも独り息子を失った. ¶intensify one's grief 悲哀を深める. ¶master (＝control) one's grief 悲しみを抑える. ¶His grief was solaced by time. 彼の憂愁は時がこれをいやした.
Q acute grief 痛切な悲しみ. ¶bitter grief 痛ましい悲しみ. ¶He was in deep grief. 彼は深い悲哀に沈んでいた. ¶There are not, on earth at least, eternal griefs. とに角現世には永遠の哀愁なるものはない. ¶He was in extreme grief. 彼は非常に悲しんでいた. ¶He died leaving his wife in great grief. 悲嘆に暮れる妻を残して死んだ.
P I was nearly driven mad by grief. 悲嘆のために私は狂気せんばかりであった. ¶he killed himself in his grief over ... 彼は...を悲しんだ余り自殺した. ¶through grief at the loss of his son 息子をなくしたのを悲しんで. ¶much to the grief of ... ...にとって非常に悲しいことには. ¶come to grief うき目を見る ‖ bring him to grief 彼をうきめに会わせる. ¶be relieved of one's grief 悲しみが消える. ¶I suppose the parents are beside themselves with grief. その両親は悲しみの余り狂気のようになっていることでしょう.
P² We had much grief at that matter. われわれはそのことで大いに心を痛めた. ¶with grief for one's death その死を悲しんで. ¶with grief in his heart 哀愁を胸に懐いて. ¶the grief of old age 老の悲哀. ¶with grief over one's death その死を悲しんで. ¶His conduct has been a great grief to me. 彼の行状は私には非常な苦痛であった.

grievance, *n.* 不平, 苦情, 不平の種.
V orators airing their favorite grievances to ever-changing and impassive listeners 絶えず変るかつ感覚の鈍い聴衆に対して例の不平を述べ立てる弁士. ¶evoke a grievance from ... ...の不平を買う. ¶have a grievance against a person 人に対して不平をいだく. ¶lay their grievances directly before ... 彼らの苦情を直接に...に持ち出す. 【類】lay before him certain grievances in regard to ... ¶pigeon-hole grievances 不平を取合わない. ¶redress grievances 弊害を改める. 【類】as a final means of redressing their grievances. ¶remedy a grievance keenly felt by ... ...が痛切に感じた不平の種を除く. ¶remove a grievance Japan harbours against America 日本がアメリカに対して懐く苦情の種を除く. ¶I must settle grievance immediately with ... 私は...との話合いで苦情を直ちに解決せねばならない. ¶give vent to one's smothered grievance うっ憤を晴らす. ¶state their grievances to the Mayor 彼らの苦情を市長に陳述する. ¶uncover and adjust grievances 苦情を探ってその対策を講じる.
Q real or fancied grievance 理由のあるまたは理由のない不平. ¶social grievance 社会の弊害.
Q² settle wage grievances 賃金に関する苦情を解決する. ¶handle worker grievances 労働者の苦情を処理する.
P² Japan's grievances against America 米国に対する日本の苦情.

grieve, *v.* 悲しませる, 悲しむ.
M feel deeply grieved 深く心痛する.
P grieve about the death of one's son 息子の死を悲しむ. ¶I am deeply grieved at your bereavement. 貴下の御不幸は心痛にたえません. 【類】I am grieved at my sister's death. / grieve at the loss of a friend. ¶I grieve for you very much. 大いに君のために悲しむ. 【類】He grieves for his wayward son. / He grieved for what he had committed. / grieve for one's sins. ¶He was grieved on hearing of his friend's death. 彼は友の死を聞いて悲しんだ. ¶grieve on the death of his father 彼の父の死を悲しむ. ¶My soul is grieved to death. 私の心は死ぬほど悲しい. ¶grieve with him in his failures and sorrows 彼の失敗や悲しみに同情する.
O I am grieved to hear such bad news. こんないやなことを聞いて悲しく思っている.

grill, *v.* きびしく尋問する.
P be grilled by newsmen on one's views toward communism 共産主義に対する意見で新聞記者連に油をしぼられる.

grimace, *n.* しかめつら.
V make grimaces at ... ...に向ってしかめ面する ‖ make funny grimaces こっけいな顔付をする.
Q a wry or derisive grimace ゆがんだ, あるいはばかにしたようなしかめ面.
P with a grimace 顔をしかめて.

grimace, *v.* しかめ面する.
P grimace at a person 人に対してしかめ面をする.

grin, *n.* 歯をむき出すこと.
Q with a broad grin にたにた歯をむき出して. ¶a flickering grin かすかな笑い. ¶with a silly grin あほらしくにたにた歯をむき出して.

grin, *v.* 歯をむき出して笑う.
M He grinned broadly at me. 彼は私ににやにや笑いかけた. ¶grin foolishly ばかみたいににやにや笑う. ¶I grinned inside. 私ははらで笑った. ¶grinning sheepishly きまり悪そうに苦笑しながら.
P grin at a person 他人に対して歯をむき出して笑う ‖ he grinned approval at ... ...に対し承知の意でにやりとした. ¶He grinned with delight. 彼はうれしいのでにたにた笑った.

grind, *n.* くそ勉強.
Q nerve-racking grind はげしい勉強.

grind, *v.* とぐ；みがく；ひく，砕く；苦しめる，しいたげる；つく，細かく搗(つ)ける；せっせと勉強する；演奏する．

M *grind **away*** 猛勉強する．¶It will not *grind **fine***. それは細かにつけない．¶when ***finely*** *ground* 細かに搗けたら．¶*grind **out*** a tune on a pipe-organ パイプオルガンで一曲ひく．¶Corn *grinds **well***. 穀物はよくつける．

M^2 The price was *ground **down***. 代金を値切られてまけた．‖people who are *ground **down*** by poverty 貧苦に悩む人人．

P *grind **at*** history and geography 歴史と地理をこつこつ勉強する．¶flour *ground **from*** barley 大麦をついた粉．¶A mill is a place where wheat is *ground **into*** flour. 製粉工場は小麦が製粉される場所だ．‖ *grind* a lesson ***into*** one's head ［教師が］レッスンをその頭にたたき込む．¶*grind* money ***out of*** the people 人民から金を搾取する．¶*grind* it ***to*** fine powder それをこまかい粉につく．【類】*grind* grain ***to*** flour ‖ Steel *grinds **to*** a sharp edge. 鋼鉄は切れるようにとげる．¶*grind* it ***under*** one's heel それを足下にふみにじる．¶*grind* glass ***with*** sand and water 砂と水でガラスをみがく．

grinder, *n.* ひく(とぐ)器具．

Q^2 a ***knife*** *grinder* ナイフとぎ器(と石)．¶a ***meat*** *grinder* 肉ひき器．

grinding, *n.* 摩擦．

P^2 the *grinding **of*** the teeth 歯ぎしり．

grindstone, *n.* ひきうす．

Q ***mounted*** (***unmounted***) *grindstone* 台のある(ない)ひきうす．

grip, *n.* 把握(はく)；会得．

V ***get*** a vice-like *grip* on ... …を万力のように握る．¶The speaker ***has*** a good *grip* of his subject. あの弁士は取扱う問題を十分のみ込んでいる．‖ ***have*** a *grip* of ... …を了解している ‖ ***have*** a *grip* on an audience 聴衆の心理をつかむ．¶***lose*** one's *grip* on ... …を手放す．【類】Suddenly, in the crowd, mother ***lost*** her *grip* on my hand. ¶***regain*** its *grip* on ... 再び…をつかむ．¶***take*** a firm *grip* of ... …をしっかり握る．¶the police ***tightened*** its *grip* upon ... 警察が…の取締りを一層厳重にした．

Q their ***deep*** and ***widespread*** *grip **of*** cinematograph upon the public 映画が公衆に及ぼす深くかつ広い影響．¶a ***friendly*** *grip* 親しい握手．¶He has a ***feeble*** *grip* of my idea. 彼には私の考えがよくわかっていない．¶have a ***good*** *grip* on an audience 大衆[の心]をうまくつかむ．¶The habit has an ***unusual*** *grip* upon some people. この癖はある人には異常に強い．

Q^2 lose one's ***iron*** *grip* on ... しっかり握っていた手を…から引離される．

P I saw two figures ***at*** *grips*. 二人の者がつかみ合っているのを見た．¶This country is now ***in*** the *grip* of an epidemic of influenza. この地方には今流行性感冒がはやっている．‖He is ***in*** the *grip* of poverty. 彼は貧苦に悩んでいる．¶shake hands ***with*** a hearty *grip* 熱心に握手する．¶those who come ***within*** the *grip* of the law 法網にかかった人々．

P^2 a building in the *grip **of*** fire 現に燃えている建物．¶the secret of his *grip **on*** the public 彼が公衆の心をつかむ秘決．¶come to *grips* (blows) ***with*** ... …とつかみ(なぐり)合いになる．

grip, *v.* しっかりつかむ．

M The brake doesn't *grip **properly***. ブレーキがうまくかからない．

grist, *n.* 粉にひく穀物；《俗》量．

V It will ***bring*** *grist* to the mill. それはもうけ仕事になる．¶The oppositionist in politics desires to ***take*** all *grist* that comes to his mill. 在野党員は何でも我田引水的に利用しようとする．

Q a ***mighty*** *grist* of rain 多量の雨．

P It would be so much *grist **to*** the mill of his enemies. それは敵にとってそれだけの利益となるだろう．

groan, *n.* うめき，うなり．

V ***give*** a loud *groan* 高いうめき声を出す．¶***heave*** a *groan* 一声うめく．

Q ***blood-curdling*** *groans* ぞっとして血が凍るようなうめき声．

P a speech interrupted ***by*** *groans* of disapproval「反対」の声でやじり倒された演説．¶He fell ***with*** a *groan*. 彼はうーんと言って倒れた．

groan, *v.* うめく，うなる，苦しむ．

M He *groaned **out*** a reply. 彼はうなって(苦しげに)答えた．‖He *groaned **out*** a sad story about himself. 彼はうめくような声で悲痛な身の上話をした．

M^2 The speaker was *groaned **down*** by the audience. 講演者はやじり倒されてしまった．

P *groan **under*** the burden of toil 苦しい重荷の下にうめく ‖ *groan **under*** a heavy load of taxation 重税の下に苦しむ．¶Every page *groans **under*** good things. どのページも有益なことが満載されている．【類】Russians *groan **under*** oppression. ¶*groan **with*** pain (toothache) 痛い(など)のでうなる．

groat, *n.* 少額，少量．

Q It is not ***worth*** a *groat*. それは一文の値打ちもない．

grocery, *n.* 《米》食料品店；《英》小間物；*pl.*《米》食料品(かん詰類など)．「《英》小間物雑貨．

Q^2 at a ***corner*** *grocery* かどの食料品店で．¶***fancy*** *grocery*

P^2 *groceries **in*** (***out of***) stock ストックのある(ない)食料品．

groove, *n.* みぞ．

Q the ***delicate*** *groove* in the Japanese eyelid 日本人の二重まぶた．¶go on in the ***old*** *grooves* 旧慣を墨守する．¶go out of the ***ordinary*** *groove* 常軌を逸する．¶keep in the ***same*** *groove* 同一てつを踏む．¶the ***social*** *groove* 社会の常軌．

grope, *v.* 盲探しする，も索する．

M *grope **blindly*** in the dark 暗中も索する．

M^2 *grope **about*** for ... …を手探りする．【類】*grope **about*** in the dark for ... / I *groped **about*** a good while to no purpose.

P *grope **after*** light 光明を探し求める．¶I *groped **for*** the door in the utter darkness. 真暗の中で入口を手探りした．‖ *grope **for*** a clue to the mystery その秘密を解くかぎをさがし求める．¶*grope* one's way ***through*** darkness くらやみの中を手さぐりで行く．¶*grope **with*** one's hands 手探りする．

groping, *n.* 手探り．

P^2 a random *groping **after*** ... …のもさく．

gross, *n.* 大体，総体；グロス(十二ダース)．

P It is unfair to condemn ***in*** the *gross*. 十ぱ一からげに非難するのは不当だ．‖The goods are valued ***in*** [the] *gross* at 20,000 yen. 商品は総体で二万円と評価される．

P ten *gross **of*** pens (buttons) ペン(など)を十グロス．

gross, *a.* 卑わいな．

P too *gross **for*** publication 余りに卑わいで公刊できない．

grouch, *n.* ふきげん．

V He ***has*** a *grouch* on. 彼はへそを曲げている．

ground, *n.* (**1**) 土地，地面，地所；地歩；*pl.* 敷地，構内．

V ***break*** *ground* for the Panama-Pacific Exposition パナマ太平洋博覧会会場の起工をする ‖ The book ***breaks*** new *ground*. その著作は新方面の開拓だ．【類】***break*** entirely new *ground* / The article ***breaks*** fresh *ground*. ¶***clear*** the *ground* 土地を切り開く．¶The *ground* is ***consecrated*** (= ***hallowed***) by the presence of a shrine. この土地は神殿があるので神聖なものとなっている．¶The *ground* is ***covered*** with deep snow. 地面には雪が深い．‖The research ***covers*** much *ground*. その研究は広い範囲にわたっている．‖The *ground* was ***covered*** in the last lecture. その点は前回の講義で述べた．¶***disinfect*** the *ground* with lime 石灰で地面を消毒する．¶He ***extended*** the *grounds* considerably beyond their original limits. 彼はもとの境界よりも余ほどその所有地を広げた．¶The movement rapidly ***gained*** *ground*. その運動は著々進捗した．【類】The doctrine (教義) ***gained*** much *ground*. / It is ***gaining*** *ground* steadily. / Rightly or wrongly the impression has ***gained*** *ground* abroad that Japan believes in military power as a means of national advancement. / the belief is ***gaining*** *ground* that the Government intends to ... / the conviction (確信) is ***gaining*** *ground* that ... / the opinion is fast ***gaining*** *ground* that ... / Such is the revolutionary view (革命思想) which has been ***gaining*** *ground* of late. ‖ ***gain*** *ground* on ... 段々と…に近づく．¶The troops ***gave*** *ground*. 軍隊は退却した．¶I ***had*** my *ground* mostly ***planted*** in fruit trees. 私は自分の地面には大抵果樹を植えた．¶***hold*** one's *ground* against ... …に相峙する ‖ It stoutly ***held*** its *ground*. それは断固として対抗した．¶***keep*** one's *ground* 自分の位置を保つ．¶***kiss*** the *ground* 平伏する．¶***lay out*** the *grounds* 地取りをする．¶The *grounds* are beautifully ***laid out*** after the native method. 庭園は土地風にならって美しく造ってある．【類】Prince Mitsukuni, generally known as Mito-Komon, ***laid out*** the *grounds* as a place in which to enjoy a calm old age after a life of labor (余生を楽しむための土地)．¶***leave*** the *ground* 離陸する．¶***level*** (= ***smooth***) the *ground* 地ならしする．¶***level*** buildings ***to*** the *ground* 建物を取りくずす．¶gradually ***lose*** *ground* 次第に地歩を失う(不利になる) ‖ ***lose*** *ground* before the growing influence of ... …の勢力増大に伴い次第に弱体となる ‖

This view has never entirely *lost* the *ground* and still counts adherents in this country. この見解は決して全く捨てられはせずこの国にはいまだにこれを固守している者がある. ¶*make up* the lost *ground* in a race 競争で後れを取り返す. ¶The horse *paws* the *ground*. 馬はひずめで地をかく(あがく). ¶*plot* the *ground* 地割りをする. ¶*plow* the *ground* for a later harvest 後作のために土地を耕す. ¶*prepare* the *ground* long and well 地盤を造る ‖ *prepare* the *ground* (=pave the way) for ... ...の準備をする. ¶If he emphasizes his modern languages a little more, he may *recover* enough *ground* to obtain a diploma. 彼はも少し近代語に力を入れれば卒業証書がもらえるほどに取返しがつくだろう. ¶*regain* (=recover) lost *grounds* 失地を取戻す. ¶*retrace* the *ground* あと戻りする. ¶*strike ground* 座礁する ‖ *strike* the *ground* with the forehead 土下座をする. ¶The ship *took* the *ground*. 船が浅瀬に乗上げた. ‖ *taking* the very lowest *ground* ごく低い見地から言っても. ¶*till* the *ground* 土地を耕す. ¶*touch ground* [足など]水底にとどく. ¶*traverse* a familiar *ground* 慣れた土地を歩き回る.

v² Historic *ground* *abounds*. 史跡が多い.

Q discussion on the *actual ground* 現地講話. ¶a pair of vases, with chrysanthemums and butterflies in color on *back ground* 背景に彩色した菊花やちょうの描いてある一対の花びん. ¶sit on the *bare ground* 地面にじかにすわる. ¶a *botanizing ground* 植物採集地. ¶a *breeding ground* for dangerous bacteria 危険な細菌の発生地. 【類】a *breeding ground* of dangerous thoughts. ¶the *ground* made *classic* by ... ...で名所となった土地. ¶a *colonizing ground* 植民地. ¶Employers and laborers will reach a *common ground* of agreement. 雇主と雇人とが妥協点を見出すだろう. ¶the dead lying in *consecrated ground* 聖地に埋葬された死者. ¶take *conservative ground* 保守的立場をとる. ¶*damp ground* 湿地. ¶a *dumping ground* for human refuse 廃人の捨て場所. ¶The building was located on *elevated ground* in the country. その建物はいなかの高台にあった. ¶compete with ... on *equal ground* ... と対等の立場で競争する. ¶an *exercise ground* 運動場. ¶a *fertile ground* (=hotbed) for crime 犯罪の温床. ¶a *filled-in ground* 埋立地. ¶This house stands on *firm ground* この家は堅い地盤に立っている. ¶The house is on *high ground*. その家は高台にある. ¶Kamakura is *historic ground*, and each shrine has its legends. 鎌倉は歴史的な土地でどの神社仏閣にもそれぞれ伝説がある. ‖ it stands on *historic ground*, the site of ... それは...の所在地だった史跡の地にある. ¶a *holy ground* 聖域. ¶a *made* (=*reclaimed*) *ground* 埋立地. ¶in *marshy ground* 湿地に. ¶in the *middle ground* at the left is ... 左の中景にあるのが...(写真の説明). ¶a *neutral ground* 中立地帯. ¶*plowed ground* 耕作された土地. ¶a *private ground* 私有地. ¶a *raised ground* 盛上げた土地; [地震などで]突起した土地. ¶It is pleasantly situated on *rising ground* in the midst of a grove of trees. それは森の中の高台の上に気持よく位置を占めている. ¶a *sacred ground* 聖地. ¶*sloppy ground* ぬかるみになった土地. ¶the *solid ground* 固い地面. ¶take *strong grounds* against ... に反対する. ¶*terraced ground* 台地. ¶with a vine in black on *red ground* 赤地に黒でぶどう模様のある. ¶*uneven* (=*rugged*) *ground* でこぼこの土地. ¶a red cross on *white ground* 白地に赤の十字.

Q² an *anchorage ground* 停泊地. ¶a *ball ground* 野球場. ¶a *breeding ground* for ... ...[野生動物など]にとっての発育地. ¶a *burial ground* for ... の埋葬地. ¶*coffee grounds* コーヒー園 ¶on *college grounds* (=campus) 大学の構内で. ¶on the *cricket ground* クリケット[球戯]場で. ¶such a soil is a suitable *culture ground* for the development of ... そのような環境は...の発展によい下地となる. ¶an *execution ground* 処刑場. ¶a *fishing ground* 漁場. ¶*flying* (=*aviation*) *grounds* 飛行場. ¶a *football ground* しゅう球場. ¶a *holiday ground* for the weekenders 週末旅行者の遊覧地. ¶a *home ground* 〖野球〗ホームグランド. ¶a *hunting ground* 狩猟場. ¶On the *grazing grounds* are many cattle. 牧場に牛が沢山いる. ¶Japan is the happy *hunting ground* for European collectors of art treasures and curios. 日本はヨーロッパの美術骨とう品収集家にとって好個のあさり場である. 【類】Kanda is the book-lovers' happy *hunting ground*. ¶a *parade ground* 練兵場. ¶a *parking ground* for automobiles and autocycles 自動車オートバイの駐車場. ¶a *pleasure ground* 遊園地. ¶a *proving ground* 〖軍〗[兵器の]実験場. ¶a splendid *recreation ground* すばらしい遊園地(保養地). 【類】A cricket match was played on the *Recreation Ground* yesterday. ¶a *riding ground* 馬場. ¶in a *school ground*. 学校ので運動場. ¶a *spawning ground* [さけなどの]産卵地. ¶a *sports* (=*sporting*) *ground* 競技場. ¶a good *starting ground* for the climber 登山家の便利な出発点. ¶a *testing ground* for ordnance 大砲試射地 ‖ a *testing ground* 試運転場. ¶Australia is a *touring ground*. オーストラリアは観光の土地である. ¶the *training ground* of our statesmen わが国の政治家養成所. 【類】The school is to be a *training ground* for those going to the East and a centre of intelligence in regard to Eastern matters for those at home.

P hell *above ground* この世ながらの地獄 ‖ Its roots are protruding *above ground*. その根が地面に露出している. ¶He was dragged *along* the *ground*. 彼は地上を引きずられた. ¶*below ground* 地下に. ¶*from* the *ground* up 根本から, 徹底的に. 【類】begin one's career anew *from* the *ground* up. / His record has to be built *from* the *ground* up. ‖ *from* the *ground* to the apex of the roof 地面から屋根の頂上まで. ¶The seed had sprouted *from under* the *ground*. その種は地下から芽を出したのであった. ¶*in* the *grounds* of the university 大学の構内に ‖ deposit a treasure *in* the *ground* 宝を地中に埋蔵する ‖ Rabbits burrow *in* the *ground*. うさぎは地に穴を掘る. ‖ cracks *in* the *ground* 地割れ. ¶The trees struck root *into* the *ground*. 木は根を張った. ‖ It is stuck *into* the *ground*. それは地中に差込んである. ¶a piece (=patch) *of ground* 一片の土地. ¶*on* the *ground* of ... ...のグラウンドで; ...の理由で ‖ *on* a *ground* of dark blue こん地に ‖ walk *on* the *ground* 地上を歩く ‖ The building is *on* the *grounds* of the College. その建物は同大学の構内にある. ‖ embroidery done *on* rich *ground* りっぱな地に施した刺しゅう. ¶dig it *out of* the *ground* それを地下から掘出す. ¶fall *to* the *ground* like a house of cards トランプ札を組んで造ったおもちゃの家のように倒壊する ‖ That suits me down *to* the *ground*. それは僕にはもってこいだ. ‖ fall flat *to* the *ground* ばったり地上に倒れる ‖ The house was burnt *to* the *ground*. 家屋は丸焼けになった. ‖ consign it *to* the *ground* それを埋める. ¶lay it *under ground* それを地下に埋める ‖ a cell *under ground* 地下の物置. ¶relieve traffic congestion by rapid transit *underneath* the *ground* 地下の迅速な輸送で交通の雑踏を緩和する. ¶it is now contained *within* the *grounds* of Mr. ... それは今...氏邸の一部になっている.

P² the *ground* *for* the building was broken by ... その建物の始工式が...によってあげられた.

(2) [しばしば *pl.*] 根拠, 理由.

V He dared to *abandon* scientific *ground* 彼は科学的根拠を放棄することをあえてした. ¶It *affords* no *ground* for complaint. それには不平を言う理由がない. ¶*find* in it some *ground* for hope that ... それが...という望みを掛ける幾分の理由になると思う. 【類】We *find* no *grounds* for contests (闘争). ¶The abusive language *formed* the *ground* of the quarrel. 悪口がそのけんかの起りであった. ¶It will *give grounds* for opposition. それが反対の理由になるだろう. 【類】It *gave ground* for suspicion. ¶he *has* no *ground* to complain of ... 彼には...の不平を言うべき理由がない. ¶steadily *maintain* the *ground* that ... ... という説を保持する. ¶The future, which is unpredictable, *offers* some *ground* for hope. 未来は予言はできないが希望を抱きうる幾分の理由がある. ¶I *see* no sufficient *ground* for ... ...の理由が私には十分分からない. ¶repeatedly *shift* one's *ground* 始終言を左右にする. ¶It *supplies* reasonable *ground* for doubt. それには疑うべき当然の理由がある.

Q I have *ample grounds* for maintaining that ... ...と主張する十分の論拠が私にある. 【類】There are *ample grounds* for anxiety. ¶the accusation has no *better ground* than ... その非難は...以上十分の根拠はない. ¶on *broad ground* 大体. ¶on *compassionate grounds* 同情心をもって. ¶Nowadays wars of nations are only fought on *economic grounds*. 今日では国家間の戦争は経済的理由がその唯一の原因である. ¶judge literary work upon *ethical* rather than upon *aesthetic grounds* 審美的論拠よりはむしろ道徳的論拠に基いて文芸品作を批評する. ¶we have fairly *good grounds* to believe that ... われわれには…と信じる相当の理由がある. ¶on *hygienic grounds* 衛生上の理由で. ¶on *insufficient grounds* 不十分な理由で. ¶on *justifiable grounds* 正当な理由で. ¶a *legal ground* 法的根拠. ¶on the *nebulous ground* that ... …というばく然とした根拠で. ¶The committee's report covered a great deal of *new ground.* 委員会の報告には大分新しい見解が盛込まれている. ¶a clause discriminatory to Japanese on *racial grounds* 人種的理由で日本人を差別した条項. ¶there is no *rational ground* for ... …に対する何ら合理的な理由はない. ¶supply *reasonable ground* for doubt 疑うべき相当な理由を与える. 【類】No *reasonable ground* could be brought towards it. / There is a *reasonable ground* for the expectation of an improvement in business. ¶cover much the *same ground* as ... …と大体同じことをいう. ¶Such a proposition would, of course, be fiercely resisted on *sentimental grounds.* 左様な提議はもちろん感情的理由で猛烈に反対されるだろう. ¶there is not the *slightest ground* for feelings of enmity between ... …間には反感を懐く少しの理由もない. ¶we are on *sounder ground* when coming to the question of ... …の問題となると大分話に確実性がある. ¶there are *strong grounds* for believing that ... …と信じる十分な理由がある. ¶go on *sure grounds* 確固とした論拠に基いて進行する ‖ I feel I am on *sure ground* in saying that ... 私の…という言説に対して私には確かな理由があると思う. ¶on *what grounds* do you think it would be better to ...? どういう理由で君は…する方がよいと思うか. 【類】On *what ground* did you pick him up for the place?

Q^2 find a *meeting ground* for the two main statements 二つの声明の妥協点を見出す. ¶on "*security grounds*" 「保安」という理由で.

P *On* these *grounds* he ought to be congratulated on the success of his experiment. これらの理由で彼の実験の成功を慶賀すべきである. ‖ *on grounds* of family expediency 家庭の都合上 ‖ He resigned *on* the *ground* of illness. 彼は病気という理由で辞職した. ‖ He bases his objection *on* five *grounds.* 彼はその反対の理由を五カ条示している. 【類】object (reject) *on* the *ground* that ... / recommend (claim, attack) it on the *ground* that ... ¶object to it *upon* humanitarian *grounds* 人道上の理由でそれに反対する.

P^2 there is *ground for* fear that ... …と心配する理由がある. 【類】just *ground for* complaint / No *grounds for* suspicion were found against any persons. ¶*grounds of* a claim 請求の原因 ‖ the *ground of* their refusal seems to have been based on ... 彼らが拒絶した理由は…に基いていたようである.

ground, *v.* 基かせる; 素質を与える; 座礁する.

M He is *well* (=*thoroughly*) *grounded* in science (French). 彼は科学(など)のりっぱな素養がある. ‖ The theory is *well* (*ill*) *grounded.* その説はたしかな論拠がある(ない). 【類】He is well *grounded in* the English language.

P *ground* a child *in* learning 子供に学問の基礎を造らせる. 【類】*ground* him *in* mathematics (chemistry) ‖ be *grounded in* a dangerous position 危険な位置で座礁している. ¶It is *grounded on* this fact. それはこの事実に基いている. ‖ The ship *grounded on* the mud, and no damage is expected. その船は泥地に乗り上げたので何ら損害ない見込み. 【類】The ship *grounded on* the rock, but got off (離礁した) again with little damage. ‖ Self-discipline is *grounded on* self-knowledge. 自己修養の土台は自分を知ることである. ‖ *ground* one's opinion *on* (=*upon*) facts その説の基礎を事実に置く.

grounding, *n.* 基礎, 根底; 手ほどき.

V They *have* a *grounding* in these sciences. 彼らにはこれらの科学の根底がある.

Q a *firm grounding* in theory 理論上の確固とした根拠. ¶The *previous grounding* in ... stood him in good stead. 前もって彼に…の素養があったのが役に立った.

ground-rent, *n.* 地代, 借地料.

P lease a piece of land *at* a *ground-rent* of £30 三十ポンドの地代で借地する.

groundwork, *n.* 地ならし.

P^2 This work is but a *groundwork for* its successor. この仕事はその後継者に対する地ならしに過ぎない.

group, *n.* 群, 集団, 組.

V rise to *address* a *group* 立ち上って会集に呼びかける. *form* a separate *group* 別種を成す. ¶We *joined* the *group.* われわれはその群と一緒になった.

V^2 The *group broke up.* 集団が解散した.

Q the *conservative* (*progressive*) *group* in a party 一党の内の保守(進歩)派. ¶a *cooperative group* 協同団体. ¶a *factitious group* よく事件を起すグループ. ¶an *incongruous* and *ill-assorted group* 不調和で不つり合な一群. ¶an *insular group* 群島. ¶the *Japanese group* (=team) of commercial mission 日本側の商業使節団. ¶a *religious group* 宗教団体. ¶This is a *small* but *troublesome group.* これは小さいがやっかいな一団だ.

Q^2 the *age group* between 40 and 50 四十から五十までの年齢層. ¶*correlation groups* 相関団体. ¶conduct a *discussion group* on a subject ある問題について討論会をやる 【類】a wireless (=radio) *discussion group* ‖ a seminar and a *discussion group* ゼミと討論グループ. ¶the head of the *Soviet embassy group* ソ連大使館員の主席. ¶the *extremist groups* of both Right and Left 左右両派の極左極右のグループ. ¶a *fireside group* 炉辺の集り. ¶a happy *family group* 楽しい家庭の集り ‖ *family groups,* headed by pater or mater, or both 父か母または両親の下にある家庭の集り. ¶a *gangster group* ギャング(集団強盗). ¶a *higher* (*lower*)*-income group* 高(低)額所得者層. ¶a *hobby group* 同趣味仲間. ¶set up an *inquiry group* 調査団を組織する. ¶a *labor* and *farmer group* 労農グループ. ¶an intellectual *leadership group* 知的指導者の団体. ¶a *left-wing group* 左翼派. ¶Cases have been in which the judgment of the *minority group* was much sounder. これまで少数派意見が正しい例もいくつかあった. ¶an *occupation group* 職業グループ. ¶a *press group* 新聞記者団. ¶the cupidity of *pressure groups* in politics 政界圧力団体の欲望. ¶in *relay groups* グループ交替制で. ¶the next *repatriation group* 次回の復員組. ¶those in the *small income group* 小額収入者. ¶a *study group* 研究班. ¶Iwo Jima is in the *Volcano Island group.* 硫黄島は火山群島の中にある. ¶a *white-collar group* 勤人階級. ¶a *world group* 世界諸国の集り.

P *in groups* [三々五々]群がって ‖ go out *in* small *groups* 小グループに分れて出かける ‖ classify them *in groups* それを分類する. ¶They fall *into* two main *groups.* それらは二大別される. ¶It comes *under* this *group.* それはこの部に属する.

P^2 a *group of* islands (children) 群島(子供の群).

group, *v.* 寄せ集める, 組合わせる; 群がる.

M They *naturally group* themselves in two main classes. それは当然二大別される. ¶*group together* this and that それとこれとを組合わせる.

P People *group about* him. 人が彼の周囲に群がる. ¶Many villages are *grouped along* the shore. その沿岸に多くの村落が集まっている. ¶The children *grouped around* the player. 子供たちは選手の回りに集った. 【類】the problems that are *grouped around* ... ¶They may be *grouped in* eleven departments as follows: それは次の十一部門に分たれる. ¶Earthquakes are *grouped,* according to their origin, *into* three classes. 地震はその原因によってこれを三種に分類する. ¶They can be *grouped under* four main topics. これを四大区分にすることができる. 【類】The languages of Africa may be *grouped* in the main *under* four heads: Bantu, Sudanic, Hamitic, and Semitic. ¶For centuries the Hungarian language was *grouped with* the European family of languages. 数百年の間ハンガリー語はヨーロッパ語の部に分類されていた.

group-leader, *n.* 司会者.

P^2 the *group-leader for* a broadcast discussion 放送討論会の司会者.

grove, *n.* 小林, 小森.

Q a *dense grove* of ... …の密生した小林.

P^2 a *grove of* evergreens (lofty cryptomeria) 常緑樹(高い杉)の木立.

grovel, *v.* 手をついてはう.

P *grovel at* their feet 彼らの足下にひれ伏す. ¶They *groveled before* their cruel lord. 彼らは残酷な主君の前にひれ伏した. ¶*grovel under* taxes 課税に苦しむ.

grow, *v.* 生じる, はえる; 生長する, 発達する, ふえる; なる; 栽培する, 作る.

M *grow* ***abundantly*** 盛んに繁茂する. ¶*grow* ***accustomed*** to … …に慣れて来る. ¶*grow* ***aged*** before one's time 早老する. ¶*grow* ***angry*** 腹を立てる. ¶The new towns are *growing* ***apace***. 新しい都市はぐんぐん発達している. 【類】The number of … is *growing* ***apace***. ¶*grow* ***better*** 段々よくなる. ¶*grow* ***chicken-hearted*** at … …におじける. ¶*grow* ***greatly*** in public favor 大分評判が良くなる. ¶His heart does not *grow* ***grey*** with years. 彼は年を取っても気が若い. ¶It is *growing* ***dark***. 段々暗くなって来る. ¶*grow* ***easy*** 楽になる. ¶He *grew* ***eloquent*** over the theme, his favorite. 彼は題目がお得意のものであったので気焔をあげた. ¶*grow* ***excited*** 興奮する. ¶*grow* ***faint*** 気が遠くなる. ¶gradually *grow* ***familiar*** with … …に段々慣れて来る. ¶*grow* ***fashionable*** 流行する. ¶*grow* ***fat*** (***thin***) 肥え(やせ)る. ¶He has *grown* [by] ***five inches***. 彼は五インチのびた. ¶The meadows *grow* ***green***. 牧場が青くなる. ¶It will *grow* ***hot*** as soon as the sun begins to shine. 太陽が照り始めると暑くなりましょう. 【類】It *grows* ***hot*** or ***cold*** according as the sun shines or gets behind the clouds. ¶*grow* ***indigenously*** 自然にはえる. ¶He has *grown* quite ***industrious*** lately. 彼は近ごろ全く勤勉になった. ¶*grow* ***intoxicated*** 酔がまわって来る. ¶*grow* ***late*** おそくなる. ¶It is *growing* ***less*** and ***less***. 段々減って来る. ¶hair *growing* ***luxuriantly*** ふさふさとはえた髪の毛. ¶*grow* ***old*** gracefully 品のよい老人になる. ¶*grow* deadly ***pale*** 真青になる. ¶*grow* ***peevish*** at … …をぐずぐず言う. ¶Leaves *grow* out from nodes. 葉は節から出る. ¶Weeds *grow* ***rankly***. 雑草が繁茂する. ¶The plant *grows* ***rapidly*** to its full size. その植物はたちまち成長しきる. 【類】Socialism had *grown* very ***rapidly*** in Japan within the past few years. ¶*grow* ***rich*** by one's own industry 自分の努力で金持ちになる ‖ *grow* rich in color 色が濃くなる. ¶*grow* ***ripe*** 熟する. ¶forest giants *growing* ***skywards*** 空の方へのびて行く森の大木. ¶*grow* ***sour*** すっぱくなる. ¶*grow* ***strong*** in health 健康になる. ¶*grow* ***tame*** 慣れて来る. ¶*grow* ***timid*** おく病になる. ¶*grow* ***tipsy*** 酔がまわる. ¶*grow* ***tired*** of … …にあきて来る. ¶The flowers *grow* ***together*** on the top of the stem. その花は茎の頂きにかたまって咲く. ¶Large cities *grow* ***underground***. 大都市は地下に発展する. ¶*grow* ***uneasy*** 心配になる. ¶*grow* ***upwards*** 上方へのびる. ¶plants *growing* ***vigorously*** 盛んにのびる草木. ¶His lips *grew* ***white***. 彼のくちびるは色が失せた. ¶The situation (question) *grew* ***worse***. 形勢(など)が段々悪化した. 【類】*grow* ***worse*** and ***worse***.

M² *grow* ***down*** 減少する. ¶the tree apples *grow* ***on*** りんごがなる木. ¶a wall *grown* ***over*** (=overgrown) with ivy つたの一面にはえた壁. ¶children *growing* ***up*** to manhood 大人に成長しつつある子供たち. ‖ *grow* ***up*** to be an idle, good-for-nothing fellow 大きくなってのらくら者になる ‖ *grow* ***up*** and learn to disbelieve it 成長してそれを信じないようになる ‖ A hostile feeling *grew* ***up*** in the community. 敵意がその社会で強まった. 【類】*grow* ***up*** into a man of strong character / She *grew* ***up*** to be a handsome woman. / America where he *grew* ***up***. / He *grew* ***up*** on a farm (農家の育ち). / He has *grown* ***up*** to be a fine young man.

P cherry-trees *growing* ***along*** the riverbank 河岸に沿うてはえている桜の木. ¶There used to be a large weeping willow *growing* ***beside*** your house. 君の家の側にもと大きなしだれ柳の木があったっけ. ¶The soy bean is *grown* ***for*** forage in the southern United States. 合衆国の南部では大豆を飼料として栽培する. ‖ It is *grown* ***for*** market. それは売るために栽培する. ¶A lily *grows* ***from*** a bulb. ゆりはゆり根からはえる. ‖ Much Manchurian tobacco is *grown* ***from*** American seed. 満州のタバコは多く米国種子で栽培する. 【類】Plants and flowers *grow* ***from*** seeds. / a leaf *growing* ***from*** the stem. ¶*grow* ***from*** adolescence ***to*** manhood 青年期から成人期に生長する. 【類】*grow* ***from*** aprons ***to*** full beards (幼年から成年まで) / *grow* ***from*** boyhood ***to*** manhood. ¶Potatoes *grow* ***in*** the ground. じゃが芋は土の中で育つ. 【類】Rice *grows* ***in*** very wet ground. / Cattails (がま) *grow* ***in*** a wet place. / Fruits *grow* ***in*** orchards. ‖ The situation *grows* ***in*** gravity. 時局が重大化する. ‖ It is manifestly *growing* ***in*** favor. それはたしかに人気が増している. 【類】As the system has continued to work successfully, it has *grown* steadily ***in*** favor. / *grow* ***in*** number[s] (数が)ふえる. / *grow* ***in*** abundance / The city has *grown* ***in*** size and importance. / It has *grown* ***in*** popularity. / *grow* ***in*** strength (stature, wisdom, knowledge, usefullness) ‖ *grow* ***in*** bunches (tufts, clumps) 房(など)になってはえる. 【類】*grow* ***in*** water (moist land, wet soil, a meadow) / *grow* wheat ***in*** the field / *grow* … ***in*** our garden (a flower-pot) ‖ The accusation *grew* ***in*** warmth. その非難の声が高くなった. ¶An egg *grows* ***into*** a bird. 卵が鳥になる. 【類】An acorn *grows* ***into*** an oak. ‖ *grow* ***into*** a habit 習慣になる ‖ The minutes *grew* ***into*** hours, but he did not make his appearance. 何十分, 何時間を待ったがそれでも彼は姿を見せなかった. 【類】Weeks *grew* ***into*** months. ‖ A neglected cold may *grow* ***into*** a serious illness. かぜもほおっておくと大病にならないとも限らない. ‖ *grow* ***into*** manhood or womanhood 大人になる. 【類】a girl *growing* ***into*** womanhood / *grow* ***into*** noble and healthy manhood ‖ *grow* ***into*** a tall youth (tree) 長じて背の高い青年(など)になる ‖ *grow* ***into*** fashion (favor) 流行してくる(人気が出る) ‖ Once such a thought has *grown* ***into*** a man's mind it is very difficult to get rid of it. こういう思想が一度心に芽ばえるとこれを捨てることははなはだ困難である. ¶the hair which *grows* ***on*** the face 顔にはえる毛 ‖ *grow* ***on*** a hill (mountain, wall, rock) 丘(など)に生じる ‖ It is *grown* ***on*** the land. それは地上に栽培される. 【類】Wheat may be *grown* to advantage ***on*** heavy clay soil (重い赤土). / a rock ***on*** which are *grown* sea-weeds / Melons (Grapes) *grow* ***on*** vines (つる). / Berries *grow* ***on*** a bush. / Money does not *grow* ***on*** trees. / Moss sometimes *grows* ***on*** trees. / An acorn (どんぐり) *grows* ***on*** an oak tree. ‖ A straw is the stem ***on*** which wheat *grows*. ストローは小麦のなる茎である. ‖ The bad habit *grew* ***on*** (=upon) him. 彼にその悪習慣がついた. ¶*grow* ***out of*** date 時代遅れになる ‖ It has *grown* ***out of*** fashion. それははやらなくなった. ‖ it *grew* ***out of*** the feeling that … それは…という感情から起った ‖ The book has *grown* ***out of*** lectures to students. その本は学生に授けた講義がもとでできた. ‖ All arts *grow* ***out of*** necessity. すべて芸術は必要から生れる. ‖ He has *grown* ***out of*** the bad habit he had when young. (年を取って)若いころの悪い癖から抜けた. ¶*grow* ***to*** man's estate 一人前になる ‖ *grow* ***to*** manhood 大人になる ‖ *grow* ***to*** full vigor 長じて十分元気よくなる ‖ Buds *grow* ***to*** blossoms. つぼみがふくらんで花と開く ‖ *grow* ***to*** maturity 成熟する ‖ the territory *grew* ***to*** an area of … その領土が…の面積に拡大した ‖ the population has *grown* ***to*** … in the year of … …年にその人口は…になった ‖ morality *grown* ***to*** habit 習慣になった徳行 ‖ The wind *grew* ***to*** a tempest. 風は強くなってあらしに変った. 【類】*grow* ***to*** perfection / Pine-trees *grow* ***to*** a great height. / The tree *grows* ***to*** a great size. ¶It *grew* ***toward*** morning. 朝に近くなった. ¶Melons are *grown* ***under*** glass. メロンは温室で仕立てる. ¶The habit *grew* ***upon*** me. 私にその習慣がついた. ‖ the feeling *grew* ***upon*** me that … …の感情が段々強まって来た. 【類】The longing for home had *grown* ***upon*** him until it became insupportable. ¶The sense of duty *grows* ***with*** age. 義務の観念は年齢とともに発達する. ‖ The place is thickly *grown* ***with*** great gloomy pines. そこにはうっそうとした松の大木がこんもりとはえている. ¶These trees *grow* ***without*** cultivation. この木は栽培せずにはえる L(自生する).

grower, *n.* 栽培者.

Q² a ***chrysanthemum*** *grower* 菊作り. ¶a ***fruit*** *grower* 果樹栽培者. ¶a ***peanut*** *grower* 南京豆栽培者. ¶a ***seed*** *grower* 種子採取業者(たね屋). ¶a ***silk*** *grower* 養蚕業者.

P² a *grower* ***of*** birds 小鳥飼育家.

growing, *n.* 栽培; 成長.

Q² ***fruit*** *growing* 果樹栽培. ¶***poultry*** *growing* 養鶏. ¶***strawberry*** *growing* (=culture) いちご栽培. ¶***stock*** *growing* (=raising) 家畜の飼養. ¶***tea*** *growing* 茶栽培. ¶***timber*** *growing* 立木の成長. ¶the *growing* ***of*** silkworms L=sericulture 養蚕.

growl, *n.* うなり声.

V The dog suddenly ***gave*** a low *growl*. その犬は突然低くうなり出した. ¶***utter*** a low *growl* 低いうなり声を発する.

growl, *v.* うなる.

M *growl* ***back*** at … …にどなり返す. ¶*growl* ***out*** one's disapproval それはいかんとどなる. ¶Lions *growl* ***savagely***. ライオンは猛烈にうなる.

P Bulldogs *growl at* intruders. ブルドッグは侵入者に向かってうなる. 【類】The dog *growled at* the cat.

grownup, *n.* 大人. 「大人を頼む.

V No children for me. *Give* me *grownups*. 子供はだめだ.

growth, *n.* 生長, 発達, 発育; 産出物; 結果.

V ***accelerate*** *growth* 発育を早める. ¶***arrest*** *growth* 発達を妨げる. ¶The oyster takes five years to ***attain*** its full *growth*. かきは十分発育するには五年かかる. ¶***check*** *growth* 発達を妨げる. ¶***complete*** its *growth* その発育を完成する. ¶Japan ***compressed*** the *growth* of centuries into a generation. 日本はわずか一世代の間に数百年の進歩を遂げた. ¶***control*** the family *growth* according to the means of support 収入に応じて産児を調節する. ¶***cripple*** the *growth* of ... …の発育を妨げる. ¶***encourage*** the *growth* of ... …の発達を奨励する. ¶***follow*** with great satisfaction its *growth* in influence and power それが勢力と権力を増すのを非常に満足して見守る. ¶***force*** the *growth* of ... …の生長を促す. ¶***foster*** *growth* 発育を助ける. ¶Men ***get*** their *growth* before they are thirty. 人の体は三十前に成熟する. ¶***halt*** the *growth* of cancer cells がん細胞の成長を止める. ¶***hamper*** the *growth* of foreign trade 外国貿易の発達を阻害する. ¶***hasten*** the *growth* of scientific knowledge 科学知識の発達を促進する. ¶The very means taken to ***hinder*** the *growth* of the movement hastened its spread. その運動の発展を阻止しようとして取った手段がかえってその拡大を促進することになった. ¶fail to ***make*** *growth* 発展し損う. ¶***produce*** a *growth* of hair 毛髪の成長を助ける. ¶The trees have ***reached*** their full *growth*. その木は十分に生長した. ¶***retard*** the *growth* of civilization 文明の発達を遅らす. ¶***show*** a steady *growth* 着実な進歩を見せる ‖ Its popularity is ***showing*** almost daily *growth*. その評判がほとんど日一日と高まりつつある. ¶***stunt*** the *growth* of ... …の生長を止める. ¶briefly ***trace*** the *growth* of the movement その運動が発達した跡を簡単に述べる. 【類】***trace*** the *growth* of a belief in immortality (不滅の信仰).

Q words of American growth アメリカで発生した語. ¶***cancerous*** *growths* がん腫(しゅ). ¶oranges of ***California*** *growth* カリフォルニア産のオレンジ. ¶a large tree, apparently of a ***century's*** *growth* 百歳ほどの大木. ¶a ***constant*** *growth* 間断ない発展. ¶plants of ***foreign*** *growth* 外国産の植物. ¶The root has put forth ***fresh*** *growth*. その根から新しい芽がでた. ¶reach its ***full*** *growth* 十分に成長する. ¶for ***further*** *growth* さらに発展するため. ¶a ***gradual*** *growth* 漸進. ¶***intellectual*** *growth* 知能の成長. ¶*Shinto* is of purely ***Japanese*** *growth*. 神道は純然たる日本の産物である. ¶a ***large*** *growth* in manufacturing during the war 戦時中製造業の大発展 ‖ We are but children of ***larger*** *growth*. われわれは大きな子供に過ぎない. ¶a ***malignant*** *growth* in a body 体内の悪質な発生物(がんなど). ¶give children chances of a ***mental*** and ***moral*** *growth* 子供らに精神的及び道徳的発達の機会を与える. ¶The custom is of quite ***modern*** *growth*. この習慣は全く最近のものである. ‖ a town of ***modern*** *growth* 近代的に発達した都市 ‖ a ***modern*** *growth* 現代の産物. ¶***moral*** and ***material*** *growth* 道徳的及び物質的発達. ¶a ***morbid*** *growth* 病的形成物(こぶなど). ¶*Shinto* is of ***native*** *growth*. 神道はこの国はえ抜きのものだ. 【類】It is of purely ***native*** *growth*. ¶the result of ***natural*** *growth* 自然に発生した結果. ¶a science of comparatively ***new*** *growth* 比較的新しく発生した科学. ¶make a ***normal*** *growth* 平常の成長を遂げる. ¶a ***parasitic*** *growth* 寄生的な発生物. ¶a period of ***rapid*** *growth* 生長の盛期 ‖ A tree of extremely ***rapid*** *growth* is generally short-lived. きわめて早く成長する木は一般に寿命が短かい. ¶a ***rapid*** and ***sustained*** *growth* じん速にして永続する発達. ¶a thought of ***recent*** *growth* 近ごろ生れた思想 ‖ The custom is a plant of ***recent*** *growth*. その習慣は近年できたものである. ¶a ***retarded*** *growth* 遅れた成長. ¶Civilization is a plant of ***slow*** *growth*. 文明は[いわば]発育のおそい木だ. ¶***spiritual*** *growth* 精神的発達. ¶show a ***steady*** *growth* 確実な成長振りを示す. 【類】the ***steady*** *growth* of anti-Japanese feelings / The trade is making a ***steady*** and ***healthful*** *growth*. ¶It is of no ***sudden*** *growth*. それは急にできたものではない. ¶It has enjoyed an ***unprecedented*** *growth* during the past year. それは去年中に空前の発達をとげた. ¶a ***vigorus*** *growth* 盛んな発達. ¶a ***wholesome*** *growth* toward the ideal of a gentleman 紳士の理想への健全な発展. ¶the introduction and ***widespread*** *growth* of ... …の導入及びその広範な発展. ¶a ***young*** (***small***) *growth* (=plant) 若い(小がらの)植木.

Q² British imperialism was a ***capitalist*** *growth*. 英帝国主義は資本主義的発達であった. ¶It has had a ***mushroom*** *growth*. それは(きのこのように)急速に成長(発展)した. 【類】The cinematograph industry has been one of ***mushroom*** *growth*. ¶The large civilized cities of the world are practically of ***nineteenth-century*** *growth*. 世界の大文化都市は実際上十九世紀に発達したものだ. ¶sustain strong ***plant*** *growth* 強力な植物の成長を支持する. ¶Bacteria are ***vegetable*** *growths*. バクテリヤは植物的生物である. ¶prevent ***weed*** *growth* 雑草の繁茂を防ぐ. ¶the new ***word*** *growth* of the new land 新しい土地の新語の成長.

P a check ***in*** *growth* 発達の妨害 ‖ trees stunted ***in*** *growth* 生長を妨げられた木. ¶***with*** the *growth* in membership 会員の増加とともに. 【類】***with*** the *growth* of civilization.

P² the *growth* ***in*** luxury つのるぜいたく ‖ *growth* ***in*** membership 会員の増加. 【類】the *growth* ***in*** popularity of ... ¶the *growth* ***of*** publications 出版業の発展. 【類】the successful *growth* ***of*** our foreign commerce.

grub, *v.* 掘る.

M ***grub out*** one's family history その家系を調べる.

M² ***grub up*** earth 土を掘返す ‖ ***grub up*** roots 根を掘りとる.

grubber, *n.* 努力家.

Q² a ***knowledge*** *grubber* こつこつ勉強する人.

grudge, *n.* 恨み, うっ憤.

V I ***bear*** him no *grudge*. 私は彼になんの恨みもない ‖ ***bear*** a *grudge* against ... …に恨みを抱く. 【類】The *grudge* he ***bears*** me is quite unwarrantable (逆恨み). ¶***earn*** one's *grudge* 人の恨みを買う. ¶***harbor*** (=***nurse***) a *grudge* 恨みをいだく. ¶He ***had*** a *grudge* against me. 彼は私を恨んでいた. ¶He ***owes*** me a *grudge*. 彼は僕を恨んでいる. ¶***settle*** the old baseball *grudge* between A nine and B nine A チームと B チーム間の昔の野球のうっ憤を解決する. ¶***work off*** a *grudge* 恨みを晴らす.

Q he had no ***deep-seated*** *grudge* against ... 彼は…に対して深い恨みをいだいていなかった.

gruel, *n.* かゆ.

V ***give*** (***take***) one's *gruel* かゆを飲ませる(飲む); [比ゆ的に] ひどい罰を与える(受ける).

Q² ***corn*** (***rice***) *gruel* とうもろこし(米)のかゆ.

grumble, *v.* 不平を鳴らす, かこつ.

M *grumble* ***out*** a protest ぶつぶつ言う.

P He is always *grumbling* ***about*** something. 彼はいつもなにか不平を鳴らしている. ¶*grumble* ***at*** a person 人に不平を鳴らす ‖ *grumble* ***at*** hot weather 暑さをこぼす ‖ *grumble* ***at*** one's lot 自分の運命をかこつ. ¶*grumble* ***over*** one's food 食事に文句を言う.

guarantee, *n.* 保証; 保証人; 担保品.

V This ***affords*** some *guarantee* that his end will be attained. これで彼の目的が達せられるだろうということが幾分確実になる. ¶refuse to ***give*** *guarantee* 保証を拒む. ¶He ***holds*** the *guarantee*. 彼は担保を保有している. ¶it ***provides*** no sufficient *guarantee* against ... それは…に対して十分の保証にはならない. ¶***require*** a *guarantee* 担保が要る. ¶***stand*** *guarantee* for ... …の保証人になる.

Q The ***best*** *guarantee* of peace is preparedness for war. 平和の最善の保証は軍備にある. ¶give ***effective*** *guarantee* of ... …の有効な保障を与える. ¶***flimsy*** *guarantee* 薄弱な保証. ¶a ***maritime*** *guarantee* 海上警備員. ¶The business is too risky without ***substantial*** *guarantee*. 実質的な担保なしにはその取引はとても危険だ. ¶a ***sure*** *guarantee* of ... …の確実な保証. 【類】A bright sky in the morning is not a ***sure*** *guarantee* of the weather for the rest of the day. ¶a ***written*** *guarantee* 保証書.

P All our goods are sold ***on*** a money-back *guarantee*. 私どもの品物はすべてお気に召さなければ代金払戻の保証付で売っています. ¶sign ***under*** *guarantee* 保証付の署名をする. 【類】Our goods are sold ***under*** *guarantee* of money-back if they fail to satisfy the customer. ¶Goods are sold ***with*** money-back *guarantee*. 商品は返金保証付で売っている. ¶a *guarantee* ***against*** ... …に対する保証. ¶be some *guarantee* ***for*** ... 幾分の…保証になる. 【類】a *guarantee* ***for*** fidelity (忠実) / men whose position ought to be a *guarantee* ***for*** their good behavior. ¶A diploma is no *guarantee* ***of*** efficiency. 卒業証書は高能率の保証にはならない.【類】His name is a *guarantee* ***of*** accuracy and intimate knowledge of the subject.

guarantee, *v.* 保証する；請合う.

M be ***fully*** *guaranteed* 十分保証されている.

P *guarantee* goods ***against*** breakage 商品の破損に対して保証する.【類】*guarantee* a person ***against*** (=***from***) loss (injury). ¶*guarantee* a watch ***for*** twelve months 時計は一カ年保証する. ¶*guarantee* payment ***to*** ... …に支払いを保証する.【類】Perfect satisfaction is *guaranteed* ***to*** our customers.

guard, *n.* 守護, 守衛；番兵, 衛兵；車掌.

V The Nio ***keep*** *guard* over the approach to the temple. 仁王がお寺の門を守護する. ‖ ***Keep*** a *guard* on your tongue. 口を慎しめ. ¶They ***maintain*** a police *guard* at the legation. その公使館には警官が守衛している. ¶***place*** a *guard* at the door 入口に番兵を置く. ¶The *guard* is ***relieved*** at intervals 衛兵は時間で交代になる.

Q He was escorted under an ***armed*** *guard*. 彼は武装した護衛兵に守られて行った. ¶a ***heavy*** *guard* of policemen 多数警官の護衛. ¶the ***Imperial*** *Guards* 近衛連隊.

Q² The diplomat abroad is the ***advance*** *guard* of commerce. 外交官は商業の前衛である. ¶a ***crossing*** *guard* 踏切番. ¶an ***honor*** *guard*=a guard of honor 儀じょう兵. ¶***Police*** *guards* stood near the room. 警官がへやの近くで立番をしていた. ¶a ***railway*** *guard*=《米》a train conductor《英》列車の車掌. ¶The cable of a liner is protected by a ***rat*** *guard*. 汽船のいかりづなはねずみの害から保護されている. ¶a ***secret service*** *guard* 平服護衛官. ¶a ***security*** *guard* 警護団員.

P when one is ***off*** *guard* 油断している時に ‖ he was ***off*** his *guard* with ... 彼は…に気を許していた ‖ being taken ***off*** one's *guard* 不意を打たれて.【類】I caught him ***off*** his *guard*. / This threw me ***off*** my *guard*. / put him ***off*** his *guard*. ¶policemen ***on*** *guard* 護衛の警官 ‖ a regiment ***on*** *guard* at ... …守備の連隊 ‖ go ***on*** *guard* 衛兵勤務に出る ‖ be ever ***on*** one's *guard* 常に油断がない ‖ let us be ***on*** our *guard* against ... われわれが…に陥らないよう警戒しよう ‖ be ***on*** *guard* with a rifle 銃を持って警戒している.【類】Be ***on*** your *guard*. / Be ***on*** your *guard* against woman. / put him ***on*** his *guard*. ¶The prisoners are ***under*** a strong *guard*. 捕虜は厳重に監視されている.

P² a *guard* ***against*** evil spirits 悪魔除け. ¶stand *guard* ***at*** the door 入口で歩しょうに立つ. ¶a *guard* ***of*** honor 儀じょう兵.

guard, *v.* 守る, 防ぐ；用心する, 警戒する.

M ***carefully*** *guard* against dangers 危険に陥らないよう十分に用心する. ¶***zealously*** *guard* their morals 彼らの道徳を注意深く守ってやる. ¶***safely*** *guard* ... 安全に…を守る. ¶a residence ***strongly*** *guarded* from thieves 賊のはいれないように厳重にしてある邸宅. ¶young men well equipped for life's duties and ***well*** *guarded* against its temptations 人生の任務を果すための十分な教養を受けかつ誘惑に打勝つだけの十分な修養を積んだ青年.

P *guard* ***against*** accidents 事故の起らないよう警戒する.【類】to *guard* ***against*** another accident / plants *guarded* ***against*** frost and snow (霜・雪害) ‖ to *guard* ***against*** [fires] 火災防止のため ‖ *guard* oneself ***against*** danger 危険に陥らないよう用心する.【類】*guard* ***against*** this error (misunderstanding). ¶We keep dogs to *guard* our houses at night ***from*** thieves and tramps. 宅では夜中盗賊やルンペンのはいれないよう犬を飼って置きます. ‖ *guard* a person (thing) ***from*** danger (accident) 危険(など)を防止する.

guardian, *n.* 保護者, 後見人, 番人.

V When the cherry-trees are in flower, they ***put*** a *guardian* in charge. 桜が咲くと番人を付ける.

Q ***legally constituted*** *guardians* of minors 未成年者の正式後見人. ¶She should be turned over to her ***natural*** or ***legal*** *guardian*. 彼女はその当然のまたは法律上の後見人に引渡さるべきである. ¶***students'*** *guardians* 学生の保護者. ¶a ***true*** *guardian* of the right その権利の真の守護者.

Q² a ***poor-law*** *guardian* 救貧法の民生委員.

P act ***as*** a *guardian* for a person 人の後見人になる.

P² become a *guardian* ***for*** ... …の後見人になる. ¶The press is a *guardian* ***of*** the public weal. 新聞紙は公益の守護者である. ‖ a "*guardian* ***of*** the welfare of humanity" 人類幸福の守護者 ‖ The diplomat is a *guardian* ***of*** the interests of a country in its international relations. 外交官は一国の国際的利益の守護者である. ¶a *guardian* ***to*** a person 人の保護者.

guardianship, *n.* 後見.

P He is still ***under*** *guardianship*. 彼はまだ後見されている. ‖ ***under*** the *guardianship* of ... …の後見の下に.

guardsman, *n.* 警備員.

Q² a ***frontier*** *guardsman* 国境警備隊員.

guess, *n.* 推量, おく測, 推しはかり.

V ***give*** a *guess* 推量する. ¶***hazard*** (=***venture*** [***on***]) a *guess* at ... …をおく測する.【類】***hazard*** a *guess* that ... ¶***make*** a *guess* at his age 彼の年をあててみる.【類】***make*** a *guess* that ... ¶***miss*** one's *guess* 当てそこなう.

Q Not a ***bad*** *guess* that! 当らずといえども遠からずだ. ¶It is not a ***baseless*** *guess*. いい加減な推量ではない. ¶make a pretty ***fair*** *guess* as to ... …についてかなりうまい推測をやる. ¶a ***happy*** *guess* 的を射た推量. ¶***hazardous*** *guesses* at the future 将来を当推量する. ¶It was a ***mere*** *guess*. それはほんの推量にすぎなかった. ¶the ***nearest*** *guess* as to ... is ... …一番事実に近い推量は…である. ¶a ***random*** *guess* あてずっぽう. ¶Only the ***roughest*** *guesses* can be made of it. それはざっとしか見当がつかない. ¶***rough-and-ready*** *guess* あてずっぽう. ¶***sagacious*** *guesses* 賢明な推測. ¶No ***satisfactory*** *guess* as to their authorship had been made until ... その著者については…まで満足な推定はなかった. ¶a ***shrewd*** *guess* 鋭い推測. ¶make a ***wild*** *guess* at ... …に対して途方もないおく測をする. ¶a ***wrong*** *guess* 見当違い.

P Age? Fifty-five to sixty ***at*** a *guess*. 年ですか, まず五十五から六十という所でしょう. ‖ I should say, ***at*** a *guess*, fifty per cent of them. まず五割でしょうね. ‖ write words ***at*** a *guess* あてずっぽうに語を書く ‖ ***At*** a rough *guess*, he may be about sixty. 大ざっぱに言ってあの人は六十位でしょう.【類】***At*** a rough *guess*, the total Jewish population of the metropolis does not fall far short of 115,000. ¶***By*** my *guess* he was about twenty-two. 私の推測では彼は二十二歳位であった. ‖ I set my watch ***by*** *guess* at half past two. あてずっぽうで時計を二時半にした. ¶***on*** a *guess* 推量で.

guess, *v.* 推量する；言い当てる.

M *guess* ***correctly*** 正しく推量する. ¶can ***easily*** *guess* らくにあてられる. ¶***Just*** *guess* it. まあ当てて見給え. ¶*guess* most ***nearly*** 最も近く言い当てる. ¶*guess* ***it out*** それを言い当てる. ¶*guess* ***right*** (***wrong***) うまく当てる(当てそこなう). ¶be ***rightly*** (***wrongly***) *guessed* 図星をさされる(当てそこなう). ¶*guess* ***wildly*** 途方もない推測をやる.

P *guess* ***at*** his meaning 彼の意味を推量する.【類】One may *guess* ***at*** the riddle many times without a solution. ¶I *guessed* it ***from*** his remarks. 私は彼の言葉でそれを推察した.

guessing, *n.* 推量.

V It ***baffles*** *guessing*. 一向見当が付かない.

guesswork, *n.* あて推量.

Q ***mere*** *guesswork* ほんの当て推量. ¶a matter of ***vague*** *guesswork* あいまいな推量.

P ***by*** *guesswork* 当て推量で.

guest *n.* 客, 旅客.

V ***accommodate*** *guests* with lodging, food, and drink 客に宿と食料と飲み物を供する ‖ The hotel can ***accommodate*** 100 *guests*. そのホテルは百人の客を収容することができる.【類】The hotel can ***accommodate*** foreign *guests*. ¶***entertain*** *guests* 来客をもてなす. ¶I ***expect*** *guests* to dinner. 晩さんに客がある. ¶***feast*** one's *guests* 客をもてなす. ¶I ***have*** a *guest*. 私には来客がある. ¶***invite*** *guests* to a party 客をパーテーに呼ぶ. ¶***put up*** *guests* 客を泊める. ¶***receive*** *guests* 客を迎える. ¶***show*** the *guests* to their seats 客を座席に案内する. ¶***slight*** (=neglect) a *guest* 客を粗末にする. ¶***take in*** *guests* 客を迎える.

V² *Guests* ***pair off***. 来客が二人ずつ手をたずさえて(食堂などに)行く.

Q an ***agreeable*** *guest* 愉快な客. ¶***belated*** *guests* 行き暮れた旅客. ¶the ***chief*** *guest* 主賓. ¶a ***complimentary*** *guest* at a hotel ホテルの無料接待の客. ¶a ***distinguished*** *guest* 貴賓. ¶***free*** *guests* at hotels ホテルの無料宿泊者. ¶He was a ***frequent*** *guest* at the famous breakfasts of Samuel Rogers. 彼はサミュエル・ロジャーズの有名な朝食会にしばし

ば客となった. ¶a most ***honored*** *guest* 主賓の一人. ¶the ***nation's*** *guest* 国賓. ¶an ***obnoxious*** *guest* いやな客. ¶an ***out-of-town*** *guest* いなか客. ¶an ***overnight*** *guest* 一晩泊りの客. ¶speed the ***parting*** (=going) and welcome the ***coming*** *guests* 去る客を送り来る客を迎える. ¶a "***paying*** *guest*" [ホテルなどの]宿泊客, 同居人(来客に対して). ¶I desire to be received as a ***paying*** *guest* (下宿人) in an English or American home. / An Oxford tutor and wife receive young foreigners as ***paying*** *guests.* ¶a ***permanent*** *guest* at a hotel ホテルに永住している客. ¶I shall bring with me two ***personal*** *guests.* 私は(会などへ)ふたり友人を連れて来ます. ¶the ***principal*** *guest* of the day その日の主賓. ¶a ***rooming*** *guest* へや借りの客(アパートやホテルなどの). ¶a ***state*** *guest* 国賓. ¶***transient*** *guests* in a hotel ホテルの一時客. ¶an ***uncalled-for*** *guest* 招かれざる客(いやな客). ¶***unwelcome*** (***welcome***) *guests* いやな客(歓迎できる客).

Q² ***fellow*** *guests* at an inn 宿屋の相客. ¶a ***flight*** *guest* 航空機乗客. ¶He was one of the ***honor*** *guests* at the luncheon. 彼は昼さん会の主賓の一人だった. ¶a ***home*** *guest* 家庭の来客. ¶a ***hotel*** *guest* ホテルのとまり客. ¶a ***resident*** *guest* in a hotel ホテルの長期滞留客. ¶a ***restaurant*** *guest* レストランの客. ¶the ***star*** *guest* [ラジオなどで]花形のお客さん. 「に招待される.

P be invited to ... ***as*** a *guest* of the nation 国賓として…

P² He is one of the *guests* [now staying] ***at*** a hotel. 彼はホテルに滞在中の客の一人だ. ‖a *guest* ***at*** a luncheon (party, dinner) 昼食(など)に招かれた客. 【類】I was a *guest* ***at*** his wedding. ¶*guests* ***in*** a hotel ホテルの客. ¶a *guest* ***of*** distinction 貴賓 ‖a *guest* ***of*** the court 国賓(王国の) ‖a *guest* ***of*** honor at a dinner 晩さん会の主賓.

guffaw, *n.* 高笑い, 大笑.

Q The company broke out into ***loud*** *guffaws* at the silly utterance. 一同はそのばか気た言草を聞いてわっと笑い出した. ¶a ***male*** *guffaw* or two 男の大きな笑い声一つ二つ.

guidance, *n.* 指導, 案内.

V ***give*** valuable *guidance* in ... …について貴重な指導を与える. ¶None of them were fit to ***give*** him *guidance* in his present strait. その内だれも彼の現在の窮境を救うに適してなかった. ¶***provide*** *guidance* for first-hand study 直接研究に対して指導をする. ¶***seek*** *guidance* in the study of English 英語研究の指導を求める.

Q thanks to the ***able*** *guidance* of ... …の手腕ある指導のお陰で. ¶under ***competent*** *guidance* 有能な指導の下に. ¶the ***Divine*** *guidance* 天助. ¶The newspaper provides an ***important popular*** *guidance.* 新聞紙は民衆の重要な指導者である. ¶***mental*** *guidance* and refreshment 精神の指導と刺激. ¶***personal*** *guidance* in the course of their studies 彼らの学習学科に対する個人指導. ¶with ***proper*** *guidance* 指導宜しきを得れば. ¶give ***rational*** *guidance* to young men as to sexual matters 性のことに関して青年を合理的に指導する. ¶under ***sympathetic*** *guidance* 同情ある指導の下に. ¶***tender*** *guidance* やさしい指導. ¶ask for ***topographical*** *guidance* 土地の模様について指導を求める. ¶***vocational*** *guidance* 職業指導.

Q² ***extracurricular activity*** *guidance* 〘教育〙科外活動ガイダンス. ¶***home-room*** *guidance* 〘教育〙ホーム・ルームの指導. ¶***student*** *guidance* 学生補導.

P a few hints ***for*** the *guidance* of the beginner 初心者の参考のための二三の注意 ‖***for*** your *guidance* 御参考のため ‖the following advice is given ***for*** the *guidance* of ... 次の注意は参考までに申上げる. ¶***under*** the *guidance* of ... …の指導の下に. ¶***without*** the *guidance* of a teacher 師につかないで.

guide, *n.* 案内者; 案内記, 手引.

V ***employ*** (=***engage***) a *guide* 案内者を雇う. ¶The book ***forms*** a complete *guide* to a very complex subject. その本は非常に複雑な問題に対するりっぱな手引になる. ¶***furnish*** a *guide* to ... …への手引になる. ¶***hire*** a *guide* for one's sightseeing 観光にガイドをやとう. ¶I ***need*** a *guide.* 私は案内者が要る. ¶It would be safer to ***take*** a *guide.* ガイドを頼んだ方が安全だろう.

Q a ***handy*** *guide* 軽便な案内記. ¶though not an ***infallible*** *guide* 完全な参考書ではないにしても. ¶an ***informative*** *guide* to ... …にとって参考になる手引. ¶a ***licensed*** *guide* 有資格案内業者. ¶their ***main*** *guide* 彼らの主立った案内者. ¶a ***postal*** *guide* 郵便便覧. ¶a ***practical*** *guide* to the language 同国語の実際的な手引. 【類】The Century Book for Mothers is a ***practical*** *guide* in the rearing of healthy children. ¶a ***professional*** *guide* 専門の案内業者. ¶a ***qualified*** *guide* 有資格の案内業者. ¶a ***registered*** *guide* 免許登録の案内業者. ¶a ***reliable*** *guide* 信頼しうる案内者. ¶a ***rough*** *guide* to the tourist (sightseer) 旅行家(など)のしおり. ¶Their advice would be a ***safe*** *guide.* 彼らの忠告は安全な指導になるだろう. 【類】Instinct is not always a ***safe*** *guide.* ¶Common sense is the ***supreme*** *guide.* 常識が最善の指針である. ¶a ***travelers'*** *guide* 旅行案内; ガイド. ¶The "Spectator" is a ***trustworthy*** *guide* to English affairs. スペクテーター誌は英国事情に関する信頼するに足る手引である. ¶an ***unerring*** *guide* 確かな手引. ¶a ***valuable*** *guide* 貴重な手引. ¶a ***welcome,*** perhaps an ***indispensable,*** *guide* ありがたいそして恐らく必須(ひっ)の手引.

Q² a ***buying*** *guide* 買物案内. ¶an ***English speaking*** *guide* 英語を話す案内人; 英会話の手引き. ¶a ***lady*** *guide* 婦人案内人. ¶a ***ready-reference*** *guide* [これは便利だ式の]便覧. ¶a ***study*** *guide* 勉学のしおり.

P ***as*** a *guide*=for one's guidance 参考のため ‖religion ***as*** a *guide* to conduct 行為の指針としての宗教.

P² Japan is a *guide* ***among*** Oriental nations. 日本は東洋諸国の指導者である. ¶a *guide* ***for*** visitors 遊覧者のための案内. ¶These philosophical views serve as a *guide* ***in*** life. これらの哲学的見解は処世の指針になる. ‖a *guide* ***in*** making money through investments 投資による金もうけの指針. ¶a *guide* ***to*** the British Museum 英国博物館案内. 【類】a *guide* ***to*** travelers. ‖Cook's *guide* ***to*** Paris クックのパリー案内記. 【類】Visitors' *Guide* ***to*** Westminster Abbey. ‖a *guide* ***to*** life insurance 生命保険案内 ‖The letters (文字) are no *guide* ***to*** the pronunciation. / publish the results already obtained, as a *guide* ***to*** future workers in the same field of research.

guide, *v.* 指導する, 案内する.

M a lighthouse *guides* ships ***safely*** to a harbor. 灯台によって船は安全に入港できる.

P *guide* his people ***along*** the path of progress 彼の部下を教導して進歩の道程をたどらせる. ¶be *guided* ***by*** common sense (principle) 常識(主義)によって導かれる. ¶we have been *guided* ***in*** the main by ... われわれは主として…を参考にした. ¶*guide* people ***into*** error 人を過誤に落し入れる. 【類】*guide* the young men ***into*** the right path / *guide* the reader ***to*** right reading ‖The public have not the requisite knowledge of the manufacture of soap to *guide* them ***to*** a proper selection. 一般の人は石けん製造について必要な知識がないから適当に石けんの選択ができない. ¶*guide* them ***toward*** a better mastery of the art of writing 彼らを指導して文章をじょうずに書けるようにする.

guide-book, *n.* 案内記, 旅行案内.

V ***consult*** a *guide-book* 旅行案内を見る.

Q a ***popular*** *guide-book* to Europe 欧州の一般向案内書. ¶a ***trustworthy*** *guide-book* 信用できる旅行案内. ¶a ***truthful*** *guide-book* うそのない案内記.

P refer ***to*** (=consult) a *guide-book* 案内書を引いてみる.

P² a *guide-book* ***for*** travelers 旅行案内. ¶Murray's *guide-book* ***to*** Japan マレーの日本案内記. 【類】a *guide-book* ***to*** (=for) foreign tourists.

guild, *n.* 組合.

Q² the ***screen Writers Guild*** 映画脚色家組合.

guillotine, *n.* 断頭台, 斬首台.

P death ***by*** the *guillotine* 断頭台での死. ¶behead the criminal ***with*** the *guillotine* 断頭台でその罪人の首を切る.

guilt, *n.* 罪, 犯罪.

V ***aggravate*** one's *guilt* その罪を一層重くする. ¶***betray*** one's *guilt* 思わずその罪を暴露する. ¶***confess*** one's *guilt* その罪を自白する. ¶***deny*** one's *guilt* その罪を否定する. ¶***lay*** the *guilt* upon ... 罪を…に着せる.

Q² ***war*** *guilt* 戦争犯罪.

P a partner ***in*** *guilt* 共犯者. ¶charge ... ***with*** *guilt* …を告訴する.

guiltless, *a.* 経験のない, 知らない.

P He is *guiltless* ***of*** the alphabet. 彼はABCも知らない. ‖He is *guiltless* ***of*** moustache. 彼は口ひげがない. 【類】a room *guiltless* ***of*** any ornamentation ‖the earth *guiltless* ***of*** the plow すきを入れたことのない土地.

guilty, *a.* 罪ある, 有罪の.

M ***doubly*** *guilty* 一層罪が重い. ¶He proved (=was

found) ***not guilty***. 彼は無罪と判明した.【類】be given the verdict of "***not guilty***" (無罪の評決).

P He is *guilty **of*** one or two slips. 彼は一二の失さくを演じた. ‖ the author is *guilty **of*** the extraordinary blunder of saying that ... 著者は…と言っているがこれははなはだしい間違いである.【類】He is *guilty **of*** a gross blunder (breach of the law (違法), an overweening presumption (ごう慢無礼), rudeness or neglect). / persons *guilty **of*** criminal acts against ... / be *guilty **of*** the offense of ... / He was found *guilty **of*** murder. / What crime was he *guilty **of***? ‖ be *guilty **of*** bad taste 悪趣味を発揮する.

guise, *n.* 様子, 姿; 身なり.

V ***penetrate*** a *guise* 見せかけを見破る. ¶The body may ***wear*** a worldly *guise,* the heart immersed in unworldly thoughts. 心は塵(じ)外の思想にひたりながら身は世俗の衣をまとうこともできよう.

Q Japan in ***ancient*** (***modern***) *guise* 昔(今)風の日本. ¶an old custom in a ***new*** *guise* 当世風にした古い風俗. ¶People will not recognize you in ***this*** *guise.* こんな風をしては人が君と気が付かないだろう.

P go ***in*** the *guise* of a monk 僧の格好をして行く ‖ be presented ***in*** the *guise* of fiction 小説の形をとって発表されている ‖ Talkies enable one to learn a foreign language ***in*** the *guise* of amusement. トーキーだと楽しみながら外国語が習える. ¶He traveled ***under*** (=in) the *guise* of a priest. 彼は僧に変装して旅をした. ‖ ***under*** (=***in***) the *guise* of friendship 友情を装って.【類】the superstition which is everywhere creeping over us ***under*** the *guise* of religion.

guitar, *n.* ギター.

V ***pick*** *a guitar* ギターをつめびきする. ¶***strum*** a *guitar* ギターをかきならす. ¶***twang*** a *guitar* ギターをぽろんとひく.

P sing ***to*** the *guitar* ギターに合わせて歌う.

gulf, *n.* 湾, 入海; 懸隔.

V ***bridge*** the *gulf* between ... ...間の橋渡しをする.【類】***bridge*** the *gulf* which separates ... from ... ¶The quarrel ***left*** a *gulf* between them. その争いで両者間が疎遠になった. ¶***widen*** the economic *gulf* between rich and poor 貧富の経済的懸隔を大きくする.【類】***widen*** the *gulf* lying between the governors and the governed (支配者と被支配者). ¶A great *gulf* ***yawned*** between business and the professions. 実業と高等職業との間に大きなへだたりがあった.【類】the deep and wide *gulf* which ***yawns*** between East and West.

Q the ***impassable*** *gulf* between the samurai and the merchant 士商間の越え難い隔り. ¶The prostitute is separated by a great and impassable ***social*** *gulf* from her married sister. 売春婦と人妻とには社会的にこゆべからざる一大懸隔がある. ¶there is a ***wide*** *gulf* as yet unbridged between ... and ... ...間には今後除かなければならぬ大きな懸隔がある ‖ a ***wide*** *gulf* of separation 大きな懸隔.

P ***in*** the *Gulf* of Mexico メキシコ湾に. ¶The Bell Mountain is situated ***on*** the *Gulf* of Suez. ベル山はスエズ湾に臨んでいる. ¶the great *gulf* ***between*** rich and poor 貧富の大懸隔.

gull, *n.* かもめ.

V *Gulls* ***wheel*** above. かもめが頭上に輪を描いて飛ぶ.

gull, *v.* あざむく, だます.

P *gull* a person ***into*** wrongdoing 人をだまして悪事をさせる. ¶He was *gulled* ***of*** his money. 彼はだまされて金を取られた. ¶*gull* a person ***out of*** his money 人の金を詐取する.

gulp, *n.* ぐい飲み, 一飲み.

P Don't swallow your meals ***at*** a *gulp.* 食事を一飲みにしてはいけない ‖ drink ***at*** a *gulp* ぐいと一杯ひっかける.【類】When a chicken drinks, it lifts its head ***at*** each *gulp.* ¶"I may have to go home," he whispered, ***with*** a *gulp* at his Adam's apple. のどぼとけをごくりとさせて彼は「私は帰らなければなるまい」とささやいた.

gulp, *v.* ぐいと飲む; 息をのむ.

M^2 *gulp* ***down*** a sob 涙を無理に抑える ‖ *gulp* ***down*** a glass of beer ビールをぐいぐい飲む.

P He *gulped* ***at*** the sad news. その凶報に彼は息をのんだ.

gum, *n.* ゴム; (米) ガム.

V ***chew*** *gum* ガムをかむ.

Q ***Arabic*** *gum* アラビアゴム.

Q^3 ***chewing*** *gum* チューインガム.

gumption, *n.* 才覚, 知恵.

V if he ***had*** the slightest *gumption,* he would find out that ... 彼に少しでも頭があれば…ということが分るのだが.

gun, *v.* 銃, 砲; (米口語) けん銃.

V ***aim*** one's *gun* at ... 銃を…に向ける. ¶The wind ***blew*** "great *guns.*" 風が烈しく吹いた. ¶***bring*** a *gun* to bear 砲を差向ける. ¶***charge*** a *gun* with powder and ball 砲に火薬と弾丸を装てんする. ¶***cock*** a *gun* 銃の引金を上げる. ¶***direct*** a *gun* against a fort 要さいに砲を向ける. ¶***discharge*** a *gun* 砲を発射する. ¶***disembark*** the *guns* and ammunition 砲弾薬を陸揚げする. ¶***dismantle*** *guns* 砲を解体する. ¶***dismount*** a *gun* 砲を砲架から降ろす. ¶***fire*** a *gun* 砲を打つ ‖ ***fire*** the opening *gun* 火ぶたを切る ‖ ***fire off*** a *gun* 砲を発射する. ¶***give*** a *gun* 発砲を命じる. ¶***handle*** a *gun* 砲を操縦する. ¶***lay*** a *gun* 砲を照準する. ¶***level*** a *gun* at ... ...に銃を向ける. ¶***load*** a *gun* 砲に装てんする. ¶***man*** the *gun* 砲員を配備する. ¶***mount*** a *gun* 砲を砲架に載せる ‖ a cruiser ***mounting*** six 6-in. caliber *guns* 口径六インチ砲を六門とう載している巡洋艦. ¶***place*** *guns* in position 砲をその位地に置く. ¶***point*** a *gun* at ... ...に銃を向ける. ¶***respond*** *gun* for gun 同数の礼砲を行う. ¶***secure*** the *guns* 砲をつなぎ留める. ¶***shoulder*** a *gun* 銃を肩にする. ¶***silence*** the *guns* 砲を沈黙させる. ¶***spike*** a *gun* 砲を廃物とする; 計画の裏をかく. ¶***taking*** a *gun* in hand [けん]銃を手にして. ¶Russian *guns* were ***turned*** on British ships. ロシア側の砲門が英国の船に向けられた. ¶***unload*** a *gun* 銃から弾丸を抜く.

V^2 The *gun* ***went off.*** 大砲が発射された. ¶naval *guns* ***roared*** as ... ...の時に艦砲がとどろいた.

Q a ***big*** *gun* 大砲. ¶a ***double-barrelled*** *gun* 双身銃. ¶a ***heavy*** *gun* 重砲. ¶with ***ready*** *gun* 銃を打つばかりにして.

Q^2 an ***anti-aircraft*** *gun* 高射砲 (an A.A.gun と略す). ¶an ***air*** *gun* 空気銃. ¶an ***anti-tank*** *gun* 対戦車砲. ¶be like a pair of ***battleship turret*** *guns* 一対の戦艦の砲塔備砲のようである(乳房がつき出ている様). ¶***breech-loading*** *guns* 後装砲. ¶a ***flint-lock*** *gun* 火打ち石銃. ¶a ***high-velocity*** *gun* 高速度砲. ¶a ***Krupp*** *gun.* クルップ砲. ¶a ***large caliber*** *gun* 大口径砲. ¶a ***life-saving*** *gun* 救難火砲(海岸から難破船へ救助なわを発送する). ¶a ***long-range*** *gun* 長距離砲. ¶a ***magazine*** (=repeating) *gun* 連発銃. ¶a ***Maxim*** *gun* マキシム[機関]銃. ¶the ***midday*** *gun*=the noongun 午砲. ¶fire ***minute*** *guns* (弔砲などの)分時砲を発する. ¶an ***old-pattern*** *gun* 旧式の大砲. ¶a ***siege*** *gun* 攻城砲. ¶a ***smooth-bore*** *gun* [銃身内部に筋のない]滑腔(こう)銃. ¶a ***spray*** *gun* (はい取りなどの)噴霧銃. ¶a ***sub-machine*** *gun* 半自動機関銃. ¶the report of the ***sunset*** (=***evening***) *gun* 夕砲の響き. ¶a ***Woolwich*** *gun.* ウーリッジ砲(英式前装砲). ¶an ***11-inch*** *gun* 十一インチ砲.

P people ***behind*** the *gun* 銃後の人々. ¶the distant boom ***of*** *guns* told that ... 遠方にとどろく大砲の音によって…と分かった. ¶shoot game ***with*** a *gun* 野鳥類を銃で打つ ‖ Take good aim ***with*** your *gun.* 銃でよくねらえ.

P^2 He was coming this way, *gun* ***in*** hand. けん銃を手にしてこっちへやってきた.

gun-fire, *n.* 砲火.

Q the throb of a ***distant*** *gun-fire* 遠方の砲声.

gunman, *n.* 砲手; (米) ピストル強盗.

V^2 Three *gunmen* ***broke in*** and killed a clerk right on the spot. 三人のピストル強盗が侵入し, 事務員を一人その場で射殺した.

Q a ***good*** *gunman* ピストルなどの名手.

gunner, *n.* 射撃手, 砲兵.

Q^2 a ***master*** *gunner* 射撃の名手.

gunnery, *n.* 射撃力.

Q ***excellent*** *gunnery* 優秀な射撃力.

gunpowder, *n.* 火薬.

V ***explode*** (=***blow up***) *gunpowder* 火薬を爆発させる. ¶The Chinese are said to have ***invented*** *gunpowder.* 中国人が火薬を発明したということだ.

Q ***blasting*** *gunpowder* 爆発火薬. ¶a ***slow-burning*** *gunpowder* 燃焼の緩慢な火薬. ¶***smokeless*** *gunpowder* 無煙火薬.

gunshot, *n.* 着弾距離.

P bring a ship ***within*** the *gunshot* of the place 船をその地点の着弾距離内に進める.

gush, *n.* 流出, 噴出.

P^2 a *gush* ***of*** anger (enthusiasm) ほとばしる怒り(熱情). ‖ a *gush* ***of*** oil (water) 油(など)の噴出 ‖ a *gush* ***of*** cold wind 一陣の寒風.

gush, *v.* わき出る.

M His nose was *gushing* ***out*** blood. 彼の鼻から血が流れ出

していた. 【類】Thick blood *gushed out* (どくどく流れ出た).

P clear water *gushing from* a spring 泉からわき出る清水.

gust, *n.* 烈風, 疾風.

Q The wind blew in *fitful gusts.* 風が気まぐれに吹いた. ¶a *violent gust* of wind 猛烈な一陣の風.

P² *gusts of* joy (rage) にわかの歓喜(怒り) ‖ a *gust* of sea breeze 一陣の海風 ‖ *gusts of* rain ざーざー降りしきるにわか雨 ‖ *gusts of* sound にわかの物音.

gusto, *n.* 趣味, 嗜好(しこう), 好み.

V *enjoy* the full *gusto* of the cool 涼味を満喫する.

P The hungry boy ate his dinner *with gusto.* 空腹の少年は舌づつみを打って食事をした. ¶in those days I could write *with* [a] *gusto* under the pen-name of ... 当時は...という雅号で会心の筆を執ることができた.

gut, *v.* 内部を焼き尽す, 破壊する.

P The building was *gutted by* fire. その建物は火事で内部が焼けた.

gutter, *n.* とい, みぞ; 《俗》貧民くつ.

V *reach* the *gutter* 零落する.

Q² a *valley gutter* 谷どい.

P rise *from* the *gutter* 卑せんから身を起す. ¶people *of* the *gutter* 細民. ¶marry a girl *out of* the *gutter* いやしい身分の女をめとる ‖ take a child *out of* the *gutter* 子供を貧民くつから救い出す.

guy, *n.* 《米俗》男, 奴.

Q a *husky guy* 《米》がん丈な男. ¶a *main guy*=a big bug 《口語》頭かぶ, かしら. ¶I've misjudged you. You're really a *nice guy* after all. 君を誤解していた, 君はやっぱりいい男だな. ¶a *regular guy* 性質のよい男. ¶a *smooth* (=fair-spoken) *guy* 《口語》冷静に話す男. ¶The fellow seems to be a *stiff guy.* やつは一癖ありそうな男だ. ¶a *swell guy* すばらしい男. ¶a *tough guy* 不死身の男. ¶a *wise guy* 利口な男.

gym[nasium], *n.* 体育館.

Q a *factory gym* for workers' recreation 工員休養施設としての工場体操場. ¶a *school* (*university*) *gym* 学校(大学)体育館.

gymnastics, *n.* 体操, 訓練.

V *perform gymnastics* on the bar 鉄棒で体操をする. ¶*practice gymnastics* 体操をやる.

Q Language study is the most stimulating *intellectual gymnastics.* 語学研究は最も刺激のある知的訓練である. ¶a *mental gymnastics* 精神訓練. ¶Massage is a *passive gymnastics.* マッサージはぶしょうな体操である.

Q² *home gymnastics* 家庭体操.

P² *gymnastics with* or *without* apparatus 器械または徒手体操.

Gypsy, gypsy, *n.* ジプシー.

P He lives the life *of* a *gypsy* (=like a gypsy). 彼はジプシーのような生活をしている.

H

habiliment, *n.* 服装.

Q² artisans and navvies in *working habiliments* 作業服をつけた職人や土方.

habit, *n.* (**1**) 習慣, 癖, 風習, 習性.

V *abandon* a *habit* 習慣を捨てる. ¶*acquire* a *habit* ... ...の習慣がつく. 【類】*acquire* a dictionary *habit* / *acquire habits* of correct speaking. ¶*adopt* European *habits* 欧州風を採用する. ¶*alter* or *root up* fixed *habits* 身についた習慣を改めるかまたはとり去る. ¶Some insane people *assume* the *habit* of dogs. 精神病者には犬のまねをするものがある. ¶try to *break* a *habit* 癖をやめようとする. 【類】*break* one's *habit* of taking bromide / The *habit* is not easily *broken.* ¶*break off* the *habit* of ... ...する習慣をやめる. ¶*break up* a *habit* ある習慣をやめてしまう. 【類】It is not easy to *break up* such *habits* when once they become fixed. ¶*build up* the *habit* of ... ...の習慣を作る. ¶This new habit has been added to the man *habits* a civilized man is *carrying* [*with*]. 文明人のもっている多くの習慣の中にこの新しい習慣が加わった. ¶*catch* the *habit* of ... from foreigners ...の癖を外人から習う. ¶*change* one's *habits* 習慣を変える. ¶*contract* a bad *habit* 悪癖がつく. ¶*correct* one's *habits* 癖を改める. ¶*create* good *habits* よい習慣を植付ける. ¶*crush* bad *habits* right at the start 初手に悪習を打破する. ¶*cultivate* a *habit* of regularity 物事を規則正しくする習慣を養う. ¶*cure* bad *habits* in writing and speech 書いたり話したりするときの悪い癖を直す. 【類】*cure* a man of bad *habits.* ¶*develop* a pernicious *habit* of ... ...という有害な癖がつく. 【類】They have *developed* the *habit* of paying a weekly visit to their nearest cinema. ¶*discard* (=give up) a *habit* 習慣を捨てる. ¶*discontinue* a *habit* 習慣をやめる. ¶*drop* a *habit* 習慣をやめる. ¶*encourage habits* of thrift 倹約の風を奨励する. ¶*eradicate* a bad *habit* and replace it by a good one 悪習を根絶させてそれを良風に変える. ¶help *establish* the *habit* 習慣を確立するようにする. ¶*form* the *habit* of saving money 貯金の習慣をつける. 【類】The *habit* is *formed* almost insensibly (知らず知らずの間に). ¶*foster* a *habit* of ... ...の習慣を助長する. ¶*forswear* a bad *habit* 悪癖を誓ってやめる. ¶*get over* a *habit* 習慣に打勝つ. ¶*give up* the tobacco *habit* 喫煙をやめる. ¶he *has* a *habit* of ... 彼には...の習慣がある. ¶*implant* (=*inculcate*) correct language *habits* in the pupils of the middle school その中学の生徒に言葉を正しく話す習慣をつけさせる. ¶*keep* regular *habits* 規則正しい習慣を守る. ¶*kill* the long-word *habit* いたずらに長い語を使う癖をやめる. ¶*know* the *habits* of wild animals 野獣の習性を知る. ¶*learn* bad *habits* 悪い癖を覚える. ¶You should *leave off* (=*discontinue*) this *habit* of idleness. このなまけ癖はやめたが良い. ¶It is easy to *maintain habits* once formed. 一遍ついた習性はたやすく続けられる. ¶*make* a *habit* of ... ...を常習とする. ¶*observe* the right *habits* of living 正しい生活法を守る. ¶*outgrow* the bad *habits* of boyhood 成長して少年時の悪癖が直る. ¶He tried very hard to *overcome* the *habit.* 彼はその習慣に打勝とうと懸命に努力した. ¶*pick up* good *habits* of study 勉学の良習をつける. ¶Lending libraries and cheap books *popularize* the *habit* of reading. 貸本屋や廉価本が読書の癖を普及させる. ¶*practice* the *habit* その風習を行う. ¶*prevent* bad *habits* 悪習を防ぐ. ¶*reform* bad *habits* 悪い習慣を改める. ¶*relinquish* a bad *habit* 悪習をやめる. ¶*remove* bad *habits* 悪習を取除く. ¶the *habit* is deeply *rooted* among ... その習慣は...の間に深く根を下している. ¶*set up* correct *habits* 正しい習慣をつける ‖ *set up* a troublesome "bromide *habit*" 厄介なブロマイド常用の癖を作る. ¶The *habit* is very hard to *shake off* when once acquired. その癖は一たん身につくと中々抜けない. ¶*spread* the reading *habit* 読書の習慣を普及させる. ¶*start* a drink *habit* 飲酒の癖をつける. ¶*stimulate* the *habit* of reading 読書の習慣を勧める. ¶*substitute* some good *habit* for a bad one 悪い習慣を良い習慣に変える. ¶*suppress* the opium *habit* アヘン常用の風習を禁じる. ¶*take on* rapidly Western *habit* of life 急に西洋風になる. ¶*take up* the *habit* of ... ...の癖がつく. ¶*throw* (=*cast*) *aside* a boyish *habit* 子供じみた習慣を捨てる. ¶*uproot habits* resolutely 断固として習慣を根絶させる.

V² The *habit grew* upon me. その習慣が私にできた.

Q *abstemious habits* 節制. ¶an *acquired habit* ついた癖. ¶Beware of the *awful habit.* 恐ろしい習慣に染まないように気をつけよ. ¶it will lead to the forming (=contracting) of a *bad habit* それで悪い癖がつく ‖ an incorrigible *bad habit* 抜けない悪癖 ‖ slide into a *bad habit* 知らず知らず悪い癖がつく. ¶*brooding reserved habits* 沈んで物を言わない習慣. ¶a *cheerful habit* (=frame) of mind 明朗な性質. ¶a *confirmed habit* of drinking 直しようのない飲酒の癖. ¶*correct habits* 正しい習慣. ¶*curious habits* of thought and speech 奇妙な考え方や話し方. ¶*deeply ingrained* (=*rooted*) *habits* こう盲に入った癖. ¶a *desirable habit* 好ましい習性. ¶fall into *dissolute habits* 身を持くずす. ¶*domestic habits* 家風. ¶Her home was unhappy on account of her husband's *drunken habits*. 彼女の家庭はその夫の飲酒癖のために楽しくなかった. ¶*Eastern* (*Western*) *habits* of thought 東(西)洋風な考え方. ¶an *evil habit* 悪習. ¶a *filthy habit* けがらわしい風習. ¶It has become a *fixed habit*. その癖が固まってしまった. ¶a *foolish habit* ばかげた習慣. ¶It strikes us as a *foreign habit*. それはわれわれには異国の習わしのように思われる. ¶*good habits* 良い習慣. ¶*harmful habits* 有害な習慣. ¶to prevent the formation of *incorrect habit* of pronunciation 間違った発音をする癖のつかないように. ¶an *incorrigible habit* of wrinkling one's nose 鼻にしわをよせるという直し難い癖. ¶his *incurable habit* of ... ...という彼の直らない癖. ¶an *ineradicable habit* 直らない癖. ¶*insidious habits* 知らず知らずつく癖. ¶create *instinctive habits* of using good English 自然に良い英語を使う習慣を作る. ¶*insular habits* and prejudices 島国的習性と偏見. ¶an *inveterate habit* 根深い習慣. ¶a man of *irregular habits* 不規則な習慣の人. ¶acquire *luxurious habits* ぜいたくになじむ. ¶a *nasty habit* いやらしい習慣. ¶He has *neat habits*. 彼はきれい好きだ. ¶*national habits* 国の習わし. ¶an *objectionable habit* 非難すべき風習. ¶an *odious habit* いやな習性. ¶Most people dislike to have their *old habits* of thought disturbed. たいていの人は従来やってきた物の考え方に干渉されるのを好まない. ¶a *pernicious habit* 有害な習慣. ¶a man of *plebeian habits* 平民的な人. ¶the *predatory habit* of guides ガイドの(観光客の)金をまき上げる癖. ¶of *profligate habits* and a drunkard 道楽ものでのん平の. ¶the *quarrelling habit* 闘争癖. ¶*queer habits* of the Indians インデヤンの変な風習. ¶a very unassuming man of *quiet habits* おとなしい少しも出しゃばらない人. ¶He was of *reckless* and *dissolute habits*. 彼は向う見ずで放らつであった. ¶the cultivation of *regular habits* in emptying the bowels 規則正しく排便する習慣の養成 ‖ make it a *regular habit* to ... ...するのを一定の習慣とする. ¶a *repulsive* (=*revolting*) *habit* いやな習慣. ¶*right habits* of study 学習の正しい習慣. ¶The *scientific habit* of mind was invented only three hundred years ago. 科学的な物の見方はわずか三百年前にできたものだ. ¶*sedentary habits* すわる習慣. ¶a *sensible habit* 賢明な習慣. ¶a *settled habit* 確立した習慣. ¶a man of *simple habits* 単純な習性の人. ¶*sober habits* 酒を飲まない習慣. ¶cultivate *social habits* 社交性を養成する. ¶*spendthrift habits* 浪費癖. ¶*studious habits* 研究癖. ¶An old *habit* is *tenacious*. 古い習慣はなかなか亡びないものだ. ¶encourage *thrifty habits* 節約の風習を奨励する. ¶an *unpatriotic habit* 非愛国的風習. ¶*vicious habits* 悪習慣. ¶develop *worth-while habits* and skills 価値のある習性や技能をのばす.

Q² the *alcohol* (*cigarette, dictionary, drinking, note-taking, reading, or whisky*) *habit* 飲酒(など)の癖. ¶cure the *cigarette habit* 喫煙の癖を直す. ¶the *club habit* クラブに出入りする習慣. ¶establish the *dictionary habit* 辞書になじむくせをつける. ¶the *dress habit* 衣装道楽. ¶a victim of the *drink* (=*drinking*) *habit* 飲酒の被害(犠牲)者. ¶a jovial person of *easy-going habits* 陽気でのんきな人. ¶*good health habits* 健康増進の習慣. ¶the *hotel habit* ホテルに止宿する癖. ¶the *life habits* of bees みつばちの習性. ¶a complete change of *living habits* 生活慣習の一変. ¶encourage the *museum habit* 博物館行きの習慣を奨励する. ¶*peace-loving habits* 柔和な風. ¶the *reading habit* 読書癖. ¶train students to the *research habit* 学生を訓練して研究癖をつけさせる. ¶the *souveniring habit* みやげ物を買う習慣. ¶the *tea habit* 茶を飲む習慣. ¶the *theater*[*-going*] *habit* 劇場通いの癖. ¶the *tobacco* (=*smoking*) *habit* 喫煙の癖. ¶fully acquire *town habits* すっかり都会生活の癖がつく. ¶a *vagabond habit* 放浪癖.

P guard *against* a *habit* of ... ...の癖が付かないように用心する. ¶confirmed *by habit* 習慣でかたまって ‖ *by* mechanical *habit* 機械的な習慣で. ¶wean him *from* a *bad habit* 彼の悪い癖をやめさせる ‖ it is only *from habit* that ... ...というのは習慣に過ぎない. ¶He is democratic and plain *in* his *habits* (=tastes). 彼は平民的で地味だ. ‖ He was *in* the *habit* of saying "I have went." 彼は I have went という癖があった. 【類】I am *in* the *habit* of brushing my teeth twice daily. / He has been *in* the *habit* of spending his summer holidays in Nikko for several years. / not *in* the *habit* of taking saké / *in* the *habit* of frequently changing her name when travelling / *in* the *habit* of rising early. ¶He fell *into* the *habit* of leaving homework untouched. 彼は宿題をそのまま放ったらかすという癖がついた. ‖ get *into* a *habit* of ... ...の癖がつく. ¶The force *of habit* is strong. 習慣の力は偉大である. ‖ a man *of* plebeian *habits* 平民的な人. ¶adhere *to* one's old *habit* 古くからの癖を捨てない.

P² a training in *habits of* order 秩序的にする習慣の訓練 ‖ the *habit of* smoking 喫煙癖. 【類】his *habit of* keen observation [of things]. ¶it is a *habit with* (=habitual to) him to ... ...するのは彼のいつもの癖である.

O make it a *habit* to ... 一つの癖として...する.

(2) 僧服; [婦人用]乗馬服.

Q robed in the *Franciscan habit* フランシスコ派の僧服をまとって. ¶a young lady in a *close-fitting habit* ぴったりした乗馬服を着た若い婦人. ¶a *monk's habit* 僧服, 法衣. ¶a *nun's habit* 尼僧の僧服. ¶in their *official habits* 役人服装で.

Q² a *riding habit* [婦人の]乗馬服.

habit, *v.* 服装をする.

P men *habited as* women 女装した男たち.

habitat, *n.* 産地.

V The banana is ever *widening* its *habitat*. バナナの産地は絶えず広がって行く.

habitation, *n.* 住所, 住宅.

V During his 56 years in Paris, Renan *had* nearly a dozen different *habitations*. ルナンはパリに五十六年住んでいる間に十二回ばかり住居を変えた.

Q people of *fixed habitations* 定住所のある人々. 【類】He has no *fixed habitation*.

habitual, *a.* 常習の.

P *habitual to* him 彼に常習の.

habituate, *v.* 慣らす.

P *habituate* oneself *to* hardship (a foreign climate) 自分を困難(など)に慣らす.

habitué, *n. F.* 常連.

Q² a *morphine habitué* モルヒネ中毒患者. ¶*movie* (*opera*) *habitués* 映画(歌劇)の常連.

hack, *n.* [文筆の]助手; 《米》タクシー.

V *hire hacks* 文筆の助手を頼む; [選挙で]運動員をやとう; 《米》タクシーを頼む.

hack, *v.* 切る, 切りさいなむ.

M *hack off* the tops of cocoanuts with a sharp knife. 鋭いナイフでココやしのこずえを切り取る.

P *hack* it *to* pieces それをずたずたに切る. ¶*hack* a person *to* death with an axe おので...を惨殺する.

hackneyed, *a.* 陳腐な.

M This kind of joke is *fairly hackneyed*. こういった冗談は相当古臭い. ¶"Whiter than snow" is an expression that sounds *rather hackneyed*.「雪より白い」という文句はちょっと響きが古めかしい.

hackwork, *n.* 下働き.

V He *does hackwork* for an encyclopedia. 彼は百科辞典の下働きをしている.

Hades, *n.* めい土.

P a river *in Hades* 三途の川.

haemorrhage, =hemorrhage.

haggle, *v.* 値切る, 口論する.

P *haggle about* prices 値切る ‖ The Germans were *haggling about* the terms of the Peace Treaty. ドイツ国民は平和条約の条項について交渉を重ねていた. ¶*haggle over* prices 値切る ‖ They are *haggling over* the matter. そのことですったもんだをやっている. ¶*haggle with* sellers 売手と交渉をする.

haggling, *n.* 値切.

V I don't like to *have* any *haggling*. 僕は一切値切るのはきらいだ.

Q after *much haggling* さんざ値切ってから.

P *after* some *haggling* over the price of goods 品をちょっと値切ってから. ¶to be accepted or rejected *without haggling* 値切らないでそのまま受けたり断わったりする.

hail, *n.* あられ, ひょう.

V² Much *hail fell*. あられが盛んに降った.

Q *soft hail* みぞれ.
P *amid* a *hail* of bullets 弾雨の中にあって.

hail, *v.* あられが降る.
P *hail* (=rain) blows *on* ... ...をぽかぽかなぐる.
O It *hails*. あられが降る.

hail, *n.* 大声で呼ぶこと.
P *beyond* (=*out of*) *hail* 声の届かない所に. ¶lie *within hail* of ... ...から呼べば聞える所にある.

hail, *v.* 呼ぶ, あいさつする.
P They *hailed* him *as* king. 彼らは王として彼を迎えた. ‖ be *hailed as* a great writer 大作家として歓迎される ‖ *hail at* the top of one's voice を声を限りに呼ぶ. ¶soldiers *hailing from* America 米国からの兵士. 【類】Hey, man! What State do you *hail from*? / My critic *hails from* Birmingham. ¶*hail to* a person to stop 人に止れと呼びかける. ¶The proposal was *hailed with* the greatest satisfaction. その提案はこの上もない満足をもって迎えられた.
O Here comes the history prof. Let's *hail* him. そら歴史の先生がやってきた. ちよっと声をかけよう. 【類】*hail* a taxi.

hair, *n.* 髪, 毛.
V *arrange* one's disordered *hair* 乱れた髪を直す. ¶*bind* the *hair* 髪を結う. ¶*bob* one's *hair* 断髪にする. 【類】the fashion of "*bobbing*" the *hair*. ¶*braid* the *hair* 髪を編む. 【類】*braid* one's *hair* into a crown (束髪). ¶*brush* the *hair* 髪にブラシをかける. ¶*caress* one's *hair* その髪をなでる. ¶have one's *hair clipped* (=cropped) *short* 髪を短く刈り込む. ¶*comb* one's *hair* 髪をすく. ¶*crop* one's *hair* 髪を短く刈る. ¶*curl* her *hair* with a curling iron こてで髪をカールにする. ¶*cut* one's *hair close* 髪を坊主刈りにする. ¶*cut* one's *hair short* 髪を短くする. ¶*cut off* her *hair* 彼女の髪を切る. ¶You *dishonor* your white *hair*. 君の白髪が泣くよ. ¶She is *doing* her *hair*. 彼女は髪を結っている. ¶*do up* one's *hair* 髪を結う. ¶*dress* her *hair* 髪を結う. ¶*dye hair black* (*reddish*) 髪を黒(赤)く染める. ¶*fix* her *hair* 髪を結う(留める). ¶*friz* and *curl hair* 毛を縮らす. ¶*get* one's *hair trimmed* 髪の手入をしてもらう. ¶*have* spare *hair* on the head 髪が薄い. ¶*groom* one's *hair* 髪を整える(なでつけたり, ブラシをかける). 【類】His *hair* was well *groomed*. ¶*have* one's *hair cut* 髪を刈ってもらう. ¶*leave* the *hair uncut* 髪を伸びるにまかせる. ¶*let down* one's *hair* 髪を解く. ¶*let* one's *hair grow* long 髪を伸ばす. ¶I am *losing* my *hair*. 私は髪が抜ける. ¶*make* one's *hair stand* on end 身の毛がよだつ思いをさせる. ¶without *moving* (=*turning*) a *hair* 髪の毛一筋も動かさないで, 落着き払って. ¶He *parts* his *hair* in the middle (at the side). 彼は髪を真中(横)で分けている. ¶*plait* the *hair* 髪を編む. ¶*pluck out* a *hair* 毛を一本抜く. ¶*protect* elaborately dressed *hair* from being ruffled 念入りに結った髪の乱れないようにする. ¶*put* her *hair up* 髪を上げる. ¶*rub down* one's *hair* 髪をなでつける. ¶*rumple* (=*tousle*) one's *hair* 髪を乱す. ¶*shave* [*off*] *hair* 頭を丸める. ¶*split* (=part) one's *hair* on the left-hand side (in the middle) 髪を左側(真中)で分ける ‖ *split hairs* over ... 〘比喩〙 ...についていやにこまかく論議を戦わす. ¶*stroke* her soft *hair* 彼女の柔い髪をなでる. ¶He howled and *tore* his *hair*. 彼は泣きわめいて髪をかきむしった. 【類】*tear* one's *hair* and cry / She *tore* her *hair*, wrung her hands, and beat her breast like a mad woman. ¶*tidy* her *hair* 髪のもつれを直す(きちんとする). ¶*hair tied* in European style 欧州風に結った髪. ¶*tie up* her *hair* in a sort of mob-cap モブ・キャップ風に髪を結う. ¶It was more than enough to *turn* my *hair*. それは私の髪の毛の色が変るほどの苦しみであった. ¶*undulate* the *hair* 髪を縮らす. ¶*wear* one's *hair long* 髪を長くている ‖ the present feminine vogue of *wearing* the *hair bobbed* 髪を断髪にする今どきの女の流行 ‖ *wear* one's *hair cut short* 髪を短くしている. 【類】*wear* one's *hair* in the latest style (最新式に).
V² Her *hair* is *coming off*. 彼女の髪が抜ける. ¶Her *hair flows* in the *wind*. 彼女の髪が風に波打っている. ¶*Hair falls out* (=*off*). 毛が抜ける. ¶*hair grows* on ... 毛が...に生える. ¶Her *hair hung* about her neck and down her back. 彼女の髪は首のあたりから背中までたれていた. ¶*hairs sprouting* on the chin あごに生えている数本の毛. ¶His *hair stood on* (=*bristled up*) at this frightful sight. この恐ろしい光景に直面して彼の髪がさか立った. ¶Her long *hair* was *streaming* in the wind. 彼女の長い髪は風に波打っていた.
Q *axillary* and *pubic hair* わき毛と陰毛. ¶Her *hair* was *black* and *glossy* as the raven's wing. 彼女の髪はからすの羽のように黒くてつやつやしていた. ¶*blonde hair* ブロンドの髪. ¶*Bobbed hair* is not passé. 断髪はまだ盛りを過ぎてはいない. 【類】*Bobbed hair* was then quite the fashion (=go, *colloq.*). ¶*bristly hair* こわい毛. ¶*brown hair* かっ色の髪. ¶*clotted hair* [油で]固めた髪. ¶*coarse hair* あらい髪. ¶*crisp* (=*curly*) *hair* 縮れ毛. ¶*cropped hair* 坊主頭. ¶*curled hair* 縮らせた髪. ¶*dark hair* 黒い髪. ¶*dishevelled hair* 乱れ髪 ‖ Her *hair* was all *dishevelled*. 彼女の髪はとても乱れていた. ¶*downy hair* うぶ毛. ¶Most film stars have *dyed hair*. 映画スターはたいてい髪を染めている. ¶a woman with glossy *fair hair* つやのよいブロンドの髪の女. ¶a person with *falling hair* 髪が薄くなって来た人. ¶wear *false hair* 入毛をしている. ¶a *few stray hairs* 二三本どうかして生えた毛. ¶*fine hair* 見事な髪. ¶*flaxen hair* 麻色の髪. ¶*frizzled hair* 縮らせた髪. ¶His *hair* is slightly *frosted*. 彼の髪は少し白くなった. ¶*fuzzy hair* 縮れ毛. ¶*golden hair* 金髪. ¶They have *good* and *profuse hair* on the head. 彼らはりっぱな房々とした髪をしている. ¶*Gray hair* is called "the flowers of the grave." 白髪は「墓の花」と言われている. ¶There is not a *gray hair* on his head. 彼は白髪一本もない. ‖ She is a dark woman with *grey curly hair*. 彼女は色の黒い女で白髪の縮れた毛をしている. ¶*grizzled hair* 白髪交りの髪. ¶She has very *heavy hair*. 彼女は随分髪の毛が多い. ¶a youth with *hoary hair* 老書生. ¶a young woman with the *jetblack hair* 真黒な髪をした若い女. ¶*kinky hair* 縮れた髪. ¶*lank hair* [縮れてない]しなやかな髪. ¶*light hair* 淡い色の髪. ¶*light auburn hair* 薄あか色の髪. ¶*long* and *flowing hair* 波打つ長髪. ¶The boy has *long, lint-white hair*. その少年は白味かかった麻色の長い髪をしている. ¶Three *more* white *hairs!* また三本しらがができたわい! ¶have *permed hair* 《米俗》髪にパーマをかけている. ¶*peroxide hair* 過酸化水素で赤くした髪. ¶*platinum-dyed hair* プラチナ染の髪. ¶with no other headcovering than their own *plenteous hair* 房々した髪の外にはなにも頭にかぶらないで. ¶the *pompadour hair* of a Japanese woman 日本の女の結ったポンパドゥール巻. ¶*raven black hair* 真黒な髪. ¶*red hair* 赤毛 *cf.* a redhead 《米》赤毛の女. ¶*rusty hair* さび色の髪. ¶*silky hair* 絹のような髪. ¶*silvery hair* 銀髪. ¶*sleek hair* つやのある髪. ¶*smooth hair* なめらかな髪. ¶*snow-white hair* 真白い髪. ¶*soft hair* 軟かい髪. ¶*spare hair* 薄い髪. ¶Whiskers are *stiff hairs*, that grow on a man's face. ほおひげは顔に生える固い毛である. ¶*straight hair* 直毛. ¶*tungled hair* 乱れ髪. ¶*thick hair* 濃い髪. ¶*thin hair* 薄い髪. ¶*tousled hair* もつれ髪. ¶a woman with her *hair undone* 髪を乱した女. ¶*waveless hair* パーマをかけていない髪. ¶*wavy hair* 波形の髪. ¶*well-groomed hair* よく手入れしてある髪. ¶He has *white hair*. 彼は白髪頭だ. ¶*woolly hair* 羊毛のような髪. ¶*yellow hair* 黄色い髪.
Q² *glass hair* ガラス繊維で造った髪. ¶have sharp *leaf hairs* [葉に]とがった針毛がある.
P seize one *by* the *hair* 人の髪をつかむ. ¶He lost the game *by* a *hair*. 彼は間一髪で勝を逸した. ¶with a flower *in* her *hair* 髪に花をさして. ¶He has a thick (thin) growth *of hair*. 彼は濃い(薄い)髪をしている. ¶The fate of the nation hung *on* a *hair*. 国家の存亡が危機一髪の所だった. ¶examine the matter *to* a *hair* その事件を微細に調べる. ¶a youth *with* hoary *hair* 髪は白いが気は若い人; 若白髪の人. 【類】*with* her *hair* in pig-tails (お下げ).
P² People wore their *hair in* queues in those days. その時分はべん髪にしていた. ¶a *hair of* the axilla submitted to the microscope 顕微鏡にかけられたわきの下の毛. ¶*hair on* the head (chest, face) 頭(など)の毛.

haircut, *n.* 散髪.
V *get* a *haircut* 髪をかってもらう.

hair-do, *n.* 《米》結髪.
Q a *modern* (*classic*) *hair-do* 最近(古典的な)髪型.

hair-splitting, *n.* 小理屈.
Q *mere hair-splitting* へ理屈. ¶Such *hair-splitting* is *worthy* of the metaphysics of the school-men. こんな小

理屈は実際にうとい学者のやることだ.

half, *n.* 半分.

V *cry halves* with one 相手に自分と半分わけにせよという. ¶*spend half* of it その半分を費す.

Q one's *better half* よき半身(すなわち「妻」) ¶the *complementary half* of an integral whole 全体の片側半分. ¶in the *first half* of the century その始めの半世紀に ‖ the *first* (*second*) *half* of the last inning 〖野球〗最後の回の表(裏). ¶the *first* (*second*) *half* of the task その仕事の前(後)半. ¶the *fairer half* of the nation 国民の大半. ¶in the *former* (*latter*) *half* of the eighteenth century 十八世紀の前半(後半)に. ¶40 years, the *larger half* of a man's life 人の一生の大半たる四十年. ¶an account of one's *past half* 半生記. ¶a *return half* of a return ticket 往復切符の復の方. ¶The *second half* of the programme was devoted to a cinema show. 余興は映画であった. ¶*Two halves* make a whole. 半分が二つで一つになる.

P I bought it *at half* its value. 私はそれを半値で買った. ¶cut down the expenditure *by half* その経費を半減する. She is too clever *by half*. 彼女は少し器用すぎる. ‖ too long (much) *by half* 半分だけ長(多)すぎる ‖ He did not do things *by halves*. 彼は物事を中途半端にしなかった. 【類】reduce *by half* the number of ... / reduce railway fares *by half*. ¶cut it *in half* それを半分に切る ‖ The party is likely to split *in half*. その党派は二派に分裂しそうだ. ¶divide it *into halves* それを二つに分ける. 【類】split *into* two *halves*.

P² *half for* fun 面白半分に. ¶About a *half of* the crop has been marketed. その作物の約半分は市場に出された. ¶devote *half of* one's time to ... その時間の半分を…に当てる. ¶say *half to* oneself だれにいうともなく言う.

O a mile and a *half*=one and a half mile 一マイル半. 【類】two pounds and a *half*=two and a half pounds.

half-dead, *a.* 半死半生の.

P be *half-dead with* cold 寒さで死にかかっている.

half-full, *a.* 半ば入った.

P a bottle *half-full of* whisky ウイスキーが半分残っているびん.

half-holiday, *n.* 半休, 半ドン.

V Students were *given* a *half-holiday*. 学生たちは半日休をもらった.

Q² a *school half-holiday* 学校の半ドン日.

half-hour, *n.* 半時間.

V *snatch* a *half-hour* of sleep in a car 車の中で三十分の睡眠を取る.

half-mast, *n.* ハーフ・マスト.

P fly a flag *at half-mast* 半旗を掲げる.

half-price, *n.* 半額.

P Children are allowed to travel *at half-price*. 子供は汽車賃は半額でいい.

O Children *half-price*. 〖掲示〗子供は半額.

hall, *n.* 会館, 広間.

Q a *bachelor's hall* 独身者の家. ¶a great *baronial hall* 大広間. ¶a *lofty hall* 天井の高い会館. ¶a *residential hall* for students 学生の寄宿舎. ¶a *servants' hall* 召使いのたまりべや.

Q² an *assembly hall* 集会室; [市会の]会議室; [学校の]講堂. ¶a *banquet hall* 会食食堂. ¶a *concert hall* 演奏会場. ¶a *county hall* 《米》郡役所. ¶a *dining hall* 食堂. ¶a *discussion hall* 談話室. ¶*drill hall* (boy scouts などの) 道場. ¶the *eating hall* at an American college アメリカの大学の食堂. ¶an *entrance hall* 玄関先, [ホテルの]ロビー. ¶a home goods *exhibition hall* 国産品陳列場(展示会場). ¶a *lecture hall* 講堂. ¶a *meeting hall* 集会場. ¶a *mess hall* 〖軍〗食堂. ¶cheap *music hall* 安もののショー劇場, 寄席. 【類】King of the Paris *music halls* (Maurice Chevalier) (ショー劇場の王様) / The first public demonstrations of jujitsu in England were given on the London *music halls* by two Japanese exponents (日本の専門家). ¶a *recreation hall* for employees 社員の娯楽室. ¶a *residence hall* 学校の寄宿舎. ¶the Sample Exhibition *Hall* 商工振興館. ¶a *town hall* 町役場; 町会議事堂. ¶ the *YMCA Hall* キリスト教青年会館.

P The lectures are to be delivered *at* the *Hall*. その講演は大講堂で催される. ¶There were over 2,000 people *in* the *hall*. その会館には二千人以上の人が集まっていた.

hall-mark, *n.* 刻印; 特徴.

Q an *infallible hall-mark* of American speech 米人の言葉を示す間違いのない刻印.

P² Courtesy and self-control are the *hall-marks of* a gentleman. 礼儀と自制は紳士の特徴(資格)である.

halloo, *interj.*, *n.* 大声でどなること.

V *call out* (=*shout*) "*halloo*" to ... …に大声で叫かける. ¶*give* a laud *halloo* 大声をあげる.

halloo, *v.* 大声に呼ぶ.

P *halloo after* (=*to*) a person 人に大声で呼びかけて注意する.

halo, *n.* かさ, 後光.

V *paint haloes* around the heads of ... …の頭の周りに後光を描く.

P² There is a sort of *halo of* sanctity surrounding the word. その言葉には一種の神聖な後光が取巻いている. ¶a *halo round* the sun 太陽の光輪.

halt, *n.* 停止, 休息.

V places by the wayside where a *halt* can be *called* for refreshments either solid or liquid 飲食物を取るためにとまる路傍の場所 ‖ It is time to *call* a *halt*. もうだまっているべきでない(やめさせなくてはいけない). ‖ He hoped the House would not consent to *call* a *halt*. 彼は下院が停会の要求に応じないことを希望した. ¶It is time to *cry halt!* 止れと号令をかけてよいときである. ¶the steamer *makes* a *halt* (=stops *or* call) at ... その汽船は…に寄港する. 【類】the party (caravan) *made* a *halt* at ...

Q The war came to a *temporary halt*. 戦争が一時休止された.

Q² make our *midday halt* 正午の休みをする.

P The train came *to* a *halt*. 列車が(一時)停車した. ‖ bring the horse *to* a *halt* 馬をとめさせる.

halt, *v.* 留まる.

M *Halt there!* とまれ.

P *halt* two days *at* ... 二日間…に留まる. ¶our train *halted between* ... われわれの列車は…間で立往生をした. ¶*halt between* two opinions 二つの意見に迷う. ¶*halt for* breath 息をつくために立どまる ‖ *halt for* the night 一晩泊る ‖ fail to *halt for* a stop sign at an intersection 交差点の赤信号に対しストップしない. ¶"Neither the Sun nor the Moon," says an old Japanese proverb "ever *halt upon* their journey." 「月日に関守なし」という日本の古い諺がある.

ham, *n. pl.* もも, ひかがみ; ハム; 《俗》しろうと.

Q² a *radio ham* アマチュア放送(通信)士.

P a slice *of ham* ハム一切れ. ¶sit *on* one's *hams*=squat ひざを折ってすわる.

Hamlet, *n.* ハムレット.

Q a sort of *French Hamlet* 一種のフランス式ハムレット.

P It would be *Hamlet with* the Prince of Denmark left out. それでは主人公抜きの芝居(骨抜き)になってしまう.

hammer, *n.* つち, 金づち(ハンマー).

V *use* a *hammer* to crack nuts 木の実をわるためにつちを使う. ¶*wield* the *hammer* of Thor 戦争する.

Q a *wooden hammer* 木づち.

Q² a *gas hammer* ガス・ハンマー. ¶a *hand hammer* 手ハンマー. ¶a *power hammer* 動力ハンマー. ¶a *sledge hammer* [製鉄所の]大ハンマー. ¶a smithy *steam hammer* かじ屋の蒸気ハンマー.

P come (=go) *under* the *hammer* at ... …で競売になる. 【類】His collection was dispersed *under* the *hammer* (=by auction). / It was sold for £100 *under* the *hammer*. ¶strike *with* a *hammer* つちで打つ.

hammer, *v.* つちで打つ; よく働く.

M The guns are *hammering away* 銃がぽんぽん発射している. ‖ *hammer away* at one's classwork 学校の勉強をこつこつやる ‖ *hammer away* at a dictionary 辞書と首引きをする. ¶*hammer out* thin たたいて薄くのばす ‖ *hammer out* a draft constitution for an institute ある学会の規則の草案を練って作る.

P *hammer at* the door ドアをどんどんたたく. 【類】Perry *hammered at* Japan's gates in 1853. ‖ *hammer at* a typewriter タイプライターを打つ. ¶*hammer in* a nail くぎを打ち込む. ¶*hammer* the idea *into* his head その思想を彼の頭にたたき込む ‖ *hammer* gold *into* thin leaves 金を薄く打ちのばす. ¶desperately *hammer on* a typewriter タイプライターをやけにたたく.

hammer-blow, *n.* ハンマーの一撃.

P It came *like* a *hammer-blow*. それはハンマーの一撃のように突然やってきた.

hammock, *n.* つり床(ハンモック).

V *lash* a *hammock* ハンモックをたたむ. ¶A *hammock* was

slung across the darker corner of the room. 一つのハンモックが暗いへやのすみにつるされた.

P sleep ***in*** a ***hammock*** ハンモックに寝る.

hand, *n.* 手, 人手; 筆跡; 求婚; 時計の針.

V ***accept*** one's ***hand*** 求婚を承諾する. ¶Some teachers are in favor of ***allowing*** a free ***hand.*** 教師の中には生徒を放任することを可とするものもある. ¶***amputate*** his right ***hand*** 彼の右手を切断する. ¶***ask*** (=***beg***) his daughter's ***hand*** in marriage 娘に求婚する. 【類】 ***ask*** the ***hand*** of ... in marriage. ¶***assume*** the controlling ***hand.*** 局に当る. ¶***bear*** a ***hand*** 手伝いをする. ¶***beckon*** one's ***hand*** to him to come back 戻れと彼に手招きをする. ¶He will later ***bless*** the ***hand*** which has chastised him. 彼は自分を苦しめた人をやがては感謝するだろう. ¶***bring*** one's ***hand*** to salute 手をあげてあいさつする. ¶***burn*** one's ***hand*** 手をやけどする. ¶***hands calloused*** by labor 労働でたこのできた手. ¶***catch*** his ***hand***=catch him by the hand 彼の手を取る. ¶***chafe*** one's ***hands*** 手をさすって暖める. ¶The house has ***changed hands.*** その家は持主が変った. 【類】 the hotel ***changed hands,*** being taken over by ... / It has ***changed hands*** at about £150. / ***changed hands*** for prices below ... (...以下で売買). ¶***claim*** her ***hand*** in the dance 彼女にダンスの相手を当然のこととして求める. ¶***clap hands*** over ears 両手で耳をはさみ打ちする ‖ ***clap*** one's ***hands*** with delight 喜んで拍手する. 【類】 They ***clapped*** their ***hands*** heartily. / pull the temple bell and ***clap*** his ***hands*** to ensure that the Gods hear the short muttered prayer and put to his credit the half-farthings he bestows. ¶***clasp hands*** with ... と固く手を握る ‖ ***clasp*** the right ***hand*** of his bride 自分の花嫁の右手を握る. ¶***clench*** (=***clinch***) the ***hand*** 手をしっかりと握り固める. ¶strike with a ***hand closed*** こぶしで打つ. ¶***cut*** onc's ***hand*** with a knife ナイフで手を切る. ¶She ***declined*** his ***hand.*** 彼女は彼の求婚を断わった. ¶The sharp eyes of critics can soon ***detect*** the amateur ***hand.*** 批評家の鋭い目にはしろうとは隠せない. ¶He ***dug*** his ***hands*** into his pocket, and started off. 彼は両手をポケットに突込んで歩きだした. ¶***distend*** one's ***hand*** 手をさしのべる. ¶I ***dried*** my ***hands*** and face with a towel. 私はタオルで手と顔をふいた. ¶The factory ***employs*** some 12,000 ***hands*** constantly, representing a weekly wage bill of £20,000. 同工場はおよそ一万二千の使用人を常用しその週給が二万ポンドになる. ¶***extend*** one's ***hand*** cordially for handshaking ねんごろに手を差しのべて握手を求める ‖ ***extend*** a helping ***hand*** to ... ...に援助を与える. ¶***fold*** one's ***hands*** patiently waiting for this miracle to pass 手を組み合わせてこの奇跡の消滅するのを気長く待つ. ¶A crowd of foreign princelings aspire to ***gain*** her ***hand.*** 多数の外国の小公子たちが彼女をものにしたがっている. 【類】 wooed a village maiden and ***gained*** her ***hand*** (うんと言わせた). ‖ ***gain*** the upper ***hand*** 勝利を得る. ¶A pickpocket ***got*** his ***hand*** into my pocket. すりが私のポケットに手を入れた. ‖ ***Get*** your ***hand*** off me. 手を離してくれ(手を掛けたのを怒って). ‖ I read everything I can ***get*** my ***hands*** on. 私は手当り次第に読む. ¶She ***gave*** me her ***hand.*** [求婚したら]彼女はうんと承知した. ¶Rare books should be handled after one's ***hands*** are carefully ***gloved.*** 珍本は用意周到に手袋をはめてから取扱うのが本当だ. ¶***grab*** one's ***hand*** しっかり手を握る. ¶***grasp hands*** and say farewell 手を握って別れを告げる. ¶***grip*** the offered ***hands*** 差出された手を握る. ¶He was seized with a desire to ***have*** a ***hand*** in the business. 彼はその仕事に仲間入りをしたいと思い込んだ. 【類】 I ***had*** no ***hand*** in the business. ‖ ***have*** one's ***hands full*** 手一杯だ. 【類】 The editor and staff ***had*** their ***hands*** too ***full*** to undertake it. ¶He ***held*** her ***hand*** in his. 彼は自分の手で彼女の手を握った. ¶***hire*** new ***hands*** 新規に人を入れる. ¶***hold out*** a ***hand*** of sympathy 手を差しのべ(握手を求め)て同情を示す ‖ ***hold out*** one's ***hands*** 両手を差出す. ¶***Hold*** 'em (=them) ***up***! [ギャングが]ホールダップ! ‖ he ***held up*** his ***hands*** in horror when he heard that ... ...だと聞いて彼は恐怖のあまり両手をあげた. 【類】 ***hold up hands*** of horror at ... / ***hold up*** one's ***hands*** in surrender (despair) 降参すると(絶望のあまり)手をあげる. ¶***immerge*** one's ***hand*** into the boiling water 熱湯に片手を突込む. ¶***introduce*** one's ***hand*** into a woman's armpit 女のわき下へ手を入れる. ¶Yokohama is the place where Japan and America first ***joined hands.*** 横浜は日米が最初に手をつないだ地である. 【類】 The East and West have ***joined hands*** in Japan. / Science and industry have ***joined hands.*** / ***join hands*** with ... / ***join hands*** to destroy... ‖ ***join hands*** in brotherhood 仲よく手を握る(協力する). 【類】 ***join hands*** in an effort ‖ ***join*** one's ***hands*** 合掌する. ¶***keep*** one's ***hand*** in ... ...との関係を続ける ‖ just to ***keep*** the ***hands busy*** ほんの手持ぶさたに ‖ It is wise for the Government to ***keep*** its ***hand*** off the affair. その事件には政府は干渉しない方が得策だ. ¶I ***know*** his ***hand*** very well. 私は彼の筆跡をよく知っている. ¶***lay*** one's ***hands*** on the pertinent documents without delay 直ちに適当な書類に手を入れる ‖ The thief ran away with some valuables that he could ***lay hands*** on. 賊は手当り次第に金目の物を持って逃げ出した. ‖ ***lay*** one's ***hands*** on the culprits その犯人を捕える ‖ I ***laid*** my ***hand*** upon the latch of death's portal. 私は棺をけに片足突っ込んだ. 【類】 Loss of time and temper may be avoided if one knows when to ***lay hands,*** at a moment's notice, upon the article wanted. / He bought up every pamphlet of the kind that he could ***lay*** his ***hands*** on (手当り次第). ¶We haven't ***laid off*** any ***hands*** yet. われわれの所ではまだ人減らしはしていない. ¶***lend*** a ***hand*** to make ... ...するために手を貸す. ¶Dogs are fond of ***licking*** one's ***hands.*** 犬は手をなめたがる. ¶***lift*** one's ***hands*** with astonishment at the very idea その思いつきに驚いて両手を挙げる ‖ ***lift*** a ***hand*** against one's master 主人に反抗する. ¶***need*** the friendly ***hand*** of guidance 親切な指導者を要する. ¶***offer*** one's ***hand*** for hand-shaking 握手のため手を差出す. ¶***oil*** a person's ***hand*** (=palm) 人にそっと金をつかませる. ¶***open*** one's ***hand*** 指をひろげる. ¶***pass*** one's ***hand*** across one's forehead 額に十字を切る. ¶***place*** one's ***hands*** on one's breast 胸に両手を当てる. 【類】 ***place*** one's ***hand*** on the table. ¶He ***possesses*** a pleasing running ***hand.*** 彼は感じのよい草書体の字を書く. ¶***press*** her ***hand*** sympathetically 同情して彼女の手を握りしめる. 【類】 "I am delighted to see you," said she, ***pressing*** my ***hand*** warmly. ¶***put*** one's ***hand*** behind one's ear to catch what is going to be said 言うことを聞きもらさないように耳の後へ手をやる ‖ Everything to which he ***puts*** his ***hand*** is good. 彼のやるものなら何でもできがよい. ‖ She ***put*** her ***hand*** on the door knob. 彼女はドアの握りに手をかけた. 【類】 There is system (休系) about everything he ***puts*** his ***hands*** to. / She ***put*** her ***hand*** tenderly on his shoulder. / ***put*** one's ***hand*** in one's pocket to pay for it / The newspaper writer must know where to ***put*** his ***hand*** on for an apt quotation. ¶She ***put out*** her ***hand*** towards me. 彼女は私の方に手を差しのべた. ¶***put up*** one's ***hand*** with a rush [生徒などが]あわてて手をあげる. ¶***raise*** one's ***hand*** as if about to strike 今にもなぐらんばかりに手をあげる ‖ ***raise*** one's ***hand*** against ... =try to beat ... ...をなぐろうとして手をあげる; ...を大いに非難する ‖ ***raise*** one's ***hand*** to heaven 天に向って手をあげる. 【類】 ***raise*** one's ***hand*** as a signal to the teacher when one has finished. ¶***reach*** [one's ***hand***] for ... ...の方に手をのばす. ¶***reach out*** a ***hand*** 手をのばす. ¶***refuse*** her ***hand*** (女が)求婚を謝絶する. ¶***rinse*** the ***hands*** 手を洗う. ¶***rub*** one's ***hands*** with glee 喜んでもみ手をする ‖ ***rub*** one's ***hands*** nervously together / ***rub*** one's ***hands*** together to get warm / He ***rubbed*** his numbed ***hands*** together and blew upon his fingers. ¶All ***hands*** were ***saved.*** 全員助かった. ¶***set*** the ***hands*** forward (backwards) 時計の針を進める(遅らす) ‖ ***set*** one's ***hand*** [and seal] to the document その書類に署名する ‖ ***set*** one's ***hand*** on (=upon) ... ...の仕事に着手する ‖ ***set*** [***hand***] to two undertakings 二つの仕事に手を着ける. ¶***set back*** the ***hands*** of progress 進行を阻止する(逆行させる). ¶***shake hands*** warmly with ... 熱心に...と握手する. 【類】 ***shake*** the ***hand*** of another / The custom of ***shaking hands*** after meals is unknown in England. ¶He ***shoved*** his ***hands*** deep into his trousers' pockets. 彼は両手をズボンのポケットに深く突込んだ. ¶***show*** their ***hands*** in a decisive matter はっきりと挙手をもって賛意を表する. ¶***shut*** one's ***hand*** 自分の手を握る. ¶***smut*** one's ***hands*** with coal 石炭で手をよごす. ¶***squeeze*** one's ***hand*** 人の手を握り縮める. ¶***stick up*** one's ***hands*** 両手をあげる. ☞ギャングがピストルを突

きつけて Stick 'em (=them) up! という. ¶*stretch* a helping *hand* to ... ...に救いの手を差しのべる. ¶*strike hands* 契約する, 手を打つ. ¶The work *suggests* an unpracticed *hand*. その作品は未熟という感じを与える. ¶*take* a *hand* in the matter そのことに関係する. ¶She *took* his *hand* warmly in hers. 彼女は彼の片手を自分の両手で固く握った. ¶*throw up hands* 両手を投げるようにあげる. ¶*thrust* one's *hand* into one's pocket 片手をポケットに突込む. ¶*tie* one's *hands together* behind one 両手を後に組む. ¶The *hand* of a master can easily be *traced* in the picture. その絵を見ると名人の作だということが分かる. ¶*try* one's *hand* at literary composition 文章道に指を染める. 【類】*try* one's *hand* at fiction (writing a play) / *try* one's *hand* unsuccessfully at journalism. / *try* one's *hand* at reform (改革) / after *trying* his *hand* at various callings (職業) / Stevenson *tried* his *hand* occasionally on the composition of fables. ¶He can *turn* his *hand* successfully to any kind of work. ¶*unglove* the *hand* 手袋をぬぐ. ¶*use* one's *hands* awkwardly 手を不器用に使う. ¶*Warm* your *hands* a bit at the fire 火で少し手を暖めなさい. ¶*wash* one's *hands* before lunch 昼食前に手を洗う ‖ *wash* one's *hands* with soap and water 石けんで手を洗う. ¶He *washed* his *hands* of the business. 彼はその仕事から手を引いた. 【類】I have *washed* my *hands* of all the share in the transaction. ¶He *waved* his *hand* at some acquaintances in the crowd. 彼は群集中二三の知人を認めこれに手を振ってあいさつした. ‖ There virgin soil *waves* its *hands* (=beckons) to us. そこには処女地が手を振ってわれわれの開拓を待っている. ¶He *wrung* his *hand* and congratulated him on his epoch-making feat. 彼の手を握りしめてその画期的な功績に対して祝辞を述べた. ¶stand *wringing* one's *hands* [心に苦しみがあるので]両手を握りしめながら立つ. 【類】tear one's hair and *wring* one's *hands*. ¶They *write hands* that are plain and legible. 彼らは分りよくて読みやすい文字を書く. ‖ He *writes* a very bad *hand*. あの人は金くぎ流だ.

v² The *hand* of the clock is *creeping* on to the half hour. 時計の針が徐々に進んで半になる. ¶The *hand* of the clock *goes round*. 時計の針が回る. ¶The girl's *hand shot up*. その少女はあわただしく手をあげた.

Q He writes an *abominable* (=a very bad) *hand*. 彼は実に悪筆だ. ¶one hears nothing but praise on *all hands* for... だれでも...をほめないものはない ‖ it seems to be allowed on *all hands* that ... 一般に...と認められているようだ. ¶an *all-accomplished hand* 円熟した腕(の人). ¶The task of writing fuller history I leave to *apter hands*. 一層完備した歴史を記述する仕事は私よりもっと適当な人にまかせる. ¶Wars are not waged with *bare hands*. から手では戦争はできない. ¶The copies are in the *binders' hands*. その本は今製本中である. ¶a *bold, frank, back hand* 大胆で率直な左かしぎの筆跡. ¶*casual hands* 臨時に働く人. ¶a *competent hand* 有能な働き手. 【類】Each chapter of the book is intrusted to a *competent hand*. ‖ a *competent guiding hand* 有能な指導の手. ¶written in a *contemporary hand* その時代の手跡で書いた. ¶a *cramped hand* いじけた手跡. ¶a sumptuous feast prepared under the *cunning hands* of the *chef de cuisine* 料理長のさえた腕で調理された山海の珍味. ¶a letter written in a *delicate female hand* 優美な女文字で書かれた手紙. ¶essays by *diverse hands* 色々な人の手になる随筆. ¶a nervous excitable wife, permanently under the *doctor's hands* 始終医者の手にかかっている神経質で興奮しやすい妻. ¶a street with shops on *either hand* 両側に店のある町. ¶We detect the *erring hand* of the lay writer in almost every paragraph. ほとんど各段にしろうとのやる誤りが見られる. ¶It is to be seen on *every hand*. それはいたる所に見られる. 【類】On *every hand* there would appear to be indications and assurances of better times in the strictly commercial sense. ¶after several years of carefully training at his *experienced hands* 彼の老練な腕で数年間みっちり仕込まれてから. ¶He is a *famous hand* at such a work. 彼はこの種のことにかけては評判の腕ききだ. ¶a good *farm hand* よく働く作男. ¶a *fine* (*large*) *hand* 細(大)字の筆跡. ¶study the subject at *first* (*second*) *hand* 直接(間接)にその問題を研究する. 【類】He is acquainted at *first hand* with things Western. / a knowledge obtained at *first hand* / investigate, at *first hand*, into ... / see things at *first hand*. ¶with *folded hands* 手をこまぬいて. ¶be in *fraudulent hands* 不正者の所有となっている. ¶He is given a *free hand*. 彼は自由行動を許されている. ¶My *hands* are *full*.=I have full hands. 私は手が一杯だ. ¶He entered the firm as a *general hand*. 彼は一般事務員として入社した. ¶The matter was dealt with by a *gentle hand*. その事件は情のある取扱方をした. ¶extend the *glad hand* of welcome to ... 喜ばしい歓迎の手を...に差しのべる. ¶*gnarled hands* 節高の手. ¶write a *good hand* 字がうまい ‖ He is a *good* (*poor*) *hand* at chess. 彼はチェスがうまい(へただ). ¶mechanics with *greasy hands* 油で汚れた手の工員たち. ¶a *green hand* 青二才. ¶The *grim hand* of consumption clutched at his life. 肺病の恐ろしい手が彼の生命をつかもうとした. ¶with a *high hand* 高飛車に出て. ¶As a mistress she carries matters with a *high hand*. 彼女は主婦として家の中をかき回す. ¶a *heavily-ringed hand* やたらに指輪をはめた手. ¶give him a *helping hand* 彼に手を貸す. 【類】A *helping hand* was extended to me. / a kind boy with a *helping hand* for the smallest fry (一番小さな子) / lend a *helping hand* to the cause (その主義). ¶a *horny hand* ごつごつした手. ¶a very *illegible hand* 非常に読みにくい筆跡. ¶The work was plainly executed by *inferior hands*. その作品はたしかに腕のない者の製作だ. ¶a *junior hand* 若い職工. ¶written in a *juvenile hand* 子供の筆跡で書いた. ¶expend money with a *lavish hand* 金を湯水のように使う. ¶He sat close on my *left hand*. 彼は私のすぐ左手にすわった. ¶write a *legible hand* 字をはっきり書く. ¶Engels had a *lighter hand* with the pen than Marx. エンゲルスはマルクスより筆が軽妙だ. ¶turn the *minute hand* [時計の]分針を回す. ¶a *moist hand* 油っ手. ¶*national hand* 一国民の書体. ¶a *new hand* 新米, 新手. ¶I am *no hand* at describing costumes. 僕は服装の解説は苦手だ. ¶He is an *old hand* at the game. 彼はその道の老練家だ. ¶... on the *one hand*, and on the other ... 一方には...そして他方には... ¶slap with the *open hand* 平手でぴしゃりと打つ. ¶A good companion with an *open hand* to people in distress. 不幸な人々を快く迎えるよい友. ¶His trade is certainly more lucrative than mine, but, on the *other hand*, more risky. あの人の商売はなるほど私のよりもうけは多いがまた危険も一層多い. ¶written in his *own hand* 自書した. ¶a *plain, clear hand* 読みやすい明りょうな筆跡. ¶The issue was then in the *printer's hands*. [雑誌の]その号は当時印刷中であった. ¶The manufactory was started (=taken up) by the State and carried on till ..., when it reverted into *private hands*. その製造所は政府に買上げられその手で経営されていたが...になって再び民業になった. ¶*pudgy hands* 《俗》短くって太った手. ¶The author placed on the raw material his *quickening hand*. 著者は材料を生かして使った. ¶The money will be deposited in *responsible hands*. その金は責任ある人に預ける. ¶his *right hand* 彼の片腕. 【類】On Marshal Oyama's *right hand* sat General Kodama, "the Japanese Kitchener," who was literally Oyama's right-hand man in every sense. 【類】sit at his *right hand* / The book should be kept at the *right hand* (座右におく) of every student of English. ¶with her own *royal hand* 女王自ら. ¶buy at *second hand* 古手を買う ‖ hear (borrow) at *second hand* また聞き(借り)する ‖ a watch with a *second hand* 秒針付懐中時計. ¶a work of *several hands* 数人の合作. ¶*shapely hands* 格好のよい手. ¶*snow-white hands* 真白い手. ¶give with a *sparing hand* 控え目に金を出す(出し惜む). ¶a *splendid hand* 達筆. ¶handle the matter with a *steady hand* しっかりした態度でその事件を取扱う. ¶The affair is controlled by a *stronger hand* than chance, providence. その事件は偶然よりはもっと手強い力すなわち天の摂理によって支配されている. 【類】unless managed by a *strong hand*. ¶We have not *sufficient hands*. 手が足りない. ¶The company is safe so long as it is led with so *sure* a *hand*. かくまでにしっかりした首脳者がある限りその会社は安全だ. ¶be admirably portrayed by a *sympathetic hand* 好意のある人の手でりっぱに描写されている. ¶a *thick* (*thin*) *hand* 肉太の(細い)筆跡. ¶The English version has been made by an *unknown hand*. その英訳は無名の人の手になった. ¶The piano was played by ***unseen hands***. ピアノは見えない者(幽霊)がひいた. ¶gain (=get) the ***upper hand*** 高飛車に出る, 優位に立つ ‖ He has the ***upper hand*** of the whole school. 彼は学校を切って回わす. ‖ Those brilliant rogues got the ***upper hand*** of the whole of the police in Paris. ¶The compilation was translated by ***various hands***. その編集物は色々な人の手で翻訳された. ¶receive a visitor with ***warm hands*** 訪問客を手厚く迎える. ¶The stock is large and in ***weak hands***. 在庫品は多量で売は弱気だ. ¶men and women of honest hearts and ***willing hands*** 真心があって進んでことに従う男女.

Q² a missing Japanese in ***Communist hands*** 共産党の手に落ちたゆくえ不明の日本人. ¶a ***deck hand*** 船荷係の水夫. ¶***dockyard hands*** ドックの職工たち. ¶one of the King's subjects in ***enemy hands*** 敵の手中に落ちた英国民の一人. ¶a ***factory hand*** 職工, 工員. ¶hire ***farm hands*** 農家の手伝(作男)を頼む. ¶scarcity of ***field hands*** 野良の手不足. ¶keep a ***firm hand*** on ... ...をがっちり握っている(支配している). ¶***Harvest hands*** are scarce. とり入れの手が足りない. ¶an ***hour*** (a ***minute, second***) ***hand*** [時計の]時(分, 秒)針. ¶the ***iron hand*** of fate 運命の鉄手(冷酷) ‖ possess an ***iron hand*** requisite in a hero 英雄に必要なくろがねの手(強力)を持つ ‖ One must have an ***iron hand*** gloved in velvet for the treatment of the psychoneurosis. 精神病院は鬼手仏心を必要とする. ¶a ***kitchen hand*** 台所働き. ¶a ***machine hand***=a mechanic 機械工. ¶a ***ranch hand*** =a ranchman《米》牧場労働者. ¶the Chinese ***running hand*** 草書 ‖ The ***running hand*** is something between the square and grass forms. 行書はかい書と草書の中間である. ‖ the Japanese ***running hand*** 平仮名. ¶a ***school-copy-book hand*** 学校の習字の手本のような筆跡. ¶"supers" and ***stage hands***〘劇〙エキストラと舞台係.

P The opening of the yachting season is near ***at hand***. ヨットのシーズンの始まるのも間近だ. ‖ Linguists are ***at hand*** to interpret the wishes of patrons. 外国語の分かるものがいて御客様の御希望を通訳いたします. ‖ Your kind information is ***at*** (=to) ***hand***. 御親切なお通知を落手致しました. ¶have ***at hand*** for assistance a reference book 参考書を座右におく ‖ I feel grateful for the kindness and attention received ***at*** his ***hand***. 私は彼から受けた好意と親切に対して感謝している. 【類】We need an English dictionary constantly ***at hand***. / Patients may be sure of the finest treatment possible ***at*** the ***hands*** of highly skilled doctors and nurses. / Graduating students receive their diplomas ***at*** the ***hands*** of the Chancellor (大学総長). ¶The letter was delivered ***by hand***. その手紙は手ずから渡された. ‖ lead a person ***by*** the ***hand*** 人の手を引く ‖ a brief memoir ***by*** the ***hand*** of his son 彼の息子によって書かれた短かい回想録 ‖ fill the blank ***by hand*** 余白に書入れる ‖ The twins were brought up ***by hand*** (on cow's milk). 双生児は親の乳(牛乳)で育った. ‖ die ***by*** one's own ***hand*** 自殺する ‖ essays ***by*** many ***hands*** 作者様々な随筆 ‖ They have this ignorance ***by*** the ***hand*** of God. 彼らは生れつきこの点は無知である. 【類】This building was largely built ***by*** the ***hands*** of Cornellians (コーネル大学出身者). / fantastic stones fashioned ***by*** the ***hand*** of time (自然の手). ¶wrestle it ***from*** his ***hand*** 彼の手からそれを強奪する ‖ Purchases are being made only ***from hand*** to mouth. 買入れは差当りの入用だけに限られている. ‖ I had spent all money in my possession and rubbed on ***from hand*** to mouth. 私は金を残らず使ってしまったのでその日暮しという有様であった. ‖ transmit it ***from hand*** to hand それを手から手へ渡す ‖ The book contains illustrative sketches ***from*** his ***hand***. その本は著者の自画がさし絵になっている. ¶go out, cane ***in hand*** ステッキ片手に出かける ‖ cash ***in hand***=ready money 手もとの現金 ‖ balance ***in hand*** 30th Nov., 1918 一九一八年十一月三十日現在手もと残高 ‖ the orders ***in hand*** 調達中の注文 ‖ the business ***in hand*** やっている仕事. 【類】finish the work ***in hand*** / I have work ***in hand***. / It is hoped that the work will soon be put ***in hand*** (=set on foot). ‖ small articles carried ***in the hand*** [旅客の]手荷物 ‖ take one's pen ***in*** one's ***hand*** ペンを手にする ‖ the liquidation is ***in*** the ***hands*** of ... 清算は...の手で行われている ‖ cry ***in*** her ***hands*** 両手で顔をおおうて泣く ‖ His life was ***in*** my ***hands***. 彼の命は私の掌中にあった. ‖ leave it ***in*** the ***hands*** of ... それを...に任せる. 【類】***In*** the artist's ***hands*** no theme is trite, no tale too old to be told anew. / The matter is ***in*** the ***hands*** of the police. / ***In*** the right ***hand*** (適当な人が使えば), that power becomes a force for good. / fall ***in*** the ***hand*** of an assassin (凶刃に) / the affairs of the firm are now ***in*** the ***hands*** of ... / The cultivation of rice in Hawaii is entirely ***in*** the ***hands*** of the Chinese. ‖ before these papers are ***in*** the ***hands*** of the readers of the Contemporary Review このコンテンポラリー・レビュー誌を読者が手にせられる以前に ‖ The MS. is ***in*** the ***hand*** [writing] of the author. その原稿は著者の自筆である. ‖ He certifies it ***in*** his own ***hand***. 彼は署名入りで証明している. ‖ walk hand ***in*** hand 手に手をとって歩く. ¶The antique fell ***into*** my ***hands***. その古物は私が手に入れた. ‖ put it ***into*** the ***hands*** of ... それを...に渡す. ¶The factory employs hundreds ***of hands***. その工場は数百の職工を使用している. ¶The work is ***off*** my ***hands***. その仕事は私の手を離れた. ¶***on hand*** 手もとに; 便利な;《米》出席して. ¶Evidences of busy activity are to be seen ***on*** every ***hand***. 活動している模様がいたる所に見えている. ‖ The street has trees ***on*** either ***hand***. その町の両側に木が植えてある. ‖ I have five fingers ***on*** my ***hand***. 手にはこの通り五本指がある. ‖ Please be ***on hand*** at 12.30 sharp. 正零時半にお出で下さい. ‖ I ordered her to be ***on hand*** that morning. その朝来ているように彼女に命じた. ‖ having a little time ***on hand*** 少し時間があるので. 【類】with plenty of time ***on hand*** / those with time ***on hand*** (=who are not pressed for time) / I had then a good deal of leisure ***on*** my ***hands***. ‖ Have you anything ***on hand*** for this evening? 今晩何か御用がおありですか. ‖ have it ***on hand*** それは手もとにある. 【類】We have too many goods ***on hand***. ‖ A large stock is kept constantly ***on hand***. 在庫品をいつも豊富に持っています. 【類】the quantity ***on hand*** / finest cigars and cigarettes ***on hand*** ‖ go ***on hand*** and knees=go on all fours 四つんばいになって行く. 【類】creep through ***on*** his ***hands*** and knees / crawl ***on hands*** and knees in a cavern (洞穴) ‖ ***On*** the thin ***hand*** is a wedding-ring. 細い手には結婚の指輪がはめてある. ‖ stand (walk) ***on*** one's ***hand*** 逆立をする(逆立をして歩く) ‖ fillip a man ***on*** the ***hand*** 人の手を指ではじく ‖ We have a fight ***on*** our ***hands*** (=are at war). われわれは戦争をしている. ‖ He is ***on*** my ***hands***. 彼は私が世話をしている. ‖ with all the members ***on hand*** (=attending)《米》全員出席して. ¶The boys have got quite ***out of hand***. その子供らは全く手に負えなくなった. ‖ It would be difficult to answer these questions ***out of hand***. これらの問題を即座に答えるのはむずかしかろう. ‖ He is hardly ever ***out of*** the doctor's ***hands***. 彼はまだ医者の手を全く離れてはいない. ¶The dwelling has passed ***through*** many ***hands***. その住宅は幾度も持主が変った. ‖ the goods that have passed ***through*** the firm's ***hands***. その社の手を経て取引された商品. ¶is not yet ***to hand*** まだ入手しない ‖ Your remittance has come ***to hand***. 御送金は入手致しました. 【類】Your telegram was ***to hand*** just in time. / the latest London papers ***to hand*** show that ... / until further instructions (訓令) come ***to hand***. ¶Given ***under*** my ***hand*** at Yokohama, Japan, this 27th day of March, 1905. 一九〇五年三月二十七日日本横浜において署名(契約書などの終りの文). ¶write ***with*** one's own ***hand*** 自筆で書く ‖ welcome it ***with*** open ***hands*** 双手を広げてそれを歓迎する. 【類】***with*** warm ***hands*** ‖ I cannot ***with*** my ***hand*** on my heart, call Mr. ... a gentleman. 私は心から...を紳士とは呼ぶ気にはなれない. ‖ ***with*** his ***hands*** tied behind him 後ろ手に縛られて.

P² He is a poor ***hand at*** figures. 彼は計算がへただ. ¶She has a ***hand for*** needlework (hairdressing). 彼女は裁縫(など)がうまい. ¶***hand in*** hand with ... ...と手をつないで, ...と提携して. ¶primeval nature little altered by the ***hand of*** man ほとんど人間が手をつけていない原始的な自然. ¶***Hands off*** my private life. 僕の私生活に干渉するな. ¶He has a bad ***hand with*** the gun. 彼は射撃がへただ.

O *Hands* off!〘掲示〙手をふれるな. ¶*Hands* up! 両手をあげろ; ホールダップ! (ギャングが gun をつきつけて).

hand, *v.* 手渡す, 伝う.

M ***hand out*** handbills ちらし(ビラ)を配る. 【類】***hand out*** leaflets to people / ***hand out*** a dismissal notice (解雇状)

to ... / *hand out* copies of resolutions (決議文のコピー).
M[2] historic relics *handed down* to our own days 現代に伝えられた歴史的参考品. 【類】*handed down* from one generation to another ‖ qualities *handed down* by heredity 遺伝による資質 ‖ *hand down* a decision (verdict) 判決を下す.【類】*hand down* its judgment on the case / *hand* it *down* to posterity (後世に) / *handed down* through the ages / custom which our fathers have *handed down* to us / the secret *handed down* from father to son / one of the heirlooms (家宝) which were *handed down* from generation to generation. ¶*hand in* one's resignation (=papers) to ... 辞表を...に差出す ‖ *hand in* a bid 入札する ‖ *hand in* a claim [損害賠償の]要求書を提出する. ¶*Hand* it *on* to each of your classmates when through. 読み終ったら級友一人々々に回してくれ. ‖ *hand on* the torch [of knowledge] 知識の灯火を後世に伝える. ¶The offender was *handed over* to the police. その罪人は警察に引渡された. ‖ *hand* it *over* to the police それ(遺留品など)を警察に届ける ‖ *hand over* a duty 当直を引渡す, 当番の交替をする ‖ *hand over* one's property to ... ...にその財産を譲る. 【類】*hand over* the premiership (総理のいす) to ... / The motion (動議) was *handed over* to a committee. / *hand over* the matter to our solicitor (事務弁護人) / *hand over* the business (商売を譲る) to his son / *hand over* the deeds of a property (資産の権利) ‖ *hand* them *over* to the custody of ... それらを...の保管に移す ‖ Mr. Attlee gave assurance that he would not *hand over* India to chaos. アトリー氏はインドを混乱状態に落し入れる気はないと確言した. ‖ He climbed the tree *hand over* hand. 彼は手を交互にくり出して木に登った. ¶*hand* it *round* in quick order 大急ぎでそれを回す ‖ *hand round* a hat for ... ...のため帽子を回す(募金など). 【類】Two waiters *handed round* the dishes (食事のさら). ¶*Hands up*, those who have the right answer. 分かったら手をあげなさい.
P *hand* a lady *into* a car 手を貸して婦人を車に乗せてやる. ¶*Hand* it *into* your classmates. それを級友に回してくれ. ¶a cablegram to *hand to* the Bank of Japan from New York 日本銀行がニューヨークから受取った電報 ‖ *hand* it *to* him それを彼に渡す.

handbill, *n.* 引札.
V *distribute handbills* 引札を配る.

handbook, *n.* 案内書; 要覧.
Q[2] a *mother-and-child handbook* 母子手帳.
P[2] a *handbook for* San Francisco サンフランシスコ案内書 ‖ a *handbook for* teachers 教師用要覧. ¶a *handbook of* physical training 体操の教本. ¶a *handbook on* India インド便覧 ‖ a *handbook on* philosophy 哲学入門. ¶a *handbook to* ethnological collections in the British Museum 英国博物館所蔵人種学収集品の手引. 【類】a *handbook to* ceramics (English literature) / a *handbook to* tourists.

hand-clap, *n.* 拍手.
V *gain* a few *hand-claps* 二三の拍手を受ける.

handclasp, *n.* 握手.
Q greet a person with a *warm handclasp* 堅い握手で人を迎える.

handcuff, *n.* 手錠.
V It took all four of us to *get* the *handcuffs* on him. 彼に手錠をはめるのにわれわれ四人総掛りでやらなければならなかった. ¶*Handcuffs* were *placed* on her wrist. 彼女の手首に手錠がはめられた. ¶*put handcuffs* on criminals 犯人に手錠をかける. ¶*slip handcuffs* on ... こっそり...に手錠をはめる. ¶*snap* the *handcuffs* on ... ぱちんと...に手錠をかける. ¶*wear handcuffs* 手錠をかけられている.

handful, *n.* 一握り.
Q a *mere handful* of students ほんの数人の学生.
V They *constitute* but a pitiful *handful* of the number. その数の中のごく少数に過ぎない.
P[2] a *handful of* rice (grain) 一握りの米(など).

handicap, *n.* ハンディキャップ.
Q *industrial handicaps* 産業上不利な条件. ¶the *physical handicaps* peculiar to women 婦人特有な肉体的ハンディキャップ. ¶a *serious handicap* 大なるハンディキャップ. ¶a *triple handicap* (=distress) 三重苦(ヘレン・ケラー女史のような).
P The business was conducted so well *against* such a *handicap*. その仕事はこうした不利があったにしては非常にうまく行ったわけだ.
P[2] a *handicap to* one's progress in school 学校における進歩の障害.

handicap, *v.* 不利な条件をつける.
M He started in life very *heavily handicapped*. 彼はきわめて不利な条件のもとに社会へ巣立った. ¶the *physically handicapped*=the disabled 身体障害者. ¶*severely handicapped* はなはだしく不利の立場に置かれて.
P people *handicapped by* illiteracy (age)=the handicapped 無学(など)による不利な条件を背負っている人々. 【類】a family *handicapped by* misfortune.

handicraft, *n.* 手職, 手芸.
V They *have* a *handicraft*. 彼らには手に職がある.
Q *artistic handicraft* 美術工芸. ¶*female handicraft* 女子の手職.

handicraft, *v.* 手細工をする.
M an object of art *painstakingly handicrafted* 細工に手の込んだ美術品.
P a sweat shirt *handicrafted by* ... 毛糸の編セーター.

handkerchief, *n.* 手ふきん(ハンケチ).
V *bind* a *handkerchief* round one's hand 手にハンケチを巻く. ¶*putting* her *handkerchiefs* to her eyes 目にハンケチを当てて. 【類】*Put* a *handkerchief* over your mouth when you sneeze. ¶*throw* a *handkerchief* over ... ...の上にハンケチをかける. ¶*take handkerchiefs* under their hats, after the fashion of the Indian puggaree インド人の帽子の日除布風に帽子の下にハンケチを巻く. ¶*wave* a *handkerchief* at ... ...目がけてハンケチを振る. 【類】Katherine *waved* her *handkerchief* to her father as long as his boat was in sight.
Q[2] a *bundle handkerchief* ふろ敷.
P bury one's face *in* one's *handkerchief* ハンケチに顔を埋める. ¶dry one's tears *on* a *handkerchief* 涙にハンケチを当てる. ¶blow one's nose *with* a *handkerchief* ハンケチで鼻をかむ.

handle, *n.* 柄, にぎり手(ハンドル).
V The *handle* is *broken off*. ハンドルがこわれている. ¶He has *got* no *handle* to his name. 彼は肩書を持たない. ¶He *has* a *handle* to his name. 彼は肩書を持っている. ¶*put handles* to one's ideas 思想を表現する. ¶*rattle* the *handle* [電話などの]にぎり手をがちゃがちゃさせる. ¶*turn* the *handle* [戸口などの]ハンドルを回す. 【類】*turn* the *handle* to the right.
Q a cup with a *broken handle* 手のとれた茶わん.
Q[2] feather dusters on *cane handles* とうの柄についた羽のちり払い.
P a man *with* a *handle* to his name [貴族の]肩書などを持つ人.

handle, *v.* 取扱う, 待遇する.
M It should be *delicately handled*. それは取扱いに用心しなければならない. ¶*handle* it *dexterously* それを巧みに扱う. ¶*duly handle* ...をよしなに取扱う. ¶This machine *handles easily*. この機械は取扱いが簡単だ. ¶*handle gently* 手柔かに取扱う. ¶He was *harshly handled* by unfriendly critics. 彼は同情のない批評家に手ひどく扱われた. ¶*handle* a person *kindly* 人を親切に取扱う. ¶if not *properly handled* へたなことをすると. ¶he was *roughly handled* by ... 彼は...にひどく取扱われた. ¶*handle* collections *scientifically* 収集品を科学的に取扱う. ¶*handle* ... *severely* ...を手きびしく取扱う.
P if *handled by* one who knows how やり方の分かっている人が扱うと. ¶*handle* people (instruments) *with* great care 人(など)を非常に慎重に取扱う ‖ Historical and chronological matters are *handled with* much license in Scott's Ivanhoe. スコットのアイバンホーには歴史的年代的事実を自由に変更してとり入れられてある.
O They *handle* groceries. あの店は食料品を扱っている.

handler, *n.* 取扱う人(器具).
V It does not *pay* its *handlers*. それは取扱っても引合わない.
Q[2] a *baggage handler* 手荷物係員. ¶a *cash handler* 現金出納係. ¶a *poultry handler* 養鶏業者.

handling, *n.* 取扱い.
V This will greatly *facilitate* the *handling* of our business. こうするとわれわれの事務取扱いが大分有利になる. ¶The matter *needs* delicate *handling*. その件は慎重な取扱いを要する. ¶*receive* rough *handlings* 手荒い取扱いをうける. ¶The situation *requires* very careful and tactful *handling*. 時局は周到にして巧妙な対策を要する. ¶*simplify handling* 取扱いやすいようにする.

Q the *diplomatic handling* of one's affairs 事件の外交的取扱い. ¶require *careful handling* 取扱いに注意を要す. ¶*four handlings* (=motions) 四回の動作. ¶*free handling* of bicycles [鉄道会社の]自転車無料取扱い. ¶The subject is worn out with too *frequent handling*. その題目はあまり度々論じられるので古臭くなっている. ¶a *fuller* and *further handling* of the subject その問題の一層徹底的評論. ¶The writer is to be admired for his *impartial handling* of the question. 筆者がその問題を公平に取扱っているのは感心すべきことだ. ¶from *improper handling* 取扱いがよろしくないので. ¶*rough handling* of goods 品物の粗瀾な取扱い. ¶*scientific handling* of materials 材料の科学的取扱い. ¶*special handling* 特別扱い. ¶his *statesmanlike handling* of the perplexing administrative problems that confront him daily 毎日出会う困難な行政上の諸問題の政治家らしい取扱い. ¶a *tactful handling* of the subject その問題の巧妙な取扱い. ¶with *unsteady handling* 危なかしい手つきで. ¶*wrong handling* 誤った取扱い.

Q² *cargo handling* 船荷扱い.

P *under* wise *handling* 賢明な取扱いの下に.

handmaid, *n.* 女中, 侍女.

P² a *handmaid to* Mrs. ... ...夫人つきの小間使い.

handshake, *n.* 握手.

Q greet each one with a *friendly handshake* 互に友情的な握手を取交わす. ¶greet him with a *hearty handshake* 心からの握手をもって彼を迎える. ¶a *limp* (=*spiritless*) *handshake* 力のない握手. ¶a *vigorous handshake* 力強い握手.

handshaking, *n.* 握手.

Q *warm handshakings* and embraces, and tender farewells 暖い握手と抱擁とそして情を込めた別辞.

handspring, *n.* 宙返り.

V *throw* a *handspring*=turn a summersault 宙返りをする. ¶*turn handsprings* とんぼ返りをする.

handwriting, *n.* 筆跡, 習字.

V He *has* a bad *handwriting*. 彼は字がへただ. ¶It *shows* the *handwriting* on the wall. われわれはこれによって反省すべきである.

Q the evolution of the *British national handwriting* 英国書風の沿革. ¶a *clear handwriting* 明りょうな筆跡. ¶Her *handwriting* is *firm* and *assured*. 彼女の筆跡はしっかりして重みがある. ¶*good handwriting* うまい筆跡. ¶*illegible handwriting* 読みにくい筆跡. ¶in his *original handwriting* 彼の真筆の. ¶*poor handwriting* 金くぎ流. ¶*readable handwriting* 読みやすい筆跡. ¶*spidery handwriting* ひょろひょろした細い字体. ¶*stiff* (=*cramped*) *handwriting* しぶった筆跡.

P The marginal notes are believed to be *in* the *handwriting* of the author himself. その本の余白書入は著者自身の筆跡だと言われている. 【類】manuscripts *in* his *handwriting* / a document signed by him *in* his own *handwriting*.

handy, *a.* 器用な, 手ごろの, 調法な.

M *extremely handy* 非常に調法な.

P The trolley-car is *handy at* the next block. 電車は次のブロックで乗れる. ¶*handy for* the pocket ポケットに入れるに便利な. ¶make it more *handy of* reference それをさらに参考に便利にする. ¶He was *handy with* the needle. 彼は針仕事が器用だった. ‖ He is *handy with* his boot. 彼はよく人をける.

hang, *n.* 《俗》呼吸(こつ).

V *get* the *hang* of the business (a machine) その仕事(など)の呼吸をのみ込む.

hang, *v.* 掛ける; つるす; ぶらさがる; 絞刑にする.

M while away (=pass away) hours which would perhaps otherwise *hang heavily* on my hands 手持ちぶさたの時間をそれでつぶす. ¶The notorious pirate Kidd was *hanged here* in the year 1701. 名うての海賊キッドが一七〇一年にこの地で絞刑に処せられた. ¶His hands *hung limply*. 彼の両手はだらりと下っていた. ¶Where do they *hang out*? 《口語》彼らはどこに住んでるんだい. ¶a splendid hall *richly hung* with tapestries つづれにしきを沢山たれたりっぱな広間.

M² *hang about* all day doing nothing 一日中ぶらぶらする. ¶*hang around* here この辺をうろつく. ¶Where have you been *hanging* [a]*round*? どこをうろつき回っていたんだ. ¶Her hair *hung down* on her shoulders. 彼女の髪は肩にたれていた. ¶She may *hang on* for years. 彼女はまだ当分は死なないでしょうよ. ‖ a cough that *hangs on* 抜けないせき ‖ *hang* (=hold) *on* to the last 最後までがん張る ‖ The lawsuit is still *hanging on*. 訴訟問題はまだ片づかない. ¶*hang up* a sign on the door, "Closed Until 12 o'clock" ドアに「十二時まで休憩」という掲示を出す. ‖ *hang up* the receiver 電話の受話器をかける, 電話を切る. 【類】*hang up* a notice / *hang up* stockings at Christmas / *hang up* a wet garment to dry / be *hung up* on the line to dry ‖ *hung up* draperies over the shelves たなに掛布をかぶせる ‖ *hung* it *up* on exhibition (show) 陳列のためそれをつるす ‖ *hang up* trimmings on a Xmas tree クリスマスツリーの飾りつけをする ‖ *hang up* a question in debate 問題の論議をあとに回す. 【類】The measure was *hung up* for the session (その期中). ‖ The scheme has been *hung up*. その計画は中止された. ‖ *hang* it *up* against the wall それを壁に掛る ‖ *hang up* one's hat [帽子をかける, から]くつろぐ, 長座する.

P *hang about* a place ある場所をうろつく ‖ *hang about* a girl 娘のしりを追い回す. 【類】The children *hung about* their grandma to hear a fairy tale. ¶the lamp *hung above* the table テーブルの上につるしたランプ. ¶A calendar *hung against* the wall. 暦が壁に掛けてあった. ¶*hang around the* home その家の近くをうろうろする. ¶Three of his works are *hung at* the Royal Academy. 彼の作品三点が王立美術院に出品してある. ‖ with a botanical case *hanging at* his side 脇に植物採集の胴乱をぶらさげて. ¶His life *hung by* a single hair (=thread). 彼の命は危機一髪であった. ¶The criminal was *hanged for* an example. その犯人は見せしめに絞刑に処せられた. ¶a picture *hanging from* the wall 壁に掛っている絵. ‖ *hang from* a strap つり皮にぶら下る. 【類】a chandelier *hanging from* the ceiling / A sunflag *hangs from* the window. ¶A full moon *hung in* the sky. 満月が空にかかっていた. ¶His portrait was *hanging on* the wall. 彼の肖像が壁にかけてあった. ‖ *hang on* a strap つり皮につかまる. ‖ Cornucopias are *hung on* Christmas trees. 三角の福袋がクリスマスツリーにぶらさがっている. 【類】A world map was *hung* [up] *on* the wall. / *hang* one's hat *on* a book / *hang* the clothes *on* the clothline (ほしもの綱). ¶I'm tired enough of *hanging on to* a strap. こうつり皮につかまっているのは閉口だ. ¶The cliff *hangs over* the road. がけが道路上につき出ている. ‖ the fear which *hangs over* the world today 今日世界にのしかかる恐怖. 【類】The war-clouds that were *hanging over* the land burst in all their terrible fury (開戦となった). ‖ There is always a mystery *hanging over* the woman. その女には絶えずある秘密がつきまとっている. ‖ Deprivation of office is *hanging over* his head. 免職が彼の身に迫っている. ¶the sweet scent that *hangs round* a plum grove 梅林にただよう芳香. ¶*hang* it *to* a raft それをいかだにつける. ¶It is *hung upon* a hook in the wall. それは壁のかぎにかけてある. ‖ the issues that *hang upon* its outcome その結果として生じる諸問題 ‖ a question *upon* which life and death *hang* 生死にかかわる問題. ¶The picture is *hung with* its face turned to the wall. その絵は表面を壁に向けてかけてある. 【類】her neck *hung with* garlands of flowers (花輪) ‖ a small closed building, *hung with* gaudy pictures from the devotees whose prayers have been answered 願がかなった信者から納めた俗っぽい絵がかけてある戸のしまった小さな建物(絵馬堂).

hangar, *n.* 格納庫.

Q² an *airplane hangar* 格納庫. ¶a *radiation-proof hangar* [原子力の]放射線しゃ断装置のある格納庫.

hanging, *n.* つるすこと; 絞首刑.

Q² *paper* (=*wall*) *hangings* 壁紙. ¶a *kakemono* for *spring hanging* 春掛けの軸.

P death *by hanging* 絞首刑.

hang-over, *n.* 残がい.

P² a *hang-over from* the old regime 旧政権の名残り.

hanger, *n.* 衣紋かけ.

Q² a *coat hanger* 衣紋かけ. ¶a *paper hanger* 経師屋.

P a dress *on* a *hanger* 衣紋かけに掛けた衣装.

hanker, *v.* 渇望する.

P *hanker after* (=*for*) ... ...を渇望する.

hankering, *n.* 切望.

V he *had* a *hankering* to show his friends ... 彼は友人に...をとても見せたがっていた ‖ I *have hankerings* for ... 私

は…を切望している.

hansom, *n.* つじ馬車.

V and then, *hailing* a *hansom*, we made our way to … それから一台のつじ馬車を呼び止めてわれわれは…へ向った.

haphazard, *n.* 偶然.

P things done *at haphazard* でたらめにやったこと.

happen, *v.* 起る, 生じる.

M as ***commonly*** *happens* よくあるように. ¶it may ***easily*** *happen* that … …ということはたやすく起きるかもしれない. ¶Does this train ***ever*** *happen* to be late? この列車が遅れるようなことがありましょうか. ¶it ***frequently*** *happens* that … …ということは間々ある. ¶***how*** does it *happen* that …? どうして…. ¶it ***so*** *happened* then that … そこへもってきて…があった. ¶it ***sometimes*** *happens* that … どうかすると…ことがある. ¶it not ***unfrequently*** *happens* that … …はありがちのことだ.

P It *happened* ***in*** my absence. それは私の留守中のことです. ‖I *happen* (=fall) ***in*** with them at mealtime. 彼らとは食事時に落合う. ¶*happen* ***on*** (=***upon***) a person 偶然人に会う. ¶It *happened* ***through*** your negligence. それは君の怠慢から起ったことだ. ¶An accident *happened* ***to*** him. 彼は遭難した. ¶What *happened* ***to*** your leg? 脚をどうなさった. ‖He's been gone long. What's *happened* ***to*** him, I wonder? ずい分おそいな, どうかしたんじゃなかろうか. ¶This *happened* ***under*** my eyes. これは私の目の前で起った.

O if I don't *happen* to reach home until … …までにもし私がうちへ帰らなかったら. ¶I *happened* to meet him. 私は偶然彼に会った.

happening, *n.* できごと.

V Occasionally short-sighted people ***have some*** remarkable *happenings*. 近眼の人はどうかすると飛んでもない目に会うことがある. ¶In old days such a phenomenon would have been regarded as ***heralding*** some unusual *happening*. 昔だったらこうした現象は何か異常なできごとの前兆と見られただろう.

Q the ***commonplace*** *happenings* of every day 日々の平凡なできごと. ¶a selection from ***current*** *happenings* 時事抄録. ¶a summary of the ***important*** *happenings* of the year 今年度重大事件の概観. ¶the most wildly ***improbable*** *happenings* とっぴょうしもないできごと. ¶a ***noteworthy*** *happening* 注目すべきできごと. ¶a series of ***singular nocturnal*** *happenings* 一連の珍らしい夜間のできごと. ¶a ***strange*** *happening* 不思議な事件. ¶an ***unexpected*** *happening* that necessitates a change of program 番狂わせ.

Q² be up on ***world*** *happenings* 世界の動きに通じている.

P² the *happenings* ***of*** the day 最近のできごと.

happenstance, *n.* 《米俗》偶然のできごと.

Q the result of ***fortuitous*** *happenstance* 偶然のできごとの結果.

happiness, *n.* 幸福, 幸運.

V feeling as though I had ***buried*** all my *happiness* すっかり幸福を失ったようにがっかりして. ¶***cloud*** (=***dim***) the *happiness* of … …の幸福をくもらす. ¶***covet*** the *happiness* of others 他人の幸福をうらやむ. ¶Serious psychoneuroses often ***destroy*** the *happiness* of individuals and of families. 重い精神神経病者はしばしば個人並びに一家の幸福を破壊することがある. ¶Every one ***envied*** their *happiness*. 皆が彼らの幸福をうらやましがった. ¶I ***find*** *happiness* in knowing that you are well. 私は君の御健康を知ってうれしい. ¶***mar*** *happiness* 幸福を傷つける. ¶***procure*** (=***secure***) true *happiness* 真の幸福を得る. ¶***produce*** *happiness* 幸福を生じる. ¶***seek*** *happiness* 幸福を求める. ¶even when *happiness* was ***snatched*** from her grasp よし幸福が彼女から奪いとられたとしても. ¶The death of his beloved wife has ***taken*** all the *happiness* out of life. 彼は愛妻をなくして世の中が少しも面白くなくなった. ¶I ***wish*** you both every *happiness* and prosperity. あなた方の幸福と繁栄を祈ります. ¶***wreck*** (=***ruin***) one's *happiness* 幸福を破壊する.

Q I think my *happiness* would be quite ***complete*** if to that were added the gift of a little child. 今の私の幸福な上に子供を一人恵まれさえすればこの上もない幸福だろうと思います. ¶have their ***conjugal*** *happiness* displayed 夫婦仲のいいところを見せつける. ¶Simple habits and ***domestic*** *happiness* reign there. そこの暮しは質素で家庭は幸福であった. ¶so innocent was her ***exuberant*** *happiness* that … 彼女のあふれる幸福は…というほど無邪気なものであった. ¶***frail*** *happiness* はかない幸福. ¶a moment of ***great*** *happiness* 大きな幸福の瞬間. 【類】make for the ***greatest*** *happiness* of the greatest number. ¶an ***illusory*** *happiness* 幻影的な幸福. ¶weep over one's ***lost*** *happiness* 幸福を失って泣く. ¶***married*** *happiness* 幸福な結婚生活. ¶***quiet*** *happiness* 静かな幸福. ¶***restful*** *happiness* 安らかな幸福. ¶a ***shortlived*** *happiness* つかの間の幸福. ¶***solid, heartfelt*** *happiness* 堅実で心からの幸福. ¶***unselfish*** *happiness* 私心なき幸福. ¶***wholesome*** *happiness* 健全な幸福.

Q² other ***world*** *happiness* あの世の幸福.

P injurious ***to*** *happiness* 幸福に害のある.

happy, *a.* 幸福な, 仕合わせな; (言いまわしが)適切な.

M I shall be ***most*** *happy* to do so. ぜひそう致したいと思います. ¶***perfectly*** *happy* 全く幸福な. ¶***supremely*** *happy* この上もなく幸福な. ¶I shall be ***very*** *happy* to see you. ぜひお目にかかりたい.

P He is *happy* ***about*** his promotion. 彼はその昇進を喜んでいる. ¶He is *happy* ***among*** his children. 彼は子供に取巻かれて仕合わせに暮している. ¶be *happy* ***at*** the news (discovery) そのニュース(など)で喜んでいる. 【類】I am *happy* ***at*** hearing that… ¶It will be *happy* ***for*** him. それは彼のために仕合わせであろう. ¶I am *happy* ***in*** the consciousness that … 私は…と知ってうれしく思う. ‖be *happy* ***in*** one's expression …こなれている ‖He was *happy* and comfortable back ***in*** his old home. 彼は生れ故郷に帰って幸福で住み心地がよかった. ¶He is *happy* ***over*** his success. 彼はその成功を喜んでいる. ¶He is *happy* ***with*** his wife (friends). 彼は細君(など)とむつまじく暮している.

O You look *happy* today. きょうはうれしそうだね.

harakiri, *n.* 切腹.

V ***commit*** (=perform) *harakiri* 切腹する. ¶He was sentenced to ***perform*** *harakiri*. 彼は切腹を仰せ付けられた. 【類】***perform*** *harakiri* according to custom (しきたりにより).

Q It was a ***magnificent*** *harakiri*! あっぱれな切腹であった.

harangue, *n.* 熱烈な演説.

Q an ***excited*** *harangue* 熱弁. ¶launch into a ***long*** *harangue* 長広舌をふるう.

harass, *v.* 困らす, 悩ます.

P *harass* a person ***by*** … …で人を困らせる.

harbinger, *n.* 前兆.

Q a ***sure*** *harbinger* of evil 必ずわざわいがあるという前兆.

P² The cuckoo is the *harbinger* ***of*** spring. ほととぎすは春の前ぶれだ.

harbo[u]r, *n.* 港, 避難所.

V ***blockade*** a *harbor* 港を封鎖する. ¶***construct*** a *harbor* 築港する. ¶***enter*** [a] *harbor* 入港する. ¶a beautiful bay ***forming*** a splendid natural *harbor* 天然の良港をなしている美しい湾. ¶***give*** *harbor* to a criminal (spy, a slave) 罪人(など)をかくまう. ¶We are expected to ***make*** the *harbor* tonight. 今夜着港のはずです. ¶***Mine*** *harbors* in case of war. 戦争になれば港湾に水雷を敷設する. ¶the hill ***overlooking*** the *harbor* of … …の港に臨んでいる小山. ¶***sound*** a *harbor* 港の水深を測量する.

Q a ***deep-water*** *harbor* 深水港. ¶Hongkong has been endowed with one of the ***finest natural*** *harbors* in the world. 香港は世界で最もりっぱな天然の港に恵まれている. ¶***good*** and ***convenient*** *harbors* 便利な良港. ¶an ***ice-bound*** *harbor* 氷鎖港. ¶a ***magnificent land-locked*** *harbor* 入江の奥のすばらしい港. ¶a ***natural*** (an ***artificial***) *harbor* 自然(人工)の港. ¶a ***peaceful*** *harbor* おだやかな港. ¶The city is situated on a ***splendid*** *harbor*. その市はりっぱな港に臨んでいる.

Q² an ***ice*** (***ice-free***) *harbor* 凍(不凍)港. ¶***New york*** *harbor* is one of the most beautiful, largest and best of the world's great ports. ニューヨーク港は世界の大港中もっとも美しい, 大きな良港の一つである.

P call ***at*** a *harbor* 寄港する. ¶The steamer is now ***in*** *harbor* at Quebec. その汽船は目下ケベック港に停泊中である. ¶The town is built ***on*** the *harbor*. その町は港に臨んでいる.

P² the *harbor* ***at*** Vladivostok ウラジオストック港. ¶a *harbor* ***of*** refuge 避難港 ‖the *Harbor* ***of*** Yokohama=Yokohama Harbor 横浜港.

harbo[u]r, *v.* 抱く; かくまう.

P The dog *harbors* fleas ***in*** his shaggy hair. その犬のむく毛の中にのみがいる.

O *harbor* a criminal (spy) 犯罪人(など)をかくまう. ¶*harbor* evil thoughts (hatred) 悪意(など)を抱く.

harbo[u]rage, *n.* 避難所.

V These vessels in storm could ***find*** *harborage.* これらの暴風におそわれた船は避難ができた.

hard, *a.* 堅い; つらい, つれない; よく勉強する.

M This book is ***rather*** *hard* to read and understand. この本は少しむずかしい. ¶Life is ***so*** *hard,* ***so*** *hard*! この世はつらい, つらい. ¶His heart must be ***very*** *hard.* あの人の心は木か石でできてるに違いない.

M² be *hard* ***up*** for money 金に困っている.

P He is *hard* ***at*** it. 彼はそれを熱心にやっている. 【類】*hard* ***at*** work (study). ¶This problem is too *hard* ***for*** me to solve. この問題はとてもむずかしくって私には解けない. ¶How *hard* ***of*** hearing he is! あの人はなんて耳の遠い人だろう. ‖ people very *hard* ***of*** understanding とても理解の悪い人たち. 【類】I am a trifle *hard* ***of*** hearing. ¶I hope you will not be *hard* ***on*** us. 何分お手柔かに願います. ‖ The dry weather has been *hard* ***on*** my garden. 雨がないので庭は台なしだ. ¶The stone is *hard* ***to*** the touch. 石は手触りが堅い. ¶He is hard ***upon*** eighty. 彼はもうじき八十だ. ‖ follow *hard* ***upon*** another 人のあとについて行く. ¶The times are very *hard* ***with*** him. あの人は昨今仲々苦しい. ‖ Things are getting *hard* ***with*** us. 世の中はだんだん暮しにくくなる.

O Grey squirrels look so much like the color of the tree that they are *hard* to see. 灰色のりすは木の色によく似ているので見つけにくい. ¶It is rather *hard* to find fault with me now. 今私を非難するのは少々酷だ. ¶He was *harder* than adamant. 彼は石より冷たい男だった.

hard, *adv.* 近くに.

P The cottage stood *hard* ***by*** the river. そのいなか家は川のほとりに立っていた.

harden, *v.* 堅くする, 堅くなる.

M He had ***utterly*** been *hardened* to all shame. 彼は全然恥を恥としない人間となってしまっていた.

P His mind was *hardened* ***against*** pity. 彼の心はかたくて情にもとけなかった. ¶*harden* it ***by*** heat それを熱で堅くする ‖ a heart *hardened* ***by*** the rubs of life 世間ずれのした人. ¶*harden* ***in*** drying かわくと固くなる. 【類】*hardened* ***in*** the sun or by fire. ‖ *hardened* ***in*** heart つれなくなっている. ¶long usage *hardened* ***into*** law 法律になった長い慣習. ¶one who has been *hardened* ***to*** public speaking 公開演説になれっこになっている人.

hardening, *n.* 硬化.

P² *hardening* ***of*** arteries 動脈硬化.

hard-heartedness, *n.* 無情.

V ***increase*** the *hard-heartedness* of the rich towards the poor 貧者に対する富者の無情をつのらせる.

hardihood, *n.* 剛毅(*), 気骨.

V He ***had*** the *hardihood* to deny. 彼は否定するだけの気概があった.

hardness, *n.* 苦難.

V ***endure*** *hardness* as a good soldier りっぱな軍人らしく苦難にたえる.

hardship, *n.* 困苦, 苦難.

V ***bear*** *hardship* 困苦にたえる. ¶***cause*** *hardship* 難渋させる. ¶***endure*** the *hardships* of ... ...の辛苦を忍ぶ. 【類】***endure*** *hardship* patiently (辛抱強く) / ***endure*** *hardship* as pioneer missionaries (宣教師の先達) / great *hardships* bravely ***endured.*** ¶***entail*** great *hardships* 非常な困苦を伴う. ¶***experience*** *hardships* つらい思いをする. ¶***inflict*** great *hardship* upon ... ...をはなはだしい苦境に立たせる. ¶This did much to ***mitigate*** the *hardships* of these long journeys. これがかかる長途の旅の苦しみを和げるために大いに役立った. ¶***suffer*** great *hardships* 非常に苦しい目に会う. ¶***undergo*** almost incredible *hardship* ほとんど信じられない位の苦しみを受ける.

Q after a voyage of ***great*** *hardship* 非常に苦しい航海を終えてから. ¶the ***increasing*** *hardships* that confront ... ...にとって増大しつつある困難.

P go ***through*** many *hardships* 幾多のかん難辛苦をなめる. ¶inured ***to*** *hardships* 困苦に慣れた.

hardware, *n.* 金物.

Q ***builders'*** (=***building***) *hardware* 建築材料の金具.

Q² ***household*** *hardware* 家庭用金もの. ¶white marble with ***silver*** *hardware* 銀の金具のついた白い大理石.

P deal ***in*** *hardware* 金物を商う.

hare, *n.* 野うさぎ.

V ***shoot down*** a *hare* 野うさぎを射ち殺す. ¶***start*** a new *hare* by saying ... ...という新説をはく.

Q a ***tame*** *hare* 飼いならした野うさぎ.

P The race was not ***to*** the *hare.* 競争はうさぎの勝とはならなかった.

hark, *v.* 聞け.

M *hark* ***away***! *hark* ***back***! *hark* ***forward***! 声を掛けて猟犬を鼓舞する叫び. ¶*hark* a hound ***back*** 猟犬を呼び戻す.

harm, *n.* 害, 損害.

V ***cause*** incalculable *harm* to ... ...にばく大な損害を及ぼす. ¶It ***does*** much more *harm* than good. それは益少く害が多い. ‖ ***do*** more *harm* than good よいどころか有害 ‖ No *harm* ***will*** be ***done*** by the delay. 遅れても一向差支えない. ‖ It will ***do*** no *harm* to tell it once more. それをもう一ぺん申上げても差支えなかろう. ¶It will ***make*** one no *harm.* それはだれにも害を及ぼさないだろう. ¶I ***mean*** no *harm.* 私には少しも悪気はない. 【類】He probably ***meant*** no *harm* to you. ¶I ***see*** no *harm* in doing so. 私はそうして差支えないと思う. ¶***suffer*** *harm* from being out in a storm あらしに外出してひどい目に会う. ¶***threaten*** bodily *harm* 身体に危害を加えられるおそれがある. ¶***work*** decided *harm* to the interests of ... たしかに...に不利を来すことになる. 【類】The American missionaries have ***wrought*** much *harm* to China.

Q It did me ***bodily*** *harm.* それは私の体を害した. ¶do ***great*** *harm* 大いに害をなす. ¶***immeasurable*** *harm* 計り知れない害. ¶do a person ***little*** *harm* 大してからだにさわらない. ¶The frost did ***much*** *harm* on the fruit farm. 霜が果樹園に大害を与えた. ¶There is ***no*** *harm* in doing so. そうして一向差支えない. ¶***serious*** *harm* ゆゆしい害. ¶***slight*** *harm* 小害. ¶***untold*** *harm* ばく大な害.

P safe ***from*** *harm* 害のない. ¶come ***to*** *harm* うき目を見る. ¶***without*** *harm* 害がなくて. ¶do *harm* ***to*** the crops 作物に害を及ぼす.

harmful, *a.* 有害な.

P That will be *harmful* ***to*** discipline. それでは示しがつかない.

harmless, *a.* 無害の.

M Some snakes are ***utterly*** (=***quite***) *harmless.* へびには全然無害のものがある.

P It is *harmless* ***for*** the health. それは健康に害がない. ¶be *harmless* ***to*** fabric [クリーニングなどの場合]生地がいたむようなことはない.

harmonious, *a.* 調和する.

P *harmonious* ***in*** color scheme ***with*** ... 色の配合が...と調和した. ¶*harmonious* ***with*** the whole 全体と調和した.

harmonize, *v.* 調和する.

P *harmonize* ***with*** a person (thing) 人(物)と調和する. 【類】The color of the curtains *harmonized* ***with*** the rooms.

harmony, *n.* 調和, 融和, 和合.

V ***establish*** *harmony* among ... ...の間に融和を確立する. ¶The enlargement of the abdomen in pregnancy ***impairs*** the *harmony* of the figure. 妊娠してお腹が大きくなると美容を損うものである. ¶***re-establish*** the disturbed *harmony* 破られた調和を回復する. ¶***secure*** *harmony* between labor and management 労使協調を確保する. ¶***spoil*** the *harmony* 調和を乱す. ¶***strengthen*** international *harmony* 国際協調を強化する.

Q the ***celestial*** *harmony* 天の音楽. ¶work together in ***complete*** *harmony* きわめて円満に協力する. ¶There is always perfect ***conjugal*** *harmony* in the household. 夫婦仲は申分がない. ¶chime in ***exact*** *harmony* with ... ...と正確に歩調をそろえる. ¶a disposition to work together in ***perfect*** *harmony* 完全に人と協調して働く性質. ¶pregnancy as evidence of a ***sexual*** *harmony* 性的和合の証拠としての妊娠. ¶get into ***spiritual*** *harmony* with the Koreans 朝鮮人と精神的に融和するようになる. ¶a ***wonderful*** *harmony* of contradictions 矛盾の不思議な融合.

Q² ***color*** *harmony* 色の調和. ¶in the interest of ***party*** *harmony* 党の平和のために. ¶insure ***world*** *harmony* 世界協調を確保する.

P act ***in*** *harmony* 協調して働く ‖ live ***in*** *harmony* with ... ...と仲よく暮す ‖ change ***in*** *harmony* with the years 時代の推移に順応する. 【類】Men are valuable just in proportion as they are able and willing to work ***in*** *harmony* with other men.—Elbert Hubbard. / ***in*** *harmony* with our age. / It is ***in*** *harmony* with tradition and general sentiment. / It is not ***in*** *harmony* with modern ideas.

¶It is ***out of*** *harmony* with Japanese habits of thought. それは日本人の考え方とは調和しない. ¶sing ***with*** perfect *harmony* 完全な諧(ちょう)調で歌う.

P² *harmony* ***between*** the old and new learnings 新旧学問の調和.

harness, *n.* 馬具.

V ***buckle on*** the *harness* 馬具を着ける. ¶***put*** the *harness* on a horse 馬に馬具を着ける.

P die ***in*** *harness* 死ぬまで仕事を続ける. ¶a set ***of*** *harness* 馬具ひとそろい.

harness, *v.* 馬具を着ける, 馬装する.

P *harness* a horse ***to*** a carriage 馬車に馬を取りつける.

harp, *n.* たて琴(ハープ).

V ***strum*** a *harp* ハープをひく.

P play ***on*** a *harp* ハープをひく. ¶a singer ***to*** a *harp* ハープに合わせて歌う歌手.

harp, *v.* くどくど繰返す.

M He ***continually*** *harps* on lack of opportunity. 彼は機会に出合わないことを始終くよくよ言う.

P *harp* ***on*** the same string 同じことをくどくど繰返す. 【類】Don't keep on *harping* ***on*** that. / He is still *harping* ***on*** the same topic. ‖ *harp* ***on*** stock points いつもの議論を繰返す.

harrow, *n.* まぐわ.

P pass through life ***under*** a *harrow* of debt 借金に苦しみながら世を渡る ‖ ***under*** the *harrow* 難渋して.

harsh, *a.* あらい, 耳ざわりな.

P *harsh* ***to*** the ear 耳ざわりな.

harshness, *n.* 荒々しさ.

V ***soften away*** *harshness* 荒々しさを和らげる.

Q ***exacting*** *harshness* てあらい当り方.

harvest, *n.* 収穫; 穀物; 所得.

V A bumper *harvest* is ***anticipated*** in Ireland this year. アイルランドでは今年は豊作の見込である. ¶The crop ***bore*** a plentiful *harvest*. 豊作であった. ¶***blight*** the *harvest* 作柄をいためる. ¶His preaching tour ***brought in*** a rich *harvest* of souls. 彼の説教旅行は多数の人を信仰生活に導くことができた. ¶***expect*** a splendid *harvest* 一大収穫を期待する. ¶***gather*** [***in***] a *harvest* とり入れをする. 【類】In that country they ***gather*** three *harvests* from the field of rice each year. ¶This year ***promises*** a good *harvest*. 今年は豊作の見込である. ¶***reap*** a good *harvest* 沢山な収穫を得る. 【類】The season is short, and the *harvest* must be ***reaped*** in the proper time. ‖ ***reap*** a *harvest* of profits 利益を収める. ¶***ruin*** French *harvests* フランスにおける作物の収穫に大害を与える. ¶The research could not fail to ***yield*** a rich *harvest* to the naturalist. その博物学者の研究は大収穫をもたらさずにはおかなかった. ¶The *harvest* ***promises*** a plentiful one. その収穫は豊富の見込みだ.

Q The seed thus sown speedily fructified and yielded an ***abundant spiritual*** *harvest*. かくてまかれた種がすみやかに実を結んで精神的に大なる収穫があった. ¶an ***ample*** *harvest* 豊作. ¶an ***average*** *harvest* 平均作. ¶a ***bad*** *harvest* 凶作. ¶an extremely ***bountiful*** *harvest* 大豊作. 【類】one of the most ***bountiful rice*** *harvests* on record. ¶a ***fair*** *harvest* 豊作. ¶reap the ***golden*** *harvest* うまい利益を得る. ¶It means a ***goodly*** *harvest* of bad debts. それだと貸倒れが沢山できる. ¶the quality rather than the abundance of the ***literary*** *harvest* 文学作品の量よりむしろ質. ¶a ***plenteous*** *harvest* 豊作. ¶reap a ***poor*** *harvest* 不作だ. ¶a ***rich*** *harvest* 豊作. ¶a ***scanty*** *harvest* 不作. ¶There is every prospect of a ***splendid*** *harvest*. 大豊作の見込み十分である. ¶a ***wretched*** *harvest* ひどい不作.

Q² The ***oyster*** *harvest* was small this year. 今年はかきはできが悪かった. ¶The ***wine*** *harvest* was the worst in many years. ぶどう作は何年来の不作だった.

P Rice will be cheap ***after*** *harvest*. 米は収穫後には安くなるだろう. ¶***at*** the grape *harvest* ぶどう収穫のころに. ¶a reaper ***in*** *harvest* 収穫の刈り手. ¶the time ***of*** *harvest* 収穫期.

harvester, *n.* 収穫機.

Q² a ***combine*** *harvester* 《米》複式収穫機(刈入れと脱穀の). ¶a ***self-binding*** *harvester* 自動緊縛機.

has-been, *n.* 《米》盛りの過ぎたもの.

V She complained, saying that her hubby ***called*** her "*has-been*." 夫が彼女を「ばあさん」と呼んだと文句を言った.

Q The hall was crowded with ***literary*** *has-beens*. 《米》その会堂は盛りの過ぎた文士で一杯だった.

hash, *n.* へま.

V ***make*** a *hash* of ... ＝spoil in dealing with ... ...でへまをやる.

haste, *n.* 急ぎ, 迅速.

V ***Excuse*** my *haste* as I have to go to the wedding of a friend. 友人の結婚式に行くので早々の乱筆おゆるし下さい. ¶***make*** all *haste* to ... 大あわてで...する. 【類】Unless you ***make*** *haste*, you won't be in time for the train. ‖ he ***made*** *haste* to add that ... 彼は急いで...と付け加えた ‖ He ***made*** *haste* to be gone. 彼は急いで立去った. ‖ ***Make*** *haste* slowly. 〖諺〗ゆっくり急げ(急がば回れ). ¶The matter ***requires*** *haste*. そのことは迅速を要する.

Q in a ***feverish*** *haste* to ... 大急ぎで...する. ¶retreat in ***hot*** *haste* あわてて退却する. 【類】send off in ***hot*** *haste*. / despatched in ***hot*** *haste* for ... ¶in the ***mad*** *haste* to ... ...しようとむちゃくちゃに急いで. ¶as a result of too ***much*** *haste* あせった結果. ¶We have made all ***possible*** *haste*. できるだけ急いだ. ¶with ***precipitate*** *haste* 急ぎに急いで. ¶make ***undue*** *haste* あせり過ぎる. ¶with ***unusual*** *haste* 特に急いで. ¶speed in ***wild*** *haste* むちゃくちゃに急ぐ.

P Marry ***in*** *haste* and repent at leisure. 〖諺〗あわてて結婚ゆっくり後悔. ‖ flee ***in*** all *haste* 一目散に逃げる ‖ ***in*** great *haste* あわを食って. ¶***with*** all *haste* 大急ぎで. 【類】ran off ***with*** *haste*. ¶***without*** *haste* 気長に.

P² make *haste* ***with*** one's task 仕事を急ぐ.

haste, *v.* 急ぐ.

P *haste* ***with*** confusion あわてふためく.

hasten, *v.* 急ぐ.

M *hasten* ***away*** down to ... ...の方に急いで行く. ¶*hasten* ***back*** 急いで帰る. ¶*hasten* ***forward*** 急いで前進する. ¶*Hasten* ***slowly***. ゆるゆる急げ(急がば回れ). ¶*hasten* ***upstairs*** 急いで二階へ上る.

P *hasten* ***by*** car 車を飛ばす. ¶*hasten* ***to*** his assistance 急いで彼の救助におもむく ‖ Directly (＝As soon as) I heard the news, I *hastened* ***to*** the spot. 私はその知らせに接して時を移さず現場へ急行した. ‖ The year is *hastening* ***to*** its close. 今年もぐんぐん終りに近づいている. ¶*hasten* ***towards*** a definite end はっきりした目標に向って急ぐ.

hasty, *a.* 急の, 気早の.

M It is ***too*** *hasty* to conclude that way. にわかにそうと断じかねる.

P be *hasty* ***in*** one's judgments 結論を急いでいる ‖ Let us not be too *hasty* ***in*** condemning him for it. われわれはにわかに彼をその故に責めてはならない. ‖ I was too *hasty* ***in*** concluding that ... 私は早合点して...と決めてしまった.

hat, *n.* 帽子.

V Emily was carefully ***adjusting*** her *hat* before a mirror. エミリーは鏡の前で帽子の格好を念入りに直していた. ¶***check*** one's *hat* 帽子をあずける. ¶***cock*** one's *hat* slightly 少し帽子を横ちょにする. ¶***doff*** (＝take off) one's *hat* and bow 帽子を取ってお辞儀をする. ¶***don*** (＝put on) a *hat* 帽子をかぶる. ¶***get*** a *hat* ***on*** 帽子をかぶる. ¶***hang*** one's *hat* on the hatpeg 帽子掛けに帽子を掛ける. ¶***have*** one's *hat* ***on*** 帽子をかぶっている. ¶***hang up*** one's *hat* 帽子を掛ける; 〖比ゆ〗長居する, くつろぐ. ¶chairs constructed to ***hold*** *hats* on the rungs 座席の下に帽子を入れるようにこしらえたいす ‖ ***hold*** one's *hat* gingerly そっと帽子を持つ. ¶He ***jammed*** his *hat* on the side of his head, and walked out. 彼は帽子を横ちょにかぶってその場を出た(憤然として職を辞するなどの場合). ¶***keep on*** one's *hat* 帽子をかぶったままでいる. ¶I don't know where I ***left*** my *hat*. どこに帽子をおき忘れてきたか覚えがない. ¶***lift*** one's *hat* [あいさつに]帽子をとる. ¶***pass*** [***round***] the *hat* [寄付金を集めるために]帽子を回す. ¶***press*** one's *hat* over his brows 目深にまゆ毛の上まで帽子をかぶる. ¶***pull*** one's *hat* over one's eyes 帽子を目深にかぶる ‖ He ***pulled*** my *hat* over my ears. 彼は僕の帽子をぐいと押しつけた(いたずらまたは腹を立てて). ¶***push*** one's *hat* ***back*** ffo one's forehead 帽子をあみだかぶりにさせる(いたずらして). ¶***put on*** one's *hat* 帽子をかぶる. ¶***raise*** one's *hat* to ... 帽子を取って...に会釈する; ...に敬意を表する ‖ ***raise*** one's *hat* in answer to ... 帽子を取って...に答礼する ‖ To shame him I ***raised*** my *hat* with mock solemnity. 彼を辱めようとして私はわざと丁寧に彼にあいさつした. ¶Ladies ***remove*** their *hats* in a concert. 婦人は音楽会では帽子を取る. ¶***snatch up*** one's *hat* 無造作に帽子を取る. ¶***take*** (＝***put***) ***off*** one's *hat* to ... 帽子を取って...に敬礼する; ...に頭を下げる ‖ I ***take*** my *hat* ***off*** to him. 全くあの人には頭が下がる. ¶***throw*** one's *hat* in the ring 拳闘の試合に出る.

¶ *tilt* a *hat* sideways 帽子を横ちょにかぶる. ¶ *tip* (=*tilt*) one's *hat* politely 帽子をかしげて会釈する. ¶ *touch* one's *hat* to ... 帽子に手をかけて…に会釈する. ¶ Milliners *trim hats*. ミリナーは婦人帽子を作る. ¶ *try on* a *hat* 帽子をかぶってみる. ¶ *turn* one's *hat* between one's hands 両手の間に帽子をひっくり返す. ¶ *wear* one's *hat* on one side 帽子を横かぶりにする.

V² This *hat* ***becomes*** you. この帽子は君に似合う. ¶ This *hat* ***fits*** me to a T. この帽子は私にぴったりだ. ¶ This *hat* does not ***suit*** me. この帽子は私には似合わない.

Q a ***chic red hat*** いきな赤い帽子. ¶ a ***cute hat*** 気のきいた帽子. ¶ attired in ***gold-bound hat*** 金モールのバンドのついた正帽をかぶって. ¶ He's quite a high *hat*. 《米》 彼は全く気どり屋だ. ¶ a ***high-crowned hat*** 山高帽. ¶ a ***lady's hat*** 婦人帽. ¶ a ***loose hat*** ゆるい帽子. ¶ Are ***low-crowned hats*** out of fashion now? 山の低い帽子は今では流行しないのですか. ¶ try a ***new hat*** on 新しい帽子をかぶってみる. ¶ a ***saucy hat*** スマートな帽子. ¶ a ***soft hat*** 中折帽. ¶ a ***soldier's hat*** 軍帽. ¶ a ***wide-brimmed hat*** つば広帽.

Q² a ***billy-cock hat*** 《英》 山高帽. ¶ a gray ***bowler hat*** ねず色の山高帽. ¶ a ***campaign*** (=***combat***) ***hat*** 戦闘帽. ¶ a ***crush hat*** たたみ帽. オペラ帽(ばねじかけでたためる). ¶ a ***Derby hat*** 《米》 山高帽. ¶ a ***felt hat*** フェルト帽. ¶ a ***field-service hat*** (=cap) 戦闘帽. ¶ Koreans' ***flytrap hats*** 韓国人のはい取り器に似た帽子. ¶ ***gipsy hat*** (=***bonnet***) ひさしの大きい婦人用帽子. ¶ a ***new-look hat*** 新型帽. ¶ an ***opera hat***. オペラ帽. ¶ a ***Panama hat*** パナマ帽. ¶ a ***picture hat*** 縁広の婦人帽(普通黒で, だちょうの羽で飾った). ¶ a ***plug hat*** 《米》 シルクハット. ¶ a ***pot hat*** 山高帽. ¶ a tall ***silk hat*** シルクハット. ¶ a ***small-size hat*** 小型の帽子. ¶ a man in the ***straw hat*** 麦わら帽をかぶった男 ‖ a broad-brimmed ***straw hat*** つば広の麦わら帽. ¶ a ***sun hat*** 日除け帽. ¶ a ***top hat*** シルクハット. ¶ a ***trilby hat*** 《英》 中折れ. 【類】 have one's ***trilby hat*** cleaned and re-blocked (新しく型どりした). ¶ a ***yatchting hat*** ヨット帽.

P a gemtleman ***in*** a tall silk *hat* 山高のシルクハットをかぶった紳士. ¶ fumble ***with*** one's *hat* 帽子を手でいじくり回す. ¶ go out ***without*** a *hat* 帽子をかぶらずに出掛ける.

P² a *hat* ***for*** women 婦人用の帽子. ¶ *hat* ***in*** hand 手に帽子を持って; うやうやしく. ¶ a *hat* ***of*** invisibility 隠れ笠. ¶ a *hat* ***with*** a high crown and a narrow brim 山が高くて縁のせまい帽子.

hatch, *n.* 昇降口, 艙(そう)口.

Q from her ***yawning hatches*** 船の大きく開いている艙口から.

Q² a ***service hatch*** [台所から食堂へ]料理を出す窓.

hatch, *v.* ふ化する; はかる.

M *hatch* ***out*** ふ化する ‖ *hatch* ***out*** into adult form ふ化して大きくなる.

P The eggs are *hatched* ***by*** the heat of the sun. その卵は太陽の熱でふ化する. ¶ *hatch* ***in*** the sun 日なたでかえる. ¶ a young man *hatching* ***into*** evil deeds 段々品行が悪くなる青年. ¶ *hatch* 12 ***out of*** 20 eggs 二十の卵から十二かえる. ¶ a plan *hatched* ***with*** secrecy 秘密に企てられた計画.

hatchery, *n.* [魚の]ふ卵所.

Q² a ***fertile hatchery*** for dangerous thought 危険思想の一大養成所.

hatchet, *n.* 手おの.

V ***bury*** the *hatchet* [比ゆ的] 和睦する; ほこを収める.

hate, *n.* 憎悪.

Q ***bitter hate*** ひどい憎しみ.

P look at a person ***with*** *hate* にくらしげに人を見やる.

hate, *v.* にくむ; きらう.

M *hate* ***bitterly*** to ... …することは非常にきらう. ¶ *hate* ... ***blindly, instinctively,*** without rhyme or reason …を訳もなく盲目的に本能的ににくむ.

P He *hates* me ***for*** it. 彼はそのために私をにくむ. ¶ *hate* drink ***like*** a viper (poison, the very devil) 飲酒をだかつ(など)のごとくきらう.

O I *hate* to study. 私は勉強がきらいだ.

hateful, *a.* にくむべき, きらいな.

P *hateful* ***to*** me 私のきらいな.

hater, *n.* 憎悪者, 嫌悪者.

Q a ***good*** *hater* 大いにきらう人.

Q² a ***woman*** *hater* 女ぎらいの人.

P He is a *hater* ***of*** marriage. あの人は結婚ぎらいだ.

hatful, *n.* 帽子一杯.

P² a *hatful* ***of*** nuts 帽子に一杯のナット.

hatred, *n.* 憎悪, 恨み.

V ***bear*** a person *hatred* 人に憎悪(ぞう)の念を持つ ‖ ***bear*** one's *hatred* towards ... …に対して憎悪の念を懐く. ¶ ***conceive*** for ... a profound *hatred* …を極度に憎む. ¶ To claim payment is to ***court*** *hatred*. 支払を要求するのは憎まれるように持掛けるようなものだ. ¶ Such an opinion will ***create*** *hatred* everywhere. こんな意見を述べるといたる所で憎まれる. ¶ ***feel*** irreconcilable *hatred* towards ... …に対していやし難い憎悪を感じる. ¶ ***harbor*** bitter *hatred* 激しい憎悪の念を懐く. ¶ ***have*** a *hatred* for ... …を憎む ‖ ***have*** a *hatred* of ... …から憎まれている. ¶ ***hold*** a special *hatred* for ... …を特にきらう. ¶ ***incur*** the *hatred* of Heaven 天の憎しみを買う. ¶ ***intensify*** their *hatred* to ... …に対する彼らの憎しみを激化する. ¶ ***nurse*** intense *hatred* against ... …に対して強烈な憎悪の念を懐く. ¶ ***stir up*** *hatred* 憎しみを起させる.

Q ***bitter*** *hatred* 強い憎悪. ¶ A ***deadly*** *hatred* prevails. すごい憎しみがみなぎっている. ¶ There is a ***deep-rooted*** *hatred* on the part of the Hungarians towards the Austrians. ハンガリー人はオーストリア人に対して根深い憎しみを持っている. ¶ ***fierce*** *hatred* 烈しい憎悪. ¶ hate him with a really ***hellish*** *hatred* 彼を徹底的に憎む. ¶ abhor with ***homicidal*** *hatred* 殺してやりたいほど憎悪する. ¶ ***implacable*** *hatred* 執念深い憎しみ. ¶ earn the ***lasting*** *hatred* of ... …からいつまでも憎まれる. ¶ there was no ***personal*** *hatred* to ... …に対して個人的な憎しみは少しもなかった. ¶ the ***resolute*** *hatred* of wrong doings 悪行に対する決然とした憎しみ. ¶ Carlyle's ***savage*** *hatred* of shames 恥ずべき行為に対するカーライルの激しい憎しみ.

Q² ***class*** *hatred* 階級的憎悪. ¶ ***party*** *hatred* 党派的憎悪. ¶ purveyors of ***race*** (=racial) *hatred* 人種的憎悪を扇動する人々.

P² *hatred* ***at*** (=***to, towards,*** or ***against***) ... …に対する嫌悪(けんお). 【類】 His *hatred* ***against*** ... was intense.

haughtiness, *a.* 高慢.

Q ***overbearing*** *haughtiness* ごう慢不そん.

haughty, *a.* 高慢な.

P *haughty* ***to*** one's inferiors 目下の者に対してごう慢な.

haul, *n.* 一網, 一たぐり.

Q a ***rich*** *haul* of sardines いわしの大漁. ¶ The fishermen had a ***successful*** *haul*. その漁師たちは大漁であった.

P ***at*** one *haul* 一網に.

haul, *v.* 引張る, 引く; 方向を変える.

M *haul* ***away*** by wagons 荷馬車で運ぶ.

M² *haul* ***down*** (***up***) a flag 旗を引降ろす(引上げる). ¶ *haul* ***in*** a rope 綱をたぐる ‖ *haul* ***in*** (=***up***) a net 網をたぐり上げる. ¶ *haul* a person ***off*** to a jail 人を刑務所に連行する. ¶ *haul* a bucket ***up*** バケツを引上げる.

P *haul* ***at*** (=***upon***) a rope 綱を引張る. ¶ You'll be *hauled* ***over*** the coals. 君ひどい目に会うぞ. ¶ The submarine fired two shots, as a summons to the steamer to *haul* ***to***. 潜水艦は二発打ってその汽船に停止を命じた. ‖ *haul* ***to*** the wind=*haul* ***on*** the wind 船首を風上に向ける.

haulage, *n.* 運搬.

Q² ***horse*** *haulage* 馬力運搬.

haunt, *n.* 巣くつ, 出没個所.

V ***make out*** *haunts* of the thieves 盗賊の巣くつを発見する.

Q a ***favorite*** *haunt* of birds 鳥が好んで集まる所. 【類】 ***favorite*** *haunts* of film people (映画人). ¶ ***popular*** *haunts* of pleasure 遊覧地, 盛り場. ¶ ***sordid*** *haunts* of drunken vice and horrid joviality 飲酒の害悪とぞっとする歓楽のきたない巣くつ.

Q² a ***holiday*** *haunt* (=resort) 休日の行楽地. ¶ the ***pleasure*** *haunts* of London ロンドンの歓楽街.

P wild beasts ***in*** their native *haunts* 自然の生活そのままの野獣.

P² a favorite *haunt* ***for*** Londoners ロンドン人の遊び場. ¶ a *haunt* ***of*** lovers 恋人同志のよく行く所.

haunt, *v.* 付きまとう.

P he was *haunted* ***by*** perpetual fear that ... 彼は…という不安に始終つきまとわれていた. 【類】 he is continually *haunted* ***by*** the suggestion that ... / *haunted* ***by*** the shade (亡霊) of ... / *haunted* ***by*** anxiety / be *haunted* ***by*** the dread of dying. ¶ *haunted* ***with*** gloomy thoughts 陰うつな考えに付きまとわれて.

have, *v.* 持つ; 食べる; 求める.

M The matter *had* ***better*** be left as it is. その件はそっとしておいた方がいいよ. ‖ In the interest of society they *had* ***better*** not have been born. 社会のためからいうとあの人た

ちは生れて来なかった方がよかった. ¶You *have* ***only*** (=***but***) to go to school for learning. 君は学校に行ってさえすればいいんだ. ¶*have* it ***out*** with ... ...とあくまで論じつくす ‖ He was making up his mind to *have* it ***out*** with Rose. 彼はローズに思いのたけを言ってやろうと決心しかけていた. ‖ I *have* it ***out*** for cleaning. それはクリーニングに出してある. ¶You can't *have* it ***so.*** そうは行かない. ‖ Rumor *has* it ***so.*** そういううわさだ. ¶You *have* me ***there.*** こりゃ参った.

M² *Have* ***after***!=Pursue! *or* Let us pursue! あとに続け. ¶She seems to *have* it ***in*** for me. 《米》彼女は私に恨みを懐いてるようだ. ¶We *have* (=There is) no heat ***on*** in this room. このへやにはヒーターがない. ‖ I *had* ***on*** two flannel shirts. 私はフランネルのシャツを二枚重ねて着ていた. ‖ the coat I *have* ***on*** 私の着ている上衣. 【類】*have* ***on*** one's overcoat. ¶waitf or a ship to *have* ***upon*** the horizon 船が水平線上に現われるのを待っている.

P *Have* you any money ***about*** (=with) you? お金をお持合わせでしょうか. ¶it does not mean that he *has* anything ***against*** ... ...に反感を持つというわけじゃない. ¶*have* English ***at*** one's finger-ends 英語に熟達している ‖ those who *have* the interest of their country ***at*** heart 憂国の士. ¶have a dictionary ***by*** one for reference 座右に字引を置いて参考する ‖ In 1890 he married ..., ***by*** whom he *had* a daughter and a son. 彼は一八九〇年に...と結婚して一女一男が生れた. ¶*have* ... ***for*** supper 夕飯に...を食べる ‖ *have* ... ***for*** one's teacher ...を師とする ‖ They are now to be *had* almost ***for*** the price of waste-paper. 今では紙くず同様の値で買える. ‖ can be *had* ***for*** a cent 一セントで買える ‖ I *have* a message ***for*** you. おことずけがあります. ‖ I *have* a surprise ***for*** you. 珍らしいもの(ニューズ)があるよ. ¶I *had* it ***from*** him. 私はそれを彼から聞いた. ‖ You had a call ***from*** Miss Jane. ジエーンさんからお電話でした. ¶I *have* some money ***in*** hand. 私は少し金を持合わせている. ‖ *have* this ***in*** mind (=view) このことを頭に入れておく ‖ *Have* some milk ***in*** your cup? ミルクを入れましょうか. ‖ *have* (=hold) foreigners ***in*** the utmost contempt 外国人をあくまで見下げている ‖ *have* one ***in*** one's power 人を自由にする. ¶It is to be *had* ***of*** all grocers. それはどの雑貨商にもある. 【類】It is to be *had* ***of*** Maruzen. ¶He *had* 100 yen ***on*** him. 彼は百円持っていた. ‖ He *has* the Bible ***on*** the tip of his tongue. 彼は聖書をそらんじている. ¶the latest information to be *had* ***on*** the subject その問題について得らるべき最近の情報. ¶He *had* a cabin ***to*** himself. 彼は一船室を独占した. 【類】*have* a table all ***to*** ourselves. / We *had* the whole compartment (列車の一室) ***to*** ourselves. ‖ *have* her ***to*** wife 彼女をめとる. ¶*have* it ***under*** lock and key それを錠を掛けて仕舞っておく. ¶I *have* no money ***with*** me. 私は金を持合わしていない. ‖ *have* a talk ***with*** ... ...と話す.

O I *have* to go. 私は行かなくてはならない. ¶you don't *have* to be very old to remember ... 大した老人でなくっても...は記憶している. ¶The man who knew Fitzgerald and did not like him *has* yet to be found. フィッツジェラルドを知って彼を好かない人はいまだかつてない.

haven, *n.* 港, 避難所.

V ***assign*** a *haven* of resort for American merchants and whaling ships アメリカの商船及び捕鯨船出入の港を指定する. ¶***have*** no *haven* for refuge 浮ぶ瀬がない.

Q the study of classics as an ***intellectual*** *haven* in one's old age 老境の知的休養としての古典研究.

Q² a ***GI rest*** *haven* 兵士用休養所. ¶Atami is a ***winter*** *haven.* 熱海は避寒に適した土地である.

P² a *haven* ***for*** disreputable people 花柳のちまた. ¶a *haven* ***of*** rest いこいの場所.

havoc, *n.* 荒廃, 破壊.

V ***cause*** (=***do***) *havoc* 荒らす. ¶***make*** *havoc* of picturesqueness はなはだしく美観を害する. ¶Too much study ***played*** *havoc* with the health of the boy. 過度の勉強がその少年の健康を大いに害した. ‖ Typhoons ***played*** *havoc* with the rice plant. 台風で米作は大被害を受けた. ¶The storm ***spread*** *havoc* and desolation throughout vast regions. その暴風のために広い地域にわたる大被害があった. ¶The sun ***worked*** *havoc* with the skin of these sea bathers. これらの海水浴客は日に当って皮膚が大分荒れていた. ‖ the *havoc* ***wrought*** by the Germans on France and Belgium ドイツ軍によってなされたフランス・ベルギー両国の荒廃.

Q The fruit fly is an insect which works the ***direst*** *havoc* among gardens in Austria. 果樹ばえはオーストリアの果樹園に大損害を与えるこん虫である. ¶the typhoon made ***sad*** *havoc* among ... その颱風は...に惨害を与えた. ¶The hailstones have done ***terrible*** *havoc.* 降ひょうが大惨害を与えた. 【類】***terrible*** *havoc* has been done through ...

hawk, *n.* たか.

V cannot ***distinguish*** a *hawk* from a handshaw 菽麦(しゅく)を弁じない.

hawk, *v.* たか狩をする.

P *hawk* ***for*** game たか狩をする.

hawk, *v.* 呼売する.

P *hawk* ***from*** house ***to*** house 家ごとに売歩く.

hawker, *n.* 呼売人.

Q ***bawling*** *hawkers* 大声でわめく呼売人.

Q² a ***kerbstone*** (=***sidewalk***) *hawker* 街頭呼売人. ¶a ***newspaper*** *hawker* 新聞売子. ¶a ***street*** *hawker* 街頭呼売人.

hay, *n.* 乾草, まぐさ.

V ***load*** the *hay* on wagons 乾草を荷馬車に積む. ¶***make*** *hay* 乾草を作る ‖ ***Make*** *hay* while the sun shines. 〖諺〗機会を逸するな. ‖ ***make*** *hay* of things 物を取り散らかす. ¶***rake*** the *hay* 乾草をかき集める.

Q the smell of ***new-mown*** *hay* 新たに刈った乾草のにおい.

P dry grass ***for*** *hay* 乾草にするために草を乾かす. ¶a mow ***of*** *hay* 一度に刈集めた乾草 ‖ a pile ***of*** *hay* 一山の乾草.

hazard, *n.* 危険.

V ***eliminate*** fire *hazard* to the utmost できうる限り火災の憂いを除く. ¶***run*** the *hazard* その危険を冒す.

Q His cause at ***all*** *hazards* must be defended. 彼の主張はどうあっても弁護せねばならない. ¶at ***every*** *hazard* どんな危険を冒しても.

Q² reduce ***fire*** *hazards* 火災の危険を減らす.

P ***at*** the *hazard* of one's life 生命をとして ‖ select ***at*** *hazard* でたらめに選ぶ.

hazard, *v.* 思い切ってやってみる.

P *hazard* one's life ***on*** the rock-climbing 岩のぼりに運命をかける.

O *hazard* a guess 当てずっぽうを言う.

haze, *n.* もや, かすみ.

Q There was a ***mournful dim*** *haze* around the moon. 月には陰気な薄もやがかかっていた. ¶A ***thin*** *haze* veiled the hills. 山々にはかすみがかかっていた. ¶look at things through a ***visionary*** *haze* 幻のようなもやを通して物を見る.

Q² thin ***summer*** *haze* 薄い夏のもや.

P I saw Mt. Fuji dimly in the *haze.* 富士がもやのなかにぼんやりかすんで見えた.

P² The low hills on the horizon wore a *haze* ***of*** dark blue. 水平線上の小山は黒ずんだ青色のもやに包まれていた.

head, *n.* 頭, 頭脳; 首領; 項目; 貨幣の表面.

V This *sake* ***affects*** the *head.* この酒は頭に来る. ¶***bang*** one's *head* on a door in the dark 暗がりで頭を戸にごつんと打ちつける. ¶***bare*** one's *head* 脱帽する. ¶***beat*** a person's *head* ***off*** さんざんに打負かす. ¶***bend*** one's *head* 頭をかがめる ‖ He walks, ***bending*** his *head* forward. 頭をかがめて歩く(老人が). ¶***bother*** one's *head* about ... ...に頭を悩ます. ¶***bow*** one's *head* to ... ...におじぎをする ‖ ***bow*** one's *head* before a meal 食事の前のお祈りをする. 【類】***bow*** one's *head* three times to the ground. / weakly ***bow*** one's head and submit to ... / instinctively (思わず) ***bow*** one's *head* / ***bowed*** one's *head* in shame (mute greeting) / ***bow*** low one's *head.* ¶***bump*** one's *head* against ... 頭を...にぶっつける. ¶We ***bumped*** *heads* ***together.*** 僕たちははち合わせをした. ¶***bury*** one's *head* in one's hands 両手で頭をかかえる. ¶***clear*** the *head* 頭をはっきりさせる. ¶It ***cost*** him his *head.* 彼はそのために命を取られた. ¶***count*** (=***figure***) *heads* 頭(人)数を調べる. ¶forget to ***cover*** one's *head* 帽子をかぶるのを忘れる ‖ I want something to ***cover*** my *head* with. 何か頭をおおうものが欲しい. ¶***cram*** one's *head* with knowledge 知識を頭に詰込む. ¶***cut off*** the *head* 首をはねる. ¶***dip*** one's *head* into the water 頭を水の中に突込む. ¶***drop*** one's *head* on one's breast 胸の辺まで頭をたれる. ¶***duck*** one's *head* to avoid a missile 弾丸などを避けようとして頭をすくめる. ¶Such an idea has never ***entered*** my *head.* そんな考えはついぞ私の頭に浮ばなかった. ¶The snake ***erected*** the *head.* そのへびはかま首を立てた. ¶He soon

gained the *head* of the class. 彼はやがて級の首席になった. ¶ ***get*** a *head* 二日酔する. ¶***give*** a *head* to beer ビールのあわを立たせる ‖ The liquor ***gave*** me a *head.* その酒で二日酔した. ¶***hang*** the *head* in shame or sorrow 恥じてまたは悲しくて首をたれる.【類】***hang*** her *head* in shamefaced confusion (恥ずかしさにどぎまぎして). ¶***hang down*** one's *head* 頭をたれる. ¶***have*** a *head* for mathematics 数学の頭がある ‖ Beware of drinking too much, or you'll ***have*** a " *head.*" 深酒をやらないようにしないと二日酔するよ. ¶This beer ***has*** a good *head* ***on.*** このビールはよくあわが立っている. ¶fall down and ***hit*** one's *head* ころんで頭を打つ. ¶***hold*** one's *head* ***erect*** 頭を真直にしている ‖ ***hold*** one's *head* ***high*** 頭を高くしている ; たかぶる ‖ ***hold*** the *head* ***natural*** (***well back***) 頭を自然の位置におく(十分後ろにそらせる). ¶***hold down*** the *head* うなだれる. ¶***Hold up*** your *head,* speak out like a man. きちんと首をのばして男らしく活発に言いなさい. ¶***incline*** one's *head* 首を傾ける. ¶***jerk*** one's *head* 首をぐいと引く. ¶Don't be excited and ***keep*** your *head.* 興奮しないで落着き給え. ‖ fight to ***keep*** his *head* above water 借金をすまいと奮闘する ‖ ***keep*** the *head* ***covered.*** 帽子をかぶったままでいる. ¶***knock*** one's *head* against a post 頭を柱にこつんと打っつける. ¶***lay*** *heads* ***together*** 相談する. ¶***lift up*** one's *head* 頭をもたげる. ¶***lose*** one's *head* 血迷う ‖ Or else you shall ***lose*** your *head.* さもないと首がないぞ.【類】He came near ***losing*** his *head.* ¶Too much drink will ***make*** your *head* ***sick.*** 深酒は気持ちが悪くなる. ‖ He nobly ***made*** *head* against the difficulty. 彼は堂々とその困難を排して進んだ. ‖ I can't ***make*** *head* or tail of the thing! こりゃ何が何だか分らない.【類】I can't ***make*** *head* or tail out of it. = It's all Greek to me (ちんぷんかんぷん). ¶His *head* was somewhat ***muddled*** by the liquor he had consumed. 彼の頭は飲んだ酒のせいで幾分にぶっていた. ¶***nod*** one's *head* in acknowledgement of his salutations 彼のあいさつに答えてうなずく. ¶Windows are flung open and *heads* are ***obtruded*** from second and third floor. 窓は開け放たれて三階や四階の窓から頭がつき出ている. ¶***perk*** one's *head* 頭をあげる. ¶The hat ***pinches*** my *head.* 帽子が頭を締めつける. ¶***poke*** one's *head* into a hornets' nest 余計な世話を焼いてひどい目にあう. ¶***pop*** one's *head* out of the carriage window 客車の窓から頭を突き出す ‖ He ***popped*** his *head* ***in*** at the door. 彼はドアから首を出した. ¶***pop out*** one's *head* 頭をひょいとつき出す. ¶***punch*** the *head* of ... ...の頭をぶんなぐる. ¶***put*** one's *head* out of the window 窓から頭を出す. ¶***putting*** her *head* ***in*** at the door 戸口から(へやの中へ)頭をつき出して. ¶***put*** their *heads* ***together*** and contemplate ... 額を集めて...を熟慮する. ¶***puzzle*** one's *head* in vain for ... ...のためにむなしく頭を苦しめる. ¶***raise*** one's *head* 頭をもたげる. ¶She ***reared*** her *head* angrily. 彼女は怒って頭を上げた. ¶It ***requires*** a steady *head.* それにはしっかりした頭脳が要る. ¶***rest*** one's *head* on the pillow まくらに頭をのせる. ¶He ***scratched*** his gray *head* 彼は白髪頭をかいた. ¶***severed*** his *head* from his body 頭と胴を切り離す. ¶***shake*** one's *head* dubiously (firmly, gravely) いぶかしげに(など)頭を振る ‖ many wiseacres ***shook*** their *heads* over the folly of ... 多数の利口ぶった人たちが...の愚さに頭を振った. ¶He ***shaved*** his *head* and became a monk. 彼は頭を丸めて坊主になった. ¶***show*** its *head* 頭を出す ‖ He has not ***shown*** much *head* for business. 彼には大して事務の才がない. ¶***slap*** the *head* 頭をぴしゃっと張る. ¶You ought to go and ***soak*** your *head.* 頭を冷しておいで. ¶***stick*** one's *head* in the office door 事務所のドアをあけて頭を突込む ‖ ***stick*** one's *head* out of the window 窓から頭を出す. ¶***strike*** one's *head* against ... ...に頭を打つける. ¶***strike off*** a criminal's *head* 罪人の首をたたき切る. ¶***take*** the *head* of the table 食卓の上席に着く. ¶***take*** (= cut) a man's *head* ***off*** 首を切る. ¶***throw*** the *head* ***foward*** 首を投げる. ¶***tip*** one's *head* to one side 首をかしげる. ¶***toss*** his *head* to show his dissent 異議を示すために首を振立てる ‖ She ***tossed*** her *head* in pride. 彼女は誇らしげに首を振立てた. ¶They fell to their knees and ***touched*** their *heads* to the ground. 皆の者は地に頭をつけた. ¶Do not ***trouble*** your *head* about that. そのことに頭を悩ますな. ¶***turn*** one's *head* toward ... ...の方に顔を向ける ‖ ***turn*** *head* over heels とんぼがえりをする ‖ The horses' *heads* were ***turned homeward.*** 馬の首を家路に向けた ‖ Success has ***turned*** his *head* (= brain). 彼は成功してうぬぼれるようになった.【類】The joy (Her kisses) ***turned*** his *head* (有頂天). / His *head* is ***turned.*** ¶***turn away*** one's *head* 側を向く. ¶***uncover*** the *head* 脱帽する. ¶***wag*** one's *head* in disapprobation 承知しないで頭を振る.

V² My *head* ***aches.*** 頭痛がする. ¶Do you wonder that my *head* ***reels?*** 私の頭がくらくらっとするのも無理がないでしょう. ¶His *head* began to ***soften.*** 《米》彼はもうろくし出した. ¶My *head* ***swims.*** 頭がふらつく.【類】It is so high that the *head* ***swims*** when you look down. / If we could conceive it, our *heads* would ***swim*** at the mere thought.

Q. the ***autocratic*** *head* of the most military nation of modern times 近代最大陸軍国の専制的君主. ¶He has a ***bald*** *head.* 彼ははげ頭だ. ¶***bandaged*** *heads* 包帯をした頭. ¶He has a ***clear*** *head.* 彼は明せきな頭脳を持っている. ‖ the secret of a ***clear*** *head* 頭脳を明せきにする秘けつ. ¶a ***close-cut*** (= ***close-cropped***) *head* 短かく刈った頭. ¶under a ***competent*** *head* 手腕ある首脳者をいただいて. ¶a ***cool*** *head* 冷静な頭脳. ¶the ***crowned*** *heads* of Europe 欧州の君主たち.【類】For many generations Wedgewood has been supplying the finest tableware to the ***crowned*** *heads* and aristocracy of Europe. ¶That story would be worth a ***double*** *head.* その(新聞)記事は二段の見出しをつける価値がある. ¶an ***egg-shaped*** *head* 卵形の頭. ¶It may be summarized under the ***following*** *heads.* それは次の諸項目に要約される.【類】consider the subject under the ***following*** *heads*: (1)...; (2)...; (3)... ¶get up a ***full*** *head* of steam 十分蒸気の馬力が出る. ¶I have a ***giddy*** *head.* 頭がぐらぐらする. ¶He has a ***good*** *head* for a political problem. 彼は政治の頭がある. ¶a ***hard*** *head* しっかりした頭. ¶keep a ***level*** *head* through it all その間ずっと冷静でいる. ¶a ***massive*** *head* 大頭. ¶a ***misshapen*** *head* 不格好な頭. ¶This child has an ***old*** *head* on young shoulders. この子は年は行かないが考えは老けている. ¶the ***present*** *head* of the family その家族の当主. ¶His ***proud*** *head* bowed to nothing. 彼は頭が自尊心が強く何物にも屈しなかった. ¶the ***royal*** *heads* of Europe ヨーロッパの元首. ¶a ***running*** *head* [本の各ページの]上部見出し. ¶He has a ***scheming*** *head.* 彼には計画性がある. ¶a bolt with ***square*** (***hexagon cheese***) *head* 角(など)頭ボールト. ¶have a ***strong*** *head* 酒が強い. ¶the ***surviving*** *head* of the great historic family 歴史的由緒ある家柄の当主. ¶a ***thick*** *head* ぼうっとした頭. ¶The subject will be treated under ***three main*** *heads.* その問題を三つの主なる項目の下に論じられよう. ¶a ***tonsured*** *head* てい髪した頭. ¶the ***two*** *heads* of the English-Speaking peoples 英語国民の二元首(国王と大統領). ¶the ***white-haired*** *head* of a family 白髪の家長. ¶a ***wide*** *head* 該博な頭脳. ¶a ***wooden*** *head* 鈍い頭.

Q² a ***banner*** *head* 新聞の八欄全長の見出し. ¶have an excellent ***business*** *head* すばらしい実業的才能がある.【類】has a keen ***business*** *head.* ¶a ***college*** (***university***) *head* 学(総)長. ¶a ***department*** *head* [学]部長; 省長官. ¶a ***division*** *head* 部長. ¶an ***executive*** *head* 社長(理事長, 幹事長など). ¶the ***family*** *head* of each household 各戸の戸主. ¶a ***figure*** *head* かいらい, ロボット. ¶a ***flower*** *head* 花冠. ¶the ***fountain*** *head* of English art 英国美術の源流.【類】the ***fountain*** *heads* (水源) of all the streams in that part. ¶a ***household*** *head* 戸主. ¶a ***magenta*** *head* 赤毛の頭. ¶that splitting " ***morning after*** " *head* 例の頭の割れそうな二日酔. ¶the ***pit*** *heads* 炭鉱の坑口. ¶a " ***scare*** *head* " 〚新聞〛「こけおどし」の大見出し. ¶a ***school*** *head* 学校長. ¶a ***section*** *head* 部課長. ¶a ***union*** *head* 労組の委員長. ¶a ***ward*** *head* 区長.

P. He went to Paris ***as*** the *head* of the delegation. 彼は派遣団の首席委員としてパリーにおもむいた. ¶Dr. Bain is ***at*** the *head* of the Illinois Geological Survey. ベイン博士はイリノイ州地質調査所の所長である. ‖ He is ***at*** the *head* of the movement. 彼はその運動を指揮している.【類】put ... ***at*** the *head* of the Government (政府の首班) / He has been 10 years ***at*** the *head* of the Society. / ***at*** the *head* of the administration (内閣) / ***at*** the *head* of the editorial staff is ... / ***at*** the *head* of a mission from ... ‖ appear ***at*** the *head* (foot) of a list 表の最初(最後)に出ている ‖ the marching of a regiment with its band ***at*** its head 楽隊を先頭に進隊の行進. 【類】The King rode proudly ***at*** the *head* of his soldiers. / place him ***at*** the *head* of the list. / The god is placed ***at*** the *head* of the pantheon (諸神). / They were ***at*** the *head* of their epoch. / They are ***at*** the *head* of the nations in industry, commerce, and in political influence. / graduated ***at*** the *head* of his class ‖ men ***at*** the *head* of affairs in Japan 日本の国事の指導的立場にある人士. 【類】those ***at*** the *head* of large business houses and Government and municipal departments / sit ***at*** the *head* of the table (卓の上席) / carve a chicken (分配のために鶏肉を切る) ***at*** the *head* of a dinner-table / The French undoubtedly stand ***at*** the *head* of all European nations in matters of art. ‖ The city is picturesquely situated ***at*** the *head* of a bay. その町は入江の奥に美しく位している. 【類】He stood ***at*** the *head* of his class. / ***at*** the *head* (=top) of the list stands … ¶You are taller ***by*** a *head* 君は首だけ高い. ‖ The ship settled down ***by*** *head.* 船首が先に沈んだ. ¶a covering ***for*** the *head* 頭のかぶり物. ¶***from*** *head* to foot=from the crown of the head to the tip of the toes 頭の先からつま先まで ‖ He trembled ***from*** *head* to foot. 彼は全身ふるえていた. ‖ the fourth ***from*** the *head* of the procession 行列の先頭から四番目. ¶feel a pain ***in*** one's *head* 頭痛がする ‖ an old man with few teeth ***in*** his *head* ろくに歯のない老人. ¶it came ***into*** his *head* that … …ということが彼の頭に浮んだ ‖ he took it ***into*** his *head* to … 彼は…しようと思いたった. ¶be ***off*** one's *head* 気の狂っている, 理性を失っている ‖ He's ***off*** his *head* about the girl. 彼はその娘に夢中だ. He is ***off*** his *head* for pride. 彼は慢心している. ¶***On*** this *head* (subject) I will speak a few words. このことに関しては一言申上げましょう. 【類】he remarks ***on*** this *head* … / my observation ***on*** this *head* ‖ strike (=hit *or* blow) a person ***on*** the *head* その頭を打つ ‖ hair ***on*** the *head* 髪の毛. ¶He is quite ***out of*** his *head.* 彼は全く気が狂っている. ‖ write ***out of*** his own *head* 自分の頭で書く. 【類】draw a picture ***out of*** one's *head* / He did it ***out of*** his own *head.* ¶The water was ***over*** my *head.* [水の中で]私のせいが立たなかった. ‖ He is ***over*** *head* and ears in love with her. 彼は彼女に首ったけだ. ‖ preach ***over*** the *heads* of the congregation 会衆の理解し得ない(高遠な)ことを言う. ‖ talk ***over*** our *heads* われわれの理解し得ないことを言う ‖ brandishing the axe ***over*** his *head* おのを頭上に振りかざして. ‖ He bought that house ***over*** the other's *head.* 彼はその人を出し抜いてその家を買った. ¶***per*** *head* of cattle 牛(家畜)一頭当り ‖ the consumption of meat and milk ***per*** *head* of the population その人口の一人当りの牛肉及び牛乳消費量. ¶He had a handkerchief ***round*** his *head.* 彼は頭にハンケチを巻いていた. ¶It may be included ***under*** this *head.* それはこの項目に入れて差支えない. ‖ problems which arise ***under*** this *head* このことに関連して起る諸問題. 【類】it comes ***under*** the *head* of … / be kept away ***under*** the *head* of "unavailable" (「不用」の部) / ***under*** this *head* fall … / The question easily divides itself ***under*** three *heads.* / … may conveniently be grouped ***under*** three *heads* / If we roughly classify …, we may group them ***under*** four *heads.* / It may, I think, be considered ***under*** three *heads*: … (1) … ; (2) … ; (3) … ¶walk ***with*** *head* proudly erect ごう然とそり身になって歩く ‖ ***with*** uncovered *head* 無帽で.

P² The ship was unable to make *head* ***against*** the storm. その船は時化(しけ)に会って進めなかった. ¶The boy has a *head* ***for*** mathematics. その少年は数学の頭がある. ‖ a man with a *head* ***for*** detail ち密な頭脳の人. ¶the *head* ***from*** a doll. 人形から抜いた首 ‖ the *head* ***of*** a reformatory 矯正院長 ‖ the *head* ***of*** a tribe しゅう長 ‖ the *head* ***of*** the expedition その探検隊の隊長 ‖ the *heads* ***of*** all states, whether monarchical or republican 君主制たると共和制たるとを問わずあらゆる国家元首 ‖ the *head* ***of*** the household (=family) 戸主. 【類】the sixteenth *head* ***of*** a family noted for its hereditary skill in this art ‖ This reservoir has a fine *head* ***of*** water. この貯水池は(水源が高いから)水の出がよい. ‖ the *head* ***of*** barley 大麦の穂 ‖ a *head* ***of*** lettuce (cabbage) ちさの葉(きゃべつの巻いた部分). ¶tumble in the air *head* ***over*** heel[s] とんぼ返りをする.

head, *v.* 向う; 先に立つ, 頭になる.

M *head* ***straight*** for … …に直行する ‖ *head* ***westward*** (***eastward***) 西(東)方に向う.

M² *head* ***off*** a race レースの先頭を切る ‖ *head* ***off*** a quarrel けんかを止めさせる ‖ *head* ***off*** another war 戦争の再発を防止する ‖ *head* ***off*** the inflation インフレを食い止める ‖ *head* ***off*** disease microbes 病菌の発生を防ぐ ‖ Fido *headed* [***off***] his flock of sheep for the pasture. [犬の]ファイドーは羊の群を牧場に導いた. ‖ I *headed* him ***off*** from making a speech. 彼が演説するのを中止させた. ¶*head* ***up*** the organization その団体の長になる ‖ *head* ***up*** the new commission [委員長として]新しい委員会を指導する.

P a tourist party *headed* ***by*** … …が団長の観光団. 【類】an education mission *headed* ***by*** Dr.— ‖ *headed* ***by*** their band 楽隊が先頭に立って. ¶factory workers *heading* ***for*** home 家路に向う工場の職工たち. 【類】weekenders *headed* ***for*** cooler seaside and resort areas / a slow boat that *headed* ***for*** the States / *head* one's boat ***for*** the shore / a ship *heading* ***for*** the Swedish coast. ¶***in*** the chapter *headed* "…", dealing with … …に関する「…」という題目の章に.

headache, *n.* 頭痛.

V ***cure*** a *headache* 頭痛をなおす. ¶***get*** a *headache* 頭痛がする. ¶It ***gives*** me a *headache.* そうすると僕は頭痛がして来る. ¶I ***have*** a *headache.* 私は頭痛がする. ¶***plead*** a *headache* for not going 頭が痛いので行かないと言いわけをする. ¶***sleep off*** a *headache* 寝て頭痛をなおす. ¶***walk off*** a *headache* 歩いて頭痛をなおす.

Q an ***awful crashing*** *headache* 頭が割れるような頭痛. ¶have a ***bad*** (***slight***) *headache* ひどく(ちょっと)頭が痛い. ¶I have got a most ***beastly*** *headache.* ひどく頭が痛い. ¶one of his ***biggest*** *headaches* 一つの大頭痛の種. ¶He suffered from ***fearful*** *headache* in after life. 彼は晩年になってひどい頭痛に悩んだ. ¶a ***heavy*** *headache* はげしい頭痛. ¶a ***raging*** *headache* 猛烈な頭痛. ¶a ***splitting*** (=***racking***) *headache* 頭が割れるような頭痛.

P suffer ***from*** a *headache* 頭痛がする. ¶She is subject ***to*** *headaches* 彼女は頭痛持ちだ. ¶I am troubled ***with*** a *headache.* 私は頭痛で悩んでいる.

P² be a *headache* ***for*** … …にとって頭痛の種である.

headdress, *n.* かぶりもの.

Q² a ***wartime*** *headdress* 戦時特別帽.

P ***off*** *headdress* 脱帽して.

headgear, *n.* かぶりもの.

Q² ***pit*** *headgear* [坑夫の]炭坑帽. ¶act as umpire ***without*** *headgear* 面をつけないでアンパイヤをやる.

heading, *n.* 表題, 題目, 見出し.

Q a ***sensational*** *heading* 刺激的大見出し.

Q² facts arranged under ***black letter*** *headings.* ゴシック活字の見出しをつけた事実. ¶***cross*** *headings*=crosshead 〖新聞〗[記事の]差込み見出し. ¶a ***side*** *heading* 側(横)見出し.

P ***under*** the *heading* "… …"「……」の見出しで ‖ come ***under*** the *heading* of "…"「…」の部類にはいる. 【類】it may be included ***under*** the *heading* of … ‖ There are no reliable statistics ***under*** this *heading.* このことに関しては何ら信じるに足る統計がない. ‖ everything which comes ***under*** the *heading* of … …と名の付くものならすべて. ¶publish an article ***with*** the above *heading* 上記の表題で一文を発表する. ¶selected this as a *heading* ***for*** this paper, because … この論文の表題としてこれを選んだわけは…

headland, *n.* みさき.

V ***double*** a *headland* みさきを回る.

head-light, *n.* 前灯.

V ***have*** their *head-lights* on [car が]前灯をつけている.

headline, *n.* 見出し.

V the paper ***carries*** the *headline,* "…" その論文には「…」という見出しが付いている. ¶The following *headlines* are ***displayed*** across two columns in a most prominent position. 次のような見出しがきわめて目につきやすい場所に二段にわたって掲げてある.

Q ***catching*** *headlines* 人目をひく見出し. ¶a ***flush*** *headline* 左側をそろえた(数行の)見出し. ¶***misleading*** *headlines* 人の誤解しそうな見出し.

Q² give ***front page*** *headlines* to … …を一面見出しで掲げる. ¶Gothic is the fat, bold type face which is used mostly for ***newspaper*** *headlines.* ゴシックは太くて厚い活字の面で多く新聞の見出しに使われる. ¶***scare*** *headlines* in newspapers 新聞の大見出し(あまり重要でない記事につけ

た). ¶the ***up-to-the-minute news*** *headlines* of the day 当日の最新ニュースの見出し.

P ***under*** the sensational *headline*, "…" 「…」という扇情的な見出しで. ¶The terrible news was published ***with*** heavy *headlines* and editorial comments in the morning issues of July 16. この恐るべきニュースが七月十六日の朝刊に大見出しと社の批評を添えて発表された.

headman, *n.* 市(村)長. 「市町長村長.

Q² the City mayor, ***Town*** *headman* or ***Village*** *headman*

headquarters, *n. sing., pl.* 本部, 本営; 本場.

V ***establish*** strike *headquarters* ストの本部を設ける ‖ His Majesty ***established*** his *headquarters* at Hiroshima. 陛下には大本営を広島におかせられた. ¶***transfer*** the Imperial *headquarters* to … 大本営を…に移す.

Q ***General*** *Headquarters* 総司令部. ¶***national*** *headquarters* 全国本部. ¶the ***tourists'*** *headquarters* 観光本部.

Q² ***IX Corps*** *Headquarters* 第九兵団司令部.

P London is recognized ***as*** the *headquarters* of the ivory trade. ロンドンは象牙取引の中心地として認められている.

P² make this hotel one's *headquarters* ***for*** a day or two このホテルを二三日の滞在所にする. ¶Corinth and Athens were the *headquarters* ***of*** the manufacture of Greek pottery. コリントとアテネはギリシアの陶器製造の中心地

headway, *n.* 前進, 進歩. Lであった.

V The fire ***gained*** *headway*. 火事が拡がった. ¶***gather*** *headway* 前進する. ¶The work is steadily ***making*** *headway*. その仕事は着々進んでいる. ‖ ***make*** little *headway* らちがあかぬ ‖ ***make*** good *headway* against … …にりっぱに対抗する. 【類】The work cannot ***make*** *headway* until it is more strongly supported financially. / a steamer trying to ***make*** *headway* against the storm.

Q The idea is making ***steady*** *headway*. その考えが着々広

heal, *v.* いやす; いえる. Lまりつつある.

P The anti-Japanese feelings have been *healed* ***by*** time. 排日思想はときの経過するにつれて自然に消失した. ¶He was *healed* ***of*** his wound. 彼は傷がいえた. ‖ The treatment *healed* him ***of*** fever. その治療で彼の熱がとれた. ¶*heal* a patient ***with*** medicine 病人を薬でなおす.

O *heal* a man with (=sick of) the dropsy 水腫(しゅ)にかかっ

healer, *n.* 治療師. Lた人をいやす.

Q a ***magic*** *healer* まじない師, 祈禱師.

Q² a ***woman faith*** *healer* 信仰治療をやる婦人.

healing, *n.* 治ゆ, 治療法.

V ***promote*** rapid *healing* 全快を早める.

Q² ***faith*** *healing* 信仰療法.

P *healing* ***without*** drugs 無薬療法.

health, *n.* 健康, 衛生.

V The climate ***affected*** his *health*. その土地の気候が彼の体にさわった. ¶***benefit*** their *health* and character 彼らの健康及び性格を益する. ¶His sufferings were so severe that his *health* was permanently ***broken***. 彼は苦しみ方がひどいのでその健康を永久に害した. ¶***cause*** ill *health* 不健康にする. ¶do nothing to ***compromise*** *health* 体にさわるようなことは何もしない. ¶***damage*** *health* 健康を害する. ¶His *health* is utterly ***destroyed***. 彼の健康は全くこわされた. ¶***drink*** *health* 祝杯をあげる ‖ Let's ***drink*** *health* to the bride. 花嫁のために乾杯しましょう. 【類】***drink*** the Emperor's *health* / The *health* of the guest was ***drunk*** in champagne. ¶***endanger*** one's *health* その健康を危くする. ¶***enjoy*** *health* and longevity 健康と長寿を享有する. 【類】***enjoy*** good *health* ‖ She was one of those patients who, having nothing else to do, live only " to ***enjoy*** bad *health*." 彼女は所在がなくいわゆる「病気のお相手をする」ためにのみ生きているような患者の一人だった. ¶***favor*** *health* 健康に益がある. ¶to ***find*** his *health* 健康回復のため. 【類】He travelled over Europe in the hope of ***finding*** *health*. / I congratulate the patient upon having ***found*** her *health*. ¶***give*** *health* to the skin 皮膚を丈夫にする ‖ I ***give*** you the *health* of General Foch. わが輩は諸君とともにフォッシュ元帥のために祝杯をあげたいと思う. ¶***guard*** one's *health* 健康に注意する. ¶***harden*** one's *health* 体を丈夫にする. ¶***have*** good *health* 体が丈夫だ. ¶This greatly ***impaired*** his *health*. これで彼はひどく健康を害した. ¶***improve*** one's *health* by exercise 運動をして健康を増進する ‖ A change in the dietary of the Japanese Navy greatly ***improved*** the *health* of the sailors. 日本の海軍の食物が変ったので水兵の健康が大層よくなった. ¶***injure*** *health* with anxiety and strain 心配や過労で健康を害する. ¶***inquire after*** his *health* 彼のごきげんうかがいをする. ¶***keep*** one's *health* ***strong*** 健康を丈夫に保つ. ¶She ***lost*** her *health* to sit up to nurse her father. 彼女は父の看病でろくに寝なかったので健康を害した. ¶***maintain*** *health* 健康を維持する. ¶***occasion*** ill *health* to … …の健康を損う. ¶He ***possesses*** good *health*. 彼は体が丈夫である. ¶***preserve*** one's *health* 健康を保持する. ¶***produce*** *health* 健康を産む. ¶Laughing ***promotes*** *health*. 笑いは健康に益がある. 【類】***promote*** the public *health*. ¶***propose*** the *health* of the guest of honor 主賓の健康を祝し乾杯を発議する. ¶***propose*** and ***drink*** *healths* 健康を祝して杯をあげる. ¶The dentifrice ***protects*** the *health* of your teeth, mouth and gums. この歯みがきは歯・口及び歯ぐきを保護する. ¶***rally*** one's *health* 健康を回復する. ¶***reap*** good *health* [その結果]健康を得る. ¶***recover*** one's *health* 健康をとり戻す. 【類】He ***recovered*** (=was restored to) his perfect *health*. / ***recover*** their robust *health* after years of suffering. ¶in order to ***recruit*** one's *health* 健康回復のため. ¶to ***recuperate*** his *health* 保養のため. ¶rapidly ***regain*** *health* and strength すみやかに健康と元気とを回復する ‖ solicitous to ***regain*** one's *health* 切に健康回復を望んで. ¶***restore*** one's impaired *health* by means of sea-air and sea-bathing 海岸の空気と海水浴とで健康を回復する. ¶***retain*** one's *health* 健康を保有する. ¶***risk*** one's *health* 健康を危くする. ¶You will ***ruin*** your *health*. それでは体がたまるまい. ¶***secure*** good *health* 体を丈夫にする. ¶He is ***seeking*** *health* in the Hakone mountains. 彼は箱根の山で養生している. ¶His *health* is completely ***shattered***. 彼は全く健康を害した. ¶***suit*** one's *health* 健康に適する. ¶The change of climate seriously ***threatened*** his *health*. 風土の相違が大いに彼の健康をおびやかした. ¶***toast*** the *health* of … …の健康を祝して乾杯する. ¶permanently ***undermine*** one's *health* 永久的に健康を害する. 【類】***undermine*** the *health* of the strongest. ¶He has ***upset*** his health for several months. 彼はここ数ケ月間からだをこわしている. ¶***wreck*** the *health* of … …の健康を破壊する.

V² My *health* has greatly ***benefited*** by the travel. その旅行は大いに私の健康を増進した. ¶His *health* ***broke*** and rapidly sank gravewards. 彼は健康を害してぐんぐん衰弱して行った. ¶Under the heavy strain, her *health* completely ***broke down***. 過労で彼女は体を台なしにした. ¶His *health* began to ***break up***. 彼の健康が衰え始めた. ¶His *health* ***failed*** [him]. 彼は健康を害した. ¶His *health* ***gave way***. 彼は健康を失った. ¶Is your *health* ***improving***? お体は段々およろしいのですか. ¶At last *health* is ***returning***. いよいよ健康が回復しかけている. ¶His *health* ***sank*** rapidly and he died in Paris. 彼はずんずん衰弱してパリーで死んだ. ¶His *health* ***suffered***. 彼は健康を害した. 【類】His *health* began to ***suffer***.

Q He is in ***bad*** *health*. 彼は体が悪い. ¶He enjoys perfect ***bodily*** *health*. 彼は申し分のない健康体である. ¶He had been in ***broken*** *health* for some time. 彼は(その時)しばらく体を傷めていたのであった. ¶those in ***delicate*** *health* 病身の人々. ¶be in ***declining*** *health* 健康が衰えている. ¶***economic*** *health* 経済的健全. ¶He is in ***excellent*** *health*. 彼はすこぶる健康だ. ¶He was in ***failing*** *health*. 彼は体をいためていた. 【類】on account of his ***failing*** *health* / ***Failing*** *health* soon drove him to Italy for a change of air. / His ***failing*** *health* exiled him to the Far West. ¶He resigned on account of ***feeble*** *health*. 彼は虚弱な体のために職を辞した. ¶***fine*** *health* 健康. ¶Her *health* is ***frail***. 彼女は病身だ. ¶enjoy ***good*** *health* 健康に恵まれている. 【類】I'm glad to find you in ***good*** *health*. ¶affect ***human*** *health* 人間の健康に影響する. ¶on account of ***ill*** *health* 病気のため. ¶the result of ***impaired*** *health* 健康をこわした結果. ¶of ***infirm*** *health* 体の丈夫でない. ¶He is still in ***mental*** and ***bodily*** *health* and vigour. 彼はまだ心身ともに壮健である. ¶a man in ***normal*** *health* 普通の健康状態の人. ¶He has returned to his ***perfect*** *health*. 彼は全快した. ¶***Physical*** *health* depends on moral health. 肉体の健康は精神の健康に依存する. ¶He was then in ***poor*** *health*. 当時彼は体を悪くしていた. ‖ He preferred a ***poor*** *health* to a remedy so heroic. そん

な荒療治よりは(このままの)弱いからだの方がよいと言った. ¶his ***precarious*** *health* 彼のおぼつかない健康. ¶his ***psychic*** *health* 彼の精神の健全. ¶guard the ***public health*** 公衆の衛生を保護する. ¶the doctor promised me ***restored*** *health* if I... 医者は私が...すれば健康回復を請合うといった. ¶This injured his naturally ***robust*** *health*. このために彼は生来丈夫な体を傷めた. ¶He was such a picture of ***rosy*** *health*. 彼はいかにも健康に見えた. ¶For some time his *health* had been not altogether ***satisfactory***. しばらく彼の健康はあまりすぐれなかったのであった. ¶be in ***strong*** (***weak***) *health* 身体が丈夫である(弱い). ¶His *health* became ***undermined***. 彼は大いに健康を害した. ¶enjoy ***vigorous*** *health* 元気盛んだ.

Q² ***student*** *health* 学生の健康.

P consult a physician ***about*** one's *health* 医者に診察してもらう. ¶inquire ***after*** one's *health* 見舞いをする. ¶try walking ***for*** one's *health* 健康のために散歩を試みる ‖ good ***for*** one's *health* 健康に益がある. ¶Morning walks are good exercises ***for*** the *health*. ¶those who are ***in*** robust *health* 強壮な人々 ‖ ***in*** *health* and disease (=illness) 丈夫な時も病気の時も. ¶He is in the best ***of*** *health*. 彼はこの上もなく健康だ. ‖ She is an incarnation ***of*** *health* and sunshine. 彼女は健康と明朗性の化身だ. ¶He was ***out of*** *health* and irritable. 彼は体が悪くていらいらしていた. ¶***owing to*** failing *health* 病気のため. ¶***To*** your *health*! 御健康を祝します(乾杯する時の語). ‖ He was restored ***to*** his usual *health*. 彼は健康を回復した. ¶He was blessed ***with*** good *health*. 彼は健康に恵まれていた. 「彼は病身であった.

P² His *health* ***in*** early youth was delicate. 少年のころの

healthy, *a.* 健康な.

M ***outwardly*** *healthy* みかけは丈夫な.

heap, *n.* [うず高い]山, かたまり.

Q² a ***dump*** *heap* ごみの山. ¶a ***helter-skelter*** *heap* of brick and iron junk 乱雑なれんがや鉄くずの山. ¶a ***refuse*** *heap* くずの山. ¶a ***sand*** *heap* 砂の山. ¶Millions of dollars go into the ***scrap*** *heap* every year. 毎年何百万ドルの価値のあるものがむだになる.

P I saw her ***in*** a *heap* under the window. 私は彼女が一塊になって窓の下にうずくまっているのを見た. 【類】lie (sit) ***in*** a *heap* ‖ pile hay ***in*** *heaps* 枯れ草を山と積む. ¶collect fallen leaves ***into*** a *heap* 落葉をかき集めて山を作る. ¶all ***of*** a *heap* どさっと, どさっと. 【類】fall all ***of*** a *heap* / be knocked (=struck) all ***of*** a *heap*.

P² The tower collapsed in a ***heap of*** ruin. その塔は崩壊して累々と山をなしていた. ‖ a ***heap of*** rubble がれきの山. ‖ The book is a dull and uninteresting ***heap of*** dry bones. その本は無味乾燥丸で白骨の堆(たい)積だ. ‖ have a ***heap of*** work to do 沢山仕事がある. ¶***heaps on*** heaps 累々と.

heap, *v.* 積み重ねる.

M² *heap* ***up***... ...を積み上げる ‖ be *heaped* ***up*** in confusion めちゃめちゃに積み重なっている.

P *heap* scorn and contempt ***on***... ...を盛んに侮り恥ずかしめる. ¶He *heaped* ***upon*** me all kinds of insult and abuse. 彼は私にありとあらゆるののしりと非難を浴びせた. ¶*heap* a dish ***with*** fruits さらに果物を盛る. 【類】*heap* a plate ***with*** food / a table *heaped* ***with*** books (bulletins, papers) ‖ a field of battle *heaped* ***with*** the dead 死がいが累々としている戦場 ‖ *heap* a person ***with*** favors 人に何くれとなく目をかけてやる.

hear, *v.* 聞く, 聞える; 聴取する.

M He hears ***badly*** in one ear and not in the other. 彼は一方の耳が遠く片方のは全然聞えない. ¶A whistle is ***dimly*** *heard*. かすかに汽笛が聞える. ¶have *heard* ***enough*** about... ...はもう聞きあきている. ¶Wait until you *hear* ***further*** from me. 私からさたするまで待て. ¶have *heard* so ***much*** about... ...はうわさに高い. ¶[I] ***never*** *heard* of that. そんなの聞いたこともない. ¶be still *heard* ***occasionally*** 今も時々聞く. ¶I have ***often*** *heard* it said that ... ...とはよく聞くことだ. ¶Please *hear* me ***out***. [話の]終りまで聞いて下さい. ‖ *hear* ***out*** a speech 演説を終りまで聞く ‖ refuse to *hear* him ***out*** 彼の話を終りまで聞こうとしない. ¶***So*** I *heard*. そうだそうです. ¶I *heard* him ***throughout***. 私は彼のいうことをしまいまで聞いた. ¶***vaguely*** *hear* of... ...のことをばく然と聞く. ¶*hear* ***wrong*** 聞き損う.

P Is there anything true in what I've *heard* ***about*** you? このあなたのおうわさはいくらか当っていますか. 【類】Have you *heard* ***about*** the robbery? ¶I *hear* ***for*** certain that the vessel has sailed. その船はもう出帆したと確かに聞いている. ¶Eight different pronunciations of the word "often" are *heard* ***from*** educated people. "often" という語には八つの異った発音が教養のある人士の間に聞かれる. ‖ I *heard* ***from*** China that ... ...と中国から私の所に消息があった. ‖ I have not *heard* ***from*** him since. それっきりたよりがない. ‖ I *hear* ***from*** a very good authority that ... 私はきわめて信ずべき筋から...と聞いた. 【類】I *heard* it ***from*** his own lips. / I've *heard* nothing ***from*** him=I haven't *heard* anything ***from*** him yet. / I should be glad to *hear* ***from*** you on the subject. ¶The firing of a gun was *heard* ***in*** the distance. 砲声が遠くに聞えた. ¶He was never *heard* ***of*** again. 彼の消息はその後絶えた. ‖ *hear* ***of*** one's death 死んだということを聞く. 【類】Every one has *heard* ***of*** the nightingale, though very many have never heard it sing. / I am very much concerned (=shocked) to *hear* ***of*** his sudden death. / Be sure and let me *hear* ***of*** your safe arrival. / She has not since been *heard* ***of***. ¶Such an expression is never *heard* ***on*** British lips. そういう言回しは英人は決して使わない. ¶The sound could be *heard* ***to*** a great distance. その音は遠くまでとどくだろう. ¶We *hear* ***with*** our ears. われわれは耳で聞く. ‖ I *heard* ***with*** astonishment that ... 私は...と聞いて驚いた.

O *Hear* him say! 彼の言うことを聞け(ヒアヒア).

hearing, *n.* 聴力; 聴取; 審問.

V the court ***adjourned*** the *hearing* till ... その裁判所は...まで審問を延期した. ¶His *hearing* is ***dimmed***. 彼は耳が遠い. ¶His theory did not ***find*** a *hearing* for many years afterwards. 彼の説は以後幾年も世間から耳を傾けられなかった. ¶***gain*** (=***get***) a *hearing* 発言の機会を得る, 聞いてもらえる. 【類】He was unable to ***gain*** a *hearing*. ¶No socialists or radical political orators can ***get*** a *hearing* in that conservative town. その保守的な町ではどの社会主義者も急進的政談演説家も耳を傾けられない. ¶Let's ***give*** him a *hearing*. 彼の言い分を聞こう. 【類】The rowdy students would not ***give*** him a *hearing*. ‖ The Minister ***gave*** the petitioners a *hearing*. その大臣は請願者に面会を許した. ¶***have*** a fair *hearing* 公平に聞いてもらう. ¶an ear-trumpet to ***help*** one's *hearing* 補聴器. ¶***lose*** one's *hearing*=become deaf 聴力を失う. 【類】She ***lost*** her *hearing* through scarlet fever. ¶His opinion ***met*** the readiest *hearing*. 彼の意見はたちまち傾聴された. ¶***obtain*** a *hearing* from ... ...に聞いてもらう. ¶*Hearing* is ***postponed***. 審問は延期された. ¶***practice*** *hearing* 耳をならす. ¶The delegation of students ***received*** a sympathetic *hearing* from the University authorities. 学生代表の陳情は大学当局から同情を持って聴取された. ¶***set*** the preliminary *hearing* for ... 予審を...に決める. ¶They ***won*** for themselves a respectful *hearing*. 彼らの言分は謹聴された.

Q The *hearing* of a dog is very ***acute***. 犬は耳がとても鋭い. ¶The speaker had an ***attentive*** *hearing*. その弁士は熱心に傾聴せられた. 【類】give an ***attentive*** *hearing* to ... ¶His *hearing* is somewhat ***bad*** (=***impaired***). あの人は少し耳が遠い. ¶Give me a ***candid*** *hearing*. [私の言うことを]公平に聞いて下さい. ¶***defective*** *hearing* 不完全な聴力. ¶give him a ***fair*** *hearing* 彼の言分を公平に聞いてやる. ¶an ***open*** *hearing* 公聴会. ¶a ***preliminary*** *hearing* 予審. ¶***public*** *hearing* 公判. ¶obtain a ***respectful*** *hearing* 大いに傾聴される. ¶a ***sharp*** *hearing* 鋭い耳. ¶get a ***wide*** *hearing* in educational circles 教育界に広く傾聴せられる.

Q² a war-contracts ***bribery*** *hearing*. 戦時契約収賄事件の審問. ¶a ***removal*** *hearing* 身柄移送のための審問. ¶An audition is a ***test*** *hearing* of a singer or an entertainer applied for the stage. オーディションとは舞台志望の歌手や芸能人の試聴会である.

P I recognized him ***at*** first *hearing*. 私は一言聞いただけであの人だなと感付いた. ¶***beyond*** *hearing* 聞えない所に. ¶***during*** the *hearing* of the case その訴訟事件の審問中に. ¶He said so ***in*** the *hearing* of the present writer. 彼はこの文の筆者が聞いている所でそう言った. ¶He is hard ***of*** *hearing*. 彼は耳が遠い. ‖ the sense ***of*** *hearing* 聴覚. ‖ it might, ***on*** first *hearing*, perhaps seem strange that ... は

じめて聞くと…ということは不思議に思われましょう. ¶***out of** hearing* 聞えない所に. ¶***under*** preliminary *hearing* 予審中. ¶discuss it ***within*** the *hearing* of … …の聞える所でそのことを話し合う. ‖ There was no one ***within*** *hearing*. 聞える所にはだれもいなかった.

P² *hearings* ***of*** a bill 議案の審議 ‖ the *hearing* ***of*** a cause

O *Hearing* was off again. 審問は再び延期された. ⌊審判.

hearsay, *n.* 風聞, うわさ.

V ***re-echo*** the *hearsay* of … …の風聞を反響する.

P I know it only ***by*** *hearsay*. 私は風聞だけでそれを知っている. ¶speak ***from*** *hearsay* 人の話を聞いて言う. ¶I know only ***through*** *hearsay*. 私はただ風聞だけで知っている. ‖ gain knowledge ***through*** *hearsay* and reading only 人の話や読書だけで知識を得る.

heart, *n.* 心臓; 心, 胸; 勇気.

V ***affect*** the *heart* 心臓にさわる. ¶This ***bespeaks*** a kindly *heart*. これで親切が分かる. ¶***Bless*** your kind *heart!* 御親切有難う. ¶***break*** one's *heart* from disappointed love 失恋のために悲嘆に暮れる. 【類】a woman ***breaking*** her *heart* for a man / a story to ***break*** one's *heart*. ¶***brighten*** one's *heart* 心を晴々させる. ¶The noise ***brought*** her *heart* up into her mouth. その騒ぎを聞いて彼女はびっくり仰天した. ¶She has ***captivated*** his *heart*. 彼女は彼の心を奪った. ¶***Cleanse*** your *hearts* of hatred. 諸君の憎しみの気持を一掃せよ. ¶***cross*** one's *heart* 胸に十字を切る ‖ ***Cross*** my *heart*, I didn't. 全く(誓って)私はそんなことはしない. ¶***crush*** the *heart* 気をくじく. ¶***cry*** one's ***heart out*** 胸が裂けるほど泣く. ¶***cultivate*** the *heart* 修養をする. ¶***deceive*** one's own *heart* 自らをあざむく. ¶***eat*** one's ***heart out***=suffer silently 悲嘆に暮れる. ¶***exchange*** *hearts* at our eyes 互に目にものを言わせる. ¶I could ***feel*** my *heart* ***go*** thump—thump—thump. 私は胸がどきどきした. ‖ The first time she threw me a kiss I ***felt*** my *heart* ***stop*** [beating]. 彼女が初めて私に接ぷんを投げたとき私は心臓が止ったかと思った. ¶The good news ***filled*** their *hearts* with joy. その吉報が彼らを狂喜させた. ¶***fix*** their *hearts* on other things 別のことに心を注ぐ. ¶***fret*** one's *heart* 心をいらだたせる. ¶***gain*** the *heart* of a pretty girl. きれいな女の子の愛情を得る. ¶***gather heart*** 元気を出す. ¶a youth to whom the maiden ***gave*** her *heart* その乙女が愛を捧げた青年. 【類】she ***gave*** her entire *heart* to … ¶The news ***gladdened*** my *heart*. その便りは私を喜ばした. 【類】***gladden*** the *hearts* of thousands of mothers. ¶fear and anxiety ***gnawing*** her *heart* 彼女の胸に食い入る恐怖と心配. ¶***harden*** one's heart 心を鬼にする, 思い切ってやる ‖ ***harden*** one's *heart* against … がん迷で…を認めない. 【類】His *heart* was ***hardened*** by a life of crime. ‖ a *heart* ***hardened*** by the rubs of life 浮世の苦しみですさんだ心. ¶With such a forlorn look I ***had*** not the *heart* to prosecute my inquiries. こうした心もとない情勢なので私は研究をしてみようという気になれなかった. ‖ ***have*** one's *heart* in one's mouth (=boots) at … …を見てはっと思う. 【類】When driving I have often ***had*** my *heart* in my mouth at a daring youngster leisurely crossing the street—just ahead of the horses. ‖ You ***have*** my *heart*. 私はあなたのものです. ‖ ***have*** no *heart* (=mind) to … …する気はさらにない. ¶***improve*** the *heart* 心をみがく. ¶***keep*** the *heart* ***beating*** 心臓の鼓動を続けさせる(生命を持続させる) ‖ ***keep*** one's *heart* ***pure*** 心を純潔に保つ. ¶***Keep*** your *heart* ***up***! 失望するな. ¶The suitor ***laid*** his *heart* at her feet. 彼は彼女に求婚した. ¶She resolved never to ***let*** her *heart* go out to anyone again. 彼女は二度とだれにも心を寄せまいと決心した. ¶***lift up*** one's *heart* in prayer 祈りで気を引立てる. 【類】***lift up*** the *hearts* of people. ¶Do not ***lose heart*** at the want of instant success. すぐさま成功しないからといって落胆するな. ‖ He has ***lost*** his *heart* to a very pretty young girl, I hear. あれはきれいな子に首ったけだとよ. ¶There are ceramics enough to ***make*** the collector's *heart* ***glad***. そこには収集家をしてすいぜんおく能わざらしめる陶磁器がある. ‖ A sudden noise ***made*** the *heart* ***gallop***. 突然音がしたのでどきっとした. ¶***mellow*** one's *heart* 気を和らげる. ¶His enthusiasm is enough to ***melt*** a *heart* of stone. 彼の熱誠には石のような心もとける. ¶It is not the eye, but the ear, that ***moves*** the *heart*. 人の心を動かすのは目ではなくて耳だ. ¶A terrible fear ***numbed*** his *heart*. 恐ろしさにぞっとした. ¶***murder*** one's *heart* 人を精神的に殺す. ¶***nerve*** the *heart* 元気づける. ¶***open*** one's *heart* to him and tell him how … 彼に胸中を打明けて…の次第を語る. ¶Mountain-climbing ***overtaxes*** one's *heart*. 登山は心臓を無理に使う. ¶***pluck up*** one's *heart* 元気を出す. ¶***put*** one's *heart* into one's work (task) 仕事(など)に熱中する ‖ The danger ***put*** her little *heart* in her mouth. その危険に出会って女の子ははっと思った. ¶***rend*** one's *heart* 断腸の思いをする. ¶I heard a sound which ***sent*** my *heart* into my mouth. 私ははっとするような音を聞いた. ¶***set*** one's *heart* at rest (=ease) 心を安んじる ‖ ***set*** her *heart* on a screen career 映画人になろうと心を決める ‖ ***set*** one's *heart* on a desire ある念願を起す ‖ ***set*** one's *heart* on earthly goods 現世の財宝に目をくれる. 【類】He has never failed in doing anything on which he had ***set*** his *heart*. ¶His *heart* was ***softened*** and melted into tears. 彼の心はやわらぎ涙にくれた. 【類】Misfortune sometimes ***softens*** the *hearts* of men and turns them toward God. ‖ Nash has ***stolen*** America's *heart*. ナッシュは全米を悩殺した. ¶***steel*** one's *heart* against … 心を鬼にして…に対する. ¶***stir*** the *hearts* of the young to a noble ambition 青年を鼓舞して高尚な志望を起させる. 【類】deeply ***stir*** the *heart*. ¶Excess in any exercise ***strains*** the *heart*. 運動が過ぎると心臓に無理ができる. ¶***take heart*** 元気を出す ‖ He had ***taken*** fresh *heart* at the little glimpse of hope that had been presented to him. 彼は一道の希望の光に接して勇気を回復し得た. ‖ a blow enough to ***take*** the *heart* out of a strong man 強い男の心臓をたたき出すくらいの一痛撃. ¶His *heart* was ***thrilled*** with secret pleasure. 彼は胸に持つ喜びで心が躍った. ¶***throw*** one's *heart* into work 仕事に熱中する. ¶The article does not ***touch*** the *heart* of the subject. その文は問題の核心に触れていない. 【類】This ***touched*** her *heart* deeply. ¶They know how to ***touch*** and ***fire*** the *hearts* of their hearers and make them laugh or cry at their wills. 彼らは聴衆を思いのままに感動させ興奮させまたあるいは笑わせあるいは泣かせる術を心得ている. ¶***train*** the *heart* 修養をする. ¶Religion ***uplifts*** the *hearts* of men in this troubled world. 宗教はこの苦しみの多い世の中で人の気を引立たせる. ¶***weaken*** one's *heart* by over-indulgence in tobacco タバコをのみすぎて心臓を弱くする. ¶***wear*** one's *heart* on one's sleeve 思ったことを言ってしまう. ¶***win*** the *heart* of … …の愛情を得る. ‖ ***win*** all *hearts* だれにも愛される. 【類】He has completely ***won*** my *heart*. ¶It ***wrings*** my *heart* to hear you! 君の話を聞くと腸を断つ思いだ.

V² My *heart* ***aches***. 胸が痛む. ¶My *heart* ***beats*** high. 私の心臓は高鳴りしている. 【類】Her *heart* ***beat*** fast in his arms. / In those lovers two *hearts* ***beat*** as one. / His *heart* ***beat*** violently. ‖ Such noble conduct moves the *heart* that ***beats*** in every human breast. こうしたりっぱな行いはいわゆる人間の胸を打つのである. ¶My *heart* ***bleeds*** for him. 私は彼のために大いに心を痛めている. ¶his *heart* ***broke*** when … …時彼は非常に悲しがった. ¶My *heart* ***died*** within me. 私は元気がくじけた. ¶My *heart* ***flutters***. 私は胸騒ぎがする. ¶My *heart* ***goes out*** to him in pity. 私はあの人をお気の毒に思う. 【類】my *heart* ***goes out*** in gratitude to … ¶His *heart* ***leaped out*** to the child. 彼はたちまちその子供に同情した. ¶my *heart* ***leaped up*** when … …したときに私の胸は躍った. ¶His *heart* ***misgave*** him. 彼は不安を感じた. ¶My *heart* ***overflowed*** with tenderness. 私は可哀そうで胸が一杯になった. ¶His *heart* ***palpitated***. 彼は動きがした. ¶My *heart* ***pounded*** with expectation. 期待で私の胸は躍った. ¶His *heart* ***pulsates*** in sympathy with the sorrows of the human race. 彼の心臓は人類の苦楽に共鳴して鼓動する. ¶His *heart* ***sank*** within him. 彼はがっかりした. 【類】Our *hearts* ***sank*** low. ¶The *heart* ***swells***. 胸が一杯になる. 【類】Elevated and humbled at the same time by so much happiness, my *heart* ***swelled*** with gratitude to God. ¶The *heart* ***throbs*** with fright. 恐ろしさで胸が躍る. 【類】His *heart* ***throbs*** violently. / my *heart* ***throbs*** with joy at the thought of … ¶Her *heart* was ***thumping*** with emotion. 彼女は感極まって心臓がどきどきしていた.

Q He has a ***badly-diseased*** *heart*. 彼は心臓をひどく悪くしている. ¶The inspiring book fired thousands of ***boyish*** *hearts* with a youthful enthusiasm. その霊感に富んだ著作

は幾千の青年の血をわかした. ¶These ***brave hearts*** left for the front leaving hearts as brave behind them. これらの勇士は自分に劣らぬ勇しい心の持主を後に残して戦地に立った. ¶a ***brave, true heart***. 勇敢で真実の心. ¶die of a ***broken heart*** 落胆して死ぬ. ¶The *heart* of England is not ***callous*** to the sufferings of her children. 英国の心は自国の人々の苦痛に無関心ではない. ¶The sufferings of the poor appealed to her ***charitable little heart***. 貧民の悩みは彼女の慈悲深い子供心に同情を起させた. ¶a ***cold*** and ***unfeeling heart*** 冷たくって無情な心. ¶a ***compassionate heart*** 同情深い心. ¶a ***cruel*** and ***pitiless heart*** 残忍冷酷な心. ¶an ***evil heart*** よこしまな心. ¶That racy letter has acted like a cordial to his ***failing heart***. そのぴりっとした手紙は彼の元気のない心に興奮剤のようにきいた. ¶a ***feeble heart*** かよわい心臓. ¶If you have a ***feeling heart***, pity him. 君に同情心があれば彼をあわれんでやれ. ¶take ***fresh heart*** 元気づく. ¶a ***generous heart*** 物惜みしない心. ¶have a ***gentle heart*** 気持ちがやさしい. ¶with a ***glad heart*** 喜んで. 【類】 with the ***glad*** heart of a man who is conscious that he has acted generously. ¶proceed with ***good heart*** to ... 満足して...におもむく. ‖ He bade me to be of ***good heart***. 彼は私に力を落すなと言った. 【類】 She had a ***good heart*** and a sound intellect. ¶a ***happy heart*** 幸福感. ¶He has a ***hard heart***. 情がない. ¶with a ***heavy heart*** 悲しい心を抱いて. ¶the manifold wickedness of the ***human heart*** 人間の心の色々な悪性. ¶an ***indomitable heart*** 不抜の志. ¶in his ***inmost heart*** 心の奥底では. ¶He has a ***kind*** (=***warm***) ***heart***. 彼は情がある. ¶A ***light heart*** lives long. のんき者は長生する. ‖ When my day's work is past I can play games with a ***light heart***. 一日の仕事が終るとのんびりした気持で運動ができる. ‖ with a ***light heart*** 浮立つ心で. ¶a ***loyal heart*** 忠義な心. ¶London is the ***mighty throbbing heart*** of political England. ロンドンは英国政治の脈うつ巨大な心臓である. ¶They have ***no heart*** for study. 彼らは勉強する気がない. ¶a ***noble heart*** りっぱな心. ¶a ***proud heart*** 誇り高い心. ¶a performance in Tokyo ever dear to the ***provincial heart*** いなか者が東京で忘れられない娯楽の一つ. ¶with a ***radiant heart*** 晴れやかな心で. ¶He has a ***responsive heart*** あの男はツーと言えばカーだ. ¶cherish in one's ***secret heart*** an ambition to ... 心ひそかに...の大望を抱く. ¶with a ***sinking heart*** 気がめ入って. ‖ support the ***sinking heart*** 沈む心を浮立たせる. ¶with a ***sorrowful heart*** 悲しい心を抱いて. ¶the ***stout hearts*** and strong arms of her sons その国の健男児. ¶a ***tender, chivalrous heart*** やさしくて義俠的な心. ¶one's ***sweet heart*** (=sweetheart) 愛人. ¶a ***throbbing heart*** 動悸(き)を打つ胸. ¶She loved him with an ***undivided heart***. 彼女は専心彼を愛した. ¶the dear possessor of her ***virgin heart*** 彼女の初恋を勝ち得た男. ¶a ***warm heart*** あたたかい心. ¶He is troubled with a ***weak heart***. 彼は心臓が弱くて困っている. ¶agree with a ***whole heart*** 双手をあげて賛成する. ‖ Perhaps he does not give his ***whole heart*** to the game when he plays with you. 多分君と勝負をするときは本気にならないのだろう. ¶His ***heart*** is ***young***. 彼は気が若い.

P a man (girl, book, an art) quite ***after*** my own *heart* 私とぴったり気のあう人(など) ‖ They succeeded in securing a house ***after*** their own *hearts*. 彼らは気に入った家が見当った. ¶have it ***at*** *heart* 真に...と思う. ¶He is ***at*** *heart* an ardent reformer. 彼は内心熱烈な改革者である. 【類】 She was not a courtesan ***at*** *heart*. / He was furious ***at*** *heart*. / He is ***at*** *heart* a skeptic (疑っている). / Now she feels sick ***at*** *heart*, because I gave it to her sister. ‖ those who have ***at*** *heart* the welfare of those who sorrow and suffer 嘆き苦しんでいる人たちの幸運を心に念じている人々. ‖ Great inventions are not brought forth ***at*** a *heart*.—Smiles. 大発明は一気にできるものでない. ‖ I felt a slight beating ***at*** the *heart*. 私は軽い胸騒ぎを感じた. ‖ situated ***at*** the *heart* of the very smartest shopping district 最も尖端的な商店街の中心にある. 【類】 ***at*** the *heart* of London. ¶I know it ***by*** *heart*. 私はそれを暗記している. ‖ get (=learn) it ***by*** *heart* それを暗記する ‖ have it ***by*** *heart* それを暗記している. ¶I thank you ***from*** my *heart*. 私は君に衷心から感謝する. 【類】 I pray for his happiness ***from*** my *heart*. ‖ ***from*** the *heart* of hearts 心の奥底から. ‖ The words were spoken ***from*** her *heart*. その言葉は彼女の真心から出たのだ. ¶pure ***in*** *heart* 心の純な. ‖ down ***in*** her *heart* 彼女の心の奥底で. ‖ feel (think) ***in*** one's *heart* that ... 心に...と感じる(など). ‖ one who was ***in*** the *heart* of affairs その衝に当った人. ‖ a free trader ***in*** *heart* 心の中は自由貿易主義者. ‖ I am a little ***in*** *heart* again. 私は少し元気がつきました. ‖ ***in*** their *heart* of hearts 心の奥底では. ‖ ***in*** the *heart* of the mountain (lake, region) 山(など)の奥まった所に ‖ One imagines that one is ***in*** the *heart* of the country. ごくいなかに行ったような感じがする. 【類】 The lake is delightfully situated ***in*** the *heart* of romantic scenery. ¶instil a principle ***into*** one's *heart* ある主義をその心に注入する. ¶She wears it ***next*** her *heart*. 彼女はそれをはだ身離さず持っている. ¶the girl ***of*** his *heart* 彼の意中の若い女. ‖ express from the bottom ***of*** my *heart* 真心をこめて言う. ¶I told him of what was ***on*** my *heart*. 私は思っていたことを彼に話した. ‖ lay one's hand ***on*** one's *heart* 胸に手をあてる. ¶His advice was firmly graven ***on*** my *heart*. 彼の忠告が堅く私の肝に銘じた. ¶He is ***out of*** *heart*. 彼は元気がない. ¶She clasped it ***to*** her *heart*. それをしっかと抱きしめた. ‖ take it ***to*** *heart* それをじっくり考えてみる. ‖ He takes her dearly ***to*** *heart*. 彼女を心から愛している. ‖ take one's failure to one's *heart* 失敗を気にする. ‖ stab one ***to*** the *heart* その胸を刺す. ‖ come home ***to*** one's *heart* 胸にこたえる. ‖ a subject close ***to*** the *hearts* of social reformers 社会改革家がいつも考えている一つの問題. ‖ get [down] ***to*** the *heart* of a matter 問題の核心に触れる. ¶***with*** a *heart* full of feeling 万感胸に迫って. ‖ a young man ***with*** his *heart* in his profession 自分の職業に熱心な青年. ‖ They parted ***with*** heavy *hearts*. 彼らは悲しい思いをして別れた. ‖ I welcome your idea ***with*** all my *heart*. 私は衷心から君の意見に賛成する. 【類】 We welcome the envoy ***with*** our whole *heart*. / do it ***with*** one's whole *heart*. ¶a man ***without*** a *heart* 情のない人.

P² the heart ***of*** the matter 事件の核心 ‖ London is the *heart* ***of*** the British Commonwealth. ロンドンは英連邦の中心である.

heartburn, *n.* 胸やけ.

V ***have heartburn*** 胸がやける.

heartburning, *n.* しっと.

V ***cause*** great *heartburnings* 大いにしっとを起す.

hearten, *v.* 元気づける.

M² ***hearten up***=cheer up 勢いを付ける, 励ます.

O This news will ***hearten*** them. その便りは彼らを元気づけるだろう.

hearth, *n.* 炉.

Q² a ***cast-iron hearth*** 〚機〛鋳鉄火床.

P There was a fire ***on*** the *hearth* burning. 炉には火が燃えていた.

P² a *hearth* ***with*** a hood 覆いのある火床.

heart-sick, *a.* 悲嘆にくれて.

P He is ***heart-sick over*** the loss of his only daughter. 彼は一人娘を失って悲嘆にくれている.

heartstrings, *n. pl.* 心の琴線.

V ***break*** one's *heartstrings* 悲痛な思いをさせる. ¶***touch*** one's *heartstrings* その心の琴線に触れる.

P pull ***at*** one's *heartstrings* 人の感情を揺り動かす.

heat, *n.* 熱, 暑さ; 交尾期.

V ***absorb heat*** 熱を吸収する. ¶***alleviate*** the *heat* of summer 暑気を和らげる. ¶to ***avoid*** the *heat* of the town 避暑のために. ¶***bear*** the *heat* 暑さを忍ぶ. ¶***enjoy*** the *heat* of a fireplace (stove) 炉(ストーブ)にあたる. ¶***escape*** the *heat* of the town 避暑に(地方へ)出掛ける. ‖ go up country to ***escape*** the summer *heat* 避暑にいなかへゆく. ¶***evolve heat*** 熱を放散する. ¶***feel*** the *heat* too much ひどく暑さを感じる. ¶***generate*** an intense *heat* 高熱を発する. ¶***get on heat*** さかりがつく. ¶***give off heat*** 熱を発散する. ¶***keep*** the *heat* at not less than 95 degrees 温度を九十五度からさがらないようにする. ¶***keep off*** the *heat* 暑さを防ぐ. ¶***laugh off*** town *heat* 都会の暑さを笑殺する. ¶The sun ***radiates*** *heat*. 太陽は熱を放射する. ¶The fish will not ***stand*** the *heat* until the following morning. この暑さでは魚は翌朝までもつまい. ‖ I cannot ***stand*** *heat*. 私は暑さには閉口だ. 【類】 Really we cannot ***stand*** such *heat* as this. ¶There were no electric fans to ***temper*** the *heat*. 暑さを和らげる扇風機が一つも置いてなかった. ¶***withstand*** extreme *heat* 極熱にたえる.

V² The *heat* has ***abated***. 温度がさがった.

Q His blood was at ***boiling heat***. 彼の血は(怒りで)沸騰していた. ¶***broiling heat*** しゃく熱. ¶a ***dead heat***=a race without result〘競馬〙互角の競争. ¶in this trying period of ***extreme*** *heat* この炎暑のきびしい時期に. ¶***fugitive*** *heats* 発散する熱. ¶a ***gentle*** *heat* とろび. ¶The great *heat* is now ***gone.*** 暑さの盛りはもう過ぎた. ¶The *heat* is really ***insupportable;*** I am knocked up. この暑さではとてもたまらない, 僕は参ってしまった. ¶***intense*** *heat* 酷暑. ¶an ***intolerable*** *heat* たえられない暑さ. ¶***lingering*** *heat* of summer 残暑. ¶Pottery is burnt at a ***moderate*** *heat.* 陶器はころあいの熱で焼く. ¶***oppressive*** *heat* 物すごい暑さ. ¶the ***parching*** *heat* of summer (the sun) 夏(など)のやきつくような暑さ. ¶***radiant*** *heat* 輻射熱. ¶a metal at a ***red*** *heat* 赤く熱した金属. ¶***scorching*** *heat* しゃく熱. ¶***steamy*** *heat* 蒸暑さ. ¶***stifling*** *heat* 息がつまる暑さ. ¶***suffocating*** *heat* 息苦しい暑さ. ¶oppressed by ***sultry*** *heat* 蒸暑さで参ってしまって. ¶notwithstanding the ***sweltering*** *heat* 汗だくだくの炎暑にもかかわらず. 【類】in the ***sweltering*** *heat* of midsummer / gasp in ***sweltering*** *heats.* ¶escape the ***trying*** *heat* of the summer たえ切れない夏の暑さを避ける. ¶The *heat* is ***unbearable.*** 暑くてやりきれない. ¶The paper was written with conviction at ***white*** *heat.* その文は確信をもって白熱した筆で書かれた. ‖The agitation continues at ***white*** *heat.* 運動は白熱的に進行している. 【類】burn at ***white*** *heat* / metal at ***white*** *heat.*

Q² preserve the ***body*** *heat* 体温を保持する. ¶human ***body*** *heat* 人間の体温. ¶during the ***midsummer*** *heat* 真夏の暑気の続く間. ¶***steam*** *heat* 蒸気熱. ¶the ***summer*** *heat* 暑気. 【類】the ***summer*** *heat* of the city.

P work ***at*** fever *heat* 熱狂的に働く. ¶A good many people have been affected ***by*** the *heat* lately. 近ごろ大分暑気にあたった人がある. ¶dry ***by*** *heat* 熱でかわく. ¶I could not sleep ***for*** the *heat.* 私は暑くて眠れなかった. ¶***in*** the *heat* of battle 戦いの最中に‖***in*** the *heat* of the day 日盛りに‖a cow ***in*** *heat* さかりのついた雌牛‖a bitch ***in*** *heat* followed by a pack of dogs 犬の群に追いかけられたさかりのついた雌犬. ¶Metals melt ***with*** *heat.* 金属は熱でとける. ‖***With*** this *heat,* everybody is more or less upset. この暑さではだれでも多少閉口する. ‖accuse a person ***with*** some *heat* 相当はげしく人を非難する. 【類】speak ***with*** great *heat* (熱を込めて). ¶She answered ***without*** *heat.* 彼女は熱のない返事をした.

P² I feel quite enervated by the *heat* ***of*** Tokyo. 私は東京の暑さにすっかり参っている.

heat, *v.* 熱する; 激する.

M Our houses or offices are ***properly*** *heated,* when the thermometer records 65° to 70° F. われわれの住居にしても事務所にしても気温は華氏の六十五度から七十度を適度とする.

M² *heat* ***up*** cold meat 冷え肉を温める‖The room was comfortably *heated* ***up.*** へやは気持ちよく温まっていた.

P In the hot-spring water is naturally *heated* ***at*** 106°. その温泉は百六度の温度がある. 【類】*heated* ***at*** 97° of Réaumur (列氏). ¶*heat* it ***over*** a brazier それを火ばちで熱する. ¶I want my bath *heated* ***up to*** ... 湯加減を…にしてもらいたい. ¶He was *heated* ***with*** passion: 彼は激怒していた.

heater, *n.* 発熱器 (ヒーター).

Q² a ***bath*** *heater* ふろがま. ¶a ***gas*** *heater* 暖房用ガスコンロ.

heathen, *n.* 異教徒.

V ***Christianize*** the *heathen* 異教徒をキリスト教に入れる. ¶***convert*** the *heathen* 異教徒を改宗させる.

Q a ***stiff-necked*** *heathen* 強情な異教徒.

heating, *n.* 暖房[施設].

Q ***central*** *heating* 暖房装置(ボイラーなどの).

Q² ***floor*** *heating* 床暖房. ¶***household*** *heating* 家庭暖房. ¶***steam*** *heating* 蒸気暖房.

heave, *v.* 持ちあげる; ふくれる, 現われる.

M *heave* a ship ***ahead*** 船を綱をたぐって前進させる. ¶*Heave* ***away*** (=ho)! よいと巻け, えいや. ¶The deck is *heaving* ***uncomfortably.*** [波で]デッキがひどく上下に動揺している.

M² He *heaved* the boy ***up.*** 男の子をどっこいしょと抱き上げた. ‖He *heaved* [***up***] his plan of going abroad. 彼は洋行をやめにした.

P The island *heaved* ***in*** sight. その島が見えてきた. ‖We were speaking of him and just then he *heaved* ***in*** sight. 彼の話をしていたところへ彼がひょっくり現われた.

O *heave* a sigh of relief ほっとため息をつく.

heaven, *n.* 天, 天国.

V ***make*** a *heaven* of hell 地獄を天国にする. ¶***move*** *heaven* and earth to ... …するために大々的努力をする. ¶*Heaven* be ***praised!*** 有難いことだ. ¶***survey*** the starry *heavens* 天体を観測する. ¶***Thank*** *Heaven!* ありがたや. 【類】I ***thank*** *Heaven* I met you in time.

V² *Heaven* ***forbid*** that ... 天帝よ願わくは…せしむるなかれ. ¶*Heaven* (=God) ***knows.*** 神ぞ知る(人には分からない).

Q in the ***blue*** *heavens* 青空に. ¶He did so little with the gifts he had received from a ***bounteous*** *heaven.* 彼は恵深い天からうけた才能をほとんど利用しなかった. ¶in the ***eastern*** *heavens* 東の空に. ¶***Good*** *heavens!* How did you get into this condition? おやおや, これはどうしたということだ. ¶She was in the ***seventh*** *heaven* of rapture. 彼女はうれしくって有頂天であった. ¶the ***starry*** *heavens* 星空.

Q² the ***midnight*** *heavens* 夜半の大空.

P I swear ***by*** *Heaven* that ... 私は神かけて…ということを誓う. ¶There came a voice ***from*** *heaven.* 天に声があった. ‖The penalty fell like a thunderbolt ***from*** *heaven.* 天罰は電光のように降ってきた. ¶I was ***in*** *heaven.* 私は有頂天だった. ‖the stars ***in*** *heaven* 空の星. 【類】Suddenly heavy clouds appeared ***in*** the *heavens.* ¶gaze up into the firmament ***of*** *heaven* 青空を仰ぎ見る‖an inhabitant ***of*** *heaven* 天人. ¶a voice came ***out of*** (=***from***) the *heaven.* 声が天から聞えてきた. ¶go ***to*** *heaven*=die 昇天する. ¶There is nothing new ***under*** *heaven.* 地上に新しいものはない.

heavy, *a.* 重い; しつこい.

M make the task ***unexceedingly*** *heavy* one その仕事をひどく骨の折れるものにする.

P The odds were *heavy* ***against*** us. われわれに到底勝味はなかった. ¶*heavy* ***for*** its size 大きさの割に重い. ¶The food is too *heavy* ***on*** my stomach. 私にはその食物は胃にもたれる. ‖He was *heavy* ***on*** beer. 彼は盛んにビールを飲んだ. ¶*heavy* ***with*** sleep 眠い‖*heavy* ***with*** perfumes 香水がぷんぷんする‖A tree *heavy* ***with*** fruit. 枝もたわわな木. ‖a woman *heavy* ***with*** child 大きなおなかをかかえた妊婦.

Hebe, *n.* 青春の女神.

Q² a ***marble*** *Hebe* 大理石で造った青春の女神.

Hebrew, *n.* ヘブライ人.

Q a ***Russian*** *Hebrew* ロシヤ系ヘブライ人.

hedge, *n.* 生垣.

V ***lay*** a *hedge* 生垣を造る. ¶***plant*** a *hedge* 生垣を造る. ¶***trim*** a *hedge* 生垣を刈込む.

Q a ***clipped*** *hedge* 刈込んだ生垣. ¶a ***dead*** *hedge* 枯枝などで作った垣.

P be ***on*** the *hedge* (=sit on the fence) 形勢を傍観する, 日より見をきめ込む.

P² a *hedge* ***of*** hawthorn さんざしの生垣.

hedge, *v.* 垣根で囲う; 束縛する.

M² *hedge* ***in*** the enemy force 敵軍の行動を妨害する‖be *hedged* ***in*** with rules and regulations 規則々々で動きのとれないようにされている‖a town *headged* ***in*** by low hills 低い山に囲まれた町. ¶be *hedged* ***off*** from the outer world 外界から隔離されている. ¶*hedge* ***up***=obstruct さえぎる, 妨害する.

heed, *n.* 注意, 留意.

V ***give*** *heed* to ... …に注意する‖He ***gave*** no *heed* to my advice. 彼は私の忠告を聞かなかった. ¶***pay*** (no) *heed* to ... …を顧みる(顧みない). 【類】***paid*** little *heed* to the results. ¶***take*** *heed* to ... …に注意する, …を顧みる. 【類】He ***took*** no *heed* of what I said. / ***take*** *heed* that ... / They ***took*** no *heed* of the consequence of the action.

Q As they have no desire to be taught, ***little*** *heed* is paid of the instruction given. 彼らは習おうという気がないのだから授業に注意しない. ¶I pay ***much*** *heed* 大いに留意する. ¶pay ***practical*** *heed* to the message he utters 彼の説く所を実地に行う.

heedful, *a.* 注意深い.

P *heedful* ***of*** instruction 授業によく注意する. ¶give ***special*** *heed* to ... 特に…に注意する.

heedless, *a.* 不注意な, 無とん着な.

P *heedless* ***of*** tradition (custom, other people, consequences) 伝統(など)にむとん着な‖*heedless* ***of*** the fact that ... …という事実を無視して.

heel, *n.* かかと.

V I was left to ***cool*** my *heels* upon the steps. 私は階段でさんざっぱら待たされた. ¶***get*** (=have) the *heels* of ... ...

を追越す. ¶He has ***had*** India-rubber *heels* to his boots. 彼は長ぐつにゴムのかかとをつけている. ¶The baby lying on his back ***kicked*** his *heels* ***up*** into the air in the delight over some toy given him. あおむけに寝かしてあったその赤ちゃんはもらったおもちゃがうれしくて足をけり上げた. ¶***lift*** (=***raise***) the *heel* against ... ...を足げにする. ¶***make*** a *heel* [馬などが]ける. ¶***show*** one's *heels* to ... ...にくびすを見せる, ...から逃げる. ¶***turn up*** one's *heels*. 死ぬ. ¶***throw*** one's *heels* higher than one's head かかとを頭より高くあげる. ¶***tickle*** the *heels* かかとをくすぐる. ¶***use*** the *heel* 歩く. ¶shoes with *heels* ***worn down*** かかとがすりへったくつ.

Q ***high*** French *heels* ハイヒールのフランスぐつ.

Q² ***Louis XVII*** *heels* [かかとの七インチもある]ハイヒール.

P arrive ***at*** the *heels* of ... ...とくびすを接して到着する ‖ shoes down ***at*** the *heel* (=*heels*) かかとのつぶれたくつ ‖ socks and stockings each out ***at*** the *heel* かかとのすり切れたソックスやくつ下 ‖ with his grey terrier ***at*** his *heels* 灰色のテリヤをつれて. ¶walk ***in*** high *heels*=walk high-heeled ハイヒールをはいて歩く. ¶come ***on*** the *heels* of ... ...のくびすに接して来る ‖ the enemy ***on*** their *heels* 彼らを追う敵 ‖ follow close ***on*** the *heels* of ... ...のすぐ後に続く ‖ tread ***on*** the *heels* of ... ...を見ならう ‖ turn ***on*** one's *heel*[*s*] くるりとくびすを回らす. ¶The thief took ***to*** his *heels* at a tremendous pace. 盗人は物すごい歩調でかけ出した. ¶***heels over*** head まっさかさまに.

P² a *heel* ***on*** a shoe くつのかかと(ヒール).

heel, *v.* [船が]傾く.

P *heel* ***to*** port (starboard) 左(右)舷に傾く.

hegemony, *n.* 覇(は)権.

V Thebes ***held*** the *hegemony* in Greece under the leadership of Epaminondas. テーベはエパミノンダス統率の下にギリシアにおける覇権を掌握した. ¶***obtain*** the *hegemony* of (=supremacy over) the rest of ... ...自余の国に対して覇権を獲得する.

Q the ***Russian*** *hegemony* in Asia アジアにおけるロシアの支配力.

P He says that the yellow races, at first ***under*** the *hegemony* of Japan and later under the leadership of the Chinese, will overrun Europe. 黄色人種は最初は日本の覇権の下に後には中国人の統率の下に欧州をじゅうりんするだろうと彼は言う.

P² the *hegemony* ***of*** European civilization in the East 東洋における欧州文明の優勢.

height, *n.* 高さ; 頂上; *pl.* 高原(地).

V ***attain*** a *height* of ... ...の高度に達する. 【類】The *sugi* is the largest tree in Japan, ***attaining*** a *height* of 120 feet and a girth of 30. ¶***clear*** a *height* of five feet at a standing jump 立跳で五フィートの高さまで飛び越す. ¶He ***has*** a good *height*. 彼は背が高い. ¶***judge*** men's *heights* by the eye 身長を目で測る. ¶***measure*** the *height* of a mountain 山の高さを測る. ¶***mount*** lofty *heights* 高山に登る. ¶***reach*** the *height* of its prosperity (power) その繁栄(など)の頂上をきわめる ‖ enthusiasm ***reached*** its *height* when ... ...の時熱情はその最高潮に達した. ¶***scale*** the *heights* of the Japan Alps 日本アルプスの頂上をきわめる. 【類】***scale*** the *height* of a mountain. ¶***take*** one's *height* 身長を計る.

Q an ***average*** *height* 平均の高さ. ¶***commanding*** *heights* 見晴らしのよい高地. ¶It is of ***considerable*** *height*. それは随分高い. ¶on the ***cool*** *heights* of Karuizawa 軽井沢の涼しい高地で. ¶at a ***dizzy*** *height* from the ground 地上からめまいのするくらいの高さで. ¶attain to an ***enormous*** *height* 非高な高さに達する. ¶look down from a ***giddy*** *height* 目のまわるような高さから見おろす. ¶***immeasurable*** *height* 測り知られない高さ. ¶of ***immense*** *height* 非常に高い. ¶He is of ***middle*** *height*. 彼は中位の背だ. ¶Many have reached ***momentary*** *heights* and have fallen to oblivion just as rapidly. 多数の人が一朝にして名をなし同じく一朝にして忘却のふちに没した. ¶a man of ***towering*** *height* 雲つくような男. ¶Taxes reach an ***unprece dented*** *height*. 諸税が異例の高率に達した. ¶at ***various*** *heights* [高低]色々の高度で. ¶a house built on a ***wooded*** *height* ある樹木の多い丘の上に建てられた家.

Q² ***Washington Heights*** ワシントン・ハイツ.

P She was rather ***above*** the middle *height*. 彼女は並よりやや背が高かった. ¶The rage was ***at*** its *height*. その流行が絶頂だった. ‖ The market is ***at*** its *height*. 市況は今景気の絶頂だ. ‖ There the season is ***at*** its *height*. そこは今一番にぎやかだ(遊覧地など). 【類】My terror was ***at*** its *heights*. / The sun is now ***at*** its *height*. / The tide was ***at*** its *height*. / The gale was ***at*** its *height*. / The banquet is ***at*** its *height*. ‖ He was then ***at*** the *height* of his popularity. 彼は当時人気の絶頂にあった. 【類】***at*** the *height* of his fame and influence / the empire when ***at*** the *height* of its power / ***at*** the *height* of good times (景気) / Under Nebuchadnezzar Babylon was ***at*** the *height* of her splendour. / the Romans ***at*** the *height* of their civilization / ***at*** the *height* of his success / ***at*** the *height* (真最中) of the war ‖ He was, then, ***at*** the *height* of his inventive ability. 彼はそのころ発明の才が最も油の乗っていた時だ. ‖ ***at*** the *height* of their perplexity 彼らが困り抜いている所へ ‖ He was caught ***at*** a *height* of about 13,000 ft. by violent air currents. 彼は約一万三千フィートの高空で猛烈な気流に出会った. 【類】***at*** a *height* (=an elevation) of ... ft. above the sea-level / photographed ***at*** a *height* of 984 feet (飛行機などから) / ***At*** a *height* of four miles the air becomes so thin that it is almost impossible to breathe. ¶***below*** the medium *height* 並の高さ以下. ¶***during*** the *height* of the crisis 危機の真ただ中に ‖ ***during*** the *height* of summer 真夏の間 ‖ ***during*** the *height* of travel season 旅行季節の盛りに. 【類】***during*** the *height* of the plague. ¶fall ***from*** a *height* of ... ...の高さから墜落する. ¶six feet ***in*** *height* 高さ六フィート ‖ ***in*** the *height* of the season [温泉場など]季節の盛りに. 【類】***in*** the *height* of the travelling season / ***in*** the *height* of summer / ***in*** the *height* of her popularity (人気) / ***in*** the *height* of the Australian gold-fever (金鉱熱) / ***in*** the *height* of one's vigor (元気) / a fresh-colored young gentleman dressed ***in*** the *height* of fashion (流行の尖端を行く). 【類】his ability to dress ***in*** the *height* of fashion. ¶***Of*** what *height* is that tree? あの木はどの位の高さか. ¶***on*** *heights* commanding ... ...を見渡せる高地の上に. 【類】a cottage ***on*** the *heights*. ¶grow ***to*** the *height* of 10 feet 十フィートの高さに成長する ‖ This raised him ***to*** the *height* of his unparalleled position. このために彼は比類ない高い地位に昇進した.

P² the *height* ***of*** absurdity ばかの骨頂 ‖ It is the *height* ***of*** folly. 愚の骨頂である. 【類】the *height* ***of*** arrogance (cruelty).

heighten, *v.* 高まる, 元気づく.

P become *heightened* ***in*** spirits 元気づく.

heir, *n.* 嗣子, 相続人.

V ***disinherit*** an *heir* 嗣子を廃嫡する. ¶Danjuro the ninth ***left*** no *heir* to his honors. 九代目団十郎にはその誉れある家門の後嗣がなかった.

Q an *heir* ***apparent*** 推定相続人. ¶a ***direct*** *heir* 直系相続人. ¶It is not her political position, but a long, slow process of evolution which has fitted Japan to take her place amongst the ***Great*** *Heirs* of the ages. 日本が時代の偉大な後継者の仲間入りができたのはその政治的地位ではなくして永い間徐々に発展をとげた結果である. ¶a ***legal*** *heir* 法定相続人. ¶the ***legitimate*** (=***right***) *heir* 嫡子相続人. ¶an *heir* ***male*** 男の相続人. ¶a ***natural*** *heir* [出生権による]自然相続人. ¶an *heir* ***presumptive*** 仮定相続人. ¶the ***sole*** *heir* to the fortune その財産の唯一の相続人.

P² an *heir* ***at*** law 法定相続人. ¶an *heir* ***by*** legal right 法定相続人. ¶She was *heir* ***to*** a large fortune. 彼女は大きな財産の相続人であった. ‖ *heir* ***to*** the title and estates of the peer その貴族の爵位と財産との後継者 ‖ *heir* ***to*** the British throne 英国王位継承者 ‖ fall *heir* ***to*** an estate 財産の相続人になる ‖ a panacea for all the ills that flesh is *heir to* 万能薬.

heirloom, *n.* 相伝の動産.

V precious *heirloom* ***handed down*** from ancestors 祖先伝来の宝物.

Q a ***national*** *heirloom* 国宝. ¶They are cherished as ***precious*** *heirlooms*. それらは先祖代々の宝として秘蔵されている. ¶He left them as ***sacred*** *heirlooms* to his children. 彼はそれらを神聖な累代の宝として子供たちに残した.

P² It became an *heirloom* ***for*** his descendants. それは彼の子孫に残した家宝となった.

hell, *n.* 地獄.

Q² a ***gambling*** *hell* とばく宿.

P fall into the bottom ***of*** *Hell* 地獄の底に落ちる. ¶I

would go ***through*** hell for him. 彼のためには水火をも辞さない. ¶Go ***to hell!*** 地獄におちろ, くたばっちまえ.

P[2] a *hell **of*** a lot of people 物すごい群集 ‖ a *hell **of*** noise (brawl) ひどい音(など). ¶It would be *hell **on*** earth. この世ながらの地獄ができよう. ¶To *hell **with*** democracy! 民主主義がなんだ.

hello, *n.* おいという呼かけ.

V ***say*** my *hello* to ... ...によろしく ‖ What are you doing with the ice box without even ***saying*** *hello?* ただ今とも言わないで冷蔵庫で何してんの(母が子供に).

helm, *n.* かじ; 支配, 権力.

V ***assume*** (=***take***) the *helm* of state affairs 国政をみる, 政権を握る. ¶***ease*** the *helm* かじを戻す. ¶***hold*** the *helm* of the Ship of State ***firm*** and guide her into port 国家という船のかじをしっかり握って港に入れる. ¶***port*** the *helm*=helm a port おもかじを取る. ¶***right*** the *helm*=helm the midship かじの柄を中央におく. ¶***shift*** the *helm* かじを変える. ¶***starboard*** the *helm*=helm a starboard 取かじにする.

P men ***at*** the *helms* of the companies 諸会社の首脳たち ‖ A premier is ***at*** the *helm* of the country's administration. 首相は国政処理の衝にある.

helmet, *n.* ヘルメット.

Q[2] wear a ***steel*** *helmet* 鉄かぶとをかぶる. ¶a ***sun*** *helmet* [南国の]ヘルメット帽.

help, *n.* 助力, 救済; 《米》使用人.

V I had to ***accept*** *help* from ... 私は...から世話を受けねばならなかった. ¶The author has the pleasant duty of ***acknowledging*** *help* from many quarters in the preparation of this book. 著者は本書の著述に当って各方面から得た助力を深謝する. ¶***ask*** (=***beg***) ***for*** *help* 助けを請う. ¶We ***derived*** *help* from the following books: われらは次の書籍を参考にした. 【類】great *help* may be ***derived*** from ... ¶I was authorized to ***engage*** such *help* as I needed. 私には必要の場合に助手を使うだけの権限があった. ¶***enlist*** the *help* of others 人の協力を得る. ¶***ensure*** a *help* 必ず救済を受けるようにする. ¶***expect*** *help* from ... ...を当にする. ¶***extend*** *help* to ... ...に援助を与える. ¶***give*** appropriate *help* to ... ...に適当な助力を与える. ¶He ***had*** four *helps*. 彼は四度おかわりをした. ¶***have*** *help* from ... ...から助けてもらう. ¶***hire*** outside *help* 人手を借りる ‖ ***hire*** some *help* 人を雇う. ¶***implore*** *help* 救助を求める. ¶***invoke*** the *help* of Heaven for ... ...のために天助を祈る. ¶***lend*** one's *help* to ... ...に手を貸す. ¶I ***need*** some *help* with my household duties. 少しく家事を手伝ってもらう人が入用だ. ‖ sorely ***need*** *help* 大いに助けを要する. ¶***obtain*** *help* 助けを得る. ¶I ***offered*** him *help*. 私は彼を助けようと申出た. ¶I cannot ***promise*** my immediate *help*. 私は今すぐ援助するという約束はできない. ¶I ***received*** much *help* from ... 私は...から大いに助けてもらった. ¶***render*** *help* in a quiet unostentatious way 地味な目立たない方法で援助する ‖ ***render*** *help* of various kinds 色々世話をする. 【類】***render*** *help* in misfortune. ¶***secure*** the *help* of ... ...の協力を得る. ¶***seek*** the *help* of ... ...の助けを求める. 【類】***seek*** *help* from ... ¶***solicit*** *help* from ... ...の助力をこう. ¶I am a beginner and ***want*** *help*. 私は初心だから人の力を借りる必要がある.

V[2] until *help* ***arrives*** 助けの人が来るまで.

Q render an ***active*** *help* to ... ...を実際助ける. ¶I find the typewriter a ***big*** *help* in my school work. タイプライターが学校のことをやるのに大変私に役に立つ. ¶seek outside ***counseling*** *help* 第三者の意見を求める. ¶the ***divine*** *help* 神の助, 天助. ¶Wanted: ***domestic*** *help* 〖広告〗女中を求む. 【類】I want a ***domestic*** *help* (女中を一人). ¶***efficient*** *help* 能率的な援助. ¶an ***every-day*** *help* 日々の助け. ¶an ***excellent*** *help* 大いなる助け. ¶ask for ***financial*** *help* to start in business 商売を始めるについて金融をこう. ¶***friendly*** *help* 親切な世話. ¶be a ***good*** *help* in ... ...に仲々役に立つ. ¶His advice was a ***great*** *help* to our success. 彼の忠言はわれわれの成功にとって大いに力になった. ¶receive ***important*** *help* from ... ...から重要な援助を受ける. ¶render ***invaluable*** *help* in ... ...に非常に貴重な援助を与える. ¶***kindly*** *help* 親切な手伝い. ¶She proved a ***loyal*** *help* to him and devoted mother to his children. 彼女は彼には忠実な内助者(手助け)であり子供たちには献身的な母となった. ¶The aim of the London Writer Circle is to provide ***mutual*** *help* among writers. ロンドン著作者クラブの目的は著作家の相互援助である. ¶We don't need any ***outside*** *help*. われわれは外部からの援助は一切必要としない. ¶***pecuniary*** *help* 金銭上の援助. ¶***printed*** *helps* 参考書類. ¶his ***scholarly*** *help* 彼の博識な援助. ¶employ ***skilled*** *help* 熟練工を雇う. ¶This volume will prove a ***solid*** *help* to them. この本は大いに彼らの参考になるだろう. ¶It is of ***special*** *help* to the beginner. それは特に初心者に役に立つ. ¶It will be a ***substantial*** *help* towards the rent. それは結構家賃のたしになるだろう. ¶a ***useful*** *help* 有用な助け. ¶Good order is a ***valuable*** *help* to the communities. 正しい秩序は社会にとって貴重なものである.

Q[2] ***business*** *help* [集合的に]事務員. ¶give ***emergency*** *help* to ... ...[緊急の際]臨時に手を貸してやる. ¶***every-day*** *help* 常雇い. ¶shortage of ***farm*** *help* 野良仕事の手不足. ¶The company is dependent on ***government financial*** *help*. その会社は政府の財政的援助を受けている. ¶a ***lady*** *help* 小間使い. ¶a ***study*** *help* 研究助手. ¶obtain ***subsidy*** *help* from the government 政府から補助金を得る.

P It is ***beyond*** *help*. それはどうにも手の下しようがない. 【類】***beyond*** all human *help*. ¶***by*** the *help* of a dictionary 辞書を使って. ¶***but for*** his *help* あの人の助けがなかったら. ¶***by*** the *help* of the electric telegraph 電信のおかげで. ¶call upon others ***for*** *help* 他人の助けをこう. ¶cry ***for*** *help* 叫んで助けを求める ‖ He often comes to me ***for*** *help*. 彼はよく助けてくれと私の所へやって来る. 【類】come to ... ***for*** financial *help* (財政上の補助). ¶This may be ***of*** *help* towards the required amount. これが所要総額のいくらか足しになるかもしれない. 【類】be ***of*** much (little) *help*. ¶Don't count ***on*** others' *help*. 人を当てにするな. ¶The patient is ***past*** medical *help*. その病人はもう医者の手に負えない. ¶***through*** one's *help* そのおかげで. ¶***with*** the help of a stick つえをついて ‖ ***with*** a (=the) *help* of a microscope (science) 顕微鏡(科学)の力で. 【類】read it ***with*** the *help* of a dictionary. ¶do it ***without*** *help* 自力でそれをやる.

P[2] there is no *help* ***for*** it but to ... それは...するより他に道がない. ¶I had no *help* ***from*** any one. 私はだれからも助けてもらわなかった. ¶*helps* ***in*** the use of good English 正しい英語の手引き ‖ fine examples collected by him as a *help* ***in*** his researches 研究材料として彼が集めた適当な例. ¶He became a *help* ***to*** his parents. 彼は両親の手助けになった. ¶a *help* ***toward*** English composition 英作文の助け. 【類】*helps* ***towards*** correct speech / The book is a *help* ***towards*** truer and higher living.

help, *v.* 助ける, 助力する.

M *help* him ***back*** to an honest life 彼を助けて正業につかせる. ¶*help* ***forward*** conversation 話が途切れないようにさせる ‖ If I can *help* you ***forward*** in any way I shall be delighted. どんなことでもお手伝いできたらうれしいんですが. ¶*help* very ***materially*** 大いに助けになる. ¶He ***kindly*** *helped* me out. 彼は私(の困っているところ)を親切にも救ってくれた. ¶I'll *help* you ***out*** with your work. 仕事を手伝ってやろう. ‖ take up side-work to *help* ***out*** with his expense 彼の費用をねん出しようとしてアルバイトをやる ‖ She *helped* ***out*** his words to speak correctly. 彼女は彼が正しく話せるように口をはさんでやった. ‖ Gesture in telephone talk cannot *help* ***out***. 電話で手まねをしても役に立たない. ‖ He didn't say a word to *help* me ***out***. 私を弁護するようなことは一言も言わなかった. ¶Do not, if you can ***possibly*** *help* it, let a child go to bed crying. できることなら子供が泣きながら寝床に行くことのないようにせよ. ¶I ***really*** couldn't *help* it. 全くどうにもならなかったのだ.

M[2] *help* a person ***down*** to the ground 人を地上に降してやる. ¶*help* a person ***in*** (***out*** or ***off***) 人を中に入れてやる(外に出してやる). 【類】He *helped* her ***off*** the train. ¶He *helped* me ***on*** (***off***) with my overcoat. 彼は僕にオーバーを着せて(ぬがせて)くれた. ¶He *helped* me ***up*** to my feet by the arm. 彼は僕の腕をつかまえて立たせてくれた.

P *help* ***in*** the right direction 正しい方向へ向けてやる(善導する) ‖ *help* a person ***in*** his work 人の仕事を手伝う. ¶*help* one ***into*** the house (carriage) 手を貸して家(など)に入れてやる. ¶*help* a person ***on*** (***off***) the horse 馬に乗せてやる(降ろしてやる) ¶*help* him ***out of*** his financial difficulties 彼の財政難を救ってやる. 【類】*help* a person ***out*** *of* clothes (a car). ¶I *helped* her *over* the fence. 私は彼女を助けてさくを越えさせた. ¶*help* him *through* the university 彼を援助して大学を卒業させる. ¶Please *help* me *to* salt. 塩をお願いします(食卓で取ってもらうとき). ‖ *help* oneself *to* bread and butter liberally 盛んにバタ付きパンを食べる ‖ *help* a person *to* a rope 人に綱を投げてやる ‖ *help to* further study さらに研究を進める場合の助けとなる ‖ An analysis of English intonation may *help* ***towards*** the acquirement of that important element of speech. 英語の音の抑揚を分析することは話しの要素たる音の抑揚を習得する上に役立つだろう. 【類】 *help* ***towards*** the attainment of this ideal (理想の実現) / *help* ***towards*** the propagation (undersanding) of ... / it will greatly *help* ***towards*** making ... / *help* ***towards*** this end. ¶*help* Japanese students ***with*** their English compositions 日本の学生の英作文を見てやる. 【類】 *help* a person ***with*** his work / My father used to *help* me ***with*** my lessons. ‖ Just *help* me ***with*** this baggage. この荷物を運ぶのですがちょっと手を貸して下さい. ‖ *help* a person ***with*** a loan 人に金を貸してやる. 【類】 He *helped* me ***with*** numerous suggestions. ‖ *help* ***with*** his financial support as well as ***with*** his sympathy 同情ばかりでなく財政的に助ける.

helper, *n.* 助力者.

V ***enlist*** willing *helpers* to aid in carrying it out その実行を進んで援助する人たちの賛助を得る. ¶***hire*** a *helper* 手伝いを雇う.

Q She was an ***effective literary*** *helper* to her husband. 彼女はその夫にとって文筆上のよい助力者であった. ¶an ***efficient*** *helper* 有能の助力者. ¶a ***safe*** *helper* 安全な助手. ¶a ***voluntary*** *helper* 自分から進んでの手伝い手.

Q² ***office*** *helpers* 事務員たち.

helpful, *a.* 助けになる.

M ***mutually*** *helpful* 相互に助けになる.

P be *helpful* ***to*** ... ...の力になる.

helping, *n.* 一盛り.

V ***Give*** me another *helping*, please. おかわりを頂だい. ¶***offer*** a second *helping* free おかわりを無料で出す. ¶***take*** a good *helping* of fresh meat so cooked as to be easily digested 消化のいいように料理した新しい肉を盛りだくさんに一人前食べる.

Q a ***generous*** *helping* of vegetables (meat) 野菜(肉)の大盛り. ¶ask for a ***second*** *helping* おかわりをする. 【類】 It was so very good that I had a ***second*** *helping*. ¶Take some more rice; you can ask for ***several*** *helpings* during the meal. もう少しご飯を召上れ, 食事中に幾度もおかわりをしてもよいのです.

helpless, *a.* 無力な; ふがいない; 助けのない.

M be ***quite*** *helpless* まるきりいくじがない. ¶How ***utterly*** *helpless!* いやはやいくじのないこと.

V ***help*** the *helpless* 無力な人たちを助ける.

O remain alone and *helpless* 一人ぼっちで無力である.

helpmate, helpmeet, *n.* 内助者, 妻(または夫).

Q a ***first-class*** *helpmeet* (=*helpmate*) 最上の協力者. ¶He is a ***good*** *helpmate* for our work. 彼はわれわれの仕事のいい協力者だ. ¶a ***model*** *helpmate* 良妻. ¶a ***noble*** *helpmate* りっぱな妻(夫). ¶For forty years she was the ***true*** and ***loving*** *helpmate* of her husband. 四十年間彼女はその夫の真実で愛情の深い内助者であった. ¶a ***worth*** *helpmate* in her husband's work 彼女の夫の仕事のりっぱな助力者.

P² a true *helpmate* ***to*** her husband 夫への真実な内助者.

helve, *n.* [道具などの]柄.

V ***throw*** the *helve* after the axe (=hatchet) 泥棒に追銭を出す.

hem, *v.* 囲む.

M *hem* (=shut) ***out*** 閉め出す.

M² a yard *hemmed* ***around*** (=about) by iron fences 鉄さくで囲んである庭. ¶*hemmed* ***in*** between ... ...の中に閉じ込められて ‖ a small lake *hemmed* ***in*** on all sides by thick leafy trees こんもり茂っている林に囲まれた小湖. ¶*hemmed* ***off*** from one another お互いに隔離されて.

P a skirt *hemmed* ***with*** golden fringe 金色のふさへりのついたスカート.

hemisphere, *n.* 半球.

Q in the ***northern*** *hemisphere* 北半球で.

hemistich, *n.* 〖詩〗 半行.

Q the ***upper*** *hemistich* 短歌などの上の句.

hem-line, *n.* 〖服飾〗 へり, ふち.

Q a dress with a ***low*** *hem-line* すその長いドレス.

hemorrhage, *n.* 出血.

V ***arrest*** *hemorrhage* 出血を止める.

Q ***cerebral*** *hemorrhage* 脳いっ血.

P² *hemorrhage* ***from*** (=***of***) the lungs 肺出血. ¶*hemorrhage* ***in*** the brain 脳出血.

hen, *n.* めんどり.

V ***feed*** *hens* めんどりにえをやる. ¶***keep*** *hens* for profit 商売に養鶏をやる. ¶On a poultry-farm, the farmhand ***sets*** the *hen*. 養鶏所では農夫がめんどりに卵をかえさす.

V² A *hen* ***cackles*** when she lays an egg. めんどりは卵を生むときここと鳴く. ¶The *hens* are beginning to ***set.*** 《米》 めんどりは抱きがつきだした. ¶The *hen* ***sits*** [on]. そのめんどりは抱きがついている.

Q a ***breeding*** *hen* ひよっこを育てるめんどり. ¶an ***idle*** (=***a non-egglaying***) *hen* 卵を生まないめんどり. ¶a ***poor laying*** *hen* 産卵の少いめんどり. ¶a ***prolific*** *hen*=a good layer 多産鶏. ¶a ***sitting*** *hen* だきのついているめんどり.

Q² a ***high-record*** *hen* 多産鶏. ¶a ***turkey*** *hen* 七面鳥の雌 (a turkey cock に対して). ¶yearlings or ***two-year*** *hens* 一年めんどりまたは二年めんどり. ¶a ***200-egg*** *hen* [一年に]二百箇産卵するめんどり.

herald, *v.* 先ぶれする.

M He is ***frequently*** *heralded* as the "potato king." 彼はよくじゃが芋王と呼ばれる. ¶make public a ***long*** *heralded* plan 久しい以前から先ぶれのしてあった計画を発表する.

herb, *n.* 草.

Q a ***medicinal*** *herb* 薬草. ¶a ***poisonous*** *herb* 毒草. ¶***poisonous*** and ***deadly*** *herbs* 猛毒草類.

P subsist ***on*** *herb* 草を食って生活する.

herbalist, *n.* 薬草研究家.

Q² Dodneus, the ***Netherlands*** *herbalist* オランダの本草家ドドニュース.

herd, *n.* 獣群; 賤(せん)民の群.

Q He was above the ***common*** *herd*. 彼は群を抜いていた. ¶the ***vulgar*** *herd* 愚民.

Q² the ***fur-seal*** *herd* on an Island 島のおっとせいの群.

P drive away cattle ***by*** *herds* 牛を群にして追う. ¶live ***in*** *herds* 群せいする.

P² a *herd* ***of*** cattle 牛の一群.

herd, *v.* 群がる.

M *herd* ***together*** 群がる ‖ prisoners *herded* ***together*** 一カ所に集合させられた捕虜.

P *herd* ***with*** men who have forced him to guilt 彼を無理やりに罪悪生活に陥れた人たちの仲間になる.

here, *n.* ここ.

P [There's] nobody else ***around*** *here*. ここには外にだれもいないよ. ¶***from*** *here* on これからは. ¶Get ***out of*** *here!* 出て行け. ¶***up to*** *here* ここまで(は).

hereafter, *n.* この後.

Q in the ***long*** *hereafter* 遠い将来において.

heredity, *n.* 遺伝.

Q ***ancestral*** *heredity* 祖先の遺伝. ¶He has a very ***bad*** *heredity*. 彼には非常に悪い遺伝がある. ¶of ***neuropathic*** *heredity* 遺伝的に神経質な. ¶***social*** *heredity* 社会的伝承.

P handed down ***by*** *heredity* 遺伝によって伝わった. ¶criminals ***from*** *heredity* 遺伝による犯罪者.

heresy, *n.* 異端, 邪説.

P a leader ***in*** *heresy* 邪説の首唱者.

heritage, *n.* 家督, 相続産.

V ***hand down*** a glorious *heritage* 光栄ある家柄を伝える. ¶He has worthily ***upheld*** the *heritage* of Leonardo, Vico, Galileo, and Volta. 彼はレオナールドやヴィーコやガリレオやヴォルタを産んだ国に恥じない.

Q Japan's ***cultural*** *heritage* 日本の文化的継承. ¶a ***glorious*** *heritage* かくかくたる継承. ¶have a rich ***historical*** and ***cultural*** *heritage* 豊富な歴史的文化的遺産を持っている. ¶a ***priceless*** *heritage* 貴重な継承.

Q² his ***England*** *heritage* 彼の英国にある遺産.

hermit, *n.* 隠者.

Q² a ***Taoist*** *hermit* 道教の隠者.

P² become a *hermit* ***from*** society 世間から離れて隠者になる.

O turn *hermit* 隠者になる.

hero, *n.* 英雄, 勇士; 主人公.

Q the world's ***celebrated*** *heroes* 世界の有名な英雄たち. ¶a ***doughty*** *hero* 勇士. ¶William the Conqueror, the ***great*** *hero* of English history 英国史上の大英雄ウイリヤム一世. ¶a ***hoar-headed*** *hero* 白髪の英雄. ¶***legendary*** *heroes* 伝説の勇士. ¶his ***literary*** *hero* 彼の愛好する文士. ¶the ***martial*** *hero* 勇壮な軍人. ¶***military*** *heroes* [戦功あ

る]軍人たち. ¶a ***mythical*** hero 神話の中に出る英雄. ¶*heroes* ***named*** and ***unnamed*** on land and sea 海陸の有名無名の勇士. ¶He was the ***national literary*** hero of his age. 彼はその時代の国家的文豪であった. ¶a ***popular*** hero 人気者. ¶***spiritual*** heroes 神霊界の英雄. ¶a ***sunburnt*** hero 日に焼けた勇士. ¶one of the "***unsung heroes***" of the war 無名の一出征勇士. ¶The man is a ***veritable*** hero. 彼は真の英雄だ. ¶a ***workaday*** hero 日常生活の勇士.

Q² the latest ***Derby*** hero 最近のダービー(英国競馬)の勝者. ¶a ***film*** hero ＝a leading man 映画の主役男優. ¶a ***football*** hero [試合で活躍した]しゅう球の選手. ¶collegiate ***gridiron*** heroes《米》フットボール(で活躍した)大学の選手たち. ¶a great popular ***war*** hero 人望のある偉大な軍人.

P He is counted ***as*** a national *hero*. 彼は国民的英雄をもって目されている. ¶the type ***of*** hero often to be seen in a fictitious story 小説(など)によく現われる型の英雄.

P² a hero ***in*** everyday life 日常生活の勇士. 【類】Prince Genji is the *hero* ***in*** the Genji Monogatari, a romance written by Murasaki Shikibu, in the tenth century of the Christian era. ¶*heroes* ***of*** faith 信仰上の英雄たち. 【類】*heroes* ***of*** peace / the *heroes* ***of*** the hour who saved a drowning child ‖ *heroes* ***of*** the day その日の勇者(ゲームに勝った人たち). ‖ *heroes* ***of*** the action film 〖映〗活劇ものの立役者たち. 【類】*heroes* ***of*** the workaday world ‖ the *hero* ***of*** a novel (story, tale) 小説(など)の主人公.

heroine, *n.* 女勇士, 女主人公.

Q ***humble*** *heroines* of family life 家庭生活に雄々しく立働くつつましい主婦たち. ¶She became a ***national*** *heroine* overnight. 彼女は一朝にして国民敬慕の的となった. ¶Joan of Arc is the ***popular*** *heroine* of France ジャンダークはフランス国民の崇拝する女傑である.

Q² a ***film*** *heroine*＝a leading woman 映画の主演女優.

P² a *heroine* ***of*** the cross キリスト教の女勇士 ‖ the *heroine* ***of*** a novel 小説の女主人公.

heroism, *n.* 義勇, 雄々しい行為.

V a monument erected to ***honor*** the *heroism* of … …の雄々しい行為をたたえるために建てた記念碑.

Q ***great*** *heroism* was shown by … …は非常な勇敢さを示した. ¶***His*** *heroism* is beyond praise. 彼の犠牲的行為は絶賛に値する. ¶***magnetic*** *heroism* 人をひきつける英雄行為. ¶the romance of ***missionary*** *heroism* 伝道者の壮烈な物語. ¶She stuck to her post with ***true Casabianca*** *heroism*. 彼女は真にキャサビアンカに劣らない壮烈さをもってその任務を守った. ¶***unconquerable*** *heroism* 打勝ち難い英雄精神. ¶the ***unexampled*** (＝***unparalled***) *heroism* of the troop その軍隊の無双の勇敢さ.

Q² ***newspaper*** *heroism* 新聞(で書き立てる)英雄行為.

herring, *n.* にしん.

V ***cure*** *herring* [くん製または塩物などにして]にしんを貯蔵する.

Q ***smoked*** (＝***smoke dried***) *herrings* にしんのくん製.

hesitancy, *n.* ちゅうちょ.

V need ***have*** no *hesitancy* in … ちゅうちょすることなく…してよい.

hesitate, *v.* ちゅうちょする.

P *hesitate* ***about*** a matter あることにちゅうちょする. ¶They *hesitated* ***at*** no deed which might increase their profits. 彼らは自分たちの利益になることならどんなことでもためらわなかった. ¶*hesitate* ***before*** replying 返事をする前にためらう. ¶*hesitate* ***between*** fighting and submitting 戦うかそれとも降服するかとためらう. ¶*hesitate* ***in*** speaking 話すときに言いよどむ. 【類】Don't *hesitate* ***in*** doing anything good and correct.

hesitation, *n.* ちゅうちょ.

V I ***felt*** some *hesitation* in accepting the invitation to write an article. 私は執筆の依頼に応じるかどうかを多少ちゅうちょした. 【類】we do not ***feel*** the least *hesitation* in saying that … ¶we ***have*** no *hesitation* in telling you that … 僕たちはちゅうちょする所なく君に…と言える. 【類】the present writer ***has*** no *hesitation* in saying (affirming) that … ¶***overcome*** one's *hesitation* 敢然として断行する.

Q She came to the point after some ***bashful*** *hesitation*. 彼女はいく分ためらってからその点に触れた.

P ***after*** much *hesitation* 随分ためらってから. ¶admit, though ***with*** some *hesitation*, that … ちょっとためらって…と認める. ¶if I am asked what is …, I answer ***without*** *hesitation* that … もし…は何かときかれたら私は一も二もなく…と答える ‖ ***without*** a moment's *hesitation* 即刻. 【類】He decided to take it ***without hesitation***.

P² *hesitation* ***in*** speaking 話すときのためらい(あの一を盛んに入れる).

hew, *v.* 切る, 切り倒す.

M a cottage *hewn* ***asunder*** by a bomb test (strong wind) 爆撃試験(強風)でばらばらになった小屋. ¶*hew* ***out*** a statue in the rock 岩に像を刻む ‖ *hew* ***out*** careers for themselves 自分の運命を開拓する.

M² *hew* ***down*** a tree [to the ground] 木を切り倒す. ¶oak trees *hewn* ***up*** by a hurricane 暴風にやられて根こそぎになったかしの木.

P a statue *hewn* ***out of*** (＝***from***) marble 大理石に刻んだ立像. ¶*hew* ***to*** pieces 寸断する, きれぎれにする.

heyday, *n.* 全盛期.

V He ***enjoyed*** such a *heyday* in social London. 彼にはロンドン社交界においてかかる全盛の時代があった. ¶It ***has had*** its *heyday*. その全盛期は終った.

P ***in*** the *heyday* of the bicyclist 自転車流行時代に ‖ an actress ***in*** the *heyday* of her genius その天分の最もよく発揮された時代の女優 ‖ He is ***in*** the *heyday* of life. 彼は男盛りだ.

hiatus, *n.* すき間, 割れ目; 〖音声〗母音接続.

P² There is a *hiatus* ***between*** the e's in pre-eminent. "pre-eminent" は e と e を分離して発音しなければならない. ¶There is a *hiatus* ***in*** the manuscript. その手記には脱落が一カ所ある. ‖ a *hiatus* ***in*** the biographical literature of the country その国の伝記文学における一つの欠陥.

hiccup, *n.* しゃっくり.

V ***have*** the *hiccups* しゃっくりをする.

P say ***with*** a *hiccup* しゃっくりをしながら言う ‖ He was affected ***with*** *hiccup*. 彼はしゃっくりを起した.

hide, *v.* 隠す, 潜む; 隠す.

M be *hidden* ***away*** in old records 古い記録の内に隠れている. ¶It was ***fortunately*** *hidden* from view. それは幸いだれにも見えない所にあった. ¶***deliberately*** *hide* the facts from the jury 故意にその事実を陪審員たちから隠す. ¶*hide* ***out*** 隠れる, ずらかる. 【類】*hide* ***out*** in the bushes.

P *hide* ***among*** the trees 木の中に隠れる. ¶*hide* ***behind*** the door 戸の後に隠れる ‖ *hide* ***behind*** one's authority 職権をかさに着る. ¶a mountain *hidden* ***by*** clouds 雲に隠れた山. ¶It is *hidden* ***from*** view in the photo. それは写真には出ていない. ‖ *hidden* ***from*** the eye 見えない. ¶She *hid* her face ***in*** her handkerchief. 彼女はハンケチで顔を隠した. ‖ *hide* something ***in*** the ground 地中に何かを隠す. ¶*hide* it ***out of*** one's sight それを人目につかないようにする. ¶*hide* ***under*** a cloak of charity 慈善の美名に隠れる. ‖ *hide* one's talent (＝light *or* candle) ***under*** a bushel 自分の才能を隠す ‖ *hide* it ***under*** bed clothing それを夜具の下に隠す.

hide, *n.* 獣皮.

Q a ***raw*** (＝***green***) *hide* 生皮.

P ***soak*** *hides* in a weak alkaline solution 獣皮を薄いアルカリ溶液の中に浸す. ¶***tan*** *hides* 獣皮をなめす.

hideous, *a.* ぞっとする.

P Though *hideous* ***in*** reality, it seemed wonderful, beautiful, seen through the veil of mist and sunset. 実際はひどいものだが夕日のもやに包まれるとすばらしくきれいに見えた.

hideout, *n.* かくれ家.

Q a ***secret*** *hideout* かくれ家.

hierarchy, *n.* 組織.

Q a propaganda hoax perpetrated by Japan's ***militarist*** *hierarchy* 日本の軍部の行った虚偽の宣伝. ¶the ***Nazi*** *hierarchy* ナチの組織(制度). ¶the ***Soviet ruling*** *hierarchy* ソ連の支配組織.

P next ***in*** the *hierarchy* are … 番付面で次には…が来る. ‖ advance a step ***in*** the *hierarchy* of the civil service 文官の階級が一段進む.

high, *n.* 天; 高所; 最高点.

V ***reach*** (＝***hit***) a new *high* 新記録を作る.

Q a ***new*** *high* (low) in three years 三年ぶりの最高(低)記録.

Q² reach an ***all-time*** *high* of … の最高記録に達する. ¶Prices are the ***postwar*** *high*. 物価は戦後最高である.

P a blessed visitation from ***on*** *high* 天よりの聖なる訪れ ‖ The day-spring from [***on***] *high* hath visited us. れい明天より訪れたり. ‖ march under the flag held bravely ***on*** *high* 勇ましく旗を高く翻して行進する ‖ While ***on*** *high* the great white clouds slid swiftly. 空には大きい白雲が速く流れていた.

high, *a., adv.* 高い, 高く.

M The sun was ***already*** *high*. 太陽はすでに高かった. ¶*as high* as the clouds 天にもとどくほど. ¶Prices there are ***incredibly*** *high*. そこでは物価が信じられないほど高い. ¶an ***uncomfortably*** *high* total [死者などの]いやになるほど多い総数. ¶aim ***too*** *high* 望みが高過ぎる ‖ be ***too*** *high* for my purpose 高過ぎて私の目的には適しない.

M^2 the river is known *high* ***up*** as ... and lower down as ... その川は上流を…といい下流を…という.

P *high* ***above*** one's head 頭上高く. ¶men *high* ***in*** politics 政界の名士 ‖ a religious dignitary *high* ***in*** office 高僧 ‖ *high* ***in*** stature 背の高い ‖ *high* ***in*** attainment 造けいの深い. 【類】*high* ***in*** price. ¶Their orders are *higher* ***than*** the law 彼らの命令は法律以上の威力を持っている.

high-colored, *a.* 色彩の強い.

M Travelers' talks are ***proverbially*** *high-colored*. 旅行談はきまって誇張が多い.

highest, *n.* 最高.

P It will not be much higher than five hundred yen ***at*** the *highest*. それはたかだか五百円をあまり出まい. ‖ I do not think prices are ***at*** their *highest* (lowest). 私は物価は最高(最低)だとは思わない. ‖ the estimate of the crop ***at*** the *highest* (lowest) 作物の最高(低)予想. 【類】when his reputation was ***at*** its *highest* / when that art was ***at*** its *highest*.

highland, *n.* 高地.

Q a ***jutting*** *highland* つき出た高地.

highlight, *n.* 呼びもの.

Q^2 ***radio*** *highlights* 放送番組中の呼びもの. ¶This week's ***TV*** (=***video***) *highlights* 今週のテレビ番組の呼びもの.

P^2 the *highlight* ***of*** his visit to ... 彼の…への訪問中の主な事.

Highness, *n.* 殿下.

Q his ***Imperial*** (***Royal***) *Highness* 殿下. ¶his ***small*** *Highness* 若宮殿下.

high-priced, *a.* 高価な.

M ***exorbitantly*** *high-priced* 滅法高い.

highroad, *n.* 大道.

P He is ***on*** the *highroad* to ruin. 彼は破滅の一路をたどっている. 【類】the *highroad* ***to*** success (fame).

highway, *n.* 大道, 公道.

V The progress of science has ***transformed*** the commercial *highway*. 科学の進歩が世界の通商路を一変した. ¶Prostitutes ***walk*** the *highway* apparently unmolested. 売笑婦が一見した所何の干渉もされずに大道を歩く.

Q ***deteriorated*** *highways* 修繕おくれの道路. ¶an ***imperial*** *highway* to fortune 正々堂々の致富の道. ¶a ***national*** *highway* 国道. ¶The ocean is an ***open*** *highway*. 大洋は公道である. ¶a ***public*** *highway* 公道.

Q^2 an ***ocean*** *highway* 大洋航路. ¶well constructed ***state*** and ***county*** *highways* りっぱな州道及び郡道.

hike, *n.* 《米俗》ハイキング; 行軍; [物価・賃金の]引上げ.

V ***take*** a *hike* ハイキングをやる.

Q^2 ***price*** *hike* 物価騰貴. ¶a ***rent*** *hike* 料金値上げ. ¶a general ***salary*** *hike* 一般給料の値上げ. ¶***industry-wide wage*** *hikes* 全産業の賃金値上げ.

P the troops were ***on*** the *hike* from ... toward ... 軍隊は…から…への行軍中であった.

hike, *v.* ハイキングする; 上昇する.

M^2 *hike* ***up*** output 生産をあげる.

P plan to *hike* ***to*** the country いなかへのハイキングをもくろむ.

hiker, *n.* ハイカー.

Q^2 ***free-ride*** *hikers*=《米》hitchhikers 通りがかりの車にただで乗せてもらうハイカー. ¶a ***mountain*** *hiker* 登山者.

hilarious, *a.* 陽気な.

M He was ***slightly*** *hilarious*. 彼はちょっと酔っていた.

hill, *n.* 丘, 小山.

V ***ascend*** a *hill* 小山に上る. ¶***climb*** a steep *hill* けわしい丘を上る. ¶***crest*** a *hill* 丘の上に登る. ¶***mount*** a *hill* 小山に登る. ¶***reforest*** denuded *hills* 裸になった小山に植林する.

Q a ***densely-wooded*** *hill* 樹木うっそうたる小山. ¶***high*** *hills* 高い丘. ¶a lake surrounded by ***low*** *hills* on three sides 三方低い丘に囲まれた湖水. ¶richly ***mineralized*** *hills* 鉱物の多い小山. ¶a ***rocky*** *hill* 岩山. ¶a ***rounded*** *hill* 円山. ¶***rugged*** *hills* 凹凸(おう とつ)の丘陵. ¶A bluff is a ***steep*** *hill*. ブラフとは急こう配の小山のことである. ¶a range of ***tree-clad*** *hills* 木の茂った一連の丘.

Q^2 an ***ant*** *hill* あり塚.

P The river rises ***among*** the *hills*. その川は源を小山に発している. 【類】some desolate outposts (さびしい前線拠点). ***amongst*** the *hills*. ¶***beyond*** the *hill* 丘の向うに. ¶go ***down*** a *hill* 丘を降りる. 【類】walk ***down*** (=to the bottom of) a *hill* ‖ dash ***down*** the *hill* 丘をかけ下る. ¶the trend ***of*** the *hills* 山なみの走る向き ‖ on the top ***of*** a *hill* 山頂に. ¶stand ***on*** a *hill* 丘の上に立つ. ¶The sun was rising ***over*** the *hills*. 太陽が山の上に登る所であった. ‖ go ***over*** the *hill* 丘を越えて行く; 《軍俗》脱走する. ¶go (walk, scramble) ***up*** a *hill* 小山に登る(など) ‖ haul a heavy load ***up*** the *hill* (=uphill) 坂に重荷を引上げる.

hillside, *n.* 小山の山腹.

V ***climb*** a steep *hillside* けわしい小山の山腹をよじ登る.

Q a house on a ***bleak*** *hillside* 吹きざらしの丘の斜面の家. ¶a ***desolate*** *hillside* 荒涼たる丘の斜面. ¶a ***rugged*** *hillside* ががたる丘の斜面. ¶a ***steep*** *hillside* 丘の急斜面. ¶a terraced *hillside* 段丘. ¶a ***woody*** (=***wooded***) *hillside* 木のおい茂っている丘の斜面. ¶a ***windy*** *hillside* 風の吹く丘の頂上.

P ***on*** a *hillside* 小山の山腹に.

hilltop, *n.* 丘の頂上.

V ***reach*** the *hilltop* 頂上につく.

P ***from*** the *hilltop* 丘の頂上から.

hilt, *n.* [刀剣の]柄.

P put one's hand ***on*** the *hilt* 柄に手をかける ‖ ***on*** the *hilt* of one's dagger 短刀の柄に. ¶***thrust*** [in] a dagger ***to*** the *hilt* つかも通れと突き刺す. ¶prove it quite ***up to*** the *hilt* それを十分に証明する.

him, *pron.* 彼に, 彼を.

P Religion is ***with him*** no outward ceremony or formal lip-service. 宗教は彼にとっては外面的な儀式でもなければ形式的な口先のお勤めでもない.

hinder, *v.* 妨げる.

P *hindered* ***by*** a difficulty 一つの困難によって妨げられ. ¶He *hindered* me ***from*** doing this. 彼が邪魔をして私にこれをさせなかった. 【類】*hinder* a person ***from*** going. / Nothing shall *hinder* me ***from*** accomplishing my purpose. ‖ Age *hinders* me ***from*** moving swiftly. 年のせいで身体の動きがにぶい. ¶*hinder* him ***in*** his progress 彼の進歩を妨げる.

hindmost, *n.* 最後.

V It was everybody for himself, and the devil ***take*** the *hindmost*. 人はどうなろうと自分さえよければといった工合であった.

hindrance, *n.* 障害, 邪魔.

V No *hindrance* must be ***placed*** in his way. 彼の妨害をしてはならない. ¶***throw*** *hindrances* in the way of ... …の邪魔をする. 【類】try to ***throw*** *hindrances* in the way of the proposed marriage.

Q It will prove a ***serious*** *hindrance* to the advancement of learning. それは学問の進歩には大なる障害となるだろう.

P He was able to complete his studies ***without*** *hindrance*, although he was somewhat slow. 彼は幾分遅鈍の方であったが首尾よく学業を終えることができた.

P^2 a *hindrance* ***to*** success (trade, happiness) 成功(など)の障害.

hinge, *n.* ちょうつがい.

Q ***strident*** *hinges* きーきーきしるちょうつがい.

P connected (=joined) ***by*** *hinges* ちょうつがいにつながれた. ¶***off*** the *hinges* ちょうつがいが外れて, 調子が狂って. 【類】The door is ***off*** its *hinges*. ¶open ***on*** *hinges* ちょうつがいで開く ‖ The door swung open ***on*** the *hinges* (ぎいと開いた). ‖ a door turning ***on*** *hinges* ちょうつがいで回転するドア ‖ a lid ***on*** a *hinge* ちょうつがいつきのふた.

hinge, *v.* …につながる.

P The argument *hinges* ***on*** this point. その議論はこの点に帰着する. ‖ My acceptance *hinges* ***on*** the terms. 私の承諾は条件次第だ.

hint, *n.* 暗示, 注意, 心得.

V a few *hints* may be usefully ***added*** here for those who ... …の人たちの参考にここに二三の暗示をつけ加える. ¶***breathe*** the faintest *hint* of ... …をほんのかすかに暗示する. ¶***convey*** a *hint* 暗示を与える. ¶***drop*** *hints* of one's designs 意向をほのめかす. 【類】He came to me and told me that he was sure she loved me, for she had ***dropped*** a *hint* that seemed to imply as much. ¶***follow up*** a *hint* 暗示をたどる. ¶***furnish*** useful *hints* 有益な暗示を与える. ¶***get*** many a helpful *hint* 多くの有益な暗示を得る. ¶Will you ***give*** me a *hint* what I ought to do? どうすればよいのか一言おっしゃって下さいませんか. 【類】Why not ***give*** him a *hint*? ¶***glean*** many *hints* from ... …から色々な暗示を拾う. ¶He ***had*** not the least *hint* or clue of suspicion of my having done so. 彼は私がそうしたこ

とについて少しも感付かずまた疑ってもいなかった. ¶a person so thick-skinned that he would not ***heed*** gentle *hints* えん曲な言回しでは気がつかないほど神経の鈍い人. ¶***receive*** a *hint* from ... …から暗示を受ける. ¶I have the honor to ***submit*** these *hints* to the consideration of Congress. これらの参考意見を国会の審議に提出する光栄を有します. ¶The *hint* was well ***taken***. その暗示がよくさとられた. ‖ too obtuse to take the *hint* 鈍感で感付かない. 【類】She ***took*** the *hint* and went out of the room. ¶***throw out*** *hints* それとなく言う. ¶perfectly ***understanding*** the *hint* よくその暗示をさとって.

Q a ***broad*** *hint* 明らかな暗示. ¶a pretty ***clear*** *hint* かなり明かな暗示. ¶a ***delicate*** *hint* 巧妙な暗示. ¶***general*** *hints* on a traveling outfit 旅行用品に関する一般的の注意. ¶I gave him a ***gentle*** (=***mild***) *hint* and he didn't get it. それとなくにおわせたんだが感づかなかった. ¶some ***helpful*** *hints* 有益な注意二三. ¶***medical*** *hints* for travellers 旅行者への医学上の注意. ¶a ***plain*** *hint* 明らさまな示唆. ¶a ***polite*** *hint* 上品な暗示. ¶***practical*** *hints* 実際的注意. ¶***suggestive*** *hints* 示唆に富んだ注意. ¶***useful*** *hints* 有益な暗示 ‖ some ***useful*** *hints* as to the requirements of good writing 好い文章を書くについて必要な二三注意すべき点. ¶***vague*** *hints* ばく然とした暗示. ¶the ***warning*** *hint*, "Beware of the Dog"「犬御用心」という警告的注意. ¶a ***welcome*** *hint* 喜ばしい暗示.

Q² ***duty*** *hints* 職務心得. ¶***money-saving*** *hints* 貯金の心得.

P² *hints* ***about*** letter writing 手紙の書き方についての心得. ¶a *hint* ***as to*** ... …についての示唆. ¶here is a *hint* ***for*** ... ここに…についての心得がある ‖ *hints* ***for*** holidays 休日(をいかに暮すべきか)に関しての参考 ‖ *hints* ***for*** further study (reading) さらに研究(など)を進めるについての注意. 【類】helps and *hints* ***for*** home study / *hints* ***for*** intending emigrants. ¶take *hints* ***from*** England 英国から暗示を得る. ¶*hints* ***on*** bivouac 露営の心得. 【類】*hints* ***on*** housekeeping (cooking) / *hints* ***on*** microphone speaking. ¶*hints* ***to*** (=for) travellers 旅行者への注意. 【類】*hints* ***to*** writers for newspapers. ¶*hints* ***towards*** Latin prose composition ラテン語作文についての注意.

hint, *v.* 暗示する

M *hint* ***darkly*** that ... 暗に…とほのめかす. ¶***dimly*** *hint* ばく然とにおわす. ¶***gently*** *hint* えん曲に暗示する. ¶*hint* ***obliquely***=insinuate それとなしに言う. ¶***openly*** *hint* 公然とにおわす. ¶*hint* ***vaguely*** at one's resignation 辞職をにおわせる.

P *hint* ***at*** his resignation 彼の辞職を暗示する. ¶He *hinted* ***to*** me nothing of his intention. 彼は自分の意中を私に少しもにおわさなかった.

hinterland, *n.* 奥地.

Q² the ***Arab*** *hinterland* アラビア奥地.

hip, *n.* しり.

V These prostitutes ***swung*** their *hips* violently as they walked. この売春婦たちは歩くとき激しくしりを振った.

Q with ***grinding*** *hips* おしりをふって. ¶***plump*** *hips* 太ったしり.

P fall ***on*** one's *hips* しりもちをつく.

hire, *n.* 賃金; 借(貸)料.

V ***pay*** the carriage *hire* to ... …へ馬車賃を払う.

P These bicycles are ***for*** *hire*. これらの自転車は賃貸する. 【類】horses (automobiles) kept ***for*** *hire* / boats (clothes, cars) ***for*** *hire* ‖ We took a ferry plying ***for*** *hire*. われわれは料金を取る渡し舟に乗った ‖ carry on illicit sexual intercourse ***for*** *hire* 金をやって不義の情交を続ける. ¶Do you keep boats ***on*** *hire?* 貸ボートがあるか. ‖ let them out ***on*** *hire* それらの貸出しをする.

hire, *v.* 賃貸(借)する,; 雇う.

M *hire* [herself] ***out*** as a maid 女中として雇われる. 【類】Though very poor, they never thought of *hiring* ***out*** to do servants' work. ‖ *hire* ***out*** boats (horses, bicycles) by the hour 一時間いくらで貸ボート(など)にする.

P *hire* a motor-car ***by*** distance (the hour) 自動車を距離(時間)で借りる. ¶*hire* ... ***for*** a day …を一日賃借する. 【類】clothing *hired* ***for*** the occasion.

hireling, *n.* 雇い人.

Q a ***mere*** *hireling* たかだか人に使われる身.

hiring, *n.* 雇入れ.

Q ***domestic*** *hiring* 下女雇入れ.

P² *hiring* ***through*** the union 組合を通じての雇用.

hiss, *v.* しっしっという.

M *hiss* ***away*** children 子供たちをしっしっと追払う.

M² The speaker was *hissed* ***down***. 演者はやじり倒された. ‖ The teacher *hissed* ***down*** his pupils. 先生は生徒を静粛にさせた.

P *hiss* ***at*** a person 人にしっしっという. ¶They *hissed* him ***off*** the stage. 皆がしっしっと言って彼を舞台から下した.

historian, *n.* 歴史家.

V ***find*** its *historian* in ... …がその歴史を書いている.

Q a ***biased*** *historian* 偏見のある歴史家. ¶a ***faithful*** *historian* 忠実な歴史家. ¶a ***painstaking*** *historian* 苦心惨たんの歴史家. ¶The ***perfect*** *historian* is he in whose work there is no hasty judgment. その著作中に速断を下していない人は完全な歴史家である.

Q² an ***amateur*** *historian* しろうと歴史家. ¶***future*** *historians* 将来の歴史家.

P² a *historian* ***of*** Marie Antoinette マリー・アントワネットの伝記を書いた人.

history, *n.* 歴史, 来歴.

V ***affect*** the *history* of the world 世界の歴史に影響を及ぼす. ¶popular phrases that ***carry*** a *history* 来歴を持つ一般使用の句. ¶It would be ***distorting*** *history*. それでは歴史的事実を曲げることになる. ¶those great men who ***filled*** *history* with their deeds その業績を歴史に残した人たち. ¶***garble*** *history* 歴史を曲げる. ¶He ***gave*** me the *history* of his fall. 彼は自分の落ちぶれた一部始終を私に話した. ¶The art of biblical miniature painting ***has*** a *history* of a thousand years. 聖書の豆画の技術には千年の歴史がある. 【類】The bank ***has*** a *history* covering a period of more than two centuries. ¶***learn*** *history* at the fountain-head 歴史をその源泉にさかのぼって研究する. ¶These are the clubs in which English *history* during the last sixty years has been largely ***made***. 過去六十年の英国の歴史は大体これらのクラブの中で作られたのである. ‖ So much *history* is being ***made*** every day. 今日は天下多事である. ¶Street names ***mirror*** *history*. 町名は歴史を反映している. ¶***rake up*** a little *history* 材料を集めてちょっとした歴史をつづる. ¶***relate*** its *history* その来歴を語る. ¶How strangely, indeed, *history* is ***repeated***! いかにも不思議に歴史は繰返されるものだ. ¶***sketch out*** the *history* of ... …の歴史を略説する. ¶***trace*** the *history* of Christianity in Japan 日本におけるキリスト教史の跡をたどる ‖ ***trace*** *history* backward 歴史を倒叙する. 【類】***trace*** its *history* through the centuries.

V² *History* ***repeats*** itself. 歴史は繰返す. ¶*history* ***shows*** that ... 歴史によると…

Q ***authentic*** history 正史. ¶***ancient*** *history* 古代史. ¶a ***brief*** *history* 小史. ¶The city has had a ***chequered*** *history*. その市は波瀾の多い歴史を持っている. 【類】The word "rationalization (合理化)" has had a ***chequered*** *history*. ¶it is ***common*** *history* that ... それは普通に見られる歴史的事実である. ¶a ***complete*** *history* 全史. ¶***contemporary*** *history* 現代史. ¶an important period in the ***cultural*** *history* of the Japanese people 日本国民の文化史上重要な時期. ¶in the ***early*** *history* of our race わが民族の上代に. ¶***English*** (***Japanese, American***) *history* 英国(日本, 米国)史. ¶tomes of ***erudite*** *history* 学術的な史書. ¶an ***eventful*** *history* 多事多端の歴史. ¶The picture has the ***following curious*** *history*. その絵には次のような奇妙な来歴がある. ¶The town has a ***glorious*** *history*. その市には輝かしい歴史がある. ¶It has an ***honored*** *history* and an illustrious present. それには誉れある過去とりっぱな現在とがある. ¶The place has had an important rôle to perform in the shaping of ***human*** *history*. その土地は人類史上において重要な役割を演じた. ¶all ***illuminating*** *history* of American journalism アメリカ新聞紙の明快な沿革. ¶without any ***illustrious ancestral*** *history* 何らの門閥もなくて. ¶an ***intellectual*** *history* of Europe from St. Augustine to Marx 聖オーガスチンからマルクスに至るヨーロッパ思想史. ¶The word has an ***interesting*** *history*. その語は興味ある歴史を持っている. ¶a ***lifelong*** *history* 一代記. ¶***local*** *history* 地方史. ¶It has had a ***long*** *history* of growth. それは古い発達の歴史を持っている. ¶The University can boast a ***long*** and ***honorable*** *history*. その大学は長年月の名誉ある歴史を誇っている. ¶***medieval*** (***modern***) *history* 中世(近代)史. ¶The ***mental*** and ***spiritual*** *history* of the Koreans is marked by the animism and Shamanism of most early forms of religion. 韓国人の思

想史及び宗教史は宗教の最古形式たる精霊説及びシャマン教によって特色づけられている. ¶ *military history* 戦史. ¶ one of the greatest figures in *modern history* 近世史における最大人物の一人. ¶ in our *national history* わが国の歴史において. ¶ a sketch of his *personal history* 彼の略歴. 【類】 He puts into the novel much of his own *personal history*. / Of his *personal history* (経歴) little is known. ¶ her *previous history* 彼女のこれまでの経歴. ¶ He believes that the greatest master of prose in *recorded history* is Plato. 彼は有史以来散文の最大作家はプラトンだと信じている. ¶ a *secret history* 秘史. ¶ *secular history* 世俗の歴史. ¶ a *succinct history* 略史. ¶ the *true history* of the affair seems to be that ... その事件の事実は...らしい. ¶ a *synoptic history* of legislation in a country ある国の立法通史. ¶ *universal history* 万国史.

Q² a big thrill in *amusement history* 興行史上の大異彩. ¶ a career of trade dominance almost unique in American *business history* 米国商業史上ほとんど比類のない貿易雄飛の経歴. ¶ a *case history* 病歴. ¶ the *family history* of the man 同人の戸籍 ‖ inquire carefully into the *family history* of an individual with whom the question of mating has arisen 結婚問題が起った者の家系を綿密に調査する. ¶ It was the first strike of its kind in *flying history*. それは航空史上最初の大成功(ヒット)であった. ¶ *poultry history* 養鶏の歴史. ¶ her *love histories* 彼女の恋の歴史. ¶ one's *life history* その経歴 ‖ study the *life history* of a new fungus 新しい菌の生態を研究する. ¶ *school histories* 数種の歴史の教科書. ¶ *railroad history* 鉄道史. ¶ a red letter event in *screen history* 映画史上記念すべき事件. ¶ a *sketch history* of ... ...小史. ¶ a *subject history* 細部門の歴史. ¶ a *United States history* 米国史. ¶ Unparalleled in the annals of *world history*. 世界史にその比を見ない. ¶ *World War History* 世界大戦史.

P ***in*** the *history* of mankind 人類史上. ¶ ***in*** the *history* of thought 思想史上 ‖ There is no other example ***in history*** of such a marvellous progress. かかる驚異的発展は史上に類がない. ‖ His achievements will go down (=abide) ***in history***. 彼の業績は歴史に残るだろう. ‖ a case that can scarcely be matched ***in history*** ほとんど歴史に類例のない事件 ‖ These scholars are possessors of Ph. D.'s ***in history***. これらの学者は歴史の博士号を持っている. ¶ before the dawn ***of*** *history* 有史前に ‖ one of the greatest volcanic disasters ***of*** *history* 史上最も悲惨な噴火の一つ. ¶ a ship ***with*** a *history* 歴史のある船 ‖ a woman ***with*** a *history* 数奇な運命をたどった女 ‖ ***with*** a romantic *history* 小説的な経歴を持って ‖ ***with*** a *history* going back to ... ...までさかのぼる歴史を持って.

P² the *history* ***of*** human thought 人類思想史 ‖ the *history* ***of*** a case 病歴 ‖ the *history* ***of*** letters 文学史 ‖ the *history* ***of*** his life 彼の経歴 ‖ The *history* ***of*** this sense appears to begin with the author. この語をこういう意味に使いだしたのはその著者が始めであった. ‖ a *history* ***of*** opinion on the question その問題に関する意見の沿革. 【類】 the *history* ***of*** opinion regarding ... ¶ *History* ***without*** illuminating maps is like a room without windows. 説明地図のない歴史は窓のないへやのようなものだ.

hit, *n.* 大当り, 的中;〖野球〗安打(ヒット).

V ***applaud*** the *hit* うまいことを言ったのを拍手かっさいする. ¶ ***make*** a *hit* あたる. ¶ He ***scored*** forty *hits* in shooting. 彼は四十発的中した.

Q one of the ***biggest*** *hits* of the season その季節中での大当りの一つ. ¶ His answer was a ***clever*** *hit*. 彼の答えは即妙であった. ¶ He made a ***good*** *hit*. 彼の計画は図に当った. ¶ It made a ***great*** *hit*. それは大当りだった. ¶ a ***happy*** *hit*. 適評; 大当り. ¶ make an ***instantaneous*** *hit* たちまち成功する. ¶ a happy ***journalistic*** *hit* 新聞のスクープ. ¶ He made a ***lucky*** *hit* in business. 彼は事業でうまく当てた. ¶ a ***mighty*** *hit* 大当り. ¶ ***scattered*** *hits* 〖野球〗散発安打. ¶ the author made a ***successful*** *hit* with ... その著作家は...で当てた. ¶ a ***timely*** *hit* [野球などの]適時安打.

Q² a ***base*** *hit* 〖野球〗塁打(単打). ¶ a ***box-office*** *hit* [映画興行の]大当り. ¶ two current ***Broadway*** *hits* 今週のブロードウェイの二つの当りもの. ¶ a ***chance*** *hit* まぐれあたり. ¶ a ***gallery*** *hit* スタンドプレー. ¶ a ***record*** *hit* 最高記録の当り. ¶ a ***record-smashing*** (=***breaking***) *hit* 記録破りの大当り. ¶ a ***sacrifice*** *hit* 〖野球〗犠打. ¶ a ***screen*** *hit* 大当りの映画. ¶ a ***scratch*** *hit* [野球などの]まぐれ当り. ¶ an outstanding "***song*** *hit*" 大当りのヒットソング. ¶ a ***stage*** musical *hit* バラエティショーの当りもの. ¶ a ***two-base*** *hit* 二塁打.

P² That was a *hit* ***at*** me. それは私への当てこすりだった. ¶ a *hit* ***by*** chance まぐれあたり. ¶ a *hit* ***for*** three (two) runs 三(二)塁打. ¶ a *hit* ***of*** a jar《俗》意外な打撃. ¶ make a *hit* ***with*** a play (book, story) 芝居(など)で当てる.

hit, *v.* 打つ, 当る.

M *hit* ***back*** 打ち返す ‖ *hit* ***back*** in strong terms 手ひどく言い返す. ¶ It *hit* ship-builders ***badly***. それは造船業者に大打撃を与えた. ¶ You've ***certainly*** *hit* it. 君は確かにうまく当てたよ. ¶ *hit* ***close*** しかと当たる. ¶ He was ***hard*** *hit* at the news. 彼にとってそのニュースは大打撃だった. 【類】 The cinema industry has been ***hard*** *hit* by the economic depression. / especially ***hard*** *hit* is the ... project (計画). ¶ *hit* ***out*** straight and hard ストレートにしかもきつく(げん骨で)打つ. ¶ *hit* it ***right*** それに適中する.

M² *hit* ***off*** a poem (words of music) 即席で作詩(詞)する ‖ *hit* ***off*** music for the words その歌詞を直ちに作曲する ‖ The hound *hit* ***off*** the scent. その猟犬は跡をかぎつけた. ‖ The Yankees *hit* ***off*** 12 runs against 5 by the Giants. ヤンキースはジャイアンツの五点に対し十二点たたき出した. ‖ be *hit* ***off*** to the life ほんものそっくりに作ら(描か)れている ‖ *hit* it ***off*** together 一緒に仲よくやる ‖ *hit* ***off*** a bank's balances 銀行預金の帳じりをうまく合わせる.

P *hit* ***against*** a person 人にぶっつかる ‖ *hit* one's head ***against*** the door 戸に頭をぶっつける. ¶ *hit* ***at*** a mark 的に向って射る. ¶ The business is hard *hit* ***by*** extra burdens of taxation. その事業は税の過当な負担でひどく打撃を受けている. ¶ The ball *hit* him ***in*** the eye. そのボールは彼の目に当った. ¶ *hit* him ***on*** the cheek 彼のほおに当る ‖ *hit* a person ***on*** the head 人の頭を打つ ‖ *hit* ***on*** (=***upon***) a device (plan, an idea, happy solution) ある工夫(など)を偶然思いつく. 【類】 *hit* ***upon*** a stratagem (計略). ¶ *hit* a person ***with*** a hammer (stone) 人をつち(など)でぶつ.

O You've *hit* it! そのものずばり, 御名答. ‖ *hit* the mark 的中する.

hitch, *n.* 故障, 差支え.

Q Everything passed off without the ***slightest*** *hitch*. 万事いささかの滞りもなく終了した. ¶ An ***unfortunate*** *hitch* occurred at the meeting. その会でとんだ番狂わせがあった.

P The programme was gone through ***without*** a *hitch*. プログラムが滞りなくすんだ. 【類】 The concert went off ***without*** a *hitch*.

P² There was not a *hitch* ***in*** the proceedings. 会の進行には少しの故障もなかった.

hitch, *v.* つなぐ.

M *hitch* ***up*** a horse [to a wagon] 馬を馬車につなぐ ‖ *hitch* ***up*** one's trousers ずぼんを引きあげる.

P *hitch* a horse ***to*** a post 馬を柱につなぐ.

hitchhiking, *n.*《米》自動車に便乗すること.

P cover a long distance ***by*** *hitchhiking* 便乗して遠距離を踏破する.

hitter, *n.* 〖野球〗打者.

Q a ***hard*** (=***heavy***) *hitter* 強打者.

Q² a ***home-run*** *hitter* 本塁打者.

hitting, *n.* 打つこと; 命中.

Q² ***hundred percent*** *hitting* 百発百中. ¶ ***place*** *hitting* 〖野球〗ねらい打ち.

hive, *n.* はちの巣.

Q The General Post Office is a ***veritable*** *hive* of industry at midnight. 真夜中の中央郵便局は確かに大車輪で活動するはちの巣だ.

P² It is a very *hive* (=centre) ***of*** the industry. それは真にその種の産業の中心地である.

hive, *v.* 群居する.

M *hive* ***off*** [みつばちが]分封する; 集結する ‖ The company immediately *hived* ***off*** to the second position. その中隊は直ちに第二陣地に集結した.

hoard, *n.* 貯蔵.

Q a ***squirrel's*** *hoard* of nuts りすの貯えた木の実.

Q² a ***rice*** *hoard* 米の貯蔵.

hoarding, *n.* 板囲; 死蔵.

V ***erect*** *hoarding* [建築場などに]板囲をする.

Q² ***gold*** *hoarding* 金の退蔵.

hoarse, *a.* しわがれた.

O grow *hoarse* しわがれ声になる.

hoary, *a.* 白髪の, 古い.

P *hoary with* antiquity 古色そう然たる ‖ a person *hoary with* age 年老いて白髪になった人.

hoax, *v.* だます.

P *hoax* a person *out of* his money 人をだまして金を取る.

hobble, *v.* びっこを引く.

M *hobble away* びっこをひきひき立去る.

M² *hobble along* びっこを引いて歩く.

hobby, *n.* 道楽.

V Every one should *have* a good *hobby.* だれでも一つの良い道楽があるべきだ. ¶ *indulge* one's *hobby* 道楽にふける. ¶ *make* a *hobby* of one's work 仕事を道楽にする. ¶ *mount* a *hobby* [趣味の]道楽をやる. ¶ He *pursued* his *hobby* of collecting old almanacs for so many years. 彼は多年古い暦を収集する道楽を続けた. ¶ Perhaps no *hobby gives* more pleasure to its rider than the collecting of old stained-glass. 恐らくはどんな趣味でも昔の焼付ガラスを収集するくらい好事家に楽しみを与えるものはなかろう.

Q an *absurd hobby* ばかげた道楽. ¶ a *curious hobby* 変った道楽. ¶ an *expensive hobby* 金のかかる道楽. ¶ a *fascinating hobby* 実に面白い道楽. ¶ an *insipid hobby* 興味の薄い道楽. ¶ Reading is the *only hobby* I can speak of. 私の趣味と言ったらまず読書ぐらいです. ¶ a *reasonable hobby* 合理的な道楽.

Q² have no *sports hobbies* スポーツをやらない.

P The autograph-hunter spent 18 years of strenuous activity in the pursuit *of* his *hobby.* そのサイン収集家はその道楽を十八年熱心にやった.

P² a *hobby for* research in history 歴史研究の道楽.

O His *hobby* was travelling. 彼の道楽は旅行だった.

hobbyist, *n.* 道楽のある人.

Q² a *motor hobbyist* 自動車道楽の人.

hockey, *n.* ホッケー.

V *play hockey* with a club クラブでホッケーをやる.

Q² *ice hockey* アイスホッケー.

hoe, *v.* くわで耕す.

M² *hoe up* (=out) weeds from about flowers 花の回りから雑草を刈りとる.

hog, *n.* 豚.

V *raise hogs* 《米》=breed pigs 豚を飼う.

V² The *hog grunts.* 豚がぶうぶう鳴く.

Q a *plump hog* 丸々太った豚. ¶ hesitate to go the *whole hog* 一辺倒をためらう.

Q² a *road hog* 《米俗》規則を守らない自動車運転手.

P *like* a *hog* on ice 〖比ゆ〗あぶなっかしく.

hoist, *n.* 引(巻)あげ; 起重機.

V *give* ... a *hoist*=give a hoist to ... …を押しあげる.

Q a *geared hoist* 巻きあげ機. ¶ a *hydraulic hoist* 水力起重機.

Q² a *clay hoist* 土塊押しあげ機. ¶ a *goods hoist* 《英》貨物昇降機. ¶ a *hand hoist* 手動巻きあげ機. ¶ a *power hoist* 動力起重機. ¶ a *steam hoist* 蒸気力起重機.

hoist, *v.* あげる.

M *hoist out* a boat [甲板から]ボートを降ろす.

M² *hoist down* a cargo 船荷を降ろす.

hold, *n.* 把持, 把握; 船倉.

V The cliff afforded no *hold* for us to *take.* がけには手がかりも足がかりもなかった. ¶ *catch hold* of (=seize) a man by the neck 人の首っ玉をつかまえる. ¶ *gain* a *hold* upon ... …を服従させる ‖ The flames had *gained* a strong *hold* before the firemen arrived. 消防夫がかけつける前に火の手はもういっぱいにひろがった. ¶ *get hold* of the game 獲物を手に入れる. 【類】 They killed all people, women and children included, whom they *got hold* of (手当り次第). / We all love to *get hold* of a new word and to spend it freely. ¶ The witchcraft still *has* a *hold* on the popular mind. 妖(ﾖｳ)術はまだ民衆の心を把持している. 【類】 The author *has* already a considerable *hold* upon the reading public. ¶ *keep* one's *hold* on ... …をとらえて放さない. 【類】 *keep* a firm *hold* on ... ¶ *lay hold* of a high-tension wire 高圧線をつかむ ‖ *lay* deep *hold* of the author's ideas その著作家の思想をしかとつかまえる. ¶ Never *leave hold* of it. 決してそれを離すな. ¶ *let go* one's *hold* of ... …から手を放す. ¶ *loosen* (=*release*) one's *hold* on ... …の手をゆるめる. ¶ *lose* one's *hold* on (=of) ... …を手ばなす ‖ *lose* one's *hold* on realities 現実をつかみそこなう ‖ The faith has never *lost* its *hold.* その信仰は決してその力を失わなかった. 【類】 The actor has *lost* his *hold* upon the playgoers (人気を失った). ¶ *maintain* (*relax*) one's *hold* over ... …に対する(取締りの)手を強(弱)める. ¶ My hands *quitted* their *hold.* 私は手を放した. ¶ the control has *relaxed* its *hold* upon ... その統制は…に対する把握をゆるめた. ¶ *relinquish* one's *hold* つかまえた手をゆるめる. ¶ It will *retain* its *hold* in the future. それは将来においてもその把持を維持するであろう. ‖ Buddhism *retains* its *hold* upon the great mass of Chinese. 仏教は依然として中国の大衆の間に勢力を持っている. 【類】 Loyalty to the Throne (忠君) *retains* its *hold* on the Japanese mind. ¶ Educational films have *secured* firm *hold* in the educational field. 教育映画は教育界にしっかりとした勢力ができた. ¶ *seize hold* of (on) ... …をとらえる. 【類】 The disease has *seized* deep *hold* on him. ¶ *strengthen* one's *hold* upon ... …を握る手を強める. ¶ It has not *taken* much *hold* upon popular esteem. それはあまり一般に流行していない. ‖ Shame *took hold* upon him. はじらいの念が彼をとらえた. ‖ *take hold* of the public fancy 世人のこのみに投じる ‖ The strong arm of the law *took hold* of the affair. 法の鉄腕によってその事件を裁くことになった. ‖ This shows the readiness of the present British Government to *take hold* of new ideas. この事は現英国政府が進んで新思想を採用する意志があることを示す. 【類】 I should not allow such a thought to *take hold* on me. ¶ *tighten* her *hold* over Manchuria 満州に対する把握の手を引締める. ¶ This *weakened* his *hold* on his audience. このために彼は聴衆をとらえる力が弱くなった.

Q These ideas have a *considerable hold* of the English rustic mind. こういう思想が英国の地方人には随分勢力がある. ¶ cling with a *convulsive hold* to ... …に武者振りつく. ¶ take a *deep hold* upon popular mind 一般人の心に深く根ざす. ¶ take *fast* (=*firm*) *hold* of ... …をしっかりつかむ ‖ a *firm hold* on theory 学理上の確実な根拠. ¶ have a *great hold* over ... …に対して大きな威力を持つ. ¶ obtain an *increasing hold* on the estimation of the public 世論によって次第に高く評価されつつある. ¶ Their writings took *powerful* (=*strong*) *hold* of the thought of Japan. 彼らの著作は日本の思想界に大勢力を持っている. 【類】 The idea of devil has taken a *powerful hold* on the mind of man. / The religion has a *powerful hold* on the life of the people. ¶ the *same hold for* ... 同じことが…に対しても言える. ¶ has *strong hold* on the English public 英国人大衆の心をとらえている. ¶ Keep *tight hold* of this, so as not to drop it again. それをまた落すといけないからしっかりつかまえておいで.

Q² a *cargo hold* [旅客機の]貨物積載室.

P *in* the *hold* of a ship 船倉内に.

P² It took a firm *hold in* the Empire. それはその帝国において大いに勢力を扶植した. ¶ The movement is taking *hold on* Japan. その運動は日本において勢力を得つつある. 【類】 They lost their *hold* (支配力) *on* the people. ¶ The idea retains some *hold over* the most enlightened souls. その考えは最も進歩した人たちにすらまだいくらかの勢力を持っている. ¶ an exposition of the subject which takes *hold* deeply *upon* thoughtful men 思慮ある人士を根深くとらえている問題の解説 ‖ Has the sentiment any *hold upon* the public opinion? その感情は世論の上に多少勢力があるか.

hold, *v.* 握る, 固執する; 信じる; 押える.

M *hold aloof* from ... …から離れている. ¶ *hold back* rising anger 立腹をおさえる ‖ *hold back* information 情報が漏れないようにする ‖ *hold back* inflation インフレを抑える ‖ *hold back* goods from market 品を市場に出さないで抑えておく ‖ *hold back* the economy of a country 国家の経済の発展を阻害する. 【類】 Producers are *holding back* supplies. ‖ *hold back* from mentioning it それを口にすることをさし控える. ¶ *hold* it too *cheaply* それを見くびる. ¶ an office *held concurrently* with the principal 兼職. ¶ *coscientiously hold* that ... 良心的に…と主張する. ¶ *hold* it *disdainfully* at arm's length それを軽べつして近づけない. ¶ *hold fast* to the resolve その決心を堅く守る. ¶ *Hold firm* until you hear from me. さたをするまでがん張れ. ‖ *hold firmly* to the rail 手すりにしっかりとすがり付く. 【類】 I *hold firmly* to the belief that ... / *hold firmly* of the dogma (独断) that ... ¶ I have no idea to *hold forth.* 私には申上げるような意見もありません. ‖ *hold forth* the possibility that ... …という可能性を示す ‖ He *held forth* (=

spoke in public) on the necessity of reform. 彼は改革の必要を唱道した. ¶*hold* ***good*** 有効である；適用される ‖ It may be feared that these remarks still *hold* ***good*** to some extent. かかる批評がまだ幾分当を得ているのではなかろうかと気づかわれるのである. ‖ the same criticism *holds* ***good*** with ... ...に対しても同様の批評が下される. ¶The weather will *hold* ***long***. この天気は当分続くだろう. ¶*hold* ***out*** one's hands towards ... ...の方に両手をさしのべる ‖ *hold* ***out*** a friendly hand 友情の手をさしのべる ‖ *hold* ***out*** a hand to literature 文学に手をのばす ‖ She *held* me ***out*** her hand and gave mine a squeeze. 彼女は(握手に)手を出して私の手をぎゅっと握りしめた. 【類】*hold* ***out*** the hand of friendship and cooperation to ... ‖ *hold* ***out*** the hope that ... ...という希望を持ち続ける. 【類】*hold* ***out*** scant hope for ... / *hold* ***out*** possibilities for a new base on life (新生面を切り開く可能性) for Europe / *hold* ***out*** the prospect of a change in American policy ‖ *hold* ***out*** a bad example 悪例を示す ‖ *hold* ***out*** against its present enemies その現在の敵にあくまで対抗する ‖ *hold* ***out*** to the last 最後までがん張る ‖ *hold* ***out*** for lower rates [為替]レートが下がるまで待っている ‖ Manufacturers are *holding* ***out*** supplies, watching for higher prices. 生産者は値上りを待って品物を出さない. ¶*hold* ***out*** against ... ...に立向かう ‖ *hold* ***out*** obstinately がん強に立向かう ‖ if their appetite *holds* ***out*** おなかが持てば ‖ The supplies will *hold* ***out*** till the end of the voyage. 食料は航海の終りまで保つでしょう. 【類】Babylon had *held* ***out*** for ten years before it was taken. ¶The subject was *held* ***over*** till the next meeting. その問題は次会まで延ばすことになった. ¶***personally*** I *hold* that ... ...私一個人としては...と思う. ¶*hold* him ***responsible*** for ... 彼に...の責任を負わせる. ¶*hold* ***together*** =not separate, *or* remain in union 結合する, 調和を保つ ‖ *hold* ***together*** by strong twine 強いより糸でつづる. ¶I *hold* very ***strongly*** that ... 私はどこまでも ... と言張る. ¶wooden staves *hold* ***together*** by hoops たがで締めたおけ木 ‖ The youths swore to each other—whatever may happen—to *hold* ***together*** in life and death. その二青年はどんなことがあろうと生死をともにすることを誓った. ‖ The meson is one of the particles that *hold* the atom ***together***. メソンは原子を結合させる微分子の一つである. ‖ The Western democracies must *hold* ***together*** for collective security. 西欧民主国群は集団保障のため結合しなければいけない. 【類】Love of country *holds* a nation ***together***. ¶*hold* ***true*** 真実である. ¶it is almost ***universally*** *held* by writers that ... ...ということは論者が広く唱道する所である.

M² *hold* ***down*** Germans ドイツ人を抑圧する ‖ Meat prices were *held* ***down*** by price control. 物価統制で食肉の値上りは抑えられた. 【類】*hold* prices and wages ***down*** ‖ *hold* ***down*** traffic accidents despite soaring traffic volume 交通量の激増にもかかわらず交通事故をふえないようにする ‖ *hold* ***down*** one's eyes 目を伏せている ‖ This is the only job I can *hold* ***down*** for life. 一生やっていける仕事といってはこれだけです. ¶*hold* ***off*** purchases 買入れを手控える ‖ The rain is still *holding* ***off***. 天気がぐずついている. ‖ *hold* ***off*** (=out) for lower prices 手控えて値下りを待つ. 【類】Buyers continue to *hold* ***off***. / be *held* ***off*** the market in hopes of getting higher prices ‖ *Hold* your dog ***off*** [from here]. 犬をここへ入れないように. ‖ His cold manner *holds* people ***off***. 彼の冷たい態度で人がよりつかない. ¶*Hold* ***on*** there! That's it! [撮影の際など]そのままに, よし. ¶*Hold* it ***on***, please. [電話口で]そのままでどうぞ. ‖ I'm pleased to find that you still *hold* (=keep) ***on*** a correspondence with her. 君はまだ彼女と文通してることを知ってうれしい. ‖ This pin *holds* the wheel ***on***. このピンで車輪がはなれない. ‖ *hold* ***on*** to the strap つり皮にぶらさがる. 【類】*hold* ***on*** to one's job / *hold* ***on*** to mother's apron / *hold* ***on*** to the railing (てすり) / *hold* ***on*** to one's principle (主義) ‖ Birds *hold* ***on*** to the trees by their feet. 小鳥は足で木にとまる. ¶Please *hold* ***over*** the rest of the goods. あとの品物は(売らないで)とっておいてください. ‖ *hold* ***over*** a bill for future consideration その内に審議することとして議案を引込ます ‖ *hold* ***over*** till one's successor is appointed 後継者が任命されるまで職にとどまる ‖ The case will be *held* ***over*** till the next hearing. その件は次回の審理まで持越しになる. ¶be *held* ***up*** by armed men 武装兵によって持ちこたえている. 【類】The position is still *held* ***up***. ‖ *hold* it ***up*** temporarily それを一時発表せずに置く ‖ *hold* ***up*** a warning finger at ... ...に気をつけろよと指で戒める ‖ *hold* ***up*** but little hopes of success あまり成功の見通しがつかない ‖ cause buyers to *hold* ***up*** バイヤーに買い控えさせる ‖ *Hold* ***up***! ホールダップ(両手をあげろ). ‖ *hold* ***up*** bank clerks 銀行員にホールダップを命じる. 【類】The bank was *held* ***up*** by an armed man. / Armed bandits sometmes *hold* ***up*** passenger trains. / At noon yesterday four unmasked men *held* ***up*** a Texas Pacific train near the town. / his automobile was *help* ***up*** in broad daylight by ... ‖ The liner was *held* ***up*** by a thick fog. 定期船は濃霧のため停船した(出航できなかった). 【類】The ship was *held* ***up*** by the strike. ‖ *hold* ***up*** an egg before a candle ろうそくの火で卵をのぞく(良不良を見るため) ‖ *hold* it ***up*** high それを高く掲げる. 【類】*hold* ***up*** a high ideal of conduct ‖ *hold* ***up*** Rangers and Commandos as heroes 遊撃隊員や奇襲隊員を殊勲者として推称する ‖ *hold* ***up*** the hands of the players (wrestlers) [選手の手をあげる, から] 声援する, 元気づける ‖ *hold* a fort ***up*** against the enemy 敵攻撃に対抗し要さいを持ちこたえる ‖ *hold* a person ***up*** to derision 人を笑いものにする(やり玉に上げる). 【類】He *held* ***up*** the government to hatred and contempt (憎悪と侮辱). / Dickens was almost alone in *holding* ***up*** to ridicule (やり玉にあげる) the potent shames of his time. ‖ *hold* it ***up*** for admiration これみよがしに示す. ¶*hold* ***up*** one's hands ***for*** astonishment びっくりして両手をあげる ‖ He was *held* ***up*** to students as a model for emulation. 彼は学生のお手本として示された. ‖ *hold* ***up*** a ture mirror to the existing state of affairs in ... ...における現状を赤裸々に示す.

P *hold* ***against*** the enemy 敵に対抗する ‖ If it hurt you, please don't try to *hold* it ***against*** me. もしそれでお気に障ったとしてもどうぞ私を悪く思わないように. ¶be *held* ***as*** hostage 人質として押えられる. ¶*hold* a stag ***at*** bay しかを追いつめる(のがさない). ¶Under the existing social conditions young women are compelled to *hold* the opposite sex ***at*** arm's length. 現下の社会状態では若い婦人は異性を余り近付けないようにせざるを得なくなる. ‖ He is *held* ***at*** the jail on a charge of murder. 彼は殺人罪で刑務所に入れられている. ‖ I *hold* him ***at*** my mercy. あの男はもうこっちのものだ. ‖ The market *holds* ***at*** ... yen. その相場は...円を保っている. 【類】Funeral services will be *held* from the family residence ***at*** two o'clock Saturday afternoon with the Rev. C.E.W. Brecht officiating (司会者となって). ¶*hold* a cigarette (pipe) ***between*** his lips 口に紙巻タバコ(など)をくわえる. ¶*hold* a person ***by*** the hand (sleeve) 人の手(など)をつかむ. 【類】He *held* it ***by*** the rope. / *hold* the sheep ***by*** the horn. ¶*hold* a person ***for*** ransom 身の代金を取るために人を押える ‖ The baggage was *held* ***for*** non-payment of rent. 間代未払のために荷物を押えられた. ¶The exhibition will be *held* ***from*** the end of this month to the end of next. その展覧会は今月の末から来月の末まで開かれる. ¶be *held* ***in*** prison (=jail) 収監されている ‖ *hold* shares ***in*** a business 商売の経営に参加する(パートナーとなる) ‖ be *held* ***in*** custody 監禁される ‖ he is *held* ***in*** deep (=great) veneration by ... 彼は...から大いに尊敬されている ‖ It is *held* ***in*** high estimation by collectors. それは収集家に珍重されている. ‖ *hold* him ***in*** high regard (=esteem, veneration) 大いに彼を尊重する ‖ *hold* it ***in*** the hollow of one's hand それを掌中に握る. 【類】In this branch of literature thieves and murderers are *held* ***in*** honor. ‖ *hold* ***in*** one's hands the whole of the Eastern trade 東洋貿易を一手に引受けている ‖ *hold* an enemy ***in*** check 敵を食い止める ‖ *hold* dancing ***in*** aversion ダンスをきらう ‖ *hold* a person ***in*** fear 恐れている ‖ be *held* ***in*** suspension 中ぶらりんになっている. ¶*hold* it ***of*** no account それをものの数とも思わない. ¶*hold* ***over*** him an umbrella 彼の上にかさを差しかける. ¶*hold* ***to*** one's rule 自分のきめた規則を固守する ‖ In my earlier years I myself *held* ***to*** this view. 私も若い時はその考えであった. 【類】*hold* ***to*** one's purpose ‖ *hold* a person ***to*** a promise (an agreement) 人に約束(など)を守らせる ‖ *hold* a person ***to*** ridicule (derision) 人をやり玉に上げる(笑いものにする). ¶*hold* them ***under*** control 彼らを支配する. ¶I *hold* ***with*** him that ... 彼同様私は...と思う.

hold-all, *n.* 合切袋.
Q^2 a *football hold-all* フットボール選手の合切袋.
holder, *n.* 入れもの；携帯者.
Q^2 a ***cigarette** holder* パイプ. ¶cottagers and ***allotment** holders* 《英》小作人と小地主. ¶a ***commutation-ticket** holder*＝a commuter 《米》定期券使用者. ¶a ***cuffs** holder* [ワイシャツの]カフスつり. ¶a ***dictionary** holder* 辞書台. ¶a ***franchise** holder* 選挙権所有者. ¶a ***key chain** holder* 鎖状かぎ差し. ¶a ***license** holder* 免許状所持者. ¶a ***fishing rod** holder* 釣ざおかけ. ¶a ***matchbox** holder* マッチ入れ. ¶a ***meal coupon** holder* 食券使用者. ¶a ***scarf** holder* スカーフかけ. ¶If slavery is a disgrace, then a ***slave** holder* must bear his full portion of obloquy. 奴隷制度が恥辱であるとするなら，奴隷所有者はあらゆる非難を甘受せねばならない. ¶a ***ticket** holder* 切符所持者；切符入れ. ¶a ***toilet-paper** holder* トイレットペーパーはさみ. ¶a ***tooth-brush** holder* 歯ブラシ入れ. ¶a ***world-record** holder* in ... ...の世界記録保持者. 「の保有者.
P^2 *holders* ***of*** lots in a concession 専管居留地における地区
holding, *n.* 固守；保有.
Q an ***obstinate** holding* on to an ultra-antiquated system 極端に旧式な方法のがん迷なる墨守.
Q^2 ***gold** holdings* in a bank 銀行の金の保有高. ¶***livestock** holdings* on the farm 農園の飼養家畜数. ¶***oil** holdings* 油
holdout, *n.* がん張り. 田の持株.
Q ***stubborn** holdout* on the issue その問題に対するしつよ
holdup, *n.* 追はぎ(ホールドアップ). うながん張り.
Q^2 a daring ***daylight** hold-up* was staged at ... 大胆きわまる白昼追いはぎが...で行われた.
hole, *n.* 穴.
V A boiler explosion ***blew*** a *hole* right through the hull. 汽かんが破裂して船体に穴があいた. ¶***block up*** a *hole* 穴をふさぐ. ¶***bore*** a *hole* through a plank 板に穴をあける ‖ stare down with eyes so bright that they seem to ***bore*** two *holes* to earth 地面に穴のあくほどぱっちりした目で見つめる. ¶A lighted cigarette ***burned*** a *hole* in his clothes. 火のついた巻タバコで彼の着物に焼穴ができた. ‖ The boy felt his loose change ***burning*** a *hole* in his pocket. 少年はポケットに小銭があるのでどうしても買いたいと思った. ¶***chop*** a *hole* in the ice for fishing 釣をするために氷に穴をあける. ¶***cover*** a *hole* [衣類などの]穴を繕う. ¶A rat ***cut*** a *hole* through the ceiling. ねずみが天井に穴をあけた. ¶***dig*** a deep *hole* in the ground 地面に深い穴を掘る. ¶***drill*** *holes* in ... ...に穴をもみあける. ¶Bookworms ***eat*** *holes* in books. しみが書物に穴を食いあける. ¶***excavate*** a *hole* 穴をうがつ. ¶***fill*** a *hole* with ... 穴を...で詰める. ¶***fill up*** a *hole* 穴を詰める. ¶***gnaw*** a *hole* かじって穴をあける. ¶The storm ***knocked*** a *hole* in her starboard bow above water-mark. あらしで船の喫水線の上の右舷前方に穴があいた. ‖ ***knock*** a big *hole* in the theory that ... ...という学説に一大痛棒を食わせる. ¶***make*** a *hole* in the safe 金庫に穴をあける(大金を使いこむ). ¶***pick*** *holes* in him 彼のあらを探す. ¶***prick*** *holes* with a thick pin 太いピンで穴をあける. ¶***puddle up*** a *hole* in the wall [下塗りで]壁穴をふさぐ. ¶***punch*** a *hole* 穴をあける. ¶***stop [up]*** a *hole* 穴をふさぐ. ¶***tear*** a *hole* in one's coat (stockings) 上衣(など)にかぎ穴があく. ¶Walking ***wore*** a *hole* in my shoe. 歩いたので片方のくつはすり切れて穴があいた.
Q I wished a ***great big** hole* would appear to swallow me up. 穴があったら入りたい気がした. ¶The fire burnt a ***large** hole* in the blanket. こげて毛布に大きな穴があいた. ¶an ***oval** hole* 卵形の穴. ¶a ***wretched** hole* to live in ひどいぼろ家.
Q^2 an ***eyelet** hole* [ひもを通す]目穴. ¶a ***finger** hole* [フルート・尺八などの]指穴. ¶a ***peep** hole* のぞき穴.
P creep ***through*** a *hole* 穴をはい抜ける. ¶It is pierced ***with*** *holes*. それにはいくつか穴があいている.
P^2 There is a *hole* ***in*** my sock. 僕のくつ下に穴があいてい
hole, *v.* 穴をあける. る.
M *hole* ***out*** 『ゴルフ』球を穴に入れる.
M^2 Bears *hole* ***up*** for the winter to go by. くまは穴の中で越冬する. ‖ the caves where Japanese soldiers once *holed* ***up*** (＝out) 日本軍がかつて入り込んでいたほら穴.
holiday, *n.* 聖日，祝祭日；《英》休暇，休日.
V In America Xmas vacation is occasionally ***called*** "the *holidays*." アメリカではクリスマスの休みを「ザ・ハラデイズ」と呼ぶことがある. ¶***celebrate*** a *holiday* 祭日を祝う. ¶***enjoy*** but one *holiday* in the year 年にたった一度の休みを楽しむ. ¶I ***finished*** my *holiday* with a voyage. 私は休暇の終りに船客をした. ¶***give*** them a day's *holiday* 彼らに一日の休みを与える. ¶He ***gave up*** *holidays* and other time off. 彼は休日その他の休みを取らなかった. ¶***have*** a *holiday* once in a while 時たま休暇をとる. 【類】I want to ***have*** a few more *holidays* for recreation. / For one month in the summer, he and his pupils ***had*** their *holidays*. ‖ ***have*** a *holiday* 一日休む ‖ ***have*** a year's *holiday* to recruit 一年間休養する. 【類】We are to ***have*** four *holidays* beginning [from] today. ¶Tokyo will ***hold*** a public *holiday* on the occasion. そのとき東京は一般に休日になる. ¶The whole city ***kept*** *holiday*, and gave itself up to pleasure. 全市をあげて祭日を祝って歓楽を尽した. ¶Let's ***make*** *holiday* for a day or two. 一二日骨休みをしよう. 【類】The average Londoner is not inclined to get up unusually early, even to ***make*** *holiday*. ¶***mis-spend*** *holidays* 休暇をへたに使う. ¶***observe*** a *holiday* 祝日を守る ‖ *holidays* officially ***observed*** 公休日. ¶***plan*** a *holiday* 休日の行楽を計画する. ¶***receive*** a *holiday* on some other day of the week as a compensation for ... ...の埋合せにその週の他の日に休日をもらう. ¶I have ***snatched*** a short *holiday* from my work to come here. ちょっと仕事のひまを盗んで参りました. ¶***spend*** a *holiday* at ... ...で休日を暮す ‖ a campaign to induce strangers to ***spend*** their *holiday* in Ireland 他国人にアイルランドを遊覧させようとする運動. 【類】***spend*** one's *holidays* at the seaside. ¶***take*** *holiday*＝《米俗》vacate 休暇をとる. 【類】***take*** a month's (week's) *holiday* ‖ He is ***taking*** a *holiday* in the country. 彼は仕事を休んでいなかへ旅行している. 【類】August and September are the months of the year during which most English people ***take*** their *holidays*. 「日.
V^2 a *holiday* ***extending*** from ... to ... ...から...にわたる休
Q I enjoyed an ***agreeable** holiday* this summer. 私はこの夏楽しい休日を過した. ¶take a ***brief** holiday* 短かい休みを取る. ¶three ***consecutive** holidays* 三日の連休. ¶a ***double** holiday* [祭日と日曜がかち合った]二重の休日. ¶a ***fortnight's** holiday* 二週間の休暇. ¶Our school had a ***half** holiday*. われわれの学校では半休だった. ¶I wish you a ***happy** holiday*. [休暇旅行などのとき]愉快に遊んでいらっしゃい. ¶an ***intellectual** holiday* 頭の休日. ¶a ***jolly** holiday* 愉快な休日. ¶a ***legal** holiday* 法定公休日. ¶***local** holidays* 地方の祭日. ¶a ***merry** holiday* 楽しい休日. ¶a ***movable** holiday* 日の一定しない祭日. ¶a ***national** holiday* 大祭日. 【類】the French ***national** holiday* (14th July, the Fall of the Bastille, 1789). ¶A ***public** holiday* was declared in honor of his arrival. 彼の到着を祝して公休日が宣せられた. ¶a ***religious** holiday* 宗教休日(クリスマス，復活祭など). ¶with a ***regular** holiday* once a month 一カ月一度の定休日があって. ¶pass a ***short** holiday* at ... ...で短い休暇を過す. ¶enjoy a ***well-earned** holiday* 天下晴れての休日を楽しむ. ¶In the L.C.C. schools Saturday is a ***whole** holiday*. エル・シー・シー(ロンドン市立)校では土曜日は全日休む. ¶our ***yearly** holidays* われわれの例年の休暇.
Q^2 a ***bank** holiday* 《英》銀行休日(一般定休日). ¶British ***bank** holiday* is called legal holiday in the United States and Canada. ¶***Christmas** holidays*＝《米》the Xmas Vacation クリスマス休暇. ¶the ***Columbus** Day holiday* コロンブス祭日. ¶Whitsuntide, the gayest of ***country** holidays* 地方の休日で一番にぎやかな聖霊降誕節. ¶the ***Easter** holidays* (＝vacation) 復活祭休暇. ¶a ***four-day** holiday* 四日間の連休. ¶the ***Fourth of July** holiday* 七月四日(米国独立祭)休日. ¶an ***official** holiday*＝a legal holiday 正式休日. ¶the ***Saturday half-day** holiday* 半どんの土曜日. ¶***School** holidays* are now with us. 学校がお休みになった. ‖ The occasion will be a ***school** holiday*. その行事の日は学校は休みです. ¶spend a ***seaside** holiday* 海岸で休日を送る. ¶spend part of their ***summer** holiday* in ... 夏期休暇の一部を...で暮す ‖ go away for the ***summer** holiday* 夏期休暇を利用して旅行する. 【類】the five weeks' ***summer** holiday*. ¶a ***three-day** holiday* proclaimed in celebration of ... ...の祝典に三日間の休日が布告された. ¶go on a ***week-end** holiday* 週末行楽に出かける ‖ I shall treat myself to a ***weekend** holiday*. 週末旅行で骨休めをしよう.
P ***after*** a brief *holiday* 短かい休日の後. ¶***at*** the Xmas

holidays クリスマスの休暇に. ¶*during* the Whitsun *holidays* 聖霊降臨祭の休日中. ¶The whole family was out *for* a *holiday*. 家族は皆休日の遊びに出掛けた. ‖ Where are you going *for* your *holidays* this summer? この夏休はどちらへお出掛けですか. ‖ a student down *for* his *holidays* 休みで遊びにいなかにきた学生. ¶*in* the *holidays* 休暇に. ¶He is off *on holiday*. 彼は休みで遊びに旅行している. ‖ while *on* a *holiday* 休日中に ‖ be away *on holiday*=《米》 be away for the vacation 休暇旅行中である. 【類】 students *on holiday* / "Tourist" in its old specific sense is a visitor *on holiday* or for pleasure. ‖ stay there *on* a *holiday* 休日にそこに滞在する. ¶*with* a day's *holiday* once a month 月に一日の公休があって.

P² Tuesday next, the Emperor's birthday, will be a *holiday at* the Custom House. 次の火曜日の天長節には税関は休みになる. ‖ take a ten days' *holiday at* Christmas クリスマスに十日仕事を休む. ¶take [a] *holiday for* the purpose of ... ...のために休む. ¶During the blossom time everyone who can do so takes some sort of a *holiday from* his work and spends the day under the blooming cherrytrees. 花時にはだれしも出来ればどうにかして仕事を休み咲いた花の下でその日を過すのである. ¶For the well-to-do a summer *holiday out of* town is not uncommon. 避暑は裕福な人たちには珍しくないことだ.

holiday-maker, *n.* 遊覧者.

V Trains *convey holiday-makers* to their playgrounds. 汽車が遊びに出かける人たちを遊覧地へ運ぶ. ¶*tempt holiday-makers* from abroad 海外から遊覧者を誘致する.

P The resort is crowded *with holiday-makers*. そこは行楽客で混雑している.

holiday-time, *n.* 休日期.

P *during holiday-time* 休日期の間. ¶*in holiday-time* 休日期に.

holiness, *n.* 神聖.

V *pollute* its *holiness* その神聖をけがす.

hollow, *n.* 穴, うつろ, くぼみ.

V *cut* a *hollow* into ... ...に穴をうがつ. ¶*make* a *hollow* in (=hollow out) ... ...をえぐる.

P A traffic manager has *in* the *hollow* of his hand, as one might put it, the traffic of the system. 運輸主任は言わばその系統の輸送をその掌中に握っている.

hollow, *v.* 穴を明ける.

P a prehistoric boat *hollowed from* a tree trunk 木の幹をえぐって造った有史前の船.

hollowware, *n.* 深い容器.

Q an *enamelled hollowware* エナメル塗のうつわ.

Q² *cast hollowware* 鋳ものの器(うつわ). ¶stamped *steel hollowware* 打ち抜き鋼鉄うつわ. ¶*solid-drawn hollowware* 引き抜きうつわ.

holocaust, *n.* 破滅.

Q² predict a *world holocaust* 世界人類の破滅を予想する.

homage, *n.* 敬意, 尊崇, 崇拝.

V *do* him *homage* 彼に敬意をささげる; 臣下の礼を尽す ‖ I *do homage* to your purity, truth, and loyalty. 私はあなたの純潔・真実・忠誠に対して敬意を表する. ¶*make homage* to the memory of ... ...の霊に敬意を表する. ¶*pay* their *homage* to the Imperial Shades 皇祖の霊を拝む. 【類】 *pay homage* to gods (the spirits of ...) / The young are still ready to *pay homage* to the old. ¶The head of the Dutch factory at Nagasaki came to Yedo once a year to *present* his *homage* to the Shogun. 長崎オランダ館長は将軍に敬意を表するため年一度江戸に来た. ¶*tender* my sincerest *homage* to ... ...に私の心からの敬意を表する.

Q pay the grandeur of nature its *due homage* 自然の偉大さにその当然受くべき敬意を表する. ¶come home to pay one's *filial homage* to one's parents 帰省する. ¶pay *grateful homage* to ... ...に謝恩の意を表する. ¶pay the *last homage* to the defunct 死者に告別をする. ¶do *posthumous homage* to ... ...に対して死後の敬意を払う.

P *in homage* to ... ...に敬意を払うために.

P² pay silent *homage before* the tomb of ... ...の墓前に默とうをささげる.

home, *n.* 家; 家庭; 生家, 故郷; 養育院, 孤児院.

V *build* a *home* 家庭を造る ‖ *build* their own *home* 自分の家を建てる. ¶*buy* a *home* 自分の住む家を買う. ¶*decorate* one's *home* 屋内を飾る. ¶*defile* the *home* of one's ancestors by introducing a singing girl as one's wife 芸者を自分の妻として先祖の家を汚す. ¶*establish* a *home* 家庭を作る. ¶*find* its *home* in ... ...がその本場になる. ¶The picture has *found* a safe and lasting *home* in the National Gallery. その絵は国立美術館に安全にかつ永久に収蔵されることになった. 【類】 The books *find* a fitting *home* there. ¶*forsake* one's *home* and live in a hotel 家をたたんでホテル住いをする. ¶He *founded* his *home* there. 彼はそこを永住の地とした. ¶*furnish* one's *home* attractively 室内装飾を体裁よくする. ¶*get home* 家に着く; 適中する. ¶*get* the *home* in order 家庭を整理する. ¶*guard* one's *home* from ... ...から家庭を防御する. ¶He *has* his *home* (=lives) at present in Switzerland. 彼は現在スイスに住んでいる. ‖ He *has* no *home* for rest. 彼には休息の家がない. ¶Experience has demonstrated that hot water or steam is the most healthful agent for *heating homes*. 経験によると湯か蒸気が家庭の暖房にはもっとも健康的である. ¶*keep* one's *home tidy* 自宅をきちんとしておく. ¶The son decided to *leave* the paternal *home*. その息子は父の家を去る決心をした. ¶*make* one's *home* at ... ...に家庭を持つ ‖ *make* one's *home* with ... ...の家に住込む. 【類】 The newly married couple have *made* their *home* at 4 Shinryudo-cho, Azabu. / The young couple will *make* their *home* at No. 67 Shinzaka Machi, Akasaka. / Mr. Waters and his bride will *make* their *home* in ... / He has *made* his *home* in a hotel up to now (ホテル住い). ‖ will *make* it their *home* for some time to come 当分そこを家にする ‖ *make* a *home* in England 英国に支社をつくる(米国雑誌について) ‖ There are a hundred ways in which glass can *make* your *home* more attractive. ガラスで家庭生活を美しくする色々の方法がある. ¶*make* and *keep* a happy *home* 幸福な家庭を作って暮らして行く. ¶With the help of a single maid she *managed* their new little *home* in modest comfort. たった一人の女中をおいて彼女は小さな新家庭を質素ながらも楽しく切盛りした. ¶*own* one's own *home* 自分の家を持つ ‖ Full a hundred New York clubs *own* their own *homes*. ニューヨークに独立した建物を持つクラブは百はたしかにある. ¶*possess* a *home* 家を持つ. ¶*provide* a suitable *home* for a collection of pictures 絵の収集を収蔵する建物を造る. ¶*save* a *home* from the sheriff's hammer 家を公売に付せられないようにする. ¶Only three *saw* their *homes* again. 生きて帰るものわずかに三人. ¶*set up* one's little *home* 小さな住居をつくる. ¶Jealousy is the chief force that *unmakes* home. しっとは家庭を破壊する主なる力である. ¶It is human nature to *want* a *home*. 家庭を欲しいと思うのは人情である. ¶the man who has *wrecked* B's *home* Bの家庭の平和を破った男.

Q the caretaker of an *all-absent home* 留守担当者. ¶an *attractive home* 住心地のよさそうな家. ¶*better-class homes* 上流の家庭. ¶the *cherished home* of foreign artists, dancers, musicians, singers, and other talented performers 外国の芸術家・舞踊家・音楽家・歌手その他すぐれた芸術家のあこがれの国. ¶The country will make a *comfortable home* for him. その国は彼にとって愉快な住み場所になるだろう. ¶peoples living together in a *common home* 一国に共同で住んでいる諸民族. ¶a *convalescent home* 病後静養所. ¶a *desolate home* 住む人のない(わびしい)家. ¶an *elegant home* 風雅な家. ¶a *fine home*=《英》 a fine house 《米》 りっぱな邸宅. ¶their *first home* was made at ... 彼らは...ではじめて家庭を持った. ¶have a *grand home* 豪壮な邸宅を構える. ¶he has a *happy home* at ... 彼は...で幸福に暮している. ¶a *humble home* 粗末な住宅. ¶build *imposing homes* 堂々たる邸宅を建てる. ¶an *industrial home* for the blind 盲人授産場. ¶its *interim home* その仮の建物(本建築でない). ¶a *joyless home* 陰気な家庭. ¶a *lavish home* 豪華な邸宅. ¶He has gone to his *long* (=*last*) *home*. 彼は永眠した. ¶his *modest home* 彼のささやかな住宅. ¶make a *new home* 新居を構える. ¶*Old homes* are being torn down. 古い家は今取こわし中だ. ¶England is the *original home* of this system. 英国はこの制度の本家本元である. ‖ the *original home* of the Greeks ギシリア人発祥の地. ¶Lessons are given in pupil's *own home*. 出張教授をします. ¶an *owner-built home* [借家でない]自分で建てた住居. ¶a *palatial home* 豪壮な家. ¶She lived with relatives far from her *parental home*. 彼女は親のもとを遠く離れて親類の所に寄留していた. ¶The new building is to serve as a *permanent home* for the Association. その新しい建物は同協会の永久事務所

になるはずだ. ¶museums, galleries and ***private homes*** 博物館, 美術館及び個人の住宅. ¶Servants carry away habits of luxury learned in a ***rich home***. 召使には金持の家で覚えたぜいたくな習慣がついて行く. ¶stay in one's ***second home*** 別邸(二号の家)にとまっている ‖ To them the club is a ***second home***. その人たちにはクラブは家庭の延長である. ¶a ***sordid home*** kept on $100 a month 月百ドルでやって行くしみったれた家庭. ¶his ***suburban home*** 彼の郊外の家. ¶***telephone-equipped homes*** 電話のある家. ¶***unhealthy homes*** 非衛生的な家. ¶a ***waterless home*** 水道の引いてない家. ¶a ***well-ordered home*** 整とんした家. ¶"Broadcasting House," the B.B.C.'s ***wonderful new home***, was then open. 放送局 B.B.C. のりっぱな新しい建物はその時事業開始した.

Q² his ***bachelor home*** 彼の独身家庭. ¶a ***beach home*** 海の家. ¶a ***beehive apartment home*** はちの巣式アパートの住居. ¶one's ***Boston home*** ボストンの本(別)宅. ¶my ***boyhood (childhood) home*** 私の少年(子供)時代の家. ¶her ***castle home*** 彼女の居城. ¶go back to one's ***city home*** [別荘から]都市の本宅に戻る. ¶a ***club home*** クラブ会館. ¶a ***common-sense home*** 実用向住宅. ¶a ***cottage home*** いなか家. ¶He died at his ***country home***. 彼はいなかの別荘で死んだ. ¶a ***dependent home*** 〘軍〙家族住宅. ¶a juvenile ***detention home*** 少年院. ¶the ***Edinburgh home*** of the Scotland Education Department スコットランド教育省のエディンバラ庁舎. ¶a low-rent ***cooperative home*** 家賃の安い協同出資住宅. ¶a ***farm home*** 農家; 農園労働者の宿泊所. ¶the ***future home*** of the company その会社の将来本部となるもの. ¶an ***infant home*** 育児所. ¶the ***Johnson home*** =《英》Mr. Johnson's ジョンソン家の住宅. ¶a ***laying home*** [養鶏の]産卵場. ¶a ***loot home*** 盗品隠匿場所. ¶a ***maternity home*** kept by a Mrs. Blaber ブレイバー夫人という人の経営している産院. ¶a ***middle-class home*** 中流家庭 ‖ come from ***middle-class homes*** 中流家庭出身である. ¶a ***nursing home*** 託児所. ¶a ***one-floor home*** 平家建ての家. ¶a ***rescue home*** 救済ホーム(自由廃業などの女のための). ¶a ***sailor home*** from sea 海員ホーム. ¶a ***seashore (=seaside) home*** 海の家. ¶a ***single-family home*** 一家族ずつの住宅. ¶one's ***summer home*** in the country いなかの夏期別荘. 【類】close one's ***summer home***, "Arthur's Seat," at ... ¶Mrs. Roosevelt left here for the ***Wilmer home***. ルーズベルト夫人はウイルマーさんのお宅に出かけた.

P He is ***at*** the ***home*** of his cousin in New York. 彼はニューヨークのいとこの家にいる. 【類】***at*** the ***home*** of her parents / the meeting will be held ***at*** the ***home*** of Mr. ... ‖ I left it ***at home***. 私はそれを家においてきた. ‖ ***at home*** and abroad 内外の ‖ cookies made ***at home***=homemade cookies 手製のクッキー ‖ a tyrant ***at home*** 内づらの悪い人 ‖ Abroad ***at Home*** 海外旅行印象記(書物の題名) ‖ Is he ***at home?*** 彼は在宅ですか. ‖ He is in, but is not ***at home***. 彼は在宅だが面会はできない. ‖ He will be ***at home*** to his friends on Friday. 金曜日は彼の面会日だ. ‖ feel ***at home*** in England 英国が自国のように感じられる. 【類】At last he was ***at home*** to a certain extent. ‖ He was ***at home*** on Scotland's mountains. 彼はスコットランドの山に精通していた. 【類】He is thoroughly ***at home*** in English literature. / He was equally ***at home*** with the brush and the pen. / become as much ***at home*** as ducks in the water あひるが水にいると同様気楽になる ‖ He is more ***at home*** with a gun than anything else. 彼は他の何よりも猟銃を持っていると機げんがよい. ‖ be quite ***at home*** on the stage すっかり舞台で板についている ‖ a lion ***at home***, but a fox in the battle (陰弁慶). ¶leave ***for home*** 家へ帰る. ¶bring their food ***from home***. 家から食物を持って来る ‖ He is absent ***from home***. 彼は家にいない. ¶A great many women in America are beginning to think that their place is ***in*** the ***home***. アメリカの大部分の女は彼らの本分は家庭にあると考え始めている. ‖ see that sex hygiene be taught ***in homes*** 性衛生が家庭で教えられるように注意する ‖ It is indispensable ***in*** the ***home***. それは家庭になくてならないものだ. ‖ The industry requires no machinery and can be carried on ***in*** the ***home***. その産業は機械がいらず家庭でできる. ¶How can I ***get to*** your ***home?*** お宅へはどう行けばいいでしょうか.

P² a ***home for*** the aged (old soldiers) 老人(など)ホーム. ¶Alaska is the ***home of*** fur seals. アラスカはおっとせいの本場である. 【類】France, ***home of*** cosmetics / the ***home*** (=headquarters) ***of*** the society その会の本部 ‖ the ***home of*** the Hawaiian Trust Company, Ltd. 有限責任ハワイ信託会社の建物 ‖ his first "***home of*** his own" 彼の始めて建てた住宅 ‖ Philadelphia is a city ***of homes***; there is a dwelling house for every five persons of the population. フィラデルフィヤは住宅の市である, そこには全住民中五人に対して一軒の割で住宅がある.

home, *ad.* わが家へ; 自国へ, 本国へ; 十分.

P get ***home by*** the Mediterranean route 地中海を経て帰国する. ¶He is ***home from*** Yale for the holidays. 彼は休暇でエール大学から帰っている. ‖ Jim is ***home from*** college for a fortnight. / just ***home from*** America. ¶I didn't get ***home till*** near one. 私は一時近くまでは家へ帰らなかった. ¶She went ***home to*** her mother. 彼女は母のもとに帰って行った. ‖ the point we wish to drive ***home to*** them is that ... 彼らに十分わからせたいと思う点は...ということである ‖ this brings ***home to*** the public mind the practical importance of ... このことが...の実際的重要性を一般の人々に十分感じさせる. 【類】it has recently been brought ***home to*** me that ...

O I want to be ***home*** when it is sent me. それが私に送られた時帰宅していたいと思う. ¶He was satisfied to be ***home*** at last. 彼はやっとのことで家に帰れたのを喜んでいた.

home, *v.* 家に帰る.

P jovial amateur cricketers or footballers ***homing from*** a Saturday's match 土曜日の試合から帰って来る快活なクリケット及びフットボールのしろうと競技者.

home-building, *n.* 家庭を持つこと.

V ***begin*** one's ***home-building*** 家庭を持ち始める.

homeland, *n.* 母国, 生国, 故郷.

Q the ***Japanese homeland*** 日本本国.

P² Yezo, the ***homeland of*** the Ainu アイヌの故郷たる蝦夷(えぞ).

homely, *a.* 質素な, 装飾のない; 不きりょうの.

M She is ***as homely*** as a telegraph pole. 彼女は電信柱のように飾りけがない.

home-maker, *n.* 家庭生活者.

Q an ***artistic home-maker*** 芸術的家庭生活者.

homer, *n.* 〘野球〙本塁打.

V ***swat (=smackout)*** three ***homers*** in a game 一ゲームにホーマーを三本かっとばす.

Q² a ***pinch homer*** 危機を救う本塁打(逆点ホーマー).

homesick, *a.* 故郷恋しい.

P be ***homesick for*** Japan 日本が恋しい.

homesickness, *n.* 郷愁.

P He returned to his native land ***of homesickness***. 彼は国が恋しくなって帰った.

homestead, *n.* 生家.

Q² the ***Edison homestead*** エディソンの生家.

homework, *n.* 宿題.

V ***do*** one's ***homework*** 宿題をやる.

honest, *a.* 正直な, 誠実な, 正しい.

M ***as honest*** as the day 白日のごとく公正な. ¶be ***foolishly honest*** ばか正直だ. ¶***painfully honest*** ばか正直な. ¶***perversely honest*** ばか正直な. ¶***transparently honest*** and sincere 徹底的に正直でまじめな.

P ***honest beyond*** belief 信じられないほどに正直な. ¶persons who are ***honest in*** their own praise and blame, and intelligent in their own discrimination ほめるにもせめるにも正直でありかつ物の弁別にそう明な人々. ¶***honest to*** goodness 真っ正直な. ¶being ***honest to*** a fault ばか正直だから ‖ be ***honest to*** absurdity あきれるほど正直だ ‖ She is ***honest to*** John, really. 彼女は全くジョンに貞節だ. ¶I must be ***honest with*** you. 私は君に隠さずに言わなければならない. ‖ to be ***honest with*** you 正直のところ ‖ Let us be ***honest with*** each other. お互いかけ引なしにしよう.

honesty, *n.* 正直, 忠実, 公正.

V ***build honesty*** into the character of a student 学生の品性に正直を植えつける. ¶***doubt*** one's ***honesty*** その正直を疑う. ¶***guarantee*** one's ***honesty*** その正直を保証する. ¶***practice honesty*** 正直を実行する. ¶***question*** one's ***honesty*** その正直を疑う. ¶***suspect*** one's ***honesty*** その正直を疑う. ¶***vouch*** one's ***honesty*** その正直を保証する. ¶***Honesty is*** the best policy. 正直は最善の政策である.

Q the virtue of ***commercial honesty*** 商売上の正直という

徳. ¶***intellectual*** *honesty* 真理に忠実な心. ¶***political*** *honesty* and straightforwardness 政治上の正直と率直. ¶Within each piece is the ***sturdy*** *honesty* that sincere craftmen fill into all Kurpen productions. クルペン(ニューヨークの写真商)の製品には一々誠実な職工の誠意がこもっている.

Q² ***business*** *honesty* 商人の正直. ¶actions of ***law*** *honesty* 法網に掛らないというだけの正直. ¶***pupil*** *honesty* 生徒の純真さ.

P I cannot ***in*** *honesty* refuse to pay the money. 僕は徳義上その金の支払を拒絶することはできない. ¶an evidence ***of*** one's *honesty* その正直に対する証明. ¶I cannot, ***with*** *honesty*, lay claim to much originality. 正直の所私はあまり独創を誇ることはできない.

P² *honesty* ***in*** business (public service) 商売(公務)上の正直.

honey, *n.* はちみつ.

V ***gather*** *honey* from the flowers 花からみつを集める. ¶***lay up*** *honey* みつを貯える.

Q² ***candied*** *honey* 糖化みつ. ¶***virgin*** *honey* 巣からとったなまのみつ; 巣から流れ出るみつ.

honeymoon, *n.* みつ月, 新婚旅行.

V The *honeymoon* is to be ***spent*** in Nikko. みつ月は日光で送ることになっている.

Q The married couple are now at Kamakura, spending a ***happy*** *honeymoon*. 新婚夫婦は今鎌倉で楽しいみつ月を送っている.

P The young couple have gone off ***on*** a *honeymoon*. 若夫婦は新婚旅行に出掛けた.

hono[u]r, *n.* 敬意; 名誉, 光栄; 体面, 面目.

V ***accord*** due *honor* to ... ...に当然の名誉を与える. ¶Thousands of its students have ***achieved*** high academic *honors*. そこの何千という学生がりっぱな学問上の名誉を得ている. ‖ The winning of the Nobel prize is one of the highest *honors* an author can ***achieve***. ノーベル賞を得ることは作家として達しうる最高名誉の一つである. ¶***add*** *honor* to ... ...の名誉になる. ¶***attain*** *honor* 光栄を得る. ¶***award*** the *honor* to ... その栄誉を...に授ける. ¶***bestow*** on him a well-deserved *honor* 彼に全く当然の名誉をになわせる. ¶***blight*** his *honor* and his fair name 彼の名誉と美名を傷つける. ¶it ***brings*** *honor* to (=reflects credit on) ... それは...の名誉になる. ¶it has done so much to ***build up*** the *honor* and prosperity of ... それは...の名誉と繁栄を築き上げるに大いに貢献する所があった. ¶He ***carried off*** the highest lawn tennis *honors*. 彼はローンテニスの最高栄冠を得た. 【類】He ***carried off*** second *honors* of $1,000 with his plan. ¶***claim*** the *honor* of originating ... ...の元祖であると主張する. 【類】he may fairly ***claim*** the *honor* of having been the pioneer of ... ¶***compromise*** one's *honor* その名誉を危くする. 【類】It will ***compromise*** the *honor* of the school. ¶***confer*** academic *honors* upon ... ...に学問上の名誉を授ける. 【類】an *honor* never before ***conferred*** upon a woman. ¶***covet*** higher *honors* より高い栄誉を望む. ¶He ***declined*** the *honor* of the Royal Gold Medal of the Royal Institute of British Architects. 彼は王立英国建築学会の王立金ぱい受賞の名誉を辞退した. ¶I ***deem*** it an *honor* to accept your invitation. 私は貴下の御招待をお受けすることを名誉に思う. ¶***deserve*** all *honor* あらゆる名誉を受ける価値がある. ¶***divide*** *honors* with A as ... ...としての名誉をAとともに受ける. ¶I will ***do*** myself the *honor* to call again in a few days. 私は数日後またお訪ねする光栄に浴します. ‖ those who ***did*** me the *honor* of replying 私に回答して下すった方々 ‖ They gathered together to ***do*** *honor* to the occasion (memory of ...). その日を祝う(...追悼の)ために集まった. ‖ to ***do*** him *honor* 彼に敬意を表するために. 【類】We dressed our ships with flags to ***do*** *honor* to the occasion / His contributions to science ***do*** *honor* to the university of which he is a member. / A bust (胸像) ***does*** *honor* to his memory in Westminster Abbey. ‖ ***do*** the *honors* of the table (house, town, castle) to ... 食卓(など)で...に対して主人役を勤める. ¶I ***enjoyed*** the *honor* of an interview with ... 私は...と会見するの光栄に浴した. ¶I ***feel*** it a great *honor* to have been the first. 私が最初であったことを非常な名誉と思う. ¶***gain*** high *honors* at a university 大学で優秀な成績を表彰される. 【類】***gain*** for themselves undying *honor*. ¶***grudge*** person *honors* 人に栄誉をいやいや与える. ¶***guard*** jealously the *honor* of the land 国の名誉を大事に守る. ¶He ***had*** the *honor* of exhibiting before many crowned heads of Europe. 彼は欧州諸国の元首の前で公演するの光栄に浴した. 【類】he ***had*** the *honor* of being the first winner of ... / The club ***had*** once the *honour* of numbering Louis Stevenson among its members. ‖ I ***have*** the *honor* of his acquaintance. 存じあげております. 【類】He ***had*** the *honor* of representing his country at the Olympic Games. ¶***heep*** *honors* upon the dead poets and dead artists 死んだ詩人や芸術家に幾多敬意の表示をささげる. ¶***keep unsullied*** the *honor* of ... ...の名誉を汚さずに保持する. ¶***lose*** one's *honor* 自己の名誉を失う. 【類】To ***lose*** *honor* is to lose more than life. ¶***pay*** *honor* to his tomb 彼の墓にもうでる. ¶if you will ***permit*** me the *honor* その名誉を私に授けて下さらば. ¶you ***pledge*** your *honor* to ... 君が...するのは君の名誉を賭けることになる. ¶***preserve*** the *honor* of the country 国の名誉を保持する. ¶***prostitute*** *honor* 名誉を汚辱する. ¶***receive*** the *honor* of knighthood ナイトの位を賜わる. ¶That ***reflects*** no *honor* on you. それは一向君の名誉にならない. 【類】It ***reflected*** *honor* on Japanese civilization. ¶***refuse*** the *honor* of knighthood ナイトの名誉を拒絶する. ¶***render*** *honor* to ... ...に敬意を表する. ¶***request*** the *honor* of his presence 彼の臨席の光栄にあずかることを願う. ¶***respect*** *honor* 恥を知る. ¶***sacrifice*** feminine *honor* and dignity 婦人の名誉と威厳を犠牲にする. ¶***satisfy*** one's [sense of] *honor* その名誉心を満足させる. ¶***save*** the *honor* of ... ...の体面を保つ. ¶***sell*** one's *honor* for money 金で名誉を売る. ¶***share*** an *honor* with ... ...とともに名誉に浴する. ¶***stain*** one's personal *honor* その一身上の名誉を汚す. ¶***survive*** one's *honor* 生恥をさらす. ¶***take*** the highest *honors* at a university 大学で誉れの学位を得る. ¶Their *honors* is in no way ***tarnished***. 彼らの名誉は決して汚されていない. ¶a stratagem to ***test*** American *honor* 米国の名誉心を試験する計略. ¶He did his part to ***uphold*** the *honor* of the old flag. 彼は歴史ある軍旗の名誉を支持すべく彼の本分を尽した. 【類】They ***upheld*** the *honor* of their Alma Mater (母校) at the front. ¶His *honor* has been ***vindicated*** after a lawsuit. 彼は裁判でその名誉を回復した. ¶He has well ***won*** the *honors*. 彼はりっぱに栄冠を獲得した. ‖ ***win*** further *honors* by ... ...によってさらに名誉を得る. 【類】***win*** *honors* (受賞する) in a show / ***win*** high academic *honors* ‖ The brilliant fool ***wins*** high *honors* by rushing in where angels fear to tread. めくらへびにおじずで大ばかがりっぱな名誉をかち得ることがある. ¶***wound*** (=***hurt***) national *honor* 国家の名誉を傷つける.

V² To Professor Morse ***belongs*** the *honor* (=credit) of being the pioneer of primitive archaeology in Japan. モールス教授は日本における考古学の先駆者たるの名誉をになう. 【類】It is to the London Missionary Society that ***belongs*** the *honor* of first undertaking a Protestant mission to the dense population to China. ¶*Honors* ***followed*** fast. 名誉が重なってやってきた. ¶the man to whom the *honor* should ***go*** was ... その栄誉をになうべき者は...であった.

Q ***commercial*** *honor* and integrity 商業上の道義と正直. 【類】The ***commercial*** *honor* of the firm is beyond suspicion. ¶It is a ***deserved*** *honor*. それは当然受けるべき名誉だ. ¶***earthly*** and ***ephemeral*** *honors* 浮世のかげろうにひとしい栄誉. ¶***empty*** *honors* 空虚な栄誉. ¶to their ***eternal*** *honor* 彼らを千歳の名誉として. ¶do ***full*** *honor* to his memory 故人に心から追悼の意を表する. ¶I deem it a ***great*** *honor* to be allowed to address you. 皆さんにお話しをする機会を与えられましたことを光栄と存じます. ¶He was graduated with the ***highest*** *honors* of his class. 彼は最優等で卒業した. ‖ The order of the Legion of Honor is regarded throughout the world as one of the ***highest*** *honors* a man can receive. [フランスの]レジョンドヌール勲章を受けることは世界最高の栄誉と見なされている. ¶It does him ***infinite*** *honor*. それは彼にとって無限の名誉となる. ¶***injured*** *honor* 不面目. ¶an ***invidious*** *honor* 人をうらやませる名誉. ¶obtain the ***long-coveted*** *honor* of ... ...という長い間待望の光栄に浴する. ¶accord ***merited*** *honors* to ... ...に当然な名誉を与える. ¶carry various ribbons of ***military*** *honor* 各種の軍事勲功章をはい用する. ¶***more*** *honor* than I deserve 身に余る光栄. ¶***personal*** *honor* 一

身上の名誉. ¶the ***premier honors*** go to ... 一等の栄冠は...に帰する. ¶the somewhat ***questionable honor*** of ... ...というささか疑わしい栄誉. ¶a ***signal honor*** 一大名誉. ¶***womanly honor*** 女の名誉. ¶***worldly honors*** 現世の名誉

Q² ***business honor*** 商業道徳. ¶the highest ***scholarship*** *honor* was captured by ... 学者として最高の名誉が...によって獲得された.

P regard it ***as*** an *honor* それを一つの名誉と思う. ¶***For*** the *honor* I bear him, I refrain from mentioning his name. 名前はその人の名誉を重んじて述べるのを差しひかえます. ‖ He will take the refused draft ***for*** the *honor* of the drawer. 彼は拒絶手形を振出人の信用のため引受けるだろう. ¶It was called (=named) ... ***in*** his *honor*. それは彼を記念するために...と命名された. 【類】 ***in*** *honor* of a soldier of peace, fallen in service. / a special number ***in*** *honor* of the anniversary of his 70th birthday / There will be a holiday ***in*** *honor* of the event (記念日). ‖ economic essays (経済論文集) contributed ***in*** *honor* of John Bates Clark / the tournament held ***in*** *honor* of ... / The temple was erected ***in*** *honor* of the soldiers who died for the country. / The driveway is so called ***in*** *honor* of the great shade trees which adorn the outer boundary. / His colleagues and former students compiled and published his essays ***in*** *honor* of his thirty years' service with the University. ‖ We gave dinner ***in*** his *honor*. われわれは彼を招いて晩さん会を催した. ‖ He graduated ***in*** *honors*. 彼は優等で卒業した. ‖ Agriculture is held ***in*** great *honor* in China. 中国では農業は非常に重んじられている. ¶a code ***of*** *honor* 社交の礼法 ‖ the old Japanese code ***of*** *honor* 日本古代の道徳律. ‖ a sense ***of*** *honor* 道義心. ¶I hereby certify ***on*** my *honor* that ... 私はここに私の名誉にかけて...ということを保証する. ‖ ***On*** my *honor*, it is true. 誓ってそれは真実である. ‖ ***On*** your *honor* I rely on you to stay here. お前は逃げるようなひきょうなことはしないだろう. 【類】 I ask you this ***on*** your *honor* as a gentleman. ¶I was ***under*** *honor* not to divulge the secret to the public. 私はその秘密をもらさないということを誓っていた. ¶***Upon*** my *honor!* 私の名誉にかけて, 断じて. ‖ The honor system places students ***upon*** their *honor*. 無監督制度は学生の名誉心に訴える. ¶play one's part ***with*** *honor* 男らしく自己の本分を尽す ‖ receive a person ***with*** *honor* 礼をもって人を迎える. 【類】 He was received ***with*** all the *honors* due to his elevated position (高官にふさわしい). ‖ He passed the examination ***with*** *honors*. 彼は優等で試験に及第した. 【類】 He graduated ***with*** high *honors*. ¶He is ***without*** *honor* in their own country. 彼は故国では重く見られていない.

P² He is an *honor* (a disgrace) ***to*** his country (nation, profession). 彼は国(など)にとっての誇り(恥辱)である. ‖ A military medal with an "accolade" is the highest *honor* possible ***to*** the French soldier. ナイトの礼をもって勲章を授与されることはフランス軍人にとってこの上もない名誉である.

hono[u]r, *v.* うやまう, あがめる; 栄誉を授ける, 礼遇する.

M I was ***exceedingly honored*** to be so treated. そういう取扱いを受けて私は大いに光栄に思った. ¶It is impossible to too ***highly honor*** him for what he has done. 彼の事業に対してはあくまで敬意を表わさねばならない. ‖ I feel ***highly*** *honored* 非常に名誉に感じる.

P He was *honored* ***as*** a model man. 彼は師表と仰がれた. ¶Tickets will be *honored* ***at*** City Hall. 市会館で切符引替えに入場料を戻す. ¶He *honored* us ***by*** attending the meeting. 彼がその会に臨席されたのはわれわれの光栄であった. 【類】 The exhibition was *honored* ***by*** the visits of many members of the Royal Family. ‖ a man *honored* ***by*** the whole world 全世界から尊敬されている人. 【類】 The Marquis was *honored* ***by*** the Emperor with a gracious message (優あくなる御言葉). ‖ This banquet is invariably *honored* ***by*** the presence of the Lord Mayor. この宴会にはいつもロンドン市長が臨席する. ¶anyone who may *honor* this book ***with*** his attention この本を注意して閲読下さる方はだれでも ‖ He was *honored* ***with*** the degree of D.C.L. by the university. 彼は同大学から法学博士の称号を受けた. ‖ They *honored* him ***with*** a military drill. 彼に敬意を表して軍事教練が行われた. 【類】 He was *honored* ***with*** an invitation. / The exhibition was *honored* ***with*** the visit of ... 「を重んじる.

hono[u]rable, *a.* 尊敬すべき; 名誉ある, 光栄ある; 体面

M I am ***too*** *honorable* to do anything of that kind. 私は体面を重んじるからそんなことはしない.

P The book is *honorable* ***to*** all concerned—to the printer, binder, and engraver. その本のできばえは関係者一同一印刷者, 製本者, 版画彫刻家一にとっての名誉である.

honorarium, *n.* 謝礼.

V ***pay*** *honorarium* to authors 著者に謝礼金を払う.

Q ***Satisfactory*** *honorarium* is to be paid upon acceptance. 採用と同時に十分な原稿料を支払うことになっている.

hood, *n.* ずきん(フード); ほろ; 〘自動車〙フード.

V The car ***has*** its *hood* for sun, wind, or rain. その車には日光風雨を避けるためにほろがついている. ¶***put*** (=***let***) ***down*** the *hood* ほろを降ろす. ¶***put up*** the *hood* ほろをかける. ¶***wear*** a *hood* on her head 頭にずきん(フード)をかぶる.

Q² a ***car*** *hood* (=bonnet) 自動車のおおい(フード).

P muffle one's faces ***in*** *hoods* and veils 頭巾やヴェールで顔を包む. ¶a sledge ***with*** a round *hood* 丸いほろのついているそり ‖ a rubber coat ***with*** a *hood* フードのついた雨がっぱ. 「torcar 自動車のフード.

P² the *hood* ***of*** an automobile=《英》the bonnet of a mo-

hood, *v.* おおい隠す. 「いる山々.

P hills *hooded* ***with*** white clouds 頂上が白雲でおおわれて

hoodlum, *n.* 《米》よたもの.

P a gang ***of*** *hoodlums* ぐれん隊. ¶crack down ***on*** *hoodlums* よたものを弾圧する.

hoof, *n.* ひずめ.

Q a ***cloven*** *hoof* [牛などの]ひずめ.

P oxen ***on*** the *hoof* まだと殺されてない雄牛. ¶***under*** the *hoof* of the conqueror その征服者にじゅうりんされた.

hook, *n.* かぎ, ホック; つり針.

V ***bait*** a *hook* つり針にえさをつける. ¶***jangle*** the telephone *hook* to call the attention of the operator 交換手の注意をうながすために電話機の受話器掛けをがちゃがちゃさせる. ¶***take*** the *hook* 食い込む.

Q a ***naked*** *hook* えさのついてないつり針.

Q² a ***fish*** *hook* つり針.

P ***above*** one's *hook* その力量以上の. ¶He wanted to earn some money ***by*** *hook* or by crook. 彼はなんとかして金を少しもうけたいと思った. ¶put food ***on*** a *hook* つり針にえさをつける ‖ ***on*** one's own *hook* 人から言われないで, 自分

hook, *v.* かぎで掛ける. 」から進んで.

M² *hook* ***in*** かき込む, なんとかして手に入れる ‖ I have been *hooked* ***in*** for a trial. 私はいや応なしに審判を受けるはめになった. ¶*hook* ***on*** to ... かぎを...に引掛ける. ¶*hook* ***up*** a big fish 大魚を釣りあげる ‖ a horse *hooked* ***up*** to a post 柱につながれた馬.

P a skirt *hooked* ***at*** the side (back) 横(背後)にフックのつい

hookup, *n.* 放送網. 」たスカート.

Q The programme was heard here throughout the ***national*** *hookup*. その番組は全国のラジオで聴取された. ‖ speak over (=on) a ***nation-wide*** *hookup* 全国(中継)放送で

hooligan, *n.* 暴力の徒. 」演説する.

Q² an ***embryo*** *hooligan* 暴力少年(不良児).

hoop, *n.* たが; [輪回しの]輪.

V ***drive*** a *hoop* 輪を回す. ¶***reel*** a *hoop* for fun and exercise なぐさみや運動に輪回しをやる. ¶***trundle*** [***along***] (=reel) a *hoop* 輪を回す.

hoop-skirt, *n.* 輪形スカート.

Q a Frenchwoman ***in*** a *hoop-skirt* 輪形(フープ)式スカートのフランス婦人.

hooray, *int.* [hurrah の変形] フレー, 万歳.

P² *Hooray* ***for*** Charlie Chaplin! チャーリー・チャプリン万

hoot, *n.* 叫び, あざけり; 汽笛の声. 」歳!

V At five o'clock precisely the steamer ***gave*** two terrific *hoots* as a notice that in a few minutes she would start. 正五時に汽船は数分の後出帆する合図にけたたましく汽笛を二度鳴らした.

V² Two more *hoots* ***came*** from the siren, and the steamer started on her journey. 汽笛がさらに二声鳴って汽船は航海の途に上った.

hoot, *v.* 野次る; ぶー(ぽー)と鳴る.

M *hoot* ***away*** an entertainer 芸人を野次って引っこませる. ¶Down by the river an owl *hooted* ***dismally***. 川しもの方

でふくろが無気味に鳴いた. ¶*hoot* him *out* 彼を野次ってひっこませる. ¶They heard a car *softly hoot* as it came nearer. 自動車がこっちへ近づきながら低くぶーと鳴らすのが聞えた.

M^2 *hoot down* a speaker 演者を野次り倒す.

P *hoot after* a person 人の後からどなる. ¶*hoot at* a speaker 演説をやじる. ¶They *hooted* the speaker *off* the platform. 聴衆が弁士をやじって演壇からひっこませた. ¶They *hooted to* the speaker to quit the platform. 彼らは弁士にやじを飛ばして演壇から引込めさせようとした.

hooting, *n.* 汽笛, 号笛, 警笛.

Q automobiles with their *ear-piercing hootings* 鼓膜を破るような警笛を鳴らす自動車.

hop, *n.* 片足飛び; 飛躍; 《米口》横断飛行; 《口語》舞踏.

Q^2 after a *six-hour hop* from … …から空路六時間かかって. ¶a *trans-Pacific hop* 太平洋横断飛行.

P *at* the first *hop* 直ちに. ¶*on* the *hop* 片足飛びで; 活躍して ‖ catch a person *on* the *hop* まさに出かけようとするところをつかまえる. ¶Let's go *to* the *hop* (＝dance party). 《米》ダンスに行こう.

hop, *n.* 〚植〛ホップ.

P^2 *hops for* beer brewing ビール醸造用のホップ. ¶the *hops of* commerce 商品のホップ.

hop, *v.* 飛ぶ, 片足で飛ぶ; 《米》離陸する.

M *hop away* on one foot 片足でぴょんぴょんとび歩く.

M^2 A robin *hops about* from tree to tree. こま鳥が木から木へとぴょんぴょんと飛び回る. 【類】Sparrow *hop about* in the snow. ¶He got hurt in the left leg and had to *hop along.* 左脚をけがしたので仕方なく[片足で]飛びながら歩いた. ¶*Hop in* and I'll take you there. [owner-driver が]乗り給え, そこへ連れてってやる. ¶*hop* (＝take) *off* from … for … 〚空〛[空路]…から…へ飛ぶ.

P *hop on* one leg 片足で飛ぶ. ¶Three rabbits *hopped out of* the basket. 三匹のうさぎがかごから飛び出した.

hope, *n.* 希望, 予期, 見込.

V *abandon* the *hope* of … …という希望を捨てる. 【類】*abandon* the *hope* they had long nursed (宿願) of … ¶*Hopes* of a better state of things are *anticipated.* 局面が好転するものと見られている. ¶*arouse* a great *hope* in the minds of … …の心に大きな望みを起させる. ¶they *attached* their *hopes* for the future to … 彼らは将来に対して…に希望をかけた. ¶*awaken hopes* 望みをいだかせる. ¶*blast* one's *hopes* 望みを失わさせる. ¶His *hopes* were *blighted.* 彼は希望を失ってしまった. ¶*brighten* the *hope* 希望の光を輝かす. ¶This *brought* new *hope* to him. これで彼は希望を新たにすることができた. ¶there are no precedents on which to *build* the *hope* of … [心強く]…という望みを立てるだけの前例がない. ¶*build up* strong *hopes* of … …という強い望みを築く. ¶*center* one's *hopes* on … その希望を…に集中する. ¶*cherish* high *hopes* 高い望みをいだく. ¶*crush* one's *hope* その希望をくじく. ¶*damp down* high *hopes* 心強い望みを薄くする. ¶*darken* the *hopes* of … …の望みを薄くする. ¶His *hopes* were all *dashed* to pieces. 彼の希望は全く水泡に帰した. ¶*defeat* the *hopes* of … …の希望をくじく. ¶*disappoint* the *hopes* they raise 彼らがいだく希望を失わせる. 【類】Thus all *hopes* were *disappointed.* ¶*dispell* the *hope* that … …という希望を消す. ¶*encourage* the *hope* that … …という望みをいだかせる. ¶we *entertain* a *hope* that … われわれは…という希望をいだく. 【類】*hopes* are still *entertained* in some quarters that … ¶*express* a *hope* that … …という望みを述べる. 【類】*express* the *hope* that … / the *hope* is also *expressed* that … ¶*extinguish* one's *hope* 絶望させる. ¶*fasten* one's *hope* on … その希望を…につなぐ. ¶My *hopes* were *frustrated* (＝*ruined*). 私の望みは無に帰した. ¶Life has failed to *fulfil* their *hopes* and their wishes. この世では彼らの望みと願いを果たし得なかった. ¶*furl hopes* 望みを捨てる. ¶*gain* fresh *hope* 新しい望みを得る. ¶He knows how to *give* his patient the *hope* of cure. 彼は病人に回復の希望を持たせるこつをのみ込んでいる. ¶*give up hope* 絶望する. 【類】*give up* all *hope* of succeeding. ¶I *hang* my *hopes* of … on him. 私は…の望みを彼にかける. ¶I *have hope* of … 私は…の望みをいだいている. 【類】*have* you any *hope* of …? / I *have hopes* that … / *have* every *hope* of … ‖ I *have* the highest *hopes* for the future of … 私は…の将来に対して最高の望みをかけている. ¶*hold out* high *hopes* that … …という大望を捨てない. ¶let us *indulge* the *hope* of a great popular success for … …に対して非常に人気のある成功を博しうる希望をいだこう. 【類】*indulge* a *hope* that … ¶*inspire* the *hope* that … …という希望を鼓吹する. ¶*kill hope* 絶望させる. ¶*lay* one's *hopes* on … …に望みをかける. ¶*lose hope* 失望する. ¶*nourish* a *hope* 希望をそだてる(捨てずにいる). ¶has long *nursed* a *hope* that … …という希望をもっている. ¶*offer hope* of realization 実現の望みを与える. ¶*pin hope* on … …に望みをかける. ¶*raise hopes* among … …間に希望をいだかせる. 【類】The severe frost *raised* the *hopes* of skaters. / Don't *raise* your *hopes* too much. ¶This *hope* has been more than *realized.* この希望は十二分に実現された. ¶*relinquish* a *hope* 希望を捨てる. ¶*revive* the *hope* of … …の希望を復活する. ¶I *see hope* for improvement. 私は改善の望みがあると思う. ‖ He *saw* all his *hopes* dashed down. 彼は絶望のふちに沈んだ. ¶This *shut off* all *hope* that they would be reconciled. このために彼らが仲直りをするだろうという望みが全くなくなった. ¶*surrender* all *hope* 絶望する. ¶*wake* the *hope* that … …という希望をめざます. ¶*wither hopes* 希望を失わさせる.

V^2 His *hope went down.* 彼は希望を失った. ¶Our *hope went up* on hearing the good news. その吉報に接してわれわれは希望が高まった. ¶The *hope* of the people *rested* on him. 人の望みが彼の上に集まった. ¶*Hopes* of returning prosperity *run high.* 景気復活の希望が盛んである. ¶Their *hopes sank,* but not their courage. 彼らの希望はくずれたが, 志気はくずれなかった.

Q an *ardent hope* 熱烈な希望. ¶the *bright-hued hope* of the future 明るい将来の希望. ¶a long *cherished hope* 宿望. ¶the plan is offered to the public with the *confident hope* that … …と確信してその案を世人に提供する. 【類】look with *confident hope* for … ¶one's *dearest hopes* その最も大事な望み. ¶one's *eager hope* その熱心な希望. ¶express an *earnest hope* that … …という熱心な希望を述べる. ¶a *faint hope* おぼつかない希望. ¶the blighting of the *fairest hopes* 最も頼もしい希望のざ折. ¶a *false hope* そらだのみ. ¶he sent a telegram expressing his *fervent hope* that …, 彼は…という彼の熱烈な希望を述べた電報を送った. ¶has *firm hopes* [大丈夫と]確信をもっている. ¶in the *fond hope* that … …を楽しみに. ‖ His *fondest hopes* will be blighted (fulfilled). 彼の一番大事な望みが失われ(満たされ)るであろう. ¶as a *forlorn hope* ただ一つの頼りとして. 【類】It seems a *forlorn hope.* ‖ cling to a piece of wood as the last *forlorn hope* はかない最後の望みとして一片の木にすがりつく. ¶There is *good hope* that the thing will turn out well. それがうまく行くだろうという十分な望みがある. ¶there are *high hopes* of … …という十分な見込がある ‖ his *highest hope* 彼の最高の望み. ¶*illusory hopes* 空虚な望み. ¶he has *little hope* of … 彼には…の望みがほとんどない ‖ There is *little hope* of his recovery. 彼は回復する望みはまずない. ¶a *naive hope* あどけない望み. ¶I have *no hope* to … 私は…する望みがない. ‖ There can be *no hope* of a revival of trade unless … …しなくては貿易再興の希望は持てない. ¶my *one* and *only hope* 私の唯一の希望. ¶the *only remaining hope* 残る唯一の望み. ¶These *hopes* were too *sanguine.* これらの望みはあまり楽天(のん気)すぎていた. ¶I have a *slight hope* of … 私は…のかすかな望みを持っている. ¶There is just a *slim hope* of success. 成功の見込みは薄い. ¶a *triumphant hope* 勝利(成功)の希望. ¶an *unfulfilled hope* 実現しない希望. ¶a *vague hope* ばく然とした見込. ¶a *vain hope* むだな望み. ¶The plan was realized beyond the *wildest hopes.* 夢にも思わなかったその計画が実現された. 【類】He has lived to see the dream realised beyond his *wildest hopes.*

Q^2 a dim *recovery hope* 薄い回復の望み.

P He waited, hoping *against hope.* 万一を期待して待っていた. ¶blind *beyond hope* of cure 治療の望みがないまでにめしいて ‖ It was *beyond* all *hope* of repair. それは全く修繕の望みがなかった. ¶I am *in hopes* that … …私は…という望みを持っている. 【類】I am *in hopes* of succeeding. / *in* [the] *hopes* of seeing him / *in* the *hope* of finding health (療養のため) / I send you, with compliments, this copy of … *in* the *hope* that it may be of use to you. / The idea of laying down (ねかしておく) a picture, so to speak, *in* the *hope* of its acquiring greater value with age was intolerable to him. / People flock to London *in* the *hope* of obtaining work as craftsmen, clerks, or in any other capacity. ‖ *in* [the] *hope* of reward 報酬を望んで. ¶whatever *of hope* might have lingered in any breast was dispelled when ... 少しでもまだ希望をいだいていた者があったにしてもそれは...の時に全く煙と消え去った. ‖ a ray *of hope* 希望の光. ¶It is *past* all *hope*. それは全く望みがない. ¶*with* the *hope* of recovering his previous losses 彼の以前の損失を取戻す目的で ‖ *with* the *hope* that ......という希望で. ¶he is not *without hope* that ... 彼は...という希望がないでもない.

P² They are all full of *hope for* the future. 彼らは皆将来に対して希望に満ちている. ‖ I fear there is no *hope for* her. どうも彼女はだめらしい. ¶*Hope of* recovery is dim. 回復の見込みは薄い. ‖ *hope of* your help 君の協力の期待. ¶With the mental type of stammering, *hopes of* a cure are much greater. 精神から来ているどもりの方は余ほど矯正の見込がある.

hope, *v.* 望む, 希望する, 期待する.

M *ardently hope* for ... 熱心に...を望む. ¶I cannot *but hope* that ... 私は...と望まざるを得ない. ¶we may *confidentially hope* that ... われわれは確信をもって...という希望を持つことができる. ¶I *devoutly hope* that ... 私は切に...と望む. ¶it is *earnestly hoped* that ... ...ということが熱心に望まれている. ¶we may *fairly hope* that ere long he will ... われわれは間もなく彼が...するだろうという希望をいだいて差支えない. ¶I *fondly hoped* that ... 私はあさはかにも...と望んでいた. ¶you can *hardly hope* to ... ほとんど...と望み得ない ‖ One can *hardly hope* anything good from it. どうせろくなことはありようはない. ¶you may *legitimately hope* that ... 君は...と望んで差支えない. ¶you may *reasonably hope* that ... ...は過大の望みではない. ¶let us *sincerely hope* that ... われわれはまじめに...であるように望もう. ¶*vainly hope* to ... いたずらに...と望む.

P *hoping against* hope for some favorable turn in affairs 事態が好転するようにと望み難きを望んで. ¶*hope for* a miracle 奇跡を待つ ‖ *hope for* success 成功を期待する. 【類】A newspaper has to win the confidence of the reading public before it can *hope for* success. ‖ if I am allowed to *hope for* more 欲を言えば ‖ Greater happiness than thou hast ever *hoped for* shall be thine. 汝の望みより大なる幸福が与えられん. ¶Both parents saw in their child the promise of genius, and *hoped* great things *from* him. 両親ともその子供が天才として発展するものと信じ大いにわが子に望みをかけた. ‖ *hope* much *from* ... ...に大いに望みをかける.

Q I *hope* you will think of that. 君がそれについて考えるようにしてほしい. ¶I *hope* it will be fine tomorrow. 私はあすは天気だと思う.

hopeful, *n.* 希望に満ちた人.

Q [the] *young hopefuls* 希望に満ちた若人たち.

hopeful, *a.* 望みをいだいている, 有望な.

P I am *hopeful of* success. 私は成功する望みをいだいている. 【類】He is *hopeful of* attaining his object. ‖ be *hopeful of* the day when ... ...という日を待ち望んでいる.

O I am *hopeful* that ... 私は...することが望ましい.

hopefulness, *n.* 希望.

Q his *persistent hopefulness* in adversity 逆境にあって変らない彼の希望.

hopeless, *a.* 望みのない.

M The project is *quite hopeless*. その計画は全く望みがない.

P *hopeless of* success 成功する望みのない.

O The doctor gave up his case as *hopeless*. 医者はその患者にさじを投げた.

hopper, *n.* 〘機〙ホッパー; 《米俗》ダンサー.

Q² a *feed hopper* 〘鉄道〙給水ホッパー. ¶Fred Astaire is the number one *show hopper* in the United States. フレド・アステーアは米国第一のショー舞踊師である.

horde, *n.* 群.

Q an *untamed horde* 生蕃(ばん). ¶the *Mongol hordes* 蒙古の大群.

horizon, *n.* 地(水)平線; 範囲; 眼界.

V *broaden* (=*extend*) the mental *horizon* 心の眼界を広げる. ¶No cloud seemed to *dim* our *horizon* of happiness. われわれの幸福の地平線を曇らす雲は少しもないように思われた. ¶*enlarge* one's *horizon* 眼界を広くする. ¶*expand* our intellectual *horizon* われわれの知的眼界を拡大する. ¶The height *gives* a larger *horizon*. その高所では眼界が広くなる. ¶You have *opened* a new *horizon* for me! あなたのお言葉で私は大いに悟る所がありました. 【類】*open* a new *horizon* to one. ¶*scan* the distant *horizon* 遠い視野を細かに見る. ¶*widen* the intellectual *horizon* of young people 青年の知的眼界を拡げる.

Q the *far horizon* はるかなる地(水)平線. ¶a *foggy horizon* もうろうとした地(水)平線. ¶Grave clouds cover the *international horizon*. 国際線上に暗雲がたなびく. ¶a man of *narrow horizon* 眼界の狭い人. ¶The question looms so large upon our *national horizon*. その問題はわが国民の視界に大きく浮き出ている. ¶a *political horizon* 政治的眼界. ¶an *unbounded horizon* はるかなる地(水)平線.

P The sun rose *above* the *horizon*. 太陽が地(水)平線上に昇った. ¶*Against* the purple *horizon*, towers the snow-capped summit of Mount Fuji. 紫色の地平線に雪を頂いた富士山がそびえている. ¶The sun has sunk *below* the *horizon*. 太陽が地(水)平線の下に没した. ¶The ship disappeared *beyond* the *horizon*. 船は水平線の彼方に消えた. ¶clouds *on* the *horizon* 地(水)平線上の雲 ‖ A new industry has appeared *on* the *horizon*. 新しい産業が出現した. ¶The sun sank *towards* the *horizon*. 太陽が地平線の方へ沈んだ.

P² enlarge one's *horizon on* some special subject ある特殊な問題に関する知識を拡大する.

horn, *n.* 角笛, 警笛(ホルン).

V *blow* a *horn* to clear the way ホルンを吹いてじゃまものをおしのける. ¶*draw in* one's *horns* 弱音を吐く. ¶*saw off horns* 角をのこで引き切る. ¶*sound* the *horn* [自動車が]警笛(ホルン)を鳴らす.

V² the *horn blew* to announce that ... ...を報じる警笛が鳴った.

Q *budding horns* 芽を出した角.

Q² an *auto* (=a motor) *horn* 自動車の警笛 ‖ with a voice like an *automobile horn* 自動車の警笛のような声で. ¶an *ear* (=a *head*) *horn* イヤホーン. ¶the *Klaxon Horn* 〘商標〙自動車のクラクション(鋭く鳴る).

P He found himself *on* the *horns* of a dilemma. 彼は板ばさみになったことに気づいた.

horoscope, *n.* 星占.

V *cast* a *horoscope* 星占をする. ¶*read* our *horoscope* われらの運勢を星で占う.

horrify, *v.* 恐怖させる.

P I was *horrified at* the thought (=notion) of ... 私は...のことを思ってぞっとした. 【類】*horrified at* the sight of...

horror, *n.* 恐怖, 戦りつ, 大なる嫌悪(けん), 惨事.

V He *has* a *horror* of a worry. くよくよするようなことが大きらいだ.

Q war and its *attendant horrors* 戦争とそれにともなう悲惨事. ¶a *foreign horror* 外国の恐ろしいもの(土人が鉄道をそう見る). ¶His book bristles with *pedantic horrors*. 彼の本はげん学気分で鼻持ちがならない.

Q² a *railway horror* 鉄道の大惨事.

P flee *in horror* 恐れて逃げる ‖ draw back *in horror* 恐れてしり込みする. ¶with a shudder *of horror* ぞっとして. ¶*To* my *horror* the child fell into the pond. 私の驚いたことにその子が池に落ちた. ¶thrilling *with horror* こわいのでぞっとして ‖ It struck me *with horror*. 私はそれが恐ろしかった.

P² the *horrors of* modern warfare 現代戦の恐しさ.

horse, *n.* 馬.

V *attach* a *horse* to gate (post) 馬を門(など)につなぐ. ¶*back* a wrong *horse* 競馬でかけ馬を見損う. ¶*bait* a *horse* 馬にかいばをつける. ¶*break in* a *horse* 馬をならす. ¶*caracole* one's *horse* 〘馬術〙乗馬を半回転させる. ¶*catch horses* with a lasso 馬を投げなわで捕える. ¶*change horse* (駅伝の)馬をかえる. ¶He does not know how to *control* a *horse*. 彼は馬の御し方を知らない. ¶*curry* a *horse* 馬の毛をすく. ¶*dismount* a *horse* 馬から降りる. ¶*drive* a *horse* 馬を御する. 【類】*drive* a *horse* to water. ¶set him to *feeding* the *horses* 馬にかいばをやれと命じる. ¶*fodder* one's *horse* 馬にまぐさをやる. ¶*flog* a dead *horse* むだ骨を折る. ¶*gallop* a *horse* 馬を走らせる. ¶*get on* (=*mount* or *ride*) one's (=the) high *horse* ごう然と構える. ¶*groom* a *horse* 馬の手入をする. ¶*harness* a *horse* 馬に馬具をつける. 【類】*harness horses* to a sleigh. ¶*hire* a *horse* 馬をやとう. ¶You can *hold* the *horse*, while I bring the saddle. 私がくらを持ってくるまで馬の口を取っておいで. ¶*keep* a *horse* 馬をかっている. ¶The driver ***lashed*** his *horse* into full speed. 御者は馬にむち打って全速力を出させた. ¶***lead*** one's *horse* 馬をひく. 【類】***lead*** a *horse* by the bridle (手綱) ‖ One man may ***lead*** a *horse* to water, but ten cannot make him drink. 〖諺〗飲まぬ馬にや水やれぬ(一人でも馬を水の飲める所に連れて行けるが十人かかってでも水を飲ませることはできない). ¶*Horses* must be ***left*** at this point. ここで馬を乗り捨てねばならない. ¶***manage*** a *horse* 馬を御する. ¶***mount*** (=ride) a *horse* 馬に乗る. 【類】***mount*** a *horse* and reduce him to docility (従順) / ***Mounting*** a splendid *horse*, he rode off. ¶***put*** one's *horse* at the fence 馬にかきねを飛び越えさせる. ¶***put*** [***in***] the *horse* to a car 車に馬をつける. ¶***put out*** one's *horse* to grass 馬を草地へ出す. ¶***rear*** *horses* 馬を飼育する. ¶***rein back*** a *horse* [手綱を操って]馬を後へ戻す. ¶***rein in*** one's *horse* 手綱を引いて馬を止める. ¶***reserve*** a *horse* 馬を借切にする. ¶***rest*** a *horse* 馬を休ませる. ¶He ***rides*** a *horse* admirably. 彼は乗馬の名手だ. ‖ ***ride*** a *horse* bareback はだか馬に乗って行く. ¶***rub down*** a *horse* 馬にブラシをかける. ¶***saddle*** a *horse* 馬にくらを置く. ¶***shoe*** a *horse* 馬に蹄鉄(ﾃｲ)を打つ. ¶***singe*** a *horse* 馬の毛焼をする. ¶The lady ***sat*** her *horse* so well. その婦人は実にうまく馬を乗りこなした. ¶***spur*** one's *horse* 馬に拍車をかける. ¶***stop*** a runaway *horse* 奔馬を止める. ¶***take*** *horses* 馬をやとう ‖ ***take*** one's *horse* to pasture 馬を牧場に連れて行く. ¶***train*** a *horse* 調馬する. ¶***try*** a *horse* 馬に乗ってみる. ¶***unharness*** a *horse* 馬から馬具をはずす. ¶***urge on*** a *horse* 馬を走らせる. ¶***water*** a *horse* 馬に水をやる. ¶***yoke up*** a *horse* 馬にくびきをかける.

V² The *horse* ***bolted.*** その馬がかけ出した. ¶My *horse* ***bucked.*** 私の馬が跳ねた. ¶The *horse* ***dashed*** along the street. その馬は通りをかけ出した. ¶The *horse* ***galloped*** at full speed. 馬が全速力でかけた. ¶*Horses* ***neigh.*** 馬がいななく. ¶the *horse* ***shied*** at the sight of ... 馬が...を見て跳びのいた. ¶His *horse* ***threw*** him. 彼は馬に振落された.

Q ride on a ***barebacked*** *horse* はだか馬に乗る. ¶a ***black*** *horse* 黒馬. ¶a ***chestnut*** (=***bay***) *horse* 栗毛の馬. ¶***cream-colored*** *horse* クリーム色の馬. ¶whip a ***dead*** *horse* 〖比ゆ〗死馬にむち打つ. ¶a ***draft*** *horse* ひき馬. ¶a ***fast*** *horse* 足の速い馬. ¶a ***four-year-old*** *horse* 四歳馬. ¶his ***favorite*** *horse* 彼の愛馬. ¶a ***frisky*** *horse* よくはね回る馬. ¶go round on the ***hobby*** *horse* メリー・ゴー・ラウンドの木馬に乗る. ¶***Hungry*** *horses* make a clean manger. 〖諺〗空き腹にまずいものなし. ¶the ***iron*** *horse*=the railway 鉄道. ¶a ***jaded*** *horse* やくざ馬; 疲れた馬. ¶a ***lean*** *horse* やせ馬. ¶a ***mettlesome*** *horse* 勇みたつ馬. ¶a ***piebald*** *horse* まだら馬. ¶a ***rangy*** *horse* やせて脚の長い馬. ¶a ***runaway*** *horse* 放れ馬. ¶a ***craggy*** *horse* 骨ばった馬. ¶a ***scrawny*** *horse* やせ馬. ¶a ***skittish*** *horse* かんの強い馬. ¶a ***sound*** *horse* 強健な馬. ¶a ***spare*** *horse* 予備の馬. ¶a ***spirited*** *horse* 元気のある馬. ¶a ***stray*** *horse* 持主の分からない馬. ¶a ***swift*** *horse* 足の速い馬. ¶a ***tractable*** (an ***untractable***) *horse* おとなしい(じゃじゃ)馬. ¶try to ride a ***vicious*** *horse* くせの悪い馬に乗ってみる. 【類】a ***vicious*** and ***dangerous*** *horse.* ¶a ***white*** *horse* 白馬.

Q² the nosebags of a ***cab*** (=***coach***) *horse* 馬車馬のかいば袋. ¶a ***carriage*** (=***wagon***) *horse* 馬車馬. ¶It is ungracious to look a ***gift*** *horse* in the mouth. もらいものの欠点をさがすのはぶしつけだ. ¶a ***harness*** *horse* 馬車馬. ¶the ***iron*** *horse* 《俗》機関車. ¶a ***mother*** *horse* 母馬. ¶a ***pack*** *horse* 駄(ﾀﾞ)馬. ¶a ***post*** *horse* 逓送馬. ¶a ***race*** *horse*=a racer 競馬馬. ¶hire a ***saddle*** *horse* 乗馬をやとう.

P She is at home ***astride*** a *horse.* 彼女は乗馬が得意だ. ¶dismount ***from*** a *horse* 馬から降りる ‖ He was thrown ***from*** his *horse.* 彼は落馬した. ¶a pair ***of*** *horses* 二頭ぞろいの馬 ‖ As captain ***of*** *horse,* he was present at the most important battles of the last war. 騎兵大尉として彼はこの度の戦役の大会戦に参加した. ¶fall ***off*** one's *horse* 落馬する. ¶I have never been ***on*** a *horse* in my life. 私はこれまで馬に乗ったことがない.

horseback, *n.* 馬の背.

P get down ***from*** *horseback* 下馬する. ¶a rider ***on*** *horseback* 馬上の人 ‖ travel ***on*** *horseback* 騎馬旅行をする ‖ It is accessible ***on*** *horseback.* そこへは馬に乗って行ける.

horseman, *n.* 騎手.

P He can ride a horse ***like*** a *horseman.* 彼は騎手のように馬を乗回せる.

horsemanship, *n.* 馬術.

Q ***daring*** *horsemanship* 冒険な馬術.

P a feat ***of*** *horsemanship* 馬術の曲芸(曲馬など).

horse-power, *n.* 馬力.

V ***brake*** *horse-power* 馬力にブレーキをかける(速度をおそくする). ¶***develop*** over 50,000 *horse-power* 五万馬力以上を出す.

Q ***indicated*** *horse-power* 公示馬力. ¶***effective*** *horse-power* 実馬力. ¶***French*** *horse-power* フランス馬力(普通の一馬力の 0.986 に当る). ¶***nominal*** *horse-power* 表示馬力.

horse-riding, *n.* 騎馬.

P be good ***at*** *horse-riding* 騎馬がうまい.

horse-sense, *n.* 《米》常識.

V ***have*** *horse-sense* 《米》要領を得ている.

horseshoe, *n.* 蹄鉄(ﾃｲ).

V ***forge*** a *horseshoe* 蹄鉄を作る.

horsewoman, *n.* 女の乗馬者, 女騎手.

Q an ***accomplished*** *horsewoman* りっぱな女騎手. ¶an ***enthusiastic*** *horsewoman* 熱心な女騎手. ¶an ***expert*** *horsewoman* 熟練した女騎手.

hose, *n.* ホース; 〖商〗[集合的] 長くつ下.

V ***attach*** *hoses* to two hydrants 二本の消火せんにホースを取つける. ¶***reel*** the *hose* リールにホースを巻く. ¶***wind*** the *hose* on a reel ホースをリールに巻く.

P a reel ***for*** the *hose* ホース巻き機(リール).

Q ***half*** *hose* 短くつ下(ソックス).

Q² ***ankle*** *hose*=anklets 短くつ下, ソックス(主に婦人用). ¶a ***fire*** *hose* 消防ホース. ¶a ***garden*** *hose* 庭園散水用ホース. ¶a ***leather*** *hose* 皮製ホース. ¶a ***rubbber*** *hose* ゴムホース. ¶***silk*** (***nylon***) *hose* 絹(ナイロン)くつ下. ¶india-rubber ***suction*** *hose* with wire inside 吸水用の針金入りゴムホース.

P In the evening, I water my garden ***with*** the *hose.* 私は夕方ホースで庭に水をやる.

hosiery, *n.* 〖集合〗くつ下.

Q² ***nylon*** *hosiery* ナイロンくつ下類. ¶***run-proof*** *hosiery* ほつれ止めくつ下類. ¶***winter*** *hosiery* 冬くつ下.

hospitable, *a.* もてなしのよい.

M ***overwhelmingly*** *hospitable* 恐縮するほどにもてなしのよい.

P *hospitable* ***to*** ... ...にもてなしのよい.

hospital, *n.* 病院.

V ***attend*** a *hospital* 病院通いをする. ¶***build*** a *hospital* 病院を建てる. ¶***enter*** (=***go into***) a *hospital* 入院する. ¶This *hospital* was ***instituted*** in 1895. その病院は一八九五年の創立である. ¶***leave*** a *hospital* 退院する. ¶***Remember*** the *Hospital* in your will. 貴下の遺言書にこの病院への寄付をお加え下さい(病院基金募集広告文). ¶***run*** (=***operate***) a *hospital* 病院を経営する. 【類】The doctor ***runs*** a *hospital.*

Q a ***general*** *hospital* 総合病院. ¶a ***mental*** *hospital* 脳(精神)病院. ¶a thoroughly ***equipped*** *hospital* 完備した病院.

Q² a ***cottage*** *hospital* 軽便病院. ¶an ***evacuation*** *hospital* 《軍》臨時病院. ¶a ***fever*** and ***smallpox*** *hospital* 熱病及び天然痘病院. ¶a ***field*** *hospital* 野戦病院. ¶a ***flying*** *hospital* 航空病院. ¶a ***foundling*** *hospital* 捨児収容所. ¶a ***garrison*** *hospital* 衛戍(ｼﾞｭ)病院. ¶an ***isolation*** *hospital* 避病院. ¶***lock*** *hospitals* 性病院. ¶a ***lying-in*** *hospital*=a maternity hospital 産科病院. ¶a ***tuberculosis*** *hospital* 結核病院. ¶a ***VD*** *hospital* 花柳病院.

P a patient ***at*** a *hospital* 入院患者. ¶He is ***in*** *hospital.* 彼は入院している. ¶inmates ***of*** a *hospital* 入院患者. ¶He will soon be ***out of*** *hospital.* 彼は近々退院する. ¶go ***to*** *hospital* 通院する ‖ send a person ***to*** [a] *hospital* 病院へ入れる ‖ He was taken ***to*** *hospital.* 入院させられた. ‖ He was carried ***to*** *hospital.* 彼は病院へ担ぎ込まれた.

P² "a *hospital* ***for*** moral diseases" 「道徳上の病人のための病院」.

hospitality, *n.* 歓待, 厚遇.

V ***abuse*** one's *hospitality* 歓待につけこむ. ¶I ***accepted*** his *hospitality* for five days. 私は五日間彼の厄介になった. ‖ Well, then, I think I may venture to ***accept*** your *hospitality.* そんなら御ちそうになりましょうか. ¶***Afford*** me the *hospitality* of your columns. 貴紙に御掲載下さるようお願いします. ¶*hospitality* ***done*** through a caterer 仕出し屋から取った御ちそう. ¶***enjoy*** richly the *hospitalities* showed upon him 彼に示された歓待を十分に楽しむ ‖ I ***enjoy*** the *hospitality* of ... 私は...の厄介になっている.

¶***exercise*** great *hospitality* 大いにもてなす. ¶we ***extended*** *hospitality* of the club to ... われわれはクラブに...を招待した ‖ ***extend*** one's *hospitality* to ... ...を招待する ‖ ***extend*** a wide *hospitality* to Americanisms [辞書が]アメリカ語法を広く採録する. ¶***give*** him *hospitality* 彼を厚くもてなす. ¶***offer*** *hospitality* to ... ...を歓待する意を示す ‖ The university generously ***offered*** the *hospitality* of its grounds and buildings. 同大学は寛大にもその校庭と建物との使用を提供した. ¶***receive*** the *hospitaliy* of kind people 親切な人々のもてなしを受ける. ¶***repay*** a person's *hospitality* by ... ...によって人の厚意に報いる. ¶***share*** the *hospitality* of ... ...の歓待にあずかる. ¶***show*** boundless *hospitality* あくまで歓待ぶりを見せる. ¶They will ***welcome*** the *hospitality* of friends in private houses. 友人たちが私宅に置いてもらうことを彼らは歓迎するでしょう.

Q a ***charming*** *hospitality* 楽しいもてなし. ¶***cheery*** *hospitality* 朗かな歓待. ¶a ***cordial*** *hospitality* 懇切なもてなし. ¶***hearty*** *hospitality* 心からのもてなし. ¶He is *hospitality* ***incarnate***. 彼は下へもおかないもてなしをする. ¶***kindly meant***, but often ***oppressive***, *hospitality* [いなかなどで経験する]好意からであってもときには押付けがましい歓待. ¶show ***lavish*** *hospitality* to ... 惜気もなく...を歓待する. ¶***magnificent*** *hospitality* 素晴しい歓待. ¶receive with an ***openhanded*** *hospitality* 大いに歓待を受ける. ¶***overwhelming*** *hospitality* 圧倒的な歓待. ¶***princely*** *hospitality* 豪華な歓待.

P ask you ***for*** the *hospitality* of your columns 投書を載せて下さるようお願いします. ¶partake ***of*** *hospitality* 歓待を受ける. ¶trespass ***on*** one's *hospitality* 人の厚遇につけ上がる.

host, *n.* 主人.

V ***play*** *host* to ... ...を招待する.

Q a ***boorish*** *host* 非礼な主人. ¶a ***charming*** *host* 魅力のある主人.

P act ***as*** *host* 主人役をつとめる.

P² he will be *host* ***at*** a cocktail party to be held at his residence at ... ...の自宅で開かれるカクテルパーティに主人役をする. ¶In 1924 Hawaii was *host* ***to*** a food conservation conference. 一九二四年ハワイは食料品保存会議の主人役を務めた.

host, *n.* 軍勢; 大勢.

V ***assemble*** a mighty *host* 大軍を集結する.

Q a ***motley*** *host* うごうの衆.

P ***for*** a *host* of other objects 他の多くの目的のために.

P² a *host* ***of*** rivals 大勢の競争者 ‖ and a *host* ***of*** other writers その他多数の作家たち.

hostage, *n.* 人質.

V ***give*** *hostages* to fortune 人または物を失う危険を冒す. ¶***Putting*** *hostages* to death was one of Germany's war crimes. 人質を殺したのはドイツが戦争で作った罪の一つであった.

hostel, *n.* 大学寄宿舎, 宿舎(ホステル).

Q ***collegiate*** *hostels* [単科]大学の寄宿舎. ¶stop for the night at a ***hikers'*** *hostel* その晩はハイカーの山小屋に一泊する.

Q² a ***Y.M.C.A.*** *hostel* on the beach (hill) ワイエムの海(山)の家. ¶a ***youth*** *hostel* 青少年専用ホステル.

P² pure free milk *hostels* ***for*** the poor of London ロンドンの貧困者に無料で純粋の牛乳を支給する宿舎.

hostelry, *n.* 宿屋.

Q² an ***out-of-town*** *hostelry* いなかの宿屋.

hostess, *n.* 女主人.

Q² an ***air[plane]*** *hostess* (=stewardess) [空の]スチュワデス. ¶a ***cabaret*** *hostess* キャバレの女給. ¶a ***dance*** *hostess* [[職業]ダンサー.

P act ***as*** *hostess* 女主人役になる.

P² She will be *hostess* ***to*** a party of seven this evening. 彼女は今晩七人の客の相手をする.

hostile, *a.* 敵対する.

M a strong party ***vehemently*** *hostile* to ... ...に猛烈に敵対している一大党派.

P *hostile* (favorable) ***to*** a person (country, nation) 人(など)に敵対する(好意を持っている). 【類】be *hostile* ***to*** the movement (運動) / be *hostile* ***to*** Christianity.

hostility, *n.* 敵意, 敵対; *pl.* 戦争.

V ***abandon*** *hostility* 敵性を放棄する. ¶***arouse*** the *hostility* of ... ...に敵意を起さす. ¶***cease*** *hostilities* 停戦する. ¶***commence*** *hostilities* 開戦する. ¶***display*** one's *hostility* 敵意を示す. ¶they ***evinced*** no *hostility* to ... 彼らは...に少しも敵意を示さなかった. ¶***excite*** great *hostility* 大いに敵意を喚起する. ¶***give up*** *hostilities* 戦闘を止める. ¶***open*** the *hostilities* 火ぶたを切る(開戦する). 【類】***open*** *hostilities* with ... ¶***precipitate*** *hostilities* 開戦を激成させる. ¶***prevent*** *hostilities* 敵対行為を防止する. ¶Do or say nothing to ***provoke*** *hostility*. 敵意を起させるようなことをしたり言ったりするな. ¶***show*** an open *hostility* to ... ...に対してあからさまに敵意を示す. ¶***suspend*** *hostilities* 停戦する. ¶***widen*** the *hostilities* 戦火を拡大する.

V² *Hostilities* ***broke out*** between the two powerful families of Minamoto and Taira. 有力な源平二氏の間に争いが起った. ¶if *hostilities* should ***occur*** もし戦争が起ったら.

Q a ***latent*** *hostility* to Europeans 欧州人への潜在的敵意. ¶***naval*** *hostilities* (=warfare) 海戦. ¶He has no ***personal*** *hostility* to me. 彼は私に対し個人的な敵意は持っていない.

P ***during*** *hostilities* 戦争中に.

P² There is much (no) *hostility* ***against*** America. 米国に対する大いに敵意がある(ない). ¶*hostilities* ***in*** Indo-China インド支那の戦闘. ¶their ignorant *hostility* ***to*** the system itself, instead of its abuses その組織の弊害に対するのではなく組織自体に対する彼らの盲目的な敵意 ‖ His *hostility* ***to*** the woman found vent in a sharp remark. 彼は婦人に対する敵意を鋭い言葉でぶちまけた.

hot, *a.* 暑い, 熱い.

M ***Awfully*** *hot*, isn't it? ずい分暑いですね. ¶***boiling*** *hot* 煮えくり返るように暑い. ¶***broiling*** *hot* 猛烈に暑い. ¶***confoundedly*** *hot* ばかに暑い. ¶The bath is ***nipping*** *hot*. ふろが痛いくらい熱い. ¶***oppressively*** *hot* 熱苦しい. ¶Hot, ***scorchingly*** *hot!* 暑い, やきつけるように熱い. ¶***unbearably*** *hot* たえられないくらい暑い. ¶***uncomfortably*** *hot* 苦しいほど暑い.

P very *hot* ***for*** the season この季節にしては随分暑い. ¶It is *hot* ***in*** Formosa. 台湾は暑い. ¶*hot* ***with*** rage (shame, zeal) 怒(など)で赤くなる.

hotbed, *n.* 温床.

P The place is a *hotbed* (=cradle *or* source) ***of*** malaria. そこはマラリヤ養成所みたいなものだ. 【類】a *hotbed* ***of*** diseases and vices.

hotel, *n.* 旅館, ホテル.

V ***erect*** a modern *hotel* 近代式ホテルを建設する. ¶The *hotel* is ***filled up*** with modern comforts. そのホテルには近代式な快適の設備がしてある. ¶*hotels* ***kept*** in Western fashion 洋式の旅館(ホテル). ¶Here the Railway Company ***maintains*** a splendid *hotel*. ここでその鉄道会社がりっぱなホテルを経営している. ¶***recommend*** a *hotel* 旅館を推奨する. ¶***run*** (=***operate***) a *hotel* 旅館を経営する. 【類】The *hotel* is ***run*** entirely in European style. / ***run*** a *hotel* on the European (American) plan.

Q a ***cheap-looking*** *hotel* 安っぽい旅館. ¶a ***commercial*** *hotel* 商人旅館. ¶a ***commodious*** *hotel* 手広い旅館. ¶a ***cozy*** *hotel* 居心地よい旅館. ¶a ***decent*** *hotel* 相当(りっぱ)な旅館. ¶a ***Japanese-operated*** *hotel* 日本人の経営するホテル. ¶a ***luxurious*** *hotel* 豪華なホテル. ¶a ***metropolitan*** *hotel* 首都のホテル. ¶***poor men's*** *hotels* 貧民ホテル. ¶boardinghouses and ***private*** *hotels* 下宿屋としろうと下宿. ¶a ***ramshackle*** *hotel* けちな旅館. ¶a ***renovated*** *hotel* 新装のホテル. ¶a ***residential*** *hotel* アパート式の(止宿客専用)ホテル. ¶a ***stately*** *hotel* 堂々たるホテル. ¶a ***swanky little*** *hotel* すばらしい小ホテル. ¶***un-Europeanized Japanese*** *hotels* in the country districts 地方の欧化されない純日本旅館. ¶The *hotel* is ***well-appointed*** (=has good furniture and arrangements). そのホテルは何から何まで設備が行届いている.

Q² an ***apartment*** *hotel* アパート式ホテル(定宿人を主とする). ¶a ***bachelor*** *hotel* 独身者ホテル. ¶a ***bath*** *hotel* 温泉宿. ¶a recognized ***conference*** *hotel* 会議を開くに便利なホテル. ¶a ***family*** *hotel* 家族向ホテル. ¶***home*** *hotels* in Germany (=Herbergen zur Heimath) ドイツの家族用ホテル. ¶a ***lake-side*** *hotel* 湖畔ホテル. ¶a fashionable ***London*** *hotel* ロンドンの一流ホテル. ¶a ***luxury*** *hotel* 豪華なホテル. ¶a ***railway*** *hotel* ステーションホテル. ¶a ***recreation*** *hotel* 休養向のホテル. ¶a ***rendezvous*** *hotel* 連れ込みホテル. ¶a ***resort*** *hotel* [海辺などの]盛り場のホテル. ¶a ***rest*** *hotel* for the Army soldiers 軍人の休息ホテル. ¶a ***summer*** (***winter***) *hotel* 避暑(寒)地のホテル. ¶a ***union station*** *hotel* 《米》[連絡線の]ステーションホテル. ¶a good ***West*** (=***Western***) ***plan*** *hotel* 西欧式食事付ホテル.

P put up (stop) ***at*** a *hotel* 宿を取る ‖ stay ***at*** a *hotel* 旅館

に泊っている ‖ get registered ***at*** a ***hotel*** ホテルに投宿する. ¶He is stopping ***in*** the ***hotel***. 彼はその旅館に泊っている.

hour, *n.* 時間.

v can only ***allow*** ... *hours* for loading 積荷の時間は…時間しか与えられない. ¶***ask*** the *hour* 時間を尋ねる. ¶***beguile*** the *hours* with dominoes and card-playing ドミノやトランプをやって時間をまぎらす. 【類】***beguile*** their *hours* of waiting. ¶The clock was ***booming out*** the *hour*. 時計が鳴り響いていた. ¶***brighten*** one's *hour* of loneliness by ... …してさびしい時をなぐさめる. ¶Clocks ***call out*** the *hour*. 時計は時を打つ. ¶I ***counted*** the *hours* till the promised day arrived. 私は指折り数えて約束の日を待っていた. ¶Cocks ***crow*** the *hour*. 鶏は時を告げる. ¶***curtail*** the working *hours* 労働時間を短縮する. ¶***doze*** (=***idle***) one's *hours* ***away*** ぶらぶらして日を送る. ¶***dream*** the *hour* ***away*** 夢うつつに時を過す. ¶***drive*** the *hours* along 日を送る. ¶I ***earned*** two *hours* today. 私はきょう二時間得をした(教師が休みのクラスがあった時など). ¶***extend*** (***reduce***) *hours* of labor 労働時間を延ばす(縮める). ¶The speech ***filled*** two *hours*. その演説は二時間かかった. ¶We ***have*** still an *hour* to spare. まだ一時間の余裕がある. ‖ We ***have*** one *hour* at noon for dinner. 正午に食事の時間が一時間ある. ‖ The old man ***has*** but a few *hours* to live. その老人は余命が二三時間しかない. ¶The cuckoo clock ***hooted*** [***out***] the *hour*. はと時計が時間を告げた. ¶He ***keeps*** early *hours*. 彼は(帰宅・朝起・就寝などが)いつも早い. ‖ habitually ***keep*** late *hours* 夜ふかしをする ‖ ***keep*** regular *hours* 寝起の時を規則正しくする. ¶***make*** regular *hours* ***seem short*** 時のたつのを忘れさせる. ¶The *hour* was ***moved*** to the afternoon. その時刻が午後に変更された. ¶The voyage ***occupies*** (=takes) eight *hours*. その航海は八時間かかる. ¶***pass*** an agreeable *hour* with ... …と楽しい一時間を送る. ¶The book may help to ***pass away*** an *hour* or so pleasantly. その本は一時間そこらを愉快に過すたしになろう. ‖ ***pass away*** the idle *hours* ひまをつぶす. ¶The *hours* from two to five are ***pledged*** to another visitor. 二時から五時まではもう一人の来訪者に約束がしてある. ¶figures ***representing*** *hours* 時間を示す数字. ¶The journey then ***required*** more *hours* than it now does minutes. 当時その旅行は現在要する何分という時以上の時間がかかった. ¶He must now ***rue*** the *hour* when he was tempted to take the step. 彼はあの時思い切ってやればよかったと今ごろは後悔しているにちがいない. ¶the way in which one ***spends*** one's leisure *hours* 暇な時間を過す方法. ¶Clocks (Bells) ***strike*** *hours*. 時計(など)が時刻を打つ. 【類】while the bell is ringing or the clock is ***striking*** the *hour* / The bell is used for ***striking*** the *hour*. / The clock began to ***strike*** the *hour* of midnight. ¶The film ***takes*** over two *hours* to exhibit. その映画は映写に二時間以上かかる. ¶***tell*** the *hour* 時刻を報じる. ¶when Big Ben ***tolls*** the *hour* of four in the morning ビッグ・ベン(英国国会議事堂塔上の大時計)が朝の四時を打つと. ¶***waste*** a full *hour* 丸一時間をむだにする. ¶***while away*** idle *hours* 暇な時間を過す. 【類】***while away*** a sunny *hour* on a seat in the garden. ¶***work*** shorter *hours* 短縮した時間で就業する.

v² I thought my *hour* had ***come***. いよいよ死ぬ時が来たなと思った. ¶The *hours* are ***hastening on***. 時間がぐんぐんたつ. ¶*Hours* ***slipped away***. 時間が知らない間に過ぎた. ¶when the first *hour* of a new day has ***struck*** 夜中の一時が鳴ると.

Q work "***after hours***" 居残りをする. ¶at ***all hours*** of the day and night 昼夜時間にかまわずいつでも. ¶at ***any hour*** of the day or night 昼間または夜間いつでも. ¶at the ***appointed hour*** 約束の時間に. ¶visit people at the ***awkward hour*** of one o'clock 午後一時という間の悪い時間(昼飯時)に人を訪問する. ¶keep ***bad*** (=late) *hours* 夜ふかし朝寝をする. ¶It was still before ***banking hours***. まだ銀行の営業時間前だった. ¶a ***bare hour*** かろうじて一時間. ¶at this ***belated hour*** 今ごろになって, 今さら. ¶He has to be at a certain place at a ***certain hour***. 彼はある時刻にある場所へ行かねばならない. ¶the ***closing hour*** of the museum その博物館の閉館時刻 ‖ just at that ***closing hour*** of light ちょうど日暮に. ¶for five ***consecutive hours*** 五時間ぶっ通しで. ¶at ***certain hours*** 定まった時刻に. ¶at this ***crucial hour*** この危急な際に. ¶in Britain's ***darkest hours*** 英国の苦境のどん底に ‖ at the ***darkest hour*** of night 真夜中に. ¶I spent two ***delightful hours*** with ... 私は…と愉快な二時間を送った. ¶at ***different hours*** 時間をかえて. ¶***difficult hours*** 都合の悪い時間. ¶kill a couple of ***dull hours*** by reading 読書で二時間退屈をしのぐ. ¶at a very ***early hour*** in the morning ごく早朝に ‖ in the ***earlier hours*** of the evening 宵の口に. 【類】Pray excuse my having come at such an ***early hour***. / A fishing vessel was sunk off ... in the ***early hours*** of yesterday. ¶at this ***eleventh hour*** この際どい時に. ¶***every alternative hour*** 一時間おきに. ¶about once ***every half hour*** 半時間毎に約一回. 【類】The medicine is to be taken ***every four hours***. ¶in an ***evil hour*** あいにく. 【類】in an ***evil hour*** for him. ¶Passengers should ascertain from [the] Company's agents the ***exact hour*** of departure. 船客は同会社の代理店で正確なる出帆時刻をお確かめ下さい. ¶at the ***extraordinary hour*** of four or five in the morning 朝の四時五時という突飛な時間に. ¶go to bed at a ***fixed hour*** きまった時間に床につく. ¶in the ***fresh hours*** of morning 朝のすがすがしい時間に. ¶at that ***ghostly hour*** 鬼気迫るうしみつ時に. ¶the ***golden hours*** [ラジオなど]ゴールデンアワー(放送の 7 時 — 9 時まで). ¶in the ***good hour*** 折よく ‖ keep ***good hours*** 夜ふかしをしない. ¶the ***grey hours*** 朝まだき. ¶a ***half hour*** (=half an hour) later《米》三十分遅れて ‖ be late by the ***half hour*** 半時間も遅い. ¶Here many ***happy hours*** can be spent. ここでは愉快に幾時間も過せる. ‖ dream the ***happy hours*** away 白河夜船である. ¶a book for an ***idle hour*** 暇つぶしに読む本 ‖ fill up her ***idle hours*** 余暇をそれに使う. ¶at an ***inconvenient hour*** 都合の悪い時に ‖ the ***last hours*** of a person 臨終の数時間 ‖ an account of his ***last hours*** 彼の臨終物語. ¶keep ***late*** (***early***) *hours* 朝寝夜ふかし(早寝早起)をする. ¶I awoke at some ***late hour*** of the night. 私は夜ふけて目が覚めた. 【類】in the ***late hours*** of night / The use of strong tea or coffee at ***late hours*** is one of the most common causes of sleeplessness. / until a ***late hour*** of the evening. ¶out of ***licensed hours*** (営業)許可時間外に. ¶for fourteen ***long hours*** 十四時間という長い時間中. ¶at the *hour* ***mentioned*** 規定の時刻に. ¶in the ***middle hours*** of the night 真夜中に. ¶for the ***next two hours*** それから二時間. ¶in ***odd hours*** ひまひまに. ¶in ***off hours*** 休息時間に. ¶at ***other hours*** 他の折に. ¶It is not a fad that has its ***passing hour***. それはちょっと騒がれてすぐ忘れられるような一時の流行ではない. ¶many ***perspiring hours*** 汗を流す(努力の)長時間. ¶We have ***punctual hours*** for meals. われわれはきちんと食事の時間をきめている. ¶eat at ***regular hours*** 時間をきめて食事をする ‖ keep ***regular hours*** 時間を正確に守る(遅刻しない). ¶I want to get home at a ***respectable hour***. 私は夜おそ過ぎない中に帰宅したい. ¶He spends his ***scanty hours*** of leisure in sport. 彼はわずかの余暇にスポーツをやる. ¶the ***shortened hours*** of labor made possible by applied science 科学の応用によって可能となった労働時間の短縮. ¶in one's ***sleeping hours*** 睡眠中に. ¶in the ***small hours*** of the morning 午前一二時ごろに. 【類】in the ***small hours*** before dawn / towards the ***small hours*** of the night / go to press (印刷にかかる) in the ***small hours*** of the morning. ¶He spoke for three ***solid hours*** without stopping. 彼は三時間ぶっ続けに演説をした. ¶in the ***spare hours*** of a busy life 多忙な生活の余暇に. ¶in the ***still hours*** of the night 夜の静寂な時間に. 【類】at that ***still hour***. ¶at the ***unearthly hour*** of 3.30 in the morning 午前の三時半という気味の悪い時刻に. ¶call at an ***unfashionable hour*** 時刻はずれに人を訪問する. ¶They arranged to get the last tram delayed for 15 minutes beyond the ***usual hour***. 終発電車を定刻より十五分遅らしてもらうように打合わせをした. 【類】Please call me (電話をかけてくれ) at the ***usual hour***. ‖ He lay in bed beyond the ***usual hour*** that morning. 彼はその朝いつもより遅くまで寝ていた. ¶spend ***weary hours*** 何時間も退屈する ‖ help to while away ***weary hours*** 退屈しのぎになる. 【類】beguile (紛らす) ***weary hours***. ¶rise at such ***weird hours*** こんな不気味な時間に起きる. ¶at ***what hour*** of the day or night it may be 日中または夜間の何時であろうと.

Q² in one's ***after-office hours*** 会社が引けてから. ¶***bank-to-bank labor hours***〖鉱〗坑内実労働時間. ¶the ***bedtime*** *hour* 就寝時間. ¶*booking office hours* 出札就業時間. ¶a flexible *breakfast hour* 定りのない朝飯時. ¶during *business hours* 営業時間中 ‖ outside *business hours* 営業時間外に. 【類】 during normal *business hours*. ¶the *closing hour* 締切[閉店]時間. ¶*consultation hours* [医者の]診療時間. ¶The engineering courses of the College of Engineering at Cornell University require 145 *credit hours* for graduation. コーネル大学の工学部の工学科は百四十五単位を履修しないと卒業できない. ¶during the *daylight hours* 日のある中に. ¶in *day[time] hours* 昼間は. ¶at the dinner *hour* 晩さん時に. ¶outside *duty hours* 仕事の余暇に. ¶one's *dying hour* 臨終. ¶The Great Flyer leaves Los Angeles at a convenient *evening hour*—6:06 p.m. 特急快速号はロスを夕方の都合よい時間すなわち六時六分に出る. ¶800 *flying hours* 滞空八百時間. ¶the *goodnight hour* [ラジオ]お休み番組. ¶the use of *leisure hours* 余暇の利用. ¶a task for his own *leisure hours* 彼の暇な時の仕事. 【類】 read books in *leisure hours* / spend one's *leisure hours* in ... ¶during the *lunch[eon] hour* 昼食時間に ‖ interrupt one's *lunch hour* 昼食時の邪魔をする. 【類】 They spend half of their *lunch hour* out of doors. ¶work through *midnight hours* 深夜作業をする. ¶during *non-working hours* 仕事のない時は. ¶in their *off-duty hours* 彼らの休息時に. 【類】 soldiers tramping the street during their *off-duty hours*. ¶out of (during) *office hours* 執務時外(内)に. 【類】 before (after) *office hours*. ¶differentiation of *office-attendance hours* 勤務時間の差別. ¶wait for the *opening hour* [銀行などの]営業開始時間を待つ. ¶*peak hours* [ラジオの]ゴールデン・アワー. ¶increase of productivity *per man hour* of work 延人員一人当りの生産性の増加. ¶*play hours* 遊び時間. ¶in the *post-midnight hours* 夜半過ぎに. ¶in *predawn hours* 夜あけ前に. ¶the *rapid service hours* [国電など]急行運転時間. ¶Seven o'clock is his *rising hour*. 七時が彼の起きる時間だ. ¶in *rush hours* ラッシュアワー(混雑時)に ‖ a *rush hour* in a restaurant レストランの混む時間 ‖ morning and evening *rush hours* 朝晩のラッシュアワー. ¶the *sailing hour* of a ship 船の出帆時. ¶after *school hours* 学校が終ったら ‖ student activities outside of *school hours* 課外活動. ¶*semester hours* [大学の]一学期の時間数. ¶after *session* (=*school*) *hours* 授業が終ってから. ¶*shop* (=*shopping*) *hours* 開店時間. ¶during one's *sleeping hours* その睡眠中は. ¶enjoy a *social evening hour* 晩の社交の時間を楽しむ. ¶I don't like to have a caller in my *study hours*. 勉強中人に来られるのは困る. ¶at her *toilet hours* 彼女のお化粧時間に. ¶all his *waking hours* 目が覚めてる間ずっと ‖ curtail the *working hours* 就業時間を短縮する. ¶your *zero hour* 君の決断すべき時 ‖ be needed at *zero hour* いざという時必要だ ‖ be waiting for *zero hour* 決戦を待っている; 《口語》危機に備えている.

P *after* an *hour* of irresolution どうしようかと一時間も考えたあげく ‖ *after* office *hours* 執務時間後. ¶*at* this *hour* of morning 朝のこの時刻に. 【類】 *at* the *hour* of six / *at* the *hour* named (指定の) / *at* the *hour* of lunch ‖ *at* this *hour* of night こんなに夜遅く ‖ *at* any *hour* of the day and night 昼夜を問わずいつでも. 【類】 *at* such an *hour* / Pray excuse my calling *at* your tiffin *hour* (昼食時間). ¶I shall be glad to see you any day *between* the *hours* of 11 and 5. 十一時から五時までの間だったら何日でも喜んでお目にかかります. ¶No one can be held *beyond* twenty-four *hours* unless a specific charge is made. 何か一定の罪科なくしてだれでも二十四時間以上拘留しておくことはできない. ¶engage a person *by* the *hour* 時間ぎめで人を雇う ‖ sit *by* the *hours* together in lecture rooms 数時間教場で講義を聞く. ¶*during* the weird *hours* of the night 気味悪い夜の時間中に. ¶*for hours* at a time 引続き数時間 ‖ *for* an *hour* or so 一時間かそこら ‖ *for hours* together 何時間も続けて ‖ *for* full[y] five *hours* 五時間たっぷり. 【類】 wait *for* an *hour* / Weather forecasts are not reliable *for* more than thirty-six or forty-eight *hours* in advance. ¶*from hour to hour* 時々刻々. ¶*in* an *hour* or two 一二時間で ‖ four thousand *in* an *hour* [製産高]一時間に四千 ‖ *in* the *hour* of the Empire's danger 帝国の危機に際して. 【類】 reveal themselves as heroes *in* the *hour* of national peril / *in* its *hour* of trial (試練) / *in* that *hour* of national darkness (暗黒) / I will help you *in* [the] *hour* of need. / *in* the *hour* of her sore need / *in* the *hour* of death / *in* the *hour* of victory. ¶sit up *into* the small *hours* of the night 夜の一二時ごろまで起きている. ¶Tell me the number *of hours* to be required. それに要する時間を言って下さい. ‖ a couple *of hours* 二時間ばかり ‖ the question *of* the *hour* 刻下の問題 ‖ the man (novel, play) *of* the *hour* 今世人の注意を引いている人(など). ¶work *out of hours* 時間外に働く. ¶fly 50 miles *per hour* 毎時五十マイルで飛ぶ. ¶*till* a late *hour* at night 夜遅くまで. ¶say *to* an *hour* [日だけでなく]時間まで(正確に)言う ‖ from eight a.m. *to* the *hour* of noon 午前八時から正午まで ‖ *to* this *hour* 今が今まで. 【類】 He worked hard almost *to* the *hour* of his death (死の真近まで). ¶High revelry was held *until* the early *hours* of the morning. 盛大な酒宴が払暁まで続いた. ¶It is *within* two *hours* by train. そこへは汽車で二時間内に行ける.

P[2] an *hour after* sunrise 日が出てから一時間 ‖ *Hour after* hour passed without rescue forthcoming. 救いの人が来ずに時間がたって行った. ¶an *hour before* sundown 日没前一時間. ¶*hour by* hour 時々刻々. ¶The steamer can only allow two *hours for* discharge. その汽船は荷おろしに二時間の余裕しかない. ¶two o'clock in the morning, the old Japanese *hour of* ghosts 午前の二時すなわち昔の日本のうしみつ時 ‖ about half past five, his *hour of* rising 彼の起床時五時半ごろ.

house, *n.* 家, 家屋; 一門, 家族; 聴衆, 観客; 議会, 議場.

V *aggrandize* the *house* その家名をあげる. ¶*alarm* the *house* 家中の者をびっくり目をさまさせる. ¶The play is still *attracting* full *houses*. その芝居はいまだに大入りである. ¶The *house* of Mr.... was *broken into* by a burglar. ...氏の家は夜盗にはいられた. ¶He *brought* the *house down*. 彼は満場のかっさいを博した. ¶*build* (=*erect*) a *house* 家を建てる. 【類】 When a builder *builds* a *house*, he contracts to build it for so much money (いくらいくらで). ¶he *bought* a *house* in ... 彼は...に家を買った. ¶*call* the *House* to order 議場の静粛を命じる. ¶*carry* the *house* 満場をうならせる. ¶*change houses* 移転する. ¶The *house* was *crowded*. その劇場は大入りであった. ¶The *houses* were *decked* with lanterns and flags. 家々には提灯や旗が掲げてあった. ¶The police *disinfected* the whole *house*. 警察ではその家中を消毒した. ¶*do up* a *house* 家を修繕する. ¶The theatre *drew* a full *house*. その劇場は満員であった. ‖ The play *drew* a good *house*. その劇は大入りであった. 【類】 The theatre continues to *draw* immense *houses* with the play. ¶I could *eat* a *house* now. 腹がぺこぺこだ(家でも食べられそうだ). ¶*enter* a *house* by force 無理に家にはいる. 【類】 Clean the shoes on a door mat before *entering* a house. ¶*equip* a *house* with furniture 家に家具を備え付ける. ¶*face* the *house* to the south to admit the sunshine 日光を入れるため家を南向きにする. ¶I am glad you *found* my *house*. よくたずねて(訪問して)下さいました. ¶*finish* a *house* 家を仕上げる. ¶He *founded* a famous and prosperous *house* of business. 彼は有名で繁盛する商店を築き上げた. ¶*fumigate* the *house* with hydrocyanic acid シアン化水素酸(青酸)で家をくん蒸消毒する. ¶*furnish* a *house* 家に家具を備え付ける. ¶*give* it a *house* それを収容する家を造る. ¶He *had* his *house broken into* by a burglar. 彼は夜盗にはいられた. ¶*have* one's *house repaired* 家を修繕させる. ¶the *house* once *inhabited* by ... かつて...が住んだ家. ¶I want to *insure* my *house*. 私は家に保険をつけたい. ¶*keep house* 世帯を持つ ‖ cook and *keep house* 料理や家政をやる ‖ She *keeps house* for my father. 彼女は私の父のために家事の世話をしている. 【類】 His *house* is *kept* by his sister. ‖ *keep* a country *house* いなかに別荘を持つ ‖ *keep* the (=one's) *house* 引きこもって家にいる. ¶*keep open house* 門戸を解放する, 来客を歓迎する. ¶*keep house together* 一緒に世帯を持つ. ¶It is not safe to *leave* one's *house* empty at night. 夜家をあけるのは物騒だ. ¶*let* a *house* at so much a month 月幾らで家を貸す. 【類】 *let* a *house* at a rent of ... ¶*light houses* by electricity 家を電灯で照明する. ¶He *makes* his *house* a hell on earth. 彼は自分の家をこの世ながらの地獄にしている. ¶stay at home and *mind* the *house* 留守居をする. ¶*mistake* a *house* 家を間違える. ¶*mortgage* a *house* 家を抵当にする. ¶*move house* 転宅する. ¶Who *occupied* this *house* before it was let to us? この家を私たちが借りる前にだれが住んで

いました. ¶*operate* a *house* of prostitution 女郎屋をやる. ¶*Houses* are *over* (*under*)-*heated.* 家の暖房が強(弱)すぎる. ¶*own* a *house* of one's own 自分の家を持つ. ¶*paint* a *house* *blue* (*white,* etc.) 家を青く(など)塗る. ¶*pass* one's *house* without dropping in その家を素通りする. ¶That *house* is well *planned.* その家は設計がよく出来ている. ¶*pull* one's *house* to pieces その家を取りこわす. ¶*pull down* a *house* 家を取りこわす. ¶*put* the *house* in order 家を整理する ‖ *put up* a *house* 家を建てる ‖ *put up* my *house* for sale 私の家を競売に付する. ¶*raise* the *house* upon the fire 家人の注意を防火に向ける. ¶*re-acoustic* the *house* in accordance with the new requirements of the talking pictures トーキー興業に順応するために家の音響的効果を改善する. ¶*rent* a *house* to live in 住宅を借りる. 【類】 *rent* one's *house* during one's absence. ¶*rob* a *house* 家をかすめる. ¶I was so ill that I had to *rouse* the *house.* 私は気分が悪かったので家人を起さなければならなかった. ¶The *house* was *sold out* for the first performance. 同劇場の第一回興行は売切れであった. ¶*set* one's *house* in order before going away or in case of death 旅行前か不幸の後で一家の整理をする ‖ *set* a *house* on fire (=in flames) 家に火をつける. 【類】 The *house* might be *set* on fire. ¶*set up houses* 世帯を持つ. ¶*sublet* a *house* 家をまた貸する. ¶*take* a *house* for the summer 夏の間家を借りる ‖ *take* a *house* in Shinagawa 品川に家を持つ. 【類】 *take* a country *house* ‖ *take* a *house* to pieces to set it up elsewhere 家を他所に移すために取りこわす. ¶*tear down* a *house* 家をこわす. ¶*tenant* a *house* 家を賃借する. ¶This *threw* the whole *house* into confusion. そのために家中大騒ぎだった. ¶*turn* (=*move*) a *house* *round* to face the south=face a house southward 家を南向きにする. ¶Several *houses* in this neighborhood were *visited* by thieves during last week. この近所で先週盗賊にはいられた家が数軒ある. ¶*wind up* the Naples *house* ナポリの家をたたむ.

V² The *house* was *bursting* with people. 劇場ははちきれんばかりの大入だった. ¶The *house* *looks S.W.* その家は西南向きだ. ¶This *house* does not *rent* so *high* as the other. この家の家賃は片方ほど高くない. ¶The *house swam* before my eyes. 家が動くように見えた(酔って).

Q the *adjoining house* 隣接する家. ¶an *ancestral house* 先祖伝来の家. ¶The above well-known hostelry is the *appointed house* for the Commercial Travellers' Association. 上記の有名な旅館は商用旅行者組合の指定宿である. ¶the *bare* and *squalid houses* of the slum dwellers 貧民くつの飾りのない見すぼらしい家. ¶Mr. ..., who is well-known as a player on a one-stringed instrument, gave a musical entertainment last night to a *big house* at the hotel. 単絃楽器の演奏者として有名な…氏は昨夜同ホテルで演奏をやって大入りであった. ¶goods produced by *British houses* (=manufacturers) 英国の工場で製産した品. ¶a *bumper house* 《俗》 大入. ¶a *burning house* 焼けている家. ¶a *burnt house* 焼けた家. ¶factories and *commercial houses* 工場と商店. ¶a *crowded* (=*packed*) *house* 大入(満員) ‖ He played to a *crowded house* at every performance. 彼は興行の度毎に大当りだった. ¶*dark, low, forbidding houses* 暗くて低くていやな家. ¶a *deserted house* 人のいない家. ¶a *dilapidated house* あばら屋. ¶keep a *disorderly house* 家で淫売をする. 【類】 the owner of *disorderly houses.* ¶a *duplex house* 《米》 二世帯家屋. ¶The *house* was almost *empty.* その家はほとんど空であった. ¶take an *expensive house* 高価な住宅を買う. ¶a well *fitted up house* 道具をりっぱに取付けてある家. ¶a *four-roomed house* 四室の家. ¶The *house* was *full.* その家は満員であった. ¶a *furnished house* 建具・家具の完備した住宅. 【類】 a partly *furnished house.* ¶It is expected that there will be a *good house* at the Kabukiza tomorrow. あすの歌舞伎座は大入りになるだろうという予想だ. ‖ If this order is not in your line kindly pass it on to a *good house* doing in this class of goods. この注文の品を扱っていないようだったら, 注文書をその方面のしっかりした店に御回しを願います. ¶Mr. Murray, head of the *great publishing house* of that name 同じ名前の大出版店の店主たるマレー氏. ¶a *half-timbered house* 一部木材建築の家. ¶take a *handsome house* in the suburbs 郊外でりっぱな家に住む. ¶a *healthy house* 健康によい家. ¶a *historic house* 由緒のある家. ¶an *ivy-covered house* つたのからまっている家. ¶a *licensed house* 娼家. ¶a *magnificent house* 宏壮な家. ¶a *mercantile house* 商店. ¶a *moderate-sized house* 中位な大きさの家. ¶a *mud godown built house* 土蔵造りの家. ¶an *old-fangled suburban house* of some midland town ある英国中部の町の郊外にある旧式の家. ¶*one* (*two*)-*storied house* 平家(二階建て). ¶"Bungalow" is an Indian word meaning a small *one-storied house.* 「バンガロー」はインド語で小さい平家のことだ. ¶The *house* is getting *packed* (=crowded). だんだんこんできた. ¶a *partially-built house* 普請中の家. ¶But certainly Nora, wonderful as her character was, could not draw *paying houses* for a week. たしかにノラの役柄は素敵ではあったが一週間と入りは取れなかった. ¶a *prefabricated house* 組立て住宅. ¶a *pretentious house*=a prefab 見掛けだけの家. ¶a *publishing house* 出版屋. ¶a *ramshackle house* 破れ家. ¶a *ready-built house* 貸(売)家建の家. ¶the *reigning house* 皇統. ¶a *reputable house* 評判のよい家. ¶the *rival houses* of Taira and Minamoto 敵対する源平二氏. ¶Come in. It's a *shabby house* to ask a man into. おはいり下さい, むさくるしい家ですが. ¶The Bill was considered in a *small House.* その案は少数出席の議会で討議された. ¶a *small rented house* 小さな貸家. ¶Theirs is a *social house.* あの家庭はお客さんによくする. ¶a *spooky house* おばけ屋敷. ¶The *house* was *thin.* 入りが少なかった. ¶the *three Imperial princely houses* of Chichibu, Takamatsu and Mikasa 秩父・高松・三笠の三皇族. ¶a *three-roomed house* 三室の家. ¶*townspeople's houses* 町家. ¶the earlier of the *two* "*houses*" per night 一夜二回興行の表. ¶an *unoccupied house* あき家. ¶his *unpretentious house* 彼の質素な家. ¶an *untenanted house* 空家. ¶a *warm, well-built house* しっかりと建てた暖い家. ¶*weather-beaten houses* 雨風にさらされた家. ¶The *whole house* was upset. 家中てんやわんやだった. 【類】 The *whole house* is a mess.

Q² an *adobe house* アドービれんが造りの家屋(昔スペイン人がアメリカで建てた). ¶an *apartment house* アパート. ¶an *assignation house* 待合. ¶a *banking house* 銀行(営業する場所). ¶a *bathing house* 湯屋. ¶her *beach house* 彼女の海岸の別邸. ¶a *beer house* ビヤホール. ¶a *bird house* 小鳥の家(巣). ¶a *branch house* 分家. ¶a *brick house* れんが建ての家屋. ¶a *brooder house* ひなの保育箱. ¶one's *business house* そのお店(私宅に対し). ¶Theatres then had *capacity houses.* 劇場は当時大入満員だった. ¶a *car house* 車庫. ¶a *chicken house* 養鶏場. ¶a *chop house*=a cheap restaurant 外食店. ¶at the *corner house* 角の家(うち)で. ¶build a *country house* いなかに別荘を建てる. ¶a *cow house* 牛小屋. ¶the *Crew House* クルー卿の邸宅. ¶a *death house* [刑務所などの]死体室. ¶a *drink house* のみ屋. ¶The robbers were using the temple as a *dwelling house.* 盗賊がその寺を住居にしていた. ¶a *dove house* はとの家(巣). ¶the *Eagle House* 《米》 イーグル館(ホテルの名称). ¶an *eating-house* 食堂, 軽食屋. ¶an *export house* 輸出店. ¶a *fertilizer house* 肥料工場. ¶a *finance house* 金融会社. ¶The freighter is a *first class house.* 貨主は一流の店だ. ¶a *first-run movie house* [映画の]第一封切館. ¶a *forcing house* [速成栽培]温室. ¶a *foreign-style house* 洋風の家 ‖ shoddy *foreign-style houses* in Japan 日本のまやかしの洋式家屋. ¶a *frame house* 《米》 木造家屋 ‖ a comfortable six-room *frame house* 感じのよい六間の木造家屋. ¶a *fraternity* (*sonority*) *house* [米大学の]友愛(女子友愛)会館. ¶a *gambling* (=*gaming*) *house* ばくち宿. ¶a *glass house* ガラス製造所; 温室; 写真撮影室(ガラス屋根の) ‖ "People in *glass houses* should not throw stones," the old saying goes. 古諺に「ガラスの家に住む人は石をほうらない」とある. ¶an *incubator house* ふ卵器(ひなの保育箱). ¶an *investment house* 投資信託会社. ¶a *jewelry house* 宝石店. ¶a low *lodging house* 下等のアパート. ¶a *log house* 丸太小屋. ¶a *mad house* 気違い病院. ¶a *mail-order house* 通信販売店. ¶a *movie house* (=theater) 映画館. ¶a "*million dollar*" *picture house* 「百万ドル」映画館. ¶a *muniment house* 証書記録保管所. ¶a first class *music house* 一流楽器店. ¶a *poor house* 貧民院. ¶*poultry houses* and their accompanying yards 養鶏所とその敷地. ¶a *publishing house* 出版屋. ¶draw a *record house* 記録的な大入りをとる. ¶a *red-brick house* 赤れんがの家. ¶a *refreshment house* 喫茶店. ¶a *rendezvous house* 待合. ¶a *residence house* 住宅. ¶a refrigerated *cinema house* 冷房装

置の映画館. ¶a ***rental*** *house* 貸家. ¶a ***rival*** *nouse* 競争店. ¶a ***road*** *house* 《米》 街道筋の旅館. ¶a ***rooming*** *house* アパート ‖ a waterfront ***rooming*** *house* 海(湖・河)岸のアパート. ¶a ***roosting*** *house* 鶏舎. ¶a ***seed*** *house* 種屋. ¶***selling*** *houses* 販売店. ¶a ***slaughter*** *house* 畜殺場. ¶a ***sod*** *house* 切り芝生を積んで壁にした家. ¶a ***sporting*** *house* 《俗》 売春宿, 魔くつ. ¶a ***sporting goods*** *house* 運動具店. ¶A policeman took him to the ***station*** *house*. 《米》 警官が彼を警察に連れて行った. ¶a ***store*** *house* 倉庫. ¶a ***supply*** *house* 用具店. ¶a ***tenement*** *house* むね割長屋. ¶a ***three-family*** *house* 三家族共住の住居. ¶a ***tool*** *house* 道具置場. ¶He has a ***town*** *house* and a country house. 彼は都市といなかに邸を持っている. ¶a great ***trading*** *house* 大貿易商店. ¶The writings of de Sade are now regarded as a ***treasure*** *house* of true observations in the domain of sexual psychology. サド侯の作品は性心理学方面の真の観察として宝庫視されている. ‖ the Arabian Nights, the ***treasure*** *house* of Oriental folklore 東洋の民族宝典アラビア夜話. ¶a ***week-end*** *house* 週末に使う別宅. ¶a ***wholesale*** [***business***] *house* 問屋. ¶a ***20-room*** *house* 二十室ある家屋.

P *around* the *house* 家の周囲に. ¶call ***at*** one's *house* 人の家を訪問する ‖ board ***at*** the *house* その家に下宿する ‖ ***at*** the corner *house* 角の家で ‖ ***at*** the third *house* from the corner 角から三番目の家で. ¶seek ***for*** a *house* 家を探す. 【類】 look about ***for*** a *house* to let. ¶shut up ***in*** a *house* 家の中にとじこもって. ¶***in front of*** the *house* その家の前で. ¶I was ***out of*** the *house* at the time. 私はその時外出していた. ¶I was shown ***over*** the *house*. 私は家中案内された. ¶The bell rang ***through*** the *house*. そのベルの音が家中に鳴り響いた.

P² a *house* ***by*** the river 河畔の住宅 ‖ the *house* ***by*** the sea 海の家. ¶*houses* ***for*** rent (=to let) 《米》 貸家. ¶a *house* ***of*** business 商店 ‖ a *house* ***of*** custody 留置場 ‖ a *house* ***of*** detention 拘置所 ‖ the *house* ***of*** Sir Isaac Pitman and Sons ピットマン卿父子の家族 ‖ a *house* ***of*** ill fame (=prostitution) 魔くつ, 青楼 ‖ the *House* ***of*** Peers (Commons) 上(下)院 ‖ The *house* ***of*** Voigtlander is the oldest optical establishment in the world. フォイクトレンデル商会は世界中で一番古い眼鏡店である. ¶a *house* ***with*** small rooms 小さなへやのある家.

house, *v*. 家に入れる, 宿らす, 庇護する.

M a people ***abundantly*** *housed*, fed, clothed, salaried and taxed 衣食住から給料も豊かで, おまけに税金まで多い国民(アメリカ). ¶***safely*** *housed* from the inclement weather 険悪な天気から安全な家に庇護(ご)されて.

P The library is *housed* ***in*** a fine building. その図書館にはりっぱな建物がある. 【類】 St. Paul's School is now *housed* ***in*** a splendid building at Hammersmith. ‖ be *housed* ***in*** an Army barrack 陸軍兵舎に収容される. 【類】 homeless people *housed* ***in*** barracks.

household, *n*. 家族, 家庭, 一家内.

V He ***aroused*** the *household*. 彼は家族の者を起した. ¶***arrange*** the *household* 家庭を整理する. ¶***direct*** the *household* 家庭の采配を振る. ¶***manage*** one's *household* その家庭を管理する. ¶It is the duty of a mistress to ***run*** a *household* effectively. 効果的に一家を経営するのは主婦の務だ.

V² late in the evening after his *household* had ***gone*** to sleep 夜ふけて家族のものが眠りについてから.

Q a ***Christian*** *household* キリスト教徒の家庭. ¶***No*** *household* is complete without a copy of the book. 戸毎に一本を備うべきだ. ¶He was brought up in a ***temeperate*** *household*. 彼は禁酒の家庭に育った. ¶a ***well-ordered*** (=***well-regulated***) *household* 整とんした家庭.

P work ***in*** a *housefold* 内職をやる. ¶the members ***of*** a *household* 一家の人々.

housekeeper, *n*. 家政婦.

Q a ***frugal*** (=***thrifty***) *housekeeper* 節約な家政婦. ¶make a ***good*** *housekeeper* いい奥さんの質を備えている.

housekeeping, *n*. 家計, 家政, 世帯.

V ***break*** (=***wind***) ***up*** *housekeeping* 家をたたむ. ¶***do*** the *housekeeping* 家政をつかさどる. ¶A better present for a young wife ***setting up*** *housekeeping* it would be hard to find. 世帯を持つ若い妻君にとってこれ以上の贈物はないだろう. ¶We ***started*** *housekeeping*, two in family with a servant. われわれは一家二人で召使を一人おいて世帯を持ち始めた.

Q ***light*** *housekeeping* 手軽な世帯. ¶the School of ***Scientific*** *Housekeeping* in New York City ニューヨークの家政学校.

housetop, *n*. 屋根, 屋頂.

P He preached naturalism ***from*** the *housetop*. 彼は声を大にして自然主義を唱道した. ‖ cry ***from*** the *housetops* 公衆に呼び掛ける. ¶The sun was beginning to catch ***in*** the *housetop*. 太陽が屋根にさし始めた.

housewarming, *n*. 引越祝い, 新宅開きの祝い.

V ***give*** a *housewarming* 新宅開きの祝いをやる.

housewife, *n*. 主婦, 家婦, 世話女房.

Q an ***orderly*** *housewife* きちょうめんな主婦. ¶***practical*** *housewives* 世話女房. ¶a ***provident*** *housewife* 心がけのよい主婦. ¶a ***servantless*** *housewife* 召使をおかない主婦.

housework, *n*. 家の仕事, 家庭経済.

V ***do*** *housework* 家事をやる. 【類】 My wife is ***doing*** her *housework* as usual. / ***do*** all the *housework* herself.

Q ***light*** *housework* 楽な家事. ¶***routine*** *housework* きまりきった家事.

housing, *n*. 住宅.

Q ***civilized*** *housing* 文化住宅. ¶***insanitary*** *housing* 衛生的でない住居.

Q² ***dependent*** *housing* 〘軍〙 家族の住宅. ¶***family*** *housing* 家族の住宅. ¶***off-campus*** *housing* 学外の住宅. ¶***rental*** *housing* 借家住宅. ¶***student*** *housing* 学生の住居. ¶***troop*** *housing* 軍隊の宿泊. ¶the dismantling and re-use of ***surplus war*** *housing* 戦時余剰家屋の一部取りこわしや転用.

hover, *v*. 空を舞う, 飛しょうする, 徘回する.

M *hover* ***high*** out of sight 高く舞い上って見えなくなる.

P *hover* ***about*** a place ある場所を徘回する. ¶The mercury *hovers* ***around*** 100°. 寒暖計は百度を上下する. ¶*hover* ***between*** life and death 生死の境をさまよう. ¶Butterflies *hover* ***from*** flower to flower. ちょうは花から花へと飛び回る. ¶*hover* ***over*** a stove ストーヴにかじりつく ‖ *hover* ***over*** the city 市の上空を飛びまわる ‖ The spirit of youth *hover* ***over*** him. 青年時代の元気がまだ彼に残っている.

how, *ad*. いかにして, どういう訳で.

P *how* ***about*** the matter of ...? ...の件はどうなりましたか.

O He did not know *how* to spell this word. 彼はこの語のつづりを知らなかった. ¶*How* on earth can I do such a thing? 一体どうして私にそんなことができましょう. ¶Hello! *How* have you been since? やあ, その後元気かい.

howl, *n*. ほえ声, 怒号, うなり声.

V The dog ***gave*** a deep *howl*. 犬が遠ぼえをした. ¶***raise*** a *howl* 悲鳴をあげる. ¶The child ***set up*** a *howl*. 子供がわっとわめき立てた.

howl, *n*. ほえる, うなる; たけり騒ぐ.

M *howl* ***down*** a speaker 怒号して弁士を黙らす. ¶The child *howled* ***horribly***. 子供が火のつくように泣いた.

Q² a ***calamity*** *howler* 《米俗》 苦労性の女.

P Many *howled* ***at*** his idea. この考えを罵倒(ば)したものが多かった. ¶The elements were *howling* ***around*** her. 風波がその船の回りに狂いたけっていた. ¶*howl* a speaker ***off*** the platform 弁士をどなって引っこめる.

hub, *n*. 中心, 中枢.

P China considered herself the *hub* ***around*** which the other nations revolved. 中国は自国をその周囲に他の国民が回転する中心だと考えていた. ¶***up to*** the *hub* 深くはまり込んで.

P² the *hub* ***of*** the universe. 万物の中心.

hubbub, *n*. がやがや.

P² the *hubbub* ***of*** life 人生のてんやわんや.

huddle, *v*. ぞんざいにやる, 早く片づける; ちぢこまる.

M *huddle* ***together*** for warmth 暖をとろうと抱き合う.

M² *huddle* ***on*** one's clothes 急いで衣服を着る. ¶*huddle* ***over*** one's work 仕事をなぐる(ぞんざいにやる). ¶*huddle* one's job ***through*** 仕事をさっさと片づける. ¶be *huddled* (=huddle oneself) ***up*** in bed 丸くなって寝る ‖ The British government *huddled* ***up*** a peace with Germany. 英政府はドイツと急ぎ平和条約を結んだ.

hue, *n*. 色, 色彩; 色合.

Q a ***blackish*** *hue* 黒ずんだ色. ¶a winter coat with a ***blackish, warm*** *hue* 黒ずんだ暖かそうな色のオーバー. ¶a ***gorgeous*** *hue* はなやかな色合. ¶a ***healthy*** *hue* 健康そうな血色. ¶a ***hectic*** *hue* 肺病のような赤ら顔. ¶see the future in an ***optimistic*** and ***roseate*** *hue* 楽観的で快活な色彩の中に将来を考える. ¶***subdued*** *hues* じみな色合. ¶a ***warm*** *hue* 暖い感じの色彩, 暖色.

Q² *rainbow hues* にじの色合.

hue, *n.* 叫び声, 非難の声.

V *despatch* a *hue* and cry after ... ...の後からごうごうたる攻撃の叫び声をかける ¶His political opponents *took up* the *hue* and cry. 彼の政敵は雷同して彼を非難した.

hug, *n.* 抱きしめ.

V *Give* me a *hug*, darling. 私を抱いてよ, ねえ.

hug, *v.* 抱く.

P They *hugged* each other *for* the victory. 勝利でみんな抱き合って喜んだ.

hum, *n.* 雑音, がやがやの声.

V The dusk came slowly down, enveloping the city and *quieting* the *hum* of day noises. 夕やみが徐々に迫ってきて町を包み日中の騒々しい声を静めた.

hum, *v.* ぶんぶん鳴る.

M The sewing machine was *busily humming.* ミシンがいそがし気に動いていた.

M² *hum along* [車が]びゅーと走る. ¶Bees are *humming around* from flower to flower. みつばちは花から花へぶんぶん飛び回っている.

human, *a.* 人の, 人間の, 人生の.

M He is *more human* in thinking than his father. 彼は父よりは考え方が人間的だ.

O To err is *human*, to forgive divine. 誤るは人, これを許すは神.

humanitarian, *n.* 人道主義者, 人道家.

Q a *sentimental humanitarian* 多感な人道家.

humanity, *n.* 人間性, 人情, 人道; 人間, 人類.

V a question *affecting humanity* 人道問題. ¶maladies that *afflict humanity* 人類を悩ます病気. ¶They did nothing to *benefit humanity* at large. 彼らは人類一般に利益を与えたことは何もなかった. ¶*disgrace humanity* 人類の名を辱しめる. ¶*elevate humanity* 人類を向上させる. ¶*serve humanity* 人類に奉仕する.

V² *Humanity progresses* very slowly. 人類は進歩が緩慢だ.

Q *afflicted humanity* 悩める人々. ¶a beach with its masses of *bathing-suit-clad humanity* 水着の人の群のいる海岸. ¶*laboring humanity* 労働社会. ¶the great mass of *obscure, suffering, inarticulate humanity* 身分低く苦難に悩み政治に参加していない人間の大群. ¶*oppressed humanity* 下積になっている人々. ¶the odor of *packed humanity* 群集のいきれ. ¶a mass of *perspiring humanity* 汗だらだらな人々の群. ¶out of *pure humanity* 全くの慈愛心から. ¶*suffering humanity* 苦難の人々. ¶*surging humanity* 波のように押寄せる群集.

P a crime *against humanity* 人道に反する罪. ¶act in the interests *of humanity* 人道のために働く ‖ in the name *of humanity* 人道の名において. ¶an outrage *on humanity* 人道のじゅうりん. ¶contrary *to humanity* 人道に反して. ¶treat animals *with humanity* 動物を愛護する.

humanization, *n.* 人間化, 教化, 感化.

V a process of *increasing humanization* 教化を増す方法.

humble, *v.* 卑しくする, 屈服する.

P *humble* oneself *before* one's creditors 債権者の前でぺこぺこする. ¶be *humbled to* nothingness 面目丸つぶれにされる ‖ be crushed and *humbled to* the dust [比ゆ的] 高い鼻をへし折られてぺしゃんこにされる.

humbug, *n.* ごまかし; ぺてん師.

O a *pretentious humbug* 正直者を装うぺてん師.

P² a *humbug in* art いかもの芸術家.

humdrum, *n.* 単調, 退屈.

P dissatisfied *with humdrum* 退屈で弱って.

humidity, *n.* 湿度.

Q *relative humidity* 比較湿度.

humiliate, *v.* へこませる.

M feel *utterly humiliated* すっかりへこまされる.

humiliating, *a.* 屈辱的な, 不面目の, 恥ずかしい.

P We feel this as *humiliating to* the national pride. われわれはこのことを国民の不面目と感じる.

humiliation, *n.* 屈辱, 屈従.

V *bring humiliation* upon ... ...の上に屈辱を招く. ¶*escape* this crowning *humiliation* この第一の屈辱を免かれる. ¶he *has* the *humiliation* of ... 彼は...という恥ずかしい目にあっている.

Q a *lasting humiliation* 末代の恥辱. ¶a *national humiliation* 国辱.

P We cannot sit down quietly *under* that *humiliation.* われわれはその屈辱を受けて黙っていられない.

humility, *n.* けんそん, 卑下.

Q approach him with *abject humility* ぺこぺこ頭を下げて彼に近づく. ¶*base humility* 卑屈. ¶*haughty humility* 口ではけんそん心では高慢, 卑下自慢. ¶*Intellectual humility* is essential for real research work. 知的謙虚は本当の研究にはなくてならないものだ.

P *in humility* 卑下して. ¶*with* profound respect and *humility* 深い尊敬とけんそんとをもって.

humo[u]r, *n.* 気質, 気性, 気分; 滑けい(ユーモア); 〖生物〗液体.

V The *humor* of the evening was *contributed* by his laugh-provoking little speech. その晩は彼のユーモアのあるちょっとした演説のために一座が笑い興じた. ¶Every man *has* his *humour.* 〖諺〗十人十色. ¶rise above annoyances and *keep over* good *humor* 困難に際し超然として元気にやって行く. ¶He failed to *see* the *humor* of the comment. 彼はその言葉のユーモアを解しかねた. ¶His *humor* is *tinged* with grimness. 彼のしゃれにはすご味がある.

V² His good *humor returned.* 彼はきげんが直った. ¶when the *humor takes* me 気が向くと.

Q He came home in a very *bad humor.* 彼はたいへん不気げんで帰宅した. ¶*cheap humor* だじゃれ. ¶*crystalline humor* 〖生物〗[目の]水晶体. ¶say in *dry humor* まじめな顔をして冗談を言う. ¶*fantastic humor* へんてこなこっけい. ¶He returned home in a rather *glum humor.* 彼はやや不きげんで帰宅した. ¶in a *good humor* 上きげんで ‖ send him away in *good humor* 気持よく彼を送り出してやる. ¶*grim humor* すご味のあるユーモア. ¶*grotesque humor* 怪奇味のあるユーモア. ¶in a very *ill humor* 非常な不きげんで. ¶*intellectual humor* 知性のユーモア. ¶*ironical* but *kind humor* 皮肉だが親切なユーモア. ¶*lambent humor* 上品なユーモア. ¶words spoken in *lead humor* 重々しい気分で言った言葉. ¶his *mordant humor* 彼の毒舌的なしゃれ. ¶I see *no humor* in your tricks. 君のやり口はどうもおもしろくないね. ¶*original* and *witty humor* 目新しい機知に富んだユーモア. ¶*pure* and *spontaneous* and *irresistible humor* 純真で, 自然で, つい引きこまれるユーモア. ¶*Rabelaisian humor* ラブレー式の(大味な)ユーモア. ¶*racy humor* きびきびしたユーモア. ¶*robust humor* 健康なユーモア. ¶*rollicking humor* ふざけ散らすしゃれ. ¶*simple humor* 単純なユーモア. ¶be in *sour humor* 不きげんである. ¶say in *sourgrape humor* ... ...と負け惜しみを言う. ¶with *unconscious humor*, he insisted that ... ...そのユーモアを意識せずに...と主張した.

P Every man [is] *in* his *humor.* なくて七癖. ‖ We were then not *in* a *humor* to appreciate. そのときわれわれは鑑賞する気分になっていなかった. ‖ He is *in* no *humor* for supper (conversation). 彼は夕飯(など)に対して気乗りがしない. 【類】They are not *in* the *humor* for work. ‖ Quit your joking! I'm *in* no *humor.* 冗談はよしてよ, 私おこってんのよ. ¶frequent flashes *of humor* 機知縦横 ‖ He has no sense *of humor.* 彼はユーモアを解しない. ‖ There was a grain *of humor* in his remark. 彼の言葉には幾分のユーモアがあった. 【類】The situation was not without a touch *of humor.* ¶He was a little *out of humor.* 彼は少し不きげんだった ‖ You may take it up with pleasure when you're *out of humor.* ふさいでいるときそれを見るときげんが直るよ. ¶The story is told *with* much *humor* and grace of style. その物語はユーモアたっぷりで文体も上品だ.

humorist, *n.* ユーモアのうまい人.

Q² a *flashlight humorist* ひらめくように冗談が口にでる人.

humorous, *a.* こっけいな.

M *irresistibly humorous* たまらなくこっけいな.

hump, *n.* [背の]隆肉, 背隆起.

P *with* a *hump* on his back 背中にこぶが一つついて.

humpback, *n.* せむし, ねこ背.

P a person *with* a *humpback* せむしの人.

hundred, *n.* 百, 百個.

V *involve hundreds* of duties 無数の色々な職務がふくまれる.

Q I only need six more to have a *full hundred.* あと六個あると百になる.

P They are sold *by* the *hundred.* それは百いくらで売る. 【類】People are flocking *by hundreds* to visit the place. ‖ They can be counted *by hundreds.* それは百をもって数えられる. ¶one *in* a *hundred* 百人の中で一人 ‖ The applications are arriving *in hundreds.* 願書はなん百とやってくる. ‖ twenty *in* every *hundred* 百につき二十ずつ ‖ Examples of ... might be quoted *in hundreds.* ...の例は何百とあげられる. ¶count from one *to* a *hundred* and backward 一から百まで数え次に逆に(百から)数える. ¶*under* a *hundred* 百以下.

P² *hundreds of* soldiers なん百という兵士.【類】*hundreds of* specimens (標本) of butterflies ‖ *hundreds of* thousands of people (spectators).

hunger, *n.* 飢餓, 空腹; 渇望, 欲.

V ***allay*** one's *hunger* 空腹をみたす. ¶***appease*** one's *hunger* 腹をこしらえる. ¶***gratify*** the *hunger* for literature 文学欲を満足させる. ¶***quicken*** *hunger* 腹をすかせる. ¶He devoured book after book to ***satisfy*** his mental *hunger*. 彼は知的渇望を満足させるため一冊また一冊とむさぼり読んだ. ‖ ***satisfy*** one's *hunger* on ... ...を食べて空腹をみたす. ¶***stay*** *hunger* 空腹を支える. ¶*hunger* ***whetted*** by mountain air 山の空気でそそられた食欲.

V² *Hunger* ***stared*** me in the face. 私は飢餓に直面した.

Q A ***great*** *hunger* for riches came upon him. 彼は強い財産欲にとらわれた. ¶***intellectual*** *hunger* 知識欲.

Q² satisfy the ***curiosity*** *hunger* 好奇心を満足させる. ¶***earth*** *hunger* 地所を持ちたい病, 領土拡張欲. ¶***excitement*** *hunger* スリルを求める欲望. ¶***General*** *Hunger* 飢餓将軍(食糧補給難の敵をひやかして).

P pressed ***by*** *hunger* 飢餓に迫られて. ¶die ***of*** (=***from***) *hunger* 餓死する. ¶faint ***with*** *hunger* 空腹のため倒れそうになって.

P² a *hunger* ***after*** knowledge 知識欲. ¶a *hunger* ***for*** reputation (fame) 名声へのあこがれ.【類】"The *hunger* ***for*** brotherhood is at the bottom of the unrest of the modern civilized world," said the great English painter of ideas—G.F. Watts. 「し.

O *Hunger* is the best sauce.〖諺〗すき腹にまずいものな

hunger, *v.* 飢える; 渇望する, 切望する.

P *hunger* ***after*** luxury ぜいたくを渇望する. ¶*hunger* ***for*** food (water, news, knowledge) 食物(など)を欲する.

hungry, *a.* 飢えている, 腹がすいて.

M ***ravenously*** *hungry* 猛烈に腹のへった. ¶***terribly*** *hungry* 非常にひもじい.

P *hungry* ***after*** wealth 富を渇望して. ¶He is *hungry* ***for*** publicity. 彼は自己宣伝に夢中である.【類】be *hungry* ***for*** honor (glory) / A Liverpool cable despatch in a trade journal reads "The world is *hungry* ***for*** cotton and cotton goods."

hunt, *n.* 狩猟, 捜索, あさり. 「つける.

Q find a job after a ***long*** *hunt* 長い間求職のあげく職を見

Q² a ***lion*** (***tiger***) *hunt* しし(とら)狩り. ¶Long ***house*** *hunt* is ended. 長い間の住宅さがしは終った. ¶a ***paper*** *hunt*〖ゲーム〗紙きれさがし. ¶a ***wild boar*** *hunt* いのしし狩り. ¶stage a ***treasure*** *hunt* 宝さがしをやる.

P ***during*** a *hunt* 狩猟中. ¶take part ***in*** a *hunt* 狩猟に加わる ‖ ***in*** our *hunt* for the beautiful in nature 自然美を求めて. ¶a detective ***on*** the *hunt* 罪人捜索の探偵.

P² a bookworm ***on*** the *hunt* 本屋あさりの愛書家.

hunt, *v.* 狩る, あさる, 捜す.

M *hunt* ***out*** 狩りだす, 探しだす. ¶*hunt* ***out*** facts on ... ...に関する事実を捜し集める ‖ *hunt* ***out*** violators 犯人をさがし出す ‖ *hunt* ***out*** the knowledge in literature 文献の知識を調べ出す.

M² *hunt* ***down*** the terrorists テロリスト(暴力革命者)を追いつめる ‖ The stag was *hunted* ***down*** in the long run. そのしかは追いつめられて遂につかまった.【類】The offender (犯人) was finally *hunted* ***down***. ¶*hunt* ***up*** words in a dictionary 語を辞書で捜しだす ‖ *hunt* ***up*** old records 古い記録を渉猟する ‖ *hunt* [***up***] the whole house ***for*** ... ...見つけるため家中を捜がす.

P *hunt* ***for*** capital 資本を求める ‖ *hunt* ***for*** the missing property ゆくえ不明の所有物を捜す.【類】*hunt* ***for*** fleas / *hunt* in vain ***for*** a job / go about *hunting* ***for*** a job / *hunt* ***for*** a house to let / *hunt* ***for*** something to eat. ¶The game is being *hunted* ***to*** the verge of extinction. 獲物が狩り立てられて絶滅しかけている.

hunter, *n.* 狩猟者; 探求者, 追求者.

Q The leopard is a ***skilful*** *hunter* ひょうはうまく(えじきの)獲物を捕える. ¶a ***trigger-happy*** *hunter* 射撃の上手な狩猟家.

Q² be pestered by ***autograph*** *hunters* サイン狂に悩まされる.【類】He was besieged by ***autograph*** *hunters* (サイン攻めにあった). ¶a surging mob of ***bargain*** *hunters* 見切品あさりに押し寄せる大群集. ¶a ***big-game*** *hunter* 猛獣狩猟家. ¶a ***book*** *hunter* 漁書家. ¶a ***fortune*** *hunter* 金が目当てで妻を捜す人. ¶***head*** *hunters* of Formosa 台湾の食人種. ¶an ***ivory*** *hunter* 文学・映画・競技の天才発見業者(米国). ¶a ***job*** *hunter* 求職者. ¶a ***professional rat*** *hunter* 本職のねずみ捕り. ¶a ***souvenir*** *hunter* おみやげあさりの人々. ¶a ***spy*** *hunter* スパイを捜す人.

P hungry ***like*** a *hunter* 猛烈にお腹がへった.

P² a *hunter* ***after*** glory 名誉を追う者. ¶He is a *hunter* ***by*** pursuit. 彼の生業は猟師.

hunting, *n.* 狩り, 狩猟.

V ***do*** the *hunting* for ... ...を求めてさがし回る.

Q² go on ***hare*** *hunting* うさぎ狩りに行く. ¶***house*** *hunting* 貸家捜し. ¶***place*** (=***job***) *hunting* 職さがし. ¶***whale*** *hunting* 捕鯨.

P divert oneself ***in*** *hunting* 狩猟で気晴しをする. ¶He is fond ***of*** *hunting*. 彼は猟が好きだ.

O Let us go *hunting*. 猟に行こう.

hunting-ground, *n.* 狩猟場.

Q Kanda is a ***happy*** *hunting-ground* for second-hand books. 神田は古本を捜すのに良い場所だ.

hurdles, *n. pl.*〖競技〗障害物(ハードル).

Q the ***high*** (***low***) *hurdles* ハイ(ロー)ハードル.

P jump (=leap) ***over*** the *hurdles* [in a race] ハードルを越える.

hurl, *v.* 投てきする, 強く投げる.

M The insults were *hurled* ***back and forth***. 互いに侮辱の言葉を投げ合った(泥試合).

M² For a month they go in for German, then something *hurls* them ***off*** to French. 一カ月ほどドイツ語をやったがちょっとしたことで急にフランス語にくら変えしてしまう(三日坊主).

P They are *hurling* reproaches ***at*** each other. 彼らは互に非難の言葉を浴びせ合っている. ‖ *hurl* a stone ***at*** ... ...に石を投げつける. ¶She *hurled* herself ***into*** the depths of the well. 彼女はその井戸に身を投げた. ¶She *hurled* herself ***on*** her enemy, the dog. 彼女(小鳥)は敵である犬に自分からぶつかって行った.

hurling, *n.* 投げること.

Q ***underhand*** *hurling* in baseball 野球の下手投げ.

hurrah, *int.* 万歳.

P *hurrah* ***for*** ...! ...万歳, ...がん張れ.

hurricane, *n.* 烈風, 暴風, 台風.

V ***had*** a *hurricane* at ...で暴風に会った.

V² A *hurricane* ***hit*** the eastern coast of the United States. ハリケーンが米東海岸に襲来した.

Q A ***severe*** *hurricane* passed over here. 猛烈な暴風が当地を通過した.

P The ship was sunk ***by*** a *hurricane*. その船は暴風で沈んだ. ¶The ship is reported foundered ***in*** a *hurricane*. 同船は暴風で沈没したと言われる.

O It blew a *hurricane*. 暴風が吹きまくった.

hurry, *n.* 早急, そう忙, あせり.

Q I'm in a ***great*** *hurry*. 私は非常に急いでいる. ‖ You should not be in too ***great*** a *hurry* to do so. 余りせいてやってはいけない. ¶Is there any ***immediate*** *hurry?* 急いでしなければなりませんか. ¶I am in ***no*** *hurry* for it. 私はそれを急いではいない.

P We are all ***in*** a *hurry* today. われわれは皆きょうは急いでいる. ‖ Nothing is ever done ***in*** a *hurry*.〖諺〗せいてはことをし損じる.【類】Do not be ***in*** a *hurry* to succeed. / ***in*** my *hurry* / Why are you ***in*** such a *hurry?* ‖ ***in*** the *hurry* of life 急がしい人生では. ¶***owing to*** the *hurry* of business 急ぎの仕事なので.

P² There is no *hurry* ***about*** it. それは急がんでよい.

O What's your (=the) *hurry?* どうしてそんなに急ぐんだ.

hurry, *v.* 急ぐ, あせる; 急がす, 促す.

M I must *hurry* ***away*** to catch the train. 私は汽車に間に合うように急がねばならない. ¶*hurry* ***back*** from Europe ヨーロッパから急いで帰る ‖ *hurry* ***back*** for ... ...をとりに急いで戻る ‖ *Hurry* ***back*** to work, boys! [一休みしてから]みんな仕事にかかれ.【類】*hurry* ***back*** to ... by plane ¶*Hurry* ***forward*** all you possibly can. できるだけ急いでくれ. ‖ Producers are *hurrying* ***forward*** supplies. 生産業者は製品を急造している. ¶*hurry* ***home*** 急ぎ帰宅する. ¶*hurry* ***out*** into the garden 急いで庭にとび出す ‖ *hurry* ***out*** into the storm あらしの中に飛込む.【類】*hurry* ***out*** (=***off***) to school. ¶*hurry quickly* through a disagreeable task いやな仕事を手早くやってしまう. ¶*hurry upstairs* (*downstairs*) 急いで階段をあがる(降りる).

M² I *hurried along* for fear I should be late. 遅れないように急いで行った. ‖ *hurry along* together 一緒に急いで行く. ¶We have no need to *hurry off*. 急いで出かける必要はない. ‖ *hurry* one's clothes *off* (*on*) 衣服を急いでぬぐ(着る) ‖ our conductor *hurried* us *off* to when ... ...車掌が...したとき急いでわれわれを下車させた. ¶Here comes our bus! Let's *hurry on*. そらバスだ. 早く乗ろう. ¶*hurry over* to ... 急いで...へ行く. ¶I'll *hurry round* to you. 急いで君のところに回ろう. ¶make a person *hurry up* to ... 人を...に急がせる.

P *hurry into* a car 急いで車に乗り込む. ¶*hurry on* (*off*) a train 列車に急いで乗る(降りる). ¶*hurry on* the business 仕事を急いで運ぶ. ¶*hurry over* one's meal あわてて食事をする. ¶*hurry through* (=do hastily) one's work 急いでその仕事を片づける. ¶*hurry to* the rescue 急いで救助におもむく. ¶*Hurry with* my order, please. 僕の注文を急いでくれ. 【類】*hurry with* one's task (home work).

hurt, *n.* けが; 損害.

V *do hurt* 傷つける ‖ it would *do* no *hurt* to you to ... ...しても君が害を受けることはあるまい. ¶He *received* no *hurt* whatever. 彼には何のけがもなかった.

Q a *bad hurt* ひどいけが. ¶*Hurts* are *slight*. けがは軽微である. 「して片輪になっていた.

P His right arm was lame *from* a *hurt*. 彼の右腕はけがを

P² a *hurt from* a blow 打撲傷. ¶*hurt in* the wide sense of the term 広い意味での損害. ¶a *hurt on* the forehead 額の傷.

hurt, *v.* けがさせる, 傷つける, 感情を傷つける; 痛む, 痛める.

M It *hurts* me *awfully* to cough. せきをするとひどく痛む. ¶*badly hurt* ひどく痛む. ¶It *hurts bitterly*. 激しく痛む. ¶though *deeply hurt* ひどく感情を害したが. ¶*hurt greatly* 非常に感情を傷つけられて. ¶He was *seriously hurt*. 彼は重傷を負った.

P *hurt at* one's conduct (word) 人の行動(など)に感情を害して. ¶He was *hurt in* a traffic accident. 彼は交通事故でけがをした.

O *hurt* one's feelings 人の感情を害する. ¶Did I *hurt* you? お気にさわりましたか.

hurt, *a.* 負傷した.

P get *hurt on* the head (*in* the leg).

hurtful, *a.* 害のある, 有害の.

P *hurtful to* health 健康に有害な.

husband, *n.* 夫, 良人, 亭主.

V *belittle* one's *husband* before others 夫を人前でけなす. ¶She failed to *catch* a *husband*. 彼女は夫を持ちそこねた. ¶*deceive* one's *husband* 情夫をこしらえる. ¶*divorce* one's *husband* 夫と離婚する. ¶*get* (=*obtain*) a *husband* 亭主を持つ. ¶They say she has *had* four *husbands*. 彼女は亭主を四人も変えたそうだ. ¶*humor* a *husband* 亭主のきげんをとる. ¶to *join* her *husband* in Paris パリーで彼女の夫と一緒になるために. ¶They *lost* their *husbands* in the service of the State. 彼女たちは国家のために夫を失った. ¶*rejoin* her *husband* 再び夫と一緒になる. ¶*take* a *husband* 亭主を持つ.

Q a *brutal husband* 残忍な夫. ¶a *devoted husband* 愛妻家. ¶a *domesticated husband* 家庭的な夫. ¶a *fiendish husband* 悪魔のような夫. ¶a *generous husband* 寛大な夫. ¶a *half-sober husband* なま酔の夫. ¶a *henpecked husband* 恐妻家. ¶an *ideal husband* 理想的な夫. ¶an *irreproachable husband* 申分のない夫. ¶a *jealous husband* やきもちやきの亭主. ¶a *second husband* 第二の夫. ¶a *true* and *loving husband* 忠実でやさしい夫. ¶an *unselfish husband* わがままでない夫. ¶a *violent husband* 手荒い夫. ¶her *would-be husband* 彼女の夫になろうとする人.

Q² an *apron husband* 世話やき亭主. ¶Mrs. Lindbergh and her *aviator husband* 飛行士のリンディとその奥さん. ¶her *movie-star husband* 彼女の映画スターである夫. ¶her *sportsman husband* 彼女のスポーツマンの夫.

P dwell together *as husband* and wife 夫婦として同せいする. ¶work *without* a *husband* 亭主を持たずに働く.

husbandry, *n.* 農業.

Q *ill husbandry* 経済のへたなこと.

Q² *animal husbandry* 畜産. ¶*dairy husbandry* 酪農業. ¶*garden husbandry* 園芸農. ¶*poultry husbandry* (=keeping, culture *or* breeding) 養鶏(など)業.

P *swine husbandry* 養豚.

hush, *n.* 無言, 沈黙; 静寂.

V *break* the *hush* 沈黙を破る. ¶A *hush fell* over the ship. 船は静まりかえった. 【類】A *hush fell* over the onlookers.

hush, *v.* 静かにさせる, だまらす, 静める.

M *hush up* the affair 事件をもみ消す. 【類】*hush up* a scandal / The matter was *hushed up*, and all the servants were forbidden to mention it.

P *hush* a baby *to* sleep [うるさい]赤ん坊を寝つかせる.

hushmoney, *n.* 口留め金, 内済金.

V *extort hushmoney* 口留め金を強制する.

husk, *n.* 皮, から, もみ.

V *remove husk* from rice paddy by pounding もみをついてからを去る. 【類】*remove husk* from (=husk) Iudian corn (とうもろこし).

P rice *in* the *husk* もみ.

hustle, *v.* 乱暴に押す; 《口語》元気よくやる.

M *hustle* a person (thing) *aside* 人(物)を横へ押しつける.

M² *hustle along* through the crowd 人ごみを乱暴にかき分けて進む. ¶*hustle around* あばれ回る. ¶He *hustled* it *through*. 彼はそれをさっさとやってのけた. ¶*hustle up* one's work 仕事をさっさと片づける.

P They *hustled* the tramps *out of* town. みんなで浮浪者を町から追い出した. ¶*hustle through* a street 人を押しのけて通行する. ¶Mother *hustled* her baby *to* bed. 母は無理に赤ん坊を寝かしつけた.

hustler, *n.* 急がしい人.

P² a *hustler after* food がつがつしている人. ¶a *hustler for* publicity 宣伝屋.

hut, *n.* 小屋, 草舎, 掘立小屋.

V *knock up* (*down*) a *hut* 小屋を急造する(とりこわす).

Q There were a few stray *fisherman's huts* along the beach. 海岸には二三の漁師の家が散在していた. ¶a *Robinson Crusoey hut* [ロビンソンクルーソー式の]そまつな小屋.

Q² a *bamboo hut* 竹造りの小屋. ¶a *one-room log hut* 一室しかない丸太小屋. ¶a *Quonset hut* 〖米軍〗かまぼこ形兵舎.

P a *hut for* pilgrims 巡礼者を泊める小屋.

hybrid, *n.* 混血児, 雑種.

P a *hybrid between* ... and ... ...と...とのあいのこ.

hydrant, *n.* 給水せん.

Q² a *fire hydrant* 消火せん.

hydrogen, *n.* 〖化〗水素.

Q *heavy hydrogen* 重水素.

hygiene, *n.* 衛生, 衛生法.

Q *mental hygiene* 精神衛生. ¶*Public* and *private hygienes* are of a negative nature—that is to say, they consist not in doing something for the health, but in not doing anything to compromise health. 公衆並に個人衛生は消極的である—すなわち健康を増進するためにするのでなく健康を害しないようにすることである. ¶*sexual hygiene* 性の衛生.

Q² *child hygiene* 児童衛生. ¶*factory hygiene* 工場衛生. ¶*maternity* and *infant hygiene* 産婦乳児衛生. ¶*school hygiene* 学校衛生.

hymn, *n.* 賛美歌, 賛歌.

V Chimes *pealed forth* the national *hymn*. 鐘楽が国歌を奏し出した. ¶*play* the national *hymn* 国歌を演奏する. ¶The birds *sang* their vesper *hymn*. 鳥は夕べの聖歌を歌った. ‖ The choir *sang* the *hymn* beginning "Heirs of unending life." 合唱隊は「尽きぬ命(いのち)の世つぎ人」で始まる賛美歌を歌った.

Q² a *Buddhist hymn* 和賛.

P² a *hymn in* honor of ... ...を賛美する歌. ¶a *hymn of* praise to God 神を賛美する歌.

hyperbole, *n.* 誇張.

Q a *foolish hyperbole* 愚かな誇張.

P *without hyperbole* 掛値なしに, 正しく.

hyper[a]esthesia, *n.* 神経過敏.

V *cultivate hyper[a]esthesia* 神経をますます過敏にする.

hyphen, *n.* 連字符, ハイフン.

P The words should be separated *by* a *hypen*. その語はハイフンで離すのが本当だ. ¶They are usually written *with* a *hyphen*. それらの語はハイフンを付けて書くのが普通だ.

hypnosis, *n.* 催眠, 催眠状態.

P a person *under hypnosis* 催眠状態にある人.

hypnotism, *n.* 催眠.

Q² *mass hypnotism* 集団催眠.

hypochondria, *n.* 憂うつ症.

V He *developed* serious *hypochondria.* 彼は病勢が募ってひどい憂うつ症に陥った.

hypocrisy, *n.* 偽善, 偽言, ねこかぶり.

Q To pretend otherwise would be ***mere*** *hypocrisy.* それと違った風(ふ)をするとそれはほんとの偽善になるだろう.

hypocrite, *n.* 偽善者, 偽君子, ねこかぶり.

V ***expose*** a *hypocrite* 偽善者をあばく. ¶***play*** the *hypocrite* ねこをかぶる.

Q a ***canting*** *hypocrite* 説教めいた物言いをする偽君子.

hypothecate, *v.* 抵当に入れる.

P *hypothecate* it ***at*** a pawnshop それを入質する.

hypothesis, *n.* 仮説, おく説.

V Notwithstanding the absence of facts, a fairly reasonable *hypothesis* can be ***built up.*** 材料の事実は得られないがかなり正当な仮説を立てることができる. ¶***confute*** a *hypothesis* 仮説を論ばくする. ¶***disprove*** a *hypothesis* 仮説を非難攻撃する. ¶***suggest*** a *hypothesis* 仮説を提言する. ¶***venture*** a *hypothesis* 仮説を立てて見る. ¶***verify*** a *hypothesis* 仮説を実証する.

Q archaeologists so fertile in ***ingenious*** *hypotheses* 仮説をたてるのがすこぶる巧妙な考古学者たち. ¶Two *hypotheses* are ***possible.*** 二つの仮説が立てられる. ¶Well, we will take it as a ***working*** *hypothesis* for want of a better. では他にこれというものもないからその説を根拠にして論じて見よう. ¶This *hypothesis* is quite ***untenable.*** この仮説は全く取るに足らない.

P ***on*** (=***upon***) this *hypothesis* he experimented with ... この仮説にもとずいて彼は...を試みた ‖ ***on*** the *hypothesis* that ... ...という仮説にもとずいて.

hysterics, hysteria, *n.* ヒステリー.

V ***go off*** (=***fall***) into *hysteria* (hysterics) ヒステリー症状を起す.

P almost ***in*** *hysterics* (=hysterical) ほとんどヒステリーになって. ¶She is affected ***with*** *hysterics.* 彼女はヒステリーにかかっている.

I

ice, *n.* 氷; 《英》アイスクリーム.

V They nodded to each other by way of ***breaking*** the *ice* of unacquaintance. 彼らは知り合いになる皮切りとして互にうなずき合った. 【類】At the social gathering the weather is the subject which usually ***breaks*** the *ice.* ¶***crush*** *ice* 氷を砕く. ¶He ***cut*** no *ice* (=figure) in stage show. 《米口》彼は舞台ではえなかった. ¶***eat*** an *ice* アイス(冷凍ジュースなど)を食べる. ¶We shall ***have*** *ice* tomorrow. あしたは氷が張るでしょう. ¶***shave*** *ice* 氷をかく(削る). ¶Will you ***take*** an *ice?* アイスクリームを召上りますか.

V² The *ice* ***cracks.*** 氷が割れる. ¶The *ice* ***formed*** early and stayed late. 早く結氷して遅くまで解けなかった. ¶The *ice* ***gave way.*** 氷が割れた[スケートのときなど].

Q Get me a glass of coke with plenty of ***chipped*** *ice* in it. 氷のぶっかきを沢山入れたコカコラを一ぱい下さい. ¶***cracked*** *ice* 割れた氷. ¶***melting*** *ice* 溶けつつある氷. ¶the ***treacherous*** *ice* 見かけは堅そうな薄氷. ¶tread on ***thin*** *ice* 薄氷を踏む.

Q² ***drift*** *ice* on the water 水上の流氷. ¶a block of ***flower*** *ice* 花氷一個. ¶***inland*** *ice* (=ice-cap) [高山などの]万年氷; [頭を冷す]氷のう. ¶***pancake*** *ice* パンケーキ氷(北海・南極などの沿岸に見る薄氷). ¶***sheet*** *ice*=ice sheet 板氷(一面に張詰めた氷). ¶a ***strawberry*** *ice* 《英》いちごアイスクリーム. ¶a ***water*** *ice* 冷凍果汁. ¶***winter*** *ice* [北極付近の]千歳氷.

P Navigation is closed ***by*** *ice.* 結氷のために航行がとだえている. ¶cool it ***by means of*** *ice* それを氷で冷やす. ¶The ship is fast ***in*** the *ice.* 船は氷に堅くとざされている. ¶Water was frozen ***into*** *ice.* 水が凍った. ¶amuse oneself ***on*** the *ice* 氷すべりをして遊ぶ ‖ He slipped ***on*** the *ice.* 彼は氷の上ですべった. 【類】skate ***on*** *ice.* ¶walk ***over*** the *ice* 氷の上を歩く. ¶He broke ***through*** the *ice.* 彼は氷が割れて落ちた. ¶Let us go ***upon*** the *ice.* 氷の上へ行こう. ¶The lake is blocked up ***with*** *ice.* 湖は結氷している.

ice, *v.* 凍らす; 氷でおおう.

M² The pond was *iced* ***over.*** 池に氷が張りつめていた. ¶be *iced* ***up*** 氷にとざされる; 氷づめにされる.

iceberg, *n.* 氷山.

V ***strike*** an *iceberg* 氷山に衝突する.

icebox, *n.* 冷蔵庫.

Q The class-room is a ***veritable*** *icebox.* その教室は全く冷蔵庫だ.

ice-cream, *n.* アイスクリーム.

V ***churn*** *ice-cream* アイスクリームをかき回す.

icon, *n.* 像.

Q² a ***Buddhist*** *icon* 仏像.

idea, *n.* 考え; 意見, 思想; 思付き; 観念.

V ***abandon*** the *idea* of ... ...の考えを棄てる. ¶***abnegate*** the *idea* of freedom 自由の思想を棄てる. ¶***absorb*** Western *ideas* 西洋思想を吸収する. ¶It takes a long time to persuade people to ***accept*** new *ideas.* 世人に説いて新思想を受入れさせるには長い年月を要する. 【類】***accept*** Western *ideas* of science and philosophy / The *idea* is not now ***accepted.*** / ***accept*** an *idea* without protestation. ¶***acquire*** a general *idea* of ... ...の概念を得る. ¶***act out*** an *idea* 一つの考えを実行する. ¶***adapt*** an old *idea* 旧思想を(新時代に)順応させる. ¶***adopt*** good *ideas* 良い考えを採用する. 【類】America's rapid industrial progress has been due to its readiness to ***adopt*** new *ideas* and to interchange information. ¶the *ideas* ***advanced*** in this present article この論文の中に開陳した思想. ¶***advocate*** the *idea* of ... ...の思想を擁護する. ¶***afford*** some *idea* of the scope of ... ...の範囲について幾分の理解を与える. ¶***allay*** a misconceived *idea* 間違った考えを打破する. ¶To judge it so is to ***apply*** to the seventeenth century the *ideas* of the twentieth. それをそう判断するのは二十世紀の思想を十七世紀に適用することになる. ¶***arrange*** *ideas* for presentation 表現のために思想を整える. ¶***assimilate*** the *ideas* of the Occident 西洋思想を同化する. ¶I could not ***bear*** the *idea* of being dependent on a man. 人に頼るという考えは私には耐えられなかった. ‖ After the European War the *idea* of a league of nations was ***born.*** 欧州戦争後に国際連盟の思想が生れた. ¶This is an *idea* ***borrowed*** from the West. この思想は西洋からの借りものだ. ¶He ***brought*** the *idea* over to Japan. 彼はその思想を日本へもたらした. ¶***carry*** an *idea* to an absurdity ばかばかしい考え方をする ‖ *Ideas* are ***carried*** from one generation to another by education. 思想は教育によってある時代から次の時代へと伝えられる. ‖ ***carry*** big *ideas* to a successful conclusion すばらしい考えを首尾よく遂行する. ¶in order to ***carry out*** one's *ideas* thoroughly その考えを実現するために. 【類】***carry out*** one's *idea* with tact and good sense (手際よく賢明に). ¶***cast aside*** a preconceived *idea* 先入思想を棄てる. ¶I guess you ***catch*** my *idea.* 私の申し上げることがお分かりでしょう. ¶They ***caught up*** the *idea* of "boys' clubs." 彼らは不良少年矯正運動に共鳴した. ¶***cherish*** the *idea* that ... ...という考えをいだく. ¶words in which to ***clothe*** one's *ideas* 思想に衣をきせる(思想を表現する)言葉. ¶***collect*** one's *ideas* (=thoughts) 考えをまとめる. ¶***color*** the popular *ideas* on ... ...に関する一般の考えに影響を及ぼす. ¶***combat*** the *idea* that ... ...という説に異論を唱える. ¶***communicate*** *ideas* 思想を伝える ‖ ***communicate*** our *ideas* to one another 互にわれわれの意思を疎通する. ¶he ***conceived*** the *idea* that ... 彼は...という考えを起した ‖ ***conceive*** one's *idea* for a painting 絵の腹案を作る. ¶***contradict*** accepted *ideas* [一般に]認められている思想に反対する. ¶***convey*** the *idea* that ... ...という思想を伝える ‖ It does not ***convey*** a correct *idea.* それでは曲解になる. 【類】Von Wenckstern's Bibliography of the Japanese Empire ***conveys*** a pretty fair *idea* of the amount of printer's ink that has been spilled (出版された文献の量) on the subject of Japan since 1859. ¶***denounce*** the *idea* that ... …という思想を排斥する. ¶***destroy*** the *idea* of class 階級思想を打破する. ¶***detest*** the *idea* of ... …の思想をきらう. ¶***develop*** this *idea* and write a book upon it この思想をおし広めて一冊の本を書く. ¶***dismiss*** the *idea* of ... …の考えを棄てる. ¶***dispel*** the mistaken *ideas* which prevail on the subject 本問題について世上に流布している誤解を一掃する. ¶***dispute*** the prevalent *idea* that ... …という世間流布の思想に反対する. ¶***disseminate*** American *ideas* アメリカ思想を伝える ‖ use the theatre as a means of ***disseminating*** radical *ideas* 過激思想を広める手段として劇場を利用する. ¶***dissipate*** the *idea* that ... …という考えを打破する. ¶***drop*** the *idea* その考えをやめる. ¶***echo*** the same *idea* 同じ思想を繰返す. ¶It ***embodies*** the latest and best *ideas* in hotel construction. それはホテルの建築における最新にしてまた最善の趣向を具体化している. 【類】 the new invention ***embodies*** the latest *ideas* in ... ¶***emphasize*** the *idea* of ... …の思想を強調する. ¶***endorse*** the *ideas* expressed in the article その論文に表明されている思想を是認する. ¶He had little power to ***enforce*** his *ideas*. 彼には自分の意見を実現させるだけの力がなかった. ¶rather ***enjoy*** the *idea* of ... むしろ…という考えを喜ぶ. ¶***enlarge*** man's *idea* of the universe 宇宙に関する人間の思想を拡大する. ¶***entertain*** a womanish *idea* めめしい考えを持つ. ¶***exchange*** *ideas* with ... on education 教育について…と意見を交換する ‖ The collectors occasionally meet to ***exchange*** *ideas* and specimens. その収集家たちは意見や標本を交換するために折々会を開く. ¶***expand*** one's *ideas* その考えをおしひろめる. 【類】 ***expand*** the *idea* of brotherhood. ¶***explain*** one's *idea* その考えを説明する. ¶it ***exploded*** many long-cherished *ideas* as to ... それは…に関して永い間持たれていた諸説をくつがえした. ¶***exploit*** new *ideas* 新思想を利用する. ¶the ability to ***express*** one's *ideas* in writing 文章の力. 【類】 ***express*** one's *ideas* agreeably and effectively (in a coherent forceful way). / ***express*** one's *ideas* or emotions musically. ¶warmly ***favor*** the *idea* 大いにその考えに賛成する ‖ indications would seem to ***favor*** the *idea* that ... 情勢が…という考えに有利であるように思われる. ¶He does not ***fit*** his *ideas* to real conditions. 彼は足が地についていない(上ずっている). ¶***fix*** the *ideas* in our minds その観念をわれわれの心に留める. ¶***follow*** the same *idea* 同じ考えを実行する. ¶the book will enable the student to ***form*** some *idea* of the salient features of ... その本によって学生は…に関する大要を幾分知ることができる. 【類】 I can now ***form*** an *idea* of it. / we can ***form*** no ideas of ... ¶***formulate*** *ideas* 思想を秩序立てて述べる. ¶***foster*** this *idea* この考えをいだく. ¶***further*** the *idea* that ... …という考えを押進める. ¶enable them to ***gain*** some *idea* of ... 彼らをして…を幾分理解させる. 【類】 ***gain*** a true *idea* of ... / an *idea* of ... may be ***gained*** from ... ¶some *idea* of the extent may be ***gathered*** from the fact that ... その範囲のことは…の事実からいく分推察できる. ¶***get*** a real *idea* of ... …を真に理解する. 【類】 picture (想像せよ) ..., and you ***get*** an *idea* of ... / I am sending you a book of views so that you can ***get*** an *idea* what the place is like. / enlighten (蒙を開く) foreigners who have ***got*** wrong *ideas* of France and its people from Paris correspondents. ¶***Give*** me an *idea* of the book. それはどんな本か話してくれ. ‖ no amount of explanation can possibly ***give*** any adequate *idea* of the importance of ... …の重要性はいくら説明しようと到底十分に了解させることはできない. 【類】 no words can ***give*** any *idea* of ... / this picture will ***give*** a good *idea* of ... / it will perhaps ***give*** some *idea* of ... ¶***give up*** the *idea* of ... …という考えを断念する. ¶***grasp*** the *idea* of ... …をのみ込む. ¶I ***hammered*** this *idea* into his head. 私はこの考えを彼の頭にたたき込んだ. 【類】 ***hammer*** into the patient's head the *idea* that he will get well. ¶I ***hate*** the *idea* of moving. 私は引越しなんてことはきらいだ. ¶I do not think he ***has*** any *idea* of doing so. 彼にそんなことをしようという気があろうとは思わない. 【類】 I had no *idea* of his conduct. ¶I ***have*** no *idea* of what it is like. 一向見当がつかない. 【類】 By Jove (驚いた)! I ***had*** no *idea* it was so late. ‖ so that one may ***have*** a better *idea* of ... …を一層よく了解するように ¶***hold*** a big *idea* 大きなことを考えている. ¶***imbibe*** Western *ideas* 西洋思想を吸収する. ¶***impart*** our own *ideas* through writing or through speaking 自分の考えを執筆または談話を通じて伝える. ¶***implant*** in the mind of ... the *idea* of ... …の心に…の思想を植えつける. ¶the dangers of ***importing*** Western *ideas* into the East 東洋に西洋思想を輸入するにともなう種々の危険. ¶***inaugurate*** the *idea* of ... …についての考えを発表する. ¶***inculcate*** *ideas* of good citizenship 善良な市民たるの概念を教え込む. ¶***inspire*** indecent *ideas* 劣情をそそる. ¶***instill*** into the mind of the student the *idea* that ... 学生の心に…という思想を注入する. ¶***interchange*** *ideas* 意見を交換する. ¶Compromise ***involves*** the *idea* of concession. 妥協は譲歩を意味する. ¶***lead*** *ideas* in another direction 思想を別の方向に導く. ¶Everybody ***likes*** the *idea* of getting something for nothing. だれもただでなにかを得たがるものだ. ‖ I don't ***like*** the *idea*. 私はその考えには賛成できない. ¶***master*** an *idea* 一つのことに通じる. ¶***nurse*** an *idea* 考えをいだく. ¶***obtain*** a precise *idea* of passing events 時事問題について正確な概念を得る ‖ to ***obtain*** a good *idea* of ... one cannot do better than visit ... …を十分理解するためには…に行くのが一番だ. ¶He ***opposed*** the *idea*. 彼はその考えに反対した. ¶***overthrow*** customary or preconceived *ideas* 従来のまたは先入の思想をくつがえす. ¶I ***owe*** the *idea* to ... 私のこの考は…から得たのである. ¶***pick up*** new *ideas* and learn new methods in their respective trades 各々の職業に応じて新しい趣向を採り新しい方法を学ぶ. ¶***popularize*** the *idea* of ... …の思想を普及させる. ¶***produce*** new *ideas* for laborsaving 労力節約の工夫に新機軸を出す ¶***propagate*** Christian *ideas* among the natives 土人の間にキリスト教の思想を広める. ¶I am glad you ***proposed*** the *idea*. 君がこの案を提議してくれてうれしい. ¶***propound*** the *idea* that ... …と説く. ¶***pursue*** the highest ethical *ideas* 最高の倫理思想を追求する. ¶He ***pushed*** the *idea* ***away*** from him as if it were a sin. 彼はそう考えるのをまるで罪悪でもあるかのように念頭から駆逐した. ¶***put*** an idea into one's head ある思想を頭に入れる. 【類】 try to ***put*** the *idea* to a test ‖ ***put*** one's *ideas* into writing (=on paper) その思想を文章に表わす ‖ ***put*** an *idea* into practice (=action *or* operation) 一つの考えを実行する. 【類】 ***put*** that idea of his into operation. ¶***put through*** a big *idea* 大きな考えをやり通す. ¶A society called "..." has been constituted to ***realize*** the *idea*. その趣旨達成のために「…」という協会が成立した. ‖ ***realize*** Swedenborg's *idea* of Heaven スエデンボルグの天国思想を悟る. ¶willingness to ***receive*** new *ideas* 進んで新思想を取入れようとする心. ¶I ***recommend*** your *ideas* on physical training. 私は体育に関する君の意見を推賞する. ¶***refute*** the foolish *idea* that ... …というばかげた考えを反ばくする. ¶***reject*** the *idea* altogether その考を全然排斥する. ¶I do not ***relish*** the *idea* of ... …の考えは私は感心しない. ¶***render*** the *idea* of war more and more repellent 戦争というものをますますきらいにさせる. ¶***repudiate*** the silly *idea* そのばか気た考えを否認する. ¶***revise*** the old *ideas* in the light of recent knowledge ちかごろの学問に照して旧思想を改める. ¶his discovery ***revolutionized*** our *ideas* as to ... 彼の発見は…についてのわれわれの思想を革新させた. ¶I ***revolved*** the *idea* round in my mind. 私はその考えについて思い回らした. ¶***ridicule*** the *idea* that ... …という考えをあざける. ¶We ***round out*** an *idea* by combining fragmentary *ideas*. われわれは断想を結び合せて一つの思想をまとめる. ¶***scorn*** the idea of ... …の考えを軽べつする. ¶***scout*** the *idea* of ... …という意見をしりぞける. ¶***scrap*** old, outworn *ideas* and welcome new ones 古ぼけた思想を棄てて新思想を歓迎する. ¶He travelled all over the world ***seeking*** fresh *ideas* in office construction and accommodation. 彼は事務所の建築及び設備に関する新趣向を求めながら全世界を旅行した. ¶***seize*** an *idea* ある思想を会得する. ¶an ability to easily ***seize*** and ***assimilate*** the *ideas* of others 他人の考えを容易にとらえて自分のものにする能力. ¶***set forth*** one's *ideas* 考えを開陳する. ¶***set in*** one's *ideas* of original sin 原罪について自分の説を述べる. ¶***shape*** an *idea* 一思想を形成する. ¶try to ***spin out*** few *ideas* 二三の思いつきを述べようとする. ¶***spread*** the false *idea* of ... …という誤れる思想を広める. ¶thoroughgoing radicals ***spurn*** the *idea* that ... 徹底的な過激論者は…と

いう思想をはねつける. ¶I cannot ***stand*** the ***idea*** of .. 私は…の考えにはがまんができない. ¶***steal*** an ***idea*** 人の思付きを盗む. ¶***strike*** an original ***idea*** 独創的な考えを出す. ¶***suggest*** the ***idea*** of … …の考えを暗示する. ¶correct so as to ***suit*** one's own ***idea*** 自分自身の考えに合うように直す. ¶willingly ***support*** this ***idea*** 進んでこの意見に賛成する. ¶***Tell*** me your ***ideas*** on the subject without any reserve. その問題についての君の意見を腹蔵なく述べてくれ. ¶***throw ideas*** into shape 思想をまとめる. ¶his failure to ***translate*** that ***idea*** into fact その考えを実行する段における彼の失敗. ¶completely ***upset*** our preconceived ***ideas*** of … …というわれわれの先入思想を完全にくつがえす. ¶***utter*** an ***idea*** 一つの考えを述べる. ¶***ventilate*** one's ***idea*** in a newspaper 自己の思想を新聞紙上に発表する. 【類】 ***ventilate ideas*** obnoxious (有害な) to … ¶***welcome*** new ***ideas*** 新思想を歓迎する. ¶***work out*** this ***idea*** with marked success この思いつきを見事に遂行する. 【類】 ***work out*** his ***ideas*** to a successful conclusion.

v² Then a bright ***idea came*** to him. そのとき彼に名案が浮んだ. ¶An ***idea crossed*** my mind. ある考えが私に浮んだ. ¶the ***idea flashed*** on him (=into his mind) that he should … …すべきだという考えが彼の心にひらめいた. 【類】 there suddenly ***flashed*** upon me the ***idea*** of … ¶The ***idea*** did not ***occur*** to him. その考えは彼れには浮ばなかった. ¶The ***idea pleased*** her. 彼女はこの考えが気に入った. ¶An ***idea seized*** upon him. 突然ある考えが彼に浮んだ. ¶The ***ideas*** have ***spread*** from west to east. その思想は西から東へと伝わった. ¶Western ***ideas streamed in.*** 西洋思想が流れこんだ. ¶An ***idea*** has ***strucked*** me. ふとある考えが浮んだ.

Q ***abstract ideas*** 抽象的観念. ¶bring his ***abstruse ideas*** within the comprehension of the lay mind 彼の幽遠な思想を大衆にのみ込めるようにする. ¶What an ***absurd idea!*** いかにもばかげた考えだ. ¶give an ***accurate idea*** of … …を正確に理解させる. 【類】 it enables us to form a fairly ***accurate idea*** of … ¶he has no ***adequate idea*** of … 彼は…をよく知っていない ‖ it is quite ***impossible*** to give an ***adequate idea*** of … …について十分に分からせることは全く不可能だ. ¶an ***admirable idea*** りっぱな考え. ¶an ***amateurish idea*** しろうと考え. ¶an ***ancient idea*** 昔の考え. ¶docks constructed after the most ***approved ideas*** 最良の設計によるドック. ¶Can you give any ***approximate idea*** of … …は大体どういった性質のものですか. ¶It wouldn't be a ***bad idea***, would it? そうするのもよかろう. ¶***basic ideas*** 根本観念. ¶a big boss with ***big ideas*** 太っ腹の大親分. ¶a ***borrowed idea*** 付焼刃(人に教えてもらった知恵). ¶***brilliant ideas*** すばらしい思いつき. ¶think up a ***bright idea*** いい考えを出す. ¶What do you say? A ***capital idea***, isn't it? どうだ, 名案だろう. ¶the ***central idea*** 中心思想. ¶a ***chimerical idea*** 夢のような考え. ¶possess ***clear ideas*** of what is wanted なにが必要かという明かな考えを持っている. 【類】 It will give you ***clearer ideas*** of the subject. ¶***clearcut*** and ***definite ideas*** 簡潔で明確な観念. ¶a ***clever idea*** 気のきいた趣向. ¶posters and handbills conveying ***communistic ideas*** 共産主義思想を伝えているポスターとビラ. ¶afford a ***comprehensive idea*** of … …の総括的概念を与える. ¶put ***conflicting ideas*** to test 矛盾する考えを試して見る. ¶***Confucian ideas*** 儒教の思想. ¶a complete shattering of ***conventional ideas*** 伝統的思想の徹底的粉砕. ¶get a ***correct idea*** of … …について正確な観念を得る. ¶the ***current ideas*** of the time on … …についての現代思想. ¶we have a very ***different idea*** of … われわれは…について非常に異った考を持つ. ¶the ***devilish idea*** that evil may be beautiful and that some ugly things are good 悪は美しいかも知れないとか醜い物の中にも良いものがあるという悪魔的な考え. ¶***dim ideas*** ばく然とした観念. ¶I have not the most ***distant idea*** of the matter. そのことはまるきり知らない. ¶the ***dominant idea*** or characteristic of the period 現代の主思潮または特徴. ¶one ***dominating idea*** 一つの要旨. ¶get quite an ***erroneous idea*** of … …について全く誤った観念を得る ‖ have an ***erroneous idea*** of … …を誤解している. 【類】 there is an ***erroneous idea*** in regard to … ¶demolish an ***established idea*** 定説を破る. ¶***European ideas*** of the country are generally hazy. その国に対するヨーロッパ人の思想は一般にもうろうとしている. ¶an ***exaggerated idea*** of one's own importance 自分自身を買いかぶった考え. ¶***exalted ideas*** 高遠な思想. ¶That is an ***excellent idea***. それはすばらしい考えだ. ‖ The pictures are sufficiently large to give an ***excellent idea*** of originals. その絵を見ると原物がよく分かる位大きい. ¶this picture gives but a ***faint idea*** of … この絵では…がはっきりしない. 【類】 give one a ***faint idea*** of … ‖ he has not the ***faintest idea*** of … 彼は…は全然知らない. ¶give a ***fair idea*** of what it is like. それがどんなものかよく分からせる. 【類】 The pictures give a ***fair idea*** of the varied beauties of the country. / can gather (=form) a very ***fair idea*** of … ¶***fallacious ideas*** 誤った考え. ¶it is based on the ***false idea*** that … それは…という誤った観念に基いている. 【類】 start from the ***false idea*** that … ¶a ***familiar idea*** 世間周知の思想. ¶a most ***fantastic idea*** すこぶるばかげた考え. 【類】 The ***idea*** that a language can be "improved" by deliberate effort (努力) is ***fantastic***. ¶to say that … is to convey but a ***feeble idea*** of the immense importance of … …といっても…の極めて重要なことをわずかにほのめかすに過ぎない. ¶try to spin out a ***few ideas*** 二三の思想を考え出そうと努める. ¶get a ***first-hand idea*** of … …を直接理解する. ¶acting under the influence of a ***fixed idea*** ある固定観念の下に行動して. 【類】 He has his ***fixed ideas***. ¶A ***foolish idea*** that! 浅ましい考えだ. ¶***foreign ideas*** 外国思想. ¶That ought to be the ***fundamental idea***. それが当然根本思想であるべきだ. ¶give a ***general idea*** of … …の概念を与える. 【類】 a ***general idea*** of it can be gathered from … / grasp the ***general idea*** of … ¶the ***get-rich-quick idea*** 一挙に金持ちになろうとする考え. ¶It is a ***good idea*** well carried out. それは思付きもよく実行方法もよい. ‖ That's a ***good idea***. それはいい考えだ. ‖ the statistics give a ***good idea*** of … その統計によって…がよく理解できる. 【類】 give one a ***good idea*** of … ¶The ***idea*** is ***good*** but is not ***workable***. その考えは良いが実行はできない. ¶The ***governing idea*** of Mr. Spencer's The Philosophy of Style is economy. スペンサーの文体論の中心思想は節約ということである. ¶an age when, in Denmark, ***great ideas*** were in the air デンマークでりっぱな思想が広く行われた時代. ¶a ***guiding idea*** 指導精神. ¶a ***hackneyed idea*** 古くさい考え. ¶a ***happy idea*** 妙案. ¶I had then only a ***hazy idea*** of how I should treat the subject. 当時私はその問題をいかに取扱うべきかはっきりした考えがなかった. ¶the ***high ideas*** of Christian religion キリスト教の高遠な理想. ¶dissipate many an ***ill-preconceived idea*** 多くの誤った先入観を駆逐する. ¶an ***ingenious idea*** 巧みな考え, 名案. ¶an ***intolerable idea*** 許しがたい考え. ¶things appealing to the ***juvenile idea*** 子供の心に興味を起させるもの. ¶the objectification of the ***latent ideas*** of a Phidias or a Michelangelo into their consummate efflorescence フィディアスやミケランジェロのような人たちのもっていた潜在的観念を具体化してらんまんと咲きにおわせること. ¶the ***leading ideas*** of Greek thought ギリシア思想の根本概念. ¶I have not the ***least idea*** of it. 私には一向見当がつかない. 【類】 no one appears to have the ***least idea*** to … ¶carry out one's ***long-cherished idea*** 素志を貫く. ¶The ***idea*** is ***ludicrous***. その考えはばからしい. ¶there is always a ***lurking idea*** in my mind that … 私の心の中に…という考えが始終ひそんでいる. ¶***main ideas*** 主な考え, 主眼. ¶dispel the ***mistaken ideas*** which prevail on the subject この問題に付帯する誤った考を一掃する. ¶Slavery is an institution so repugnant to ***modern ideas***. 奴隷制度は近代思想に大いにそむく制度である. ¶***morbid ideas*** 病的な考え. ¶a ***musty idea*** かびの生えた考え. ¶a ***narrow-minded idea*** けちな考え. ¶a ***national idea*** 国民思想. ¶introduction of ***new ideas*** from the Occident 西洋から新知識の移入. 【類】 We are ready to welcome ***new ideas*** and go with the times. ¶a man of ***new*** and ***progressive ideas*** 考えの新しい進歩的な人. ¶I had ***no idea*** it would take so long. それがそんなに永くかかろうとは思わなかった. ‖ He has ***no idea*** of his own. 自分の考えというものがない. ‖ He has ***no idea*** of time. 彼は時間の観念がない. 【類】 you can have ***no idea*** how … ‖ I have ***no idea*** of changing my position. 勤めを変えようという考えは僕にはない. ‖ It gives ***no idea*** of the labor involved in its production. それではその製作に要した労力を一向に明かにしていない. ¶a ***novel idea*** 目新しい趣向. ¶***noxious ideas*** 害毒思想. ¶***obsessive ideas*** 止むに止まれない思い. ¶The *old idea* that ... is exploded. ...という古臭い考えは打破された. ¶an *old-fashioned idea* 旧式な考え. ¶a challenge of an *old long-accepted idea* 古くから承認されている思想への挑戦. ¶He is full of *original ideas*. 独創に富んでいる. 【類】The *original idea* was developed in his brain. その最初の思いつきが彼の頭の中で発展した. ¶an *outworn idea* 古臭い考え. ¶Is that not a *peachy dandy idea?* それはすてきな考えじゃありませんか. ¶a *pet idea* 得意の考え. ¶*pet ideas* 得意の思想. ¶Their *political ideas* are elementary. 彼らの政治思想は幼稚だ. ¶Dried specimens convey but a *poor idea* of the living examples. 干からびた標本は生きた見本の面影をわずかに伝えるだけだ. ¶the *popular idea* of ... ...についての一般の考え. ¶a *praiseworthy idea* 賞すべき考え. ¶He was influenced by *preconceived ideas*. 彼は先入観念に支配されていた. ¶a *prevailing idea* 広く行きわたっている考え. ¶be dominated by *previous ideas* (=notions) 先入主となっている. ¶men of *progressive ideas* 進歩的な考えの人々. ¶the *prominent idea* 要旨. ¶a *rash idea* 突飛な考え. ¶*ready-made ideas* でき合の考え, 既成観念. ¶only a very few people possess the *remotest idea* of ... ほんの少数の人が...について極めてばく然たる考をもっているに過ぎない. ¶*revolutionary ideas* that would be dangerous to the body social 社会に危険な革命思想. ¶have a *rough idea* of ... ...について大体分かっている. ¶the *ruling idea* of a generation 一時代の主思潮. ¶*sane ideas* 健全な考え. ¶a *sensible idea* 気のきいた考え. ¶a man of *shrewd ideas* 識見のある人. ¶convey *similar ideas* in different words 同じ思想を違った言葉で述べる. ¶The ruins give us some *slight idea* of their original magnificence. その廃虚は昔の豪華な面影を幾分しのばせる. ‖ I haven't the *slightest idea*. 全然見当がつかない. ‖ none but who have witnessed it can have the *slightest idea* of ... それを実見したもの以外には...についてはだれにも分かりっこはない. ¶*smart, crisp, humorous* and *original ideas* 気がきいて, きびきびして, ユーモラスで独創的な考え. ¶*some idea* of the magnitude of this industry can be had when we realize that ... われらが...ということを頭に浮べるときこの工業のいかに巨大なものであるか幾分わかるのである. 【類】*some idea* of ... may be gained by ... / may convey *some idea* of ... ¶*speculative* ideas 思索的な思想. ¶give a *splendid idea* of ... ...を十分に了解させる. ¶The book abounds in *startling ideas* expressed with originality and power. その本は独創的に力強く述べられた奇想に満ちている. ¶They have a *strange idea* of female beauty. 彼らは女性美について変った考えを持っている. ¶have *strict ideas* about smoking 喫煙についてやかましい考えをもつ. ¶a *sudden idea* 不意の思いつき. ¶give a *sufficient idea* of ... ...について十分その意を伝える. ¶The *idea* of ... is *superannuated*. ...という考えは陳腐だ. ¶That's a *swell idea*. そいつあいい考だ. ¶*threadbare ideas* 古臭い思想. ¶a jumble of *unrelated ideas* 関係のない思想の雑集. ¶a *utopian idea* 夢想. ¶have some *vague idea* of history and philosophy 歴史と哲学はそら覚えである. ¶*vague* and *hazy ideas* 空々ばくばくたる考え. ¶The *very idea!* まさか! ¶gain a remarkably *vivid idea* of ... ...について極めて鮮明に知る. ¶a *vulgar idea* 俗説. ¶a *whimsical idea* 酔狂. ¶a *wholesome idea* 健全な考え. ¶a *wicked idea* 太い了見. ¶a *wild idea* 突飛な考え. ¶a *wise idea* 利口な考え. ¶his *world-wide ideas* 彼の世界的思想. ¶get *wrong ideas* 誤った考えを持つ. 【類】give a *wrong idea* to ... / articles which have given quite a *wrong idea* of French morals and character.

Q² *class-struggle idea* 階級闘争の観念. ¶an efficient *management idea* 有効管理の観念. ¶a *germ idea* 思想の芽. ¶Once this *key idea* had been found the plan was rapidly developed. この根本思想が確立すると計画は早く発展した. ¶carry the *money-making idea* too far 金もうけ主義に走り過ぎる. ¶the *root idea* 根本概念.

P *according to* European *ideas* ヨーロッパ風の考えによると. ¶I shuddered *at* the bare *idea* of ... 私は...を思っただけでぞっとした. ¶We're all *for* the *idea*. われわれは皆それに賛成である. ‖ He was exiled from his country *for* his political *ideas*. 彼は政見のために自国から追放された. ¶It is far *from* the Japanese *idea* of beauty. それは日本人の美の観念とは大いにかけ離れている. ¶It entered *into* my *idea* (=head). 私の心にその考えが浮んだ. ¶a train *of* *ideas* 一連の考え ‖ commerce—the dissemination *of* commodities and *ideas* 通商すなわち商品と思想の伝播(ぱ). ¶act *on* this *idea* この考え通り行動する. 【類】based *on* the *idea* that ... ¶*to* our *ideas* われわれから見ると. ¶add *to* the *idea* of it the implication of ... その観念の外に...の意を持つ. ¶acting *under* this *idea* この考えに基いて. ¶study *with* the *idea* of becoming an artist 芸術家になる積りで勉強する. ¶*without* any *idea* of the whole 全体については少しも考えないで.

P² a sporting fellow with no *ideas about* politics 政治は少しも分からないスポーツマン. ¶His *ideas as to* right and wrong were somewhat hazy. 正邪に関する彼の観念は幾分不明りょうだった. ¶the *idea behind* this was ... このかげに潜む目的は...だった. ¶There is an *idea for* a sonnet there. そこには一篇の短詩に値する情趣がある. ¶an *idea from* America 米国から得た考え. ¶the *idea in* going to America was to ... 渡米の目的は...するためだった ‖ the most fundamental *idea in* his philosophy 彼の哲学における最も根本的な理念. ¶*ideas of* the uninitiated しろうと考え ‖ the Hegelian *idea of* the ultimate identity of thought and being 思想と実在とが結局は同一だというヘーゲル派の理念 ‖ That's the *idea of* it. その通りだ. ‖ Nonsense! That *idea of* yours! You are humbugging us! ばかな! そんなこと! 君は僕たちをだましているんだ! ‖ The *idea of* saying as much! そんなこと言うなんてひどいぞ. 【類】American *ideas of* comfort. ‖ The *idea of* ... began to present itself. ...という考えが現われてきた. ¶Mr. Johnson's *ideas on* naval expansion 海軍拡張に関するジョンソン氏の考え ‖ new *ideas on* inorganic chemistry 無機化学に関する新説.

O The *idea!* まさか. ¶my *idea* is that ... 私の考えは...である ‖ What's the *idea?* 一体どうしたというんですか.

ideal, *n*. 理想, 典型.

V *approach* the *ideal* of the perfect man 完全な人という理想に近づく. ¶*attain* the *ideal* that ... ...という理想を実現する. ¶*cherish ideals* of justice and peace 正義と平和の理想をいだく. ¶an *ideal* they deemed worth *cherishing* and *defending* 彼らが心にいだいてこれを擁護するに足ると考えていた理想. ¶*establish* high *ideals* 高い理想を樹立する. ¶*follow* the Teutonic *ideal* of ... ...というチュートン民族の理想を追う. ¶*fulfil* high *ideals* 高い理想を達成する. ¶*hold up* an *ideal* ある理想を掲げる. ¶*meet* one's *ideal* 理想にかなう. ¶They *possess* a high *ideal* of love. 彼らは愛という崇高な理想をもっている. ¶*pursue* an *ideal* 理想を追求する. ¶*raise* the *ideal* of national education to its highest point 国民教育の理想を最高水準まで高める. ¶*reach* one's *ideal* 理想に達する. ¶*realize* the *ideal* best 最もよく理想を実現する. ¶a youth who *represented* her *ideal* 彼女の理想にかなった青年. ¶*set* before one an *ideal* of ... その前に...という典型を示す. ¶*set up* the *ideal* of a finer civilization よりよい文明という理想を立てる.

Q a *false ideal* 誤まった理想. ¶a perfectly *feasible ideal* 十分に実現のできる理想. ¶hold up *fake ideals* 間違った理想を掲げる. ¶*fundamental ideals* 基本的な理想. ¶a *hazy ideal* of human brotherhood 四海同胞というはっきりしない理想. ¶the shedding of illusions or *false ideals* 迷想や誤った理想からの脱皮. ¶a *lofty ideal* of life 人生の高遠な理想. 【類】instil *lofty ideals* into the minds of the young. ¶the *Mohammedan ideal* of woman eternally submitting 女は永久に服従するというマホメット教の理想. ¶an *ideal possible* of realization in our time 現代において実現可能な理想. ¶a *sordid ideal* 下劣な理想. ¶an *unattainable ideal* 実現不可能な理想. ¶an *unselfish ideal* 私心なき理想.

P *below* the *ideal* 理想に達しない.

P² a scholar *of* high *ideals* 理想の高い学者 ‖ the cradle *of* so many *ideals* 幾多理想の発祥地.

idealist, *n*. 理想家.

Q an *enlightened idealist* 進歩せる理想家.

idealize, *v*. 理想化する.

P The essential qualities of gentleness have in Christian times been *idealized in* Mary, the Mother of Jesus. しとやかさの要素はキリスト教が行われて以来エスの母マリアにおいてこれが理想化されて来た.

identical, *a*. 同一の.

P *identical in* our views (form) 意見(形式)の全く同じな ‖ seem *identical in* signification 意義が同じであるように見

える. ¶Good will is *identical* ***with*** friendship. 好意は友情と同じものだ. 【類】Ancient Chinese astronomy is *identical* ***with*** ancient Chaldean astronomy.

identification, *n.* 鑑定; 提携.
V The body ***awaits*** *identification.* その死体は検死を待っている.
Q a system of ***criminal*** *identification* 犯罪鑑定法 ‖ materials of ***criminal*** *identification* 犯罪鑑識資料.
Q^2 ***fingerprint*** *identification* 指紋鑑識.
P *identification* ***through*** fingerprints 指紋による鑑識. ¶He is free from *identification* ***with*** either party. 彼はどの党派にも属していない.

identify, *v.* 同一視する; 同定する; 利害関係を一にする.
M He is ***actively*** *identified* with our plans. 彼は大いにわれわれの計画に協力している. ¶be not ***clearly*** *identified* as yet まだはっきりと身元が判明していない. ¶It is ***closely*** *identified* with prostitution. それはりっぱに売春屋と見なされている. ‖ The Christian converts were ***generally*** *identified* with the reform party. キリスト教改宗者は一般に改革派に属するものと見られていた. ¶men ***prominently*** *identified* with ... …に関係の深い人々.
P the body has been *identified* ***as*** that of ... その死体は…のものと判明した ‖ *identify* a corpse ***as*** the person hunted after 死体は捜索中の人だと分かる. ¶The porters may be *identified* ***by*** their red caps. 赤帽は赤い帽子で見分けがつく. ‖ The child was *identified* ***by*** its clothing. 着ていた衣服でその子だということが分かった. ¶*identify* oneself ***with*** the party その党派に関係する ‖ He has been *identified* ***with*** the Japanese tea trade for years. 彼は多年日本茶の取引をやっている. ‖ the agitation ***with*** which she is *identified* 彼女の関係した騒じょう ‖ *identify* religion ***with*** religious rites 宗教と宗教的儀式とを同一視する. 【類】the two men most prominently *identified* ***with*** (と縁故が深い) this new publication were ... / He has been *identified* ***with*** Harvard as student and teacher since 1910. 【類】The legislature (立法部) should be *identified* in interest ***with*** the people. / the practice of *identifying* the more important articles in an encyclopedia ***with*** their authors by means of initials (頭文字).

identity, *n.* 同一; 身元, 正体.
V ***betray*** one's *identity* 本性を現わす. ¶He changed his name to ***conceal*** his *identity.* 彼は身元をかくそうとして名を変えた. 【類】***conceal*** one's *identity* under initials. ¶***determine*** his *identity* 彼の身元をつき留める. ¶***disclose*** one's *identity* 身元を明かす ‖ a gentleman, whose *identity* I think may ***disclose,*** Mr. ... その名前を出しても差支えなかろうと思う…氏が… ¶***discover*** the *identity* of the author 著者の何者であるかをさがし当てる. ¶***divulge*** the *identity* of ... …の正体をあばく. ¶The police were unable to ***establish*** her *identity.* 警察は彼女の身元を確めることができなかった. ‖ ***establish*** *identity* by a passport 旅行免状で身元を証明する ‖ ***establish*** the *identity* of stolen goods 盗品がかくかくの品に相違ないことを確かめる. ¶***prove*** one's *identity* その身元を明かにする ‖ Passports are frequently serviceable in ***proving*** the *identity* of the traveller. 旅券は旅行者の身元証明の役に立つことが往々ある. ¶***reveal*** his *identity* その匿名をあばく. ¶he prefers to ***veil*** his *identity* under the pseudonym "..." 彼は…の匿名を用いて本名を名乗ることを避けている.
Q a ***lost*** *identity* 身元の分からないこと. ¶a case of ***mistaken*** *identity* 人違い. ¶a benefactor whose *identity* is ***unknown*** 無名の篤志家.
P unless you are sure ***of*** their *identity* その身許がはっきりしなければ. ¶There is no clue ***to*** the *identity* of the murderer. その殺人犯人を調べる何の手がかりもない.

ideology, *n.* イデオロギー.
Q slaves of ***bourgeois*** *ideology* ブルジョア・イデオロギーの奴隷. ¶American ***capitalist*** *ideology.* アメリカ資本主義思想. ¶Russian ***Communist*** *ideology* ロシア共産主義思想. ¶***Fascist*** *ideologies* フアッショ思想. ¶***Marxist*** *ideology* マルクス思想. ¶an exposition of ***Soviet*** *ideology* ソビエト思想の解説.

idiocy, *n.* 白痴.
V ***feign*** *idiocy* 白痴を装う.

idiom, *n.* 慣用語; 語風.
V These ***constitute*** peculiar *idioms.* これらは独特な慣用句である. ¶***linguistic*** *idiom* 言語上の慣用. ¶foreign-born Americans who have not yet ***mastered*** the *idiom* of the English language まだ英語の慣用句をこなし得ない外国生れのアメリカ人. ¶***violate*** *idiom* 慣用語法を破る.
Q We cannot quarrel with ***accepted*** *idioms.* われわれは認められている慣用句をとや角言うことはできない. ¶the ***correct*** *idiom* is ... 正確な慣用法は…である. ¶speak in the ***cultivated*** *idiom* of the capital 首都の言葉で話す. ¶should be accepted as ***established*** *idiom* 確立した慣用語として承認すべきだ. ¶use a perfectly ***good*** *idiom* when we say that ... われわれが…と言って少しも語法に合わないようなことはない. ¶***homely*** *idioms* 親しい慣用句. ¶***national*** *idiom* 国民一般の慣用語法(地方的に対して). ¶***widely recognized*** *idioms* 広く認められた慣用句. ¶a jumble of ***unintelligible*** *idioms* 分からない慣用語の混交.
P This expression is ***against*** *idiom.* この言葉使いは慣用に反している. ¶express ***in*** English *idioms* 英語の慣用句で言表わす.

idiosyncrasy, *n.* 特質.
Q treat each animal according to its ***peculiar*** *idiosyncrasies* それぞれ動物の特性を考えて取扱う.
P^2 an *idiosyncrasy* ***of*** a single writer たった一人の作家の独特の表現法.

idiot, *n.* 白痴者, あほう.
Q a ***drooling*** *idiot* よだれたらしのあほう. ¶a ***perfect*** *idiot* 手のつけようのない白痴.
P He is next door ***to*** an *idiot.* 彼はほとんど白痴だ.

idle, *v.* 怠ける, 怠けて過ごす.
M *idle* ***away*** one's time 時間を空費する.
M^2 *idle* ***about***＝be lazy ぶらぶらして暮らす ‖ They did nothing but *idle* ***about.*** 彼らは怠けてばかりいた.

idle, *a.* むだな.
Q It would be *idle* to attempt to estimate the result, but one thing is quite certain. 結果を予想しようとしてもそれはむだであるがただ一つだけ全く確かなことがある.

idleness, *n.* 怠惰, 安逸, 無為.
Q The history of invention is the history of ***applied*** *idleness.* 発明の歴史は閑暇利用の歴史である. ¶***enforced*** *idleness* 仕方なしの無職. ¶***sweet*** *idleness* and rest 甘美な安逸と休息.
P lose time ***by*** *idleness* 怠けて時を空費する. ¶He is all right except ***for*** his *idleness.* 彼は良い人だが怠けるのがきず. ¶A man, like a sword, rusts ***in*** *idleness.* 人も刀と同じに使わないとさびる. ‖ spend time ***in*** *idleness* 無為に日を送る. ¶fall ***into*** *idleness* 怠惰になる. ¶spend days in next ***to*** *idleness* ほとんで何もしないで日を送る.

idler, *n.* 怠け者.
Q an ***inveterate*** *idler* 始末に負えない怠け者. ¶a ***loafing*** *idler* of the parish その教区ののらくら者.

idol, *n.* 偶像.
V ***worship*** *idols* 偶像を崇拝する.
Q a ***fallen*** *idol* 崇拝者を失った偶像(人気の落ちた人). ¶the ***national*** *idol* 国民崇拝の的. ¶become a ***popular*** *idol* 一般の崇拝する所となる. ¶Georges Charpentier, the ***pugilistic*** *idol* of France フランスけん闘界の人気者たるジョルジュ・シャルパンティエ.
Q^2 a popular ***screen*** *idol* 人々に好まれる映画の人気俳優.
P^2 the *idol* ***of*** his countrymen 彼の国人の偶像. 【類】He was the *idol* ***of*** his parents.

idolater, *n.* 崇拝者.
Q ***eager*** *idolaters* of mammon 熱烈な富の崇拝者.

ignominy, *n.* 恥辱.
V ***bring*** *ignominy* to one's country (family) その国(家名)をはずかしめる.

ignoramus, *n.* 無識者, あきめくら.
Q a ***complete*** *ignoramus* as to ... …については全く無知な人. ¶a ***dull*** *ignoramus* 鈍物. ¶an ***honest*** *ignoramus* 正直な無学者. ¶an ***utter*** *ignoramus* 全く無知の人.

ignorance, *n.* 無学, 無知, 無識.
V ***abuse*** one's *ignorance* その無知に乗じる. ¶***affect*** *ignorance* 知らん振りをする. ¶***betray*** one's own palpable *ignorance* 無知を明白に暴露する. ¶***confess*** one's *ignorance* 正直に知らないという. ¶***counterfeit*** *ignorance* 知らない顔をする. ¶***display*** one's *ignorance* 無学を表明する. ¶***exhibit*** one's gross *ignorance* of ... …に対するそのはなはだしい認識不足を示す. ¶***exploit*** the popular *ignorance* 一般人の無知を利用する. ¶***expose*** one's *ignorance* その無学をさらけ出す. ¶It is no use ***feigning*** *ignorance.* 知らないふりしてもだめだ. ¶***flaunt*** one's *ignorance* その無知を振り回す. ¶he ***had*** the *ignorance* to confound ... with ... 彼は…と…とを混同するくらい認識不足であった. ¶***mend***

one's *ignorance* 無学を改める. ¶***plead*** *ignorance* 知らないと主張する. ¶***pretend*** *ignorance* about … …について知らない振りをする. ¶***profess*** *ignorance* 知らないとはっきり言う. ¶They ***reveal*** their complete *ignorance* of the subject. 彼らはその問題について全くの無知をさらけ出している.

Q ***abysmal*** *ignorance* はなはだしい無知. ¶display an ***amazing*** *ignorance* in … …に驚くべき無知を表わす. ¶***assumed*** *ignorance* そ知らぬ顔. ¶in ***blissful*** *ignorance* of … …を知らぬが仏で. ¶***dense*** *ignorance* of simple, elementary principles of … …の単純で初歩の原則に対するはなはだしい無知. ¶A ***deplorable*** *ignorance* on this subject has resulted in a serious consequence. この問題に関する嘆かわしい無知はその結果由々しいことになった. ¶These erroneous ideas are due to an ***excusable*** *ignorance*. これらのあやまちは無知によるもので許さるべきだ. ¶***gross*** *ignorance* 全くの無知. ¶***hygienic*** *ignorance* 衛生上の無知. ¶***innocent*** *ignorance* 罪のない無知. ¶***journalistic*** *ignorance* 新聞雑誌記者の無知. ¶Such *ignorance* is truly ***laughable***. かかる無知は全く笑うべきだ. ¶***palpable*** *ignorance* 明かな無知. ¶***profound*** *ignorance* はなはだしい無学文盲. ¶Such an attitude comes from ***sheer*** *ignorance*. かかる態度は皆目の無知から生じる. ¶***stupendous utter*** *ignorance* 全く驚くべき無知. ¶***Such*** *ignorance* (breach of etiquette, etc) is indeed to be blamed. こういう無知(失礼なこと…)は実にけしからん. ¶To spell incorrectly is a mark of ***vulgar*** *ignorance*. つづりを間違えるのは見苦しい無学の印だ. ¶the ***widespread*** *ignorance* of the true action of alcohol 酒精の真の作用についての一般人の無知.

Q^{2} ***sex*** *ignorance* 性に対する無知.

P It was ***from*** *ignorance*. それは無知から生じたことだ. ‖ error ***from*** *ignorance* 無知からでた誤り. ¶The matter was not taken into consideration ***in*** our *ignorance*. われわれの認識不足からそのことを考慮に入れなかった. ‖ keep him ***in*** *ignorance* of … 彼に…を知らさないでおく. ¶take advantage ***of*** one's *ignorance* その無知に乗じる. ¶***out of*** sheer *ignorance* 全然知らないために. ¶***through*** *ignorance* of the law 法律を知らないため. 【類】***through*** one's *ignorance* of foreign customs.

P^{2} *Ignorance* ***of*** the law excuses no man. 法律を知らないことは言訳にはならない. 【類】his *ignorance* ***of*** German. ¶one's *ignorance* ***on*** this matter このことに関する無知.

ignorant, *a.* 無知な.

M ***amazingly*** *ignorant* of … …についてびっくりするくらい無知な. ¶***blissfully*** *ignorant* of … …を知らぬが仏で. ¶almost ***childishly*** *ignorant* of … …について無知なことは子供同然. ¶***densely*** *ingorant* of … …についてはなはだしく無知な. ¶***entirely*** *ignorant* of … …に全然無知な. ¶***grossly*** *ignorant* of … …にはなはだ無知な. ¶***pitiably*** *ignorant* of … …に気の毒なくらい無知な. ¶be ***quite*** *ignorant* regarding … …に関して全く無知である. ¶He is ***too*** *ignorant* of the ways of the world. 世の中を知らないにもほどがある. ¶***woefully*** *ignorant* about … …についてはなはだ無知な.

P be *ignorant* ***of*** the world (affairs, matter, language, fact) 世間(など)を知らない. ¶*ignorant* ***upon*** the subject その問題について無知な.

ignore, *v.* 無視する, 不問に付する.

M ***criminally*** *ignored* 刑法上不問に付された. ¶***diplomatically*** *ignore* the fact 外交的にその事実をわざと無視する. ¶***politely*** but ***firmly*** *ignore* 丁重にしかも断固として無視する. ¶***rudely*** *ignore* 無礼にも無視する. ¶***utterly*** *ignore* it それを全く無視する. ¶***wrathfully*** *ignore* the modern world 憤然として近代の世界を無視する.

ill, *n.* 害; 悪事; 困難; 病気.

V ***cure*** the *ills* of society 社会の害悪を矯正する. ¶***do*** (=***work***) *ill* to him 彼に害を加える. ¶***experience*** all the *ills* of poverty 貧乏のあらゆる辛苦を経験する. ¶***imprecate*** *ill* on … …に禍あれと祈る. ¶I can ***think*** no *ill* of him. 私にはあの人に悪いことがあるとは思われない.

Q the ***common*** *ills* of mankind 普通の病気. ¶***deep-rooted*** *ills* 内部の病気. ¶the ***multitudinous*** *ills* that flesh is heir to 人間がかかる諸病. ¶a ***psychic*** *ill* 精神上の病気.

ill, *a.* 病気の, 不快な.

M ***chronically*** *ill* 病気が慢性になって. ¶***critically*** *ill* 危篤な. ¶He is ***dangerously*** *ill*. 彼は危篤だ. ¶***incurably*** *ill* with cancer of the stomach 不治の胃がんにかかって. ¶***seriously*** *ill* with heart disease ひどい心臓病にかかって ‖ ***seriously*** *ill* of nervous break-down ひどい神経衰弱にかかって. ¶he was ***so*** *ill* that he ***could*** not … 彼は大分健康がすぐれなかったので…することができなかった. ¶At length he became ***very*** *ill*. 遂に彼はひどい病気になった.

P It made me *ill* ***at*** ease. そのために私はぎごちない感じがした. ¶He made himself *ill* ***by*** drinking. 彼は酒を飲んで病気になった. ¶I am *ill* ***from*** want of sleep. 私は睡眠不足で気分がすぐれない. ‖ be *ill* ***from*** tuberculosis 結核にかかっている. ¶He fell *ill* ***of*** measles (a fever). 彼ははしか(など)にかかった. ‖ He is *ill* ***of*** a fever. 彼は熱病にかかっている. ¶He was taken *ill* ***through*** grief. 彼は悲嘆の余り病気になった. ¶He was *ill* ***with*** scarlet fever. 彼はしょう紅熱であった. ‖ He is *ill* ***with*** fever. 彼は熱がある. ‖ He seems to go *ill* ***with*** his seniors. 先輩とはうまく行かないらしい.

ill-effect, *n.* 悪結果; 副作用.

V ***produce*** no *ill-effects* 副作用を起さない. ¶without ***suffering*** any *ill-effects* なんらの悪結果をこうむらずに.

Q ***subsidiary*** *ill-effects* 副作用.

ill-feeling, *n.* 悪感情, 反感.

V ***bear*** no *ill-feeling* towards … …に対して悪感情を持っていない. ¶***have*** no *ill-feeling* against … …には反感はもっていない. ¶***manufacture*** *ill-feeling* against America 米国に対して反感を起させる. ¶***stir*** *ill-feeling* abroad against … 外国で…に対する反感を扇動する.

P ***through*** *ill-feeling* against … …への反感から.

ill-fortune, *n.* 不運, 不幸.

P ***by*** *ill-fortune* 不幸にして.

ill-health, *n.* 不健康.

V ***induce*** *ill-health* 不健康をきたす. ¶He ***pleaded*** *ill-health* and advancing years for his resignation. 彼は辞職の理由として健康のすぐれないことと老齢を持ち出した. ¶***suffer*** *ill-health* 不健康に悩む.

Q owing to ***continued*** *ill-health* 引続き健康がすぐれないので.

P resign one's office ***through*** (=***owing to***) *ill-health* 不健康のために辞職する.

illiberal, *a.* 狭量な.

P He is *illiberal* ***to*** (=***towards***) his subordinates. 彼は部下に対して狭量だ.

illiteracy, *n.* 無学, 文盲.

V a campaign to ***abolish*** *illiteracy* 無学絶滅運動. ¶***wipe up*** *illiteracy* 無学を一掃する.

illiterate, *a.* 無学の.

M ***densely*** *illiterate* 無学文盲な.

illness, *n.* 病気.

V He ***bore*** his *illness* admirably. 彼はりっぱに病気にたえた. ¶go to office ***braving*** his *illness* 病気を押して出勤する. ¶he ***brought on*** *illness* by … 彼は…のために病気になった. ¶He ***contracted*** an *illness* from which he never recovered. 彼は病気にかかってそれで死んでしまった. ¶***feign*** (=***pretend, or sham***) *illness*=sham sickness 仮病をつかう ‖ He received me in bed, ***feigning*** *illness*. 彼は病気を装って寝たまま私に会った. ¶He ***got over*** his *illness* quickly. 彼の病気はじきに直った. ¶He ***had*** a bad *illness* at fifteen. 彼は十五の年に重病にかかった. ¶***plead*** *illness* 病気を言訳する. ¶***stave off*** an *illness* 病気を予防する. ¶***survive*** one's *illness* 病気に打勝つ. ¶***throw off*** one's *illness* 病気をいやす. ¶He ***transmitted*** the *illness* to his wife. 彼はその病気を妻に感染させた.

V^{2} His *illness* will soon ***pass away*** (=***off***). 彼の病気はじきに直るだろう.

Q ***bodily*** *illness* 肉体上の不快. ¶after a ***brief*** *illness* しばらく病気した後. ¶a ***depressing*** *illness* 気を腐らすような病気. ¶contract a ***fatal*** *illness* 死病にとりつかれる. ¶an ***infectious*** *illness* 伝染病. ¶in his ***last*** *illness* 彼が命を取られた病気. ¶a ***lingering*** *illness* 長びく病気. ¶a ***long-continued*** (=***prolonged***) *illness* 長わずらい. ¶after a ***protracted*** *illness* 長わずらいの後で. ¶A ***serious*** *illness* befell him. 彼は重病にかかった. ¶a ***severe*** *illness* 重い病気. ¶after a ***short*** *illness* ちょっと病気した後で. ¶a ***slight*** *illness* 軽い病気. ¶a ***sudden*** *illness* 急病. ¶at the time of his ***unfortunate*** *illness* in New York 彼がニューヨークで運悪く病気にかかったとき.

P He died ***after*** an *illness* of 10 days. 彼は十日わずらって死んだ. ¶He was pulled down ***by*** his *illness*. 彼は病気で衰弱した. ¶***during*** his *illness* 彼の病気中. ¶He is in ***for*** an *illness*. 彼は病気で引こもっている. ¶recover ***from*** one's *illness* 病気が回復する ‖ He is still weak ***from*** his late *illness.* 彼はこの間の病気でいまだに弱っている. ¶a stage ***in*** an *illness* 病気の一段階. ¶***in consequence of*** one's *illness* その病気の結果. ¶He is cheerful ***in spite of*** his *illness.* 彼は病気でも元気だ. ¶I've had a bit ***of*** *illness* for the past two weeks and I have to be careful. この二週間ちょっと病気したので気をつけなければならない. ¶***on account of*** one's *illness* 病気のために. ¶liable ***to*** *illness* 病気にかかりやすい. ¶He was seized ***with*** an *illness.* 彼は突然病気にかかった. 「後.

P² after an *illness* ***of*** several months 五六カ月の病気の

O Children should be quiet when there is *illness* in the house. 家族に病人があるときは子供たちは静かにしていなければいけない.

illogical, *a.* 論理に合わない, 不合理な.

M ***marvellously*** *illogical* 驚くほど不合理な.

ill-treatment, *n.* 虐待.

V She nobly ***bore*** the *ill-treatment* of her husband. 彼女は夫の虐待をりっぱに忍んだ.

illuminate, *v.* 照らす, 照明する; 鮮明にする, 飾る.

M That *illuminates* me ***a great deal.*** 大へん参考になります. ¶*illuminate* ***electrically*** 電気照明をする.

P *illuminate* a subject ***by*** many pleasant touches of humor ユーモア味たっぷりで主題をにぎやかにする. ¶streets *illuminated* ***for*** the celebration 祝賀で電飾した街路. ¶*illuminated* ***with*** electricity 電気で照明をした ‖ *illuminate* a statement ***with*** examples 例をあげて所説の解明を与え

illuminating, *a.* 解明する. └る.

M be ***exceedingly*** *illuminating* 大変参考になる.

illumination, *n.* 照明, 光輝; 飾光; 解明.

V ***cast*** *illumination* upon the social life in which we have our being われわれの生存している社会を明朗にする. ¶An electric installation ***provides*** *illumination* for the use of the school. 電気設備があって同校の照明用に供している.

Q ***correct*** (***faulty***) *illumination* よろしきを得た(得ない)照明. ¶***electric[al]*** *illumination* 電灯照明. ¶***grand*** *illumination* of a building 建物の大々的電飾(なにかの記念など

Q² ***flood*** *illumination* 投光照明. └で).

P² the *illuminations* ***at*** the East India Railway Offices, Calcutta カルカッタの東インド鉄道事務所にある電飾. ¶*illumination* ***of*** obscure facts (results) 不明な事実(など)の

illusion, *n.* 幻影, 幻想, 迷夢. └解明.

V ***break*** an *illusion* 迷夢を破る. ¶***cherish*** the *illusion* that ... ...という錯覚を持つ. ¶to ***complete*** the *illusion* どこまでも現実感を深くして(実物に)見せようとして. ¶A picture of a fall ***creates*** the *illusion* of coolness. 滝の絵は涼しい感じを与える. ‖ ***create*** the *illusion* of space 広く見せる. ¶***destroy*** thc *illusion* of reality 現実感を打破する. ¶***dispel*** *illusions* concerning ... ...に関する迷想を打破する. 【類】It is worth while to ***dispel*** this *illusion.* ¶Lead shot rolled about in a drum ***gives*** the *illusion* of a rough sea. 太鼓の中で鉛の小球を転がすと海が荒れるような感じがする. 【類】This ***gives*** a visitor the *illusion* of being in his own home. ¶***have*** an *illusion* 錯覚を起している. 【類】He ***had*** an *illusion* that the porter was a general. ¶***intensify*** the *illusion* 幻想を深める. ¶he ***shares*** the *illusion* that ... 彼もまた...という迷想をいだいている. ¶***spoil*** the *illusion* (折角の)幻想をめちゃくちゃにする.

Q the ***fondest*** *illusions* of our youth われわれ青年時代に最も好んで描く幻想. ¶indulge in the ***pleasing*** *illusion* that ... ...という楽しい幻想にふける. ¶a ***shattered*** *illusion* 打ちこわされた幻想. ¶a ***sweet*** *illusion* 楽しい幻想.

P labor ***under*** the *illusion* that ... ...という迷想をいだく ‖ he is ***under*** the *illusion* that ... 彼は...という錯覚を持っている. 【類】He is ***under*** *illusions* on this point.

illustrate, *v.* (**1**) 明かにする, 説明する, 例証する.

M ***aptly*** *illustrate* 適例を示す. ¶*illustrate* most ***eloquently*** 最も雄弁に説明する. ¶the anecdote ***forcibly*** *illustrates* ... この逸話は...を力強く例証する. ¶it ***pointedly*** *illustrates* how ... それは...の次第を明らかに物語っている.

P to *illustrate* this ***by*** a familiar example 卑近な例でこれを説明すると ‖ *illustrate* ***by*** facts 事実によって説明する. ¶*illustrate* this ***from*** one's personal experience 自分の体験からこれを説明する. ¶be *illustrated* ***in*** photogravure 写真版で説明してある.

(**2**) 図解する, さし絵(写真など)を入れる.

M a book ***attractively*** *illustrated* 美しいさし絵のある本. ¶***beautifully*** *illustrated* in color and black-and-white 彩色や白黒(写真など)で美しくさし絵のしてある. ¶***copiously*** *illustrated* 豊富にさし絵を入れてある. ¶The book is ***freely*** *illustrated* from the author's own collection. その本は著者自ら収集したさし絵をたくさん入れてある. ¶be ***fully*** *illustrated* from photographs 写真版のさし絵がたくさん入れてある. ¶be ***handsomely*** *illustrated* from original watercolors 肉筆の水彩画から取ったさし絵で美しく飾られている. ¶be ***heavily*** *illustrated* 沢山に絵が入れてある. ¶***lavishly*** *illustrated* by reproductions of ... and photographs ...の複写や写真をふんだんにそう入してある. ¶***liberally*** *illustrated* 豊かにさし絵を施した. ¶a guide ***photographically*** *illustrated* 写真をさし絵に入れてある案内書. ¶be rather ***poorly*** *illustrated* さし絵がわずかだ; 説明が下手だ. ¶be ***profusely*** *illustrated* with facsimiles from ... ...からの複写が沢山入っている. 【類】be ***profusely*** *illustrated* from cover to cover (巻頭から巻末まで). ¶***satisfactorily*** (=***richly***) *illustrated* by photographs 十分に写真をそう入した. ¶be ***sumptuously*** *illustrated* ぜいたくにさし絵が入れてある. ¶***superbly*** *illustrated* りっぱなさし絵が入れてある. ¶It is *illustrated* so ***well*** in Fig. No. 2 that detailed description will be unnecessary. それは第二図で十分くわしく看取されるから別に説明を要しないだろう. ¶***well*** and ***amply*** *illustrated* 十分豊富にさし絵がはいっている.

P *illustrated* ***by*** charts and diagrams 図や図表によって解説してある. 【類】be *illustrated* ***by*** half tones (写真版の絵) / be *illustrated* ***by*** about fifty designs (図版) ‖ lectures *illustrated* ***by*** lantern slides (=stereopticon views) 幻灯板(実物幻灯)を援用した講演 ‖ *illustrated* ***by*** artists 画家によってさし絵を施された. ¶*illustrated* ***from*** sketches and photographs by ... ...の手になるスケッチや写真をさし絵に入れてある ‖ *illustrated* ***from*** old prints and pictures 古い版画や絵をそう入してある. ¶his remarks were *illustrated* ***with*** magic lantern views of ... 彼の解説には...の幻灯を添えた ‖ *illustrated* ***with*** excellent photographs (the reproductions of rare photographs) りっぱな写真(など)がそう入してある. 【類】*illustrated* ***with*** a picture (sketches) by

illustration, *n.* (**1**) 説明, 解説, 例証. └...

V we need to ***add*** no further *illustrations* to show that ... ...ということを示すにはこの上の説明を加える必要がない. ¶***adduce*** *illustrations* 例を引く. ¶it ***affords*** an *illustration* of Emerson's remark "..." それは「...」というエマースンの言葉を説明する ‖ The events I am now going to relate ***afford*** a striking *illustration* of this. 私が今述べようとする事件はこのことの顕著な例証になる. ¶***furnish*** a good *illustration* よい例証を提供する. ¶It is needless to ***multiply*** *illustrations.* 色々と例証をあげる必要はない. 【類】I could ***multiply*** *illustrations* to infinity. / *Illustrations* might be ***multiplied*** indefinitely. ¶for instance, to ***take*** an *illustration* 例えば一つの実例を示すと. 【類】to ***take*** another *illustration.*

Q an ***amusing*** *illustration* おもしろい(笑わせるような)説明. ¶an ***apposite*** *illustration* 適切な例. ¶an ***apt*** *illustration* 適例. ¶A ***brief*** *illustration* will make it clear. ちょっとした例を示すとこのことが明白になるであろう. ¶***concrete*** *illustration* 具体的な例証. ¶***consummate*** *illustrations* of fortitude and self-sacrifice 堅忍と犠牲の完全な実例. ¶a ***curious*** *illustration* of this is afforded by ... これについて興味ある実例が...によって示されている. 【類】a ***curious*** *illustration* of the old saying about (...に関する古い諺). ¶It serves as an ***extreme*** *illustration.* それは極端な例として役立つ. ¶to give a ***familiar*** *illustration* 通俗な例をあげれば. ¶a ***favorite*** *illustration* よく持ち出される例証. ¶a ***flagrant*** *illustration* 著しい悪例. ¶a ***forcible*** *illustration* 力強い例. ¶the following case is a ***good*** *illustration* of ... 次の例は...の適例である ‖ a ***good*** *illustration* of our racial peculiarities will be found in ... われわれの人種的特異性のよい実例が...に見出される. ¶to take ***homely*** *illustration*: ありふれた例をあげて見ると. ¶an ***obvious*** *illustration* 明白な実例. ¶one of the most ***pointed*** *illustrations* of the truth of Aristotle's remark that ... ...というアリストテレス説の真理を示す最も適切な例の一つ. ¶a ***salient*** *illustration* of the fact that ... ...という事実の顕著な例. ¶to give a ***simple*** *illustration* 早い

話が. ¶a ***striking*** *illustration* of the theory that ... ...という説の著しい例証. 【類】 the most ***striking*** *illustration* of this is to be ... ¶a ***telling*** *illustration* 一つの適例. ¶The book is valuable as a ***vivid*** *illustration* of the Yedo in the time of Iyeyasu. その本は家康時代の江戸を眼前にほうふつさせる貴重な文献である.

P ***by way of*** *illustration* 例として. ¶if, ***for*** *illustration*, ... 例えば...とするも. ¶a case ***in*** *illustration* 解説となる一例. 【類】 an instance cited ***in*** *illustration* of it ‖ Blackwood is the last periodical to be cited ***in*** *illustration* of it. その例としてブラックウッド誌は決して適切でない. ‖ There are many current stories, authentic and otherwise, that might be quoted ***in*** *illustration* of this point. この点を明かにするため引用しうる色々のうわさがあるがそれには根拠のあるのもあればないのもある. 【類】 a story ***in*** *illustration* of the fact. ¶describe ***with*** *illustration* 例をもって説明する.

P^2 an *illustration* ***from*** the book その本からの例証. ¶an *illustration* ***of*** that fact その事実の例証 ‖ as an *illustration* ***of*** the foregoing remarks, we may take ... 前説の一例として...をあげ得る.

(**2**) さし絵, 図解.

V An *illustration* of it is ***given*** in the accompanying cut. その絵がさし絵に出ている. ¶beautiful *illustrations* for the story will be ***made*** by ... その物語のために...が美麗なさし絵をかく.

Q ***abundant*** *illustrations* 豊富なさし絵. ¶as shown in the ***accompanying*** *illustration* これに付随している図解に示してあるように. ¶***black-and-white*** and ***colored*** *illustrations* ペン画と彩色のさし絵. ¶a ***brilliant*** *illustration* さん然たるさし絵. ¶***colored*** *illustrations* 彩色を施したさし絵. ¶an ***exquisite*** *illustration* 精妙なさし絵. ¶***hair-raising*** *illustrations* of war 身の毛がよだつ戦争画. ¶an ***original*** *illustration* 原画のさし絵. ¶***photographic*** *illustrations* 写真のさし絵. ¶***pictorial*** *illustrations* さし絵. ¶good and really ***useful*** *illustrations* 良く描けていて, 真に有用なさし絵 ‖ *Illustrations* are often more ***useful*** than definitions in teaching the meaings of words. 言葉の意味を教えるのにさし絵が定義よりも有用なことがしばしばある. ¶"***wash***" *illustrations* in the Strand Magazine ストランド誌の「洗ってもはげない」さし絵.

Q^2 a ***cover-page*** *illustration* 表紙の絵. ¶The numerous ***facsimile*** *illustrations* add greatly to the value of the catalogue. 沢山の複写画はこのカタログの価値を非常に増している. ¶a ***full-color*** *illustration* 極彩色さし絵. ¶***full-page*** *illustrations* 一ページ大の絵. ¶Each lecture will have ***lantern*** *illustrations*. 講演にはそれぞれ幻灯画がつく. ¶a ***process*** *illustration* 写真版さし絵. ¶a ***whole*** (=***full***) ***page*** *illustration* 一ページ大のさし絵.

P as shown ***in*** *illustration* 図に示したように.

P^2 *illustrations* ***from*** (= ***after***) original drawings and photographs 原画及び写真を複製にしたさし絵. 【類】 *illustrations* ***from*** frescoes (壁画). ¶*illustrations* ***of*** a rule 規則を説明する諸例. ¶*illustrations* ***in*** photogravure 写真凹版のさし絵. ¶*illustrations* ***to*** his book 彼の本のさし絵.

illustrative, *a.* 明かにする, 解き明かす, 例証する.

P quotations *illustrative* ***of*** the case of words 言葉の使用を説明する引用句 ‖ The pictorial illustrations are strictly *illustrative* ***of*** the text. さし絵は本文を精確に解明している.

illustrious, *a.* 著名な.

P ***among*** them the most *illustrious* were ... 中にも最も有名なのは...であった. ¶a man *illustrious* ***in*** learning and wealth 学問と富で著名な人.

ill-will, *n.* 悪意, えん恨.

V ***bear*** *ill-will* towards ... ...を恨んでいる. 【類】 ***bear*** no *ill-will* toward ... ¶***excite*** hatred and *ill-will* between nations 国民間に憎悪(ぞ)えん恨を激成する. ¶***incur*** some one's *ill-will* だれかの恨みを招く. ¶***stir*** one's *ill-will* 人のえん恨を喚起する.

P inspired ***by*** *ill-will* えん恨に刺激されて.

image, *n.* 像, 肖像, 彫像; 生写し.

V ***make*** an *image* out of snow 雪だるまを作る. ¶***obtain*** a sharp *image* of ... の鮮明な肖像を手に入れる. ¶***produce*** *images* in the camera カメラに物像が現われる. ¶***throw*** an *image* on ... ...に像を投射する.

Q a ***colossal*** *image* of Buddha 仏陀の巨像. ¶***dim-remembered*** and ***dream-like*** *images* うろ覚えの夢のような姿. ¶a ***gigantic*** *image* of Buddha 大仏. ¶stand like a ***graven*** *image* 彫像のように立つ. 【類】 worship a ***graven*** *image*. ¶***haunting*** *images* and thoughts 胸に去来する幻影と思念. ¶The picture is the ***living*** *image* of his father. その絵は彼の父親の生写しだ. ¶a ***rock-cut*** *image* of the Buddha 岩に刻んだ仏陀の像. ¶obtain a ***sharp*** *image* of ... はっきり...の姿を認める. ¶***standing*** and ***seated*** *images* of Buddha 仏陀の立像及座像. ¶***visual, auditory,*** and ***olfactory*** *images* 視覚・聴覚・嗅(きゅう)覚の影像. ¶He is the ***very*** *image* of his father 彼は父親そっくり.

Q^2 a ***snow*** *image* 雪だるま.

P^2 an *image* ***in*** the mind 心像.

imaginary, *a.* 想像上の, 空想の.

M The distinction is ***more*** *imaginary* than real. その区別は真実というよりはむしろ想像上のものだ.

imagination, *n.* 想像, 空想; 想像力.

V ***allow*** the *imagination* its full play 想像をたくましくする. ¶***awaken*** one's *imagination* 人の想像力を喚起する. ¶***cast*** our *imagination* back into the misty past 遠い昔に思いをはせる. ¶***defy*** the *imagination* 想像に絶する. ¶***excite*** the *imagination* of ... ...の血を沸かす. ¶***fire*** (=***kindle or stir***) the *imaginations* of one's pupils 教え子たちの血を沸かす. 【類】 ***fire*** the youthful *imagination* / his young *imagination* was ***fired*** by the tales of ... recounted (話された) by ... ¶by ***giving*** the *imagination* a little play, one can easily imagine oneself to be ... 少しく想像力を働かすと容易に自分が...だと思うことができる. ¶he ***has*** a dull *imagination* indeed if he cannot picture to himself ... 彼にして...が想像できないなら全く鈍感な男だ. ¶***impress*** the popular *imagination* 人気を取る. ¶***inflame*** the *imagination* 想像力を燃やす. ¶***pamper*** *imagination* 想像をほしいままにする. ¶How all this was done ***passes*** the *imagination* to conceive. このこと全部をどうしてやったかは想像に苦しむ. ¶with fruit of a sort to ***stagger*** the *imagination* 想像に余りある一種の成果を収めて ‖ The vast scope of the debris clearance job ***staggers*** the *imagination*. [戦災都市の]崩壊物清掃は想像に及ばない大仕事だ. ¶***stimulate*** and ***enrich*** *imagination* 想像力を刺激しかつ豊富にさせる. ¶***surpass*** all *imagination* どうにも想像のできない ‖ at a speed ***surpassing*** all *imagination* at this time 今日では想像もつかない速度で. ¶it does not ***take*** much [stretch of] *imagination* to realize that ... ...ということを実感するには大した想像力を要しない.

V^2 his active *imagination* ***conjured up*** ... 彼の盛んな想像力は...を作り出した. ¶*imagination* ***fails*** to conceive what this must have been when ... ...の場合に果してこれがどうなったかは想像さえできない. ¶her *imagination* ***pictured*** what would become of her if ... 彼女はもし...したなら自分はどうなるだろうかと想像して見た.

Q no ***active*** *imagination* is required to guess ... ...を推量するには大して想像力を働かす必要はない. ¶***brilliant*** *imagination* すばらしい想像力. ¶The ***constructive*** *imagination* is the greatest of human powers. 建設的想像力は人間の力の中で最も偉大なものである. ¶a man of ***creative*** *imagination* 独創的想像力の持主 ‖ the power of ***creative*** *imagination*. ¶Real or imaginary dangers assume an excessive importance in the morbidly ***excited*** *imagination*. 病的に興奮した想像力においては事実あるいは空想的の危険が過度の重要性を持つのである. ¶the wide knowledge and ***fertile*** *imagination* of the writer その作家の広い知識と豊かな想像力. ¶***glowing*** *imagination* 白熱した想像力. ¶with a ***little*** *imagination* one is conscious of ... 少し想像をたくましくすれば...ということが自覚される. ¶Fiction is a record of the ***national*** *imagination*. 小説は国民想像の記録である. ¶He has ***no*** *imagination*. 彼は想像力を欠いている. ¶the very antithesis of that conjured up by the ***popular*** *imagination* 世人の想像の正反対. ¶it must be a ***sluggish*** *imagination* which is not quickened by the sight of ... ...の光景を見て刺激されないような想像力は鈍いといわざるを得ない. ¶***strong*** *imagination* 強烈な想像力. ¶possess an unbounded and ***vigorous*** *imagination* 自由なそして強い想像力を持つ. ¶***vivid*** *imagination* ありありと想像する能力.

P vital ***beyond*** all *imagination* 全く想像以上に重要な. 【類】 be successful ***beyond*** *imagination*. ¶perhaps colored ***by*** *imagination* 気のせいか. ¶***in*** *imagination* he could picture ... 彼は心の中に…を思い浮べることができた || let us try to conceive *in imagination* the difference between ... ...間の相違を想像して見よう || be fertile *in imagination* 想像力が豊かである || I can see *in imagination* that ... ...が想像で私に浮んで来る. ¶ give play *to* one's *imagination* その想像を働かす || give full play *to* one's *imagination* 想像をたくましくする.

P² What followed must be left to the *imagination of* the reader. それからどんなことが起ったかは読者の想像にまかせねばならない.

imagine, *v.* 想像する, 仮定する; 推量する.

M It can be ***better imagined*** than described. それは説明するより推量にまかした方がよい. ¶ ***dimly imagine*** おぼろげに想像する. ¶ It can ***easily*** be ***imagined***. それは容易に想像し得られることだ. ¶ You can ***little imagine*** my surprise. 私がどんなに驚いたかあなたにはちょっと想像ができないでしょう. ¶ I ***never imagine*** that ... 私は決して…とは思わない. ¶ I can ***quite imagine*** that ... ...ということは私にもよく想像ができる. ¶ I ***imagined*** myself [to be] ***safe***. 私は私自身無事だと思った. ¶ ***vividly imagine*** ありありと想像する. ¶ His elation may ***well*** be ***imagined***. その得意思うべしである. 【類】I can ***well imagine*** how pleased your parents will be. ¶ *imagine* him ***to be*** an enemy 彼を敵だと思う || *Imagine* yourself ***to be*** in his place. 彼の身になって考えて見給え. 「とができよう.

P it might be *imagined* ***from*** ... それは…から想像するこ

O I cannot *imagine* how ... どうして…か想像がつかない.

imbecile, *n.* 虚弱者, 低能者.

Q ***intellectual*** *imbeciles* 低能者.

imbed, *v.* 埋める.

P It was found *imbedded* ***in*** the earth. それは土中に埋まっていた. || thet ruth that is *imbedded* ***in*** these lines これらの詩に込められた真理.

imbibe, *v.* 吸収する.

P Roots *imbibe* fluids ***from*** the soil. 根は土から水分を吸収

imbue, *v.* 浸込ませる; かぶれさせる. 」する.

M The people are ***deeply imbued*** with a military spirit (an adventurous spirit). 国民には深く軍国精神(など)が浸込んでいる. ¶ ***thoroughly imbued*** with the spirit of ... ... の精神に徹し.

P *imbue* the idea ***into*** the students その思想を学生に植付ける. ¶ *imbue* it ***with*** moisture それを湿らす || *imbue* a person ***with*** ambition (patriotism, a new idea) 人に功名心(など)を植付ける. 【類】*imbue* the minds of youth ***with*** good principles / He is *imbued* ***with*** modernism. / He is *imbued* ***with*** the true ideals of education. / He is *imbued* ***with*** the spirit of social service (社会奉仕の精神).

imitate, *v.* まねる.

P a style *imitated* ***from*** another 他から模倣した型.

imitation, *n.* 模倣; 模造品.

V It ***deserves*** *imitation* in Tokyo and other large cities. 東京その他の大都市においてもこれにならう価値がある. ¶ ***second*** the *imitation* その模倣を奨励する.

Q ***awkward*** *imitations* of the freedom of foreign manners 外国人のゆう容迫らない態度をへたにまねたもの. ¶ a ***base*** *imitation* of a man 人非人(人面獣心). ¶ a ***blind*** *imitation* of ... ...の盲目的模倣. ¶ Beware of ***bogus*** *imitations*. 模造品に注意せよ. ¶ a ***clever*** *imitation* 巧みな模造品. ¶ ***deleterious*** *imitations* 有害な模造品. ¶ ***fraudulent*** *imitations* of American trade-marks 米国商標の詐欺的模造. 【類】make a document or write a signature in ***fraudulent*** *imitation*=forge a document or a signature. ¶ a ***mere*** *imitation* 全くの模造品. ¶ ***nasty*** *imitations* いやなまがい物. ¶ ***parrot-like*** *imitation* おうむのような模倣. ¶ Beware of ***poor*** (=***inferior***) *imitations*. いか物に用心せよ. ¶ the ***servile*** *imitation* of ... ...の卑劣な模倣. ¶ ***shoddy*** *imitations* まやかし物. ¶ a ***slavish*** *imitation* of the West 西洋の卑屈な模倣. ¶ ***spurious*** *imitations* にせ物. ¶ a ***transparent*** *imitation* 見え透いた模造品. ¶ Beware of ***worthless*** *imitations*. つまらない模造品に注意せよ.

Q² ***paste*** *imitations* of precious stones ねり物の人造宝石.

P made ***in*** *imitation* of shark-skin さめ革まがいの(模様など). 【類】It is beautifully speckled (美しい斑紋がある) ***in*** *imitation* of tortoise-shell. || built ***in*** *imitation* of ... ...まがいの(建物など).

P² an *imitation* ***from*** the original pattern 原型から作った模造品. ¶ an *imitation* ***of*** this fabric この織物の模造品 || an *imitation* ***of*** life 実物の模倣.

imitative, *a.* まねる.

P He is *imitative* ***of*** his master. 彼は主人をまねる.

imitator, *n.* 模倣者.

Q They are very ***clever*** *imitators* and adopters. 彼らは極めて巧妙な模倣者でありまた応用者である. ¶ ***incompetent*** *imitator* 拙劣な模倣者. ¶ ***milk-and-watery*** *imitators* 貧弱な模倣者. ¶ a ***servile*** *imitator* 卑劣な模倣者. ¶ a ***slavish*** *imitator* 卑屈な模倣者.

immaterial, *a.* 重要でない; 関係のない.

M be ***almost*** *immaterial* ほとんど用がない. ¶ It is ***wholly*** *immaterial* whether he ... or not. 彼が…しようがしまいがそんなことは一向重きをおくに足りないことだ.

P it is quite *immaterial* ***to*** me whether ... ...か否かは私から言うとどうでもよい || *immaterial* ***to*** the theme [小説など]テーマには関係のない.

immediately, *ad.* 直ちに, すぐ. 「でしょう.

M He will be here ***almost*** *immediately*. 彼はもうすぐ来る

P *immediately* ***after*** his arrival 彼の到着後直ちに. ¶ the period *immediately* ***before*** the festival of ... ...祭の直前. ¶ *immediately* ***on*** his beginning to speak 彼が話し始めると 」とすぐに.

immerse, *v.* 浸す; たんできさせる.

M he is ***deeply*** *immersed* in a study of ... 彼は…の研究に熱中している.

P *immerse* the body (bottle) ***in*** water 体(など)を水につける || He sat, *immersed* ***in*** the profoundest contemplation. 彼はすわってじっと考え込んだ. 【類】*immersed* ***in*** study (pleasure, business) / *immerse* oneself ***in*** mathematics / He is *immersed* ***in*** gross sensuality (野卑な肉欲).

immersion, *n.* 浸入; たんでき, 専心.

P baptize one ***by*** *immersion* 水に浸して洗礼を授ける. ¶ *immersion* ***in*** study (business, mathematics) 勉学(など)に専心. ¶ *immersion* ***into*** water 水中へ浸入.

immigrant, *n.* (外国からの)移住者.

Q Hawaiian sugar planters were contemplating the importation of ***Russian*** *immigrants* to solve the labor problem in the islands. ハワイの砂糖栽培者は同島における労働問題の解決策としてロシア移民の移入をもくろんでい

Q² ***quota*** *immigrants* 割当の移住民など. 」た.

P² *immigrants* ***from*** South Asia 南アジアからの移民.

immigrate, *v.* [他国から]移住する.

P *immigrate* ***into*** the country その国に来住する.

immigration, *n.* [他国からの]移住.

V ***assist*** *immigration* to New South Wales ニュー・サウス・ウエールズへの移住を援助する.

Q ***alien*** *immigration* to England 他国人の英国移住.

P a law ***against*** the *immigration* of Asiatic peoples アジア人入国禁止法. ¶ Asiatic *immigration* ***into*** Australia アジア人の豪州移住. 「本人の合衆国移住.

P² the *immigration* ***of*** Japanese ***to*** the United States 日

immolate, *v.* 犠牲にする.

P *immolate* one thing ***to*** another 一物を他物の犠牲にする.

immoral, *a.* 不道徳な, 不行跡な.

M ***flagrantly*** *immoral* 恐ろしく不徳義な. ¶ ***scandalously*** *immoral* 外聞の悪いほど不行跡な.

immorality, *n.* 不道徳, 不行跡.

V ***encourage*** *immorality* 不道徳に拍車をかける. ¶ This rather serves to ***popularize*** *immorality* instead of checking it. それは不倫を抑制せずにかえってこれを流行させることになる. ¶ ***practice*** *immorality* as a trade 色を売

Q ***glaring*** *immorality* 目に余る不行跡. 」る.

P² a life ***of*** *immorality* 不行跡の生活.

immortality, *n.* 不滅, 永遠性, 不朽.

V Some thought that the donor was ***seeking*** *immortality* for too modest an equivalent. その寄贈者は少しの寄付で名を永世に残そうという虫のよい考えであったと評するもの

immortalize, *v.* 不朽にする. 」もあった.

P be *immortalized* ***by*** a poet 詩人によって永久に伝えられる. 【類】Christ's Hospital, the famous "Bluecoat School" (「青服学校」) *immortalized* ***by*** Charles Lamb in the Essays of Elia.

immune, *a.* 免かれている; 免疫の.

P persons rendered *immune* ***against*** (=to) the attacks of scarlet fever しょう紅熱に免疫となった人. ¶ *immune* ***from*** foreign competition [貿易など]外国の競争を免かれている

‖ to be *immune from* the charm of woman 女難よけに ‖ *immune from* a disease (the contagion, poison) 病気(など)に免疫になっている. 【類】*immune from* punishment (penalty, taxation) / I am *immune from* the malady, for I had it once. ¶*immune to* the disease その病気に対して免疫になっている ‖ become *immune to* ... ...に免疫になる.

immunity, *n.* 免除; 免疫.

V *bring immunity* against the disease その病気に対して免疫にする. ¶injection of antitoxin for *conferring* temporary *immunity* 一時的の免疫性を与えるための抗毒素注射 ‖ *confer* an *immunity* on the patient (流行病などが)患者を免疫にする. ¶*enjoy immunity* from taxation 免租される. ¶*gain immunity* from conscription 徴兵を免除される. ¶*receive immunity* from taxation 課税を免除される. ¶*secure immunity* from mistakes 間違いをしないようになる.

Q *acquired immunity*〖医〗後天免疫性.

P the period *of immunity* 免疫期間. ¶*immunity from* a disease 免疫 ‖ *immunity from* military service 兵役免除.

immure, *v.* 監禁する.

P He is *immured in* prison. 彼は監禁されている.

impact, *n.* 衝撃.

V His return from abroad will *have* great *impact* on the political world.

Q America's *diplomatic* and *ideological impact* on Russia ロシアに対するアメリカの外交及び思想上の衝撃. ¶its *immediate impact* upon ... ...に対する直接の迫力.

P² the *impact of* sound (light) on the ear (eye) 耳(目)に対する音(光)の衝撃 ‖ the *impact of* two worlds 二つの世界の圧迫. 【類】The *impact of* the two swords threw off little sparks (火花).

impale, *v.* 突き刺す.

P butterflies *impaled on* small pins 小さなピンで刺した

impair, *v.* そこなう. ちょう.

P *impair* it *by* friction それを摩擦していためる.

impart, *v.* 伝える, 知らせる.

P *impart* information *to* a person 人に消息を伝える.【類】*impart* skill (knowledge) *to* another / I have nothing of importance to *impart to* you. ‖ Her presence *imparts* an air of elegance *to* the meeting. 彼女がいると会合に優雅な感じを与える.

impartial, *a.* 公平な.

P He is *impartial in* his opinions. 彼の説は公平だ. ¶He is *impartial to* his pupils. 彼は生徒に公平だ.

impartiality, *n.* 公平.

V he failed to *exercise* his usual *impartiality* in ... 彼は...に対していつもの公平振りを発揮しかねた.

Q with *rigid impartiality* あくまで公平に.

P *with* perfect *impartiality* 十分公平に.

impassable, *a.* 通行のできない.

P "Roads *impassable to* motors." 自動車通行止.

impasse, *n.* 袋小路.

Q *political impasse* 政治的行きづまり.

impatience, *n.* こらえられないこと, 短気, 性急.

V Some *impatience* was *exhibited* owing to the non-arrival of the speaker. 弁士が見えないので多少やきもきしていた. ¶He *has* a keen *impatience* with the dull. 彼は鈍物は大きらいだ. ¶*restrain* one's *impatience* じっと我慢する. ¶without *showing impatience* いらいらしないで気長く.

Q in *savage impatience* [まどろっこいので]やけになって.

P *out of impatience* 我慢しきれないで. ¶*with* some *impatience* 多少いらいらして ‖ wait *with impatience* やきもきして待つ.

P² *impatience of* restraint 束縛に対する焦慮 ‖ *impatience of* hypocrisy 偽善に対する憤慨.

impatient, *a.* こらえきれない; 待ちかねる.

M The discharge is *greatly impatient* by bad weather. 荷卸しは悪天候のため大いに妨げられている.

P wax (=grow) a trifle *impatient at* his long pleading 彼の長たらしい弁論にはいささかじれったくなる. ¶I am *impatient for* his arrival. 私は彼の着くのを待ちかねている. ‖ He was *impatient for* his holidays (payment). 彼は休暇(など)を待ちかねていた. ¶He is *impatient of* (=*at*) delay. 彼は遅いのをじれったがっている. ‖ *Impatient of* heat, he left town for the country. 彼は暑さにたえられないで避暑にでかけた. 【類】He is *impatient of* results. / He was *impatient of* reproof (非難). / He was *impatient of* views which did not agree with his own. ¶He was *impatient under* his sufferings. 彼は苦難にたえ切れなかった. ¶He is *impatient with* his servants. 彼は奉公人に対してよく腹を立てる.

impeach, *v.* 非難する, 弾劾する.

P He was *impeached for* treason. 彼は反逆罪で弾劾された. ¶they *impeached* him *of* ... 彼らは...で彼を問責した. ¶*impeach* a person *with* an error その過失を問責する.

impede, *v.* 妨害する.

P He was *impeded in* his work. 彼は仕事を妨害された.

impediment, *n.* 妨害, 故障.

V He *has* an *impediment* in his speech. 彼はどもる. ¶*put impediments* in the way of ... ...に邪魔を入れる.

P an *impediment to* progress (trade) 進歩(など)の妨げ.

impedimenta, *n.* 荷物, 用器入れ.

Q² The Londoner with his *golfing impedimenta* is a familiar spectacle on the railway platform of the Metropolis. ゴルフ器具をたずさえたロンドンの人は同市の駅のプラットフォームでよく見かける風景である.

impel, *v.* 駆る; 促す.

P He was *impelled by* strong passion. 彼は激情にかられた. ‖ *impelled by* sudden thought 突然の思い付きで. ¶The heart *impels* the blood *through* arteries. 心臓は動脈中に血液を送り込む. ¶necessity *impelled* him *to* the performance of ... 彼は必要にかられて...をした. 【類】Hunger *impels* one *to* crime. ‖ The premises *impel* us *to* the conclusion. その前提からこの結論に到達する.

impend, *v.* 差迫る; 差しかかる.

P Danger *impends over* his head. 危険が彼に迫っている. 【類】Destruction is *impending over* his head. ‖ A great rock *impends over* the lake. 大きな岩石が湖上に差しかかっている.

impenetrable, *a.* はいり込めない, 通らない; がん固な.

M Aristocracies are *naturally impenetrable* by new ideas. 貴族には当然新思想が分からない.

P clay *impenetrable by* the roots of plants 植物の根の入らない堅い粘土. ¶*impenetrable to* (=by) heat (light, the rain) 熱(など)の通らない. 【類】woods *impenetrable to* sunlight / a mind *impenetrable to* (=*by*) new ideas (がん固な人).

imperative, *a.* やむを得ない.

P It is *imperative on* us to do so. そうすることはわれわれに取って万やむを得ない. 【類】It is *imperative on* him to return.

imperceptible, *a.* 感知し難い.

P *imperceptible to* the senses 感覚には感じない.

imperialism, *n.* 帝国主義.

Q² American "*dollar imperialism*" アメリカの「ドル帝国主義」. ¶the *Red imperialism* 赤の帝国主義. ¶the menace of *United States* "*imperialism*" いわゆるアメリカ帝国主義の脅威. ¶Communist elements denounced it as *Yankee* "*imperialism*." 共産分子はこれをアメリカ帝国主義として非難した.

imperialist, *n.* 帝国主義者.

Q a *staunch imperialist* 忠実な帝国主義者.

impersonal, *a.* 個人には関係のない.

M My remarks are intended to be *quite impersonal*. 私は別にだれ彼と指していう訳ではない.

impersonality, *n.* 非人格性.

Q *polite impersonality* 個人関係を考慮に置かない丁寧で職務的な態度.

impersonate, *v.* ...の役を勤める; [声・スタイルなど]まねる.

P He *impersonates* Hamlet *with* great skill. 彼はハムレットの役が非常にうまい.

O *impersonate* a well-known vocalist 有名な声楽家のまねをする ‖ Abe Lincoln impersonates the ideal American. リンカーンは理想的な米国人の典型だ.

impertinence, *n.* 無礼.

V he *had* the *impertinence* to ... 彼は無礼にも...した. ¶Please *pardon* the *impertinence* of a perfect stranger in thus addressing you. 一面識もないのにこんなことを申上げて無礼の段は幾重にもおわび致します.

P a piece *of impertience* 一つの無礼.

impertinent, *a.* 無礼な, 生意気な.

M he was *so impertinent* as to ... 彼は...するほど無礼であった. ¶He pas *impertinent enough* to talk back to older people. 彼は生意気にも年長者に対し口返答をした.

P He is *impertinent to* his master. 彼は主人に無遠慮だ.

impervious, *a.* 通さない; 鈍感な.

P He is *impervious to* criticism. 彼は人の非難などは耳にも入れない. ‖ *impervious to* heat (light, water) 熱(など)を

通さない.

impetus, *n.* 刺激, 勢い.

V It ***gained impetus*** every moment as a moving body on an incline. それは斜面を転下する物体のように一刻ごとに力を増した. ¶The new treaty has ***given*** an *impetus* to trade. 新条約で貿易が活気づいてきた. ‖ ***give*** a fresh *impetus* to … …に新しい刺激を与える. 【類】 ***give*** an *impetus* to individual energy. ¶***lend*** an *impetus* to movement (progress) 運動(など)に気勢を添える. ¶***receive*** *impetus* from an outside quarter 外部からの刺激を受ける.

Q receive an ***additional*** *impetus* from … さらに…から刺激を受ける. ¶It gave an ***enormous*** *impetus* to the movement. それが運動にばく大の刺激を与えた. ¶receive a ***fresh*** *impetus* from … …から新しい刺激を受ける. ¶a ***huge*** *impetus* 非常な刺激. ¶a ***powerful*** *impetus* 力強い刺激. ¶it will help lend ***some*** *impetus* to … それで…を幾分でも促進させることになろう. ¶a ***timely*** *impetus* was given to the movement by … …がその運動に与えた刺激は時宜を得たものであった.

P The two trains came into collision ***with*** great *impetus*. 両列車は非常な勢いで衝突した.

P[2] an *impetus* ***from*** the souls of the departed 死者の霊魂からの与える力.

implant, *v.* 植付ける; 扶植する.

M The desire was ***deeply*** *implanted* in his breast. その欲望は彼の胸中に深く植付けられた.

P *implant* seeds or trees ***in*** the garden = implant the garden with seeds or trees 種または木を庭園に植込む ‖ The teeth are *implanted* ***in*** the alveoli of both jaws. 歯は両あごの歯槽に植付けられている. ‖ *implant* virtue (a desire, a good principle) ***in*** one's mind = implant one's mind ***with*** virtue (a desire, a good principle) 徳(など)をその心に扶植する.

implement, *n.* 器具, 道具.

V ***provide*** a useful *implement* for … …に必要な器具を支給する.

Q ***agricultural*** *implements* 農具. ¶a rudely ***conducted*** *implement* 構造の粗略な道具. ¶a ***writing*** *implement* 写字用具.

Q[2] a ***farm[ing]*** *implement* 農具. ¶***flint*** and ***bronze*** *implements* made by primitive people 原始人の作った石器及び銅器. ¶a ***household*** *implement* 調度品. ¶a ***kitchen*** *implement* 台所の器具類. ¶a ***war*** *implement* 戦争用具.

P[2] *implements* ***of*** divination 占い用具 ‖ an *implement* ***of*** restraint 戒具.

implementation, *n.* 履行, 遂行.

P ordinances issued ***in*** *implementation* of directives from the Allied Forces Headquarters 連合軍司令部の命令実施のため発せられた法令.

P[2] the *implementation* ***of*** the terms of surrender 降伏条件の履行.

implicate, *v.* 連座させる; 錯そうさせる.

P *implicate* one ***in*** the murder (robbery, fraud) 謀殺(など)に人を連座させる ‖ He was *implicated* ***in*** a plot (= conspiracy). 彼は陰謀に連座した. ¶*implicate* one's interest ***with*** (= in) those of others その利害を他の利害と錯そうさせる. 【類】 the interests of individuals *implicated* ***with*** those of the community ‖ He is *implicated* ***with*** others in the crime. 彼は他の者と連累だ.

implication, *n.* 含蓄, 含意.

V The term ***carries*** no derogatory *implications*. その言葉には何ら軽べつ的な意味は含まれていない. ¶It ***implies*** deeper *implications*. それはさらに深長な意味を含んでいる.

Q An *implication* is often more ***important*** than the direct statement. 含蓄は明言よりも一層重要なことが間々ある. ¶It has an ***opprobrious*** *implications*. それには侮辱的な意味が含まれいる. ¶The incident had ***political*** *implications*. その事件には政治的な含みがあった.

P ***by*** *implication* 暗々の内に. 【類】 it means ***by*** *implication* that …

implore, *v.* 懇願する.

P *implore* aid (pardon, mercy) ***from*** him 彼に扶助(など)を懇請する. ¶she *implored* him ***with*** tears in her eyes to … 彼女は涙ながらに彼に…を懇願した.

imply, *v.* 暗示する.

P as *implied* ***by*** (= ***in***) the name その名称の示すように.

O Her smile *implied* that she had forgiven us. 彼女のほほえみはわれわれを許したことを意味した.

impolite, *a.* 不作法な, 失敬な.

P it is very *impolite* (= rude) ***of*** you to … …するのは非常に失礼である. ¶take care not to be *impolite* ***to*** customers 客にそそうのないように気をつける.

import, *n.* (**1**) 意義, 意味; 重要.

V ***fathom*** its deeper *import* そのさらに深長な意義をさぐる. ¶I fail to ***grasp*** the *import* of … 私には…の意味がつかめない.

Q a matter of ***great*** *import* 重大な事柄. ¶a word of ***like*** *import* 同じような意味の言葉. ¶a word of ***noble*** *import* 高尚な意味の言葉. ¶an affair of ***no small*** *import* 容易ならない事件. ¶exchange a few words of ***tender*** *import* 優しい二三の言葉を取交す.

P a question ***of*** vital *import* 大問題.

P[2] the *import* ***of*** words 言葉の意義.

(**2**) 輸入, 輸入品.

V The *import* of this article is ***prohibited*** here. この品物の輸入はここでは禁止になっている. ¶***wear*** French *import* フランスからの輸入品を身に着ける. ¶Our *imports* ***fall*** short of our exports. わが国の輸入品は輸出品と同額に達していない.

Q ***direct*** *import* 直輸入. ¶***foreign*** *import* to the port of New York ニューヨーク港における外国からの輸入. ¶a list of ***main*** *imports* 主要輸入品の一覧表. ¶It was not more than one-sixth of the ***total*** *import* of foreign produce. それは外国品の総輸入額の六分の一を出なかった. ¶Rubber is a ***useful*** *import*. ゴムは重要な輸入品である.

Q[2] ***food*** *imports* 輸入食料品. ¶***overseas[s]*** *imports* 海外からの輸入品.

P the excess ***of*** *imports* ***over*** exports 輸入超過. ¶the taxes ***on*** *imports* 輸入品税.

P[2] the *imports* ***from*** Australia ***to*** Japan 豪州から日本への輸入品. ¶the principal *imports* ***into*** Japan from abroad 日本への主要輸入品. ¶the *import* ***of*** foreign articles 外国品の輸入.

import, *v.* 輸入する; 重大な関係を有する.

M It is a question that *imports* us ***nearly***. それはわれわれに密接な関係のある問題だ.

P The woolen goods were *imported* ***at*** Shimonoseki. その毛織物は下関に輸入された. ¶*import* goods ***from*** a country 某国から商品を輸入する. ¶*import* an irrelevant matter ***into*** a discussion 議論に見当違いのことを持込む ‖ *import* cotton ***into*** Japan ***from*** India インドから棉花を輸入する. ¶*import* goods not in stock ***to*** order 注文によって持合わせていない品を輸入する.

importance, *n.* 重要性, 大切; 身分の貴いこと; 尊大.

V the *importance* of the study of English has been ***accentuated*** when he said that … 彼は…と言って英語研究の重要性を強調した. ¶***acquire*** a greater *importance* 一層重要視される. 【類】 ***acquire*** *importance* ‖ The manufacture of … is ***acquiring*** *importance* as an industry. …の製造は工業として重要視されてきた. ¶***assume*** considerable industrial *importance* 産業的にかなりの重要性を帯びる. ¶***attach*** great *importance* to this subject この問題を重要視する. 【類】 ***attach*** little *imortance* to … / I refrain from ***attaching*** much *importance* to … / Orientals ***attach*** great *importance* to numbers. ¶Electro-chemistry ***attained*** considerable *importance*. 電気化学はかなり重要になった. ¶***discriminate*** the relative *importance* 重要性をそれぞれ識別する. ¶***emphasize*** one's [own] *importance* もったいぶる ‖ strongly ***emphasize*** the *importance* of … 大いに…の重要性を強調する. 【類】 I cannot too greatly ***emphasize*** the *importance* of giving a practical character to the study of English. ¶***enforce*** the *importance* of … …の重要性を力説する. ¶***exaggerate*** the *importance* of … …の重要性を誇張する. ¶***exalt*** the *importance* of … …の重要性を高める. ¶***give*** *importance* to … …に重きをおく. ¶it ***has*** much *importance* to … それは…にとってきわめて大切だ. ¶***kill*** the commercial *importance* その商業上の重要性をそぐ. ¶***lend*** additional *importance* to the statement that … …という声明に一層の重要性を加える. ¶It is day by day ***losing*** its *importance*. それは日一日とその重要性を失いつつある. ¶***magnify*** the *importance* of … …の重要性を増す. ¶***measure*** one's *importance* by one's income 収入によって人の貫禄を度(はか)る. ¶The *importance* of … cannot be ***overemphasized***. …の重要性は誇張し過ぎるということはない. ¶We are apt to ***overrate*** their *importance*. われわれはややもすれば彼らを買いかぶる. ¶The *importance* of this idea cannot be ***overstressed***.

この考えの重要さはいかに強調しても強調し過ぎるということはない. ¶***overvalue*** the *importance* of ... ...を重要視しすぎる. ¶***place importance*** on ... ...に力こぶを入れる. ¶***realize*** the *importance* of ... ...の重要性を実感する. 【類】the *importance* of it is at once ***realized*** when one reflects on the serious consequences that might result from ... / the *importance* of the question will be ***realized*** when we consider ... ¶Its *importance* is generally ***recognized.*** その重要性は一般に認められている. ¶***revive*** its dwindling *importance* as a port for export trade 輸出貿易港としてのその衰勢をばん回する. ¶***show*** the relative *importance* of the players by varying the type 活字(の大きさ)を変えて演技者の相対的重要性を示す. ¶***stress*** the *importance* of ... ...の重要性を強調する. ¶Nobody with a grain of sense ***underestimates*** the great *importance* of good cooking. 少しでも物の分かった人は優良な料理法が大事だと思わないものはない. ¶***underrate*** the *importance* of the subject その問題を軽視する. ¶***urge*** the *importance* of ... ...の重要性を切論する.

Q The point is of ***basic*** *importance.* その点が根本的に大切なのだ. ¶It is of ***capital*** *importance.* それは最も大切なことだ. ¶of ***cardinal*** *importance* 枢要な. ¶a place of much ***commercial*** *importance* 商業上の要地. ¶of ***crucial*** *importance* 断然重要な. ¶be of ***enormous*** *importance* 非常に大切なことである. ¶of ***especial*** *importance* 特に重要な. ¶attach ***exaggerated*** *importance* to ... ...を過大に重視する. ¶be of an ***extreme*** *importance* to ... ...にとってきわめて重要である. ¶It may prove of ***far-reaching*** *importance* to education. それは教育上種々の点において重要なものとなるであろう. ¶a matter (question) of the ***first*** *importance* 最も重要な件(など). 【類】Repeated practice is of the ***first*** *importance* to students. ¶a journal of ***first*** or of ***second-rate*** *importance* 一流または二流の新聞. ¶it is of ***first-rate*** *importance* that ... ...ということが最も大切だ. ¶assume a ***fresh*** *importance* since ... ...以来新たに重要性を持つ. ¶it is of ***fundamental*** *importance* to ... ...するのが根本的に必要だ. ¶a matter of such ***grave*** *importance* かくまで重大な件. ¶a matter of ***great*** *importance* 重要な件 ‖ with an air of ***great*** *importance* えらそうな風をして. ¶***growing*** *importance* 増大する重要性. ¶a matter of the ***highest*** *importance* 最も重要な件. ¶objects (places) of ***historic*** *importance* 歴史的に重要な品(など). ¶The place has ***historic*** and ***present*** *importance.* その土地は過去においてもまた現在においても重要な場所である. ¶a matter of ***hygienic*** *importance* 衛生上重視すべきこと. ¶countries which are of the chief ***industrial*** *importance* 主要産業国. ¶an event of ***international*** *importance* 国際的に重要なできごと. ¶be of ***key*** *importance* きわめて重要である ‖ all types of goods of ***international*** *importance* 国際的価値のある各種の商品. ¶a matter of the ***last*** *importance* 最も重大な事. ¶of ***leading*** *importance* きわめて重要な. ¶It is of the ***least*** *importance* to me. それは私にとってはちっとも重きをおく必要のないものだ. ¶the Saturday Evening Post, or other magazines of ***like*** *importance* サタディ・イーヴニング・ポストまたは他の同様重要な雑誌. ¶of very ***little*** *importance* ほとんど重要視する必要のない. ¶***military*** *importance* 軍事的重要性. ¶of ***minor*** *importance* さほど重要でない. ¶be of ***momentous*** *importance* to us われわれにきわめて大切である. ¶men of ***more*** or ***less*** *importance* 多少とも勢力のある人々. ¶attach ***more*** *importance* of ... ...に一層重きをおく ‖ matters of the ***most*** *importance* 最も重要な件. ¶an article of food of ***national*** *importance* 国家的に重要な食品. 【類】a manufacture (subject) of ***national*** *importance.* ¶people of ***national*** and ***local*** *importance* 全国的にも地方的にも重要な人々. ¶We attach ***no*** *importance* to the report. われわれはそのうわさには少しも重きをおかない. ¶They are classed in the order of ***numerical*** *importance.* それらは数の順序に分類してある. ¶discoveries of ***outstanding*** *importance* ひときわ重要な発見. ¶assert one's ***own*** *importance* 幅をきかす. ¶an event of ***overshadowing*** *importance* 圧倒的に重大な事件. ¶of ***paramount*** *importance* 最も重要な. ¶a subject of ***permanent*** *importance* to such a nation as ours われわれのような国民には永久に重大な問題. ¶the ***practical*** *importance* of the industry to the human race 人類に取ってその産業の実際的重要性. ¶of ***present*** *importance* 差当って重要な. ¶This is of ***primary*** *importance.* これは根本的に必要だ. ¶These topics are of ***prime*** *importance.* これらの問題は重大だ. ¶various points of ***prime commercial*** *importance* 商業上主要な種々の点. ¶it is of ***profound*** *importance* to ... それは...に取ってはなはだ必要なことである. ¶see that the ***proper*** *importance* is given to ... ...の軽重を誤らないように注意する. ¶it is of ***real*** *importance* that ... ...は真に重要なことだ. ¶a question of ***relative*** *importance* 比較的重要な問題 ‖ discriminate the ***relative*** *importance* 相対的な重要性を弁別する. ¶The question becomes of almost ***secondary*** *importance.* その問題の重要性はほとんど二次的なものになって来る. ¶a matter of very ***small*** *importance* 重要性の少ないことがら. ¶His family seems to have been of ***some*** *importance.* 氏の家族は世間からは多少重んぜられていたらしい. ¶be of ***sovereign*** *importance* 最高の重要性がある. ¶the great ***strategic*** *importance* of Alaska as a defense area 防御地域としてアラスカの大なる戦略的重要性. 【類】It possesses the highest ***strategical*** *importance.* ¶of ***subordinate*** *importance* 付随的に必要な. ¶of ***superior*** *importance* 特に重要な. ¶of ***supreme*** *importance* 最も重要な. ¶an article of ***timely*** *importance* 時にとって必要な論文. ¶You cannot attach ***too much*** *importance* to practice. 練習というものはどこまでもこれを重んじなければならない. ¶be of ***trifling*** *importance* 余り重要でない. ¶attach ***undue*** *importance* to ... ...を重視し過ぎる. ¶It is of ***urgent*** *importance* to the well-being of a very large number of people. それは大多数の国民の幸福に切に必要なものだ. ¶discuss some matter of ***urgent international*** *importance* 国際的に緊要なある問題を論議する. ¶it is of the ***utmost*** *importance* to ... ...するのが最も必要なことだ. ¶of ***vital*** *importance* 根本的に重要な. ¶a happening of ***worldwide*** *importance* 世界的に重要性のあるできごと.

Q^2 the ***business*** *importance* of English 英語の商業上の重要性. ¶***world*** *importance* 世界的な重要性.

P He poisoned his mind ***by*** *importance.* 彼は地位が高いのが彼の心に禍をした. ¶first ***in*** *importance* comes ... 一番大切なことは... ‖ increase (=grow) ***in*** *importance* 重要性を増す. ¶Nothing ***of*** *importance* resulted from the movement. その運動は大して成果があがらなかった.

P^2 the *importance* ***of*** being well dressed 身なりを良くすることの重要さ. 【類】The *importance* ***of*** the matter has been brought home to me (しみじみ分かった). ¶They discussed several matters of *importance* ***to*** the association. 彼らは同協会に取って重要な諸件を討議した.

important, *a.* 重要な.

M ***highly*** *important* 非常に重要な. ¶***less*** *important* それほど重要でない. ¶***numerically*** *important* 数が多いので重要な. ¶***supremely*** *important* きわめて重要な. ¶***too*** *important* to be neglected はなはだ重要で無視できない.

P *important* ***before*** everything 何よりも重要な. ¶it is *important* ***for*** us to ... ...するのはわれらにとって大切なことである.

importation, *n.* 輸入, 輸入品.

V^2 *Importations* from abroad have greatly ***declined.*** 海外よりの輸入が大いに減少した. ¶flour *importations* have ***diminished*** by ... 小麦粉の輸入が...だけ減じた.

Q an ***American*** *importation* 米国からの輸入品. ¶a ***foreign*** *importation* 舶来品. ¶The cook is a ***recent*** *importation* from Paris. その料理人は最近パリから呼び寄せたものだ.

P we are dependent upon *importation* ***from*** foreign countries for ... われわれは...を外国からの輸入に頼っている. ¶Alchemy was an *importation* ***from*** Greece ***by way of*** Bactria. 錬金術はバクトリアを経てギリシアから輸入されたものであった.

importer, *n.* 輸入者.

Q^2 a ***diamond*** *importer* ダイアモンド輸入者. ¶Shriro, the ***sundry goods*** *importers* 雑貨輸入商のシュリロ.

importune, *v.* うるさくせがむ.

P *importune* him ***for*** money 彼に金をくれとうるさくせがむ. ¶He *importuned* me ***with*** requests. 彼は私にうるさく頼んだ.

Q I was not only invited but *importuned* to buy. 私は買ってくれるように勧められただけでなくうるさくせがまれた.

importunity, *n.* しつよう.

P He requested me ***with*** *importunity.* 彼はうるさく私に

要求した. ¶the *importunities* ***of*** the beggars こじきのあつかましさ.

impose, *v*. 課する; 欺く.

M ***sportively*** *impose* upon ... …を面白半分にだます.

P They will not so easily *impose* ***on*** me. 私はそう容易に彼らにだまされはしまい. ‖ *impose* ***on*** the multitude 世間の人をだます ‖ I *imposed* ***on*** his kindness by asking for ... 私は彼の親切に甘えて…を頼んだ. ¶the fine of two thousand yen shall be *imposed* ***upon*** ... …に二千円の罰金刑を科する ‖ *impose* bad wine ***upon*** customers 悪い酒をおしつける ‖ *impose* ***upon*** those who do not possess the knowledge requisite to detect the fraud その詐欺を看破るだけの知識のない人たちをだます. 【類】 *impose* ***upon*** the public.

imposition, *n*. 賦課.

P[2] the *imposition* ***of*** limitation 制限を設けること ‖ the time for the *imposition* ***of*** sentence upon ... was fixed for ... …に対する判決申渡の時日は…と決定した.

impossibility, *n*. 不可能のこと.

V ***perform*** *impossibilities* 不可能なことをする.

Q an ***absolute*** *impossibility* 全然あり得ないこと. ¶a ***logical*** *impossibility* 論理上不可能のこと. ¶a ***physical*** *impossibility* その物の性質上不可能なこと. ¶Aristotle speaks of a "***probable*** *impossibility*" as being more convincing than an "improbable possibility." アリストテレスはがい然的不可能は非がい然的可能より一層明確なものだと論じている. ¶a ***sheer*** (=an utter) *impossibility* 全然不可能なこと.

P ask ***for*** *impossibilities* 不可能のことを要求する.

O It is an *impossibility* to change lead into gold. 鉛を金に変えることは不可能だ.

impossible, *n*. 不可能事.

V ***accomplish*** (=***achieve***) the apparently *impossible* 一見不可能なことをなし遂げる. ¶***attempt*** the *impossible* 不可能事を試みる. ¶try to ***do*** the *impossible* できないことをやろうとする. ¶***make*** the *impossible* possible 不可能を可能にさせる. ¶To discover the source of the Nile was for many centuries the standing expression for ***performing*** the *impossible*. ナイル川の水源発見は幾世紀にわたって不可能なことをなすという意味に転用されて来た. ¶***try*** the *impossible* できないことをやってみる.

impossible, *a*. 不可能な.

M it is ***absolutely*** *impossible* to ... …することは絶対的に不可能である. ¶***manifestly*** *impossible* 明かに不可能な. ¶it is ***mathematically*** *impossible* that ... …ということは数理上不可能なことだ. ¶promises ***obviously*** *impossible* of fulfilment 明白に履行不可能な約束. ¶***practically*** *impossible* 実際上不可能な. 【類】 Despite the accuracy of modern technology, it remains ***practically*** *impossible* to make a number of things absolutely uniform. ¶it was ***quite*** *impossible* to ... …することは全く不可能であった. ¶I thought such was ***utterly*** *impossible*. よもやそんなことはなかろうと思っていた. ¶***well-nigh*** *impossible* ほとんど不可能な. ¶***wholly*** *impossible* 全然不可能な.

P Without diligence it is *impossible* ***for*** any one to learn a foreign language. 努力しないではだれにだって外国語は学べない. ¶He will attempt what others have declared to be *impossible* ***of*** attainment. 彼は他の人が達成不可能だと言切ったことを試みるだろう. ‖ *impossible* ***of*** fulfilment (definition) 遂行(など)が不可能な. ¶*impossible* ***to*** him 彼に取っては不可能な.

O It is regarded as *impossible*. それは不可能と見なされている. ‖ find it *impossible* to ... …することはできないことが分かる.

impostor, *n*. 詐欺師.

V ***show up*** an *impostor* 詐欺師の化けの皮をはぐ.

Q a ***daring*** *impostor* 大詐欺師. ¶He is a ***regular*** *impostor*. 彼は全くの詐欺師だ. ¶a ***thorough*** *impostor* 徹底的な詐欺師.

Q[2] a begging ***letter*** *impostor* 無心の手紙を書く詐欺師.

P regard him ***as*** an *impostor* 彼を詐欺師と見る.

imposture, *n*. 詐欺.

Q a ***hollow*** (=***thorough***) *imposture* 《口語》 全くの詐欺.

impracticable, *a*. 実行不可能な; 通れない.

M be ***altogether*** *impracticable* for ... 全然…には不向である.

P The pass is *impracticable* ***for*** jinriki or horse. その山道は人力車や馬では通れない. ‖ it is *impracticable* ***for*** me to ... …することは私にはできない.

imprecate, *v*. のろう.

P *imprecate* curses ***upon*** him 彼をのろう.

impregnate, *v*. 飽和する, 浸みこます.

M ***strongly*** *impregnated* with iron 鉄分を多量に含んだ.

P the air *impregnated* ***with*** a pleasant perfume ふくいくたる香気に満ちた空気. 【類】 water *impregnated* ***with*** salt.

impress, *n*. 印象; 特徴.

V All great virtues ***bear*** the *impress* ***of*** self-denial.—Channing. りっぱな徳はいずれも自制という特徴をもっている. ‖ His countenance ***bore*** the *impress* of high intelligence. 彼の容貌には高い知性が現われていた. ¶a genius that has ***left*** its *impress* on the world to the end of time 名を永久に残した英才. 【類】 ***leave*** the *impress* of one's remarkable personality upon ... その異常の人格を…に躍如たらしめる.

Q leave a ***deep*** *impress* on the minds of ... …の心に深い感銘を与える. ¶Her art bears a ***distinctive*** *impress*. その国の美術は明かに特徴をもっている. ¶leave a ***permanent*** *impress* upon the country その国に不朽の足跡を残す. ¶He left ***small*** *impress* on the world. 彼は大した仕事もやらないで世を去った.

impress, *v*. 感動させる, 印象を与える.

M be ***deeply*** *impressed* by ... …の印象が焼きつけられる. ¶*impress* him ***favorably*** 彼に好印象を与える. 【類】 This matter ***favorably*** *impressed* the investigating authorities (捜査当局). / I was ***favourably*** *impressed* by his appearance. ¶*impress* a fact ***forcibly*** on the consciousness of ... 事実を…の心に強く止める. ¶I am ***greatly*** *impressed* with ... 私は…に大いに感動した. ¶*impress* ***indelibly*** on the mind of ... …の心にうち消し難い印象を与える. 【類】 *impress* itself ***indelibly*** upon the memory of all visitors. ¶what *impresses* ***most*** the student of ... …の研究者に最も深い感銘を残すもの. ¶It is ***strongly*** *impressed* on my memory. それは私の記憶にはっきりと残っている. 【類】 these experiments ***strongly*** *impressed* him with the belief that ...

P He *impressed* me ***as*** a man of great ability. 彼は私に大手腕家だという印象を与えた. ¶one cannot help being *impressed* ***by*** ... 人は…によって印象を受けずにはいない. ¶*impress* ***on*** parents the importance of ... 親たちに…の重要性を印象づける ‖ *impress* ***on*** the pupils that ... 生徒らに…という事を銘記させる ‖ *impress* ***on*** one's mind 心に印象を与える. 【類】 It will *impress* words better ***on*** the memory. ¶It should be *impressed* ***upon*** intending insurers that they cannot be too careful in the selection of an office. 保険契約をしようと思う者は会社の選択には細心の注意を要することを銘記せねばならない. 【類】 *impress* ***upon*** public attention the supreme importance to the nation of ... ¶I remained long *impressed* ***with*** this sight. 私はこの光景に胸を打たれて永い間忘れることができなかった. ¶He is *impressed* ***with*** that notion and desires to *impress* it on me. 彼はその考えがしみ込んでそれを私につぎ込みたいのだ. ‖ Judges *impress* the people ***with*** the dignity of law by wearing a false head of hair. 判事はかつらをかぶって国民に法の尊厳を示す. ‖ be very much *impressed* ***with*** ... …で非常に深い印象を受けている. 【類】 no one can look at ... without being *impressed* ***with*** the truth of ...

impression, *n*. 印象, 感想, 意見; 刷り.

V ***acquire*** new *impressions* 新しい印象を得る. ¶He ***brought back*** many interesting *impressions* of his trip. 彼は旅の面白いみやげ話を沢山持ち帰った. ¶***carry away*** *impressions* both pleasant and regretful 好印象と悪印象とが心に残る. 【類】 It is probably true that the *impression* a traveller ***carries away*** from England is that it is a land of first-rate scenes and third-rate hotels. ¶***cause*** a painful *impression* 痛ましい印象を与える. ¶***chronicle*** the first *impressions* 第一印象を記録する. ¶it ***confirms*** the *impression* that ... それは…という印象を強める. ¶***convey*** the *impression* that ... …という印象を与える. ¶***correct*** that wholly false *impression* その全然誤った印象を是正する. ¶***create*** the *impression* that ... …という印象を与える. ¶***deepen*** the *impression* that ... …という印象を深くする. ¶the *impressions* which he ***derived*** from the tour 彼がその旅行から得た印象. ¶***dispel*** this untoward *impression* この面白くない印象を一掃する. ¶***dissipate*** that *impression* その印象を解消させる. ¶we are anxious to ***efface*** the *impression* caused by ... われわれは...のために生じた印象を消滅させたいと思う. ¶He intends to ***embody*** the *impressions* of his present journey in a book. 彼は今度の旅行の印象をまとめて一冊の本にするつもり. ¶***express*** one's *impressions* 感想を述べる. ¶I shall never ***forget*** the *impression* made upon me. 私がうけた印象は決して忘れない. ¶***gain*** the *impression* from it that ... それから...という印象を受ける. 【類】 *impressions* ***gained*** during his trip. ¶***get*** vivid *impressions* 鮮かな印象を受ける. ¶***give*** a vivid *impression* of local color 地方色を眼前に躍如たらしめる ‖ ***give*** a totally false *impression* of ... ...を全然誤解させる. ¶***have*** (=***exercise***) a favorable *impression* upon ... ...に好印象を与える. ¶It seemed to ***leave*** a favourable *impression* upon every one present. それは全出席者に良い印象を与えたようだ. 【類】 It ***leaves*** an *impression* on the visitor not easily forgotten. / it ***left*** an *impression* behind it as though ... ¶Although he is twenty-four years old, he ***makes*** the *impression* of a young man of eighteen. 彼は二十四歳になっているのだけれど十八歳の青年のような印象を与える. 【類】 ***make*** a deeper *impression* on our minds / ***made*** a very bad *impression* on thoughtful hearers / an *impression* ***made*** strongly on my mind. ¶His speech ***produced*** a great *impression* on the audience. 彼の演説は聴衆に大なる感銘を与えた. ¶***record*** *impressions* in black and white 印象を書きつづる. ¶one ***receives*** the *impression* that ... われらは...という印象を受ける. 【類】 That's the *impression* I ***received***. ¶***remove*** a false *impression* with regard to ... ...について誤った印象を排除する. ¶***strengthen*** the gloomy *impression* 陰気な印象を濃厚にする. ¶***take*** *impressions* of ... with dry inkstone rubbed over Japanese paper placed over them その上におかれた日本紙の上を鐘墨で擦って乾拓を取る. ¶***voice*** one's *impression* of ... ...についての印象を発表する.

v² the *impression* ***prevails*** among young men that ... 青年など一般は...と思っている.

Q an ***agreeable*** *impression* 好印象. ¶It created a very ***bad*** *impression* throughout the country. それは国中に極めて悪い印象を与えた. ¶give a ***biased*** *impression* 一方に偏した印象を与える. ¶my ***confident*** *impression* is that ... 私の所信は...だ. ¶make a ***deep*** *impression* 深く感動させる ‖ leave a ***deep*** *impression* upon ... ...に深い印象を残す. ¶a ***deep*** and ***lasting*** *impression* 深い永続的な印象. ¶It made an ***enduring*** *impression* on me. それは私に容易に忘れられない印象を与えた. ¶receive an ***erroneous*** *impression* 間違った印象を受ける. ¶The news has made an ***excellent*** *impression* here. その報道が当地ではすばらしい印象を与えた. ¶it made an ***extraordinary*** *impression* on ... それは...に異常な印象を与えた. ¶it created a ***false*** *impression* of ... それは...について誤った印象を与えた. 【類】 convey a very ***false*** *impression* to ... / give ***false*** *impressions* of American life / have a ***false*** *impression* of him (誤解). ¶It can hardly make a ***favorable*** *impression* upon the public opinion of Japan. それは日本の世論に好印象を与えることはほとんどできない. ¶one's ***first*** *impressions* of ... 人の...に対する第一印象. ¶the ***first-hand*** *impression* of the Middle East 直接得た近東の印象. ¶it is a ***general*** *impression* that ... ...というのが一般の印象である. 【類】 the ***general*** *impression* of the applicant / the ***general*** *impression* produced by the book is that ... ¶make a ***good*** *impression* on ... ...に好印象を与える. 【類】 Business letters should be so prepared as to carry a ***good*** *impression* of organization by which they are sent out. / A cheerful voice creates a ***good*** *impression*. ¶His speech produced an ***immense*** *impression* on the audience. 彼の演説は聴衆に深甚な印象を与えた. ¶It left ***indelible*** *impressions* on my mind. それは私の心に忘れ難い印象を残した. ¶***ineffaceable*** *impressions* 消えない印象. ¶make an ***ineradicable*** *impression* upon ... ...に消えない印象を与える. ¶leave (=make) a ***lasting*** *impression* on ... ...に永続的な印象を残す. 【類】 remain as a ***lasting*** *impression*. ¶it was sufficient to create a ***loose*** *impression* that ... それは...という大体の印象を与えるには十分であった. ¶one of the ***main*** *impressions* left upon me after knowing him for many years is that ... 彼を知って数年後私の心に残っている主な印象の一つは...である. ¶under the ***mistaken*** *impression* ... ...という間違った考えから. ¶it does not make ***much*** *impression* upon ... それは...に大した印象を与えない. ¶give one a quite ***new*** *impression* of ... 人に...の全く新しい印象を与える. ¶some ***outstanding*** *impressions* ある著しい印象. ¶it may be so, but my ***own*** *impression* is that ... そうかも知れないが私自身の印象は...である. ¶cause a ***painful*** *impression* 痛ましい印象を与える. ¶It does not leave upon the mind any very ***permanent*** *impression*. それは心に永続的な印象を留めない. ¶on the basis of one's ***personal*** *impressions* その個人的印象に基づいて ‖ carry away ***pleasant*** *impressions* [読書など]愉快な印象をそれから得る. ¶a ***pleasing*** *impression* 愉快な印象. ¶He carried away with him a very ***poor*** *impression* of the service of the hotel. ホテルのサービスがよくないという印象を受けて立った. ¶an *impression* is widely ***prevalent*** in this country that ... この国では...という考えが広く行われている. ¶It made a ***profound*** *impression* upon me. それは私に深い印象を与えた. 【類】 The affair created a ***profound*** *impression* when it became known in the city. ¶it would make the ***same*** *impression* on ... as ... would on ... それは...が...に与えると同じような印象を...に与えるであろう. ¶make a ***sympathetic*** *impression* upon the reader 読者の同情を引く. ¶It is creating the most ***unfavorable*** *impression*. それは最も不利な印象を与えている. 【類】 efface the ***unfavorable*** *impressions* thus produced. ¶This impression is ***universal***. この印象は一般に持っている. ¶I have a ***vague*** *impression* that ... 私には...というぼんやりした印象がある. ¶give a ***vivid*** *impression* of local color 地方色の生々した感じを与える. ¶We carry away with us a ***vivid*** and ***lasting*** *impression*. われわれは生々とした印象をいつまでも持ち続ける. ¶the ***wide-spread*** *impression* that ... という一般に流布している意見. ¶convey a ***wrong*** *impression* 間違った印象を伝える. ¶create a ***wrong*** or ***deceitful*** *impression* 間違ったまたは虚偽な印象を持たせる.

Q² ***chance*** *impressions* 偶感. ¶the ***eye*** (***ear***) *impression* 目(耳)の印象. ¶instruments of ***mass*** *impression*: the press, radio, screen, platform, schools 大衆に印象づける施設—新聞, ラジオ, 映画, 講演, 学校. ¶a ***parting*** *impression* 別離の感想. ¶have not made a ***pin's point*** *impression* on my heart 私の心にはピン先ほどの印象も与えなかった.

P conclude ***from*** the first *impressions* that ... 第一印象によって...と思い込む. ¶I was ***under*** the *impression* that ... 私は...だと思っていた ‖ ***under*** the *impression* that it will prove of utility to ... それは...にはためになるという考えで. ¶He left it ***with*** an *impression* which was to linger in his memory for years. 彼は幾年も彼の記憶に残るべき印象をいだいてそこを去った.

P² his *impressions* ***about*** ... ...についての彼の印象. ¶a woman's *impression* ***at*** a boxing-match けん闘仕合を見ての女の印象. 【類】 my *impressions* ***at*** Koya-san. ¶*impressions* ***from*** Japan 日本から受けた印象 ‖ an *impression* ***from*** a plate 金属版刷り. ¶*impressions* ***of*** his recent trip abroad 彼が最近外遊中に得た印象. 【類】 His *impressions* ***of*** the country were not so favorable. ¶A British writer's *impressions* ***on*** Japan 日本に関する一英人記者の印象.

impressiveness, *n.* 印象の深いこと, 荘厳さ.

v This ***gives*** *impressiveness* to what he says. このことが彼の言うことの印象を深める. ¶***lend*** *impressiveness* and dignity to the scene その光景に荘厳と威儀を与える.

imprint, *n.* なつ印; 印刻.

v His writings ***bear*** the *imprint* of a genius. 彼の書いたものには天才のひらめきがある. ‖ ***bear*** an *imprint* of originality 独創性を示す. ¶Suffering ***left*** its *imprint* on her face. 彼女の顔には苦悩のしわがよっていた.

Q² books bearing the A ***Company*** *imprint* A 会社の名が出ている書籍.

imprint, *v.* 押印する, 印する, 印刻する.

P *imprint* a postmark ***on*** an envelope 封筒に消印を押す. 【類】 *imprint* a kiss ***on*** one's brow. ‖ it is deeply *imprinted* ***on*** the minds of ... それは...の心に深く銘記してある. ¶The name of the firm is often *imprinted* ***with*** a rubber stamp. その商社の名がしばしばゴム判で押してある.

imprison, *v.* 幽閉する, おし込める.

v He had been *imprisoned* ***down there*** for years. 彼はそこに何年間も幽閉されていた.

imprisonment, *n.* 入所, 禁固; 幽閉.

v The culprit ***got*** several weeks' *imprisonment* for arson.

犯人は放火のとがで数週間の禁固に処せられた. ¶He repeatedly ***suffered imprisonment*** for this offense. 彼はこの犯罪でしばしば禁固に処せられた. 【類】***suffer*** lengthened *imprisonment* with forfeiture of houses and property (財産は没収せられ). ¶he ***underwent*** eighteen months' *imprisonment* for ... 彼は...のため十八カ月の禁固に処せられた. 【類】He is ***undergoing imprisonment***.

Q He lives in ***close imprisonment***. 彼は幽閉されている. ¶***limited*** *imprisonment* 有期禁固.

Q^2 be sentenced to ***life imprisonment*** 終身禁固に処せられる.

P sentenced ***to*** *imprisonment* with three years' hard labor 三年の懲役に処せられる.

P^2 *imprisonment* ***for*** life 終身禁固. ¶five years' *imprisonment* ***with*** hard labor 五カ年の懲役.

improbability, *n.* ありそうもないこと.

Q ***glaring*** *improbabilities* てっきりありそうもないこと.

improbable, *a.* ありそうもない.

M it is ***highly*** *improbable* that he should ... よもや...はしまい.

improbity, *n.* 不正直, 不誠実.

Q ***commercial*** *improbity* 商業上の不正直.

improper, *a.* 不適当な.

P *improper* ***to*** the occasion その折に不適当な.

impropriety, *n.* 不穏当; 非礼, 不作法.

V ***commit*** an *impropriety* 不作法なことをする. ¶girls in their teens ***see*** no *impropriety* in drinking publicly with men companions. 十代の少女たちが男を相手に公然飲酒して何とも思わない.

P ***without*** *impropriety* 妥当を欠くことなく, 当然.

improve, *v.* 改善する, 改良する, 上達させる; 向上する.

M It can ***hardly*** be *improved* upon. それには改善の余地がない. ¶***How much*** you have *improved!* 大進歩だ. ¶***materially*** *improve* 実質的に改善する. ¶He has ***much*** *improved* in health. 彼は大いに健康を回復した. ¶be anxious to *improve* oneself ***professionally*** 職業資格を強化しようと努めている. ¶He played it with a brilliancy and fire that could ***scarcely*** be *improved* upon. 彼はほとんど改善の余地のないまでにりっぱにかつ熱心にそれを演じた. ¶He is *improving* ***slowly*** from the effects of a fall he had recently. 彼は最近ころんでけがをしたが段々よくなっている.

P *improve* ***by*** study 勉強によって向上する ‖ The situation will not *improve* ***by*** waiting. 現状は待っていたのでは好転しない. ¶*improve* it ***for*** his own end 自分の目的のためにそれを利用する. ¶*improve* ***in*** appearance after successive washings 洗えば洗うほど外観が良くなる. 【類】*improve* ***in*** knowledge / *improve* ***in*** appearance / *improve* ***in*** physique / *improve* ***in*** price / *improve* ***in*** skill. ¶This thought was *improved* ***into*** a resolution. この考えをいよいよ実行することにした. ¶try to *improve* ***on*** it それをさらに良くしようとする ‖ Publications, like men, *improve* ***on*** the constructive counsel of friend and associate. 出版物は人間同様友人などの建設的な助言で良くなる. ‖ He *improves* ***on*** acquaintance, I think. 彼はつき合って見ると益々良い人のように思われる. ‖ *improve* ***on*** the inventions of others 他人の発明を改良する. 【類】I was unable to *improve* ***on*** his translation. ‖ *Improving* ***on*** the plan of Cromwell, every night he slept in a different quarter of London.—De Quincey. クロムウェルの故知にならって彼は毎夜ロンドンで場所を替えて寝泊りをした. ¶*improve* one's English ***with*** constant use 絶えず使って英語を上達させる ‖ *improve* ***with*** acquaintance 知れば知るほど良くなる ‖ Wine *improves* ***with*** age. ぶどう酒は時がたつと段々良くなる.

improvement, *n.* 改善, 改良; 進歩, 上達.

V ***bring about*** *improvement* 改良を施す. ¶***carry out*** *improvement* 改善を実行する. ¶***contemplate*** *improvements* 改善を企てる. ¶He more than any other single person is instrumental in ***effecting*** the *improvements*. 彼は他の何人よりもその改善の達成にあずかって力がある. ¶***embody*** the latest *improvements*. 最新の改良を具体化する. 【類】These are some of the *improvements* ***embodied*** in this issue. ¶I ***expect*** an *improvement* soon. 近々改善されるはずである. ¶***hasten*** the *improvement* 改善を促進する. ¶it ***has*** many *improvements* over ... それは...よりも良くなっている所が多い. ¶***initiate*** *improvements* 改善に着手する. ¶We have ***introduced*** various *improvements* in our new machines. 手前どもの新しい機械は各種の改善が施されています. ¶***make*** *improvements* in technique 技術を改善する. 【類】***make*** extensive *improvements*. ¶This ***marked*** a distinct *improvement* in the cleanliness of the streets. この時から市街が見違えるほど清潔になった. ¶***note*** a great *improvement* in ... ...が大いに改善されたことを示す. ¶***produce*** an *improvement* 改善をきたす. ¶***propose*** *improvements* 改良を提案する. ¶***show*** *improvement* in profits over the previous year of some 15% 前年に比し約一割五分だけ利益が増したことを示す. 【類】***show*** a decided *improvement* on ... / ***show*** an *improvement* in demand. ¶It would be difficult to ***suggest*** any *improvement*. 何らかの改良を提言することは困難であろう. ¶***undergo*** successful *improvements* 首尾よく改善される. ¶***work*** an *improvement* 改善を施す.

V^2 if no *improvement* ***results*** その結果良くならなければ. ¶*Improvement* ***took place*** slowly. 徐々に改善された.

Q It will be an ***appreciated*** *improvement* upon the present state of things. それは現下の状態に対して著しい改善となるであろう. ¶***considerable*** *improvements* 著しい改善. ¶a ***decided*** *improvement* on the previous arrangement 以前の設備に対して断然たる進歩. ¶a ***distinct*** *improvement* in railway comfort 列車設備上格段の改善. 【類】mark a ***distinct*** *improvement* in the cleanliness of the streets / Bailey's dictionary was a ***distinct*** *improvement* on its predecessors. ¶contemplate an ***extensive*** *improvement* 広汎な改善を企てる. ¶It has undergone ***frequent*** and ***various*** *improvements*. それにはひんぴんと種々改善が施された. ¶a ***further*** *improvement* それ以上の改善. ¶***gradual*** *improvement* ***of*** the mass 大衆の向上. ¶On the whole there is ***great*** *improvement*. 大体において非常な進歩だ. 【類】I consider it a ***great*** *improvement*. / It is no ***great*** *improvement* on his past work. ¶with the ***latest*** *improvements* 最新の改善を加えて. ¶a ***major*** *improvement* 主な改善. ¶It shows a ***marked*** *improvement* on his other works. それは彼の他の作品に出し著しい進歩を示している. 【類】***marked*** *improvements* over the original edition (原版). ¶***minor*** *improvements* さ細の改善. ¶***moral*** *improvement* 道徳的進歩. ¶***necessary*** *improvements* 必要な改善. ¶The *improvement* is scarcely ***perceptible***. その改善はほとんど気がつかない. ¶make ***rapid*** *improvement* 迅速な改善を行う. ¶a ***revolutionary*** *improvement* over ... ...に対する一大改革. ¶bring about a most ***salutary*** *improvement* in the conditions of ... ...の状態にはなはだ有効な改善をもたらす. ¶a ***significant*** *improvement* 顕著な改善. ¶a ***slight*** *improvement* 少しの進歩. ¶make ***steady*** *improvement* (=expansion) ぐんぐんのびる. ¶It is showing signs of ***steady*** though ***slow*** *improvement*. それは遅々としてはいるが着実な進歩の跡を示している. ¶a ***substantial*** *improvement* 実質的改善. ¶a ***vast*** *improvement* in taste and comfort 趣味及び快適の点における設備上の大改良.

Q^2 ***city*** (=***civic***) *improvements* 都市の改善. ¶***day to day*** *improvements* 日々の改善. ¶***language*** *improvement* 言語改良. ¶***river*** *improvement* 河川改修事業. ¶***street*** *improvement* 区画整理. ¶***town*** *improvement* 都市改善. ¶***vocabulary*** *improvement* 語彙(ごい)増大.

P Are there any prospects ***of*** *improvement?* 改善の見込があるか. ‖ show no signs ***of*** *improvement* 何ら進歩の跡を示さない. ¶a step ***towards*** social *improvement* 社会改善への一歩.

P^2 *improvements* ***in*** the typewriter タイプライターの改善 ‖ *improvement* ***in*** accommodation at country hotels いなかホテルの設備改善. ¶the *improvement* ***of*** health 健康の増進. ¶an *improvement* ***on*** the old rules (system) 旧規則(など)の改善. 【類】London at Christmas time today is a great *improvement* ***on*** the Christmas London of the past. / *improvements* ***on*** one's own inventions / *improvement* ***on*** traffic service. ¶*improvement* ***through*** breeding 飼育による改善. ¶an *improvement* ***upon*** its predecessors それ以前のものに比しての進歩.

improvidence, *n.* 不用意な行為.

Q ***hopeless*** *improvidence* 矯正の見込みのない不注意な金使い.

improvise, *v.* (詩などを)即席に作る, にわか作りする.

P a comical story *improvised* ***for*** the moment 一時の間に合わせに作ったこっけい物語.

imprudence, *n.* 不注意, 不用意, 軽率.

V He ***had*** the *imprudence* to say so. 彼は軽率にもそんなことを言った.

impudence, *n.* 鉄面皮, 厚顔, 図々しさ.

V he *had* the *impudence* to ... 彼は鉄面皮にも...した.

Q *Such impudence!* 何を小しゃくな. ¶*unruffled impudence* 平然たる鉄面皮.

P He said *with* cool *impudence*. 彼はずうずうしく落付き払って言った.

P² the *impudence of* a servant *to* his master 主人に対する下男のずうずうしさ.

impulse, *n.* 衝動, はずみ, 刺激; でき心.

V *feel* an irresistible *impulse* to ... ...しようという抑えがたい衝動を感じる. ¶*follow* a sudden *impulse* 一時のでき心でやる. ¶*follow out* their own *impulses* 彼ら自身の衝動に従う. ¶*give* a great *impulse* forward or backward 前進または退歩の大なる刺激を与える. 【類】*give* an *impulse* in that line (=direction) / Rivalry *gives* an *impulse* to trade. ¶*gratify* the sexual *impulse* 性欲を満足させる. ¶*heighten* the sexual *impulse* 性欲を増す. ¶*obey impulse* of curiosity 好奇心に駆られてする. ¶*receive* a great *impulse* 非常な刺激を受ける. ¶*resist* the *impulse* 一時のでき心を抑える. 【類】He does not know how to *resist* his *impulse*.

V² an irresistible *impulse arose* to ... ...しようという抑え難い衝動が起った.

Q *charitable impulses* 慈善的衝動. ¶*creative impulse* 創作熱. ¶He gave the *first strong impulse* to a study of this subject in Japan. 彼は日本におけるこの学科の研究に対し最初の強い刺激を与えた. ¶receive a *fresh impulse* owing to ... ...のために新しい衝撃を受ける. ¶a *generous impulse* 寛大な心のはずみ. ¶an *imperial impulse* 非常に大きな衝動. ¶pressed by an *irresistible impulse* 抑え難い衝動に駆られて. 【類】He is dominated by an *irresistible impulse* to count everything. / feel an *irresistible impulse* to jump overboard. ¶He committed these acts from a *morbid impulse* he could not control. 彼は抑えきれない病的衝動からこれらのことをやった. ¶a spokesman of *national impulse* 国民的感激の代弁者. ¶give a *new* and *powerful impulse* to the progress of ... ...の進歩に対して新しく力強い刺激を与える. ¶a *noble impulse* 気高い衝動. ¶an *overmastering impulse* 非常に強い衝動. ¶His marriage was the result of *rash impulse*. 彼の結婚は無鉄砲なでき心の結果であった. ¶a *slight impulse* 軽い衝撃. ¶A *sudden impulse* came over him. 不意にそういう気になった. ¶a *suicidal impulse* 自殺しようとする衝動. ¶keep under subjection the *unruly impulse* of the flesh 意馬心猿を制御する. ¶the *writing impulse* 執筆の刺激.

P A mob is more urged *by impulse* than by reason. 暴民は理屈よりも衝動で動く方が多い. ¶a man *of impulse* 衝動的な人. ¶*on impulse* [心の]はずみで. 【類】*on* the *impulse* of the moment. / acting *on* a moment's *impulse*. / A woman acts more *on impulse* than a man [does]. ¶*upon* a sudden *impulse* でき心で.

P² an *impulse of* enthusiasm 熱意の衝撃.

O the *impulse* to travel 旅行したいという衝動.

impunity, *n.* 無罰; 無難.

Q with *comparative impunity* 比較的無難に. ¶with *perfect impunity* 少しの危険もなく.

P go *with impunity* 〖比ゆ〗大手を振って歩く ‖ It is all in accordance with natural laws that may not be defied *with impunity*. それはすべて自然の法則に合致しているのでこれを犯せば罰を免れない. ‖ These are sane literature, which can be read *with impunity* by young men and women. これらは清浄な文学で青年男女が読んで差支えない.

impurity, *n.* 不潔, 不浄.

V *burn off impurities* 不浄物を焼却する. ¶*eliminate impurity* 雑物を取去る. ¶*remove impurities* 不純物を除く.

V² The *impurity falls* from one by doing so. そうするとその汚れが取れる.

imputable, *a.* 帰しうる.

P It is *imputable to* one's own fault. それは自身の落度である. ‖ a cause not *imputable to* oneself 自分の責に帰すべからざる事由.

impute, *v.* 帰する, 負わす.

P *impute* the fault *to* him その過失を彼にきせる.

in, *prep., ad.* 中に.

P *in between* them 彼ら二人の間に. ¶He is *in for* an illness. 彼は病気のために引きこもっている.

inability, *n.* 不可能, 無能.

V Here I must *confess* my *inability* to understand. ここにいたって僕は了解しかねることを告白しなければならない.

P² *inability through* old age 老朽.

inaccessible, *a.* 近づき難い.

P The library is *inaccessible to* the people at large. その図書館は一般公衆には閲覧させない. 【類】materials *inaccessible* (入手できない) *to* Western students.

inaccuracy, *n.* 不正確, 誤り.

V *rectify inaccuracies* 不正確の個所を改める.

Q *glaring inaccuracies* 歴然たる誤り. ¶*grave inaccuracies* はなはだしい不正確. ¶a *slight inaccuracy* ちょっとした不正確さ. ¶fall into *occasional inaccuracies* 折々誤りをおかす.

inaccurate, *a.* 不正確な.

M *wholly inaccurate* 全然不正確な.

inactivity, *n.* 不活発.

P² the *inactivity*, the passivity *of* the East 東洋の不活動と受動性.

inadequate, *a.* 不十分な, 不適当な.

M *absurdly inadequate* お話にならないほど不十分な. ¶*lamentably inadequate* なさけないくらい不備な. ¶The legislation is *obviously inadequate*. 法律は明かに不備である. ¶be *wholly inadequate* to meet the demand とうてい需要に応じられない.

P *inadequate for* the needs of a new time 新時代の要求に添わない. 【類】be *inadequate for* the purpose intended. ¶*inadequate to* the occasion (end) その場(目的)に役立ちかねる ‖ The remuneration is *inadequate to* the services. 報酬はその仕事に対し不十分だ.

inadmissible, *a.* 許容されない.

M be *absolutely inadmissible* 絶対に許されない.

inadvertence, *n.* 手落ち, 粗相.

Q through *sheer inadvertence* 全くの疎漏で.

P *by* an *inadvertence* 手落ちからして. 【類】errors made *by inadvertence* or by insufficient ingenuity. ¶*Through inadvertence* the name has been omitted from the list. 手落ちからその名がその表から漏れた.

inappreciation, *n.* 不満.

V *show inappreciation* of ... ...を喜ばない.

inattendance, *n.* 不行届.

V *report inattendance* of employees 雇人の不行届を申告する.

inattentive, *a.* 不注意の, むとんちゃくの.

P be *inattentive to* one's classwork 教室の勉強に対してうわのそらでいる. 【類】*inattentive to* one's appearance.

inaudible, *a.* 聞きとれない.

P It was almost *inaudible to* me. それは私にはほとんど聴きとれなかった.

inaugurate, *v.* 就任式を行う.

P He was *inaugurated as* President. 彼は大統領に就任した.

inauguration, *n.* 開始; 就任式.

V The Cunard Line recently *announced* the *inauguration* of a new service between Boston and London, with a sailing every three weeks.—Travel. キューナード汽船会社は三週間に一回就航するボストン・ロンドン間の新航路開始を最近公表した.

inborn, *a.* 生得の.

P *inborn* (=congenital) *in* him 彼に生得の.

incapable, *a.* 無能の, 役に立たない.

M render it *functionally incapable* それを官能的に無能にする.

P *incapable of* performing one's duties その本分を尽すことのできない ‖ *incapable of* learning (work) 習うこと(など)のできない ‖ be *incapable of* becoming a mother 不妊症である.

incapacitate, *v.* 無能力にさせる.

P Illness *incapacitated* him *for* work (duty). 彼は病気で仕事(など)ができなかった. 【類】Cold *incapacitated* him *for* the enjoyment of life for a fortnight. ¶*incapacitate* a person *from* working 人に仕事をできなくさせる.

incapacity, *n.* 無能, 無力.

Q *functional incapacity* 機能的な無能. ¶*legal incapacity* 法律上の無能力. ¶*reproductive incapacity* in women 女性における生殖無能(不妊).

P² *incapacity for* work 仕事に対する無能力. ¶*incapacity from* working 仕事の不能.

incarcerate, *v.* 監禁する.

P He was *incarcerated in* the local jail. 彼はその土地で収監された.

incarceration, *n.* 監禁.

V The physician *recommended* his *incarceration* in a lunatic asylum. かかりの医師は彼を精神病院に監禁することを勧めた.

incarnate, *v.* 体現する.

P *incarnated in* human form 人間の形に体現した.

incarnation, *n.* 権化(ゲ), 化身.

Q in a *previous incarnation* 前世では.

P² the *incarnation of* health 健康の化身(そのもの). ¶be

the *incarnation of* avarice 欲の鬼である.

incase, *v.* 包む.

P *incased **in*** paper wrappers 包紙に包んだ ‖ their feet *incased **in*** stout topboots がん丈な乗馬ぐつをはいた足.

incasement, *n.* 箱.

Q ***triple*** *incasement* of coffins 三重の棺.

incendiarism, *n.* 放火.

V ***commit*** *incendiarism* 放火する.

incense, *n.* 香.

V ***burn*** *incense* in a temple お寺で焼香する. 【類】*incense* was ***burned*** to the spirit of ... / ***burn*** one's *incense* to an idol. ¶***kindle*** *incense* 香をたく. ¶***offer*** *incense* 焼香する.

V^2 The *incense* has never ceased to ***smoke*** before the tomb. その墓前に香の煙が絶えない.

Q ***spirit-calling*** *incense* 反魂香.

incense, *v.* 怒らす.

P He was *incensed **against*** the slanderer. 彼はつげ口した者を怒った. ¶He was *incensed **at*** the insult offered. 彼は侮辱されて怒った. ‖ He became *incensed **at*** this invasion of his prerogatives. 彼はこうして自分の特権を侵害されたのを憤慨した. 【類】He was much *incensed **at*** the statement published yesterday. ¶He was *incensed **by*** this remark. 彼はこの言葉に憤慨した. ¶become *incensed **with*** ... ...を怒る.

incentive, *n.* 刺激, 動機.

V ***give*** an *incentive* to ... ...を刺激する.

Q It may prove an ***additional*** *incentive*. それが一段の刺激になるであろう. 【類】an ***additional*** *incentive* to travel in Switzerland. ¶the ***best*** *incentive* to ... ...にはこよなき刺激. ¶one of the ***chief*** *incentive* 主な刺激の一つ. ¶give an ***increased*** *incentive* for higher scholarship 一層学力をつけようとする刺激を与える. ¶Scientific object is the ***main*** *incentive* of the expedition. 科学的目的がその探検の主要な動機である. ¶there is not ***much*** *incentive* for them to ... 彼らが...することに対する励みは多くない. ¶afford a ***powerful*** *incentive* to ... ...に有力な刺激を与える. ¶a ***real*** *incentive* 真実の動機. ¶This will give Japanese students a ***special*** *incentive* to literary expression in English. これが日本の学生に英語による文学的表現への刺激を与えるであろう. ¶***spurring*** *incentive* to ... ...を奮起させる刺激. ¶a ***strong*** *incentive* 強い刺激. 【類】Competition is the ***strongest*** *incentive* to industry. / The clash of opinion is the ***strongest*** *incentive* to thought.

Q^2 ***Wartime*** *incentive* no longer spurs us. 戦時の刺激は今やわれわれを奮起させない.

P^2 an *incentive **to*** exertion 努力への刺激. 【類】the *incentives **to*** human action / an *incentive **to*** increased efficiency (能率増進) by workers / *incentives **to*** lust (情欲).

O an *incentive* to do their best 彼らに最善をなさしめる一刺激.

inception, *n.* 始め, 発端.

P ***from*** the *inception* of the book その本の著作に着手して. ¶a friend of the movement ***since*** its *inception* その運動のそもそもの始めからの同志. 【類】***since*** its *inception* (創立以来) two or three years ago.

inch, *n.* インチ.

V ***having*** no *inch* of steel on one's person 身に寸鉄も帯びず.

Q He is ***every*** *inch* a king. 彼はどう見ても王者だ. ‖ He knows ***every*** *inch* of the land. 彼はその土地をくまなく知っている. ‖ He is a gentleman, ***every*** *inch* of him. 彼はどう見ても紳士だ. 【類】Great crowds thronged ***every*** *inch* of the route (立すいの余地ないほど).

P die ***by*** *inches* じりじりと死ぬ ‖ ***By*** *inches* the water shallows. 少しずつ水が浅くなる. ¶***In*** *inches* he was not a giant. 彼は背の高さは大男というほどではなかった. ¶at intervals ***of*** a few *inches* 二三インチおきに. ¶He told the height accurately ***to*** an *inch*. 彼は一インチもたがわずその高さを言い当てた. ¶Rates were cut down ***within*** an *inch* of ruin by the railways in competition. 競争のため鉄道会社は料金をほとんど破滅の境まで引下げた. ‖ He ought to be licked ***within*** an *inch* of his life! 彼を打って半殺しにしなくっちゃいかん. 【類】He was flogged (むち打たれた) ***within*** an *inch* of his life. / come ***within*** an *inch* of being killed (すんでのことで).

P^2 Their skirts are the regulation four *inches **below*** the knee. 彼らのスカートはひざ下規定の四インチである.

O He is an *inch* or two shorter than you. 彼は君より一二インチ背が低い.

inch, *v.* 少しずつ動く.

M *inch **in*** (***out***) にじり入る(出る).

incident, *n.* できごと, そう話, 付帯的事物.

V And the *incident* (fight, dispute) was ***closed***. そしてその事件(など)は片がついた. ¶***epitomize*** the principal *incidents* of the affair その事件の主なできごとを概説する. ¶a touching *incident **happened*** (=***occurred***) when ... ... のときに人の心を打つできごとが起った.

Q an ***amusing*** *incident* 面白いできごと. ¶***brilliant*** or ***salient*** *incidents* 花々しいまたは顕著なできごと. ¶a ***casual*** *incident* ちょっとしたこと. ¶a ***comic*** *incident* こっけいなできごと. ¶Apparent dullness is a quite ***common*** *incident* to youthful genius. 一見愚鈍に見えるのは若い天才にあり勝のことだ. ¶a ***commonplace*** *incident* 平凡なできごと. ¶***dramatic*** *incidents* 劇的事件. ¶***exciting*** *incidents* in a novel 小説のやま. ¶an ***extraordinary*** *incident* 異常なできごと. ¶a ***horrible*** *incident* 恐ろしいできごと. ¶a ***humorous*** *incident* こっけいなそう話. ¶an ***inspirational*** *incident* 感激的なできごと. ¶the ***main*** *incidents* in the history of the war その戦史上の主なできごと. 【類】follow very closely the ***main*** *incidents* in the life of ... ¶a very ***notable*** *incident* 極めて著しいできごと. ¶There has been a most ***painful*** *incident* in his family history. 彼の家族では過去に非常に痛ましいできごとがあった. ¶a very ***pitiable*** *incident* 非常に哀れなできごと. ¶a ***recent*** *incident* 最近のできごと. ¶a ***singular*** *incident* 珍事. ¶a ***stirring*** *incident* 目ざましい事件. ¶a ***thrilling*** *incident* はらはらさせるできごと. ¶***topical*** *incidents* 話題になるできごと. ¶a ***touching*** *incident* 人を感動させるできごと. ¶a ***trifling*** *incident* ささいなできごと. ¶a very ***trivial*** *incident* ごくつまらないできごと. ¶an ***unfortunate*** *incident* 不幸なできごと. ¶passing over ***unimportant*** *incidents* of the voyage, I will proceed at once to narrate ... 航海中のこまごまとしたできごとは飛ばして直ちに...のことを物語ることにする. ¶without ***untoward*** *incident* 無事に.

Q^2 the ***China*** *incident* (affair, emergency) シナ事変. ¶the ***Lukouchiao*** *incident* 盧溝橋事件.

P the agent ***in*** the following *incident* 次のできごとの主人公. ¶The night passed, however, ***without*** an *incident*. しかしその夜は無事に過ぎた.

P^2 one *incident **from*** Napoleon's biography ナポレオンの一生における一そう話. ¶*incidents **in*** the life of ... ...の一生のできごと. ¶the *incidents **of*** a journey 旅のできごと. ¶an *incident **to*** a train 列車のできごと.

incident, *a.* 起るべき.

P evils *incident **to*** human society 人間社会にありがちの弊害. 【類】calamities *incident **to*** human life.

incidental, *a.* 付帯の.

P Whatever expenses *incidental **to*** purchasing it I shall be very glad to reimburse you. それをお買いになる費用はいくらでも喜んで御返済致しましょう. ‖ *incidental **to*** the main issue (=question; matter) その主要な問題(など)に付帯せる. ¶benefits *incidental **to*** office 役徳.

incipiency, *n.* 発端, 初期.

P ***from*** its *incipiency* その発端から. ¶a typical case of dementia praecox ***in*** *incipiency* 早発性痴呆症の代表的初期患者.

incision, *n.* きざみ.

V ***make*** an *incision* in ... ...にきざみをつける.

incite, *v.* 扇動する; 励ます.

P *incite* them ***against*** ... 彼らを扇動して...に反対させる. ¶*incite* people ***to*** violations of law and order 民衆を扇動して法律及び秩序を乱させる.

incitement, *n.* 奨励.

P^2 an *incitement **to*** study 研究の奨励.

incivility, *n.* 無作法.

Q a ***gross*** *incivility* ひどい無作法.

inclination, *n.* 傾向, 好み.

V ***feel*** an *inclintion* to doubt 疑わしいと感じる ‖ I ***felt*** no *inclination* to contract another marriage. 私は再び結婚する気にはなれなかった. ¶I ***had*** no *inclination* in that way. そういう気は私にはなかった. 【類】He ***had*** no *inclination* to contract another marriage (再婚する). ¶***manifest*** a strong *inclination* for religious life 宗教生活への強い念願を示す. ¶They ***show*** very little *inclination* to buy further at present. 彼らは今の所それ以上買いそうもない. 【類】The English student does not ***show*** an *inclination* to studies. ¶when the *inclination* ***prompted*** 気が向いたとき.

Q a ***benevolent*** and ***beneficent*** *inclination* 慈悲慈善の傾向. ¶promote the ***bookish*** *inclination* of the nation 国民の読書し好を増進する. ¶My ***natural*** *inclination* is towards archaeology and history. 私の生来の好みは考古学と歴史にある. ¶He has ***studious*** *inclinations* and is fond of books. 彼は学究的な傾向があって書籍が好きだ.

P it is very much ***against*** my own *inclination* to say this to you, but ... はなはだ不本意ながら... ¶He has an *inclination* ***for*** study. 彼は勉強が好きだ. ¶She declares that she has never felt any *inclination* ***to*** a man. 彼女はいまだかつて男に心を寄せたことはないときっぱり言っている.

P *inclination* to steal 盗癖.

incline, *n.* こう配.

Q run down a ***steep*** *incline* 急坂を走り下る.

P ***at*** an *incline* of ... degrees ...度のこう配で.

P² an *incline* ***of*** 20 in 100 百分の二十のこう配.

incline, *v.* 傾く, 心を向ける; 傾ける.

M be very ***favorably*** *inclined* towards ... ...の方に非常に好意的である. ¶be ***not*** (***little***) *inclined* to ... ...するのは(あまり)気が進まない.

P I strongly *incline* ***to*** the view that ... 私は...という見方に強く心が傾く. ‖ *incline* ***to*** luxury ぜいたくに流れる ‖ *incline* the ear ***to*** a request 要求に耳を傾ける ‖ orange *inclining* ***to*** yellow 黄色がかったオレンジ色. ¶You are too much *inclined* ***towards*** pleasure. 君はあまり快楽に走りすぎる. ‖ I *incline* ***toward*** the second alternative. 私は二つの中第二の方に心が向く.

O I am *inclined* to agree. 私はなるほどそうだと思う. ¶He is not *inclined* to go there. 彼はそこへ行く気がない. ¶He appears to be *inclined* to going. 彼は行く方に傾いているらしい. ¶I am *inclined* to think that ... 私は...と考えたい.

include, *v.* 含む.

M under this title are ***generally*** *included* such items as ... この名の下に...のごとき品目も通例含まれている.

P It is *included* ***among*** the number. それはその数に含まれている. 【類】I *include* you ***among*** my friends. ¶It is *included* ***in*** the new budget for 1937-1938. それは一九三七年度の新予算に計上されている. ‖ More than eighty persons are *included* ***in*** the party. 八十人以上その仲間に加わっている. ‖ It is to be *included* ***in*** the same category. それは同じ種類に属すべきものだ. ‖ the society *includes* ***in*** its membership ... その会の会員中に...がいる. 【類】The last order is *included* ***in*** the previous. / I hesitate to *include* a pork chop ***in*** a catalogue of light refreshments. ¶It is *included* ***under*** the somewhat vague designation of "..." それは「...」という幾分ばく然とした部類に入れてある. ‖ It may be *included* ***under*** this head. それはこの項目に入れてよかろう. ‖ Synecdoche is now usually *included* ***under*** metonymy. 〘修辞〙提ゆ法は今は換ゆ法の中に通例含まれている. ¶German "mild steel" is in England *included* ***with*** puddled bars. ドイツの軟鋼は英国では棒状ねり棒の部に入れてある.

inclusion, *n.* 包含.

P her *inclusion* ***among*** the great Powers その国の列強への仲間入.

inclusive, *a.* 含める.

P A calendar year is ***from*** January 1 ***to*** December 31 *inclusive.* 暦年は一月一日から十二月三十一日までである. ¶*inclusive* ***of*** ..., but exclusive of ... ...は含むが...は含まない. 【類】*inclusive* ***of*** expenses (cost, persons).

incognito, *n.* 匿名, 微行.

V ***keep*** one's *incognito* 本名をあかさない.

Q an ***august*** *incognito* 微行の貴顕.

P protected ***by*** *incognito* 微行して. ¶***in*** the strictest *incognito* 最も厳重な微行で.

income, *n.* 収入, 所得.

V A Greek saying has this: "First ***acquire*** an independent *income,* and then practice virtue."「先ず独立の生計を立てて然る後に徳を施せ」とギリシアの諺にある. ¶a position which ***brings*** you a comfortable *income* 君に相当な収入になる地位. ¶***bring in*** *income* 収入を得させる. ¶***derive*** a good *income* from ... ...から好い収入を得る. ¶***draw*** an *income* of ... a year from ... ...から年収...を得る. ¶***earn*** a princely *income* すばらしい収入を得る. ¶***enjoy*** an annual *income* of ... 年収...を得る. ¶His expenses ***exceeded*** his *income.* 彼の支出が収入を超過した. ¶***gain*** a good *income* よい収入を得る. ¶The lord ***granted*** him an *income* of five hundred *koku* a year. 藩主は彼に年五百石の知行を与えた. ¶***have*** an *income* of ten dollars a week 一週十ドルの収入がある. ¶find how to ***increase*** the *income* without increasing the outgo どうしたら出費を増さないで収入をふやすことができるかを研究する. ¶an author who is bent on ***making*** a big *income* rather than a great book りっぱな書物を作るよりも多額の収入をかせごうとしている著作家. ¶He ***obtains*** an *income* of over £10,000 a year from his enterprises. 彼はその事業から年収一万ポンド以上を得ている. ¶***overlive*** one's *income* 収入以上の暮しをする. ¶***produce*** an *income* 収入がある. ¶Formerly Japanese *incomes* were ***reckoned*** in rice as their homes are measured by mats. 昔日本人の収入はその家の大きさを畳数で言うように米で言ったものだ. ¶***secure*** a comfortable *income* 相当の収入を得る. ¶***stabilize*** one's *income* その収入を一定する. ¶These will ***swallow up*** all my *income.* これで私の収入が残らず出てしまう. ¶***use*** the *income* of the fund only, permanently investing the principal 元金を永久的に投資据置にしてその資金からの収入だけを使う. ¶***yield*** an *income* of ... ...の所得を産む.

Q make a ***comfortable*** *income* out of writing 文筆で相当の収入を得る. ¶a ***fixed*** *income* 定収入. ¶***fluctuating*** *income* 一定しない収入. ¶have a ***good*** *income* from ... ...からよい収入を得ている. ¶a ***gross*** *income* 総収入. ¶earn a ***handsome*** *income* かなりな収入を得る. ¶acquire an ***independent*** *income* 自分の収入を得る(親からの仕送りでなく). 【類】Instead of having an ***independent*** *income* he had to work for his living. ¶earn a ***large*** *income* 多大の収入を得る. ¶fowls noted for giving a ***liberal*** *income* 豊かな収入が得られるので評判の鶏(産卵率が高いので). ¶people with ***limited*** *incomes* 所得の少ない人々. ¶a ***meagre*** *income* 乏しい収入. ¶a ***monthly*** *income* 月収. ¶the ***net*** *income* of ... ...の純収入. ¶earn a very ***precarious*** *income* きわめておぼつかない収入を得る. ¶it is quite a ***princely*** *income* in the eyes of ... それは...から見ると実にすばらしい収入である. ¶a ***prospective*** *income* 予想収入. ¶a ***scanty*** *income* 貧弱な収入. ¶They have pitiably ***small*** *incomes.* 彼らは気の毒なくらい収入が少ない. ¶a ***snug little annual*** *income* ちょっとした年収. ¶a ***superb*** *income* すばらしい収入. ¶the ***total*** *income* from farms last year was ... 昨年の農場からの全所得は...であった.

Q² ***cash*** *income* 現金収入. ¶add to the ***family*** *income* by making ... ...を作って家庭の収入を増加する. ¶His business is not large enough to furnish a ***living*** *income.* 彼の営業は生活ができるだけになっていない. ¶average ***per capita*** *income* 平均一人当り収入. ¶***property*** *income* 資産収入. ¶a ***retirement*** *income* 退職支給の所得. ¶***service*** *income* 勤労所得.

P These daughters dress ***above*** their father's *income.* これらの娘は父の収入以上に着飾る. ¶live ***beyond*** one's *income* 収入以上に暮す. ¶a person ***of*** small *income* 収入の少ない人. ¶persons living ***on*** "unearned *incomes*"「不労所得」で暮している人々. ¶He was suddenly stranded ***with*** no *income* at all. 彼は急に全然収入がなくなって困った. ‖ men ***with*** small *incomes* 収入の少ない人々. ¶live ***within*** one's *income* 収入内で暮す.

P² the *income* ***of*** an insurance company ***from*** premiums 保険会社の掛金による収入. ¶He has an *income* ***of*** ¥ ... a year. 彼は年に...円の収入がある. 【類】the *income* ***of*** a successful physician (はやる医師) / *income* ***from*** land (property).

incompatibility, *n.* 相克, 矛盾.

P *incompatibility* ***of*** temperament 気の合わないこと.

incompatible, *a.* 矛盾せる.

M ***utterly*** *incompatible* with ... ...とは全く両立しない.

P *incompatible* ***with*** civilization 文明と両立しない ‖ *incompatible* ***with*** each other 相入れない.

incomplete, *a.* 不完全な.

M ***woefully*** *incomplete* はなはだ不完全な.

incomprehensible, *a.* 不可解な.

P It is quite *incomprehensible* ***to*** me. それは私には全然分からない.

incongruous, *a.* 調和しない.

P conduct *incongruous* ***with*** one's principles その主義にそぐわない行為.

inconsiderate, *a.* 考えの浅い.

M be ***abominably*** *inconsiderate* 無分別きわまる.

inconsistency, *n.* 矛盾.

Q *strange inconsistency* 奇妙な矛盾.
P *inconsistency in* ... ...における矛盾.

inconsistent, *a.* 矛盾する.

P It is *inconsistent **with*** the spirit of the age. それは時代精神と矛盾する.【類】loyalty *inconsistent **with*** filial duty.

inconstant, *a.* 浮気の.

P be *inconstant **in*** love 浮気をする.

incontinence, *n.* 不貞; [大小便の]失禁.

V Continental Europe traditionally ***condones*** *incontinence* on the part of the male sex. 欧州大陸では伝統的に男子の不貞を大目にみている.
Q ***nocturnal*** *incontinence* 夜尿[症].

inconvenience, *n.* 不便, 不自由.

V make arrangements to ***avoid*** *inconvenience* as much as possible できるだけ差支えを避けるような手配をする. ¶***bear*** (=put up with) *inconveniences* 不自由を忍ぶ. ¶***cause*** *inconvenience* to ... ...に不便を与える.【類】as long as it ***causes*** no *inconvenience.* ¶***endure*** *inconveniences* 不自由を忍ぶ. ¶***experience*** *inconvenience* 不便を感じる. ¶***give*** *inconvenience* to ... ...に不便をかける. ¶***have*** *inconvenience* 不自由な思いをする. ¶it threatens to ***give*** much *inconvenience* to ... それは...に大層不便を与えるおそれがある. ¶***mitigate*** the growing *inconvenience* ますます増大する不便を緩和する. ¶go far to ***obviate*** the *inconveniences* arising from ... ...から生じる不便を除く上に大いに助けになる. ¶***suffer*** no *inconvenience* 少しも不自由を感じない ‖ ***suffer*** *inconvenience* from ... ...から迷惑をこうむる.
Q ***grave*** *inconvenience* 大不便. ¶cause ***great*** *inconvenience* 大不便を与える. ¶***intolerable*** *inconvenience* たえられない不便. ¶It caused a ***serious*** *inconvenience.* それは非常な不便を与えた. ¶a ***slight*** (=***trifling***) *inconvenience* ちょっとした不便.
P I did it ***at*** some *inconvenience* to myself as I was exceedingly busy at the time. その折非常に忙しかったので私には幾らか迷惑であったがやった. ‖ He attended the meeting ***at*** great *inconvenience.* 彼は万障繰合してその会に出席した. ¶You must have been subjected ***to*** much *inconvenience.* 随分不自由だったでしょう. ¶***without*** *inconvenience* 都合も悪くなく.【類】***without*** the least *inconvenience.*
P² even at a little personal *inconvenience **to*** herself 彼女自身には少々迷惑ではあっても.

inconvenient, *a.* 迷惑な.

P *inconvenient **to*** him 彼に迷惑な.【類】if not very *inconvenient **to*** you.

incorporate, *v.* 合同する, 結合する.

P It was *incorporated **as*** a limited company. それは有限責任会社として法人組織になった. ¶It has been *incorporated **in*** the present pages. それは現在の書物の中に編み込まれた.【類】Your idea will be *incorporated **in*** the plan. / The American principles of finance was *incorporated **into*** the fiscal system of the country. ‖ *incorporate* one thing ***into*** another 甲を乙に結合する.【類】two volumes *incorporated **into*** one / Part of Germany was *incorporated **into*** Poland according to the Treaty of Versailles. ¶be *incorporated **on*** a legal basis 法律によって合併される. ¶it was *incorporated **under*** the laws of the State of New York for the purpose of ... それを...という目的でニューヨーク州の法律によって法人組織にした. ¶a firm *incorporated **with*** another 他社と合併した会社.【類】Transylvania was *incorporated **with*** Hungary in 1713. ‖ The additions and corrections are *incorporated **with*** the body of the work. 追加と修正が著作の本文中に編入された.

incorporation, *n.* 編入.

P² *incorporation **of*** a society 協会法人設定 ‖ the centenary of the *incorporation **of*** Toronto ***as*** a city トロント市制実施百年記念祭.

incorrect, *a.* 誤った.

M ***absurdly*** *incorrect* 途方もなく誤った. ¶***grossly*** *incorrect* reports 非常に誤った報告. ¶be ***totally*** *incorrect* 全く誤っている.
P *incorrect **in*** figures 数字の不正確な.

incorrectness, *n.* 誤り, 不正確.

Q ***logical*** *incorrectness* 論理上の誤り.

increase, *n.* 増加.

V What has ***caused*** the *increase?* その増加の原因は何か. ¶***check*** any further *increase* in his family 彼の子供がその上ふえないようにする. ¶The strikers ***demand*** an *increase* in wages of 20 per cent. 同盟罷業者は賃金の二割値上を要求している. ¶***exhibit*** an *increase* of 30 per cent. 三割の増加を示す. ¶***get*** an *increase* in salary 増給してもらう. ¶***give*** an *increase* of salary 増給する. ¶***have*** an *increase* in salary 給料が増加する. ¶***promote*** the *increase* of friendly relations between employers and employed 雇主と雇人との関係の親善を助長する. ¶***receive*** an *increase* of salary 昇給する ‖ the company's performance over that of last year ***represents*** an *increase* of 82 per cent 会社の成績は昨年より八割二分の増加を示している. ¶The registration of the university ***shows*** (=***exhibits***) an *increase* of ... over last year. 大学の入学は昨年より...増加している.【類】***show*** a decided *increase* over ...
V² An *increase* has ***occurred.*** 増加した.
Q show a ***considerable*** *increase* 著しい増加を示す. ¶a ***continuous*** *increase* 間断ない増加. ¶an ***enormous*** *increase* ばく大の増加. ¶a ***fivefold*** *increase* 五倍の増加. ¶a ***further*** *increase* in the size of the family この上の家族の増大. ¶the ***gradual*** *increase* in the cost of living 生活費漸増. ¶an ***immoderate*** *increase* in population 過度の人口増加. ¶show ***marked*** *increase* 著しい増加を示す. ¶The production had only a ***moderate*** *increase.* 生産においてほんの少しの増加を見ただけであった. ¶***natural*** *increase* of population 人口の自然増加. ¶make a ***positive*** *increase* of knowledge 明らかに知識が増進する. ¶show ***progressive*** *increase* 累進的増加を示す. ¶a ***qualitative*** (***quantitative***) *increase* 質(量)の増進. ¶there has lately been a ***rapid*** *increase* in ... 近ごろ...の急速な増加があった. ¶***seasonable*** *increases* in the prices of milk and eggs 牛乳及び卵の値段の季節的騰貴. ¶a ***sevenfold*** *increase* in nine years 九年間に七倍の増加. ¶a ***sharp*** *increase* 激増. ¶a ***sizable*** *increase* 割合に大きい増加. ¶show a ***slight*** *increase* over 1907 一九〇七年に対してわずかの増加を示す. ¶a ***startling*** *increase* 驚くべき増加. ¶the ***steady*** *increase* of wealth 富の堅実な増加.【類】There was a ***steady*** *increase* in population. ¶a ***substantial*** *increase* 相当の増加. ¶a ***sudden*** *increase* 突然の増加. ¶show a ***wonderful*** *increase* over ... ...に対して驚くべき増加を示す. ¶The imports show a ***yearly*** *increase.* 輸入は年々の増加を示す.
Q² to avoid ***budget*** *increase* 予算の増加を避けるため. ¶a ***fare*** *increase* on the city subways 市の地下鉄の運賃値上げ. ¶rapid ***pay*** *increases* 短期の増給 ‖ a yearly ***pay*** *increase* 年々の増給. ¶Wage increases will soon be offset by ***price*** *increases.* 賃銀増加は物価騰貴でじきに帳消になるだろう. ¶***production*** *increase* 増産. ¶***salary*** *increases* and promotions 増給と昇格.【類】demand a $500-a-year ***salary*** *increase.* ¶a ***ten-yen*** *increase* in his salary 彼に対する十円の増給. ¶a ***wage*** *increase* of 18 cents an hour 一時間十八セントの賃銀増加.【類】refuse to grant ***wage*** *increases* to ... / an hourly ***wage*** *increase* of 30 cents / an 18 1/2 cents an hour ***wage*** *increase.* ¶This represents a ***46 percent*** *increase* over the preceding year. これは前年に比し四割六分の増加になる. ¶a ***$25*** *increase* in salary.
P ***at*** no *increase* in price 価格を増加しないで. ¶the rate ***of*** *increase* 増加率. ¶Picture house attendances are distinctly ***on*** the *increase.* 映画の観覧客は明かに増加しつつある.【類】The membership of the club is ***on*** the *increase.* / It is visibly (目に見えて) ***on*** the *increase.*
P² an *increase **by*** natural growth 自然増加. ¶an *increase **in*** body-weight 体重の増加.【類】get an *increase **in*** speed (population). ¶*increase **of*** production 増産 ‖ *increase **of*** salary 昇給.【類】There was an *increase **of*** weight from eighty-two to one hundred pounds. / an *increase **of*** ... per cent on the year preceding. ¶The membership of the association is a large *increase **over*** last year. その協会は昨年よりも大いに会員数が増した.

increase, *v.* 増す.

M His infirmities were ***daily*** *increasing* 彼の衰弱が日々増していた. ¶The town is ***fast*** *increasing* in population. その市はどんどん人口が増加しつつある. ¶Trade is ***gradually*** *increasing* (decreasing). 商売は漸次に増加(減少)している. ¶***greatly*** *increase* in value 価値が大いに増す. ¶***highly*** *increase* 非常に増加する. ¶Italy has ***largely*** *increased* her population. イタリアはその人口が大いに増した. ¶***materially*** *increase* 著しく増加する. ¶*increase **proportionally*** to ... ...に比例して増加する. ¶*increase **pro rata*** あん分

比例的に増す. ¶*increase* ***rapidly*** in popularity 急速に人気が増す. ¶They have ***remarkably*** *increased* in number. それは著しく数を増した. ¶***slightly*** *increase* ちょっと増加する. ¶*increase* ***steadily*** 着々増加する.

P *increase* ***by*** 38 per cent. 三割八分だけ増加する ‖ *increase* ***by*** 400 四百だけ増加する. 【類】The number *increased* ***by*** over 17,000. ¶The company has *increased* the capital stock ***from*** £10,000 ***to*** £20,000. 同会社は資本金を一万ポンドから二万ポンドに増加した .¶It has *increased* 20 per cent ***in*** price. その値段が二割上った. 【類】*increase* ***in*** power (violence, number, wages) ‖ *increase* ***in*** lawlessness ますます無法行為にでる. 【類】*increase* ***in*** number materially / The attack *increased* ***in*** vehemence. / The export *increased* ***in*** volume by 20 percent over last year. / His reputation has *increased* more and more ***in*** brilliancy. ¶Drinking and smoking among women is *increasing* ***to*** an alarming extent in America. 米国では婦人間の飲酒や喫煙が驚くほどの増加を示しつつある. ‖ *increase* one's salary ***to*** $300 その月給を三百ドルに上げる. ¶The success of the book has been *increasing* ***with*** years. その本の売れ高は年とともに増加しつつある.

incredulity, *n.* 懐疑.

V This statement need not ***arouse*** the reader's *incredulity*. かく言っても読者は懐疑の念を起すに及ばない.

incredulous, *a.* 信じない, 軽信しない.

M I am ***wholly*** *incredulous* of the truth of that story. 私はその話は全然信用していない.

P I am *incredulous* ***of*** ...＝I do not believe ... 私は...を信じない.

increment, *n.* 増大, 利得.

Q an ***unearned*** *increment* 不労所得.

incrust, *v.* 皮をかぶせる, 外装する.

P *incrusted* ***with*** ... ...で外装した.

inculcate, *v.* 教え込む, じゅんじゅんと教える.

P *inculcate* an idea ***into*** one's mind ...にある観念を教え込む. ¶he *inculcated* ***on*** us the duties of ... 彼は...の義務をわれわれにじゅんじゅんと説いた.

incumbency, *n.* 職に在ること; 在職期.

Q Sign the form personally and follow signature with your ***present*** *incumbency*. 御自身で用紙に署名してその次に貴下の現職を付記して下さい.

P ***during*** his *incumbency* 彼の在職中.

incumbent, *n.* 在職者.

Q the ***present*** *incumbent* of the presidential chair of the company その会社の現社長.

P² the *incumbent* ***of*** a temple 寺の住職.

incumbent, *a.* よりかかっている; 義務的な.

P it is *incumbent* ***on*** me to ... ...することは私の義務である ‖ duties *incumbent* ***on*** office 役に付帯した務め. ¶this makes it *incumbent* ***upon*** him to ... これで...することは彼の義務となる.

incur, *v.* 招く, こうむる.

P all expenses which may be *incurred* ***in*** ... ...のため要すべき一切の費用. ¶He *incurred* a heavy loss ***through*** you. 彼は君のために大損をした.

incursion, *n.* 乱入, 侵入, 入寇(こう).

V ***make*** an *incursion* into ... ...に侵入する.

Q the time for the ***great*** *incursion* of pilgrims 参けい者がどっと押寄せて来るとき. ¶a ***predatory*** *incursion* 掠奪的侵入. ¶The schoolboy makes ***rude*** *incursions* into art on his slate or the fly-leaf of his schoolbook. 学校児童は石板や教科書の飛ページにやたらに絵とも何ともつかないものを描き散らす.

P *incursion* ***into*** the enemy's country 敵国への侵入.

indebted, *pa.* 恩義をこうむっている, 負うている.

M be ***deeply*** *indebted* to him for ... ...について彼に負う所が多大である. ¶I should be ***greatly*** *indebted* (＝obliged) if you would ... ...して下さらば幸甚に存じます. ¶be ***heavily*** *indebted* to ... ...に負う所が多大である. ¶we are ***lastingly*** *indebted* to ... われわれは永久に...のお陰をこうむっている. ¶I am ***much*** *indebted* for your useful criticism. 私は貴下の有益な批評に対して感謝にたえない.

P I am *indebted* ***for*** the honor of your visit. 御訪問いただき感謝にたえません. ¶I am *indebted* ***to*** him ***for*** valuable assistance. 私は貴重な援助に対し彼に負う所がある. 【類】***for*** these statistics I am *indebted* ***to*** the courtesy of (の好意で) ‖ We are *indebted* ***to*** [the kindness of] Mr ... ***for*** your name. 御芳名は...氏から承っています. 【類】I feel greatly *indebted* ***for*** ...

indebtedness, *n.* 恩を受けていること; 負債があること, 「負債権.

V gratefully ***acknowedge*** one's *indebtedness* to ... for ... ...に対して...に負う所を有難く思う. 【類】desire to ***acknowledge*** my *indebtedness* to ... ¶***cancel*** one's *indebtedness* to ... ...に対するその借金を帳消しにする. ¶The author desires to ***express*** his *indebtedness* to ... for suggestions and information. 著者は注意及び情報に対して...に負うことを表明します. 【類】I am glad to take this opportunity to ***express*** my great *indebtedness* to ... ¶***feel*** one's *indebtedness* to him その恩義を感じる. ¶I must ***record*** my *indebtedness* to ... 私は...に対する私の感謝を記録せねばならない.

Q Germany's ***foreign*** *indebtedness* ドイツの外債.

P be ***under*** *indebtedness* to ... ...の世話になっている ‖ place one ***under*** *indebtedness* 恩にきせる.

indecency, *n.* 非礼, 無作法, 不体裁.

V ***protest*** the *indecency* of talking politics at official ceremonies 公の儀式で政治を語る不穏当を抗弁する.

Q ***indescribable*** *indecency* 名状しがたい無作法.

indecision, *n.* 不決断, 不決定, ためらい.

V ***manifest*** the usual *indecision* in making a purchase 買物をするとき例のごとくぐずぐずする.

Q owing to the ***official*** *indecision* 当局の優柔不断で.

indefatigable, *a.* 根気のよい, うまない, 不屈不とうの.

P Do not fear to apply to him; he will be *indefatigable* ***for*** you. 彼に頼むことを恐れてはいけない, 彼は君のために労を惜しまないから. ¶be *indefatigable* ***in*** their endeavors to ... 彼らの...しようとする努力は不屈である.

indefensible, *a.* 弁解の立たない.

M ***legally*** *indefensible* 法律上弁解のできない.

indemnification, *n.* 賠償, 補償.

P in *indemnification* ***for*** ... ...の賠償に ‖ *indemnification* ***for*** damage 損害賠償.

indemnify, *v.* 保証を与える, 損害賠償を保証する.

P *indemnify* a person ***against*** any loss 損害賠償を人に保証する. ¶*indemnify* the owners ***for*** damages 所有主に損害賠償を保証する. ¶*indemnify* ***to*** a person ***for*** damages 損害に対して人に賠償を保証する.

indemnity, *n.* 賠償, 補償, 賠償金.

V ***claim*** *indemnity* for ... ...に対し賠償を請求する. ¶***collect*** a large *indemnity* 多額の賠償金を取立てる. ¶***concede*** an *indemnity* 賠償金を譲与する. ¶***exact*** an *indemnity* of ... ...の賠償金を強請する. ¶***give*** an *indemnity* 賠償をする. ¶***obtain*** an *indemnity* for ... ...の賠償を得る. ¶***pay*** a heavy *indemnity* 巨額の賠償金を払う. ¶***receive*** *indemnity* for a damage done 損害の賠償を受取る. ¶***secure*** a large *indemnity* 多大の損害賠償を得る. ¶***wring*** *indemnity* from ... ...から賠償を強制的にとる.

Q a ***big*** *indemnity* 多額の賠償金.

Q² a ***war*** *indemnity* 戦争の賠償金. ¶***war loss*** *indemnity* 戦争による損失の賠償.

P sue a person ***for*** *indemnity* 損害賠償で人を訴える.

indent, *n.* 〖商〗注文書.

V ***cancel*** all standing *indents* 未済の注文を全部取消す.

indent, *v.* 鋸(きょ)歯状に刻む.

P The coast is *indented* ***by*** tiny bays. その沿岸は小さな入江が幾つかあって屈曲が多い.

indenture, *n.* [正副二通の]契約書; 年期奉公契約書.

V ***break*** one's *indentures* その契約書を破棄する.

P go to him ***under*** *indenture* 年期奉公の契約で彼のもとに勤める.

indenture, *v.* 契約して年期奉公に入れる.

P he was *indentured* ***to*** ... 彼は...の所に年期奉公にはいった.

independence, *n.* 独立, 自立, 自主.

V The country formally ***declared*** *independence*. その国は正式に独立を宣言した. 【類】The colonies ***declared*** their *independence* from England. ¶***enjoy*** an *independence* 独立を享有する. ¶***gain*** one's *independence* その独立を獲得する. ¶***give*** legislative *independence* to ... ...に立法上の独立を与える. ¶***leave*** him full *independence* 彼に思う存分やらせる. ¶***lose*** its *independence* その独立を失う. ¶***maintain*** *independence* 独立を維持する. ¶***proclaim*** its *independence* その独立を宣言する. ¶I ***preferred*** the *independence* of a hotel to being a guest of a friend of mine. 私は友人の所に厄介になるよりホテルの方が気楽でよかった. ¶***recover*** her *independence* その国の独立を回復す

る. ¶*regain* her *independence* その国の独立を復活する. ¶*safeguard* the national *independence* 国家の独立を護る. ¶*threaten* our *independence* わが国の独立をおびやかす. ¶when they *won* their *independence* from England 彼らが英国から独立したとき.

Q the *economic independence* of women 女子の経済的独立. ¶*fiscal independence* 財政権の独立. ¶*intellectual* and *artistic independence* 学問と芸術の独立. ¶*national independence* 国の独立. ¶Japan's *newly-regained independence*. 日本の新たに回復した独立. ¶formally declare their *political independence* 正式に政治上の独立を声明する.

P the movement for the *independence of* India インド独立運動.

independent, *a.* 独立の, 自主の, 自立の.

M *economically independent* 経済的に独立して. ¶be *financially independent* 財政的に独立している.

P A wife can have property *indendent of* her husband. 妻は夫から独立して財産を所有しうる. ‖ *independent of* one's father 親の厄介にならずに.

independently, *ad.* 独立して.

P His opinion is formed *independently of* any proof. 彼の意見はなんら証拠なしに立てられたものだ.

index, *n.* みだし, 索引.

V *compile* an *index* 索引を作る. ¶Manner of walking *gives* an *index* to one's character. 歩き方で人の品性がうかがわれる.

Q an *alphabetical index* to ... ...の ABC 順の索引. ¶a nicely *arranged index* うまく作成した索引. ¶a *copious index* 豊富な索引. ¶it cannot be taken as a *reliable index* to ... それは...の信頼できる指標として受入れることができない. ¶an *authors' index* 著者索引(図書館などの).

Q² the *Consumer Price Index* 消費者物価指数. ¶maintain a high *business index* 高営業指数を維持する. ¶a *name index* 氏名索引.

P² an *index to* a book 本の索引 ‖ writing as an *index to* temperament 気質を知る手段としての筆跡 ‖ the *index to* the current issues of publications 現在出版物発行の指標.

index, *v.* 索引を付ける.

P *index* it *under* ...それを...の項下に索引を出す.

Indian, *n.* インド人, アメリカインディアン.

Q *American Indians.* アメリカ土人. ¶*Pueblo Indians.* メキシコ及びアリゾナにおける共同村に住むインド人の一団. ¶*Red Indians* 北米土人.

india-rubber, *n.* インドゴム, 弾性ゴム.

P rub out *with india-rubber* ゴムで消す.

indicate, *v.* 指す, 示す, 指摘する.

M *clearly indicate* one's intention to ... ...しようという意志を明らかに示す. ¶this *indicates* very *decidedly* that ... これは...ということをはなはだ明確に示している. ¶*indicate incontestably* that ... 議論の余地なく...ということを示す. ¶*indubitably indicate* that ... 疑いもなく...を示す.

P the scope of the book is *indicated in* its title: it is ... この本の範囲はその表題にあらわれている. すなわちそれは...である.

indication, *n.* 表示, 指示; 徴候, 形跡.

V Her face *bore* all the *indications* of nobility of soul and a cheerful disposition. 彼女の顔には高貴の精神と明朗な気質がよく現われていた. ¶his face *gave* no *indication* of ... 彼は...の色を顔に出さなかった. ¶*show* (=give) *indications* of ... ...の徴候を示す.

V² all *indications point* to ... 大勢は...に傾いている.

Q *auspicious indications* 縁起のよい徴候. ¶a *certain indication* of rain たしかな雨模様. ¶a *cheering indication* 愉快な徴候. ¶a *conclusive indication* 決定的な徴候. ¶there seems to be *every indication* that ... ...という十分の徴候があるように思われる ‖ It has *every indication* of being genuine. それはどう見ても本物のようだ. ¶a *fair indication* of the trend その傾向の明かなあらわれ ‖ There are *fair indications* that the improvement is likely to continue. その改善は継続するらしいことはほぼ明かである. ¶the *first indication* of ... ...の第一の徴候. ¶a *few indications* of main points 二三の主な点の指摘. ¶give *frequent indications* of one's true composition 時々その本性を現わす. ¶*hopeful indications* 有望な徴候. ¶an *infallible indication* of ... ...の間違いのない徴候. ¶There are *many indications* that there will be no war in the next ten years. 今後十年間に戦争はあるまいという形勢が大分認められる. ¶give *plain indications* of ... ...の明確な徴候を示す. ¶there is a *strong indication* that ... ...という著しい徴候がある. ¶it is a *sure indication* that ... これは...という確かな証拠である. ¶a *routing indication* on a letter 手紙の経由筋の指示 (via Suez などと). ¶there are not *wanting indications* that ... ...という徴候が見られる. ¶a *welcome indication* that ... ...といううれしい徴候.

P *according to* all *indications* 情勢を総括すると.

P² The newspaper is unreliable as an *indication of* public opinion. 新聞紙は世論の表示として信頼し難い. ‖ an *indication of* popular feeling 民衆の感情表示. 【類】There are *indications of* a good (poor) trade.

O the *indications* generally are that ... 大勢は...である.

indicative, *a.* 表示する, 指示する.

P faces *indicative of* the joy of living 生活の享楽を表示する顔 ‖ His features are *indicative of* his intelligence. 彼の容貌は聡明さを示している. ‖ *indicative of* one's good nature お人よしの, しおらしい.

indicator, *n.* 指示者, 指示器.

Q a *trustworthy indicator* of wealth 信頼できる富の尺度.

Q² an *air-speed indicator* 飛行速力表示器. ¶a *direction indicator* 方向表示器. ¶a *stock indicator*=a stock-printer 株式相場(自動)指示器. ¶a *household wants indicator* 入用品表示器(家庭用品の名が列記してあって入用の所へ peg を差すようになっている板).

P² the *indicator of* the current direction 電流方向指示器.

indict, *v.* 告訴する, 告発する.

P *indict* a person *as* a rioter 治安ぶん乱者として人を告訴する. ¶be *indicted for* murder (treason, bigamy) 殺害(など)のかどで告訴される. ¶be *indicted by* a grand jury 大陪審によって告発される. ¶be *indicted on* a charge of ... ...のかどで告訴される.

indictment, *n.* 告訴, 起訴, 告発.

V The grand jury *found* an *indictment* against him. 大陪審が彼を有罪と認めた. ¶*lay* the *indictment* at the door of ... その告発を...がしたものとする.

Q a *bitter indictment* 痛烈な告発. ¶a *scathing indictment* しゅん烈な起訴. ¶make a *supplementary indictment* 追起訴する. ¶a *true indictment* 正当の告訴.

P *on* an *indictment* for forgery 偽造に対する告発で. ¶He was *under indictment* for embezzlement at the time of his election. 彼が選挙されたとき公金を費消したかどで告訴されていた.

P² an *indictment for* murder 殺人罪の告発. ¶an *indictment of* American rule in the Philippines フィリピン群島における米国統治の非難.

indifference, *n.* 冷淡, むとん着, 無関心.

V *feign indifference* むとん着を装う.

Q receive one with *absolute indifference* 全く冷淡に人を迎える. ¶a *callous indifference* to the sufferings of others 他人の苦痛に対する無情な冷淡. ¶an attitude of *calm indifference* 冷静な態度. ¶a *cold indifference* 冷やかなむとん着さ. ¶a *contemptuous indifference* 人を食った冷淡さ. ¶with *frigid indifference* 冷酷に. ¶a *gentle indifference* やさしいむとん着さ. ¶affect a *haughty indifference* ごう然としてむとん着の風をよそおう. ¶show an *icy indifference* to ... 冷やかなむとん着さを示す. ¶an *incredible indifference* to ... ...に対する信じられないほどのむとん着さ. ¶He received my remonstrance with *perfect indifference.* 彼は私の苦言を空うそぶいて聞いていた. ¶with a *philosophical indifference* to ... ...に対して虚心坦懐に. ¶treat a person with *scornful indifference* 人を軽べつし冷淡に扱う. 【類】He looked aside with *scornful indifference.* ¶endure it with *stoical indifference* 苦痛を意としないむとん着さをもってそれにたえる. ¶look on at it with *stupid* and *openmouthed indifference* あほらしい口あんぐりの体でそれを眺める. ¶in *supreme indifference* to the fact that ... ...の事実にとん着せず涼しい顔をして. ¶*thoughtless indifference* to truth 真理に対する無思慮な冷淡さ. ¶in *utter indifference* to the fact that ... ...という事実に全然むとん着で.

P *in* calm *indifference* to ... ...に対して冷静に. ¶view it *with indifference* それを無関心に眺める.

P² *indifference about* success or failure 成否についての無関心. ¶*indifference as to* one's personal appearance 自分の服装についてのむとん着. ¶the *indifference of* the general public *towards* education 教育に対する一般人の無関

心. ¶*indifference* ***to*** the pain of others 他人の苦痛に対する冷淡. 【類】*indifference* ***to*** money.

indifferent, *a.* むとん着な, 冷淡な.

M be ***quite*** *indifferent* 一向平気である. ¶be ***utterly*** *indifferent* to one's appearance 風さいには全く無関心である.

P *indifferent* ***about*** one's welfare (success or failure) その幸福(など)についてむとん着な. ¶*indifferent* ***to*** one's study 自分の勉強に不熱心な ‖ He is *indifferent* ***to*** his dress. 彼は服装にむとん着だ. 【類】be *indifferent* ***to*** public criticism / be *indifferent* ***to*** praise or blame (毀誉ほうへん) / *indifferent* ***to*** worldly gain (浮世の利益).

indigenous, *a.* その国土に特有の.

P the religion *indigenous* ***to*** Japan 日本に固有な宗教 ‖ *indigenous* ***to*** China 中国に特有な. 【類】Kangaroos are *indigenous* ***to*** Australia.

indigestion, *n.* 不消化, 消化不良.

V ***give*** one *indigestion* 人を消化不良に陥らせる. ¶***induce*** one's *indigestion* 消化不良をきたす. ¶***promote*** *indigestition* 消化不良に陥らせる.

Q ***Bad*** *indigestion* comes from lack of mastication. 消化不良はそしゃくの不足から起る. ¶***intellectual*** *indigestion* 知識の不消化. ¶***mental*** *indigestion* 精神上の不消化 (physical indigestion に対して).

indignant, *a.* 怒っている, 憤慨している.

M ***hotly*** *indignant* upon hearing that ... ...と聞いてぷんぷん怒って. ¶becoming ***somewhat*** *indignant* やや色をなして.

P he was *indignant* ***about*** the incident of ... 彼は...の事件について憤慨していた. ¶he got *indignant* ***at*** the suggestion that ... 彼は...と言う注意を受けて憤慨した. 【類】*indignant* ***at*** the insult (injustice) / I was *indignant* ***at*** their mean actions (卑劣な行為). ¶*indignant* ***beyond*** measure 非常に憤って. ¶*indignant* ***over*** the treatment he received 彼が受けた待遇に憤慨して. ¶*indignant* ***with*** ... ...に対して憤慨して.

indignation, *n.* 公憤, 義憤, 憤怒.

V ***arouse*** popular *indignation* and disgust 人々の憤怒とけんおを呼び起す. ¶***cause*** great *indignation* on the part of ... ...を非常に憤怒させる. ¶***excite*** general *indignation* throughout the country 国中に広く義憤を呼び起す. 【類】***excited*** much *indignation* here. ¶***invite*** another's *indignation* 人の怒りを招く. ¶He ***kept*** his *indignation* to himself. 彼はその憤怒を外に現わさなかった. ¶***raise*** the *indignation* of ... ...の憤怒を高める. ¶***repressing*** his righteous *indignation* 彼の義憤を抑えて. ¶***rouse*** the *indignation* of ... ...の憤怒を呼び起す. ¶***stir up*** considerable *indignation* 非常に憤怒を引き起す.

V² *Indignation* ***broke out*** everywhere. いたる所に義憤が起った.

Q a storm of ***public*** *indignation* 公憤のあらし. ¶excite much ***natural*** and ***justifiable*** *indignation* 無理のない正当な義憤を大いに呼び起す. ¶by ***noble*** *indignation* 気高い義憤によって. ¶***oratorical*** *indignation* against ... ...に反対の気炎. ¶expend a certain amount of ***moral*** *indignation* on ... ...に多少の義憤をもらす. ¶a ***virtuous*** *indignation* 義憤. ¶excite ***widespread*** *indignation* 一般の憤りを買う.

P withdraw ***in*** *indignation* 憤然として引きさがる. ¶a storm ***of*** *indignation* 憤怒の爆発. ¶***to*** my deep *indignation* 私が大に憤ったことには. ¶My blood boils ***with*** *indignation*. 私の血は憤怒で煮えくりかえる.

P² his *indignation* ***with*** the public for its inadequate recognition of his deserts 世間が彼の功績を十分認めないのでそれに対する彼の憤慨.

indignity, *n.* 下劣さ.

P subject a person ***to*** *indignities* 人にぶじょくを加える. 【類】The bandits subjects us ***to*** all sorts of *indignities*.

P² *indignity* ***of*** one's speech (=language) 品のない言葉使い.

indiscretion, *n.* 無分別, 無思慮; 軽率, 不きん慎.

V ***commit*** a grave *indiscretion* 大失策をする. ¶he ***had*** the *indiscretion* to ... 彼は無分別にも...した.

Q her ***youthful*** *indiscretion* 彼女が若気の無分別.

P² *Indiscretion* ***in*** eating and drinking brings on such troubles. 乱暴な飲食がこうした病気を招く. 【類】*indiscretion* ***in*** choosing one's friends.

indispensable, *a.* 不可欠の, 緊要な.

P *indispensable* ***for*** ... ...にとって欠くことのできない. ¶Health is *indispensable* ***to*** all. 健康はだれにも欠くべからざるものである. ‖ Fresh air during sleep is *indispensable* ***to*** health. 睡眠中新鮮な空気を呼吸することは健康上不可欠必須のことである.

indispose, *v.* 不適当にする, 加減悪くする, 不きげんにする.

M I am ***suddenly*** *indisposed.* 私は急に気分が悪くなった.

P It will *indispose* a person ***for*** work. それは人をして仕事に不適当ならしめる. ‖ I am *indisposed* ***for*** any work. 私はどんな仕事にも気が進まない. ¶He is *indisposed* ***with*** a chill. 彼は悪寒がして加減が悪い.

indisposition, *n.* 不快, 不気分; いや気.

V in spite of *indisposition* ***caused*** by a chill さむけがして加減が悪かったが.

Q a ***slight*** *indisposition* 軽病.

P² *indisposition* ***for*** ... ...に対するいや気.

indistinguishable, *a.* 区別されない.

M ***practically*** *indistinguishable* from new [古手であるが新も同様な.]

P They are *indistinguishable* ***from*** one another. 彼らはいずれがいずれとも見分けがつかない.

individual, *n.* 個人, 個体.

V ***fit*** the *individual* for ... その人を...に適するように仕込む.

Q ***disease-proof*** *individuals* 病気にかからない人々. ¶He is one of those ***gifted*** *individuals* who can detect indecency in almost everything. 彼はほとんど凡てのものに不適当を見出すことのできるといったたちの人である. ¶a ***good, kindly*** *individual* 善良な親切気のある人. ¶a universally ***known*** *individual* 世界的人物. ¶These ***lawless*** *individuals* first robbed and then killed him to prevent future complications. これらのろうぜき者はまず彼から略奪して後難をさけようと彼を殺害した. ¶***middle-aged*** *individuals* 中年の人々. ¶***obscure*** *individuals* 無名の士. ¶an ***odious*** *individual* いやな人. ¶***old*** *individuals* 老人たち. ¶a ***particular*** *individual* その人個人. ¶***private*** *individuals* 私人.

Q² the ***subject*** *individual* 本人.

individualism, *n.* 個人主義.

Q ***co-operative*** *individualism* 協力個人主義. ¶***sturdy British*** *individualism* がん強な英国人の個人主義.

individuality, *n.* 個性, 個人性, 人格.

V ***cultivate*** (=***develop***) one's *individuality* おのれの個性をのばす. ¶Dress ***expresses*** the wearer's *individuality*. 服装はその人の個性を表示する. ¶***give*** a marked *individuality* to ... ...にはっきりした個性を与える. ¶***lose*** one's *individuality* その個性を失う. ¶***preserve*** one's *individuality* 個性を失わない. ¶***repress*** *individuality* 個性を抑制する. ¶***respect*** *individuality* 個性を尊重する. ¶***stamp*** his *individuality* upon ... 彼の個性を...の上に刻みつける ‖ Art, as of old, should ***stamp*** a nation's *individuality*. 芸術は昔のように国民の持味を明かに出すべきである. ¶***work out*** one's own *individuality* 自分の個性を発揮する.

Q These subjects are treated very much in the Corot style, but with a ***distinct*** *individuality*. これらの題材は大分コロー風に取扱われているがしかもそこに著しい個性が現われている. ¶He is wanting in ***fixed*** *individuality*. 彼は固定した個性を欠いている. ¶a man of ***marked*** *individuality* はっきり個性を持つ人. ¶His writings are marked by ***strong*** *individuality* of style. 彼の著作は個性を強く発揮した文体がその特徴だ.

indolence, *n.* 怠惰, ものぐさ, 遊惰.

P pass one's day ***in*** *indolence* 怠惰にその日その日を送る.

indolent, *a.* 怠惰な, ものぐさな, 無性な.

P *indolent* ***about*** ... ...について怠惰な.

indorse, *v.* =endorse.

induce, *v.* 誘致する, 生じさせる, 引き起す.

M ***artificially*** *induced* pearl 養殖真珠.

P the taciturnity *induced* ***by*** the pipe of tobacco タバコに気を取られて生じた沈黙. ¶*induce* many owners ***to*** dispose of their collections その収集を売立てるように多くの所有主を説きつける.

O *induce* a person to ... 人を誘って...させる.

inducement, *n.* 誘導, 誘因, 動機.

V he ***felt*** a strong *inducement* to ... 彼は熱心に...しようという気になった. ¶he ***has*** a strong *inducement* to ... 彼は大いに...しようという気になっている. ¶These attractions ***hold out*** alluring *inducements* to travel in that country. これらの魅力が大いにその国の旅行を誘致する. ¶What *inducement* have you to ***offer***? どんな有利な条件を提供できますか.

V² We will start work as soon as sufficient *inducement*

offers. われわれは十分その見込のつき次第仕事を始めよう.

Q a *gentle inducement* for a tip それとなく祝儀を出させようとする持掛け. ¶offer *good inducement* [買わせるなどの]魅力がある. ¶see *great* (*no*) *inducement* 大いに乗気にさせるものがある(何ら…ない). ¶offer *greater inducements* 一層魅力のあることを持ち出す. ¶an *irresistible inducement* 飛びつかずにはおれないような好餌(ゞ). ¶it has *no inducement* to … それには…するようにひき付けるものがない. ¶This job offers them sufficiently high *pecuniary inducements.* この仕事は高い報酬が得られると言って彼らを誘致する. ¶a *small inducement* あまり気の進まないこと. ¶a *strong inducement* 力強い誘致. ¶The offer is not *sufficient inducement.* その提供には十分の魅力がない. 【類】There is not *sufficient inducement* to establish an agency.

P² as an *inducement to* the cigarette-smoking public 愛煙家連の心を引き付ける一つの方法として ‖ They held out repeated *inducements to* foreign artisans to come over. 彼らは外国の職工にしばしば好餌をもって渡来を促した.

induct, *v.* 就任させる.

M He was *formally inducted into* the office. 彼は正式にその役に就任した.

induction, *n.* 帰納; 誘導.

Q *magnetic induction* 〖物理〗磁気誘導.

P² an *induction from* observations 観察からの帰納. ¶the *induction of* foreign capital into Japan 日本への外資導入.

indulge, *v.* 好きなようにさせる, ふける.

M Smoking may be *freely indulged* in. 喫煙は自由にできる. ‖ He *indulged* himself too *freely* with wine. 彼は酒を飲み過ぎた. ¶He *seldom indulges* in a holiday. 彼はめったに休まない.

P *indulge in* dreams of the time when … …時代の夢想にふける. 【類】*indulge in* drunkenness, boisterousness (どんちゃん騒ぎ), loud-talking, and other actions causing annoyance to … / *indulge in* alcoholic liquors habitually / *indulge in* dissipation / *indulge in* luxuriousness to one's heart's desire (思う存分) / *indulge in* one's sloth (怠惰) / *indulge in* the habit of … / *indulge in* needless conversation / *indulge in* sarcasm (皮肉) / *indulge in* luxury ‖ *indulge in* reminiscence 昔をしのぶ ‖ *indulge in* a little speechifying (=idle talk) 少し弁舌をろうする. 【類】*indulge in* needless verbosity (だ弁) / *indulge in* eulogistic remarks (賛辞) ‖ It is too early to *indulge in* pessimism. 悲観するのはまだ早過ぎる. ‖ One cannot afford to *indulge in* such idle thoughts. そんなのんきなことは言っていられない. ‖ sports and pastimes *indulged in* by Englishmen 英国人のやる運動娯楽. 【類】Fishing, bathing, and dancing can be *indulged in* there. ¶*indulge* his globe-trotting propensities *to* the full 彼の世界漫遊癖を十分満足させる.

indulgence, *n.* 放縦, たんでき; 大目にみること.

V I *ask* your *indulgence* for … …私は…に対しあなたのご許しを願います. ‖ I must *ask* the reader's kind *indulgence* for any inaccuracies and omissions that may possibly occur. あるいは誤り脱漏があるかも知れずこの点読者諸氏のお許しをこわねばならない. ¶*crave* the *indulgence* of … …のお許しを願う. ¶*solicit* the *indulgence* of our readers 読者諸君のお許しを願う.

Q *alcoholic indulgence* 飲酒. ¶ask his *considerable indulgence* 彼の格別の許しを願う. ¶*fleshly indulgence* 肉欲にふけること. ¶give *full indulgence* to the vagaries of imagination 盛んに空想にふける. ¶*moderate indulgence* in "hard" liquor 強烈な酒の適度の飲用. ¶regard love as a *permissible indulgence* 恋愛を許容しうる道楽と見なす. ¶*Such indulgence!* 不埒千万. ¶*unbridled indulgence* 手のつけられない放縦. ¶*uncontrolled indulgence* 野放らつ(無礼講などの). ¶*worldly indulgences* 現世の快楽.

P kill a child *with indulgence* 放任しておいて子供を台なしにする ‖ treat *with indulgence* 手柔らかに取扱う.

P² *indulgence in* strong tea こい茶の好み ‖ *indulgence in* wine ぶどう酒好き. ¶the *indulgence of* one's tastes 自分の趣味にふけること.

indulgent, *a.* ふける; 寛大な, 甘い.

M His parents are *too indulgent.* 両親が甘すぎる.

P *indulgent in* wine (gambling). ぶどう酒にふけって. ¶*indulgent towards* others 他人に寛大な. ¶be *indulgent with* women 女に甘い.

industrialism, *n.* 産業主義, 工業熱.

V *Industrialism leapt* into existence. 工業熱がさかんになった.

Q² *machine industrialism* 機械産業主義.

industrialist, *n.* 生産業者, メーカー.

Q² an *aviation industrialist* 飛行業者. ¶a *big*(*small*)-*time industrialist* 大(小)メーカー.

industrialization, *n.* 工業化.

P² *industrialization of* atomic energy appliances 原子力機械の工業化.

industrialize, *v.* 産業化する.

M Cotton spinning is the most *completely industrialized* of Japanese industries. 紡績は日本の産業中で最も完全に産業化している.

industrious, *a.* 勤勉な, 孜々(し)たる.

P *industrious about* … …について勤勉な. ¶*industrious in* one's business 自分の業務に勤勉な.

industry, *n.* (**1**) 工業, 産業, 実業.

V *assist* the crippled *industry* その無能力の産業に助力を与える. ¶Ship-building and the fisheries *constitute* the chief *industries* of Plymouth. 造船業と漁業とはプリマスの主要な産業になっている. ¶*cripple* the *industry* 産業を無能力にさせる. ¶*develop* an important *industry* 重要な産業を開発する. ¶War *dislocates* the *industries* of a country. 戦争は一国の産業を混乱させる. ¶The *industry* was *established* in 18—. その産業は千八百幾年かに創設された. ¶*expand industry* and commerce 商工業を拡張する. ¶the district *has* a new *industry* as a result of … その地方には…の結果として新しい工業が起った. ¶*kill* (=*destroy*) certain home *industries* ある種の国内産業を死滅させる. ¶*open up* new *industries* 新しい産業を開発する. ¶*practice* an *industry* 一つの産業を経営する. ¶*preserve* the *industry* from extinction その工業の衰亡を防ぐ. ¶*promote industries* 産業を振作する. ¶He *pursued* the *industry* of farming until the age of 19 years. 彼は十九歳まで農業に従事していた. ¶*rationalize* the *industry* その産業を合理化させる. ¶*revolutionize industry* 産業に革命を起す. ¶*ruin* the *industry* その産業を衰退させる. ¶The *industry* was *transplanted* from Korea. その産業は朝鮮から伝わったものだ. ¶*trustify* the *industry* その産業をトラストにする.

V² The *industry* once *flourished* remarkably in the country. その国では昔その工業が非常に栄えた. ¶New *industries sprang up.* 新しい産業が興った.

Q² *basic* (=*key*) *industries,* such as textiles and coal 織物・石炭などの基本産業. ¶a heavily *capitalized industry* 多額の資本を投じた工業. ¶The *chief industry* of the town is the … manufacture. 同市の主な産業は…の製造である. ¶the *colossal cinematographic industry* of our times 現代のぼう大な映画事業. ¶a *decaying industry* 衰亡しつつある産業. ¶a *domestic industry* 家庭工業. ¶an *extensive industry* 範囲の広い工業. ¶*extractive industries* [鉱・農・漁などの]生産業. ¶a once *flourishing* but now *obsolete rural industry* かつては繁盛したが今は衰微している一つの地方産業. ¶Switzerland's *greatest industry* is the entertaining of tourists. スイスの最大産業は観光客を接待することだ. ¶*heavy* (*light*) *industries* 重(軽)工業. ¶Agriculture is an *important industry.* 農業は重要な産業である. 【類】The sea fisheries are an *important industry* in Norway. ¶Italy has a *large industry* in silk weaving and reeling. イタリアは絹織物や繰糸業を盛んに営んでいる. ¶*machine-driven industry* 機械工業. ¶The tourist business is one of the *major industries* of the West. 観光業は米国西部の主要な産業の一つである. 【類】The press has become a *major industry.* ¶create *new industries* 新産業を興す. ¶*pastoral* and *agricultural industries* 牧畜及び農業. ¶*productive industry* 生産工業. ¶This led to the growth of a *profitable industry.* これで有利な産業の発達を見るにいたった. ¶the inauguration of two *promising local industries* 二つの有望な地方産業の創始. ¶*remunerative industries* 有利な産業. ¶the chief branch of *rural industry* 地方産業の主要な部門. ¶a highly *skilled British industry* which is in danger of extinction 高度の技術を持ちながら衰亡の危機にひんしている英国の一産業. ¶a *spoon-fed* (=an artificially encouraged) *industry* 助成産業. ¶The collection and distillation of camphor is one of the *staple industries* of Formosa. しょう脳の収集と蒸留とは台湾の主要産業の一つである. ¶*sweated industry* 搾取産業. ¶those essential to *various industries* 産業界の要

人. ¶Agriculture is the world's greatest and most ***vital industry***. 農業は世界の最大にして最も緊要な産業である.
Q² the ***air industry*** 飛行産業. ¶the ***amusement*** (=***entertainment***) ***industry*** 演芸事業. ¶the ***atomic bomb industry*** in Tennessee テンネシーの原子爆弾工業. ¶the ***auto*** [***mobile***] ***industry*** 自動車工業 ‖ the shut-down of much of the ***automobile industry*** 自動車工業の多数閉鎖(中止). ¶the American ***aviation industry*** アメリカ航空機工業. ¶The "***beauty industry***" ranks fourth in American economic life. 美粧業はアメリカ経済生活の第四位にある. ¶the ***book industry*** 書籍出版業. ¶Thus is the ***brewing industry*** carried on. 醸造業の現状は以上のようである. ¶The [radio] ***broadcasting industry*** 放送事業. ¶the ***building industry*** 建設事業. ¶the ***capital goods industry*** 資本財産業. ¶the ***capitalist industry*** 資本主義産業. ¶revitalize the ***coal industry*** 石炭事業を復活させる ‖ the bituminous ***coal industry*** 有煙石炭業. ¶the ***commercial vehicle industry*** 商業用の車両製造業. ¶the ***construction industry*** 建(築)事業. ¶***defense industries*** 国防諸事業. ¶***export industries*** 輸出諸産業. ¶***factory industry*** in twelve-hour shifts 十二時間交代の製造工業. ¶the ***farm*** (=***farming***) ***industry*** 農業. ¶the ***furniture making industry*** 家具製造業. ¶protect ***home*** (=***household***) ***industries*** 家内工業を保護する. ¶be still an ***infant industry*** なお幼稚な産業である. ¶the ***iron*** and ***steel industry*** 鉄鋼事業. ¶the ***knit fabric industry*** メリヤス工業. ¶a ***large-scale industry*** 大規模産業. ¶the ***lightmetal industry*** 軽金属産業. ¶the ***livestock industry*** 畜産業. ¶***manufacturing industries*** 諸種製造業. 【類】a famous center of ***manufacturing industry***. ¶Chicago is the heart of the ***meat industry***. シカゴは食肉産業の中心である. ¶the ***meat packing industry*** 食肉かん詰業. ¶***men's wear industry*** 男子服装業. ¶the ***motion picture*** (=***movie***) ***industry*** 映画事業. ¶***munition industries*** 軍事産業. ¶Japan's ***newspaper industry*** 日本の新聞事業. ¶***packing industry*** かん詰業. ¶***peace***[***-time***] ***industries*** 平和産業. ¶***peasant industries*** 農民産業. ¶the ***plastics industry*** プラスチック工業. ¶the ***poultry industry*** 養鶏業. ¶basic ***production industries*** 基礎生産事業. ¶Viscount Masatoshi Okochi, former head of the ***Riken industries*** 旧理研工業の社長であった子爵大河内正敏. ¶the ***Ruhr industries*** ドイツルール地方の諸産業. ¶communications, transport, utilities or other public ***service industries*** 交通運輸公益事業またはその他公共産業. ¶the decline of the French ***shipping industry*** フランス海運事業の衰退. ¶the ***silk textile industry*** 絹織物工業. ¶***steel industries*** 鋼鉄諸工業. ¶***synthetic fiber industries*** 合成繊維諸産業. ¶the ***tourist industry*** 観光事業. ¶the ***toy-making industry*** おもちゃ製造業. ¶The ***travel industry*** entered 1937 with steady rising traffic 観光業はますます高まる旅行熱を前にして 1937 年を迎えた. ¶the ***trucking industry*** トラック運送業. ¶the ***type-setting industry*** 製版業. ¶***utility industries*** 公益事業. ¶***war industries*** 戦時諸産業. 【類】the former Japanese ***war industry*** in Manchuria / the decline of major ***war industries*** / the closing of ***war industries***. ¶the ***wine*** and ***dairy industries*** ぶどう酒及び酪農産業.
P an important branch ***of industry*** 産業の重要な一部門.
(**2**) 勤勉.
Q his truly ***herculean industry*** 彼の真に精力的な勤勉. ¶win success by ***honest industry*** 正直に働いて成功する. ¶a monument of ***misdirected*** and ***mistaken industry*** 方針を誤った努力の記念物. ¶a man of ***indefatigable industry*** 不屈不とうの人. ¶the ***loyal*** and ***tireless industry*** 忠実にして辛抱強い勤勉. ¶***misapplied industry*** 目的を誤った努力. ¶***steady, unfaltering industry*** 着実にして断固たる努力. ¶with ***unremitting industry*** 間断ない努力をもって. ¶a man of ***untiring industry*** うまざる努力の人. ¶by ***unwearied industry*** 根気よく.
P gain one's position ***by industry*** 勤勉によってその地位を得る. ¶gain the prize ***through*** (=by means of) one's ***industry*** 勤勉によってその賞を得る. ¶One cannot succeed ***without industry*** 勤勉なくしては成功は得られない.
P² ***industry in*** the collection of materials 材料収集の努力.

inelegancy, *n*. 無趣味, 無風流.
Q use ***colloquial inelegancies*** 不体裁な俗語を使う.

ineligible, *a*. 選ぶに足らない
P ***ineligible for*** service (membership, office) 職務(など)に選ばれる資格のない.

inequality, *n*. 不同, 不平等.
V There is nothing like an ocean trip to ***level off*** social *inequalities*. 社会的差別の撤廃には大洋航海にしくはない.
P² the ***inequality between*** the rich and [the] poor 貧富間の懸隔. ¶great ***inequalities of*** wealth 富の大なる不平等. ¶***inequality of*** treatment 差別待遇.

inertia, *n*. 不活発, ゆるみ.
Q ***institutional inertia*** 制度上の不備. ¶a ***mental inertia*** and want of energy 精神のゆるみと精力の欠乏.

inevitable, *n*. 不可避のこと.
V ***accept*** the *inevitable* with philosophy さとってあきらめる. ¶***face*** the *inevitable* 不可避の運命に直面する.

inevitable, *a*. 不可避の.
M it was ***almost inevitable*** that ... ...ということはほとんど避け得られなかった.

inevitableness, *n*. 不可避.
V ***explain*** the *inevitableness* of the circumstances 因果を含める.

inexperienced, *pa*. 経験のない.
P He was *inexperienced* ***in*** women. 彼は女に無経験であった. ‖ be *inexperienced* ***in*** the world 世間なれしていない.

infallibility, *n*. 不過誤.
V No dictionary-maker can ***claim*** *infallibility*. 辞書編集者はだれも過失がないと主張することはできない.
Q ***papal infallibility*** 教皇の無謬(カトリック教では教皇は神の代表で誤りをなすことなしと主張する).

infamy, *n*. 不名誉, 汚名.
V in order to ***escape*** the *infamy* of detection 露顕の汚名を免れるために.

infancy *n*. 幼年, 幼年期.
Q in his ***earliest infancy*** 彼がほんの幼稚な時代に.
P ***during*** the *infancy* of its national life その国民生活の幼稚な時代に. ¶sightless ***from infancy*** 幼少から盲目な ‖ ***from infancy*** to old age 幼年時代から老年時代まで. ¶die ***in infancy*** 幼少のころに死ぬ ‖ the motor-car ***in*** its *infancy* 初期の自動車. ¶***since*** one's *infancy* 幼年時代から.

infant, *n*. 赤児, 幼児.
V a mother who is ***suckling*** an *infant* at her breast 幼児に授乳している母. ¶She ***nurses*** her own *infant*. 彼女は自分で赤ん坊を育てる. ¶***wean*** one's *infant* 赤児を乳離れさせる.
Q prematurely ***born infants*** 月足らずで生れた赤ん坊. ¶a ***breast-fed infant*** 母乳で育った児. ¶a ***hand-reared infant*** 牛乳で育った赤児. ¶a ***new-born infant*** 生れたての赤児. ¶a ***lisping infant*** 片言交りの幼児. ¶like the ***spoiled infant*** that must be constantly tossed up and down or have something shaken before its eyes 断えずゆすぶったり目の前になにか振ってやらなくてはならない悪いくせをつけた赤ん坊のように.
P ***from*** an *infant* 幼少から. ¶an *infant* ***at*** the breast 母乳を飲んでいる幼児. ¶an *infant* ***in*** her arms 彼女に抱かれた幼児.

infantry, *n*. [団] 歩兵.
Q be in command of a ***mounted infantry*** 乗馬歩兵を指揮している.
P the First Regiment ***of*** *Infantry* 歩兵第一連隊.

infatuate, *v*. 有頂天にさせる.
P be *infatuated* ***by*** (=***with***) a woman 女にうつつを抜かす. ¶become *infatuated* ***with*** the study of ... ...の研究に夢中になる. 【類】*infatuated* ***with*** gambling.

infatuation, *n*. 有頂天, 惑でき, ほれ込み.
V ***display*** *infatuation* for a woman ある女の愛におぼれる. ¶he ***had*** an *infatuation* for ... 彼は...に惑できした. ¶***show*** *infatuation* for a woman ある女にうつつを抜かす.
Q recover from an ***absurd infatuation*** 目(迷い)が覚める.
P² his *infatuation* ***for*** an actress 彼が女優にうつつを抜かしたこと.

infect, *v*. 病毒を伝える, 伝染する; 感染させる.
M become ***easily infected*** by disease germs 病菌に容易に感染する. ¶young men ***venereally infected*** 性病にかかった青年たち.
P The whole room was *infected* ***by*** the smell of coal. 室中に石炭の臭気が浸み込んでいた. ¶*infected* ***with*** the revolutionary fever 革命熱にかぶれて ‖ *infected* ***with*** tuberculosis (malady) 結核(など)に感染して. 【類】be *infected* ***with*** the evils of society.

infection, *n*. 伝染, 伝染病; 伝染病毒.
V ***bring*** the *infection* その伝染病毒を持って来る. ¶***catch***

the *infection* of skiing スキー熱にかぶれる. ¶The mosquito ***communicates infection.*** 蚊が伝染病毒を伝える. ¶***disseminate*** (=***spread***) *infection* 病毒を広める. ¶***prevent*** (=***keep off***) *infection* 伝染病を予防する. ¶***receive*** two *infections* of ... 二度...に感染する. ¶increase the power to ***resist infection*** 伝染病に抵抗する力を増す. ¶***take*** the *infection* 病毒に感染する.

Q The ***typhoid*** *infection* may be spread through a whole neighbourhood owing to neglect of disinfection. 消毒を怠ったために腸チブスが付近に流行するかも知れない. ¶the danger of ***venereal*** *infection* 性病にかかる危険.

Q² a serious ***eye*** *infection* 重い眼病の感染.

P precaution ***against*** *infection* 伝染に対する警戒. ¶The disease comes ***from*** *infection.* その病気は伝染から来る.

P² *infection* ***from*** yellow fever 黄熱の病毒.

infelicity, *n.* 不幸, 不吉; 不適切.

Q victims of ***domestic*** *infelicity* 家庭の不仕合わせに悩む人々.

P² *infelicities* ***of*** expression 表現の不適切.

infer, *v.* 推論する, 推測する, 推知する.

M ***infer a priori*** that ... ...と演えき的に推定する. ¶from this we may ***certainly*** *infer* that ... これによってわれわれは...ということを確かに推定することができる.

P *inferring* ***from*** that それから押して. ¶it was *inferred* ***from*** the message that ... その通信から...ということが推測された. 【類】may be *inferred* ***from*** the fact that ... / it will be *inferred* ***from*** what we have said that ...

inference, *n.* 推論, 推理, 推測.

V ***draw*** an *inference* from ... ...によって推定する ‖ ***draw*** their own *inference* 彼ら独自の判断を下す. 【類】***draw*** *inferences* from facts / ***draw*** *inferences* not authorized by facts (事実の裏づけのない).

Q a ***fair*** *inference* from a statement ある陳述からの公平な推定. ¶***legitimate*** *inference* from known facts 既知の事実からの正当な推理. ¶a ***natural*** *inference* 当然な推測. ¶draw ***sinister*** *inference* 筋違いの推断を下す.

P² The *inference* ***from*** these facts is quite (=perfectly) obvious. これらの事実からの推断は極めて明確である. 【類】one *inference* ***from*** the above might be that ...

inferior, *n.* 劣等者.

Q a ***social*** *inferior* (superior) 社会的に地位の低(高)い人.

P look down ***upon*** one's *inferior* 目下をさげすむ.

inferior, *a.* 劣っている, 下位の, 劣等の.

M be ***decidedly*** *inferior* 明かに劣っている. ¶***mentally*** *inferior* to ... ...よりも精神的に劣っている. ¶be better armed but ***numerically*** *inferior* 装備はまさっているが兵数は劣っている. ¶***socially*** *inferior* to ... 社会的に...より劣っている.

P *inferior* ***in*** quality (degree) 質(など)が劣等の. ¶Woman is *inferior* ***to*** man in some respects. ある点では女は男より劣っている.

inferiority, *n.* 劣等.

V ***admit*** *inferiority* 〖比ゆ〗シャッポをぬぐ.

P have a sense ***of*** *inferiority* 劣等感をもつ.

inferno, *n.* 地獄.

Q a ***twentieth-century*** *inferno* 二十世紀に見る地獄.

infest, *v.* 群をなして横行する, 出没する.

P places *infested* ***by*** snakes へびの出没する場所 ‖ This neighbourhood is *infested* ***by*** thieves. この道は物騒である. ¶regions *infested* ***with*** bandits ひ賊の出没する地方. 【類】a big city *infested* ***with*** pickpockets / The house is much *infested* ***with*** mice. / clothes *infested* ***with*** lice / The warehouse was *infested* ***with*** rats.

infidelity, *n.* 不忠, 不貞, 不義.

V ***repeat*** *infidelity* 不貞をくり返す.

Q the hotbed of ***conjugal*** *infidelity* かんいんの温床地. ¶***marital*** (=***matrimonial***) *infidelity* 結婚者の不貞.

P a cause ***of*** *infidelity* 不信の原因.

infiltration, *n.* 浸透.

Q² ***Communist*** *infiltration* into ... 共産主義の...への侵潤.

P advance ***by*** *infiltration* 浸透する(軍隊などが).

infinite, *a.* 無限の.

P be *infinite* ***in*** number 数限りなくある.

infinitive, *n.* 〖文法〗不定詞.

Q a ***split*** *infinitive* 分割不定詞.

infinity, *n.* 無限, 無窮, 無数.

P² There exists between these forms an *infinity* ***of*** intermediate forms. これら両形式の間に無数の中間形式がある.

infirmary, *n.* 治療所.

Q² an ***eye*** *infirmary* 眼科治療所.

infirmity, *n.* 欠点, 弱点.

V ***gibbet*** the social *infirmities* of the day 今日の世の中のあらを捜す. ¶have the *infirmities* of old age 老衰している.

V² *Infirmity* ***comes*** with old age. 年をとると衰弱する.

Q his ***growing*** *infirmities* 彼の寄る年波.

inflame, *v.* 火をつける, 燃やす.

P *inflamed* ***with*** anger (love, crying, desire) 怒り(など)に燃えて.

inflammation, *n.* 激興; きん衝, 炎症.

V ***allay*** *inflammation* 激興を静める. ¶***reduce*** the *inflammation* きん衝を緩和する. ¶***set up*** (=***start***) the *inflammation* of ... ...の炎症を起させる. 【類】***set up*** acute *inflammation.*

P² an *inflammation* ***of*** the eyelids まぶたの炎症.

inflation, *n.* インフレ[ーション].

V ***check*** *inflation* インフレを防止する. ¶***fan*** price *inflation* 物価高をあおり立てる.

Q a ***galloping*** *inflation* 急性インフレ. ¶owing to the ***post-war*** *inflation* of Japan 日本の戦後インフレーションにより.

Q² the continuing ***currency*** *inflation* 連続する通貨インフレーション. ¶the ***post-World War 1*** *inflation* 第一世界大戦後のインフレーション. ¶***wartime*** *inflation* 戦時インフレーション.

inflection, *n.* 音調の変化; 〖発音〗語尾変化.

Q ***natural*** and ***cheery*** *inflections* 自然で気持のよい音調変化. ¶a ***rising*** (***falling***) *inflection* 上昇(降下)音調.

P² the old *inflection* ***for*** the possessive case 所有格に対する昔の語尾変化.

inflict, *v.* 加える, こうむらす, 課する.

P *inflict* a defeat ***on*** the enemy 敵を敗北させる. ¶*inflict* punishment ***upon*** a person 人に罰を加える.

inflow, *n.* 流入.

Q encourage American ***capital*** *inflow* 米国資本の流入を奨励する.

P² the *inflow* ***of*** German tourists ***into*** Switzerland ドイツ観光客のスイスへの流入.

influence, *n.* 影響, 感化; 勢力, 権勢.

V ***acquire*** great *influence* over ... ...に対して大なる勢力を得る. ¶***assert*** one's *influence* 幅をきかせる. ¶***avert*** evil *influences* 魔を除ける ‖ The act is believed to ***avert*** malign *influences.* そうすると魔よけになると信じられている. ¶***bespeak*** his *influence* in getting a government position for his son 彼の権勢に物を言わせて息子を官庁に就職させる. ¶his *influence* was ***brought*** to bear upon ... 彼の権勢を借りて...を威圧した. 【類】***bring*** outside *influence* to bear upon ... ¶***cost*** one's *influence* in favor of this movement この運動達成のためその勢力を用いる. ¶***destroy*** his *influence* 彼の勢力をくじく. ¶***direct*** all its *influence* to the furtherance of ... その全力を...の発達に向ける. ¶***efface*** the *influence* of education 教育の力をまっ殺する. ¶The teacher has succeeded in ***establishing*** an *influence* (=a prestige) over his pupils. その教師は生徒から尊重されるようになった. ¶close the country completely so as to ***exclude*** all alien *influences* 外国の影響を全然受けないように鎖国する. ¶***exercise*** his *influence* in favor of peace 平和のために尽力する ‖ the *influence* which the mind ***exercises*** on the functioning of our organs 精神がわれわれの諸器官の活動に及ぼす影響. 【類】It ***exercised*** a strong *influence* towards goodwill between the two great English speaking peoples. ¶***exert*** *influence* 感化を及ぼす ‖ ***exert*** a favorable *influence* upon ... ...に好影響を及ぼす. 【類】***exert*** her *influence* with ... / ***exert*** a most harmful *influence* on ... / The good *influence* ***exerted*** by her work was even more powerfully felt by those who came into direct communication with her personality. ¶***expand*** one's *influence* 勢力を拡張する. ¶***extend*** the *influence* of ... ...の勢力を伸展する. ¶***fix*** American *influence* in the East 米国の勢力を東洋に扶植する. ¶***forfeit*** the *influence* 勢力を失う. ¶he ***gained*** an *influence* over ... 彼は...を動かした ‖ ***gain*** predominating *influence* 優勢を占める. ¶Might I ask you to get him to ***give*** me his *influence?* 彼の勢力を借りるように貴下からお願いができますまいか. ¶a language whose literary treasures have ***had*** so great an *influence* on the shaping of English literature その豊富な文学が英文学を作る上にあずかって力のあった国語. 【類】***have*** a great *influence* on international cordiality / The country ***had*** no *influence* on a European knowledge. / He ***has*** a great *influence* with the people (lower class, company). / ***have*** an important *influence* upon ... ‖ I ***have*** some *influence* with ... 私は…には少し幅がきく. ¶ ***impair*** the *influence* of the local authority 地方当局の勢力をそこなう. ¶ ***invoke*** the *influence* of ... …の援助を請う. ¶ ***lend*** one's helpful *influence* to ... …に助力を貸す. ¶ ***lessen*** the *influence* of ... …の影響をそぐ. ¶ Morals and will-power entirely ***lose*** their controlling *influence*. 道徳や意志の力は全くその統制力を失う. ¶ ***make*** one's *influence* felt 幅をきかせる. ¶ He ***obtained*** great *influence* with the local businessmen. 彼は土地の実業家の間に大勢力を揮った. ¶ in order to ***offset*** this bad *influence* この悪影響を相殺するために. ¶ ***outlast*** the *influence* of ... …の勢力にめげずその地歩を維持する. ¶ ***produce*** a telling *influence* on ... …に有効な感化を及ぼす. ¶ Every single soul is ***radiating*** an *influence* for good or for evil on all about him. 人はだれでもその周囲のすべての人によかれ悪かれ感化を及ぼしている. ¶ ***ruin*** the *influence* of ... …の力を失わせる. ¶ ***scare away*** evil *influences* 魔を払う. ¶ I can not ***secure*** the *influence* of ... 私は…の力を借りることができない. ¶ ***sell*** one's *influence* 自分の勢力を売物にする. ¶ The works of these decorators ***show*** a Japanese *influence*. これらの装飾家の作品は日本人の影響を受けている. ¶ ***suppress*** Axis *influence* 枢軸勢力を抑圧する. ¶ ***throw*** all one's *influence* on the side of ... …の側にその全力を傾ける. ¶ ***undergo*** European *influence* ヨーロッパの影響を受ける. ¶ ***undermine*** his *influence* at court 宮中における彼の勢力をくつがえす. ¶ ***use*** one's *influence* 顔をきかせる. ¶ would you be good enough to ***use*** your *influence* to ...? どうかあなたのお力添で…していただけませんか. 【類】I will ***use*** all my *influence* in your favor. / beseech him to ***use*** his *influence* to prevent this / Please ***use*** all the *influence* you can get. / ***use*** its *influence* towards minimizing the possibilities and dangers of fire / He has promised to ***use*** all his *influence* in your favor. / ***use*** one's *influence* for peace / they are ***using*** all their *influence* against ... / ***use*** *influence* in (=on) behalf of ... ¶ ***ward off*** evil *influences* 悪影響を防止する ‖ ***ward off*** demonic *influences* 魔よけをする. ¶ ***widen*** one's *influence* 顔を売る. ¶ He ***wields*** a vast *influence* over his countrymen. 彼は同胞間に非常な勢力を持っている. ¶ ***withstand*** corrupting *influences* 腐敗的影響に抵抗する. ¶ Your name will ***work*** a lot of *influence* with the American officials. あなたの名前は米国官吏に対して大いに幅がきくであろう.

V² His *influence* is ***waning***. 彼の勢力は衰へつつある.

Q exert an ***active*** and ***animating*** *influence* 進んで効果的の努力をする. ¶ ***adverse*** *influence* on ... …に対する不利な影響. ¶ exert an ***aggravating*** *influence* upon ... …に悪影響を及ぼす. ¶ untouched by ***alien*** *influences* 少しも外国の影響を受けずに. ¶ ***ancestral*** *influence* 遺伝. ¶ ***atmospheric*** *influences* 大気の諸影響. ¶ have a ***bad*** *influence* on young people 青年に悪影響を及ぼす. ¶ ***baleful*** *influence* 有害な勢力. ¶ exert terribly ***baneful*** *influence* upon ... …に恐ろしく有害な影響を及ぼす. ¶ will have a ***beneficial*** (=***benign***) *influence* on ... …に有益な影響を及ぼすであろう. ¶ have a ***broadening*** and ***educative*** *influence* 視野を広めかつ教育的な力を持つ. ¶ ***civilizing*** *influences* 文化力. ¶ ***climatic*** *influences* 気候の影響. ¶ The party exercises ***considerable*** *influence* in national and municipal affairs. その政党は国政及び市政上に著しい勢力がある. 【類】His works had a ***considerable*** *influence* on nineteenth-century thought. ¶ a ***constructive*** *influence* 建設的な力. ¶ ***Contrary*** *influences* have been at work. 反対の力が働いていた. ¶ ***controlling*** *influences* 抑制力. ¶ withstand ***corrupting*** *influence* 堕落的勢力に対抗する. ¶ After 1700 waves upon waves of ***cultural*** *influences*, arising in England, swept over France and the rest of Europe. 一七〇〇年後は英国に起った文化の波がフランスその他欧州全部に押寄せた. 【類】the ***cultural*** *influence* of Holland. ¶ the ***curative*** *influence* of an idea 一つの思想の医療的効果. ¶ It will have a more ***dangerous*** *influence* on the money. それは金融の上に一層危険な影響を及ぼすであろう. ¶ a ***debasing*** *influence* 悪影響. ¶ exert such a ***decisive*** *influence* on the issue 結果の上に決定的な影響を及ぼす. ¶ exert a ***deep*** *influence* on ... …に深い影響を与える. ¶ have a most ***demoralizing*** *influence* upon the minds of young boys 青年の心に非常な悪影響を及ぼす. ¶ it had a ***depressing spiritual*** *influence* upon ... それは…を悲観させた. ¶ a ***desirable*** and ***effective*** *influence* 望ましい有効な影響. ¶ ***destructive*** *influences* 破壊的影響. ¶ have a ***direct*** *influence* on ... …に直接影響する. ¶ attribute it solely to ***divine*** *influence* それを全然天意に帰する. ¶ exert a profound ***economic*** *influence* 深甚な経済的勢力を揮う. ¶ The development of Japanese ***educational*** *influence* extended to China, India, and Siam. 日本の教育的勢力が発展して中国・インド及びタイにまで及んだ. ¶ an ***elevating*** and ***ennobling*** *influence* 気高く向上せしめる感化力. ¶ a little place utterly unspoiled by ***European*** *influence* ヨーロッパの影響に全然そこなわれていない一小区. ¶ exercise an ***evil*** *influence* 悪影響を及ぼす. ¶ ***external*** *influences* 外部の影響. ¶ their ***farreaching*** *influence* for good 彼らの広汎(こう)にわたるよい影響. ¶ bring some ***favorable*** *influences* to bear upon the soul of the delinquent 違犯者の心によい影響をもたらす. ¶ the Chinese insensibility to ***foreign*** *influences* 外国の影響に対する中国人の無感覚. ¶ ***formative*** *influences* in his early life 彼の少年時代における精神発育に及ぼす力. ¶ lose ***former*** *influence* 以前の勢力を失う. ¶ under a ***genial*** *influence* of a glass of whiskey ウイスキー一杯傾け陶然として. ¶ ***geographical*** *influence* in history 歴史に及ぼす地理的影響. ¶ have a very ***great*** *influence* in ... …について非常に大なる勢力をもつ. ¶ have a ***great*** and ***growing*** *influence* 大きい, しかも増大する勢力をもつ. ¶ a ***harmful*** *influence* 有害な影響. ¶ predisposed, through ***hereditary*** *influences*, to ... 遺伝に依って…する傾向を持った. ¶ Flying will prove one of the greatest ***humanizing*** *influences* known to history. 飛行は史上最も大なる教化力の一つとなるであろう. ¶ when udner ***hypnotic*** *influence* 催眠術にかかっている時 ‖ hold her under a ***hypnotic*** *influence* 彼女を催眠状態にしておく ‖ exercise a ***hypnotic*** *influence* over ... …に催眠術を施す. ¶ ***hypnotizing*** *influence* 催眠力. ¶ have a more ***immediate*** and ***vital*** *influence* 一層直接にして重要な影響を及ぼす. ¶ an ***improving*** *influence* 改善力. ¶ the ***inhibitory*** *influence* of reason 理性の制止力. ¶ an ***injurious*** *influence* 有害な影響. ¶ an ***inspiriting*** and ***invigorating*** *influence* 鼓舞激励する力. ¶ the educational value of an educational institution as a center of ***intellectual*** and ***moral*** *influence* 知的及び道徳的感化の中心としての学校の教育的価値. ¶ yield to the ***intoxicating*** *influence* of Romanticism ロマンティシズムの陶酔的影響を受ける. ¶ the steady speed of ***Japanese*** *influence* 日本勢力の着実な進展. ¶ ***lasting*** *influences* 永続的な影響. 【類】exercise a ***lasting*** *influence* over human life. ¶ It has had ***little*** *influence* on Western civilization. それは西洋文明にほとんど何の影響をも及ぼさなかった. ¶ due to ***male*** *influence* [共学などの場合]男子の影響によって. ¶ a ***malignant*** *influence* 有害な影響. ¶ the product of ***many*** and ***diverse*** *influences* 多種多様の影響の所産. ¶ The nose of Cleopatra had a ***marked*** *influence* on the destinies of the ancient world. クレオパトラの鼻は古代世界の運命に顕著な影響を及ぼした. ¶ the ***mephitic*** *influence* of jealousy in society 社会におけるさい疑心の悪影響. ¶ It has a ***moderating*** *influence* on the situation. それは時局を緩和する力がある. ¶ a ***moral*** *influence* 道徳的感化. ¶ a ***neutralizing*** *influence* 中和的勢力. ¶ I have ***no*** *influence* over that man, and therefore my advice has ***no*** *influence* on his action. 私はあの人に対して威力がないので私の忠告は彼の行為には影響を及ぼさない. ¶ ***parental*** *influences* 親の感化. ¶ exercise a ***permanent*** *influence* upon ... …に永久的感化を及ぼす. ¶ exercise a ***pernicious*** *influence* in this respect こういった有害な勢力を及ぼす. ¶ make effort to restore her ***reduced*** *influence* 同国の衰微した勢力を回復しようと努める. ¶ one's ***personal*** *influence* over ... その…に対する人格的影響. ¶ some ***phenomenal disturbing*** *influence* ある異常なかく乱的影響. ¶ the most ***potent*** *influence* of all 最も有力な影響. ¶ exert a most ***powerful*** *influence* for good in ... …に非常に有力な好影響を及ぼす. 【類】Example has a more ***powerful*** *influence* over the minds of men than precept. ¶ exercise on the masses a ***powerful*** and ***educative*** *influence* 大衆に有力な教育的感化を及ぼす. ¶ a ***predominant*** *influence* 有力な影響. ¶ have a ***preponderating*** *influence* in politics 政治において優越した勢力を持っている. ¶ the ***profound*** *influence* which plague has exercised upon the course of human history 人間の歴史の動向に疫病が及ぼした甚大な影響. ¶the ***protective*** *influence* of vaccination against the ravages of small-box 天然痘の流行に対する種痘の予防力. ¶***psychic*** *influence* 精神的影響. ¶quietly exercise a ***reciprocal*** *influence* upon ... ...に知らず知らず相互的感化を及ぼす. ¶the ***refining*** *influence* of literature 文学が精神を高める力. ¶acquire a ***remarkable*** *influence* over ... ...に対して非常な勢力を得る. ¶exercise a ***salutary*** *influence* over ... に健全な影響を及ぼす. ¶***seductive*** *influence* of comrades 仲間の誘惑的感化. ¶a ***serious*** *influence* 由々しい影響. ¶***sinister*** *influences* 面白からぬ影響. ¶by the ***sinister occult*** *influence* of ... ...の邪悪な魔力で. ¶It exercised but ***slight*** *influence* over the minds of the masses. それは大衆の心にほんのわずかな影響を与えたにすぎなかった. ¶the ***sobering*** *influence* of responsibility 責任の人を覚醒させる力. ¶***softening*** *influence* 軟化的影響. ¶under the ***sole*** *influence* of ... 全然...の影響で. ¶a ***solvent*** *influence* 溶解力. ¶a ***soothing*** *influence* 慰撫(いぶ)力. ¶the ***steadying*** *influence* of Chinese classics 漢学の心を堅固にする力. ¶a ***tremendous*** *influence* 驚くべき勢力. ¶use ***unfair*** *influence* 不正に力を使う. ¶an ***uplifting*** *influence* 人を向上させる力. ¶the ***vivifying*** *influence* of the spring rain 春雨の活気を生む力. ¶a ***wholesome*** *influence* 健全な影響. ¶it never had a really ***wide*** *influence* upon ... それは決して...に本当に広大な影響を与えなかった. 【類】It exerted a ***wide*** *influence* in creating a better understanding of Japan in America. ¶a ***wide-spread*** *influence* 広はんな影響. ¶It had undoubtedly a ***wonderful*** *influence* over young minds. それは青年の心に確かに驚くべき感化を与えた.

Q² Insidious ***Communistic*** *influences* were penetrating China. すきをねらう共産党の勢力が中国に浸透しつつあった. ¶the ***local boss*** *influences* 地方的顔役の勢力. ¶a question of ***family*** *influence* 家庭(の)感化力の問題. ¶***home*** *influence* 家庭の影響.

P ***as*** an *influence* for good よい影響力として. ¶affected ***by*** the *influence* of the Gulf Stream メキシコ湾流の影響を受けて ‖ ***by*** the *influence* of magic 魔法の力で. ¶powerful (feeble) ***in*** *influence* 勢力が強い(弱い). ¶a man ***of*** great *influence* 大なる感化力のある人. ¶***owing to*** European *influence* ヨーロッパの影響を受けて. ¶***through*** the *influence* of example 範例の力で ‖ ***through*** the *influence* of some of her friends 彼女の友人中二三の力添えによって. 【類】largely ***through*** the *influence* of ... / ***through*** the *influence* of circumstances / ***through*** the *influence* of the political bosses. ¶***under*** the *influence* of alcohol (=liquor *or* drink) 酒に酔って. 【類】while ***under*** the *influence* of opium / ***under*** the *influence* of Buddhism / He did so ***under*** the *influence* of a passing emotion (一時の感情で). / ***under*** the *influence* of an idea (anger) / a woman ***under*** the *influence* of her periods (月経) / ***under*** the *influence* of his agitation (扇動) / The industry of primitive pottery is fast dying out everywhere ***under*** the *influence* of "civilization." / ***under*** the *influence* of indignation and revenge (憤怒と復しゅう心) ‖ a design ***under*** Western *influence* 西洋風の意匠 ‖ ***under*** the *influence* of his hallucinations 錯覚に陥って ‖ ***under*** the *influence* of modern life 現代生活の影響の下に ‖ He came ***under*** the *influence* of Herbert Spencer. 彼はハーバート・スペンサーの感化を受けた. ¶***within*** one's *influence* その勢力範囲内に.

P² The idea has *influence* ***among*** statesmen. その思想は政治家の間に勢力がある. ¶The Anglo-Japanese alliance was a potent *influence* ***for*** the peace and development of the East. 日英同盟は東洋の平和と発展にとって甚大な力であった. ‖ an *influence* ***for*** good 良い影響. ¶use one's *influence* ***in*** bringing it about その実現に努力する. 【類】*influences* ***in*** European art. ¶the *influence* ***of*** America in the world 世界におけるアメリカの勢力 ‖ the *influence* ***of*** environment 環境の影響. ¶the *influence* ***of*** the East ***on*** the West 西洋に及ぼす東洋の影響. 【類】the *influence* ***of*** the minds ***on*** the body / the *influence* ***of*** mythology ***on*** literature. ¶labor's *influence* ***over*** Congress 議会に対する労働者の勢力. ¶His *influence* ***upon*** those around him was unbounded. 周囲の人に対する彼の勢力は無限であった.

influence, *v.* 影響を及ぼす, 感化する, 左右する.

M ***profoundly*** *influence* ... ...に深甚の影響を及ぼす.

P The Japanese people are quickly *influenced* ***by*** new ideas. 日本国民は容易に新思想に感化される. ‖ *influenced* ***by*** a bribe わいろに動かされて ‖ be *influenced* ***by*** bad examples 悪いお手本に左右される. ¶he was *influenced* ***for*** good ***by*** ... 彼は...に善導された. ¶*influence* young people ***in*** the choosing of their mates 青年が友だちを選ぶ上に影響する.

influenza, *n.* 流行性感冒, 悪性感冒.

V ***contract*** *influenza* 流感にかかる. ¶***have*** *influenza* 流感にかかっている.

Q ***malignant*** *influenza* 悪性の感冒.

P suffer ***from*** *influenza* 流感にかかる. ¶an epidemic ***of*** *influenza* 流感の流行.

O *Influenza* is an infectious disease. 流感は伝染病だ.

influx, *n.* 流入, 流れ込み, 入来.

Q a ***great*** *influx* of laborers 労働者の大挙入国.

P² an *influx* ***of*** visitors 訪問客の目白押し. ¶the *influx* ***of*** Japanese settlers ***into*** Australia, the United States, and Canada 豪州・合衆国及びカナダへの日本移民の流入. 【類】an *influx* ***of*** wealth (gold) / an *influx* ***of*** correspondence.

inform, *v.* 通報する; 告発する, 密告する.

M he ***coolly*** *informed* me that ... 彼は冷静に...と私に告げた. ¶I am ***credibly*** *informed* that ... たしかな筋から...ということを聞いた. ¶be ***little*** *informed* 余り物を知らない. ¶be ***officially*** *informed* that ... 正式に通告される. ¶I was ***reliably*** *informed* that ... 私は...との信用のできる報告を受けた. ¶I am ***rightly*** *informed* that ... 私は...という間違いのない報告に接した. ¶be ***vaguely*** *informed* of ... ...についてほのかに聞いている. ¶He is remarkably ***well*** *informed.* 彼は非常によく物を知っている. ‖ be seemingly ***well*** *informed* 事情通らしい ‖ keep us ***well*** *informed* of ... ...についてわれわれによく知らしておいてくれる. ¶be ***widely*** *informed* 物知りだ. ¶You have been ***wrongly*** *informed.* 君は間違っていることを教えられたのだ.

P He is well *informed* ***about*** the matter. 彼はそのことをよく知っている. ¶*inform* ***against*** a suspicious person 疑わしい人を密告する ‖ *inform* a tax office ***against*** ... ...の脱税を摘発する ‖ *inform* ***against*** the thief その賊を訴える. ¶*inform* a person ***concerning*** ... ...に関して人に告げる. ¶be better *informed* ***of*** law business 法律事務に一層通じている. ¶I shall be sincerely grateful to all those who are good enough to *inform* me ***of*** any mistakes or omissions which they may happen to detect. 誤びゅう・脱漏を発見されて私にお知らせ下さる方には心から感謝いたします (編集者などの言葉). 【類】Did you *inform* the post-office ***of*** the change of your address? / *inform* him ***of*** the fact / be *informed* ***of*** the current movements in the world. ¶I must be kept *informed* ***on*** (=***upon***) the affairs (situation). 私はその事柄(など)について絶えず報道を受けなければならない. 【類】keep him *informed* ***upon*** current events.

informal, *a.* 非公式の, 表立たない, 略式の.

P We are very *informal* ***among*** ourselves. 私たち内輪同志ではごく略式にやります.

informality, *n.* 略式.

Q Present-day writers of fiction rely more and more on ***colloquial*** *informality* of expression. 今日の小説家はくだけた口語体をますます用いる.

informant, *n.* 通知者, 通報者.

Q an ***intelligent*** *informant* 要領を得た報告者.

P ... is our *informant* ***on*** the point ...はこの事項の出所(人)です.

O So said my *informant.* 私に教えてくれた人がそう言った.

information, *n.* 通報, 報告; 音信, 消息; 知識, 見聞; 告発.

V I ***accumulated*** much *information* both from him and from other sources. 私は彼に及び他の方面から沢山報告を集めた. ¶***acquire*** *information* relative to ... ...に関して知識を得る. ¶***amass*** a great amount of curious *information* 珍らしい見聞を沢山集める. ¶***bring together*** in (=into) one work *information* concerning ... ...に関する知識を一書にまとめる. 【類】***bring together*** *information* scattered through various books and periodicals. ¶***centralize*** *information* with regard to ... ...に関する情報を一つの中心から出るようにする. ¶***classify*** *information* according to ... 情報を...に従って分類する. ¶***coax forth*** *information* 情報をつり出す. ¶***collate*** a large amount of *information* relating to ... ...に関する多大の情報を校合する. ¶*collect information* 情報を集める. ¶*information communicated* to me by him relative to the subject under investigation 調査中の題目に関して彼から私に通信してくれた事項. ¶The *information* has been *confirmed.* その報道は確実となった. ¶The book *contains* much useful *information,* imparted with great clearness and impartiality. その本の中には非常に明りょうにかつ公平に述べた多くの有益な知識が盛られている. ¶*convey information* 知識を伝える. ¶From what source did you *derive* the *information?* その情報の出所はどこです. ‖ From what source do you *derive* their *information?* どんな方面から君はそれらに関する知識を得るか. ¶those *desiring* fuller *information* on (=about=regarding) ... are requested to apply to ... ...に関してさらに詳しく知りたい人々は...へお申出下さい. ¶*diffuse information* 知識を広める. ¶*digest* the *information* その知識を整理する. ¶*disclose* the *information* そのことを発表する. ¶*disseminate information* concerning (=in regard to) a cure for burns やけどの治療に関する知識を広める. 【類】*disseminate* financial *information.* ¶*divulge information* 報道を漏らす. ¶*draw* much curious *information* from ... ...から多くの珍らしい知識を得る. 【類】*draw* one's *information* from the authors best qualified to give it. ¶*duplicate information* 通知(など)を再発する(第一回のが逸失したので). ¶*elicit* the *information* that ... ...という報道をつり出す ‖ *elicit information* by enquiry 尋問して知ってることを言わせる. ¶*extract information* from ... ...から知識を得る. ¶those who are in a position to *furnish information* concerning ... ...に関する知識を提供できる立場にある人々. ¶*gain* additional *information* from ... ...からその上の知識を得る. 【類】*gain* a little useful *information* in a pleasant manner. ¶*gather information* at first hand 直接に報道を収集する. ¶get authentic *information* as to ... ...に関して正しい知識を得る. ¶These scholars have *given* no new *information* to the world. これらの学者は何ら新知識を世人に与えていない. ‖ *give information* upon ... ...に関して情報を与える ‖ A table *gives information* in shorter space than would be possible if full sentences were used. 表は文より狭い紙面で用が足りる. 【類】The *information* was *given* at the police-station. / *give* the *information* sought. ¶refuse to *give out information* on ... ...ついて報道を発表するのを拒む. ¶*impart information* 知識を与える. ¶Kindly *issue* this *information* in your next publication. どうかこの報道を今度発行の分にのせて下さい. ¶We *lack* definite *information* on this point. この点については確実な知識が欠けている. ¶*lay* an *information* 告発する. ¶*locate information* on a given subject in an encyclopaedia ある問題を百科全書で調べる. ¶Do not *make* the *information* public. その報告を公表してはいけない. ¶*obtain* all the *information* you can as to ... ...に関してできるだけ調査せよ ‖ I could not *obtain* any *information.* 私は何らの報道をも得ることができなかった. 【類】Investors may *obtain* further *information* by making use of the coupon (質問券を利用して) / indicate the sources whence he can *obtain* fuller *information* respecting ... ¶*Pick up* all the *information* you can while travelling. 旅行中できるだけの見聞を集めよ. ¶*place* the *information* in the right quarter その報道を適当な方面に配付する. ¶On this subject we *possess* but very incomplete *information.* われわれはこの問題に関してはほんの不完全な知識しか持ち合わせていない. ¶*present* much *information* 多大の報道を提供する. ¶*provide* free *information* to ... ...に無料で報道を提供する. ¶*receive* private *information* 内密の報道を受ける. ¶*report information* to ... concerning ... ...に関して...へ報道する. ¶his letter *requesting information* as to ... ...についての報道を求める彼の手紙. ¶I have *secured information* to the effect that ... 私は...という意味の報道を得た. 【類】the difficulty of *securing* precise *information* on ... ‖ For those *seeking information* on (=about=respecting) these matters there is no better book than this history. これらのことに関して知りたいと思う人にとってこの歴史ほどよい本はない. ¶*select* and *organize* the scattered *information* about ... ...に関して散逸する知識を選択して組織立てる. ¶*send information* to ... ...に通報する. ¶*spread* before my reader the *information* I have so far collected on the subject この問題に関して私がこれまで収集した見聞を読者の前に展開する. ¶*supply information* regarding ... ...に関する知識を提供する. 【類】*supply* every *information* available. ¶*tip information* to ... ...にちょっと教えてやる. ¶*tip off* one's *information* ちょっと情報を漏らす. ¶*transmit* the *information* to the proper person 関係の人にその情報を伝える. ¶*volunteer information* 進んで情報を与える.

V[2] another piece of *information* from ... *states* that ... ...からのも一つの報道に...とある. ¶No *information* has *transpired* as yet. まだ何とも報告が出ていない.

Q We are in a position to give *accurate* and absolutely *unbiassed information.* われは正確にして全く不偏な報道をなしうる地位にある. ¶supply *accurate* and *up-to-date information* of ... ...の正確にして最新な知識を提供する. ¶give *advanced information* about ... ...について前もって報道する. ¶*authentic information* 確実な情報. ¶*authoritative information* justifies the statement that ... 権威ある報道によって...という言説の正しいことが分かる. 【類】sources (出所) of *authoritative information* on ... ¶the *available information* on the subject is limited. この件について手に入れられる知識は限られている. ¶*biased information* 偏した知識. ¶*commercial information* 商報. ¶*confidential information* 秘密の通報. ¶*correct information* 正しい報道. ¶give *definite information* 確報をする. ¶get *definite* and *reliable information* on ... ...に関する確かな信頼のできる情報を得る. ¶We wish somewhat more *detailed information.* も少し詳しい報告が欲しい. ¶More *exact information* follows by mail. 正確な報道は追って郵送する. ‖ furnish *exact* and *reliable information* about trade conditions 商況について正確にして信頼できる報道を提供する. ¶The book will not give the *exhaustive information* you require. その本では貴下の必要とするような徹底的な知識は得られないであろう. ¶facts and *fair, unprejudiced information* 事実と公平にして不偏な報道. ¶the dissemination of *fasle information* 虚報の宣伝. ¶gain *first-hand information* about (=as to) ... ...について直接の見聞を得る. ¶*full information* may be obtained from ... 十分の知識が...から得られる. 【類】send *full information* about / He has *full information* at hand. / *Full information* is as yet lacking. ‖ supply those concerned with *full information* of ... 関係者に...のあらゆる情報を提供する ‖ The reader is referred for *fuller information* to the following books. もっと詳しく知りたい読者は次の書について見られたい. ¶for *further information* address or apply to ... さらに詳細を知りたい方は...に手紙その他で照会して載きたい. 【類】*Further information* may be obtained by addressing the Secretary of Columbia University. ¶pick up a vast fund of *general information* 一般知識を多量に収集する. ¶*geographical information* 地理的知識. ¶*gratuitous information* 無報酬の情報. ¶*hackneyed guide-book information* 月並の案内書から得た知識. ¶it will give you much *helpful information* on ... ...について沢山の有益な知識を与えてくれるだろう. ¶*immediate* (=*first-hand*) *information* 直接の情報. ¶give us but *imperfect information* われわれにきわめて不完全な知識を与える. ¶contain a good deal of *interesting information* 面白い記事がたくさん載っている. 【類】pick up some *interesting information.* ¶secure *instantaneous information* on ... ...について即時の報道を得る. ¶the *latest information* on ... ...に関するごく最近の情報. ¶buy *military information* from ... ...から軍事情報を買いとる. ¶so *much information* packed in so small a compass 小さな範囲の中につめ込んだ多くの報道. ¶The book contains *much new information.* 同書には沢山の新しい知識が盛ってある. ¶furnish ... with *necessary information* ...に必要な情報を提供する. ¶incorporate the *new information* 新しい報道をその中に付加する. ¶*occupational information* 職業情報. ¶*official information* 公報. ¶*out-of-date information* 古臭い情報. ¶"*personally conducted*" *information* 直接本人に与える通知. ¶*practical information* on ... ...に関する実際的知識. ¶ask for *private information* as to ... ...について内密の報告を求める ‖ This is for your *private information* only. これはただあなただけの参考に申しあげる. ¶the most *recent* and *authentic information* on ... ...に関する最も新しい確

かな情報. ¶I can get no ***reliable information*** concerning ... 私は...に関してなんら信用するに足る情報を得ることができない. 【類】according to ***reliable information*** / Our patrons can always depend on ***reliable information*** and courteous attention (丁重な取扱い). ¶We have only ***scanty information*** of his life. 彼の一生についてわれらの知る所はほんのわずかしかない. ¶books of ***secondary information*** 根本資料によらないで編集した書物. ¶***secret information*** against ... ...に関する不利な密告. ¶***solid information*** 着実な報道. ¶glean a good deal of ***sound information*** concerning ... ...に関して確実な報道を沢山集める. ¶***statistical information*** 統計的知識. ¶***trustworthy information*** published in the Press 新聞に発表された信頼すべき情報. ¶get ***unbiassed information*** on ... ...について公平な報道を得る. ¶he would be glad to hear from any of our readers who happen to possess any ***unpublished information*** in regard to ... 彼は...について未発表の情報をもち合わせている読者からの投書を歓迎します. ¶***up-to-date*** and ***accurate information*** 最近の正確な知識. ¶gain much ***useful information*** from ... ...から沢山有益な知識を得る. 【類】***useful information*** in fishing / a mine of (豊富な) ***useful information*** ‖ You will find in the book a great deal of ***useful information*** packed in a small space. その本には簡約した沢山の有益な事項がある. ¶***vague information*** ばく然たる知識. ¶a mass of interesting and ***valuable information*** on ... ...に関する面白く価値のある一連の知識. ¶a storehouse of ***varied information*** 諸方面の知識の倉. ¶He says that he has some ***vital information*** for your ear alone. あなただけに聞かせる重大な報道を持っていると彼は言っています.

Q² ***expert information*** as to customs duties 関税に関する専門的知識. ¶***hearsay information*** 人から聞いた情報. ¶***labor market information*** 労働市場情報. ¶***out-of-the-way information*** 珍らしい情報. ¶***trade information*** of various-kinds 各種の商報. ¶supply vital ***war information*** to ... ...に重大な戦事報道を供給する.

P ***according to*** recent ***information*** 最近の報道によれば. ¶just ***for information*** ほんの参考のため. 【類】I enclose ***for*** your ***information*** a copy of a letter (手紙の写し) from ... ‖ ***for*** the ***information*** of such inquirers こういうことを知りたいと思う人々の参考に ‖ Thank you ***for*** your ***information***. 知らせて下さって有難うございます. ¶***from information*** received we prefer to ... 入手した情報から考えてわれわれは...したいと思う. ¶a very useful piece ***of information*** 一つの非常に有益な情報 ‖ a mine ***of information*** 知識の宝庫. 【類】The book is a mine ***of information*** on matters scientific, legal, etc. ¶act ***on information*** received 聞込みによって動く. ¶He obliged me ***with information***. 彼は私に知らして下さった. ¶I am speaking ***without*** firsthand ***information***. 私の言っていることは直接に聞いたことではない.

P² ***information about*** ... may be obtained, without charge, by communicating with ... ...に関する情報は...に問合わせると無料で得られる. ¶lay an ***information against*** a person 人を告訴する. ¶***information as to*** (= ***concerning or respecting***) ... ...についての報道. ¶***information for*** passengers 旅客への報道. ¶paucity of ***information on*** the subject その問題に関する知識の少ないこと. 【類】the distribution of ***information on*** matters of the theatre 演劇に関する知識の普及. ¶for ***information regarding*** ... apply to ... ...に関して知りたい方は...に申し出て下さい.

informer, *n*. 告発人, 密告人.

P² an ***informer against*** a thief 賊の密告人.

infraction, *n*. 違犯, 抵触.

V intention of ***committing*** an ***infraction*** 犯意. ¶acts which do not ***constitute*** a punishable ***infraction*** 違犯として罰するまでにならない行為. ¶***Infractions*** of these rules are ***punished*** by imprisonment for not more than 6 weeks. これらの規則違犯者は六週間以下の禁固に処せられる.

Q They felt it as a ***serious infraction*** of their monopoly. 彼らはそれを彼らの専売権をはなはだしく侵害するものと感じた.

P ***without*** any ***infraction*** of the laws なんらの法律違犯なしに.

P² ***infractions of*** the club-house rules クラブの規則違犯 ‖ ***Infractions of*** these laws are visited by punishment. これらの法律に違犯すると罰せられる. 【類】***infraction of*** the law should be punished by a fine of ...

infringe, *v*. 犯す, 違犯する, 侵害する.

P ***infringe on*** nation's sovereignty 国家の主権を侵害する. 【類】The government ***infringed on*** the freedom of the press. / ***infringe on*** (=***upon***) a person's rights (人権).

infringement, *n*. 違犯, 違背; 侵害.

V It ***constitutes*** an ***infringement*** of the patents. それは特許権の侵害になる.

Q a ***serious infringement*** of ... ...の重大な侵害.

P² ***infringement of*** the laws of health 不衛生 ‖ an ***infringement of*** the copyright 著作権の侵害. ¶***infringement on*** human rights 人権侵害.

infuse, *v*. 注入する, 吹込む, 鼓吹する.

P ***infuse*** a spirit ***into*** one's mind 人の心に一つの精神を鼓吹する ‖ ***infuse*** new blood ***into*** the old generation 古い世代の人々に新しい血を注入する. 【類】***infuse*** fresh courage ***into*** soldiers / ***infuse*** new patriotism ***into*** the hearts of ... ¶***infuse*** them ***with*** the new idea of democracy 彼らに民主主義の新思想を注入する.

infusion, *n*. 注入, 注出; 浸し(汁).

Q They have a ***rich infusion*** of Mongol blood. 彼らには蒙古族の血がたくさん混っている.

P² an ***infusion of*** salted cherry-blossoms 桜湯.

ingenuity, *n*. 器用, 発明の才, 巧妙, 工夫.

V Nature ***baffles*** human ***ingenuity*** and foresight. 自然は人間の機知と先見を失敗に終らせる. ¶***demand ingenuity*** 新工夫を要する. ¶***display*** great ***ingenuity*** in ... ...に偉大な発明の才を示す. ¶***exercise*** one's ***ingenuity*** to ... ...すべく手を尽す. 【類】All ***exercise*** the utmost ***ingenuity*** in beautifying their surroundings. / a problem ***exercising*** the ***ingenuity*** of ... ¶***exert*** one's ***ingenuity*** 工夫をこらす. ¶In trying to solve the problem we seem to have ***exhausted*** all the ***ingenuity*** that the brain of man could suggest. この問題解決の試みにわれわれは人間の頭で思いつきうるあらゆる工夫をこらしたように思われる. ¶a task ***requiring*** no little ***ingenuity*** 少なからぬ工夫を要する仕事. ¶He ***showed*** much ***ingenuity*** in making it. 彼はその製作に多大の工夫を示した. ¶***tax*** the ***ingenuity*** of experts 専門家の考案を必要とする. 【類】***tax*** one's ***ingenuity*** (= brains) to ...

Q ***diplomatic ingenuity*** 巧妙な外交策. ¶it will require ***no little ingenuity*** to ... ...するには少なからぬ工夫がいるだろう. ¶***Yankee ingenuity*** 米人的策略.

P ***with*** devilish ***ingenuity*** 悪魔のような技巧をもって.

P² exercise one's ***ingenuity upon*** the selection 選択の上に工夫を凝らす.

ingot, *n*. 地金(の固まり).

P zinc ***in ingot*** 亜鉛塊.

ingratiate, *v*. ...に取入る.

P ***ingratiate*** himself ***into*** his favor うまく彼の歓心を買う. ¶***ingratiate*** himself ***with*** rich or influential people 金持または有力者に取入る.

ingratitude, *n*. 忘恩, 義理知らず.

Q To neglect to do this would be ***base ingratitude***. これを怠ればあきれ果てた義理知らずとなるだろう. ¶This is ***black ingratitude***! よくよくの恩知らずだ. ¶***fiendish ingratitude*** 鬼畜にひとしい恩知らず.

P reproach a person ***with ingratitude*** 恩知らずだと言って人を非難する.

P² ***ingratitude to*** a person 人に対する忘恩.

ingredient, *n*. 成分, 要素.

Q a ***bitter ingredient*** in the sweets of ... ...の甘味における一つの苦味(楽しい中の苦しみ). ¶the ***chief ingredient*** of ... ...の主成分. ¶It has ... for its ***main ingredient***. それは...が主成分になっている. ¶That night he seemed to be the ***necessary ingredient*** to make the party. その晩彼は会にとってなくてならない人であるらしかった. ¶***pernicious ingredients*** 有害な成分. ¶the ***principal ingredients*** of ... ...の主要成分.

P² the ***ingredients of*** a cake 菓子の成分. 【類】the ***ingredients of*** a mixture (混成物).

inhabit, *v*. 住む, 生息する, 居住する.

M a district ***sparsely*** (***densely***) ***inhabited*** 人煙まれな(人口密な)地方.

P an island ***inhabited by*** wild beasts 野獣の住む島.

inhabitant, *n*. 住民, 居住者.

V Vancouver, which began as a lodging camp, now

numbers over 300,000 *inhabitants*. [伐木者の]足だまりとして始まったヴァンクーヴァーは今では人口三十万を数える都会となった. 「*itant* 原住民.

Q an *indigenous inhabitant* 土着民. ¶an ***original*** *inhab-*

P a small town ***of*** 5,000 *inhabitants* 人口五千の小さな町. ¶Glasgow, ***with*** over one million *inhabitants*, has only about 100 miles of tramway. 人口百万を超過するグラスゴーは約百マイルの電車線路を有するに過ぎない.

P² an *inhabitant* ***of*** the town その町の住人.

inhale, *v.* 吸込む, 吸入する. 「込む.

P *inhale* smoke ***from*** one's cigarette 巻タバコから煙を吸

inherent, *a.* 固有の, 生来の; 付随している.

P be *inherent* ***in*** human nature 人間の本性である ‖ *inherent* ***in*** the French character フランス国民性特有の. 【類】 bear the burden of duty and danger *inherent* ***in*** the soldier's profession / the imitative qualities *inherent* ***in*** man. ¶the difficulties *inherent* ***to*** (=attending) the study of ... ...の研究に付随する困難.

inherit, *v.* 受け継ぐ, 相続する, 伝承する.

M ***ancestrally*** *inherited* 先祖伝来の.

P He *inherited* a large fortune ***from*** his father. 彼は父から大きな財産を受け継いだ. ‖ *inherit* a taste (quality) ***from*** another person 他人から趣味(など)を受け継ぐ.

inheritance, *n.* 継承, 相続; 遺伝; 遺産.

V ***seize*** an *inheritance* 遺産を横領する. ¶The *inheritance* ***passed over*** to the dynasty of Austria. その王位の継承はオーストリアの王朝に帰した. 「なった青年.

P a young man rich ***by*** *inheritance* 財産を相続して金持に

P² *inheritance* ***of*** family pride 家柄の誇りの継承 ‖ the *inheritance* ***of*** criminal tendencies 犯罪傾向の遺伝.

O The ability to cook is sometimes an *inheritance*. 料理の才は往々遺伝である.

inhibit, *v.* 押える, 妨げる.

O A sense of duty *inhibited* him to quit his work. 彼は責任感から職場を離れなかった.

inhibition, *n.* 抑制.

V ***increase*** the *inhibition* 抑制の力を増大させる.

Q ***social*** *inhibitions* 社会的制裁.

inimical, *a.* 反する, 害になる.

P Bad habits are *inimical* ***to*** success. 悪習慣は成功の敵である. 【類】 *inimical* ***to*** health. ¶Modern city life is in certain respects *inimical* ***to*** childhood. 現代都市生活はある点において子供に有害である.

initial, *n.* 首字, 頭字. 「する(記する).

V ***carve*** (***mark***) their *initials* on ... 彼らの頭字を...に彫刻

Q proper names which have attained the ***small*** *initials* 小文字に(普通名詞に)なった固有名詞. 「の).

Q² ***identification*** *initials* 頭字確認票(商業文で筆者名など

P He writes ***over*** the *initial* "V.R.S." 彼は V.R.S. の首字を記名して文を書く.

initial, *v.* 頭字で書く(署名する).

P The document was *initialed* J.A.S. ***by*** John Allen 「Smith.

initiate, *v.* 手ほどきする; 引入れる.

M He was ***sexually*** *initiated* at the age of 14. 彼は十四歳のとき異性を知った. ¶he has not yet been ***thoroughly*** *initiated* into the mysteries of ... 彼は...の神秘がいまだ十分分かっていない.

P He was *initiated* ***into*** the duties of his place. 彼は自分の職責の何物たるかを教えられた. ‖ *initiate* them ***into*** the mysteries of ... 彼らに...の秘けつを伝授する. 【類】 He was *initiated* ***into*** the technical mysteries of his trade. / My wife *initiated* her ***into*** the complicated way of putting on a kimono (着物の着方). / *initiate* students ***into*** the world of science.

initiation, *n.* 手引, 手ほどき.

P ***at*** the *initiation* of ... ...の手引で.

initiative, *n.* 発端, 手始め, 率先, 創始, 発議権, 率先権.

V ***destroy*** *initiative* 進んでやる精神を喪失させる. ¶The city ***displayed*** a laudable *initiative* in the fight against tuberculosis. その市が率先して結核撲滅運動を起したのは感心なことだ. ¶***have*** the *initiative* 先手をとっている, 主導権がある. ¶***lose*** the *initiative* 受身になる. ¶***take*** the *initiative* 率先してやる, 先手を打つ. 【類】 They are accustomed to ***taking*** the *initiative* in things. / the *initiative* was ***taken*** by ... / The position of ... is favorable for ***taking*** the *initiative* in the matter. ‖ ***take*** the *initiative* away from ... ...から主導権を奪う.

Q ***American*** *initiative* 米国人の発意力. ¶by ***individual*** *initiative* 銘々の発意で ‖ leave little to ***individual*** *initiative* ほとんど個人の主動を抑制する. ¶upon one's ***own*** *initiative* 自発的に. ¶***private*** *initiative* 民間の発意.

Q² stifle ***business*** *initiative* 商業の自主性を封じる.

P ***of*** one's own *initiative* 自発的に. ¶act entirely ***on*** his own *initiative* 全く彼一個の考えでやる ‖ ***on*** (=***upon***) the *initiative* of ... ...の発議で. ¶mainly ***owing to*** his *initiative* 主として彼の発議で.

P² she took the *initiative* ***among*** the nations of the world in ... その国は他国に率先して...した. ¶take the *initiative* ***in*** courtship 先に求婚する.

inject, *v.* 注入する, 注射する.

P *inject* cocaine ***into*** the broken leg 骨折した脚にコカインを注射する ‖ *inject* a remark ***into*** a conversation 話しの中へくちばしを入れる ‖ *inject* Communist propaganda ***into*** motion pictures 映画に共産党の宣伝を入れる. 【類】 *inject* a solution (溶液) ***into*** ... ¶*inject* medicines ***under*** the skin 皮下注射をする.

injection, *n.* 注入, 注射.

V ***get*** (=***have***) *injection* under the skin (in the arm) 皮下(など)注射をしてもらう. ¶***make*** (=***give***) an *injection* 注射する.

Q ***hypodermic*** (= ***subcutaneous***) *injection* 皮下注射. ¶***rectal*** *injection* 直腸注射.

Q² administer two ***camphor*** *injections* カンフルを二回注射する. ¶a ***spine*** *injection* 脊(せき)骨注射.

P² an *injection* ***of*** morphia モルヒネ注射. ¶an *injection* 「***to*** the bowels 腸注射.

injector, *n.* 注入器.

Q an ***automatic*** *injector* 自動注入器.

injudicious, *a.* 思慮のない, 無分別な.

P it would be *injudicious* ***of*** the government to ... ...したなら政府の無分別となろう.

injunction, *n.* 命令, 禁止.

V ***give*** strict *injunction* 厳重な命令を発する.

Q ***admonitory*** *injunctions* 訓戒的禁止. ¶a ***parting*** *injunction* 告別訓示. ¶a ***solemn*** *injunction* 厳命. ¶a ***superfluous*** *injunction* 余計な訓示.

Q² defy a ***court*** *injunction* to ... ...せよとの裁判所の命令を無視する. ¶***Government*** *injunctions* forbidding ... ...を禁じる政府の命令. ¶***police*** *injunction* to the crowd 群集への警官の命令. 「と注意すれば.

P ***upon*** the simple *injunction* of the nurse 看護婦がちょっ

injure, *v.* 害する, 傷つける, けがをさせる.

M ***mortally*** *injured* 致命的の負傷をして. ¶***permanently*** *injured* 一生のけがをして. ¶more or less ***seriously*** *injured* 重軽傷を負うて ‖ *injure* oneself ***seriously*** 重傷を受ける. ¶be ***severely*** *injured* in the crash of a passenger plane 乗客機の事故で重傷を受けている. ¶***shockingly*** *injured* about the face 顔のあたりにぞっとするようなけがをして. ¶***slightly*** *injured* 軽傷を負って.

P It was *injured* ***by*** an earthquake. それは地震でこわれた. ¶be *injured* ***in*** a fire 火事で傷を受ける. ¶He was badly *injured* ***on*** both legs. 彼は両脚をひどくけがした.

injurious, *a.* 害になる, 有害な, 毒の.

P *injurious* ***to*** health 健康に有害な ‖ be *injurious* ***to*** credit 信用にかかわる. 【類】 *injurious* ***to*** social order / be *injurious* ***to*** the best interests of the Japanese people / be *injurious* ***to*** the cause of freedom.

injury, *n.* 害, 損害, 危害, けが.

V ***avenge*** an *injury* to ... or a murder of ... upon ... ...に危害を加えられまたは...を殺害されたあだを...に報いる. ¶***do*** *injury* to ... ...に害を加える. ¶***dress*** an *injury* けがに包帯する. ¶***escape*** *injury* 傷害を免れる. ¶We cannot ***estimate*** the *injury*. 損害の見積りがつかない. ¶No *injuries* were ***incurred***. 負傷者なし. ¶***inflict*** *injury* on ... ...に傷を負わせる. ¶***pay back*** an *injury* 害に報復する. ¶***prevent*** *injury* to ... ...への損害を予防する. ¶He ***received*** a serious *injury* to a knee. 彼はひざに重傷を負った. ¶***redress*** the *injury* done to ... ...に対して加えられた損害を賠償する. ¶***repair*** *injury* 損害を賠償する. ¶***repay*** an *injury* 意趣返しをする. ¶No personal *injury* was ***reported***. 人体の損傷は無かったということだ. ¶***retaliate*** an *injury* on an enemy 敵に損害の復しゅうをする. ¶***suffer*** *injuries* 負傷する. 【類】 ***suffer*** fractures (挫傷) and other grave *injuries*. ¶He *sustained* such *injuries* that he very soon afterwards died. 彼は重傷を負って間もなく死んだ. ¶it ***worked*** great *injury* to the friendly relations of ... and ... それが...と...間の親善関係に大きな危害を及ぼした.

V² No *injury* has ***occurred.*** 何らの損害もなかった.

Q do a person a ***deadly*** *injury* 人に致命傷を加える. ¶***ghastly*** *injury* 恐ろしいけが. ¶do some ***grave*** *injury* to our health われわれの健康に非常な害を及ぼす. ¶It resulted in ***great*** *injury.* その結果大損害になった. ¶It is doing ***incalculable*** *injury* to Japan's prestige in Europe. それはヨーロッパにおける日本の威信に計り知れないほどの損害を与えている. ¶receive ***internal*** *injuries* 内傷を受ける. ¶a ***major*** *injury* 大損害. ¶receive ***minor*** *injuries* ささいの損害をこうむる. ¶a serious ***physical*** *injury* 重大な負傷. ¶work ***reciprocal*** *injury* 双方の損害になる. ¶receive a ***severe*** *injury* to his head 彼の頭に重傷をこうむる. ¶receive a ***slight*** *injury* to his knee 彼のひざに軽傷をこうむる. ¶***substantial*** and ***irreparable*** *injury* 重大かつ回復できない傷害. ¶***terrible*** *injuries* 恐ろしい損害. ¶one who does oneself a ***wilful*** *injury* 自分にわざと傷を負わせる者. ¶It was fortunate that he escaped without ***worse*** *injuries.* その位のけがで済んだのは彼の幸運であった. ¶suffer a ***skull*** *injury* in a fall ころんで頭がい骨に傷を受ける.

P though ***to*** his own *injury* 自分は損害をこうむっても. ¶***without*** *injury* to quality 品質を落さないで ‖ escape ***without*** *injury* けがをせずにのがれる.

P² *injury* ***by*** fire 火災による損害. ¶*injury* ***to*** health and life 健康と生命に対する害. ¶inflict serious *injury* ***upon*** ... ...に重大な損害を加える.

injustice, *n.* 不正, 不義, 非行.

V ***commit*** a great *injustice* 一大不正を犯す. ¶he has ***done*** all *injustice* to ... 彼は...に対してあらゆる不公正をやった. ¶Strong nations have never hesitated to ***perpetrate*** *injustices* on weaker ones when their economic interest so demanded. 強国民は経済上の利益に迫られると弱国民に不正を加えて顧みなかった. ¶***redress*** (=***remedy***) *injustice* 不正を正す ‖ ***remedy*** this *injustice* to ... ...に対するこの不正を正す. ¶***remove*** an *injustice* 不正を除く.

Q This is ***gross*** *injustice.* これははなはだしい不正義だ.

P An expurgated edition is ***in*** *injustice* to the author. 削除版は著作者に対する不正義である. ¶***without*** *injustice* to any of the parties concerned 関係者のだれにも不公平にならないで.

P² the *injustice* ***of*** the law 法の不備.

ink, *n.* インキ, 墨汁; いか墨.

V ***dry*** *ink* with (=on) a blotting-paper 吸取紙でインキを吸取る. ¶***get*** *ink* on one's dress 衣にインキがつく. ¶***make*** some *ink* more ***Japonica*** 墨をする. ¶Over the question much *ink* has already been ***shed.*** その問題は大分文筆上の議論がやかましかった. ¶***sling*** serious *ink* at ... ...をむきになって攻撃する. ¶He ***spilt*** his *ink* on the desk. 彼はインキを机上にこぼした. ¶The cuttlefish ***spurts*** the *ink* as a means of defense. いかは防衛策として墨を吹き出す.

V² In hastily printed sheets the *ink* ***smears*** when they are moved. 急速に印刷したものはずれるとインキが散る.

Q ***Indian*** *ink* 唐墨. ¶***marking*** *ink* (布などに)印しをつけるインキ. ¶An odor of ***printer's*** *ink* is perceptible. 印刷用インキのにおいははっきり分る. ¶***washable*** (permanent) *ink* 洗って落ちないインキ. ¶***writing*** *ink* 筆記用インキ.

Q² a ***permanent record*** *ink* 万年インキ.

P be ***in*** red *ink* 赤インキで書いてある; 《米》赤字である ‖ printed (written) ***in*** red *ink* 赤インキで印刷し(書い)た ‖ The business is ***in*** [the] red (black) *ink.* 商売は赤(黒)字だ. 【類】The net results of American foreign trade, in April, had to be recorded ***in*** red *ink* for the first time in nearly two years. ¶write clearly ***with*** *ink* インキではっきり書く. 【類】A pen is an instrument used in writing ***with*** *ink.* ‖ a table cloth stained ***with*** *ink.* インキでよごれたテーブルかけ.

ink, *v.* インキをつける.

M² *ink* ***in*** 下絵をインキで描く.

inkling, *n.* 暗示, 風示.

V ***get*** an *inkling* of the fact that ... ...という事実の暗示を得る. ¶***have*** no *inkling* as to the real cause 実際の原因につき一向わかっていない ‖ not to ***have*** the least *inkling* that ... ...ということは少しも気付かない. 【類】I ***had*** not the slightest *inkling* that anything of the kind was in progress. ‖ ***have*** some *inkling* of a headache ちと頭痛がする.

Q the ***first*** *inkling* I had that ... came when ... ...のときに初めて...ということに感づいた.

inkstick, *n.* 墨.

V ***rub*** the *inkstick* against the inkstone 墨をする.

inlaid, *a.* 象眼した, 切りはめた.

P *inlaid* ***into*** wood 木に象眼した. ¶*inlaid* ***with*** gold and silver 金銀を象眼した.

inlay, *v.* 象眼する, 切りはめにする.

P *inlay* it ***on*** metal それを金属に象眼する. ¶*inlay* it ***with*** gold それを金で象眼する.

inmate, *n.* 同居人, 同宿人.

V ***turn out*** the *inmates* of homes of prostitutes upon the streets あいまい屋の女どもを町へ野放しにする.

Q the ***other*** *inmates* of the apartment-house アパートの他の居住者たち. ¶He is kept in the asylum as a ***permanent*** *inmate.* 彼はその養育院で一生世話を受ける身となっている.

Q² ***concentration-camp*** *inmates* 集団抑留所収容者.

inn, *n.* 旅館, 宿舎, 旅宿.

V He ***keeps*** an *inn* there. 彼はそこで旅館をやっている.

Q a ***lake-side*** (***river-side***) *inn* 湖(河)畔の宿屋. ¶a small ***roadside*** (=***wayside***) *inn* 小さい路傍の宿屋. ¶an ***old-time*** *inn* 昔風の宿屋.

P put up ***at*** an *inn* 宿を取る ‖ stop ***at*** an *inn* 旅館に泊っている ‖ servants ***at*** an *inn* 旅館の召使.

inning[s], *n.* 〖野球〗回; 番. ☞英は常に複数, 米は単数形をとる.

V ***has*** his *innings* 番が回って来る ‖ Now the Conservatives will ***have*** the *innings.* 今度は保守党が政権をとる番だ.

Q ***extra*** (=***extended***) *innings* 〖野〗補回. ¶The Yankees won by 12 runs and ***one*** *inning.* ヤンキースが十二点アルファで勝った. ¶score a run in the first (second) half of the ***third*** *inning[s]* 第三回の表(裏)で一点をあげる.

innocence, *n.* 無罪, 潔白; 無邪気.

V ***destroy*** the *innocence* of a child 純真な童心を傷つける. ¶***maintain*** one's *innocence* 無罪を主張する. ¶stoutly ***proclaim*** one's *innocence* がん強にその無罪を声明する.

Q his ***defenseless*** *innocence* 彼の無警戒の無邪気さ.

P thinking ***in*** my *innocence* that ... 私は無邪気にも...と考えて ‖ It may become, ***in*** all *innocence,* a cause of annoyance. 少しもその積りはなくともそれが迷惑にならぬとも限らない. ¶wear an air ***of*** *innocence* 何食わぬ顔をする.

innocent, *a.* 罪のない, 潔白な; 無邪気な; 《俗》...を欠いている.

M ***as*** *innocent* as a lamb 小羊のように無垢(ㇰ)な. ¶a face ***childishly*** *innocent* 子供っぽい無邪気な顔.

P He is *innocent* ***of*** this crime. 彼にはこの罪がない. 【類】The truck-driver was proved *innocent* ***of*** manslaughter. ‖ cow-skin boots *innocent* ***of*** polish みがいたことのない牛皮の長ぐつ ‖ be *innocent* ***of*** the craft of fiction 小説を書く法を知らない. 【類】a French servant, *innocent* ***of*** English.

innovation, *n.* 改新, 革新.

V he ***antidated*** by nearly a century the *innovation* of ... 彼は...の改革をほとんど百年前に先べんを着けた. ¶***establish*** an *innovation* 更新する. ¶***introduce*** an *innovation* 革新を実行する. ¶***make*** *innovations* 種々改革をやる. ¶***oppose*** *innovation* 改新に反対する.

Q ***conservative*** *innovation* 保守的改進. ¶It was a ***decided*** *innovation* in those days. それは当時としては確かに新しい試みであった. ¶an ***ill-advised*** *innovation* 無分別な改革. ¶a great ***journalistic*** *innovation* 新聞事業の一大改革. ¶a ***new-fangled*** *innovation* 最新の改革. ¶a ***novel*** *innovation* 目新しい試み. ¶***radical*** *innovations* 急激な革新. ¶ice-cream sodas—a ***recent*** *innovation* in China 近ごろ中国のやり出したアイスクリームソーダ. ¶the most radical ***technical*** *innovation* of this war この戦争の最も根本的な技術的変革. ¶an ***unheard-of*** *innovation* 空前の改新. ¶a ***welcome*** *innovation* 喜ぶべき改新.

P² an *innovation* ***in*** religion 宗教改革 ‖ introduce an important *innovation* ***in*** publishing 出版界に重要な革新を起す.

inoculate, *v.* 接種する, 種痘する.

P be *inoculated* ***against*** typhoid (small-pox, malaria). 腸チフス(など)の予防注射を受ける. ¶*inoculate* ... ***with*** an anticold vaccine ...に感冒予防のワクチン注射をする. 【類】*inoculate* a person ***with*** an idea (思想).

inoculation, *n.* 注射.

Q ***anti-typhoid*** *inoculation* 腸チフス予防注射. ¶an ***ex-***

perimental inoculation 試験的接種. ¶***preventive inoculation*** against disease 病気予防注射. ¶***protective inoculation*** for cholera コレラ予防注射.

Q² *rabies inoculation* 恐水病予防接種.

P² *inoculation **against*** typhoid 腸チブス予防注射.

inoperative, *a.* 無効な.

P certain clauses of the treaty became *inoperative **as*** the result of the hostilities between ... and ... 同条約のある箇条は…間の戦争の結果無効になった.

inpouring, *n.* 流入.

Q a ***steady*** *inpouring* of fresh air and outpouring of stale air 断えざる新鮮な空気の流入とよごれた空気の排出.

inquest, *n.* 尋問, 審理, 取調べ.

V ***conduct*** an *inquest* on the body その死体の検査を行う. ¶an *inquest* was ***held*** on the body of ... …の死体検査が行われた.

P² an *inquest **on*** the body of ... …の死体検査. ¶a coroner's *inquest **over*** the body of ... …の死体に対する検死官の調査.

inquietude, *n.* 不安.

Q be attacked by an ***infinite*** *inquietude* 底知れぬ不安の念にかられる.

inquire, enquire, *v.* 調査する, 尋ねる, 問う, 求める.

M *inquire **cautiously*** 細心の調査をする. ¶*inquire* too ***closely*** about ... …について綿密すぎるほど調査する. ¶*inquire* more ***deeply*** into the matter その事件をもっと突込んで調べる. ¶*inquire **demurely*** しかつめらしく尋ねる. ¶*inquire **gruffly*** ぶっきら棒に尋ねる. ¶*inquire **out*** the plans of an enemy 敵の計画をかぎつける.

P I *inquired **about*** the battle. 私はその戦について尋ねた. ¶*inquire **after*** (=for) him 彼の安否を尋ねる. 【類】He came to *inquire **after*** your health. ¶I will *inquire* again ***as to*** that matter. その事についてもう一ぺん聞いて見ましょう. ¶*inquire **at*** the post-office 郵便局で尋ねる. ¶*inquire **by*** telephone 電話で尋ねる. ¶*inquire* (=ask) ***for*** goods in a shop 店で商品がないかと尋ねる. 【類】*inquire **for*** a certain book ***at*** a bookseller's / On *inquiring **for*** a room, I again met with the ominous word "Full up (満員)." ‖ *inquire **for*** ... …はおいでかと尋ねる ‖ I am the person you *inquire **for***. 私がお尋ねの本人です. 【類】*inquire **for*** (=after) his health. ¶*inquire **into*** that affair その事件を調査する ‖ send the account to the Psychical Research Society to have the matter *inquired **into*** その記事を心理研究会に送ってその事件を調査してもらう. 【類】I have just called on you to *inquire **into*** the affair. / The matter is now being *inquired **into*** (目下調査中). / *inquire **into*** the circumstances of ... ‖ *inquire **into*** the will of God 神にうかがいを立てる. ¶*inquire* it ***of*** a person 人にそれを問う. 【類】I *inquired **of*** the soldier about the battle. / I *inquired **of*** the librarian if she had any literature (文献) on ... / I *inquired **of*** the person about the matter. ‖ I *inquired* the reason ***of*** his long absence. 私はなぜ彼が長く不在であったかを尋ねた.

inquirer, *n.* 尋問者, 調査人, 研究者.

Q a ***curious*** *inquirer* 好奇心の強い質問者. ¶an ***honest*** *inquirer* まじめな研究者. ¶a ***scientific*** *inquirer* 科学研究者.

inquiry, *n.* 問い, 尋問, 照会, 問合わせ.

V for all particulars ***address*** *inquiries* to ... 詳細は…にあてて照会して下さい ‖ all *inquiries* should be ***addressed*** to ... 質問はすべて…あてにしていただきたい. 【類】***address*** *inquiries* to leading scholars. ¶***answer*** an *inquiry* 問合わせに答える. ¶A rigid *inquiry* has been ***begun***. 厳重な審問が始まった. ¶***bark*** (=***smother***) *inquiry* 質問をやじり倒す. ¶***carry out*** many *inquiries* as to ... …について幾多の調査を実行する. ¶***conduct*** an *inquiry* into the possibility of ... …の可能性を調査する. ¶The *inquiry* has not yet been ***finished***. まだ調べがつかない. ¶*inquiry **freed*** from prejudice and artificial restraints of church and state 教会及び国家の偏見及び不自然な抑制を免れた研究. ¶***handle*** *inquiries* 質問を処理する. ¶***have*** an *inquiry* for ... …(商品など)に対する問合わせがある. ¶***hold*** an *inquiry* relative to ... …に関する調査を行う ‖ ***hold*** an *inquiry* into the circumstances of ... …の事情を調査する. 【類】***hold*** an *inquiry* into the proposed scheme. ¶***institute*** an *inquiry* into ... …の調査を始める. 【類】***institute*** proper *inquiry* into the case / ***institute*** *inquiries* of his own 自分で研究する. ¶***invite*** *inquiries* from ... …からの質疑を促す. ¶***make*** *inquiries* about ... …で照会する. 【類】The Chinese Government is ***making*** *inquiries* on the subject. ‖ He ***made*** no further *inquiry* into the matter. 彼はその段階で事件の調査を打切った. ‖ ***make*** *inquiries* as to irregularities of mail delivery (郵便物遅着など) / *inquiry* should be ***made*** at ... prior to ... ¶An *inquiry* has now been ***opened*** into the Paris police scandals. パリ警察疑獄事件の審問が開始された. ¶***promote*** the *inquiry* その研究を促進する. ¶***prosecute*** *inquiries* into ... …の調査を実行する. ¶***provoke*** *inquiry* 質疑を引き起す. ¶He ***pursued*** *inquiries* that resulted in his writing an authoritative book. 彼はその研究を続けその結果権威ある著述をするに至った. ¶***receive*** *inquiries* for ... …の照会を受ける. 【類】Several other firms have ***received*** the same *inquiry*. ¶He did not all ***relish*** the impertinent *inquiries* which were made into his family history. 彼は自分一家の事情に立入って無作法な質問をされるのをまことに心苦しく思った. ¶***send out*** an *inquiry* for ... の照会を出す. ¶***stifle*** *inquiry* 調査をさせないようにする. ¶***stimulate*** (=***urge***) scientific *inquiry* 科学の研究を奨励する. ¶he has ***summed up*** his *inquiries* in the conclusion that ... 彼はその研究を概括して…という結論を下した. ¶the members of the Commission appointed to ***undertake*** the *inquiry* その調査を行うべく任命された委員会の委員. ¶***welcome*** *inquiries* 質問を歓迎する.

V *inquiry **proves*** that ... 調べて見ると…と分かった.

Q I must reserve it for ***another*** *inquiry*. これは別の研究として残しておかなければならない. ¶There is already a ***brisk*** *inquiry* for the goods. すでにその品に対し盛んに問合わせがある. ¶make ***confidential*** *inquiries* 内密の調査をやる. ¶without ***due*** *inquiry* into their antecedents 彼らの履歴についてしかるべき調査もせずに. ¶a very ***doubtful*** *inquiry* (買入に対する)非常に疑わしい(物になりそうもない)問合わせ. ¶look at each other with ***dumb*** *inquiry* 無言の中に聞きたいようすで顔を見合わす. ¶in reply to your ***esteemed*** *inquiry* of June 10 六月十日付のお問合わせに対し. ¶an ***ethical*** *inquiry* 倫理的な一考察. ¶make ***exhaustive*** *inquiries* 八方手を尽して調べる. ¶institute a ***fresh*** *inquiry* into ... …に対する新研究をやる. ¶a ***full*** *inquiry* will be made into ... …の十分な調査が行われるであろう. ¶We have good stock on hand with ***good*** *inquiry*. 小店には優秀な手持の品がありまた有望な問合わせもあります. ¶for ***further*** *inquiry* 再調査のために; 再照会を待って ‖ The bill was tabled for ***further*** *inquiries*. 議案は再調査のため懸案となった. ¶a ***historical*** *inquiry* 歴史的な一考察. ¶He made ***many*** *inquiries* into these matters. 彼はこれらの事柄を色々研究した. ¶make ***minute*** *inquiries* into the matter その件を詳細に研究する. ¶***modern*** *inquiry* into ... …に関する近代の研究. ¶The market closed firmer (duller) with ***more*** (***less***) *inquiry*. 市況は問合わせが増して(減って)強(弱)調で終了した. ¶have ***much*** (***no***) *inquiry* for ... …について多くの問合わせがある(ない). ¶he is in receipt of ***numerous*** *inquiries* on ... 彼は…について幾多の照会を受けている. ¶***Parliamentary*** *inquiry* 議事上の質疑. ¶Mr. S has summed up his ***philosophical*** *inquiries* in the conclusion that the universe is the outcome of an infinite and eternal energy. S氏は彼の哲学研究を概括して宇宙は無限にして永久性を持つ力の結果であるという結論を下した. ¶A ***preliminary*** *inquiry* into a murder case closed yesterday. 殺害事件の予審はきのう終結した. ¶I have failed to reach them by ***postal*** *inquiries*. 私は郵便問合わせをしたが先方に通じなかった. ¶make ***proper*** *inquiries* as to ... …について然るべき問合わせをする. ¶institute ***proper*** *inquiry* into the case この件について然るべき審査を行う. ¶deal with ***public*** *inquiries* through the post 一般公衆の質問を郵便で処理する. ¶a ***sarcastic*** *inquiry* whether ... …か否かの皮肉な質問. ¶a ***scientific*** *inquiry* into the subject 同問題に関する一つの科学的研究. ¶A ***searching*** *inquiry* will be held. 厳密な取調べが行われるだろう. ‖ would be found on a ***searching*** *inquiry* to ... 丹念に取調べて見たら…ということが分かるだろう. ¶He has made ***special*** *inquiries* into the matter. 彼はその件を特に調査した. ¶by ***statistical*** *inquiry* 統計的調査によって. ¶a ***suave*** *inquiry* as to ... …について丁寧な質問. ¶a ***superfluous*** *inquiry* 余計な調査.

Q² ***telephone*** *inquiries* 電話の問合わせ.

P ***by*** postal *inquiries* 郵便で問合わせて. ¶I learned ***on***

inquiry that ... 私は問合わせて見たら...と分かった. ¶I found ***upon*** *inquiry* that ... 私は調べたら...と分かった. 【類】***upon*** *inquiry* it was ascertained that ...

P² make *inquiry* ***about*** it それについて調査する. ¶I will make *inquiries* ***among*** my friends. 私は友人の間で調べて見よう. ¶*inquiries* ***as to*** ... should be made at ... ...についての問合わせでは...せねばならない. ¶I am writing to make *inquiry* ***concerning*** (=***respecting***) ... 私はこの手紙で...に関するお問合わせをしたいのです. ‖ an *inquiry* ***concerning*** ... ...に関する一考察. ¶institute an *inquiry* ***into*** the cause of ... ...の原因調査を始める ‖ an *inquiry* ***into*** socialism 社会主義の研究 ‖ an *inquiry* ***into*** his personality will reveal that ... ...素性(すじょう)を洗って見ると...が分かるだろう. 【類】*inquiry* ***into*** the varying views of people about the life after death. ¶an *inquiry* ***on*** ... ...についての研究 ‖ I made a personal *inquiry* ***on*** the spot. 私は現場で自ら調査した.

inquisition, *n.* 宗教裁判.

Q another ***Spanish Inquisition*** スペインの宗教裁判の二の舞.

inquisitive, *a.* 聞きたがる, 知りたがる.

P be *inquisitive* ***about*** another's affairs 他人のことを聞きたがる.

inroad, *n.* 侵入, 侵略.

V ***make*** an *inroad* upon a country ある国に侵入する ‖ ***make*** *inroads* in the export market in Mexico メキシコにおける輸出市場に進出する.

Q English makes ***steady*** *inroads* upon French as the language of diplomacy and upon German as the language of science. —H.L. Mencken. 英語は外交語としてフランス語を科学の語としてはドイツ語を着々侵食しつつある.

P² Japanese goods making *inroads* ***into*** the British market 英国の市場に進出する日本品. ¶Japanese *inroads* ***on*** Latin American markets 日本のラテンアメリカ市場への進出.

insane, *a.* 狂気の, 気違いじみた.

P He went *insane* ***from*** the tragedy. 彼はその悲劇のために気が狂った. ¶be *insane* ***on*** a subject ある問題に関して気違いじみている.

insanitary, *a.* 不衛生の.

M ***grossly*** *insanitary* はなはだしく不衛生な.

insanity, *n.* 狂気, 発狂, 精神錯乱.

V ***cause*** *insanity* 発狂させる. ¶***produce*** transient *insanity* 一時的な乱心をきたす.

Q ***climacteric*** *insanity* (女性などの)変換期に起る精神病. ¶***partial*** *insanity* 偏執狂. ¶regard free love as ***social*** *insanity* 自由恋愛を社会的狂気ざたと見なす. ¶Such talk would be ***stark*** *insanity*. そんなことをいったらそれこそ狂気のさたであろう. ‖ ***strict*** *insanity* 本物の狂気. ¶suicide during ***temporary*** *insanity* 一時的狂乱中の自殺.

P a violent outburst ***of*** *insanity* 突然の発狂. ¶a strong tendency ***to*** *insanity* 精神錯乱への著しい傾向.

insatiable, *a.* あくことのない, 足るを知らない.

P *insatiable* ***of*** fame 名誉を欲してあくことのない.

insatiate, *a.* 足るを知らない, あくことのない.

P *insatiate* ***of*** fame 名誉を欲してあくことのない.

inscribe, *v.* 書く, 記す, 彫る, 刻みつける.

M His exploits are *inscribed* ***indelibly*** in stone. 彼の勲功は深く石に刻みつけられてある.

P pin to his coat a large ticket with the words "..." *inscribed* ***in*** bold characters 太い字で「...」と書いた大きな札を彼の上衣にピンで留める ‖ Their names are *inscribed* ***in*** letters of gold. 彼らの名前は金文字で記してある. ‖ *inscribe* one's name ***in*** a book 本に名を記す. 【類】be *inscribed* ***in*** one's memory. ¶The names were *inscribed* ***on*** the memorial tablet＝The memorial tablet was inscribed ***with*** the names. その記念碑にはそれらの名前が刻んであった. ¶*inscribe* a book ***to*** a friend 書物に題記して友に寄せる. ¶the name *inscribed* ***upon*** the pedestal of the statue 像の台座に刻んだ名. ¶It is *inscribed* ***with*** a poem. それには詩を彫りつけてある. 【類】*inscribe* a marble ***with*** a legend (伝説) / The pictures in the gallery are *inscribed* ***with*** the title, the name of the painter, and the school. / a sun-dial (日時計) *inscribed* ***with*** Roman figures—Shiogama—1783—presented by Rin Shihei ‖ a small, unpretentious structure, *inscribed* ***with*** the legend "His Majesty's Customs"「陛下の税関」と表札の記してある小さくて質素な建物. 【類】*inscribed* ***with*** Chinese characters, signifying the English, "..."

inscription, *n.* 記名, 題名, 碑名.

V The *inscription* is ***affixed*** to the door. その彫刻文字が入口に付いている. ¶a slab of marble ***bearing*** this *inscription* この彫刻文字の付いている大理石板. 【類】The stone ***bears*** on its face the following *inscription*. / it ***bears*** an *inscription* to the effect that ... / it ***bears*** over its door an *inscription*, both in Russian and English capitals, signifying that ... / the memorial ***bears*** an *inscription* stating (=recording) the fact that ... / The engine ***bears*** the *inscription* 1889, built in Glasgow. ¶An *inscription* to his memory was ***carved*** upon a rock on Mount Heng. ヘング山上の岩に彼の遺名を伝える碑文が刻まれた. ¶The statue ***contains*** (=bears) no *inscription*. その像には銘がない. ¶***decipher*** a mutilated *inscription* き損した碑文を判読する. ¶The donor ***engraved*** the following *inscription* upon it. その上に寄贈者が次の碑銘を刻んだ. ¶These stones ***have*** Egyptian *inscriptions*. これらの石にはエジプト文字が刻んである. ¶***have*** an *inscription* ***put up*** 碑銘を掲げさせる. ¶***incise*** an *inscription* on a stone 石の上に碑文を刻む. ¶with the following *inscription* ***pinned*** upon it: "..." その上に次の「...」という文句をくぎ留めにして. ¶On the grave this *inscription* is ***placed***. 墓にこの碑文が記してある. 【類】with this *inscription* ***placed*** over the doorway. ¶with an *inscription* ***recording*** its gift to the church at ... それを...にある教会へ寄付する旨の刻文の付いている.

Q an ***appropriate*** *inscription* 適当な碑文. ¶The book contains a ***contemporary*** *inscription* stating that it was a presentation copy. その本には献本であるという同時代の記入がある. ¶The present bore the ***following courteous*** *inscription*: その贈物には次の丁重な文句が付いていた. ¶a ***puzzling*** *inscription* 難解な碑文. ¶bearing a ***suitable*** *inscription* 適切な碑文のある. ¶a ***touching*** *inscription* on a monument 記念碑上の人を感動させる碑文.

Q² a ***postmark*** *inscription* 郵便消印の標語. ¶a ***signboard*** *inscription* 看板の文句. ¶a ***stone*** *inscription* 石碑文.

P send him a novel ***with*** the *inscription* on the fly-leaf, "From..." 飛ページに「...から」と記して小説を彼に送る.

P² There was an *inscription* ***in*** Chinese characters ***over*** the arch. アーチの上に漢字で題字があった. ¶the *inscription* ***on*** (=***upon***) his tombstone (=gravestone) 彼の墓碑銘. 【類】an *inscription* ***upon*** a banner.

insect, *n.* [一般に]虫; こん虫.

V Flowers ***attract*** *insects*. 花はこん虫をひき付ける. ¶***collect*** *insects* こん虫を採集する.

Q ***beneficial*** *insects* 益虫. ¶a ***blight-causing*** *insect* 草木を枯らす害虫. ¶a ***familiar*** *insect* ありふれたこん虫. ¶a ***harmful*** *insect* 害虫. ¶a ***hopping*** *insect* 跳躍するこん虫. ¶an ***injurious*** *insect* 害虫. ¶a ***parasitic*** *insect* 寄生虫. ¶a ***singing*** *insect* 鳴く虫. ¶a ***tiny*** *insect* 微小なこん虫. ¶Gnats are very ***troublesome*** *insects*. [あかまだら]蚊は非常にうるさい虫だ.

Q² ***enemy*** *insects* 諸害虫. ¶mosquitos, bed bugs, and other ***household*** *insects* 蚊, 南京虫その他屋内のこん虫類. ¶a scale *insect* 貝殻虫.

P a swarm ***of*** *insects* 一群のこん虫. ¶feed ***on*** *insects* こん虫を食とする. ¶trees infested ***with*** *insects* こん虫のついた木.

insecurity, *n.* 不安全, 不安定.

Q ***economic*** *insecurity* caused by the depression 不景気から生じた経済的不安.

Q² ***world*** *insecurity* 世界の不安.

P² the *insecurity* ***of*** footing in the solfatara その硫気坑における足場の不安定.

insensibility, *n.* 無知覚, 無感覚, 無とん着.

Q ***artistic*** *insensibility* 芸術に対する無感覚.

P² the Chinese *insensibility* ***to*** foreign influence 外国の影響力に対する中国人の無感覚.

insensible, *a.* 無感覚の; 人事不省の.

P *insensible* ***of*** the beauties of art 芸術の美に無感覚な. 【類】*insensible* ***of*** the danger of losing one's life. ¶grow *insensible* ***to*** discomfort 不快を感じないようになる ‖ Mars is never *insensible* ***to*** the glance of beauty. 英雄色を好む. 【類】*insensible* ***to*** the influence of the hour / *insensible* ***to*** music (pain) ‖ *insensible* ***to*** (=***of***) shame 恥知らずな. 【類】*insensible* ***to*** color.

insensitive, *a.* 無感覚な, 冷淡な.

P callous or *insensitive to* … …に対して無情冷淡な.

inseparable, *a.* 分けられない, 分離し得ない.

P his name is *inseparable from* the history of … 彼の名は…の歴史から切離すことができない. 【類】be *inseparable from* each other.

insert, *v.* 入れる, はめる, 差し込む.

P *insert* a word ***between*** two words 二語の間に一語をそう入する. ¶*insert* an advertisement (a portrait) ***in*** a newspaper 新聞に広告(など)を載せる. 【類】I wish to *insert* ***in*** the contract the following. ¶*insert* one's head ***under*** the curtain 窓かけの下に頭を突込む.

insertion, *n.* そう入, 差込.

V ***make*** an *insertion* そう入する. 【類】The following *insertion* has been ***made*** in the contract.

Q When used the ***customary*** *insertion* of a credit line "Courtesy Great Northern Line" will be published. 使用の場合は「グレート・ノーザン・ラインの厚意による」と付記します(宣伝用の写真を会社が雑誌などに贈ってきた場合).

inset, *n.* そう入図.

P It is shown ***in*** the *inset* above. それは上にあるそう入図に示してある.

inside, *n., ad.* 内部(に), 内側(に).

V men who have never ***seen*** the *inside* of a school (=an institution of learning) in their lives 学校経歴のない人.

P ***for*** the *inside* of a week 一週間以内に. ¶the White House ***from*** the *inside* 内部から見た白亜館. 【類】Mr. Baring is one of the few critics who know Russia ***from*** *inside*. ¶overcoats fur-lined ***on*** the *inside* 毛裏の外とう ‖ paint fares ***on*** the *inside* of a car 電車の内側に賃金表をペンキで書く ‖ The measurement is ***on*** the *inside*. 寸法は内のりです. ¶a door locked ***upon*** the *inside* 内から錠を下したドア.

P^{2} the *inside* ***of*** prohibition 酒類製造販売禁止の内幕 ‖ *Inside* [***of***] the mouth there are 32 teeth, 16 in each jaw. 口の中に上下あご各十六枚合わせて三十二枚の歯がある. ‖ We were there *inside* [***of***] eight minutes. われわれは八分たたない内にそこへ着いていた. ☞米口語では inside が within の意に使われる. I'll be back *inside of* an hour.

Q prohibition *inside* out 表へ出した禁酒の内幕. ¶turn one's coat *inside* out 上衣を裏返しにする. 【類】wear kimono *inside* out.

insight, *n.* 洞察, 看破, 眼識.

V ***afford*** an excellent *insight* into … 何々へすぐれた見通しを与える. ¶***gain*** an *insight* into this very difficult problem このはなはだ困難な問題を洞察する. ¶***get*** an *insight* into lives and customs of other peoples 他国民の生活習慣を洞察する. ¶***give*** a person a good *insight* into … 人をして…をりっぱに洞察させる ‖ ***give*** an *insight* into the past of … 何々の過去を見通しさせる. ¶I managed to ***have*** an *insight* into main facts. 私はどうやら主な事実を洞察することができた.

V^{2} The highest *insight* ***dawned*** on him. 彼は大悟徹底した.

Q with a ***clear*** and ***admirable*** *insight* he says that … 明達でりっぱな識見をもって彼は…と言っている. ¶***critical*** *insight* 批判力. ¶gain a ***deeper*** *insight* into … …をさらに深く洞察する. ¶get a ***fair*** *insight* into … …への良い見通しができる. ¶give a ***fresh*** *insight* into … …への新しい見方を示してくれる. ¶show a lack of ***historic*** *insight* 史眼の欠けていることを示す. ¶The author has a remarkably ***keen*** *insight* into human nature. 著者は人間性について際立って鋭い洞察力をもっている. ¶a ***marvelous*** *insight* into human nature 人間性への驚くべき洞察. ¶his penetrating *insight* into human nature and human motives 人間性と人間の動機への彼の透徹した洞察力. ¶She has a woman's ***quick*** *insight* into character. 彼女は人物を早く見抜くという女性固有の眼力を持っている. ¶a lack of ***sympathetic*** *insight* 同情的観察の欠乏.

insignia, *n.* 記章.

Q ***armorial*** *insignia* 紋章, 旗章.

Q^{2} signet rings bearing their ***division*** *insignia* 部門の記章のある指環. ¶the ***railway service*** *insignia* 鉄道従業員記章. ¶a red ***hammer-and-sickle*** *insignia* [ソ連の]赤い槌(つち)と鎌(かま)の記章.

insignificance, *n.* 無価値.

Q it is dwarfed into ***comparative*** *insignificance* by … それは…に比べるとつまらないものになってしまう. ¶in spite of their ***numerical*** *insignificance* 彼らは数の上では取るに足らないが.

P fade ***into*** *insignificance* ぼけて見えなくなる ‖ fade ***into*** *insignificance* in comparison with (=by the side of) … …に比べると取るに足らないものになる.

insincere, *a.* 不実な, 不誠実な, 誠意のない.

P *insincere* ***with*** another person 他人に対して不誠実の.

insincerity, *n.* 不誠実.

Q ***sickening*** *insincerity* 軽べつすべき不誠意.

P^{2} *insincerity* ***in*** speech 言葉の不まじめさ.

insinuate, *v.* 巧みに取入る.

P *insinuate* oneself ***into*** the mind (=good grace) of … …に巧みに取入る.

insinuation, *n.* 風刺, ぐう話, ほのめかし.

Q with a ***gentle*** *insinuation* that … …という軽い風刺で.

insist, *v.* 主張する, 言い張る, 固執する.

M ***strenuously*** *insist* upon … 力強く…を固執する.

P *insist* ***on*** the original demand 初めの要求を主張する. 【類】*insist* ***on*** an opinion / *insist* ***on*** one's innocence / *insist* ***on*** the importance of … ‖ I *insist* ***on*** your taking his money. 君は彼の金を是非受けなさい. ‖ if you *insist* ***on*** it たってとあれば. 【類】*insist* [***on*** the fact] that one is innocent / *insist* ***on*** going out. ¶*insist* ***upon*** payment 支払を固執する. 【類】The school rightly *insists* ***upon*** a very high standard of ability among its teachers. / There is a gentleman who *insists* ***upon*** seeing you on important business. / *insist* ***upon*** the fulfilment of a contract.

insistence, *n.* 主張, 固執, 無理じい.

V too much *insistence* cannot be ***laid*** on the fact that … …ということをどこまでも主張する必要がある.

P ***at*** his *insistence* 彼の主張で. ¶urge ***with*** some *insistence* 少し強硬に主張する.

insistent, *a.* 言い張る, 固執する.

P he is *insistent* ***in*** the advocacy of … 彼は…を強硬に主張する. ¶He was very *insistent* ***upon*** this point. 彼はこの点で頗る強硬だ.

insolence, *n.* 横着, 横柄, ごう慢.

V he ***had*** the *insolence* to do … 彼は横着にも…した. ¶***push*** their *insolence* and arrogance to intolerable lengths 我慢し切れないほど横着ごう慢を押し通す. ¶I cannot ***suffer*** his *insolence*. 彼の横着はがまんができない.

Q an ***unheard-of*** *insolence*. もっての外の横柄.

insolent *a.* 横柄な, 横着な, ごう慢の.

P *insolent* ***to*** customers (one's inferiors) 顧客(など)に対して横柄な.

insolubility, *n.* 不解決.

Q ***psychological*** *insolubility* 割り切れないもの.

insoluble, *a.* 溶けない.

P *insoluble* ***in*** water 水に溶けない.

insomnia, *n.* 不眠症.

Q a ***persistent*** *insomnia* がん強な不眠症.

P suffer from *insomnia* 不眠症でなやむ.

inspect, *v.* 調査する.

P be *inspected* ***by*** an outside body [経理など]外部団体によって調査される.

inspection, *n.* 検査, 検閲, 視察.

V ***bear*** *inspection*. よく見てもらっても欠点が出ない. ¶***hold*** an *inspection* of … …を検閲する. ¶we ***invite*** *inspection* of our extensive show rooms where may be seen a large stock of … …が豊富に取そろえてある弊店の手広い陳列室の御一覧を願います. ¶***make*** an *inspection* of a school (factory) 学校(など)を視察する. ¶***undergo*** *inspection* 点検を受ける. 【類】***undergo*** a medical *inspection* (身体検査).

Q on ***closer*** *inspection* it proved (=turned out) to be … よく調べて見るとそれは…であると分かった. 【類】***closer*** *inspection* revealed the fact that … ¶a ***formal*** *inspection* of … …の正式な検査. ¶***official*** *inspection* 検視. ¶a ***personal*** *inspection* of the situation 現状の実地調査. ¶***postal*** *inspection* 郵便物に対する郵便局の検査. ¶***sanitary*** *inspection* 衛生検査. ¶***searching*** *inspection* 厳密な検査.

Q^{2} ***acceptance*** *inspection* 領収検査. ¶***customs*** *inspection* 税関検査. ¶the ***food*** *inspection* of the poor 貧民の食料検査. ¶***house-to-house*** *inspection* 戸別検分. ¶***meat*** *inspection* 食肉検査. ¶***quarantine*** *inspection* 検疫. ¶***safety*** *inspection* [自動車などの]安全検査.

P The exhibition was honored ***by*** the *inspection* of the Emperor. その展覧会は天覧の光栄に浴した. ¶a tour ***of*** *inspection* 視察旅行. ¶it was found, ***on*** *inspection*, to be … 検分したら…と分かった.

inspector, *n.* 検査者, 検閲官.

V an *inspector* is ***stationed*** in … 検閲官が…に駐在している.

Q^{2} a ***health*** *inspector* 健康診査官. ¶a ***police*** *inspector* 警

視. ¶a *school inspector*=《米》a school commissioner 視学官.

inspiration, *n.* 霊感, 天来の感興, 入神.

V *derive inspiration* from ... …から霊感を得る. ¶*draw inspiration* from its setting その環境から霊感を得る.【類】*draw* their *inspiration* from alien sources. ¶*find* the greatest *inspiration* from the works of ... …の作から最大の霊感を得る.【類】the poet (artist) *found* an *inspiration* in ... / It is the work of a scientist who has *found inspiration* and joy in his work. ¶*get inspiration* from ... …から霊感を得る. ¶Suddenly he *had* an *inspiration*. 彼は急に霊感を得た. ¶*need inspiration* 霊感を必要とする. ¶he *owes* his *inspiration* on ... 彼はその霊感を…から受けた. ¶He *received inspiration* in his dream. 彼は夢に霊感を受けた. ¶*seek inspiration* at the shrine of ... …神社にもうでて霊感を求める.

Q an *alien inspiration* 外国の刺激. ¶He had a *brilliant inspiration*. 彼にすばらしい考えが浮んだ. ¶Her son was a *constant inspiration* to her. 息子は母にとって不断の感激であった. ¶*forced inspiration* しいて起された霊感. ¶a *perennial inspiration* 永続的霊感. ¶*spontaneous inspiration* 自然に発した霊感. ¶have a *sudden inspiration* 突如として霊感を得る.

Q² *platform inspiration* 演壇上の霊感.

P *by* the *inspiration* of Chicago's example シカゴの例に激励されて. ¶*on* a sudden *inspiration* 突然の霊感で. ¶*under* the *inspiration* of his patriotic conception of ... …についての彼の愛国思想に刺激されて.【類】Saint Paul, writing *under* the *inspiration* of God, says: ¶*with* a sudden *inspiration* 突然の霊感で.

inspire, *v.* 鼓吹する, 激励する.

M The news *instantly inspired* the troops with redoubled courage. その報道は直ちに兵士らを鼓吹してその勇気を倍加させた.

P I guess you have been *inspired by* somebody else? あなたはだれかから入知恵されましたね.【類】be greatly *inspired by* reading the life of a great man. ¶*inspire in* a person a love *for* learning 向学心を人に鼓吹する. ¶*inspire* him *to* further efforts 彼を激励してさらに努力させる. ¶His bravery *inspired* his soldiers *with* confidence in himself. 彼の勇敢な行為は部下を感激させ彼を信頼させた. ‖ *inspire* a person *with* patriotism (courage, hope) 人の愛国心(など)を鼓舞する.【類】*inspire* us *with* a great admiration for his powers.

instability, *n.* 不確定.

P² the *instability of* water 水の不定形性.

instal[l], *v.* 着座させる; 就任させる.

M *instal* oneself *comfortably* in a seat in the second class car 二等車の席にゆったりおさまる.

P be *installed as* chairman of the committee 委員会の長として就任している.【類】Have you *installed* Y *as* your household servant? ¶He has been *installed in* his office. あの人は就任した.

installation, *n.* 施設, 設備, 装置.

V All steamers with accommodations for fifty passengers or more, entering or clearing from American ports, are required by law to *carry* a wireless *installation*. 米国の港に出入する船舶で五十人以上の乗客を収容するものはすべて法律によって無電の設備をする規定になっている. ¶All large ships now *have* a wireless *intallation*. 今日では大きな船にはすべて無電装置がある.

Q² American *air force installations* in China 中国にあるアメリカ空軍諸施設. ¶*Army installations* 陸軍の諸設備.【類】*Army* and *Navy installations*. ¶a *lighting* (*heating*) *installation* 照明(暖房)装置. ¶*plant installations* 器械装置. ¶a *steam turbine installation* 蒸気タービン装置. ¶*telephone installations*, operated by the Chinese Government, are found at Canton, Chefoo, ... 中国政府が運営する電話装置は広東チーフーなどにある. ¶demilitarize *wartime installations* 戦時施設の武装を解除する.

P All modern vessels of any size are fitted *with* wireless *installations*. 大小を問わず現代の船舶はすべて無電装置がしてある.

instal[l]ment, *n.* 分割払, 掛金, 一回分.

V *keep up* the *installments* 分割払を続ける. ¶*pay instalments* when they become due 賦払金を期日通り仕払う. ¶The Century *prints* a first *instalment* of Mr. John Morley's Life of Oliver Cromwell. センチュリー誌はジョン・モーレー氏のオリヴァー・クロムウェル伝の第一回分を載せている.

Q Payment may be made in *annual instalments*, if desired. 支払は希望により年賦で差支えない. ¶the *first instalment* of a paper on ... …に関する論文の第一回分. ¶It is payable by *monthly instalments* of $50. それは五十ドルの月賦払いができる. ‖ pay off by *monthly instalments* of $20 二十ドルの月賦で完済する. ¶a *valuable first instalment* of reform 改革の貴重な第一歩. ¶the system of payment by *weekly* or *monthly instalments* 週賦または月賦払制.

P Payment *by instalments* can be arranged. 分納支払に応じます.【類】Arrangements may be made for payment *by instalments*. / the system of payment *by instalment* / purchase one's own dwelling *by instalments* spread over a series of years. ¶a story that appeared *in installments* 続きもので出た小説.【類】a serial story *in* six *installments*. ‖ apply fertilizer *in* two *instalments* 二回に分けて施肥する ‖ repay *in instalments* over a specified number of years 特定の期間に年賦償還する.【類】The sum will be paid *in instalments* covering a period of five years. / payable *in* monthly *instalments* of $7.50. ¶sold *on instalments* 月賦で売った.

P² as an *instalment of* the results of my investigations, I published in 1894 ... 私の調査の結果の一部として一八九四年に…を公にした. ¶an *instalment on* a house 家屋に対する一回分の賦払い.

instance, *n.* 例, 実例, 例証.

V *adduce instances* 例をあげる. ¶*afford* an *instance* of ... …の一例を示す. ¶A striking *instance* was *brought* to my notice the other day. 私は先日顕著な一例に気がついた. ¶to *cite instances* 例をあげると.【類】to illustrate by *citing* a few *instances* from life ‖ *cite* one or two more illustrative *instances* さらに一二の実例を引く. ¶*ferret* (=*search*) *out instances* for the purpose of condemning ... …を攻撃する目的で例を捜し出す. ¶*furnish* abundant *instances* of ... …の豊富な例を提供する. ¶*give* an *instance* 一例を示す. ¶I might *multiply instances* of ... 私は…の例をあげようとすれば幾らでもあげることができる.【類】such *instances* might be *multiplied* indefinitely, but sufficient have been mentioned to show that ... / *instances* could be *multiplied*, but these will suffice to show that ... / *instances* of the same sort could easily be *multiplied*. / It is needless to *multiply instances* of this kind. / we must go on *multiplying instances* for ever of ... ¶*instances* have been *observed* in which ... …という例がこれまで人の目に触れた. ¶*quote instances* in illustration 説明に例を引く.【類】Numerous other *instances* might here be *quoted*. ¶He *relates* the following *instance* of which he was an eyewitness. 彼はその実見した次の実例を語っている. ¶no better *instance* of the spirit of ... can be *shown* than the fact that ... …の事実ほど…の精神をよく示すものはない. ¶to *take* (=cite *or* give) only one *instance* ただ一例だけをあげれば.【類】to take a *single instance* / for example, to *take* but one *instance*.

V² *instances* have *occurred* in which ... …という場合の数例がある.

Q an *authentic instance* 確実な実例. ¶to take a *concrete instance*, we will consider the example of ... 具体例をあげるために…の例を考えて見よう. ¶*countless instances* 数限りない例. ¶an *exceptional instance* 例外. ¶to give a *familiar instance* 早い話が. ¶except in a *few isolated* and *brilliant instances* 二三の珍らしいりっぱな例を除いては. ¶I thought so too in the *first instance*. 私も始めはそう思った.【類】the problem arose in the *first instance* from ... / the cause has to be found in the *first instance* in ... ‖ act in the *first instance* 率先してそのことに当る ‖ as ordered in the *first instance* 最初に注文した通り ‖ a court of *first instance* 第一審判決裁判所. ¶the most *flagrant instance* 最も醜く感じられる例. ¶For the sake of illustration, I cite the *following instance*. 例証のために次の例を引こう. ¶adduce a *historical instance* of ... …の歴史上の例を示す. ¶to give an *illustrative instance* from sport 例をスポーツに取れば. ¶And this is no *isolated instance*. そしてその実例は他にもある. ¶a *lamentable instance* of extravagance ぜい沢の一つの悪例. ¶the *leading instance* 最も著しい例. ¶In *most instances*, the use of new terms is dictated by necessity or utility. たいていの場合新語を使う

のは必要があるかまたは役に立つかによるのである. ¶a ***notable*** *instance* 顕著な例. ¶a ***notorious instance*** (悪い意味で)有名な例. ¶in ***numberless instances*** 無数の事件において. ¶in ***numerous*** *instances* 多数の場合において. ¶This is only ***one*** *instance* of his devotion to the cause. 彼のその主義に忠実なことは万事この行き方である. ¶I wish to add, entirely at my ***own*** *instance* (=request), that ... 私は全く自分の意志で…とつけ加えておきたい. ¶***parallel*** *instances* 類例. ¶only in ***rare*** *instances* まれな場合だけ. ¶to give a ***ready-at-hand*** *instance* 早い話が. ¶***regrettable*** *instances* 遺憾な例. ¶a ***shining*** *instance* of youthful piety 青年信仰の模範. ¶to take a ***similar*** *instance* 類似の例を示す. ¶a ***single*** *instance* out of many 数多い中のただ一つの例. ¶a ***solitary*** *instance* ただ一つの例. ¶***some detached*** *instances* 二三の個々別々の例. ¶to take a ***striking*** *instance* 著しい例をあげれば. ¶***striking*** *instances* of longevity 著しい長命の例. ¶this *instance* is but ***typical*** of ... これは全く…の代表的な例である. ¶*instances* are not ***wanting*** in which ... …という例はある.

P ***As*** an *instance* the following may be quoted. 一例として次のものを引用できよう. ¶***at*** his *instance* 彼の発議で. 【類】***at*** the *instance* of local authorities / It is ***at*** your *instance* that I have undertaken this commission. ¶in London, ***for*** *instance* ロンドンなどでは. 【類】Intemperance is so highly destructive that the expectation of life of the intemperate, at the age, ***for*** *instance*, of thirty, is only 13.8 years.—Darwin. ¶***in*** one *instance* ある場合においては ‖ ***in*** every *instance* あらゆる場合に. 【類】***in*** the present *instance* / ***in*** some *instances*.

P² *Instance* ***after*** instance might be given, but these suffice. 幾らでも例をあげることができるがこれで十分だ. ¶an *instance* (=a case) ***of*** good out of evil 禍転じて福となる例 ‖ an *instance* ***of*** a good deed done 美談 ‖ Spitting in public is an *instance* ***of*** vulgarity. 公衆の前でつばを吐くことは下品の一例である.

O This is merely an *instance*. これはほんの一例に過ぎない.

instance, *v*. 例にひく.

M this may be ***familiarly*** *instanced* in ... 卑近の例を示せば...

instant, *n*. 瞬間, 寸時, 即刻.

Q in ***another*** *instant* 間もなく. ¶in ***that*** *instant* 即刻.

P ***at*** that *instant* その瞬間. ¶it is not to be compared ***for*** an *instant* with ... それは到底…とは比較にならない ‖ I did not lose my presence of mind ***for*** an *instant*. 私は少しも心を乱さなかった. ¶He was ordered to leave the room ***in*** an *instant* (=instantly). 彼は即刻へやを出ろと命じられた. ‖ ***in*** the *instant* of crossing the threshold 敷居をまたごうとする瞬間. 【類】He was back with us ***in*** an *instant*. ¶awake ***on*** the *instant* (=at once) 即座に目をさます ‖ judge ***on*** the *instant* that ... 即座に…と判断する.

instead, *ad*. 代りに.

P *instead* ***of*** ... please read ... …は…の誤り(正誤の場合) ‖ The steamer will arrive in port on the 18th of this month, *instead* ***of*** the 25th. 船は今月二十五日ではなく十八日に入港する.

O If you cannot go, let him go *instead*. 君が行けないなら彼を代りにやりなさい.

instigate, *v*. そそのかす, 教唆する, 扇動する.

P the violence was *instigated* ***by*** ... その暴行は…によって扇動された. ¶*instigate* a person ***to*** some evil deed 人を扇動してある悪事を働かせる.

O *instigate* a person to do ... 人をそそのかして…をさせる.

instigation, *n*. 扇動, 教唆.

Q ***social*** *instigation* or compulsion 社会の教唆または圧迫.

P undertake a journey ***at*** the *instigation* of ... …におだてられて旅行をやる ‖ The riot broke out ***at*** the *instigation* of a certain politician. その騒動はある政治家の扇動で起った.

instigator, *n*. 教唆者, 扇動者.

Q one of the ***chief*** *instigators* 主なる扇動者の一人. ¶the war and its ***Imperial*** *instigator* その戦争とこれを教唆した皇帝.

instill, *v*. 浸み込ませる, 注入する.

P *instill* ***in*** them the sentiment that ... …という感情を彼らに注入する ‖ *instill* ***in*** them an enterprising spirit 彼らに企業的精神を吹込む. ¶*instill* ***into*** the minds of the public the importance of ... …の重要性を公衆に吹込む. 【類】*instill* ***into*** the mind of the student the idea that ...

instinct, *n*. 本能, 本性, 天性; 直覚.

V ***awaken*** the lowest *instincts* 最も卑しい諸本能を目覚ます. ¶***correct*** *instinct* by reason 理性をもって本能を矯正する. ¶***excite*** gambling *instinct* 賭博心を刺激する. ¶try to ***fight*** one's *instincts* by religion その本能を宗教で抑制しようと試みる. ¶***follow*** blindly the *instincts* of nature 自然の本能に盲従する. 【類】***follow*** simply a brute *instinct* (劣情). ¶He ***has*** a highly developed art *instinct*. 彼は著しく発達した芸術本能を持っている. ¶***possess*** the journalistic *instinct* 新聞記者の勘がある. ¶***rouse*** every evill *instinct* a man possesses 人が持っているあらゆる悪性を呼びさます. ¶***satisfy*** the just patriotic *instinct* of the nation 国民のごく自然な愛国心を満足させる. ¶***show*** a sound *instinct* for ... …に対する健全な本能を示す.

Q the ***acquisitive*** *instinct*=the desire to possess 所有欲. ¶pander to the ***base*** *instincts* 卑俗な本能に迎合する. ¶true to ***boys'*** *instinct* 少年の天性そのままに. ¶They have the ***commercial*** *instinct* greatly developed. 彼らには大分商売気がある. ¶the ***conservative*** *instinct* of man 人間の保守的本能. ¶Vices are such acts as are repugnant to the ***cultivated*** *instincts* of society. 悪徳とは社会の常識的本能がいみきらう所の行為を指すのである. ¶The English have a ***deep*** *instinct* for affairs. 英国人は事務の才に富んでいる. ¶a sort of ***dim*** *instinct* 一種のかすかな本能. ¶The ***dramatic*** *instinct* is obviously very strong in the nursery. 演劇本能は幼少時代に非常に盛んであることは明かだ. ¶***egoistic*** *instincts* 自我的本能. ¶the ***fine*** pioneering *instinct* which inspired the forefathers of British commerce 英国人の祖先に商業を鼓吹したあのりっぱな企業的精神. ¶the ***fundamental*** *instincts* upon which life is built 人生の築かれる土台たる本能. ¶***hereditary*** *instinct* 遺伝的本能. ¶***inborn*** *instinct* 生得の本能. ¶***linguistic*** *instinct* 言語的本能. ¶the ***lowest*** *instincts* of mankind 人間の最も下劣な本能. ¶***master*** *instincts* of life 人生の主な本能. ¶***maternal*** *instinct* 母性. ¶***old-time*** *instinct* 昔ながらの本能. ¶appeal to the ***pictorial*** *instinct* 芸術的本能に訴える. ¶man's ***polygamous*** *instinct* 男の一夫多妻的本能. ¶a reversion to the ***primitive human*** *instinct* 原始的人間本能への逆転. ¶with a sort of ***prophetic*** *instinct* 一種の予言的天性のある. ¶***roving*** *instincts* 放浪性. ¶the ***sexual*** *instinct* 性の本能. ¶with the ***true*** *instincts* of the poet 詩人たる真の本能で. ‖ It is a ***true*** *instinct* which refuses to put a word between preposition and noun. 前置詞と名詞の間に言葉をはさむのを不可とするのは真の本能からきている.

Q² The Russian woman has keen ***gambling*** *instinct*. ロシア婦人は天性かけごとが大好きだ. ¶***homing*** *instinct* 帰巣本能(はとなどの). ¶the physiological age when the ***mating*** *instinct* is strongest 結婚をしたいという本能の最も強い年齢. ¶appeal to the ***play*** *instinct* of a cat ねこの遊戯本能に訴える. ¶manifest the ***setting*** *instinct* [鶏が]卵をかえす本能を示す.

P guided ***by*** *instinct* 本能に導かれて. ¶know ***from*** *instinct* that ... 本能的に…と知る. ¶***With*** the *instinct* of a poet, he saw in it effective material for a drama. 彼は詩人の持つ直覚で劇の好材料をその中に見付けた. ¶He has an *instinct* ***for*** art. 彼は生来芸術に向いている. 【類】have an *instinct* ***for*** outdoor sports.

institute, *n*. 会, 院, 学会, 協会.

Q a ***collegiate*** *institute* 学院.

Q² a ***guidance*** *institute* 講習会. ¶the ***Pasteur Institute*** パスツール研究所. ¶a ***research*** *institute* of ceramics 窯(よう)業研究所. ¶the ***Science Talent*** *Institute* [アメリカ]科学技能研究所.

institute, *v*. 設ける, 起す, 始める.

P *institute* a suit ***against*** a person (firm) 人(など)を相手取って訴える. ¶The present English statute mile was *instituted* ***in*** the time of Elizabeth. 現在英国の法定マイルはエリザベス女王のときに制定された.

institution, *n*. 学会, 学校; 団体; 制度; 慣習.

V Her alumni are now privileged to ***enter*** *institutions* in Europe and America for post-graduate work without examination. 同校の卒業生は今日では欧米大学院に無試験入学ができる. ¶***evaluate*** *institution* for the purpose of accreditation 公認の目的で建設物を評価する. ¶All the leading government *institutions* are ***quartered*** here. あらゆる主要な官庁はみなここに集中している. ¶***remodel*** the social *institutions* of each age in response to the demands of the new generation 新時代の要求に応じて時代時代に社会制度を改める. ¶***study*** Western business *insti-*

tutions 西洋の商業制度を研究する. ¶*upbuild* a lasting *institution* of worth 永久性のあるりっぱな制度を築き上げる.
Q the American spirit and ***American** institutions* 米国魂と米国諸制度. ¶a ***bogus** institution* インチキな団体. ¶The Times is as much a distinctly ***British** institution* as are Parliament, roast beef, and bulldogs. タイムズ紙は議会や焼肉やブルドッグが英国の名物であると同様確かに一つの名物である. ¶The Committee of Conservators of *Closed Institutions* 閉鎖機関管理委員会. ¶Dartmouth is not a ***co-educational** institution.* ダートマス(大学)は男女共学の学校ではない. ¶The Theatre Français is a most ***conservative** institution.* テアトルフランセーは最も保守的な機関である. ¶a purely ***Continental** institution* 純然たる欧州大陸の制度. ¶administrators of ***correctional** institutions* 感化院の管理者たち. 【類】a State (州) ***correctional** institution.* ¶a ***disinterested** institution* for public service 社会奉仕の非営利的機関. ¶an ***educational** institution* 学校. ¶The University of Chicago is a privately ***endowed** institution.* シカゴ大学は個人の寄付による学校である. ¶a heavily ***endowed** institution* 基金の豊かな学校(など). ¶a critic and enemy of ***established** institutions* 既存制度の批評家ならびに敵. ¶The Times Atlas has now become an ***established*** and ***recognized** institution.* タイムズ・アトラスは今や世間から認められた押しも押されもしない出版物となった. ¶all the ***financial** institutions,* which make up the financial structure of society 社会の財政組織を成すあらゆる金融機関. ¶***highest** institutions* of learning 最高学府. ¶***human** institutions,* political and social 人間の政治及び社会制度. ¶***individual** institutions* 個人の機関 ¶an ***invaluable** institution* きわめて貴重な制度. ¶***kindred** institutions* in Europe 欧州における同種の団体. ¶Poultry raising is not a ***modern** institution.* 家禽(かきん)飼養は近代に始まったことではない. ¶Who's Who is a ***national** institution.* 紳士録は国家的刊行物である. ¶The newspaper is a ***necessary modern** institution.* 新聞は近代の必要な機関である. ¶a ***permanent** institution* 永久的な機関. ¶It began as a ***philanthropic** institution.* それはもともと慈善機関であった. ¶***private** institutions* 私立の団体. ¶***public** institutions* 公共団体. ¶The "Boy Scouts" are now a ***recognized** institution* in the land. ボーイ・スカウトは今日ではこの国において一般から認められている制度である. ¶The library is a ***reputable** institution.* その図書館は評判が良い. ¶Marriage is a ***sacred** institution.* 結婚は神聖な制度である. ¶a ***self-maintaining** institution* (収支償う)自活の団体. ¶lodgings in private, club and ***semi-private** institutions* しろうと家・クラブ及び半しろうと家における宿泊. ¶plant a ***similar** institution* in England イギリスに同様な公共団体を設ける. ¶school as a ***social** institution* 社会的機関としての学校. ¶a ***state-protected** institution* 国家の保護する制度. ¶***state-supported** institutions* of higher learning 国立高等教育機関. ¶***time-honored** institution* of the Senior Wranglership 昔から伝わっている(ケンブリッジ大学の)数学一級及第資格制度. ¶such ***trade-promoting** institutions* as the chamber of commerce and industry and the commercial museum 商工会議所及び商品陳列館のごとき商業奨励機関. ¶*Seppuku* is a ***unique** institution* in the history of nations. 切腹は世界史上独特な習慣である. ¶***venerable** institutions* 古い歴史のある諸団体.
Q² New York's ***amusement** institutions* seat over 1,000,-000. ニューヨークの娯楽場には百万以上の座席がある. ¶a ***banking** institution* (=establishment) 金融機関. ¶a ***business** institution* 商業設立物(銀行・会社). ¶***Carnegie** Institution* カーネギー財団 (Andrew Carnegie が 1902 年に創設したもの). ¶a ***charity** institution* 慈善団体. ¶***city** institutions* 市の諸機関. ¶a ***correction** institution* 感化院. ¶the abolition of the ***family** institution* 家族制度の廃止. ¶***Government** institutions.* 諸官庁. ¶a ***parent** institution* 母体. ¶a ***teacher-training** institution* 師範学校. ¶a ***teaching** institution* 学校. ¶the ***Tenno** institution* 天皇制.
P² a charitable *institution **for*** the education of young children 児童教育の慈善団体. ¶an *institution **of*** secondary or higher education 中等または高等教育の学校 ‖ the celebration of the fiftieth anniversary of the *institution **of*** the Japanese post and telegraph service 日本郵便電信事務創設の五十年記念祝賀 ‖ they favored the *institution **of*** a savings bank at ... 彼らは...における貯蓄銀行の創設を支持した ‖ *institution **of*** public action 〘法〙 公訴提起.

instruct, *v*. 教授する, 教育する, 指図する.
M unless ***otherwise** instructed* 別に指令を受けていなければ.
P *instruct* a class ***by*** lecturing 講義によって教授する. ¶*instruct* students ***in*** botany 学生に植物学を教える. 【類】*instruct* a class ***in*** history ‖ *instruct* students ***in*** English 学生に英語を教える.

instruction, *n*. (**1**) 教授; 教訓.
V ***attend** instruction* (=school) 学校に出席する. ¶***broaden*** technical *instruction* 工業教育を拡張する. ¶***combine** instruction* with amusement 教授と娯楽を結び付ける. ¶***derive*** much *instruction* from ... ...によって大いに啓発される所がある. ¶***draw** instruction* from ... ...によって教えられる所がある. ¶*instruction* directly ***enjoyed*** in his laboratory and the class-rooms of the professor その教授の研究室並に教場で親しく受けた授業. ¶***gain** instruction* on such subject こうした題目について教えを受ける. ¶***give*** musical *instruction* to ... ...に音楽を教授する. 【類】*instruction* ***given*** both personally and by the post (通信で) / *Instruction* is ***given*** in English. ¶He has ***had*** very little formal *instruction.* 彼は正式の教育をほとんど受けなかった. ¶***impart** instruction* 教授する. ¶self-educators unable to ***obtain*** viva voce *instruction* 教師から口頭で教授を受けることができない独学者. ¶the school ***offers** instruction* in ... その学校は...の教育を授ける. ¶Japan ***owed*** its first *instruction* in it to British officers. 日本はそれを最初に英国士官から習った. ¶A university should ***provide** instruction* in the Fine Arts. 大学は美術の教授をなすべきである. ¶***receive** instruction* in drawing from ... ...から図画の教授を受ける ‖ ***receive*** some *instruction* as to ... ...について少し教授を受ける. ¶***seek** instruction* in music 音楽の授業を求める. 【類】Kobo Daishi visited China in 804 A.D. to ***seek** instruction* in Buddhist mysteries (奥義). ¶*Instruction* was ***suspended*** for some time owing to the strike of teachers. 教師罷業のためしばらく休校した. ¶***take*** one's *instruction* 教授を受ける. ¶***transmit** instruction* 教えを伝える. ¶he is ***undergoing*** *instruction* from ... 彼は...から教えを受けている.
V² the *instruction **includes*** ... 教授学課は...を含む.
Q give ***advanced** instruction* in ... ...の高等知識を授ける. ¶***all-round** instruction* 一般にわたる授業. ¶***clinical** instruction* 臨床教授. ¶receive ***collegiate** instruction* at ... ...で大学教育を受ける. ¶ten to fifteenth years of ***fruitful** instruction* 十年ないし十五年にわたる有効な教授. ¶***military** instruction* 軍事教育. ¶seek ***personal** instruction* from ... ...から親しく教授を仰ぐ. ¶***practical** instruction* in home-building and mother-craft 家政及び母性の実際教育. ¶***printed** instructions* 印刷した説明書. ¶I believe in ***sane*** and ***wholesome sex** instruction* to the rising generation. 私は青年男女に健全な性教育を施すことが良いと信じる. ¶***Sound** instruction* in English is the best foundation for successful study of other languages. 英語を完全に学ぶことは他の国語をりっぱに修得する最善の基礎である. ¶***theoretical** instruction* in ... ...の理論的教授. ¶Dr. Clyde Fisher, curator of ***visual** instruction* and director of astronomy, the American Museum of National History, New York City ニューヨーク市米国博物館の実物教授監督者並に天文学の指導者たるクライド・フィッシャー博士. ¶practical ***vocational** instruction* 実用的職業教育. ¶Such knowledge cannot be conveyed by ***written** instruction.* かかる知識は文字では授けられない.
Q² ***broadcast** instruction* 放送による教授. ¶***class-room*** *instruction* 教室授業. ¶***group** instruction* 集団授業. ¶***mail** instruction* 通信教育. ¶***mass** instruction* 大量授業(大きなクラス等での). ¶***night** instruction* 夜学. ¶***science** instruction* 科学教授.
P Carlyle says, "Often I have found a portrait superior ***in*** *instruction* to half a dozen written biographies." カーライルいわく「余は一枚の肖像画の教える所数冊の伝記にまさる場合あるを知れり」と. ¶There over 300 pupils are ***under*** *instruction.* その学校では三百人以上の生徒が教授を受けている. ¶***without*** *instruction* 教わらないで.
P² *instruction **by*** lecturing 講義による教授. ¶*instruction **in*** essay-writing 論文作法教授. 【類】*instruction **in*** dancing (written English) ‖ receive *instruction **in*** rudiments

手ほどきをされる.

(2) *pl.* 指図, 注意, 訓示; 用法.

V *await instructions* 指図を待つ. ¶*carry out* his *instructions* carefully and loyally 細心にまた忠実に彼の言付を実行する. ¶*cancel instructions* 指図を取消す. ¶His *instructions* were *carried out.* 彼の指図を実行した. ¶*esteem* one's kind *instructions* その親切な指図を尊重する. ¶*follow instructions* 指図に従う. 【類】Failure is impossible if the *instructions* given are carefully *followed.* ¶I resolved to *follow out* the teacher's *instructions* to the letter. 私は先生の注意を厳守しようと決心した. ¶*give instructions* 指図を与える. ¶*issue instructions* in that effect その意味の訓令を発する ‖ *instructions issued* by ... relative to ... …に関して…の発した訓令. ¶the deceased *left* express *instructions* to ... 故人は特に…という遺言をした. ¶*observe instructions* 訓示を守る. ¶*See instructions* on reverse side. 裏面の用法を御覧下さい. ¶*shout instructions* 大声で指図する. ¶*take instructions* 指図を受ける. ¶*violate instructions* 言付にそむく. ¶*wire instructions* to ... …に訓電を発する.

V² *instructions governing* ... …に関する訓示.

Q follow the *above instructions* 上の指図を守る. ¶*detailed instructions* as to ... …について詳細な指図. ¶give *explicit instructions* on this point この点について明白な指図を与える. ¶have *full instructions* regarding ... …に関して詳細な指図を受けている. ¶receive *fresh instructions* さらに指図を受ける. ¶wait until *further instructions* さらに指令のあるまで待つ. 【類】await *further instructions.* ¶*general instructions* 一般的注意事項. ¶*minute instructions* on ... …に関する詳細な指示. ¶*oral instructions* 口頭の指図. ¶issue *rigorous instructions* 厳命を下す. ¶*routine instructions* きまりきった指図. ¶give *special instructions* to ... …に特別の指令を授ける ‖ except under *special instructions* 特に注意を受けている場合の外は. ¶*specific instructions* 特別の指図. ¶issue *written instructions* 文書の指令を発する.

Q² *forwarding instructions* [注文の品]発送上の指図. ¶under *Moscow instructions* モスコー指令の下に. ¶*packing* and *shipping instructions* 荷作り並びに積出の指図. ¶*renewal instructions* 継続通知(雑誌購読など).

P *on* your *instructions* 貴下の指図で. ¶act *under instructions* from ... …の指図通り行動する ‖ protest, *under instructions* from ..., against ... …の訓令で…に抗議する. ¶stop selling *until* further *instructions* 再命のあるまで販売を停止する.

P² *instructions as to* (=*concerning*) ... …についての指図. ¶*instructions for* use 使用上の注意 ‖ issue *instructions for* the release of the prisoner その囚人を釈放する指令を出す. ¶by *instructions from* one's Government 政府の指令により. ¶*instructions to* voters 投票者への注意.

instructor, *n.* 教授者, 教師.

Q an *able* and *experienced instructor* 有能にして経験ある教授者. ¶a *foreign instructor* in English 英語の外人教師.

Q² a *foreign language instructor* 外国語教師. ¶a *gymnastic instructor* 体操教師. ¶a *part-time instructor* 時間給の教師. ¶a *swimming* (*football*) *instructor* (=coach) 水泳(しゅう球)教師. ¶a *sword instructor* 剣道師範. ¶a *trade instructor* 手の職を練習する人.

P *under* good *instructors* 適当なる教師の(指導の)下に.

P² *instructor in* chemistry at Dartmouth College ダートマス大学の化学教授. 【類】A.H. Feller, *instructor in* International Law, Harvard Law School. / He is my *instructor in* music.

instructorship, *n.* 教師の職.

V *take* an *instructorship* in mathematics 数学教師の職につく.

instrument, *n.* 器械, 器具, 道具; 方便, 媒介; 人の手先; 「証券; 楽器.

V *discard* the *instrument* その器具を廃物にする. ¶*install instruments* 器具を備付ける. ¶I cannot *play* any *instrument.* 私は何も楽器の演奏ができない. ¶*turn out* (=*produce*) an *instrument* 器具を製作する.

Q an *admirable instrument* of culture 修養のりっぱな手段. ¶Reading is one of the *chief instruments* of study. 読書は勉学の主な手段の一つである. ¶a *clocklike instrument* 時計式な器具. ¶be made a *convenient instrument* by ... …に道具に使われる. ¶the knowledge of English as a *cultural instrument* 修養の手段としての英語の知識. ¶a rather *dangerous instrument* of intellectual training やや危険な知的訓練法. ¶a *delicate instrument* 精巧な器械. ¶the value of the novel as an *educational instrument* 教育手段としての小説の価値. ¶The United Nations is an *effective instrument* for maintenance of peace. 国際連合は平和維持への有効な機関である. ¶a precision *mechanical instrument* 精密器具. ¶play on *musical instruments* 楽器を奏する. ¶*negotiable instruments* 流通証券. ¶The Greek language is deemed by many as the most *perfect instrument* of expression that mankind has ever known. ギリシア語は多くの人によってかつて人類に知られた最も完全な意志発表の媒介物であると考えられている. ¶Is every newspaper published in Japan used as a *political instrument?* 日本の新聞は皆政党の機関紙ですか. ¶a *second instrument* of communication 第二の通信機関.

Q² a *boring instrument* 穴明け器. ¶a *brass instrument* 管楽器. ¶a *cutting instrument* 切断器. ¶a *fire control instrument* 防火器. ¶underwrite the U.N. as an international *peace-keeping instrument* 国際連合を国際平和保持の機関として推薦する. ¶*orchestra instruments* オーケストラの諸楽器. ¶a *percussion instrument* 打音楽器. ¶a *precision instrument* 精密器具. ¶a *radiation checking instrument* 放射能測定器. ¶a *string instrument* 弦楽器. ¶a *wind instrument* 風力測定器. ¶a *writing instrument* 筆記器具(万年筆など).

P the renunciation of war *as* an *instrument* of national policy 国策遂行の手段としての戦争放棄.

P² an *instrument for* the formation of character 品性陶やの一手段. ¶he was an *instrument in* the introduction of ... 彼は…輸入の媒介者であった. ¶*instruments of* production 生産機関 ‖ an *instrument of* torture 責道具 ‖ use the Conference as an *instrument of* co-operative study その会議を協力研究の機関とする.

instrumental, *a.* 手段となる, 助けとなる, 役に立つ, あずかって力ある.

M He was *chiefly instrumental* in introducing Shakespeare to the Japanese public. 彼はシェークスピアを日本の一般公衆に紹介するにあずかって力があった. ¶*mainly instrumental* in ... 主として…にあずかって力ある.

P *instrumental in* carrying a business to good order. 【類】He was *instrumental in* my finding work. / Commodore Perry, who first visited these shores in command of the American fleet in 1854, was *instrumental in* opening Japan to foreign intercourse.

instrumentality, *n.* 助け, 手段, 道具.

V *use* every *instrumentality* at its disposal to investigate these charges. その機関を総動員してこれらの非難を取調べる.

P in a great degree *through* his *instrumentality* 主として彼の力をかりて. 【類】*through* the kind *instrumentality* of ... ‖ shall be effected *through* the *instrumentality* of ... …によりこれをなすべきものとす.

insubordinate, *a.* 不従順な, 服しない.

P *insubordinate to* one's superiors 長上に不従順の.

insubstantial, *a.* もろい; 非現実的な.

M A cobweb is *very insubstantial.* くもの巣は弱々しい.

P The plan is *insubstantial from* any point of view. その案はどう見ても現実的ではない.

insufficiency, *n.* 不足, 不十分, 不適当.

Q the *miserable insufficiency* of the system of examination 試験制度のはなはだしい欠陥.

insufficient, *a.* 不足な, 不十分な.

M *wretchedly insufficient* in salaries 俸給が気の毒なほど少ない.

insularity, *n.* 島国根性, 狭量.

V *have* one's *insularity reformed* 狭量を矯正してもらう.

insulation, *n.* 絶縁物.

V Rats *eat away* the *insulation* from wires and so cause fires. ねずみが電線の絶縁物をかじって火事を出す.

insulator, *n.* 〖電〗絶縁器.

Q² a *globe insulator* 球形がい子.

insult, *n.* 侮辱, 無礼.

V This is very much like *adding insult* to injury. これは踏んだりけったりするようなものだ. ¶*avenge* the *insult* 侮辱された恨みを晴らす. ¶I cannot *bear* the *insult* any longer. もうこの侮辱は我慢できない. ¶*bray forth insults* さん

ざんば倒する．¶He would not ***brook*** an *insult* from any one. 彼はだれからの侮辱でも甘受しなかった．¶***heap*** *insults* upon him 彼に数々の侮辱を加える． ¶it ***implies*** an *insult* to the understanding and the talents of ... それは…の理解力及び才能を暗に侮辱することになる．¶***level*** *insults* at ... …に侮辱を加える．¶***offer*** one an *insult* 人に侮辱を加える．¶***pocket*** (=***swallow***) an *insult* 侮辱を忍ぶ．¶***revenge*** an *insult* 侮辱を受けた恨を晴らす．¶***shower*** *insults* upon one's name めちゃめちゃにその名誉を傷つける．¶***suffer*** these *insults* in silence これらの侮辱を無言で忍ぶ．

Q indulge in ***calumnious*** and ***vulgar*** *insults* 悪口非難をほしいままにする． ¶a ***deadly*** *insult* 猛烈な侮辱． ¶a ***deliberate*** (=an ***intentional***) *insult* 故意の侮辱． ¶a ***gratuitous*** *insult* 理由なしに受けた侮辱． ¶consider it a ***gross*** *insult* それを大なる侮辱と考える． ¶He was subjected to ***humiliating*** *insults.* 彼は赤恥をかいた．¶a ***public*** *insult* 公然の侮辱． ¶***scurrilous*** *insult* 口ぎたない侮辱． ¶a ***studied*** *insult* 念の入った侮辱．¶***unpardonable*** *insult* 許し難い侮辱． ¶a ***wanton*** *insult* 無茶な侮辱．

P enraged ***at*** the *insult* 侮辱を憤慨して．

P[2] an *insult* ***to*** his intelligence 彼の知能に対する侮辱．【類】it is an *insult* ***to*** an intelligent child to tell him that ... / an *insult* ***to*** the intelligence of the nation / It is an *insult* ***to*** an audience made up of cultured people.

insult, *v.* 侮辱する．

P *insult* ... ***by*** language …を言葉で侮辱する． 【類】The enemy *insulted* the flag ***by*** throwing mud at it.

insupportable, *a.* たえられない．

P *insupportable* ***to*** me 私にはたえられない．

insurance, *n.* 保険, 保険料, 保険契約．

V *Insurance* is not ***accepted*** against war risks in those waters. その近海の戦時損害に対しては保険契約には応じない． ¶he ***carries*** a life *insurance* amounting to ... 彼には契約高…の生命保険が付いている． ¶***contract*** *insurance* with laborers 労働者と保険を契約する． ¶***effect*** a life *insurance* 生命保険をつける． 【類】***effect*** a new *insurance* / *insurances* ***effected*** in seventy-two offices. ¶They ***gave*** an *insurance* upon his life. 彼らは彼に生命保険を付けた．¶set fire to the house to ***obtain*** the *insurance* 保険金を取るために家に放火する． ¶***pay*** the *insurance* upon one's life 生命保険金を支払う．¶***receive*** a large *insurance* for a house burnt 家の焼失のために多額の保険金を受取る．¶***take out*** marine *insurance* through American insurance firms 米国保険会社に海上保険を付ける．

V[2] Fire *insurance* ***covered*** the property damage. その焼けた家財には火災保険が付いていた．¶The *insurance* on it ***ran out*** three weeks before the fire. その保険契約は火事の三週間前に切れていた．

Q[2] ***accident*** *insurance* 傷害保険． ¶***burglary*** *insurance* 盗難保険． ¶***casualty*** *insurance* 傷害保険． ¶a satisfactory ***crop*** *insurance* 好収穫保険． ¶***endowment*** *insurance* 養老保険．¶***fidelity*** *insurance* 信用保険．¶***fire*** *insurance* 火災保険．¶***health*** *insurance* 健康保険．¶***life*** *insurance* 生命保険． ¶***marine*** *insurance* on American property placed with companies outside the United States 合衆国以外の会社と契約した米国人の財産に対する海上保険． ¶***post-office life*** *insurance* 簡易生命保険． ¶***State*** *insurance* against illness or unemployment 病気または失業に対する国家保険． ¶***theft*** *insurance* 盗難保険．¶***transport*** *insurance* 運輸保険． ¶***unemployment*** *insurance* 失業保険．

P partly covered ***by*** *insurance* 一部保険が掛けてある．¶*insurance* ***against*** railway accident and loss of baggage 鉄道事故お及荷物損失に対する保険． ¶About 20,000 yen of the damage was covered ***by*** *insurance.* 損害高の中約二万円は保険が付けてあった．

P[2] an *insurance* ***of*** 1,000,000 yen on his life 百万円の彼の生命保険． ¶*insurance* ***on*** ships and merchandise 船舶商品に対する保険．【類】Mr. Rodman Wanamaker of Philadelphia is the most heavily insured man in the world, carrying $4,000,000 *insurance* ***on*** his life. / *insurance* ***on*** lives (houses, goods) / the *insurances* ***on*** the two damaged buildings amount to ...

insure, *v.* 保険をつける, 保証する．

M The goods are ***fully*** *insured.* 品物は十分に保険がついている． ¶He is ***heavily*** *insured* against death. 彼は巨額の生命保険を付けている． ¶*insure* ***provisionally*** 仮保険を付ける． ¶It is ***wholly*** (***partly***) *insured* with companies. 会社に全部(一部)保険がつけてある．

P be insured ***against*** loss (damage, injury, death, theft, fire) 損失(など)に対して保険を付けてある ‖ *insure* its premises ***against*** fire その家屋に火災保険を付ける．【類】The traveller is *insured* ***against*** accident. / cargoes *insured* ***against*** loss at sea / At what rate can you *insure* ***against*** all risks (一切の危険)? ¶The premises are *insured* ***among*** 28 different companies for a total sum of 15 million francs. その建物は二十八会社に総計一千五百万フランの保険を付けてある． ¶*insure* ***at*** a low premium 安い掛金で保険を付ける． ¶How much was the house *insured* ***for***? その家にはどれだけの保険が付けてあったか．【類】My house is *insured* ***for*** two-thirds of its value. ¶*insured* ***in*** that [insurance] company その会社に保険契約をして．¶*insured* ***on*** a valuation of $... 価格…ドルの保険を付けて．¶be *insured* ***with*** a local company その土地の会社と保険契約がしてある．

insurrection, *n.* 反乱, 暴動, 一揆(き)．

V ***lead*** an *insurrection* 暴動の首領となる． ¶***put down*** an *insurrection* 一揆を静める． ¶***raise*** an *insurrection* of the peasants 百姓一揆を起す．「を起した．

Q They burst out into ***open*** *insurrection.* 彼らは公然暴動

insusceptible, *a.* 感じのない, 無感覚の．

P *insusceptible* ***to*** pain 苦痛を感じない．

intact, *a.* そっくりそのままの．

P The plane was left *intact* ***after*** the crash. 同機は墜落後そのままにしてある．

intake, *n.* 吸込み(摂取)量; [収入の]上り高．

Q the daily ***caloric*** *intake* of the average citizen 平均市民の日々カロリー摂取量．

Q[2] a big ***box-office*** *intake* 〚劇場〛大した切符の上り高．¶lift the ***food*** *intake* of millions of people above the starvation level 数百万人の食物摂取量を飢餓線以上に高める．¶the ***per capita*** caloric *intake*＝the intake of calories per person 一人当りカロリーの摂取．

integration, *n.* 統合．

Q ***racial*** *integration* 人種の統合(特に黒・白人間の)．

P[2] the *integration* ***of*** races＝racial integration.

O *Integration* or segregation is a big problem in the South. [黒・白の]統合か分離かは南部の大問題である．

integrity, *n.* 完全, 保全; 正直, 清廉．

V ***defend*** the *integrity* of a country 一国の独立保全を守る． ¶***impugn*** the *integrity* of the officials concerned 不正行為に対して関係役員を弾劾する． ¶***maintain*** China's territorial *integrity* 中国の領土保全を維持する．¶***preserve*** the *integrity* of China 中国の保全を計る． ¶***threaten*** the *integrity* of a state 国の保全を脅かす(独立国たるの面目を失わせるおそれがある)．

Q a man of the ***cleanest*** *integrity* 最も清廉な人． ¶lack of ***commercial*** *integrity* 商業道徳の欠如． ¶a strong sense of ***moral*** and ***social*** *integrity* 道徳及び社会正義の強い意識． ¶***political*** *integrity* 政治上の廉直． ¶customs preserved in ***primitive*** *integrity* 原始的な純真さをもって保存された風俗． ¶the preservation of the ***territorial*** *integrity* of China 中国の領土保全．

P adopt it ***in*** its *integrity* そっくりそのまま採用する．¶***with*** *integrity* and grit, and intelligence and the fear of God 誠実勇気知慮と敬神の心をもって． ¶a man ***of*** *integrity* 廉直の士．

intellect, *n.* 知, 知力, 知能．

V ***blunt*** the *intellect* 知力を鈍らす．¶***broaden*** one's *intellect* 知識を広める．¶The *intellect* is not ***clouded.*** 気は確かだ． ¶***cramp*** one's *intellect* 知能の働きを妨げる．¶***distrust*** his *intellect* and morality 彼の知能と品行を信用しない．¶***feed*** one's *intellect* upon the great masters of human thought 偉大な思想家の著書を学んで自己の知力を養う．¶***sharpen*** the *intellect* 知能をみがく． ¶***train*** the *intellect* 知能を練磨する．

Q a man of ***brilliant*** *intellect* さん然たる知能の人．¶with ***clear*** *intellect* 明せきな知力のある．¶a man of ***colossal*** *intellect* 鬼才．¶***keen*** *intellect* 鋭い英知． ¶Ambitious ***provincial*** *intellects* are ever attracted to the national capital. 大望のある地方の英才はいつも国都に引付けられる．¶the ***quicker*** *intellects* けい敏な人． ¶the ***slower*** *intellects* 知能の遅鈍な人．

P barren ***in*** *intellect* 知的に貧弱な ‖ gigantic ***in*** *intellect*

知力の非常にすぐれた. ¶a man *of intellect* 知者.

intellectual, *n.* そう明な人, 知者, 識者.

Q *bright young intellectuals* 若い秀才. ¶*political intellectuals* 政界の知識人.

intelligence, *n.* (1) 知識, 見聞; 通信, 情報.

V the latest mail *brought intelligence* of ... 最近の郵便船が…の報告をもたらした. ¶*collect* trade *intelligence* abroad 海外の商況を収集する. ¶A contemporary has attacked the paper for *disseminating* false *intelligence*. 同業の新聞がその新聞が虚報を伝えることを攻撃した. ¶This *intelligence* is *given* by the Times. この報道はタイムスが伝えた. ¶*pick up* their *intelligence* on the subject その問題に関して彼らの見聞を広める. ¶*receive .intelligence* of the event at ... …でその事件の報道を受ける.

Q *accurate intelligence* 正確な報道. ¶*authoritative intelligence* 信頼すべき報知. ¶*circumstantial intelligence* 詳細の情報. ¶*false intelligence* 誤報. ¶*market intelligence* 市況. ¶*recent intelligence* from ... reports ... …からの最近の情報によると…とのことである. ¶have *secret intelligence* of the enemy's plans 敵の計画の秘密の情報を入手している. ¶*unbiased intelligence* 公平な報道.

Q² *market intelligence* 市況.

P² *intelligence from* ... relates that ... …からの報道が…と伝えている.

(2) 知能, 理知.

V *bring* one's *intelligence* to bear upon household duties (=housekeeping) その知能を家庭の仕事に働かす. ¶*increase intelligence* 知能を増す. ¶I will not *insult* the *intelligence* of the reader by explaining the moral of my story. 私は賢明な読者諸君に対し私の物語の教訓を説明するようなことは致しません. ¶*measure intelligence* 知能を測定する. ¶*task* the *intelligence* of thinking men 思想家の頭を悩ます.

Q a man with *average intelligence* 普通の知能のある人. 【類】obvious to *average intelligence*. ¶acutely *critical intelligence* 鋭く批評的な知能. ¶restitution of *decayed intelligence* 衰えた知力の回復. ¶*far-seeing intelligence* 先見の明. ¶a person of *high intelligence* 高(低)い知能の人. ¶have a *keen intelligence* 鋭い知能を持つ. ¶a boy who shows very *little intelligence* 知力の著しく低い少年. ¶At school he displayed a *mediocre intelligence*. 学校では彼は凡庸な才を示した. ¶a woman of *much intelligence* 理知のすぐれた女. ¶Anybody with *ordinary intelligence* and no special training can fill the position. 普通の知能があれば特別の訓練のない人でもその地位につける. ¶insult *public intelligence* 公衆の知能を侮辱する(大衆を愚ろうする). ¶*puny intelligence* 薄弱な知能. ¶guidance of some *supervising intelligence* ある監督者の分別ある指導.

P persons defective *in intelligence* 理知を欠いている人々. ¶a person *of* ordinary *intelligence* 普通の知能の人. ¶*with* ordinary *intelligence* 普通の才能のある.

intelligent, *a.* 知性のある.

M a *decidedly intelligent* woman 知性に富んだ婦人.

O She looks *intelligent*. 彼女は利口そうだ.

intelligentsia, *n.* 知識階級.

P *among* the *intelligentsia* 知識階級の間に.

intelligible, *a.* わかりやすい.

P *intelligible to* the initiated 初心者にもわかりやすい.

intemperance, *n.* 不節制.

P² *intemperance in* eating or drinking 飲食上の不節制.

intend, *v.* 欲する, 志す; 図る, もくろむ.

M *mainly intended* as ... 主に…を意図した. ¶as *originally intended* 最初の計画通り. 【類】All other conditions must remain as *originally intended*. ¶as if *intended otherwise* それとなく. ¶*primarily intended* for ... 主として…を目的とした. ¶as if not *so intended* それとなしに.

P This is not *intended as* a pleasantry. これは冗談ではない. ¶*intended by* Providence as a compensation to ... …に対する埋合わせとして神が作られた. ¶a record of a journey whether *intended for* publication or merely as a memorandum 出版のためあるいは単に備忘のための旅行の記録 ‖ *intended for* the career of a merchant 商人にしようとした. 【類】Father *intended* me *for* a soldier. ‖ His remark was *intended for* me. 彼の言葉は私に向って吐いたものであった.

O The building was *intended* (=designed) to be a museum. その建物は博物館にする計画であった. ¶*intend* going to ... …に行く積りである.

intended, *n.* 《口語》婚約者(男・女とも).

P May I present you *to* my *intended*? 私の婚約者に紹介しようか.

O She is my *intended*. 彼女は私の婚約者だ.

intensity, *n.* 強度; 熱烈.

V *gather intensity* 熱烈さを増す. ¶*heighten* the *intensity* of effect 効果を高める.

Q There are few strong situations or moments of *dramatic intensity*. 劇的強烈さの強い場面または瞬間はほとんどない. ¶The heat continues with *increased intensity*. 暑気は引続き激しい. ‖ in view of the continually *increasing intensity* of the struggle for existence 生存競争がますます激烈になるにかんがみて. ¶with *twofold intensity* 二倍の強度をもって.

P study *with intensity* 激しく勉強する.

P² *intensity of* illumination 照度.

intent, *n.* 意志, 意向; 計画.

Q with the *avowed intent* to ... …しようとの断固たる決心をもって. ¶with *burglarious intent* 夜盗の目的で. ¶with the *deliberate, purposeful intent* of ... 計略的に…しようとする目的で. ¶with *felonious intent* 犯意を持って. ¶with *good* (*malicious*) *intent* 善(悪)意で. ¶from *suicidal intent* 自殺する考えで. ¶*true intent* and real meaning of ... …の本当の意志と真実の意義.

P He was *to* all *intents* and purposes boycotted. 彼はつまりボイコットされたのだ. ¶*with intent* to do grievous bodily harm 恐ろしい肉体上の危害を加えようとの意志で. 【類】*with intent* to cheat another.

intent, *a.* 熱心な, 専心な, 余念のない.

M *deeply intent* on a problem ある問題に専心して.

P *intent on* carrying out the mighty work of reconstruction 復興の大事業を実行しようとの熱意に燃えて. 【類】be *intent on* (=upon) learning French. ¶*intent upon* a book entirely oblivious of his surroundings 自分の周囲を全く忘れて本に読みふけって. 【類】*intent upon* (=on) working at one's typewriter.

intention, *n.* 意志, 意向, 目的, 趣旨.

V I definitely *abandoned* my *intention* of ...ing 私は…しようという意志を断然放棄した. ¶*accomplish* one's *intention* 所思を遂行する. ¶*announce* one's *intention* of ...ing ... …しようという意志を発表する. ¶He did not *carry out* his *intention*. 彼はその志を実行しなかった. ¶*change* one's *intention* その意向を変える. ¶*cherish* an *intention* of ... …の志をいだく. ¶carefully *concealing* the *intention* of ... …を気どられないように十分注意して. ¶*declare* one's firm *intention* to ... …しようとする確固たる意志を宣言する. ¶Ineffective means often *defeat* the best *intentions*. 手段が効果的でないとしばしば最善の計画も失敗に終る. ¶to begin with, let me *disclaim* any *intention* of ...ing ... 第一に私は…しようという意志のないことを言明する. ¶*disclose* one's *intention* to ... …しようとの意中を発表する. ¶*disguise* one's *intention* 意志を見せない. 【類】*disguise* one's mean *intention* (卑しい考え). ¶*express* one's *intention* of standing as a candidate for ... …議員立候補の意志を発表する. ¶*form* the *intention* to ... …しようという意志を起す. 【類】*form* a secret *intention* to ... ¶I doubt whether he *has* any *intention* of ... 少しでも…しようという意志を彼が持っているかどうか私は疑う. 【類】Germany *had* no *intention* of violating our neutrality. ¶he has *intimated* his *intention* of ...ing 彼は…しようという意志を示した. ¶the government has *made known* its *intention* shortly to ... 政府は近々…しようとする意志を発表した. ¶clearly *reveal* one's *intentions* その意志を明白にもらす. ¶*signify* one's *intention* of ...ing ... …しようという意志を表わす. 【類】He *signified* his *intention* to be present at the meeting. / His Majesty was graciously pleased to *signify* his *intention* to ...

Q With the *best intentions*, he has gone the wrong way to work. その志は良とすべきだが彼はそのとるべき途を誤った. ¶a *bona-fide intention* 誠意. ¶by *deliberate intention* 故意に. ¶fulfil one's *ever-present intention* その素志を貫く. ¶by his *express intention* 特に彼の意志により. ¶with very *good intention* はなはだ善意に. ¶abandon one's *hastily formed intention* その急速に立てた目的を放

棄する. ¶His *intentions* are ***honorable***. 彼の志はりっぱだ. ¶Many thanks for your ***kind*** *intentions*. 色々御親切ありがとうございます. ¶Teaching was my ***original*** *intention*. 教師となることが私の始めの考えでした. ¶***peaceable*** *intentions* おだやかな考え. ¶***praiseworthy*** *intention* 奇特な意図. ¶***sincere*** *intention* 誠意あること. ¶we have not the ***slightest*** *intention* on our part to ... われわれには...しようという考えは毛頭ない. ¶each try to fathom the ***unexpressed*** *intention* of the other お互に腹の探り合いをする. ¶***warlike*** *intention* 戦闘意志.

P an act good ***in*** *intention* 志は良しとすべき行為. ¶***with*** the *intention* of doing ... ...をする積りで ‖ inspect goods in a store ***with*** no *intention* to buy 店をひやかす. ¶***without*** the least *intention* of doing so そうしようという意志は毛頭なくて.

intentioned, *pa.* ...の意のある, たくらまれた.

M he is ***well*** ***(ill)*** *intentioned* (=disposed) towards ... 彼は...に対して好(悪)意がある. 【類】however ***well*** *intentioned* it may be.

inter, *v.* 埋葬する, 葬る.

P The body was *interred* ***at*** ... Cemetery. その遺骸は...墓地に葬られた. ¶The baby was *interred* ***with*** his mother. その赤ん坊は母とともに埋葬された.

interact, *v.* 相互に作用する.

P *interact* ***on*** each other 相互に作用し合う.

interaction, *n.* 相互作用.

Q in ***complete*** *interaction* with ... ...と完全な連絡を保って.

intercede, *v.* 仲裁する, 仲にはいる.

P *intercede* ***for*** a person 人のために仲裁する ‖ *intercede* ***for*** his life 彼の命ごいをする. ¶*intercede* ***with*** a person on behalf of ... ...のために人に対して仲裁する ‖ *intercede* ***with*** Christ [牧師が信者を]キリストにとりなす. 【類】*intercede* ***with*** a person ***for*** a pardon.

intercept, *v.* 妨害する, 止める.

P *intercept* a radio message ***at*** ... ...で無電通信を傍受する. ¶*intercept* a stream ***between*** ... and ... ...と...との間で流れを止める. ¶*intercept* light ***from*** ... ...から光線をさえぎる.

interception, *n.* 妨害; 傍受.

P[2] the *interception* ***of*** communications 通信の妨害. 【類】the *interception* ***of*** radio communications (無電通信).

interceptor, *n.* 妨害者; 迎撃機.

V ***fly*** *interceptors* against enemy raiders. 敵機来襲に対して迎撃機をくり出す.

Q[2] a ***radio*** *interceptor* 放送傍受者.

intercession, *n.* 仲裁, 調停, とり成し.

Q His *intercession* was ***successful***. 彼の仲裁は成功した.

P his life was spared ***on*** *intercession* of ... ...の仲裁で彼の命は助かった. ¶***through*** his *intercession* 彼の調停で.

P[2] an *intercession* ***for*** rain 雨ごい.

interchange, *n.* 交換, 交易, 交代.

V ***encourage*** a fraternal *interchange* of ideas 思想の隔意なき交換を奨励する. ¶***facilitate*** the *interchange* of views between ... and ... ...間の意見交換に便宜を与える.

Q ***cultural*** *interchange* between the two countries 二国間文化交流. ¶encourage a ***fraternal*** *interchange* of ideas 友愛的思想の交換を奨励する. ¶***free*** *interchange* of ideas 思想の自由な交換. ¶***fruitful*** *interchange* of inspiration 有益な霊感の交換. ¶***intellectual*** *interchange* 知識の交換. ¶an ***official*** *interchange* of views 公式な意見の交換. ¶a ***personal*** *interchange* of views 個人的な意見の交換. ¶a ***pleasant*** *interchange* of courtesies 気持のよい礼儀の交換.

P ***after*** an *interchange* of civilities あいさつを取交わした後.

P[2] an *interchange* ***in*** the mental products of nations 世界国民の思想的産物の交換. ¶*interchange* ***of*** thought (personnel) 思想(人員)交換 ‖ an *interchange* ***of*** courtesies and presents 礼儀と進物の交換. ¶an *interchange* ***of*** glances ***between*** ... and ... ...と...の二人の間で互に見交わすこと.

intercommunication, *n.* 相互の交通.

P[2] a greater *intercommunication* ***of*** nation ***with*** nation 国民間のさらに親密な交通 ‖ an *intercommunication* ***of*** man with nature 人と自然の霊交.

intercourse, *n.* 交際, 交通.

V ***cultivate*** friendly *intercourse* among ... ...間の親交を計る. ¶***discontinue*** *intercourse* 絶交する. ¶***foster*** mutual *intercourse* 相互の親交を計る. ¶***have*** *intercourse* with foreign friends 外国人の友人と交際している. 【類】those who have not ***had*** much *intercourse* with him. ¶***hold*** *intercourse* with departed spirits 死者と霊交する ‖ ***hold*** human *intercourse* 交際する, 人中に出る ‖ ***hold*** *intercourse* with port (the shore) 港(など)と交通する. ¶***intercept*** the *intercourse* between ... and ... ...間の交通を禁止する. ¶***open*** *intercourse* with Japan 日本と交通を開く ‖ ***open*** a commercial *intercourse* with ... ...と商取引を開始する. ¶***preserve*** harmonious *intercourse* 親密に交際を続ける. ¶***promote*** *intercourse* beween ... and ... ...間の交際を助成する ‖ ***promote*** social *intercourse* 親交を計る. ¶***renew*** one's *intercourse* with ... ...との旧交を暖める. ¶***resume*** *intercourse* with Europe 再びヨーロッパと交通する. ¶***stimulate*** friendly *intercourse* among ... ...の間に親密な交際を奨励する.

Q have ***carnal*** *intercourse* with ... ...と関係(肉交)する. ¶expressions used in ***colloquial*** *intercourse* 口語に用いる語句. ¶the ***commercial*** *intercourse* of Japan with ... 日本と...との通商. ¶under the influence of ***continental*** *intercourse* 大陸との交渉の影響を受けて. ¶the growth of ***foreign*** *intercourse* 外国と交際の進展. ¶preserve ***harmonious*** *intercourse* 円満な交際を維持する. ¶have ***illicit*** *intercourse* with ... ...とかん通をする ‖ be charged with an ***illicit*** *intercourse* with ... ...との不義のとがをもって問われる. ¶***indirect*** *intercourse* with foreign nations 外国と間接の交際. ¶English and French are more widespread and more used in ***international*** *intercourse* than German. 英語とフランス語はドイツ語より分布が広く一層国際語として用いられている. ¶***mutual*** *intercourse* of nations 国民間相互の交際. ¶***oral*** *intercourse* with other people 他人との言葉の上の交際. ¶There is no ***particular*** *intercourse* between the two. 両者の間に特別な交際はない. ¶***personal*** *intercourse* (手紙の交際に対し)直接の交際. 【類】This led to the withdrawal of the Mikado from ***personal*** *intercourse* with his subjects. ¶***physical*** *intercourse* 肉交. ¶***psychical*** *intercourse* 精神的交際. ¶have ***sexual*** *intercourse* with ... ...と性交する. ¶Acquaintance and friendship are two degrees of ***social*** *intercourse*. 知己関係と友人関係とは社交の二段階である. ¶enter into ***spiritual*** and ***bodily*** *intercourse* with ... ...と精神的及び肉体的交渉を始める. ¶look forward to years of ***unchanged*** *intercourse* 長年にわたる変らぬ交際を期待する.

Q[2] ***everyday*** *intercourse* with one's friend 友人との毎日の交際.

P[2] *intercourse* ***among*** ... ...間の交際. ¶*intercourse* ***between*** young men and women 若い男女の交際. ¶*intercourse* ***by*** correspondence 手紙での交際. ¶cut oneself off from all *intercourse* ***with*** one's friends 友人とあらゆる関係を絶つ.

interdependence, *n.* 相互依存.

Q because of the ***delicate*** *interdependence* of credit-built finance 信用に基く財政には微妙な相互依存関係があるので.

P ***owing to*** the *interdependence* of the financial world 財界の相互依存関係で.

P[2] the *interdependence* ***of*** ecclesiastical and secular history 宗教史及び一般史の相互関係.

interdependent, *a.* 相互依存する.

M These two matters are very ***closely*** *interdependent*. これら二つのことはきわめて緊密に相依存している.

interdict, *n.* 禁止, 禁令.

V ***issue*** an *interdict* against ... ...の禁令を発する. ¶***remove*** the *interdict* 禁令を解く. ¶***withdraw*** an *interdict* 職権禁止令を撤回する(ローマ教皇の).

interdict, *v.* 禁止する, 禁制する.

M ***peremptorily*** *interdict* 厳重に禁止する.

P *interdicted* ***by*** law 法律によって禁止されて. ¶*interdicted* ***from*** acting 行動を禁止されて.

interest, *n.* (**1**) 興味, 趣味, 感興, 関心.

V The subject ***absorbs*** much *interest*. その題目は非常に興味を引く. ¶it ***acquires*** additional *interest* from the fact that ... それは...という事実のためにさらに興味を引く ‖ ***acquire*** a real *interest* 真の興味を感じる. ¶the circumstance ***adds*** special *interest* to ... この事情が...に特別の興味をそえる. ¶***allow*** *interest* at the rate of ... ...の割合で利子を付ける. ¶He will ***appreciate*** your *interest*. 彼は貴下の御厚意を有難く思うでしょう. ¶***arouse*** *interest* in travelling to Japan 日本への旅行に興味を持たせる. 【類】***arouse*** *interest* in marine topics ‖ ***arouse*** the *interest* of the audience / ***arouse*** an *interest* in the study of ... / ***arouse*** a deeper *interest* in the study of English on the part of ... / Great *interest* has been ***aroused*** throughout the country. / It has ***aroused*** a great deal of *interest*. / great *interest* has been ***aroused*** by ... ¶Some historical *interest* is ***attached*** to those streets. それらの町には歴史的興味が幾分付随している. ¶***attest*** the *interest* that is still felt in ... ...に対してなお興味を持っていることを証明する. ¶***awaken*** a world *interest* 世界の興味をよび起す. ¶this ***awoke*** the *interest* of ... これは...の関心を引いた. 【類】 this first ***awoke*** my *interest* in ... / ***awaken*** an *interest* in the problem of ... / The most remarkable result of the new method is the *interest* it ***awakens*** in the pupils. ¶***blunt*** one's *interest* in ... ...に対するその興味をにぶらす. ¶***capture*** the reader's *interest* 読者の興味を捕える. ¶And what thing in particular ***caught*** your *interest*? そしてなにが特に君の興味を喚起したか. ¶***cherish*** a special *interest* in ... ...に特別の興味を持つ. ¶The subject naturally ***claims*** our *interest* and our study. われわれがその題目に対して興味を持って研究するのも当然だ. ¶***command*** *interest* 興味を起させる. ¶***compel*** *interest* 無理に興味をおしつける. ¶***create*** a vivid *interest* and desire to travel 旅行しようという熱心な興味と願望を起させる. ¶***create*** and ***promote*** *interest* in ... ...に対する興味を喚起してこれを増進させる. ¶He ***cultivated*** this *interest* so that it developed a large part of his life work. 彼のこの興味はますます深化して遂にそれは彼の一生の仕事の大部分となった. ¶***deaden*** *interest* 興味をそぐ. ¶***deepen*** *interest* 興味を深める. ¶***develop*** an *interest* in a subject ある問題に対する興味を増進する. ¶A mother cannot ***disclaim*** *interest* in the welfare of the fruit of her womb. 母親はその子の福祉に付いて関心を持たずにはいられない. ¶***display*** much *interest* in the subject of religion 宗教の問題に大なる興味を示す. ¶***draw*** *interest* 関心をひく. ¶***engage*** the *interest* of ... ...の興味を引きつける. ¶***engender*** *interest* in study 研究に興味を生じさせる. ¶I thank you for the *interest* you ***evinced*** in that affair. あの事件に関心をお持ち下さってありがとうございます. 【類】 Great *interest* is already being ***evinced*** in the forthcoming event. ¶***evoke*** *interest* in ... ...に興味を起させる. 【類】 ***evoke*** intense *interest* / This remarkable natural phenomenon ***evoked*** much *interest*. ¶***excite*** much *interest* 評判をとる. 【類】 ***excite*** the *interest* of the public in the question / It ***excited*** immense *interest* not only in London but on the Continent. / ***excite*** most public *interest* than usual. ¶***express*** great *interest* in the scheme その計画に多大の興味を示す. ¶He ***feels*** an *interest* on these subjects. 彼はこれらの問題に興味を持つ. 【類】 continue to ***feel*** an *interest* in the subject / ***feel*** much (no) *interest* in ... / ***feel*** quite a parental *interest* in ... / ***feel*** a special *interest* in ... ¶***feign*** an *interest* 関心を持つような風を装う. ¶***find*** a fresh *interest* 新たに興味を持つ. ¶***fix*** universal *interest* and attention 広く世界の興味と注意をひきつける. ¶the reader desirous of ***following*** his *interest* further 興味を持ったのでさらにその問題を研究しようと思う読者. ¶***foster*** the *interest* of ... ...の興味を涵養する. ¶the question ***gains*** a special *interest* at the present moment, when ... その問題は...なる矢先に興味を引く. ¶***get*** an *interest* in ... ...に興味を持つ. ¶It ***gave*** him a new *interest* in life. それは人生に対する新しい興味を彼に与えた. ¶***have*** a real *interest* in ... ...に対する真の興味を持つ. ¶***hold*** the reader's *interest* 読者の興味をひきつけておく. ¶***impair*** the *interest* of ... ...の興味をそこなう. ¶***increase*** the *interest* in Japan 日本に対する興味を増大させる. ¶***induce*** *interest* 興味を持たせる. ¶***keep up*** *interest* 興味を持続する. 【類】 ***keep up*** a permanent *interest* in ... ¶***kill*** one's *interest* その興味をそぐ. ¶***kindle*** anew public *interest* in the subject その問題に新に一般の関心をそそる. ¶this ***kindled*** and ***fostered*** my *interest* in ... これが...に対する私の興味を喚起しかつそれを助長した. ¶this fact ***lends*** *interest* to ... この事実によって...興味が起ってくる. 【類】 this fact ***lends*** a special *interest* to ... ¶People are ***losing*** *interest* in it. 人々はそれに対する興味を失っている. 【類】 He ***lost*** all *interest* in life. ¶***lower*** (***heighten***) one's *interest* in ... ...に対する興味を減じる(増す). ¶Our *interest* is ***maintained*** to the end. われわれの興味は最後まで持続する(小説などの場合). ¶***make*** *interest* 乗気にならせる. ¶he is beginning to ***manifest*** (=take) an *interest* in ... 彼は...に興味を持ちかけている. 【類】 ***manifested*** a special *interest* in natural history / ***manifest*** deep *interest* / ***manifest*** much *interest* in the matter. ¶I never let my *interests* be ***narrowed*** to one thing. 私は決して私の興味を一事に局限しない. ¶***offer*** (=show) special *interest* 特に興味を示す. ¶***owe*** its *interest* to the fact that ... ...のために興味をひく. ¶***possess*** an antiquarian *interest* 古物に興味を持つ. 【類】 ***possess*** a keen *interest* in the problems of youth / It ***possesses*** little *interest* beyond that which is inevitably attached to "firsts" of anything. ¶***promote*** an *interest* in good spech 良い言葉に対する関心を増進する. ¶***quicken*** public *interest* in ... ...に一般の興味をそそる. ¶***reawaken*** *interest* in ... 再び...に興味を喚起する. ¶***receive*** added *interest* because of ... ...のために一層興味がある. ¶***rekindle*** *interest* in ... ...再び興味を持つ. ¶***relax*** one's *interest* in ... ...に対する興味を薄くする. ¶***renew*** one's *interest* in ... ...に対する興味を新たにする. ¶***retain*** one's *interst* その興味を持続する. ¶***revive*** *interest* in ... ...に対する興味を復活する. ¶***rouse*** our *interest* われわれの興味を喚起する. ¶***show*** an *interest* in poetry 詩に興味を示す ‖ Students do not ***show*** an *interest* in the subject. 学生はその問題に関心を持たない. 【類】 He has ***shown*** *interest* in the Society by requesting admittance to membership. / ***show*** little (a great) *interest* in ... ¶***stimulate*** one's *interest* in geography (Japanese travel) 地理学(など)に対する興味をそそる. 【類】 ***stimulate*** public (a world) *interest*. ¶***stir up*** *interest* in ... ...に対する興味を起させる. ¶Throughout these stirring and eventful pages the *interest* is well ***sustained***. これらの興奮的な事件を多く取扱ったページを通じて興味がよく持続されている. ¶***take*** an *interest* in ... ...に気乗りがする. 【類】 ***take*** little *interest* in ... / he has produced a work which deserves to be read by all who ***take*** an *interest* in ... / He early began to ***take*** an *interest* in public affairs. / come to ***take*** an *interest* in ... / those who ***take*** an *interest* in these problems.

V² a special *interest* ***attaches*** to it as it is ... それは...であるが故にそれに対して特に興味がある. ¶the greatest *interest* ***centred*** around ... ...が一番の呼物であった ‖ these are noteworthy, but *interest* ***centres*** in ... これらは注目に値するが...が一番注意を引く(名所など). ¶*Interest* ***diminishes***. 興味が減少する. ¶The *interest* ***dropped***. 関心が薄らいだ. ¶Our *interest* in this story never ***flagged*** for a moment. この物語に対するわれわれの興味は瞬時も決して薄らがなかった. ¶he felt ***growing*** upon him an *interest* in ... 彼は...に対する興味が段々自分にわいて来るのを感じた. ¶The *interest* in the United States in the civilization of China and Japan has ***increased*** enormously in recent years. 中国及び日本の文明に対する合衆国の興味は近年著しく増大した. ¶the *interest* of these cases ***lies*** in ... これら事件の興味は...の点にある. ¶Never has *interest* in it ***run*** so high as it does today. それに対する興味が今日ほど上昇したことはない.

Q the book has an ***abiding*** *interest* as ... その本は...であるからいつまでも興味が失せない. ¶an event of ***absorbing*** *interest* 人の心を引きつける事件 ‖ read with an ***absorbing*** *interest* 熱中して読む. ¶a question of more ***academic*** *interest* 一層学究的な問題. ¶take an ***active*** *interest* in business affairs 商売に大いに興味を持つ. ¶***acute*** *interest* 鋭い興味. ¶it gives ***additional*** *interest* to ... そのことが...に一層興味を与える. 【類】 The excellent illustrations lend ***additional*** *interest* to the article. ¶about ***all*** the *interests* of the human minds 人心を引き付けるあらゆる題目. ¶It has an ***antiquarian*** *interest* for the rising generation. それは現代青年に対して考古的な興味がある. ‖ objects of ***antiquarian*** *interest* 考古参考品. ¶***avocational*** and ***recreational*** *interest* 合の手といった気分転換の興味. ¶with ***breathless*** *interest* 固ずをのんで. 【類】 a matter of ***breathless*** *interest*. ¶***chief*** *interests* in life such as woman, money, etc. 女・金など主として人の心を引き付けるもの. ¶names of ***commanding*** *interest* 圧倒的興味ある人々の名. ¶feel ***common*** *interest* in ... ...にひとしく興味を感じる. ¶of ***compelling*** *interest* 関心を持たずにはいられない. ¶study it with a ***concentrated*** *interest* それを熱心に研究する. ¶await with ***considerable*** *interest* 非常な興味を持って

待つ. 【類】 foster a ***considerable interest*** in ... ¶those who have a ***continuous interest*** in it それに引続き興味を持つ人々. ¶take a ***cordial interest*** in ... ...に熱心な興味を持つ. ¶a matter of ***current interest*** 目下興味のある問題. ¶feel a ***deep interest*** in its welfare その幸福に深い関心を持つ ‖ take a ***deep interest*** in ... に深い興味を持つ. ¶matters of ***deep*** and ***abiding interest*** 深くかついつまでも興味を感じさせる事柄. ¶a widely ***diffused*** and ***keen interest*** 広く行きわたった強い興味. ¶feel an ***earnest interest*** in ... ...に熱心な興味を感じる. ¶there is now such ***enhanced interest*** in ... 今...に対し大分興味が高まっている. ¶stories of ***enthralling interest*** 魅惑的な興味のある物語. ¶be of more than ***ephemeral interest*** 一時的興味以上のものがある. ¶be of ***exceptional interest*** 特に興味がある. ¶It must prove of ***extraordinary interest*** to every one who reads it. それはだれでもそれを読む人には確かに非常に興味あるものに相違ない. ¶it has an almost ***fascinating interest*** for those who ... それは...という人々にはほとんど魅力的といってよい興味がある. ¶display a ***fatherly interest*** in ... 親身になって...を世話する. ¶***far-reaching interest*** 遠大な興味. ¶a subject of the greatest ***general interest*** today 今日最も一般的に興味ある題目. 【類】 There is a ***general interest*** in sports. ¶take a ***genuine interest*** in ... ...に真の興味を感じる. ¶One of his ***great intersts*** was education. 彼の大なる関心の一つは教育であった. ‖ take a ***great interest*** in pictures 絵画に大なる興味を持つ. 【類】 take a ***greater interest*** in ... / It should be of ***great interest*** at the present moment. / It cannot fail to be of the ***greatest interest***. ¶be of ***high interest*** 強い興味のあるものである. ¶a spot of ***historic interest*** 史跡. ¶a museum of rare and curious objects of ***historical interests*** connected with medicine and the allied sciences 医学及び同系の科学に関係ある珍奇な歴史的興味ある物を収蔵している博物館. ¶His activity was watched with ***hostile interest***. 彼の活動は敵意をもって注視された. ¶features of news value or ***human interest*** 報道価値のあるまたは人情的興味のある記事. 【類】 a study of deep ***human interest***. ¶of ***immense interest*** to ... ...に取って絶大な興味のある. ¶a wife's ***insufficient interest*** in the home 家庭に対する妻の不十分な関心. ¶arouse the ***intellectual interest*** of the young people 青年の知的関心を引き起す. ¶He urged the need for ***intelligent interest*** in the military forces by civilians. 彼は一般国民が軍隊に理解ある興味を持つことの必要を説いた. 【類】 It is likely to be useful to tourists who take an ***intelligent interest*** in what they see. ¶At this remark the children manifested ***intense interest***. この話を聞いて子供たちは熱心な興味を示した. ¶It aroused ***international interest*** and discussion. それは世界の興味と論議とを呼び起した. ¶be of ***inthralling interest*** われ知らず引入れられるほど興味のあるものである. ¶***intrinsic interest*** そのものの持つ人を引きつける力. ¶take a ***keen*** and ***active interest*** in ... ...に熱心にして盛んな関心を持つ. ¶He looked at it with ***kindling interest*** that grew to admiration. 彼は崇拝とまで高まった燃えるような興味を持ってそれをながめた. ¶show ***kindly interest*** 親切に世話する. ¶awaken more than a ***languid interest*** もっと活気のある興味を呼び起す. ¶The number has two or three articles of ***literary interest***. [雑誌の]その号には文学的興味のある二三の記事が載っている. 【類】 places of ***literary interest***. ¶subjects about which people feel ***little interest*** 人々がほとんど興味を感じない問題. ¶This points to a ***lively interest*** in Japan. このことは日本に対して活発な関心のあることを示している. 【類】 I take a ***lively interest*** in all kinds of intellectual work (athletic affairs, educational matters). / He evinces a ***lively interest*** in art. ¶a man whose ***main interest*** is art and beauty 主として芸術や美に関心を持つ人. ¶He has ***many-sided interests***. 彼は多方面な興味を持つ. ¶films of ***medical*** and ***scientific interest*** 医学及び科学から見て興味ある映画. ¶The place has a ***melancholy historical interest***. その土地には悲しい歴史上の思い出がある. ¶take ***more interest*** 一層の関心を持つ. ¶She took a ***motherly interest*** in him. 彼女は母のように彼を世話した. ¶take ***much interest*** in the subject その問題に大いに興味を持つ. ¶He takes ***no interest*** in his clothes. 彼は辺幅を飾らない. ¶feel a ***particular interest*** in ... ...に特に興味を感じる. ¶take more than ***passing interest*** in ... ...に通り一遍以上の興味を持つ. 【類】 a subject of ***passing interest***. ¶be of ***peculiar interest*** at the present juncture 時節柄特に興味がある. ¶Diaries and letters have a ***permanent interest***. 日記や手紙には永久的な興味がある. 【類】 books that have been found to possess a ***permanent interest***. ¶take a ***personal interest*** in ...に親しく興味を持つ. ¶awaken only a ***pitiful interest*** ほんのわずかの興味を呼び起すにすぎない. ¶It is of ***poignant interest***. それには強い興味がある. ¶the fact lends ***pointed interest*** to an article which appeared in a recent number of ... その事実が最近発行の...誌の記事に対し特別な興味を呼び起させる. ¶He did much to awaken a ***popular interest*** in this science. 彼はこの科学に世人の興味を呼び起すべく大いに尽力した. ¶The question presents a ***practical*** as well as a ***theoretic[al] interest***. この問題は理論的並に実際的の興味がある. ¶questions of ***practical*** and ***pressing interest*** 至急解決を要する実際問題の種々. ¶of ***present*** and ***prospective interest*** 現在及び将来にわたって興味のある. ¶a revival of ***public interest*** in ... ...に対する世人の興味の復活. 【類】 arouse ***public interest*** in ... ¶take a ***renewed interest*** in poetry 再び詩に興味を持つ. ¶a point of ***scenic interest*** 風光明美な地点. ¶rich in ***scenic*** and ***historic interest*** 名所旧跡に富んだ. ¶take a ***serious interest*** in the grave problem of the day 刻下の重大問題に対し真剣になる. ¶The subject has but ***slender interest*** for me. 私にはその題目は興味が薄い. ¶Her tragic death lends a ***somber interest*** to any memorial of her. 悲惨な最後を遂げたので彼女の思出にはいつも陰うつな気持が伴う. ¶Among them this possesses ***special interest***. 彼らの間にこれが特別な興味がある. 【類】 it has a ***special interest*** from the fact that ... / show ***special interest*** in ... ¶take a ***strong interest*** in ... ...に大なる興味を持つ. ¶quicken ***students' interest*** 学生の興味を促進する. ¶These subjects are of ***superior interest*** to the majority of the Japanese people. これらの問題は大多数の日本人に特に興味がある. ¶be of ***surpassing interest*** 際立って興味がある. ¶***sympathetic interest*** and valuable suggestions 同情的関心と貴重な示唆. ¶It has ***theoretical interest*** only. それは理論上の興味しかない. ¶***thrilling interest*** わくわくさせる感興. ¶monographs (news items) of ***topical interest*** 時節柄興味ある専攻論文(など). ¶with ***unabated interest*** 薄れない興味をもって. ¶arouse ***uncommon interest*** 非常な興味を呼び起す. ¶I read the book from start to finish with ***unflagging interest***. 私はその本を始めから面白くて一気に読んだ. ¶an object of ***unique interest*** 独特の興味ある物. ¶a topic of ***universal interest*** だれもが興味をもつ問題. ¶questions of ***vital interest*** きわめて重要な関係のある諸問題. ¶take a ***vivid interest*** in ... 大いに...に興味を持つ. ¶take a ***warm interest*** in a person 人に同情を持つ. ¶manifest a ***warm interest*** in ... ...強い興味を持つ. ¶He has a ***wide interest*** in human affairs. 彼は人事に広く関心を持つ. ¶the ***widened interest*** in ... ...に関する一般化した関心. ¶in view of the ***widening interest*** by the general public in it 一般公衆がそれにますます広く関心を持つことから考えて. ¶***wide-spread interest*** has been aroused by ... ...によって広く興味が呼び起された. ¶an event of ***world-wide interest*** 世界的に興味あるできごと.

Q[2] pictures of ***adult interest*** and content 成人の興味と満足を得る映画. ¶a film full of ***child interest*** 子供が非常におもしろがる映画. ¶***heart interest*** 人情味. ¶a story with a ***love interest*** in it 恋愛小説. ¶Selection has been guided by ***student interest***. 選定は学生の興味で決められた. ¶of peculiar ***time interest*** 時節柄特に興味のある. ¶stimulate a ***world interest*** 世界の興味をそそる. ¶a Mecca of ***world interest*** 世界の興味の中心(地). ¶America has become the center of ***world interest***. アメリカは世界の関心の中心となった.

P I speak ***from interest*** in you. 私はあなたに関心を持っているから話すのです. ¶it may be ***of interest*** to note (= mention) in this connection that ... これに関連して...ということを述べるのは興味があろう. 【類】 stories ***of interest*** to women / a subject ***of*** deep ***interest*** to a student of history / a subject ***of interest*** to persons working in the fields of education and sociology ‖ excite a good deal ***of interest*** 大なる興味を呼び起す. ¶It will be read ***with interest*** by every one who takes it up. それを手に取る人は

だれも皆興味をもって読むであろう. ¶gaze ***with*** deep *interest* at … 深い興味を持って…をながめる. 【類】begin a study of … ***with*** new *interest*.

P² *interest* ***in*** the present 現在に対する興味. 【類】take *interest* ***in*** the subject / there is a great deal of *interest* ***in*** this subject among … / arouse in the child an *interest* ***in*** school studies / His *interest* ***in*** languages became deeper than ever. ‖ *interest* ***in*** the elections is heightened 選挙熱が高まる.

(**2**) 利益, 利害; 関係, 利害関係.

V ***advance*** one's own *interests* 自分の利益を増進する. 【類】***advance*** the *interests* of the people (a firm). ¶***affect*** one's *interests* その利害関係に影響する. ¶***benefit*** their *interests* 彼らの利益を増す. ¶The *interests* of China are so closely ***bound up*** with those of Japan. 中国の利害は日本のそれときわめて密接に関係している. ¶***conserve*** the *interests* of … …の利益を保持する. ¶***consider*** first the *interests* of … 第一に…の利害関係を考慮する. ¶***consult*** one's best *interests* 何が一番その得になるかを考える. ¶***defend*** their *interests* 彼らの利益を保護する. ¶***develop*** modern manufacturing *interests* 現代製造工業の利益を増進する. ¶***espouse*** the *interests* 利益をはかる. ¶succeed in bringing England better acquainted with China, and ***establishing*** a more lively *interest* in its claims 英国をして一層中国と接近させてその要求に対する一層大なる関心を呼び起すことに成功する. ¶***extend*** one's *interests* in … …の事業を拡張する ‖ ***extend*** his *interest* to … 彼の事業の手を…へ延ばす. ¶***forward*** the *interests* of the empire 帝国の利益を助長する. ¶He is ready to do anything to ***further*** his *interests* in life. 彼はこの世における彼の利益を増進するために何でもやる考えでいる. 【類】in recognition of his life-long service in ***furthering*** the *interests* of submarine telegraph / ***further*** the best *interests* of the State / ***further*** the *interests* of the British trader / We will ***further*** your *interest* as far as possible. ¶***give up*** worldly *interests* 浮世の利害を捨てる. ¶***grant*** permanent proprietary *interests* in mining lands to … …に鉱山の永久所有権を付与する. ¶***guard*** one's *interests* その利益を保護する. ¶***hamper*** the *interest* of … …の利益を阻害する. ¶***harm*** Japan's commercial *interest* 日本の商業上の利益を侵害する. ¶***have*** an *interest* to the extent of … (株を持っている場合など)…の程度まで利害関係を持つ ‖ those who ***have*** the *interest* of their country at heart 憂国の士 ‖ all the Powers ***having*** *interests* in the Far East 極東に利害関係を持つすべての国. 【類】I ***have*** not any *interest*, direct or indirect, in any tramway company. ‖ a paper that ***has*** its own *interests* to serve 機関新聞 ‖ They ***have*** an important *interest* in the matter. 彼はその件には重大な関係を持っている. ¶***investigate*** the commercial *interests* of Japan 日本の商業上の利害を調査する. ¶if you ***make*** my *interests* your interests あなたが私の利益をもってあなたの利益とするならば. ¶***meet*** the legitimate *interests* of its workers その職工の合理的な利益を計るようにする. ¶***monopolize*** *interests* in China 中国における利益を独占する. ¶***obstruct*** American *interests* 米国の利益を妨害する. ¶***postulate*** the *interests* of … …の利益を要求する. ¶***promote*** the *interests* of civilization 文明のためを計る. 【類】every effort was done to ***promote*** the *interest* of … / ***promote*** the best *interests* of the young / ***promote*** their common *interests* / ***promote*** the public *interest* (公益). ¶***protect*** our *interests* throughout the whole transaction 全取引を通じてわれわれの利益を保護する. ¶***protect*** and ***advance*** the *interests* of … …の利益を保護しかつ増進する. ¶***pursue*** one's own *interest* 自分のためをはかる. ¶***push*** one's *interests* to the utmost あくまで自己の利益を助長しようとする. ¶***realize*** a fair *interest* on the capital invested 投じた資本に対して相当な利益を得る. ¶***rebuild*** her commercial *interests* in China 中国におけるその商業上の利益を建て直す. ¶***root out*** German *interests* in the Far East 極東におけるドイツの利益を根絶する. ¶***ruin*** her commercial *interests* in the Far East 極東におけるその国の商業上の利益を破壊する. ¶***sacrifice*** the national *interests* to those of the world 世界のために国家の利益を犠牲にする 【類】***sacrifice*** one's permanent *interests* for the gratification of a momentary pride / ***sacrifice*** one's own selfish *interests* for the larger welfare of society as a whole. ¶***safeguard*** the *interests* of … …の利益を保護する. ¶***serve*** the *interests* of peace (Japan) 平和(など)のために尽す. 【類】***serve*** the best *interests* of education / ***serve*** our common *interest* in the best possible way ‖ ***serve*** American *interests* 米国のためになる. ¶The *interest* of the individual and the class should be ***subordinated*** to that of the community as a whole. 一般社会の利益を主とし個人や階級の利益は従とせねばならない. ¶***take on*** new *interest* with the latest turn of affairs 最近の局面展開とともに新たな興味が生じる. ¶Please attend the meeting and ***watch*** our *interests*. 会に出席してわれわれの利害関係に御配慮下さい.

V² Their *interests* ***clash***. 彼らの利害関係が衝突する. ‖ American *interests* do not ***clash*** with those of Japan. 米国の利害は日本の利害と衝突しない. ¶Their *interests* ***harmonize***. 彼らの利害関係は一致する.

Q It is for the ***best*** *interests* of the public. そうするのが一番一般の利益になる. ¶investigate the ***commercial*** *interests* of the country その国の商業上の利益を調査する. ¶have topics of ***common interest*** to talk about 話があう ‖ persons with a ***common interest*** 同志. 【類】Travelling is in the ***common interest***. ¶He has ***financial interests*** in many companies. 彼は多数の会社に財政上の関係がある. ¶I have an ***important*** *interest* in the matter. 私はその事件に重要な利害関係がある. ¶backed by ***influential British*** *interests* 有力な英国の事業家を後だてに持った. ¶It is to be on ***joint interest***. それは共同の利益という建前でやることになっている. ¶have ***large interests*** in common. ともに大なる利害関係を有している. ¶a subject of purely ***local*** *interest* 全く地方的利害関係の問題 ‖ The information is of more than ***local*** *interest*. この報道は単に地方的な関係に止らない. ¶***material*** and ***spiritual*** *interests* of the people 物質的及び精神的に国民に関係する事柄. ¶enter into agreement for their ***mutual interest*** 彼ら相互のために協定する. ¶for the advancement of their ***national*** *interests* 彼らの国家的利益増進のために. ¶be against the ***national*** *interest* 国利に反するものである. ¶the ***naval*** *interests* in that country その国における海軍の利害関係. ¶for their ***own interests*** 彼ら自己の利益のために. 【類】in his ***own interests***. ¶for his own ***personal*** *interest* 彼一個の利益のために. ¶subordinate one's own ***private*** *interests* for the welfare of the nation 国民の幸福のために自己の利害を従属させる. 【類】sacrifice ***private*** *interests* for the public weal / place the public weal above one's ***private*** *interests*. ¶in the ***public interest*** 一般公衆のために. 【類】affect the ***public interest*** / involve matters of ***public interest*** / become the subject of ***public interest*** / work against the ***public interest*** / a subject of general ***public interest***. ¶has only a ***remote*** *interest* ただ間接の利害関係をもつ. ¶He has no ***selfish financial*** *interests* to subserve. 彼はなんら財政上自分のためを計ろうという考えを持っていない. ¶in the ***sole*** *interest* of … 全く…のために. ¶He has the ***true*** *interest* of his people at heart. 彼は真に彼の国民の利益を念願としている. ¶the ***ultimate*** *interest* of … …の終局の利益. ¶***vested*** *interests* of various kinds 種々の既得権. ¶adequate recognition of Japan's ***vital*** *interests* 日本の死活問題に対する十分の認識.

Q² protect the ***business*** *interests* of the manufacturers in that country その国の製造業者の営業権を保護する. ¶It is to the ***self*** *interest* of this country to help feed the work in its slow comeback from war. 戦争から緩慢な回復をなすにあたり事業進捗(ちょく)を援助することはこの国自身の利益となるのである. ¶respect ***United States*** *interests* in the Far East 極東における米国の利益を尊重する.

P it is ***for*** the best *interest* of … to … …することは…にとってなによりためになる ‖ He has no regard ***for*** their *interests*. 彼は彼らの利益を顧みない. ¶it is ***in*** his *interest* to … …するのは彼のためになる ‖ I am speaking entirely ***in*** your own *interests*. 私は全くあなたのために話しているのだ. 【類】He is about to make trips abroad ***in*** the *interest* of his business. / I will do the best ***for*** your *interests*. / ***in*** the *interest* of national security / ***in*** the *interest* of Shakespearean research / ***in*** the *interest* of science (humanity, truth, international peace, the peace of the world, public order and decency) / it is not desirable ***in*** the *interest* of the State or of the race that …

should ... / They are working *in* the *interest* of peace throughout the world. / do much service *in* the *interests* of peace / His voyage was made *in* the *interests*, not of trade or conquest, but of scientific curiosity. / a monthly publication issued *in* the *interests* of the salmon fisheries, etc. / the exploitation of ... *in* the *interests* of a small section of capitalists / the rule of the minority *in* the *interests* of that minority / *in* the *interests* (=cause) of civilization (public peace, public health, public safety) / The names are arranged in alphabetical order *in* the *interest* of ready reference (検索の便) / act *in* the *interests* of ... / work sincerely *in* the *interests* of .... ¶ be ***of interest*** to ... ...に利益である. ¶ It is [*to*] your *interest* to do so. そうすることは君の利益になる. 【類】You will find it ***to*** your *interest* to consult him.

P² a conflict of *interests* ***between*** father and daughter 父と娘の間の利害の衝突. ¶ I have not any *interest*, direct or indirect, ***in*** any electric tramway company. 私は市電会社には直接にしろ間接にしろ一切関係がない. ¶ The *interest* ***of*** Mr. ... ***in*** the journal has closed. その新聞は…氏の手を離れた.

(**3**) 利子, 利息.

V Five per cent *interest* is ***allowed*** on deposits. 預金には五分の利子を付ける. ‖ *interest* will be ***allowed*** at the rate of ... ...の割で利子が付く. ¶ The bonds ***bear interest*** at the rate of five to six per cent. 同公債には五分ないし六分の利子がつく. ‖ a loan to ***bear interest*** at 6 per cent with issue price at 94 per 100 yen face value 額面百円につき発行価格九十四円の六分利付公債. 【類】***bear*** 5 per cent *interest*. ¶ ***carry*** an annual *interest* of ... ...という年々の利子を生む. ¶ At present the English law allows a money-lender to ***charge*** what *interest* he likes. 現在英国の法律は金貸業者に勝手な利子を取ることを許している. ¶ ***compute*** (=***reckon***) *interest* 利子を計算する. ¶ ***draw*** *interest* at 6% [公債など]六分の利子を生みだす ‖ a deposit ***drawing*** six per cent *interest* 六分の利子がつく預金. ¶ ***earn*** a safe *interest* on capital 資本に対して安全な利息をもうける. ¶ ***figure*** *interest* 利息勘定をやる. ¶ ***pay*** *interest* on a loan (=borrowed money) 借りた金に利子を払う. ¶ ***realize*** a fair *interest* on the capital invested 投資に対し割のよい利子を得る. ¶ ***yield*** compound *interest* 複利を生みだす ‖ an investment safe and ***yielding*** highrate *interest* 安全高利回りの投資.

Q ***accrued*** *interest* 〘商〙繰延利子. ¶ a ***bare*** *interest* for the capital 資本に対する僅少の利益. ¶ reckoning ***compound*** *interest* 複利勘定をして. ¶ at ***high*** *interest* 高利で. ¶ ***moderate*** *interest* 低廉な利子. ¶ *interest* ***payable*** (***receivable***) 借人(貸付)金利子.

Q² borrow money at ***six per cent*** *interest* 六分の利子で金を借りる. ¶ pay ***3%*** *interest* on the loan 三分の利子を払う. ¶ ***ex*** *interest* 利息落ち.

P lend money ***at*** *interest* 利息を取って金を貸す ‖ loan out (=put out) ***at*** *interest* 利子を取って貸す. ¶ return a blow (kiss) ***with*** *interest* 殴打(など)を一層強く仕返す ‖ ***with*** *interest* at five per cent. 五分利付で. ¶ pay a loan ***without*** *interest* 利息を付けずに借金を返す.

P² *interest* ***for*** a single day 日歩. ¶ *interest* ***from*** investments 投資からの利子. 【類】*interest* ***from*** a loan. ¶ *interest* ***on*** a deposit 預金に対する利子. 【類】*interest* ***on*** investments (投資) / *interest* ***on*** a principal (元金) / *Interest* ***on*** this loan is charged at 50 per cent. / *interest* ***on*** (=***upon***) the money borrowed by ...

(**4**) 株, 持株; 権利.

V ***buy*** an *interest* in a business ある事業の株を買う. 【類】***buy*** a half *interest* in the newspaper. ¶ He ***owns*** an *interest* in a firm. 彼はその店に出資している. ¶ ***sell*** one's *interest* in a company (an enterprise) ある会社(など)の持株を売る.

(**5**) 利害関係者, 事業団体; …側.

V ***represent*** all the *interests* concerned 関係事業団体を代表する.

Q the ***landed*** *interest* 地主側.

Q² the ***banking*** *interest* 銀行団. ¶ a center of ***bookselling*** *interest* 書籍販売業の中心. ¶ ***hotel*** *interests* ホテル業者. ¶ ***iron*** (***steel***) *interests* 鉄(鋼)業者. ¶ various ***travel*** *interests* in Japan 日本の各種観光事業団. ¶ the ***management*** (***labor***) *interest* 経営(労働)者側. ¶ the ***shipping*** *interests* 海運業者. ¶ They control sugar refining *interests* in California. 彼らはカリフォルニア州の精糖業を牛耳っている.

interest, *v.* 関係させる, 興味を起させる.

M be ***actively*** *interested* in ... 盛んに…に活動している. ¶ That will ***certainly*** *interest* you. これはきっとあなたにはおもしろいと思われるでしょう. ¶ He is ***heavily*** (=***deeply***) *interested* in the company. 彼はその会社に大分出資している. ¶ I have been ***greatly*** *interested* to note that ... ...を見て私は非常に興味を感じた. ¶ You know ***how*** *interested* I am in everything you do. 私はあなたのすることにはなんでも興味をもっていることをあなたは御存じでしょう. ¶ the parties ***immediately*** *interested* 直接関係のある当事者. ¶ ***intensely*** *interested* in ... ...深く興味を持って. ¶ ***keenly*** *interested* in ... ...に非常に興味を感じて. 【類】subjects which *interest* them ***keenly***. ¶ I was ***much*** *interested* to ... 私は…するのが非常におもしろかった. ¶ some question in which people are ***warmly*** *interested* 人々が大いに興味を持っているある問題.

P try to *interest* men of means ***in*** the question of ... 財産家に…の問題に興味を持たせるように努力する ‖ I became *interested* ***in*** old maps. 私は古い地図に興味を持つようになった. 【類】*interested* ***in*** botanical studies / deeply *interested* ***in*** female education / anyone *interested* ***in*** the subject ... / An enthusiast is a person who is *interested* ***in*** a cause, sometimes unwisely so. ‖ some enterprising gentleman *interested* ***in*** real estate 不動産業に関係のあるある企業家の紳士. ‖ I cannot arbitrate, being *interested* ***in*** the matter. 私はこの件には利害関係があるから仲裁することができない. 【類】*interested* ***in*** the crime problem. ¶ I was much *interested* ***by*** your magazine article on ... ...に関するあなたの雑誌に書かれた文を非常におもしろく拝見致しました. ¶ The boy seemed deeply *interested* ***over*** the dog. その少年はその犬に深い興味を持っているらしかった.

interesting, *a.* 興味ある.

M it is ***chiefly*** *interesting* as having been the birth-place of ... それは…が生れた所だというので主として興味がある. ¶ ***deeply*** *interesting* relics 非常に興味ある遺物. ¶ it is ***doubly*** *interesting* because ... それは…故に二重に興味がある. ¶ be ***fascinatingly*** *interesting* おもしろくてたまらない. ¶ ***intensely*** *interesting* 非常におもしろい. ¶ matters which are ***perennially*** *interesting* to humanity 人間に永久的に興味のある事柄. ¶ be ***piquantly*** *interesting* 切実なおもしろ味がある. ¶ No object ***really*** *interests* us but man. 人間以外真にわれわれに興味を起させるものはない.

P It is chiefly *interesting* ***for*** the ruins of an old castle. それは主として古城の廃虚なるが故に興味が深い. ¶ matters *interesting* ***to*** us われわれには興味のある事柄.

interfere, *v.* 干渉する.

M It can not ***possibly*** *interfere* with the business. それは決してその仕事の妨害にはならない. ¶ It will ***seriously*** *interfrere* with the progress of the work. それは大いに仕事の進行の邪魔になるだろう.

P You have no right to *interfere* ***between*** us. 君は僕たち二人のことに口ばしを入れる権利はない. ¶ *interfere* ***in*** general elections 総選挙に干渉する. 【類】This is not a matter for you to *interfere* ***in***. / He has no right to *interfere* ***in*** the matter. / Do not *interfere* ***in*** other people's business. ¶ This addition may *interfere* ***with*** the symmetry of the book. これを付け加えるとその本の均斉を妨げるかもしれない. ‖ *interfere* ***with*** our industrial development わが国産業の発展を妨げる ‖ He *interfered* ***with*** the matter by freely exercising his frateral authority. 彼はやたらに兄貴風をふかせてそのことの邪魔をした. ‖ *interfere* ***with*** an official in the performance of his duty 公務員の職務執行を妨害する. 【類】The demands of the war rather *interfered* ***with*** the collection of funds. / The interests of Japan and America do not *interfere* ***with*** each other. / I intended to go, but some visitors interfered. / Something always *interferes* ***with*** my going there.

interference, *n.* 干渉, 邪魔.

V ***brook*** no *interference* by ... ...の邪魔を容赦しない. ¶ will ***suffer*** no *interference* 干渉させないだろう.

Q The problem requires ***governmental*** *interference* for its solution. その問題の解決には政府の干渉を要する. ¶ These efforts have been hampered by ***official*** *interference*. これらの努力は官憲の干渉で妨害された. ¶ ***outside*** *interference* 外部からの干渉. ¶ ***personal*** *interference* 個人

的な干渉. ¶He was prevented by ***timely interference*** from committing suicide. 彼は折よく邪魔をされて自殺ができなかった. ¶make ***uncalled-for interference*** 余計なお節介をする. ¶***unwise interference*** 知恵のない干渉.

Q² ***discountenance*** *interference* 干渉を排斥する. ¶***Government interference*** 政府の干渉. ¶***State interference*** in trade by way of customs duties 関税による国家の干渉.

P² *interference* ***in*** politics 政治上の干渉. ¶*interference* ***with*** her internal affairs その国の内政干渉.

interim, *n.* 暫時.

P ***in*** the *interim* その間.

interior, *n.* 内部, 内地.

V ***embellish*** the *interior* of a church with ... 教会の内部を...で飾る. ¶***penetrate*** the *interior* of ... ...の内地にはいり込む.

Q various semi-independent military chiefs in the ***distant*** *interior* of China 中国奥地の幾多の半ば独立した領将たち.

Q² the ***house*** *interiors* 室内.

P travel ***in*** the *interior* of China 中国奥地を旅行する.

interjection, *n.* 叫び声.

V² All these *interjections* ***broke*** from him. これらの叫び声が皆彼の口から出た.

interlard, *v.* 混入する.

P He richly *interlarded* his speech ***with*** many foreign words. 彼はその演説に外国語を盛んにそう入した.

interleave, *v.* 間に紙をはさむ.

P *interleaved* ***with*** blank paper 白紙をはさんでとじた.

interlocutor, *n.* 対話者.

Q the ***chief*** *interlocutor* in a dialogue 対話の主役.

interlude, *n.* 幕間(まい)狂言.

V ***enjoy*** an *interlude* of repose 仕事の合間を楽しむ.

Q a ***comic*** *interlude* 幕間の喜劇.

intermarriage, *n.* 雑婚.

Q a prejudice against ***white*** and ***yellow*** *intermarriages* 黄白人種の雑婚に対する偏見.

P those children coming ***out of*** *intermarriages* resulted from two World Wars 二回の大戦による国際結婚によって生じたこれらの子供たち.

P² *intermarriage* ***of*** races 諸人種の雑婚.

intermarry, *v.* 雑婚する.

P *intermarry* ***with*** a royal house 高貴な家柄と縁を結ぶ.

intermediary, *n.* 媒介者.

Q² a ***peace*** *intermediary* 平和の媒介者.

intermediate, *a.* 介在する.

P a being *intermediate* ***between*** the ape and man さると人間との中間にある生物.

interment, *n.* 埋葬.

V ***make*** *interments* 埋葬する.

intermingle, *v.* 混合する.

P *intermingle* ***with*** each other 互いに混り合う ‖ Salt and sugar *intermingle* ***with*** each other. 塩と砂糖は混る.

intermission, *n.* 中絶.

P ***in*** the *intermissions* of his business life 実業界の仕事の合間合間に. ¶***with*** a short *intermission* now and then 時折短かい間をおいて. ¶***without*** *intermission* 間断なく.

P² an *intermission* ***for*** supper 夕食のための中休み.

intermix, *v.* まざる, 混じる.

P *intermix* ***with*** ... ...とまざる.

intern, *n.* 〖医〗インターン.

P serve (=act) ***as*** an *intern* インターンとして勤務する. ¶wind up the duties ***of*** an *intern* インターンの勤務を修了する.

internee, *n.* 被抑留者.

Q ***civilian*** *internees* 軍人以外の被抑留者たち.

interpellation, *n.* 質問.

V ***address*** an *interpellation* 質問演説をする.

P the Socialist *interpellation* ***on*** the increase in the cost of living 生活費の増加に関する社会党員の質問.

interplay, *n.* 相互作用.

Q a ***free*** *interplay* of influences 影響の自由な相互作用.

interpose, *v.* 間に入る, 口を出す.

P *interpose* ***between*** the combatants 二人の闘士の間に立って仲裁する. ¶*interpose* ***in*** the matter その事件に口を出す ‖ *interpose* a barrier ***between*** ... ...間に境界をつける.

interposition, *n.* 仲裁, 干渉.

Q a ***direct*** *interposition* of Providence 神の直接仲裁.

interpret, *v.* 解釈する, 通訳する.

M ***falsely*** *interpreted* 誤って解釈された. ¶***rightly*** *interpreted* 正しく解釈された. ¶It may be ***so*** *interpreted.* そうも取れる. ¶a very vague term that may be *interpreted* ***variously*** 色々に解釈されるきわめてあいまいな語.

P *interpreted* ***as*** a concession 譲歩と解される. ¶*interpret* ***between*** two persons 二人間を通訳する. ¶when *interpreted* ***in*** this way こんな風に解釈されると ‖ *interpret* a dream ***in*** one's favor 夢を自分に都合のいいように判断する. ¶can be *interpreted* ***into*** ... ...と解釈できる. ¶*interpret* Japan ***to*** the West 日本を西洋に紹介する.

interpretation, *n.* 解釈.

V ***bring about*** a better *interpretation* of the East to the West and of the West to the East 西洋に東洋を東洋に西洋を一層よく理解させる. ¶This spirit ***found*** *interpretation* in the art of that time. その精神が当時の芸術に現われている. ¶***give*** a friendly *interpretation* to ... ...に友情的な解釈を与える. ¶He advised his students not to ***place*** too liberal an *interpretation* upon the Bible. 彼は自分の学生に聖書にあまり自由な解釈を下すなと忠告した. ¶***put*** some other *interpretation* on ... ...に何か別な解釈をする ‖ ***put*** a wrong *interpretation* upon the advice of one's superiors 先輩の忠告を悪くとる. 【類】***put*** one's own *interpretation* on ...

Q the ***current*** *interpretation* of college life given in Hollywood-made movies ハリウッド製映画に現われた大学生活の現代的解釈. ¶***delusional*** *interpretations* 誤った解釈. ¶It has given rise to most ***diverse*** *interpretations.* それには非常にまちまちな解釈が与えられた. ¶a ***hasty*** or ***one-sided*** *interpretation* 速断的なまたは片寄ったな解釈. ¶His life was so much a ***living*** *interpretation* of the De Pauw ideal of service. 彼の一生はいかにもデポー大学の奉仕の理想を具現したものであった. ¶***materialistic*** *interpretation* of history 唯物史観. ¶***perverted*** and ***distorted*** *interpretations* of positions and views of opponents 相手の立場や意見の曲解. ¶It is not capable of ***precise*** *interpretation.* それを正確に解釈することはできない. ¶a ***rationalistic*** *interpretation* of myths 神話の合理的解釈. ¶The passage may be given ***several*** *interpretations.* この一節は色々に解釈ができる. ¶a ***strained*** or ***fantastic*** *interpretation* こじつけまたは気まぐれの解釈. ¶***uncritical*** *interpretations* 眼識のない解釈. ¶put an ***unfavorable*** *interpretation* upon ... ...に対して不利な解釈を下す. ¶be susceptible of ***various*** *interpretations* 色々に解釈できる. 【類】***Various*** *interpretations* may be placed to this article. ¶It is capable of very ***wide*** *interpretation.* それはきわめて広義に解釈ができる.

Q² a piece of ***life*** *interpretation* 一つの人生観.

P² a new *interpretation* ***of*** the meaning of ... ...の意味の新しい解釈. 【類】Japan's *interpretation* ***of*** the world's affairs / the *interpretation* ***of*** statutes (法令). ¶an *interpretation* ***of*** the Orient ***to*** the Occident 西洋への東洋紹介.

interpreter, *n.* 通訳, 解説者, 解釈者.

V ***bring*** an *interpreter* along with ... 通訳を連れて来る. ¶***employ*** an *interpreter* 通訳を雇う. ¶***find*** their *interpreter* in ... ...が彼らの説明者である(...がその説明に当る). ¶we have ***lost*** Japan's best *interpreter* to the West in the death of ... ...の死去によって日本は西洋に対するその最良の解説者を失った. ¶***procure*** an *interpreter* 通訳を雇う.

Q ***creative*** *interpreters* of music 音楽の独創的な解釈者. ¶a ***faithful*** *interpreter* of the actual usage 日用語を使用する忠実な解釈者. ¶He was one of the ***greatest*** *interpreters* of Japan to the Western world. 彼は日本を西洋へ紹介した最も偉大な人物の一人だった. ¶an ***official*** *interpreter* 通訳官. ¶one's ***personal*** *interpreter* その人個人の通訳. ¶a ***reliable*** *interpreter* 信頼するに足る通訳. ¶a ***respectable*** *interpreter* りっぱな通訳. ¶***uniformed*** *interpreters* 制服の通訳.

Q² a ***student*** *interpreter* 見習通訳官; 学生通訳.

P serve (=act) ***as*** *interpreter* for ... ...の通訳をつとめる. ¶His speech was translated into English ***by*** his *interpreter*. 彼の演説は通訳によって英語に訳された. ¶He spoke ***through*** his *interpreter*. 彼は通訳を通して語った.

P² *interpreters* ***of*** their own life and culture to the other world 自国の生活と文化とを外国に解説する者.

interrelation, *n.* 相互関係.

P² *interrelations* ***of*** historical events 歴史事件の相互関係.

interrelationship, *n.* 相互関係.
Q the *intimate* (=*close*) *interrelationship* of the well-known Indo-European tongues 一般に知れているインド・ヨーロッパ諸語の緊密な相互関係.
P^2 the *interrelationships between* business and public 商業と公衆の相互関係.
interrogate, *v.* 尋ねる, 尋問する. 「人的に尋ねる.
M *interrogate personally* on the point その点について個
P being *interrogated as to* ..., he said ... …について質問されて彼は…と言った. ¶I *interrogated* him *on* the subject of ... 私は…の問題について彼に尋ねた. ‖ *interrogate* him *on* this point 彼にこの点を尋ねる.
interrogation, *n.* 質問, 質問書.
V *conduct interrogation* on ... …に対して質問する. ¶*present* an *interrogation* to the government 政府に質問書を提出する. ¶*quit* an *interrogation* 質問をやめる.
P in reply *to* an *interrogation* 質問に答えて.
interrogatory, *n.* 質問.
Q a *written interrogatory* 質問書.
interrupt, *v.* 妨げる, さえぎる.
M His speech was *constantly interrupted* by applause. 彼の演説は始終かっさいで妨げられた. ¶*interrupt* oneself *suddenly* [やっていたことを]急にやめる.
P *interrupt* a person *in* his talk 人の話を邪魔する.
O I don't want to be *interrupted.* 人に邪魔されたくない. ¶*interrupt* one's work to answer a telephone 電話に出るため仕事を中止する.
interruption, *n.* 邪魔, 妨害.
Q an *annoying interruption* うるさい邪魔.
P *amidst* many *interruptions* 幾多の妨害にあって. ¶I want to engage in work secure *from interruption.* 私は邪魔をされないで仕事をしたい. ¶*without interruption* of service 休業せずに.
P^2 *interruption of* communication 交通妨害 ‖ *interruption of* procedure 訴訟手続の中断. ¶*interruption on* the cable between Shanghai and Tientsin 上海・天津間の海底 └電信の妨害.
intersect, *v.* 横切る.
P Streets usually *intersect at* right angles. 通りは普通直角に交叉する. ‖ The railway *intersects with* each other *at* this place. その鉄道はこの所で交叉している.
intersection, *n.* 交叉点.
Q^2 at *street intersections* 街の交叉点で.
P *at* the *intersection* of trade routes (six streets) 通商路 └(など)の交叉点に.
intersperse, *v.* まき散らす.
P He *interspersed* cherry-trees *among* the willows. 彼は柳の間に桜を植込ませた. ¶His speech was *interspersed with* touches of humor. 彼の演説にはユーモアが交った. ‖ The grass is *interspersed with* beds of flowers. 芝地に花 └壇が配してある.
interval, *n.* 間隔, 期間.
Q at *brief intervals* 少し間をおいて. ¶a *fine interval* 晴れ間. ¶at *frequent* (*infrequent*) *intervals* ちょいちょい(珍しく)度々. 【類】Catalogues are issued at *frequent intervals.* / The occasion is notable inasmuch as this is the first complete European concert company presented in Japan at *infrequent intervals.* ¶at *long intervals* 長い間をおいて. 【類】I am delighted to see you after so *long* an *interval.* ¶a *lucid interval* 正気に帰った期間(狂人の). ¶Further volumes will be issued at *monthly intervals.* 以下月々続刊される. ¶at *quarterly intervals* 三月目に(年四回). ¶followed at *rapid intervals* 矢つぎ早に続けられた. ¶The novelist produces at *rare intervals.* その小説家は寡作家だ. ¶at *regular* (*irregular*) *intervals* 一定の間をおいて(不規則に). 【類】appear at *regular six-monthly intervals.* ¶at *rhythmic intervals* 律動的な間をおいて. ¶at a *short interval* of time 短い時間をおいて. 【類】be followed at *short intervals.* ¶at *stated intervals* 所定の間をおいて. ¶at *successive intervals* 次々と間をおいて. ¶*uninspired intervals* of poets, novelists, etc. 詩人・小説家などの霊感を受けない(筆の進まない)期間. ¶at a *week's interval* 一週間の間をおいて.
Q^2 after *two-week* (=two weeks') *intervals* 二週間の間をおいて. ¶Trains are running at *15-minute intervals.* 列車は十五分間隔で運転されている. ¶a *meal interval* 食事休息時間 ¶at *six-month intervals* 六カ月間隔で. ¶the visit of the King and Queen of Italy to the Pope after a *ten-year interval* 十年間をおいてイタリアの国王と女王が教皇への御訪問.
P *after* an *interval* of three months 三月の間をおいてから. 【類】*after* ten minutes' *interval.* ¶*at* an *interval* of ten minutes=with ten minutes' intervals 十分おきに. 【類】The railway service between Yokohama and Tokyo will increase so that trains will be run *at intervals* of 15 to 20 minutes. / *at intervals* of two hours / report *at intervals* for further treatment / recur *at intervals* of about eighty years / *at* three or four hour *intervals* / *at* an *interval* of two months. ¶This work was continued *by intervals.* この仕事は間をおいて継続した. 【類】Work at the studio (撮影所) starts early, stops late, and is broken only *by* a very short luncheon *interval.* ¶*during* the *intervals* between the acts 幕合に. ¶*in* the *intervals* of leisure from other duties 他の勤務の合間に ‖ *in* an *interval* 合間に. 【類】*in* the *intervals* of his business (official labors) / done *in intervals* of other duties. ¶*with* an *interval* of one day 一日あいだをおいて ‖ *with* but a short *interval* of time between ... and ... …と…のきわめて短い合間をおいて. ¶*without interval* のべつに.
P^2 When jealousy is at hand, peace is only an *interval between* two wars. しっとがあると平和は闘争の合間たるにすぎなくなる. ¶Work for them is only an *interval in* play. 彼らには働くことは遊びの合間に過ぎない. ¶There was two hours' *interval to* the next train. その次の汽車までには二時間の間があった.
intervene, *v.* 間にはいる, 干渉する.
P the period which *intervened between* ... and ... …と…との間にはさまる期間. ¶we have no intention of *intervening in* the internal affairs of ... われわれは…の内政に干渉する意思はない.
intervention, *n.* 調停; 干渉; 介在. 「けるために.
V to *escape* the *intervention* of the police 警察の干渉を避
Q This led to the *armed intervention* of England. この結果英国の武力的干渉を招くにいたった. ¶*international intervention* 国際的干渉. ¶on whose *kind intervention* その人の親切な仲裁で. 「*vention* 国家の干渉.
Q^2 *Government intervention* 政府の仲介. ¶*State inter-*
P *on* the *intervention* of ... …の仲裁で. ¶*through* the *intervention* of friends 友人の調停で. ¶*without* the *intervention* of an interpreter 通訳なしで.
interview, *n.* 会見(インタビュー), 引見.
V *ask* (=*beg*) *for* an *interview* with ... …との会見を求める. ¶*give* an *interview* to the daily papers (newsmen) 新聞記者に会見する. ¶When will you *grant* me an *interview?* いつ御面会が願われましょうか. ¶*have* an *interview* with (=interview) the President 大統領と会見する. ¶*hold* an *interview* with ... …と会見する. ¶I failed to *obtain* an *interview.* 私は会見できなかった. 【類】I finally *obtained* an *interview* with ... ¶*refuse* all *interviews* on the subject この問題については一切面談を拒絶する. ¶*request* an *interview* 面会をこう. ¶I *secured* an *interview* on the subject with ... 私はこの問題について…と会見した. ¶*seek* an *interview* with ... …に面会を求める.
Q *chatty interviews* 肩のこらない会談. ¶a *delightful interview* 愉快な会見. ¶a *personal interview* 面談. ¶a *pointless interview* 要領を得ない会見. ¶at a *second interview* 二度目の会見で. ¶a *stolen interview* 密会.
Q^2 an *application interview* 求職者面接. ¶a *job interview* 求職面接. ¶at a *press interview* 記者会見で. ¶a *sales interview* 売込面会. ¶a *story interview* 新聞の記事にするための会見. ¶a *telephone interview* 電話での会談.
P The matter cannot be discussed except *at* a personal *interview.* その件は直接面会の上でなくては話せない. ‖ *at* our last *interview* われわれのこの前の会見で.
P^2 an *interview between* ... and ... …と…との会見.
interview, *v.* 会見する.
M *personally interview* 親しく会見する.
interweave, *v.* 織合わす, 関連させる.
M be *closely interwoven* with ... …と密接に関連している.
P *interweave* it *with* ... それを…と織合わせる
intestine, *n.* 腸.
P pain *in* the *intestines* 腸の痛み.
intimacy, *n.* 親密, 親交, 懇意.
V *break off* the *intimacy* 情交を断つ. ¶he *enjoyed* the closest *intimacy* with ... 彼は…と最も親密であった.

¶gradually ***establish*** (=*form*) an *intimacy* with ... ...と段々懇意になる. ¶*foster intimacies* among students 学生間の親睦を助成する. ¶***have*** a sexual *intimacy* with ... ...と性関係がある. ¶those who do not ***profess*** *intimacy* with Greek and Latin ギリシア語やラテン語は不得手と言っている人たち. 「あった.

V^2 *intimacy* ***existed*** between ... and ... ...と...とは親密で

Q ***artistic*** (***literary***) *intimacy* 芸術(文学)上の友人関係. ¶have ***no*** *intimacy* with ... ...と懇意にしていない.

P^2 the *intimacy* ***between*** the two 両人間の親密. ¶I felt a sense of *intimacy* ***with*** him. 私は彼に対して心安さを感じ └した.

intimate, *a.* 親しい.

P *intimate* ***with*** ... ...と親しい.

intimate, *v.* 暗に知らす.

P he *intimated* ***to*** me his intention of ... 彼は...の意図を └私に暗に知らせた.

intimation, *n.* 通知.

V *intimation* was ***given*** to him that ... 彼に...の旨を通知した. ¶***issue*** an *intimation* 通告を発する. ¶having ***received*** *intimation* that ... ...という情報に接して.

Q An ***early*** *intimation* of acceptance will be obliged. お受取の節はお早く御一報下さい. ¶since the ***last intimation*** この前の通告以来. ¶there has been no ***previous*** *intimation* of ... ...についてなんらの予告もなかった.

P^2 I received a copy of a letter ***with*** an *intimation* that ... 私は...の旨を報じた手紙の写しを受取った.

P give early *intimation* ***as to*** ... ...について早くから通知す └る.

intimidate, *v.* おどす.

P *intimidate* ... ***by*** threats ...を威嚇する. ¶He was *intimidated* ***into*** silence. 彼はおどかされて黙ってしまった. ¶It was *intimidated* ***out of*** existence. それは威嚇の結果その影を消すにいたった. ¶*intimidate* a person ***with*** threats 人 └を威嚇する.

intimidation, *n.* 威嚇, おどし.

P ***by*** *intimidation* or threats 威嚇または脅かつで.

intolerable, *a.* たえられない.

M ***really*** *intolerable* to ... ...には実にたえられない.

P *intolerable* ***to*** us われわれにはたえられない.

intolerance, *n.* がん迷, 不寛容. 「見せない.

V ***show*** no *intolerance* to ... ...に対してがん迷さを少しも

intolerant, *a.* 我慢のできない, 許さない, 雅量のない.

P He was *intolerant* ***of*** laziness and somewhat impatient of incapacity. 彼は怠惰には我慢ができずまた無能に対しては幾分もどかしがった.

intonation, *n.* 語調(イントネーション).

Q The student talked English with a ***solid Japanese*** *intonation* that I could not recognize it as English. その学生は英語と思われなかったほど日本語の語調丸だしで英語を話した.

Q^2 develop a ***sing-song*** *intonation* 単調な抑揚となる.

P English spoken ***with*** a Japanese *intonation* 日本語の語調で話された英語.

P^2 the *intonation* of conversational style of English 会話体英語のイントネーション.

intoxicate, *v.* 酔う.

P *intoxicated* ***from*** wine 酒に酔って. ¶*intoxicated* ***with*** (=***by***) success 成功に酔って. 【類】 *intoxicated* ***with*** joy └(victory).

intrench, entrench, *v.* 侵害する.

P *intrench* ***on*** (=***upon***) one's rights 権利を侵害する.

intrepidity, *n.* 剛勇.

Q with ***laudable*** *intrepidity* あっぱれな剛勇をもって.

intricacy, *n.* 錯そう.

V The book though difficult is a mine of wealth to those who have the patience to ***explore*** its *intricacies*. その本は難解ではあるがその錯そうした内容を探究するだけの辛抱強い人々には知識の庫である. ¶***master*** the *intricacies* of business 複雑な事務に精通する.

intrigue, *n.* 密通, 陰謀.

V ***carry on*** an *intrigue* with a woman 女と密通する.

Q a ***diplomatic*** *intrigue* 外交上の陰謀.

Q^2 a ***love*** *intrigue* 色仕かけ.

intrigue, *v.* 通じる. 「ど)と通じる.

P *intrigue* ***with*** the opposite party (a person) 反対党(な

introduce, *v.* 紹介する; 輸入する; 提出する.

M Vaccination for small-pox was ***first*** *introduced* into the United States in 1792 by Dr. William Yates. 種痘は一七九二年ウィリヤム・イェーツ博士によって初めて米国に輸入された. ¶***parenthetically*** *introduce* ... 合の手に...をはさむ.

P Christianity was *introduced* ***among*** the Anglo-Saxons at the opening of the seventh century. キリスト教は七世紀の初めにアングロ・サクソン人の間に広められた. 【類】 *introduce* civilization ***among*** the people out of respect to their feelings (感情を害しないように). ¶he *introduced* her ***as*** his daughter, ... 彼は彼女を自分の娘...と紹介した ‖ It was originally *introduced* ***as*** a term of reproach. それは非難の言葉として使用されたのが始まりである. ¶The Bill was *introduced* ***by*** ... in the Parliament of 1901. その議案は一九〇一年...によって議会に提出された. ¶Buddhism was *introduced* ***from*** India in the third century B.C. 仏教は紀元前三世紀にインドから伝来した. ‖ ***From*** Cathay (=China) the abacus was *introduced* in Korea and Japan. そろ盤は中国から朝鮮及び日本に伝わった. ¶*introduce* a question ***for*** debate 論議のため問題を提出する. ¶The Bill will be *introduced* ***in*** the next session of the Diet. この案は次期の議会に提出されるであろう. ‖ Jonas Hanway *introduced* the umbrella ***in*** London. ジョーナス・ハンウェーがこうもりがさをロンドン人に紹介した. ‖ Are you the gentleman *introduced* ***in*** this letter? あなたがこの紹介状の方ですか. ¶Porcelain-manufacture was *introduced* ***into*** Japan from China about 1513. 磁器の製造は一五一三年ごろ中国から日本に輸入された. 【類】 Potatoes were *introduced* ***into*** Eupope from America. / Buddhism was *introduced* ***into*** China about A.D. 67. / Walking-sticks were first *introduced* ***into*** fashion by effeminate Henry II. of France. ‖ *introduce* phonetics ***into*** the list of subjects to be studied in the training colleges 音声学を師範大学の学科目中に入れる ‖ *introduce* a young lady ***into*** society 若い淑女を社交界に紹介する. 【類】 They have *introduced* me ***into*** their charming social life and their home life. ‖ He was *introduced* ***into*** a backroom. 彼は奥のへやに案内された. ¶We *introduced* them ***to*** all our friends. 僕たちは彼らを僕たちの友人に紹介した. 【類】 Let me *introduce* you ***to*** Mr. Hida. / it is my pleasure to *introduce* ***to*** you with this letter Mr. ... / I should like to be *introduced* ***to*** her. / since the Dictionary was first *introduced* ***to*** the public.

introduction, *n.* 紹介; 緒論, 序文.

V he succeeded in ***getting*** an *introduction* to ... 彼は首尾よく...に紹介をしてもらえた. ¶***make*** a formal *introduction* 正式の紹介をする. ¶He ***needs*** no *introduction* to the music loving public. 彼は音楽愛好家には紹介の必要がない(既に知られているから). 【類】 Dr. Gulick ***needs*** no *introduction* to readers in Japan. ¶***require*** no *introduction* to readers interested in ... ...に興味をもつ読者には紹介するまでもなく周知のことである. ¶***seek*** an *introduction* from the hostess 女主人から紹介してもらう.

Q a ***biographical*** *introduction* 経歴の紹介. ¶a ***critical*** *introduction* 批評的序文. ¶on a ***first*** *introduction* 始めて紹介されたとき. ¶a ***gracious*** *introduction* 丁寧な紹介. ¶a ***historical*** *introduction* 歴史的序論. ¶Television is a ***later*** *introdurction* than the radio. テレビの出現はラジオより新しい. ¶a ***popular*** *introduction* to ... ...への一般の紹介. ¶a ***protracted*** *introduction* 長文の緒言. ¶The word is supposed to be of very ***recent*** *introduction*. その語はごく最近できたものと思われている. ¶a ***valuable*** and ***illuminating*** *introduction* 価値のある啓もう的の緒論.

P ***in*** this *introduction* この緒論において. ¶***on*** a first *introduction* はじめて紹介されたとき. 【類】 ***on*** the *introduction* from ... ‖ It proved, ***on*** *introduction*, not to be so useful as expected. 採用して見ると思ったほどに便利でなかった. ¶transact their business with a limited clientele procured ***through*** *introduction* 紹介で得た少数のお得意で営業する. ¶***with*** an *introduction* from ... ...からの紹介で.

P^2 *introduction* ***of*** European knowledge ***among*** the people その国民間におけるヨーロッパの学問の紹介. 【類】 the *introduction* ***of*** Western knowledge (the study of European languages) ***among*** the people. / the *introduction* ***of*** fire-arms ***among*** the Japanese ‖ The *introduction* ***of*** steel made high buildings easy to build. 鋼鉄材を使うようになって高層家屋の建築が容易になった. ¶the *introduction* ***of*** ... at Rome ***from*** the East 東洋からローマへの...の輸入. ¶the *introduction* ***of*** vaccination ***into*** Japan 種痘の日本への輸入. 【類】 the *introduction* ***of*** Christianity ***into*** the Far East. / the *introduction* ***of*** chess into Arabia. ¶the *in-*

troduction **of** foreign capital **to** Japan 外資の日本輸入 ‖ an *introduction* **to** a well-known professor 著名な教授への紹介 ‖ An *introduction* **to** English Grammar [書名]英文法の手引.

introspective, *a.* 内省的な.

M *morbidly introspective* 病的なくらい内省的な.

intrude, *v.* 押入る, 邪魔する.

P *intrude* **into** one's room (house, territory) へや(など)に押入る ‖ *intrude* more and more **into** the economy of modern life 現代生活の経済と関係がますます深まる. ¶*intrude* **on** one when one is busy 人が忙しいときに邪魔をする. 【類】Really, I am ashamed of thus *intruding* **on** (=**upon**) your time. ‖ May I *intrude* **on** your privacy? お邪魔をしてもよろしゅうございますか. ¶I am *intruding* **upon** you at a very busy time.

intruder, *n.* ちん入者.

Q an **unwelcome** *intruder* 歓迎のできないちん入者.

intrusion, *n.* 侵入, ちん入.

Q a **bold** *intrusion* on one's privacy 人の秘密への大胆な立入り.

P² the *intrusion* **of** women **into** the masculine sphere of influence 男性の勢力範囲内への女性の侵入.

intuition, *n.* 直覚.

Q a kind of **subconscious** *intuition* 一種の潜在的直覚.

P **by** *intuition* 直覚によって.

inundate, *v.* みなぎらす.

P *inundated* **with** flood こう水ではんらんした ‖ He has been *inundated* **with** telegrams and letters of congratulations. 彼のもとに祝電祝状がこう水のように押寄せた. 【類】I was *inundated* **with** requests from ...

inundation, *n.* こう水.

V A sudden *inundation* **rose** during the night. その夜突然こう水がでた.

inure, *v.* 慣らす; 役立つ.

P We are *inuring* ourselves **to** fatigue. われわれは自分自身を労役に慣らしている. ‖ *inured* **to** hardship (misfortune, work) 困苦(など)に慣れた. 【類】be early *inured* **to** danger ‖ The agreement *inures* **to** the benefit of the employers. その協定は使用者側に有利である.

invade, *v.* 侵略する.

P My house was *invaded* **by** a crowd of visitors. 大勢来客に押しかけられた. ¶*invade* a country **in** full force 大挙侵入する.

invalid, *n.* 病人.

V² The *invalid* is **picking up.** その病人は段々よくなっている. ¶The *invalid* **feels** easier now. その病人は今は少しよい.

Q a **bed-ridden** *invalid* 床についている病人. ¶a **chronic** *invalid* 慢性の病人. ¶a **confirmed** *invalid* 長わずらいの病人. ¶a **consumptive** *invalid* 肺病患者. ¶an **imaginary** *invalid* 気のせいで病気になっている人. ¶a **perennial** *invalid* 長年の病人.

Q² a **war** *invalid* 戦争の傷病者.

P families **with** *invalids* 傷病者のある諸家族.

invalid, *v.* 病身にする, 傷病兵として兵役を免除する.

M He was *invalided* **home** with enteric 彼は腸チフスで帰国を許された.

M² be *invalided* **down** to ... 病兵として...へ送る.

P he was *invalided* **for** a month after ... 彼は...のために一カ月の間病気だった. ¶He was *invalided* **out of** the Army. 彼は病気で陸軍を免役された. ¶the soldier was *invalided* down **to** ... その兵士は病気で...へ送られた.

invaluable, *a.* 非常に貴重な.

P *invaluable* **for** reference 参照に貴重な. ¶This book is *invaluable* **to** me. これは私には貴重な本だ.

invasion, *n.* 侵略, 侵入.

V Japan **knows** no foreign *invasion* except that of the Mongols. 日本は蒙古襲来以外に外国からの侵略を受けたことがない. ¶**prevent** the foreign trade *invasion* 外国の商業上の侵入を防ぐ. ¶**repel** an *invasion* 侵略を撃退する.

Q an **Eastern** *invasion* of Western markets 東洋の西洋市場進出. ¶**religious** *invasions* 宗教の侵入.

Q² a **blitz** *invasion* 電撃的侵入. ¶the **Broadway** *invasion* of Hollywood [映画製作業における]ハリウッドのブロードウェイ進出(ハリウッドはカリフォルニアに, ブロードウェイはニューヨーク市にある). ¶an **immigrant** *invasion* 移民の侵入.

P² an *invasion* **of** constitutional rights 憲法上人権の侵害.

invective, *n.* 悪口.

V Moralists **exercised** the *invectives* against prostitution. 道徳を論じる人たちは売春をののしった. ¶*invectives* are no longer **hurled** against those who ... ...する人たちにもう悪口を浴びせるものはない. ¶**utter** *invectives* against ... ...をののしる.

inveigh, *v.* ののしる.

P *inveigh* **against** militarism (democracy, fascism, injustice) 軍国主義(など)に極力反対する.

inveigle, *v.* だます, そそのかす.

P successfully *inveigle* some publisher **into** bringing out a book ある出版業者をだまして本を出させる ‖ He *inveigled* the lieges **into** revolt by a false assertion. 彼は虚言を用いて臣下をそそのかしそれをそむかせた.

invent, *v.* 発明する.

M So runs a story which, if not true, is at least **smartly** *invented.* これがその話の筋であるが事実でないにしてもとにかくうまく考えたものだ.

P *invented* **by** ... or annexed from abroad ...によって創作されたかまたは外国から輸入された.

O *invent* an excuse (a false story) うまい言い抜け(など)をでっちあげる.

invention, *n.* 発明, 発明品; 作りごと.

V **back** an *invention* financially 財政的に発明を後援する. ¶**claim** original *invention* for ... ...を最初に発明したと主張する. ¶**commercialize** one's *invention* その発明を営利化する. ¶the *invention* of ... is **credited** to ... ...の発明は...に帰せられている. ¶**find** the new *invention* useful その新発明が有用なことを認める. ¶**make** great *inventions* 大発明をする. ¶He duly **patented** the *invention.* 彼は正式にその発明品の専売特許を得た. ¶**perfect** (=**complete**) an *invention* 発明を完成する. ¶He is **producing** a new *invention.* 彼は新発明品を考案中だ. ¶**promote** *invention* 発明を奨励する. ¶get capital enough to **put** one's *invention* on the market 発明品を市場に出せるだけの資本を得る ‖ **put** his *invention* to practical use 彼の発明を実用化する. 【類】**put** one's *invention* on commercial basis (営業化). ¶**spread** the *inventions* abroad 無根のことを言いふらす. ¶**try** a new *invention* 新発明品を試用してみる. ¶Sneers, rather than cheers, **welcomed** the *invention.* その発明を世人はかっさいよりもむしろちょう笑をもって迎えた. ¶**work out** one's *invention* その発明を成就する.

Q The sash-window is an **English** *invention.* かまち窓は英人の発明だ. 【類】Sound photography (発声写真) is a **German** *invention.* ¶**gross** *inventions* はなはだしい虚構. ¶an **ingenious** *invention* 巧妙な発明品. ¶the **numerous** *inventions* of Thomas Edison トマス・エディソンの数多の発明. ¶claim **original** *invention* for ... ...を最初に発明したと主張する. ¶a recently **patented** *invention* 最近特許になった発明品. ¶**poetic** *invention* 詩作の才. ¶The whole story is a **pure** *invention.* その話は一切全くの作りごとだ. ¶bc of **recent** *invention* 近ごろ発明したものである. ¶a **ridiculous** *invension* ばかげた作りごと. ¶commercially **useful** *inventions* 商業的に有用な発明品. ¶a **valuable** *invention* 貴重な発明. ¶It's a **wild** *invention.* それは出たらめなうそである.

Q² an **Edison** *invention* エディソン発明品の一つ. ¶a **patent** *invention* 特許を得た発明. ¶**twentieth-century** *inventions* 第廿世紀の諸発明. ¶**Yankee** *inventions* (=notions) アメリカ人独特の小さい発明品.

P skilful **in** *invention* 発明の巧みな. ¶**of** his own *invention* 彼自身の発明にかかる. ¶Necessity is the mother **of** *invention.* 必要は発明の母なり. ¶The *invention* **of** glass took place in prehistoric times. ガラスの発明は有史前のことだ.

inventor, *n.* 発明家.

Q a **heaven-born** *inventor* 天賦の発明家. ¶a **mechanical** *inventor* 機械発明家. ¶a **prolific** *inventor* 多産な発明家. ¶a **silver-thatched** *inventor* 白髪の発明家. ¶a **versatile** *inventor* 万能の発明家.

Q² a **shorthand** *inventor* 速記術発明家.

inventory, *n.* 財産目録, 商品目録.

V **make** an *inventory* of their loss 彼らの損害の程度を調べる. ¶**take** an *inventory* of one's characteristics その特徴を一々調べあげる.

Q make a **careful** *inventory* of a year of graduate study 研究科一年間の仕事を入念に細目調べをする. ¶take a **minute** *inventory* of ... ...を細密に調査する.

P² make an *inventory* **of** one's resources その知能をしぼる ‖ his *inventory* **of** the woman 彼のその女の面相のたな下し(総評).

inverse, *n.* 逆のもの.

P² Evil is the *inverse of* good. 悪は善の逆だ.

invert, *n.* 性欲異常者.

Q a *sexual invert* 性欲異常者, 同性愛者.

invest, *v.* (**1**) 着せる; 与える; 資格を与える.

M The crown prince was ***fully invested.*** その皇太子は正式にさく立された.

P He was ***invested with*** full powers. 彼は全権を与えられた. 【類】 be ***invested with*** the power of administration (行政権) / The military governor has been ***invested with*** full authority. ‖ he was ***invested with*** the title of ... 彼は...の称号を与えられた ‖ places ***invested with*** memories of his early life 彼の若い日の思い出多い土地. 【類】 The castle is ***invested with*** mystery and romance.

(**2**) 投資する.

M he has ***invested heavily*** in ... 彼は...に多額の投資をしている. ¶He has ***recently invested*** in (=bought) an automobile. 彼は最近自動車を買った. ¶capital can be ***safely invested*** in ... 資本を...に安全に投下ができる. 【類】 The funds are ***safely*** and ***soundly invested.***

P Today he has close upon (=nearly) a million sterling ***invested in*** his business. 彼は今日では自分の事業にかれこれ百万ポンド投資している. ‖ the inevitable drop in income from the stocks and bonds ***in*** which the scholarship funds are ***invested*** 奨学資金を投資している株や公債からの収入の不可避的減退 ‖ ***invest in*** physic 薬の御厄介になる. 【類】 ***invest in*** a project (silver mine).

investigate, *v.* 調査する, 研究する.

M ***investigate at first-hand*** 直接に調査する. ¶***rigidly investigate*** 厳密に調査する. ¶***thoroughly investigate*** the cause of the accident その事故の原因を徹底的に調査する.

P ***investigate into*** an affair ある事件を調査する.

investigation, *n.* 調査, 研究.

V still ***await investigation*** なお調査を待つ. ¶from motives which would not ***bear*** close ***investigation*** 厳重な取調には堪えないような動機から. ¶***begin*** an ***investigation*** of ... ...の調査を始める. ¶***carry*** one's ***investigation forward*** (=***ahead***) 研究を進める. ¶***carry*** one's ***investigation farther*** 研究をさらに進める. ¶***carry on investigations*** in ... in the seminary of Prof ... at the University of ... ...大学の...教授の研究室で...について研究する. ¶***carry out investigations*** into ... ...の研究をやりとげる. ¶***conclude investigation*** 研究を終了する. ¶***conduct investigations*** into ... ...の研究をする. 【類】 an ***investigation conducted*** in the true scientific spirit. ¶I ***invite investigation*** of the matter. 私の方からその調査をしてくれと言いたい. ¶***make investigations*** on the subject of literature in China 中国文学の題目について研究する. 【類】 an ***investigation*** should at once be ***made*** into the facts of the situation with a view to ... ¶***prosecute*** vigorous ***investigation*** into ... ...に対する熱心な研究を遂行する. ¶***pursue*** an ***investigation*** 研究(調査)を進める. 【類】 The police are ***pursuing investigations*** in the matter. / Important studies and ***investigations*** are being ***pursued.*** / ***pursue investigations*** with great ardour (熱心). ¶***put*** the ***investigations*** into the hands of the police その調査を警察の手にゆだねる. ¶This subject is now ***receiving*** scientific ***investigation.*** この問題は今や科学的に研究されている. 【類】 It has not yet ***received*** full ***investigation.*** ¶***start*** an ***investigation*** with a view to ...ing ... ...の目的で研究を始める. ¶***take up investigation*** 研究に着手する. ¶The question is now ***undergoing*** a searching ***investigation*** at the hands of the Department. この問題は目下その省で厳密に調査されている. ¶a casual ***investigation undertaken*** for curiosity's sake, demonstrated that ... 好奇心から着手された偶然の調査によって...ということが証明された.

V² A secret ***investigation*** has been ***proceeding.*** ある研究が秘密に進められている. ¶the ***investigation*** into ... goes to ***show*** that ... ...の研究は...を示している.

Q ***advanced investigation*** 高度の研究. ¶***antiquarian investigations*** 考古的研究. ¶***close*** and ***diligent investigation*** 苦心惨たんたる研究. ¶on ***closer investigation*** よく調べて見ると. ¶***criminal investigation*** 犯罪捜査. ¶a very ***elaborate*** and ***scholarly investigation*** of ... ...のきわめて念入りで学究的な研究. ¶make ***exhaustive investigations*** in the field of ... ...の方面において徹底的な研究をする. ¶the result of ***extensive investigation*** 広はんな研究の結果. ¶***first-hand investigation*** 直接の調査. ¶***fruitful investigations*** 効果的な調査. ¶there is need of ***further investigation*** 一層進んだ調査をする必要がある. 【類】 It is a point worthy of ***further investigation.*** ¶a ***globe-girdling investigation*** of ... 全世界にわたる...調査. ¶rouse the authorities to ***keen investigation*** into the causes その原因を鋭意調査するように当局の注意を呼び起す. ¶the art of ***historical investigation*** 歴史的研究法. ¶a ***laborious*** but ***fruitless investigation*** 労多くして功少い調査. ¶***Little investigation*** has been made. あまり調査をしていなかった. ¶***original investigations*** in untrodden fields 前人未踏の分野における独創的な研究. ¶***pioneer investigation*** 率先した研究. ¶***recent investigations*** on the subject その問題に関する最近の研究. ¶start a ***rigid investigation*** to find out ... ...を見きわめるため厳密な調査を始める. ¶prosecute ***rigorous investigations*** into ... ...に厳重な調査を行う. ¶***scientific investigation*** of the subject その問題の科学的調査. ¶a ***scholarly investigation*** 学究的研究. ¶make a ***searching investigation*** into ... ...を徹底的に調査する. ¶make a ***statistical invesigation*** of ... ...を統計的に研究する ‖ it is shown by ***statistical investigation*** that ... ¶It has never been the subject of a ***systematic*** and ***exhaustive investigation.*** それはこれまで組織的な徹底的な研究題目にはならなかった. ¶***technical investigations*** 技術上の調査. ¶make a ***thorough investigation*** of vice conditions in that city その市の犯罪状況を徹底的に調査する. ¶his ***valuable investigation*** on ... ...に関する彼の貴重な研究.

Q² ***field investigation*** [飛行機事故などの]現場調査. ¶a ***full-scale investigation*** is under way into 大規模の調査が行われている. ¶"***loyalty***" ***investigations*** of Federal workers 連邦職員の「忠誠」(米国政府にそむく意志があるか否かの)調査. ¶an ***on-the-spot investigation*** 現地調査. ¶place a firm under ***police investigation*** 会社を警察の手で調査する. ¶conduct ***spot investigations*** 現地調査を行う.

P ***According to*** official ***investigation,*** the population of Tokyo numbered 1,705,028 in 1902. 公式の調査によると東京の人口は一九〇二年に百七十万五千二十八人を算した. ¶***by*** his careful ***investigation*** of ... ...についての彼の綿密な研究によって. ¶the subject ***of*** an ***investigation*** conducted by ... ...の行った研究題目 ‖ a line ***of investigation*** 研究の方面. ¶***on*** closer ***investigation*** it will be found that ... 一層詳しく調べると...ということが分かるだろう ‖ ***on*** a fuller ***investigation*** on the subject その問題をもっとよく調べると. ¶The matter is ***pending investigation.*** まだ調べがついていない. ¶knowledge gained ***through*** one's own careful ***investigations*** 自身の注意深い研究によって得た知識. ¶the subject ***under investigation*** 研究中の問題. ¶***upon investigation*** I ascertained that ... 研究の結果私は...ということを確かめた.

P² an ***investigation as to*** the comparative utility of the motor-bus and tram-car 乗合自動車と電車との効用比較についての調査. ¶an ***investigation by*** ... shows that ... ...の調査によると...である. ¶a statistical ***investigation concerning*** ... ...についての統計的研究. ¶***investigations in*** folk psychology 民族心理学における研究. ¶a scientific ***investigation into*** the possibilities of gas-turbines ガスタービンの可能性についての科学的研究 ‖ ***investigations into*** the causes of ... ...の諸原因調査. ¶an ***investigation of*** health conditions 健康状態の調査 ‖ ***investigation of*** reliability 身もと調査. ¶***investigations on*** the relation of the house-fly to disease はえと疾病との関係に関する調査 ‖ during the progress of the ***investigations on*** the dynamo 発電機に関する研究中に.

investigator, *n.* 研究家.

V The question is one which has ***exercised*** many ***investigators.*** その問題は幾多の研究家が手に掛けたものである.

Q an ***earnest investigator*** 熱心な研究家. ¶an ***experienced investigator*** of twenty years' standing 二十年の経験ある研究家. ¶a "***get-wise-quick***" ***investigator*** 一夜づけの研究家. ¶a ***juvenile investigator*** 少年研究家. ¶***previous investigators*** (=one's predecessors) in this field この方面研究の先輩. ¶a ***scientific investigator*** 科学的研究者. ¶a staff of ***trained investigators*** 訓練を経た研究家グループ.

Q² a ***juvenile inverstigator*** 少年保護司.

P² an ***investigator of*** street signs 街頭看板の研究家.

investiture, *n.* 叙任, 授与; 冊立.
V *obtain investiture* from ... ...から任命される.
P² the *Investiture of* the Prince of Wales 英国皇太子のさく立. ¶*investiture with* a title 称号の授与.

investment, *n.* 投資.
V The industry ***has*** large *investments* of capital. その事業には多大の資本が下してある. ¶***make*** an *investment* in ... ...に投資する ‖ You are certain that you are ***making*** a sure *investment*. 君はその投資で損をする気づかいはない. ¶***protect*** one's *investments* その投資を保護する. ¶This colossal undertaking ***represents*** an *investment* of 10,000,000 dollars. この大企業の資本金は一千万ドルである.【類】***represent*** an approximate *investiment* of ...
Q His savings were nearly all wiped out by a ***bad*** *investment* in a store. 彼の貯蓄はある商店の経営が失敗したのでほとんど全部飛んでしまった. ¶By ***careful*** *investment*, he obtained a big profit. 慎重な投資で彼は巨利を得た. ¶make a ***considerable*** *investment* in ... ...に金を掛ける. ¶a ***doubtful*** *investment* 疑わしい投資. ¶A good antique is a ***good*** *investment*. たしかな古物を買うのは利回のいい投資(好利殖法)になる. ¶***profitable*** *investment* 有利な投資. ¶***gilt-edged*** *investment* 確実な投資. ¶The industry represents a ***huge*** *investment*. その産業にはばく大な投資がしてある. ¶a ***lucrative*** *investment* 有利な投資. ¶***mercantile*** *investment* 商業上の投資. ¶make it a ***paying*** *investment* それを引合う投資にする. ¶a ***poor*** *investment* もうけの薄い投資. ¶a ***risky*** *investment* of money 危険な投資. ¶It is a ***safe*** *investment* to dress well. 服装をよくするのは安全な投資だ(損にならない). ¶a ***safe*** and ***sure*** *investment* 安全確実な投資. ¶a ***solid*** *investment* 確実な投資. ¶a ***sound*** *investment* 健全な投資. ¶a dangerously ***speculative*** *investment* 投機的で危険な投資. ¶a ***wise*** *investment* 賢明なる投資.【類】It will always be found a ***wise*** *investment*.
Q² make a ***long-range*** *investment* 長期にわたる投資をする. ¶a ***long-term business*** *investment* 長期商業投資. ¶Japan's ***overseas*** *investment* 日本の海外投資.
P a promising field ***for*** *investment* 有望な投資方面. ¶He would rather place his money ***in*** the best *investment* there is. 彼は一番いい投資に金をつぎ込みたいと思っている.
P² *investment* ***in*** real estate (stocks) 土地(など)への投資. ¶an *investment* ***of*** $500 ***in*** war bonds 戦時公債に五百ドルの投資.

investor, *n.* 投資者.
Q a ***bona-fide*** *investor* 善意の投資者. ¶a ***speculative*** *investor* 山師的な投資者. ¶a ***timid*** *investor* おく病な投資者.

invisible, *a.* 目に見えない.
M ***completely*** *invisible* 全く見えない.
P *invisible* ***from*** here ここから見えない. ¶*invisible* ***to*** the naked eye 肉眼では見えない.

invitation, *n.* 招待状, 招待, 勧誘.
V He has ***accepted*** an *invitation* to take charge of the glass works. 彼はそのガラス工場の監督を持掛けられてこれを承諾した. ‖ ***accept*** an *invitation* to be present at ... ...に出席の招待を承諾する.【類】***accept*** an *invitation* with pleasure.【類】Twenty nations have ***accepted*** *invitations* to attend the Congress. / I ***accepted*** an *invitation* to dine with him. / ***accept*** the *invitation* tendered (与えた) to him. ¶***decline*** an *invitation* to dinner 正さんの招待を断る.【類】***decline*** an *invitation* with regrets (遺憾ながら) ‖ To my great regret I must ***decline*** your *invitation*. ¶You will therefore please ***disregard*** the *invitation* for Thursday afternoon. それゆえ木曜日の午後の招待は御放念下さい. ¶***extend*** a cordial *invitation* to (=for) them to ... 彼らに...するよう丁重な招待状を送る.【類】A cordial *invitation* has been ***extended*** to all to be present. / An *invitation* to attend this lecture is ***extended*** by the Society to all persons interested. ¶***get*** an *invitation* to dinner 晩さんに招かれる. ¶***give*** a pressing *invitation* to ... ...にしきりに勧める. ¶I ***had*** an *invitation* to tea from ... 私は...からお茶の会によばれた. ¶***issue*** *invitations* for the marriage of her daughter to ... ...に娘の結婚の招待状を出す.【類】***issue*** *invitations* to ... to attend ... ¶She ***kept*** a standing *invitation* to visit her. 彼女は絶えず人の訪問を受けていた. ¶***recall*** (=***cancel***) *invitations* 招待を取消す. ¶***receive*** an *invitation* to a party ある宴会に招待を受ける. ¶It would be very rude to ***refuse*** his *invitation* a second time. あの人の招待を二度断っては大変失礼になろう. ¶***send*** an *invitation* by post or by a messenger 郵便または使いで招待状を送る. ¶***send out*** *invitations* for a luncheon in his honor 彼のための午さんの招待状を出す. ¶***withdraw*** an *invitation* 招待を取消す. ¶***write*** one's *invitations* on paper 招待状を書く.
V² an *invitation* ***came*** from ... to dinner ...から晩さん会の招待が来た.
Q The *invitation* is a very ***appealing*** one and I should be happy to accept it if it were possible for me to do so. その御招待は非常にうれしいのでできることならお受け致したいのですが. ¶extend a most ***cordial*** *invitation* for the representation of ... ...代表者派遣に対する最も懇篤な招請を発する. ¶receive a ***distasteful*** *invitation* 迷惑な招待を受ける. ¶the ***kind*** *invitation* extended in your letter of ... 貴方の...付手紙による御親切な招待. ¶a ***not-to-be-refused*** *invitation* to a dinner-and-theater party 万障繰合わして出席をこうという食事付観劇会招待券. ¶an ***urgent*** (=a ***pressing***) *invitation* 緊急の招き. ¶a ***written*** *invitation* 招待状.
Q² accept a ***dinner*** *invitation* 晩さんの招待を承諾する.
P ***at*** the *invitation* of the Carnegie Peace Foundation カーネギー平和財団から招待されて ‖ ***at*** his *invitation* 彼から招待されて. ¶***by*** *invitation* of ... ...の招待で. ¶Many thanks ***for*** your *invitation*. 御招待下さいましてありがとう. ¶***On*** (=***Upon***) the *invitation* of ..., he returned to Japan. ...に勧められて彼は日本に帰った.【類】He joined the staff (部員) ***on*** my *invitation*. ¶in compliance ***with*** an *invitation* from ... ...の勧めに従って.
P² accept an *invitation* ***for*** tomorrow's dinner 明日の晩さん会の招待を受諾する. ¶an *invitation* ***from*** ... ...からの招待. ¶an *invitation* ***to*** dinner (a party) 正さん(など)への招待.

invite, *v.* 招待する, 勧める.
M The public is ***cordially*** *invited*. 一般公衆の出席を切に願う. ‖ Inspection is ***cordially*** *invited*. 是非御一覧下さい (店の陳列など). ¶***earnestly*** *invite* 懇請する. ¶*invite* (=ask) him ***out*** to dinner 彼を正さんに招く. ¶Inspection ***respectfully*** *invited*. 是非御来観下さい [店などへ].【類】the patrons are ***respectfully*** and ***earnestly*** *invited* to contribute their criticisms, whether favorable or otherwise, on ... to ... ¶You are ***urgently*** *invited* to attend ...
M² It was nice of you to *invite* me ***over***. わたしをお客さんに呼んで下さってありがとう.
P *invite* a person ***into*** the house 人を家に招く. ¶*invite* a person ***to*** a wedding (party, dinner) 人を結婚式(など)に招待する ‖ He *invited* me ***to*** a seat in a boat. 彼はボートに乗れと私に言ってくれた.
O She is seldom *invited* to go out. 彼女は滅多に人の家に招待されない. ¶*invite* him to assist at the ceremony 彼にその式へ出席するように勧める.

invocation, *n.* 祈願.
V ***chant*** the *invocation* "Namu Amida-Butsu!" 南無阿彌陀仏と称名を唱える. ¶***muttering*** the omnipotent *invocation* "Namu Amida-Butsu! NAB" 南無阿彌陀仏, 南無...と無量の功徳ある念仏をつぶやきながら. ¶The Right Rev. G. Ashton Oldham, Bishop of Albany, ***pronounced*** the *invocation* at the dedication. アルバニーの監督アシュストン・オールダム猊下(げいか)がその献堂式で祈とうをした. ¶***repeat*** the *invocation* three times 三度祈りを繰返す.【類】ceaselessly ***repeat*** the same *invocation*, "*Namu myoho renge kyo! Namu myoho renge kyo!*"
Q utter the ***holy*** *invocation* お題目を唱える.
P ***with*** an *invocation* for Divine guidance and aid 神のお導きとお助けをお祈りして.

invoice, *n.*〖商〗送り状, 仕切状(インボイス).
V ***accept*** an *invoice* 送状を受理する. ¶***check*** an *invoice* 送状を付合わす. ¶***obtain*** from the United States Consul a consular *invoice* in quadruplicate 合衆国領事から正副四通の領事仕切状を入手する.
V² *invoice* ***covering*** goods shipped to ... ...向の積荷記載の送状.
Q a ***duplicate*** *invoice* = an invoice in duplicate 送状副本. ¶an ***export*** (***import***) *invoice* 輸(出)入送状. ¶an ***original*** *invoice* 送状正本.
P state ***on*** an *invoice* 送状に明記する.

invoke, *v.* 呼びよせる.
P *invoke* evil spirits ***on*** ... ...に悪霊を取付かせようとする.

involve, *v.* 包む; 巻き込む; 陥れる.

M be ***perpetually involving*** oneself in lawsuits 始終訴訟にわずらわされている. ¶be ***successively involved*** in war 相次いで戦争に参加する. ¶be spared exasperation and delay ***usually involved*** 普通その結果起る焦慮と遅延とを免れる.

P The early history of pavements is ***involved in*** obscurity. 舗道の初期の歴史はよく分かっていない. ‖ I was once ***involved in*** an argument with a Canadian on the question. 私はこの問題でかつて一カナダ人と議論した. ‖ be ***involved in*** a case ある事件に引合に出される. 【類】The firm is *involved* (=implicated) ***in*** the failure. / *involve* him ***in*** expenses (a trouble) / *involve* him ***in*** no obligation to ... ‖ become ***involved in*** financial difficulties 財政難に陥る ‖ The origin of this word is ***involved in*** obscurity. この言葉の起りは不明である. ‖ The buildings were ***involved in*** the same ruin. その建物もひとしく残がいとなった(地震などで). ‖ He is deeply ***involved in*** debt. 彼は借金を山ほど背負っている. ‖ He was ***involved in*** working out a puzzle. 彼はなぞを解こうと一生懸命だった. ‖ Without *involving* the reader ***in*** too much technical language, it may be stated thus. 術語を使ってはかえって読者をわずらわすことになるので次のように述べる. ¶He said that no person was ***involved with*** him in his crimes. 彼は自分の犯罪には連累者は一人もないと言った.

inwardness, *n.* 真相.

Q learn the ***true inwardness*** of ... ...の真相を知る.

ion, *n.* 〔理〕イオン.

Q a ***negative*** (***positive***) ***ion*** 陰(陽)イオン.

iota, *n.* 僅少.

V ***contribute*** one ***iota*** to ... ...に一片の微力を尽す.

P without disturbing ***by*** one ***iota*** ... 少しも...をかく乱せずに.

ire, *n.* 怒り.

V ***arouse*** the ***ire*** of ... against ... ...に対して...の憤怒の念を起させる. ¶***brave*** the paternal ***ire*** 父の怒りを無視する. ¶***draw*** on oneself the ***ire*** of ... ...の怒りを招く. ¶***excite*** the ***ire*** of ... ...を怒らす. ¶***rouse*** the ***ire*** of ... ...を怒らす. ¶***vent*** one's ***ire*** on うつ憤を...にぶちまける.

iridescence, *n.* 真珠色.

Q glass with the ***soft iridescence*** of a pearl 柔らかい真珠色をしたガラス.

iron, *n.* 鉄; アイロン.

V ore ***containing iron*** 鉄分を含有する鉱石. ¶Don't try to ***keep*** too many ***irons*** in the fire. 余り色々のことに手を出すな. 【類】He ***had*** many ***irons*** in the fire, and he kept them all hot. ¶***leave*** one's ***iron*** on アイロンをかけっぱなしにしておく.

Q ***cast iron*** 鋳鉄. ¶***corrugated iron*** 波状鉄板. ¶an ***electric iron*** 電気アイロン. ¶***galvanized iron*** 亜鉛引鉄板. ¶Strike while the ***iron*** is ***hot***. 〔諺〕鉄は熱い中に打て(好機を逸するな). ¶***meteoric iron*** いん鉄. ¶use a ***moderate iron*** ほどよい温度のアイロンを使う. ¶***waving*** (=***curling***) ***iron*** [髪などの]カール用アイロン. ¶***wrought iron*** 鍛鉄.

Q² ***bar iron*** 条鉄. ¶***fire irons*** 炉用鉄具(ひのしなど). ¶***L angle iron*** L 形鉄. ¶***pig iron*** 銑鉄. ¶***plate iron*** 延板の鉄. ¶a ***polishing iron*** つや付アイロン. ¶be starring for ***scrap iron*** 屑鉄を渇望している. ¶***sheet iron*** 鉄板. ¶***Tee iron*** T 字形鉄. ¶an electric ***waffle iron*** 電気ワッフル製造器.

P a worker ***in iron*** かじ屋. ¶a man ***of iron*** 意志強固の人.

iron, *v.* アイロンをかける; 障害を除く.

M ***iron out*** some knotty problems 難問題を円満に解決する ‖ ***iron out*** misunderstandings 誤解を解く. 【類】***iron out*** dispute among ... / ***iron out*** conflicting viewpoints. 【類】There are many practical difficulties to be ***ironed out***. / ***iron out*** differences on various national problems.

ironwork, *n.* 鉄製品.

Q ***galvanize ironwork*** 鉄製品に亜鉛メツキする. ¶***painted ironwork*** ペンキ塗の鉄製部.

P² ***ironwork for*** buildings 建物の鉄製品.

irony, *n.* 風刺, 皮肉, 反語.

V It ***illustrates*** the ***irony*** of fate. それは運命の皮肉の一例になる.

Q condemn ... in ***biting irony*** 辛らつな皮肉で...を非難する. ¶a ***bitter irony*** 辛らつな皮肉. ¶by the ***curious irony*** of chance 不思議な回り合せで. 【類】by a ***curious irony*** of fate. ¶***diabolical irony*** 極悪非道な皮肉. ¶with a ***fine irony*** 巧みな風刺で. ¶***life's ironies*** 人生の皮肉. 【類】life's ***little irony***. ¶***malicious irony*** 意地悪な皮肉. ¶a ***quiet irony*** 穏かな風刺. ¶strike the note of ***scathing irony*** 辛らつな皮肉を飛ばす. ¶By ***some irony*** of fate, Nature gave the weaker sex strong hair—the stronger sex weaker hair. 皮肉な運命で自然は女に強い毛を男に弱い毛を与えた(男のははげるから). ¶by a ***strange irony*** of fate 奇妙な回り合わせで.

P I was stricken dumb ***by*** his ***irony***. 彼の皮肉でぎゃふんと参った. ‖ ***by*** the ***irony*** of fate 皮肉なことには. ¶a delightful stroke ***of irony*** 痛快な皮肉の一撃. ¶There was a touch ***of irony*** in his speech. 彼の演説にはちょっと風刺があった. ¶***with*** abundant ***irony*** and sarcasm 風刺や皮肉沢山で.

P² It was the ***irony of*** fate that in taking up arms against Germany Japan should have appeared to be aiding Russia. ドイツと戦争することになった日本がロシアに加担する形となったのは運命の皮肉であった.

irreconcilability, *n.* 和解不能.

Q² the ***Kuomintang-Communist irreconcilability*** 国民党と共産党の和解不能.

irreconcilable, *a.* 和解し難い.

P ***irreconcilable to*** (=***with***) a person ... 人と和合し難い.

irregular, *n.* 不正規兵, ゲリラ兵.

Q a ***Chinese irregular*** 中国不正規兵.

irregular, *a.* 不規則の.

P be ***irregular in*** one's attendance 出席が不規則である ‖ ***irregular in*** shape 不正規な形の.

irregularity, *n.* 不規則.

Q ***incorrigible irregularity*** of habits 矯正し難い不規律な習慣. ¶***postal irregularities*** 郵便事務の不整とん.

P² ***irregularities in*** books 帳簿の不正 ‖ ***irregularities in*** connection with rental of city-owned piers 市有桟橋使用料に関する不規律(料金のまちまち). 【類】***irregularities*** (でこぼこ) ***of*** the earth's surface.

irrelevant, *a.* 筋違いの.

M be ***altogether irrelevant*** もっての外である.

P ***irrelevant to*** the present problem 今の問題とは筋違いの.

irresolution, *n.* 優柔不断, 無定見.

V ***display*** (=***show***) considerable ***irresolution*** 大いに心がまどう.

irrespective, *a.* 無関係の.

P ***irrespective of*** their nationality 国籍のいかんにかかわらず. 【類】***irrespective of*** cost / ***irrespective of*** color (民族) / ***irrespective of*** duty status (職務) / ***irrespective of*** their length / ***irrespective of*** sex (age, social status) / ***irrespective of*** size / ***irrespective of*** creed, race, or nationality ‖ newspapers ***irrespective of*** party affiliations 不偏不党の新聞 ‖ ***irrespective of*** the time of day 時間にお構いなしで(いつであろうと).

irresponsibility, *n.* 無責任.

P² the ***irresponsibility of*** the report 該報告書の無責任.

irresponsible, *a.* 責を負わない.

M That sounds ***rather irresponsible***. それは少し無責任のように聞える. ¶be ***utterly irresponsible*** 無責任きわまる.

P He is utterly ***irresponsible for*** what he says. 彼は全然無責任なことを言う.

irrigate, *v.* かんがいする.

P a land ***irrigated by*** streams 沢山の流れでかんがいされた土地.

irrigation, *n.* かんがい.

Q ***intestinal irrigations*** かん腸.

P² About 170,000 acres of land have been brought ***under irrigation***, as the result of constructing the canal. その疎水工事が竣成したため約十七万エーカーの土地がかんがいされるようになった.

irritability, *n.* 短気, かんぺき.

Q ***explosive irritability*** 怒りっぽい気短かさ. ¶***nervous irritability*** 神経のいらだち. ¶***sulky irritability*** 気むずかしさ. ¶***touchy irritability*** かん癖.

irritate, *v.* 怒らす, いらいらさせる.

P He was ***irritated against*** you. 彼は君に対して腹を立てていた. ¶Do not be ***irritated at*** my sadness. 私の悲嘆を気に掛けて下さるな. ‖ ***irritated at*** ill-treatment 虐待を憤慨して. ¶***irritated by*** (=***with***) him 彼に対して腹を立てて.

O Sunburn ***irritates*** our skin. 日焼けははだをひりひりさせる.

irritation, *n.* 刺激, きん衝, 痛み.

V ***allay*** the ***irritation*** of the skin 皮膚の痛みを和らげる. ¶***relieve irritation*** 痛みを軽減する.

Q² a gargle to relieve minor ***throat irritations*** due to colds かぜのため軽いのどの痛みを緩和するうがい薬でのうがい.

island, *n.* 島.

V The *island* was *discovered* at about 4 a.m. on the 25th of March. 三月二十五日の午前四時ごろにその島が見えた. ¶*inhabit* an *island* 島に住む.

Q an *artificial island* 造った島. ¶shipwrecked on a *desert island* 無人島に難船して. ¶a *desolate island* 無人島. ¶Bayuca, a *fabled island* of the Indians, in which they stated there was a fountain of eternal youth 不老の泉があるというインド人の架空的な島ベイユーカ. ¶*floating islands* of ice and snow 氷と雪の浮流島(流氷). ¶the *Japanese Islands* 日本諸島. ¶*lonely islands* さびしい島. ¶the *main island* of Japan 日本本土. ¶an *outlying* (=*offlying*) *island* 離れ島. ¶*pine-clad islands* 松の生えている島々. ¶a *savage island* 蛮人の住む島. ¶a *spooky island* 幽霊島. ¶an *uninhabited island* 無人島.

Q² an *atoll* [*island*] 環礁島. ¶a *coral island* さんご島. ¶the Japanese *home islands* 日本人の故国の島々. 【類】outside the *home islands* of Japan. ¶the former Japanese *mandate islands* the Marshalls, the Carolines, and the Marianas 旧日本委任統治諸島(マーシャル, カロリン, マリアナ群島). ¶the *South Pacific Islands* 南太平洋諸島. ¶a *volcano island* 火山島.

P the noted Valley of Death *in* the *island* of Java ジャヴァ島の名高い死の谷 ‖ *in* the *island* of Shikoku 四国に. ¶Not a Russian was then *on* the *island* of Sakhalin. 当時樺太にはロシア人は一人もいなかった. 【類】The home of the famous Venetian glass is *on* the *island* of Murano, a mile north of Venice. / Benten's shrines are mostly situated *on islands*. / The American metropolis is built *on* the *Island* of Manhattan. / Pearl Harbor, *on* the *island* of Oahu in Hawaii, is destined to become the great naval base of the Pacific. / Opposite Kure, *on* Etajima, stands the Naval College. / He has a residence *on* Long *Island*, N.Y., but does business in New York City.

P² the *island* *of* Great Britain 大英国島(イングランド, スコットランド, ウエールスを含めたもの). ¶an *island off* the east coast of ... ...東海岸沖の島.

islander, *n.* 島民.

Q² *Pacific islanders* 太平洋諸島民. ¶*Solomon islanders* ソロモン群島民.

isle, *n.* 島.

Q the *British Isles* 英国諸島(イングランド, アイルランド及びその周辺の小島を含めて).

Q² in these *sea-girt isles* これらの海に囲まれた島では. ¶our *time-girt isle* of life 人生という時間に囲まれた島.

P *in* the British *Isles* 英国諸島に. ¶*on* the *Isle* of Man マン島に.

ism, *n.* 主義.

Q an *alien ism* 外国の主義.

isolate, *v.* 隔離する.

M *telegraphically isolated* 電信不通の.

P *isolated from* the world (another person) 世界(など)から孤立した. 【類】The patients should be *isolated* (隔離する) *from* the rest.

isolation, *n.* 孤立.

Q a policy of *dictatorial isolation* 衆議によってことを決しない政策. ¶a *feudal isolation* of Japan 日本の封建的孤立. ¶a *geographical isolation* 地理上の隔離. ¶*international isolation* 国際的孤立. ¶*political isolation* 政治的孤立. ¶*rigorous isolation* of the diseased ones 病人の厳重な隔離. ¶a *splendid isolation* 光栄ある孤立. ¶stand in *sublime isolation* 崇高な孤立状態をなす.

P keep a patient *in isolation* 患者を隔離する.

isolationist, *n.* 《米》孤立主義者.

Q He is known as a *stubborn isolationist*. 彼はがん固な孤立主義者として知られている.

issuance, *n.* 発行.

Q² new *currency issuance* 新貨幣発行.

issue, *n.* (**1**) 発行.

V The publisher has found it impossible to *maintain* the weekly *issue*. 出版者はその週刊を続けることは不可能だということを知った. ¶I never *miss* an *issue* 私は毎号必ず買う.

Q in its *current issue* その今月(週)号に. ¶This *enlarged issue* of the Vigilance Record takes the place of the normal *issues* for June and July. ヴィジランス・レコードは増大号を発行して六月と七月号の普通号に代えることにした. ¶an *extra special issue* 臨時特集号. ¶the *largest issue* 最もページ数の多い号. ¶it was printed in the *May 21, 1919, issue* of an English trade-paper called ... それは...という英国の商業新聞の一九一九年五月二十一日号に掲載された. ¶in the *New Year's issue* 新年号に. ¶in a *recent issue* of the Hochi 最近発行の「報知」に. ¶I've just finished reading your *special issue* on Africa. 私はアフリカに関する貴誌の特別号を今読み終った所です. 【類】Congratulations on your special *African issue*.

Q² a *bond issue* 公債発行. 【類】a $50,000,000 *bond issue*. ¶the *April 5 issue* of "Life" 四月五日発行の「ライフ」誌. ¶make a *debenture issue* 社債を発行する. ¶the *Govenment issue* of military outfits to soldiers 兵士に対する政府の用品給与. ¶in its *May issue* for 1955 一九五五年五月号に. ¶be clothed in *regulation issue* 正規の服装だ. ¶a special *stamp issue* 特別郵便切手発行.

P in an article *in* the *issue* for Feb. 21, 1882 一八八二年二月二十一日発行の分の記事に. 【類】The next article will appear *in* an early *issue*. ¶The price *of issue* is par. 発行価格は額面通り. ¶commencing *with* the February *issue* 二月号から始めて.

P² a new *issue of* a book 書籍の新刊行.

(**2**) 問題, 争点.

V *complicate* the *issue* 問題を複雑にする. ¶*decide* the *issues* raised by ... ...から起る問題を解決する ‖ That *issue* must be *decided* before any other questions can be dealt with. その問題は他の問題を処理する前に解決されねばならない. ¶The question *involves* immense *issues*. その問題は重大な争点を含む. ¶we are not *joining issue* with him when we say ... われわれが...というからとて彼と議論を戦わそうとしているのではない. ¶*leave* the *issue* in higher hands 問題をもっと上の人の手にゆだねる. ¶*raise* complicated *issues* 複雑な問題を引き起す ‖ It is a pity to *raise* a metaphysical *issue* of this kind. こんな哲学問題をかつぎ出すのは遺憾である. ¶*resolve* an *issue* 問題を解決する. ¶*settle* amicably the *issue* in dispute 係争中の問題を友誼的に解決する. ¶*take issue* on this point この点で論争する ‖ *take* (=*join*) *issue* with ... ...を向うに回して議論する.

V² No big *issues came* up. 大問題は起らなかった.

Q Whether ... or ... is a *debatable issue*. これかあれかは討議のある問題だ. ¶raise *fake issues* せん気筋の議論をする. ¶raise *false issues* せん気筋の議論を引き起す. ¶the *general issues* of a labor dispute 労働争議の一般問題. ¶a *grave issue* 重大問題. ¶child labor, one of the *great political, industrial, social* and *moral issues* of today 少年労働即ち今日の政治的・産業的・社会的及び道徳的大問題の一つ. ¶the *hottest political issue* in France フランスの緊急政治問題. ¶offer an *ideal* campaigning *issue* 選挙戦に理想的な題目となる. ¶new books on *international issues* 国際問題に関する新刊書. ¶*larger issues* of national life 国民生活のより大なる問題. ¶a question of *live issue* 《米》当面の問題. ¶The question of the wisdom of coeducation is yet a *living issue*. 男女共学の可否はいまだに議論が尽きない. ¶a *momentous issue* 重要な問題. ¶a *past issue* 過去の問題. ¶the No. 1 *political issue* 第一の政治問題. ¶a *serious issue* 大切な問題. ¶steer clear of a *thorny issue* 当りさわりのある問題に触れない. ¶a *universal issue* 世界的問題.

Q² The *inflation issue* is a touchy one. インフレは複雑な問題である. ¶a *side issue* 付帯(枝葉の)問題. ¶a *wage-price issue* 賃銀物価問題. ¶the major *world issue* of the day 今日重大の世界問題.

P the point *at issue* 問題点 ‖ the question *at issue* 当面の問題 ‖ we are entirely *at issue* with those who maintain that ... われわれは...と主張する人々と全く意見を異にしている. ¶the question *in issue* 争議されている問題.

P² The submarine *issue between* the United States and Germany has been settled. 米ドイツ間の潜水艦問題は解決された. ¶*issues of* the day 時事諸問題.

(**3**) 子孫.

V He *had* no *issue*. 彼には子がなかった. ¶He *left* no *issue*. 彼が死んで後に子供がなかった.

Q One out of every six marriages in the United States now fails to result in *live issue*. 現今米国では六組の結婚中一組は夫婦間に子ができない. ¶He is without *male issue*. 彼には男の子がない.

P He died *without issue*. 彼は子なしで死んだ. ‖ Her union with him proved *without issue*. 彼女と彼との間には子ができなかった.

(**4**) 結果.

V *abide* (=*face*) the *issue* その結果を甘受する. ¶*await* the *issue* of the events 事件の成行を待つ.

Q of *doubtful issue* 結果の疑わしい. 【類】 The *issue* is extremely *doubtful*. ¶conduct the matter to a *triumphal issue* その事件を成功させる.

P *in* the *issue* 結局は.

P^2 since the successful *issue from* the Russian campaign 首尾よくロシア征戦に勝って以来. ¶The *issue of* marriage has been five children. その結婚で結局五人の子供ができた.

(5) [軍需品などの]給与, 配給.

Q a *new issue* 新給与.

Q^2 articles of the *Army* (*Government*) *issue* 軍隊(など)給与品.

issue, *v*. 発する, 生じる; 振りだす.

M smoke *issuing forth* from a volcano 火山からふきだす煙.

Q policies *issued against* damages by fire 火災保険証書. ¶Return tickets are *issued at* a fare and a half. 往復切符が片道賃金の五割増で発行されている. 【類】 Through (Excursion) tickets (通し(回遊)切符) are *issued at* principal stations. ‖ The loan, though *issued at* par, was covered over twenty-four times. 額面通りに発行された公債の応募額が二十四倍以上になった. ¶The maximum amount *for* which a single money order may be *issued* in America is $100. 米国では一回の郵便為替の最高金額は百ドルだ. ¶An Army Order was *issued from* the War Office. 軍令が陸軍省から発せられた. ‖ a stream *issuing from* (=taking its rise in) a lake 湖水から流れでる小川. 【類】 all the works *issued from* his pen / the number now *issuing from* the press (目下出版中) / periodical tickets (定期乗車券) are *issued from ... to ...* ¶*issue* passports *to* persons going abroad 洋行する人に旅券を発行する ‖ be prepared to *issue to* the public 公衆に配布のために発行する用意ができている. 【類】 *issue* the volume *to* subscribers (読者) at the price of 40s. / *issue* a book *to* the world (=public) ‖ Cheap return tickets are *issued to* all South Coast resorts. 南海岸の観光地行割引往復切符が発行されている.

italic, *n*. イタリック(斜体活字).

P printed *in italics* イタリックで印刷された.

itch, *n*. かゆみ; かいせん; 渇望.

V *have* the *itch* かいせんにかかっている ‖ He *has* the scribbler's *itch*. 彼はやたらに書きたがる.

Q with a most *pronounced itch* in his palm のどから手がでるように欲しがる(わいろ・心付などを).

P^2 an *itch for* money 金銭欲.

itch, *v*. 渇望する.

P My fingers *itch for* a fray. [けんかしたさで]この腕がむ鳴る.

O My hands *itch* to do it. 僕はそれをやりたっくて腕がむずずしている.

item, *n*. 箇条, 項目, 内訳; 種(品)目; 一片の記事.

V It *forms* a serious *item* of expenditure. それは大変入費がかかる. ¶*state items* of an account 勘定の内訳をする.

V^2 an *item appeared* in one of the gossip papers to the effect that ... よた新聞の一つに...という記事が出た.

Q Steamship rates are the *biggest item* of a trip to Europe. 船賃が欧州旅行費の最大項目になる. ¶the *chief item* in the week of festivities 一週間の祭典の主な種目. ¶a *heavy item* of cost 大きな費目. ¶an *important item* in the export returns 輸出統計表中の重要な項目. ¶a batch of *informing items* 一括した有益な事項. ¶*local items* 〖新聞〗 地方記事. ¶those *minor items* of sport events 競技中のそういった小さい種目. ¶the most *momentous items* of intelligence 情報の最も重要な項目. ¶a *negligible item* 言うに足らない費目. ¶There is many a *tempting item* upon the programme. そのプログラムには人を引付ける種目が沢山ある.

Q^2 move to the next *agenda item* 会議の次の項目に進む. ¶*city items* 〖新聞〗 市内地方版の記事. ¶kill a *budget item* 予算の項目を削る. ¶*business items*=items of business 営業種目. ¶*clothing items* 衣料品. ¶*consumer items* of minor importance 重要性の低い消費物資. ¶a *credit item* 貸方項目. ¶a *debit item* 借方項目. ¶a chief *export item* of Scotland スコットランドの主な輸出品. ¶vital *food items* 重要食料品 ‖ allocation of *food* and *other relief items* 食料その他救助項目の割当. ¶a *front-page item* 〖新聞〗 第一面記事. ¶*furniture items* 家具の項目. ¶*handicraft items* 手芸項目. ¶3,500 *import items* 三千五百の輸入品. ¶major *living-cost items* 主な生活費. ¶*luxury items* ぜいたく品. ¶*market-basket items* 市場の買物. ¶a $450 *million item* for the further development of atomic energy 原子力開発のために四億五千万ドルの(予算の)項目. ¶a *news* item 〖新聞〗 一片のニュース.

P item *by item* 逐条に, 一品一品(数える).

P^2 *item of* expenses 費目. ¶*items on* the programme プログラムの諸種目 ‖ How many *item* are there *on* the list? そのリストには何品目はいっていますか.

iteration, *n*. くどくど言うこと.

Q with *tiresome iteration* くどくどと.

itinerary, *n*. 旅程, 路筋.

V *arrange* one's *itinerary* 旅程を作製する. ¶*draw up* an *itinerary* 旅程を作成する. ¶*make out* an *itinerary* 旅程を作成する. ¶*make* (=*map*) *up itinerary* 旅程を作る. ¶*prepare* (=draw up) *itineraries* for side trips 付けたり旅行の日程を作る. ¶an *itinerary covering* over six months 六カ月以上にわたる旅程.

Q a *detailed itinerary* of one's proposed journey 計画旅行の詳細な日程. ¶*full itineraries* of all tours あらゆる旅行の詳細な案内記. ¶a *tentative itinerary* (決定的でない)暫定的な旅程.

P Include these places *on* your *itinerary*. あなたの旅程にはこれらの場所を加えなさい.

itself, *pron*. それ自身.

P Put it *by itself*. それを別にしておけ. ¶The matter speaks *for itself*. そのことは言わずとも明かだ. ¶The dictionary is a library *in itself*. その辞書はそれ自体一つの文庫である ‖ The door closed *of itself* 戸が自然にしまった ‖ The candle went out *of itself*. ろうそくは自然に消えた.

ivory, *n*. 象牙.

Q *animated ivory* 生きた象牙(雪のはだ).

Q^2 *imitation ivory* 模造象牙.

P chessmen *in ivory* 象牙の駒(こま). ¶the tower *of ivory* =the ivory tower 象牙の塔(学問の殿堂). ¶carved *on ivory* 象牙に彫った.

ivy, *n*. つた.

Q^2 *poison ivy* and sand fleas つたうるしと砂のみ.

J

jab, *n*. 一撃(パンチ).

Q have a *nasty jab* on the cheek ほおにすごいパンチを受ける.

jabber, *n*. おしゃべり.

Q the *incomprehensible jabber* of a child 子供のわけのわからないおしゃべり.

P^2 the *jabber of* foreigners 外人のちんぷんかんぷんの会話.

jabber, *v*. しゃべる.

M^2 *jabber along* for hours 数時間しゃべり続ける.

jack, Jack, *n*. 男; 男の子.

Q *Every jack* has his Jill. 男の子は皆彼女をつれている.

Q^2 This is *Brother Jack*. これが兄(弟)のジャックです. ¶*Every* man *Jack* says so. だれだってそう言っている. ¶the *Union Jack* 英国の国旗.

P a *Jack of* all trades=a jack-of-all-trades 何でもやる器用な男.

jack, *n*. てこ(ジャッキ).

Q^2 a *lever jack* てこ仕掛の起重機. ¶a *lumber jack* 木材人足. ¶a *screw jack* ネジで動かす起重機.

jack, *v*. ジャッキで上げる.

M^2 He *jacked up* the car and changed the back tire. 彼はジャッキで車を上げて後輪タイヤを換えた. ¶*jack up* living *costs* a few percentage points 二三パーセント生活費を上げる.

jacket, *n*. ジャケツ; [本の]ジャケット.

Q a *strait jacket* 狂人の縮めジャケツ.

Q² an *Army battle jacket* 陸軍戦闘服. ¶a *book jacket* 書物のジャケット. ¶a *cork jacket* コルク衣(浮袋). ¶a *dinner jacket* 通常えん尾服の尾のない上衣(宴会の略服). ¶a *duty jacket* [制服式の]職場ジャケット. ¶a *fatigue jacket* 作業用のジッケツ. ¶a *shooting jacket* 遊猟着. ¶a *smoking jacket* 喫煙服. ¶a *sports jacket* 運動着. ¶wear a *sweater jacket* 袖のないセーターを着る. ¶in a "*Tuxedo*" *jacket* タキシードジャケツを着て. ¶a *work jacket*＝an overall 労働作業衣.

jade, *n.* 玉(ぎょく), 硬玉.

Q² *green* and *white jade* ひすいと玉. ¶*true jade* ほんとの玉.

jade, *n.* あばずれ女; やせ馬.

V I'm sure I don't know how to *handle* such a *jade*. あんなあばずれは私には手がつけられない.

Q Memory is a *fickle jade*. 記憶は当てにならない. ¶a *saucy jade* すれっからし. ¶a *sorry jade* やせ馬.

jag, *v.* ぎざぎざをつける.

M² *jag in* のこぎり形に刻む, ぎざぎざをつける.

P The wall was *jagged on* its top and sides. 壁は上も側もぎざぎざになっていた.

jail, *n.* 監獄, 刑務所.

V *break jail* 脱獄する.

Q² a *detention jail* 留置場. ¶a *police jail* 警察留置場.

P He is held on a charge of murder *at* a *jail*. 彼は殺人の罪で刑務所に収容されている. ¶Men who are *in jail* are sometimes made to work out of doors. 囚人は刑務所外で働くことがある. ‖ He is confined *in jail*. 彼は収監されている. 【類】a fine of $40 and two months *in jail* / put him *in jail* / I'll have him *in iail* (刑務所へぶち込んでやる) for this. ¶He was sent *to jail*. 彼は刑務所へ入れられた.

jam, *n.* ジャム; 混雑.

V *spread jam* on slices of bread＝spread slices of bread with jam 切ったパンにジャムを付ける.

Q² eat *raspberry jam* on one's bread パンにきいちごジャムをつけて食べる. ¶a terrific *traffic jam* 交通地獄.

jam, *v.* 詰込む, 押込む; つぶす.

M It's *jammed full*. (電車などが)満員だ.

M² Crowds *jammed in* for seats when the train pulled up. 列車が止まると群集は席を得ようと雑とうした. ¶The road was *jammed up* with motor-vehicles. 道路は自動車ですし詰であった.

P *jam* one's finger *in* a train door 列車の戸で指をつぶす. ¶a street-car *jammed to* suffocation 息が詰まるくらい詰込まれた電車 ‖ The hall was *jammed to* its doors. その会館は立すいの余地がなかった. ¶The corridor was *jammed with* people. 廊下は人で一杯だった.

jamboree, *n.* ボーイスカウトの大会.

Q a *juvenile jamboree* ボーイスカウトの大会; 《米》若人の愉快な会合.

janitor, *n.* 門衛.

Q a *bullying* or *browbeating janitor* 威張りちらしたりしかりとばしたりする門衛.

January, *n.* 一月.

V he *spent* all *January* at ... 彼は一月中を…で送った.

P *during January* 一月中. ¶*from January* to about May 一月から五月ごろまで. ¶in the course *of January* 一月中に ‖ on the first *of January* 元旦に.

Japan, *n.* 日本.

Q *postwar Japan* 戦後の日本. ¶*sporting Japan* スポーツ日本.

Japanese, *n.* 日本人.

Q Roy Saeki, a *Hawaiian-born Japanese* and one of Japan's leading baseball writers, ... ハワイ生れの(日本人で)日本の主なベースボール記者ロイ佐伯. ¶*kimono-clad Japanese* 着物を着た日本人.

Q² *second-generation Japanese*＝Nisei [Japanese] 二世日本人.

jar, *n.* 不調和.

Q We felt a *slight jar* when the engine joined the train. 汽関車が列車に連結した時私たちは少し震動を感じた.

Q² a *family jar*＝a matrimonial quarrel 夫婦げんか.

P be *at* [a] *jar* 仲たがいしている. ¶The door is *on* the *jar* (＝ajar). 戸が少し開いている.

jar, *n.* つぼ.

Q a *covered jar* ふた付きつぼ.

Q² a *glass jar* ガラスびん. ¶an extra-large, *economy size jar* 特大徳用びん. ¶a *stoneware jar* 石焼のかめ.

P² a *jar of* pickles つけ物一びん.

jar, *v.* 耳にさわる.

M The door *jarred open*. ドアがぎーっと開いた. ¶*jar unpleasantly* on the ear 耳ざわりである.

P *jar on* my ears (nerves) 私の耳(かん)にさわる. ¶I hope that difference of opinion may not *jar with* literary brotherhood. 私は意見の相違から文学上の交誼に影響を及ぼすことのないように望む.

jargon, *n.* 通語, 隠語.

V to *use* the *jargon* of the oculist 眼科医の専門語で言えば.

Q use a *technical jargon* 一般人には分からない専門語を使う. ¶a *barbarous jargon* 耳ざわりなたわ言.

Q² in the *trade jargon* of today 今日の商売上の隠語(符ちょう)では.

P express oneself *in* the *jargon* of one's science その専門の術語で表現する.

jaunt, *n.* 遠足, 遊山.

Q a month's *pleasure jaunt* 一カ月の楽しい遊山旅行.

jaunt, *v.* 遊山旅行する.

P *jaunt through* Europe ヨーロッパを遊山旅行する.

jaw, *n.* あご.

V *dislocate* one's *jaw* あごをはずす. ¶Then just *hold jaw* (＝tongue). それならちょっと待って下さい[相手の言葉をさえぎるとき]. ¶Oh, *shut* your *jaw!* だまれ! ¶*wag* one's (＝the) *jaw[s]* うるさくしゃべる.

Q The lion drags along a lamb between his *strong jaws*. ライオンは強いあごでくわえて小羊を引きずって行く. ¶a person with *prominent jaws* あごの張った人.

P the socket *in* the *jaw* あごの穴. ¶throw oneself *into* the *jaws* of death 身をていして死地に入る. ¶a man *with* tireless *jaw* つかれを知らない弁舌家.

P² be in the *jaws of* death 死にひんしている ‖ the *jaws of* a vise 万力のつかみ.

jaw-breaking, *a.* 〖米口〗発音しにくい.

M The name is *really jaw-breaking* [to pronounce]. その名前は本当に発音しにくい.

jay, *n.* かけす; 《米俗》いなかもの.

Q a *blue jay* かけす; 《俗》いなか者.

jazz, *n.* ジャズ.

Q *hot jazz* 新しいジャズ.

jazz, *v.* ジャズ的に騒ぐ.

M² They were all gay and *jazzing up* after a round of beers. 彼らは愉快でビールを一回り飲むとジャズ的に騒いだ.

jealous, *a.* しっと深い.

M *bitterly jealous* of ... …を大いにねたましく思って. ¶*madly jealous* しっと心で夢中になって. ¶*mortally jealous* とてもしっと深い.

P She's *jealous of* my new bonnet, I guess. あの人は私の新しい帽子がうらやましいに違いない. ‖ *jealous of* one's reputation (honor, good name) 人の名声(など)をうらやむ ‖ He is *jealous of* his rivals. 彼はその競争者をねたんでいる.

jealousy, *n.* しっと.

V *display jealousy* しっとを示す. ¶*exhibit* (＝*show*) *jealousy* of one's wife 妻をしっとする. ¶*invite* the *jealousy* of ... …のしっとを招く. ¶*nurse jealousy* or grudge against ... …にしっとまたは恨みを抱く. ¶*overcome jealousy* しっとを抑える. ¶*provoke* the *jealousy* of ... …のしっと心を起させる. ¶*rouse* one's *jealousy* しっとを起させる. ¶*show* great *jealousy* of one's success その成功を大いにねたむ. ¶*stir jealousies* しっとを起させる.

Q *burning jealousy* 燃えるようなしっと. ¶*long-pressed jealousy* 長らく抑えていたしっと. ¶It was the *natural jealousy* of trade. それは商売敵で無理もないことであった. ¶*personal jealousy* 個人的なしっと. ¶Of course there may be *professional jealousy* at the bottom of the question. もちろんその問題の底には同業者のしっとがあるかもしれない.

Q² *intra-office jealousies* 役所内のしっと. ¶adandon minor *intraparty jealousies* 小さな党派内のねたみを捨てる. 【類】There was no whisker of any *intra-party jealousy* or strife. ¶*race jealousies* 人種間のそねみ.

P He was spurred up *by jealousy* to commit a crime. 彼はしっとに駆られて罪を犯すに至った ‖ tormented *by jealousy* しっとにもだえて. ¶arouse a feeling *of jealousy* しっと心を起させる. ¶act *out of* (＝*from*) *jealousy* しっと心からやる. ¶burning *with jealousy* しっとに燃えて. ¶turn yellow *with jealousy* しっとで黄色になる(黄はしっとの表象).

P² the *jealousy of* class-feeling 階級観念から出たしっと.

jeans, *n. pl.* あや織(デニム)のずぼん.

Q a pair of *old, faded blue jeans* 古い色のあせた青いデニムのずぼん. ¶co-eds *in* blue *jeans* 《米》青いデニムのずぼ

んをはいた男女共学校の女学生(男子にはまれに用う).

jeer, *v.* あざける.

P *jeer at* the idea of ... ...という考えをあざける ‖ *jeer at* a person 人をあざける. ¶He was *jeered at* by his audience. 彼は聴衆にやじられた. ☞米語用法は He was jeered *by* his audience. ¶*jeer off* the idea その考えを一笑に付す.

jelly, *n.* ゼリー.

Q^2 *plum jelly* のし梅.

jeopardy, *n.* 危険.

P He was often *in jeopardy* of his life. 彼はしばしば生命の危険に陥った. ‖ place commercial interests *in jeopardy* 通商上の利益を危険にさらす.

jerk, *n.* ぐいと引くこと.

V *give* a violent *jerk* 強くぐいと引く ‖ *give* the string a *jerk* ひもをぐいと引っぱる. ¶*Put* a *jerk* into it! 《俗》しっかりやれ!(応援のかけ声).

Q pull with a *sudden jerk* 不意にぐっと引く(手綱などを).

P move *by jerk* ぴくぴくと動く ‖ stimulate the flow of a fountain-pen *by jerks* 万年筆を振ってインキの出をよくする. ¶His conscience works *in jerks* (=by fits and starts). 彼の良心は気まぐれに働く. ¶move *with jerks* ががたがた動く ‖ A tram-car starts *with* a *jerk*. 電車ががたんと動き出す. ‖ pull ... *with* a *jerk* ...をぐいと引く.

jerk, *v.* 急に引く(押す).

M The door *jerked open*. ドアがぐいと開いた. ¶*jerk out* one's words とぎれとぎれに言い出す.

M^2 The train *jerked along*. 列車はがたがた進んだ.

P She was *jerked into* the lap of a gentleman in a street car. 彼女は電車内で紳士のひざの中によろけ込んだ. ¶The train *jerked to* a stop. 列車はがたんと停った.

jest, *n.* 冗談, しゃれ, ひやかし.

V *break* a *jest* 冗談を言う. ¶*drop* a *jest* しゃれを言う. ¶*make* a *jest* of ... ...をからかう. ¶*speak* a *jest* to ... ...に冗談を言う.

Q a *biting jest* とげのある冗談. ¶a *dry jest* だじゃれ. ¶a story-teller of *infinite jest* こっけい百出の落語家. ¶a *light jest* 軽いしゃれ. ¶a *merry jest* おもしろい冗談. ¶an *off-hand jest* 当意即妙のしゃれ. ¶a *popular jest* among his friends 彼の友人間の一つの笑い草. ¶a *sharp jest* 毒を含んだしゃれ. ¶a *standing jest* おきまりの冗談.

P say *by way of jest* 冗談に言う. ¶half *in jest* I inquired ... 私は冗談半分に...と尋ねた ‖ more *in jest* than in earnest 冗談まじりに ‖ spoken *in jest* 冗談に言った.

jest, *v.* 冗談を言う, 茶化す.

P *jest at* a person 人をひやかす ‖ *jest at* one's misery 人の不幸をひやかす ‖ *jest at* one on one's poverty 人の貧乏をからかう.

jester, *n.* 冗談をいう人.

Q gently rebuke an *uncouth jester* ぶしつけな冗談を言う人をたしなめる.

Q^2 a *court jester* 王様の太鼓持.

jet, *n.* 噴出; 出口; ジェット機.

V The fountain *sends up* a *jet* of water twenty feet high. その噴泉は二十フィートの高さまで水を吹き上げる.

Q at a *single jet* たった一発で. ¶a *supersonic jet* 超音速ジェット機.

Q^2 a flickering *gas jet* ちらちらするガスの灯. ¶Eight or nine *gas jets* are burning. 八つか九つの火口からガスが燃えている.

jetty, *n.* 桟橋.

Q A bit of *broken jetty* ran out from ... とぎれた桟橋の一端が...から突出ていた.

Jew, *n.* ユダヤ人.

Q formerly "*stateless*" *Jews* 以前国家のなかったユダヤ人たち.

Q^2 *upper-class English Jews* 上流階級の在英ユダヤ人.

jew, *v.* 値切る.

M^2 I wanted $200 for my car, but he *jewed* me *down* to $150. 私は自動車を売って二百ドル欲しかったが彼は百五十ドルに値切った.

jewel, *n.* 宝石.

V *add* another *jewel* to his crown of glory 彼の名誉に一段の光彩を添える. ¶She *makes* a *jewel* of her son. 彼女は息子を宝石のように大切にする. ¶*put on jewels* 宝石を身につける. ¶*set* a *jewel* 宝石をはめる. ¶*set off* a *jewel* 宝石を引立たせる.

Q *cheap* and *gaudy jewels* 安くてけばけばしい宝石. ¶*cut* and *uncut jewels* みがいたまたはみがかない宝石. ¶*glittering jewels* さんらんたる宝石. ¶the *historic jewels* which form the heirlooms of the Crown 皇室伝来の宝物たる歴史的宝玉. ¶a *precious jewel* 高価な宝石 ‖ the most *precious jewel* of Italian beauty, Venice イタリア美の極致ヴェニス市. ¶*superb jewels* きわめて美しい宝石.

P bedecked *with jewels* 宝石で飾り立てた ‖ a ring set *with* a *jewel* 宝石入の指輪 ‖ *with jewels* around her neck 首に宝石をつけて.

P^2 the *jewel of* his collection 彼の収集中の至宝 ‖ a *jewel of* a son 大事な男の子.

jewel, *v.* 宝石で飾る.

P *jewelled with* precious stones 宝石で飾った ‖ a sky *jeweled with* stars 星をちりばめた空.

jewel[le]ry, *n.* 宝石類.

V *wear jewelry* 宝石類を身に着ける.

Q *conspicuous* and *cheap jewelry* 目立って値の安い宝石. ¶*sham jewellery* にせ宝石. ¶*trashy jewelry* 安もの宝石.

Q^2 *imitation jewelry* of little value 価値のない模造の宝石. ¶*silver jewelry* 銀装飾品.

P articles *of jewelry* 宝石細工.

jiff[y], *n.* 瞬間.

P I'll make another *in* a *jiffy*. すぐにもう一つ作りましょう. ‖ The portable dressing table holds all the necessary cosmetics and implements, ready for use *in* a *jiffy*. この携帯用の鏡台には即座に使える必要な化粧品や諸道具が残らず入れてある.

jingle, *n.* りんりん.

P sound *with* a *jingle* りんりんと響く.

jingle, *v.* ちりんと鳴る.

M The sleigh *jingled away* on the snow. そりが雪中をちりんちりん鈴を鳴らして去った. ¶Bells *jingle merrily*. 鈴の音が愉快に鳴る.

M^2 *jingle off* 落ちる; ちゃりんと落ちる.

P Money *jingled in* his pocket. 金が彼のポケットの中でじゃらついた.

jingling, *n.* ちりんちりん.

P^2 the *jingling of* sleigh bells そりの鈴の音.

jinrikisha, *n.* 人力車.

V *call* a *jinrikisha* 人力車を呼ぶ. ¶*hire* a *jinrikisha* 車を雇う. ¶*mount* a *jinrikisha* 人力車に乗る. ¶*order* the *jinrikisha* 人力車を呼ぶ. ¶*take* a two-man *jinrikisha* 二人引きの車に乗る. 【類】*jinrikishas* can be *taken* from ... to ...

P go *by jinrikisha* 車で行く. ¶go to ... *in* a *jinrikisha* 車に乗って...へ行く. 【類】ride *in* a *jinrikisha*.

P^2 a *jinrikisha with* two men 二人引きの車.

job, *v.* 仕事, 請負仕事.

V *boss* the *job* 牛耳を執る. ¶*bungle* a *job* できそこなう, 不手際をやる. ¶He had to *chuck* the *job* like a hero or get fired. 彼は男らしく辞職するかくびになるかであった. ¶*do* odd *jobs* about the house 家庭の雑用をする ‖ It will not *do* the *job* required. それは役に立つまい. ¶the strategy of *finding job* 仕事を見付ける作戦. ¶He *got* a *job* with a real estate firm. 彼は土地会社に就職した. ¶*have* no *job* 職がない. ¶*hold* a *job* 仕事を持っている. ¶*hunt* (=*look out for*) a *job* 仕事を捜す. 【類】*hunt* another *job*. ¶They *lost* their *jobs*. 彼らは失業した. ¶He *made* a satisfactory *job* of the business. 彼はその仕事で満足な成績をあげた. ‖ Well, to *make* a short *job* of it, it ended in a failure. そこで手っとり早く申上げればそれは失敗したという訳です. ¶*perform* odd *jobs* 内職をする. ¶*pick up* a *job* here and there あちこちで仕事を拾う. ¶*quit* his *job* and look for something better 彼の今の仕事をやめて何かよい仕事を捜す. ¶*rush* one's *job* 仕事を急ぐ. ¶*take* a *job* 就職する. ¶He often *shifts jobs*. 彼はよく仕事を変える. 【類】He *took* a *job* as office boy with a law office in New York. / Do you want to *take* the *job*? ¶*throw up* one's *job* 仕事をやめる. ¶I *want* a *job* with your company. 私は貴会社に就職を希望しています.

V^2 *Jobs* as stewardess in most cases *go* to the widows and relatives of sailors, and the outsider has no chance. 船の女給仕の仕事は多くの場合船員の未亡人や親せきの者がこれに採用されるので他の者は就職の機会がない.

Q a tremendously *backbreaking job* 恐ろしく骨の折れる仕事. ¶a *bad job* つまらない仕事. ¶a *big job* 大仕事. ¶a *delicate job* 頭を使う仕事. ¶it is an *easy job* to ... ...することはやさしい ‖ It is not the *easiest job* in the world それは決して楽じゃない. ¶A crooked politician presents his friends with *fat jobs*. 不正な政治家はその仲間にもうけ仕事をあてがう. ¶He thrust himself into a *highly paid job*. 彼は高給の仕事にありついた. ¶find a *good job* よい職につく. ¶a *hard job* 困難な仕事. ¶give it up as a *hope-*

less job それを望みのない仕事として放棄する. ¶The police thought the theft to be an ***inside*** *job*. 警察では盗難を内部の者の仕わざとにらんだ. ¶It is a ***jolly good*** *job* that you came. 君が来てくれてほんとによかった. ¶the newspapers' ***main*** *job* 新聞の重な仕事. ¶do a ***miserable*** *job* in ... に不手際をやる. ¶This is a ***nice little*** *job*, isn't it? これは仲々細工がいいね. ¶do an ***odd*** *job* or two for a private customer 店の仕事の片手間仕事をやる[下請の仕立屋など]. ¶hold a ***permanent*** *job*. ¶It's a ***pretty*** *job*, I can tell you. 君骨だぜ. ¶a ***put-up*** *job* たくらんだ仕事(やお長). ¶make ***satisfactory*** *job* of the business その仕事を物にする. ¶a ***slipshod*** *job*, done to order in a hurry 大急ぎにやったぞんざいな請負仕事. ¶a ***side*** *job* アルバイト. ¶a ***soft*** *job* 楽な仕事. ¶a ***troublesome*** *job* 面倒な仕事. ¶a ***tough*** *job* 骨の折れる仕事. ¶a most ***thankless*** *job* 極めて栄えない仕事. ¶You have a very ***unpleasant*** *job*. 君は非常におもしろくない仕事している(家捜しなどしている人に). ¶He is now employed on an ***urgent*** *job*. 彼は今急ぎの仕事にかかっている.

Q² take a "***business***" *job* 金になる仕事を始める. ¶the great industrial centres where ***chance*** *jobs* may be most easily picked up 半端仕事がちょいちょいある大工業中心地. ¶a ***city-day-laborer*** *job* 市の日雇い仕事. ¶a ***construction*** *job* 土建業(おもに家屋建築業). ¶a ***desk*** *job* 書記の仕事. ¶take ***factory*** *jobs* 工場仕事をする, 職工になる. ¶a ***full-time*** (***part-time***) *job* 専任(嘱託の)職. ¶bar Communists from ***Government*** *jobs* 官庁仕事から共産党員を除外する. ¶a ***high quality*** *job* 高尚な仕事. ¶an ***office*** *job* 事務の仕事. ¶He's too busy with ***pay*** *jobs* to do his school work. アルバイトに急がしくて学校の方はお留守だ. ¶their lost ***pre-service*** *jobs* 兵役につく前に勤めていた仕事. ¶***reporting*** *job* 通信業(新聞記者などの). ¶handle ***routine*** *jobs* おきまり仕事(常務)を扱う. ¶Some ***sales*** *jobs* are dead end. ある売方仕事は昇進の途が開かれていない. ¶a ***steady-for-life*** *job* under the Government 一生安定した官吏の職. ¶a ***summer*** *job* 夏の仕事. ¶a ***two-man*** *job* 二人がかりの仕事. ¶a ***union*** *job* 労組の業務. ¶It is not the aim of education to prepare students for ***white-collar*** *jobs*. 学生を月給取りの仕事にそだてるのは教育の目的ではない.

P They are paid ***by*** the *job*. [一仕事いくらという]請負で支払われる. ¶change ***for*** a softer *job* もっと楽な仕事にかわる ‖ apply ***for*** a *job* ***to*** ... ...に職を申込む. ¶The Osaka department stores are full of school girls ***on*** summer *jobs*. 大阪のデパートには夏の臨時雇の女学生が沢山いる. ‖ He is constantly ***on*** the *job*. 彼はそれからそれと仕事をしている. ‖ a machine ***on*** the *job* 機械運転中. ¶be ***out of*** [a] *job* 失業している.

job, *v.* 賃仕事に出す.

M *job **out*** 仕事を下請に出す.

P *job **in*** elections 選挙でひともうけする.

M² *job **off*** [製品を]もうけて売る; ごまかす.

jobber, *n.* 《英》問屋業者.

Q a ***dishonest*** *jobber* 不正直な問屋.

jobless, *n.* 失業者.

V ***mobilize*** the *jobless* for public works 公共事業のため失業者を動員する.

job-placement, *n.* 職につかせること.

Q² ***youth*** *job-placement* 青年の就職あっ旋.

jockey, *n.* 騎手.

Q² a ***disk*** *jockey* 〖ラジオ〗レコード音楽解説者.

jog, *v.* 揺れて行く.

M *jog **away*** (=***off***) 去る, 退く.

M² Matters *jog **along*** somehow. 事はどうにか運んでいる. 【類】*jog **along*** without a moment's stopping.

joggle, *v.* 揺れて進む.

P² The omnibus *joggled **down*** the street. 乗合馬車は街路を徐々とゆれて進んだ.

join, *v.* 加わる, 加入させる; 接合する.

M He proposed a Chicago yell in which all present *joined **heartily***. 彼がシカゴ大学のエールを発議したら出席者が皆熱心に参加した. ¶All of us *joined **lustily*** in the chorus. われわれ一同熱心にその合唱に加わった. ¶The doctor has told me that in his dictionary the words "nervous" and "curable" are always *joined **together***. その医者は彼の考えでは「神経性」のものは必ず「全治しうる」と私に語った.

M² He *joined **up*** in 1915 and was sent out to India. 彼は一九一五年に入隊しインドに派遣された.

P *joined **by*** a hinge ちょうつがいで継ぎ合わされた ‖ pipes *joined **by*** cement セメントで継いだ管 ‖ be *joined **by*** the conjunction *and* 接続詞 and でつながれる. ¶*join **in*** a contest (game of cards, campaign, movement, chorus) 競技(など)に参加する ‖ My younger brother *joined* me ***in*** partnership in 1904. 一九〇四年に弟は私の社の社員になった. ‖ My wife *joins* me ***in*** very kind regards. 妻からも是非よろしくと申しました. ‖ *join **in*** the nation's war effort 国策の線に沿う ‖ send Latin to *join* Greek ***in*** the limbo of "useless" studies ギリシア語同様ラテン語も「役に立たたない」学科として廃棄する. 【類】His friends *joined* him ***in*** his search. / *join **in*** the stream of people / *join **in*** the march / All Japan *joins **in*** these celebrations. / *join **in*** his happiness / *join **in*** a movement / *join **in*** a joyous song / *join **in*** a speculation / *join **in*** a labor strike / *join **in*** a game of ping-pong / Father, mother, and grandmother *joined **in*** the fun. / He came up to *join* us ***in*** a drink. / My sister *joins* me in affectionate remembrance to you. ¶*join* an island ***to*** the mainland with a bridge 橋で島を本土へつなぐ ‖ High character, *joined **to*** ability, is bound to win success in any work of life. 才能に加うるに高潔な人格をもってすれば人生の事業になに一つ成功しないものはない. ‖ *join* oneself ***to*** the opposite party 反対党にはいる. ¶*join **with*** me ***in*** drinking the health of ... 私と一緒に...の健康を祝して幹杯して下さい. 【類】*join **with*** me ***in*** expressing these good wishes. / *join **with*** you ***in*** the hope that ... / All the world went to Harvard University to *join **with*** it ***in*** keeping its 300th birthday. / We *joined **with*** the rest ***in*** the general hilarity provoked by the farcical antics of the performers.

joinder, *n.* 〖法〗併合.

P² a *joinder **of*** offenses (defendants) 犯罪(被告)の併合.

joiner, *n.* 指物師.

P² a *joiner **by*** trade 商売は指物師.

joint, *n.* 継目(ジョイント), 節, 関節; 輪切肉.

V ***set*** a *joint* 接骨する. ¶***solder*** a *joint* 継目をはんだ付けにする. ¶A *joint* has ***started***. 継目が離れた.

Q tough steak and ***badly-cooked*** *joints* 堅いビフテキと料理のまずい輪切肉. ¶***bolted*** *joint* ボールトで締めた継ぎ合わせ. ¶the ***middle*** *joint* of a finger 指の中関節. ¶a ***rheumatic*** *joint* リューマチ性の関節.

Q² a ***bamboo*** *joint* 竹の節. ¶a ***flange*** *joint* フランジ継手. ¶a ***scarf*** *joint* [木材の]おっかけ継ぎ.

P with small sheaths ***at*** the *joints* 節のところに小さなさやのある. ¶a *joint **in*** a lead pipe 鉛管の継目 ‖ aching ***in*** every *joint* 節々の痛む. ¶His loin was ***out of*** *joint* from cowardice. 彼はおく病で腰を抜かした. ‖ His knee is ***out of*** *joint*. 彼のひざの骨が外れている. ‖ The times are ***out of*** *joint*. 現代は調子が狂っている. 【類】That put my arm *out of joint*.

joint, *v.* 結合する.

P *joint* efforts ***for*** the common good 公益に協力する.

joint-editorship, *n.* 共同編集.

P ***under*** the *joint-editorship* of ... and ... 甲乙両氏の共同編集の下に.

joke, *n.* 冗談, しゃれ.

V ***cap*** a *joke* 負けずに冗談を言い返す. ¶***carry*** a *joke* too far 冗談が過ぎる. ¶***cast*** a *joke* at ... ...をからかう. ¶***crack*** a *joke* 冗談を言いだす ‖ ***crack*** *jokes* with ... ...に冗談を言う ‖ ***crack*** *jokes* at the expense of ... ...を冷かす. ¶***cut*** *jokes* with ... ...に冗談をいう. ¶***dislike*** practical *jokes* 悪ふざけをきらう. ¶He always ***enjoyed*** a *joke* against himself. 彼はいつ自分が冷かされても一緒におもしろがった. ¶***fire*** (=***let***) ***off*** a *joke* しゃれを言う. ¶***get off*** one's *joke* on ... ...に冗談をいう. ¶He ***had*** a *joke* on her. 彼は彼女をからかった. ¶He ***levelled*** his *jokes* at her. 彼は彼女に向って冗談を言った. ¶***love*** a *joke* しゃれを好む. ¶***make*** quite a good *joke* うまいしゃれを言う ‖ ***make*** *jokes* at the expense of ... ...をからかう. ¶He at once ***perceived*** the *joke*. 彼はすぐそのしゃれが分かった. ¶***perpetrate*** a *joke* on his colleagues 同僚を冷かす ‖ Some wag ***perpetrated*** the following *joke* in a newspaper paragraph. あるこっけい家が新聞の断片記事で次のような冗談を言った. ¶***play*** a *joke* on each other お互に冗談を言う. ¶***relish*** a *joke* 冗談をおもしろがる. ¶He ***saw*** the *joke* quickly and joined in the general merriment caused by the prank. 彼はそのしゃれが即座に分かって皆と一緒に打興じた. ‖ I wonder if he ***saw*** the *joke*. 彼にそのしゃれが分かったかしら. ¶He knows how to ***take*** a *joke*. 彼はうまくしゃれを受流す. ¶You can ***talk*** a *joke!* 君は話せる.

V² The *joke* ***fell*** upon strong ground. その冗談が相手に分からなかった. ¶This *joke* has ***gone*** a little too far. この冗談は少し言い過ぎだ. ¶*Jokes* ***passed*** to and fro at table. 食卓で冗談があちこち飛んだ.

Q He is notorious for his ***bad*** and ***moth-eaten*** *jokes*. 彼は古臭いだじれゃを言うので有名だ. ¶***cheap, rubber-stamp*** *jokes* 味のない紋切形のしゃれ. ¶a ***coarse*** *joke* 下品な冗談. ¶It was a ***colossal*** *joke*. それはこつけいのきわみであった. ¶a ***current*** *joke* at the time 当時流行のしゃれ. ¶a ***dull*** *joke* だじゃれ. ¶a ***first-rate*** *joke* すばらしいしゃれ. ¶a ***foolish*** *joke* ばかげた冗談. ¶a ***heartless*** *joke* 残酷な冗談. ¶treat it as a ***huge*** *joke* それをすてきな冗談として取扱う. ¶How can you be angry at such an ***innocent*** *joke?* こんな罪のない冗談になんだって怒るんです. ¶It is ***no*** *joke* to be a popular singer. はやりっ子の歌手というものは大したものだ. ‖ ***No*** *joke* in this case. 冗談ごとじゃない. ¶play a ***practical*** *joke* on ... ...に悪ふざけをする ‖ In old Japan badgers were believed to be players of ***practical*** *jokes*. 昔日本ではたぬきはいたずら者だと信じられていた ‖ English coinage is a ***practical*** *joke*. 英国の貨幣[制度]は全くひどい(複雑なので). ¶***primeval*** *jokes* 原始的な冗談. ¶crack ***ribald*** *jokes* at ... ...に下品な冗談を言う. ¶***rich*** *jokes* うま味のある冗談. ¶a ***smutty*** *joke* みだらな冗談. ¶a ***spicy*** *joke* うがった冗談. ¶a ***stale*** *joke* 古臭い冗談. ¶a ***standing*** *joke* amongst ... ...間のいつも持ちだされる笑い草. ¶a ***stock*** *joke* with the French comic papers フランスのこっけい新聞によく見る陳腐なしゃれ. ¶a ***subtle*** *joke* 巧妙なしゃれ. ¶an ***unintended*** *joke* しゃれのつもりでないしゃれ. ¶***untranslatable*** jokes 翻訳のできないしゃれ. ¶a ***worn-out*** *joke* かびの生えたしゃれ. ¶***wretched*** *jokes* つまらない冗談. ¶None of ***your*** *jokes*. 冗談言うな.

P ***as*** a *joke* 冗談に ‖ The table laughed ***at*** the *joke*. 食卓の人々はその冗談で笑った. ¶It is ***beyond*** a *joke*. それは冗談ごとではない. ¶***by way of*** a *joke* I named it ... 私はおもしろ半分にそれに...と名をつけた. ¶I was only doing this ***for*** a *joke*. 私はこれを冗談にやったまでだ. 【類】I said it just ***for*** a *joke*. ¶what I said ***in*** *joke* 私が冗談に言ったこと ‖ ***in*** *joke* (=jest *or* fun)=out of sport 冗談に ‖ half ***in*** *joke* 半ば冗談に.

P² a *joke* ***in*** bad taste 悪ふざけ. ¶a *joke* ***on*** Bismarck ビスマークに関する笑話.

joke, *v.* 冗談を言う, からかう.

M ***joking apart*** (***aside***) 冗談はさておき. ¶*joke* ***teasingly*** (=rally) with ... うるさく...をからかう.

P *joke* a man ***on*** his baldness 人のはげ頭をからかう. ¶It is not a subject to *joke* ***upon***. それは冗談ごとではない. ¶He *joked* ***with*** me ***about*** the matter. 彼はそのことで私に冗談を言った.

O You are *joking*, sir! 御冗談でしょう.

joker, *n.* こっけい家.

Q a ***confirmed*** *joker* 冗談ばかり言う人, しゃれの名人. ¶an ***inveterate*** *joker* 常習的なかいぎゃく家. ¶***Practical*** *jokers* delight in the embarrassment of their victims. いたずら者は相手が当惑するのをおもしろがる.

joking, *n.* 冗談.

P but seriously ***without*** *joking* しかし冗談でなくまじめに.

jolly, *a.* 陽気な.

P He was *jolly* ***from*** (=***in***) drink. 彼は一杯きげんであった.

jolt, *n.* がたん.

P The car stopped ***with*** a *jolt*. 車はがたんと揺れて止まった.

jolt, *v.* がたんと揺れる.

M The car *jolted* ***badly*** over the rough road. 車は悪路でひどくがたついた.

jolting, *n.* 揺れ.

V The car ***received*** a tremendous *jolting*. 車は大揺れを食った.

jostle, *v.* 押す.

P ***jostled by*** a crowd 群集に押されて ‖ We were *jostled* ***by*** the big crowd at the entrance. 入口で大群集に押しもまれた. ¶The crowd *jostled* ***into*** the theatre. 群集は押されて劇場になだれ込んだ. ¶*jostle* ***through*** a crowd 人ごみの中を無理やりに通り抜ける. ¶*jostle* ***with*** each other for ... ...のために互いに争う.

jot, *n.* 微少.

O not a *jot* みじんも. 【類】I don't care a *jot*.

jot, *v.* ちょっと書きとめる.

M² *jot* them ***down*** in one's notebook (on paper) 手帳(など)にそれを書留める.

jotting, *n.* 略記.

Q ***brief*** *jottings* on the backs of envelopes 封筒の裏に手短かに書いたもの.

journal, *n.* (**1**) 日刊新聞, 定期刊行物.

V ***start*** a new *journal* 新しい新聞(雑誌)を刊行する.

Q a ***daily*** (***biweekly, weekly, bimonthly, monthly***) *journal* 日刊(週二回, 週刊, 月二回, 月刊)新聞(雑誌). ¶a ***first-class*** *journal* 一流の新聞. ¶an ***illustrated*** *journal* 絵入新聞(雑誌). ¶an ***influential*** *journal* 有力な新聞紙(雑誌). ¶the ***ministerial*** *journal* 政府の機関新聞. ¶a ***minor*** *journal* 小新聞. ¶a ***scholarly*** *journal* 学究的な新聞. ¶***scurrilous*** *journal* 三文(悪口)新聞(雑誌). ¶a ***semi-official*** *journal* 半官的新聞.

Q² a ***class*** *journal* 階級機関紙. ¶a ***college*** *journal* 大学新聞. ¶a ***home*** *journal* 家庭雑誌. ¶a ***snippet*** *journal* のりとはさみで編集する雑誌. ¶a ***socialist*** *journal* 社会主義新聞. ¶a ***society*** *journal* (=newspaper) 上流社会のできごとを報道する新聞紙. ¶one of the ***staid*** and ***thoughtful*** ***London*** *journals* まじめで思慮深いロンドンの新聞の一つ. ¶a ***trade*** *journal* 貿易新聞.

P For a time he worked as reporter ***on*** The New York Evening *Journal*. 一時彼はニューヨーク・イヴニング・ジャーナルの記者をやった.

(**2**) 日記, 仕訳帳.

V ***keep*** a *journal* 日記(仕訳帳)をつける.

P A *Journal* ***from*** Japan [書名]日本日記.

journalism, *n.* [新聞・雑誌の]経営(編集); 新聞・雑誌界.

V ***enter*** *journalism* 新聞(雑誌)記者(または業者)になる. ¶***follow*** *journalism* as a profession 職業として新聞(雑誌)業にたずさわる. ¶Forsaking medicine, he ***took up*** *journalism*. 彼は医者をやめて新聞記者になった.

Q ***admirable*** *journalism* りっぱな新聞(雑誌)経営(編集). ¶***conscientious*** *journalism* 良心的な新聞(雑誌)経営. ¶***daily*** *journalism* 日刊新聞業. ¶***ephemeral*** *journalism* すぐつぶれる新聞(雑誌). ¶***personal*** *journalism* 個人経営の新聞事業. ¶***sensational*** *journalism* 扇情的態度の新聞(雑誌)編集. ¶***yellow*** *journalism* 黄色(安っぽい扇情的)新聞編集.

Q² ***evening*** *journalism* 夕刊編集. ¶***magazine*** *journalism* 雑誌編集. ¶***side-walk*** (=***claptrap***) *journalism* 人気取りの新聞(雑誌)業.

P² . books which are only *journalism* ***between*** boards ボール紙にはさまれた(単行本という形式だけで)新聞・雑誌的(高級著作の香の乏しい)内容.

journalist, *n.* 新聞(雑誌)記者.

Q ***best-informed*** *journalists* 最も消息に通じた記者. ¶He is a ***brilliant*** *journalist*, but not a seer or poet. 彼は才気縦横の記者であって達見の士とか詩人とかいうのではない. ¶a very ***eminent*** *journalist* 卓越した記者. ¶a ***shallow*** *journalist* 浅薄な新聞記者. ¶a ***vile*** hooligan *journalist* 卑劣な不良記者. ¶a ***visiting English*** *journalist* in America 米国訪問中の英国記者.

Q² a ***free-lance*** *journalist* フリーランサーの新聞記者. ¶a ***labor*** *journalist* 労働記者.

journey, *n.* 旅行, 行程.

V ***accelerate*** a *journey* 旅行を早める. ¶***accomplish*** (=finish) a *journey* 旅を終える ‖ The *journey* may be ***accomplished*** by rail on the ... railway. その旅行は...鉄道でできる. ¶***begin*** one's *journey* 旅立つ. ¶***break*** one's rail *journey* (=stop over) at ... ...で途中下車する. ¶***continue*** (=***pursue***) one's *journey* 旅行を続ける. ¶She is expected under favorable conditions to ***do*** the *journey* in 2 hours. 天候が順調だと船は二時間で目的地に着く. 【類】We have ***done*** a good *journey*. ¶These cut flowers can ***endure*** a long *journey*. この切花は長途の行程にたえる. ¶***enliven*** a dull railway *journey* 退屈な鉄道旅行に活気を添える. ¶***extend*** one's *journey* to ... ...まで旅を続ける(足を延ばす). ¶***finish*** a *journey* covering a distance of ... 行程...の旅を終える. ¶I hope you ***had*** a pleasant *journey* back to your fatherland. 無事御帰国のことと存じます ‖ We ***have*** a long *journey* before us. われわれはこれから長途の旅行にでかける. ¶***lose*** a *journey* 旅行がむだになる. ¶***make*** a *journey* to ... on Government business 公用で...へ旅行する. 【類】***make*** a *journey* through a tract of the earth's surface / He ***made*** several *journeys* across Kyushu. ¶***map out*** a *journey* 旅行の計画を立てる. ¶Busy people ***measure*** their *journeys* not by miles but by time. 忙しい人は旅行をマイル(距離)でなくて時間で計算する. ¶The rest of the *journey* must be ***performed*** on foot. それから先の旅は徒歩でなく

てはできない. ¶*make* a *journey* to the world beyond あの世へ旅立つ. 【類】*make* a *journey* around the world. ¶when *planning* a *journey* 旅行を計画しているときに. ¶*postpone* a journey 旅行を延ばす. ¶*pursue* one's *journey* 旅行を続ける. ¶The newly opened railway service *reduces* the *journey* to ... by one and a half days. 汽車開通で...への旅行が一日半だけ早くできるようになった. ¶*repay* the *journey* to ... ...への旅行をする価値がある(得る所があるから). ¶*resume* the *journey* (途中下車または滞在した後)再びその旅を続ける. ¶The picturesque view *rewards* a tiresome *journey* to the place. その美景がそこまでの退屈な旅を償う. ¶*shorten* one's *journey* その旅行を短縮する. ¶The fish *stood* the *journey* very well. 魚はその輸送中少しも悪くならなかった. ¶*take* one's *journey* into a far country 遠い国へ旅する. 【類】*take* a *journey* for pleasure. ¶*undertake* a *journey* 旅をする. ¶*vary* the return *journey* 行きと違った経路で帰る ‖ the *journey* can be *varied* by returning via ... 帰りの旅は路を変えて...経由とすることもできる. 【類】the return *journey* may be *varied* by taking motorbus from ... ¶I *wish* you a good *journey*. 道中御無事を祈ります.

Q a *bridal journey* 新婚旅行. ¶a *brief journey* 小旅行. ¶an *exciting* and *beautiful journey* 興味をそそる美しい旅. ¶on the *forward* (=*going*) *journey* 往きの旅に. ¶make *frequent jouneys* over to America アメリカへ何回も旅行する. ¶You will only embark upon a *fruitless journey*. 君は無だ足をするだけのことになるだろう. ¶*life*['*s*] *journey* 人生の旅. ¶go [on] a *long journey* 長い旅に出る. ¶*outward* and *homeward journeys* 往きの旅と帰りの旅. ¶perform a *penitential journey* to Jerusalem エルサレムへざんげの旅をする. ¶venture on a *perilous journey* 敢然として危険の旅行に立つ. ¶I hope you had a *pleasant journey* back to your Fatherland. あなたがお国への旅行はさぞ愉快だったでしゅうね. ¶I wish you a *prosperous* (=*favorable*) *journey*. 道中御無事に. ¶make a *rapid journey* through Japan, Korea, and China 日本・朝鮮・中国を大急ぎで旅行する. ¶undertake a *round-the-world journey* 世界一週旅行をする. ¶I wish you a *safe journey*. 道中御安全を祈ります. ¶a *single journey* 片道旅行. ¶The *journey* was *tedious*. その旅は退屈だった. ¶her *triumphant journey* to her home land 故国ににしきを着て帰る旅. ¶make an *urgent journey* 大急ぎの旅をする.

Q² make a *business journey* into the country いなかへ商用で旅行をする. ¶a *honeymoon* [*journey*] 新婚旅行. ¶a *land* (*sea*) *journey* 陸(海)の旅行. ¶an *overland journey* 陸路の旅. ¶begin a *railway* (=*train*) *journey* 鉄道旅行を始める. ¶on his *return journey* from ... ...からの旅の帰りに. 【類】The *return journey* was made over the same route. / the *return* (=homeward) *journey* is made over the route or via ... / on my *return journey* from ... ¶a *school journey* 修学旅行. ¶an outfit for a *skiing journey* スキー旅行の装備. ¶take a *train* (=*railway or railroad*) *journey* 汽車旅行をする ‖ a 200-mile *train journey* 二百マイルの汽車旅行. ¶a *twenty-mile journey* 二十マイルの旅行. ¶a *wedding journey*=a honeymoon 新婚旅行.

P *during* his return *journey* from ... ...から帰りの旅行中に. ¶The ticket is good *for* the entire *journey*. その切符は全旅行に有効である ‖ be well equipped *for* one's *journey* 旅行の準備が十分できている. ¶*in* my *journey* 私の旅行中に. ¶set forth *on* one's *journey* 旅に出る ‖ the time occupied *on* the *journey* between ... and ... is ... ...間の旅行に要する時間は...だ. 【類】a pleasant companion *on* a *journey*. ¶Let us proceed *with* our *journey*. さあ旅に出かけよう. ¶It is *within* five days' *journey* of Tokyo. そこまでは東京から五日の旅だ.

P² make a *journey across* the country (desert, the continent) その国(など)を横断旅行する. ¶a *journey by* train (steamer) 汽車(など)旅行 ‖ It is about a day's *journey by* boat from ... それは...から汽船で約一日の旅行だ. ¶a *journey from* Foochow *to* Wenchow through Central Fuchien 福建省の中央を通過して福州から温州までの旅. ¶a *journey in* Manchuria 満州の旅行. ¶a *journey* far *into* Asia アジアの奥地への旅行. ¶a *journey through* the country その国を通過する旅行. ¶a *journey to* Europe by way of Siberia シベリア経由による欧州への旅行. ¶the return *journey towards* London ロンドンへの帰り旅. ¶a *journey with* him 彼と連れの旅.

journey, *v.* 旅行する.

M *journey abroad* to get information 見聞を広くするために海外に旅行する. ¶*journey far* from ... ...から遠方に旅行する. ¶*journey home* 旅から帰途につく. ¶*immediately journey* to ... 早速...へ旅行する.

M² *journey on* 旅を続ける.

P *journey by* water (land, rail) 海路(など)により旅行する. ¶*journey in* a ship 船で旅行する. ¶*journey into* India インドの内地へ旅する. ¶*journey on* foot 徒歩で旅行する ‖ *journey on* water 水上を旅行する. ¶*journey over* [the] sea 海上を旅行する.

joviality, *n.* 愉快, 陽気.

Q speak with an *artificial joviality* 快活をよそおって話す.

joy, *n.* 歓喜.

V it *brings* twofold *joy*—there is the joy of ... and of ... それは二重の喜びをもたらす, すなわち...の喜びと...の喜び. ¶The glad news *carried joy* into hearts of all. その吉報は皆のものの心を喜ばせた. ¶I need hardly *describe* the *joy* of his parents, nor the pleasure with which villagers welcomed him back. 彼の両親のうれしさや彼の帰郷を歓迎する村人の喜びは申すまでもない. ¶*feel* the *joy* of life 人生の喜びを感じる. ¶*find joy* in ... ...を喜ばしく思う. ¶He *had* the *joy* to see his expectation realized. めでたくも彼の期待は実現された. ¶*know* life's deep *joy* 人生の深い喜びを知る. ¶She *looked* the *joy* she felt. 彼女はその喜ばしさを顔に見せた. ¶I don't *see* much *joy* and mirth in that. 私はそんなことはあまりおもしろいともおかしいとも思わない. ¶*share joys* and sorrows with ... ...と悲喜をともにする. 【類】*share* the *joys* and sorrows, and cares and responsibilities of ... ¶The crowd *took* a brutal *joy* in heaping insults upon his venerable head. 群集は残酷にも尊敬すべきこの老翁の上にさんざん侮辱を加えて喜んだのである. ¶*taste* the *joys* of ... ...の喜びを味う. ¶I *wish* you *joy*. おめでとう. 【類】We *wish* you *joy* of the occasion (このたびのことの).

Q *demoniacal joy* 悪魔的な喜び. ¶The flowers give me *great joy*. 私はその花が大好きだ. 【類】*Great joy* was felt among his friends for his success. ¶*healthy joy* over the coming of new order 新制度の実現に対する健全な喜び. ¶*heavenly joys* 有頂天の喜び. ¶with an *immeasurable joy* 千万無量の喜びをもって. ¶an *ineffable joy* 包みきれない喜び. ¶a burst of *inexpressible joy* 筆紙に尽し難い歓喜の爆発. ¶There is *more joy* in pursuit than in possession. 持つことよりは持とうとすることに喜びがあるのだ. ¶The tired eyes and the tightly-drawn cheeks show that there is not *much joy* in his life. つかれた目・引締ったほおはその人の生活に余り喜びのないことを示す. ¶a *neverfailing* (=an *everlasting*) *joy* 決して衰えない喜び. ¶his eyes shining with *sudden* and *overwhelming joy* 不意のそして圧倒的な歓喜に輝く彼の目. ¶a *proud joy* 誇らしい喜び. ¶*social joys* 交際の喜び. ¶feel some *strange joy* 少し変ったよろこびを感じる. ¶taste the *sweetest joy* of life 人生の最も楽しい喜びを味う. ¶a *transient joy* つかの間の喜び. ¶*unmarried joys* 未婚者の喜び. ¶with *unutterable* (=*unspeakable*) *joy* 口に出せない喜びをもって. ¶Your magazine is a *weekly joy* to me. あなたの雑誌は私にとっては毎週の楽しみです. ¶with a cry of *wild joy* 狂喜のあまり声をあげて.

P cry *for* (=with) *joy* うれし泣きをする. 【類】dance *for* (=*with*) *joy* ‖ The dog wagged his tail *for joy*. 犬は尾を振って喜んだ ‖ leap (=jump) *for joy* 喜んで飛び回る. ¶*in* my great *joy* at the tidings その知らせに接して大喜びのあまり ‖ They have been good friends both *in joy* and in sorrow.彼らは苦楽ともにした親友であった. ¶a chuckle *of joy* 喜びの含み笑い ‖ through excess *of joy* うれしさの余り. ¶At last, in the far distance, *to* his great *joy*, he spied a light. 彼はついにはるか遠方に一つの光りを見て喜んだ. ¶wild *with joy* over ... ...に対して狂喜して. 【類】He was mad *with joy* at the news. / They clapped their hands *with joy*. / He jumped *with joy*. ‖ welcome him *with* great *joy* 大喜びして彼を歓迎する ‖ He was beside himself *with joy*. 彼は喜んで気も狂わんばかりであった.

P² The *joy of* joys is the joy that joys in the joy of others. 喜びの中の喜びは他人の喜びを喜ぶその喜びである. ‖ the *joy of* buying 物を買う喜び. 【類】the *joy of* triumph (victory). ¶a *joy to* the eye 目の正月.

joyful, *a.* 喜ばしい.

P be *joyful* ***of*** ... ...をうれしがる. ¶*joyful* ***to*** one ... ...にとって喜ばしい.

jubilant, *a.* 歓喜する.

P *jubilant* ***over*** ... ...を歓喜して.

jubilee, *n.* 五十年祭.

V With this edition the book ***attains*** its *jubilee*. 今次の版でその本は初刊以来五十年に達する. ¶The school ***celebrated*** its *jubilee* this week. その学校は今週創立五十周年の祝典をあげた. 【類】This year (1929) ***celebrates*** the golden *jubilee* of psychology, since it might be said that before 1879 there was no organized science of psychology in the world. ¶***keep*** its *jubilee* その五十年祭を挙行する.

Q[2] the ***diamond*** *jubilee* of the Midland Railway ミッドランド鉄道創立六十年祭. 【類】commemorate the Queen's ***Diamond*** *jubilee*.

P Thomas A. Edison's ***golden*** *jubilee* of discovery of electric light トーマス・エジソンの電灯発明五十年祭.

judge, *n.* 裁判官, 鑑定人, 審査員.

V ***name*** *judges* 審査員を指名する.

Q an ***assistant*** *judge* 判事補. ¶***capable*** *judges* 有能な判定家. ¶a ***commissioned*** *judge* 正判事. ¶It is deemed (=pronounced) by ***competent*** *judges* to be the best. それは専門家から最上だと言われている. ‖ a ***competent*** *judge* of music りっぱな音楽批評家. ¶a ***fine*** *judge* of verse けい眼な詩の批評家. ¶He is a ***good*** *judge* of the fine arts. 彼は美術品の目がきく. ¶a ***harsh*** *judge* of men 手きびしい人物評論家. ¶***impartial*** *judges* 公平な審判者. ¶He is by no means an ***infallible*** *judge*. 彼は決していつも正しい批判者ではない. ¶a ***keen*** *judge* of human nature (feminine beauty) 人間性(女性美)をよく理解している人. ¶He is ***no bad*** *judge* of talent. 彼は人の才能を仲々よく見抜く. ¶Be your ***own*** *judge*. 自分自身で判断せよ. ¶a ***poor*** *judge* 判断のへたな人. ¶a ***presiding*** *judge* 裁判長. ¶a ***superintending*** *judge* 監督判事. ¶he would be a ***rash*** *judge* who would say that ... ...だという人はその批判の軽卒なることを免れないであろう. ¶a ***sagacious*** *judge* そう明な批判者. ¶a ***shrewd*** *judge* of character 鋭い人物批評者. ¶a very ***sound*** *judge* of pictures きわめて正しい絵画の鑑定家. ¶an ***unrelenting*** *judge* 仮借しない批判者. ¶a ***venal*** *judge* 無節操な判事.

Q[2] an ***army*** *judge* 軍法官. ¶an ***associate*** *judge* 陪席判事. ¶a ***beauty*** *judge* 美人コンクールの審査員. ¶a ***circuit*** *judge* 巡回裁判判事. ¶a ***distance*** *judge* 艇差判定員 (boat race の一着と二着の距離を判定する役員). ¶a ***registration*** *judge* 登記判事.

P The offender was tried ***by*** a *judge*. 犯人は判事に取調べられた.

P[2] a *judge* ***at*** a fair 博覧会の審査員. ¶I am not a *judge* ***of*** paintings. 私には絵の批判はできない.

judge, *v.* 判断する, 批判する, 裁判する.

M *judge* ***candidly*** 無遠慮に批判する. ¶*judge* ***equitably*** 公平に判断する. ¶*judge* ***fairly*** and ***kindly*** of ... ...について公平にしかも親切に批判する. ¶*judge* ***harshly*** 苛酷に批判する. ¶Do not *judge* others ***hastily***. 他人を軽卒に判断するな. ¶American opinion will ***infallibly*** *judge* that ... 米国の世論は必ず...と正しい判断を下すだろう. ¶He was *judged* ***innocent***. 彼は無罪と判決された. ¶*judge* ***rightly*** 正しく判断する. ¶***rigidly*** *judge* according to ... ...に準拠して厳格に判断する. ¶*judge* ***unfairly*** 不公平に判断する.

P *judge* ***at*** first sight 一見して判断する. ¶*judge* ***between*** the combatants 競技者の成績を判定する ‖ *judge* ***between*** two pronunciations 二通りの発音についてその良否を判定する. 【類】*judge* ***between*** the beauty of ... and ... ¶to *judge* ***by*** the results 結果によって判断すると ‖ *judged* ***by*** the barks of the Communist press 共産党新聞ががなり立てているところから見ると ‖ a test ***by*** which to *judge* 判断の根拠を成す試験法 ‖ *judge* a member's diligence ***by*** the number of times his name appears in the newspapers 会員の勤勉振りを新聞にその名の出る回数で判断する. 【類】*judged* ***by*** the standards of today / *judge* ***by*** externals (皮相) / *judging* ***by*** appearances (one's looks, one's dress) / It is unfair to *judge* primitive people ***by*** the standards of our present day civilization. ¶I will leave you to *judge* ***for*** yourself. 御自分の判断にお任せします. ¶*Judging* ***from*** his saying such stupid things, I should say he is not very intelligent. こんなばかげたことを言うようではあの人は利口じゃない. ‖ *judged* ***from*** this point of view この観点から判断して. 【類】She didn't appear to be poor, *judging* ***from*** the way in which she was dressed. / *Judging* ***from*** reports, his character is not without blemishes. / *judging* ***from*** statistics recently made public / *judging* ***from*** the lesson of the past. ¶*Judge* ***of*** its merits and faults for yourself. 君自身でその長短を判断せよ. ‖ You may *judge* ***of*** a book by its effect upon your mind. 君が読んでどういう感じを持つかで書物を判断して差支えない. ‖ *judge* [***of***] people ***by*** their appearances 見掛けで人を判断する ‖ One is at a loss to *judge* ***of*** its contents ***from*** the title. 題名からはその内容の判断がつかない. ‖ how to *judge* ***of*** a picture 絵の見方. ¶It is best not to *judge* ***on*** first appearances. 一見しただけで判断をしないことが何より大切なことだ. 【類】It is not fair to *judge* ***of*** people by the acts of a few undesirables.

Q I *judged* it prudent to stay at home. 私は家にいるのが無事だと考えた. 【類】I *judge* him to be good and honest.

judg[e]ment, *n.* (**1**) 判断, 判断力, 見識.

V He never allows partizanship to ***affect*** his *judgment*. 彼は党派心のために判断が狂うようなことはない. ¶***avoid*** hasty *judgment* 早のみ込を避ける. ¶***bias*** one's *judgment* 判断をかたびいきにする. ¶***bring*** superficial *judgment* to the study of ... ...の検討において皮相の判断を下す. ¶***cloud*** one's *judgment* of ... ...に対する判断力を曇らす. ¶The superior quality of the goods ***compelled*** a favorable *judgment* from all. その商品が優秀であるために勢い一般の好評を得るようになった. ¶So many things to be taken into consideration ***confuse*** prompt *judgment*. 色々と考慮すべき点があるので急速には判断がつかない. ¶***correct*** (=***right***) one's *judgment* その判断を正す. ¶***delay*** one's *judgment* 断定を延ばす. ¶To be successful a gardener must ***exercise*** *judgment* in deciding upon the proper date to plant his crop. 成績をあげるには栽培者は作物の植え付に適当の日を選ばなくてはいけない. ¶***exhibit*** a judicious *judgment* 分別ある判断力を示す. ¶***follow*** one's own good *judgment* 自分のよいと思う通りにする. ¶Appearances are deceitful; but it is on them that we ***form*** our *judgments*. 表面だけではあてにならないものだがわれわれの判断はそれに基くのである. ‖ The book has the defects of *judgments* ***formed*** by a traveler on a country through which he passes in an express train. その本には急行列車で通過した国に対する旅行者に見られる判断の誤りがある. 【類】***form*** a *judgment* upon facts / ***form*** a fresh *judgment* about ... / I leave the readers to ***form*** their own *judgment*. / so far as I can ***form*** a *judgment* / material for ***forming*** a *judgment* on ... ¶He ***has*** good *judgment*. 彼にはりっぱな判断力がある. ¶***lead*** one's *judgment* ***astray*** 判断を迷わす. ¶***let*** one's *judgment* be influenced by ... その判断を下すにあたって...に左右される. ¶***lose*** one's *judgment* 判断力を失う. ¶***mislead*** the *judgment* 判断を誤らせる. ¶***modify*** one's *judgment* その判断を修正する. ¶He is apt to be moved by a strong impulsive obsession which ***overpowers*** his *judgment*. 彼はとかく強烈な発作的強迫観念のためにその判断力を失いやすい. ¶Don't ***pass*** *judgment* on a man until he has died. 棺をおおうまで人物を論じるな. 【類】One must be very slow (慎重に) to ***pass*** *judgment* in these cases. / a consensus of opinion of those qualified to ***pass*** *judgment* / it is yet too soon to ***pass*** *judgment* upon ... ¶I do not feel competent to ***pronounce*** *judgment* on the matter. 私にはこの問題について断案を下すに足る資格があるように思えない. ¶Posterity will ***ratify*** the *judgment*. 後世の人がこの判断を是認するだろう. ¶It ***represents*** the mature *judgment* of the best leaders. それは最もすぐれた指導者の円熟した判断である. ¶***require*** careful *judgment* 慎重な判断を要する. ¶But it is well to ***reserve*** *judgment* on these points until more accurate information is to hand. しかしもっと正確な報道が手に入るまで断案を下さないがよい. ¶after due reflection has ***ripened*** and ***matured*** my *judgment* よく思案して私の判断が熟してから. ¶***show*** better *judgment* それ以上の見識を示す. 【類】***show*** excellent *judgment*. ¶***stay*** (=reserve) *judgment* till one hears both sides 双方の言い分を聴くまで判断を控える. ¶***submit*** one's *judgment* to others with modesty 謙そんの態度で自分の判断を他人に持ち出す. ¶***suspend*** one's *judgment* 断案を下すのを見合わせる. ¶***Use*** your *judgment* in selecting a substitute. 慎重に代理をお選びなさい. ‖ Unless specific instructions accompany the order we shall ***use*** our best *judgment* as to the method of shipment. 特に御指図がなければ発送の方法については当方で万全を期しましょう. ¶*judgment* ***warped*** by self-interest (patriotic prejudice) 私利(など)にゆがめられた判断. ¶carefully ***weigh*** *judgments* 注意深く異なる判断を比較考査する. ¶***win*** the favorable *judgment* of the world 世人から是認される. ¶It is wise to ***withhold*** *judgment* when the data are obviously incomplete. 材料が明かに不備の場合は判断を差控えるのが賢明なやり方だ.

Q form an ***adequate*** *judgment* on ... …に対し適当な判断を下す. ¶those best entitled to ***authoritative*** *judgment* その判断に最大権威ある人々. ¶Brutus: a good man with ***bad*** *judgment* ブルータスすなわち判断に欠けた善人. ¶a consensus of the ***best*** *judgment* of the English-speaking world 英語を話す社界の最良な判断の総合. ¶against one's ***better*** *judgment* うっかりと. ¶He has a ***clear*** and ***settled*** *judgment*. 彼は明敏にして着実なる判断力を持つ. ¶***common sense*** *judgment* 常識判断, しろうと考え. ¶***cool*** *judgment* 冷静な判断. ¶form ***correct*** *judgment* of ... …を正しく批判する. ¶pass ***critical*** *judgment* 批評的な判断を下す. ¶with ***excellent*** *judgment* 卓抜した判断力をもって. ¶pass a ***fair*** *judgment* on ... …に公正な判断を下す. 【類】A ***fair*** *judgment* can now be pronounced on it. ¶pass ***final*** *judgment* on ... …に対して決定的判断を下す. ¶He meets all the exceptional situations with ***good*** *judgment*. 彼はあらゆる異常な局面をすぐれた判断力で処理する. ¶Beware of ***hasty*** *judgment*. 速断に失しないように御注意. ¶Time is the sure corrector of all aberrations of ***human*** *judgment*. 時はすべての人間の判断の誤りを確実に訂正してくれる. ¶his ***impeccable*** *judgment* 彼の間違いのない判断力. ¶arrive at an ***independent*** *judgment* on a question ある問題について一家の説を立てる. 【類】form one's own ***independent*** *judgment*. ¶on one's ***individual*** *judgment* 個人的判断に基いて. ¶***infallible*** *judgment* 誤らざる判断. ¶form an ***intelligent*** *judgment* as to ... …について理解ある判断をする. ¶acquire a ***keen*** *judgment* as to ... …に関して鋭い判断力を得る. ¶has no ***literary*** *judgment* 文学的判断力がない. ¶exhibit not a ***little*** *judgment* in dealing with a vexed question 難問題を取扱うのに相当の判断力を示す ‖ he must have ***little*** *judgment* or great obstinacy who does not confess that ... …と自白しない人は判断力が乏しいか非常に強情な人に相違ない. ¶***mature*** *judgment* 円熟した判断. ¶***Moderate*** and ***balanced*** *judgments* often pass unheeded. 穏健中正な判断はよく無視される. ¶He is to be admired for the courage which enables him to form ***original*** *judgments*. 彼に独創的判断を下す勇気のあるのは感服だ. ¶in my ***personal*** *judgment* 私一個の考えでは. ¶***Quick*** *judgments* are hazardous. 早急な判断は危険だ. ¶His *judgment* is soundly ***sane***. 彼の判断はきわめて健全だ. ¶lose one's ***sober*** *judgment* 血迷う. ¶the consensus of ***sound*** *judgment* 正しい判断の一致. ¶***subjective*** *judgment* 主観的判断. ¶acquire a ***sure*** *judgment* as to ... …に関して確実な判断をつける. ¶***Suspended*** *judgment* is the greatest triumph of intellectual discipline. 容易に断定を下さないことは知的訓練の最大勝利である. ¶a ***sweeping*** *judgment* 一掃的な(細部を考慮しない)判断. ¶an ***unbiassed*** *judgment* 偏見のない判断. ¶a ***wholesome*** *judgment* 健全な判断. ¶***wise, temperate*** *judgment* 賢く穏当な判断.

Q² ***aptitude*** *judgment* 適性判断(テスト). ¶use ***business*** *judgment* in making one's purchases 買入れに商業的判断力に従う. ¶***value*** *judgment* 価値判断.

P ***in*** my *judgment* 私の考えでは. 【類】He is wanting ***in*** *judgment*. / ***in*** the *judgment* of posterity (後世の人) ‖ I am unable to sit ***in*** *judgment*. 私は批評するだけの器量がない. ¶act ***on*** one's own *judgment* 自分自身の判断で行動する. ¶The matter is left entirely ***to*** your *judgment*. その件はすべて君の判断に任せる. ¶act ***with*** *judgment* 思慮ある行動をする.

P² exquisite *judgment* ***in*** art 鋭い芸術批評. ¶pass *judgment* ***on*** a question ある問題に対して判断を下す.

(2) 判決, 裁判.

V ***affirm*** the *judgment* of a lower court 下級裁判所の判決を確認する. ¶***annul*** *judgment* 裁判を取消す. ¶***attack*** a *judgment* 裁判に不服を称える. ¶***deliver*** *judgment* 宣告を下す ‖ *Judgment* was ***delivered*** in the ... case in favor of the defendant. …事件は被告の勝訴となった. 【類】in a *judgment* ***delivered*** in the Supreme Court. ¶***give*** (= render) a *judgment* 判決を言渡す ‖ ***give*** *judgment* in a case ある事件に判決を下す. ¶***make*** a *judgment* 《米》判決を下す. ¶***pronounce*** a *judgment* on a case 一事件に対して判決を言渡す. ¶***render*** *judgment* 判決を言渡す. ¶***reserve*** *judgment* 判決を猶予する. ¶***reverse*** the *judgment* of the lower court 下級裁判所の判決をくつがえす. ¶***revise*** a *judgment* 判決を再審する. ¶***squash*** a *judgment* 判決を破棄する. ¶***uphold*** the *judgment* of the lower court 下級裁判所の判決を支持する.

Q reserve ***final*** *judgment* until ... …まで結審を保留する. ¶a ***foreign*** *judgment* 外国判決. ¶a ***full*** *judgment* 判決全文. ¶an ***irrevocable*** *judgment* 決定判決. ¶quash an ***original*** *judgment* 原判決を破棄する. ¶it is ***poor*** *judgment* to ... …するのは考えが足りない(まずい). ¶the ***sober*** *judgment* of courts 裁判所の公平な判決.

Q² enderr a "***default*** *judgment*" 欠席裁判を宣告する.

P sit ***in*** *judgment* on ... …をさばく.

P² a *judgment* ***of*** acquittal 無罪判決 ‖ a *judgment* ***of*** conviction 有罪判決. ¶It is a *judgment* ***on*** you for getting up late. それは君が寝坊した罰だ. ¶a *judgment* ***upon*** ... *obstance verdicto* …に対する評決無視の判決.

jug, *n.* ジョッキ.

P² a *jug* ***of*** beer ジョッキー杯のビール.

juggle, *n.* 手品.

V ***practice*** (=***perform***) some *juggle* ちょっと手品をやる.

juggle, *v.* 手品をやる.

P *juggle* ***with*** words 言葉でごま化す.

juggler, *n.* 奇術師.

Q² a ***dagger*** *juggler* 短刀使いの手品師. ¶an expert ***word*** *juggler* 巧妙な言葉の手品師(新聞記者など).

P one of the most expert ***of*** *jugglers* in the profession その仲間で最も老練な一奇術師. ¶a *juggler* ***in*** statistics has figured out that ... 統計家の複雑な計算によると…

juggling, *n.* 手品; 詐欺.

P² He was charged with some dishonest *juggling* ***with*** his master's accounts. 彼は店の帳尻をごま化したという罪科を負わされた. ‖ It needs some *juggling* ***with*** various railway systems before you reach your destinaton. 目的地にお着きになるまでに込入った乗替がある.

juice, *n.* 汁, 液; 《米俗》電流.

V ***express*** the *juice* of the grape ぶどうの汁をしぼり出す. ¶***extract*** the *juice* from lemons レモンから汁をしぼる. ¶***generate*** the gastric *juice* 胃液を出させる. ¶***squeeze*** *juice* from a lemon レモンの汁をしぼる. ¶***suck up*** all the *juice* from the poor 貧乏人の汁をことごとく吸い取る.

Q ***gastric*** *juice* 胃液. ¶[There is] ***no*** *juice* on. 《俗》停電だ. ¶a ***sweet watery*** *juice* 水のような甘い汁.

Q² canned ***fruit*** *juices* かん詰め果物液. ¶***orange*** (***grapc***) *juice* オレンジ(グレープ)ジュース.

P a pear full ***of*** *juice* 水気の多いなし.

jumble, *n.* 混乱.

Q a ***curious*** *jumble* of date 妙な時代(日付)違い.

P Things are all ***in*** a *jumble*. 何もかも乱雑になっている.

jumble, *a.* 乱雑な.

P a study *jumble* ***with*** books 書物で乱雑な書斎.

jumble, *v.* 乱雑にする.

M Toys, boots, and books were all ***jumbled together*** in a cupboard. おもちゃ・くつ・書物が戸だなの中にごたまぜにしてあった. ¶***jumble up*** everything in a drawer to find something 何かをさがしに引出しをかき回す.

jump, *n.* 跳躍.

V He ***has*** (=***gets***) the *jump* on me. 彼に出し抜かれた. ‖ ***have*** a *jump* on any competitors in trade いかなる商業上の競争者よりもはるかに有利な位置に立つ. ¶Prices ***take*** a *jump*. 物価が暴騰する.

Q a ***broad*** *jump* 幅とび. ¶at ***full*** *jump* 《米》=at full speed 全速力で. ¶a ***high*** *jump* 高飛び. ¶a ***running high*** (***broad***) *jump* 走り高(幅)とび.

Q² a ***parachute*** *jump* パラシュート降下. ¶a ***pole*** *jump* 棒飛び. ¶a ***ski*** *jump* スキー跳躍[場]. ¶a 100 ***per cent*** *jump* in the five-cent subway fare 地下鉄の五セント運賃を百パーセント引上げ.

P ***at*** a *jump* 一躍して. ¶He took the rest of the steps ***in*** a *jump*. 彼はあとの階段を一飛びに上った. ‖ the fund rose ***in*** three *jumps* to ... 資金が三口の多額寄付で...の額に達した. ¶The cat seized it ***with*** a *jump*. ねこが飛んでそれを捕らえた.

jump, *v.* 飛ぶ.
M *jump* ***aside*** 飛びのく. ¶*jump* ***overboard*** 甲板から飛降りる.
M[2] He *jumped* ***down***, falling head foremost. 彼はまっさかさまに飛降りた. ‖ *jump* ***down*** one's throat 閉口させる(議論などで). ¶a *jump* ***in*** prices 値段の騰貴. ¶*jump* ***off*** before the train stopped moving 列車が止まる前に飛降りる ‖ We cannot *jump* ***off*** our shadows, and as little can we escape the influence of the society in which we live.—Froude. われわれは自分の影法師から離れることができないと同様にわれわれの住む社会の感化を免れることはできない. ¶*jump* ***on*** to the stage 舞台に飛上がる. ¶*jump* ***up*** behind 引受手形の裏書をする ‖ *jump* ***up*** over the fence 垣を飛越える. 【類】 The dog *jumped* ***up*** at the meat in his master's hand. / *jump* ***up*** from the grass / *jump* ***up*** on a chair.
P *jump* ***across*** crevices 破れ目を飛越える. ¶*jump* ***at*** a conclusion 速断する ‖ He *jumped* ***at*** the proposal (invitation). 彼は喜んでその申出(など)に応じた. ‖ He *jumped* ***at*** the offer like a hungry dog. 彼はこの申出に飢えた犬のようにとびついた. ¶*jump* ***for*** joy (=delight) こおどりして喜ぶ. ¶*jump* ***from*** a railway train 汽車から飛おりる. ¶*jump* ***in*** a street car 電車に飛乗る. ¶*jump* ***into*** a train just as it is starting 発車しかけている列車に飛乗る. 【類】 She was stopped by a constable in an attempt to *jump* ***into*** the Sumida River. / commit suicide by *jumping* ***into*** the river ‖ The new invention *jumped* ***into*** popularity. その新発明品が急に評判になった. ¶*jump* ***off*** a car [while] in motion 進行中の車から飛降りる. 【類】 *jump* ***off*** a wheel (自転車) ‖ *jump* ***off*** a bridge ***into*** the river 橋から川へ飛込む. ¶*jump* ***on*** a car (train) 車(など)に飛乗る. ¶*jump* ***out of*** bed 寝床から飛出す ‖ *jump* ***out of*** harm's way 飛のいて危険を避ける ‖ *jump* ***out of*** one's skin for joy 喜んで有頂天になる. ¶*jump* ***over*** a fence (ditch, brook) 垣(など)を飛越す ‖ *jump* a horse ***over*** a fence 馬に垣を飛越えさせる ‖ *jump* ***over*** a page or two while reading 読書中一二ページ飛ばす. ¶*jump* ***to*** one's feet 急に立ち上る ‖ He *jumped* ***to*** the door. 彼は戸口へ飛んで行った. ‖ *jump* ***to*** a quick (=hasty) conclusion 早のみ込みする. ¶The teacher *jumped* ***upon*** (=***on***) the inattentive pupil. 教師は不注意な生徒に急に向った. ¶He *jumped* ***with*** a splash into the river. 彼は川の中へざんぶとばかり飛込んだ. ‖ *jump* ***with*** joy 小おどりして喜ぶ.

jumper, *n.* 飛ぶ人; 〖服飾〗ジャンパー.
V ***wear*** a *jumper* to protect one's coat 上衣がよごれないようにジャンパーを着る.
Q[2] a ***ski*** *jumper* スキーの跳躍者(選手).

jumping *n.* 跳躍.
Q[2] ***sheet*** *jumping* 帆索飛び.

junction, *n.* 接合, 交差点.
V at this point the railway line ***effects*** a *junction* with ... この地点でその鉄道は...と連絡する.
P It stands ***at*** the *junction* (=fork) of two rivers. 二つの川の落合う所にある. 【類】 ***at*** the *junction* of Chancery Lane with Fleet Street.

juncture, *n.* 時, 急場.
Q at a ***critical*** *juncture* 危急の際に. ¶at ***important*** *junctures* 大切な時に. ¶at an ***opportune*** *juncture* 都合のよい折に. ¶at the ***present*** *juncture* この際. 【類】 at the ***present*** *juncture* of affairs.
P It was ***at*** this *juncture* that he arrived upon the scene. 彼が現場にあらわれたのはこの時だった.

jungle, *n.* 密林(ジャングル).
Q the gross vegetation of the ***tropical*** *jungles*. 熱帯ジャングルの繁茂する草木.
Q[2] near the ***wild-beast haunting*** *jungles* 野獣の住むジャングルに近づく.
P wander ***through*** a *jungle* 密林の中をさまよう.

junior, *n.* 年少者.
P She is my *junior* ***by*** seven years. 彼女は私より七つ年下だ. ¶I am his *junior* ***in*** life. 私は彼の後輩です.

junior, *a.* 年下の, 官位の下の.
P He is *junior* ***to*** me. 彼は私の下役だ.

junk, *n.* ジャンク(中国船).
V ***fit out*** a *junk* with a cargo worth ... 価額...の荷を積込んだジャンクを仕立てる.

jurisdiction, *n.* 裁判権, 管轄権.
V ***exercise*** *jurisdiction* 司法権を行使する. ¶This office does not ***have*** *jurisdiction* over advertising matters. 宣伝はこの役所の管轄ではない. 【類】 The office ***has*** *jurisdiction* over the district. ‖ ***have*** no *jurisdiction* to hear this case この事件をさばく権限を持たない ‖ courts ***having*** *jurisdiction* of marriage licenses, divorces, registration of wills, etc. 結婚許可・離婚・遺言の登記などを管轄する裁判所 ‖ He ***has*** *jurisdiction* over 425,000 enlisted men and 47,000 officers. 彼は 425,000 の兵士と 47,000 の士官を部下に持っている.
Q under the ***direct*** *jurisdiction* of ... ...直轄の. ¶***appellate*** *jurisdiction* 上訴審の裁判権. ¶***exclusive*** *jurisdiction* 専属管轄. ¶***extraterritorial*** *jurisdiction* 治外法権による裁判管轄権. ¶***material*** *jurisdiction* 事物管轄. ¶***original*** *jurisdiction* 第一審の裁判権. ¶***territorial*** *jurisdiction* 土地管轄.
P it falls ***beyond*** (***within***) the *jurisdiction* of ... それは...の管轄外(内)になる. ¶it is ***outside*** the *jurisdiction* of ... それは...の管轄外である. ¶subject ***to*** the *jurisdiction* of ... ...の管轄を受ける. ¶The Personnel Board is ***under*** the *jurisdiction* of the Cabinet. 人事院は内閣の所轄である. ¶It is ***within*** the *jurisdiction* of the military authorities. それは陸軍当局の管轄内にある. ‖ The business is ***within*** the *jurisdiction* of this office. その事務は当所の管轄に属している.
P[2] *jurisdiction* ***over*** foreigners 外人に対する司法権.

juror, *n.* 審査官.
Q an ***alternate*** *juror* 補充陪審員.
P[2] a *juror* ***of*** the Patent Bureau 特許局の審査官.

jury, *n.* [団]陪審員.
V The *jury* were ***disagreed***. 陪審員の意見が一致しなかった. ¶The *jury* were ***divided*** in opinion. 陪審員は意見の一致を見なかった.
V[2] the *jury* ***held*** that ... 陪審員は...との決定を下した.
Q a ***grand*** *jury* 大陪審. ¶a ***petty*** *jury* 小陪審. ¶a ***trial*** *jury* 公判陪審.
P a trial ***by*** a *jury* 陪審裁判. ¶serve ***on*** a *jury* 陪審員をつとめる ‖ sit ***on*** a *jury* 陪審員になる.

just, *a.* 正しい, 公正な.
P *just* ***in*** one's dealings 処置の公正な. 【類】 He is fair and *just* ***in*** judgment. ¶be *just* ***to*** one's engagement 約束を守る. ¶deal with the matter so as to be *just* ***to*** all the people concerned 関係者一同に対して公平であるようにその事件を取扱う.

just, *ad.* 正しく.
P *just* ***at*** present ちょうど今. ¶a person *just* ***from*** abroad 外国から帰朝したばかりの人. ¶*just* ***in*** time ちょうどいい時に.

justice, *n.* (**1**) 正義, 公正; 裁判, 賞罰.
V ***administer*** *justice* to ... ...を裁く. ¶***deny*** one *justice* 人を公平に取扱わない. ¶a government able to maintain peace and ***dispense*** (=administer) *justice* 平和を維持し曲直を分明にしうる政府. ¶***do*** *justice* to ... ...を公平に取扱う; ...を十分に評価する ‖ to ***do*** him *justice* 彼を公平に言うと ‖ ***do*** oneself *justice* 腕前を十分に発揮する ‖ I ***do*** you *justice*. お気持はよく分かっています. ‖ It is impossible to ***do*** *justice* to the subject in a short article. 短かい論文では十分にその問題を取扱うことはできない. ‖ *Justice* has been ***done***. 裁判が下った; 正当なことが行われた. ‖ when I had ***done*** *justice* to all the good things ごちそうをやたら頂戴してから. 【類】 To ***do*** *justice* to this subject would require far more space than can be given in an ordinary magazine article. / This photo does not ***do*** her *justice* (似ていない). / The title of this work hardly ***does*** *justice* to it. ¶try to ***escape*** *justice* by flight 警察の手から逃げようとする. ¶The courts ***give*** *justice* to the people. 裁判所は人民を公平に裁判する. ‖ The portrait does not ***give*** him *justice*. この肖像画は彼にあまり似ていない. ¶he ***met*** retributive *justice* at the hands of ... 彼は...にあだを取られた. ¶***mete out*** *justice* 賞罰を行う. ¶***obtain*** *justice* 正しい裁きを受ける. ¶We ***realize*** the complete *justice* of your claim. われわれはあなたの要求が全く正しいことを認める. ¶***receive*** ample *justice* 十分な応報を受ける. ¶***secure*** even-handed *justice* 公平な裁きを得る. ¶I ***saw*** the *justice* of his remarks. 私は彼の言うことの正しいのが分かった. ‖ I fail to ***see*** the *justice* of his accusal. 私には彼が告訴さ

れた理由が分からない. ¶*justice* can best be ***served*** by ... ...によって最も公平となる. ¶***take*** *justice* into one's own hands 法律の手を経ないで勝手に処分する. ¶*justice* ***tempered*** with mercy 慈愛を加味した正義. ¶***violate*** *justice* 正義を破る.

Q do ***ample*** *justice* to a feast ごちそうを十分いただく. ¶it is the ***barest*** *justice* to him to say ... ...と言うのは彼に対して是を是とするに過ぎない. ¶No halftone reproduction can do ***entire*** *justice* to any photograph or painting. どんな網版の複写でも写真や絵にそっくり似させることはできない. ¶We did ***full*** *justice* to the excellent meal provided for us. われわれは用意してくれた結構な食事を十分頂戴した. ‖ do ***full*** *justice* to his brilliant gifts 彼のすばらしい天才を十分に発揮する. 【類】 the question would not, however, have ***full*** *justice* done to it if attention were not called to ... ‖ The papers have done ***full*** *justice* to that topic. 諸新聞はその題目について盛んに書きたてた. ‖ Art can do ***full*** *justice* to a sunset and poetry to a battle. 美術は日没を詩は戦争を十分に描き出すことがきる. ¶a court of ***international*** *justice* 国際裁判所. ¶There is ***no*** *justice* in the censure. その非難には正しい根拠がない. ‖ Such a cursory survey can do ***no*** *justice* to the subject. こんな概説ではその問題を十分に論じたとは言えない. ¶***providential*** *justice* 天罰. ¶do ***scant*** *justice* to ... ...に対して認識不足である ‖ we would be doing the subject ***scant*** *justice* did we omit to mention ... 仮に...の説明を省略したとするとその問題を十分に論じたことにならないだろう. ‖ Unfortunately, the photographic reproduction does it ***scant*** *justice*. 不幸にしてその写真の複写はあまり原画に似ていない. ¶in ***simple*** *justice* to us われわれに対する当然の行為として. ¶the establishment of ***social, political*** and ***economic*** *justice* 社会的・政治的・経済的正義の確立. ¶***summary*** *justice* 即決裁判.

P a person with a great love ***for*** *justice* 大いに正義を愛する人 ‖ join in the fight ***for*** *justice* 正義の戦に加わる. ¶You must, ***in*** *justice* to yourself, see the Hillman before deciding on your new car. あなたは新車購入を決心なさる前にぜひヒルマン車を御覧にならねばなりません. ‖ ***in*** *justice* it must be said (=I must say) that ... ぜひ...と申さなければならない. ¶miscarriage ***of*** *justice* 裁判の失当. ¶give oneself up ***to*** *justice* 自首して出る. ¶bring a person ***to*** *justice* [犯罪に対して]人を裁判にかける. ¶*Go* may ***with*** *justice* be considered more difficult than chess. 碁は確かに西洋将棋よりもむずかしい. ‖ Switzerland has been described, ***with*** some *justice*, as the political laboratory of Europe. スイスがヨーロッパの政治的実験室と評されたのはもっともな所がある. ¶It is not altogether ***without*** *justice*. それは全然名分が立たないという訳ではない. ¶*justice* ***to*** (=***for***) the oppressed しいたげられた者への正義.

(**2**) 判事, 裁判官.

Q a ***chief*** *justice* 《米》 裁判長 (a presiding judge) ‖ the Chief *Justice* of the United States 米国最高裁判所長官.

Q^2 an ***associate*** *justice* of the United States 最高裁判所判事. ¶a ***circuit*** *justice* 巡回裁判官. ¶a ***police*** *justice* 簡易裁判所判事.

P^2 a *justice* ***of*** the peace 保安判事.

justifiable, *a.* 正当な.

M It is ***not*** *justifiable* to say so. そう言うには当らない.

justification, *n.* 弁明, 正当とすること.

V this judgment ***finds*** ample *justification* in the fact that ... この見解は...ということ事実に徴して十分に正しいことが分かる. 【類】 *justification* is ***found*** in this fact that ...

Q with ***considerable*** *justification* 誠にもっともなことで. ¶it is an altogether ***insufficient*** *justification* for ... それは...には全く申しわけが立たない. ¶the ***moral*** *justification* of prostitution 売春の道徳的是認. ¶There is ***no*** *justification* for it. それでは義理がたたない. ¶his ill health is the ***only*** *justification* for ... 彼の病気が...の唯一の言訳である. ¶***rationalistic*** *justification* 合理的弁明. ¶It is quite ***sufficient moral*** *justification*. それは全く十分な道徳的弁明だ. 【類】 There is not ***sufficient*** *justification* for it.

P say ***in*** *justification* of ... ...を弁解のためにいう ‖ without any valid reason ***in*** *justification* of the act その行為を弁護する何ら正当の理由なく. ¶You might use that adjective ***with*** full *justification*. 君はその形容詞を使って少しも差支えない. ¶attack a person ***without*** *justification* 人を理由なく攻撃する.

P^2 *justification* ***by*** faith 信仰による正当化(他力本願). ¶there is no *justification* ***for*** ... ...してよい訳はない. ¶the *justification* ***of*** the means by the end 目的による手段の正当化.

justify, *v.* 正当たるを証する, 証明する.

M It is ***amply*** *justified* by the result. それは結果によって十分に正当なことが証明されている. 【類】 His conduct is ***amply*** *justified* on these grounds. ¶The act, I think, was ***barely*** *justified* by the circumstances. 周囲の事情から察してその行為はどうやら正当だったと思う. ¶one seems ***fairly*** *justified* in concluding that ... ...と結論してもよいような気がする. ¶He was ***fully*** *justified* in leaving the matter untouched. 彼がその事を捨ておいたのについては十分に正当の理由があった.

P I do not think this criticism is *justified* ***by*** the facts. 私はこの非難は事実が証明していないと思う. ‖ people who live with more show than is *justified* ***by*** their income 収入不相応に見えを張った生活をする人々. ¶*justify* oneself ***for*** one's conduct 自己の行為を弁明する. ¶The Germans are largely *justified* ***in*** their fear of Russia. ドイツ国民がロシアを恐れるのはまことにもっともなことだ. ‖ Was I *justified* ***in*** this course of action? 私がこういう行為に出たのは正しかったか. ¶he is *justified* ***in*** his deduction that ... 彼は...と推定して正しい.

jut, *v.* 突き出る.

M a bit of land *jutting* ***out*** into the sea (bay) 海(など)に突き出ている地の一角 ‖ a large rock which *jutted* ***out*** little way into the water 水中へ少しつきだしている大きな岩.

P a pine-tree *jutting* ***beyond*** the walls へいの外に突き出ている松の木. ¶I saw a gun *jutting* ***out of*** the bushes. そのやぶから銃口が出ているのを見つけた.

juvenile, *n.* 少年.

P books ***for*** the *juvenile*=juvenile books 少年向読物.

juxtaposition, *n.* 並列.

P^2 the *juxtaposition* ***of*** grinding poverty ***with*** the most striking manifestations of modern wealth 近代における富の最も顕著な表現と極貧との並立.

K

kaleidoscope, *n.* 万華鏡.

Q Image followed image in my ***mental*** *kaleidoscope*. 私の心の万華鏡に後から後へと像が現われた. ¶the ***political*** *kaleidoscope* 政局の万華鏡.

karma, *n.* 因果応報.

Q by the ***evil*** *karma* of that action その行いの報いで.

keel, *n.* 竜骨.

V The *keel* of the "Great Western" was ***laid*** in 1836. グレート・ウエスターン号は一八三六年に起工された. 【類】 During that time the *keels* were ***laid*** for eight motor vessels for a total of 25,300 tons. ¶***lay down*** the *keel* 造船の起工をする.

keen, *a.* 鋭い, 強い.

M ***as*** *keen* ***as*** razors かみそりのように鋭い ‖ ***as*** *keen* ***as*** mustard 非常に熱心な.

P He is *keen* ***after*** money-making. 彼は金もうけに抜目がない. ¶He is so *keen* ***about*** his game as to forget everything else. 彼はゲームに夢中になって何でも忘れるほどだ. ¶*keen* ***of*** scent (hearing) きゅう覚(など)の鋭い. ¶He is *keen* ***on*** stamp collecting. 彼は切手収集に熱心だ. ‖ He is *keen* ***on*** her. 彼はあの女にほれている. ‖ I am not very *keen*

on a hot place. 私は暑い所は余り感心しない.
o There the competition was *keener* than steel. そこは競争が非常に激しかった.

keenness, *n.* 鋭敏; 熱心.
P² the *keenness* ***of*** the school ***on*** things athletic その学校の運動に対する熱心.

keep, *v.* 続ける; 守る; 養う; しまっておく; 経営する.
M *keep* ***abreast*** with (=of) the times 時勢におくれないようにする.【類】No student who wishes to *keep* ***abreast*** of the times can afford to ignore German publication. / *keep* ***abreast*** of the swift motion of the time / *keep* ***abreast*** of the latest developments in the theatre / *keep* ***abreast*** of developments in Europe and America / It is the duty of a good teacher to acquaint himself with his subject, become a master of its literature (文献), and *keep* ***abreast*** of the latest development in his subject. / *keep* ***abreast*** of the progress of technology (工芸学). ¶*keep* ***alive*** international animosities 国際的えん恨を忘れさせないようにする. ¶*keep* ***aloof*** from the crowd 群集から離れている. ¶Better *keep* them ***apart***. 彼らを離しておいた方がよい. ¶*keep* ***away*** from bad companions 悪友から遠ざかる ‖ *keep* colds ***away*** with ... ...(薬)をのんで感冒にかからないようにする. 【類】*keep* ***away*** evil spirits (悪霊) / What's *kept* you ***away*** so long? ¶*keep* ***back*** the crowd 群集を制止する(前に出ないように) ‖ It is very difficult to *keep* ***back*** one's *tears* when deeply moved. 激しく感動したときは涙を抑えるのが中々むずかしい. 【類】*keep* ***back*** youngsters from social evils ‖ Receipts from the interior are *kept* ***back*** by snowstorms. 内地からの受荷がふぶきのため滞っている ‖ *keep* dinner ***back*** for an hour 一時間食事を遅らす ‖ I knew he was *keeping* something ***back*** from me. 彼が私に何か隠しているのを私は知っていた. 【類】I have nothing to *keep* ***back*** from you. ¶It *kept* me so ***busy***. そのために私は非常に忙しかった. 【類】*keep* children ***busy*** all the time. ¶*Keep* ***clear***. この中に入るべからず. ¶*keep* it ever ***clearly*** in mind それをいつも明確に記憶している. ¶*keep* ***close*** to ... ...から離れないでいる. ¶it is to be *kept* ***constantly*** in mind that ... 絶えず心に止めておくべきことは...である. ¶*keep* ***cool*** 冷静にしている. ¶*keep* it ***dry*** それを湿らないようにする. ¶Their promises were ***faithfully*** *kept*. 彼らの約束は忠実に守られた. ¶*keep* ***firmly*** in your mind the fact that ... ...という事実を銘記せよ. ¶That's the way to *keep* ***fit***. それが健康法である. ¶the store is *kept* ***going jointly*** by ... その店は...が共同でやっている. ¶The meat will *keep* ***good*** till tomorrow. 肉はあすまでもつでしょう. ¶*keep* dictionaries ***handy*** (=on hand) 辞書を手もとにおく. ¶He could ***hardly*** *keep* himself from bursting out laughing again. 彼は再び吹き出さずにはいられなかった. 【類】I could ***hardly*** *keep* from laughing. ¶*keep* ***inactive*** 怠けている. ¶Milk curdles when *kept* too ***long***. 牛乳はあまり長くおくとかたまる. ¶*keep* it ***moist*** by sponging それを海綿で絶えずしめしておく. ¶*Keep* ***out***!〖掲示〗立入るべからず. ‖ *keep* ***out*** [the] cold 風のはいらないようにする ‖ *Keep* ***out*** from the vestibule.〖掲示〗車体の連結部に立たないこと. 【類】*keep* ***out*** the heat arising fom the sun's rays / get the gangsters out of town and *keep* them ***out***. ¶*keep* the headquarters ***posted*** as to the army's movements その軍隊の行動について本部に絶えず知らせる. ¶The date must be ***punctually*** *kept*. 時日は正確に守らなければならない. ¶*keep* ***quiet*** about ... ...について黙っている. ¶His words *kept* ***ringing*** in my ears. 彼の言ったことが私の耳に残っていた. ¶*keep* the windows ***shut*** (***open***) 窓を締めて(あけて)おく. ¶*keep* ***silent*** (=***still***) 静かにしている. ¶He confided it to me as a secret to be ***solemnly*** *kept*. 彼は極秘としてそれを私に打明けた. ¶*Keep* ***straight on*** until you come to ... and turn to the left. ...に出るまでまっすぐに行ってそれから左にお曲りなさい. ¶*keep* ***strictly*** within one's income あくまで収入だけで生活をする ‖ *keep* ***strictly*** to one's native language 自国語しか使わないでいる. ¶The garden is ***well*** *kept*. 庭園はよく手が入れてある.
M² *keep* ***down*** weeds 雑草を延びないようにする ‖ *keep* ***down*** the cost of production 生産費が上らないようにする. 【類】*keep* the speed ***down*** / *keep* ***down*** the water from overflowing / *keep* ***down*** gas bills / *keep* ***down*** unemployment / *keep* ***down*** taxes / We would rather see prices *kept* ***down*** than wages rise. / *keep* ***down*** the plague of rats (ペスト) / *keep* ***down*** irritation (いらいらした感じ). ¶be *kept* ***in*** by the rain 雨に降り込められる ‖ The doctor *kept* me ***in*** for a week. 医者は一週間私に外出を禁じた. 【類】be *kept* ***in*** with flu. ¶*keep* ***in*** with one's superiors 先輩と折合って行く. 【類】*keep* ***in*** with ladies. ¶*keep* ***off*** the heat 暑気をよける. 【類】*keep* ***off*** bad men (悪人を避ける) / *keep* ***off*** infection (伝染) ‖ *keep* hands ***off*** 手を触れないようにする ‖ *keep* a person ***off*** balance 人が立っていられないようにする. 【類】*keep* ***off*** enemy ships / use an umbrella to *keep* ***off*** the rain. ¶if the rain *keeps* ***on*** もし雨がやまなければ ‖ School *keeps* ***on*** till four o'clock. 学校は四時までである. ¶*keep* a person ***on*** at his work 人にその仕事を続けさせる ‖ *keep* ***on*** breathing 呼吸を続ける ‖ He *kept* his hat ***on***. 彼は帽子をかぶったままでいた. 【類】You may *keep* your topcoat ***on***. / *keep* one's shirt ***on*** with sleeves rolled down ‖ *Keep* cover ***on*** tight. ふたをしっかりしておくこと. ¶*Keep* them ***over***, please, till he calls for them. 彼が品物を取りに来るまで預っておいて下さい. ¶The firemen managed to *keep* the fire ***under***. 消防夫の力で鎮火した. ¶The old custom is still *kept* ***up*** in that district. その地方ではその古い風俗がなお存続している ‖ *keep* ***up*** the rotation of blooms 花が後から後へと咲いているようにする ‖ *keep* ***up*** conversation 談話を続ける ‖ *keep* them ***up*** to the standard その(商品)の規格を落さないようにする. 【類】Monkeys *kept* ***up*** their chatter. / *keep* ***up*** our reputation as ... / *keep* ***up*** troop morale (士気) / *keep* ***up*** present dietary standards (現在の栄養) ‖ *keep* ***up*** the fight 戦を続ける. 【類】*keep* ***up*** the pace (歩調) / *keep* ***up*** with the times (world) / I still keep ***up*** my acquaintance (交際) with him. / *keep* ***up*** a regular correspondence with ... / *keep* ***up*** relations with ... / *keep* prices ***up*** / be carefully *kept* ***up*** to date / *keep* ***up*** with the progress of the times / *keep* ***up*** with modern changes in school practices and methods ‖ I am *keeping* you ***up*** with my story. 話が長くなりました ‖ *keep* ***up*** a home 世帯を持続ける(崩さないで) ‖ demand for wage rises sufficiently to *keep* ***up*** with the rising living costs 生活費の向上に十分対応しうるだけの賃金引上の要求 ‖ *Keep* the right side ***up***.〖掲示〗横積無用. ¶He *kept* me ***waiting*** for two hours, without a word of excuse. 彼は一言の言訳もしないで私を二時間待たせた. ¶*keep* it ***warm*** さめないようにする. ¶try to *keep* ***well*** 病気にならないようにがん張る.
P *keep* it ***about*** one's person それを身につけておく. ¶*keep* one's head ***above*** water 借金をしないようにする, 破産しないようにする. ¶*keep* a castle ***against*** the enemy 敵に対抗して城を守る. ¶*keep* it ***as*** a remembrance それを形見に取っておく. ¶*Keep* ***at*** it! これを辛抱しろ(根よく働け). ‖ grow tired of *keeping* ***at*** one and the same thing 全然同じことをたゆまず続けるのに飽きてくる ‖ *keep* it ***at*** hand for reference 参考用にそれを手近におく ‖ *keep* a person ***at*** arm's length 人と余り懇意にならないようにする ‖ They *kept* ***at*** him for payment. 彼らは払いを得るため彼にくっついて行った. ‖ *keep* the temperature ***at*** 80° F. 温度を華氏八十度にしておく. ¶I *keep* it ever ***before*** my mind. 私はいつもそれを念頭においている. ¶be *kept* ***for*** reference 参照のため保存してある(統計などが) ‖ *keep* a seat ***for*** him 彼のために席を取っておく 【類】I've *kept* seats ***for*** you all. ‖ My sister *keeps* house ***for*** me. 私の妹(姉)が家事を世話してくれます. ‖ *keep* hens ***for*** profit from their product 利益のために鶏を飼う. ¶I could hardly *keep* ***from*** smiling. 私は微笑せずにはいられなかった. ‖ God *keep* my children ***from*** all harm. 神よ子供らの危難を守り給え. 【類】The rain (cold) *kept* us ***from*** going out. ‖ *Keep* this ***for*** Mr. Brown, please. どうぞこれをブラウン氏の分としてしまっておいて下さい. ‖ I really must not *keep* you ***from*** your work. 私は絶対にお仕事の邪魔なんかしてはならない. ‖ *keep* the police and the law courts ***from*** bribery 警察や裁判所に収賄行為のないようにする. ¶*keep* it ***in*** mind それを忘れないでいる ‖ be *kept* ***in*** bed 床についている ‖ *keep* a rabbit ***in*** a box うさぎを箱にかう ‖ *keep* it ***in*** one's possession それを手離さずにいる ‖ *keep* her ***in*** life 彼女を生かしておく ‖ Every siege or shipwreck or polar expedition brings out some hero who *keeps* the whole company ***in*** heart. ろう城とか難船とか極地探検とかには必ず全員の元気を支える英雄が現われるものだ. ‖ *Keep* ***in*** your school until you have finished its curriculum. 卒業するまで学校に

いなさい. ‖ *keep in* position 地位を保持する ‖ *keep* a person *in* constant fear 人をたえずこわがらせる. ‖ *keep* them *in* check 彼らを食い止めておく ‖ His story *kept* us all *in* suspense. 彼の話がどうなるかとみんなやきもきした. ‖ chickens *kept in* confinement 囲い飼いのひな ‖ *keep* it *in* stock それが品切れにならぬようにする ‖ *keep in* (=restrain) a horse 馬を御する ‖ *keep in* touch with the world 世の中と接触を保っている. 【類】*keep* most of his equals *in* some awe of him / He *kept in* very close touch with everything that affected his firm. ‖ *keep* her *in* hand for loading 積荷のため船を手離さずにおく. 【類】butter *kept in* the refrigerator / finished goods *kept in* a storehouse ‖ be *kept in* motion 運転されている ‖ She will *keep* him *in* order. 彼女は彼を「おとなしく」させておくだろう. ‖ Everything can be *kept in* proper order. 物は何でも適当に整理しておくことができる. ‖ *keep in* communication with ……と文通を続ける. ¶*Keep off* the grass. 芝生に入るべからず. ‖ *keep off* the sun 日をよける ‖ to *keep* my mind *off* my troubles 苦労を忘れるために. ¶periodicals *kept on* file とじ込になっている定期刊行物 ‖ *keep* him *on* gruel 彼にかゆを食わせておく ‖ *keep on* beaten track 従来のやり方を続ける ‖ *keep* check (=tab) *on* a statement 計算書を調べる. ¶*keep* them *out of* mischief (=harm's way) 彼らに危害のないようにする. 【類】*keep out of* a quarrel ‖ *keep out of* sight 隠れている ‖ *keep out of* his way 彼を避ける. 【類】*keep out of* bad company / *keep out of* the way of the tram cars ‖ Shall I *keep* him *out of* school? 彼に学校を休ませようか. ‖ the only way to *keep out of* trouble is to … そばづえを食わないただ一つの方法は…である. ¶*keep to* one's bed ずっと床についている ‖ *keep to* the pledge 誓約を守る ‖ *keep* the matter *to* oneself そのことを秘しておく ‖ *keep to* the middle path 中庸をとる ‖ adopt the "*keep to* the right" rule for pedestrians 歩行者右側通行の規則を採用する ‖ *keep to* the regulations 規則を守る. 【類】*keep to* one's determination / *keep to* the truth ‖ *keep* oneself *to* oneself 交際を避けて独りでいる. 【類】He *kept* himself very much *to* himself. ‖ *keep to* one's office for long 長く職についている. ¶*keep* India *under* subjection インドを支配下におく ‖ *keep* it *under* lock and key それを錠前のかかる所にしまっておく. 【類】her parents' precious darling who is *kept under* lock and key (箱入娘) ‖ He was *kept under* arrest for three days. 彼は三日間拘留された. ‖ The dogs were *keeping with* him. 犬が彼に付いて行った. ¶*keep* step (=pace) *with* him 彼と歩調を合わせる. 【類】I *kept* as much *with* him as I could. ‖ *keep* company *with* a person 人と交際を続ける. ¶*keep within* one's income (budget) 収入(予算)内で暮らす ‖ *keep* people *within* bounds 人々に度を過さないようにさせる ‖ *keep within* the bounds of truth and dignity 誠実と権威をそこなわぬようにする.

keeper, *n.* 番人, 保管人.

Q^2 a *coffee-house keeper* コーヒー店経営者. ¶a *level-crossing keeper* 踏切番人. ¶a *lighthouse keeper* 灯台守. ¶a *lodging-house keeper* 下宿屋. ¶a *poultry keeper* 家きん飼養者. ¶a *store keeper*=《英》a shopkeeper 店主.

keeping, *n.* 保管, 保存; 釣合.

P erect a fire-proof building *for* the safe *keeping* of art treasures 重要美術品を安全に保管するために耐火建物を造る. ¶It is *in* my *keeping*. それは私が保管している. ¶be in *safe keeping* in … …に保管してある ‖ *in keeping* with modern needs 現代の要求に添うようにして. 【類】have status (格式) *in keeping* with their significant (重大な) responsibilities. / *in keeping* with the tone of a business letter. ¶This color is *out of keeping* with the room. この色はへやと調和しない. ‖ be *out of keeping* with one's taste 自分の趣味と合わない. ¶a hostelry in *keeping with* the grandness and beauty of the Nation's Capital 首府の壮大と美麗にふさわしいホテル ‖ in *keeping with* the traditions of … …の伝統にふさわしい ‖ a state of things more in *keeping with* civilization 一層文化的な事態.

keepsake, *n.* 形見.

P keep it *as* a *keepsake* 形見にそれをもっている.

keg, *n.* のみ口.

Q^2 put a *beer keg* on tap ビールだるにのみ口をつける.

ken, *n.* 視界.

P *beyond* (*out of*, *outside*) one's *ken* 視界を越えて. ¶*in* (*within*) one's *ken* 視界に. 【類】come *within* one's *ken*.

kerb, *n.* [街路などの]辺石(ふちいし).

P stand *at* the *kerb* 辺石に立つ. ¶a beggar *by* the *kerb* 辺石のそばにいるこじき.

kerbstone, *n.* 辺石(ふちいし).

P *on* the *kerbstone* 辺石の上で.

kettle, *n.* 薬かん, 湯沸かし.

V *put* a *kettle* over the fire 薬かんを火にかける.

V^2 The *kettle boils*. 薬かんの湯がわく. ¶The *kettle sings*. 湯沸かしがちんちんいう.

Q Here is a *pretty kettle* of fish. 困ったことになった.

P^2 A *kettle of* ice water sweats on a hot day. 氷水の容器は暑い日には汗を出す.

key, *n.* (**1**) かぎ; 秘決; のど.

V It *affords* (=*offers or* furnishes) the *key* to an understanding of the situation. それは時局を理解するかぎである. ¶When we consider …, we at once *discover* a *key* to his proceedings. …を考慮するとすぐに彼の行為の動機を了解することができる. ‖ *discover* (=*find*) the *key* to the closed secret その秘密のかぎを見出す ‖ *find* a *key* to good writing 文章をよく書くこつが分かる. ¶*fit* a *key* to a lock かぎを錠前にはめる. ¶It *furnishes* the true *key* to the question. それはその問題を正しく解釈するかぎになる. ¶*give* the *key* a turn かぎを一回まわす. 【類】He *gave* the *key* a slow turn when the door swung open. ‖ the title, " … ", *gives* the *key* to its intentions …という題名はその目的のかぎとなる. ¶He *holds* the *key* of the casket. 彼はその小箱のかぎを持っている. ‖ The port *holds* the *key* to the trade. その港はその貿易のかぎを握っている. ‖ *hold* the *key* to the situation 局面打開のかぎを握る. ¶*leave* the *key* in the lock 錠前にかぎを差したままにしておく. ¶The scientists do not yet *possess* the *key* to one of the most obscure of Nature's problems—the earthquake. 科学者には自然界の諸問題中最もあいまいなものの一つである地震の説明がまだできない. ¶*pound* (=strike) the *keys* of a typewriter タイプライターのキイを打つ. ¶*put* the *key* in the lock かぎを錠前にはめる. ¶*strike* the right *key* 正しい音調を打出す; 肯けいにあたる. ¶*tap* the *keys* of a typewriter タイプライターの文字盤を打つ. ¶He hung his coat over the keyhole after he had *turned* the *key*. 彼はかぎをかけてかぎ穴の上に上衣を掛けた. ¶*turn* the *key* in the lock 錠にかぎをかける. ¶The *key grated* in the lock. かぎが錠前の中でぎーぎー鳴った.

Q The book is an *admirable key* to the stores of knowledge behind it. その本はその問題に関する豊富な文献に対する良い手引である. ¶a *duplicate key* 合いかぎ. ¶a *false key* 合いかぎ. ¶it serves as the *golden key* to unlock … それは…を開ける合いかぎとして役立つ. ¶Each locker has its own *individual key*. ロッカーにはそれぞれ専用のかぎがある. ¶This is the only *key* to the mysteries of his character. これが彼の性格の神秘性を明かにする唯一のかぎである. ¶the *right key* for the solution of the problem その問題解決の正しいかぎ. ¶a *three-toothed key* 三つ歯のかぎ.

Q^2 the *cross keys* 十字かぎ(居酒屋の看板・ヨーク大僧正の紋章). ¶a forgotten *hotel key* 返すのを忘れたホテルのへやのかぎ. ¶a *latch key* はじき錠のかぎ(家の入口にある). ¶Transport has always been the *master key* of trade. 輸送は常に貿易の親かぎであった. ¶a *skeleton key* 合いかぎ.

P It is believed that the thief entered the house *by means of* false *keys*. 泥棒は合いかぎを用いてその家にはいったと信じられている. ¶a bunch *of keys* 一束のかぎ. ¶It furnishes a *key for* the solution of the problem. それはその問題解決のかぎを与える.

P^2 the *keys of* one's baggage 手荷物のかぎ. ¶Uraga was the *key of* the capital. 浦賀は首府ののどに当る所であった. ‖ the *key of* the position 要害の地. ¶the *key to* success 成功の秘けつ ‖ The *key to* good health is to eat and sleep regularly. 健康の秘けつは規則正しく食って規則正しく寝ることである. ‖ a *key to* abbreviations 略語の解説. 【類】the *key to* his doctrine / He has the *key to* the whole secret. / Knowledge is a treasure, but practice is the *key to* it. / Education is the *key to* power. / the *key to* modern history / a *key to* the solution of the question / Humor is the *key to* the hearts of men.—Mark Twain. / A living language is a *key to* the better understanding of a foreign people. ‖ The outer is the *key* ***to*** the inner man. 外ぼうは内心のしおりである.

(**2**) 調子.

Q The music was in a ***low key***. 音楽は低い調子であった. ¶say in ***plaintive key*** 訴えるような調子で言う.

P Her voice is ***in*** a high *key*. 彼女の声は調子が高い. 【類】poem written ***in*** a melancholy *key*. ¶His voice was ***out of*** *key*. 彼の声は調子外れだ.

key, *v*. 調子を整える.

M² *key* ***up*** (***down***) 調子を上げ(下げ)る. 【類】The coach *keyed* ***up*** the team for the big game. / *key* a piano ***up*** to concert pitch ‖ *key* ***up*** an offer (demand) 申出(など)を強調する.

keynote, *n*. 基調, 骨子; 主要点.

V In this essay we ***have*** the *keynote* to philosophy. この論文によってわれらは哲学の眼目を知る. ¶Do you ***know*** the *keynote* of London? 君はロンドンの特徴を知っているか. ¶The first essay, which gives its title to the volume, ***strikes*** the *keynote* of the book. その書の表題になっている一番始めの論文がその本の骨子をなしている. ‖ ***strike*** the *keynote* of one's life's work 一生の仕事の基調をなす.

P² Life and energy seemed to be the *keynote* ***of*** the city. 活気と活動力とがその都会の基調のように思われた. ‖ This is the *keynote* ***of*** his speech. これが彼の演説の骨子だ. 【類】The *keynote* ***of*** her life is its womanliness. / Sobriety (渋さ) is the *keynote* ***of*** Japanese taste. / Today the *keynote* ***of*** the wedding gown is simplicity. / This is a *keynote* ***to*** the character of the man.

keystone, *n*. かなめ.

P² Novelty is the *keystone* ***of*** success in all things. 目新しいということがあらゆる物の成功のかなめ石である.

kibitzer, *n*. 《米口》お節介な傍観者.

P assume the air ***of*** a *kibitzer* お節介な傍観者的態度をとる.

kick, *n*. けること; 《米口》興奮, スリル.

V ***administer*** a stiff *kick* 激しくける. ¶***deal*** *kicks* to disturbers 妨害者をける. ¶I ***got*** a big *kick* (=stimulus) out of knowing that ... 私は......と知って非常に興奮した. 【類】I ***got*** a *kick* from the game. ¶***give*** a *kick* to ... ...をける. ¶I ***received*** a *kick* from a horse. 私は馬にけられた.

Q² the ***corner kick*** 〚蹴球〛コーナーキック.

P² give a *kick* ***at*** ... ...をける. ¶give a *kick* ***on*** the shin 向うずねをける.

kick, *v*. ける.

M *kick* the fire ***out*** 火を踏み消す.

M² *Kick* not ***down*** the ladder which raiseth thee. 出世を助けた友を捨てるな. ¶*kick* ***off*** one's shoes くつをけって脱ぐ. ¶*kick* ***up*** the devil's delight. 騒ぎを引き起す.

P *kick* ***against*** the pricks 抗すべからざる者に反抗して傷を受ける ‖ *kick* ***against*** authority 権力に反抗する. 【類】*kick* ***against*** political restraints (政治的拘束). ¶*kick* ***at*** a dog 犬をける ‖ *kick* ***at*** decision (judgment) 決定(など)に言いがかりをつける ‖ *kick* ***at*** (=against) one's duty 本分を尽すことをきらう. ¶He was *kicked* ***by*** a horse. 彼は馬にけられた. ¶be *kicked* ***for*** his pains 苦心をしてけ飛ばされる(骨折損のくたびれもうけ). ¶*kick* a person ***in*** the chest (stomach) 人の胸(など)をける. ¶*kick* a person or thing ***into*** a river 人または物を川へけ落す. ¶I *kicked* him ***on*** the head. 私は彼の頭をけった. ¶*kick* a person ***out of*** the house (company, army) 人を家(など)からけり出す. ¶*kick* a person ***to*** death 人をけ殺す. ¶*kick* a person (thing) ***with*** boots 長ぐつで人(など)をける.

kid, *n*. 《口語》子供.

Q a ***cute*** (=***lovely***) *kid* かわいい子.

Q² shabbily clad ***DP kids*** 見すぼらしい着物を着た浮浪児(戦争の) ☞ D.P. は displaced person の略. ¶a film for ***school kids*** 児童向映画. ¶undernourished ***slum kids*** 栄養不良の貧民くつの子供たち. ¶verminous (=lousy) ***war kids*** しらみたかりの戦争孤児たち.

kidney, *n*. 腎臓; 性質.

Q a man of his ***own kidney*** 自分とはだ合のあった人. ¶two fellows of the ***same kidney*** (=mind) 同志二人.

P a very dangerous disease ***of*** the *kidneys* 非常に危険な腎臓病.

kill, *n*. [狩の]獲物.

Q There was a ***plentiful kill*** of wild animals. 野獣の沢山の獲物があった.

kill, *v*. 殺す, 殺害する; [時を]費す; [配合を]こわす.

M ***infallibly kill*** 確かに殺す. ¶He was *killed* ***instantaneously*** (=***outright***). 彼は即死した. ¶*kill* oneself ***intentionally***=suicide 自殺する.

P He was *killed* ***by*** a thunderbolt. 彼は落雷で死んだ. 【類】He was *killed* ***by*** a sudden accident. / He was *killed* ***by*** surprise. / He *killed* himself ***by*** poison. / He was *killed* ***by*** a fall from the horse. ¶He was *killed* ***for*** his money. 彼は金をねらわれて殺害された. ‖ be fatted to be *killed* ***for*** meat と殺して食用にするためふとらせる(豚など). ¶mothers and widows of those *killed* ***in*** the war 戦死者の母親や未亡人たち. 【類】He was *killed* ***in*** action (=engagement). / He was *killed* ***in*** a railway accident. ‖ The proposal was *killed* ***in*** the House. その提案は議会で握りつぶされた. 【類】The bill was *killed* ***in*** the Parliament. ¶*kill* oneself ***on*** the railway 鉄道自殺をする. ¶Most of the insect pests were *killed* ***off*** by the recent heavy frost. 害虫の大部分は近ごろの大霜で全滅した. ¶He was *killed* ***through*** falling from his machine at a height of 3,000 ft. 彼は三千フィートの上空で機体から落ちて死んだ. ‖ He was *killed* ***through*** getting entangled in the machinery. 彼は機械に巻込まれて死んだ. ¶The regiment were *killed* ***to*** a man. その連隊は全滅した. ¶He was *killed* ***with*** a sword (knife, weapon). 彼は刀(など)で切り殺された.

O *kill* time たいくつをまぎらす. ¶*kill* a bill 議案を葬る. ¶The play was funny enough to *kill* us all. その劇はおかしくてどうにもがまんができなかった. ¶One color may *kill* the harmony of the other colors. ある色が他の色の色調を乱すことがある.

killer, *n*. 殺す人.

Q² a ***fly killer*** はえたたき. ¶a ***germ killer*** 殺菌剤. ¶a ***lady killer*** 女たらし.

killing, *n*. 殺すこと.

Q² ***mercy killing*** 安楽死(一服盛って).

kiln, *n*. かまど.

Q² a ***pottery kiln*** 製陶のかまど.

kimono, *n*. 着物.

Q in ***beautiful kimono*** きれいな着物を着て. ¶a freshly ***laundered*** cotton *kimono* 洗たくしたばかりの木綿着物.

P appear ***in*** *kimono* 着物で出る.

kin, *n*. 血族.

V ***claim*** *kin* with ... ...の仲間だという.

kind, *n*. 種類; 種属.

V ***love*** one's *kind* 同類を愛する. ¶***multiply*** (=***propagate***) their *kind* その種属を繁殖させる. ¶***produce*** their *kind* 彼らと同種のものを産する. ¶The tame rabbit ***reproduces*** its *kind* six to seven times annually. かいうさぎは年に六七回子を産む. 【類】The existing organism (有機物) endeavors to ***reproduce*** its *kind*.

Q hats of ***all kinds*** あらゆる種類の帽子 ‖ He shouted ***all*** *kind* of abuse. 彼を口をきわめてののしった. ¶it is ***another*** *kind* of ... それもまた...の一種. ¶the ***best*** *kind* of houses 最上級の家. ¶Show me a ***better*** *kind*. もっといいのを見せてくれ. ¶the ***common*** *kind* of ... ...の普通の種類. ¶of very ***different*** *kinds* 非常に種類の異った. ¶lighter and more ***ephemeral*** *kinds* of writing もっと軽く一時的な文章. ¶of ***every*** *kind* あらゆる種類の. ¶a ***gigantic*** *kind* of ... ...の巨大な種類. ¶thought of a ***healthy*** *kind* 健全な思想. ¶an idiot of the most ***hopeless*** *kind* 絶望的なばか者. ¶the young of the ***human*** *kind* 人間の子供. ¶A semidesert is an ***inbetween*** *kind* of country, half prairie and half desert. 半さばくとは大草原とさばくの中間である. ¶an ***inferior*** *kind* 劣等な種類. ¶a thing of the ***like*** *kind* 類似の物. ¶the ***only*** *kind* of ... ...の唯一の種類. ¶a tragedy of the most ***pathetic*** *kind* 最も痛ましい悲劇. ¶Wedding preparations are a ***pleasant*** *kind* of "worry." 結婚準備は愉快な「心づかい」というべきものだ. ¶anti-Japanese feeling of a ***pronounced*** *kind* むきだしの排日. ¶a narrative of a purely ***psychological*** *kind* 純然たる心理的物語. ¶a ***rare*** *kind* of ... ...の珍種. ¶books of a ***rare old*** *kind* きこう書. ¶European furniture of a ***rough*** *kind* 粗雑なヨーロッパ風の家具. ¶headaches of a ***skull-bursting*** *kind* 頭の破れそうな頭痛. ¶a ***solitary*** *kind* of life 孤独的生活. ¶a reply of ***some*** *kind* 何らかの返答. ¶The work of the agent is of a most ***varied*** *kind*. その代理店の仕事は非常に多種多様である. ¶the censorship of ***various*** *kinds* of literature 色々の種類の文献の検閲. ¶***What*** *kind* of a man would you like for a husband? 夫にはどんな方がお好きですか. ¶this ***wonderful*** *kind* of humanity この驚嘆すべき人物(天才など).

Q² The wolf is an animal of the ***dog*** *kind*. おおかみは犬

類の動物である. ¶The sardine is a small fish of the ***herring kind***. いわしはにしんと同じ種類の小魚である. ¶the ***horse kind*** 馬類. ¶a ***Philippine kind*** of banana フィリピン種のバナナ. ¶The bamboo is a plant of the ***reed kind***. 竹はあし類の植物である. ¶an animal of the ***tiger kind*** とらの類の動物. ¶a winding instrument of the ***trumpet kind*** らっぱの種類の吹奏楽器.

P similar ***in kind*** 同種類の ‖ be different ***in kind*** 種類を異にする ‖ be unprecedented ***in kind*** 先例のない種類のものである ‖ donations to the Red Cross ***in kind*** 赤十字社への物品寄付. ¶I have heard something ***of*** the ***kind***. 私もそういったようなことを聞いています. ‖ I am one ***of*** the ***kind*** that, when they can't say anything good about people, don't say anything at all. 私は人のことをよく言えない時には何も言わずにいるという人間だ. ¶This is the best ***of*** its ***kind***. これがこの種では一番上等品です. 【類】It is the only journal ***of*** its ***kind*** published in the English language. / the only one ***of*** its ***kind*** in London. / an animal ***of*** this (that) ***kind*** ‖ He has genius ***of*** a ***kind***. 彼にはちょっとした天分がある. ‖ This box will make a table ***of*** a ***kind***. この箱はテーブルの代りになる. ¶it is ***with*** a ***kind*** of shock that we realize that ... 衝撃といった感じでわれわれは...ということを知った.

P² He is the ***kind of*** man who ... ...というたちの男だ. ‖ This ***kind of*** thing shouldn't be allowed. そういったことは許すべきでない. ‖ I still have a ***kind of*** suspicion about it. 私はまだそれに付て多少の疑がある. ‖ He said he would do any ***kind of*** work assigned to him. 彼はどんな仕事でもやりましょうと言った. ‖ You look ***kind of*** tired. 君は疲れているようだ ‖ I was feeling ***kind of*** homesick. 私は郷愁といったものを感じた. ☞ ***kind of***＝sort of《口語》「...みたい, ちょっと...のよう」の意, kinda, kind o', kinder とも書く. 例: I ***kind of*** hope he'll join us. / He ***kind of*** expected it. / I'm ***kinda*** tired.

kind, *a.* 親切な.

M Nature is a mother ***kind alike*** to all. 自然は総ての物に親切な母のようなものだ. ¶an ***embarrassingly kind*** welcome 迷惑するほど丁重な歓迎. ¶He was ***kind enough*** to take me over the city. 親切にも市を案内してくれた. 【類】Be ***kind enough*** to hold your tongue (だまる).

P It's very ***kind of*** you. どうもご親切ありがとう. 【類】It's awful ***kind of*** you to come to meet us. ¶They are always ***kind to*** us. 彼らはわれわれにはいつも親切だ. 【類】Be ***kind to*** old people. ¶He is very ***kind towards*** his neighbors. 彼は隣人にはなはだ親切だ. ¶He was ***kind*** and gentle ***with*** his wife and children. 彼は妻子に親切でやさしかった.

kindhearted, *pa.* 親切な.

M ***incorrigibly kindhearted*** どこまでも親切な.

kindle, *v.* [情を]動かす.

P ***kindle*** him ***to*** courage 彼の元気をつける. ¶***kindle*** him ***with*** passion 彼の熱情を燃やす.

kindly, *a.* 親切な.

P ***kindly by*** nature 生れつき親切な.

kindness, *n.* 親切, 好意.

V ***abuse*** one's ***kindness*** 人の親切につけこむ. ¶***accept*** his hospitable ***kindness*** 彼のねんごろな好意を受ける. ¶I take this opportunity of ***acknowledging*** the numerous ***kindnesses*** I have received at your hands since I came here. 私が当地へ来てから皆さんから受けた多大な御好意に対して謝辞を申述べます. ¶I much ***appreciate*** your ***kindness*** in using your influence for me. 私のためにお骨折下すったあなたの御親切を厚くお礼申上げます. ¶An injustice may ***cancel*** the previous ***kindness***. 不公平なことをすると前の親切がむだになるかも知れない. ¶***disregard*** one's ***kindness*** 人の親切をむだにする. ¶***Do*** me the ***kindness*** to hold your tongues. 皆さんどうぞ黙っていて下さい. ¶Would you ***have*** the ***kindness*** to pull up the window? すみませんが窓を上げて下さいませんか. ‖ I have ***had*** so many ***kindnesses*** shown to me by him. 私はあの人に色々お世話になりました. ¶I ***received*** many ***kindnesses*** from ... 私は...から色々お世話をしてもらった. ¶Some day I will ***reciprocate*** your great ***kindness*** to me. いつか私はあなたが大層ご親切にして下すったご恩返しをしたいと思います. ¶***repay*** the ***kindness*** 親切に報いる. ¶***return*** a ***kindness*** 親切に報いる. ¶He has ***shown*** great ***kindness*** to me. 彼は私に大変親切にしてくれた. ¶***Kindness*** is ***thrown away*** upon him. 彼に親切にしてやってもむだだ. ¶Their ***kindness*** has not been ***wasted***. 彼らの親切は無にならなかった.

Q a ***cruel kindness*** 親切から出た荒療治, 仏心鬼手. ¶you would do me a ***greater kindness*** if you would ... ...何々して下されば一層ありがとうございますが. ¶***helpful kindness*** 助けになる親切. ¶***human kindness*** 温情 ‖ lacking ***human kindness*** 不人情. ¶***loving kindness*** 慈愛心. ¶with ***outward kindness*** 親切ごかしに. ¶out of ***pure kindness*** of heart 純真な親切心から. ¶***ready kindness*** 速応する親切心. ¶***reproachful kindness*** 戒しめる親切心. ¶***self-interested kindness*** おためごかしの親切. ¶***simple kindness*** 他意なき親切. ¶do a ***small kindness*** ちょっとした親切を尽す. ¶***thoughtful kindness*** of the giver 寄贈者の好意ある心づかい. ¶***true kindness*** 真実の親切. ¶I thank you for the ***uniform kindness*** you show to my son. せがれがいつもお世話になりましてありがとうございます. ¶***unremitting kindness*** いつもながらの親切. ¶with the ***utmost kindness*** この上もなく親切に.

P ***by*** the ***kindness*** of ... ...の好意で ‖ He was greatly moved ***by*** your ***kindness***. 彼はあなたの御親切にひどく感動した. ¶I owe you a lot ***for*** many ***kindnesses*** I have received from you and I want to repay them. 私はあなたに随分お世話になっていますのでご恩返しをしたいと思っています. 【類】I am much obliged to you ***for*** your ***kindness*** yesterday. / Many thanks ***for*** your ***kindness*** in seeing me off at Yokohama. ¶a gentleman, whose name we must ***in*** all ***kindness*** withhold, ... 一人の紳士が—その名は特に預っておくが—... ¶perform a little act ***of kindness*** ちょっとした親切なことをする ‖ a good deal ***of kindness*** 非常な親切. ¶act ***out of kindness*** 親切からする. ¶it was ***owing to*** his ***kindness*** that ... ...したのは彼のお陰だった. ¶***through*** your ***kindness*** あなたのおかげで. ¶treat him ***with kindness*** 彼に親切にしてやる. ¶words ***without kindness*** 無慈悲な言葉.

P² ***kindness to*** a stranger 見知らぬ人への親切 ‖ His ***kindness to*** animals and birds was nearly divine. 彼の獣や鳥に対する親切は神の業に近かった.

kindred, *n.* 血族.

V ***claim kindred*** with a rich person ある金持と親類筋だと言う.

Q a ***near kindred*** 近親者.

kindred, *a.* 類似の, 同性の.

P ***kindred to*** ... ...に類する.

king, *n.* 王.

V ***checkmate*** the ***king*** [将棋]王を詰める. ¶The ***king*** was ***cheered***. 王様が万歳を唱えられた. ¶***crown*** him ***king*** 彼を王にする. ¶***depose*** (＝***discrown or dethrone***) a ***king*** 王を廃する. ¶We will ***have*** a ***king*** over us. われらはわれらのいただく王を立てよう. ¶overthrow their ***king*** 彼らの王を廃する. ¶They ***made*** him ***king***. 彼らは彼を王にした. ¶They ***proclaimed*** him ***king***. 彼らは彼を王と宣言した. ¶***put*** the ***king*** in check [将棋]王手と出す. ¶God ***save*** the ***king***! 王様万歳! ¶Long ***live*** the ***king***! 王様万歳.

Q ***half-legendary kings*** 半ば伝説的な諸王. ¶the ***late king*** 先王. ¶the ***then king*** 当時の王. ¶Voltaire, the ***uncrowned king*** of his age 彼の時代の無冠の王ヴォルテール.

Q² a ***homerun king***〘野球〙ホームラン王. ¶a ***money king*** 大財産家. ¶a ***potato*** (***cotton***) ***king*** じゃがいも(など)王. ¶John D. Rockefeller, the ***oil king*** of America 米国の石油王ジョン・D・ロックフェラー.

P in presence ***of*** the ***king*** 王の御前に. ¶***under*** Henry I., *King* of England 英国王ヘンリー一世の下に.

P² a ***king among*** his mates 彼の仲間の大将. ¶He is a ***king in*** name, but not in reality. 彼は王と言っても名だけで実はない. ¶the *King* ***of*** Hades えん魔大王. ¶the *King* ***of*** Kings 王の中の王(キリスト). ¶"The ***king of*** soaps and the soap of kings." 石けんの王にしてまた王者の石けん(Pears 石けんの広告の文句). ‖ ***king of*** the gamblers 博徒の親玉. 【類】He was then considered a ***king of*** painters. ¶He is a ***king with*** all, all existing for him and him alone. 彼は皆のものの王である, 皆のものは彼のため, そして彼だけのために生存しているのである.

kingdom, *n.* 王国.

V ***establish*** the ***kingdom*** of God on the earth 地上に神の王国を建設する. ¶***overthrow*** a ***kingdom*** 王国を滅ぼす. ¶***solidify*** a ***kingdom*** 王国の基礎を固める.

Q the ***milliennial kingdom*** of Christ キリストの千年後の

王国. ¶lowly members of ***nature's kingdom*** 自然界の下等生物. ¶a ***seagirt little kingdom*** 海に囲まれた小王国.

Q² the ***animal kingdom*** 動物界. ¶the ***kitchen kingdom*** 台所王国. ¶a ***pocket*** (=***toy***) ***kingdom***=a tiny State 小国.

kingship, *n.* 王位.

V ***resign*** the *kingship* of ... ...の王位を捨てる.

kink, *n.* ねじれ; もつれ.

V He ***has*** a *kink* in his mind. 彼は量見がねじくれている. 【類】he ***had*** a *kink* in him that ...

Q He is all right save for a ***little kink*** or two. ちょっと妙な所はあるが気は確かだ.

kinship, *n.* 血族関係, 類似.

V those who ***claim kinship*** with the Stuarts スチュアート家と血族関係があるという人々. ¶those who ***feel*** a ***kinship*** with Hitler ヒトラーの同志. ¶***see*** the *kinship* of ... with ... ...と...と関係があると認める. 「血族関係.

Q the ***ethnological kinship*** of the races 民族の人種学上の

P The two things are not ***without kinship***. その二つの間には関係がないこともない.

P² the ***kinship of*** human nature 人間性の類似.

kinsman, *n.* 親戚.

Q a ***near kinsman*** to ... ...の近親. ¶a ***spiritual kinsman*** of Emerson エマソンの同志.

kiosk, *n.* 亭, 小室.

Q² a ***telephone kiosk*** 公衆電話室.

kiss, *n.* 接ぷん, キッス.

V ***exchange kisses*** キッスを取交わす. 【類】They ***exchanged*** the first lover's *kisses*. / ***exchange kisses*** with ... ¶***Give*** me a ***kiss***, won't you? キッスしてよ. ¶***have*** her first *kiss* はじめて彼女とキッスする. 【類】Let me ***have*** your *kiss*. ¶***implant*** a *kiss* on ... ...にキッスする. ¶***imprint*** a *kiss* on her beautiful forehead 彼女の美しい額にキッスする. ¶***lavish kisses*** and caresses on a woman 女をめちゃめちゃにキッスして愛ぶする. ¶***press*** a *kiss* upon one's lips くちびるにキッスする. 【類】***press*** a hearty *kiss* on her soft cheek. ¶***print*** a long *kiss* on her cherry lips 彼女の赤いくちびるに長くキッスする. ¶***receive*** the first good-morning *kiss* of the opening day 朝の最初のお早うのキッスをうける. ¶***send*** a *kiss* [別れゆく人などに]キッスを送る. ¶***snatch*** a *kiss* from her lips 彼女のくちびるに不意にキッスする. ¶***steal*** a *kiss* from ... ...にこっそりキッスする. ¶***throw*** a *kiss* at ... ...に投げキッスをする. 【類】***throw*** *kisses* to each other on parting / wave her handkerchief and ***throw*** him a *kiss*.

Q a ***clinging kiss*** 吸い付くキッス. ¶after some ***hearty*** *kisses* of leave 別れの熱いキッスをしてから. ¶***horizontal kisses*** 平面キッス(顔を重ねてくちびるを合わせた). ☞このキッスは映画に出すことを禁止している所がある. ¶a ***leech-like kiss*** [ひるのように]吸い付くキッス. ¶a ***maternal kiss*** 母親のキッス. ¶Where is the ***old-fashioned, juicy, long-drawn-out kiss*** in the close-up? 大写しに出る昔風の, みずみずしい長いキッスはどうなってしまったのか(今日は見られなくなった). ¶a ***resounding kiss*** 音をたてるキッス. ¶the ***sexual kiss*** 性的な接ぷん. ¶a ***smacking kiss*** 高い音をたてるキッス. ¶***Stolen kisses*** are sweet. 気づかれずにしたキッスは甘露の味. ¶a ***sweet kiss*** 甘いキッス. ¶a ***vertical kiss*** 側面のキッス. ¶a ***voluptuous kiss*** いやらしいキッス.

Q² a ***farewell kiss*** 告別のキッス. ¶a ***parting kiss*** 別れのキッス. ¶a ***stage kiss*** 舞台のキッス. ¶a ***movie*** (=***screen***) ***kiss*** 映画のキッス.

P² a *kiss* ***on*** the cheek (mouth) ほお(など)のキッス.

kiss, *v.* キッスする.

M ***kiss affectionately*** 愛情をこめてキッスする. ¶***kiss*** and ***kiss again*** 何度も何度もキッスする. ¶***kiss*** a toothache ***away*** キッスして歯痛を取ってやる. 【類】Mother ***kissed away*** his tears. / May angels ***kiss*** your agony ***away*** at your dying hour! ¶***kiss fervently*** 激しくキッスする. ¶***kiss*** her ***fondly*** 彼女に愛のキッスをする. ¶***kiss*** her ***passionately*** on the mouth 彼女の口に熱烈にキッスする. ¶***kiss tenderly*** やさしくキッスする. ¶***kiss wildly*** 猛烈にキッスする.

P ***kiss*** her ***on*** the mouth (lips, forehead) 彼女のくちびる(など)にキッスする. 【類】***kiss*** a baby ***on*** its cheek.

O A soft wind ***kissed*** the treetops. そよ風が木ずえをなでした.

kissing, *n.* キッスすること.

Q² ***hand kissing*** 手のキッス.

kit, *n.* 用具一式; 袋.

V The following articles ***constitute*** a *kit* taken by Captains Speke and Grant in their journey, 1860-63, from Zanzibar to Egypt. 次の諸品が一八六〇年から六三年にかけてスペケ, グラント両大尉がザンジバールからエジプトへの旅行に携帯した用具一式である.

Q² a ***beauty kit*** 化粧品入れ ‖ Be sure to include it in your ***camp kit*** this summer. この夏はあなたのキャンプ用品の中にそれを忘れずに入れて下さい. ¶provide ***comfort kits*** to the soldiers at the front 戦線にある兵士に慰問袋を持たせる. ¶a ***first-aid kit*** 《米》応急手当用具入れ. ¶a ***sewing kit*** 針箱. ¶a ***shaving kit*** ひげそり道具.

kitchen, *n.* 台所.

V ***modernize*** a *kitchen* 台所を近代化する.

Q a ***diet kitchen*** 患者まかない所; 貧窮患者まかない所. ¶a ***sick-diet kitchen*** 患者まかない所. ¶a ***municipal kitchen*** 市設食堂.

kite, *n.* たこ; とび.

V ***draw in*** a *kite* たこを引きおろす. ¶***fly*** (=***let out***) a *kite* たこをあげる. ¶***let up*** a *kite* with the wind 風でたこをあげる.

Q a ***long-tailed kite*** 尾長とび.

Q² a ***picture kite*** 絵だこ.

kitten, kitty, *n.* 子ねこ.

V ***kitten*** three *kitties* 三匹子ねこを産む.

Q a ***frisky kitten*** よくじゃれる子ねこ.

knack, *n.* こつ, 呼吸, 妙; くせ.

V ***acquire*** (=***catch***) the *knack* of ... ...のこつをのみ込む. ¶***develop*** so much *knack* for management 大いに経営に妙を得る. ¶He has a *knack* ***for*** employing to advantage all odd moments. 彼は零細な時を利用する「こつ」を知っている. 【類】A good many husbands ***have*** the unhappy *knack* of being more kind and polite to other women than to their wives. ‖ he ***has*** a *knack* amounting to genius for ... 彼は天才といってよいほど...に対して妙を得ている. ¶***learn*** the *knack* of ... ...の呼吸をのみ込む. ¶He ***possesses*** the *knack* at languages which is born into some men. 彼はある人たちが先天的に知っている言語修得のこつをのみ込んでいる.

Q He has an ***admirable knack*** of teaching arithmetic. 彼は算術教授にすばらしく妙を得ている. ¶he has a ***happy knack*** of ... 彼は...することに妙を得ている. ¶by a ***peculiar knack*** 独特なこつで. ¶R. L. Stevenson had a ***pretty knack*** of describing the places he had visited. R. L. スティブンスンは彼が行った場所を美しく描くに妙を得ていた.

P² workmen who have a certain *knack* ***at*** handling tools いくらか道具を扱うこつを心得ている職工. ¶a *knack* ***for*** business 商売のこつ. ¶the *knack* ***of*** selling more 売上高を多くするこつ.

knapsack, *n.* 背のう.

V ***throw*** one's *knapsack* on the floor 床へ背のうを投げ出す. ¶***wear*** a *knapsack* on one's back 背のうを背負う.

knave, *n.* 悪漢.

V ***play*** the *knave* 悪事を働く. 「悪党.

Q an ***arrant knave*** 極悪人. ¶a ***scheming knave*** たくらむ

P² a *knave* ***in*** broadcloth 羽織ごろ.

knee, *n.* ひざ, ひざ関接, ひざ頭.

V ***bend*** the *knee* ひざを折る. ¶***blow*** (=bend) the (=one's) *knee* to=respect=worship ... ...にひざを屈する. ¶***dislocate*** the *knee* ひざ関接を脱臼(ﾀﾞｯｷｭｳ)する. ¶***get knee*** to knee with him 彼とひざを交えて語る. ¶***give*** a *knee* to ... ...を助(ﾀｽ)ける. ¶***hurt*** one's *knee* ひざにけがをする. ¶***lose*** the *knee* ひざがわななく. ¶***slap*** one's *knee* ひざをぴしゃりと打つ. ¶***wear out*** the *knees* of one's trousers ズボンのひざ頭をすり切らす.

V² Her *knees* ***failed***. 彼女のひざが役に立たなくなった. ¶my *knees* ***shook*** under me as ... ...したとき私のひざががくがくした. 「じられたひざ.

Q on ***bended knees*** ひざを折曲げて. ¶a ***wrenched knee*** ね

P The water came ***above*** the *knees*. 水がひざの上まできた. ¶The boy was laid ***across*** the mother's *knee* and spanked. その児は母親のひざの上に横にされてぴしゃぴしゃと打たれた. ¶learn the language ***at*** its mother's *knee*. 【類】No words can ever come home to a man's mind with the force of those he learned ***at*** his mother's *knee*. / a child ***at*** its mother's *knee* ‖ The boy was amputated ***at*** its *knee*. その少年はひざのところから切断された. ¶He was struck ***below*** the *knee*. 彼はひざの下をぶたれた. ¶He was wounded ***in*** the *knee* by a fall. 彼はころんでひざをけ

がした. ¶fall (drop *or* go down) ***on*** their *knees* ひざまずく ‖ Suddenly he fell ***on*** his *knees* to thank God. 急にひざまずいて神に謝した. ‖ be ***on*** the *knees* of the gods＝be still undetermined まだ決定していない ‖ I begged her forgiveness ***on*** my *knees*. 私はひざまずいて彼女のゆるしをこうた. ‖ a babe ***on*** its mother's *knee* 母のひざの上の赤ん坊 ‖ go down ***on*** one's *knee* ひざまずく ‖ They were brought ***to*** his *knees*. ついに彼らは彼に降参した. ¶kneel ***upon*** one's *knees* ひざまずく. ¶***with*** suppliant *knees* 七重のひざを八重に折って.

kneel, *v.* ひざまずく.

M ***kneel down*** at the entrance of a shrine 神社の入口でひざまずく. ¶He ***knelt reverently*** in prayer. 彼はうやうやしくひざまずいて祈った.

P ***kneel at*** his feet 彼の足もとにひざまずく. ¶***kneel in*** prayer ひざまずいて祈る. ¶***kneel on*** (＝upon) the floor 床にひざまずく. ¶***kneel to*** him 彼にひざまずく.

knell, *n.* 葬る鐘.

V ***ring*** the *knell* for the old era 旧時代を送る鐘を鳴らす ‖ His refusal ***rung*** the *knell* of our hopes. 彼の拒絶で万事休すだった. ¶The opening of the ports ***sounded*** this death *knell* of the ancient regime. 開港は旧制度を葬る鐘の響きであった. ‖ The *knell* of ... was being ***sounded***. ...を葬る鐘が鳴り響いていた(滅びんとしていた). ¶***toll*** the *knell* for ... ...を葬る鐘を鳴らす.

Q² be the ***death knell*** for ... ...がおじゃんになる.

knickerbockers, *n. pl.* 短ずぼん.

Q² ***chessboard knickerbockers*** 縦横しま短ずぼん.

knife, *n.* 小刀.

V I ***got*** my *knife* into him. 私は彼にえん恨をいだいた. ¶***open*** one's *knife* 小刀をあけて刃を出す. ¶***plunge*** a *knife* into ... ...に小刀を突き刺す. ¶***sharpen*** a *knife* on a whetstone と石で小刀をとぐ. ¶***whet*** a *knife* 小刀をとぐ.

Q a ***dull knife*** 切れない小刀. ¶play a ***good*** (***capital***) ***knife*** and fork たらふく食う. ¶a ***sharp knife*** 切れる小刀. ¶a ***surgeon's knife*** メス.

Q² a ***bowie knife*** 両刃の猟刀. ¶a ***butcher knife*** 肉切り包丁. ¶a ***clasp knife*** 畳みナイフ. ¶a ***desert knife*** 食後の果実などに用いるナイフ. ¶a slender ***fish knife*** 刺身包丁. ¶a ***pocket knife*** ポケット用ナイフ. ¶a ***sheath knife*** さや付ナイフ.

P Catholicism has declared war ***to*** the *knife* against modern culture. カトリック教は近代文化に対して血戦を宣言した. ¶He was ***under*** the *knife* for about half an hour. 彼の手術は約三十分間かかった. ‖ go (＝pass) ***under*** (＝submit to) the surgeon's *knife* 手術を受ける ‖ He underwent an operation for a liver trouble, and died ***under*** the *knife*. 彼は肝臓病で手術を受け手術中に絶命した. ¶cut it ***with*** a *knife* それを小刀で切る. ¶a ***knife with*** a thin blade 薄刃のナイフ.

knight, *n.* 騎士(ナイト).

P² a ***knight of*** the pen 文士 ‖ a ***knight of*** the razor 理髪師 ‖ a ***knight of*** the knife 巾着切り.

knight, *v.* ナイトに列する.

P He was ***knighted for*** his services to the law. 彼はその法律に尽した功労に対してナイトに叙せられた.

knighthood, *n.* 勲爵士たること, 勲爵士の位.

V ***knighthood*** has been ***conferred*** to ... ...にナイトの位が授けられた. ¶***receive*** a ***knighthood*** from the king 王からナイトの爵位を受ける ‖ He ***received*** his ***knighthood*** in 1866 for his work in the laying of Atlantic cable. 彼は大西洋海底電線敷設工事のために一八六六年勲爵士の位を受けた.

knit, *n.* 編むこと.

Q² ***rib knit*** じゃば編み. ¶***run-proof knit*** 空どけのしない編み方.

knit, *v.* 編む.

M ***knit*** them ***together*** それを編み合わせる ‖ people ***knit together*** by common interests 同志 ‖ ***knit together*** in co-operative action the poorly directed activities of ...

M² The sweater was smartly ***knit up***. そのセーターは気がきいた編方がしてあった.

P ***knit by*** hand (machine) 手(機械)編みの. ¶***knitted in*** wools 毛編みの.

knitting, *n.* 編物.

V ***take up*** her ***knitting***彼女の編物を始める.

knob, *n.* ノップ, 引き手.

V² This ***knob*** dosen't ***work***. このハンドルはきかない.

Q² a ***door knob*** (＝doorknob) 戸の引き手.

knock, *n.* 戸をたたくこと, ノックすること.

V ***hear*** several ***knocks*** on the wall 壁を何べんもたたく音を聞く. ¶I will teach the rascal to ***play*** this runaway *knock* on this door. あいつ戸をたたいて逃げて行くなんてどうしてくれるか見ていろ.

V² While they were talking there ***came*** a ***knock*** at the street door. 彼らがそこで話しているうちに表の戸口にノックがした. ¶A ***knock sounded***. 戸をたたく音がした.

Q There came a ***lively knock*** at the door. はげしくドアをたたく音がした. ¶a ***loud knock*** 音の高いノック. ¶He got a ***nasty knock*** on the head when he fell. 彼は倒れたとき頭をしたたか打った. ¶a ***postman's knock*** 郵便集配人のたたくノック(とんとんとんと三度). ¶a ***timid knock*** おずおずしたノック.

P The door of manager's office opened to her ***at*** the first *knock*. 支配人事務室の戸口が最初のノックで開かれて彼女は迎えられた.

P² There was a ***knock at*** the door. 戸口にノックの音がした. 【類】hear a *knock* or two ***at*** (＝***on***) the door.

knock, *v.* 打つ, たたく.

M ***knock*** a person ***back*** into his senses たたいて正気に返らせる. ¶***knock hard*** at the door 激しく戸をたたく. ¶be ***knocked out*** (＝KO'd) 打倒される, 負ける ‖ I'll ***knock*** your brains ***out***. 脳みそが出るほどやっつけるぞ. ¶***knock softly*** on (＝at) ... ...を静かにたたく. ¶***knock together*** a rough box 粗末な箱をにわかごしらえする. ¶I ***knocked together*** a few necessaries and started off. 私は二三の必要品をとりまとめて出掛けた.

M² Where have you been ***knocking about*** ever since? その後どこをうろついていたのか. ‖ be ***knocked down*** by a bullet 銃弾で打倒される ‖ ***knock down*** an old building 古い家を取こわす ‖ be ***knocked down*** by a blow in the face 顔を打たれて倒される. 【類】He was ***knocked down*** and got one leg run over by a truck. / ***knock down*** one's pipe now and again / ***knock down*** icicles (つらら) ‖ a book ***knocked down*** for $99 九十九ドルで競売された本. ¶it was ***knocked down*** at Count ...'s sale to ... それは...伯爵家の競売売立で...の手にはいった. 【類】The article was ***knocked down*** at the auction. / I ***knocked*** his price ***down*** (まけさせた) to $45. ‖ an object ***knocked down*** 落札物. ¶***knock*** (＝strike) ***in*** a nail くぎを打ち込む ‖ They ***knocked in*** the victuals and drink till they could hold no more. 彼らは食ったり飲んだりついに正体がなくなった. ¶***knock off*** smoking 喫煙をやめる ‖ ***knock*** the ash ***off*** one's pipe パイプから灰を落とす. 【類】***knock*** the dust ***off*** his coat ‖ Let's ***knock*** (＝leave) ***off*** our work here and have a rest. ここで仕事を止めて一休みしようではないか. ‖ ***knock off*** verses 詩を早く書く ‖ ***knock off*** 10% for cash 現金は一割引. 【類】***knock off*** 10 cents from the price ‖ the men now go to work at six in the morning and ***knock off*** at twenty minutes to seven. 職人は今は朝六時に職場に出て七時二十分前にやめる. ¶He was completely ***knocked over*** on the floor after a long fight. 彼は長い格闘の後床に完全に打のめされた. ‖ I clumsily ***knocked over*** a cup of tea. 私は粗こつにも茶わんをひっくりかえした. ¶He ***knocked under*** to his fate. 彼はその運命に降服した. ¶Very sorry to ***knock*** you ***up***, Mr. T. T さんあなたをたたき起してすみません. ‖ ***knock up*** against ... ...につきあたる ‖ I'm completely ***knocked up*** from overwork. 私は過労で全く疲れている. 【類】In passing the sands without a guide, his horse had ***knocked up***. / be ***knocked up*** with a day's work / It is the heat that ***knocks*** him up. / This heat is really insupportable, I am ***knocked up***. ‖ Every literary man, however great is his success, will ***knock up*** in the end. いかにえらい成功をした文筆の人でも皆しまいには種切れになるだろう.

P ***knock about*** the world 世界を放浪する. ¶***knock*** one's head ***against*** a post 柱に頭を打ちつける. 【類】***knock against*** a person / ***knock at*** the front door / since Perry ***knocked at*** the door of slumbering Japan ‖ Cruel, biting poverty ***knocks at*** the door. 痛ましい赤貧がその家を見舞う. ¶***knock for*** admittance to ... ...へ入れてくれとノックする. 【類】***knock for*** admission at the portal of ... ¶***knock*** it ***from*** his hand 彼の手からそれをたたき落す. ¶a double room ***knocked into*** one ぶっこ抜きの二間 ‖ He received a blow that ***knocked*** him ***into*** a cocked hat. 彼は一発食ってぺちゃんこになった. ¶I ***knocked*** him clean ***off*** his feet. 私は彼を見事にはり倒した. ¶*knock* ***on*** the door of his apartment 彼のへやの戸口をたたく ‖ You had better *knock* ***on*** wood! (やくよけのおまじないに)木の上をたたいたらよいでしょう. ‖ Let's *knock* ***on*** wood. 縁起でもない. ‖ The bad weather *knocked* all other forms of holiday-making ***on*** the head. 天気が好くないので他のあらゆる種類の行楽をすっかりだめにしてしまった. ¶*knock* sleeping people ***out of*** their beds 眠っている人を寝床からたたき起す. 【類】*knock* ash ***out of*** one's pipe. ¶*knock* ... ***to*** atoms ... を粉みじんに打ち砕く. ¶*knock* ***upon*** one's door その家の戸をたたく.

knocking, *n.* たたく音, ノック.

V ***answer*** his *knocking* 彼のノックに応じる.

P² Belshazzarish *knocking* ***of*** the knees ベルシャザール王のようにひざをがたがたふるわすこと.

knot, *n.* (**1**) 節, むすび目; 難問.

V ***cut*** a Gordian *knot* 一刀両断の処置に出る. ¶About three out of eight boards ***have*** *knots* in them. 八枚の板の中三枚ばかりは節がある. ¶***loosen*** a *knot* 結び目をゆるめる. ¶***make*** a *knot* tight (loose) 結び目を締める(ゆるめる). ¶***tie*** a *knot* in the end of a thread 糸の端に結び目を作る. 【類】***tie*** a *knot* in a rope = tie a rope in a knot / ***tie*** a *knot* in one's handkerchief to keep from forgetting a thing. ¶***undo*** (= ***untie***) a *knot* 結び目を解く.

V² The *knot* has ***slipped***. 結び目が解けた. 【類】The *knot* ***slipped*** easily.

Q an ***intricate*** *knot* 複雑な結び目. ¶a ***running*** *knot* ずっこけ. ¶an ***S-shaped*** *knot* S 字結び. ¶a ***tight*** *knot* 容易に解けない結び目.

Q² a ***love*** *knot* 愛結び(愛を表わす結び方). ¶a ***man-rope*** *knot* 綯(な)い合わせ結び. ¶***true-love*** (= ***true-lover's***) *knot* 比翼結び.

P They stood about ***in*** *knots* chattering. 三々五々かたまってしゃべっていた. 【類】They were gossiping together ***in*** a *knot* by the door. ‖ tie ... ***in*** a *knot* ...に結び目をこしらえる. ¶timber ***without*** a *knot* 節なしの材木.

P² a *knot* ***in*** wood 木の節. ¶a *knot* ***of*** politicians 一群の政治家. ¶a *knot* ***on*** a tree 木のこぶ.

(**2**) 海里(ノット).

V break the world's record for speed by ***attaining*** 36 *knots* per hour 時速三十六ノットを出して速力の世界記録を破る. ¶The steamer ***makes*** twenty-four *knots* an hour. その汽船は時速二十四ノットを出す. ¶She can ***steam*** 20 *knots* an hour with natural draught. その船は普通の船脚で時速二十ノットを出せる. ‖ a ship designed to ***steam*** 21 *knots* 二十一ノットを出せるように設計された船.

P steam ***at*** ... *knots* ...ノットの速力で進む.

know, *n.* 知ること.

P He is ***in*** the *know* about it. 彼はその道に明るい. ¶to those ***in*** the *know* その道の人からいうと.

know, *v.* 知る, 覚える, 区別する.

M I do not *know* ***any more*** than ... 私は...同様に知っていない. ¶*know* Japan ***at first hand*** 日本を(親しく見て)直接に知る. ¶*know* ***beforehand*** about ... ...について前もって知る. ¶he *knows* ***better*** than to ... 彼は...するようなばかなまねはしない ‖ people who should *know* ***better*** もっと物の分かっておるべき人たち. ¶You *know* ***best***, Anton, I trust you. アントン, 君が一番よく知っている, たしかに. ¶I *know* him only ***casually***. 私はほんの偶然彼を知っているだけだ. ¶Of the number of ..., failing an official census, nothing can be ***certainly*** *known*. ...の数については政府の国勢調査ができていないので確実には分からない. ¶be ***commercially*** *known* as ... ...として商人の間に知られている(商品など). ¶let you *know* ***definitely*** 確報を致します. ¶As ***far*** as I *know*, he is good and honest. 私の知る限り彼は善良で正直だ. ¶Had I *known* it ***earlier***! 私がもっと早くそれを知っていたらよかった. ¶*know* ***exactly*** 正確に知る. ¶I do not think it is very ***generally*** *known* that ... ...ということがきわめて広く知れているとは私は思わない. ¶He ***hardly*** *knew* where he was. 彼はほとんど自分の立場が分からなかった. ¶I *know* ***how*** to do it. 私はその仕方を知っている. 【類】I do not *know* ***how*** to ride a bicycle. ¶Let me *know* ***immediately*** by telephone. すぐ電話で知らして下さい. ¶*know* ***instinctively*** 本能的に知る. ¶I *know* him ***intimately***. 私は彼と親しくしている. ¶The name is ***little*** *known* here. ここではその名を知る人はほとんどない. 【類】languages of which I *know* ***little*** or ***nothing***. ¶*known* ***locally*** as ... その地方で...と言っている. ¶Have you *known* him ***long***? あの方と長らく御懇意ですか. ¶those who wish to *know* ***more*** are referred to ... さらにその上に知りたい方は...に問合わせて下さい. ¶He probably *knows* ***most*** about it. 彼は多分そのことについては最もよく知っているだろう. ¶I *know* as ***much***. それ位のことは知っている. ¶be *known* ***nation-wide*** 国内で知られている. ¶and I *knew* ***no more*** それから先のことは夢中だった. ¶be ***officially*** *known* as ... 正式には...として知られる. ¶***otherwise*** *known* as ... 別名... ¶*know* ***personally*** or by name 直接または名前だけで知っている. ¶be ***popularly*** *known* as "Two penny Tube" 俗にタペニーテューブ(二ペンス地下鉄)という. ¶*know* ***positively*** that ... ...と確かに知っている. ¶***presently*** (= ***readily***) *know* it それはすぐに分かる. ¶I ***scarce*** *know* how to express my thoughts. 私には自分の考えをどう言っていいかほとんど分からない. ¶I *know* him very ***slightly***. 私は彼とはほんのちょっとした知合いだ. ¶Even a child *knows* ***some*** of it. 子供でさえいくらかそのことを知っている. ¶*know* ***thoroughly*** 十分に知る. ¶*know* ... ***through*** and ***through*** (= ***out and out***) ...を知り抜いている. ¶the world will ***ultimately*** *know* that ... 世人は結局...ということを知るようになるだろう. ¶*know* full ***well*** 十分知っている. 【類】It happened that they *knew* each other ***well***. / a lady whom he *knew* too ***well***. ¶heaven only *knows* ***why*** ... = only God *knows* ***why*** ... ...のわけは神のみぞ知る. ¶become ***widely*** *known* because ... ...のために広く知られるようになる.

P I don't *know* ***about*** that. 私はそのことについては知らない. ‖ I'll let you *know* all ***about*** it later on. その件はあとで万事お知らせする. ¶know all there is to *know* ***about*** ...について知るべきことは皆知っている. 【類】I *know* practically nothing ***about*** it. / *know* ***about*** a matter (person) / Do you *know* anything ***about*** astronomy? ¶I *know* nothing ***against*** him. 私は彼について悪いことは聞いていない. ¶Whom do you *know* ***among*** them? 君は彼らの中だれを知っているか. ‖ I *know* him ***as*** a man of ability. 私は彼を手腕家と思っている. ¶We *know* a policeman ***by*** the clothes he wears. 警官は服装で分かる. ‖ *know* him ***by*** reputation その人のことは評判には聞いている ‖ He *knew* the songs ***by*** heart. 彼はその歌を暗記していた. 【類】*know* ***by*** hearsay / I *know* him ***by*** reputation, but not ***by*** sight. / I *know* him ***by*** name. / I *know* him ***by*** his voice. / *know* this ***by*** (= from) experience. ¶*know* ***for*** a dead certainty しかと心得ている ‖ I *know* ***for*** a fact that ... ...を事実と心得ている. ‖ I *knew* him ***for*** a German. 私は彼がドイツ人だと知っていた. 【類】I *know* it ***for*** certain (確かに). ¶*know* ***from*** experience that ... 経験から...を知る. 【類】we *know* ***from*** history that ... / I *know* it ***from*** the paper. / we *know* ***from*** history that ... ‖ Persons who will become famous in after life may generally be *known* ***from*** their childhood. 栴檀(だん)は二葉より芳し. 【類】I *know* him ***from*** the photograph. ‖ I don't *know* him ***from*** Adam. 私は彼を全く知らない. ‖ *know* good ***from*** evil 善悪の区別を知る. 【類】A fool may easily be *known* ***from*** a wise man. / *know* a friend ***from*** an enemy / It's not so easy to *know* right ***from*** wrong. / They are twins and it's difficult to *know* one ***from*** the other. ‖ do not *know* chalk ***from*** cheese 物の区別がつかない ‖ *know* a town ***from*** end to end 町をすみからすみまで知っている. ¶I *know* more ***of*** the world than you do. 僕は君よりも世間のことはよく知っている. 【類】How did you come to *know* ***of*** it? / I *know* ***of*** a case in which ... ‖ I *knew* ***of*** his presence in the other room. 私は別のへやに彼がいたことを知っていた. 【類】if we want to *know* more ***of*** it we can turn to ... ‖ *know* absolutely nothing ***of*** ... ...のことは全く何も知らない ‖ I want to buy a pair of shoes; do you *know* ***of*** a good store anywhere? くつを一足欲しいのですがどこかいいくつ屋をご存知ですか. 【類】Do you *know* ***of*** any teacher who would suit me? ¶*know* who's who ***on*** the screen 映画俳優のことに通じている. ¶be *known* all the country ***over*** 全国に知れわたっている.

O I *know* him to be a gentleman. 私はあの人は紳士だと思っている. ¶The summer was gone before I *knew*. 夏がいつの間にか過ぎてしまった. ¶He is living God *knows* where, subsisting on God *knows* what. 彼はどこでどうして暮していることやら. ¶as every schoolboy *knows* 三歳

の童子も知っているように. ¶You ought to *know* better. 君は世間を知らんね.

know-how, *n.* 《米》事情; 秘けつ.

V *have* the *know-how* of the business その商売のこつを心得ている.

Q *scientific know-how* 科学的処理法.

knowing, *n.* 知ること.

M There is ***no knowing*** what he will be up to next. 彼がこの次に何を仕でかすか分からない. 【類】Otherwise, with this wind, there's *no knowing* how the fire would have raged.

knowledge, *n.* 知識, 学識.

V ***accumulate*** *knowledge* 知識を蓄積する. ¶***acquire*** a reading *knowledge* of foreign languages 外国語を読めるだけの知識を得る. 【類】*knowledge* ***acquired*** in the course of a flying visit. ¶***advance*** *knowledge* 知識を進める. ¶***air*** one's *knowledge* 知識を誇示する. ¶***assimilate*** the *knowledge* one acquires 獲得した知識を消化する. ¶***assume*** a previous *knowledge* of ... ...の予備知識があるものと仮定する. ¶***broaden*** one's *knowledge* of ... ...の知識を広める. ¶***broaden*** and ***enrich*** the *knowledge* of ... ...の知識を広めかつ豊富にする. ¶make use of the gramophone as a means of ***brushing up*** and ***improving*** their *knowledge* of the language 言語の知識をみがきかつ進歩させる手段として蓄音機を利用する. ¶***build up*** accurate *knowledge* 正確な知識を築きあげる. ¶An ideal teacher ***combines*** a thorough *knowledge* of his subject with skill in teaching. 理想的教師はその専門学科の十分な学識と教授法の熟練とを兼備する. ¶***communicate*** one's *knowledge* to ... ...に知識を伝える. ¶***correct*** and ***amplify*** *knowledge* 知識を修正しかつ拡大する. ¶***cultivate*** a *knowledge* of their goods in the consumer's mind 彼らの商品の知識を消費者に植え付ける. ¶***deepen*** one's *knowledge* of ancient thought 古代思想の知識を深める. ¶The variety theatre entertainment does not ***demand*** a great *knowledge* of the language. 寄席興業を見るには言葉をよく知っていなくともよい. ¶He ***denied*** any *knowledge* of this check. 彼はこの小切手については自分は何も知らないといった. ¶***derive*** one's *knowledge* from ... ...からその知識を得る. ¶To ***develop*** the *knowledge* of one another among the peoples of the world is an essential factor in the preservation of peace. 世界各国民相互の理解を深めることが平和保持の基本的要素である. ¶The publication contributes to ***diffuse*** the *knowledge* and study of the subject. その出版物はその部門の知識及び研究を広めるに寄与する所がある. 【類】***diffuse*** among the American people a more accurate *knowledge* of the people of Japan. ¶***discover*** new *knowledge* 新知識を発見する. ¶a *knowledge* of this fact should be widely ***disseminated*** among ... この事実は...間に広く普及さすべきである. ¶***distribute*** *knowledge* 知識を広める. ¶***enlarge*** one's *knowledge* of ... ...に対する自分の知識を広める. 【類】***enlarge*** scientific *knowledge.* ¶considerably ***enrich*** our now scanty *knowledge* of ... ...についてのわれわれの現在の貧弱な知識を著しく豊富にする. ¶further ***extend*** our *knowledge* of ... さらにわれわれの...についての知識を拡大する. ¶***gain*** a first-hand *knowledge* of ... ...について直接の知識を得る ‖ practical *knowledge* ***gained*** by experience. 経験で得た実際的知識. ¶***gather*** much *knowledge* 多くの知識を集める. ¶Many Japanese in Japan are studying European languages in order to ***get knowledge*** of facts from European sources. 多くの日本人はヨーロッパの本源から知識を得ようとしてヨーロッパ語を修める. ¶***give*** a fuller *knowledge* of Japan 日本についてのさらに深い知識を与える. ¶***has*** a *knowledge* of short-hand 速記の心得がある. 【類】These are languages of which I ***have*** a practical *knowledge.* / They ***have*** little *knowledge* of the ways of society (世間のこと). / I ***have*** no *knowledge* of his whereabout (彼の居所). ¶***imbibe*** book *knowledge* 書籍から知識を吸収する. ¶***impart*** useful *knowledge* 有用な知識を与える. 【類】***impart*** one's *knowledge* through the medium of books, lectures, etc. ¶***improve*** one's *knowledge* of English 英語の知識を向上させる. 【類】***improve*** a general *knowledge* of the subject. ¶***increase*** *knowledge* by original investigations and study either in science or literature 科学または文学における独創的な調査研究によって知識を増進させる. ¶***make popular*** the *knowledge* which is now almost restricted to specialists 現在ほとんど専門家が独占している知識を普及させる. ¶***obtain*** the *knowledge* required for one's future triumph 将来の成功に必要な知識を得る. 【類】***obtain*** a *knowledge* of the art of ... ‖ a means of ***obtaining*** *knowledge* 学問修得の手段. ¶***organize*** and ***codify*** *knowledge* 知識を組織し体系づける. ¶***parade*** one's *knowledge* 知識を見せびらかす. ¶***pick up*** *knowledge* on ... ...のことを知る. 【類】for the purpose of ***picking up*** *knowledge* on the porcelain manufactures of Paris and other places. ¶***popularize*** *knowledge* 知識を普及させる. ¶he ***possesses*** special *knowlege* of ... 彼は...について特殊の知識を持っている. ¶***presuppose*** a *knowledge* of grammar 文法の知識を有するものと見なしてかかる. ¶Such a method of teaching will never ***produce*** an efficient *knowledge* of a language. こうした教授法では到底有効な語学の知識を養い得ないであろう. ¶***promote*** a *knowledge* of preventive method of conception 避妊法の知識を普及させる. 【類】***promote*** a *knowledge* of Russia and Russians / ***promote*** historical *knowledge* ‖ an incorporated organization devoted to ***promoting*** a *knowledge* of ... ...の知識奨励を目的とした法人組織の団体. ¶***propagate*** a *knowledg* of ... ...の知識を広める. ¶***pursue*** *knowledge* for its own sake 知識それ自体のために知識を求める. ¶***refresh*** one's *knowledge* of history 歴史の知識を新たにする. ¶***require*** specialized *knowledge* 専門知識を要する. 【類】it does not ***require*** a very keen *knowledge* of mathematics to understand that ... ¶Reading *knowledge* can best be ***secured*** through speaking knowledge. 読書力を増進するのは会話力によるのが最も良い. ¶***spread*** the *knowledge* of ... ...の知識を広める. ¶***store up*** *knowledge* 知識を蓄える. ¶***summarize*** the present *knowledge* concerning ... ...についての現在の知識を摘要する. ¶***test*** *knowledge* by its application 知識を応用して試みる. ¶***turn*** to account one's *knowledge* of English 英語の知識を役に立たせる. ¶***utilize*** one's *knowledge* in ... ...その知識を...に利用する. ¶***widen*** one's *knowledge* and experience 知識と経験とを広める. ¶***work out*** new *knowledge* from the unknown 未知の世界から新知識を造り出す.

V^2 A *knowledge* of ... has become widely ***diffused***. ...の知識が広まった. ¶My *knowledge* ***ends*** there. 私はそれ以上のことは知らない. ¶as far as our present *knowledge* ***goes*** 現在われわれが知っている限りでは.

Q ***abstract*** *knowledge* 抽象的知識. ¶It is purely ***academic*** *knowledge* and is not based upon facts of life. その知識は全く机上論で生きた事実に立脚していない. ¶get his mass of ***accumulating*** *knowledge* into the permanence of books 彼の蓄積した知識を著作によって後世に伝える. ¶an ***accurate*** *knowledge* of ... ...の正確な知識. ¶***actual*** *knowledge* 実際の知識. ¶an ***adequate*** *knowledge* of ... ...の十分な知識. ¶have ***ample*** *knowledge* of ... ...をよく知っている. ¶his ***antiquarian*** *knowledge* 彼の好古的知識. ¶***assimilated*** *knowledge* 同化した知識. ¶a ***basic*** *knowledge* 基礎知識. ¶a ***book*** *knowledge* of a subject ある問題の書籍による知識. ¶one should have a ***broad*** *knowledge* of ... われわれは...についての広い知識を持つべきだ. 【類】Feeling the necessity of a ***broader*** *knowledge* of the subject than could be acquired in this country, he decided to go abroad. ¶have ***carnal*** *knowledge* of ... ...と性交する. 【類】punish ***carnal*** *knowledge* of a girl under fourteen. ¶we have no ***certain*** *knowledge* of ... われわれは...について確かなことは何も知らない. ¶Hokusai succeeded in conveying so much ***close*** *knowledge* of form, character, and expression in such simple and apparently careless strokes of the pen. —Phil May. 北斎は簡単で一見無造作と思われる運筆で形体・特徴・表現に対するきわめて適切な知識を伝えることに成功した. ¶it is a [matter of] ***common*** *knowledge* that ... 周知のごとく... ¶has a ***competent*** *knowledge* in ... ...に相当の心得がある. ¶gain a ***comprehensive*** *knowledge* of ... ...についての該博な知識を得る. ¶he has a ***correct*** *knowledge* of ... 彼は...の正確な知識を持つ. ¶fond of ***curious*** *knowledge* 珍奇な知識を好む. ¶a ***deep*** *knowledge* of ... ...の深い知識. ¶acquire a ***deep-seated*** *knowledge* of the principles その原則につき根深い知識を得る. ¶a ***difficult*** *knowledge* 困難な学問. ¶***documentary*** *knowledge* 文献による知識. ¶This ***dusty*** *knowledge* needs brushing up after the passage of years. このほこりだらけの学問は年数を経ているからブラシをかける(再研究の)必要がある. ¶Such a method of teaching will never produce an ***efficient*** *knowledge* of language. こうした教授法では言語の功果的知識は決して得られまい. ¶an ***elementary*** *knowledges* of botany 植物学の初歩知識. ¶***empirical*** *knowledge* 経験的知識. ¶***encyclopedic*** *knowledge* 百科全書的知識(間口は広いが奥行は浅いという意). ¶when ***European*** *knowledge* was gaining a footing in Japan ヨーロッパの学問が日本で地歩を占めつつあった時に. ¶an ***exclusive*** *knowledge* of ... ...の専門的の知識. ¶possess an ***extensive*** *knowledge* of ... ...の広い知識を有する. ¶have a ***fair*** *knowledge* of five languages 五カ国語について相当の知識がある. ¶Modern civilization is indebted to the Orient for its ***first*** *knowledge* of the art of inoculation for the prevention of smallpox. 近代文化は種痘の技術に対する最初の知識を東洋から得たのである. ¶***first-hand*** *knowledge* of things Japanese 日本の事物に対する直接の知識. 【類】They had a ***first-hand*** *knowledge* of the language by study abroad. ¶He has a ***fluent*** *knowledge* of eight languages. 彼は八カ国語を流ちょうに話す. ¶in ***full*** *knowledge* of the circumstance その事情をよく知っていながら; みすみす. 【類】with the ***full*** *knowledge* and concept of ... ¶A ***general*** *knowledge* of Japanese adds greatly to the pleasure of foreign tourists travelling in Japan. 一通り日本語を知っていると外国の観光者は大層おもしろく日本の旅行ができる.【類】possess a ***general*** *knowledge* on this head (この件につき). ¶add much to ***geographical*** *knowledge* 地理上の知識を大いに増す. ¶A ***good*** *knowledge* of one language is better than a bad knowledge of many. 一つの国語を十分に知ることは多くの国語をいい加減に知るよりましだ.【類】obtain a ***good*** *knowledge* of the English language / I would prefer a ***good*** *knowledge* of a few things to a bad *knowledge* of many. ¶innocent of ***grammatical*** *knowledge* 文法の知識のない. ¶a man of ***half*** *knowledge* 半可通の人. ¶***hard-won*** *knowledge* 研究の結晶. ¶add to the ***historical*** *knowledge* of the world 世界歴史の知識に寄与する. ¶sound ***historical*** *knowledge* 堅実な歴史の知識. ¶the progress of ***human*** *knowledge* 人間知識の進歩. ¶***humanized geographic*** *knowledge* 人文化した地理の知識. ¶his ***immense*** *knowledge* 彼の博学. ¶have an ***intimate*** *knowledge* of ... ...を熟知している. ¶a ***literary*** *knowledge* of ... ...の文学上の知識. ¶She has ***little*** *knowledge* of sexual matters. 彼女は性のことはほとんど知っていない. ¶They have ***little direct*** *knowledge* of conditions in the East. 彼らは東洋の状態についてほとんど直接の知識をもっていない. ¶a ***manysided*** *knowledge* of English life and thought 英国人の生活と思想についての多方面な知識. ¶his ***masterly*** *knowledge* of English 英語についての彼の精通. ¶He is possessed of but a ***meagre*** *knowledge* of banking. 彼は銀行事務について貧弱な知識しかもたない. ¶***military*** *knowledge* 軍事上の知識. ¶***modern*** *knowledge* and old beliefs 近代知識と昔の信仰. ¶He has no ***musical*** *knowledge*. 彼は少しも音楽の知識がない. ¶***new*** *knowledge* on old foundation 旧基礎の上に立つ新知識. ¶the application of ***new scientific*** *knowledge* to industrial problems 科学的新知識の産業問題への応用. ¶His *knowledge* of ... is ***nil***. 彼の...の知識はゼロだ. ¶I have ***no*** *knowledge* of his whereabouts. 私は彼の居所を知らない. ¶a ***one-sided*** *knowledge* of ... ...の一方に偏した知識. ¶The old professor was a repository of ***out-of-the-way*** *knowledge*. 老教授はかけ離れた珍奇の知識の泉であった. ¶His *knowledge* is ***over-specialized***. 彼の知識は偏し過ぎている. ¶***partial*** *knowledge* 部分的な知識. ¶to my ***personal*** *knowledge* 私の親しく知っている所では. 【類】be based upon the ***personal*** *knowledge* of ... ‖ be within the ***personal*** *knowledge* of ... ...を直接に知っている. ¶acquire a ***practical*** *knowledge* of a language (writing technique) 一国語(文章道)の実用的知識を得る. 【類】The past quarter-century has witnessed an amazing evolution in man's ***practical*** and ***cultural*** *knowledge*. ¶a ***practical*** as well as a ***scholarly*** *knowledge* of a language 言語の学究的のみならず実用的知識. ¶with some ***previous*** *knowledge* of ... ...に関する幾分の予備知識を持って. ¶I have no ***previous*** *knowledge* of the subject. 私はその問題について予備知識をもっていない. 【類】Some ***previous*** *knowledge* of chemistry is necessary. ¶without ***prior*** *knowledge* 予備知識なく. ¶His *knowledge* is ***prodigious***. 彼の学識はすばらしい. ¶***professional*** *knowledge* 職業的の知識. ¶a ***profound*** *knowledge* of archaic literature 古代文物についての深遠な学識. ¶his ***profound*** *knowledge* of the subject 彼のこの問題に関する深遠な知識. ¶It is almost a matter of ***public*** *knowledge*. それはほとんど世間周知のことだ. ¶the ***recorded*** *knowledge* of man 記録された人類の知識. ¶a ***rudimental*** *knowledge* of mechanics 機械学の初歩の知識. ¶Sexual knowledge is a ***sacred*** *knowledge* concerning the great truths of life. 性の知識は人生の大真理に関する神聖な知識である. ¶diffuse ***sanitary*** *knowledge* 衛生思想を普及させる. ¶a ***scholarly*** *knowledge* of ... ...の学究的知識. ¶for the increase of ***scientific*** *knowledge* 科学知識を増進するために. 【類】the advance in ***scientific*** *knowledge* / accumulated ***scientific*** *knowledge* of the world / application of ***scientific*** *knowledge*, methods, or research / it is ***scientific*** *knowledge* that ... ¶acquire a very ***serviceable*** *knowledge* of the language 言語のきわめて実用的な知識を得る. ¶He has ***shrewd*** and ***practical*** *knowledge* of the world. 彼は世の中についてぬけ目のない実用向の知識を持っている. ¶has a ***sizable*** *knowledge* of Latin and Greek ラテン語ギリシア語に相当の心得がある. ¶a ***sound*** *knowledge* of the technicalities of writing 作文の仕方に関する確かな知識. ¶acquire ***special*** *knowledge* on a subject ある問題に関する特殊な知識を得る.【類】On this matter I have some ***special*** *knowledge*. ¶***specific*** *knowledge* 特殊の知識. ¶establish ***sufficient*** *knowledge* and understanding of the principles of the Constitution 憲法の原則の十分な知識と了解を確立する. ¶has a ***sufficient preliminary*** *knowledge* of ... ...の十分な予備知識を有する. ¶have a ***superficial*** *knowledge* of English 英語の浅薄な知識をもつ. 【類】Europeans write and talk about China so often from quite ***superficial*** *knowledge*. ¶***superficial*** and ***scrappy*** *knowledge* 浅薄な断片的知識. ¶***superior*** *knowledge* 優秀な知識. ¶He has only a ***theoretical*** *knowledge* of the language. 彼はその国語の理論的知識しかない. ¶acquire a ***thorough*** *knowledge* of English 英語の徹底的な知識を得る. 【類】a ***thorough*** *knowledge* of one language first / a ***thorough*** *knowledge* of all foreign conditions. ¶***universal*** *knowledge* 普遍的な知識. ¶promote "***useless*** *knowledge*" いわゆる「無用な知識」を増進する. ¶his ***wide*** *knowledge* of Indian life インドの生活についての彼の広い知識 ‖ a teacher of ***wide*** *knowledge*, pure taste, and sound judgment 見聞が広く趣味が良く判断が確かな教師. ¶the lump sum of the ***world's*** *knowledge* today 今日の世界知識の総和. 【類】an important contribution to the ***world's*** *knowledge* of Japan. ¶a ***working*** *knowledge* of English 役に立つ英語の知識. ¶lack of ***worldly*** *knowledge* 世間見ず. ¶In these fields our *knowledge* is still very ***young*** (=in a state of infancy). この方面ではわれわれの知識はまだ幼稚だ.

Q² ***background*** *knowledge* 予備知識. ¶***Bible*** *knowledge* 聖書の知識. ¶acquire ***book*** *knowledge* 読書からの知識を得る. ¶***business*** *knowledge* 商業の知識. ¶have the rudiments of ***engineering*** *knowledge* 工学の初歩を知る. ¶have really ***expert*** *knowledge* of ... ...の真の専門的な知識をもっている. ¶***fact*** *knowledge* 事実の知識. ¶a ***foundation*** (=basic) *knowledge* of ... ...の基礎知識. ¶***grammar*** *knowledge* 文法の知識. ¶possess an ***outline*** *knowledge* of ... ...の大要を知る. ¶acquire a ***reading*** *knowledge* of English 英語の読書力を得る. 【類】In America, to be graduated from college the student must have a ***reading*** *knowledge* of at least one modern foreign language. / good ***reading*** *knowledge* of one or two foreign languages. ¶***recognition*** *knowledge* 見たら分かるという(認識)知識(読書力). ¶***reproduction*** *knowledge* 複成ができる知識(作文力). ¶disseminate ***scripture*** *knowledge* by means of books 書籍によって聖典の知識を広める. ¶the spread of the ***sex*** *knowledge* 性知識の普及. ¶a practical ***speaking*** and ***reading*** *knowledge* of English 話したり書いたりする実用英語の知識. 【類】have a perfect ***speaking*** *knowledge* of ... ¶***world*** *knowledge* 世界情勢の知識.

P five years ***after*** our first *knowledge* of him 彼を始めて知ってから五年たって. ¶It is ***beyond*** my *knowledge*. それは私には分からない. ¶a thirst ***for*** *knowledge* 知識欲. ¶speak it ***from*** his own *knowledge* 彼自身知ってそれを話す. ¶advance ***in*** *knowledge* 知識が進む. ¶the spread ***of*** *knowledge* 知識の普及 ‖ a branch ***of*** *knowledge* 一学科 ‖

have not an ounce *of knowledge* of ... ...は皆目知らない. ¶It was altered ***out of*** all *knowledge*. それは見違えるくらい変った. ¶***To*** my *knowledge*, there are no adequate books on the subject. 私の知る所ではその問題についてはしっかりした著作がない. ‖ ***to*** my certain *knowledge* 私が確かに知っている所では. 【類】 ***to*** our *knowledge*=so far as we know / This has never been done before, ***to*** the writer's *knowledge*, at least, by any of his predecessors who have travelled over the same field. / It has never before, ***to*** my *knowledge*, been translated into English. ‖ it has come ***to*** my *knowledge* that ... 聞く所によると. 【類】 This somehow came ***to*** the *knowledge* of the police. ‖ There is no royal road ***to*** *knowledge* 学問に近道はない. ¶***with*** varied *knowledge* and experience 色んな知識と経験によって ‖ ***with*** the mother's *knowledge* 母が承知で ‖ ***with*** [the] *knowledge* of ... ...と話合いで. ¶***within*** the writer's *knowledge*=so far as the writer knows 筆者の知っている所では. ¶***without*** my *knowledge* 私の知らない間に. 【類】 ***without*** his full *knowledge* / Did you do it ***without*** the *knowledge* of your father?

P[2] His *knowledge* ***about*** the subject is very extensive. 彼のそのことに関する知識はきわめて広い. ¶It is common *knowledge* ***among*** the German rank and file that ... ...ということはドイツの兵士間にあまねく知れわたっている事実である. ¶gain further *knowledge* ***as to*** ... ...についてさらに研究する. ¶acquire a *knowledge* ***of*** practical life 実生活の知識を得る. 【類】 a *knowledge* ***of*** cooking and sewing / a *knowledge* ***of*** these facts / a *knowledge* ***of*** the geography of the locality. ¶a very valuable addition to our *knowledge* ***on*** the subject その問題についてわれわれの知識へのきわめて貴重な貢献の一つ. 【類】 His *knowledge* ***on*** the subject seems to be on a par with my own (私と似たもの).

known, *pa.* 知られた.

M Mr. ... ***better*** *known* as "..." 「...」で通っている...氏. ¶an ascent *known* ***colloquially*** as ... 俗に...と言っている坂. ¶Of his life very little is ***definitely*** *known*. 彼の一生についてははっきりしたことはほとんど知られていない. ¶It is ***favorably*** *known* by its users. それは使用者間に評判がよい. ¶as is ***generally*** *known* 周知のごとく. ¶The ship ***hitherto*** *known* as ... has been rechristened. 今まで...と言っていた船が改名された. ¶***internationally*** *known* artists 国際的に知名な芸術家. ¶***little*** is *known* of him except that he was the son of ... その人については...の子息だったということ以外にほとんど何も知られていない. 【類】 ***little*** is *known* by the public concerning ... ¶***locally*** *known* as "Rag Fair" 地元では「ぼろ市」と言っている. ¶***nationally*** *known* persons 全国に知られている人. ¶***otherwise*** *known* as ... またの名は... ¶a woman ***personally*** *known* to me 私が直接知っている女. ¶***popularly*** *known* as ... 一般に...として知られた. ¶an actress ***professionally*** *known* as ... ...という芸名の女優. ¶***publicly*** *known* 公に知られた. ¶***technically*** *known* as ... 技術的には...で通っている. ¶a thing ***universally*** *known* わかり切ったこと ‖ as is ***well*** *known* 周知の通り. 【類】 a writer so ***well*** *known* as ... ¶goods ***well*** and ***favourably*** *known* throughout the world 全世界にけん伝された商品. 【類】 so ***well*** and ***favorably*** *known* to the English and American travelling public. ¶He is ***well*** and ***honorably*** *known* to us all. 彼はわれら一同にはよく知られまた尊敬されている. ¶a person ***widely*** *known* for his literary genius その文才で広く知られている人.

P carbon photographs *known* ***as*** the brown autotypes ブラウン・オートタイプと言っているカーボン写真. 【類】 He is *known* ***as*** "Long Tom" from his great height. / The Hongkew Settlement of Shanghai is *known* by some ***as*** the American Settlement. ¶it is *known* ***by*** the name of ... それは...の名で通っている. ¶That is *known* ***for*** truth. それは事実として知られている. 【類】 He was *known* ***for*** many acts of charity. ‖ France is suffering from the worst tourist business *known* ***for*** at least a generation. フランスは少くとも三十年振りの観光業不振に悩んでいる. ¶He is greater than any other name *known* ***in*** literature. 彼の文名は他のだれよりも偉大である. ¶It is *known* ***in*** history ***as*** the Sakuradamon Incident. 世にこれを桜田門の変という. ‖ The wheat is *known* ***in*** England ***under*** the name of Dreadnought. その小麦を英国ではドレッドノートと言っている. ¶He is *known* all ***over*** the world (=the world over). 彼は世界的に知られている. ¶*known* ***throughout*** the land 国内に聞えた. ¶the most costly *known* ***to*** commerce 商品として最も高価な物 ‖ painted with every color *known* ***to*** the palette 絵の具で現わせる限りの色彩で描いた. 【類】 It is *known* ***to*** foreign residents ***as*** Camp Hill. / be little *known* ***to*** the world at large / He has been *known* ***to*** us all ***as*** a story writer. / long before she was *known* ***to*** fame ***as*** a successful writer of fiction ‖ The red pine of Japan is *known* ***to*** science ***as*** Pinus densiflora. 日本の赤松は学名をピヌス・デンシフロラと言う. ‖ be *known* ***to*** literature ***by*** his initials A.K.H.B. 彼の頭文字 A.K.H.B. の首字で文学界に知られている. ¶who is *known* ***under*** her *nom de guerre* of ... ...という彼女の仮の名で知られている...

knuckle, *n.* ひざ関節.

V ***bend up*** one's *knuckles* ひざを屈する.

P be down ***on*** the *knuckle* せっせと働いている.

knuckle, *v.* 指の節で打つ.

M[2] *knuckle* ***down*** to one's work 仕事に精を出す. ¶*knuckle* ***under*** to a person 人に屈服する.

L

label, *n.* 張紙, 張札, レッテル.

V ***attach*** a *label* to ... ...にレッテルを付ける. ¶The sign "Pay here" on a *label* is ***pinned*** to the curtain. カーテンにピンで留めた紙片に「支払はここで」と書いてある. ¶***place*** forged *labels* on bottles びんににせのレッテルを張る. ¶***put*** (***paste***) a *label* on a box 箱にレッテルを張る(のりで張る). ¶A *label* is ***tied on*** to a trunk. 札紙がトランクに付けてある.

V[2] as the *labels* of their luggage ***denote*** 荷札が示すように. ¶trains with *labels* ***showing*** their destinations 行先を示す標示板の付いた列車.

Q ***adhesive*** *labels* のり付レッテル. ¶***explanatory*** *labels* in a museum 博物館の説明札. ¶a ***forged*** *label* bearing the name of a German firm ドイツ商会の名の付いたにせレッテル. ¶paste a ***gummed*** *label* on ... ゴム引の張札を...に着ける. ¶***official*** *labels* 官位. ¶a ***regional*** *label* 地域別を示す表示(米語英語など). ¶plainly ***worded*** *labels* 平易に書かれた張札.

Q[2] ***Latin*** *labels* of botanical specimens 植物標本のラテン名札. ¶be labelled with a red "***Not-to go***" *label* 赤で「不良車」の標示をする. ¶a "***poison***" *label* 毒薬というレッテル. ¶a ***union*** *label* 組合レッテル.

P describe ***on*** a *label* 張札の上に解説する. ¶a bottle ***with*** a white *label* 白いレッテルつきのびん. ¶*labels* ***on*** pictures 絵についた札.

label, *v.* レッテルを張る.

P[2] be *labeled* ***as*** an Americanism アメリカ語として分類する ‖ be *labeled* ***as*** slang in the dictionary 辞書に俗語と記してある.

laboratory, *n.* [化学の]実験室, 研究所.

Q a magnificently ***appointed*** *laboratory* 設備の完備した実験室. ¶national university and ***private*** *laboratories* 国立大学及び私設の実験室. ¶a ***shabby*** *laboratory* 貧弱な研究所. ¶a ***well-equipped*** *laboratory* 設備のよい実験室.

Q[2] a ***chemistry*** *laboratory* 化学研究所. ¶a ***crime*** *laboratory* 犯罪研究所. ¶the ***Crime Detection*** *Laboratory* 科学捜査研究所. ¶a ***crime investigation*** *laboratory* 犯罪調査研究所. ¶equip a ***research*** *laboratory* 研究所に必要な設

備をする. ¶a ***science*** *laboratory* 科学研究所.
P ***from*** *laboratory* to life 実験室から実生活へ.

labo[u]r, *n.* **(1)** 労力; [団] 労働者; *pl.* 苦心.

V ***abridge*** *labor* 労力を省く. ¶***assign*** her *labor* of public utility 地道の仕事を当てがう(免囚の売春婦などに). ¶rise early in the morning to ***begin*** the *labor* of a new day 朝早く起きて新しい一日の仕事を始める. ¶***command*** the *labor* of 5,000 hands 五千の労働者を使役する. ¶It ***cost*** him infinite *labor*. そのために彼は多大の労力を費した. ¶Success ***crowned*** his *labors*. 彼の労苦は成功した. ¶***deem*** one's *labor* as wasted 骨折損と考える. ¶***devote*** much *labor* to the task 大いにその仕事のために尽す. 【類】The author has ***devoted*** the *labor* of eighteen years to the work. / ***devote*** the *labor* of a lifetime. ¶***direct*** into proper channels the *labors* of ... ...の労力を適当な方面に向ける. ¶***do*** manual *labor* 手先の仕事をする. ¶***draw labor*** from ... ...から労働者を寄せる. ¶the work ***embodies*** the lifelong *labors* of ... その著作は...の一生の仕事の結晶である. ¶***employ labor*** 労働者を使役する. ¶***entail*** too much *labor* to be practicable 実行不可能なほど労力を要する. ¶***expend labor*** for nothing むだ骨を折る. 【類】All the *labor* that I have ***expended*** on the case will be thrown away. ‖ The editor of the guidebooks will ***extend*** his *labors* to Japan. その案内記編集者は日本の案内記も編集することになるであろう. ¶I waited patiently for time to ***fructify*** my *labors*. 私は自分の努力が実を結ぶときを辛抱強く待った. ¶To some students such work is a task ***involving*** more *labor* than the subject deserved. 人によってはそのような勉強はその学科不相応な努力を要する. ¶***lavish*** *labor* on ... ...に労力を惜まない. ¶A good library ***lessens*** (=***lightens***) the *labor* of investigators. 良い図書館があると研究者の労力が軽減する. ¶***lighten*** their *labor* 彼らの負担を軽くする. ¶***lose*** one's *labor* 骨折り損をする. ¶*Labor,* too, is not only more expensive but it is very difficult to ***obtain***. また労力もその価が一層高いのみならず非常に得難いのである. ¶***perform*** the Herculean *labors* involved in ... ...に必要な非常に骨の折れる仕事をする. ¶***protect*** our *labor* against cheap foreign labor 労銀の低廉な外国の労働者に対してわが国の労働者を保護する. ¶***pursue*** one's *labors* 勉強(仕事)をする. ¶***put*** one's *labor* against ... ...に対抗する. ¶***receive*** hard *labor* 苦役を受ける. ¶Sweet thoughts ***refresh*** my *labors*. 楽しい考えで私は骨の折れるのを忘れる. ¶These books amply ***repay*** the *labor* of reading. これらの本は読む価値が十分ある. ¶The task ***requires*** much hard *labor*. その仕事は大いに労力を要する. ¶A rich harvest will ***reward*** your *labors*. 君の骨折りは大いに報いられよう. ¶It is a labor which will ***save*** much *labor* to others. その仕事で大分他人の手が省かれるだろう. ¶***share*** one's *labor* with ... ...と労苦をともにする. ¶***shun*** *labor* 骨惜みをする. ¶***simplify*** and ***abridge*** *labor* 仕事を簡易にしかつ省略する. ¶***spare*** no *labor* upon ... ...に努力を惜しまない. 【類】No *labor* has been ***spared***. ¶The work ***summarizes*** the *labors* of a lifetime. その本は一生の仕事(研究)の総くくりである. ¶***undertake*** a *labor* so Herculean そんなに骨の折れる仕事を企てる.

Q ***apostolic*** *labors* 使徒の労苦. ¶***arduous*** *labors* 骨の折れる仕事. ¶an abundant supply of ***cheap*** *labor* 低廉な労働力の豊富な供給. ¶***cheap*** and ***plentiful*** *labor* 低廉で豊富な労力. ¶the dreariest and most ill-paid of all kinds of ***clerical*** *labor* 机の仕事としては最も無味な最も報酬の薄いもの. ¶the product of the ***combined*** *labors* of a staff of scholars 一団の学者の共同労作. ¶***compulsory*** *labor* 強制労働. ¶devote the most ***conscientious*** *labor* for public good 社会のためにもっとも良心的な努力を傾注する. ¶the ***Cyclopean*** *labors* of Zola ゾラの巨大な仕事. ¶a ***difficult*** *labor* 難産. ¶***editorial*** *labors* 編集の苦心. ¶***effective*** and ***well-directed*** *labors* 有効で指導よろしきを得た労力. ¶***enthusiastic*** *labors* 熱烈な努力. ¶***evangelical*** *labors* 布教事業. ¶***forced*** *labor* 強制労働. ¶***fruitless*** *labor* むだ骨. ¶by ***hand*** *labor* 手仕事で. ¶It was plain ***hard*** *labor*. それは全く重労働だった ‖ was sentenced to four years at ***hard*** *labor*=《英》was sentenced four years' ***hard*** *labor* 四年間の重労働を宣告された. 【類】confinement at ***hard*** *labor* for 10 years / Such an offense shall be punished by detention in prison or at ***hard*** *labor*. ¶***hard muscular*** *labor* 苦しい筋肉労働. ¶***heavy*** *labor* 骨の折れる仕事. ¶a ***Herculean*** *labor* 非常に骨の折れる一つの仕事. ¶***hired*** *labor* 賃金労働. ¶maintain oneself by ***honest*** *labor* 正業について生活する. ¶***human*** *labor* 人間の働き. ¶an ***ill-requited*** *labor* 余り報いられない仕事. ¶***immense*** and ***unremunerative*** *labor* 非常に大きなしかも金にならない労力. ¶the result of years' ***incessant*** *labor* 数年間の絶えざる苦心の結果. ¶with ***infinite*** *labor* 非常に骨を折って. ¶Every one knows the almost ***inhuman*** *labor* falling to the lot of the primary school teacher. 小学校教師の仕事が人間業でないほどに骨の折れることはだれも知っている. ¶the ***irritating*** *labor* of composition 作文における産みの悩み. ¶engaged in ***light*** *labor* 楽な仕事をしている. ¶the value of one's ***linguistic*** *labors* その語学的努力の価値. ¶with as ***little*** *labor* as possible できるだけ骨を折らないで. ¶A teacher of low salary has to make out the rest by ***literary*** *labor*. 薄給の教師は文筆の働きで収入の埋合わせをしなければならない. ‖ the background of his ***literary*** *labor* 彼の作中に取入れた土地の風物. 【類】in appreciation of his ***literary*** *labors* (文学上の功労). ¶give it up as ***lost*** *labor* むだ骨だったとあきらめる. ¶be completed after ***long*** and ***conscientious*** *labor* 長期にわたる良心的な努力によって完成される. ¶***manual*** *labor* 力わざ. ¶women sharing in ***masculine*** *labors* 男の仕事を一緒にやる女. ¶***monotonous*** *labor* 単調な仕事. ¶a ***necessary*** and ***useful*** *labor* 必要にして有用な労力. ¶***no slight*** *labor* かなりの仕事. ¶leaders of ***organized*** *labor* 組合労働者の指導者. ¶***painstaking*** *labor* 骨の折れる仕事. ¶the fruit of your ***patient,*** I would say, ***heroic*** *labors* あなたの辛抱強いそして雄々しいとも言える努力の結果. ¶devote one's wisdom and ***persevering*** *labor* to the study of ... ...の研究に英知とたゆまない努力とを捧げる. ¶perform ***physical*** *labor* 肉体労働をする. ¶thanks to the long-continued and carefully ***planned*** *labors* 多年にわたり細心に計画された労力のおかげで. ¶The book has been my ***pleasant*** *labor* of more than three years. その本の著作は三年以上にわたる私の愉快な仕事だった. ¶the fruits of a ***prodigious*** *labor* 巨大な労力の成果. ¶***productive*** *labor* 生産的労働. ¶The *labor* is very ***severe***. その仕事は非常に苦しい. ¶***skilled*** *labor* 熟練労働. ¶The book is the product of ***some nine years'*** *labor*. その本は約九年間の努力の産物だ. ¶***statistical*** *labors* 統計事業. ¶***statute*** *labor* 賦役. ¶***strength-sapping*** *labor* 精力をすり減らす仕事. ¶go home after a day's ***strenuous*** *labor* 終日骨の折れる仕事をしてからうちに帰る. ¶***sweated*** *labor* and low wages 搾取労働と低賃金. ¶***trained*** *labor* 熟練労働. ¶***unproductive*** *labor* 不生産的労働. ¶the ***unremitting*** *labor* of many years 多年の絶えざる努力. ¶***unskilled*** *labor* 不熟練労働. ¶the fruit of the ***unwearying*** *labor* of many years 営々として多年苦心した成果. ¶***virtuous*** *labor* 堅気の仕事. ¶The mountain was the product of the earth in ***volcanic*** *labor*. その山は噴火の結果できたものだ.

Q² the piteousness of ***child*** *labor* 児童労働のいたいたしさ. ¶alien ***contract*** *labor* 契約による外人労働. ¶***day*** *labor* 日雇労働. ¶There is a shortage of ***farm*** *labor*. 農園で手が足りない. ¶soil tilled by ***hand*** *labor* 手で耕作された土地 ‖ with the least ***hand*** *labor* 手はほとんど使わないで ‖ the relative productive power of ***hand*** and ***machine*** *labor* 手工業と機械工業の比較生産力. ¶***machine*** *labor* 工場労務. ¶***midnight*** *labor* 深夜業. ¶***missionary*** *labor* 伝道事業. ¶***office*** *labor* 事務の仕事. ¶***plantation*** *labor* 栽培園労働. ¶***prison*** *labor* 囚人労働. ¶***slave*** *labor* in pits 坑内の重労働. ¶prevent ***Sunday*** *labor* 日曜勤労を止める. ¶***surplus*** *labor* 過剰労働. ¶***sweat shop*** *labor* 搾取労働. ¶The millers are confident that they can carry on with ***volunteer*** *labor*. 工場主は有志労働者でもってやってゆける自信がある.

P pose a problem ***between*** *labor* and management 労使間に問題を提起する. ¶gain ***by*** *labor* 働いて得る. ¶money gained ***from*** *labor* 働いて得た金. ¶The hours ***of*** *labor* are from 7.30 to 12 and from 1 to 5.30 o'clock. 労働時間は七時半から十二時, 一時から五時半までである. ‖ a division ***of*** *labor* 分業 ‖ the claims (rights) ***of*** *labor* 労働者側の要求(など). ¶***through*** the *labors* of ... ...の骨折りで. ¶produced ***with*** *labor* 骨を折って生産した. ¶laborers ***without*** *labor* 仕事のない労働者.

P² translate it as a *labor* ***of*** love 楽しみにそれを翻訳する ‖ a *labor* ***of*** duty 務め.

(2) 分べん.

V *secure* easy *labor* お産を軽くする.

Q *easy, quick,* and almost *painless labor* 軽くって早くほとんど無痛の分べん. 【類】*easy labor* and easy deliverance. ¶in her *first labor* 初産に. ¶have very *rapid labors* 常にお産が早(軽)い.

P a woman *in labor* 産婦 ‖ It was a case of a mountain *in labor* [bringing forth a mouse]. それは大山鳴動[してねずみ一匹]の一例であった.

labo[u]r, *v.* 働く; 努力する, 苦心する; 分べんする.

M *assiduously labor* 営々として働く. ¶*earnestly labor* 熱心に働く. ¶*labour fruitfully* 成績をあげて働く. ¶*labor heroically* for the eternal happiness of others 他人の永久幸福のためにけなげに働く. ¶*labor indefatigably* 根気よく働く. ¶*labor industriously* (=*enthusiastically*) 勤勉に働く. ¶*labor unceasingly* 絶間なく働く.

Q *labor at* the problem その問題の解決に苦心する ‖ *labor at* a piece of work ある仕事をする. 【類】*labor at* a typewriter. ¶*labor for* breath 息苦しい; 困難を訴える ‖ *labor for* the good of our fellows 仲間のために尽す. ¶*labor in* a great cause 大義のために働く. ¶He *labored* thirty years *on* his book. 彼はその著書に三十年苦心した. ‖ a single small-holder *laboring on* his spot 自分の土地を耕作している独身の自作農. ¶He *labored over* it far into the night. 彼は深更までそのことに骨を折った. ¶You must be *laboring under* some misapprehension. 君は何か考え違いをしているに違いない. ‖ *labor under* a grave defect 重大な欠陥に苦しむ. 【類】*labor under* a great mistake (=error) / I've been *laboring under* a great misconception hitherto. / *labor under* a difficulty / *labor under* many disadvantages / *labor under* the disadvantage of ... ‖ *labor under* a delusion 錯覚に陥る ‖ *labor under* a difficulty of speech 口がよくきけない. ¶*labor with* child 分べんする.

labo[u]rer, *n.* 労働者.

V *laborers thrown* out of employment 解雇された労働者.

Q *agricultural laborers* 農業労働者. ¶*seasonal laborers* ある季節だけの(臨時)労働者.

Q[2] a *bond laborer* どれい, 農奴. ¶*construction laborers* 土工. ¶a *contract laborer* 契約労務者. ¶a *day laborer* 日雇労務者. 【類】a casual *day laborer*. ¶a *farm laborer* 農園労務者. ¶an *immigrant laborer* 移民労働者. ¶a *plantation laborer* 栽培園労働者(普通園内に居住している). ¶a boss *road laborer* 道路人夫頭. ¶use them as *slave laborers* 彼らをどれいとしてこき使う. ¶a *wharf laborer* 港湾人夫.

labyrinth, *n.* 迷路.

P be involved *in* a *labyrinth* of perplexities紛糾の渦中に巻込まれて. ¶The work is ramified *into* a *labyrinth*. その仕事は迷路のように細かく分かれている.

lace, *n.* ひも, レース.

V *undo* the *lace* of boots くつのひもを解く.

Q a piece of *exquisite lace* 一枚の優美な高級レース. ¶a dress trimmed *with lace* レースのふち飾りのついたドレス.

P[2] *lace for* a dress ドレス用のレース.

lace, *v.* レースを付ける; ひもでしばる.

M *lace in* [one's waist] ひもで(腰を)しめる. ¶*lace up* a dress 着物にレースを付ける ‖ *lace up* one's shoes くつのひもを結ぶ.

lack, *n.* 欠乏, 不足.

V *display* one's utter *lack* of intelligence most plainly in dialectal English 方言的な英語で自分の無知ぶりを歴然とさらけ出す. ¶*feel* a *lack* of ... ...の不足を感じる. ¶*have* no *lack* of money 金は不自由しない(十分ある). ¶That *shows* a *lack* of common sense. それは非常識だ. ‖ an attitude *showing lack* of restraint 不謹慎な態度. ¶*supply* a *lack* 補欠する.

Q a *complete lack* of sympathy and understanding 同情と理解の完全な欠如. ¶a *conspicuous lack* of these qualities これら諸性質の顕著な欠乏. ¶There is a *regrettable lack* of the sense of proportion. 遺憾ながら良識に欠けている. ¶show a *singular lack* of self-restraint 明かに自制心を失っている.

P *for lack* of brains 頭がないので ‖ It cannot be discussed here *for lack* of space. そのことは紙面が許さないからここでは論じられない. 【類】The house could not be finished *for lack* of funds (金). / leave it out *for lack* of space (ページが取れないのでそれを省く) / No. 3 on the programme was passed out *for lack* of time. / be acquitted *for lack* of evidence (証拠不十分) / No one needs to be lonely *for lack* of company (相手がなくても). / The plants withered *for lack* of water. / I am calling it "..." *for lack* of a more exact term. / The papers made the most of it *for lack* of news. ‖ The service had to be abandoned *for lack* of sufficient patronage. その事業はお客が思うようにつかずやめることになった. ‖ It may be called (=styled) "..." *for lack* (=want) of a better word (=term). 適当の語がないから仮に...としておく. ¶find the evening tedious *from lack* of occupation 仕事がないので夕方を退屈に感じる ‖ atrophy *from lack* of exercise 使用しないための萎縮(いしゅく). 【類】*from* (=through) *lack* of nourishment. ¶*owing to* a *lack* of proper protection 然るべき保護施設がないので. ¶*through lack* of experience 経験不十分のため ‖ paralyse *through lack* of use 使わないので麻ひする.

P[2] *lack of* confidence 不信任 ‖ *lack of* contact with the progress of the world 世界の進歩と没交渉 ‖ his *lack of* logic 彼の非論理 ‖ *lack of* aptitude 無器用 ‖ *lack of* attention うわのそら ‖ *lack of* coordination 不調整, 片びっこ. 【類】*lack of* discipline (しつけ) / *lack of* energy (vitality, vigor) ‖ *lack of* foresight お先まっ暗 ‖ *lack of* forethought 行き当りばったり ‖ *lack of* information うかつ ‖ *lack of* initiativeness 引込思案 ‖ *lack of* latitude 動きが取れない ‖ a *lack of* method 無秩序, でたらめ. 【類】*lack of* consideration for the feelings of others / *lack of* ability to ... / *lack of* order (秩序) / *lack of* prudence (慎重さ) / a *lack of* resourcefulness / *lack of* sincerity / *lack of* understanding / *lack of* union (=unity) てんでんばらばら ‖ *lack of* variety 千篇一律 ‖ All is due to my *lack of* virtue. みんな私の不徳の致す所です.

lack, *v.* 欠く, 不足する.

M It is *conspicuously lacking* at the present time. それは今の所著しく欠けている. ¶He must be *sadly lacking* in intelligence. 彼は余ほど知恵が足りないに違いない. ¶The contributions *still lack* about $10,000 of the sum required. 寄付はまだ必要額には一万ドルほど足りない. ¶*utterly lack* ... 全然...を欠いている. ¶*woefully lacking* in common sense 情けないほど常識を欠いている.

P They do not *lack for* funds (customers). 彼らは資金(など)には事欠いていない. ¶*lack in* moral courage (energy) 気骨(など)を欠く. 【類】be *lacking in* the element of the picturesque / persons *lacking in* serious character / *lack in* literary distinction (=merit) / Edison was *lacking in* mathematical training. ¶It *lacks* 3 yen *of* a thousand yen. 千円に三円足りない. ‖ It *lacks* ten minutes *of* eight. 八時十分前.

lacquer, *n.* 漆.

Q *scraped lacquer* (漆工の)とぎ出し.

P He was poisoned *with lacquer*. 彼は漆にかぶれた. ‖ varnish it *with lacquer* それを漆で塗る.

lacquer, *v.* 漆で塗る.

P a case *lacquered in* black (vermilion) 黒(朱)漆で塗った箱.

lacuna, *n.* 欠陥.

V *fill* a *lacuna* in our knowledge of ... われらが有する...の知識の欠陥を補う.

lad, *n.* 若者, 青年.

Q a *goggle-eyed lad* 眼玉の小僧. ¶a *neglected lad* 大事にされなかった若者. ¶a *promising lad* 有望な青年. ¶a *uniformed lad* 制服を着けた青年. ¶a *young lad* 若者.

Q[2] act as an *office lad* in a lawyer's office 法律事務所で書生をやる.

P[2] a *lad of* eighteen 十八の青年 ‖ a *lad of* brain 頭の働く青年.

ladder, *n.* はしご.

V *climb* [*up*] a *ladder* はしごを登る. 【類】*climb* the *ladder* of success. ¶*climb down* a *ladder* against ... ...にたてかけたはしごを降りる. ¶*kick away* (=*down*) the *ladder* 恩をあだで返す(出世の道を開いてくれた人を見捨てる). ¶*lean* a *ladder* against ... ...にはしごを掛ける. ¶*let down* a *ladder* はしごをおろす. ¶*mount* a *ladder* はしごを登る. ¶*place* (=*rest*) a *ladder* against ... ...にはしごを掛ける. ¶*put* (=*set*) *up* a *ladder* はしごを掛ける. ¶*run up* a *ladder* はしごをかけ登る. ¶*Steady* the *ladder* while I get on. 私が登っている間はしごをしっかり押えていてくれ.

Q an *aerial ladder* 繰出しはしご. ¶a lamp cleaner with his *light, portable ladder* 軽い携帯用のはしごを持ったランプ掃除人. ¶The *ladder* is not *secure*. そのはしごは安全でない. ¶An emperor is at the top of the *social ladder*.

皇帝は社会層の頂点に位する. ¶an unsafe (=unsteady) ladder 危ないはしご.

Q² an accommodation ladder 〘航〙タラップ.

P descend on a ladder はしごで降りる ‖ get one's foot on the ladder 仕事を始める.

lade, *v.* 積む, 載せる.

V be laden with heavy responsibility 重い責任を負っている ‖ The air is laden with the delicious aroma of the newly-cut golden grain. あたりは刈り取ったばかりの黄金色の穀物でよい香がぷんぷんしていた. ‖ orange trees laden with fruit 実がなっているオレンジの木 ‖ a ship laden with grain (coal, cotton) 穀物(など)を積んだ船 ‖ a heart laden with sorrow 悲しみで一杯の胸. 【類】a newly returned gentleman laden with wisdom.

M a tree heavily laden with friut 枝もたわわの果樹.

lading, *n.* 積荷.

P² a bill of lading 船荷証券; 〘鉄道〙荷為替.

lady, *n.* 貴婦人, 淑女, 婦人.

V conduct ladies to their carriages under cover of an umbrella 淑女たちにかさをさしかけて馬車まで送る. ¶court a lady 淑女に言寄る. ¶escort a lady home 淑女を宅まで送る. ¶give up (=jilt) a lady [婚約の]女を捨てる. ¶lead a lady out 女に付添って出る. ¶marry the lady of one's choice 自分で選んだ女と結婚する. ¶take a lady in (=down) to dinner 淑女を晩さんの席に案内する.

Q a highly accomplished lady 才芸の高い淑女. ¶a bed-ridden old lady 病床の老婦人. ¶a dainty little lady 細腰のかわいい娘. ¶an elderly lady 中年の貴婦人. ¶a fashionable lady 社交界の淑女. ¶a fair and frail lady かよわい麗人. ¶the First Lady of the United States 米国第一婦人(大統領の夫人の別称) ‖ the first lady of the theatre 舞台のナンバーワン. ¶a freckle-faced young lady そばかすのある若い娘. ¶gentle maiden ladies of uncertain age 年齢不詳の良家の未婚の淑女. ¶elegantly gowned lady 優美に装った淑女. ¶the great ladies of the Court of France フランス宮中の高貴の女官. ¶a large assemblage of handsome and agreeable ladies 美しくて感じのよい多数の淑女たちの集り. ¶high-born ladies and gentlemen 名門の紳士・淑女. ¶the honored lady on this occasion この場合の光栄ある婦人[船の命名式などにおいて式事に参加した場合などの]. ¶a leading lady (=woman) 〘映〙主役女優. 【類】leading ladies of the day ‖ the leading lady of a dramatist [劇作家の]脚本に現われた女主人公. ¶a maiden lady 未婚婦人. ¶a married lady 既婚婦人. ¶painted ladies おしろいをつけた婦人たち. ¶a perfect lady 申分のない淑女. ¶a middle-aged stout lady 中年のでっぷり太った婦人. ¶a young lady お嬢さん ‖ a neurotic young lady ノイローゼにかかった若い婦人. ¶a perennially youthful lady 万年娘. ¶a vivacious lady 快活な婦人.

Q² a court lady 女官. ¶a New York lady of great wealth ニューヨークの大富豪の婦人. ¶chorus or small-part ladies コーラスガールすなわち端役の女たち. ¶a fine society lady りっぱな社交界の婦人 ‖ a fashionable society lady 上流の社交婦人. ¶the sovereign ladies of Europe ヨーロッパの王座を占める婦人. ¶a wash lady=a washwoman 洗たく女. ¶a widow lady [身分の高い人の]未亡人.

P light summer suits for ladies 婦人用夏向き軽装スーツ.

P² a lady of high station 身分の高い婦人 ‖ a lady of position 地位の高い淑女. 【類】the lady of the house (主婦) ‖ a lady of fashion 流行の先端を行く婦人 ‖ ladies of pleasure 売春婦.

ladyship, *n.* 貴婦人の身分.

P Good night to your ladyship. [貴婦人に向って]おやすみなさい.

lag, *n.* 遅れ.

Q² a time lag 時間的ずれ. 【類】There is something else to consider about it—a time lag, for example.

lag, *v.* 遅れる.

P Japan lags far behind other countries in ... 日本は…の点において他国よりはるかに遅れている. ‖ We cannot afford to lag behind other nations in the exploitation of the air. われわれは航空の点において他国に遅れるようなことがあってはならない.

lair, *n.* 獣の巣.

Q We saw lions not in iron cages, but in their native lairs. われわれは鉄製のおりの中でなく自然の巣の中にいるライオンを見た.

lake, *n.* 湖, 湖水.

V The lake is fed by rivers. その湖水には数条の川が流れ込んでいる.

V² Not a breeze stirred the lake. 湖水をかき乱す微風すらなかった. ¶The lake has dried up. 湖水が干上った. ¶The lake teems with fish. その湖水は魚が豊富だ.

Q a placid lake 穏かな湖水. ¶a sapphire lake 紺ぺきの湖水.

Q² a crater lake 火口湖. ¶a fossil (=dead) lake 死湖(太古の湖水の干上ったもの). ¶a glacier lake 氷河湖. ¶a pleasure lake レクリエーション向きの湖水.

P There is land all around a lake. 湖水は陸で囲まれている. ¶a villa by the lake その湖畔の別荘. ¶The river rises from a lake. その川は湖水から発する. ¶fishing in the lake その湖水の魚釣り. ¶a village at the head of the lake その湖水の上手の村 ‖ on the immediate shore of the lake 湖水に隣接した岸辺に. ¶a boat race on Carnegie Lake カーネギー湖上のボート・レース. 【類】Let's have a row on a lake. / sunset on the lake / steamers used on the American Great Lakes / Boats can be obtained for excursions (遊覧) on the lake. ¶boating upon the lake 湖上のボート遊び.

P² the Lake of Biwa=Lake Biwa 琵琶湖.

O The lake becomes an immense mirror in which the mountains are outlined. その湖水が大きな鏡になって山々の影を映している.

lake-side, *n.* 湖畔.

P² a hotel on the lake-side=a lake-side hotel 湖辺のホテル.

lamb, *n.* 小羊.

V² Lambs bleat. 小羊が鳴く.

Q² roast lamb 焼小羊. ¶one's ewe lamb 〘聖書〙一番大事にしているもの.

lame, *a.* びっこの.

P He is lame in the left foot. 彼は左足がびっこだ. ¶lame of one leg (both legs) 片足(両足)がびっこの.

O go (=fall) lame びっこになる ‖ walk lame びっこを引く.

lament, *n.* 悲嘆.

Q make pathetic lament over one's loss 自分の不幸(死別などの)に対し非常に残念がる.

lament, *v.* 嘆く.

M deeply lament the death of ... …の死を深くいたむ.

P He died lamented by all. 彼は皆に嘆かれて死んだ. ¶lament for the death その死を嘆く.

lamentation, *n.* 悲嘆, 号泣.

V set up a great lamentation 大きな悲嘆の声をあげる. ¶take up a lamentation for ... …を悲しむ声をあげる.

lamp, *n.* ランプ.

V blow down (=out) a lamp ランプを吹消す. ¶extinguish a lamp ランプを消す. ¶The lamp is fixed to the wall. ランプが壁に取付けてある. ¶hang a lamp from a hook in the ceiling 天井のかぎにランプをつるす. ¶hoist a lamp ランプをつり上げる. ¶The servant was told to light the lamp. 召使はランプをともせと言付けられた. ¶lower a lamp ランプを引下げる. ¶put out (=extinguish) a lamp ランプを消す. ¶screw a lamp into its socket 電球をソケットにはめる. ¶screw up the lamp ランプの心を出す. ¶shade a lamp with one's hand 手でランプをかざす. ¶trim a lamp ランプの心を切る. ¶When light is not needed, always turn the lamps down. あかりがいらなければいつも心を小さくしてお置き. ¶turn a lamp too high ランプのしんをあげ過ぎる. ¶turn up the lamp ランプの心を出す. ¶upset a lamp ランプをひっくりかえす.

V² The lamp flames. ランプが輝いている. ¶The lamp flares. ランプの灯が出過ぎる. ¶The lamp flickers. ランプの灯がちらつく. ¶The lamp smokes. ランプが煙る.

Q a clear lamp 透明電灯. ¶colored [electric] lamps 着色電球. ¶a dying lamp 消えかかっているランプ. ¶The "Eternal Lamps" kept burning in synagogues. いわゆる万年灯はユダヤ人の教会に絶やさないようにしてあった. ¶a frosted lamp つや消し電球. ¶an incandescent lamp 白熱電灯(今の普通の電灯). ¶a phosphorescent lamp (=light) 螢光電灯. ¶a used-up lamp 電灯の廃球.

Q² an alcohol (=spirit) lamp アルコールランプ. ¶an arc lamp アーク灯. ¶a coal oil lamp 石油ランプ. ¶a desk lamp 電気スタンド. ¶a floor lamp フロアランプ(床上スタンド). ¶a lighted gas lamp 点火しているガス灯. ¶by (=in) the light of a kerosene (=an oil) lamp 石油ランプの光で. ¶study by the midnight lamp 夜半ランプ(電灯)の光で勉強する. ¶a naphtha lamp ナフサ(揮発)油ランプ. ¶Mazda lamps are sold in exchange for used-up lamps. マツダランプは廃球と交換販売制です. ¶an old petroleum lamp 古

びた石油ランプ. ¶a ***reading*** *lamp* 読書用ランプ. ¶a ***safety*** *lamp* [鉱山用]安全灯. ¶a ***standard*** *lamp* 台付ランプ, 台ランプ. ¶a ***student*** *lamp* 明暗調節自在の読書用ランプ. ¶a ***sun*** *lamp* 〘映〙サンランプ(撮影用). ¶a ***tungsten*** *lamp* タングステン灯. 「下を照す灯だ.
P^2 The word is a *lamp* ***to*** my feet. その言葉はわれらが脚

lamplight, *n.* 灯光.
Q ***dim*** (***bright***) *lamplight* うす暗い(明るい)電灯.
P work done ***by*** *lamplight* ランプ(電灯)の光でやった仕事.

lamppost, *n.* 電灯柱. 「立つ.
P stand leaning ***against*** a *lamppost* 電灯柱によりかかって
O be as tall as a *lamppost* 電柱みたいなのっぽだ.

lance, *n.* やり.
V ***break*** a *lance* with ... ...と仕合をする; ...と議論をする. ¶Knights ***carried*** *lances* in hand. 騎士は手にやりを持っていた. ¶***tilt*** a *lance* against ... ...をやりで突く.
Q a ***free*** *lance* 野武士; 自由職業者; 専属でない芸能人(な
P pierce ... ***with*** a *lance* やりで...を突き刺す. Lど).

land, *n.* 土地, 陸, 国土.
V We are ***approaching*** *land.* 陸が近くなった. ¶He ***bought*** the *land* for the purpose of building on it. 彼は家を建てるつもりでその土地を買った. ¶***clear*** *land* 土地を切り開く. ¶***depopulate*** the *land* その地の住民を絶やす. ¶***enrich*** the *land* 土地を肥沃(ひよく)にする. ¶***enter*** the *land* of strangers 未知の国に入る. ¶In Holland great dikes are built that the sea may not ***flood*** the *land.* オランダでは海水が陸地に浸水しないように大堤防が築かれている. ¶I ***have*** *land* of my own. 私は自分の土地を持っている. ¶***improve*** waste *land* 荒地を開拓する. ¶***irrigate*** *land* 土地をかんがいする. ¶***join*** the *land* in one 国内を統一する. ¶***lease*** *land* 土地を借りる. ¶***make*** the *land* 陸地を認める. ¶***measure*** *land* 土地を測量する. ¶***nationalize*** the *land* 土地を国有にする. ¶the right to ***own*** Japanese *land* in fee-simple 永代借地で日本の土地を所有する権利. ¶The *land* was ***plotted.*** その土地の地取りがされた. ¶***possess*** *land* 土地を所有する. ¶Japanese subjects cannot now ***purchase*** or ***acquire*** *land* in California. 日本人は今ではカリフォルニア州で土地を買ったり獲得したりすることはできない. ¶***reach*** *land* 陸に着く. ¶***reclaim*** the arid *lands* 乾燥した土地を開墾する. ¶***sight*** *land* in the far distance 遠くに陸地が見えて来る. ¶***survey*** *land* 土地を測量する. ¶***till*** (=***cultivate***) the *land* for the bean crop 豆をとるため土地を耕す. ¶***touch*** *land* 陸に接触する. ¶***turn*** *land* into a forest 土地を森林に仕立てる. ¶I found a farmer ***working*** his *land.* 私は農夫が畑を作っているのが目に付いた.
Q his ***adopted*** *land* 彼の帰化国. ¶Proletarians of ***all*** *lands,* unite! 世界のプロレタリアよ, 団結せよ! ¶***arable*** *land* 適耕地. ¶a ***barbaric*** *land* 蛮地. ¶***barren*** *land* 不毛の地. ¶***beautiful rolling*** *land* 美しく起伏した土地. ¶a ***classic*** *land* 古典的国土. ¶a very ***cold*** *land* 極寒地. ¶Germany, the ***cradle*** *land* of the Reformation 宗教改革の発祥地ドイツ. ¶the transformation of wild into ***cultivated*** *land* 荒野の耕作地への転換. ¶in ***diverse*** *lands* and in diverse ages 各時代の諸地方に. ¶learning to swim on ***dry*** *land* 畳の上の水練. ¶***examination-ridden*** *lands* as England 英国のような試験の盛んに行われる国. ¶***fertile*** *lands* 沃(よく)土. ¶a ***far-away*** *land* 遠国. ¶some ***far-off*** *land* どこか遠い国. ¶men from ***foreign*** *lands* 外国から来た人 ‖ roam in ***foreign*** *lands* 外国を放浪する. 【類】a tourist in ***foreign*** *lands* / It was difficult to realize that we were in a ***foreign*** *land.* ¶***forested*** *land* 森林地. ¶***grazing*** *land* 牧地. ¶in our ***home*** *land* 本国で. ¶***kindred*** *lands* 属国. ¶a rich country gentleman with ***large*** *lands* 富めるいなかの大地主. ¶***leased*** *land* 借地. ¶a ***long longed-for*** *land* 永い間のあこがれの国. ¶***Mohammedan*** *lands* 回教国. ¶one's ***native*** *land* 故国. ¶He lies unmarked somewhere in ***No Man's*** *Land.* 彼はどこかざんごうの間に墓標もなく埋められている. ¶a ***newly broken*** *land* 新開墾地. ¶in ***our own*** and ***other*** *lands* 国の内外において. ¶a ***peaceful happy*** *land* 平和で幸福な国. ¶***public*** *land* 公有地. ¶***rank swampy*** *land* 雑草のはびこる沼地. ¶***rich, agricultural*** *land* 豊じょうな農業地. ¶***rough, stony*** *land* でこぼこした石だらけの土地. ¶a ***sacred*** *land* 聖地. ¶It was a ***sealed*** *land* to Western people. それは西洋人には開放されない国であった. ¶go into a ***strange*** *land* 未知の国に入る. ¶***thick-timbered*** *land* 密林地. ¶***undulating*** *land* 起伏のある土地. ¶***unproductive*** *land* 不毛の地. ¶a ***vacant*** *land* あき地. ¶timberplanting on ***waste*** *land* 荒れ地の造林. ¶in ***Western*** *Land* 西洋で. ¶reclaim ***wet*** *land* 湿地を開墾する.
Q^2 ***bounty*** *lands* 下賜地(米国で軍人軍属に与える公有地). ¶a ***coal*** *land* 炭田. ¶a ***daughter*** *land* 属国. ¶redistribute the ***farm*** *lands* on an equitable basis 耕作地を公平に再配分する. ¶***grass*** *land* 草地. ¶a ***grazing*** *land* 放牧場. ¶open the ***hermit*** *land* of Japan to Western commerce 孤立日本を西欧と通商のため開国する. ¶drain ***marsh*** *lands* 湿地を干拓する. ¶***mountain*** *land* 山地 ¶***oil*** *lands* 石油諸地帯. ¶the ***Pacific*** *lands* 太平洋に面する地方. ¶***pasture*** *land* 牧場. ¶rolling ***prairie*** *land* うねる大平原. ¶a ***school*** *land* 学校所有地. ¶***state*** *lands* 国有地, 公有地. ¶a ***sunshine*** *land* 日当りのよい土地. ¶a ***tax-free*** *land* 免税地. ¶a ***timber[ed]*** *land* 木材採集地. ¶a ***vacation*** *land* [休暇旅行に適する]観光地(カナダなど). 【類】Japan as a ***vacation*** *land.*
P Some came ***by*** *land* and some by water. ある者は陸路で, ある者は海路でやってきた. ‖ Korea is connected with China ***by*** *land.* 朝鮮は中国とは陸続きである. ¶far ***from*** the *land* of their birth 彼らの生れ故郷から遠く離れて. ¶***in*** *lands* afar 遠い国で ‖ ***in*** the *land* of the stars and stripes 星条旗の国(米国)において ‖ He flung himself on a couch and was quickly ***in*** the *land* of dreams. 彼は寝床に横になるとすぐ夢の国の人となった. ‖ ***in*** all *lands* あらゆる国で. ¶a desirable lot ***of*** *land* 買入れたいと思う地所 ‖ a strip ***of*** *land* 帯状の地所 ‖ a plot (=tract) ***of*** *land* 小区域. 【類】own 200 acres ***of*** *land.* ¶Autos run ***on*** the *land.* 自動車は陸上を走る. ‖ the houses ***on*** the *land* belong to ... その地所の家作は...のものだ. 【類】live ***on*** *land* / travel ***on*** *land* and sea. ¶An epidemic of cholera spread ***through*** the *land.* コレラが国中に流行した.
P^2 the *lands* ***about*** the Mediterranean Sea 地中海沿岸諸国. ¶the *lands* ***of*** their origin 彼らの本国 ‖ a *land* ***of*** revolutions and political instability 革命や政治的不安の国. ‖ the *Land* ***of*** the Blest ほうらいの島, 天国 ‖ the *land* ***of*** citizenship 国籍国(本国) ‖ a *land* ***of*** contrasts あべこべ国(新旧などのように相反するものが共在している). 【類】the *land* ***of*** the gods ‖ a *land* ***of*** continual summer とこ夏の国 ‖ the *Land* ***of*** Promise=the Promised Land 〘旧約聖書〙カナンの地; 希望の国. 【類】a *land* ***of*** liberty. ¶put a piece of *land* ***under*** wheat 一片の土地に小麦をまく.

land, *v.* 上陸する, 着陸する; 陥る; 当てる.
M ***Where*** did you *land?* あなたはどこに上陸しましたか.
P *land* ***at*** Yokohama (a port) 横浜(など)に上陸する ‖ After sailing for an hour, we *landed* ***at*** a beach. 帆走一時間後にある浜に上った. ¶embark and *land* ***at*** wharf ふ頭で船へ乗降りする. 【類】The boat *landed* ***at*** Cherbourg (フランスのシェルブール). ¶*land* passengers and cargo ***from*** a vessel 船から客貨を降ろす. ¶*land* ***in*** Japan (=on Japanese soil) 日本に上陸する. 【類】*land* ***in*** a country ‖ It may *land* you ***in*** prison. そんなことしたら刑務所へぶち込まれるかもしれない. ‖ He was *landed* ***in*** difficulties. 彼は困難に出会った. 【類】One of these petty officials almost *landed* me ***in*** jail. / The pilot *landed* the airliner ***in*** the field (着陸させた). ¶*land* ***on*** Japanese soil (=our shores) 日本に上陸する ‖ *land* ***on*** an airport 空港に着陸する ‖ *land* a punch ***on*** the upper jaw 上あごにパンチを食わせる. ¶the aliens who *land* ***upon*** our shores わが国に上陸する外人. 【類】*land* ***on*** the Japanese coast / *land* ***on*** the coast of ... / *land* ***on*** an island.

landing, *n.* 上陸, 着陸; [階段の]踊り場.
V ***effect*** a *landing* 上陸する. ¶We hadn't been up long before we were lost in the fog over the Channel and were forced to ***make*** a *landing* on the French coast, causing a delay of two hours. われわれは離陸後間もなくイギリス海峡で霧に襲われて余儀なく二時間遅れてフランスに着陸した.
Q ***blind*** *landing* 盲目着陸. ¶make a ***forced*** *landing* 不時着する. ¶make a ***graceful*** (***awkward***) *landing* 見事な(まずい)着陸をする. ¶make a ***perfect*** *landing* 完全な着陸をする. ¶make a ***safe*** *landing* 無事着陸する.
Q^2 attempt an ***emergency*** *landing* at ... ...に不時着を試みる. ¶a ***fire escape*** *landing* 非常降口. ¶make a ***para-***

chute landing パラシュート着陸をする. ¶a ***steamboat*** *landing* 蒸気船乗場.

P He paused for breath ***on*** the *landing*. 彼は階段の踊り「場でちょっと一息ついた.

P² *landing* ***in*** the face of the enemy 敵前上陸. ¶*landing* ***of*** the pilgrims ***at*** Plymouth 清教徒のプリマス上陸[米国史の]. ¶the *landing* ***of*** a hostile enemy ***on*** our shores 敵のわが国上陸. ¶Such was my first impressions on my *landing* ***on*** the island of Saghalien. これが樺太上陸に際しての私の第一印象であった.

landing-ground, *n.* 着陸地.

Q² an ***emergency*** *landing-ground* for the benefit of planes 航空機用の不時着地.

landing-place, *n.* 上陸場.

V It ***affords*** a good *landing-place* for boats. それは船舶のよい上陸地をなしている.

landlady, *n.* [下宿屋などの]おかみ.

Q² a ***lodging-house*** ***(boarding-house)*** *landlady* 下宿屋の「おかみ.

P² the *landlady* ***of*** a roadhouse 街道にある宿屋のおかみ.

landlord, *n.* 地主; [下宿屋などの]亭主.

Q a ***cruel*** *landlord* 無慈悲な地主. ¶a ***profiteering*** *landlord* 暴利をむさぼる地主.

Q² an ***absentee*** *landlord* 不在地主. ¶an ***apartment*** *landlord* アパートの経営者. ¶a ***slum landlord*** 貧民アパートの「持主.

landlordism, *n.* 地主制度.

Q² ***absentee*** *landlordism* 不在地主制度.

landmark, *n.* 目標; 史上著名な出来事.

V It ***forms*** a *landmark* that may be seen for many miles around. それは数マイル四方から見える目標となっている. ¶Visitors will ***miss*** many old *landmarks*. 見物人は多くの古い目標が消失していることに気付くであろう.

Q ***ancient*** *landmarks* dear to the antiquarian 好古家にとって貴重な古跡. ¶The chimney forms a ***conspicuous*** *landmark*. その煙突はいい目標になる. ¶preserve ***historic*** *landmarks* 史跡を保存する. ¶a ***literary*** *landmark* 文学史上注目すべき作品など. ¶a ***noble*** *landmark* 貴重な目標(㊟). ¶The book stands out as one of the ***notable*** *landmarks* in the progress of modern science. その本は近代科学の進歩における一つの顕著な著作として高い位置を占めている. 【類】Professor Wyld's book is a ***notable*** *landmark* in the new movement for treating English grammar as the grammar of a living tongue. ¶The pagoda forms a ***picturesque*** *landmark*. その塔は絵のような美しい目標となる. ¶The building is a most ***striking*** *landmark*. その建物は非常に目立った目標である.

P an entertainment that will stand ***as*** a *landmark* in the annals of the talking screen トーキー映画史上画期的な地位を占める一映画.

P² *landmarks* ***in*** world's history 世界史上の大事件. 【類】a *landmark* ***in*** the history of civilization.

landowner, *n.* 地主.

Q² ***absentee*** *landowners* who subsist on the rent in kind from their holding 所有地からの物納によって生活する不在「地主たち.

landscape, *n.* 風景, 風景画.

V ***disfigure*** *landscape* with advertisements 広告で風致を害する. ¶The group of Titans ***dominates*** the *landscape* for miles around. 巨大な群峰が数マイル四方の風景を支配している. ¶lofty derricks ***dotting*** the *landscape* in an oil field 油田において風景のあちこちに立っている高い油井やぐら. ¶a desolate *landscape* ***enlivened*** by autumnal tints 秋色に色どられた荒涼とした風景.

Q its ***beautiful surrounding*** *landscape* その周囲の美しい景色. ¶a ***coastal*** *landscape* 海岸の景色. ¶an ***English*** *landscape* 英国の風景. ¶the three ***famous*** *landscapes* of Japan 日本三景. ¶a ***lovely*** *landscape* 美しい景色. ¶a ***sunlit*** *landscape* 日光を浴びた景色. ¶A cloud steals over a ***sunny*** *landscape*. 雲がこっそり出て日のあたった景色に影をさす. ¶a ***superb*** *landscape* 壮麗な風景.

Q² look out over the peaceful ***summer*** *landscape* 穏かな夏景色を見渡す. ¶a ***spring*** *landscape* 春景色.

P² a *landscape* ***in*** oil 油絵の風景画. ¶a *landscape* ***of*** snow 雪景色. ¶*Landscape* ***with*** (=and) Figures (Sheep, Cattle, Waterfall) 人物(など)のある風景[画題].

landslide, *n.* 《米》地すべり; 《米》大勝利.

Q a ***Democratic*** *landslide* [選挙で]民主党の大勝利.

lane, *n.* 小路.

Q a ***crooked*** *lane* まがった小路. ¶These trees make a pleasant ***shady*** *lane* in summer time. その樹木があるので夏は気持よい日かげの小路になる. ¶a ***single*** (double) *lane* 片道だけの(往復できる)道. ¶the ***tributary*** *lanes* of Fleet Street and Strand フリート街とストランド街に通じる小路. ¶***winding, tree-shady*** country *lanes* 曲りくねった木かげの多い小さないなか路.

Q² an ***air*** *lane* 《米》航空路. ¶an ***ocean*** *lane* 航路. ¶clear ***sea*** *lanes* of mines 航路から爆雷を除去する. ¶a ***ship*** *lane* 航路. ¶The island is off ***shipping*** *lanes*. 同島は航路から「はずれている.

language, *n.* 言語, 国語.

V ***acquire*** a *language* ある国語を習得する. 【類】a *language* ***acquired*** by study (habit). ¶***boycott*** the *language* of the enemy 敵国の言語を学ばないようにする. ¶***drop*** a sign *language* 話の中にちょっと手まねを入れる. ¶***employ*** a violent *language* 激語を使う. ¶***encourage*** and ***diffuse*** the English *language* 英語を奨励し普及させる. ¶***couch*** one's *language* so that ... ...というように表現する. ¶The works of Joseph Conrad Korzeniowski ***enriched*** the English *language*. コンラッドの作品は英語を豊富にした. ¶***exchange*** *language* 言葉を交わす. ¶It was Talleyrand, I think, who said that "*Language* was ***given*** us to conceal our thought."「言語はわれわれの思想を隠すために与えられたものだ」と言ったのはタレィランだったと思う. ¶***interpret*** the *language* of the treaty after their own fashion 条約の文句を自己流に解釈する. ¶people who ***know*** no *language* but his own 自国語の外は何も知らない人々. ¶Germans or Russians coming to England generally ***lose*** their *language* in the first generation and always in the second. ドイツ人またはロシア人は英国にきてから概して一代の中に自国語を話さなくなり, 二代には必ず話さなくなる. ¶***master*** a *language* ある国語に熟達する. ¶***mince*** its *language* その言葉を遠慮して言う. ¶***murder*** the English *language*=speak broken English なっていない英語を使う. ¶Art is universal and ***needs*** no *language*. 美術は普遍的であって何らの言葉を要しない. ¶It has been remarked that soldiers quartered in a foreign country will ***pick up*** a *language* without effort. 外国に駐留する兵士は言葉をわけなく聞覚えするものだと言われている. ¶***portray*** a *language* in its natural and full outlines 国語をその自然のままの全形で示す(辞書編集者の目標). ¶***preserve*** the English *language*, whether spoken or written, in its pure state 口語体であれ文語体であれ英語をその純粋の姿のまま保存する. ¶***purify*** the German *language* from French words 国語純化のためにドイツ語中のフランス語を除去する. 【類】***purify*** the national *language* from all foreign words. ¶He can ***read*** no foreign *languages* but English. 彼は英語以外の外国語は何も読めない. 【類】***read*** two foreign *languages* well. ¶***record*** the Ainu *language* in written form アイヌ語を文字で記録する. ¶a delicacy which ***shames*** the *language* of eulogy—the baked potato いかなる賞嘆の言葉も及ばない美味—焼きじゃが芋. ¶***speak*** a foreign *language* with a native accent 外国語を自国語の口調で話す. 【類】***speak, read,*** and ***write*** the English *language* with ease and accuracy. ¶***take up*** a foreign *language* to learn 外国語を習い始める. ¶***understand*** a foreign *language* directly 外国語を直解する. ¶***use*** *language* before women for which he desires to be promptly kicked 女の前でたちまち蹴られるような言葉を好んで使う‖It is not every one who can learn to ***use*** *language* well. 巧みな言葉使いはだれにでも会得されるという訳にはいかない. 【類】able to ***use*** the English *language*. ¶There was no sincerity in the *language* that he ***wielded***. 彼の用いた言葉は誠意を欠いていた. ¶The Japanese ***write*** their own *language* in Chinese characters. 日本人は自国語を漢字で書く. 【類】The *language* that we ***write*** will always differ somewhat from the language that we speak.

Q use ***abusive*** (=violent) *language* against ... ...に暴言を吐く. ¶clothe one's thoughts with ***accurate*** and ***appropriate*** *language* 思想を正確適切な言葉で表現する. ¶describe it in *language* ***adequate*** to its beauty その美を十分伝えるような言葉でそれを記述する. ¶***ancient*** *languages* 古代語. ¶in ***appreciative*** *language* 美しい言葉で. ¶tell in ***approved*** baby *language* 赤ん坊らしい言葉で言う. ¶use ***bad*** *language* 悪い言葉を使う. ¶***bitter*** and ***sarcastic*** *language* 辛らつで皮肉な言葉. ¶use ***bitter, scornful*** *language*

辛らつで, 軽べつ的な(または非難する)言葉を使う. ¶***boastful*** *language* ごう慢な言葉. ¶***classic*** *language* 古典語, 雅語. ¶in ***clear*** and ***gay*** and ***delightful*** *language* はっきりとして快活でそして気持のよい言葉で. ¶express in ***clear*** and ***simple*** *language* 簡単明りょうな言葉で述べる. ¶use ***coarse*** *language* 粗暴な言葉を使う. ¶English, Dutch, and German are ***cognate*** *languages*. 英・蘭・独語は同族語である. ¶in ***colloquial*** *language* 口語で. 【類】express it in terse ***colloquial*** *language*. ¶***commercial*** *language* 商用語. ¶***continental*** *languages* 大陸語. ¶***conventional*** *language* 月並な言葉. ¶***correct*** and ***beautiful*** *language* 正確で美しい言葉. ¶a ***dead*** *language* 死語(ラテン・ギリシア語など). ¶He expressed himself in ***decided*** *language* on the subject. 彼はそのことについてきっぱりと言切った. ¶French is still considered the ***diplomatic*** *language*. フランス語はまだ外交語と考えられている. ¶indulge in ***disquieting*** (***sensational***) *language* 不穏(扇情的)な言辞を用るい. ¶***elevated*** *language* 高尚な言葉. ¶inability to use the ***English*** *language* correctly 正確に英語を使えないこと. ¶***every*** *language* known to civilization あらゆる文明国の国語. ¶***expressive*** *language* 意味の強い言葉. ¶in ***financial*** *language* 財政の術語で言えば. ¶use ***fine*** *language* 文を飾る. ¶the displacement of French by German as a ***first*** *language* 第一国語としてフランス語に代えるにドイツ語をもってすること. ¶a ***flexional*** *language* 語尾変化の多い国語. ¶A ***foreign*** *language* is a consciously acquired one. 外国語とは意識的に習得した言葉である. 【類】The man who does not know a ***foreign*** *language* does not know his own.—Goethe. ¶***gross*** *language* 下卑た言葉. ¶***harsh*** *language* 粗暴な言葉. ¶in ***highflown*** *language* 大げさな言語で. ¶in ***highly-polished*** *language* よく洗練された言葉で. ¶in ***homely*** *language*＝in common parlance 平たい言葉で. ¶***indecent*** *language* みだらな言葉. ¶be couched in ***inflated*** *language* 誇張した言葉で表現されている. ¶an ***inflected*** *language* 屈折語. ¶***ill*** *language* 悪口. ¶***kindred*** *languages* 同族語. ¶use ***insulting*** *language* 侮辱的な言葉を用いる. ¶English is the ***leading*** *language* of commerce. 英語は主な商用語だ. ¶Chinese was a ***literary*** *language* in the Edo period. 漢文は江戸時代の文語であった. ¶***living*** *languages* 現代語. ¶use ***low*** *language*, language unfit for decent company 下品な言い方すなわち上品な人々には合わない言葉を使う. ¶His *language* is a trifle ***lurid***. 彼の言葉使いはちょっとすご味がある. ¶in ***metrical*** *language* 韻文で. ¶a ***modern*** *language* 近代語. ¶a ***national*** *language* 国語. ¶there is ***no*** *language* to tell how ... ...の次第を告げようにも言葉がない. ¶***obscene*** *language* 卑わいな言葉. ¶use ***offensive*** *language* 腹の立つ言い方をする. ¶in ***official*** *language* 公用語で. 【類】The conference has no ***official*** *languages*. ¶in the ***ordinary*** *language* 普通の言葉で言えば. ¶read "Don Quixote" in its ***original*** *language* 原語で「ドン・キホーテ」を読む. ¶***philosophical*** (＝***a priori***) *languages* 哲学的な言葉. ¶penned in somewhat ***picturesque*** *language* 美文めいた筆で書いた. ¶in ***plain*** *language* 平たく言えば. ¶***Poetic*** *language* is largely figurative. 詩語は比ゆ的のものが多い. ¶the ***polite*** *languages* 上品な言葉(ギリシア語とラテン語). ¶in ***popular*** *language* 平たく言えば. ¶in ***present-day*** *language* 現代語で言えば. ¶The ***prevailing*** *language* in Luxemburg is German. ルクセンブルグで一般に話されている言葉はドイツ語だ. ¶***profane*** *language* のろいやののしりの言葉. ¶the ***quaint*** *language* of the Authorized Version きん定聖書の古い言い回し. ¶if in ***restrained*** *language* 表現は控え目ではあるが. ¶***Romanic*** *languages* ラテン系統の言語. ¶Russian is a ***second*** *language* in China. ロシア語は中国では第二の国語だ. 【類】acquire English as a ***second*** *lauguage* / take up a ***second*** *language*. ¶a ***second native*** *language* 第二の母国語. ¶denounce him in ***severe*** *language* 激烈な言葉で彼を非難する. ¶the idea, in ***simple*** *language*, is ... 平たく言えばその思想は...だ. 【類】in such ***simple*** *language* as children can understand. ¶The story is told in ***simple*** and ***elegant*** *language*. その物語は平易で優美な言葉でつづられている. ¶in ***simple*** and ***lucid*** *language* 平易明確な言葉で. ¶in ***simple, untechnical*** *language* 専門語を使わず分かりやすい言葉で. ¶***spoken*** *language* 口語. ¶***stereotyped*** *language* 紋切形の言葉. ¶speak a ***strange*** *language* 異国人の言葉を話す. ¶He objected in ***strong*** *language*. 彼は言葉強く反対した. ¶You shouldn't use such ***strong*** *language*. そんな乱暴なことを言うものではない. ‖ That is ***strong*** *language*, friend B! ビー君! それはひどい. ¶in ***technical*** *language* 術語で. ¶use ***threatening*** *language* おどし文句を使う. ¶***turgid*** *language* 大げさな言葉. ¶Tagore is a poet in ***two*** *languages*. タゴールは二国語を使う詩人である. ¶"Refuse" is no ***uncertain*** *language*.「拒絶」は決してあいまいな言葉ではない. ¶Music is everybody's language or you may call it a ***universal*** *language*. 音楽は万人の言葉, すなわち世界語と呼んでもよい. 【類】a ***universal second*** *language* (第二国語). ¶I guessed what he said in an ***unknown*** *language*. 私に分からない国語で彼が何を言ったかを私は推察した. ¶tell ... in most ***unmistakable*** *language* that ... きっぱり...と言う. ¶***unparliamentary*** *language* 議場では許されない言葉. ¶an ***unprintable*** *language* 印刷にはされない(野卑な)言葉. 【類】The boss called his servant and told him many things in ***unprintable*** *language*. ¶expressed in ***unscientific*** *language* 非科学的に言えば. ¶in ***untechnical*** *language* 通俗な言葉で. ¶the ***vernacular*** *languages* in India 数種のインド母国語. ¶use ***vile*** *language* 毒舌を揮う. ¶use ***violent*** *language* 暴言をはく. ¶in ***vulgar*** *language* 俗語では. ¶decry in the ***wildest*** *language* as acts of violence on the part of ... ...の側の暴力行為として口をきわめて非難する. ¶pictures of the ***wordless universal*** *language* 言葉のない世界語たる絵画. ¶***Written*** *language* is expected to be more careful and exact than spoken language. 文章語は口語よりも一層綿密で正確なものとされている.

Q^2 the ***book*** *language* 文章体の言葉. ¶***code*** *language* 暗号の言葉. ¶***cousin*** *languages* 近似国語. ¶written in ***everyday*** *language* 日常語で書かれた. ¶The deaf and dumb use ***finger*** *language* to express their ideas. ろうあ者は指話する. ¶"***flash***" *language* 一時の流行語(ぱっと現われてぱっと消える). ¶speak English as one's ***home*** *language* 英語を家庭語として話す. ¶the ***mandarin*** *language* [中国]官話. ¶the same ***parent*** *language* 同一語系の言語. ¶a ***prefix*** *language* 接頭国語(アフリカ語のような). ¶The Indians soon overtook him, and in ***sign*** *language* ordered him to dismount. インディアンはやがて彼に追ついて手まねで馬から下りろと命じた. ‖ All communication was by ***sign*** *language*. 用をたすのは一切手まねでやった. ¶***sister*** *languages* 姉妹語. ¶In ***slang*** *language* M.P. stands for Military Police or Mounted Police. 俗語では M.P. は憲兵[隊]または騎馬警官[隊]の意だ. ¶***street*** or ***popular*** *language* 街の言葉, すなわち通俗語. ¶the ***underworld*** *language* ギャングの言葉. ¶create artificially a ***world*** *language* 人工的に世界語を創造する.

P ***in*** the *language* of Shakespeare シェークスピアの言葉を借りて言えば ‖ ***in*** the *language* of the underworld ギャング仲間の言葉で言うと. 【類】***In*** the *language* of today he was a "mixer."(「他人と折合のよい人」) ‖ ***in*** the *language* of the street (＝ordinary life) 俗に言う ‖ speak not ***in*** the *language* of the platform, but of the smoking-room 演壇の(四角ばった)言葉でなくて喫煙室の(くだけた)言葉で話す. 【類】***in*** a *language* not his own / What is this called ***in*** your *language*? / writers ***in*** the English *language* / ***in*** the *language* of poetry (雅語) ‖ one may say ***in*** the *language* of sincere compliment that ... 人はお世辞でなく...と言うであろう. ¶the study ***of*** *language* 語学研究 ‖ a teacher ***of*** *language*＝a language teacher 語学教師. ‖ murder the beauty ***of*** a *language* 言語の美をそこなう.

P^2 use the *language* ***of*** the day 現代語を使う ‖ the *language* ***of*** literature and the *language* ***of*** the masses 文語と口語 ‖ The *language* ***of*** fact is more convincing than the language of fiction. 事実は作りごとより一層力がある. ‖ the *language* ***of*** the street corner 通俗語 ‖ the *language* ***of*** fine clothes よそ行きの言葉. 【類】until recently French was considered the *language* ***of*** diplomacy (外交語).

languish, *v.* あこがれる, やつれる.

P *languish* ***for*** her in secret 密かに彼女に思い焦れる. ¶*languish* ***in*** a prison 監獄で苦悶する. ¶He was *languished* ***to*** skin and bones. 彼は衰弱して骨と皮になった.

languor, *n.* 倦怠(ｹﾝﾀｲ).

V ***feel*** *languor* 倦怠を感じる.

Q the ***delicious*** *languor* of a sun bath 日光浴の快いけだるさ. ¶an atmosphere of ***extradinary*** *languor* 非常に重苦

しいふん囲気.

P² the *languor of* the sky 空のうっとうしさ.

lantern, *n.* ちょうちん.

V *carry* a lighted *lantern* 灯をともしたちょうちんを持って行く. ¶ *have* (=*hold*) a *lantern* ちょうちんを持つ. ¶ *light* a *lantern* ちょうちんに灯をともす. ¶ The rear guard *wears* a green *lantern*. 後部車掌は緑色の合図灯を下げている.

Q a garden illuminated with *colored lanterns* 色ちょうちんで飾った庭園.

Q² a *shadow-picture lantern* 走馬灯. ¶ an avenue of votive *stone lanterns* 石灯ろうの並んでいる通り.

P like a *lantern in* the dark やみ夜の灯のように.

lap, *n.* ひざ.

P sit down *in* (=on) the *lap* ひざにすわる ‖ You can easily use the typewriter *in* your *lap*. そのタイプライターはひざの上で楽に使える. 【類】let one's book *lie* unopened *in* one's *lap* ‖ I was brought up *in* the *lap* of luxury at home up to the age of twelve. 私は十二の年まで家でぜいたくに育った. ‖ a person *in* the *lap* of Fortune 幸運に恵まれた人. ¶ a child sitting *on* the *lap* of his mother 母のひざの上にすわっている子供. 【類】sit under a tree with a book *on* one's *lap*.

lap, *v.* しゃぶる, [波が]寄せる.

M² Cats and dogs *lapped up* water. ねこと犬は水をぴちゃぴちゃ飲んだ. 【類】*lap up* a plate of soup ‖ *lap up* compliments (flattery) お世辞(おべっか)をそっくりそのままとる.

P be *lapped in* luxury ぜいたくにふけっている ‖ Waves were *lapping on* the beach. 波が岸辺にひたひたと寄せていた.

lapel, *n.* 折えり.

Q² bear a badge on a *coat lapel*. 折えりに記章をつけている.

P wear a ha'penny rose *in* the *lapel* of one's coat 上衣の折えりに半ペニーのばらをさす.

lapse, *n.* 経過; 間違い; 堕落.

V It *requires* the long *lapse* of a century. それは百年の長い年月の経過を要する.

Q *linguistic lapses,* spoken or written 話したり書いたりする言葉の間違い. ¶ a *momentary lapse* of attention ちょっとの間の不注意. ¶ a *moral lapse* 堕落. ¶ He had *occasional lapses* into slang. 彼は話の間にちょいちょい俗語を使った. ¶ There are *unfortunate lapses* in style in his composition. 彼の作文には所々ミスがある.

Q² after a *three-month lapse* 三カ月経過後.

P even today, *after* the *lapse* of many centuries 幾百年後の今日ですら ‖ *after* the *lapse* of a certain period of grace 一定期の猶予の後. ¶ *by lapse* of time 時の経過によって. ¶ *in* the *lapse* (=in course) of two years 二年たって. 【類】*in* the *lapse* of a little time before one is quite aware of it. ¶ *with* the *lapse* of time 時が経過するにつれ忘れ.

P² *lapses of* centuries 数世紀の流れ ‖ *lapse of* memory 胴忘れ.

lapse, *v.* 経過する; 堕落する.

M *lapse backward* in a march 進軍で落後する.

P *laspe from* good manners 次第に行儀が悪くなる. ¶ *lapse into* idleness 知らない間に怠け出す ‖ *lapse into* quietude 静まる ‖ *lapse into* unconsciousness 無意識に陥る ‖ *lapse into* nothingness 世間から忘れられる ‖ *lapse into* the vernacular いつか自国語が出る(外国語を話しているとき).

larceny, *n.* 窃盗.

Q *small larcenies* こそ泥事件.

lard, *n.* ラード.

V *use lard* for cooking ラードを料理に使う.

larder, *n.* 食料室.

Q a *half-empty larder* 貯蔵品の少ない台所戸だな. ¶ a *peripatetic larder* 弁当, 行厨(こうちゅう).

large, *n.* 一般.

P The drunkard is as much a danger to society as a lunatic *at large,* which he is. 大酒飲は野放しの狂人同様に社会をおびやかすものであるが彼はその適例だ. ‖ a prisoner who is *at large* on bail 保釈で出てきている囚人 ‖ be delighted to be once more *at large* もう一度しゃばの風にあたって喜んでいる. 【類】The prisoner is still *at large.* ‖ give a question to class *at large* クラス全体に質問する. 【類】benefit not only his own country but the world *at large* / the public *at large* ‖ scatter imputations *at large* やたらに中傷をやる. ¶ done *in large* (=on a large scale) 大規模になされた.

large, *a.* 大きい.

M *conspicuously large* 著しく大きな. ¶ *proportionately larger* than ... ...とは比べて割に大きい. ¶ *slightly larger* than ... ...よりちょっと大きい. ¶ *unusually* (=*extraordinarily*) *large* 並外れて大きな.

P One is *larger* than the other *by* a few inches. 一方は他方より数インチ大きい. ¶ a person *large of* limbs 手足の大きい人. ¶ One of her hips is *larger than* the other. 彼女のおしりは片方が大きい.

lark, *n.* ひばり.

V² A *lark carols.* ひばりがさえずる. ¶ *Larks soar.* ひばりが空高く舞上る. ¶ The *larks* were *trilling* away overhead. ひばりがさえずりながら上空に飛上って行った.

Q a *blithe lark* 楽しげなひばり. ¶ *lively larks* 陽気なひばり. ¶ a *mounting lark* 上げひばり.

P rise *with* the *lark* ひばりと一緒に起きる.

O as lively as a *lark* ひばりのように陽気な.

lash, *n.* むち.

V The criminal was sentenced to *receive* one hundred *lashes* (=strikes=blows). 罪人は百たたきの刑を宣告された.

Q a sentence of *twelve lashes* 十二むち打ちの刑.

P strike a prisoner *with* a *lash* 囚人をむちで打つ.

lash, *v.* むち打つ, [風波などが岸などに]ぶっつかる.

M He *lashed* his horse *hard.* 彼は馬をひどくむちで打った. ‖ The rain *lashed hard* against the windows. 雨は窓を強く打った. ¶ They pulled the sail in to the boom and *lashed* it *securely* with rope. 彼らは帆を帆げたに引きよせロープでしっかり縛りつけた. ¶ *lash out* a horse 馬を急がせる ‖ He *lashed out* at his book reviewer. 彼は自著の批評家にさんざんに食ってかかった.

P *lash at* ... ...をむち打つ. ¶ *lashed by* a strong easterly wind 強い東風に吹きつけられて. ¶ The gale *lashed* the seas *into* fury. 暴風が荒波を立てた. ¶ *lash* one *on* the back その背を打つ. ¶ *lash* a boy *with* a whip 少年をむちで打つ.

lass, *n.* 小娘.

Q a *blooming lass* of fresh eighteen 水々しい十八娘. ¶ a *bonnie* (=*bonny*) *lass* 美しい小娘. ¶ a *cherry-looking lass* さくらんぼのようなほおをした小娘. ¶ *Scots lasses* スコットランドの娘っ子たち.

Q² the "*Hallelujah Lasses*" of the Salvation Army 救世軍の女士官たち.

lassitude, *n.* けだるさ.

V *produce lassitude* だるくさせる.

Q an *agreeable lassitude* 気持のよいけだるさ. ¶ *physical lassitude* 肉体のけだるさ.

last, *n.* 最後.

V He peacefully *breathed* his *last.* 彼は安らかに息を引取った. 【類】She *breathed* her *last* in peaceful ending to a troubled life. ‖ *breathe* its *last* [会など]解散する. ¶ *look* one's *last* 見納めをする. ¶ Scientists estimate that another century will *see* the *last* of the Australians. 科学者は次の世紀に豪州土人が絶滅することを予想している. ‖ *see* the *last* of her on the screen 銀幕上での彼女の見納めをする.

Q It is beginning, at *long last,* to have the attention of the public. それは漸くのことで一般から注意され出した.

P He will come *at last.* 彼はいよいよ来るだろう. 【類】His chance came *at last.* / He died *at last.* ¶ All men were against him, but he kept his courage *to* the *last.* あらゆる人が彼に反対したが彼は最後までがん張り通した. 【類】He held out *to* the *last.* / fight *to* the *last* / hold on *to* the *last* (しがみつく) ‖ die defending the castle *to* the *last* 城をまくらに討死する ‖ Every hero becomes a bore *at last.*—Emerson. どの英雄でも最後には鼻につく. ‖ strip her *to* the very *last* 彼女を最後の一線まで裸かにする. ¶ I am planning a little trip about the *last of* this month. 私は本月の末ごろちょっと旅行しようと思っている.

last, *a., ad.* 最後の(に).

O When did you *last* write a letter to him? 彼にこの前手紙を出されたのは何日ですか. ¶ since I *last* saw him この前会って以来. ¶ *last* but not least 順序は最後でも重要さは前に述べた事に劣らない. 【類】*last,* but far from least, is ...

last, *v.* 続く.

M It *lasted all night.* それは夜通し続いた. ¶ His speech *lasted an hour.* 彼の演説は一時間続いた. ¶ *last forever* 永

久に続く. ¶The strike is expected to *last long*. このストは長期にわたるものと思われている. 【類】This weather won't *last* much *longer*. ‖ It *lasts longer*. それは一層もちがよい. ¶*last out* 続く. ¶*last* full *six months* まる六カ月続く.

P *last about* an hour 約一時間続く. ¶The trial *lasted for* ten consecutive days. 裁判は十日間継続して行われた. ‖ The blockade is likely to *last for* some time. 封鎖は当分続きそうだ. ‖ I have enough tobacco to *last* me *for* ten more days. あと十日位のむだけのタバコがある. ¶*last from* autumn *to* spring 秋から春まで続く. ¶*last from* five o'clock *until* seven 五時から七時まで続く. ¶It covered the whole of the seventeenth century, and *lasted* well *into* the eighteenth. それは十七世紀の全部にわたり十八世紀になっても相当の所まで続いた. ‖ The heat of a wonderful summer *lasted into* September. 驚くべき夏の炎熱が九月まで続いた. ¶*last through* the winter 冬中続く. ¶*last throughout* the year その年中続く. ¶the exhibition *lasts till* ... 博覧会は…まで続く. ¶Such discouragement has never *lasted with* me. こんなけちを付けられても私は決してこれに屈しなかった.

O while my money *lasts* 金の続く限り.

lat., =latitude 緯度.

P at long. 66 E. *by lat*. 83 N. 東経六十六度, 北緯八十三度で.

latch, *n*. 錠, かけがね(ラッチ).

Q² a *thumb latch* 押錠.

P a door *on* (*off*) the *latch* ラッチをかけてある(ない)ドア.

latch, *v*. かけがね(ラッチ)をかける.

M *latch* a door *click* ドアにかちんとラッチをかける. ¶This door won't *latch properly*. このドアはうまくかけがねがかからない.

late, *a*., *ad*. おそい, おそく.

M *Better late* than never. おそくともしないよりはいい. ¶So sorry, I'm so *dreadfully late*. どうもおそくなった(招待されて). ¶should be forwarded *not later* than ... …より前に発送すべきものである. ¶It is never *too late* to mend. 改めるにおそ過ぎるということはない.

P "Exhibitions of photographs in stereoscopic machines have become very common *of late*. 立体写真機による写真の展覧会は近ごろきわめて普通になった. 【類】I have been busy *of late*. / He hardly ever goes there *of late*. ¶He won't be home *till late*. 彼はおそくならなければ家に戻らないだろう. 【類】sit up *till* (=*until*) *late* at night / The inspiration to write did not come to her *until late*. ¶come home *late at* night 夜おそく家に帰る. 【類】be *late at* school (登校). ¶be *late for* school 学校(の授業)に遅れる. 【類】be *late for* work / I was two hours *late for* my engagement. / Don't be *late for* the train. / The season a little too *late for* the fishing. ¶He had often been *late from* the city. それより以前彼は時々町からの帰りがおそかった. ‖ You are *late from* the office tonight. 今夜あなたは会社からお帰りがおそい[妻の苦情]. ¶*late in* life 晩年に ‖ She is *late in* her teens. 彼女は十八九だ. 【類】*late in* spring (autumn). ¶sit up *late into* the night 夜おそくまで起きている. 【類】Often I read from 4 o'clock in the afternoon until *late into* the night. ¶He is *late of* getting up in the morning. 彼は朝寝坊だ. ‖ ..., *late* (=formerly) *of* the Bengal Civil service 前ベンガル国民軍所属の… 【類】John Smith, *late of* Boston (最近までボストンにいた). ¶*late to* school (office) 学校(など)に遅れる.

O applications must be posted to reach us not *later* than ... 申込書は当方に…前に届くように出さなくてはいけない. ¶his own room, *late* his uncle's 最近まで伯父のへやであった彼の自室.

lately, *ad*. 近ごろ.

M until *comparatively lately* 比較的最近まで.

latent, *a*. 潜在する.

P the good *latent in* him 彼に潜在する善玉.

latest, *a*. [late の最上級] 最後の, 最近の.

P I shall be back by five o'clock *at latest*. おそくも私は五時までには帰ります. 【類】In a few days *at* [the] *latest* I will return.

lathe, *n*. 旋盤, ろくろ.

Q² a *foot lathe* 足踏み旋盤. ¶a *four-spindle lathe* 四錘旋盤. ¶a *screw-cutting lathe* ねじ切り旋盤. ¶a *shafting lathe* 軸回り旋盤. ¶a *spinning lathe* 紡糸旋盤. ¶a *turret lathe* ターレット旋盤.

P turn ... *in* a *lathe* 旋盤の中で…を回す. ¶turn out the shapes of the pottery *on* the *lathe* ろくろで陶器の形を作り出す.

Latin, *n*. ラテン語.

Q² in *dog Latin* めちゃくちゃなラテン語で. ¶*law Latin* 法律用ラテン語.

P² What he says are all *Latin* and Greek *to* me. 彼のいうことはちんぷんかんぷんだ.

Latinist, *n*. ラテン語学者.

Q *skilled Latinist* 老練なラテン語学者.

latitude, *n*. 緯度; 地方; 自由.

V *allow* a little *latitude* in the matter of ... …の件に関し少しの自由を与える. 【類】*allow* a person more *latitude* / No *latitude* is *allowed* in that case. ¶*lack latitude* 動きが取れない, 融通性がない.

Q Polar bears live in the *cold latitude*. 北極ぐまは寒帯地方に住む. ¶*high* (*low*) *latitudes* 高(低)緯度地方, 赤道より遠い(近い)地方.

P *at* approximately the same *latitude* ほぼ同緯度に. ¶this district is *in* the same *latitude* as ... この地方は…と同緯度にある.

latrine, *n*. 便所.

Q² a *camp latrine* 兵舎の便所. ¶a *trough latrine* とい状連接便所.

lattice, *n*. 格子(つくり).

Q a *barred lattice* of bamboo すだれ.

Q² a *wrought-iron lattice* [錬鉄の]鉄格子.

laugh, *n*. 笑い, 笑声.

V The happy joke *brought* an honest *laugh*. そのうまい冗談でわれわれ一同心から笑わせられた. ¶*cause* a *laugh* 笑わせる. ¶*create* a *laugh* by ... …で笑わせる. ¶*draw* a *laugh* 笑いを招く. ¶We *enjoyed* a big *laugh*. われわれは大笑いをした. ¶*excite* (=raise) a *laugh* 笑わせる. ¶*force* a *laugh* 無理に笑わせる. ¶*get* a *laugh* 笑わせる. ¶*give* a hysteric *laugh* ヒステリックに笑う. ¶He *had* quite a *laugh* over it. 彼はそのことで大笑いをした. ‖ *have* a *laugh* at a person 人を冷笑する ‖ You *have* the *laugh* on me this time. 今度は君が僕を笑う番だ. ¶*laugh* a hearty *laugh* 心から笑う. ¶*provoke* a *laugh* 笑いを催させる. ¶*raise* a good *laugh* 盛んに笑わせる.

V² How their *laugh rings out*! 彼らの笑声がどんなに強く鳴響くことか.

Q an utterly *abandoned laugh* 全くたわいもない笑い. ¶an *affected laugh* 作り笑い. ¶an *agreeable laugh* 快い笑い. ¶an *amused, noiseless laugh* 楽しい静かな笑い. ¶a *boisterous* and *noisy laugh* 騒々しい笑い. ¶a *broad laugh* 無遠慮な笑い. ¶a *cackling laugh* きゃっきゃっという笑い. ¶an *empty laugh* そら笑い. ¶Catullus said long ago that "Nothing is more foolish than a *foolish laugh*." 昔カタラスは「ばか笑いぐらいばか気たものはない」と言った. ¶have a *good laugh* 大笑いをする. ¶provoke (=excite) a *hearty laugh* 心から笑わせる. ¶He answered with a *high laugh*. 彼はからからと笑って答えた. ¶bring an *honest laugh* 心から笑わせる. ¶an *infectious laugh* [一人が笑うと]伝染する笑い. ¶a *loud, hollow laugh* うつろな高笑い. ¶a *low, rippling, musical, joyous laugh* 低くて波打つ音楽的な楽しい笑い. ¶the *merry laugh* of children 子供たちの楽しそうな笑い声. ¶a *mirth-provoking laugh* 楽しくさせる笑い. ¶a *mischievous laugh* 意地悪な笑い. ¶a *nervous laugh* 神経質な笑い方. ¶an *open* and *explosive laugh* だれはばかるところない爆笑. ¶She burst into one of her *rich laughs*. 彼女はいつもながらにぎやかに笑いくずれた. ¶give a *shy little laugh* はずかしそうににちょっと笑う. ¶a *smothered laugh* 忍び笑い.

Q² a *society laugh* お愛想笑い.

P burst *into* a *laugh* ふき出す. 【類】turn away one's face *with* a *laugh* / say *with* a *laugh*.

laugh, *v*. 笑う.

M *laugh aloud* in the fullness of his content 会心の余り大いに笑う. ¶*laugh* one's fear *away* 心配を笑い消す ‖ *laugh away* one's tears 涙を笑いでごまかす. 【類】He talked and *laughed away* his leisure hours (時間をつぶした) / *laugh away* another's apprehension (心配). ¶*laugh boisterously* 騒々しく笑う. ¶*laugh causelessly* わけもなく笑う. ¶*laugh consumedly* (=*excessively*) 大いに笑う. ¶*laugh foolishly* 他愛なく笑う. ¶*laugh heartily* and *wholly* 心の底から笑う. ¶*laugh lightly* うれしそうに笑う. ¶*laugh derisively* ばかにして笑う. ¶*laugh good-humoredly* 上きげんに笑う. ¶*laugh grimly* にたりと笑う. ¶*laugh heavily* 大いに笑う. ¶*laugh hugely* 大いに笑う.

¶*laugh* almost *hysterically* 気違いじみた笑い方をする. ¶*laugh immoderately* 度外れに笑う. ¶*laugh maliciously* 意地悪げに笑う. ¶*laugh merrily* 楽しげに笑う. ¶*laugh out* 吹きだす, からからと笑う. ¶*laugh outright* 無遠慮に笑う. ¶*laugh rudely* (=jeer) at ... ...を冷笑する. ¶We can only *laugh scornfully* at the folly of such a proposition. そんな提言のばかばかしさをあざ笑うだけだ. ¶*laugh uproariously* at nothing 何でもないことをげらげら笑う. ¶*laugh wryly* 口をゆがめて笑う.

M² About this her brother *laughed* her *down*. このことで兄が笑ったので妹は沈黙した. ¶*laugh* it *off* 一笑に付す. 【類】*laugh off* suggestions that ... / *laugh off* (=*away*) one's embarrassing situation (人の困っている状態) / *laugh off* a warning / The trouble was too black and terrific to be *laughed off*.

P *laugh about* a mistake 過失を笑う. ¶*laugh against* one's will 思わず笑う. ¶*laugh at* a person 人をあざわらう ‖ *laugh at* the notion of going abroad 洋行するのを笑う.【類】*laugh at* a funny story (こっけいな話) / *laugh at* a joke ‖ Love *laughs at* a distance. ほれて通えば千里も一里. ‖ He was *laughed at* for his pains. 骨折損のくたびれもうけをした. 【類】He was *laughed at* by his friends. / He was *laughed at* for being so foolish. / I don't want to be *laughed at* in company. / We *laughed at* his fancy. ‖ I regretted your absence very much, there was, indeed, enough to *laugh at*. 君が欠席したのはいかにも残念だった, 会は随分おもしろかった. ¶I have known him *laugh for* nothing. 私は彼が何でもないことを笑う男だということを知っている. ¶He *laughed in* his sleeve. 彼はかげで笑った(舌を出した) ‖ *laugh in* scorn あざ笑う ‖ *laugh in* one's face 面と向って笑う. ¶*laugh* at him *into* silence 彼を笑って黙らせる ‖ *laugh* oneself *into* convulsions 腹を抱えて笑う. ¶*laugh like* an idiot ばか笑いをする. ¶*laugh on* the other (=wrong) side of one's mouth《口語》[えびす顔が]急に泣き顔になる(失敗して). ¶Perhaps they have been *laughed out of* the habit by this time. 多分彼らは人から笑われてもはやその癖も直ったろう. ¶*laugh over* (=at) a trifle (joke) つまらないこと(など)を笑う. ¶*laugh under* one's breath くすくす笑う. ¶soil *laughing with* harvests 豊作で笑顔を呈する大地 ‖ *laugh with* scorn at ... ...をさげすんで笑う.

O He *laughed* till the tears ran down his face. 彼はあまり笑ったので涙が出てきた. ‖ *laugh* until one's sides ache 横っ腹が痛くなるほど笑う ‖ *laughed* until we cried. ¶He did nothing but *laugh*. 彼は笑ってばかりいた.

laughing, *n.* 笑うこと.

V *burst out laughing* 爆笑する. ¶We could not *help laughing* われわれは笑わないではいられなかった. ¶*hold* one's *laughing* 笑いたさをこらえる.

P We nearly died *with laughing*. われわれは死ぬほど笑った.

laughing-stock, *n.* 笑草.

V *make* a *laughing-stock* of oneself 笑いものになる. 【類】*make* oneself a *laughing-stock* for the world.

P He is the *laughing-stock of* everybody. 彼は皆の笑草だ. 【類】This made him the *laughing-stock of* the whole school. / become the *laughing-stock of* ... ¶a *laughingstock to* the world 世間の笑草.

laughter, *n.* 笑い, 高笑い, 笑声.

V *create laughter* 笑い出させる. ¶*excite laughter* 笑いを催させる. 【類】*excite* the *laughter* of an audience by saying ... / The universal element of human imperfection—alike in all ages and places—*excites* at once our *laughter* and our tears. ¶He *moved* the *laughter* of his audience. 彼は聴衆を笑わせた. ¶*provoke laughter* あざけりを促がす. ¶A *laughter* was *raised* against him. 彼はちょう笑された. ¶Her *laughter tinkled* pleasantly. ほゝゝという彼女の笑い声は耳に快かった. ¶He can only amaze the ignorant and *wake* the *laughter* of the erudite. それは無学の者を驚かし博学の士を笑わせるだけだ. ¶*Laughter swept* the House. 笑声が議院全体にどよめいた.

Q The audience received it with *boisterous laughter*. 聴衆はそれを聞いてどっと笑った. ¶a *contagious laughter* 伝染する笑い. ¶a *convulsive laughter* 腹を揺する大笑い. ¶a *diabolical laughter* 悪魔的な笑い. ¶an *explosive laughter* 爆笑. ¶a *gay laughter* ほがらかな笑い. ¶a *hearty, merry laughter* 心からの愉快な笑い. ¶His lower jaw became dislocated by *immoderate laughter*. あんまり笑ったので彼の下あごが外れた. ¶a *loud laughter* 高笑い. ¶a *sardonic laughter* 冷笑. ¶have a *side-splitting laughter* 腹を抱えて笑いこける. ¶a *sincere laughter* 心からの笑い. ¶an *unprovoked laughter* 何とはなしの笑い. ¶This utterance of his was greeted with bursts of *uproarious laughter*. 彼のこの言葉に聴衆はどっと笑い出した.

P burst *into laughter* どっと笑い出す. ¶At that there was a great roar *of laughter*. それで皆がどっと笑った. ‖ peals *of laughter* 笑声. ¶*with laughter* or with tears 笑ったり泣いたり. ¶roll about *with laughter* over Weller and Dowrer (in *Pickwick Papers*) ウェラーやダウラーの文句を読み腹を抱えて笑う.

launch, *n.* 進水; ランチ.

V *board* a *launch* ランチに乗る. ¶*make* a *launch* into the wide world 広い世間に乗出す.

Q² a *steam launch* 汽艇.

launch, *v.* 進水する; 乗出す.

M *launch out* in praise of her beauty 彼女の美の礼賛を始める ‖ *launch out* into extravagance 放縦生活に入る ‖ He *launched out* into an extended defense of his administration. 彼は自分の施政の弁護を長々と述べ立てた. ‖ *launch out* into strong language 暴言をはき始める ‖ *launch out* into a series of experiments 次々と色々な実験を始める ‖ *launch out* on a voyage of discovery 発見への航海に乗り出す. ¶be at last *really launched* いよいよ軌道に乗る. ¶be *successfully launched* 首尾よく進水する, 仕事のすべり出しがよい.

P She was *launched at* Belfast for the ... Company. ...会社注文のその船はベルファーストで進水した. ¶The Iyo Maru was *launched from* the Mitsubishi Shipbuilding Yard at Nagasaki on the 24th inst. 伊予丸は今月二十四日三菱長崎造船所で進水した. ¶*launch into* politics 政界に乗出す ‖ I had scarcely entered, when he *launched into* abuse against me. 私が室にはいるかはいらないのに彼は私にののしりを浴びせかけた. 【類】*launch into* a business or professional career. ¶*launch on* an ocean vayage 大洋航海に出帆する. ¶the ship was *launched under* the sponsorship of... 同船は...の後援の下に進水した. ¶books now being *launched upon* the world 世に送り出されつつある書物 ‖ Japan is already well *launched upon* her world career. 日本はすでに世界的活動に十分乗出している.

launcher, *n.* 発射器.

Q² a *rocket launcher* ロケット発射機.

launching, *n.* 進水.

P² the *launching of* a battleship *from* a shipbuilding yard ある造船所での一戦闘艦の進水(式).

laundry, *n.* 洗たく; 洗たくもの.

V *Laundry* may be *done* there. そこで洗たくができる. ¶He *runs* a *laundry*. 彼は洗たく屋をしている.

Q *soiled laundry* 汚れた洗たく物.

Q² *steam laundry* 蒸気洗たく.

P send linen *to* the *laundry* リンネル物を洗たくに出す. 【類】Send them over *to* the *laundry*.

laundrying, *n.* 洗たく.

P It can be removed *for laundrying*. それは洗たくのために取はずしができる.

laurel, *n.* 月けい樹; 名声, 栄冠.

V He went on to *add laurels* to his crown. 彼は次々に名声が高まっていった. ¶*earn* fresh *laurels* 新たな栄冠を得る. ¶The actress *gained* many *laurels* in the Imperial Theater. その女優は帝国劇場で幾多の名声を博した. ‖ He *gained* for German scholarship bright *laurels* in this field. 彼はこの方面で大いにドイツの学問上の名声を高めた. ¶*reap* (=win) one's *laurels* 名声を博する. ¶to *retrieve* the *laurel* which has been lost in the Pacific 太平洋上で失われた栄冠を取戻すために. ¶*Seeking* new *laurels*, he came to America in 1832. 彼は新しい名声を求めて一八三二年アメリカにきた. 【類】He does not *seek* the *laurels* of the original investigator. ¶He *won laurels* in the war with China. 彼は中国との戦いで名を揚げた.

P a crown *of laurel* 月けい冠. ¶Even were he in future to add nothing *to* his *laurels* in his work, he would remain an author of great permanence. 彼はたとえ将来の著述によって名声を高めることがないにしても不朽の著述家たることを失わないであろう.

lavage, *n.* 洗浄.

V *give lavage* of the stomach 胃を洗う.

lavatory, *n.* 便所.

Q² a *flush lavatory* (=toilet) 水洗便所.

lavish, *a.* 浪費する, 過多の.

P *lavish in* one's compliments (expenditure) お世辞(など)の多過ぎる. ¶*lavish of* one's money 金使いの荒い. ¶too *lavish with* one's money 金を使い過ぎる.

lavish, *v.* 浪費する.

P *lavish* money *upon* a person 人のためにむやみに金を出す ‖ *lavish* praise (favors) *on* a person 人をむやみにほめる(ひいきにする). 【類】She *lavished* kindness *on* her guests. / *lavish* money *on* (=*upon*) luxries (ぜいたく品).

law, *n.* 法律; 法則, おきて.

V *abrogate* (=*repeal, cancel or rescind*) a *law* ある法律を廃止する. ¶*administer* a *law* 法律を執行する. ¶skilfully worded to *avoid* the *law* 法網をくぐるために言葉使いを巧みにした. ¶*break* the *law* 法律を破る ‖ be accused of *breaking* the *laws* 違法のかどで訴えられる. ¶He found a number of ways of *circumventing* the *law*. 彼は法網をくぐる幾多の手段を案出した. ¶*codify* the *laws* 法律を編成する. ¶*declare* martial *law* 戒厳令を布く. ¶*defy* the *law* 法律にそむく. ¶*discover, prove,* and *apply* the *laws* 法則を発見し, 証明しかつ応用する. ¶*disregard* the *laws* of humanity in their treatment of prisoners 人道を無視して囚人を取扱う. ¶The old *law* has been *done away with*. 古い法律が廃された. ¶*enact* and *administer* a *law* 法律を制定しこれを執行する. ¶It is the business of the police (executive part of a government) to *enforce* the *laws*. 法律を励行するのが警察(など)の本務である. 【類】inexorably *enforce* a *law*. ¶*enter* the *law* 弁護士になる. ¶Any attempt to *evade* the *law* will be followed by the confiscation of the objects. 法網をくぐらんとするものはすべてその物件を没収される. ¶*evade* and *dodge laws* 法網をくぐる. ¶*execute laws* 法律を執行する. ¶scientists are trying to *find out* the *law* which regulates ... 科学者は...を支配する法則を発見しようと試みている. ¶*fix* immediate *laws* 緊急法律を定める. ¶*flout* (=*mock*) *law* 法律をばかにする. ¶Social evolution *follows* its own *laws* in its own fashion. 社会進化は特有の様式で特有の法則に従がうものである. ¶*formulate* (=*frame*) a *law* 法則を作る. ¶we *have* a *law* under which people are required to ... 一般人に...することを要求する法律がある ‖ I will *have* the *law* on you. 君を訴える. ¶*infringe* the *law* of literary copyright 著作権を侵害する. ¶*institute* a *law* 法律を制定する. ¶The judicial part of a government *interprets* the *laws*. 政府の司法部が法律の解釈をする. ¶Street noises have become such maddening minor worries to Londoners of late years that the *law* has been *invoked*. 近来市内の騒音がロンドン人の物狂わしい小さな悩みとなったのでこれを取締る法律が要望されて来た. ¶*keep* the *law* 法律を守る. ¶*lay down* a new *law* 新法律を定める. ¶*let* the *law* vigorously *enforced* on its violators 法律違反者を厳格に法律で処分する. ¶*maintain law* and order 安寧秩序を維持する. ¶*make laws* against ... ...を禁じる法律を作る. 【類】*make* a *law* expelling the Jews from Spain ‖ It was *made law*. それは法律になった. 【類】They *made* a *law* that all the people should be taxed. / *make* it a *law* to ... ¶*obey* the *law* of the country 国法を遵守する. ¶*observe* the *law* to the letter 法を厳守する. ¶*Laws* are sometimes *outlived* rather than *repealed*. 法律は廃止されたというよりはむしろ有名無実になることがある. ¶*override* the *law* of the land 国法を犯す. ¶*pass* a *law* against ... ...禁止の法律を制定する ‖ The *law* was *passed* by a two-thirds vote. その法案は三分の二の多数によって国会を通過した. 【類】they have *passed* a *law* in France making it legal to ... / The *law* has recently been *passed* in the Diet. ¶Lincoln was very poor when he began to *practice law*. リンカーンが弁護士を開業したときは非常に貧乏だった. ¶Martial *law* has been *proclaimed* in Petrograd and [its] vicinity. ペトログラード並にその付近に戒厳令が布かれた. ¶*promulgate* stringent *laws* against ... ...を禁じる厳重な法律を公布する. ¶*relax* or *suspend* the *law* against ... ...を禁じる法律を緩和または停止する. ¶*shape* the *law* to conform to ... ...に準じて法律を作る. ¶*square* the *law* with practice 法を実際と一致させる. ¶*study* the *law* 法律を研究する. ¶*take* the *law* into his own hands 法を勝手に曲げる, 私刑を加える. ¶*transgress* the *law* of morality 道徳のおきてを犯す. ¶*uphold* the *law* 法律を守る. ¶*violate* the *law* of the land 国法を犯す. ¶*wrest* the *law* to suit oneself 勝手に法を曲げる.

V² the *law allows* a person to ... 法律は人が...するのを許している. ¶the *law forbids* a person to ... 法律は人が...するを禁じている. ¶English *law prohibits* a man from ... ing ... 英国の法律では人が...するのを禁じている. ¶The *law provides* that a parent should send his child to school. 法律は親がその子を通学させなければならないことを規定する. ¶the *law requires* ... to ... ...することは法の命じるところである. ¶the *law steps in* to protect the interests of ... ...の利権保護のために法律が干渉する.

Q They cannot be accepted as *binding laws*. それは拘束力のある法律としては承認できない. ¶*civil law* 民法. ¶under the *common law* 慣習法によって ‖ robbery as understood at *common law* 慣習的に認められている夜盗行為. ¶the fundamental principles of *criminal law* 刑法の根本原則. ¶follow *definite laws* 一定の法則に従う. ¶break a *divine law* 神のおきてを破る. ¶*elaborate laws* were framed for (against) ... ...のために(を禁じる)念の入った法律が作られた. ¶the *eternal laws* of the moral world 道徳界永久のおきて. ¶under *existing law* 現行法により. ¶*Federal laws* 《米》 連邦法. ¶according to a *German law* ドイツの法律では. ¶it is a *great law* of nature that ... ...は自然の大法則である. ¶Order is *Heaven's first law*. 秩序は第一の天則である. ¶*immovable laws* of nature 不易の自然律. ¶lay down *immutable laws* 鉄則を作る. ¶It is an *inevitable law* of nature. それは避けられない自然の法則だ. ¶The *inexorable law* of change which rules our social life われわれの社会生活を規定する変化という鉄則. ¶There is no one *inflexible law* that can be laid down as a guide for them all. ただ一箇条で彼ら全体の手引となるような不動のおきてはない. ¶an *inviolable law* 不可侵の法律. ¶all foreigners placed under *Japanese law* 日本の法律の支配下にある全外国人. ¶the *Judaic Law* ユダヤ法. ¶*local laws* 地方法規. ¶put the city under the *martial law* その市に戒厳令を布く ‖ The city is now under *martial law*. 同市には目下戒厳令が布かれている. ¶*milder laws* 一層寛大な法律. ¶violate the *moral law* 道徳のおきてを犯す. ¶transgress a great *natural law* 自然の大法則を犯す ‖ the workings of *natural law* 自然法則の発動. ¶transgress *Nature's laws* 自然の法則を犯す. ¶in accordance with the *Naval Law* enacted in 1910 一九一〇年に制定された海軍法によって. ¶an *obnoxious law* 不都合な法律. ¶*Penal law*, like every other social phenomenon, is evolved according to the momentary exigencies of society. 刑法は他のあらゆる社会的現象と同じく社会の時々刻々の変化に準じて進展するのである. ¶a *proposed law* 法案. ¶*rudimentary* (=*elementary*) *law* of health 基本的健康法則. ¶make *severe laws* against prostitution 売春禁止の厳法を設ける. ¶the *silent laws* of usage 慣用という沈黙の法(語法など). ¶The constitution is the *sovereign law* in the administration of the state 憲法は国政の最高法律である. ¶*special laws* 特別法. ¶The Constitution is the *supreme law* of the land. 憲法は一国の最高法律である. ¶the *unalterable law* that ... ...という千古不易の法則. ¶a *universal law* 世界の慣行. ¶by some *unwritten law* or unpublished code of manners ある不文律すなわち暗黙の間に守られる慣例によって. ¶*wise laws* 賢明なおきて. ¶a *written law* 成文律.

Q² the *Anti-closed Shop Law* クローズド・ショップ禁止法. ¶the *Anti-Subversives Law* 破壊防止法. ¶the *antitrust laws* 独占禁止法. ¶*canon law* 教会法. ¶*city laws* 都市法. ¶the *Employment Security Law* 職業安定法. ¶*equity law* 衡平法(慣習法に対し). ¶the *espionage law* スパイ取締法. ¶the Chinese *exclusion laws* 中国人排除法. ¶the *Family Registration Law* 戸籍法. ¶*Game laws* protect wild life. 狩猟法によって野鳥を保護する. ¶the *Government Service Payroll Law* 官吏俸給令. ¶the *Habeas Corpus Law* 人身保護法. ¶ease the *immigration laws* 移民法を緩和する. ¶the *Imperial House Law* 皇室典範. ¶the abolition of the *iron laws* of wages 賃金の鉄則の廃止. ¶the *Labor Standard Law* 労働基準法. ¶*land laws* 土地に関する諸法 ‖ the Alien *Land Law* 外国人土地

法. ¶***lynch*** *law*=mob law 私刑. ¶enact a ***manhood suffrage*** *law* 普通選挙法を制定する. ¶the ***Maxwell distribution*** *law* 《理》マックスウエル式配分法. ¶the ***National Public Service*** *Law* 国家公務員法. ¶under the new ***naturalization*** *law* 新帰化法によって. ¶the ***Occupational Disease*** *Law* 職業病法. ¶an ***omnibus*** *law* 数個の法律を一つに盛り込んだ法律. ¶a ***peace preservation*** *law* 治安維持法. ¶terminate the present ***press*** and ***security*** *laws* 現行新聞法及び保安法を停止する. ¶the ***Public Service*** *Law* 公務員法. ¶the ***Resources Investigation*** *Law* 資源調査法. ¶observe ***speed*** *law* 速度制限規則を守る. 【類】The motorist was guilty of breaking the ***speed*** *laws*. ¶in some ***State*** *laws* it is enacted that ... ある州の法律には…と規定してある. ¶there is a ***statute*** *law* requiring a company to ... 会社は…すべきことを規定した成文律がある. ¶the ***Subversive Activities Prevention*** *Law* 破壊活動防止法. ¶under Japanese ***tariff*** *laws* 日本関税法により. ¶***traffic*** *laws* 交通規則. ¶***war-time*** *laws* 戦時法.

P The moral is ***above*** the civil *law*. 道徳は法律の上に位する. ¶The highest persons in the State are ***above*** and ***outside*** the *law*. 国家最高の貴顕は法律を超越し法律の圏外におかれる. ¶They sentenced him to death ***according to*** the *law* at that time. 当時の法律によって彼を死刑に処した. ¶it is ***against*** the *law* to ... …することは法律違反である ‖ It is ***against*** the *laws* which regulate the physical universe. それは物理的な宇宙を規定する法則に反する. 【類】There is a *law* ***against*** spitting in the streetcar. ¶an attorney ***at*** *law* 《米》弁護士(訴訟事務を取扱う). ¶a counselor [***at*** *law*] 《米》法廷弁護士 ‖ a suit ***at*** *law*=a lawsuit 訴訟事件 ‖ an offense ***at*** *law* 法律上の罪(人) ‖ ***At*** *law*, the members of a partnership are always treated as individuals. 法律では合名会社の役員は常に個人として取扱われる. ‖ curious cases and amusing actions ***at*** *law* 変った訴訟事件と珍裁判ざた ‖ entitled ***at*** *law* or in equity (=law of equity) to ... …法律上または衡平法では…の権利がある. ¶the absolute equality of all creeds ***before*** the *law* in Japan 日本における法律上あらゆる信教の絶対平等. 【類】We are equal ***before*** the *law*. ¶we are prohibited ***by*** *law* from ... ing ... われわれは法律で…するのを禁じられている ‖ regulated ***by*** *law* 法律で規定された ‖ stipulated (=provided) ***by*** *law* [条項など]規約された. 【類】The Turks are now compelled ***by*** *law* to use the Roman alphabet / openly ***by*** *law* / it is required ***by*** *law* to ... / ***By*** *law* the Bodleian Library is entitled to a copy of every copyright book printed in the United Kingdom. ¶There is no provision ***in*** the *law* on this point. この点に関しては何ら法律上の規定がない. 【類】***in*** a *law* passed in 1908 / A day ***in*** *law* includes the whole twenty-four hours. ‖ a sister-***in***-*law* 義妹. ¶infraction ***of*** the *law* 法律違犯 ‖ a more rigid enforcement ***of*** the *laws* governing the sale of poisons 毒薬販売取締法の一層厳重な励行 ‖ The machinery ***of*** the *law* was set in motion. 法律の機関が活動を開始した. ‖ He was at last caught in the meshes ***of*** the *law*. 彼はとうとう法網にかかった. ‖ The aid ***of*** the *law* is invoked to enforce fulfilment. 強制的決行のために法律の助けを要望している. ‖ The letter ***of*** *law* should harmonize with the spirit of the law. 法律の条文は法律の精神と一致すべきだ. ¶try to make money ***outside*** the *law* 非合法に金もうけをする. ¶without recourse ***to*** *law* 法律に訴えないで. ¶***through*** the *law* of association of ideas 連想の法則によって. ¶equal justice ***under*** *law* 法律上の公正. 【類】be authorised to act ***under*** the *law* / he is entitled ***under*** the *laws* of Japan to ... / ***under*** existing Japanese *law*. ¶***within*** the *law* 法律の認める範囲内で.

P^2 *law* ***against*** professing Christianity キリスト教信仰の禁令. 【類】*Laws* ***against*** contraception (避妊) have existed in America since the seventies (一八七〇年代) and in France since 1920. /The *law* ***against*** opium-smoking is in force in Formosa. / There is a *law* ***against*** black-marketeering (やみ取引禁止の). / There is a *law* ***against*** truancy (無断欠席). ¶Work is Heaven's *law* ***for*** all men. 働くことはあらゆる人間の守るべき神のおきてである. ‖ a *law* ***for*** life and conduct 生活と行為のおきて. ¶the *law* ***of*** succession 相続法 ‖ the *law* ***of*** demand and supply 需要供給の法則 ‖ *laws* ***of*** motions 〘理〙運動の三法 ‖ the *law* ***of*** nations 国際法 ‖ *laws* ***of*** nature 自然の法則 ‖ the *law* ***of*** gravity 引力の法則 ‖ the *laws* ***of*** motion [ニュートンの]運動の三法則 ‖ violations of the *laws* ***of*** war 戦事法の違反. ¶The *laws* ***on*** Sunday observance are based on the moral principles of early Colonial times when even travel was forbidden. 日曜(安息日)遵守についての諸法令は旅行さえ禁じた初期の植民時代の道徳的原理にもとずいている. ¶In these matters every man must be a *law* ***unto*** himself. これらのことについてはそれぞれ自分の判断で行かなければならない. 【類】Shelley's genius, being purely lyrical, was often a *law* ***unto*** itself (往々一般の標準では批判ができない). / Italy in 1850 was a land of many petty states, each more or less a *law* ***unto*** itself (それぞれ独自性のある). ¶go to *law* ***with*** a person ある人を訴える. ¶The police *law* ***with regard to*** ... is very strict. …に関する警察の取締は厳格だ.

O The Bill has become a *law*. その議案は法律になった.

law-abiding, *a*. 法に忠実な.

M ***more*** (***less***) *law-abiding* さらに法に(不)忠実な.

lawbreaking, *n*. 違法.

Q ***international*** *lawbreaking* 国際法違反.

lawful, *a*. 適法の.

P It is *lawful* ***for*** him to ... 彼が…するのは適法行為である.

lawlessness, *n*. 無法.

Q a struggle between ***organized*** *lawlessness* and forces of order 組織立った不法行為と秩序ある勢力との争闘.

lawn, *n*. 芝生.

V ***mow*** the *lawn* 芝を刈る.

Q a ***dewy*** *lawn* 露を置いた芝生. ¶a ***grassy*** *lawn* 芝地. ¶a ***sloping*** *lawn* 傾斜をなす芝生. ¶a ***verdant*** *lawns* 緑の芝生.

Q^2 a ***tennis*** (***croquet***) *lawn* テニス(クローケー)場.

P lie ***on*** the *lawn* 芝生に横たわる. ¶walk ***over*** a *lawn* 芝生を歩く.

lawsuit, *n*. 訴訟.

V ***bring*** a *lawsuit* against him for ... …のために彼を相手取って訴訟を起す. ¶***enter*** (=***bring in***) a *lawsuit* against ... …に対して訴訟を起す. ¶***face*** a *lawsuit* 訴えられる. ¶***gain*** a *lawsuit* 訴訟に勝つ. ¶he ***had*** a *lawsuit* on hand with ... about ... 彼は…のことで…を相手取って訴訟を起していた. ¶***lose*** a *lawsuit* 訴訟に負ける. ¶***win*** a *lawsuit* 訴訟に勝つ.

V^2 Then ***followed*** a *lawsuit*, which consumed many months and a good deal of money. それから何カ月もかかり金も相当食う訴訟事件が始まった.

Q a ***tedious*** *lawsuit* 長びいてあきあきする訴訟.

P the parties ***in*** a *lawsuit* 訴訟の当事者. ¶pay the cost ***of*** the *lawsuit* その訴訟費用を支払う.

P^2 a *lawsuit* ***with*** ... …との訴訟.

lawyer, *n*. 法律家, 弁護士.

V ***employ*** (=***hire***) a *lawyer* 弁護士を雇う. ¶His parents intend to ***make*** a *lawyer* of him. 両親は彼を弁護士にしようとしている.

Q engage a very ***able*** *lawyer* すこぶる有能な弁護士を頼む. ¶a ***brilliant*** *lawyer* りっぱな弁護士. ¶Some of the most ***eminent*** *lawyers* will try the case. 一流法律家が何人かこの事件審理に当るだろう. ¶a ***pettifogging*** *lawyer* 三百代言. ¶a ***practicing*** *lawyer* 開業弁護士. ¶He is known as a ***successful*** *lawyer*. あの弁護士ははやるという評判だ.

Q^2 ***brother*** *lawyers* 兄弟弁護士. ¶a ***canon*** *lawyer* 教会法学者. ¶a ***crown*** *lawyer* 英国皇室付弁護士; 刑事弁護士. ¶a ***labor*** *lawyer* 労働弁護士. ¶a ***one-time*** *lawyer* 元弁護士. ¶It is enough to puzzle a ***Philadelphia*** *lawyer*. それはどんな知恵者でも困る難題だ. ¶a ***shyster*** *lawyer* 《米》三百代言. ¶a ***trial*** *lawyer* 法廷弁護士.

P He practices ***as*** a *lawyer*. 彼は弁護士をやっている. ‖ set up ***as*** a *lawyer* 弁護士になる.

P^2 He is a *lawyer* ***by*** profession. 彼の職業は弁護士. ¶Who is to act as *lawyer* ***for*** him? だれがあの人の弁護士になるのです.

lax, *a*. しまりのない.

P He is *lax* ***in*** morals. 彼は道徳堅固でない. ‖ be *lax* ***in*** discipline (morals) 志気(道徳)がたるんでいる ‖ men who are inclined to be *lax* ***in*** such things こうしたことに無精な人々.

laxative, *n*. 下剤.

Q phenolphthalein, a supposedly ***mild*** and ***inoffensive*** *laxative* 緩慢で副作用のないと仮定されている下剤フェノルフタレン.

laxity, *n*. 弛緩(しかん), 放縦.

Q ***moral*** *laxity* 道徳の弛緩. ¶the ***prevailing*** *laxity* of morals in the matter of ... …についての一般の放縦.

¶*sexual laxity* 性的放縦.

Q² *police laxity* in connection with gambling and vice と博や犯罪に対する警察の手抜かり.

P² *laxity **in*** personal cleanliness 身体の清潔に関する不注意. ¶*laxity **of*** supervision 監督の不行届 ‖ a *laxity **of*** moral fiber 道徳心のゆるみ.

lay, *v.* 置く, 横たえる, 配置する; 課する; 横たわる [lie の誤「用」; [卵を]生む.

M a book of continuous and enthralling charm, which, once opened, it is hard to *lay **aside*** 一度巻を開くと容易にやめられないほど魅力のある本 ‖ *lay* it ***aside*** with disappointment 失望してそれを放棄する ‖ He is *laid **aside*** by illness. 彼は病気のために休んでいる. ¶*lay* it ***away*** in a drawer それを引出しに仕舞込む. ¶*lay* it ***bare***=uncover (=reveal) it それをむき出しにする, 暴露する. 【類】*lay **bare*** one's chest / *lay **bare*** one's secret (feelings). ¶If *laid **end to end***, they would reach around the globe. 縦に並べておくとそれは地球を一回りする長さになるだろう. ¶when *laid **low*** by typhoid fever チフスで寝ていた時に ‖ He *laid* the tree ***low***. 彼はその木を切り倒した. ¶*lay* it ***out*** for sale それを売物として陳列する ‖ *lay **out*** pictures for a magazine 雑誌のため写真をレーアウト(編集)する ‖ The pattern was *laid **out*** for the next German try for world supremacy. 世界征はのため次のドイツの計画のお膳立てができた. ‖ The hill has been *laid **out*** as a small park. その岡は小公園になった. 【類】*lay **out*** a garden for flowers / The plots are *laid **out*** in orchards. ‖ a ground tastefully *laid **out*** 体裁よく手を入れてある地面 ‖ His money is well *laid **out***. 彼の金はうまく投資してある.【類】He *laid **out*** all his gains in purchasing land. ¶The land has been *laid **open***. その土地は立木が切り払われた. ¶*lay* the matter ***squarely*** before him その事件を彼に正直に打明ける. ¶*lay* it ***waste*** それを荒廃させる.

M² *lay **down*** a volume 本を下におく. ¶*lay **down*** arms ほこを収める. 【類】Will he *lay **down*** his power (権力)? / *lay **down*** the pen and take up the sword / He will not *lay* it ***down*** until it is finished. / *lay **down*** one's life for truth / *lay **down*** one's life for a great cause (大義) ‖ *lay **down*** gas pipes ガスパイプを敷く. 【類】*lay **down** (**up**)* a railway ‖ *lay **down*** a plant for ... ...のために工場を建設する. 【類】*lay **down*** a *plant* of sufficient capacity / *lay **down*** a solid foundation for the construction of a new Japan ‖ *lay **down*** a decision 決意を固める ‖ it is *laid **down*** in the law that ... ...と法律に規定されている ‖ *lay **down*** the law that ...という法則を立てる. 【類】*lay **down*** a general *policy* (大綱) / no rule can be *laid **down*** / act as *laid **down*** in Rule 217 / the principles (原則) therein *laid **down*** / This is one of those matters on which no general rule can safely be *laid **down***. / as *laid **down*** in the foregoing paragraph ‖ She endeavored to *lay **down*** (=establish) for herself a future course of action. 彼女は自分で将来行く道を定めた. ‖ *lay **down*** the land in grass 土地に芝生を植える. 【類】The land was *laid **down*** with red and white / be sentenced to punishments *laid **down*** by law ‖ Torpedoes have been *laid **down***. 水雷が敷設された. ¶*lay **in*** money for future use 将来の必要のため金をためる. 【類】*lay **in*** a stock for the winter. ¶*lay **off*** employes during a slack period 不況の期間雇人を一時解雇する. 【類】I was *laid **off*** last week because we haven't enough work for all the men. / *lay **off*** most hands in their employ ‖ One of the leading works in the district has been *laid **off*** by a strike. その地域のある一流工場はストのため閉鎖した. ¶The telephone is *laid **on***. 電話がしかれている. 【類】In modern life, water and gas are *laid **on***. ‖ The color is thickly *laid **on***. 色が濃く塗られている. ‖ Well-bred cattle *lay **on*** flesh quick. 飼料のよい牛はすぐ太る. ‖ *lay **on*** a new tax 新税を課す. ¶I have been *laid **up*** with the cold. かぜで床についていた. ‖ *lay **up*** a store of conveniences against ... ...に備えて有用なものをたくわえる. 【類】*lay **up*** money against a rainy day (他日ことある場合に備えて) / *lay **up*** money enough to send for mother / food *laid **up*** against a day of want (困ったとき) ‖ a lot of arable land *laid **up*** in ridges うねを作ってある一耕地 ‖ *lay* it ***up*** in one's heart 心に留めておく ‖ There were forty acres of grass *laid **up*** for hay. 四十エーカー(約十八町歩)の牧草地は干草に当ててあった. ‖ I have been *laid **up*** with a bad cold for three weeks. 私はひどいかぜのため三週間寝ていました.

P *lay **about*** a person with a whip むちで人を手当り次第に打つ. ¶A bridge is *laid **across*** the river. その川に橋がかけてある. ¶*Lay* these pots ***along*** the veranda. これらのはちを縁側に並べてお置き. ¶*lay* the blame ***at*** the doors of ... その罪を...にきせる ‖ He *lays* this misfortune ***at*** my door. 彼はこの不幸を私のせいにした. 【類】The failure will be *laid **at*** your door. ¶The book was first *laid **before*** European readers. その本は最初ヨーロッパで出版された. ‖ The bill has been *laid **before*** the House of Commons. その議案が下院に提出された. 【類】*lay* the case ***before*** the State Department / *lay* it ***before*** the next meeting of ... ¶we *lay **behind*** most countries in the world in ... われわれは...では世界の大抵の国に遅れている ‖ He had heard that you were *laid **by*** the heels. 君がつかまったと言うことは彼は知っていたよ. ¶His wife *laid* the table ***for*** the evening meal. 彼の妻は夕食の支度をした. ¶a chair *laid **in*** the way 邪魔になるいす ‖ he was *laid **in*** his tomb at ... 彼は...の墓に埋葬された. ¶The earthquake and fire *laid **in*** ruins the nation's capital and its most important seaport. 地震と火災とが首都と最重要港とを崩壊した. ‖ It was *laid **in*** (=reduced to) ashes. それは灰じんに帰した. ¶This maxim deserves to be *laid **on*** heart. この金言は心に銘記するに足る. ‖ *lay* him ***on*** his bed 彼をベットに寝かせる ‖ *Lay* it ***on*** the table. それをテーブルの上におけ. 【類】If you *lay* a finger (指一本でも指そうものなら) ***on*** Miss ... I'll kill you. ‖ *lay* one's hands ***on*** ... ...に手をつける(着手する) ‖ *lay* a person ***on*** the lips キッスする ‖ *lay* it ***out of*** account それを採算外におく. ¶These are words of encouragement that may well be *laid **to*** heart. これら激励の言葉は十分銘記する値打がある. 【類】a word worth *laying **to*** heart ‖ He has been *laid **to*** rest at the cemetery. 彼はその墓地に葬られた. ‖ *lay* it ***to*** the account of ... それを...の勘定につける ‖ be *laid **to*** the door of ... 責任を...に帰する. ¶He seems to have *laid* the libraries and museums in all the four corners of the earth ***under*** contribution. 彼は世界中の図書館と博物館で材料をあさったらしく思われる. ‖ I *laid* myself ***under*** obligation to him for ... 私は...に対し彼の恩義に預った. ‖ *lay* it ***under*** contribution to one's own benefit 自家薬ろう中のものとする. ¶I *laid* myself ***upon*** the bed. 私は寝床に横になった. ‖ the injunction *laid **upon*** ... ...に与えた指令. ¶Most streets are paved with wood or stones, or *laid **with*** asphalt. 大抵の通りは木や石が敷いてあるかまたはアスファルトで舗装されている.

layer, *n.* 層; 敷くもの(人); [卵を産む]めんどり; れんが工; 敷設船.

Q in ***alternate*** *layer* 交互の層を成して. ¶an ***impervious*** *layer* of rock 水の浸透しない層. ¶the ***middle*** *layers* of society 社会の中間層. ¶a ***phenomenal*** *layer* すばらしく卵を産むめんどり. ¶All soft fruits such as strawberries should be spread in ***single*** *layers* on shallow dishes, otherwise the under fruit will not keep firm and good. いちごのようなやわらかい果実は浅いさらに一重ねに盛らねばならない, そうしないと下になったのがやわらかくなっていたむ. ¶***thin*** *layers* 薄い層.

Q² a ***brick*** *layer* れんが工. ¶a ***mine*** *layer* 爆雷敷設船.

P separate ***in*** *layers* 層になって分離する.

layman, *n.* 俗人.

Q to the ***ordinary*** *layman* 凡俗には.

layoff, *n.* 《米》休止; 《米》[一時的の]解雇.

Q² a ***three-hour work*** *layoff* 三時間の仕事休止. ¶***war-industry*** *layoff* 戦時産業の人員整理.

layout, *n.* 配列; 設計.

V This map ***shows*** the *layout* of the plant. この地図を見ると工場の設計が分かる.

P² the *layout **of*** magazine pictures 雑誌写真の配列(レーアウト).

layover, *n.* 途中下車.

Q² We had a ***four-hour*** *layover* at Chicago. われわれはシカゴで四時間途中下車した. ¶a ***one-night*** *layover* (=stop-over) 一晩の途中下車.

laziness, *n.* 怠惰.

V ***overcome*** our *laziness* われわれの遊惰心に打ち勝つ.

lazy, *a.* 怠惰な.

M ***intolerably*** *lazy* 手のつけられないほど怠惰な.

P He is *lazy **in*** the study of English. 彼は英語の研究を怠けている.

lead, *n.* 指導; 首位(リード); 模範; 主役; 〖トランプ〗真先に出す札.

V Yale spurted madly at the finish, ***cutting down*** the *lead.* エールは最後になって懸命にぐんぐんのして先頭を切った. ¶***follow*** the British *lead* 英国の範にならう. 【類】***follow*** her *lead* in naval matters. / The *lead* thus given was quickly ***followed.*** / Covertly (=Secretly) ***follow*** the *lead* of another singer. / ***follow*** the *lead* set by ... / ***follow*** the *lead* of American in the field of mechanical invention. ¶***gain*** (***lose***) the *lead* in a game 競技でリードする(リードを奪われる). ¶Japan ***gave*** the *lead* to other Powers in ... 日本は…において率先して諸強国に範をたれた. ‖ I ***gave*** him a *lead* in setting the problem. 私は彼が後から続くようにその問題を解決する手段を講じた. ¶***have*** the *lead* in a game 競技でリードを奪う. ¶still ***hold*** the *lead* 依然首位を占めている. ¶She ***played*** *leads* in several popular pictures. 彼女は幾つかの評判の映画に主役を演じた. ¶***return*** one's *lead* 受札を出す(ダイヤが出たらダイヤを). ¶The government ***takes*** the *lead* and the people follow. 政府が先に立ち国民がこれに従う. ‖ ***take*** the *lead* in civilization (educational reform) 文明(など)の牛耳をとる. 【類】***take*** the *lead* in protesting / ***take*** the *lead* in the first three innings (最初の三イソニソグ) / easily ***take*** the *lead* among ... / The crew ***took*** the *lead* at once and held it comfortably the whole way. / He passed ... and ***took*** the *lead* for the rest of the course. / France then ***took*** the *lead* in the politics of Europe. / In the study and manufacture of perfumes Germany and France have ***taken*** the *lead* in recent times. / In woolen manufacture the United Kingdom ***takes*** the *lead,* with France second, the United States third, Germany fourth, and Austria-Hungary fifth.

Q Chicago had an ***early lead,*** but in the closing rounds Waseda was fighting hard, scoring seven runs in the last two innings. シカゴは早くからリードしていたがゲームの終りに早稲田は善戦し最終の二回で七点を獲得した. ¶hold a "***friendly lead***" [ビヤホールなどで]死んだ友だちの遺族などのために金を集める. ¶get a ***good*** (=***long***) *lead* on ... 競技で…をぐんと引き離す. ¶a ***summary lead*** 結論. ¶follow this ***wise lead*** この賢明な手本にならう.

P Harvard was ***in*** the *lead* from the first. [ボート・レースなどで]ハーヴァードは最初から先頭だった. ‖ English is far and away ***in*** the *lead* as a world-speech. 英語は世界語として断然リードしている. ¶***under*** the *lead* (=guidance, leadership, *or* direction) of ... …の指導のもとに.

P² blindly follow the *lead* ***of*** London in sanitary matters 衛生施設の問題で盲目的にロンドンの範にならう.

lead, *v.* 導く, [ダンスで相手を]リードする; 至る.

M These false ideals *lead* men ***astray*** and blind them to a sense of the real truth. これらの間違った理想は人を迷わし真理に対する感覚を失わしめるものである. 【類】The lad was *led* ***astray*** by evil companions (悪友). ¶be *led* ***away*** from danger 危険から立去らせる ‖ Officer, *lead* the prisoners ***away.*** だんな, 囚人どもを引っ立てて行って下さい. ¶*lead* them ***back*** to the right way 彼らを正道に立帰らせる. ¶*lead* up ***convincingly*** to this なるほどと思わせるようにこのことに持って行く. ¶this *led* ***eventually*** to an intimate friendship between ... and ... これが縁で結局…と…とが親密になった. ¶he was ***gradually*** *led* to believe that ... 彼は次第に…と信じるようになった. ¶*lead* ***forward*** cautiously 用心深く案内する. ¶Military expansion ***inevitably*** *leads* to military strife on an ever-widening scale. 軍備拡張は必然的にますます大規模の戦争を引起すようになる. ¶a passage *leading* ***inward*** 内部への通路. ¶one is ***naturally*** *led* to ... 自然…ということになる. ¶indulge in wild talk, which *leads* ***nowhere*** まとまりのつかない空談にふける. ¶*lead* a person ***out*** 外へつれ出す. 【類】The stable-boy wanted to *lead* ***out*** one of the housemaids to country dancing. / *lead* ***out*** a lady to a dance. ¶be *led* ***solely*** by one's love of truth 全く真理への愛によって導かれる. ¶Its study does not ***visibly*** *lead* either to fame or fortune. その研究は名声や富をもたらすことがはっきりしたものでない. ¶***Where*** does that road *lead?* あれはどこへ行く道か.

M² *lead* ***off*** a dance 先に立ってダンスを始める ‖ *lead* ***off*** the batting order 〖野球〗先頭打者になる. 【類】He *led* ***off*** with his companion in a sort of quick-step. ¶He was *led* ***in.*** 彼は中に案内された. ¶I've *led* her ***on*** to tell her secret. 私は彼女に秘密をしゃべらせるように持ちかけた.

P The general *led* the army ***against*** the city. 将軍は軍を率いてその市を攻めた. ¶*lead* one ***by*** the hand 人の手を取って導く ‖ Intelligent people cannot be *led* ***by*** the nose. 頭のある人々を勝手に引回すことはできない. ‖ the revolt *led* ***by*** ... …の率いる暴動 ‖ The boat (=crew) *led* ***by*** two lengths. そのボートは二艇身リードした. ¶a railway *leading* ***from*** ... ***to*** ... …から…に通じる鉄道. ¶He *led* ***in*** all his classes during his college career. 彼は大学在学中いつもクラスの首席を占めた. ‖ America *leads* ***in*** tooth carpentry (=dentistry). 歯科では米国が第一. 【類】*lead* ***in*** oil (coal) production. ¶a large gate *leading* ***into*** the court 中庭に通じる大きな門 ‖ This *led* him ***into*** error. このために彼は間違いをやった. ‖ *lead* them ***into*** the right path 彼らを善導する ‖ *lead* the youngman ***into*** a better way その青年を改心させる ‖ He has been *led* ***into*** the wrong course by a friend. 彼は友人のために邪道にはいった. ‖ *lead* a person ***into*** the house 人を家の中に案内する ‖ a course which can only *lead* one ***into*** trouble 人を踏み誤らせるに過ぎない生き方 ‖ *lead* the United States ***into*** entanglements in the Far East 合衆国を極東の紛争に巻込む. ¶He *led* us ***over*** the factory compound. 彼はわれわれを工場のあちこちに案内した. ¶The way *leads* ***through*** fields and hamlets. 道は野や部落の中を通る. ¶The wording is likely to *lead* ***to*** ambiguity. その語句は不明確の恐れがある. ‖ This *led* ***to*** an action for divorce. このために離婚の訴訟ざたになった. ‖ Poverty *led* her ***to*** prostitution. 彼女は貧にせまって肉を売るに至った. ‖ Drunkenness invariably *leads* ***to*** laxness of moral restraint in woman. 女は酒を飲むと必ず道徳の堅固がくずれる. ‖ these symptoms *led* the physician ***to*** the diagnosis of ... これらの症状からその医者は…と診断した ‖ *lead* them ***to*** action 彼らを行動に移らせる ‖ will probably *lead* ***to*** a general election. おそらくは総選挙になるだろう ‖ information *leading* ***to*** the arrest of the offender その犯人逮捕に役立つ情報. 【類】It will *lead* ***to*** a considerable simplification of formalities in this connection. / The error of a points-man *led* ***to*** a fatal railway disaster. / *lead* ***to*** much inconvenience ‖ His proceedings *led* ***to*** no result. 彼の処置は不首尾に終った. 【類】I don't think it will *lead* ***to*** a good (the best) result. / It will not *lead* ***to*** any practical result. / *lead* ***to*** serious consequences / events *leading* ***to*** the war / it *led* ***to*** the belief that ... / it *led* ***to*** the discovery that ... / the conclusion ***to*** which the arguments *lead* / *lead* ***to*** hostilities (戦乱) / *lead* ***to*** misunderstanding / will *lead* ***to*** a good result / The event *led* ***to*** the great revolution (大革命). ‖ The inquiry will *lead* ***to*** business. 照会はやがて取引きになる. 【類】This may *lead* ***to*** a good business. / The offerings are too high to *lead* ***to*** business. / be likely to *lead* ***to*** destruction (破滅) / full courses *leading* ***to*** bachelor's degree (バチェラーの学位) / *lead* ***to*** the superfluity and disappearance (発展的解消) of ... / this *leads* ***to*** the conclusion that ... / This *led* ***to*** considerable friction. (不和) / *lead* ***to*** endless confusion / This *led* ***to*** more widespread appreciation of its value and mission. / a new course *leading* ***to*** the degree of Bachelor of Science in Administrative Engineering / This road *leads* ***to*** wealth. / All paths *lead* ***to*** Rome. / Delinquent children *led* ***to*** the rupture of family ties (一家の破滅). ¶the conditions (=circumstances) which *led* ***up to*** the war 戦争を引起した情勢 ‖ the incident *leading* ***up to*** the principal event 主要事件を誘発する付随事件 ‖ the negotiations *leading* ***up to*** the convention of ... …の仮条約を締結するまでに至った談判 ‖ *lead* ***up to*** it in a strategic manner かけ引でつぼへはめ込む ‖ *lead* ***up to*** a conclusion 結論に導く ‖ He *led* ***up to*** his favorite topic. 彼は自分の得意な問題にと引張って行った. 【類】This *led* ***up to*** the arrest of the criminal. / This event *led* ***up to*** the establishment of a republic. / the sequence of events that has *led* ***up to*** ...

leader *n.* 指導者, 指揮者, 首領; 論説; 水の樋(ひ).

V ***appease*** the *leaders* of the revolt その反乱の指揮者をなだめる. ¶The paper ***devotes*** a *leader* to the matter. その新聞はその事件を論説で取扱っている. ¶the ability to ***recognize*** *leaders* when they appear 指導者が現われたときそ

れを認識する能力. ¶Who ***writes*** *leaders* for the newspaper? その新聞にはだれが論説を書いているか.

Q an ***able*** *leader* of modern thought 近代思想の有能な指導者. ¶an ***acknowledged*** *leader* 定評ある指導者. ¶a ***big industrial*** *leader* 偉大な産業指導者. ¶***blind*** *leaders* of the blind おろかな大衆の盲目的指導者. ¶a ***born*** *leader* of men 生れながら人の上に立つ者. ¶the ***commercial*** and ***industrial*** *leaders* of the nation 同国商工業界の巨頭連. ¶***distinguished*** *leaders* of opinion 知名の世論指導者. ¶***eminent*** *leaders* of religious thought 宗教界の名士. ¶***ethical*** *leaders* 道徳上の指導者. ¶a ***gallant*** and ***inspiring*** *leader* 勇壮で人を感激させる指導者. ¶pay homage to a ***great*** *leader* 大指導者に敬意を払う. ¶the ***intellectual*** *leaders* of the coming age 次の時代の知的指導者. ¶an ***intrepid*** *leader* 大胆な指導者. ¶the erstwhile ***Japanese military*** *leaders* 以前の日本軍部指導者連. ¶***legislative*** *leaders* 立法府の巨頭. ¶a ***natural*** *leader* of men 人の上に立つように生れついた者. ¶the ***potential*** *leaders* of the country 将来国の指導者たるべき人々. ¶one of the ***prominent*** *leaders* of thought of the day 現代思想の卓越した指導者の一人. ¶***public*** *leaders* 公けの指導者たち. ¶***regional*** *leaders* 土地の有力者たち. ¶***revolutionary*** *leaders* 革命の首領. ¶gradually subdue the ***rival rebellious*** *leaders* 反乱の指揮者を徐々に鎮圧する. ¶***secondary*** *leaders* 少壮指導者たち. ¶the ***trusted*** *leader* of a party 信任の厚い政党の首領. ¶The Japanese are the ***unquestioned*** *leaders* of the Asiatic races. 日本人は確かにアジア人種の指導者である. ¶***virtuous, learned, able,*** fully ***reliable*** *leaders* of men 有徳で学問があり有能で十分に信頼のできる民衆の指導者. ¶a ***vocational*** *leader* 求職指導員.

Q[2] the ***Administration*** *leaders* in Congress 米議会の行政指導者たち(政府側の幹部). ¶a ***band*** *leader* 楽隊指揮者, バンドリーダー. ¶a ***cheer*** *leader* 応援団長. ¶a ***business*** *leader* 一流実業家. ¶a ***choir*** *leader* 教会の合唱隊の指揮者. ¶ministers and other ***church*** *leaders* 牧師たち及び他の教会長老たち. ¶underground ***Communist*** *leaders* 地下にもぐった共産党指導者連. ¶***Congress*** *leaders* 米議会指導者たち. ¶the ***Fascist*** *leaders* of Italy and Germany イタリア及びドイツのフアッショ指導者たち. ¶a ***fashion*** *leader* 流行を作る人. ¶the ***floor*** *leader* 院内総務. ¶a ***forum*** *leader* 公開討論会の司会者. ¶a ***gang*** *leader* [土工など]組長. ¶***Government*** *leaders* 政府の有力閣僚など. ¶the ***House*** *leader* 院内(米では下院)総務. ¶***industry*** *leaders* 一流産業人たち. ¶a ***labor*** *leader* 労組幹部員. ¶***left-of-center*** *leaders* 左翼の指導者たち. ¶the ***majority*** (***minority***) ***floor*** *leader* 多(少)数党院内総務. ¶a ***merchandising*** *leader* 販売部長. ¶an ***opposition*** *leader* 《英》野党々首; 野党指導者. ¶an ***orchestra*** *leader* 演奏会指揮者. ¶***party*** *leaders* 党首脳連. ¶a ***rain*** *leader* たてどい. ¶a ***purged Red*** *leader* 追放された赤の指導者. ¶a ***ring*** *leader* 暴力団の団長. ¶***Senate*** (***House***) ***minority*** *leaders* 米上(下)院少数党首脳連. ¶an eminent ***Socialist*** *leader* 著名な社会党指導者. ¶***society*** *leaders* 社交界を牛耳る人たち. ¶a ***Strike*** *leader* スト指導者. ¶the ***Soviet*** *leaders* and their adherents ソ連指導者とその追随者. ¶a ***suffrage*** *leader* 参政権運動の指導者. ¶***top-ranking war*** *leaders* 最高戦争指導者. ¶***union*** *leaders* 労組幹部連. ¶a ***war*** *leader* 戦争指導者. ¶a ***wartime*** *leader* 戦時指導者. ¶prominent ***woman suffrage*** *leaders* 著名な女子参政権指導者たち.

P He is widely recognized ***as*** a *leader* in research and investigation. 彼は調査・研究の率先者として広く知られている. 【類】be respected ***as*** a spiritual *leader*.

P[2] a *leader* ***among*** men 人の上に立つ人. ¶*leaders* ***in*** the world's thought, action, and culture 世界の思想・行為・文化の指導者 ‖ a *leader* ***in*** the movement to ... ...しようとする運動の首領. ¶a *leader* ***of*** fashion 流行のさきがけをする人. 【類】a *leader* ***of*** opinion / *leaders* ***of*** industry, commerce, and labor / *leaders* ***of*** medical thought in this country and abroad / *leaders* ***of*** modern thought ‖ "Like it or not, America is the *leader* ***of*** the free world. 好むと好まざるとを問わずアメリカは自由世界の指導者だ.

leadership, *n.* 指導, 指揮, 統率.

V ***accept*** his *leadership* 彼を首領と仰ぐことを承諾する. ¶***assume*** the *leadrship* of ... ...統率の任に当る. ¶The virile teacher is expected to go beyond the confines of his school routine and ***carry*** his intellectual *leadership* into the community. その活動力盛んな教師は学校で日々の教べんを取る以外にその知的指導を一般社会にまで及ぼすことを期待されている. ¶***exercise*** *leadership*＝rule the roast 牛耳をとる. ¶***follow*** the *leadership* of ... ...の指揮に従う. ¶He ***has*** the *leadership* of the bar of the capital within his grasp. 彼は首都法曹界の牛耳をとっている. ¶***maintain*** their *leadership* as ... ...として彼らの指導を維持する. 【類】***maintain*** the *leadership* it has held for 16 years. ¶***resign*** the *leadership* of a party 党の指導者の地位を退く. ¶***show*** *leadership* in a question ある問題で腕を見せる. ¶***take*** the *leadership* in ... ...の牛耳をとる. ‖ He has consented to ***take*** the *leadership* of the meetings. 彼はその諸会合を司会することを承諾した.

Q an expedition under the ***able*** *leadership* of Prof. ... ... 教授の手腕ある統率の下にある探検隊. 【類】The association is flourishing under ***able*** *leadership*. ¶***better*** *leadership* in the business 事業界における一層有力な統率. ¶***poor*** *leadership* さえない指揮的手腕. ¶***Powerful*** *leadership* is essential. 有力な指導が是非必要だ. ¶***public*** *leadership* [社会]一般の指導権.

Q[2] The tasks are organized and carried out under ***student*** *leadership*. その仕事は組織化され学生の指導の下に遂行される. ¶the ***world*** *leadership* of the United States 米国の世界指導権.

P The Glee Club, ***under*** the *leadership* of Eric Dudley, then sang the Alma Mater. グリークラブはエリク・ダッドレイの音頭取りで母校の校歌を歌った.

P[2] his personal *leadership* ***in*** the movement その運動に対する彼自身の指導.

leading, *n.* 指導.

P Bass viol was played ***in*** the *leading* of the singing. ベース・ビオルが歌のリードとして演奏された.

leading-string, *n.* 拘束; 指導.

V ***shake off*** the *leading-strings* 拘束を脱する.

P ***in*** *leading-strings* 人の指導を受けて, 一本立ができないで. 【類】childen kept ***in*** *leading-strings* by their parents.

leaf, *n.* (**1**) 木の葉.

V ***blow off*** the *leaves* 木の葉を吹落す. ¶Many of the trees had ***dropped*** all their *leaves*. 多くの木はすっかり落葉していた. ¶An evergreen does not ***lose*** its *leaves* as other plants do. 常緑樹は他の木のように落葉しない. ¶Worms ***nibble*** the green *leaves*. 虫が青葉を食う. ¶The trees began to ***put forth*** *leaves*. 木の葉が出初めた. 【類】Every tree was ***putting forth*** its young *leaves* and rich blossoms. ¶Deciduous trees ***shed*** their *leaves* annually. 落葉樹は毎年木の葉を落す. ¶The *leaves* are ***shrivelled up*** by the heat. 木の葉が暑さでしなびた.

M[2] *Leaves* ***fall off***. 葉が落ちる. ¶The young *leaves* ***sprout*** early in spring. その若葉は早春に出る. ¶The *leaves* ***stir***. 葉が揺れる.

Q tinted ***autumnal*** *leaves* 秋の紅葉. ¶a ***brown*** *leaf* かっ色の葉. ¶rip off ***dead*** *leaves* 枯葉をつみとる. ¶***deciduous*** *leaves* 落葉樹の葉. ¶a ***dry*** *leaf* 枯葉. ¶Spinach is a ***green*** *leaf*. ほうれん草は緑葉である. ¶put forth ***new*** *leaves* 若葉を出す. ¶***quivering*** *leaves* in a cold wintry wind 寒い冬の風に震える木の葉. ¶a ***sear***[***ed***] (＝***dried up***) *leaf* 枯葉. 【類】***sear*** (＝***sere***) *leaves* of autumn. ¶***shiny*** *leaves* 陽光を受けて輝く木の葉. ¶***Shivering*** *leaves* of "quivering aspen" trees made dancing shadows over us. 震えるポプラの葉がわれわれに踊る影を投げかけた. ¶Sparrows are fond of eating the ***tender*** *leaves* of early plants. 雀は若草の軟かい葉が好きだ. ¶the ***truncate*** *leaf* of the tulip チューリップの截(せつ)形葉. ¶***yellow*** *leaves* 黄葉. ¶***young*** *leaves* 若葉.

Q[2] rinse the ***tea*** *leaves* out of a tea-pot 茶の出がらしをきうすからゆすぎとる. ¶a ***fern*** *leaf* しだの葉. ¶the ***fig*** *leaf* いちじくの葉. ¶a ***maple*** *leaf* かえでの葉. ¶an ***oak*** *leaf* かしの木の葉.

P London ***in*** *leaf* 青葉のロンドン ‖ The trees are ***in*** *leaf*. 木は青葉になった. ¶spring ***into*** *leaf* 葉を出す.

P[2] *leaves* ***from*** trees 木から取った(落ちた)葉. ¶the *leaf* ***of*** an oak tree かしの木の葉.

(**2**) [本などの紙の]一枚.

V ***borrow*** a *leaf* from its rivals 競争者の知恵を借りる. ¶***detach*** a *leaf* from a book 本から一枚抜取る. ¶***double over*** a *leaf* to mark the page そのページの目印に紙を折返す. ¶***rumple*** the *leaves* 本の紙をしわにする. ¶***take*** a *leaf* out of one's book 人を見習う. ¶*tear* a few *leaves* of a book 本の数葉を破り取る. 【類】A *leaf* has been ***torn out.*** ¶***turn*** a new *leaf* 本心に立返る. 【類】I am going to ***turn*** a new *leaf* and never drink sake again. ‖ ***turn*** *leaves* to chapter five ページをめくって第五章をあける. 【類】on ***turning*** the *leaves* of the telephone book. ¶He sat down to read at the page where he had ***turned*** the *leaf* ***down.*** 彼は紙を折返しておいた所を読もうとして腰をおろした. 【類】a book with a *leaf* ***turned down.*** ¶I found that letter while I was ***turning over*** the *leaves* of a book. 私は本のページを繰っている時にその手紙を見付けた. ‖ He has ***turned over*** a new *leaf*. あの人は心を入れ替えた. ¶The book ***wants*** two *leaves*. その本は二枚(四ページ)抜けている.

Q a book with ***uncut*** *leaves* 紙の端の切ってない本.

P a delicate flower pressed ***between*** the *leaves* of a book 本の紙の間に押した優美な花. ¶It is given ***over*** *leaf*. それは裏面に書いてある.

P² a *leaf* ***from*** Japan's book of flower arrangement 日本生花の本の一ページ(生花の見本の絵の説明).

leafage, *n.* [団]木の葉.

Q The ***fresh*** *leafage* and the blue sky made me feel that the world has just been created. 新緑と青空で世界が今造られたように感じた.

leaflet, *n.* 小冊子, ビラ.

V ***fold*** *leaflets* together バラの印刷物を折りたたむ.

Q² ***advertising*** *leaflets* 広告ビラ. ¶an ***air-drop*** *leaflet* 空中散布のビラ. ¶a ***guide*** *leaflet* [博物館などの]案内ビラ. ¶a ***propaganda*** *leaflets* 宣伝ビラ.

league, *n.* 同盟.

V ***form*** a *league* 同盟を作る.

Q² an ***art purity*** *league* 清純芸術連盟. ¶a good ***citizenship*** *league* 良民連盟.

P You are ***in*** *league* with rebels. 君は謀反人と結託している.

P² the *league* ***between*** the two powers その二強国間の同盟. ¶the *League* ***of*** Nations 国際連盟.

league, *v.* 同盟する, 団結する.

P *league* ***against*** the common enemy 団結して共同の敵に当る. ¶*league* ***with*** the country その国と同盟する. 【類】*leagued* ***with*** each other.

leak, *n.* 漏口, 漏り.

V ***find*** and ***stop*** *leaks* 漏りを見つけて穴をふさぐ. ¶The roof ***has*** a bad *leak*. 屋根がひどく漏る. ¶***plug up*** a *leak* 漏る穴を詰め物してふさぐ. ¶The roof ***sprang*** a *leak*. 屋根が漏り出した. ¶***start*** (=***spring***) a *leak* 漏口ができる. ¶***stop*** *leak* 漏口をふさぐ.

V see where the *leak* ***starts*** 漏りを見つける.

Q cause a ***considerable*** *leak* 大いに水漏れを生じさせる. ¶There are ***some*** *leaks* in the roof. 屋根から雨漏りがする. ¶a ***small*** *leak* 小さな漏口.

P² a *leak* ***in*** the roof 屋根の漏り. 【類】*leak* ***in*** the gas bag.

leak, *v.* 漏る.

M The roof *leaks* ***badly.*** 屋根がひどく漏る. ¶Water *leaks* ***out.*** 水が漏れる. ‖ The news *leaked* ***out.*** その情報が漏れた. 【類】It *leaked* ***out*** to the world. / The secret *leaked* ***out.*** / but enough *leaked* ***out*** to indicate that ... ‖ *leak* ***out*** through ... ...を通して漏れる. ¶the information *leaked* ***through*** to ... その情報が...に漏れた.

P The information may have *leaked* ***in*** England. その情報は英国に漏れたかもしれない. 【類】The roof *leaked* ***in*** two or three places.

O The roof is *leaking*. 屋根から雨漏りがしている.

leakage, *n.* 漏れ.

V ***cause*** *leakage* 漏らす.

Q ***electric*** *leakage* 漏電. ¶***premature*** *leakage* 早過ぎた漏えい(発表すべき時になっていない).

P *leakage* ***in*** French War Office secrets フランス陸軍省の機密漏えい. ¶a *leakage* ***of*** military secret 軍機の漏えい事件.

leaking, *n.* 漏えい.

V ***prevent*** *leaking* 漏えいを防ぐ.

lean, *a.* 乏しい.

P *lean* ***of*** results 結果が思わしくない.

lean, *v.* もたれる, 傾く, 曲る.

M *lean* ***back*** in one's chair いすにそり返える. ¶*lean* ***backward*** 後方へそる. ¶*lean* ***forward*** 前に屈む. ¶*lean* ***out*** at the window 窓からからだを乗り出す.

P *lean* ***across*** the counter 勘定台越しに寄りかかる. ¶*lean* ***against*** the wall (door, lamp-post) 壁(など)に寄りかかる. 【類】*lean* one's arm ***against*** the railing. ¶*lean* ***in*** the direction of ... ...の方に傾く. ¶*lean* ***on*** a false hope 当てのない希望を当てにする ‖ *lean* ***on*** a broken reed 空頼みをする ‖ *lean* ***on*** a walking stick つえにすがる. 【類】*lean* ***on*** the desk / She *leaned* ***on*** her lover's arms. ‖ *lean* ***on*** (=***upon***) others for help (advice) 他人の助け(など)を期待する ‖ *lean* ***on*** one's own advice 自分だけで考えを決める(人に頼らないで). ¶It is dangerous to *lean* ***out*** [***of***] the window. [汽車など]窓の外へもたれ出るのは危険だ. ¶*lean* ***over*** the table (railing, desk) テーブル(など)にもたれる. ¶It *leans* ***to*** one side. それは一方に片寄っている. ‖ The path *leans* ***to*** the left (north). 道が左(など)に曲る. ‖ He *leans* ***to*** that opinion. 彼はその意見に傾いている. 【類】hitherto (今までのところ) I have *leaned* ***to*** the opinion that ... ¶The tree was *leaning* ***towards*** the south. その木は南の方へ傾いていた. ‖ *lean* ***toward*** communism 赤化の傾向がある. 【類】His inclination *leans* ***toward*** golf. ‖ The old man rested a while on the way, *leaning* ***upon*** his staff. その老人は途中でしばらくつえにすがって休んだ.

leaning, *n.* 傾向, 好み.

V He ***has*** a *leaning* towards music. 彼には音楽趣味がある. ¶He ***showed*** a *leaning* towards alien ways. 彼には外国好みの癖があった.

Q a political party with ***Democratic*** *leanings* 民主々義的色彩の政党.

Q² an organization with ***Communist*** *leanings* 共産主義的傾向をもつ団体. ¶have ***fascist*** *leanings* ファッショの色彩がある. ¶his extreme ***left-wing*** *leanings* 彼の極端な左傾. ¶one's ***party*** *leanings* その政党色. ¶his alleged ***pro-Communist*** *leanings* 彼のいわゆる容共主義.

P² his *leaning* ***to*** the left 彼の左傾. ¶a *leaning* ***toward*** pacifism 平和主義への傾向.

leap, *n.* 飛び, 飛躍.

V ***fetch*** a *leap* 一飛び飛ぶ. ¶The carp ***gave*** a *leap*. そのこいが一はね飛んだ. ¶He ***took*** the *leap* of 100 feet to the hard earth below. 彼は百フィートの高さから固い地上へ飛下りた. 【類】The dying Hume said he was about to ***take*** a *leap* in the dark.—C. Hodge.

Q The company took an ***enormous*** *leap* forward. その会社は一大躍進をした. ¶take a ***perilous*** *leap* 冒険的飛躍を試みる. ¶a ***sensational*** *leap* to fame 名声への目ざましい飛躍.

P ***at*** a *leap* 一足飛びに. 【類】It cannot be reached ***at*** a single *leap*. / ***at*** every *leap*. ¶Nature, according to Linnæus's famous maxim, never goes ***by*** *leaps*. リンネの有名な格言によると自然は決して躍進するものではない. ‖ ***by*** *leaps* and bounds とんとん拍子に. 【類】His progress is not steady, but goes ***by*** *leaps* and bounds. / Within the lifetime of a single generation Japan seems to have travelled ***by*** *leaps* and bounds over all the stages which Western countries have covered in centuries of slowly graduated and almost imperceptible transformation. ¶***in*** one *leap* 一飛びで. ¶Swedish industry has of late years grown ***with*** *leaps* and bounds, but the labor troubles have increased at an almost still more rapid rate. スエーデンの工業は近年急激に発展したがしかし労働争議がほとんどそれ以上の早さで増加した.

P² a *leap* ***in*** the dark 後先の考えもない行為, 暴挙.

leap, *v.* 飛ぶ.

M *leap* ***blindly*** めくら滅法に飛ぶ. ¶*leap* ***easily*** to the conclusion that ... 難なく...という結論に飛躍する. ¶He *leaped* ***suddenly*** into fame in 1872 with "..." 彼は一八七二年の「...」で一躍有名となった.

M² My heart *leaps* ***up*** when I behold the rainbow in the sky. 大空にかかっているにじを見ると僕の胸はおどる.

P The dog *leaped* ***at*** the stranger. 犬はその見知らぬ人に飛びついた. ‖ *leap* ***at*** a chance 機会に飛付く. ¶She *leaped* ***for*** joy at the good news. 彼女はその吉報を得て喜んでこおどりした. ¶*leap* ***from*** a third-storey window 三階の窓から飛降りる ‖ *leap* ***from*** one's horse 馬から飛降りる. ¶*leap* ***into*** a taxi タクシーに飛乗る ‖ *leap* ***into*** the sea (a stream) 海(など)に飛び込む ‖ His heart almost *leapt* ***into*** his mouth. びっくり仰天した. ‖ *leap* up ***into*** its master's lap [ねこが]主人のひざに飛乗る. ¶*leap* ***off*** a tower 塔から飛降りる. ¶*leap* ***on*** him 彼に飛びつく ‖ *leap* ***on*** one leg 片足で飛ぶ ‖ *leap* ***on*** a horse 馬に飛乗る. ¶*leap* ***out*** *of* a chair いすから飛立つ ‖ ***leap out of*** one's skin うれしくて飛立つ ‖ ***leap out of*** the pan into the fire 小難を逃れて大難に会う. ¶***leap over*** a fence (obstacles, ditch) へい(など)を飛越える. ¶***leap through*** a window 窓から飛出る. ¶***leap to*** fame たちまち名声を得る. ‖ He ***leaped to*** his death on the pavement below. 彼は舗道へ飛降りて死んだ. ‖ In 1930 the number ***leaped to*** 150,000,000. 一九三〇年にはその数は一億五千万にはね上った. ‖ *leap* (=jump) to a conclution 結論にとびつく, 速断する. 【類】He ***leaped to*** its conclusion. ¶salmon ***leaping up*** the falls 滝を飛上っているさけ. ¶He ***leaped upon*** me like an enraged panther. 彼は怒れるひょうのように私に食って掛った. ¶***leap with*** delight (=joy) 喜んで飛立つ.

learn, *v.* 学ぶ, 習う, 聞く.

M He is ***learning fast.*** 彼は学力が進む. ¶I am ***learning how*** to do it. 私はその仕方を習っている. ¶Men almost ***invariably learn*** by experience. 人間は大抵経験によって悟るのだ. ¶***learn later*** of the accident あとでその事件の発生を聞く. ¶***learn*** as ***much*** as possible of ... ...をできるだけよく学ぶ. ¶we ***now learn*** that ... 今度はわれわれは...であることを知る. ¶***learn out*** 見破る. ¶***learn quickly*** (=***rapidly***) 覚えが早い. ¶foreign events ***learned scrappily*** by telegraph 電報で断片的に知った海外のできごと. ¶***learn slowly*** through experience 経験を通してだんだん分かって来る. ¶He will ***soon learn*** to speak English. 彼はじき英語を話せるようになるだろう. ¶***learn*** it ***thoroughly*** それを徹底的に学ぶ.

M² ***learn*** it ***off*** それを覚えてしまう.

P he has ***learned*** much ***about*** the work of ... 彼は...の仕事を大分習った. 【類】***learn about*** the duties of a weather observer. ¶Men almost invariably ***learn by*** experience too late. 人間はほとんどすべての場合もう間に合わない時になって経験で知るものだ. ‖ ***learn by*** imitation まねで習う ‖ He has ***learned*** it ***by*** heart. 彼はそれを暗記している. ‖ ***learn by*** the mistake of others 他人の間違いを見て悟る ‖ ***learn by*** sheer memory 全く記憶力で覚える ‖ ***learn*** English ***from*** the home study course 英語を講義録で学ぶ ‖ You will ***learn*** much ***from*** association with him. 彼とつき合うと君は色々物が覚えられるだろう. ¶We seem to ***learn*** nothing ***from*** experience in this respect. われらはこの点では経験からは何も学ぶことがないようだ. ‖ we ***learn from*** an American paper that ... 米国の一新聞の報道する所によると... ‖ ***learn from*** the kindness of ... ...の好意で知る ‖ I ***learned*** English ***from*** (=***with or under***) a foreign teacher. 私は外人の教師から英語を習った. ¶It should be read by all willing to ***learn of*** the wisdom of the East. その本は東洋の学問に志す者はだれも読まなければならない. ‖ ***learn of*** the results of ... ...の結果を知る ‖ ***learn of*** (=from) Mr. ... that ... ...氏から聞いて...を知る. ¶***learn*** English ***with*** zeal 熱心に英語を学ぶ.

O I have not yet ***learned*** to like the sweet bean paste. 私はようかんはまだ好きになれない. ‖ His acquaintances ***learned*** to avoid him because of his bad character. 彼の知人たちは人物がよくないので彼を避けるようになった. 【類】***learn*** to estimate its value / You will in time ***learn*** to tell whether the antique is genuine or not. / ***learn*** to do it by doing / We have ***learned*** to esteem him for his public virtues. / The printers of the Clarendon Press have performed an exacting task with the skill and precision which we have ***learned*** to expect from them. / Babies ***learn*** to speak at two. ¶earn while you ***learn*** 習いながら金をもうける ‖ ***learn*** how to ride a horse (bicycle) 馬(など)の乗り方を覚える.

learned, *pa.* 学問のある.

P He is ***learned beyond*** his years. 彼は年の割に学問がある. ¶doctors ***learned in*** the law 法律に通じた学者など. ‖ a scholar ***learned in*** Sanskrit サンスクリット語に明るい学者. 【類】scientific men ***learned in*** zoology.

learner, *n.* 学習者.

V This difficulty tends to ***baffle learners.*** この困難な点がややもすれば学習者を悩ます. ¶the sort of difficulty which ***besets*** the ***learner*** 学習者を悩ますような困難. ¶***mislead*** the ***learner*** 学習者を誤らせる. ¶***warn learners*** not to ... ...しないように学習者を戒める.

Q ***alert learners*** 鋭い学習者. ¶***apt learners*** さとい学習者. ¶a ***bad learner*** 成績のあがらない学習者. ¶an ***enthusiastic learner*** 熱心な学習者. ¶***foreign learners*** of English 外国[英米以外]の英語学習者. ¶a ***quick*** (***slow***) ***learner*** 覚えの早(おそ)い生徒. ¶a ***would-be learner*** 学者の卵.

Q² an ***adult learner*** 成人学習者.

P a ***learner in*** the first stage 初学者.

learning, *n.* 学問, 学識.

V ***absorb*** the ***learning*** of one's time その時代の学問を吸収する. ¶***display*** one's ***learning*** 自分の学問を誇示する. 【類】***display learning*** and insight (識見). ¶***encourage learing*** 学問を奨励する. ¶***exhibit*** one's ***learning*** 自分の学識を誇示する. ¶***further*** one's ***learning*** 学問を進歩させる. ¶***like learning*** 学問を好む. ¶***parade*** one's ***learning*** 学問を鼻にかける. ¶***possess learning*** both broad and deep 広くて深い学問を有する. 【類】He ***possesses*** great ***learning.*** ¶***pursue learning*** 学問に精進する. ¶***require*** little ***learning*** 大した学問はいらない. ¶***respect learning*** 学問を尊重する. ¶***teach*** dead ***learning*** 役に立たない学問を教える. ¶***wear*** one's ***learning*** lightly 学者振らない.

Q institutions for ***advanced learning*** 高等教育の府. ¶illustrate a thesis with great ***archaeological learning*** 一つの題目を深遠な考古学の力で証明する. ¶Oxford University, one of the centres of ***British learning.*** 英国学問の一中心たるオクスフォード大学. 【類】By the death of ... ***British learning*** (学界) loses one of the most remarkable of its younger men. ¶In those days ***Chinese learning*** was held in the highest reverence. その時代には漢学が最も重んじられた. ¶***copious learning*** combined with deep humility 深い謙そんと結びついた豊かな学問. ¶a man of ***extensive learning*** 博学者. ¶institutions of ***higher learning*** 高等教育機関. ¶covering the most important branches of ***human learning*** (=knowledge) 人知の中で最も重要な部門にわたって. ¶his ***immense*** and ***multifarious learning*** 彼の深遠で多種多様な学識. ¶the ***occult learning*** of the Chaldeans カルデヤ人の神秘な学問. ¶***profound learning*** 深遠な学識. ¶learners of ***slow learning*** and quick forgetting 覚えるのがおそく忘れるのが早い学習者. ¶remain the groundwork of all ***sound learning*** あらゆる健全な学問の土台となっている. ¶***unconscious*** or "***natural***" ***learning*** 無意識すなわち自然的な修得. ¶a gentleman of ***unexcelled antiquarian learning*** 比肩する者のない考古学者. ¶***unproductive learning*** 不生産的な学問. ¶***vast learning*** 該博な学問. ¶His writings have a tincture of ***Western learning.*** 彼の書いたものには西洋学の臭味がある.

Q² the "Kultur" of ***book learning*** 書物の学問のいわゆる"文化" ‖ the limitations of ***book learning*** 読書による知識の限界. ¶***heart learning*** 心学. ¶"***memoriter learning***" 詰込み学問.

P slow ***at*** (=***in***) ***learning*** 物覚えの鈍い. ¶***in point of learning*** 学問の点では. ¶a man ***of*** considerable ***learning*** 博学な人. ¶a man ***without learning*** 無学な人.

P² ***learning by*** a passive absorption 受動的な吸収による学問. ¶the ***learning of*** linguistic facts inductively, as the child does 子供が帰納的にやるような言語事象の修得 ‖ Though he has never visited the Occident, his ***learning of*** Western matters, gathered from extensive reading, is by no means meagre. 彼は西洋へ行ったことはないが多読で得た西洋事情の知識は決して貧弱ではない.

lease, *n.* 租借, 租借期限, 賃貸借契約.

V ***extend*** the ***lease*** for ninety-nine years 租借期限を九十九カ年に延長する. ¶be ***given*** a new ***lease*** on life 命拾いする; 更に寿命が延びる. ¶***grant*** a ***lease*** of a piece of ground 土地を貸下げる. ¶***obtain*** a 99 years' ***lease*** of territory 九十九カ年の土地租借権を得る. ¶***owe*** its new ***lease*** of popularity on the German stage to ... ドイツの舞台へのりっぱなカムバックは...のお陰である. ¶I cannot see our way clear to ***renew*** your ***lease*** on the old terms. 私はもとの条件では貸地契約を書換えかねる. ¶***secure*** the ***lease*** of grounds 土地を賃借する. ¶***take*** a ***lease*** for two years from ... of the building known as No. 881 Fifth Avenue 五番街の八百八十一号の建物を...から二年間借りる ‖ ***take*** a new (=fresh) ***lease*** on (=of) life [更生する意から]再び健康体になる, [失職・破産などから]立直る. ¶His ***lease expires*** on May 31st. 彼の借地期限はこの五月三十一日に切れる.

Q² under ***government lease*** 政府との賃貸契約で.

P hold land ***by lease*** 土地を賃借している. ¶take a furnished house *on* a long *lease* 長期賃貸借契約で造作付の家を借りる. 【類】take a piece of land *on* a *lease* of ten years. ‖ The house is offered *on lease*. その家は貸家になっている. ‖ He is *on* new *lease* of life. 彼は健康が回復している. ¶fall *out of lease* 借地期限が切れる. ¶put out (=offer) land *to lease* 土地を賃貸する. ¶Japanese have 17,596 acres of land *under lease* in California. 日本人は加州で一万七千五百九十六エーカの土地を租借している. ‖ It is held *under lease* for ninety-nine years from the Chinese Government. それは中国政府から九十九ケ年の契約で借りている. ‖ a piece of land held *under* a *lease* having 68¾ years to run あとまだ六十八年九カ月の契約で借りている土地.

P² a *lease of* life 寿命.

lease, *v.* [土地などを]貸す, 借りる.

M *lease* it *out* for a fixed percentage 一定の歩合でそれを賃貸する.

P It is *leased to* Japan. それは日本に租借されている.

leash, *n.* 皮ひも.

V *slip* the *leash* 束縛を脱する.

P hold (=have) ... *in leash* ...を拘束する. ¶a dog *on* a *leash* 皮ひもにつながれた犬.

least, *n.* 最小.

V It is, to *say* the *least*, unsatisfactory. それはごく控え目に言っても不十分である. ‖ Lying is a bad habit, to *say* the *least* of it. ごく穏かに言ってもうそつきは悪い癖だ. 【類】I thought his excuse conventional (紋切形), to *say* the *least* [of it].

P You'll need ten thousand yen *at least*. 君は少くとも一万円はいるだろう ‖ lay down, *at* the *least*, £100 per annum 少くとも年に百ポンドを貯金する. ¶He is not *in* the *least* concerned about it. 彼はそのことは少しも気にしていない. 【類】They do not *in* the *least* understand this. / We were not *in* the *least* thinking of it. ‖ without being *in* the *least* disconcerted 少しも騒がず.

leather, *n.* 皮, 革.

V *curry leather* 皮を調製する. ¶*lose leather* 皮膚をすりむく. ¶*soften leather* 皮を柔らかくする.

Q *genuine leather* 本皮.

Q² a book bound in *Morocco leather* モロッコ皮で装ていした本. ¶*patent leather* 保険製革(仮うるしを密に塗った特別なめし皮). ¶*Russia leather* ロシア皮. ¶a *strong leather* 強い皮.

P It is bound *in leather*. それは皮の装ていだ.

leave, *n.* 許可; 休暇, 暇ごい.

V *ask leave* (=permission) 許しをこう ‖ without *asking leave* 無断で. ¶*beg leave* to ... ...の許しをこう. ¶He has *got leave* [of absence]. 彼は賜暇を得た. 【類】*get leave* and go back to ... ‖ *get* one's *leave* 暇を出される. ¶In case you *give* me *leave*, I will start at once. お許しが出れば私は今にも出発します. ¶*Grant* me *leave* of absence for a week. 一週間の欠席をお許し下さい. ¶you may *have leave* till ... ...までお前に暇をやる ‖ You may *have* my *leave* to visit the factory. 君に工場を見学する許可をあげよう. ¶*obtain leave* for him to ... 彼が...する許しを得る. 【類】*obtain leave* from the authorities (当局). ¶The trooper *overstayed* his *leave*. その兵士は賜暇期間以上に滞留した. ¶*request leave* to ... ...の許しをこう. ¶She *took* her *leave* of (=said good-bye to) me. 彼女は私にいとまを告げた. 【類】I *took leave* of him at the door and took a car. ‖ at *taking leave* 告別の際. 【類】He solemnly *took* his *leave* of them. / I will *take* my *leave* for today. / he *took* his *leave*, and set out for ...

Q take an *affectionate* (=a *passionate*) *leave* of ... ...に情のこもったいとまごいをする(別れを惜しむ). ¶take *formal leave* of ... ...と正式に別れを告げる. ¶take *four months' leave* 四カ月の暇を取る. ¶a *physiological leave* 生理休暇. ¶*sabbatical leave* 安息賜暇. ¶be on *sick leave* 病欠中である. ¶take a *sorrowful leave* of one's friends 友人と悲しい別れを告げる. ¶take the most *tender leave* of ......にきわめて情のこもったいとまごいをする. ¶a *terminal leave* 〘軍〙除隊休暇(除隊直前の).

Q² a *maternity leave* 分べん休暇. ¶on *one-year leave* of absence from one's job 一年間の休職で. ¶sailors on *shore leave* 許可を得て上陸中の船員 ‖ be denied *shore leave* 上陸許可が出ない. 【類】Half the crew were given *shore leave*.

P *by* your *leave* 御免をこうむって. ¶ask one *for leave* to go to ... ...へ行く許しを人にこう. ¶a soldier home *on leave* from the front 戦地から賜暇帰国中の兵士 ‖ He is coming home *on leave* of absence. 彼は賜暇帰国の途にある. 【類】The American Ambassador will go home *on leave*. / He is back in Japan *on leave*. ¶Give me that gun! you have no right to take it *without leave*. その銃をよこせ! 君は無断でそれを持って行くという法はない.

P² Thirty days' *leave of* absence per year with pay is usually granted to civil service employees in America. 米国では通例年に三十日の有給賜暇が文官に与えられている. 【類】The professor has *leave of* absence from her work for the coming year. / In 1831 he was granted a *leave of* absence to England for his health.

leave, *v.* 残す, 去る; そのままにしておく.

M *Leave* us *alone*, please. 私たちに構わないで下さい(邪魔は遠慮して下さい). ‖ be *left alone* with ... ...と二人きりになる ‖ They are *left* severely *alone*. 彼らには一切かまわないで(相手にせずに)いる. ¶*leave aside* the question of ... ...の問題を差しおく. ¶I was *left behind*. 私はおきざりにされた. ‖ things *left* [*behind*] 忘れ物 ‖ It was *left behind* in a hurry. それは急いだのでおき忘れてきた. 【類】passengers' belongings that have been *left behind* by mistake ‖ He was *left behind* in the race. 彼はその競争に落後した. ‖ He *left* his wife and children *behind*. 彼は妻子をあとに残して死んだ. ¶*leave blank* 白紙のままにしておく, [用紙など]書き込みをしないでおく. ¶The matter is *left entirely* to your arrangement. この件は一切あなたの御配慮にお任せします. ¶*leave half-finished* 未完成のままにしておく. ¶*leave* it *optional* with him whether he will ... or not ... するかどうかは彼の随意にさせる. ¶*leave out* (=omit) a word or name in writing 書き物に一語または一つの名前を抜かす ‖ *leave out* part of a letter 手紙の一部分を削除する ‖ be *left out* in the cold 寒気の中に放っておかれる; わざと放ったらかされる(冷遇される). 【類】Violets will flower in January, though they are *left out* all the winter. ‖ call a person *leaving out* the title of honor 呼びすてにする ‖ *leave out* half one's words 半分だけしか文句を言わない. ¶The difficulty has been to decide what to *leave out* rather than what to *leave in*. 困難は何を入れるかよりもむしろ何を除くかを決するにあった. ¶*leave* the city *permanently* or *transiently* 永久にまたは一時的に市を去る. ¶one must *leave* it *there* それ以上追究できない ‖ *leave* the rest pages *uncut* そのあとのページを切らないでおく. ¶*leave* it *undone* それをせずにおく ‖ It might well be *left undone*. よせばいいのに. ¶*leave unsaid* what one would rather say 言いたいことを言わないでおく. ¶This had perhaps better be *left untold*. これは言わぬが花だろう. ¶*leave* no plan *untouched* あらゆる立案をする. ¶We *left* no plan *untried*. われわれは百方手を尽してみた. ¶*leave* no stone *unturned* to ... ...百方手を尽して捜す. ¶They were *left* (=kept) *waiting*. 彼らは待たされた. ‖ It may be very *well left* to the reader to discover. その発見は当然読者に任せておいた方がよいであろう.

M² *leave off* the habit in disgust いやになってその習慣を止める ‖ They *left off* work earlier than usual. 彼らはいつもより早目に仕事を切上げた. ‖ begin where another has *left off* 人が中止したところから始める. 【類】Where did we *leave off* last time? / Let's *leave off* here for lunch. / *leave off* talking ‖ He *left off* all his friends and acquaintances and went over to South America. 彼は友人知人を捨てて南アメリカへ行った. 【類】He was *left off* (見離された) by his family doctor. ¶Ah, lucky me, fifty dollars *left over* this month. やれ, ありがたや, 今月は五十ドル残ったぞ. ‖ He thought the matter might be *left over* for the present. 彼はその件は当分手をつけない方がよかろうと考えた.

P *leave* a few guineas *as* a guarantee 手付に数ギニーを預ける. ¶I *left* my trunk *at* the station. 私はトランクを停車場に預けた. ¶His wife *left behind* her two little girls. 彼の妻は二人の娘を後に残して死んだ. 【類】Zola has *left behind* him thirty or forty books. ‖ His humor was of that nature which exhilarates and enlivens without *leaving behind* it a sting. 彼のユーモアはおもしろくって陽気で毒があとにちっとも残らないといった種類のものであった. ¶He was *left* rich *by* his father. 彼は父が死んだので金持

になった. ‖ *leave* **by** the 4.30 train from ... 四時半の列車で...を出発する. ¶the newly married couple *leaving* **for** their honeymoon 新婚旅行に出発する新郎新婦. 【類】 *leave* Tokyo **for** a trip in Hokkaido / *left* England **for** a tour of the world ‖ They *left* him **for** dead. 死んだものとしてあきらめた. ‖ Despair? Pshaw! *Leave* (=Save) that **for** cowards. 絶望? ちぇっ! そんなことは臆病者のやることだえ. ‖ She *left* a note **for** her husband. 彼女はちょっと書いたものを夫に残した. ‖ He *left* business **for** literary work. 彼は実業界を去って文筆を執る身となった. ‖ It was *left* **for** him to complete it. 彼に至って始めてそれが大成された. ‖ He *left* her **for** another woman. 彼は彼女を他の女と見かえた. ‖ *leave* nothing to be desired **for** ... ...のためには申し分なしである. ¶The question of remuneration I *leave* entirely **in** your hands. 報酬の件はあなたに一任する. 【類】 I am willing to *leave* it **in** your hands to do the best. ‖ He *left* it **in** my keeping (=charge). 彼はそれを私に預けておいた. ‖ *leave* it **in** one's care それを人に預ける ‖ He *left* me **in** the dark about the case. その件では彼は私に何も言ってくれなかった. ‖ They will not *leave* you **in** the lurch. あの人たちは窮境に立つ君を見捨てるようなことはあるまい. ‖ I trust that you *left* Mr. M. **in** good health. M さんは定めしお元気でしたろうね. ‖ *leave* one's family **in** comfort [死んだ後]遺族が楽に暮せる ‖ *Leave* me **in** peace. 邪魔をしないで下さい. ‖ Several vessels had to *leave* **in** ballast. 数隻は空荷で出帆しなければならなかった. ¶He *left* Cardiff in 1912 **on** a lengthy voyage. 彼は一九一二年にカーディフを出発して長い航海に上った. ‖ previous to *leaving* **on** a trip to Europe 欧州の旅に立つ前に ‖ They *left* their guns **on** the field. 彼らは大砲を戦場に残して行った. ¶*leave* it **out of** consideration (=account) それを度外視する ‖ *leave* **out of** count 計算に入れない ‖ He was *left* **out of** the race. 彼はその競走で落後した. 【類】 They *left* me entirely **out of** the conversation. ¶*leave* the choice **to** you その選択は君に任せる. 【類】 It was *left* **to** chance. / I *leave* it **to** your consideration. / It may be safely *left* **to** his judgment. / *leave* it **to** guess work (勝手に推量) / *leave* it **to** conjecture / it **is** *left* to the discretion of (の裁量に) / What followed must be *left* **to** the imagination of the reader. / Much is *left* **to** the imagination. / I *leave* it **to** your judgment. (御判断に) / I *leave* the prices to you. / The matter was *left* **to** public derision (世間のちょう笑). ‖ Members of the party were *left* **to** their own devices. 党員は銘々の考えで行動するよりほかなかった. ‖ He was *left* **to** himself (=his own devices). 彼の勝手にさせておいた(干渉しなかった). 【類】 They *left* me **to** myself. ‖ He *left* it **to** the world as his legacy. 彼はそれを彼の遺産として世に残した. ‖ I will not *leave* you **to** your fate. 僕は君を見殺しにはしない. ¶the impressions *left* **upon** them by ... ...が彼らに与えた印象. ¶She *left* word **with** her servant that she should not be back until evening. 彼女は晩まで帰れないと召使に言い残した. ‖ *leave* a card **with** the servant 召使に名刺をおいて去る ‖ I will *leave* the matter **with** you. 君にお任せする. 【類】 I will *leave* the book **with** you. / He *left* a widow **with** three children to take care of. / I must go at once, but I have no one to *leave* the baby **with**. / I am prepared to *leave* it **with** you as my security (それを担保として). ‖ I am *left* **with** no alternative but to ... 私には...するより他に道がない.

O *leave* it to perish それを破滅するままに捨てて顧みない. ‖ The foundation stone is all that is *left* to tell where once the castle stood. 礎石が昔の城の名残を留めているだけだ. ‖ The weather *left* nothing to be desired. 天気は申分なしであった.

leaven, *n.* 酵母; 潜勢力.

V^2 New *leaven* is **working** in society. 社会に新しい酵母(潜勢力)が発酵しつつある.

leaven, *v.* 発酵させる.

P public opinion liberally *leavened* **with** anti-Japanese sentiment 抗日感情を大いに根に持つ世論.

leaving, *n.* 立去ること.

Q **pre-time** *leaving* of work (office) 早引け.

leavings, *n.* 残り物.

V **have** his *leavings* 彼のお残りを頂戴する.

lecture, *n.* 講義, 講演; 小言.

V All the (=The whole of the) students **attended** the *lecture*. 全学生がその講演に出席した. ¶The students **boycotted** all *lectures*. 学生はすべての講義をボイコットした. ¶in **concluding** this *lecture* I would venture to say that ... この講演を終了するに当り私はあえて...と申上げたい. ¶**cut** a *lecture* 《米》講義に出ない. ¶**deliver** a *lecture* on the subject of ... ...の題下で講演をする. 【類】 **deliver** a *lecture* at the university taking as his subject "..." / the *lectures* were **delivered** in the French language ‖ a *lecture* **delivered** before a society ある会で行った講演. ¶intelligently **follow** a *lecture* 理解しつつ講義を聞く. 【類】 They could not **follow** the *lecture*. / The *luctures* are **followed** by discussions, and questions may be asked. ¶**give** *lectures* before our universities and scientific societies わが国の大学及び科学協会で講演する ‖ Mr. T **gave** us a long *lecture*. T 氏はわれわれに長いお説教をした. 【類】 My father **gave** (=read) me a *lecture* on my conduct. ‖ **give** a person a *lecture* on chivalry 人に士道(特に婦人に対する尊敬)を説く. 【類】 I **gave** him a little medical *lecture* (医学上のこと). ¶The *lecture* was **greeted** with the appreciation and applause it merited. その講演はそれが当然受くべき称賛とかっさいとで迎えられた. ¶The *lecture* was **illustrated** throughout with lantern views (slides). その講演は全部幻灯を使用した. ¶**patch up** a *lecture* 間に合わせの講演をする. ¶**his published** *lectures* on ... ...彼の...に関する公刊された講義. ¶he **read** me a *lecture* when I ... 私が...したらお説教をきかせた(意見をされた). 【類】 I **read** him a long *lecture* on the folly of living alone. ¶**water** [**down**] one's *lecture* to last another hour 講演をもう一時間続くように引延ばす.

Q an **alfresco** (=**outdoor**) *lecture* 屋外講義. ¶an **extra-curriculum** *lecture* 科外講義. ¶an **illustrated** *lecture* [幻灯使用などの]絵入講演. ¶a **moral** *lecture* お説教. ¶a **smart** *lecture* 気のきいた講演.

Q^2 a **curtain** *lecture* 奥さんの寝床の小言. ¶a **film** (=**motion picture**) *lecture* on Morocco モロッコに関する映画による講義. ¶a [**magic**] **lantern** *lecture* 幻灯使用の講演. 【類】 give a **lantern** *lecture* on English home life. ¶an **orientation** *lecture* ガイダンス講義(外国留学生などに). ¶free **public evening** *lectures* on French literature フランス文学に関する無料公開夜間講座. ¶a **radio** (**TV**) *lecture* ラジオ(テレビ)放送講演. ¶a **read** *lecture* 朗読講演.

P appear **at** *lectures* 講義に出る ‖ There was a good attendance **at** the *lecture*. その講演には相当の聴講者があった. ¶attend a course **of** *lectures* 連続講義に出る ‖ establish a course **of** *lectures* at the university by the will of ... ...の遺言でその大学に連続講座を設ける. 【類】 He will start his series **of** *lectures* on November 1st. ¶he gave a *lecture* **at** ... **on** ... 彼は...で...について講演した.

P^2 a *lecture* **in** English 英語での講演. ¶*lectures* **on** commerce (economics, religion, the situation) 商業(など)に関する講義. ¶his recent *lecture* **to** the Society of Arts 美術協会における彼の最近の講演. ¶a *lecture* **upon** history 歴史の講演.

lecture, *v.* 講演する, 講義する; 説論する.

M *lecture* a boy rather **mildly** for being lazy 男の子が怠けているのをやわらかく小言を言う. ¶I *lectured* him **severely** on the matter. 私はそのことについて手きびしく彼に言っておいた.

P *lecture* **before** a crowded audience 多数の聴衆を前にして講演する ‖ while *lecturing* **before** a class in the University 大学の一クラスで講義中. ¶He *lectured* **on** the foreign affairs in the Imperial presence. 同氏は海外事情について御前講演を行った. 【類】 in *lecturing* **on** his experiences / *lecture* her **on** her behavior ‖ I only know about it enough to *lecture* **on**. 私はそのことについてどうやら講演ができるくらいしか知らない.

lecturer, *n.* 講演者; 講師.

V The *lecturer* could not be **heard**. [発音の調子が変ってるなどで]その講演は分かりかねた.

Q a **delightful** *lecturer* 愉快な講演者. ¶He is no **dry-as-dust** *lecturer*. 彼は決して無味乾燥な講演者ではない. ¶**extra-academic** *lectures* 科外講義の講師. ¶an **illuminating** *lecturer* on world affairs 世界の事情に関し大いに蒙を開くに足りる講演者. ¶an **itinerant** *lecturer* 巡回講演者. ¶He is a **non-resident** *lecturer* on journalism at Cornell University. 彼はコーネル大学の新聞学科外講師である. ¶a **popular** *lecturer* 人気のある講演者. ¶**silver** (**leaden**)

***tongued** lectures* 銀鈴のような(重くるしい)音調の講演者. ¶a ***special** lecturer* at Columbia University コロンビア大学特別講演者.

Q² an ***anti-tobacco** lecturer* 禁煙を説く人. ¶a ***career** lecturer* 職業講演者. ¶a ***college** lecturer* 大学講師. ¶an ***exchange** lecturer* to (from) Japan ...から日本への(からの)交換講師. ¶a ***radio** (**TV**) lecturer* ラジオ(テレビ)放送講演者.

P² There is a *lecturer **in*** diplomatics at Oxford. オクスフォードでは古文書学の講師がいる. ¶a *lecturer **on*** English literature at Tokyo University 東京大学英文学講師. 【類】 Daniel Jones, *lecturer **on*** phonetics at University College, London. / *lecturers **on*** scientific subjects.

lectureship, *n.* 講座, 講師の職.

V ***establish** a lectureship* on citizenship 公民権についての講座を設置する. ¶***found** a lectureship* on pathology 病理学の講座を設ける.

P² He was appointed a *lectureship **on*** government at Harvard. 彼はハーヴァード大学の政治学講師に任ぜられた.

ledger, *n.* 元帳.

Q a ***bulky** ledger* 大型の元帳.

Q² a ***sales** ledger* 販売元帳.

P An entry was made ***in** a ledger*. 元帳に一項目が記入された.

leech, *n.* ひる.

V ***apply** leeches* ひるを(患部に)当てる.

leer, *v.* 色目を使う, 横目でみる.

M *leer **archly*** at ... ...を意味ありげに横目で見る.

P *leer **at*** a girl 娘に色目を使う.

left, *n.* 左, 左側.

P See the map ***at** left*. 左側地図参照. ‖ His address is given ***at** the left* of the card. 彼の住所はその名刺の左側にある. ‖ The figures ***at** the left* of the decimal point indicate the volume; those at the right, the page. 小数点より左の数字は巻を, 右のはページを示す. ‖ he had ***at** his left* Mr. ... 彼の左に...氏がいた. 【類】 The new building ***at** the left* is the home of a prominent life insurance company. / standing ***at** the left*. ¶visible ***on** the left* 左手に見える. 【類】 ***on** his left* stands ... / "Walk ***on** the left*." / I sat ***on** his left*. / ***on** the left* of this picture may be seen ... / the store ***on** the left*. ¶wear *kimono* right ***over** left* 着物を左前に着る ‖ He is a smart guy—***over** the left*. 彼はさかさに利口だ(本当はばかだ). ¶***To** the left* of the Marquis sat General Kuroki. 侯爵の左に黒木大将が着席した. ‖ a little ***to** the left* of ... is ... ...の少し左方に...がいる. 【類】 The Admiral is seated in the center, ***to** his left* is his wife, to his right his daughter, and close behind him two sons. ‖ Keep ***to** the left*. 左側通行. ¶*left **on*** entering the building is on show ... その建物にはいると左に...が陳列してある.

leftist, *n.* 左派の人.

Q² ***non-Communist** leftists* 共産党に属さない左派.

leg, *n.* 脚.

V ***amputate** one's leg* 片脚を切断する. ¶***bend** one's legs* at the knees backward 両脚をひざで背後に曲げる(ひざを折る). ¶He ***broke** his leg* in his fall. 彼は転んで片脚を折った. 【類】 fall off a ladder and ***break** one's leg*. ¶***carry** one's legs* off 立ち去る. ¶He was so intoxicated that he had difficulty in ***controlling** his legs*. 彼は大分酔っていたので足の運びがうまく行かなかった. ¶His *legs* were ***crossed*** while one foot poised in the air. 彼の両脚は組合わされて片脚は宙に浮いていた. ‖ sit with one's *legs **crossed*** (=one leg over one's knee) 脚を組合わせて腰をかける. ¶***cut off** one's leg* below the knee 片脚をひざ下から切断する. ¶applaud, on the screen, Josephine Baker, ***displaying** her undraped legs* 裸脚を見せてジョセフィン・ベイカーが銀幕に現われるのを拍手かっさいする. ¶***find** one's legs* 歩けるようになる. 【類】 I couldn't ***find** my legs* any farther. ¶He ***fractured** his left leg* below the knee by falling from the back of a horse. 彼は落馬して左脚をひざの下から折った. ¶***get** one's sea legs* 動揺する船の甲板の上が歩けるようになる. ¶He has ***had** both legs **amputated*** from below the knee. 彼は両脚をひざの下から切断した. ‖ ***have** the legs* of ... ...に追いつく. ¶***jiggle** one's legs* 脚をゆさぶる. ¶***keep** one's legs* ころばないでいる. ¶***keep on** one's legs* 立ち続ける. ¶***knock** one's legs* from under one そのすねを払う. ¶From Bombay we ***made** a long leg* to Singapore. ボンベイからシンガポールまで直航した. ¶***pluck off** legs* of a fly はえの脚をもぐ. ¶Are you trying to ***pull** my leg?* 君は僕をだまそうとしているのか. ¶***recover** one's legs* 立ち上る(倒れてから). ¶***scrape** a leg* 脚をかく. ¶***set** a broken leg* 折れた脚を接骨する. ¶***stretch** one's legs* 足を延ばす; 歩き出す(長座してから) ‖ ***stretch** one's legs* on the platform [汽車から]プラットホームに降りる. ¶***stretch out** one's legs* to their full extent 足を十分に延ばす. ¶They ***thrust** their legs* into long boots and their heads into helmets. 彼らは長ぐつに脚を突込み頭にヘルメットをすっぽりかぶった.

V² He ran away as fast as his *legs* could ***carry*** him. 彼は足のつづく限り急いで逃げのびた. 【類】 Go as fast as your *legs* can ***carry*** you. ¶The *legs* and feet ***felt*** heavey. 足が上から下まで重くなった. ¶One's *legs **sleep.*** 足がしびれてきかない.

Q ***bandy** legs* がにまた. ¶a funny little man with ***bow** legs* 脚の曲ったこっけいな小男. ¶be laid up with a ***broken** leg* 片脚が折れて床についている. ¶a chair with ***flaring** legs* 脚が外側に開いたいす. ¶walk upright on his ***hind** legs* [くまなどが]あと脚で立って歩く. ¶The bishop seemed quite on his ***last** legs*. 僧正は死にひんしていた. ¶He is a tall and spare man, with very ***long** legs*. 彼は背が高くやせていて脚が長い. ¶The airman has accomplished the ***second** legs* of his round-the-world trip. その飛行家は世界一週の第二段階を終った. ¶***stockingless** legs* くつ下をはかない脚. ¶He has a ***weak** leg*. 彼は足が弱い. ¶a man with a ***wooden** leg* 義足をした人. ¶a ***wounded** leg* 負傷した足.

Q² a ***game*** (=***lame***) *leg* 《口語》 びっこ. ¶the hem at the bottom of the ***trouser** leg* ずぼんのすそのへり.

P catch him ***by** the leg* 彼の脚をとらえる. ¶fetters ***for** the legs* 足かせ. ¶a hurt ***in** his leg* 彼の脚の傷 ‖ He was wounded ***in** the leg*. 彼は脚を傷めた. 【類】 He got hurt ***in** the leg*. / The tiger bit his daughter ***in** the leg*. ‖ The New York-Los Angeles route of the aerial post is laid out ***in** three legs* (=stages). ニューヨーク・ロス・アンゼルス間の航空郵便路は三段飛行になっている. ¶He is lame ***of** a leg*. 彼は片ちんばだ. ¶I was never ***off** my legs*. 私は少しも足を休めなかった. ¶a cut ***on** the leg* 脚の切傷 ‖ He is a text-book ***on** two legs*. あの人は二本足の(生きた)教科書だ(よく教科書を頭に入れている). ‖ He was bitten ***on** the leg* by a dog. 彼は犬に脚をかまれた. ‖ hop ***on** one leg* 片脚で飛ぶ ‖ get ***on** one's legs* (=feet) 立ちあがる ‖ You're old enough to stand ***on** your own legs*. もうお前も独り立ちできる年だ. ‖ A columnist is ***on** his legs* all the time collecting news. [特別欄担当の]新聞記者はたねとりにいつも歩き回っている. ¶rise ***to** one's legs* 立上る ‖ take ***to** one's legs* (=heels) 逃げ出す. ¶stand ***upon** one leg* 一本脚で立つ. ¶a jump ***with** both legs* 両脚そろえての跳躍. ¶a chair ***without** legs* 脚のないいす.

P² *legs **of*** imitation horse [芝居などの]馬の脚.

legacy, *n.* 遺産.

V ***bequeath** a noble legacy* to one's country その国にりっぱな遺産を残す. ¶***inherit** a legacy* 遺産を相続する. ¶***leave** a legacy* 遺産を残す. ¶***realize** the legacy* as a fact 現に遺産が手に入る. ¶***receive** a legacy* 遺産をもらう.

Q an ***ancestral** legacy* 先祖からの伝来物. ¶the ***best** legacy* of the old civilization 古代文明最上の遺産. ¶a ***handsome** legacy* 相当な遺産.

legalize, *v.* 適法化する.

P be *legalized **by*** the Japanese consul 日本の領事によって正式に認められる(旅券など).

legend, *n.* 伝説; 銘, 題語.

V signboard ***bearing** the legend*, "..." ...という文句の看板. 【類】 The gravestone ***bears** the legend* "One of the Pioneers of Civilization in Oregon." ¶articles ***carrying** the legend*: "Made in Japan"「日本製」の銘のある商品. ¶A huge bill ***containing** the same legend* was put up in the shopwindow. 同文の大きなビラが飾窓に出してあった. ¶the *legend **displayed*** outside the house 屋外に掲示した題語. ¶The *legend* "strawberries and cream" is ***inscribed*** outside the windows of a fruiterer's shop.「いちごクリーム」という看板がくだ物屋の窓のとびらの外側に出ている. 【類】 the *legend **inscribed*** over many a riverside door announcing "Tea and hot water 9d." ¶He ***made** the legend* into a beautiful ballad. 彼はその伝説を美しい俗謡に作った. ¶***reject** the legend* as unfounded 根拠のないものとしてその伝説を排斥する. ¶He has ***taken** the* *legend* for the subject of one of his poems. 彼はその伝説を材料にして一篇の詩を作った.

V² hence a *legend* ***arose*** that ... そこで…という伝説が起った. ¶many *legends* have ***gathered*** about ... …については色々なうわさがある. ¶the *legend* that has ***grown up*** (=been woven) around it それに付まとう伝説. ¶The *legend* ***says*** (=***goes***) that Fuji arose in a night. 伝説によると富士は一晩の中にできたのだそうだ.

Q There is a ***framed*** *legend* on the wall, which runs: "..." 壁にわく入れの告知板があってそれに「…」と書いてある. ¶a ***local*** *legend* avers that ... 地方の伝説には…とある. ¶the ***obstinate*** *legend* still runs that ... 相変らず…という伝説が消えない. ¶it is founded on an ***old*** *legend* attaching to ... それは…についての古くからの伝説にもとずいている. ¶There is a ***real old*** *legend* connected with the antique. その古物にはたしかに古い折紙が付いている. ¶A notable sign in one of Boston's busiest streets bears the ***remarkable*** *legend,* "Cole and Wood, dealers in Wood and Coal." ボストンの繁華街のある有名な看板に「薪炭商コール・アンド・ウッド」というすてきな文句がある.

P ***according to*** one *legend* ある伝説によると.

P² the *legend* ***concerning*** ... …についての伝説.

O there is a *legend* that ... …という伝説がある.

leggings, *n. pl.* きゃはん.

V ***unbuckle*** one's *leggings* きゃはんを脱ぐ.

Q² ***canvas*** *leggings* カンヴァス地のきゃはん.

legion, *n.* 軍隊; 多数.

V ***organize*** a *legion* (=band) of death 決死隊を組織する.

Q the ***American*** *Legion* アメリカ在郷軍人団.

Q² a ***Nazi*** *legion* ナチス軍団.

P² the *Legion* ***of*** Honor [フランス]レジョンドヌール勲章. ‖ a *legion* ***of*** people=a large crowd 大群衆. 【類】*legions* ***of*** insects.

O Its uses are *legion.* その用途は多種多様である. ¶Though books upon the subject are *legion,* a really good one is yet to be written. その問題に関する書籍は無数あるが本当に良い本は未だ著作されていない.

legislate, *v.* 法律を制定する.

P *legislate* ***against*** it most stringently 最も厳重にそれを禁止する法律を制定する. ¶those who are to lead and to *legislate* ***for*** the people of a country 一国の国民を指導しかつこれに対し法律を制定すべき人々.

legislation, *n.* 法律, 法制.

V ***enact*** *legislation* for ... …のために法律を制定する. ¶*legislation* designed to ... has been ***introduced*** in the Congress in the form of two bills …を目的とする法の制定は二法案として議会に提出された. ¶endeavor to ***obtain*** *legislation* against ... …を禁止する法律制定の実現に努力する.

V² No *legislation* has ***occurred*** since the above resolution was adopted. 上記の決議が採択されてから何らの法律も制定されなかった.

Q the threatened or actual enactment of ***adverse*** *legislation* abroad 外国におけるそれと反対の法律実現の恐れまたは実現. ¶in the event this ***dissatisfactory*** *legislation* is enacted このおもしろからぬ法律が制定される場合には. ¶It is a crime to be suppressed by ***drastic*** *legislation* ruthlessly enforced. それはきびしい法律を何ら仮借なく励行して圧迫すべき罪悪だ. ¶in harmony with the most ***enlightened European*** *legislation* 最も進歩したヨーロッパの法制と合致して. ¶designed to supplement or amend ***existing*** *legislation* 現行法律を補正もしくは修正の目的で. ¶pass ***restrictive*** *legislation* against ... …を弾圧する法案を立法化する. ¶***superficial*** *legislation* 皮相的な法制. ¶one of the most remarkable specimens of ***wise*** *legislation* 賢明な法律の最も著しい一つの標本.

Q² ***class*** *legislation* 階級立法(一階級のためにする立法). ¶***education*** *legislation* 教育立法. ¶***emergency*** *legislation* 非常時立法. ¶***factory*** *legislation* 工場法. ¶***labor*** *legislation* then pending in Congress 当時米議会で審議中であった労働立法. ¶sort from the bills introduced "***must***" *legilation* for the session 提出議案の中今議会通過をぜひ必要とするものを選定する. ¶***State*** *legislation* 一国の立法; 《米》州の立法. ¶***war*** (=***wartime***) *legislation* 戦時立法.

P contrary to the spirit ***of*** *legislation* 立法の精神に反して. ¶***under*** *legislation* at the last session of Parliament 前英国議会を通過した法律によって.

legislature, *n.* 立法府.

Q² a ***State*** *legislature* 国の立法府; 《米》州の立法府.

legitimacy, *n.* 正当(合法)性.

V ***question*** the *legitimacy* of ... …の合法性を問題にする.

legman, *n.* 〖新聞〗取材記者.

Q Today an editor himself is his ***own*** *legman* in my view. 今日では私の見るところで編集者自身が取材記者である.

legwork, *n.* 〖新聞〗取材活動.

Q ***Diligent*** *legwork* has been done by W.B., NATO correspondent 北大西洋条約機構の通信記者によって根気強い取材活動がなされた.

leisure, *n.* 暇, 好都合.

V ***beguile*** one's *leisure* with reading 読書で暇つぶしをする. ¶He took up the occupation in the hope of ***buying*** *leisure* for his real vocation. 彼はそれによって天職を尽す暇を得る見込でその職についた. ¶***devote*** the *leisure* of a lifetime to ... 一生を通じての暇の時間を…に費す. ¶***employ*** one's *leisure* wisely 暇を生かして使う. ¶he ***found*** *leisure* to ... 彼は…する暇を見出した ‖ He ***found*** more *leisure* and opportunities for pleasure. 彼はより多くの遊ぶ暇と機会を見付けた. ¶I cannot ***get*** any *leisure*. 私は少しも暇がない. ¶I ***have*** no *leisure* to ... 私は…する余暇がない. ¶***obtain*** a little *leisure* 寸暇を得る. ¶***occupy*** one's *leisure* with studies on ... …余暇を…の研究に当てる. ¶***pass*** one's *leisure* in idleness 安逸に日を送る. ¶It is not a wise way to ***spend*** one's *leisure*. それは暇を使う賢明なやり方ではない. ¶***turn*** their *leisure* to profit 暇を利用して金もうけをする. 【類】***turn*** their *leisure* to account by making the acquaintance of the Museums, the Art Galleries, etc. ¶***wait*** [***on***] one's *leisure* その人の都合のつくまで待つ.

Q ***commercialized*** *leisure* 営利化された閑散時[公衆娯楽機関など]. ¶a life of ***easy*** *leisure* 安逸の一生. ¶What ***little*** *leisure* was left is devoted to his studies in Pali. 彼はわずかの暇があればそれでパーリ語を研究した. ¶a ***moment's*** *leisure* ちょっとの暇. ¶enjoy ***salaried*** *leisure* 俸給をもらって閑散の身となる(洋行など命じられた場合). ¶articles scribbled in the ***scant*** *leisure* of an Indian subeditor インドにおける新聞の編集次長がわずかの暇に書きなぐった文章. ¶***undigested*** *leisure* 利用できない暇. ¶the first fruits of the author's ***well-earned*** *leisure* 著者のりっぱに獲得した閑散が産んだ最初の著述 ‖ He is now enjoying a ***well-earned*** *leisure* from his arduous labors in the capital. 首都における骨の折れる仕事を終えて彼は閑散の身となっている. ¶women who had a life of ***well-fed*** *leisure* 暇で食物のおごった暮しをした女たち.

P when I am ***at*** *leisure* 私の暇のときに. 【類】I shall be ***at*** *leisure* the day after tomorrow and will join the excursion with pleasure. / You can do it ***at*** your *leisure.* ¶live ***in*** *leisure* 閑居する. ¶a man ***of*** *leisure* 閑人. ¶a civilization that does not degenerate ***under*** *leisure* 閑散のために堕落しない文化. ¶people ***with*** scanty *leisure* 暇にとぼしい人々.

P² You would, in that case, have *leisure* ***for*** your work. 君もそうなると暇ができよう. ¶He has some *leisure* ***from*** his studies. 彼は研究の合間にいくらか暇がある.

lemon, *n.* レモン.

V ***pare*** a *lemon* very thin レモンの皮をごく薄くむく.

P Tea has a good flavor with a slice ***of*** *lemon* in it. レモンの薄片を入れると紅茶は香りがよくなる.

lemonade, *n.* レモン水.

V ***drink*** *lemonade* through a tube ストローでレモン水を飲む.

lend, *v.* 貸す, [力などを]貸す.

M It *lends* itself ***admirably*** to a literary treatment. それは文学的に取扱うのに大いに適している. ¶The brain is an organ which does not ***easily*** *lend* itself to study. 頭脳は直ぐには研究しにくい機関である. ‖ a subject that does not *lend* itself ***easily*** to popular treatment ちょっと通俗化のできない問題. ¶*lend* ***out*** money 金を貸しつける ‖ *lend* ***out*** books 本を貸出す. ¶Skyscrapers, railroads, and cotton mills do not *lend* themselves ***readily*** to conventional poetic treatment. 摩天楼, 鉄道, 紡績工場などは従来の詩の扱い方ではちょっと問題にならない. ‖ methods that *lend* themselves ***readily*** to the instruction of ... …の教授に容易に適用のできる方法.

P He *lent* me money ***as*** a favor. 彼は好意で私に金を貸

してくれた. ¶*lend* money ***at*** high interest 高利で金を貸す. ¶I *lent* him a hand ***in*** doing it. それをするについて私は彼に手を貸した(加勢した). ¶*lend* money ***on*** goods 品物を抵当に金を貸す. ¶*lend* one's aid ***to*** the project その計画に手を貸してやる ‖ *lend* one's helping hand ***to*** ... ...に救いの手をさしのべる ‖ This will *lend* itself ***to*** the readers. これを見れば読者の参考になるだろう. ¶*lend* a hand ***with*** the work その仕事に手を貸す ‖ Please *lend* a hand ***with*** my luggage. 荷物を運ぶんですがちょっと手を貸して下さい.

lender, *n.* 貸す人.

Q^2 a ***money lender*** 金貸し, 金融業者.

length, *n.* 長さ; 程度, 度合.

V ***add*** much *length* of life to ... ...を長く持たせる. ¶***attain*** a *length* of three feet 三フィートの長さに達する. ¶***find*** (=***know or get***) the *length* of one's foot その短所(弱点)を見抜く. ¶They did not ***give*** the *length* of wear (=durability) previously secured with British manufactures. それらには以前もっていた英国製品のような耐久力がなかった. ¶He ***went*** the *length* of saying it. 彼はそんなことまで言った. ‖ The Japanese ***go*** the *length* of omitting personal pronouns in almost all cases. 日本人はほとんどすべての場合と言っていいほど人称代名詞を省略する. ¶the river ***has*** a *length* of ... その川の長さは...である. ¶***increase*** their *length* of life [船・器具など]長く持たせる. ¶***measure*** the *length* 尺を取る ‖ He ***measured*** his *length* (=fell at full length) on the slippery, muddy road in endeavouring to evade an automobile fast moving. 彼は疾走している自動車を避けようとしてすべる泥だらけの道に大の字に倒れた. ¶***reach*** (=attain) a *length* of ... ...の長さに達する. ¶***reduce*** the *length* of the process by more than one half 工程を二分の一以上短縮する.

Q be carried to ***absurd*** *lengths* 行き過ぎである. ¶They have an ***aggregate*** *length* of about 2,000 feet. それらは全長約二千フィートある. ¶He went ***all*** *lengths* to attain his goal. 彼は自分の目的を達するためあらゆる手段を試みた. ¶keep people at ***arm's*** *length* 人を近づけない. ¶***assorted*** *lengths* 長短取合わせたもの. ¶a ***boat's*** *length* 一艇身. ¶It is explained at ***considerable*** *length*. それはすこぶる詳細に説明されている. 【類】a passage of ***considerable*** *length*. ¶It is of ***convenient*** *length*. それは手ごろの長さだ. 【類】cut it in any ***convenient*** *lengths*. ¶of any ***desired*** *length* どんなにも望みの長さの. ¶of ***equal*** *length* 長さのひとしい. ¶the ***focal*** *length* (distance) of a lens レンズの焦点距離. ¶describe at ***full*** *length* 十分くわしく解説する ‖ stretch out one's legs at ***full*** *length*. 足を長々と延ばす. 【類】stretch oneself [at] ***full*** *length*. ¶a recital at ***great*** *length* 長々と述べた説話 ‖ England will never go to any ***greater*** *length* than a protest. 英国は精々抗議をするくらいが関の山だろう. ¶Oxford was first, ***half*** a *length* ahead. [ボート・レースで]オックスフォードが第一位で半艇身リードしていた. ¶Ten is an ***hour's*** *length* distant. 十時にはまだ一時間ある. ¶reach an ***inordinate*** *length* [記事などが]法外な長さに達する. ¶expound a theory at ***inordinate*** (=***excessive***) *length* きわめて詳細に学説を解釈する. ¶***intended*** *length* of stay 滞在の予定の長さ. ¶***moderate*** *length* 適度の長さ. ¶They are of the ***same*** *length*. それらは同じ長さである. ¶write at ***some*** *length* on ... ...に関しやゝ詳細に書く. ¶the ***total*** *length* of ... ...の全長. ¶for a ***vast*** *length* of time 非常に長い期間.

Q^2 ***radio wave lengths*** ラジオの波長. ¶measure one's ***sleeve length*** そでたけを計る. ¶a ***three-block length*** (=distance) [通りの]三丁の距離.

P dwell ***at*** *length* on ... ...を詳説する ‖ space is not available for dealing ***at*** *length* with ... ...を詳細に論じる余白がない. 【類】The letter is too long to be printed ***at*** *length*. ‖ The matter is scarcely important enough to dwell upon ***at*** any *length*. そのことはなんら詳細に論じるほどの価値がない. ‖ ***At*** *length* his longings were satisfied. いよいよ彼の願がかなった. 【類】***At*** *length* the Monday evening arrived. ¶The crew won ***by*** two *lengths*. そのクルーは二艇身の差で勝った. 【類】The horse won ***by*** a half *length*. ¶pieces of wood cut ***in*** *lengths* of about 2 ft. 約二フィートの長さに切った木片 ‖ It measures twenty feet ***in*** *length*.=It is twenty feet long. それは長さが二十フィートある. 【類】***In*** what *length* must the rails be? / It can be made ***in*** any *length*. ‖ increase ***in*** *length* 長さがます ‖ papers of 5 to 7 pages ***in*** *length* 全体で五ページから七ページまでの論文. 【類】Each paper should be accompanied by a summary not exceeding 400 words ***in*** *length*. ¶They are ***of*** the same *length*. それらは同じ長さだ. ¶***over*** the whole *length* and breadth of the Empire 全帝国にわたって. ¶***throughout*** the *length* and breadth of the land 国中いたる所. ¶Most people would go ***to*** any *lengths* to avoid a skunk. 大抵の人は零敗をまぬがれようとしてどんな事でもやるものだ. ‖ show ***to*** what *lengths* "freedom" is permitted to go 自由の限界を示す ‖ It is dreadful to think of the *lengths* ***to*** which jealousy will go in time of crisis. 危急の際におけるしっと心の活動力はこれを考えるのも恐ろしいことだ. ¶***with*** a *length* of 100 ft. 長さ百フィートの. ¶***within*** an arm's *length* 手の届くところに.

P^2 the *length* ***of*** a reign 統治の期間 ‖ When women get once out of compass, there are no *lengths* ***of*** licentiousness that they are not capable of running. 女が一度脱線するとその不身持の無軌道振りは止めどがない.

lengthen, *v.* 延ばす, 延びる.

M The list might be *lengthened* out ***indefinitely***. それは枚挙にいとまがない.

P Days *lengthened* ***into*** weeks, and weeks into months, and months into years. 日は週に週は月に月は年にと移って行った. ¶Her stay *lengthened* ***to*** four weeks. 彼女の滞在は四週間に延びた.

O His walking pace was quickened and *lengthened* as he neared the scene. 彼は現場に近づくにつれ足なみが早くなり大またになった.

leniency, *n.* 寛大.

V ***show leniency*** 寛大さを示す.

lenient, *a.* 寛大な.

M ***mischievously*** *lenient* かえってためにならないくらい寛大な.

P They have been *lenient* ***in*** the treatment of war prisoners. 彼らは捕虜を遇するに寛大だった. ¶French public opinion is *lenient* ***to*** abortion. フランスの世論は堕胎に対して寛大だ. ¶*lenient* ***towards*** (=to) ... ...に対して寛大な. ¶The judge was *lenient* ***with*** him. 裁判官は彼に寛大だった.

lens, *n.* レンズ.

Q an ***achromatic*** *lens* 無色レンズ. ¶a ***convex*** (***concave***) *lens* 凸(凹)レンズ.

leprosy, *n.* らい病.

V I wonder if *leprosy* ***runs*** in the family. あの家はらい病の血統ではないだろうか.

P afflicted ***with*** *leprosy* らい病にかかった.

lessen, *v.* 減らす.

M My energy *lessens* ***gradually*** with age. 年とともに精力が衰える.

P the number was *lessened* ***by*** ... その数は...だけ減らされた.

lesser, *n.* より少い方.

P^2 the *lesser* ***of*** the two evils その二つの悪の中ではましの方.

lesson, *n.* (**1**) 学課, 課業.

V ***assign*** *lessons* 課業を割当てる. ¶It is needless for him to ***attend*** my *lessons*. 彼は(よくできるから)私の授業に出る必要がない. ¶***conduct*** a *lesson* in a foreign language 外国語で授業する. ¶***do*** *lessons* 予習(復習)をする. ¶I needn't say how we ***did*** our *lessons* that day. (放課後におもしろい遊びがあるので)その日はどんな勉強ぶりだったかは言うに及ぶまい. ¶***dodge*** a *lesson* ある学課の時間を抜かす. ¶We ***exchanged*** *lessons* in our respective languages. われわれは言葉の交換教授をやった. ¶Have you ***finished*** your *lessons* for tomorrow? あしたの学課の予習はすみましたか. ¶I am trying to ***get*** my *lesson* today so that I shall not have to do it tomorrow. 私は学課の予習を明日やらずに済むように今日やって仕舞おうとしているのです. ¶I have ***got through*** my *lessons*. 私は予習を済ました. ¶He ***gives*** English *lessons* at four hundred yen an hour. 彼は一時間四百円で英語を教える. 【類】*Lessons* ***given*** on Monday, Wednesday and Friday afternoons. ‖ Proverbs ***give*** us the best *lessons* in the art of expression.—John Burroughs. ことわざはわれらに最もよく表現の技巧を教える. ¶***give up*** the *lesson* to come to the lecture その講演を聞くためにその授業を放棄する. ¶***grave*** this *lesson* on his consciousness この教訓を彼にたたきつける. ¶I wish to ***have*** *lessons* in ... 私は...を習いたいと思う. 【類】We ***have*** no *lessons* this afternoon. 【類】The pupils have ***had*** six months' *lessons*, of two hours a day, of five days a week. ‖ He ***had*** his *lesson* at his fingers' ends. 彼はその学課の予習をよくやっていた. ¶He will not ***hold*** a *lesson* this afternoon. 彼は今日午後の授業はやらないだろう. ¶*impose* long-night home *lessons* on very young children ごく幼い児童に夜おそくまでかかる宿題を課する. ¶I *know* my *lesson*. 私は予習をやってきている. ¶No reduction is made for a pupil *missing* a *lesson* for his own convenience. 自分の勝手で授業を休む生徒に対して割引をしない(個人教授などの場合). ¶*neglect* one's *lessons* 自分の勉強をおろそかにする. ¶*prepare* and *review lessons* 学課の予習復習をする. ¶After *reading* this *lesson* let the pupils reproduce it orally. この学課を読んだ後で生徒に口頭で言わせるようにせよ. ¶*receive lessons* by mail in a correspondence school 通信学校の通信教授を受ける.【類】*receive lessons* from ... / He has never *received* a single *lesson* on the subject. ¶He seemed rather to be *repeating* a *lesson* learned by heart than relating a fact from his own knowledge. 彼は自分の知っていることを話すというよりはむしろ暗記した学課を繰返しているように思われた. ¶Can you *say* your *lesson*? お前は予習ができているか. ¶*study* one's *lesson* 学業を勉強する. ¶*take lessons* in English 英語の教授を受ける.【類】*take lessons* to be a professional stage dancer / I am *taking* (=have been taking) *lessons* on the piano. ‖ He *took* a few *lessons* in printing. 印刷技術を少し習った.

Q a *conversational lesson* 会話のけいこ. ¶We had *daily lessons* in dancing. 僕たちは毎日ダンスのけいこがあった. ¶a *dull lesson* おもしろくない学課. ¶It can be learned in one *easy lesson*. それはやさしい一回の課業で覚えられる. ¶I am *one lesson* ahead of him in ... 私は...では彼より一日の長がある. ¶*oral lessons* 口頭教授. ¶taught by *postal lessons* 通信教授で教わった. ¶recite a *prepared lesson* 準備した学科を復唱する. ¶give *private lessons* in English 英語の自宅(個人)教授をする.【類】I am open to accept engagements to give *private lessons* to ladies and gentlemen. ‖ give *private lessons* in piano and violin ピアノ及びヴァイオリンの個人教授をする. ¶take *vocal lessons* from ... ...について声楽のけいこをする. ¶*What lesson* do we have in the first hour? 一時間目は何の授業ですか.

Q² *class lessons* クラスの課業. ¶*composition lessons* 作文のレッスン. ¶take *fencing* (*swimming*) *lessens* フェンシング(水泳)を習う. ¶give *film lessons* 映画を用いて授業をする. ¶*history lessons* at school 学校の歴史の課業. ¶prepare *home lessons* 宿題をやる. ¶*music lessons* 音楽のけいこ. ¶an *object lesson* on ... ...についての実物教授.【類】witness an *object lesson* in English. ¶practice their *piano lessons* ピアノの練習をする. ¶take *riding lessons* 騎馬(オートバイ乗りなど)のけいこをする. ¶a *scripture lesson* バイブル・レッスン.

P *after* the *lessons* 授業が終ってから. ¶*during* the *lesson* 授業中に. ¶I thank you *for* the *lesson* you gave me. 勉強させて頂きありがとうございます.【類】Thanks *for* the *lesson* in shopping (買い物の仕方). ¶We are *through* our *lessons*. 授業(レッスン)は終了した.

P² add interest to one's *lessons by* appropriate illustration 適当な図解によって授業に興味を加える. ¶It is a *lesson in* culture to read a French author. フランスの本を読むことは教養の一学課である. ‖ *lesson* one (=the 1st lesson) *in* home decoration 住宅装飾法第一課. ¶*lessons on* literature 文学に関する課業.【類】first *lessons* (手ほどき) *on* the violin. ¶*lessons upon* the art of living 処世法に関する課業.

(**2**) 教訓, 実物教訓.

V In some respects this will *afford* a *lesson* to Western nations. これはある点で西洋諸国民の参考になるだろう. ¶*draw* a *lesson* from ... ...から教訓を得る. ¶*drive home* a *lesson* 一つの教訓を徹底させる. ¶*furnish lessons* for the future 未来の教訓になる. ¶A valuable *lesson* may be *gleaned* from it by those who have eyes to see. 具眼の士だったらその中から尊い教訓を拾いとるだろう. ¶The *lesson* was *impressed* on the pupils' minds with great force by the teacher. 先生のその教訓は生徒の心に深い感銘を与えた. ¶*learn lessons* from the ablest, in age as well as in youth 老若を問わず最も有能なものから教訓を学ぶ.【類】What *lesson* you have *learned* from this story? / *learn* a *lesson* from experience / *learn* a *lesson* of incalculable value (測りようのない尊い教訓) / *learn* a *lesson* by failure ‖ We are just beginning to *learn* that *lesson* in Japan. ようようそのことが日本に分かってきた. ¶*point* a *lesson* [引例によって]教訓を強調する. ¶*provide* an object *lesson* on this point この点についての実物教訓を提供する.【類】*provide* a fine object *lesson* in favor of ... (...に有利な). ¶*read* them a *lesson* 彼らをこらす ‖ *read* aright the *lessons* of history 歴史の教訓を正しく理解する. ¶*swallow* a bitter *lesson* 苦い教訓を我慢して受入れる. ¶*take* a *lesson* from ... ...にかんがみる ‖ In popular education, too, the Russians *took lessons* from the English. 大衆教育においてもまたロシヤは英国に習った. ‖ He *took* the *lesson* to heart. その教訓が彼の身にこたえた. ¶It will *teach* him a *lesson*. それは彼の薬になるだろう. ‖ He must be *taught* a *lesson*. 彼を一つこらさねばならない. ¶I'm going over and *teach* that guy a *lesson*. 出かけて行ってきゃつに目にもの見せてやる. ‖ Nature teaches *beautiful lessons*. 自然は美しい教訓を与える.【類】The people of Japan *teach* foreigners a *lesson* in this respect.

Q take to heart the *bitter lesson* taught by history 歴史の教える苦い教訓を銘記する. ¶one of the *chief lessons* to be learned from his life is ... 彼の一生から学ぶべき主な教訓の一つは...だ. ¶a *good lesson* 一つの好訓戒. ¶learn the *grim lesson* that ... ...といういかめしい教訓を得る. ¶an *instructive lesson* to all だれにもためになる教訓. ¶teach them a *lasting lesson* 彼らに永く忘れられない訓戒を与える. ¶The spoiled child had not learned *life's lesson* of relative values. そのだだっ子はものには相対的価値というものがあることを当時未だ心得ていなかった. ¶carry a *moral lesson* 道徳的な教訓を含む ‖ have a *moral lesson* in view 道徳的教訓を目的とする. ¶the *old, old lesson* that there's no place like home 家庭にまさる所なしという古い古い教え. ¶What has happened in Great Britain is a *salutary lesson* for other countries as well. 大英国内に起ったことは他国にとってまた他山の石となる. ¶learn a *severe lesson* = have a bitter experience ひどい目に会う ‖ You shall have a *severe lesson*. こっぴどくしかられるぞ. ¶learn thereby one of the most *useful lessons* of life それによって最も有用な一つの人生教訓を学ぶ. ¶read a *valuable lesson* ためになるお説教をする. ¶a *valuable* and *lofty lesson* 貴重にして崇高な教訓.

Q² vivid *object lessons* 生々した実物教訓 ‖ as is shown by an *object lesson* 実物が示す通り ‖ offer a living *object lesson* to ... ...にとって生きた実物教育になる.【類】this will serve as an excellent *object lesson* regarding ... / It was built as an *object lesson* by the Government. / A visit to the Fall is an *object lesson* in geography. / furnish an instructive *object lesson* / a striking *object lesson* from Germany ‖ Those short measure baskets were all burned as an *object lesson*. これら貫目不足のかごは全部見せしめのため焼却された.

P It serves *as* a *lesson* to him. それは彼にとって一つの教訓になる.

P² a *lesson for* Great Britain 英国にとっての一教訓. ¶one *lesson from* such an accident as this is that ... こういう事件から受ける教訓は...だ ‖ England's *lesson from* France 英国がフランスから得た教訓. ¶a *lesson of* warning 警告の意味の教訓 ‖ learn the *lesson of* patience 忍耐すべきだということを覚える ‖ the *lesson of* the book is that ... その本から得られる教訓は...ということである ‖ the *lessons of* the past 過去の教訓 ‖ some *lessons of* the yellow fever 黄熱病流行から得る教訓. ¶an object *lesson on* the danger of walking on railroad tracks 鉄道線路歩行の危険についての実物教訓. ¶It was a *lesson to* me. それは私の戒めとなった. ‖ Let this be a *lesson to* you to thieve in future. 君はこれにこりて今後は盗みなどしないようにしたまえ.

lesson, *v.* 教える.

P If the war has taught us anything, it has *lessoned* us *in* the economic solidarity of the world. その戦争がわれらに何物かを教えたとすればそれは世界の経済的連帯性ということであった.

let, *n.* 故障.

P pass off *without let* or hindrance 無事に済む.

let, *v.* ...せしめる; 貸す.

M *let* him *alone* 彼に構わないでおく. ¶*let fall* words うっかりしゃべる. ¶*let go* of her hand 彼女の手を離す ‖ *let go* [of] one's hold 手を離す.【類】*Let go* of me, please! ¶*let loose* one's fury 猛烈に怒り出す. ¶*let* bicycles *out* on hire 自転車を賃貸する ‖ Do not *let* the fire *out*. 火を消えないようにせよ. ¶*let slip* an opportunity 機会を逸する.

M² *let down* blinds (curtains) よろい戸(など)をおろす.

¶*let down* its gangways タラップをおろす.【類】You may put up the screen (仕切りの幕) or *let* it *down* at will (自由に). ‖ *let down* restrictions on ... …に制限を加える ‖ You may count on me not to *let* you *down*. 大丈夫失望させるようなことはないよ.【類】I hope you won't *let* me *down* again. ¶*Let* me *in* under your umbrella. かさに入れて下さい. ‖ *Let* him *in* as a member of our club. 彼をこのクラブに入会させ給え. ‖ This pair of shoes *let in* water. このくつは水がしみ込む. ‖ Open the window to *let in* fresh air. 窓をあけて新鮮な空気を入れよ. ‖ *Let me off* at the 5th floor. 五階でおろしてくれ(エレベーターガールに). ‖ *let off* the steam by ... …によってうっぷんを晴らす ‖ *let off* debt (punishment) (=remit) 負債(など)を免除する ‖ be *let off* with a reprimand 訓戒の上放免してやる.【類】*let* one *off* without punishment (罰しないで) ‖ *let off* fireworks 花火をあげる.【類】*let off* a gun / *let off* the charge in a firearm (火器) ‖ His blow *let* the balloon *off* with a pop. 彼がぷっと吹いたので風船玉がぱんと破裂した. ‖ The house was *let off* in sets of chambers. その家屋はへやをいくつかに区切って貸した. ¶*let* it *up* in the sky [風船玉など]それを空へ飛ばす.

P It *lets at* 70 yen a month. それは月七十円で貸せる. ‖ *Let* me *at* him! 僕にやらせてくれ(人をいじめる時など). ¶*let* one's house *for* ... yen 家を…円で貸す. ¶*let* him *into* the office (house) 彼を事務所(など)に入れる ‖ *let* one *into* a home by the backdoor 裏門から入れる. ¶*let* him *out of* prison 彼を刑務所から出す ‖ Don't *let* it *out of* your sight. それから目を離さないでいてくれ.

O *let* this come to a boil これを煮立てる. ¶*Let* it not be objected that I am contradicting myself. 私が自己矛盾だという異議を持ち出されては困る. ¶*let* it be known that ..., and ... …ということが世間に知れると… ¶I thought I had better *let* them stand as they were. そのままにしておくのがよいと私は考えた. ¶*Let* go! *let* go! 放せ! 放せ!

letter, *n.* **(1)** 手紙, 書状; 書面.

V Why did you not *acknowledge* the *letters* I sent you a week ago? 一週間前に出した手紙を受取ったとなぜ知らせなかったか. ¶*address* a *letter* 手紙のあて名を書く ‖ properly *address* a *letter* あて名を正確に記す.【類】The *letter* was wrongly *addressed*.【類】*address* a *letter* to ... = write [to] ... / *letters addressed* to and from ... ¶*answer* (=reply to) a *letter* 手紙の返事を出す.【類】I rarely *answer* my *letters* at home. ¶*assort letters* 手紙を分類する. ¶Let me *begin* my *letter* by thanking you for your great kindness. まず始めにあなたの御親切に対し感謝致します. ¶*cash* a *letter* of credit 信用状を現金化する. ¶*close* a *letter* 手紙の筆をおく. ¶*compose* a *letter* 手紙の文をつづる. ¶*cut up* a *letter* 手紙の封を切る. ¶*date* a *letter* 手紙に日付を書く. ¶*deliver letters* to their addresses 手紙をそのあて先に配達する. ¶*dictate letters* to a typist タイピストに手紙を口述する. ¶*direct* a *letter* 手紙の名あてを書く. ¶See to it that this *letter* is *dispatched* at once. この手紙を至急出すようにしてくれ給え. ¶*drop* a *letter* into a pillar-box 手紙を投かんする.【類】*drop* the *letters* and other mail into the letter-box at the front door. ¶*exchange letters* for mutual study 相互の学習のために手紙を交換する. ¶*file letters* 手紙をとじ込む. ¶*fling* a *letter* into the wastebasket 手紙を紙くずかごに投げ込む. ¶*fold* a *letter* and put it carefully back into the envelope 手紙を畳んでそれをもと通り丁寧に封筒に仕舞う. ¶*forward* him a *letter* 手紙を彼に転送する. ¶*give* him a *letter* 彼に手紙を出す ‖ Would you kindly *give* me a *letter* of introduction to Mr. ...? …氏に紹介状を書いて頂けないでしょうか. ¶*glance over* a *letter* 手紙をざっと見る. ¶*hand* him a *letter* 手紙を彼に手渡しする. ¶I *had* a *letter* from him yesterday saying (=in which he says) that ... きのう彼から…という手紙をもらった. ‖ I *have* your *letter* of October 5 with ... 君の十月五日付の…の手紙を入手した. ¶*indite letters* in English 英文で手紙を書く. ¶Your *letter* is evidently *intercepted* somewhere. お手紙はどうもどこか途中で紛失したものらしい. ¶a circular *letter* has been *issued*, signed by ... …の署名した回状が発せられた. ¶*leave* a *letter* for ... …に渡す手紙を残す. ¶*mail* a *letter* at the post box 手紙をポストに入れる.【類】I'll have my sister *mail* your *letter*. ¶*mislay* a *letter* 手紙を置忘れる. ¶*open* a *letter* 手紙を開封する. ¶He *poetized* his *letter* to her. 彼女への手紙を詩の形で書いた. ¶*post* (=mail) a *letter* 手紙を出す. ¶*prepay* a *letter* 郵税を前納する. ¶*present* a *letter* of introduction 紹介状を呈示する. ¶*purchase letters* of credit 信用状を買う. ¶*put* a *letter* in[to] an envelope 手紙を封筒に入れる.【類】*put* a *letter* into a mail-box = post a letter ‖ *quote* a *letter* as it stands 手紙の文をそのまま引用する. ¶he *received* a *letter* informing him of ... 彼は…のことを通知する手紙を受取った ‖ a *letter* has been *received* from him intimating that ... 彼から…を知らせる手紙を受取った ‖ *receive letters* of inquiry from ... asking ... …から…を問い合わす照会状を受取る ‖ have a *letter registered* 書留にしてもらう ‖ *Letters* containing a valuable document should be *registered*. 貴重書類入りの手紙は書留にしなくてはいけない. ¶*send* him a *letter* 彼に手紙を出す. ¶*send off* (=*away*) a *letter* 手紙を出す. ¶*sign* a *letter* 手紙に署名する. ¶*smuggle* a *letter* out of a prison [手を回して]監獄からこっそり手紙を出す. ¶*stamp* a *letter* 手紙に切手を張る. ¶*submit letters* for signature 署名のため書状を(責任者に)提出する. ¶A mailman (=postman) is a man who *takes letters* to people's homes. 郵便配達は手紙をみんなの家に持って行く人である. ‖ He *took* a *letter* out of his pocket. 彼はポケットから手紙を取出した.【類】*Take* this *letter* with you. ¶*take out letters* of credit from ... …から信用状を取る. ¶*tear open* a *letter* 手紙を裂いて開ける. ¶*write* a *letter* home 家に手紙を書き送る ‖ *write letters* to the papers 新聞に投書する.【類】Please *write* me a *letter* once in a while and tell me about yourself and your work. / *write* a *letter* from London / I will *write* you a good *letter* (良いたより) one of these days.

V² *Letters cross* [each other]. 手紙が行違う. ¶The *letter went* astray. その手紙が途中で紛失した. ¶The *letter miscarried* in the mail (=was lost in transit). その手紙を郵送中に紛失した. ¶*letters* which have *passed* between ... and ... …と…との間に取交わした手紙. ¶Your esteemed *letter* has just *reached* me. 御芳書正に落手致しました. ¶The *letter runs* thus. その手紙にはこう書いてある.

Q a very *angry letter* 非常に怒った手紙. ¶receive an *anonymous letter* 差出人不明の手紙を受取る ‖ an *anonymous letter* informed the Metropolitan Police that ... ある人が匿名で…と警視庁へ知らせた. ¶an *appreciative letter* 感謝の手紙. ¶an *autobiographical letter* [就職のため]自分の履歴を書いた手紙. ¶in your *before-last letter* 君の前々回の手紙に. ¶a *brief letter* 短い手紙. ¶a *confidential letter* 親展書状. ¶a *consolatory letter* 悔み状. ¶a *crawling scraggy letter* ひじきの行列の手紙. ¶a *dry* and poorly *worded letter* 味のない文句のまずい手紙. ¶write him an *enthusiastic letter* 彼に熱誠こもる手紙を出す. ¶*familiar letters* (儀式張らない)日常の書簡. ¶*formal letters* 形式的な書簡. ¶a *friendly letter* 親切な手紙. ¶a *graceful letter* of thanks 丁重な感謝状. ¶I received a *gracious letter* of acknowledgment. 私は丁寧な礼状を受取った. ¶a very *guarded letter* 細心の注意を払って書いた手紙. ¶a *heart-rending letter* 胸も張りさけるような手紙. ¶an *illiterate letter* 無学者の手紙. ¶I have *important letters* to mail. 重要な手紙を郵便に出さなくてはならない. ¶an *impudent letter* 厚かましい手紙. ¶*incoming letters* 来状. ¶He wrote an *indignant letter* to The Times on the subject. 彼はその問題でタイムス社に激烈な手紙を送った. ¶your *kind letter* あなたの親切なお手紙. ¶his *latest letter* from Italy 彼のイタリアからの最近の通信. ¶address a *long letter* to ... …にあて長い手紙を出す. ¶find a *missing letter* 紛失した手紙を見つける.【類】try to trace the *missing letter*. ¶a *newsy letter* 《俗》ニュースの沢山ある手紙. ¶He wrote me back such a *nice letter*. 彼は実に親切な返事をよこした. ¶an *obliging letter* ねんごろな手紙. ¶an *offensive letter* 失礼な手紙. ¶an *official letter* 公用の手紙. ¶an *open letter* 公開状. ¶an *outgoing letter* 出す手紙. ¶a *personal letter* 私信. ¶a *personal* business *letter* 私用向の手紙. ¶A *preliminary letter* is advisable. まず手紙で照会した方がよい. ¶a *private letter* 私信. ¶by *registered letter* 書留郵便で. ¶a *scathing* and *scornful letter* しゅん烈で侮辱的な手紙. ¶a *short* but *sweet letter* 短いがうれしい手紙. ¶a *smoothly worded* and *conciliatory letter* 用語が穏かで折れて出た手紙. ¶a *spite-hot letter* 火のように激した手紙. ¶*sympathizing* letters 慰問状. ¶She sends him ***tender letters.*** 彼女は彼にやさしい手紙を寄せる. ¶a ***threatening*** *letter* that the furniture will be seized and sold 家具を差押えて売払うという脅迫状. ¶a ***typewritten*** *letter* with a signature underneath 署名入りの印書々状. ¶an ***unstamped*** *letter* 切手の張ってない手紙. ¶a ***vigorous*** *letter* of complaint 猛烈な苦情の手紙.

Q² an ***adjustment*** *letter* 調停の手紙. ¶an ***air mail*** *letter* 航空郵便による手紙. ¶an ***application*** *letter* [就職などの]申込書状. ¶an ***autograph*** *letter* of Keats キイツの自筆の手紙. ¶a ***begging*** *letter* 無心の手紙. ¶***boyhood*** *letters* 少年時代の手紙. ¶a ***business*** *letter* 商用の手紙. ¶a ***chain*** *letter* (連鎖式)幸運の手紙. ¶send out a ***circular*** *letter* to … …に回状を出す. ¶a ***covering*** *letter* 同封の手紙, 添状. ¶a ***claim*** *letter* [貿易の](損害などに対する)クレームの手紙. ¶a ***fan*** *letter* ファン・レター. ¶a ***home*** *letter* 家からの手紙. ¶an ***imitation*** typewritten *letter* 一見タイプしたような印刷書状. ¶a ***love*** *letter* ラブレター, 恋文. ¶a ***night*** *letter* 夜間々送電報. ¶a ***referential*** *letter* from a responsible person 責任ある人からの照会応答の手紙(求職者採用の際). ¶a ***Roosevelt*** *letter* ルーズベルト氏からの手紙. ¶a ***six*** or ***eight page*** *letter* 六ページないし八ページの手紙.

P apply ***by*** *letter* 書面で申込む ‖ ***by*** *letter* or telegram 手紙か電報で. ¶***in*** a *letter* reached home he says … 自宅への手紙に彼は…と言ってよこしている ‖ The invoice was omitted ***in*** your *letter*. 貴書状には仕切状が抜けていました. 【類】he says ***in*** his *letter* that … ‖ It is expressed ***in*** *letters* on the land question which he addressed through the Daily Mail to Mr. Churchill. それを彼はデイリィ・メールを通じてチャーチル氏にあてた土地問題に関する書簡の中に述べている. ¶the postscript (=P.S.) ***of*** a *letter* 手紙の追伸 ‖ I have a lot ***of*** *letters* to answer. 私は返事を出す手紙が沢山ある.

P² Any *letter* ***for*** me today? きょうは僕に手紙は来ませんか. ¶The Chairman read a number of (=some) *letters* ***from*** friends who were unable to be present. 議長は出席のできなかった仲間から送られた手紙を朗読した. ¶a *letter* ***of*** condolence on the death of … …の死を悔む手紙 ‖ a *letter* ***of*** apology 謝罪状 ‖ a *letter* ***of*** attorney 委任状 ‖ a *letter* ***of*** advice 通知状 ‖ with a *letter* ***of*** guarantee 保険証付きの ‖ a *letter* ***of*** inquiry 照介状 ‖ a *letter* ***of*** marque 商船捕獲免状 ‖ a *letter* ***of*** sympathy (=condolence) 悔み状 ‖ a *letter* ***of*** transmittal 送付状 ‖ a *letter* ***of*** verdict 〘法〙評決状 ‖ a *letter* ***of*** appreciation 感謝状 ‖ my *letter* ***of*** some days ago 先日出した小生からの手紙. ¶I have received from him a *letter* ***on*** the matter. 私はその問題に関係した手紙を彼から受取った. ¶*letters* ***to*** and ***from*** her 彼女とやりとりした手紙.

(**2**) 文字, 字義; 符号.

V He ***has*** many *letters* after his name. 彼は名前に沢山肩書が付いている. ¶He does not ***know*** his *letters*. 彼は目に一丁字もない. 【類】You don't ***know*** your *letters* even. ¶*Letters* are ***put*** in italic type to show that they are not sounded. 無声音を示すために文字がイタリック体になっている. ¶***read*** aloud the *letters* of the test types through the trial glasses 視力検定用の活字を眼鏡越しに読上げる.

V² The *letters* ***dance*** and I can not understand what I am reading. 私は文字が躍って読んでいることが分からない.

Q Birds in flight wrote upon the sky the ***bi-forked*** *letter* of the Greeks. 飛鳥が空にまたのあるギリシア文字を書いた. ¶be printed in ***black*** *letters* ゴシック活字で印刷されてある. ¶printed with (=in) ***capital*** *letters* 頭文字で印刷された. ¶The promises remained a ***dead*** *letter*. その約束はほご同然であった. 【類】The treaty has become a ***dead*** *letter* (=scrap of paper). / Laws aiming at punishing … are practically ***dead*** *letters*. / The law of supply and demand is not a ***dead*** *letter* here. ¶Many mysterious rays are being discovered in such numbers that soon there will not be ***enough*** *letters* in the alphabet to name them all. 不明な各の放射線は次から次へと発見されるのでやがてこれに命名する字母の不足を感じるであろう. ¶There is a key on the board for ***every*** *letter* in the alphabet. その盤にはアルファベットのすべての文字に対するけん板がある. ¶Navy Day spelled in ***human*** *letters* 人体(の列)でつづったNavy Day. ¶the ***initial*** *letters* of the name 姓名の頭文字. ¶write in ***large*** *letters* 大文字で書く. ¶a notice in ***prominent*** *letters* はっきりした文字で出した掲示. ¶writing Japanese in ***Roman*** *letters* 日本語のローマ字つづり. ¶write in ***small*** *letters* 小文字で書く. ¶a ***syllabic*** *letter* 仮名.

Q² Name and address only to be written here. Please write in ***block*** *letters*. 住所氏名はここに書いて下さい. (分かりよいように)活字体に書いて下さい. ¶***call*** *letters* 〘ラジオ〙呼び出し符号 (JOAK, NBC など). ¶***ribbon*** *letters* リボン結びに形どった装飾活字または文字.

P It was blazed ***in*** *letters* of fire on my memory for all time. それは永久に消えない火の文字となって私の記憶に焼付けられた. ‖ carry out the law both ***in*** *letter* and spirit その法律を文字及び精神の両方面にわたって施行する ‖ in spirit as well as ***in*** *letter* 文字上のみならず精神においても. ¶carry out instructions ***to*** the *letter* 言付けを厳守する ‖ interpret the clauses ***to*** the strict *letter* of the law 法文通り厳密にその条項を解釈する. 【類】obey ***to*** the *letter* the injunction (命令) as to… / This order is ***to*** be obeyed ***to*** the *letter*. / Such charges may not be believed ***to*** the *letter* by persons of even average common sense. ¶engraved ***with*** *letters* 文字を彫った.

P² in *letters* ***of*** gold 金文字で; 美しい文章で.

(**3**) *pl.* 文学.

V ***forsake*** *letters* for politics 文学を政治にくら替する.

Q His death is a loss to ***Irish*** *letters*. 彼の死はアイルランド文学にとって損失だ.

P his interest ***in*** *letters* 彼の文学趣味. ¶He has become famous in the world ***of*** *letters*. 彼は文壇の名士となった. ¶Mr.… as a man ***of*** *letters* 文学者としての…氏.

letter, *v.* 文字で書く.

P *lettered* ***in*** gold (本の背などに)金文字で印刷した.

letter-box, *n.* 《英》郵便箱, ポスト.

V a postman ***clearing*** a *letter-box* 郵便箱をあけている集配人 ‖ The *letter-box* is ***cleared*** five times a day. 郵便箱は一日に五回開かれる. ¶***put*** a *letter* into a letter-box = post (=mail) a letter 手紙を投かんする.

lettered, *pa.* 文字入れの.

P a book *lettered* ***in*** gold 金文字入りの本.

letterhead, *n.* 書簡紙頭部の印刷文字, 頭部に字句を印刷した書簡紙.

V ***use*** (=***write on***) the *letterhead* of the University 頭部に同大学の文字入りの便せんを使用する.

Q² a ***business*** *letterhead* 商用文の頭部(発信人の住所などを印刷した).

P a letter ***under*** the *letterhead* of "The Diversity Theatre" 頭部にダイヴァーシティ劇場という文字入りの用紙に認めた手紙.

lettering, *n.* 文字.

Q the ***gilt*** *lettering* on their caps (水兵などの)帽子の上の金文字. ¶written in ***tiny*** *lettering* 小さな字で書いた.

P² explanation of the *lettering* ***on*** the plan 図面に示した(符号)文字の説明.

letterpress, *n.* 印刷した字句.

Q pictures with ***descriptive*** *letterpress* 解説付の絵.

level, *n.* 水平, 水準; 平面.

V ***attain*** a high *level* of culture 高度の文化水準に達する. ¶***draw*** *level* 並行して先を争う. ¶***find*** one's true *level* 真面目を発揮する. ‖ Water goes to ***find*** its *level*. 水は水平を求める(低きに流れる). ¶I have done my best to ***keep*** *level* with the latest results of foreign investigation. 私は外国における最近の研究結果と同一水準を保つために最善を尽した. ¶***lift*** the *level* 水準を高める. ¶***maintain*** a *level* ある水準を保つ. ¶They ***occupy*** a very low *level* when regarded purely as literature. それらは純文学の見地から論じるときわめて低い水準を占めることになる. ¶***raise*** the *level* of the human race (=humanity) 人類の地位を高める. 【類】***raise*** the moral and intellectual *level* of the people / ***raise*** the *level* of performances (演技). ¶***reach*** a high *level* of merit 高い価値を持つようになる. 【類】***reach*** higher *levels* of success in academic work (学業) / maintain his generally ***high*** *level* of excellence. ¶***touch*** a *level* of ¥12,000,000 千二百万円台に達する.

Q a ***dead*** *level* 平原. ¶below the ***general*** *level* 普通の水準以下. ¶people on a ***higher intellectual*** *level* より高い知的水準にある人々. ¶at a ***lower*** *level* もっと低い水準に. ¶he is on a higher ***moral*** *level* than … 彼は…より高い道徳的水準にある. ¶be far above the ***ordinary*** *level* of the fiction 一般小説の水準をはるかに上まわっている. ¶attain its ***prewar level*** 戦前の水準に達する.【類】Production of consumer goods (消費物資) is far from reaching ***prewar level***. ¶persons who live above a certain ***social level*** ある社会的水準以上の生活をしている人々. ¶be on the ***topmost level*** [式典などの]最高段にある. ¶people on ***various levels*** of culture 文化の水準を異にした人たち.

Q^2 at prices below ***black market levels*** やみ相場より低い値段で. ¶from 60 to 70 semester hours of study on the ***college level*** 大学程度の一期六十時間から七十時間の学修時間. ¶raised it up to the ***eye level*** of him それを自分の目の高さにあげた. ¶pictures produced mainly on the ***comprehension level*** of children 大体子供にも分かる程度の絵画. ¶British coal supply is below the ***danger level*** 英国の石炭生産は既に危険状態にはいっている. ¶Many clerks in government work settle down to routine work and soon seem unable to resist the pull of the ***dead level***. 多くの官吏は紋切形の仕事に落付きやがてはその単調さに反抗する力も抜けてしまうようだ. ¶The courses are on both ***high school*** and ***college level***. 課程は高校程度と大学程度とある. ¶be upon the same ***knowledge level*** with ... ...と同等程度の知識を持っている. ¶a higher ***nutrition level*** より高い栄養度. ¶Prices are now at ***peak levels*** or hovering in that neighborhood. 物価は今や最高を示しているかもしくはそれに近い状態である. ¶He has never occupied a position on a ***policy making level***. 彼は政策立案の地位を占めたことはない. ¶the general advance in ***price levels*** 一般物価水準の上昇.【類】the changes of the ***price level*** / two ***price levels***—the officially established ones and black-market prices (丸公とやみ値). ¶the slump to a ***record level*** 最底記録への暴落. ¶the ***salary level*** 給与ベース. ¶The speed of sound is 760 miles per hour at ***sea level***. 音の速度は水平面で一時間七百六十マイルである. ¶exist on a bare ***subsistence level*** かろうじて生きている程度である.【類】a standard of living (生活標準) gradually approaching the bare ***subsistence level***. ¶be below ***tide level*** あげ潮の高さには達しない. ¶fix a new ***wage level*** at ¥8,358 新賃金ベースを八千三百五十八円に決定する.【類】set the ***wage level*** at ¥3,791. ¶attain the ***world level*** 世界的水準に達する.

P He stood very far ***above*** the ordinary ***level*** of humanity. 彼は普通の人間の水準よりはるか上に立っていた. ¶among the nations ***at*** higher ***levels*** of culture より高い文化の水準にある諸国民の間に.【類】***at*** low ***levels*** of civilization ‖ lie down on a bed with the head and feet ***at*** the same ***level*** 頭と足を同じ高さにして寝台の上で横になる. ¶nations ***above*** (***below***) the ***level*** of civilazition 文明の水準以上(下)の国々. ¶A *hanamichi*, or a runway is ***on*** a ***level*** with the stage. 花道は舞台と同じ高さだ. ‖ The river water rose now until it was ***on*** a ***level*** with the banks. 河水は今や両岸にあふれる程度まで増水した. ‖ The snowfall measured nine inches ***on*** the ***level***. 積雪は平地で九インチあった. ‖ people who stood ***on*** a low ***level*** of civilization 文明の低い水準に立った人々. ¶***out of level*** 平らでない. ¶Such disgraceful conduct put them on a ***level with*** the beasts. かかる恥ずべき行為によって彼らは獣類の列に堕したのである.

level, *v.* 水平にする, 同等にする; 倒かいさせる; ねらう.

M^2 ***level down*** (***up***) the prices (their salaries) 物価(など)引(上)下げでででこぼこを直す. ¶His popularity is ***levelling off***. 彼の人望は下り坂だ. ¶***level*** a road ***up*** 道路を平らにする ‖ The older officials with smaller salaries applied to have them ***levelled up*** to the salaries of the new-comers. 低収入の古参職員はならして新入者の給料までの昇給を申入れた.

P ***level*** all abuses ***against*** (=***at***) ... あらゆる悪口雑言を...に浴せかける. ¶Some of the criticism ***levelled against*** us are not altogether fair. われわれに向けられた非難の中には当っていないものもある. ¶a great deal of criticism has been ***levelled at*** ... おびただしい非難が...に浴せかけられた ‖ ***level*** a pistol ***at*** ... ...にピストルを向ける. ¶It was ***levelled in*** the dust. それは倒かいされた. ¶***level*** a building ***to*** (=***with***) the ground 建物を地上に倒す. ¶The palace is now ***levelled to*** the dust. ¶Her masts ***level with*** the spires of churches. その船の帆柱が教会のせん塔と同じ高さになっている.

level[l]ing, *n.* 地ならし.

Q^2 ***ground levelling*** 地ならし.

lever, *n.*〖機〗てこ(レバー).

Q^2 a ***contact lever*** コンタクト・レバー. ¶a ***control lever***〖空〗操縦かん. ¶a ***foot lever***〖空〗フート・レバー.

leviathan, *n.* 海の巨獣(鯨など); 大財産家.

V Thou canst not ***draw out*** a ***leviathan*** with a hook. かぎで鯨はつるべくもない.

Q^2 Hence the eventual concentration of all the wealth of the nation in the hands of a few ***billionaire leviathans***. そこで国富のすべてが結局はその億万長者の手に集まることになる.

levity, *n.* 軽卒.

Q I hope there will be ***no levity*** here. (重大な場合であるから)この席では何ら軽卒にわたることがないようにしたい.

P treat a serious subject ***with levity*** 重大問題を軽卒に処理する.

levy, *n.* 賦課.

Q collection of ***capital levy*** 資本課税の徴収.

Q^2 ***excise levies*** 物品(消費)税.

P a ***levy of*** 8% ***on*** certain war profits ある種の戦時利得に対する八分の課税.

levy, *v.* (税などを)課する.

P ***levy*** tax ***against*** ... ...に課税する. ¶the rate of the taxes ***levied on*** incomes 所得税率 ‖ a tax ***levied on*** inherited property 相続税.【類】the tax of ... is ***levied on*** visitors who stay more than a week at ... ¶***levy*** blackmail ***upon*** ... ...を強請(ゆす)る.

levying, *n.* 課税.

Q^2 ***tax levying*** 徴税.

lewdness, *n.* いん欲.

Q be given to ***indiscreet lewdness*** 無分別ないん欲にふけっている.

lexicographer, *n.* 辞書編集者.

Q He was a ***great lexicographer*** of the day. 彼は当時の辞書編集の大家であった.

lexicon, *n.* 辞書.

P a ***lexicon to*** a classic author 古典作家の解釈辞書.

liability, *n.* 責任, 債務; 傾向.

V do not ***accept liability*** for loss or damage to ... ...に対し喪失または損傷の責を負わない. ¶***acknowledge*** the ***liability*** 責任を認める. ¶***deny*** one's ***liability*** 責任を否認する. ¶***hold*** no ***liability*** for ... ...の責を一切負わない. ¶***leave*** behind one unsecured ***liabilities*** amounting to ... 総計...に達する無担保の債務を彼に残す. ¶***liquidate*** one's ***liabilities*** 負債を清算する. ¶***meet*** one's ***liabilities*** 責務を弁済する. ¶***repudiate*** the ***liability*** その責務を拒絶する. ¶No ***liability*** is ***undertaken*** for any error or omission. 誤記または脱落に対しては何らの責を負わない.

V^2 my ***liability ceases*** on ... 私の責任は...日で終る.

Q ***limited*** (***unlimited***) ***liability*** 有(無)限責任.

Q^2 ***union liability***〖労〗[経営者側に対する]労組の義務(契約の不履行, ストなどによる損害補償など).

P be ***under*** no ***liability*** to ... ...すべき何らの責任もない.

P^2 ***liability for*** an accident 事故に対する責任.【類】***liability for*** military service. ¶***liability to*** an illness 病気にかかりやすいこと ‖ ***liability to*** noseblood 鼻血の出やすいこと.

liable, *a.* 責を負うべき, ...しやすい, ...の傾向のある.

M As a rule, men are ***more liable*** to insanity than women. 概して男は女より発狂しやすい.

P be ***liable for*** damages 損害に対する責任のある ‖ I am not ***liable for*** other people's debts. 私は他人の借金の責は負わない.【類】The master is ***liable for*** the faults of his servant. ¶Prices are ***liable to*** alteration in accordance with the fluctuation of exchange. 物価は為替の変動で変る. ‖ Hotel charges are ***liable to*** frequent variation. ホテルの料金は変動しがちだ. ‖ The steamers between ... and ... are ***liable to*** suspension in winter owing to ice. ...間の汽船は冬は結氷のために欠航しがちだ.【類】Every man is ***liable to*** error. ‖ be illegal and ***liable to*** seizure 不正だから差押えはまぬかれない ‖ Any one who ... is ***liable to*** a fine and imprisonment. ...する者はすべて罰金及び禁固に処せられる.【類】such a person is ***liable to*** a fine of ... / A violation of this regulation is ***liable to*** punishment. ‖ any person who ... is ***liable to*** proceedings for infringement of patent rights ...するものは特許権侵害として訴えられる.【類】Any person who ... is ***liable to*** an action at law (法のさばき).

O ***liable*** to catch cold かぜを引きやすい.【類】He is *lia-*

ble to lose his temper (=get angry).

liaison, *n.* 不倫, 私通; 連絡.

V ***effect*** [a] *liaison* with ... ...とわたりをつける(連絡を取る). ¶He ***formed*** a number of *liaisons* with women. 彼は数人の女と不倫行為があった. ¶***keep up*** a *liaison* with ... ...と醜関係を続ける.

Q ***inter-theatre*** *liaison* 戦地区間の連絡. ¶***perfect*** *liaison* between ... and ... ...間の完全な連絡.

liar, *n.* 虚言者.

Q a ***colossal*** *liar* 大うそつき. ¶a ***big*** (=***great***) *liar* 大うそつき. ¶a ***gratuitous*** *liar* 不必要にうそをつく人. ¶an ***incorrigible*** *liar* 手のつけられないうそつき. ¶a ***notorious*** *liar* 札つきのうそつき. ¶the ***tallest*** *liar* この上もない大ぼら吹き. ¶***What*** a *liar* (he is)! (彼は)何というらそつきだ.

libation, *n.* 神酒.

V ***pour*** *libations* on their gods 彼らの神像に神酒を注ぐ.

libel, *n.* 非難文, 侮辱.

V ***spread*** *libels* against ... ...非難の文を散布する. ¶***write*** a *libel* against ... ...を非難する一文を草する.

Q a ***gross*** *libel* 大侮辱. ¶It is a ***shameful*** *libel* on our national character. それはわが国民性に対するとんでもない侮辱である.

P^2 a *libel* ***against*** a person (=one's character) ある人に対する非難. ¶a *libel* ***on*** art and artists 芸術と芸術家に対する侮辱. 【類】a *libel* ***on*** human nature (人間性).

liberal, *a.* 自由な, 豊富な, 寛大な, 物惜みしない.

P *liberal* ***in*** opinion (thought, view) 意見(など)の自由主義的な ‖ *liberal* ***in*** supply 供給の豊富な ‖ *liberal* ***in*** giving 惜気もなく与える. ¶*liberal* ***of*** one's money 金に大まかな. ¶He has shown himself *liberal* and friendly ***to*** the West. 彼は西洋に対して寛大で友情的態度を示した. ‖ *liberal* ***to*** an opponent 反対者に寛仁な ‖ *liberal* ***to*** profusion 大ざっぱ過ぎるくらいな. ¶*liberal* ***with*** tipping チップを惜しまない ‖ He is *liberal* ***with*** his purse (=money). 彼は金惜しみをしない.

liberalism, *n.* 自由主義.

V ***defend*** *liberalism* 自由主義を守る.

P an advocate ***of*** *liberalism* 自由主義の擁護者.

Q ***economic*** *liberalism* 経済的自由主義.

Q^2 ***eighteenth*** and ***nineteenth century*** *liberalism* 十八・九世紀の自由主義.

liberate, *v.* 釈放する, 放出する.

M *liberate* little birds ***out*** into the sky 小鳥を大空に離してやる. ¶***provisionally*** *liberated* from the necessity of ... 一時...する必要から解除された.

P *liberate* him ***from*** bondage 彼を釈放する. 【類】*liberate* ... ***from*** the slavery (どれい制度) / *liberate* them ***from*** the pressure (圧制) of ... ‖ *liberate* the water ***from*** the pond 池の水を放出する.

liberation, *n.* 釈放.

V ***demand*** the *liberation* of ... ...の釈放を要求する.

Q ***provisional*** *liberation* 仮出獄(所).

P ***On*** his *liberation*, the prisoner had some money. 釈放された時その囚徒はいくらか金を持っていた.

liberty, *n.* 自由, 無遠慮.

V cannot ***allow*** the *liberty* of ... ...する自由は許されない. 【類】They are ***allowed*** great *liberties* at this season. ¶People often ***confuse*** *liberty* with licence. 人はとかく自由と放縦を混同する. ¶***defend*** one's *liberties* その自由を擁護する. ¶You will ***excuse*** the *liberty* I take in writing to you. 失礼ながら一筆申上げます. ¶***gain*** one's *liberty* 自由を獲得する. ¶*Liberty* to appeal was ***given***. 控訴の自由が与えられた. ‖ Fowls are ***given*** the *liberty* of the fields. 家きんは放し飼いにされている. ‖ Lincoln ***granted*** *liberty* to slaves. リンカンはどれいたちに自由を与えた. ¶they ***have*** the *liberty* to ... 彼らは...することができる. 【類】You ***have*** no *liberty* of choice (選択). ¶***recover*** one's *liberty* 自由を回復する. ¶I ***take*** the *liberty* of telling you this. 失礼ですが君にこのことをお話します. ‖ He ***took*** the *liberty* of using my dictionary while I was absent. 彼は私の留守中勝手に辞書を使った. 【類】we are ***taking*** the *liberty* to remind you that ... ‖ ***take*** small *liberties* with the strict order of facts 多少事実を曲げる. 【類】***take*** some *liberties* with the original in translation ‖ He has ***taken*** the *liberties* with my property. 彼は私の財産を横領した. ‖ ***take*** *liberties* with women 女に悪ふざけする. 【類】You must not ***take*** *liberties* with older people. / allow a man to ***take*** *liberties* with her. ¶***uphold*** *liberty* and justice 自由と正義を支持する. ¶***use*** one's personal *liberty* sensibly 個人の自由を賢明に使う. ¶***violate*** personal *liberty* 個人の自由を侵害する. ¶***win*** *liberty* for ... ...の自由を獲得する. ¶***yield*** all *liberty* to ... ...にすべての自由を許す.

Q enjoy to the full the ***civil*** *liberties* which belong to American citizens. 米国市民の持っている市民の自由を十分に享有する. ¶restrict the ***glorious*** *liberty* of English public-school education 英国私立学校教育の光栄ある自由を制限する. ¶take ***naughty*** *liberties* with ... ...に悪ふざけする(女などに). ¶***personal*** *liberty* 個人の自由. ¶***political*** and ***religious*** *liberty* 政治及び宗教の自由. ¶***unbounded*** *liberty* 無限の自由.

P be ***at*** *liberty* to use 使用自由である ‖ I am not ***at*** *liberty* to tell any bit of it. 私はその話は一切禁じられています. ‖ set a person (slave) ***at*** *liberty* 人(など)に自由を与える ‖ I shall be ***at*** *liberty* (=free) this afternoon. きょうの午後はひまの予定です. 【類】You are ***at*** *liberty* to go or stay. / Each member will be ***at*** *liberty* to state his own views. / I do not feel ***at*** *liberty* to mention the name of the school. / You are ***at*** perfect *liberty* to use this letter as you think fit. / All dogs ***at*** *liberty* without being muzzled and labelled shall be seized (口輪や札を付けないで). ¶***with*** *liberty* to ... 勝手に...することができて.

P^2 *liberty* ***of*** instruction=freedom of teaching 教授の自由 ‖ *liberty* ***of*** speech (the press, religious worship, thought and action) 言論(など)の自由 ‖ The *liberties* ***of*** the people are extremely *limited*. 人民の自由は極度に制限されている.

librarian, *n.* 司書.

Q^2 an ***acquisition*** *librarian* 図書収集担当の司書. ¶a ***catalogue*** *librarian* カタログ(目録)作成担当の司書. ¶***music*** *librarians* of a radio station 放送局の音楽資料係. ¶a ***reference*** *librarian* 参考図書館員(司書).

library, *n.* 図書館, 文庫; 蔵書.

V He has ***accumulated*** a *library* of 17,000 volumes. 彼は一万七千巻の蔵書を集めた. ¶***build up*** a private *library* 私用の図書収集をする. ¶***catalogue*** a *library* 文庫の目録を作る. ¶***collect*** a *library* of books dealing with ... ...関係の本を収集する. ¶The *library* is ***consulted*** annually by about 65,000 persons. その図書館は毎年約六万五千の読者に利用される. ¶His *library* is now being ***dispersed***. 彼の蔵書は昨今散逸しつつある. ¶The *library* is ***equipped*** with ample funds for its support. その図書館は維持資金が豊富にある. ¶***erect*** a *library* 図書館を建設する. ¶The society has ***formed*** a *library*. その会は文庫を設けた. ¶***frequent*** a *library* 図書館にしばしば出入する. ¶He ***has*** (=***possesses***) a *library* of 100,000 volumes. 彼は十万冊の蔵書がある. ¶***house*** a *library* 蔵書を(安全な場所に)入れる. ¶***maintain*** a large *library* 大図書館を維持する. ¶These published in English alone would ***make*** a *library* of some hundreds of volumes. 英語で出版されるものだけで数百冊の多数に上るだろう. 【類】He has published enough to ***make*** a small *library*. ¶***open*** a *library* for children 子供向きの図書館を開く. ¶***own*** a *library* of ten thousand volumes 家に万巻の書を擁する. ¶***set*** one's *library* to rights 蔵書を整理する.

V^2 The whole culture of rubber is a science round which a *library* has already ***accumulated***. ゴム栽培といえばそのあらゆる文献がすでに一集書をなしている一科学である. ¶The *library* ***comprises*** about 13,000 volumes. その図書室は約一万三千冊を収蔵している.

Q the lost ***alexandrian*** *library* 消滅したアレキサンドリアの図書館. ¶an ***audio-visual*** *library* 視聴覚ライブラリー. ¶It is to be found in any ***considerable*** *library*. それは相当の図書館には備付けてある. ¶the ***extensive*** *library* of the late ... 故...の大蔵書. ¶a ***fine*** *library* collected by his father 彼の父の集めたりっぱな蔵書. ¶a ***free*** *library* 無料図書館. ¶The ***Home University*** *Library* [書名]家庭大学双書. ¶The university possesses a ***magnificent*** *library* of Chinese books (=works). その大学には漢籍のすばらしい蔵書がある. ¶***private*** *library* 私設図書館. ¶***public*** and ***institutional*** *libraries* 公開並に団体付属の図書館. ¶a ***select little*** *library* of chemical literature 化学文献の精選した小文庫. ¶a ***well-selected*** *library* 選択よろしきを得た双書.

Q² a *circulating library* 貸出し専門の文庫. ¶a *college* (*university*) *library* 大学図書館. ¶a *home library* 家庭双書. ¶a *daughter library* 付属図書館. ¶a *lending library* 貸出し図書館. ¶the *luxurious Rylands Library* at Manchester マンチェスターの豪華なライランド図書館. ¶a *reference library* 参考資料図書館. ¶a *research library* 研究図書館. ¶a *room library* 書斎.

P books *from* the *library* of ... ...の旧蔵(手沢本).

P² the people's *library of* literature 国民文学双書 ‖ a *library of* Buddhist Sutras 仏典の書庫.

license, licence, *n.* (1) 免許; 免許状, 許可証, 鑑札.

V ***apply for*** a *license* 免許状下付を申請する. ¶***award*** a *license* 免許状を授与する. ¶***forfeit*** a *license* 免許状を取上げられる. ¶***get*** a *license* 許可証を得る. ¶***grant*** (=***give***) *license* to ... ...に許可を与える ‖ ***grant*** *licenses* for a patent 特許許可を与える. 【類】***grant*** him a *license* empowering him to ... ¶He ***has*** a *license* to keep a dog. 彼は畜犬の鑑札を持っている. ¶***hold*** a *license* 許可証を持っている. ¶***issue*** listeners' *licenses* ラジオ聴取許可証を発行する. ¶***lose*** one's *license* 免許状を失う. ¶***obtain*** a *license* from ... ...から免許を受ける. ¶He was ***refused*** a *license*. 彼は免許下付が不認可になった. ¶***reissue*** a *license* 免許証を再発行する. ¶***renew*** a *license* 免許証を書換える. ¶No *license* is ***required*** in Scotland for salmon or trout fishing. スコットランドではさけ及びますの漁には鑑札がいらない. ¶***revoke*** a *license* to practice [医師などの]免許状を取上げる. ¶***secure*** secondary school teacher's *license* without examination 無試験で中等教員免状を取る. ¶***Show*** me your *license*. 免許状を見せろ. ¶His *license* was ***suspended*** for six months. 彼は六カ月間免許状の使用を停止された. ¶***take out*** a *license* to fish salmon さけ猟鑑札を受ける ‖ guides who have ***taken out*** their *licenses* 許可を得ている案内業者.

Q a ***chauffeur's*** *license* 自動車運転手免状. ¶A "ship of the red seal" means a vessel possessing an ***Imperial*** *license* to trade. 御朱印船というのは貿易の官許を得ている船ということである. ¶Deviation from historic truth is the ***natural*** *licences* of the romancer. 史実から逸脱することは小説家当然の権利である. ¶obtain from ... a ***special*** *license* to ... ...から...の特許を得る. ¶a ***temporary*** *license* 仮免(許証).

Q² renew one's ***dog*** *license* 飼犬の鑑札を更新する. ¶a ***driving*** *license* 運転免許証. ¶without a ***government*** *license* 政府の許可なしに. ¶secure a ***hunting*** (=***shooting***) *license* 狩猟許可をとる. 【類】applicants for ***hunting*** *licenses*. ¶revocation of ***liquor*** *licenses* 酒類販売許可証の取消し. ¶issue a ***marriage*** *license* 結婚許可証を発行する. ¶a ***mining*** *license* 採鉱許可証. ¶Have you got a ***schooling*** *license?* 教員免状をお持ちですか.

P The term ***of*** *license* has expired. 免許期間が満了した. ¶It is prohibited except ***on*** *licenses* from the Government. それは政府の許可がなくてはできない. ¶except ***under*** special *license* 特許による以外は ‖ do trading business ***under*** Government *license* 政府の許可をとって貿易をやる. ¶He was summoned for driving a motorcar ***without*** a *licence*. 彼は無免許で自動車を運転したために召喚された.

P² a *license* ***from*** customs authorities 税関の許可.

(2) 放縦.

Q ***sexual*** *licence* 性的放縦. ¶***unbridled*** *licence* 手のつけられない気まま. ¶***wild*** *license* of fashionable society 上流社会の乱脈.

license, *v.* 許可する, 認める.

P The premises are *licensed* ***for*** dancing その建物ではダンスすることが許されている.

lichen, *n.* こけ.

P stones covered ***with*** *lichens* こけの蒸した石.

P² a *lichen* ***on*** tree-trunks 木の幹に生えたこけ.

lick, *v.* なめる.

M² The flames *licked* ***up*** a row of buildings in a second. 炎がたちまち一ならびの建物をなめ尽した. 【類】The flames *licked* ***up*** everything that was combustible. ‖ The cat *licks* ***up*** milk with the tongue. ねこが舌で牛乳をなめる.

P *lick* it ***into*** shape それにどうにか目鼻をつける.

lid, *n.* ふた.

V ***lift*** the *lid* of the box 箱のふたを開ける. ¶***open*** the *lid* ふたを開ける. ¶***put on*** the *lid* ふたをする. ¶***take off*** the *lid* ふたを外す. ¶***undo*** a *lid* ふたを開ける. ¶***wrench*** the *lid* out of place 無理にふたをはずす. ¶***wrench off*** the *lid* ふたをねじ取る.

P covered ***with*** a *lid* ふたをした.

lie, *n.* うそ, 虚偽.

V ***act*** a *lie* [行為で]あざむく. ¶He ***detests*** a *lie* in any form. 彼はうそと名のつくものは一切これをきらう. ¶***give*** the *lie* to ... ...に(面と向って)うそをとがめる ‖ ***give*** a person the *lie*=accuse a person of lying 人の言うことをうそだといって非難する. 【類】Every one would ***give*** you the *lie*. ¶***invent*** a *lie* about ... ...についてうそをねつ造する. ¶***refute*** a *lie* うそを実証する. ¶Don't ***tell*** a *lie!* うそを言うな. ¶***write*** monstrous *lies* 途方もないうそを書く.

Q ***abominable*** *lies* 憎むべきうそ. ¶an ***absolute*** *lie* 全くのうそ. ¶a ***barefaced*** *lie* 真赤なうそ. ¶a ***bald-faced*** *lie* しらじらしいうそ. ¶a ***black*** *lie* 悪質なうそ. ¶tell a ***circumstantial*** *lie* その場の都合でうそをつく. ¶a ***cowardly*** *lie* ひきょうなうそ. ¶a ***deliberate*** *lie* 念の入ったうそ. ¶a ***downright*** *lie* あからさまなうそ. ¶a ***favorite*** *lie* いつものうそ. ¶a ***heartless*** *lie* 冷酷なうそ. ¶***hollow*** *lies* 見えすいたうそ. ¶an ***impudent*** *lie* 人をばかにしたうそ. ¶a ***medical*** *lie* [医者の]方便としてのうそ. ¶an ***outrageous*** *lie* けしからぬうそ. ¶a ***palpable*** *lie* 明白なうそ. ¶a ***plausible*** *lie* まことしやかなうそ. ¶a ***transparent*** *lie* 見えすいたうそ. ¶***unscrupulous*** *lies* 厚かましいうそ. ¶a ***white*** *lie* 悪意のないうそ. 【類】even the smallest or the ***whitest*** *lie*. ¶tell a ***whopping*** *lie* 大それたうそをつく.

Q² tell ***business*** *lies* 商売上のかけ引きを言う.

P tell all sorts ***of*** *lies* うそ八百をならべる.

P² It is a *lie* ***out of*** the whole truth. それは真赤なうそだ.

lie, *v.* うそをつく, あざむく.

M *lie* ***intentionally*** 故意にうそをつく. ¶*lie* ***knowingly*** (***unknowingly***) わざと(うっかり)うそをはく. ¶*lie* ***prodigiously*** 大うそをつく. ¶*lie* ***readily*** すらすらとうそをつく.

P She *lied* ***about*** you to me. 彼女は僕に君のことについてうそをついた. ¶*lie* ***in*** one's teeth (=throat) 真赤なうそをつく. ¶*lie* a person ***into*** ... 人をだまして...に落し入れる. ¶*lie* a person ***out of*** his money 人をだましてその金を奪いとる. ¶There's no use trying to *lie* ***to*** me. 僕をだまそうとしたってだめだ. 【類】She *lied* ***to*** her husband. / You're *lying* ***to*** me.

lie, *v.* 横たわる, 寝る; 停泊する, 存在する.

M *lie* ***abed*** 寝床についている. ¶It *lies* too far ***afield*** (=***away***) for a three-days' trip. そこは三日の旅には遠すぎる. ¶*lie* ***along*** 長々と横たわる. ¶*lie* ***awake*** 目をあけて寝ている. ¶*lie* ***back*** in the armchair 安楽いすにどっかとそり返る ‖ Laboratories *lie* ***back*** of all the business enterprises of today. 研究所は今日のあらゆる事業の背後の力になっている. ¶He *lies* ***buried*** here. 彼はここに葬られている. ¶His horse *lay* ***dead*** on the road. 彼の馬は路上に死んでいた. ¶It will *lie* pretty ***deep*** today. きょうの雪は大分積る. ‖ The principle *lies* ***deep*** in our human nature. その原則はわれわれの人間性に根ざしている. ¶the strength that *lies* ***dormant*** 潜在している力. ¶Don't *lie* ***flat***. ばったりと寝るな. 【類】*lie* ***flat*** on the ground. ¶*lie* ***hard*** (=heavy) on ... ...を圧迫する. ¶The food *lies* ***heavy*** (=***cold***) on the stomach. その食物は腹にもたれる. ‖ The hours *lay* ***heavy*** on my hands. 時間をもてあました. ¶His money *lies* ***idle*** in the bank. 彼の金は銀行で遊んでいる. ¶*lie* ***idly*** on one's oars 仕事を怠けてぶらぶらする. ¶a person who *lies* ***late*** in bed 朝寝坊する人. ¶*lie* ***lazily*** in bed 長々とベットに横になる. ¶The shadows *lie* ***long***. [夕日で]影が長く映っている. ¶*lie* ***low*** 平伏する. ¶it *lies* ***near*** to suppose that ... ...と想像するのももっともだ. ¶The book *lay* ***open*** on the desk. 本は机上に開いたままになっていた. ¶*lie* ***prostrate*** ひれ伏す. ¶*lie* ***scattered*** 散らばっている. ¶*lie* ***sleeping*** 横になって眠っている. ¶*lie* ***still*** 静かにふしている. ¶*lie* ***stretched out*** as if dead まるで死んだようにのされている.

M² *lie* ***down*** to ... 戦わずして...に降服する ‖ *lie* ***down*** and take it easy 横になって身体を楽にする. 【類】*lie* ***down*** for a rest. ¶The black bear *lies* ***up*** during the day in caves or amongst rocks. 黒くまは日中は洞穴か岩かげにひそんでいる. ‖ I have a bad cold, and must *lie* ***up*** for a day or two. 私はひどいかぜをひいて一両日は寝ていなければならない.

P Sheets of paper *lie* ***about*** the room. 紙がへやに散らばっている. ¶The village *lies* ***across*** the river. その村は川の向う側にある. 【類】A narrow bridge *lay* ***across*** the stream. ¶Accusation of theft *lay **against*** him. 彼は窃盗の罪に問われた. ¶The path *lies **along*** a stream (the shore). 路は小川(など)に沿うている. ¶The hot springs *lie **among*** pretty scenery. その温泉は風光明美である. ‖ The choice *lies **among*** A, B, C, and D. A, B, C 及び D の内どれでも選択することになっている. ¶The lake *lies **amongst*** the mountains. その湖水は山中にある. ¶The blame *lies **at*** his door. 責は彼が負うべきものだ. ‖ Luck *lies **at*** your very door. 幸運の神は君の手中にある. ‖ The bones *lie **at*** rest in the soil of the island. 遺骨はその島に葬られている. ‖ The matter *lies **at*** my heart. 私はそのことが気にかかる. ‖ The ship *lies **at*** anchor in the harbor. 船はその港に停泊している. ‖ *lie **at*** full length on a couch 長いすに大の字に寝る ‖ Drinking *lies **at*** the foot of his deseases. 彼の病気の根源は飲酒にある. 【類】 the philosophy that *lies **at*** the base of their activities. ¶A happy future *lies **before*** you. 幸福な未来が君の前途に横たわっている. ¶What mystery *lay **behind*** the disappearance of the girl? その少女失そうの裏面にはどんな秘密が潜んでいたのだろうか. ¶The truth *lies **between*** extremes. 真理は両極端の中間に存する. 【類】 He *lay* for a long time ***between*** life and death. ¶His conduct *lies **beyond*** all question and reproach. 彼の行為は明々白々で疑いようもなければ非難のしようもない. ¶He has the Mss. *lying **by*** him for the next number. 次号に載せる原稿が彼の所にある. ¶*lie **in*** bed with a bad cold ひどい感冒で床についている ‖ The charm of travel *lies **in*** its new experiences. 旅の妙味はその新しい経験に存する. 【類】 She *lay **in*** bed with her baby's head nestling in sleep against her breast (ふところに抱かれて). / The charm of it *lay* more ***in*** telling than ***in*** the tale. / its chief interest to most people *lies **in*** the fact that ... / The greatest charm of the bride's costume *lies **in*** its simplicity / The chief difficulty *lies **in*** ... / Happiness *lies **in*** contentment. / Woman's strength *lies **in*** her weakness. / ***In*** that *lie* both its strength and weakness. / The cause *lies **in*** the fact that ... / a familiar example (卑近な例) *lies **in*** the case of ... ‖ The city *lay **in*** ruins after the battle. その市は戦争でひどく荒廃していた. ‖ as much as *lies **in*** one's power 力の及ぶ限り ‖ *lie* [***in*** wait] for ... ...を待ち伏せる. 【類】 Roving bands of robbers infest the roads and many other dangers *lie **in*** wait (いろいろな危険が横っている). ‖ *lie **in*** ambush 待伏せる. ‖ *lie **in*** the way 邪魔になる ‖ the secret of the trick *lies **in*** the fact that ... その手品の種は...だ ‖ the pleasure which *lies **in*** the denial of pleasure 快楽否定の中に存在する快楽 ‖ contribute as much as ***in*** us *lies* to ... われわれの力の及ぶ限り...に寄与する. ¶The ship is *lying **off*** the mouth of the river. その船は河口の沖合に停泊している. ¶*lie **on*** the floor (desk, table) 床(など)の上にある. 【類】 *lie* on the bed and sleep / *lie **on*** a sickbed ‖ *lie **on*** one's face (back, side) うつむき(仰向き, 横)になる. 【類】 *Lying **on*** his back was torture. ¶though the subject *lies **outside*** our present inquiry, it should be added that ... この問題は当面の研究の範囲外ですが...のことをつけ加えておくべきであろう. ¶A white mist *lay **over*** London. 白い霧がロンドンにかかった. ¶*lie **towards*** ... ...によりかかる. ¶*lie **under*** deep obligations to ... ...に大いに負う所がある ‖ *lie **under*** the suspicion of corruption 収(贈)賄の疑いがある ‖ the fault *lies **with*** ... その罪(過失)は...にある. 【類】 The fault does not *lie* ***with*** the government officials. / The choice *lies **with**.* you ‖ the interest of the book *lies **with*** the little band of men who ... この本に興味を感じるものは...という小数のグループにある ‖ *lie **with*** a woman 同きんする.

lien, *n.* 財産留置権.

V He ***has*** a *lien* on the cargo. 船荷の取得権が彼にある. ¶***place*** a *lien* on goods 品物の取得権を決める.

P² a prior *lien **on*** property (income, earnings) 財産(など)先取権.

lieu, *n.* 代り.

P A guaranteed security will do ***in*** *lieu* of a cash deposit. 保証担保をもって現金預金に替えてもよい. ‖ grant a new certificate ***in*** *lieu* of and as a substitute for her original certificate of registry その船の最初の登録証明書の原本に代るものとして新しい証明書を下付する.

lieutenant, *n.* 陸軍中尉; 副官.

Q Lassalle and his ***faithful*** *lieutenants* ラサールとその忠実な副官. ¶a ***first*** (***second***) *lieutenant* 〖陸軍〗中(少)尉. ¶his ***great*** *lieutenants* 彼の有名な幕僚. ¶his ***principal*** *lieutenant* 彼の片腕.

life, *n.* 生命; 生活, 生計; 活気; 人; 伝記.

V ***abandon*** hotel *life* ホテル生活をやめる. 【類】 The girl decided to ***abandon*** her licentious *life* (放縦な生活). / ***abandon*** her *life* of prostitution (泥水商売). ¶***abbreviate*** one's *life* 命を縮める. ¶learn to ***accept*** one's *life* 現在の境遇に満足する, 足るを知る. ¶***add*** *life* to ... ...の活力を増す. ¶***adjust*** our *life* accordingly われらの生活をこれに準じて調節する. ¶***adopt*** the simple *life* 簡易生活を行う ‖ ***adopt*** a *life* of prostitution 売春婦になる. ¶***ameliorate*** the *lives* of the workmen 労働者の生活を改善する. ¶***amend*** one's *life* 処世法を改める. ¶***approach*** middle *life* 中年に近づく. ¶The unhappy girl has ***attempted*** her own *life*. その不幸な娘は自殺をしようとした. ¶***attribute*** one's long *life* to ... 長命は...がその原因だとする. ¶Arts ***beautify*** *life*. 芸術は人生を美化する. ¶***beg*** one's *life* 命ごいをする. ¶***begin*** *life* as a clerk in a bank 銀行員として始めて実社会に立つ. ¶There are a great number of youths who ***begin*** *life* with the idea that the way to success lies through a college education. 成功への道は大学教育にありという考えを抱いて世に出る青年が非常に多い. ‖ He ***began*** *life* with nothing. 彼は無一文で世に出た. 【類】 young fellows who have just ***begun*** *life* with plenty of leisure and a little money ‖ ***begin*** *life* again (=anew) 生活のまき直しをする. 【類】 ***begin*** a *life* entirely fresh and new. ¶He ***bled*** his *life* ***away***. 彼は出血の結果死んだ. ¶***blight*** her whole *life* 彼女の一生にたたる. ¶***brighten*** one's *life* 生活を明朗化する. ¶This ***brought*** his *life* to a premature close. このために彼は若死した. ¶***carry*** his *life* in his hands 命がけの仕事をする. ¶***cast*** away *life* 命をなげうつ. ¶***change*** *life* and start afresh 人生の新規まき直しをする. ¶***choke*** the *life* out of a person 絞殺する. ¶The traffic accident ***claimed*** 21 *lives*. 交通事故で二十一名の死者を出した. ¶***close*** one's *life* at the age of ... ...歳で一生を終る. ¶This event ***colored*** his entire *life*. この事件が彼の一生に影響を及ぼした. ¶***consecrate*** one's *life* to the service of the poor, the suffering, and the oppressed 貧しい者, 苦しむ者, しいたげられた人々のために一生を捧げる. 【類】 henceforth my *life* shall be ***consecrated*** to ... ¶***consider*** *life* freed from early bias 以前の偏見を捨てて人生を考察する. ¶There are instances of men who on becoming blind have ***continued*** their active *life*. 盲目になっても活動的生活を続けた人の例がある. ¶The engineering work ***cost*** many *lives*. その工事は多数の死者を出した. ¶those who ***count*** their official *life* by months 数カ月まえに就任した人々. ¶***cover*** a *life* of sin with outward sanctity 外観は神聖らしく見せかけて罪深い生活を隠す. ¶This sad news ***crushed*** the life out of her. この悲報に接して彼女は失望のふちに沈んだ. ¶***create*** a new *life* 新生命を創造する. ¶***curse*** one's *life* 人生をのろう. ¶Death suddenly ***cut*** short the *life* of his promising career. 死のために突然彼の有望な前途が絶たれた. ¶His *life* was ***darkened*** by disease. 彼の生活は病気で暗いものになっていた. ¶***dedicate*** one's *life* to science 科学に一生を捧げる. ¶***depart*** this *life* この世を去る ‖ on the point of ***departing*** this *life* いまわのきわに. ¶***desert*** *life* 死ぬ. ¶Three grains of that poison is sufficient to ***destroy*** *life*. その毒は三ゲレーンで優に人を殺す. 【類】 The fire ***destroyed*** hundreds of *lives* and many million dollars worth of property. ¶***devoted*** his *life* and wealth to ... ...に彼の一生と富とを捧げた. 【類】 men and women ***devoting*** their *lives* for the advancement of civilization / a man whose whole *life* was ***devoted*** to the service of his country / ***devote*** one's whole *life* to the service of humanity. ¶***disregard*** one's own *life* 自分の生命を軽んじる. ¶***dream away*** one's *life* 人生を夢のように暮す. ¶***eat*** one's *life* ***away*** 生命をすり減らす. ¶This led to scenes of jealousy which ***embittered*** the *life* of both. このために両人の生活を苦しめたしっとの場面を現出した. ¶persons who ***ended*** their *lives* in (=by) leaping from buildings 建物から飛下りて死んだ人々. 【類】 ***end*** one's *life* with poison / the serious illness which ***ended*** his *life*. ¶***endanger*** *life* 生命にかかわる. ¶help to ***endure*** *life* 生き抜くための役に立つ. ¶***enjoy*** a *life* of happiness 幸福に暮す.

【類】*enjoy life* fully (=to the full) / *enjoy life* to the fullest possible degree / He is *enjoying* a happy (cheery) *life*. ¶*enrich* the *life* of the people 国民の生活を豊かにする. 【類】*enrich* the corporate *life* (共同生活). ¶*enrich* and *deepen life* 生活を豊かにかつ深くする. ¶*enter* married *life* 結婚生活にはいる. ¶*expose* one's *life* 生命をかける. ¶*find life* unattractive 世の中がおもしろくなくなる. ¶*fashion* one's *life* along another's lines 人を見習って自分の生活を改造する. ¶*finding life* a bore 世の中にあきて. ¶For over half a century he has *followed* the *life* of a naturalist. 彼は五十余年間博物学者としての生活を続けた. 【類】*follow* a *life* which descended to the lowest depths of human degradation (堕落のどん底生活) ‖ Gautama *followed* the *life* of a mendicant as he proceeded from place to place instructing his disciples. 釈迦は弟子たちに教えながら所々方々を転々してこじきの生活を送った. ¶He commanded all Christians in his domain to become Saracens or *forfeit* their *lives*. 彼はその領土の全キリスト教徒に対して回教徒になれと命じこれにそむくものは生命を奪うと言渡した. 【類】Iemitsu forbade the construction of ships over a certain size, and decreed that every Japanese who left the country should *forfeit* his *life*. ¶*fortify* life 身体を丈夫にする. ¶*frighten* (=*scare*) the *life* out of ... ...をおどかして気絶させる. ¶*get life* from God 神から生命を受ける. ¶*give* one's *life* to ... 一生を...に捧げる ‖ *given* fresh *life* 新しい元気を得て. 【類】*give* it entirely new *life* ‖ the sons of Cornell University who *gave* their *lives* in (=during) the World War 世界大戦に命を捧げたコーネル大学生. 【類】*give* one's *life* for one's country ‖ His achievements *gave* him a *life* beyond his years. 彼の業績は彼の名を後世に残した. ‖ She *gave* her *life* to save her child. 彼女はその子を救うために命を捨てた. ‖ *give* a picture *life* and spirit 絵に生命と気魄(ᵏ)とを与える. ¶*give up* one's *life* for a cause ある主義のために命を捨てる. ¶*guard* the *lives* and property of foreigners 外国人の生命財産を保護する. ¶*guide* one's *life* by the principle その主義を処世の方針とする. ¶*have* long *life* [物が] 長持ちがする ‖ live together and *have* a *life* together 同居して一身同体の生活をする ‖ Children *have* as many *lives* as a cat. 子供はねこと同様中々死なないもの. ¶*hazard* one's *life* in saving ... 命をかけて...を救う. ¶I cannot *imagine life* without her. 彼女なしの人生は考えられない. ¶*imperil* the *lives* of passengers 乗客の生命を危くする. ¶*infuse life* into ... ...に新生気を吹込む. ¶*instill* (=put) new *life* into ... ...を復活させる. ¶*insure* one's *life* heavily 巨額の生命保険をつける ‖ *insure* one's *life* for ... yen ... 円の生命保険をつけ. 【類】By annual payments of premiums to an insurance company we may *insure* our *lives* and properties. ¶He somehow manages to *keep life* together on the salary. 彼はその給料でどうにかやっている. ¶He *laid* his *life* as the price of progress. 彼は進歩の代価として生命を犠牲にした. ¶They *laid down* their *lives* for their country. 彼らは国のために生命を捨てた. 【類】*lay down* one's *life* to serve one's prince / We are all ready to *lay down* our *lives* for the country. / He was willing to *lay down* his *life* rather than survive in disgrace. ¶The couple *has* a *life* of ideal happiness. その夫婦は理想的な幸福の生活を送っている. ¶*lead* a *life* of shame [売春など] 恥かしい生活をする. 【類】*lead* the *life* of a drunkard (酔っぱらい) / He had *led* the *life* of a saint (聖者). / *lead* a *life* of well-fed leisure / *lead* an easy *life*= live a life of ease / how to *lead* simple *life*. ¶*leave* (= quit) a *life* of sin 罪悪の生活を捨てる ‖ *leave* one's *life* of worldly pleasure 浮世を捨てる. ¶To save time is to *lengthen life*. 時間を節約することは寿命を長くすることだ. ‖ *lengthen* the *life* of a machine (an electric bulb) 機械(など)を長くもたせる. ¶*live* a *life* of a hermit (the poor) 隠者(など)の生活を送る ‖ life and how to *live it* 人生と処世法 ‖ *live* a *life* of separation from the world 世間から離れた生活をする. 【類】*live* a *life* of idleness, without work and without regular occupation / *live* the *life* of a religious recluse (修道士のような生活) / have no leisure to *live* a *life* of original inquiry (独創的研究). / They have *lived lives* of severe bodily exertion (激しい筋肉労働の生活). ‖ *live life* to the full 充実した生活を送る. ¶*live out* one's *life* 一生を終る ‖ *live out* a natural *life* 天寿を全うする. ¶He was in great danger of *losing* his *life*. 彼はすんでのこと命を取られる所だった. ‖ He nearly *lost* his *life*. 彼は危く死ぬところだった. 【類】He came very near to *losing* his *life*. / *lose* one's *life* in an attempt to ... (...しようとして) / *lose* one's *life* by shipwreck (難船) / *lose* one's *life* by an accident (事故で生命を失う) / He was reluctant to *lose* his *life*. / Many *lives* were *lost* in the earthquake. ¶*maintain life* 生をつなぐ. ¶By jealousy and ill-temper he *makes* his *life* a hell. 彼はしっとと不きげんで地獄の生活をしている. ‖ *life* was *made* a burden to him by ... 彼は...のために人生を悲観した. ¶*mix* one's *life* with theirs 自分の生活を彼らの生活にとけ込ませる. ¶You are my saviour—I *owe* my *life* to you! What can I do for you? あなたは私の命の親だ—あなたのおかげで私は助かったのだ, どうお礼をしたらよいでしょう. ¶*pass* one's *life* in idleness 怠けて一生を暮す ‖ become an old man before one has scarcely *passed* middle *life* まだ中年なのに老人になる. ¶*pick up* their *lives* 彼らの命を救う. ¶*prefer* single *life* 独身生活を選ぶ. ¶He honestly tried to *present life* as he saw it—that is the secret of his literary fame. 彼は人生を見たままに表現しようと忠実に試みた—それが彼の文名の秘けつだ. ¶*prolong* the *life* of the teeth 歯の寿命を長くする ‖ the art of *prolonging life* 長寿法. ¶*pursue life* of pleasure and gaiety 道楽三まいに日を送る. 【類】*pursue* a marchant *life*. ¶*put life* into the picture 絵に生気を吹込む. ¶*quit* a *life* of shame 泥水商売から足を洗う. ¶*rationalize* human *life* 人類の生活を合理化する. ¶after *reaching* adult *life* 成年に達してから. ¶*review* one's past *life* with satisfaction 満足して過去を回顧する. ¶*risk* one's *life* on thin ice あぶない橋をわたる ‖ *risk* his valuable *life* against the murderous burglar 貴重な生命をかけて殺人強盗に手向う. ¶*ruin* one's *life* 人生を棒に振る. ¶They *sacrificed* their *lives* in the great cause. 彼らは大義のためにその生命を犠牲にした. ‖ a ceremony as a memorial to the animals whose *lives* were *sacrificed* in the interest of scientific research 科学研究のために殺された動物の追善供養. 【類】Young and helpless *lives* are often *sacrificed* to lust and shame (泥水稼業). ¶*save* his *life* 彼の命を救う. ¶persons wishing to *secure* their own *lives* 自分の生命の安全を欲する人々. ¶*see life* as a whole 人生の全ぼうを見る. ¶He *sought* her *life* (=wanted to kill her). 彼は彼女の生命をねらった. ‖ enemies that *seek* his *life* 彼の命を取ろうとする敵. ¶The soldier was resolved on *selling* his *life* as dearly as he could. その兵士はできるだけ多くの敵をたおして死ぬ決心をした. 【類】He saw in an instant to what a pass (危機) things had come and determined to *sell* his *life* dearly. ¶He has *served* a long and useful *life*. 彼は長くて有益な一生を送った. ¶*shape* one's *life* to the new conditions 生活を新しい情勢に適合させる. ¶*shorten* the *life* of ... ...の寿命を縮める. ¶*sigh away* one's *life* ため息ついて暮す. ¶*simplify life* 生活を簡素化する. ¶*sleep* one's *life away* 眠って暮す. ¶*spare* the *life* of ... ...の命を助けてやる. ¶*spend* one's *life* in good work りっぱな仕事をして一生を送る. 【類】He *spent* his early *life* on a farm. ¶*stain* a *life* 一生に泥を塗る. ¶He *started life* on the last rung of the ladder, and worked himself up. 彼は低い地位から立身出世した. ‖ *start life* with the woman of his choice 望みの女と一緒に世帯を持つ ‖ The Woman's Magazine *started* its *life* two years ago with a man as editor-in-chief. ウーマンス・マガジン誌は二年前一人の男性を主筆にして世に出た. 【類】He *started life* with about $1,600 in the bank. / *start life* in a coal-mine. ¶They *steered* their *lives* amidst the foaming whirlpools of those troubled times with consummate art. 彼らは当時乱れた世のあわ立つ渦巻の中をあっぱれな手並で乗切った. ¶*study life* from its late side 夜の生活を研究する. ¶*suck* all the *life* out of ... ...の生気を吸い尽す. ¶We did not have sufficient food to support *life*. われわれは生きるに足るだけの十分の食料がなかった. ¶*surrender* one's *life* to the guidance of emotion 感情の導くままに行動する. ¶*sustain life* 命をつなぐ. 【類】The act of eating is not merely for the purpose of *sustaining life*. ¶*take* one's own *life*=commit suicide 自殺する ‖ *take* one's *life* by strategem だまし討ちにする. 【類】She *took* her own *life* by leaping from the bridge into the river. / *take* human *life* / be not afraid to *take* one's *life* into one's hands (生命を賭する). / Those photographs were made by men who ***took*** their ***lives*** in their hands to get them. ‖ ***take*** the ***life*** out of the leather 皮の耐久力を害する. ¶***take life easy*** 人生をのんきに考える. ¶***take up*** the studious ***life*** 学究生活に入る. ¶***threaten*** the ***life*** of ... ...の生命を脅かす. ¶***throw away*** one's ***life*** for the sake of one's master 主人のために命を捨てる. 【類】***throw away*** one's ***life*** in battle / ***threw*** their ***lives away*** at the Kegon waterfall. ¶***trace*** his ***life*** from boyhood upwards 彼の一生を少年時代からずっとたどってゆく. ¶***translate life*** into line and color 人生を絵にかく. ¶***trust*** one's ***life*** to an unskilful doctor へたな医者に生命を託する. ¶***try*** a country ***life*** 田園生活をやっている. ¶***understand life*** 世間を知っている. ¶She ***used*** her ***life*** well. 彼女はりっぱな一生を送った. ¶if he ***values*** his ***life*** 彼にして命が惜しければ. ¶the habit of ***viewing life*** philosophically 哲学的に人生を観察する習慣. ¶They ***walk*** their ***life*** alone. 彼らは独りで人生(の旅)を歩む. ¶***waste*** valuable ***lives*** 貴重な人命を浪費する. ¶***whistle away*** one's ***life*** 口笛を吹いて(のんきに)一生を暮す. ¶I would ***yield*** my ***life*** rather than to ... 私は...するよりは命を捨てた方がよい.

v² She walked on quickly, crushing the wild flowers under her feet, hastening as though ***life depended*** on her speed. 彼女は足取り早く野の花を踏みつけ一所懸命に急いだ. ¶***Life*** was ***ebbing*** fast. ひん死の状態であった. ¶His ***life*** was fast ***ebbing away***. 彼は刻々死にひんしつつあった. ¶His ***life hangs*** by a thread. 彼の命は風前の灯である. ¶In a large town ***life moves*** with a rush. 大都会では生活がせわしい. ¶A new ***life opened out*** to the solitary man. 新しい人生がその孤独の人に開けた. ¶The presses in the neighborhood of the Fleet may fairly claim to be the main arteries through which ***pulsates*** the intellectual ***life*** of England. フリート街付近の諸新聞は英国の知的生命が脈うつ大動脈だと言っても過言ではない. ¶Man's ***life vanishes*** like the dew. 人生朝露のごとし. ¶This is how ***life*** (=the world) ***wags*** on. 人生ってこんなものだ.

Q an ***abstemious life*** 節制ある生活. ¶live an ***abundant life*** 豊かな生活をする. ¶enter ***active life*** 活社会にはいる. 【類】lead a physically ***active life***. ¶an ***active*** and ***courageous life*** 活動的な勇気ある生活. ¶photographs taken from ***actual life*** 実写物 ‖ in ***actual life*** 現実の社会では ‖ He has seen next to nothing of ***actual life***. 彼は世間というものをほとんど見ていない. ¶in ***adult life*** 成年に. ¶die in ***advanced life*** 高齢で死ぬ. ¶a very ***adventurous life*** きわめて冒険的な生活. ¶It will stand him in good stead in ***after*** (=later) ***life***. それが後になって彼の役に立つだろう. 【類】Only a few of the students will have occasion to speak and write English in ***after life***, the majority being satisfied if they can read English books with ease, intelligence and pleasure. ¶an ***agricultural life*** 農村の生活. ¶an ***aimless life*** 目的のない一生. ¶***amatory life*** 恋愛生活. ¶***American life*** and ways アメリカ人の生活並に風習. ¶an ***ascetic life*** 禁欲生活. ¶They lead ***austere*** and ***ascetic lives***. 彼らは厳格な行者の生活をしている. ¶The ***average life*** of a film is three months. 映画の平均寿命は三カ月だ. ¶the ***awakening sexual life*** 目ざめつつある性生活. ¶how ***barren life*** would be if there were no ...! ...がなかったら人生はどんなにつまらなかろう. ¶lead a ***better life*** よりよい生活を送る. ¶a ***better*** and ***higher life*** よりよくより高い生活. ¶a ***blameless life*** 非の打ち所のない生活. ¶lead the ***Bohemian life*** [伝統にとらわれない]自由奔放な生活を送る. ¶protect ***British lives*** and interests from mob violence 暴民の危険から英国の人命と権益を保護する. ¶Her ***life*** was ***burdensome*** to her. 彼女は生きているのが苦になった. ¶lead a ***bustling life*** of it 煩雑な生活をする. ¶live a ***busy life*** 多忙な生活を送る. ¶a ***busy-a-day life*** of a big city 大都市の多忙の生活. ¶an intensely interesting chronicle of a ***busy*** and ***eventful life*** 多忙にして多事多端な一生のすこぶる興味ある年代記. ¶The ***care-free life*** of his classmates, by its very contrast, generates a strange bitterness within his heart. 彼の級友の気苦労のない生活はその対照のはなはだしさが彼の心に異様な悲哀を起させる. ¶have (=bear) a ***charmed life*** 不死身である(シェイクスピアのマクベスから). ¶a ***chaste life*** 貞節な一生. ¶his ***chequered life*** 彼の数奇をきわめた一生.

¶***civic life*** 市民生活. ¶useless to the army but far from useless in ***civil life*** 軍隊には無用だが一般社会生活には決して無用でない. ¶the pleasures and the comforts of ***civilized life*** 文明生活の娯楽や歓楽. 【類】the tension of highly ***civilized life***. ¶a ***clean moral life*** 潔白な道徳生活. ¶a day in my ***clerical life*** 私が聖職にあった当日. ¶the ***cloistral life*** とん世生活. ¶live a ***colorful life*** 数奇な生活を送る. ¶a ***commercial life*** 商業界の生活. ¶Chicago's ***commercial*** and ***industrial life*** シカゴの商工業生活. ¶the ***complex life*** of a great city 大都市の複雑な生活. 【類】***Life*** has today become much more ***complex***. ¶Her ***conjugal life*** was profoundly troubled. 彼の結婚生活に一大かっ藤を生じた. ¶a ***contented life*** 満足の生活. ¶a ***continent life*** 禁欲生活. ¶***corporate life*** 団体生活. ¶the ***corrupt social life*** of the times 現代の腐敗した社会生活. ¶an exceptionally ***crowded*** and ***varied life*** 異例に変化の多い一生. ¶***cultural life*** 文化生活. ¶the village where he used to live his ***daily life*** 彼が日常生活を送った村. ¶They swam for ***dear life***. 彼らは必死となって泳いだ. ¶a ***decent life*** 恥しくない生活. ¶a ***desultory life*** without regular occupation 定職のない不規則な生活. ¶a ***dissipated life*** 放とう生活. ¶a ***dissolute life*** 放とう三まいな生活. ¶The death of Dr. ... ended a most ***distinguished*** and ***useful life***. ...博士の死によって非常に秀でた有用な一生が終った. ¶a ***diversified life*** 変化に富んだ一生. ¶***domestic life*** in Japan 日本の家庭生活. ¶a ***double life*** 二重生活. ¶the ***dual life*** of the Japanese 日本人の二重生活. ¶a ***dull, monotonous domestic life*** 退屈で単調な家庭生活. ¶while yet in ***early life*** まだ若かった時分. ¶an ***easy life*** 気楽な暮し. ¶its contribution to the ***educational life*** of its community その社会の教育方面への貢献. ¶Forty buildings are devoted to the ***educational*** and ***social life*** of Demison students. 四十の建物がデミソンの学生たちの教育的及び社交的生活に提供されている. ¶the ***emotional life*** of a nation as reflected in its literature and art その国の文学及び美術に反映している国民の情緒生活. ¶***English provincial life*** 英国の地方生活. ¶the ***erotic life*** of women 女の性生活. ¶the ***eternal life*** 永遠の命. ¶***everyday Russian life*** ロシアの日常生活. ¶a young man of ***exemplary life*** 模範的生活をしている青年. ¶an ***exemplary Christian life*** キリスト教徒としての模範的生活. ¶She wanted to see her son before ***life*** is ***extinct***. 彼女は息がある内に息子に会いたがっていた. ¶He ruined himself by an ***extravagant life***. 彼はぜいたくな暮しをして身を滅ぼした. ¶a ***fallen life*** 堕落した生活. ¶her ***fast life*** 彼女の放縦な生活. ¶At the middle of the fifth month of ***fetal life*** occurs the phenomenon of the "quickening." 妊娠五カ月目の中ほどに「胎動」現象が起る. ‖ during the ***fetal life*** of a child 小児の胎内生活の中に ‖ the influence of the factors which have acted upon the child in ***fetal life*** 胎教. ¶enjoy the ***free life*** in the open air 戸外で自由に羽根をのばす. ¶a ***frugal life*** 質素な暮し. ¶a ***fruitful life*** 業績に富む生活. ¶a ***life full*** of misery and shame 悲惨や恥辱に満ちた生活 ‖ a ***life full*** of vicissitudes はらんの多い一生. ¶a ***fuller, brighter***, and ***nobler life*** より充実した, より輝かしい, よりりっぱな生活. ¶a ***God-fearing life*** 信心深い生活. ¶a ***good*** and ***virtuous life*** 善良で正しい生活. ¶a ***happy life*** 幸福な暮し. ¶lead a ***happier***, or at least a less ***unhappy, life*** それより一層幸福なせめてそれほど不幸でない生活をする. ¶bring back to a ***healthy life*** 健康体に戻す. ¶the ***hectic life*** of the capital 首都のにぎやかな生活. ¶a marriage in ***high life*** 上流社会の結婚. ¶turn to a ***holy life*** 神聖な生活に向う. 【類】lead a ***holy life*** by forsaking secular employments and family relations. ¶lead (=live) an ***honest*** and ***useful life*** 正直で有用な生活を送る. 【類】an ***honest*** and ***virtuous life***. ¶an ***honorable life*** りっぱな生活. ¶a busy ***housewife's life*** 忙しい主婦生活 ‖ in another region of ***human life*** 社会の別の方面において. ¶The war cost heavily in ***human life*** and treasures. その戦争は大いに人命と財貨を消費した. ‖ the advent of ***human life*** on this planet この惑星における人類の出現 ‖ an unconditional respect for ***human life*** あくまで人命を尊重すること. ¶a man of ***humble life*** 身分の低い人. ¶Wordsworth's doctrine that the richest source to poetic material is to be found in ***humble*** and ***rustic life*** 詩の材料の最も豊富な源泉はいやしい田園生活の

中に見出されるというワーズワースの説. ¶a ***hygienic life*** 衛生的生活. ¶an ***idle, purposeless life*** 怠惰で目的のない生活. ¶an ***impure*** and ***immoral life*** 不純で不倫な生活. ¶The structure has a practically ***indefinite life***. その建物は事実上永久的のものだ. ¶lead an independent ***life*** 独立の生活を営む. ¶conditions of ***industrial life*** 労働者の生活状態. ¶the ***inner life*** of the House of Commons 下院の内部生活. ¶an ***isolated life*** 孤独生活. ¶He began his ***journalistic life*** on the *Penny Illustrated Paper*. 彼はペニー・イラストレイテッド紙で記者生活にはいった. ¶Cancer is a disease of ***later life***. がんは晩年の病気だ‖in a ***later life*** 晩年に. ¶***lazy life*** 怠惰な生活. ¶a ***licentious*** and ***abandoned life*** 気随気ままな生活. ¶It will be found to have a ***limited life***. それは持ちが悪い. ¶a romance of ***literary life*** 文筆生活のロマンス. ¶Only the best books represent the accumulated exprerience of actively ***lived lives***. 最良の書だけが活動生活によって蓄積した経験を示すのである. ¶a ***lonely life*** 孤独の生活. ¶He spent a ***lonely*** and ***friendless life***. 彼は孤独な友人のない一生を送った. ¶***Long life***, happiness and prosperity to all of you. 諸君の全てに長寿と幸福と繁栄とを祈ります. 【類】We wish you a very ***long life***.‖a ***long life*** to ...! ...万歳. ¶***low life*** 下層生活. ¶live a ***luxurious life*** ぜいたくをする. ¶He lived ***many lives***; he was a traveller, an explorer, a mighty hunter, a soldier, and a sailor. 彼は実に色んな生活をした. 旅人であり, 探検家であり, すぐれた狩猟家であり, 軍人であり, 船乗りでもあった. ¶a ***married life*** 結婚生活. ¶a ***mediocre life*** 平凡な生活. ¶***mental life*** 精神生活. ¶women in ***middle life*** 中年女. 【類】reach ***middle life***. ¶the tragedy of a ***misfit life*** 不似合な生活の悲劇. ¶the luxuries of ***modern life*** 現代生活のぜいたく品. 【類】the rush (忙しさ) of ***modern life*** / the whirl of ***modern life*** in a large city. ¶a ***moderate*** and ***simple life*** ほどよい簡易な生活. ¶a ***moral*** and ***God-fearing life*** 道徳的な信心深い生活. 【類】a ***moral, healthy***, and ***comfortable life***. ¶***national*** and ***world life*** 国民的及び世界的生活. ¶Cats have ***nine lives***. ねこは命が九つある(仲々死なない). ¶***No lives*** were lost. 一人も死者を出さなかった. ¶a ***noble life*** 気高い生活. ¶take up a ***normal life*** 常人の生活をする. ¶It is not a "***novelized***" ***life*** as most biographies have been. それは多くの伝記のように小説化された伝記ではない. ¶enter ***official life*** 官吏生活にはいる‖others high in ***official life***=other high functionaries 他の高官たち. ¶He is no ordinary man and has lived no ***ordinary life***. 彼は非凡で決して平凡な生活をしなかった. ¶an ***outdoor*** (=***out-of-door***) ***life*** 戸外生活. ¶***over-strenuous life*** 奮闘し過ぎる生活. ¶This nearly cost him his ***own life***. 危く自分の生命を失うところだった. ¶his ***past life*** 彼の過去の生活. ¶a ***pastoral life*** 田園生活. ¶***perpetual life*** 永遠の生命. ¶quit ***political life*** 政界を去る. ¶***political*** and ***public life*** 政治生活と公人生活. ¶***post-school life*** 卒業後の生活. ¶***Practical life*** brings all kinds of annoyances to us. 実際生活ではわれわれにはありとあらゆる煩累がつきまとう.‖in ***practical life*** 実生活では. ¶His ***life*** is ***precarious***. 彼の生活は不安定だ. ¶the ***pre-institution life*** of a prisoner 囚人の収容前の経歴. ¶during its ***prenatal life*** 胎内にいる時に. ¶an invasion of ***private life*** by newspapers 新聞が私生活に立入ること‖an interruption into the house and ***private lives*** of the great 偉人の家庭や私生活へ立入ること. 【類】Thelma Herrick, in ***private life***, Mrs. Hall Herrick / the irregularities (乱脈) of one's ***private life***‖relegation of the daimyos to ***private life*** 諸大名を私生活へ移すこと(廃藩). ‖Hands off my ***private life***. 私の私生活に干渉しないでくれ. ¶his ***private*** and ***public life*** 彼の私的並に公的生活. ¶The time has come when it is no longer excusable that our medical students should enter ***professional life*** without a knowledge of scientific psychology. わが医学生が科学的心理学の知識なくして開業することはもはや言訳の立たない時代となった. ¶***psychic life*** 精神的生活. ¶He has been for about half a century in ***public life***. 彼は約五十年の公人生活をした. 【類】a man in ***public life***. ¶happenings in ***real life*** 実生活のできごと‖the ***real life*** of the day 当時の実生活. ¶a ***regular*** and ***temperate life*** 規則的な節制ある生活. ¶the essentials of the ***religious life*** 宗教的生活の本質. ¶a very ***restful life*** きわめて安らかな生活. ¶a ***restless, wandering life*** 落着のない放浪生活. ¶a ***retired life*** 隠とん生活. ¶lead a ***riotous life*** すさんだ生活を送る. ¶the ***rough lives*** of seafaring people 船乗りの荒っぽい生活. ¶scenes of ***rural life*** 田園生活の風景. ¶lead a ***rustic life*** 田園生活をする. ¶the ***sailor's life*** 船乗り渡世. ¶a ***saintly life*** 聖者のような生活. ¶those who live ***respectful*** and ***respectable lives*** りっぱな尊敬に値する生活を送る人々. ¶***savage life*** 野蛮な社会. ¶take to a ***seafaring life*** 船乗り渡世を始める. ¶a ***secluded life*** 隠退生活. ¶live their ***secluded, old-world life*** in the suburb 郊外に引きこもって昔ながらの生活をする(欧州からの移民など). ¶a ***sedentary life*** [仕立屋の職人のような]座業の生活. ¶spend a ***sedentary life*** 座業の生活を送る. ¶***seething, bubbling life*** 生気はつらつたる生活. ¶a ***self-supporting, law-abiding life*** 一本立ちの良心的な生活. ¶a ***sequestered life*** 隠とん生活. ¶***sexual life*** 性生活. ¶The magazine had but a ***short life*** of three numbers. その雑誌はわずか三号で廃刊になった. ¶an advocate of the ***simple life*** 簡易生活の主張者. 【類】live a ***simple*** and ***contented life***. ¶live the ***single life*** 独身生活をする. ¶***slave-holding life*** in the South [アメリカ]南部のどれい所有者の生活. ¶lead a ***sober, hard working life*** まじめで勤勉な生活をする. ¶The ***social life*** has become more manifold. 社会生活が一層複雑になった. 【類】various phases of ***social life*** / ***social life*** in America. ¶various phenomena in ***social*** and ***economic life*** 社会生活及び経済生活における種々な現象. ¶***social*** and ***royal life*** of Great Britain 大英国の社会生活と王室生活. ¶the ***soldier's life*** 軍人生活. ¶lead a ***solitary life*** 孤独の生活を送る. ¶his life, his ***soul's life***, in his poems 彼の詩の中の彼の生活すなわち彼の魂の生活. ¶the ***squalid life*** of the poor 貧乏人のみすぼらしい生活. ¶a ***sterile life*** 業績のない生活. ¶a ***stern moral life*** 厳格な道徳生活. ¶a ***still life*** 静物. ¶He ended a very ***strenuous life*** in a tragic way. 彼は非常に奮闘的な生活を悲劇的に終えた. ¶the ***sub-human life*** of the world どん底の生活. ¶a ***succinct life*** 略伝. ¶secrets of a ***successful life*** 処世の秘けつ. ¶***Life*** is ***sweet***, we cannot die yet. 命は惜しい, まだ死なれない. ¶a ***temperate life*** 酒を飲まない生活. ¶a man of wide experience in every phase of ***theatrical life*** 芝居生活のあらゆる方面にわたって広い経験のある人. ¶a ***tranquil domestic life*** 円満な家庭生活. ¶***transitory life*** はかない人生(浮世). ¶a ***turbulent public life*** はらん重畳の公生活. ¶a very ***uneventful life*** きわめて平穏無事な生活. 【類】live the ***uneventful lives*** of the English middle class (中産階級) / His ***life*** was comparatively ***uneventful***. ¶an ***unfortunate married life*** which terminated in divorce 離婚に終った不幸な結婚生活. ¶an extremely ***unhappy married life*** 非常に不幸な結婚生活. ¶***urban*** and ***rural life*** 都会生活と田園生活. ¶a ***useful life*** 有用な生活. ¶the ***uterine life*** of a fetus 胎児の胎内生活. ¶a ***vagrant life*** 放浪生活. ¶a ***varicolored life*** (=career) はらん重畳の生活. ¶a ***varied*** and ***adventurous life*** 変化の多い冒険的生活. ¶her ***veiled*** and ***secluded life*** 彼女の世を忍ぶ生活. ¶a ***vicious life*** 邪悪の生活. ¶spring into ***vigorous, palpitating life*** きびきびしたどきどきと脈うつ生活に飛込む. ¶a ***virtuous life*** 正しい生活. ¶come to ***vivid life*** 生々してくる, 活気が出る. ¶a ***wandering life*** 放浪的生活. ¶during their ***wedded life*** of nearly sixty years かれこれ六十年の結婚生活の間. ¶***Welsh life*** in London centres chiefly in the chapels. ロンドンにおけるウェールズ人の生活は礼拝堂が中心になっている. ¶devote one's ***whole life*** to ... 一生を...に捧げる. ¶a ***wild life*** 放縦生活. ¶***work-a-day lives*** あくせくした生活. ¶a ***wretched life*** みじめな生活. ¶Statistics show that dementia præcox is chiefly a disease of ***young life***. 統計によると早発性痴呆(ほう)症は主として年の若い者の病気である.

Q[2] ***adult life*** 成人生活. ¶Landseer has painted ***animal life*** excellently. ランドシア卿は動物の生態のすばらしい絵を書いた. ¶***animal*** and ***plant life*** 動植物の生態. 【類】The desert island had almost no ***animal*** or ***vegetable life***. ¶like ***Army life*** 陸軍の生活のように(規則正しい). ¶the ***art life*** of the country その国の美術生活. ¶***back-stage life*** 楽屋生活. ¶***barrack life*** in India インドの兵営生活. ¶gems of ***bird life*** 鳥類中の珍種. 【類】the study of ***bird life***. ¶***brothel life*** 売春婦の生態. ¶enter

business** life* 実業界に入る. ¶"campus** life*" in America アメリカの大学生活. ¶lead a ***cat-and-dog** life*《俗》犬猿(えん)の生活を送る；[夫婦など]けんか生活をおくる. ¶the "***behind-the-scenes**" life* of a political party 政党の内幕. ¶***campus*** (=college) *life*《米》大学生活. ¶***child** life* in America アメリカの児童生活. ¶gay ***city** life* はなやかな都会生活. 【類】Without a good water supply ***city** life* would be impossible. ¶***club** life* クラブ生活. ¶He enjoys "***college** life*" more than academic work. 彼は学問よりはむしろいわゆる大学生活(学生運動)そのものを楽しむ. ¶***community** life* 社会生活. ¶try a ***country** life* 田園生活をやってみる. 【類】A simple ***country** life* has many pleasures. / writings describing ***country** life* / ***Country** life* is better than city life to a child predisposed to hysteria (ヒステリー気味の子供). ¶a picture of ***Eskimo** life* エスキモー生態の絵. ¶drudgeries of ***everyday** life* 日々の雑事. 【類】too remote from ***everyday** life*. ¶tired of insipid ***family** life* 無味な家庭生活にあきあきして ‖ re-knit their ***family** life* in Europe at the side of husbands serving with the Army of Occupation 占領陸軍部隊に勤務している夫君とともに欧州における自分らの家庭生活を再建する. 【類】The ***family** life* is always charming. ¶ideas of ***future** life* 将来の生活設計. ¶enjoy the ***group** life* 団体生活をする. ¶***home** life* 家庭生活. ¶abandon ***hotel** life* ホテル生活を切り上げる. ¶bygone ***London** life* 過ぎ去ったロンドンの生活. ¶a screen star without a ***love** life* ロマンスのない映画スター ‖ No more meddling in my ***love** life*. 私の恋愛生活にはこの上口を出さないで下さい. ¶a study of lower ***middle-class** life* in London ロンドンの下級中流生活の研究. ¶***navy** life* 海軍の生活. ¶the lure of gay ***night** life* (chorus girl などの経験する)はなやかな夜の生活への誘惑 ‖ watch the colorful ***night** life* 色々な夜の生態をながめる. ¶lead an ***open-air** life* 野外生活を送る. 【類】free ***open-air** life*. ¶an ***out-of-door** life* 戸外生活. ¶enjoy ***recreation** life* リクリエーションを楽しむ. ¶studies of sex in ***savage** life* 蛮人の性生活研究. ¶***school** life* 学校生活. ¶a ***sea-faring** life* 海上生活. ¶the ***sex** life* of the lobster えびの性生活. 【類】Indulge in ***sex** life*. ¶a luxurious ***society** life* ぜいたくな社交生活. ¶***student** life* 学生々活. ¶"***till-dawn**" **night** life* 不夜城生活. ¶He did not like ***town** life*, so he has gone to live in the country. 彼は都会の生活がきらいでいなかに行った. ¶during his second year of ***university** life* 大学生活二年目に. ¶***upper-class** life* 上流階級の生活. ¶his ***vagabond** life* in America 彼のアメリカにおける放浪生活. ¶static ***village** life* 静かな農村の生活. ¶wild ***West** life*《米》あらあらしい西部の生活.

P value honor ***above*** *life* 名を命以上に惜む. ¶***during*** my *life*=while I live 私の存命中. ¶It was a principle with him, ***for*** *life*, never to be in debt. 決して借金しないというのが彼が一生守った主義だった. ‖ crippled ***for*** *life* 一生不具の ‖ an invalid ***for*** *life* 一生不治の病人. ¶be imprisoned ***for*** *life* 無期懲役となる ‖ If a child be taught to rise early, it will make him an early riser ***for*** *life*. 子供に早起を教え込むと一生早起になるだろう. ‖ He ran ***for*** his *life*. 彼は一所懸命逃げた. ‖ I cannot ***for*** the *life* of me remember where I met her. 一体どこで彼女に会ったのかどうしても思い出せない. ‖ ***for*** two *lives* 二代の間. ¶a portrait [taken] ***from*** *life* 写生の肖像画 ‖ rescue her ***from*** a *life* of vice and infamy 罪の生活から彼女を救う ‖ cut off so long ***from*** the general mental *life* of the world 世間普通の精神生活からそんなに久しく引離されて. ¶He has never seen Japan or the Far East ***in*** his *life*. 彼は生れてからまだ日本または極東を見たことがない. ‖ ***in*** early *life* 若いころに ‖ go out ***in*** *life* 世に出る ‖ men who knew him ***in*** the *life* 在世中の彼を知っていた人々 ‖ only once ***in*** my *life* 後にも先にもただの一遍 ‖ believe ***in*** a *life* beyond the grave 来世を信じる. ¶the duration ***of*** their *life* 彼らの寿命 ‖ He is in the prime ***of*** *life*. 彼は男盛りだ. ‖ misrepresentation ***of*** British *life* in American films アメリカ映画におけるイギリス生活の誤った描写 ‖ a primitive mode ***of*** *life* 原始的生活様式 ‖ He has passed the middle-mile post ***of*** *life*. 彼は人生の半ばを過した. ‖ in every walk ***of*** *life* あらゆる職業において ‖ attain lofty pinnacles ***of*** *life* 人生の高峰に達する. ¶Is there any *life* ***on*** the planet Mars? 火星に生物がいるか. ¶all ***through*** *life* 一生を通じて ‖ She longs to be his companion ***through*** *life*. 彼女は彼の一生の伴りょたることを切に願っている. ¶***throughout*** his whole *life* 彼の一生を通じて. ¶go back ***to*** private *life* 野に帰る ‖ be true ***to*** *life* 本ものそっくりだ, 生き写しだ. ¶narrowly escape ***with*** one's *life* 命からがら逃げ出す. ¶The kerosene market is ***without*** *life*. 石油市場は活気がない.

P² He began *life* ***as*** a photographer (coal merchant). 彼は写真屋(など)として世に出た. 【類】he began *life* ***as*** an apprentice to ... / he started *life* ***as*** an assistant in the firm of ... ¶*life* ***at*** a Zoo 動物園での生活 ‖ The boy of this well-to-do class begins *life* ***at*** a public school. この有産階級の少年は予備学校が実生活の始まりである. ¶higher *life* ***for*** working people 労働者のさらに向上した生活. 【類】a clean *life* ***for*** man and woman. ¶social *life* ***in*** the insect world こん虫界における群居生活 ‖ He began *life* ***in*** journalism. 彼は新聞(雑誌)記者から身を起した. ¶a *life* ***of*** pleasure (dissipation and frivolity) 遊惰(など)の生活 ‖ a *life* ***of*** many griefs 悲しみの一生 ‖ a *life* ***of*** hand to mouth その日暮し ‖ Activity is the *life* ***of*** the hen. 活動はめんどりの生命である. ‖ a *life* ***of*** shame 恥辱の生活(売春など). 【類】a *life* ***of*** crime / a *life* ***of*** prostitute / a *life* ***of*** vice / a *life* ***of*** sexual abstinence (禁欲) / a *life* ***of*** temperance and chastity (節制と貞節) / retire to a *life* ***of*** study, contemplation and learned ease at ... / lead a *life* ***of*** luxury (ease, poverty and labor, self-sacrifice, charity) / live a *life* ***of*** mere existence / live the *life* ***of*** a recluse (隠者). ¶That millionaire began *life* ***with*** nothing. その百万長者は裸一貫で世に出た. ‖ he started in *life* ***with*** a belief that ... 彼は...という信念を抱いて世に出た.

O as large as *life* 実物大の. ¶*Life* is but a walking shadow. 人生は夢のごとし. 【類】*Life* is but an empty dream. ‖ *Life* is likened to a voyage. 人生航路のごとし.

(**2**) 伝記.

Q a ***succinct*** (=***brief***) *life* of ... ...の略伝.

P² Boswell's "*Life* ***of*** Johnson" ボスウエルの「ジョンスン伝」. ‖ "The *Lives* ***of*** the English Poets" by Dr. Johnson. ジョンスン博士の「英国詩人列伝」.

life-blood, *n.* 生血；活力.

V ***infuse*** new *life-blood* into its fast drying bones そのどんどんかれて行く老骨に新血(新精力)を注入する. ¶***suck*** the *life-blood* from ... ...の生血を吸う.

P² Confidence is the *life-blood* ***of*** trade and commerce. 信用は通商貿易の生命である. 【類】Good publicity (宣伝) is the *life-blood* ***of*** any business. / Good books are the *life-blood* ***of*** civilized people.

lifeboat, *n.* 救命艇.

V ***lower*** a *lifeboat* 救命艇を降ろす.

lifebreath, *n.* 生命.

P² The flair for the dramatic is the very *lifebreath* ***of*** journalism. 劇的な事件に対する鋭い眼識がジャーナリズムの生命である.

life-line, *n.* 生命線, 命のつな.

V ***cut*** Britain's *life-line* to America [英国へ物資を給供する]米国との生命線を断つ.

P² Oil has become the *life-line* ***of*** civilization. 石油が文明の生命線となった.

life-study, *n.* 一生の研究.

V He ***made*** a *life-study* of this question. 彼はこの問題を一生の研究課題にした.

lifetime, *n.* 一生.

V he ***devoted*** a *lifetime* to the study of ... 彼は...の研究に一生を捧げた ‖ ***devote*** a *lifetime* of labor to ... ...に一生の労力を捧げる. 【類】He ***devoted*** a *lifetime* of thought and work to the cause. / ***devote*** the whole *lifetime* to the task. ¶***give*** a *lifetime* of study to ... ...を一生研究する. ¶It will ***last*** a *lifetime*. それは一生もつだろう. ¶***live*** an ordinary *lifetime* 普通の人だけ生きる. ¶It would ***require*** more than a *lifetime*. それは一生かかってもできないだろう. ¶He has ***spent*** a *lifetime* over this book. 彼はこの本に一生を費した. 【類】***spend*** a *lifetime* in the study of ... ¶The making of such a work ***takes*** a *lifetime*. こうした著作を完成するには一生かかる.

Q within a ***single*** *lifetime* 一人の生涯(がい)中に.

P ***during*** a whole *lifetime* 全生涯の間に. ¶This book of his has become a classic ***in*** his *lifetime*. この彼の著作は彼の生存中に永久性のある名著となった. ‖ at least ***in*** our own *lifetime* 少くともわれわれの時代には. ¶It may be realized ***within*** the *lifetime* of men now living. それが現在生きている人間の生存中に実現されるかも知れない.

P² These are words which may not be seen again in a *lifetime* ***of*** reading. これらは一生を通じての読書に二度と出くわさない語かもしれない.

lifework, *n.* 一生の仕事.

V ***make*** ... one's *lifework* ...を一生の仕事にする.

lift, *n.* 乗車; 《英》エレベーター.

V My machine has broken down. Could you ***give*** me a *lift* to the next village? 私の自動車(など)がこわれたのですが次の村まで乗せてって下さいませんか. ¶He ***offered*** me a *lift*. 彼は私に(その自動車に)お乗りになりませんかと言った.

Q ***Electric*** *lift* to all floors.=Electric elevators serve all floors. [掲示]エレベーターが各階に通じております.

P go up ***in*** a (=***by***) *lift* エレベーターで上る.

lift, *v.* 揚げる.

M The tower *lifts* its pinnacles ***skyward.*** 塔のせん端が空高くそびえている.

M² *Lift* ***up*** your heart. 元気を出せ. ‖ *lift* ***up*** one's heart in reading ... ...を読んで沈んだ気持を引き立てる. 【類】be *lifted* ***up*** in spirit ‖ *lift* ***up*** one's eyes 目をあげる ‖ *lift* ***up*** one's voice 声を張り上げる ‖ *lift* ***up*** one's voice against ... ...に対して抗議する, 反抗する ‖ *lift* ***up*** one's head 頭をあげる, 頭角を現わす ‖ *lift* up (=prick) one's ears きき耳を立てる.

P This *lifts* it ***above*** the common herd. これあるがためにそれは群を抜いているのである. 【類】There is something original in his work that *lifts* him ***above*** other authors. ¶*lift* a hand ***against*** one's master 主人に手向う. ¶*lift* ***at*** a heavy weight 重いものをもち上げようとする. ¶*lift* a pan ***by*** the handle 取手でなべを持ち上げる. ¶*lift* an anxiety (a sorrow) ***from*** (=***out of***) a person 心配(悲しみ)を取除いてやる. 【類】*lift* them ***out of*** barbarism (野蛮状態). ¶He was rapidly *lifted* ***into*** power. 彼はたちまち権勢にありついた. ‖ He *lifted* the child ***into*** his arms. 彼は子供を抱きあげた. ¶He *lifted* it ***to*** his head. 彼はそれを頭におしいただいた. ‖ This discovery has *lifted* him ***to*** world fame. この発見で彼は世界的名声を博した.

lifting, *n.* 持ち上げること; 見識.

Q ***heavy*** *lifting* 持上げるに骨が折れること. ¶the ***occasional*** *lifting* of one's glass to one's lips 時々杯を口に持ってゆくこと.

light, *n.* 光; ともしび; あかり; 見方; 花形.

V His opinion ***adds*** a new *light* to the question. 彼の意見はその問題に新たな光明を添える. ¶Without a shade, the lamp ***affords*** only a garish *light*. かさをかけないと電灯が目に強く当る. ¶***blow out*** a *light* 灯火を吹き消す. ¶***brighten*** a *light* 灯を明るくする. ¶***Bring*** me a *light*. 私の所にあかりを持って来い. ‖ The scientists will ***bring*** *light* to the subject. 科学者がこの問題を究明するであろう. ‖ ***bring*** the *light* of true philosophical criticism to bear on ... 真の学理的批判の光をもって...を考察する. ¶***burn*** artificial *light* 灯をともす. ¶he ***carried*** the *light* of gospel to ... 彼は...に福音の光をもたらした. ¶***cast*** *light* on ... ...を明かにする. ¶Our electric *light* was ***cut off*** by a storm last night. 昨夜は暴風で停電して灯が消えた. ¶***dim*** a *light* 灯を暗くする. ¶The ship ***displays*** a red *light*. その船は赤色灯を掲げている. ¶***emit*** a brilliant *light* さん然たる光を放つ. ¶The lighthouse ***exhibits*** a green *light*. その灯台の光色は緑だ. ¶The public ***expects*** *light* and leading from him. 大衆は彼から光明と指導とを期待している. ¶***extinguish*** the *light* 灯を消す. ¶***flash*** a *light* upon ... ...に光をぱっと当てる. ¶The subject will ***get*** (=***receive***) some *light* from his researches. その問題は彼の研究で幾分光明を得るだろう. ¶***give*** *light* 光る. 【類】This bulb ***gives*** a pale (green) *light*. ‖ Please ***give*** me a *light* (タバコの)火を貸して下さい. ¶***give off*** (=***out***) a *light* 光を発する. ¶Electric *lights* and bells are ***installed*** throughout. 全部電灯や電鈴が備付けてある[ホテルなど]. ¶***light*** the *lights* 灯をつける. ¶***lower*** *lights* 灯を弱める. ¶Some lanterns use oil to ***make*** the *light*. カンテラの中には点灯用に油を用いるものもある. ‖ ***make*** the *light* ***dim*** (***bright***) あかりをくらく(明るく)する. ¶***obscure*** the *lights* 光を暗くする. ¶***obstruct*** the *light* 採光を妨げる. ¶***obtain*** a *light* 光明を得る. ¶a case of ***putting*** a *light* to powder. [粉に火を付けるように]らちのあかないこと. ¶***Put*** the *light* ***on*** (***off***). 灯をつけ(消し)てくれ. ¶***Put out*** the *lights* before leaving a room. へやを出るとき灯を消しなさい. ¶***reflect*** the *light* into ... ...の中に光を反射させる. ¶***screen*** *lights* 光をさえぎる. ¶***secure*** a good *light* from above 上から十分な明りを採る. ¶***see*** the *light* of day ひの目を見る, 世に出る ‖ It is not known when the book first ***saw*** the *light*. その本の出版されたのはいつだか分からない. 【類】Practically all the best essays in the English language have first ***seen*** the *light* in the periodical press (定期刊行物). / The author died before his book had ***seen*** the *light* (=appeared). / The articles have already ***seen*** the *light* in various English papers and periodicals. / A new book by the author is to ***see*** the *light* this autumn. / The publication was never intended to ***see*** the *light* of day. / The 1938 edition will soon ***see*** the *light* of day. ‖ In an upper window of that house I ***saw*** a *light* burning. その家の上の一つの窓に私は灯がともっているのを見た. ¶The moon was ***shedding*** its full *light*. 月はこうこうと照っていた. ‖ ***shed light*** on the question whether ... ...かどうかの問題の解決に役立つ ‖ The genius of ... ***shed*** a new *light* on the subject. ...の天才はその問題に新しい光を投げた. 【類】***shed*** further *light* on what has remained a mystery. ¶The lighthouse is intended to ***show*** (=exhibit) the *light*. 灯台は光を放つようにできている. ¶***soften*** the *light* 光をやわらげる. ¶***shun*** the *light* 光を避ける. ¶We ***sighted*** *lights* in the distance. 遠方に灯が見えた. ¶***spread*** a pale *light* 薄暗い光を放つ. ¶***strike*** a *light* チッマをする. ¶***switch off*** (=***out***) all the electric *lights* 電灯をすべて消す. ¶***switch on*** electric *light* 電灯をつける. ¶Illustrations ***throw*** *light* upon the text. 図解は本文の説明を助ける. ‖ Modern investigations have ***thrown*** great *light* upon this question. 近代の研究によってこの問題は大いに明らかにされた. 【類】***throw*** great *light* upon many of the dark problems of ... / ***throw*** *light* upon some phases of Irish history / ***throw*** no *light* on ... / ***throw*** a little *light* on ... ‖ ***throw*** much additional *light* upon ...の問題をさらにはっきりさせる. ¶***turn*** a *light* ***on*** 灯を点ける ‖ a *light* ***turned low*** 細くした灯. ¶***turn out*** (=***out***) the *light* 灯を消す. ¶We ***want*** more *light* in this room. このへや屋をもっと明るくしてほしい.

V² While he wept, *light* ***began*** to dawn in his thoughts. 彼が泣いている間に光明が彼の心の中に見え始めた. ¶*Light* is ***breaking.*** 夜が明け始める. ¶The *light* is ***dawning*** little by little. 段々と夜があける. ¶*light* ***came*** to me through reading a passage in ... ...の一節を読んで悟るところがあった. ¶the electric *light* ***failed*** 電灯が消えた. ¶The electric *light* ***flickers.*** 電灯が明滅する. ¶The *light* ***glimmered*** on the lake. 灯火が湖面に弱い光を映していた. ¶The *light* ***goes out.*** 灯が消える. ¶The electric *light* ***went out*** and an electrician put it right. 電灯が消えたので電気屋が直してくれた. ¶Cross quickly when green *light* ***shows.*** 青が出たら急いで渡れ. ¶The *light* ***streams*** into the room. 光がへやに流れ込む. ¶*Light* ***struck*** on his face. 光線がぱっと彼の顔にさした.

Q ***All*** *lights* have to be out by eleven. 灯は全部十一時までに消さねばならない. ¶The lamp gave a very ***bad*** *light*. ランプは非常に暗かった. ¶make him appear in a ***bad*** *light* [比ゆ的に]彼を不利な立場におく ‖ see things in a ***bad*** *light* 物事を悪く解釈する. ¶The doctor is one of the ***brightest*** *lights* in the profession. その医師は同業者中最も令名高い一人である. ¶work in too ***brilliant*** *light* 強過ぎる光の中で仕事をする. ¶in the ***broad*** *light* of day 真昼間. ¶My lantern cast a ***clear*** *light* into the cave. 私のカンテラはほら穴の中をずっと照した. ¶throw a ***clear impartial*** *light* on the subject その問題にはっきりした公平な解釈を与える. ¶***colored*** *lights* 着色灯. ¶throw ***considerable further*** *light* upon ... ...にさらに著しい光明を投げる. ¶***dazzling*** *light* まばゆい光. ¶They saw things in a ***different*** *light*. 彼らは別の見方をした. ¶a ***dying*** *light* 消えかかってる灯火. ¶Mt. Fuji in the ***early*** *light* あけぼのの富士. ¶***Electric*** *lights* and bells throughout. 全室電灯とベル装置[ホテルなど]. 【類】In 1879 Mr. Edison invented the ***electic*** *light*. ¶***emergency*** *lights* [船などの]非常灯. ¶Circumstances put him in a ***false*** *light*. 色々な事情で彼は誤解された. ‖ view things in a ***favorable*** *light* 物事を自

分に都合よく解釈する. ¶All this I could see by the pleasantly ***flickering light*** of the three bronze lamps. 私は三個の青銅のランプの快くゆらめく光でこれをすっかり見ることができた. ¶***fluorescent light*** 螢光灯. ¶throw a ***fresh light*** on ... …に新しい光明を投げる.【類】throw (=shed) some ***fresh light*** on ... ¶We at last came in sight of the ***friendly lights*** of the village. われわれはとうとうその村のうれしい灯が見えるところまできた. ¶in the ***full light*** of day 白昼に ‖ in the ***full light*** of public notice 大っぴらに ‖ the moon threw a ***full light*** on ... 月が…を照した. ¶the ***high lights*** (=highlights) in the Academy's catalogue 美術展覧会目録中目ぼしい出品 ‖ some ***high lights*** (=salient events) of history 歴史の重要事件. ¶viewed in an ***historic light*** 歴史に照して見ると.【類】important ***historical light*** is thus shed upon the origin of ... ¶***incandescent light*** 白熱灯(普通の電灯). ¶work with ***insufficient light*** 不十分な明りで働く. ¶he has thrown so much ***interesting light*** upon ... 彼は…にすこぶる興味ある光明を投げた. ¶***lambent light*** 薄明り. ¶Prof. Wilson, a ***leading light*** of the university その大学の権威たるウィルソン教授 ‖ his ***leading light*** 彼の方針. ¶and other ***lesser lights*** of literature その他群小文学者. ¶***literary lights*** (=luminaries) of the day 当代の文豪. ¶***lowered lights*** 弱められた灯. ¶cast a ***lurid light*** on ... …が物すごく見えるような説明をする. ¶he has thrown much ***needed light*** on ... 彼は…にすこぶる重要な光明を投じた. ¶Don't look for an escape of gas with a ***naked light***. はだかろうそく(など)でガスの漏れを探してはいけない. ¶a ***new light*** on ... is thrown by ... …によって新しい光明が…に投げられた.【類】shed ***new light*** upon / throw a ***new*** and ***powerful light*** on natural laws. ¶even viewing the prospects of ... in the most ***optimistic light*** ...の前途を最も楽観的に見ても. ¶To be opened in ***ruby light*** only. [フィルムやネガなど]赤色灯の下でのみ開くこと. ¶The moon cast a ***pale light***. 月は青白い光を投げた. ¶He has a tendency to look at everything in a ***pessimistic light***. 彼は何ごとでも悲観的に見る傾向がある. ¶read in a ***poor light*** 薄暗い灯で読書する ‖ view it in a ***poor light*** それを低く評価する. ¶see the world in a ***proper light*** 世間を正しい目で見る ‖ present it in a ***proper light*** それを正しく紹介する. ¶***red*** (***blue, orange***) ***light*** 赤(など)の光. ¶put it in the ***right light*** それを正しく評価する.【類】understand ... in its ***right*** (=true) ***light*** / I never saw things in the ***right light*** till I heard his sermon. ¶see things in a ***rosy light*** 物事を楽観的に見る. ¶look in the ***same light*** as ... …と同じような見方をする. ¶From the first his case was looked upon in a most ***serious light***. 最初から彼の容体は非常に危険視されていた. ‖ consider the matter in a ***serious light*** そのことをまじめに考える. ¶a ***shining light*** of the team そのチームの花形.【類】I don't think I should be a ***shining light*** (権威) in music. ¶***side light*** on the history of ... …側面史. ¶All the world was flooded with a ***soft golden light***. 全世界はやわらかい黄金色の光で包まれた. ¶a ***spiritual light*** 霊の光. ¶throw a ***strong light*** on that dark subject そのはっきりしていない問題に強い光明を投げる. ¶view a matter in its ***true light*** ことの真相を知る. ¶This placed everyone concerned in an ***unfavorable*** (a ***favorable***) ***light*** このために関係者一同は面目を失した(具合よく行った).

Q² a ***beacon light*** [港内や飛行場などの]標識の灯火. ¶She looked under twenty by ***candle light***. 彼女は夜目には二十以下に見えた. ¶a ***ceiling light*** 天井灯. ¶***cinema lights*** 映画のスターなど. ¶***city lights*** [かがやかしい]都会の灯. ¶***day light*** 日の光り.【類】Summertime is intended to save ***day*** light. ¶in the failing ***evening light*** 暗くなる(かすかな)夕方の明りで. ¶***flash light*** せん光 ☞ a flash-light《米》懐中電灯. ¶***floor light*** 床光. ¶in cheery glamor of ***gas light*** ガス灯の心地よい光で.【類】glisten under the ***gas light***. ¶***heat light*** 夏日の夕暮に地平線上に見えるいなずま. ¶a ***lamp light*** ランプの灯. ¶be brightly lit up with ***neon light*** ネオンの光で明るく照らされている. ¶a reflecting ***pavement light*** 鋪道反射灯. ¶a ***rush light*** 灯明, 灯心の火. ¶***sheet light***=sheet lightning 幕電. ¶jump a ***stop light*** 赤信号を無視する. ¶***summer light***=heat lightning [夏期の]無声電. ¶When the ***traffic light*** is green, we cross the street by the crosswalk. 信号が青になるとわれわれは横断歩道を通って街路の向うに渡る. ¶***zigzag light*** 折電(稲光の).

P ***according to*** his ***light*** 彼の見解に従えば. ¶get up ***before light*** 夜が明けないのに起きる. ¶***between*** the ***lights*** たそがれに. ¶illuminated ***by*** electric ***light*** 電灯で照明された ‖ write one's despatches ***by*** electric ***light*** 電灯でその通信を書く ‖ read ***by light*** of fireflies or reflection of snow 螢雪の光. ¶it is interesting ***for*** the ***light*** it throws on ... …に投げている光明のためにそれは興味がある. ¶viewed ***in*** this ***light*** こういう風に見ると ‖ reconsider it ***in*** the ***light*** of criticism 批評を参考にしてそれを再考する ‖ ***in*** the ***light*** of precedents 前例に徴して.【類】study the present in the ***light*** of the past / in the ***light*** of recent researches (modern knowledge, present knowledge) / ***in*** the ***light*** of reason and experience / ***in*** the ***light*** of more recent discoveries / The facts are presented ***in*** the ***light*** of recent views of language. / ***in*** the ***light*** of these facts it is clear that ... / ***in*** the ***light*** of this fact we are led to wonder whether ... / It is to be regarded as excusable ***in*** th ***light*** of circumstances. / when we regard it ***in*** this ***light***, we see that ... / if we regard ... ***in*** this ***light***, we find the astonishing fact that ... ‖ I never think of it ***in*** that ***light***. 私はそのことについてどうしてもそんな風には考えられない. ‖ ***In*** the ***light*** of a full moon we got a gorgeous view of London. われわれは満月の光で華麗なロンドンの景を見た. ‖ ***in light*** and darkness 明るいときにも暗いときにも. ¶A Royal request is invariably considered by the recipient ***in*** the ***light*** of a command. 王の申し出はこれを受ける人からは必ず命令という風に考える.【類】These quotations, though independent of the context, are perfectly intelligible ***in*** their own ***light***. ¶the discovery cast a flood ***of light*** on ... その発見は…に大なる光明を投げた.【類】shed a flood ***of light*** on the subject. ¶bring it ***to light*** それを明るみに出す ‖ it has come ***to light*** through investigation that ... …ということが調査の結果明かになった. ¶fit up a new home ***with*** electric ***lights*** 新しい家に電灯を取付ける ‖ One is dazzled ***with*** electric ***lights***. 電灯で目がくらむ.

P² The ***light of*** the moon flooded gently on the blue-white roofs of the vast slumbering city. 月の光が眠っている広い町の青白い屋根におだやかにあふれた. ‖ The ***light of*** the true One's message has penetrated. ただ一人の神の光が行渡った. ¶An investigation of ... may throw some ***light on*** the subject. …を調べてみるとその問題の理解に幾分助けになるかもしれない. ¶the book is full of new ***lights upon*** the character of ... その本は豊富な新説をもって…の人格を批判している.

light, *v*. 点火する; [顔など]晴々する.

M ***brilliantly lighted*** こうこうと灯のともった. ¶The room was ***brightly lit*** up. へやは明るく電灯がついていた. ¶a room ***dimly lit*** up 電灯のうす暗いへや. ¶***discreetly lit*** ほどよく灯をともして. ¶***lighted entirely*** by artificial light 全部人工照明を用いた. ¶The buildings are ***lighted throughout*** with electricity. その建物にはどこもかも電灯がつけてある.

M² ***light up*** an oil lamp 石油ランプを点火する ‖ ***light up*** one's imagination ... その想像力に点火する ‖ The flash of lightning ***lit up*** part of the sky. 稲光で空の一部が明るくなった.【類】This room ***lights up*** well. / The sky ***lights up*** at sunset. / The burning house ***lit up*** for miles around. ‖ A smile ***lit up*** her face. 彼女の顔は微笑で輝いた.【類】Her face ***lighted up*** and shone with gaiety. / Her face ***lighted up*** when she saw you. / a face ***lit up*** with joy ‖ a theatre ***lit up*** by electricity 電灯照明の劇場.

P ***lit by*** gas or electricity ガス灯や電灯のついた.【類】rooms ***lighted by*** electricity and heated by hot water. ¶Attendants ***lighted*** his way ***with*** pine torches. 従者は彼の行手をたいまつで照した. ‖ ***lighted with*** electric light 電灯照明を用いた.

O offices electric-***lighted*** and steam-heated 電灯照明とスティーム暖房の事務室.

light, *a*. 軽い.

P ***light in*** weight 目方の軽い.【類】make it as ***light in*** weight as possible. ¶***light of*** heart 心のすがすがしい ‖ ***light of*** weight 目方の軽い ‖ make ***light of*** all troubles (the most formidable obstacles) あらゆる労苦(など)を苦

にしない.
O as *light* as a feather 羽毛のように軽い.

light, *a*. 明るい.
P be *light* ***in*** color 色彩が明るい.
O He works as long as it is *light*. 彼は明るい間働く.

light, *v*. 降りる; [鳥などが]とまる; ふと起きる.
P The bird *lighted* ***from*** the tree. その鳥が木から降りた. ¶He *lighted* ***on*** a happy idea. 彼はよい思いつきがふと胸に浮んだ. ‖ *light* ***on*** a solution 解決が胸に浮ぶ ‖ He *lighted* ***on*** a passage which attracted his attention. 彼はその注意を引いた一節にふと行当った. ‖ His hand *lighted* ***on*** the hilt of his dagger. 彼の手は思わず短刀の柄にふれた. ‖ A bird *lighted* ***on*** the tree. 一羽の鳥がその木にとまった.

lighten, *v*. 軽くする.
P *lighten* a ship ***of*** her cargo 船の荷を降ろす.

lighter, *n*. ライター; 点火夫.
V He lit up his cigar with a small gadget ***called lighter***. 彼はライターと称する小道具でシガーに火をつけた.
Q² a ***cigar lighter*** ライター. ¶a ***gas lighter*** ガス灯の点灯夫. ¶a ***one-hand lighter*** 片手ライター.

light-hearted, *a*. のんきな.
P be *light-hearted* ***to*** excess あまりのんき過ぎる.

lighting, *n*. 照明.
V ***install*** electric *lighting* 電灯を装置する.
Q ***electric*** *lighting* 電灯照明. ¶***incandescent*** *lighting* 白熱灯(普通の電灯)の照明. ¶***natural*** *lighting* 採光.
Q² ***arc*** *lighting* アーク灯の照明. ¶***stage*** *lighting* 舞台照明. ¶Gas was formerly used for ***street*** *lighting*. ガスは以前街灯に使用されていた.
P The use of electricity ***for*** *lighting* and traction. 照明及び動力としての電気使用.

lightness, *n*. 軽さ.
P ***with*** the *lightness* of ... ...のように軽い.

lightning, *n*. 電光, 稲妻.
V The rod ***diverts*** *lightning* into earth or sea. 避雷針は電光を土地または海へそらす.
V² The *lightning* ***flashed***. 稲光がした. ¶The sky was overcast, the *lightning* ***leaped*** from cloud to cloud. 空が曇っていて稲妻が雲から雲に飛んだ. ¶*Lightning* ***plays*** in the sky. 稲妻が空にぴかぴかしている. ¶The *lightning* ***splintered*** a big pine tree. 大きな松の木に落雷して木が裂けた. ¶The *lightning* ***struck*** him dead. 彼は落雷に打たれて死んだ. ‖ The *lightning* ***struck*** the ground (a tree, building). 落雷した.
Q ***forked*** *lightning* 折電(分裂する稲光). ¶The *lightning* was ***vivid***. 稲光がひどかった.
Q² ***chain*** *lightning* 連鎖電光. ¶***flashing*** *lightning* 稲光り. ¶***heat*** *lightning* [夏期の]無声電. ¶***sheet*** *lightning* 幕電(折電による). ¶***summer*** *lightning*=heat lightning. ¶***zigzag*** *lightning* 折曲電光.
P He was struck dead ***by*** *lightning*. 彼は雷に打たれて死んだ. ¶She moves ***like*** *lightning*. 彼女は稲妻のように素早く動く. ‖ His eyes glared ***like*** *lightning*. 彼の目は電光のように光った. ¶a stroke ***of*** *lightning* 雷の一撃. ¶The whole sky was lurid ***with*** *lightning*. 稲妻で空は一面にすさまじくなっていた.
O as quick as *lightning* 稲妻のように素早く.

like, *n*. 同様の人または物.
V Like ***begets*** *like*. かえるの子はかえる. ¶Like ***likes*** *like*. 〘諺〙類は友を呼ぶ. ¶I have never ***seen*** the *like*. こんなのは今まで見たことがない. ‖ Shall we ever ***see*** the *like* again of ...? ...のような人(または物)がまたとあるだろうか.
P The average British schoolboy is said to be more intelligent and ready-witted than the majority ***of*** his *like* on the Continent. 英国小学校の生徒は平均して大陸における多数の同程度の生徒より利口で気がきいているそうだ.
P² the *like* ***of*** you and me われわれふぜい.
O tradesmen, such as a baker, a tailor, a shopkeeper, and the *like*. パン屋, 洋服屋, 店主といった商売人たち.

like, *v*. 好く, 好む.
M Take any book that you *like* ***best***. 君の一番好きな本をどれでもお取り. ¶*like* it ***exceedingly*** それを非常に好む. ¶I ***hardly*** *like* to ... 私は余り...したくはない. ¶***How*** do you *like* it? いかが. ¶I should very ***much*** *like* to see it. それをぜひ見たいものだ. ¶I would ***naturally*** *like* to ... もちろん私は...したいと思う.
O I should *like* to have been there. 僕はそこへ行きたかった. 【類】I'd *like* to see Mr. Johnson.

likelihood, *n*. ありそうなこと.
Q there is ***every*** *likelihood* that ... どうも...なるらしい. ¶in all ***human*** *likelihood* 十中八九. ¶There is ***little*** *likelihood* of their giving consent to it. 彼らはそれを承諾しそうもない.
P ***in*** all *likelihood* どう見ても.
P² There is always a *likelihood* ***of*** such a thing happening. いつもそういったことがありそうに思われる.

likely, *a*. ありそうな, ...らしい.
M It is ***hardly likely*** that I shall be able to present on the occasion. 私はどうもその席へは出られそうもありません. ‖ I am ***hardly likely*** to finish it within a week. 私は一週間内にそれを仕上げられそうもありません. ¶I thought it was ***least likely*** that he would be the man. よもやあの人だとは思っていなかった. ¶be ***little likely*** to ... ...はちょっとありそうもない. ¶***most likely*** 十中八九ありそうな. ¶it is ***quite*** *likely* that ... ...ということは全くありそうなことだ. ¶It is ***very likely*** that he will not consent. 彼はどうも承知しそうもない.

like-minded, *n*. 同志.
V His lofty morality ***attracts*** the *like-minded*. 彼は徳が高いので同じような人を引きつける.

like-minded, *pa*. 同志の.
P a body of men and women *like-minded* ***with*** himself. 彼自身と同じ心の一群の男女 ‖ others who are *like-minded* ***with*** himself 彼の同志たち.

liken, *v*. たとえる.
P Man's life is ***often*** *likened* to sea voyage. 人の一生はしばしば航海にたとえられる. ¶Man has been *likened* well ***to*** a diamond which can be polished only in its own dust. 人はそれ自身の粉末によってのみみがかれるダイヤモンドのようなものだとはよく言ったものだ. 【類】The relations of sovereign and people can well be *likened* ***to*** those of parent and child.

likeness, *n*. 類似; 肖像.
V ***bear*** a striking *likeness* to ... ...に著しく似ている ‖ Most colonial stamps ***bear*** some family *likeness* to the stamps of the mother country. 植民地の切手は大抵母国の切手と幾分血族的類似があるものだ. ¶***have*** some physical and mental *likeness* with ... ...といくらか肉体的及び精神的に似ている. ¶***have*** one's *likeness* (=picture) ***taken*** 写真をとってもらう. ¶The statue ***shows*** an unmistakable *likeness* to himself. その立像は彼自身に生写しだ. ¶***take*** one's *likeness* その人の写真を取る.
Q It is a ***bad*** *likeness*. それはよく似ていない(肖像画など). ¶a ***deep*** (=***strong***) *likeness* よく似ていること. ¶an ***exact*** *likeness* of ... ...とうり二つだ. ¶The bust is an ***excellent*** *likeness*. その胸像は実によく似ている. ¶a ***framed*** *likeness* of ... ...の額になった肖像. ¶a ***good*** *likeness* よく似た肖像. ¶his ***remarkable*** *likeness* to his brother 彼の兄(弟)との酷似. ¶***speaking*** (=***lifelike***) *likeness* 生写し. ¶a ***splendid*** *likeness* of ... ...のすばらしい肖像. ¶a ***striking*** *likeness* 著しく似ていること. ¶be a ***true*** *likeness* of ... ...生写しだ. ¶He is the ***very*** *likeness* of his father. お父さんそっくり.
Q² ***family*** *likeness* 親子兄弟の似た点 ‖ false ***family*** *likeness* 他人のそら似.
P² *likeness* ***between*** ... and ... ...と...の間の類似. ¶a *likeness* ***in*** color 色の類似. ¶a *likeness* ***of*** a person ある人の肖像. ¶You have a *likeness* ***to*** him. 君はあの人に似ている.

liking, *n*. 好み.
V He ***bears*** (=has) a *liking* for Japanese food. 彼は日本食が好きだ. ¶***develop*** a *liking* for ... ...が好きになる. ¶***evince*** a *liking* for De Quincey ド・クィンシーに対する愛好を示す. ¶***follow*** one's personal *liking* 自分の好きなことをやる. ¶***form*** a *liking* for ... ...が好きになる. ¶***have*** a *liking* for ... ...を好む. 【類】He ***has*** a great *liking* for English people. / select subjects which appeals to one, and ignore those for which one ***has*** no *liking*. ¶***profess*** a *liking* for ... ...が好きだと言明する. ¶***show*** a *liking* for arithmetic 算術が好きらしい. ¶he has ***taken*** the greatest possible *liking* to ... 彼は...が非常に気に入った. 【類】suddenly ***take*** a *liking* to intellectual pursuits.
Q mold it a bit to his ***better*** *liking* [文章など]もう少し自分の気に入るように練りあげる. ¶***individual*** *likings* 個人的な好み. ¶I have no ***particular*** *liking* for ... 私は...を別段好きではない. ¶one's own ***personal*** *likings* 自分個人

の趣味. ¶I have taken a ***prodigious liking*** to her. 私はとても彼女が気に入った. ¶have a ***special liking*** for ... 殊に...を好く.

P I can accommodate ***to*** your *liking*. 僕は君の好みに応じることができる. ‖ It was most ***to*** my *liking*. それはもっとも私の気に入った. 【類】Things can not be always ***to*** one's *liking*.

P² He has a great *liking* ***for*** travel. 彼は旅行が大好きだ 【類】have a *liking* ***for*** good, stirring, healthy fiction. ‖ with a *liking* ***for*** drawing 絵の好きな.

lily, *n*. ゆり.

V To comment upon this would be to ***paint*** the *lily*. これを説明するのは蛇足(だそく)というものだ.

Q the one ***fair lily*** in all this rank grass この雑草中ただ一つの美しいゆりの花. ¶as the ***spotless lily***, unsoiled by the mire in which it grows どろに染まないはちすのように.

Q² an ***Easter lily*** [復活祭に使う]白ゆり. ¶a water garden with lotus and various ***pond lilies*** はすや色々な水蓮のある水公園(池).

P² the *lily* ***of*** the valley 鈴らん.

limb, *n*. 手足(腕・脚など).

V ***amputate*** a *limb* 足を切断する. ¶***break*** a *limb* 足を折る. ¶He ***lost*** a *limb* in [the] battle. 彼は戦で手(または足)を一本なくした. ¶***make*** the *limbs* ***quail*** 手足をすくめる. ¶***stretch*** one's aching *limbs* 痛む手足を延ばす. ¶His *limbs* immediately ***sank*** from under him. 彼はたちまち腰が抜けた.

Q the ***lower limbs*** limply stretched out 力なく延ばした両脚. ¶***sound limbs*** 完全な四肢. ¶***stout limbs*** がん丈な四肢. ¶***weak*** and ***puny limbs*** 弱くて小さな四肢.

P trembling ***in*** every *limb* 手足を震わせながら.

P² the *limbs* ***of*** a cross 十字の腕木.

limbo, *n*. 地獄の辺土; 忘却.

Q² send one into ***political limbo*** 人を政界から葬る.

P sink ***into*** the *limbo* of oblivion (=forgotten things). 忘却のふちに落込む, 世人に忘れられる.

limelight, *n*. 脚光.

Q² be in the ***world limelight*** 世界の脚光を浴びている.

P Franklin's life was lived from first to last ***in*** the *limelight* of the world. フランクリンの生活は始めから終りまで世界環視の中にあった. 【類】The Baroness has been ***in*** the *limelight* in Europe for the past six or seven years. ¶be fond ***of*** the *limelight* 《口語》 人前に出たがる. 【類】Politicians are very fond ***of*** the *limelight*.

limit, *n*. 限界, 極度, 範囲, 制限; 指し値.

V ***advance*** the *limit* to ... 限界を...に拡大する. ¶***alter*** the *limit* 限界を変更する. ¶***cut out*** the age *limit* 年齢の制限を削除する. ¶The age *limit* is not strictly ***enforced***. 年齢の制限は厳しく励行されていない. ¶***exceed*** the *limits* of decorum 無礼にわたる. ¶***fix*** the *limit* 限界を定める. ¶Everything ***has*** its *limit*. 物には限界というものがある. ¶***increase*** the *limit* to ... 限度を...に高める. ¶His ambition ***knows*** no *limits*. 彼の野心は底止する所を知らない. 【類】Avarice (欲) ***knows*** no *limits*. ¶You ought to ***learn*** the *limits* of your ability. 自分の能力の限界を知るべきだ. ¶***lower*** the *limit* to ... 制限を...に下げる. ¶***narrow down*** the *limits* 範囲を狭める. ¶The city has ***outgrown*** its *limits*. その市は従来の範囲では狭くなった. ¶***overstep*** the *limits* imposed by ... ...の設けた制限を越える. 【類】***overstep*** the normal (正常の) *limit*. ¶***pass*** the *limits* of moderation 適度の限界を越える. ¶***place*** a *limit* upon ... ...に制限を設ける ‖ ***place*** (=***set***) the *limit* at ... 制限を...に置く. ¶the law ***prescribing*** a *limit* of age for professors 教授連の停年に関する法律. ¶***raise*** a *limit* for ... ...の制限を緩和する. ¶the parcel-post has ***raised*** the weight *limit* from ... to ... 小包郵便の重量の制限が...から...に増大された. 【類】We must ***raise*** the *limit* for discount (割引) to compete with opponents. ¶***reach*** the *limit* of one's resources 方策がつきる. 【類】***reach*** the *limit* of one's patience. ¶***reduce*** one's *limit* to ... その指値を...に下げる. ¶The law ***sets limits*** on juvenile labor. 法律は少年労働に制限を設けている. ‖ ***set limits*** to lawlessness 無法を抑制する. ¶The boom ***surpasses*** all normal *limits*. にわか景気で異状のすさまじさだ.

V² The *limit* of perpetual snow ***occurs*** at 18,600 ft. on its S. side and at 18,000 ft. on its N. side. 万年雪の限界はその南側では高度一万八千六百フィートから見られ北側では一万八千フィートから見られる.

Q exceed ***certain limit*** ある限度を越える. ¶***economic limit*** 経済的限界. ¶The ***extreme limit*** of human life probably does not extend very far beyond the hundred-year mark. いくら長生しても人間の寿命はおそらく百歳の線はあまり越えられまい. ¶within the ***final limit*** of the ticket その切符の有効期間内に. ¶***fixed limit*** 定限. ¶the ***highest*** (***lowest***) ***limit*** 最高(最低)限度. ¶be reduced almost to the ***last limits*** of starvation 餓死一歩手前まで押しやられる. ¶within ***legal limits*** 法律の許す範囲内で. ¶the ***maximum*** (***minimum***) ***limit*** 最大(最小)限度. ¶within ***narrow limits*** せまい範囲内に. ¶there is ***no limit*** to ... ...に制限はない. 【類】there appeared to be ***no limit*** to ... ¶define the ***proper limits*** of ... ...の適当な制限を規定する. ¶Owing to the ***rigid limits*** of space, the book is necessarily a mere outline of the subject. 紙数にきびしい制限があるので本書はやむを得ずその問題の大略しか述べられない. ¶Fifty students for a class is the ***utmost limit***. ひとクラスは最大限五十人である. ¶within its ***territorial limits*** その領土内で.

Q² set ***age limit*** 年齢の制限を設ける ‖ retire under the ***age limit*** 停年で退職する. ¶live outside the ***boundary limit*** for telegrams 電報の配達区域外に住む. ¶within the ***city limits*** 市の境界内に(で). ¶raise the ***exemption limit*** for estate duty from ... to ... 資産税の免税点を...から...に上げる. ¶a theme with a ***length limit*** 長さに制限のある作文. ¶***off limits*** to women 女人禁制 ‖ ***off limits*** to unauthorized personnel 許可なしに出入り禁止. ¶under a ***one-hour time limit*** [意見の発表など]一時間以内という制限で. ¶before the expiration of the final ***return limit*** of the ticket その切符の最終帰着期限満了前に ‖ a ticket with a ***return limit*** on Monday 帰途が月曜までに制限されている切符. 【類】the ***return limit*** of an excursion ticket. ¶***Speed limit***: 20 MPH. 『掲示』 速度制限: 毎時二十マイル(以内). 【類】put a ***speed limit*** on ... / exceed the ***speed limit*** of 30 miles per hour / drive automobiles under the ***speed limit*** (制限速度内で). ¶within the ***three-mile limit*** 三マイルの範囲内に. ¶***time limit*** of delivery (注文品などの)納期. 【類】before the ***time limit*** is up / fix a definite ***time limit*** for ... / with a ***time limit*** of four days for the answer / There is no ***time limit*** on the tests. / a ticket with a 15-day ***time limit***.

P ***above*** *limit* 制限を越えた. ¶sell (buy) ***at*** *limit* 指値で売る(買う). 【類】We have only been able to buy ***at*** your *limit*. / We cannot execute your order ***at*** your *limits*. ¶buy ***below*** (***above***) one's *limits* 指値以下(以上)で買う. 【類】We have sold slightly ***below*** your *limits*. ¶***beyond*** the *limits* of reason 無理に ‖ His reputation as a phonetician extends far ***beyond*** the *limits* of this country. 発音学者としての彼の名声は遠く外国にまで及んでいる. 【類】the exodus (進出) of our people from the narrow area of their Mother Land to new and wider regions ***beyond*** the *limits* of the four seas. ¶***in*** the *limits* of a single chapter 一章の範囲内で. ¶outside ***of*** the city *limits* 市外. ¶restaurants placed ***on*** *limits* [駐留軍など]立入り自由の料理店. ¶We could accomplish nothing ***on account of*** the *limit*. われわれは制限されているので何もできなかった. ¶***outside*** the *limits* of the practical 実際的の範囲外に(で). ¶***to*** the very *limit* ぎりぎりの線まで. ¶He retired ***under*** the age *limit*. 彼は停年で引退した. ¶***up to*** the *limit* of the law 法律の許す範囲まで. ¶keep ***within*** *limits* 制限内にとどめる ‖ ***within*** the city *limits* of ... ...の市内に. 【類】***within*** the *limits* of human intelligence / it is not possible ***within*** the *limits* of this work to ... / ***within*** the *limits* of the wider Metropolitan area / ***within*** the *limits* of one's authority (権限内) ‖ compress ***within*** the *limits* of the space allowed (紙面の許す限り) ‖ ***within*** the *limit* of $200 in cost in any one instance 一口二百ドルの範囲内で. ¶***without*** *limit* 制限なしに.

P² the *limit* ***of*** my space is not favorable to the consideration of ... 紙数に限りがあるので...に触れることは適当でない. ¶There is a *limit* ***to*** a man's energy. 人間の精力には限りがある. ‖ There is a *limit* ***to*** everything. すべて物には限りがある.

limit, *v*. 制限する.

M His knowledge about it is ***rather limited***. 彼のそれに

ついての知識は割合狭い.

P The personnel is *limited at* (=*to*) 6,000. 人員は六千名に制限されている. ¶Membership is not *limited by* sex. 会員資格に男女の制限はない. ¶people *limited for* time 時間が十分にない人たち. ¶Our standing army is *limited in* members. わが常備軍は数に限りがある. ‖ be *limited in* one's knowledge of the world 世事にうとい. 【類】Each speaker was *limited in* time—two minutes. ¶The membership of the union, *limited* at present *to* 500, is open to all interested in the matter. その組合員は今のところは五百人に限られてはいるが一般関係者は会員になれる. 【類】The edition is *limited to* 1000 copies priced at five shillings. / Speeches were *limited to* 15 minutes each. / The expenses should be *limited to* what you can really afford (支払可能の程度).

limitation, *n.* 制限, 限界.

V It would *exceed* the *limitations* of this article if discussed adequately. その問題はくわしく論じるとこの論説では論じ尽せないだろう. ¶Free composition as an exercise *has* its *limitations*. 練習としては自由作文には都合の悪い点がある. ¶*raise* the *limitation* to ... 制限を...に緩和する. ¶I *recognized* his *limitations*. 私は彼の弱点を知った.

Q because of *budgetary limitations* 予算に制限があるので. ¶make a *drastic limitation* of the birth-rate 出生率を大々的に制限する. ¶the question of *naval limitation* 海軍軍備制限問題. ¶*voluntary limitation* of offspring 自主的産児制限.

Q^{2} *arms limitation* 軍備制限. ¶*family limitation* 家族(出生)数の制限.

P trade *under* very rigid *limitations* きわめて厳重な制限下に行われる取引. ¶*within* a *limitation* of 50 per cent 五割の範囲内で. ¶free to build merchant ships *without* any *limitation* on their tonnage トン数に制限のない商船建造の自由な.

P^{2} the *limitations of* translations 翻訳の限界(不完全性). ¶*limitations on* Japanese immigrants 日本移民の制限.

limitless, *a.* 無限の.

M His ambition is *practically limitless*. 彼の野心は実際底知らずだ.

limp, *n.* びっこひくこと.

Q have a *bad limp* ひどくびっこを引く.

P walk *with* a *limp* びっこを引いて歩く.

limp, *v.* びっこを引く.

M *limp away* びっこを引き引き去る. ¶*limp badly* ひどくびっこを引く.

M^{2} *limp along* びっこを引き引き歩く.

limp, *a.* 元気のない, ぐにゃぐにゃの.

M His character is *rather limp*. 彼の性格はかなり弱い.

P All the flowers look *limp in* such hot weather. この暑さでは花はみんな勢がない.

line, *n.* (**1**) 線; 電信(話)線; 戦線.

V *cut* the *line* of retreat 退路を断つ. ¶It is impossible to *draw* an exact *line* in all cases. あらゆる場合に正確に区別することは不可能だ. 【類】It is hard to *draw* a *line* between things so similar. / *draw* no *line* of distinction between ... / If we are to distinguish these classes at all, a *line* must be *drawn* somewhere. / It is impossible to *draw* an exact *line* in all cases. / *draw* a *line* parallel (平行線) to ... ¶I do not see that a hard and fast *line* can be *established* in the matter at all. その問題には全く一定の標準が立てられないと思う. ¶dogmatically *fix* a *line* of demarcation between ... 独断的に...間の境界線を決める. ¶*follow* the *line* of least resistance 一番楽なことをやる. 【類】*follow* a *line* of research / *follow* the same *line* of reasoning. ¶*form* a *line* 列を作る ‖ *form* battle *lines* 戦線を布く. ¶*Hold* the *line*, please. [電話で]そのままお待ち下さい. ¶The magazine article *passes* the *line* of decency. その雑誌記事は風俗壊乱にわたる. ¶*pursue* a *line* of argument itself calculated to deepen mistrust それ自体が不信任を増すような論法をたどる. ¶*rule lines* on paper 紙にけいを引く. ¶Traffic will always *seek* the *line* of least ultimate resistance. 交通は結局最小抵抗線を常に求めるものである. ¶*settle* the *line* of demarcation between ... and ... ...間の境界線を設定する. ¶*take* (=*follow*) the *line* of least resistance 最小抵抗線につく. ¶*understand* the *line* of argument 議論の筋を理解する.

Q an *aerial line* 架空線. ¶[The] *line* is *busy*. 《米》=[The] number is engaged 《英》お話中です. ¶there is no *clear line* of division between ... and ... ...と...との間には明確な区別はない. 【類】separate them by a *clear line* of demarcation from ... / a *clear* and *distinctive line* of division runs across ... ¶establish a *clear cut line* of authority and responsibility 権限及び責任の帰するところを明かにする. ¶show the relief of the land by *contour lines* 等高線によって土地の盛上げを示す. ¶a *curved line* 曲線. ¶the *dead line* 締切期. 【類】establish a *dead line*. ¶very clearly *defined line* of demarcation separating them それらを分かつきわめて明白な境界線. ¶No *definite line* of demarcation can be drawn. 明確に区別ができない. ¶*delicate lines* and perfect proportions 優美な線と完全なつり合. ¶a sharp drawing of the *dividing line* between ... and ... ...と...とを克明に区別すること. ¶The coupon is to be torn out on *dotted line*. クーポンは点線から切取る. ‖ the Air Force, the country's *first line* of defense 国防の第一線たる空軍. 【類】The *first line* was raided by the enemy bombers. ‖ A paragraph has its *first line* indented. [文の]節の書き始めは端を引込める. ¶the *front line* 前線. ¶Between the two no *hard-and-fast line* can well be drawn. 二者の間には画然たる区別がよくつけられない. ¶draw a *hazy line* of demarcation between ... ...の間をあいまいに区別する. ¶an *imaginary line* 虚線. ¶an *isobathic line* 〖地理〗等深線. ¶an *isoseismal line* 〖地震〗等震度線. ¶a *lean line* 肉細の線. ¶The cars were standing still in a *long line*. 電車が幾台もつながって停止していた. ¶a very *narrow line* divides it from ... それと...とは壁一重. ¶run on *parallel lines* 平行線上を走る. 【類】The development of wireless telephony runs along roughly *parallel lines* with that of ordinary telegraphic communication. ¶Tear on this *perforated line*. 点線のところを切り取ること. ¶draw a *perpendicular line* 垂直線を引く. ¶it is quite impossible to draw a *sharp line* of demarcation between ... and ... ...と...の間にはっきり区分を立てることは全く不可能だ. 【類】originally no *sharp line* of distinction existed between ... and ... / There is no *sharp line* of demarcation between the two groups. / a *sharp dividing line*. ¶a *single* (*double*) *line* of rails [鉄道の]単(複)線. ¶a *slant line* 斜線. ¶*solid line* 実線. ¶*some line* must be drawn between ... and ... ...と...との間に何か区別をつけねばならない. ¶in a *straight line* 直線をなして ‖ His life has been a *straight line*. 彼の一生は終始一貫していた. ¶no *strict line* can be drawn between ... ...間に明確な分界線を引くことはできない. ¶The first *telegraphic line* in Japan was opened to traffic in 1869. 電信線が開通した. ¶a *thick line* 肉太の線. ¶in an *unbroken line* 連綿として. ¶words underscored with a *wavy line* 下に波線を引いた語. ¶in a *zigzag line* ジグザグに(なって).

Q^{2} an *advance line* of defense 国防の第一線. ¶draw *battle lines* in an all-out fight over the housing problem 住宅問題と真剣にとり組むための背水の陣を布く. ¶fly in a *bee line* (=beeline) 《英》直線に飛ぶ ‖ make a *bee line* for ... ...の方向へ直線に進む. 【類】The distance between them is five miles in a *bee line*. ¶the *Blackston line* ブラッキストン・ライン(津軽海峡の日本の南北動物分界線). ¶the *border line* between the two 二者の境界線. 【類】it is just on the *border line* which separate ... from ... ¶the *boundary line* between ... ...間の境界線. ¶a *clothes line* 物干ひも. ¶The university does not draw the *color line*. その大学は人種の区別はしない. ‖ cross the *color line* from Negro to white=be classed as a white 黒人と白人との人種の区別をする(白人の部に入れられる). ¶clog *communication[s] lines* 交通線を防害する. ¶construct new *defense lines* along the border 国境に沿うて新しい防衛線を設ける. ¶the *demarcation line*=the line of demarcation 境界線. ¶a *distribution line* [電力の]送電線. ¶the *finish line*=the goal 決勝点. ¶send men to the *firing line* 第一線に兵を送る. 【類】the gunners (砲手) on the *firing line*. ¶a *gas line* ガス管線. ¶the *horizon line* 水平線. ¶America's expanded "*life line*" アメリカの拡大した「生命線」. ¶form a *march line* 勢ぞろいする. ¶a *party line* [電話の]共同線; [政党の]政策方針. 【類】*Party lines* have been swept away. ¶draw a *pencil line* across a board 板の上に鉛筆で線を引く. ¶establish *picket lines* =place pickets 〖労〗ピケ・ラインを引く. 【類】violence (暴力) on *picket lines* / cross a tight *picket line* of striking workers. ¶the ***Plimsoll line*** 〖航海〗満載喫水線. ¶a ***pole line*** 電柱の線. ¶break through (＝cross) a ***police line*** 警戒線を突破する. ¶construct a ***power line*** from ... to ... [電力の]送電線を...から...まで建設する. 【類】The gale destroyed ***power lines***. ¶hold the ***price line*** その価格を維持する. ¶the ***shore line*** 海岸線. ¶a ***sky line*** [地形や都会の建物など]空に映じた輪郭. ¶a ***sounding line*** [水深を計る]測鉛線. ¶return to the ***starting line*** and begin all over again 新規まき直しをやる. ¶a ***steam line*** スチーム管. ¶The ***telegraph line*** between the two cities is interrupted. 両都市間の電信線は故障している. 【類】The ***telegraph line*** is not open to the public. ¶establish ***telephone lines*** 電話線を引く. 【類】find oneself on a crossed ***telephone line*** (混線). ¶a ***transmission line*** [電力の]送電線. ¶A five cent fare holds on all, except one, ***transport lines*** in New York. 五セントの乗車賃はニューヨークでは一つの線を除き他のすべての輸送線で有効である. ¶a ***trunk*** (＝key) ***line*** 幹(本)線‖The telephone is on a ***two-party line*** その電話は共用線に接続している. ¶***walkway lines*** 横断歩道の白線. ¶the ***water line*** 喫水線(船舶の).

P all ***along*** the ***line*** 全線に沿って‖The changes have been ***along*** the ***line*** of progress. その変化は進歩の線をたどってきている. ¶His working merits are just ***above*** the ***line***. 彼の仕事の成績は普通なみよりやや上だ. ¶***at*** high water ***line*** 満潮時に. ¶stand ***in*** a ***line*** 一列にならぶ‖Soldiers marched in column and attacked ***in line***. 兵士は縦隊で進み横隊になって攻撃した. ¶The pass is not good ***on*** this ***line***. そのパスはこの線では無効です.‖***on*** the ***lines*** that had been lain down すでに決定ずみの線に沿って. ¶His picture was hung "***on*** the ***line***." 彼の絵は目の高さの所にかけられた(特選画など). ¶Man's eyes are ***out of line*** in two cases out of five. 人の目は五人中二人は(かっこうよく)並んでいない.

P² The ***line of*** demarcation between ... and ... is somewhat indeterminate. ...と...との境界線は幾分明確さを欠く.‖***lines of*** communication 〖軍〗交通線‖the ***line of*** thought 考え方‖his ***line of*** argument 彼の論法. ¶the ***line of*** future development 将来進出の線‖the ***line of*** attack they will follow in the campaign [選挙運動の際]攻撃すべき線.

(2) 行; 書状, 証書; 詩句; せりふ.

V ***drop*** him a ***line*** 彼に一筆送る. ¶***forget*** one's ***lines*** 自分のせりふを忘れる. ¶***scrawl*** a few ***lines*** 二三行なぐり書きをする. ¶***send*** a ***line*** of thanks 一筆礼状を出す. ¶***speak*** one's ***lines*** せりふを言う. ¶***lines suggested*** by ... ...が折にふれて作った詩. ¶I will just ***write*** him a ***line***. 彼に一筆書こう.‖at the very moment that I am ***writing*** these ***lines*** この文を丁度書いている時に. ¶The ***line jingles*** in my head. その詩句が私の頭の中にりんりん鳴っている. ¶***scratch*** a few ***lines*** [手紙など]二三行走り書きする. ¶***stagger*** the ***lines*** [新聞の見出しで]行を少しずつ右にずらす.

Q write in ***alternate lines*** 一行おきに書く. ¶the ***celebrated line*** 有名な詩句. ¶There is not a ***dull line*** in the whole of it. その全体の中でつまらない所は一行もない. ¶I received a few ***icy lines***. 私はそっけない返事をもらった. ¶***oft-quoted lines*** よく引用される詩句. ¶the ***opening line*** of a novel 小説の書出し. ¶***pathetic*** and ***soul-stirring lines*** 哀切人の心を打つ詩句.

Q² ***marriage lines*** 結婚認可証.

P read ***between*** the ***lines*** 言外の意をくみとる‖read reproaches ***between*** the ***lines*** of a friendly letter 表面友情のこもった手紙の中に非難の調子を感得する.

P² a poem ***of*** six ***lines*** 六行詩. ¶in the sixth ***line of*** the twelfth page ***from*** the beginning 十二ページの上から六行目に. ¶The actor was not sure ***of*** his ***lines***. その俳優は自分のせりふに自信がなかった.

(3) 航路, 空路, 線路; 会社(鉄道・汽船・航空など).

V ***block*** a ***line*** 航路または線路をふさぐ. ¶***construct*** a double ***line*** of railway 鉄道の複線を敷設する. ¶***establish*** a special ***line*** of steamers between ... and ... ...と...との間に臨時の航路を設ける. ¶the orchard ***flanks*** the railway ***line*** between ... その果樹園は...間の鉄道線路に隣接している. ¶***join*** the Vladivostock ***line*** ウラジオ線に接続する. ¶***operate*** street-car ***lines*** 《米》市内電車線を経営する. ¶The railway ***rejoins*** the main ***line*** at ... その鉄道は...で再び本線に連絡する. ¶***run*** a train ***line*** 《英》電車線路を経営する. ¶the steamship company will ***strike*** a new ***line*** from ... その汽船会社は...からの新航路を開くことになるだろう.

V² the ***line ascends*** the valley of ... to 線路が...のけい谷を上って...へ向っている. ¶From here the ***line branches away*** to the west. ここから線路が西方へ分かれている. ¶a ***line branches off*** here to ... 線路がここから...へ分かれている. ¶steamship ***lines operating*** from ... to ... ...から...へ通う航路. ¶from this point a branch ***line runs*** (＝***extends***) to ... この地点から......へ支線がある. ¶the ***line strikes*** north towards ... 線路が...へと北に向っている.

Q ***existing lines*** 既成線. ¶the ***Interurban Line*** 都市間連絡線. ¶join the ***main line*** (支線が)本線に接続する. ¶***projected lines*** 計画線. ¶***proposed lines*** 予定線. ¶a ***regular line*** to Australia 豪州への定期航路. ¶a ***single*** (***double***) ***line*** of rails 単(複)線鉄道.

Q² an ***air line***＝an airline 航空系統, 航空会社; 《英》航空路 (airway)‖a network of ***air lines*** 航空路網‖One U.S. ***air line*** recently completed the haul in about 100 flying days. 最近一米国航空会社がその輸送を空輸百日で完了した. ¶Both railroads and ***bus line*** are strike-bound. ストで鉄道もバスも運転休止している. ¶the ***Cunard Line*** キューナード汽船会社. ¶the ***loop line*** [鉄道の]ループ線; [電車などの]環状線. ¶the ***North Atlantic Air Lines*** 北大西洋航空会社. ¶a ***rail*** and ***water line*** 鉄道及び水路線(汽車汽船連絡の). ¶cities and towns in ***railroad lines*** 鉄道で結ぶ市や町. ¶***railway lines*** buckled by the great heat of the sun 太陽の高熱でゆがんだ鉄道の軌条. ¶the ocean traversed by several ***steamer lines*** 幾つかの航路で横断された大洋. ¶a ***suburban line*** 郊外鉄道. ¶lay down a ***surface-car line*** 路面電車線を敷く. ¶a ***trunk*** [***line***] 《米》幹線.

P run ***off*** the ***lines***＝jump the rails＝《米》jump the track 脱線する. ¶boats now running ***on*** the ***line*** 現在その航路についている汽船‖The new steamer will be run ***on*** the N.Y.K. Australian ***line***. その新造船は日本郵船豪州航路につくだろう.

P² a ***line to*** Australia＝an Australian ***line*** 豪州航路.

(4) 血統.

V, V² He ***founded*** a ***line*** of Egyptian kings. 彼はエジプト王統の開祖である. ¶The ***line*** has ***died out***. その血統が絶えた.

Q he has a ***clear line*** of descent from ... 彼は確かに...の子孫である. ¶The succession to the throne is in the ***direct line***. 皇位継承は直系に依って行われる.‖in a ***direct line*** of succession from ... to ... 血統が...から...まで連綿と続いて. ¶a ***divine dynastic line*** 神授の王統. ¶on the ***female*** (***male***) ***line*** 女(男)子の血筋に(で). ¶the ***Imperial Line*** unbroken from prehistoric ages 有史前の時代から連綿たる皇統. ¶The family is extinct in the ***male line***. その家族は男子の血統が絶えている. 【類】the extinction of the ***male line*** of the house of ... ¶the ***maternal ancestral line*** 母方の祖先の血統. ¶the ***paternal ancestral line*** 父方の祖先の血統. ¶the ancestress of the ***royal line*** of Stuart スチュアート家王統の女子祖先. ¶an ***unbroken line*** of sovereigns 連綿たる王統.

Q² fowls which have good ***blood lines*** behind it 血統(毛すじ)のよい家きん. ¶trace back one's ***family line*** 血統調べをする.

P He comes ***of*** a good ***line***. 彼は血統がよい.

P² a ***line of*** emperors unbroken for ages eternal 万世一系の皇統‖The ***line of*** Yoritomo ended in 1219. 頼朝の家系は一二一九年に絶えた.

(5) 方面, 方針, 方法, 傾向; 政策; 職業.

V Though comparatively modern, they ***follow*** with substantial accuracy the ***lines*** of the original buildings. それらは比較的近代的ではあっても実質的には原物の建築法を正確に踏襲している. ¶it was continued along the same ***lines laid down*** by ... それは...が立てた同一方針で続けられた‖One cannot ***lay down*** a hard and sharp ***line***. 一定不変の区別を立てることはできない. ¶***map out*** the ***lines*** of our campaign carefully われらの運動の方法を周到に立案する. ¶***open*** new ***lines*** of inquiry 新方面に調査を進める. ¶***seek*** new ***lines*** of activities 新方面に活躍しようとする. ¶***take*** one's ***line*** 方針を定める.

Q He's rather in the ***alcoholic line*** (＝on the alcoholic side). 彼はどっちかというと上戸の方だ. ¶The enterprise developed along more ***ambitious lines***. その事業が一層大規模に発展した. ¶They stock only the ***best line*** (＝kind) of hats. あの店では帽子は高級品だけ仕入れている. ‖ The ***best line*** of approach in studying English is to learn to speak it. 英語研究はまず話すことを習うのからするのが一番よい. ¶banking in its ***broad lines*** and general principles その広範な諸方面及び一般的原則における金融業. ¶one's ***chosen line*** of work 自分で選んだ職業. ¶follow ***conventional lines*** 在来のやり方を踏襲する. ¶there are several ***converging lines*** of evidence which point to the deduction that ... 種々な方面の証拠から推して...と結論することができる. ¶practice on ***correct lines*** 正しい方法によって練習する. ¶take a ***decided line*** 断固として決行する. ¶in the ***different lines*** of study それぞれ異なった研究方面で. ¶The life of the officer runs on very ***different lines***. 士官の生活は(兵士などのに比べて)その趣を異にしている. ¶lay down a ***definite line*** of investigation 一定の研究案を立てる. ¶an ***entrenched line*** of thought 固定した考え方. ¶in ***every line*** of human endeavor 人間活動のあらゆる方面において. ¶hotels conducted on ***foreign lines*** 外国式に経営するホテル. ¶reorganization of the Turkish Army on ***German lines*** ドイツ式によるトルコ陸軍の再編制. ¶the ***main line*** of historical development 歴史的発展の大綱. ¶She has a ***good line***. 彼女は姿がいい. ¶***hard lines*** 苦境, 不運. ¶a very ***important line*** of research 非常に重要な研究方面. ¶one of its ***major lines*** of work その事業の主要項目. ¶soldiers (teachers) trained along ***modern lines*** 近代式に訓練された軍人(など). 【類】organize along ***modern lines*** / the development of Japan along ***modern lines*** / steamships built and fitted on ***modern lines*** / reconstruct it on the most ***modern lines***. ¶a story written on an entirely ***new line*** 全く新しい書きかたをした小説. ¶Business was continued along the ***old lines***. 営業は旧式な方法で継続された. ¶conducted on ***original lines*** 独創的な方法で経営された. ¶the rapid advance of knowledge along ***particular lines*** 特殊な方面の知識の急激な進歩 ‖ men with special knowledge along ***particular lines*** 特殊な方面の専門知識を有する人々. 【類】your ***particular line*** of interest ‖ Geology is his ***particular line***. 地質学が彼の専攻です. ¶the reconstruction of the city on modern ***planning lines*** 近代式計画案による同市の再建. ¶on thoroughly ***progressive lines*** 全く進歩的な方法で. ¶teaching on ***reform lines*** 改良方法による教授. ¶along the ***same lines*** これにならって ‖ be in the ***same line*** of thought 同じ思想傾向(考え方)にある. 【類】those interested in the ***same line*** of investigation. ¶The hospital is run on ***scientific lines***. その病院は科学的方法で経営されている. 【類】overhaul their management on ***scientific lines***. ¶I carry on the work as a ***side line***. 私はかたわらその仕事をしている. ¶on ***similar lines*** 同じ方針の下に. ¶a ***skilful line*** of tactics to pursue under such circumstances かかる事情のもとに取るべき巧みな策略. ¶his ***special line*** of work 彼の専門. ¶built on the most ***up-to-date lines*** 最新式に建造された. ¶***What line*** are you in? 君のお仕事は何ですか.

Q^2 He is in the ***banking*** (***broker***) ***line***. 彼は銀行(ブローカー)業者である. ¶decide on the "***party line***" 政党の政策を決定する.

P It is ***along*** this ***line*** that we hope to make our chief contribution to education in general. われわれが一般の教育に専ら寄与したいのはこの方面においてである. ‖ ***along*** approved scientific ***lines*** 世間から認められた科学的方法で. 【類】develop ***along*** the ***lines*** of ... / I shall be glad to help any woman who feels the need of advice ***along*** these ***lines***. ¶a recognized leader of instruction ***in*** his ***line*** 彼の専門方面の教育で有名な指導者 ‖ Business is poor generally ***in*** our ***line***. 私たちの商売は一体に不景気です. ‖ ***in*** the ***line*** of ... ...の方面では. 【類】the most extensive manufactures ***in*** our ***line*** in the world / If not ***in*** your ***line***, kindly pass on to a good house doing in this class of goods. ‖ ***in line*** with ... =along with ... ...とともに, ...に添うて. 【類】In addition to supervising the work of Takata & Co. he has taken a course of studies ***in line*** with his profession at the Columbia University. / ***in line*** with the government policy / somewhat ***in line*** with such work in European countries ‖ The umpire stands so as to be ***in line*** with the winning post and the winning horse. 審判者は決勝点と勝馬とを見通すように立っている. ‖ something ***in*** one's ***line*** その性に合うもの. 【類】It's more ***in*** my ***line***. / That's not much ***in*** my ***line***. ‖ This is quite ***in*** the ***line*** of historical precedent. これは全く歴史の伝統に合致するものである. ¶The paper is conducted ***on lines*** independent of party politics. その新聞は政党政治に関係なく経営されている. 【類】the school is to be conducted ***on lines*** similar to those of ... ‖ ***on*** the ***lines*** of a French chateau フランスの別荘式に ‖ The hotel provides good accommodation ***on*** the European ***lines***. そのホテルはヨーロッパ方式で上等のサービスをする(止宿料に食事を含む式). ‖ I am doing Latin as much as possible ***on*** these ***lines***. 私はこの方法でできるだけラテン語を勉強している. 【類】be made ***on*** the same ***line*** / write another book ***on*** the ***lines*** of "Quo Vadis." / a society founded ***on*** the ***lines*** of this plan / Action will be taken ***on*** the ***lines*** indicated. ‖ ***on*** the ***lines*** that were laid down. ¶be ***out of line*** with ... ...とは一致しない(別種のものである) ‖ be ***out of*** one's ***line*** 畑違いである.

P^2 in this ***line of*** literature 文学のこの方面では.

(6) 品目.

V the ***lines*** we ***handle*** are ... 弊店が扱っている品目は...です. ¶We ***have*** a full ***line*** of photographic supplies. 弊店には写真用品が十分取そろえてあります. ¶its ***lines*** of production ***range*** from ... to ... その製品の種目は...から...に及ぶ.

Q He carries the ***best line*** of shoes in town. 彼は市内で一番上等のくつを仕入れている. ¶We carry a ***full line*** of canned goods. かん詰なら何でもおいています. ¶***important lines*** of merchandise 重要商品.

Q^2 the ***dry-goods*** (***grocery***) ***line*** 太物(食料品)商. ¶***luxury lines*** of goods ぜいたく品類. ¶They are more or less ***in*** the ***line*** of luxury. 多少ぜいたく品の部に属する.

(7) 列.

V ***cross*** the ***line*** of a procession 行列を横切る. ¶***form*** [a] ***line*** [兵隊などが]列を作る. ¶***join*** the bread ***line*** 市の無料給食をもらう仲間にはいる.

Q In the ***receiving line*** stood the bridal couple and the parents of the bride and groom. 接待の列に新郎新婦とその両親が立った. ¶There we have ***waiting lines***. そこでは待っている人が列を作っている. 【類】a ***waiting line*** at a theatre.

Q^2 Those cars are just off the ***assembly line***. それらの自動車は組立工場から出たばかりの新車である. ¶ban ***nylon lines*** in the shopping districts 商店街におけるナイロンものを買あさる列を禁じる.

P ***in*** a ***line*** 一列に.

(8) 釣糸.

V Many anglers ***cast*** their ***lines*** in this river. この川には釣師が大勢出る.

Q ***frayed out lines*** 弱った綱.

P fish ***with*** a rod and ***line*** 釣ざおで魚を釣る.

line, *v.* 線を引く; しわをきざむ; 整列する; 裏打ちをする.

M a face ***deeply lined*** with worldly cares 浮世の苦労が深く刻み込まれている顔.

M^2 ***line off*** 線で画する. ¶troops assembled on the parade-ground and ***lined up*** for inspection 練兵場に集められて検閲のために整列した兵士 ‖ Have them ***line up***. 整列させよ. 【類】All ***lined up*** along my way to the station. / Housewives ***lined up*** at butcher shops and delicatessens. / ***line up*** for a roll call (点呼) / ***line up*** for seats in a cinema / eager buyers who ***lined up*** at daybreak / ***line up*** for the night game / Cars were ***lining up*** along the road for a mile ‖ ***line up*** against the influence of Soviet Russia 連携してソ連の勢力に対抗する.

P ***line through*** (=cross out) an entry 一つの記入事項をまっ殺する. ¶an avenue ***lined*** on both sides ***with*** trees 両側に立木が列んだ道 ‖ The boxes are ***lined with*** lead. 箱は内側に鉛が張ってある. ‖ ***lined*** inside ***with*** white tiles 内側を白いタイルで張った ‖ ***lined with*** india-rubber ゴム裏の ‖ an overcoat ***lined with*** silk (fur) 絹(毛)裏のオーバー. ‖ His study is ***lined with*** books to the ceiling. 彼の書斎は天井まで届く書だなで取巻かれている. 【類】***line with*** paper (cloth) / The avenue is ***lined with*** rows of over-arching trees. / The long street is ***lined with*** closely set blooming cherry-trees, which meet in flowery canopy overhead. / The river-bank (street) was ***lined with*** people. / The whole route was ***lined with*** military and naval troops. ‖ drive on a road ***lined with*** signboards.

lineage, *n.* 血統, 系統.
Q a person of *ancient* (*lofty*) *lineage* 旧家(など)の人. ¶a woman of *high lineage* 名門の婦人. ¶sons (daughters) of *illustrious lineage* 名門の息(など). ¶men of *noble lineage* 名門の士. ¶men of *royal lineage* 皇族の方々.

lineament, *n.* 容ぼう.
V I could not well *distinguish* the *lineaments* of his face. 私には彼の容ぼうの見分けがよくつかなかった.

linen, *n.* リンネル; [集合的] リンネル製品.
V *bleach linen* リンネルをさらす. ¶*change* one's *linen* リンネルの下衣などを替える. ¶*iron* the *linen* リンネルにアイロンをかける. ¶*put on* fresh *linen* (=clean sheets) on the bed 寝床に新しいリンネルの敷布をかける. ¶*starch* the *linen* リンネルにのりを付ける.
Q *personal linen* はだ着.
Q[2] *bed linen* シーツやピローケース(まくらおおい)など. ¶*table linen* リンネルのテーブル掛.

liner, *n.* 定期船; [定期]旅客機.
V companies *operating* the great transpacific *liners* 太平洋横断の定期巨船を持っている諸会社.【類】It is *operating liners* to Australia.
Q *luxurious liners* 豪華な定期船. ¶*palatial liners* 豪華定期船.
Q[2] war-seized *luxury liners* 戦争で捕獲された諸豪華客船. ¶a *mammoth* (=*monster*) *liner* 巨大な定期船. ¶a big *ocean liner* 外洋航路の大型定期船. ¶a *passenger liner* 客[定期]船. ¶a *President liner* プレジデント汽船会社の定期船.

liner, *n.* 政策に忠実な人;〘野球〙ライナー.
V *drive* a *liner* into outfield 外野にライナーをとばす.
Q[2] a *party liner* 政党の政策に忠実な人.

lineup, *n.*〘スポーツ〙ラインナップ.
V *announce* the *lineups* on both sides 両側のラインナップを発表する.

linger, *v.* ぐずぐずする, 長引く, 残る.
M This will *linger longest* in his memory. それが彼の記憶に最も長く残るだろう. ¶*linger out* (=*away*) one's days on a sickbed だらだらといつまでも病床で日を送る.
M[2] He still *lingered about* after everyone else had left. 彼はみんなが去ったあともなおぶらついていた. ¶The custom is still *lingering on* in the rural districts. その習慣はまだ地方には残っている. ‖ *linger on* past visiting hours 訪問時間が過ぎてもぐずぐずして帰らないでいる.
P *linger around* a park 公園をぶらつく. ¶*linger at* the door 入口でためらう. ¶*linger between* life and death 生死の間をさまよう. ¶*linger by* the wayside 路傍でうろつく. ¶The regard for ... still *lingered in* the popular mind. ...に対する尊敬の念がまだ一般人の心に残っていた. ‖ His last words still *linger in* our ears. 彼の臨終の言葉がまだわれわれの耳に残っている. ¶*linger on* dinner 食卓をいつまでも離れずにいる ‖ *linger on* the lawn 芝生をぶらつく. ¶*linger over* one's lager ビールをゆっくりと飲む ‖ *linger over* one's work ‖ *linger over* one's desk when writing 物を書くときには長い時間を費す.【類】After dinner, we *lingered over* our coffee. ¶*linger upon* a problem ある問題を長々と論じ立てる.

lingo, *n.* [専門語, 外国語など] 分からない語, ちんぷんかんぷん.
V I can *speak* their *lingo*. 私は[人に分らない]彼らの言葉が話せる. ¶I can *understand* his *lingo* no better than Sanskrit. 彼のしゃべることは僕にはサンスクリット同様ちんぷんかんぷんだ.
Q use a *strange lingo* 人に分からない言葉を使う.

linguist, *n.* 語学者.
Q He was an *excellent linguist*, speaking the principal languages with fluency and ease. 彼は主要国語をすらすら話すすぐれた語学者であった. ¶an *excellent English linguist* すぐれた英語学者. ¶They are not naturally *good linguists*. 彼らは語学の天才じゃない.

linguistics, *n.* 言語学.
Q *comparative linguistics* 比較言語学. ¶*general linguistics* 一般言語学.

lining, *n.* 裏地.
V I can *see* the silver *lining* in the dark clouds which have hung over Europe for the last four years. 過去四年間ヨーロッパの空にかかった黒雲すなわち大戦の中にも光明の半面を私は認めることができる.
Q a beach bag with *rubberized lining* ゴム裏の海水浴場用「ビーチバッグ.
Q[2] *rayon crepe linings* 人絹クレープの裏地. ¶There was a *silver lining* to the dark cloud. その凶事には光明の半面があった. ‖ a *silver lining* in a gloomy picture 憂いの中の一喜.【類】dark clouds edged with a *silver lining*. ¶*zip-in lining* [外とう・ジャンパーの]チャック付裏.

link, *n.* 環, かん, 連鎖.
V This *constitutes* a *link* in the broken chain. これは切れた鎖の連鎖をなすものである. ¶*establish* a *link* between ... and ... ...と...との連絡をつける. ¶*find links* of connection between events それらの事件の連絡をたどる. ¶*form* a *link* between ... and ... ...と...の間のつながりになる.【類】this *forms* a natural *link* with ... ¶It *marks* an important *link* in the chain of development. それは発展の連鎖における重要な一環をなしている. ¶*pluck* the *link* asunder 環を抜きとる. ¶By the death of ... a *link* with ... has been *removed*. ...の死によって...との連鎖が断たれた. ¶*sever* a *link* that binds us to ... われらを...に結んでいる連鎖を断ち切る. ¶The last *link* with ... was *snapped*. ...との最後の連鎖が切り離された. ¶one of the last *links* that *bind* us to the quaint and picturesque past われらを奇異な絵のように美しい過去に結びつけている最後の連鎖の一つ.
Q a *connecting link* between ... ...の間を結ぶ連環. ¶ancient works of art and other *cultural links* with the past 古美術品やその他の過去との文化的連鎖. ¶an *intermediate link* between ... and ... ...と...との中間を結ぶ連鎖. ¶the *lower links* of the chain of animal life 下等動物. ¶supply the *missing links* in the chain of development 進化の道程において喪失した連鎖を補う. ¶there is thus a *slight link* between ... and ... かくして...と...との間にはわずかなつながりがある. ¶the *spiritual link* connecting the Orient and the Occident 東洋と西洋とを結ぶ一脈の精神的交渉. ¶A chain is no stronger than its *weakest link*. 鎖の中一つでも弱い所があれば全体が弱くなる.
P[2] the *links between* the past and the present times 過去の時代と現代とのつながり. ¶*links in* a chain of causation 因果関係における連鎖. ¶a *link with* the past 過去とのつながり.

link, *v.* つなぐ.
M His fame is *linked closely* with the march of English civilization. 彼の名声はイギリス文明の進歩に密接な関係がある. ¶the name of ... is *indissolubly linked* with the name of ... ...の名は...の名と不可分に結ばれている. ¶*inexorably linked* to ... ...にしっかりとつながれた. ¶*inseparably linked* with ... ...と切っても切れない関係のある. ¶These are *subtly linked* together. それらは微妙にからみ合っている. ¶be *linked together* by interest 利害関係で結ばれる.
M[2] *link* it *up* with ... それを...と抱合わせる(品物など) ‖ *link up* the Empire 全帝国を連結する.
P names forever *linked with* ... ...と永久に結ばれた名 ‖ the work *linked with* his name 彼の名と結び付けられた事業 ‖ The welfare of the whole nation is closely *linked with* industry. 全国民の幸福は産業と密接な関係がある.

links, *n. pl.* ゴルフ場.
P He has been spending every morning and afternoon *on* the golf *links*. 彼はゴルフ場で朝夕送ってきた.

linotype, *n.*〘印刷〙一行式植字鋳造機(ライノタイプ).
P This book has been set *on* the *linotype*. この本はライノタイプで組まれたものだ.

lion, *n.* しし(ライオン); 人気者.
V a woman almost naked and *bestriding* a *lion* ほとんど裸体でライオンにまたがる女. ¶*cage* a *lion* ライオンをおりに入れる. ¶This continually *causes* the British *lion* to roar. このことのためにいつも英国は怒ってほえた. ¶A small *lion* was *cubbed* in the Zoo. 動物園でライオンの子が生れた. ¶He has been *made* a *lion* (=lionized[3]) among young ladies. 彼は若い婦人たちの間でもてはやされている. ¶*tame* a *lion* for the circus ライオンをサーカス用に調練する.
V The *lion went* for him. ししが彼に飛びついた. ¶*Lions roar*. ししがほえる.
Q a *performing lion* 芸をするライオン. ¶a *social lion* 引っぱりだこ. ¶He was received as a *young lion* in London society. 彼はロンドン社交界の若い花形として歓迎された.
P fight *like* a *lion* 奮戦力闘する.
P[2] a *lion in* a cage おりの中のライオン. ¶the *lion of* the evening その晩の人気者 ‖ the *lion of* literature 花形文士.
O as bold as a *lion* ライオンのように勇敢な.

lionize, *v.* 大騒ぎする.

M The celebrity was ***enthusiastically lionized.*** その名士は大もてであった.

lip, *n.* くちびる.

V ***apply*** one's *lips* to … くちびるを…にあてる. ¶***bite*** one's *lip* じっとくちびるをかむ(がまんする). 【類】***bite*** one's *lip* in anger. ¶***compress*** one's *lips* くちびるを結ぶ. ¶In spite of himself, a smile ***curled*** his *lip*. 思わず彼は笑って口をほころばせた. ¶Not a complaint ***escaped*** his *lips*. 彼は不平を一言も漏らさなかった. 【類】He did not allow any word to ***escape*** his *lips*. ¶Their *lips* ***glued*** fast ***together***. 二人のくちびるがぴったり吸いついた. ¶We ***hung on*** his *lips*. 僕たちは彼の話に聞き入った. ¶We welcomed wine as a means of ***loosening*** our *lips*. われわれは口ほごしの(打融ける)手段として酒を歓迎した. ¶***make*** a *lip* 口をとがらす. ¶***open*** our *lips* to speak 口を開けて話す. ¶girls who ***paint*** their *lips* 口紅をつける女たち. ¶That was the only remark that ***passed*** his *lips*. それだけが彼の口から出た言葉であった. ¶***pinch*** their *lips* 彼らのくちびるをつねる. ¶She ***placed*** her *lips* against mine. 彼女は私のくちびるにキッスした. ¶***pout*** one's *lips* くちびるをとがらす. ¶She ***pressed*** her *lips* to mine. 彼女のくちびるを私のくちびるに押付けた. ¶***purse*** [*up*] the *lips* 口をつぼめる. ¶He hesitatingly ***put*** his *lips* on hers. 彼はおずおずと彼女のくちびるにキッスした. ¶***put*** one's *lips* to another's ear [ささやきの際]口を人の耳につける. ¶Trained deafmutes can ***read*** the *lips* with facility. 訓練されたろうあ者は容易に人のくちびるの動きで意味を察しる. ¶***rouge*** one's *lips* 口紅を塗る. ¶***shoot out*** the *lips* くちびるを突出す(軽べつの表情). ¶***smack*** one's *lips* over … …に舌づつみを打つ. ¶***stain*** one's *lips* with a curse 悪態をついて自分の身を傷つける. ¶***thrust out*** (=pout) the *lips* くちびるをとがらせる. ¶***unite*** their *lips* in a kin くちびるを接してキッスする. ¶***wet*** one's *lips* くちびるをぬらす.

V² Their *lips* ***met***. 彼らはキッスした. ¶Her *lips* slightly ***parted***. 彼女のくちびるが少し開いた. ¶His *lips* ***twitched***. 彼のくちびるがぴくぴく動いた.

Q ***amorous*** (=***lascivious***) *lips* 好色なくちびる. ¶***chapped*** *lips* 荒れたくちびる. ¶***cracked*** *lips* ひびが切れたくちびる. ¶***drawn*** and ***retracted*** *lips* 引締ったくちびる. ¶***dry*** *lips* かわいたくちびる. ¶***dry*** and ***parched*** *lips* かわいてかさかさした口びる. ¶Their *lips* are ***dumb***. 彼らはくちをとじている. ¶***everted*** *lips* むき出たくちびる. ¶***hot*** and ***wet*** *lips* [恋人などの]熱いぬれたくちびる. ¶***inverted, thin*** and ***retracted*** *lips* 外にまくれた薄くて引締ったくちびる. ¶bite one's ***lower*** *lip* 下くちびるをかむ. ¶***luscious*** *lips* 甘美なくちびる. ¶***moist*** *lips* ぬれたくちびる. ¶***pouting*** *lips* とがらしたくちびる. ¶***prominent*** *lips* 突き出たくちびる. ¶***quivering*** *lips* ふるえるくちびる. ¶***red, inverted***, and ***thick*** *lips* 赤くってまくれた厚いくちびる. ¶***ripe*** *lips* 熟し切ったくちびる. ¶***rosy*** *lips* 赤いくちびる. ¶thickly ***rouged*** (=***painted***) *lips* 真赤に塗ったくちびる. ¶***rouge-faded*** *lips* ルージュのはげたくちびる. ¶***shapely*** *lips* 格好のよいくちびる. ¶***slacken*** *lips* しまりのない口. ¶***slim*** (=***thin***) *lips* 薄いくちびる. ¶***thick*** and ***inverted*** *lips* 厚くて外にまくれたくちびる(黒人などの).

Q² ***cherry*** *lips* 真赤なくちびる. ¶a ***crater*** *lip* 火口のふち. ¶a ***hare*** *lip*= harelip みつくち.

P moisten one's thumb and fingers ***at*** one's *lips* くちびるで指をぬらす. ¶believe in God in our hearts, not only ***by*** our *lips* 口先ばかりでなく心から神を信じる. ¶we have it ***from*** Mr….'s own *lips* that … …ということを直接…から聞いた. 【類】***From*** the *lips* of an Ainu seventy years old, on the northern Kuriles, Torii has recorded the story of how pots were previously made there, chiefly by women. / I heard it ***from*** his *lips*. ‖ Such words fell ***from*** their *lips* (=were said by them). こんな言葉が彼らの口から出た. ¶the Christianity ***of*** the *lips* 口先だけのキリスト教. ¶He died with a prayer for England's welfare ***on*** his *lips*. 彼は口に英国の隆盛を祈って死んだ. ‖ move about with songs ***on*** their *lips* 歌を歌いながら歩く ‖ words which are daily ***on*** our *lips* 常用語 ‖ with a cold smile ***on*** her *lips* くちびるに冷笑を浮べて ‖ The name of neurasthenia is ***on*** everybody's *lips*. 神経衰弱ということをだれもかも言っている. 【類】Democracy is a word ***on*** everybody's *lips*. / The song was ***on*** (=***upon***) everybody's *lips*. / His name is much ***on*** men's *lips* today. ‖ His name arises first ***on*** every bookseller's *lips* as being a bibliomaniac. どの本屋も書狂として真先に彼の名をあげる. ¶I learned it ***through*** the *lips* of … 私は…の口からそれを聞いた. 【類】The secret got out ***through*** the *lips* of his servant. ¶These were words that rose ***to*** his *lips*. これが彼の口から出た言葉であった.

liquefy, *v.* 液化する.

P ***liquefy*** it ***by*** heat それを熱で液化する.

liquid, *n.* 液体.

V ***distill*** *liquids* 液体を蒸留する.

Q an ***oily*** *liquid* 油のような液体. ¶the ***resultant*** *liquid* そうしてできた液. ¶the vapors of ***various*** *liquids* 色々な液体から出る水蒸気.

Q² ***fermenticide*** *liquid* 発酵殺菌液.

P wash … ***by*** a *liquid* …を液体で洗う. ¶small particles ***in*** a *liquid* 液体中の微粒子. ¶a film ***on*** a *liquid* 液体面の薄皮.

liquidation, *n.* 清算.

Q ***complete*** *liquidation* (解散会社の)残務完了. ¶***developmental*** *liquidation* of a party 会の発展的解消.

P The Pall Mall Gazette declares that the whole system of constitutional politics in Europeanized Japan is now ***in*** [the stage of] *liquidation*. ペル・メル・ガゼット紙はいわく「欧化された日本における立憲政治の全制度は今や清算の段階にある」と.

P² the *liquidation* ***of*** property 財産の清算.

liquor, *n.* 液体; 飲料, 酒.

V We youngsters thought it was manly to be able to ***carry*** one's *liquor* well. われわれ若者は酒に酔わないのが男らしいと思っていた. ¶He couldn't ***hold*** his *liquor*. 酔っ払わずにいられなかった. ¶***sell*** intoxicating *liquors* without licence 無免許で酒類を販売する. ¶***use*** intoxicating *liquors* 酒類を用いる.

Q ***alcoholic*** *liquors* 酒精飲料. ¶***fermented*** *liquor* 発酵させた飲料. ¶***hard*** *liquor* アルコール分の強い飲物 ☞ *soft drink*. ¶an ***intoxicating*** *liquor* 飲むと酔う飲物(酒). ¶***neat*** *liquor* 生一本の酒. ¶***spirituous*** *liquors* 酒精飲料. ¶***strong*** *liquors* 強い酒類. ¶***vinous*** *liquor* ぶどう酒.

Q² Beer is a ***malt*** *liquor*. ビールは一種の麦芽の酒である.

P He is ***in*** *liquor*. 彼は酔っている. ¶He that keeps warm ***on*** *liquor* is like a man who pulls his house to pieces to feed the fireplace.—H. W. Beecher. 酒でからだを暖めている人はまるで自分の家をぶちこわして暖炉にくべているようなものだ.

list, *n.* (**1**) 表, 目録, 名簿.

V The *lists* were ***closed*** yesterday. 募集は昨日締切になった(債券など). ¶***compile*** a long *list* of … …の長い目録を作る. ¶the above *list* might be ***continued***, but sufficient examples have been given to show that … なお列記すれば数多いことであるが以上で十分…ということを示すことができる. ¶the *list* has been ***curtailed*** by … …のためその数が減った. ¶***draw up*** a *list* of one's debts 債務を表に作る. 【類】***draw up*** a *list* of the best hundred novels illustrating history / It would not now be possible to ***draw up*** a *list* of the ten greatest British novelists without placing on it the names of two or three women, at the least. ¶This table does not ***exhaust*** the *list*. この表は全部の品目を載せたものではない. ‖ ***exhaust*** the *list* of purgatives [便秘者などが]下剤の数々を試用しつくす. ¶It would not be difficult to ***extend*** the *list*. なおいくらでもあげられる. 【類】The *list* could be largely (indefinitely) ***extended***. / The *list* is continually being ***extended***. ¶The dangerous mountain ***has*** a long *list* of victims. この危険な山はこれまで多数の犠牲者を出している. ‖ The ship ***has*** a distinguished passenger *list*. その船には知名な船客が乗っている. ¶He ***heads*** a *list* of pro-Japanese men of prominence. 彼は知名な親日派の首位を占めている. ‖ Of all agreeable things to the thirsty man cold water ***heads*** the *list*. のどのかわいた者にとっては冷水が何よりだ. 【類】He ***heads*** the *list* of subscribers with $1,000,000 out of his own pocket. / ***headed*** the subscription *list* with the sum of … ¶***increase*** the civil *list* of a king 国王の王室費を増加する. ¶***issue*** a class *list* クラス名簿を出す. ¶***keep*** a *list* of the names of … …の名簿を保存する ‖ ***keep*** a word *list* [書き込んで]単語帳を作る. ¶He ***leads off*** the subscription *list*. 彼はその寄付帳のトップを切っている. ¶***make*** a *list* of … …の表を作る. 【類】***Make*** a *list* of the twenty-five largest cities in the world, and you will find that more than a third of them are in Asia. / ***make*** a full *list* (全表) of ... ¶***make out*** a *list* of persons 人名表を作成する. ¶***make up*** a *list* 表を作る. ¶The school has ***obtained*** a long *list* of successes at the various examinations. その学校は各種の試験において多数の合格者を出した. ¶***open*** a subscription list to secure the fund necessary for carrying out the work of the society その会の事業を行うに必要な資金を得るための資金募集をする. ¶***prepare*** a *list* of ... ...の一覧表を作成する. ¶You can ***prolong*** the *list* indefinitely. その他数うるにいとまがない. ¶***revise*** a *list* 表を改訂する. ¶***top*** the *list* of performers 出演者中の筆頭である. ¶***write out*** a *list* 表を作る.

v² The *list* of applications for the entrance examination will ***close*** on the 21st. 入学試験の申込は二十一日に締切る.

Q an officer on the ***active*** *list* 現役名簿にのっている将校. ¶an ***alphabetical*** *list* of advertisements ABC 順の広告一覧表. ¶Let it remain on your ***black*** *list*. それを君のブラック・リスト(注意人物名簿)にのせたままにしておけ. ¶a ***brief*** *list* 列記名の少ない表. ¶make a ***complete*** *list* of ... ...の完全な表を作る. ¶place goods on the ***contraband*** *list* 商品などを輸出入禁止表に入れる. ¶draw up a more ***copious*** *list* of ... ...の一層内容豊富な表を作る. ¶We hope that we may be placed on your ***exchange*** *list* for all printed matter issued by you. 貴所御発行の印刷物全部を当方のものと交換せられることを希望します. ¶an ***exhaustive*** *list* (遺漏のない)完全表. 【類】I have merely mentioned here a few names, without pretending to give an ***exhaustive*** *list*. ¶in the ***foregoing*** (=***above***) *list* 上記の表の中に. ¶a ***formidable*** *list* of ... ...の恐るべき多数の表. ¶The new tariff places ... on the ***free*** *list*. 新関税率は...を免税品目表の中に入れている. ¶it would take too long to give a ***full*** *list* of ... ...全部を表示することになると余り紙面を使い過ぎることになる. ¶a ***geographical*** *list* of members 会員の地方別表. ¶It is a ***goodly*** *list*, and one which anyone with a good memory can easily extend. それは相当数え上げたものであるが記憶のよいものならだれでもその上つけ加えることは容易なことである. ¶a ***graded*** *list* 番付. ¶one can make an ***interminable*** *list* of ... ...は枚挙にいとまがない. ¶the ***itemized*** *list* of contents 内容の項目別表. ¶a ***long*** (***small***) *list* 長(短か)い表 ‖ a ***long*** *list* of applicants 志願者の長い名簿. 【類】Baedeker's guidebook (ベデカーの案内記) on Holland, Belgium, and the Rhine published in 1839 was the precursor of the ***long*** *list* of similar works. ¶a ***partial*** (***complete***) *list* 一(全)部の表. ¶prominent on the ***passenger*** *list* are ... 船客の主なものは...である. ¶a ***pencilled*** *list* of one's requirements 鉛筆で書いた買物の控え. ¶His name appeared in the ***published*** *list* of bankrupts. 彼の名が破産公告名簿に出た. ¶he was placed on the ***retired*** *list* with the rank of ... 彼は...官位で退役となった. ¶a ***second-hand book-seller's*** *list* 古本屋名簿. ¶a ***selected*** *list* 選抜した表. ¶a ***shocking*** *list* of fatalities 死亡者の驚くべき数. ¶put him on the ***sick*** *list* for several days 数日間彼を(その名簿にのせて)病人として取扱う. ¶a ***tabulated*** *list* 一覧表. ¶a ***topographical*** *list* 地域別表. ¶a ***well-selected*** *list* 選択よろしきを得た表.

Q² an ***adoption*** *list* of text-books 採用教科書表. ¶firms on ***Admiralty*** and ***War Office*** *list* 海軍省及び陸軍省御用の商社. ¶a current ***best-seller*** *list* 今年度ベストセラー表. ¶a ***burgess*** *list* 市公民名簿(英国で救貧委員の調製する). ¶She has a great many fashionable people on her ***calling*** *list*. 彼女の訪問者の中には多数の上流人士がいる. ¶the ***casualty*** *list* includes ... 死傷者名簿に乗っているものは...である. ¶a ***check*** *list* 照合用の表(選挙人名簿など). ¶an ***election*** *list* 選挙人名簿. ¶the store has more than one thousand men and women on its ***employment*** *list*. 同店には一千人以上の男女使用人がいる. ¶The last man on the ***honors*** *list* at Cambridge is called "the Wooden Spoon" ケンブリッジ大学の優等生のびりを「木の・スプーン」という. ¶The closure of the ***enrolment*** *list* is near at hand. 締切の期日が迫っている[入学などの]. ¶be placed on a "***lynch*** *list*"「リンチ名簿」にのる(リンチされる) ‖ Please place my name upon your ***mailing*** *list*. 私の名前を発信簿に載せて下さい. ¶a ***membership*** *list* 会員名簿 ‖ an official ***membership*** *list* 職員名簿. ¶a "***must***" *list* ぜひ実現すべき項目. ¶a "***master these words***" *list* 単語覚え帳. ¶the ***passenger*** *list* included ... 乗客名簿には...の名がのっていた. 【類】The blue ribbon liner Rex sailed on June 23 with a record ***pasenger*** *list* (最高記録数の船客) of 1,942. ¶employees on the regular ***pay-roll*** *list* 正式社員. ¶be on a ***priority*** *list* 優先名簿にのっている(重点的資材配給を受ける). ¶a ***price*** *list* of the principal articles in stock 主な在庫品の物価一覧表. ¶those whose names do not appear on the ***prize*** *list* 受賞者名簿に名前の載らない人々. ¶be on the ***purge*** *list* パージになっている. ¶books on the required ***reading*** *lists* of schools 学校の必修図書目録にある書籍. ¶a ***refernce*** *list* 参考用一覧表. ¶Their names did not appear on ***registration*** *lists*. 彼らの名前は新入学籍簿になかった(不合格となった). ¶the ***registry*** *list* 登記名簿. ¶be placed on the ***reserve*** *list* 予備に編入される. ¶Put it on your ***shopping*** *list*. それを買物帳につけなさい. ¶Enter your name on our ***subscription*** *list*. この寄付帳に御記名下さい. 【類】a ***subscription*** *list* was opened for the purchase of ... ¶a ***tabulation*** *list* 一覧表. ¶Food, of course, continues to rank first on the ***urgent want*** *list*. もちろん食料が相変らず緊急物資表の第一位を占めている. ¶the ***visiting*** *list* 訪問客の名簿. ¶those who are on the ***waiting*** *list* [参加]希望者. 【類】a big ***waiting*** *list* of applicants for vacancies in a firm / Every university has a long ***waiting*** *list*. / There is always a full ***waiting*** *list* (満員).

P ***Among*** the *list* of contributors we notice many well-known names. 寄付者の中に多数の名士の名が見える. 【類】***Among*** the casualty *lists* (死傷者表) appear the names of two distinguished officers. ¶He was eighteenth ***in*** a *list* of about 100 contestants. 約百名の競技参加者中十八番目であった. ‖ We did not find the name ***in*** the *list*. 名簿の中にその名前が見当らなかった. 【類】the names ***in*** *List* I. / the names included ***in*** the *list* of ... / names enumerated ***in*** the *list* / A large number of the steamers ***in*** this *list* are available for time charter (臨時の用船契約). ‖ ... constitute important items ***in*** the *list* of sporting fish ...は釣の方では重要な魚になっている. ¶first ***on*** the *list* comes ... 表の筆頭に...が来る. 【類】appear second ***on*** the *list* / lowest ***on*** the *list* is ... / it stands fourth ***on*** (=in) the *list* of ... / The next important item ***on*** the calligrapher's *list* is ink. / We have his name ***on*** the *list*. / He came [out] first ***on*** the *list* of successful candidates. / He should be placed first ***on*** the *list*. ‖ Japan stands fairly high up ***on*** the *list* as regards ... 日本は...についてはかなり高い地位を占めている. 【類】let this reform be high ***on*** the *list* / pre-eminent ***on*** the *list* is ... / It comes seventh ***on*** the *list* of British railways in length. / He stands high ***on*** the *list* of new graduates. / His name is the newest ***on*** the *list*. ‖ the last book ***on*** our *list* 当方の目録の最後の本. ‖ be ***on*** the *Echo list* of contributors エコー誌の投稿者の一人になっている. ¶***To*** the *list* the name of ... has now been added. ...もその仲間にはいった.

P² The *list* ***for*** subscriptions is now closed. 申込みはもう締切りました. ¶a *list* ***of*** the killed and the wounded = a casualty list. ‖ a *list* ***of*** particulars 明細表 ‖ a large *list* ***of*** subscribers 寄付者総名簿. 【類】the world's *list* ***of*** famous astronomers (天文学者).

(**2**) 傾斜.

V The ship ***had*** a *list*. 船がかしいだ.

(**3**) *pl.* 仕合場, 競争場.

V ***enter*** the *lists* in a competition [入札などの]競争に加入する ‖ he ***entered*** the *lists* for ... 彼は...の弁護をした ‖ ***enter*** the *lists* with ... ...と論戦する. 【類】I do not ***enter*** the *lists* to defend ... / ***enter*** the *lists* against ... ¶He ***left*** the *lists* absolutely defeated by the foe. 彼は敵に惨敗して引さがった. ¶He ***quit*** (=left) the *lists* without scoring a single success. 彼は勝負のすむまで負け通しだった.

list, *v.* 名簿に記入する, 表に加える, 徴募する.

M as *listed* ***above*** (***below***) 上(下)記のように. 【類】in the examples *listed* ***below***.

P those *listed* ***among*** the "immortals" 名を万世にたれる者の中に数えられた人々. ¶He was *listed* ***as*** a private [soldier]. 彼は一兵士として徴募された. ¶It is *listed* ***at*** $3,000. それは三千ドルと定価表にのっている. ¶It is *listed* *in* the catalogue. それはカタログに記入してある. ¶this should be *listed with* ... これは...の部に記すべきものだ.

list, *v*. 傾く.

P *list to* port or starboard 左舷(さげん)または右舷に傾く.

listen, *v*. 傾聴する, 耳を傾ける.

M *listen **attentively*** 傾聴する. 【類】When the teacher explains the lessons, the scholars ought to *listen **attentively*** to what he says. ¶*listen **carefully*** 注意して聞く. ¶*listen **closely*** じっと聞入る. ¶*listen **cynically*** to the protestations of ... ...の抗議をあざけるように聞く. ¶He *listened* only ***distractedly*** to my counsels. 彼は私の忠告をほんの上の空で聞いていた. ¶*listen **eagerly*** 熱心に聞く. ¶*listen **impatiently*** もどかしく聞く. ¶*listen **intently*** 熱心に耳を傾ける. ¶***Just** listen.* ちょっと聞け. ¶*listen **patiently*** じっと聞く. 【類】*listen **patiently*** and ***attentively***.

M² *listen **in*** on the radio (to music) ラジオ(の音楽)を聞く.

P *listen **at*** key-holes かぎ穴に耳を寄せて聞く. ¶*listen **for*** a footstep 足音に耳を澄ます ‖ *listen **for*** an answer どう答えるかと耳を澄ます. 【類】The mother *listens **for*** her baby's cry. / He kept still, *listening **for*** any more noise to come. / *listen **for*** the watch to tick time. ¶*listen **to*** a lecture 講義を傾聴する ‖ *listen **to*** a talk from ... ...の話を聞く ‖ willingness patiently to *listen **to*** views which differ from his own 彼自身と説を異にする意見を謹聴すること ‖ *listen **to*** reason 理性に従う ‖ *listen **to*** the suggestions of wisdom 知者の言に耳を傾ける ‖ Pardon, mademoiselle, I wish to *listen **to*** your heart. お嬢さんちょっと聴診させて頂きます. ‖ *listen **to*** the beating of one's heart 心臓の鼓動を聞く ‖ He won't *listen **to*** me. 彼は私の言を聞こうとしない. ‖ *listen **to*** the breathing of a sleeper 寝息をうかがう. 【類】*listen **to*** the music of the band / this afternoon we are to *listen **to*** ... / *listen* to the teacher ‖ ¶*listen **with*** outstretched neck and distended eyes 首を延ばし目をみはって聞く ‖ *listen* very attentively ***with*** halfclosed eyes 半ば目を閉じてきわめて熱心に聞く ‖ *listen **with*** strained ears 耳をそばだてて聞く. 【類】*listen **with*** interest and respect ‖ *listen **with*** all one's mind 念を入れて聞く.

listener, *n*. 傾聴者; [ラジオの]聴取者.

V ***bore*** one's *listener* 聞き手を退屈させる. ¶He ***carried*** his *listeners* along with unbroken interest. 彼は聴者を間断ない興味で引き付けて行った.

Q He is a brilliant talker and an ***accomplished** listener*. 彼は話手としてもりっぱなものでありまた聞手としても堂に入ったものだ. ¶***appreciative** listeners* 目の高い聞き手. ¶his ***awe-struck** listeners* 彼の話にあっけに取られた聞手. ¶a ***good*** (***bad***) *listener* 聞きじょうず(べた). ¶an ***intelligent** listener* そう明な聞き手. ¶This class of conversation is peculiarly irritating to ***well-informed** listeners*. この種の談話は消息通の聞き手には特に心苦しいものだ.

Q² a ***radio** listener* ラジオ聴取者. ¶a ***student** listener* [教育放送のなど]聴学生.

P He has been admitted ***as** listener*. 彼は聴講生として許可された.

listening, *n*. 聞きとり.

Q² ***radio** listening* ラジオ聴取.

P words ***worth** listening* to 傾聴に価する言葉.

literacy, *n*. 読書作文力.

Q ***national** literacy* 国民の読書作文の力.

P² *literacy **for*** the mass 一般民衆の読書作文力.

literary, *a*. 文学的な.

M a ***purely** literary* work 純文学的作品. ¶***too** literary* [文体が]あまり堅過ぎる.

literati, *n*. 文士たち.

P² the *literati **of*** Great Britain 英国の文士たち.

literature, *n*. 文学; 文献; 著述, 印刷物.

V ***adopt*** (=***follow***) *literature* as a profession 職業として文筆業に携わる. ¶The subject can ***boast of*** an extensive *literature*. その問題を取扱った文献は多い. ¶***build up*** a characteristic *literature* of her own その国特有の文学を建設する. ¶*literature **cited*** 参考書目. ¶***develop*** a patriotic *literature* 愛国的な文学を発達させる. ¶***encompass*** most of the Freudian *literature* フロイドの(精神分析)文献は大ていそろっている. ¶Those are novels with (=by) which he ***enriched*** English *literature*. それらの小説は彼がよってもって英国文学を豊富にした作品である. 【類】He ***enriched*** English *literature* with valuable and permanent contributions (寄与). ¶***form*** a voluminous *literature* [事実などが]大冊な文献をなしている. ¶Japan ***has*** a *literature* dating from A.D. 712 in the Kojiki, or sacred book of Shintoism. 日本には古事記すなわち神道の聖典という紀元七百十二年から始まる文献がある. ¶***interpret*** the *literature* of the Japanese to the Western world 日本文学を泰西に紹介する. ¶The Chinese ***possess*** an extensive *literature*. 中国人は広範な文献を持っている. ‖ Japanese ***possesses*** a *literature* dating from A.D. 712. 日本語の文献は西暦七百十二年から始まる. ¶He has ***produced*** a *literature* treating different phases of the subject. 彼はその題目の諸方面を論じた著述を出版した. ‖ The advance of the motor car is ***producing*** an extensive *literature* of its own. 自動車の発達につれ自動車関係の文献がますます多くなりつつある. ¶I ***searched*** Japanese *literature* in vain for ... 私は...の日本の文献を求めたが徒労に終った. ¶Patterns and *literature **sent*** post free on request. [広告] 希望者には見本と印刷物とを無料で郵送します. ¶***study*** English *literature* 英文学を研究する. ¶The *literature **supplied*** there is not always of a very wholesome kind. そこに備付の新聞雑誌は余り健全なもののみとはいえない. ¶***summarize*** the early *literature* concerning the subject その問題に関する初期文献の内容を要約する. ¶***talk** literature* 文学を談じる.

V² A considerable *literature* already ***exists*** on the subject. その問題にはすでにかなり多くの文献が現存している. ¶the considerable *literature* which has ***grown up*** round the subject その問題をめぐって生じた相当多い文献. 【類】Quite a *literature* has ***grown up*** on this subject. ¶The *literature* of the subject has ***passed*** beyond enumeration. その題目の文献が数えきれないほど多い.

Q It produced an ***abundant** literature*. そのために沢山の文献を生んだ. ¶The library contains about 180,000 volumes of ***ancient*** and ***modern** literature* in various languages. その図書館は種々の国語で書いた約十八万冊の古代及び現代文学を収蔵している. ¶a hiatus in the ***biographical** literature* of the country 同国伝記文献の盲点. ¶The *literature* on ... is simply ***boundless***. ...に関する文献は全く無数だ. ¶***catch-penny** literature* [売れさえすればいいという]三文文学. ¶the spread of ***cheap** literature* 安価文学の普及. ¶***Chinese** literature* is one of the most voluminous in the world. 中国文学は世界で最もぼう大なものの一つだ. ¶circulate ***clandestine** literature* against the regime 反政府的な秘密文書を散布する. ¶the ancient ***Chinese** literature* on alchemy 錬金術に関する古代中国の文献. ¶***classical*** and ***modern** literature* 古典及び現代文学. ¶***clean** literature* 清浄な文学. ¶The language has a ***considerable** literature* of its own both in prose and verse. その国語には散文・韻文の文学が相当にある. ¶***contemplative** literature* 観照文学. ¶***contemporary** literature* on Afghanistan アフガニスタンに関する現代の著作. ¶The question has given rise to an extensive ***controversial** literature*. その問題に関して多数の論争的著述が生れた. ¶The English language possesses a ***copious** literature*, which goes as far back as the end of the eighth century. 英語には豊富な文学があり遠く八世紀の末にさかのぼる. ¶in the field of ***creative** literature* 創作の方面で ‖ masters of ***creative** literature* (=novelists) 創作の大家. ¶***descriptive** literature* 解説的文献. ¶The Greeks gave the world a great ***dramatic** literature*. ギリシア人は偉大な劇文学を世に伝えた. ¶the ***early** literature* of this subject この問題に関する初期の著述. ¶the ebb tide in ***English** literature* 英文学の退潮 ‖ Prof. Y, Lecturer in ***English** Literature* at Edinburgh University エジンバラ大学英文学講師 Y 教授. ¶good ***English prose** literature* 英国のすぐれた散文文学. ¶No people can be intellectually great without an intimate acquaintance with an ***ennobling** literature*. 何人も高尚な文学に親しまないでは知的に偉大であることはできない. ¶writers of ***ephemeral** literature* その著作の生命が短かい文学者. ¶***epistolary** literature* 書簡文学. ¶***equivocal*** (=***questionable***) *literature* and lascivious dramatic representations いかがわしい書物とわいせつな劇. ¶***erotic** literature* エロ文学. ¶an ***extensive** literature* on the subject in all tongues あらゆる国語で書かれたその問題に関する広範の文献. 【類】an ***extensive** literature* has accumultated round ... / Sanskrit is the language of an ***extensive*** and ***important*** *literature*. ¶the author of incomparably the ***finest*** *literature* of the year その年の群を抜いた傑作の作者. ¶There is a ***flourishing*** *literature*, translated and original, in Esperanto. エスペラント語には翻訳並に創作の文献が沢山存在している. ¶the poverty of the stock of ***foreign*** *literature* contained in the majority of free libraries 大半の無料図書館に不足している外国文学の蔵書. ¶***foul*** *literature* 反道徳文学. ¶"***freak***" *literature* 「気まぐれ」文学. ¶wide reading of ***good*** *literature* りっぱな文学の広い読書. ¶a writer of ***great*** *literature* 大文豪. 【類】The country has a ***great*** *literature* of its own. ¶the rapidly ***growing*** *literature* on ... ...に関し急速に増加している文献. ¶***hawker's*** *literature* 行商人のちらし. ¶in the field of ***imaginative*** *literature* 純(創作)文学の領域で. ¶***immoral*** *literature* わいせつ文学. ¶***inflammatory*** *literature* 扇情的文献(怪文書). ¶***inspirational*** *literature* 感情的文学. ¶there is a ***large*** *literature* relating to ... ...についておびただしい著書がある. ¶***light*** *literature* 軟文学. ¶There is very ***little*** *literature* in the field. その方面の文献はきわめて乏しい. ¶cases recorded in ***medical*** *literature* 医学の文献に記録された病例. 【類】New words are constantly being added to ***medical*** *literature*. ¶the ***mighty*** *literatures* of Greece and Rome ギリシャ及びローマの大文学. ¶create a ***national*** *literature* 国民文学を創作する. 【類】the ***national*** *literature* in relation to other literatures. ¶The Chinese language contains many thousand volumes of ***original*** *literature*. 中国語は数千冊の創作文学を持っている. ¶***periodical*** *literature* 定期出版物. ¶***physical*** (***chemical***) *literature* 物理(化学)に関する文献. ¶the place occupied by women in the ***poetic*** *literature* of the world 世界の詩文学において女性の占めている地位. 【類】study the ***poetical*** *literature* of the Japanese. ¶***polite*** (=***belletristic***) *literature* 純文学. ¶***popular*** *literature* 大衆文学. ¶***pornographic*** *literature* エロ本. ¶The ***present*** *literature* on the subject is enormous. その問題に関する現代の著述ははなはだ多い. ¶***printed*** *literature* 印刷物. ¶***profane*** *literature* 俗悪文学. ¶"***proletarian***" *literature* いわゆる「無産者」文学. ¶dreamers and writers of ***prophetic*** *literature* 夢想者と予言文学の作家. ¶***pure, uplifting*** *literatures* 純粋で向上性ある文学. 【類】***pure, true,*** and ***ennobling*** *literature*. ¶a concise summary of the ***recent*** *literature* on social research 社会研究に関する最近著作の簡潔な摘要. ¶English ***romantic*** *literature* 英国ロマン派文学. ¶The *literature* on the subject has been very ***scanty***. その問題に関する文献は従来すこぶる乏しかった. ¶A History of the Art of Printing is a substantial contribution to ***serious*** *literature*. その印刷史は堅い著作への一大貢献である. ¶***solid*** *literature* (=readings) かたい文学. ¶***standard*** *literature* 模範文学. ¶***tabooed*** *literature* 禁書. ¶***tutorial*** *literature* 配布教材. ¶a dealer in ***uncurrent*** *literature* 珍書書店. ¶***unsuitable*** *literature* 不適当な文献. ¶***unwholesome*** *literature* 不健全な文学. ¶the ***vast*** *literature* of the Revolution その革命に関するぼう大な文献. ¶There is a ***voluminous*** *literature* on the subject. その問題には多数の文献がある. ¶***weighty*** *literature* 重要な文学. ¶***yellow-covered*** *literature* 黄表紙文学.

Q² ***anti-Occupation*** *literature* 反占領軍的文書. ¶quotations from ***Buddhist*** *literature* 仏典からの引用句. ¶***campaign*** *literature* 選挙に関する文書. ¶"***dangerous thought***" *literature* 危険思想文書. ¶***English-world*** *literature* 英語世界の文学. ¶***garbage*** *literature*=literary garbage くだらない読物. ¶***government*** *literature* 政府刊行文献. ¶The book is a valuable and important contribution to ***Hegel*** *literature*. 同書はヘーゲル[哲学]文献に関する重要な貢献である. ¶***newspaper*** and ***magazine*** *literature* 新聞・雑誌(ジャーナリズム)の文学. ¶the advertisements or the ***pamphlet*** *literature* of charlatans and quacks あやし気な山師や医者たちの宣伝広告または小冊子文献. ¶publish ***party*** *literature* 党の文書を公刊する. ¶***folk*** *literature* 民俗文学. ¶***poultry*** *literature* 養鶏に関する文献. ¶***sales*** *literature* 販売のための文献. ¶pernicious "***tell-tale***" *literature* 有害な「暴露」小説. ¶***trade*** *literature* [カタログなど]商業上の文献.

P Essex ***in*** *literature* 文学上のエセックス ‖ ***in*** the *literature* of European countries 欧州諸国の文献には. 【類】***in*** the *literature* of the subject, we find numerous references to the fact that ... 【類】These expressions are seldom met with ***in literature***. / men eminent ***in literature***. ¶the type ***of*** *literature* stocked at the book-store その本屋が持っている本の種類 ‖ a critical review ***of*** the *literature* on the subject そのテーマに関する著書の評論 ‖ lesser lights ***of*** *literature* それ以下の文士連. ¶amenities ***of*** *literature* 文学の楽しみ.

P² The *literature* ***about*** faked antiques will fill any library. にせ骨とう品に関する著書は汗牛充棟もただならぬものがある. ‖ a most welcome addition to the *literature* ***about*** books 書物に関する文献に対する非常に喜ばしい追加. ¶a *literature* ***concerning*** ... ...に関する文献. ¶the splendour of British *literature* ***in*** the nineteenth century 十九世紀の英文学の豪華 ‖ a comprehensive survey of the *literature* ***in*** English 英語で書かれた(その題目の)文献の総覧. ¶enable the student to keep up with the *literature* ***of*** the subject 学生をしてその問題の著書に親しませる ‖ *literature* ***of*** digression 閑文学 ‖ the *literature* ***of*** entertainment 娯楽読物類 ‖ the *literature* ***of*** travel 旅行に関する文献(旅行記など) ‖ the *literature* ***of*** the day 現代の文学. 【類】There was a *literature* ***of*** botany as far back as the time of Plato and Aristotle. / The *literature* ***of*** the subjects touched upon in this book is, in most instances, voluminous. / I have made, I suppose, the largest private collection in the world of the *literature* ***of*** heredity, genetics, and eugenics (遺伝・実験遺伝学及び優生学の文献). ¶the *literature* ***on*** the subject その問題に関する著書 ‖ Japanese *literature* ***on*** philately is practically nil. 切手収集に関する日本の文献は事実上絶無だ. 【類】the *literature* ***on*** Japan in English / *literature* ***on*** language methodology (言語方法論). ¶in the *literature* ***relating*** (=***pertaining***) ***to*** ... ...についての著書中に. ¶The *literature* ***upon*** this subject is very large. この問題に関する文献はきわめて多数だ. ‖ the growth of *literature* ***upon*** ... ...に根を張った文学の成長.

O It is not, of course, *literature*; it does not pretend to be literature. それはもちろん文学でもなくまた文学と見せようともしてない.

litigant, *n.* 訴訟人.

P² the *litigants* ***in*** a lawsuit 訴訟人.

litigation, *n.* 訴訟.

V ***avoid*** *litigation* 裁判ざたを避ける.

Q a court of ***administrative*** *litigation* 行政裁判所.

Q² the subject of ***court*** *litigation* 起訴題目.

P² *litigation* ***over*** damages 損害賠償の訴え. ¶he was in *litigation* ***with*** ... ***over*** the partnership returns from ... 彼は...からの組合の利益について...と訴訟中だった.

litter, *n.* [獣などの]一腹の仔; 乱雑.

V A female rat may ***have*** five or six *litters* yearly, and an average of nine per litter. ねずみは年々五六回子を産み一回の平均は九匹である.

Q dogs of the ***same*** *litter* 一腹の犬.

P ***in*** a [state of] *litter* とり散らして. 乱雑になって.

litter, *v.* まき散らす, 取乱す.

P a fire-place *littered* ***with*** cigarette ends 巻タバコの吸いがらで散らかった暖炉. 【類】a room *littered* ***with*** books / a desk *littered* ***with*** the latest official orders and notifications / The table was *littered* ***with*** remains of eatables (食物).

little, *n.* 少し, 暫時.

V She ***knows*** *little* of the world. 彼女は世間知らずだ. ¶***make*** *little* of (=belittle) worldly honor 浮世の名利をくさす. 【類】***make*** *little* of the value of education.

P ***after*** a *little* 暫くの後. ¶***by*** *little* and little=little by little 次第次第に ‖ gain a victory ***by*** a *little* 少差で勝つ ‖ gain in health little ***by*** *little* 少しずつ丈夫になる. 【類】The water oozes out little ***by*** *little*. ¶***for*** a *little* [while] 暫時. 【類】Can you spare it ***for*** a *little*? / Let me have the book (貸して下さい) if you can spare it ***for*** a *little*. ¶The paragraph is really an essay ***in*** *little*; it contains almost every element contained in an essay in large. その一節は実は一個の小論文をなしており長い論文のもつあらゆる要素を備えている. ‖ the world's knowledge ***in*** *little* 世界知識の縮図. 【類】Leo Tolstoy: an interpretation done ***in*** *little*. / So, ***in*** *little*, we see the birth of a new capitalism. / observe ***in little*** all the features familiar on a grander scale.

little, *a.* 少しの, 小さい.

M ***ridiculously little*** ばかばかしく少い. ¶***vastly little*** 物すごくちょっぴり. ¶***very little*** ほんのわずか.

littleness, *n.* 僅少.

P^2 It realizes to us, in a way which nothing else can, the *littleness* ***of*** human intelligence. それはわれわれに他のものをもってしてはなし得ない方法で人知の貧弱さを悟らせる.

littoral, *n.* 沿岸地方.

Q the ***Caspian littoral*** 裏海沿岸地方.

live, *v.* 住む, 生きる, 暮す.

M *live* ***abroad*** 外国に住む. ¶*live* ***again*** 生き返る. ¶*live* ***alone*** 独りで暮す. ¶He *lives* ***apart*** from his wife. 彼は妻と別居している. ¶He *lives* too long ***away*** from home. 彼はあまり永く本国を離れている. ¶can ***barely*** *live* 辛うじて生活ができる. ¶*live* ***chastely*** 禁欲生活をする. ¶*live* ***close*** (=***near*** *or* ***hard***) ***by*** 近所に住む. ¶foreigners who *live* ***closely*** with ... ...と親密にしている外人. ¶They can not *live* ***comfortably*** together. 彼らは愉快に同居ができない. ‖ A thrifty family can *live* quite ***comfortably*** on that sum at least a year. 倹約な家庭ならそれだけの金で少くも一年は何不足なく暮せる. ¶*live* ***comfortably*** (=in comfort) 楽に暮す. ¶*live* ***contentedly*** in one's conditon 自分の地位に満足して暮す. ¶*live* ***continently*** 自制して暮す. ¶He is paid barely enough to *live* ***decently***. 彼はどうにか相当に暮してゆけるだけの給料をもらっている. ¶Chinese can *live* ***down*** Japanese. 中国人は[生活程度が低いので]日本人を駆逐することができる. ¶I cannot afford to *live* ***expensively***. 私はぜいたくな暮しはできない. ¶*live* ***far off*** 遠方に住む. ¶*live* ***fashionably*** 当世向に暮す. ¶*live* ***fast*** 放とうする. ¶*live* ***forever*** 永久に残る. ¶*live* more ***frugally*** もっと質素に暮す. ¶He ***lived happily*** with her. 彼は彼女と仕合わせに暮した. ‖ They ***lived happily*** ever after (=afterwards). めでたしめでたし(おとぎ話の結びの言葉. ¶*live* ***happy*** 幸福に暮す. ¶*live* ***high*** on one's large income 多大の収入でぜいたくに暮す. ¶*live* ***holily*** 清浄に暮す. ¶*live* ***honestly*** 正直に暮す. ¶Children *live* ***intensely*** in the present. 子供たちは強く現在に生きる. ¶*live* ***long*** after one's death [名声など] 死後長く残る. ¶*live* ***luxuriously*** ぜいたくに暮す. ¶***nobly live*** and bravely die りっぱに生き雄々しく死ぬ. ¶Who *lives* ***nearest*** to the school? だれが学校に近い所にいるか. ¶He *lives* ***next-door*** to me. 彼は私の隣りに住んでいる. ¶It is feared that the patient will not *live* ***out*** the summer. 病人は夏中もちそうもない. ‖ *live* ***out*** West《米》西部に住む ‖ She *lives* ***out*** as a cook. 彼女は通いコックだ. ¶*live* ***perilously*** near to starvation ほとんど餓死せんばかりのきわどい暮しをする. ¶*lived* ***pleasantly*** to the age of ninety-two 九十二歳まで幸福に生きた. ¶*live* ***precariously*** 食うや食わずの暮しをする. ¶*live* ***simply*** 簡易生活をする. ¶《英》*live* ***single***=《米》keep bach 独身生活をする. ¶*live* ***temperately*** 控目に暮す. ¶*live* ***together*** harmoniously むつまじく同居する. 【類】*live* ***together*** peacefully in communities. ¶*live* ***wastefully*** むだの多い暮しをする. ¶We manage to *live* ***well*** and ***comfortably*** on $600 a year. われわれは年六百ドルで結構不自由なく暮している. ¶*live* ***worthily*** りっぱに暮す.

M^2 *live* ***down*** South《米》南部に住む ‖ *live* ***down*** the fault (sin) of the past 善行によって旧悪を償う ‖ *live* ***down*** the past 過去を忘れるような生活をする ‖ *live* ***down*** their reputation as a party 公党としての名誉を忘れるようになる ‖ *live* ***down*** a scandal (prejudice, false step) 汚職(など)をあとの行為で償う ‖ He *lives* ***down*** in Hampshire. ハンプシャに住んでいる. ¶*live* ***in*** 住み込む(女中や弟子など). 【類】*live* ***in*** as a cook (maid, houseboy). ¶He *lives* ***on*** in spite of the accident. 彼はその事故で命を失うこともなく生きている. ¶*live* ***up*** East《米》東部に住んでいる. 【類】He *lives* ***up*** north. ‖ *live* ***up*** to one's father's reputation 父の名を恥ずかしめないようにする ‖ *live* ***up*** to one's promises 約束を守る. 【類】*live* ***up*** to one's name / *live* ***up*** to our agreement / Students are expected to *live* ***up*** to certain standards of behavior. / The work does not *live* ***up*** to our expectations. / the country's failure to *live* ***up*** to the treaty / *live* ***up*** to one's ideal / *live* ***up*** to one's principle (主義) /*live* ***up*** to international commitments (国際的義務) / *live* ***up*** to the laws / *live* ***up*** to the motto (標語) / *live* ***up*** to its traditions (伝統) / *live* ***up*** to the conditions imposed (課せられた条件通り) / *live* ***up*** to its past reputation (過去の名声を傷つけないように) / make effort to *live* ***up*** to a high praise.

P *live* ***above*** oneself 分不相応の生活をする ‖ *live* ***above*** one's position (=means) 身分(資産)不相応の暮しをする. ¶*live* ***across*** the road (river) 道路(川)の向う側に住む. ¶*live* ***after*** foreign models 外国風な生活をする ‖ *live* ***after*** another's death 人に先に死なれる ‖ The good which he did will *live* ***after*** him. 彼がなした善事は彼の死後に残るだろう. ‖ *live* ***after*** the world's opinion 世界の世論に従って行動する. ¶*live* ***among*** strangers 見知らぬ人に交って住む. ¶Do you think you could *live* ***as*** a gentleman on £2 a week? 一週二ポンドで紳士として暮してゆけると思いますか. ¶He *lives* ***at*** No. 20 in this street. 彼はこの街の二十番地に住んでいる. ‖ *live* (=stay) ***at*** a hotel ホテル住居をする ‖ *live* ***at*** rest 静かな生活をする. 【類】*live* ***at*** one's uncle's / He is now *living* ***at*** home. / *live* ***at*** a small town. ¶*live* ***beyond*** one's income (salary, means) 収入(など)以上に暮す ‖ *live* ***beyond*** seventy 七十過ぎまで生きる. ¶He *lives* ***by*** his novels. 彼は自分の小説で食っている. ‖ *live* exclusively ***by*** the pen ペンだけで食って行く ‖ *live* ***by*** toil (=muscular labor) 労働して暮す ‖ *live* ***by*** the sweat of one's brow 額に汗して暮す ‖ What does he *live* ***by***, I wonder? あの人は何をして食ってるんだろう. 【類】*live* ***by*** literature (文筆) / *live* ***by*** writing (one's pen) / *live* ***by*** swindling industry (いかさま事業). ¶*live* ***for*** higher aspirations より高い望みを抱いて暮す ‖ They *live* ***for*** no purpose. 彼らは目的なしに生きている. ‖ have something to *live* ***for*** 生きて行く目標がある. 【類】I have nothing worth *living* ***for***. / *live* ***for*** others / They are amenities (楽しみ) which make life worth *living* ***for***. ¶*live* ***from*** hand ***to*** mouth その日暮しをする ‖ *live* ***from*** day ***to*** day その日暮しをする. ¶*live* ***in*** the country in summer 夏はいなかに住む ‖ I *lived* ***in*** lodgings before I got married. 私は結婚前は下宿住居だった. ‖ *live* ***in*** close friendship with ... ...と親密に暮す ‖ Their names will echo round the world, and *live* ***in*** history. 彼らの名は世界中に鳴り響いて歴史に残るだろう. ‖ The speech will *live* ***in*** history because of its simplicity. その演説は純真のために後世に伝わるであろう. 【類】*live* ***in*** rear tenements (裏長屋) / *live* ***in*** affluence (=opulence) (裕福に) / *live* ***in*** comfort and peace (安楽に) / *live* ***in*** luxury (poverty) / *live* ***in*** great plenty (austerity) / *live* ***in*** idleness / *live* ***in*** privation (窮乏) / *live* ***in*** a state of poverty / *live* ***in*** obscurity / *live* ***in*** retirement (=seclusion) / His name will *live* for ever ***in*** the history of Japan (English literature). ‖ *live* ***in*** the memory of ... / It still *lives* ***in*** my memory. ‖ Children proverbially *live* ***in*** the present. 子供は現在に生きるものとなっている. ‖ *live* ***in*** the future (past) 将来(過去)に生きる ‖ the only place worth *living* ***in*** 住んでよい唯一の場所 ‖ *live* ***in*** a small way つましく暮す ‖ *live* ***in*** her 彼女に夢中になる ‖ the complicated age ***in*** which we are *living* われわれの住んでいるこの複雑な時代 ‖ There are very few people who do not *live* ***in*** quotation-marks most of their lives. 人生の大半を人のまねをせずに(独創力を発揮して)暮す人はきわめて少ない. ¶*live* ***in*** peace ***with*** all one's neighbors 隣人と平和に暮す. ¶*live* ***like*** a brute 畜生のような暮しをする. ¶He *lives* ***near*** Odawara. 小田原在に住んでいる. ¶*live* ***on*** land (***in*** the water) 陸上(水中)に生息している ‖ *live* ***on*** rice (fish, vegetable, fruit) 米(など)を常食とする ‖ The sight of food had made him sick, and he had *lived* ***on*** tea and soup. 食物を見ると胸が悪くなるので茶とスープを用いていた. ‖ the habit of *living* ***on*** plain food 粗食の習慣 ‖ *live* ***on*** one's pension (annuity, retiring allowance) 年金(など)で暮す ‖ How to *live* ***on*** 24 hours a day [書名] 一日二十四時間の生活法. 【類】have to *live* ***on*** a small income / How he manages to *live* ***on*** that salary! / *live* ***on*** the proceeds of one's own writings / *live* ***on*** the earnings of a girl / people who *live* ***on*** investments / *live* cheerfully ***on*** a legacy of fifty thousand which his uncle left him / schools which *live* ***on*** the fees of their students / *live* ***on*** three pence a day ‖ It is said that two can *live* ***on*** less than one. 二人(夫婦)になると一人の時より経済的だといわれてい

る ‖ *live **on*** gifts 恩給(など)もらって生活する. 【類】*live **on*** alms (施物), which they begged from door to door / *live **on*** charity / He is at the age when one might be doing very well for himself, and not *living* like that ***on*** his parents ‖ Nara *lives **on*** its vistors. 奈良は遊覧客で立って行く. ‖ *live **on*** credit 借金して暮す. 【類】*live **on*** one's savings ‖ Work is the tenure ***on*** which we *live*. 仕事(労働)はわれわれの食わんがための無形の財産である. ‖ *live **on*** the cross (square) 《俗》不正行為をして(しないで)暮す ‖ *live **on*** a friend 友人のやっかいになっている ‖ It is a historic town *living **on*** the memories of its past. それは過去の思い出に生きる歴史的な市である. ‖ *live* forever ***on*** the memories of man 永久に人から記憶される ‖ *live **on*** the run 活動的生活をする ‖ *live **on*** a street 通りに住んでいる. 【類】I was *living **on*** the back streets. / *live **on*** the other side of a street (river). ¶He *lived **out of*** the world. 彼は世間から離れて暮していた. ¶In this autobiography the patient, brilliant, and triumphant inventor *lives **over*** his eighty-five years again. この自叙伝においてこの辛抱強くて才気があって意気揚々とした発明家の八十五年の生活が細大漏らさず書かれている. ‖ *live **over*** the street 道の向い側に住む ‖ I *live **over*** the school, at the tailor's. 私は学校の向うの洋服屋に同居している. ¶*live **through*** financial difficulties 財政上の困難を切抜ける ‖ It was said that he had small chance to *live **through*** the night. 彼の命は夜明までもちそうもないといわれた. ‖ Do you think I'll *live **through*** it, Doctor? 生命に別条はありませんか, 先生. ¶*live **to*** a hundred 百まで生きる ‖ *live **to*** some purpose 意義ある生活をする. 【類】*live **to*** a good old age / She *lived **to*** the age of eighty-eight, able to care for herself almost till the day she died. / *lived **to*** a great (good old, ripe old) age / *live **to*** the great age of eighty-two years / *live **to*** so green (かくしゃくたる) and so buoyant (陽気な) an old old age. ¶*live **under*** the same roof 同居する ‖ *live **under*** the sheltering wing of Great Britain 英国の保護のもとに生存する ‖ The American flag gives freedom and justice to all *living **under*** it. 米国の国旗はその下に生活するすべての人に自由と正義とを与える. ‖ he was *living **under*** the assumed name of ... 彼は…と名を変えていた ‖ He *lives **under*** petticoat government. 彼の家は奥さん天下だ. ‖ She *lives **under*** her paternal roof. 彼女は父(両親)のひざ下にある(生娘だ). ‖ He *lives **under*** the cat's foot, so to speak. 彼はいわば人の手先に使われている. ‖ We are discovering more and more that the world is an inter-dependent world and that no one country can *live **unto*** (=to) itself. われらは世界は相互依存の世界であっていかなる国もその国だけではやってゆけないことをますます悟りつつあるのである. ¶*live **up to*** a rule 規則通りに行動する ‖ try to *live **up to*** the lofty standard (ideal) we set before us われわれが定めた高いレベル(など)に到達しようと努める. 【類】He *lived **up to*** the highest standard of membership. ‖ *live **up to*** one's duty (obligations, motto) / try to *live **up to*** the heroes / *live **up to*** one's income. ¶*live **upon*** the coarsest fare ごく粗食する ‖ *live **upon*** women 女を食い物にする ‖ *live **upon*** other people's money 人から金をもらって暮す ‖ *live **upon*** its past reputation その過去の名声で生きる ‖ He *lived **upon*** a great wheat farm in Kansas. 彼はカンサス州の大小麦畑を経営していた. ¶A good many students *live **with*** their families. 学生は家族と一緒に住んでいる者が相当ある. 【類】Grandmother *lives **with*** the family. ‖ *live* "doubled up" ***with*** friends or relatives 友人または親類と同居する. ¶*live **within*** one's salary (income, means) 俸給(など)の限度内で暮す ‖ a people *living **within*** themselves 鎖国の国民.

O Few men *live* to be eighty. 八十まで生きる者はまれだ. ¶we may *live* to know that ... われわれの時代に…が分かる日が来る. ¶He did not *live* to finish the work 彼はその仕事を仕上げるまで生きていなかった. 【類】He did not *live* to see its success.

livelihood, *n.* 生計, 暮し, 糊(こ)口の道.

V It ***affords*** a *livelihood* to a great number of people. 多数の人がそれによって生計を立てている. ¶***draw*** one's *livelihood* from ... …によって生計を立てる. ¶***earn*** a *livelihood* by ... …によって暮してゆく ‖ the difficulty of ***earning*** a *livelihood* 生活難 ‖ persons unable to ***earn*** a *livelihood* 生計を立て得ない人々. 【類】It became necessary for her to ***earn*** her own *livelihood*. / turn to teaching as a means of ***earning*** a *livelihood*. ¶***eke out*** a slender *livelihood* 細い煙を立てる. ¶***eliminate*** *livelihood* 生活の道を奪う. ¶in order to ***gain*** a *livelihood* 食わんがため(生活をしのぐために). ¶***get*** an artistic (a literary) *livelihood* 絵(文章)で飯を食う. ¶***make*** a *livelihood* by ... …によって生計を立てる. ¶***obtain*** a *livelihood* 生計を立てる. ¶***pick up*** a scanty *livelihood* わずかに暮しを立てる. ¶It ***promises*** a *livelihood* to countless families. 無数の家族がそれによって生計を立てられる見込がある. ¶***receive*** one's *livelihood* from parents 両親から生計費を受ける. ¶***seek*** a *livelihood* in ... …に生活の道を求める. 【類】***seek*** a *livelihood* by [means of] ... ¶***take away*** the *livelihood* of millions 幾百万人の生計を奪う. ¶***wring*** a *livelihood*, copper by copper, in the fair way of trade 小銭をかせいで地道にどうやら生活を立てる.

V² Their *livelihood* ***depends*** upon the labor of their hands. 彼らは手仕事で生活している.

Q gain a ***bare*** *livelihood* 漸く生計を立てる. ¶a ***decent*** *livelihood* 相当な暮し. ¶an ***easy*** *livelihood* 楽な生計. ¶those who have a ***fixed*** *livelihood* 定収入あるもの. ¶earn a very ***good*** *livelihood* きわめてゆったりした生計を立てる. 【類】It will give a ***good*** *livelihood*. ¶earn a ***handsome*** *livelihood* 相当な生活をする. ¶earn an ***honest*** *livelihood* 正しい暮しを立てる. ¶a means to an ***honest***, if not ***honorable***, *livelihood* りっぱとまでは行かなくともとに角正しい生活の道. ¶We do not recognize prostitution as a ***legitimate*** *livelihood*. われわれは売春を正業とは考えない. ¶make a ***moderate*** *livelihood* 中庸の生活をする. ¶poor people earning a ***precarious*** *livelihood* 不安な生活をする貧民. 【類】Their *livelihood* is so often ***precarious***. ¶earn a ***scanty*** *livelihood* 細々と煙を立てる. ¶earn ***small*** and ***precarious*** *livelihood* 細々と危うげな暮しを立てる.

P ***for*** a *livelihood* 生活のために. ¶lose the means ***of*** *livelihood* 生活の道を失う.

liveliness, *n.* 活発.

V This ***gave*** temporary *liveliness* to the trade. このために商況が一時活気を帯びてきた.

Q This gave ***temporary*** *liveliness* to the trade. これで貿易も一時活気を呈するに至った.

P when the meeting (festival) was ***at*** its *liveliness* 会(など)のたけなわなとき.

lively, *a.* 活気ある.

M The market is ***quite*** *lively* (very dull) 市場はすこぶる活気がある(ない).

M² move *lively* ***about*** 活発に動く.

liven, *v.* 陽気にする.

M² *liven* ***up*** a dull day 退屈な一日を陽気にする. 【類】Things are beginning to *liven up* (景気よく).

liver, *n.* 生活者.

Q a ***fast*** *liver* 放とう者. ¶a ***good*** *liver* 豊かな生活者. ¶the ***grave*** *liver* of a simple life 単調な生活を送るまじめな人. ¶a ***hearty*** *liver* 大食家. ¶a ***high*** *liver* ぜいたくな生活者.

liver, *v.* 肝臓.

Q a person of ***white*** *liver*=a coward おく病者.

livery, *n.* そろいの衣服; 飼料を出して馬を預けること.

V a butler ***wearing*** his full *livery* 仕着せで着飾った給仕長.

P horses kept ***at*** *livery* 料金を取って預っている馬. ¶servants ***in*** *livery* 仕着せを着た召使. ¶servants ***out of*** *livery* 自服の召使.

living, *n.* 暮し, 生計, 生活.

V ***afford*** a substantial *living* to those who are engaged in it それに従事している人々に相当な生活を与える. ¶She ***earns*** her own *living*. 彼女は自活している. 【類】***earn*** one's own *living* as an artist / I was faced with the problem of ***earning*** my *living*. / ***earn*** a *living* chiefly by writing (sewing) / He ***earns*** a *living* with his violin. / ***get*** a *living* with the pen (文筆). ¶He manages to ***eke out*** a *living*. 彼はどうにか食っている. 【類】***eke out*** a *living* by this way / ***eke out*** a *living* on a tiny (わずかな) income. ¶***find*** a decent *living* かなりな暮しをする ‖ ***find*** a *living* in literature 文筆で生計を立てる. ¶***gain*** a *living* 暮しを立てる. ¶***get*** one's *living* honestly 正しい道を踏んで生計を立てる ‖ work hard [in order] to ***get*** a *living* 食って行くために懸命に働く. ¶He ***has*** a good *living*. 彼は相当の暮しを

している. ¶try to ***make*** her own *living* 独立しようと努める. 【類】***make*** his *living* as a teacher of French / ***make*** a *living* by the sweat of one's brain instead of the sweat of one's brow / ***make*** a *living* by taking boarders (同居人をおいて) / know how to ***make*** a *living* (世渡り) / use one's pen to ***make*** a *living* ‖ ***make*** a *living* a burden to ... ...にとって生活を重荷にさせる. ¶as a means of ***obtaining*** a *living* 生活の手段として. 【類】Novel-writing is a very precarious mode of ***obtaining*** a *living*. ¶***pick up*** a *living* 暮しを立てる. ¶***scrape*** a *living* かつかつに暮す. ¶***seek*** a *living* for oneself 自活の道を求める. ¶***win*** a *living* on four acres 四エーカの土地で生計を立てる.

Q ***abstemious*** or even ***frugal living*** 節制のある質素なくらいの生活. ¶only a ***bare living*** 辛うじて食ってゆけるだけの生活. 【類】earn a ***bare living***. ¶goods necessary to ***civilized living*** 文化生活の必要品. ¶She is now earning ***comfortable living***. 彼女は今相当に暮している. 【類】make a ***comfortable living*** out of ... / lack nothing for ***comfortable living*** (何不自由ない). ¶To prepare us for ***complete living*** is the function which education has to discharge.—Herbert Spencer. われわれをして完全な生活の準備をなさせることが教育の果さねばならない職務である. ¶***correct*** (=***right***) ***living*** 正しい生活. ¶improve one's ***daily living*** その日常生活を改善する. ¶for what they consider ***decent living*** 彼らの考える人間らしい生活をするために. ¶make a very ***decent living*** for a poor widow 貧しい未亡人としてはりっぱな暮しをする. ¶make a ***fair living*** かなりな暮しをする. ¶can make a ***good living*** よい金がとれる ‖ earn a ***good living*** for their families by ... 家族が楽に暮せるだけの生計費を...によって得る ‖ ***Good living*** and little exercise inclined him to obesity. 彼は美食と運動不足のために肥満した. ¶can get a ***handsome living*** by writing fiction りっぱに作家として食って行ける. ¶***happy*** and ***useful living*** 世間で有益な生活. ¶a country characterized by ***high living*** and enormous material prosperity 高い生活程度と巨大な物資によって特色づけられた国. ¶earn an ***honest living*** まじめな生活をする. ¶get a ***hungry living*** as clerk in the church 教会書記として貧しい暮しを立てる. ¶***lavish living*** ぜいたくな暮し. ¶earn ***meagre living*** 貧弱な生計を立てる. ¶earn a ***modest living*** as ... ...として質素な暮しを立てる. ¶***modern living*** 文化生活. ¶sound thinking and ***noble living*** 健全な思索と高尚な生活. ¶***plain living*** and high thinking 質素な暮しと高い思索. ¶the little rules of pleasant and ***agreeable living*** 楽しく気持ちよい生活のちょっとした法則. ¶earn a ***poor living*** as a day laborer 日やといとして貧乏暮しをする. ¶earn a ***precarious living*** おぼつかない生計を立てる. ¶***rational living*** 合理的生活. ¶earn a ***scant[y] living*** 細々と暮す. ¶***simplified living*** 簡易生活. ¶***strenuous living*** 奮闘的生活. ¶***thrifty living*** 節約生活. ¶Today, in ***urban living***, children seldom see their fathers around except on weekends. 今日の都会生活では週末以外には子供が父親と一緒にいることは滅多にない. ¶***wise living*** 賢明な生活. ¶Life is ***worth living***. 世の中はおもしろい. ¶***wrong living*** 正しくない生活.

Q² those who earn less than a ***subsistence living*** 食うに足りない生活費を得る人々. ¶continue a ***hand-to-mouth living*** その日暮しを続ける. ¶***everyday living*** 日々の生活.

P What does he do ***for*** a *living?* 彼の生業は何ですか. ‖ A shoemaker makes shoes ***for*** his *living*. くつ屋は生活のためにくつを造る. ‖ They depend on rice ***for*** *living*. 彼らは米を常食としている. ¶the style (=mode) ***of*** *living* 生活様式 ‖ the art ***of*** *living* 処生法 ‖ standards ***of*** *living* 生活水準. ¶***through*** high *living* ぜいたくな生活のために.

P² earn one's *living* ***at*** some humble but honest occupation つまらなくとも正しい仕事で生計を立てる. 【類】They are earning their *living* ***at*** some type of engineering (一種の技術). ¶earn one's own *living* ***by*** the use of one's bones and muscles 重労働で自活する. 【類】make a *living* ***by*** frippery (外見のよい安物衣類) / make a *living* ***from*** literary work (文筆). ¶He was virtually driven to this, because he could not earn a *living* ***in*** any legitimate way. 彼は正当な方法で生計を立てられなかったために結局こんな破目になった. ‖ Staying at the hotel is like *living* ***in*** the pages of "Who's Who." その旅館に泊ることは紳士録の中で暮すのと同じだ(色々な人と知り合いになる).

¶make a *living* ***out of*** the sale of ... ...の販売で暮しを立てる. 【類】make a *living* ***out of*** curious jobs (妙な仕事).

load, *n*. 荷, 重荷, 一担ぎ.

V the aeroplane is capable of ***carrying*** a *load* of ... その飛行機の積載量は...だ. ¶A truck built to ***haul*** the average *load* speedily is the most profitable trackless transportation unit. 通常の荷を迅速に運搬するように造られたトラックは最も有利な無軌道輸送機関だ. ¶***remove*** the *load* of misinterpretation which is laid upon ... ...に関するはなはだしい誤解を除く. ¶***shoot*** its *load* (車などが)荷をすべり落す. ¶***take*** a *load* off one's mind 心の重荷をおろす. ¶***transport*** heavy *loads* over long distances 長距離間に重荷を運ぶ.

Q girders to stand a ***distributed*** (***concentrated***) ***load*** of ... tons 平均した(重点的な) ... トンの重さに堪えるガード(橋けた). ¶lift ***heavy loads*** 重荷を持上げる ‖ with a ***heavy load*** on one's shoulders 重荷(責任)を負って. ¶a ***huge load*** 巨大な荷.

Q² All trains left with ***capacity loads***. 列車はすべて積載量一杯の荷を積んで出発した. ¶transfer a ***car load*** from ... to ... 車一台の荷を...から...に転送する. ¶her ***deck load*** 同船の甲板積. ¶with only ***one-third loads*** 三分の一しかない船の積載量で. ¶a big ***shoulder load*** かつぐには骨の折れる荷. ¶the student's ***study load*** 学生の学習負担. ¶reduce ***tax loads*** 課税の負担を軽減する. ¶a ***truck load*** of vegetables トラック一台分の野菜. ¶a ***two-horse load*** 二駄分の荷. ¶a whole ***wagon load*** 貨車の全積載量.

P The porter carries as much as ... pounds ***at*** one *load*. その運搬夫は一かつぎで...ポンドを持運ぶ. ‖ ***at*** full *load* 満載で. ¶groan ***under*** a heavy *load* of taxation 重税にうめく.

P² *Loads* ***upon*** loads of furniture arrived in numberless carts. 家具の荷が無数の車に積まれて続々到着した.

load, *v*. 荷を積む; 装填する.

M the water carrier *loaded* ***down*** with the weight of his earthen-vessels その土器の重みで腰の曲った水運搬人. ¶*load* ***up*** 積荷する. 【類】Have you finished *loading* ***up*** yet?

P the steamer is *loading* ***for*** ... その汽船は...行の荷を積込んでいる. ¶The revolver was *loaded* ***in*** five chambers. その五連発のピストルは充弾してあった. ¶be *loaded* ***onto*** a wagon 貨車に積込まれる. ¶He has been *loaded* ***to*** the muzzle with new knowledge. 彼は新知識をぎっしり詰込まれた. ‖ greyhound bus *loaded* ***to*** its full capacity of thirty-three passengers 三十三人の乗客で満員の快速バス. ¶*loaded* ***upon*** a waggon (cart) 荷馬車(など)に積載された. ¶boats *loaded* ***with*** all sorts of produce あらゆる種類の産物を積載した船 ‖ *load* her ***with*** presents 彼女を贈物攻めにする ‖ a vessel *loaded* ***with*** cargo (timber, coal) 荷物(など)を積んだ船 / be *loaded* ***with*** all possible despatch (じん速に) ‖ air *loaded* ***with*** carbonic acid gas 炭酸ガスで飽和した空気 ‖ The boughs of cherry-trees are *loaded* ***with*** blossoms. 桜の枝は満開の花をつけている. ‖ be *loaded* ***with*** honors 多大の光栄に浴する. 【類】a heart *loaded* ***with*** sorrow / *load* a ship ***with*** a cargo of cotton / They *loaded* him ***with*** all manner of reproaches. / The audience *loaded* him ***with*** the most extravagant applause. (熱烈なかっさい). / He left us, *loaded* ***with*** kind messages and hearty thanks to his wife. ‖ *loaded* ***with*** years and honors, he retired into private life at ... 彼は年に不足もなく功成り名遂げて...で隠退生活にはいった.

loading, *n*. 荷積み.

Q ***homeward*** (***outward***) ***loading*** 本国(外地)向け荷積み. ¶***prompt loading*** じん速な荷積.

loaf, *n*. 一塊.

Q² a ***two-pound loaf*** of bread 二ポンドのパン一個.

P² a *loaf* ***of*** bread 一塊の食パン(一斤, 二斤, または四斤の).

loaf, *v*. 遊び暮す.

P *loaf* ***around*** saloons 酒場を飲み回る. ¶*loaf* ***on*** the job in textile mills 織物工場で怠業する. ¶*loaf* ***through*** life ぶらぶらして一生を送る.

loafer, *n*. 浮浪人.

Q a ***grimy***, ***grubby loafer*** in the street 街のきたないけがれた浮浪人.

Q² ***street loafers*** 街の浮浪人(ルンペン)たち. ¶a ***night*** (***day***) ***loafer*** 夜(昼)の浮浪者.

loan, *n.* 貸付; 公債; 借金.

V *conclude* a *loan* of ... yen with a bank 銀行から…円借入の約束を結ぶ. ¶The country *contracted* a large foreign *loan.* その国は外国と大借款を締結した. ¶*float* a *loan* of forty million dollars 四千万ドルの公債を募る. ¶*get* the *loan* of money from ... …から金を借りる ‖ *get* the *loan* of a book 本を借りる. 【類】*get* a *loan* from an insurance company on one's policy (保険証書を抵当に). ¶*have* a *loan* of money 金を借りる. 【類】Can I *have* the *loan* of it? ¶*issue* a *loan* 公債を発行する. 【類】A *loan* for ... will be *issued* shortly on this market. ¶*liquidate* a *loan* 負債を清算する. ¶*make* a *loan* on an easy-payment plan なしくずし(月賦)で金を借りる. 【類】*make* a *loan* on a pledge (抵当で). ¶The company has *negotiated* a *loan* of 15 million yen with an English syndicate. 同社は英国のシンディケートと千五百万円の借入を協定した. ¶*obtain* the *loan* of money from ... …から…金を借りる. 【類】*obtain* the *loan* of a building. ¶The *loan* of the water supply of the town has been *oversubscribed.* その公債の応募は募集金額を超過した. ¶*pay off* (=*repay*) a *loan* 負債を返済する. ¶*place* a *loan* before the public for subscription 一般から公債を募集する. ¶*raise* a *loan* 公債を募集する. 【類】*raise* a *loan* of ... yen to be expended in the improvement (市の給水改良のため). ¶*renew* the *loan* on the same terms as before 従来と同一条件で借金を書替える. ¶*solicit* a *loan* of money from a friend 友人に借金を頼む. ¶I *want* a *loan* of £100. 僕は百ポンドを借りたい.

Q an *agricultural loan* 農民貸付け. ¶contract a *big loan* 大借款を締結する. ¶obtain *cheap loans* from savings-banks 貯蓄銀行から低利資金を借りる. ¶The Government has decided to raise a fourth *domestic loan* of £20,000,000. 政府は二千万ポンドの第四回国債募集に決した. ¶a *foreign loan* 外債. ¶an *illegal loan* extended to ... …への浮貸. ¶an *internal loan* 内国債. ¶a *long* (*short*)-*term loan* 長(短)期貸付. ¶subscribe to a *popular loan* 好評のある公債に応募する. ¶a *public loan* 公債. ¶*unpaid loans* 未済の借金.

Q² *call loan* 当座貸付金. ¶an *emergeney loan* 非常時(臨時)公債. ¶*inter-library loan* 図書館仲間の(本の)貸借. ¶a *long-range loan* 長期公債. ¶a *long-term government loan* 長期の政府公債. ¶a *short-term loan* 短期公債. ¶a *war loan* (=bond) 戦時公債.

P call at one's house *for* a *loan* of ... …の金を借りにその家を訪問する. 【類】He came to me *for* a *loan* of money. ¶I asked him *for* the *loan* of a book. 私は彼にある本の借用を申入れた. ¶It has been *on loan* for many years at the museum. それは多年その博物館に貸与してあった. ¶*with* a *loan* of £15,000 upon it その品に対し一万五千ポンド貸付けてある.

P² a *loan from* another language 他国語からの借用語. ¶a *loan of* ... on bottomry bond 〘海〙船底書入貸借証を抵当に…の借款. ¶a *loan on* security 担保貸付.

loan, *v.* 貸す, 金を貸す.

M *loan out* to ... …に貸出す. 【類】*loan out* books.

P I would rather *loan* a million dollars *on* character than on any other collateral in the world.—J.P. Morgan. 私はどんな担保よりもその人の人格を見込んで百万ドルでも貸付けよう. ‖ How much will you *loan on* this watch? この時計でいくら貸してくれる. ¶articles supplied and *loaned to* policemen 巡査給与品及び貸与品.

loathe, *v.* にくむ.

O *loathe* the smell of grease 油のにおいがきらいだ.

loathing, *n.* 嫌悪(ｹﾝｵ).

P regard it *with loathing* それを非常にきらう. ‖ treat one *with* a bitter *loathing* 人をひどくきらう.

lobbing, *n.* 〘テニス〙ロッブ.

Q *nice* (*poor*) *lobbing* じょうず(へた)なロッブ.

lobby, *n.* [ホテルなどの]ロビー; 《米》[議会の]院外団.

Q a *strong lobby* (議案の通過または阻止に対する)強力な院外団.

Q² a *hotel lobby* ホテルのロビー. ¶the main *street-floor lobby* 一階の大広間(ロビー). ¶a *union* (*cotton*) *lobby* 労組(綿花業者)の院外団.

lobby, *v.* 《米》議案通過の運動をする.

M They are *actively lobbying* for (against) the bill. 彼らはその議案通過(阻止)にやっきとなっている.

lobbyist, *n.* 《米》[議会の]院外団(陳情者).

P act *as* a *lobbyist* 陳情者の役をやる.

lobe, *n.* 耳たぶ.

Q² prominent *ear lobes* 福耳.

locality, *n.* 所在地, 場所.

Q Rheumatism affects people living in *damp localities* リューマチはじめじめした土地に住む人を冒す. ¶vary in *different localities* 地域々々で異なる. ¶live in a *fashionable locality* 上流社会の居所に住む.

Q² the *bourgeois locality* 中産階級の住宅地区. ¶a *working-class locality* 労働者の住宅区域.

P *in* your *locality* あなたのいらっしゃる所では.

P² the *locality of* residence 居住地.

locate, *v.* [建物を]おく, 位する; 見つける; 《米》居住する.

M *locate somewhere* on the Pacific coast 太平洋岸のどこかに居住する.

P the hotel is centrally *located at* ... そのホテルは…市の中心にある. ¶The office is *located in* a business center. その事務所は商業の中心地にある. ‖ *locate* a leakage *in* a tank タンク漏れを見つける. ¶*locate* a place *on* a map 地図で場所を見つける.

location, *n.* 場所, 位置; 〘映画〙野外撮影(ロケーション).

V The college *outgrew* its *location.* その大学は地域の狭隘(ｷｮｳｱｲ)をきたした. ¶*secure* the *location* for a middle school 中学校の敷地を買う. ¶Points in red *show location* of railway hotels of the Canadian Pacific Railways. 赤の点はカナダ太平洋鉄道経営の鉄道ホテルの所在を示す.

Q photographed on the *actual location* in Asia アジアの現地で撮った. ¶hang up the posters in *advantageous location* 目につきやすい位置にポスターを掛ける. ¶a most *delightful location* すこぶる好い場所. ¶difficulties experienced in making motion pictures in *far-away locations* 遠く離れたロケーションで経験した映画製作上の困難. ¶*geographical location* 地理的位置. ¶an exceedingly *happy location* for the monument その記念碑にはうってつけの場所. ¶Immigrants were warned against *hasty location.* 移民たちは居住地を早まって決めないように忠告された. ¶*ideal* and *central location* 理想的な中心の位置. ¶The *location* is exceptionally *poor*, viewed from a sanitation point. その位置は衛生的見地からいうと非常にまずい. ¶a *quiet location* 閑静な土地.

Q² a *large-scale location* at ... …における大規模のロケーション.

P be *on location* in Italy イタリーでロケーション中.

P² the *location of* a place on a map 地図上でのある場所の位置.

locator, *n.* 探知器.

Q² a *radio locator*=a radar 電波探知器. ¶a *sound locator* 音波探知器.

loch, *n.* 湖水.

Q blue *sparkling lochs* embosomed among the hills. 丘に囲まれた青白く輝いている(スコットランドの)湖水.

lock, *n.* 錠.

V *break* a *lock* 錠をこわす. ¶*break open* a *lock* 錠をこじ開ける. ¶*fasten* a *lock* 錠をおろす. ¶a key to *fit* the *lock* 錠に合うかぎ. ¶*hamper* a *lock* 錠を狂わす. ¶The trunk *has* a good *lock.* そのトランクには丈夫な錠が付いている. ¶*open* a *lock* with a key=unlock かぎで錠をあける. ¶*pick* a *lock* 錠をこじ開ける. ¶*wrench off* a *lock* 錠をねじ切る.

V² The *lock clicked shut* (*open*). 錠はカチンとしまった(あいた).

Q² a *burglar-alarm lock* 警報錠. ¶a *Yale lock* エール錠(ドアに用いる).

P turn a key *in* a *lock* かぎで錠をあける(しめる). ¶*off* the *lock* 錠を掛けないで. ¶*on* the *lock* 錠を掛けて. ¶keep one's money *under lock* and key 錠をおろして金をしまっておく.

P² ¶There was no *lock on* the door. 戸口には錠が付いていなかった. ¶a *lock to* a gate 門の錠.

lock, *v.* 錠をおろす; 拘留する, しまい込む; 抱き締める.

M carefully *lock away* the records 記録を大事にしまい込む. ¶She *locked* me *out.* 彼女(妻)から締出しを食った. ‖ The workers had been *locked out* before they went on strike. 労働者たちはストをやる前に工場閉鎖を食った. ¶*securely locked* ちゃんと錠をおろした.

M² be *locked in* へやに閉じこめられる ‖ *lock* oneself *in* 閉じ込もる. ¶*lock up* a house (yard, trunk) 家(など)にかぎをかける. ¶*locked up* in the punishment cells (police station) 監房(など)に監禁された ‖ *lock **up*** a prisoner 囚人を監禁する. 【類】 be *locked **up*** in a room / He *locked* himself ***up*** (閉じこもって) in the study / *lock* it ***up*** in a strong-room (金庫) of a bank / *lock* things ***up*** for safety / *lock **up*** ... in a box / *lock* them ***up*** in a separate compartment of the brain.

P All the doors had been *locked **from*** the outside. ドアーは皆外から鍵をおろしてあった. ¶He *locked* her ***in*** a room for a whole day. 彼は彼女をまる一日一室に監禁した. ¶She *locked* a child ***to*** her breast. 彼女は子供を胸に抱き締めた.

O This door won't *lock*. このドアは錠がかからない.

lock, *n.* 髪毛.

Q ***lank** locks* of hair [ちじれ毛でない]長い髪の巻毛. ¶***uncombed** locks* of hair くしを入れてない髪.

locker, *n.* かぎ戸だな(ロッカー).

V ***break open*** a *locker* ロッカーをこじあける.

Q ***individual** lockers* 個人別の錠前付携帯品置場.

Q² a ***checkroom** locker* 一時預所の手荷物保管箱. ¶a ***foot** locker* 手もとにおく保管箱. ¶a ***steel** locker* 鋼鉄のロッカー. ¶a ***wall** locker* かべにはめこんであるロッカー.

P I have not a shot ***in*** the *locker*. 私は懐中無一物だ.

lockout, *n.* 〘労〙 工場閉鎖.

V A *lockout* was ***declared*** against 19,000 metal workers in Leipzig and Thuringia, Germany. ドイツのライプチッヒ及びチューリンゲンにおける一万九千の金属労働者に対して工場閉鎖(ロックアウト)が宣言された.

Q² a ***factory** lockout* 工場閉鎖.

locomotion, *n.* 移動; 交通機関.

Q ***aerial** locomotion* 空中輸送.

Q² the problem of ***London** locomotion* ロンドンの交通の問題. ¶***steam** locomotion* by land and sea 陸や海の蒸気交通機関.

P a mode ***of*** *locomotion* 輸送の方法.

locomotive, *n.* 機関車.

V ***drive*** a *locomotive* 機関車を運転する.

V² The *locomotive* has ***broken down.*** その機関車はこわれた. ¶The *locomotive **goes puffing along.*** 機関車があえぎながら進む.

Q two ***electric** locomotives*—one pulling and one pushing 二台の電気機関車—一台は引張り一台は押す.

Q² a ***bogie** locomotive* (=engine) ボギー(回転)式機関車. ¶a ***coal-burning steam** locomotive* 石炭蒸気機関車. ¶a ***compressed-air** locomotive* 圧気機関車. ¶an ***express** locomotive* 急行列車用機関車. ¶a ***goods** locomotive*=《米》a freight engine 貨物列車専用機関車. ¶a ***passenger** locomotive* 旅客列車専用機関車. ¶a ***shunting** locomotive* 入換機関車. ¶a ***steam** locomotive* 蒸気機関車. ¶***super-power electric*** and ***oil-burning*** *locomotive* 超過熱電気及び石油機関車. ¶a ***tank** locomotive* 給水車付の機関車. ¶a ***tender** locomotive* 炭水車付の機関車.

P A train pulled ***by*** two *locomotives* is called a double header. 二両の機関車を連結した列車を二頭列車と呼ぶ. ¶burn coal (oil) ***on*** a *locomotive* 石炭(など)を機関車にたく.

locution, *n.* 言葉使い, 話し振り.

V ***use*** a ponderous *locution* 重苦しい言葉使いをする.

Q a ***barbarous** locution* 下品な言葉使い.

Q² translate Japanese ***slang** locutions* into English expressions of corresponding degree of vulgarity 日本語の俗語調の言い方を同じ程度の俗語調の英語に翻訳する.

lode, *n.* 鉱脈.

V Those writers have ***struck*** a rich *lode.* それらの文士は文学の沃(ﾖｸ)土(好材料)にぶつかった.

lodge, *n.* 宿る小屋.

Q a ***caretaker's** lodge* 番小屋.

Q² a ***hunting** lodge* 狩人の宿る小屋.

lodge, *v.* 寄寓する, 下宿する; くい入る, 倒す; はさまる; 届出る.

M All his manners showed that he was *lodged **pretty much*** at large. 彼は全く面食ったという風情であった.

P *lodge* a complaint ***against*** him 彼を告訴する. ¶*lodge **at*** different houses in ... ...の別々の家に泊る ‖ *lodge* papers ***at*** ... 書類を...に差出す ‖ *lodge* a charge ***at*** a police station against him 彼を相手取って警察に訴える. ¶remove matter *lodged **between*** teeth 歯の間にはさまった物を取る. ¶A ball has *lodged **in*** his breast. 弾丸が彼の胸にささった. 【類】 The bullet *lodged **in*** the neck (brain). ‖ The soldiers are *lodged **in*** private houses. その兵隊たちは民家に宿泊している. ¶*lodge **with*** relatives or friends 親類または友人の家に寄寓する ‖ *lodge **with*** the Johnsons ジョンスンさんの家に下宿する.

lodger, *n.* 下宿人.

V ***take** lodgers* 下宿人をおく.

Q² his ***fellow** lodgers* 同じアパート住いの人たち.

lodging, *n.* 宿泊, 下宿, 貸間.

V ***change*** one's *lodgings* 下宿を変える. ¶***hire** lodgings* 間借りをする. ¶***seek** lodgings* 下宿を探す. ¶***share** lodgings* with ... ...と共同で間借りをする. ¶He ***took*** a *lodging* for me. 彼は私のために間を借りておいてくれた. ¶***take up*** one's *lodgings* 宿を取る.

Q ***dry** lodgings* まかないなしの下宿. ¶he died in ***obscure** lodgings* in ... 彼は...の名もない下宿で死んだ. ¶I intend to take ***private** lodgings* soon. 僕は近いうちにしろうと下宿に引越そうと思っている. ¶a young man in ***shabby** lodgings* しがないアパート暮しの青年.

P call ***at*** one's *lodgings* 人のアパートを訪問する. ¶I was ***at*** your *lodgings* just now. 今し方僕は君の下宿に行った. ¶live ***in*** *lodgings* 下宿住居をする. ¶Send them over ***to*** my *lodgings.* [買物など]それを私のアパートに届けて下さい. ¶a hired hand ***with*** *lodging* 住込みの雇人 ‖ ***with*** board and *lodging* [下宿など]食事つきで. ¶***without** lodging* 通いで.

lodging-house, *n.* 下宿屋.

Q a ***cheap** lodging-house* 木賃宿.

Q² an ***open-all-night** lodging-house* 夜通し出入自由のアパート.

loft, *n.* はと小屋.

Q² a ***pigeon** loft* はと小屋.

lofty, *a.* 高い, 高慢な.

P *lofty **of*** mien 風さいの高慢ちきな. ¶*lofty* almost ***to*** giddiness めまいがするくらい高い.

log, *n.* 丸太; 〘海〙 測程器.

V ***crop** logs* in the mountains 山奥で丸太を伐る. ¶***heave*** (=***throw***) a *log* 測程器を投げて船の速度を測る. ¶***roll** logs* for ... ...のために骨を折る. ¶***saw** logs* into boards のこぎりで丸太を板にひく. ¶***saw up** logs* 丸太をひく. ¶***score** logs* for building a logcabin 丸木小屋を造るために丸太に刻み目をつける.

Q a ***patent** log* 特許測程器.

Q² a ***Christmas*** (=Yule) *log* クリスマスにたく木株.

P sleep ***like*** a *log* 熟睡する.

loggerhead, *n.* ばか者.

P They are ***at*** *loggerheads.* 彼らはけんかをしている. ¶fall (=go) ***to*** *loggerheads* 殴り合いになる.

P² ***at*** *loggerheads **with*** ... ...と争って.

logic, *n.* 論理学; 論理, 論法.

V ***chop** logic* へりくつを言う.

Q It is far ***better** logic* to suspend judgment until we can obtain some further light upon the matter. その問題については何かそれ以上の光明が得られるまでは判断を下すのを見合わすのがはるかに理屈に合っている. ¶***deductive*** (***inductive***) *logic* 演繹(ｴｷ)(帰納)論理学. ¶***examine*** the *logic* of ... ...の論理を吟味する. ¶***follow*** no *logic* 理屈を無視する. ¶***formal** logic* 形式論理学. ¶by the ***inevitable** logic* of event ことの成行上避けられないこととして. ¶***pure** logic* 純粋論理学. ¶***sound** logic* 健全な論法. ¶His *logic* seems ***unanswerable*** (=incapable of being refuted). 彼の論理は反ばくできそうもない. ¶the ***unrelenting** logic* of the rational mind 合理的の頭に働く仮借ない論理.

P governed ***by*** *logic* 筋の通った. ¶***with*** the same *logic* they might demonstrate to us (=as well argue) that ... その筆法で行けば...とも言えるわけだ.

logical, *a.* 論理的.

M ***thoroughly** logical* どこまでも論理的な.

logician, *n.* 論理学者, 評論家.

Q a ***shaky** logician* 理路の立たない評論家.

loin, *n.* 腰.

V ***gird up*** one's *loins* 腰に帯を締める; 緊こん一番する. 【類】 the *loins* are ***girded*** fresh for ...

P spring ***from*** one's *loins* その子として生れる. ¶fruit (=child) ***of*** one's *loins* 自分に生れた子供.

loiter, *v.* 方々をさまよう.

P He was arrested while *loitering **about*** the court house this afternoon. 彼はきょう午後裁判所付近をぶらついている所をつかまった. ¶*loiter **around*** a street corner 町角をうろつく. ¶*loiter **on*** the road 道草を食う.

loiterer, *n.* ぶらぶらする人.
Q² a ***home-returning*** *loiterer* 家に帰る途中道草を食っている人.

loitering, *n.* ぶらつき.
Q ***No*** *loitering* in this compound. このさく内をうろつくべからず.

loll, *v.* だらりと横になる.
M *loll* ***comfortably*** in his splendid carriage すばらしい車に心地よげに横たわる. ¶*loll* ***out*** its tongue [犬など]舌をだらりと出す ‖ Little girls *loll* ***out*** on the grass. 小娘たちが芝生の上にだらりと横になっている.

London, *n.* ロンドン.
Q ever ***dear*** *London* いつもなつかしのロンドン.

loneliness, *n.* 孤独.
Q a life of ***proud*** *loneliness* 孤高の生活.

long, *n.* 長きもの.
V It will not ***take*** *long*. 長くはかからないだろう.
Q He did not have to wait ***that*** (=so) *long*. 彼はたいして長く待たずにすんだ.
P ***before*** *long* ほどなく. ¶Eucken's influence as a thinker has ***for*** *long* been felt far beyond the borders of his native land. 思想家としてのオイケンの影響は久しい以前から遠く国外にまで及んでいる. 【類】He will not remain ***for*** *long*.
P² the *long* and short ***of*** it is that ... かいつまんでいうと...となる.

long, *a., ad.* 長い(く).
M ***disproportionately*** *long* 不均衡に長い. ¶I have lived *long* enough. 年に不足はない. ¶Maybe he didn't go to school *long* ***enough***. 多分彼は学校を早くやめてしまったのだろう. ¶***How*** *long* have you been a smoker? タバコをお吸いになってからどのくらいになりますか. ¶***no*** *longer* もはや...でない. 【類】He is ***no*** *longer* alive. ¶The address was ***thirty-seven minutes*** *long*. その演説は三十七分間だった.
M² ***as*** (=so) *long* as ... ...する限りは(以上は) ‖ Stay ***as*** *long* as you like. いつまでもごゆっくりして下さい.
P I am not *long* ***about*** the job. 私はその仕事にかかってまだ長くない. 【類】Do not be *long* ***about*** it (ぐずぐず). ¶*long* ***before*** the war ずっと戦前に ‖ The occasion was not *long* ***in*** coming. 機会はほどなくやって来た. ¶He is *long* ***in*** returning. 彼は帰りが遅い.
O It was not *long* before he came up. まもなく彼が姿を現わした.

long, *v.* 切望する, あこがれる.
P *long* ***about*** ... ...を切望する. ¶*long* ***for*** the city (her country) その市(など)にあこがれる ‖ *long* ***for*** masculine companionship 男性との交際を欲する ‖ *long* ***for*** (=***after***) fame 名誉を渇望する. 【類】*long* ***for*** peace.
O I'm *longing* to see him. 彼に会いたい.

longest *n.* 最長.
P ***at*** [the] *longest* [長くとも]せいぜい ‖ Life is short even ***at*** its *longest*. 人生はいくら長く生きたところで短いものだ.

longevity, *n.* 長命.
V ***attribute*** one's *longevity* to the fact that ... その長命を...という事実に帰する. ¶***enjoy*** *longevity* 長生きする.
P an instance ***of*** *longevity* 長寿の一例.

longhand, *n.* 普通の書方.
P write ***in*** *longhand* 普通の書方で書く(速記でなく).

longing, *n.* 切望, あこがれ.
V ***feel*** a *longing* toward ... ...にあこがれを感じる. ¶I ***had*** an unaccountable *longing* for the sea. 私は何となく海にあこがれをもっていた. ‖ I ***have*** a great *longing* for home. 私は故郷を非常に恋しく思っている. ¶He has beautifully ***voiced*** this *longing* in one of his poems. 彼はこのあこがれをその詩の一つに美しく言い表わした.
Q the ***divine*** *longing* within us われわれの胸にある聖なるあこがれ. ¶***stifled*** *longings* of our hearts 抑制したわれわれの心のあこがれ. ¶***ungovernable*** *longings* 抑え切れないあこがれ.
P² He has a great *longing* ***for*** liberty. 彼は自由を切望している.

look, *n.* 顔つき, 目付, 様子; 一見.
V ***bend*** one's *look* upon ... ...に顔を向ける. ¶***exchange*** *looks* 互いに顔を見合わせる ‖ ***exchange*** a *look* of intelligence 互に顔を見合わせてそれとさとる. ¶***fasten*** one's *looks* upon ... ...を見詰める. ¶***get*** a good *look* into one's face 人の顔をしげしげとながめる. 【類】***get*** a good *look* at ... ‖ ***get*** a last *look* at the placid face of the sweet sleeper かわゆく眠っている者(死んだ子供など)の穏かな顔の見納めをする. ¶***give*** a *look* around ずっと一遍見回す ‖ ***give*** new *look* to ... =furnish up ... ...に新装を施す ‖ He ***gave*** me a *look* with his black eyes. 彼は恐ろしい目をして私を見た. 【類】he was ***given*** a *look* of thanks by ... ¶May I ***have*** a *look* at it? それを見せて頂けませんか. ‖ ***have*** a *look* over a ship 船内を見物する ‖ I ***had*** another good *look* at it, and saw plainly enough that it was an imitation. 私はそれをもう一度よく見たら模造品ということが明かに分かった. ‖ He ***has*** the *look* of a bit tired, deflated facsimile of Adolf Hitler. 彼はくたびれてぺちゃんこになったヒットラーといった顔つきをしている. 【類】It ***has*** the *look* of being genuine. ¶***impair*** to serious extent their good *looks* 大いに彼女らの容色を害する. ¶***improve*** her *looks* きりょうをよくする. ¶***keep in*** her good *looks* 美ぼうを落さないでいる. ¶I don't ***like*** his *looks*. 私はあの人の顔付を好かない. ¶Even a pretty woman would ***lose*** her good *looks* with such a coiffure. たとい美人でもあの髪の結方ではきりょうが落ちよう. ¶He ***put on*** a serious *look*. 彼はまじめな顔をしていた. ¶***set*** one's best *looks* 最もよく化粧する. ¶***steal*** a *look* at ... ...を盗み見する. ¶***take*** a *look* at ... =look at ... ...を見る ‖ ***take*** another *look* at ... ...をもう一度見る. 【類】***take*** a good *look* at ... / May I ***take*** (=have) a *look?* ‖ ***take*** a last *look* at the features (=face) of ... ...の見納めをする ‖ His eyes ***took*** a downcast *look*. 彼は目を伏せた. ¶***throw*** a *look* of contempt at ... ...にばかにしたような目付をする ‖ He ***threw*** me a furious *look*. 彼は私をはったとにらんだ. ¶***turn*** a *look* of keen reproach on ... ...に対して激しい非難の表情を見せる. ¶***wear*** a puzzled *look* of amazement はとが豆鉄砲を食ったような顔付をする.
V² A wild *look* ***came*** into his eyes. 険悪の相が彼の目に現われた. 【類】A frightened *look* ***came*** over her face. ¶A *look* of disappointment ***passed*** over his face. 失望の色が彼の顔に浮んだ.
Q put on ***amorous*** *looks* 色目をつかう. ¶He gave me an ***awful*** *look* as he passed. 彼は通り過ぎざま私に恐ろしい目付をした. ¶a ***backward*** *look* 後への振向き. ¶There was a ***blank*** *look* in his face. 彼はぽかんとした顔つきをしていた. ¶a ***brave*** *look* 勇ましい顔付. ¶He has a ***challenging*** *look*. 彼はちょう戦的な顔付をしている. ¶take a ***close*** *look* at ... ...をしげしげ見る. ¶after a ***critical*** *look* 批判的に見てから. ¶with a ***disconsolate*** *look* なぐさめかねた顔付で. ¶have a ***fierce*** *look* on one's face その面上には恐しい様相が浮んでいる. ¶have a ***first-hand*** *look* at ... ...を実見する. ¶a ***frowning*** *look* 不興顔. ¶a ***glassy*** *look* どんよりしたまなざし. ¶have ***good*** *looks* きりょうがよい ‖ Mother Nature has favored them with the ***good*** *looks*. 彼女たちは美ぼうに生れついている. ¶take a ***hasty*** *look* into ... ...を急いでのぞき込む. ¶a ***hungry*** *look* 空腹の顔付. ¶an ***imperious*** *look* ごう慢な顔付. ¶***incredulous*** *looks* 不審な面もち. ¶with an ***inquiring*** *look* けげんそうな面もちで. ¶take (=have) a ***last*** *look* at the port before sailing for foreign ports 外国の港へ向けて出帆する前にその港に見納めをする. 【類】Napoleon's ***last*** *look* at France. / take a ***last, parting*** *look* at her husband. ¶take a ***longing*** *look* at ... ...をなつかしそうに見る. ¶There is nothing that gives a room such a delightfully ***lovable*** *look* as plenty of well-filled book-shelves. およそへやにぎっしり詰った書だなが沢山あるくらいそのへやに心地よく落着けそうな気分を出させるものはない. ¶a ***malignant*** but ***coward*** *look* 悪意はあるがしかしおじけた顔付. ¶give him a ***meaning*** *look* 彼に意味ありげな目付をする. ¶has a ***neglected*** *look* だらしなく見える. ¶the ***new*** *look* of current Broadway plays 今興業中のブロードウェー劇のニュールック ‖ take on a ***new*** *look* 新生面を呈する. ¶an ***open*** and ***straightforward*** *look* 明けっぱなしで卒直な顔付. ¶their ***pale*** *looks* 彼らの青ざめた顔付. ¶with a ***peculiar*** *look* 妙な様子をして. ¶He gave me a ***puzzled*** *look*. 彼は私に当惑した目付をした. ‖ shoot a ***puzzled*** *look* at ... ...に困った顔を向ける. ¶She gave a ***queer*** *look*. 彼女は妙な顔をした. ¶have a ***rapid*** *look* at the sights of a city 大急ぎで市中を見物する. ¶a ***sapient, vacant*** *look* 利口だがぼんやりした顔付. ¶a ***scornful*** *look* ばかにした顔付. ¶a ***searching*** *look* せんさく的な目付. ¶take a ***second*** *look* at ... ...をもう一度見る. ¶One would probably not give him a ***second*** *look*. [興味を引くものがないから]恐らくだれも二度と彼の顔を見ようとはすまい. ¶He has a ***set*** *look* on his face. あの人はきか

ない顔付をしている. ¶a ***sharp*** *look* 鋭い目付. ¶a ***sour*** *look* 渋面. ¶I threw a ***startled*** *look* at her. 私は驚いて彼女を見やった. ¶has a ***stern*** *look* きびしい面もちをしている. ¶wear a ***sullen*** *look* (=countenance) 不機げんな顔をしている. ¶with a ***suspicious*** *look* けげんな顔をして. ¶wear a ***troubled*** *look* 困った顔をする. ¶Things took on an ***ugly*** *look*. 事態が険悪になった. ¶There is such an ***uncanny*** *look* about the place. その場所は何となく薄気味が悪い. ¶a ***wide*** *look* 広々としたながめ. ¶The ***worried*** *look* had passed from his eyes. 困ったという顔付はもう彼の目から去っていた. ¶women with a ***young-old*** *look* 若いのか年よりか分からないような女たち.

Q² with a pleading don't be ***angry-with-me*** *look* in her eyes 怒らないでねといった訴えるような目付で. ¶have a ***hangdog*** *look* げすな顔をしている. ¶a ***wartime*** *look* 戦時色.

P Do not judge of a man ***by*** his *looks*. 人を見かけによって判断してはならない. ¶They weep a little just ***for*** the *looks* of the thing (=appearance's sake). 彼らは体裁でほんのちよっと泣くだけだ. ¶***from*** the *look* of the sky 空模様から(考えると). ¶superior ***in*** *looks* 容ぼうのすぐれた. ¶***with*** a *look* of anxiety upon one's face 顔に憂色を浮べて ‖ ***with*** a *look* of indecision on his face どちらとも決しかねた面もちで ‖ ***with*** *looks* of great composure 落着き払って ‖ ***with*** *looks* not at all pleased 一向浮かない顔で. 【類】***with*** a *look* of eager inquiry.

P² take a *look* ***into*** a well 井戸をのぞく. ¶have a *look* ***of*** age 古く見える ‖ a *look* ***of*** expectation したり顔. 【類】The ranks seem filled from the lowest peasantry, and one seeks in vain in a long line of faces for a *look* ***of*** intelligence.

look, *v*. 見る, 注目する; 期待する; 考える.

M *look* ***about*** for a house 家を捜す. ¶*look* ***abroad*** for more business それ以上に海外取引を求める. ¶*look* far ***ahead*** into the future ずっと先を見越す. ¶England *looks* ***ahead*** to a prosperous 1939. 英国は好景気の一九三九年を予期している. ‖ The wise statesman *looks* ***ahead*** for the inevitable reaction. 賢明な政治家は必ず反動が来るものと予想する. ¶*look* ***alarmed*** びっくりした様子をする. ¶*Look* ***alive*** and get a move on it. しっかりしてそれをてきぱきやれ. ¶He *looks* ***angry***. 彼は怒っているようだ. ¶*look* ***around*** for a house to let 貸家を捜す. ¶He *looked* ***aside*** when I spoke to him. 彼に話しかけたら横を向いた. ¶*look* ***askance*** at ... ...を横目に見る. ¶*look* ***austere*** 厳格な様子をする. ¶She *looked* ***away*** from him. 彼女は彼から顔をそむけた. ¶You *look* ***awful*** in those tweed pants. そのツイードのずぼんをはくととてもおかしい. ¶*look* ***back*** at a person 人を振返って見る ‖ *look* ***back*** into our history わが国の歴史にさかのぼる ‖ *looking* ***back*** on (=upon) the past I can now see that ... 過去を追想して私は今...と悟ることができる. 【類】*looking* ***back*** on my childhood, I can remember that ... / She *looked* ***back*** on the course of vice she had run. / pause to *look* ***back*** over the days since the end of the war / if one *looks* ***back*** over the past hundred years or more / *look* ***back*** over a chapter ‖ *look* ***back*** to ... with satisfaction (pleasure) ...を満足して(喜んで)...を追想する ‖ *look* ***back*** through the mist of time (=years) to the scenes of childhood 歳月の霞を通して子供のころの有様を追想する. 【類】I try to *look* ***back*** over the years and to remember my childish impressions. ¶One portion of my life is not very pleasant to *look* ***back*** to. 私の一生には回想してあまり愉快でない時代もあります. ¶*look* ***backward*** for its causes and forward for its effects その原因にさかのぼりその将来の結果を考えて見る ‖ *looking* further ***backward*** さらに過去にさかのぼって. ¶Things are *looking* a little ***better***. 事態がやや好転しつつある. ‖ You *look* ***better*** in that new suit. その新調の服を着ると男振りがあがる. ¶My father had just died and things *looked* ***black*** for my mother, for my sister, and for my little brother. そのころちょうど父が死んだので母や姉や弟の前途は暗たんたるものであった. ¶*look* ***blank*** ぼんやりしている. ¶*look* ***blankly*** at ... ぼんやり...をながめる. ¶*look* ***blue*** 憂うつそうだ ‖ You *look* ***blue*** with cold. 君は寒いので顔が青ざめている. ¶*look* it ***carefully*** それを注視する ‖ *look* ***carefully*** into the papers 書類をよく調べる. ¶*look* ***cautiously*** round こわごわあたりを見回わす. ¶*look* ***closely*** into the causes その原因を精査する ‖ *look* ***closely*** at ... ...をじっと見る. ¶*look* ***coldly*** upon the proposal その提案を冷視する. ¶We may ***confidently*** *look* toward the time when ... われわれはきっと...のときの来るべきことを期待できる. ¶*look* ***critically*** at ... ...を批判的に見る. ¶He *looks* ***decidedly*** a dandy. 彼は断然ハイカラだ. ¶*look* ***deep*** into the hearts of other people 他人の意中を深く推察する. ¶*look* ***dignified*** 品があるように見える. ¶*look* ***disapprovingly*** at ... ...をにらむ. ¶The weather *looks* ***doubtful***. 天気が怪やしい. ¶He *looked* ***dubious***. 彼はけげんな顔をした. ¶I am *looking* ***eagerly*** for the February number. 私は二月号を待ち焦れている. ¶He *looks* ***every inch*** a gentleman. 彼はどこからどこまでも紳士だ. ¶*look* ***fixedly*** じっと見る. ¶The exercises *looked* ***foolish*** to him. その練習は彼にはばかげて見えた. ¶He is fifty years old, but he *looks* only ***forty***. 彼は五十だが四十にしか見えない. ¶we may *look* ***forward*** to a time in the near future when ... われわれは近き将来...のときを期待してよい. 【類】I *look* ***forward*** with interest how he will deal with it. / *look* ***forward*** with confidence to ... / *look* ***forward*** to increased trade between the two countries / few of us *look* ***forward*** with eagerness to the day when ... / travelers *looking* ***forward*** to arrival at home / *look* ***forward*** to the day, not far distant I hope, when ... / We *look* ***forward*** to more prosperous times (好景気). / I have been *looking* ***forward*** to the pleasure of seeing you. / *look* ***forward*** hopefully to ... / *looked* ***forward*** to the ordeal (試練) with considerable anxiety / We *look* ***forward*** to hearing from you favorably in the matter at an early date. / I can assure you that I shall always *look* ***forward*** to news of your doings (御起居の消息) with great pleasure. / she is *looking* ***forward*** with keen anticipation (切に) to ... / *look* ***forward*** with keen interest and pleasure / *look* ***forward*** with the deepest apprehension (非常に心配して) ‖ It will be *looked* ***forward*** to with interest by all theatergoers. それは劇愛好家に興味を持って期待されよう. ¶*look* at one ***freezingly*** 人を冷淡に見やる. ¶*look* the questions of the day ***fully*** and ***fearlessly*** in the face 時事問題をまともにかつ恐れずに直視する. ¶*look* ***funny*** へんに見える. ¶*look* ***glum*** 気むずかしく見える. ¶*look* ***good-natured*** お人よしに見える. ¶*look* ***grave*** 真顔になる. ¶You *look* pretty ***green***. 君は大分顔色が悪いよ. ¶*look* ***guilty*** 有罪らしい. ¶*looked* ***haggard*** やつれた様に見えた. ¶*look* ***halfway*** between ... and ... ...と...との中間のように見える. ¶*look* ***hard*** at ... ...をじっと見る. ¶*Look* ***here***! いいかね. ¶I say! *Look* ***here***! あのね. ‖ *Look* ***here***, this is playing it very low (=behaving meanly) down on us! おい, おれたちを卑劣な手段で一杯食わそうというのだな. ¶*look* ***hideous*** 恐ろしく見える. ¶One must *look* ***higher*** and ***further***. もっと高く大局から見なければいけない. ¶*look* ***inquiringly*** 尋ねるように見る. ¶She *looks* ***intelligent***. 彼女は利口そうだ. ¶*look* ***intently*** at ... ...をじっと見る. 【類】*look* ***intently*** into the darkness of the forest. ¶***joyfully*** *look* forward to ... ...を楽しみに待ちもうける. ¶*look* at him ***keenly*** 彼をじっと見る. ¶He *looked* most ***kindly*** at me. 彼は非常に親切気に私を見た. ¶*look* ***longingly*** at ... ...をなつかしそうに見る. ¶I saw him *looking* ***lovesick***. あの人は恋わずらいでもしているように見えた. ¶He doesn't *look* ***much*** like a hunting dog. あれは見た所あまり猟犬らしくもない. ¶*look* ***narrowly*** into ... ...をつぶさに調べる. ¶*look* ***nervously*** at ... 心配そうに...を見る. ¶You *look* ***nice*** with that hair-do. その髪はよく似合います. ¶*look* ***obliquely*** 斜めに見る. ¶*look* ***out*** across the lake 湖水を見晴らす ‖ I will *look* ***out*** for you. お目にかかれるでしょう(同じ汽車で行くと言った時などのあいさつ). ‖ *Look* ***out*** for pick-pockets! すりに御注意. 【類】*Look* ***out*** for the people entirely destitute of religion. ‖ "*Look* ***out*** for the squall!" cried the sailor. 「そらスコールだ」と船員が叫んだ. ‖ Please *look* ***out*** for a good teacher for me. 私に良い教師を見つけて下さい. ‖ *look* ***out*** for an agency for ... ...の代理店をさがす. 【類】He is always *looking* ***out*** for number one. ‖ He will be able to *look* ***out*** for himself. 彼は一人立ができるだろう. ‖ with the windows *looking* ***out*** on the Sumida River 隅田川を見晴す窓のある. 【類】The windows *looked* ***out*** on a garden. / a house *looks* ***out*** upon (=on) ... ‖ *look* ***out*** defiantly on the world 世間をちょう戦的に見る ‖ I *looked* ***out*** over the audience with folded arms. 私は腕を組んで聴衆を見渡した. ¶*look* ***out*** through a window 窓(ガラス)を通して外を見る. ¶*look* it ***over*** hurriedly それを急いで一読する. ¶*look* ***questioningly*** 不審そうにながめる. ¶*look* ***quizzically*** じろじろ見る. ¶*look* ***reproachfully*** 非難の目付で見る. ¶*looking* ***scornfully*** at ... …をしり目にかけて. ¶Rugs soon get to *look* ***shabby***. 敷物はすぐ見すぼらしくなる. ¶*Look* ***sharp***! 気をつけろ. ‖ I hope you will *look* ***sharp*** (=make haste) about this. これを早くやってもらいたい. ¶*look* ***sharply*** at a person 人をじろっと見る. ¶She *looked* ***shyly*** around her. 彼女はこっそりあたりを見回した. ¶*look* ***sideways*** at ... …を横から(または斜めに)見る. ¶The ship *looked* ***spick-and-span*** in a glistening coat of white paint. その船はぴかぴかする白ペンキでよそおって真新しく見えた. ¶*look* him ***squarely*** in the eye 彼を直視する. ¶*look* ***steadily*** at ... …をじっと見る. ¶*look* the other ***straight*** in the face 相手の顔をまともに見る. ¶*look* ***strange*** 奇妙に見える. ¶*look* ***strangely*** at ... …を不思議そうに見る. ¶*Look* ***there***, Ma! Trees, houses and everything are flying backward so fast. ほらお母ちゃん. 木でもお家でも何でもとても速く後へ飛んで行くよ. ¶*look* ***through*** (=inspect) our large assortment of ... 店内にある…の沢山取そろえた品に目を通す ‖ His eyes were so brilliant that he really seemed to be *looking* one ***through***. 彼の目は真に人を見抜くと思われるほどらんらんとしていた. ¶He saw that things were beginning to *look* very ***ugly***. 彼は事態がきわめて重大になりつつあると見て取った. ¶*look* ***unconcerned*** 無関心な風をする. ¶The river *looked* very ***unpromising***. その川は見た所つれそうもなかった. ¶*look* ***upward*** 仰ぎ見る. ¶*look* ***vacantly*** at his questioner 彼の質問者をぼんやりながめる. ¶He *looks* ***villainous***. 彼は悪党づらをしている. ¶*look* ***well*** 丈夫そうに見える. ¶*look* ***wise*** 利口そうに見える. ¶*look* ***wistfully*** at ... …をあこがれの目で見る. ¶***yearningly*** *look* あこがれてながめる. ¶She *looks* ***young*** (***old***) for her age. 彼女は年にしては若く(ふけて)見える.

M² *look* ***about*** for one's hat 帽子を捜す. ¶The last time I saw him he was *looking* ***about*** for something to do. この前彼に会ったときは彼は何か仕事を捜していた. ‖ if a person *looks* ***about*** a bit, he will find that ... ちょっとあたりを見回せば…ということが分かるだろう. ¶*look* ***around*** for help 助けをさがし求める ‖ *look* ***around*** every corner for ... すみずみまで…を捜しまわる. ¶*look* ***before*** and ***after*** 前後を見回す. ¶*look* ***down*** on the lake 湖水を見下ろす. ¶*look* ***down*** on a thing 物を見下ろす.【類】I have found that by reading in the common way—*looking* ***down*** on the book—I can only read for a comparatively brief time without feeling my eyes tired. But by looking up at a book (あお向きで本を見る) I can read all day without fatigue.—Hearn. ‖ *look* ***down*** upon the poor 貧乏人をべつ視する ‖ *look* ***down*** at ... …を見下ろす ‖ *look* ***down*** from an aeroplane over a city 飛行機から市を見下ろす.【類】a room *looking* ***down*** on a river (stream) ‖ *look* ***down*** into the street 通りを見下ろす ‖ *look* ***down*** below.【類】*look* ***down*** from a high place on ... ‖ *look* ***down*** with an air of scorn upon ... 人をばかにしたような様子で…を見くだす.【類】much *looked* ***down*** upon by ... ‖ Who, when the shares *look* ***down***, try to sell? 株が下っている時に売りに出るものがあるか. ¶He *looked* ***in*** to see anybody else around. 彼はだれかいるかとのぞいてみた. ‖ promise to *look* ***in*** 立寄るように約束する.【類】*look* ***in*** at mother's house / He *looks* ***in*** on us once in a while. / I will *look* ***in*** upon him after breakfast. ¶*look* ***on to*** the future 将来の事を考える. ¶*look* a boy ***over*** 少年をよく見る ‖ *look* them ***over*** ざっと目を通す. ¶*look* ***round*** for ... …を捜して見回す.【類】*look* ***round*** for a publisher. ¶His eyes glared at the stranger with a gaze that seemed to *look* him ***through*** and ***through***. 彼はその旅人を奥の底まで見通すといった凝視でねめつけた. ¶*look* ***up*** at the roof 屋根を見上げる ‖ *look* ***up*** at ... defiantly …をいどむように見上げる.【類】*look* ***up*** at the stars / *look* ***up*** into the heavens / *look* ***up*** from a book one is reading ‖ *look* ***up*** into the sky 空を見上げる.【類】*look* ***up*** to heaven ‖ I hope you will *look* me ***up*** (=call on me). どうぞお出かけ下さい. ‖ Prices are *looking* (=going) ***up***. 物価が立直ってきた.【類】Business is *looking* ***up***. / Things are *look-ing* ***up***. ‖ *look* ***up*** to a person as a head 人を頭領と仰ぐ.【類】The United States is always *looked* ***up*** to as the Patriarch of the Americas. ‖ *Look* him ***up*** in "Who's Who." あの人を紳士録で調べて御覧. ‖ *look* it ***up*** in the dictionary それを辞書で調べる ‖ *look* ***up*** numbers in the telephone book (=directory) 電話帳で番号を調べる ‖ I'm *looking* ***up*** jobs in the want ads. 求人広告で職を捜してるのさ. ¶*look* a person ***up*** and ***down*** 人を上から下までじろじろ見る.

P I went out to *look* ***about*** me. 私はあたりの様子を見に出掛けた. ¶It is not a good sign when men *look* so much ***above*** themselves for a wife. 男が妻をもらうのに自分より上を見過ぎるのは感心したことではない. ¶The window *looks* ***across*** the garden seawards. 窓は庭越に海の見晴しがある. ¶*look* ***after*** visitor's luggage 客の荷物を世話する ‖ He *looks* ***after*** my business. 彼が私の仕事を(代って)やる. ‖ *look* ***after*** sheep 羊の番をする. ‖ Please *look* ***after*** him on arrival. 着いたら彼をよろしく頼む. ‖ *look* ***after*** the interests of ... …の利権を守る ‖ *look* ***after*** the affairs of ... …の件を引受ける ‖ The police *look* ***after*** all breaches of the peace. 警察では一切の治安妨害を監視する.【類】He *looks* ***after*** my home and children while I'm away. ¶He *looked* ***at*** me piercingly. 彼は私を鋭く見詰めた. ‖ He *looked* ***at*** me with a strong glare. 彼は私をきっとねめつけた. ‖ *look* ***at*** it in its true light (=proper aspect) それの正しい見方をする ‖ on *looking* ***at*** the illustration it will be observed that ... そのさし絵を見ると…ということが分かるでしょう ‖ *looked* ***at*** through the dim vista of six centuries 六百年のおぼろげな歳月を通覧する.【類】The doctor *looked* ***at*** the tongue. / *look* ***at*** the clock to see what time it is / *look* ***at*** each other anxiously / She is pretty to *look* ***at***. / *Look* ***at*** this matter seriously. / *look* ***at*** the world with an Eastern eye / I *looked* ***at*** the watch, and soliloquized on the length of night (夜長をかこった). / *look* only ***at*** the surface of ... / *looked* ***at*** from this point of view / But if we *look* ***at*** the matter from a wider standpoint, our conclusion must be very different. / *look* ***at*** the problem more broadly / As a physician I *look* ***at*** the situation in another way. / *look* ***at*** everything in a pessimistic (optimistic) light / *look* ***at*** a person incredulously (懐疑的に) ‖ so *looked* ***at*** その角度から見て. ¶He *looked* aimlessly ***before*** him. 彼は前途をあてどもなくながめた. ¶*look* ***behind*** one 後を振向く. ¶*look* ***below*** the surface 皮相でない観察をする. ‖ *Look* ***below*** you! 下を見よ(上を見れば限りがない). ¶*look* ***beyond*** the narrow horizon of the present 現在というせまい範囲を越えて見る ‖ *look* ***beyond*** the grave あの世のことを考える. ¶*look* ***down*** the well 井戸をのぞく. ¶He trudged on the streets *looking* in vain ***for*** employment. ‖ He was wrong to *look* ***for*** fruit from a tree that only bore flowers. 彼が花しか咲かない木から果実を求めようとするのは間違いだった. ‖ One has not to (=need not) *look* very far ***for*** an answer. その問題の解決は手近にある. ‖ *Look* ***for*** my spectacles. 僕の眼鏡を捜してくれ. ‖ *look* with interest ***for*** the arrival of ... …の到着を今か今かと待つ.【類】*look* ***for*** a job / *look* ***for*** no recompense (報酬) / *Look* ***for*** it on your favorite newsstand. / *look* ***for*** a great victory / I don't *look* ***for*** much profit from the business. / Otherwise only very moderate results may be *looked* ***for***. ¶*looked* ***from*** this point of view この見地から言うと ‖ *look* ***from*** the window into the neighbor's garden 窓からお隣の庭を見おろす. ¶*look* ***in*** a dictionary 辞書を引く ‖ *Look* ***in*** a mirror=*Look* at yourself in the mirror. 鏡をご覧. ‖ *look* ***in*** one's bureau drawers たんすの引出を捜す ‖ *look* a person ***in*** the face 人の顔をじっ見る ‖ *look* ***in*** one's eyes その目を見入る.【類】*look* people frankly (率直に) ***in*** the eye ‖ *look* ***in*** that direction その方向を見る ‖ Don't *look* a gift horse ***in*** the mouth. もらいもののあらを捜すな(馬の口を見ると年齢が分かることから). ‖ *look* ***into*** the face 顔をのぞき込む ‖ I will certainly *look* ***into*** that right away. よろしゅうございます早速そのことを調べて見ます. ‖ *look* ***into*** one's antecedents その経歴を調べる ‖ *look* ***in[to]*** a hand-mirror 手鏡をのぞく ‖ *look* ***into*** a room へやをのぞく.【類】*look* ***into*** a shop windows / *look* ***into*** darkness 暗がりをすかして見る ‖ *look* ***into*** the past history of patients 患者の病歴を

調べる ‖ *look* ***into*** newspapers and magazines 新聞や雑誌に目を通す ‖ *look* ***into*** a school and see pupils at work 学校を参観して生徒の勉強振りを見る. 【類】*look* ***into*** the matter at the first opportunity (できるだけ早い機会に) / Let us *look* ***into*** this point. / He promised to *look* ***into*** it as soon as he could. ‖ *look* ***into*** the square [窓から]広場をのぞく ‖ *look* ***into*** the street 通りをながめる ‖ *look* up ***into*** one's face その顔を見上げてじろじろ見る. 【類】*look* down ***into*** one's face ‖ *look* ***into*** the future 将来を見通す. 【類】*looking* ***into*** the future I can see ... ¶It *looks* ***like*** rain. 雨が降りそうだ. ¶The city *looked* ***like*** a dream coming true. その市は夢が実現したもののように見える. 【類】He *looks* ***like*** a soldier. / *look* ***like*** new ‖ Some pansies (三色すみれ) *look* ***like*** faces. ¶*look* ***off*** one's book 書物から目をそらす. ¶a house looking ***on*** the street 通りに面した家. 【類】a cottage *looking* ***on*** the sea (lake, park). ‖ He always *looks* ***on*** the surface of things. 彼は万事物ごとの表面を見る(皮相な観察をする). ‖ *look* ***on*** your map of Japan ***for*** ... 日本地図を見て...を捜して見給え. 【類】*Look* ***on*** the map of Netherlands and you will see many names ending in "trecht" or "tricht," which is the local corruption of the old Latin "trajectum," or ford (浅瀬). ‖ *look* ***on*** the bright (dark) side of things 物の光明(暗黒)の方面を見る, 楽(悲)観する ‖ They *look* ***on*** it askance. 彼らはそれをいぶかしげに見る. ‖ I *look* ***on*** (=consider) that as useless. それを役に立たないと思う. ‖ *look* ***on*** a diploma as a passport or certificate necessary to get a "job" 卒業証書を就職に必要な旅券すなわち証明書と見なす ‖ *look* ***on*** ... aghast ぼう然として...をながめる. 【類】The New York Times *looks* ***on*** a lost subscriber as a lost friend. ‖ *look* ***on*** a person with favor 好意をもって人を見る. 【類】We always like to know why the subscription was discontinued. / *look* ***on*** ... with suspicion / *look* with interest ***on*** ... ‖ *Look* ***on*** the reverse side of this jacket. この本のカバーの裏面を見よ. ¶*look* ***out of*** the window 窓の外を見る ‖ *look* ***out of*** the corner of one's eye 横目を使う. ¶The children were sitting at the table *looking* ***over*** their lessons for the morrow. 子供たちは机に向ってあくる日の学課を調べていた. ‖ *look* ***over*** a list 表に目を通す. 【類】*look* ***over*** an account (計算書) / *look* ***over*** the examination papers (試験の答案) ‖ She *looked* ***over*** her spectacles. 彼女は眼鏡越しに見た. ‖ *look* ***over*** one's shoulder 人の肩越しに見る ‖ *look* ***over*** one's faults その過失を看過する. ¶*look* ***through*** the window down ***into*** the street 窓から通りを見降ろす ‖ *look* ***through*** a book 本を通読する ‖ *look* ***through*** the key-hole かぎ穴からのぞく ‖ *look* ***through*** a telescope 望遠鏡で見る ‖ He *looked* in ***through*** a crack on the wall. 彼は壁のすき間から中をのぞいた. ‖ The world is too wise and it can *look* ***through*** any of your cheap tricks. 世間は利口だから君のちゃちな計略は何でも見破ってしまう. ¶The house *looks* ***to*** the south. その家は南向だ. 【類】a window *looking* ***to*** the west ‖ *look* [***to***] right and left 右や左に目を配る ‖ *look* (=see) ***to*** it that ... ...するように心掛ける ‖ These circumstances *look* ***to*** an alliance. こういう事情のため同盟成立の気運に向っている. ‖ rouse the careless householder to *look* ***to*** his fastenings 戸締りの悪い居住者を起して戸締りをするように注意する ‖ *look* ***to*** the water-bottles to see that they do not leak 漏らないかどうか水筒を調べて見る ‖ Let me *look* ***to*** that. 考えて見よう. ‖ *look* ***to*** the face まともに見る ‖ *look* ***to*** one's own safety 自己の安全に注意する ‖ *look* ***to*** (=expect) him for help (assistance, advice, a loan of money) 彼の援助(など)を期待する ‖ men ***to*** whom we *look* for leadership (guidance) われわれが首領と仰ぐ人たち. ¶stand *looking* ***towards*** ... ...の方に向って立つ ‖ *look* ***toward*** the east 東の方を見る ‖ The photograph is *looking* ***towards*** the Pacific. この写真は太平洋に向っているようにとったものだ. ¶*look* ***upon*** (=regard) ... as ... ...を...と見なす ‖ The kind employers do not *look* ***upon*** their employees merely as so many machines. 親切な雇主はその雇人を皆機械だという風には見なさない. ‖ The programme must not be ***looked upon*** as cast iron. その計画は動きのとれないものと考えてはならない(多少変更がきく). ‖ they *look* ***upon*** it as their task to ... 彼らは...するのを彼らの仕事だと考えている. 【類】They *looked* ***upon*** him as a father. / I *look* ***upon*** ... as my second home. / They *look* ***upon*** me as their inferior. / Pasteur is *looked* ***upon*** as one of the greatest benefators of humanity. / he is *looked* ***upon*** as unneighbourly by ... ‖ *look* ***upon*** oneself as ... ...と自任する ‖ *look* ***upon*** the face of ... ...の顔を見る ‖ Her countenance when smiling is not most delightful to *look* ***upon***. 彼女の笑顔はそうよくはない. ‖ The house *looks* ***upon*** the river (lake, sea). その家は川(など)に臨んでいる. ¶*look* ***with*** pity (amusement) ***at*** ... 同情(興味)をもって...を見る. 【類】*look* ***with*** scorn (suspicion) ***upon*** ... / *look* ***with*** considerable suspicion ***upon*** ... ‖ The Hindus *look* ***with*** horror ***upon*** the meat-eater, that makes his body a grave for the corpses of animals. インド人は肉食者は自分の身体を動物の死体を葬る墓にするものだとしてこれをこわがっている.

looking-glass, *n.* 鏡, 姿見.

V ***confront*** a *looking-glass* 姿見に向う.

lookout, *n.* 警戒.

V ***give*** a good *lookout* for ... ...を十分用心する. ¶I'll ***keep*** a *lookout* over myself in future. 今後は気を付けます.

Q keep a ***proper*** *lookout* しかるべく警戒する. ¶take (=keep) a ***sharp*** *lookout* for ... ...を厳重に警戒する.

P I will telephone you when to expect me.—Very good; I'll be ***on*** the *lookout* for you. 「いつお伺いするか電話で申上げましょう」「よろしい, それではお待ちしております」. ‖ He is always ***on*** the *lookout* for young capable men. 彼はいつも若くって役に立つ人を捜している.

loom, *n.* 織機.

Q² a ***hand*** *loom* 手織機. ¶a ***linen*** *loom* リネン織機. ¶a ***power*** loom 機械織機. 「機織仕事をして.

P weave ***at*** one's *loom* 機を織る. ¶at work ***on*** the *loom*

loom, *v.* ぼんやり見える, ぼーっと浮き出る.

M fears (worries, cares) *looming* ***ahead*** 前途に横わる心配(など). ¶Outstanding office buildings and sky-scrapers *loom* ***conspicuously*** in the sky-line. 高壮な事務所用建物や摩天楼が目ざましく空に浮かぶ. ¶The clock tower *loomed* ***large*** in the fog. 時計台が霧で大きく見えた.

M² All these questions and others are *looming* ***up*** more or less distinctly for settlement. (世人の注意を呼び起す度合には)それぞれ差はあってもこれらの問題やその他多くの問題が明らかに解決を求めている. ‖ A ship *loomed* ***up*** in the distance. 遠くに船がぼんやり見えた.

P They looked up at the black mountain that *loomed* ***above*** them. 彼らは頭上ほのかに浮かび出ている黒い山を見上げた. ¶*loom* ***in*** sight ぼんやり見える. ¶*loom* ***on*** the scene その場面に現われる. ¶*loom* ***out of*** ... ...から除々に現われる. ¶a steeple that *looms* ***through*** the mist (clouds) もや(など)の中からぼーっと見えるせん塔.

loop, *n.* 宙返り飛行.

V The airman "***looped*** the *loop*." その飛行士が宙返りをした. ¶***turn*** *loops* 宙返りをする.

loophole, *n.* 抜け穴.

Q² plug a ***tax*** *loophole* 脱税の抜け穴をふさぐ.

loose, *n.* 解放, 放任.

V ***give*** a *loose* to one's fancy 想像をほしいままにする.

P Her husband is ***on*** the *loose*. 彼女の亭主は不身持だ.

loose, *a.* ゆるい.

P I am *loose* ***in*** the bowels. 私は下痢している.

O let *loose* one's anger かんしゃく玉を破裂させる. ¶A boat broke *loose* and shot down the stream. ボートはとも綱がとけて矢のように下った.

looseness, *n.* ゆるみ.

Q ***sexual*** *looseness* いんとう.

P² *looseness* ***of*** the bowels 下痢.

loosing, *n.* 解くこと.

Q a ***liberal*** *loosing* of the purse-strings 気前よく財布のひもをゆるめること.

loot, *n.* 盗品.

P The burglar ran out of the house ***with*** his *loot*. 盗賊は盗品を持ってその家から逃出した.

lop, *v.* 切り取る.

M² *lop* ***off*** a bough 枝を切取る. 【類】*lop* ***off*** some little branches from the vine to make it grow better and bear more fruit ‖ Our colonial possessions have been *lopped* ***off***. わが国は植民地を失った.

lord, *n.* 領主; 神; 亭主.

V *Lord knows.* 神ぞ知る.

Q the **feudal** *lord* of the clan その藩主. ¶my [**noble**] *lord* 御前様. ¶the **outside** *lord* 外様(ﾄｻﾏ). ¶**pampered** *lords* わがままなとの様. ¶a very **wicked** *lord* 非常に悪いとの様.

Q^2 a **liege** (=sovereign) *lord* 君主, 藩主. ¶battlegrounds of **war** *lords* 群雄の戦場. 【類】people liberated from their **war** *lords*.

P live **like** a *lord* 王侯の暮しをする.

P^2 the *lord* **of** her bosom 彼女の大事なだんな様(夫).

lord, *v.* 威張る, わが物顔をする.

P *lord* it **over** ... …君臨する. 【類】The whites *lord* it **over** the natives.

lore, *n.* 学問; 伝説集.

Q wise in **antiquarian** *lore* 古代の学問に通じた. ¶Hakui and Shukusei, the loyal brothers of **Chinese** *lore* 伯夷・叔斉すなわち中国の書物に伝わる忠義な兄弟. ¶"Notes and Queries" is a store-house of **curious** *lore*.「ノーツ・アンド・クィーリーズ」(英国の質疑応答雑誌)は興味深い知識の宝庫である. ¶**fascinating traditional** *lore* きわめて興味ある伝説. ¶a vast collection of **human** *lore* 人間知識の一大集成. ¶a display of **literary** *lore* 伝承文学の展示. ¶delve patiently into the **quaint** and **curious** *lore* of the past 過去の変り種の珍しい伝説を根気よく調べる.

Q^2 **mountain** *lore* 山に関する伝承的知識. ¶a **nursery** *lore* おとぎ話. ¶a study of **proverb** *lore* 民間伝承のことわざの研究.

lorry, *n.* トロッコ; 《英》トラック.

Q^2 a **motor** *lorry*=a truck 《英》トラック.

P a train **of** *lorries* トロッコ連結車.

lose, *v.* 失う, 損する, 負ける.

M *lose* oneself **easily** in a maze of platforms ホームの迷路でよく戸まどいする. ¶*lose* a battle **heavily** 戦いに大敗する. ¶It is **irretrievably** (=**irrevocably**) *lost*. 取返しがつかない. ¶I've **just** *lost* his name. 彼の名をちょっと忘れた. ¶He **nearly** *lost* his eyesight. 彼はほとんど失明した. ¶*lose* **out** a game 勝負に負ける ‖ be *lost* **out** in consumption 肺病でひどく衰弱する. ¶The captain was *lost* **overboard.** 船長は海中に姿を没した. ¶the art of ... is **practically** *lost* …の技術はほとんど滅びている. ¶**rarely** *lose* by comparison with ... …に比べて見劣りすることはめったにない. ¶Such a treasure one will not **willingly** *lose*. こうした宝は失って喜ぶものはない.

P The crow was *lost* **among** the trees. からすは林の中に姿を消した. ¶The ship was *lost* (=wrecked) **at** sea. その船は海上で遭難した. ¶He was *lost* **before** God. 彼は神から見離されていた. ¶He *lost* **by** 800 votes. 彼は八百票の差で敗れた. ‖ He *lost* her **by** death. 彼は彼女に死別れた. ‖ I hear that he is *losing* **by** his business. 聞く所によると彼は商売で損をしているようだ. ¶He was recently *lost* **for** four days in dense woods. 彼は最近密林中で四日間ゆくえ不明であった. ¶A few books have been *lost* **from** the library. 数冊の本が書庫から紛失した. ¶be *lost* **in** the darkness 暗がりに見えなくなる ‖ The lad was *lost* **in** the crowd. その若者は人ごみの中にまぎれ込んだ. ‖ be *lost* **in** the woods 森の中で道に迷う ‖ The original of the Olympic games was *lost* **in** [the mists of] antiquity. オリンピックゲームの起原はぼうばくとして知る由もない. 【類】The mysterious Gipsies, whose origin is *lost* **in** antiquity, have penetrated even into Mongolia. / Its origin is lost **in** [the twilight of] obscurity. ‖ He was *lost* **in** deep thought for a few minutes. 彼は二三分間思案に暮れていた. ‖ *lost* **in** ecstasy うっとりとして ‖ *lost* **in** silent meditation めい想にふけって. 【類】He was *lost* **in** this delicious reverie (=brown study) (快い空想). ‖ he stood *lost* **in** wonder at ... 彼は…を考えぼう然として立っていた.【類】*lost* **in** astonishment / quite *lost* **in** admiration / We were so *lost* **in** each other that we forgot the passing of the time. ‖ *lose* **in** beauty 美しさを失う. 【類】it *loses* **in** ... but gains in ... ‖ The country *lost* over 150,000 **in** killed and wounded. その国は死傷者十五万を出した. ‖ *lose* **in** a contest (competition, battle, game) 勝負(など)に負ける. ¶The advice was *lost* **on** them. その忠言も彼らには何の効もなかった. ‖ this fact is not *lost* **on** ... …がこれを知らない訳ではない ‖ *lose* something **on** the ball 球威を失う. ¶the money he had *lost* **over** the transaction 彼がその取引で損をした金 ‖ *lose* one's head **over** a woman ある女に迷う. ¶The ship was speedily *lost* **to** view. (出港する)船がみるみる消えて行った. ‖ women who have become *lost* **to** all considerations of decency 全然女のたしなみのない女性 ‖ Another genius *lost* **to** the world, and all through a woman. また一人の天才がこの世から失われた, しかも全く一女性のために. ‖ be *lost* **to** history 知る由もない, 伝わらない. 【類】The art was *lost* **to** the world forever. ‖ This masterpiece of art has been *lost* **to** the nation. その美術の名品はその国になくなった(外人に買われなどして). ‖ *lost* **to** shame 恥を知らない. 【類】*lost* **to** virtue ‖ He is *lost* **to** all sense of propriety. 彼には礼儀作法という観念が全然ない. ‖ Though *lost* **to** sight, to memory dear. もう見ることはできないがなつかしい. ¶This lesson has not been *lost* **upon** him. この(にがい)経験に彼はこりた. ‖ The joke was *lost* **upon** the audience. そのしゃれは聴衆には分からなかった. ¶It is said **with** Francis Thompson we *lost* the greatest poetic energy since Browning. フランシス・トムスンの死によってブラウニング以後最大の詩人を失ったと言われる.

O give a person up for *lost* 死んだものとあきらめる. ¶The program has *lost* its interest. その番組はおもしろくなくなった.

loser, *n.* 損失者, 失敗者.

Q a **bad** (**good**) *loser* きたない(きれいな)負け方をする人. 【類】Everybody respects a **good** *loser*. ¶the **heaviest** *losers* by the storm その暴風で一番損害を受けたもの. ¶a **sure** *loser* 必ず失敗する者.

Q^2 A bargain hunter is a **money** *loser*. 安物買の銭失い.

P^2 a *loser* **at** bridge-whist 〖トランプ〗ブリッジ遊びで負けた者. ¶China will be a *loser* **by** his death. 中国は彼の死によって損失をこうむるだろう.

loss, *n.* 損失, 損害; 死亡, 喪失.

V **balance up** a *loss* 損失を埋合わす. ¶**bear** a *loss* 損害賠償をする. ¶**cause** a big *loss* [結果は]大損失となる. 【類】The volcanic eruption **caused** enormous *losses*. ¶The *loss* caused by the fire was amply **covered** by insurance. その火災による損害は保険金で十分償えた. ¶**cover up** a *loss* 損害を埋合わせる. ¶**deplore** his *loss* 彼の死をいたむ. ¶**entail** a heavy *loss* 大損害となる. ¶it is impossible to **estimate** the *loss* to the nation arising from ... …から生じる国家の損失はこれを見積ることが不可能である. ¶**extenuate** his *losses* 彼の損失を軽減する. ¶**face** a temporary *loss* 一時の損失をおかしてやる. ¶she cannot **get over** the *loss* of ... 彼女は…の死をあきらめかねている. ¶**incur** a great *loss* of life and property 生命財産に大損失をきたす. ¶**inflict** great *losses* on the enemy 敵軍に大損害をこうむらせる. ¶It **involves** a serious financial *loss*. それは財政上の大損失になる. ¶the venture **leaves** a *loss* (profit) of ... その事業は…の損失(利益)になる. ¶**make** a *loss* 損をする. ¶**make good** all *losses* 損害を全部弁償する. ¶**make up** [for] a *loss* 損害を埋合わせる. ¶It **means** *loss* to sell for that much. そんな値で売っては損が立つ. ¶It **means** an irreparable *loss* of prestige. そうすると取返しのつかない威信の毀損となる. ¶He leaves a wife and four children to **mourn** his *loss*. 彼は妻と四人の子供を後に残して(最近)死んだ. ¶The gain hardly **offset** the *loss*. 利益はほとんど損失を償うに足らなかった. ¶**prevent** the *loss* of morale in a fighting force 士気のくじけるのを防ぐ. ¶**recompense** (=**indemnify**) a *loss* 損害を賠償する. ¶In trying to **recoup** (=compensate for) the *losses* he made still more unfortunate investments. 彼は損失の埋合わせをしようとしてさらに不運な投資をした. 【類】with the hope of **recouping** his previous *losses*. ¶**recover** the *loss* 損失を埋合わせる. ¶**repair** a *loss* 損を償う. ¶It would not be so easy to **replace** to our company the *loss* of so sweet a member of it. われわれの仲間から言うと実に良い一会員を失った訳でその後がまに据える人を得ることはちとむずかしかろう. ¶**restore** one's *loss* 損失を償う. ¶try to **retrieve** their previous *losses* in gambling (business) ばくち(など)でこうむった前の損失を取り返そうとする. ¶I can not sub-contract without **showing** a *loss* of ... …の損失を明かにして始めて下請負いができます. ¶**split** the *loss* (profit) with ... 損失(利益)は…と折半する. ¶**sow** *loss* and reap gain 損をして得を取る. ¶**stand** a *loss* 損害にたえる. 【類】**stand** any *loss* which may occur through ... ¶**suffer** great *losses* 大損害を受ける ‖ He has just **suffered** an irreparable *loss* in the sudden death of his brother. 彼はその兄の突然の死で取返しのつかない損失をこうむったばかりの所だ. 【類】Russia lost a fine battleship, but she **suffered** a heavier *loss* in the death of a man who seemed to make her fleet a real factor in the struggle. / The expedition has ***suffered*** no *loss* of life. / He ***suffered*** the *loss* of his only child. ¶***sustain*** great *losses* 大損害を受ける.【類】the world of letters (文壇) ***sustained*** a painful *loss* by the death of ... ¶***turn loss*** into gain 欠損を転じて利益にする.

Q We are now running at an ***actual loss.*** 今の所われわれの商売は現に欠損だ. ¶the ***appalling loss*** of life and property 生命財産の驚くべき損失. ¶It is ***China's loss.*** それは中国の損になる. ¶***complete loss*** of intellect 白痴状態. ¶a ***dead loss*** [埋合わせのつかない]丸損. ¶show ***decided loss*** in vigor まるっきり元気がない. ¶a ***distinct loss*** to art 芸術にとって明白な損失. ¶The business is carried on at an ***enormous loss.*** 大犠牲を払って商売を続ける. ‖ ***enormous loss*** of life and property 生命財産の大損失. ¶What is the ***estimated loss?*** 損害の概算はどの位ですか. ¶a ***financial loss*** 財政上の損失.【類】a store that runs at a great ***financial loss*** / It will prove a great ***financial loss.*** ¶a ***frightful loss*** of life in war 戦争における人命の恐るべき損失. ¶sell promptly to avoid ***further loss*** この上の損害を避けるため直ちに売却する. ¶a ***grave national loss*** 国家の大損失. ¶***great loss*** of life and destruction of property 生命の大損失と財産の破壊.【類】His death is a ***great loss*** to the country. ¶a ***grievous*** and ***irreparable loss*** to the cause of labor and freedom 労働者と自由のために痛ましい取返しのつかない損失. ¶His death inflicts a ***heavy loss*** on his country. 彼の死は自国に大損失を与える. ¶this means ***heavy losses*** to ... これは...にとって結局大損害になる.【類】Many have suffered ***heavy losses,*** and some even bankruptcy (破産). ¶run a paper at a ***heavy annual loss*** 年々大欠損をして新聞を経営する. ¶***industrial losses*** 産業上の損失. ¶an ***irredeemable loss*** 償い得ない損失. ¶the educational world sustained an ***irreparable loss*** in the death of ... 教育界は...の死で取返しのつかない損失をこうむった. ¶with the ***least loss*** of time できるだけ早く. ¶***material loss*** 物質的損失. ¶find oneself at a ***momentary loss*** for words ちょっとうまい言葉が出て来ない. ¶His death is regarded as a ***national loss.*** 彼の死は国家の損失と見られている. ¶an ***overwhelming loss*** [取返しのつかない]大損失. ¶a ***partial (total) loss*** 部分的(完全)な損失. ¶***pecuniary loss*** 金銭上の損失.【類】entail no ***pecuniary loss*** on ... ¶a ***real loss*** to the nation 国にとて真の損失. ¶a ***ruinous loss*** 途方もない損失. ¶They suffered a ***sad loss*** through the death of their fifth son. お気の毒なことに五男がなくなられた. ¶a ***severe loss*** to the industry その工業にとっての一大損失. ¶a ***small loss*** 小さな損失. ¶***stupendous losses*** 巨大な損失. ¶many deaths and ***terrible loss*** of property 多数の死と財産の驚くべき損失. ¶a ***total loss*** 全損. ¶a ***tremendous loss*** of lives 非常に多数の人命の損失. ¶a ***trifling loss*** 軽微な損失.

Q² ***crop losses*** were put at ... 作物の損失は...と見積られていた. ¶***fire loss***=loss by fire 火災による損失.【類】The ***fire loss*** will be paid by the insurance company. ¶try to shun the ***future loss*** 将来の損失を避けようとする. ¶The country suffered terrible ***manpower losses*** during the war. 同国は戦争でおびただしい人的損害をこうむった. ¶***money losses*** 金銭上の損失. ¶***property loss*** is estimated at ... 財産の損失は...と概算されている. ¶***revenue loss*** 収入の減少. ¶***soil*** and ***crop losses*** from floods 洪水による土壌と作物の損失. ¶***strike losses*** ストによる損失. ¶***war [time] losses*** 戦争による損失.【類】recoup (弁償する) ***wartime losses.*** ¶eliminate ***waste losses*** むだを省く. ¶These strikes affected 5,000,000 workers and caused ***1.6 per cent loss*** of working time in all industries. これらのストに五百万の労働者が参加し全産業で 1.6 パーセントの労働時間の損失となった.

P I am ***at*** a *loss* what to do. 私はどうすればよいのか当惑している. ‖ I found myself ***at*** a *loss* for words of consolation. 慰る言葉もなかった.【類】He was ***at*** a *loss* what to say. / He was ***at*** a *loss* for a suitable reply (=a proper answer). / One is ***at*** a *loss* to suggest a possible improvement. ‖ through grief ***at*** the *loss* of his son 息子の死を悲しむ余り ‖ sell ***at*** a *loss* 損をして売る ‖ That would be selling ***at*** a *loss.* その値では損が立つ.【類】It can only sell ***at*** a *loss.* / run a factory ***at*** a *loss* / The operations (事業) have been carried on ***at*** a *loss.* ¶It was attended ***by*** considerable *loss* of life. それは大分人死にがあった. ¶He was for a long time inconsolable ***for*** the *loss* of his wife. 彼は妻に死なれて久しく意気消沈していた. ¶It resulted ***in*** a *loss.* それは結局損になった. ‖ The company suffered a succession ***of*** *losses.* その会社は赤字続きだった. ¶deterioration ***through*** *loss* of function 機能喪失による退化. ¶The enemy was routed ***with*** heavy *loss.* 敵は大損害をこうむって敗走した. ‖ The business is conducted ***with*** an enormous *loss.* その事業は大欠損をして経営されている.【類】His army was utterly routed, ***with*** a *loss* of from 15,000 to 20,000 men. / They were defeated ***with*** great *loss.* / be repulsed ***with*** great *loss* / ***with*** the *loss* of ... lives / Luckily I got off ***with*** a small *loss.* / ***with*** the *loss* of three killed and seven wounded. ¶It is desirable to consult a doctor ***without*** *loss* of time. 早速医者に見てもらう方がよい. ‖ He knows how to be vivacious ***without*** *loss* of dignity. 彼は威厳を失わないで陽気になれる術を心得ている.【類】***without*** *loss* of life / ***without*** the *loss* of a single life.

P² The town suffered serious *losses* ***from*** the floods. その町は洪水で大損害を受けた. ¶*losses* ***in*** business 商売の損失 ‖ there is a *loss* ***in*** weight of ... ...の目減りがある. ¶The ship was wrecked with great *loss* ***of*** life. 同船は難破して多数の死者を出した. ‖ *Loss* ***of*** health is worse than *loss* ***of*** wealth. 健康の損失は富の損失より悪い. ¶with *loss* ***on*** cost 元値を切って ‖ the *loss* ***on*** the building is expected to be ... その建物の損害は...の見込. ¶His death is a *loss* ***to*** the cause of international understanding and good will. 彼の死は国際間の理解と親善のために惜しむべきことだ.【類】a *loss* ***to*** the nation / *losses* ***to*** literature / His absence (不出場) is a great *loss* ***to*** the team. ¶incur *loss* ***upon*** loss 損失に損失を重ねる.

lot, *n.* (**1**) 運命,(生活)状態.

V people who ***bear*** their hard *lot* so well よく不運にたえる人々. ¶to ***better*** one's *lot* 運命を開拓するために.【類】try to ***better*** their *lot* in life / ***better*** the *lot* of labor (労働者). ¶Their cruel *lot* is thus greatly ***brightened*** by science. かくして彼らの悲惨な運命が科学によって大いに明るくなる. ¶***cast*** (=***throw***) ***in*** one's *lot* with ... ...と運命をともにする. ¶She ***endures*** her *lot* with patience. 彼女は辛抱強く自己の運命にたえる. ¶***improve*** one's *lot* 運命を開拓する.【類】a method of ***improving*** the *lot* of the working men. ¶***join*** their *lot* with ... ...と運命をともにする. ¶instigate them to ***throw*** their *lot* with us in this war 彼らをそそのかしてこの戦争にわれわれと運命をともにさせる ‖ The two companies have ***thrown*** their *lots* together. その二会社は合併した.

Q an ***enviable lot*** 結構な身分. ¶a ***hard lot*** 辛い運命. ¶It is ***man's lot*** to suffer. 苦しむのは人の運命だ. ¶Husbands are a ***sorry lot.*** 亭主族はつらい.

P It fell ***to*** my *lot* to take Miss ... in to dinner. 私が思いがけなく...嬢を食堂に案内することになった.【類】Great happiness fell ***to*** his *lot.* ¶happy ***with*** their *lot* 彼らの運命に満足して.

(**2**) くじ.

V ***draw*** (=***cast***) ***lots*** for ... ...のためにくじを引く ‖ ***draw lots*** to see who will ... だれが...するかをきめるためにくじを引く.【類】***draw lots*** for turns (順番をきめるために). / ***draw lots*** for choice (選択) / ***draw lots*** for military service (入営) ‖ ***draw*** a bad *lot* 貧乏くじを引く.

V² The *lot* ***fell*** on (=upon) me. くじに当った.

P ***by*** *lot*=by the drawing of lots 抽せんで ‖ distribute (decide) ***by*** *lot* 抽せんで分け(決定す)る.【類】It is to be previously determined ***by*** *lot.* / be chosen ***by*** *lot.*

(**3**) 地所;《米》『映』スタジオ.

Q a ***built-over lot*** 家屋のある敷地. ¶a ***vacant lot*** 空地.

Q² ***building lots*** in good position 場所の良い敷地 ‖ ***building lots*** to let 貸地 ‖ assign a ***building lot*** to each settler [建物の]敷地を各居住人に割当てる. ¶Families are clearing the wreckage fom their ***home lots*** to scratch vegetable gardens. 各家族は自分たちの屋敷をならして野菜畑に換えようと破壊物を片づけている. ¶a ***house lot*** 宅地. ¶an underground ***parking lot*** 地下の自動車置場.【類】She went to the cottage, cutting across the ***parking lot,*** the shortest way over there. ¶a ***studio lot*** 《米》映画撮影所.

P He found me a job ***on*** the Paramount (M-G-M) *lot.*

彼は私のためにパラマウント(など)撮影所に仕事を見付けて
(4) 一口;[商品の]一組, 一山. └くれた.
Q *another lot* 別口. ¶I cannot possibly ship the ***whole*** *lot* by the first steamer. 今度の船便では到底商品全部を発送することはできない.
Q² supply vegetables in ***carload*** *lots* 野菜を貨車定量に分けて供給する. ¶Cattle are being fatten in ***feeding*** *lots* for market. 食用牛を市場向けに特設牧場で太らせる. ¶***job*** *lot* 込売(買)品. ¶Special prices on ***quantity*** *lots*. 大口買入れは特別に安くします. ¶buy food in ***wholesale*** *lots* 食料を卸し値で買う.
P sell ***by*** *lots* 口をわけて売る. ¶How much ***for*** the *lot?* その口は皆でいくらだ. ¶***in*** a *lot* 一まとめにして,一括して ‖ ship goods ***in*** *lots* 商品を(一括でなく)分送する ‖ They were offered (=put up) all ***in*** one *lot* and sold. それは全部一口として提供されそして売却された. ‖ Such an expenditure ***in*** one *lot* will affect the safety of living. 一遍にそんな金を出しては生活に響いて来る. ¶divide ***into*** small *lots* 小口に分ける.
P² This *lot* ***of*** oranges is not so good as the last. この口のオレンジは前のほどおいしくない.
(5) 沢山.
Q an ***awful*** *lot* of trouble 大へんな苦労. ¶My daughter's piano lessons cost a ***fearful*** *lot*. 娘のピアノのけいこはえらく金がかかる. ¶He had a ***vast*** *lot* of adventures. 彼はあらゆる冒険をやった.
P² after a *lot* ***of*** thinking, I decided that ... よく考えてから...に決めた ‖ I have quite a *lot* ***of*** novels. 私は随分沢山の小説をもっている. 【類】I have a *lot* ***of*** letters to answer. / He has had a vast *lot* ***of*** adventures. ‖ We had *lots* ***of*** fun. 本当に愉快だった. 【類】I think it's quite a *lot* ***of*** fun to ... ‖ The store has a *lot* ***of*** trade. その店は繁盛している. ‖ There were *lots* ***of*** prospects around. 買いそうな客が沢山いた. ‖ You got a *lot* ***of*** nerve, huh? 相当な
(6) 一団, グループ. └心臓だね(図々しい).
Q a ***fine*** *lot* of companions 愉快な仲間. ¶a ***heartless*** *lot* └薄情な連中.

lot, *v.* 小口に分ける; 分割する.
M *lot* ***out*** [土地を]分割する, [品物を]区分する.

lottery, *n.* 富くじ, 福引.
V ***countenance*** a *lottery* 富くじを容認する. ¶***draw*** a *lottery* くじを引く. ¶a Chinese Government *Lottery* ***instituted*** for the purpose of raising funds for the development of civil aviation and construction of highways throughout China 民間飛行の発達と中国全土を通じて国道建設を目指し資金募集のために設定した中国政府の富くじ. ¶***run*** a *lottery* 富くじを起す. ¶***hold*** a *lottery* 福引をする.
V² The *lottery* ***took place***. 富くじが行われた.
Q² The article shows how the French ***State*** *lotteries* are worked. この記事を見ればフランス国営富くじのやり方が分かる.
P take a draw ***in*** a *lottery* 富くじを引く ‖ win a prize ***in*** a *lottery* 富くじに当る ‖ I'm lucky (unlucky) ***in*** *lottery*. 私はくじ運がいい(悪い).

loud, *a.* 声が大きい; はでな.
M Her dress is ***too*** *loud* for her age. 彼女の服装は年に似合わぬはでなものだ.
P people who are *loudest* ***against*** the reform その改革に最も強く反対する人々. ¶he is *loud* ***in*** his praise of ... 彼は口をきわめて...を賞める. 【類】*loud* ***in*** their praises of ... / he is *loud* ***in*** denouncing (非難する) / be *loud* ***in*** one's approval of ... ¶Don't be *loud* ***of*** voice in the public. 人中で大声を出すな.

loudspeaker, *n.* 拡声器.
V Wireless *loudspeakers* which are ***played*** too loud, too long, and too late, are a source of constant complaint to suffering neighbours. 声が余り大きかったり, 余り永く続いたり, また時刻が余りおそくなったりするのでラジオの拡声器使用に対しては近所のものから絶えず苦情が出る.
P announce it ***over*** the *loudspeaker* ラウドスピーカー(拡声器)でそれをアナウンスする.

lounge, *n.* 遊び場; 休けい室; 寝いす.
Q a ***favorite*** *lounge* of students 学生の好んで遊ぶ場所.
Q² We regard the theatre as something more than an ***after-dinner*** *lounge*. 劇場を食後の休憩室以上のものと見ている. ¶a ***cocktail*** *lounge* コクテル酒場のあるへや. ¶a ***sun*** *lounge* サンルーム.
P lie down ***on*** a *lounge* 寝いすに横たわる.

lounge, *v.* ぶらぶら歩く; ぐったりと横になる.
P *lounge* ***about*** streets 街をぶらつく. ¶*lounge* ***at*** their ease くつろぐ. ¶*lounge* ***into*** the station ゆうゆうと停車場にはいる. ¶*lounge* ***on*** a sofa ぐったりと長いすに横になる.

louse, *n.* しらみ.
V ***crush*** a *louse* with one's fingernail しらみをつぶす. ¶***have*** *lice* on the hair 髪にしらみがたかっている. ¶***remove*** *lice* from (=delouse) ... ...からしらみを駆除する.
Q² a ***plant*** *louse* 木じらみ.
P hair infested ***with*** *lice* しらみのたかっている髪.

love, *n.* 愛, 恋愛, 愛情; 愛人.
V ***acquire*** a scholarly *love* of learning 学問を学究的に愛するようになる. ¶***arouse*** *love* 愛情を起す. ¶***awaken*** in him a new *love* for the beauty of nature 彼に自然美に対する新たな愛を呼び起す. ¶***conceive*** *love* for ... ...を愛するようになる. ¶It ***cost*** me her *love*. それで私は彼女の愛を失った. ¶***declare*** one's *love* to ... ...に恋を打明ける. ¶My wife ***desires*** her kind *love* to you. 妻があなたによろしくと申しました. ‖ the beautiful youth whose *love* she ***desired*** 彼女がその愛を得たいと思いこがれた美ぼうの青年. ¶***develop*** in all classes of people a *love* for the beautiful in music, literature, and art あらゆる階級の人々に音楽・文学・美術の美に対する愛を啓発する. ¶***doubt*** his *love* for ... ...に対する彼の愛を疑う. ¶***earn*** his *love* 彼の愛をかち得る. ¶***encourage*** a *love* of animals 動物愛を助長する. ¶***feel*** no *love* for ... ...に少しも愛を感じない. ¶***forfeit*** (=lose) her *love* 彼女の愛を失う. ¶seek to ***gain*** her *love* 彼女の愛を得ようとする. ¶She ***gave*** her *love* from gratitude. 彼女は恩に感じてその愛を捧げた. ¶***Give*** my best *love* to your parents. くれぐれも御両親によろしく. ¶***gratify*** one's *love* of ancient art 古代美術の趣味を満足させる. ¶She ***has*** a great *love* for cats. 彼女はねこが大好きだ. ‖ He ***has*** much *love* for this child of old age. 彼はこの晩年の著作を大いに愛している. ¶A long absence of her love from the country ***healed*** her *love*. その愛人が長らく国を離れていたので彼女の恋は消えてしまった. ¶***inspire*** in his pupils a *love* for right conduct 生徒に正しい行為に対する愛を鼓吹する ‖ ***inspire*** a deeper *love* for one's country もっと深い祖国愛を鼓吹する. 【類】***inspire*** a *love* of study. ¶***lose*** her husband's *love* 夫の愛を失う. 【類】Darwin himself confessed and lamented that in the course of his scientific investigation he had altogether ***lost*** his *love* of poetry. ¶***make*** *love* with ... ...に思いを寄せる ‖ ***make*** *love* to a girl 女をくどく. ¶***reciprocate*** his *love* 彼の愛に報いる, 相愛する. ¶***renew*** one's *love* [一遍捨てた女との]よりを戻す. ¶His *love* was ***requited***. 彼の愛が報いられた. ¶***retain*** the *love* of one's husband in spite of his ill use つれなくされても夫に対する愛情を失わない. 【類】***retain*** her *love* for her former husband. ¶He did not ***return*** her *love*. 彼は彼女の愛に報いなかった. 【類】She ***returned*** his *love* passionately (熱烈に). ¶***receive*** his *love* 彼から愛される. ¶***sanctify*** and ***divinize*** sexual *love* 性愛を神聖化する. ¶***Say*** my *love* to Jack. [女性から]ジャックによろしく. ¶All ***send*** *love*. 皆からよろしく. ‖ He has ***sent*** *love* to all my family. 彼からみんなによろしくと言ってきた. ¶***show*** *love* 愛情を示す. ¶***win*** her *love* 彼女の愛を得る.
V² The old *love* ***blazed up*** anew. 昔の愛情が新たに燃えあがった. ¶*Love* ***grew up*** between them. 二人は恋仲になった.
Q conceive a ***burning*** *love* for ...に対し熱烈な慕情を抱く. ¶***chaste*** *love* 純潔な愛. ¶***conjugal*** *love* 夫婦愛. ¶***dawning*** *love* 次第に深まり行く恋. ¶His *love* for me was ***dead***. 私に対する彼の愛はなくなった. ¶stirred by a ***deep*** *love* for ... ...に対する深い恋心に動かされて. ¶***disappointed*** *love* 失恋. ¶***erotic*** *love* 性的愛. ¶***everlasting*** *love* いつまでも変らない愛情. ¶***fanatic[al]*** *love* of country 熱狂的な祖国愛. ¶He remained true to his ***first*** *love*. 彼は初恋を捨てなかった. ¶***filial*** *love* 親に対する子の愛. ¶His was no ***fleeting*** *love*. 彼のはすぐにさめるような恋ではなかった. ¶***free*** *love* 自由恋愛. ¶***guilty*** *love* 邪恋. ¶show a ***genuine*** *love* of literature 文学に純真な愛着を示す. ¶inspired by the ***genuine*** and ***enlightened*** *love* of one's country 祖国に対する純真なそして明達な愛に激励されて. ¶children with an ***inborn*** *love* of mischief 天性いたずらっぽくできている子供たち. ¶have an ***intense*** *love*

of music はなはだ音楽を好む. ¶***inverted*** *love* [同性愛など]倒錯した愛. ¶Light loves are not ***lasting*** *loves*. 浮いた愛は永く続く愛ではない. ¶his ***lost*** *love* 彼の亡くなった愛人. ¶***maternal*** *love* 母性愛. ¶from ***mere*** *love* of it 単にそれが好きだという理由から. ¶firmly united by ***mutual*** *love* 相愛で堅く結ばれた. ¶***onesided*** *love* 片思い. ¶his ***only*** *love* 彼の唯一の愛人. ¶***Parental*** *love* is deep and true. 親の愛は深く真実だ. ¶He had a most ***passionate*** *love* for flowers. 彼は花を非常に好んだ. ¶***physical*** *love* 色情. ¶***Platonic*** *love* 精神的恋愛, 純愛. ¶for the ***pure*** *love* of science 真実科学を愛するために. ¶noted for their ***quixotic*** *love* of adventure 空想的な冒険好きで有名な. ¶***reciprocal*** *love* 相思. ¶***reciprocated*** *love* 報いられた恋. ¶replace ***sensual*** *love* by the pure relationship of brother and sister 肉欲的な愛に代えるに純真な兄妹の関係をもってする. ¶***spiritual*** *love* 精神的恋愛. ¶his ***spurned*** *love* 彼をはねつけた彼の女. ¶her ***steadfast*** *love* for a faithless husband 不貞な夫に対する妻の変らぬ愛. ¶She is my ***sweetest*** *love*. 彼女は私の最も愛する愛人だ. ¶a *love* ***unabated*** by time or absence 時がたっても留守をしても衰えない愛. ¶He has an ***unconquerable*** *love* for liquor. 彼は酒を見ると我慢ができない. ¶***unfortunate*** *love*. 不幸な恋 ¶an ***unrequited*** (=***unreturned***) *love* 報いられない恋. ¶***unsatisfied sexual*** *love* 満されない性愛. ¶make ***violent*** *love* to ... ...に激しく言寄る. ¶***virgin*** *love* 初恋. ¶He had no ***vulgar*** *love* of money. 彼にはいやしい金銭欲がなかった. ¶***wild*** *love* 無軌道の恋. ¶***wounded*** *love* 傷ついた恋.

Q^2 ***cupboard*** *love* 欲から出た愛情. ¶his ***lady*** *love* 彼の恋人. ¶***mother*** (=maternal) *love* 母性愛.

P cemented ***by*** *love* 愛で結ばれた. 【類】 inspired ***by*** *love*. ¶marry ***for*** *love* not for money 金でなく, 愛情で結婚する. ¶marry ... ***for*** *love* ...と愛のために結婚する ‖ a suicide ***for*** *love* 情死者 ‖ grow melancholy (or mad) ***for*** *love* 恋わずらいをする ‖ Few men go into teaching ***for*** the *love* of it. 教えることが好きで教師になるものは少ない. 【類】 ***for*** the *love* of mankind. ¶He stayed on in the navy ***from*** *love* of the profession. 彼は好きで海軍に踏み止まった. ¶fall ***in*** *love* with ... ...と恋に落ちる ‖ be deeply ***in*** *love* with a woman 女に夢中になる ‖ be desperately ***in*** *love* with each other 首ったけにお互いが愛し合っている. ¶turbulently ***in*** *love* 猛烈に恋して ‖ a rival ***in*** *love* 恋がたき. 【類】 he fell wildly (=madly) ***in*** *love* with ... ‖ a teacher ***in*** *love* with his profession 教えるのが好きな教師. ¶***out of*** *love* with life 人生がいやになって ‖ He is ***out of*** *love* with her. 彼女との熱もさめている(いや気がさした). ‖ He did so ***out of*** *love*. 彼は愛情からそうした. ‖ ***out of*** *love* for the good old days 昔なつかしさに. ¶she pined away ***through*** *love* for ... 彼女は...に恋わずらいした. ¶***with*** my *love* [手紙の末尾に]さようなら ‖ city people ***with*** a *love* for the soil 土に愛着を持つ都会人 ‖ blind ***with*** *love* 恋に夢中の.

P^2 *love* ***between*** parent and child 親子の愛. ¶a *love* ***for*** pictures (mountains, Shakespeare, truth and beauty, scholarship) 絵画(など)に対する愛好 ‖ citizens with a *love* ***for*** the Constitution and a reverence for the flag 憲法を愛し国旗を尊重する国民. 【類】 her *love* ***for*** her fellowman (同胞愛). ¶from a *love* ***of*** danger 冒険が好きで ‖ his *love* ***of*** truth / *love* ***of*** cleanliness / *love* ***of*** nature ‖ *love* ***of*** the poetical (風流). ¶Give my *love* ***to*** all. 皆様によろしく. ¶***with love*** [手紙の結尾に]愛をもって ‖ a man of letters in *love* ***with*** life 人生を愛好する文学者. 【類】 They were in *love* ***with*** each other (相思の仲).

love, *v.* 愛する, 恋する.

M ***ardently*** *love* 熱愛する. ¶*love* ***blindly*** 盲目的に愛する. ¶She ***dearly*** *loved* her son. 彼女は息子を大層可愛がった. ¶***deeply*** *love* 深く愛する. ¶*love* her ***devotedly*** 彼女を熱愛する. ¶*love* ***divinely*** 神々しい愛を捧げる. ¶*love* ***faithfully*** and ***lastingly*** 忠実にまた永続的に愛する. ¶*love* her ***loyally*** 彼女を真心こめて愛する. ¶*love* ***passionately*** 熱烈に愛する. ¶*love* ***sincerely*** 誠実に愛する. ¶***tenderly*** *love* やさしく可愛がる. ¶a girl who *loved* ***unwisely*** 分別もなく恋をした娘. ¶*love* ***warmly*** 熱烈に愛する. ¶*love* ***wildly*** 無軌道に恋する.

P He *loves* money ***above*** everything else. 彼は何より金が好きだ. ¶He was *loved* devotedly ***by*** his people. 彼は彼の臣民に非常に敬愛された. ¶*love* ***to*** extraction 首ったけ恋をする ‖ She *loved* him ***to*** the day of her death. 彼女は死ぬ日まで彼を愛した. ¶*love* one's country ***with*** one's whole heart 専心国を愛する.

loveliest, *n.* 美の絶頂.

P The season is now ***at*** its *loveliest*. 季節は今が一番よい.

loveliness, *n.* 美しいこと.

Q ***dreamy*** *loveliness* of her face 彼女の顔の夢のような美しさ. ¶the ***fresh green*** *loveliness* of the countryside 愛すべきいなかの新緑.

lovely, *a.* 愛らしい, 美しい.

M be ***exceedingly*** *lovely* 愛くるしい. ¶***How*** *lovely!* 何ていいんでしょう[花や景色など]. ¶almost ***too*** *lovely* to use 使うにはちょっと惜しい位.

P voice *lovely* ***to*** the ear 聞いてほれぼれする声.

lover, *n.* 恋人, 情夫; 愛好者.

V a book which cannot but ***fascinate*** all *lovers* of the sea 海を愛する者はだれでも引きつけずにはおかない本. ¶She ***has*** a *lover* on the sly. 彼女は秘密の愛人を持っている. ¶***jilt*** (=***desert***) her *lover* 恋人を見捨てる. ¶prostitutes who ***support*** their *lovers* 彼らの情夫にみつぐ売春婦たち.

Q an ***ardent*** *lover* of truth 熱烈に真理を愛する者. ¶a ***deep*** *lover* of nature 自然の深い愛好者. ¶a ***devoted*** *lover* of music 音楽を熱心に愛好する者. ¶a ***devout*** *lover* of Thackeray サッカレー(作家)の熱心なファン. ¶a ***fervent*** *lover* of ... ...の熱烈な愛好者(ファン). ¶She is a ***general*** *lover*. 彼女は八方美人の恋をする. ¶[a couple of] ***guilty*** *lovers* 不義の恋人同士. ¶two ***happy*** *lovers* 幸福な恋人同士. ¶a ***jealous*** *lover* of truth 真理の熱心な愛好者. ¶a ***middle-aged*** *lover* full of fire 火のように燃えきった中年の恋人. ¶two ***neurotic*** and ***decadent*** *lovers* 二人のノイローゼ気味で退廃的な愛人. ¶a ***passionate*** *lover* of knowledge 知識の熱烈な愛好者. ¶a ***rejected*** *lover* ふられた男. ¶a ***slighted*** and ***despondent*** *lover* ばかにされて元気のない愛人. ¶***star-crossed*** *lovers* 不幸な恋人. ¶a ***thoughtful, dispassionate*** *lover* of his country, not a blind idolater 盲目的な崇拝者でなくて思慮深い冷静な愛国者.

Q^2 a ***cat*** *lover* ねこ好き. ¶a ***cricket*** *lover* クリケット愛好者. ¶a ***mountain*** (***nature***) *lover* 山(など)好きな人. ¶a ***music*** *lover* 音楽愛好者. ¶a ***peace*** *lover* 平和愛好者. ¶her bronzed ***sailor*** *lover* 彼女の愛人である赤銅色の船員. ¶a ***sensation*** *lover* 人をあっと言わせることの好きな人. ¶a ***story*** *lover* 小説好き.

P^2 a great *lover* ***of*** sports 大のスポーツ・ファン ‖ a *lover* ***of*** ceramics 陶器の愛好者 ‖ a *lover* ***of*** his family 自分の家庭を大事にする人 ‖ a *lover* ***of*** pleasure 遊び好き.

O a *lover* and his girl 彼氏と彼女.

love-relationship, *n.* 恋愛関係.

V ***form*** a *love-relationship* with ... ...と恋仲になる.

low, *n.* 低いこと, 低調.

Q^2 Carping critics yearly declare that the pictures exhibited in the Royal Academy are an ***all-time*** *low*. 口やかましい批評家たちは王立美術館に陳列される絵はもっとも低調だというのが毎年の例である. ¶a ***record*** *low* [温度など]記録破りの低さ.

low, *a.* 低い, 弱い, 乏しい.

M an ***astonishingly*** *low* ratio 驚異的低率. ¶***mentally*** *low* 低能な. ¶His wife is ***very*** *low*. 彼の細君は大層弱っている.

P *low* ***in*** funds 資金の乏しい ‖ steel *low* ***in*** carbon content 炭素成分の少ない鋼鉄 ‖ a woman *low* ***in*** social standing as a geisha 芸者風情.

lower, *v.* 下げる.

M The barrier to foreign trade was ***slightly*** *lowered*.

P the price was *lowered* ***from*** ... ***to*** ... 値段が...から...に下げられた.

lowness, *n.* 低いこと.

P^2 Navigation is suspended in consequence of the *lowness* ***of*** water in the river. 川の水位が低いので航行は中止されている.

loyal, *a.* 忠義な, 忠誠な, 忠実な.

M be ***unflinchingly*** *loyal* to ... ...に対する忠誠はゆるがない.

P *loyal* ***in*** one's love 恋に忠実な. ¶*loyal* ***to*** one's programme (country, religion) 主義(など)に忠実な. 【類】 *loyal* ***to*** the king (throne) / a husband *loyal* ***to*** his wife / be *loyal* ***to*** a cause (主義).

loyalty, *n.* 忠実, 忠義.

V ***encourage*** *loyalty* ***to*** employers 雇主への忠勤を奨励する. ¶without in any way ***losing*** one's *loyalty* to one's own country 少しも祖国に対する忠誠は失わずに. ¶They pledged their loyalty to the cause of the Allies. 彼らは同盟国のために忠誠を誓った. ¶practice loyalty 忠誠を尽す. ¶retain their loyalty to the countries of their birth 生国に対して忠誠を持続ける. ¶sarcifice loyalty to ... …のために節操を曲げる. ¶show their loyalty 忠誠を示す.

Q divided loyalty ふたごころ. ¶intense loyalty to the throne and deep affection for the country 君への熱烈な忠義と深甚の愛国心. 【類】intense loyalty to their own code (仲間の規約). ¶a noble loyalty of heart 高潔な心の誠. ¶the self-sacrificing loyalty of a sister to her erring brother 心得違いの兄への妹の献身的な忠実. ¶his steadfast loyalty to his friends 友人に対する彼の不動の誠実. ¶his unmeasured loyalty to his word 言明したことに対する彼の限りない忠実. ¶unquestioning loyalty 絶対的忠実. ¶cling with unshakable loyalty to ... ゆるぎない忠誠をもって…を擁護する. ¶unswerving loyalty 生一本の忠節.

Q² labor loyalties split politically 政治的に分裂した労働者の忠誠. ¶party loyalty 愛党心.

P unparalleled in bravery and loyalty 忠勇無比の. ¶out of loyalty to the Emperor 天皇への忠義から.

P² loyalty of the people for their Emperor and the country 皇帝及び国家に対する国民の忠誠. ¶loyalty to self (his friends) 自我(など)に対する忠実 ‖ loyalty to high aims 高い目的に対する忠実 ‖ loyalty to today without loyalty to tomorrow あすのことは考えずにきょうだけに対する忠実.

lubricity, *n.* いん奔.

Q veiled lubricity 体裁をまとったいん奔.

lucidity, *n.* 明るさ, 明りょう; 正気.

V The lucidity is but slightly if at all affected. かりに気が狂っているとしてもほんのちょっとだ. ¶promote lucidity of thought and expression 思想及び表現の明確さを増す.

Q write prose of rare beauty and of perfect lucidity 非常に美しくかつきわめて明確な文を書く. ¶with remarkable lucidity 非常に明確に.

P set forth with great lucidity the laws which govern the forces of nature 自然力を支配する法則を明快に述べる.

P² the lucidity of his thought 彼の思想の透徹.

luck, *n.* 運, 縁起, 好運.

V bewail one's luck 不遇をかこつ. ¶in the superstitious belief that it will bring good luck それは好運をもたらすだろうという迷信的な考え方で. 【類】The charm (護符) is supposed to bring good luck and prosperity to the owner (=possessor or wearer). / bring bad luck. ¶in order to change the luck 縁起直しに. ¶deserve a good luck 幸運に恵まれるのが当然. ¶envy one's good luck 人の幸運をうらやむ. ¶fetch a person some bad luck 人に不仕合わせをもたらす. ¶we had the luck to ... われわれは運よくも…した. 【類】we had the ill luck to ... ‖ May you have better luck next time! 今度は成功を祈ります. ‖ I never have any luck that way. 私はそういうことには運が悪い. ¶keep off bad luck 災難をよける. ¶prognosticate good luck 幸運を前兆によって予知する. ¶try one's luck in the country その国へ行って運命を開拓する ‖ try one's luck in that stream [つり師などが]その川で試みる. 【類】I'm going to try my luck at fishing. / try her luck in the matrimonial lottery (結婚の富くじ). ¶I heartily wish all good luck to the movement. 私はその運動の成功を衷心から祈る. ‖ I wish you good luck in getting a job. 首尾よく君が就職できるように.

V² Luck goes against him. 彼には運がない. ¶no worse luck can happen to a man than to ... …する位不幸なことはない. ¶His luck still held and escaped death. 彼はまだ運があって死をのがれた. ¶Oh, if this luck would only hold up! この運が続いてくれるといいのだが. ¶The luck ran terribly against me. 僕は運がすこぶる悪かった. ‖ Each asked the other how the luck was running. 二人はうまく行ってるかどうかとお互に尋ねた. ¶The luck has turned in our favor. 運が向いてきた.

Q bad luck 不運 ‖ avert bad luck 災難をよける. ¶blind luck もっけの幸. ¶We had capital luck. とても運がよかった. ¶false luck (実際は不幸な)表面上の幸福. ¶Good luck [to you]! お元気で(別れるとき). ‖ Diligence is the mother of good luck. 勤勉は福の神. ‖ this first good luck encouraged me to ... この幸先のよいのに勢いづいて私は…した ‖ regard the calamity as good luck (=a blessing) in disguise 不幸を偽装した幸運と見る ‖ as good luck would have it 運よく. ‖ With good luck I might succeed. うまく行けば私は成功するかも知れない. ¶rage within at one's hard luck 心中その不運を怒る. 【類】I'm in hard luck, I need five dollars badly and I haven't the least idea where I can get it. ¶I am in ill luck to-night. 僕は今夜は運が悪い[勝負事など]. ‖ I was too late as ill luck would have it. 私は運悪く間に合わなかった. ¶My companion's luck was poor. 私の連れは運がよくなかった(釣など). ¶by pure, undeserved luck もっけの幸で. ¶by rare luck 幸運にも. ¶have tough (=hard or bad) luck 運が悪い.

Q² his fishing luck [つり師の]魚運. ¶pot luck [来客への食事などの]有合わせの品. ¶Is there such a thing as telephone luck? 電話運なんてものがあるかね(直にかかるかからないなど).

P by good luck 幸運にも ‖ by [a stroke of] bad luck 運悪く. ¶wear it for luck 縁起にそれを身に着ける. ¶You are in luck, let me tell you! それはあなたが運が好いのですよ. ‖ be in bad luck=be down on one's luck 運が悪い. ¶repeated strokes of luck 好運続き. ¶people out of luck 不遇な人々. ¶I got it through pure luck. 全くの幸運でそれを手に入れた. ¶He has at last come to luck. やっとあの人に運が向いてきた.

P² with luck on his side 彼が運よく行けば. ¶Good luck to you both. [結婚式などに]お二人の御幸福を祈ります. 【類】Good luck to the author!

O Luck was against us. 運がなかった. ¶Luck is with us. 運がある.

lucky, *a.* 運のよい.

M How lucky. 何て間がいいんだろう. ¶a marvellously lucky youth すばらしく幸運な若者. ¶I was lucky enough to meet him there. 運よくそこで彼に会った.

P He who is lucky at cards is unlucky in marriage. トランプに運のよい者は結婚に運が悪いものだ. ¶it is lucky for you that ... …したのは君には仕合わせだ. ¶say that one is lucky in love のろける ‖ I don't seem to be lucky in the matter of finding him. 会いに行って彼に会えるということはどうも僕にはうまく行かないようだ.

lucre, *n.* 利益.

Q be greedy for filthy lucre 不正利得に汲々としている.

ludicrous, *a.* ばかげた.

M irresistibly ludicrous 実にばかげた.

luggage, *n.* 荷物, 手荷物; 《米》からのかばん.

V I left it behind unwilling to burden his luggage with so heavy a weight. 私は彼の荷物がかさ張るのでそれを後へ残してきた. ¶carry one's luggage 手荷物を運ぶ. ¶My luggage has been checked right through to Kobe. 私は手荷物を神戸までまっすぐチッキにした. ¶have one's luggage labeled 手荷物に付せんをつける. ¶have one's luggage registered—《米》have one's bgagage checked 手荷物をチッキにする. ¶label one's luggage for ... 手荷物に…行の札を張る. ¶leave one's luggage with a porter 手荷物を赤帽にあずける. ¶sell traveling bags and luggages 《米》かばん類を売る. ¶He stored his luggage at the station. 彼はその駅に手荷物をあずけた. ¶take (=carry) luggage with one 荷物を持ってゆく. ¶weigh one's luggage 手荷物の目方を計る. ¶his luggage consisted of ... 彼の荷物は…でぁあった.

Q excess luggage 超過手荷物. ¶lost or missing luggage 遺失または紛失手荷物. ¶personal luggage 手荷物. ¶railway passengers' luggage 鉄道旅客の手荷物.

Q² hand luggage 手荷物. ¶a sale of unclaimed railway luggage 鉄道の遺失品の処分販売.

P the contents of the luggage その手荷物の中味.

lukewarmness, *n.* 微温.

P Let it cool to lukewarmness. それをなまぬるくなるまで冷せ.

lull, *n.* なぎ, 小康, 小止(ぉ).

Q in a temporary lull 一時のなぎに.

P during a lull in their work 彼らの仕事の手すきに. 【類】during a lull in a storm (rain).

P² a lull in business (a conversation, political life, traffic) 商売(など)の小止み.

lull, *v.* 寝かしつける; 静まる, 静める.

M The wind (rain) [was] lulled awhile. 風(など)がちょっとないだ.

P lull a child to sleep (=rest) 子供を寝かしつける.

O lull one's fears (suspicions, worries) 人の恐怖(など)を静める.

lullaby, *n.* 小守歌.

V The south wind had been ***humming*** a *lullaby*. 南風がそよそよと吹いていた. ¶***sing*** a *lullaby* to the baby 赤ん坊に小守歌を歌ってやる.

lumber, *n.* 《米》製材(板など); 《英》未加工木材.

V ***cut*** *lumber* to lengths 丸太を一定の長さに切る.

Q ***warpy*** or ***knotty*** *lumber* ひずみのあるあるいは節の多い木材.

Q^2 ***building*** *lumber* 建築用材. ¶***redwood*** *lumber* アメリカ杉材.

P a dealer ***in*** *lumber* 材木屋.

lumber, *v.* がたがたと音をたてる; どしんどしんと歩く.

M The bear *lumbered* ***away*** after sniffing at the dead body. そのくまはその死体をかいでからのそりのそり立ち去った. 【類】A cart *lumbered* ***away*** (=***off***).

M^2 A heavy truck *lumbered* ***by*** (***past, along***). 重いトラックががたがた通り過ぎた.

lumber, *v.* 木を切出す; [場所を]ふさぐ.

M^2 *lumber* ***up*** 場所ふさぎになる. 【類】a room *lumbered* ***up*** with all sorts of rubbish.

P *lumber* ***for*** the market 市場向け製材をする.

lumbering, *n.* 伐採.

Q ***unwise*** *lumbering* [木材の]不得策な伐採.

luminary, *n.* 発光体; 大家.

Q ***legal*** *luminaries* 法律の大家. ¶the ***lesser*** *luminaries* who followed in their train 彼ら(大家)より一段格がおちる連中. ¶These names are not ephemeral flashes but ***permanent*** *luminaries*. これらの名前はたちまち消えるせん光でなくて永久に輝く発光体だ.

lump, *n.* 塊, こぶ.

V ***feel*** a *lump* in one's throat 胸が一杯になる. ¶***get*** a *lump* over one's eye 目の上にこぶをこしらえる. ¶***swallow*** the *lump* in one's throat せき上げてくる感じを抑えて胸が詰った.

V^2 a *lump* ***came*** into one's throat, looking at ... ...を見る.

Q a ***ridiculous*** *lump* would rise in my throat every time I thought of ... ...のことを思う度におかしさがこみあげてくる. ¶She is a ***sheer*** *lump* of fat. 彼女は丸々と太っている.

P sell them ***by*** the *lump* それをひとまとめにして売る. ¶take them ***in*** the *lump* (=collectively) それを全体として考慮する ‖ take one's money ***in*** a *lump* 金をまとめて受取る.

P^2 I thanked him with a *lump* ***in*** my throat. 私は胸一杯で彼に感謝した. ¶a *lump* ***of*** sugar (coal, clay) 一塊の砂糖(など).

lump, *v.* ひとまとめにする.

M *lump* the work ***together*** 仕事をまとめる ‖ He *lumped* foreigners ***together*** as a race who ... 彼は外国人を...する手合として片付けてしまった. ¶The expenses ought to be *lumped* ***together***. 経費は一括して計算すべきだ.

P *lump* the contents of ... ***in*** a single volume ...の内容を一冊の単行本にまとめる. ¶*lump* ***under*** the title of ... ...の名称下にまとめる. ¶*lump* [in] ***with*** ... ...と同類に入れる.

lunatic, *n.* 狂人.

Q ***escaped*** *lunatics* 脱走した狂人. ¶He was regarded as ***mild-mannered*** *lunatics*. 彼は軽い狂人位に扱われた. ¶a ***raging*** *lunatic* 猛り狂う狂人. ¶a ***raving*** *lunatic* たわ言を言う狂人. ¶a ***violent*** *lunatic* 凶暴性の狂人.

Q^2 a ***pauper*** *lunatic* 貧窮の狂人.

P He was regarded ***as*** a *lunatic*. 彼は狂人に見られた.

lunch, *n.* 昼食; 《米》軽食.

V ***carry*** cold *lunches* 冷飯弁当を持ってゆく. ¶***eat*** *lunch* between meals 《米》食事の間に軽食(おやつ)をとる. ¶***give*** him a *lunch* to carry to school 学校へ持って行く弁当を彼に与える. ¶Let us ***have*** (=take) *lunch*. 昼飯を食べよう. ☞昼飯の意味では luncheon の方が上品な言葉. ¶Stay longer. I'll ***fix*** you *lunch* ごゆっくりして下さい, お昼を仕度しますから. ¶***prepare*** *lunch* for ... ...のためお昼の仕度をする. ¶***put up*** *lunches* 弁当をこしらえる. ¶***take*** *lunch* with ... at ... ...と...で昼飯を食べる ‖ You'd better ***take*** a *lunch* ***along***. 弁当を持って行った方がいい. ¶***unpack*** the *lunch* 弁当箱の包みを解く. ¶***wrap up*** one's *lunch* 弁当を包む.

Q ***cold*** *lunch* 弁当. ¶We had a ***fine*** *lunch*. われわれはりっぱな昼食をとった. ¶This ticket entitles you to a ***free*** *lunch*. この券御持参になればお弁当を差上げます. ¶a ***light*** *lunch* 軽い昼食. ¶a ***quick*** *lunch* 簡単な昼食. ¶***semi-European*** *lunch* 合の子弁当. ¶a ***slight*** *lunch* 軽い昼食.

Q^2 a ***basket*** *lunch* 《英》駅弁. ¶***Box*** *lunches* will be provided. 折詰弁当を差上げます. ¶a ***five-decker*** *lunch* 五重箱入弁当. ¶My ***noon*** *lunch* does not take a very long time. 私が昼の弁当をつかうのは余り長くかかりません. ¶an ***open-air*** *lunch* 野外での弁当. ¶***school*** *lunch* 学校の弁当.

P ***after*** *lunch* 昼食後. ¶I was ***at*** *lunch* when he called. 彼が訪問したとき私は昼食中だった. ‖ drink a pot of porter ***at*** *lunch* お昼に黒ビールを一杯のむ. ¶What will you have ***for*** *lunch?* お昼に何を食べますか. 【類】eat sandwiches ***for*** *lunch*. ¶Stay ***to*** *lunch* please. ゆっくりしてお昼を食べていらっしゃい. ¶Are you through ***with*** your *lunch?* 昼飯はすみましたか.

lunch, *v.* 昼飯をとる.

M *lunch* ***together*** 一緒にお昼を食べる.

lunchbox, *n.* 弁当箱.

V ***fill*** (=***pack***) a *lunchbox* 弁当を詰める.

luncheon, *n.* 昼食, 午さん; 弁当.

V ***eat*** one's frugal *luncheon* 粗末な昼飯を食べる. ¶***give*** a *luncheon* tomorrow in honor of ... ...のために午さん会を催す. ¶***have*** *luncheon* on the way 途中で弁当を使う. ¶***hold*** a *luncheon* 午さん会を催す. ¶We ***took*** our *luncheon* at the drug-store across the street. われわれは通りの向う側の売薬兼軽食店で昼飯を食べた.

Q They were tendered a ***complimentary*** *luncheon* as the guest of the hotel manager. 彼らはホテルの支配人のお客として昼飯のごちそうにあずかった. ¶A ***standing cold*** *luncheon* was served. 立食のきょう応があった. ¶a ***substantial*** *luncheon* ごちそうのある昼飯.

Q^2 a "***hen*** *luncheon*" 女だけの午さん会. ¶a ***stand-up*** *luncheon* 立食会.

P entertain him ***at*** *luncheon* 彼に昼飯のもてなしをする. ¶go [out] ***for*** *luncheon* 昼飯を食べに外出する. ¶sit down ***to*** *luncheon* 午さんの席につく.

P^2 a *luncheon* ***of*** fresh bread and butter 新鮮なバタ付き[の焼たての]パンのランチ.

luncheon-hour, *n.* 昼飯時.

Q One o'clock is the ***conventional*** *luncheon-hour* of the English public. 一時は慣例上英国一般の昼飯時となっている.

lunchroom, *n.* 食堂.

Q^2 ***factory*** *lunchrooms* 工場の[昼]食堂. ¶a ***school*** *lunchroom* 学校の食堂.

lune, *n.* 弓形.

Q^2 a ***sand*** *lune* 砂丘.

lung, *n.* 肺.

V ***affect*** one's *lungs* 肺を悪くする. ¶***sound*** the *lungs* 肺を打診する.

Q^2 F. Snyte, the polio victim, spent 12 years in an "***iron*** *lung*." スナイトは小児まひで十二年間「鉄の肺」に閉込められた.

P breathe deep ***into*** the *lungs* 肺に空気を吸い込む. ¶injurious ***to*** the *lungs* 肺に悪い.

lunge, *v.* 一突きする.

P *lunge* ***at*** one's opponent 相手を一突きする(剣道やけん闘で).

lurch, *n.* 不意の傾斜; 不利な立場.

V ***give*** a sudden *lurch* in rounding a curve (船などが)曲線を描いている中に不意に傾く. 【類】The car ***gave*** a *lurch* and upset.

P leave a person ***in*** the *lurch* 人を見殺しにする.

lurch, *v.* よろめく.

M *lurch* ***forward*** 前へのめる.

P *lurch* ***against*** a table 机にぶつかってよろめく.

lure, *n.* 魅力.

V ***feel*** the *lure* of the sea 海の魅力を感じる.

Q a ***sexual*** *lure*=a sex appeal 性的魅力. ¶an ***uncontrollable*** *lure* どうにも打勝ち難い誘惑.

Q^2 a land of ***travel*** *lure* 観光的魅力のある国.

P^2 the *lure* ***of*** the shops (buried treasure) (飾り立てた)店(など)の持つ魅力. ¶the *lure* ***of*** the antique 古物の味. 【類】the *lure* ***of*** adventure. ¶a *lure* ***to*** the other sex 異性への性的魅力.

lure, *v.* 誘惑する, おびき出す.

M *lure* her ***away*** from husband and home 彼女を夫の手と家からおびき出す. ¶*lure* ***back*** their old customers 以前の顧客を引き戻す.

P *lured* ***by*** a curiosity to see ... ...を見たいという好奇心に駆られて. 【類】*Lured* ***by*** the lust of gold, the pioneers pushed onward. ¶*lure* ... ***into*** a trap ...をわなにおびき寄せる ‖ *lure* a person ***into*** a false sense of security 人を間違った安全感に陥らせる ‖ Our troops were *lured* ***into*** a dangerous position. わが軍は危地に誘い込まれた. ¶Every spring and fall the lights along the coast *lure* countless birds ***to*** destruction. 毎年春と秋には海岸の灯火に誘われて無数の小鳥が死ぬ. 【類】 *lure* a person ***to*** his doom ⌊(死).

lurk, *v.* 潜む, 潜伏する.

P there *lurks* ***in*** my memory ... 私の記憶に…が潜んでいる ‖ Hostile ships were *lurking* ***in*** that vicinity. 敵艦がその付近に潜伏していた.

lust, *n.* 欲, 欲望.

V ***gratify*** one's *lust* その欲望を満たす. ¶The *lust* of men must not be ***overdone.*** 人間の欲はこれを抑制しなくてはいけない.

Q ***carnal*** (=***fleshly***) *lust* 肉欲. ¶***fiendish*** *lust* 悪魔的な欲. ¶his ***wicked*** *lust* for gold 彼のよこしまな金銭欲.

Q² ***blood*** *lust* 残忍性.

P² flesh *lust* ***against*** the spirit 魂にそむく肉欲. ¶the *lust* ***for*** world domination 世界支配の欲望 ‖ a *lust* ***for*** power 権勢欲. 【類】 It is no exaggeration to say that man's *lust* ***for*** wealth has always been a dominant passion. / the *lust* ***for*** gold. ¶the *lust* ***of*** lucre 金銭欲 ‖ the *lust* ***of*** conquest 征服欲.

lust, *v.* 欲する.

P *lust* ***after*** riches 富を欲する ‖ *lust* ***after*** human blood 血に渇く. ¶*lust* ***for*** gains (gold) 利益(など)を欲する.

luster, lustre, *n.* 光, 光彩, 光沢.

V ***add*** *luster* to the name of ... …の名に光彩を添える. ¶***give*** a *lustre* to ... …の光沢を出させる. ¶***heighten*** *luster* 光彩を増す. ¶Her eyes ***lost*** their *lustre.* 彼女の目はその光沢を失った. ¶***preserve*** the *luster* of his memory 彼の遺烈を汚さないようにする. ¶Edward Caird ***shed*** a peculiar *luster* on the University of "the second city of the Empire." エドワード・ケアードは帝国第二の大都市(グラスゴー)の大学に独特な光彩を添えた. ¶***sully*** the *luster* of the day's exploit その日の勲功の光をそぐ. ¶***take on*** a new *lustre* 新たに光彩を添える. ¶Lapse of time cannot ***tarnish*** the *luster* of his memory. 時がたっても彼の遺烈を曇らすことはできない. ¶throw ***new*** *luster* on an honorable family 名家に一段の栄光を添える.

Q a ***fine, glossy*** *luster* 美しい光沢. ¶a ***metallic*** *luster* 金属的な光沢. ¶the ***parting*** *luster* of the sun 斜陽の名残の光. ¶a ***satiny*** *luster* しゅすのような光沢. ¶opals of ***splendid*** *luster* and fire 見事な光沢とせん光のたん白石.

P² the *luster* ***of*** pearls (porcelain) 真珠(など)の光沢.

luxuriance, *n.* 繁茂.

Q The word lover rejoices in the ***tropical*** *luxuriance* of the vast realm of English words. 言語愛好者は英国言語の巨大な領域における熱帯的な繁茂に対して喜びを感じる. ¶The foliage was in its ***utmost*** *luxuriance.* 木の葉は最もよく茂っていた.

luxuriate, *v.* ふける.

P *luxuriate* ***in*** the hot baths in a hotspring resort 温泉場で浴湯気分にふける ‖ The lover of classic lore *luxuriates* ***in*** the pages of Greek or Roman poets, philosophers, or historians. 古典的な学問の愛好者はギリシアまたはローマの詩人・哲人または歴史家の著書をたん読する.

luxurious, *a.* ぜいたくな.

P *luxurious* ***in*** diet (clothing) 食物(など)にぜいたくな.

luxury, *n.* ぜいたく, ぜいたく品; 愉快.

V ***abandon*** *luxury* ぜいたくをやめる. ¶Few could ***afford*** the *luxury.* そのぜいたくのできるものは少ない. ‖ I cannot ***afford*** the *luxury* of a telephone. 私には電話を引くようなぜいたくはできない. ¶***ape*** the *luxuries* of the wealthy 金持のぜいたくをまねる. ¶***buy*** *luxuries* ぜいたく品を買う. ¶***deny*** oneself the *luxury* of ... …のぜいたくを避ける. ¶***enjoy*** the *luxury* of a bath 気持のよい湯にはいる. 【類】 can ***enjoy*** few *luxuries* in life. ¶***feast*** the *luxury* of the eye 目を喜ばす. ¶***for[e]go*** all *luxuries* あらゆるぜいたくを控える. ¶***throw away*** our *luxury* われわれのぜいたくを捨てる. ¶Their homes ***typify*** *luxury* at its very best. 彼らの住宅は最高級のぜいたくとはいかなるものかを示すものである.

Q the ***crowning*** *luxury* 最上のぜいたく. ¶the ***enervating*** *luxuries* of the rich 人間を骨抜にする(気力をまひさせる)金持のぜいたく. ¶Next to women and automobiles, research is the most ***expensive*** *luxury* in American life.—Dr. Charles P. Grayson. アメリカの生活では研究が女と自動車に次いで最も金のかかるぜいたくだ. ¶***personal*** *luxuries* 装身用のぜいたく品. ¶enjoy ***sensuous*** *luxury* [物質的に対し]美的なぜいたくにふける. ¶A swimming bath was a well-nigh ***unknown*** *luxury* to dwellers in the metropolis. 水泳浴場は首都の市民たちにはほとんど未知のぜいたくな物だった.

Q² be highly prized as a ***table*** *luxury* 食卓の珍味として非常に賞美されている.

P live ***in*** *luxury*=live a life of luxury ぜいたくに暮す. 【類】 travel ***in*** *luxury* / be cradled ***in*** *luxury* / grew up lapped ***in*** *luxury* / wallow ***in*** *luxury* / He was brought up ***in*** *luxury.* ¶leisure ***without*** *luxury* ぜいたくのない閑散.

P² the greatest *luxury* ***in*** life 人生における最大の楽しみ. ¶*luxuries* ***of*** civilization 文明の快楽 ‖ I cannot pay for the *luxury* ***of*** a private tutor at home. 私には家庭へ教師に来てもらうというぜいたくはできない. ¶It is a *luxury* ***to*** me. それは私にはぜいたく品だ. ‖ treat oneself ***to*** the *luxury* of ... …というぜいたくをやる.

O What a *luxury* it is to be alone! 独身でいるのは実に結構なものだ.

lyre, *n.* 古ギリシアのたて琴; 詩情.

V ***awaken*** the *lyre* of ... の詩心を動かす.

M

machination, *n.* 計略.

V ***counteract*** the *machinations* of ... …の計略の裏をかく.

P² the *machination* ***of*** a scoundrel 悪漢の陰謀.

machine, *n.* (1) 機械; 自転車, 自動車, 飛行機.

V ***assemble*** a *machine* 機械を組立てる. ¶***control*** a *machine* 機械を制御する. ¶***feed*** the *machine* with cotton (紡績工場で)機械に綿をかける. ¶***handle*** a *machine* properly 機械を正しく取扱う. ¶***have*** a *machine* in operation 機械を運転させる. ¶***instal*** a *machine* 機械を据えつける. ¶***invent*** a *machine* 機械を発明する. ¶He knows how to ***handle*** (=***manage***) a *machine.* 彼は機械の扱い方を知っている. ¶***Let*** the *machine* ***alone.*** 機械に触れるな. ¶***manipulate*** *machines* in telegraphy 電信の機械を巧みに扱う. ¶he ***mounted*** his *machine* (=bicycle) and dashed off to ... 彼は自転車に乗って…の方へ突走った. ¶***operate*** (=***run***) a *machine* 機械を運転する. ¶The *machine* was ***piloted*** by a sub-lieutenant. その(飛行)機は少尉が操縦した. ¶***plan*** a *machine* 機械の設計をする. ¶This *machine* is ***protected*** by American and foreign patents. この機械はアメリカその他諸国の専売特許の保護を受けている. ¶***put together*** a *machine* 機械を組立てる. ¶***put*** a *machine* ***up*** 機械を組立てる. ¶The *machine* can be ***regulated*** at pleasure. その機械は自由に調節ができる. ¶***remount*** one's *machine* 自転車に再び乗る. ¶I can ***run*** my *machine* faster or slower at will. 私は自転車(または自動車)をもっと早くもおそくも思うようにできる. ¶***set*** a *machine* to work 機械を運転する. ¶***start*** a *machine* 機械を運転させる. ¶***take*** a *machine* to pieces 機械を分解する. ¶***take down*** a *machine* 機械を分解する. ¶***tend*** (=***look after***) a *machine* 機械を扱う. ¶***test*** a *machine* 機械を試験する. ¶***work*** a *machine* 機械 ⌊を扱う.

V² The *machine* ***works*** well. 機械の具合がよい.

Q an ***automatic*** *machine* 自動機. ¶a highly ***efficient*** *machine* 高性能の機械. ¶a ***hand-operated*** *machine* 手動機. ¶a cog in a ***magnificent*** and highly ***energized*** *machine* すばらしく性能の強大な機械の一輪. ¶the most ***modern*** and ***efficient*** *machine* 最新型高性能機. ¶a unit in a highly organized machine きわめて精妙に組織された機構の一単位. ¶a semiautomatic machine 半自動式の機械.

Q[2] an adding machine 加算器. ¶an addressing machine 名あて印刷機. ¶a boring machine 中ぐり盤. ¶these ancient machines これらの昔の機械. ¶a computing machine 計算器. ¶a dishwashing machine 自動さら洗い機. ¶a drilling machine ボール盤. ¶a flour-dressing machine 精粉機. ¶a flying (=an air) machine 飛行機. ¶a gear-cutting machine 歯切り盤. ¶a hand-power drilling machine 手動ボール盤. ¶a hand-punching machine 手動押抜き機. ¶a heavier (lighter)-than-air machine 〖空〗航空機(航空船). ¶a horse-power (hand-power) thrashing machine 馬力(手動)脱穀機. ¶an ice-making machine 製氷機. ¶keyboarding machine けん盤(キーのついた機械). ¶a linotype machine ライノタイプ機. ¶a mowing machine for crops 刈取り機. ¶a milling machine フライス盤. ¶a numbering machine ナムバリング・マシン. ¶a planing machine 平削り盤. ¶a plate-bending machine 板曲げ盤. ¶a printing machine 印刷機. ¶Images of the stars are thrown on the interior of the dome-shaped ceiling by a complicated projection machine (planetarium). 星の映像が複雑な投影機(プラネタリウム)によって円形天井の内部に映される. ¶a punching machine=a puncher 押抜き機; 刻印機. ¶a reaping machine 刈入れ器. ¶a rice-polishing machine 精米機. ¶a scrap-shearing machine スクラップせん断機. ¶a screwing (=screw) machine ねじ切り盤. ¶a sewage-liming machine [どぶの]石灰散布機. ¶run a sewing machine by foot ミシンを足で踏んで使う ‖ The sewing machine is humming busily. ミシンがかたかたと忙しそうに動いている. ¶a shaping machine=a shaper 形削り盤. ¶a shearing machine はさみ盤; 毛刈器. ¶a "silk" dressing machine 絹巻き機. ¶singeing machine 毛焼き機. ¶a [penny-in-the-]slot machine 自動(販売)機(銅貨を入れる). ¶a slot-drilling machine みぞ穴ボール盤. ¶a stenotype machine ステノタイプ. ¶a thrashing (=threshing) machine=a thrasher (=thresher) 脱穀機. ¶a ticket-punching machine 切符穴あけ器. ¶a ticket vending machine 自動切符販売機. ¶a talking machine 蓄音器. ¶an efficient transportation machine 高能率の運輸機関. ¶a try-your-strength machine 握力計量器. ¶a typing machine=a typewriter. ¶a vending machine 自動販売器. ¶a welding machine 溶接機. ¶build a war machine 兵器を組立てる. 【類】a modern war machine. ¶a washing machine 洗たく器. ¶a weighing machine 計量機. ¶a woolen spinning machine 紡毛機.

P manufactured by machine 機械製の. ¶He lost control of his machine. 彼は機械(自動車, 飛行機など)を操縦しきれなくなった. ¶Keep off the machine. 機械に触れるな.

P[2] a machine for cleaning rice 精米機.

(**2**) 機構, 機関; ((米)) [政党などの]黒幕.

V throw our economic machine out of balance わが経済機構を乱す.

Q the social and political machine of a country 一国の社会政治機構.

Q[2] a party machine 政党幹部会.

P His methods were quite different from those of the party boss, for he never worked through a "machine." 彼のやり方は党首のとは違っていた, 彼は政党機関内で活動した人ではなかったから.

P[2] the machine of government 政治機構.

machinery, *n.* (**1**) [集合的に]機械.

V The factory contains much machinery. その工場には沢山の機械がある. ¶design machinery 機械を考案する. ¶dismantle machinery 機械を取りはずす. ¶The machinery is driven by electricity. その機械は電気で運転する. ¶fit out (=up) machinery 機械を取付ける. ¶build a mill and install some machinery 工場を建て若干の機械を取付ける. ¶put together machinery 機械を組立てる. ¶select, install, operate and maintain machinery 機械を選び取付け運転しかつこれを維持する. ¶set the machinery in motion 機械を運転させる. ¶set up (=erect or fix) machinery 機械を組立てる. ¶Very little machinery is used. ほとんど機械を使わない. 【類】use foreign machinery. ¶warm up machinery 機械運転の用意をする.

Q goods manufactured by automatic machinery 自動機製の商品. ¶dissemble and assemble complicate machinery 複雑な機械を分解したり組立てたりする. ¶crude machinery 粗製の機械. ¶a mass of expensive machinery 沢山の高価な機械. ¶industrial machinery 工業用機械. ¶testing machinery 試験中の機械. ¶up-to-date machinery 最新式の機械. ¶machinery, working and still 使用中及び使用休止の機械. ¶woolen machinery 紡毛機.

Q[2] bolt and nut-making machinery ボールト・ナット工作機械. ¶cotton-mill machinery 製綿機. ¶farm machinery 農耕作機. ¶flour-mill machinery 製粉工場用機械. ¶labor-saving machinery 労力節約機. ¶lend-lease machinery from the United States 米国からの武器貸与法による機械. ¶oil mill machinery 油井用機械. ¶ordnance machinery 兵器工作機. ¶ore-dressing machinery 鉱石仕上げ機. ¶plate-bending machinery 板曲げ機. ¶refrigerating machinery 冷凍器. ¶rivetting machinery びょう打機. ¶rope-making machinery ロープ製造機. ¶woodworking machinery 木工機.

P It was made by machinery. それは機械製だ[手製に対して]. ¶with the precision of machinery 機械のように正確に. ¶hosiery made on machinery 機械製メリヤス製品. ¶equipped with new machinery 新型機を備えつけて.

(**2**) 機関, 機構.

V create machinery 機関を創設する. ¶establish machinery to ... …する機関を設ける. ¶blandly ignore the machinery of law 平気で法律の機関を無視する. ¶Our college, like all the rest, maintained the machinery of vocational guidance. われわれの大学でも他校同様職業指導の機関を設けた. ¶those who set in motion the machinery of the State 朝に立つ人々.

V[2] the creation of suitable machinery which will be able to function effectively in the interests of these nations これら諸国民のために有効に働く適当な機関の創設.

Q the administrative machinery 行政機関. ¶the deliberative machinery of the church at work 教会の審議機関の運用. ¶improvements in educational machinery 教育機関の改善. 【類】It has become an effective part of the educational machinery of our country. ¶information-gathering machinery 情報機関. ¶powerful machinery 有力な機関.

Q[2] the Communist propaganda machinery 共産党宣伝機関. ¶create enforcement machinery which no single nation, however powerful, dare defy いかなる強国も一国では対抗できないほど強力な実施機関を新設する. ¶government machinery 政府機構. ¶establish grievance machinery 苦情機関を設ける. ¶law enforcement machinery 法施行機関. ¶The black market was steadily being replaced by "orderly" trade machinery. やみ市場は次第に「秩序ある」貿易機関によってとって代えられた. ¶effective peace machinery 効果的平和機構. ¶relief machinery 救済機構.

machinist, *n.* 機械工.

Q[2] an aviation machinist 航空機械工.

mad, *a.* 気の違った; ((口語)) 怒った; ((口語)) 熱狂して; 心が乱れて.

M He is as mad as a hornet. 彼はくまばちのように怒っている. ¶He was rather mad (=annoyed) at missing his train. 彼は汽車に乗り後れて相当気をいらいらさしていた. ¶He is really mad about her. 彼は彼女に首ったけだ. ¶He is stark mad. 彼は全く気違いだ. ¶He goes simply mad over baseball. 彼は野球に夢中だ. ¶be zealously mad on (=about) ... …に全く夢中だ.

P I am mad about the stage. 僕は演劇に夢中だ(熱狂している). ¶He ran mad after music. 彼は音楽に熱中した. ¶He is mad (=angry) at me. 彼はすごく僕のことを怒っている. ¶He was nearly driven mad by grief. 彼は悲しみの余り気が狂いそうになった. ¶be mad for fame (honor, reputation) 名声(など)を得ようとやっきになっている. ¶He is mad with anger (=rage, envy). 彼は非常に腹を立てている(など). ‖ He is mad with liquor. 彼は酒に酔っぱらっている. ‖ He is mad with pain (disappointment). 彼は痛み(など)にもだえた. ‖ The spectators were as if mad with the desire to see blood. 見物人は殺気立っていた.

O He has gone mad. 彼は気が違った. ¶He must be mad to do such an imprudent thing. そんな不謹慎なことをするとは気が違っているに相違ない.

madman, *n.* 狂人.

P They were wild over the victory, crying and dancing like so many madmen. 勝利に気が立って, 狂人のようにど

なったりおどったりしていた. ¶He is next door ***to*** (=***near-ly***) a *madman.* 彼はほとんど狂人だ.

madness, *n.* 狂気.

V ***feign*** *madness* admirably 見事に狂気を装う.

Q It would be ***downright*** (=***sheer***) *madness* to do such a thing. こんなことをするからには本当の気違いだ. ¶There was ***hereditary*** *madness* in his family. 彼の一家は気狂いの系統だった. ¶Anger is a ***short*** *madness.* 立腹は一時の狂気だ. ¶he declared it ***utter*** *madness* to ... 彼は…するのは全くの気違いざただと言った.

Q^2 ***mountain*** *madness* 登山狂.

P He was driven ***to*** *madness* by it. それが原因で彼は気が狂った. ‖ He was stung ***to*** *madness.* 彼は狂気のごとく激こうした.

P^2 a *madness* ***for*** flowers 花に対する熱愛.

magazine, *n.* (**1**) 雑誌.

V It has recently ***absorbed*** another *magazine.* その雑誌は最近一つの雑誌を買収した. ¶***bind*** *magazines* into volumes 雑誌を合本にする. ¶***bring out*** (=***publish***) a *magazine* 雑誌を発行する. ¶The firm has succeeded in ***carrying*** (=***tiding***) the *magazine* over the war. その社は戦時(の不振)中どうにか雑誌の出版を維持した. ¶The *magazine* will be ***discontinued*** in future. その雑誌は今後廃刊になるだろう. ¶***edit*** a *magazine* "for their health" いわゆる「道楽に」雑誌を編集する. ¶***take*** [***in***] a *magazine* 雑誌を取る. 【類】I have ceased ***taking*** the *magazine.*

V^2 The *magazines* ***carries*** a couple of long political articles. その雑誌には二三の長い政治記事がのっている. ¶The *magazine* is still ***running.*** その雑誌はまだ出ている.

Q the ***best*** and most ***dignified*** *magazine* 一番良くて最も気品のある雑誌. ¶a ***cheap*** *magazine* 低級雑誌. ¶***fine-print*** *magazines* 細字印刷の雑誌. ¶an ***illustrated weekly*** *magazine* 絵入週刊雑誌(グラフィック). ¶This is the ***latest*** *magazine.* これが最近発行の雑誌です. ¶style rules of ***leading*** *magazines* 一流雑誌の文体規程. ¶***monthly*** (***weekly, fortnightly, bi-monthly***) *magazines* 月刊(など)雑誌. ¶a ***non-political*** *magazine* 政治を取扱わない雑誌. ¶a ***pictorial*** *magazine* 絵入り雑誌. ¶a ***semi-annual*** *magazine* 半年毎に出す雑誌. ¶a ***serious*** *magazine* まじめな雑誌. ¶an ***unillustrated*** *magazine* さし絵のない雑誌.

Q^2 an "***action***" *magazine* [西部ものなど]活劇ものの雑誌. ¶an ***alumni*** *magazine* 校友会誌. ¶a ***campus*** (=***college***) *magazine* 大学雑誌. ¶a ***dime*** *magazine* 十セント雑誌(安雑誌). ¶an ***eight-page*** *magazine* 八ページ雑誌. ¶a ***fan*** *magazine* 映画愛好者の雑誌. ¶a ***fiction*** *magazine* 小説雑誌. ¶a ***highbrow*** (=highgrade) *magazine* [インテリ向]高級雑誌. ¶a ***membership*** *magazine* 同人雑誌. ¶a ***pulp*** *magazine* 安雑誌. ¶a ***quality*** *magazine* 高級雑誌. ¶a ***student*** *magazine* 学生雑誌. ¶a ***teen-age*** *magazine* 少年少女の雑誌. ¶a ***trade*** *magazine* 貿易雑誌. ¶a ***true-story*** *magazine* 実話雑誌.

P write ***for*** *magazines* 雑誌に寄稿する ‖ subscribe ***for*** a *magazine* 雑誌を予約(年ぎめ)でとる. ¶I learned ***from*** a *magazine* that ... 私は雑誌で…を知った. ‖ The extract is ***from*** the ... *magazine* of 1849. その抜粋は一八四九年の…雑誌に出たものだ. ¶an article ***in*** a *magazine* 雑誌掲載の一文. ¶in the latest issue ***of*** the *magazine* 同誌の最近号に. ¶contribute ***to*** a *magazine* 雑誌に寄稿する.

P^2 an American *magazine* ***on*** the Orient 東洋に関する米国の一雑誌.

(**2**) 倉庫; 火薬庫.

V ***explode*** a *magazine* 火薬庫を爆発させる.

Q an ***explosive*** *magazine* 火薬庫. ¶an ***inexhaustible*** *magazine* 無尽蔵の倉庫.

magazinist, *n.* 雑誌編集者.

Q a ***well-known*** *magazinist* 有名な雑誌編集者.

magic, *n.* 魔術; 魅力.

V ***break*** the *magic* of ... …の魔術を破る, …の魅力を損じる. 【類】The most beautiful woman in the world, if she has a strident, harsh, and upleasant voice, ***breaks*** the *magic* of her charm with a word (一こと言うと).

P appear as if ***by*** *magic* 魔術でやったように現われる ‖ It was done ***by*** *magic.* それは魔術でやったのだ. ‖ be hit ***by*** the *magic* of music (scenery) 音楽(など)の魅力に打たれて. ¶It is used ***in*** *magic.* それは魔術に使う. ¶***like*** *magic* 不思議なように.

magician, *n.* 魔術師, 手品師.

Q^2 an ***expert*** *magician* 本職の魔術師. ¶a ***sleight-of-hand*** *magician* 達者な手品師.

magistrate, *n.* 治安判事; 行政官.

Q The President is the ***chief*** *magistrate* of the United States. 大統領は米国の最高行政官である. ¶a ***civil*** (***judicial***) *magistrate* 文政(司法)官. ¶a ***stipendiary*** *magistrate* 《英》有給治安判事.

Q^2 a ***committing*** *magistrate* 拘留官. ¶a ***police*** *magistrate* 簡易裁判所判事. ¶a ***trial*** *magistrate* 審判官.

magnanimity, *n.* 寛容.

V They seldom ***have*** the *magnanimity* to acknowledge their mistake. 彼らは自分の誤りを認めるほどの寛容さを示すことは滅多にない.

magnate, *n.* お歴々, おえら方, …王.

Q ***commercial*** *magnates*=merchant princes 豪商. ¶a ***feudal*** *magnate* 大名. ¶a ***financial*** *magnate* of importance 財界の巨頭. ¶***industrial*** and ***financial*** *magnates* 工業界や財界の巨頭. ¶a ***landed*** *magnate* 大地主. ¶a ***literary*** *magnate* 文豪. ¶a ***veteran industrial*** *magnate* 工業界の元老.

Q^2 a ***mining*** *magnate* 鉱山王. ¶a ***railroad*** *magnate* [私設]鉄道の大立物. ¶a ***ship-building*** *magnate* 造船界の巨頭.

P^2 a leading *magnate* ***in*** industrial circles 工業界の大立物. ¶*magnates* ***of*** a town 町の有力者たち.

magnet, *n.* 磁石; 人を引きつけるもの.

Q one of the ***best*** *magnets* to attract patronage to ... …に客を引付ける最良なものの一つ.

Q^2 a ***bar*** *magnet* 棒磁鉄. ¶a ***horseshoe*** *magnet* てい鉄形磁鉄.

P^2 a *magnet* ***for*** tourists 観光客を引きつけるもの.

magnetism, *n.* 磁力; 魅力.

Q ***physical*** *magnetism* 磁力. ¶He is gifted with ***strong personal*** *magnetism.* あの人は強く人を引きつける力を持っている.

magnification, *n.* 拡大.

Q the ***unlovely*** *magnification* of the mouth by a singer 歌手の見っともなくあける大口.

magnificence, *n.* 壮麗.

Q ***costly*** and at the same time ***refined*** *magnificence* 高価であると同時に上品な豪華.

P^2 wonder at the *magnificence* ***of*** Niagara Falls ナイアガラ瀑布の壮観に感嘆する.

magnificent, *a.* 壮麗な.

P It is *magnificent* ***in*** the extreme. それはきわめて壮麗だ.

magnifier, *n.* 拡大鏡.

Q^2 a ***hand*** *magnifier* 虫眼鏡.

P see ... ***through*** a *magnifier* 拡大鏡を通して…を見る.

magnify, *v.* 拡大する; 誇張する.

M bacteria, ***greatly*** *magnified* 高度に拡大されたバクテリヤ. ¶very ***highly*** *magnified* 極度に拡大した.

P *magnify* oneself ***against*** ... …を見くびる, 軽べつする. ¶*magnify* ... ***to*** the size of ... …を…の大きさに拡大する.

magnitude, *n.* 重要, 重大.

V The industry has ***assumed*** greater *magnitude.* その工業が盛大になった. ¶the evil ***attained*** such a *magnitude* as to call forth ... その悪弊は…を呼び起すほど重大になった.

Q a task of ***considerable*** *magnitude* かなり重要な仕事. ¶a star of the ***first*** *magnitude* 一等星. ¶The opening of Parliament is an official and social function of the ***first*** *magnitude.* 議会の開会は官辺及び社会のすこぶる重要な機能である. 【類】a movie star of the ***first*** *magnitude* (大スター). ¶a matter of ***immense*** *magnitude* きわめて重大な問題. ¶a question of ***national*** *magnitude* 国家的重要性ある問題. ¶a task of ***no mean*** (=***small***) *magnitude* 侮り難い仕事. ¶a view of ***surprising*** *magnitude* 驚くほど重大な見解. ¶a matter of ***tremendous*** *magnitude* すばらしく重要な問題.

P a historic event ***of*** such great *magnitude* かくも重大な歴史的事件.

P^2 the *magnitude* ***of*** the fact of domestication 野獣の家畜化という事実の(文化史上における)重大性.

magpie, *n.* かささぎ.

V^2 *Magpies* ***chatter.*** かささぎがぎゃーぎゃー鳴く.

mahogany, *n.* マホガニー.

Q^2 ***genuine*** (***imitation***) *mahogany* 本物(偽物)のマホガニー.

Mahomedanism, *n.* 回教.

V ***adopt*** *Mahomedanism* 回教を信仰する.

maid, *n.* 処女; 女中.

V ***abduct*** a *maid* 処女を誘かいする.

Q a hard-featured ***old*** *maid* with a voice like a file やす

りのような声の持主である恐ろしい御面相のオールドミス‖ How do you get to be an ***old maid***? あなたどうしてオールドミスにならなくっちゃならないの.

Q² a ***house-parlor maid*** 部屋付女中. ¶a ***kitchen maid*** 下女. ¶a ***house maid***=a housemaid 女中.

P² a *maid* ***of*** all work 雑働きの女中‖a *maid* ***of*** honor 花嫁につき添う処女.

maiden, *n.* 少女.

Q a ***blushful maiden*** はにかむ少女. ¶a ***convent-bred*** *maiden* 修道院育ちの処女. ¶a ***love-lorn maiden*** 失恋した少女. ¶a ***modern maiden*** 現代式の少女. ¶a ***white-robed*** *maiden* 白衣の少女. ¶a ***winsome*** (=***charming***) *maiden* 愛きょうのある少女.

P² a *maiden* ***of*** bashful fifteen はにかむ十五歳の少女‖a *maiden* ***of*** sixteen summers 十六歳の少女.

maidenhead, *n.* 処女性.

V She has ***lost*** her *maidenhead* (=virginity). 彼女は純潔を失った.

maid-servant, *n.* 女中.

V ***dismiss*** a *maid*[-servant] 下女に暇をやる.

mail, *n.* 《米》郵便, 郵便物; 郵船; 郵便車.

V ***address*** *mail* to ... 郵便を...あてに送る. ¶it was given an order by the government to ***carry*** *mail* between ... and ... それは...間に郵便物を輸送するように政府から命じられた. ¶***catch*** that *mail* その郵便に間に合わせる. ¶***embark*** *mails* and passengers 郵便物や客を上船させる. ¶pamphlets of instruction with which governmental bureaus ***flood*** the *mail* 政府諸官庁の盛んに郵送する訓令の印刷物. ¶***forward*** one's *mail* to ... ...あてに郵便を転送する. ¶He ***handled*** the royal *mail* for upwards of twenty years. 彼は二十年以上英国郵便事務に携わった.【類】More than 30,000 persons are employed to ***handle*** the *mail* in New York. ¶***miss*** the *mail* 郵便の締切に間に合わない. ¶***open*** the morning *mail* 朝の来状を見る. ¶***rob*** the *mails* 郵便物を盗む.

V² Nearly all the *mails* for England ***go*** by Siberia now. 英国行の郵便物は今は大抵シベリアを経由する. ¶When does the next *mail* ***go out*** (***come in***)? この次の郵便はいつ出るか(はいるか). ¶When does the Canadian *mail* ***sail***? カナダ行の郵船はいつ出るか.

Q ***Any*** *mail* for me today? きょうは手紙が来ていませんか. ¶***domestic*** (***foreign***) *mail* 国内(外)郵便. ¶per ***first*** (***last***) *mail* 第一(最後の)便で. ¶I send you, by the ***same*** *mail* as this, ... これと同じ船であなたに...を送付する. ¶*Mails* are ***uncertain***. 郵便はけんのんだ(紛失することがある). ¶an ***up*** (a ***down***) *mail* 上(下)りの郵便. ¶a ***voluminous*** *mail* 沢山の郵便.

Q² by ***air*** *mail* 航空郵便で. ¶an ***express*** *mail* 速達便. ¶receive much ***fan*** *mail* ファンレターを沢山受取る. ¶begin ***flying*** *mail* 航空郵便を始める. ¶***incoming*** *mail* 受取郵便. ¶a ***night*** *mail* 夜行郵便列車. ¶***outgoing*** *mail* 発送郵便 ¶reply per ***return*** *mail* 折返し返事をする.【類】I shall be glad to hear from you by ***return*** *mail*.

P send a message ***by*** *mail* 郵便で便りをする‖Subscriptions will be received ***by*** *mail*. 寄付の申込は郵便で受付ける. ¶The letter may have been lost ***in*** [the] *mails*. その手紙は郵送中に紛失したのかも知れない.【類】receive a check (小切手) ***in*** the *mail*. ¶***go over*** one's *mail* 配達された手紙に目を通す. ¶personally or ***through*** the *mail* (=by letter) 本人自身または書面で‖send it ***through*** the *mails* それを郵送する.

P² All the *mail* ***for*** England is landed at Liverpool. 英国行の郵便物は全部リヴァプールで陸揚げする.

mail, *v.* 《米》郵便で出す.

M *mail* ***back*** 折返し返事の手紙を出す. ¶*mail* ***out*** to ... 2,000 copies of ... ...に...を二千部郵送する.

O *mail* X'mas cards クリスマス・カードを郵送する.

mailbox, *n.* 《米》郵便ポスト, 郵便受け.

Q a freshly ***painted*** *mailbox* ペンキ塗り立ての郵便ポスト.

P mail a letter ***at*** a *mailbox* 《米》手紙をポストに入れる.

mailman, 《米》郵便屋.

V² The *mailman* ***comes*** around twice a day. 郵便屋は二回まわってくる.

Q There was no telephone and ***no*** *mailman* all day. 一日中電話もかからなければ郵便も来なかった.

main, *n.* 本土; 本管; 大体.

Q the ***Spanish*** *main* スペイン系アメリカ本土(南米カリブ海沿岸地方).

Q² a ***fire*** *main* 消火本管. ¶a ***supply*** *main* 給水管. ¶A ***water*** *main* bursted. 水道のもと管が破裂した.

P This statement is, ***in*** the *main*, true (=accurate *or* correct). この陳述は大体において正しい.【類】The facts are correctly stated ***in*** the *main*. / The results are, ***in*** the *main*, satisfactory. / conform ***in*** the *main* to ... / I accept it as ***in*** the *main* correct. ‖it is due ***in*** the *main* to ... それは大体...に基因する‖the theory is based, ***in*** the *main*, on ... その学説は大体...に論拠している.【類】it represents ***in*** the *main*, the opinion of ...

mainland, *n.* 本土.

P² the *mainland* ***of*** California [島に対して]カリフォルニア本土.【類】Typhoon Kitty (キティー台風) hit the *mainland* ***of*** Japan (本州).

mainspring, *n.* 主因.

P² the *mainspring* ***of*** the success その成功の主因.

mainstay, *n.* 柱石.

P The disaster to the household was caused by the untimely death ***of*** its *mainstay*. その家族の不幸は大黒柱が若死したことであった.

P² Agriculture is the *mainstay* ***of*** a country. 農は国の本である.

maintain, *v.* 固守する, 主張する; 維持する.

M Quotations are ***barely*** *maintained*. 相場価格は辛うじて保たれている. ¶The price has been ***consistently*** *maintained*. その価格はずっと変らない. ¶***rigidly*** *maintain* ... ...を厳守する. ¶He ***stoutly*** *maintained* his innocence. 彼はがんとして自分の無罪を主張した.

P *maintain* one's ground ***against*** the enemy 敵に対して己が地歩を維持する. ¶a school *maintained* ***by*** the theatre 劇場付属の学校. ¶The railway is *maintained* ***out of*** public money. その鉄道は公共の金で維持されている.【類】a research laboratory (研究所) *maintained* ***by*** a firm of London manufacturers.

O ***maintain*** the policy to be wrong=maintain that the policy is wrong その政策が誤っていると主張する. ¶***maintain*** one's family 家族を養う.

maintenance, *n.* 維持.

Q² ***building maintenance*** 営繕. ¶***law maintenance*** 法の維持. ¶***vehicle maintenance*** [自動車などの]車の保全.

P ***by*** the *maintenance* of justice 正義を保持して. ¶***for*** the *maintenance* of order 秩序維持のために.

P² *maintenance* ***of*** equipment 設備の保全‖the *maintenance* ***of*** prisoners of war 捕虜収容‖*maintenance* ***of*** way 〘鉄道〙保線.

majesty, *n.* 威厳, 尊厳.

P Parliamentary politics ***bear*** a precarious *majesty* in the House of Commons. 議会政治は衆議院においてわずかにその威厳を保っている. ¶***revere*** the sacred *majesty* of law 法律の尊厳を尊重する. ¶***serve*** his *Majesty* 陛下に奉仕する. ¶***uphold*** the *majesty* of the law 法律の威厳を維持する.

Q his ***late*** (***present***) *Majesty* 先帝(今上)陛下. ¶Deep rivers flow with ***silent*** *majesty*. 深い川は静かにおごそかに流れる. ¶a peak rising in a ***single*** *majesty* 厳然としてそびえる孤峰.

major, *a.* 大なる.

P *major* ***to*** ... ...より大なる[数・量など].

major, *v.* 《米口》専攻科目とする.

P *major* ***in*** mathematics 数学を専攻科目とする‖*major* ***in*** English and minor in French 英語を専攻にフランス語を副攻にする. ☞英語用法は specialize in ...

majority, *n.* 多数, 過半数; 《米》投票の得点勝差; 陸軍少佐の位; 成年.

V He has ***attained*** (=***got*** *or* reached) his *majority*. 彼は成年に達した. ¶***command*** a *majority* 多数を制する.【類】The party ***commands*** an absolute *majority* in the House. ¶***compose*** the *majority* 多数派を構成する. ¶The proposal failed to ***find*** a *majority*. その提案は過半数の賛成者を得るに至らなかった. ¶***form*** the *majority* 大多数をなす. ¶The government ***got*** their *majority* at the last election. 政府党は前の選挙で過半数を占めた. ¶The Liberal party ***has*** a *majority* in the House. 自由党が議会で過半数を占めている. ¶The party at present ***holds*** the *majority* in the Reichstag. 今その党派はドイツ共和国の議会で過半数を占めている.【類】The company ***holds*** a *majority* of the stock (株の過半数). ¶***join*** the *majority*=die 亡き数に入る(死ぬ). ¶That party which ***obtains*** the *majority* of seats in the House is called the Government. 議院で過半数の議席を得る党派を与党という. ¶He polled a *majority* of 100 polls against 20 for his rivals.

彼は相手の二十に対し百の多数票を獲得した. ¶***possess*** a comfortable *majority* in the Diet 議会で優に過半数を占める. ¶***reach*** the legal *majority* 法律上成年に達する. ¶***receive*** a *majority* (plurality) of votes over those cast for ... ...への投票数に対し過半(大多)数の得票を得る. ¶***win*** a *majority* at a Congress《米》議会で過半数を占める. ☞ 米語用法の majority は次例による: If A received 15,000 votes, B 7,000, and C 5,000, A had a *majority* of 3,000.

Q This gives the Government an ***assailable*** *majority*. これで政府は攻撃することのできない多数を占めたことになる. ¶by a ***bare*** *majority* わずかの差で. ¶The Government has a ***comfortable*** *majority* in the Diet. 政府側は国会で優に過半数を制している. ¶in the ***crushing*** *majority* of cases (=instances) 圧倒的に多数の場合に. ¶by a ***decided*** *majority* 断然多数で. ¶by a ***decisive*** *majority* 決定的大多数で. ¶by an ***enormous*** *majority* 非常に大多数で. ¶with the aid of a ***fortuitous*** *majority* 意外に多数の援助者を得て. ¶Six to one is a ***good*** *majority*. 一に対する六は相当の多数である. ¶the ***great*** *majority* of people 大多数の人々. ¶in the ***great*** *majority* of cases 大多数の場合. ¶an ***immense*** *majority* 非常な多数. ¶an ***inferior*** *majority* わずかの多数. ¶He was returned by a ***large*** (***small***) *majority*. 彼は大多数(わずかの差)で議員に選出された.【類】The resolution passed by a ***small*** *majority*. ¶by the ***narrow*** *majority* of 139 to 131 百三十一対百三十九のわずかの差で.【類】remain in office (政権を維持する) with a ***narrow*** *majority* in Parliament. ¶Parliament accepted the Bill by an ***overwhelming*** *majority*. 議会は圧倒的多数で該議案を承認した.【類】The Bill was rejected in a ballot by an ***overwhelming*** *majority*. ‖ in the ***overwhelming*** *majority* of cases 大多数の場合に. ¶The result of the elections is expected to give the Cabinet a ***sweeping*** *majority* in the Lower House. 選挙の結果下院では与党が圧倒的大多数を占めるものと予想される. ¶in the ***vast*** *majority* of cases 最も多くの場合に.

Q² ***committee*** *majority* 委員会の過半数. ¶defeat a competitor by ***landslide*** *majority* of ... votes 相手を...票という圧倒的多数で破る. ¶The House passed a drastic labor bill by a ***three-to-one*** *majority*—308—107. 下院は三百八対百七という三対一の多数で画期的な労働法案を可決した. ¶A ***two-thirds*** *majority* is required. 三分の二の多数が必要である.【類】have a ***two-to-one*** *majority*. ¶their ***twenty-six-seat*** *majority* in the House 下院の過半数議席二十六.

P He was elected ***by*** a *majority* of 120 against 70. 彼は七十票に対する百二十票の多数で当選した. ‖ decision ***by*** *majority*. 多数決.【類】He was elected ***by*** a *majority* of nearly 7,000 votes over his opponent. / The bill was defeated ***by*** 141 to 108—*majority* 33. / The bill passed ***by*** a *majority* of 28. / The resolution was rejected ***by*** a *majority* of 68, the figures being 586 for and 654 against. / The resolution was adopted ***by*** a *majority* of ... ¶***in*** the *majority* of cases 多くの場合 ‖ They are ***in*** the *majority*. 彼らは多数者の中に加わっている.【類】***in*** the *majority* were Mr. ... and Mr. ... ¶go over ***to*** (=join *or* enter) the *majority* 死ぬ.

P² It is probable that women are in *majority* ***among*** centenarians. 百歳の人の間では婦人が多数を占めているだろう. ¶the party that has a *majority* ***in*** the House of Commons 下院で過半数を占めている党派. ¶a *majority* ***of*** people 多数の人々. ¶his *majority* ***over*** his competitors 競争者の合計得票に対する彼の超過数.

O The *majority* will go ***to*** him. 大多数の投票は彼に行くだろう. ‖ The *majority* is for (against) him. 大多数は彼に(不)賛成だ.

make, *n.* 作り, こしらえ; 形状, 体格; 気質; 製作, でき.

Q cigars of ***American*** *make* 米国製の葉巻タバコ. ¶suits for gents of ***British*** *make* 英国製の紳士服. ¶of ***cheaper*** *makes* もっと低れんな製作の. ¶pianos of ***different*** *makes* 色々型の違ったピアノ. ¶garments of ***domestic*** *make* 手製の着物. ¶of ***English*** *make* 英国製の. ¶This is of ***home*** (***foreign***) *make*. これは国産(外国製)だ. ¶***inferior*** *makes* of fountain pens 悪い万年筆. ¶a man's ***mental*** *make* 人の頭のでき具合. ¶This cap is of quite a ***new*** *make*. この帽子は全く新型だ. ¶a man's ***physical*** *make* 人の体格. ¶The *make* is very ***poor***. できがきわめてまずい. ¶He is of a ***smooth*** (***contentious***) *make*. 彼は気だてがおだやか(けんかずき)だ. ¶of ***small*** *make* 小形の. ¶a box of a ***specific*** *make* 特製の箱. ¶planes of a ***standard*** *make* 標準型の飛行機. ¶articles of ***top-grade*** (=first-class) make 第一級品. ¶secondhand machines of ***various*** *makes* 色々型の違ったふる手の機械. ¶***Whose*** *make* is it? それはだれの作か.

P She is slender ***in*** *make*. 彼女はきゃしゃにできている. ‖ cheap ***in*** *make* 粗製の. ¶machines ***of*** other *makes* 別口の機械. ¶writers ***on*** the *make* やがて文士として立つ人々.

P² the *make* ***of*** a garment 着物の仕立.

make, *v.* つくる, 作る; ...ならしめる, ...にする; [...を]...にする; 考える; 了解する; 歩く, 行く; [程度など]進む.

M *make* ***away*** with a book 本を手離す(売渡す) ‖ *make* ***away*** with (=kill) oneself 自殺する ‖ *make* ***away*** (=***off***) with money 金を持ち逃げする. ¶*make* ***believe*** (=pretend) that ... ...であるように見せかける.【類】He always *makes* ***believe*** to work hard. / *make* ***believe*** to be a scholar. ¶I *make* ***bold*** to ask favor. 厚かましくもお願い致します. ‖ I have *made* ***bold*** to call on you. 思い切ってお伺いしました.【類】I further *make* ***bold*** to say that ... / He *made* ***bold*** to express his opinion in no flattering terms of certain of their faults and failings. ¶It *makes* everything ***clear***. それですっかりはっきりした. ¶Can't you *make* it ***clear***, John? ジョン, はっきり説明してくれ. ¶*make* ***colorful*** one's conversation 会話につやをつける. ¶articles ***conscientiously*** *made* 親切にできた品. ¶*make* ***enough*** of a comeback to ... ...するに足りる復興振りを示す. ¶*make* ***even*** 清算する, 貸借なしにする. ¶*made* ***expressly*** for the purpose 特にそのために作られた. ¶*make* ***fast*** しっかりくくりつける ‖ The tide *makes* ***fast***. 潮がずんずん差して来る. ¶*make* one's power ***felt*** めにもの見せる. ¶a work by which his reputation was ***first*** *made* 彼の出世作. ¶*make* him ***free*** 彼を自由の身にする. ¶*make* him ***glad*** 彼を喜ばせる. ¶The servants have been *making* ***free*** with the sugar lately. 召使などは近ごろ砂糖を勝手に使っている. ¶*make* ***good*** one's promise 約束を果たす ‖ *make* ***good*** one's purpose 目的を遂げる ‖ *make* ***good*** the loss of ... ...の損害を埋合わせる(弁償する).【類】I have said that Anthropology has not yet *made* ***good*** its title to be ranked as an independet science.—A. Macalister. / I'll *make* ***good*** your loss. / It is likely to be *made* ***good***. ‖ Salary $50,000 to begin with; $100,000 a year after *making* ***good***. 俸給は始めのうちは五万ドル; いよいよいということになってからは年に十万ドル. ¶Let us *make* ***home*** the best we can. できるだけ急いで家へ帰りましょう. ¶*make* one ***immune*** against ... ...に対して人を免疫にさせる ‖ Winter is *making* ***in earnest***. 段々本格の冬になってきた. ¶The decision is ***irrevocably*** *made*. =The die is cast. もう動きのない所(本ぎまり)となった. ¶Advertising rates are to be *made* ***known*** on application. 広告料は申込に応じて通知することになっています. ¶He *made* ***light*** (***much***) of the difficulty. 彼はその困難を軽(重要)視した.【類】Almost **everywhere she** was well treated and *made* ***much*** of. ¶*make* ***merry*** over their victory 彼らの勝利ではしゃぐ. ¶Have you *made* it ***out***? それがお分かりになりましたか. ‖ How do you *make* that ***out***? そりゃどういうわけです. ‖ You can *make* it ***out*** with a telescope. 望遠鏡で見れば分かるでしょう.【類】I can't *make* ***out*** what it's all about! / His speech from the balcony could with difficulty be *made* ***out*** in the din. / as far as this reporter can *make* ***out*** / all I can *make* ***out*** is that ... ‖ *make* ***out*** a copy 複本を作製する ‖ *make* ***out*** a check 小切手を書く ‖ *make* ***out*** a record 記録を作る ‖ The bills of lading (船荷証券) are *made* ***out*** to order. / *make* ***out*** a report ‖ *make* ***out*** a budget / *make* ***out*** an order for books (本の注文書) / *make* ***out*** a bill (勘定書) ‖ *make* ***out*** the deficiency out of ... ...から不足を補う ‖ *make* ***out*** on a small wage わずかの賃金でどうやら暮す ‖ How are thing *making* ***out***? 景気はどうかね. ¶*make* it ***popular*** それを一般向きにする. ¶*make* it ***public*** それを公にする. ¶*make* ***ready*** 用意する. ¶*make* oneself ***responsible*** for ... ...に対して責任を負う. ¶It will *make* you ***ridiculous*** in their eyes. 君がそんなことをしたらあの人たちの笑い物になるだろう. ¶Wealth *makes* many men ***selfish***. 金ができると多くの人は利己主義になる. ¶***solidly*** *made* がっし

り作られた. ¶*make* ***straight*** for … …に直行する. 【類】he *made* ***straight*** towards … ¶*make* oneself ***strange*** 勝手が分からない振りをする. ¶pains should be taken to *make* ***sure*** that … …ということを確めるために骨を折るべきだ ‖ I *made* ***sure*** that he would do so, but am disappointed. 彼は大丈夫そうするだろうと思っていたが失望した. ¶*make* oneself ***understood*** 自分の意志を了解させる.

M² The eldest girl's frocks can be *made* ***down*** for her sisters. 《俗》長女の上着は妹たちのに小さく仕立て直される. ¶rapidly (stealthily) *make* ***off*** 急いで(そっと)立去る ‖ *make* ***off*** (=away) with public money 公金をもって逃げる. ¶he has *made* ***over*** his property to … 彼はその財産を…に譲渡した ‖ This coat will have to be *made* ***over*** (=remade). この服は改造する必要がある. ¶*make* ***up*** a list of … …の表を作製する ‖ All these will *make* ***up*** a long list. これを並べると長い表になる. ‖ *make* ***up*** a prescription 処方箋を作る ‖ *make* ***up*** the accounts to date きょうまでの計算をする ‖ *make* ***up*** a fire 火をおこす. 【類】*make* ***up*** a good fire (勢のよい火) / *make* ***up*** a bed ‖ *make* ***up*** (=edit) a magazine 原稿を編集する ‖ *make* ***up*** a train of cars 列車を編成する. 【類】*make* ***up*** a party to go to a dance / *make* ***up*** only 20 percent of the total population / They amounted to 5-million dollars, *making* ***up*** 15 per cent of the total imports. / a quality that goes to *make* ***up*** a perfect teacher ‖ She was slow in *making* ***up*** her mind. 彼女は仲々決心がつかなかった. ‖ with the mind so *made* ***up*** そう腹をきめて. 【類】*make* ***up*** one's mind on the question of … / I could not *make* ***up*** my mind which to choose. / *make* ***up*** one's mind in one's own way (自分流に) / People want more information in order to *make* ***up*** their minds (もっと詳しく知りたがる). ‖ *make* ***up*** a marriage 結婚を取きめる ‖ facts that go to *make* ***up*** the civilization of the West 西欧文明の基礎になる事実 ‖ Your letter was unreadable having been *made* ***up*** wet. お手紙はすっかりぬれていて読めなかった. ‖ more than *make* ***up*** for the loss 損失を償って余りがある ‖ *make* ***up*** [for] this loss この損害を補う ‖ *make* ***up*** the lost ground 失地を回復する ‖ *make* ***up*** the deficit 赤字を埋める ‖ *make* ***up*** in quantity what it lacks in quality 質の悪いのは量で補う. 【類】*make* ***up*** natural deficiency / She has reared her children, *making* ***up*** by loving instinct what she lacked in knowledge. 【類】*make* ***up*** for lost time (時間の遅れ) ‖ *make* ***up*** for leeway 遅れを取戻す, 苦境を脱しようとする ‖ By dint of hard study he *made* ***up*** for his want of ability. 彼は猛勉強によって能力の不足を補った. ‖ She *makes* ***up*** for the defects of her person by the sweetness of her manner. 彼女は肉体の不美を態度の魅力で補う. 【類】raise wages to *make* ***up*** for the increased cost of living / I will *make* ***up*** in diligence what I lacked in natural gift. / But what she lacks in size she *makes* ***up*** in nerve (勇気). ‖ *make* ***up*** cloth into a suit 布地をたってスーツを仕立てる ‖ flowers *made* ***up*** into beautiful and artistic arrangements 美しく芸術味豊かに生けた花 ‖ be *made* ***up*** of many factors 色々な要素から成っている. 【類】The train was *made* ***up*** of 15 coaches. / a conservative government—a government *made* ***up*** of men of old Japan. / a crowd *made* ***up*** of priests and soldiers and common people ‖ Each quiz will be *made* ***up*** of from 5 to 10 questions. 各テストは五問から十問の質問を含むことになろう. ‖ *make* ***up*** galley of type into pages 〘印刷〙棒組からページにメーキャップする ‖ *make* ***up*** to one's senior office 上役に取入る ‖ He wanted to *make* ***up*** to the cute housemaid. 彼はその美しい女中に言い寄ろうとした ‖ *make* it ***up*** with him to be friends again 彼と仲直りしてまた仲よしになる ‖ Jack is down here to *make* ***up***. ジャックが仲直りしようとここへ来ている. 【類】Bill, Jack is coming to *make* ***up*** with you. ‖ The set of his followers *made* ***up*** a gang with him as leader. 彼の子分らは彼を統領として一団を作った. ‖ *make* ***up*** (=proceed) to … …に進み寄る ‖ *make* ***up*** to (=flatter *or* try to gain the favor of) … …に取入る ‖ The two friends quarrelled, but they *made* it ***up*** [again]. その二人はけんかしたが仲直りをした. ‖ an actor *made* ***up*** for the part of an old man 老人に粉した俳優 ‖ She was then slightly *made* ***up***. 彼女は当時薄化粧していた. 【類】She *made* herself ***up*** for outing. ¶an old man *made* ***young*** again 若返った老人.

P He *made* ***after*** the boy. 彼はその子供を追いかけた. ¶It is *made* ***by*** art, not by nature. それは自然の力でなく人工でできている. ‖ This is *made* ***by*** hand (machinery). これは手細工(機械製)だ. ¶He looks a sturdy fellow, one who was *made* ***for*** action. 彼は筋骨たくましく活動に適した人のように見える. ‖ This *makes* (=conduces) ***for*** efficiency. こうすると能率が上がる. ‖ They *make* ***for*** chaos, not cosmos. それらのことは破壊的であって建設的ではない. ‖ *make* ***for*** … as hard as one can run 一生懸命かけて…に向う ‖ The treaty was *made* ***for*** peace in the Far East. その条約は極東の平和のために結ばれた. ‖ He *made* ***for*** the door. 彼は戸口の方へ行った. ‖ We *made* ***for*** home together. われわれは一緒に家に帰った. 【類】Next we *made* ***for*** the Albert Memorial (アルバート記念館). ‖ it will *make* ***for*** the good of … それは…の利益になるだろう. 【類】It is true that war *makes* ***for*** national welfare in a sense. / This alliance *makes* ***for*** peace. / *make* much ***for*** the peace of the world / That doesn't *make* ***for*** your case. / the virtues that *make* ***for*** success in commercial life / Absence of competition *makes* ***for*** sloth (ものぐさの風). ‖ The hat was *made* ***for*** you. その帽子は君にピッタリだ. ‖ *make* allowance ***for*** circumstances 事情をしん酌する ‖ *make* room ***for*** an old lady 老婦人のために席をあけてやる ‖ *make* way ***for*** others [to go by] 人が通れるようにあけてやる. ¶Gas is *made* ***from*** coal. ガスは石炭から造る. 【類】a man *made* ***from*** snow=a snow-man / Havana, a cigar *made* ***from*** Cuban tobacco. / Brandy is *made* ***from*** grapes. / curry-powder *made* ***from*** the original Indian recipe / We *make* our clothes ***from*** cloth. / Butter is *made* ***from*** cream. / Bread is *made* ***from*** flour. / Cereal (《米》穀粉で作った朝食) is *made* ***from*** grain. / Cheese is *made* ***from*** milk. / Tea is *made* ***from*** dried tea leaves. / Cloth is *made* ***from*** cotton. / Grape jelly (ぶどうジェリ) is *made* ***from*** sugar and grape juice. / Nylon is *made* ***from*** air, coal and water. / Oatmeal is *made* ***from*** oats (カラス麦). / Rubber is *made* ***from*** sap (樹液). / Saccharin (サッカリン) can be *made* ***from*** coal tar. / We *make* flour ***from*** wheat. ‖ *make* a living ***from*** literary work 文筆によって生計を立てる. ¶*made* ***in*** Great Britain 大英国製. 【類】Automobiles are *made* ***in*** a factory. ‖ *make* a difference ***in*** tariff 料金に違いが出る ‖ *make* a name ***in*** the world 世の中で名をあげる. 【類】*make* a speech ***in*** public. ¶Wool is *made* ***into*** cloth and yarn. 羊毛はらしゃや毛糸になる. ‖ *make* hide ***into*** leather 生皮をなめし皮にする / The skin of the walrus (せいうち) is *made* ***into*** leather. / Sour grapes are *made* ***into*** raisins (干ぶどう) or wine. ‖ *make* them ***into*** bundles それをたばねる ‖ *make* milk ***into*** butter and cheese 牛乳でバターやチーズを造る. 【類】*make* a story (小説) ***into*** a play (戯曲) / *make* it ***into*** a stock (=jointstock) company (株式会社) ‖ *make* them ***into*** slaves 彼らをどれいにする. ¶Cloth is *made* ***of*** (=out of) cotton (silk, wool). 布は綿(など)で作る. ‖ a pillow *made* ***of*** down 羽根まくら ‖ *make* a cat ***of*** cloth for the baby 赤ん坊に布でねこを作ってやる. 【類】A football is *made* ***of*** leather. / a cord *made* ***of*** human hair / The Eskimos eat the flesh of the polar bear and *make* clothes ***of*** its splendid fur. / God *made* man ***of*** clay. / Concrete is *made* ***of*** cement, sand, stones, and water. / *make* a box ***of*** wide boards / Some roads are *made* ***of*** gravel (砂利) / Articles *made* ***of*** metal are called hardware (金物). / Some shoes are *made* ***of*** cloth. / Bed sheets (シーツ) are *made* ***of*** white cloth. / Lemonade (レモン水) is *made* ***of*** lemon juice, sugar, and water. / *make* a wreath (花輪) ***of*** flowers / Many tools (器具) are *made* ***of*** iron. / Crackerjack is *made* ***of*** popcorn (はぜきび). / Flour is *made* ***of*** wheat. / Furniture is *made* mainly ***of*** wood. ‖ One of the boatmen, *making* a megaphone ***of*** his hands, roared, "…". 舟子の一人は両手でメガフォンをこしらえて「…」と叫んだ. ‖ He was *made* ***of*** different stuff. あの男は他の人とできが違っている. ‖ Good manners are *made* ***of*** petty sacrifices. ささいな犠牲でりっぱな行儀ができ上る. ‖ *make* a man ***of*** him 彼を一人前の男にする ‖ *make* a friend ***of*** an enemy 敵を味方にする ‖ *make* game ***of*** a person 人をおもちゃにする. 【類】I intend to *make* a lawyer ***of*** my son. ‖ *make* nothing ***of*** others' opinion 人の意見を無視する ‖ I can *make* nothing ***of*** his words. 私には彼の言ったことが一向分からない. ‖ What do you *make of* this, of her coming? 彼女が来るというのは一体どうした訳だろう. 【類】 One doesn't exactly know what to *make of* (=judge) him. ‖ Attention is the stuff that memory is *made of*. 注目は記憶のもとである. ‖ Don't *make* a fool *of* me. 人をばかにするな. ‖ *make* the best *of* abad bargain 損して徳とる ‖ be *made* an idol *of* by one's admirers 崇拝者(ファン)に神様扱いにされる ‖ What an object you have *made of* yourself! 何というだらしのないことだ. ‖ He was *made* a lion *of* among women. 彼は女に大もてであった. ‖ *make* the most *of* an opportunity 機会をせいぜい利用する ‖ *make* a show *of* (=display) leather goods くつ製品を陳列する ‖ *make* a show *of* (=show off) one's talent 自分の才能を見せびらかす ‖ *make* a poor show *of* oneself ひどい目に合う, へまをやる ‖ I can *make* no sense *of* wnat he says. あれの言うことはさっぱり分からない. ‖ *make* good (the best) use *of* … …を(最大限に)利用する ‖ Though my bed was not long enough for me, I had to *make* a virtue *of* necessity. 私の寝台は私には長さが足りなかったがぜいたくを言わずにそれで満足した. ‖ How much do you think would be *made on* the business? この取引でどの位もうかりましょうか. 【類】 *make* a jack-o'-lantern (お化けちょうちん) *out of* a pumpkin ‖ What can you *make out of* this stuff (この材料)? / The box is *made out of* cedar wood. ‖ He *made* a great fortune *out of* ale. 彼はビールで大身代をこしらえた. ‖ *make* much profit *out of* it それで大いにもうける ‖ *make* merry *over* another's mishap 人の災難をうれしがる. ¶clothes (shoes) *made to* one's measure 寸法に合わせてこしらえた着物 ‖ My clothes are *made to* order. 私の服は注文仕立だ. 【類】 It was a day *made to* order (おあつらえの) for such a spectacle (観艦式など), with brilliantly clear sky and the miracle of Fujiyama against the western sky.—Eliza Ruhamah Scidmore. ¶He *made* (=stepped) *toward* home. 彼はわが家へと歩を進めた. ¶This is *made with* a knife. これは小刀で作ったものだ. ‖ What do you *make with* flour? 粉で何をこしらえるか. 【類】 The bow is *made with* a stick and a string. / Strawberry cake is *made with* biscuits and strawberries. ‖ Revolutions are not *made with* rose-water. 革命はなまやさしいことでは遂げられるものでない. ‖ an agreement *made with* … …と結んだ協定 ‖ They *made* terms *with* him which amounted complete submission. 彼らは彼と妥協したがそれは完全な降服も同様なものであった. ‖ *make* a quarrel *with* … …と口げんかをする ‖ *make* friends *with* … …と友人になる.

O He was *made* to do it. 彼はそれをさせられた. 【類】 The bear was *made* to dance. ¶Why, what *makes* you think that? まあ何だってそんなことを考えるのか. ¶the politics which *made* and unmade Rome ローマを起したと同時にローマを亡ぼした政略. ¶*make* believe (=pretend) to throw a ball 球を投げるまねをする.

maker, *n.* 作成者.

Q made by a ***respectable maker*** たしかな製造業者の手になる.

Q² a ***cosmetics maker*** 化粧品製造業者. ¶a ***curriculum*** *maker* 教課編成者. ¶a ***dictionary maker*** 辞書編集者. ¶a ***garden*** *maker* 庭園師. ¶Krupp, the great ***German gun*** *maker* ドイツの大兵器製作者クルップ. ¶a ***holiday maker*** 休日行楽者. ¶***Opinion*** *makers* in the publishing world are people who know the best in literature and appreciate the best in life. 出版界で世評を作る人とは文学において最高を知りまた人生における最高を正しく評価する人々である. ¶top ***government policy makers*** 政府の最高政策立案者たち. ¶a ***path maker*** 開拓者. ¶a ***trouble maker*** よく事件を起す人. ¶a ***wine maker*** ぶどう酒醸造業者.

makeshift, *n.* 臨時策.

Q purely ***temporary*** *makeshifts* 全く一時のまにあわせ策.

make-up, *n.* ふん装; 構造; 気質.

Q in a ***laughter-provoking*** *make-up* 腹の皮をよらせる顔作りで. ¶It is a part of his ***mental*** *make-up*. 彼の性格にはそんな所もある. ¶the ***physical*** or ***mental*** *make-up* of a man 人の肉体的または精神的構造.

Q² ***pancake*** *make-up* パンケーキ(固形おしろい)によるお化粧. ¶***society*** *make-up* 社会の構成. ¶the art of ***theatre*** *make-up* 劇のメーキアップ技術. ¶He is ***of*** a nervous *make-up* (=disposition). 彼は神経質な男だ.

P² *make-up of* Congress [米国の]議会構成.

makeweight, *n.* 足し前, 埋草.

P He was attached to the Embassy merely ***as*** a *makeweight*. 彼は補充員に加わるだけで大使館付となった.

making, *n.* 製作; 素質, 器.

V He ***has*** the *making*[*s*] of a general in him. 彼は将たる素質をそなえている. 【類】 He ***has*** in him the *making*[*s*] of a great cartoonist (漫画家). / In his opinion the Chinese ***have*** the *making* in them of good and valiant soldiers.

Q ***new*** *making* [着物の]仕立おろし.

Q² ***collection*** *making* コレクション(収集)の仕方. ¶time spent in ***home*** *making* 家事に費す時間. ¶***rain ~aking*** 人口降雨. ¶***road*** *making* 道路建設.

P a land where civilization is still ***in*** the *making* 今なお文化未完成の国 ‖ The child of today is the man of a future day ***in*** the *making*. 今日の小児が将来大人になるのである. ‖ a criminal, either actual or ***in*** the *makıng* (=incomplete³) 既遂または未遂の犯人. 【類】 He is still ***in*** the *making*. / a dictionary ***in*** the *making* / The dictionary was thirty-four years ***in*** the *making* (三十四年の歳月を要した). / mankind ***in*** the *makıng*. ¶My poverty is ***of*** my own *making*. 私の貧乏は自業自得だ. ‖ These thoughts are not ***of*** his own *makıng* or discovery. これらの考えは彼自身案出または発見したものではない.

P² This misfortune was the *making of* him. この不幸がかえって彼の成功の因となった. ¶the *makings* (=earnings) ***out of*** one's work《口語》その仕事からのかせぎ高.

maladjustment, *n.* 不調和.

Q ***social*** *maladjustment* 社会の不調節.

malady, *n.* 疾病.

V This ***set up*** (=caused) the *malady* from which he died. このために彼の死因となった病が起った.

Q a ***deadly*** *malady* 命とりの病気, 死病. ¶Toothache is an ***excruciating*** *malady*. 歯痛は非常に苦しいものだ. ¶that ***incurable*** *malady* of trout fever ます釣り熱というあの不治の病. ¶***social*** *maladies* (=evils) 社会悪. ¶a ***torturing*** *malady* 非常に苦しい病気.

Q² an ***infant*** *malady* 小児病.

malaria, *n.* マラリア.

V ***stamp out*** *malaria* マラリヤを撲滅する.

malcontent, *n.* 不平家.

Q a ***grumbling*** *malcontent* ぶうぶういう不平家.

male, *n.* 男性.

Q² ***adult*** *males* (females) 成人男性(女性).

malediction, *n.* 悪口, 悪態.

V ***utter*** a *malediction* 悪口をはく.

maleficent, *a.* 害をなす.

P *maleficent* ***to*** a person 人に害をなす(魔物など).

malevolent, *a.* 悪意のある.

P *malevolent* ***to*** a person 人にあだする.

malice, *n.* 悪意; えん恨.

V It is wrong to ***bear*** *malice*. 恨みをいだくのは良くない. ‖ I ***bear*** you no *malice*. 私は君を恨んではいない. ¶***harbour*** *malice* 悪意をいだく.

P He did it ***of*** *malice*. 彼は悪意でそれをやった. ¶***in*** the *malice* of destiny 運命のいたずらで. ¶***through*** *malice* 悪意から.

P² *malice against* a person 人に対する悪意. ¶bear *malice* (=ill-will) *to* (=***towards***) … …に対して悪意をいだく.

malign, *a.* 悪意のある.

P *malign to* (=***towards***) a person 人に対して悪意を持つ.

malignant, *a.* 悪意ある.

P *malignant to* (=***towards***) a person 人に対して悪意のある.

malnutrition, *n.* 栄養不良.

Q² ***wartime*** *malnutrition* 戦時栄養失調.

P sallow, undersized, and ill-shaped children ***from*** *malnutrition* and want of exercise 栄養不良や運動不足のため血色の悪い発育不良な格好のとれていない子供たち.

maltreatment, *n.* 乱用, 虐待.

P² the *maltreatment of* idiom 慣用語句の乱(誤)用 ‖ *maltreatment of* animals 動物の虐待.

mammal, *n.* ほ乳動物.

Q the ***higher*** (***lower***) *mammals* 高等(下等)ほ乳動物.

man, *n.* 人, 人間; 男; 大人; 一かどの男; 雇人; 配下; 良人; 『将棋』こま.

v ***act*** the *man* against oppressors of the weak 弱者に迫害を加えるものに対して男気を出す. ¶***allow*** a *man* to take liberties with her はだを許す. ¶***appoint*** a *man* to an office 人をある職に任命する. ¶***call in*** a medical *man* 医師を迎える. ¶***crown*** a *man* 王位につかせる; 駒(こま)を王にならす. ¶*Men* are often ***deceived*** by what they see. 人は往々自分の目にだまされる. ¶***draw*** a *man* from retirement 隠退した人を引っ張り出す. ¶***electrify*** his *men* 彼の部下に深い感化を与える. ¶***estimate*** a young *man* accurately in an interview 会見して青年の人物を正確に見定める. ¶***fillip*** a *man* on the hand 人の手を指ではじく. ¶Education ***fits*** a *man* for social life. 教育は人を社会生活に適するようにつくり上げる. ‖ ***fit*** young *men* into the world 青年を世の中で役に立つように仕込む. ¶***get*** her *man* [女に]恋人ができる. ¶We cannot ***get*** suitable *men*. われわれは適当な人が得られない. ¶He knows how to ***handle*** *men*. 彼は人間の取扱い方を心得ている. ¶You can't ***hate*** a *man* you know. 知っている人は憎めない. ¶My cook ***has*** a young *man*. うちの(女)コックには若い恋人がある. ¶He ***held up*** a *man*, robbed him of £50 and a watch and chain. 彼は辻強盗をやってある人から五十ポンドと時計をくさりぐるみ奪った. ¶***identify*** the *man* その人がだれだか(身もとを)確かめる. ¶***impersonate*** a noble *man* [俳優など]貴人にふんする. ¶She ***knows*** no *man*. 彼女はまだ男のはだを知らない. ¶The masters ***locked out*** all the *men*. 雇主たちは従業員を一斉に閉め出した(ストの際). ¶***make*** a *man* of him 彼を一人前の男にする ‖ qualities that ***make*** a *man* ひとかどの人間に必要な資質 ‖ ***make*** a new *man* of him 彼を生れ変らせる. 【類】You have ***made*** another *man* of me. ‖ I will ***make*** *men* pay! 男どもどうするか見ていろ! (男の犠牲になった女ののろいの声). ¶***marry*** a *man* for his worth 人物を見込んで結婚する. ¶ability to ***pick out*** good *men*, and assist them to get on 人材を抜てきしこれを助けて成功させる能力. ¶Indeed, professors are the last *man* an omniscient God would ***pick up*** for the job. 全知の神がその仕事をさせる人を教授連から選ぶなどは思いも寄らないことだ. ¶To ***place*** a new *man* suddenly in a position of command is a risk which is often worth the while. 新人を突然主任の地位にすえることは往々試みる値打のある冒険である. ¶***play*** the *man*=act manly 男らしく振舞う. ¶a gift that ***pleases*** every *man* 万人向の進物. ¶He has entirely ***put off*** that old *man*. 彼はあの老人をまんまと一杯食わせた. ¶The dinner is ***put off*** "the old *man*" and ***put on*** "the new *man*." それは年忘れの会であった. ¶the great doctrines which ***raise*** *man* to higher levels 人類を向上させる大教理. ¶ Can I ***recognize*** the *man?* 私がその人に会ってその人だと分かりましょうか. ¶a better system of ***recruiting*** able *men* for public service 改善された官吏登用法. ¶***seek out*** the *man* その人を捜し出す. ¶I did not intend to ***slight*** that *man*. 私にはあの人を侮る積りはなかった. ¶The people of Calvert County can ***spot*** a *man* from St. Mary's or Anne Arundel, as soon as he opens his mouth. カルヴァート州の人はセント・メリーまたはアン・アランデルからきた人を一言聞けばすぐそれと感付く. ¶***start*** a *man* in business 人に商売を始めさせる ‖ This *man* I have ***started*** in life. この人を私は引立ててやった. ¶***station*** *men* at ... 人員を...に配置する. ¶***trace*** *men* who are "wanted" お尋ね者を捜し出す. ¶***train*** a *man* for a lawyer 人を法律家に仕込む. 【類】Our colleges are charged with failings to ***train*** *men* for citizenship. ¶***turn*** (=***send***) ***out*** *men* [大学など]卒業生を出す. ¶***unman*** the *man* その人をめめしくする.

v² *Men* do ***expect*** purity and goodness from women. 男子は純潔と善良とを女子に期待する. ¶as *men* ***go*** 世間並の人物標準から見れば. ¶*Man* ***proposes***; God disposes. 〖諺〗ことを計るは人, ことを為すは神.

Q an ***able-bodied*** *man* 屈強な男子. ¶***active*** and ***strong*** *men* 活動的で強壮な男子. ¶***alcoholic*** *men* and women 酒を愛する男女; アルコールに中毒した男女. ¶an ***all-round*** *man* 多芸多能の人. ¶an ***American*** *man* 男のアメリカ人. ¶He's quite ***another*** *man*. 彼はすっかり変った(別人の観がある). ¶an ***austere*** *man* 厳格な人. ¶an ***average*** *man* 並の人. 【類】The ***average*** *man* in the street is unable to tell the distinctive features of the wood of oak from that of chestnut. / These words are beyond the vocabulary of the ***average*** *man*. / knowledge beyond that possessed by the ***average*** *man*. ¶a ***bearded*** *man* ひげのある人. ¶I consider him the ***best*** *man* for the place. 彼は正にはまり役だと思う. ¶one of the ***best-hated*** *men* in Japan 日本で一番憎まれ者の一人. ¶a ***big dark*** *man* 大柄な色黒の人. ¶the type of those ***breezy*** *men* of action あの活発な働き手の典型. ¶a ***brisk*** *man* 活気のある人. ¶a ***burly, good-natured*** *man* たくましい善良な人. ¶He is a ***busy*** *man*. 彼は忙しい人だ. ¶a ***caclulating*** *man* 勘定高い人. ¶a ***city-bred*** *man* 都育ちの人. ¶the ***civilized*** *man* of today 今日の文明人. 【類】diseases peculiar to ***civilized*** *men*. ¶It is the belief of some of the ***clearest-visioned*** *men* of England. 英国のけい眼者の一部はそう信じている. ¶a ***cold*** (***hot***)***-blooded*** *man* 冷(熱)血漢. ¶***college-bred*** *men* =college graduates 大学出の人. ¶a ***competent*** and ***efficient*** *man* 申分のない有為の人. ¶a ***complete*** *man* 申分のない人. ¶a ***courteous kindly*** *man* いんぎんで親切な人. ¶a ***dead*** *man* 余分な人員. ¶a ***disagreeable*** *man* いやな男. ¶a ***dying*** *man* ひん死の人. ¶The Maya Temple is the greatest achievement of ***early*** *men* in America. マーヤ人の寺院はアメリカにおける初期の人間の手になる最大功績である. ¶an ***educated*** and ***accomplished*** *man* 教養ある人. ¶eminent ***literary*** *men* 著名な文士たち. ¶an ***enlisted*** *man* (=EM) 下士官兵 ‖ terminal leave pay for ***enlisted*** *men* 兵に対する期末休暇手当. ¶an ***enterprising*** *men* やり手. ¶one of the most ***erudite*** *men* of his age 彼の時代の大学者の一人. ¶a ***European*** *man* ヨーロッパ人. ¶an ***exacting*** *man* やかまし屋. ¶an ***excellent*** *man* of business すぐれた事務家. ¶***ex-service*** *men* 軍隊に籍をおいた人. ¶a ***fastidious*** *man* 気むずかしい人. ¶a ***feeble-minded*** *man* 低能. ¶the ***first*** *men* in the South 南部地方における第一流の人士. ¶Sir Aurel Stein, absolutely the ***first ranking*** *man* in his line その社会では断然第一人者であるオーレル・スタイン卿. ¶a ***first-rate*** *man* of business 第一流の実業家. ¶a woman and three ***foreign*** *men* 一人の婦人と三人の男の外国人. ¶one of the ***foremost*** *men* in ... ...における一流の人物の一人. ¶children earning the wages of a ***full-grown*** *man* 大人の給金をもらう子供. ¶Between the two, I prefer the has-been to the ***going-to-be*** *man*. 二者の中で私は何々たらんとする人よりも何々たりし人の方を採る. ¶a ***good*** and ***honest*** *man* 善良で正直な人. ¶This *man* is [a] ***good-for-nothing***. この人は何の役にも立たない. ¶a ***good-proportioned*** *man* [からだの]均整のとれた人. ¶a ***Grand Old*** *Man* of science 科学の老大家. 【類】Mr. Takahashi, Japan's "***Grand Old*** *Man*" of finance. / Prof. Abe, the ***grand old*** *man* of baseball in Japan. / this ***grand old*** *man* who is still hale at the age of ninety. ¶a ***grave-faced*** *man* まじめな顔をした人. 【類】a ***grave-looking*** *man* in a black coat (モーニング). ¶He will make a ***great*** *man* in future. 彼は将来大人物になる. 【類】one of the ***greatest*** *men* of his time. ¶He is a ***grown*** *man* now. 彼はもう大人だ. ¶*men* ***grown gray*** in literary pursuits 文壇の老大家. ¶a ***haggard-faced*** *man* 顔のやつれた人. ¶He's not ***half*** the *man* he was. 彼は大いに変った. ¶Who is the ***happy*** *man?* おむこさんはだれですか. ¶You are a ***hard*** *man* to deal with. 君は気むずかしい人だ. ¶a ***hard-hearted*** *man* 薄情者. ¶a ***healthy old*** *man* 達者な老人. ¶***highly-placed*** *men*=men of high standing 身分の高い人たち. ¶an ***honorable*** *man* りっぱな人物. ¶satisfy (=fortify) the ***inner*** *man* [食事をして]腹をこしらえる. ¶an ***insignificant little*** *man* つまらない人間. ¶an ***illiterate*** *man* 無筆の人. ¶an ***illustrious*** *man* 有名な人. ¶an ***impetuous*** and ***excitable*** *man* 性急で激しやすい人. ¶an ***indignant*** *man* 憤慨している人. ¶***innocent*** *man* 無邪気な人. ¶an ***intelligent*** *man* そう明な人. ¶an ***intemperate*** *man* 不節制な人. ¶a ***just*** *man* 正しい人. ¶a ***keen*** *man* of business 鋭敏な実務家. ¶a ***kind-hearted*** *man* 親切な人. ¶a ***kindly*** *man* 心のやさしい人. ¶quite a ***ladies'*** *man* 女にちやほやする男. ¶I am the ***last*** *man* in the world to ... 私は断じて...はしない. 【類】He was the ***last*** *man* I suspected of it. ¶a ***law-trained*** *man* 法律の頭ができている人. ¶a ***lazy*** *man* 怠け者. ¶They cast him as ***leading*** *man* in the film. 彼がその映画の主役に選ばれた. ‖ a ***leading*** *man* in an action play 活劇ものの主役. ¶we ***lesser*** *men* われわれ雑輩. ¶a ***light-handed*** *man* 手先の器用な人. ¶a ***light-headed young*** *man* of fashion 時流を追う軽薄な青年. ¶a ***light-hearted*** *man* 気軽な人. ¶a ***light-***

fingered man すり. ☞ 総称は the light-fingered gentry. ¶a *literary man* 文学者. ¶a *little man* 子供; つまらない人. ¶a *lonely man* [独りぼっちで]さびしい人. ¶a *long-headed man* 賢明な人. ¶What kind of a *looking man* is he? どんな風さいですか. ¶The historian is a *looking-back man*. He has nothing to do with what is coming. 歴史家は回顧の人である. 彼は未来には何の関係もない. ¶get wild like a *mad man* 気違いのように暴れる. ¶He is no *man's man*. 彼は人の配下に立つ人間ではない. ¶like *many another man* and woman before him 彼以前に同じ例が多くあったように. ¶a *marked man* 注意人物. ¶a *married man* 妻帯者. ¶a *medical man* 医者. 【類】consult a *medical man* / send for a *medical man*. ¶a *meek-looking man* おとなしそうな人. ¶a *mere man* 凡人. ¶the top A.S. *military man* in the Far East 極東米軍最高の軍人. 【類】a *military* or *naval man*=a service man. ¶It has been said that the most *miserable man* in the world is one who has no friends. 友人のない人が世の中で一番みじめな人だと言われている. ¶*military men* 軍人. ¶a *moneyed man* 富者. ¶almost everything that a *mortal man* can desire およそ人間の望みうるほとんどすべての物 ‖ *Man* is *mortal*. 人は死ぬものだ. ¶*multi-millioned men* 数百万の富を有する人々. ¶He has done more for the navy and for his country than any *naval man* since the days of Nelson. 彼はネルソンの時代この方どの海軍々人よりも海軍及び国家のために尽す所が多かった. ¶a *necessary man* 有用の人物. ¶the *new man* 今度の人. ¶a *non-educated man* 教育のない人々. ¶an *old man* 老人; 隊長, 大将(社長など) ‖ a malevolent *old man* 意地の悪い老人. ¶an *ordinary man* 平凡な人. ¶an *ordinary laboring man* 普通の労働者. ¶an *outspoken man* 遠慮なく物を言う人. ¶an *over-mannered man* is like an overdressed lady. 行儀の良過ぎる男子は着飾り過ぎた婦人のようだ. ¶I am not now my *own man*. 私は今は自主自由の身ではない. ¶a *pale man* 青びょうたん. ¶a *pivotal man* in the firm その店の中心人物. ¶a *powerful man* 有力者. ¶a *prepossessing man* 人好きのする人. ¶*primitive* (=dawn) *man* 原始人. ¶a *princely man* 君子. ¶a *professional man* 専門家, くろうと. ¶*progressive* and *enlightened men* 進歩的で明敏の人. ¶Your *practical man* will sneer at ... 例の実際家は…に対してせせら笑うだろう. ¶*prominent men* of the time 当世の名士 ‖ *prominent men* of affairs 知名の実務家. ¶a *pushing, ambitious man* 気鋭の野心家. ¶a *quiet, studious man* 落着いた篤学者. ¶a *reading man* 読書家. ¶a *recently-blinded man* 最近失明した人. ¶a *red-blooded* young *man* 元気はつらつたる若者. ¶a *remarkable man* 非凡な人. ¶*representative men* in the business and in the professions 実業界及び専門家社会の代表的人物. ¶seek out the *right man* 適材を捜す. 【類】get the *right men* in the right place. ¶a *right-handed man* 右ききの人. ¶a *righteous man* 正義の人. ¶a *right-thinking man* and woman 考えの正しい男女. ¶a *rising man* 日の出の勢の人. ¶a *safe man* 信頼すべき人. ¶no *sane man* thinks that ... いやしくも正気な人は…と思わない. 【類】No *sane man* can be opposed to trade union (労働組合). ¶*Men* are *scarce* (*plentiful*). 人手が容易に得られない(いくらもある). ¶a *self-contained* and *silent man* 打解けない無口の人. ¶a *self-made man* 自力でやり上げた人. ¶a *self-possessed man* 落着いた人. ¶a *sensible man* 物の分かった人. ¶He is a very *set* (=*obstinate*) *man*. あの男はなかなか強情だ. ¶a *shining well-groomed* and *well-tailored young man* 身支度も好く服装もきちんとしてひときわ目立つ青年. ¶a *short man* 背の低い人. ¶*shrewd men* of business 機敏な実業家. ¶a *simple, homely man* 一本気でじみな人. ¶a *single man* 独身者. ¶a *smart man* 利口な人. ¶a *smooth-spoken man* 口のうまい人. ¶a *sober-minded man* 冷静な人. ¶You are quite a *sociable man*. 君は社交家だ. ¶a *tall, spare man* やせてのっぽの人. 【類】He is *tall* and *lean*. ¶a *solemn-faced man* いかめしい顔の人. ¶one of those *sorry men* こういう不幸な人. ¶a *sound business man* 着実な実業家. ¶a *straightforward man* 卒直な人. ¶a *tactful man* 気のきいた人. ¶a *thin* (*thick*) *man* やせた(太った)人. ¶*thinking men* in the States are realizing that ... 米国の識者に…ということが理解されて来た. ¶a *thriving man* (商売などの)当り屋. ¶a *titled man* 肩書のある人. ¶*top men* 頭株, 領袖(りょう). ¶a *travelled man* 経験ある旅行家. ¶a *trusted man* 信頼されている人. ¶a *trustworthy man* 信頼するに足る人. ¶an *uncultivated man* 修養のない人. ¶the burdens of the *under man* 下積の人の重荷. ¶a most *undesirable man* もっとも好ましくない男. ¶*university-bred* (=*trained*) *men* 大学仕込みの人. ¶*untried men* まだ気心の分からない人. ¶an *untutored man* 野人. ¶the *very man* 正にその人. ¶a *weedy young man* ひょろひょろした若者. ¶a *well-conducted man* 素行のよい人. ¶a *well-dressed man* りっぱな服装した人. ¶a *well-educated man* 十分に教育された人. ¶a *well-groomed young man* 髪の手入の行き届いた青年. ¶a *well-informed man* 物知り. ¶a *well-read* and *intelligent man* 博識そう明の人. ¶a *well-set-up young man* 格好の良い若人. ¶*wild men* about town 放とう者. ¶a *working man* 労働者. ¶her *young man* 彼女の若いつばめ. ¶I didn't like to say anything while *your man* was about; but the fact is ... 彼氏がいたので何にも言わずにいたが事実は…なのだ.

Q[2] an *adult man* or woman 成人男女. ¶a *bronze man* with a book in hand 本を手にした銅像. ¶a Chicago *business man* シカゴの実業人. ¶a *small-business* (*big-business*) *man* 小(大)企業家 ‖ businesslike *business man* てきぱきやる実務家. ¶a *call man* 随時的召集員 (fire department の). ¶a *Cambridge man* ケンブリッジ出身者(在学生). ¶a *career man* 《米》はえ抜きの外交官. 【類】a *career man* of long experience / a Government "*career man*." ¶a *cattle man*=a cattleman 《米》牧牛業者; 牧夫. ¶Papa is a *City man*, who goes early to business. パパは下町(金融街)に事務所があって朝早く家を出ます. ¶a *college man* 《米》大学生. ¶a *color man*=a colorman 黒人. ¶a *commission man* 仲買人, ブローカー. ¶a *committee man*=committeeman 委員. ¶a *con man* 《米俗》=a confidence man. ¶a *confidence man*=a bunko steerer とり込みさぎ師. ¶He is now in Paris as a foreign *contact man* for Pathé. 彼は目下パリにあってパテ映画会社の外国交渉を担当している. ¶a *credit man* [銀行などの]信用調査係. ¶a *department-store man* デパートの従業員. ¶a *duty man* 当直員. ¶an *efficiency man* 能率係. ¶Hans Andersen was a famous *fairy-tale man*. ハンス・アンデルセンは有名なおとぎ話作者だった. ¶a *family man* 家庭持ち; 家庭的の人物 ‖ He is the only *family man* in our group. われわれ仲間で家族のあるのは彼だけだ. ¶a *fighting man* 戦闘員; 戦士. ¶a *four minute man* [米国の大戦当の]四分間新聞会見という宣伝係の人. ¶Japan's *front-rank man* 日本の第一線級の人. ¶a *fruit man* くだもの屋(売る人). ¶a *garbage man* ごみ屋(特に台所の). ¶*Government men* announced recently that ... 政府筋では最近…と発表した. ¶American military *government men* 米軍政府当局. ¶a *grain man* 穀物を扱う人. ¶a *high-point man*=a high-pointer 『軍』従軍点数の高い兵士; [一般に]高点者. ¶a *holdup man* 追いはぎ. ¶a *hotel man* ホテル従業員. ¶a *junk man* (=junkman) くず屋. ¶*key men* in peace industry 平和産業の中心人物 ‖ a *key man* in a conservative party 保守党の中心人物. 【類】The farmer is a *key man* in the situation today. ¶The Japanese are the *know-how men* of the Far East. 日本人は極東における技術者である(日本は極東における工業国である). ¶a *laboratory man* 研究所員. ¶the earnings of *laboring men* and women 勤労男女の収入. ¶a *Lancashire man* [英国の綿業中心地]ランカシャ人. ¶a *liaison man* 連絡(渉外)係. ¶a *life man* 生命保険会社員. ¶a *London man* = a Londoner. ¶place "*look-out*" *men* at ... 警備員を…に配置する. ¶a *low point man*=a low-pointer 『軍』従軍点数の低い人; [一般に]得点の低い人. ¶a *maintenance man* 営繕掛員. ¶a machine *maintenance man* 機械営繕係員. ¶a "*medicine man*" [土人の]まじない師, きとう師. ¶a *quack medicine man* やぶ医者. ¶a *merchandise man*=merchandiser 商品係. ¶a *movie man* 映画人. ¶About fifteen *neighborhood men* and boys quickly gathered. 十五人ほどの近所の大人や子供が大急ぎで集った. ¶Walter Lippmann is one of America's greatest *newspaper men*. ウォルターリップマンはアメリカ最大の新聞人の一人である. ¶a *newsreel camera man* 時事映画のカメラマン ‖ a *newsreel* and *radio man* 時事映画・放送関係者. ¶a *night-soil man* おわい屋. ¶The new ambassador to Tokyo is a "*non-career man*." 新駐日大使は外交畑出身じゃない. ¶a

non-college man 大学出でない人. ¶a ***nose*** and ***throat man*** 鼻とのどの専門医. ¶an ***odd job man*** 雑用夫. ¶an ***old clothes man*** 古着商人. ¶a ***Parliament man***=a member of Parliament 英国々会議員. ¶a ***peace-at-any-price man*** 徹底的平和主義の人. ¶a ***plain-clothes man*** 私服の警官(捜査係). ¶a ***press liaison man*** 新聞記者との連絡係. ¶a ***production man*** 生産者. ¶a ***publicity man*** 宣伝係. ¶a ***public relations man*** 渉外係. ¶a ***pushcart man*** [やお屋など]手押車の行商人. ¶a ***radio man*** 放送関係者. ¶a ***railroad man***=《英》a railway man 鉄道員. ¶a ***repair man*** 修繕係. ¶a ***research man***=a researcher 調査員. ¶a ***rewrite man*** 〘新聞〙[記事を書直す]整理部員. ¶his ***right-hand man*** 彼の右腕. ¶a ***route man*** 〘新聞〙発送係. ¶a ***safety man*** 安全掛. ¶a ***salvage man*** at the door of a burnt-out place 焼失家屋の戸口にいる焼跡始末係員. ¶a returned ***service man*** 帰還兵. 【類】Discharged ***service men*** are coming back to their jobs. ‖ a distinguished ***service man*** 殊勲者. ¶the ***Shilling Man*** [英国]雑誌を読む中流階級の人. ¶a ***sleight-of-hand man*** 手品師. ¶a ***society man*** 社交界の紳士. ¶a ***still-camera man*** [映画に対し]普通のカメラマン. ¶a ***speed-up man*** 進行係. ¶a ***stunt man*** [空中サーカスなど]曲芸人. ¶a Waseda ***trained man*** 早稲田出の人. ¶be regarded as a "***Taft man***" タフト系と見なされている. ¶a ***tea*** and ***coffee man*** 紅茶・コーヒー商人. ¶a ***temperance man*** 禁酒家. ¶a ***thinking man*** 思想家. ¶a ***ticket-of-leave man*** 仮出獄人. ¶a ***tip-off man*** [競馬などの]情報屋. ¶a ***tobacco man*** タバコ屋(販売人); タバコ業者. ¶a ***university*** (=***varsity***) ***man*** 《英》大学生. ¶a ***utility man*** 雑用をやる人. ¶a ***vegetable man*** 《米》やお屋. ¶a ***washing*** (=***laundry***) ***man*** 洗たく屋. ¶a ***weather man***=a weatherman. 【類】the ***weather man*** said the skies would be clear. ¶His aides were merely ***yes men***. 彼の側近者は単にイエスマンに過ぎなかった. ¶a ***60-point man***=a 60-pointer 〘軍〙従軍点数六十点の人々; [一般に]六十点とった人.

P names foremost ***among*** Chicago business *men* シカゴ実業家間の名流. ¶live together ***as*** *man* and wife 夫婦として同居する. ¶the multiplicity of trades carried on ***by*** one *man* alone 個人経営による多数の商売. ¶astronomy ***for*** the *man* in the street しろうと分かりのする天文学. ¶The function of the appendix ***in*** *man* is not understood. 人の盲腸は何の役に立つか分かっていない. ¶It is the *man* ***behind*** the gun that is important. 機構よりもこれを運営する人が大切だ. ¶the rights ***of*** *man* 人権 ‖ Birds strut about quite fearlessly heedless of the presence ***of*** *man*. 鳥は人がいても少しもこわがらないでそりかえって歩いている. ¶The members of the Cabinet, ***to*** a *man*, objected. 閣僚こぞって反対した. 【類】the police ***to*** a *man* believe that ... / Almost ***to*** a *man* they are supporters of the policy. / They applauded it ***to*** a *man*. / They were perished ***to*** a *man*. ‖ They fought ***to*** the last *man*. 彼らは最後の一人まで戦った. ‖ ***to*** the average *man* it is astonishing that ... 普通の人にとって...は驚くべきことである.

P^2 a *man* ***about*** town 道楽者, 通人. ¶the *man* ***behind*** the camera=the cameraman カメラマン. ¶He is the right *man* ***for*** the position. 彼は適任者だ. ‖ He is the *man* ***for*** the job. 彼はその仕事にはあつらえ向の人だ. ‖ the *man* ***in*** (=***on***) the street [通行人, から]一般大衆. 【類】The *man* ***in*** the street knows little of him. / the speech of the "*man* ***in*** the street" / What can the *man* ***in*** the street (門外漢) be expected to know of it? ‖ There were two *men* ***in*** his character. 彼には二つの異った性格があった. ‖ send for the *man* ***in*** blue 警官を呼びにやる. ¶a *man* ***of*** ability 手腕家 ‖ a *man* ***of*** talent (genius) 才能のある人(天才) ‖ a *man* ***of*** age and experience 老練家 ‖ a *man* ***of*** birth 門閥家 ‖ a *man* ***of*** breeding 育ちの良い人. 【類】a *man* ***of*** birth and breeding ‖ a *man* ***of*** fame and mark 知名の士 ‖ a *man* ***of*** firm character 堅実な性格の人 ‖ a *man* ***of*** great vitality and working force 力の充実した人 ‖ a *man* ***of*** high station 身分のある人 ‖ a *man* ***of*** rank 高位の人 ‖ a *man* ***of*** hobbies 色々道楽のある人 ‖ a *man* ***of*** letters 文士 ‖ *men* ***of*** mettle 気骨のある人々 ‖ a *man* ***of*** narrow views 見解のせまい人 ‖ some young *men* ***of*** little account ほとんど取るに足らない青年たち ‖ a *man* ***of*** iron 鉄の意志の人; 冷酷な人. 【類】He is a man ***of*** iron under any conditions. ‖ a *man* ***of*** parts 才能のある人. 【類】a young *man* ***of*** parts and ambition ‖ a *man* ***of*** pleasure 道楽者 ‖ a *man* ***of*** wealth 富者 ‖ a *man* ***of*** substance 資産家. 【類】a *man* ***of*** no financial substance ‖ *men* ***of*** tact and experience 老巧経験の士 ‖ the *man* ***of*** the moment (=the day) 時の人 ‖ a *man* ***of*** the world 世なれた人. 【類】the great *men* ***of*** the world ‖ a *man* ***of*** wide influence 顔役 ‖ a *man* ***of*** action 活動家 ‖ a *man* ***of*** decision 決断力のある人 ‖ a *man* ***of*** impulse 感情家 ‖ a *man* ***of*** integrity 正しい人 ‖ a *man* ***of*** leisure ひまな人 ‖ *men* ***of*** note 有名人たち ‖ a *man* ***of*** peace 平和主義の人 ‖ a *man* ***of*** sense 分別のある人 ‖ a *man* ***of*** resources 知謀に富む人 ‖ a *man* ***of*** stability 沈着な人 ‖ a *man* ***of*** one book 一つの方面に精しい専門家 ‖ a *man* ***of*** means and position 資産も地位もある人 ‖ I dislike a *man* ***of*** that stamp (=type). ああいう型の人はきらいだ. 【類】*men* ***of*** the stamp of university professors (大学教授型) ‖ a *man* ***of*** straw わら人形; [比ゆ的に]架空の人物, ロボット, 節操のない人, 財力の伴わない人 ‖ a *man* ***of*** virtue 徳の高い人 ‖ a *man* ***of*** will 意志の人 ‖ a *man* ***of*** imperious will 我を通す人 ‖ a *man* ***of*** his words 約束の堅い人 ‖ a *man* ***of*** few words 口数の少い人 ‖ a *man* ***of*** worth 君子 ‖ marry the *man* ***of*** her choice 自分で選んだ男と結婚する. ¶a *man* ***on*** the beam 時代の波に乗った男. ¶a *man* ***of*** sturdy (slender) build からだのがっちりした(か細い)人. 【類】It is not too much to say that the vast fabric of British overseas trade is in a large measure due to the exertions of the "*man* ***on*** the spot (現地在住者)."—The Times. ‖ It is quite forgotten by the *man* ***on*** the street. それは一般の世人から全然忘れられている.

O whether *man* or woman 男にせよ女にせよ.

man, *v*. 人を備える.

M^2 Mining and agriculture are the most vital industry which we must *man* ***up***. 鉱山と農業はわれわれが人力を供給すべき最重要な産業である.

P *man* a ship ***with*** able hands 船に屈強の水夫を乗組ませる.

O Sailors *man* a ship. 船員が乗船する. ¶*man* the guns 砲座につかせる.

manage, *v*. 処理する, 管理する; 操縦する; どうにかして...する, 首尾よく...する.

M He *managed* it ***all right*** (***badly***). 彼は手際よく(悪く)そのことをまとめた. ¶*manage* ***artfully*** 巧みに処理する. ¶The hotel is ***badly*** *managed*. そのホテルは管理が行届いていない. ¶You must *manage* ***better*** in future. 今後はもっとうまくやらなくちゃいけない. ¶That store is *managed* ***honestly***. あの店は正直だ. ¶***How*** do you *manage* to keep out of debt? どうして借金せずにやって行くか. 【類】He knows ***how*** to *manage* a horse. ¶The plan will succeed or not according as it is ***judiciously*** *managed*. その計画は処理のよろしきを得ると否とで成否が分かれるだろう. ¶Do you ***often*** *manage* to cut yourself when you shave? 顔をそる時切ることがしょっちゅうありますか. ¶if not ***properly*** *managed* へたをすると. ¶I will *manage* it ***somehow***. 何とかやってみましょう. ¶He ***successfully*** *managed* to get it through. 彼は首尾よくそれをやり遂げた.

P He is *managed* ***by*** his wife. 彼は細君のしりに敷かれている. ‖ be *managed* ***by*** a board of three directors 三人理事会で管理されている. ¶*manage* ***on*** one's income 収入でやりくりする. ¶He *managed* her ***to*** his own views. 彼は彼女を思い通りに操縦した. ¶*manage* ***with*** delicacy 手際よく処理する.

O I *managed* to make him understand it. 私はどうにかこうにかあの人に了解させた. ‖ He *manages* to subsist. 彼はどうにか暮している.

management, *n*. 処理, 処置; 管理, 経営; 操縦.

V ***direct*** the *management* of a company 会社を管理する. ¶***exercise*** the general *management* and supervision of ... ...の総監督に当る. ¶The society ***has*** the *management* of the exhibition. その展覧会はその会の主催だ. ¶***introduce*** scientific *management* 科学的管理法を取入れる. ¶***loose*** *management* だらしない管理(経営). ¶***reorganize*** the *management* of a company 会社の経営法を改める. ¶It ***requires*** very careful *management*. それは用意周到の取扱いを要する. ¶***take over*** the *management* of a magazine 雑誌の経営を引受ける. 【類】***take over*** the *management* of the business under the style (名義) of ... ¶the *manage-*

ment of the Society's affairs shall be ***vested*** in a Council consisting of six members, viz. ...同協会事務管理の権能は…の六名からなる評議員会に与えられる.

Q ***adroit*** *management* 巧みな処置. ¶Robert College at Constantinople is an excellent institution under ***American*** *management*. コンスタンチノープルのロバート学院はアメリカ人の経営になるりっぱな学院だ. ¶***Bad*** *management* was a cause of the failure. 経営が悪かったのが失敗の原因の一つだった. ¶***clumsy*** *management* まずい管理. ¶The modern university is a collection of colleges and specialized schools under one ***common*** *management*. 近代の大学は一つの共同管理下にある分科大学と専門学校との集合体である. ¶***dexterous*** *management* 巧妙な処置. ¶a store under the ***direct*** *management* of ... ...の直営店. ¶***efficient*** *management* 能率的経営. 【類】Their action, we are afraid, is not consistent with really ***efficient*** and ***economical*** *management*. ¶***energetic*** and ***capable*** *management* きびきびした手腕の現われた経営振り. ¶thanks to ***excellent*** *management* りっぱな経営のおかげで. ¶a service bureau under ***experienced*** *management* 老練な管理下にある代理部. ¶***faulty*** *management* 欠陥のある管理. ¶The business is under ***foreign*** *management*. その業務は外国人の管理下にある. ¶with ***good*** *management* 経営よろしきを得れば. ¶under ***better*** *management* 一層よい管理の下に. ¶***intelligent*** and ***able*** *management* そう明で有能な経営. ¶under Japanese-Chinese ***joint*** *management* 日支合弁で. 【類】the "Franconia" World Cruise, under the ***joint*** *management* of the Cunard White Star Line and Thos. Cook & Son. ¶***judicious*** (=***proper***) *management* 無理のない経営. ¶It will require some ***little*** *management*. それは多少手加減がいる. ¶under ***new*** *management* 新経営者の手で. ¶***poor*** (=***incompetent***) *management* まずい経営. ¶a school under ***private*** *management* 私立学校. ¶under the favorable influence of a ***progressive*** *management* 進歩的経営法の好影響を受けて. ¶under ***proper*** *management* 適当の処置の下に. ¶***rational*** *management* of the drink and amusement traffic 飲酒並に娯楽業者の合理的監理. ¶***rational*** and ***scientific*** *management* 合理的で科学的な監理. ¶***systematic*** *management* 組織立った管理. ¶***unbusiness-like*** *management* 非能率的な経営. ¶Under his ***vigorous*** *management* the school attained great prosperity. 彼の敏腕でその学校は大いに発展した.

Q^2 the actual ***day-by-day*** *management* 日々の管理. ¶***factory*** *management* 工場経営. ¶***household*** (=house) *management* 家政. ¶***personnel*** *management* 人事管理. ¶a ***railroad*** *management* that lives in the past 旧式な鉄道経営.

P ***by*** reckless *management* 無謀な経営法で. ¶The hotel has been left ***to*** our *management*. そのホテルはわれわれが経営することになった. ¶The store is ***under*** English *management*. その店は英人が経営している. 【類】The firm is ***under*** new *management*. ‖bring various stores ***under*** one *management* and ownership 多くの商店を買占めて一手に経営する. 【類】a group of restaurants operated in various parts of the city ***under*** one *management*.

manager, *n.* 処理者, 支配人; 監督.

Q an ***assistant*** *manager*=a sub-manager 副支配人; 〖野球〗助監督. ¶an ***athletic*** *manager* 運動競技監督. ¶His wife is a ***bad*** (***poor***) *manager*. 彼の妻は家政がへただ. ¶a ***general*** *manager* 総支配人. ¶a ***capable*** *manager* 有能な支配人. ¶a ***resident*** *manager* [銀行などに]居住の支配人. ¶a ***technical*** *manager* 技術部長.

Q^2 an ***advertising*** *manager* 宣伝部長. ¶a ***billet*** *manager* 軍人宿舎の管理者. ¶a ***branch*** *manager* 支店長. ¶a ***business*** *manager* 支配人; 営業部長. ¶a ***business promotion*** *manager* [会社などの]営業部長. ¶a ***campaign*** *manager* 選挙運動の選挙長. ¶a personal ***campaign*** *manager* 候補者個人の選挙長. ¶a ***company*** *manager* 会社の支配人. ¶a ***concert*** *manager* 演奏会のマネージャー. ¶a ***department*** *manager* 部長. ¶an ***employment*** *manager* 雇用係長. ¶a ***factory*** *manager* 工場長. ¶a ***floor*** *manager* 《米》舞踊場の支配人. ¶a ***hotel*** *manager* ホテル支配人. ¶a ***houses-to-let*** *manager* 差配. ¶a ***labor*** *manager* 勤労部長. ¶a ***lecture*** *manager* 講演仲介者. ¶a ***personnel*** *manager* 人事部長. ¶a ***plant*** *manager* 工場長. ¶a ***playing*** *manager* 〖野球〗選手をかねる監督. ¶a ***pro-ball*** *manager* 職業野球監督. ¶a ***PX*** *manager* PXの支配人. ¶the ***resident*** *manager* of a theatre 劇場管理人. ¶a ***sales*** *manager* 販売部長. ¶a ***stage*** *manager* 舞台監督. ¶a hard-boiled ***store*** *manager* がん固な商店経営者. ¶the most matchless ***traffic*** *manager* in the world, the London policeman 世界無比の交通整理者たるロンドンの警官. ¶a ***works*** *manager* 工場経営者.

P act ***as*** *manager* 支配人役を代行する.

managership, *n.* 支配人の職.

V he ***resigned*** *managership* of ... 彼は…の支配人の職を辞した. ¶***take on*** the *managership* of her home 自家の家政に当る.

mandate, *n.* 命令, 諭告; 委任統治; 選挙区民から議院などに向って発する要求.

V After protracted consideration the National government has decided to ***ask*** a *mandate* from the people. 長らく考慮を重ねた上で国民政府は遂に民意を問うことに決定した. ¶***assign*** the *mandate* of ... to ... ...の委任統治を…に割当てる. ¶***carry out*** a *mandate* 委任統治を行う. ¶dare ***disobey*** his *mandates* あえて彼の訓令に背そむ. ¶***exercise*** a *mandate* 委任統治権を行使する. ¶Japan has ***held*** a *mandate* in the South Seas for many years. 日本は数年来南洋の委任統治権を握ってきた. ¶***maintain*** her *mandate* for Yap ヤップ島に対する委任統治権を保持する. ¶Japan ***secured*** the *mandate* over the islands. 日本はこれら諸島の委任統治権を獲得した. ¶***transfer*** the *mandate* to ... 委任統治権を…に移す.

Q^2 be placed under the ***United Nations*** *mandate* 国際連合の委任統治下におかれてある.

P They are ***under*** the *mandate* of Japan. それは日本の委任統治下にある. 【類】The Marshall, Caroline, and Ladrone groups are governed by Japan ***under*** *mandate*. / territories ***under*** *mandate* / hold the islands ***under*** *mandate*.

P^2 The *mandate* ***for*** the former German North Pacific islands has been granted to Japan by the Peace Conference. 旧ドイツ領であった北太平洋諸島の委任統治権は平和会議で日本に譲渡された.

mane, *n.* たてがみ.

V Angry animals ***erect*** the *mane*. 怒った動物はたてがみを逆立てる. ¶That horse ***has*** a thin *mane*. あの馬はたてがみが薄い. ¶The horse ***tossed*** his *mane*. 馬がたてがみを振った.

manes, *n.* 亡霊.

V ***appease*** (=***propitiate***) the *manes* of ... ...の霊をなぐさめる.

manger, *n.* かいばおけ.

P The horse is tied up ***to*** the *manger*. 馬はかいばおけにつないである.

maneuver, *n.* 演習.

Q ***anti-air-raid*** *maneuvers* 防空演習. ¶use every ***crafty*** *maneuver* あらゆるこうかつな手段を用いる. ¶an ***extensive*** *maneuver* 大演習. ¶carry out ***grand*** *maneuver*. 大演習を挙行する.

Q^2 hold an ***army*** (***navy***) *maneuver* 陸(海)軍演習を行う.

P^2 a *maneuver* ***between*** two sides 対抗演習.

maneuver, *v.* 策略を使う.

P *maneuver* the enemy ***into*** (***out of***) position 策略で敵を陣地内(外)に誘う. 【類】*maneuver* him ***into*** a marriage with her.

manhole, *n.* マンホール.

V a seaman ***descending*** a *manhole* マンホールを降る水夫.

P be vaporing ***through*** a *manhole* マンホールから湯気が上っている. 【類】fall down ***through*** a *manhole*.

manhood, *n.* [一人前の]男子たる資格; 大人, 成人; 勇気.

V ***attain*** *manhood* 大人になる. ¶***reach*** (=arrive at) *manhood* 成年に達する.

Q He is a ***budding*** *manhood*. 彼は成年期に達しかけている. ¶They are still in ***early*** *manhood*. 彼らはまだ大人になったばかりだ. ¶Pessimists declare that the ***nation's*** *manhood* is degenerating. 国民の元気が衰退しつつあると悲観するものがある. ¶***virile*** *manhood* 男らしさ.

P grow ***into*** *manhood* 大人になる. ¶He is in the prime ***of*** *manhood*. 彼は男盛りだ. ¶He could not live ***to*** *manhood*. 彼は成人せずに死んだ.

manhunt, *n.* 人捜し, 捜索.

Q launch a ***nationwide*** *manhunt* for the murders of ... ...の殺人事件で犯人の全国捜査を始める.

mania, *n.* 熱中, 心酔; ...狂, ...熱.

V He ***has*** a *mania* for gambling (music, ballgames,

stamp collecting). 彼はばくち(など)狂だ.

Q a ***perfect*** *mania* for ... swept [over] the country ...の大流行が全国に拡がった. ¶a ***suicidal*** *mania* 自殺狂.

Q² the ***collecting*** *mania* 収集癖. ¶a ***gold-speculation*** *mania* 金鉱熱. ¶a ***photo*** *mania* 写真狂.

P a *mania* ***for*** [possessing] rare books 希覯(きこう)書の収集熱 ‖ a *mania* ***for*** English ways 英国かぶれ. 【類】He has a *mania* ***for*** tearing buttons off people's clothes. / there is quite a *mania* ***for*** ...

manicure, *n.* マニキュア.

V ***have*** a *manicure* マニキュアをやってもらう.

manicure, *v.* マニキュアを施す.

M *manicure* ***artfully*** 巧みにマニキュアを施す.

O *manicure* finger-nails 指のつめにマニキュアを施す.

manifest, *a.* 明確な.

P It is *manifest* ***at*** a glance. それは一目りょう然だ. ¶It is *manifest* ***to*** every impartial mind. それは公平な人には明らかなことだ.

manifestation, *n.* 表明, 表示.

Q the ***aesthetic*** *manifestation* of a great people 大国民の美的方面の発現. ¶the Japanese spirit and its ***manifold*** *manifestations* 日本精神とその多様の表現. ¶Beauty is worthy when it is the ***outer*** *manifestation* of a beautiful nature. 美ぼうは美質の外面的表示である場合に価値がある. ¶***physical*** *manifestations* of love 愛の物質的表示. ¶a ***stormy*** *manifestation* of patriotism 猛烈な愛国的精神の発露. ¶***unseemly*** and ***ill-considered*** *manifestations* of feelings 感情の露骨で無分別な表明.

Q² a ***surface*** *manifestation* 表面的現象. ¶***war*** *manifestations* 戦時の諸現象.

P² a *manifestation* ***of*** a resolution 決意の現われ ‖ an outward *manifestation* ***of*** wealth and position, such as the automobile 例えば自動車といった富や身分の外面的表示.

manifesto, *n.* 布告, 宣言.

V ***issue*** a *manifesto* 布告を出す. ¶The party ***set out*** its *manifesto* yesterday. 政党がきのうその綱領を発表した.

Q a ***political*** *manifesto* 政綱. ¶a ***pre-election*** *manifesto* released by the party その党から発せられた選挙前党対策声明.

manipulation, *n.* 掛引, 操作.

Q ***adroit*** *manipulation* of stocks 株式の機敏な操作.

Q² ***currency*** *manipulations* 通貨政策.

manipulator, *n.* 策士.

Q² a ***price*** *manipulator* 物価の変動を画策する人. ¶a ***Wall Street*** *manipulator* [ニューヨークの]ウオール街(金融界)の策士.

mankind, *n.* 人類, 人間.

V ***afflict*** *mankind* 人類を悩ます. ¶***benefit*** all *mankind* 人類全体を益する. ¶*Mankind* is (*or* are) ***corrupted.*** 人類は腐敗している.

P² *mankind* ***at*** large (=in general) 一般の人類.

manliness, *n.* 剛毅(ごうき).

V ***cultivate*** *manliness* 剛毅の気性を養う. ¶***foster*** *manliness* 剛毅の気性を養う.

Q ***honest*** *manliness* 素ぼく.

manner, *n.* 仕方, 仕振り; 挙動, 態度; 流儀; 種類; *pl.* 行儀, 作法.

V ***ape*** (=***copy***) foreign *manners* 外国風をまねる. 【類】***ape*** the *manners* of the West. ¶try to ***attain*** a quick and composed *manner* 沈着な風を養おうとする. ¶All *manner* of repairs is ***carried out*** by experienced workmen. あらゆる種類の修繕が老練な職工の手で施されている. ¶***catch*** the *manner* of ... ...にならう. ¶***cultivate*** good *manners* 好い行儀を習う. ¶***develop*** a *manner* of one's own 一流儀を作る. ¶Moving pictures sometimes ***distort*** national *manners*, customs and characteristics. 映画はときに国民の風俗習慣や特徴を誤り伝える. ¶He ***has*** the *manner* of tactful men of the world. あの人には如才のない世間なれた人の態度がある. ‖ He ***has*** no *manners*. 彼は行儀が悪い. ¶Children should ***learn*** *manners*. 子供は行儀を覚えなければならない. ¶***make*** all *manner* of grumbles at ... ...に対して盛んに不平を言う. ¶***practice*** good *manners* towards ... 礼を厚くして...に対する.

Q his ***abrupt*** and often ***antagonizing*** *manner* 彼のぶっきらぼうで往々反抗的な態度. ¶in a very ***acceptable*** *manner* 非常に感じのよい態度で. ¶***all*** *manner* of things (people) あらゆる種類の物(人々). ¶He has an ***awkward*** *manner*. 彼は態度がぎごちない. ¶in an ***amicable*** *manner* 和協的態度で. ¶it is considered ***bad*** *manners* to ... ...するのは不作法となっている. ¶shouting and singing in a ***boisterous*** *manner* 騒々しく叫んだり歌ったりして. ¶***brusque*** *manners* そっけない挙動. ¶in a ***business-like*** *manner* 事務的に, てきぱきと. ¶***calm*** and ***collected*** *manner* 泰然自若. ¶She has ***charming*** *manners*. 彼女の動作には愛きょうがある. ¶in a ***clean*** and ***straightforward*** *manner* りっぱに堂々と. ¶***coarse*** (=***wild***) *manner* 粗野な態度. ¶in a ***concise*** *manner* 簡潔に. ¶in a ***confused*** *manner* うろたえて. ¶in a ***cordial*** *manner* 懇篤に, 熱誠をこめて. ¶***courteous*** *manners* いんぎんな挙動. 【類】her ***courteous, cheerful*** *manner*. ¶affect a ***cultured*** *manner* of speech 教養のある人のような口のきき方をする. ¶read in a ***cursory*** *manner* ぞんざいに読む. ¶in the ***customary*** *manner* 例のごとく. ¶in a ***cut-and-dried*** *manner* 味もそっけもなく. ¶***decisive*** and ***blunt*** *manner* 断固としてそっけない態度. ¶in a ***definite*** and ***uniform*** *manner* はっきりと一様に. ¶continue in a very ***desultory*** *manner* 漫然と続ける. ¶in a very ***dignified*** *manner* すこぶる重々しい態度で. ¶in a ***disorderly*** *manner* 乱雑に. ¶in an ***earnest*** *manner* 熱誠をこめて. ¶in an ***easy*** *manner* ものなれた態度で. ¶***engaging*** *manners* 人を引きつける挙動. ¶***evil*** *manners* 悪行. ¶She has ***fair*** *manners*. 彼女は身だしなみがいい. ¶a ***fascinating*** *manner* 人を魅する挙動. ¶in a ***formal*** *manner* 正式に ‖ His *manner* is always ***formal***. あの人はいつも四角張っている. ¶his ***frank*** and ***courteous*** *manner* あけっぱなしでいんぎんな態度. ¶endeavor to get it settled in a ***friendly*** *manner* 友好的に解決しようと努める. ¶speak in a ***general, abstract*** *manner* 一般的で抽象的な言い方をする. ¶his ***gentle*** *manners* 彼の物柔かい態度. ¶in his ***gentleman-like*** *manner* 紳士らしい態度で. ¶***good*** *manners* and good morals よい作法とよい品行. ¶her ***gracious*** *manners* 彼女の優雅なもの腰. ¶an impostor who conducts affairs in a ***grand*** *manner* 物事を大仕掛にやる山師. ¶in a ***high-handed*** *manner* きわめて高飛車に. ¶Things are no longer done in a ***hit-and-miss*** *manner*. 今日では手当りばったりで物をやるようなことはない. ¶***homespun*** *manners* 洗練されていない振舞. ¶words written in an ***illiterate*** *manner* 金くぎ流に書いた字. ¶in a most ***imperturbable*** *manner* 少しも動ぜず. ¶in a very ***improper*** *manner* すこぶる乱暴に. ¶an ***insinuating*** *manner* うまく取入る態度. ¶***kind*** *manners* 親切な態度. 【類】***kind*** and ***gentle*** *manners*. ¶in a ***knowing*** *manner* 万事心得顔に. ¶in a ***lifelike*** *manner* 真に迫って. ¶in ***like*** *manner*=in the same way 同様に. ¶an answer uttered in a ***lukewarm*** *manner* なま返辞. ¶in a ***masterly*** *manner* 手際よく. ¶***mild*** and ***courteous*** *manners* 温和で丁寧な態度. ¶have ***nice*** (=good) *manners* 行儀がよい. ¶His *manner* is ***offensive***. 彼の態度はしゃくにさわる. ¶in a ***playful*** *manner* ひょうきんな態度で. ¶***polite*** *manners* 上品な作法. ¶in a very ***pronounced*** *manner* きわめて目に立つように. ¶labor in a ***quiet*** and ***unobtrusive*** *manner* こっそりと目立たないように働く. ¶***refined*** *manners* 洗練された態度. ¶in a sort of ***regular*** *manner* いわば普通のことになっていて. ¶***repulsive*** *manners* いやらしい挙動. ¶spend their holidays in a ***roistering, boisterous*** *manner* わいわい言って休日を暮す. ¶in a ***rough, clumsy,*** and ***unskilful*** *manner* ぞんざいで不器用に. ¶His ***rude*** *manners* grated on me. あいつの乱暴な態度がしゃくにさわった. ¶***rustic*** *manners* いなかくさい挙動. ¶after the ***same*** *manner* as ... ...と同じように. ¶in a ***satisfactory*** *manner* 満足のできるように. ¶in a ***scientific*** *manner* 科学的に. ¶He was killed in a ***shocking*** *manner*. 彼はひどい殺され方をした. ¶in a most ***skilful*** *manner* 非常に巧妙に. ¶do work in a ***slipshod*** *manner* だらしなく仕事をする. 【類】The subject is taught in a ***slipshod*** *manner*. ¶in a ***startling*** *manner* 人を驚かすように. ¶He was a man of commanding appearance, and of ***suave*** and ***courteous*** *manners*. 彼は風さいは堂々としていて挙動は優雅で丁寧なものであった. ¶the task has been accomplished in a highly ***successful*** *manner* by ... その仕事は...によってきわめて好成績に成し遂げられた. ¶in ***such*** a *manner* こんな風に. ¶in the most ***surprising*** *manner* 実に驚くばかりに. ¶carry on research in a ***systematic*** and ***well-organized*** *manner* 研究を秩序的に整然と進めて行く. ¶***tardy heavy*** *manner* 気の進まない沈うつな態度. ¶The Duke of Wellington was credited with having written war dispatches in the most ***telling manner***. ウェリントン公は最も有効に軍事公文書を書いたと言われていた. ¶He handles people in a ***tender manner***. 彼は物柔かな態度で人を扱う. ¶die in a ***tranquil manner*** やすらかに死ぬ. ¶***turbulent manners*** 乱暴な挙動. ¶in a ***typical Chevalier manner*** シュヴァリエー流のやり方で. ¶in ***unceremonious manner*** うちとけた態度で. ¶in an ***ungainly*** (=***awkward***) ***manner*** 武骨に. ¶***ungentlemanly manners*** 紳士にあるまじき不作法. ¶in an ***unostentatious manner*** 目立たないように. ¶in the ***usual manner*** 相変らず. ¶***What manner*** of man is he? 彼はどういう人か. ‖ in ***what manner***=how どういう風に. ¶He has most ***winning*** (=charming) ***manners***. 彼はほんとに愛きうがある. ¶in a ***winsome manner*** あいそよく.

Q² the ***capitalist manner*** of production 資本家的な生産方式. ¶***company manners*** (人前だけにやる)社交的作法. ¶elaborate ***drawing-room manners*** 念のいった応接間の作法. ¶sound something like a ***novel manner*** 何か耳新しく聞える. ¶***platform manners*** 演説の態度. ¶Most motorists have no "***road manners***." 自動車乗用者連は大抵道路の作法をわきまえていない. ¶***table manners*** 食卓の作法.

P ***after*** the ***manner*** of ... ...流に. ¶***after*** this ***manner*** こういう風に. ¶The story is ***beyond*** any ***manner*** of doubt. その話は何ら疑いを入れる余地がない. ¶by all ***manner*** of means もちろん, たしかに ‖ He does not look thirty-two ***by*** any ***manner*** of means. 彼はどうしても三十二とは見えない. ¶be affable ***in manner*** あいそがよい ‖ ***in*** a ***manner*** not justified by the law 非合法的なやり方で. 【類】***in*** the ***manner*** above explained / It is ***in*** a ***manner*** worthy of the highest praise. / He is great ***in*** a ***manner***. ‖ ***in*** a ***manner*** of speaking=so to speak いわば ‖ differ ***in*** all ***manner*** of ways 様々の点で異なる ‖ This picture is ***in*** the ***manner*** of Raphael. これはラファエル風の絵だ. ‖ ***in*** the ***manner*** now described 今述べたように. 【類】***in*** the ***manner*** already explained (sketched) / the solution of a problem ***in*** a ***manner*** likely to be generally satisfactory / ***in*** this ***manner*** ‖ rough ***in*** their ***manners*** 態度の荒々しい. ¶the Yankee ***to*** the ***manner*** born きっすいの米人 ‖ like one ***to*** the ***manner*** born はえ抜の人のように. ¶a person ***without manners*** 礼儀を知らない人.

P² ***manners in*** a community 一つの社会の風習. ¶one's ***manner of*** speaking (walking) 話し(歩きっ)振り. 【類】There is something awkward ***in*** his ***manner*** of speaking. / the ***manner of*** execution ‖ all ***manner*** (=sorts) ***of*** diseases 種々の病気.

mannerism, *n.* 旧型墨存(マンネリズム); 癖.

V ***have*** the ***mannerism*** of ... のくさ味がある.

Q a ***foreign mannerism*** of Milton ミルトンの外国語法準用の一例.

mannish, *a.* 男性的な.

P She is very ***mannish in*** her manners. 彼女は動作がきわめて男性的だ.

manoeuvre, *n.* =maneuver.

mansion *n.* 邸宅.

Q a ***lordly mansion*** 堂々たる邸宅. ¶a ***palatial mansion*** 豪華な邸宅. ¶a ***private mansion*** 私邸. ¶one's ***second mansion*** 別宅. ¶a ***stately mansion*** 堂々たる邸宅.

Q² an imposing ***white granite mansion*** 堂々たる大理石の邸宅.

mantle, *n.* 外衣; 衣はつ; [ガス灯などの]マントル.

V No successor promises to ***assume*** her ***mantle*** or the sceptre of her sway over the public. どんな後継者にも彼女の衣はつを継いで民衆を統治することはできそうもない. ¶Consciously or unconsciously the young Wordsworth ***inherited*** the ***mantle*** that fell from Cowper's shoulders. 意識的にか無意識にか少年ワーズワースはクーパーの衣はつを継いだ. ¶he worthily ***wore*** the ***mantle*** of ... 彼はりっぱに...の衣はつを継いだ.

V² his ***mantle fell*** upon ... 彼の衣はつは...によって継がれた.

Q Tokyo under the ***first mantle*** of snow 初雪に埋もれた東京. ¶an ***incandescent mantle*** 白熱灯.

Q² an ***asbestos mantle*** [ガスストーブなど]石綿のマントル.

mantle, *v.* おおう, 包む.

M peaks ***heavily mantled*** with snow 深雪におおわれた峰々.

P the whole district ***mantled in*** loveliest white 一面の銀世界. ¶peaks heavily ***mantled with*** snow 白一色の峰々 ‖ a goblet ***mantling with*** foam あわ立つ杯.

manual, *n.* 便覧.

Q a ***reliable manual*** of reference 確かな参考書. ¶a ***teacher's manual*** 教師用参考書.

Q² a ***desk manual*** 卓上便覧. ¶a ***pocket reference manual*** ポケット型参考書. ¶a ***ready-reference manual*** of ... for students 学生のための...便覧.

P² a ***manual for*** students 学生用参考書. ¶a first ***manual of*** composition 作文入門書.

manufactory, *n.* 製造所, 工場.

V ***set up*** a ***manufactory*** 工場を建てる.

Q The whole civilized world is a ***co-operative manufactory*** of knowledge. 全文明世界は知識の共同製作所だ.

manufacture, *n.* 製造; 製品.

V ***forbid*** the ***manufacture*** of ... ...の製造を禁止する. ¶the city ***has manufactures*** of many kinds of commodities 同市は多種の商品の生産地である. ¶***ruin*** the ***manufactures*** 製造業を衰微させる.

Q of ***domestic*** (=***home***) ***manufacture*** 内国製の. ¶mostly of ***English manufacture*** 主に英国製の. ¶tiles of ***excellent manufacture*** 製作優秀のタイル. ¶It is of ***foreign manufacture***. それは外国製だ. ¶specimens of ***Japanese manufacture*** 日本製の標本. ¶jams of ***reputed manufactures*** 有名な製造所のジャム. ¶Men and equipment are the two essentials of ***successful manufacture***. 労働者と設備とは製造業の成功に欠くべからざる二要素である. ¶Lacquer ware is a ***well-known Japanese manufacture***. 漆器は有名な日本の製品だ.

Q² ***by-products manufacture*** 副産物生産. ¶***cloth*** (***silk***) ***manufactures*** 綿(絹)製品. ¶***home manufacture*** 国内生産. ¶***iron*** (***steel***) ***manufacture*** 製鉄(鋼). ¶a center of the ***pottery manufacture*** 製陶業の中心地.

P goods ***of*** foreign (Japanese) ***manufacture*** 外国(日本)製品.

P² the ***manufacture of*** artificial ice 人工製氷 ‖ noted for its ***manufacture of*** earthen ware. 土器製造で有名な.

manufacture, *v.* 製造する.

P It is ***manufactured at*** Osaka. それは大阪製だ. ¶It is ***manufactured by*** machinery (hand). それは機械(手)製だ. ¶Sheffield steel is ***manufactured from*** Swedish iron. シェフィールドの鋼鉄はスエーデン産の鉄で製する. ¶It is ***manufactured in*** Germany. それはドイツ製だ. ¶***manufacture*** rags ***into*** paper ぼろを紙に製造する.

manufacturer, *n.* 製造業者, 製作者.

V ***ruin*** the ***manufacturer*** 製造業者を破滅におとしいれる.

Q an ***enterprising manufacturer*** 企業心に富む製造業者.

Q² an ***aircraft manufacturer*** 飛行機製作業者. ¶***alkali manufacturers*** and their subsidiaries アルカリ工場とその下受け工場. ¶an ***aviation manufacturer*** 飛行機製作業者. ¶a ***freezer manufacturer*** 冷凍機製造家. ¶a ***leather manufacturer*** 製皮業者. ¶a ***motor-vehicle manufacturer*** 自動車類製作業者. ¶a ***munitions manufacturer*** 兵器製造業者. ¶a ***pencil manufacturer*** 鉛筆製造業者.

P² Mr. K, ***manufacturer of*** ... ...本舗 K 氏.

manure, *n.* 肥料.

Q ***artificial manure*** 人造肥料. ¶***nitrogenous manure*** 窒素肥料.

Q² ***cow manure*** 牛ふん肥料. ¶***farmyard manure*** たい肥.

P Dung is used ***as manure***. ふんは肥料として用いられる. 【類】valuable ***as manure***.

manure, *v.* 施肥する.

P ***manure with*** dung ふんを肥料にする. 【類】vegetable grown on fields ***manured with*** sewage or other fecal matters (汚物) containing germs of disease.

manusrcipt, *n.* 原稿, 写本; 手写.

V a ***manuscript classified*** "available" 採用に決定した原稿. ¶***copy manuscript*** 原稿を写す. ¶***send*** one's ***manuscript*** to the printer 原稿を印刷者に送る. ¶***submit manuscripts*** to an editor 編集者に原稿を送る. ¶***write*** one's ***manuscript*** in one's own hand 自筆で原稿を書く.

V² a ***manuscript bearing*** as a title ... ...と表題の付いた原稿. ¶The ***manuscript*** will ***go to press*** early next month. 原稿は来月早々印刷に付せられる.

Q ***beautiful manuscripts*** 美しい写本. ¶a ***blue-penciled manuscript*** for the magazine [編集のため]青鉛筆で削られた雑誌原稿. ¶a ***hand-written manuscript*** 手写した原稿. ¶I have seen ***medieval manuscripts*** in which a given word is spelled four different ways on a single page! 一ページ中に一つの単語が四通りにつづられている中世紀の筆写本を見た. ¶***pen-written manuscripts*** ペン書の原稿. ¶a ***rejected*** (=an ***unaccepted***) ***manuscript*** 没書. ¶a ***spurious*** *manuscript* にせの手写本. ¶a ***typewritten manuscript*** タイプライターで打った原稿. ¶At his death he left a great mass of ***undigested manuscripts***. 彼は整理のついていない多量の原稿を残して死んだ. ¶an ***unfinished manuscript*** 未完成の原稿. ¶an ***unpublished manuscript*** 未刊の原稿. ¶***unsolicited*** *manuscripts* 持込み原稿.

Q² the original ***holograph manuscript*** of ... 全文自筆の最初...の原稿. ¶a ***parchment manuscript*** 羊皮紙の手記.

P a book ***in manuscript*** 写本 ‖ The work is already complete ***in manuscript***. その著作はすでに脱稿した.

many, *n.* 大勢, 多数.

V I did not ***find many***. 私が見たのは多くはなかった.

M I have five books of the kind, but I need ***as many again***. その本は五冊あるがもう十冊ほしい. ¶there are ***so*** *many* who ... ...という人は多い.

P It was believed ***by many***. それは多数の人に信じられていた.

P² ***Many of*** them are not ripe. 全部が熟しているわけではなかった.

many, *a.* 多くの, 多数の.

M I waited for fifteen minutes—they seemed ***as many*** hours to me. 私は十五分待ったがそれが十五時間ぐらいに思われた. 【類】It was decided to send 20 students to Japan and about ***as many*** to Europe and America. / I found six mistakes in ***as many*** lines. / Take ***as many*** as you want. ‖ There are ***as many*** minds as there are men. 十人十色. ¶***ever so many*** どっさり. ¶a ***great*** (***good***) *many* people 非常に(かなり)多数の人々. ¶***How many?*** 幾つ, 幾人. ¶The boys are climbing like ***so many*** monkeys. 子供たちはさるのように登って行く. ‖ ***So many*** men, ***so many*** minds. 十人十色. ¶There is one ***too many***. 一つ余る. ‖ be ***too many*** to enumerate 枚挙にいとまない.

Q *Many* a day did I wait for his return. 私は彼の帰りを幾日も待った. ¶for *many* a long year 幾年も幾年も長い間. ¶*Many* a man has made the same mistake. 同じ失錯をした人は幾人もある.

map, *n.* 地図.

V ***consult*** a *map* 地図を調べる. ¶***draw*** a *map* 地図を描く. ¶***hang up*** a *map* on the wall 地図を壁にかける. ¶***reconstruct*** the *map* of the globe 世界の地図を塗りかえる. ¶***roll*** [***up***] a *map* 地図を丸く巻く. ¶***search*** the *map* for Singapore 地図でシンガポールを捜す. ¶***study*** the *map* of South America 南米の地図を調べる.

V² *maps* ***dealing*** with ... ...関係の地図. ¶*maps* ***showing*** ... ...を示す地図.

Q a ***good modern*** *map* りっぱな近代地図. ¶an ***outline*** *map* 輪郭地図. ¶a ***perspective*** *map* of a city 都市の配景図. ¶a ***pictorial*** *map* 絵入りの地図. ¶Eire is called Ireland on ***recent*** *maps*. アイレは近ごろの地図にはアイルランドとなっている. ¶a ***rough*** *map* 略図.

Q² an ***automobile road*** *map* of the country around New York ニューヨーク付近の自動車道路地図. ¶a ***catchment-basin*** *map* 流域図. ¶a ***city*** *map* 市内地図. ¶a ***contour*** *map* 等高線地図. ¶a ***folding*** *map* 折たたみ地図. ¶an ***inset*** *map* 差込図(大きな地図の中に差込んだ). ¶a ***large-scale*** *map* 拡大地図. ¶an ***outline*** *map* 略図. ¶a large scale ***reference*** *map* 拡大参考地図. ¶a ***route*** *map* to ... ...に至る経路図. ¶a ***sketch*** *map* 見取り図. ¶a ***spot*** *map* of the country 点で関係個所を示した図. ¶a Japanese ***Staff*** *map* of Manchuria 日本参謀部の満州地図. ¶a ***three-miles-to-the-inch*** *map* 三マイルを一インチで示した地図. ¶a ***touring*** *map* 旅行地図. ¶an ***up-to-the-minute*** *map* 最新版地図. ¶a ***wall*** *map* of the world 掛ける世界地図. ¶a ***weather*** *map* 天気図. ¶a ***world*** *map* 世界地図.

P ***According*** to the *map* this is the spot. この地図によると, これがその地点だ. ¶You can see it ***in*** the *map*. それは地図にある. ‖ Look it out ***in*** the *map*. それを地図で捜しなさい. ¶Look it up ***on*** your *map*. その地名を地図で調べなさい. ‖ countries represented ***on*** (=***in***) a *map* 地図に出ている国々 ‖ point it out ***on*** the *map* それを地図上で示す ‖ It is only a speck ***on*** an ordinary *map*. それは普通の地図では一つの点に過ぎない. 【類】Point out ***on*** the *map* the chief cities of France. / Show it to me ***on*** the *map*. / look ***on*** (=search) the *map* for ... / It looks small ***on*** the *map*. / The place is not found ***on*** any *map*. ‖ The battlefield is designated ***on*** the *map* by a cross. 戦場は地図面に十字記号で示してある.

P² a *map* ***from*** original survey 実地測量の地図. ¶place-names on *maps* ***of*** China 中国地図の地名. ¶a *map* ***on*** a reduced scale 縮尺図.

map, *v.* [計画などを]立てる, 企画する.

M ***map out*** plans for ... ...の計画を作る ‖ ***map out*** a city plan 都市計画を立てる. 【類】***map out*** a definite plan / ***map out*** a schedule for the trip / ***map out*** a piece of work / ***map out*** an agenda (議事日程) / ***map out*** a program / ***map out*** its next steps 次の手順をきめる / ***map out*** one's future その将来の計画を立てる / ***map out*** one's traveling schedule (旅行日程) / ***map out*** its strategy (戦略) for ... / ***map out*** a new career (新生活) / ***map out*** plots of ground (土地区画をする) to be used as places of recreation for the children ‖ ***map out*** a route 道順を定める.

maple, *n.* かえで.

Q a ***flaming*** *maple* 燃えるようなかえで. ¶***reddening*** *maples* 紅葉しつつあるかえで.

mar, *v.* 害する. そこなう.

P *mar* the happiness (harmony) ***of*** ... ...の幸福(調和)を破る. ¶*mar* the beauty ***of*** city streets 街路の美観をそこなう. ¶the Japanese effect ***marred by*** modern incongruities 近代的なもので殺風景になった日本的効果.

marble, *n.* 大理石; *pl.* おはじき(玉).

V Let's ***play*** *marbles*. おはじきをやろう. ¶***quarry*** *marble* 大理石を切り出す. ¶***shoot*** *marbles* おはじき玉をねらってはじく.

P carve ***in*** *marble* 大理石に彫る ‖ a statue (bust) ***in*** *marble* 大理石立(胸)像. ¶It is made (=built) ***of*** *marble*. それは大理石製だ. 【類】The floor is ***of*** *marble*.

march, *n.* 進軍, 行進; 行程; 進歩, 発展; 歩調; 行進曲.

V ***beat*** a *march* on one's drum 行進曲の太鼓を打つ. ¶intelligently ***follow*** the *march* of events in recent years 近年における事件進展のあとを理解してたどる. ¶***gain*** (=***get***) a *march* on ... ...よりも一日の行程だけ先になる. ¶I have ***had*** a long *march* of it. 私は長い旅行を続けて来た. ¶It will ***make*** a full day's *march*. それはたっぷり一日の里程になる. ¶***measure*** the *march* of the stars 星の運行を測定する. ¶He ***pursued*** his *march* upon Yamaguchi. 彼は山口を指して歩を進めた. ¶They ***resumed*** their *march* at a quick step. 彼らは再びかけ足で行進を続けた. ¶They ***started up*** their long *march* to Peking. 彼らは北京への長途の旅行に出発した. ¶He ***stole*** a *march* on (=upon) me. 彼は僕を出し抜いた. ¶The drums ***struck up*** a *march*. 太鼓が進軍の合図を打ち出した.

Q a ***dead*** (=***funeral***) *march* 葬列. ¶soldiers on a ***forced*** *march* 強行軍中の兵士. ¶the ***forward*** *march* (=progress) of civilization 文明の進歩. ¶an ***hour's*** *march* 一時間の行程. ¶the ***inevitable*** *march* of events 避くべからざる大勢. ¶a ***long*** *march* 長途の行軍. ¶He desired that his nation might, by rousing from the coma of centuries, take its rightful place in the ***onward*** *march* of civilization. 彼はその国民が数百年の眠りからさめて文明の進歩に貢献せんことを念願とした. ¶a *march* ***past*** 分列式. ¶a ***quick*** *march* 速歩(はやあし). ¶They made their ***triumphal*** *march* through the city. 一同はがい旋行進で市街を練って歩いた.

Q² Bataan's ***death*** *march* バターンの死の行進. ¶a ***frog*** *march* がん強なあるいは泥酔した囚人を下向にして四肢を持って運ぶ法. ¶a ***funeral*** *march* 葬送行進[曲]. ¶organize a ***hunger*** *march* 飢餓行進隊を組織する. ¶a ***six-hour*** *march* 六時間の進軍. ¶play a ***wedding*** *march* 結婚行進曲を奏する.

P ***after*** a three days' *march* 三日間行進の後に. ¶***at*** slow *march* 徐行々進で. ¶It proved a new era ***in*** the *march* of civilization. それは文明の進歩において一新紀元を画するものとなった. ‖ ***in*** (=with) the *march* of time 時がたつにつれて. ¶the strains ***of*** the *march* 進軍の曲. ¶troops ***on*** (=***in***) *march* 行進中の軍勢. 【類】The regiment was ***on*** the *march*. / education ***on*** the *march*. ¶in line ***with*** the *march* of events 事態の進展と歩調を合わせて ‖ keep abreast ***with*** the *march* of the times 世の進歩に遅れないようにする.

P² on the *march* ***against*** (=toward) ... ...に向って行進中の. ¶a *march* ***into*** the country その国への行進 ‖ the *march* ***of*** the glass industry ***into*** new fields of public service and convenience ガラス産業の公益的新方面への進出. ¶a *march* ***of*** twenty miles 二十マイルの行進 ‖ the *march* ***of*** soldiers to a tune 楽曲に合わせた兵士の行進 ‖ the *march* ***of*** affairs 事件の進展 ‖ The *march* ***of*** time and

civilization has, however, altered things considerably. とはいえ時勢と文明の進歩は著しく事物を変更した. 【類】the *march of* intellect / the *march* (=growth) *of* population. ¶a *march on* ... ...への行進. ¶troops on the *march through* a village 村落を通って行進中の軍隊. ¶a *march towards* socialism 社会主義への発展.

march, *v.* 行軍する, 行進する; 送る.

M *march hand in hand* 手に手を取って進む. ¶The soldiers *marched out.* 兵士がくり出した. ‖ *march out* the soldiers 兵士をくり出す. ¶*march past* 分列行進をする. 【類】*march past* the commanding officer. ¶The procession *marched slowly on.* 行列は徐々に行進した.

M² *marched down* through the peninsula 半島を南下する ‖ *march down* on Gibraltar ジブラルタルに向って南下する. ¶*march in* くり込む. ¶*march off* 進み去る ‖ *march* war prisoners *off* to prison 戦犯者を刑務所に送る. ¶Science *marches on.* 科学は進む.

P *march against* the enemy 敵軍に攻めよる. ¶The procession *marched along* the highway. 行列は街道を行進した. ¶*march as far as* Kobe 神戸まで進む. ¶*march at* double-quick かけ足で行進する. ¶*march in* fours 四列で進む ‖ *march in* procession 列を作って行進する ‖ *march in* step with others 他人と足並をそろえて進む ‖ *march in* the van of thought 思想界の先頭に立って進む. ¶He *marched into* Kyushu at the head of a large force. 彼は大軍を率いて九州に攻め入った. 【類】*march into* a walled city in China. ¶*march on* a fotress 要さいに向って進軍する. 【類】The general was *marching on* the town, when news of its capture (陥落の報) reached him. ¶*march out of* the fort ほう塁から進み出る. ¶*march through* the streets with measured steps 歩調をとって市中を行進する. ¶*march to* Peking 北京へ進む ‖ *march to* the defence of ... ...の防御のために行進する ‖ *march to* the piping of Henry George or Edward Bellamy ヘンリー・ジョージまたはエドワァド・ベラミーに共鳴して運動する ‖ *march to* a tune on the bugle らっぱの吹奏に合わせて進む. ¶The soldiers *marched towards* Berlin. 軍隊はベルリンへ向って進んだ. 【類】German soldiers *marched towards* Danzig. ¶*march under* the American flag アメリカの国旗の下に行軍する ‖ Religion or philosophy, it matters little which flag one *marches under,* provided that it is held bravely high. 宗教にせよ哲学にせよ旗のぼりを高く掲げて勇敢に進むならばいずれの旗下に立つも大した変りはない. ¶*march upon* the capital 首都に向って進撃する.

mare, *n.* めす馬.

V *ride* (=*go on*) Shank's (=Shanks' *or* shanks's) *mare* 「ひざくり毛で行く.

Q The *gray mare* is the better horse. 細君が夫をしりにしいている(かかあ天下).

Q² a *timber mare* [兵営の刑具として用いる]木馬.

P² Shanks' *mare on* the Tokaido [Road]. 東海道をひざくり毛.

margin, *n.* ふち; 欄外, 余白; 余裕, 余地; 利さや, [マージン]; 開き; 限界.

V *afford* (*leave*) a wide *margin* of free activity 大いに自由活動の余地を与える(残す) ‖ The price *leaves* no *margin* of profit. その値段ではもうけの余地がない. ¶*allow* a good *margin* of profit for the importer 輸入商のために十分な利益の開きを与える.

Q He expected the House to pass the bill by a *comfortable margin.* 彼はその案が相当の多数で議会を通過するものと見ていた. ¶have a *fair margin* of profit 相当もうけ(利ざや)がある. ¶an *insufficient margin* for safety 十分でない安全さ. ¶A *large margin* of profit is looked for. 大きな利益の開きが期待される. ¶Sound business allows one only a *narrow margin* of profit. 堅い商売はもうけが薄い. ‖ win only by a *narrow margin* and after a hard-fought struggle きわどくしかも悪戦苦闘の後に勝つ. 【類】He was elected (当選した) by a *narrow margin.* ¶a *slim* (=narrow) *margin* [of profit] 薄い利ざや, わずかのマージン. ¶in the *small margin* of leisure 寸暇を得て. ¶a *wide margin* of profit 多い利ざや.

Q² lower the *loss margin* 損失高を少くする. ¶the bank's *note-issuing margin* 銀行の紙幣発行限界. ¶wholesale and retail *price margins* 卸しと小売の値段の開き. ¶The bill was overwhelmed by a *2-to-1 margin.* 議案は二対一の差で圧倒的に否決された.

P write down *in* the *margin* of a book 本の余白に書き込む. ¶go *near* the *margin* 際どい所まで行く. ¶*on* a *margin* 余白に. 【類】notes (注) *on* the *margin* of the page ‖ He is *on* the *margin* of bare subsistence. 彼は食うや食わずの境遇にある. ¶buy *with* a good *margin* 十分(売値との)開きを付けて買う.

P² the *margin of* a lake (river, wood) 湖水(など)のふち.

marine, *n.* 海運; [the M-] 海兵隊.

V *develop* a mercantile *marine* 商船の数を多くする.

Q² a *merchant marine* 商船. ¶the *U.S. Marines* 米海兵隊.

mariner, *n.* 海員.

Q² a *master mariner* 商船または漁船の船長.

mark, *n.* こん跡; はん点; 印し, 記号; 標識, 標的; 特徴, 特色; 点数, 標準点; 名声.

V One hundred extra *marks* are *accorded* to every pupil present on the opening day. 第一日に出席した生徒にはすべて別に百点を与える. ¶*achieve* superior scholastic *marks* in all the subjects studied すべての履修科目で優等の点を取る. ¶*marks allotted* for the subject その科目の設定点数. ¶*alter* the *mark* 印を変更する. ¶*assign* the highest *marks* 最高点を付ける. ¶*assume* some *mark* of virtue 幾分有徳の人であるかのごとく見せかける. ¶*attain* full *marks* 満点を取る. ¶*award* high *marks* 高点を与える. 【類】*award* grades and *marks* (等級と点数) ‖ Handwriting will be considered in *awarding marks.* 筆跡を採点に加味する. ¶The monument *bears* the *marks* of age. その記念碑は見たところ大分古い. 【類】*bear marks* of use 使用した形跡を示す / *bear marks* of brutality (ひどい虐待) / *bear marks* of great antiquity / His hands *bear marks* of the bullet. / His hands *bear marks* of toil (労働したあと). / *bear* the *marks* of Hellenistic influence (ギリシア文芸) / The poem *bears* the *mark* of youth. ‖ He *bears* the *mark* of his office. 彼は官職の記章を着けている. ¶*displace* punctuation *marks* 句読点をつけそこねる. ¶*earn* high *marks* 優良点を取る. ¶*exceed* the 1,000-*mark* 一千台を上まわる. ¶*gain* 70 *marks* 七十点を取る. 【類】*gain* a *mark* of 65 to 75 (六十五点ないし七十五点). ¶*get* a *mark* of 100% in three subjects 三科目に満点を取る. 【類】*get* good *marks* at school. ¶The new teacher *gave* me high *marks.* 今度きた先生は僕に良い点をくれた. ¶*hand out* good *marks* [教師などが]良い点をつける. ¶He *has* good *marks* for English. 彼は英語の点がよい. ‖ This Bible *has* the *mark* of frequent use. この聖書はよく使ってある(相当よごれている). ¶You *hit* the *mark.* うまく当てた, 図星だ. 【類】he *hit* the *mark* in stating ... ¶Twelve o'clock but (=only) *indicates* the highwater *mark* of the evening's festivities. 十二時になって始めて夜のにぎやかさが盛りになる. ¶those who have *left* a *mark* in (=on) history 青史に名を残した人々. 【類】men who have *left* their *mark* in the history of France ‖ His teaching *left* a deep *mark* (深い印象) upon the great mass of average readers. ¶*make* a high *mark* 高点を得る ‖ the work in which he first *made* his *mark* 彼の出世作 ‖ *make* one's *mark* (=name) in the world 天下に名を成す. 【類】He had already *made* his *mark* in philological studies (言語学の研究で). / In the domain of thermo-dynamics (熱力学の分野で) he *made* a *mark* that will not be forgotten. / He was at Cambridge where, as at school, he *made* his *mark* in football. / As the creator and ruler of the Congo, he has *made* his *mark* in history. ¶*miss* one's *mark* 的をはずす ‖ entirely *miss* the *mark* 丸で見当違いをやる. ¶*obtain* 82 *marks* out of a possible 100 最高点百点のうちから八十二点を取る. 【類】High *marks* are often *obtained* by second-rate grinds (余り頭のよくない勉強家). / Their business is to *obtain* as many *marks* as possible with the least amount of effort. / Papers *obtaining* 110 *marks* will be passed with distinction. ‖ *overshoot* the *mark* (=oneself) 標的を射越す(度を過ごす). ¶*pass* the million *mark* 百万ドル台を突破する. 【類】The population of the city has now *passed* the 4-million *mark.* ‖ *pass* the four-score *mark* 八十を越す. ¶Tradesmen *place* a private *mark* on their goods to denote price. 商人は商品に符帳を付ける. ¶Don't *put* chalk *mark* on fences or buildings. へいや建物に白墨で落書きするな. ‖ *put* a large query *mark* against ... ...を大いに疑う ‖ *put* a black *mark* against a man 人に(注意人物として)黒点を付ける. ¶*put in* punctuation *marks* 句読点

を付ける. ¶ *reach* the half-century *mark* [米俗] 五十台に達する ‖ *reach* the zero *mark* 零点に達する. 【類】 *reach* the seven figure *mark* (百万台). ¶ *receive* the lowest *marks* in the subject その科目で最劣等点をもらう. 【類】 He *received* low (high) *marks*. / The boy *received* one hundred *marks* in every study. / *receive marks* according to the merit of the answers (答案の成績によって). ¶ *represent* the highwater *mark* of ... ...の最高水準を示す. ¶ *rub off* (=*out or erase*) chalk *marks* チョークのあとを消す. ¶ *score* 70 *marks* 七十点とつける. ¶ *secure* high *marks* in one's examination 試験で優等点を取る. ¶ *set* the *mark* high 望みを大にする ‖ *set* a *mark* of reprobation upon ... ...に罰点をつける. ¶ The building *showed marks* of hasty erection. その建物にはにわか造りのこん跡があった. ¶ *take* one's *mark* amiss ねらいを誤る. ¶ Our exports *touched* (=reached) highwater *mark*. わが輸出額は高潮に達した. ¶ *use* quotation *marks* 引用符を用いる. ¶ *win* the full 100 *marks* 満点を取る. ¶ a *mark* **wrought** into paper 紙にすきこんだマーク.

Q *additional mark* will be given for ... ...に対してさらに点を与える. 【類】 give *additional marks* for ... ¶ a *bad mark* 劣等点. ¶ have the *best marks* 最高点を取っている. ¶ *characteristic marks* 特徴. ¶ *collectors' marks* 蔵(書)印. ¶ *Diacritical marks* are used to show how words are pronounced. 語の発音を示すには区分発音符が用いられる. ¶ words with no "*discountenancing mark*" about them 悪い意味の付随していない語 ‖ set a *discountenancing mark* upon ... ...に罰点をつける. ¶ As a mission field Japan's *distinctive mark* is her combination of her heathenism with Western civilization. 布教地として日本の特徴は従来の異教々義と西洋文明とが互に混合している点にある. ¶ Command of the mother tongue is the most *distinguishing mark* of the educated man or woman. 母国語の練達が教育ある男女の最も著しい特徴である. ¶ Tom had *good marks* on his report card. トムは通知簿の成績はよかった. ¶ secure (give) *full marks* 満点を取(与え)る. ¶ pass an examination with a *high mark* 高点で試験をパスする. 【類】 The *highest mark* was 55.1%. ¶ bear *indubitable marks* of painstaking care 疑うべからざる苦心の跡が見える. ¶ make an *international mark* 国際的に名をあげる. ¶ a *late mark* 遅刻点. ¶ get *low marks* 劣等点を取る. ¶ It's a *mere mark* of my best regards. それはほんのご気げん伺いの印です. ¶ The *minimum marks* for a pass 最小限度の及第点. ¶ make *more marks* 一層名をあげる. ¶ He made *no mark* in history. 彼は歴史に名を残さなかった. ‖ a fellow of *no mark* 匹夫. ¶ have no *outer mark* of gentility 外面少しも上品な所がない. ¶ receive a *passing mark* in an examination 試験で合格点をとる. 【類】 I will give him a *passing mark*. ¶ get *poor marks* 悪い点を取る. ¶ get 75 per cent of the *possible marks* 最高点の七割五分を取る. ¶ As the *previous mark* obliterated, it was re-marked. 前につけた印が消えたので再び印をつけたのです. ¶ have *separate marks* for ... ...にはそれぞれ別々のマークがつけてある. ¶ as a *special mark* of his personal esteem 特に彼の敬意の印として ‖ as a *special mark* of favor 特旨をもって. ¶ *telltale marks* 隠そうとして隠されないこん跡.

Q² an *accent mark* アクセントの符号. ¶ go over the *billion dollar mark* 十億台を越える ‖ Japan's foreign commerce is now near the *billion-dollar mark*. 日本の外国貿易は今や十億ドル近くである. ¶ a *birth mark* あざ. ¶ the turning of a *century mark* 世紀の変り目. ¶ A hyphen is a *division mark* between syllables. ハイフェンはシラブル(音節)の区切りの印である. ¶ "Success" in our present age seems to be reckoned by the *dollar mark*. 現代のいわゆる成功はドルの標準で計られるもののようだ. ¶ a high *examination mark* 高い試験の評点. ¶ a *factory mark* of pottery 陶器の窯印. ¶ a *failure mark* 落第点. ¶ windows spotted with *fly marks* はえのふんなどがそこここについている窓. ¶ step down life's course almost to the *half-century mark* ほとんど五十の坂を越える. ¶ reach the *halfway mark* 目標の半ばに達する. ¶ the *high-water mark* 高潮線; 最高水準 ‖ the *high-water mark* of prosperity 繁栄の絶頂 ‖ reach the *high-water mark* of its perfection その完成の高潮に達する. 【類】 the *high-water mark* of ... English poetry / reach its *high-water mark* in the work of ... / touched his *high-water mark* of literary popularity with the publication of ... / Has the influence of Moscow already passed its *high-water mark* in western Europe? ¶ Her clothing bore no *identification marks*. 彼女の衣服にはその身もとの分かるようなものは何も着いていなかった. ¶ an *interrogation mark* 疑問符. ¶ an *intonation mark* 〖音声〗抑揚の符号. ¶ a *laundry mark* on a handkerchief ハンカチについている洗たく屋の印. ¶ a *low-water mark* 干潮線; 最低度. 【類】 reach the *low-water mark* of trading business. ¶ secure *demerit marks* 罰点をもらう. ¶ as the year neared the *midway mark* 一年も半ばを終ろうとしたとき. ¶ *mildew marks* かびの[はえた]あと. ¶ be close to the *million mark* 百万台に近い. 【類】 be well over the two *million mark* / touch the *million-dollar mark*. ¶ erase *pencil marks* 鉛筆書きを消す. ¶ a *per-cent mark* 歩合標(%). ¶ *punctuation marks* 句とう点. ¶ on a scale below the *prewar mark* 戦前[の水準]以下の規模で. ¶ Craigie *pronunciation marks* クレーギー式発音符号. ¶ The manuscript was found not up to the *publication mark*. その原稿は出版する価値がないと見られた. ¶ a word enclosed in *quotation marks* ‖ He is still a *question mark*. 彼はなお疑問の人物だ. ‖ the largest *question mark* is ... 最大の疑点は...である. 【類】 one big *question mark* must be set against ... / be still an undeveloped *question mark*. ¶ implant *red lip marks* on ... ...に赤いくちびるの跡をつける. ¶ explanation of *reference marks* 参照符(★や☞など)の説明. ¶ *school marks* and other criteria of scholastic achievement 学業の成績を示す学校の評点及び色々な基準. ¶ a *smallpox mark* ほうそうのあと, あばた. ¶ a *strawberry mark* 赤あざ. 【類】 The sailor has a *tattoo mark* on his left wrist. / those indelible (消えない) *tattoo marks*. ¶ a *trade mark* of excellence 一流品の商標 ‖ None are genuine unless bearing the above *trade marks*. 上掲の商標のないものは皆にせ物です.

P *as* a *mark* of their appreciation 彼らの感謝の印として ‖ The seal was carried *as* a *mark* of authority. [昔中国で]その印章は権威の印として携帯された. 【類】 the exhibition of the buttocks *as* a *mark* of contempt / given to ... *as* a *mark* of special favor by ... / To ... *as* a *mark* (=proof) of admiration, respect and esteem. / *as* a *mark* of honor (敬意) / *as* a *mark* of affectionate esteem (敬愛) / *as* a *mark* of recognition (功労認識) / *as* a *mark* of honorary distinction for public services / *as* a *mark* of the respect which is felt for his character and achievements by ... ¶ fire *at* a *mark* 標的を射撃する ‖ aim *at* a *mark* 標的をねらう. ¶ *below* the *mark* 標準以下で, コンマ以下で ‖ those falling *below* a *mark* of 65 in the examination 試験成績六十五点以下のもの ‖ a desolate region lying *below* high-water *mark* 高潮線下にある荒れ果てた地帯. 【類】 be *below* the $1,000 *mark*. ¶ That is quite *beside* the *mark*. それは丸で見当違いだ. 【類】 it will not be *beside* the *mark* to say that ... ¶ *between* the *marks* of parenthesis 括弧の間に. ¶ *beyond* the *mark* 標準以上に, 過度に. 【類】 go *beyond* the *mark*. ¶ It is far *from* the *mark*. それは見当違いだ. ¶ words *in marks* of parenthesis 括弧内の語 ‖ A woman, writing to a stranger, should prefix to her signature her title, "Mrs." or "Miss," *in marks* of parenthesis. 未知の人に文通する場合に婦人は署名の前に括弧に入れて "Mrs." とか "Miss" とかその称呼を付記すべきものだ. ¶ we should be *near* the *mark* in saying that ... ...と言えばほぼ核心に近いだろう. 【類】 "..." is not quite the word, perphaps be *near* the *mark*. ¶ a man *of mark* 知名の士 ‖ a man *of* no *mark* 名もない人 ‖ a theologian *of mark* 著名な神学者 ‖ must attain a certain required percentage *of marks* 点数は規定の率に達しなければならない ‖ fall short *of* the *mark* 的に達しない; 失敗に終る ‖ go wide *of* the *mark* 的を大分はずれる; 飛んだ見当違いをする. ¶ The discussions are *off* the *mark*. 討議が要点に触れていない. ¶ I am not far *over* the *mark* in saying ... ...と言うもあえて過言ではない. ¶ The estimate is *under* the *mark*. 見積りが内輪になっている. ¶ As a matter of fact, this rough estimate appears to be rather *under* than *over* the *mark*. 実はこの概算は標準以上といわんよりはむしろ標準以下であるらしい. ¶ come *up to* (=reach) the ... *mark* ...の水準に達する. 【類】 My English is not *up to* the *mark*. ‖ I am not *up to* the *mark* (=out of sorts) today. 僕はきょうはからだの具合が悪い. ‖ These goods do not come ***up to*** the *mark*. この品は標準に達していない. ‖ They run well ***up to*** the 100 *mark*. 結構百以上の数になる. ¶He was received ***with*** great *marks* of favor. 彼は大いに優待された. ‖ send him away ***with*** a *mark* of disapprobation 彼に非難を加えて追出す ‖ loading him ***with*** every *mark* of affection 彼に能う限りの愛情を浴びせて. ¶speak ***within*** the *mark* 急所にあたる ‖ we shall be well ***within*** the *mark* if we estimate the cost at ... その費用を...と見積れば大丈夫だろう.【類】we shall be ***within*** the *mark* if we assume that ... / must be well ***within*** the *mark* when he predicts that ... ¶***without*** the least *mark* of emotion 激する様子がいささかもなく.

P² obtain a required number of *marks* ***at*** an examination 試験で所要の点数を取る. 【類】get good *marks* ***at*** school. ¶You are bound to make some *mark* ***behind*** you. 諸君は後世に多少の足跡を残す義務がある. ¶the *mark* ***for*** a channel 水路標識 ‖ The maximum number of *marks* ***for*** the subject is 100. その科目の満点は百点だ. ¶high *marks* ***in*** examinations 試験の優等点 ‖ *marks* ***in*** a game 競技の得点 ‖ make a *mark* ***in*** letters 文士として名をなす ‖ make one's *mark* ***in*** life 世間に名をあげる. 【類】My *marks* ***in*** history were 80/100. ¶There were no *marks* ***of*** violence on the body. 死体には暴行を加えられたこん跡が少しもなかった. ‖ a *mark* ***of*** ignorance 無知の印. 【類】a *mark* ***of*** inferiority. ¶*marks* ***of*** parenthesis 括弧 ‖ a *mark* ***of*** wisdom 知恵のある証拠 ‖ Politeness is a *mark* ***of*** good breeding. しとやかなのは育ちのよい証拠だ. ‖ with bruises and other *marks* ***of*** ill-usage 打撲傷やその他暴行の跡 ‖ a *mark* ***of*** your true friendship 君の真の友愛のしるし. ¶a manufacturer's *marks* ***on*** his wares 製作品に付けた製造者のしるし ‖ *marks* ***on*** pottery [製陶所の]かまじるし ‖ Have I a *mark* ***on*** my face? 僕の顔にあとが付いているか. ‖ leave its *mark* ***on*** history 歴史上にその名を残す ‖ have a *mark* ***on*** the ground (a stone, a scrap of paper) 地上(など)にこん跡を残す. ¶make one's *mark* ***upon*** the age その時代に名をあげる.

mark, *v*. 記号をつける; 点数をつける; 指定する; 特徴をなす; 分画する; 計画する.

M *Mark* ***carefully*** how it is to be done. やり方をよく見ていなさい. ¶Classics are *marked* ***high***. 古典文学は貴い物とされている. ¶***leniently*** *mark* a difficult paper むずかしい試験問題に対し手やわらかに採点する. ¶*mark* ***out*** the good and the bad 善悪をわかつ ‖ *mark* ***out*** courses for contest 競技のコースを線を引いて区画する. ¶*mark* ***out*** a building 建物の設計をする ‖ *mark* ***out*** plots of ground 地割りをする ‖ *mark* ***out*** a plan 計画を立てる ‖ *mark* ***out*** oxen (=bulls) for slaughter と殺すべきものとして雄牛をえり抜く.【類】The ring-leaders (首領) were *marked* ***out*** for punishment. ¶*mark* a pupil ***perfect*** 生徒に満点を付ける. ¶***rigorously*** *mark* an easy paper やさしい試験問題に対して厳しく採点する. ¶The wrinkles about the eyes are ***strongly*** *marked*. 目の回りのしわが著しく目立つ.

M² *mark* ***down*** しるし(マーク)をつける; [定価の]値引きをする.【類】*mark* ***down*** to a third of its price ‖ *mark* ***down*** a sale (credit) 売上(掛売)を記帳する. 【類】All the textile prices have been *marked* ***down***. / *mark* ***down*** goods. ¶a place *marked* ***off*** for people to ... ...する人たちのため仕切りをした場所 ‖ This type is clearly *marked* ***off*** from the rest. この型は他のものとはっきり違っている. 【類】These manners and customs *mark* ***off*** from the brutes. / This is the only feature that *marks* him ***off*** from others. ‖ *mark* ***off*** a tennis court テニスコートの位置を線で示す. 【類】be difficult to *mark* it ***off*** from ... / *mark* them ***off*** from the rest. ¶*mark* ***up*** prices 値を高くする ‖ *mark* ***up*** goods 値上の札をつける; 〚商〛原価に利益と諸掛りを加える.

P His cruelty *marks* him ***as*** a brute. 彼の残忍なことといったら丸で畜生だ. ¶Mathematics was *marked* ***at*** zero. 数学は零点を付けられた. ‖ are *marked* ***at*** ten dollars 十ドルと値段がつけてある. ¶*mark* him ***below*** zero 彼をコンマ以下に扱う. ¶be *marked* ***by*** few events of interest [その間の歴史には]あまり面白い事件がない. ‖ His manner was *marked* ***by*** great quietness. 彼の態度には非常な落着きがあった. ‖ *marked* ***by*** smallpox あばたのある ‖ the year was *marked* ***by*** ... その年...があった ‖ In certain parts *marked* ***by*** signs at the roadside, cameras are forbidden. 路傍に標識のある一定の場所では撮影は禁じられている. ¶be *marked* off ***by*** quotation *marks* 引用符号で囲ってある. 【類】It is *marked* ***by*** a small cross (小十字記号). / Byron's writings are *marked* ***by*** passionate fire. / These attempts are *marked* ***by*** many failures and few successes. ¶*mark* a person ***for*** punishment 人を罰することにきめる ‖ *mark* ***for*** the scrap-heap 廃物にするしるしをつける ‖ *mark* chicks ***for*** identification [識別の便利のため]ひよっこにしるしをつける. ¶*mark* ***in*** pencil 鉛筆で印を付ける. 【類】Every article is sold at a fixed price (正札値段), *marked* ***in*** plain figures (はっきり数字で) on the article itself. ¶*mark* ***with*** an asterisk (a cross, a plus sign, a number) 星印(など)を付ける ‖ The breast is *marked* ***with*** initials in colored thread. 胸部には色糸で頭字が縫付けてある. ‖ cloth *marked* ***with*** light blue spots 水玉模様の布地. 【類】It was *marked* ***with*** rose-shaped spots. / baggage *marked* ***with*** labels (荷札) ‖ a placard *marked* ***with*** the destination 届先の記してある張札. 【類】All packages must be *marked* ***with*** the name and destination of the owner. ‖ He is slightly *marked* ***with*** the small-pox. 彼は薄あばたがある. 【類】a face *marked* ***with*** small-pox ‖ The boundaries of provinces and countries are *marked* ***with*** dotted lines. 州と郡の境界は点線で示してある. ‖ It is expected that 1930 will be *marked* ***with*** (=see) outstanding achievements in this field. 一九三〇年にはこの方面の業績に著しいものがあるだろうと期待されている.

marker, *n*. 標識; 採点者.

Q² ***lenient*** (***rigorous***) *marker* 点のあまい(きびしい)人. ¶a ***road*** *marker* 道路の標識.

market, *n*. 市場; 市況, 販路; 市価, 相場.

V ***acquire*** and ***exploit*** new *markets* 新に市場(販路)を獲得してこれを開拓する. ¶I wonder how it will ***affect*** the *market*? それがどう市況に影響するかしら. ¶the *market* is ***affected*** by ... 市場は...の影響を受けている. ¶The stock will ***bear down*** the *market*. その株は市場を圧倒するだろう. ¶***boycott*** a *market* ボイコット(不買同盟)する. ¶***broaden*** their *markets* それら商品の販路を拡げる. ¶gradually ***build up*** a *market* for a product 漸次生産品の販路を築き上げる. ¶***capture*** a new *market* 新市場を獲得する. ¶***cheapen*** the *market* 市価を下げる. ¶The *market* is ***closed*** rather quiet. 市場の引けはやや閑散であった. ¶***command*** the *market* 自由に商品がさばける. ¶The De Beers Company ***controls*** the diamond *market* of the world. デ・ビーアズ会社が世界のダイヤモンド市場を左右している. ¶***corner*** the *market* 株(または商品)を買占める. ¶sell goods at a loss with a view to ***creating*** a new *market* 新販路開拓のため損をして品を売る. ¶***cultivate*** a New York *market* ニューヨークにおける販路を開拓する. ¶Bears are selling to ***depress*** the *market*. 〚相場〛思わく売りで市場は不況である. ¶***destroy*** their *market* その売行きを悪くする. ¶a manufacturer wishing to ***develop*** his foreign *market* 外国の販路拡張を望んでいる製造家. ¶***enlarge*** the *market* for their products その生産品の販路を拡張する. ¶***engross*** the *market* 市場を独占する. ¶***extend*** its *markets* その販路を拡張する. ¶***find*** a *market* for ... ...のはけ口を捜す ‖ I can ***find*** a *market* for it elsewhere. それは他にはけ口がある. ‖ The product will ***find*** a *market* in America. その生産品は米国にはけ口ができるだろう. 【類】***find*** a *market* for ... ...のさばけ口を捜す / The company's manufacturers are ***finding*** a very large *market* all over the world. / British makes (=manufactures) would probably ***find*** a *market*. ¶***flood*** the *market* with ... 市場を...ではんらんさせる. ¶***glut*** the *market* 商品を市場に持込過ぎる(在荷過多にする). ¶***hold*** a *market* 市を立てる ‖ ***hold*** the *market* by offering goods cheaply 商品を安価に提供して市場を左右する. ¶***influence*** the stock *market* 株式市場を左右する. ¶***lose*** one's *market* 商機を失う. ¶Good wares ***make*** quick *markets*. 良い品はじん速にさばける. ‖ ***make*** a *market* 人気を引立てる ‖ a mother who is base enough to ***make*** a *market* of her own flesh and blood 娘を売物にするような下等な母. ¶***manipulate*** the *market* 相場を人為的に狂わせる. ¶***meet*** a ready *market* よくさばける. ¶***mend*** one's *market* その商売の景気を直す. ¶The city ***offers*** a good *market* for foreign manufactures. その市は外国製品の好市場である. ¶***open up*** a

market in the Far East for Australian products 豪州品のために極東に市場を開く. ¶***overrun*** one's ***market*** 売惜みをして売る時機を失う. ¶***overstand*** one's ***market*** 高いことを言って売損う. ¶***overstock*** the ***market*** 市場に商品を入れ過ぎる.【類】The *market* is ***overstocked*** with those goods. ¶The tremendous drop in silver ***paralysed*** the ***market***. 銀の暴落が市場をまひさせた. ¶***play*** the ***market***《米》相場に手を出す, 相場をやる. ¶***reach*** a quality ***market*** hitherto untouched 従来手のつけてない上流社会に売込む. ¶***regain*** her lost ***markets*** その国の失った販路を回復する. ¶***rig*** (=manipulate prices in) the ***market*** 人為的に相場を狂わせる. ¶***secure*** Asiatic ***markets*** for German products ドイツ生産品のためにアジアの市場を手に入れる. ¶***seek*** a new ***market*** for his manufactures 彼の製作品の新販路を捜す.【類】***seek*** an enlarged ***market*** for products. ¶***spoil*** the ***market*** for ... ...の市場を荒す. ¶a ***market*** fully ***stocked*** 仕入の豊富な市場. ¶***study*** the ***market*** in a most careful manner きわめて慎重に市況を調査する. ¶***supply*** a ***market*** with ... 市場に...を供給する ‖ a ***market*** poorly ***supplied*** 品不足の市場. ¶Bulls are buying to ***sustain*** the ***market***. 強気筋が相場をくずさないため買いあおる. ¶***tap*** the ***markets*** of Asia アジアの市場を開拓する. ¶***tighten*** the money ***market*** 金融をひっ迫させる.

V² The ***market*** is ***advancing***. 相場は上向きだ. ¶The ***market is*** now at a standstill. 市況は今や行詰っている. ‖ ***Markets are*** in a very sensitive state. 市場は非常に神経過敏になっている. ¶The ***market continues*** very strong. 市況は引続き強気だ. ¶The ***market*** is ***drooping***. 相場は小ゆるみになりつつある. ¶***Markets*** are ***falling***. 相場は下向きだ. ¶The ***market remains*** the same. 市況に変動はない. ¶The ***market*** has ***revived***. 市場が活気づいてきた. ¶The ***market*** is ***rising fast***. 市価はどんどん騰貴しつつある. ¶The ***market rules*** high (low). 相場は高価(安値)保合(もちあい)である. ¶The ***market sags***. 相場がじり安になっている. ¶The ***market stiffens***. 市況が引締まる(物価が高くなる).

Q an ***active market*** 活発な市況. ¶an ***advancing market*** 上向きの市況. ¶The ***market*** is very ***bad***. 市況ははなはだ不良だ. ¶***bearish*** (***bullish***) ***market***=bear (bull) market 弱(強)気相場. ¶The U.S.A. is the ***best market*** for Brazil's coffee. 米国はブラジルコーヒーの最上の市場だ. ¶New York City and other high-consuming areas have ***black markets*** in meat. ニューヨーク市とか消費の多い地域では食肉のやみ市がある. ¶There is a ***brisk market*** for cotton. 棉花の景気がよい. ¶a ***buyers'*** (***sellers'***) ***market*** 買(売)手市場. ¶buy in the ***cheapest market*** and sell in the ***dearest*** 一番安い相場で買って一番高い相場で売る. ¶a ***city market*** 市設市場. ¶a ***consuming market*** 消費市場. ¶The ***market*** is utterly ***depressed***. 市況は全然不振だ. ¶not to be sold or distributed on the ***civilian market*** 軍隊内部以外の販売または配布は禁じられて. ¶***domestic*** (=home) ***markets*** 内国の市場. ¶The ***market*** is ***dull***. 市況は不振だ. ¶the modern ware made for the ***European market*** 欧州の市場目当てに造った現代式の器物. ¶The ***market*** is much ***excited*** owing to rumors of war. 戦争のうわさで市場は高気配だ. ¶The ***market*** is ***fair***. 市況は順調だ. ¶a ***falling market*** 下向きの市況. ¶regain her trade in ***Far Eastern markets*** 極東の市場におけるその国の貿易を回復する. ¶the ***market*** is ***firm*** in consequence of ... ...の結果市況はしっかりしている.【類】The ***market*** is very ***firm*** with an upward tendency (上向相場). ¶a ***flat market*** 引立たない市況. ¶place a loan on the ***foreign market*** 外債を募集する. ¶in a ***free market*** 自由市場で. ¶seek ***fresh markets*** 新販路を求める. ¶The goods are now on the ***general market***. その品は今一般に販売している. ¶a ***gilt-edged market*** 確実な一流市場. ¶a ***glutted market*** 供給過多の市場. ¶The ***market*** is ***good***. 市況は良好. ‖ There is a ***good market*** for these articles. この品はよくさばける. ¶find a ***good lucrative market*** for ... ...の有利な良いさばけ口を見付ける. ¶a ***gray market*** in metals 金属のやみ類似市場. ¶there is a ***great*** and ***growing market*** for ... ...の売行はばく大で段段に増大しつつある. ¶This year the tea ***market*** is very ***hopeful***. 今年は茶が有望だ. ¶an ***inactive market*** 不振の市況. ¶undersell the foreigners in the ***international market*** 国際市場で外人より安く売る. ¶The ***market*** is very ***irregular***. 市況は不安定だ. ¶There was a ***large market*** today. きょうの市場は大取引があった. ¶may be bought in ***open market*** 一般市場で買える.【類】Money is scarce (plenty) on the ***open market***. ¶the American ***literary markets*** 米国の原稿市場. ¶the most ***lucrative market*** in the world 世界中で一番有利な市場. ¶Japanese coals have displaced Australian coals in so ***many markets***. 大多数の市場で日本の石炭が豪州品を駆逐した. ¶a ***narrow market*** 狭い販路. ¶carry goods to ***near-by markets*** 最寄りの市場に商品を持って行く. ¶a ***new market*** for ... ...の新販路. ¶There is ***no market*** for the goods. この品ははけ口がない. ¶study ***overseas markets*** 海外の市況を調査する. ¶The ***market*** is ***quiet***. 市況は平静だ. ¶A ***ready market*** is always available. いつでもすぐに売れる ‖ find (=command) a ***ready market*** すぐさばける. ¶a ***rising market*** 上向きの市況. ¶The ***market*** is very ***sluggish***. 市況はきわめて緩慢だ. ¶The ***market*** is ***steady***. 市況はしっかりしている. ¶The ***market*** is ***strong***. 市況は強調だ. ¶compete in the ***sugar markets*** of the world 世界の砂糖市場で競争する. ¶English books have the advantage that, owing to the widespread knowledge of the English language throughout the world, a ***vast market*** is open to them. 英語が世界中に普及しているので英書には販路がばく大であるという利益がある. ¶with a ***vast potential market*** ばく大の販路を占められる可能性を有して. ¶The ***market*** is decidedly ***weaker***. 市況は明かにますます軟調を呈している. ¶a ***wild market*** 乱調の市況. ¶in the ***world's market*** 世界の市場で.

Q² a ***bear*** (***bull***) ***market***〘株〙下向き(上向き, 強気)相場. ¶The ***coal market*** is very excited. 石炭相場は大いに活気がある. ¶the ***coffee*** (***corn***, ***cotton***) ***market*** コーヒー(など)市場. ¶***contract market***〘相場〙先物契約市場. ¶The ***discount market*** is very unsettled. 割引相場はすこぶる不安定だ. ¶an ***exchange markets*** 為替市場. ¶an expansion of our ***exports markets*** わが国の輸出市場の拡張. ¶a ***grain*** (***vegetable***, ***fish***) ***market*** 穀物(青物・魚)市場. ¶***holiday markets*** 休日開場の市場. ¶They are selling well in our ***home*** (=domestic) ***market***. 国内で結構さばけています. ¶an ***import*** (***export***) ***market*** 輸入(出)市場. ¶an ***investment market*** 投資市場. ¶the ***labor market*** 労働需給市場. ¶quotations on the ***London market*** ロンドン市場の付け値(相場). ¶a ***meat market*** 食肉市場. ¶a loose (tight) ***money market*** 放漫金融(金づまり)市況.【類】The ***money market*** is getting tight (loose). ¶purchased them on the ***New York market*** ニューヨーク相場でそれらを買った. ¶an ***open-air market*** 青空市場. ¶explore ***overseas markets*** 海外市場を開拓する. ¶a ***second-hand market*** 古もの市. ¶The ***security market*** is steadly going down due to the tightening money situation. 証券取引市場も金づまりで次第に下向きになっている. ¶there is a panic in the ***silk market*** 絹糸市場には恐慌がある. ¶a ***spot market***〘相場〙現物市場. ¶a ***stock market*** 株式市場. ¶The ***tobacco export market*** gets shaky. タバコ輸出市場は動揺している. ¶a ***wheat market*** 小麦市場. ¶flood the ***world market*** with ... 世界市場に...をはんらんさせる.

P buy fish ***at*** the ***market*** 市場で魚を買う ‖ Mother is ***at*** the ***market***. 母は市場へ買物に行っている. ‖ a covered stall ***at*** the ***market*** 市場の屋台店. ¶goods fit ***for*** the ***market*** 市場向きの品 ‖ goods ***for*** the Shanghai ***market*** 上海向きの品 ‖ pack fish ***for market*** 市場へ出す魚の荷ごしらえをする. ¶His house is ***in*** the ***market***. 彼の家は売物に出ている.【類】Brewery property (醸造所) in many parts of the country is ***in*** the ***market***. / On July 6th, 1925, I found that a Gutenberg Bible was ***in*** the ***market***. / It has just been placed ***in*** the ***market***. / This is the best article ***in*** the ***market***. / one of the best-selling books ***in*** the American ***market*** / have no serious competitor ***in*** the ***market*** of the world / A crisis is threatening ***in*** that ***market***. ‖ There is quite a panic ***in*** the money ***market*** owing to ... ...ため金融市場は全く混乱状態だ. ‖ We are always ***in*** the ***market*** for good listeners. こっちの話をよく聞いてくれる人はいつでも歓迎する. ‖ We are ***in*** the ***market*** for short stories of an original nature. 本社は独創に富んだ短編小説の原稿を手に入れようとしている. ‖ The company is ***in*** the ***market*** with an issue of $40,000,000 in 4½ per cent mortgage debenture stock. その会社は四分五厘利付発行の社債四千万ドルを募集している. ¶bring (=put) ... ***into*** the ***market*** ...を売物に出す ‖ come ***into*** the ***market***=be offered for sale 売物に出る ‖ They will soon find their way *into* world *market*. それらはすぐ世界市場に販路を見出すだろう. ¶ the cultivation *of* the *markets* in that section of the world 世界のその地方における市場の開拓. 【類】 the cultivation *of* the Siberian *market*. ¶ Japanese goods *on* the Australian *market* 豪州市場の日本品 ‖ the best of its kind *on* the *market* その種の売物ではこの上なしの品 ‖ The goods are being undersold by others *on* the *market*. その品は目下市場でそれ以下の値段で販売されている. 【類】 The Roneo Litho is the simplest duplicating machine (謄写器) *on* the *market*. / Reader's Digest is a magazine of condensed reprints culled from all the publications *on* the *market*. / a surprisingly strong demand for Swedish goods *on* foreign *markets*. / There is not a satisfactory French Dictionary *on* the *market*. ‖ a house *on* the *market* 売家 ‖ a drug *on* (=in) the *market* ストック品. 【類】 There are numberless patterns of the kind *on* the *market*. / There is now *on* the *market* a paper towel (紙手ぬぐい), and for it many advantages are claimed. ‖ It has appeared (=made its appearance) *on* the *market*. それは市場に出始めた. 【類】 Desirable residences sometimes go *on* the *market*. / place it *on* the *market* / new inventions put *on* the *market*. ¶ bring ... *to market* ...を売物に出す ‖ go *to market* 買物に行く ‖ go badly *to market* 売(買)損する.

P² The *market for* English wool continues very firm. 英国羊毛の相場は引続き非常に堅調である. ¶ supersede the English goods on the most important *markets of* the world 世界の重要市場で英国品に取って代る.

marketeer, *n.* 《米》 市場商人.

Q become pawns in the hands of *black marketeers* やみ屋の手先きに使われる.

marketeering, 《米》 市場の取引.

Q *black marketeering* やみ取引.

marketing, *n.* 買物; 取引.

V *do* our evening *marketing* われわれの夕方の買物をする.

Q *cooperative marketing* 協同取引.

marking, *n.* 点ずけ.

V *receive* a zero *marking* 零点を取る.

Q He is *generous* (*poor*) in *marking*. 彼は点が甘(辛)い.

P² the *marking of* the selling price *upon* each article 商品全部に値札をつけること.

marksman, *n.* 射手.

Q an *accurate marksman* ねらいの確かな射手. ¶ I am a *poor marksman*. 僕はねらいがへただ.

maroon, *v.* [孤島などに]おきざりにする.

P be *marooned by* the flood 洪水に囲まれてとり残される. ¶ He was *marooned on* a desert island. 彼は孤島におきざりにされた.

marriage, *n.* 縁組, 結婚; 夫婦の縁.

V *accept marriage* 結婚を受諾する. ¶ The *marriage* was *annulled*. その結婚は取消された. ¶ *arrange* a *marriage* between A and B 甲乙間の結婚を取持つ. ¶ *break* (=dissolve) a *marriage* 離婚する. ¶ The *marriage* was *broken off*. 結婚を解消した. ¶ The *marriage* has been *celebrated* (=*solemnized*) quietly in the presence of a few persons. その結婚式は少数の人が立合って物静かに行われた. ¶ He *concluded marriage* of convenience with a lady. 彼はある婦人と政略結婚をした. ¶ young people *contemplating marriage* 結婚しようと思っている若い人たち. ¶ *contract* a *marriage* 結婚する. 【類】 *contract marriage* with ... / He was prevented from *contracting* a *marriage* by pecuniary want. ¶ *defer* one's *marriage* until one's income becomes larger 収入がふえるまで結婚を延ばす. ¶ *dissolve* her *marriage* with ... ...との彼女の結婚を解消する. ¶ The match-maker has succeeded in *effecting* the *marriage*. 媒酌人はうまくその縁組をまとめた. ¶ *forswear marriage* 結婚しないことを誓う. ¶ *legalize* a *marriage* 結婚の法律上の手続きをふむ. ¶ He *made* a respectable *marriage*. 彼は恥かしからぬ縁組をした. 【類】 after *making* a good *marriage* / He *made* a *marriage* of convenience with a lady of good family. / There were five *marriages made* here yesterday. ¶ *negotiate marriage* 結婚の交渉をする. ¶ It is now fashionable to *perform marriages* in the afternoon. 午後に婚礼を行うのが当世風だ. ¶ *propose marriage* 結婚を申込む. ¶ *reject marriage* 結婚を拒絶する.

Q a *barren* (=*sterile*) *marriage* 子のない結婚. ¶ a *bogus marriage* 怪しげな結婚. ¶ a *childless marriage* 子のない結婚. ¶ In America the laws hold a religious marriage to be just as binding as a *civil marriage*. 米国の法律では宗教結婚は非宗教結婚(牧師の手を借りず官吏などの立会で行う結婚)と同様の効果がある. ¶ a *coercive* (=*forced*) *marriage* 強制的結婚. ¶ a *companionate marriage* 友愛結婚. ¶ *consanguineous marriages* 血族結婚. ¶ a *consensual marriage* 合意の結婚. ¶ *deferred marriage* 晩婚. ¶ *delayed marriage* 日を後らした結婚. ¶ force her into a *distasteful marriage* 無理やり彼女にいやな結婚をさせる. ¶ an *early marriage* 早婚. ¶ *easy-going marriages* のんきな結婚. ¶ a *fictitious marriage* 虚偽の結婚. ¶ a *free marriage* 自由結婚. ¶ a *fruitful* (*fruitless*) *marriage* 子の多い(ない)結婚. ¶ a *happy* (an *unhappy*) *marriage* 仕合わせな(不幸な)結婚. ¶ an *ill-assorted marriage* 不つり合いの縁組. ¶ an *immoral marriage* 不義の結婚. ¶ *improvident marriages* 不用意な結婚. ¶ an *imprudent marriage* 不用意の結婚. ¶ *indifferent marriages* 気の乗らない結婚. ¶ *international marriages* 国際結婚. ¶ a *left-handed marriage* 身分違いの結婚; にせの結婚. ¶ a *legal* (an *illegal*) *marriage* 正式の結婚(なれ合いの結婚). ¶ a *loveless marriage* 愛のない結婚. ¶ a *low marriage* 身分の低いものとの結婚. ¶ *mercenary marriages* 欲得ずくの結婚. ¶ a *mixed marriage* 異人種間の結婚. ¶ *monogamous marriage* 一夫一婦. ¶ a *morganatic* (=*left-handed*) *marriage* 身分違いの結婚. ¶ *plural* (=*polygamous*) *marriage* [モルモン教などの]一夫多妻. ¶ a *religious marriage* 宗教結婚. ¶ an unceasingly *stormy marriage* 風波の絶えぬ夫婦生活. ¶ a *successful marriage* 上首尾の結婚. ¶ an *unfortunate marriage* 不仕合わせな結婚. ¶ a *valid marriage* 正当の手続きをふんだ結婚. ¶ a *virtuous marriage* 正しい結婚. ¶ a *wealthy marriage* 有福な結婚. ¶ a *well-assorted marriage* 似合いの縁組.

Q² a *common-law marriage* 内縁. ¶ a "*G I*" *marriage* 《米》 [占領軍の]兵隊結婚. ¶ a *love marriage* 恋愛結婚. 【類】 She made an unhappy *love marriage* beneath her. ¶ a *near-kin marriage* 近親結婚. ¶ an *oak-and-ivy marriage* 非常に年の差の大きい結婚(老いらくの恋). ¶ a *pair marriage* 一夫一婦. ¶ a *picture marriage* 写真結婚. ¶ a *spite marriage* あてつけの結婚. ¶ a *trial marriage* 試験結婚.

P sterility *after marriage* 結婚後に子のないこと. ¶ A marriage portion is property given to a daughter *at marriage*. 持参金は結婚の際娘に与える財産だ. ‖ the age *at marriage* 結婚年齢. ¶ a relation *by marriage* 姻戚 ‖ a child *by* a previous *marriage* 先妻(夫)の子 ‖ his uncle *by marriage* 妻の伯父. ¶ a girl ripe *for marriage* 結婚適齢の娘. ¶ He asked my sister *in marriage*. 彼は僕の妹をもらいたいと申出た. ‖ give one's daughter *in marriage* 娘を嫁にやる ‖ unite *in marriage* 結婚する. 【類】 she was given *in marriage* to ... / the promise of his daughter *in marriage* / take her *in* (=*into*) *marriage*. ¶ *in* and *out of marriage* 結婚生活及び未婚生活において. ¶ *on* her *marriage* with ... ...と結婚したとき. ¶ the dissolution *of* his *marriage* with ... 彼の...との結婚解消 ‖ *Of* this *marriage* there are two sons, both adults. この結婚で二人の男子が生れいずれも成年に達している. ‖ a proposal *of marriage* 結婚申込 ‖ There was one child *of* the *marriage*, a daughter, born in July, 1915. 夫婦の間には一九一五年七月生れの一人の女の子があった.

P² *marriage by* proxy 代理結婚. ☞ 戦時中に米国で新郎の出征兵士に代って結婚式をやったもの. ¶ a *marriage for* love 愛の結婚 ‖ a *marriage for* money 欲得ずくの結婚. ¶ a *marriage of* reason [情実でない]合理的結婚 ‖ the *marriage of* A to B AとBの結婚. 【類】 *marriage of* (=*between*) A and B. ¶ Her *marriage to* ... was celebrated yesterday. 彼女の...との結婚はきのう式が挙行された. ¶ live in a happy *marriage with* a young woman 若い婦人と幸福な結婚生活を送る ‖ a *marriage with* a deceased wife's sister 亡妻の妹との結婚. ¶ *marriage without* boredom and without cradle 子供がなく倦怠を知らない結婚生活.

married, *pa.* 結婚した.

M She is *already married*. もう人妻です. ¶ She is *happily* (*unhappily*) *married*. 彼女は幸福(不幸)な家庭を持っている.

marrow, *n.* 髄.

P He is an aristocrat *to* the very *marrow* in his bones. 彼はあくまで貴族的な人だ. ‖ a London wastrel *to* the very *marrow* きっすいのロンドン浮浪児. 【類】 a Communist *to* the *marrow* [of his bones].

marry, *v.* 結婚する；めとる，…に嫁する；縁づかせる，めあわす；[僧などが]…の結婚式を行う。

M *marry early* 早婚する. ¶*marry late* in life 晩婚する. ¶*marganatically marry* 身分不つり合の結婚をする. ¶a *properly married* couple 天下晴れての夫婦. ¶she was *secretly married* to … 彼女はこっそり…と結婚した. ¶she was *twice married,* first to … and afterwards to … 彼女は最初…にその後…にと二度片付いた ‖ He was *twice married,* and his second wife survived him. 彼は二度結婚して後妻の方は彼より長生きした. ¶It is well known that *geisha* occasionally *marry* extremely *well.* 芸者は非常に良いところへ片付くことが往々あることは世人のよく知る通りである. ‖ He *married well* and *happily* and was a devoted father and husband. 彼は良縁を得て幸福な家庭を作り忠実な父でもあり夫でもあった. 【類】 He has a daughter very *well married* there. ¶*When* did he get *married?* 彼はいつ結婚したか. ¶He has been *married two years.* 彼は結婚して二年になる. 【類】 Mr. S, aged 24, *married 5 years* (結婚後五年), sterile.

M² *marry* her *off* to a rich merchant 金持の商人の許に娘「をかたずける.

P *marry* his daughter *above* (*below*) him 自分より身分の高(低)い者に娘を縁づける. ¶*marry against* one's will いやいや結婚する. 【類】 She *married against* her relatives' wishes. ¶*marry among* themselves 内輪で結婚する. ¶Your father *married,* as people say, *beneath* him. お前のお父さんは世間でいう身分下の結婚をした. ¶*Marrying for* mere lucre would surely ruin thy career. 単に欲得ずくの結婚はたしかになんじの一生を滅ぼすに至るであろう. ‖ *marry for* money 金を目当てに結婚する ‖ *marry for* mere lucre 金が目当で結婚する ‖ *marry* him *for* love 彼と愛の結婚をする ‖ *marry* a girl *for* her pretty face (beauty) 美ぼうにほれて少女をめとる ‖ A girl used to *marry* a man *for* better or worse, now marries him for more or less. 昔は女は苦楽をともにしようとして結婚したが，今では金の有無を見定めて結婚する世の中となった. ¶She hoped that she could *marry into* some family of rank. 彼女はどこか地位の高い家へ片付きたいと望んだ. 【類】 *marry into* a country family ‖ *marry into* the purple 玉のこしに乗る. ¶He is not able to *marry on* his present salary. 彼は今の俸給では結婚はできない. ¶She is *married to* a foreigner. 彼女は外国人のところに片付いている. 【類】 *married,* very happily, *to* a rich doctor. / one of his daughters is *married to* …, another is the wife of … / he was *married to* a daughter of … / He wished to *marry* his daughter *to* a peer. / The clergyman *married* Mary Jones *to* John Smith.

marsh, *n.* 沼沢.

V *drain* a *marsh* 沢地の水をはかせる.

Q a *reedy marsh* あしの多い沼.

marshal, *n.* [陸軍]元帥；隊長.

Q² a *field marshal* 元帥. ¶a *fire marshal* 《米》消防隊長. ¶a *provost marshal* 〖陸軍〗憲兵司令官；〖海軍〗未決監長.

P² a *Marshal of* France フランスの陸軍元帥.

marshal, *v.* 排列する.

P an honor guard *marshaled for* a review 閲兵のため整列した名誉衛兵隊. ¶*marshal* people *into* a long line 人々を列べて長い行列を作らせる.

marshal[l]ing, *n.* 排列.

P² the *marshaling of* ideals (作文のときの)思想の排列.

mart, *n.* 市場.

Q a *busy mart* 繁華な市場. ¶*international marts* (=markets) 国際市場. ¶Chicago is the *largest mart* of the Middle West. シカゴは中西部最大の市場だ. ¶an *official mart* 公営市場(税関没収品などを政府で公売する所). ¶Nagasaki was once the *sole mart* of the foreign trade of Japan. 長崎はかつて日本の外国易貿の唯一の市場であった.

martyr, *n.* 殉教者，殉難者，犠牲者.

V *burn* a *martyr* at the stake 殉教者を火刑に処する. ¶*die* a *martyr* to one's principle 主義に殉じる. ¶*make martyrs* 犠牲者を出す ‖ *make* a *martyr* of a man 人を悩ます ‖ *make* a *martyr* of oneself 自己を犠牲にする.

P² He was a *martyr for* his faith. 彼は信仰に殉じた. ¶He became the *martyr of* liberty. 彼は自由の殉教者となった. ¶a *martyr to* business 事業の犠牲者. ‖ a *martyr to* a cause (one's religion, Christianity) 大義(など)のために身命を捨てた人. 【類】 *martyr to* love / *martyr to* duty / a *martyr to* science / a *martyr to* the truth ‖ He was a lifelong *martyr to* rheumatism (gout, asthma). 彼は一生リウマチス(など)に悩んだ.

martyrdom, *n.* 殉難，殉死；苦難.

V *dare* and *endure martyrdom* 苦難を冒してこれに堪える. ¶He *suffered martyrdom* with great heroism. 彼は雄々しく苦難を忍んだ. ‖ He caused his whole family to *suffer martyrdom.* 彼はその家族全体に苦難の巻添えを食わせた. 【類】 He *suffered martyrdom* on account of his Christian faith.

P² *martyrdom for* the cause その主義のために一命を捨てることをした.

marvel, *n.* 不思議な物，驚異すべき物(人).

V He has *done* (=*performed*) *marvels.* 彼は色々不思議なことをした.

Q one of the *great marvels* in the world 世界大奇観の一.

Q² a *tennis marvel* テニス界のきりん児.

P² a *marvel of* minuteness 驚くほど微細なもの ‖ a *marvel of* beauty 絶世の美人 ‖ a *marvel of* lightness 軽妙の極致 ‖ a *marvel of* perfection 完全の極致. 【類】 *marvels of* science (nature) ‖ Napoleon is a *marvel of* history. / A Japanese house is a *marvel of* neatness. ¶How I have succeeded in my business is still a *marvel to* me. 私がどうして事業に成功したのか今なお不思議です.

marvel, *v.* 驚嘆する.

P *marvel at* one's skill その手練に感嘆する ‖ make a person *marvel at* … …に対して人を驚嘆させる.

marvelous, *a.* 驚嘆すべき.

M How *marvelous!* すてきすてき. ¶*Simply marvelous!* すてき.

Marxist, *n.* マルクス主義者.

Q a *full-fledged Marxist* 本格的マルクス主義者.

Mary, *n.* マリア，メリー.

Q² the *Virgin Mary* 処女マリア.

mascot, *n.* マスコット.

V The cat was *made* a *mascot* among the sailors. そのねこは船員たちのマスコットにされた.

mash, *n.* すりえ.

Q feed *dry* (*wet*) *mash* 乾いたえさ(すりえ)をやる.

Q² *chicken mash* for my chicks ひよっこにやる鶏のえさ.

mash, *v.* ほれさせる.

P He is *mashed on* (=has sentimental admiration for) her. 彼は彼女に参っている(ほれている).

mask, *n.* 覆面，仮面；かこつけ.

V *assume* (=*put on*) the *mask* of … …の仮面をかぶる. ¶*drop* (=*cast aside, pull off or tear off*) one's *mask* 仮面をぬぐ；本音をはく. 【類】 *cast aside* the *mask* of hypocrisy (虚偽の仮面). ¶He *threw off* the *mask* he had been wearing up to this time. ここに至って彼は本音をはいた. ¶*wear* a *mask* [over one's face] 仮面をかぶる.

Q wear a *black mask* 黒の覆面をする(盗賊など). ¶under the *deceptive mask* of … …にまぎらして.

Q² an *anti-gas mask* 防毒面. ¶the history of the *death mask* デスマスクの歴史. ¶a *fencing mask* 剣術の面. ¶a *flu mask* 流行性感冒よけマスク.

P "…" was the *mask behind* which he was hiding. 「…」は彼がその陰に隠れていた仮面であった. ¶poison *in* the *mask* of medicine 薬と見せかけた毒. ¶*under* the *mask* of … …の仮面をかぶって，を口実にして ‖ He did it *under* the *mask* of charity. 彼は慈善にかこつけてそれをやった. ‖ conquer a people *under* the *mask* of religion 伝道にかこつけて国を取る ‖ an old friend *under* a new *mask* 新しい仮面をかぶった古い友.

mask, *v.* 仮面をかぶる.

P brothels *masking as* massage rooms 表面はマッサージ治療所の売春くつ. ¶*mask* one's real character *behind* an assumed manner 体裁をつくろって本性をかくす. ¶*mask* one's enmity *under* an appearance of friendliness 友人顔して敵意をかくす.

masquerade, *n.* 仮装舞踏会.

P join *in* a *masquerade* 仮装舞踏会に加わる.

masquerade, *v.* 仮装する，いつわる.

P *masquerading as* Admiral Togo (Adolf Hitler) 東郷大将(など)に紛する ‖ a fair woman *marquerading as* a man 男装の麗人 ‖ a professional *masquerading as* an amateur しろうとと振れ込む(いつわる)専門家. 【類】 *masquerade as* respectable citizens (れっきとした市民) / an old idea *masquerading as* new. / a rushlight (灯心ろうそく) *masquerading as* a star. ¶*masquerade under* the good name of … …の美名に隠れて. ¶The "friendship" is simply love or flirtation *masqurading under* another name. 友情

というのは恋愛かいちゃつきが別名の仮面をかぶったものに過ぎない.

mass, *n.* かたまり; 群, 集団; 大半, 大多数.

V I decided to give my life to the task of ***educating*** and ***uplifting*** the *masses*. 私は大衆の教育と向上とに一身を捧げることに決心した. ¶***elevate*** the *masses* 大衆を向上させる. ¶***hold*** the *mass* together 大衆を糾合する. ¶***incite*** (=***agitate***) the *masses* to overturn the British political system 民衆を扇動して英国の政治組織をくつがえす. ¶***influence*** the *mass* and scholars 一般人と学者とを左右する. ¶***serve*** the *masses* 民衆に奉仕する.

Q a ***confused*** *mass* of things ごちゃごちゃになった物. 【類】 a ***confused*** *mass* of unrelated notions ちぐはぐの思想. ¶a ***floating*** *mass* of ice 流氷塊. ¶the ***great*** *mass* of people 人民の大半 ‖ a ***great*** *mass* of buildings 多数の建物の集団. ¶He spent a ***huge*** *mass* of treasure. 彼はばく大の金銭を費した. ¶A ***new*** *mass* of hot air hit the Midwest. 新しく発生した一団の熱風が米国の中西部を襲った. ¶an ***indistinct*** *mass* もうろうとしたひとかたまり. ¶millions of the ***laboring*** *masses* 数百万の労働大衆. ¶the ***toiling*** *masses* 労働下層民. ¶the ***vocalized*** and ***articulated*** *mass* 意見を持ってこれを発表することのできる大衆.

Q^2 a frigid ***air*** *mass* 冷凍した空気.

P There is not real militarism ***among*** the French *masses*. フランスの民衆間には真の軍国思想というものはない. ¶receive a sum ***in*** a *mass* 一口にある金を受取る ‖ buy (sell) ... ***in*** [the] *mass* ...をまとめて買う(売る) ‖ taken ***in*** the *mass* and on the average 大ざっぱに平均をとって見ると ‖ look at them ***in*** *mass* from an altitude それを高所から大観する. ¶collect ***into*** a *mass* ひとまとめにする.

P^2 He was a *mass* ***of*** bruises. 彼は全身打撲傷だらけだった. ‖ He says that religion is a *mass* ***of*** falsehood (incongruities). 宗教はうそ(矛盾)のかたまりだと彼は言う. ‖ Within twenty minutes the whole building was a *mass* ***of*** flames. 二十分以内に建物全部が火炎のかたまりとなった. ‖ a *mass* ***of*** iron (stone, earth) 鉄塊(など). 【類】 a *mass* ***of*** people / a *mass* ***of*** troops / *masses* ***of*** dark clouds ‖ The azalea made a *mass* ***of*** color in the garden. 庭にはつつじがあざやかに咲いていた.

mass, *n.* 〖宗教〗 法会, 法事, 回向(えこう), ミサ.

V ***attend*** *mass* in a cathedral 本山の法会に出席する. ¶***hold*** a Buddhist *mass* 法事を営む. ¶***say*** (=***read***) *mass* ミサをささげる. 【類】 ***say*** *masses* for the dead.

Q^2 be present at a ***death*** *mass* 死者のミサに出席する. ¶In Roman Catholic a ***requiem*** *mass* is said for the death. ローマカトリック教では死者に対しミサを捧げる.

P^2 a *mass* ***for*** the repose of one's soul 供養.

mass, *v.* 集合する.

P Troops are *massing* ***in*** the frontier. 軍隊は国境線に集結している.

massage, *n.* マッサージ.

Q ***facial*** *massage* 顔面マッサージ.

Q^2 ***scalp*** *massage* 頭部マッサージ.

mast, *n.* マスト.

V^2 The *mast* ***snapped***. マストがぽきっと折れた.

Q the forest of ***lofty*** *masts* 林立する高いマスト.

Q^2 a ***fore-top*** *mast* 〖航〗 前マストから二番目のマスト.

P serve ***before*** the *mast* 水夫になる.

master, *n.* 主人; 学者, 教師; 達人, 大家; 〖教育〗 [しばしばM-] 修士; [呼びかけ] ぼっちゃん.

V He ***eclipsed*** his *master*. 彼は出藍(らん)の誉があった. ¶No man can ***serve*** two *masters*. 人は二人の主人に仕えることはできない.

Q They were ***absolute*** *masters* of themselves under fire. 彼らは砲火の下にあって自若としていた. ¶a ***consummate*** *master* of the English language 申分のない英語の大家. ¶a ***complete*** *master* (mistress) of an art. 一芸の奥義をきわめた人. ¶an ***extraordinary*** *master* of oratory 非凡な演説の大家. ¶***great*** *masters* of knowledge 大学者 ‖ a ***great*** *master* of [literary] style 名文家. 【類】 a ***great*** *master* of prose / the ***greatest living*** *master* of poetry. ¶a ***hard*** *master* やかましい主人. ¶***illustrious*** *masters* 著名な巨匠たち. ¶an ***inferior*** *master* 二流どこ. ¶American ***literary*** *masters* 米国の文豪たち. ¶a ***masterful*** *master* 専横な主人. ¶an ***old*** *master* in new phrasing 新語句の名人. ¶become one's ***own*** *master* 一本立になる ‖ He is his ***own*** *master*. 彼は自分の思う通りにできる(自由の身だ). 【類】 He was his ***own*** *master* enough to do it. ¶a ***past*** *master* in the art of timing. 〖演劇・音楽〗 タイミングの老手 ‖ a ***past*** *master* of the arts of pen and sword 文武両道の達人. ¶a ***severe*** *master* きびしい主人. ¶My *master* is very ***strict***. 主人はばかにきびしい. ¶He is a ***thorough*** *master* of the subject. 彼はその問題には徹底的に明るい. ¶***topmost*** *masters* 第一流の大家. ¶They are placed under ***well-trained*** and ***competent*** *masters*. 彼らはりっぱに訓練されかつ手腕のある教師についている. ¶***Young*** *Master* George ジョージぼっちゃま.

Q^2 an ***assay*** *master* 試金官(金銀塊または貨幣を吟味する官吏). ¶a ***concert*** *master* 合奏長(指揮者の代理). ¶a ***dancing*** *master* ダンス教師. ¶The ***Globe*** *Master* 地球支配者(飛行機名). ¶a ***music*** *master* 音楽の教師. ¶a ***riding*** (***fencing***) *master* 乗馬(など)の教師. ¶a ***ring*** *master* [サーカスの]団長. ¶a ***writing*** *master* 書道の先生.

P The disciple is not ***above*** the *master*. あの弟子は師匠以上ではない. ¶She studied painting ***under*** *masters*. 彼女は数名の教師について絵を習った ‖ He worked ***under*** a strict *master*. 彼はきびしい主人のもとで働いた. ¶He learned Latin ***without*** a *master*. 彼はラテン語を独学でやった.

P^2 a *master* ***in*** lacquer うるし細工の名人. 【類】 a *master* ***in*** literature 文学の大家. ¶make oneself a *master* ***of*** an art 一芸をきわめる ‖ a *master* ***of*** arts 修士 ‖ He must be *master* ***of*** himself in order to adapt himself to the requirements of the moment. 臨機応変の処置を取るには落着いていなくてはいけない. ‖ He is *master* ***of*** strategy. 彼は戦略の達人だ. ‖ a great *master* ***of*** the art of make-up ふん装術の名人 ‖ a *master* ***of*** ceremonies 《米》 [ショーなどの]司会者. 【類】 He is *master* ***of*** ceremonies at a picture house in Detroit. ‖ be *master* ***of*** one's destiny 自己の運命を自由に変えられる ‖ One must be *master* ***of*** one's circumstances. 人は境遇に勝たなくてはいけない. 【類】 be *master* ***of*** the situation ‖ a *master* ***of*** exposition 名解説者 ‖ a *master* ***of*** that speciality その道の専門家 ‖ a *master* ***of*** his craft この道の達人 ‖ one of the greatest *masters* ***of*** English style 英文大家の一人 ‖ be *master* ***of*** one's own time 自分の時間を自由に使える ‖ He is the *master* ***of*** a factory (shop). 彼は工場(店)主だ.

P He is *master* ***of*** himself. 彼はよく自己を制する. 【類】 He is a *master* ***of*** music (painting). / *masters* ***of*** their respective subjects / be *master* ***of*** one's trade / a *master* ***of*** wordcraft (文章) ‖ *Master* ***of*** Arts (Science) 文(理)学修士.

master, *a.* 達人の, 優れた.

M He was not then ***fully*** *master* of his nerves. その時彼はあまり気がしっかりしていなかった.

master, *v.* きわめる, 修める.

M *master* ***completely*** the situation 困難な状況を完全に克服する. ¶***thoroughly*** *master* ... 徹底的に...をきわめる.

masterpiece, *n.* 傑作.

V ***create*** a *masterpiece* in painting 絵画の傑作を出す. ¶***hear*** a musical *masterpiece* murdered 名曲をだいなしにした演奏を聞く.

Q an ***enduring*** *masterpiece* 不朽の傑作. ¶***living*** *masterpieces*=excellent pictures in tableaus vivants 活人画の傑作. ¶***nature's richest*** *masterpieces* 自然の最も貴重な傑作(自然美). ¶a ***scenic*** *masterpiece* 絶景.

Q^2 a ***world*** *masterpiece* 世界的名作.

P^2 a *masterpiece* ***by*** Turner ターナーの傑作. ¶*masterpieces* ***in*** English literature 英文学の傑作 ‖ a *masterpiece* ***in*** divorce 奇抜な離婚ざた. ¶*masterpieces* ***of*** the cartoonist's art 漫画芸術の傑作 ‖ *masterpieces* ***of*** French romance フランス浪漫派小説の傑作 ‖ a *masterpiece* ***of*** learned research and a monument of untiring labor 学者的研究の傑作たると同時にうまざる努力の記念碑 ‖ a *masterpiece* ***of*** persuasive reasoning and lucid exposition 理路整然として名文の解説.

masterwork, *n.* 傑作.

Q This is one of his ***latest*** *masterworks*. これは彼の最近の傑作の一つだ.

mastery, *n.* 支配; 熟達, 通暁; 優勝.

V ***acquire*** a *mastery* of a foreign language 外国語に熟達する. ¶Every man should ***exercise*** *mastery* over his own fortune. 人は皆自己の運命を支配すべきである. ¶We ***gained*** (=got or obtained) the *mastery* of the enemy. われらは敵に打勝った. ¶He has ***got*** the *mastery*. 彼は勝を

制した. ¶He ***has*** complete *mastery* over his employees. 彼は使用人をよく監理している. ¶***make mastery*** of ... ...を自分のものにする. ¶***obtain*** the most complete *mastery* of ... ...に通暁する ‖ The flames soon ***obtained*** the complete *mastery* of the ship. 火炎は間もなく船全体に燃え広がってしまった. ¶***possess*** a *mastery* of the English language 英語に通暁している. ¶***secure*** the *mastery* of the seas 海上のは権を握る.

Q the ***admirable*** *mastery* of the technique りっぱな技術の精通. ¶an ***artist's*** *mastery* of color 画家の絵具の使い方の巧妙. ¶be short of ***complete*** *mastery* 精通というほどには行かない(幾分未熟な). 【類】achieve ***complete*** *mastery* of ... ¶man's ***increasing*** *mastery* over disease 人間の段段に進捗する病気の征服. ¶The translation shows a perfect contempt for the English idiom combined with an ***imperfect*** *mastery* over the French. その翻訳を見ると訳者が英語の語法を無視しかつ(原文の)フランス語法をよく理解していないことがわかる. ¶acquire a ***sufficient*** *mastery* of English 英語に十分熟達する. ¶get a ***thorough*** *mastery* of ... ...に精通する. ¶acquire a ***thorough practical*** *mastery* of English 英語を十分に活用しうるようになる. ¶His *mastery* of chess is really ***wonderful***. 彼のチェスの腕前は全くすばらしい.

P strive ***for*** *mastery* 雌雄を争う. ¶employ ***with*** equal *mastery* the two languages of French and English 英仏両国語を同じように達者に使う. ¶***Without*** a proper *mastery* of English, it is impossible to speak it with any approach to correctness. 英語に相当熟達していなくってはそれを正確に話すことはできない.

P^2 *mastery* ***of*** environment 環境の征服 ‖ *mastery* ***of*** fear 恐怖の克服. 【類】*mastery* ***of*** evil passions and emotions (情欲や衝動) / the *mastery* ***of*** moods (むら気). ‖ the *mastery* ***of*** the ability to read and write 読書力及び作文力の熟達. ¶the *mastery* ***over*** words 言葉を自由に駆使する力. 【類】man's *mastery* ***over*** nature / His *mastery* ***over*** the English language is wonderful. / gain a swift *mastery* ***over*** new details.

masthead, *n.* マストの先.

P The flags fly (=flutter) ***at*** the *masthead*. 旗がマストの上にひるがえる.

mat, *n.* 畳(マット).

V ***comb*** the *mat* off the dog's hair マットから犬の毛をすきとる. ¶***re-cover mats*** 畳の表替えをする. ¶They ***shake*** *mats* dustily, a work that the city laws will not permit at a later hour. その人たちはマットを振ってほこりを立てるがこれは市の規則で早朝でなくては許されないことになっている. ¶***take up*** the *mats* 畳を上げる.

Q^2 a ***door*** *mat* ドアー・マット. ¶a ***floor*** *mats* 床上に敷くマット. ¶a ***table*** *mat* テーブル敷き.

P walk ***over*** the *mat* マットの上を歩く.

P^2 a *mat* ***of*** weeds ござ.

match, *n.* マッチの棒.

V ***apply*** a *match* to gunpowder 火薬にマッチを付ける. ¶***light*** a *match* マッチをつける. ¶***scratch*** a *match* on the sole of one's slipper 上ぐつの底でマッチをする. ¶***strike*** (=light) a *match* マッチをする ‖ Some *matches* will ***strike*** anywhere. マッチにはどこですっても付くのがある.

Q a ***lighted*** *match* 火の付いたマッチ.

Q^2 a ***friction*** *match* (普通の)すりマッチ. ¶a ***safety*** *match* 安全マッチ(普通のマッチ). ¶a ***sulfur*** *match* 硫黄マッチ.

P a box ***of*** *matches* マッチ一箱 ‖ a pack ***of*** *matches* マッチの小箱. 【類】a small package ***of*** *matches*. ¶burn ***with*** a *match* マッチで燃やす. 【類】light a cigar ***with*** a *match*.

O This *match* won't catch fire. このマッチはなかなか火がつかない.

match, *n.* 敵手; よく似合う人または物; 配偶; 婚姻; 試合, 競技.

V ***arrange*** a *match* between ... and ... ...と...の縁談を取まとめる. ¶***break off*** the *match* 縁組を破談にする. ¶He has ***found*** his *match*. 彼は好敵手を見付けた. ‖ I ***find*** my *match* in him 彼は好敵手だ. ¶***have*** (=***hold***) a *match* 試合をする. ¶***look round for*** a suitable *match* for her son 息子のために適当な嫁を捜し回る. ¶***lose*** the *match* その試合に負ける. ¶***make*** a *match* 媒酌をする. 【類】Master Cupid (月下氷人) proceeds to ***make*** a *match*. ‖ She has ***made*** a good *match*. 彼女は良い人に嫁した. ‖ opportunities for ***making*** a good *match* 良縁を結ぶ機会. ¶***meet*** (=find) one's *match* 好敵手に出会う ‖ He never ***met*** his *match*. 彼は負けたことはない. ¶***play*** a *match* against ... ...と試合をする. ¶he ***proved*** no *match* for ... 彼は...にはかなわないことが分かった. ¶***row*** a *match* ボートレースをする. ¶***run*** a *match* 競走する. ¶We shall never ***see*** his *match*. 彼に匹敵する人は二度と見られないだろう. ¶I ***watched*** the *match* with great interest. 私は非常な興味をもてその試合を見た. ¶***win*** the *match* その試合に勝つ.

V^2 The *match* ***came off*** last week. 先週その試合が催された. ¶The *match* ***ended*** in a tie. その試合は同点に終った.

Q a ***good*** *match* 良縁. 【類】He (She) is a ***good*** *match*. ¶there was ***no*** *match* for ... ...にはだれもかなわなかった ‖ I am ***no*** *match* for him. 彼にはとてもかなわない. ¶a ***runaway*** *match* かけ落結婚. ¶play a ***scratch*** *match* ハンディキャップなしの競技をやる. ¶a ***suitable*** *match* 好配偶. ¶an ***uneven*** *match* つり合わない(互角でない)勝負.

Q^2 have an ***all-night*** *match* with playing-cards トランプをやって夜を明かす. ¶a ***championship*** *match* 選手権試合. ¶a ***consolation*** *match* 慰藉(しゃ)(残念)競技. ¶a ***cricket*** (***fencing, wrestling***) *match* クリケット(など)の試合. ¶an ***exhibition*** *match* 模範試合, オープン戦. ¶a list of the ***first-day*** wrestling *matches* すもうの初日の取組. ¶a pure ***love*** *match* 純粋の恋愛結婚. 【類】a true (pure) ***love*** *match*. ¶a ***play-off*** *match* [同点の]決勝試合. ¶a ***return*** *match* 〘拳闘〙リターンマッチ(選手権をとられた場合九十日以内に奪回戦を行うことになっている). ¶a ***soccer*** (***rugger***) *match* ア式(ラ式)しゅう球試合. ¶a ***walking*** *match* 競歩.

P Our side beat the other ***in*** the *match*. われわれの方が試合に勝った.

P^2 He was more than my *match* ***in*** diplomatic shrewdness. 外交にかけては彼は私より役者が一枚上であった. ¶play a *match* ***against*** ... ...と試合をする. ¶a *match* ***at*** shooting 射撃の試合 ‖ play a *match* ***at*** tennis (cricket, football) テニス(など)の試合をする. ¶a baseball *match* ***between*** the teams of Waseda and Keio 早稲田対慶応の野球試合. ☞一般に英語用法は match で, 米語用法は game という: a baseball (football) *match*=《米》a baseball (football) *game*. ¶a *match* ***for*** a prize 懸賞試合 ‖ I am no *match* ***for*** him. 彼にはかなわない. 【類】be more than a *match* ***for*** ... ‖ The hat is a *match* ***for*** the coat. その帽子は上衣によく似合う.

O He found me more than his *match*. 彼は僕にはかなわないことを知った.

match, *v.* 添わせる; 取組ませる; 匹敵する; つり合う; 連添う.

M They are ***equally matched*** in their knowledge of English. 彼らは英語の学力では互角だ. ¶The colors *match* ***well***. その色はうつりが良い. ‖ jewels ***well*** *matched* in color 色のつり合いの取れた宝石. ¶a ***well-matched*** couple 似合の夫婦.

P *match* the American baseball-players ***against*** Japanese school teams アメリカの野球団を日本の学生チームと試合させる. ¶it is more than (thousand times) *matched* ***by*** ... それより...の方が(断然)まさっている ‖ be *matched* only ***by*** ... 敵するものは...あるのみである. ¶I will *match* you ***in*** a race (game, fencing). 競走(など)では僕が君の相手になるぞ. ‖ No one can *match* him ***in*** argument. 議論では彼に匹敵するものはない. ‖ It cannot be *matched* ***in*** our country. わが国にそれに匹敵するものがない. ¶It *matches* so well ***with*** the other things. それは外の物と大層よくつり合う. ‖ These ribbons do not *match* ***with*** your hat. 【類】*match* one competitor ***with*** (=against) another / This color does not *match* ***with*** that. ‖ Let beggars *match* ***with*** beggars. 〘諺〙われなべにとじぶた, 牛は牛づれ.

O a carpet with curtains to *match* カーテンと釣合った敷物.

match-box, *n.* マッチ箱.

P^2 a *match-box* ***of*** a house マッチ箱のような家.

mate, *n.* 配偶; [手袋などの]片方.

V A vast number of men and women who wish to marry cannot ***find*** *mates*. 結婚を望んでいる男女でその配偶が見当らないでいるものが非常に多い.

V^2 I've found one, but its *mate* is still ***missing***. 片方は見つけたが, もう片方が見えない.

Q the most ***fit*** *mates* 最もふさわしい配偶. ¶a ***life-long*** *mate* 偕(かい)老同穴の連合い. ¶one's ***running*** *mate* 立候補仲間. ¶English quotation-marks are not exacly ***sym-***

metrical mates. 英語の引用符(“ ”)はきちんとつり合った対(ふ)ではない.
Q^2 ***school** mates*=schoolmates 学友.
P^2 the *mate **for*** him 彼の配偶. ¶Find me the *mate **of*** (=*to*) this glove. この手袋の片方を見つけてくれ.

mate, *v.* 添わせる; 交わる; 連れ添う.
P I will not *mate **with*** him. 僕は彼と交わるまい. ‖ *mate **with*** a man (woman) 男(女)に連れ添う ‖ *mate* a woman ***with*** a man 女を男に添わせる ‖ *mate* one's words ***with*** deeds 言行を一致させる.

material, *n.* 原料; 資料, 教材; [織物の]地.
V ***afford*** ample *material* 十分に材料を供給する. 【類】***afford*** the best *material* for ... ¶***alphabetize*** *material* 材料を ABC 順に並べる. ¶***amass*** *materials* for ... ...の材料を集める. ¶***assemble*** *meterials* into a structure 材料をまとめて一つの建築に作り上げる. ¶***bring together*** and ***arrange*** chronologically this *material* so as to form a continuous story 連続した物語を成すようにこの資料をまとめて年代順に配列する. ¶There is so much *material* to ***choose*** from ... ...から選び出す材料が非常に多い. ¶***collect*** *material[s]* for a biography of ... ...の伝記の資料を集める. 【類】***collect*** *materials* having reference to ... / He ***collected*** his *materials* at first hand (じかに). ¶***collect*** and ***put together*** *materials* 材料を集めて組立てる. ¶***digest*** the *material* collected 集めた材料をこなす. ¶***dig out*** *material* 材料を掘出す. ¶Post ***discolors*** delicate *materials.* いたみやすい材料は郵便で送ると色がさめる. ¶***draw*** *material* from ... ...から材料を取る ‖ nearly the whole of the *material* is ***drawn*** from ... 材料のほとんど全部は...から取ったのだ. ¶***face*** a *material* with ... ...で上張りする. ¶***feed*** *material* into a machine 機械に材料を送り込む. ¶***furnish*** valuable *materials* to ... ...に貴重な材料を提供する ‖ He ***furnishes such*** limited *materials* for biography. 彼の一生には伝記の材料になるものが実に乏しい. ¶***gather*** *materials* upon some topic ある題目に関する資料を集める. 【類】***gather*** *materials* with which to write ... / for the purpose of ***gathering*** *materials.* ¶***get*** *material* for stories 物語の資料を採る. ¶***get together*** my *material* 自分使用の材料を収集する. ¶***glean*** *materials* from ... ...から材料を集める. ¶***handle*** the *material* adroitly 巧みに材料を処理する. ¶***hunt up*** *material* for an essay 随筆の資料を捜し出す. ¶***make*** raw *materials* into useful forms 原材で有用な器具を作る. ¶The *materials* must be carefully ***picked.*** 材料は精選するを要する. ¶***prepare*** *material* for publication 出版のために資料を用意する. ¶***provide*** *materials* of instruction 教材を準備する. 【類】***provide*** *materials* for carrying on an enterprise / It will certainly ***provide*** *material* for much discussion and deliberation. ¶***put*** the *material* into permanent form 材料を永久的のものに作り上げる. ¶***reduce*** raw *materials* into a form suitable for use 原料を役に立つような形に仕上げる. ¶***secure*** *materials* for production 生産資材を確保する. ¶***use*** *material* culled from Japanese and Chinese books 和漢の書からえり抜いた資料を使う. ¶***use up*** all the *material* in hand 手持ちの材料を使い切る. ¶***work up*** (=***expend***) *materials* 材料を製作に使う. ¶Experiments have ***yielded*** interesting *material.* 実験から興味ある資料を得た.
Q ***abundant*** *material* 豊富な材料. ¶have ***adequate*** *materials* 十分材料がある. ¶***all*** *materials* 一切の材料. ¶***basic raw*** *materials* 基本原料. ¶***cheaper*** *materials* もっと安価な材料. ¶a ***constructive*** *material* 構材. ¶***critical*** *materials* 重要資材. ¶a loose kind of graduate's gown in ***dark*** *material* 黒の服地で作っただぶだぶした卒業式の礼服風のもの. ¶***discarded*** *materials* 廃物. ¶The ***fecal*** *materials* are the dross of the digestion. ふんの材料は消化の残りかすである. ¶Japan accepted the offer of the ***fissionable*** *material* by the United States 日本はアメリカからの核分裂資材の供給申出を受諾した. ¶***fragrant*** *materials* 香料. ¶wealth of ***illustrative*** *material* 豊富な説明資料. ¶***incentive*** *materials* 報奨物資. ¶***indigestible*** *material* 消化できない(ほど多量の)材料. ¶***inflammable*** *material* 可燃物. 【類】Celluloid is a highly ***inflammable*** *material.* ¶One half of all ***known*** *materials* consist of oxygen. われわれの知っている物質の半ばは酸素から成る. ¶***massive*** *material* ぼう大な資料. ¶***mimeographed*** *material* 謄写版の刷り物. ¶a new combinations of ***old*** *material* 古材料の新しい組合わせ. ¶***photographic*** *meterials* 写真材料. ¶***printed*** *material* 印刷物. ¶***promising*** *materials* 物になるような材料(文学の). ¶There is a dearth of ***published*** *material* on the subject. その問題に関する出版物は不足している. ¶***raw*** *materials* used in glass manufacture ガラス製造に使用する原料. 【類】***raw*** *materials* of commerce / ***raw*** *material* for chemical goods / process ***raw*** *matirials* (加工) / There are those who maintain that Whitman's compositions are not finished poems but merely the ***raw*** *material* untranslated into poetry ‖ the ***raw*** *material* for a book instead of the finished product (内容が消化した本になっていない)完成品でなく著作の素材. ¶the ***requisite*** *materials* of ... ...に必要な材料. ¶***scarce*** *materials* 希少物資. ¶The book embodies a large amount of ***scattered*** *material.* その本には諸方から集めた多量の材料が載せてある. ¶***semi-fabricated*** *material* 半製原料. ¶***semi-finished raw*** *material* 半製原料. ¶***shoddy*** *materials* ざつな品. ¶***statistical*** *materials* 統計資料. ¶***strategic[al]*** *materials* 戦略物資. ¶a soft *material* for dressing wounds ほうたい用の柔かい材料. ¶the admission of ***unfit*** *materials* 進学不適当者の入学. ¶an ***unpromising*** *material* for poetry 詩には不向の材料. ¶We use no ***unsolicited*** *material.* 本誌では依頼原稿以外のものは使用しない(任意投稿謝絶). ¶***vital*** *material* 主要資材. ¶the elimination of ***waste*** *material* 廃物の除去. ¶***welcome*** *material* to editors 編集者が歓迎する原稿. ¶a ***woolen*** *material* for ladies' dresses 婦人服向の毛織物. ¶***written*** or ***printed*** *material* (筆記または印刷した)文献.
Q^2 ***binding*** *material* [料理]つなぎ. ¶***building*** *materials* 建築資材. ¶***clothing*** *materials* 服飾材料, 服地. ¶***coloring*** *materials* 着色材. ¶***construction*** *materials* 建設資材. ¶obtain permission to use ***copyright*** *material* 版権使用の許可を得る. ¶***drawing*** *materials* 製図材料. ¶***dress*** (=clothing) *material* 衣料 ‖ steam-smoothed ***dress*** *material* 湯気で柔かにした服地. ¶a new ***fabric*** *material* 新型織地. ¶***fertilizer*** *materials* 製肥原料. ¶***fire-resisting*** *material* 防火用資材 ¶***flooring*** and ***roofing*** *materials* 床屋根資材. ¶***food*** *materials* 食料. ¶***key*** *materials* 主要資材. ¶***packing*** *material* 荷造り資材. ¶***paving*** *materials* 舗装道路用資材. ¶***polishing*** *materials* 研磨材. ¶***practice*** *material* 練習用資材. ¶***printing*** *materials* 印刷用資材. ¶***railroad construction*** *materials* 鉄道建設資材. ¶***rainproof*** *material* 防水資材. ¶***reading*** *material* 読みもの. 【類】the usual ***reading*** *material* of adult Americans / grasp the contents of ***reading*** *material.* ¶Few libraries have such ***research*** *material.* こんなに研究資料の豊富な図書館は多くない. ¶***rote*** *material* 暗記物. ¶***sewing*** *materials* 裁縫材料. ¶a thin ***silk*** *material* 薄い絹物. ¶***source*** *material* 根本資料. ¶***steel*** *materials* 鋼鉄材. ¶***story*** *material* 話の種. ¶***teaching*** *materials* 教材. ¶***war*** *materials* 戦争資材. 【類】Food is a vital ***war*** *meterial.* / the stockpiling (蓄積) of vital ***war*** *mateials* such as tin and manganese. ¶***waterproof*** *material* 防水材料. ¶***writing*** *materials* 文房具.
P make it ***from*** raw *materials* 原料でそれを作る. ¶***in*** *material* and workmanship 材料及び細工の点において.
P^2 *material* ***for*** clothing 被服材料 ‖ *materials* ***for*** the manufacture of paper 製紙材料 ‖ *materials* ***for*** the History of Great Japan 大日本史資料. 【類】*materials* ***for*** Japanese history in European archives (古文書庫). ¶*material* ***of*** war 軍需品. ¶*material* ***of*** conversation 話の種. ¶*material* made ***of*** cotton and wool 木綿と毛でできた織物. ¶*material* ***on*** Japanese history 日本史資料

materialism, *n.* 唯物論.
Q a ***Godless*** *materialism* 無神論的唯物論. ¶***historical*** *matersialism* 唯物史観.

materialization, *n.* 実現.
P^2 the *materialization* ***of*** one's ideas 自分の考案の実現.

materialize, *v.* 実現する, 具体化する.
M The project has ***never*** *materialized.* その案は全然具体化しなかった.
P Business at last *materialized* ***with*** Hongkong. ついにホンコンと商談がまとまった.

maternity, *n.* 分べんすること.
Q matrons who fear ***late*** *maternity* 晩年の分べんを恐れる妻たち.

mathematician, *n.* 数学者.
Q He is the ***best*** *mathematician* in our class. 彼はクラスで一番数学ができる. ¶a ***great*** *mathematician* 大数学者.

¶I am a *poor mathematician*. 僕は数学は不得手だ.
Q² you don't have to be an *expert mathematician* to figure that ... 君が...を計算するには熟練な数学者たるを要しない. ¶Mary Somerville, the great *woman mathematician* of any age 古今まれな偉大な女流数学者メリー・サマビル.

mathematics, *n*. 数学.
Q from the view-point of *cold mathematics* 冷静な数学的見地から見ると. ¶the *native mathematics* of Japan. 和算. ¶His *mathematics* is *wrong*. 彼の統計(など)には誤りがある.

mating, *n*. 配偶; 配合.
Q *monogamous mating*, or mating of one man to one woman for life 一夫一婦制すなわち一人の男が一生一人の女と連添うこと.
P² the *mating of* white *with* black 黒人と白人の配合.

matriculate, *v*. [大学に]入学する.
P *matriculate at* a university 大学に入学する ‖ *matriculate at* an institution of higher learning 上級の学校(大学)に入学する. ¶students to *matriculate in* college 大学に入学する学生たち ‖ *matriculate in* Cornell University コーネル大学にはいる. 【類】 those who were *matriculated in* ...

matriculation, *n*. 入学入学.
P apply *for matriculation* 入学を申込む.

matrimony, *n*. 結婚.
V *enter matrimony* (=marry) at an early age 若いときに結婚する.

matron, *n*. [年配の]既婚の女, 奥方, 夫人.
Q a *bulky matron* 大柄な細君. ¶a *stout matron* でっぷり肥った中年の婦人. ¶a *virtuous matron* 貞淑な妻. ¶a *withered matron* うば桜.
Q² a *society matron* 社交界に出る既婚婦人.

matter, *n*. (**1**) 物質, 物; 原稿; うみ, ふん尿.
V The book *contains* much useless *matter*. この本の中には無用のことが多い. ‖ A package (=parcel) must not *contain* any written *matter* whatever. 小包の中にはいかなる文書も封入してはならない. ¶*eat* fecal *matter* くそを食う(犬が). ¶*let* the *matter* out うみを出す.
Q "The Record of *Ancient Matters*" 古事記. ¶*animal* (*vegetable*) *matter* 動(植)物質. ¶the effluvia from *decomposing matter* 腐敗物の臭気. ¶*excrementitious matter* ふん尿. ¶*fecal matter* 便. ¶The newspaper contains *good matter*. その新聞には良いことが載っている. ¶A mailplane carries *mailed matter*. 郵便機は郵便物を運ぶ. ¶*mineral matter* 鉱物質. ¶*obscene matter* 風俗壊乱もの. ¶When the bowels are emptied only every second or third day, *poisonous matters* are being continually absorbed into the blood. 通じが一日おきか二日おきにだけしかないと毒素が絶えず血液中に吸収される. ¶*postal matter* 郵便物. ¶the baser *printed matter* of today 今日の低俗な印刷物. ¶*printed* or *written matter* 印刷物または筆記物. ¶it is the mark of an ignoramus in *publishing matters* to say that ... ...というのは出版に関する無知の証拠である. ¶*purulent matter* うみ. ¶*putrid matter* 腐敗物. ¶*third-class matter* 第三種郵便物(定期刊行). ¶a hundred pages of *well-written matter* きちんと書いた百ページの原稿. ¶*written*, *printed* or *typewritten matter* 筆記・印刷または印書した物. ¶utilize a very considerable amounts of *unpublished matter* 大量の未刊行資料を使用する. ¶*waste matter* 廃物.
Q² *coloring matter* 色素. ¶*living matter* 生物. ¶*mail matter* 便郵物 ‖ sorting of *mail matter* 郵便物の区分. ¶*print* (=printed) *matter* 印刷物. ¶furnish good *reading matter* よい読物を提供する ‖ ten million words of *reading matter* 二千万語の読物 ‖ prurient *reading matter* みだらな読物. ¶periodical publications on *theatre matters* 劇に関する定期刊行物(雑誌など).
P three states *of matter* 物体の三態(固体・液体・気体).
(**2**) 材料; ...のたね; ...ほど; 事柄; 事件, 問題; 重大事.
V *adjust* the *matter* そのことを適当に処理する. 【類】 *matters* might have been peacefully (穏やかに) *adjusted*, but ... ¶*afford* much *matter* (=food) for thought 思想のかてを多く与える. ¶*aggravate* a *matter* ことを荒立てる. ¶*allow* the *matter* to drag for a long time その問題をずるずるにしておく. 【類】 *allow* the *matter* to drag out so long that ... ‖ The *matter* was *allowed* to rest for 1,500 years. その問題は千五百年間そのままになっていた. ¶It is too late to *alter* the *matter* now. 今さらそれを変えようとしてもおそい. ¶Endeavor to *arrange matters* amicably. 万事穏便に取計らうように努力する. 【類】 *arrange* the *matter* to one's satisfaction / He is at his wits' end to *arrange matters*. / having thus *arranged matters* satisfactorily. ¶The *matter* has not yet been *ascertained*. そのことはまだ確かめてない. ¶*brave* the *matter out* そのことを敢然やり通す. ¶*brazen* the *matter out* そのことを鉄面皮にやり通す. ¶this *brought matters* to such a pass that ... このため...という羽目に立ち至った ‖ *bring* the *matter* to his attention その問題に彼の注意を引く ‖ *bring* the *matter* to a point その問題のらちをあける ‖ *bring matters* to such a pass こうした土壇場まで持って来る. ¶the *matter* was *brought up* at a meeting of ... ...の会でその問題が持ち出された. ¶*carry* this *matter* to a foolish extent この事件をあまり大げさにする ‖ the *matter* has been *carried* a stage *further* by the formation of ... その事件は...の組織によってさらに一段の進展を見た ‖ I will *carrry* the *matter* to its logical conclusion. 僕はそれを徹底的にやる. ¶*clear up matters* 事情を明かにする. ¶*clinch* the *matter* after three years' careful inquiry 三年間にわたる慎重調査の後にその問題を決着させる. ¶*commend* this *matter* to the attention of the public この問題に世人の注意を呼ぶ. ¶*commit* a *matter* to a lawyer 事件を弁護士に委任する. ¶confidentially *communicate* the *matter* in writing to ... その事件を書付に書いて秘密に...へ伝える. ¶That will *complicate matters*. そうするとことが面倒になる. ¶*consider* the *matter* in a scientific way 科学的にその問題を研究する. ¶*control matters* connected with ... ...に関する事項を監理する. ¶*cut* the *matter short* その問題を簡単に処分する. ¶The *matter* is quite *decided*. 事件は全く決定するに至った. ¶*defer* (=put off) *matters* ことを延ばす. ¶But the *matter* can not be *determined* in this way. しかしこのことはこういう風にはきめられない. ¶*discuss* the *matter* in detail 詳細にその事件を審議する. 【類】 He *discussed* the *matter* with his friends. / *discuss* a *matter* case by case. ¶*dismiss* the *matter* from one's mind そのことを心に留めない ‖ *dismiss* the *matter* summarily あっさり片付ける. ¶*draw* the *matter out* to a tedious length 事実をくどくどしく引延ばして言う. ¶*expedite* the *matter* greatly 大いにことをはかどらせる. 【類】 That will *expedite matters*. ¶That *explains matters*. それで訳が分かる. ‖ It serves to *explain* the *matter* more fully. それで事件の真相が一層明確になる. ‖ the *matters* being satisfactorily *explained* 事情がよく分かったので. ¶we can *express* the *matter* more simply by saying that ... そのことは...と言えば一層簡単に言表わされる. ¶It will greatly *facilitate matters* with us. それでわれわれの事件もすらすらと運ぶだろう. ¶I *find* much *matter* for reflection in this book. この本には思想のかてとなるものが沢山ある. ¶I doubt if he has ever *given* the *matter* a thought. 一体あの男がそのことを少しでも考えて見たかどうか怪しいものだ. ‖ *give* the *matter* careful thought そのことを慎重に考える. 【類】 He *gave* the *matter* no further thought. ¶*handle* detective *matters* 探偵事件を手がける. ¶The police now *have* the *matter* in hand. 警察では目下その事件に手を着けている(調査中). ¶You must *have* the *matter put* into legal form. 君はその事件に対し法律上の手続をふまなくてはいけない. ¶Words will not *help matters*. 口で言うだけでは何の益もない. 【類】 It is well enough to say that ..., but saying so does not *help* the *matter*. ¶*ignore* a *matter* of the first importance 最も緊要な事柄を閑却する. ¶make efforts to *improve matters* 諸事改善に努力する. ¶*interlard* important *matter* with uninteresting trivialities 重要問題におもしろくもない小さなことをはさむ. ¶*investigate* the *matter* minutely その事件を詳しく調べる. ¶Kindly *keep* the *matter* before you. その問題をお考えの中において下さい. ‖ We succeeded in *keeping* the *matter* from being noised abroad. われわれはその問題をうまく世間から騒ぎ立てられないで済んだ. 【類】 *keep* this *matter secret* from ... ¶*lay* the *matter* before the committee その問題を委員会の審議にかける ‖ *lay* the *matter* before the Emperor その事件を奏上する. ¶*leave* the *matter* absolutely in the hands of ... その事件を...に全く一任する ‖ I *leave* the *matter* entirely to your arrangement. あなたの計らいに一切お任せする ‖ *leave* the *matter undecided* ずるずるべったりにしておく. ¶*let* the *matter drop* =leave the matter as it is 手を引く, そのままにする ‖ *Let*

the *matter drop*, and say no more. もうその話はやめにして下さい. ‖ *let* the whole *matter fall* through 全部を失敗に終らせる. ¶ *let* the *matter go* そのままにしておく. ¶ I never *let* the *matter pass* my lips. 口外した覚えはない. ¶ *Let* the *matter rest* until you hear from me again. そのことは私から便りをするまでそのままにしておけ. ¶ *Let* the *matter stand over*. そのことは居すわりにしておけ. ¶ It *makes* no *matter*. たいしたことはない. ‖ *make* the *matter public* 表立てる. ¶ to *make* the *matters worse* 一層困ったことには, おまけに. ¶ Crying will not *mend matters*. 泣いても追っつかない. ¶ That will not *mend* or *mar matters*. それは毒にも薬にもならぬ. ¶ pardon my *mentioning* the *matter*, but ... こう申しては失礼ですが ... ¶ to *mince* the *matter* 内輪に言えば ‖ not to *mince matters* はっきり(露骨に)言えば. 【類】 without *mincing* the *matter*. ¶ You have *overdone* the *matter*. 君少し薬がきき過ぎた. ¶ *place* (=leave) the *matter* in the hands of ... そのことを...に委せる. ¶ This would *precipitate matters* to a most undeniable climax. こうすると何もかもすぐ滅茶苦茶になってしまうだろう. ¶ *press matters* to extremities 物ごとを極端まで特って行く. 【類】 *press* the *matter* to that degree. ¶ *push* the *matter forward* 事件を押進める. ¶ *push* the *matter* a little *further* もう少し問題を押し進める. ¶ *push* a *matter* in a business like-manner てきぱきはかどらせる. ¶ to *put* the *matter* briefly 簡単に言えば ‖ to *put* the *matter* in a nutshell (=word) 一口にこれを言えば, せんじ詰めれば ‖ to *put* the *matter* in the language of the psychologist 心理学者の口ぶりをまねて言えば ‖ *put* the *matter* before the tribunal その事件を裁判に出す ‖ *put* the *matter* in its proper light ことの真相を明かにする. ¶ *put* the *matter right* 是正する. 【類】 it may be only *putting* the *matter* in a different form (別の言い方に) to say that ... ¶ He *put off* the *matter* from day to day with excuses and evasions. 彼は言を左右に託し日一日と事件を延ばした. ¶ *reconsider* the *matter* そのことを考え直す. ¶ *refer* the *matter* to arbitration その件を仲裁に任せる. 【類】 *refer* the *matter* to a committee (委員付託) / The *matter* will be *referred* to the Diet for approval. ¶ *regard* a *matter* in a serious light 問題をまじめに考える. ¶ *report* the *matter* to the police 事件を警察に報告する. ¶ *set* the *matter* to rights (=in order) 事件を片付ける ‖ *set matters right* きまりを付ける ‖ That will *set* all *matters right* again. それで万事都合よくなるだろう. ¶ present him with a sovereign to *settle* the *matter* 事件の片を付けるために彼に一ソヴリン(一ポンド金貨)を贈る ‖ *settle* a *matter* by mutual concession 歩み寄ってことをきめる. 【類】 *settle* the *matter* by arbitration (調停で) / *settle* the *matter* as he wishes / Can you manage to call here this evening to *settle matters* (片をつける)? ¶ *show* the *matter* in its true light その真相を示す. ¶ That will *simplify matters*. それで問題は簡単になる. ¶ This will *square matters*. これで文句はないだろう (損害や借金などを払ったときなど). ¶ *state* the *matter* as it is ありていにその旨を述べる. ¶ *stave off matters* for five years more これから先五カ年間万事繰延べにする. ¶ *straighten matters out* ことを適当に処置する. ¶ *submit* the *matter* to arbitration (committee) その件を仲裁に任せる(委員付託とする). 【類】 *submit* the *matter* to inquiry (審査) by ... ¶ He *sums* the *matter up* thus: 彼はその問題をかく概括する. ‖ to *sum up* the *matters* つまり. ¶ *summarize* the *matter* as follows:— その事件を次のごとく摘要する. ¶ He *tackled* the *matter* in London "Sporting Life." 彼はロンドンスポーティング・ライフ誌上でその問題を取扱った. ¶ *take* the *matter* in hand その事件に着手する ‖ *take matters easy* 物事をのん気に考える ‖ *take matters* philosophically 物事を冷静に考える ‖ *take* (=bring) the *matter* to court その事件を法廷に持出す ‖ That will *take matters* out of sequence. それでは話が前後する. ¶ *take* the *matter up* at once with ... ...と一緒にその件を取上げる. 【類】 I trust you will *take* the *matter up*, and try to get an explanation. / The police *took* the *matter up* in earnest. / *take* a *matter up* for discussion (investigation) ‖ *take* this *matter up* very strongly with ... ...とこのことで大いに談判する ‖ It is expected that the authorities will *take up* the *matter* vigorously. 当局者は厳重にその事件の取調をするはずだ. ¶ We *talked* the *matter over* among ourselves. われわれは一同相談した. ¶ *think* a *matter over* とくと思案する. 【類】 *think* the *matter* carefully *over*. ¶ *throw* the *matter up* in despair やけになって問題を投げ出す. ¶ *transfer* (=transmit) all *matters* to ... 万事を...の手に移す. ¶ *treat* the *matter* in much the same tone as ... と大体同じような筆法でその事件を扱う. ¶ *turn* the *matter over* in my mind その問題を反覆考慮する. ¶ the principles *underlying* the *matter* その件の基礎をなす原理. ¶ *unravel* the *matter* 問題を釈明する. ¶ Far-Eastern minds *view* these *matters* differently. 極東の人々はこれらの問題に対して別の見方をする. ‖ I do not *view* the *matter* in that light. 僕はそうは思わない. 【類】 You do not *view* the *matter* in the proper light. ¶ endeavor to *work matters* to the advantage of ... 万事...のためになるように努める.

v^2 the *matter* having *become* thus *complicated* ことがこんなに面倒になったので. ¶ By May 1877 *matters* have *begun* to move. 一八七七年の五月までにはすでにその気運に向っていた. ¶ But this year *matters* have quite *changed*. しかしことしは事情が一変した. ¶ if *matters come* to an extremity いよいよという時になったら. ¶ *Matters went on* very smoothly. 事は支障なく進行した. 【類】 *Matters* were not *going* smoothly. ‖ So *matters went* with him from bad to worse. そういう訳で彼の立場はますます悪化して行った. ¶ The *matter* has *progressed* to that stage. 話がそこまで進んでいる. ¶ Thus you will see how the *matter stands*. これで実情が分かるだろう. ‖ as *matters stand* today (=at present) 今日のところでは ‖ seeing how *matters stood* そのときの情勢を見て. 【類】 It is sad, but that is how *matters stand*. / there the *matter stood* until ... / I saw how *matters stood*. ¶ as *matters* have now *turned out*, I am not at all sorry that ... こういうことになって見れば私は...をちっとも後悔していない.

Q It is quite *another matter*. それは全く別問題だ. ¶ a *cardinal matter* 一つの重要なこと. ¶ discuss *classified matters* 機密事項を論じる. ¶ *commonplace matters* 平凡な事柄. ¶ *curious, quaint*, and *out-of-the-way matters* 珍奇で風変りで飛び離れた事項. ¶ *current matters* of interest 興味ある時事問題. ¶ *Matters* are *different* in Japan. 日本は事情が違う. ¶ a *difficult matter* 難事. ¶ an *easy matter* 朝飯前. ¶ a *fundamental matter* 根本的な問題. ¶ It is no *great matter* for wonder[ment]. それは驚くに足らない. ‖ a *great matter* of statecraft 国政上の大事件 ‖ That is a *great* (*small*) *matter*. それは大(小)事だ. ¶ a wealth of *historical matter* [沢山の]歴史的事項. ¶ *household matters* 家庭の事項. ¶ I have an *important matter* to attend to. 私は大事な用件を控えている. 【類】 an *important public matter*. ¶ an *impractical matter* できない相談. ¶ in *international matters* as well as in personal *matters* 私事におけると同様国際的問題においても. ¶ But this is a *later matter*. しかしこれは今論ずべきことでない. ¶ The expenses of 2,000 yen were no *light matter*. 二千円という入費はばかにできない金であった. ¶ *main* (=important) *matters* 主要な件. ¶ in the *mere matter* of number 単に数の点では. ¶ a *minor matter* 一小事. ¶ *no matter* how rich he is 彼がどんなに金があっても ‖ It is *no matter* what happens. 何事が生じても構わない. 【類】 *no matter* what it may be / *no matter* what he says, I ... / You should go to the country for a change, *no matter* where. ¶ it is *no easy matter* to ... ...するのは容易なことでない. ¶ the Law of Procedure in *Non-contentious Matters* 非訴訟事件手続法. ¶ conversation on *personal matters* 個人問題についての会話(ゴシップ). ¶ *matters political* 政治問題. 【類】 They did not take up any *political matter*. ¶ The *matter* is *pressing*. そのことは緊急を要する. 【類】 handle the most *pressing matters* first. ¶ It ceased to be a *private matter*. それは私事ではなくなった. ¶ a *public matter* 公事. ¶ It is a *pure matter* of form ほんの形式だけのことだ. ¶ *quoted matter* 引用された事項. ¶ *sanitary matters* 衛生事項. ¶ a *secondary matter* 第二次的事項. ¶ a *serious matter* 重大事. ¶ a definitely *settled matter* 確定事項. ¶ He is indirect and evasive in the *simple matter* of fact. 彼は簡単な事実問題にも遠回しで不得要領だ. ‖ it would be a *simple matter* to ... ...するのは簡単なことだろう. ¶ a *slight matter* 些(さ)事. 【類】 it is no *slight matter* to ... ¶ A *small matter* divided the friends. 小さなことでその友人たちは仲たがいをした. ¶ a *sorrowful matter* 悲しむべきこと. ¶bring ***statistical matter*** down to date 統計に最近のことまで載せる. ¶is largely a ***stylistic matter*** 主として文体上の問題である. ¶***suggestive matter*** 示唆に富む事項. ¶speak of ***trifling matters*** seriously and of serious matters as triflingly つまらないことを真剣に語りそして重大なことを軽々しく語る. ¶a ***trivial matter*** ささいなこと. ¶some of the ***vital*** *matters* of life 人生における重要事項のあるもの.【類】It is a ***vital matter*** to us. ¶discuss ***weighty matters*** 重要問題を論議する. ¶He is extremely negligent in ***worldly matters***. 彼は俗事には極端に無とん着だ.【類】She has little understanding in ***worldly matters***.

Q[2] ***Army tactic matters***. 陸軍の戦術問題. ¶in ***every-day matters*** 日常のありふれたことで. ¶***family matters*** 家庭の事情. ¶It is no ***laughing matter***. 笑いごとじゃない. ‖ make ***laughing matter*** of ... ...を冷かす. ¶These are all ***long-range matters***. これらはいずれも遠大な問題である. ¶***love matters*** 恋愛問題. ¶lack of knowledge of ***marine matters*** 海事に対する認識不足. ¶meanness in ***money matters*** 金銭にきたないこと. ¶view ***sex matters*** in a new light 性問題を新しい角度から見る. ¶the ***subject matter*** of debate 論議の主題 ‖ bear upon the ***subject matter*** of the complaint 該異議事項に関係している ‖ the ***subject matter*** of a litigation 訴訟事項.【類】Simple enough in style (文体) for younger children, but interesting in ***subject matter*** (内容) to any age.

P I will ask some one ***about*** that *matter*. そのことをだれかに聞いて見よう. ‖ We have consulted him ***about*** the *matter*. その件について彼に相談した. ‖ I know nothing ***about*** the *matter*. そのことは何も知らない. ¶***as*** a *matter* of convenience, we invite ... to ... 便宜上われわれは...を...に招待する ‖ take it ***as*** a *matter* of course それをもちろんのことと思う ‖ ***as*** a *matter* of fact 実際の所は, 実は.【類】***as*** a *matter* of actual fact / ***as*** a *matter* of cold fact / ***as*** a *matter* of simple (=pure) fact / ***as*** a *matter* of principle / ***as*** a *matter* of experience / simply ***as*** a *matter* of habit / whatever, then, one may hold ***as*** a *matter* of theory, it is clear that, ***as*** a *matter* of practice, ... / regard the love of women (女を愛すること) ***as*** a *matter* of life and death ‖ now ***as*** a *matter* of history これを歴史に徴するに, そもそも ‖ just ***as*** a *matter* of precaution 用心に如くはなしと. ¶This discussion is ***beside*** the *matter* in hand. この議論は本件に関係がない. ¶***For*** that *matter* I am another. その点は僕もお仲間だ. ‖ Such a thing is so ridiculously simple that few students—or adults, ***for*** that *matter*—have ever thought of it. こんなことはばかばかしく簡単なのでこれまでそれに考えを向けた学生は—その点においては大人も—多くなかった.【類】We do not sufficiently cultivate in children, or, ***for*** that *matter*, in ourselve either, the sense of Beauty.—Lord Avebury. / Few physicians, individually, few institutions ***for*** that *matter*, possess enough radium to treat satisfactorily even the lesser run of ordinary ailments (簡単な病気). / The first duty of every man, or every woman, ***for*** that *matter*, is to see to it that society is in no respect burdend by his existence.—James H. Canfield. ¶***in matters*** of detail 詳細の点では ‖ ***in matters*** of money 金の点では ‖ ***in*** a *matter* of hours (weeks) 数時(週)間で ‖ his extreme parsimony ***in*** all *matters* of finance およそ金銭にかけては極端な出し惜しみ ‖ Consult your own convenience ***in*** that *matter*. そのことは君の都合のよいようにし給え.【類】Japan lags (=goes) behind other nations ***in*** the *matter* of ... / faultless ***in*** *matters* of fact / his ignorance ***in*** *matters* of psychology / He has not too good a reputation ***in*** the *matter* of honesty. / ***in*** *matters* pertaining to ... / ***In*** the *matter* of apparel (服装), his taste is highly commendable. / We are of one mind ***in*** this *matter*. / He is concerned ***in*** that *matter*. ¶***in regard to*** this *matter* この点に関しては. ¶I will go ***into*** the *matter* carefully. 慎重に取調べよう. ¶He was busy and her existence was ***of*** no *matter* to him. 彼は多忙であり彼女の存在などは彼にとって問題でなかった. ‖ The translations contain articles of great value to students ***of*** Japanese *matters*. その翻訳には日本問題の研究者に取って非常に有益な記事がのっている. ¶***on*** all *matters* 一切の事項につき ‖ I came ***on*** a *matter* of business. 僕は用件があってやってきた. ¶quarrel ***over*** a trifling *matter* くだらないことでけんかする. ¶***touching*** (=***concerning***) that *matter* そのことについて. ¶***with*** *matters* in this condition 諸事こんな情勢で. ¶***within*** a *matter* of hours 数時間以内に.

P[2] on all ***matters appertaining to*** ... ...に関するあらゆる問題について. ¶It is a *matter* ***for*** congratulation. それはめでたいことだ.【類】It is indeed a *matter* ***for*** mutual congratulation. ‖ think of child-bearing as a *matter* ***for*** pride and joy 出産を喜び誇るべきことと考える ‖ it is a *matter* ***for*** wonder that ... ...ということは不思議なことだ. ‖ a *matter* ***for*** debate 討論の余地がある問題 ‖ It is [a] *matter* ***for*** tears (smile, regret). それは涙(など)の種だ.【類】it is not a *matter* ***for*** wonder when we recollect that ... / a *matter* ***for*** regret (rejoicing, surprise, indignation, lamentation, complaint, satisfaction, consideration, anxiety) / a *matter* ***for*** sincere regret / It is a *matter* ***for*** interesting psychological deduction. / *matters* ***for*** teaching=teaching materials / His words supplied plenty of *matter* ***for*** thought (思想のかて). / a *matter* ***for*** conjecture. ¶the *matter* ***in*** dispute (=issue) 問題の事件 ‖ I have no books bearing upon the *matter* ***in*** hand. 調査中の事項に関する本は一冊も私は持っていない. ¶a *matter* ***of*** amusement to ... ...から見るとおかしなこと ‖ a *matter* ***of*** choice 自由に選択しうる件.【類】it is a *matter* ***of*** common experience that ... ‖ It is a *matter* ***of*** common knowledge. それは世間周知のことだ.【類】it is well known, but it may be less a *matter* ***of*** common knowledge that ... ‖ That is a *matter* ***of*** common sense. それは常識だ. ‖ a *matter* ***of*** very grave concern to ... ...に取ってきわめて重大な件.【類】a *matter* ***of*** national concern / a *matter* ***of*** no small concern to Japan / a *matter* ***of*** more vital concern than ... ‖ it is a *matter* ***of*** congratulation for ... それは...に取ってめでたいことだ.【類】a *matter* ***of*** hearty congratulation ‖ entirely (largely) a *matter* ***of*** conjecture 全然(大部分)当て推量.【類】it must remain largely a *matter* ***of*** conjecture ‖ I find it a *matter* ***of*** consolation that ... 私に取って...はせめてもの慰めである. ‖ it is a *matter* ***of*** convenience that ... ...とは便利なことだ ‖ That is a *matter* ***of*** course. それは当然のことだ.【類】It is a *matter* ***of*** course when a man cannot pay his debt that he should smash up. ‖ purely a *matter* ***of*** courtesy 純然たる儀礼の問題. ‖ a *matter* ***of*** decades 数十年(など)を要すること ‖ It is now not a *matter* ***of*** days, but of hours. 今は日の問題ではなくて時間の問題だ. ‖ The examination is very brief—a *matter* ***of*** seconds, not minutes. その試験はごく短かい—何秒の問題で何分とはかからない. ‖ It seems to be little more than a *matter* ***of*** time. それはほとんどときの問題に過ぎないように思われる.【類】it is but a *matter* (=question) ***of*** time when ... / it would be a *matter* ***of*** time and opportunity for the United States to ... / it was a *matter* ***of*** some difficulty to ... ‖ Its authorship is a *matter* ***of*** dipute. その作者はだれであるかは議論のある問題だ.【類】a *matter* ***of*** disspute among economists / a *matter* ***of*** discussion ‖ Morality is altogether a *matter* ***of*** doing. 道徳は全く実行の問題だ. ‖ The present pronunciation of those words is a *matter* ***of*** doubt or controversy. それらの言葉の現在の発音は疑問や議論のある所だ. ‖ It is a *matter* ***of*** economy also. それはまた経済になる ‖ a *matter* ***of*** history 史実 ‖ It is a *matter* ***of*** chronology. それは時代の違いである ‖ a *matter* ***of*** everyday occurrence (experience) 日常茶飯事.【類】This is a *matter* ***of*** everyday observation. ‖ Age is a *matter* ***of*** feeling, not of years.—G. W. Curtis. 年齢というのは年数の問題ではなくて気持の問題だ.【類】It is a *matter* ***of*** fact, not a *matter* ***of*** opinion. / a *matter* ***of*** form / It is a *matter* ***of*** habit / as a *matter* ***of*** policy / a *matter* ***of*** joy / a *matter* ***of*** importance (=moment) / a *matter* ***of*** ruitine / a *matter* ***of*** rejoicing to ... / it is a *matter* ***of*** safety to ... / It is a *matter* ***of*** speculation rather than fact. / In those days a journey to that town was entirely a *matter* ***of*** *jinrikisha* and *kago*. / It is only a *matter* ***of*** money. / a *matter* ***of*** national character / become a *matter* ***of*** necessity / That is a *matter* ***of*** no consequence (=importance). ‖ Here, preference is a *matter* ***of*** temperament. さて選り好みはその人の気質による. ‖ In the *matter* ***of*** hotel accommodations Milwaukee is hard to beat. ホテルのサービスでは

ミルウォーキー(米国)はすばらしい. ‖ Health is much more a *matter* ***of*** habits and of diet than of medicine. 健康は医薬によるよりも習慣や食物による方が余ほど多い. ‖ Question of taste is after all a *matter* ***of*** individuality. 趣味(好み)の問題は結局各個性の問題だ. ‖ a *matter* ***of*** more than ordinary interest 非常に興味ある問題. ‖ It is a *matter* ***of*** knowledge to the people of this country. それはこの国の人民には隠れもない事実である. ‖ It is liable to become a *matter* ***of*** legal and unpleasant procedure. それはややもすれば不愉快な裁判ざたともなりかねない. ‖ a *matter* ***of*** life and death to ... ...に取っての死活問題 ‖ *matter* ***of*** literary history 文学史に記録すべきこと ‖ a *matter* ***of*** looks 体裁 ‖ a *matter* ***of*** notoriety [悪い意味で] 有名なこと ‖ It is a *matter* ***of*** opinion. それは人々の考え次第だ. ‖ a *matter* ***of*** peculiar difficulty 特に困難なこと ‖ a *matter* ***of*** private agreement between ... and ... ...と...との間で内々話のまとまっている問題 ‖ it is a *matter* ***of*** regret that ... ...というのは遺憾なことだ. 【類】It is a *matter* ***of*** deep regret. ‖ a *matter* ***of*** remark throughout the country 全国の評判の種 ‖ a *matter* ***of*** self-interest as well as duty 義務の問題たると同時に利欲の問題. 【類】a *matter* ***of*** shame / a *matter* ***of*** some surprise / That is a *matter* ***of*** taste. / Dinner coats and evening dress are worn by many at dinner on shipboard, but this is a *matter* ***of*** individual taste (銘々の好き好き). / It is a *matter* ***of*** tradition. / It is a *matter* ***of*** universal knowledge (だれもが知っている). / It should be regarded as a *matter* ***of*** urgency. ‖ it becomes a *matter* ***of*** wonder how ... どうして...したか不思議に思われる ‖ it was a *mattre* ***of*** talk among the neighboring tradesmen that ... ...というのは近所の商人仲間の話題であった ‖ It sold for a *matter* ***of*** (=about) fifty dollars. それは五十ドルばかりで売れた. ‖ a *matter* ***of*** seven miles off 七マイルばかりへだった所. 【類】We covered the whole distance, a *matter* ***of*** 10,000 miles. / The party walked the whole way to Kamakura, a *matter* ***of*** fifteen miles or so. / stretching for a *matter* ***of*** one hundred and fifty yards or so along Thames Street. / The voyage to ... is only a *matter* ***of*** about seventy hours. / The best way to reach Portugal is by boat from Southampton to Lisbon, a *matter* ***of*** three days' run (約三日間の航行). ¶take the *matter* ***under*** consideration その問題を考慮する. ¶Is [there] anything the *matter* ***with*** the engine? エンジンがどうかしたか. 【類】What is the *matter* ***with*** you? / There is nothing (=Nothing is) the *matter* ***with*** me. / Is there anything the *matter* ***with*** her? / Something is the *matter* ***with*** the machine. / Something is the *matter* ***with*** your lungs. / He must have something the *matter* ***with*** his feet. / There is something the *matter* ***with*** my watch. / There's something the *matter* ***with*** the old thing.

matter, *v.* 関係する, 重要だ.

M it doesn't *matter* ***at all*** whether ... ...でもどうでもちっとも構わない. ¶It *matters* ***little*** to me who is elected. だれが当選しようと私には大した関係はない. 【類】it *matters* ***little*** whether ... ¶It *matters* ***much*** to a character where a man is born. 生地は人格に重大な関係がある. ¶It *matters* ***nothing*** to me. それは私には何んでもない. ¶Having heard the true way in the morning, ***what*** *matters* it if one should come to die at night? 朝に道を聞きて夕に死すとも可なり.

P It does not *matter* ***to*** me which side may win or lose. どっちが勝っても負けても私は構わない.

matting, *n.* むしろ.

Q² ***fancy*** *mattings* 花むしろ.

mature, *a.* 成熟した.

P those more *mature* ***in*** years もっと老熟した人.

O The fruit is getting *mature* (=ripe). くだものがだんだん熟して来る.

mature, *v.* 成熟する; 完成する; 熟させる.

M His mind was not of the type that *matures* ***early***. 彼は早熟の型ではなかった(大器晩成の方だった). ¶His character has ***greatly*** *matured* during these years. この数年間彼の人格は大いに円満になった. ¶***sexually*** *mature* 性的に成熟する. ¶His genius *matured* ***slowly***. 彼の天びんは晩成した. ¶Plans for the building of liners are ***well*** *matured*. 定期船建造案は首尾よく実現した. ¶The Portuguese blood *matures* ***young***. ポルトガル人は早熟だ.

P wine *matured* ***by*** age 年月をかけてじゅくさしたぶどう酒 ‖ *mature* ... ***by*** artificial heat ...を人工熱で熟させる.

maturity, *n.* 成熟, 完成; 満期日.

V the period at which the body ***attains*** *maturity* 身体の成熟する時期. ¶***hasten*** *maturity* 完成を早める. ¶***reach*** *maturity* 満期になる. 【類】***reach*** full *maturity*.

Q attain ***complete*** *maturity* 完全に成熟する. ¶reach ***mental*** *maturity* 知能が成熟する. ¶mental powers at ***ripe*** *maturity* 円熟した精神能力. ¶***sexual*** *maturity* 性的成熟.

P pay ***at*** *maturity* 満期日に支払う ‖ meet a payment promptly ***at*** *maturity* 支払期日には遅怠なく支払う. ‖ ***at*** the *maturity* of ... ...の満期日に. ¶come (=grow) ***to*** *maturity* 成熟する. ¶the shortness of human life for the attainment of *maturity* ***in*** art 芸術完成が期せられない人生の短かさ.

maxim, *n.* 格言, 訓言; 主義.

V ***adapt*** an old homely *maxim* 古来の俗諺を改作する. ¶***follow*** the *maxim* "When in Rome, do as the Romans do" 「郷に入りては郷に従え」という格言通りやる. ¶***lay*** the *maxim* to our heart 格言を心に留める. ¶***lay down*** a *maxim* 格言を作る.

Q an ***established*** *maxim* 動かない格言. ¶a ***golden*** *maxim* 金言. ¶There is an ***old Greek*** *maxim* saying that a large book is a great evil. 古ギリシアの格言に大きな本は大きな弊害なりというのがある ¶***lofty*** *maxims* 高尚な格言. ¶a ***moral*** *maxim* 道徳上の格言. ¶it is an ***old*** *maxim* that ... ...は古来の格言だ. ¶a ***sagacious*** *maxim* 金言. ¶a thoroughly ***sound*** *maxim* in political philosophy 政治哲学における至言. ¶a ***time-honored*** *maxim* 古くからの格言.

P act ***on*** the *maxim* that ... ...という格言を服ようする.

maximum, *n.* 最大量; 極度.

V The speed limit is 40 miles an hour. Don't ***exceed*** this *maximum*. 速度制限は四十マイルだ. この制限を超えてはいけない. ¶***find*** the *maximum* of efficiency with the minimum of labor 最小の労力で最大の能率をあげる. ¶***reach*** a *maximum* 極限に達する. ¶***realize*** the *maximum* of success in ... ...に最大の成功を遂げる.

P The excitement was ***at*** its *maximum*. 興奮はその極度に達した. ¶mark examination papers ***on*** the *maximum* of 100 points 百点満点で試験の採点をする.

P² the *maximum* ***of*** wage for the minimum of work 最小の労働に対する最高の賃金.

mayor, *n.* 市長.

Q² a conference of ***city*** *mayors* and town managers 市長町村長会議. ¶the ***Lord*** *Mayor* of London ロンドン市長.

P² a *mayor* or a headman ***of*** city, town, or village 市町村長.

mayoralty, *n.* 市長たること.

P ***during*** the *mayoralty* of ... ...の市長時代に. ¶***Under*** his *mayoralty* the city thrived. 彼が市長をしていた時代その市は隆盛となった.

maze, *n.* 迷路; 紛糾.

Q I seemed to be in an ***inextricable*** *maze*. 私は抜けて出られない迷路にはいったような気がした. ¶through a most ***intricate*** *maze* of narrow streets and courts せまい往来と路地の非常に入組んだ迷路を通って. ¶a ***perplexing*** *maze* 非常な紛糾.

P He is ***in*** *maze*. 彼は途方にくれている(当惑している). ¶fail to find one's way out ***through*** a *maze* 迷路から抜け出られない.

me, *pron.* [I の目的格] 僕(私)に.

M ***Me too.*** 《口語》 僕もだ.

Q ***Poor me!*** 情けない.

P ***After me*** the deluge, you know. あとは野となれ山となれさ. ¶This is ***between*** you and *me*. これは内しょだがね.

meadow, *n.* 草地, 牧草地.

V, V² The *meadow* is not yet ***mown***. その草地はまだ刈ってない. ¶Vast *meadows* ***stretched*** to the eastward. びょうぼうたる草原が東の方に広がっていた.

Q a ***fertile*** *meadow* 肥よくな牧場. ¶a ***fragrant*** *meadow* よいにおいのする草地. ¶a ***lush*** *meadow* 青々した牧場.

Q² a ***beaver*** *meadow* 海狸が掘り崩した湿地の乾けるよく地. ¶a ***hillside*** *meadow* 丘の斜面の牧場.

P The plant grows ***in*** *meadows*. その植物は草地にはえる. ¶on a knoll ***in*** the *meadow* 牧場の小山に. ¶***on*** the *meadow* below the hill 丘の下の草原に.

meager, *a.* 貧弱な.

M Those hospitals are ***pathetically meager***. それらの病院は実に貧弱だ.

meal, *n.* 食事, 食物.

V A friend and I lived together, and ***cooked*** our own *meals*. 僕は友人と二人で自炊生活をやった. ¶***despatch*** a hasty *meal* 食事を急いで済ます. ¶***eat*** a hearty *meal* 腹一杯食べる. ¶He even ***forgets*** his *meals*. 彼は三度の食事さえ忘れる. ¶We can ***get*** a fair *meal* for twenty cents. 二十セントでかなりの食事ができる. ¶He ***has*** his *meals* elsewhere. 彼はよそで食事をする. ‖ I've ***had*** a hearty *meal* of … …をたらふく食べた. ¶Though honey is sweet, one can't ***make*** a *meal* of it. みつは甘くとも常食にはならない. ‖ ***make*** a hearty *meal* of … …を満腹する. 【類】***make*** a *meal* of honey. ¶No reduction is made if one has ***missed*** a *meal*. [下宿屋などで]一食事を抜かしても割引はしない. ¶It is possible to ***obtain*** excellent *meals* at any hour of the day or night. 昼夜いつでもりっぱな食事が得られる. ¶Soup generally ***opens*** a *meal*. 食事は普通スープで始まる. ¶He ***ordered*** his own *meal* at random. 彼は出任せに自分の食事を注文した. ¶Let us ***partake of*** a *meal* before we start. 出発前に食事をしよう. ¶***prepare*** a *meal* 食事の準備をする. ¶***serve*** a full *meal* for only 20c. わずか二十セントで腹一杯食わせる. ¶He cannot ***stand*** a heavy *meal*. 彼は(胃腸が弱いから)腹に応える食物は食べられない. ¶Don't ***swallaw*** your *meals* at a gulp. 食物をうのみにしてはいけない. ¶***take*** three *meals* a day =《米》eat three times a day 一日三食とる. 【類】***take*** (=eat) one's *meal* / ***take*** one's *meals* at a restaurant (in the municipal kitchen). ¶Lodgers ***take*** their *meals* ***out***. 下宿人はよそで食事をする(外食する).

V² usually their *meals* ***consisted*** of … その人たちの食事は普通…であった.

Q ***daily*** *meals* 三度三度の食事. ¶at ***each meal*** 食事ごとに. ¶an ***elaborate meal*** こった食事. ¶cook their ***evening*** *meal* 彼らの夕食を調理する. ¶Eat fruits or vegetables and bran-containing bread with ***every meal***—this will help to cure your constipation. 果物または野菜とふすま入のパンを食事ごとに食べなさい—これは便泌の薬になる. ¶obtain an ***excellent meal*** すばらしい食事をとる. ¶eat a ***foreign meal*** 洋食を食べる. ¶after a ***frugal meal*** 簡単な食事を済ませて. ¶a ***good meal*** 結構な食事 ‖ make a ***good*** (poor) *meal* よく食べる(あまり食べない). ¶***after*** a ***hasty*** *meal* 食事もそこそこで. ¶refresh oneself with a ***hearty*** *meal* of … …をたら腹食べて元気を出す. ¶a ***heavy*** (=***substantial***) *meal* 腹ごたえのある食物. ¶eat a ***hurried meal*** 急いで食事をする. ¶***inexpensive*** *meals* 安直な食事. ¶a small restaurant providing ***light meals*** 手軽な食事のできる小料理店. ¶a ***nice meal*** 美食. ¶a ***noon meal*** 昼飯. ¶a ***nutritious*** (=***nourishing***) *meal* 栄養食. ¶I am afraid you have made a ***poor meal***. どうもお粗末でした. ¶Their ***principal meal*** is potatoes. 彼らの主要食物はじゃがいもだ. ¶obtain a "***sent-in meal***" 外から食事を取る. ¶take a ***simple meal*** at a restaurant 飲食店で簡単な食事をする. ¶a ***spare meal*** つつましい食事. ¶a ***square meal*** 十分な食事. ¶***three meals*** a day 日に三度の食事 ‖ take ***three regular hearty meals*** きちんと三度十分に食事をする. ¶***well-cooked meals*** 調理の行届いた食事.

Q² a ***fish meal*** 魚料理. ¶a ***full-course meal*** 正式のさら数の出る食事. ¶a ***meat meal*** 肉の食事 ‖ a substantial ***meat meal*** 腹ごたえのある肉の食事. ¶eat one's ***midday meal*** 昼飯をとる. ¶a ***morning*** (an ***evening***) *meal* 朝(夕)食. ¶a ***poultry meal*** 鶏肉料理. ¶the provision of ***school meals*** 学校給食. ¶***restaurant meals*** 料理屋の食事. ¶a ***three-course meal*** 三さら出る食事.

P eat three eggs ***at*** a *meal* 一度の食事に卵を三つ食べる. ¶eat ***between*** *meals* 間食をする. 【類】eat a snack (おやつ) ***between*** *meals* / drink milk ***between meals***. ¶***during*** a *meal* 食事中に. ¶drink wine ***to*** one's *meal* 食事にぶどう酒を飲む. ¶lodging ***with*** *meals* 食事付きの間借り.

P² a *meal* ***at*** noon-time 昼飯.

mean, *n.* (**1**) 中庸.

V ***follow*** the golden *mean* 中庸を守る. ¶***overstep*** the *mean* 中庸を破る. ¶***represent*** a *mean* for … …の平均を示す. ¶***strike*** a *mean* between … …の中を取る. ¶***take*** the *mean*=split the difference 中を取る.

Q ***golden*** (=***happy***) *mean* 中庸 ‖ adopt the ***golden mean*** =go middle 仲を取る ‖ a ***happy*** *mean* between … …の中庸がある.

P² There is a *mean* ***in*** all things. 何事にもほどというものがある.

(**2**) [*sing., pl.* 同型 -s] 手段, 方法; 機関.

V ***adapt*** *means* to end 目的に応じて手段を変える, 人を見て法を説く. 【類】He knows how to ***adapt*** *means* to ends. ¶***adopt*** some effective *means* 何か有効な手段を採る. ¶***advise*** some *means* of escape from … …からのがれる方法を教える. ¶***afford*** the *means* of … …の手段になる. ¶***consider*** a new *means* of livelihood 新たな生計手段を考える. ¶she ***derives*** her *means* of livelihood from … 彼女は…によって衣食している. ¶***devise*** a *means* of … …の道を講じる ‖ endeavor to ***devise*** *means* by which to … …すべき方法を案出しようと努める. 【類】***employ*** all possible *means* / ***employ*** such *means* as one considers best. ¶***exhaust*** every *means* あらゆる手段を尽す. ¶***find*** a *means* for increasing his income 収入増加の途を講じる ‖ ***finding*** all other *means* unavailing 他の手段は皆無益と悟って. 【類】*means* must be ***found*** to … / ***find*** other *means* to … / She ***found*** *means* of livelihood after she had dropped her burden (身二つになってから). ¶we ***have*** in our power the *means* of … われわれには…の手段が取れる ‖ I ***have*** no *means* of asceratining it. 私にはそれを確かめる方法がない. 【類】I ***have*** no *means* of remittance (送金) from here. ¶Ends ***justify*** *means*. 目的のためには手段を選ばない. ¶***leave*** no *means* untried (=stone unturned) in … …に百方手を尽す ‖ No other *means* is ***left***. もう外に取るべき手段がない. ¶***make*** it a *means* of self-advertisement それを売物(自己宣伝)にする. ¶He ***pressed*** all *means* into his service. 彼はそのために色々の手段を取入れた. ¶***take*** every possible *means* できる限りの手段をつくす. ¶or, *means* will be ***taken*** to compel them to do so そうしなければその分にはおかない. ¶***try*** every *means* of …ing … …するに百方手を尽す. 【類】***try*** some other *means*. ¶must ***use*** every *means* to … …すべくあらゆる手段を講じなければならない. 【類】***use*** all the *means* at one's command to … / ***use*** all possible *means* to … / ***use*** unfair *means* at an examination / the *means* ***used*** for this end.

Q by ***aggressive*** *means* 侵略的手段によって. ¶by ***any*** *means* 何とかして. ¶an ***available*** *means* 実行し得られる手段. 【類】every *means* ***available***. ¶a ***base*** *means* of making money 金をこしらえる卑劣な手段. ¶***cheap*** *means* of transit 低廉な運送機関. ¶a ***cheap*** and ***rapid*** *means* of locomotion 安くて速い旅行機関. ¶a ***curative*** *means* 治療法. ¶His effort to accomplish this end by ***diplomatic*** *means* failed. 外交手段によってこの目的を果そうとする彼の努力は失敗に帰した. ¶a most ***effective*** *means* of … …のきわめて有効な手段. ¶adopt ***energetic*** *means* 精力的な手段をとる. ¶put into activity ***every*** *means* of tracing her 彼女のゆくえを百方手を尽して捜す. ¶***every modern*** *means* of ballyhoo (=publicity)《米》現代式のあらゆる宣伝方法. ¶an ***excellent*** *means* of self-cultivation in English 英語独習の良法. ¶by ***fair*** *means* or foul 手段を選ばず. ¶The novel remains now the ***favorite*** *means* of expression for the bulk of imaginative writers. 小説は今は想像に富む多数文士の好んで用いる表現の手段となっている. ¶by ***foul*** *means* 不正手段によって. ¶use ***fraudulent*** *means* of expropriating other people's money 他人の金銭を奪うような詐欺行為をする. ¶***improved*** *means* of travel 改良された交通機関. ¶***inadequate*** *means* of transportation 不十分な運輸機関. ¶They tried to realise the plan through the ***insidious*** *means* at their command. 彼らはあらゆる陰険な手段によってその計画を実現しようとした. ¶take ***legal*** *means* 適法(正当)な手段を取る. ¶obtain a ***moderate*** *means* of livelihood どうにか暮らせるようになる. ¶the closer contact brought about by ***modern means*** of communication 近代の交通機関が生んだ一層密接な接触. ¶take the ***necessary*** *means* 必要な手段を取る. ¶their only ***one*** *means* of livelihood 彼ら唯一の生活手段 ‖ as ***one*** *means* to this end この目的を達する一つの手段として. ¶seek the settlement of the dispute by ***pacific*** *means* 平和的手段によってその紛争の解決を求める. ¶by ***peaceful*** *means* おだやかな手段によって. ¶a ***popular*** *means* of suicide 世間でよくやる自殺法. ¶use all ***possible*** *means* to … …のためにあらゆる手段を取る. ¶The motion picture is a ***powerful*** *means* of diffusing ideas. 映画は思想普及の有力な機関である. ¶a ***precarious*** *means* of gaining a livelihood おぼつかない生活手段. ¶a ***preventive means*** 予防法. ¶by ***questionable means*** いかがわしい手段で. ¶He has no ***regular means*** of existence. 彼にはきまった収入がない. ¶***several*** (=***various***) ***means*** 種々の手段. ¶The business gives him but a ***slender means*** of getting a living. その商売で彼はようよう生活を立てているに過ぎない. ¶take ***prompt means*** 急策を講じる. ¶explore all ***reasonable means*** of attaining the object 目的達成のためのあらゆる合理的手段を検討する. ¶by ***revolutionary means*** 過激な手段で. ¶by ***some means*** [or other] どうにかして ‖ help him by ***some means*** or other 何とかして彼を援助する. ¶take the ***surest means*** to ... ...のために最も確実な手段を取る. ¶The complete isolation of Peking continued, ***telegraphic***, ***postal***, and ***railway means*** of communication being stopped. 電信も郵便も鉄道も不通で北京は依然孤立の姿であった. ¶by ***unfair means*** 不正手段で. 【類】 employ ***unfair means*** at an examination. ¶use ***unjust means*** 不正手段を用いる. ¶Metaphor is a ***valuable means*** of giving vividness to a statement. 隠喩(いんゆ)は叙述を鮮明にする貴重な手段である. ¶by ***violent means*** 手荒い手段で. ¶without ***visible means*** of subsistence これというはっきりした生活の手段もなく. ¶by a ***warlike means*** 武力で.

P the merits of the radio ***as*** a ***means*** of international communication 国際伝達の手段としてのラジオの効果. 【類】 Fiction writing ***as*** a ***means*** of living is no easy task. / take a walk ***as*** a ***means*** of exercise / the bicycle ***as*** a ***means*** of pleasure / ***as*** a ***means*** of precaution (用心) / the film ***as*** a ***means*** of propaganda. ¶the increase of population ***beyond*** the ***means*** of subsistence 生活力を越える人口の増加. ¶***by*** some ***means*** or other 何とかして ‖ the treatment of the mind ***by means*** of conversational methods 対話による精神療法 ‖ He has made a fortune ***by means*** of industry. 彼は努力の結果財産をこしらえた. ‖ ***by*** all the ***means*** in one's power 力の及ぶ限りの手段を尽して ‖ it ***by*** no ***means*** follows that ... 決して...とはならない. 【類】 Thoughts are expressed ***by means*** of speech. / A series of charming views illustrating the lecture were shown ***by means*** of the epidiascope (万能幻灯映写機). / express our thoughts ***by means*** of words / The story is told chiefly ***by means*** of conversation. / He escaped ***by means*** of a back window. ‖ The income of the shop girl was utterly insufficient to support life, and she had to supplement it ***by means*** not approved by the moralists and usually referred to as the oldest profession (昔の商売, すなわち売春). / ***by*** all ***means*** do not neglect doing ... / be ***by*** no ***means*** negligible / His knowledge of English is ***by*** no ***means*** despicable. ¶The plan is only waiting ***for means*** of accomplishment. その計画は実行を待つ段になっている. ¶***through*** (=by) ***means*** of ... ...によって. ¶She is ***without*** the ***means*** of existence. 彼には生活の道がない.

P² the best ***means for*** doing it それをなす最良の手段 ‖ as a ***means for*** the expression of thought 思想表現の方法として. ¶***means of*** extending one's trade 商売を拡張する手段 ‖ ***means of*** subsistence 生計手段 ‖ The ***means of*** communication between here and ... are interrupted. 当地と...との通信は途絶している. ‖ ***means of*** conveyance 輸送機関. 【類】 Esperanto as a ***means of*** international communication / ***means of*** transport (=transportation) / ***means of*** locomotion, such as the elevated railway, the surface cars, and the subway ‖ be deprived of ***means of*** transit (交通停止で)足を取られる. ¶a ***means to*** the desired end 目的に達する手段 ‖ Wealth is a ***means to*** an end, not the end itself. 富は目的その物ではなくて目的に達する手段だ. ‖ a ***means to*** prosperity 繁栄への道. 【類】 as ***means to*** this end / as a ***means to*** the end in view / Grammar is a ***means to*** an end, not an end itself.

(3) *pl.* 資力, 資産, 収入.

V he ***accumulated*** the ***means*** that enabled him to ... 彼は自分で...のできるだけの資力を蓄えた. ¶He ***has*** not ***means*** to keep a motor-car. 彼には自動車を持つだけの余裕がない. ‖ He ***has*** private ***means***. 彼には私財がある. 【類】 I ***have*** not the ***means*** for purchasing the O.E.D. ¶to ***increase*** the ***means*** of his family 彼の一家の生活の足しに. ¶***obtain*** a moderate ***means*** of livelihood 相当の生計を立てるだけの資力を得る. ¶***possess*** ample ***means*** 豊かな資産を有する. ¶***provide means*** for ... ...の資力を支給する. ¶***secure means*** of earning a livelihood 生計の資を得る.

V² as far as his ***means allow*** 彼の資力の許す限り.

Q people of ***considerable means*** かなりの資産家. 【類】 The company is possessed of some ***considerable means***. ¶He has ***independent means***. 彼は人の世話にならないで食って行ける. ¶a vagrant without ***legitimate means*** of support 一定の仕事のない浮浪者. ¶students of ***limited means*** 学資の乏しい学生 ‖ His ***means*** of support are ***limited***. 彼は財政が豊かでない. ¶The cinema is suitable for the enjoyment of those of ***moderate*** as well as ***expensive means***. 映画は有福人にも余り有福でない人にも向く娯楽である. ¶The firm has not ***much means***. その会社は資力がない. ¶men and women of ***narrow means*** 資産の乏しい男女. ¶a man of no ***ordinary means*** 並以上に資力のある人. ¶lack ***private means*** 私財がない. ¶men of ***scanty*** (=***slender***) ***means*** 収入の乏しい人々. ¶A person of my ***small means*** cannot afford to buy such things. 僕のような金のないものにはこんなものは買えない. 【類】 a collector (収集家) of ***small means***.

P live ***above*** (=***beyond***) one's ***means*** 収入以上(身分不相応)の生活をする. ¶every man ***according to*** his ***means*** だれも彼もその資力に応じて. ¶a gentleman ***of means*** 資産家. ¶His expenditure is not in proportion ***to*** his ***means***. 彼は身分不相応な金使いをする. ¶a young lady ***with means*** 若い有産婦人. 【類】 men ***with*** small ***means***. ¶live ***within*** one's ***means*** 収入内で暮す ‖ It is procurable at a cost well ***within*** your ***means***. それはあなたが楽にお買いになれる代価です. ¶***without*** ample ***means*** 資力が乏しいので.

mean, *a.* けちな, 卑しい; 気分の悪い.

M I feel ***awful mean*** today. きょうはとても気分が悪い. ¶He is a ***very mean*** fellow. あの男は実にいやな人間だ. ‖ He is ***very mean*** (=rough) to us. [先生など]彼はとてもわれわれにひどく当る.

P He is ***mean about*** money. 彼は金銭には卑しい. ¶***mean*** (=poor) ***in*** appearance 外見の貧弱な.

mean, *v.* 思う; あてる, きわめる; 意味する.

M It ***means a great deal***. それには大いに意味がある. ¶To look up 10,000 words in a dictionary ***means at least*** 300 hours' work. 辞書で一万語を捜すのは少くとも三百時間の仕事だ. ¶I ***mean*** it ***definitely***. たしかにそうだ. ¶His words ***mean much***. 彼の言葉には大いに含蓄がある. ‖ it ***means much*** to ... ...することは大いに役立つ. ¶I did not ***really mean*** it. 僕は本気ではなかった. 【類】 You ***really mean*** it? / The words do not ***really mean*** that. ¶it ***means roughly*** ... 大体をいうと...となる. ¶I wonder whether it is ***meant seriously***. それは本気で言ったのかしら. ¶He ***means well*** (***ill***) towards me. 彼は僕に対して好意をもっている(いない).

P He ***meant*** it ***as*** a kindness. 彼はそれで親切の積りだったのだ. ¶What do you ***mean by*** it? それはどういう意味か. ‖ Whom do you ***mean by*** a friend? 友だちとはだれのことか. 【類】 What do you ***mean by*** this word? ¶What he said was ***meant*** only ***for*** himself. 彼はただ自分のことを言ったのだった. 【類】 It is ***meant for*** a joke. ‖ He took internally what was ***meant for*** external application. 彼は外用薬を飲んでしまった. ‖ This parcel is ***meant for*** her. これは彼女にやる包だ. ‖ I ***meant*** it ***for*** your good. それは君のためを思ってしたのだ. ‖ What is this ***meant for***? これはどうするのか. ‖ Is that bell ***meant for*** my train? あのベルは僕の乗る列車のかい. ‖ There is no knowing how much he ***means for*** what he says. どこまでが本心か分かったものじゃない. ‖ He was ***meant*** (=intended) ***for*** soldier. 彼は軍人になることになっていたのだ. ‖ It ***means*** something ***for*** him. それは彼にとっては意味がある(大事だ). ¶You don't realize what fire would ***mean to*** you? 火事に会ったらどんなだか君には分かっていない.

O Poor teeth ***mean*** poor digestion and poor digestion ***means*** poor nutrition. 歯の悪いのは消化が悪いということになり消化の悪いのは栄養不良ということになる. ¶Anyhow, I ***mean*** to go. とにかく僕は行く積りです. ¶***Meaning*** what they say and saying what they mean—such is modern diplomacy. 口に出したことは腹にあり腹にあることは口に出して言う—これが近代の外交だ. ¶When I say yes, I ***mean*** it. 私は本気でよしと言ってるんだ. ¶Forgive me please. I didn't ***mean*** it. 失礼しました. そういう積

りではなかったのです.

meander, *v*. 曲折する.

P meander ***a long way off*** to the sea 長々と曲りくねって流れ海に達する. ¶A stream of clear water ***meanders amid*** roses, orange trees, lemons, pomegranates, and grapevines. 一条の清い流れがばら・だいだい・レモン・ざくろ・ぶどうの木の中をうねりくねって流れる. ¶***meander through*** hills and fields 丘や野原を横切ってくねくねして流れる.

meaning, *n*. 意味, 意義; 主旨.

V ***acquire*** (=take on) a new *meaning* [言葉など]新しい意味を持つようになる. ¶***attach*** a *meaning* of his own to the terms he uses 彼が用いている言葉に彼独特の意義を付ける. ¶The word ***bears*** (=has) a double *meaning*. その言葉には二重の意味がある. ‖ ***bear*** a hidden *meaning* 言外の意味を持つ. ¶***bring out*** the *meaning* distinctly 意義を明確にする. ¶***catch*** the *meaning* at once 直ちに意味をさとる. 【類】In the case of Chinese words (漢語) in Japanese it is sometimes difficult to ***catch*** the *meaning* by sound. ¶words that have ***changed*** their *meaning* 意味の変った言葉. ¶***comprehend*** the *meaning* of ... ...の意義を会得する. ¶***contain*** this symbolic *meaning* この象徴的意義を含む. ¶exactly ***convey*** one's *meaning* 正確に意味を伝える. 【類】Words sometimes fail to ***convey*** fully the desired *meaning*. ¶***darken*** its *meaning* その意味をあいまいにする. ¶***determine*** the true *meanings* of words 言葉の真の意義を決定する. ¶***dig*** the *meaning* out of an English passage 一節の英文の意味を追究する. ¶***distort*** one's *meaning* 人の底意を曲解する. ¶***elucidate*** the *meaning* 意味を釈明する. ¶***extract*** its net *meaning* その純意義を摘出する. ¶***fathom*** his *meaning* 彼の底意を測る. ¶choose the word which extractly ***fits*** one's *meaning* 自分の思いにきっちり合う言葉を選ぶ. ¶***gain*** (=***attain***) a new *meaning* of a word 語に新しい意味がつく. ¶This composition contains many sentences from which it is difficult to ***gather*** *meaning*. この作品には意味の取りにくい文章が沢山のっている. ¶***get*** the real *meaning* of the text 本文の真意をつかまえる(会得する). ¶We now ***give*** a new *meaning* to the word. 今日ではその言葉に新しい意味をつけるようになった. 【類】***give*** a moral *meaning* to a story. ¶***grasp*** the *meaning* of ... ...の意味をつかむ. 【類】***grasp*** instantly the *meaning* that lies behind the figures (比ゆ) / I fail to ***grasp*** your *meaning*. ¶It ***has*** some hidden *meaning*. それにはある隠れた意味がある. ¶***hit*** the *meaning* 意義を知り当てる. ¶The following anecdote will ***illustrate*** my *meaning* better than any explanation. 次の一つ話はどんな説明よりも私の真意を明かにするだろう. ¶***impart*** (=***add***) a new *meaning* to ... ...に新しい意味をつける. ¶***infer*** its *meaning* from context 文脈から推してその意味を解する. ¶Words are said to be used in a literal sense when they ***keep*** their regular *meaning*. 言葉が文字通りの意味に用いられるというのはそれが普通の意義を失わない場合を言うのだ. ¶The young that have not ***learned*** the *meaning* of a gun and its danger are easy to shoot. 鉄砲とその危険を知らない幼獣(鳥)はこれを射留めるのが容易だ. ¶***list*** the *meanings* of a word in the order of historic development 一語の意味を歴史的発展の順序に配列する(ウブスター大辞典のように). ¶***look up*** the *meaning* of the word in a dictionary 辞書で言葉の意味を捜す. ¶hackneyed phrases that have ***lost*** *meaning* その意味を失った陳腐な文句. ¶to ***make*** my *meaning* ***clear*** 私の趣旨を明かにするために. ¶***misapprehend*** one's *meaning* 人の真意を誤解する. ¶He ***mistook*** my *meaning*. 彼は私の言うことを取り違えた. ¶***perceive*** the full *meaning* of ... ...の意味を十分飲込む. ¶***pervert*** the *meaning* 意味を曲げて取る. ¶***put*** a wrong *meaning* on ... ...に間違った意味をつける. ¶***puzzle out*** (=***work out or solve***) the *meaning* of a sentence 文の意味を判読する. ¶He could ***read*** no *meaning* into them. 彼にはその真意が分かりかねた. ¶***seize*** the full *meaning* of ... ...の意味を十分に会得する. ¶***shade*** the *meaning* a little 意味を少しぼかす. ¶punctuate so as to ***show*** the *meaning* best 意味がはっきりするように句とう点を打つ. ¶***strain*** the *meaning* of a word 語意を曲解する. ¶***take*** its *meaning* to heart その意味を心に銘じる. ¶***take on*** a new *meaning* under these circumstances こうした事情で新しい意味を持つようになる. ¶***twist*** the *meaning* of ... ...の意味を曲解する. ¶***understand*** (=comprehend *or* grasp) the *meaning* 意味を了解する. ¶The chief aim of punctuation is to ***unfold*** the *meaning* of sentences, with the least trouble to the reader. 句読点の主な目的は最少の労力をもって読者に文章の意義を表明することにある.

Q They are not "..." within the ***accepted*** *meaning* of the word. それらは本当の意味の「...」ではない. ¶convey an ***ambiguous*** *meaning* あいまいな意義を伝える. ¶an ***apparent*** *meaning* 表面の意義. ¶the ***central*** *meaning* of the word その語の中核をなす意義. ¶It has a ***cryptic*** *meaning* capable of different interpretations. それには色々に解釈のできる神秘的意義がある. ¶a ***deeper*** *meaning* of life [皮相でない]より深い人生の意味. ¶It has a ***deep*** and ***subtle*** *meaning*. それには深奥な意味がある. ¶The word has no ***definite*** *meaning*. その語にはこれというはっきりした意味はない. ¶the use of the same word by various people with ***different*** *meanings* その語の人によって意味の相違している用法. ¶the ***essential*** *meaning* of the dispute その争議の要点. ¶He is a gentleman in ***every*** *meaning* (=sense) of the term. 彼はその語のあらゆる意味において(どう見ても)紳士である. ¶the ***exact*** *meaning* the sentence is intended to convey その文が持つ正確な意味. ¶have ***exoteric*** and ***esoteric*** *meaning* 表面の意義と内面の意義とがある. ¶an ***extended*** *meaning* 広義. ¶What is its ***figurative*** *meaning?* その比ゆ的の意味(転義)は何か. ¶a verb of ***full*** *meaning* 本動詞(助動詞に対し) ‖ get the ***full*** *meaning* of ... ...の意味を十分会得する. ¶a ***hidden*** (=***latent***) *meaning* 裏の(隠れた)意味. ¶facts of nature and their ***human*** *meanings* 自然界の事実とその人間から見た意義. ¶convey an ***indecent*** *meaning* to the minds of the readers 読者の心にわいせつな意味を伝える. ¶an ***inner*** *meaning* 隠れた意味 ‖ the forms and their ***inner*** *meaning* 形式とその内面的の意義. ¶My *meaning* was ***innocent***. 私は悪気で言ったのではなかった. ¶It has an ***intelligible*** *meaning*. それには明確な意味がある. ¶the ***intended*** *meaning* 目指した意味. ¶a word of ***like*** *meaning* 類語. ¶Railway transportation in the ***modern*** *meaning* of the term began with the Stockton and Darlington Railway. 現代の意味における鉄道運輸は[英国の]ストックトン・ダーリントン鉄道から始まったのだ. ‖ old events and ***modern*** *meanings* 過去のできごととその現代から見た意義(温古知新). ¶the ***multiplied*** *meanings* of words 語の分岐した意味. ¶a ***new*** *meaning* of an old word 古語に付加された新義. 【類】give a ***new*** *meaning* to ... ¶***obsolete*** *meanings* of common words 一般語のすたれた意味. ¶He cared nothing for success in the ***ordinary***, ***worldly*** *meaning* of that term. 彼は普通世俗的の意味でいう成功なるものには一向とん着しなかった. ¶It has an ***opprobrious*** *meaning*. それには悪い意味がある. ¶From the ***original***, ***literal*** *meaning* of a word arises its figurative meanings. 語の本来の文字通りの意味からその比ゆ的意味が生れる. ¶an ***outer*** *meaning* 表面の意味. ¶lose its ***primary*** *meaning* そのもとの意味を失う. ¶It has a ***profound*** *meaning*. それには深長な意味がある. ¶acquire a ***quasi-technical*** *meaning* 術語のような意味を持つようになる. ¶the ***racial*** *meaning* of mother love 母性愛の民族的意義. ¶the ***radical*** *meaning* of the word その言葉の原義. ¶the ***real*** *meaning* 真の意義. ¶words of ***similar*** and ***opposite*** *meanings* 同意語と反意語. ¶sense a ***special*** *meaning* in ... ...の特別の意味を感知する. ¶acquire a ***special*** or ***peculiar*** *meaning* 特別のあるいは変った意味を持つ. ¶***symbolic*** *meanings* of flowers 花の象徴的意味(花言葉に見られる). ¶This word has no ***technical*** *meaning* in law. この語には法律上何ら専門的の意味はない. 【類】the drawback (弱味) of using a word with a popular sense in a ***technical*** *meaning* / Many words in law have ***technical*** *meanings* different from those which they bear in ordinary speech. ¶the ***unfathomable*** *meaning* of the song その歌の測るべからざる(深長な)意味. ¶The collocation has a ***unitary*** *meaning*, as if one word. その連語用法は一語のように単一の意味を持つ. ¶The word is not a code word; it has its ***usual*** *meaning*. その語は暗号じゃなく普通の意味を持っている. ¶a ***wide*** *meaning* 広い意味.

Q² the ***core*** *meaning* of a word 一語の中心の意味(他はそれから分岐したもの). ¶the ***root*** *meaning* of a word 語の根本的意味. ¶the ***slang*** *meaning* of a word 語の俗語的な意味. ¶***surface*** *meaning* 表面の意義. ¶fail to grasp ***word*** *meanings* 語の意義をつかみ損う.

P I cannot come ***at*** (=understand) the *meaning* of this word. 私にはこの言葉の意味が分からない. ¶a word not clear ***in meaning*** 意味の不明な語 ‖ The room to which the street-walker retires with her prey is not a brothel ***in*** the *meaning* of the law. 売春婦がかもを連込むへやは法律上の売春宿ではない. ‖ The words of God are deep and multiplied ***in meaning***. 神の言葉は意味は深長複雑である. ¶a word ***of*** kindred *meaning* 類似の意味の語. ¶It has a world ***of meaning***. それには沢山意味がある. ¶***with meaning*** 意味ありげに ‖ each ***with*** a separate *meaning* 各別々の意味があって. ¶***within*** the *meaning* of these articles (of this statute) 本条(本法)に規定するところの ‖ be ***within*** the *meaning* of this maxim この金言が当てはまる. ¶***without meaning*** in the least to brag 大口をたたくわけではないが. 【類】***without meaning*** to depreciate or belittle ...

P^2 There is no *meaning* ***in*** what he says. 彼の言うことは無意味だ. ¶look up in a dictionary the *meaning* ***of*** a word 単語の意味を辞書で引く.

meanness, *n.* 卑劣.

V He cannot ***brook meanness***. 彼は卑劣なことを黙って見ていられないたちだ.

P He is ***above*** such *meanness*. 彼はそんな卑劣なことをするような男じゃない. ¶never stoop ***to meanness*** 決して卑劣なことはしない.

meantime, *n.* その間.

P He will be back ***in*** the *meantime*. 彼はその内に戻って来るだろう. 【類】***In*** the *meantime* [the] day had dawned. / ***In*** the *meantime* let us do the things we can.

meanwhile, *n.* その間.

P ***in*** the *meanwhile* our story returns to ... そこで話は...に戻る.

measles, *n.* はしか.

V It ***has*** the *measles*. 子供がはしかにかかっている.

V^2 *Measles* ***broke out***. はしかが流行し出した.

Q ***German*** *measles* 軽いはしか.

P^2 *measles* ***in*** man (swine) 人(豚)のはしか.

measure, *n.* (**1**) 尺度, 度量, 寸法; 度量器, 物差; 標準; 程度, 限度.

V ***achieve*** the highest *measure* of success 大成功を収める. ¶a play that ***affrods*** a full *measure* of entertainment 十分に楽しめる劇. ¶***attain*** a *measure* of success 一応成功を収める. ¶I ***got*** good *measure*. 尺(量)はたっぷりあった. ¶***take*** a person's *measure* 寸法をとる; 人物を見る ‖ ***take*** *measure* of the finger for a ring 指輪を合わせるために指の寸法を取る. 【類】The tailor ***took*** my *measure* for a new suit. / Will you ***take*** my *measure?* ‖ I soon ***took*** his *measure* (=understood his character). 私はすぐあの人の気性をのみこんだ.

Q ***broad*** (***long***) *measure* 幅(長さ)の寸法. ¶examine it with a ***certain*** *measure* of fullness 幾分細かに論じる ‖ There is a ***certain*** *measure* of justice in what you say. 君の言うことには幾分道理がある. ¶in ***considerable*** *measure* 大いに. ¶a ***dry*** *measure* of Spain スペインの乾量(ます). ¶This looks like penny-wise, pound-foolish in an ***exaggerated*** *measure*. これは極言すれば文惜しみの百知らずというべきだろう. ¶meet with a ***fair*** *measure* of success 相当に成功する. ¶It did not meet with the ***full*** *measure* of success it deserved. それはそれ相応の十分な成功はしなかった. ¶Throw that in for ***good*** *measure*. ついでにそれもおまけに入れとけ. ‖ with ... thrown in for ***good*** *measure* おまけに...まで入れて(もり沢山に). ¶in a ***great*** (=large) *measure* 大いに. ¶I will help though in a ***humble*** *measure*. 私は及ばずながら尽します. ¶It was doubtless in ***large*** *measure* due to the fact that ... それは疑いもなく...の事実に起因するところが多かった. ‖ depend in ***large*** *measure* upon ... 大半...に依存する. 【類】The history of geographical discovery in America is in ***large*** *measure* a history of conquest. ¶***metric*** *measure* メートル度量法. ¶in ***no small*** *measure* 少なからず. ¶possess in ***rich*** *measure* the remarkable and exceptional talent of ... ...の非凡な才能を豊富に持っている. ¶I got ***short*** *measure*. 尺(量)が不足だった. 【類】The shopkeeper gave me ***short*** *measure*. ¶The report is in ***some*** *measure* true. その話は幾分は事実だ. ¶my thanks are due in ***special*** *measure* to ... 私は特に...に感謝せねばならない.

Q^2 a ***cloth*** *measure* 呉服尺. ¶***liquid*** *measure* 液量. ¶a ***pint*** *measure* 一パイントます. ¶***standard*** *measure* 正規の量器. ¶a ***tape*** *measure* テープ尺. ¶a ***waist*** *measure* of about sixty-two inches 腰回りの寸法約六十二インチ ‖ take one's ***waist*** *measure* ウエストの寸法をとる. ¶a ***yard*** *measure* ヤードさし.

P Perhaps the development of the work of the post-office may be regarded ***as*** a *measure* of a country's civilization. 恐らく郵便事務の発達いかんは一国の文化の尺度と見なすことができよう. ¶He loves his work ***beyond*** *measure*. 彼は非常に自分の仕事を愛する. 【類】Her joy was ***beyond*** *measure*. / Your exploits tonight astounded me ***beyond*** *measure*. / I was amazed ***beyond*** all *measure*. / He is rude ***beyond*** *measure*. ¶***by*** *measure* (数や目方でなく)寸法によって ‖ They sell wine ***by*** the *measure*. ぶどう酒をはかり売りにする. ‖ ***By*** all *measure* Shelley is unquestionably one of the great lyrical poets of England. たしかにシェリーは英国の一大叙情詩人であることは疑うべくもない. ¶***in*** *measure* 適度に ‖ ***in*** a great (=large) *measure* 大いに ‖ ***in*** some *measure* 幾分か ‖ He is selfish ***in*** a *measure*. 彼は幾分手前勝手の所がある. ‖ That happiness he experienced ***in*** a *measure* granted to few men. その幸福を彼は滅多に得られないほど享有した. ¶He was astonished ***out of*** *measure*. 彼は途方もなく驚いた. ¶My coat is tailored (=made) ***to*** *measure*. 僕の上衣は寸法を合わせてこしらえた. 【類】a suit of clothes made ***to*** *measure*. ¶***within*** *measure* 適度に, ほどよく. ¶***without*** *measure* 非常に, 過度に.

P^2 a *measure* ***for*** liquids 液体の量器. ¶Ton is a *measure* ***of*** weight. トンは重量を示す. ‖ a *measure* ***of*** four inches 四インチの物差 ‖ a *measure* ***of*** 10 litres 十リットルの量器 ‖ attain a *measure* ***of*** success 幾分の成功を収める ‖ Money is the *measure* ***of*** worth. 金銭は価値の量器(標準)だ. ‖ A *measure* ***of*** indulgence is due to children. 子供はある程度のわがままはしかたのないものだ.

(**2**) 手段, 方法, 処置; 政策, 法案.

V ***adopt*** decisive *measures* 断固たる手段を採る. ¶***advise*** remedial *measures* 救済策(善後策)を授ける. ¶***approve*** a *measure* (=bill) 議案を承認する. 【類】We ***approve*** the *measure* of the administration. ¶***bring in*** a *measure* 案を(会議などに)付議する. ¶rigorously ***carry out*** these *measures* これらの方策を励行する. ¶***discuss*** *measures* of relief 救済策を論議する. ¶***enact*** repressive *measures* 圧迫手段を講じる ‖ The *measure* was recently ***enacted*** by Congress. 同議案は最近(米)国会で立法化された. ¶***enforce*** Draconian *measures* きびしい方策を励行する. ¶***give*** him first-aid *measures* 彼に応急手当を施す. ¶***have*** hard *measures* 残酷に取扱われる. ¶***institute*** legal *measures* against ...=take [the] law measure on ... [colloq.] ...に対して訴訟を起す. ¶***organize*** preventive *measures* 予防策を立てる. ¶***press*** *measures* against ... ...の対策を強行する. ¶***provoke*** *measures* of retaliation 報復手段を激成させる. ¶This *measure* must not be ***pushed*** to excess. この政策は極端に押し進めてはいけない. ¶***push forward*** an important legislative *measure* 重要法案が通過するように運動する. ¶***reject*** a *measure* 議案を否決する. ¶The Government has ***taken*** *measures* to preserve order. 政府は秩序維持の方法を講じた. 【類】The Government ***took*** *measures* to promote domestic industry. / *Measures* must be ***taken*** to meet this situation (時局に対する). / They ***took*** severe *measures* against the wrongdoers (ごろつき). ¶proceed to ***take*** the necessary *measures* 進んで必要な手段を取る. ¶***thwart*** a *measure* ある方策に邪魔を入れる. ¶***use*** preventive *measures* 予防手段を採る.

Q as an ***alternative*** *measure* he advocated ... その代り彼は...を唱道した. ¶the ***best possible*** *measure* 万全の策. ¶the observance of ***certain hygienic*** *measures* 一定の衛生規則の遵守. ¶resort to ***coercive*** *measures* 高圧手段に出る. ¶a ***compulsory*** *measure* 強制処分. ¶adopt ***concerted*** *measures* 協定案を採用する. ¶use ***corrupt*** *measures* with ... ...を買収する. ¶take ***counter*** *measures* to ... ...の対策を講じる. ¶a ***curative*** *measure* 救治策. ¶a ***desperate*** *measure* 無謀な策. ¶***drastic*** *measures* 荒療治. ¶take ***effectual*** *measures* to correct social evils 社会悪をなくすため効果的な措置をとる. ¶the most ***effective prophylactic*** *measure* against fever 熱病の最も有効な予防法. ¶take ***every possible*** *measure* あらゆる可能な方法をとる. ¶as an ***extreme*** *measure* 苦しまぎれに ‖ ***Extreme*** *measures* are necessary in a crisis. 危急存亡のときには極端の手段が必要だ. ¶a ***faltering*** *measure* 弱腰の手段. ¶***foolish*** *measures*

愚策. ¶take a very ***generous measure*** with regards to ... ...に関してきわめて寛大な処置を取る. ¶I am in favor of ***gentle measures.*** 穏当な処置に賛成だ. 【類】by ***gentle,*** and sometimes by ***drastic, measures.*** ¶despise ***half measures*** なま半可なことをきらう. 【類】reject ***half measures*** / ***Half measures*** do not succeed. / ***Half-way measures*** will not be sufficient. ¶***hard measures*** 強硬手段. ¶take ***heroic measures*** 男らしい処置を取る. ¶take a ***high-handed measure*** 高圧手段をとる. ¶The *measure* is ***ill-timed*** (***well-timed***). その処置は時機を失している(機宜を得ている). ¶as an ***immediate measure*** 応急手段として. ¶adopt an ***incentive measure*** 報奨措置を講じる. ¶an ***infallible measure*** 万全の策. ¶the ***last measure*** 最後の手段. ¶***legislative measures*** 法案. ¶a ***lukewarm measure*** 手ぬるい手段. ¶***makeshift measures*** 間に合わせの策. ¶a ***mistaken measure*** 誤った方法. ¶a ***philanthropical measure*** 慈善事業. ¶a ***political measure*** 政策. ¶a ***potent measure*** in bringing about industrial harmony and prosperity 工業の調和と繁栄とをもたらすに有力な方法. ¶take ***precautionary measures*** 予防策を講じる. 【類】as a ***precautionary measure.*** ¶***Preventive measures*** are being taken. 予防策が講じられつつある. ¶employ ***prophylactic measures*** 予防策を講じる. ¶take a ***proper*** and ***effective measure*** 適当で効果的な措置をとる. ¶a ***prudent measure*** 用心深い方法. ¶***Quick measures*** were needed. 応急措置が必要であった. ¶resort to ***radical measures*** 抜本的措置に出る. ¶a ***rash measure*** 無分別なやり方. ¶send her to Europe as a ***recuperative measure*** 病後療養のため彼女をヨーロッパへやる. ¶a ***remedial measure*** 救治策. ¶***remedial*** and ***preventive measures*** 救済予防法. ¶a ***repressive measure*** 抑圧的措置. 【類】***repressive*** police ***measures.*** ¶as a ***retaliatory measure*** against ... ...に対する報復手段として. ¶a most ***rigid measure*** もっともきびしい手段. 【類】***Rigid measures*** are being taken to suppress the movement. ¶***rigorous measures*** to suppress the evil 厳重な弊害撲滅策. ¶a ***severe measure*** 厳重な方策. ¶***strict sanitary measures*** 厳重な衛生方策. ¶take ***stringent measures*** to prevent ... ...予防の厳重な処置を取る. ¶a ***sudorific measure*** 発汗させる方法. ¶a ***measure suitable*** to the occasion 時宜に適した処置. ¶as a ***tentative measure*** 成案として. ¶***temporary measures*** 臨時措置. ¶***therapeutic measures*** 治療法. ¶***timely measures*** 時宜を得た方法. ¶actuate him to a ***tragic measure*** 彼をたきつけて悲惨な方法を取らせる. ¶an ***untrustworthy measure*** 信頼できない方法. ¶***useful measures*** 有用な手段. ¶a most ***valuable hygienic measure*** きわめて有益な衛生手段. ¶a ***vexatious measure*** めんどうな措置. ¶take ***vigorous measures*** of disinfection 消毒を強力にやる. 【類】take ***vigorous measures*** in this direction. ¶take ***vigorous repressive measures*** 強力な抑圧手段を取る.

Q² an ***Administration measure*** 政府案. ¶***agrarian reform measures*** 農地改革諸案. ¶an ***anti-inflation measure*** インフレ対策. ¶a ***companion measure*** to ... ...の姉妹案. ¶Mr. Attlee's program of ***crisis measures*** アトリー氏の非常措置プラン. ¶a ***de-control measure*** 統制撤廃案. ¶as an ***emergency measure*** 非常措置として. 【類】a temporary ***emergency measure.*** ¶***emergency*** economic ***measures*** 非常経済措置. ¶***farmland reform measures*** 農地改革諸案. ¶as a ***health control measure*** 保健策として. ¶as an ***interim measure*** 臨時措置として. ¶obstruct the implementation of ***land reform measures*** 土地改革案の実施を妨害する. ¶a ***military*** (***traffic***) ***safety measure*** 軍備充実(交通安全)策. ¶***party measures*** 政党政策. ¶as a ***preparedness measure*** 国防上の一策として. ¶a ***relief measure*** 救済策. ¶as a ***wartime measure*** 戦時の一方策として.

P ***as*** a ***measure*** of hygiene 衛生的手段として. ¶To his amazement the members, to a man, objected ***to*** the ***measure.*** 彼の驚いたことには会員は一人残らずその案に反対した.

P² Government ***measures for*** relief are already under way (=being carried on). 政府の救済策がすでに実行されている. 【類】***measures for*** the relief of the poor. ¶a ***measure of*** reprisal 報復手段 ‖ a ***measure of*** execution 執行処分.

measure, *v.* 計る, 量る; 寸法を取る; 測れば...ある; じろじろ見る; 比べる; つり合わせる.

M ***measure out*** food to the poor 貧民に食物を配給する.

M² ***measure up*** to (=meet) the great task《米》その大事業を引受けるに 足りる ‖ He ***measures up*** to his job in every way. 彼はあらゆる点において適材である. ‖ It doesn't ***measure up*** to specifications. それは仕訳書と合わない. 【類】Any product bearing the name of the manufacturers ***measures up*** to the high standards. / The paper did not ***measure up*** to the standard of merit.

P Russia could not ***measure*** herself ***against*** Austria. ロシアはオーストリヤの敵ではなかった. ¶I can ***measure*** a person ***at*** a glance. 私は一目で人物がわかる. ¶I only ***measured*** it ***by*** the eye. 目分量です. ‖ Time is ***measured by*** the hour, minute, and second. 時は時・分・秒で計る. 【類】***measure*** a person ***by*** one's school career (学歴で) / It is ***measured by*** a certain standard (一定の標準). / ***measure by*** weight (目方で). ¶I want you to ***measure*** me ***for*** a new coat. 新調の上衣の寸法を取ってもらいたい. ‖ I was ***measured for*** boots (a suit of clothes). 私はくつ(など)の寸法を取ってもらった. ¶***measure*** a person ***from*** top ***to*** bottom 人を頭のてっぺんから足の先までじろじろ見る. ¶***measure*** 7 inches ***in*** diameter (height, length) 直径(など)七インチある ‖ There the snowfall is ***measured,*** not ***in*** inches, but ***in*** feet. そこでは降雪量はインチで計るのではなくてフートで計る. ‖ It cannot be ***measured in*** terms of money. それは金銭では計られない. ¶***measure*** one's desires ***to*** one's fortune 欲望を財産につり合わせる. ¶He ***measured*** me ***with*** his eyes. 彼は私をじろじろ見た. ‖ ***measure*** one's strength (skill) ***with*** a rival (foe) 対手(など)と力(など)を比べる.

measurement, *n.* 測量; 大きさ, 量; 寸法.

V ***Give*** me your ***measurements,*** please. あなたの寸法をどうぞおっしゃって下さい(とらして下さい). ¶***make*** the ***measurements*** 寸法を取る. ¶***take*** an accurate ***measurement*** of ... ...を正確に計る.

Q ***fine measurements*** 精密な寸法. ¶***precise measurements*** 精確な寸法. ¶***inside measurement*** 内法(うちのり).

Q² take ***chest*** (***bust, waist***) ***measurement*** 胸囲(など)を計る.

P Ocean freight is usually ***by measurement,*** not by weight. 大洋運賃は普通目方でなくて大きさで取るのだ. ‖ two hundred yards ***by*** actual ***measurement*** 実測で二百ヤード. ¶take ***measurements with*** a rule 物差で寸法を取る.

meat, *n.* 肉; 食事 (meal).

V The dog ***bit meat*** off the bone. 犬が骨から肉をかみ取った. ¶***carve meat*** 肉を切る. ¶***chew meat*** 肉をかむ. ¶***cut meat*** 肉を切る ‖ ***cut*** the ***meat*** off a bone 骨から肉を切取る. ¶***do meat*** 肉を料理する. ¶***eat meat*** 肉を食う. 【類】***eat*** less ***meat*** and more vegetables. ¶***fletcherize meat*** 肉を十分かんで食べる. ¶***gnaw*** the ***meat*** off a bone 骨から肉をかみ取る. ¶***heat up*** cold ***meat*** 冷肉を暖める. ¶***mince meat*** 肉をこまかに切る. ¶***pick*** the ***meat*** off a bone 骨から肉をむしり取る. ¶***steam meat*** 肉を蒸す. ¶***stuff meat*** 肉を詰める. ¶***trim meat*** 肉を調理する.

V² This ***meat*** does not ***agree*** with me. 僕はこの肉を食べるとあたる. ¶The ***meat*** has ***gone bad.*** 肉が悪くなった. ¶The ***meat*** won't ***go round.*** 肉が全体の人数に行渡るまい. ¶***Meat keeps well*** here. 肉はここにおくと持つ. 【類】***Meat*** will not ***keep overnight*** in such hot weather. ¶This ***meat smells bad.*** この肉はにおいが悪い. ¶***Meat*** will ***spoil*** if kept too long. 肉は長くおくと腐る. ¶The ***meat*** won't ***suffice*** for us all. 肉は皆に回りきるまい. ¶This ***meat*** is ***turning bad.*** この肉は悪くなりかけている.

Q ***Australian cold storage meats*** 豪州の冷蔵肉. ¶horse-flesh and other even ***baser meats*** 馬肉及び他のもっと下等な肉. ¶***broken meat*** 食い残りの肉. ¶***butcher's meat*** 肉屋で売っている肉. ¶***canned*** (=***tinned***) ***meat*** かん詰肉. ¶***chilled meat*** 冷蔵肉. ¶***fat meat*** 脂肉. ¶***fresh meat*** 新鮮な肉. ¶***lean meat*** 脂肪のない肉, 赤身. ¶***potted meat*** びん・かん・瀬戸物などに詰めた味付け肉. ¶***preserved meats*** 貯蔵肉. ¶***putrid meat*** 腐れ肉. ¶***raw meat*** なま肉. ¶***roasted meat*** ロース焼の肉. ¶***Salted meat*** keeps a long time. 塩肉は長く保(も)つ. ¶***second*** (***third***)***-grade meat*** 二(三)等肉. ¶***smoked meat*** くん製肉. ¶***sound meat*** いきのよい肉. ¶***tender meat*** 柔かい肉. ¶This ***meat*** is quite ***tough.*** この肉は実にこわい. ¶***snake meat*** へび肉.

Q² ***fish*** and ***shell meat*** 魚貝の肉. ¶***horse meat*** 馬肉.

P Say grace ***before meat.*** 食前のお祈りをささげなさい. ¶a piece ***of meat*** 肉片 ‖ a good cut ***of meat*** 上肉のひと切れ.

P² *meat of* prime quality 最上肉.

mechanic, *n.* 機械工.

Q² an *auto* (=*automobile*) *mechanic* 自動車技工. ¶an *aviation mechanic* 航空機技工. ¶a *farm mechanic* 農場技工. ¶a *garage mechanic* 自動車庫技工.

mechanism, *n.* 機械; 機構.

V *adjust* the receiving *mechanism* of a wireless apparatus 無線の受信機を調節する.

Q a highly *complex mechanism* of the United Nations 国際連合のきわめて複雑な機構. ¶a *rusty mechanism* which works only with difficulty かろうじて運転しているさびた機械装置.

Q² *clock-work mechanism* ぜんまい仕掛の機構. ¶*office mechanisms* 事務用器具.

P *by* an ingenious *mechanism* 巧妙な機構で.

P² the *mechanism of* voice production 音声発生の機構.

mechanization, *n.* 機械化.

Q² the spread of *farm mechanization* 農村機械化の普及.

medal, *n.* メダル.

V For this service he was *awarded* a *medal*. この功労のために彼は賞はいを授けられた. ¶He *carried off* the first-class gold *medal* for both painting and sculpture at the Paris Exhibition of 1900. 彼は千九百年のパリ博覧会で絵画と彫刻とに対して一等賞金ぱいを受領した. ¶*cast medals* in honor of his memory 彼の記念はいを鋳造する. ¶*confer* a service *medal* on … …に功労章を授ける. ¶he *deserves* gold *medals* for … 彼は…に対して金ぱいを受ける価値がある. ¶this *medal*, which has been *established* in memory of …, is awarded annually to … …の記念に設けられたこの賞はいは毎年…に授与されることになっている. ¶*found* (=*cast or mold*) a gold *medal* 金メダルを鋳造する. ¶Western Australian wool *obtained* five gold *medals* and three diplomas of honor at the Franco-British Exhibition, 1908. 西部オーストラリアの羊毛は一九〇八年の英仏博覧会で金ぱい五個と賞状三通を得た. ¶the gold *medal offered* by the Jiji 時事新報の金ぱい. 【類】*offer* a gold *medal* for competition. ¶*receive* a silver *medal* 銀ぱいを受領する. 【類】He *received* the congressional *medal* of honor for gallantry on battle-field at the siege of Port Hudson. ¶*stamp* a *medal* with a crown 賞はいに王冠を刻印する. ¶*strike medals* to commemorate the event その事件の記念に賞はいを鋳造する. ¶*take* the first *medal* 一等賞はいを受領する. ¶*win* a *medal* 賞はいを得る.

Q All competitors are presented with *commemorative medals*. 競争参加人は皆記念はいを贈られる.

Q² a *Blue Ribbon Medal* 緑授章. ¶*Distinguished Service Medal*〘米軍〙戦時功労章. ☞英軍では Distinguished Service Order. ¶carry off the firstclass *gold medal* for painting at an exhibition 展示会で絵画の一等金ぱいを獲得する. ¶a *Good Conduct Medal*〘米軍〙善行勲章. ¶a *madonna medal* くびにかける聖母像の記章. ¶award a *merit medal* to … …に有功章を贈る. ¶The company took the *prize medal* at the Los Angeles World Fair. 同社はロスアンゼルス世界博覧会で賞はいを受領した.

P the letters *on* a *medal* 賞はいの文字 ‖ stamp a crown *on* a *medal* 賞はいに王冠を刻印する. ¶He was honoured *with* a *medal*. 彼は賞はいを授与された.

P² a *medal for* bravery 戦功章. ¶*Medals of* merit they have bravely won are scattered freely upon their broad breasts. 彼らが授与された勲章を沢山胸にぶら下げている.

medalist, *n.* 賞はい受領者.

Q² *Victoria gold medalists* of the Royal Geographical Society 王立地理学協会のヴィクトリア金ぱい受領者たち.

meddle, *v.* 干渉する, 手を出す.

M *meddle too much* 余り干渉をし過ぎる.

P *meddle in* everything 一々干渉する. 【類】He is inclined to *meddle in* other people's affairs. / *meddle in* politics / I will not *meddle in* the matter. ¶Little boys should not *meddle with* guns. 子供らは鉄砲をいじってはいけない. 【類】*meddle with* politics (philosophy).

meddlesome, *a.* 干渉的な, お節介な.

M *disagreeably* (=*uncomfortably*) *meddlesome* 不愉快なほど干渉的な.

meddling, *n.* 干渉.

Q *needless meddling* 余計なお節介. ¶make *uncalled-for meddling* いらざるお節介をする.

Q² *Government meddling* in … …における政府の干渉.

mediate, *v.* 仲裁する.

P *mediate between* two persons or countries 二人または二カ国の間を調停する.

mediation, *n.* 調停.

V *offer mediation* with a view to … …の目的をもって居中調停を申し出る.

Q² *grievance mediation* 紛争調停.

P *through* the *mediation* of … …の調停で.

mediator, *n.* 仲介者.

P² The Iranians were the great *mediators between* the West and the East. イラン人は西洋と東洋との間の偉大な仲介者だった. ‖ a *mediator between* lover and beloved 月下氷人.

medicament, *n.* 薬剤.

V *apply* a *medicament* to … …に薬をつける.

medication, *n.* 医療.

Q *drugless medication* 無薬医療. ¶*Various medications* were successively tried, but without success. 色々治療をやって見たがだめだった.

medicine, *n.* 医学(特に内科の); 医薬, 薬.

V *administer medicine* by the mouth (per rectum) 口(直腸)から薬を入れる ‖ *administer* one's *medicine* その人の薬を盛る. 【類】*administer medicine* to a sick child. ¶*ask for medicine* for a cold 感冒の薬を求める. ¶*compound* a *medicine* 薬を調合する. ¶Doctors of the better class seldom *dispense* their own *medicines*. 一流の医師はめったに自身で調剤しない. 【類】*dispense medicines* gratuitously (無料で). ¶*drink* the wrong *medicine* 間違った薬を飲む. ¶*furnish medicine* to the sick 病人に薬を与える. ¶*make up* a *medicine* 薬を調合する. ¶*mix* a *medicine* 調剤する. ¶*practice medicine* without proper qualification 無資格で医者を開業する. 【類】be indicted for *practicing medicine* without a licence (無免許で) ‖ licenses to *practice medicine* 医院開業免許. ¶*prepare medicines* from Russian prescriptions ロシアの処方で調剤する. ¶*prescribe medicine* 処方を書く. ¶*put* a *medicine* in one's mouth 口に薬を入れる. ¶*serve out medicine* to the poor 貧困者に施薬する. ¶He has never been known to *taste medicine*. 彼が薬をのんだということは聞かない. ¶*study medicine* and surgery 内外科を研究する. ¶*take medicine* 薬をのむ. 【類】Are you *taking medicine* for your cold? / *Take* the *medicine* with hot water. / *take* so many *medicines* as to convert human stomachs into drug-stores. ¶If you would *try* this *medicine*, you would find that it would soon cure you. この薬を用いれば直ちに治るということが分かるでしょう.

V² A *medicine acts* (=*operates* or *works*). 薬がきく. ¶This *medicine* has *taken effect*. この薬はきいた.

Q an *agreeable medicine* のみよい薬. ¶a *bad-tasting medicine* まずい薬. ¶*clinical medicine* 臨床医学. ¶a *dangerous medicine* 危険な薬. ¶*domestic medicine* しろうと療治. ¶an *efficucious medicine* よくきく薬. ¶A *good medicine* tastes bitter. 良薬口ににがし. ¶*internal* (*external*) *medicine* 内(外)服薬. ¶take *opening medicine* 通じ薬をのむ. ¶books on *popular medicine* 通俗医書. ¶a *powerful medicine* 強い薬. ¶*practical medicine* 実地医学. ¶*preventive medicine* 予防医学. ¶a *proper medicine* for … …の適薬. ¶a *proprietary medicine* 家伝薬. ¶a *purgative medicine* 下剤. ¶a *quack medicine* いんちき薬. ¶a *sedative medicine* 鎮静剤. ¶a *specific medicine* 特効薬. ¶a *strong* (*weak*) *medicine* 強(弱)い薬.

Q² *cure-all* [*medicine*] 万能薬. ¶a *patent medicine* 売薬.

P It is used *as* a *medicine*. それは薬に用いる. ‖ He drinks brandy *as* a *medicine*. 彼はブランディーを薬に飲む. ¶It is used *in medicine* for its stimulant quality. それは興奮性があるので薬として用いる. ¶He has never had a bottle *of medicine*. 彼は一びんの薬も飲んだことはない. ‖ a dose (three doses) *of medicine* 一服(三服)の薬 ‖ the operation *of* a *medicine* 薬の作用. ¶heal *with medicine* 薬で直す. ¶The cough will pass away *without medicine*. せきは薬を飲まないでも止まる.

P² a *medicine for* external application 外用薬 ‖ a *medicine for* fever (indigestion, diarrhoea) 熱(など)の薬. ‖ a *medicine for* the cold かぜ薬 ‖ There is no *medicine for* curing a fool. ばかにつける薬はない. 【類】a *medicine for* loosening the bowels (通じを付ける) / a *medicine for* expelling worms (虫下し).

mediocrity, *n.* 普通, なみ.

Q *mental mediocrity* 平凡な頭.

P, P^2 His talent is ***above*** (***below***) ***mediocrity***. 彼の才能は普通以上(下)だ. ¶*mediocrity* ***of*** capacity 凡才.

meditate, *v.* 沈思する, 黙想する.

P He *meditates* ***on*** his past life. 彼は自分の過去の生活を回想する. ‖ *meditate* ***on*** one's misfortunes わが身の不運を思う.

meditation, *n.* 沈思, めい想.

Q after ***deep*** (=***profound***) *meditation* 沈思黙考の後に. ¶a ***solitary*** *meditation* 独居めい想.

P He sat alone ***in*** *meditation*. 彼は独座めい想にふけった. ‖ be absorbed ***in*** *meditation* 思索にふけっている.

medium, *n.* 媒介物; 中間, 中庸.

V it ***constitutes*** a *medium* for an exchange of ideas by … …の意見交換の機関となっている. ¶The magazine serves to ***establish*** a *medium* of intercourse between the two peoples. その雑誌はその二国民の交際機関として役立つ. ¶***hit*** the happy *medium* うまく中庸を得る. ¶***strike*** the *medium* between two extremes 両極端の中間を取る.

Q Scott had little conception of language as an ***artistic*** *medium*. スコットは言語を芸術的媒介物としてはほとんど考えていなかった. 【類】Joseph Conrad, a Pole by birth, chose English as his ***artistic*** *medium*. ¶a ***circulating*** *medium*=a medium of circulation 通貨. ¶Mandarin is the ***colloquial*** *medium* of two-thirds of the Chinese people. 官話は中国人の三分の二の会話の用語になっている. ¶a ***common*** *medium* of communication 普通の交通機関. ¶a ***cultural*** *medium* 一つの文化機関. ¶The printed page is the ***great universal*** *medium* of information. 印刷物は一般的の大報道機関である. ¶strike the ***happy*** *medium* うまく中を取る. 【類】A ***happy*** *medium* is always best. ¶an ***international*** *medium* of communication 国際的交通機関. ¶the rival merits of the drama and the novel as ***literary*** *mediums* 文学的表現法として戯曲及び小説の相匹敵する長所.

Q^2 an ***advertising*** *medium* 広告機関. 【類】an effective ***advertising*** *medium* / a very expensive ***advertising*** *medium*. ¶an ***art*** *medium* 芸術家の表現仲介物. ¶a ***voting*** *medium* 票決手段.

P the English language ***as*** a *medium* of instruction 教授の用語としての英語. ¶***by*** (=***through***) the *medum* of … …の手を経て, …によって. ¶***through*** that *medium* その手段によって ‖ ***through*** *medium* of electricity 電気の力で ‖ ***through*** the *medium* of your columns 貴紙を通じて. 【類】***Through*** the *medium* of the Syrians Greek culture penetrated Persia. / ***through*** the *medium* of a forwarding agent (運送店) / All children like to express themselves ***through*** the *medium* of form and color.

P^2 the just *medium* ***between*** familiarity and austerity 心安だてと厳格との中庸. ¶a *medium* ***for*** (=of) advertising 一つの広告手段. 【類】the sandwich-board (背と腹に掛けた看板) as a *medium* ***for*** advertisement ‖ The air is a *medium* ***for*** sound. 空気は音の媒体である. ¶There is a *medium* ***in*** all things. 何ごとにも中庸ということがある. ¶a *medium* ***of*** publicity 宣伝機関 ‖ a *medium* ***of*** intercourse 交際機関 ‖ a *medium* ***of*** exchange 交易の媒介物.

medley, *n.* 雑集, ごもく.

Q Faces of every conceivable type pass you in ***bewildering*** *medley*. ありとあらゆる型の顔が目まぐるしいように雑然と前を通って行く. ¶an ***interesting*** *medley* (=miscellany) on Oriental subjects 東洋の諸題目に関する雑記.

P^2 a *medley* ***of*** contradictions 矛盾だらけ ‖ What a *medley* ***of*** races there is in New York! ニューヨークには何と色々な人種が集ってるんでしょう.

meed, *n.* 〘詩〙報酬, ほう賞.

V ***accord*** a person a great *meed* of praise … に大なる賞賛を与える. ¶His conduct ***deserves*** the full *meed* of praise. 彼の行動は十分賞賛に価する. ¶it would be unjust not to ***give*** due *meed* of praise to … …に報いるに賞賛をもってするのが当然でそうなければ不公平であろう ‖ ***give*** a *meed* of praise where praise is due 当然ほむべきものをほめる. ¶***lay*** our *meed* of profound sympathy at the feet of the widowed lady その未亡人に対してわれわれの深い同情を寄せる.

meet, *n.* 集合, (運動)競技会.

V Our school ***held*** a field (=an athletic) *meet* yesterday. きのう僕たちの学校に運動会があった.

Q an ***athletic*** *meet* 陸上競技会.

Q^2 manage a ***swimming*** *meet* 水泳会を開く. ¶a ***track and field*** *meet* 陸上競技大会.

meet, *v.* 会う, 出会う, 出迎える.

M ***accidentally*** *meet* 偶然に会う. ¶Let's *meet* ***again*** up there at Parkinson's. パーキンスン氏のお宅でもう一度会いましょう. ¶*meet* ***every other week*** 隔週に会う. ¶I *met* him ***face to face***. 私は彼と顔をつき合わした. ¶*meet* ***fortuitously*** ひょっくり出会う. ¶*meet* him ***half way*** 彼に譲歩する. ¶She *met* me ***joyfully***. 彼女は喜んで私を迎えた. ¶when we *met* ***last*** われわれがこの前会ったとき. ¶He will *meet* us ***later*** in the banquet. 彼はのちほど晩さん会の席で一緒になるだろう. ¶Such an article is ***rarely*** *met* with. そのような品は滅多にない. ¶*meet* ***squarely*** 堂々とこれに当る. ¶*meet* ***together*** at … …で会合する. ¶***Well*** *met*! ***Well*** *met*! Mr. … …さん, よい所でお会いしました.

M^2 *meet* ***up*** with … …と偶然に会う ‖ *meet* ***up*** face to face with … …とばったり出くわす.

P They did not *meet* ***as*** strangers. 彼らの会見はよそよそしくはなかった. ¶They *met* ***at*** New York in annual convention. その協会の会員は例年の会をニューヨークで開いた. 【類】they *met* ***at*** the residence of … ¶We were *met* ***by*** … at the station. われわれは駅で…の出迎えを受けた. ‖ We *met* together ***by*** accident (=chance). 僕たちは偶然会った. ‖ the method ***by*** which the situation can best be *met* その状況に最も適した方法 ‖ My offer was *met* ***by*** a flat refusal. 私の申出は断固拒絶された. ¶They *met* ***in*** consultation. 一同が相談会を開いた. ‖ They *met* ***in*** conference (=convention). 彼らは会議を開いた. ‖ *meet* ***in*** secret 秘密に会合する ‖ *meet* ***in*** (=***on***) the street 町で会う ‖ unfamiliar words *met* ***in*** one's reading 読書中に出会った未知の語. ¶I *met* her ***on*** the road. 私は路上で彼女に会った. ¶this belt won't *meet* ***round*** my waist. このバンドは私のウエストには合わない(短か過ぎる). ¶*meet* ***with*** … …の経験をする; 得る; 偶然出会う ‖ *meet* ***with*** their approbation of … 彼らから…の是認を得る ‖ *meet* ***with*** a polite but decided rebuff 丁重だが手ごわく断わられる ‖ The suggestion *met* ***with*** disfavor. その提議は否決された ‖ The change has *met* ***with*** general acceptance. その変更は一般に受けがよかった. 【類】The arrangements will not *meet* ***with*** approval. ‖ *meet* ***with*** little (no) opposition / *meet* ***with*** a reaction / *meet* ***with*** opposition from certain quarters / *meet* ***with*** a refusal (ひじ鉄砲) / *meet* ***with*** a reprisal (報復) / *meet* ***with*** universal sympathy / The attempt has *met* ***with*** scant (=little) success. / *meet* ***with*** more or less success / I hope it will *meet* ***with*** the success it so richly merits. / It will *meet* ***with*** the success your sincere efforts deserve. / So far their efforts have *met* ***with*** no tangible success (目に見えるほどの成功). / *meet* ***with*** a hearty welcome / *meet* ***with*** a splendid reception / *meet* ***with*** a misfortune / It *met* ***with*** a large sale. / The army *met* ***with*** a reverse. / The ship *met* ***with*** a mishap. ‖ This appeal *met* ***with*** a satisfying response. この哀訴は満足な応答に接した. ¶Similar efforts *met* ***with*** the same failure. 同じような努力をして同じような失敗をした. ‖ *meet* ***with*** destruction 亡びる ‖ *meet* ***with*** one's doom 運の尽きになる ‖ *meet* ***with*** the wishes of … …の望みに応じる ‖ *meet* ***with*** the support of … …の援助を受ける ‖ He *met* ***with*** a sensational death. 彼は人騒がせな死に方をした. ‖ he *met* ***with*** a violent death at the hands of … 彼は…の手で非業の最後を遂げた ‖ *meet* ***with*** gratifying result 満足な結果を見る. 【類】*meet* ***with*** a new experience ‖ *meet* ***with*** similar fate / In this I have never *met* ***with*** a failure. 【類】*meet* ***with*** a strange adventure (珍事) / *meet* ***with*** a street accident / She *met* ***with*** the wrong man (とんでもない者). 【類】at a considerable distance from where I *met* ***with*** him / Immediately on my return I shall *meet* ***with*** you to discuss the matter. ‖ words *met* ***with*** only in books 書物の上だけで見られる語 ‖ 'Onto' (as one word) is occasionally *met* ***with*** in print. 一語とした onto は印刷物にときどき見られる. ‖ *meet* force ***with*** force 腕力に報いるに腕力をもってする ‖ *met* ***with*** a very large sale 大量の販売ができた ‖ *meet* ***with*** marked hostility from … …からはっきり敵意を示される ‖ His like is rarely *met* ***with*** the wide world over. この広い世間でも彼みたいな人は滅多にない. 【類】Such a person is rarely to be *met* ***with*** today.

meeting, *n.* 会合, 会見; 会, 会議, 集会.

V *address* a *meeting* 会衆にあいさつする ‖ *address* public *meetings* 公開の席で演説する. ¶*adjourn* a *meeting* for 18 days 会を十八日間延期する. 【類】The *meeting* was *adjourned* to November 17. ¶*appoint* a *meeting* 面会日を指定する. ¶*arrange* a *meeting* with ... ...と会合を打合わせる. 【類】The *meeting* has been *arranged* for Thursday evening. ¶*attend* a *meeting* 会に出る. ¶The *meeting* was *broken up* by the sudden entrance of a mob. 暴民の乱入で会は散会した. ¶try to *bring* the *meeting* to a vote 票決の段取りにしようとする ‖ A vote of thanks to the lecturer *brought* the *meeting* to a close. 講演者に感謝の意を表しここにその会は閉会を告げた. ¶*call* a *meeting* 会を召集する. ‖ A *meeting* shall be *called* by the president twice a year. 会は年二回会長によって召集される. ‖ *call* a *meeting* of a committee 委員会を開く ‖ *call* a *meeting* to order 開会を宣言する. ¶*call for* a *meeting* 集会を要求する. ¶The *meeting* has been *changed* to Monday. その会は来週月曜日に変更された. ¶*close* a *meeting* 閉会する. ¶*conduct* a public *meeting* 公けの集会を主催する. ¶*convene* a *meeting* 集会を催す. ¶*convoke* an urgent *meeting* 緊急会議を召集する. ¶*disperse* a public *meeting* 集会を解散する. ¶we *had* a *meeting* with ... われわれは...と会合した ‖ We *had* a very crowded *meeting*. われわれの会は非常に盛会であった. ¶*hold* a *meeting* 会を催す. ¶A *meeting* was *given* in camera. 秘密会が開かれた. ¶the Chairman, in *opening* the *meeting*, stated that ... その会を開くに当って議長は...と述べた. ¶*organize* a *meeting* 会を組織する. ¶*preside over* a *meeting* 司会をする. ¶*proclaim* a *meeting*=name it as illegal 会合を違法と宣する. ¶*rally* a political mass *meeting* 《米》政治大会を開く. ¶A Cabinet *meeting* was *summoned*. 閣議が開かれた.

V² The *meeting* was *assembling*. その会は開催中であった. ¶when the *meeting broke up* 散会になったとき. ¶The *meeting came off* (=*took place*) yesterday. その会はきのう催された. ¶The *meeting consisted of* two morning sessions and one afternoon concert. その会は午前二度の会議と午後一度の音楽演奏から成っていた. ¶The *meeting fell through*. その会はお流れになった. ¶the *meeting opened* with an address of welcome by ... その会は...の歓迎の辞で始まった. ¶The *meeting terminated* at midnight. その会は夜半に終った.

Q our *accidental meeting* われわれの偶然の会合. ¶I intend to attend (=be present at) the *annual meeting*. 私は年次例会に出席するつもりです. ¶a largely *attended meeting* 出席者の多い会合. ¶a *commemoration meeting* 記念会. ¶at a *crowded meeting* of businessmen 実業家の大勢出席した会合で. ¶an *enthusiastic meeting* 熱心な集会. ¶*face-to-face friendly meetings* 顔つき合わせての親ぼく会. ¶the *first* and *subsequent meetings* 第一回及びそれ以後の会議. ¶the *following meeting* 次期会議. ¶a *fortuitous meeting* 偶然の会合. ¶call a *general meeting* of shareholders 株主総会を開く. 【類】an ordinary (=regular) *general meeting* / an extraordinary *general meeting*. ¶a *graduates' meeting* 同窓会. ¶a *great meeting* 大会. ¶a *huge* monster *meeting* [何万という]驚くべき多数の大会. ¶a *joint meeting* of Congress 《米》議会の両院合同協議会. ¶a *large meeting* 大会. ¶have a *merry meeting* 愉快な会合をやる ¶at the *monthly meeting* of ... ...の月次例会で. ¶a monster *native meeting* 地方民の大会. ¶in an *open meeting* 公開の会合で. ¶a *patriotic meeting* 愛国的会合. ¶address a *political meeting* 政治的会合で演説する. ¶a *regular meeting* 例会. ¶Postponement of the *scheduled meeting* brought veiled charges from the press of procrastination on the part of Britain. 予定会議延期に関し新聞は英国側が引き延しをしたのだという意味のえん曲な非難をした. ¶call a *special meeting* 臨時会を召集する. ¶a *stormy meeting* [政談演説会などの]騒々しい会合. ¶My best wishes for a *successful meeting*. 御盛会を祈る. ¶a *teetotal meeting* 酒抜きの会合. ¶a *vast public meeting* 民衆大会. ¶an exceedingly *well-attended meeting* きわめて出席良好な会合.

Q² an *ad hoc meeting* 特別会議. ¶an *alumni meeting* 同窓会. ¶an *American college prep meeting* before a football game しゅう球試合前の米予科生の会合. ¶a *Big-3 meeting* 三巨頭会談. ¶a *business meeting* 商談. ¶a *casual meeting* 偶然の会合. ¶a *chance meeting* 偶然の会合. ¶a *committee meeting* in camera 秘密委員会. ¶the report of a *company meeting* 会社会合の報告書. ¶a *council meeting* 協議会. ¶This is not to be a *dinner meeting*. 事務だけの会で食事はない. ¶an *emergency meeting* 非常集会. ¶a *faculty meeting* 教授会. ¶a *fellowship meeting* of students and faculty 教員生徒の懇親会. ¶a *Four-Power meeting* 四カ国会議. ¶a *graduates meeting* 卒業生の会合. ¶a public *indignation meeting* [政府・国策に対する]公憤大会, 国民総けっ起大会. ¶an admission-paid *lecture meeting* 有料講演会. ¶a *liaison meeting* 打合わせ会. ¶an unlawful *love meeting* 不義の密会. ¶hold a *luncheon meeting* 昼さん会を開く. ¶call a *mass meeting* 大会を招集する ‖ a *mass meeting* of medical practitioners 開業医大会. ¶a *membership meeting* 会員大会. 【類】call a full *membership meeting*. ¶a *monster meeting* 大会. ¶an *open-air meeting* 戸外の集会(青空大会). ¶hold its *opening meeting* その開会式を開く ‖ An *overflow meeting* was held. 満員のため入場できなかった者のために別に集会が開かれた. ¶a "*play*" *meeting* 余興の会. ¶a *propagandist meeting* 宣伝者たちの会合. ¶attend a *Saturday meeting* 土曜会に出る. ¶a *school meeting* 学校の会. ¶a *strike meeting* ストライキ会議. ¶hold a *three-day meeting* 三日間の連続会議を開く. ¶a *town meeting* 町の会合. ¶a routine *White House meeting* [米国の]定例閣議.

P The proceedings *at* a *meeting* are usually recorded. 会の議事々項は通例記録を取る. ‖ *at* (=in) the *meetings* of our English society われわれの英語会の会合で. ‖ Were you *at* the *meeting* last Sunday? この前の日曜日は会に出られましたか. ‖ *at* the *meeting* of two roads 交差路(追分け)で. ¶*before* a crowded *meeting* 大集会に臨んで ‖ a question *before* a *meeting* 会議に提出された問題. ¶take part *in* a *meeting* 会に出席する.

P² the *meeting between* ... and ... took place in ... ...間の会見は...に行われた. ¶address a *meeting of* one's constituents 彼の選挙区民にあいさつを述べる. ¶at the *meeting on* January 21, 1858 一八五八年一月二十一日の会で. ¶remember a *meeting with* a person 人との会見を想起する.

meeting-place, *n*. 会合所, 会合地.

P² Vienna is most interesting, perhaps, as the *meeting-place between* East and West. ウインナは東西両洋間の会合地として恐らく最も興味ある所であろう.

meeting-point, *n*. 会合点.

P² a *meeting-point of* two civilizations—Oriental and Occidental 東西両文明の会合点.

megaphone, *n*. 伝声管, メガホン.

V *put* the *megaphone* to his mouth 彼の口にメガホンを当てる.

Q² a *conch megaphone* ほら貝.

P give instructions *through* the *megaphone* メガホンを通じて指令する.

melancholy, *n*. 気うつ, 憂うつ.

V *dissipate melancholy* うさを晴らす.

Q a *morbid melancholy* seizes me on reading ... 僕は...を読むと病的な憂うつにかかる. ¶*sweet poetic melancholy* 美しい詩的憂愁.

P² There is some *melancholy in* his mirth. 彼の笑いには「何か暗い影がある.

mellowness, *n*. 軟熟; 耳ざわりのよいこと.

V *give* a *mellowness* to sound 音声に軟か味を与える.

Q *smooth mellowness* 芳じゅん.

melody, *n*. 旋律, 節, かい調.

V The sun *kindled* all the *melodies* and harmonies of light on the mountain top. 太陽が出て山頂のあらゆる種類あらゆるかい調の光にぱっと点火した. ¶The ballad singer *made* a doleful *melody*. その俗謡歌手は調子のよい悲しい音を出した.

Q, Q² a *harmonized melody* かい調の曲. ¶*popular Negro melodies* 流行の黒人歌. ¶a *sacred melody* 神聖な旋律.

melon, *n*. まくわうり, メロン.

V *cut* a *melon* 《俗》利益を配分する.

Q² a *honeydew melon* 甘露メロン.

P eat a piece *of melon* 一片のメロンを食べる.

melt, *v*. とける, とかす, 融解する, 心がとろける, 消える.

M The crowd *melted away*. 群衆が漸次消え去った. ‖ My, your story really *melts away* my soul. まあ, あんたのお話には本当に感激するわ. 【類】The snow soon *melted away* when the sun came out. ¶The mist *melted rapidly* in the morning sun. 霧は朝日を受けてたちまち消えた.

M² *melt down* metal 金属を溶かす. ¶The ice of the lake *melted off*. 湖水の氷は溶けた. ¶*melt up* metal scrap《米》くず金属を溶解する.

P Glass *melts at* a great heat. ガラスは高熱でとける. ¶Houses *melted before* the flames. 幾多の建物がめらめらと火炎になめられた. ¶Lead *melts* in the fire. 鉛は火中でとける. 【類】The snow *melts in* the sun. / *melt in* the haze / Sugar *melts in* tea. ¶*melt into* tears 心和らいで涙を催す ‖ *melt* a statue *into* cannon 銅像をとかして大砲を鋳る ‖ *melt into* insignificance 世間から忘れられる ‖ be *melted into* sympathy 同情に変る. ¶Ice *melts with* heat. ⌊氷は熱で溶ける.

member, *n.* 会員, 議員.

V The society *claims* 2,000 *members*. その協会は会員二千を数えている. ¶The committee *comprises* five *members*. 同委員会は五人の委員から成っている. ¶*draw* its *members* mainly from the ranks of ... その会員を主として...の間から集める. ¶The society *enrolls* 250,000 *members*. その会は二十五万の会員を持っている. ¶*gather* its *members* together at a festive annual dinner 毎年の祝宴にその会員を集合する. ¶"*hammer*" a *member* [株式取引所で]所員を失格者と宣言する. ¶The association *has* 700 *members* (=a membership of 700). 同会には七百人の会員がある. ¶It now *numbers* many thousands of *members*. 会員は現在幾千という数を示す. ¶*post members* 会員の名を掲示する. ¶*reinstate* a *member* 会員に復する. ¶The county *returns* three *members* to the House of Commons. その県から三人の国会議員を出す.

Q an *accredited member* 信任状所有会員. ¶an *annual member* 一年会員. ¶an *associate member* 組合会員. ¶an *assured member* 生命保険に加入した人. ¶a *burdensome member* of the community 社会の厄介者. ¶the *chief member* of the commission 委員長. ¶*co-opted members* 互選会員. ¶a hightly *esteemed member* of a society 非常に尊敬を受けている会員. ¶the *feathered members* of the collection その収集物中の鳥類. ¶the *female* (*male*) *members* of a family (party) 一家(など)の女(男)たち. ¶The book is the *final member* of the series. その本は同双書中最後のものである. ¶The captain is the *first member* of a ship's crew. 船長は船員の長である. ¶*hard-up members* of the aristocracy 貧困貴族. ¶an *honorary member* 名誉会員. ¶*illustrious members* of this school この派の幹部. ¶a *junior member* 少年会員. ¶a great number of the *leading members* of the European and other communities ヨーロッパ及びその他の団体の主なる大勢の人々. 【類】*leading members* of the profession. ¶She is expecting the arrival of a *new member* of her family. 赤ん坊が産れる. ¶a *non-regular member* of the staff 嘱託. ¶a *non-resident member* of the community その地のとう留客. ¶500-*odd membbers* 五百有余の会員. ¶the *older members* of a family 家族中の年長者たち. ¶*parliamentary members*《英》国会議員. ¶*prescribed members* 規定の会員. ¶a *prominent members* 有名な会員. ¶A gardener is a *regular member* of the crew. その乗組員の中にはきまって園丁が一人いる. ‖ the *regular members* of the dictionary staff 辞書編集部員. ¶the *representative member* of a company 会社の代表社員. ¶the less *reputable* and *responsible members* of the business community 商業界で評判のよくない無責任な店. ¶*resident members* of the community その土地に住んでいる人々. ¶a *respectable member* of society 真人間. ¶*respected* and *honored members* of society りっぱな人物. ¶the *second member* of the triangle 三角関係の第二者. ¶make him into a *self-supporting member* of society 彼を社会の自活者にさせる. ¶*sustaining members* 維持会員, 賛助員. ¶a *useful member* of society 社会の有用な一人. ¶one of the most *useful* and *respected members* of the community その社会の最も有用にして尊敬されている人々の一人. ¶*valued members* of the Japan Society 日本協会の重立った人々. ¶*well-to-do* and *respected members* of society 裕福で尊敬されている人々. ¶transform criminals into *worthy members* of society 罪人をりっぱな人に改造する.

Q² an *armed service member* 軍人. ¶a *Cabinet member* in Mr. Asquith's Administration アスキス内閣の閣員. ¶a *charter member* 設立会員(法人団体の). ¶a *church member* 教会員. ¶a *class member* クラス員. ¶*coal-miner members* of the United Mine Workers of America 全米炭鉱夫組合所属の炭鉱夫たち. ¶a *commission member* 委員. ¶a *Communist party member* 共産党員. ¶a class *committee member* クラス委員. ¶a *Congress member*=Congressman《米》下院議員. ☞米では上院議員は Senators. ¶a *country member* 地方会員. ¶*country* and *town members* 地方及び町村役員. ¶*crew members* 乗組員. ¶*Diet members*=Dietmen 国会議員. 【類】women *Diet members* =Dietwomen ‖ a *Diet lower member* 下院議員. ¶a full time *faculty member*《米》専任教職員. 【類】*faculty members* usually retire at 65. ¶the *family members* of Mr. D.D 氏の家族たち. ¶a *fire-brigade member* 消防隊員. ¶a *fraternity* (=*frat*) *member*《米》男子学生友愛会員. ☞ fraternity はその会員の資格審査がやかましく, 学生は frat member になることを誇りとしている. 女子会員は a sorority sis (=member). ¶a *House Steering Committee Member*《米》下院運営委員会. ☞米国では the House は下院, 上院は the Senate. ¶a *household member* of ... ...家の一人. ¶a British *Labor Member* of Parliament 英議会の労働党議員. ¶*left-wing members* of the government 政府の左派に属する人々. ¶a *life member* of the Red Cross Society 赤十字社の終身会員. ¶a *Lower House member* 下院議員. ¶a non-regular *staff member* 嘱託. ¶a *party member* 党員. ¶*rank-and-file members* 平の会員, 陣がさ連. ¶a *Socialist member* 社会党員. ¶a debating *society member* 討論会の一員. ¶*school board members* 地方教育局委員. ¶a *staff member* of a business company (the Times) 会社(など)の正社員. 【類】a former *staff member* of the Toa Shimbun / *staff members* of a leading museum ‖ a union *staff member* 労組役員. ¶a *star member* of a troupe (circus) [サーカス]一座の花形. ¶a former *teaching member* of the faculty 前教諭. ¶a *team member*=a teammate 〖競技〗チーム・メンバー. ¶a *United Nations member* 国際連合加盟国. 【類】The General Assembly admitted 16 nations as new *U.N.* (=United Nations) *members*. ¶a *veteran member* of the Tokyo bar 東京弁護士会の古参会員.

P be accepted *as* a regular *member* of ... ...の正会員と認められる. 【類】*as* a *member* of the family of free nations (自由国家群).

P² a respectable, if not very respected, *member of* a community ある社会での, 尊敬されないまでもしっかりした一員 ‖ a *member of* a music society 音楽部員 ‖ a *member of* the cast 配役の一人 ‖ become a *member of* ... ...の会員になる. 【類】*members of* her household. ¶Japan is a *member to* the Postal Union. 日本は万国郵便連合加盟国である.

membership, *n.* 会員の資格, 会員たること; 会員全体.

V *ask membership* in a party 入党を申出る. ¶Bishops, Cabinet Ministers, and judges are entitled to *claim membership* of the Athenaeum as a matter of right. 僧正・内閣々僚・判事は当然の権利としてアテネウムの会員たる資格がある. ¶*compose* its *membership* その会員を構成する. ¶honorary *membership* will be *conferred* upon ... 名誉会員の資格が...に与えられる. ¶*desire membership* in a society ある会に入会を望む. ¶with a *membership drawn* from all parts of the country その国の各方面から選んだ会員があって. ¶*forfeit* (=*lose*) one's *membership* 会員として失格する. ¶it *has* a *membership* of over ... それには...人以上の会員がある. 【類】An urban church (都市の教会), *having* a *membership* of three hundred and fifty, pays its pastor a salary of one thousand dollars a year. ¶*hold membership* in a club あるクラブの会員となっている. ¶*increase* the *membership* of the Association 同協会の会員を増加する. ¶The *membership* is *limited* to 2,000. 会員数は二千人に制限してある. ¶they are planning to *obtain* a *membership* of ... ...人の会員を得ようと計画している. ¶*possess* a *membership* exceeding ... ...人以上の会員を有する. ¶*renew* one's *membership* in a society ある会の会員資格を復活する. ¶*resign* one's *membership* 退会する. ¶*seek membership* in the United Nations 国連に加入を求める.

V² The *membership amounted* altogether to nearly 400 persons, belonging to 23 nations. 会員数は二十三カ国にわたり全部で約四百人を数えた. ¶the *membership* of the society *numbers* ... その会の会員は...人ある. ¶The present *membership* of club *totals* 80. その会の会員現在数は総

計八十人である.

Q retire from ***active membership*** of the Academy 学士院の現役会員を辞する. ¶possess a very ***considerable membership*** 非常に多数の会員を有する. ¶***efficient membership*** in a community ある団体における有力な人々. ¶the ***entire membership*** of the Council 参事会の全会員. ¶admit a person to ***full membership*** ...を正式会員と認める. ¶***honorary membership*** is open to ... ...は名誉会員たることを得る. ¶The League has now a ***large*** and ***increasing membership***. 連盟の加盟国は多数でかつ漸次増加しつつある. ¶a small bibliographical society with a strictly ***limited membership*** 厳重に制限した会員を有する小さな書誌学会. ¶be elected to ***non-permanent membership*** 有期会員に選出される. ¶The ***original membership*** was 112. 創立当時会員数は百十二人であった. ¶***partial membership*** 準会員資格. ¶seek a ***wide membership*** among the nation 広く会員を募る.

Q² ***Class membership*** is limited to from 12 to 15. クラス総員は十二名から十五名に限られている. ¶be granted an honorary ***life membership*** 名誉終身会員の資格を与えられる. ¶an ***organized union membership*** 組織労組の組合員. ¶the ***rank and file membership*** of a party 平党員. ¶apply for ***U.N. membership*** 国連加盟を申込む.

P there are ***among*** its ***membership*** ... ...がその会員になっている. ¶apply ***for membership*** in the ... Academy ...会の会員を申込む. ¶Starting ***with*** a ***membership*** of 50, it has now no less than 727. それは始めは会員数五十名であったが目下七百二十七名となっている.

P² advantages of ***membership in*** the Nippon Automobile Club 日本自動車クラブの会員の特典.【類】***Membership in*** the club is open to men and women of all nationalities / He was dismissed from ***membership in*** the organization. ¶***Membership of*** the Society is open to all who are in sympathy with its aims. 同会々員たるの資格はその目的に共鳴する人にはだれでも与えられる. ¶***membership on*** an entertainment committee 余興委員たち.

memento, *n.* かたみ, 記念物.

V ***destroy*** the ***mementoes*** of the old love 昔の恋のかたみを破棄する. ¶***form*** most artistic ***mementoes*** of ... ...の非常に芸術的な記念物となっている.

Q ***interesting mementoes*** of ... ...の興味ある記念物. ¶a very ***suitable memento*** はなはだ適切な記念物.

P built ***as*** a ***memento*** of a person ある人の記念として建造した ‖ ***as mementoes*** of the occasion その折の記念に ‖ ***as*** a ***memento*** of those happy days spent together 一緒に暮した当時の思い出に.

memo, *n.* 覚え(メモ).

V ***make*** a ***memo*** in one's date-book メモに記入する.

memoir, *n.* 言行録, 回想録, 実録; 論文.

V ***publish memoirs*** on the subject of his investigation 彼が調査した問題の研究報告を発表する.

Q write a ***complete historical memoir*** on ...についてまとまった歴史上の論文を書く. ¶a ***secret memoir*** 秘録.

Q² ***war memoirs*** 戦争記録.

P in his ***memoir on*** Lowell 彼のローウェル回想録の中に.

memorandum, *n.* 備忘録, 覚書(メモ).

V ***make memoranda*** of newly-acquired English words 新しく修得した英語の備忘録を作る ‖ ***make*** notes and ***memoranda*** 注や覚え書を作る.

Q Under ***Administrative Memorandum*** No. 41 政府覚書第四十一号によって. ¶***penciled memoranda*** 鉛筆で書いた覚書.

Q² He was purged by ***SCAP memorandum*** No. 15. 彼は連合軍総司令官覚書十五号によって追放された.

P ***as*** a ***memorandum*** of it その覚書として. ¶noted ***on*** a ***memorandum*** 備忘録に記した.

P² A ***memorandum on*** the subject has been submitted to the Minister of Education. その問題に関する覚書が文部大臣に提出された. ‖ a ***memorandum on*** currency 通貨に関する参考覚書.

memorial, *n.* 建白書, 請願書; 記念物, 記念碑.

V ***address*** a ***memorial*** to the legislature 立法府に建白書を出す. ¶***erect*** a ***memorial*** to (=in honor of) ... のために記念碑を建てる. ¶***establish*** some fitting ***memorial*** for ... ...のために何か適切な記念物を設立する. ¶***forward*** a ***memorial***, to which ... signatures are attached, to ... ...人の署名を付した建白書を...に出す. ¶***raise*** a ***memorial*** to the late ... 故...の記念碑を建てる. ¶***sign*** a ***memorial*** 建白書に署名する. ¶***unveil*** a ***memorial*** to ... ...記念碑の除幕式を行う.

Q an exhibition of ***interesting memorials*** 興味ある記念物の展覧会. ¶a ***lasting memorial*** to the genius of ... ...の天才を永遠に記念するもの. ¶a ***national memorial*** to ... ...に寄せた国家の記念物. ¶The relics of Rome dot the landscapes of Europe, a ***perpetual memorial*** of that mighty empire. ローマの遺跡がヨーロッパの所々に点在してその大帝国の名残を永遠に留めている. ¶a ***proper*** and ***fitting memorial*** 相当で適切な記念品. ¶a ***standing memorial*** to ... ...を絶えず記念する物. ¶erect a ***suitable memorial*** 適切な記念物を建てる.

Q² a ***parting memorial*** 別れの記念品. ¶The arch was erected as a ***war memorial***. そのアーチは戦争記念に建設されたものであった.

P the college was founded ***as*** a ***memorial*** of ... その大学は...の記念に設立したものだ. ¶***for*** a ***memorial*** 記念のため.

P² as a thank-offering and ***memorial of*** the victory 戦勝の感謝と記念に.【類】This sixth volume of the N.E.D. is a ***memorial of*** the munificence of the worshipful Company of Goldsmiths who have generously contributed five thousand pounds towards its production. ¶as a ***memorial to*** the name and fame of Shakespeare シェークスピアの名声の記念として.【類】as a ***memorial to*** his father / as a ***memorial to*** the seamen who lost their lives during the war.

memoria, *n.* 記念.

P ***In Memoriam***. 亡き人の記念に(墓碑または死亡者の小伝などの見出し).

memorization, *n.* 記憶.

O ***imperfect memorization***, resulting in hesitancy, confusion, etc. ためらい・ろうばいなどに終る不完全な記憶.

memorize, *v.* 記憶する.

M ***carefully memorize*** ... よく...を記憶する. ¶***memorize*** ... ***word by word*** ...を一語一語記憶する.

memory, *n.* 記憶, 記憶力, 追想, 回想; 遺名, 霊.

V ***aid*** the ***memory*** 記憶を助ける. ¶***arouse*** his dormant ***memory*** 彼の潜在記憶を呼び起す. ¶***assist*** the ***memory*** 記憶を助ける. ¶***awaken memories*** in the minds of those who ... ...した人々の心に記憶を呼び起す ‖ ***awaken*** happy ***memories*** 楽しい記憶を呼び起す ‖ ***awaken*** many far back ***memories*** 古い記憶の数々を呼び起す. ¶I must always ***bless*** his ***memory***. 私はいつも彼のめい福を祈らなければならない. ¶***bring back memories*** of the days when ... ...の当時を回想する ‖ ***bring back*** many cherished ***memories*** to "old timers" 古くから住んでいるものに昔恋しいという色色な感じを呼び起す ‖ ***bring back*** the ***memory*** of persons, places, or events that happened long ago 人や場所や久しい以前に起った事件を回顧する. ¶Of all the senses that of smell has the most power of ***calling up*** ancient ***memories***. 五感の中で嗅覚が昔の記憶を呼び起す一番強い力を持っている. ¶visitors to ... ***carry away*** pleasant ***memories*** of ... ...を訪れる人は...の愉快な思出をみやげにして帰る. ¶***carry*** the ***memory back*** to the palmy days of ... ...の得意の時代を回顧する. ¶***celebrate*** the ***memory*** of ... = memorize ... 《米》 ...を記念する. ¶all who ***cherish*** his ***memory*** 彼の遺名を慕う人は皆 ‖ ***cherish*** the ***memory*** of ... in the highest esteem (=respect) ...の遺名をこの上なく慕う ‖ The ***memory*** of the late ... is still ***cherished*** in many hearts. 故...の思い出はいまだに多くの人々の心に深く秘められている. ¶though age has ***clouded*** his ***memory*** 年老いて彼の記憶はおぼろげになったが. ¶***conjure up memories*** of ... ...をしのばせる. ¶***cram*** the ***memory*** with facts 事実を頭に詰め込む. ¶***cultivate*** the ***memory*** of him whom she loved heartily 彼女が心から愛した男を追憶する ‖ ***cultivate*** a good ***memory*** 記憶力を養う. ¶***defame*** the ***memory*** of a deceased person 故人の遺名を汚す. ¶***develop*** (=cultivate) one's ***memory*** 記憶を良くする ‖ ***develop*** a strong ***memory*** 強健な記憶力を養う. ¶Age ***dims*** one's ***memory***. 年を取ると記憶力が鈍る. ¶***discipline*** the ***memory*** 記憶力を鍛る. ¶***drive away*** all unpleasant ***memories*** あらゆる不愉快な記憶を消失させる. ¶This ***endears*** her ***memory*** in the hearts of English-speaking peoples. このために英語を話す国民(英米など)は心に彼女の思出をいとしく思う. ¶The ***memory*** is ***enshrined*** in many hearts. その思出は幾多の人々の心に秘められている. ¶It entirely ***escaped*** my *memory*. それを私はすっかり忘れていた. ¶***exercise*** one's *memory* 記憶力を錬磨する. ¶***fill up*** (=***stimulate***) one's *memory* その記憶を促す. ¶***freshen*** one's *memory* as to ... ...について人の記憶を新たにする. ¶The book ***gives*** us some *memories* of youth. その本に彼の若いころの思い出がのせてある. ¶a scene that ***haunts*** the *memory* しばしば記憶によみがえる光景. ¶***help*** the *memory* 記憶を助ける. ¶***hold*** the *memory* of ... in grateful remembrance ...に対して謝恩の念をいだく ‖ I ***hold*** his *memory* ***dear***. 私は彼の思出を大事なものにしている.【類】his *memory* is ***held*** in high esteem by ... ¶***honor*** the *memory* of Nelson ネルソンを追慕する ‖ visit the grave to ***honor*** the *memory* of ... ...の墓にもうでる ‖ it has been so named to ***honor*** the *memory* of ... ...を記念するためにその名を付けた.【類】***honor*** the *memory* of ... and his work for education by a memorial banquet / The *memory* of ... has been ***honored*** by a bronze memorial tablet. (青銅の記念はい). / This is not the greatest reason for our ***honoring*** Spenser's *memory*. ¶***impair*** one's *memory* 記憶力を衰退させる. ¶***impress*** our *memory* われわれの記憶に銘する. ¶***improve*** one's *memory* 記憶をよくする. ¶***jog*** the *memory* 記憶を呼び起す. ¶***keep*** the *memory* 記憶を持続する.【類】His generosity, without his genius, is sufficient to ***keep*** his *memory* green. ¶The trip has ***left*** such haunting *memories* of the good times that I never get over longing to go back again. その旅行は楽しく日を送った忘れ難い記憶を残したので私はもう一度行って見たくてたまらない. ¶***lessen*** the *memory* 記憶を減退させる. ¶***lose*** one's *memory* 記憶力を失う. ¶***overburden*** the *memory* 記憶力を過重に使う. ¶to ... I ***owe*** a happy *memory* of discussions bearing upon this book この本に関して議論した楽しい思出が私にあるのは...のお陰である. ¶The fierceness of the storm ***passed*** all *memory*. その暴風はだれの記憶にもないほど猛烈なものであった. ¶***perpetuate*** the *memory* of ... ...の思出を永久に伝える. ¶***plead*** a poor *memory* 記憶が悪いのを口実にする. ¶The ruins of Port Zelandia in Tainan ***preserves*** the *memory* of Dutch rule in Formosa. 台南のゼランデイア城あとは台湾におけるオランダ人の支配をしのばせる. ‖ I ***preserve*** no *memory* of the dream. 私はその夢は覚えていない.【類】***preserve*** a very vivid *memory* of the things one saw. ¶It ***recalls*** the *memory* of days now irretrievably past. それを見ると今は帰らない昔の思出を心に呼び戻す. ‖ No one can doubt the power of scents to ***recall memories*** of the past. 香料に過去の思出を呼び起す力のあることを何人も疑わない. ¶***refresh*** one's *memory* as to ... ...について記憶を新たにする ‖ ***refresh*** historic *memories* 昔をしのぶ. ¶***respect*** his *memory* 彼を追慕する. ¶***resurrect*** the *memory* of the past 過去の記憶をよみがえらす. ¶The old woman ***retains*** her keen *memory* of early events. そのお婆さんは若い時代のことをよく覚えている. ¶***revere*** the *memory* of ... ...を追慕する.【類】They ***revere*** the *memory* of their ancestors. ¶***revive*** the fragrant *memories* of Florence Nightingale フローレンス・ナイチンゲールの遺烈を忍ぶ. ¶***run*** our *memory* ***back*** over the pages of history 過去の歴史にさかのぼる. ¶His name has ***slipped*** my *memory*. 彼の名を私は失念した. ¶***strengthen*** the *memory* by special exercises for the purpose of ... ...のため特殊の練習で記憶力を強健にする. ¶severely ***tax*** the *memory* 記憶力を激しく使う. ¶a specialist in the art of ***training*** the *memory* 記憶術の専門家. ¶***treasure*** its *memory* その思出を大事に胸にしまっておく. ¶***trust*** our *memories* われわれの記憶を信頼する. ¶You ***wake*** the *memory* in me. 君にそう言われたので僕は思い出した. ¶Some enduring monument should be erected to ***wake*** the *memory* of this great man. この偉人をしのぶために永久的な記念碑を建設すべきだ.

V² Around it many happy *memories* ***cluster***. それには色色楽しい昔の思い出がまつわっている. ¶names that *memory* ***conjures up*** 思出に浮ぶ名前. ¶His *memory* is steadily ***declining***. 彼は段々記憶力が衰える. ¶*Memories* ***die out***. 記憶がうせる. ¶My *memory* is ***failing***. 私は記憶が段々悪くなる. ¶*Memory* is ***gone*** and cannot recollect it in the least. 記憶がうせてそのことは少しも思い出せない. ¶His *memory* ***played*** him false here. 彼はこの点で記憶違いをしていた. ¶*Memories* of ... ***return*** to me. ...の思い出が私によみがえる. ¶if my *memory* ***serves*** me aright=if I remember rightly 私の記憶に誤りがなければ.

Q in ***affectionate*** (=loving) *memory* of ... 愛する...の追憶に. ¶the ***auditive*** *memory* of musicians 音楽家の聴覚の記憶. ¶Most pepole confess to a ***bad*** *memory*. 大体の人は記憶の悪いことをこぼす. ¶a ***bitter-sweet*** *memory* にがくて甘い思い出. ¶***black*** *memories* of the days when ... ...時代の暗たんたる思い出. ¶The following pictures may bring back many ***cherished*** *memories* to "old timers." 次に掲げた写真は古い在住者にはなつかしい思い出の数々を呼び起すことであろう.【類】The kind and pleasant treatment given to me while there will always remain a ***cherished*** *memory* with me. ¶I have a ***clear*** *memory* of the dream. 私はその夢をはっきり覚えている. ¶a ***confused*** *memory* of ... ...のめちゃめちゃな記憶. ¶have a ***decent*** *memory* 相当よい記憶力を持っている. ¶a ***defective*** *memory* 不完全な記憶力. ¶It will ever remain a ***delightful*** *memory*. それはいつも愉快な記憶として残るであろう. ¶It seems already a ***distant*** *memory*. それはもはや遠い昔のことのように思われる. ¶awaken many ***far-back*** *memories* 色々昔の記憶を呼び起す. ¶It will always remain with me a ***fond*** *memory*. それはいつも楽しい思い出として私の心に残るでしょう. ¶***fugitive*** *memories* わずかに記憶に残るもの. ¶I have a ***good*** (=retentive) *memory*, so I learn much more quickly than other people. 僕は物覚えが良いから他の人より余ほど早く覚える. ‖ be born with a ***good*** *memory* 生れつき記憶がよい. ¶He has a ***good auditory*** *memory*. 彼は聞き覚えがよい. ¶a ***good old*** *memory* 昔なつかしい思い出. ¶His name will live long in the ***grateful*** *memories* of their future countrymen. 将来その同国人は深く彼に感謝し長くその名を忘れないであろう. ¶His *memory* is still ***green*** (=***fresh***) in the hearts of his friends. 彼の思い出は彼の友だちの心に今なお新しい. ¶a place fraught with ***hallowed*** *memories* 聖なる思出の多い場所. ¶It yields ***interesting*** *memories* for after days それは楽しい後の思い出になる. ¶within ***living*** *memory* 生きている人(われわれ)の記憶にある. ¶It is the gift of Harrison D. McFaddin "94" in ***loving*** *memory* of his parents. それは一八九四年卒業ハリソン・ディー・マクファデン氏が両親の記念に寄付したもの. ¶a ***marvelous*** *memory* 驚異的な記憶力. ¶revive ***old*** *memories* 古い記憶をよみがえらす. ¶have a ***pleasant*** *memory* of ... ...の愉快な思出がある.【類】His eventful past is a storehouse of ***pleasant*** *memories* which so much enrich his days of humdrum routine (単調な生活). ¶have a ***poor*** *memory* 記憶が悪い. ¶a ***powerful*** *memory* for 強大の記憶力. ¶he has a ***prodigious*** *memory* for ... 彼は...に対してすばらしく記憶がよい. ¶He has a ***proud*** *memory* of a visit paid to him by the late King Edward. 彼には故エドワード皇帝が御臨幸になったという誇らしい思出がある. ¶a person of ***quick*** *memory* 覚えの早い人. ¶***resurgent*** *memory* よみがえる記憶. ¶a man of wide reading and a ***retentive*** *memory* 博覧強記の人.【類】a remarkably ***retentive*** *memory*. ¶His *memory* will be ***sacred*** to us as that of a scholar of high ideals, a teacher of great merits, and a genial friend. 故人は理想の高い学者, 力量のある教師, そして快心の友として世人から敬慕されるだろう. ¶have a ***short*** (***long***) *memory* 忘れっぽい(仲々忘れない)人 ‖ a long tongue and a ***short*** *memory* 長広舌と弱い記憶力.【類】All advertisers are well aware of the ***short*** *memory* of the public. ¶a name of ***sinister*** *memory* to ... ...に取って縁起の悪い思い出の名. ¶a ***sound*** *memory* しっかりした記憶力. ¶You have a ***splendid*** *memory*. 君の記憶力はすてきだ. ¶have a ***strong*** (***weak***) *memory* 記憶がたしかだ(弱い). ¶It has a ***tenacious*** *memory* for persons. 彼は人のことをよく覚えている. ¶a ***treacherous*** *memory* あてにならない記憶. ¶dates of ***uncertain*** *memory* 記憶の不確実な年代.【類】he has a very ***uncertain*** *memory* for ... ¶It is among my ***unforgettable*** *memories*. それは私にとって忘れることのできないものの一つだ. ¶an ***unreliable*** *memory* 当にならない記憶. ¶the ***visual*** *memory* of painters [風景・人物など]画家の目の記憶. ¶He has ***vivid*** *memories* of the man. 彼はその人をはっきり覚えている. ¶Her *memory* is ***unimpaired***. 彼女の記憶は衰えていない. ¶have ***vivid*** *memories* of ... ...をはっきり覚えている. ¶a ***wandering*** *memory* 確実性を欠く記憶.

Q² learn by ***ear*** *memory* 聞いただけで覚える.

P Past events sweep ***across*** one's *memory*. 過去のできごとがそれからそれと記憶に浮ぶ. ¶It is ***beyond*** my *mem-*

ory. それは私には覚え切れない. ‖ It is ***beyond*** the *memory* of man. それは人間の記憶を絶した(遠い昔の)ことである. ¶repeat it ***from memory*** 暗誦する ‖ drop (=fade *or* slip) ***from memory*** 忘れられる. 【類】die away ***from*** the *memory* of the world / a sketch redrawn and perfected ***from memory*** / make a speech ***from memory*** (原稿なしで). ¶***in memory*** of the men who offered their lives in defense of their country 国家のために生命を捧げた人々を記念するために. 【類】a poem composed ***in memory*** of his friend ... ‖ his name will live ***in*** the *memory* of ... 彼の名は...の記憶に生きるであろう ‖ a school founded ***in memory*** of ... ...の記念のために設立した学校. 【類】Her look at that time lives ***in*** my *memory*. / It may live ***in*** the *memory* for lifetime. / This visit will always remain ***in*** my *memory*. / an experience salient ***in*** my *memory* / still fresh ***in*** our *memories*. / Her name is held ***in*** loving *memory* all through China. ¶photograph it indelibly ***on*** one's *memory* それをその記憶に深く銘じる ‖ engrave ***on*** one's *memory* その記憶に刻みつける. ¶He is only a *memory* ***to*** me now. その人は今はない. ¶a banquet ***to*** the *memory* of ... 故...記念の晩さん会. 【類】a monument erected ***to*** the *memory* of ... ‖ It has stuck ***to*** my *memory*. それは私の記憶に焼付けられた. ‖ the shrine is sacred ***to*** the *memory* of ... その社は...の霊に捧げたものだ. ¶to impress itself ***upon*** the *memory* of ... ...の記憶にはっきり残るように. ¶***with*** the *memory* of ... fresh upon him 彼の心に新しい...の思い出を持って. ¶It is well ***within*** the *memory* of old men living today. 今日存命の老人は十分それを記憶している[あまり昔のことでない]. ‖ time was—and that ***within*** recent *memory*—when ... 以前—しかも余り遠くない以前に... 【類】***within*** the *memory* of men still living=within living memory / ***within*** the *memory* of men still active in business / ***within*** the *memory* of man.

P² I have a good *memory* ***for*** faces. 私は人の顔をよく記憶する. ¶We are a people of short *memories* ***in*** some things. われわれはあることに関しては忘れっぽい国民である. ¶a *memory* ***of*** my boyhood 私の少年時代の思い出. 【類】It brought back to him *memories* ***of*** the days fifty years ago. / The *memory* ***of*** those happy days is still vivid to me. / The *memory* ***of*** the insult rankled in his mind. / It will soon be a *memory* ***of*** the past. / *memory* ***of*** our friendship.

menace, *n*. 脅迫, 威かく.

V become a *menace* ***to*** the countries in Asia アジアの脅威となる. ¶It ***constiutes*** a standing (=constant) *menace* to the peace of the world. それは世界の平和に対する不断の脅威である. ‖ It ***constitutes*** a *menace* to her existence. それはその国の存立に対する脅威となる. ¶It looks as if man is at last in a position to ***defeat*** the *menace* of malaria. 人間がマラリアの恐怖から遂にのがれたらしい(特効ある新薬が出てきたので). ¶***put*** one's *menace* into execution 脅迫を実行する. ¶The symptoms which he presents ***render*** him a *menace* to himself, to others, or to the public peace. 彼が示す(精神病的などの)症状は彼自身に取っても他人に取ってもまた公安に取っても危険なものである.

Q a ***brown*** *menace* 黒人禍. ☞ a yellow peril 黄人禍. ¶Fire is an ***ever-threatening*** *menace* to his business. 火災は彼の事業における不断の脅威である. ¶a ***grave menace*** to ... ...に取って重大なる脅威. ¶He considers the unregulated birth-rate the ***greatest*** *menace* of civilization. 彼は産児不調節は文化の最大脅威であると考えている. ¶a ***growing*** *menace* to ... ...に取って益々加重する脅威. ¶a ***national*** *menace* 害を国民に及ぼすおそれあるもの. ¶a ***positive*** *menace* to the safety of the nation 国家の安全にとって明かな脅威. ¶a ***potential*** *menace* to life ありうべき生命への危険. ¶a ***remote*** *menace* to ... 行く行くは...に取って危険となるもの. ¶It will become a ***serious*** *menace* to the safety and integrity of the Empire. それは帝国の安全と保全とに取って重大な脅威になるであろう. ‖ a ***serious*** *menace* to the health of the community その団体の衛生に取って由々しい脅威. ¶a ***skilful legal*** *menace* to society 巧みに法網をくぐる悪漢の社会に与える脅威. ¶an ***unmeaning*** *menace* 知らずに行う脅迫.

Q² the ***Red*** *menace* 赤の恐怖.

P They were forced, ***under*** *menace*, to this act. 彼らは脅迫されて余儀なくそうした. ‖ live ***under*** a constant *menace* of ... 始終...を恐れて生活する.

P² a *menace* ***against*** one's reputation その名声に対する脅威. ¶a *menace* ***to*** the lives of many people 多数の生命に対する脅威. 【類】It is a *menace* ***to*** the existence of a country. / a *menace* ***to*** world peace (the public peace, the stability of society, public welfare).

menace, *v*. おびやかす, おどす, 脅威する.

M such nations as ***constantly menaced*** by war 絶えず戦争におびやかされているような国家.

P *menace* a person ***with*** a revolver (sword) ピストル(など)で人をおどかす.

mend, *n*. 修繕; 改善.

P Conditions at present certainly are ***on*** the *mend*. きょうの状態はたしかに良い方に向いている.

mend, *v*. 直す, 繕う, 修繕する.

M The patient is *mending* ***nicely***. その人の病状は順調である. ¶Least said ***soonest*** *mended*. 〘諺〙口はわざわいのもと.

O I had my watch (shoes, clothes) *mended*. 私は時計(など)を直させた. ¶***mend*** one's manners (=ways) 行状をあらためる.

mending, *n*. 修繕.

V The shoes ***need*** *mending*. そのくつは修繕を要する.

menses, *n. pl*. 月経.

V Her *menses* ***recur*** with regularity. 彼女の月経は順当である.

menstruation, *n*. 月経.

V Her *menstruation* ***ceased***. 彼女は月のものを見なくなった.

P during the periods ***of*** *menstruation* 月経時に.

mentality, *n*. 知力, 精神能力, 精神状態.

V ***change*** the *mentality* 心機を一転させる. ¶***develop*** the child's *mentality* その子供の精神能力を開発する. ¶He ***has*** a *mentality* of 12 years. 彼の精神状態は十二歳の子供のようである. ¶***study*** the *mentality* of the delinquent 非行者の精神状態を研究する.

Q ***abnormal*** *mentality* 精神異常. ¶a person of ***average*** *mentlaity* 普通の能力の人. ¶He possesses a ***childish*** *mentality*. 彼は子供っぽい考えを持っている. ¶the correction of the ***hysterical*** *mentality* ヒステリー的精神状態の矯正. ¶deviation from ***normal*** *mentality* 正常精神状態からの逸出(精神病者となること). ¶***warped*** *mentality* 心の歪(ゆがみ).

mention, *n*. 陳述, 挙示, 言及.

V ***add*** [a] *mention* of ... to ... ...に...のことを付記する. ¶should ***claim*** first *mention* 筆頭に述べるだけの値打がある. ¶the records ***contain*** no *mention* of ... その記録は...に言及していない. ¶Such instances are rare enough to ***deserve*** *mention*. こうした例はまれであるからここに述べる価値がある. ‖ ***deserve*** special *mention* from the fact that ... ...という事実から見て特に述べる価値がある. ¶All these names ***find*** *mention* here. これらの名は皆ここに誌してある. ‖ we ***find*** a *mention* of it as early as ... in ... そのことは...のころすでに...に記録してある ‖ I ***find*** no *mention* of ... in the records of ... ...の記録には...のことが述べてない. ¶it ***has*** no *mention* of ... それは...に言及していない. ¶***make*** *mention* of ... ...を述べる. 【類】***make*** a short *mention* of ... / of which *mention* is ***made*** below / no *mention* is ***made*** of ... / the book does not ***make*** any *mention* of ... / supplementing ... *mention* must be ***made*** of ... / in one of the early numbers of Literature *mention* was ***made*** of ... / *mention* has already been ***made*** of ... / *mention* should also be ***made*** of ... ¶we never ***meet*** any *mention* of ... in ... ...の中には...に関する記事が一向見当らない. ¶He ***obtained*** honorable *mention* [展覧会などで]彼はほう状をもらった. ¶The event ***received*** only very brief *mention* in the paper. そのことは同紙にはほんのちょっとしか出ていなかった. ‖ ***receive*** honorable *mention* 賀辞を受ける ‖ The *mention* of his name was ***received*** with hisses. 彼の名が出たので(聴衆は)これをやじった.

V² in the book there ***occurs*** a *mention* of ... この本の中に...のことがのっている.

Q only a ***bare mention*** can be made of ... についてはほんのちょっと述べうるだけだ. 【類】There is only a ***bare mention*** of it in the book. ¶It deserves ***brief mention***. そのことはちょっと述べる価値がある. ¶deserve special ***complimentary mention*** 特に推賞に値する. ¶***detailed mention*** should be made of ... ...に関しては詳述せねばならない. ¶the one who deserves the ***first mention*** いの一番にあげる価値のあるもの ‖ The point, of ***first mention*** in this article, is here reconsidered. その文で最初に言った点をさらにここで考案して見よう. ¶The ***first known*** *mention* of the word occurs in Kojiki. その語が始めて使われた個所は古事記である. ¶***frequent*** *mention* is made of ... ...に関ししてしばしば述べられている. ¶a list of those whose work entitles them to ***honorable*** *mention* and encouragement その事業に対して賛辞と奨励を受ける資格のある人々の名簿. 【類】in the long list of ... he deserves most ***honorable*** *mention* for ... ‖ make ***honorable*** *mention* of the papers forwarded by ... ...が送った論文を秀逸と認める. ¶He received a diploma (=certificate) of ***honorary*** *mention*. 彼はほう状を授与された. ¶***incidental*** *mention* has already been made of ... ...についてはすでに少し述べておいた. ¶A ***mere*** *mention* of his name angered her. ちょっと彼の名を言っただけでも彼女は怒った. ¶***meritorious*** *mention* ほう状(賞はいを受けない場合の). ¶there is ***no*** *mention* of ... ...に関して述べていない. ¶***particular*** *mention* must be made of ... ...について特に述べねばならない. ¶deserve more than ***passing*** *mention* ざっと述べるだけでは足りない. ¶make ***some*** *mention* of ... ...のことを少し述べる. ¶single it out for ***special*** *mention* それについて特筆する. 【類】There is nothing worth ***special*** *mention*. ‖ obtain ***special*** *mention* in an examination 試験で優等をとる.

P He pales even ***at*** the *mention* of these things. 彼はこういうことを言われただけで青くなる. 【類】instinctively one thinks of ... ***at*** [the] *mention* of ... ¶That man is ***beneath*** *mention*. あの男はお話にならない. ¶Fears are evoked ***by*** the very *mention* of ... ...の名を聞いただけでおびえる. ¶this account would be incomplete ***without*** a *mention* of ... この場合一言ぜひ...のことを述べておかなくてはならない. 【類】no sketch of his services to the community could be complete ***without*** *mention* of his very useful work as ...

P² the first *mention* ***of*** the earthquake in literature 地震に関する文献における最初の記事 ‖ I do not find any *mention* ***of*** this in the Japanese sources. 日本の文献にはこのことが述べてない.

mention, *v.* 陳述する, 記載する, 挙示する.

M He produced from his pocket the letter ***already*** *mentioned*. 彼はポケットから最前の手紙を取り出した. ¶*mention* it, by name, downright 名を指してそれをはっきり言う. ¶we may *mention* ***en passant*** that ... ついでに...と言ってよかろう. ¶I might ***incidentally*** *mention* that ... ちなみに記す... ¶too numerous to *mention* ***individually*** あまり例が多過ぎて一々述べられない, 枚挙にいとまない. ¶My husband has ***often*** *mentioned* you to me. あなたのことは宅からよく聞いております. ¶be ***strongly*** *mentioned* as candidate for the post of ... ...の候補として呼声が高い.

P ***as*** *mentioned* above 前記の ‖ it may be *mentioned* ***as*** an instance of ... それは...の一例と見なされる. 【類】***as*** *mentioned* in the previous chapter / ***as*** *mentioned* in the preceding article. ¶it is *mentioned* ***at*** (=***on***) page 108 それは百八ページにのっている. ¶too numerous to *mention* ***by*** name 非常に多数なので一々あげることができない. 【類】He *mentions* them ***by*** name. / *mention* them only ***by*** their Christian names ‖ *mention* imports ***by*** countries 輸入品名を国別に示す. ¶He is being *mentioned* ***for*** the place (=office *or* position). 彼はその地位(の候補者)に名をあげられている. ¶They are not to be *mentioned* ***in*** the same breath. それらは同日の論じゃない(比較にならない). ¶***of*** which we shall *mention* further on それについては追って述べるとしよう. ¶*mention* the matter ***to*** him そのことを彼に言う.

O to *mention* only a few examples of ... 二三...の例をあげれば. ¶without *mentioning* ... =not to *mention* ... ...は言うに及ばず.

menu, *n.* 献立; 料理.

V In the restaurant both Japanese and European *menus* are ***provided***. その料理屋では和洋両食ができる.

V² The usual *menu* ***consists*** of soup, meat, vegetables and dessert. 普通の献立はスープ・肉・野菜及び食後の茶菓から成る.

Q It is a great aid to the humble house-keeper in varying the ***daily*** *menu*. それは毎日の献立に変化を添える点において貧しい家政婦に取って大なる助けになる. ¶a ***light*** *menu* 軽い料理.

merchandise, *n.* 商品, 商貨.

V ***express*** *merchandise* to ... ...へ商品を急送する, ¶***make*** *merchandise* of oneself わが身を売物にする[売春婦など]. 【類】a woman who ***makes*** *merchandise* of her body. ¶***sell*** Japanese *merchandise* 日本商品を売る.

Q ***general*** *merchandise* 一般商品 (特別の valuable merchandise 以外の). ¶***returned*** *merchandise* 返品. ¶throw ***valuable*** *merchandise* overboard to save the vessel in a storm 暴風雨の際船を救うため貴重な商品を海に投じる.

Q² ***gift*** *merchandise* 寄贈用商品.

P treat it ***as*** *merchandise* それを商品として扱う.

merchandising, *n.* 売買, 商売.

P Marshall Field & Company, a leader ***in*** finer *merchandising* 上等な品物販売の随一たるマーシャル・フィールド会社.

merchant, *n.* 商人, 商売.

V ***become*** a *merchant* 商人になる.

Q a ***broken-down*** *merchant* 破産した商人. ¶an ***enterprising*** *merchant* 進取的な商人. ¶an ***ever-watchful*** *merchant* 抜目のない商人. ¶a ***faithless*** *merchant* かん商. ¶a ***hard, money-loving, purse-proud, wealthy London*** *merchant* がん固で締り屋で金自慢な金持のロンドン商人. ¶***peripatetic*** *merchants*=pedlars 行商人. ¶an ***unreliable*** *merchant* 信用のできない商人. ¶a ***wily*** *merchant* こうかつな商人.

Q² an ***area*** *merchant* 仕切屋. ¶a ***brass-plate*** *merchant* 《俗》石炭売込仲買商. ¶***City*** *merchants* ロンドン商業区の商人たち. ¶a ***coal*** (***lumber, grocery, leather goods***) *merchant* 石炭(など)商. ¶a ***kerbstone*** (=***curbstone***) *merchant* (=broker) 〖株式〗場外取引の商人. ¶a ***small town*** *merchant* 小都市の商人. ¶a ***wholesale*** (***retail***) *merchant*=a wholesaler (retailer) おろし(小売)商人.

P He set up ***as*** a *merchant*. 彼は商人として身を立てた.

merciful, *a.* 慈悲深い, 情深い.

P *merciful* ***to*** others 他人に対して慈悲深い.

mercury, *n.* 水銀; 水銀柱.

V ***fix*** *mercury* 水銀を固める.

V² The *mercury* ***indicated*** 85 degrees in the shade. 寒暖計は室内で八十五度を示した. ¶The *mercury* in thermometer ***mounted up*** (=***rose***) to 115 degrees. 寒暖計の水銀は百十五度に上った. ¶The *mercury* ***registered*** 65 degrees. 寒暖計は六十五度を示した. ¶The *mercury* ***stood*** at nearly 90°. 寒暖計は約九十度であった.

mercy, *n.* 慈悲, 仁慈, あわれみ.

V ***allow*** no *mercy* かしゃくしない. ¶He ***begged*** the *mercy* of silence concerning the episode. 彼はそのできごとについては人に話さないようにと懇願した. 【類】In an agony of shame he ***begged*** the *mercy* of silence concerning the episode. ¶***have*** *mercy* on ... ...をあわれむ. ¶***implore*** the *mercy* of God upon ... ...の上に恵みを垂れ給えと神に祈る. ¶***show*** *mercy* on (=to) every thing 万物をあわれむ. 【類】He ***shows*** little *mercy* to the poor. ¶***take*** *mercy* on a person 人をあわれむ.

Q We should be thankful even for ***small*** *mercies*. よしどんなわずかの同情でも感謝すべきだ. ¶***tender*** *mercy* 深い慈悲.

P be ***at*** the *mercy* of the circumstances 環境に左右されている. 【類】Primitive man was always very much ***at*** the *mercy* of his environment. / For a fortnight the captain and his men roved adrift ***at*** the *mercy* of wind and waves (波のまにまに). ¶ask Heaven ***for*** *mercy* on one's sin その罪に対して天のあわれみをこう ‖ beg ***for*** *mercy* 慈悲をこう ‖ ***for*** *mercy*=for mercy's sake 後生だから. ¶***in*** *mercy* かわいそうだと思って. ¶spare one ***out of*** *mercy* かわいそうと思って人を許してやる. ¶abandon one's ship ***to*** the *mercy* of the waves その船を波のなすがままに任せる. ¶***without*** *mercy* 容赦なく.

merge, *v.* 沈む, のまれる, 没入する; 合併する.

M *merge* ***imperceptibly*** into ... 区別のつかないまでに...に融け込む, いつのまにか...となる.

P *merge* an antagonism ***in*** a larger, wider, and nobler consciousness さらに大にさらに広くさらに高尚な自覚を振作して敵意を忘れる ‖ the bureau is now *merged* ***in*** ... その局は今は...と合併した. ¶Twilight *merged* ***into*** darkness. たそがれから次第に暗やみになった. ‖ *merge* ***into*** ... with no clear line of demarcation はっきりした限界を見せずに...と融合する ‖ This business he *merged* ***into*** a banking-house. 彼はこの店を銀行と合併した. 【類】Anglo-Saxon and Norman-French had gradually *merged* ***into*** Modern

English. ¶The Equitable Trust Company of New York was *merged with* the Chase National Bank in 1930. ニューヨークのエクィタブル信託会社は一九三〇年にチェース国立銀行と合併した.

meridian, *n.* 頂点, 絶頂, 盛り.

V His power has ***passed*** the *meridian*. 彼の勢力は下り坂になった. ¶During the Victorian era the novel ***reached*** the *meridian* (=zenith) of its power in the hands of a brilliant group of writers. ヴィクトリア朝の間に小説は一群の優秀作家の手で全盛時代に達した.

P He was then ***at*** the *meridian* of his intellectual power. 彼は当時その知力の頂点にあった.

merit, *n.* 手柄, 功績; 価値.

V ***accept*** the *merit* その価値を認める. ¶***acquire merit*** 値打が出る. ¶***appreciate*** its *merits* その価値を認める. ¶***belittle*** the *merit* of … …を軽んじる. ¶***claim*** the *merit* of … …に価値ありと主張する. ¶***compare merits*** and demerits 長所短所を比較する. ¶***determine*** relative *merits* 優劣を決する. ¶He ***disclaims*** his own *merit* in favor of others. 彼は自分の功績を人に譲った. ¶***discuss*** the relative *merits* of Beethoven and Wagner in the peculiar jargon of the musical critic 音楽批評家独特な言葉でベートーヴェンとワグネルの優劣を議論する. ¶***evacuate*** the *merits* of … …の価値をなくする. ¶***extol*** his *merit* as an orator 彼の雄弁振りを嘆美する. ¶He ***has*** the *merit* of offending none. あたりさわらずというのが彼のよい所だ. ‖ ***have*** both *merits* and demerits 長所短所をもっている. ¶seriously ***impair*** the *merits* of … …の長所をひどく損う. ¶By one day's service the worshipper ***obtains*** as much *merit* as if he had served thirty-three thousand days. 一日のお勤めで三万三千日だけの功徳がある. ¶***overestimate*** the *merit* (value) of … …を買いかぶる. ¶***overrate*** one's own *merit* 自分の値打を高く評価する(うぬぼれる). ¶***possess*** high *merit* 大いに価値がある. 【類】It ***posseses*** considerable *merit* as a work of art (芸術品). ¶***set forth*** (=***bring out***) the *merit* of … …の価値を示す. ¶The picture ***shows*** much artistic *merit*. その絵には大いに芸術的価値がある. ¶without any desire to ***underestimate*** the *merit* of … …の価値を見くびろうとして言うではないが…である.

V² But there its *merit* ***stops***. けれどもその長所はそれきり

Q the ***architectural*** *merits* of a literary production 文学作品の構想的価値. ¶passmen of more than ***common*** *merit* 《英》普通以上の成績の卒業生. ¶***comparative merits*** and demerits of … and … …と…の優劣. ¶of ***conspicuous*** *merit* 目立って功労のある. ¶a ***counter-balancing*** *merit* [短所の]埋合わせになる特徴. ¶writers of ***decided*** *merit* 断然すぐれた文士. ¶of ***distinctive merit*** 功績顕著な, 抜群の. ¶a scholar of ***doubtful*** *merit* いかがわしい学者. ¶***false merit*** にせの手柄. ¶the ***great*** *merit* of the book その本の大なる強み. ¶his ***internal*** *merit* 彼の心の美. ¶an evidence of ***intrinsic*** *merit* 真価のある一つの証拠. ¶Duma's style shows its ***light*** *merits* in dialogue. ジューマは特に会話にすぐれている. ¶***literary*** *merit* 文学的価値. ¶a poet of no ***mean*** *merit* 非凡な詩人. ¶the ***outstanding*** *merit* of the story その小説の著しい長所. ¶one's ***personal*** *merit* その人の特性 ‖ be reduced to one's naked ***personal*** *merit* 裸一貫になる. ¶he has the ***saving*** (=redeeming) *merit* of … 彼には…というう め合わせとなる長所がある. ¶a work of no ***small*** *merit* なかなかの佳作. 【類】Were pen-drawing something to be mastered in a week or a month there would be ***small*** *merit* in the accomplishment. ¶its ***surpassing*** *merit* is that … その卓越した特徴は…である. ¶have the ***unique*** *merit* of … …という独特の価値がある.

P ***according to*** one's *merit* その手柄に応じて. ¶the principle of promotion ***by*** *merit* 成績による昇進法. ¶a man ***of*** *merit* 勲功ある人 ‖ a method ***of*** high *merit* 非常に価値のある方法. ¶judge a matter ***on*** its *merits* of a case= judge a case on its merits 〘法〙本件に基づきある件を裁判する.

P² a *merit* ***in*** a person 人の美点.

O Those who know the Boer system of warfare know that it is not favoritism but *merit* that selects the officers. ブーア人の戦法を知る者はブーア人が将校を選ぶに私情によらずして手柄によることを知る.

merit, *v.* 功によって得る, …を受ける価値がある.

M He ***richly*** *merits* such a distinction. 彼にはかかる名誉を受ける価値が十分ある. ¶His conducts ***well*** *merit* the award. 彼の行為は受賞の資格が十分ある.

mermaid, *n.* 人魚; 《米》女子の水泳選手.

Q a ***soaring*** *mermaid* in mid-air 空中ダイヴィングをやっている女子水泳家. ¶They are ***veritable*** *mermaids*. 彼女などは全くかっぱの親類である.

P² *mermaids* ***in*** a swimming pool プールの女かっぱども.

merriment, *n.* 快楽, 歓楽, 陽気.

V The parlor game ***caused*** much *merriment*. その室内遊戯で大いに陽気になった. ¶***provoke*** *merriment* 興を起させる.

Q ***after-dark*** *merriment* 夜の歓楽. ¶***demoniac[al]*** *merriment* 乱痴気騒ぎ. ¶a source of ***sarcastic*** *merriment* 皮肉な笑いを催させる種. ¶It convulsed the assembly with ***spontaneous*** *merriment*. そのために一同がおかしさのあまり思わずどっと吹出した. ¶***straiend*** *merriment* わざとらしい笑い. ¶They shook with ***uncontrollable*** *merriment*. 皆のものがおかしくてたまらず笑いこけた.

P provoke a baby ***to*** *merriment* 赤ん坊をあやして笑わせる.

merry, *a.* 楽しい, 陽気な, 愉快な.

P He was *merry* ***over*** his cups. 彼は杯をかさねながら陽気にやっていた. ‖ Those children are making *merry* ***over*** that game. あの子供たちはその競技をやって面白く遊んでいる.

O Let us make *merry!* 陽気にやろうぜ.

merry-go-round, *n.* 遊園地.

Q² a ***carnival*** *merry-go-round* 子供遊園地. ¶the ***Washington*** *Merry-go-round* [新聞の題名]ワシントンだより.

merry-maker, *n.* 陽気に遊ぶ人, 浮かれ騒ぐ人.

Q The place was alive with ***light-hearted*** *merry-makers*. そこは陽気な連中でにぎやかだった.

Q² ***weekend*** *merrymakers* 週末のうかれ者ども.

merrymaking, *n.* 浮かれ騒ぐこと.

Q ***hilarious*** *merrymaking* 浮れ騒ぎ. ¶***wild*** *merrymaking* どんちゃん騒ぎ.

mess, *n.* 会食; ごっちゃ; へま; 不潔.

V He managed (=was stupid enough) to ***make*** a *mess* of it. 彼はどうやらみそをつけた. ‖ He contrived to ***make*** a *mess* of the whole thing. 彼は何もかもめちゃくちゃにしてしまった. ¶***sweep up*** a *mess* ごみをかく.

Q make an ***awful*** *mess* of it. ひどい不手際をやる. ¶His clothes were in an ***indescribable*** *mess*. 彼はなんとも言えないひどい装(なり)をしていた. ¶What a ***jolly*** *mess* I am in! 〘反語〙いやはやひどい事になった! ¶make a ***pretty bad*** *mess* of it かなりへまをやる.

P officers ***at*** *mess* 会食中の将校. ¶They were [placed] ***in*** a *mess*. ごっちゃになっていた. 【類】The room is ***in*** a *mess*.

mess, *v.* 食する, 会食する; ごっちゃにする.

M² They just *messed* everything ***up***. あの人たちはめちゃくちゃにしてしまった.

P *mess* ***with*** … …と会食する.

message, *n.* 口上, 伝言(メッセージ); 使命; 《米》大統領の教書.

V ***address*** a *message* to Congress 《米》[大統領・州知事が]教書を議会に出す. ¶the chairman ***announced*** several *messages* of greeting from … 座長は…からの五六の祝詞を発表した. ¶***bear*** the *message* to … …への通信を持って行く. ¶The servant ***brought*** him the *message* that some one wanted to speak with him over the telephone, presumably his wife. 召使は「どなたからか, 多分奥様と思いますが, 電話がかかりました」という知らせを彼にもたらした. ‖ His new work ***brings*** a *message* for this and the coming-generation. 彼の新著は現代及び次代へ使命をもたらす. ¶***cable*** a *message* 海外へ電命を発する. ¶The package ***carries*** no written *message*. その包みには通信文がはいっていない. ¶***code*** a *message* 普通電報を暗号に直す. ¶***communicate*** a *message* 通信する. ¶***convey*** a *message* from … …からの伝言をする. ¶***deliver*** a *message* 伝言する ‖ The magazine ***delivers*** its *message* independently and fearlessly. その雑誌は独立して大胆にその使命を伝える. ¶***dispatch*** a *message* 電命を発する. ¶***do*** *messages* 使命を果す. ¶This ***drew*** from him a *message* of thanks. このことで彼から感謝状をもらった. ¶***file*** a *message* at a wireless telegraph office 無線電信局で電文を差出す. ¶***forward*** one's *message* to … その通信を…に転送する. ¶***Give*** him my *message*. 彼によろしく言ってくれ. ‖ ***give*** a *message* to the young men of the present day 現代の青年に所思を伝える. ¶I ***have*** a *message* to deliver to you. 私はあなたに伝言を頼まれている. ¶He ***left*** a *message* for him written on a visiting card. 彼は名刺に書いた彼への伝言をおいて来た.

ǁ *leave* a *message* with the servant 召使に言いおく. ¶*radio* a *message*=send a *message* by radio《米》無線通信をする. ¶*receive* a *message* of encouragement from ... …から激励の手紙を受取る. ¶*route* a wireless *message* via Sable Island セーブル島経由の無電で送る. ¶*run* (=*send*) a *message* for a person 人のために使いをする ǁ *send* a *message* post-haste to ... 大急ぎで…に通知を出す. 【類】*send* a *message* of sympathy to ... / He *sent* a *message* of congratulation to ... on their silver wedding. ǁ *send messages* over a long distance by means of one or more columns of smoke 一個または一個以上の煙柱(のろし)によって長距離に通信する. ¶liners fitted with the necessary apparatus for *tapping* wireless *messages* at sea 海上で無電を送信するに必要な設備のある定期船. ¶*transmit messages* through a cable 海外電報を出す. ¶*wire* a *messages* to ... …に電報を打つ.

Q a *coded message* 暗号電報. ¶a *complimentary message* あいさつの言葉. ¶a *congratulatory message* 祝詞. ¶a *courteous message* 丁重な式詞. ¶an *inspiring message* 感激させる式辞. ¶Give them my *kindly message*. みなさんによろしく伝えて下さい. ¶the *last message* of a dying soldier 死にひんする軍人の臨終の言葉. ¶a *loyal message* 尽忠の言葉. ¶a *secret message* 秘密の通信. ¶*telegraphic messages* received at ... …への入電. ¶a *verbal message* 口頭の伝言. ¶The news was sent by a *wireless message*. その知らせは無電で送られた. ¶a card with a *written message* 用向の書いてある名刺.

Q^2 receive a *cable message* from America アメリカから海底電報を受取る. ¶a *farewell message* 告別の辞 ǁ send a *farewell message* of thanks to ... …に告別の謝辞を送る. ¶bring a *goodwill massage* to ... …に親善メッセージをもたらす. ¶a *pigeon message* 伝書ばとによる通信. ¶a *radio message*《米》無電通信. ¶The President's *State of the Union message*《米》大統領の議会に送る教書(正式の呼称). ¶take a *telephone message* 電話の口ずてを聴取する. ¶get a *teletype message* on ... …に関するテレタイプの通信を受取る.

P He mentioned this fact *in* his *message* to the people. 彼は同国民に述べた彼の所感の中でこのことに触れた. ¶He was bound for ... *on* a *message*. 彼はある使命を帯びて…に行くのであった. ¶Will you go to your mother *with* a *message* from me? 私からの伝言を持ってあなたのお母さんの所へ行ってくれませんか.

P^2 a *message between* two persons or nations 二人または二国間の通信. ¶*message by* wireless (mail, telegraph) 無線(など)による通信. ¶I have a *message for* you from my mistress. 私の所の奥様からあなたにことづけがあります. ¶a *message from* a person (place) ある人(など)からの通信. ¶send a *message of* condolence (=sympathy) 弔詞を送る. 【類】a *message of* encouragement from her mother. ¶the President's *message to* Congress 大統領の議会への教書 ǁ Here's a *message to* you. あなたへの伝言です. 【類】Here's a *message of* hope for your success from Uncle George.

messenger, *n.* 使者, 伝令使.

V *despatch* a *messenger* with orders 命を授けて使者を急派する. ¶*get* a *messenger* 使いの者を雇う. 「認用達し.

Q *God's messenger* 神のお使い. ¶a *licensed messenger* 公認用達し.

Q^2 a *doll messenger* of friendship 人形の親善使節. ¶a *good-will messenger* from Washington, D.C. ワシントン府からの親善使節.

P send a letter *by* a *messenger* 使いを立てて手紙をやる.

P^2 a *messenger from* ... bearing a command to ... …の命令を持って…からきた使者. ¶The robin is the *messenger* (harbinger) *of* spring. こま鳥は春の先ぶれである. ¶a *messenger of* the gospel of Christ *to* the Japanese 日本人への福音の伝道者.

metal, *n.* 金属.

V Rust *frets metal*. さびは金属を腐食する. ¶The train *left* the *metals*. その列車が脱線した. ¶*refine* a *metal* 金属を精錬する. ¶*roll metal* 金属にローラーをかける. ¶*rust* or *corrode* a *metal* 金属をさびさしたり腐食さしたりする.

Q *alloyed metal* 合金. ¶coins of *base metal* 卑金属製のぜに. 【類】Alchemy (錬金術) is a process by which *baser metals* could be turned into gold. ¶*light* (*heavy*) *metal* 軽(重)金属. ¶*molten metal* 溶解した金属. ¶a *precious metal* 貴金属. ¶a *rare metal* 希金属. ¶a *refractory metal* とけにくい金属. ¶*road metal* [道路の]しき砂利.

Q^2 *antifriction metal* 減磨メタル(軸受け用の). ¶*cast-off metal* くず金, スクラップ. ¶*Muntz metal* マンツメタル(銅と亜鉛の合金). ¶be stripped and crushed for *scrap metal* 付属品をはずしてスクラップにする. ¶*sheet metal* 板金. 「一片(枚)の金属.

P a worker *in metal* 金工. ¶a piece (=sheet) *of metal* 一片(枚)の金属.

metamorphose, *v.* 変化する, 変形する.

P *metamorphosed into* ... …に変形した.

metamorphosis, *n.* 変形, 変性, 変態.

V *undergo metamorphosis* 形態が変化する.

V^2 Such a *metamorphosis* cannot *take place* in a day. こうした激変は一朝にしてでき得べきでない.

Q a *mental metamorphosis* 心機一転. ¶go through *several metamorphoses* [こん虫などが]数回変形する.

metaphor, *n.* 〖修辞〗隠ゆ, 比ゆ.

V *drop metaphor* in expressing it 隠ゆによらないでそれを表現する.

Q a *quaint metaphor*, but a solid fact 奇妙な隠ゆではあるが確かな事実. ¶*racy metaphor* きびきびした隠ゆ. ¶expressed in a *well-worn metaphor* 陳腐な比ゆで表現した.

Q^2 a *slang metaphor* 俗語的隠ゆ.

P talk *by metaphor* 比ゆで話す.

P^2 a *metaphor from* chemistry 化学から借用した比ゆ.

metaphysician, *n.* 形而上学者, 純正哲学者.

Q Few men combine, as he does, the intuitions of a poet with the logical precision and exact thought of a *trained metaphysician*. およそ彼ほど詩人の直感と円熟した純正哲学者の明確な理論並びに正確な思想とを兼備している者は少い.

metaphysics, *n.* 形而上学, 純正哲学.

Q *Buddhistic metaphysics* 仏教の哲理.

mete, *v.* 裁く; 分け与える.

M *mete out* justice to ... [法に照して]…を裁く. 【類】*mete out* stern justice ǁ *mete out* flogging as punishment むち打ちの刑に処する ǁ *mete out* a sentence to ... …に判決を下す. 【類】*mete out* a ten-year sentence to ... ǁ *mete out* happiness 幸福を分け与える. 【類】*mete out* rewards to ... / the treatment *meted out* to those who ...

meteor, *n.* 流星.

V^2 a *meteor* is seen *darting* through the sky. 流星が飛ぶ.

Q one of those *literary meteors* which burst suddenly upon the sight, often to disappear again as suddenly あの突然出現してよくまた突然消えてしまう流星のような文士の一人.

meter, *n.* 〖詩〗詩脚.

Q written in the *ordinary* 7, 5, 7, 5 *meter* 普通の七五調で書いた.

meter, *n.* メートル, …計.

Q^2 an *ampere meter* 〖電〗アンペア計. ¶a *gas meter* ガスのメートル. ¶*grain meter* 自動量穀器. ¶the takings per annum from the *slot meters* [硬貨を入れる]自動計量器から得た一年の収入. ¶a *speed meter* 速度計.

methane, *n.* 〖化〗メタン.

V^2 *Methane comes* from marshes. メタンは沼沢から生じる.

method, *n.* 方法, 法式, 法則; 手段, 手続.

V *adopt* the same *method* with regard to ... as with ... …について…と同様の手段をとる. ¶*apply* the same *methods* to ... …に同じ方法を適用する. 【類】*apply* German *methods* to English philology ǁ successfully *apply* a *method* 効果的にある方法を用いる. ¶*change* one's *method* drastically 根本からやり方を変える. ¶this *constitutes* the best *method* of ... これが…の最も良い方法である. ¶He *developed* the *method* which bears his name. 彼は彼の名を冠する方法を案出した. ¶*devise* a better *method* 一層良い方法を工夫する. 【類】*devise* some *method* which will accomplish this result. ¶*essay* (=try) various *methods* 色々な方法を試みる. ¶It is necessary for the company to *establish* more economical *methods*. その会社はもっと経済的な方法を立てる必要がある. ¶*follow* the same *method* of inquiry 同じ研究方法をとる. 【類】The author *follows* the same *method* of treatment on the subject. / the only *method* then to be *followed* was to ... ¶*inaugurate* a new *method* of teaching 新教授法を始める ǁ *inaugurate* a new *method* of teaching a foreign language 外語教授の新案を始める. ¶*initiate* novel and startling *methods* in the art of war 戦術にざん新にして驚異すべき方法を創始する. ¶*introduce* the French *method* of grape culture フランス式のぶどう栽培法を採用する. 【類】the factory has *introduced* many modern *methods* / *introduce* a *method* into one's reading. ¶*invent* a simple *method* 簡単な方法を発明する.【類】***invent*** an ingenious *method* of popularizing ... ¶No particular *method* can be ***laid down*** as the best 特に善の善なるものとして立て得べき方法がない. ¶avert revolution and ***preserve*** constitutional *methods* 革命を避けて立憲政治を維持する. ¶***pursue*** a *method* ある方法を取る. ¶***renew*** their *methods* 彼らの方法を革新する. ¶***reverse*** the *method* usually followed 普通に取る方法を逆に行く. ¶***scrap*** old *methods* and adopt new ones 古いやり方を捨てて新しい方法を採用する. ¶***study*** business *methods* 商業実務を研究する. ¶***try*** a new *method* of study 新研究法を試みる. ¶the principle ***underlying*** the *method* その方法の原則. ¶***use*** Western *methods* and weapons of war 西洋の戦法と武器とを採用する. 【類】***use*** birth control *methods* (産児制限法) / ***use*** this *method* with ... (...と併用する). 「といいと思う.

v² I hope this *method* will ***spread*** このやり方が普及する

Q go to an ***alternate*** *method* 別法をとる. ¶a new ***anaesthetizing*** *method* 新麻酔法. ¶stick to ***antiquated*** *method* 古臭い方法にかじりつく ‖ ***antiquated*** *methods* of traveling 旧式の旅行法. ¶by the most ***approved*** *method* 最善と見なされた方法で. ¶the ***best*** *method* of procedure 最善の手段. ¶a ***clinic*** *method* of teaching 臨床式教授法. ¶***conservative*** *methods* 保存的手段. ¶The *method* is exceedingly ***cumbrous***. その方法はきわめてわずらわしい. ¶The book pursues a ***different*** *method* in its treatment of the problem. その本はその問題を異った方法で取扱っている. ¶the ***direct*** *method* of language teaching 語学の直接教授法. ¶a ***dishonest*** *method* 不正手段. ¶Nature's ***drastic*** *method* 自然の激烈なやり方. ¶***economic*** *methods* of language learning 語学修得の経済的方法. ¶an ***effective*** *method* 有効な手段. ¶an ***efficient*** *method* 能率的なやり方 ¶by ***exact scientific*** *methods* 正確な科学的方法で. ¶the ***experimental*** *method* その実験方式. ¶a ***fallacious*** *method* of getting at the facts 事実に到達する誤った方法. ¶a ***faulty*** *method* 欠点のあるやり方. ¶One of the ***favorite*** *methods* of investigation in educational research is the questionary. 教育学上の研究でよくやる調査法の一つは質問回状による方法である. ‖ one's ***favorite*** *method* その慣用手段. ¶the ***grammatical*** *method* 文法による語学教授学習法. ¶***graphic*** *methods* for presenting facts 図解式の事実提示法. ¶It is left to most ***haphazard*** *methods*. それは全く手当り次第の方法に任せられてある. ¶a ***hazardous*** *method* いいかげんのやり方. ¶an almost ***ideal*** *method* ほとんど理想的な手段. ¶***immediate*** (***ultimate***) *methods* 暫定(決定)的方法. ¶the ***impressionistic*** *method* of portraiture 印象主義の人物描写法. ¶a ***legitimate*** *method* 合法的手段. ¶a ***methodless*** *method* 方式を立てない方法. ¶after ***modern*** *methods* 近代的方法によって. 【類】***modern*** *methods* of student personnel work (厚生法) ‖ one of the ***modern, most approved*** *methods* of ... 新しくてもっとも広く認められている...法の一つ. ¶***multiform*** (=***various***) *methods* 様々の方法. ¶be on the ***new*** *method* 新方式によっている. 【類】I was taught by an entirely ***new*** *method* devised and developed by ... ¶His talk has ***no*** *method*. 話に筋が立っていない. 【類】There is ***no*** *method* in his teaching. ¶a ***novel*** *method* 新奇なやり方. ¶an ***oldfashioned*** *method* 古臭い方法. ¶The examination is conducted by the ***oral*** *method*. その試験は口頭で行われる. ¶his ***pedagogic*** *method* 彼の教授法. ¶a feature of the ***political*** *method* of the country その国の政治のやり口の一方面. ¶***popular superficial*** *method* of etymologizing 通俗的で浅薄な語源研究法. ¶one of the ***practical*** and ***sensible*** *methods* of learning a foreign language 実際的で賢明な外国語学習法の一つ. ¶the most ***practicable*** *method* is to ... ...するもっとも実際的な方法は...である. ¶***President Truman's*** new *method*. トルーマン大統領の新政策. ¶follow the ***primitive*** *method* in the manufacture of ... ...の製作に原始的なやり方をする. ¶a ***pure direct*** (***modified***) *method* of language teaching 語学の[翻訳によらない]純直接(折衷)教授法. ¶a ***quaint*** *method* 奇妙なやり方. ¶the ***rigorous*** *method* of science 精密な科学の研究方法. ¶pursue ***roundabout*** *methods* う遠な方法を取る. ¶a ***routine*** *method* きまりきったやり方. ¶a ***second-hand*** *method* of acquiring knowledge 知識を獲得する間接の方法. ¶a ***self-correcting*** *method* of composition 作文の自己添削方法. ¶***short-sighted*** *methods* 近眼者流の方法. ¶adopt a ***similar*** *method* 同様な手段を採る. ¶***slipshod*** *methods* ずさんな方法. ¶a ***slow*** and ***sure*** *method* 安全着実な方法. ¶A ***specific*** and ***sure*** *method* of treatment has yet to be found. 確実な特効療法がまだ見つからない. ¶it would be contrary to ***scientific*** *method* to ... ...するのは科学的方法に反するだろう.【類】the applications of ***scientific*** *method* to Government departments. ¶a new ***therapeutic*** *method* 新療法. ¶a ***time-worn*** *method* 老朽(古くさい)手段. ¶shift from ***traditional*** to progressive *methods* 伝統的なやり方から進歩的なやり方に切換える. ¶***various*** *methods* are followed in ... ...では色々な方法が試みられている. ¶a ***violent*** *method* of expressing contempt 軽べつを示す猛烈なやり方 ‖ use ***violent*** or ***warlike*** *methods* 暴力的なあるいは好戦的な手段を用いる. ¶adopt ***Western*** *methods* 西洋式を採用する.

Q² ***bolshevist*** *methods* 過激主義者のやり方. ¶study ***business*** *methods* 商売のやり口を研究する.【類】Their ***business*** *methods* are above suspicion (ガラス張り). / the ***business*** *methods* followed by European governments. ¶a modern ***campaign*** *method* 近代的運動法. ¶a ***classroom*** *method* of procedure 教室での操縦教授法. ¶sound recording by either ***disc or film*** *method* 音盤または映画法による録音. ¶the ***grammar-translation*** *method* in language study 語学修得における文法・翻訳法. ¶a demonstration of American ***fire fighting*** *methods* 米国式消防活動の実演. ¶the ***flint*** and ***steel*** *method* of fire production ひうち石と鋼鉄による発火法. ¶the ***hand-to-mouth*** *method* of living その日暮し. ¶by "***hit-or-miss***" *method* 一か八かで, 運を天に任せて ‖ follow the ***hit-or-miss*** *method* of investigation でたらめな調査法をやる. ¶study a foreign language by an easy ***home-study*** *method* 外国語を楽な自修法で習う. ¶the ***hunt-and-hit*** *method* of typewriting with one finger of each hand. 両方の手の一本指でポッツリポッツリとタイプをすること. ¶adopt the rough "***kill or cure***" *method*「殺すか生かすか」の手荒い方法を採る. ¶the ***lowpoint*** *method* of scoring in a debating contest 討論の減点採点法(欠点をマイナス点で表わす). ¶by ***mass production*** *method* 大量生産式に. ¶***merchandising*** *methods* 取引の方法. ¶the ***perambulator*** *method* of education [世話を焼き過ぎる]乳母日がさ式の教育法. ¶modern ***police*** *methods* 近代警察方式. ¶modern ***police laboratory*** *methods* 近代的警察実験方式. ¶***piece-rate*** and ***bonus*** *methods* of payment 仕事のでき高及び特別手当による(給料)支払法. ¶"***police state***" *methods* いわゆる警察国家方式. ¶adopt efficient ***production*** *methods* 能率的な生産方式を採用する. ¶gather information by the ***questionnaire*** *method* アンケートによって情報を集める. ¶study the American ***railroad*** *method* アメリカの鉄道方式を研究する. ¶a ***reducing*** *method* やせる法. ¶***research*** *methods* 種々の調査法. ¶a ***rule-of-thumb*** *method* 大ざっぱな(目分量の)やり方. ¶use modern ***sales*** *methods* 近代的販売方式を採る. ¶a ***suicide*** *method* 自殺の手段. ¶adopt a new ***teaching*** *method* 新しい教授法を採用する. ¶use the ***telegraph*** *method* in writing 文を簡潔にする. ¶***terrorist*** *methods* 色々のテロ戦術. ¶In the ***touch*** *method* all fingers are used. [タイプの]キータッチングは全指を動かす. ¶excellence of ***training*** *methods* 訓練方法の優秀さ. ¶by ***trick*** *methods* いんちきで. ¶an efficient ***working*** *method* 能率的な作業方式.

Q ***up-to-date*** *methods* of fire fighting 最新の消火法.

P give one's age ***according to*** the Japanese *method* 日本風の数え方(数え年)で年齢を言う. ¶a first French book ***after*** the natural *method* 自然式によるフランス語入門書 ‖ ***after*** the English *method* 英国流に ‖ Pupils are required to perform a series of actions ***after*** the Gouin *method*. 生徒にグーアン教授法にならって(外国語を話しながら)連続的な行動をさせる. ‖ ***after*** the same *method* 同じ方法で. ¶***by*** the inductive *method* 帰納法によって. ¶We turn to German ***for*** *method*, go to France for culture. われわれは方法ならドイツに文化ならフランスに求める. ¶I will answer your question ***in*** the Socratic *method*. 君の問はソクラテスの問答法によって答えよう. ¶a man ***of*** *method* きちょうめんな人. ¶a history of architecture ***on*** the comparative *method* 様式比較法を根拠とした建築史. ¶***Under*** old *methods* of learning a language, rules are memorized but correct habits are not formed. 言語学習の古い方法

では規則は記憶できるが正しい言語習慣は作られない. ¶*through* the only *method* possible 取りうべき唯一の方法で. ¶work *with method* 順序を立てて仕事する. ¶*without method* でたらめに.

P^2 new *methods* ***for*** the study of literature 文学新研究法. ¶There is no *method* ***in*** his way of thinking. 彼の考え方はでたらめだ. ¶*methods* ***of*** teaching (instruction) 教授法. ¶society's *methods* ***of*** dealing with some of its hampered members 社会が厄介者を取扱う方法 ‖ new *methods* ***of*** approach to its study その新しい研究法 ‖ His *methods* ***of*** raising money were more than objectionable. 彼の資金あつめの方法は実にひどいものであった.

O That's his *method* (=way). それがあいつのやり口だ.

methodologist, *n.* 方法学者, 方法論者.

Q a ***linguistic*** *methodologist* 言語教習方法学者.

metropolis, *n.* 首都; 《口語》主要都市.

Q a ***cosmopolitan*** *metropolis* 世界的な都市. ¶the ***roaring, surging*** *metropolis* 騒然と人波寄せる首都. ¶Paris, a ***super-refined*** *metropolis* 非常に洗練された首都パリー. ¶a ***vast*** *metropolis* 広大な首都.

Q^2 a ***giant*** *metropolis* 巨大都市.

P ***at*** the *metropolis* 首都において.

P^2 Putney is the *metropolis* ***of*** boating men. パトニー(テムス河畔)はボート人の本場である. ‖ Chicago is the *metropolis* ***of*** the Middle West. シカゴは中西部の主要都市である.

mettle, *n.* 勇気, 血気, 気力.

P a man ***of*** *mettle* 気概のある人.

mezzotint, *n.* メゾチント版.

V ***scrape*** a *mezzotint* メゾチント版に彫る.

miasma, *n.* 悪気, 毒気.

V^2 *miasma* ***rising*** from a swamp 沼沢から立ちのぼる悪気.

Q the ***deadly*** *miasma* of the slum 貧民くつの恐ろしい悪気.

mickle, *n.* たくさん, 多量.

V Many a little ***makes*** a *mickle*. ちりも積って山となる.

microbe, *n.* 微生物, 細菌.

Q ***malignant*** *microbes* 有毒細菌.

microcosm, *n.* 縮図.

P^2 a *microcosm* ***of*** English history 英国史の縮図.

microphone, *n.* 送話器; マイク.

Q^2 In ***hand*** *microphones* the receiver and transmitter are in one piece. 手動送話器では受送話器は一組になっている.

P speak ***at*** a *microphone* マイクに向って話す. ¶speak ***through*** a *microphone* マイクを通じて話す.

microscope, *n.* 顕微鏡.

V ***focus*** the *microscope* upon ... …に顕微鏡の焦点を合わせる, …を批判する. ¶the *microscope* will ***reveal*** ... 顕微鏡で見ると…が見える.

Q a ***high-powered*** *microscope* 高度の顕微鏡. ¶examine ... through a ***powerful*** *microscope* 高度の顕微鏡で…を調べる.

Q^2 an ***electron*** *microscope* 電子顕微鏡.

P seen under a high power ***of*** the *microscope* 高度の鏡微鏡で見ると. ¶visible only ***through*** a *microscope* 顕微顕でしか見えない. ¶a close examination ***under*** the *microscope* shows ... 顕微鏡でよく見ると…が分かる. 【類】 ***under*** the *microscope*, it proved to ... / put it ***under*** the *microscope* (検鏡する) / analyzed ***under*** a *microscope* (分析する) / when placed (=seen) ***under*** the *microscope* / observe ... ***under*** the *microscope*. ¶examine ***with*** a (=the) *microscope* 顕微鏡で調べる.

mid-air, *n.* 宙天.

P a beautiful rainbow hanging ***in*** *mid-air* 宙天にかかる美しいにじ.

midday, *n.* 日中, 正午.

Q^2 on ***Sunday*** *midday* 日曜の真昼に.

P the ship left here ***at*** *midday* on the 5th inst. [bound] for ... 同船は今月五日正午…に向けて当地を出帆した. ¶He will be back ***by*** *midday*. 彼は正午までには帰るだろう. ¶It is now ***past*** *midday*. 今は正午過ぎだ.

middle, *n.* 中央, 真中, 中ごろ.

P ***about*** the *middle* of next month 来月の半ばごろ. ¶He ranks somewhat ***above*** the *middle* of his class. 彼の席次はまず中以上だ. ¶***at*** about the *middle* of the 19th century 十九世紀の半ばごろに. 【類】 ***at*** the *middle* of the present year. ¶She burst out laughing ***in*** the *middle* of our discussion. 彼女はわれわれが話し合っている最中わっと笑い出した. ‖ She sat quite still ***in*** the *middle* of her bed. 彼女は床の真中にじっとしてすわっていた. ‖ She sailed mysteriously ***in*** the *middle* of the night for a secret destination. その船は奇怪にも真夜中にどこともも知れずこっそりと出帆した. ‖ part the hair ***in*** the *middle* 髪を真中で分ける. 【類】 He came ***in*** the *middle* of [the] day. / ***in*** the *middle* of the stream. ¶thrust ***into*** the *middle* of ... …の真中に割り込む.

P^2 in the *middle* ***between*** ... …の真中に. ¶in the *middle* ***of*** winter = in midwinter 真冬に.

middle-aged, *a.* 中年の.

M a stout lady, ***apparently*** *middle-aged* でっぷりした一見中年の婦人.

middle-class, *n.* 中流社会, 中産階級.

Q ***educated*** *middle-class* 教育ある中産階級. ¶the ***lower*** (***upper***) *middle-class* 下層(上層)中産階級. ¶the ***workaday*** *middle-class* 中産勤労階級.

middleman, *n.* 仲買人, 媒介者.

V direct trade ***eliminating*** the *middleman* 仲買人の手を抜く直接取引.

middling, *a.* 中位の.

M It is ***just*** *middling*. 丁度中ほどである.

midget, *n.* こびと.

P^2 a *midget* ***in*** a show 見世物のこびと.

mid-life, *n.* 中年.

P ***at*** *mid-life* 中年で. ¶***in*** late *mid-life* 中年後期に.

midnight, *n.* 夜半, 真夜中.

P ***about*** *midnight* 真夜中ごろ. ¶sit up till a little ***after*** *midnight* 真夜中少し過ぎまで起きている. 【類】 till twenty minutes ***after*** *midnight*. ¶on July 13th ***at*** *midnight* 七月十三日の真夜中に. ¶just ***before*** *midnight* 真夜中ちょっと前に. ¶***near*** *midnight* 真夜中近く. ¶study till ***past*** *midnight* 夜半過ぎまで勉強する. 【類】 It was well ***past*** *midnight*. ¶work in one's study ***until*** *midnight* 真夜中まで勉強する.

midshipman, *n.* 士官候補生.

P^2 a ***naval academy*** *midshipman* 《米》海軍大学々生.

midst, *n.* 中, 真中, 中間.

P ***in*** the very *midst* of ... …の真最中 ‖ Japan is ***in*** the *midst* of a transformation from an agricultural to an industrial nation. 日本は農業国から工業国へ転換の最中である. ‖ a rest-house ***in*** the *midst* of the mountains 山中の茶店 ‖ ***in*** the *midst* of a general hubbub あたりが騒々しい中で. 【類】 We are now ***in*** the *midst* of the most severe economic disaster of modern times. / ***in*** the *midst* of a pleasant dream, he was roused by the sound of ... / depart ***in*** the *midst* of a heavy rain (a storm, war) / ***in*** the *midst* of this altercation / The diplomat undertook what he regarded as a sacred duty—the writing of a book, ***in*** the *midst* of engrossing public work (公務に専念するかたわら). ‖ fundamental similarities ***in*** the *midst* of great superficial differences 表面大いに相違して見えるが根本的には類似している点 ‖ We have ***in*** our *midst* a great man of letters from England. 英国の文豪が来朝している. ‖ He was but recently ***in*** our *midst*. 彼はほんの先ごろまで生きていた. ‖ the foreigners ***in*** our *midst* 来朝中の外国人. ¶We rode ***into*** the *midst* of the forest. われわれはその林の中に馬を乗り入れた.

midsummer, *n.* 真夏.

P ***in*** *midsummer* 真夏に.

midway, *a., ad.* 真ん中の(に), 中途の(に).

P *midway* ***between*** ... and ... …間の中途 ‖ a style *midway* ***between*** ... and ... …と…の中間の様式. 【類】 situated *midway* ***between*** ... and ...

midwife, *n.* 助産婦, 産婆.

Q a ***certified*** *midwife* 免許状のある助産婦.

mien, *n.* 顔色, 風さい, 容姿, 態度.

Q her ***aristocratic*** *mien* 彼女の貴族的な容姿. ¶a man of ***proud*** *mien* ごう慢な態度の人. ¶***truculent*** *mien* どう猛な顔色. ¶his ***warlike*** *mien* 彼の闘争好きな態度.

P ***with*** an indignant *mien* 憤然たる様子をして.

might, *n.* 力, 勢力, 威勢, 腕力.

V ***muster*** that *might* その力を結集する.

Q ***armed*** *might* 武力.

P ***beyond*** one's *might* 自分の力に負えない. ¶the supremacy ***of*** *might* rather than of right 正義よりはむしろ腕力の優勢. ¶***with*** *might* and main 力の限り. 【類】 ***with*** all one's *might* [and main].

migrate, *v.* 移り住む, 移住する, 転住する.

M These birds *migrate* ***northwards*** in spring and ***southward*** in fall. これらの鳥は春は北へ, 秋は南へ移住する.

P *migrate* ***from*** Africa ***to*** Spain アフリカからスペインに

移住する ‖ *migrate* ***to*** their winter haunts 彼らの冬のすみかに移る.【類】the labouring classes who have *migrated* ***to*** town ***from*** rural districts.

migration, *n.* 移住, 移動.

Q The ***annual migration*** from towns to the seaside and other holiday resorts have already set in. 例年の都人士の海岸やその他の遊覧地への出遊びがもう始まった.

Q^2 ***bird migration*** 鳥類の移住. ¶***summer migration*** to the seaside 夏季(都人士の)海岸地帯への移動.

P^2 ***migration of*** culture 文化の移動.

mild, *a.* 温和な.

Q The weather is warm and *mild* ***in*** this part. この辺は天候が温暖だ.

O draw it *mild* 《口語》内輪に言う.

mike, *n.* マイク. ＝microphone.

P address one's audience ***through*** a (=***over*** the) *mike* マイクを通じて聴衆に呼びかける.

mildew, *n.* かび.

V ***show*** *mildew* かびがはえる.

V^2 *Mildew* ***grew*** and ***killed*** the rosebuds in the garden. かびがはえて庭のばらがだめになった.

P covered ***with*** *mildew* かびだらけで.

mildew, *v.* かびを生やす.

M get *mildewed* ***all over*** 一面かびだらけになる.

mile, *n.* 英里, マイル.

V He ***covered*** many *miles* on his bicycle. 彼は自転車で何マイルも走った.【類】The ten *miles* from ... to ... are ***covered*** in ... hours. ¶The train ***does*** the $44^1/_2$ *miles* in forty-three minutes. その汽車は四十三分で四十四マイル半走る.【類】***do*** some hundred *miles* on the English railways. ¶You ***have*** three *miles* more to go. あと三マイルあります. ¶A ***kurumaya makes*** about four *miles* an hour. 人力車は一時間に約四マイル走る. ¶The Northern Pacific Railway ***operates*** 6,655 *miles* of main and branch lines. 北太平洋鉄道は幹支線を合して六千六百五十五マイルを経営している. ¶***travel*** many *miles* a day 一日数マイルを旅行する.

Q a ***long*** *mile* by boat 小舟で一マイルとちょっと. ¶three ***marine*** *miles* 三海里. ¶a ***nautical*** *mile* 一海里. ¶a ***short*** *mile* distant 一マイルたらず離れた. ¶a ***slant*** *mile* [空中などから]斜めに一マイル. ¶***three*** and a ***half*** *mile*＝three miles and a half 三マイル半.

Q^2 be ninety ***airline*** *miles* from ... …から九十航空マイルある. ¶a ***passenger*** *mile* 〘鉄道〙輸送マイル(乗客一人一マイルを計算基礎とする).

P go a little ***beyond*** a *mile* 一マイルのちょっと先きへ行く. ¶travel ***for*** a hundred *miles* 百マイル旅行する ‖ all the neighbors ***for*** a *mile* round 一マイル四方の近隣は全部 ‖ ***for*** *miles* around 周囲数マイルにわたって. ¶***per*** *mile* 一マイルごとに. ¶***within*** three *miles* of ... …から三マイル以内のところに.

P^2 My house is two *miles* ***from*** the sea. 私の家は海岸から二マイルある. ¶*miles* ***of*** rubble [空襲後など]荒野原. ¶Here you will find *mile* ***upon*** *mile* of silver sand. ここには銀砂が何マイルも続いている.

mileage, *n.* マイル数, マイル程.

Q^2 Its ***route*** *mileage* is 108,681. その道路マイル数は十万八千六百八十一マイルとなっている. ¶the total ***single track*** *mileage* 単線総マイル数.

milestone, *n.* マイル標石.

V this ***marked*** the first *milestone* in his struggle to ... これが彼の…しようとする努力の第一歩であった ‖ This ***marked*** another *milestone* in the history of the organization. これがまたその団体の歴史における一画期的事件であった.

Q^2 reach its third ***quarter-century*** *milestone* (=the 75th anniversary) その七十五週年に達する.

P^2 a *milestone* ***on*** the road towards ... …に至る道の一マイル標.

militant, *n.* 闘士.

Q^2 a ***Communist*** *militant* 共産党闘士(行動隊員).

militarism, *n.* 軍国主義, 武断政治.

V ***abolish*** *militarism* 軍国主義を廃する. ¶***dethrone*** *militarism* 軍国主義を撤廃させる. ¶*Militarism* cannot be ***killed*** by warfare. 軍国主義は戦争によって絶滅するものではない.

Q ***patriotic*** *militarism* 愛国的軍国主義.

militarist, *n.* 軍国主義者.

Q the ***powerful*** *militarists* 軍閥.

militate, *v.* 働く, 作用する.

P this argument can *militate* ***against*** ... この議論は…を反ばくするに足りる ‖ His bad manners will *militate* ***against*** his success in business. 彼の無作法が彼の商人としての成功の妨げになるだろう. ¶The weather *militated* ***in favor of*** the crops. 天候がその作がらに幸いした.

milk, *n.* 乳, 牛乳; ミルク.

V ***adulterate*** *milk* with 25 per cent of water 牛乳に二十五パーセントの水を混ぜる. ¶***boil*** and ***sterilize*** *milk* 牛乳を煮沸し殺菌する. ¶Acid ***curdles*** *milk.* 酸は牛乳を凝結させる. ¶***deliver*** *milk* 牛乳を配達する. ¶***dilute*** *milk* with water 牛乳に水を割る. ¶***doctor*** (=adulterate) *milk* 牛乳に混ぜものをする. ¶***feed*** cow's *milk* to a baby＝feed a baby on cow's milk 赤ん坊に牛乳を飲ませる. ¶Cows ***give*** *milk.* 雌牛から乳がとれる. ¶The lap-dog is ***lapping*** *milk.* ちんころが牛乳をぴしゃぴしゃなめている. ¶***lick up*** the spilt *milk* こぼれた牛乳をすっかりなめる. ¶The gland ***secretes*** *milk.* 腺(せん)が牛乳を分泌する. ¶***sip*** *milk* 牛乳をすする. ¶Do not ***sip*** the *milk.* 牛乳をすすって飲むな. ¶***skim*** the *milk* 牛乳の上皮をすくい取る. ¶The babe ***sucks*** *milk.* 赤ん坊は乳を吸込む. ¶***take*** cow's *milk* 牛乳を飲む. ¶The warm weather has ***turned*** the *milk* [sour].＝The warm weather has made the milk go bad. 陽気が暖かいので牛乳が悪くなった. ¶A baby ***vomits*** *milk* from repletion. 赤ん坊が乳をあます.

Q ***bacteria-free*** *milk* 細菌のない牛乳. ¶***condensed*** *milk* 練乳. ¶***contaminated*** *milk* 不純な牛乳. ¶***dehydrated*** *milk* 粉ミルク. ¶the ***mother's*** *milk* 母乳. ¶***pasteurized*** *milk* 低温殺菌牛乳. ¶***skimmed*** *milk* 上皮を除いた牛乳. ¶***sour*** *milk* すい牛乳. ¶It is too late to cry over ***spilt*** *milk,* of course. もち論過ぎ去ったことはくよくよしても追付かない. ¶***sweet*** *milk* 甘い牛乳. ¶***watery*** *milk* 水っぽい牛乳. ¶***whole cow's*** *milk* 全乳.

Q^2 ***breast*** *milk* 母乳.

P nourish a baby ***on*** mother's *milk* 母乳で赤ん坊を育てる.【類】feed a puppy ***on*** *milk.*

milk, *v.* 乳をしぼる; 乳が出る; ぴんはねする.

M The treasurer *milked* the club fees ***dishonestly.*** 会計係が会費を不当にぴんはねした. ¶Cows are not *milking* ***well*** at this time of year. 今時分は牛乳の出がよくない(しぼれる量が少ない).

milk-and-water, *a.* 味のない, 気力のない.

Q *Sake* is ***mere*** *milk-and-water* to it. それに比べると酒などは水みたいなものだ.

mill, *n.* 水車場, 製粉所.

V ***run*** a *mill* 水車場を経営する ‖ a *mill* to ***run*** by water and hand 水力と手動で動かす水車.

Q^2 a ***cane*** *mill* [さとうきびの]精糖工場. ¶a ***corn*** *mill* とうもろこし精粉工場. ¶a ***cotton spinning*** *mill* 綿紡績工場. ¶curb overproduction by the "***diploma*** *mills*" いわゆる「免状工場」による生産過剰を防ぐ. ¶a row of ***flour*** *mills* on the river front 河岸に並ぶ製粉工場群. ¶a ***grinding*** *mill* 製粉機. ¶a ***hand*** *mill* ひきうす. ¶a ***lumber*** (=***timber***) *mill* 製材所. ¶an ***oil*** *mill* 製油所. ¶a ***paper*** (***steel***) *mill* 製紙(鋼)所. ¶a ***rice-grinding*** *mill* 製米工場. ¶a ***rice-pearling*** *mill* 精米工場. ¶a ***rice sweep*** *mill* 精米機. ¶a ***saw*** *mill* 製材所; [同所の]のこぎり. ¶a ***silk-reeling*** *mill* 絹糸機; 絹糸工場. ¶a ***spinning*** *mill* 紡績工場. ¶a ***starch*** *mill* でん粉工場. ¶a ***steel*** *mill* 製鋼所. ¶a ***textile*** *mill* 織物工場. ¶a ***wind*** *mill* [製粉の]風車小屋. ¶a ***wire*** *mill* ワイヤ工場. ¶a ***wood*** *mill* 木工場.

P be ground ***in*** a *mill* 製粉される. ¶men who have been "***through*** the *mill*" 実地経験のある人々.

P^2 a *mill* ***with*** sixteen wings 十六翼のある風車.

millennium, *n.* 至福の時期, 至福千年.

V ***bring in*** the *millennium* 至福千年をもたらす.

O the *millennium* will be on when ... …という時こそ世は極楽だ.

millet-seeds, *n.* きび.

V *millet-seeds* are ***formed*** on the skin はだえにあわを生じる.

milliner, *n.* 婦人帽子屋(製造人).

Q^2 a ***man*** *milliner* 男の婦人製帽師.

milling, *n.* 製粉.

Q^2 ***corn*** *milling* とうもろこしの製粉. ¶***flour*** *milling* 製粉作業.

million, *n.* 百万, 大数, 無数.

V Can you ***count*** one *million?* 百万まで数えることができるか. ¶***expend*** *million* upon million on ... …に何百万

と金を使う. ¶The firm ***handles millions***. その店は何百万という金を取扱う. ¶***involve millions*** of outlay 何百万という出費を要する.

Q China's fast ***awakening millions***. 中国のどんどん目覚めて行く何百万の民衆. ¶***countless millions*** 無数の民衆. ¶for a ***million million*** of years 数億年間. ¶London's ***teeming millions*** ロンドンのうようよする大衆.【類】the life of the ***teeming millions*** of a great city. ¶the ***toiling millions*** of America アメリカ幾百万の労働者. ¶***uncounted*** (=***untold***) *millions* of people 無数の大衆.

P The estimated exportation for 1929 is ***around*** one *million*. その一九二九年度の輸出額は百万がらみと見積られている. ¶***by*** [the] *millions* 何百万となく. ¶science ***for*** the *million* 百万人の科学. ¶scale: one ***in million*** ...尺比例(縮尺)...百万分の一.

P² Through his books he reached ***millions of*** people. 彼は著書を通じて無数の大衆に接触した.【類】thousands and ***millions of*** people.

millionaire, *n*. 百万長者, 大富豪.

Q a ***company-promoting*** *millionaire* 新会社発起の百万長者. ¶a ***mammoth*** *millionaire* 大富豪. ¶Black-market operators were the ***new*** *millionaires* of Japan. やみ商人が日本の新興財閥であった. ¶***prewar*** (***postwar***) *millionaires* 戦前(後)の百万長者. ¶a ***public-spirited*** *millionaire* 公共心のある富豪. ¶a *millionaire* ***several times over***=a multimillionaire 幾百万の大富豪.

Q² a ***vampire*** *millionaire* 吸血鬼的百万長者. ¶a ***war*** *millionaire* 戦争成金.

O He was born a *millionaire*. 彼は百万長者に生れた.

millstone, *n*. 磨石, ひきうすの石; 重荷.

P grind corn ***on*** a *millstone* ひきうすで穀物をひく.【類】be ground ***on*** a large *millstone*.

P² It is a *millstone* ***around*** his neck. それは彼を苦しめる重荷である.

mimicry, *n*. 物まね, 人まね.

Q ***apish*** *mimicry* さるまね. ¶***protective*** *mimicry* 〖動物〗擬態. ¶***vocal*** *mimicry* ものまね, 声帯模写.

mince, *v*. 切りきざむ; 遠慮して言う.

P He *minced* no words ***in*** his accusation. 彼はかしゃくなく責めたてた.

O not to *mince* matters (=words) はっきり言えば.

mind, *n*. (1) 心, 精神, 心知, 知力.

V ***absorb*** the *mind* of ... ...の心を奪う. ¶***activate*** and ***inspire*** the *minds* of the people 民心を鼓舞激励する. ¶***affect*** one's *mind* その心に影響する. ¶The question ***agitates*** his *mind*. その問題が彼の心をかき乱す. ¶induce them to ***alter*** their *minds* 彼らの考えを変えさせようとする. ¶***apply*** the *mind* to books 心を書籍に向ける. ¶It had value in ***arousing*** the sluggish *mind* of the masses. それは大衆のなまけ心にむち打つという効果があった. ¶***attune*** one's *mind* to ... ...にその心を調和させる. ¶***baffle*** the Western *mind* 西洋人を面食らわせる. ¶***bend*** one's *mind* on the task of ... の仕事に専念する. ¶***bias*** one's *mind* その心をかたよらせる. ¶To the right understanding of a subject, it is necessary to ***bring*** an unbiassed *mind*. 一つの問題を正しく理解するためには公平な心を持つことが必要だ. ¶***broaden*** one's *mind* by a liberal education 高等教育によってその心を広くする. ¶***burden*** the reader's *mind* with unnecessary details 不必要な細かいことまで書いて読者の心を悩ます. ¶***change*** one's *mind* その考えを変える. ¶anyone who has ***cleared*** his *mind* of the obsession of tradition will agree that ... 伝統にとらわれない人はだれでも...に同意するだろう. ¶***cloud*** one's *mind* その心を曇らす. ¶***collect*** one's disordered *mind* 乱れた心を取り直す. ¶***compose*** one's *mind* 心を落着ける. ¶***concentrate*** one's *mind* on some thought ある思想に凝る. ¶His *mind* is ***contracted***. 彼は量見がせまい. ¶***corrupt*** and ***debauch*** the *mind* and morals of ... ...の心も道徳も堕落させる. ¶***cram*** one's *mind* with ... ...[知識など]を頭につめ込む. ¶This thought ***crossed*** her *mind* as she ... 彼女が...した時にこの考えが胸に浮んだ ‖ Two instances ***cross*** my *mind* at this moment. 今二つの例が私の心に浮ぶ. ¶To ***cultivate*** the *mind* is to make it bear fruit in a realization of the best that is latent within it. 精神の修養ということはその内に潜在する最善のものを実現して実を結ぶようにさせることである. ¶***debase*** the *mind* 心を卑しくする. ¶***depress*** the *mind* 落胆させる. ¶Education ***develops*** the *mind*. 教育は心知を開発する. ‖ ***develop*** the international *mind* 国際心を啓発する. ¶***disburden*** one's *mind* to ... ...に心を打明ける. ¶***discipline*** the *minds* of man in virtue 道徳的に精神を鍛錬する.【類】Grammar ***disciplines*** the *mind* and develops the logical faculty (論理的能力). ¶***distract*** one's *mind* その心を迷わす. ¶***disturb*** one's *mind* その心を乱す. ¶***divert*** one's *mind* from the thought of ... ...の考えを他に転じさせる. ¶***divest*** one's *mind* from one's worries その心の悩みを忘れさせる. ¶***dwarf*** the *mind* 心をいじけさす. ¶***ease*** one's *mind* 心を安んじる. ¶***educate*** the public *mind* 社会人を教育する ‖ It is blatant mockery to speak of ***educating*** *minds* that dwell in anaemic bodies. 貧血した虚弱の者を教育するなどと口にするのは徒らな放言に過ぎない. ¶***elate*** the *mind* 得意がらせる. ¶***engross*** the *mind* of ... ...の心を奪う. ¶***enlarge*** a *mind* 眼界を広くする. ¶***enlighten*** the public *mind* 民心を啓発する. ¶***ennoble*** the *mind* 精神を高尚にする. ¶***enrich*** one's *mind* 心を豊富にする.【類】with *mind* ***enriched*** by his experiences. ¶A bold thought ***entered*** his *mind*. 大胆な考えが彼に浮んだ. ¶*minds* ***enthralled*** by convention 因襲にとらわれた心. ¶The question ***exercises*** the *minds* of the scientists. その問題は科学者連の研究が必要だ. ¶a question now very much ***exercising*** the Japanese *mind* 日本人が今大いに頭を使っている問題.【類】The question is ***exercising*** the *minds* of the British industry very actively. ¶Knowledge ***expands*** the *mind*. 知識は視野を広くする. ¶***fix*** one's *mind* on ... ...に専念する.【類】***fix*** the *mind* continually on ... ¶***follow*** his own *mind* 彼自身の考えに従う. ¶***give*** one's *mind* to gambling (drinking) ばくち(など)に凝る. ¶***guess*** one's *mind* その心を推察する. ¶Phantoms constantly ***haunted*** my *mind*. 幻影がひっきりなしに私の心に去来した. ¶I ***have*** a *mind* to do it. 私はそれをやりたい気がする. ‖ I ***had*** half a *mind* to continue the dispute. その論議を続けたいような気もあった.【類】I ***have*** no *mind* to ... ¶His *mind* is ***impaired*** by age. 彼は年のせいで精神力が弱っている. ¶***improve*** one's *mind* and enlarge one's faculties by reading and reflection 読書と反省によって知をみがき能力を増進する. ¶***initiate*** the infant *mind* into the first mysteries of number 幼児の心に数の不可思議を教え込む. ¶***interest*** the child's *mind* 子供の心に興味を持たせる. ¶***interpret*** the *mind* of a nation 国民の心を判断する. ¶He came back from the trip, his *mind* ***invigorated*** for the whole week. 彼はその旅行から帰ってきて一週間ずっと元気づいた. ¶***keep*** one's *mind* on ... ...に注意を怠らない ‖ burn incense ***keeping*** one's *mind* upon the memory of ... ...のことを心に念じて香をたく. ¶She is too young to ***know*** her own *mind*. 彼女はまだ若いから自分で自分の心が分からない.【類】I ***know*** her constant *mind* (変らない心). ¶***Let*** your *mind* dwell on it. よくそのことを考えて見なさい.【類】***Let*** her *mind* dwell on these ideas. ¶We must ***lift*** our *minds* above the mere national standpoint. われわれはただ国家的な立場ばかりでなくそれ以上の高所から考えねばならない. ¶I'm afraid she may ***lose*** her *mind*. 彼女は発狂するのではなかろうか. ¶She ***made up*** her *mind* to die rather than be defeated in her purpose. 彼女は目的が遂せられなければ死ぬ決心をした.【類】I ***made up*** my *mind* that something should be done. ¶There is a penetrating dampness about the London drizzle that seems gradually to ***mildew*** the *mind*. ロンドンの長雨には身にしみ込むような湿気があってそれが漸次心を腐らしそうに思われる. ¶***narrow*** one's *mind* 心を狭量にする. ¶The drama is now ***occupying*** the public *mind*. その劇が今や一般人の心を引きつけている. ¶***open*** the *mind* 胸きんをひらく. ¶***open up*** one's *mind* freely 自由に意中を語る. ¶***polish*** (=improve) one's *mind* 心をみがく. ¶***pollute*** the *mind* 心を汚す. ¶He ***possesses*** a cultivated *mind*. 彼は精神の修養ができている. ¶Constantly ***practice*** and ***train*** one's *mind* 絶えず心をみがききたえる. ¶however far I ***project*** my *mind* into the future, I cannot foresee a time when ... いかに遠く将来に思いをはせても...なる時を予想することはできない. ¶***puzzle*** one's *mind* with the thought, "..." ...と考えて不審に思う. ¶***raise*** the *mind* above low cares 俗事に超越する. ¶He ***reads*** *mind* like a book. 彼は本を読むように人の心を読む. ¶try to ***read*** one's *mind* その腹をさぐる. ¶***recreate*** one's *mind* 考えを新たにする. ¶Works of taste ***refine*** the *mind*. 高尚な作品は心を清くする. ¶It ***reflects*** the official's *mind* of Tokyo. それは東京の役人の

心を反映する. ¶forget his work and ***rest*** his ***mind*** 彼の仕事を忘れて心を休ませる. ¶He ***reveals*** a ***mind*** fresh with vigour and full of the joy of life. 彼は見たところ元気に満ち人生の喜びにあふれている. ¶***rid*** the patient's ***mind*** of the idea of ... 病人に...の考えを捨てさせる. ¶This notion ***seized*** his ***mind***. 彼はこの考えを持つに至った. ¶You may ***set*** your ***mind*** at rest about that. そのことについては御安心なさい. ‖ He has ***set*** his ***mind*** on acting. 彼は俳優になることに決心した. ‖ ***set*** one's ***mind*** at rest 精神を休める. ¶It has ***slipped*** my ***mind*** entirely. 私はそれを全然忘れてしまった. ¶***solace*** the ***mind*** 心をなぐさめる. ¶concerning ... he ***speaks*** his ***mind*** emphatically ...に関して彼は自分の意中をきっぱりひれきしている. 【類】***speak*** one's ***mind*** vigorously about ... / ***speak*** one's ***mind*** too strongly / He always ***speaks*** his ***mind*** freely. / ***speak*** one's ***mind*** frankly / He is a fool who ***speaks*** all his ***mind***. ¶***steep*** the student's ***mind*** in an atmosphere of English thought 学生の心を英国思想のふん囲気の中に浸す. ¶***stimulate*** the ***mind*** to originality of thought 心を刺激して独創性を発揮させる. ¶***stock*** one's ***mind*** with a large number of valuable facts, opinions, and ideas 幾多の貴重な事実や意見や思想を心に取入れる. ¶***stuff*** the ***mind*** with facts 事実を頭に詰め込む. ¶***sublimate*** our ***minds*** to their original purity われわれの心をもとの純潔さまで高める. ¶***Switch*** your ***mind*** on to some other thought when an unwelcome thought arises. 不愉快な考えが起ったときは心を他に転じるようにせよ. 【類】***switch*** your ***mind*** away from ... ¶***take*** one's ***mind*** out of one's accustomed groove その心を新方面に向ける(心機一転). ¶***take*** one's ***mind*** off the thoughts 気を紛らす. 【類】***take*** one's ***mind*** off the work. ¶***tickle*** the ***minds*** 心をくすぐる ‖ the puzzle that is ***tormenting*** the ***minds*** of all other countries すべての他の国民の心を悩ましているなぞ. ¶The thought ***tortured*** my ***mind***. そう考えて私は心を悩ました. ¶an instrument for ***training*** the ***mind*** 心を練磨する道具. ¶***trouble*** one's ***mind*** 心にかける, 心配する. ¶***turn*** one's ***mind*** to ... ...に心を向ける. 【類】***turn*** their ***minds*** to its consideration. ‖ His ***mind*** was ***turned*** by his losses. 損をしたので彼の心が狂った. ¶***unbalance*** the ***mind*** ろうばいさせる. ¶desire to ***unbend*** one's ***mind*** from business 仕事を休もうと願う. ¶***unburden*** one's ***mind*** to ... ...に心を打明ける. ¶***unfold*** the ***mind*** 心中をひれきする. ¶Joy at his sudden recovery nearly ***unhinged*** his ***mind***. 急に回復した喜びで彼はちょっと気が変になる位だった. ¶***unsettle*** the ***minds*** of people 人々の心をかき乱す. ¶These problems ***vex*** the ***mind*** of Europe. これら諸問題が欧州人士の心を悩ましている. ¶***weary*** the ***mind*** けん怠を覚えさせる.

v² His ***mind became affected*** at his brother's disgraceful death. 兄(弟)が不名誉な死を遂げたので彼は気が変になった. ¶The ***mind*** often ***dwelled*** on voluptuous images. 心にみだらなことが浮ぶことが度々あった. ¶Our ***minds*** can ***travel*** when our bodies are forced to stay at home. 身体は余儀なく家にあっても心は自由にかけ回る. ¶the ***mind turns*** to ... 心が...の方に向く. ¶My ***mind wandered***. 私は心が乱れた. ¶My ***mind*** doesn't ***work*** that way. 私はその方面の仕事へは向かない.

Q I was dazzled by the scintillations of his ***academic mind***. 私は彼の学才のけんらんさにげん惑された. ¶What the speech reporter needs most is an ***alert mind***. 演説を報道する記者には鋭敏な頭が一番必要だ. ¶the ***ancient*** and the ***medieval mind*** 古代人及び中世人の考え. ¶He has an ***antiquated mind*** 彼はあたまが古い. ¶a ***balanced mind*** 平均のとれた心. ¶a ***candid, pouncing mind*** 淡白で遠慮のない心. ¶He has a ***capable mind***. 彼には手腕がある. ¶of a ***charitable mind*** 慈悲心のある. ¶to the ***childish mind*** 幼な心に. ¶a ***clear*** and ***active mind*** はっきりした活動的な頭. ¶a ***constructive mind*** 建設的な心. ¶the product of a ***cultured mind*** 教養ある人の頭の産物. ¶be of a ***curious mind*** 好奇心がある. ¶a ***deliberative mind*** 物をよく考える性質. ¶He has a ***deranged mind***. あの人は気が狂っている. ¶a ***disciplined mind*** 訓練された心. ¶The vapors of a ***disordered mind*** 頭の狂った人の空想. ¶the ***Divine mind*** 神意. ¶the expression of an ***earnest*** and ***candid mind*** 熱心にして率直な心の表現. ¶Discernment is one of the tests of the ***educated mind***. 判断力は教育ある人の証拠の一つだ. ¶an ***elevated mind*** 高潔な心. ¶He has an ***English mind***. 彼は英国人の心を持っている. ¶a man of ***feeble mind*** うすのろの人. ¶the ***feminine mind*** 女心. ¶a ***fertile mind*** 創意の豊かな心. ¶She is of a ***frugal mind***. 彼女はつましい. ¶I have a ***good mind*** to ... 私はぜひ...したいと思っている. ‖ possession of a ***good mind*** (=intelligence) 知性を持つこと. ¶I had ***half*** a ***mind*** to continue the dispute. よっぽど議論を続けようかと思った. ¶with ***happy*** and ***carefree minds*** 愉快で心配のない心で. ¶a ***harmonious mind*** 調和的な心. ¶the ***historical mind*** 歴史精神. ¶the ***immature minds*** of children 子供の未熟な心. ¶to ***impartial minds***, it will seem pretty clearly apparent that ... ...公平に考える人々にとっては...ということはかなり明らかであると思われるであろう. 【類】give an ***impartial mind*** to the inquiry. ¶an ***impure mind*** 不純な心. ¶a man of very ***independent mind*** 独立心の強い人. ¶In the kindergarten the ***infantile mind*** is first taught to use its awakening powers of reason. 幼稚園でまず幼児の心は漸次目ざめて来る理性の力を用いることを教えられる. ¶They have ***inquiring minds***. 彼らは研究心がある. ‖ be of an ***inquring mind*** せんさく好きだ. ¶think and speak with an ***international mind*** 国際精神を持って考えかつ話す. ¶You must not have an ***irresolute mind***. 君はぐらついた考えを持ってはいけない. ¶the ***keenest minds*** 最も鋭い頭の人々. ¶discuss subjects of interest with ***kindred minds*** 興味ある問題を同志と論議する. ¶the ***juvenile mind*** 童心. ¶avoid the use of technical terms unfamiliar to the ***lay mind*** しろうとに不なれな術語の使用を避ける. 【類】the ***lay mind*** understand little of ... ¶have a ***logical mind*** 論理的な頭をもっている. ¶a ***marvelous mind*** 驚くべき知力. ¶So many men, so ***many minds*** 世はさまざま. ¶a ***mature mind*** 成熟した頭. ¶a ***mean*** and ***narrow mind*** 卑しく狭い心. ¶strange as it may seem to the ***modern mind*** 近代人から見ると妙に見えるかも知れないが. 【類】The ***modern mind*** is liable to misunderstand the real significance of ancient customs. / appeal to the ***modern mind***. ¶a ***nimble mind*** よく働く頭. ¶with an ***open mind*** 偏見なしに. ¶an ***original mind*** 独創的な心. ¶It appeals to the ***popular mind***. それはしろうと好きがする. ¶a ***prejudiced mind*** 偏見. ¶the custom of deifying all things which the ***primitive mind*** was unable to grasp 原始人の心に解釈し得なかったことは何でも神様扱いにする習慣. ¶a ***prurient*** (=an impure) ***mind*** 好色な心. ¶cultivate the ***public mind*** 公共心を養う ‖ the education of the ***public mind*** 公衆教育. ¶have a ***quick mind*** 頭の働きが早い. ¶a ***reasoning mind*** 理性的な頭. ¶young men and women of the ***rebellious*** and ***original mind*** 御しにくい独創的な心の青年男女. ¶No man in his ***right mind*** would pass up such a bargain. 正気の人ならだれだってそんなに安い品物を見のがさないだろう. ‖ Are you crazy?—I am quite in my ***right mind***. 君は気が狂ったのか—私は全く気は確かだ. ¶The author has true sympathy with the ***rural mind***. その著者はいなかの人に真の同情を寄せている. ¶his ***scholarly mind*** 彼の学者はだ. ¶a ***scientific mind*** 科学的な心. ¶a ***small mind*** けちな心. ¶He is alleged to have been of ***sound mind*** at the time of the offense. 彼はその罪を犯したとき気が確かであったということである. 【類】One wonders whether he is of ***sound mind*** (正気のさた). ¶a ***statesmanlike*** and ***liberal mind*** 政治家のようで寛大な心. ¶a person of ***systematic mind*** 考えが秩序的な人. ¶spur and whip the ***tired mind*** into action 疲れ切った心にむちを与えて(鼓舞激励して)行動させる. ¶keep a ***tranquil mind*** 心を平静に保つ. ¶***unbalanced mind*** 平衡の取れていない心. ¶with ***unbiased minds*** 一方に偏しない心で. 【類】with an ***unbiased mind***. ¶an ***unperturbed mind*** 動じない人. ¶to the ***unprejudiced mind***, however, it is clear that ... しかし公平な見方をする人には...ということは明らかである. ¶the ***unscientific mind*** 非科学的な心. ¶The jury returned a verdict of suicide while of ***unsound mind***. 陪審官たちは精神に異状を呈しての自殺という評決を下した. 【類】a man of ***unsound mind***. / The suicide was of ***unsound mind*** when he committed the deed. ¶have a ***vacant mind*** ぼうっとしている. ¶a ***vigorous*** and ***alert mind*** 元気鋭敏な人. ¶a person of ***weak mind*** 精神耗弱者. 【類】those with ***weak*** or ***feeble minds***. ¶a ***well-balanced mind*** 平均のとれた頭. ¶a ***well-poised mind*** つり合のとれている心. ¶an unusually ***well-stored mind*** 非凡な物知り ‖

the resources of his ***well-stored*** *mind* 彼のうんちく. ¶throw one's ***whole*** *mind* into the work 全精神をその仕事に打込む.

Q² a child with an ***adult*** *mind* and vice versa 大人じみた考えの子供とその逆. ¶people with "***grasshopper*** *minds*" nibble at everything and master nothing 何でも屋で何一つ物にしない人たち. ¶a ***master*** *mind* 主たる精神; 偉人. ¶a man with a ***one-track*** *mind* 一筋道(一本気)の人. ¶a ***propaganda-proof*** *mind* 宣伝に惑わされない心(人). ¶even the ***twentieth-century*** *mind* is staggered by ... 二十世紀の人ですら...にはぎょっとする. ¶the ***world*** *mind* 世界心(世界を考慮に入れた考え方).

P The conviction flashed ***across*** his *mind*. 彼は急に心に確信ができた. ‖ A sudden idea flashed ***across*** my *mind*. 急にある考えが私の胸に浮んだ. ¶When we think of Napoleon Bonaparte a world (=huge number) of visions and memories rise ***before*** the *mind*. われわれがナポレオン・ボナパルトを思うとき幾多の幻想や記憶が目前に浮かんで来る. 【類】keep it constantly ***before*** one's *mind* / if you call it ***before*** your *mind*. ¶deeply engraved ***in*** his *mind* 彼の心に深く銘じて ‖ venture to speak what one has ***in*** *mind* 思っていることを口に出す. 【類】we have it ***in*** *mind* when we speak of ... ‖ the memory which could not fail to rankle ***in*** the *minds* of ... ...の骨髄に徹するうらみ ‖ say it ***in*** one's *mind* はらの中でそういう ‖ Say it over and over till it is written ***in*** your *mind*. それをあなたの心に刻み付けられるまで繰返し繰返しお言いなさい. ‖ he was ***in*** two *minds* as to whether to ... or not 彼は...をすべきかすべからざるかの二筋道に迷った ‖ sound ***in*** *mind* 気のたしかな. ¶in a happy (sad) frame ***of*** *mind* 幸福(悲しい)気分で. ¶I asked him what was ***in*** and ***on*** his *mind*. 一体何を考え何を言おうとしたのかと彼に尋ねた. ¶high powers ***of*** *mind* 非常にすぐれた知能 ‖ No two men are ***of*** a *mind*. 十人十色. ‖ When a woman gives you a piece ***of*** her *mind* it's because she cannot keep the piece. 女が君に心を打明けて言うのは胸に秘めておけないからだ. ‖ I am ***of*** the same *mind* with you on the question. この問題については僕は君と同意見だ. ¶I cannot get this thing ***off*** my *mind*. 私はこのことを忘れることができない. ‖ have the matter ***off*** one's *mind* そのことを忘れる. ¶I have troubles ***on*** my *mind*. 私は心に悩みがある. ¶I made him tell me what was ***on*** his *mind*. 私は彼が気になっていることを話させた ‖ Shoot! What's ***on*** your *mind?* 《俗》言っちまえ! 何を言おうとしているんだ? 【類】have ... constantly ***on*** one's *mind*. ‖ It is (=weighs) ***on*** my *mind*. それが気がかりだ. ‖ a weight ***on*** one's *mind* 心の悩み ‖ I know what he has ***on*** his *mind*. 彼の心中は分かっている. 【類】I have had the matter ***on*** my *mind* for a long time. ‖ I have something ***on*** my *mind*. ¶go ***out of*** *mind* in time 時がたつと忘れる ‖ He seems quite ***out of*** his *mind*. 彼は全く気が狂ったようだ. ‖ Great Scott! You're ***out of*** your *mind*. これゃ驚いた. 君はどうかしている. ‖ Out of sight, ***out of*** *mind*. 〖諺〗去る者は日々にうとし. ¶I cannot this minute call it ***to*** *mind*. ちょっと胴忘れをした. ‖ ***to*** my *mind* 私に言わせると. 【類】***to*** our *mind* / There is nowhere like Tokyo ***to*** my *mind*. / His workmanship is not much ***to*** my *mind*. ‖ ***to*** the lay *mind* it would seem that ... しろうと考えでは...と思われるだろう. ¶Two hours of constant study, daily, ***with*** a concentrated *mind*, are worth years of random reading. 毎日続けて熱心に二時間あて勉強すると手当り次第に多年読書するのにまさる.

P² events uppermost in the *minds* ***of*** the audience 見物人が一番期待している競技.

(2) 人間.

V No question has ever ***attracted*** so many minds as this. この問題ほど多数の人の心をとらえたものはない. ¶satisfy ***critical*** *minds* 批評家を満足させる.

Q an ***aspiring*** *mind* 大望をもつ人. ¶the ***best creative*** *minds* of the times その時代の最もすぐれた独創的な人々. ¶***brilliant*** *minds* 頭のいい人々. ¶a ***commonplace*** *mind* 平凡な人. ¶***Congenial*** *minds* are disposed to associate. 〖諺〗類は友を呼ぶ. ¶one of the ***greatest*** *minds* of the century その世紀の大偉人の一人. ¶a most ***illuminated*** *mind* of his age 彼の時代の最も賢明な人. ¶a ***little*** *mind* 小人. ¶a ***methodical*** *mind* きちょうめんな人. ¶***No two*** *minds* think alike. 人間の考えはそれぞれ違う. ¶a ***plastic*** *mind* 感化を受けやすい人. ¶***Western*** *minds* 西洋の人たち(の心).

P appeal ***to*** the public *mind* 一般大衆に訴える. ¶***youthful*** *minds* 若人たち.

P² the best *minds* ***in*** Japan 日本のもっともすぐれた人たち.

mind, *v.* 心に留める, 気にする.

P Never *mind* ***about*** that. それにはお構い下さるな.

O Do you *mind* my smoking? タバコをのんでもよろしゅうございますか. ¶I have no objection, *mind* you, but I think it's unwise. 私は反対じゃないだがね, しかしそれはまずいと思うね.

minded, *a.* ...する気のある, ...する意向の, ...の気のある.

M ***auditorily*** *minded* 聴覚型の. ¶***commercially*** *minded* people 商売気のある人たち. ¶more ***internally*** *minded* 一層内省的な心の. ¶***internationally*** *minded* Americans 国際的なアメリカ人. ¶***like-minded*** people 同志. ¶those who, like Pestalozzi, are "***psychologically*** *minded*" ペスタロッチのように物を心理学的に考える頭のある人々. ¶if he is ***so*** *minded* 彼がその気なら. 【類】those who are ***so*** *minded*. ¶***theoretically*** *minded* Europeans 理論的傾向のあるヨーロッパ人.

mindful, *a.* 心に留める, 気をつける.

P be *mindful* ***of*** ... ...によく注意する ‖ be *mindful* only ***of*** one's own interest 自分のことばかり考える. 【類】He was so heroically *mindful* ***of*** his task and his responsibilities. / *mindful* ***of*** one's duties.

mine, *n.* 鉱山, 鉱坑; 機雷; 富源.

V ***blow up*** a *mine* 鉱坑を爆破する. ¶The book ***contains*** a *mine* of (=rich³) information. その本には豊富な知識がのっている. ¶***develop*** a *mine* 鉱山を開発する. ¶***explode*** a *mine* in the sea 機雷を海中で爆発させる. ¶He ***found*** a *mine* of wealth in the narratives of forgotten Englishmen. 彼は忘れられた英国人の物語の中に収入(稿料)の種を見出した. ¶***lay*** (=***place***) a *mine* 水雷を敷設する. ¶***open up*** a *mine* 鉱山を開発する. ¶***operate*** (=***work***) a *mine* 鉱山を採掘する(経営する). ¶***promote*** a *mine* 鉱山採掘を企画する. ¶***run*** a *mine* 鉱山を経営する. ¶***shut down*** a *mine* 鉱山の採掘を休止する. ¶***strike*** a *mine* 機雷に触れる. 【類】She ***struck*** a German *mine* in the Baltic.

Q an ***abandoned*** *mine* 廃坑. ¶***drifting*** *mines* 浮流水雷. ¶The steamer struck a ***floating*** *mine*. その汽船は浮流水雷にかかった. ¶He is a ***perfect*** *mine* of learning. 彼は実に博識だ. ¶It is a ***rich*** *mine* of quaint names. それには珍らしい人名がたくさんのせてある. ¶a ***submerged*** *mine* 敷設水雷. ¶a ***valuable*** *mine* of ... ...の貴重な宝庫. ¶a ***veritable*** *mine* of historical data 全く無尽蔵な史料.

Q² a ***diamond*** (***gold, silver, copper***) *mine* ダイヤ(など)鉱山. ¶a ***wildcat*** *mine* いんちき鉱山.

P the yield (=output) ***of*** a *mine* 鉱山の産額.

P² a *mine* ***of*** statistics and information bearing on ... ...関係の統計や事項をのせた出版物. 【類】a *mine* ***of*** curious information.

miner, *n.* 鉱夫, 坑夫.

V ***safeguard*** *miners* 鉱夫を保護する.

Q ***entombed*** *miners* 埋没した鉱夫.

mineral, *n.* 鉱物, 鉱石.

Q ***metallic*** *minerals* 金属鉱物. ¶a ***rare*** *mineral* 珍らしい鉱物.

P the United States is rich ***in*** *minerals*. アメリカ合衆国は鉱物に富む.

mingle, *v.* 混じる; 交ざる, 入りまじる.

M *mingle* ***harmoniously*** with ... 折合よく...と交際する.

P *mingle* ***in*** crowds 群衆に交じる ‖ They *mingle* very little ***in*** society. 彼らはあまり人と交際しない. ¶with astonishment *mingled* ***with*** amusement 面白がると同時に驚いて ‖ ***With*** his piety *mingled* a fair amount of worldly cunning. その信仰心にはかなりの現世的なずるさも交っていた.

O by *mingled* gentleness and firmness 温良に加うるに決断をもってして.

mingling, *n.* いりまじり.

Q ***free social*** *mingling* between men and women of the upper classes 上流社会における男女の自由な社交的接触.

miniature, *n.* 小さい物; 小形; 小規模; 縮図.

Q an ***exact*** *miniature* of ... ...の小さいだけのもの.

P He is indeed a Hercules ***in*** *miniature*. 彼は実際ハーキュリーズを小形にしたようなものだ. ‖ the world ***in*** *miniature* 世界の縮図, 小世界. 【類】Shanghai is a little world, where all China ***in*** *miniature* may be studied at close range. / It is represented here ***in*** *miniature*. / present ***in*** *miniature* all the features of ... / The waterchestnut has a remarkable resemblance to the head of the buffalo ***in*** *miniature*. ひしは水牛の頭を小さくしたものによく似ている.

minimum, *n*. 最小限, 最小量, 最小額.

V They wish to ***inflict*** a *minimum* of hardship on the public. 彼らは公衆にできるだけ困難を掛けないようにしたいと思っている. ¶***spend*** a *minimum* of both time and money 時と金をできるだけ少なく費す. ¶***state*** the irreducible *minimum* of ... ...を最小極限に言う.

Q the ***irreducible*** *minimum* of a demand 要求の最小限度 ‖ shed everything but " the ***irreducible*** *minimum* " 除かれるだけ除く. 【類】 bring expenses to the ***irreducible*** *minimum* / the ***irreducible*** *minimum* of a boy's education before specialisation begins. ¶be reduced to the ***lowest*** *minimum* 最低限度に縮少される.

P ***at*** a *minimum* of expense 最小限度の費用で. 【類】 ***at*** a *minimum* of cost and trouble / the maximum of luxury ***at*** the *minimum* of cost. ¶reduce expense ***to*** the *minimum* 費用を最小限度に減らす. ¶***with*** a *minimum* of inconvenience to ... ...にできるだけ不便をかけないで ‖ the power of giving a maximum of expression, ***with*** a *minimum* of means 最小限度の方便をもって最大限度の発表をやる力. 【類】 ***with*** a *minimum* of effort (trouble, eyestrain and fatigue) / Boys go through college today ***with*** a *minimum* of education and a maximum of evasion (回避). / ***with*** the *minimum* of effort and the maximum of results.

P² The airship is constructed on the principle of reducing it to a *minimum* ***of*** weight consistent with the strength. 飛行船は耐力を低下させずに重量を最小限度まで減らすということを原則にして建造される.

minion, *n*. ちょう児.

P² a *minion* ***of*** fortune = a lucky person 運命のちょう児.

minister, *n*. 大臣; 公使; 伝道者.

V ***accredit*** a *minister* to a foreign government 公使に信任状を授けて外国へ派遣する. ¶He was ***appointed*** Japanese *minister* to Mexico. 彼はメキシコ駐さつ日本公使に任命された. ¶The Emperor ***met*** his *ministers* and discusses the affairs of state. 天皇は各大臣に謁を賜わり国務を議論された.

Q Sir John Jordan, ***British*** *minister* in Peking 北京駐さつ英国公使ジョン・ジョルダン卿. ¶a ***competent*** *minister* 主務大臣. ¶a ***former*** *Minister* of Foreign Affairs 前外務大臣. ¶Envoy Extraordinary and *Minister* ***plenipotentiary*** for Great Britain to ... ...駐さつ英特命全権公使. ¶the ***prime*** *minister* 首相 ‖ ***prime*** *ministers* from Asiatic countries アジア諸国からきている首相たち.

Q² ***inner-Cabinet*** *ministers* 閣内閣僚(経済閣僚など). ¶an ***interior*** *minister* 内政相. ¶***key*** *ministers* of the Cabinet 主要閣僚. ¶a full-time ***Transportation*** *minister* [兼任などに対し]専任運輸相.

P² the Chinese *Minister* ***at*** Tokyo 東京駐さつ中国公使. the *Minister* ***for*** Communications 郵政大臣 ‖ Signor Balbo, *Minister* ***for*** Air 航空大臣バルボ氏. ‖ the *Minister* ***for*** Home (Foreign) Affairs 内(外)務大臣. ¶*Minister* ***from*** the United States to ... ...駐さつ米国公使. ¶the *Minister* of Justice 法務大臣 ‖ the *Minister* ***of*** Native Affairs 土民事務大臣 ‖ a *minister* ***of*** religion 牧師(伝導師) ‖ *ministers* ***of*** wisdom = books 知恵を伝えるもの(すなわち書籍) ‖ a *minister* ***of*** the gospel 福音の伝道者.

minister, *v*. 奉仕する, 助けとなる, 貢献する.

P *minister* ***to*** the wants of man 人間の用を達する ‖ *minister* ***to*** one's vanity (whims) 人の虚栄心(など)を満足させる ‖ The modern poet often *ministers* ***to*** the weaker side of human nature. 現代詩には人間性の弱点を謳歌するものがよくある. ‖ Those who *minister* ***to*** others are happier than those who think only of themselves. 他人に奉仕する人は自分のことばかり考える人よりは幸福である. ‖ *minister* ***to*** his needs 彼の世話をする. 【類】 *minister* ***to*** the educational needs of ... / *minister* ***to*** the necessities of the indigent / I *ministered* ***to*** him in his last hours (臨終の際) / Loving hands and hearts *ministered* ***to*** her to the last.

ministration, *n*. 牧師の職務, 伝道.

P² He is engaged in *ministrations* ***among*** the poor, the afflicted, and the irreligious. 彼は貧しいもの悩めるもの無宗教のものの間に伝道をやっている.

ministry, *n*. 内閣; [政府の]各省.

V The *ministry* will be ***defeated*** on that question. その問題では内閣は敗北するだろう. ¶***enter*** the *ministry* of the Presbyterian church 長老教会の聖職につく. ¶***form*** a new *ministry* 新内閣を組織する. ¶***join*** the *ministry* of ... ...内閣の班に列する.

Q a ***bureaucratic*** *ministry* 官僚内閣. ¶the ***competent*** *ministry* 主務省. ¶a ***mosaic*** *ministry* 寄合内閣. ¶Quakers reject a ***paid*** *ministry* 清教徒は有給の聖職を排斥する.

Q² the ***Agriculture-Forestry*** *Ministry* 農林省. ¶the ***Commerce-Industry*** *Ministry* 商工省. ¶***key*** *ministries* [政府の]重要各省. ¶a ***party*** *ministry* 政党内閣. ¶the ***Postal Service*** *ministry* 郵政省. ¶the ***service*** *ministries* 陸海軍省. ¶the ***Telecommunications*** *Ministry* 電通省. ¶the ***Transportation*** *Ministry* 運輸省.

P a change ***in*** the *Ministry* 内閣更迭. ¶He worked ***under*** the *Ministry* of Education in Egypt. 彼はエジプトの文部省に奉職していた.

P² the British *Ministry* ***of*** Food 英国食料省.

mink, *n*. ミンク(いたち属).

Q an ***expectant mother*** *mink* 妊娠しているミンク.

minor, *n*. 未成年者, 未丁年者.

P in the case ***of*** a *minor* 未成年者の場合は.

minority, *n*. 未成年, 未成年; 少数; 少数党.

V The party ***forms*** a small *minority* in the House of Commons. その党は下院の少数党を成している.

Q an ***active*** *minority* 積極的活動的な少数分子. ¶a ***considerable*** *minority* 相当数の多い少数派. ¶the ***discerning*** *minority* 少数の具眼者. ¶They are in a ***decided*** *minority*. 彼らは断然少数である. ¶opposition on the part of the ***educated*** *minority* 教育ある少数の者の方での反対. ¶a ***hysterical*** *minority* やっきとなっている少数派. ¶an ***important*** and ***intelligent*** *minority* 重要にして賢明な少数派. ¶a ***large*** *minority* 数の相当ある少数派. ¶a ***respectable*** *minority* of thinking persons in England 英国における尊敬すべき少数の思想家たち. ¶***small*** *minorities* 小会派. ¶a ***superior*** *minority* 質のすぐれた少数派. ¶a ***tyrannous*** *minority* 専横な少数派.

P ***during*** one's *minority* 未成年の期間に. ¶Such persons are certainly ***in*** the *minority*. そうした人々は確かに少数である. ‖ They are ***in*** a small *minority*. 彼らは少数である. ‖ they are ***in*** the *minority* in proportion to ... 彼らは...に比べて少数である ‖ girls still ***in*** their *minority* 未成年の少女 ‖ ***in*** a *minority* of cases 僅少の場合において.

mint, *n*. 造幣局; 財源, 富源.

V ***coin*** (= ***make***) a *mint* of money 巨万の富を作る. ¶He ***has*** a *mint* of money. 彼はばく大な金を持っている.

Q² Economy is the ***household*** *mint*. 経済は家庭の宝だ.

P Coins are struck ***at*** the *mint*. 貨幣は造幣局で鋳造する.

mintage, *n*. 造語.

Q These phrases are ***fresh*** *mintages*, peculiar to himself. これらの句は彼独特の新しい新造語である.

minute, *n*. **(1)** 分, 少刻, 一瞬.

V I ***enjoyed*** every *minute*. 私は一刻一刻皆楽しかった. ¶if you can ***find*** a few *minutes* to spare 君にちょっとお暇があれば. ¶I've just ***got*** ten *minutes* to catch my train. 汽車にはあと十分しかない. ¶Between ... and (= What with ... what with ...) they seem to ***have*** scarcely an idle *minute*. ...やら...やらで彼らには一分の暇もないらしい. ¶It ***lacks*** three *minutes* of (= to) two. 二時に三分前です. ¶if you can ***spare*** a *minute* ちとお手すきなら. ¶It ***wants*** eleven *minutes* to (= of) four. 四時に十一分前.

V² as the *minutes* ***flew away*** 一分一分と時がたって行くに.

Q I thought ***every*** *minute* that the big elm would go. 今にもそのにれの大木が折れはしないかと思った. ¶***Few*** *minutes* of buses to all parts 諸方面のバスまで二三分(貸間の広告中の文句). ¶in the ***last*** *minute* of a game 競技の最後のどたん場で. ¶Come here, ***this*** *minute*! すぐお出で. ¶All this work was done in ***odd*** *minutes* at night. これらの仕事は皆夜間零砕の余暇にやったのだ.

P He is a methodical person: he catches up the same train every morning and leaves the house each day ***at*** exactly the same *minute*. 彼はきちょうめんな人だ, 毎朝同じ汽車に乗り毎日一分も違わず家を出る. ¶***during*** every *minute* of the twenty-four hours day 一日二十四時間の各

分間. ¶wait ***for*** a few *minutes* 数分間待つ ‖ ***for*** a *minute* you would imagine that they were ... 一見した所では…と思われる ‖ Let's stop ***for*** a *minute* to think it over. ¶The train leaves ***in*** ten *minutes*. その汽車は十分後に出ます. ¶In Japan it is the custom for guests to come ahead of time instead of ***on*** the *minute*. 日本では来客が時間きっちりでなくその前に来るのが普通である. ¶come home at five o'clock ***to*** the *minute* 一分も違わず五時かっきりに帰宅する ‖ reach one's office ***to*** the *minute* 丁度時間に事務所に着く ‖ I was so much excited that my pulse, whose ordinary action is scarcely 60 beats ***to*** the *minute*, was accelerated to 80 or 85. 私は非常に興奮していたので普通一分間やっと六十の脈はくが八十ないし八十五に増進していた. ‖ Phillips Brooks sent for an avalanche of words at the rate of two hundred or more ***to*** the *minute*. フィリップス・ブルックス氏は一分間二百語以上の割合でとうとうと弁じた. ¶***up to*** the *minute*＝up to date 現在まで.

P[2] We arrived there a few *minutes* ***ahead of*** the time. 二三分前に到着した. ¶five *minutes* ***before*** (***behind***) time 時刻より数分早(おそ)い. ¶the ten *minutes* ***between*** periods 授業十分の休み. ¶ten *minutes* ***of*** five《米》五時十分前. ¶It is twenty *minutes* ***past*** ten. 十時二十分過です. ¶It is five *minutes* ***to*** seven. 七時五分前です. ☞ 米語では before ten, after ten の形もよく使われる.

(2) 筆記, 覚書, 控.

V It was how this *minute* was ***caused*** to be entered in our records. この記事がわれわれの記録にのるようになった次第は以上の通りである. ¶***make*** (＝***draw up***) a *minute* of a meeting 会議の覚書を作る.

minute, *a.* 微細な, 詳細な.

P *minute* ***to*** tediousness いやになるほど詳細な.

minuteness, *n.* 微細, 詳細.

Q ***laborious*** *minuteness* of technical skill 技巧のせん細. ¶***tedious*** *minuteness* うんざりするほどの詳細.

miracle, *n.* 奇跡.

V ***accomplish*** *miracles* of self-restraint 奇跡的な自己抑制をやる. ¶***achieve*** a *miracle* 奇跡を示す. ¶***do*** *miracles* 奇跡を行う. ¶***perform*** *miracles* 奇跡を行う. ¶***represent*** *miracles* as the fundamental proof of religion 宗教の根本的な証明として奇跡を説く. ¶Only God can ***work*** a real *miracle*. 神のみが真の奇跡を行いうる. 【類】***work*** various (numerous) *miracles*. ¶A *miracle* is ***wrought***. 奇跡が行われる.

V[2] suppose a *miracle* ***happened*** and ... 仮りに奇跡が起って…としたら. ¶Unless a *miracle* ***intervened***, this was a certainty. 奇跡でも起らない限りこれは確かなことであった. ¶Such a *miracle* has never ***occurred*** before! こんな奇跡はいまだかつて起ったためしがない. ¶A *miracle* ***presented*** itself. 奇跡が起った. ¶unless a *miracle* ***prevents*** 奇跡でも起って(それを)妨げない限り.

Q a ***familiar*** *miracle* shown by everyday heroism 日常生活の勇士によって示された珍らしくない奇跡. ¶A ***modern*** *miracle* is the building of a house within the original estimates. 最初の見積価格以内で家が建つと今日では不思議なことになる. ¶a ***psychological*** *miracle* 心理学上の奇跡.

P ***by*** some *miracle* 何かの奇跡で ‖ He escaped ***by*** a *miracle*. 彼は奇跡的に免れた. ¶***with*** a *miracle* of patience 驚くべき忍耐心をもって.

P[2] The cutting of the Panama Canal is a *miracle* ***of*** human perseverance. パナマ運河の開さくは奇跡的な人間の忍耐力を示したものである.

miraculous, *a.* 奇跡のような, 神業の.

V ***perform*** the *miraculous* 奇跡を行う. ¶***work*** the *miraculous* 奇跡的なことをやる.

mire, *n.* 泥沼.

P be stuck ***in*** the *mire* 動きがとれない.

mire, *v.* 泥にはまり込む.

P be *mired* ***in*** a ditch みぞにはまりこむ.

mirror, *n.* 鏡, 反射鏡.

V ***fix*** a *mirror* to ... …に鏡を取りつける. ¶***hold*** a small *mirror* before one's face to correct one's pronunciation 発音を正しくするために小さな鏡を手に持つ ‖ ***hold*** the *mirror* ***up*** toward ... …の方に手にした鏡を向ける ‖ ***hold*** the *mirror* ***up*** to nature 自然のままを写す. ¶He ***held up*** the satiric *mirror* to his degenerate countrymen. 彼は堕落した同胞を皮肉に描写した. 【類】***hold up*** a true *mirror* to the existing state of affairs in Russia.

Q a ***clouded*** *mirror* 曇った鏡. ¶a ***cracked*** *mirror* ひびの入った鏡. ¶a ***distorting*** *mirror* ゆがんだ鏡. ¶a ***flattering*** *mirror* うぬぼれ鏡. ¶The newspapers are a ***good*** *mirror* of the times. 新聞は時代のよい鏡である. ¶a ***level-edged*** *mirror* 縁を削った鏡.

Q[2] a ***burning*** *mirror* 天日とり鏡. ¶a ***hand*** *mirror* 手鏡. ¶a ***parlor*** *mirror* 応接間の大鏡. ¶a ***plane*** *mirror* 板鏡.

P look ***in*** the *mirror* 鏡をのぞく ‖ see ***in*** a *mirror* 鏡に映るのを見る ‖ It is reflected ***in*** the *mirror*. それは鏡に映っている. ‖ Look at yourself ***in*** the *mirror*. 鏡で自分の姿を御覧. ‖ national life and character ***in*** the *mirror* of early English literature 昔の英文学に映じた国民生活と品性. ¶hold an object ***up to*** a *mirror* 物を鏡に映す.

P[2] a *mirror* ***of*** the times in which he lived 彼の時代の写生(写し出したもの).

Q a sea as placid ***as*** a *mirror* 鏡のように平穏な海.

mirror, *v.* 鏡に映す, 反射する, 反映する.

M *mirror* more ***faithfully*** the modern heart 近代人の心を一層忠実に描く.

P Towering castles crowning vine-clad hills *mirrored* ***in*** romantic rivers greet you in beautiful Germany. 美しいドイツに行くとぶどうの木のおい茂る小山に高くそびえる城が詩趣のある川に映るのが見られる.

mirth, *n.* 歓楽, 愉快.

V ***evoke*** *mirth* 笑いを催させる. ¶She insisted on knowing what ***occasioned*** his *mirth*. 彼女は彼が何でおかしいのか知りたいものだと言張った. ¶His comic appearance ***provoked*** *mirth* rather than admiration. 彼のこっけいなようすは賞賛よりはかえって笑いを買った. ¶with ***suppressed*** *mirth* 笑うにも笑えず. ¶***vulgar*** *mirth* 下卑た笑い.

Q ***gentle*** *mirth* 穏かな歓楽. ¶provoke a ***lively*** *mirth* 大いに興じさせる. ¶One is moved to a little ***quiet*** *mirth* by such a remark. こんなことを言われるとちょっとおかしく感じられる.

P It is good ***for*** *mirth* to the Europeans. それはヨーロッパ人を面白がらせることができる. ¶ripples ***of*** *mirth* 歓楽のざわめき. ¶a matter ***of*** *mirth* 笑いの種.

misadventure, *n.* 不幸, 不運, 災難.

P ***by*** *misadventure* 運悪く, 誤って. ¶***by*** mere *misadventure* 全くのそそうで. ¶He reached there ***without*** any *misadventure*. 彼は無事にそこに着いた.

misapplication, *n.* 誤用.

P[2] *misapplication* ***of*** a principle 原則の誤用.

misapply, *v.* 誤用する.

P He *missapplied* his talents ***in*** a manner of speaking. いわば彼は才能の使い方が悪かった.

misapprehension, *n.* 誤解, 思い違い.

V to ***avoid*** *misapprehension*, it should, however, be added that ... しかし誤解をさけるために…ということを付加えねばならない. ¶Such information is liable to ***cause*** *misapprehension* owing to its ambiguity. そういう報道はあいまいであるので誤解を引起しやすい. ¶***dispel*** the current *misapprehensions* 世間の誤解を一掃する.

P plain ***beyond*** *misapprehension* 誤解の余地なく明確な. ¶lay oneself open ***to*** *misapprehension* 自分に誤解を招くようなことをする. ¶they are ***under*** a *misapprehension* in your view that ... 彼らは…という君の考えを誤解している.

misbehavio[u]r, *n.* 不品行, 不行儀, 不身持.

Q ***sexual*** *misbehavior* 不身持.

miscalculation, *n.* 勘定違い; 見当違い.

V he has ***made*** many *miscalculations* about ... 彼は…について色々と見当違いをやった.

miscarriage, *n.* 失策, 失敗.

Q a ***gross*** *miscarriage* of justice 大変な誤審.

P[2] a *miscarriage* ***of*** one's plan (attempt) 計画(など)の失敗 ‖ a *miscarriage* ***of*** goods (mail) 誤配 ‖ a *miscarriage* ***of*** justice〖法〗誤審.

miscarry, *v.* 失敗する.

M All his plans have ***sadly*** *miscarried*. 彼の計画はすべて散々な失敗に終った.

mischance, *n.* 不幸, 不運, 不仕合わせ.

V That's one of the *mischances* one has to ***endure*** on a journey. それは旅行中がまんしなければならない厄介の一つである.

P ***by*** *mischance* 運悪く. 【類】***by*** some unhappy *mis-*

chance. ¶end *without mischance* 無事に済む.

mischief, *n*. 害, 禍, 災害, いたずら.

V *brew mischief* いたずらをたくらむ. ¶A little neglect may *cause* great *mischief*. ちょっとした怠慢から大災害が起ることがある. ¶It *did* so much *mischief* (=harm). それは大いに害になった. ¶*inflict* untold *mischief* on the community 社会に測り知れない損害を与える. ¶*make mischief* =excite quarrels 不和の種をまく, 仲を悪くさせる. ¶*perpetrate* an unintentional *mischief* 思わない害を与える. ¶*play* the *mischief* with ... ...にいたずらをする, ...をめちゃめちゃにする. 【類】Don't *play* the *mischief* with the cards I have arranged. ¶*work mischief* いたずらをする.

Q *Great mischief* was wrought by the storm. あらしの災害は大きかった.

P The children are *after* some *mischief*. その子供たちは何かいたずらをしようとしている. ¶*by* wanton *mischief* 気紛れに. ¶He is fond *of mischief*. 彼はいたずらが好きだ. ‖ a boy brimful *of mischief* いたずら盛りな男の子. ¶keep children *out of mischief* 子供にいたずらをさせないようにする.

mischievous, *a*. いたずら好きの.

M *as mischievous* as a monkey さるのようにいたずら好きな.

P There is something *mischievous in* his eyes. いたずらっぽい目つきをしている.

misconception, *n*. 誤解, 誤認.

V to *avert misconceptions* it may be stated at the outset that ... 誤解の起らないように初めに...と述べておく方がよいと思う. 【類】to *avert* possible *misconceptions*. ¶*correct* the *misconceptions* 誤謬を訂正する. ¶*dispel* gross *misconceptions* from their minds 彼ら自身の大きい誤解を一掃する. ¶All possible *misconceptions* have been *precluded*. 万誤解のないように手はずをした. ¶*remove* such *misconceptions* そうした誤解を取除く.

V² I have again to repeat emphatically, as so much *misconception exists* on this point, that ... この点に関しては随分誤解があるので私は...ということを繰返して力説せねばならない.

P It is founded *on* a complete *misconception*. それは全然誤解から生じている.

P² their *misconception about* Japan 日本に関する彼らの誤解. ¶Can't it be a *misconception on* your part? それはもしかしたらあなたのお考え違いではないでしょうか.

misconduct, *n*. 不行儀, 不行跡.

V *commit misconduct* with ... ...と不義(かん通)する.

P scandalized (=offended) *by* his *misconduct* 彼の不行跡に憤慨して. ¶He got the sack *for* his *misconduct*. 《俗》行状が悪いので首になった. ¶when detected *in misconduct* 非行を見つけられる.

P² her *misconduct with* Mr. ... ...氏と彼女との不行跡.

misconduct, *v*. 処置を誤る.

P *misconduct* oneself *with* another 他人に対してわが身の処置を誤る.

O *misconduct* one's business affairs その仕事の処置を誤る.

misconstruction, *n*. 誤解.

V *place* (=*put*) a *misconstruction* on an order 言付を誤解する.

misconstrue, *v*. 誤解する.

O *misconstrue* one's idea (conduct, actions, words) 考え(など)を誤解する.

misdeed, *n*. 失行.

Q *glaring misdeeds* 不らち. ¶city officials charged with *gross misdeeds* 非常な失行を非難された市吏員.

misery, *n*. 不幸, 災害.

V *abate* this *misery* この不幸を減じる. ¶*alleviate* the *misery* その災害を軽くする. ¶*bear* the *misery* of poverty 貧窮にたえる. ¶War *causes* universal *misery*. 戦争は全人類を不幸にする. ‖ This *causes* half the social *miseries* of the time. 現代社会の悲惨はその半分はこれに起因している. ¶to *complete* the *misery* 泣面にはちで. ¶*create misery* 不幸を産み出す. ¶*entail* great *misery* and privation 非常な不幸と窮乏とを引き起す. ¶*forget*, for a time, thus ever-present *misery* 一時この絶えず付まとうかん難を忘れる. ¶*produce misery* 不幸を産む. ¶*relieve misery* 困窮を救う. ¶*sow misery* 不幸の種をまく. ¶I *suffered* untold *misery* from mosquito bites. 私は蚊に攻められてひどい目に会った.

Q in *abject misery* うちしおれて. ¶be in the *deepest misery* ひどくふさぎ込む. ¶a *life-long misery* 一生の不幸.

P die *in* great *misery* 非常に窮乏して死ぬ. 【類】She died *in misery* in a convent (尼寺). / live *in misery* and want. ¶fall *into* great *misery* 大不幸に陥る. ¶He was in the depth *of misery*. 彼は不幸のどん底にあった.

misfit, *n*. 不適当; 不似合な衣服.

V I have never *had* a *misfit* with that tailor. 私はあの洋服屋にこしらえさせて合わなかったということはない. ¶*linguistic misfits* 語学的無能力者.

misfortune, *n*. 不運, 不幸, 災害.

V *accept* a *misfortune* with resignation 不運をあきらめる. ¶*avert misfortune* 不幸を避ける. ¶*bear misfortune* cheerfully 快く不運を忍ぶ. 【類】*bear misfortunes* with equanimity (平然と) / *bear* the *misfortune* calmly, philosophically (平静にかつ自若として). ¶*bewail* one's *misfortunes* 自分の不幸をなげく. ¶*bring* their *misfortunes* under the notice of the public 彼らの不幸を世人に知らせる ‖ *bring misfortune* on one's family その一家に不幸をもたらす. ¶to *complete* his *misfortune* その上不幸なことに. ¶*escape misfortune* 不幸を免れる. ¶no matter what *misfortune* he may *experience* 彼はどんな不幸な目に会おうとも. ¶*have* the *misfortune* to ... 不運にも...する. 【類】Sir, you are, I think, the biggest ass that I ever *had* the *misfortune* to set eyes upon. / I *have* always the *misfortune* to be out when you come; I am really very sorry. ¶*invite misfortune* 不幸を招く. ¶He *met* his *misfortune* like a man. 彼は男らしく彼の不幸に耐えた. ¶*mitigate misfortunes* 不幸を軽減する. ¶*regret* one's *misfortune* その不運を遺憾に思う. ¶*suffer* some *misfortune* ある不幸な目に会う.

V² *misfortune* that is *befalling* ... ...の身に降りかかる不幸. ¶*Misfortunes* never *come* single. 〖諺〗泣き面にはち. ¶the greatest *misfortune* that can *happen* to a young man 青年の身にふりかかる最大の不幸. ¶A great *misfortune* is *impending*. 一大不幸が差迫っている.

Q *crushing misfortune* 一大不幸. ¶*domestic misfortunes* 家庭の不幸. ¶He met with a *double misfortune*. 彼は二重の不幸に会った. ¶a *financial misfortune* 財政上の不幸. ¶a *heavy misfortune* 一大不幸. ¶an *impending misfortune* さし迫っている不幸. ¶an *irredeemable misfortune* 何とも補いのつけられない不運. ¶*national misfortunes* 国家の不幸. ¶a *singular misfortune* 奇禍. ¶a *sudden misfortune* 奇禍. ¶a *terrible misfortune* 一大災禍. ¶quite an *unexpected misfortune* 飛んだ災難.

P to provide *against* any *misfortune* 万一の不幸に備えるために. ¶depressed *by* his *misfortune* 彼の不幸のために意気そそうして. ¶a man *in misfortune* 不幸な境遇にある人 ‖ She deserted me *in* my *misfortunes*. 彼女は私の不運の最中に家出した. ¶victims *of misfortune* 災禍の犠牲者. ¶cry *over* one's *misfortune* 不幸をなげき悲しむ. ¶labor *under* the heaviest *misfortune* 最大不幸の下に悩む. ¶weighed down *with* his *misfortune* 彼の不幸に悩まされて.

misgiving, *n*. 疑惑, 懸念.

V *dispel misgivings* 疑惑を一掃する. ¶*express misgivings* 懸念を言明する. ¶*feel misgivings* 懸念を感じる. ¶*have* a *misgiving* about ... ...を不安に思う.

P² there were many *misgivings as to* ... ...について色々懸念があった.

O *Misgiving* is often a cause of international infidelity. 疑惑がしばしば国際間の不信を引き起す.

misguide, *v*. 惑わす, 誤らせる.

M a *ridiculously misguided* opinion ばかばかしいくらい誤った意見.

P *misguided by* a false story デマに惑わされて.

mishap, *n*. 不幸, 不運, ちん事.

V² no *mishap befell* us except that ... ...以外には何らの不幸もわれわれに起らなかった.

Q *industrial mishaps* 生産の事故. ¶through some *unavoidable mishap* 思いがけない不幸に出会って.

Q² an "*unloaded*" *gun mishap* いわゆる空砲のちん事(弾丸が込めてあったので). ¶a *traffic mishap* 交通事故.

P *owing to* a *mishap* to the machinery 機械の故障のために. ¶perform *without mishap* 滞りなくなし遂げる. 【類】We reached our destination *without* further *mishap*.

P² the haps and *mishaps of* life 人生の禍福. ¶a *mishap to* a pleasure-steamer 遊覧汽船のちん事.

misinform, *v*. 知らせ違える, 誤報する.

M I found myself *grossly misinformed* of it. 私はその件について非常な誤解をしていた.

P I find I was *misinformed about* it. 私はそれを聞き違えていたことが分かった.

misinformation, *n*. 誤報, 誤伝.

V *print misinformation* about Japan 日本について誤報を伝える.

misinterpret, *v.* 誤解する.

M be ***grossly*** *misinterpreted* ひどく誤解される.

O *misinterpret* one's idea (motives) その考え(など)を誤解する.

mislay, *v.* おき忘れる.

M I've ***unhappily*** *mislaid* his letter. あいにく彼の手紙をしまいなくした.

mislead, *v.* 誤らす, 迷わす, 邪路へ導く.

M Credulous people are ***easily*** *misled* by false advertisements. 信じやすい人たちはでたらめな宣伝にすぐ迷わされる.

P I was entirely *misled* ***about*** the matter. そのことについて私は考え違いをしていた. ¶he is *misled* ***by*** the preconception that ... 彼は...という先入思想にとらわれている. 【類】*misled* ***by*** bad companions. ¶be *misled* ***into*** the belief that ... ...と誤信する.

misleading, *a.* 誤らせる.

M The statement is ***grossly*** *misleading.* その所信は非常に人を惑わしやすい.

mismanagement, *n.* 不取締, 不始末.

Q ***serious*** *mismanagement* in the direction of the company's affairs 同会社の事務取扱上における大失策.

misnomer, *n.* 名称誤用, 誤称.

Q an ***absurd*** *misnomer* 名の実に伴わない一例. ¶Was there ever a ***greater*** *misnomer?* これほど名実相反するものがかつてあったろうか.

misplace, *v.* おき場所を誤る.

O You may have *misplaced* it. それをどっかへおき忘れたんだろう.

misprint, *n.* 印刷上の間違い, 誤植.

Q ***ridiculous*** *misprints* ばからしい誤植.

P The book is not entirely free ***from*** *misprints.* その本には全然誤植がないわけではない.

P[2] it is a *misprint* ***for*** "..." それは「...」の誤植 ‖ possibly a *misprint* ***for*** ... 多分...の誤植.

mispronounce, *v.* 発音を誤る.

M words ***often*** *mispronounced* by the illiterate 無学者がよく誤って発音する語.

mispronunciation, *n.* 発音の誤り, 誤読.

Q a ***gross*** *mispronunciation* 大きな誤読.

misread, *v.* 誤読する.

O *misread* one's motives その真意を誤解する.

misreading, *n.* 誤読.

Q a ***strange*** *misreading* of Roman history ローマ史に対する妙な曲解.

misreport, *v.* 誤り伝える.

M The event was ***grossly*** *misreported.* そのできごとははなはだしく誤り伝えられた.

misrepresentation, *n.* 誤説, 誤伝; 偽言.

V Such *misrepresentations* are widely ***circulated.*** そうした誤伝が世間に広まっている. ¶***expose*** *misrepresentations* 誤説を反ばくする.

Q ***hysterical*** *misrepresentations* ヒステリックな偽言. ¶***plausible*** *misrepresentations* of ... ...のまことしやかな誤説.

misrule, *n.* 悪政, 暴政.

P centuries ***of*** *misrule* 数百年にわたる悪政.

miss, *n.* 令嬢, お嬢さん.

V She has ***changed*** *Miss* for Mrs. 彼女は奥さんになった.

Q an ***elderly*** *miss* オールドミス. ¶a ***pert*** (=***saucy***) *miss* なまいきな小娘. ¶a ***perky*** *miss* はつらつとした娘. ¶a ***slim*** *miss* 《米》柳腰のお嬢さん. ¶Hya, ***young*** *miss!* 《米口語》やあ, お嬢さん.

Q[2] a ***bread-and-butter*** *miss* 《俗》食い気盛りの娘, 若い娘っ子. ¶***school*** *misses* and college girls 女生徒と大学女学生.

P most glamorous dress coats ***for*** *misses* and juniors [広告]お嬢さん向きのもっともすばらしいドレスコート.

miss, *v.* 失う, 逸する, 乗りはぐれる; ...のいないのをさびしく思う.

M We have *missed* you ***badly*** since you were gone. お別れしてからほんとに寂しうございました. ¶I ***just*** *missed* being run over by a truck. すんでのところでトラックにひかれるとこだった. ¶The ball ***narrowly*** *missed* him. 弾丸が少しのところでそれた. ¶He ***never*** *missed* attending the lectures. 彼はその講義には一ぺんも欠席しなかった. ¶He ***seldom*** *misses* his aim. 彼はめったにねらいをはずさない(あいつがねらったらまず最後だね). ¶He will be ***sorely*** *missed* by a circle of personal friends. 彼がいなくなると知人たちが非常にさびしがるだろう. 【類】He will be ***sorely*** *missed* in the political world of ours.

P He attempted the smile of genial indulgence and *missed* it ***about*** a yard. 彼は寛大な微笑をもらそうとしたが仲々うまく行かなかった. ¶It *missed* me ***by*** a couple of inches. それは一二インチの差で私にあたらなかった. ‖ *miss* a train ***by*** one minute 一分のところで汽車に乗りそこなう. 【類】The bullet *missed* me ***by*** a hair's breadth (間一髪). ¶He *missed* his umbrella ***from*** the stand. 彼がかさ台に入れたかさがなくなっていた. ‖ The boy had been *missing* ***from*** his home for some days. その少年は数日家出してゆくえが分からなかった. 【類】The exhibit was *missed* ***from*** the museum. / The funds (金) are *missing* ***from*** the safe (金庫). / He was *missed* ***from*** the steamer. ¶I *missed* him ***in*** his usual seat. 彼はいつもの席にいなかった. 【類】I *missed* the notice ***in*** the paper. ‖ those *missing* ***in*** action 出征生死不明者たち.

O Oh, really! I am sorry we shall *miss* you. ああそうですか. 私どもはあなたがいなくなってさびしくなるでしょう. ¶No student of contemporary art who is in Tokyo this autumn should *miss* seeing the Teiten. この秋東京にいる現代美術の研究家はだれでも帝展を見のがしてはならない. ¶a book with some leaves *missing* 落丁のある本. 【類】There is a volume (page) *missing.*

missile, *n.* 飛道具, 弾丸, ミサイル.

Q a ***guided*** *missile* 誘導弾. ¶an ***intercontinental*** (***intermediate-range***) ***ballistic*** *missile* 大陸間(中距離)弾導弾 (=ICBM, IRBM). ¶a ***projectile*** *missile* 飛道具.

Q[2] advance ***air-to-air*** guided *missiles* 長時間継続誘導ミサイルを発達させる. ¶a ***rocket*** *missile* 自動発射物(ロケット・無人機など). 【類】A ***rocket*** *missile* flew across the sky.

missing, *a.* ゆくえ不明の.

P He is ***among*** the *missing.* 彼もゆくえ不明の一人だ. ¶He is reported ***as*** *missing.* 彼はゆくえ不明を伝えられている.

mission, *n.* 使命, 任務, 天職; 特派員; 布教, 伝導; 公使館.

V Without a moment's hesitation he ***accepted*** the *mission.* 少しもちゅうちょせず彼はその使命を引受けた. ¶***accomplish*** a *mission* 使命を果す. 【類】It has ***accomplished*** its historical *mission* (=rôle). ¶***carry out*** one's *mission* おのれの使命を全うする. ¶He ***confirmed*** his divine *mission* with miracles. 彼は奇跡によってその神聖な使命を明らかにした. ¶He ***discharged*** that delicate *mission* with skill. 彼はその困難な使命を手際よく果した. ¶***dispatch*** a special *mission* to Japan 特使団を日本に派遣する. ¶the delicate *mission* to ... was ***entrusted*** to ... ...という困難な使命は...が引受けることになった. ¶He ***executed*** his *mission* well and wisely. 彼はその使命をりっぱにかつ賢明に果した. ¶***follow*** the sacred *mission* 布教師になる. ¶***found*** a *mission* 布教事務所を創設する. ¶***fulfil*** their *mission* 彼らの使命を全うする. 【類】***fulfil*** its *mission* as ... / ***fulfil*** one's *mission* in life / ***fulfil*** the *mission* with complete success. ¶He ***made*** a *mission* to Moscow for this purpose. このため自分でモスコーに出かけた. ¶the *mission* was well ***performed*** by ... その使命は...によって首尾よく果された. ¶The church has ***planted*** its *mission* in every land. 同教会はすべての国にその布教所を設立した. ¶***send out*** a *mission* to ... for the purpose of ... ...のために使節団を...へ派遣する. ¶The store faithfully ***serves*** a *mission* of cheapness. その店は忠実に廉売の任務を果している. ¶***take up*** (=***assume***) this *mission* この使命をになう.

Q a ***civilizing*** *mission* 文化的使命. ¶a ***commercial*** *mission* 貿易使節団. ¶He was unfitted for the ***delicate*** *mission* with which he has been entrusted. 彼はその委任された微妙な使命を果すに適していなかった. ¶charged with a ***diplomatic*** *mission* 外交上の使命を帯びて. 【類】a ***diplomatic*** *mission* to the Pope. ¶The building has a ***double*** *mission.* その建物は二重の目的に使用される. ¶a U.S. ***educational*** *mission* 米教育使節団. ¶***Foreign*** *missions* 〖宗教〗外国伝道. ¶fulfil one's ***great*** *mission* その大きい使命を果す. ¶charged with a ***high*** *mission* りっぱな使命を帯びて. ¶on an ***official*** *mission* of study and investigation 研究調査の官命を帯びて. ¶their ***particular*** *mission* in life is to ... 彼らのこの世での使命は特に...することである. ¶He has been sent (=despatched) to ... on a ***political*** (***secret***) *mission.* 彼は政治上(秘密)の任務を帯びて...に遣わされた. ¶the ***prostitutes'*** *mission* in society 社会における売春婦の使命. ¶visit ... on a ***religious*** *mission* 宗教上の使

命を帯びて…におもむく. ¶he was sent on a ***special mission*** to ... 彼は特命を帯びて…に派遣された.【類】despatch a ***special mission*** to Japan / He believed that the English race, above all those in existence, had a ***special mission*** from Heaven to subdue and occupy the earth. ¶a ***sublime mission*** 崇高な使命.

Q² on a ***bombing mission*** 爆撃の任務を帯びて.【類】a dangerous ***bombing mission.*** ¶on ***business mission*** 商用で. ¶The bomber was returning from a ***combat mission*** over ... 同爆撃機は…に対する戦闘行為から帰還の途上にあった. ¶the recent visit to the United States of five young Japanese ladies on a ***goodwill mission*** 親善使節としての五人の日本娘の最近の訪米. ¶***Home Missions*** 〚宗教〛国内伝道. ¶the ***Soviet Mission*** in Japan 駐日ソ連代表部. ¶a ***trade mission*** to South Asia 南アジアへの貿易使節団. ¶send a ***training mission*** コーチ団を派遣する.

P He left England ***on*** this *mission.* 彼はこの使命を帯びて英国を出発した. ¶He believed that thus he would best secure a successful issue to the delicate ***mission with*** which he had been charged. かくして彼は自分に委任された困難な任務をりっぱに果すことができると信じた.

P² Japan's *mission* ***in*** the Pacific 太平洋における日本の使命. ¶a special correspondent of the Times on a *mission* ***to*** the Far East 使命を帯び極東派遣中のタイムズ特別通信員.

missionary, *n.* 宣教師, 伝道師.

Q a ***devoted missionary*** 熱心な宣教師. ¶a ***Christian missionary*** キリスト宣教師. ¶Morrison, the ***first missionary*** to China 中国最初の宣教師モリスン. ¶a ***foreign missionary*** 外人宣教師. ¶a ***one-time missionary*** 一時宣教師であった人. ¶a ***returned missionary*** 外国から帰ってきた宣教師.

mission-house, *n.* 伝道館.

P² a *mission-house* ***for*** foreign sailors 外国水夫の伝道所.

misspell, *v.* 誤ったつづりをする.

M These words are ***often misspelled*** even among British people. これらの語は英国人の間でさえしばしばスペルを誤られる.

misstatement, *n.* 言い誤り, 誤述.

V ***spread misstatements*** 誤報を伝える.

Q an example of ***biographical misstatement*** 伝記の誤述された例. ¶a ***glaring misstatement*** 顕著な誤述. ¶a ***wilful misstatement*** 故意の誤述.

mist, *n.* 霧, かすみ, もや.

V ***clear mist*** もやを晴らす. ¶The sun ***dispelled*** the *mist.* 太陽が出てかすみが消散した. ¶The *mist* has entirely ***cleared off.*** 霧がすっかり晴れた. ‖ The *mist* ***clears off*** (= ***away***). 霧が散じる. ¶The morning *mists* were still ***hovering*** over the field. 朝霧がまだ野にたれ込めていた. ¶***Mist rests*** upon the surrounding scenery. 霧があたり一面立ち込めている. ¶The ***mist rises.*** 霧が立昇る. ¶A ***mist spreads*** before my eyes. 目がくらむ.

Q ***gauzy morning mists*** 紗(しゃ)のようなうすい朝霧. ¶see through the ***roseate mist*** created by imagination 楽観の色眼鏡を通して見る. ¶a ***thick mist*** 濃霧.

P The view was blotted out ***by mist.*** 景色が霧に隠れて見えなかった. ¶veiled ***in*** a *mist* 霧に閉されて. ¶see ***through*** the *mist* 霧を通して見る.【類】see the glimmer of distant lamps ***through*** the *mist.*

P² A ***mist of*** prejudice spoiled his judgment. 偏見のゆがみが彼の判断を狂わせた. ¶the *mist* ***on*** the mountains 山上の霧.

mistake, *n.* 間違い, 誤り, 誤びゅう.

V ***admit*** a *mistake* frankly 率直に間違いを認める. ¶***avoid*** *mistakes* 間違いを避ける. ¶***detect*** the *mistake* その誤びゅうを発見する. ¶***duplicate*** the *mistakes* of Napoleon and Hitler ナポレオンやヒットラーの誤りを繰返す. ¶***eradicate*** *mistakes* 誤びゅうを根絶する. ¶***find out*** one's *mistake* その誤りを発見する. ¶***make*** a *mistake* 間違える.【類】Do not be afraid of ***making mistakes.*** ‖ one ***makes*** no *mistake* in saying that ... …と言っても決して間違いではない ‖ ***make*** the *mistake* of ... …のようなばかをやる.【類】***make*** the *mistake* of getting several times as much as one needs / don't ***make*** the *mistake* of judging that ... …と判断するような間違いをするな.【類】he ***made*** no *mistakes* in the choice of ... / ***make*** a *mistake* in one's estimate of ... (見込違い) / ***make*** *mistakes* in calculations (計算). ¶He is apt to ***note*** another's *mistake.* 彼はよく人の誤りに気がつく. ¶one of the most popular *mistakes* ***perpetrated*** by Japanese students of English 日本の英学生がやる最も普通な誤りの一つ. ¶***rectify*** (=***correct***) a *mistake* 誤りを正す. ¶***repeat*** the *mistake* of ... …の誤りを繰返す. ¶*Mistakes* are ***scored*** in red ink. 誤りの所には赤インキで下に線を引く.

V² when no *mistakes* could ***arise*** 間違いが起らないようだったら. ¶*mistakes* ***creep*** into ... 知らない間に…の中に誤りができる.

Q make an ***awful*** (a ***terrible***) *mistake* 恐ろしい間違いをやる. ¶***bad mistakes*** 悪い間違い. ¶a ***comical mistake*** こっけいな間違い. ¶***common misakes*** よくある間違い. ¶a ***deplorable mistake*** 悲しむべき誤り. ¶a ***disastrous mistake*** 危険な間違い. ¶a ***fatal mistake*** 飛んでもない間違い. ¶a ***foolish mistake*** ばからしい間違い. ¶a ***ghostly mistake*** 物すごい間違い. ¶a ***glaring mistake*** 目に立つ間違い. ¶a ***grand mistake*** 大間違い. ¶a ***grave mistake*** 由々しい間違い. ¶a ***gross mistake*** ひどい間違い. ¶a ***huge mistake*** 大間違い. ¶an ***inexcusable mistake*** ゆるし難い間違い. ¶***laughable mistakes*** ばかばかしい間違い. ¶a ***monumental mistake*** とてつもない誤り. ¶surely, and ***no mistake*** 大丈夫, 間違いなし.【類】Are you certain that there is ***no mistake?*** ¶***outrageous mistatkes*** もっての外の間違い. ¶***pretended mistakes*** わざとやるあやまち. ¶a ***regrettable mistake*** 残念な間違い. ¶a ***ridiculous mistake*** ばかばかしい誤り. ¶it is a ***sad mistake*** to think that ... …と考えることは悲しむべき誤りだ. ¶I cannot but think that the adoption of such a course would be a ***serious mistake.*** こうした方針を取ることは大きな誤りだろうと私は思わざるを得ない. ¶a ***silly mistake*** ばかげた間違い. ¶There is not a ***single mistake*** in it. そのにはただの一つの誤りもない. ¶a ***slight mistake*** ちょっとした間違い. ¶a ***social mistake*** 社交上の失錯. ¶a ***stupid mistake*** あほらしい間違い. ¶a ***terrible mistake*** とんでもない間違い. ¶a ***trifling mistake*** ささたる誤びょう. ¶an ***ugly mistake*** 見苦しい間違い. ¶an ***unfortunate mistake*** 間の悪い間違い. ¶an ***utter mistake*** 全くの誤り. ¶a ***vital mistake*** 致命的な間違い.

P It was Mr...., ***beyond*** *mistake.* それは確かに…氏だった. ¶A letter for me, left ***by*** *mistake* at my neighbor's house, was kept for two days and then given back to the postman. 私にあてた手紙が間違って隣りに配達されて二日たってから配達人に返された.【類】He boarded the wrong train ***by*** *mistake.* ¶apologize ***for*** one's *mistake* その間違いをわびる. ¶a dictation free ***from*** *mistakes* 間違いのない書取り. ¶He carried my umbrella ***in*** *mistake* for his. 彼は私のかさを間違えて持って行った. ¶fall ***into*** a *mistake* 誤りに陥る. ¶***through*** careless *mistakes* 不注意から.【類】***Through*** *mistake* he took my hat instead of his own. ¶I was laboring ***under*** a *mistake.* 私は勘違いして(余計な)骨を折っていた. ‖ ***under*** a *mistake* of facts 事実を勘違いして. ¶His compositions bristle ***with*** *mistakes.* 彼の作文は間違いだらけだ.

P² I will make no ***mistake about*** it. 私はそれを間違いなくやります. ¶There is some *mistake* ***between*** us. 僕らの間に何か手違いがある. ¶He made a *mistake* ***by*** not dying. 彼は死なないのは間違いであった. ¶*mistakes* ***in*** grammar (conversation, pronunciation, psychology) 文法(など)の誤り.

mistake, *v.* 誤る, 間違える, 誤解する.

M *mistake* it ***away*** それを間違えて持って行く. ¶You are ***decidedly mistaken.*** 君は確かに考え違をしている. ¶if I am not ***greatly mistaken*** たしか. ¶you are ***grossly mistaken*** if you think that ... 君が…と思うならそれは飛んでもない間違いです. ¶***Surely*** he is *mistaken.* 確かに彼は勘違いしている.

P You are ***mistaken about*** (=***in***) him. 君は彼について思違いをしている. ¶*mistake* one ***for*** the other [二者の中]一方を他方と間違える ‖ They *mistook* license ***for*** liberty. 彼らは放縦を自由と思い込んだ.【類】I *mistook* him ***for*** his brother. / I was ***mistaken for*** a spy. / *mistake* an umbrella ***for*** one's own / He *mistook* you ***for*** somebody else. ¶***mistake with*** a problem 問題に関して考え違いをする.

mistress, *n.* 主婦; 情婦.

V ***keep*** a *mistress* めかけをおく.

Q a ***kept mistress*** and her keeper 二号とそのだんな. ¶an inexperienced ***young mistress*** 経験の浅い若奥さん ‖ home dresses for ***younger mistresses*** 若奥様向きの家庭着.

P² be a ***mistress of*** all the feminine arts あらゆる女の道一切に通じている.【類】She is a ***mistress of*** the feminine arts of adornment (美容術). / *mistress* (=master) of the situation ‖ Venice used to be the *Mistress of* the Adriatic. ベニスはかつてアドリア海を支配していた.

mistressship, *n.* 覇(は)権.

P² hold the *mistresship of* the seas 海上の覇権を握っている.

mistrust, *n.* 疑惑, 不信, 懐疑.

V *deepen mistrust* 疑いを深める. ¶*dispel* one's *mistrust* その疑いを晴らす.

Q² the sources of ***present-day*** *mistrust* 現代不安の源泉.

mistrustful, *a.* 疑い深い, 信じない.

P *mistrustful of* ... …を疑って.

misunderstanding, *n.* 誤解, 誤認.

V *break down misunderstandings* 誤解を解く. ¶*combat misunderstanding* and misinformation 認識や報道の誤りを正そうとする. ¶*correct* a *misunderstanding* among … …間の誤解を正す. ¶*dispel* the *misunderstandings* of Japan and America 日米間の誤解を一掃する. ¶*dissipate misunderstandings* existing between the two peoples 二国民間に現存する誤解を除く. ¶*explain misunderstanding* 誤解を説明する. ¶so as to ***leave*** no *misunderstanding* in his mind as to … …について彼に何ら誤解の残らないように. ¶*produce misunderstandings* 誤解を生じる. ¶*remove misunderstanding* and establish good-will among the nations around the Pacific 太平洋を取巻く諸国民間の誤解を去って親善を確立する.

V² *Misunderstandings* sometime ***arise.*** 時には誤解も起る.

Q a ***gross*** *misunderstanding* はなはだしい誤解. ¶remove ***international*** *misunderstandings* 国際間の誤解を除く. ¶***irritable*** *misunderstandings* 感情を害する誤解. ¶in order that there may be ***no*** *misunderstanding* 誤解の起らないように.

P ***through*** a stupid *misunderstanding* on the part of … …の方にばかげた誤解のあるために.

P² have *misunderstanding* ***about*** a matter or a person 事件または人について誤解している. ¶by an amusing *misunderstanding* ***between*** … and … …間のこっけいな誤解によって.

misuse, *n.* 誤用, 濫用.

V It ***constitutes*** *misuse* of power. それは権力の濫用になる.

P protest ***against*** *misuse* of one's name その名を濫用したことに対して抗議する. ¶To call it … is a *misuse* ***of*** the word. それを…と言うのは言葉の誤用である.

mite, *n.* 微少, さ少, わずか.

V ***contribute*** one's *mite* to … …に対してその微力を尽す. ¶***give*** one's *mite* to charity 貧者の一灯を捧げる.

Q the ***widow's*** *mite* 貧者の一灯. 【類】contribute a *widow's mite* to …

mitt, *n.* 長手袋(指なしの); 〘野球〙ミット.

V ***wear*** *mitts* 長手袋をはめる.

Q a ***catcher's*** (***first baseman's***) *mitt* キャッチャー(ファースト)ミット.

mix, *v.* 混ぜる; 混合する, 交際する.

M *mix* ***much*** with the natives 土着民と大いに交際する. ¶These colors *mix* ***well.*** これらの色は配合の具合がよい. ‖ These people do not *mix* ***well.*** この人たちは折合がよくない. ‖ be not ***well*** *mixed* up yet まだよく混じっていない. 【類】*mix* up ***well*** with each other.

M² *mixed* ***up*** in an affair (a quarrel, war, revolution) 事件(など)にかかりあって. 【類】Don't get *mixed* ***up*** in politics. / *mix* ***up*** with something shady (いかがわしいこと).

P *mix* ***in*** the highest cicles 高貴の間に交際する ‖ *mix* much ***in*** society 始終社交界に立入る. ¶I wondered how he would *mix* ***with*** the others. あの人が人とうまく折合うかどうか私は懸念していた. ‖ *mix* poison ***with*** wine ぶどう酒に毒をまぜる. 【類】*mix* water ***with*** whisky / Oil doesn't *mix* ***with*** water. / It's like trying to *mix* oil ***with*** water. / Don't *mix* business ***with*** pleasure. ‖ *mix* ***with*** strange companions 知らない友と交わる.

mixer, *n.* 混合器; 交際家; ミキサー.

Q He is a ***good*** (***bad***) *mixer.* 《米》彼は人づき合がよい(悪い). ¶He is a ***wonderful*** "*mixer.*" あの人は大の交際家だ.

Q² a ***cement*** *mixer* セメント混合機.

mixture, *n.* 混合, 混和; 混合物.

V ***Stir*** the *mixture* a little. その混合物をちょっとかき回しなさい.

Q a ***chemical*** *mixture* 薬品の混合物. ¶a ***curious*** *mixture* of beauty and ugliness 美と醜の奇妙な取合わせ ‖ There was a ***curious*** *mixture* of feelings all at once. 万感こもごも至るという気持であった. ¶a ***gaseous*** *mixture* ガス体の混合物. ¶The group were a ***queer*** *mixture* of good and evil. その一団は善悪の不思議な混合体であった. ¶a ***singular*** *mixture* of boyish simplicity and the venerableness of age 子供らしい単純さと老人の尊厳さとの不思議な混和. ¶a ***strange*** *mixture* of civilization and savagery 文明と野蛮との不思議な混合.

P corrupt ***by*** *mixture* 混和して悪くする.

P² Air is a *mixture* ***of*** gases. 空気は気体の混合物である. ‖ with a *mixture* ***of*** joy and anxiety かつ喜びかつ心配して ‖ a *mixture* ***of*** tragedy and comedy 悲劇と喜劇の合の子.

moan, *n.* うなり, うめき.

Q² ***ocean*** *moan* 大洋のうなり(海鳴り).

P He sank back ***with*** a *moan* of pain. 彼は一声苦痛のうめきとともにどっかと倒れた.

P² the *moan* ***of*** the autumn wind 秋声.

moan, *v.* うめく.

M² *moan* ***about*** the pain 苦痛でうめき声をあげる. ¶*moan* ***over*** the death of … …の死を悲しみ嘆く.

moat, *n.* 大堀.

V ***fill up*** *moats* 大堀を埋める.

P We feasted our eyes on the fine pines ***along*** the *moat.* 私たちは大堀に添うて生えている美しい松を見て目を楽しませた. ¶a castle surrounded ***with*** a *moat* 堀で取巻かれた城.

mob, *n.* 暴徒, 暴民, 一揆(き).

V ***disperse*** a *mob* 暴民を追い払う. ¶The *mob* was ***excited.*** 群集はいきり立った. ¶***put down*** the *mob* 暴徒を鎮圧する.

V² *Mobs* ***gathered*** round the court. 法廷の周囲に暴民が集った.

Q a ***clamorous*** *mob* わめき立つ群衆. ¶a ***good-natured*** *mob* 善良な群集. ¶an ***organized*** *mob* against the government 反政府の組織化された暴民. ¶***packed*** *mob* ぎゅうぎゅう詰の群衆. ¶***Rowdy*** *mobs* gathered in the leading thoroughfares. 乱暴な群衆が大通りに集った. ¶not an army but an ***undisciplined*** *mob* 軍隊ならぬう合の衆. ¶an ***unruly*** *mob* 無統一の(めちゃめちゃな)暴民.

P² a *mob* ***of*** rioters 暴徒の一群.

mobility, *n.* 浮動性.

P² The *mobility* ***of*** the population 人口の浮動性.

mobilization, *n.* 動員, 出兵.

Q ***industrial*** *mobilization* 産業動員. ¶***rapid*** *mobilization* じん速な動員.

Q² a ***surprise*** *mobilization* 急激な動員.

P Orders ***for*** the *mobilization* of the German Army were issued at 5:15 p.m. Aug. 1. ドイツ軍の動員命令は八月一日午後五時十五分に発せられた.

mock, *n.* 愚弄(ろう).

V ***make*** public *mock* of … …を人中で愚弄する.

mock, *v.* あざける, あざ笑う.

P Here are colors and gradations of tint which *mock* ***at*** all efforts of the painter's art to imitate them. ここにはあらゆる画家の技巧努力をもって模倣しようとしても到底及ばないとりどりの色彩がある. ‖ *mock* ***at*** craving for honors 名誉欲をあざける. 【類】*mock* ***at*** one's misfortune / The thoughtless then *mocked* ***at*** the commercial possibilities of flight. ¶He was *mocked* ***with*** false (deceitful) hopes. はかない夢と終った.

mockery, *n.* あざけり, 侮慢.

Q a ***mere*** *mockery* ほんの嘲ろう. ¶it is a ***sad*** *mockery* to call that … それを…といっては名実が相伴わない.

P ***after*** a *mockery* of a trial 形だけの裁判で.

P² a *mockery* ***in*** terms 名実相伴わない一例.

mode, *n.* 方法, 様式; 時好, 流行.

V ***follow*** the *mode* (=fashion) 流行を追う. ¶***invent*** new *modes* of expression 新しい表現法を考案する.

Q ***civilized*** *modes* of living 文化生活. ¶this ***evil*** *mode* of living この悪い生活の道 [prostitution などを指していう]. ¶a ***formal*** *mode* of address (Your Royal Highness など) 正式な呼び方の様式. ¶***incidental*** and ***intentional*** (=informal and formal) *modes* of education 偶発的及び有意的(すなわち非公式または正式の)教育. ¶the ***peculiar*** *modes* of their thought and its manifold expression 彼らの独特な考え方とその多様な表現. ¶the ***proper*** *mode* of living 普通の生活様式. ¶a ***terse*** and ***succinct*** *mode* of stating one's views 簡潔平明な思想表現法. ¶***stereotyped*** *modes* of speech 紋切型の言い方. ¶the ***two*** *modes* of thought 二つの思想形式. ¶his ***usual*** *mode* of procedure [盗人など

の]いつものやり口. ¶*various modes* of inquiry 種々の調査法. ¶a *weak mode* of procedure 手弱いやり方.

Q^2 a change in *living modes* of Japanse people 日本人の

P *in mode* (=fashion) 流行して. ⌊生活様式の変化.

P^2 The "chair" is a *mode of* locomotion in mountainous districts. かごは山岳地方における一つの交通機関である. ‖ their *modes of* thought 彼らの思想形式. ¶Heat is a *mode of* motion. 熱は運動の一種である.

model, *n.* 模型, ひな型; 模範, 手本; モデル.

V ***complete*** a working *model* of a machine 機械のひな型を完成する. ¶here was no *model* which could be ***followed*** お手本にするような型がなかった. ¶***Make*** him your *model.* 彼を君の模範とせよ. ¶***make*** a *model* of ... ...を模範にする. ¶***supply*** a *model* for ... ...にお手本を示す, ...のお手本になる. ¶***use*** a *model* モデルを使う.

Q an ***artist's*** *model* 芸術家のモデル. ¶a ***fit*** *model* for the sculptor 彫刻家にとって適切なモデル. ¶a school founded on a ***foreign*** *model* 外国の例にならって創立した学校. ¶a ***good*** *model* of speech and pronunciation 口語と発音のよい手本. ¶the ***latest*** *models* of Ford cars 最近型のフォード. ¶a ***moving*** (=***working***) *model* 動く模型. ¶There was ***no*** *model* to follow. 見ならうべき手本がなかった. ¶an ***out-of-date*** *model* 時代遅れの型. ¶a ***relief*** *model* of the Japan Alps 日本アルプスの凸(ぼ)状模型.

Q^2 a ***fashion*** *model* ファッション・モデル. ¶a ***gypsum*** *model* of ... ...の石こうの模型. ¶a ***nude*** *model* posing for a class of art students 美術学校のクラスでポーズをとる裸体モデル女. 【類】employ a ***nude*** *model* for ... ¶a ***pilot*** *model* 試作見本. ¶a ***snow*** *model* 雪だるまなど. ¶a ***utility*** *model* 簡便型. ¶a ***working*** *model* 作業型. ¶The trucks were ***1945*** *models.* そのトラックは一九四五年型だった.【類】a Chrysler of the '58 *model*=a '58 Chrysler.

P live ***after*** foreign *models* 外国風に生活する.【類】be built ***after*** the same *model.* ¶it will serve ***as*** a *model* to ...それは...に取って一つの手本になる ‖ act ***as*** a *model* モデルになる.【類】pause ***as*** a *model* for ... ¶make separate studies on paper ***from*** nude *models* 裸体モデルから紙上に種々なクロッキをとる. ¶design ***on*** the *model* of ... ...を手本として設計する.【類】***on*** the *model* of the example above ‖ make ***on*** the *model* of ... ...にならって造る ‖ frame one's sentences ***on*** the *model* of ... ...を手本として文を作る ‖ Operas ***on*** the Italian *model* first appeared in England in 1705. イタリアを手本としたオペラは一七〇五年始めて英国に現われた.【類】We organized our navy ***on*** an English *model.* ¶fit up an establishment ***upon*** the *model* of ... ...を手本として制度(など)をつくる.

P^2 a *model* ***for*** copying 複写の手本, 習字手本. ¶a *model* ***in*** wax ろうで作った模型. ¶a *model* ***of*** discretion 模範的な分別 ‖ The book is a *model* ***of*** compression. その本は簡潔の点で模範的である.【類】a *model* ***of*** architectural beauty ‖ The student is a *model* ***of*** diligence and conscientious work. その学生は勤勉とまじめな努力のお手本である. ‖ His life was a *model* ***of*** Christian virtue. 彼の生活はキリスト教道徳の典型であった.【類】be a *model* ***of*** lucidity (明快) / He is a *model* of the virtues (美徳).

model, *v.* 模型を作る, 模型に合わせて作る.

M be ***beautifully*** *modelled* after the original りっぱに原型を写している. ¶The features were ***delicately*** *modeled.* その顔立はたおやかにできていた.

P The schooling of today is a great hopper grinding out thousands of young men *modelled* ***after*** one pattern. 現代の学校教育は一定の型に造った多数の青年を送り出す大じょうごのようなものだ. ¶a woman's features *modelled* ***in*** clay 粘土で造った女の顔. ¶The system was *modelled* ***on*** that now in use in America. その制度はアメリカ現行のものの模倣である.【類】The present Yokohama Park is the oldest one in Japan *modelled* ***on*** parks of Western countries. / The Japanese Constitution was *modelled* ***on*** the German. / The system is *modelled* ***on*** that in use in Berlin. / The political Constitution of Canada is *modelled* ***on*** that of the Mother Country. / Throughout the past 30 years Japan, greatly to the advantage of her development, has largely *modelled* herself ***on*** (=***upon***) Germany. / *model* one's discourse (講演) ***on*** the style of

moderate, *a.* 節度のある, 穏和な, 適度の. ⌊...

P The hotel is *moderate* ***in*** its charges. そのホテルは料金もかっこうです. ‖ Be *moderate* ***in*** all things. 万事に中庸を守れ. ‖ He is *moderate* ***in*** drinking. 彼は適度に酒を飲む.

moderation, *n.* 節制, 節度; 中庸, 適度.

V ***exercise*** *moderation* 中庸を得る. ¶***lack*** *moderation* 度を過ごす. ¶***use*** great *moderation* in drinking 大いに節酒する.

Q use tobacco (alcoholic drinks) in ***strict*** *moderation* タバコ(酒類)を十分控え目に用いる.

P drink *sake* ***in*** *moderation* 酒を適度に飲む.【類】drinking (bicycling) ***in*** *moderation.*

P^2 *moderation* ***in*** charges 料金の手ごろ ‖ *moderation* ***in*** prosperity and fortitude in adversity 繁栄におごらず逆境にもひるまないこと.【類】*moderation* ***in*** eating and drinking ‖ *moderation* ***in*** all things 万事控え目.

modernism, *n.* 現代思潮(モダニズム).

Q paintings representing ***distorted*** *modernism* モダンア

modernity, *n.* 当世風, 現代主義. ⌊ート派の絵画.

V ***detect*** the *modernity* of a fake antique 今できの古物を看破する.

Q the fashion of ***extreme*** *modernity* 極端な現代風(カリプ

modernization, *n.* 近代化. ⌊ソスタイルなど).

P^2 the *modernization* ***of*** an outmoded factory setup 旧式な工場設備の更新.

modernize, *v.* 現代風にする.

M ***abominably*** *modernized* いやに現代化した.

modest, *a.* 謙そんな, 遠慮勝ちな, 質素な.

P *modest* ***in*** one's behavior (speech) 態度(など)の謙そん

O for a few *modest* yen わずか二三円で. ⌊な.

modesty, *n.* 謙そん; 控え目.

V Chinese women ***have*** their *modesty* in their feet. 中国婦人は足を見せるのを恥ずかしがる.

Q ***abnormal*** *modesty* 並はずれた謙そん. ¶***false*** *modesty* ねこかむり.【類】***false*** *modesty,* created by custom and prejudice. ¶***inherent*** *modesty* 生れつきのつつましさ. ¶***immodest*** *modesty* 度を過した謙そん. ¶***maiden*** *modesty* 乙女のはじらい. ¶***virgin*** *modesty* 処女の恥じらい.

P ***with*** a *modesty* that must be admired 賞賛に値する謙

modicum, *n.* 僅少, 少額. ⌊そんさで.

V The statement ***had*** a *modicum* of veracity. その陳述にはほんの少しは真実な点もあった.

Q with a ***mere*** *modicum* of clothing 裸に近い格好で.

modification, *n.* 変更, 改修, 修正.

V ***introduce*** *modifications* 修正を施す. ¶Some substantial *modifications* will have to be ***made.*** 少しく実質上の改変を加えねばならない. ¶it has ***received*** important *modifications* since ... それは...以来重要な改変をこうむった. ¶***require*** a *modification* 修正を要する. ¶***suggest*** a *modification* 変更を提示する.

Q a very ***effective*** *modification* of the British system 英国式をはなはだ効果的に改正したもの. ⌈るかも知れない.

P This law is subject ***to*** *modification.* この法律は変更され

P^2 *modification* ***of*** a motion [動議の]変更.

modifier, *n.* 《文法》修飾語.

Q an ***essential*** *modifier* of a noun 名詞の重要な修飾語.

modify, *v.* 変える, 改める; 制限する.

M *modify* ***materially*** 実質的に改める.

P a specimen of Chinese architecture *modified* ***by*** Japanese designers 日本の設計者によって改修された中国建築の

modulate, *v.* 〖無電〗周波数を変える. ⌊一例.

O *modulate* radio waves ラジオ(無線)の周波数を変える.

modulation, *n.* 抑揚; 変調.

Q^2 ***frequency*** *modulation* 〖無電〗周波変調.

P^2 "tones" or *modulation* ***of*** the voice 《中国語》四声.

moist, *a.* ぬれている, 湿った.

P *moist* ***with*** dew 露にぬれている.

moisten, *v.* しめらす, ぬらす.

M The plaster sticks if it is ***slightly*** *moistened.* そのこう薬はちょっとしめすとくっつく.

P *moistened* ***by*** rain 雨にぬれた.

moisture, *n.* 湿気, 水分.

V ***absorb*** *moisture* 湿気を吸う, 陽気を食う. ¶***knead out*** *moisture* [洗たくのとき]しぼって水気をとる. ¶The air ***took up*** more *moisture.* 空気に一層水分が加わった. ¶***wipe off*** the *moisture* from the panes 窓ガラスから湿気をぬぐい取る. ⌈出た.

V^2 *Moisture* ***started*** from my forehead. 私の額から汗が

Q There is *much moisture* here. ここは湿気が多い.
P soften *by moisture* 水分で柔かにする. ¶keep it free *from moisture* 湿気を受けないようにしておく. ¶*through moisture* 湿気のために.

mo[u]ld, *n.* 型, 模型.
V *break* the old *molds* of style 古風な型を破る.
Q a man of *gentle mold* やさしいたちの人. ¶be cast in a *heroic mold* 英雄型の人だ. ¶It appears that a *uniform mold* for teachers is one of the essentials of education in America. 教師を同じ型に入れることが米国教育の一つの要点らしい.
Q² a *sand mold* for casting metals 鋳物用砂型.
P the form received *from* a *mold* 型から取った形態. ¶cast *in* a *mold* 型で鋳た.

mo[u]ld, *v.* 形を作る, 模する, 型どる.
P *molded after* the fashion of ... ...流の. ¶*mold in* wax ろうで型どる. ¶*mold* clay *into* a bust こね土で胸像を作る. 【類】be *molded into* the form of ... ¶writings *moulded on* older literature 擬古文. ¶*mold* a statue *out of* bronze (clay) 青銅(など)で像を作る. ¶*mold* one's style *upon* the best of modern writers 一流現代作家を手本にして文体を練る.
Q² *leaf mold* 腐葉土.

mo[u]ld, *n.* かび.
V *gather mold* かびが生える. 【類】During the rainy season in Japan all organic textures quickly *gather mold*, through combined heat moisture.
Q *blue* (*green*) *mold* 青かび.
P there is a film *of mold* over ... ...の上に薄いかびがはえている. ¶covered *with mold* all over かびだらけの.

mo[u]lding, *n.* 型造り.
Q *plastic* (*rubber*) *goods molding* プラスチック製品のかた造り.
P² the *molding of* dishes (vases) *from* clay こね土によるさら(など)の型造り.

moment, *n.* 瞬間, 片時, せつな ; 時機.
V before it has *acquired* a dangerous *moment* 危険な時機に達しない中に. ¶He has a knack for employing to *advantage* all odd *moments*. 彼はわずかな時間を有効に使うことがうまい. ¶*await* the propitious *moment* 好機を待つ. ¶*await* and *seize* the psychological *moment* to ... 機をねらって...する. ¶*beguile* the dull *moments* of a lazy holiday することのない休日の退屈さを紛らす. ¶*brighten up* dull *moments* 退屈を慰める. ¶*devote* every spare *moment* to ... 暇さえあれば...をやる. ¶I am *enjoying* each *moment*. 私は寸時でも愉快に暮している. ¶The on-lookers *had* an anxious *moment*. 見物人は気が気でなかった. ¶*lose* the psychological *moment* 好機を逸する. ¶*save* many a precious *moment* 多くの大切な寸時を節約する. ¶*steal* a few *moments* of time from other more weighty and pressing duties 他の一層大切で急がしい務めから数分の暇を盗む. ¶*while away moments* of inanity or fatigued waiting by ... ...をやって無為のときまたは退屈な人待の時間を忘れる.
V² Then *came* the crucial *moment*. それから裁決の時機がやってきた. ¶The *moment seemed* opportune. その時機が熟したように思われた.
Q in *all moments* of stress 一切の緊急の際に. ¶It may occur [at] *any moment*. それは今にも起るかも知れない. ¶come at an *apt moment* いい時にやって来る. ¶He arrived at an *awkward moment*. 彼はまずい時に着いた. ¶at his *best moment* 彼の全盛のときに. ¶a *bewildering moment* 途方に暮れるとき. ¶the Dutchman in his more *boisterous* and *convivial moments* of relaxation 一層騒々しい陽気な宴会のときにおけるオランダ人. ¶at a *critical moment* 危機に際して. ¶at a *crucial moment* 瀬戸ぎわに ‖ as the *crucial moment* approaches いよいよというときになると. ¶the *decisive moment* for ... ...にとって決定的なとき. ¶in one's *defenceless* (=unguarded) *moments* うっかりしている時に. ¶He was in one of his *didactic moments*. 彼のお説教が始まった. ¶it was a *dramatic moment* when ... それは...というような目ざましいときであった ‖ a *dramatic moment* in life (Japanese diplomacy) 一生(など)の劇的瞬間. ¶brighten up *dull moments* 退屈なときを明るくする. ¶an *embarrassing moment* 困惑するとき. ¶We expect him up here *every moment*. 今か今かと彼を待っている. ¶in a *few moments* しばらくすると. ¶for one *fleeting moment* ほんの一瞬間. ¶in *gay moments* after dinner 食後の愉快なときに. ¶We live in a *great moment* in history. われわれは歴史的に重大な時期に生きている. ¶one of the *happiest moments* of my life 私の一生で最も楽しいときの一つ. ¶in *heated moments* 激したときに. ¶the *historic moments* when the fate of nations hung in the balance 諸国民の運命が決せられた歴史的な時機. ¶an *idle moment* 無為のとき. ¶in my *illogical moments* 僕の頭がはっきりしてい(論理的に働か)ないとき. ¶in his *inferior moments* 彼の栄(は)えないときに. ¶at the most *inopportune moment* 折も折とて, あいにく. ¶This was what he said in his *last moments*. これが彼の臨終の言葉であった. ‖ His courage failed him at the *last moment*. いよいよというとき彼の勇気がくじけた. 【類】defer a visit until the *last moment*. ¶in his *lucid moments* 彼(精神病者)が正気のときに. ¶work in *odd moments* 合間合間に働く ‖ a book for *odd moments* for busy people 忙しい人が暇を見ては読む本. 【類】in *odd moments* after her housework was done / carry a book in the pocket to read at *odd moments* / put to use one's *odd moments*. ¶in his *off moments* 彼の仕事の休みの時 ¶I don't doubt your word for *one moment*. 私はあなたの言うことを少しも疑っていない. ¶He came at an *opportune moment*. 彼が折よくやってきた. ¶If an appointment must be broken, notification should be given at the earliest *possible moment*. 約束が履行できない際はできるだけ早く通告しなければいけない. ¶One can thereby save many a *precious moment*. 大いに貴重な時間をはぶくことができる. ¶at the *prescribed moment* 規定のときに. ¶at this *present moment* 今この時. ¶it was a *proud moment* for him when ... それは彼が...するという得意のときであった. 【類】the *proudest moment* of his life. ¶The *psychological moment* has at last come for him to launch the scheme. 彼がその計画を実行する好機がいよいよやってきた. ¶at just the *right moment* 今だというときに. ¶My whole soul is with you and your family at this *sad moment*. 今回の御不幸に対し私は衷心からあなたとあなたの御家族に同情を捧げます. ¶at the *same moment* 同時に. ¶in *spare moments* 余暇に. ¶devote every *spare moment* to ... ひまさえあれば...をやる. ¶a very *stirring moment* in English history 英国史上非常に人心の沸騰した時代. ¶Flushed and excited, this is one of the *supreme moments* of his life. 得意で感激に満ちた今は彼の一生中最良のときの一つあでる. ¶a *tense moment* 緊張したとき. ¶a *terrible moment* for the young, unpracticed ... 年若く経験に乏しい...にとって恐ろしいとき. ¶a *thrilling moment* 血わき肉躍るとき. ¶at a *tragic moment* 悲劇的な瞬間に. ¶at this *uncomfortable moment* この不愉快なときに. ¶in one's *unguarded moments* うっかりしているときに. ¶at this *very moment* 今この瞬間に. ¶in *wakeful moments* 目がさえて(眠れない)とき. ¶in *waking moments* 目ざめているときに, 警戒しているときに. ¶I was prevailed upon, in a *weak moment*, to ... うっかりしていた折に...するように説き伏せられた. ‖ in one of my *weaker moments* うっかり. 【類】I was prevailed upon, in a *weak moment*, to air my views upon ... ¶at his *worst moment* 彼の最も振わないときに.
Q² in one's *leisure moments* そんな暇なときに. 【類】devote one's *leisure moments* largely to theological study (神学の研究).
P *at* the *moment* of writing この文を書いているときに ‖ the fashionable word *at* the *moment* 昨今流行している語. ‖ *at* the *moment* of death 臨終のときに ‖ *At* this *moment* the book is a document of special interest. 時節柄その本は特に興味のある記録である. ‖ I can't tell you *at* this *moment*. 今は言われない. ‖ There are approximately two billion human beings alive on this earth *at* the present *moment*. 現在約二十億の人間がこの地上に住んでいる. ¶*during moments* of melancholy 気のふさいでいるときに. ¶I am not *for* one *moment* saying that ... 私は決して...と言っているのではない. ‖ I forget *for* the *moment*. 私は今ちょっと忘れました. 【類】whose name *for* the *moment* I have forgotten ‖ Let me speak *for* a *moment*. 一言申上ますが. ‖ He paused *for* a *moment*. 彼はちょっとためらった. 【類】Won't you come in *for* a *moment?* ‖ I do not *for* a *moment* suggest (think) that the stories are true. その物語は決して本当だとは言(思)わない. 【類】I do not *for* one *moment* wish to be understood to advocate it. ¶*from*

the first *moment* 最初から ‖ *from* the present *moment* 今から. ¶ The evil once done cannot be undone *in* a *moment*. 一旦やってしまった悪いことはすぐもとに返すことはできない. ‖ *in* a *moment* of time 瞬時に ‖ he said *in* a *moment* of petulance that ... 彼はむっと怒ったときに...と言った. 【類】 *in* a *moment* of discouragement he remarked that ... / Today, when *in moments* of retrospect I consider all that has passed,—they seem the echoes from a past as distant as a former existence (隔世の感). / *in* the *moment* of danger or deep distress. ¶ the book *of* the *moment* is ... 目下世人の注意を引いている本は...である ‖ the man *of* the *moment* ときの顔役. ¶ *on* the *moment* 即時に. ¶ maintain one's calm *to* the last *moment* 最後まで平静を続ける ‖ Nothing has been heard of ... *to* this very *moment*. 今という今まで...の消息は一向分からない. ¶ up *to* this very *moment* この瞬間まで ‖ *up to* the *moment*, nothing has been heard of ... 今日に至るまで...の消息は分からない. ¶ They are concerned with immediate practical problems, *with* the *moment* and not with eternity. 彼らは目下の実際問題, すなわち永遠ではなく現在のことに関心を持っているのである.

P² It might be said that no *moment in* the life of a ship is quite so important as her christening and launch. 船の歴史ではその命名式や進水式のときほど大切なときはないと言ってよかろう. ¶ in the *moment of* peril 危険に際して ‖ the *moment of* death 断末魔.

O I came out to meet you the *moment* I saw you coming. あなた方がお出でになるのを見るとすぐにお迎えに出てきました. ¶ Just a *moment*, please. ちょっとお待ち下さい.

(2) 重要.

P a matter *of moment* 重要な事柄 ‖ It is *of* no small *moment*. 決して小さいことではない. ‖ There is no transactions *of moment* to record. 記録に留めるほどの重要な取引けない. 【類】 a matter *of* the greatest *moment* / an affair *of* no (little) *moment*.

momentous, *a.* 大切な.

P *momentous to* ... ...にとって重要な.

momentum, *n.* 動力, はずみ.

V *add momentum* to ... ...に拍車をかける. ¶ *gaining momentum* はずんできて; 次第に重要性を増して. ¶ *gather momentum* はずんで来る. ¶ A falling object *gathers momentum* as it falls. 落下物体は落下するに従ってはずみ(加速度)がつく.

P *on* the *momentum* of business boom 好景気に乗じて. ¶ with this *as* a *momentum* これを契機として.

monarch, *n.* 君主, 元首; 大立物.

Q the *financial monarch* of the world 世界の金融王. ¶ an *uncrowned monarch* 無冠の帝王.

Q² a *boy monarch* 少年君主(幼君).

P² a *monarch of* the forest 森の王[オークの木など].

monarchy, *n.* 立憲政治, 君主政体.

V *discard* the *monarchy* 王国制を廃棄する.

Q The system of government of the Russian Empire was that of the *absolute monarchy*. ロシア帝国の政治組織は専政君主政体であった. ¶ an *autocratic monarchy* 専制君主政体. ¶ a *constitutional parliamentary monarchy* 立憲君主政体.

monastery, *n.* 僧院, 修道院.

V *join* a *monastery* 僧院にはいる.

Monday, *n.* 月曜日.

V *keep* Saint *Monday* 月曜にくたびれ休みをする.

Q The Reading Circle meets on *alternate Mondays*. その読書会は一つおき(隔週)の月曜日に会合する. ¶ *Easter Monday* 復活祭の翌日.

money, *n.* 貨幣, 金銭; 富, 財産, 金力.

V The school is ready to *accept money* from any source, however tainted. その学校はどんな金でもどんなに不浄な金でも平気でその寄付を受ける. ¶ *accumulate money* with sweat of one's brow 額に汗して金をためる. ¶ *advance money* 前金で渡す ‖ *advance money* at low interest without security 担保を取らずに低利で金を用立てる. 【類】 *advance money* for the necessary expenses. ¶ He cannot *afford* the *money* for a long journey. 彼は長途の旅行をやる費用にたえない. ¶ *amass money* 金を蓄える. ¶ *bank money* 金を銀行にあずける. ¶ Money *begets* (=*makes*) *money*. 〔諺〕金が金を産む. ¶ I hate to *borrow money*. 私は金を借りるのがきらいだ. 【類】 *borrow money* from ... ‖ *borrow money* on one's furniture 家具を抵当に金を借りる. ¶ I will *break* the *money* with you. 君に金を分けてやろう. ¶ *bring* new *money* into the country 外国人に金を落させる. 【類】 *bring in money* by invisible import (観光事業などで). ¶ *change money* 両替する. ¶ *club* our pocket *money* together われわれの小使銭を出し合う. ¶ He is *coining money*. 彼は盛んにもうけている. ¶ *collect money* in small sums from ... ...から少額の金を集める. 【類】 *collect* the *money* on delivery of goods (代金と引換え) / I've come to *collect money* from you. ¶ *consider* the *money* well spent その金をうまく使ったと思う. ¶ *contribute money* to charity 慈善事業に金を寄付する. ¶ *cost* much *money* 金が大分かかる. 【類】 It must have *cost* a great deal of *money*. ¶ *count out money* 金を取り出しながら数える. ¶ *covet money* 金を欲しがる. ¶ *deliver up* the stolen *money* 盗んだ金を差出す. 【類】 *deliver up* all the *money* he has. ¶ storm the box-office *demanding* their *money* back 切符売場を襲って彼らが払った料金の返済を要求する. ¶ *deposit money* in (=at) a bank 銀行に金をあずける. ¶ *divert* public *money* into their own pockets 公金を流用する. ¶ go to one's bank to *draw money* 金を引出しに取引銀行へ行く. 【類】 *draw* what *money* you require from ... ‖ *draw money* in advance 前(内)借する. ‖ *draw* [*out*] *money* from a bank 銀行から金を引出す. ¶ *earn* one's *money* earnestly 正直に金をもうける. 【類】 The store is never *earning money* enough to pay its operating expenses (営業費). ¶ *eat money* 金がかかる. ¶ *embezzle* public *money* 公金を私消する. 【類】 *embezzle money* from a person (bank). ¶ *exchange* American *money* into English 米ドルを英国のポンドに換える. ¶ *expend money* on ... ...に金を使う. ¶ with intent to *extort money* from ... ...から金をゆする考えで. ¶ I cannot *find* the *money* to buy it. 私にはそれを買う金がない. ¶ *fool away* one's *money* 金をむだに使い果す. ¶ *forfeit* the *money* paid 払込んだ金を没収される. ¶ *fork over* (=*out*) the *money* 金を払う, 金を渡す. ¶ *furnish* the *money* その金を当てる. ¶ *gain money* 金をもうける ‖ *money gained* from business 事業利得金. ¶ *get* big *money* 大金を手に入れる. ¶ *get back* the *money* その金を取戻す. ¶ *get together* (=raise) sufficient *money* to ... ...するに十分な金を募る ¶ *give* all the *money* he has with him 財布の底をたたいて与える. ¶ he never *grudges money* for ... 彼は...に対して決して金を惜しまない. ¶ *handle money* 金を扱う. ¶ He *has money* in a bank. 彼は銀行に金をあずけている. 【類】 He *had* some *money* in his pocket. / I *have* no *money* about (=with) me. / We must first *have* the *money* for it. ¶ If it fails, you can *have* the *money back*. もしそれが失敗したなら金は取戻すことができる. ¶ *hoard up money* 金を死蔵する. ¶ He *holds* the *money* in trust. 彼はその金を信託にしている. ¶ *husband money* 金を倹約する. ¶ *invest money* in ... ...に投資する. ¶ He *keeps money* in a bank 彼は銀行に預金している. ¶ *lavish* (=squander away) one's *money* on ... ...に金を浪費する. ¶ *lay by money* 金をためる. 【類】 the need of *laying by money* against a rainy day (まさかのときに備えて). ¶ *lay out* (=spend) *money* 金を使う. ¶ *lay up money* 金を貯える. ¶ He died and *left* his *money*. 彼はあとに金を残して死んだ. ¶ *lend money* on land 土地(を抵当)に金を貸す. 【類】 *lend money* in advance=advance money / *lend money* at reasonable rates (相当の利率で) / *lend money* upon real security (物上担保). ¶ *loan money* upon an insurance policy as collateral 保険証書を担保に金を貸付ける. 【類】 *loan money* at high interest (高利で) / *loan money* on (を担保に) diamonds and other valuables at 2 per cent. ¶ *lock up* one's *money* 金をかぎのかかる所にしまっておく, 金を死蔵する. ¶ The pawn-shop *lost* the *money* lent upon it. その質屋はそれを質に取って損をした. 【類】 *lose money* on the stock market / You give me your lowest price, but don't *lose money* on me. / He *lost money* by the business. ¶ *make money* rapidly=coin money 急に金をもうける ‖ "war profiteers" who have *made* their *money* in various ways, allowable and unallowable 正当または不当なやり方で金をもうけた戦争成金 ‖ *make money* in cart-loads 山ほど金をもうける ‖ We could *make* some *money* on him. 彼にいくらかの金を出させることができよう. ‖ *make money* "hand over hand" ぬれ手であわのつかみどり. ¶ *marry money* ドル箱と結婚する. ¶ *muddle*

away money 湯水のように金を使う. ¶***obtain money*** by falsifying books (=accounts) 帳簿を誤魔化して金をとる‖The *money* is being ***obtained*** by a continued increase in his debts. 金はどしどし借金をして手に入れている. ¶***owe*** him the *money* 彼にその金を借りている. ¶***pay back*** the borrowed *money* 借りた金を返す. ¶***pay out money*** 金を支払う. ¶***pilfer money*** from the alms chest 慈善箱から金をくすねる. ¶***place*** one's *money* in a bank 銀行に預金する. ¶I ***planked down*** my *money*. [卑] 僕は現金で払った. ¶***present*** ready *money* 現金で支払う. ¶The *money* is to be ***provided*** out of the city purse. その金は市から支給するはず. ¶***put money*** in a bank 銀行に金をあずける‖***put*** the *money* at interest その金に利がつくようにする‖***put money*** to a good use 金を有効に使う. 【類】***put*** so much *money* into a mere hobby. ¶***put away*** one's *money* 金をしまっておく‖***put money by*** against a rainy day まさかのときの用意に貯金する. ¶I ***put up*** some *money* and set him in business. 私は若干の金を用意して彼に商売を始めさせた. ¶***raise money*** on the security of ... …を担保にして金をこしらえる. 【類】***raise money*** on cheaper terms (もっと有利な条件で) / The *money* was ***raised*** by popular subscription. ¶***reap*** much *money* and fame from ... …によって大金と名声を獲得する. ¶The Belgian *money* is ***reckoned*** in francs and centimes. ベルギーでは金をフランとサンチームで計算する. ¶He will promptly ***refund*** your *money* without argument, delay or question. 彼は苦情も遅滞も異議もなく即刻君の金を払うだろう. 【類】***refund*** the *money* if the buyer is not satisfied (品物が気に入らなければ). ¶Foreign *money* is ***refused***. 外国貨幣は受取りません. ¶***remit money*** through a bank 銀行を通じて金を送る. ¶***render up*** the stolen *money* 盗んだ金を引渡す. ¶***repay money*** 金を返す. ¶***require*** much *money* 大金を要する. ¶***return money*** 返金する. ¶***save money*** on postage 切手代を節約する. ¶***save up*** one's *money* 金を貯蓄する. 【類】***save up money*** by dint of persevering thrift (一生懸命節約して). ¶***scatter money about*** vulgarly つまらなく金を浪費する. ¶***scrape together*** some *money* for ... …のために若干の金をまとめる. ¶***screw money*** out of ... …から金をしぼり上げる. ¶***send money*** by postal order 郵便為替で金を送る. ¶***sink*** one's *money* in a business venture 商業的企業に金を投じる. ¶***solicit money*** from a passerby 通行人から金をせびる. ¶***sparing*** no *money* 金にあかして‖As I can ***spare*** the *money* for the time being, I'll accommodate you with it. 当分その金はいらないから用立てましょう. ¶***spend money*** most lavishly 非常に派手に金を使う. 【類】***spend*** one's *money* wisely (cautiously) / Everywhere men who suddenly attain prosperity ***spend money*** foolishly.‖*money* ***spent*** for (=expended in) travel 旅費. 【類】***spend money*** on curios (jewels, a race) / ***spend money*** with a free hand (ぱっぱっと). ¶***squander*** [***away***] *money* 金を浪費する. ¶***squeeze money*** out of ... …からさく取する. ¶***stake money*** on a race 競馬に金をかける. ¶***take money*** 金を取る. ¶***throw money*** [over one's shoulder] on things that do not last 長続きしないことに金を捨てる. ¶***throw away*** one's *money* 金を浪費する. ¶***trifle away*** one's *money* 金を浪費する. ¶He ***turned*** his *money* to good account. 彼は自分の金を生かして使った.‖This tradesman ***turns*** his *money* rapidly. この商人は資金回転が早い.‖***turn*** one's *money* and undertake some fresh enterprise 資金を回収して何か新しい事業を始める‖***turn*** their ***money over*** quietly at a small profit わずかの利益で彼らの金を地味に運転する. ¶***use money*** 金を使う. ¶the town ***voted*** the *money* necessary for ... 同市は…に必要な資金の支出を可決した. ¶*Money* is frequently ***waged*** on the result of a game. 競技の結果に対して金をかけることがよくある. ¶***worship money*** 金を拝む. ¶***waste*** one's *money* upon ... …に金を浪費する. ¶***withdraw*** one's *money* from a bank 銀行から金を引出す. ¶***wring money*** out of ... …から金をゆする.

Q ***counterfeit money*** 偽造貨幣. ¶***earned money*** 働いてもうけた金. ¶give (=deposit) ***earnest money*** with ... 手金を…に打つ. ¶earn ***easy money*** 《米》楽に金をもうける. ¶save ***enuogh money*** to buy ... …が買えるだけの金をためる. ¶***fat money*** 肥満した金. ¶earn ***good money*** 大分金をもうける. ¶***hard money*** 硬貨. ¶make ***honest money*** 正直に金をもうける. 【類】earn one's ***honest money***. ¶investment of ***idle money*** 遊び金の運用. ¶***illgotten money*** (riches) あぶく銭. ¶I sold my books to raise a ***little money***. 少々金をつくるため本を売った. ¶***long*** (***short***) ***money*** 長(短)期借. ¶deposit all ***loose money*** in a bank 小銭を全部銀行にあずける. ¶***lost money*** 紛失した金. ¶There is not ***much money*** in books written for teachers. 教師用の本は大して金にならない. ¶expressed in sovereigns without ***odd money*** 端銭を捨ててソヴリン(英金貨)で言うと.

V² *Money* doesn't ***avail*** in a desert. 金もさばくでは用を為さない. ¶*Money* will undoubtedly ***become*** cheaper (dearer). 金はたしかに安(高)くなるだろう. ¶*Money* ***gets*** easier. 金融が段々小緩みになる. ¶My *money* was soon ***gone***. 私の持金はじきに消えてしまった. ¶*Money* ***talks***. 金が物を言う. ¶It means ***much money*** invested. 大分金がかかっている.‖I do not know how ***much money*** it is worth. それがどの位の価値のものか分からない.‖***No money*** is available to meet it. それに向ける金が得られない. ¶***ready money*** 現金, 即金. 【類】We need a large stock of ***ready money***. ¶***soft money*** 紙幣. ¶I have not ***sufficient money*** in hand. 手もとに十分の金がない. ¶get ***surplus money*** 金をのこす. ¶***tainted money*** 汚れた(不正手段で得た)金. ¶*Money* is ***tight***. 金融ひっ迫である. ¶***unearned money*** あぶく銭. ¶***uninvested money*** 遊金.

Q² ***admission*** [***money***] 入場料. ¶assign ***allotment money*** 配当金を指定する. ¶***bail money*** 保釈金. ¶***blood money*** 償金. ¶***bronze money*** 青銅(銅)貨. ¶***call money***〖商〗コールマネ(借入金). ☞ call loan (当座貸)に対し, call money (当座借). ¶***caution money*** 保証金. ¶***charity money*** 慈善寄付金. ¶***city money*** 市公金. ¶earn ***college money*** 大学の学費をかせぐ. ¶***concession money*** 権利金. ¶***conscience money*** 罪滅ぼしの寄付金. ¶***consolation money*** 慰藉料, 涙金. ¶"***death money***" 弔慰金. ¶***deposit money*** 預金. ¶***gold*** (***silver***) ***money*** 金(銀)貨. ¶***guarantee money*** 保証金. ¶***holiday money*** 休日に使う金. ¶***hush*** (=***silence***) ***money*** 口留め料, 鼻ぐすり. ¶hand over the ***insurance money*** to ... 保険金を…に手渡する. ¶***key money*** 権利金, 保証金. ¶GI's ***leave money*** 兵隊の休暇手当. ¶***lunch money*** 弁当代. ¶the ***nation's money*** 国民の金(公金). ¶a bundle of ***paper money*** 札束. ¶print ***paper money*** 紙幣を印刷する‖irredeemable ***paper money*** 回収不可能の紙幣. ¶The ***passage money*** has been fixed at £5 per head. 船賃は一人頭五ポンドと定められた. ¶***pin money*** [妻などの]へそくり. ¶***play money*** おもちゃの金. ¶pay out of one's ***pocket money*** 小使いから支払う. 【類】make extra ***pocket money*** (余分の小使銭). ¶obtain the ***policy money*** from the insurance company 保険会社から契約の保険金を受取る. ¶***prize money*** 賞金. ¶***security money*** 保証金. ¶***show money*** 見せ金(洋行などの場合の). ¶***spot money*** 即金. ¶"***stop-tear***" ***money*** 涙金, 縁切金. ¶***tax money*** 税金. ¶***time money*** 定期貸付.

P a soul ***above money*** 金で買えない心. ¶He was ***after money***, and money only. 彼は金だけを求めた. ¶Be on your guard ***against*** false *money*. にせ金に用心し給え. ¶He did it ***for money***. 彼は金もうけのためにそれをやった.‖marry ***for money*** 金のために結婚する‖be pressed ***for money*** 金に困っている. ¶pay ***in money*** 金で支払う‖£146 ***in money*** and credit 金と信用で百四十六ポンド‖a gift ***in money*** 金子の贈物. ¶a sum ***of money*** was appropriated for ... ある金額が…に充当された‖He laid by (=saved) a large sum ***of money***. 彼は大金を貯えた.‖A large amount ***of money*** is going up in smoke. 大金が煙になって消えている.‖He lost a lot ***of money*** on the races. 彼は競馬で大分金をなくした.‖I am short ***of money***. 私は金が欠乏している. ¶interest on *money* 金利. ¶He is ***out of money***. 彼は金に困っている.‖He was cheated ***out of money***. 彼はだまされて金をとられた.‖It is a long time to be ***out of*** one's *money* for so small a profit. そんな薄利で金の回収がそれほど長くかかるのではやりきれない. ¶He has run ***through*** all his *money*. 彼は所持金を使いはたした. ¶Good physical conditions can never be bought ***with money***. 身体の健康は決して金では買えない.‖Down ***with*** your ***money***. 金をすぐ出せ.

P² He has *money* ***in*** the public funds. 彼は公債で金を持っている. ¶You can thus save *money* ***on*** your purchases. そうすると安く買物がおできになる.‖put *money* ***on*** a horse race 競馬にかける.

money-market, *n.* 金融市場, 金融界.
V *Money-market* is ***easy*** (***stringent***). 金融市況は緩慢(ひっ迫)だ. ¶***unsettle*** the *money-market* 金融市場を動揺させる. ¶***upset*** the *money-market* 金融市場をかく乱する.
Q ***easy*** *money-market* 緩慢な金融市場. ¶***stringent*** *money-market* ひっ迫した金融市場. ¶***tight*** *money-market* 金づまりの金融市場.
P there is quite a panic ***in*** the *money-market* owing to ... ...のために金融市場はかなり恐慌をきたしている.
monger, *n.* つまらないことをやる人.
Q² a ***company*** *monger* 会社設立を種にして金もうけをする人. ¶a ***gossip*** *monger* 金棒引き, ふいちょう屋. ¶an ***iron*** *monger* 金物屋(人). ¶a ***money*** *monger* 金貸. ¶a ***news*** *monger*=a gossip monger. ¶a ***war*** *monger* 戦争扇動屋.
mongering, *n.* 吹いちょうすること.
Q² ***scandal*** *mongering* 金棒引き. ¶***war*** *mongering* 戦争ちょう発(行為).
monitor, *n.* 学級委員(級長); 監視者(器).
Q² a ***Class B*** *monitor*=a moniter to Class B B クラスの学級委員. ¶a ***radio intelligence*** *monitor* ラジオ電波調整係.
monitoring, *n.* 監視.
Q² ***radio*** regulatory *monitoring* 電波監視.
monk, *n.* 僧.
V It is not the "habit" which ***makes*** the *monk*. 僧を作るのは僧衣ではない(中味が大切だ).
V² *Monks* ***live*** in a monastery. 僧は僧院に住む.
Q a ***celibate*** *monk* 独身の僧, 出家. ¶a ***holy*** and ***pious*** *monk* 聖僧, 上人. ¶a ***rascal*** *monk* 悪僧.
monkey, *n.* さる.
V *Monkeys* ***chatter*** (=***clatter***) さるはきゃっきゃっと鳴く.
Q a ***chattering*** *monkey* きゃっきゃっというさる.
O as mischievous as a *monkey* さるのようにいたずら好きな.
monocle, *n.* 片眼鏡.
V ***place*** a *monocle* in their eye 彼らの目に片眼鏡をつける.
monogamy, *n.* 一夫一婦制.
V set up an ethics which ***encourages*** *monogamy* 一夫一婦制を強調する(倫理を確立する).
monogram, *n.* 組合せ文字, 花押.
P The pottery is marked A.K. ***in*** *monogram*. その陶器には組合わせ文字で A.K. という銘がある.
monograph, *n.* 一記事, 専門論文.
V ***write*** a *monograph* on ... ...について専門論文を書く.
Q a ***learned*** *monograph* on archaeological subjects 考古学に関する専門書. ¶a ***scientific*** *monograph* 科学上の専門論文.
P² Harvard *monographs* ***in*** education ハーヴァード大学刊行教育研究書. ¶a *monograph* ***of*** the Shinto religion of the Japanese 日本神道に関する研究書.
monoplane, *n.* 単葉飛行機.
Q² a ***2-seater Blériot*** *monoplane* 複座のブレリオ単葉飛行機.
P make a great flight ***by*** (=in a) *monoplane* 単葉飛行機で大飛行をやる.
monopoly, *n.* 専売権, 独占.
V ***acquire*** the *monopoly* of the trade その商売を独占する. ¶***break*** the Spanish *monopoly* of Oriental commerce スペインの東洋における商業独占を打破する. ¶***enjoy*** a *monopoly* of trade 商売を独占する. ¶***establish*** a government *monopoly* in salt 塩の専売を開始する. ¶The company ***has*** a *monopoly* of that trade. 同会社がその商売を独占している. ¶The Government ***holds*** a *monopoly* for tobacco. 政府がタバコの専売権を有している. ¶***make*** a *monopoly* of ... ...を専売する. ¶***secure*** a *monopoly* of ... ...の専売権を獲得する. ¶***set up*** (=***establish***) a *monopoly* of ... ...を独占する.
Q have a ***practical*** *monopoly* of ... ...を事実上独占している. ¶make a ***private*** *monopoly* of ... ...の一手販売をやる. ¶establish a lucrative ***trading*** *monopoly* in ... ...では有利な商業的独占の地位を確立する.
Q² The tobacco business is a ***government*** *monopoly* in Japan. タバコは日本では政府の専売になっている. ‖ Tobacco has been made a ***Government*** *monopoly*. タバコが政府の専売となった. ¶a ***state*** *monopoly* 国家の独占. ¶Originally a South American product, rubber has now become a virtual ***world*** *monopoly* of the East Indies. 元来南アメリカ産であったゴムは今は東インド諸島が事実上世界を独占するようになった. ¶the ***zaibatsu*** *monopoly* on fertilizer 財閥の肥料独占.

P² Fiction is not a *monopoly* ***of*** England. 小説は英国の一手販売ではない.
monosyllable, *n.* 単音つづり語.
P reply ***in*** a *monosyllable* 無愛想な返事をする.
monotone, *n.* 単音, 単調.
Q in a ***boring*** *monotone* うんざりするような一本調子で. ¶the ***deadly*** *monotone* of everyday existence 日常生活のたえ難い単調.
monotonous, *a.* 単調な, 一本調子の.
M ***terribly*** *monotonous* 恐ろしく単調な. ¶***unbearably*** *monotonous* たえ切れないほど単調な.
monotony, *n.* 単調, 千篇一律.
V to ***avoid*** *monotony* 単調を避けるために. ¶***break*** the *monotony* with ... ...で単調を破る ‖ Art ***breaks*** the *monotony* of one's prosaic existence into a prismatic variety. 芸術は無味乾燥な生活の単調を破って色々変化ある生活を与える. ¶***escape*** the *monotony* of a long sea trip 長い海上旅行の単調さを免れる. ¶***relieve*** *monotony* 単調をやわらげる. 【類】***relieve*** the *monotony* of exsistence. ¶***vary*** the *monotony* by ... ...して目先をかえる.
Q the ***dead*** *monotony* of work 仕事のつまらない一本調子. ¶the ***dull*** *monotony* of semi-starvation in a slum 貧民くつの飢餓に等しい物憂い単調. 【類】the ***dull*** *monotony* of a country life. ¶the ***gray*** *monotony* of a prison life 刑務所生活のくすんだ単調さ. ¶***wearisome*** *monotony* 飽き飽きする単調さ.
P² the *monotony* ***of*** a country life 田園生活の単調さ. 【類】breaking the *monotony* ***of*** a long voyage.
monsoon, *n.* 季節風.
Q the ***famous*** *monsoons* of the Indian Ocean インド洋の「有名な季節風
monster, *n.* 怪物, 妖怪; 人非人.
Q a ***geographical*** *monster* 地理的怪物(「三才図会」の人物など). ¶an ***inhuman*** *monster* 残忍な人非人. ¶The pumpkin is a ***real*** *monster*. そのかぼちゃはでっかすぎてまるでお化けだ. ¶an ***ugly*** *monster* 醜くて巨大な怪物.
Q² a ***sea*** *monster* 海の巨大の怪物.
P² a *monster* ***of*** cruelty 鬼人 ‖ a *monster* ***of*** omniscience 超人的な博識.
monstrosity, *n.* 奇形, 巨怪物.
Q an ***architectural*** *monstrosity* 奇怪な建築.
month, *n.* [暦の上の]月.
V It will ***occupy*** you many *months*. それは幾月もかかる. ¶It ***requires*** several *months* of hard study in some library. どこかの図書館で五六カ月懸命に勉強することが必要だ. ¶I ***took*** a *month* about my task. 私の仕事に約一カ月かかった. 【類】I ***took*** me (=It took me) a *month* to go into the papers (書類調べに). ¶She ***wants*** some *months* of eighteen. 彼女は満十八には二三カ月足りない.
Q The "English Studies" is published every ***alternate*** *month*. 「英語研究」は隔月発行する. ¶during the ***cold*** *months* 寒い(冬の)期間中. ¶the ***coming*** *month* 来月, 今度の月. ¶during the ***cooler*** *months* 涼しい季節に. ¶the ***current*** *month* 今月. ¶May and June are usually ***dull*** *months* in any business. どの商売でも五月六月は閑散な月だ. ¶for the ***ensuing*** *month* その次の一カ月間. ¶She was, at that time, within a few *months* of her confinement. 彼女は当時お産の二三カ月前であった. ¶in a ***few short*** *months* わずか二三ケ月で. ¶April is the ***fourth*** *month* of the year. 四月は第四の月である. ¶the ***leafy*** *month* of June 新緑の六月. ¶in the ***off*** *months* [シーズンでない]季節はずれに. ¶during the ***opening*** *months* of the operation その作業を始めてから数カ月の間. ¶in the ***passing*** *month* この一月間に. ¶in the ***past twelve*** *months* この十二カ月間に. ¶the ***rainiest*** *month* of the year 一年中一番雨の多い月. ¶"***r***"***-less*** *months* r 字のつかない月 (May, June, July, August). ¶a ***stormy*** *month* よく荒れる月. ¶March is a ***windy*** *month*. 三月は風の吹く月だ.
Q² the ***calendar*** *month* 暦の月 (一月, 二月, 三月など) ‖ every six ***calendar*** *months* 六カ月ごとに. ¶the ***fall*** *months* 秋季. ¶proclaim a "***Go to Church*** *Month*" 「教会行勧誘月」を発表する(「...デー」「...週間」のように). ¶May was the ***peak*** *month* in 1945 for typhus. 一九四五年度の五月はチフスの大流行の月だった. ¶to avoid the ***rush*** *months* of May and June 五六の混雑月を避けて. ¶throughout the ***snow*** *months* 降雪の期間中ずっと. ¶in the ***summer*** *months* 夏季(三カ月)に. ¶during the ***vacation*** *months* [学校の]夏期休暇中. ¶in early ***war*** *months* 戦争の初期には. ¶all through the cold ***winter*** *months* 寒い冬の間ずっと.

P It will continue *about* a *month.* それは約一カ月継続する. ¶*after* two *months* of existence [会など]誕生後二カ月に. ¶You may draw upon me for the amount, *at* three *months.* 三カ月後払でその金額を当方に振出して下さい. ‖ payable *at* three *months* 三カ月後払い. ¶board *by* the *month* 月幾らでまかなう. ¶*during* the *month* of October 十月中. ¶*for months* past 過去数カ月間 ‖ *for* a few *months* ahead 今後数カ月間 ‖ *for months* at a time 引続き数カ月にわたって. 【類】They had resided there *for* six *months* or upwards. ‖ This is the last meeting *for* the *month.* 今月はこれが最後の会合だ. ¶*in* a single *month* the total was reduced to ... たった一カ月に総数が...に減じた. ¶This is the most unusual book we have read *in months.* これは過去数カ月に見ないくらい出色の著作だ. ‖ the last Saturday *in* the *month* その月の最後の土曜日. ¶*within* the *month* その月の中に ‖ He is *within* a few *months* of seventy years. 彼はもう二三ケ月で七十歳になる.

P² the *month after* next 来々月. ¶the *month before* last 先々月. ¶*month after* month 来る月も来る月も. ¶June, the *month for* roses ばらの六月 ‖ April, the last of the R-*months for* eating the succulent oyster, is here. 肉付のよいうまいかきを食うR字付の最後の月四月がやって来た.

O *month* in and *month* out 来る月も来る月も.

monthly, *n.* 月刊誌.

Q an *American monthly* "Fortune" アメリカ月刊誌「フオーチュン」. ¶a tastefully *printed monthly* 凝った印刷の月刊誌.

Q² a *penny monthly* 月刊の安雑誌.

monument, *n.* 記念碑, 石碑, 記念物.

V *build* a *monument* to ... ...のために記念碑を建てる ‖ We *built* a loving *monument* to their memory. われわれは彼らのかたみとして愛情のこもった記念碑を建てた. ¶*dedicate* a *monument* in memory of ... ...の追憶に記念碑を建てる. 【類】a *monument dedicated* to the victims of the S.S. Hitachi Maru disaster. ¶a *monument erected* as a memorial to ... ...へのかたみに建てた記念碑. 【類】In 1901 a *monument* was *erected* at Kurihama, near Uraga, to mark the landingplace of Perry. ¶He *left* behind him an enduring *monument* of his genius. 彼はその死後にその天才を永遠に伝える記念物を残した. ¶*put up* (=*set up or erect*) a *monument* to the memory of ... ...のために記念碑を建てる. 【類】the *monument* was *put up* by ... in honor of ... ¶*raise* a *monument* to his memory 彼のために記念碑を建てる ‖ A *monument* was *raised* to his memory by his surviving pupils. 師のかたみとしてその死後生徒たちによって記念碑が建てられた. ¶*rear* a *monument* to commemorate the fact その事実を記念する碑を建てる. ¶*unveil* a *monument* 記念碑(像)を開幕する. 【類】The *monument* erected to commemorate the sailing of the Pilgrim Fathers from Southampton on August 15, 1620, was *unveiled* by the American Ambassador on Friday last.

Q In spite of its antiquity, Marseilles has few *ancient monuments.* 古い歴史があるにかかわらずマルセーユには昔の記念物がほとんどない. ¶an *enduring monument* to ... ...への永遠に続く記念碑. ¶a *fine monument* りっぱな記念碑. ¶*great architectural monuments* 建築上の偉大な記念物. ¶an *imperishable monument* to his genius 彼の天才を永遠に伝える記念物. ¶early *literary monuments* of the language その国語で書いた昔の文学上の著作 ‖ *literary monuments* which have perished 失われた古文献. ¶a *modest monument* 質素な記念碑. ¶a *simple monument* 質素な記念碑.

Q² the proposed *Gladstone monument* 提案のグラッドストーン記念像. ¶a huge *monolith monument* 巨大な一本石の記念碑. ¶a national *service monument* 報国碑.

P it can only be looked upon *as* a *monument* of the incapacity of ... それは...の無能を後世に伝える物でしかない.

P² *monument in* commemoration of ... ...を記念する碑. ¶a *monument of* scholarship 不朽の業績 ‖ a *monument of* erudition 不朽の学術書. 【類】The professor's researches are *monuments of* learning. / The old Egyptians have left behind them *monuments of* industry (勤勉). / The book is one of the great *monuments of* English learning. ¶a *monument to* British work and material 英国の工作と材料を後世に伝えるもの.

mood, *n.* 気分, 心持, 機げん.

V She will *dispel* your gloomy *moods* by her bright smiles. 彼女はその晴やかな笑で君のふさいだ気分をふっ飛ばしてしまうだろう. ¶He *found* the *mood* to travel. 彼は旅行する気になった. ¶*indulge* my *mood* 私の気の向くままにする. ¶faithfully *interpret* one's *mood* その情調を忠実に解釈する. ¶He *maintained* his *mood* of extreme reserve. 彼はそのきわめて遠慮勝な態度を持続した.

V² That *mood came* over me. その気分が私に起った. ¶She treated him with arrogance or levity, as her *mood* might *dictate.* 彼女の気分の向くままに彼をあるいはごう慢にあるいは軽率に取扱った. ¶I watch the moon sinking toward those dimly white mountains, and as I gaze my *mood promises* to crystallize in the form of a poem. 私はあのかすかに白い山々の方へ月が沈んで行くのを見つめる, そして私がそれをながめ入る間に私の気分は結晶して詩になって行くように思われる. ¶He works leisurely, as the *mood strikes* him. 彼は気の向くままにゆっくり仕事をする.

Q in an *angry mood* 腹立たしくなって. ¶He was in an *argumentative mood.* 彼は議論をしようという気持になっていた. ¶She was then in one of her most *awe-inspiring moods.* そのとき彼はその最もりりしい気象を発揮していた. ¶I was not in the *buying mood.* 私には買いたい気持がなかった. ¶to meet the *changing moods* of a fickle public 始終移り変る世人の好みに応じるため. ¶He was in a *communicative mood.* 彼は話相手が欲しいようだった. ¶His *mood* was most *conciliatory* and *ingratiating.* 彼の気立ては非常に和協的で人に好かれるものであった. ¶He was in the *critical mood.* 彼は批判的気分であった. ¶a *devotional mood* 敬けんな気持. ¶an *economical mood* 経済的にやる気. ¶an *ecstatic mood* うれしくて無我夢中な気持. ¶nature in *fancy mood* 気まぐれな自然. ¶be in a *gloomy mood* 気がふさいでいる. ¶be in a *good* (*bad*) *mood* きげんがいい(悪い). ¶He loafs about how and where the *hour's mood* may lead him. 彼はその時々の気分に従ってどことなくうろつき回る. ¶a lady of *incalculable moods* 気まぐれな婦人. ¶be in a *jittery mood* いらいらしている. ¶in a *joyful mood* 喜こびあふれる気分で(うれし気に). ¶in a *laughing mood* 笑い興じて. ¶a *lyrical introspective mood* 叙情的で内省的な気分. ¶a *meditative mood* 思いに沈んだ気分. ¶Her *mood* is apt to become *melancholy.* 彼女はふさぎ勝ちだ. ¶in a *merry mood* 浮々として. ¶Paris was in a *military mood.* パリは軍隊色で塗りつぶされていた. ¶I was in *no mood* for ... 私は...しようという気分になっていなかった. ¶in a *pensive mood* ふさぎ込んで. ¶when in the *pessimistic mood* 悲観的な気分のときに. ¶in a *playful mood* ふざけ半分に. ¶The ancient name of Naniwa is still used for Osaka when the *poetic mood* is on. 詩的気分が乗って来ると大阪の代りに昔の浪速(なにわ)という名称がいまでも用いられる. ¶a *refractory mood* 反抗的気分. ¶say in a *reprimanding mood* しかりつけるような心持で言う. ¶a *self-reproachful mood* 自責の気持. ¶in a *social mood* 相手ほしやで. ¶a *statesmanlike mood* 政治家らしい気持. ¶He went away in a *sullen mood.* 彼はむっとして出て行った. ¶relapse into a *thoughtful mood* また考え込む. ¶fall into a *truculent mood* 残忍な心持になる. ¶He is in an *ugly mood.* 彼は大いに機げんが悪い. ¶an *uncommercial mood* 商売気を離れた気持.

Q² the crowd of merrymakers out in a *holiday mood* 休日気分で出遊している連中の群.

P Sadness prevailed *among* her *moods.* 悲しみが彼女の気分を支配した. ¶at last, *in* a *mood* of desperation 遂に捨ばちの気分で ‖ He is *in* no *mood* to tolerate it. 彼はそれを勘忍する気がない. ‖ nature *in* all her *moods* あらゆる姿における自然. 【類】be *in mood* for work / I'm *in* no *mood* for joking. / I'm in *no mood* to attend the party. / be *in* the *mood* for love / I'm *in* the *mood* for a game of bridge / *in* the *mood* to ... ¶a man *of moods* 気むずかしい人.

moon, *n.* 月, 太陰.

V *admire* the *moon* 月見をやる. ¶*bay* the *moon* いたずらに怒号する, むだ骨を折る. ¶Won't you come out somewhere to *view* the *moon?* 月見にどこかへ出掛けませんか. 【類】*view* the *moon* through a telescope. ¶*watch* the *moon* rising.

V^2 The *moon* had ***arched*** across the zenith and was slipping down the western sky. 月は中天を横ぎて西の空に傾いていた. ¶The *moon* ***arose.*** 月が昇った. ¶The *moon* ***came out.*** 月が出て来た. ¶The *moon* ***came up.*** 月が昇った. ¶The *moon* was ***declining.*** 月が傾いていた. ¶The *moon* ***died off.*** 月がかけてしまった. ¶The *moon* was ***rising*** high. 月が高く昇っていた. ‖ At what time does the *moon* ***rise***? 何時に月が出ますか. ¶The *moon* is ***setting.*** 月が落ちかけている. ¶How the *moon* ***shines!*** まあ明るい月だこと. ¶The *moon* ***wanes*** (***waxes***). 月はかける(満ちる).

Q a ***cold, wintry*** *moon* 寒々した冬の月. ¶the ***crescent*** *moon* 三日月. ¶***dark*** *moon* 月の出ない期間. ¶It is ***full*** *moon* now. 今は満月です. ‖ a bright ***full*** *moon* (=full-moon) 明るい満月. ¶What a ***glorious*** *moon* we have tonight? 今夜はなんといい月だろう. ¶the ***half*** *moon* 半月. ¶a ***new*** *moon* 新月. ¶an ***old*** *moon* 弦月. ¶a ***rising*** *moon* 昇る月. ¶Above the horizon soared the ***round, yellow*** *moon.* 水平線上に丸い黄色な月が上った. ¶There was a ***young*** *moon* half way up the sky. 空の中ほどに新月がかかっていた. ¶a ***waning*** *moon* かけてゆく月.

Q^2 a ***dim, morning*** *moon* 光の失せた朝の月. ¶A ***full*** *moon* is an ***allnight*** *moon.* 満月は一晩中出ている. ¶the ***autumn*** (=***fall***) *moon* 秋の月. ¶the ***harvest*** *moon* 仲秋明月. ¶a ***June*** *moon* 六月の月. ¶the ***silver*** *moon* 銀月.

P sing passionate love-songs ***beneath*** the *moon* 月下に情熱的な恋歌を歌う. ¶the man ***in*** the *moon* 月の男. ☞月のうさぎに当る. ‖ There is a man ***in*** the *moon* who carries a heavy load on his back. 月の中には重い荷物を背負った男がいる. ¶lighted ***by*** the *moon* 月に照されて. ¶He took a walk with her ***under*** the *moon.* 彼は月下に彼女と散歩した. ‖ ***under*** a California *moon* カリフォルニアの月下に.

moonlight, *n.* 月光.

V^2 The *moonlight* ***danced*** on the ripples of the lake. 月光が湖水のさざ波にゆれていた.

Q ***bright*** *moonlight* 輝く月光. ¶the ***brilliant*** *moonlight* prevailing at the time そのとき月光がくまなく照り渡って. ¶sit in the ***calm*** *moonlight* and talk of ... 静かな月光に座して...を語る. ¶walk in the ***glorious*** *moonlight* of an Italian summer night イタリアの夏の夜照り渡る月下を散歩する. ¶***mellow*** *moonlight* やわらかで豊かな月光. ¶in the ***quiet*** *moonlight* やわらかな月の光で.

P the Sumida ***by*** *moonlight* 月夜の隅田川. 【類】"The Brook ***by*** *Moonlight.*" (画題). ‖ view cherry blossoms ***by*** *moonlight* 月光で桜花を見る. 【類】travel ***by*** *moonlight.* Mt. Fuji ***in*** the *moonlight* 月光を浴びる富士. 【類】dance on the lawn ***in*** the *moonlight* / ***In*** the *moonlight* the beautiful lake sparkles like crystals. ¶The Devil's Bridge ***in*** the *moonlight,* Switzerland スイスの月下の悪魔橋. ¶***in*** the flood of *moonligh* 月光を浴びて. ¶plum blossoms ***under*** *moonlight* 月下の梅花. 【類】***under*** the silvery *moonlight.*

moonlit, *a.* 月光で照した.

M a garden ***brightly*** *moonlit* 月光で明るい庭.

moor, *n.* 荒野.

Q ***rolling*** *moors* 起伏する荒野.

P a stretch ***of*** *moors* 一帯の荒野. ¶the soldiers who left their bones ***upon*** the *moor* 骨を荒野に残した兵士たち.

moor, *v.* 停泊する, 繫留する.

P The ship was *moored* ***alongside*** the pier at Yokohama. その船は横浜の桟橋に横付けになった. ‖ The Chichibu Maru is *moored* ***at*** the pier. 秩父丸は桟橋についている. ¶It was *moored* ***to*** a buoy. それは浮標につないであった.

mooring, *n. pl.* 停泊所, 繫留所.

V ***take up*** *moorings* at Buoy No. 2 第二番ブイに停泊する.

P ships that lie ***at*** their *moorings* 停泊所に横たわる船舶. ¶part ***from*** her *moorings* その繫留所から去る.

moorland, *n.* 荒野, 沼地.

Q a desolate and sparsely ***inhabited*** *moorland* 荒れ果てて人煙希薄な荒地.

mop, *v.* ふく, 吸収する, 平らげる.

M^2 *mop* ***up*** the floor 床をぞうきんでふく ‖ *mop* ***up*** a rebellion 反乱軍を平らげる ‖ *mop* ***up*** the remnants of the enemy 残敵を掃とうする ‖ *mop* ***up*** purchasing power 購買力を吸収する ‖ *mop* ***up*** whisky, glass after glass 一杯一杯とウイスキーを平らげる. 【類】*mop* ***up*** rears of work (残業).

P *mop* one's face ***with*** a handkerchief.

mope, *v.* ふさぎ込む.

M *mope* ***away*** one's time (life) うつうつとして日(一生)を送る.

M^2 *mope* ***about*** all day 終日ふさぎ込む.

moping, *n.* ふさぎこみ.

Q ***gloomy*** *mopings* ふさぎ込み.

moral, *n.* ぐう意; 教訓; *pl.* 風紀, 身持ち.

V ***attach*** a *moral* to a story 物語に教訓を盛る. ¶***contaminate*** the *morals* 風紀を乱す. ¶***corrupt*** *morals* 風俗を壊乱する. ¶***debase*** (=***degrade***) the *morals* 風儀をみだす. ¶There is more than one *moral* to be ***drawn*** from this story. この物語には幾多の教訓が含まれている. ¶***follow*** the easy *morals* of the world 世間並のずるいやり方をする. ¶***hurt*** their *morals* 彼らの徳性を傷つける. ¶***improve*** public *morals* 風紀を良くする. ¶***inculcate*** *morals* くりかえして道徳を説く. ¶***make*** a *moral* out of ... ...を教訓の材料にする. ¶Confucianism ***moulds*** the *morals* of Japan. 儒教は日本人の徳性を作る. ¶a story intended to ***point*** a *moral* 一つの教訓を盛った物語 ‖ ***point*** one's *moral* with a modern instance 最近の例によって自分の道徳観を説く. ¶This ***raised*** the *morals* of the soldiers in the most wonderful manner. これが実に不思議なくらい軍紀を振作した. ¶***read*** *moral* into this remarkable story この有名な物語に含まれている教訓を会得する. ¶***safeguard*** public *morals* 社会道徳を擁護する.

V^2 the *moral* ***seems*** to be that ... これによって得られる教訓は...であると思われる.

Q Western men with ***Eastern*** *morals* 東洋道徳を有する西洋人. ¶women of ***easy*** (=loose) *morals* 不身持ちの女, ふしだらな女. ¶***lax*** (=loose) *morals* 不身持ち. ¶a man of ***loose*** *morals* 身持ちの悪い男 ‖ in this age of ***loose*** *morals* この道徳のすたれた時世に. ¶***public*** *morals* 社会の風紀, 世道人心. ¶***social*** *morals* 公徳. ¶a person of ***strict*** *morals* 道徳堅固な人.

Q^2 ***sea-port*** *morals* 港町の風紀.

P injurious ***to*** public *morals* 公衆道徳上有害な.

P^2 The *moral* (=lesson) ***of*** the story is "Look before you leap." その物語の教訓は「ころばぬ先のつえ」である.

morale, *n.* 士気.

V ***affect*** the *morale* of the soldiers 兵士の士気を左右する. ¶He knew how to ***bring up*** the *morale* of the troops. 彼は士気を振作させる呼吸をのみ込んでいた. ¶***heighten*** the *morale* of ... の士気を向上させる. ¶This ***improved*** the *morale* of the troops. このために士気が振った. ¶***keep up*** the *morale* 士気を落さないようにする. ¶***maintain*** *morale* 士気を維持する. ¶The army ***preserved*** its *morale.* 軍はその士気を維持した. ¶***raise*** *morale* 士気をたかめる. ¶This terrible defeat ***shook*** the *morale.* この大敗北に士気がぐらついた. ¶***stiffen*** the *morale* of the troops 軍の士気を鼓舞する. ¶***tone up*** the *morale* of a patient 病人の元気を付ける.

Q The *morale* of the troops is ***low*** (***perfect***). 軍の士気が振わない(申分ない).

Q^2 stimulate the ***Army*** *morale* 陸軍の志気を鼓舞する. ¶***fighting*** *morale* 士気. ¶The ***Navy*** *morale* sags. 海軍の士気がそそうする. ¶sink ***party*** *morale* 党の士気をそそうさせる. ¶improve ***student*** *morale* 学生の士気を高める. 【類】The ***student*** *morale* there is very low.

P improvement ***in*** the *morale* 士気の振作. ¶The defeat robbed the army ***of*** its *morale.* その敗戦で軍の士気はそそうした.

morality, *n.* 道徳, 道義, 道念; 品行, 行状.

V ***injure*** public *morality* 社会の道徳を害する. ¶***question*** the *morality* of ... ...が道徳的であるかどうかを問題にする. ¶***transgress*** *morality* 道徳を破る.

Q ***commercial*** (=business) *morality* 商業道徳. ¶the ***conventional*** *morality* 慣習的道徳. ¶***doubtful*** *morality* いかがわしい行状. ¶women of ***easy*** *morality* ふしだらな女. ¶be of ***unimpeachable*** *morality* 道徳上非難すべき点がない. ¶***lax official*** *morality* 乱れた官紀. ¶His ***lofty*** *morality* attracts the like-minded. 彼の高潔な徳性が同志をひきつける. ¶***national*** *morality* 国民道徳. ¶***private*** *morality* 個人の道徳. ¶***prudential*** *morality* 細心の道義心. ¶injure ***public*** *morality* 公衆道徳を毒する. ¶a ***sickly*** *morality* 病的な道義心.

Q^2 ***fig-leaf*** *morality* 体裁をつくろう式の道徳. ¶***sex*** (=sexual) *morality* 性道徳.

P^2 This is the *morality* ***of*** traffic. これが交通道徳である.

moralization, *n.* 道徳化.

Q ***severe*** *moralization* 厳格な訓育.

moralize, *v.* 道徳を語る.

P *moralize over* the story (*on* the matter) その物語(など)を土台にして道徳を語る.

moratorium, *n.* 支払猶予.

V *grant* a *moratorium* 支払猶予を許す.

more, *a., ad.* さらに多い; さらに多く.

M Nations are not to be judged by their size *any more* than individuals. 国家は個人と同様大きさで判断すべきものではない. ¶It is *even more* a poem than a picture. それは絵というよりはむしろ詩である. ¶He is *no more.* 彼はもはや存命していない. ‖ He is *no more* than a policeman. 彼は一警官にすぎない. ¶I will take *one more* glass. 私はもう一杯飲みましょう.

O The *more* he has, the *more* he wants. 彼は持てば持つほど欲しがる. ¶I have no *more* to say. それ以上言うことはない.

morgue, *n.* 死体置場.

Q a *temporary morgue* 臨時死体置場.

morn, *n.* [詩]朝, 夜明け.

Q a *dewy morn* 露しげき夜あけ.

P *from morn* till dusk 夜あけより日暮れまで. ¶*from* early (=grey) *morn* to dewy eve 朝早くより露おく夕べまで.

morning, *n.* 朝, 午前; 初期.

V I *spent* a profitable *morning* in the Museum. 私は博物館で有益な朝の時間を過ごした.

V² as the *morning advanced* 朝の移るにつれて ‖ when the *morning* has far (=is well) *advanced* 朝も大分おそくなって. ¶The *morning broke* fair and calm. 夜が明けて晴れた静かな朝となった. ¶when (=as) *morning came,* I found that ... 朝になって…ということが私に分かった. ¶as *morning dawned* 夜が明けて.

Q It's been raining *all morning* and all afternoon. 午前午後中ずっと降り続けだ. ¶It often happens that a *balmy morning* passes into a chilly afternoon. 朝陽気がよくって午後になって冷々する天気になることが往々ある. ¶A *bright morning* was breaking when I came to myself. 私が正気づいたときは朝日がきらきら輝いていた. ¶a *bright health-giving morning* on the beach 海辺の健康によい明るい朝. ¶one *cold wintry* (=winter) *morning* ある寒い冬の朝. ¶from *early morning* 朝早くから. 【類】in the *early* (=early in the) *morning.* ¶*every morning* 毎朝. ¶I awoke one *fine morning* to find that ... ある天気の良い朝目を覚まして見ると… ¶[on] the *following morning* 翌朝. ¶one *fatal morning* ある不吉な朝. ¶one *foggy morning* ある霧深い朝. ¶a *frosty morning* 霜の降りた朝. ¶a *glorious morning* 晴れやかな朝. ¶the *next morning* 翌朝. ¶*one morning* early ある朝早く. ¶the *previous morning*=the morning before その前の朝. ¶an olfactory image of the fragrance of a *rural morning* 鼻に残るいなかの朝の芳しいかおり. ¶the *second morning* out 二日目の朝(航海中など). ¶on the *succeeding* (=following *or* next) *morning* その次の朝. ¶I have seen him *this morning.* 私はけさ彼に会いました. ¶on a *wet* (=*rainy*) *morning* 雨降る朝.

Q² today, on this *April morning* 今日この四月の朝に. ¶one scorching *August morning* 焼けつく八月のある朝. ¶a nice, cool *autumn morning* さわやかな秋の朝. ¶It was *Christmas morning* クリスマスの朝だった. ¶one *Easter morning* ある復活祭の朝. ¶a cold *fall morning* 寒い秋の朝. ¶a foggy *January morning* 霧深い一月のある朝. ¶a *sailing morning* 出帆の朝. ¶on a blue *spring morning* 空の晴れた春の朝に. ¶one warm *Sunday morning* in May 五月のある暖い日曜の朝. ¶a raw *winter morning* 湿冷のある冬の朝.

P a bird's note *at morning* 朝鳴く鳥の調べ. ¶*before* the *morning* まだ夜が明けない中に. ¶*between* the *morning* and noon 朝と正午の間に. 【類】*between* early *morning* and late night. ¶*from morning* till late at night 朝から夜おそくまで ‖ *from* early *morning* on 早朝からずっと. 【類】*from* early *morning* till nightfall (late at night). / *from morning* to (=till) noon. / *from morning* till night. ¶go to school *in* the *morning* 朝学校に行く. 【類】early *in* the *morning* of Monday, April 24 ‖ After a good night's rest, we started early *in* the *morning* on the 25th of July. 一晩ゆっくり休んでわれわれは七月二十五日の朝早く出立した. ¶get up early *of* a *morning* 朝早く起きる ‖ He determined to break himself of a bad habit of lying in bed late *of* a *morning.* 彼は朝おそくまで寝ている悪い習慣を打破しようと決心した. ¶*on* the *morning* of Jan. 2 一月二日の朝 ‖ *on* this *morning* of all the mornings of the year 日もあろうに特にこの朝. 【類】at half past four *on* the *morning* of Jan. 2 / *on* the third *morning* / *on* the early *morning* of Dec. 6 / *on* Tuesday *morning* / *on* a warm *morning* in May. ¶I have not seen him *since morning.* 朝から彼の姿を見ない. ¶*towards* [early] *morning* 明け方近く.

P² I feel dizzy this *morning after* the spree of last night. けさはゆうべの宴会で頭がふらふらする. ¶an early *morning in* winter 冬の早朝. ¶The *morning of* the 13th broke forth most gloriously. 十三日の朝がいとも晴れやかに明けた. 【類】early on the *morning of* July 15th, 1928. ‖ Youth is the *morning of* life. 青年期は人生の朝だ.

O Traffic is heavy hereabout, *mornings* and evenings. この辺は朝晩非常に交通が激しい. 【類】It's much cooler now *mornings* and evenings. ¶Practice this exercise *morning* and evening each day. この練習を毎日朝晩けい古しなさい. ¶The weather that *morning* was beautiful. その朝は上天気だった.

morrow, *n.* 翌日, 次の日.

P *on* the *morrow* of ... …の翌日. ☞ on the eve of の対句で主として詩に用いる.

morsel, *n.* 一口, 一片, 少量.

V *eat* (=*take or have*) a *morsel* of food 食物を一口食う.

Q a *dainty morsel* for his evening meal 彼の夕飯の御馳走. ¶eat to the *last morsel* 最後の一口まで食う.

mortal, *n.* 人間.

Q He was one of the *best-hated* and *best-abused mortals* 彼は人から最も憎まれ最もば倒されたものの一人であった. ¶a *common mortal* 普通の人間. ¶a *deified mortal* 神格化された人物. ¶*fallible mortals* 間違いがちな人間. ¶unless we are more than usually *favored mortals* われわれにして普通以上に恵まれた人間でなければ. ¶*happy mortals* 幸福な人たち. ¶*minor mortals* 小人ども, つまらない人間. ¶we, *poor mortals,* ... われわれ哀れな人間どもは.... ¶a *thirsty mortal* 《俗》のんべい.

mortal, *a.* 死すべき.

P all that is *mortal of* her is resting in ... 彼女のなきがらは…に葬ってある.

mortality, *n.* 死すべきもの; 死亡率.

V The city *has* an infant *mortality* of 71 per 1,000. その町の幼児死亡率は千人につき七十一人である. ¶*lower* infantile *mortality* 幼児の死亡率を低下させる. ¶*reduce* the *mortality* from typhoid fever 腸チブスの死亡率を減じる.

V² It is said that this *mortality* is *rising.* この死亡率は高まりつつあるとのことだ. ¶The city *suffered* fearful *mortality* from this epidemic. その市はこの流行病で多数の死者を出した.

Q *early mortality* 幼時の死亡. ¶a *high* (*low*) *mortality* 高(低)い死亡率. 【類】The *mortality* was as *high* as eighty per cent before Dr. Flexner's discovery. ¶There will be a *large mortality.* 多数の死亡者を出すであろう. ¶*Mortality* is *small.* 死亡数は少ない. ¶*universal mortality* 自然界のはかなさ.

Q² The *infant mortality* is shockingly high. 幼児の死亡率は驚くほど高い. 【類】terrible *infant mortality.*

P² the *mortality from* phthisis fell from ... to ... 肺結核の死亡率は…から…へと低下した.

mortgage, *n.* 質, 抵当, 抵当権.

V The bank refused to *accept* any *mortgage* on land. その銀行は土地の抵当は一切拒絶した. ¶The bank *foreclosed* a *mortgage* on the property. その銀行はその財産を抵当流れにした. ¶His house *has* a heavy *mortgage* on it. 彼の家は多額の抵当にはいっている. 【類】He *has* a *mortgage* on the vessel. ¶*hold* a *mortgage* on land and property 土地財産を抵当に取っている. ¶*lend* a *mortgage* 抵当を出す. ¶He *offered* a *mortgage* on house property as security. 彼は家屋担保に金を貸そうと言出した. ¶*pay off* the *mortgage* on one's farm 農場を抵当に借りた金を返す. ¶I want to *place* a *mortgage* on my house. 私は家屋を抵当に金を借りたいと思う. ¶He was obliged to *raise* a *mortgage* on some property in order to get the money. 彼はその金を得るために財産を抵当に入れなければならなかった.

Q *cutthroat mortgage* とりきり抵当. ¶a *double mortgage* 二重抵当. ¶a *first mortgage* 一番抵当. ¶Money is lent out at interest on *suitable mortgages.* 相当の抵当で利息付の金が貸し出される.

Q² a *chattel mortgage* 動産抵当.
P a house *in mortgage* 抵当に入ってる家屋.
P² There is a *mortgage of* ... yen *on* the house. その家は...円の抵当にはいっている.

mortgage, *v.* 抵当にする, 質に入れる.
P It is *mortgaged to* ... *for* a large sum. それは...へ巨額の抵当にはいっている.

mortification, *n.* 屈辱, 不面目, 胸の悩み.
V he *had* the *mortification* of being ... 彼は...たることの屈辱を受けた.
P *in mortification* of his defeat 彼の失敗を恥じて ‖ shed tears *in* his *mortification* くやし涙をこぼす.

mortify, *v.* 残念に思わせる, 胸をいためさせる.
P He was *mortified at* finding the house shut. 彼はその家が締めてあるのを見て残念に思った. ¶He is *mortified by* his failure (mistake). 彼は失敗(など)をくよくよ思っている.

mosquito, *n.* 蚊.
V *drive off mosquitoes* 蚊を駆除する. ¶*feed* the *mosquitoes* 蚊に食われる. ¶*fan off* (=*away*) *mosquitoes* 蚊をうちわで追う. ¶*smoke out mosquitoes* 蚊をいぶし出す.
V² *Mosquitoes bite.* 蚊は食う. ¶*Mosquitoes buzz.* 蚊はぶんぶんいう. ¶*let* a *mosquito feed* [on the leg] 蚊にくわせておく.
Q² the *anopheles* (=*malarious*) *mosquito* マラリア蚊.
P I was bitten *by mosquitoes.* 私は蚊に食われた. ¶a swarm *of mosquitoes* 一群の蚊.

mosquito-net, *n.* 蚊帳(ﾞ).
V *hang up* (=*put up, spread or suspend*) a *mosquito-net* 蚊帳をつる. ¶*take down* a *mosquito-net* 蚊帳をはずす. ¶*use* a *mosquito-net* 蚊帳をつる.
P a bed enclosed *by* a *mosquito-net* 蚊帳に囲まれた寝床. ¶sleep *under* a *mosquito-net* 蚊帳をつって寝る.

moss, *n.* こけ, こけ類.
V A rolling stone *gathers* no *moss.* 〘諺〙 ころがる石にこけむさず(転々と職をかえると出世ができない). ¶*Moss grows* on a rock. 岩にこけがはえる.
P stones covered *with moss* こけのむした石.
P² the green *moss on* the tree 木についてる緑のこけ.

most, *n.* 最多, 最大, 極大.
V *get* the *most* of (=out of) life 人生を最大限に利用する. ¶The occasion only comes once in five years, and they naturally *make* the *most* of it. その日は五年にたった一度しか来ないので彼らはあくまでその日を享楽するのも当然である. 【類】He had a peculiar talent for *making* the *most* of the labor of other people. / those who are eager to *make* the *most* of themselves (自己の最善を発揮する) / *make* the *most* of one's opportunity / *make* the *most* of the situation one is placed in / There are the hard-working boys and girls out for a holiday trip; you can see that they mean to *make* the *most* of every minute (歓を尽す).
P I think he was fifteen *at* the *most.* 彼はせいぜい十五歳であったと思う. 【類】For the average man life is not long enough to master more than his own language; *at most,* one in addition to his own.
P² *Most of* the people are aware of it. その人たちは大抵その事を知っている. ‖ He was ill *most of* the time. 彼はその間大抵病気だった.

mot, *n.* 警句.
V *throw out mots* 警句をはく.

mote, *n.* ちり; きず.
V One is apt to *notice* a *mote* in another's eye. 人のなら小さな欠点でも気が付くものだ. ¶*pull* the *mote* out of their brother's eye 彼らの兄(弟)のあら捜しをする. ¶Try to *take* the *mote* out of your own eye before trying to take the beam out of others. 他人の小過失をとがめる前にまず自分の大過失を改めることに努力せよ.
Q *motes dancing* in the sunbeam 陽光に踊るちり.

mother, *n.* 母; 根源.
V *lose* one's *mother* 母に死に別れる. ¶*pester mother* for pocket money 母に小ずかいをせがむ.
V² The *mother sang* her child to sleep. 母は歌を歌ってその子を眠りにつかせた.
Q Christ and His *Blessed mother* キリストとその聖母. ¶a *devoted mother* 子供思いの母. ¶*disconsolate mother* (息子の死などを)あきらめられない母. ¶a child spoiled by a *doting mother* 子煩悩の母親に甘やかされた子供. ¶an *expectant mother* 妊婦 ‖ Tripping and falling is a very serious accident for the *expectant mother.* つまずいたりころんだりすることは妊婦にとっては重大な事故である. ¶a *fond mother* 子煩悩な母. ¶an *indulgent mother* 子に甘い母親. ¶her *invalid* (=*sick*) *mother* 彼女の病気の母. ¶a *laundry-conscious mother* 洗たくを気にする母親. ¶a *loving mother* 慈愛深い母. ¶a *nursing mother* 授乳する母. ¶She treats her step-children as their *own mother* would. 彼女はまま子を本当の母がするように扱う. ¶the *sorrowing mother* 悲しみのマリア. ¶China, once Japan's *spiritual mother* かつては日本の精神上の母であった中国. ¶my *tender mother* 私のやさしい母. ¶*unmarried mothers* and fathers 正式の結婚をしない父母 ‖ children of *unmarried mothers* 私生児. ¶an *unwed mother* 内縁の妻である母. ¶the *virgin mother* of the Son of God 神の子の聖母. ¶his *widowed mother* 未亡人となった彼の母. ¶a *worthy mother* and an unworthy son 有徳の母に不徳の子.
Q² his *actress mother* 女優をしている彼の母. ¶a *lying-in mother* 産じょくの母. ¶a *prison mother* 子持の母の女囚. ¶the *Queen Mother* 皇太后. ¶a dowager *queen mother* 太皇太后.
P He takes *after* his *mother.* 彼は母親似である. ¶the son of a Chinese pirate *by* a Japanese *mother* 日本人を母にした中国の海賊の子.
P² Diligence above all is the *mother of* good luck. ことに勤勉は幸運の母である. ‖ a *mother of* five children 五人の子を持つ母 ‖ Necessity is the *mother of* invention. 〘諺〙 必要は発明の母である. ‖ Contentment is the *mother of* happiness. 満足は幸福の母である. ¶She was a *mother to* the poor. 彼女は貧民の慈母であった.

mother-in-law, *n.* しゅうとめ.
Q an *aggressive mother-in-law* さしでがましいしゅうとめ.

mothlike, *a.* がのような.
P *mothlike to* the flame, he ventured into ... 火中に飛込むがのように彼は大胆にも...をあえてした.

motif, *n.* 主旨, 主題(モチーフ); 意匠.
V It *supplied* a fruitful *motif* to artists and literary men. それは芸術家と文人に豊かな題材を供給した.
Q The cloud is a *favorite motif* in Chinese rugs. 雲は中国の敷物によく見る意匠だ. ¶the *author's motif* 著者のモチーフ.
Q² *cover motif* 表紙のデザイン.
P² the *motif in* music (art, literature) 音楽(など)の主題.

motion, *n.* (1) 動議, 発議.
V the conference *adopted* a *motion* by 101 votes to 42 in favor of ... 同会議は四十二対百一票で...の動議を可決した ‖ The *motion* was *adopted* by a large majority. その動議は大多数で可決された. ‖ The *motion* was *adopted* with no dissentient (=without a dissenting voice). その動議は異議なく採択された. ¶*bring forward* a *motion* before a meeting 会に動議を提出する. ¶The *motion* was *carried* by 31 votes to 17. その動議は三十一対十七票で成立した. ¶The *motion* was *defeated* by a single vote. その動議はたった一票の差で否決された. ¶*lay* a *motion* on (off) the table 動議を提出する(却下する). ¶Their *motion* was *lost* (=negatived) by a large majority. 彼らの動議は大多数で否決された. ¶*make* a *motion* to ......しようとする動議を出す. 【類】on a *motion made* by ... / I *made* a *motion* that we stop and rest a while. ¶leave to *modify* a *motion* 動議修正の許可. ¶*negative* a *motion* 動議を否決する. ¶*offer* a *motion* 動議を出す. ¶*place* a *motion* before a conference 会議に動議を提出する. ¶*propose* a *motion* at a meeting 会に動議を提出する. ¶*put* a *motion* to a standing vote 動議(の成否)を起立で決する. ¶*reconsider* a *motion* 動議を再考する. ¶*reject* (=*turn down*) a *motion* 動議を否決する. ¶*second* a *motion* 動議に賛成する. 【類】in *seconding* the *motion,* he said ... ¶*support* a *motion* 動議に賛成する. ¶*throw out* a *motion* 動議を否決する. ¶*withdraw* a *motion* 動議を撤回する.
Q a *dilatory motion* ぐずぐず動議. ¶a *main motion* 主要動議 ‖ an incidental *main motion* 臨時重要動議. ¶he proposed entirely of his *own motion* that ... 全く自分の考えで...と提議した. ¶a *privileged motion* 優先動議. ¶a *secondary motion* 従属動議. ¶an *undebatable motion* 討議し得ない動議.
Q² introduce an *urgency motion* 緊急動議を出す. ¶a *want-of confidence motion* brought forward by ... ...の

提出した不信任の動議.

P the mover **of** the *motion* 動議の提出者 ‖ **of** its own *motion* その発意により ‖ rejection **of** a *motion* 動議の否決. ¶**on** the *motion* of the Chairman 座長の発議で ‖ **on** *motion*, duly seconded and unanimously carried 正規の賛成を得て満場一致可決された動議に基いて. 【類】 **on** *motion* of the German delegate it was voted to be the desire of the Conference that ... / a resolution of confidence in ... was passed, **on** the *motion* of ... / dismiss a case (事件を撤回する) **on** one's own *motion*. ¶**upon** the *motion* of ... …の動議に基いて.

P² a *motion* **for** adoption (rejection, adjournment) 採用(など)の発議. ¶a *motion* **in** favor of ... …を可とする動議.

(**2**) 運動; 便通.

V **eliminate** *motions* 手を抜く. ¶**follow** the *motions* of the flagship＝follow the admiral's motions 旗艦の行動に準じる. ¶**force** *motion* upon ... …に行動をしいる. ¶**give** *motion* to a machine 機械を運転させる. ¶every time he **has** a *motion* 彼の便通の度ごと ‖ I have not **had** a *motion* for several days. 私は五六日便通がなかった. ¶**impart** a forward *motion* to ... …に前進運動を起させる(便通の). ¶look carefully at the *motions* **passed** by the patient 患者の排せつした便をよく検査する. ¶**set up** a rotating *motion* 回転運動を起させる. ¶Babies **watch** people's *motions* carefully. 赤ん坊は人々の行動を注意して見つめる.

Q the **accelerated** *motion* 〘物理〙 加速度. ¶the **double** *motion* of the earth 地球の二重運動. ¶false *motions* むだな動作. ¶a **rapid** *motion* 早い運動. ¶with **regular rhythmic** *motions* 一定の律動をもって. ¶a **screwlike** or **rotary** *motion* ら旋すなわち回転的動作. ¶a **slow** *motion* 緩慢な運動. ¶an **up-and-down** *motion* 上下運動. ¶a **wavy** *motion* 波状運動.

Q² a **straight line** *motion* 直線運動.

P a body **in** *motion* 運動中の物体 ‖ be brisk (＝swift) **in** *motion* 動作が機敏である ‖ The ship was **in** *motion*. 船は進行していた. ‖ put (＝set) a machine **in** *motion* 機械を運転させる. ¶study the laws **of** *motion* 運動の法則を研究する.

motion, *v*. 動作で意を示す; 動作で指導する.

M, M² He *motioned* me **out** (**in**). 出て行け(入れ)と合図した. ¶**quietly** *motioning* him to ... 静かに彼の注意を…の方へ向けて.

P *motion* one's visitor **to** a seat 来客にお掛けなさいと動作で示す.

motivate, *v*. 刺激を与える, 動かす.

M That man's actions are **entirely** *motivated* by his desire for happiness is a doctrine which has been called "theological utilitarianism". 人間の行動は全く幸福追求にあるというのはいわゆる神学的功利主義の原則である.

P respect *motivated* **by** fear 恐怖から来る尊敬. ¶*motivated* **by** kindness (love) 情のこもった.

motive, *n*. (**1**) 動機; 目的, 意志, 本意; 誘因.

V He would **assign** no *motive* for his deed. 彼は自分の行動に対して何らの意志もないと言い張った. ¶**conceal** one's true *motive* その真意を隠す. ¶**diagnose** the underlying *motive* 真意を探る. ¶**fathom** the *motive* その動機を探る. ¶They **have** no ulterior *motive*. 彼らに何らの底意がない. ¶**impute** base *motives* to ... …を卑しい動機から出たのだとする. ¶**infer** a criminal *motive* 犯罪の動機を推測する. ¶I **misjudged** his *motives*. 私は彼の動機を誤解した. ¶**penetrate** one's *motives* その動機を見抜く. ¶**probe** the *motives* of ... …の動機を探る. ¶**question** one's *motive* その動機を疑う. ¶**respect** the *motives* of ... …の動機を尊重する. ¶**reveal** hidden *motives* 隠れた動機を明かにする. 【類】 **reveal** *motives* hitherto obscure and explain conduct hitherto misinterpreted or imperfectly understood. ¶**see** sinister *motives* in ... …を不正の動議によるものとにらむ. ¶**trace** the *motives* of ... …の動機を探る.

V² *motives* which **actuate** these men to this sort of endeavor これらの人々を刺激してこの種の努力をなさしめる動因.

Q It is difficult to see any **adequate** *motive* for the action. その行為に対するはっきりした動機がよく分からない. ¶**altruistic** *motives* 愛他的な動機. ¶the **animating** *motive* それを鼓舞する動機. ¶**base** *motives* 卑劣な動機. ¶**charitable** *motives* 慈善心. ¶Their **chief** *motive* was the desire of gain. 彼らの主な動機は利益欲であった. ¶His *motive* in going abroad was **clear**. 彼の洋行の動機は明らかだった. ¶a **complex** *motive* 複雑な動機. ¶infer a **criminal** *motive* 悪心ありと察する. ¶from **different** *motives* 色々な動機から. ¶inspired by truly **disinterested** and **patriotic** *motives* 真に利欲をはなれた愛国的な動機に刺激されて. ¶the **dominant** *motives* 最も有力な動機. ¶It is not from such a **frivolous** *motive*. そんな浮いた考えからじゃない. ¶**egoistic** *motives* 利己的な動機. ¶**gain-seeking** *motive* 利益を得ようという意志. ¶not always moved by the **highest** *motives* 必ずしも至高な動機に動かされずに. ¶prompted by **humane** *motives* 人情的な動機に刺激されて. ¶the **impelling** *motive* 推進力. ¶an **impure** *motive* 不純な動機. ¶**inner** *motives* ふくみ. ¶supply **live** *motives* for ... …に対する活動力を与える. ¶from a **low** *motive* いやしい動機から. ¶the **main** *motive* 主な動機. ¶actuated by **mercenary** *motives* 欲得ずくで. ¶from **mingled** *motives* 色々な動機で. ¶assassinations from **patriotic** *motives* 愛国的動機による暗殺. ¶They had **personal** *motives* for their acting 彼らの行為には私的な動機があった. ¶men of **philanthropic** *motives* 慈悲心の深い人. ¶from **prudential** and **other** *motives* 用心深い考えやその他の考えから. ¶**religious** *motives* 宗教的動機. ¶**selfish** *motives* 利己的な考え ‖ actuated by **slefish** or **unworthy** *motives* 利己的なまたはつまらない考えに刺激されて. ¶from a mixture of **several** *motives* 色々交った動機から. ¶conceal one's **true** *motive* 真意を隠す. ¶He had no **ulterior** *motives*. 彼にはそれ以外の動機はなかった. ¶have an **underlying** *motive* 野心がある ‖ see through the **underlying** *motive* 底意を看破する. ¶by some **unexplained** *motive* ある何とも分からない動機で. ¶solely driven by **unselfish** *motives* 全く無私無欲の動機から.

Q² the "**bread-and-butter**" *motive* of study パンを得るための勉強. ¶prompted by **economy** *motives* 節約のため. ¶a **profit** *motive* 利欲の念.

P dictated **by** high *motives* 高尚な動機に励まされて. ¶**from** a true *motive* of piety 真に敬けんな動機から. 【類】 **from** *motives* of sentiment (kindness, economy, expediency) / **from** *motives* of delicacy (遠慮して), he refrained from ... / **from** *motives* of national interest / **from** one's own *motives*. ¶**out of** (＝through) *motives* of ... …の考えから. ¶do ... **through** (＝from) *motives* of kindness 親切な考えから…をやる. ¶**with** no deeper *motive* ただそれだけの動機で. ¶**without** any selfish *motive* 何ら利己的な動機なしに.

P² the *motive* or inspiration **behind** the giving 贈与の背後にある動機または感激. ¶that great *motive* **of** action, the sex passion かの行動の一大動機たる情欲.

(**2**) 題材.

V **borrow** *motives* from nature 自然から題材を借りる.

Q a **favorite** *motive* of Japanese art 日本芸術によく取扱われる題材 ‖ a **favorite** *motive* with Japanese painters 日本画家の好んで使う題材.

motor, *n*. 発動機, 原動機; 動因.

V **reverse** the *motor* 発動機を逆に動かす. ¶**start** a *motor* モーターを動かす.

Q **prime** *motors* 主なる動因.

Q² a **gas** *motor* ガス発動機. ¶a **single-phase** *motor* 単相電動機.

P² The *motor* **of** the limousine purred softly. リムジン車のモーターが静かにぶんぶん回っていた.

motor, *v*. 自動車を駆る.

M *motor* (drive) **away** 自動車で去る.

M² *motor* **off** to ... …にドライブする. ¶*motor* **over** to ... …へ自動車で行く.

P We *motored* **to** Yokohama last Sunday. 僕たちは前の日曜日に自動車で横浜へ行った. 【類】 *motor* **to** their work every day.

motor-car, *n*. 自動車.

V **drive** a *motor-car* 自動車を駆る. ¶She knows how to **handle** (＝**manage**) a *motor-car*. 彼女は自動車の操縦を心得ている. ¶**hire** *motor-cars* 自動車をやとう. ¶He **keeps** a (＝his) *motor-car*. 彼は自動車を持っている. ¶**park** a *motor-car* 自動車を駐車場におく. ¶**take** a *motor-car* for ... 自動車で…へ行く. ¶**work** (＝**control**) a *motor-car* 自動車を操縦する.

V² The *motor-car* has **gone all wrong**. 自動車に大故障を生じた. ¶The *motor-car* is **running** at full speed. 自動車は全速力で走っている. ¶This *motor-car* **travels** ... miles an hour. この自動車は一時間…マイル走る. ¶A *motor-car* **whirred by**. 一台の自動車がびゅーっと通り過ぎた.

Q A jeep is a ***small, multi-purpose, military** motor-car.* ジープは小型で多能な軍用自動車である.

P He was knocked down (=over) ***by*** a *motor-car.* 彼は自動車にひき倒された. ¶start off ***in*** a *motor-car* for a journey 自動車で旅行に出掛ける ‖ have a ride ***in*** a *motor-car* 自動車に乗る.

motorcycle, *n.* 《英》オートバイ.

P go ***by*** *motorcycle* オートバイで行く. ¶ride [*on*] a *motorcycle* オートバイに乗る.

motor-engine, *n.* モーター・エンジン.

Q² a ***six-cylinder*** *motor-engine* 六気筒のモーター・エンジン.

motoring, *n.* 自動車に乗ること.

P They have a liking ***for*** *motoring.* 彼らは自動車に乗ることが好きだ.

motorist, *n.* 自動車乗り, 自動車常用者.

Q a ***keen*** *motorist* 大の自動車愛用者.

motor-vehicle, *n.* モーター付き車.

P Speed limits: 20 MPH ***for*** all *motor-vehicles.* 〖掲示〗速度制限: モーターづき車はすべて時速二十マイル以内.

mottle, *v.* まだらにする, 雑色にする.

P ***mottled with*** white spots 白点でまだらになって.

motto, *n.* 標語, 座右の銘.

V ***adopt*** a *motto* for ... ...に対して標語を採用する.

Q a ***fitting*** *motto* for ... ...に対する適切な標語. ¶a ***good*** *motto* for a young man 青年にとって好い標語. ¶live up to the ***old*** *motto* その古語通りの生活をする.

P The club has ***for*** its *motto* "Freedom finds fulfilment in service." そのクラブの標語は「自由の実現は奉仕にあり」である.

P² the *motto* ***on*** the banner 旗に記した標語.

mould, *n.* =mold.

mould, *v.* =mold.

mound, *n.* 小山; 〖野球〗投手盤.

V ***take*** the *mound* 投手盤に立つ.

Q ***fluttering*** *mounds* of quicksilver 魚の山(海岸の砂上の).

P² *mounds* ***of*** death 累々たる死体.

mount, *n.* 《俗》乗用馬, あん馬.

V The jockey ***had*** his first *mount.* 騎手は初めて馬に乗った.

Q his ***favorite*** *mount* 愛馬. ¶a ***little*** *mount* 小さな乗用馬.

mount, *v.* 上る, 乗る, 乗馬する; はめる, 表装する.

M The red *mounted* ***slowly*** to his cheeks. 彼のほおにはだんだんと赤味がさして来た. ¶The cost of living is *mounting* ***steadily.*** 生活費はじり上りである. ¶a map ***strongly*** *mounted* on linen リンネルで丈夫に裏打ちしてある地図.

M² The population is *mounting* ***up*** steadily. 人口がどしどしふえて行く. ‖ Even 1d. a day *mounts* ***up.*** 一日一ペンスでも積れば大したものになる.

P bullets *mounted* ***as*** souvenirs 記念品に造った小銃弾. ¶a diamond *mounted* ***in*** platinum プラチナにはめたダイヤ ‖ combs *mounted* ***in*** the latest designs 最新意匠のくし. ¶*mount* [*on*] a horse (bicycle, wall) 馬(など)に乗る ‖ The child was *mounted* ***on*** his shoulders. その子供を肩車にのせた. ‖ be *mounted* ***on*** wheels 車台にとりつけてある. 【類】children *mounted* ***on*** stilts (竹馬). ¶A pink glow *mounted* ***to*** his cheeks. ほおがほんのりと赤くなった ‖ His debts *mounted* up ***to*** thousands of dollars. 彼の負債は数万ドルに上った. 【類】In 1906 the trade between the United States and Australia had *mounted* ***to*** the respectable figure (高額) of £11,000,000. ¶*mounted* ***upon*** silken cloth 絹布で表装した. ¶a crown *mounted* ***with*** diamond ダイヤで飾った王冠.

mountain, *n.* 山, 山岳.

V ***ascend*** a *mountain* 山に登る. ¶***climb*** [*up*] a *mountain* 山に登る. ¶***cultivate*** *mountains* 山を開拓する. ¶***descend*** (=***go down***) a *mountain* 山を下る. ¶***have*** *mountains* of difficulties 幾多の困難がある. ¶The "tengu" is a long-nosed goblin supposed to ***inhabit*** the *mountains.* 「天狗」は山に住むと思われている鼻高の妖怪である. ¶Do not ***let*** your *mountain* in labor ***bring forth*** a mouse. 大山鳴動してねずみなどと言われないようにしたまえ. ¶***make*** a *mountain* out of a molehill 針小を棒大にする. ¶Firm determination ***moves*** *mountains.* 堅い決意は山をも動かす. ¶***pierce*** a *mountain* by tunnel 山にトンネルを掘る. ¶***scale*** a *mountain* 山に登る.

V² *mountains* ***looking*** beyond かなたにそびえ立つ山々. ¶The *mountain* ***rises*** 6,000 feet above sea-level. その山は海抜六千フィートである.

Q a ***bare*** *mountain* はげ山. ¶a ***bleak*** *moutain* 荒涼たる山. ¶dimly ***defined*** (=***outlined***) *mountains* かすかに輪郭を描いた山々. ¶***forested*** (***deforested***) *mountains* 森林のある(はだかの)山々. ¶***forest-clad*** *mountains* 樹木のある山山. ¶***heaven-kissing*** *mountains* 天にそびえる山々. ¶a ***huge*** *mountain* 大山. ¶an ***imposing*** *mountain* き然とそびえる山. ¶***jagged*** *mountains* けわしい山々. ¶***lofty*** *mountains* 高峰. ¶***loose*** *mountains* of lobsters, mussels, whelks [たる入でなく] ばらで山になっているえび, 貽貝(いがい), あかにし. ¶He wanted to be back once more among his ***native*** *mountains.* 彼はも一度故山に帰りたかった. ¶There are several remarkable waterfalls in the ***neighbouring*** *mountains.* 付近の山々には五六の有名な滝がかかっている. ¶***purple*** *mountains* 青紫色の山々. ¶a ***rocky*** *mountain* 岩山. ¶a ***rugged*** *mountain* 岩だらけの山. ¶***snow-capped*** (=***-crowned, -topped*** or ***-clad***) *mountains*=mountains capped with snow 雪をいただいた山々. ¶***snow-streaked*** *mountains* 雪がしまをなした山々. ¶a ***snowy*** *mountain* 白雪におおわれた山. ¶***sun-kissed*** *mountains* 陽光に輝く山山. ¶a ***timbered*** *mountain* 樹木の茂る山.

Q² a big ***ice-cream-cone*** *mountain* 大きな円すい形の山. ¶a ***table*** *mountain* 平頂山. ¶a ***3800-foot*** *mountain* 三千八百フィートの山.

P travel ***across*** *mountains* 山越しに旅行する. 【類】go west ***across*** the *mountains* 山また山を越えて西に行く. ¶***amid*** the *mountains* 山々の間に. ¶He and his family are spending the summer ***among*** the *mountains.* 彼とその家族は山間に夏を過している. ‖ lonely walks ***among*** the *mountains* 山間のさびしい道. ¶***beyond*** the *mountains* 山の彼方に. ¶***in*** a *mountain* 山中に ‖ a fortnight ***in*** the *mountains* 山中の二週間 ‖ A sojourn ***in*** the *mountains* brought only slight relief. 山に行っていたらちょっとよくなった. 【類】***in*** the *mountains* as well as on the plains / The shrine is hidden ***in*** the *mountains.* / his old home ***in*** the *mountains* (山国の彼の故郷) / live deep ***in*** [the heart of] the *mountains* (山奥深く) / Once upon a time there was an old farmer who cultivated a field ***in*** the *mountains.* / the mineral springs (鉱泉) of Miyanoshita ***in*** the Hakone *mountains* / a resort ***in*** the *mountains*=a mountain resort / interesting places ***in*** the Rocky *Mountains* / climbing ***in*** the *mountains.* ¶at the foot ***of*** a *mountain* 山のふもとに ‖ in the heart ***of*** a *mountain* 山奥に ‖ a range ***of*** *mountains*=a mountain range 山脈. ¶spend two nights ***on*** the *mountain* 山上で二週間を過ごす ‖ The Chinese have a direct supply of musk ***on*** their *mountains.* 中国人は自国の山にいるじゃこうじかから直接にじゃ香を取る. 【類】This flower grows ***on*** a high *mountain* (高山植物). / The man has been lost ***on*** (=in) the *mountains* near the village since Tuesday. ¶The road passess ***over*** a steep *mountain.* その路は急な峠になっている. ‖ We're now flying high up ***over*** the *mountains.* われわれは目下山脈の上空を飛行中である. ¶run ***up*** a *mountain* 山をかけ上る. 【類】make one's way ***up*** a *mountain.*

P² The Kumano-gawa rises in the *mountains* ***of*** Yoshino. 熊野川は吉野山に源を発する. ‖ a *mountain* ***of*** waves 山のような波 ‖ a *mountain* ***of*** rubbish ごみの山. 【類】a *mountain* ***of*** debts (difficulties, worldly cares).

mountain-climbing, *n.* 登山.

Q ***Good*** *mountain-climbing* may be obtained in Wales, the Lake Districts and Scotland. ウェールスや湖水地方やスコットランドでは興味ある登山ができる.

mountain-path, *n.* 山道.

Q a ***rough*** *mountain-path* でこぼこの山道.

mountain-range, *n.* 山脈.

Q The Himalayas are the world's ***highest*** *mountain-range.* ヒマラヤ山系は世界最高の山脈である.

mountain-side, *n.* 山腹.

P ***on*** the *mountain-side* 山腹に.

mourn, *v.* 悲しむ, 嘆く, 哀悼する.

P It grieves me to see that poor old woman *mourning* ***for*** the death of her son. かわいそうにあの老婦人が息子の死を嘆いているいを見ると私は悲しくなる. ‖ She *mourned* ***for*** him so constantly that she became seriously ill. 彼の死を始終なげき悲しんだので彼女は重い病気になった. ¶*mourn* ***over*** one's loss (failure) 損失(など)を嘆き悲しむ. 【類】He *mourned* ***over*** the death of his wife. / The whole nation *mourned* ***over*** the death of the veteran statesman.

mourner, *n.* 哀悼者.

Q the *chief mourner* 喪主.

mourning, *n.* 愁傷, 哀悼; 喪; 喪服.

V *leave off* (=*go out of*) *mourning* 喪が明く, 喪を終える. ¶*observe mourning* 喪に服する. ¶*put on* (=go into) *mourning* 喪服を着ける. ¶*wear mourning* for ... ...のために喪服を着けている.

Q *court mourning* 宮中喪. ¶in *deep mourning* 深く哀悼して. ¶a woman in *light* (=*second*) *mourning* 軽い喪服を着た婦人. ¶*national mournings* 国民一般の喪.

P The family is *in mourning*. その家族は喪中である.【類】Denmark today is *in mourning* for Professor Finsen, who died yesterday. / an old lady *in mourning* (喪服). ¶go *into mourning* from ... until ......から...まで喪に服する.【類】go *into mourning* for the deceased.

P^2 the time of *mourning for* a father 父の喪に服する期間.

mouse, *n.* 二十日ねずみ.

V^2 A *mouse gnaws*. 二十日ねずみはかじる. ¶A *mouse nibbles*. 二十日ねずみはちびちびかむ. ¶*Mice squeak*. 二十日ねずみはちゅーちゅー鳴く.

Q^2 be as poor as a *church mouse* 赤貧洗うがごとし. ¶a *field mouse* 野ねずみ. ¶a *meadow mouse* 牧場のねずみ.

P swarm *with mice* 二十日ねずみが沢山いる.

moustache, *n.* =mustache.

mouth, *n.* 口.

V *close* the *mouth* 口を結ぶ. ¶*contract* the *mouth* 口をつぼめる. ¶*cram* the *mouth full* ほお張る. ¶*gargle* one's *mouth* with ... ...でうがいする. ¶*gargle* and *rinse* one's *mouth* がらがらやって口をすすぐ. ¶*keep* one's *mouth shut* =keep mum 口をつぐむ; 秘密を口外しない. ¶the words had scarcely *left* his *mouth* before ... 彼がそれを言い終るか終らないうちに. ¶*make mouths* in a glass [娘などが]鏡に向って顔をゆがめる. ¶That *makes* my *mouth water*. それを見るとよだれが出る(食指が動く).【類】There are two strong holds at the mint to *make* a poor man's *mouth water*. / such things as it *makes* the *mouth water* even to name. ¶He *opened* his *mouth* to speak. 彼は口を開いて話し出そうとした. ‖ with his eyes and *mouth opened* in wonder 彼はあっけにとられて目も口もあけっ放しで. ¶*pout* one's *mouth* 口をつぼめる. ¶*rinse* the *mouth* after each meal 毎食後口をすすぐ.【類】*rinse* the *mouth* thoroughly. ¶*rinse out* the *mouth* うがいする. ¶*screw up* one's *mouth* ちょぼ口をする[酸っぱい果物でも食べたときなど]. ¶*shut* one's *mouth* 口をつぐむ. ¶*stop* the *mouths* of critics 批評家の口を封じる. ¶*wash* [*out*] one's *mouth* 口をすすぐ. ¶*wipe* one's *mouth* with the back of his hand 手の甲で口をふく.

V^2 one's *mouth waters* as one looks upon ... ...をながめるとよだれが出る(食欲をそそられる).【類】It is commonly said that one's *mouth* "*waters*" when one contemplates a particularly appetizing dish. / My *mouth waters* for it. / The *mouth waters* at the smell, or sight, or thought of delicious morsels.

Q the *belching mouth* of a cannon はきだす大砲の口. ¶a *determined mouth* きりっとした口元. ¶the words in *everybody's mouth* (=on everybody's lips) だれでも口にする言葉.【類】Later on, some of these faces will be pictured in every shop window, some of these now unknown names will be in *every Londoner's mouth*. ¶with a *gaping mouth* 口あんぐりで. ¶There are so *many mouths* to feed. 扶養すべき者が非常に大勢いる. ¶The *mouth* is *parched*. 口がかわいた. ¶a *pretty mouth* 美しい口. ¶a *small mouth* ちょぼ口. ¶with a *sweet mouth* かわいい口もとをして. ¶a smile with a nervously *twitching mouth* 神経質に口をひきつらせた微笑. ¶with a *wry mouth* 口をゆがめて.

Q^2 a *Cupid's bow mouth* キューピッドの弓のようなくちびるの口. ¶a *rabbit mouth* 三つ口(うさぎ口). ¶at the *river mouth* 河口に. ¶a girl with a *rosebud mouth* ばらのつぼみのような口もとの少女.

P foam *at* the *mouth* 口からあわを吹く ‖ The town is situated *at* the *mouth* of the river. その町は河口に位している ‖ a bottle narrow *at* the *mouth* 細首のびん. ¶*By mouth* and by telegraph, he sent forth his mandates. 口頭や電報で彼は訓令を発した. ‖ The patient takes nothing *by mouth*. その病人は口から何も食べない. ‖ a thought expressed *by* the *mouth* 口で言表わした思想. ¶It was whispered *from mouth* to mouth. それは口から口へとささやき伝えられた.【類】The word sounds better *from* man's *mouth* (男性的な言葉). ¶Good medicine is bitter *in* the *mouth*. 良薬口に苦し. ‖ down *in* the *mouth*=depressed 意気そそうして ‖ The story is *in* every one's *mouth*. その話はだれでも口にする. ¶*Out of* the *mouth* comes evil. 禍は口より. ‖ speak it *out of* one's own *mouth* 自分の口でそれを話す. ¶bitter *to* the *mouth* 味がにがい. ¶live from hand *to mouth* その日暮しをする. ¶a vessel *with* a small *mouth* 口の小さな器物 ‖ *with* his *mouth* watering よだれを流して.

P^2 The Dutch word "Brandewijn" became corrupted to "Brandy" in the *mouth of* the English. オランダ語の「ブランデウィーン」という言葉が英語でなまって「ブランデー」になった.

mouthful, *n.* 一口.

V *get* the first *mouthful* into one's mouth 最初の一口を食べる. ¶*Having* a *mouthful* of breakfast, he hurried out. 朝食もそこそこにあわてて出かけた. ¶*take* a big *mouthful* of ... ...をほお張る. ¶*swallow* a *mouthful* of ... ...を一口でのみ下す.

Q It is so abbreviated, as it is a *big mouthful*. それでは長くって言いにくいから略してそういうのだ.

P *at* a *mouthful* 一口で.

P^2 a *mouthful of* food 一口の食物.

mouthpiece, *n.* [器具などの]口; 代弁者, 代表者.

Q^2 American newspapersmen who served as *radio mouthpieces* for the Nazisナチス宣伝の代弁者的役割を勤めたアメリカの新聞記者.

P cigarettes *with mouthpieces* 口付巻タバコ.

P^2 It serves as a *mouthpiece for* ... on all important subjects. それはすべての重要問題に対し...の代弁者として役立つ. ¶the *mouthpiece of* a tobacco pipe キセルの吸い口 ‖ Such a man as Tagore is the *mouthpiece of* a national aspiration. タゴールのごとき人は国民的抱負の代弁者である.【類】act as the *mouthpiece of* a government / the *mouthpiece of* his party.

mouthwash, *n.* うがい剤.

Q a *safe, pleasant antiseptic mouthwash* 安全で気持のよい防腐性うがい薬.

movable, *n. pl.* 動産; *pl.* 道具.

V *pack* one's *movables* 道具を包装する.

Q *corporeal movables* 有体動産.

move, *n.* 動き, 行動; 動議; 転居.

V *get* the *move* on 《俗》急いで行く; てきぱきやる ‖ *Get* a *move* on you! ぐずぐずするな.【類】*get* a *move on* in an elevator. ¶*favor* a *move* やり口を支持する. ¶He *knows* every *move*. 万事抜け目がない(如才がない).【類】He *knows* a *move* or two. ¶He *made* a *move* to go out of the door. 彼は入口から立去る様子を見せた. ‖ *make* the first *move* toward reconciliation 再建の第一歩を踏み出す ‖ *moves* are being *made* towards ... ...への行動を取っている ‖ In "Sugoroku" *moves* are *made* by throwing dice. すご六ではさいを投げてこまを進める.

Q make an *adroit move* 機敏に行動する. ¶in still *another move* さらに別の方面の進出において. ¶make a *bad move* へまなことをやる. ¶make a *clever move* 巧妙な手を打つ. ¶It was not until 1906 that any *definite move* was made in the idea. その考えは一九〇六年になってからやっと具体化したのである. ¶Be careful about *every move* you make. 君の一進一退に注意せよ. ¶make a *false move* 措置を誤る. ¶our *first move* was ... われわれは第一着に...をやった. ¶a *forward move* of an army 軍の進出. ¶That's a *great move forward*. それは一大進展である. ¶The selection was a *happy move*. その選択はよろしきを得た. ¶the *next move* to make 次の手.【類】He returned to his hotel, pondering on his *next move*. ¶It's a *nice move*. [将棋などで]それはいい手だ. ¶the *opening move* 第一の行動, 手始め. ¶That measure was perhaps the cleverest *political move* ever made by American diplomacy. その手段はアメリカがその外交政策として取った中での恐らく最も賢明なものであったろう. ¶the *practical move* is to ... ...するのが実際的なやり口だ. ¶a *safe move* 安全な行動. ¶a *shrewd move* in business 抜け目のない商売上のかけ引.

Q^2 make a *peace move* 平和的行動をとる. ¶as a *reprisal move* 報復措置として. ¶the *Truman move* トルーマン政策(the Fair Deal など).

P *after* two *moves* 二回移転の後. ¶He is always *on* the

move (=moving about). 彼は少しもじっとしていない(活動家だ). ‖ You are ***on*** the *move* very early. お早いお出かけですね(往来で会ったときなどのあいさつ). ‖ The newspaper is the book of the day's history, the story of mankind ***on*** the *move*. 新聞は一日の歴史を書いた本, 人類活動の物語である.
P² the first *move* ***of*** the game その競技の先手.

move, *v.* 動かす; 感動させる; 動く.

M He is ***actively moving*** about. 彼は盛んに活動している. ¶*move* ***ahead*** 前進する. ¶*move* ***away*** (=***off***) 立ち去る ‖ *move* ***away*** from ... ...から引越す. ¶She *moved* ***beautifully*** into the dance. 彼女は美しくその舞踊を演じ出した. ¶We see people ***busily*** *move* in and out. 人々が忙しげに出たり入ったりしてるのが見える. ¶He was ***deeply*** *moved*. 彼は深く感動した. ¶Women are more ***easily*** *moved* to tears. 女の方が一層涙もろい. 【類】I am ***easily*** *moved* to emotion (情にもろい). ¶*move* house ***frequently*** よく引越をする. ¶*move* ***far*** 遠方へ移転する. ¶***merely*** *moved* by self-interest 単に自分の利益という動機で. ¶It reveals another step in the path by which man has *moved* ***onward*** and ***upward***. それもまた人間が向上進歩の途をたどった一歩を示すものである. ¶*move* ***noiselessly*** 音を立てないように動く. ¶*move* ***out*** into a new house 新しい家に引越す ‖ *move* ***out*** to sea 出航する. ¶*move* ***slowly off*** ゆっくり立去る. ¶*move* ***pari passu*** (=***simultaneously***) with ... ...と歩調をそろえる. ¶*move* ***seaward*** from port 船が港から出帆する. ¶Snails *move* ***slowly***. かたつむりはのろのろ動く. 【類】The train *moved* ***slowly*** into (out of) the station.

M² *move* ***about*** 動き回る; 始終引っ越しをやる. ¶"*Move* ***along***, please!" said the bus conductress. 「中へお進み願います」とバスの車掌が言った. ¶I've just *moved* ***in***. 今引越したばかりです. 【類】We will *move* ***in*** on the first of next month. / He and his family have *moved* ***in*** somewhere near his office. ¶*move* ***off*** towards ... ...の方向に進んで行く ‖ Will you just *move* ***off***? ちょっとどいて下さい. ¶Don't halt there. *Move* ***on***, *move* ***on***! そこに止まっちゃいかん. 進め進め. ‖ be free to *move* ***on*** to his own course 勝手に自分の方向に進める(何でも自由にできる). 【類】The policemen *moved* us ***on***. ¶Prices have *moved* ***up***. 物価は上った. ‖ *move* ***up*** into a higher form 上級に進む. 【類】*move* ***up*** to the next grade (a higher class). ¶*move* ***up*** and ***down*** 上ったり下ったりする.

P *move* ***about*** the class-room 教室を動き回る. ¶*move* ***against*** the enemy 敵に向って進撃する. ¶*move* ***along*** the road 道路に沿うて動く ‖ this development *moves* ***along*** lines parallel with ... この発展は...に歩調を合わせている. ¶He was *moved* ***at*** the story. 彼はその話を聞いて感動した. ¶I was *moved* ***by*** his earnestness (kindness, pity). 私は彼の熱心(など)に動かされた. ‖ hanging signs *moved* ***by*** the wind 風に動いた掛け看板. ¶*move* ***from*** one's house 家を引越す. ¶various personages who *moved* ***in*** the circle of Louis XIV ルイ十四世をめぐって活動した色々な人々 ‖ *move* ***in*** the highest society 最高上流社会に出入する. 【類】*move* ***in*** a fashionable society (club) ‖ The market price *moved* ***in*** his favor. 市価が彼に有利に動いた. ¶We have *moved* ***into*** the suburbs (country). 私たちは郊外(いなか)に引越した. 【類】The newly married couple *moved* ***into*** their new home. / He *moved* ***into*** his new quarters. / *move* pieces of furniture ***into*** another room ‖ *move* ***into*** another person's shoes その後継者となる. ¶a house *moving* ***on*** wheels 移動住宅 ‖ The conference *moved* ***on*** schedule. 会議は予定通りに進行した. ¶*move* ***out of*** a house 家移りをする. 【類】Tenants rarely *move* ***out of*** this apartment. ¶The moon and the stars *move* ***through*** the sky. 月と星は大空を運行する. ¶He *moved* yesterday ***to*** Omori. 彼はきのう大森へ引越した. ‖ be *moved* ***to*** pity 同情するようになる ‖ These inspiring words were sufficient to *move* them ***to*** action. その激励の言葉は彼らを立たしめるに十分であった. ‖ The question will not *move* one inch nearer ***to*** solution. その問題は一歩も解決に近づかないだろう. ‖ Such a story *moves* us ***to*** strong emotions. こういった話はわれわれを深く感動させる. 【類】be *moved* ***to*** anger (=wrath) / be *moved* ***to*** safety ‖ All those present to listen to his sad tale were *moved* ***to*** tears. そこにいて彼の悲話に耳を傾けた者は皆泣いた. ¶He *moved* ***toward*** an inner room. 彼は奥の間の方へ行った. ¶slow to *move* (=keep pace) ***with*** the time 時代とともに動くことが緩慢な ‖ *move* ***with*** an inevitable trend of event 抗し難い大勢とともに推移する ‖ We were *moved* ***with*** admiration and awe at her faith and courage. われわれは彼女の信念と勇気に対して感嘆と畏敬の念に打たれた. ‖ *move* ***with*** grace 優雅な起居振舞いをする ‖ be *moved* ***with*** compassion at another's fortune その(悲惨な)運命に対し同情の念に駆られる. ‖ It *moved* ***with*** its own momentum. それは破竹の勢いで進んだ. 【類】You must *move* ***with*** greater vivacity (もっと活発に).

O Let's be *moving*, pal. おい出かけよう.

movement, *n.* (**1**) 運動, 移動, 動作, 行動; 機械装置.

V ***begin*** a *movement* for ... ...の運動を始める ‖ They ***began*** a *movement* in behalf of systematic spelling in geographical names. 彼らは地名を組織的につづらせる運動を開始した. ¶***conduct*** a *movement* ある運動をやる. ¶***cripple,*** if not ***destroy,*** the *movement* その運動を破壊とまでは行かなくともざ折させる. ¶***direct*** a revolutionary *movement* 革命運動を指揮する. ¶***enter*** the *movement* その運動に参加する. ¶***espouse*** a *movement* 運動を擁護する. ¶***favor*** a *movement* by throwing the weight of one's influence on the side of ... ...の側に自己の勢力の重圧を加えて運動を後援する. ¶***forward*** a *movement* 運動を助成する. ¶***hail*** the *movement* with enthusiasm その運動を熱狂的に歓迎する. ¶***head*** a *movement* for ... ...運動の牛耳をとる. ¶***help along*** the Esperanto *movement* エスペラント運動を援助する. ¶***impede*** a forward *movement* 進歩を阻害する. ¶***inaugurate*** a national *movement* against the rat 全国的なねずみ撲滅運動を起す. 【類】***inaugurate*** a popular philanthropic *movement* (博愛運動). ¶***initiate*** a *movement* 運動を起す. ¶Similar *movements* have been ***instituted***. 同種の運動が色々起された. ¶***join*** the pure food *movement* 食料品混物反対運動に参加する. ¶***make*** a *movement* of irritation じりじりした様子をする. ¶***oppose*** a *movement* 運動に反対する. ¶***organize*** a strong *movement* 強力な運動を組織する. ¶***push*** the *movement* forward その運動を推進する. ¶This *movement* was ***regarded*** as dangerous and revolutionary. この運動はけんのんで反逆的だと見られた. ¶***scout*** the enemy's *movements* 敵の行動を偵察する. ¶a *movement* has recently been ***set*** on foot among ... 最近ある運動が...の間に始められた. ¶That *movement* has been ***snuffed out***. その運動は弾圧された. ¶***start*** a *movement* against a person ある人の排斥運動を起す. 【類】The reform *movement* was ***started*** long ago. ¶***stimulate*** a peristaltic *movements* 腸のぜん動を刺激する. ¶***suppress*** a *movement* 運動を抑圧する. ¶***take*** to pieces the *movement* of a watch 懐中時計の機械装置を分解する. ¶***watch*** one's *movements* closely その動静を厳重に看視する.

V² The *movement* soon ***died away***. その運動はやがてやんだ. ¶The *movement* rapidly ***gained*** ground. その運動はたちまち地歩を得た. ¶The *movement* has ***materialized*** in legislation. その運動の趣意が法律となって実現した. ¶The *movement* ***revived***. その運動が復活した.

Q ***accelerated*** *movement* 破竹の勢い. ¶an ***anti-alien*** *movement* 排外運動. ¶a ***backward*** *movement* in civilization 文明の退歩. ¶the operations of the various forces in their ***forward*** *movement* towards ... ...に向う前進運動の色々な力の作用. ¶Her *movements* are very ***graceful***. 彼女の動作は実に優美です. ¶the ***heavy*** *movement* of traffic 大した人出. ¶one of the most ***hopeful*** *movements* of the age is ... 現代の最も有望な運動は...である. ¶an ***interdenominational*** *movement* 宗派間の運動. ¶a ***militant*** *movement* 戦闘的な運動. ¶the ***modern social*** and ***intellectual*** *movements* that are reflected in periodical journals and the daily press 新聞雑誌などに反映している現代の社会的及び知的諸運動. ¶The era of disbelief may conceivably be needful for the ***new onward*** *movement*. 不信仰の時代は新なる前進運動に取って必要だと考えてもよい. ¶a ***patriotic*** *movement* 愛国運動. ¶a ***political*** *movement* 政治運動. ¶a ***retrograde*** *movement* 退歩. ¶there is a ***strong*** *movement* on foot (=afoot) to ... ...しようとする強大な運動が始まっている. ¶the ***vast*** *movement* of human travel for pleasure or enlightenment 娯楽または教養を目的とする旅行の大活況. ¶the ***westward*** *movement* of the American people アメリカ人の西部移動. ¶the ***whole onward*** *movement* of the human race 人類全体の進歩. ¶a ***world-wide*** *movement* 全世界的運動. ¶The *movement* is still ***young***. その運動はまだ新らしい.

Q[2] the surface, subsurface, or ***air movements*** of the naval craft 海軍艦艇の海上, 水中あるいは空中活動. ¶an ***anti-alcohol movement*** 禁酒運動. ¶an ***anticruelty movement*** 動物愛護運動. ¶the ***anti-foot-binding movement*** [中国の]てん足禁止運動. ¶a ***back-to-the-farm movement*** 帰農運動. 【類】a ***back-to-the-soil movement***. ¶the ***back-to-work movement*** (ストの)職場に帰れ運動. ¶the ***better babies movement*** 健康児運動. ¶a ***boycott movement*** against … …不買運動. ¶the "***Buy American***" ***movement*** [アメリカの]国産品使用運動. ¶the "***Buy-War-Bond***" ***movement*** 戦時国債奨励運動. ¶a ***buyers' resistance movement*** 買い手側の抵抗運動(不買同盟など). ¶a ***city-beautiful movement*** 都市美化運動. ¶a ***class movement*** 階級運動. ¶a world-wide ***Communist movement*** 全世界の共産党運動. ¶a ***co-op*** (＝co-operative society) ***movement*** 消費組合運動 ¶the ***dry movement*** 《米》禁酒運動. ¶anti-Japanese ***economic disruption movement*** in Shanghai 上海の反日経済打倒運動. ¶***enemy movements*** 敵軍の動静. ¶head of the ***Esperanto movement*** in France フランスのエスペラント運動の主動者. ¶international ***gold movements*** 国際的金の移動. ¶a ***good road movement*** 道路改善運動. ¶***heart movements*** 心臓の働き. ¶"the ***little theatre***" ***movement*** 「小劇場」運動. ¶a vigorous "***made-in-Japan***" ***movement*** 盛んな「日本品」奨励運動. ¶a ***mass movement*** 大衆的運動. ¶India's ***nationalist movement*** インドの国民会議派運動. ¶restrict unnecessary ***population movements*** 不必要人口移動を制限する. ¶***price movements*** 物価の動き. ¶a ***reform movement*** 革新運動. ¶strong ***rightist movements*** 強力な右翼派運動. ¶***safety first movement*** 安全第一運動. ¶the America's ***Self-Contained movement*** アメリカの自給自足運動. ¶***ship*** (＝***shipping***) ***movement*** 船舶の出入. 【類】London has a ***shipping movement*** of some sixteen million tons annually. ¶a ***signature collecting movement*** 署名運動. ¶the ***Socialist movement*** in England 英国の社会主義者運動. ¶a ***state-ownership movement*** 国有化運動. ¶***steamer movements*** 船舶の出入. ¶the ***temperance movement*** 禁酒運動. ¶***Transportation movement*** was seriously hampered. 輸送状態がひどく阻害された. ¶halt all ***troop movements*** 兵の移動を一切中止する. ¶the ***tourist movement*** in its national and international aspects. 国内的及び国際的面における観光客の動き. ¶a ***unification movement*** 統一運動. ¶an ***underground Fascist movement*** ファシストの潜行運動. ¶an ***undergound resistance movement*** 地下抵抗運動(政府反対の潜行運動). ¶***wind movement*** 風の動き. ¶a ***woman movement*** 婦人運動. ¶the pioneers of the ***women's suffrage movement*** 婦選運動の開拓者. ¶a ***world movement*** 世界運動. ¶the ***youth movement*** in Italy イタリアの青年運動.

P Many prominent women are ***behind*** the ***movement***. 多数の女流名士がその運動を後援している. ¶graceful ***in movement*** 物腰がしとやかな. ¶the pioneer ***of*** the ***movement*** その運動の開拓者 ‖ the initiators ***of*** the ***movement*** その運動の発起者 ‖ the proponents ***of*** the ***movement*** その運動の提案者. 【類】Nothing is known ***of*** his ***movements*** (動行) after he boarded the Flushing boat express. (急行船). ¶Fix your eyes ***on*** his ***movements***. 彼の行動に目をつけよ. ‖ leaders ***on*** the ***movement*** その運動の指導者. ¶the words of a young man in earnest ***over*** a social ***movement*** 社会運動に熱心なある青年の言説.

P[2] a ***movement against*** a person (policy) 人(など)の排斥運動. ¶the ***movement for*** the independence of India インド独立運動 ‖ a ***movement for*** the abolition of … …廃止運動. ¶***movements in*** thought and science 思想及び科学における進展. ¶a ***movement of*** revolt, at first amorphous, now definitely communistic 最初は無定形であったが今や明確に共産主義化した革命運動 ‖ the ***movement of*** pity toward … …同情の運動. ¶There is a ***movement on*** foot there, carried forward by him. そこで彼が推進しているある運動が始まっている. ¶This is a ***movement toward*** economy in this respect. それはこの点における節約への第一歩である. ‖ the ***movement*** of antagonism ***towards*** … …反対(排斥)運動.

(**2**) 便通.

V I have ***established*** a daily ***movement*** at a regular hour. 私は毎日一定の時間に通じがあるようになった. ¶***have*** a ***movement*** 通じがある. 【類】Her constipation (便秘) was obstinate, so that she often ***had*** only one ***movement*** a week, in spite of enemas and laxatives (がん腸や緩下剤).

Q have ***regular movements*** 便通が滞りなくある. ¶have a ***spontaneous movement*** 下剤なしに通じがつく.

Q[2] ***bowel movements*** 便通.

mover, *n.* 運動者, 発議者.

Q the ***chief mover*** in … …の主動者. ¶the ***main movers*** in the matter その問題の主動者. ¶He was the ***prime mover*** in executing it. 彼がそれを実行した主動者であった. 【類】the ***prime mover*** in bringing about the Bill.

movie, *n.* 《米口》映画, 映画館.

V ***attend*** the ***movies*** 映画を見に行く. ¶the ***movie*** will be ***directed*** by … その映画は…が監督することになろう. ¶***enjoy*** American ***movies*** アメリカ映画を見て楽しむ. ¶***judge movies*** intelligently 映画(の善悪)を賢明に判断する. ¶***make*** a ***movie*** of (＝filmize) a story ストーリーを映画化する. ¶the Hollywood methods of ***turning out*** "***movies***" 映画を製作するハリウッドのやり方. ¶***sexy movies*** エロがかった映画. ¶***vicious movies*** 悪徳映画. ¶***vulgar movies*** 低俗映画.

Q[2] a ***crime movie*** 犯罪映画(スリラーもの). ¶a ***war theme movie*** 戦争をテーマにした映画.

P go ***to*** the ***movies*** 映画に行く. 【類】He has been ***to*** a ***movie***.

P[2] ***movies for*** the lowbrow ミーハー向きの映画. 【類】***movies*** proper (＝good) ***for*** children.

movie-goer, *n.* 映画ファン.

Q an ***intelligent movie-goer*** インテリの映画ファン. ¶a ***thoughtful movie-goer*** 思慮深い映画ファン.

moving, *n.* 運動.

V jump off before the train ***stopped moving*** 汽車が止まらない中に飛び降りる.

Q ***conservative*** and ***slow moving*** 保存的で緩慢なやり口.

Q[2] ***air moving*** 空気の動き.

P It's time ***for moving***. もう出かける時間だ.

moving, *a.* 感動的な.

M Her story was ***really moving***. 彼女の物語には全く感動した.

O Her ***moving*** plea for help. 彼女の心を動かす嘆願.

mow, *v.* 刈る; なぎ倒す.

M[2] Nearly all the troops were ***mown down*** in a battle. ほとんど全兵士が一回の戦闘で全滅した. 【類】They were ***mowed down*** with machinegun fire like grass under a mower.

O ***mow*** the grass (grain, lawn, field) 草(など)を刈る.

mower, *n.* 草刈器.

Q[2] a ***lawn mower*** 芝刈器.

moxa, *n.* [日本]もぐさ.

V ***apply moxa*** きゅうをすえる.

P cauterize ***with*** the ***moxa*** きゅうをすえる.

MSS., Mss., *pl.* [単数は MS., Ms., ms.＝manuscript], *n.* 写本, 原稿.

V The editor carefully ***collated*** the six best *Mss.* 編者は六つの最もすぐれた原稿を校合した. ¶***prepare mss.*** for the market 売文のための原稿を作る.

Q ***MSS. available*** 採用原稿. 【類】*MSS.* not ***available***. ¶***unprinted Mss.*** 稿本. ¶The magazine does not as a rule pay for ***unsolicited Mss.*** その雑誌社では概して依頼しない原稿は買わない.

Q[2] the ***autograph Mss.*** of … …の肉筆原稿.

much, *n.* 多大, 多量, 多額.

V He has ***accomplished much*** for the welfare of the society. 彼はその会のため大いに尽した. ¶I ***admit*** that ***much***. そこまでは認める. ¶it will ***do much*** to … それは…に大いに役立つ. 【類】they do and have ***done much*** towards making … ¶I ***have much*** to say about … 私は…について言うべきことが多々ある. ¶We have ***had*** too ***much*** of war. 戦争はまっぴら. ¶It ***leaves much*** to be desired. まだ大いに申し分がある. ¶He ***makes much*** (little) of his children. 彼は子供をかわいがる(かわいがらない). ‖ He was ***made much*** of on that account. 彼はそれで大いに持てた. ¶***Much*** can be ***said*** on both sides. 双方に大いに言い分があろう. ¶I haven't ***seen much*** of him lately. このごろあの人にあまり会わない. 【類】He has ***seen much*** of the world. ¶***think much*** of … …を尊敬する, 大事にする.

Q ***How much*** of this paper have you? この紙をどれだけ持っているか. ¶but ***this much*** is certain, that … だが…というこれだけは確かだ. ¶there is ***thus much*** of truth in the thesis that ... その命題には…というだけの真理は含まれている.

P He is younger than I *by much*. 彼は私よりはずっと若い.

much, *ad.* 多く, 大いに, 沢山.

M *How much* do you charge per month? 一カ月幾らですか. ¶*So much* for today. [教師が]きょうはこれでおしまい. ‖ at *so much* a head 一人当りいくらで. 【類】at *so much* a week ‖ He is not *so much* a scholar as a teacher.＝He is rather a teacher than a scholar. 彼は学者というよりはむしろ教師だ. ¶That's *too much*. あんまりだ. ‖ He is *too much* for me あの男は手に負えない. ‖ The stove is *too much* of a good thing. そのストーブは暖か過ぎる. ‖ She is *too much* of a fine lady for me. あの女は好かない, いやにお上品ぶっている. ‖ it is perhaps *too much* to hope that ... …と望むのは少し無理かも知れない.

M² half *as much* again as ... …のもう半分だけ余計(一倍半) ‖ *as much* again as ...＝twice as much ... …の二倍. ‖ *as much* as you like いくらでもお好きなだけ.

P pay too *much by* a dollar 一ドルだけ余計に払う. ¶He is not *much of* a journalist. 彼は大した新聞記者じゃない ‖ He was *much of* a fighter in his younger day. 彼は若いときは闘志満々であった. 【類】I am not *much of* a rider and I am out of practice.

mucus, *n.* 粘液, 鼻汁.

V *loosen* the *mucus* from the lungs たんを出やすくする. ¶*secrete mucus* 粘液を分泌する.

Q *nasal mucus* 鼻汁.

mud, *n.* 泥.

V *scrape* the *mud* off one's shoes くつの泥をかき落す. ¶*spurt mud* on to ... …に泥を飛ばす. ¶*throw* (＝*sling*) *mud* at ... …に泥をぬる, 中傷する. 【類】*throw mud* at one's competitors.

Q a *nice soft unctuous mud* 美しく柔くて油のような泥.

Q² *General Mud* ぬかるみ将軍(進撃をはばむ雪解けなどの擬人). ¶*sulphur mud* 湯の花.

P The motor-car [got] stuck *in* the *mud* of the road. 自動車が道路の泥にはまりこんだ. ¶The coat is covered *with mud*. コートが泥まみれになった.

muddle, *n.* 混乱.

Q Here is a *nice muddle*. こりゃ無茶苦茶だ.

muddle, *v.* へたをやる.

M² *muddle on* (＝*along*) どうにかこうにかやって行く.

P *muddle over* a problem 問題と取っ組む. ¶*muddle through* [a difficulty] 苦労して難関を切抜ける. 【類】Britain will manage somehow to *muddle through*. ¶*muddle with* one's work へまをやる.

mud-flinging, *n.* 泥の投合い.

Q *mutual mud-flinging* 泥試合.

muffle, *n.* おおうもの.

Q² an *ear muffle* 耳かけ.

muffle, *v.* 包む. おおう.

M² *muffle* oneself *up* からだ(頭)を包む ‖ *muffle up* one's throat [えりまきなどで]のどを包む.

P *muffled in* a cloak 外とうにくるまって.

mufti, *n.* 私服, 略服.

P *in mufti* (＝plain clothes) 略(私)服を着て.

mug, *n.* 湯のみ; 一杯.

Q² a *shaving mug* ひげそり用のうつわ.

P² a *mug of* soup 一わんのスープ.

mulch, *n.* 根おおい.

Q² a *soil mulch* 〖農耕〗土かけ.

mule, *n.* らば.

O stubborn (＝obstinate) as a *mule* きわめてがん迷な.

mull, *v.* かんをする.

M *slightly mulled sake* ちょっとかんをした酒.

multiple, *a.* 多種多様の.

V *cover multiple* sins 数多くの罪を包み隠す(欠点が補われる).

multiplication, *n.* 繰返し.

V Such instances are too well known to *need multiplication* here. こうした例は枚挙にいとまがない.

multiplicity, *n.* 幾多, 多数; 集合.

P Despite his vigorous constitution his health began to fail *under* the *multiplicity* of duties. がん丈な身体であったが多方面の仕事に従事したのでその健康がすぐれなくなり出した.

P² a *multiplicity of* ... 幾多の…

multiply, *v.* 増す, ふやす; ふえる.

M Flies *multiply enormously*. はえは恐ろしくふえる. ¶*multiply over-fruitfully* ばかばかしく増加する. ¶Efficiency would be *multiplied several-fold*. (そうすると)能率が数倍するだろう.

P *multiply* one number *by* another 甲の数に乙の数を掛ける ‖ *multiply* 6 *by* 5 六に五を掛ける ‖ *multiply* twice *by* itself 二回自乗する. ¶*multiply into* the thousands 数千にふえる.

O Cares *multiply* as one gets older. 年をとるに従って苦労がふえる.

multitude, *n.* 多数, 幾多, 大数, 大勢.

V Fair skin *covers* the *multitude* of sins. 色の白いは七難隠す. ¶The book will *find* a *multitude* of readers. その本は多数のものに読まれるであろう. ¶A great *multitude gathered* in the streets. 街路に非常な群衆が集った. ¶*multitudes thronged* to see ... 群衆が…見物に集った.

Q the *half-educated multitude* of the present day 現時の教育未完成の大衆. ¶arrive in *surprising multitude* 驚くほど大勢到着する. ¶he told the *surrounding multitude* that ... 彼は周囲の大衆に…と語った. ¶the *uneducated multitude* 無学の大衆. ¶a *vast multitude* of facts 無数の事実.

P *amid* cheerful *multitudes* 歓喜する群衆の中で. ¶*In* the *multitude* of counsellors there is wisdom. 三人寄れば文珠の知恵. ‖ *in* the *multitude* of new interests and images that have occupied my stay abroad 洋行中色々屈託があったのでそれに取紛れ.

P² a *multitude of* readers (admirers, counsellors) 多数読者(など) ‖ There are *multitudes of* islands on the Pacific. 太平洋上には多数の島がある.

mumble, *v.* もぐもぐ物を言う, 口ごもる.

P The old man *mumbled* a great deal *to* himself. その老人はしきりにもぐもぐ独言をいった.

munch, *v.* むしゃむしゃかむ.

P *munch at* a cake (an apple) 菓子(など)をむしゃむしゃ食べる. ¶Those people are seen all the time *munching* something *on* the street or *in* a train car. この連中はいつでも通りや列車でむしゃむしゃやっている.

municipality, *n.* 自治市; 市区.

P The fête was prepared *by* the *municipality*. その祭は市が催したものだ.

Q a *small municipality* 小都市(自治体).

Q² the *Paris Municipality* パリ市当局(市役所).

O It will become a *municipality* in a few years. 二三年たつとそこに市制が布かれるだろう.

munificence, *n.* 大まかな施し.

P the laboratory was founded chiefly *by* the *munificence* of ... その研究所は主として…の寄付で設立された. ¶*through* the *munificence* of ... …の寄付によって.

murder, *n.* 殺害, 人殺し.

V *avenge* (＝*revenge*) the *murder* of ... …の殺害を復しゅうする. ¶*commit murder* 人殺しをやる. 【類】He *committed* three *murders*. ¶*conceal* one's *murder* その殺害を隠す. ¶*disclose* one's *murder* その殺害をあばく. ¶*discover* a *murder* 殺害を発見する. ¶It is a grievous sin to *do murder*. 人殺しをすることは大罪である. 【類】*did* two more *murders*. ¶*plot* the *murder* of ... …の殺害をはかる.

Q an *attempted murder* 殺人未遂. ¶commit a *cold-blooded murder* 残忍な殺害をやる. 【類】One cannot have pity in the case of such a *cold-blooded murder*. ¶a *double* (*triple*) *murder* 二(三)人殺し. ¶*frustrated murder* 殺人未遂. ¶He considers that war is, and always must be, a system of *licensed murder*. 彼は戦争は公認された殺人であり常に必ずそうなると考えている. ¶Nothing will justify the bombing! It's *a sheer murder*. その投爆は全く許しがたい. 全く殺人行為だ. ¶*political murders* 政治上の殺害. ¶a *wilful murder* 故意の殺害.

Q² a diabolical *mass murder* 悪魔的大量殺人. ¶the *second degree murder* 故殺. ¶*sex murder* 痴情殺人.

P *for* the *murder* of ... …殺害のために. ¶on a charge *of murder* 殺人罪で. ¶a case *of murder* 殺人事件.

P² *murder for* gain 欲からの殺人. ¶*murder with* consent 承諾殺人.

murder, *v.* 殺害する, 謀殺する.

M be *barbarously murdered* 惨殺される. ¶be *fiendishly murdered* 極悪非道な殺され方をする. ¶be *foully* (＝*wickedly*) *murdered* 毒刃に倒れる.

P *murder* ... *by* suffocation …を絞殺する.

murderer, *n.* 殺害者, 謀殺者.

V The *murderer* was at once ***apprehended.*** その殺人者は直ちに逮捕された. ¶The *murderer* was ***caught*** red-handed. その殺害者は現行犯中捕われた. ¶The *murderer* was ***put*** to death. その殺害者は死刑に処せられた.

Q a ***ruthless*** *murderer* 残忍な殺害者.

Q² a ***boy*** *murderer* 殺人少年. ¶an ***infant*** *murderer* 幼児殺し. ¶a ***wife*** *murderer* 人妻の殺人.

P a gang ***of*** *murderers* 一隊の殺害者.

murmur, *n.* ささやき; つぶやき, 不平の声.

Q a ***low*** *murmur* breaking from the lips of ... ...の口びるをもれるかすかなささやき.

P go ***without*** a *murmur* ぶつぶつ言わずに行く. 【類】huge prices are paid ***without*** a *murmur* for ... / The Japanese will die ***without*** a *murmur* at his post.

P² To his ear came a *murmur* ***of*** conversation from a distant room. 離れたへやからのささやき声が彼の耳についた.

murmur, *v.* ささやく, 不平を言う.

M *murmur* ***coyly*** はにかんでささやく.

M² A brook is *murmuring* ***down*** through low hills. 低い山の間を小川がさらさらと流れている.

P *murmur* ***about*** ... ...についてつぶやく. ¶They *murmured* ***at*** (=***against***) the treatment they had received. 彼らは自分たちの受けた待遇に対してぶつぶつ不平を言った. 【類】The people *murmured* ***against*** the government. ¶*murmur* ***over*** it その上で(じゅ文などを)小声で唱える. ¶He *murmured* words of love ***in*** her ear. 彼女に愛の言葉をささやいた. ¶*murmur* ***under*** one's breath 小声でささやく.

murmuring, *n.* つぶやき; ささやき.

P the ***confused*** *murmuring* of human voices ががやがやした人声.

P² the *murmuring* ***of*** a brook 小川のささやき.

murmurous, *a.* ざわめく, 低声の.

P The air is subtly *murmurous* ***with*** music. 空気は微妙な音楽をかすかにささやいている.

Muschik, *n.* 農民.

Q a ***Russian*** *Muschik* [帝政時代の]ロシアの農民.

muscle, *n.* 筋肉, 筋力.

V ***enervate*** the *muscles* 筋肉を弱くする. ¶***harden*** *muscles* 身体をきたえる. ¶***have*** strong *muscles* 強壮な筋肉を有する. ¶***loosen*** *muscles* 筋肉をゆるめる. ¶He did not ***move*** a *muscle*. 彼はびくともしなかった.

Q the ***chief*** *muscles* in the leg 脚の主要筋. ¶***flaccid*** (=***limp***) *muscle* 軟弱な筋肉. ¶a man of ***strong*** *muscle* 筋骨たくましい人. ¶***taut*** and ***strained*** *muscles* 引締って緊張した筋肉. ¶a ***voluntary*** (an ***involuntary***) *muscle* 随意(不随意)筋.

P useful in the development ***of*** *muscle* 筋肉の発達を助ける. ¶a great strain ***on*** the *muscles* 筋肉の過労. ¶a man ***with*** *muscle* 腕っ節の強い人.

Muse, *n.* ミューズ神, 文芸美術の神.

Q the ***British*** *Muse* 英国の詩神. ¶His *Muse* became ***dumb.*** 彼の詩神は沈黙した(詩を作らなくなった).

muse, *v.* 沈思する, 熟思する, めい想する, つくづく眺める.

P *muse* ***on*** ... ...をしのぶ. ¶*muse* ***over*** the far-distant past 遠い昔をしのぶ. 【類】*muse* ***over*** memories of the past. ¶It is useless to *muse* ***upon*** past errors. 過去の失策を思っても益はない. 【類】*muse* ***upon*** the unfairness of Fate / *muse* ***upon*** some dangerous plot ‖ *muse* ***upon*** a distant view 遠景をながめる.

museum, *n.* 博物館; 陳列場.

V ***install*** a *museum* 博物館を設立する. ¶The *museum* has been ***thrown open*** to the public. その博物館は公開された. ¶A *museum* containing Ainu relics ***stands*** in Sapporo. アイヌの遺物をおさめている博物館が札幌にある.

Q the ***Imperial*** *Museum* 帝室博物館. ¶a ***maritime*** *museum* 海事博物館. ¶a ***well-arranged*** *museum* 整備した博物館.

Q² a ***dime*** *museum* 料金の安い見せ物. ¶the Tokyo ***Foreign Trade*** *Museum* 東京貿易館. ¶a ***history*** *museum* 史料博物館. ¶a ***police*** *museum* 警察博物館.

P² To the majority the churches are only *museum* ***for*** dead religions. 多数の人から見て教会は死んだ宗教の博物館に過ぎない.

mushroom, *n.* きのこ.

V She asked us to come with her to ***pick*** [*up*] *mushrooms.* 彼女はわれわれをきのこ狩りに誘った.

P New religions have appeared ***like*** so many *mushrooms.* 新興宗教が雨後のたけのこのように現われた.

mushroom, *v.* きのこ狩りをする; きのこが生える; 急に広がる.

M The town *mushroomed* almost ***overnight.*** その町はほとんど一夜にして出現した. ¶The fire started in the cellar and *mushroomed* ***upstairs.*** 地下から発した火は階上に燃え広がった.

O go [out] *mushrooming* きのこ狩りに行く.

music, *n.* 音楽, 音曲; 美音, 好調.

V ***compose*** *music* 作曲する. ¶A military band ***discoursed*** sweet *music*. 軍楽隊は甘美な音楽を演奏した ‖ The band creditably ***discoursed*** *music*. 音楽隊は手際よく演奏した. 【類】*Music* is ***discoursed*** by the organist until the last seat is vacated (一同退場するまで). ¶I ***enjoyed*** the *music* of the verse. 私はその歌の調子を楽しんだ. ¶***face*** the *music*=accept the situation at its worst 進んで難局に当る. ¶The Marine band ***furnished*** the *music*. 海軍々楽隊が演奏した. ‖ The orchestra ***furnishes*** *music* for all hotel functions. その管弦楽団はすべてホテルの会の招請に応じる. ¶He ***has*** *music* in his soul. 彼は音楽を解する. ¶***love*** *music* 音楽を愛好する. ¶The birds ***make*** *music* all [the] day. 鳥は終日音楽をかなでる. 【類】A band of one of the Guards regiments (近衛連隊) ***made*** *music* ¶The girl was ***manufacturing*** *music* with a diminutive harmonium. その少女は小型のオルガンで音楽をやっていた. ¶***perform*** *music* 奏楽する. ¶The military band began to ***play*** cheerful *music*. 軍楽隊が明朗な音楽を奏し始めた. 【類】An enjoyable selection of *music* was ***played*** by the city band at the music stand yesterday. ¶The *music* ***poured*** from the tiny throats of invisible singers. 目に見えない歌い手の小さなのどから音楽が流れてきた. ¶be faithful in ***practicing*** her *music* 音楽の練習に忠実だ. ¶***provide*** *music* for the occasion その折に音楽が奏される. ¶***render*** *music* 演奏する.

V² the *music* ***started*** playing "..." 「...」の曲を奏し始めた.

Q make ***beautiful*** *music* 美音を発する. ¶***bright*** and ***tuneful*** *music* 晴れやかで調子の好い音楽. ¶"***canned***" *music* (トーキーやレコードなどの)いわゆるかん詰音楽. ¶***delicious*** *music* 調子の好い音楽. ¶a bit of ***dreamy*** *music*. 夢見るような節の小曲. ¶***flippant*** *music* [ジャズ式の]うわついた音楽. ¶***glorious*** *music* すばらしい音楽. ¶***instrumental*** *music* 器楽. ¶This good news was ***joyful*** *music* to him. この吉報は彼に取って耳よりな話であった. ¶***merry*** or ***sentimental*** *music* 楽しいまたは感傷的な音楽. ¶***modern*** *music* 近代音楽 (classic に対しするもので, ジャズなどではない). ¶***operatic*** *music* 歌劇(オペラ)音楽. ¶make ***raucous*** *music* to advertise ... ...を広告するため耳ざわりの音楽をやる. ¶***secular*** and ***sacred*** *music* 俗界及び宗教上の音楽. ¶***sensuous*** *music* 感覚音楽. ¶***syncopated*** *music* [ジャズなどの]切分音楽(語を一部省略するもの). ¶***vocal*** *music* 声楽. ¶***vulgar*** *music* 野卑な音楽.

Q² ***band*** *music* バンド・ミュージック. ¶***chamber*** *music* 室内楽. ¶***dance*** *music* ダンス音楽. ¶***disc*** (=***disk*** or ***canned***) *music* レコード音楽. ¶***juke-box*** *music* 《米》自動電蓄音楽(五セント白銅を入れると鳴り出すもの). ¶***part*** *music* 〖音楽〗二つ以上の声部からなる楽曲. ¶***organ*** *music* オルガン音楽. ¶***solo*** and ***choral*** *music* 独奏と合唱. ¶play ***State-side*** *music* [日本駐留軍など]アメリカ音楽を演奏する.

P I have no ear ***for*** *music*. 私には音楽を聞く耳がない. ¶delight ***in*** good *music* 好い音楽を聞いて楽しむ. ¶a band ***of*** *music* (音)楽隊 ‖ a lover ***of*** *music* 音楽愛好家 ‖ The following programme ***of*** *music* will be rendered by the City Band in Hibiya Park. 次のプログラム通り日比谷公園で市の音楽隊が演奏する. ¶dance ***to*** the *music* of ... ...の音楽に合わせて舞踏する ‖ set a song (poem) ***to*** *music* 歌(詩)を音楽に合わせる ‖ The song goes ***to*** *music*. その歌は調子が合う. ¶We were entertained ***with*** *music*. われわれのために音楽の演奏があった. ‖ ***with*** *music* by ... ...作曲で. ¶play ***without*** *music* 楽符なしで演奏する.

P² the *music* ***by*** the band=band music. ¶the *music* ***for*** the dance=dance music. ¶the *music* ***of*** the pines 松韻 ‖ The *music* ***of*** his machine is disquieting. 彼の乗物(自動車・自転車など)はいやな音がする. ‖ the *music* ***of*** the band=band music. ‖ the *music* ***of*** their songs その歌の楽曲(小鳥の歌声など) ‖ the *music* ***of*** the spheres 天界の交響楽 ‖ the *music* ***of*** his words 彼の調子のよい言葉. 【類】the *music of* little birds. ¶A young herdsman made sad *music on* a reed pipe. 若い牧童はあし笛で悲しい音楽をかなでた. ¶To hear that Consols are rising steadily is so much *music to* ears long accustomed to the perpetual talk of depression. 英国整理公債がじりじり上りになっているという話はしょっちう不景気ばかり聞いているものには誠に耳よりなことだ.

musicale, *n.* 《米》[社交用の]室内音楽会.

V The *musicales*, given during the winter after formal dinners, are ***held*** in this room. 冬季正式の晩さん会後の音楽会はこのへやで行われます.

musician, *n.* 音楽家, 作曲家; 《米》[バンドなどの]楽師.

Q an ***accomplished musician*** たん能な音楽家. ¶a ***blind musician*** 盲人音楽家. ¶a ***celebrated*** (=***noted***) ***musician*** 有名な音楽家. ¶***itinerant musicians*** 旅回りの楽師たち. ¶***strolling musicians*** 門づけの音楽家. ¶a little army of ***well-trained musicians*** 熟達した音楽家の一群.

Q^{2} a [jazz-] ***band musician*** [ジャズの]バンドの楽士. ¶***color[ed] musicians*** 《米》黒人の楽師(歌手). ¶a ***master musician*** 音楽の巨匠(名手). ¶a ***radio musician*** 放送音楽家(普通バンドの楽士をいう). ¶a ***street musician*** 門付けの楽師.

musicianship, *n.* 演奏力.

Q^{2} ***piano musicianship*** ピアノの演奏力.

musing, *n.* 沈思, 熟思.

Q ***deep musing*** 沈思黙考. ¶***fanciful musing*** 空想にふけること. ¶***solitary musings*** 独りさびしい熟思.

musk, *n.* じゃ香.

P a strong scent ***of musk*** 強いじゃ香のにおい. ¶scented ***with musk*** じゃ香のにおいがする.

m[o]ustache, *n.* 口ひげ.

V ***cultivate*** (=***grow***) one's *mustache* ひげを生やす. ¶***curl*** one's *mustache* ひげをひねる. ¶The policeman made his appearance, ***fingering*** his small *mustache*. 警官は短いひげをひねりながら現われた. ¶He ***has*** a slight *mustache*. 彼は薄いひげを生やしている. ¶***let*** one's *mustache* ***grow*** ひげをのばす. ¶***raise*** a *mustache* ひげを生やす. ¶***shave off*** one's *mustache* 口ひげをそり落す. ¶***start*** a *mustache* ひげをはやし初める. ¶***stroke*** one's *mustache* ひげをなでる. ¶***twirl*** (=***twist***) one's *mustache* ひげをひねくり回す. ¶***wear*** (=***keep***) a *moustache* ひげを生やしている.

Q laugh behind one's ***big mustache*** その長いひげのかげで笑う. ¶a ***black, bushy moustache*** 黒いもじゃもじゃしたひげ. ¶a ***bristling mustache*** もじゃもじゃに生えたひげ. ¶a lad with the first faint signs of a ***budding mustache*** 初めてかすかにひげの生えかかっている若者. ¶a ***clipped moustache*** 短く刈ったひげ. ¶a ***drooping moustache*** たれ下っているひげ. ¶a ***faint mustache*** ほんの少しのひげ. ¶a handsome young fellow with a ***fair*** (=***fine***) ***mustache*** 美事なひげを生やした美しい若者. ¶a ***false mustache*** つけひげ. ¶a carefully ***groomed mustache*** 手入れの行届いたひげ. ¶a ***heavy moustache*** 濃いひげ. ¶a ***long, dignified mustache*** 長いりっぱなひげ. ¶a ***short mustache*** ちょびひげ. ¶a ***small mustache*** ちょびひげ. ¶a ***stubby mustache*** 短く刈ったひげ. ¶a ***thin*** (***thick***) ***moustache*** 薄(濃)い口ひげ.

Q^{2} a ***Colman mustache*** コールマンひげ. ¶a small "***tiger-claw***" ***mustache*** 小さなどじょうひげ.

P a lip covered ***with*** a *mustache* ひげで隠れているくちびる.

mustard, *n.* からし.

V *Mustard* ***stings***. からしはぴりっとする.

muster, *n.* (**1**) 人員検査, 人員点呼.

V the minimum qualification which makes it ***pass muster*** as ... is ... それをして...に合格させる最小限度の資格は...である‖It can hardly ***pass muster***. それはちょっと物にならない. (**2**) 検閲.

V ***pass muster*** 検閲を通る, 合格する‖***pass*** Mrs. Grundy's *muster* 悪いうわさをされずにすむ.

muster, *v.* 集まる, 勢ぞろいする.

M^{2} *muster* ***in*** (***out***) 《米》入(除)隊させる.

P The boys *mustered* strong ***on*** that occasion. 少年たちはその折に盛んな勢ぞろいをした.

musty, *a.* かびた, かび臭い.

O grow (=get) *musty* かび臭くなる. 【類】This bread smells *musty*.

mutilate, *v.* 手足を切りとる; めちゃめちゃにする.

M ***horribly mutilated*** 物すごく手足がばらばらになって.

O The censor *mutilated* (=slashed) the article (film). 検閲係がその論文(など)の一部を削除した.

mutter, *v.* ぶつぶつ言う, 不平を鳴らす.

M ***mutter rebelliously*** 不平顔につぶやく.

muttering, *n.* つぶやき, 不平.

Q ***incoherent muttering*** うわごと.

muzzle, *n.* 口かせ具.

V The dog ***has*** a *muzzle* over his mouth. その犬は口輪をはめている. ¶***put*** a gold *muzzle* on the English press 英国の諸新聞に口止め料をやる.

myopia, *n.* 近視眼.

V It tends to ***induce*** *myopia*. そうすると近眼になりやすい.

P^{2} *myopia* ***of*** four diopter or more 四度またはそれ以上の近視.

myriad, *n.* 一万; 無数.

P Overhead there were *myriads* ***of*** stars. 頭上には無数の星が出ていた.

myself, *n.* → -self.

mystery, *n.* 神秘, 不可思議.

V ***bare*** the *mystery* to ... ...に神秘をあかす. ¶***clear up*** a *mystery* 神秘の正体を明かにする. ¶***disclose*** a *mystery* 秘密をあばく. ¶***dispel*** a *mystery* 神秘を破る. ¶***elucidate*** the *mystery* その神秘を明らかにする. ¶jealously ***guard*** a *mystery* 一所懸命秘密を守る. ¶***make*** a *mystery* of ... ...を神秘化する. ¶***make out*** (=***fathom***) a *mystery* 神秘をさぐる. ¶It ***presents*** a baffling *mystery*. それは探知し得ない不可思議である. ¶***probe*** the *mystery* to its depths (=the bottom) その不可思議を奥底までさぐる. 【類】***probe*** the *mystery* of life. ¶How it eventually found its way to a sale must ***remain*** an unsolved *mystery*. どうしてそれが売立品の中に入れられるようになったかは永久のなぞであろう. ¶***solve*** a *mystery* 神秘を解く. ¶the youth whithin whom sex is ***unfolding*** its *mysteries* 性の神秘が目ざめかけている青年. ¶***unravel*** a *mystery* 秘密を解く.

V^{2} The *mystery* has ***become deeper*** than ever. その不思議はますます深くなった. ¶The *mystery* still ***deepens***. その神秘はさらに深くなって行く. ¶There was a *mystery* ***hanging*** over her antecedents. 彼女の素性が分からなかった. ¶but the *mystery* still ***remains*** to be explained how ... しかしどうして...なるかの不思議はいまだに解けない. 【類】But the *mystery* ***remained*** and still ***remains***. / The *mystery* still ***remains*** unsolved.

Q The ***baffling*** *mystery* has been solved. そのむずかしい秘密が解けた. ¶It is a ***complete*** *mystery*. それは全く不思議だ. ¶there is ***considerable*** *mystery* in connection with ... ...については随分不思議なことがある. ¶***familiar mysteries*** 人のよく知る種々の不可思議. ¶an ***impenetrable mystery*** 端げいすべからざる神秘. ¶an ***insoluble mystery*** 解し難い不可思議. ¶Life is after all a ***profound mystery***. 人生は結局底知らずの神秘だ. ¶an ***unsolved mystery*** 未解決の不可思議.

Q^{2} an unsolved ***murder mystery*** 迷宮入りの殺人事件. 【類】a sensational ***murder mystery***.

P The case is shrouded ***in*** *mystery*. その事件は秘密に包まれている.

P^{2} the *mysteries* ***of*** nature (life) 自然(人生)の神秘.

mysticism, *n.* 神秘, 玄妙.

Q ***Eastern*** (=***Oriental***) ***mysticism*** 東洋の神秘.

mystification, *n.* 神秘.

V ***express*** *mystification* as to why ... ...の理由について不審がる.

myth, *n.* 神話, 神代物語.

V Around him *myths* relating probably to some ancestor or ancestors have ***crystallized***. 恐らくその一人または数人の先祖に関する荒唐無けいな伝説が彼に結び付けられたのであろう. ¶The *myth* has been ***exploded***. その話は根拠ないものと分かった.

Q The story is a ***pure*** *myth*. それは全く跡形もないことだ.

mythology, *n.* 神話, 神話学.

Q demons in ***Greek mythology*** ギリシア神話の悪魔.

N

nab, *v.* 《口語》捕える.

P The thief was *nabbed* (=arrested) ***by*** the police. 盗賊は警察に逮捕された.

O The batter was *nabbed*. 〖野球〗打者は三振した(凡打に打取られた).

nag, *v.* がみがみ言う.

P *nag* ***at*** a person 人に小言を言う. ¶She *nagged* him ***into*** doing what she wanted. 彼女は彼に小言をいって自分の望むことをさせた.

nail, *n.* (**1**) つめ.

V ***bite*** (=***gnaw***) one's *nails* つめをかむ. ¶***cut*** (=***trim***) the *nails* つめを切る. ¶***dye*** the *nail* つめを染める. ¶***have*** one's *nails* ***pared*** つめを切ってもらう. ¶***pare*** one's *nails* つめを切る.

Q ***concave*** *nails* そったつめ. ¶***filbert***[***-shaped***] *nails* はしばみ形のつめ. ¶***flat*** *nails* 平らなつめ. ¶***pink-tipped*** *nails* 先をもも色にしたつめ. 【類】her fingers, slender and white, with ***pink-pointed*** *nails*. ¶taper fingers with ***rosy*** *nails* 桜色のつめをした先の細い指. ¶***spatulate*** *nails* へら形のつめ.

Q² biting of the ***finger*** *nails* (=fingernails) つめをかむこと.

P the sum is to be paid down ***on*** the *nail* upon delivery of ... 金額は...と引換えに即金で支払うことになっている. ¶scratch the back ***with*** *nails* 背中をつめでかく.

(**2**) くぎ.

V ***draw out*** a *nail* くぎを抜く. ¶***drive*** a *nail* home by repeated blows of a hammer 金づちで幾度も打ってくぎを打ち込む. 【類】***drive*** a *nail* into a sure place (きく所へ). ¶***hammer in*** a *nail* くぎをたたき込む. ¶he ***has*** the *nail* on the head, when he said that ... 彼が...といったのは急所を突いている. ¶***hit*** the *nail* on the head [くぎの頭を打つ意から]正しいと思うことを言う(する). ¶***knock in*** a *nail* くぎを打ち込む. ¶***pull*** (=***draw***) ***out*** a *nail* くぎを抜く. ¶***run*** a *nail* into one's foot 足にくぎを通す. ¶The *nail* has ***started***. くぎが抜けた.

V² The *nail* doesn't ***fix fast***. くぎがよくきかない.

Q The *nail* is ***loose***. くぎがゆるんでいる. ¶a ***wrought*** *nail* [特殊用]飾りくぎ.

Q² a ***bamboo*** *nail* 竹くぎ. ¶a ***screw*** *nail* ら旋くぎ.

P ***on*** the *nail* その場で, 直ちに.

nail, *v.* くぎづけにする.

M² *nail* it ***down*** それをくぎづけにする. 【類】The lids were not *nailed* ***down***. ¶Isn't that box *nailed* ***up*** yet? この箱はまだくぎづけにしてありませんか. 【類】*nail* ***up*** a window / All the doors were *nailed* ***up***. ‖ *nail* ***up*** a notice on a tree 掲示をくぎ付けにする.

P The shopman is *nailed* all day ***behind*** the counter. その店員は終日帳場につきっきりだ. ¶The picture is *nailed* [up] ***on*** the wall. 絵は壁にくぎ付けになっている. 【類】*nail* a lid ***on*** a box. ¶*nail* it ***to*** the door 戸にそれをくぎで打ちつける ‖ *nail* a shelf ***to*** the wall 壁にたなをくぎづけにする ‖ Surprise *nailed* him ***to*** the spot. 驚きの余り彼はその場にくぎづけになった.

naked, *a.* はだかの.

M He is ***stark*** *naked*. 彼は真裸だ. 【類】***stark*** *naked*, just as she came out of the hands of pure nature (生れたままの姿で).

M² ***as*** *naked* as my mother bore me 生れたままの丸裸で.

P *naked* ***of*** comforts 慰安を与える物のない. ¶*naked* ***to*** the waist はだを脱いだ ‖ I was left *naked* (=subject) ***to*** injury. 私は害を受けるがままになっていた.

name, *n.* 名, 名称, 名義; 名声, 名誉; 著名の人; 悪口; 虚名, 空名.

V The *name* of ... may well be ***added*** to this list. ...の名はこの表に入れて差支えない. ¶***adopt*** the *name* of ... ...という名をつける. ¶***adore*** the *name* of God 神を礼拝する. ¶***affix*** one's *name* to a document 書類に署名する. ¶***allow*** one's *name* to be used as ... ...としての名義を貸す. ¶***append*** one's *name* to a paper 書類に名を付記する.【類】***append*** the *names* of authors to extracts (抜粋した文). ¶The *name* of ... is ***applied*** to it. それを...と呼んでいる. ¶***ascertain*** the *name* of the firm その商店の名を確かめる. ¶His *name* should always be ***associated*** with the university. 彼の名はいつもその大学と連想さるべきである. ¶***assume*** another's *name* 他人の名を詐称する. 【類】His *name* was probably ***assumed***. / ***assume*** a fictitious *name*. ¶His *name* is much ***banded about*** in literary columns. 彼は大分文学欄のうわさに上っている. ¶those who ***bear*** wellknown *names* 有名な人々. 【類】Sir Hiram Maxim, the inventor of the famous gun which ***bears*** his *name* (その名を取ってつけた) / the town ***bearing*** his honored *name* / the picture (映画) ***bears*** the *name* of ... / Tom Thumb is the *name* that has been ***borne*** by several famous dwarfs. / His *name* is ***borne*** by the street. / works that ***bear*** his *name* / These institutes ***bear*** the *name* of Pasteur. ‖ The list of members ***bears*** his *name*. 会員名簿に彼の名がのっている. ‖ I asked what *name* he ***bore***. 私は「お名前は」と彼に聞いた. ‖ formerly ***bore*** the *name* of ... ...以前は...という名前であった. ¶***bequeath*** a good *name* to children 名誉ある家名を子孫に伝える. ¶***blacken*** the *name* of one's family その家名を汚す. ¶Her *name* is ***blessed*** in the Red Cross world. 彼女の名は赤十字社会では尊敬されている. ‖ we have cause to ***bless*** the *name* of ... われわれは...に対して感謝すべきだ. ¶Her fair *name* was never ***breathed upon*** (=***tarnished*** *or* sullied). 彼女の令名は一度もはずかしめられなかった. ¶This ***brought*** his *name* to the front. このために彼は世人の注目を引いた. ‖ ***bring*** one's *name* into disrepute by ... ...で恥をかく. 【類】The matter has just ***brought*** his *name* prominently forward. ¶***call*** one's *name*=call one by one's name その名前を呼ぶ ‖ ***call*** one's *name* without title 人を呼び捨てにする ‖ ***call*** *names* 悪口をいう. 【類】He ***called*** me all *names*. / Boys should not ***call*** *names* each other. ‖ I ***called*** that *name* to the telephone. 私はその人を電話口に呼んだ. ¶***call off*** *names* [先生などが]指名点呼する. ¶***call out*** one's *name* 人の名を呼び上げる. ¶I cannot ***call up*** (=***remember***) his *name*. 私は彼の名が思い出せない. ¶He had no son to inherit his well-stocked farm and ***carry on*** the old *name*. 彼には沢山元手の入った農場を継いで従来の名義を継続してやってゆく息子というものがなかった. ¶I am sure you did not ***catch*** my *name*. 私の名をお聞取りにならなかったでしょう. ¶***change*** one's *name* from ... to ... ...を...と改名する. 【類】A woman ***changes*** her *name* when married. / the *name* (=title) was ***changed*** to ... ¶***communicate*** *names* to us for correspondence 通信するためその人々の名をわれわれに知らしてもらう. ¶***compromise*** the fair *name* of ... ...の令名を傷つける. 【類】If you keep company with such rough, coarse fellows, you will ***compromise*** your good *name*. ¶The ledger ***contained*** many *names* both humble and famous. その原簿には幾多の有名無名な人々の名がのっていた. 【類】The list ***contains*** many *names* of eminence. ¶***cross*** one's *name* off the list. その名前に線を引いて名簿から削除する. ¶***cut*** one's *name* on ... with a knife ナイフで...に名をきざむ. ¶***demand*** the student's *name* and school 学生の名前と学校とを聞きただす. ¶***deny*** one's *name* 名を言うことをこばむ. ¶the town ***derived*** its *name* from ... その市の名は...から来た. ¶***drag*** the *name* of the family through the mud. 家名を汚す. ¶He is the only poet that ***deserves*** the *name*. その名に恥じない詩人は彼ばかりだ. ‖ It is called irresponsibility, but ***deserves*** a harder *name*. それは無責任と言われているが実はそれ以上である. ¶***dim*** the fair *name* of ... ...の名折れになる. ¶***disclose*** one's *name* 名をあかす. ¶He refused to ***divulge*** the *name*. 彼はその名を漏らすことをこばんだ. 【類】The Minorca (ミノルカ川) ***derives*** its *name* from the Island of Minorca (=the same name). ¶***drop*** the *name* of

... and take to calling themselves "..." ...の名称を廃して自ら...と称する ‖ *drop* a *name* from a list 名簿から除名する. ¶*embellish* one's parents' *names* 両親の名を飾る. ¶Her *name* was *engraven* on the ring. 彼女の名を指環に彫りつけた. ¶I *enquired* his *name*. 私は彼の名を聞いた. ¶*enroll* one's *name* in a register その名を名簿に登録する. 【類】Please *enroll* the following *name* as a subscriber to The Boys' and Girls' Newspaper for one full year (24 issues), including my club pin (会員記章). ¶please *enter* my *name* as a subscriber to ... ...の購読申込者として小生の名を御記入願います. 【類】*Enter* your *name* in the visitors' book. / *enter* the *names* on the list of membership. ¶*erase* one's *name* from ... ...からその名を削る. ¶He *established* his *name* in literature. 彼は文士として一家をなした. ¶*exchange names* and addresses [新しい知人など] 名前と住所を交換する. ¶All *names* are *filed* in a continuous alphabet scheme. 氏名は全部 abc 順にとじ込んである. ¶*Fill* your *name* and address in this blank space. この余白へあなたの住所姓名を書き込んで下さい. ¶*fill in* one's *name* in a card カードに名を書き込む. ¶*gain* a *name* 名声を博する. ¶I cannot *find* the vessel's *name* in the Register. [ロイドの]船名簿に船名がない. ¶*gain* a great *name* 高名を博する. ¶*get* a *name* 名をあげる. ¶He *gave* his *name*. 彼は自分の名をつげた. ‖ He *gave* the *name* of Bragard. 彼はブラガードだと名乗った. 【類】She refused to *give* her *name*. / *give* one's *name* and address / *give* one's real *name* ‖ This has *given* him a *name* over the world. このために彼の名声が世界に響いた. ‖ he has invented a machine to which he *gives* the *name* of ... 彼は...と称する機械を発明した ‖ *give* a false *name* 偽名を用いる ‖ *give* a *name* to ... ...に名を付ける ‖ *give* big *names* to little things 小さい物に大きな名を付ける ‖ Hirado *gives* its *name* to a celebrated variety of blue and white porcelain. 有名な染付けの磁器は平戸という名で通っている. ¶*hand down* one's *name* to posterity 名を後世に残す. 【類】His *name* will be *handed down* for generations (幾世代も). ¶He *had* the *name* of (=was called) an eccentric. 彼は変人だと言われている. ‖ A clockwatch *has* its *name* because it strikes the hours and quarters the same as a clock automatically. 時打ち懐中時計の名はそれが柱時計同様自働的に毎時十五分おきに打つところから来ている. ‖ *have* one's *name* on the register of the university 同大学に籍をおく. 【類】He *has* his *name* in "Who's Who" (紳士録). / a hundred flowers of the field for which I *have* no *names* / a balm that *has* no *name* (得もいわれない). ¶*have* one's *name enrolled* on the mailing list 郵便発送簿中にその名をのせてもらう. ¶The contributor asks to *have* his *name withheld*. 寄付者は名を出してもらいたくないという希望を述べている. ¶Tricksters *hurt* Japan's good *name*. 悪人たちが日本の名声を傷つける. ¶The work has *immortalized* his *name*. その作品が彼の名を不朽にした. ¶*include names* of the highest standing in the country in science, literature, and art 科学・文学・美術界におけるその国の一流どころを網らする. 【類】The list of the guests present *included* many famous *names* in Japan. ¶*injure* one's fair *name* その名声を傷つける. ¶*inscribe* one's *name* on a rock 岩にその名を刻む. ¶*invent* fanciful *names* for ... ...につけるしゃれた名を考え出す. ¶It *involves* the good *name* of the nation. それは一国の名誉にかかわる. ¶They *joined* their *names* to a circular of appeal to the people of Great Britain. 彼らは大英国民に訴える回章に自分たちの名を書き添えた. ¶*Keep* my *name* on your list. 名簿にある私の名をそのままにしておいて下さい. ¶His *name* would be *known* to many of you, were I to mention it. 彼の名を言えばお分かりになる方が多いでしょう. 【類】a journalist whose *name* I *know* but *forgot*. ¶*leave* a *name* in history as ... ...として名を歴史に残す. 【類】He *left* a *name* behind of a man richly endowed with original ideas (独創力の豊かな人). ¶When Sir Henry Bessemer died, he *left* a *name* behind of a man singularly endowed with original ideas and a rare inventive capacity. ‖ Did he *leave* his *name*? [訪問者など]名を言って行ったか. ¶*lend* one's *name* to a scheme ある事業に名義を貸す. 【類】ask a number of distinguished people to *lend* their *names* as patrons. ¶*link* one's *name* with a scandal 疑獄に連座する. ¶*list* the *names* of ... ...の名を名簿に記入する. ¶I've just *lost* his *name*. 彼の名前をちょっと忘れた. ¶a special booklet giving information on ... will be sent to any person *mailing* his *name* and address to ... ...へ住所姓名を御一報下されば...のことを記述した特集小冊子をどなたにもお送り致します. ¶*maintain* the good *name* of ... ...の声価を維持する. ¶*make* a *name* for oneself by ... ...によって独力で名をなす. 【類】*make* a *name* in literature / The boy who sat at the class sometimes *makes* his *name* in after life. ¶He *made* his *name familiar* all over the world. 彼は自分の名を世界中に広めた. ‖ *make* his *name a household word* その名を人口に広く知らせる ‖ It is a monument which will *make* his *name imperishable*. 彼の名を不滅にする記念物だ. ¶Did not somebody *mention* my *name* just now? 今しがたただれか私の名を呼びませんでしたか. 【類】*Mention* some great French *names* in the arts and sciences. ¶*merit* the *name* of ... ...の名にそむかない. ¶I have a letter from him, but have unfortunately *mislaid* his *name* and address. 彼から手紙をもらったがあいにくどこかへおき忘れて住所氏名が分からない. ¶It *obtains* its *name* from a similar hill in the neighbourhood of Kyoto. その名は京都付近の形の似た丘から来ている. ¶have unanimously decided to *offer* the *name* of ... for the president of ... 満場一致で...を...の会長に推すことに決した. ¶a certain man whose *name* shall be *omitted* here (=who shall be nameless) 名は明さないがある人が. ¶his fair *name* is rapidly being *overcast* by ... 氏の名声は急速に...のために圧倒されつつある. ¶it *owes* its *name* to the fact that ... その名の起原は...の事実による. ¶It is enough to *perpetuate* his *name*. それは彼の名を後世に伝えるに足る. ¶*place* one's *name* on the subscription list 予約者名簿に名を記入する. 【類】*place* one's *name* on a mailing list (郵便発送簿) ¶*post* the *names* on the screens 名を幕に張出す. ¶She still *prefaces* her *name* with Miss. 彼女はまだ自分の名の前にミスとつけている. ¶*pronounce* one's own *name* 自分の名を言う. 【類】*pronounce* visitors' *names*. ¶*publish names* 名を公表する. ¶I *put* my *name* to the document. 私はその書類に署名した. ¶I have *put down* my *name* as a subscriber for the newspaper. 私はその新聞の購読者として記名した. ‖ *Put* my *name down* for two tickets. 切符二枚私の名でつけて下さい. ¶I cannot *recall* his *name* right now. 彼の名はちょっと思い出せない. 【類】It happens that we often fail to *recall* a *name* which we are sure we know. ¶The mountain *received* the *name* "...". その山は...と命名された. ‖ Tobacco is said to have *received* its *name* from Tobacco, a province of Yucatan, Mexico. タバコの名はメキシコのユカタン地方のトバッコという地名からきているそうだ. 【類】it *receives* its *name* on account of the imaginary resemblance it bears to (に似ていると思われる所から...). ¶I *recognize* many of the *names* of passengers. 私は乗客の氏名を多数知っている. ¶*record names* in the visitors' books 参観人名簿に名を記す. ¶*recover* one's good *name* 名誉を回復する. ¶*register* one's *name* 記名する ‖ *names registered* with ... ...[職業紹介所など]に登録してある人名. ¶*release* the *name* of ... 何々の名前を発表する. ¶*remove* his *name* from the roll of knights 勲爵士名簿から彼の名を削除する. ¶The real thief was discovered later and his good *name* was *restored*. ほどへて本物の泥棒が見つかって彼は名誉を回復した. ¶*retain* one's *name* on a subscription list 予約者名簿にその名を保留する. ¶His *name* is still *revered*. 彼の名は今なお尊崇されている. 【類】*revere* and *honor* his *name*. ¶He jealously *safeguards* the honored *name* and great position that he has won in the past. 彼は過去においてかち得た名誉と地位とをどこまでも擁護する. ¶(*save* the *name*!) (その人に幸福あれ!) [そう入句]. ¶*scrawl* one's *name* in a book 書物に自分の名前をなぐり書する. ¶work for the serene joy of *seeing* their *names* in print 自分の書いたものが印刷物に出るという地味な楽しみのために執筆する. ¶*seek* a sweeter *name* for a spade [率直でなく]飾って言おうとする. ¶*send in* my *name* as ... 私の名前は...だと取次人に通じる ‖ The porter *sent in* a visitor's *name*. 門衛は訪問者の名を取次いだ. ¶I *sent up* my *name*. 私は名刺を通じた. ¶He *set* his *name* to it. 彼はそれに署名した. ¶*sign* one's *name* on one's photo. その写真に署名する. 【類】*sign* one's *name* to a letter. ¶It ***sounds*** a Japanese ***name***. それは日本人の名らしい. ¶He ***spoke*** her ***name***. 彼は彼女の名を呼んだ. ¶***stain*** a ***name*** 名を汚す. ¶His ***name*** was ***struck*** from the peerage. 彼は華族から除名された. ¶***submit*** the ***name*** of an appointee for confirmation 確認のため選ばれる人の名を提出する. ¶***subscribe*** one's ***name*** to a document 文書に署名する. ¶Your ***name*** has been ***suggested*** to Mr. ... in connection with this matter. このことをあなたに相談したらよかろうと…さんへ注意しました. ¶This ***sullied*** his ***name*** with a stigma that time will not wash away. このために彼は末代までの汚名を受けた. ¶***take*** (=derive) its ***name*** from ... …からその名が出ている. 【類】 *Eau de Cologne* (オードコロン) ***takes*** its ***name*** from the place. ‖ He ***took*** the ***name*** of Augustin at his (=in) baptism. 彼は洗礼のときオーガスティンの名をもらった. ‖ the League now ***took*** the ***name*** of ... その連盟は…と改名した ‖ He became a disciple of Buddha, ***taking*** the ***name*** of Hoshu. 彼は仏門に入って名を宝秀と称した. ‖ Do not swear "By God! I will." It is an act of blasphemy to ***take*** the Lord's ***name*** in vain.「神に誓って致します」と言うものでない, みだりに主の名を呼ぶはとく神の行為である. ‖ ***take*** the chauffeur's ***name*** and address 運転手の名と宿所を書留める ‖ Who is that ***taking*** my ***name*** in vain? 僕のうわさをするのはだれですか. 【類】 The proprietor of the intelligence office ***took*** my ***name*** and asked me what he could do [for me]. / ***take*** to oneself the ***name*** of ... ¶***take*** (=***note***) the ***name down*** その名を手帳に控える. ¶***take*** one's ***name off*** the list 名簿からその名を削除する. ¶What ***name*** shall I ***tell*** him? どなた様とお名前をお通し致しましょうか(女中が訪問客に). ¶***translate*** their ***names*** into English equivalents 彼らの名を英語の相当語に直す. ¶***turn*** in their ***names*** 彼らの名を申告する. ¶***turn*** (=***look***) ***up*** a ***name*** in the dictionary 辞書で名を引いて見る. ¶***uphold*** the fair ***name*** of their nation 国民の名声を落さないようにする. ¶Do not ***use*** my ***name***. 私の名を出して下さるな. ‖ He kindly allowed me to ***use*** his ***name*** as approving the scheme. 彼は賛助員となることを承諾した. ¶My ***name*** was ***uttered*** by someone near me. 私の近くにいただれかが私の名を言った. ¶I don't ***want*** my real ***name*** to appear. 私は自分の本名を出したくない. ¶He ***won*** the ***name*** of a second Samson. 彼はサムソン第二世(怪力士)という名をかち得た. ‖ he justly ***won*** for him the ***name*** of ... 彼が…の名をかち得たのは当然だ. ¶He does not ***wish*** his ***name to be known***. 彼は自分の名を知られたくない. ¶He asks that his ***name*** be ***withheld***. 彼は自分の名を公にしてくれるなという. 【類】 a donor whose ***name*** was ***withheld***. ¶He cannot ***write*** his own ***name***. 彼は自分の名も書けない. 【類】 He was so unlettered that he could hardly ***write*** his ***name***. / Japan has ***written*** her ***name*** large in the history of the world during the first decade of the 20th century.

V² His ***name*** often ***figures*** in the newspapers. 彼の名は何度も新聞に出る. 【類】 people whose ***names*** always ***figure*** in literary journals (文学雑誌) / His ***name figured*** on the programme of the conference. ¶his ***name*** will ***go down*** for many generations as ... …としての彼は幾代も忘れられないであろう. 【類】 his ***name*** will ***go down*** not only as ... but as ... ¶as its ***name imparts*** その名の意味するごとく. ¶as its ***name indicates*** (=***denotes***) その名の示すごとく. 【類】 Mr. Macdonald, as his ***name indicates***, was a Scotchman. ¶His ***name*** will ***live*** in the history of English literature. 彼の名は英文学に残るだろう. 【類】 his ***name*** chiefly ***lives*** by virtue of ... ¶the first ***name*** that will ***occur*** to most of us is ... われわれの多数の頭にまず第一に浮ぶ名は…だ. ¶Roson is a "haiku" poet as the ***name shows***. 蕗村はその名でも想像がつくように俳人である. ¶as its ***name signifies*** その名の示すごとく. ¶his ***name stands out*** in the history of ... as one of ... 彼の名は…史上に…の一人としてきわ立って見える. ¶doctors whose ***names*** have ***vanished*** from the register その名が登録簿に見えなくなった医師たち.

Q retain their ***aboriginal names*** 生来の名を保持する. ¶***added names*** 号. ¶... was his ***alleged name*** 自称…であった. ¶an ***alternative name*** 別の名. ¶"Fuso" is an ***ancient name*** for Japan. 扶桑は日本の古名. ¶Bolshevism is but ***another name*** for anarchy and savagery. 過激主義とは無政府及び残忍の別名に過ぎない. 【類】 Larva is ***another name*** for caterpillar. / In such a case, "morality" is ***another name*** for ignorance, timidity, hypocrisy, prudery (ねこかぶり), coarseness, and lack of conscience. / His "friendship" was from the first simple love or flirtation masquerading under ***another name***. ¶write under the ***assumed name*** of ... …という仮名で執筆する. ¶have a ***bad name*** 評判が悪い ‖ That would give him a ***bad name***. そうしたらあの人の名にかかわる. ‖ call him ***bad names*** いろいろ悪口を言う. ¶***Big Names*** 大御所. 【類】 become a ***Big Name***. / P.A.S. Franklin is a ***big name*** in steamship circles. ¶***botanical names*** 植物学上の名称. ¶the ***bride's name*** 新婦の嫁入先の名. ¶***Christian*** (=***baptismal***) ***name*** 洗礼名. ¶***names classic*** to Japanese ears 日本人の耳には古典的な名. ¶the ***collective name*** for a group of peaks 群峰の総称. ¶It is a ***colloquial name*** of the place. それはその土地の俗称である. ¶a ***common name*** 通称. ¶a ***convenient name*** 便宜上の名称. ¶a ***corporate name*** 会社などの法律上の名. ¶a ***current name*** for ... …の通り名称. ¶under the ***delusive name*** of ... …というまぎらわしい名称で. ¶We like to call it "..." in order to lend it a ***dignified name***. その名に重みをつけるために「…」と呼びたい. ¶the most ***eminent names*** in this movement この運動の参加者中で最も著名な人々. ¶a writer with an ***established name*** 一家をなした作家. ¶a ***euphemistic name*** for ... …のえん曲な名称. ¶Rouben Mamoulian is a ***euphonious name***. ルーバン・マムーリアンとは語ろのよい名前だ. ¶under a ***false name*** 偽名で. ¶men bearing ***names famous*** in the land その土地で著名な人々. ¶***famous*** stage ***names*** 有名な芸名. ¶a ***fanciful name*** of ... …をしゃれていう名. ¶a ***felicitous name*** よい名. ¶take a ***fictitious name*** 偽名を使う. ¶call things by ***fine names*** 口前がうまい ‖ to give it a ***finer*** (***hard***) ***name*** よく(悪く)言えば. ¶the ***first name*** [姓名の]最初の名. 【類】 call each other by the ***first name***. ¶John Dewy's is undoubtedly the ***foremost name*** in the American philosophical world. ジョン・デューイーは確かに米国哲学界の第一人者である. 【類】 The membership of the society includes some of the ***foremost names*** in England. / the ***foremost-names*** in American literature. ¶The ***former name*** of Tokyo was Yedo. 東京の旧名を江戸といった. ¶one's ***full name*** [略さずに]姓名全部. 【類】 Sign here your ***full name***, please. ¶a ***general name*** including ... …を包括する総体の名. ¶a ***given*** (=Christian) ***name*** 《米》名(姓に対する). ¶He has robbed me of my ***good name***. 彼は僕の名誉を傷つけた. ‖ for the protection of Japan's ***good name*** 日本の名誉保護のために. 【類】 guardians of Japan's ***good name*** / maintain the ***good name*** of a firm ‖ for lack of a ***better name*** it may be described as ... 良い名がないので仮にそれを…としておこう. ¶It was what they call kleptomania now, but we had no ***grand names*** for crimes when I was young. それは今日窃盗狂と称するものであったが私の若い時分には各種の犯罪に対してぎょうぎょうしい名称は一つもなかった. ¶people whose ***names*** are ***great*** in the city その市で有名な人々. 【類】 Saigo, Kido, and many other ***great names*** were there. / critics of ***great name*** / make ***great names*** by the doing of great deeds ‖ a ***great name*** in confectionery 菓子では有名店 ‖ Shakespeare is the ***greatest name*** in English literature. シェイクスピアは英文学最大の巨星である. ¶known by the ***gruesome name*** of Tombstone トゥームストーン(墓石)という気味の悪い名の. ¶to give it a ***hard name*** 悪く言えば. ¶***high-sounding names*** えらそうな名前. ¶The pass is not issued in the ***holder's name***. そのパスは所有者の名で発行しない. ¶the ***holy name*** of Jesus 神聖なヤソの名. ¶known to the elect by the ***homely name*** of ... 消息通の間には…という通り名で知れている. ¶an ***honorable name*** 美名. ¶a ***humorous name*** for ... …をこっけい的に呼んだ名. ¶She still uses her ***husband's name***. 彼女はまだ夫の名を名乗っている. ¶have an ***ill name*** 評判が悪い ‖ call [***ill***] ***names*** 悪口をいう. ¶an ***ill-sounding name*** 聞かれてよくない名前. ¶the bearer of an ***illustrious name***. 著名の人. ¶He has left ***imperishable-name***. 彼は不滅の名を残した. 【類】 he made an ***imperishable name*** by ... ¶The elephant had the ***individual name*** of Jumbo. その象にはジャムボーという名がついてい

た. ¶he has made an ***international name*** for himself by … 彼は…によって国際的に名をなした. ¶such ***jawbreaking names*** as … 《米》…というような発音しにくい名前. ¶publish a work in the ***joint names*** of … and … …と…の連名で著作を刊行する. ¶call a person by his ***last name*** only その人の姓を呼び捨てにする. ¶a ***Latinized name*** ラテン語風にした名. ¶the ***literary name*** of … …の雅号. ¶London is a ***local name***. ロンドンは地名だ. ¶She continues to bear her ***maiden name***. 彼女は依然結婚前の姓名を名乗っている. ¶take a ***male name*** and costume 男の名を名乗り男の服装をする. ¶a god of ***many names*** 色々異名のある神. ¶a ***masculine personal name*** (Frank, John, Henry のような)男の名. ¶a ***mere name*** 名だけのこと. ¶the ***middle name*** (Jerome Klapka Jerome の Klapka のような)中間の名. ¶He has made a ***national name*** in baseball. 彼は野球では全国的に有名だ. ¶the ***native Philippine name*** of the plant その植物のフィリッピン固有の名. 【類】"Banana" is the ***native name*** in Guinea. ¶shout ***naughty names*** at … …をののしる. ¶assume the ***new name*** of … …新たに…という名をつける. ¶a man of ***no name*** 氏も素性もない人 ‖ Cruel is ***no name*** for it. 無残などでは表現不足. ¶a ***notable name*** 有名な人. ¶an ***obsolete name*** for … …の旧名. ¶an ***odd name*** おかしな名. ¶the ***official name*** for … …の正式の呼称(略称, 通称でなく). ¶an ***old name*** for … …の古い名 ‖ They registered it in the ***old name*** as a private company. 彼らはそれを個人会社として古い名で登録した. ¶an ***opprobrious name*** 汚名. ¶it took its ***original name*** from … その原名は…から取った. ¶call a person an imoster and ***other names*** 人をかたりだの何んのという. ¶a ***pet name*** 愛称 ‖ Bunny is a ***pet name*** for a rabbit. バニーはうさぎの愛称である. ¶give a ***picturesque name*** to … …にしゃれた名をつける. ¶"D'Aulby" is not a count at all. His ***name*** is ***plain*** George Daulby and he is the son of an English tailor. D'Aulby などとえらそうにつづっているがドールビは伯爵でも何んでもなく無位無官のジョージ・ドールビで英国の仕立屋のせがれだ. ¶a ***playful name*** 戯名. ¶Helvetia is a ***poetical name*** of Switzerland. ヘルヴィシアというのはスイスの詩的名称だ. ¶a ***popular name*** for … …の俗称. ¶Jesuits is the ***popular*** and ***abbreviated name*** of the Soiety or Company of Jesus, an organization founded during the period of the Reformation. エスイタ派というのはヤソ会の通俗的略称で宗教改革時代に起った団体である. ¶the ***posthumous name*** of … …の戒名. ¶His ***precious good name*** would be gone for ever. 彼の名誉はあたら地に落ちてしまうだろう. ¶a man rejoicing in the ***pretty name*** of … …という美しい名の付いている人. 【類】In America marble dust is used under the ***pretty name*** of "snowflake." ¶the actor is better known by his ***professional name*** of "…" その役者は「…」という芸名で言った方がよくわかる. ¶a ***proprietary name*** (Multigraph, Leika, Kodac などのような)登録品名. ¶a very ***proud name*** in Scotland スコットランドでは非常に幅のきく名前. ¶The lias is an English ***provincial name*** given to an argillaceous limestone. リアスというのは陶土質の石灰岩につけた地方的な英語の名だ. ¶a ***pseudonymous name*** 匿名. ¶a ***quaint name*** 奇抜な名. ¶write an article under one's ***real name*** 本名を使って文を書く ‖ I don't want my ***real name*** to appear. 本名は出したくない. ¶The ***name*** of England is used not only for the country itself, but as the ***representative name*** of the United Kingdom, of which it is the predominant partner. イングランドという名はその国を指すだけでなくまた中心をなす一員として全連合王国の代表の名としても用いられる. ¶in the ***sacred name*** of science 科学という神聖な名において. ¶bear the ***same name*** 同じ名がついている. ¶call one by his ***second name*** みょう字で人を呼ぶ. ¶***simple, unembroidered names*** 肩書なしのはだかの名. ¶***stellar names*** [映画などの]スターの名. ¶find a ***suitable*** trading ***name*** 適当な商号を見つける. ¶a ***sullied name*** 汚名. ¶***Technical*** and ***botanical names*** are translated into ordinary English. 専門的な植物学の名が通俗の英語に和らげてある. ¶it is known under the ***tender name*** of … それは…という優しい名で知られている. ¶***top-notch names*** in the business world 《米》実業界における大立物. ¶***unpronounceable names*** 発音しにくい名. ¶too ***unwieldy*** a ***name*** いかにも長くって読みにくい名. ¶Semasiology is a ***variant name*** for semantics. Semasiology (語義学)というのは semantics の別名だ. ¶They called him ***vile names***. 彼らはさまざまに彼をののしった. ¶call … by a ***wrong name*** …の名を間違えて呼ぶ ‖ give a ***wrong name*** and address でたらめの名と宿所を告げる.

Q² a ***business name*** 商業用の名. ¶The children have adopted his ***family name***. 子供は彼の姓を名乗った. 【類】His ***family name*** is Brown. / disgrace one's ***family name*** / He brought the ***family name*** to such shame as this. ¶a ***fancy name*** for … …の雅名. 【類】These islands bear ***fancy names***. ¶Under the ***firm name*** of George Smith and Company ジョージスミス商社という社名で. 【類】He went into business for himself under the ***firm name*** of … & Co. / he commenced his business under the ***firm name*** of … ¶***first-class names*** 一等品. ¶one's ***pen name*** 筆名. 【類】take a ***pen name***. ¶the rulings of the United States Geographic Board in the spellings of ***place names*** 地名のつづり方に関するアメリカ地理局の規定. ¶***place, river*** and ***mountain names*** 土地山川の名. ¶a ***race name*** 人種名. ¶the ***stage name*** 芸名, 源氏名. ¶Every corner bore the ***street name*** in Roman characters (=letters). 街の角々にはローマ字で町名がついている. ¶a ***trade name*** 商標名. 【類】A good ***trade name*** is necessary for a commercial product. ¶The ***Wadsworth name*** was stamped in the case of the watch. ワズウァースの(会社)名が懐中時計のふたに刻印してあった.

P He had ***against*** his ***name*** a long list of heartless cruelties. 彼が犯した残忍行為が非常に多い. ¶Brown ***by name*** 姓はブラウン. ‖ address the prisoner ***by name*** 名をあげて囚人に話しかける ‖ mention them ***by name*** 彼らの名をあげる ‖ passing ***by*** the ***name*** of … …の名で通っている ‖ He is a chairman only ***by*** (=in) ***name***. 彼はただ名のみの社長である. ‖ There is nobody here ***by*** that name. その名前の人はここにはいない. ‖ I know him only ***by name***. 名前だけは知っている(会ったことはない). 【類】He passes ***by*** the ***name*** of Black. / a Chinese student at Columbia ***by*** the ***name*** of … ¶He is a scholar ***in name*** but not in fact. 彼は有名無実の学者だ. 【類】patriots ***in name*** only / We are free in reality as well as ***in name***. / do business ***in*** his wife's ***name*** (妻の名義) ‖ ***in*** the ***name*** of … …の名において; の美名にかくれて. 【類】many crimes were committed ***in*** the ***name*** of … / ***In*** the ***name*** of France I greet you. / Business is done ***in*** another ***name*** (人の名義で). / sign it ***in*** Lady Geraldine's ***name*** / ***in*** the ***name*** of justice (liberty) ‖ ***in*** one's own ***name*** 自己の名義で, 自分一個で ‖ issue invitations ***in*** the ***name*** of … …の名義で招待状を出す. 【類】the agent of a shipper signing ***in*** the ***name*** of his principal (荷主) / He took possession of (占領した) an island ***in*** the ***name*** of Portugal. / take possession of the Pacific ***in*** the ***name*** of Spain ‖ ***in*** the ***name*** of Christianity キリスト教の名をかりて. 【類】Horrible cruelties and frightful crimes were perpetrated ***in*** the ***name*** of religion. / the crimes committed ***in*** the ***name*** of civilization ‖ Halt ***in*** the ***name*** of the law. 動くな御用だ. 【類】the atrocities perpetrated ***in*** the ***name*** of commerce and expansion / Some say that the Comintern should be ostracized ***in*** the ***name*** of humanity and justice. / ***In*** the ***name*** of Heaven, where was she? / What, ***in*** the ***name*** of all that's horrible, is that appalling noise going on upstairs? / Young man, if you haven't a natural store of initiative, ***in*** the ***name*** of all that's necessary, start now and develop it. ‖ ***in*** God's ***name***=on earth, in the world 一体全体(語勢を強める句). 【類】What, ***in*** the ***name*** of goodness (fortune, common sense, God), are you about? ¶***of*** the ***name*** of …=named … …という名の(人または物). 【類】he had by her a child ***of*** the ***name*** of … ‖ Shimonoseki is situated on the strait[s] ***of*** the same ***name***. 下関は同名の海峡上にある. ‖ He called me all kinds ***of names***. 彼は散々僕に悪口を言った. ‖ Her name, ***of*** all ***names***, is Angelia! あんなわがまま者でも名だけはアンジェリアさ! ¶He has published a book ***over*** his own ***name***. 彼は(匿名でなく)自分の姓名を署して本を出版した. ¶He had not a dollar ***to*** his ***name***. 彼は自分の金というものは一ドルもなかった. ‖ He is not entitled ***to*** the ***name*** of scholar. 彼は学者と称するに足りない. ‖ true ***to*** one's ***name*** その名にそむかず ‖ May I ask what ***name*** he answers ***to***? あの人の名前は何というのですか. ¶***under*** this *name* are included ... この名称の下に…が含まれる ‖ He carried the business on ***under*** his own *name* till 1894, when he retired in favor of his sons. 彼は一八九四年まで自分の名義で商売をやっていたがその年に息子たちのために隠退した. 【類】The business continued ***under*** the *name* of R. H. Macy & Co. ‖ it went down in history ***under*** the*name* of "..." それは歴史上のいわゆる「…」であった. ‖ alternately known ***under*** the *name* of ...=otherwise known as ... またの名は… ‖ Self-control is only courage ***under*** another *name*. 自制は勇気の別名に過ぎない. ‖ He cheated me ***under*** the *name* of friendship. 彼は友情と称して私をだました. ‖ he became a Japanese subject of the Japanese Empire ***under*** the *name* of ... 彼は…という名で日本に帰化した. ‖ The British Museum catalogue has sixty-eight entries ***under*** his *name*. 英国博物館目録には彼の名のところに六十八の記入がある. ‖ write ***under*** one's own *name* 署名して文を書く ‖ form an association ***under*** the *name* of ... …という協会を設ける ‖ publish books ***under*** their own *names*. 【類】trade ***under*** the *name* of ... ... ‖ A Japanese magazine published ***under*** the *name* of the ... 何々という名で発行した日本の雑誌. 【類】***under*** the *name* of ... they took up their abode in lodgings (宿を定めた) in the house of a tailor named ... / a letter addressed to her ***under*** the *name* of "Mrs. Pink" / Iyeyasu is worshipped ***under*** the *name* of Toshogu. / Norma Talmadge, when visiting Europe usually registers ***under*** the *name* of (と記名する) Mrs. Joseph Schenck. / The *name* ***under*** which he had passed was Ferdinand Hansen. / the *name* ***under*** which she was best known was ... / The first glimpses that we have of the notions which the Greeks possessed of the shape and the inhabitants of the earth are afforded by the poems passing ***under*** the *name* of Homer. / The Queen of Roumania is a poetess ***under*** *name* of Carmen Sylva. / old things ***under*** new *names* / sell ***under*** the *names* of brandy, whisky, and champagne. ¶I do not know any one ***with*** such a *name*. 私はそういう名の人は一人も知らない. ‖ stamp ***with*** *names* 名を押す. ¶a man ***without*** [a] *name* (=of no name) 無名の士.

P² Conrad's is an honored *name* ***among*** all Poles. コンラッドの名はポーランド人全部が尊敬している名である. ¶he gave his *name* ***as*** ... 彼は自分の名は…だといった. ‖ He made a *name* ***as*** a naturalist. 彼は博物学者として名をなした. ¶If he dies, he will leave an illustrious *name* ***behind*** [him]. 彼は死んでもかくかくたる名が後に残る. ¶What is the English *name* ***for*** "sakura"? 桜を英語で何といいますか. ‖ He has a *name* ***for*** honesty. 彼は正直だという評判だ. ‖ He has a great *name* ***for*** training horses. 彼は調馬にかけては有名だ. ¶it has its *name* ***from*** ... その名は…からきている. ¶a *name* ***in*** full=a full name 氏名. ¶He took the *name* ***of*** Anthony at his baptism. 彼は洗礼のときにアントニーという名をもらった. ‖ There was only the *name* ***of*** friendship between them. 彼らは名ばかりの友人だった. ‖ The *names* ***of*** "Punch" and Tenniel have long been synonymous. ポンチとテニエルの名は長い間切っても切れない関係を持っていた. ‖ the *name* ***of*** a number 数の名称(百と千とかいう) ‖ What is the *name* ***of*** this place? ここはどこですか. ‖ Mark a circle on the *name* ***of*** the person for whom you wish to vote. 君が選びたいと思う人の名にまる印をつけなさい.

O an author little more than a *name* ほとんど名ばかりの著者. ¶To enumerate all of the points that would be interesting to visitors to see, would be impossible, for their *names* are legion. [著者は]観光客が見ておもしろい場所を皆あげることはできない, 何しろ数が非常に多いのだから.

name, *v.* 名ずける, 称する; 指名する.

M It is ***appropriately*** *named*. それは適当な名だ. ¶it is ***fancifully*** *named* "..." それに「…」というしゃれた名がついている. ¶it was ***provisionally*** (=for the present) *named* "..." 仮にそれを「…」と命名した. ¶***so named*** from ... ... からそういう名がついた.

P Our eldest son was *named* George ***after*** his uncle. われわれの長男にはおじの名を取ってジョージとつけた. 【類】England was *named* ***after*** the Angles. / The two active volcanoes were *named* ***after*** his ships. ¶He was *named* ***as*** chairman. 彼は議長に指名された. ¶The boy is *named* ***for*** (=after) his uncle. その男子には伯父の名を取ってつけた. 【類】Rhodesia is a territory in South Africa *named* ***for*** (の名にちなんで) the late Cecil John Rhodes, by whose efforts it was added to the British Empire. ‖ *name* a day ***for*** a wedding 結婚の日を定める ‖ Winds are *named* ***for*** the direction from which they come. 風はその来る方向によって名づけられる. ¶Japanese pottery is *named* usually ***from*** the province where manufactured. 日本の陶器は通常その産地の名を取ってつける. 【類】The Cadogan Club was so *named* ***from*** Lady Cadogan, its patroness. / Calicoes were *named* ***from*** Calicut. ¶the person *named* ***in*** the document その文書に指名してある人 ‖ the beneficiary *named* ***in*** an insurance policy 保険証書に明記された保険金受取人 ‖ The wistaria was *named* ***in*** honor of Casper Wistar, an American anatomist who lived between 1761 and 1818. ウイステーリア(藤)という名は米国の解剖学者 Casper Wistar (1761-1818) を記念するために付けたのだ. ¶be *named* ***to*** chairmanship 議長に指名される.

O *Name* anything you want, it will be yours. 何でも欲しいものがあったら言いなさい, あげますから. ‖ Mr. Johnson, I presume?—Yes, that's my *name*. ジョンスンさんですね.—はあ, そうです.

name-plate, *n.* 名札.

V ***fasten*** a *name-plate* to a gate post 門柱に名札を取つける.

Q² a ***street*** *name-plate* 町名標札.

namesake, *n.* 同名の人.

Q his ***greater*** *namesake* 彼と同名のさらに有名な人.

nap, *n.* **(1)** 仮眠(ｶﾐﾝ), 昼寝.

V ***catch*** a *nap* まどろむ ‖ ***catch*** cat *naps* ちょっとうたたねする. ¶try to ***get*** a *nap* 一睡しようとする. ¶We ***played*** *nap* to keep our minds off the discomfort. 不愉快を去るため仮眠をした. ¶***take*** (=***have***) a *nap* 仮眠する, 昼寝する.

Q² take an ***evening*** (***afternoon***) *nap* よいに一睡する(午睡する). ¶take a ***short*** *nap* ちょっとまどろむ.

(2) けば.

V ***raise*** a *nap* on cloth 布にけばを立てる.

P woolen cloth ***with*** a rough (fine) *nap* けばのあらい(こまかい)らしゃ.

napkin, *n.* ナプキン.

V ***fold*** a *napkin* after eating one's dinner 食事の後にナプキン(食用の)をたたむ. ¶***lay*** one's *napkin* across one's lap ひざにナプキンを掛ける. ¶***tuck*** one's *napkin* into one's collar [食事の際など]えりの中へナプキンの端を押込む.

P He hid his intellectual talent ***under*** a *napkin*. 彼はその才を発揮しなかった.

narcotic, *n.* 麻酔剤, 催眠剤.

V ***get*** *narcotics* through illegal channel 麻薬をやみで手に入れる. ¶***smuggle*** *narcotics* from (=out of) ... …から麻酔剤を密輸入する.

P stupefy ***by*** a *narcotic* 麻酔剤で麻酔させる. ¶sleep with the aid ***of*** a *narcotic* 催眠剤で眠る.

narrate, *v.* 話す, 述べる.

M The story is ***well*** *narrated* in his new book. 彼の新著はその話を巧く述べている.

narration, *n.* 叙述.

Q a ***graphic*** *narration* 絵を見るような叙述.

narrative, *n.* 物語, 話.

V ***continuing*** his *narrative*, he said: 話を続けて彼は言った. ¶He ***gave*** a *narrative* of his journey. 彼は旅行談をやった. ¶Here my *narrative* ***ends***. ここで私の話は終る.

Q an ***animated*** *narrative* 快活な物語. ¶a ***clear*** and ***consecutive*** *narrative* 明確な連続している物語. ¶in the form of a ***connected*** *narrative* 関連した物語の形式で. ¶in a ***continuous*** *narrative* 筋の続いた物語で. ¶a ***disjointed*** *narrative* 筋道の立たない話. ¶a ***false*** *narrative* うその話, デマ. ¶a ***historical*** *narrative* 歴史的物語. ¶a ***personal*** *narrative* 身の上話. ¶a ***spirited*** and ***entertaining*** *narrative* 活気があっておもしろい話.

Q² ***Bible*** *narratives* 聖書の諸物語.

P² a *narrative* ***in*** prose (verse) 散文(韻文)の物語.

narrow, *a.* 狭い.

M be ***uncomfortably*** *narrow* せせっこましい. ¶***too*** *narrow* to pass through 狭くて通れない.

P The path is too *narrow* ***for*** a truck to pass. 路が狭過ぎてトラックが通れない. ¶He is *narrow* ***in*** opinion. 彼は

見解が狭い.

narrow, *v.* 狭くなる.

M² *narrow down* profit 利潤を少くする.

P The sea *narrows into* a strait. 海がせまって海峡になっている. ¶*narrow to* ... miles ...マイルにせばまる.

nation, *n.* 国民; 国家, 国; 人種; 民族.

V ***bring*** the *nations* into brotherly accord 諸国民を一致和合させる. ¶***build up*** a just and God-fearing *nation* 正しい敬けんな国民を作り上げる. ¶***convulse*** the *nation* 国家をかく乱する. ¶***fire*** a whole *nation* with enthusiasm 全国民の血を沸かす. ¶***guide*** the *nation* through its recent struggle その近来の争闘を切抜けて国民を指導する. ¶Washington annually ***leads*** the *nation* in lumber production. ワシントン州は木材の生産は毎年国内で第一位である. ¶the dominant ideals which ***make*** or ***unmake*** a *nation* 国民を作りもすれば滅ぼしもする支配的な理想. ¶Over fifty *nations* are ***represented*** in the population of New York. ニューヨークには五十カ国以上の国民が住んでいる. 【類】Fifty *nations* are ***represented*** by over 200 athletes in the Olympic Games. ¶ways to ***serve*** the *nation* 報国の道. ¶Prejudiced or interested writers ***vilify*** other *nations*. 偏見があるかまたはためにするところある文士は他国民を非難する.

V² The British *nation* has not ***sprung up*** in a generation. 英国民は一代で起ったものではない.

Q an ***advanced*** *nation* 先進国. ¶with ***all*** *nations* of the world 万邦とともに. ¶***Asian*** (=***Asiatic***) *nations* アジア諸国民. ¶the ***awakening*** *nations* of the East 東洋の目ざめつつある諸国民. ¶***backward*** *nations* 後進国民. ¶The Japanese are becoming a ***beer-drinking*** *nation*. 日本人はビールを飲む国民になりかけている. ¶a ***bilingual*** *nation* 二国語を話す国民. ¶lead ***Caucasian*** *nations* in ... ...において白人の先駆をなす. ¶***civilized*** *nations* 文明国民. ¶a ***conquering*** *nation* 戦勝国. ¶a ***conquered*** *nation* 敗戦国. ¶a ***conscript*** *nation* 徴兵制度の国家. ¶a ***decadent*** *nation* 退廃期の国家. ¶a ***decaying*** (=***declining***) *nation* 没落しつつある国. ¶the peoples of ***different*** *nations* 別個の国々の人々. ¶allocation of ***each*** *nation* to its proper field 各国をしてその所を得させる. ¶the highest representatives of the two great ***English-speaking*** *nations* 二大英語国民の最高代表者. ¶***every*** *nation* in the world 世界の各国民. ¶an ***exclusive*** *nation* 排外的な国家. ¶an ***exporting*** *nation* 輸出国. ¶the histories of ***extinct*** *nations* 亡びた諸国民の歴史. ¶a ***fighting*** *nation* 戦闘国民. ¶the ***foremost*** *nations* 先進国. ¶the comity of ***free*** *nations* 自由国家間の礼譲. ¶a ***friendly*** *nation* 親交国民. ¶a ***great commercial*** *nation* with world-wide interests 全世界に利害を有する大商業国. ¶an ***industrial*** *nation* 工業国. ¶***industrialized*** *nations* 産業化した国民. ¶with a methodicity characteristic of this highly ***intellectual*** *nation* このきわめて知的な国民独特の秩序性をもって. ¶***kindred*** *nations* [英国と米国のごとき]同血属の国民. ¶the ***leading*** *nations* of the world 世界の一流国民. ¶the ***major*** (***minor***) *nations* of the world 世界の大(小)国民. ¶the ***maritime*** *nations* of the world 世界の海国民. ¶the most ***favored*** *nation* 最恵国. ¶***neutral*** *nations* 中立国. ¶As an ***Occidental*** *nation* in the Orient Japan now stands alone. 東洋における西洋主義の国民として日本は今や孤立の姿である. ¶***peace-loving*** *nations* of the world 世界の平和愛好国民. ¶so ***polite*** a *nation* as France フランスのごとく礼儀ある国. ¶The English are the most ***practical*** and ***common-sense*** *nation* of the world. 英国民は世界で一番実際的で常識的な国民である. ¶***progressive*** *nations* 進歩的国民. ¶The Japanese are a ***receptive*** *nation*. 日本人は受容性に富んだ国民だ. ¶In normal times Burma is the largest ***rice-exporting*** *nation* in the world. 平年にはビルマは世界最大の米穀輸出国である. ¶***senior*** *nations* 先進国. ¶a ***small*** and ***weak*** *nation* 弱小国. ¶Japan is once again a free member of the family of ***sovereign*** *nations* 日本は再び主権国家団体の自由な一員となっている. 【類】re-establish Japan as a ***sovereign, independent*** *nation*. ¶***sport-loving*** *nations* 運動好きの国民. ¶a ***strong*** and ***well-knit*** *nation* 強大堅固の国民. ¶a ***tax-free*** *nation* 無税の国家. ¶a ***thriving*** *nation* 発展しつつある国民. ¶the ***two mighty*** *nations*, England and America 英米の二大国. ¶a ***trivial*** *nation* 小国. ¶a ***vanquished*** *nation* 敗戦国. ¶***warring*** *nations* 交戦中の国家. ¶***Western*** *nations* 西洋諸国. ¶a ***workaday*** *nation* of large families 大人口を擁してその日暮しをする国家. ¶a ***whole*** *nation* 全国民.

Q² an ***aggressor*** [*nation*] 侵略国. ¶the ***anti-Soviet*** *nations* 反ソヴィエト諸国. ¶former ***Axis satellites*** *nations* 以前枢軸国に従属した諸国. ¶the ***Big Four victor*** *nations* 四大戦勝国. ¶a ***claimant*** *nation* 有権国. ¶***cold-bath*** *nations* 冷水浴を好む国民. ¶***Cominform*** *nations* コミンフォルム所属国(共産諸国). ¶a ***conqueror*** *nation* 戦勝国. ¶a ***creditor*** (***debtor***) *nation* 債権(務)国. ¶a ***debtor*** *nation* toward Britain of about £370,000,000 英国に対して約三億七千万ポンド債務ある国. ¶the ***entente*** *nations* 協商国. ¶an ***ex-enemy*** (=former enemy) *nation* 旧敵国. ¶all ***Far East*** (=Far-Eastern) *nations* 全極東諸国. ¶a ***food-deficit*** *nation* 食料不足国. ¶the so-called "***have-not***" *nations* いわゆる「持たざる」国. ¶the citizens of the ***host*** *nation* 主催者側の国民(国際会議などの). ¶five ***key*** *nations* 五主要国. ¶a ***little island*** *nation* 小島国. ¶For a time Japan was a totally ***unprotected island*** *nation*. 日本は一時全く無援孤立の島国であった ¶a ***machine*** *nation* 広く機械を用いる国. ¶the "***Marshall plan***" *nations* マーシャル復興案適用の諸国. ¶***master*** *nations* of the day 現時の主要国民. ¶the 47 ***member*** *nations* of the UNRRA (United Nations Relief and Rehabilitation Administration) 国際連合救済復興局の四十七局員国. 【類】The Far Eastern Commission (極東委員会) is composed of eleven ***mermber*** *nations*. ¶the ***mother*** *nation* 母国. ¶***neighbor*** *nations* 隣邦. ¶the ***North Atlantic Pact*** *nations* 北大西洋条約加盟国. ¶a ***reading*** *nation* 読書好きの国民. ¶a ***rival*** *nation* 競争国. ¶Russian ***satellite*** *nations* ロシアの衛星国. ¶the ***sister*** *nations* of the British Empire 英帝国の姉妹国. ¶a ***spectator*** *nation* 傍観国(直接利害関係のない). ¶a ***sponsor*** *nation* 主催国. ¶the right of a ***victor*** *nation* 戦勝国の権利. ¶***white*** (***yellow***) *nations* 白(黄)色民族 ‖ the five ***white*** *nations* of the British Empire 英帝国の五白色民族(インドを除く). ¶among the ***world*** *nations* 世界諸国中.

P ***Across*** the *nation* labor demanded "cost-of-living" increases. 全国にわたって労働者は生活費の増加を要求した. ¶co-operation ***among*** the *nations* of the world 世界の国民間の協力 ‖ a millionaire ***among*** *nations* 富国. ¶Japan is ***behind*** European *nations* in the matter of ... 日本は...では欧州諸国に遅れている. ¶men ***of*** our own *nation* われわれ同胞 ‖ be received into the comity ***of*** *nations* 国際親交国の仲間に入れられる. ¶a cordial understanding ***with*** other *nations*. 他国民と意思のそ通.

P² a *nation* ***in*** arms 武装した国民. ¶The Swiss are the *nation* ***of*** hotel-keepers. スイスは旅館経営の盛んな国である. 【類】a *nation* ***of*** newspaper readers / the *nations* ***of*** Christendom=Christian nations.

national, *n.* 国民(一人); 同胞.

Q Occupation and other ***Allied*** *nationals*. 占領諸国民(米国人及びその同盟諸国民). ¶***French*** *nationals* in China 在中国フランス人. ¶one's ***own*** *nationals* 同胞.

Q² a ***fellow*** *national* (=countryman *or* a compatriot) 同国人. ¶a ***third-power*** *national* 第三国人. ¶***United Nations*** *nationals* 国連所属の諸国民.

P² *nationals* ***from*** various parts of the world 各国から集った人々. 【類】*nationals* ***from*** England, Germany, France, Italy, Brazil, and America. ¶*nationals* ***of*** the following countries (=States) 次の国々の人. ¶a consul's powers ***over*** his own *nationals* その国人に対する領事の権限.

nationalism, *n.* 国家主義.

V ***preach*** French *nationalism* フランス国家主義を唱道する.

Q ***extreme*** *nationalism* = ulta-nationalism 超国家主義. ¶***sane*** (***reasonable***) *nationalism* まじめ(理論的)な国家主義. ¶***sentimental*** *nationalism* 感情的国家主義.

nationalist, *n.* 国家主義者.

Q a very ***ardent French*** *nationalist* きわめて熱烈なフランス国家主義者.

nationality, *n.* 国民; 国民性; 国籍.

V ***acquire*** foreign *nationality* 外国の国籍を獲得する. ¶May I ***ask*** your *nationality*, sir? あなたのお国はどちらですか. ¶***betray*** one's *nationality* 自分の国籍を見すかされる. ¶***change*** one's *nationality* 国籍を変える, 帰化する. ¶***constitute*** a *nationality* 国家を組織する. ¶***disguise*** one's *nationality* その国籍をいつわる. ¶***guess*** the *nationality* of ... ...の国籍をいい当てる. ¶He ***lost*** his American *nationality*. 彼はアメリカの国籍を失った. ¶***regain*** one's *nationality* 国籍を回復する. ¶a crowd ***representing*** almost every *nationality* in Europe 欧州におけるほとんどあらゆる国から来ている群衆 ‖ Fourteen or fifteen *nationalities* were ***represented*** there. そこに十四五カ国の人がいた. ¶***reveal*** one's *nationality* 知らず識らずその国籍を示す.

Q men of ***all*** *nationalities* 各国の人々. 【類】people of ***all*** *nationalities* living together in New York City / They are of ***all nationalities.*** ¶foreigners of ***different*** *nationalities* 国籍の違った外国人. ¶Jews of ***divers*** *nationalities* まちまちの国籍のユダヤ人. ¶a ***double*** *nationality* 二重の国籍. ¶***dual*** *nationality* 二重国籍. ¶a meeting composed of ***every*** *nationality* under the sun 世界の各国民からなる会合. ¶ladies and gentlemen of ***exotic*** *nationality* 外国の紳士淑女たち. ¶visitors of ***foreign*** *nationality* 外国人の客. ¶He is of ***French*** (***German***, ***Irish***) *nationality*. 彼はフランス人(など)だ. ¶There is ***no*** *nationality* or politics in business. 実業には国境も政治もない. ¶men of the ***same*** *nationality* 同国人. ¶a plane of ***unknown*** *nationality* 国籍不明の飛行機. ¶men of ***various*** *nationalities* さまざまの国人.

P exhibits grouped ***according to*** *nationality* 国別にした出品. ¶delegates gathered ***from*** twenty-six *nationalities* 二十六カ国から集まった代表者. ¶Americans ***in*** *nationality*, but Germans in blood 国籍はアメリカ人だが血統はドイツ人. ¶persons ***of*** British *nationality* 英国民 ‖ regardless ***of*** *nationality* 国籍に関せず. 【類】***of*** one's own *nationality* / a melting-pot (るつぼ) ***of*** all races and *na-*

P² the *nationality* ***of*** a ship 船の国籍. ⌊*tionalities*.

nationalization, *n.* 国有化.

V ***extend*** *nationalization* into the fields of ... 何々の方面に国有化を拡張する. 「支持者たち.

Q² the supporters of ***land*** *nationalization* 土地国有化の

P² the *nationalization* ***of*** key industries (railways) 重要産業(など)の国有化.

nationalize, *v.* 国営化する. ⌊産業(など)の国有化.

O *nationalize* key industries (railroads, bus service) 重要産業(など)を国営にする.

native, *n.* 土人, 土着の人; 原産物.

V ***evangelize*** the *natives* 土人に伝道する.

Q ***brawny*** *natives* 屈強の土民. ¶a ***returned*** *native* 帰朝者. ¶The cherry-tree is a ***true*** *native* of Japan. 桜は日本が本家本元だ.

P² Are you a *native* ***of*** this place? ここのお生れですか. ‖ The turkey is a *native* ***of*** North America. 七面鳥は北米

native, *a.* 土産の, 原産の. ⌊の原産である.

P Potato is *native* ***to*** America. じゃが芋はアメリカが原産地だ. ‖ persons *native* ***to*** the region 土着の人々 ‖ festivals *native* ***to*** Japan 日本固有の祭. 【類】Beri-beri (かっけ) is *native* (=particular) ***to*** Japan. / be *native* ***to*** our air (わ

natural, *a.* 当然の; 生来の. ⌊が国土).

M ***quite*** (=***perfectly***) *natural* きわめて当然な.

P It is *natural* ***for*** him to think so. 彼としてはそう考えるのが当然だ. ¶sagacity *natural* ***to*** the mind 生れつきの

naturalism, *n.* 自然主義. ⌊利口.

Q be anxious to express thought in language of the ***closest*** *naturalism* 最も自然の言葉で思想を表現しようと努

naturalization, *n.* 帰化. ⌊める.

Q ***collective*** *naturalization* resulting from transfers of territory 領土移譲による集団帰化.

P a British subject ***by*** *naturalization* 帰化英国人.

P² the *naturalization* ***of*** aliens 外人の帰化. 「る.

naturalize, *v.* 国籍に入れる, 帰化させる; [独立]国家にす

P The Poles were *naturalized* ***after*** the war of 1914-18. 第一次大戦後ポーランドは独立国家になった. ¶He was *naturalized* ***as*** a Japanese subject. 彼は日本に帰化した. 【類】These are not yet *naturalized* ***as*** English words (英語化). ¶a Japanese *naturalized* ***from*** British birth 日本に帰化した英人. ¶He became *naturalized* ***in*** the United States in 1921. 彼は一九二一年に米国に帰化した. ¶Sporting terms have been *naturalized* ***in*** many languages. スポーツ用語は多くの国語中に移植されている. 「る.

O become a *naturalized* British subject 帰化英国人とな

nature, *n.* 性質, 本性; 質(たち), 種類; 天性; 体力; 自然; 当然の理.

V ***approach*** *Nature* with reverence 敬けんの念をもって自然に接する. ¶***arouse*** one's better *nature* 本心に立帰らせる. ¶***Ascertain*** the *nature* and extent of the damage sustained. 受けた損害の性質及び範囲を確かめる. ¶The poet ***beautifies*** all *nature*. 詩人は一切の自然を美化する. ¶***betray*** their real *nature* 彼らの本性を現わす. ¶*Nature* is ***commanded*** by obeying her.—Bacon. 自然を支配するにはまずこれに服従すべきである. ¶***copy*** (=***imitate***) *nature* 自然を模倣する. ¶***ease nature*** 便通する. ¶***flout*** *nature* 自然を侮る. ¶***harness*** *nature* [水力・風力などの]自然力を動力に利用する. ¶It ***has*** the *nature* of glue. それにはにかわの性質がある. ‖ Man ***has*** a dual *nature*. 人間は二重の性質を備えている. ¶This is ***following*** *nature*. これは自然の法則にかなっている. ¶***improve*** *nature* 自然を利用する. ¶***let*** *nature* ***take*** its own course 自然の成行に任せる. ¶Long and painful practice ***makes*** second *nature*. 長い間の困難な習慣は第二の天性となる. ¶failing to ***recognize*** the *nature* of the occasion 場所柄も考えずに. ¶***relieve*** *nature* 小(大)便をする. ¶***reveal*** one's (its) real *nature* その化の皮を現わす. ¶the folly of ***setting*** *nature* at naught 自然を無視するの愚. ¶He ***stated*** the *nature* of his errand. 彼は使の用向を述べた. ¶***suit*** one's *nature* 性に合う. ¶Such diet will not ***support*** *nature*. こんな食物では体がもたない. ¶without ***taking*** the *nature* of the occasion into consideration 場所柄も考えないで. ¶By means of the pot-plant we ***transfer*** *nature* to the inside of the house. 盆栽を飾って自然を屋内に持込む. ¶Work has a singular power to ***unfold*** and ***develop*** our *nature*. 仕事にはわれわれの天性を開発してこれを発展させる特殊の力がある.

V² *Nature* ***failed*** at last. とうとう体力が続かなくなった. ¶a beautiful face through which a beautiful *nature* ***shines*** 美しい天性に輝く美しい顔. ¶*nature* ***teaches*** us to ..., but civilization dictates that ... 自然はわれわれに...せよと教えるが一方文明は...を命令する. ¶*Nature* ***wakes***. 自然が目ざめる.

Q ***All*** *nature* looks gay. 万象ことごとく陽気に見える. ¶a ***base*** *nature* 人格の下劣な人. ¶***bounteous*** (=***bountiful***) *nature* 寛仁な性質. ¶a ***brutal*** *nature* 獣性の人. ¶The ***ceremonial*** *nature* on the occasion made free conversation impossible. 儀式の場所なので勝手に話をすることができなかった. ¶soils of ***clayey*** *nature* 粘土質の土. ¶a man of his ***cold*** *nature* 彼のように冷淡な性分の人. ¶medals and diplomas of ***commendatory*** *nature* 推奨的性質の記念章と免許状. ¶owing to the ***confidential*** *nature* of the papers 書類が秘密のものであるために. ¶a ***constructive*** *nature* 建設的性質. ¶of a ***contaminating*** *nature* 悪化性の. ¶of a ***damaging*** *nature* 損害を与える性質の. ¶of a ***dangerous*** *nature* 危険性の. ¶of a ***destructive*** *nature* 破壊的性質の. ¶Cats and dogs have entirely ***different*** *natures*. 犬とねこは各々全く違った天性を持っている. ¶goods of a ***dutiable*** *nature* [関税など]有税品. ¶matters of an ***economic*** or ***financial*** *nature* 経済または財政関係の事項. ¶of an ***erotic*** *nature* 性欲的な. ¶of ***evil*** *nature* たちの悪い. ¶matter of a ***fictitious*** and ***factitious*** *nature* 虚構及び技巧の事柄. ¶***fundamental*** *nature* 本質. ¶He is of a ***generous*** *nature*. 彼はおう揚な質(たち)だ. ¶He is [of] a ***gentle*** *nature*. 彼はおとなしい人だ. ¶***good*** *nature* 温良, 温順. ¶***gross-grained*** *natures* 粗野な性質の人々. ¶appeal to our ***higher*** and ***nobler*** *nature* われわれの一層高尚な本性に訴える. ¶owing to the very ***hilly*** *nature* of the country その地方には非常に丘が多いので. ¶a part of ***human*** *nature* 人情の一部. 【類】That is the way ***human*** *nature* works (人情の動き). / Hindus ***human*** *nature*. / ***human*** *nature* in a variety of aspects ‖ ***Human*** *nature* forbids. 情において忍びない. ¶***ill*** *nature* 意地悪. ¶two ***impassioned*** and ***enthusiastic*** *natures* 感激して熱心な両人. ¶of an ***impulsive*** *nature* 短慮な. ¶of an ***inflammable*** *nature* 激しやすい性質の. ¶plans of an ***impractical*** *nature* 実用に適しない諸計画. ¶one's ***inner*** *nature* 人の内心. ¶a ***kindly***, ***good-humored*** *nature* 親切気があってお人よしの. ¶numerous works of a ***kindred*** *nature* それに似寄った性質の種々の作品. ¶... and other matters of a ***like*** *nature* ...及びこれに類する他の事柄. ¶the ***moral*** *nature* 徳性. ¶of a ***negative*** *nature* 陰性の. ¶the ***noncommercial*** *nature* of the enterprise その事業の非商業的な性質. ¶be not of an ***official*** *nature* 公式のものではない. ¶music of an ***Oriental*** *nature* 東洋

風の音楽. ¶be of a ***permanent nature*** 永続的なものである. ¶gossip of a ***personal nature*** 個人関係の世間話. ¶a ***pessimistic nature*** 苦労性. ¶a work of a ***philosophical nature*** 哲学的の書. ¶of a ***political nature*** 政治的性質の. ¶useful information of a ***practical nature*** 有益な実際的知識. ¶determine the ***precise nature*** of ... …本質を確かめる. ¶settle where *nature* was ***propitious*** 自然の利のある所に定住する. ¶by reason of its ***protean nature***［他に職業がありかたわら売色をしている場合など］一定の形を備えていないので. ¶the ***puerile nature*** of these pieces of research これら研究のたわいなさ. ¶hues of ***quieter nature*** もっと落ちついた色合. ¶He is of a ***quieter*** and more ***retiring nature***. 彼はもっと静かで出しゃばらない. ¶***rational nature*** 理性. ¶one's ***real nature*** その本性. ¶of ***receptive nature*** 感じやすい性質の. ¶a ***reserved nature*** 底意の知れない人. ¶a ***responsive nature*** 感じやすい性質. ¶be a wrench to our ***softer natures*** 人情の忍び得ないことである. ¶be of the ***same nature*** 類を同じくするものである. ¶***sanguine natures*** 楽天的な人々. ¶the ***savage nature*** of the wild beasts of the jungle ジャングルの野獣の蛮性. ¶words of a ***scientific*** and ***technical nature*** 科学的及び専門的の言葉. ¶Habit is a ***second nature***. 習慣は第二の天性である.【類】Newspaper-reading has become, as we say, ***second nature***. ¶a ***sensitive, introspective nature*** 敏感で内省的な性格. ¶maladies of a ***serious nature*** 重い病気‖problems of a very ***serious nature*** attending upon ... …に付随するきわめて重大な諸問題. ¶a ***shy, timid*** and ***retiring nature*** 小胆でおく病で引込み勝ちな人. ¶a work of a ***similar nature*** 同様な作品. ¶persons of ***small natures*** 器の小さい人々. ¶He was of a ***sociable*** and ***kindly nature***. 彼はつき合いやすく親切な性質であった. ¶***Some natures*** cannot appreciate poetry. 詩歌を解しないたちの人がある. ¶foods of a ***starchy nature*** でん粉性の食物. ¶they are of ***such*** a *nature* that ... それは…といった風(性質)のものである. ¶her ***sunny*** and ***light-hearted nature*** 彼女の陽気で気軽な性分. ¶We instinctively look up to a ***superior nature***. われわれは人物のすぐれた人を自然尊敬する. ¶His duties are largely of a ***supervisory nature***. 彼の仕事は主に監督といった性質のものだ. ¶of a ***temporary nature*** 一時的性質の. ¶an undertaking of a ***thankless nature*** 縁の下の力持ち的な仕事. ¶betray one's ***treacherous nature*** その陰険な本性を現わす. ¶***two opposite natures*** 二つの反対の性質. ¶of ***unknown nature*** えたいの知れない. ¶He was of a ***versatile nature***. 彼は融通のきくたちだ. ¶of a ***vicious nature*** 悪質の. ¶from the ***very nature*** of things その性質上.【類】it is indeed implied in the ***very nature*** of the thing that ...

Q² the ***animal nature*** 獣性. ¶the humorous and appealing aspects of ***cat nature*** ねこの性質のこっけいで人の心を引付ける方面. ¶parents who do not know ***child nature*** 小供の本性を知らない親. ¶The discussion was largely of a ***courtesy nature***. 討議は主に儀礼的のものであった. ¶a masterpiece of ***Mother Nature*** 大自然の一大傑作. ¶the ***public utility nature*** of the enterprise その事業の公益性.

P ***according to*** the *nature* of case 事件の性質によって. ¶But this is ***against nature***. しかしこれは不自然だ.‖***against*** human *nature* 人間性に反して. ¶***by*** the *nature* of his office その役柄から言って. ¶It is made ***by nature***, not by art. それは芸術でなく自然の作ったものだ.‖he is endowed ***by nature*** for ... 彼は生得…に向いている‖He is frank (reserved) ***by nature***. 彼は生来淡白(内気)だ.【類】Man is ***by nature*** a social animal. / strong (weak, timid, brave, frank) ***by nature*** / I am ***by nature*** very methodical (きちょうめん). / Children are imitative ***by nature***. / Men, at their birth, are ***by nature*** radically good. / ***By nature***（地形から言って）Canada belongs to America. / an orator ***by nature*** or art. ¶painting ***from nature*** 写生.【類】sketch (draw, paint) ***from nature***‖***From*** its *nature*, there is no plural in the German indefinite article. その性質上ドイツ語の不定冠詞には複数がない. ¶a change ***in nature*** 性質の変化‖There is, ***in nature***, such a thing as hell.［世に］事実上地獄といったようなものがある.‖It is not ***in*** my *nature* to do such cruel things. 私の性質としてそんな残酷なことはできない.‖***in*** (＝by *or* from) the *nature* of things 物の道理として, 道理上‖The compensation was ***in*** the *nature* of a fee. その賠償金は報酬の性質を帯びていた.【類】changes which are more ***in*** the *nature* of adaptations and improvements than revolutions. ¶the beauties ***of*** *nature* 自然の美‖She is ***of*** quiet *nature* 彼女は天性温和.【類】things ***of*** this *nature*. ¶It is the ***nature of*** fire to burn. 燃えるのが火の本性だ.‖The injury is ***of*** a permanent *nature*. その傷害は永続性のものである.‖The children were all in a state of nature, so to speak. 子供たちはまるで生れたまま(丸裸)だった. ¶This picture is true ***to nature***. この絵は真に迫っている.

P² *nature of* injuries 負傷の性質.

naught, nought, *n.* 皆無, ゼロ.

V *make naught* of ... …が眼中にない.

P He set my advice ***at naught***. 彼は僕の忠告を無視した.【類】set a law ***at naught***. ¶***for naught*** (＝nothing) むだに. ¶bring one's kindness ***to naught*** 人の親切を無にする‖You have brought all my labors ***to naught***. 私の折角の骨折りが君のために徒労になった.‖My efforts have come ***to naught***. 僕の努力は水泡に帰した.‖He set ***to naught*** any advice or suggestion from outside. 彼は人の忠言や提言を無視した. ¶A thousand is written ***with*** a one and three *naughts*. 千は一と三つの零とで書き表わす.

nausea, *n.* むかつき, はき気.

V *cause nausea* はき気を催させる. ¶***feel nausea*** 胸がむかつく. ¶***provoke nausea*** はき気を催させる.

nauseate, *v.* はき気を催す.

P *nauseate* ***at*** food (work) 食物(など)で胸が悪くなる.

nauseous, *a.* はき気を催すような.

P The food is *nauseous* ***to*** the taste. その食物ははき気を催すような味がする.

O That makes me feel *nauseous*. それを見ると(聞くと)胸がむかつく.

navigable, *a.* 船が通れる.

P The river is *navigable* ***for*** large steamers. その川は大汽船が通れる.

navigate, *v.* 航行する.

M *navigate* ***home*** 復航する.

P *navigate* ***between*** two places［船が］両地間を航行する. ¶*navigate* ***on*** a river［船が］河上を航行する. ¶*navigate* ***under*** water 潜航する.

navigation, *n.* 航海, 航行, 運航; 航海術.

V *Navigation* is now ***closed*** for the season. 当季の航海はもう休航になっている. ¶***establish*** aerial *navigation* between New York and Liverpool ニューヨーク・リヴァプール間に航空を開始する. ¶The *navigation* is not ***expected*** to be open for some days yet. 航行はここ数日は開始しそうもない. ¶They built lighthouses to ***facilitate*** the *navigation* of the seas. 航海を容易ならしめるために灯台を建てた. ¶The stream ***hinders*** its *navigation*. 水流がその航行を妨げる. ¶***open up*** steam *navigation* between ... and ... …間に汽船航行を開始する. ¶*Navigation* (Traffic) will shortly be ***resumed***. 航行(交通)は近く再開されるだろう. ¶All *navigation* is now ***stopped*** on account of the ice. 結氷のため航行はすべて停止されている. ¶***study navigation*** 航海術を学ぶ. ¶*Navigation* is ***suspended*** in consequence of the lowness of water in the river. 河水が少ないので航行は当分中止.

V² before the *navigation* ***closes*** 航行の終止前に. ¶as soon as the *navigation* ***opens*** 航行が開かれるや否や.

Q ***aerial*** *navigation* 航空術, 航空.

Q² the resumption of ***full-scale*** *navigation* on the Great Lakes 大湖上の完全な航行の再開. ¶***inland*** (＝***internal***) *navigation* 内海航行. ¶***ocean*** *navigation* 遠洋航海. ¶***smooth-water*** *navigation* 平水航行. ¶a history of ***steam*** *navigation* 汽船交通の歴史.

P² *Navigation* ***on*** the Hudson River has at last been closed by ice. ハドソン河の航行は結氷のため遂に停止された. ¶*Navigation* ***through*** the canal is suspended. 運河の通航は中止している.

navigator, *n.* 航海士.

Q an ***aerial*** *navigator* 航空士. ¶a ***seasoned*** *navigator* 熟練した航海士.

navy, *n.* 海軍; 艦隊, 船隊.

V ***build*** a new *navy* 新艦隊を建造する. ¶***enter*** (＝***join***) the *navy* 海軍にはいる. ¶She ***has*** a magnificent *navy*. その国には堂々たる海軍がある. ¶***maintain*** a *navy* 海軍を維持する. ¶We ***organized*** our *navy* on an English model. われわれは英国にのっとってわが海軍を編成した.

Q a midshipman in the ***British Navy*** 英国海軍の士官候補生. ¶has a ***magnificent navy*** 壮大な海軍を保有する. ¶a

mercantile navy 商船隊. ¶a *powerful navy* 有力な海軍. ¶a *strong navy* 強大な海軍. ¶a *volunteer navy* 義勇艦隊.
Q² the ships of the ***British merchant navy*** 英国商船隊の船舶.
P He serves ***in*** the *navy*. 彼は海軍に勤めている. 【類】an officer ***in*** the *navy*=a navy officer.

near, *a., ad., prep.* 近い(く); ほとんど.
M ***as near*** as I could guess 私の察する所では. ¶He lives ***quite near***. 彼はごく近くに住んでいる. ¶He came ***very near*** being drowned. 彼はすんでのことにおぼれる所だった. ‖ The surmise comes ***very near*** the truth. その推察は当らずといえども遠からずだ.
P be *near* ***at*** hand 手近にある. ¶The hotel is *near* ***by*** the station. 旅館は駅の近くだ. ¶*near* ***in*** place (time) 場所(時間)が近い. ¶The houses stand *near* (=close) ***to*** each other. 家が立込んでいる. ‖ come (go) *near* ***to*** ... すんでのとこで...するところだ. 【類】They all came *near* [*to*] ruining themselves (身の破滅). ‖ The scheme is very *near* ***to*** achievement. その計画は成就しかかっている. ‖ I live *nearer* ***to*** the school than you. 僕は君より学校に近い.
O The sun was *near* setting. 太陽は没しようとしていた. ‖ He was *near* losing his life. 彼は死ぬところだった. ‖ the great English writers and the *near* great イギリスの大作家並に二流の大家 ‖ He came *near* being drowned. 彼はすんでのとこで溺れるとこだった. ¶It was *near* six o'clock. 六時に近かった.

near, *v.* 近づく.
M The ship was ***rapidly nearing*** the land. 同船は刻々陸地に近づいていた.
O The work is *nearing* completion. その事業は完成に近づいている.

neat, *a.* きちんとした, ちゃんとした.
M She is ***always neat*** and tidy. 彼女はいつもきちんとしている.
P *neat* ***in*** appearance 風さいのちゃんとした.

necessary, *n.* 必要品.
V If you ***have*** the *necessaries* of life, do not complain. 生活必需品をもっているなら不平を言うな. ¶He has enough money to ***obtain*** the *necessaries* of life. 彼は生活必需品を得るだけの金は持っている. ¶***provide*** the *necessary* 必要な物資を提供する.
Q ***all*** *necessaries* for a jobbing forge 賃仕事をする鍛冶場の全備品. ¶the ***bare*** *necessaries* of life ようよう間に合うだけの日用品. 【類】the ***barest*** *necessary* of life. ¶***daily*** *necessaries* 日用品. ¶***elementary*** *necessaries* 根本的必要品.
Q² ***household*** *necessaries* 家庭日用品.

necessary, *a.* 必要な.
M It is ***absolutely*** *necessary* for you to go. 君が行くのが絶対に必要だ. ‖ No alterations should be made unless ***absolutely*** *necessary*. 絶対的必要でない限り変更すべきでない. ¶it is not ***always*** (=entirely) *necessary* to us that ... ...することは必ずしも(絶対に)必要とは限らない. ¶***hardly*** *necessary* ほとんど必要のない. ¶***highly*** *necessary* 大いに必要な. ¶***imperatively*** *necessary* ぜひ必要な. ¶be rendered ***indispensably*** *necessary* 必要欠くべからざるものとなる. ¶we think it ***most*** *necessary* that ... ...はきわめて必要だと私は思う. 【類】what is ***most*** *necessary* in life is to ... ¶be ***positively*** *necessary* ぜひ必要である. ¶render it ***strictly*** *necessary* to ... ...することを必須とする.
P Was it *necessary* ***for*** you to go yesterday? 君はきのう行かなければならなかったのか. ‖ all the appurtenances *necessary* ***for*** house-keeping 世帯道具一切. 【類】things *necessary* ***for*** our daily life / Decision is *necessary* ***for*** a commander. / It is *necessary* ***for*** you to obey. / Passports are *necessary* ***for*** all who visit this country. ¶great care is *necessary* ***in*** ... ...には大いに注意を要する. ¶Sleep (=To sleep) is *necessary* ***to*** health. 睡眠は健康に必要だ. 【類】It is *necessary* ***to*** the future of the country. / Repose (休息) is *necessary* ***to*** hard work.

necessity, *n.* 必要; 切迫; 要件; 必要物.
V ***accomplish*** a natural *necessity*=respond to the call of nature 小(大)便をする. ¶I cannot too strongly ***advise*** the *necessity* of ... 私は...の必要をいかに強調しても差支えない. ¶this ***avoids*** *necessity* of ... これで...の必要がなくなる. ¶an income just barely enough to ***buy*** the *necessities* of life 辛うじて日用品が買えるだけの収入. ¶***emphasize*** the *necessity* for preserving our natural resources わが天然資源保存の必要を力説する. ¶***feel*** the *necessity* of ... ...の必要を感じる. ¶fully ***grasp*** the *necessity* of ... ...の必要を十分のみ込む. ¶We cannot ***ignore*** the *necessity* of the times. 時勢の急務を無視することはできない. ¶***meet*** immediate *necessities* 眼前の必要に応じる. ¶The *necessity* of going is thus ***obviated***. だから行くには及ばない. ¶***preclude*** the *necessity* of ... ...の必要がないようにする. ¶***realize*** the *necessity* of ... ...の必要をさとる. ¶***recognize*** the *necessity* for ... ...の必要を認める. ¶***relieve*** their pressing *necessities* 彼らの非常な困窮を救う. ¶***remove*** the *necessity* for ... ...の必要を除く. ¶***save*** the *necessity* of ... ...の必要がなくなる. ¶I do not ***see*** the *necessity* of ... 私には...の必要が認められない. ¶He ***succoured*** my *necessity* by a well-timed assistance. 彼は折よく僕の窮乏を救ってくれた. ¶***suit*** the changing *necessities* 新しい要求に応じる. ¶***supply*** the barest *necessities* ぜひ必要な物だけを給与する.
V² when the *necessity* ***arises*** 必要な場合に ‖ should the *necessity* ***arise*** 万一その必要が起れば. 【類】if ever the *necessity* ***arises***. ¶unless *necessity* ***compels*** (***prompts***) us 必要に迫られなければ. ¶except *necessity* ***drives*** 必要にかられる場合の外は.
Q It is an ***absolute*** *necessity* for the beginners. それは初学者には絶対に必要である. ‖ Unless compelled by ***absolute*** *necessity* 絶対必要ということでなければ. ¶Is there ***any*** *necessity* for ...? ...の必要があるか. ¶the ***bare*** *necessities* of life ほんの生活必需品. 【類】supply the ***barest*** *necessities*. ¶***basic*** *necessities* 基本的必需品. ¶suit the ***changing*** *necessities* 変遷する必要に対応する. ¶a matter of ***cold financial*** *necessity* 全くの財政上の問題. ¶Armies and navies are the world's most ***costly*** *necessity*. 陸海軍は世界の最も費用のかかる必要物である. ¶a ***crying*** *necessity* 焦眉(び)の急. ¶the ***day-to-day*** *necessity* of writing 日々執筆するの必要. ¶when ***dire*** *necessity* arises ぜひそうしなくてはならない場合に ‖ he was driven by ***dire*** (=sheer) *necessity* to ... 彼はやむを得ず...した. ¶I am under the ***disagreeable*** *necessity* of ... 私は...しなければならないという具合の悪い立場にある. ¶Religion is an ***eternal*** *necessity* of human nature. 宗教は人間性が永久に求める所のものだ. ¶What back-to-the-land propaganda failed to do in twenty years, ***economic*** *necessity* accomplished in six months. 土に返れの宣伝が二十年かかってできなかったことを経済的要求は六カ月でしとげた. ¶It is of ***ever-increasing*** *necessity*. それはますます必要になりつつある. ¶articles of the ***first*** *necessity* 第一に必要な品々. ¶the ***first*** *necessity* of being a poet is that one should be ... 詩人たるべき第一の資格はその人が...であるべきであるということである. ¶There is ***great*** *necessity* for ... ...が大いに必要である. ¶an ***imperative*** *necessity* まぬかれ得ない必要 ‖ I am under the ***imperative*** *necessity* of ... 私はぜひ...しなければならない. 【類】a matter of ***imperative*** *necessity*. ¶***insistent*** *necessity* for ... ...の根強い必要. ¶a ***national*** *necessity* 国家の必要. ¶To him alcoholic drink is an ***organic*** *necessity*. 彼は酒を飲まないと体の具合が悪い. ¶a ***painful*** *necessity* 苦しいが(やむを得ない)必要なこと. ¶suffer under the ***perpetual*** *necessity* of ... 絶えず...が必要なのに悩む. ¶for the gratification of the "***physical*** *necessities*" of men 人類の物質的要求を満足させるために. ¶Talking seems to be almost a ***physiological*** *necessity* to some women. おしゃべりはある女にとっては生理的必要があるらしい. ¶a ***positive*** *necessity* 絶対的必要. ¶***pressing economic*** *necessities* 差迫る経済上の必要. ¶articles of ***primary*** *necessity* 主要な必需品. ¶It is a ***prime*** *necessity*. それは主要物だ. ¶Even in Spain the study of English became a ***recognized*** *necessity*. スペインですらも英語研究の必要が認められて来た. ¶suddenly overcome by a ***sexual*** *necessity* 性欲にかられて. ¶from ***sheer*** *necessity* 万やむを得ず. ¶the ***social*** *necessity* of prostitution 売笑の社会的必要. ¶***special*** *necessities* of the regions 該地方独特の事情. ¶an ***unavoidable*** *necessity* 避くべからざる必要. ¶an ***unhappy*** *necessity* おもしろ(うれし)くない必要. ¶as a matter of ***unpleasant*** *necessity* [やらなければならないので]いやいやながら. ¶be in a state of ***urgent*** *necessity* 差迫った必要の下にある. ¶the ***vital*** *necessity* of ... ...の根本的必要.
Q² The telephone is now a ***household*** *necessity*. 電話は今日では家庭に必要な物だ ‖ ***household*** *necessities* 家庭日用品. 【類】become a ***household*** *necessity*. ¶a ***war*** *nec-*

essity 戦時の必要.

P He was driven (=compelled) by necessity to change the plan. 彼はせっぱ詰って計画を変更した. ‖ unless compelled by absolute necessity 万やむを得ない場合の外は. ¶from (=out of) necessity やむを得ず. ¶live in necessities 貧しく暮らす. ¶in accordance with the necessities of the times 時勢の急務に応じて. ¶in case of necessity 必要な場合に. ¶It must of necessity be so. ぜひそうならざるを得ない. ‖ A small vocabulary is almost of necessity a vague vocabulary. 語彙が少ないと必然的に表現が不明確になる. ‖ It does not of necessity bring increased efficiency in its train. それは必ずしも効果の増進を伴うものでない. 【類】 He will of necessity hear what you have to say. ¶out of necessity 必要上. ¶through necessity 余儀なく. ¶yield (=submit) to necessity しかたがないとあきらめる ‖ He has been reduced to necessity. 彼は貧乏になった. ¶I am under the necessity of leaving home. 私は余儀なく家出しなければならない. 【類】 His little store of money began to melt (そろそろ欠乏し出した) under the necessities of his wife and family. ¶He is faced with the urgent necessity of ... ing. 彼は...の急務に直面している.

P[2] There will be no necessity for that. その必要はなかろう. ‖ I cannot too strongly urge upon young men the necessity for ...ing. ...の必要は青年にはいくら強調してもよい. 【類】 The necessity for ... is absolutely imperative. / There is a necessity for immediate action. ¶the necessities of the country この国の窮状 ‖ the necessity of sacrificing one part of womanhood to preserve the rest 女性の一部を犠牲にして他を保護するの必要. 【類】 he has seen clearly, and urged upon the nation, the necessity of ... ¶Space is a necessity to the existence of matter. 空間は物質の存在に取っての一要件である. 【類】 Trees and fresh air are necessities (必要物) to his constitution. / Death is a necessity (必然) to life.

neck, *n.* 首.

V bend the neck 首をこごめる. ¶break one's neck 頸(けい)骨を折る ‖ break the neck of the day's work 一日の仕事の大部分を終る. ¶crane one's neck to see ... 首を延ばして...を見ようとする. ¶She embraced his neck (=fell upon his neck *or* threw her arms round his neck). 彼女は彼の首に抱きついた. ¶I have a stiff neck. 私は首がこわばっている. ¶place her neck under the domestic yoke [召使など]主人の家庭の束縛を受ける. ¶risk one's neck 危険に身をさらす, 危険を冒す. ¶stretch one's neck 首を延ばす. ¶wring the neck of a hen めんどりの首をしめる. ¶His neck is sunk in his shoulders. 彼は首が短かい.

Q a man with heavy neck and chin がっちりした首とあごのある人. ¶a long, slender neck 長い細いくび. ¶a scraggy neck やせこけた首. ¶with a thick neck 太い首をした. ¶In European folk-lore the thick, bull neck is regarded as a sign of strong sexuality. 欧州の俗説では太(ふと)い首は性欲おう盛の印と見なされている.

P She put her arms about his neck. 女は彼の首を抱いた. ¶seize a person by the neck 人の首っ玉をつかまえる ‖ win a race by a neck 首の長さだけ早くゴールに入る. ¶He was stabbed in the neck with a knife. 彼はナイフで首を刺された. ¶take a person by the scruff of the neck えり首をつかまえる ‖ the nape of the neck うなじ, えり首 ‖ the two arteries of the neck 二つの頸(けい)動脈. ¶The poor mother fell on her daughter's neck. 不びんな母親は娘の首をだきしめた. ¶wear a collar round one's neck 首のまわりにカラーを着ける. ¶plunge into the water up to one's neck 首の所まで水の中に飛込む.

P[2] the neck of a bottle=a bottleneck 徳利のくび.

necklace, *n.* ネックレース.

V She wears a necklace. 彼女は首飾りをつけている.

Q[2] a negligee necklace 略服用のネックレース.

necktie, *n.* ネクタイ. → tie.

V tie a necktie ネクタイを結ぶ.

Q Your necktie is crooked. あなたのえり飾りがゆがんでいる.

need, *n.* 必要; 急場; 必要物; 困窮.

V do one's needs 必要の仕事をする; 大小便をする. ¶emphasize the need for ... ...の必要を強調する. ¶The need for ... was envisaged at the outset. 真先に...の必要が認識された. ¶feel the need of better education もっと高い教育の必要を感じる ‖ feel a need of reliable information on ... ...に関する信頼すべき報道の必要を感じる ‖ He was beginning to feel the need of a respite from his labors. 彼は静養の必要を感じ始めた. ¶fill a new-felt need 新たに感じた必要を満たす. ¶fit the needs of today 現時の必要に適する. ¶we have need to be proud of ... われわれは...を誇りとすべきだ ‖ I have need of money (a friend). 私は金(友人)が欲しい. 【類】 we have most need of ... / You have no need of ... / You have no need to be ashamed of. ¶indicate and supply the needs 入用物を指摘しかつ供給する. ¶meet the needs of the age (community) 時代(社会)の必要に応じる. 【類】 meet the crying needs (さし迫っての急) of the poor / The school meets the need clamouring at its doors. ¶be alert to perceive the needs of the times 時代の必要に対して敏感である. ¶satisfy the need deep rooted in human nature 人性に深く根ざしている必要を満たす. ¶save the need of ... ...の必要をはぶく. ¶they did not see the need of ... 彼らは...の必要を認めなかった. ¶sense the need of the hour 刻下の所要を感知する. ¶serve the everyday needs 日常の必要を満たす ‖ serve one's need well=stand one in good stead 大いに役立つ. 【類】 serve the needs of the world / It has become altogether inadequate to serve its growing needs. ¶just suit the need 出ず入らずである ‖ suit the needs of the time 時代の要求に適合する. ¶supply a long-felt need 長らく感じられた必要を満たす. 【類】 amply supply the need. ¶urge the needs of haste 急ぐ必要ありと主張する. ¶voice their needs 彼らの要求を発言する.

V[2] if need arises 必要の場合には. ¶if need be=if it is necessary 必要ならば.

Q our animal needs われらの肉体的要求. ¶one of her basic needs その国の根本的必要物の一. ¶meet the changing needs of life 人生の移り変わる必要に応じる. ¶have constant need of ... ...が絶えず要(い)る ‖ The machine is in constant need of repairs. その機械は始終修繕の必要がある. ¶a crying need さし迫っての急 ‖ the most crying need of the world 世界が最も要求していること. 【類】 the crying need of the time / stand in such crying need of ... / seize hold of the crying needs of the day. ¶He is in desperate need of money. ひどく金に窮している. ¶What are your daily needs? 君の日常(生活)の必要物は何か. ¶He has dire need of money. 彼は大いに金に困っている. ‖ He is in dire need of work. 彼は目下仕事がなくって非常に困っている. 【類】 He took to this work out of dire need. (万やむを得ず). ¶the educational needs of the hour 刻下教育上の急務. ¶meet an evident need まぎれもない必要に応じる. ¶feminine needs 婦人必要品(化粧品・薬品など). ¶My needs are few. 私はぜいたくは言わない. ¶stand in great need of ... 大いに...に窮している. ¶satisfy immediate needs 目前の要求を満たす. ¶be not in immediate need 差当り不要のものである. ¶a great insistent need in American scholarship today 目下アメリカ学界が切望していること. ¶the young learner's needs 少年学習者の要求. ¶there is little need to speak of ... ...について語る必要はほとんどない. ¶Material need is the most important of the causes of prostitution. 物質的要求が売春の原因中最も重要性のあるものである. ¶There is much need of it. 大いにその必要がある. ¶man's natural needs [食物など]人間自然の必要. ¶education adapted to the new needs of a new age 新時代の新要求に適した教育. ¶feel no need of ... ...の必要を少しも感じない. 【類】 There's no need of your hurry. / There is no need of doing so. ¶occupational needs 職業上の必要. ¶The paramount need for clarity is too often neglected. [文章で]第一に明確であることの必要が遺憾ながらしばしば省みられない. ¶serve a passing need 一時の間に合う. ¶to suit its own political need 政争の具に供するため. ¶He stands in present need. 彼は現在困っている. ¶the pressing need of the hour 刻下の差迫った必要. 【類】 The need of ... has become pressing. ¶the prime need もっとも必要な事. ¶a profound subjective human need 根深く主観的な人類の要求. ¶continue to meet a real need 引続き真の必要に応じている. 【類】 extend aid where real need exists. ¶the religious needs of man 人間の宗教的要求. ¶in the hour of her sole need 彼女はのっぴきならなくなって. ¶meet the superstitious needs of the people 民衆の迷信を満足させる. ¶meet a twofold need 二重の必要に応じる. ¶the most urgent *needs* 焦眉の急. ¶fill a ***vital need*** 根本的必要を満たす.

Q² Before the war, Britain provided about 32 per cent of Europe's ***coal needs***. 戦争前には英国はヨーロッパの石炭需要の約三十二パーセントを供給した. ¶the actual ***composition needs*** of the students 学生が作文学習に関して実際必要を感じている諸事項. ¶***emergency needs*** 突発的必要事項. ¶serve ***every-day needs*** 日常の必要に応じる. 【類】 their ***every-day needs*** for good English—spoken or written. ¶determine ***food needs*** 必要とする食物の量を決定する. 【類】 take care of its own ***food needs*** (自分で始末する) / be considered adequate to meet the ***food needs*** of the Japanese people. ¶the ***housing needs*** of World War II veterans 第二世界大戦参加者に住宅給与の必要. ¶***kitchen needs*** 台所必需品. ¶***peacetime needs*** 平時の必要事項. ¶meet ***present-day needs*** 現代の要求に応じる. ¶their high ***priority need*** in war それら物資の戦時における優先的必要. ¶meet the nations' ***security needs*** 国民保安上の必要に応じる. ¶***student needs*** 学生の求める所のもの. ¶the ***talent needs*** of the company その会社の人材的必要. ¶***traffic needs*** 交通上の必要. ¶***war-time needs*** 戦時必要品. ¶The greatest ***world need*** is for international agreement to give all peoples access to the wealth of the world. 世界の最大必要事はすべての国民が世界の富源にあずかることができるようにさせる国際協定を結ぶことである.

P ***according to*** the *need* 必要に応じて. ¶He is ***above*** the *need* of finding work. 彼は求職の必要がない. ¶***at*** one's *need* まさかの時に. ¶He is ***beyond*** all *need* of help. 彼は援助の必要が少しもない. ¶unless they have some means or other to enable them to provide ***for*** their *needs* 彼らが必要とするものを補給する何らかの手段がない限り. ¶He is ***in need*** of help. 彼は救助を要する. ‖ The ships stand ***in need*** of repairs. 船は修繕を要する. 【類】 His handwriting stands ***in need*** of improvement. / He is badly ***in need*** of a hair-cut (shave). / It has so long been ***in need*** of reform. / be much ***in need*** of ... / be ***in need*** of information respecting ... / When you are ***in need*** of money write to me. / be ***in*** great ***need*** of help ‖ They failed him ***in*** his ***need***. 彼らはまさかの時に彼を見棄てた. 【類】 They are thankful that they have him to turn to (彼に頼れること) ***in*** their ***need***. ‖ The watch (clock) is ***in need*** of oiling. 時計の油が切れている. ¶***In case of*** need, I will help him. 必要の場合私は彼を助けよう. ¶***without*** *need* of any fresh effort 一切新たに努力せずに.

P² There is urgent *need* ***for*** a reform. 至急改革の必要がある. ‖ the *need* ***for*** birth control 産児制限の必要 ‖ There is no *need* ***for*** him to work. 彼は働く必要がない. ‖ There is no *need* ***for*** (=of) assistance. 少しも援助の必要がない. ¶the ***needs of*** time 時代の要求 ‖ the ***need of*** defecation 排便の必要 ‖ He stands in no ***need of*** recommendation. 彼は推薦を要しない.

need, *v*. 要する, 必要とする.

M We ***badly needed*** a vacation. われわれは大いに休暇の必要を感じた. ¶*need* money ***desperately*** ぜひとも金がいる. ¶it ***need hardly*** be said that ... ほとんど...と言う必要はない. 【類】 I ***need hardly*** say that ... / you ***need hardly*** be told that ... ¶I ***scarcely need*** call to your attention that ... ...はほとんど君に注意する必要がない. ¶The reform is most ***imperatively needed***. 改革はぜひとも必要だ. ¶Help is ***sorely needed***. 救助が痛切に必要だ. ¶Fund is ***urgently needed***. 資金が至急必要だ.

P This ticket is merely a reminder and is not *needed* ***for*** admittance as there is no charge. 料金が要(い)らないのだからこの切符はおぼえだけのもので入場には必要がない. 【類】 He has not all the equipment *needed* ***for*** his task. / Some of the simplest and most common terms *needed* ***for*** daily use. / He is the very man we *need* ***for*** the vacancy.

needful, *a*. 必要な.

P ***needful to*** (=***for***) ... ...に必要な. 【類】 Air and water are ***needful for*** living things (生物).

needle, *n*. 針.

V You can ***magnetize*** a *needle* by rubbing it with a magnet. 針を磁石で摩擦すると磁気が伝わる. ¶***run*** a *needle* into one's hand 手に針を立てる. ¶***stick*** a *needle* into the spine 針を背骨に刺す. ¶***thread*** a *needle* 針に糸を通す.

V² The *needle* ***snapped***. 針がぽきっと折れた.

Q a ***sharp*** *needle* 鋭い針.

Q² ***ice needles*** [霜柱などの]針状の氷. ¶She laid her ***knitting needles*** on the table. 彼女はテーブル上に編み針をおいた. ¶***pine needles*** 松葉. ¶a ***sewing needle*** 縫針.

P make one's living ***by*** one's *needle* 針仕事で生計を立てる. ¶sew ***with*** a ***needle*** 針で縫う. 【類】 lace made ***with*** *needles* / be busy ***with*** her *needle* and thread.

needless, *a*. 不要な.

M it is ***almost needless*** to say that ... ...はほとんど言うには及ばない.

needlework, *n*. 針仕事.

Q² ***art needlework*** 手芸的な針仕事.

P sit ***at*** *needlework* 腰を掛けて針仕事をする. ¶She is engaged ***in*** some *needlework*. 彼女はなにか針仕事をやっている.

needy, *a*. 貧乏な.

V ***help*** the *needy* 貧民を助ける. ¶***relieve*** the *needy* 貧民を救う.

P watch ***over*** the *needy* 貧民を保護する.

negation, *n*. 否定.

P Shaking the head is a sign ***of*** *negation*. 頭をふるのは「ノー」というしるしだ.

negative, *n*. 否定; 〖文法〗否定語; 不承知の返答; 反対決議.

V ***express*** a polite *negative* 丁寧に断る. ¶***give*** a direct *negative* to an applicant 応募者にはっきり断りの返事を出す. ¶My request ***received*** a *negative*. 私の申出は断られた. ¶I ***upheld*** the *negative*. 私は反対決議を支持した.

Q ***double*** *negatives* 二重否定語. ¶the rashness of such a ***sweeping*** *negative* かかる全面的否定の無謀さ. ¶***Two*** *negatives* make an affirmative. 二つの否定語は肯定語になる.

P The answer is ***in*** the *negative*. 返事は「ノー」です. 【類】 answer (reply) ***in*** the *negative*. ¶answer ***with*** an unhesitating *negative* 断固として否定する.

negative, *a*. 否定的の.

M ***flatly*** *negative* ... ...を全面的に否定的な.

neglect, *n*. 等閑, 怠慢; 無視; 不あしらい.

V ***Excuse*** my *neglect* in returning your book. 本をお返ししないで申訳がありません. ¶He ***showed*** no *neglect* of duty. 彼は少しも職務を怠らなかった.

Q it would be a ***criminal*** *neglect* of my duty as ... if I did not ... もし私が...しなければ...として職務怠慢の罪に問われるだろう. ¶be dismissed for ***culpable*** *neglect* of duty はなはだしい職務怠慢のため免職される. ¶He is guilty of a ***gross*** *neglect*. 彼ははなはだしい怠慢をしている. ¶***scandalous*** *neglect* 恥ずべき怠慢. ¶***studied*** *neglect* 故意の怠慢. ¶He has fallen into almost ***total*** *neglect*. 彼はほとんど閑却し去られてしまった.

P He was dismissed ***for*** *neglect* of public duty. 彼は公務怠慢のために免職された. ¶***from*** the *neglect* of the laws of health 衛生に不注意なために. ¶be dismissed ***owing to*** *neglect* of duty 職務怠慢のため免職される. ¶It was entirely ***through*** your *neglect* that we were late. われわれがおくれたのは全く君の怠慢のためだ. ¶treat a guest ***with*** *neglect* 客をおろそかに取扱う.

P² The failure may be attributed to ***neglect of*** this precaution. 失敗はこの用心を怠ったためだといえる. ¶***neglect of*** the child ***by*** the parent 親の子に対する怠慢. ¶There was *neglect* ***on*** the part of the master. 主人の方に怠慢があった.

neglect, *v*. 等閑にする; 怠る.

M Agriculture has been ***awfully*** *neglected* in the past. 過去において農業ははなはだしく等閑に付せられた. ¶***carelessly*** *neglect* 不注意に閑却する. ¶The study of the subject has ***shamefully*** *neglected*. その研究が閑却されていたのは恥ずべきことだ. ¶Its study has ***undeservedly*** been *neglected*. その研究が閑却されていたのは不都合である. ¶The goods have been ***utterly*** *neglected*. これらの商品は全く顧みられずに来た. ¶***wilfully*** *neglect* ... 故意に...を怠る.

P a child *neglected* ***by*** his teacher 教師が面倒を見なかった児童. ¶*neglect* one's business ***for*** politics 政治運動のために自分の仕事をおろそかにする.

neglectful, *a*. なげやりの.

P He is ***neglectful of*** his duties (business, friends). 彼は自分の職務(など)をなおざりにする.

negligence, *n*. 怠慢, 落度; 無とん着.

Q ***contributory*** *negligence* in the accident そのできごとを突発させるに至った怠慢. ¶the accident was due to ***culpable*** *negligence* on the part of .. その事故の原因は...の方に不届きな態度があったためだ. ¶by ***gross*** *negligence* はなはだしい怠慢によって.

P ***owing to*** one's *negligence* その怠慢のために. ¶It happened ***through*** his *negligence.* それは彼の怠慢から起った. 【類】The accident came ***through*** *negligence* on their part.

P² *negligence* ***in*** dress (manner) 衣服(動作)に対する無とん着. ¶*negligence* ***of*** the term 条項履行の怠慢.

negligent, *a.* 怠慢な.

M be ***rather*** *negligent* in dress 服装にやや不注意である.

P He was *negligent* ***in*** attending to his duties. 彼は職務を怠った. ‖ He is *negligent* ***in*** his business (work). 彼は商売(仕事)を怠る. ¶He was *negligent* ***of*** his duties. 彼は職務を怠った.

negotiate, *v.* 交渉する, 談判する; 《口語》[難局などを]切り抜ける.

M ***cautiously*** *negotiate* a difficulty 細心に困難を切り抜ける. ¶*negotiate* ***directly*** with ... …と直接交渉する. ¶It requires care and skill to *negotiate* ***safely*** a dangerous road. (自動車など)安全に危険な道路を切り抜けるには注意と熟練とを要する.

P the new series of treaties *negotiated* ***by*** Japan ***with*** foreign Powers 日本が諸外国と連続的交渉の結果になる新条約. ¶*negotiate* ***for*** the loan (purchase) of ... …借用(購入)の交渉をする. ¶*negotiate* ***over*** ... …に関して交渉する. ¶*negotiate* ***with*** the landlord ***about*** the rent 家主と家賃について交渉する ‖ *negotiate* ***with*** a foreign minister ***for*** a treaty 外国公使と条約について交渉する. 【類】*negotiate* a treaty ***with*** another nation / *negotiate* buying prices (買値) ***with*** ... / They *negotiated* ***with*** the management (使用者側) for the amendments of labor terms (労働条件改善).

negotiation, *n.* 相談, 談判, 交渉.

V ***accelerate*** our *negotiation* in connection with ... …に関するわれわれの交渉を促進する. ¶***begin*** *negotiations* for ... …の交渉を始める. ¶***break off*** *negotiations* with ... …との交渉を断絶する(破談にする). ¶***carry*** *negotiations* to success 話をまとめる. ¶***Cease*** *negotiations* until you hear from us. 当方から通知するまで交渉を中止せよ. ¶after the *negotiations* are ***closed*** 折衝が終ってから ‖ ***close*** *negotiations* with ... for ... …のための…との交渉を打切る. ¶***commence*** *negotiations* for ... …の交渉を始める. ¶*Negotiations* have just been ***completed.*** 交渉が丁度まとまった所だ. 【類】*Negotiations* are practically ***completed.*** ¶The *negotiations* are ***concluded.*** 交渉が済んだ. ¶***conduct*** *negotiations* 交渉する. 【類】The *negotiations* were ***conducted*** throughout in English. ¶***continue*** *negotiations* with ... …との交渉を続ける. ¶***enter into*** *negotiations* with ... …と交渉を開始する. 【類】*negotiations* were officially ***entered into*** with ... ¶***initiate*** *negotiations* 交渉を開始する. ¶***open*** [***up***] *negotiations* with ... …と交渉を開始する. ¶***postpone*** all further *negotiations* until ... その後の交渉を…まで延す. ¶***prolong*** *negotiations* 交渉を長引かせる. ¶***reopen*** *negotiations* between labor and management 労資間の交渉を再開する. ¶*Negotiations* have long been in progress, but have not yet ***terminated.*** 交渉は長い間進行してきたがまだ終らない.

Q *Negotiations* are ***underway*** (=going on). 交渉は進行中. 【類】*Negotiations* are ***underway*** for the issuance of a Japanese loan to France.

V² The *negotiations* ***came*** to an end. その交渉は局を結んだ. ¶The *negotiations* between ... and ... have ***failed*** (=resulted in a rupture). …間の交渉は不調に終った. ¶*Negotiations* with a Dutch shipbuilding company have ***fallen through.*** オランダ造船会社との交渉は不調に終った. ¶*Negotiations* ***proceeded*** for some weeks. 交渉は数週間続いた. 【類】*negotiations* are ***proceeding*** with the Government concerning ... / *Negotiations* are ***proceeding*** for representation in Japan of certain important American firms.

Q after ***considerable*** *negotiations* 幾多の交渉を重ねた後. ¶***diplomatic*** *negotiations* 外交の折衝, 談判. ¶get into ***direct*** *negotiation* 直接交渉に入る. ¶***fruitless*** *negotiation* 不成績に終った交渉. ¶after spending some months in ***futile*** *negotiations* with ... …と無益の交渉に数カ月を費した後. ¶***long*** and ***fruitless*** *negotiations* 長引いたむだな交渉. 【類】the product of ***long*** and ***patient*** *negotiations* among ... ¶***official*** *negotiations* are pending between ...and ... …間の正式交渉が進行中である. ¶enter into ***preliminary*** *negotiations* with ... …との予備交渉に入る. ¶after ***protracted*** ***negotiations*** 長引いた交渉の後. 【類】There had been ***protracted*** *negotiations.* ¶after ***repeated*** *negotiations* between the police and the ward office. 警察と区役所と押問答の末. ¶***tedious*** *negotiations* らちの明かない交渉.

Q² ***Loan*** *negotiations* are now under way. 借款交渉が目下進行中である. ¶***peace*** *negotiations* 和平交渉. ¶***truce*** *negotiations* 休戦交渉.

P ***after*** much *negotiation* 色々交渉の結果. ¶***by*** skilful *negotiation* 巧妙な談判によって. ¶we are ***in*** *negotiations* with ... われわれは…と交渉中. ¶the rupture ***of*** *negotiations* 談判の決裂. ¶The proposal is now ***under*** *negotiation.* その提議は目下相談中だ.

P² The matter is now the subject of *negotiation* ***between*** Japan and America. その事件は今や日米間の交渉問題となっている. ¶*negotiation* ***for*** peace 講和談判. ¶*negotiation* ***with*** Russia ロシアとの交渉. ¶commence *negotiations* ***with regard to*** ... …に関して交渉を開始する.

Negro, negro, *n.* 黒人.

Q ***American*** *Negroes* are not all black or dark-skinned; some are less dark than South-Asians, and still some are even "white" as far as their skin color is concerned. アメリカのニグロは必ずしも黒色または黒ずんだ皮膚をしていない, 南アジア人ほど黒ずんでいない者もあり, 中には皮膚の色だけでは「白い」者さえある.

P work ***like*** a *negro* 真黒なって働く.

neighbo[u]r, *n.* 隣人, 隣家.

V ***backbite*** one's *neighbors* 隣人のかげ口をいう. ¶Thou shalt ***love*** thy *neighbor* as thyself. なんじ自身を愛するごとくなんじの隣人を愛せ.

Q ***congenial*** *neighbors* 気持のよい(気の合った)近所の人たち. ¶our ***fair*** *neighbor* to the north わが北方の秀麗国[アメリカからカナダを指す]. ¶Our ***female*** *neighbor* has much money. 隣の女は金持ちだ. ¶a ***good*** (***bad***) *neighbor* 良い(きらいな)近所の人 ‖ Let us be ***good*** *neighbors.* お互に仲よくしましょう. ¶A ***good*** *neighbor* is better than a brother far off. 遠い親類より近くの他人. ¶my ***immediate*** *neighbor* 私の家のすぐ隣りの人. ¶She is one of my ***little*** *neighbors.* あれは私の近所の子です. ¶a *neighbor* ***named*** ... …という隣人. ¶***near*** *neighbors* 近隣の人たち. 【類】Today the peoples of the earth are all ***near*** *neighbors.* ‖ her ***nearest*** *neighbor* その国の一番近い隣国. ¶a ***nearby*** *neighbor* 近くに住んでいる人. ¶my ***nextdoor*** *neighbor* すぐ隣の人. 【類】Do you not know me? We are ***next-door*** *neighbors.* ¶an ***obliging*** *neighbor* 親切な近所の人. ¶The *neighbors* are very ***pleasant.*** 近所の人たちは実に気持がよい.

Q² China's ***island*** *neighbor* 中国の隣りの島国(日本). ¶my ***right-hand*** *neighbor* 右隣に住んでいる人. ¶our ***trans-Pacific*** *neighbor* 太平洋の彼方の隣国(米国など).

P Towering up ***above*** its *neighbors* stood a tall gingko-tree. 群を抜いて高くそびえる一本のいちょうの木があった. ¶I want ***as*** a good *neighbor* to tell you that ... 隣人のよしみに…をお話したい.

P² our *neighbors* ***beyond*** the Rhine ライン川の向側の国国. ¶our *neighbor* ***on*** the north 北方隣接国. ¶our *neighbor* ***to*** the south of us 南方の隣国.

neighbo[u]red, *a.* 隣接している.

M a ***beautifully*** *neighbored* villa 付近の美しい別荘. ¶***ill*** *neighbored* 隣近所の悪い.

neighbo[u]rhood, *n.* 近所, 付近; 付近の人々; 近隣のよしみ; 部落.

V The fire ***alarmed*** the whole *neighborhood.* 火事で近所の人々は大騒ぎをした.

Q I live in an ***aristocratic*** *neighborhood.* 私の近所には貴族的な人々が住んでいる. ¶The house is in a very ***good*** *neighborhood.* その家の近所は非常に良い. ¶I live in a ***healthy*** *neighborhood.* 私の住んでいる付近は健康によい. ¶He lives in the ***immediate*** *neighborhood.* 彼はすぐ近所に住んでいる. ¶girls from ***low*** *neighborhoods* 付近の貧民くつからやって来た少女. ¶in the very ***near*** *neighborhood* すぐ近所に. ¶Now the whole world is ***one big*** *neighborhood.* 今日全世界は一つの大きな隣近所になっている. ¶Is this a ***quiet*** *neighborhood?* この近所は静かですか. ¶a ***rough*** *neighborhood* わいわい連の住んでいる近所. ¶a "***smart***" *neighborhood*「新らしがりや」たちの住んでいる近所. ¶a ***squalid*** *neighborhood* 貧民部落. ¶Boston and the ***surrounding*** *neighborhood* ボストン及びその近在. ¶There is no good school in the ***whole*** *neighborhood.* この近所にはどこにも良い学校がない.

Q[2] ***low-class*** *neighborhoods* 下層階級の住んでいる付近.

P villages ***in*** the *neighborhood* of Paris パリー付近の村々 ‖ I am stranger ***in*** this *neighborhood.* この辺は不案内です. 【類】 ***In*** the Wall Street *neighborhood,* ground costs about £60 a square foot. / Is there a house to let ***in*** your *neighborhood?* ‖ The actual figures are ***in*** the *neighborhood* of (=about) $750,000. 実際の数字はおよそ七十五万ドルである. 【類】 Her average sea speed (航行速度) is ***in*** the *neighborhood* of 23 knots. / He lost a sum ***in*** the *neighborhood* of $500. / The population of Osaka is ***in*** the *neighborhood* of three millions. ‖ live ***in*** the *neighborhood* of death 死線をさまよう.

nemesis, *n.* 因果.

V[2] *Nemesis* ***fell!*** 因果応報だった.

nephew, *n.* おい.

P[2] He is a ***nephew of*** the governor. 彼は知事のおいだ. ¶He is *nephew* ***to*** the governor. 彼は知事のおいだ.

nerve, *n.* 神経; 精力, 胆力, 勇気.

V ***affect*** the *nerves* 神経にさわる. ¶***brace*** one's *nerves* 気を引締める. ¶***exhaust*** one's *nerves* 神経をつかれさせる. ¶those who ***have nerve*** more than they need and those who have less than they need 必要以上に胆力のある人々と必要だけの胆力もない人々. ‖ But I didn't ***have nerve*** enough to mention it to anybody. しかし私はそれをだれにも言うだけの勇気がなかった. ‖ ***have*** the ***nerve*** to ... ...するほどに心臓が強い. 【類】 I ***have*** no ***nerve*** to ... ¶***irritate*** one's *nerves* 神経をいら立たせる. ¶***jar*** the *nerves* 神経をいら立たせる. ¶***keep*** one's *nerve* at high tension 神経を十分に緊張させておく. ¶He is ***lacking nerve.*** 彼は意気地がない. ¶He ***lost*** his *nerve* (=presence of mind). 彼は度を失った. ¶***quiet*** one's *nerves* 神経を静める. ¶***recover*** a little our badly shattered *nerves* 取乱した心を少し落着ける. ¶***shatter*** one's *nerves* [大損失などして]精神を狂わせる. ¶***strain*** every *nerve* to ... ...しようと全力をふるう ‖ Their *nerves* were somewhat ***strained.*** 彼らは幾らか逆上(のぼ)せていた. ¶***string*** one's *nerves* 気を引締める. ¶Here *nerves* that have been ***tightened*** for years slowly relax. ここで多年引締めてきた気力が徐々にゆるみ出す. ¶***unsettle*** one's *nerve* 神経をいら立たせる.

Q ***accessory*** *nerves* 副神経. ¶He has a ***cool*** *nerve.* 彼は落着きがある. ¶I seek joys keen enough to thrill his ***dull*** *nerves* 彼の鈍感な神経を刺激するに足りるほどの喜びを求める. ¶***optic*** *nerves* to ... ...するだけの視神経. ¶***shattered*** *nerves* 散々痛みつけられた神経. ¶Only men of ***steady*** *nerve* can work at such dizzy heights. 胆力のすわった人でなければこんな目まいのするような高所では働けない. ¶***untiring*** *nerve* 疲れることを知らない精力. ¶persons of ***weak nerves*** 気の弱い人たち. ¶***What*** a *nerve!* まあずうずうしい. 【類】 ***What*** a *nerve* do you have to say so?

Q[2] ***accelerator*** *nerves* 〖解〗加速筋. ¶He has ***examination*** *nerves.* 彼は試験度胸がある. ¶He has ***iron*** *nerves.* 彼は鉄の神経(度胸)を持っている. 【類】 a man of ***iron*** (=***steel***) *nerves.*

P a severe pain ***in*** the *nerves* 神経の激しい痛み. ¶A harsh voice jars ***on*** my *nerves.* きーきーいう音は神経にさわる. ‖ The waiter is getting ***on*** my *nerves.* あの給仕人が気にさわる(何んだかいやなやつだ). ‖ This hard work is a great strain ***on*** the *nerves.* この仕事は非常に神経を疲らせる(辞典の校正や組版など). ¶injurious ***to*** the *nerves* 神経に有害な ‖ trying ***to*** one's *nerve* 神経にこたえる.

O He is all *nerves.* 神経をとがらせている.

nerve, *v.* 元気をつける. 「一度やってみなさい.

P *Nerve* yourself ***for*** another attempt. 元気を出してもう

nervous, *a.* 神経過敏の.

P be *nervous* ***about*** the result 結果を気にしている. ¶get *nervous* ***at*** an examination 試験のときに神経過敏になる.

nervousness, *n.* 神経質.

V ***allay*** *nervousness* 神経の興奮を静める. ¶***conquer*** one's *nervousness* 神経質を直す. ¶***lose*** one's *nervousness* 物事を気にしなくなる. ¶***overcome*** one's *nervousness* 神経質でなくなる. ¶***show*** *nervousness* 神経質になる.

Q He looked forward to the operation with ***considerable*** *nervousness.* 彼は手術を大分気にしていた.

P He failed to answer some questions ***through*** *nervousness.* 彼は(神経質に)固くなってある問題に答えられなかった.

nest, *n.* 巣; 巣くつ.

V ***bring*** a hornets' *nest* about one's ears [比ゆ的に]めんどうなことを引き起す. ¶***build*** a *nest* 巣を作る. 【類】 some birds ***build*** their *nests* in birdhouses. ¶I ***entered*** the *nest* of filthy streets. 私は不潔な町のごみごみしている所へはいった. ¶***feather*** one's own *nest*=promote one's own interest 私利を計る. ¶***leave*** a *nest* 巣立つ. ¶***rob*** a bird's *nest* 鳥の巣を盗む. ¶***make*** a *nest* 巣食う. ¶***stir up*** (=***arouse***) a hornets' *nest* (=a net of hornets) はちの巣をつつく, 混乱をまき起す ‖ he ***stirred up*** a hornets' *nest* by an attempt to ... 彼は...しようとしてやぶへびに終った.

Q The cuckoo lays its eggs in ***another's*** *nest.* ほととぎすは他の鳥の巣に卵をうむ. 「くまんばちの巣.

Q[2] an ***ant*** *nest* ありの巣. ¶a ***hornet*** *net*=a net of hornets

P young blackbirds ***in*** a *nest* 巣にこもっているつぐみのひな. ¶a female blackbird ***on*** a *nest* 巣についている雌のつぐみ ‖ a hen sitting ***on*** a *nest* of eggs 卵を暖めているめんどり. ¶A bird flies back ***to*** its *nest* toward evening. 鳥は夕方その巣に戻る.

P[2] a *nest* ***of*** pirates (thieves, traitors, criminals) 海賊(など)の巣くつ ‖ a *nest* ***of*** vice (crime, infamy) 悪事(など)の発生所. 【類】 a *nest* ***of*** social evils / a *nest* ***of*** vipers.

nest, *v.* 巣をかける.

P *nest* ***in*** trees (holes, bushes) 木(など)に巣をかける.

nestle, *v.* 巣に入れる; すりよる; 巣ごもる; (なごやかに)横たわる.

M A baby bird *nestles* ***close*** to its mother. 子鳥は親鳥により添うている. ¶*nestle* ***cosily*** amongst trees [家屋など]木に囲まれてこんもりした中にある.

M[2] *nestle* ***down*** in the grass among the leaves. 草(木の葉)かげに巣ごもる.

P a gay little village *nestling* ***among*** the mountains 山間に囲まれたにぎやかな小村. 【類】 temples *nestling* ***among*** the hills. ¶A few houses *nestle* ***at*** the foot of a hill. 二三の家屋が山のふもとにちんまり立っている. ¶an infant *nestling* ***in*** mother's bosom 母親のふところに抱かれている乳児 ‖ Temples *nestled* ***in*** mountain nooks. いくつかの寺が山のすみにちんまりと立っていた. 【類】 a village *nestling* cosily ***in*** a nook of the mountains / *nestle* oneself ***in*** one's bed. ¶The child *nestles* his head ***on*** his mother's breast. 子供が母親の胸に頭をすり寄せる. ¶The children *nestled* ***to*** the mother. 子供らが母親にすりよった. 【類】 She was *nestling* up ***to*** her lover.

net, *n.* 網; くもの巣; 網わな.

V ***cast*** a *net* widely 広く網を打つ. ¶***drag*** *nets* 網を引く. ¶***draw up*** (=***in***) a *net* 網を引上げる. ¶***hang up*** a mosquito *net* かやをつる. ¶***haul in*** a *net* 網を引上げる. ¶***lay*** a *net* 網を張る. ¶***make*** a *net* 網を造る. ¶***open out*** the *nets* 防御網を張る. ¶***pitch*** a *net* 網を張る. ¶***put up*** a tennis *net* 庭球網(ネット)を張る. ¶***set*** a *net* to catch wild ducks かも網を張る. ¶***shoot*** a *net* in a river 川に網を打つ. ¶Spiders ***spin*** (=weave) *nets.* くもが網を張る. ¶***spread*** a *net* 網をひろげる. ¶***weave*** a fish *net* 魚網を編む. ¶***withdraw*** the *nets* 網をはずす.

Q He has been entangled in ***amorous*** *nets.* 彼は女の問題でもめごとを起した.

Q[2] a ***drift*** *net* 流し網. ¶an ***emergency*** *net* 非常救助網(電車の). ¶a ***hair*** *net* ヘアネット. ¶a ***mosquito*** *net* かや. ¶The thief escaped the ***police*** *net.* 盗人は警察の網を脱け出た. 【類】 The ***police*** *net* was widely cast. ¶a ***safety*** *net* 救助網(電車の前などにあるもの). ¶a lesson in casting a ***throw*** *net* 投網のけいこの一回.

P play a good game ***at*** the *net* [庭球で]見事なゲームを見せる. ¶catch fish ***in*** a *net* 網で魚を捕える. 【類】 a wild duck trapped ***in*** a *net.* ¶protect chickens ***with*** a *net* put up all around 周囲に網を張って鶏のひなを保護する.

P[2] a *net* ***for*** the face [婦人の]顔網.

netting, *n.* 網.

Q[2] ***fish*** *netting* and ropes 魚網と綱. ¶***wire*** *netting* 金網.

nettle, *v.* 腹を立たせる.

P I was somewhat *nettled* ***by*** the air of superiority he assumed. 彼にえらそうな態度をされて少ししゃくにさわった.

network, *n.* 網細工; 網状組織.

V The lines of railway ***form*** a complete *network* over the face of the country. 鉄道線路はこの国全土にわたって完全な網状組織を成している.

Q an amazingly ***complex subterranean*** *network* びっくりするほど複雑な地下鉄道線路網.

Q² the ***blood-vessel*** *network* 血管網. ¶The ***communications*** *network* greatly expanded. 交通網が非常に拡張した. ¶the ***intelligence*** *network* 情報網. ¶a ***radio (TV)*** *network* ラジオ(テレビ)の放送網. 【類】The address was broadcast on the Armed Forces' *radio network* to all American troops in Japan. / His voice was recently heard here over the NBC *radio network*. ¶a worldwide ***radiophoto*** *network* 世界にわたる無線写真網. ¶the ***railroad (=railway)*** *network* of the country 同国の鉄道網. ¶the ***Red*** *network* 赤化網.

P formed ***like*** *network* 網目状をした.

P² A *network* ***of*** railways has been spread over the islands. 鉄道網が島中に拡められた.

neutral, *a.* 中立の.

V try to ***act*** the "*neutral*" in the battle between democracy and communism 民主共産間の戦いにいわゆる中立の役を演じようと努める.

O remain *neutral* 依然中立を守る.

neutrality, *n.* 中立, 局外中立.

V ***declare*** *neutrality* 中立を宣言する. ¶***maintain*** a *neutrality* 中立を持続する. ¶***observe*** (=***keep***) a strict *neutrality* 厳正中立を守る. 「*ity* 厳正中立を守る.

Q ***armed*** *neutrality* 武装中立. ¶observe a ***strict*** *neutral-*

P a violation ***of*** *neutrality* 中立違反.

new, *a.* 新しい; 新来の.

M He has something ***absolutely*** *new* to say. 彼はある全く新しい考えを持っていてそれを言おうとしている. ¶The United States is a ***comparatively*** *new* country. 米国は比較的新しい国である. ¶a revised edition, ***entirely*** *new* 改訂新版. ¶This work is ***quite*** *new* to me. 私はこの仕事は全然不案内だ. ¶something ***totally*** *new* to one's experence 全く経験のないこと.

P What's *new* [***to*** us]? 何か変ったことでもあるか. ‖ What's *new* ***about*** that? それはどこに新味があるのか. ¶a youngster *new* ***at*** the game その仕事に不慣れな若者. 【類】You will have to excuse our clumsiness! We're *new* ***at*** this business. ¶a young man *new* ***from*** the country いなかから出たばかりの青年. ¶I am *new* ***to*** the business. 私はその仕事にまだなれていない. ‖ an unpracticed simpleton, who is perfectly *new* ***to*** life 世間見ずでうすのろの青二才. 【類】an American lady, *new* ***to*** China / it may be well to inform the traveller who is *new* ***to*** American ways that ... ‖ words *new* ***to*** the language その国語には今までなかった語. 【類】scenes *new* ***to*** us in poetry / a countryman *new* ***to*** Town. ¶The idea is not *new* ***with*** us. その思いつきはわれわれには新しくもない.

newcomer, *n.* 新来者.

V ***introduce*** a *newcomer* to all those with whom he or she will come in contact 新任者をこれから触接する人々に紹介する.

P² *newcomers* ***from*** the stage lured to Hollywood by the talkies 発声映画によって劇壇からハリウッドへ引付けられた新顔. ¶a *newcomer* ***in*** the business この商売の新参. 【類】a *newcomer* ***in*** the country. ¶words that are *newcomers* ***into*** the language その国語の新語. ¶a *newcomer* ***to*** the city この市への新来者.

news, *n.* [単・複同型] 珍談; 報道, ニュース; 消息, 便り.

V The *news* has been ***anticipated***. その報道は予想されていた. ¶***ascertain*** a *news* from home 家からの音信を確かめる. ¶***bear*** good *news* 吉報を伝達する. ¶The *news* was ***blazed*** abroad. その話が言触らされた. ¶***break*** *news* gently to ... …に遠回しに話を打ち明ける. 【類】***break*** a bad (=an ill) *news*. ¶he ***brought*** *news* of ... 彼が…の報道をもたらした ‖ ***bring*** glad *news* to ... …へ吉報をもたらす. ¶***celebrate*** our first good *news* of the war わが軍最初の戦勝の報を祝う. ¶***communicate*** the *news* of ... to ... …のことを…に知らせる. ¶***concoct*** (=***cook up***) false news デマをでっちあげる. ¶***control*** *news* 報道を取締る. ¶***convey*** the joyous *news* to ... …に快報を伝える. 【類】***convey*** the sad *news* to ... ¶***discuss*** the latest *news* 最近のできごとについて語り合う. ¶***disseminate*** *news* 報道を伝える. ¶***distort*** *news* 報道をまげる. ¶***doctor*** *news* 報道をでっち上げる. ¶***falsify*** *news* to one's own end 自分の都合の好いように報道を作り上げる. ¶The *news* was ***flashed*** over Japan. その報道は日本全体に電報された. ¶***gather*** and ***edit*** local *news* ローカルニュースを収集して編集する. ¶***give*** the *news* to the world その報道を世界に発表する. ¶When do you expect to ***have*** *news*? いつ通知を受取るはずになっていますか. ‖ I ***have*** no later *news* to give you. その後お知らせすることはない. ¶Have you ***heard*** the *news*? 君はそのことを聞いたか. ¶***keep back*** the *news* from the people そのことを一般に知らせないようにする. ¶***learn*** the *news* of ... …の消息を知る. 【類】I ***learned*** the bad *news* by telegram. ¶***make*** *news* 新聞種をつくる. 【類】anything that ***makes*** *news*. ¶***manufacture*** (=***invent***) false *news* 虚報をこしらえる. ¶***mobilize*** *news*=bring news into circulation ニュースを流す. ¶***proclaim*** glad *news* of victory うれしい戦況を公報する. ¶***publish*** a terrible *news* 恐ろしい知らせを公表する. ¶How did she ***receive*** the *news*? 彼女がその知らせを聞いてどんなでした. 【類】The *news* was ***received*** throughout the British Empire with profound grief. / until we ***receive*** *news* of ... / prepare her to ***receive*** the bad *news*. ¶the *news* is ***repeated*** that ... …の話が繰返されている. ¶***retail*** the *news* その報道をふれ回る. ¶I ***see*** the *news* in your face. あなたを一目見てそのことが分かる. ¶I will ***send*** you further *news* in a day or two. 一両日中に重ねて申上げます. ¶***spread*** the *news* from mouth to mouth 口から口にその話を伝える. ¶***suppress*** *news* 報道を差止める. ¶She did not ***survive*** the *news* a whole month. 彼女はその知らせがあってから丸ひと月と生きていなかった. ¶***take*** the bad *news* to ... …に凶報をもたらす. ¶***twist*** *news* 報道を曲げる. ¶Can you ***verify*** the *news*? その報知は確かめられますか. ¶the *news* will be ***welcomed*** by all that ... …という報道はすべてに歓迎されるだろう.

V² *news* has ***reached*** us that ... …の報道がわれわれの手もとに達した. ¶The *news* ***spread*** like wildfire. その話は野火のように伝わった. ‖ somehow or other, the *news* ***spread*** abroad that ... いつの間にか…という報道が一般に伝わった. ¶The *news* ***traveled*** fast. その話はじん速に伝わった. 【類】*News* ***traveled*** quickly aboard the ship. ‖ *News* ***travels*** fast. ニュースは早く伝わる.

Q Is there ***any*** *news*? なにか変ったことがありますか. ¶I have had ***bad*** *news*. 私は悪い知らせをもらった. ¶This is ***big*** *news*. これはビッグ・ニュースだ. ¶***colored*** (=***distorted***) *news* 事実を曲げた報道. ¶***conflicting*** *news* 矛盾する報道. ¶***current*** *news* 時報. ¶no ***definite*** *news* has been received regarding ... …に関しなんら確報に接していない. ¶***dire*** *news* 凶報. ¶***distressful*** *news* 悲報. ¶a ***fateful*** *news* 凶報. ¶The *news* is ***favorable*** this morning. けさはいった通知は吉報だ. ¶***fictitious*** or ***manufactured*** *news* printed in a newspaper 虚構の, つまりでっち上げの新聞記事. ¶***foreign*** *news* in brief 海外短信. ¶wait for ***further*** *news* 後報を待つ. ¶***garbled*** *news* 手を入れた報道. ¶***general*** *news* 雑報. ¶break ***glad*** *news* to ... 耳よりの話を…にする. ¶The *news* are ***good***. それは良い話だ. ‖ This is the ***good*** *news* with which this week opened. これが今週皮切りの吉報だ. ¶come home with ***great*** *news* すてきな便りを持って帰る. ¶***Happy*** *news*? 吉報かい. ¶today's ***highlighted*** *news* きょうの目ぼしい報道. ¶a ***hopeful*** *news* 有望な報道. ¶a ***horrible*** *news* 恐ろしい報道. ¶***hot*** *news* 最近のニュース. ¶a piece of ***ill*** *news* 一片の凶報. ¶Is there any ***interesting*** *news* in the paper? 新聞になにか面白い記事がありますか. ¶The ***latest*** (=***last***) *news* is less favorable. 最近の消息はそれほど結構でない. 【類】the ***latest*** *news* we have had so far of it is ... ¶***local*** *news* 〖新聞〗地方版にのせるニュース. ¶***marine*** *news* 海事通信. ¶***mournful*** *news* 悲報. ¶That is ***no*** *news*. それはなにも珍しいことでない. ¶an ***official*** *news* from London ロンドンからの公報. ¶***political*** *news* 政治的ニュース. ¶***reliable*** *news* 信頼すべき報道. ¶break the ***sad*** *news* to ... 悲報を…に知らせる. ¶a very ***satisfactory*** *news* has been received from ... きわめて満足な報道が…からはいった. ¶***sensational*** *news* 扇情的な報道. ¶Let me have now and then ***some*** *news* from you. ときどきお便りをして下さい. 【類】I expect to have ***some*** *news* or other before long. ¶***staggering*** *news*

仰天するニュース. ¶ ***stale** news* to ... …には古臭い話. ¶ ***telegraphic** news* from ... …からの電報. ¶ "***tendentious*** " *news* 底意(ɪ)のある報道. ¶ break to a lady ***tragic** news* of her bereavement just received by wireless 無線で丁度今受信した(夫が死亡したという)悲報を一貴婦人に告げる. ¶ ***uncolored** news* 事実そのままの報道. ¶ ***unexpected*** and ***startling** news* 予期しない, びっくりするような知らせ. ¶ very ***unhappy** news* 非常に不愉快な通信. ¶ ***warlike** news* 軍事に関する報道. ¶ That's ***welcome** news.* それはうれしい便りだ. ‖ The official announcement that ... is very ***welcome** news* ...の公表は耳よりの話だ.

Q² A city editor is in charge of ***city** news,* having the direct control of local reporters. シティー編集長は地方通信員を直接に監督して市の通信を担当する. ¶ For many days it was ***first-page** news* in nearly every paper in the land. そのことは数日間国内のほとんどすべての新聞紙の第一面記事であった. ¶ ***front-page** news* 第一面記事. ¶ ***headline** news* 大見出しのニュース. ¶ ***last minute** news* 締切り間ぎわの報道. ¶ ***radio** news* 放送ニュース. ¶ ***spot** news* 〘ラジオ〙さしこみ広告のアナウンス (spot announcement). ¶ ***spot press** news* 〘新聞〙最終さし込みニュース. ¶ ***war** news* 戦況報道.

P ***according to** news* received here 当地に達した便りでは ‖ ***according to*** the latest *news.* ¶ He wept ***at*** the *news.* 彼はその話を聞いて泣いた. ‖ I was shocked ***at*** (=by) the *news.* 私はその知らせでびっくりした. ¶ just ***before*** the *news* of ... was given out …の報の発表寸前に. ¶ I was almost knocked out ***by*** the *news.* 私はその報道でほとんど腰を抜かした. ¶ distribute the "news ***behind*** the *news*" (ニュース通信社などが)新聞の種を卸す. ¶ a batch ***of** news* ひとまとめの新しい報道 ‖ a piece ***of** news* 一片のニュース ‖ a summary ***of*** the *news* of the world is daily bulletined in ... 世界の新聞の大要は日々…にのる. ¶ good *news* ***for*** disabled soldiers 廃兵には結構な話. ¶ *news* ***from*** the front 戦地便り. 【類】 *news* ***from*** America / *news* ***from*** Stateside. ¶ That is *news* ***to*** me. それは初耳だ. 【類】 ***to*** those who ..., it will be *news* that ... / it may be *news* ***to*** many of our readers that ...

newsboy, *n.* 新聞売子.

V² A *newsboy* was ***crying*** at a street corner, "Extra, Extra, Extra!" 新聞売子が町角で「号外々々」とどなっていた. ¶ A *newsboy* ***sells*** or ***delivers*** newspapers. 新聞配達人は新聞を売りまたは配達する.

newsman, *n.* 《米》新聞記者 (pressman).

Q ***data gathering** newsmen* 新聞の種取り. ¶ a ***veteran** newsman* 老練記者.

Q² a ***radio** newsman* 放送記者.

P begin one's career ***as*** a *newsman* 新聞記者を振出しに人生を踏出す.

newspaper, *n.* 新聞(紙).

V ***clip** newspapers* for one's scrapbook 張込帳に収めるために新聞を切抜く. ¶ The *newspaper* has been ***closed.*** 新聞が締切になった. ¶ ***despatch** newspapers* 新聞を発送する. ¶ ***edit*** a *newspaper* 新聞を編集する. ¶ ***hold up*** one's *newspaper* so as to hide one's face 顔が隠れる位に新聞紙を持ち上げる. ¶ ***keep** newspapers* 新聞紙を保存しておく. ¶ ***launch*** a *newspaper* 新聞を創刊する. ¶ a *newspaper* ***made*** for gentlemen by gentlemen 紳士が紳士のために作った(高級な)新聞. ¶ New York ***prints*** 43 daily *newspaper.* ニューヨークでは四十三種の日刊新聞が発行されている. ¶ ***publish*** a *newspaper* 新聞を発行する. ¶ What *newspaper* do you ***read?*** なに新聞をお読みですか. ¶ ***run*** a *newspaper* 新聞を経営する. ¶ ***spread** newspapers* on the seats 新聞を席に拡げる(野球などを見るとき). ¶ ***sue*** a *newspaper* for libel 誹謗罪のかどで新聞を訴える. ¶ ***take*** [*in*] a *newspaper* 新聞を取る. ¶ What do you do when you ***take up*** the daily *newspaper?* 日刊新聞を手にした場合どうなさいますか. ¶ ***unfold*** a *newspaper* 新聞をひろげる. ¶ A *newspaper* ***wrapped*** around the body under the coat is as good as an overcoat for warmth. 上衣の下に新聞紙で体をくるむと外とうを着た位あたたかい.

V² The *newspaper* ***carries*** a fine article. その新聞にはよい記事が一つのっている. ¶ one *newspaper,* under the heading "...", ***printed*** the following: 「...」の見出しで某新聞は次の記事を公にした. ¶ today the *newspaper* ***said*** that ... きょうその新聞に…と出ていた.

Q ***daily*** and ***weekly** newspapers* 日刊と週刊新聞. ¶ an ***English-written*** (=***English-edited***) *newspaper* 英字新聞. ¶ One need not suffer from insufficient clothing, day or night, if a ***few** newspapers* are at hand. 新聞が二三枚手もとにあれば(それを着物の下に入れるから)夜でも昼でも薄着で困るようなことはない. ¶ a ***financial** newspaper* 経済新聞. ¶ the Sphere, an ***illustrated weekly** newspaper* 絵入週刊のスフィア. ¶ one of the ***leading** newspapers* of Tokyo 東京大新聞の一. ¶ a great ***little** newspaper* 勢力のある小新聞. ¶ Are there ***no** newspapers* besides these? これよりほかに新聞はありませんか. ¶ a ***semi-official** newspaper* 半官半民新聞. ¶ ***sensational** newspapers* 扇情的(世間騒がせな)新聞.

Q² a ***backwoods** newspaper* いなか新聞. ¶ a ***campus*** (=***college***) *newspaper* 大学新聞. ¶ an official ***government** newspaper* 官報. ¶ the ***Hearst** newspapers* ハースト系新聞紙. ¶ ***penny** newspapers* 一ペニー新聞(安新聞). ¶ an ***ocean** newspaper* 海上新聞. ¶ The Isis, ***Oxford student*** weekly *newspaper* オックスフォード学生週刊新聞「イスィス」. ¶ ***school** newspapers* 学内新聞. ¶ a correspondent of the ***Scotsman** newspaper* スコッツマン新聞の通信員. ¶ "The ***Times*** " *newspaper,* ever since its foundation in the year 1785, has maintained its position not merely as a great English national newspaper, but as one of the greatest newspapers in the world. タイムス紙は千七百八十五年その創立以来英国民の大新聞たるのみならず世界の最大新聞の一としてその地位を保持して来た. ¶ an ***undergraduate** newspaper* 大学学生新聞. ¶ a ***wall** newspaper* 壁新聞.

P ***according to*** the *newspapers* 新聞によれば. ¶ ***between*** the *newspaper* and breakfast 新聞を読むときと朝飯を取るときの間に. ¶ He was traduced ***by*** a *newspaper.* 彼はある新聞でたたかれた. ¶ He writes leading articles ***for*** the *newspaper.* 彼はその新聞の論説を書いている. ‖ He corresponds ***for*** a *newspaper.* 彼は新聞に通信している. 【類】 He writes (寄書する) ***for*** a *newspaper.* ‖ subscribe ***for*** a *newspaper* 新聞を予約する ‖ Please go ***for*** a *newspaper* 新聞を買って来て下さい. ¶ a notice ***in*** a *newspaper* 新聞の通知広告. 【類】 an article ***in*** a *newspaper* = a newspaper article / It appears ***in*** the *newspapers.* / It was published ***in*** the *newspapers.* / I read it ***in*** a *newspaper.* ¶ You are ***on*** a *newspaper?* 君は新聞に御関係ですね. ‖ He began his career as a reporter ***on*** a weekly *newspaper.* 彼は週刊新聞の探訪記者として人生を踏み出した. ¶ keep the matter ***out of*** the *newspaper* そのことが新聞に出ないようにする.

newspaperman, *n.* 《米》新聞記者.

Q a ***bona-fide** nawspaperman* working for a bona fide newspaper 良心的な新聞社に勤めている良心的な記者.

newspaperwoman, *n.* 《米》婦人記者.

Q She is a ***veteran** newspaperwoman* in charge of the women's section of the paper. 彼女はその新聞の婦人欄担当の古顔の婦人記者だ.

newsstand, *n.* 《米》新聞売店.

P It is on sale ***at*** the *newsstand.* それは新聞売場で売っている. ¶ The March number is now ***on*** the *newsstand.* 三月号が今新聞売場に出ている.

New Year, *n.* 新年.

V ***celebrate*** the *New Year* 新年を祝う. ¶ ***enter*** the *New Year* 新年に入る. ¶ ring out the Old Year and ***ring in*** the *New* [*Year*] 旧年を送り新年を迎える. ¶ ***toast*** the *New Year* at the stroke of midnight 除夜の鐘を聞いて新年の祝杯をあげる. ¶ ***welcome*** the *New Year* 新年を迎える. ¶ ***wish*** [a] happy *New Year* めでたい新年を賀する.

Q on ***Chinese** New Year* 中国の新年に. ¶ a ***happy*** and ***prosperous** New Year* 幸福なめでたい新年. 【類】 I wish you a ***happy** New Year.* ¶ at the ***Jewish** New Year* ユダヤの新年に.

P street scenes ***at** New Year* 新年の街頭風景. ¶ ***during*** the *New Year* week 松の内. ¶ at the start ***of*** the *New Year* 年の始めに. ¶ give a joyous welcome ***to*** the *New Year* 楽しく新年を迎える.

next, *a., prep.* ...に次ぐ; 次に, 隣りに.

P *next* ***of*** kin 最近親族. 【類】 He is *next* ***of*** kin to me (=the next of my kin). ¶ It is *next* ***to*** (=almost) impossible. それはほとんど不可能だ. ‖ My house is *next* ***to*** the temple. 宅は寺の隣です. ‖ I learned *next* ***to*** no astronomy. 私は天文学はほとんどやらなかった. ‖ I got *next* ***to*** nothing. ほとんど得る所がなかった. ‖ in *next* ***to*** no time

ほとんどすぐに ‖ buy (sell) it for ***next to*** nothing ほとんどただで買う(売る) ‖ wear a bathtowel ***next to*** the skin 素はだに湯上りタオルをかける. 【類】I worked for ***next to*** no wages (=nothing). / he accomplished ***next to*** nothing in ... ‖ *Next **to*** rice, what is the grain most largely used by the Chinese race? / *Next **to*** hunger and thirst, love is the strongest human emotion. / *Next **to*** the Bible he likes Shakespeare best of all his books. / He placed his chair *next* [*to*] mine. / I always wear flannel *next* [*to*] the skin. ‖ get ***next to*** ... 《米口》...を知るようになる, ...と親しくなる ‖ put a person ***next to*** ... 人に...を知らせる. 【類】I'll put you next ***to*** the real state of things.

next-door, *n.* 隣.

P He lives *next-door **to*** the school. 彼は学校の隣に住んでいる. 【類】My house is ***next-door to*** the church. ‖ He is *next-door **to*** a fool (madman). 彼はばか(気違い)に近い.

nibble, *v.* 少しずつかむ.

P ***nibble at*** a bait [魚など]えさをつっつく ‖ ***nibble at*** another's books 他人の著書のあらをほじくる.

nice, *a.* 小やかましい; 気持のよい; [反語的に]やっかいな.

M Not ***altogether nice***, is it? あまりぞっとしないね. ¶He is ***too nice*** about the means. 彼は手段を吟味しすぎる.

P It was *nice **of*** the Woodleys to invite us for bridge tonight. 今夜のトランプの会にウドレー夫妻が僕たちをよんでくれたのはありがたかったね. ¶He is really *nice **to*** the guests. 彼は本当に客を親切に扱う.

O Here's a *nice* mess. 《口語》困ったことになった.

nicety, *n.* 微妙な点; きちょうめん; 精巧.

V ***acquire*** the *niceties* of pronunciation and grammatical construction in English 英語の発音と措辞の微妙な点を会得する. ¶***observe niceties*** of syntax 構文法の微妙な点を考察する.

Q a point of ***great*** *nicety* きわめて微妙な点.

P The coat fits ***to*** a *nicety*. 上衣がきっちり合う. ‖ I found my room arranged ***to*** a *nicety*. 私のへやがきちんと整とんしていた. ¶do ***with*** a *nicety* 正確にやる.

niche, *n.* 凹(おう)壇; おき所; 地位; 適所.

V She ***carved*** a special *niche* for herself. 彼女は独特の天地を開拓した. 【類】The dialogue writer has ***carved*** a new *niche* in the new scheme of talking-picture production. ¶He ***deserves*** (=***earned***) a *niche* in the temple of Fame. 彼は不朽の名声に値する. ¶***find*** one's *niche* [適材などが]適所を得る. ¶Women ***have*** certain occupational *niches* in factories, offices and stores into which they fit better than men do. 工場・役所・商店には仕事によっては婦人の方が男子よりも一層適任と思われるものがある. ¶He richly ***merits*** a *niche* in the Temble of Fame. 名を後世に残すだけの功績がある. ¶***occupy*** a *niche* in glory's temple 名誉の殿堂に合祀される ‖ it ***occupies*** a *niche* of its own among ... ...中に地歩を占めている. 【類】His work ***occupies*** a *niche* not touched by any other publication. ¶a *niche **prepared*** by God for you 神があなたのために作った名誉の席. ¶People must be made to acquire the habit of reading a certain paper before it can ***secure*** a firm *niche* in the community. ある新聞が社会において確実な地歩を占めるにはまず人々にその新聞を読む習慣を作らせなくてはならない. ¶He ***won*** his *niche* in the temple of thrift and self-help. 彼は勤倹力行の名士の中に列せられた.

Q He occupies a not ***inconspicuous*** *niche* in the temple of science. 彼は科学界で相当顕著な地位を占めている. ¶one's ***occupational*** *niche* その職場. ¶They do not yet know [in] ***what*** *niche* in life they can best fill themselves. 彼らはまだ人生のいかなる地位が自分らに一番適するかが分からない.

P be placed ***in*** a *niche* 神だな(誉れの席)に据えられる.

nick, *n.* 好時機; [せと物の]かけ目.

V ***make*** a *nick* in the corner of a saucer コーヒーざらのふちをかく.

P ***in*** the *nick* of time=just in time 丁度いいときに, 丁度間に合って. 【類】He came ***in*** the *nick* of time.

nickel, *n.* ニッケル; 《米》[五セントの]白銅貨.

V May I ***have*** a *nickel*, ma? ママ, 五セント頂だい.

P coated ***with*** *nickel* ニッケルメッキをした.

nickname, *n.* あだ名.

V he ***achieved*** the *nickname* of ... 彼は...のあだ名を得た. ¶***acquire*** a *nickname* あだ名を付けられる. ¶***get*** the *nickname* of ... というあだ名をつけられる. ¶***fasten*** a *nickname* upon ... ...にあだ名を付ける. ¶he ***had*** the *nickname* of ... 彼には...というあだ名があった. ¶to this he ***owed*** his *nickname* of ... 彼に...のあだ名のあるのはこのためであった.

P² Rob is a *nickname **for*** Robert. ロッブというのはロバートのあだ名だ.

nickname, *v.* あだなを付ける.

M "Japs," as they ***jokingly*** *nickname* us 彼らがふざけていういわゆるジャップ(日本人).

niggardly, *a.* けちな.

P I am not *niggardly*, I believe, ***of*** money. 私は金銭にはけちけちしない積りだ.

night, *n.* 夜, 一夜; 日暮; 夜陰.

V ***attend*** first *nights* 初日公演に出席する. ¶***have*** a *night* on the railway 汽車で一晩寝る ‖ ***have*** a good *night* 一晩よく眠る ‖ He was ***having*** a very late *night* of it with some friends. 彼は二三の友人と夜ふかしをしていた. ‖ ***have*** a *night* out 一夜を外ですごす. ¶***make*** a *night* of it ... 一晩浮かれ(飲み)明かす. ¶He will not ***outlive*** this *night*. 彼は明朝まで保(も)つまい. ¶***pass*** a *night* at ... ...に一泊する ‖ ***pass*** the *night* in the open air 野宿をする. 【類】***pass*** the *night* in prayer / ***pass*** the *night* in anxiety. ¶After ***sleeping*** the *night* she rose early to attend mass in a church close by. その夜を過してから彼女はすぐ近所の教会のミサに出席するために朝早く起きた. ¶She ***smiled*** a good *night* to all. 彼女は一同に向って「おやすみなさい」の積りで微笑した. ¶I ***spent*** a *night* in London. 私はロンドンに一泊した. ¶***turn*** *night* into day [赤ん坊などが]夜を昼と取違える.

V² as the *night* ***advances*** 夜がふけて行くと. ¶when *night* ***approached*** 夜が近づくと. ¶*Night* was ***closing in*** as we reached there. われわれがそこに着いたときに日が暮れかかっていた. ¶as *night* ***came on*** 夜になって. ¶when *night* ***comes*** (=falls) 夜になると. ¶as *night* ***drew on*** 夜が近づくにつれて. ¶Meanwhile the *night* ***fell***, and we had to bivouac on the ground. その間に日が暮れてわれわれは露営しなければならなかった. 【類】as *night* is ***falling***. ¶as the *night* ***glides on*** 夜がふけるにつれて. ¶The *night* ***grows*** late. 夜がふける. ¶The *night* has ***grown old***. 夜がふけた. ¶The *night* was ***pressing up*** against the windows; only the fire-light now fought the darkness in the wainscoted room. 夜陰がひしひしと窓に迫り今は独り炉の明りが羽目張りの室内で暗黒と戦った. ¶In these valleys *night* ***reigns***. あたりのけい谷は一帯に夜に包まれている. ¶as the *night* ***settles in*** 夜がふけるにつれて. ¶as the *night* ***wears on*** 夜が段々ふけるにつれて ‖ So the *night* ***wears on***. こうして夜はふける.

Q ***all night*** [long] 終夜 ‖ ***all night*** through 一晩中, 夜通し. 【類】He was up ***all night***. / We watched ***all night*** (day) long. ¶pass an ***anxious*** *night* 心配して一夜を明かす. ¶The Commodore is famous for its ***Big Nights***. [ニューヨークの]コンモドア・ホテルは盛んな夜の宴会があるので有名だ. ¶a ***black*** *night* 暗夜. ¶on the ***bridal*** *night* 婚礼の晩に. ¶on a ***charming moonlight*** (=***moonlit***) *night* 美しい月夜に. ¶a ***chill*** *night* うすら寒い夜. ¶a ***chilly*** *night* はだ寒い夜. ¶on a ***clear*** *night* 晴れた晩に. ¶on an extra ***cold*** *night* 特に寒い晩に. ¶one ***cold wintry*** *night* ある寒い冬の晩. ¶in the ***comfortless*** *night* 退屈な夜に. ¶on a ***dark, rainy*** *night* 暗い雨の夜に. ¶a ***dark*** and ***stormy*** *night* やみの暴風雨の晩. ¶It was ***deep*** *night* when he came back. 彼が戻ってきたのは真夜中であった. ¶the ***deepening*** *night* ふけ行く夜. ¶a ***dirty*** (=stormy) *night* 暴風雨の晩. ¶Do this ***each*** *night*. [その期間]毎晩これをしなさい. ¶***early*** *night* よいの口. ¶***every*** *night* 毎晩. ¶pass a ***fearful*** *night* 恐ろしい一夜を明かす. ¶a ***few*** *nights* ago 二晩三晩前に. ¶a ***first*** *night* [芝居などの]顔見世 ‖ on the ***first*** *night* 最初の晩に. ¶on a ***foggy*** *night* 霧の夜に. ¶a ***freezing*** *night* 凍りつくように寒い晩. ¶What a ***glorious*** *night!* 何んとすばらしい晩だこと. ¶I have had a ***good*** *night*. よく眠った. ‖ I wish you a ***good*** *night*. お休みなさい. ‖ He waved "***good night***" to them all. 彼はみんなに「おやすみ」の意味で手を振った. ☞ "good night" は必ずしも日本語の「おやすみ」には当らない. 夕方別れて帰宅する際などの "good night" は「ご気げんよう」位か. ¶on a ***hot sweltering*** *night* 暑苦しい晩に. ¶a ***jet-black*** *night* まっ暗な夜. ¶***last*** *night* ゆうべ ‖ his ***last*** *night* alive 彼の死の前夜. ¶sit beside him through the ***livelong*** *night* 長い長

い夜通し彼の傍にすわる. ¶What a *lovely night!* 何んと好い晩だこと. ¶a *merry night* 楽しい夜. ¶pass a *nervous night* 神経を悩まして一夜を明かす. ¶the *next night* その翌晩に. ¶*one night* ある晩. ¶*one black winter night* ある冬の暗夜. ¶a *pitch dark* (=*black*) *night* まっ暗な晩. ¶on the *previous night* その前夜に. ¶pass *restless nights* 落着かない幾夜を過ごす. ¶for *several nights* 幾夜も. ¶on *several consecutive nights* 幾夜も続いて. ¶I have passed a *sleepless night*. 夜通し眠れなかった. ¶on a *snowy night* 雪の降る夜に. ¶a *star-filled* (=*starlight*) *night* 星明りの夜. ¶a *starry night* 星空の夜. ¶a *still* (=*silent*) *night* 静かな夜. ¶a *stormy night* あらしの夜. ¶the two *succeeding nights* 二晩続いて. ¶a *tempestuous night* 暴風の夜. ¶pass an *uneasy night* 不安の一夜を明かす. ¶a *wakeful night* 目ざめ勝ちな夜. ¶the *whole night* 一晩中. ¶The *night* is *young*. まだよいの口だ.

Q^2 one *autumn night* ある秋の夜. ¶a *Christmas night* クリスマスの晩. ¶a *guest night* [クラブなどで]接待会のある晩. ¶a *horse night* cap《俗》目隠し帽(死刑囚の顔にかぶせる). ¶her first *marriage night* 彼女の結婚初夜. ¶on a cold *November night* 十一月の寒い晩に. ¶celebrate the *opening night* of a club クラブ開設の夜を祝う.【類】the *opening night* of the season. ¶late on *Saturday night* 土曜の夜おそく. ¶a wakeful *summer night* 眠れない夏の夜. ¶have a "*Television Night*" テレヴィジョンの夕を持つ. ¶on *Wednesday night* 水曜の夜に.

P Mr. Jenkins complained that he could not sleep *at nights* because of the crowing of Mr. Knight's cocks. ジェンキンスさんはナイトさんの鶏が鳴くので夜眠れないとこぼした. ‖ Heavy dews fell *at nights*. 深い露が幾夜も降りた. ‖ soldiers on duty *at night* 夜間当番の兵.【類】illuminated by natural light during the day and by artificial light *at night* / Tokyo *at night* / work *at night* / go to bed early *at night* / He came home late *at night*. ¶*before night* 夜になる前に. ¶travel *by night* 夜の旅行をする ‖ London *by night* 夜のロンドン. ‖ flee (=fly) *by night* 夜逃げする.【類】The City (ロンドンの旧市内) is the busiest part of London by day and the quietest *by night* / Bats come out *by night*. / China town *by night* is a maze of attractiveness, while, by day it devolves into dirt and cheap tardiness without a saving feature (取柄のない汚なくて平凡で活気のない街に変ってしまう). / *By night* as by day, the scene is one of rare restfulness and unique beauty. / work *by night* / The moon and stars give light *by night*. ‖ *by night* and day 昼夜の別なく. ¶*during* the *night* 夜間. ¶before we retired *for* the *night* 寝間に引込まない内に.【類】The tradesman had just shut up his shop *for* the *night*. ‖ bivouac *for* the *night* 野宿する ‖ put up [at an inn] *for* the *night* 宿を取る.【類】Could you put me up *for* the *night?* ‖ *for* three *nights* running 三晩続けて. ¶The legends say that Fuji rose *in* a *night*. 伝説では富士山は一夜にでき上ったことになっている. ‖ I awoke three times *in* a *night*. 私は一晩に三度目をさました. ‖ It was built *in* a single *night*. それは一夜の中に造られた. ‖ become famous *in* a *night* 一夜で有名になる ‖ *in* one *night* 一晩に ‖ There was a big fire *in* the *night*. 夜中に大火があった. ¶far *into* the *night* 夜ふけまで. ¶in the dead (=hush) *of night* 深更に ‖ in the shades *of night* 夜陰に ‖ go home *of* a *night* 夜分帰宅する ‖ go earlier to bed *of* a *night* 夜早寝する ‖ sleep soundly *of nights* without dreaming of ... ...の夢も見ず夜な夜なぐっすり眠る ‖ Who's there at this time *of night?* 夜中今時分そこにいるのはだれだ. ¶*on* the *night* of his return 彼が帰った晩.【類】*on* the bridal *night* / *On* dark *nights* a white light can be seen farther than any color; *on* bright *nights* red takes the first place. / late *on* Saturday *night* / *on* the *night* of the fourth of July. ¶stay *over night* 一泊する.【類】This fish will not keep *over night*. ¶bedroom, breakfast and attendance, from 8/6 *per night* per person 寝室と朝飯と給仕付で一人一晩八シリング六ペンスから. ¶The storm lasted *through* the *night*. あらしが夜通し続いた.【類】all *through* the *night*. ¶Street-cars run *throughout* the *night* on New-Year's eve. 電車は大みそ日には終夜運転する. ‖ The conflict lasted *throughout* the *night*. 戦争は夜通し続いた. ¶the subscription amounted to ... down *to* last *night* 昨夜までに寄付金は...に達した. ¶It is growing *towards night*. 日が暮れてきた.

P^2 *night after* night 毎夜. ¶the *night before* last 一昨夜. ¶*nights of* fathomless blackness 底知れない暗やみの数夜.

O There a strong wind was blowing *night* and day. そこでは夜となく昼となく強風が吹いていた.

nightfall, *n.* 日暮, 夕暮.

P *after nightfall* 日没後. ¶*At nightfall* they started again. 夕暮に彼らはまた出かけた. ¶They will arrive there *before nightfall*. 彼らは日のある内にそこに着くだろう. ¶I shall be back *by nightfall*. 私は日暮までには戻って来ます. ¶*toward[s] nightfall* 日没ごろ.

nightingale, *n.* ナイチンゲール(夜うぐいす).

V *Nightingales sing* (=*warble*). ナイチンゲールはさえずる.

Q Jenny Lind, the *Swedish nightingale* スエーデンの女流声楽家ジェニー・リンド.

nightmare, *n.* 悪夢.

V *have* [a] *nightmare* うなされる.

P He is troubled *by* (=*with*) *nightmare*. 彼はうなされるので困っている. ¶suffer *from nightmare* 悪夢におびえる.

P^2 The *nightmare of* the disaster (sad event, war, fire) その災難(など)の悪夢.

night-quarters, *n.* 宿泊所.

V *obtain night-quarters* at a hotel 旅館に宿泊する.

nine, *n.*《米》『野球』チーム.

P cheer *for* a [baseball] *nine* チームを応援する.

nip, *n.* 一つねり, 一さし.

V *feel* a *nip* in the air 空気はぴりっとはだをさす感じだ.

P^2 There is a *nip in* the air on a frosty morning. 寒いしもの朝の空気はぴりっとはだにしみる. ¶a *nip of* brandy ブランデーのごく少量.

nip, *v.* 痛める; ざ折する.

M, M^2 *nip away* (*along, off*)《英》急いで行く. ¶The wind *nipped hard* this morning. けさははだを刺すような風が吹いた.

P The buds have been *nipped by* the frost. つぼみが霜で痛んだ. ¶The scheme (=plan) has been *nipped in* the bud. その計画は出鼻をくじかれた. ‖ I got one of my fingers *nipped in* a train door. 私は指を列車のドアにはさまれた.

nipple, *n.* 乳首.

Q *rosy nipples* ばら色の乳首.

Nirvana, *n.* ねはん.

V *attain* (=*earn or enter into*) *Nirvana* 入寂する.

P Buddha's entry *into Nirvana* 仏陀の入寂.

nitrate, *n.* 硝酸.

Q^2 *ammonium nitrate* 硝酸アンモニア.

P^2 *nitrate of* soda 硝酸ナトリウム.

no, *n.* 否定, 断り, ノー.

V You *mean no*, mother?—I *mean no!* お母さん, いけないの?—いけませんよ. ¶*say* "*no*"「ノー」と言う, 承知しない ‖ I *say no*, once for all. 断然いやです. ¶He will not *take no* for an answer. 彼はノーの返事では承知しまい.

Q I am compelled to answer a *bold* "*No.*" 私は思い切って「いいえ」と答えた. ¶He dismissed me with a *curt* "*No.*" 彼は私に「だめだ」と言ってあっさり片付けてしまった. ¶*Two noes* make a yes. 二つの否定は肯定になる.

P He is sure to cut him off *with* a curt *no*. 彼はそっけなく断って氏との交渉を打切るに相違ない.

no, *a.*, *ad.* 否定の.

M *Absolutely* (=*Positively*) *no!* 断然ノーだ.

nobility, *n.* 高貴, 高雅; 貴族.

V He can *boast* no *nobility* of lineage. 彼は自慢できるような家柄ではない. ¶*degrade* the *nobility* of histrionic art 演劇の高貴性を低める.

Q^2 a *Court nobility* 公卿.

P^2 *nobility of* features 目鼻だちの上品さ ‖ *nobility* and sublimity *of* thought 思想の気高さと高尚さ.

nobody, *n.* 取るに足らない者.

V She *married* a *nobody*. 彼女は平凡な人と結婚した. ¶He *slights nobody*. 彼は人をそらさない.

Q The actress was a *humble nobody* a few years ago. その女優は数年前には名もない者だった. ¶I'm a *mere nobody*. 私は名もない男です.

O somebodies and *nobodies* 有名無名の人々.

nod, *n.* うなずき.

V *bestow* condescending *nods* on ... ...に対して大風にう

なずく. ¶He *gave* me a *nod* when he came in. 彼は入って来たとき私に默礼した.

P call a man *by* a *nod* うなずいて人を招く. ¶He answered *with* a *nod*. 彼はこっくりした; うなずいた.

nod, *v*. うなずく; いねむりする.

M *nod affably* to ... 愛想よく...にうなずく. ¶*nod drily* 無「愛想にうなずく.

P *nod at* (=*to*) a man 人にうなずく(辞儀する). ¶She sat *nodding by* the fire. 彼女は炉辺にすわっていねむりしていた. ¶*nod in* assent 承知だとうなずく. ¶He *nodded* me *into* his room. うなずいて私をへやに入れた. ¶*nod over* one's work 仕事をしながらいねむりをする. ¶*nod to* a person with a smile 微笑しながら人にうなずく. 【類】He *nodded to* me as he passed. 「うなずいた.

O He *nodded* to show his understanding. 彼は分かったと

noise, *n*. 音, 声, 響; 評判; 騒音.

V *abate* the *noise* 音響をやわらげる. ¶*hear* a *noise* of scratching 引っかく音を聞く ‖ I *hear* a crackling *noise*. ぱちぱちいう音が聞える. ¶*keep up* a continual *noise* 絶えず音を立てる. ¶Don't *make* a *noise*. やかましい. 【類】the *noise made* by the passing trains ‖ *make* a *noise* (=sensation) in the world 世間の評判になる ‖ He *made* no *noise* about it. 彼はそのことをやかましく言わなかった. 【類】Don't *make* a *noise* about trifles. ¶*produce* a thundering *noise* ごう音を発する. ¶Much *noise* is *raised* about democracy. 民主主義について世間がやかましくいう.

V² The *noise abated*. 雑音が静まった. ¶The *noise kept* me awake all night. その騒音で一晩中眠れなかった. ¶The *noise subsided*. 音響が静まった.

Q The *noise* is very *annoying*. その音が非常にやかましい. ¶make a *curious noise* 奇妙な音を出す. ¶a *deafening noise* 耳がつんぼになりそうな騒音. 【類】The *noise* in the place was *deafening*. ¶The *noise* is very *disturbing*. その音は実にうるさい. ¶a *harsh noise* 耳ざわりな音. ¶make a *hideous noise* 恐ろしい音を立てる. ¶Jazz music produces a *lively noise*. ジャズはにぎやかな音を出す. ¶make a *loud noise* 大きな音を立てる. ¶the *nerve-racking noise* and tumult of modern cities 近代都市の神経を悩ます騒音とけん騒. ¶a *rumbling noise* ごろごろ鳴る音. ¶a *shrill loud noise* かん高い音. ¶Then there was a *terrific noise* in his ears. それから恐ろしい音が聞えた. ¶with a *tremendous noise* すさまじい音を立てて.

Q² *city noises* 市の雑音. ¶away from *street noises* 町の雑音を離れて. ¶*traffic noises* 交通騒音.

P The horse took fright *at* the *noise*. 馬はその音に驚いた. ¶I cannot sleep *for* the *noise*. 私はその音で眠れない. ¶It burst [out] *with* a *noise* like thunder. それはごう然破裂した. ‖ open the door *with* a *noise* がたんとドアをあける.

P² *noise in* the ear 耳鳴り. ¶the *noise of* railways 鉄路「の響.

noise, *v*. 言いふらす, うわさする.

M it was *noised abroad* that ... ...といううわさがぱっと立った.

M² It was soon *noised about* that he was there. 彼がそこにいるということがたちまち言いふらされた. 【類】The news of his arrival was soon *noised about*.

noisy, *a*. やかましい; 《口語》はでな.

M Good gracious, children, why are you *so noisy* today? [子供に向って]まーお前たちはきょうはどうしてそんなにやかましいの.

P The night was *noisy with* bugles. その晩はらっぱでや「かましかった.

O *noisy* (=loud) color けばけばしい色.

nomenclature, *n*. 命名法; 術語.

V *harmonize* the *nomenclature* with that by other writers 術語を他の執筆者のものと一致させる. ¶or ..., to *substitute* a modern *nomenclature* すなわち, 現代の術語で言

Q *legal nomenclature* 法律用語(括称). 「えば...

Q² *plant nomenclature* 植物命名法.

P the standardization *of* the *nomenclature* of ... ...用語

nominal, *a*. 名だけの. 「の統一.

M *merely nominal* 有名無実の. 【類】I paid him a *merely nominal* rent for the cottage.

nominate *v*. 任命する; 推薦する.

P He was *nominated by* H.M. the Emperor member of the House of Peers. 氏は貴族院議員に勅選された. ¶*nominate* him *for* the position of ... 彼を...に任命する. 【類】He was *nominated for* an office (the presidency). / He was *nominated for* the Mayoralty (市長の職). / be *nominated for* the presidency (大統領候補者). ¶He was *nominated to* the Upper House. 氏は上院(議員)に推薦された. 【類】He was *nominated to* the vacant post (欠員).

nomination, *n*. 任命, 指名; 推薦.

V *accept* the *nomination* of ... ...の任命を拝命する. ¶*close nomination* 指名権(推薦)を終る. ¶*secure* a *nomination* 任命される. ¶He *won* the Democratic *nomination* for the Senate over ex-Gov. ... by a majority of 56,022 votes. 氏は五万六千二十二票の多数で...前知事を抜いて上院議員として民主党から指名された.

Q *imperial nomination* 勅選. ¶a candidate for the *Presidential nomination* in the election of 1916 一九一六年の選挙における大統領候補指名の候補者(政党大会における).

P² *nomination of* a person *to* a post ある職への任命(指名) ‖ *nomination of* a candidate 候補者指名.

nominee, *n*. 受任者. 「選議員.

Q an *Imperial nominee* to (=in) the House of Peers 勅

non-attendance, *n*. 不参, 欠席. 「に欠席の断り状.

V a letter *excusing* his *non-attendance* at a meeting 会合

P² *non-attendance at* school (church) 学校(など)の欠席.

nonce, *n*. 現時, 当時.

P *for* the *nonce* その時だけ, さし当り.

nonchalance, *n*. 無とん着.

P *with nonchalance* 平気で. 【類】He heard the news *with nonchalance*.

none, *pron*. なにも(またはだれも)...ない.

V Have you any money left? I *have none* left. 金がいくらか残っているか. 少しも残っていない. ‖ He would *have none* of such things. 彼はそんなことはいやだと言った. ‖ Let me *have none* of your chat. もうおしゃべりはやめてくれ. ¶*None* were *permitted* to enter by this gate. だれもこの門からはいることを許されなかった.

Q *None* are completely *happy*. 完全に幸福な者はない. ¶*none other* than he can ... 彼の外だれも...できない.

P *None but* Napoleon could have done it. ナポレオンならではできないことであった. ¶These goods are second *to none*. これらの品はほかのどれにも劣らない.

P² *None of* that! よせよ ‖ *None of* your impudence! 失敬なことを言うな ‖ It is *none of* your business. お前の知ったことじゃない. 【類】*None of* your joking! ‖ *None of* them came. その人たちはだれも来なかった. 【類】His English is *none of* the best. / *None of* them are of any use to me. / He is *none of* my friends.

none, *ad*. [the+比較級, too などと併用して]少しも..., 決して...

M *none the less* それでもなお. 【類】He is *none the less* happier for his wealth. ¶He is *none the better* for it. だからといってちっともよくはない. ¶I got home *none too early*. 丁度いい時に帰宅した. 【類】The pay is *none too high*. 「かった.

O I slept *none* that night. 《米口》あの晩はちっとも眠れな

nonessential, *n*. 重要でないもの.

V *whittle nonessentials* from the budget 予算から主要で

non-performance, *n*. 不履行. 「ないものを除く.

P² *non-performance of* a contract 契約不履行.

nonplus, *v*. 当惑させる, 閉口させる.

M look *utterly nonplused* 全く閉口の体である.

P He was *nonplused for* a moment. 彼はちょっと閉口した. ¶He was very much *nonplused over* the matter. 彼はその件では大いに当惑した.

nonsense, *n*. たわごと, ばかげたこと.

V *make nonsense* 無意味なことをする. ¶*speak* (=talk) *nonsense* たわごとを言う. ¶I intended to *stand* no *nonsense* from him. 私は彼からばかにされるものかと思った. 【類】I can *stand* no more of his *nonsense*. ¶Don't *talk nonsense*! ばか言え. ¶Contact with other boys will *take* the *nonsense* out of him. 他の子供に接するとあの子の気ままが直る. ¶I will not *tolerate* such *nonsense*. こんなたわ言を言わせてはおかない. ¶*utter nonsense* ばかなことをいう.

Q talk *absurd nonsense* ばかげたことを言う. ¶What *arrant nonsense!* なんというたわごとだ. ¶*drivelling nonsense* 無茶苦茶. ¶it would be *ludicrous* (=*ridiculous*) *nonsense* to say that ... ...というのはばかげたたわごとだ.

¶*palpable nonsense* 明かなたわ言. ¶*sheer nonsense* 全くのたわごと. ¶an *utter nonsense* 全く意味のない言葉.
P talk a lot ***of*** *nonsense* 盛んにたわごとをならべる ‖ volumes ***of*** *nonsense* 沢山のたわごと.
P² see the *nonsense* ***of*** national frontiers in such matter こうしたことには国境など無意味であることを認める.
O *Nonsense!* つまらない, よせ.

non-use, *n.* 使用しないこと.
P allow a substance to rot ***through non-use*** 使わずにおいて物を腐らす.

noodle, *n.* ヌードル, うどん.
Q² ***macaroni*** and ***buckwheat noodles*** マカロニやそば.

nook, *n.* 片いなか.
Q a ***cosy*** and ***comfortable nook*** 居心地のよい快適なすみ.
Q² a ***breakfast nook*** in the kitchen 朝飯を食べる台所の片すみ.

noon, *n.* 正午, 真日中.
Q a ***cloudless noon*** 晴れ渡った真日中. ¶at ***high noon*** 正午に ‖ in the ***high noon*** of a scorching day 炎熱焼くような日の真日中に. ¶at a ***hot summer noon*** 暑い夏の真日中に.
P ***about noon*** 正午ごろ. ¶adjourn for an hour ***at noon*** 正午に一時間休会する. ¶Snow fell ***before noon.*** 午前に雪が降った. 【類】a little ***before noon.*** ¶He will return ***by noon.*** 彼は昼までに帰る. ¶***from noon*** to evening 昼から夕まで. ¶He left home a little ahead ***of noon.*** 彼は正午少し前に家を出ました. ¶It is ***past noon.*** 昼過ぎだ. ¶from morning ***till noon*** 朝から昼まで. ¶It is now ***toward noon.*** もう昼に近い.
P² at the *noon* ***of*** life 年盛りに.

noonday, *n.* 正午.
P Vice stalks about ***at noonday.*** 悪徳の百鬼が白昼横行する. 【類】be dark even ***at noonday*** ‖ His guilt is as clear as the sun ***at noonday.*** 彼の罪は白日のごとく明々白々だ.

nooning, *n.* 昼休み.
Q² ***one hour nooning*** (工場などの)一時間の昼休み.

noon-time, *n.* 昼時.
P ***at noon-time*** 正午に.

noose, *n.* ずっこけ; 輪なわ.
Q a ***hangman's noose*** 絞首刑用の首なわ.
Q² a ***running noose*** ずっこくり.
P catch ... ***in*** a *noose* 輪なわで...を捕える.

norm, *n.* 標準, ノルマ.
V ***reach*** the *norm* 標準に達する.

normal, *n.* 常態.
P ***above normal*** 普通以上. ¶***below*** [the] *normal* コンマ以下. 【類】His temperature is a little ***below*** the *normal.*

north, *n.* 北, 北方; 北地.
Q bound for Nikko, Karuizawa, *or further north* 日光軽井沢方面(以北)行.
P a big battle ***at*** the *north* of the Liaotung Peninsula 遼東半島の北部における大合戦 ‖ Hiyeizan is ***at*** the *north* of Kyoto. 比叡山は京都の北にある. ¶a view of ... ***from*** the *north* 北方からの...のながめ ‖ a wind ***from*** the *north* 北風. ¶up ***in*** the *north* 北に ‖ The white bear lives ***in*** the cold *north.* 白ぐまは寒い北地に住む. ‖ Russia is ***in*** the *north* of Europe. ロシアはヨーロッパの北部にある. ¶Oji is ***on*** the *north* of Tokyo. 王子は東京の北にある.
P² *north* ***by*** east 北微東. 【類】***north by*** west. ¶three miles *north* ***of*** ... ...の三マイル北. ¶Omiya lies ***to*** the *north* of Tokyo. 大宮は東京の北に当る.

north, *a., adv.* 北の(に).
M The park is ***due north*** from the city. 公園は同市の真北に当る.
O go (sail, look, face) *north* 北に向う(など).

nose, *n.* 鼻; きゅう覚.
V ***apply*** one's *nose* to ... ...に鼻をあてる. ¶He ***blows*** his *nose* with a handkerchief (his fingers). 彼はハンケチ(手)で鼻をかむ. ¶***bury*** one's *nose* in a quart pot 一クォート(六合余)びんに鼻をうめる(飲酒家など). ¶***clamp*** the *nose* 鼻をつまむ. ¶Don't ***cut off*** your *nose* to spite your face! 短気は損気. ¶***flatten*** one's *nose* against the window 窓に鼻を押付ける. ¶***follow*** one's *nose* [鼻の向く方へ]真すぐに行く ‖ ***Follow*** your *nose.* 気の向き放題にやれ. ¶The aroma of coffee ***greeted*** (=***reached***) his *nose.* コーヒーの香りが鼻にぷーんときた. ¶The dog ***has*** a good *nose.* 犬は鼻がよくきく. ‖ He always ***has*** his *nose* in a book. 彼は始終書物に読みふけっている. ¶***hold*** one's *nose* (悪臭を避けるために)鼻をつまむ. ¶***make*** a long *nose* (=cut, cock *or* make a snook) at ... ...をあざわらう(おや指を鼻にあて他の四指をひろげて). ¶***pick*** the *nose* 鼻くそをほじくる. ¶***pinch*** the *nose* ***together*** 鼻をつまむ. ¶He ***pokes*** (=thrusts) his *nose* into everything. 彼は何にでも頭を突込む. ¶***pull*** one's *nose* 鼻を引張る. ¶***punch*** the *nose* 鼻にげんこを食わす. ¶***put*** one's *nose* out of joint 人の鼻を明かす. ¶***show*** one's *nose* in a shop 店に顔を出す. ¶He ***sticks*** his *nose* into everything. 彼は何ごとにも出しゃばる. ¶My *nose* is ***stuffed up,*** and I cannot smell. 鼻が詰ってにおいが分からない. ¶He ***sticks*** his *nose* into everything. 彼は世話好きだ. ¶***suffer*** a broken *nose* 鼻柱を折られる(主にけん鬪のとき). ¶I should like to know why she always ***thrusts*** her *nose* among my papers. 一体あの女はどうして私の書類をかき回すのだろう. ¶***thumb*** the *nose* 鼻へ親指をあてる(侮辱するときなど). ¶***turn up*** one's *nose* at ... ...を鼻先であしらう. ¶***tweak*** one's *nose* behind one's back 後ろから鼻をつまむ. ¶***wipe*** one's *nose* with a clean handkerchief きれいなハンカチで鼻をふく. ¶***wrinkle*** one's *nose* (悪臭などで)鼻にしわをよらせる ‖ an incorrigible habit of ***wrinkling*** one's *nose* 鼻にしわを寄せるという直らない癖.
V² My *nose* began to ***bleed.*** 私は鼻血が出だした. ¶a child whose *nose* ***runs*** はなを垂らす児.
Q an ***accipitrine*** (=***aquiline or eagle***) *nose* とんび鼻(わし鼻). ¶He came off with a ***bleeding nose.*** 彼は鼻血を出して立ち去った. ¶suffer a ***bloody*** *nose* 鼻血を出す. ¶a ***broad, squat*** *nose* だだっぴろくて平たい鼻(ししっ鼻). ¶a ***button-shaped*** *nose* 団子鼻. ¶an ***elevated nose*** 高い鼻. ¶famous for his ***enormous*** *nose* 大きな鼻で有名な. ¶a ***flat*** *nose* しし鼻. ¶a ***Greecian*** *nose* ギリシア人型の鼻. ¶a ***high*** *nose* 高い鼻. ¶have a ***high-bridged*** *nose* 鼻筋が通っている. ¶You must have a ***keen*** *nose* to detect it. それをかぎ出すには余ほど鼻がきかなければならない. ¶a ***long*** *nose* 鼻すじの通った鼻. ¶a ***long, high*** *nose* 鼻筋が通った高い鼻. ¶with a ***long, shapely*** *nose* 鼻筋が通って格好のよい鼻. ¶a ***narrow*** *nose* 幅のせまい(鋭い)鼻. ¶a ***prominent*** *nose* 隆起した鼻. ¶a ***pronounced*** *nose* 目立つ鼻. ¶a ***pugnacious*** *nose* けんか好きの鼻. ¶a ***Roman*** *nose* わし鼻. ¶have a ***running*** *nose* 水鼻が出る. ¶a ***saucy*** *nose* 高慢ちきな鼻. ¶a ***sharp*** *nose* とんがり鼻. ¶a ***short*** *nose* [鼻すじの通らない]短い鼻. ¶a ***short, flat*** *nose* 短く平べたい鼻. ¶a ***snub*** *nose* つまんだような鼻. ¶have a ***straight*** *nose* 鼻すじが通っている. ¶a ***turned-up*** *nose* 上を向いた鼻. ¶an ***upturned*** *nose* 上を向いた鼻. ¶a ***well-cut*** *nose* 格好の好い鼻. ¶a ***wry*** *nose* 曲った鼻.
Q² a ***bottle*** *nose* (飲酒家の)赤鼻. ¶a ***pug*** (=turned-up) *nose* ししっ鼻. ¶a ***potato*** *nose* だんごっ鼻. ¶a ***ridge*** *nose* すじの通った鼻.
P bleed ***at*** the *nose* 鼻血が出る. ¶***before*** one's *nose* 面前に. ¶He has never been trained to see ***beyond*** his *nose.* 彼はすぐ鼻先のことしか見えない. ¶He is led ***by*** the *nose.* 彼は自由に引回わされている. ‖ perceive ***by*** the *nose* 鼻で感じる. ¶Bleeding ***from*** the *nose* is common. 鼻血は珍らしくない. ¶have a cold ***in*** the *nose* 鼻風を引いている ‖ pain ***in*** the *nose* 鼻の痛み. ¶a pimple ***on*** the *nose* 鼻の上の吹出物. ¶He speaks (=talks) ***through*** the *nose* (has a nasal twang). 彼は言葉が鼻にかかる. ¶It happened ***under*** our *nose[s].* それはわれわれの目の前で起った. 【類】Such things were in progress ***under*** their *noses.* ¶examine ***with*** the *nose* [香りなどを]鼻で調べる ‖ persons of short stature and ***with*** long *noses* せいの低い長い鼻の人たち. 【類】a man ***with*** a high *nose.*
P² Those correspondents have the proverbial "*nose* ***for*** news." その通信員たちは例のニュースをかぎつける鼻を持っている.

nose, *v.* かぐ; 探す; 突進する.
M *nose* (=smell) ***out*** another's secret 人の秘密をかぎ出す. 【類】The cat ***nosed out*** a rat.
M² I'll just go and *nose* ***about*** a bit. 私は出て行って少し捜して見よう.
P *nose* ***after*** (=***for***) ... ...を捜す. ¶*nose* ***at*** (=***about***) ... ...をかぐ. ¶The train ***nosed into*** the station. 列車は停車場へはいった. ‖ *nose* ***into*** bureau drawers たんすの引だしに頭をつきこむ(その中味を調べる). ¶The plane ***nosed*** its way ***through*** the fog. 飛行機が霧の中を突き進んだ. ‖ *nose* ***into*** another's affairs 他人のことに口ばしを入れる.

nostril, *n.* 鼻孔.
V A strange odor ***assailed*** the *nostrils.* 妙なにおいが鼻をついた. ¶***pinch*** the *nostrils* together 鼻をつまむ. ¶A faint but not at all disagreeable odor ***saluted*** my *nostrils.* かすかではあるが決して気持の悪くない香が私の鼻を

ついた.

P stink ***in*** one's *nostrils* 鼻をつく, 鼻につく.

notability, *n.* 名士.

Q ***Japanese artistic*** *notabilities* 日本美術界の名士連.

P *notabilities* ***in*** literary circles 文壇の名士たち. ¶The *notabilities* ***of*** the city were present. 市の諸名士が列席した.

notable, *n.* 有名人.

V^2 Many *notables* ***came*** to the President's reception. 有名人が多数大統領の招宴に集った.

notable, *a.* 有名な.

P a name that is *notable* ***in*** letters 文学で有名な名.

notary, *n.* 公証人.

Q a [***public***] *notary* 公証人.

notch, *n.* 《米》度, 点.

Q reach the ***highest*** (=***top***) *notch* 最高度に達する. ¶Prices are at the ***lowest*** *notch*. 物価はどん底だ.

note, *n.* (**1**) 注, 注釈; [通例 *pl.*] 覚書, 手控(ノート); 略記; 手紙; 通達, 通告.

V I ***addressed*** a *note* to him, in which I construed ... 彼に一筆書き送って...を説明した. ¶***arrange*** one's *notes* for publication 刊行のためにノートを整理する. ¶I ***carry*** a *note* from him. 私は彼からの書状を持参している. ¶We ***compared*** our *notes* with tea-spoons clicked against cup and saucer. ¶in ***compiling*** the *notes* I have been greatly indebted to ... この注釈の編集について私は...に負う所が多かった. ¶***do*** one's school *notes* on a typewriter タイプライターで学校で取ったノートを写す. ¶*Notes* have been ***exchanged*** between both parties. 両当事者間に覚書が交換された. ¶I ***got*** a further *note* from him detailing more fully ... 私は彼からさらに...に関する詳細の書面をもらった. ¶***issue*** a Circular *Note* to the Powers (政府などが)列強に回文を発する. ¶Let me ***have*** your history *notes* for a while. しばらく貴君の歴史の筆記を見せてくれ. ¶***jot down*** a *note* on piece of paper 紙片に書き留める. 【類】***jot down*** *notes* from day to day. ¶***leave*** a *note* [behind] 書きおきをする. ¶He ***lost*** all his lecture *notes* in a fire. 彼は火事で講義ノートを全部焼いてしまった. ¶***make*** a *note* to that effect in the memorandum そのことを手帳に控えておく ‖ ***make*** a *note* of ... ...のメモを取る. 【類】When I hear a funny name (奇妙な名), I ***make*** a *note* of it. / ***make*** *notes* for one's own use / *notes* ***made*** on a tour through ... / He ***made*** *notes* in his book. / ***make*** *notes* on a lecture. ¶***pen*** a *note* to one's friend 友人にやる手紙を書く. ¶***pencil*** a *note* 手紙を鉛筆で書く. ¶***present*** a *note* to the British Government 英国政府に覚書を提出する. ¶***receive*** a *note* from him 彼から書状を落手する. ¶***seal*** [***up***] a *note* 手紙を封じる. ¶I ***sent*** him a *note* of remonstrance, saying that ... 彼に意見状を送って...と述べた. ¶***set down*** *notes* 注釈を記入する. ¶cannot ***sing*** a *note* 少しも歌えない. ¶***sound*** a *note* of warning on ... ...について警告を発する. ¶His speech ***strikes*** the *note* of genius. 彼の演説は天才の風がある. ¶***strike*** a new *note* by ... ...して新手を打つ. ¶Your editorial today ***strikes*** the right *notes*. 君のきょうの社説は大いにわが意を得たものだ. ¶***take*** *notes* on (=of) ... ...のノートをとる. 【類】***take*** a *note* of topic, book, and page / The policeman ***took*** *notes* from one of the spectators. / ***take*** *notes* of a public address (公開演説) / I will ***take*** a *note* of your address in case I may communicate with you at any time. / diligently ***take*** *notes* on a lecture / ***take*** *notes* intending to write an article ‖ put into shape some *notes* ***taken*** during the trip 旅行中の手控えを(単行本などに)まとめる. ¶***take down*** *notes* of ... ...と書きつける. ¶***write*** a *note* to ... ...を一筆書く. 【類】***write*** a *note* of invitation / ***write*** a careful *note* on ...

Q a ***bibliographical*** *note* of sources 出所を示した注. ¶***Careful*** *notes* should be made of this fact. この事実はていねいに控えておくべきだ. ¶the ***complete*** *notes* of the human gamut ありとあらゆる喜怒哀楽の情趣. ¶prepare ***copious*** *notes* 豊富な注を作る ‖ with ***copious*** *notes* illustrating the text of ... ...の本文を説明するこまかい注釈付で ‖ get into connected form the ***copious*** *notes* he has made 彼が取った豊富なノートをまとめる. ¶***crude*** *notes* of a journey 旅行の略記. ¶a ***diplomatic*** *note* 外交文書. ¶***elucidatory*** *notes* 備考. ¶***explanatory*** *notes* on ... ...の備考. 【類】French books printed in England with ***explanatory*** *notes* for use in schools and colleges. ¶send a ***hurried*** *note* to ... 急いで...に書状を出す. ¶an ***identic*** *note* 同文通牒. ¶I have very seldom been more gratified than by the very ***kind*** *note* which I have just received from him. 彼から受取ったばかりの親切な手紙ほど私を満足させたものはほとんどほかにない. ¶a ***marginal*** *note* 傍注, 本の書き入れ. ¶make ***mental*** *notes* of ... ...を注意する(心に留める) ‖ Do you make ***mental*** *notes* for your next picture? 次の絵の腹案をお作りですか. ¶take ***occasional*** *notes* on one's cuff カフスに必要に応じて折々書きつける. ¶a shorthand-writer to take an ***official*** *note* of the proceedings 議事録速記者. ¶in a ***penciled*** *note* on the MSS. 原稿に鉛筆で書いた注に. ¶a ***personal*** *note* sent by wire from the American President 米大統領の親電. ¶a ***prefatory*** *note* 序言. ¶take ***rapid*** *notes* 早く覚書を取る. ¶***rough*** *notes* 略注. ¶***scanty*** *notes* 少ない注. ¶prefix a ***short*** *note* to ... 短い説明を...の前に書く. ¶***shorthand-writer's*** *notes* 速記録. ¶take ***special*** *note* of ... ...を特に覚えておく. ¶make ***voluminous*** *notes* おびただしくノートを取る.

Q^2 an ***accommodation*** *note* 融通手形. ¶issue a ***circular*** *note* to the Powers 列国へ同文通ちょうを発する. ¶***classroom*** *notes* 教室のノート. ¶a ***cover*** *note* 説明の手紙. ¶Send me a ***debit*** *note*. 借方票をお送り下さい. ¶send an "***excuse me***" *note* 断りの手紙を出す(招待など). ¶keep ***field*** *notes* of work performed 実行した仕事の現場覚書を作る. ¶***foot*** *notes* to an article 一文の脚注. ¶copy one's ***history*** *notes* その歴史のノートを写しとる. ¶***interpretation*** *notes* 注解. ¶numerous marginal ***Ms.*** *notes* 数多の傍注筆記. ¶***News*** *notes* 編集者の言葉 (N.Y. Times などの通信の後に添付した). ¶a ***sale*** *note* 売上控え. ¶***specie*** *notes* 紙幣. ¶***stray*** *notes* 漫筆. ¶a ***short-term*** *note* 短期払手形. ¶a ***treasury*** *note*. 大蔵証券. ¶spread a ***warning*** *note* in the nation 国民に警戒を与える.

P speak ***from*** *notes* 草稿演説をする. ¶It is explained ***in*** the *notes*. それは注に説明してある. ¶the works of Milton ***with*** *notes* 注釈付のミルトンの著作 ‖ ***with*** a few *notes* about each 各自について二三の注を施して ‖ ***with*** a long *note* of thanks 長文の感謝状を添えて. ¶speak ***without*** *notes* (a single *note*) (一切)草稿なしで演説する.

P^2 *notes* ***for*** study 学習用の注解 ‖ with *notes* ***for*** teachers 教師用の注釈つき[教科書など]. ¶*notes* ***from*** my diary 私の日記からの略記. ¶*Notes* ***from*** Washington ワシントン便り. ¶*Notes* ***of*** the Day 時事短評(新聞の欄名) ‖ There was a *note* ***of*** anxiety in her voice. 彼女の声には心配の調子が出ていた. ¶*notes* ***on*** the competition papers 応募答案に対する審査評語 ‖ *notes* ***on*** Shakespeare シェークスピアの注釈. ¶*Notes* ***to*** Chapter III 第三章の注釈 ‖ in a *note* ***to*** the passage その節の注に. 【類】Burton, in the *notes* ***to*** his Arabian Nights, mentions ... ¶*notes* ***upon*** the daily life of Japan 日本の日常生活に関する短い記事.

(**2**) 音調, 調子; 声; 〖音〗音符; 符号; 特色, 特徴.

V ***add*** a delightful grace *note* to ... ...に楽しい装飾音を加える ‖ ***add*** a *note* of newness [調子に]新味を添える. ¶***change*** one's *note* ことばの調子を変える. ¶***emit*** a clear, shrill *note* [らっぱなど]明朗な調子の高い音を出す. ¶The songs of birds ***fling*** their silvery *notes* upon the air. 鳥がすずのような美音で歌う声が空から聞える. ¶He ***gave*** two or three *notes* on his bugle. 彼は二声三声らっぱを鳴らした. ¶***give off*** a *note* (楽器など)音を出す. ¶Her apparel ***has*** a *note* of exotic fantasy. 彼女の服装には異国好みの所がある. ¶***sing*** a false *note* 調子はずれな歌を歌う. ¶***slur*** *notes* 譜に連結線をつける. ¶***sound*** the *notes* of the scale 音階の音符を奏する. ¶***strike*** a new *note* 新機軸を出す. 【類】***strike*** no *note* of novelty ‖ ***strike*** the *notes* ピアノの鍵(けん)を打つ. ¶***touch*** *notes* 音符を奏する.

V^2 It has its ***distinctive*** *note*. それにはその特色がある. ¶the ***distinguishing*** *note* of Chinese proverbs 中国のことわざの特徴. ¶the only ***discordant*** *note* in the whole German press is ... ドイツの全新聞紙で異説を唱えているのは...だけである. ¶boldly sound a ***discordant*** *note* in the concert of praise 賞賛の声の中に敢然不賛成の声を発する. ¶"I" should rarely be the ***dominating*** *note* in a letter. 手紙では "I" という代名詞が余り目立たないようにせよ. ‖ the ***dominating*** *note* of his novels 彼の小説を一貫している特徴. ¶There were no garlands of gay flowers to strike a ***festive*** *note*. お祭り気分を出す花輪といったものは一つも

なかった. ¶the ***flamboyant note*** of the yellow paper その黄色新聞の麗々しい調子. ¶strike a ***fresh note*** 新鮮味のあることを言う. ¶He is inclined to strike rather a ***high note*** of alarm. 彼はどちらかといえばいたずらにその声を大にして人騒がせをやりたがる方だ. ¶strike a ***jarring note*** ぎーぎーいう音をたてる. ¶a ***mellow note*** of the cuckoo かっこうの美しい鳴き声. ¶It strikes the ***major*** rather than the ***minor note*** in one's "troubled lot below." それは現世苦について小乗的でなくむしろ大乗的な見方をしている. ¶strike a ***new note*** in daily journalism 日刊新聞に新機軸を出す. ¶There is no ***original note***. 月並(例によって例のごとし)である. ¶The mellow ***notes*** of the organ ***peal forth***. オルガンの快美な音が鳴り出す. ¶The author would like to add here a ***personal note***. 著者自身のことについて一言述べておきたい. ¶A modernistic ***note prevails***. 近代調が著しい. ¶His statement strikes the ***right note***. 彼の説は急所を突いている(正しい). 【類】he strikes a ***right note*** when he says that ... ¶there is a ***strong personal note*** in every book written by ... …の書いた本には皆彼一流の特徴がある. ¶the ***sweet notes*** of harps. たて琴の美しい音(ね). ¶a warbler's ***trilling note*** 小鳥のさえずる声. ¶the ***vibrant notes*** of a violin ヴァイオリンの震える音. ¶a ***whole note*** 全音符.

Q The ***booming notes*** of temple gongs punctuate the clamour that rises above Peking. 遠雷のごとき寺のどらの音(ね)が北京の空高く上がるわめきに折々まざった. ¶a big cheer not without a ***certain note*** of irony 何となく皮肉な調子のないでもない大かっさい. ¶***deep*** and ***melodious notes*** 沈んだ調子のよい音(ね). ¶Merriment is the ***dominant note***. 歓興がその特徴だ. 【類】the ***dominant note*** of the people.

Q[2] full of peaceful ***organ notes*** 平和なオルガンの音のあふれた.

P He strikes no great personal ***note as*** a painter. 彼は画家として大した個性を出していない. ¶mellow ***notes from*** an old organ 古いオルガンから出る快美な音(ね). ¶a ***note of*** correction 訂正符号. ¶His untimely death has a ***note of*** tragedy. 彼の若死には涙をしぼらせるものがある. ¶There was a ***note of*** self-satisfaction in his speech. 彼の演説には得意の調子が出ていた.

(3) 注目, 注意; 顕著, 著名.

V ***take note*** of ... = take notice of ... = pay attention to ... …に注目する ‖ My mind was so fully occupied that it ***took*** no ***note*** of time. 私は気を取られていたので時のたつのに気が付かなかった.

Q take very ***grave note*** of the facts 事実を重大視する. ¶writers of ***less note*** than ... …ほど有名でない作家. ¶Mirabeau and a host of others of ***lesser note*** ミラボー以下多数無名のやから. ¶a man of ***little note*** あまり名のない人. ¶an author of ***some note*** いくらか名の知れた著者.

P a singer ***of*** some ***note*** 多少名のある歌手. 【類】a man ***of note***. ¶a new ***note in*** literature 文壇の新声. ¶an event worthy ***of*** (=deserving) ***note*** 注目すべき事件.

(4) 《英》紙幣; 手形.

V ***notes*** are ***cashed*** by ... 手形は…で正金と引換えられる. ¶***issue notes*** 手形(紙幣)を発行する. ¶***redeem notes*** 手形を償還する.

Q a ***promissory note*** 約束手形. ¶***well-handled notes*** つかれた札(紙幣).

Q[2] a ***bank note***=《米》a bank bill 銀行券, 紙幣. ¶a ***five-pound note*** 五ポンド紙幣. ¶issue ***large denomination notes*** 高額紙幣を発行する.

P Give me the change ***in notes***, not in silver. 銀貨でなく札でつり銭を下さい.

P[2] a ***note of*** hand 約束手形.

note, *v*. 書き留める; 注解する; 着目する.

M The contents of the letter have been ***carefully noted***. その手紙の内容を丁寧に拝見しました. ¶it may be ***noted parenthetically*** ... …であるということを付記するのがよかろう. ¶Naval critics ***please note***. このことに対し海軍批評家諸君の注意を促したい. ¶These should be ***thoughtfully noted***. これは大いに注意しておくべきだ.

M[2] ***note down*** everything that is worth remembering 覚える価値のあるものはすべて書付けておく. 【類】***Note down*** what I'm going to say next.

P a man ***noted for*** skill in drawing animals 動物を描くのがうまいので有名な人. ¶we ***note*** (=learn) ***from*** your letter that ... 御書面で…と拝察します. ¶***note*** it ***on*** ... …に書入れる.

note-book, *n*. ノート.

V ***slip*** one's ***note-book*** into one's pocket ポケットの中へ手帳を入れる.

Q[2] a ***loose-leaf note-books*** 抜取自在ノートブック. ¶a ***shorthand notebook*** 速記帳.

noted, *pa*. 有名な.

P The Philippine Islands are ***noted for*** their fine sunsets. フィリピン群島はその夕日の美しさで有名だ. ‖ a woman ***noted for*** her vice いん婦. 【類】The azaleas (つつじ) here are ***noted for*** their beauty. / a man ***noted for*** skill in drawing animals / men ***noted for*** the brilliance (巧みさ) of their conversation / The bar is ***noted for*** the excellence of its liquors.

note-taking, *n*. 控えを取ること.

P[2] ***note-taking of*** (=***on***) lectures given in English 英語の講義の筆記.

nothing, *n*. 何も…ない, 少しも…しない; 虚無; ないも同然のもの.

V men who ***add nothing*** to the productive resources of the country, but are great consumers of the fruits of the labor of the lower classes その国の生産的資財には何も寄与するところなく下層社会の労働の成果を大いに消費する人々. ¶***ask nothing*** in return 何ら報酬を求めない. ¶It'll ***avail*** you ***nothing***. それは君には何の役にもたたないだろう. ¶***bring nothing*** in 何らの収入にならない. ¶I ***care nothing*** for your threats. 僕は君のおどかしなんか何とも思わない. ¶He ***did nothing*** but laughter. 彼はただ笑うばかりであった. ‖ ***Nothing doing***! どうしようもない. ¶***Nothing*** can be ***found*** to identify the wreck. 難船を確かめる何物も発見されない. ¶There is ***nothing*** I should ***enjoy*** more. 私はそれが何よりおもしろい. ¶***gain nothing*** by ... …によって何も得るところがない. ¶Except this letter he ***gave*** me ***nothing***. 彼はこの手紙より外に何も渡さなかった. ¶***get nothing*** for one's pains 骨折損のくたびれもうけ. ¶He ***has nothing*** in him. 彼は能なしだ. ‖ He ***had nothing*** to do but die. 彼は死ぬより外に道がなかった. ‖ he ***had nothing*** on except ... 彼は…の外何も着ていなかった ‖ ***having nothing*** smaller 小銭がないので ‖ She ***has nothing*** of the lady about her. 彼女は少しも淑女らしい所がない. 【類】He ***has nothing*** of the gentleman in him. ‖ He ***has nothing*** to gain by it. そうしても彼には何も益するところはない. ‖ I regret that I ***have nothing*** better to offer. こんな物しかなくて相済みません. ‖ I ***have nothing*** to say to you. 僕は君に言うことはない ‖ ***have nothing*** to do with ... …とは関係はない. 【類】Chance ***has nothing*** to do with his present success. 【類】I ***have nothing*** to please you. ¶I've ***heard nothing*** from him yet. まだ何の便りもない. ‖ ***Nothing*** more will be ***heard*** about it. もうその消息は聞かれまい. ¶I ***know nothing*** except this. この外私は何も知らない. ‖ I ***know*** practically ***nothing*** about ... 私は…については何も知らないも同然だ. ¶***leave nothing*** to chance 何ごとも運任せにしない(なおざりにしない) ‖ It ***leaves nothing*** to be desired. 申分がない. ¶It ***makes nothing*** in his favor. それは一向彼の利益にならない. ¶***make nothing*** of domestic cares 家事の世話を苦にしない. 【類】He ***makes nothing*** of getting up at five in the morning. ‖ He ***made nothing*** of my abilities. 彼は僕の手腕を軽視した. ‖ I can ***make nothing*** of it. それはどうも私には分からない. ¶He ***means nothing*** rude. 彼には乱暴なことをする積りは少しもない. ‖ I ***received nothing*** beyond what you owed me. 私はもらうべき物の外には何ももらいはしなかった. ¶You ***risk nothing***. そうしても君には少しも危険はない. ¶I ***said nothing*** of the matter. 私はそのことは何にも言わなかった. ‖ to ***say nothing*** of ... …は別として, …はもとより. ¶I ***see nothing*** humorous in it. それにはこっけいな所が少しもないと私は思う. ¶***think nothing*** of ... …を問題にしない. ¶I can ***wish nothing*** better than ... …以上のことは望まない.

V[2] *Nothing* ***arrived*** by mail. 郵便は何も来なかった. ¶*Nothing* ***came*** of the matter. それはものにならなかった. 【類】I have done my best for his sake but *nothing* ***comes*** of it. ¶but *nothing* ***happened*** しかし何の反応もなかった. ¶*nothing* good ***proceeds*** from ... …しても何の役にもたたない. ¶*Nothing* ***sounds*** more ridiculous. そんなばかな話はない. ¶*Nothing* can ***spread*** more rapidly than a bad gossip. 悪いうわさほど早く広まるものはない.

Q *Nothing* can be more ***attractive*** (=***charming***) to the eye. これ以上美しいものはない. ¶having *nothing* ***better*** to say 別に言うこともないから. ¶*Nothing* ***great*** is easy.

何でも大きなことは容易でない. ¶When searched *nothing incriminating* was found on him. 彼(の身体)を調べたときには犯罪の証拠となるようなものはなかった. ¶He was *nothing loath*. 決していやではなかった. ¶Pay no attention to it; it is a *mere nothing*. ほおっておきなさい, ほんのつまらないことですから. ‖ He is a *mere nothing*. 彼は取るに足らない人間だ. ¶He is *nothing more* than a dreamer. 彼は空想家に過ぎない. ‖ *Nothing more* came of the affair. それでことずみになった. ¶They are *nameless nothings*. 彼らは名もないやからだ. ¶There is *nothing* particularly *new*. 別段新らしい所はない. ¶I have *nothing particular* to do. 私は別に用事はない. ¶I can see *nothing remarkable* in him. 私から見ると彼には別に変ったところはない. ¶It is *nothing serious*. 大したことでない. ¶Is there *nothing strange* today? きょうは何も珍らしいことはないか. ¶*Nothing* could be *sweeter* to the ear. これ以上耳に快いものはない. ¶*trifling nothings* へのようなこと. ¶*Nothing* can be more *unequal* than the equal treatment of unequals. 不平等のものを平等に取扱う位不公平なことはない.

P How goes with your business?—*Nothing much*. 商売はどうかね, 一大したことはないね. ¶I am *at nothing*, I am only reading. 何もしてはいない, 本を読んでいるだけだ. ¶Your blame counts *for nothing*. 君の小言は何んにもならない. ‖ All my trouble went *for nothing*. 私の骨折は一切むだになった. 【類】 His work has been *for nothing* after all ‖ It isn't *for nothing* that he is a teacher. 先生だけのことはある. ‖ He is good *for nothing*. 彼はやくざだ. 【類】 This book is good *for nothing*. ‖ ride on a railway *for nothing* 鉄道の無賃乗車をやる ‖ I cannot give instruction *for nothing*. 私は無料では教えられない. ‖ sell *for* practically *nothing* ただ(無代価)みたいに売る. 【類】 spend 5,000 yen *for nothing*. ¶*Out of nothing*, nothing comes. 〖諺〗まかぬ種ははえぬ. ‖ *make* something *out of nothing* 無から有を作る. ¶He sticks *to nothing*. 彼は何ごとにもねばりがない. ¶He is poor and possesses next *to nothing*. 彼は貧乏ではとんど何も持っていない. 【類】 He fished all day, but he caught next *to nothing*. / The scheme has come *to nothing*.

P² I know *nothing about* it. 私はそのことは何も知らない. ¶They regard me *as nothing* (=nobody). 彼らは私をむしけら同様に見ている. ¶The Westerners say we Japanese are *nothing at* inventions. 西洋人はわれわれ日本人は発明にかけてはゼロだという. ¶It is *nothing but* a joke. ほんの冗談だ. 【類】 He is *nothing but* a student. ¶There is *nothing for* it but to surrender. 降参するより外はない. 【類】 There is *nothing for* it but to do what is required (要求されたことをする). ¶There is *nothing in* what you say. 君のいうことはつまらない. ¶There is *nothing like* keeping out of harm's way. 危険には近寄らないに越したことはない. ‖ There is *nothing like* home. わが家にしくものはない. ‖ There is *nothing like* blue serge for men's wear. 男子の方には紺サージが一番よく似合います. ¶Did I mean to insult him? *Nothing of* the kind (=sort). 僕が彼を侮辱する積りだって? 決してそんなことはありやしない. 【類】 Did you see the comet?—I saw *nothing of* the kind. ‖ *Nothing of* any significance was noted. 別にどうということもなかった(異状なし). ¶It is *nothing to* me. 僕には何でもない. 【類】 His failure is *nothing to* me (僕には痛くもかゆくもない). ‖ This storm is *nothing to* what I saw in England. この暴風は英国で出会ったのとは比べものにならない.

nothing, *ad.* ちっとも…[でない].

P care *nothing about* … …はちっともかまわない. ¶differ *nothing from* … …とはちっともちがわない.

O This will help you *nothing*, I'm afraid. これは何の役にも立たないかも知れん.

nothingness, *n.* 虚無, 皆無.

P dissolve *into nothingness* とけてなくなってしまう ‖ pass *into nothingness* 無に帰する, むだになる.

P² general *nothingness of* everything 諸行無常.

notice, *n.* 注意; 認識; 予告, 警告; 通知; 掲示, 張札; 短評, 紹介.

V *attract* the *notice* of the managing partner of the company 会社の専務取締役の注意を引く. 【類】 The grand building *attracted* the public *notice*. / The shops are decked out so as to *attract notice*. / The shops were all decorated so as to *attract notice*. ¶*bring* a *notice* to the attention of students 学生に掲示する. ¶This fact *deserves* some *notice*. この事実は幾分注目に値する. 【類】 *deserve* special *notice* for … ¶*direct* one's *notice* to the fact that … …の事実に注意を向ける. ¶*disregard* a *notice* 通告を不問に付する. ¶*draw notice* to … …に注意を引く. ¶*escape* one's *notice* 人目に留まらない(見落される); 人目を避ける. 【類】 This fact often *escapes notice*. ‖ He is very observant, nothing *escapes* his *notice*. 彼は非常に注意深いから何んだって見落しはしない. ‖ She left the theatre by a back door to *escape* the *notice* of the crowd. 彼女は群衆の目を避けるために裏口から劇場を出た. ¶a *notice exhibited* at … …に出した掲示. ¶We always *expect* a fortnight's *notice*. 必ず二週間前に予告して下さい. ¶*fasten* a *notice* by thumb-tacks 止めびょうで張札をとめる. ¶*get notice* of … …の通知を受ける. ¶*give notice* of inability to attend 欠席届けを出す ‖ I *gave* him *notice* then and there. その場で暇をやった. ‖ The whistle *gave notice* that the boat was about to leave. 船が出るという合図の汽笛がなった. 【類】 *give notice* of a strike / *give notice* of some alteration in the plan / Please *give* me *notice* in good time. / this is to *give notice* that … / *give notice* beforehand (=in advance) ‖ I must *give* my landlord *notice*. 家主に引越すことを知らしておかねばならない. ‖ *give notice* to the authorities 当局に届け出る. 【類】 *give notice* in writing (書面で). ¶*give out* a *notice* 公告する. ¶*hang* a *notice* in a conspicuous place 目抜きの場所に掲示を下げる. ¶*hang* (=post) *up* a *notice* at the station to indicate that … …通告のために停車場に掲示をする. ¶*have notice* 通知を受ける. ¶Please *insert* this *notice* in tomorrow's paper. 明日の新聞にこの広告を御掲載下さい. ¶*issue* a *notice* that … …という通告を発する. ¶*meet* one's *notice* その目に留まる. ¶*merit* peculiar *notice* 特に注意する値打がある. ¶*nail* a *notice*, "Hand off" 「手を触るべからず」の張札をくぎ付けにする. ¶The tenants of these dwellings have long *overstayed* their *notice* to quit. この住宅の借家人は明渡しの予告を受けながら長い間立退かずにいた. ¶*paste* a *notice* on a bulletin-board 掲示板にはり紙をする. ¶He ceased to *pay notice* to what I told him. 彼は私の言うことに注意しなくなった. ¶*place notices* where all may see them みんなの目につく所に掲示をする. ¶*post* a *notice* on a board 掲示板に掲示する. 【類】 a *notice* was *posted* calling upon the men to meet at … ‖ *post up* a *notice* at … …に張札を出す. ¶*Notice* was *printed* and *posted* in the town. 告示を印刷して町に張出した. ¶*put* a *notice* on a door 戸口に張札をする ‖ *put* a *notice* outside: "Museum, twenty-five cents admission" 屋外に「入場料二十五セント一博物館」の張札を出す. ¶*put up* a *notice* on a bulletin-board 掲示板に掲示する. 【類】 *put up notices* in their entrance-halls (玄関) to the effect that … / *put up* a *notice* in the yard (構内). ¶*receive notice* of a storm 暴風雨の予報を受ける. 【類】 *receive* a *notice* to quit (立退通告) ‖ he will *receive notice* later その人のことは後に説く. ¶*send notice* to … …に通知する. ¶*send off notice* 通知を発する. ¶*serve notice* of appearance 出頭の通知を出す ‖ *serve notice* that … …と知らせる, …と警告する. ¶*set up* a public *notice* at a place 公衆のためにある場所に掲示を出す. ¶you are requested to *take notice* that … …を御承知おき願います. ‖ I warned him, but he *took* little *notice* of it. 彼に警告したが彼は余り心に留めなかった. 【類】 the law *takes* no *notice* of … / I *took* no *notice* of it when he said it. / *taking* no *notice* of the interruption. ¶*win* world-wide *notice* 全世界に認識される.

Q A *day's notice* is required. 前日に通告を要する. ‖ give four *days' notice* 四日前に通告する. ¶after *due notice* has been given of … …について適当な警告を発した上. ¶on a *few days' notice* 予告を出してから二三日中に. ¶give *formal notice* to hold him responsible 彼に責任を負わせるという正式の通告を発する. ¶till (=until) *further notice* 追って何分のさたがあるまで. ¶give *immediate* (=*prompt*) *notice* of … …を即刻通告する. ¶This phase of the subject receives *inadequate notice* in that book. 問題のこの方面はその書中に十分説いてない. ¶give *legal notice* 合法の通告をする. ¶I am ready to start at a *minute's notice*. 通知のあり次第に出発の用意が私にはできている. ¶He came at a *moment's notice*. 彼は即刻やって来

た. ¶give a ***month's notice*** 一カ月前に知らせる ‖ If you please, madam, I wish to give a ***month's notice*** to leave. 奥様一月後にお暇をいただきとう御ざいます. 【類】give a ***month's notice*** from this minute. ¶an ***official notice*** was posted stating that … …のむねの告示が張出された ‖ They received ***official notices*** to send in their names to the authorities immediately. 彼らは即刻当局に氏名を届出るべきむねの正式の通知を受けた. ¶I did not take ***particular notice***. 私は別に注意しなかった. ¶The subject deserves a ***passing notice***. その問題は一通り注意する価値がある. ¶a ***peremptory notice*** 〚法〛催告. ¶a ***prefatory notice*** 前書き. ¶by giving ***previous notice*** 予告をして ‖ subject to at least ninety days' ***previous notice*** 少なくも九十日前に通告するという条件で. ¶a ***printed notice*** 印刷した通知書. ¶give ***proper notice*** 正当の通告をする. ¶a ***public notice*** in a newspaper 新聞の通知広告. ¶upon ***reasonable notice*** being given 相当の期間予告すれば. ¶The doctor came on ***short notice***. 医者がすぐに来た. ‖ at ***short notice*** and with limited study 短期間にしかも大した勉強もせずに ‖ We serve meals to guests at any time on ***short notice***. お客様はてっとり早くいつでもお食事ができます. 【類】make a speech on ***short notice*** / He gave me very ***short notice*** of his visit. / You have given me very ***short notice***. ‖ at the ***shortest notice*** 突然. ¶he did not take the ***slightest notice*** of … 彼は…に少しもとん着しなかった. ¶deserve a ***special notice*** 特別の注意に値する. ¶***theatrical notices*** 劇評. ¶send ***timely notice*** to … 好い時機に…に通知する. ¶Special trains can be arranged at ***two*** or ***three hours' notice***. 二三時間の猶予で特別列車が仕立てられる. ¶***underlying notice*** 下心. ¶The landlord gave a ***week's notice*** from next Friday. 家主は来週金曜日から一週間目に貸家明渡しを申入れた. ¶send a ***written notice*** to … …に書面で通知する.

Q² ***advance notice*** of time of arrival 到着時間の予報. 【類】without ***advance notice***. ¶***book notices*** 新刊紹介(新聞の). ¶a ***danger notice*** 危険注意. ¶hand a ***dismissal notice*** to … …に解職通告を渡す. ¶serve them an ***eviction notice*** その人たちに立退通知をする. ¶get only a ***few hours notice*** of … たった二三時間前に予告を受ける. ¶fail to receive ***voting notices*** 選挙通知書が来ない.

P He may be dismissed ***at*** a day's ***notice***. 一日前に予告すれば解雇してもよい. ‖ ***at*** an hour's ***notice*** 一時間の猶予で ‖ may be obtained ***at*** a moment's ***notice*** 即刻手に入る. 【類】It is not always possible there to find a car ***at*** a moment's ***notice***. ¶bring it ***before*** the ***notice*** of … それに対して…の注意を求める. ¶The fellow is quite ***beneath notice***. あいつは相手にするに足らない. 【類】Pretty though she is, she is ***beneath*** your lordship's ***notice***. ¶***in*** so short a ***notice*** そんな急に. ¶come ***into notice*** 人目に留まる. ¶It is worthy ***of notice***. それは注目に値する. ¶***on notice*** being given to … …に通知すれば ‖ ***on*** four days' ***notice*** being given 四日前に通知すれば ‖ It is available to … ***on*** a moment's ***notice***. 即刻…に間に合う. ¶bring the matter ***to*** the ***notice*** of … そのことを…に知らせる ‖ come ***to*** the ***notice*** of … …に知られる(認められる). ¶in regard to the matter ***under notice*** この事件(問題)につき ‖ the number ***under notice*** contains … その号には…がのっている[雑誌など] ‖ My servant is ***under notice*** to leave at the end of the month. 今の召使は月末に暇を取ることになっている. 【類】The late occurrence brought this fact ***under*** my ***notice***. / the most practical and complete English grammar which has come ***under*** my ***notice*** / It fell ***under*** my ***notice***. ¶absence ***without notice*** 無断欠席 ‖ ***without*** further ***notice*** この上通告せずに ‖ The prices in this catalogue are subject to change ***without notice***. この目録に掲げてある定価は予告せずに変更することがあります. 【類】dismiss a person ***without notice***.

P² a ***notice in*** writing＝a written notice 届書; 通知状. ¶The newspaper contains ***notice of*** births, deaths, etc. 新聞には出産・死亡などの通知が出る. ‖ send ***notice of*** refusal 断りの通知を出す ‖ give the gas company ***notice of*** removal ガス会社に転居を通知する ‖ a ***notice of*** an action 訴訟告知 ‖ a ***notice of*** appeal 上訴申立書 ‖ a ***notice of*** release 放免の通知. ¶a ***notice to*** mariners issued by … advises that … …の発した水路告示は…を報じている ‖ A ***notice to*** that effect shall be posted not less than three days beforehand. そのむねの掲示は少くとも三日前に出すこと.

notice, *v.* 目につく, 気がつく; 紹介する.

M as ***noticed beforehand*** 前もって通告した通り. ¶The book was ***favorably noticed*** in literary magazines. その本は文学雑誌で好評を博した.

P I ***noticed by*** yesterday's papers that … きのうの新聞紙で…が目についた.

O I didn't ***notice*** my purse missing till I got home. 私は家へ帰るまで財布がなくなっていたのに気がつかなかった. 【類】I ***noticed*** a little boy toddling (よちよちと) into the garden.

noticeable, *a.* 目立った.

M become ***glaringly noticeable*** 著しく目に立って来る.

P be ***noticeable from*** the fact that … …の事実から察せられる.

notice-board, *n.* 掲示板.

V ***disdain*** the warning ***notice-board*** of danger [通路などの]危険標示板を軽視する.

P put up an alarm ***on*** a ***notice-board*** 掲示板に警報を出す. ¶He passed by ***without noticing*** me. 彼は私に気がつかないで通り過ぎた.

notification, *n.* 告示; 届, 通知.

V the London Gazette ***contains*** a ***notification*** that … ロンドン・ガゼットに…の告示がのっている. ¶The ***notification*** must be ***made*** within … hours of birth. 届は誕生後…時間以内に出さなければならない. ¶***receive notification*** from … …から通告を受ける.

Q ***previous notification*** 予報. ¶service by ***public notification*** 公示送達.

Q² a ***government notification*** 政府示達. ¶a ***moving-in (moving-out) notification*** 転入(出)届.

P² ***notification of*** moving (＝removal) 転居届.

notify, *v.* 通知する.

M I was ***abruptly notified*** that a half-hour speech was expected of me. だしぬけに三十分間の演説をして下さいと言われた. ¶***notify briefly*** … 簡単に…と通知する.

P ***notify*** him ***in*** writing 書面で彼に通知する ‖ ***notify*** a sale ***in*** the newspaper 販売広告を出す. ¶I have been already ***notified of*** your coming. あなたのいらっしゃることは前に案内がありました. 【類】***notify*** the police ***of*** the loss (damage). ¶we have been ***notified*** [***to*** the effect] that … …のむね当方に通知があった.

notion, *n.* 観念; 考え, 見解, 意見; 《米》小間物類.

V ***bear*** this ***notion*** in mind この考えを心に留める. ¶***convey*** a ***notion*** of comparison 比較という観念を起させる. ¶***destroy*** the preconceived ***notions*** 先入観念を打破する. ¶***disprove*** the old ***notion*** that … …という古い考えに不賛成である. ¶***entertain*** a ***notion*** 考えを抱く. ¶The ***notion*** that … is still firmly ***entrenched***. …という観念は依然確立している. ¶***eradicate*** preconceived ***notions*** 先入観念を根絶する. ¶***express*** the ***notion*** of … …という考えを述べる. ¶***favor*** the ***notion*** that … …という考えを起させる. ¶***follow*** one's own ***notions*** 自分の考え通りにやる. ¶He has ***got*** (＝***taken***) a ***notion*** into his head. 彼はある考えを起した. ¶it ***gives*** a fair ***notion*** (＝good idea) of … それで…が結構会得される. ¶he ***had*** a ***notion***, not uncommon in his day, that … 彼は彼の時代には珍らしくない…という考えを持っていた ‖ I ***have*** no ***notion*** to do it. 私にはそれをする考えはない. ‖ ***have*** no ***notion*** (＝idea) of … …の気持ちはない, …は分からない. ‖ An adverbial noun ***has*** a ***notion*** of time, place, or manner. 副詞的名詞は時, 所または方法の概念を含む. 【類】They ***have*** no ***notion*** of honor, honesty, or courage. / He ***has*** no ***notion*** of risking his money. / What does this mean? I ***have*** not a ***notion*** of it. ¶get out of our ***heads*** all ***notion*** of … 一切…の概念をわれわれの頭から一掃する. ¶***hold*** strange ***notions*** 不思議な意見を持っている. ¶The ***notion*** of time is ***impaired***. 時間観念が弱められている(精神病者など). ¶The prefix "be" ***intensifies*** the ***notion*** of a verb. 接頭語 be は 動詞の概念を強調する. ¶***nurse*** a strange ***notion*** about … …について不思議な意見をいだく. ¶***ridicule*** the ***notion*** (＝idea) その考えをひやかす.

V² He was not a learned man, as the ***notion goes***. 彼は世間でいう学者ではない. ¶The ***notion*** that he would be angry did not ***occur*** to me. 彼が怒っているだろうという考えは私には浮ばなかった. ¶in some quarters the obsolescent ***notion*** still ***prevails*** that … 所によっては…という旧式の考えを持っているものがある ‖ some erratic ***notions*** seem to ***prevail*** as to … …で誤った考えが行われているらしい.

Q ***abstract notions*** 抽象的観念. ¶***airy notions*** 空想. ¶The

American notion of ... is not a bad idea. ...という米国人の考えは悪くない. ¶a person of ***antiquated** notions*=a fogy 旧弊家. ¶***bizarre** notions* 奇怪な考え. ¶it is very important at the very outset to get ***clear** notions* as to ... まず第一に...について明確な考えを持つことがきわめて大切である. ¶The ***common European** notion* is that the American husband is the slave of his wife. アメリカの亭主は妻のどれいだというのが普通の欧州人の考えである. ¶he has but an extremely ***confused** notion* of ... 彼は...については実にとりとめのない見解を持っている. ¶***crazy** notion* 狂気のさた. ¶it was a ***current** notion* in ancient China that ... ...ということは古代中国に行われた普通の見解であった. ¶a ***delusive** notion* 紛らわしい見解. ¶some very ***erratic** notions* seem to exist as to ... ...に関してきわめて奇矯な考えを持っているものがあるらしい. ¶no *notion* can be more ***erroneous*** than ... ...くらい誤った見解はあるまい. ¶the most ***exaggerated*** and ***absurd** notions* are abroad as to ... ...に関して最も大げさなばかげた考えが行われている. ¶he has but a ***faint** notion* of ... 彼は...についてただぼんやりした考えを持っているだけだ ‖ Nobody has the ***faintest** notion* that we can live under water. われわれが水中に住みうるとは何人も夢にも考えていない. ¶hastily ***formed** notions* 未熟な考え. ¶a ***freakish** notion* 酔狂な考え. ¶***fundamental** notions* 根本観念. ¶the ***general** notion* of ... ...の概念. ¶wage war with all our ***habitual** ntoions* われわれの習慣的な考えと戦う. ¶he has some ***hazy** notion* as to ... 彼は...に関してあるぼんやりした考えを持っている. 【類】entertain only a ***hazy** notion* concerning ... ¶His *notion* of the distinction between active and passive verbs is ***indistinct.*** (ラテン語など)能動態の動詞と受動態の動詞の区別について彼ははっきり分かっていない. ¶I never had the ***least** notion* of your knowing it. 君がそれを知っているとは少しも思わなかった. ¶a ***ludicrous** notion* ばかげた考え. ¶under the ***mistaken** notion* that ... ...という誤った考えで. ¶an ***odd** notion* 奇怪な考え. ¶the ***old mistaken** notion* that ... ...という従来の間違った見解. ¶approach it with no ***preconceived** notions* 虚心にこれに接する ‖ destroy the ***preconceived** notions* 先入観念を打破する. ¶a very ***prevalent*** and ***erroneous** notion* きわめて普通の誤った見解. ¶People had such ***queer** notions* in those days. 当時の人たちはこうした変った考えを持っていた. ¶a ***romantic** notion* 小説的な考え. ¶***scientific** notions* 科学的な考え. ¶Her head is full of ***silly** notions.* 彼女の頭は愚かしい考えで一杯だ. ¶have not the slightest *notion* of ... ...は夢にも思わない. ¶a ***stupid** notion* 愚かな考え. ¶a ***superstitious** notion* 迷信的な考え. ¶The *notion* may appear as rather ***Utopian.*** その考えはやや空想的に見えるかも知れない. ¶have only a ***vague** notion* of ... ...についてほんのばく然たる考えを持っている. ¶There is a ***widelyspread** notion* among the poorer classes, that rice, as an article of food, prevents the increase of the population. 貧民階級の間には米を食料品とすると人口増加を妨げるという見解が一般的に行われている. ¶***Yankee** notions* 《米》アメリカ独特の考案品(細工物).

P he is very fossilized ***in*** his *notion* of ... ...氏は...の意見にいつまでもこだわっている. ¶our fall sale ***of** notions* 《米》当店の小間物秋の売出し. ¶no one has hit ***on*** the *notion* of ... だれも...に思い付かなかった. ¶***under*** the *notion* of ... ...の概念の下に. ¶more consonant ***with*** American *notions* of hospitality 厚遇という事についてのアメリカ人の考えと一層一致して.

P² a *notion **of*** deity 神の観念 ‖ The *notion **of*** my marrying her is quite absurd. 僕が彼女と結婚するなんてばかげきっている.

notoriety, *n.* (概して悪い)評判, 隠れない悪名, 《古》著名.

V ***achieve** notoriety* 悪名をうたわれる. ¶Rightly or wrongly, in the press, in literature and in public repute, Japan has ***acquired*** an unenviable *notoriety* for defective business morality. その当不当はとに角として新聞にも書物にも世評にも日本は商売道徳に欠けているというありがたくない評判を取っている. ¶***court** notoriety* 好んで悪評を招く. ¶***earn*** for himself an unenviable *notoriety* ありがたくもない評判を立てられる. ¶***enjoy*** great *notoriety* 大変な悪評を受ける. ¶it ***gained** notoriety* for ... それは...で悪名をとどろかせた. ¶***obtain*** an unenviable *notoriety* in the newspapers 新聞でいやな評判を立てられる. ¶***win** notoriety* かんばしくない評判を取る.

Q gain an ***evil** notoriety* 悪名をうたわれる. ¶gained ***much** notoriety* among ... on account of ... ...のために...間に大変な悪評を招いた.

Q² ***newspaper** notoriety* 新聞上での悪い評判.

P ***for the sake of** notoriety* 売名のために.

notorious, *a.* 悪名高い, 名うての; 《古》名高い.

P the place has become *notorious **as*** the home of ... その地は...の本場として悪名が高い ‖ He is *notorious **as*** a "dead beat." 「ふみ倒し屋」で通っている. ¶The neighbourhood is *notorious **for*** robbery. その辺は強盗が出るので有名だ. 【類】He is *notorious **for*** his crimes. / He is *notorious **for*** his absent-mindedness (うっかり屋として). / a city *notorious **for*** its luxury.

noun, *n.* 〖文法〗名詞.

Q an ***attributive** noun* 形容詞的名詞 (*boy* soprano の boy など). ¶an ***antecedent** noun* 先行名詞.

nourish, *v.* 養育する; 助長する.

P *nourish* the baby ***on*** healthy mother's milk 健康な母親の乳で赤児を養育する. ¶*nourish* an infant ***with** milk* 牛乳で幼児を養育する.

O *nourish* a feeling of hatred 憎しみをいだく ‖ *nourish* the soil (land) 土じょうを肥やす. 【類】Freedom *nourishes* self-respect.

nourishment, *n.* 栄養物.

Q ***imperfect** nourishment* 栄養不良. ¶***solid** nourishment* 固形食物.

novel, *n.* 小説.

V ***adapt*** a *novel* to the stage 小説を劇に改作する. ¶***do*** a *novel* 小説を作る. ¶***dramatize*** a *novel* 小説を脚色する. ¶***make*** a *novel* into a movie=filmize a movel 小説を映画化する. ¶***pick up*** a *novel* only to lay it down 小説を読みだし(おもしろくないので)やめてしまう. ¶***read*** trashy *novels* ろくでもない小説を読む. ¶***run** novels* as serials in British and other newspapers 英紙その他の新聞に小説を続き物として出す. ¶***write*** a *novel* 小説を書く.

Q an ***argumentative*** and ***exhortative** novel* 理屈っぽく訓戒的な小説. ¶a ***clever*** and ***readable** novel* 巧妙で読むに足る小説. ¶a ***didactic** novel* 教訓小説, 勧善懲悪小説. ¶an ***episodic** novel* そう話的小説. ¶an ***epistolary** novel* 書簡体の小説. ¶an ***epoch-making** novel* 画期的小説. ¶an ***equivocal** novel* (内容の)いかがわしい小説. ¶an ***experimental** novel* 実験小説. ¶a ***frothy** novel* 他愛ない小説. ¶a (an) ***historical** novel* 歴史小説. ¶a ***hot** novel* 卑わいな小説. ¶an ***interesting*** and ***entertaining** novel* おもしろく楽しい小説. ¶a ***light** novel* 軽快な小説. ¶a ***mediocre** novel* 平凡な小説. ¶England is the birthplace of the ***modern** novel.* 英国は近代小説の発祥地である. ¶***nauseous** novels* はきけを催させる小説. ¶an ***original** novel* 独創性に富む小説. ¶a ***popular** novel* 大衆小説. ¶a ***realistic** novel* 写実小説. ¶a ***second-rate** novel* 二流小説. ¶the thrilling denouement of a ***sensational** novel* 扇情小説の胸を躍らせる大団円. ¶***serial** novels* of prodigious length すてきに長い連続小説. ¶a ***stirring** novel* 気を引立てる小説.

Q² a ***best-seller** novel* 最もよく売れる小説. ¶a ***blood-and-thunder** novel* 血なまぐさい小説. ¶the American ***crook** novels* 米国犯罪小説. ¶a ***detective** novel* 探偵小説. ¶a ***dime** novel* 十セント(本の)小説 ‖ A beautiful binding cannot change a ***dime** novel* into a scholarly masterpiece. 美しい表装をしても三文小説は傑作文学にはならない. ¶a ***Kipling** novel* キップリングの小説. ¶differ from the ordinary "***live happy ever after***" *novel* 普通のめでたしめでたし小説とは違う. ¶a ***mystery** novel* 推理小説. ¶a ***penny-a-line** novel* 低俗な小説. ¶a ***problem** novel* 問題小説. ¶a ***Pulitzer-Prize** novel* [米国の]ピューリッツアー賞を得た小説. ¶a ***sex** novel* 性小説. ¶a ***six-shilling** novel* 六シリング小説. ¶a ***society** novel* 社会小説. ¶a ***sporting** novel* スポーツ小説. ¶a ***three-decker** novel* 《俗》[三巻ものの]長編小説. ¶a ***three-volume** novel* 三巻小説. ¶a ***tendency** novel* 傾向小説. ¶a ***yellow-back** novel* 黄表紙小説(安小説).

P the plot ***of*** a *novel* 小説の筋.

P² a *novel **in*** three volumes=a three-volume novel. ‖ the *novel **of*** problem 問題小説 ‖ a *novel **of*** society 社会小説. ¶the *novel **with*** (=*of*) a purpose=the purpose novel 目的小説.

novel, *a.* 珍らしい.

P You will see a great many things which will be very *novel* ***to*** you. 貴下に珍らしい物が沢山に見られるでしょう.

novelist, *n.* 小説家.

Q one of our ***leading novelists*** 一流小説家の一人. ¶a ***living novelist*** 現存の小説家. ¶a ***prolific novelist*** 多作の小説家. ¶a ***rising novelist*** 新進の小説家. ¶one of our most ***successful novelists*** 最も成功した小説家.

Q² a ***dime novelist*** 三文小説家. ¶a ***lady novelist*** 女流小説家. ¶an ***English*** writing ***novelist*** 英文で書く小説家. ¶a ***society novelist*** 社会小説家.

P² a ***novelist of*** rising fame 売出しの小説家 ‖ a ***novelist of*** power long known to the better public インテリ読者層に以前から知られていた有力な小説家.

novelty, *n.* 新奇; 珍物; 新柄(がら).

V London does not ***appreciate novelty*** like New York or San Francisco. ロンドンではニューヨークやサンフランシスコのようには新奇を賞美しない. ¶***buy novelties*** for gifts みやげ物に珍らしいものを買う. ¶***crave novelties*** ひたすら新奇な物を求める. ¶In some respects the adult seems to ***dread novelty***. ある点において大人は新奇を恐れるらしい. ¶***lose*** (=***outgrow***) its ***novelty*** 珍らしくなくなる.

V² Fine while the ***novelty lasts***. 珍らしい間が花. ¶The ***novelty*** has ***worn off***. もう珍らしくなくなった.

P an ***architectural novelty*** 変った建築. ¶***latest novelties*** ごく目新しいもの. ¶it is a ***welcome novelty*** to find that ... …という新味に接するのはうれしい.

P² It is still a ***novelty in*** the place. それはその地ではまだ珍らしい. ‖ ***novelties in*** terminology 新造の術語.

novice, *n.* 新参者, 新まい; しろうと.

Q the ***rankest novices*** in the business その仕事のほんの初心者. ¶the ***veriest novice*** cannot fail to ... 本当のかけだしでも必ず…する.

P² He was a ***novice at*** the art. 彼はその技術にはしろうとだった. ¶as yet a ***novice in*** the art of ... まだ…術にかけては未熟な. 【類】***novices in*** history / no ***novice in*** affairs of this sort / the ***novice in*** writing may be counselled to ...

now, *n.* 今.

P I have heard that ***before now***. そのことはもっと前に聞いた. ¶[***between***] ***now*** and then 時折. ¶Has it been returned to the owner ***by now?*** それはもう持主へ返してしまいましたか. ¶it ought ***ere now*** to have been made familiar to ... それはすでに…によく知られておるべきはずだ. ¶I will study hard ***from now*** on. これからは一生懸命勉強します. ‖ about a year ***from now*** (=hence) 今から約一年. ¶***Until*** (=***Till***) ***now*** it has not ceased raining. 今まで降り続けた. ¶***up to now*** 今日まで.

now, *ad.* 今.

M ***but*** (=***even***) ***now*** たった今. ¶***just now*** 今しがた; 丁度今 ‖ I saw him ***just now***. 私は今しがた彼に会った. ‖ They're leaving ***just now***. 今みんな出かけるところだ. ‖ Do it ***right now***. 今すぐやれ.

O *Now* [that] I'm older, I've changed my mind. 私も年をとったので気持が変った. ¶*Now* rising, *now* falling, who knows the price for tomorrow? 値が上ったり下ったりであすの値は見当もつかない.

nowhere, *n., ad.* どこにも…ない[所].

V He ***had nowhere*** to go. 彼はどこへも行き所がなかった.

P The rumor came ***from nowhere***. そのうわさはどこからともなくやってきた.

O All he has done so far will get ***nowhere***. 彼が今までやったことは全然失敗だろう.

nucleus, *n.* 中心; 〖理〗原子核.

V It ***constitutes*** (=***forms***) the ***nucleus*** of the story. それが話の中心を成している.

Q an ***atomic nucleus*** 原子核. ¶the Kaiseijo, the ***historical nucleus*** of the present Tokyo University 今日の東京大学の始めであった開成所.

P ***as*** the ***nucleus*** of a fund 資金の基本として.

P² In Japan the family is the ***nucleus of*** the community. 日本では家族が社会の中心だ.

nude, *n.* 裸体; 裸体姿.

Q the ***ignoble nude*** いやらしい裸体姿.

P ***In*** the ***nude***, class differences disappear. 裸体では階級差別がなくなる. ‖ paint her ***in*** the ***nude*** 彼女の裸体画を描く.

P² the ***nude in*** art [絵画・彫刻に表わされた]裸像 ‖ the ***nude in*** nature [動・植物など]自然のままの姿. 【類】a scene representing the ***nude*** in nature ‖ a ***nude in*** a frame picture 額ぶちに入れられた裸体画.

nude, *a.* 裸体の.

M as ***nearly nude*** as the law will allow 法律に触れない程度までの裸体で.

P Nudism is the practice of going ***nude for*** hygienic reasons. 裸体主義は健康法として裸体生活をすることである.

nudge, *n.* 軽く突くこと.

Q give him a ***friendly nudge*** 心安だてに(ひじなどで)軽く突く.

nudge, *v.* 軽く突く.

P ***nudge to*** a person [注意を引くためなど]人をこずく.

nudity, *n.* はだか.

Q in ***complete nudity***=stark naked まっ裸で.

Q² ***stage nudity*** 舞台の裸体.

P almost in a state ***of nudity*** (=naked) ほとんど裸で.

nugget, *n.* 天然金塊.

Q full of ***suggestive*** and ***illuminating nuggets*** of wisdom 暗示に富み啓もう的な言葉に満ちた.

nuisance, *n.* 妨害; 邪魔物; 非行; [人の]迷惑になること.

V ***abate*** a ***nuisance*** 〖法〗安居妨害を緩和する. ¶They ***cause*** a ***nuisance***. 彼らは害をする. ¶As long as ... no number of laws will ***check*** the ***nuisance***. …である限りどんなに沢山の法律をもってしてもその非行を阻止することはできない. ¶***Commit*** no ***nuisance***!=Decency forbids! 小便無用. ¶***constitute*** a ***nuisance*** 邪魔となる. 【類】constitute a ***public nuisance***. ¶they ***experienced*** a considerable ***nuisance*** from ... 彼らは…のために少なからぬ妨害を受けた. ¶There was no danger that he would ***make*** a ***nuisance*** of himself. 彼が人の迷惑になるような恐れはない. ¶***mitigate*** the ***nuisance*** 妨害を緩和する. ¶Surely the police should be able to ***put down*** this ***nuisance***. この妨害はたしかに警察の手で制止できるはずだ. ¶***remove*** (=***do away with or destroy***) a ***nuisance*** 妨害を除く. ¶Something must be done to ***stop*** this ***nuisance***. この妨害を阻止するように何か方法を講じなければならない.

Q experience a ***considerable nuisance*** from ... …から非常に迷惑をこうむる. ¶it has become an ***intolerable nuisance*** to ... それが…に取ってははなはだしい迷惑に感じられ出した. ¶They are a ***perfect nuisance***. 彼らにはほとほと困る. ¶The miser is a ***public nuisance***. けちん坊は社会の邪魔物だ.

Q² In some of the cities of Northern China the ***dust nuisance*** is as pronounced as in Tokyo. 北中国の都市では東京同様ごみとほこりにひどく悩まされる. ¶The common cold is the greatest ***health nuisance***. 普通のかぜは健康の大敵である. ¶be a ***neighborhood nuisance*** 近所迷惑になる. ¶***noise nuisance*** 迷惑な雑音. ¶abate the ***smoke nuisance*** ばい煙の害を緩和する. ¶***street nuisances*** 街路の邪魔物(ごみなど). ¶I never have any trouble with the ***tipping nuisance***. 私はチップ(祝儀)で心をいためたことはない.

P ***without nuisance*** to others 他人に迷惑を掛けずに.

P² Gas-works are often a ***nuisance to*** the neighborhood. ガス工場は往々近所迷惑だ. 【類】You must not make yourself a ***nuisance to*** others. / be a ***nuisance to*** the general public.

numb, *a.* かじかんだ.

P My fingers are ***numb with*** cold. 寒さで私の指がかじかんでいる.

numb, *v.* 無感覚にする.

P Her heart was ***numbed with*** grief. 彼女は悲嘆にくれた.

number, *n.* 数; 〖文法〗数; 数字, 数詞; 番号; *pl.* 美術; [雑誌の]号; *pl.* 〖音楽〗曲目; 仲間; 連中.

V ***ascertain*** the ***number*** 数を確かめる. ¶endeavor to ***attract*** the greatest possible ***number*** of tourists to one's own country 自国にできるだけ多数の観光客を引付けようとする. ¶It ***brings*** in its train a ***number*** of troubles. それに関連して色々面倒が起る. ¶this ***brings up*** the ***number*** to ... これで数が…に増す. ¶***calculate*** the ***number*** 数をかぞえる. ¶What ***number*** is ***calling***? そちらの電話番号は. ¶***call off numbers*** 番号を呼ぶ. ¶***call up*** his ***number*** [電話で] その番号を呼び出す. ¶***count*** the ***number*** of people 人を数える. ¶***dial*** one's ***number*** on the desk phone 卓上電話をかける(ダイヤルを回して). ¶***double*** a ***number*** 数を二倍にする. ¶The ***number*** is ***doubled*** and ***trebled***. 数が二倍になり三倍になっている. ¶***employ*** a great ***number*** of laborers 労働者を多数使用する. ¶***enlarge numbers*** 数をふやす. ¶***equal*** the ***number*** of ... …の数にひとしい. ¶***Find*** me the ***number*** in the phone book. 電話帳でその番号を見つけてくれ. ¶***form*** a goodly ***number*** かなりな数に達して

いる ¶***get*** the winning *number* in a lottery 富くじに当る. ¶***give*** the exact *number* 正確な数を示す. ‖ She ***gave*** four *numbers* of Spanish dances. 彼女はスペインダンスを四番演じた. ¶***increase*** one's *numbers* of domestic fowl kept 飼ってある鶏の数を増す. ¶***keep down*** the *number* of students per teacher 教師一人当りの学生数が多くならないようにする. ¶***lessen*** the *number* of ... …の数を減らす. ¶***limit*** the *number* 数を制限する. ¶***look up*** the *number* in the phone book 電話帳で番号をさがす. ¶***lower*** the *number* 数を減らす. ¶They ***made up*** the largest *number*. 彼らが最多数を占めた. ¶***multiply*** the *number* to a still greater extent さらにその数を増す. ¶***obtain*** the highest *number* of marks 最高点を得る. ¶***obtain*** the *number* of persons required 入用な頭数をそろえる. ¶the article which ***opens*** this *number* [雑誌など]本号巻頭の文. ¶Today the Evening News ***publishes*** its 10,000th *number*. 今日でイブニング・ニュース紙は一万号になる. ¶***put forth*** the "extra Christmas *number*" クリスマスの臨時号を発行する. ¶Please be sure to ***quote*** the following *number* when replying to this letter. 御返書には次の番号を御記入下さい. ¶***raise*** the *number* of Commissioners from five to ten 委員の数を五名から十名に増す. ¶***rattle off*** the *numbers* up to ten 十までの数を早口で言う. ¶***reach*** its fourth *number* =run into four figures 四位の数(千台)に達する. ¶***reckon*** the *number* 数を取る. ¶***reduce*** the *number* 数を減らす. ¶***reduce*** by half the *number* of ... …の数を半減する. ¶***regulate*** the *number* of one's family 産児を調節する. ¶the *number* of ... was ***returned*** as ... …の数は…と報告された. ¶He ***rang*** my *number* ***up***. 彼は(電話で)私(の番号)を呼び出した. ¶He succeeded in ***saving*** quite a *number*. 彼はかなり沢山の貯金ができた. ¶***sing out*** their *numbers* at a roll-call 点呼の際彼らの番号を大声で呼ぶ. ¶***spell numbers out*** 数を文字につづる. ☞ use figures (数字で書く) に対する. ¶***swell*** the *numbers* 数をふやす(数がかさむ). ¶***thin*** [***off***] the *numbers* 数を少くする. ¶***weigh*** a certain *number* of pounds 一定の体量を有する. ¶Can you ***write*** the *numbers* from 1 to 15? 一から十五まで数を書けますか.

V² the *number* of ... ***attains*** to the enormous figure of ... …の数は…というばく大な数字に達する. ¶the *number* cannot ***fall*** far short of ... その数は大して…より下る気づかいはない ‖ The *number* has ***fallen*** greatly. 数が非常に減った. ¶The *number* continually ***fluctuates***. 数が絶えず変動する. ¶Now the *number* ***grows***. 今では数が段々ふえる. 【類】the *number* has ***grown*** (=***increased***) to ... / The *number* has gradually ***grown***. ¶A fair *number* ***presented*** themselves. 相当の数の出席者があった. ¶the *number* has ***risen*** to ... 数は…に上った. ¶Their *number* now ***stands*** at 709. その数は現在七百九になっている. ¶their *number* ***swelled*** to ... その数は…にふえた.

Q I want to know the ***accurate*** (=***exact*** or ***precise***) *number* of motor-vehicles now on the job. 今就業中の自動車の正確な数字を知りたい. ¶the ***actual*** *number* 実数. ¶the ***aggregate*** *number* of ... …の総数. ¶in an ***amazing*** *number* 驚くほど沢山に. ¶***Any*** *number* will do. いくつでもよろしい. ¶an ***appalling*** *number* of ... …という驚くべき数. ¶in ***astonishing*** *numbers* 驚くべき数で. ¶ransack ***back*** *numbers* of ... [雑誌など]旧号を調べる ‖ He is a ***back number***. 《口語》彼は時代後れだ. ¶a ***bewildering*** *number* 驚くべき数. ¶a ***certain*** *number* of ... 一定数の… ¶a ***compound*** *number* 複名数. ¶in ***considerable*** *numbers* かなり多数に. ¶Inventions and discoveries in ***countless*** *numbers* have vastly complicated modern life. 無数の発明や発見が現代生活を非常に複雑にした. ¶a ***current*** *number* 今月(週)号. ¶a ***double*** *number* [雑誌の]倍大号. ¶The next article will appear in an ***early*** *number*. この続稿は近号に掲載します. ¶in seemingly ***endless*** *numbers* 見た所では数限りなく. ¶an ***estimated*** *number* 概算数. ¶an ***even*** *number* 偶数. ¶in ***ever-increasing*** *numbers* ますます多く. ¶a ***fair*** *number* 相当の数. ¶a ***favorite*** *number* 好きな数. ¶perform the work in the ***fewest*** *number* of moves 動作を最も少なくしてその仕事をやる. ¶the ***final*** *number* 終刊号. ¶a ***fixed*** *number* of ... 一定数の… ¶a ***fractional*** *number* 分数. ¶the ***full*** *number* of ... …の全数. ¶a ***good*** *number* of ... かなり沢山の… ‖ The magazine this month is an exceedingly ***good*** *number*. その雑誌の今月号は非常によい. ¶a ***goodly*** *number* of interested spectators 興味をもって見ているかなり沢山の見物人. ¶Italy has exported her people in ***great*** *numbers*. イタリーは沢山移民を(海外へ)出した. ‖ in the ***greater*** *number* of ... …の過半数. ¶***high*** *numbers* (百万千万などの)高位数. 【類】The *number* of ... is as ***high*** as 700. ¶Unemployed men are found in ***huge*** *numbers*. 非常に多数の失業者がある. ¶Three is the ***ideal*** *number* in difficult mountain climbing. 困難な登山には三人が理想だ. ¶an ***immense*** *number*. of ... 無数の… ¶the ***inaugural*** (=***initial***) *number* 創刊号. ¶The *number* remains ***inconsiderable***. 数は相変らず大したことはない. ¶in ***increasing*** *numbers* 数がますます増大して. ¶an ***indefinite*** *number* 不定数. ¶with ***inferior*** *numbers* 少数(寡兵)をもって. ¶an extremely ***interesting*** *number* 非常に興味ある号(雑誌など). ¶in a ***large*** *number* of cases 多数の場合. 【類】a ***large*** *number* of hungers-on (食客) / in a surprisingly ***large*** *number* of cases ‖ the ***larger*** *number* of ... …の過半数 ‖ make up the ***largest*** *number* 最大多数を占めている. ¶The *number* of ... is ***legion***. …の数はきわめて多い. ¶a ***lesser*** *number* より少ない数. ¶the ***license*** *number* of a machine 機械の特許番号. ¶a ***limited*** *number* 限られた数(少しだけ). 【類】He was not called to speak as the *number* of orators was necessarily very ***limited***. ¶for a ***long*** *number* of years thereafter その後多年にわたって. ¶A ***low*** *number* is preferable (=desirable). [電話など]若い番号の方がいい. ¶The ship is carrying her ***maximum*** *number* of passengers. 船は最大限度の乗客をのせている. ¶a ***memorial*** *number* [雑誌などの]記念号. ¶contain the maximum of information in a ***minimum*** *number* of words 最小数の言葉の中に最大量の知識を含む. ¶***odd*** *numbers* 奇数. ¶read in an ***old*** *number* of The Times of ... 古いタイムス紙で…の記事を読む. ¶What is Lincoln's ***ordinal*** *number* in the line of American presidents?=What is Lincoln's number of presidency? アメリカ大統領の中でリンカーンは何代目ですか. ¶The enemy was in ***overwhelming*** *numbers*. 敵は優勢であった. ¶***previous*** *numbers* [雑誌などの]既刊号. ¶a ***prodigious*** *number* ばく大な数. ¶the ***real*** *number* 実数. ¶an easily ***remembered*** *number* 容易に覚えられる数. ¶obtain the ***required*** *number* of person 頭数をそろえる. ¶give it in ***round*** *numbers* それを概数で示す ‖ to put it in ***round*** *numbers* 概算して. ¶***serial*** *numbers* 定期刊行の号数. ¶a ***single*** *number* (=an issue) (新聞雑誌などの代価を示す場合)一册(部). ¶the ***singular*** *number* 単数. ¶once or a ***small*** *number* of times 一度または二三度. ¶a ***small select*** *number* of students 少数えり抜きの学生. ¶a ***special*** *number* 特集号. ¶for a ***stated*** *number* of years 一定の数年間. ¶in ***sufficient*** *numbers* たっぷり. ¶an ***undetermined*** *number* 不定の数, 若干. ¶an ***uneven*** (=odd) *number* 奇数. ¶an ***untold*** *number* 無数. ¶an ***unusual*** *number* 非常な数. ¶a ***vast*** *number* of pigs 沢山の豚 ‖ in a ***vast*** *number* of cases 大多数の場合に. 【類】Sheep are reared in ***vast*** *numbers*. ¶the ***whole*** *number* 全数. ¶a ***wrong*** *number* [電話の]番号違い ‖ ***Wrong*** *number*, I'm sorry. 番号が違います.

Q² a ***badge*** *number* [赤帽, 給仕人など]記章番号. ¶his ***car license*** *number* 彼の自動車番号. ¶the ***case*** *number* [商品など]こん包番号. ¶a ***Christmas*** *number* [雑誌など]クリスマス号. ¶a ***class*** *number* 部門番号(図書館の). ¶Home Journal's ***fall*** *number* ホームジャーナル誌の秋季号. ¶a ***five-digit*** (=place) *number* [一万から始まる]五けたの数. ¶***future*** *numbers* [雑誌などの]未刊号. ¶a ***house*** *number* 番地. ¶a ***licence*** *number* 自動車の許可番号. ¶a ***hundred-page*** *number* 百ページ号. ¶a ***Junuary*** *number* 一月号. ¶The dog wears a ***metal*** *number* on his collar. 犬は首に金属の番号札をつけている. ¶a ***motor-car*** *number* 自動車番号. ¶make sure that the ***page*** *numbers* run consecutively ページ数が順序よくそろっている(乱丁がない)かを確かめる. ¶one's ***party*** *number* 自分の組の番号. ¶a ***pass*** *number* 無料通行券の番号. ¶a ***peak*** *number* of ... …という最高数. ¶give one's ***phone*** (=telephone) *number* その電話番号を知らせる. ¶She gave two ***piano*** *numbers* at the concert. 彼女はその音楽会でピアノを二曲演奏した. ¶***prefix*** *numbers* on number plates of motor vehicles 自動車数字板の前方の数字 (6-1230 に見るような). ¶assign ***priority*** *numbers* to ... 優先番号を割当てる. ¶a ***reception*** (***receipt***) *number* 受付番号. ¶a ***reference*** *num-*

ber 参照番号(手紙の中で指示するに便利のように記した番号). ¶a ***registration number*** 登記番号. ¶What's your ***room number?*** あなたのおへやは何番ですか. ¶a ***seat number*** 座席番号(劇場などで). ¶the ***September number*** of *Time* タイム誌の九月号. ¶a ***six-figure number*** 六けた数(すなわち十万台). ¶the ***solo numbers*** of an opera 歌劇の独唱部. ¶a ***street number*** 街路番号(米国には Fifth Street などの名がある).

P there are many persons, myself ***among*** the *number*, who ... ...した人は多数あるが私もその一人だ ‖ included ***among*** the *number* are ... その中に...もはいっている. ¶The house is situated ***at No.*** 24. 家は二十四番地にある. ¶They were overwhelmed ***by numbers.*** 彼らは数で圧倒された. 【類】being at length overcome ***by numbers*** / The enemy won ***by*** [force of] ***numbers.*** ‖ refer to it ***by number*** その番号をいう. ¶***for*** a ***number*** of years (minutes) 数年(分)間. ‖ be like sands of the sea-shore ***for number*** 浜のまさごのように多い. ¶They exceed us ***in number.*** 彼らは数の上ではわれわれ以上だ. ‖ grow (=increase) ***in number***[*s*] 数を増す. 【類】small (large, few, three) ***in number*** ‖ ***in*** steadily decreasing ***numbers*** 数が段々減って ‖ be skilled ***in numbers*** 算数がうまい. 【類】They are found here ***in numbers.*** / Mysterious rays are being discovered ***in*** such *numbers* that soon there will not be enough letters in the alphabet to name them all. ‖ ***In*** the *number* of Literature for Feb. 25 二月二十五日号のリテラチュア誌において. ¶They are ***of*** this ***number.*** 彼らはこの類に属する. ‖ He is not ***of*** our ***number.*** 彼はわれわれの仲間ではない. ¶Without his continual help and inspiration ***over*** a ***number*** of years, this book would never have been attempted. 多年にわたる氏の間断なき助力と激励とがなかったなら本書のくわだては起らなかったであろう. ¶***to*** the ***number*** of (=numbering) about 1,000 約一千の数まで. 【類】Books, ***to*** the ***number*** of not more than eight at one time, may be taken out of the Library by any member. ‖ William Blake is one of the few poets that appeal ***to numbers*** who are indifferent to poetry. ブレイクは詩に無とん着な連中(読者)でも共鳴する少数詩人の一人だ. ¶stars ***without number*** 数知れない星. 【類】Examples ***without number*** could be quoted, but one must suffice by way of illustration.

P² a ***number of*** people 若干(多数)の人々 ‖ ***numbers of*** people 多数の人々 ‖ a ***number of*** times 幾回も ‖ The ***number of*** the house is 101. 番地は百一だ. ‖ The ***number of*** deaths was very high. 死亡数が非常に多かった. ‖ The ***number of*** jobless people grows. 失業者の数が段々ふえる. 【類】The ***number of*** collectors is growing apace (ずんずん). / the ***number of*** the staff / the ***number of*** lives lost. ¶the first ***number on*** the program プログラムの一番目.

number, *v.* 数える; 数え込む; (...の)数.

M ***number consecutively*** from 1 to 16 一から十六まで順次に数える. ¶The men ***numbered less*** than five hundred. 部下は五百に足りなかった.

M² Soldiers ***numbered off*** one by one from left to right. 兵士は左から右へと一人一人番号を言った.

P The club ***numbers*** prominent physicians ***among*** its members. そのクラブは知名の医師が会員になっている. ‖ He is ***numbered among*** the poets. 彼はその詩人仲間の一人に数えられている. ‖ ***Among*** the promoters are ***numbered*** some of the most distinguished men in the capital. 発起人の中には首都の名士も数名加わっている. ‖ men and women who are ***numbered among***[*st*] the foremost of their respective lands 彼ら各自の国では第一人者に数えられている男女. 【類】He is ***numbered among*** the best in that circle. / The school ***numbered among*** its graduates many eminent men. ¶***number between*** sixty and seventy 六七十の間を算する. ¶popular newspapers whose readers are ***numbered by*** millions 愛読者数百万を数える通俗新聞. 【類】They can be ***numbered by*** [the] thousands. ¶They ***number into*** the hundreds (thousands). 彼らは数百(千)にのぼる. ‖ ***number*** them ***from*** one and upward それを一から順次数をつける. ¶the man but for whom his son would have been ***numbered with*** the dead 彼の子息が命拾いをした恩人. ¶The students ***number over*** 2,000. 学生の数は二千以上だ. ¶I am ***numbered with*** its staff. 私はその部員の一人だ.

numbering, *n.* 番号.

Q ***consecutive numbering*** 通し番号.

numberless, *a.* 無数の.

M be ***almost numberless*** ほとんど数が知れない.

numeral, *n.* 数字; 〚文法〛数詞.

Q the ***Arabic numerals*** アラビア数字. ¶the ***cardinal*** (***ordinal***) ***numerals*** 基(序)数詞. ¶the ***Roman numerals*** ローマ数字(V, X など).

numerous, *a.* 多数の.

M fifteen times ***more numerous*** than ... ...よりも十五倍も多い. ¶***too numerous*** to enumerate (=count) 多くて数えきれない ‖ ***too numerous*** for recital 枚挙にいとまない. 【類】***too numerous*** to recapitulate (列挙する) here / be ***too numerous*** to mention.

nuptials, *n. pl.* 婚礼.

P on his ***nuptials with*** a beautiful virgin 彼の美しい乙女との結婚式のとき.

nurse, *n.* 乳母; 看護婦; 養成者, 養成所.

Q a ***chief*** (=***head***) ***nurse*** 婦長. ¶a ***dry nurse*** [乳をやらない]うば, 育児婦. ¶a ***firm*** and ***stern nurse*** しっかりした厳格な看護婦. ¶the ***supervising nurse*** [看護]婦長. ¶a ***sympathetic nurse*** 思いやりのある看護婦. ¶a ***trained nurse*** 有資格看護婦(看護婦学校出の). ¶a ***wet nurse*** 乳児のうば. ¶a ***white-robed nurse*** 白衣の看護婦.

Q² a ***graduate nurse*** 《米》=a trained nurse. ¶a ***hospital nurse*** 病院看護婦. ¶an ***intern nurse*** 病院専属の看護婦. ¶a special ***night nurse*** 特別夜勤看護婦. ¶a ***Red Cross nurse*** 赤十字看護婦.

P She had placed him out ***at nurse*** in a village. 彼女は彼(子)をいなかへ里子に出した. ¶put out a child ***to nurse*** 子供を里子に出す. ¶leave a child ***with*** a ***nurse*** 子供を乳母にあずける.

P² Difficulty is the ***nurse of*** greatness. かん難なんじを玉にす. 【類】Ancient Greece was the ***nurse of*** learning (学問の温床).

nurse, *v.* 看護する, 介抱する; [恨みなどを]いだく; [弱い火を]盛んに燃えさせる.

M ***nurse*** a person ***back*** to health 人を介抱して健康を回復させる ‖ ***nurse back*** to a flame the flickering spark of life [でき死者などを]介抱して命を取止めさせる. ¶He was ***kindly nursed.*** 彼は親切に看護された. ¶She ***nursed*** him ***together*** through his last days. 彼女は氏の晩年死に至るまでともども氏を介抱した.

P ***nurse*** a grudge ***against*** ... ...に対し恨みをいだく. ¶He has been ***nursed in*** luxury. 彼はぜいたくに育った. ¶***nurse*** embers ***into*** a flame 余じんを燃え上がらせる.

O ***nurse*** a plant (young tree) 植物(など)を育てる. ¶***nurse*** a bad cold 悪性感冒を直そうと努める. 【類】***nurse*** one's sore arm ‖ ***nurse*** one's knees ひざをかかえる.

nursery, *n.* 養成所.

Q an ***official nursery*** 官吏養成所.

Q² leave a boy to the care of a ***day nursery*** 男の子を保育所にあずける. ¶a ***reforestation nursery*** 植林育種場.

P universities as ***nurseries for*** specialists and technical scholars 専門家及び技術家の養成所としての大学. 【類】This world is an admirable ***nursery for*** great minds. ¶Idleness is the ***nursery of*** vice. 怠惰は悪徳の温床だ.

nursing, *n.* 看護.

V She ***took up nursing*** as a career. 彼女は看護婦を自分の職業として選んだ.

Q ***sick nursing*** 病人看護. ¶by ***skilful*** and ***assiduous nursing*** 熟練した熱心な看護によって.

Q² ***home nursing*** 家庭の看護.

nurture, *v.* 育てる.

M a ***delicately nurtured*** girl ひよわい娘.

nut, *n.* くるみ, 堅果; 《俗》頭; *pl.* 《俗》熱心.

V ***crack*** a ***nut*** くるみを割る. ¶***gather nuts*** 木の実を拾う.

Q It is a ***hard nut*** for him to crack. それは彼にとって難問題だ.

Q² ***ground nuts***=monkey nuts, earthnuts 南京豆. ☞米国では peanuts という方が普通.

P He is ***nuts*** (=crazy) ***about*** her. 彼女に夢中だ. ¶She is a bit ***off*** her ***nut.*** 彼女はちとどうかしている.

P² We are ***nuts on*** 'the strange.' われわれは何でも珍しいもの好きです.

nutrition, *n.* 栄養.

P take care ***of*** the ***nutrition*** of children 子供らの栄養に注意する.

nutshell, *n.* 堅果の殻; 簡単な語句.

P present it ***in*** a ***nutshell*** それを簡単に述べる. 【類】to put the matter ***in*** a ***nutshell.*** / This is the whole matter in a nutshell / the case has been put in a nutshell in his speech at ... / sum up the situation in a nutshell, thus: "..." / The whole matter lies in a nutshell. ¶The matter can be put into a nutshell, thus: その事件はかいつまんで言うとこうだ.

nuzzle, *v.* [動物が]鼻をこすりつける. ...

M The horse *gently* nuzzled my shoulder. 馬がそっと私の肩に鼻をすりつけた.

M² nuzzle up close to ... ...にすり寄る.

nylon, *n.* ナイロン; *pl.* ナイロンのくつ下.

P in nylons ナイロンのくつ下をはいて.

O Nylon is a synthetic material derived from coal, water and air. ナイロンは石炭・水・空気から作った人工繊維である.

O

oak, *n.* オークの木(かし, かしわ類).

Q *English oak* 英国産オーク材. ¶This is a romance of "an *old oak* and tender ivy." これは「老いらくの恋ものがたり」である.

Q² an acorn which has fallen from its *mother oak* 親のオーク樹から落ちたどんぐり.

oar, *n.* かい; こぎ手.

V *back* the oars 逆漕する. ¶*boat* the oars かいを収める. ¶*feather* oars かいを斜にする(一かきして元に戻すとき). ¶*pull* an oar かいでこぐ‖*pull* a good oar うまくこぐ. ¶*put in* one's oar 口ばしを入れる, おせっかいをする. ¶*ship* the oars [こぎ始めの用意]かいをクラッチに乗せる. ¶*take* the laboring oars 骨の折れるかいをこぐ; 難局に立つ. ¶*toss* the oars [敬礼の意味で]かいを立てる. ¶*trail* the oars かいをかい架から外して流す. ¶*unship* the oars かいを外す.

Q He is a *good* oar. 彼はうまいこぎ手だ.

P rest *on* one's oars 一休みする. ¶a boat propelled *with* oars かいを使う船.

oasis, *n.* オアシス.

Q offer an *ever-verdant* oasis ときわの沃地となる.

P² This is my only oasis *in* city life. ここが都会生活での私の唯一のいこいの場所だ.

oat, *n.* からす麦.

V *sow* one's wild oats 若気の至りから道楽をやる. 【類】He has *sown* all his wild oats. ‖He settled down to the drama after *sowing* his wild literary oats. 彼は文学の道楽を色々やったあげく劇に落着いた.

Q *hulled* oats もみを除いたからす麦.

oath, *n.* 誓い, 誓約; のろい, ののしること.

V *administer* an oath to some one だれかに宣誓させる‖*administer* the oath of office 就任の宣誓をする. ¶*break* one's oath その誓いを破る. ¶*drop* an oath 誓いを棄てる. ¶*make* [an] oath that ... ...という誓いを立てる. ¶*rap out* an oath のろってどなる. ¶*make oath* 誓いをする. ¶*swear* an oath 誓いを立てる. 【類】*swear* an oath on the Bible / *swear* an oath of allegiance to a government / *Swear* to me the oath of fidelity that you will not betray the secret. ‖*swear* the oath 畜生呼ばわりをする. ¶*take* oath 誓う, 宣誓する‖*take* the oath of office 服務の宣誓をする. 【類】There Washington *took* his oath of office as President. / *take* an oath before ... to ... / *take* an oath by kissing the Testament (聖書に接ぷんして) / He was willing to *take* his oath to all what he said. / *take* the oath of allegiance (忠誠) as a British subject‖*take* an oath of secrecy 秘密を守るという誓言をする‖*take* the oath of allegiance at naturalization 帰化の際に恭順の誓言をする.

Q swear a *false* oath 偽りの誓いを立てる. ¶swear an *inviolate* oath 神聖な誓いを立てる. ¶take the *legal* oath 法律上の誓言をする. ¶a *round* oath 率直な誓言. ¶On my *solemnest* oath, what I tell you is true. どこまでも誓って私の言うことは本当です.

Q² the *Five-Article Charter* Oath 五カ条の御誓文.

P bind themselves *by* a solemn oath to ... 神聖なる誓いを立てて...することを約する. ¶declare *on* oath 誓って断言する‖he stated *on* oath that... 彼は誓って...と述べた. 【類】have a statement taken *on* oath / make a declaration *on* oath‖You swear that?—*On* my oath. 誓ってか.—誓ってでございます. ¶make a statement *under* oath 誓いを立てて供述する‖say *under* oath that ... 誓って...という. ¶exclaim *with* an oath 怒りの叫びを発する.

P² take a solemn oath *to* the effect that ... ...という意味のおごそかな誓いを立てる.

obduracy, *n.* 無情, がん固, がん迷.

V *subdue* the obduracy of ... ...のがん迷をくじく.

obedience, *n.* 服従, 従順, 恭順.

V *compel* obedience 服従をしいる. ¶*command* obedience 服従させる. ¶*demand* obedience from ... ...の服従を要請する. ¶*enforce* obedience on ... ...を無理に服従させる. ¶*exact* obedience from ... ...に服従を強要する. ¶*give* a complete obedience to one's authority その権威に全く服従する. ¶*maintain* obedience 恭順を保持する. ¶*owe* no obedience to ... ...に服従の義務がない. ¶*refuse* obedience to ... ...への服従を拒む. ¶obedience is *required* to ... ...に服従することが必要だ. ¶*yield* obedience to ... ...に服従する.

Q *cheerful* obedience 心から喜んでの服従. ¶*filial* obedience 孝行. ¶exact *implicit* obedience to arbitrary orders 専横な命令に対して盲従を強要する. ¶*no* obedience is due to ... ...に服従する必要はない. ¶*ready* obedience 即座の服従. ¶a *steady* obedience 確実な服従.

P *in* obedience to the law 法律に従って. 【類】*in* obedience to an order issued by the police authorities‖in obedience *to* a gesture 手まねに応じて‖in obedience *to* the law 法律の命じる所に従って. 【類】obedience *to* a rule (custom).

obedient, *a.* 従順な, 忠順な, 順良な.

M *passively* obedient 恭順して.

P obedient *to* one's parents (superiors, dictator, ruler) 両親(など)に従順な.

obeisance, *n.* 敬礼, 礼, お辞儀.

V *do* obeisance to ... ...に敬礼する. ¶the ceremony of *making* an obeisance before the Emperor's portrait 御真影拝賀式. 【類】*make* profound obeisance to Their Majesties.

obelisk, *n.* 塔.

Q² an *advertising* obelisk 広告塔.

obey, *v.* 服従する, 命に従う.

M *meekly* obey おとなしく従う. ¶*promptly* and *cheerfully* obey an order じん速にかつ喜んで命に服する. ¶*readily* and *strictly* obey the orders of one's superiors in rank 上官の命に直ちにかつ厳密に服する. ¶obey *unmurmuringly* the commands of the spirit 魂の命令に遅疑せず服従する.

P obey *for* fear of punishment 罰せられるのが恐ろしいので服従する. ¶obey *from* fear 恐怖心から服従する. ¶obey *under* protest 反抗しながら従う. ¶obey him *with* fear and trembling 戦々兢々として彼に服従する.

obiter dictum, *L.* 漫言; 〖法〗付随的意見.

Q an *epigrammatic* obiter dictum 寸鉄的漫語. ¶*witty* obiter dicta 機知に富む漫言.

object, *n.* 目的; 事物, 物体; 対象.

V *accompany* the object with a written message 品物に手紙を添える. ¶*accomplish* the object one has so much at heart 大いに念願としている目的を果す. 【類】An army not backed by the people can never *accomplish* its object. / these objects can best be *accomplished* by ... ¶*achieve* its object その目的を果す. ¶*advance* objects 目的達成を進める. ¶*attain* the object of one's efforts 奮闘の目的を達する. ¶*call* the object into operation その物を使用する. ¶*carry out* the object その目的を遂行する.

¶ *compass* an *object* 目的をなしとげる. ¶ This will *defeat* the *object* it was intended to promote. このために達成せんとする本来の目的に反することになるだろう. ¶ *effect* its *object* その目的を成しとげる. ¶ *objects excavated* 出土品. ¶ *extend* the *object* 目的を拡大する. ¶ It will tend materially to *facilitate* his *object*. それは彼の目的を達成する上に大いに助けになるだろう. ¶ The mountain *forms* a striking *object* in the landscape. その山は風景の大立物になっている. ¶ *forward* its *objects* in every way その目的達成をあらゆる点において進める. ¶ *fulfil* the *object* that I assigned myself 自分で定めた目的をなしとげる. ¶ *further* the object of the society その会の目的を助ける. ¶ *gain* one's *object* その目的を達する. ¶ *hasve* an *object* in view 目的がある ‖ *have* no *object* in life but to ... ...の外には世の中に目的がない. 【類】 an organization *having* for its *object* the promotion of science. ¶ *objectify objects* 実物を示す. ¶ *obtain* one's *object* 目的を達する. ¶ *promote objects* 目的を助成する. ¶ *pursue* an *object* 目的を追求する. ¶ *realize* one's *object* その目的を達する. ¶ *redeem* (=*recover or take out*) a pledged *object* 質物を受出す. ¶ It helps in *securing* this *object*. それはこの目的を達する助けになる. ¶ *seek objects* 目的物を求める. ¶ *specify* the *object* of a meeting 集会の目的を明細に記す.

V² Our ultimate *object lies* beyond. われわれの終局の目的はそれより先にある.

Q regard girls as *beautiful objects* 少女を美しい品物と見なす. ¶ this *cherished object* of his life 彼のこの大事な生がいの目的. ¶ the *chief object* of interest 主な見もの. ¶ a *concrete object* 具体的な目的. ¶ a *conspicuous object* 顕著な目的. ¶ Such a person may be properly made a *constant object* of police surveillance. こういう人は常に警察から監視されるのが本当であろう. ¶ The society was founded in 1921 with the following as its *constitutional objects:* その協会はその規約に明記した次のような目的を持って一九二一年に設立された. ¶ made with a *deeper object* 一層深い目的で造られた. ¶ What a *disgusting object!* なんといやな物だろう! ¶ with a *double object*; to ... and to ... ...し, また...するという二重の目的で. ¶ *external objects* 物象. ¶ *Falling objects* gain momentum. 落下物は加速性を増す. ¶ What *fearful object* is a tipsy woman! 酒に酔った女と来ては始末に負えないものだ. ¶ the *first object* of murder まっさきに殺す目標. ¶ an *inanimate object* 無生物. ¶ *internal objects* 心像. ¶ *juster objects* of compassion 一層同情を寄せらるべきもの. ¶ a *laudable object* 賞めるに足るもの. ¶ make history one's *main object* (= subject) of study 歴史を研究の目的とする. 【類】 The study of ... was the *main object* of his life. / the *main object* to be aimed at in ... ¶ a *natural object* 自然物 ‖ a precious *natural object* 貴重な天然記念物. ¶ Expense was *no object*. 入費はいくらでも掛けた. ‖ Time [is] *no object*. 時間はいくらかかってもよい. ‖ Money *no object*. [求職広告]当方給料の額は問わず. ¶ with *no other object* than to ... ...の外には目的がない. ¶ the *original object* 本来の目的. ¶ a festival with the *pious object* of averting the floods of the river その川のはんらんを防ごうという信心深い目的で行う祭礼. ¶ Its ascent is a *popular object* of pilgrimage and holiday diversion. その登山は一般の参けい者や遊山に行く者が目的とする所である. 【類】 a highly *popular object* of worship with the lower classes. ¶ one of the most *precious objects* in my possession 私の所蔵品中一番貴重なものの一つ. ¶ a *prehistoric object* 有史以前の物体. ¶ its *primary object* その主要目的. ¶ the *prime object* of Japanese statesmanship 日本政治家の第一眼目. 【類】 one *prime object* of education is to ... ¶ the *principal object* 主な目的. ¶ make large gifts to *public objects* 公共の目的に多額の寄付をする. ¶ the *ruling object* 主眼. ¶ a *sacred object* 神聖な目的. ¶ a *secondary object* 第二次的の目的. ¶ He has a *similar object* in view. 彼も同様なことを目標にしている. ¶ for *some hidden ulterior object* なにか魂胆があって. ¶ with the *specific object* of ... ...という特殊の目的で. ¶ a *tangible object* (手でさわれる)形のある物. ¶ He has a *threefold object* in mind (=view). 彼には三つの目的がある. ¶ a *tiny object* 微小物. ¶ It was suspected that he had *ulterior objects*. 彼には他に思惑があるとけん疑がかかった. ¶ its *ultimate object* その究極の目的. ¶ a *worthy object* of ambition りっぱな大目的.

Q² an *art object*=an object of art 美術品. ¶ common *household objects* 普通家庭用の品. ¶ a *miniature art object* 小物芸術品.

P it has *as* (=for) its *object* ... ...をその目的とする. ¶ having *for* its *objects* ... その目的は...であって. ¶ *with* the sole *object* of ... ...をただ一つの目的として. 【類】 *with* that *object* in view.

P² What is your *object for* coming here tonight? なんのために今夜ここへおいでになったのですか. ¶ the *object in* preparing this book この本を編集する目的. 【類】 the *object in* studying literature. ¶ become an *object of* pity みじめなものになる ‖ the *object* of keenest care 大いに目をかけている者(物). 【類】 an *object of* aversion to his master and an *object of* pity or disdain to his fellow-officers / an *object of* envy (great penetration, fear and superstition) ‖ become the *object of* popular odium 人々の憎悪の的になる ‖ They were made the *object of* the enemies' laughter. 彼らはその敵の冷笑の的にされた. ‖ an *object of* suspicion 注意人物 【類】 make these things an *object of* scientific study / the *object of* an interview / an *object of* love / it may be made the *object of* a day's excursion from ... ‖ *objects of* virtue (高尚な)古器物 ‖ *objects of* art and antiquity 美術品や古器物. ¶ an *object to* a verb 動詞の目的.

O make oneself "an *object*" 自分を人の笑いものにする.

object, *v*. 反対する, 異議を唱える.

M I most *decidedly object* to it. 私は断然これに反対する. ¶ *formally object* to ... ...に対し正式に反対を述べる. ¶ *object strongly* to ... 猛烈に...に反対する.

P I don't *object to* a good glass of wine. 上等のぶどう酒を一杯やるのは結構だ. 【類】 He *objects to* the idea which some people seem to entertain that England owes everything to outside initiative. / Her parents *objected to* the marriage. / Do you *object to* (=mind) my opening the door?

objection, *n*. 反対, 異議, 苦情.

V *address* a grave *objection* to ... ...に対し大いに異議を唱える. ¶ The *objection* cannot be *admitted*. その反対は認めることはできない. ¶ energetically *combat* the *objections* raised by ... ...の持ちだした異議と盛んに戦う. ¶ *enter* a formal *objection* in writing 書類で正式の異議を申立てる. ¶ no such *objection* shall be *entertained* unless ... ...でなければそうした苦情は一切受理しない. ¶ I *got* no *objections*. 私の言ったことに異議は出なかった. ¶ I have no *objection* to it. 私はそれに異議はない. ¶ *interpose* an *objection* 故障を入れる. ¶ *lodge* (=*utter*) an *objection* against ... ...に対し異議を申立てる. ¶ *make objection* to ... ...に反対する ‖ *make* no *objection* upon ... ...になんら異議を唱えない. ¶ to *obviate objections* 反対されないように. ¶ *offer objection* to it on the ground that ... ...という論拠で反対を唱える. ¶ The judge *overruled* the *objection*. 審判官は反対論を棄却した. ‖ my *objection* that ... was *overruled* on the grounds, first, that ...; and, secondly, that ... ... という私の抗議は第一に...の理由でまた第二に...の理由で却下された. ¶ They *presented* strong *objections* against his appointment. 彼らは彼の任命に大反対を唱えた. ¶ *raise* an *objection* to ... ...に苦情を申立てる. 【類】 at first an *objection* was *raised* to ... / He *raised* an *objection* against the proposal, saying that ... / It is too late now to *raise* any *objection*. ¶ *resent* as meddlesome their *objections* to ... ...に対する彼らの苦情を余計なお世話と怒る. ¶ Personally, I *see* no *objection*. 自分一個としては私に何ら異議はない. ¶ *take objection* to ... ...に対し異議を唱える. 【類】 no *objection* is *taken* of ... ‖ a list of subjects to which the censors *take objection* 検閲官が承認しない主題の表[映画など]. ¶ one of the *objections* sometimes *urged* against the reform method その改良法に対して時々持出される異議の一つ. ¶ *Objection* to it has been *voiced* so many times in recent years. 近年それに対して何度も異議が唱えられて来ている. 【類】 no *objection* has been *voiced* here against ... / they began to *voice* their *objections* to ... ¶ *waive* one's *objection* 抗議を撤回する. ¶ *withdraw* one's *objection* 反対を撤回する.

V² on examination this *objection falls* to the ground, for ... 考査して見るとこの抗議も失敗に帰する, その訳は...

Q an *aesthetic* (=*esthetic*) *objection* to ... ...に対する美

学上の反対. ¶The ***chief objection*** to the story is its tediousness. その物語に対する主な非難は その退屈さにある. ¶the ***constant*** *objection* that is brought against ... ...に対していつも持出される反対. ¶a ***flimsy objection*** 薄弱な反対. ¶The *objection* is well ***founded***. その反対には十分の根拠がある. ‖ a properly ***founded objection*** 相当理由のある反対. ¶raise ***frivolous objections*** 軽率な異議を唱える. ¶be open to ***grave objections*** 重大な非議をまぬかれない. ¶***immaterial*** *objections* 重きをおくに足りない反対論. ¶take ***legal*** *objection* to ... ...に法律上反対を唱える. ¶the ***main*** *objection* to ... ...に対する主要な反対. ¶***no*** *objection* can possibly be taken of ... ...については何ら反対の余地がない. ¶there is ***one objection*** to this, in that ... ...という一つの厄介がある. ¶The action is open to ***serious obection***. その処置には大いに言分がある. ¶I have not the ***slightest*** *objection*. 私には少しの異議もない. ¶raise a ***strong*** *objection* to ... ...に対して強硬な反対を唱える. 【類】present a ***strong*** *objection* against ... ¶a ***strong aesthetic*** *objection* 強力な審美上の反対. ¶a ***stubborn*** *objection* 強硬な反対. ¶raise ***valid objections*** to the scheme その計画に有力な反対の声をあげる. ¶***weighty*** *objections* 有力な反対. ¶a ***wholesome*** *objection* ためになる反対.

P² *objection **against*** one's marriage (plan) その結婚(など)に対する反対. ¶*objection **to*** further consideration 再審議反対. 【類】There can be no *objection **to*** your doing so. / *objection **to*** smoking.

objectionable, *a.* 異議のある, 言分のある.

M ***highly*** *objectionable* 大いに不都合な. ¶be ***less*** *objectionable* まだしもである.

objective, *n.* 目標, 目的; 目的地.

V In his 23 years of service as president, he has ***achieved*** practically all the *objectives* he set forth in his inaugural address. 総長二十三年の在職中彼は就任式のあいさつで述べた計画をことごとく実現した. ¶***carry out*** these *objectives* これらの目的を達成する. ¶***have*** a certain *objective* in view ある目的をもっている. ¶***mark*** our *objective* われわれの目標を示している. ¶***reach*** our *objective* われわれの目的地に達する.

Q the ***chief*** *objectives* 主な目標. ¶***military*** *objectives* 軍事的目標.

Q² a ***long-range*** *objective* 長い先の目標.

P² my *objective **for*** the present is to ... 今のところ私としては...するつもりである. ¶the *objective **of*** the Japanese Communists 日本共産党の進む道.

objectivity, *n.* 客観性, 対象性.

V ***gain*** that *objectivity* of attitude that science embodies 科学の主眼であるあの客観的な態度を会得する. ¶***give*** scientific *objectivity* to the subject of ... ...の主題に科学的な客観性を付与する.

object lesson, *n.* 〖教育〗実物教課.

V ***make*** an *object-lesson* of ... ...を実物教訓にする.

Q The motion picture is an ***educational*** and ***entertaining*** *object lesson*. 映画は教育上及び娯楽上の実物教授である. ¶a ***striking*** *object lesson* 著しい実物教育.

objector, *n.* 反対者, 抗議者.

Q a ***conscientious*** *objector* 良心的[戦争]反対者.

oblation, *n.* 供物.

V ***make*** *oblation* to ... ...に供養(くよう)をする.

obligate, *v.* 義務を負わす.

M be ***legally*** *obligated* to ... 法律上...する必要がある.

obligation, *n.* 義務, 恩義, 義理.

V the author frankly ***acknowledges*** his *obligations* to ... 著者は...に負う所あるむねを率直に表明します(序文の文句) ‖ without ***acknowledging*** the *obligation* その恩義を謝することなく. ¶***cancel*** the *obligation* 義務を解消する. ¶***disown*** or ***conceal*** one's *obligations* to ... ...に対してその負う所あることを否認しまたは隠す. ¶This ***entails*** no *obligation*. これがために何らの責任関係も起って来ない. ¶I wish to ***express*** my *obligations* to ... for ... ...の恩義に対して私は...に感謝を述べたいと思う. ¶***fulfil*** an *obligation* 義務を果す. 【類】fail to ***fulfil*** its *obligations*. ¶Your inspection will not ***imply*** the slightest *obligation* to purchase. お買上げ下さらなくとも結構でございますから品物を御一覧下さい. ¶***impose*** an *obligation* to ... ...という義務を負わせる. ¶***incur*** *obligations* 義理を生じる ‖ I have ***incurred*** other *obligations* to ... for ... 私は...に対し...という色々の恩義をこうむっている. ¶***lay*** an *obligation* on ... ...に責任を負わせる. ¶***meet*** one's *obligations* punctiliously 自分の義理をきちんと果す. 【類】delay ***meeting*** an *obligation*. ¶***owe*** an *obligation* to ... ...に恩義を受けている. ¶***place*** an *obligation* on ... ...に義務を課する. ¶***realize*** one's corresponding *obligations* これに対する自分の責任を感得する. ¶slow to ***recognize*** its *obligation* to posterity それが後世の人に対する義務を認識するに緩慢な. ¶***undertake*** the *obligation* 義務を果す.

V² The *obligation **falls*** upon us all. その責任はわれわれ一同にかかっている.

Q he is not under any very ***binding*** *obligation* to ... 彼は...に対し何ら大した義務を負うていない. ¶realize one's ***corresponding*** *obligations* 従って生じる義務を認識する. ¶I desire to express my ***deep*** *obligation* to ... 私は...に対して大いに感謝の意を表したい. 【類】I am under ***deep*** *obligation* to ... / an acknowledgment of one's ***deep*** *obligations* to ... ¶***ethical*** *obligation* 道徳的義務. ¶fulfil ***financial*** *obligations* 財政上の義務を果す. ¶be absolved from ***further*** *obligation* 今後の義務から解除される. ¶the author wishes to express his ***grateful*** *obligation* to ... 著者は...に対して負う所あるむねを表示したい. ¶I am under ***great*** *obligations* to ... 私は...に非常に世話になっている. ¶He has placed me under a ***heavy*** *obligation*. あの方には大分恩になっている. ¶an ***international*** *obligation* such as participation in an exhibition 博覧会参加などの国際的義務. ¶a ***legal*** *obligation* 法律上の義務. 【類】be under a ***legal*** *obligation* to ... ¶a ***moral*** *obligation* 道徳上の義務. ¶he is under ***no*** *obligation* to ... 彼は...に対し何ら義務がない. ¶***mutual*** *obligation* 相互の義務. ¶***reciprocal*** *obligations* 相互の義務. ¶***solemn*** *obligations* of international understandings 国際間の約諾に基づく厳正な義務. ¶a ***social*** *obligation* 社会的義務. ¶I am under ***special*** *obligations* to ... for critically reading the manuscript and making valuable suggestions. 原稿を批判的に読んだり貴重な暗示を与えて下されたことに対して私は特に...のお世話になっている. ¶the book lays us under a ***strong*** *obligation* by offering us ... その本はわれわれに...を提供してくれて非常にありがたい. ¶***written*** *obligations* 書面に認めた義務.

Q² one's ***citizenship*** *obligations* その市民たる義務. ¶Japan's ***reparations*** *obligations* 日本の賠償義務. ¶China's ***treaty*** *obligations* 中国の条約上の義務.

P free one ***from*** (=***of***) an *obligation* ... ...の義務を解除する. ¶He placed me ***under*** *obligation* by the kind way in which he supplied me the information desired. 彼は親切にも私の希望する情報を供給してくれたので私はその恩義を感じた. ‖ I'm ***under*** many *obligations* to you for ... ...に対し私はあなたに色々なご厄介になっている. ‖ He feels ***under*** *obligation* to no man. 彼は何人にも恩になっていると思っていない. ‖ He once laid me ***under*** an *obligation*. 私は一度彼の厄介になったことがある. 【類】This puts me ***under*** no *obligation* to buy or subscribe.

P² my *obligations **to*** my predecessors in the same field of research 私と同じ方面の研究をやった先輩に対し私の負う所.

obligatory, *a.* 義務的な, やむを得ない.

P It is *obligatory **by*** law. それは法律上必ずそうしなければならないことだ. ¶Obedience is *obligatory **on*** a soldier. 服従は軍人にまぬかれない義務だ.

Q Evening dress is *obligatory*. ぜひイーヴニングコートを着用しなければならない.

oblige, *v.* 余儀なくする, せざるを得ないようにさせる, 義務を負わせる, 喜ばせる.

M I should be most ***deeply*** *obliged* if you could ... ...して下さらば誠にかたじけなく存じます. ¶I should feel ***exceedingly*** *obliged* if you would ... ...して下されば千万かたじけなく存じます. ¶By so doing you will ***greatly*** *oblige* us. そうして下さるなら誠にありがたい. ¶not ***legally*** *obliged* to ... 法律上...する義務がない. ¶I am ***much*** *obliged* [to you] for all your kindness. 色々ご親切にあずかり誠にありがとうございます. ¶***reluctantly*** *obliged* to ... いやいやながら...せざるを得ないことになって.

P You will *oblige* us ***by*** doing so. そうして下さればありがたいです. ¶Self-preservation *obliged* the people ***to*** these severities. 自己保全のために人民はこれらのきびしい道を講

じなければならなかった. ‖ I am very much *obliged to* you. あなたに深く感謝します.【類】I shall be much *obliged to* you for an early reply. ¶*oblige* a person ***with*** an answer (loan, favor) 返事(など)を与えて人を喜ばせる ‖ You will *oblige* me ***with*** your name and address. あなたのご姓名とご住所をお知らせ下さい.【類】*Oblige* us ***with*** your company at dinner.

V Sorry I can't *oblige* you. 遺憾ながらお望みに応じ兼ねます. ¶I was *obliged* to go yesterday. 私はきのう出かけねばならなかった.

obliging, *a.* 親切な.

M She was one of the ***most*** *obliging* of all my old acquaintances. 彼女は昔なじみの中でも一番親切だった.

P² be *obliging* ***to*** every person 人をそらさない.

obliterate, *v.* 消す, まっ殺する, 削除する.

M He ***carefully*** *obliterated* his name from the page. 彼は紙面から彼の名を念入りにまっ殺した.

P Holland was practically *obliterated* ***from*** the map of the world, and the Dutch flag continued to be unfurled only at Deshima. 事実上オランダは世界地図から消えてオランダの旗はただ出島だけに翻っていた.【類】It was *obliterated* ***from*** the memory.

oblivion, *n.* 忘却; 隠滅, 埋没.

Q But for his painstaking investigations it would have been consigned to ***lasting*** *oblivion*. 彼の忍耐強い調査がなかったならそれは永久に忘れられてしまったであろう.

P rescued ***from*** *oblivion* 隠滅をまぬかれて. ¶buried ***in*** *oblivion* 隠滅に帰して ‖ lost ***in*** *oblivion* 忘却されて. ¶fall (=sink) ***into*** *oblivion* [世の中に]忘れられる.

oblivious, *a.* 忘れがちの, 健忘の; 不注意な.

M ***evidently*** *oblivious* that ... 確かに...ということを忘却して. ¶***happily*** *oblivious* to the fact that ... 幸にも...ということを忘れて.

P *oblivious* ***of*** appearances 体裁かまわず. ¶*oblivious* ***of*** duty (fact, the past) 義務(など)を忘れて ‖ He seemed totally *oblivious* ***of*** my presence. 彼は私のいることを全く忘れている様子であった. ‖ *oblivious* ***of*** everything around him that is not connected with his own act 前後を忘れて. ¶*oblivious* ***to*** all extraneous matters, changes in the weather included 天候の変化はいうまでもなくあらゆる外界のことを忘れて.【類】*oblivious* ***to*** all sense of public duty 公務の念を全然忘却して.

obnoxious, *a.* 気にさわる, いやらしい.

P His foul mouth has made him *obnoxious* ***to*** us. あの男は口が悪いのでわれわれにきらわれている. ‖ a man *obnoxious* ***to*** his neighbors 近所の鼻つまみもの.

obscenity, *n.* いんわい, わいせつ.

Q a ***disgusting*** *obscenity* 実にいやらしいわいせつさ.

P the *obscenities* ***of*** the play その劇の卑わいさ.【類】*obscenity* ***of*** one's speech.

obscure, *a.* 不分明な, あいまいな.

M The name of "lock-hospital" is ***etymologically*** *obscure*. ロックホスピタル(性病々院)という名の語原は不明である.

P causes *obscure* ***to*** us われわれに不明な諸原因.

obscure, *v.* 暗くする, 不分明にする.

P ends *obscured* ***by*** means 手段のためにくらまされた目的 ‖ His fame was *obscured* (=overshadowed) ***by*** that of his great father. 彼の名声は父の大きな名声の影に隠された.

obscurity, *n.* あいまい, 不明, もうろう; 微せん.

V ***endure*** the *obscurity* 名の知れないのを苦にしない. ¶to ***prevent*** *obscurity* 明確を欠くことのないように. ¶***produce*** *obscurity* あいまいとなる.

Q ***Considerable*** *obscurity* attaches to its origin. それの起源ははなはだあいまいである. ¶try to force him out of ***self-sought*** *obscurity* 自ら求めた微せんを脱却させようと努める. ¶The press has removed the vest of ***stately*** *obscurity* which used to conceal the personality of rulers from the eyes of subjects. かつては臣下の目から主権者の人格を隠したあのいかめしい覆面を新聞が取り除いてしまった.

P emerge ***from*** *obscurity* 微せんから身を起す. ¶die ***in*** *obscurity* 落ちぶれて死ぬ ‖ be shrouded (=involved) ***in*** *obscurity* あいまいの中に包まれている.【類】content to live ***in*** *obscurity*. ¶sink ***into*** *obscurity* 世に埋もれる ‖ retire ***into*** *obscurity* 隠退する, 片いなかに引込む. ¶throw light ***on*** *obscurities* 不明の点に光明を投げる.

obsequies, *n. pl.* 葬式, 葬儀.

Q the ***Imperial*** *obsequies* 御大葬.

obsequious, *a.* おもねる, へつらう, 追従する.

M The waiters were ***expectantly*** *obsequious*. 給仕人などはもらい物を目当にぺこぺこしていた.

P *obsequious* ***to*** one's superiors 上官にぺこぺこして.

observance, *n.* 遵守, 遵奉; 式礼.

V ***compel*** *observance* 遵守をしいる. ¶strictly ***enforce*** the *observance* of the neutrality laws 中立法の遵守を厳重に励行する.

Q Yesterday Empire Day was celebrated with ***becoming*** *observances* throughout the world-wide dominions of King George VI. 昨日のヴィクトリア女皇誕生記念日(五月二十四日)の式典はジョージ六世陛下のしろしめす満天下にりっぱにとり行われた. ¶a ***careful*** *observance* of the simplest laws of health 健康の最も簡単な法則の遵守. ¶a ***centennial*** *observance* 百年祭. ¶in ***due*** *observance* of the anniversary of the beginning of the great war 大戦開始の記念日に相当する儀式を行って. ¶the ***faithful*** *observance* of the doctor's directions 医師の指図を忠実に守ること. ¶a ***religious*** *observance* 宗教的儀礼. ¶the ***rigid*** *observance* of these principles これらの主義の厳守. ¶***social*** *observances* 社会の慣例. ¶days of ***special*** *observance* [交通デーなど]特別励行の日. ¶***superstitious*** *observances* 迷信的慣習.

Q² ***Army Day*** *observances* 陸軍記念日遵守事項.

P² in due *observance* ***of*** the customs of chivalry 武勇の慣習を遵守して ‖ the *observance* ***of*** the mandates 委任の実行.【類】the *observance* ***of*** the sabbath (安息日).

observant, *n.* [法などの]遵奉者.

P² *observants* ***of*** rules (laws, the Constitution) 規則(など)の遵奉者.

observant, *a.* 注意深い, 観察している, 守る, 遵守する.

M be ***keenly*** *observant* of nature 自然を鋭敏に観察している.

P a person who is *observant* ***in*** these matters これらの事柄に心を用いる人.

observation, *n.* 観察, 注視, 注目; 言説.

V ***avoid*** *observation*=skulk 人目を忍ぶ. ¶These questions, however, ***await*** more careful and extended *observation*. しかしこれらの問題はなお一段の慎重考慮を要する. ¶***carry out*** *observations* 観測をする. ¶***compel*** *observation* 注目を余儀なくさせる. ¶***devote*** much *observation* and study to the question その問題を専心観察研究する. ¶***elude*** *observation* 見られずに済む. ¶***escape*** his *observation* 彼に見られずに済む ‖ influences which ***escape*** ordinary *observation* ちょっと目につかない影響 ‖ it has not ***escaped*** the close and accurate *observation* of ... それは...の綿密正確な観測をまぬかれはしなかった. ¶***Have*** you any further *observations* to make on the subject? その問題についてなお御意見がおありですか. ‖ he ***has*** some pertinent *observations* to make on the subject of ... 彼は...の問題について二三の適切な意見を述べている. ¶***keep*** *observation* upon ... ...を注視している. ¶the *observation* was ***made*** by ... こうした観察を下した人は...であった ‖ As for ... I should like to ***make*** this *observation*. ...については私はこのことを述べたいと思う. ‖ he laughingly ***made*** *observations* that ... 彼は笑いながら...と言った ‖ ***make*** personal *observations* 親しく観察する. ¶I ***owe*** him some valuable *observations*. 彼が二三の貴重な注意を与えてくれた事に感謝している. ¶***record*** one's *observations* of the world as one has seen it 世事を観察した通りに記録する. ¶***require*** more or less careful *observation* 多少注意深い観察を必要とする. ¶***take*** ***observations*** at sea 海上で観測する.

V² unless my *observation* ***deceives*** me 僕の観察にして誤りがなければ. ¶as far as my limited *observations* ***go*** 私の管見からすると.

Q take ***accurate*** *observations* [天文学者など]正確な観測をする. ¶by ***actual*** *observation* 実地の観察によって.【類】speak from ***actual*** *observation*. ¶an ***ancient*** *observation* 昔から気付かれていたこと. ¶***astronomical*** *observation* 天文学的観測. ¶an ***astute*** *observation* うがった観察. ¶require ***careful*** *observation* 注意深い観察を要する.【類】the power making ***careful*** and ***exact*** *observations* and records. ¶It is a ***common*** *observation* of jailers that prisoners who are the worst out of jail are often the best behaved within. 世間では最もどう猛な囚人も刑務所内では模範囚となることは看守のよく経験する所である. ¶make *critical observations* 評言を述べる. ¶a tour of *economic (commercial) observation* 経済(商業)視察旅行. ¶founded on *exact observations* 正確な観察に基づいて. ¶an *exhaustive observation* 余す所ない観察. ¶make *first-hand observations* for oneself 自分で直接に視察する. ¶He made the *following observations*. 彼は次の所見を述べた. ¶a *foolish observation* ばからしい意見. ¶*general observations* 概説. ¶an *ill-timed observation* 時宜を得ない言説. ¶*keen observation* combined with brilliant speculation すぐれた思索に加うるに明敏な観察. 【類】a work displaying proof of profound knowledge and *keen observation*. ¶the *like observation* applies to ... 同様な実説が...にも当てはまる. ¶have a wide range of *marine observation* 海に関することを広く観察している. ¶be sent to a hospital for a *mental observation* 精神状態検査のため病院へやられる. ¶make a *meteorological observation* 気象を観測する. ¶*narrow* (=*close*) *observation* 精細な観察. ¶speak from *ocular observation* of ... ...の目撃談をやる. ¶his *patient* and *minute observation* 彼の忍耐強い詳細な観察. ¶an important work based upon *personal observations* 実地の観察に基づく重要な著作. 【類】The plant is known to me from *personal observation*. / check it up (対照する) by *personal observation*. ¶make some *pertinent observations* respecting ... ...に関して二三の適切な所見を述べる. ¶*piquant personal observations* きびきびした体験談. ¶a *pregnant observation* 含蓄の多い所説. ¶some *preliminary observations* ある予備的な説明. ¶the subject of the *present observation* この文(話)の主人公. ¶*quick observation* 敏しょうな観察. ¶*scientific* and *popular observations* 科学的ならびに通俗的観察. ¶a *shrewd observation* 鋭い観察. ¶a *similar observation* would apply to ... ...に対しても同様のことが言える. ¶His conclusion is the result of *steady observations* and thoughtful study. 彼の結論はたゆまざる観察と考え深い研究の結果である. ¶*stimulating observations* (人を)刺激する言説. ¶*sundry observations* 雑感. ¶*superficial observations* 皮相の観察. ¶It is a *true observation*. それは正しい見方である. 【類】The writings of De Sade are now regarded as a treasure house of *true observations* in the domain of sexual psychology (性の心理).

Q² *mass observation* 全体としての観察.

P *according to* my *observation* 私の観察によれば. ¶I cannot prove this *from* personal *observation*. 私は自分自身の観察ではこれを証明し得ない. 【類】I can attest it *from* personal *observation*. / They are known to me *from* personal *observation*. ¶he is correct *in* his *observation* that ... 彼が...と述べたのは正しい. ¶his power *of observation* 彼の観察力. ¶build a theory *on observations* 観測に基づいて理論を組立てる. ¶cases that have come (=fallen) *under* his *observation* 彼の目にとまった事例 ‖ keep a prisoner *under observation* 囚人を看視する ‖ the period *under observation* 観察期間.

P² his *observations on* Chinese life and character 中国人の生活と性格に関する彼の所見. 【類】*observations on* the habits of ants (bees).　「述べる.

observe, *v*. 観察する, 観測する; 遵守する, 遵奉する; 言う,

M *observe accurately* 正確に観測する. ¶*anxiously observe* the sky 心配そうに空をながめる. ¶*observe closely* よく観察する. ¶he *cogently observed* that ... 彼は力強く...と言った. ¶*conscientiously observe* the law 良心的に法律を遵奉する. ¶*observe half-jokingly* 半ば冗談に言う. ¶*keenly observe* するどく観察する. ¶*observe* the rules *meticulously* 小心翼々として法則を守る. ¶read extensively and *observe narrowly* 広く読み精密に観察する. ¶he *parenthetically observed* that ... 彼は付言的に...と述べた. ¶*observe sagely* 物知り顔に言う. ¶*sedulously observe* the utmost brevity 努めてできるだけ簡潔にする. ¶*ungallantly observe* that ... 女に対する同情なく...と言放つ. ¶as he *well observes* 彼がそうとうなずけるように言っている通り.

P It was *observed as* a general holiday by more of the citizens and many of the business houses of New York. その日はニューヨーク市民の多くの人々や商店が一般に休業した. ¶*observed from* this point of view その見地から観察すると. 【類】It will be *observed from* these figures that the bachelors in California outnumber the unmarried women by 30 per cent. ¶considerable variation and some contradiction may be *observed in* the writings of different authors in describing ... ...を説明している色々な作家の著述には随分相違や矛盾が見受けられる.

O He pretended not to *observe* it. 彼はそれを見て見ない振りをした. ¶I *observed* that he was very pale, and asked him what was the matter with him. 私は彼の顔色が大変悪いのを見てどうしたのかと尋ねた.　「ー.

observer, *n*. 観察者, 観測者; 遵奉者; [会議の]オブザーバ

V *lead* some *observers* to believe that ... 観察者たちに...と信じるようにさせる. ¶*strike* the *observer* 見る者の心を打つ.

Q an *accurate observer* 正確な観察者. ¶an *acute observer* and thinker 鋭敏な観察者にして思想家. ¶an *aloof observer* 局外の観察者. ¶an *astronomical observer* 天文観測者. ¶It would appear to the *casual observer* that ... 不用意な観察者には...と思われよう. ¶a *clear observer* 頭脳明せきな観察者. ¶a *close observer* of the customs and manners of the country その国の風俗習慣の綿密な観察者. ¶a *competent* and *careful observer* 有能にして注意深い観察者. ¶a *cool-headed observer* 冷静な頭の観察者. ¶a *diligent observer* 勤勉(熱心)な観察者. ¶a *dispassionate* (=*impartial or fair*) *observer* 公平無私な観察者. ¶*experienced observers* 経験のある観察者. ¶a *flippant observer* of men and manners 人と風俗の軽率な観察者. ¶an *intelligent observer* そう明な観察者. ¶a *keen observer* of human nature 人間性の鋭敏な観察者. ¶This was noted by many *medical observers*. これは多数医学者の観察に上った所である. ¶He served as *military observer* in the Russo-Japanese War. 彼は日露戦役の際の観戦武官であった. ¶a *neutral observer* 中正の観察者. ¶continue to have its fascination for the *philosophic observer* 哲学的な観察者にとって相変らず魅力を持っている. ¶a *political observer* 政治上の観察者. ¶a *sane* and *level-headed observer* 健全にして鋭敏な観察者. ¶the eye of a *scrutinizing observer* 精査する観察者の目. ¶a *shrewd observer* 活眼の観察者. ¶To a *skilled observer* it is often easily possible to detect it. 熟練な観察者であればそれを容易に発見できることが往々ある. ¶a *subtle observer* 細かい所に目が届く人. ¶a *superficial observer* 皮相的観察者. ¶*unprejudiced* (=*unbiased*) *observers* 偏見のない観察者.

Q² qualified *aviation observer* 飛行偵察の有資格者, 有資格の飛行評論家. ¶an *expert observer* 専門の観察者. ¶a *nonexpert observer* しろうとの観察者.

P *as* an outside *observer* I should say that ... 第三者の立場で私は...と言おう. ¶congress seats *for observers* 会議のオブザーバーの席. ¶attend the conference in the capacity *of observer* オブザーバーの資格でその会議に出席する.

P² recent *observers from* abroad tell us that ... 近ごろ外国を視察して帰った人々は...と言っている. ¶one of the greatest *observers of* modern life 現代生活の最もすぐれた観察者の一人. ¶an *observer with* an imagination 想像力のある観察者.

obsess, *v*. [魔物などが]取りつく.

P be *obsessed by* the idea that ... ...という観念にとりつかれる. ¶*obsessed with* the idea of approaching death and suicide 死が接近したとか自殺をしようなどという考えに取りつかれて.

obsession, *n*. 強迫観念, 魔の襲い.

Q a sense of mental liberation from an *overmastering obsession* おさえつけられるような強迫観念から解放された感じ. ¶an *unconquerable obsession* 征服し難い強迫観念.

P² An *obsession for* uniting is a fundamental characteristic of the human mind. 結合を欲する観念は常に人間に付きまとう根本的な特性である.

O Since 1916 the fear of gas had been an *obsession*. 千九百十六年(第一大戦)以来(そのときまで)毒ガスに対する恐怖が忘れられることができなかった.

obstacle, *n*. 障害(物), 妨害, 邪魔.

V We have found some way of *circumventing* the *obstacle* which we were unable to surmount. われわれは征服し得なかった障害をうまく切抜ける手段を見つけた. ¶*clear away* every *obstacle* which has beset ... ...を取巻くあらゆる障害物を除く. ¶*climb* the *obstacle* 障害物をよじ登る. ¶It *constitutes* an *obstacle*. それが一つの障害を成している. ¶*encounter* formidable *obstacles* 恐ろしい障害物に出会う. ¶*get obstacles* out of the way 邪魔物を取除

く. ¶He ***has*** still tremendous *obstacles* to encounter. 彼はまだ恐ろしい障害物に遭遇せねばならない. ¶Courage ***knows*** no *obstacle*. 勇気に障害なし. ¶***meet*** an *obstacle* to the achievement of a goal 目標遂行の妨害に出会う. ¶he is not likely to ***offer*** any *obstacles* against ... 彼は…に邪魔を入れそうもない. ¶***oppose*** an *obstacle* to ... …へ邪魔を入れる. ¶***overcome*** all *obstacles* あらゆる障害に打勝つ. ¶***place*** *obstacles* in the way of ... …の邪魔をする. ¶***prevent*** *obstacles* 邪魔を防ぐ. ¶He ***put*** every *obstacle* in my way. 彼は私にあらゆる障害を加えた. ¶***remove*** *obstacles* out of the way 通行の障害物を除く. 【類】the preservation of the friendship of a neighboring nation by ***removing*** the *obstacle* threatening to imperil it. ¶***surmount*** every *obstacle* あらゆる障害に打勝つ. ¶***sweep away*** *obstacles* 障害を一掃する. ¶***throw*** *obstacles* in the way of ... …に邪魔を入れる.

V^2 *obstacles* ***standing*** squarely in the way of ... …の真っ正面に立っている障害物.

Q International suspicion is the ***chief*** *obstacle* to world peace. 国際間のさい疑が世界平和の主な妨害となる. ¶overcome ***every*** *obstacle* すべての障害に打勝つ. ¶a ***fatal*** *obstacle* to ... …にとって致命的な障害. 【類】throw ***fatal*** *obstacles* in the path of the project. ¶***formidable*** *obstacles* 至難の障害物. ¶in spite of ***immense*** *obstacles* 絶大の障害にもかかわらず. ¶in spite of almost ***insurmountable*** *obstacles* ほとんど打勝ち難い障害にもかかわらず. ¶an ***insuperable*** (=***insurmountable***) *obstacle* to the success of the plan その計画の成功にとって打勝ち難い障害. ¶remove the ***outside*** *obstacles* to learning 学校施設の改善をする. ¶a ***serious*** *obstacle* to ... …にとって重大な障害. ¶have ***tremendous*** *obstacles* to encounter 絶大な妨害に対抗することになる. ¶an ***unexpected*** (=***unforeseen***) *obstacle* 予期しない障害.

P ***amid*** many *obstacles* 沢山の障害の中で.

P^2 an insuperable *obstacle* ***in*** the way of ... …の前途に横たわる打勝ち難い障害. ¶an *obstacle* ***to*** progress (achievement, success) 進歩(など)にとっての障害.

obstinacy, *n.* がん固, 強情, 執よう.

Q^2 with ***bulldog*** *obstinacy* ブルドックのようながん固さで.

obstinate, *a.* がん固な, 強情な, 片意地な.

P *obstinate* ***in*** one's conduct その行いにおいてがん固な.

O be as *obstinate* ***as*** a mule 牛のように強情である.

obstruct, *v.* 妨げる, 邪魔する, ふさぐ.

P The road is *obstructed* ***by*** a landslide. 道路は山くずれでふさがっている.

obstruction, *n.* 妨害, 阻止.

V ***cause*** *obstruction* to traffic 往来の妨害になる. ¶without ***meeting*** any *obstruction* 少しの障害もなく. ¶***offer*** little *obstruction* ほとんど妨害にならない. ¶***remove*** an *obstruction* 障害を除く.

P^2 the *obstruction* ***of*** world peace by prejudices 偏見による世界平和の阻害. ¶an *obstruction* ***to*** peace (progress) 平和(など)にとっての妨害.

obstructionism, *n.* [議事などの]妨害主義.

Q ***Russian*** *obstructionism* ロシアの議事進行妨害主義.

obstructive, *a.* 妨げになる, 妨害する.

P *obstructive* ***to*** one's design (progress) その計画(など)の妨げになる.

obtain, *v.* 得る, 手に入れる, 取る.

M can *obtain* it ***cheaper*** もっと安くこれを手に入れられる. ¶***fraudulently*** *obtained* orders 詐欺で取った注文. ¶it can be *obtained* ***free*** upon application at ... それは…に申込むと無料で得られる.

P he *obtained* it ***at*** the price of ... 彼は…の値段でそれを手に入れた. ¶*obtain* money (goods) ***by*** fraud (false pretenses) 詐欺(など)で金(など)を得る ‖ *obtain* renown ***by*** deeds of valor 勇敢な行為で名声を得る ‖ information *obtained* ***by*** inquiry 聞き込み. ¶It may be *obtained* ***for*** one dollar. それは一ドルで手に入れられる. ¶*obtain* ***from*** abroad 外国から手に入れる. ¶*obtain* a loan ***of*** a person 人から借金する. ¶It can be *obtained* ***of*** a seller ***at*** the following prices: それは次の値段で商売人から手に入れることができる. ¶may be *obtained* ***through*** ... or direct[ly] from ... …を通じてまたは…から直接に手に入れることができる. 【類】*obtain* knowledge ***through*** books / *obtain* one's position ***through*** the influence of ... ¶It can be *obtained* ***to*** order on short notice. それはちょっと前に注文すれば手に入る.

obtainable, *a.* 手に入れられる, 得られる.

M be ***easily*** *obtainable* for the sum それだけ出せば容易に手に入る.

P *obtainable* ***for*** 1/- each 単価一シリングで手に入れられる. ¶It is *obtainable* ***of*** (=***through***) Maruzen. それは丸善から取り寄せられる. ‖ *obtainable* ***of*** all dealers in high-class perfumes どの高級香料商からでも手に入れることができる.

obtrude, *v.* 出しゃばる.

M ***frequently*** *obtrude* oneself しばしば差出がましくする.

P *obtrude* oneself ***on*** the notice of others 他人の目につくように出しゃばる. 【類】*obtrude* (=intrude) ***on*** another's attention. ¶*obtrude* one's opinions ***upon*** others 自説を人に押しつける.

obtuse, *a.* 鈍い, のろい.

P We have been exceedingly *obtuse* ***in*** not discovering it long ago. われわれがずっと前にそれを見つけなかったのは全くうかつであった.

obverse, *n.* [貨幣などの]表面.

P ***on*** the *obverse* 表面に.

obvious, *a.* 明かな, 明白な, 知れ切った.

M ***grossly*** *obvious* 分かり切っている. ¶it is ***perfectly*** *obvious* that ... …ということは全く明かである. ¶***quite*** *obvious* 全く明白な. ¶The error is ***too*** *obvious* to require a particular refutation. その誤りは明らかであって特に反ばくする必要もない.

P but that this is the case is *obvious* ***from*** the fact that ... しかしこれがそうだということは…の事情によって明白である ‖ The meaning of these compounds is *obvious* ***from*** the component parts. これらの成語の意味はその構成素を見れば明白である. ¶*obvious* ***to*** everybody だれにも明白な. 【類】*obvious* even ***to*** the dullest mind / *obvious* ***to*** average intelligence (人並の知能のある者).

occasion, *n.* 時, 節, 場合, 機会; 必要.

V I cannot ***allow*** the *occasion* to pass without ... 私はこの機会に乗じて…しないわけにはいかない. ¶say things ***befitting*** the *occasion* その場合に適したことを言う. ¶***celebrate*** the *occasion* by having a dinner at a restaurant 料理店でごちそうを食べて当日を祝賀する. 【類】***celebrate*** the *occasion* with a dinner. / We ***celebrated*** the *occasion* for mere form's sake (ほんの形だけ). ¶***commemorate*** an *occasion* その日を記念する. ¶The band ***enlivened*** the *occasion* with cheerful music. 楽隊は快活な音楽を奏してその場に活気を添えた. ¶***find*** *occasion* to ... …する機会を見つける. ¶The language did not ***fit*** the *occasion*. 用語がその場に適当でなかった. ¶***forfeit*** the *occasion* 機会を失う. ¶***furnish*** a suitable *occasion* for ... …に対する適当な機会を与える. ¶***give*** him *occasion* to find fault with you 彼に君のあらを捜させるようなことをする ‖ ***give*** *occasion* to great anxiety 非常な心配を引起す ‖ Do not ***give*** *occasion* to scandalous tongues to speak of you. 口の悪い人からとやかく言われないようにせよ. ¶***have*** *occasion* to mention it そのことを述べる機会に出会う ‖ I've ***had*** frequent *occasion* to find fault with you of late. 私は近ごろ再々君に小言を言わざるを得なかった. ‖ ***have*** *occasion* to consult its pages それを調べて見る必要がある(参考書など). 【類】I never have ***had*** *occasion* to use it. / ***have*** no *occasion* for ... / persons who ***have*** *occasion* to speak in public / Whenever I ***have*** *occasion* to make a present, the opportunity is gone while I am thinking of what to give. / Most persons have probably ***had*** *occasion* to observe the susceptibility of dogs to music. / I have never ***had*** *occasion* to look into this treatise myself. / I may ***have*** *occasion* to say something about it. ¶***honor*** the *occasion* with his presence 彼が臨席して当日に光栄を添える. ¶***improve*** the *occasion* その機会を利用する. 【類】He ***improved*** the *occasion* to dwell on the evils of drinking. ¶The presentation of honors for the act of devotion was ***made*** the *occasion* for a public function. 献身的行為に対する表彰会が催された. ¶they ***marked*** the *occasion* of twenty-first birthday by ... 設立二十一年記念に…をやった ‖ the exercises ***marking*** the *occasion* 記念式. 【類】the *occasion* was ***marked*** by an entertainment given to ... ¶***observe*** the *occasion* 当日を祝う. ¶***offer*** a splendid *occasion* to ... …にすばらしい機会を与える. ¶***open out*** fresh *occasion* for ... …に対して新しい機会をつくる. ¶***orna-***

ment the *occasion* by one's presence その臨席によって当日に美観を添える. ¶***recall*** the *occasion* その折を思い出す. ¶***seize*** the *occasion* of his absence to ... 彼の不在に乗じて...する. ¶It ***suits*** the *occasion*. その場合にふさわしい. ¶***take*** the *occasion* to refer to ... その機会を利用して...に言及する ‖ in the progress of a speech in the debate of ..., he ***took*** *occasion* to dub him "..." ...の議論の最中に彼は機会をとらえて彼を「...」と呼んだ. 【類】***take*** *occasion* to remark that ... / ***take*** *occasion* to severely criticize.

V² should *occasion* ***arise*** 機会があったら. 【類】if *occasion* ***arises*** / as (=when) *occasion* ***arises*** / until some opportune *occasion* (好機会) ***arises***. ¶when *occasion* ***demands*** 必要とあれば. ¶as *occasion* ***occurs*** 折があったら. ¶whenever *occasion* ***offered*** 機会があるごとに. ¶whenever *occasion* ***requires*** 必要があるごとに.

Q on this ***annual*** *occasion* この毎年の祝典に. ¶on ***another*** *occasion* 別の機会に. ¶an ***auspicious*** *occasion* めでたい折. ¶on a ***certain*** *occasion* ある折に. ¶a ***festal*** *occasion* 祝祭日. 【類】on ***festal*** *occasions*. ¶on the ***festive*** *occasion* of ... ...の祭礼の際に. ¶a ***formal*** *occasion* 晴れの場所. ¶on ***countless*** *occasions* 幾度となく. ¶on the ***first*** *occasion* 折があり次第. ¶a ***formal*** *occasion* 改まった席. ¶I have had ***frequent*** *occasion* to ... 私は...する必要がたびたびあった. ¶a ***gala*** *occasion* お祭り日, お祭り騒ぎ. 【類】His visits were always ***gala*** *occasions*. ¶It will probably be a ***great*** *occasion*. その日は盛んなことでしょう. ¶on their ***happy domestic*** *occasion* [会・祭など]彼らの楽しい家庭の祝い日に. ¶a great ***historical*** *occasion* 歴史的に大切な日. ¶on ***joyful*** *occasions* 楽しい折に. ¶a ***joyous*** *occasion* 喜ばしい折. ¶on the ***last*** (***first***) *occasion* 最後(最初)の機会に. ¶he has had ***no*** *occasion* to ... 彼には...する機会がなかった. ¶on ***one*** *occasion* ある時. ¶on ***particular*** *occasions* 特別な折に. ¶on a ***previous*** (=former) *occasion* 前の折に. ¶on a ***public*** *occasion* ある公の席で. ¶on a ***rare*** *occasion* まれに. ¶The New Year is a ***secular*** rather than a ***religious*** *occasion*. 新年は宗教的というよりは俗事的な行事である. ¶on ***several*** *occasions* 数度に及んで. ¶on ***similar*** *occasions* 同様な場合に. ¶Sales are ***stuffy*** and ***restless*** *occasions*. 売立というものはせせっこましいごたごたしたものだ. ¶ceremonial dress for ***swell*** (=***splendid***) *occasions* 晴の折のための式服.

Q² on ***state*** *occasions* 公式の会で.

P The mind, deprived of the guidance of voluntary attention, drifts ***at*** the *occasion* of various external impressions without ever becoming fixed. 心は自発的な注意力の指導を欠くといつになっても安定せずに色々な外からの影響によって動くものだ. ‖ ***at*** the *occasion* of a visit from her mother 彼女の母親から訪問を受けた折に ‖ ***at*** all *occasions* あらゆる場合に. ¶***for*** the *occasion* その折のために ‖ He has sent us a message ***for*** this *occasion*. 彼はわれわれのこの会のために式辞を寄せられた. ¶***of*** all *occasions* 折もあろうに. ¶***on*** *occasion* 折にふれて. 【類】***on*** *occasions* of ceremony ‖ He officiated ***on*** the *occasion*. 彼はその時の司会を務めた. ‖ ***on*** the *occasion* of my visit to ... 私が...を訪問したとき. 【類】***on*** the *occasion* of his birthday ‖ a speech delivered by ... ***on*** the *occasion* of the thirteenth anniversary festival of ... / ***on*** many *occasions* / ***on*** *occasions* such as these / ***on*** *occasions* of ceremony / ***on*** the *occasion* when ... / ***on*** the *occasion* I am now speaking of ... ‖ All the greater Public Schools are not represented ***on*** these *occasions*. これらの日には大きな私立中学校が全部代表者を出している訳ではない. ‖ ***on*** all *occasions*, mournful and joyous 祝儀無祝儀すべての場合に. ¶rise ***to*** the *occasion* 機に応じて善処する ‖ equal ***to*** the *occasion* ことに当って動じない. ¶***upon*** *occasion* 時折 ‖ It is a threadbare device, but useful ***upon*** *occasion*. 平凡なもくろみだが時に役立つこともある.

P² an *occasion* ***for*** feasting and rejoicing きょう宴歓喜の時. 【類】an *occasion* ***for*** entertainment and general rejoicings / an *occasion* ***for*** anxiety. ¶The completion to a boy's sixteenth year was the *occasion* ***of*** a festival at Athens in ancient Greece. 古代ギリシアでは少年が満十六歳になるとアテネで祝祭が行われた.

occasion, *v.* 起さす, 引起す, 生じる.

P disaster *occasioned* (=caused) ***by*** an earthquake 地震によって生じた災害. ¶*occasion* anxiety ***to*** a person 人に心配をかける.

O *occasion* a riot (an accident) 暴動(など)を引起す.

Occident, *n.* 西洋.

P ***in*** the *Occident* 西洋では.

occupancy, *n.* 占有期間.

P ***during*** the *occupancy* of one's post 在職中.

occupant, *n.* 占有者; 居住者.

Q the ***former*** *occupants* of the house 前の居住者たち. ¶the ***present*** *occupant* of the throne, his Illustrious Majesty 今上陛下. ¶At present its ***sole*** *occupants* are rats. 今住んでるのはねずみばかりだ.

P² the *occupants* ***of*** an apartment house アパートの居住者たち.

occupation, *n.* (**1**) 職業, 仕事.

V ***change*** one's *occupation* その職業を変える. ¶One-half of the population ***finds*** its *occupation* in agriculture. その人口の半数は農業に従事している. ¶***follow*** the same *occupation* 同じ職業に従事する ‖ ***follow*** the *occupation* of their fathers 彼らの父の職業に従う. ¶He ***has*** no fixed *occupation*. 彼は定職を持たない. ¶*occupations* not yet ***invaded*** by women まだ女が侵入していない職業(男子専業). ¶***learn*** some *occupation* 何か職業を習う. ¶***lose*** their *occupation* 彼らの職を失う. ¶***take up*** an *occupation* 職につく.

Q an ***auxiliary*** *occupation* 副業. ¶a ***dangerous*** *occupation* 危険な職業. ¶people without ***definite*** *occupations* 定職のない人々. ¶There is no more ***delightful*** *occupation* than to train those who are anxious and eager to learn. 熱心に学ぼうとする人々を教える以上に楽しい職業はない. ¶It is characterized as a ***female*** *occupation*. それは特に女の職業となっている. ¶has no ***fixed*** *occupation* 定職がない. ¶a ***futile*** *occupation*=a useless task 無益の業. ¶a ***gainful*** *occupation* 営利的職業. ¶a ***healthful*** *occupation* 健康的な職業. ¶***healthy*** *occupations* 健康的な職業. ¶active employment in ***intellectual*** *occupations* 知的職業における活動. ¶Their ***leading*** *occupation* is agriculture. その主な職業は農業である. ¶***literary*** *occupation* 文筆に親しむこと. ¶The ***main*** *occupation* is sacrificed. 本職がお留守になる. ¶a ***manufacturing*** *occupation* 製造業. ¶a ***minor*** or ***irregular*** *occupation* 副業的または臨時の職業. ¶those who shall have no ***other*** *occupation* 専任者. ¶an ***outdoor*** (=***out-of-door***) *occupation* 戸外の職業. ¶his ***present*** *occupation* as a movie actor 映画俳優としての彼の現職. 【類】if his ***present*** *occupation* fizzles out somewhere along the line. ¶The ***principal*** *occupation* of the inhabitants is to feed peacefully on tourists. 住民の主な職業は観光客を相手に楽に暮して行くことである. ¶engage in ***productive*** *occupations* 生産的職業に従事する. ¶Reading is a ***profitable*** *occupation* for our moments of leisure. 読書は閑暇を使う有益な方法である. ¶He has no ***regular*** *occupation*. 彼には定職がない. ¶a ***sedentary*** *occupation* 座業. ¶carry on ***several*** *occupations* at a time [雑務など]あれもこれも同時にやる. ¶the ***sole*** *occupation* 唯一の職業. ¶a ***subsidiary*** *occupation* of farms 農家の副業. ¶follow ***such*** and ***such*** an *occupation* しかじかの職業に従事する. ¶I cannot imagine a more ***trivial*** *occupation*. こんなつまらないことは外に類がない. ¶an ***unhealthy*** *occupation* 健康によくない職業. ¶To undertake to reform them would be an ***unprofitable*** *occupation*. 彼らを改心させようと企てるのはむだなことであろう.

Q² Gardening is an ***all-year-round*** *occupation*. 園芸は年中無休の仕事である. ¶The sanitary inspector has vetoed fur-pulling—that is, pulling the fur off rabbit skins—as a ***home*** *occupation*. 衛生視察官は毛を抜くこと—うさぎの皮から毛を抜取ること—を内職として禁止した. ¶a ***side-line*** *occupation* 副業. ¶a ***spare time*** *occupation* 片手間の仕事(アルバイト). 【類】those to whom writing is a ***spare time*** *occupation*. ¶***street*** *occupations* 街路職業.

P He is a pedlar ***by*** *occupation*. 彼の商売は行商人です. ¶an American ***of*** no *occupation* 無職のアメリカ人. ¶serving the country ***through*** *occupation* 職域奉公. ¶men ***without*** *occupation* 無職の人々.

(**2**) 占領, 占有.

Q a ***continued*** *occupation* 引続いての占領. ¶These houses are completely furnished and ready for ***immediate*** *occupation*. これらの家は家具が全部ついていてすぐ住めるようになっている. ¶***military*** *occupation* 軍隊の占

領 ‖ the allied *military occupation* 連合軍占領.

Q² be under *enemy occupation* 敵の占領下にある. ¶the *U.S. occupation* of West Germany 西独の合衆国占領.

P In this house, *after* nineteen years' *occupation*, he drew his last breath. この家に十九年住んでから彼は最後の息を引取った. ¶a territory *in occupation* 占拠地域 ‖ the army is *in occupation* of ... 軍隊は…を占領している. ¶an army *of occupation* 占領軍. ¶a territory *under* hostile *occupation* 敵の占領地区.

P² the *occupation of* a city by the enemy 敵の都市占領.

occupationaire, *n.* 占領軍人.

Q² *Tokyo Occupationaires* 東京占領軍の人々.

P procured goods *for* the *occupationaires* 占領軍用調達物資.

occupier, *n.* 居住者.

P² the *occupiers of* a house 住宅の現住者.

occupy, *v.* 占領する; 従事させる.

M I am too *busily occupied* with some important business to go to the play. 私は肝要な用があるから芝居見物に行くどころじゃない. ¶he was *deeply occupied* in thinking of ... 彼は深く…のことを考え込んでいた ‖ he is *fully occupied* in ...ing 彼は…に没頭している ‖ The berth here is *fully occupied* at present. 船(寝床)は今満員です. ¶I am more *importantly occupied* otherwise. それどころじゃない. ¶Its inhabitants are *occupied mainly* with agriculture. その住民は主に農業に従事している. ¶While I was *so occupied*, half an hour had passed. そうこうするうちに三十分たってしまった. ¶be *solely* (=wholly) *occupied* with ... …で余念がない.

P a dwelling *occupied by* them 彼らの住んでいる家屋. ¶in territory *occupied by* troops 軍隊の占領地域内に. ¶*occupy* an important position *in* the Foreign Office 外務省の重要な地位にある ‖ *occupy* oneself *in* doing something 何かやっている. 【類】be *occupied in* carpentering (writing). ¶He was *occupied with* his work. 彼は仕事で忙がしかった. ‖ *occupy* oneself *with* a deep study of ... …を深く研究する. 【類】be *occupied with* literary work.

occur, *v.* 起る, 現われる; ふと心に浮ぶ.

M It shall not *occur again*. こんなことが二度と起らないようにします. ¶the disease *occurs endemically* in ... その病気は…に風土的に発生する. ¶This is the instance that *occurs first* to one's mind. これが第一に思い当る例である. ¶*frequently occur* ひん発する. ¶Such a thing *hardly occurs*. こんなことは滅多にない. ¶The French *u* does not *normally occur* in English. フランス語の u の音は英語では普通使わない. ¶this will *readily occur* in the mind of ... これは…には容易に思い出せることであろう. ¶cholera *occurs sporadically* in ... コレラが…にちらほらある.

P A leap-year *occurs at* every four years. うるう年は四年ごとにある. ¶It *occurs* more often *in* women than *in* men. それは男よりも女に余計起る. ¶it *occured to* me that ... …が胸に浮んだ ‖ It does not *occur to* me now. それを今私は思い出せない. ‖ losses or damages *occurring to* goods 品物の受ける損失または破損. 【類】it never *occurred to* my friend that ... / in those days it never *occurred to* anyone that ... / It *occurred to* my mind. / His name did not *occur to* my memory.

occurrence, *n.* 起ること, 発生事, 事件.

V I *had* a somewhat similar *occurrence*. 私にちょっとそれと同じようなことがあった. ¶*predict* the *occurrence* of an earthquake 地震の発生を予言する.

Q Flood is practically an *annual occurrence* in this district. この地方では洪水は全く年中行事みたいなものです. ¶a matter of *common occurrence* よくあること ‖ This is a *common occurrence*. これはよくあることです. ¶Accidents are of *constant occurrence*. 不時のできごとは絶えず起るものだ. ¶Conflicts were of *daily occurrence*. 衝突は毎日起った. ¶a *deplorable occurrence* 悲しべきできごと. ¶the date of its *earliest-known occurrence* in the New England records ニューイングランド記録に最も古くのった年代. ¶the *first known occurrence* in print of a word or phrase [印刷物に]語または句の始めて印刷になったと考えられている物. ¶It's a very *fortunate occurrence*. それはまことに結構なことです. ¶Snow is of *frequent occurrence*. 雪はしばしば降る. 【類】words of most *frequent occurrence*. ¶It is of *habitual occurrence* in daily life. それは日常生活によく起ることだ. ¶a not *infrequent occurrence* かなりひんぱんに起ること. ¶a thing (an experience) of *rare occurrence* まれにあること(など). ¶*recent occurrences* 近ごろのできごと. ¶It is no *uncommon occurrence*. それは珍らしいことじゃない. ¶an *unexpected occurrence* 思いがけないできごと. ¶those *unforeseen occurrences* which we call accidents われわれがちん事と呼ぶあの予知し難いできごと. ¶The Conference was a *unique* and *unprecedented occurrence*. その会議は比類のない未曽有のできごとであった. ¶They are now almost *weekly occurrences* in London. それは今日ロンドンでほとんど毎週のようにあることだ.

Q² It is an *everyday occurrence*. それは毎日のできごとだ. 【類】a matter of *everyday occurrence*.

P *on* the *occurrence* of a vacancy 空位が生じたときに.

ocean, *n.* 大洋, 大海.

V *clear* the *ocean* of pirates 大洋から海賊を一掃する. ¶*cross* the *ocean* in a boat 小舟に乗って大洋を渡る. ¶*dragnet* the *ocean* 大洋を掃海する. ¶One can't *lap up* the *ocean* with a shell. 貝がらで大海を呑み干すことができない. ¶*sail* the *ocean* 大洋を帆走する; 航海する. 【類】He ventured to *sail* over the Atlantic *ocean* to Europe in a 20-feet canoe-like boat. ¶It is like the old woman's broom with which she would *sweep back* the *ocean*. それは老婆がほうきで大海を払いのけようとするようなむだなことだ.

Q a *billowy ocean* 波立つ大海. ¶the *boundless ocean* はてしない大洋. ¶a *deep ocean* 深い大洋. ¶They are as drops of water in a *mighty ocean*. それはそう海の一粟のようなものだ. ¶the chief Russian naval station on the *Pacific ocean* 太平洋上主なロシア海軍鎮守府 ‖ the north[-ern] (south[ern]) *Pacific Ocean* 北(南)太平洋. ¶an *unbounded ocean* 無限の大洋. ¶sail in a *vast ocean* 広大な大洋を航海する.

P He has made several trips *across* the Pacific [*Ocean*]. 彼は太平洋を五六度渡った. ‖ his country *across* the *ocean* 大洋の彼方にある彼の国. ¶countless islands *in* the Pacific *ocean* 太平洋にある無数の島々. ¶descend to the floor (=bed) *of* the *ocean* 大洋の底に下る(海底のもくずとなる). ¶an island *on* the *Pacific* 太平洋上の島. 【類】the largest and fastest vessels *on* the Pacific *Ocean* / The bay of San Francisco is probably the most magnificent harbor *on* the Pacific [*Ocean*]. / What is the influence of the moon *on* the *ocean?* ¶by means of wires laid *under* the *ocean*=by cable 海底電信で.

P² an *ocean of* time (money) ありあまるほどの時(金). 【類】*oceans of* difficulties (doubts, worries, etc.).

ocean liner, 大洋定期船.

O a *three-decker ocean liner* 三層甲板の大洋航路船.

o'clock, *n.* …時.

Q *eight-fifteen* (8:15) [*o'clock*] 八時十五分.

P He arrived *after* seven *o'clock*. 彼は七時過ぎに着いた. ¶sharp *at* two *o'clock* 正二時に ‖ *at* ten *o'clock* at night 夜の十時に. ¶His train is due *by* five *o'clock*. 彼の乗っている汽車は五時までに到着のはず. 【類】I will be back *by* nine *o'clock*.

octave, *n.* 〖音楽〗オクターブ.

V a tone (note) that *sounds* half an *octave higher* 半オクターブ高く響く音調.

octavo, *n.* 八つ折り.

P books printed *in octavo* 八つ折判で印刷した本.

odd, *a.* 端(は)の, 半端の.

O He has been wearing a moustache fifteen years *odd*. 彼は十五年余ひげを生やしている. 【類】It cost me 10 pounds *odd*. ¶forty-*odd* corporations 四十いくつかの会社. 【類】the 140-*odd* prisons of the Empire / twenty-*odd* years ago / twenty-*odd* volumes / her fifty *odd* years of literary labor.

oddity, *n.* 奇異, 奇怪.

P struck *by* the *oddity* of ... …の奇異に驚いて.

P² smile at some *oddity of* dress 服装が少し風変りなのを笑う ‖ *oddities of* spelling 変ったつづり.

oddly, *ad.* 妙に, 変に.

M *oddly enough* 変なことだが.

odds, *n.* [単・複同型] 不同; 不和; 勝目, 勝.

V He *gave* the *odds* of 10 to 1 against "Three Stars." 彼は Three Stars (馬の名)に対して一対十の割合でかけた. ¶*have* the *odds* against one 一人に対して大勢いる ‖ It *has* all the *odds* in its favor. それの方に勝目がある. ¶**lay** (=**give**) the *odds* 相手に有利な条件でかけを申込む(碁で何目置かせる, など).

Q against **hopeless** *odds* 勝つ見込のない大敵に対して. ¶fight against **terrible** (fearful) *odds* 恐ろしい大勢を向うに回して戦う.

P The attack on ... was made **against** enormous *odds*. ...の攻撃は恐ろしい大敵に向って加えられた. ¶he has been **at** *odds* with ... 彼は...と不和であった. ¶She is now **at** *odds* with fate. 彼女は今運命と戦っている. ‖ they are **at** *odds* in regard to ... 彼らは...に関して互に反目している. 【類】Opinions are **at** *odds* over ... ¶the finest and **by** all *odds* the most fascinating contemporary volume on education 教育に関する現代の著書中最もすぐれてずぬけて魅力のある本. 【類】The human machine is **by** long *odds* the most perfect mechanism that has ever happened on the earth. / Child-welfare, both pre- and post-natal, is **by** all *odds* the most hopeful direction of public-health activities. ¶read **in** *odds* and ends of time 零細な時間に読書する.

O the *odds* (=chances) are ... 大てい...という結果になるだろう. 【類】The *odds* are against us.

ode, *n.* 叙情詩, 短歌.

V **compose** an *ode* 叙情詩を作る.

P² an *ode* **to** a nightingale ナイチンゲールに寄せる小詩.

odious, *a.* いやな.

P *odious* **to** a person 人にとっていやな.

odium, *n.* 憎しみ, 憎悪, いみきらうこと.

V **incur** *odium* 憎悪を招く.

odo[u]r, *n.* 香, におい.

V As he talked, a gentle breeze blew from the harbor. It **bore** the *odor* of fish. 彼が話していたとき港から微風がそよ吹いてきた. それは魚のにおいを帯びていた. ¶He **carries** the *odor* of sanctity about him. 彼はどこからとなく聖徒らしい所がある. ¶instantly **destroy** foul *odors* すぐにいやな臭気を消す. ¶**diffuse** a sweet *odor* 芳香を発散する. ¶**emit** (=give out) an *odor* 香を放つ. ¶**exhale** an offensive *odor* いやな臭気を発散する. ¶**exude** a characteristic *odor* 特徴のあるにおいを出す. ¶**give off** (=**out**) no *odor* 少しもにおいがない. 【類】**give** (=**send**) **out** a bad *odor*. ¶All perspiration **has** an unpleasant *odor*. 汗はすべて不愉快なにおいがする. ‖ It **has** an *odor* of trickery. それは臭い. ¶**impart** a pleasant *odor* to clothes 衣類に気持のよいにおいが付く. ¶**inhale** the savory *odors* of the cooked meat 料理した肉のよいにおいをかぐ. ¶**leave** no unpleasant *odor* いやなにおいを残さない. ¶**smell** the *odor* of putrefaction 腐敗したにおいをかぐ.

V² *odor* **emanates** from ... ...からにおいがでる. ¶The *odor* **stifles** me. その臭気は息がつまる.

Q an **axillary** *odor* わきが. ¶a nauseating **bad** *odor* 胸の悪くなる悪臭 ‖ He is in **bad** *odor* with the authorities. 彼は当局に評判が悪い. ¶The smelt has a **cucumber-like** *odor*. うぐい(魚)はきゅうりのようなにおいがある. ¶**delicious** *odor* うまいにおい. ¶the **dim** *odor* of lavender ラヴェンダーのかすかな香. ¶It has an **evil** *odor*. それは悪臭がある. ¶the **excretal** *odor* ふんのにおい. ¶**fetid** *odor* むれくさいにおい. ¶The air is impregnated with **filthy** *odors*. あたりは悪臭がただよっている. ¶It has a **fine** *odor*. それはよい香がする. ¶**foul** *odor* 悪臭. ¶**fragrant** *odor* 芳香. ¶**indelicate** (**dainty**) **personal** *odor* いやな(気持のよい)体臭. ¶**irritant** *odor* 刺激性のにおい. ¶a **musky** *odor* じゃこうの香. ¶a **noisome** *odor* 有毒なにおい. ¶**offensive** *odor* いやなにおい. ¶**pleasant** (**unpleasant**) *odor* 気もちのよい(不快な)におい. ¶a room filled with **pleasing** (=**delicious**) *odors* 芳香に満ちた室. ¶**pungent** *odor* 刺激性のにおい. ¶**repulsive** *odor* いやなにおい. ¶the **resinous** *odor* of trees 樹脂のような樹木のにおい. ¶a **savory** *odor* 芳香. ¶**sharp** *odor* of medicine 薬のつんとするにおい. ¶**sickening** *odor* 胸が悪くなるようなにおい. ¶cosmetic in **six** *odors* 六種の香のコスメチック(化粧料). ¶a **stuffy, unpleasant, animal** *odor* むっとするいやな動物性のにおい. ¶notice a **subtle** *odor* of perfume 香料の微妙なにおいに気付く. ¶What a **sweet** *odor!* あぁいいにおいだ. ¶the **true** *odors* of fresh flowers 新鮮な花の本当のにおい. ¶emit **unbearable** *odor* たえ難い悪臭を発散する.

Q² **body** *odor* 体臭 (B.O. と略すことがある). ¶**bouquet** *odors* 花束のにおい. ¶the **onion** *odor* ねぎのにおい. ¶**perfume** *odor* 香水の香. ¶**telltale** *odor* 移り香.

P die **in** the *odor* of sanctity 聖者高徳の名声高くして死ぬ. ¶He is in bad (good) *odor* **with** a person (party). 彼は人(党派)に受けが悪い(善い). ¶The word has an *odor* **of** antiquity about it. その語には古風なにおいがある.

odorous, *a.* 臭気のある.

P breath *odorous* **with** alcoholic fumes ぷんぷん酒くさい「息.

off, *ad.* あちらに, 向うへ, 離れて.

M be **badly** (=**poorly**) *off* まずく行く, 暮しがよくない. ¶be **better** (**worse**) *off* [前より]暮し向がよい(悪い). ¶be **comfortably** *off* 安楽に暮している. ¶His house is **far** *off*. 彼の家は遠く離れている. ¶It is a **long way** *off*. それは遠く離れている. ¶be **well** *off* 暮し向きがよい.

P He is to be *off* **by** the train. 彼はその汽車で立つはずだ. ¶My hat is *off* **to** him. 私は彼に敬意を表する(彼には頭が下がる). 【類】Where are you *off* **to**? / I'll be *off* **to** the Fort tomorrow morning. ¶Be *off* **with** you! 去れ! ‖ *Off* **with** your hats! 帽子を取れ.

O visit there *off* and on 折々そこを訪問する.

offal, *n.* くず肉.

Q² **fish** *offal* 魚のくず.

offence, *n.* =offense.

offend, *v.* 怒らす, 立腹させる; 罪を犯す.

M The sense of hearing is more **easily** *offended* than the sense of color. 不調和に対して聴感は色感より一層敏感である. ¶**mortally** *offended* 大いに立腹して. ¶so as to *offend* **none** 当りさわりなく. ¶*offend* **unintentionally** 思わず気にさわる. ¶*offend* **unwillingly** 心ならず気にさわる.

P *offend* **against** decency or morality 礼儀道徳を犯す ‖ *offend* **against** grammar, syntax and everything else appertaining to the writing of correct English 文法・措辞その他正しい英語を書くことに関する一切の規則を破る. 【類】*offend* **against** custom (law, rule, act, grammatical usage, refinement or good taste) / *offend* **against** good taste ‖ *offend* **against** "the sense of shame" (恥知らずなこと). ¶He was *offended* **at** my joke. 彼は私の冗談で気を悪くした. 【類】He is *offended* **at** my long silence. / Why are you *offended* **at** me? / I felt almost *offended* **at** his remarks. ¶*offended* **by** his blunt speech 彼のぶしつけな言葉に立腹して. ¶*offended* **over** a matter あることで気を損じて. ¶He is *offended* **with** me. 彼は私を悪く思っている.

offender, *n.* 犯罪者, 罪人, 違犯者.

V **bring** the *offender* to justice 犯罪者を法廷につき出す ‖ **bring** an *offender* before the court [告訴して]違反者を法廷に立たせる. ¶**try** an *offender* 犯人を審理する.

Q **chronic** *offenders* 常習犯. ¶**first** *offenders* 初犯者. ¶a **flagrant** *offender* 重犯人. ¶a **habitual** *offender* 常習犯. ¶**hardened** *offenders* 常習犯. ¶an **inveterate** *offender* したたかもの前科者. ¶a **juvenile** *offender* 非行少年. ¶**occasional** *offenders* 偶発性犯罪者. ¶the **principal** *offender* 正犯. ¶a highly **probable** *offender* 有力な容疑者. ¶a **professional** *offender* 専業的犯罪者. ¶a **sexual** *offender* 性犯罪者.

Q² a **child** (=juvenile) *offender* 非行少年. ¶the **subject** *offender* 本犯. ¶a **thought** *offender* 思想犯. ¶a **traffic** *offender* 交通違反者.

P² an *offender* **against** the state 国事犯人. 【類】an *offender* **against** the law of the country ‖ an *offender* **against** the scientific doctrines of heredity 科学的遺伝説の攻撃者.

offense, 《英》**offence,** *n.* 罪, 罪科, 犯罪; 立腹, 不興.

V **cause** *offense* to ... ...の反感をよぶ ‖ **commit** the *offense* in relation to ... ...に関し違反行為をする ‖ **commit** an *offense* against public decency 風俗を壊乱するようなことをする ‖ an *offense* **committed** against the state 国事犯 ‖ **commit** *offenses* under § ... and § ... of the Criminal Code 刑法第...条及...条の罪を犯す. ¶**condone** an *offense* 罪を許す. ¶It **constitutes** a punishable *offense*. それは罰せられる罪になる. ‖ facts **constituting** an *offense* 罪となるべき事実. ¶**expiate** an *offense* 罪をつぐなう. ¶No *offense* was **designed**. 悪気はなかった. ¶**forgive** an *offense* 罪を許す. ¶**give** *offense* 気を悪くする ‖ It will **give** *offense* to no one. そうすると当りさわりがない. 【類】decline so as not to **give** *offense*. 【類】he **gave** great *offense* by declaring his disbelief in ... / **give** *offense* to the will of God. ¶**heighten** the *offense* その罪を大きくする. ¶**overlook** one's *of-*

ense その罪を見のがす. ¶***repeat*** an *offense* 罪を重ねる. ¶I hope he will not ***take offense*** if I ask it back. それを返してくれと言っても彼は怒らないだろう. ‖ be quick to ***take offense*** じきにむかっぱらを立てる. 【類】***take offense*** at one's speech / I hope you will not ***take*** any *offense* at my words. / He will ***take offense*** at the refusal, however delicately expressed. ¶***Whitewash*** no *offenses*. 罪をごまかしてはいけない.

Q Farrar states that in Holland it was once a ***capital offense*** to kill a stork. オランダでは昔こうの鳥を殺すと死刑であったとファーラーが言っている. ¶***concurrent*** *offense* 併合罪. ¶commit no ***criminal*** *offense* 犯行をしない. ¶***first*** *offenses* 初犯. ¶a ***flagrant*** *offense* 凶悪犯. ¶very ***grave*** *offenses* 非常に重い罪. ¶***heinous*** *offenses* against ... ...に対する極悪の罪. ¶***indictable*** *offenses* 告発しうべき罪科. ¶***lesser*** *offense* 軽犯罪. ¶give ***little*** *offense* to the ear 余り耳ざわりにならない. ¶***minor*** *offenses* 軽犯罪. 【類】Drunkenness, begging, assault, and larceny are ***minor*** *offenses* against the law. ¶a ***moral*** *offense* 性犯. ¶Such a conduct will give very ***natural*** *offense*. こんなことをしては(先方が)怒るのは当然なことだ. ¶a ***penal*** *offense* 刑法上の罪. ¶a ***petty*** *offense* 軽犯罪. ¶a ***punishable*** *offense* 罰すべき罪. ¶in the case of a ***repeated*** *offense* 重犯の場合は. ¶The police warned that his license would be taken away for a ***second*** *offense*. 警察では再犯になると鑑札を取上げると警告した. ¶commit a ***serious*** *offense* against elegance 優雅をはなはだしく損じる. ¶a ***weighty*** *offense* 重い罪.

Q^2 a ***rape*** *offense* 強かん罪. ¶a ***State*** *offense* 《米》州の罪科(各州の法律が異なる).

P He was brought to court ***for*** a trivial *offense*. 彼はちょっとした罪で法廷に引出された. ¶One cannot hear such a remark ***without*** *offense*. こんなことを言わはれたんでは平気では聞いていられない.

P^2 an *offense* ***against*** their laws その国の法律にそむく罪 ‖ *offense* ***against*** morality (=public decency) 風俗壊乱 ‖ an *offense* ***against*** good manners 不作法 ‖ *offenses* ***against*** discipline 規律違反. 【類】an *offense* ***against*** law / *offense* ***against*** good taste / it is an *offense* ***against*** the rules of ... ‖ *offense* ***against*** person (property) 人身(財産)に対する犯罪. ¶an *offense* ***to*** the eye 目ざわり. ¶He was indicted for an *offense* ***under*** the Bankruptcy Act. 彼は破産法の罪で起訴された.

offensive, *n.* 攻勢.

V ***assume*** (=***take***) the *offensive* against assailants 襲撃隊に対して攻勢に出る.

Q a ***concerted*** *offensive* 歩調をそろえた攻勢.

Q^2 ***labor*** *offensive* 労働攻勢. ¶a new ***mass*** *offensive* 新大衆攻勢. ¶assume a "***peace*** *offensive*" いわゆる平和攻勢をとる. 【類】the so-called ***Communist peace*** *offensive*. ¶a ***propaganda*** *offensive* against ... ...に反対の宣伝攻勢. 【類】an intensified ***propaganda*** *offensive*. ¶a ***trade*** *offensive* 貿易攻勢.

P Troops are ***on*** the *offensive*. 兵は攻勢に出ている. ¶an *offensive* ***against*** the enemy (rival) 敵(など)に対する攻勢的行動.

offensive, *a.* 攻撃的な; しゃくにさわる, 気にさわる.

M a sight ***too*** *offensive* ***to*** look at 目に余る光景.

P *offensive* ***to*** our sense of propriety われわれの礼儀的観念を傷つけるような. 【類】*offensive* ***to*** European sense / writings, pictures, and other objects *offensive* ***to*** public morals / be *offensive* ***to*** good taste or religious feelings / be *offensive* ***to*** morality ‖ words *offensive* ***to*** the ear=offensive words 耳ざわりな言葉 ‖ *offensive* ***to*** a person 人の気にさわる.

offer, *n.* 申入れ, 申出, 提供; 付値.

V Do not ***accept*** the *offer* until you hear further from me. 追って私がさたをするまではその申出に応じてはいけない. 【類】***accept*** (=***comply with*** *or* ***agree to***) an *offer* / We ***accept*** the *offer* subject to the following alterations. / gratefully ***accept*** the *offer* of ... / The *offer* was thankfully ***accepted***. ¶***cancel*** an *offer* made 申込を取消す. ¶***decline*** an *offer* 申出を断る. ¶***esteem*** an *offer* 提供をありがたく思う. ¶We ***have*** other *offers* in hand. 他からも申込があります. ¶*Offers* ***invited***. 希望者は買値を通知せられたし[広告]. ¶***make*** a special *offer* at greatly reduced prices 大割引で特別提供をやる. ¶***obtain*** (=get) an *offer* 申込を受ける. ¶***provoke*** an *offer* 提供する気にさせる. ¶***receive*** an *offer* of marriage from ... ...から結婚の申込を受ける. ¶He ***refused*** my *offer*. 彼は私の申出を拒んだ. ‖ She has ***refused*** several *offers* of marriage. 彼女は数度の縁談を断った. ¶***reject*** an *offer* 申込を拒絶する. ¶*offers* are ***requested*** for the purpose of ... ...のための提供が求められている. ¶***slight*** one's *offer* その申出を軽視する. ¶The *offer* was ***snapped up***. その申出にわれ勝ちに応じた. ¶***take back*** one's *offer* その申出を引込める. ¶Your quotation does not ***tempt*** a counter *offer*. お申越の価格では折返し当方からの申込指値は致し兼ねます. ¶An *offer* ***wanted***. [売物など]希望者はお申出下さい. ¶***withdraw*** the *offer* その申込を取消す.

V^2 an *offer* ***came*** from ... to ... ...しようという申込が...から来た.

Q a very ***advantageous*** *offer* はなはだ有利な提供. ¶***alarming*** *offers* びっくりするような申込. ¶***conditional*** *offers* 条件付の申出. ¶make a ***definitive*** *offer* 確実な申込をする. ¶We have no wish to sell, but if you make a ***fair*** *offer* it shall have attention. 当方では売る考えはないが正当な買値をつけてくれるなら考えて見ます. ¶receive a ***firm*** *offer* 確定した申込を受ける ‖ with a ***firm*** *offer* I can fix 確実な申込があれば取きめができます. ¶an ***introductive*** *offer* 始めての申込(結果がよければ引続き取引する). ¶a ***liberal*** *offer* 寛大な申出. ¶cannot make a ***lower*** *offer* than ... ...よりも低い値段の提供はできません. ¶have ***numerous*** *offers* 沢山の申込がある. ¶a ***prepublication*** *offer* 予約募集. ¶make a ***reasonable*** *offer* 相応の値をつける. ¶cannot obtain a ***suitable*** *offer* 適当の申込が得られない. ¶He has declined to sell it, although ***tempting*** *offers* have been made. 随分よい買値が出たけれども彼はそれを売ることを断った.

Q^2 a ***bargain*** *offer* 安売の提供. ¶try a ***counter*** *offer* [先方の申込に対し当方の考え通り] 折返し申込をして見る. 【類】submit a ***counter*** *offer* ‖ It is useless making a ***counter*** *offer*; our ideas are widely different. 折返しのお申込は無用です, 思惑に大分開きがありますから. ¶special ***introduction*** *offer* on ... ...の特価販売. ¶a free ten-day ***trial*** *offer* 十日間無料試用申込.

P He jumped (=snapped) ***at*** my *offer*. 彼は喜んで私の申出に応じた. ¶entice them away ***by*** the *offer* of higher salaries さらに高給の提供で彼らをつり出す. ¶There is only inferior quality ***on*** *offer*. 売物に出ているのは劣等品だけだ. ¶be ***under*** *offer* with option of refusal until ... ...まで拒絶する権利のある申込を受けている.

P^2 an *offer* ***of*** purchase 買入の申出.

offer, *v.* ささげる, 持出す, 提供する; 申込む.

M *offer* a gift ***back*** 出した進物を引込める. ¶***gratuitously*** *offer* to the travelling public 一般旅行者に無料で提供する. ¶he has very ***kindly*** *offered* to ... 彼ははなはだ親切にも...しようと申出た. 【類】Thank you for the suggestions you ***kindly*** *offered* us. ¶be ***specially*** *offered* at ¥... 特に...円で提供されている.

M^2 *offer* ***up*** one's prayer to ... ...に祈とうをささげる ‖ *offer* ***up*** a sacrifice いけにえを神に供える. 【類】*offer* [***up***] prayers for the repose of his soul (めい福を祈る).

P *offer* ... ***as*** first prize 一等賞として...を提供する ‖ he *offered* ***as*** an apology that ... 彼は言訳に...と言った ‖ *offer* oneself ***as*** a candidate for ... ...の候補者として打って出る. ¶*offer* goods ***at*** low prices 品物を廉価で提供する ‖ The book was *offered* ***at*** an American book sale. この本はアメリカの書籍売立てに出された. ‖ *offer* (=make an essay or attempt) ***at*** an undertaking ある事業をやってみる. ¶*offer* a prayer ***before*** the deity 神の前に祈とうをささげる. ¶*offer* goods ***for*** sale 品物を売りに出す. 【類】They are *offered* ***for*** sale at $15.00 each. / It is *offered* ***for*** 5s. (五シリング) ‖ *offer* oneself ***for*** a position (=place) ある職務を買って出る, 自薦する. ¶*offer* ***in*** sacrifice いけにえに供える ¶*offer* one's life ***on*** the altar of the country 国家のためにその生命をささげる. ¶*offer* ***to*** a lady ある婦人に縁談を申込む ‖ the cheapest complete Tennyson that has ever been *offered* ***to*** the public 今までに売出されたテニソン全集のうち一番廉価なもの ‖ increase the economic rewards *offered* ***to*** teachers 教師の俸給を増加する ‖ Should emergency arise, *offer* yourselves ***to*** the State. 一たん緩急あらば義勇公に奉ずべし.

offering, *n.* 奉納, 奉納物, 供物.

V ***deposit*** their votive *offerings* 彼らの奉納物を供える. ¶***leave*** votive *offerings* at a temple 堂に奉納物をおいて行く. ¶***make*** *offerings* to the departed spirit 故人の霊に供物をする. 【類】 *offerings* ***made*** to the Goddess. ¶***present*** some little *offering* to the spirit of a shrine 神社にささやかな供物をする.

Q the ***academic*** *offerings* of the university その大学の教科. ¶a ***burnt*** *offering* 燃やす供物. ¶a ***devotional*** *offering* 神仏への供物. ¶It is a very ***feeble*** *offering* compared to the gratitude I feel, but at least is a wee bit more tangible than just saying thanks. それは私の感じている謝恩の念に比べれば取るに足らない進物ではありますが少くともただ感謝を口で述べるよりとにかくちっとはましです. ¶***floral*** *offerings* 花の供物. 【類】 be presented with a ***floral*** *offering*. ¶It is supported by ***freewill*** *offerings*. それは随意の寄進で維持されている. ¶a morsel of food offered as a ***pious*** *offering* to an ancestral ghost 祖先のみたまにうやうやしく供えた一口の食物. 【類】 a ***pious*** *offering* to avert an evil (厄除けのため). ¶a new ***theatrical*** *offering* 新しい劇の出しもの. ¶through that ***vicarious*** *offering* その身代りの犠牲を通して. ¶a ***votive*** *offering* in thanksgiving for … …の願がかなったお礼の奉納.

Q² ***amusement*** *offerings* 娯楽の出しもの. ¶***curriculum*** *offerings* 学科課程. ¶***drink*** *offerings* 提供しうる飲物類. ¶a ***freewill*** *offering* 自由意思の提供. ¶***general market*** *offerings* 一般に市販している品. ¶***real estate*** *offerings* 土地家屋の売物.

P² a thanksgiving *offering* ***for*** safe childbirth 安産に対する感謝の供物. ¶an *offering* ***of*** flowers to the spirit 霊前への花の供物. ¶*offerings* ***to*** God (an image) 神(など)への供物.

offertory, *n.* 献金.

P² money given as an *offertory* ***to*** a temple 寺院への奉納金.

office, *n.* (**1**) 職務; *pl.* 世話, あっ旋.

V ***abdicate*** *office* 辞職する. ¶***accept*** *office* 就職を受諾する. ¶***administer*** one's *office* 職務をとる. ¶The Tokugawa family ***assumed*** *office* in 1603. 徳川家は一六〇三年に将軍職についた. ‖ ***assume*** an *office* 就任する ‖ I am not going to ***assume*** the *office* of critics in good usage. 私は文章の批評家をもって任じている訳ではない. ¶***decline*** an *office* offered on account of one's feeble health 不健康を理由として申出られた職を断る. ¶He ***desired*** my friend's good *offices* to introduce him to me. 彼は自分を私に紹介してくれるように私の友人にあっ旋を頼んだ. ¶***discharge*** an *office* 役目を果す. ¶***do*** all the kind *offices* in one's power できるだけの尽力をする. 【類】 He ***did*** me many good *offices*. ¶Japan ***exercised*** her good *offices* with … in behalf of … 日本は…のために…に対してあっ旋の労をとった. ¶he has ***filled*** the *office* of Lord Mayor since … 彼は…以来(ロンドン)市長の職にあった ‖ He ***filled*** several *offices* under Sir Robert Walpole. 彼はロバート・ウォルポール卿の下に色々の職についた. ¶***get*** some *office* in Tokyo 東京で何かの役につく. ¶***hold*** an *office* ある役を持つ ‖ ***hold*** two *offices* 二役勤める. 【類】 In France the President ***holds*** *office* for seven years. ‖ while ***holding*** the *office* of … …に在職中. 【類】 ***hold*** *office* for life (five years) / The qualities he has revealed have established his position as one of the greatest British Prime Ministers who have ever ***held*** *office*. / They shall ***hold*** *office* until the next regular election. / He ***held*** *office* under the Government (官吏). / He ***held*** the *office* of Silliman Lecturer in 1907. / He ***held*** the *office* from 1896 to 1903. / He ***held*** that *office* five times. ¶***keep*** *office* 在職する. ¶***lay down*** one's *office* with one's life 職に殉じる. ¶***leave*** (=resign) *office* 辞任する. ¶***misuse*** public *office* 公職を乱用する. ¶***perform*** the *office* of … …の任を果す ‖ ***perform*** menial *offices* 従僕の役をする. ¶***receive*** an *office* 役につく. ¶***reciprocate*** friendly *offices* 厚情にむくいる. ¶***resign*** an *office* 辞職する. 【類】 Feeling himself overtaken by age, he ***resigned*** his *office*. / he ***resigned*** his *office* as Chairman of … / I am commanded by His Majesty to say that it is with regret to learn that you feel you must ***resign*** the *office* of president of the Royal Geographical Society. ¶***retain*** the *office* of Chief Secretary 書記官長の職に留まる. ¶***seek*** public *office* 公職を求める. ¶He ***served*** the *office* of sheriff in 1905-6. 彼は一九〇五年から六年にかけて郡長の職を奉じた. ¶***solicit*** their good *offices* on his behalf 彼の引立をその人たちに懇請する. ¶***take*** *office* 就任する ‖ The elected Governor died before ***taking*** *office*. 当選した知事は就任しないうちに死んだ. 【類】 ***take*** *office* in the Cabinet. ¶***throw up*** one's *office* 職をなげうつ. ¶***use*** its good *offices* to see that … …するようにあっ旋する. ¶in succession to …, who will ***vacate*** *office* in the autumn この秋に退職する…の後任として.

Q a ***busy*** *office* 忙しい職務. ¶hold a ***difficult public*** *office* 困難な公職につく. ¶an ***elective*** *office* 選挙で定められる職. ¶thanks to the ***good*** *offices* of … …の尽力のおかげで ‖ continue their ***good*** *offices* by making suggestion of improvement, etc. 改善について注意を与えなどして引続き厚意を示す. ¶those holding ***high*** *office* or position 高位高官の人々. ¶accept the ***imperial*** *office* 帝位につく. ¶hold a ***private*** *office* 専用の室を持っている. ¶hold ***public*** *office* 公職にある. 【類】 He held, with distinction, ***public*** *offices*. / He was charged with corrupt robbery and speculation while in ***public*** *office*. ¶a ***sound-absorbing typist's*** *office* 防音装置のあるタイプライター室. ¶a ***technical*** *office* 専門の職. ¶the ***tender*** *offices* of the ladies of mercy 慈善のために働く婦人などのやさしい世話. ¶an ***unpretentious*** *office* 地味な職務.

P ***during*** *office* 在職中. ¶candidates ***for*** high *office* 高官の候補者 ‖ apply ***for*** an *office* 就職を申込む. ¶retire ***from*** *office* 職を辞する. ¶die ***in*** *office* 職にあって死ぬ ‖ the party ***in*** *office* 与党 ‖ whether ***in*** *office* or in opposition 朝にあっても野にあっても. 【類】 since the present Government has been ***in*** *office* / He is no longer ***in*** *office*. ¶come ***into*** *office* 就任する. ¶He was deprived ***of*** his *office*. 彼は職を免ぜられた. ‖ the Chancellor of the Exchequer in his black and gold robe ***of*** *office* 黒と金の官服を着けた大蔵大臣. ¶He is ***out of*** *office* now. 彼は目下失職している(浪人だ). ‖ The Labor Party is now ***out of*** *office* (=power). 労働党は今野にある. ¶***through*** your good *offices* あなたのあっ旋で. ¶election ***to*** a high *office* 高官への選任.

P² on taking *office* ***as*** the new president of the University of California カリフォルニア大学総長として就任するに当って ‖ He says that the *office* ***of*** Mayor is larger than that of Governor. 市長の職は知事のそれよりも重いと彼は言っている. ‖ it is not the *office* ***of*** a dictionary like this to … …することはこの種の辞書の本領ではない ‖ an *office* ***of*** honor (profit, *or* trust) 名誉(利益, 信任)の職.

(**2**) 事務所(オフィス).

V ***attend*** the *office* 事務所に出る. ¶The offices of the French consulate were ***closed***. フランス領事館は閉鎖された. ¶***establish*** an *office* 事務所を設立する. ¶He ***has*** his *office* in downtown Tokyo. 彼は下町に事務所を持っている. ‖ ***head*** the new branch *office* 新設支店(局)の長になる. ¶He ***has*** an *office* in the building. 彼はそのビルに事務所を持っている. ‖ The firm ***has*** its *office* in London. その社はロンドンに店をもっている. ¶The company ***maintains*** an *office* in Paris. その会社はパリに支社がある. ¶***open*** *offices* in … …に事務所を開く. ¶***set up*** (=establish) branch *offices* 支店を設ける. ¶***take over*** the New York *office* ニューヨークの事務所を引受ける.

V² our *office* ***opens*** at … o'clock and ***closes*** at … われわれの事務所は…時に開いて…時に閉じる.

Q an ***advisory vocational*** *office* 就職指導事務所. ¶Take this to Mr. ***Brown's*** *office*. ブラウンさんのオフィスにこれを持って行ってくれ. ¶a ***central*** *office* 中央事務所. ¶the ***detached*** *office* of the Ministry of Finance 大蔵省別館. ¶***diplomatic*** and ***consular*** *offices* 在外諸公館. ¶a ***fat*** *office* 実入りのよい役. ¶through the ***good*** *offices* of … …のあっ旋で. ¶work in a ***lawyer's*** *office* 弁護士事務所で働く. ¶the ***main*** *office* of a company 本社. ¶the seat of a ***prefectural*** *office* 県庁所在地. ¶knock before entering a ***private*** *office* 専用室に入る前に戸をたたく. ¶open a ***temporary*** *office* at … …に仮事務所を開く. ¶a ***well-appointed*** *office* よく装備された事務所.

Q² an ***administration*** *office* 事務総局. ¶an ***assay*** *office* 試験所. ¶a ***booking*** *office* [駅の]出札所. ¶a ***box*** *office* 〖劇〗 切符売場 ‖ the performance proved good ***box*** *office*. その興業は大当りだった. ¶a ***branch*** *office* 支店. ¶a ***business*** *office* 営業所. ¶a ***circumlocution*** *office* お役所風, 繁文じょく礼. ¶a ***complaint*** *office* 修理請求受付所. ¶a ***court clerks*** *office* 裁判所書記課. ¶a ***dead-letter*** *office* 配達不能郵便取扱所. ¶a ***deposit*** *office* 供託局. ¶an ***employment*** *office* 職業

安定所. ¶an *engineering office* 工務所. ¶the ***Ex-prisoners' Aid Committee** Office* 司法保護委員事務局. ¶a ***field** office* 作業所(建設会社の). ¶a ***fire** office* (=a fire insurance office) 《英》火災保険会社. ¶a ***general affairs** office* 総務室. ¶all ***Government** offices* (=agencies) 一切の官庁. ¶***government** and other **public** offices* 官公庁. ¶the ***head** office* 本部(社). ¶a ***home** office* 本社. ¶an ***inquiry** office* 案内所. ¶an ***intelligence** office* 職業紹介所. ¶an ***intendant** office* 監督局. ¶a ***juvenile classification** office* 少年鑑別所. ¶the ***Juvenile Protection** Office* 少年審判所. ¶a ***law** office* 法律事務所. ¶a ***liaison** office* 連絡所. ¶a ***life** office* 《英》生命保険会社. ¶a ***loan** office* 質屋; 金融店. ¶our ***London** office* 本社のロンドン支店. ¶The ***Lost Property** Office* 遺失品部(ロンドン警視庁). ¶an ***M-G-M Tokyo** office* メトロゴールドウィンメーヤー(映画会社)東京支社. ¶a ***mid-town** office* 市内営業所. ¶a ***money-order** office* 郵便為替管理局, 郵便為替取扱郵便局. ¶a ***newspaper** [**publishing**] office* 新聞社. ¶a little ***one-room** office* 一室の小オフィス. ¶an ***outer** office* 控所. ¶a ***patent** office* 特許局. ¶a ***placement** office* [学校などの]就職課. ¶a ***public employment security** office* 公共職業安定所. ¶the ***Public Procurators** Office* 最高検察庁. ¶a ***rat** office* 《俗》組合職工を使わない印刷所. ¶a ***receiving** office* 郵便受取所. ¶a ***registry** office* 職業紹介所. ¶a ***semi-branch** office* 出張所. ¶a ***stationery** office* 文具供給局(英国の諸官庁の文具を供給し, 報告の印刷などをする). ¶a ***supply** office* 用度課. ¶a ***ticket** office* 切符売場.

P in one's room ***at*** the *office* 事務所のその人の室で. ¶I asked for Mr. Ito, but he was not ***in*** (=at) the *office*. 伊藤さんはいますかと尋ねたが事務所にはいなかった. ‖ take a nap ***in*** one's *office* 事務所で居眠りをする. ¶The *offices **of*** the Institution are all established within the walls of this building. 同協会の事務所は全部この建物内にある.

office-bearer, *n.* 《英》官(公)吏.

Q a presiding *office-bearer* 主任級の人.

office-holder, *n.* 《米》官(公)吏.

Q an ***influential*** *office-holder* 有力な官吏.

Q^2 an ***absentee*** *office-holder* [職名給与はあるが]不在公務員.

officer, *n.* 役人, 公務員; 役員; 士官.

V The *officer* was ***degraded*** by being reduced to the ranks. 同士官は懲罰で兵卒にされた. ¶***elect*** *officers* 役員を選挙する.

Q an ***administrative** officer* 行政官. ¶a ***bonded** officer* 保証された(保証金を納めた)役員. ¶the ***civil** and **military** officers* 文武官. ¶the ***commanding** officer* of the Sugamo Prison 巣鴨収容所長 ‖ by order of ***commanding** officer* 部隊長の命により.【類】The ***commanding** officer* gave them specific orders to sneak into the enemy's camp. ¶***executive** officers* 幹部の人々. ¶***gold-laced** officers* 金モールの士官. ¶***high** officers* 高級役員. ¶***high-ranking** officers* 高級武官. ¶***incompetent** officers* 無能な役員. ¶a ***junior** officer* 下級武官. ¶a ***leading** officer* 指導的役員. ¶these ***principal** officers* of the corporation are ... その会社の主な役員は...である. ¶a ***presiding** officer* 社長(理事長). ¶***prominent naval** officers*, serving and retired 目ぼしい現役及び予備の海軍将官. ¶***salaried** officers* 有給の役員. ¶a ***senior** officer* 上席役員. ¶a ***subordinate** officer* 属僚. ¶***superior** officers* of the Army and the Navy 陸海軍の高級士官. ¶***top** officers* in the Army 陸軍の最高武官たち.

Q^2 an ***air** officer* 飛行将校. ¶***Air Base** officers* 飛行基地将校たち. ¶an ***Army** officer* 陸軍将校.【類】a high ***Army** officer*. ¶a ***brother** officer* 同僚士官. ¶a ***Cabinet** officer* (=member) 閣員. ¶a ***cipher** officer* 暗号事務官. ¶a ***class** officer* クラス委員. ¶a ***combatant** officer* 戦闘将校. ¶a ***commanding** officer* 部隊長(C.O. と略す). ¶a ***communications** officer* 通信士官. ¶a British ***Councillor** officer* 英国大使館参事官. ¶a ***customs** officer* 税関官吏. ¶a ***disbursing** officer* 出納官. ¶a ***duty** officer* 当番役員. ¶a big ships' ***engineer** officer* 大汽船の機関士. ¶an ***excise** officer* 物品税務官. ¶an ***ex-police** officer* 前警察官. ¶one's ***fellow** officer* 同僚士官. ¶a ***flag** officer* 海軍将官. ¶a ***flight** (=**flying**) officer* 飛行士官, [機長の]副長. ¶a ***full-time** officer* 専任役員. ¶a ***gun-room** officers* 尉官 (gun-room は少壮士官室). ¶the city's ***health** officers* 市の保健係員. ¶a ***hygiene** officer* 保健官. ¶an ***immigration** officer* 入国移民係員. ¶a ***language** officer* 翻訳官. ¶a ***law enforcement** officer* 法律施行官. ¶He acted as ***liaison** officer* with foreign press correspondents. 彼は外国新聞通信員との連絡係として勤務した. ¶a ***line** officer* 《米》軍艦内の戦闘及び動力に関係のある士官. ¶a ***morale** officer* 風紀係の士官. ¶a ***noncommissioned** officer* 下士官 (a noncom と略す). ¶a ***parade** officer* 置物将校(連隊事務儀礼などに通じているだけの無能将校). ¶***probation** and **parole** officers* 監視及び仮釈放事務士官. ¶a ***party** officer* 党役員. ¶a ***peace** officer* 治安官(警察官治安裁判官など). ¶a ***personnel** officer* 人事事務官. ¶a ***placement** officer* 職業配当官. ¶a plain ***clothes** officer* of the Tokyo Metropolitan Police 警視庁私服(角そで)警官. ¶a squad of twenty ***police** officers* 二十人の警官隊 ‖ a judicial ***police** officer* 司法警察官. ¶a ***press relations** officer* 新聞記者係員. ¶a ***prison** officer* 刑務官. ¶a ***probation** officer* 監視官(刑の施行を猶予したもの). ¶a ***public relations** officer* 官庁の事業の内容を人民に知らせる官吏. ¶the ***ranking** officer* of a march. 行軍の高級士官. ¶a ***receiving** officer* 接待士官. ¶a ***revenue** officer* 税務官. ¶a ***reviewing** officer* 〖法〗再調査官(下級裁判所の判決を再調査する). ¶a ***safety** officer* 保安官. ¶a ***service** officer* 現役将校. ¶a ***staff** officer* 参謀将校. ¶a key ***staff** officer* 主要参謀将校. ¶a ***supervision** officer* 保護観察官. ¶a ***town** officer* 市吏. ¶put special ***traffic** officers* on duty 特別交通係員を配置する. ¶a ***warrant** officer* 準士官.

P the orders ***of*** superior *officers* 上官の命令.

P^2 *officers **in*** the Army and Navy 陸海軍の士官. ¶an *officer **of*** State=a government official 官吏 ‖ an *officer **of*** the law 司法官 ‖ an *officer **of*** the day (week) 日直(週番)士官. ¶an *officer **on*** probation 士官候補生 ‖ *officers **on*** the active (reserve) list 現(予備)役将校.

O *officers* and workers of a society ある会の役員及び平の使用人. ¶*officers* and men 将兵.

officer, *v.* 引率する.

P be ***officered by*** ... ...(将校)に引率される.

office-seeker, *n.* 猟官運動者.

Q a ***disappointed*** *office-seeker* 失望した猟官運動者.

official, *n.* 官吏, 公吏; 役員, 事務員.

V ***dismiss*** an *official* 役人を免職する. ¶***elect*** an *official* 役人を選ぶ. ¶***suspend*** an *official* 官吏を停職する.

Q an ***able** and **efficient** official* 腕があって役に立つ官吏. ¶an ***assistant** official* of public procuration 検察補佐官. ¶The ***chief** official* of a district. 一地方の主要な役人. ¶a ***competent** official* 有能な官吏. ¶an ***estimable** and **diligent** official* 勤勉優秀な官吏. ¶a ***Government** official* 官吏. ¶a ***high** official* 高官. ¶***higher** officials* 高官たち. ¶a ***key** official* 主要官吏. ¶***military** and **civilian** officials* 文武官. ¶***national** or **municipal** officials* 官公吏. ¶a ***paid** official* 有給役員. ¶***postal** officials*=mail clerks 郵便局の職員. ¶a ***public** official* 公務員. ¶a ***responsible** official* 責任ある位置の官吏. ¶a ***wise** and **honest** official* 賢明かつ正直な官吏. ¶remove a ***worthy** official* 有能官吏をやめさせる. ¶a ***subordinate** official* 属官. ¶a ***sworn** official* 宣誓した官吏. ¶a ***technical** official* of court 裁判所技官. ¶an ***upright** official* amid so much corruption 周囲が皆腐敗している中に独り廉直を守る官吏. ¶a ***city** official* 市の役員.

Q^2 a ***civil service** official* 文官. ¶a ***city transport** official* 市の交通係員. ¶a ***court** official* 裁判所役員. ¶an ***embassy** official* 大使館役員. ¶***emigration** and **immigration** officials* [出国・入国の]移民事務官. ¶an ***executive** official* 行政官. ¶a ***Government** official* 官吏.【類】a high ***government** official*. ¶a ***grain-exchange** official* 農作物取引所役員. ¶a ***health** official* 保健官. ¶a ***job-finding** official* 職業紹介所の所員. ¶a ***judicial research** official* 裁判所調査官. ¶a ***law-enforcement** official* 司法事務官. ¶a ***matter-of-fact** official* 実務家はだの役人. ¶an ***occupation** official* 占領事務官. ¶a ***police** official* 警察官. ¶***policy-making*** high *officials* 政策作成にあずかる高官たち. ¶a ***railroad** official* 鉄道官吏. ¶a poor ***relief** official* 民生委員. ¶***SCAP** officials* 最高司令部属公務員たち. ¶a Japanese "***thought***" *official* 日本人思想関係の官吏. ¶a ***top-level** official* 高級官吏. ¶a ***union** official* 労働組合の役員. ¶train ***state** officials* 国家公務員を養成する. ¶a ***welfare** official* 厚生事務役員.

P^2 an *official **in*** the Department of Foreign Affairs 外務省官吏. ¶*officials **of*** the *sonin* rank 奏任官吏. ¶an *official **of*** a firm 商社の役員.

officialdom, *n.* 官界.

V ***challenge*** *officialdom* 官僚(団体)に挑戦する.

Q² hold a key post in the hierarchy of ***company officialdom*** 会社の役員団中に主要な地位を占める. ¶ ***Zionist officialdom*** ユダヤ教徒系官僚界.

officiate, *v.* 職務を行う, 勤務する; 司会する.

P She *officiates* ***at*** the organ in Sunday service. 日曜の礼拝で彼女はオルガン演奏を勤める. ‖ *officiate* ***at*** a wedding [ceremony] 結婚式の司会をする.

officious, *a.* おせっかいな.

P *officious* ***in*** one's attentions 色々といらない世話を焼いて.

offing, *n.* 沖, 沖合.

P ***in*** the outer *offing* 沖合に. ¶ Numbers of corpses are seen floating ***in*** the *offing*. 多数の死体が浮んでいるのが見える沖. 【類】a steamer ***in*** the *offing*.

offset, *n.* 相殺, 差引勘定.

P² *offset* ***to*** a loss 損失に対する相殺.

offset, *v.* 埋合せする.

M be ***fully*** *offset* by ... ...で十分埋合わせができる.

P Part of the profit was *offset* ***by*** the loss. 利潤の一部は...で帳消になった.

offspring, *n.* [団]子, 子孫.

V parents who are able to ***direct, control*** and ***teach*** their *offspring* intelligently 自分の子供を賢明に指導し制御し教育できる両親. ¶ ***limit*** their *offspring* (=children) 彼らの産児を制限する. ¶ ***produce*** *offspring* 子孫を産む.

Q ***healthy*** *offspring* 健康な子供. ¶ The ***sole*** *offspring* of the marriage was a daughter. その結婚で二人の間にできたのはたった一人の娘であった.

P regulation of the number ***of*** *offspring* 産児制限.

P² the *offspring* ***of*** the poor 貧乏人の子供 ‖ the *offspring* ***of*** this union この結婚で生れた子供たち. 【類】the *offspring* (成果) ***of*** modern civilization.

often, *ad.* しばしば, 度々.

M ***often enough*** 随分ひんぱんに. ¶ "Without political significance" is ***too*** *often* the cry of the blind. 「政治的意味なしに」という言葉はあまりにもひんぱんな盲まいな人たちの叫びである.

O *often* and *often* again 随分たびたび.

oil, *n.* 油, 油絵.

V ***burn*** the midnight *oil* (=study late into the night) over English lessons 深更まで英語を勉強する. ¶ ***express*** *oil* from ... ...から油をしぼる. ¶ ***extract*** *oil* from bean-cakes 豆かすから油を取る. ¶ ***feed*** *oil* to ... ...に油を注ぐ. ¶ an *oil* ***obtained*** from peanuts 南京豆からしぼった油. ¶ ***pour*** (=put) *oil* into a lamp ランプに油を注ぐ ‖ ***pour*** *oil* upon the waters 水に油を注ぐ; 激こうを緩和する. ¶ ***press*** *oil* from walnuts くるみから油をしぼる. ¶ ***put*** *oil* on the wheels 車輪に油を注ぐ. ¶ ***strike*** *oil* 《米俗》やま(投機)を当てる. 【類】That hotel has ***struck*** *oil*. ¶ ***throw*** *oil* on a fire (=the flams) 火に油を注ぐ ‖ ***throw*** *oil* on the troubled waters 紛争を緩和する. ¶ The watch ***wants*** a little *oil*. その(懐中)時計は少し油をさす必要がある. ¶ ***waste*** the midnight *oil* 夜半に油を浪費する.

V² The lubricating *oil* does not ***clog*** or ***gum***. その機械油はかたまったりべとついたりしない. ¶ *Oil* and water do not ***mix***. 油と水とはまざらない. ¶ The *oil* is ***running short***. 油が段々少くなる. ¶ The lubricating *oil* has ***turned rancid***. 機械油が腐った.

Q abstract metal from ***crude*** *oil* 原油から金属を抜取る. ¶ fry in ***deep*** *oil* (多量の油の中で)揚げる. ¶ ***edible*** *oil* 食用油. ¶ ***essential*** (=***volatile***) *oils* 揮発油. ¶ ***fatty*** *oils* 脂肪油. ¶ ***fixed*** *oils* 不揮発油. ¶ ***heavy*** (***light***) *oil* 重(軽)油. ¶ ***holy*** *oil* 聖油. ¶ ***illuminating*** *oil* 照明用の油. ¶ ***refined*** *oil* 精製油.

Q² ***cocoa-nut*** *oil* やし油. ¶ ***engine*** *oil* 機械油. ¶ ***fuel*** *oil* 燃料油. ¶ ***hair*** *oil* 毛髪油. ¶ ***lamp*** *oil* 灯油. ¶ 123 drams of ***linseed*** *oil* アマ油百二十三ドラム. ¶ ***lubricating*** *oil* 潤滑油. ¶ full of epigrams, redolent of ***midnight*** *oil* 深更のめい想をしのばせる警句の連発で. ¶ a crude ***mineral*** *oil* 粗製の鉱物油. ¶ ***mustard-seed*** *oil* からし油. ¶ ***olive*** *oil* オリーブ油. ¶ ***palm*** *oil* しゅろ油; 《俗》わいろ; 心ずけ; その下. ¶ ***safety-lamp*** *oil* 安全灯油. ¶ ***sardine*** (***herring***) *oil* いわし(にしん)油. ¶ ***table*** *oil* サラダ・オイル. ¶ ***vegetable*** *oil* 植物油. ¶ ***whale*** *oil* 鯨油. ¶ ***wood*** *oil* 木から抽出した油.

P a costly portrait [done] ***in*** *oils* 高価な油絵の肖像画 ‖ fry fish ***in*** *oil* 油で魚を揚げる.

P² as *oil* ***on*** a rough sea 荒海上の(波を静める)油のように. ¶ I don't want to kill myself ***with*** midnight *oil*. 私は深更まで勉強して命を縮めたくない.

oil, *v.* 油をさす, 滑かにする.

O *oil* one's (the) tongue ぺらぺらおべっかを言う ‖ oil a bicycle (watch).

ointment, *n.* 軟こう.

Q² boric ***acid*** *ointment* ほう酸軟こう.

O.K., *n.* 承認.

V He ***got*** an *O.K.* on it. 彼はその承認を得た.

OK, *v.* 〚米〛承認する.

O The Bill was *OK'd*. その議案は通過した.

old, *a.* 老いている, 年寄った; ...歳の; 古い.

M ***almost*** (=***nearly***) ***ninety years*** *old* ほとんど九十歳の. ¶ He is *old* ***enough*** to know better. 彼はもっと物分かりがしてよいはずの年ごろだ. ¶ He is *old* ***enough*** to be more prudent. いい年をしているのだからもっと分別がありそうなものだ. ¶ a baby a ***few months*** *old* 生れて数カ月の赤ん坊. 【類】A cheese ***seventy-one days*** *old* is said to contain 800,000 bacteria per gramme. ¶ ***How*** *old* are you? お年はおいくつですか. ¶ a tree ***incalculably*** *old* 勘定できないほど古い木.

O He is *older* than I by five years. 彼は僕より五つ年上だ. ¶ *older* than history 有史以前の. ¶ I see by the papers that poor *old* Waseda has lost twice against the Chicago team. 私は新聞で早稲田がシカゴ野球団と戦って気の毒に二度も負けたことを知った. ¶ The building is five years *old*. あの建物は五年になる.

old, *n.* 古昔, 往時.

P as ***of*** *old* 昔のように ‖ the sage ***of*** *old* 古の聖人 ‖ as the Athenians ***of*** *old* 昔のアテネ人のように ‖ Things are very different now from what they used to be ***of*** *old*. 万事昔と今とでは非常に違っている. ‖ They said ***of*** *old* that all roads led to Rome. 古人は天下の道はローマに通じると言った.

old-fashioned, *a.* 古風な, 旧式の.

M he is *old-fashioned* ***enough*** to think that ... 彼は...と考えるほどに頭が古い.

omen, *n.* 前兆, 徴候, 縁起.

Q a ***bad*** (=an ***evil***) *omen* 不吉の徴候. ¶ a ***black*** *omen* 悪い前兆. ¶ a ***cheering*** *omen* よい前兆. ¶ ***encouraging*** *omens* 気を引立たせる前兆. ¶ thinking it a ***favorable*** *omen* 幸先よしと考えて. ¶ a ***felicitous*** *omen* めでたい前兆. ¶ If ..., *omen* is ***good***. もし...なら縁起がよい. 【類】greet it as a ***good*** *omen*. ¶ a ***happy*** (=***propitious***) *omen* 吉兆. ¶ an ***ill*** *omen* 凶兆. ¶ a ***lucky*** *omen* 吉兆. ¶ an ***unlucky*** *omen* よくない前兆.

P The superstitious regard it ***as*** an unfavorable *omen*. 迷信家はそれを悪い縁起と見ている.

P² it is [a] happy *omen* ***for*** ... それは...にとって吉兆である. ¶ an *omen* ***of*** disaster 凶事の前兆.

ominous, *a.* 前兆の, 予示する.

P *ominous* ***of*** good (evil) 善(悪)の前兆で.

omission, *n.* 脱漏, 脱落, 省略, 手落ち.

V quite a number of *omissions* to be ***found*** through the pages 各ページに見出される相当の省略. ¶ Several friends ***lamented*** the *omission* of this chapter from the third edition. 数人の友人が三版にこの章が省かれているのを惜しんだ. ¶ ***point out*** an important *omission* from a list 表から大事な項が脱けているのを指摘する. ¶ ***rectify*** these *omissions* これらの遺漏を正す. ¶ ***supply*** the *omission* その脱落を補う.

Q a ***glaring*** *omission* はなはだしい脱落. ¶ a ***grave*** *omission* 重大な遺漏. ¶ an ***intentional*** *omission* 故意脱漏. ¶ a ***serious*** *omission* はなはだしい脱漏. ¶ an ***unintentional*** *omission* 無意識の脱漏.

P sins ***of*** *omissions* [なすべきことをなさなかった]怠慢の罪. ¶ ***through*** an *omission* 手ぬかりのために. ¶ ***without*** *omission* もれなく.

P² *omission* ***from*** ... ***of*** ... ...から...の脱落.

omit, *v.* 落す, 抜かす; 省く, 略す.

M an enclosure is ***apparently*** *omitted* from your letter of ... 添付物があなたの...(日付)手紙に入れ忘れてある. ¶ ***inadvertently*** *omit* the word "..." 過って「...」という言葉を落す. ¶ I ***stupidly*** *omitted* to tell him to ... 私はうっかり彼に...と言うことを忘れていた.

P *omit* the name ***from*** the list of subscribers 購読者の名簿からその名を落す ‖ These are *omitted* ***from*** this count. これらは数に入ってない. ‖ Don't *omit* ***from*** your visiting-cards your title, Mr., Mrs., or Miss. 名刺から氏, 夫人, 嬢という称号を省くな. 【類】*omit* an item ***from*** the list.

O *omit* to write 書き落す.

omnibus, *n.* 乗合自動車.
V *take* (=*get in*) an *omnibus* 乗合自動車に乗る.
V² The *omnibus goes* (=*runs*) every five minutes. 乗合自動車は五分ごとに出る.
Q² a *horse omnibus* 乗合馬車. ¶a *motor omnibus* 乗合自動車.
P travel a great deal *by omnibus* 乗合自動車で随分旅行する. ¶go to ... *in* the (=an) *omnibus* 乗合自動車で...へ行く.

once, *ad., n.* 一度, 一回.
Q *This once* I will pardon you. 今度だけゆるしてやろう.
P come (go) *at once* すぐ来る(行く) ‖ all *at once* にわかに. ¶The Siberian Railway is *at once* the longest and best known railroad in the world. シベリア鉄道は世界で最長であると同時に最も有名である. ‖ It *at once* pleases and disappoints us. そのためわれわれは喜びもし失望もする.【類】I was *at once* comforted and terrified by this thought. ‖ between vanity and humiliation *at once* 得意と失意とを同時に味わって. 【類】No great changes should ever be made *at once*. ‖ one should not conclude *at once* that ... ...だと早合点してはいけない. ¶*for once* in one's life 一生に一度だけ. ¶more *than once* 一度ならず. ¶*once* [and] *for* all 今度限り ‖ *for* this *once* これ一回だけ ‖ The Japan-China War of 1894 abolished *once for* all the Chinese claims to suzerainty over Korea. 一八九四年の日清戦争で中国は朝鮮に対する覇(は)権を永久に失った. ‖ write each item *once for* all to avoid repetition 反覆を避けるために各項目をこれを最後にはっきりと記す.【類】Let me say it *once* and *for* all. ¶*once in* a year=once a year 一年に一度 ‖ *once in* a while たまに.

one, *n.* 一つ, 一方; 一の数; 同一物, 同じこと; 人, もの.
V *exchange one* for the other [二つの中]一方を他と交換する.
Q It's *all one* to me. それは僕にとって同じことだ. ¶a *bad one* 悪いもの. ¶The fish I had lost was quite a *big one*. あの落した魚は大きかった. ¶His lot is an *enviable one*. あの人はうらやましい身の上だ. ¶It isn't *every one* who has the good fortune to succeed in it. だれもかも運よくそれに成功するとは限らない. ‖ *Every one* loves his mother. 人はだれでも母を愛する. ¶You're a *fine one!* 君はえらいよ(皮肉). ¶The show seems a very *good one*. その見世物は大変いいようだ. ‖ Buy a *good one* if you buy at all. どうせ買うなら良いのを買いなさい. ¶mutually very *helpful one* to the other 相互的に非常に助けになる. ¶*knowing ones* in the trade その道の消息通. ¶Show me *larger* (*smaller*) *ones*. ¶It is the *last one* I have. もうそれだけになった. ¶my dear *little ones* うちのかわいい子供たち. ¶A hangman's job is a very *nasty one*, isn't it? 死刑執行人の役はいやですね. ¶I have a Panama hat, —a very *old one*. 私はパナマ帽を持っています—非常に古いのです. ¶*No one* knows. だれも知りません. ¶This is the *only one* we have at hand. 持ち合わしているのはこれだけです. 【類】the copy in the Bodleian being the *only one* that is known to exist ボドリーアン図書館(英国オクスフォードの)にある本が唯一の物として知られている. ¶The theory is a *probable one*. その理屈は正確らしく思われる. ¶a *single one* たった一つ. ¶The city tramway men's strike was a *systematic one*. 市電従業員の同盟罷業は秩序的であった. ¶Which do you take, *this one* or that? これとあれとどちらをお取りになりますか. ¶a *wrong one* そうでないもの. ¶my *young ones* 私の子供たち. ¶Begin with *number one*, I say. まず隗(かい)より始めよだね. ¶*page* (*chapter*) *one* 第一ページ(章). ¶*public enemy No. 1* 第一の公衆の敵. ¶*section one* 第一項. ¶*World War 1* 第一次世界大戦.
P be *at one* with ... ...と同意見である. ¶He took out a pack of cigarettes and puffed *at one*. 彼は巻タバコを一包取りだして一本ふかした. ¶the last line *but one* 最後から二行目. ¶They came out *by ones* and twos. 一人, 二人と(ぽつぽつ)出て来た. ¶I, *for one*, won't agree. 私も賛同しない一人です.【類】I *for one* don't believe a word of it. ¶be different *from one* another 各々相違してる. ¶serves as a knife, a can-opener, and a screwdriver all *in one* 小刀, かん切, ねじ回し兼用です. ¶ten *to one* 十中の八九は.
P² *one after* another 順々に ‖ *one after* the other 交互に. ¶*one at* a time 一度に一つ. ¶*one by one* 一つずつ. ¶He is a *one for* baseball. 彼は野球に目がない. ¶*One from* five leaves four. 五から一を引くと四が残る. ¶*one in* a thousand 千人中一人. ¶She is now like *one of* the family. 彼女は今ではうちの人も同様だ. ‖ The chances are *one to* thousand. 千番に一番のかねあい. ¶I felt myself to be *one with* nature. 私は自然の中にとけこんでしまったという感じがした. ‖ I'm [at] *one with* you on that point.=I'm with you on that. その点では同意見です.
O the *one* and the whole ことごとく, 全部. ¶*one* and the same 全く同一物.

oneness, *n.* 単一性.
Q the *essential oneness* of mankind 根本において人類が一つであること. ¶a *singular oneness* of aim and purity of intent まれに見る専念と意向の純真.

oneself, *n., pron.* 自身, 自分. →-self.
P *by oneself* ただ一人で. ¶*for oneself* 独力で. ¶*of oneself* ひとりでに.

onion, *n.* ねぎ.
Q *autumn-sown onions* 秋まきのねぎ. ¶the *common onion* 玉ねぎ.
P His breath stinks *of onions*. 息が玉ねぎくさい.

onlooker, *n.* 傍観者.
Q remain a *passive onlooker* to ... ...に対して腕こまぬいて傍観する.

only, *ad.* ただただ, 単に.
M *not only* ... but [also] ... ...のみならずまた...

onset, *n.* 進撃, 攻撃; 着手.
V *delay* the *onset* of fatigue 早く疲労しないようにする. ¶*inhibit* the *onset* of the disease その病の進入を防ぐ.
P She was twenty-five years old *at* the *oneset* of her illness. 彼女は発病当時二十五歳であった. ¶*with* the *onset* of puberty 思春期に達して.

onslaught, *n.* 攻撃, 突撃.
V *make* a vigorous *onslaught* on ... ...を猛烈に攻撃する.
Q a *fresh onslaught* on ... 新たに...に対する攻撃.
P an *onslaught on* the enemy 敵に対する進撃.

onus, *n.* 負担, 重荷.
V *lay* the *onus* [of responsibility] on ... 責任を...に帰する.

ooze, *v.* にじみ出る, 分泌する.
M Juice *oozes out*. 汁がにじみ出る ‖ At last the secret *oozed out*. 秘密がとうとう漏れた.

opal, *n.* オパル(宝石).
Q The sky burned like a *heated opal*. 空は熱したオパルのように燃えた.

open, *n.* 戸外, 露店.
P We are all lovers of the life *in* the *open*. われわれは皆戸外生活の愛好者である. ‖ Why don't they come out and fight *in* the *open?* なぜかれらは出て来て戸外で戦わないのか.

open, *a.* 開いている, 公開の, 公然の; 未決の.
M It is not *so much open* to objection. それはそんなに反対を受けそうもない.
P a public reading room is now *open at* ... 一般読書室は今...で公開している. ¶Whether or not it would be possible for ... is *open for* demonstration (=doubtful). それが...にとって可能であるか否かはまだ証明の余地がある. ‖ The ship is *open for* charter. その船は用船契約に応じることができる. ‖ The arena will be *open for* all competitors. 飛入勝手次第. 【類】The hotel would be *open for* guests next June or July. / The telegraph office is *open for* public business. / The exhibition will be *open for* two weeks. ‖ The river is *open for* navigation. 川が開航された. ¶The two rooms are *open into* one another with a very wide door-way between them. その二室は大層広い入口で互に出入ができるようになっている. ¶a room *open to* sunshine from the west 西日のさすへや ‖ The factory is always *open to* visitors. その工場はいつも縦覧随意である. ‖ I am *open to* a proposal (negotiation, contract, competition) 私は提案(など)を受ける用意がある. 【類】The clinic is *open to* outsiders as well as employees and their families. / the hours in which public buidings are *open to* visitors / The competition is *open to* all (一般の参加を許す). / The races are *open to* "All England" (英国人ならだれでも). / The meeting is *open to* the public. / be *open to* contract for coal / be manifestly *open to* doubt / His conduct is *open to* criticism. / The matter is still *open to* discussion. / Educational opportunities are now *open to* all. / Membership in the Society is *open to* any one interested in the objects of the Society. / occupations *open to* women / the first college *open to* women ‖ prizes *open to* amateurs only アマチュアだけに与えられる賞品 ‖ The points most *open to* adverse criticism (反論) are three in number. / The hotel is now *open to* guests. / All offices are *open to* those who deserve (実力次第で). ‖ All our privacies are *open to* God.

われわれの秘密はすべて神が知っている. ‖ a place *open to* the sky (地上に木や建物のない)からっとした土地 ‖ The sewer is *open to* the air. 下水みぞはふたがない. ‖ *open to* the view 眼界の開けた ‖ It is *open to* this objection. それにはこうした異議を唱える余地がある. 【類】It is *open to* public inspection. / the railway will be *open to* traffic on and after July 1. ‖ It still remains *open to* question. それはいまだに疑う余地がある. 【類】Whether ... or not seems *open to* question. / it is certainly *open to* question that ... / It is *open to* doubt. / a question *open to* grave doubt ‖ The band is *open to* engagement. その楽隊は招待に応じる. ‖ The question is still *open to* research. その問題はまだ研究の余地がある. ‖ *open to* misconception 誤解を招きやすい. ‖ Still I am *open to* conviction. 私にはまだ納得ができない. ‖ Its fate is still *open to* conjecture. その運命はどうなるかまだ分からない. ‖ This view, however, is *open to* contention. しかしこの見解は議論の余地がある. ‖ He has three courses *open to* him. 彼の取りうべき手段は三つある. ‖ The sittings of the commission shall not be *open to* the Press. 委員の会議は新聞記者の傍聴を許さない. ¶I will be *open with* you about it. それについて腹蔵なくお話し致しましょう.

open, *v*. 開く, あける, 公開する; 始める.

M It will be ***formally opened*** tomorrow. 明日その開場式がある. ¶The railway was ***fully*** (***partially***) *opened* to traffic. その鉄道は全部(一部)開通になった. ¶The Prince of Wales ***officially*** *opened* the dock. 英国皇太子殿下は開渠(きょ)式を行わせられた. ¶The windows ***open out*** into a garden. 窓は庭に向いている. ‖ the veranda ***opens out*** upon the bay of ... 縁側は…湾に面している ‖ ***open out*** a mine 鉱山を開発する ‖ ***open out*** fresh occasion for ... …に新しい機会を与える ‖ the future will ***open out*** a bright prospect for ... りっぱな前途が…の将来に展開するであろう. 【類】He was just *opening* ***out*** from childhood into manhood. ¶All doors *open* ***outward***. 戸は全部外側へ開く. ¶The season *opens* ***propitiously*** (unfavorably). 季節が有望(思わしくなく)に始まった. ¶*open* the door ***softly*** 静かに戸を開ける. ¶The exhibition will *open* ***tomorrow***. 博覧会はあす開かれる. ¶*open* one's mouth ***wide*** 口を大きくあける.

M² *open* ***up*** a canal (mine) 運河(など)を開さくする ‖ *open* ***up*** a rich country 資源の豊かな国を開発する. 【類】*open* ***up*** underdeveloped land ‖ *open* ***up*** an office 事務(営業)所を開く ‖ *open* ***up*** steam navigation between ... and ... 何と何間に汽船通航を開く ‖ *open* ***up*** a country to trade 国を国際貿易に開く. 【類】Commodore Perry, who *opened* ***up*** Japan to the Western world. ‖ It *opened* ***up*** a new world to me. それが私に新天地を開拓してくれた. 【類】*open* ***up*** a new field of enterprise (in science) ‖ *open* ***up*** some very interesting problems 二三の非常に興味ある問題を持ち出す ‖ *open* ***up*** correspondence with ... …と文通を始める. 【類】*open* ***up*** direct telegraphic communication with ... ‖ *open* ***up*** one's mind freely わだかまりなく心を打明ける ‖ *open* ***up*** a wound for treatment 治療のため傷口を開く.

P all mouths began to be *opened* ***against*** ... 皆のものが…に反対の声を揚げ始めた. ¶*Open* the book ***at*** page 25. 本の二十五ページをあけなさい. 【類】School *opens* ***at*** 8 in the morning. ¶*open* the door ***by*** force 無理にドアを開ける. ¶The country was formally *opened* ***for*** intercourse with the outside world. その国は正式に他国との修交を始めた. ‖ The railway will be *opened* ***for*** (=open to) traffic. 近々その鉄道が開通になるだろう. ‖ The hospital has been *opened* ***for*** the reception of patients. 病院が患者の収容を始めた. ‖ The shooting season *opens* ***for*** deer and moose hunters. しかや大じかの猟期が始まった. ¶*open* ***from*** within 内側から開く. ¶The sitting-room *opened* ***into*** a bedroom. 居間は寝室に行けるようになっていた. ‖ The door *opens* ***into*** the passage. 戸を開くと廊下に出られるようになっている. ¶with windows that *open* ***on*** the street 通りに面している窓のある ‖ The story *opens* ***on*** a trading vessel bound for England. 話は英国行の貿易船内のできごとから始まる. ¶*open* a new road ***through*** the country その地方に道路を新設する. ¶*open* a book ***to*** page 10 十ページをあける ‖ *open* Japan ***to*** the world 日本を開国する ‖ The sanctum sanctorum is *opened* ***to*** worshippers twice a year. 年二回お開帳がある. ‖ The canal was *opened* ***to*** (=for) traffic. 運河が開通した. 【類】The subway was *opened* ***to*** traffic last year. / A new era began when Japan was *opened* ***to*** commerce and intercourse with the United States. ‖ The window *opens* ***to*** the west. 窓は西向です. 【類】The window *opens* ***to*** the sea. / A beautiful prospect *opens* ***to*** the northward. / It was *opened* ***to*** public inspection. / The hotel restaurants are *opened* ***to*** non-residents (短期の泊り客). ¶The back of the premises *opens* ***upon*** a pretty little garden. 構内の裏側は美しい小さな庭に面している. ‖ The twentieth century *opened* ***upon*** a scene of great activity in every part of the vast dominions of the Tsar. 二十世紀にはいったころロシア皇帝の大領土は至るところ活気を呈していた. ¶a letter which *opened* ***with*** this phrase この文句で書き始めた手紙. 【類】the book *opens* ***with*** a chapter on ... / Part III *opened* ***with*** ... / the lectures were *opened* ***with*** ... / the magazine *opens* ***with*** a drawing of ... by ... / the book *opens* ***with*** ... and closes with ...

opener, *n*. 開く物, せん抜き.

Q² a ***bottle*** *opener* せん抜き. ¶***business letter*** *openers* and closers 商業文の書き始めと書き終りの文句. ¶a ***can*** (=***tin***) *opener* かん切り. ¶a ***cap*** *opener* せん抜き. ¶***wooden letter*** *opener* 木製書状開封器.

opening, *n*. 開始, 着手, 開業; 発端; 間隙; すき間, 穴.

V formally ***celebrate*** the *opening* of a new building 正式に新築開きをする. ¶***mark*** the *opening* of a new era 新紀元を画する. 【類】The year may be declared approximately to ***mark*** the *opening* of the era of decadence (退廃期). ¶***offer*** an *opening* to ... …する機会を与える.

Q a ***capital*** *opening* 開始絶好の機会. ¶***ceremonial*** *opening* of a university 大学開校式. ¶get out through a ***narrow*** *opening* 狭い路を通って出る.

Q² Flames burst out through ***building*** *openings*. 火炎が建物のすき間から舌を出した. ¶a capital ***business*** *opening* 絶好の取引機会. ¶***chess*** *openings* and endings 将棋の序盤と終盤のさし方. ¶a ***foreign trade*** *opening* 外国貿易の好機. ¶a steady increase in ***job*** *openings* 勤め口の漸増.

P soon ***after*** the *opening* of the month その月にはいってからじきに. ¶***at*** the *opening* of the market 市場の開始時に. 【類】***at*** the *opening* of Parliament / ***at*** the *opening* of the college year (wrestling season). ¶***since*** the *opening* of the twentieth century 二十世紀になってから.

P² an *opening* ***among*** trees=a glade 樹間の空地. ¶an *opening* ***for*** a business 商売の機会 ‖ a good *opening* ***for*** a young man 青年にとってよい勤め口. ¶the *openings* ***from*** the rectum and the bladder 直腸及びぼうこうからの孔口. ¶the *opening* ***of*** Japan ***to*** the world 日本の開国. 【類】The *opening* ***of*** the first subway (地下鉄) in New York occurred [on] October 27, 1904. ‖ the *opening* up ***of*** motor-roads 自動車道路の開通.

opera, *n*. 歌劇, オペラ.

Q ***comic*** *opera* 喜歌劇. ¶***grand*** *opera* グランド・オペラ, 正「歌劇.

Q² a ***horse*** *opera* 〘映〙西部もの, 活劇もの. ¶a ***soap*** *opera* 〘ラジオ〙連続放送劇.

P an evening ***at*** the *opera* オペラの一夕. ¶sing ***in*** *opera* 「オペラに出て歌う.

operate, *v*. 仕事する, 工作する, 働く, 操縦する, 運転する; 効果を生じる; 外科手術をする.

M This road *operates* five trains ***a day***. 《米》この線は一日五本列車が出る. ¶The air line service is to *operate* ***daily***. その定航は毎日営業することになる. ¶***directly*** *operate* in ... 直接…に作用する. ¶Marriage *operates* ***fortuitously*** (=is a lottery). 結婚は運次第だ. ¶The medicine ***gradually*** *operated*. その薬が段々きいてきた. ¶The elevator is not *operating* ***properly***. エレベーターの具合が悪い. ¶*operate* ***psychologically*** as an incitement 精神的刺激になる.

P it will *operate* ***against*** (=affect²) the popularity of ... それは…の人気に悪い影響を及ぼすだろう ‖ A strong force was sent to *operate* ***against*** the insurgents. 暴徒に対抗すべく強力な軍隊が派遣された. 【類】the reasons which *operate* ***against*** the growth of ... ¶*operate* ***at*** pirate 海賊を働く. ¶Machinery is *operated* ***by*** electricity. 機械は電気で運転する. ¶He was *operated* on ***for*** a disease. 彼は患部の手術を受けた. ‖ Speculators are *operating* ***for*** a rise (fall). 投機業者は上昇(低下)操作をしている. ¶*operate* *from* ... ...を策源地として活動する. ¶*operate* ***on*** a patient 患者に手術を行う. 【類】*operate* a patient ***on*** the head / I had my nose *operated* ***on***. / He was *operated* ***on*** (=upon) for a tumor (はれもの). ¶*operate* (=launch operations) ***out of*** a place (port) ある場所(など)を根拠地にして行動を起す. ¶be *operated* ***under*** Dr. ... ドクトル...の手術を受ける. ¶The body *operates* very powerfully ***upon*** the soul both for good and evil. 身体は良くも悪くも精神に大なる影響を及ぼす. ‖ It has been found impossible, in view of his condition, to *operate* ***upon*** him. 彼の容体が容体なので手術を施すことは不可能と分かった.

operation, *n.* 動作, 作業; 運用, 運転; 手術; 施行, 実施; 有効期間; [しばしば *pl.*] 作戦.

V The company will soon ***begin*** *operations*. 会社は近々開業するだろう. ‖ We ***began*** *operations* at dawn. われわれは暁天作戦を開始した. ¶***carry*** (=***keep***) ***on*** *operation* 作戦を継続する. ¶The war temporarily ***closed*** the *operations* of the school. 戦争のためにその学校は一時休校をした. ¶The railway line has ***commenced*** *operations*. 鉄道が開通した. ¶***conduct*** *operations* on a large scale 大規模で作業をやる. ¶materially ***curtail*** the *operation* 事業を余ほど縮小する. ¶***expand*** one's *operation* 事業を拡張する. ¶***extend*** its *operations* to the Far East その事業を極東にまで広げる. ¶He ***had*** an *operation*. 彼は手術を受けた. ¶***inspect*** the actual *operation* 実況を調査する. ¶***perform*** an *operation* on (=upon) a patient 患者に手術を行う. 【類】***perform*** an *operation* under chloroform (クロロホルムをかけて) / The surgeon successfully ***performed*** the *operation*. / ***perform*** a difficult *operation* / In January, 1885, the first *operation* for appendicitis (虫垂炎) was ***performed*** at St. Luke's Hospital, Denver, Colorado. / ***perform*** a surgical *operation* on the rectum (直腸). ¶***reverse*** the *operation* その行動を逆にやる. ¶It cannot ***survive*** the *operation* of logical analysis. それは論理的分析の結果消滅してしまう. ¶***speed*** *operations* 仕事をはかどらせる. ¶***start*** the *operation* of ... ...の工作を開始する. 【類】***start*** mining *operation*. ¶***undergo*** an *operation* for appendicitis 虫垂炎の手術を受ける ‖ He ***underwent*** an *operation* for a liver trouble, and died under the knife. 彼は肝臓病の手術を受けてその手術中に死んだ. 【類】recovering from a surgical *operation* recently ***undergone*** at ...

Q the influence is in ***active*** *operation* その影響は積極的に働いている ‖ a line in ***active*** *operation* 開通している線路. ¶inspect the ***actual*** *operation* of ... ...の実際の作業を視察する. ¶***aggressive*** *operations* 攻撃的行動. ¶large-scale ***airborne*** (=***air-lift***) *operations* 大規模な空中輸送作業. ¶perform ***arithmetical*** *operations* 算術の運算をやる. ¶a ***brilliant*** *operation* 成功した大手術. ¶extend one's ***commercial*** *operations* in ... その商売を...に広げる. ¶the ***company's*** *operations* その会社の事業. ¶one ***continuous*** *operation* 流れ作業. ¶The University of Chicago has always been thought of as a model of ***economical*** *operation*. シカゴ大学は常に経済的経営の模範と考えられて来た. ¶***effective*** *operation* 効果的作業. ¶***electric*** *operation* 電気運転. ¶in ***full*** *operation*=in full swing 盛に活動して. ¶the four ***fundamental*** *operations* in arithmetic 算術の四則(加減乗除). ¶an ***illegal*** *operation* 不法な行動. ¶casualties arising from the ***Korean*** *operation* 朝鮮作戦中の死傷者. ¶a ***major*** (***minor***) *operation* 大(小)手術. ¶eliminate ***manual*** *operations* 手の仕事を不用にする. ¶***Military*** *operations* are taking place there. そこでは戦争をやっている. ¶mechanized ***mining*** *operations* 機械化した採鉱作業. ¶Such monopolies serve to restrict the ***natural*** *operation* of the law of supply and demand. こうした独占は需要供給の法則の自然的運行を阻止することになる. ¶***naval*** *operations* against the Russians 露軍に対する海軍の行動. ¶in ***one*** *operation* instead of four 四回でやったものを[ただの]一回で. ¶a ***painful*** *operation* 苦しい手術. ¶a ***remarkable*** *operation* 手際のよい手術. ¶after many months of ***salvage*** *operations* 引揚作業に幾月も費した後. ¶***scientific*** *operations* 科学的作業. ¶perform a ***slight*** *operation* on ... ...にちょっと手術を行う. ¶He has undergone a ***successful*** *operation* and is doing well. 彼はうまい手術を受けて経過良好である. ‖ keep the college in ***successful*** *operation* その大学を巧みに経営し続ける ‖ Vigorous action looking to the suppression of opium smoking is in ***successful*** *operation* in China. アヘン撲滅の大運動が中国で好成績をあげている. ¶a simple ***surgical*** *operation* 簡単な外科手術. ¶an ***unsuccessful*** *operation* to restore his sight 彼の失明を治そうとして不成功に終った手術.

Q² ***appendix*** *operation* 虫垂炎手術. ¶***Blackmarket*** *operations* were common. やみ取引は普通であった. 【類】He made millions of yen through ***black market*** *operations*. ¶***blasting*** *operations* 爆破作業 ‖ during ***blasting*** *operation* at a quarry 石切り場で火薬爆破の作業中. ¶***brick-burning*** *operations* れんが焼作業. ¶***building*** *operations* 建築作業. ¶***bullion*** *operations* 地金運用(外国貿易の際地金を運用して金融の円滑を謀る). ¶***capacity*** *operation* 全力操業. ¶a ***full-scale*** *operation* of a plant 工場の全面的操業. ¶***garden*** *operations* 園芸作業. ¶***guerrilla*** *operations* ゲリラ(遊撃)戦. ¶a ***land*** *operation* 陸地戦. ☞ land operation には「土地経営」の意もある. ¶***lightning*** *operation* 電撃作戦. ¶conduct ***mine-sweeping*** *operations* 水雷掃海作業を行う. ¶***mopping-up*** *operations* 掃海作業; 掃とう作戦. ¶***railway traffic*** *operation* 〘鉄道〙運転作業. ¶***rescue*** *operations* 救助作業. ¶***research*** *operations* in industry 工業の調査活動. ¶***rice processing*** *operations* 米穀加工作業. ¶***round-the-clock*** *operations* 二十四時間連続作戦. ¶***salvage*** *operations* [難破船・船荷の]引揚作業. ¶***Steel*** *operations* were down to 43.6 percent of capacity. 製鉄作業は全能力の 43.6 パーセントまで低下した. ¶the ***turnback*** *operation* of cars 〘鉄道〙車両の折返し運転. ¶Air superiority is the prerequisite of all ***war-winning*** *operations*. 制空はあらゆる戦勝工作中最も必要なものである. ¶be engaged in ***whaling*** *operations* in Antarctic waters 南氷洋に捕鯨作業に従事している.

P He died ***after*** an *operation* from appendicitis. 彼は盲腸炎の手術後死んだ. ¶***at*** one *operation* 一度の手術で ‖ do the necessary work ***at*** one *operation* 一作業ですませる. ¶***by*** *operation* of law 法律の運用によって. ¶a machine ***in*** *operation* 運転中の機械 ‖ A circulating library is ***in*** *operation* there. そこには巡回図書館がある. 【類】railways (=railway lines) ***in*** *operation* ‖ The plant is ***in*** full *operation*. その工場は全能力をあげて操業している. ‖ The school has now been ***in*** *operation* for several years. その学校は開校後五六年になる. ‖ ***in*** one *operation* 一挙に, 同時に. ¶bring rules ***into*** *operation* 規則を実施する. 【類】The orders will come ***into*** *operation* on the 15th inst. / The law has been put ***into*** *operation*. ¶the mode ***of*** *operation* やり方 ‖ a base ***of*** *operations* 作戦根拠地. ¶***on*** *operation* it was found that ... 手術して見たら...と分かった. ¶He was submitted ***to*** an *operation*. 彼は手術を受けた. ¶be ***under*** surgical *operation* 外科手術を受けている.

P² ships in *operation* ***between*** ... and ... ...と...間を航行している船. ¶the *operation* ***of*** a hotel (railroad) ホテル(など)の経営. ¶an *operation* ***on*** the abdomen (head) 腹部[(など)の手術.

operative, *a.* 働く, 動作する.

P That spirit is *operative* ***in*** every one of us. その精神はだれの心にでも働いている.

operator, *n.* 運用者, 技手; 仲買人.

V The political aspect ***causes*** *operators* on the Bourse to act with hesitation. 政治的様相が取引所の業者にちゅうちょする行動を取らせた.

Q² a ***blackmarket*** *operator* やみ業者. ¶a private ***bank*** *operator* 私立銀行経営者. ¶a ***chain stores*** *operator* 連鎖店経営者. ¶a ***coal*** *operator* 石炭業経営者. ¶a ***commercial air*** *operator* 商業航空業者. ¶an ***elevator*** *operator* エレベーター係. ¶a ***farm*** *operator* 農場経営者. ¶a ***filling station*** *operator* 給油所(自動車の)経営者. ¶a ***hotel*** *operator* ホテル経営者. ¶a ***kinema*** (=cinema) *operator* 撮影技師. ¶a ***land*** *operator* of Los Angeles ロスの土地経営者. ¶a big ***lumber*** *operator* 大木材経営者. ¶a ***lunch stand*** *operator* ランチ・スタンド経営者. ¶a ***machine*** *operator* 機械工. ¶a ***mimeograph*** *operator* 謄写版刷り屋. ¶a ***mine*** *operator* 鉱山経営者. ¶a ***telephone*** (=***phone***) *operator* 電話交換手. ¶a ***radio*** *operator* 無線技手; 放送技師 ‖ an amateur ***radio*** *operator*=a ham アマチュア無線通信者. ¶a ***realty*** *operator* 土地ブローカー. ¶a ***ship*** *operator* 船舶業経営者. ¶a ***shipping line*** *operator* 船舶航路経営者. ¶a ***switchboard*** *operator* 配電盤係; 《米》電話交換手. ¶a ***telephone*** *operator* 電話の交換手. ¶a ***train*** *operator* 列車運

転手. ¶a ***trolley-car operator*** 市内電車(登山電車)運転手. ¶CAA control of "***wildcat plane operators***" 無免許飛行士の民間飛行局 (Civil Aeronautics Authority) の統制.

operetta, *n.* 軽歌劇.

P[2] an *operetta* ***on*** the air 放送中の軽歌劇.

opinion, *n.* 意見, 説, 所見; 批判.

V ***accept*** an *opinion* overtly 公然と意見に賛成する. ¶***advance*** an *opinion* 意見を述べる. ¶Public *opinion* was greatly ***agitated.*** 世論ごうごうたるものがあった. ¶***air*** one's *opinion* その意見を述べる ‖ He ***aired*** a few moldy *opinions* about domestic ethics. 彼は家庭道徳について二三の陳腐な説をはいた. 【類】this extraordinary *opinion* was ***aired*** at a meeting of ... ¶This completely ***altered*** their *opinion.* これで彼らの説は一変した. ¶in order to ***arouse*** public *opinion* 世論を喚起するために. 【類】***arouse*** public *opinion* to the needs and benefits of self-containment / public *opinion* should be ***aroused*** to put an end to ... ¶I came to ***ask*** your *opinion* about it. 御意見を伺いに参りました. 【類】I ***asked*** his valued *opinion* upon ... ¶***base*** one's *opinion* on these facts これらの事実を基礎として自分の意見を立てる, 【類】the creation of an enlightened public *opinion,* ***based*** on accurate knowledge. ¶Experience does not seem to ***bear out*** their *opinion.* 経験に照らすとこの説は間違っているようだ. ¶it has ***called forth*** the following *opinions* from ... それによって次の説が...から出た. ¶***canvass*** the *opinions* of ... with regard to ... ...に関する...の意見を求める. ¶***change*** one's *opinion* 説を変える. ¶***cherish*** a poor *opinion* of one's abilities 自分は才能が乏しいと思う ‖ firmly and deliberately ***cherish*** the *opinion* that ... ...というしっかりした自信を持っている. ¶***combat*** an *opinion* 説を非難する. ¶***compromise*** one's *opinion* 意見を妥協する. ¶***conciliate*** public *opinion* 世論を緩和する. ¶***consult*** the best Japanese and foreign *opinions* 内外名士の意見をたたく. ¶They have diligently sought to ***control*** public *opinion* on the subject in their interest. その問題に関する世論を彼らのためになるようにしようと熱心に努力した. ¶***correct*** somewhat the erroneous *opinions* which have been current as to ... ...について行われている間違った説の幾分を訂正する. ¶***corroborate*** one's *opinion* その意見を裏書きする. ¶***countenance*** an *opinion* 説を援助する. ¶***create*** a saner public *opinion* さらに健全な世論を作る. ¶***crystallize*** public *opinion* 世論をまとめさせる. ¶He certainly was at no pains to ***cultivate*** or ***consult*** public *opinion.* 彼はたしかに与論を啓発したりこれに耳を傾けるようなことを少しもしなかった. ¶They ***debated*** their *opinions* with a warmth which would not disgrace a less austere-looking body. 一同はそれほどに謹厳でない団体においてすらその体面を傷つけることのないような熱誠をもって彼らの意見を戦わした. ¶***defend*** his *opinions* 彼の説を擁護する. ¶***deliver*** an offhand *opinion* 即席の意見を述べる. ¶***discard*** an *opinion* 考えを捨てる. ¶This *opinion* has not at present been conclusively ***disproved*** or ***refuted.*** この説は現在決定的に否認ないし反ばくされてはいない. ¶a matter on which *opinions* are ***divided*** 意見まちまちな問題. 【類】*opinion* is ***divided*** among those who have studied this condition as to ... / *opinion* is ***divided*** in Japan as to whether ... or not. ¶***dominate*** public *opinion* 世論を支配する. ¶***earn*** golden *opinions* among ... for ... ...に対し...の間に絶賛を博する. ¶It ***echoes*** the *opinion* of the best observers. それは最もすぐれた観察者の説を反映している. ‖ In saying so, I am only ***echoing*** in essence the *opinions* of most positive authorities on the subject. かく言う私はこの問題について最も確実な大家の説を本質的に反響しているにすぎない. ¶***educate*** public *opinion* on (=regarding *or* as to) this subject (in this matter) この問題(など)について世論を指導する. ¶***elicit*** the *opinions* of ... ...の意見を徴する. 【類】***elicit*** *opinions* on the subject from ... ¶petitions ***embodying*** such *opinions* as these were presented to ... 大体こうした意見の嘆願書が...に提出された. ¶***embrace*** a like *opinion* 同様な意見を抱く. ¶***enlarge*** an *opinion* 意見を敷延する. ¶***entertain*** an *opinion* 意見を持つ. ¶After ***exchanging*** our intimate *opinions* we became friendlier. お互いに腹蔵ない意見を交換してからわれわれは一層親密になった. 【類】***exchange*** *opinions* with ... on ... ¶***excite*** public *opinion* 世論を刺激する. ¶We cannot ***expect*** an unbiassed *opinion* from the rivals. 競争者たちからは公平な意見を期待し得ない. ¶It is very bold of us to venture to ***express*** an *opinion* on such a matter. こうしたことに意見を述べようとするのはわれわれとして大胆きわまる. ‖ someone competent to ***express*** an *opinion* in regard to ... ...方面の専門家. 【類】Many *opinions* have been ***expressed*** on this subject. / he further ***expressed*** the *opinion* that ... / ***express*** one's individual *opinion* (私見) / ***express*** an *opinion* on some matter of public interest / I hardly dare ***express*** an *opinion.* / the *opinion* is often ***expressed*** that ... / We ***express*** no *opinion* about (=as to) the wisdom or unwisdom or effectiveness or ineffectiveness of the measure. / ***express*** an *opinion* in writing on ... (文書をもって) / the *opinion* is ***expressed*** in political circles that ... ¶***form*** *opinions* 説を立てる ‖ I cannot ***form*** an *opinion* either way. 私はどちとも考えを定めかねる. 【類】We are in a position to ***form*** an *opinion.* / those who are in the best position to ***form*** an *opinion* / He is incompetent (= in no position) to ***form*** any *opinion* on the matter. / they are old enough to ***form*** *opinions* respecting ... / help in ***forming*** the *opinion* of the public / ***form*** one's own *opinions* on all kinds of things / ***form*** *opinions* based, not on the facts, but on somebody else's view of the facts / I ***formed*** a high *opinion* of his capacity. / I do not think that sufficient ground for ***forming*** an *opinion.* ¶***formulate*** an *opinion* as to ... ...について意見を立てる. ‖ ***formulate*** certain *opinions* regarding ... ...に関してある説を立てる. 【類】his *opinion* ***formulated*** in a report. ¶***gather*** someone's *opinion* だれかの意見を徴する. 【類】***gather*** various *opinions* on ... ¶***get*** one's *opinions* from books (talk) 書物(話)によってその意見を立てる ‖ ***give*** one's *opinion* on ... ...について意見を発表する ‖ he ***gave*** his *opinion* that ... 彼は...という意見を述べた. 【類】I am not qualified to ***give*** an *opinion* on the matter. / I was asked to ***give*** an *opinion* on it. / ***give*** one's written *opinion* on the subject (文書で). ¶***ground*** one's *opinion* on the fact that ... その意見を...という事実に基づいて述べる. ¶The majority of them ***have*** no *opinion* at all. 彼らの大多数は全然意見を持っていない. 【類】You and I ***have*** different *opinions* on that subject. ¶***hazard*** an *opinion* on the subject その問題に関して大胆に意見を述べる. 【類】one might ***hazard*** the *opinion* that ... ¶They utilized his presence to ***hear*** his *opinion* on the subject. 彼らは彼の出席を利用してその問題について意見を聞いた. ¶those who ***hold*** this *opinion* この説を主張する人々. 【類】I ***hold*** that *opinion.* / we venture to ***hold*** that *opinion* ***on*** in spite of ... / ***hold*** an *opinion* of one's own (自分独自の考え). ¶***impose*** one's *opinion* on ... ...にその説を押付ける. ¶***influence*** [the] public *opinion* 世論を左右する ‖ ***influence*** *opinion* against ... ...の意見を動かしてそれに反対させる. ¶converse and ***interchange*** *opinions* 会談して意見を交換する. ¶if it is permissible to ***interpolate*** a personal *opinion,* I may say that ... 自分一個の意見をはさむことができるなら私は...と言おう. ¶***intrude*** one's *opinion* (=view) upon others 人に自分の意見を押しつける. ¶***invite*** the *opinions* of scientists on the subject その問題に関して科学者の意見を徴する. ¶There is, however, no evidence to ***justify*** such an *opinion.* しかしそんな説を正しいとすべき何らの証左もない. ¶You may ***keep*** your *opinion,* and I'll keep mine. 意見の点では君は君僕は僕だ. ‖ Let him ***keep*** his own *opinion.* 彼に逆らわないでおけ. ¶We ***know*** your *opinion* on that matter. 私たちはその問題に対するあなたの意見を承知している. ¶***lead*** public *opinion* towards ... 世論を...の方へ導く. ¶***let*** his *opinions* ***crystallize*** 彼の説を固定させる. ¶***lose*** the good *opinion* of the world 列国から排斥される. ¶***mold*** public *opinion* through the press 新聞によって世論を作る. ¶***mold*** and ***guide*** and ***vitalize*** public *opinion* 世論を作り指導しかつこれに生気を与える. ¶public *opinion* has been ***moved*** by ... 世論は...のために動かされた. ¶***obtain*** his *opinion* as to ... ...に関する彼の説を聞く. 【類】***obtain*** the *opinion* of high authority on ... ¶***offer*** an *opinion* to ... ...に対して意見を述べる. 【類】I have no *opinion* to ***offer.*** / He is exceptionally well qualified to ***offer*** an *opinion.* / ***offer*** as a counsel (忠告として) to others an *opinion* which ... / We are not inclined to ***offer*** any *opinion* on that point. / outsiders cannot ***offer*** an *opinion* upon ... ¶I wish to ***pass*** no *opinion* on (=as to) ... 私は...について意

見を述べたくない. 【類】I do not find it easy to agree with the *opinion* ***passed*** by ... upon ... ¶***press*** (=***force***) *opinions* upon ... ...に意見を押付ける. ¶highly ***prize*** America's good *opinion* 米国の好評を大いに有難がる. ¶the need of ***producing*** an educated public *opinion* 教育ある人々の世論を作り出すことの必要. ¶***proffer*** an *opinion* 意見を述べる. ¶best qualified to ***pronounce*** an *opinion* on the subject その問題に関して意見を述べる最もよい資格のある. 【類】before ***pronouncing*** any *opinion* it would be wise to ... ¶***propound*** an *opinion* 説を立てる. ¶***publish*** one's *opinions* その意見を公表する. ¶***put forth*** an *opinion* 意見を提出する. ¶I can find nothing in it to induce me to ***qualify*** the *opinion* I have already expressed on his book. 私が彼の本に関してすでに述べた意見を変えねばならないような誘因をその中に見出し得ない. ¶***quote*** an *opinion* ある説を引用する. ¶I shall be glad to ***receive*** your *opinion* on the subject of ... 私は...の問題について君の意見を拝聴したい. 【類】This *opinion* must be ***received*** with caution. ¶***reconcile*** conflicting *opinions* 異論を調和させる. ¶***reflect*** the *opinion* of considerably large sections of the community 社会の大部分の意見を反映する. 【類】This decision truly ***reflected*** the desires and *opinions* of the overwhelming majority of the Russian laboring people. ¶That is an *opinion* which may almost be ***regarded*** as extinct. それはほとんど死滅したと見てよい説である. 【類】His *opinions* have long been ***regarded*** as authoritative. ¶***reject*** his *opinion* 彼の説を排撃する. ¶***render*** their *opinions* 彼らの説を吐く. ¶***represent*** majority *opinion* 多数者の意見を代表する. ¶one whose *opinion* I ***respect*** その説を私が尊重する人. ¶***reverence*** the *opinion* of ... の説を尊重する. ¶***reverse*** one's *opinion* 説を翻す. ¶***revolutionize*** the *opinion* on ... ...に関する説を一変させる. ¶***rouse*** public *opinion* for (against) a policy 政策に対して賛成(反対)の世論を喚起する. ¶my *opinion* was ***sought*** as to ... ...について私の意見を徴された. ¶***set up*** (=***establish***) a new *opinion* 新説を立てる. ¶*opinion* is not definitely ***settled*** as to ... ...についてまだ意見が確定していない. ¶try to ***shake*** his *opinion* 彼の意見をぐらつかせようと努める. 【類】***shook*** the *opinion* I had previously entertained. ¶I fully ***share*** your *opinion*. 私は全く君と同意見だ. 【類】I ***share*** on this point the *opinion* of ... ¶***sound*** [***out***] a person's *opinion* 人の意見をたたく. ¶***state*** one's *opinion* freely and forcibly 意見を十分にかつ力強く述べる. ¶***stir up*** public *opinion* 世論を喚起する. ¶***summarize*** the *opinions* of others from periodicals or books 雑誌や本にでた他人の説を概括する. ¶He was called upon to ***supply*** an *opinion*. 彼は意見を徴された. ¶seem to ***support*** that *opinion* その説を支持するように見える. ¶They were made to ***swallow*** *opinions* handed down from on high by authority. 彼らは天降り式の意見をうのみにさせられた. 【類】***swallow*** an *opinion* as offered. ¶***sway*** (=lead) public *opinion* 世論を指導する. ¶***swing*** (=shake) public *opinion* 世論を動かす. ¶***take*** the *opinion* of the members as to the desirability of ... ...の可否について会員の意見を徴する. ¶***Tell*** (=Give) me your *opinion* of (=on) it. それについての君の説を聞かしてくれ給え. ¶***treat*** one's *opinions* lightly その説を軽くあしらう. ¶***utter*** *opinions* 説を述べる. ¶contrary to *opinions* recently ***ventilated*** in the newspapers 近ごろ新聞に現われた説と反対に. ¶he ***ventured*** the *opinion* that ... 彼は...でもあろうかと言った. 【類】I will not ***venture*** an *opinion* upon it. / I do not hesitate in ***venturing*** the *opinion* that ... ¶One who is deputed to ***voice*** the *opinions* of others is called a spokesman. 他人を代表して意見を述べる人を代弁者という. 【類】I'm in no position to ***voice*** any *opinion* of my own about it. / ***voice*** (=***mention***) one's *opinion* as to ... / The *Kokumin* and the *Asahi* ***voice*** similar *opinions*. ¶***volunteer*** an *opinion* 進んで意見を述べる. ¶this *opinion* is further ***warranted*** by the fact that ... この説はさらに...という事実によって裏書されている. ¶***weigh*** every *opinion* impartially あらゆる説を一々公平に比較考量する. ¶***wish*** an expert *opinion* upon one's purchase その買物について専門家の意見を希望する. ¶he has ***won*** golden *opinions* among ... as ... 彼は...の間に...として絶賛を博した ‖ ***win*** the good *opinion* of ... ...の好評を博する.

v² Since then *opinion* has ***altered***. その後人の考え方が変った. ¶the *opinions* ***divide*** on the question of ... ...の問題に関して意見がまちまちである. ¶As to its origin, *opinions* ***differ***. その起源については説が一定していない. ¶there ***exists*** an *opinion* that ... ...という説がある. ¶some [*opinions*] ***hold*** that ... ある人は...と主張する. ¶Learned *opinion* ***inclines*** more and more to the recognition of their truth. 識者間にはますますそれらの真実なることを認める傾向がある. ¶Our *opinions* always ***jar***. われわれの考はいつも合わない. ¶public *opinion* ***objects*** to ... 世論は...に反対である. ¶an *opinion* ***prevailed*** that ... ...という説が流行した. 【類】an *opinion* ***prevails*** that ... ¶this *opinion* stated that ... この説は...と述べている. ¶*Opinion* is ***traveling*** in that direction. 世論はその動向をたどっている. ‖ *Opinion*, particularly on economic matters, has ***travelled*** a long way in the last few years. 殊に経済については世人の考えがここ二三年間に大分進んだ.

Q an ***abdicated*** *opinion* 人に捨てられた説. ¶contrary to the generally ***accepted*** *opinion* 一般に容認されている説と反対に. ¶***accidental*** *opinion* 付帯的な説. ¶***advanced*** *opinions* 進んだ説. ¶***adverse*** *opinions* 反対意見. ¶one entitled to an ***authoritative*** *opinion* on the subject その問題に関する権威者. ¶give one a ***candid*** *opinion* 公平な説をその人に述べる. 【類】those who wish to form a ***candid*** *opinion* on this question. ¶***civilized*** *opinion* 文化的意見. ¶it is a ***common*** *opinion* that ... ...ということは一般の説である. ¶***confirmatory*** *opinions* それを確かめる意見. ¶there is little ***conflicting*** *opinion* concerning ... ...に関して意見の衝突はほとんどない ‖ *Opinions* on this point are very ***conflicting***. この点に関する説には異論が多い. ¶His *opinion* was quite of the ***contrary***. 彼は全く意見が反対であった. 【類】two ***contrary*** *opinions* as current in his day. ¶ask one for a ***critical*** *opinion* on ... ...に関して人に批判を求める. ¶***crude*** *opinions* 未熟な意見. ¶***crude*** and ***ill-informed*** *opinions* 生硬で見聞の狭い意見. ¶***cut-and-dried*** *opinions* 味もそっ気もないおきまりの意見. ¶have no ***decided*** *opinion* 決定した考えをもたない. ¶the spread of ***dangerous*** *opinions* 危険な説の横行. ¶it is one of my ***decided*** *opinions* that ... ...ということは私の定説の一つである. ¶a ***determined*** *opinion* 確定意見. ¶I was of a ***different*** *opinion* a few years back. 私は二三年前はそれと違った考えをしていた. ¶despite a few ***discordant*** *opinions* 二三の反対説はあるが. ¶a ***dissenting*** *opinion* 異論, 異説. ¶hold ***divergent*** *opinions* まちまちの意見 ‖ On this point *opinions* are ***divergent***. この点に関して意見の一致を欠いている. ¶a ***dominant*** *opinion* 有力な意見. ¶a ***dominating*** *opinion* 支配的な意見. ¶***editorial*** *opinions* 新聞の論調. ¶an ***educated*** *opinion* 教育ある人士の説. ¶an ***enlightened*** *opinion* そう明な意見. ¶have an ***exaggerated*** *opinion* of ... ...を買かぶる. ¶an ***extreme*** *opinion* 極端な意見. ¶I have a ***favorable*** *opinion*. 私は好意的な考えを持つ. ¶***fearless*** *opinions* 思い切った意見. ¶recant one's ***first*** *opinion* 初めの意見を取消す. ¶He had no ***fixed*** *opinion* on the question. 彼はその問題に付いて一定した考えがなかった. ¶the ***formal*** *opinions* of the Attorney General issued during the year その年発表された法務長官の正式意見. ¶the general substratum of ***foreign*** *opinion* 外国の意見の根底. 【類】***foreign*** *opinion* is well-nigh unanimous in recommending ... ¶give one's ***frank*** and ***full*** *opinion* in the question asked 尋ねられた問題に関して率直で思う存分の説を述べる. ¶a ***general*** *opinion* 一般の説. 【類】The ***general*** *opinion* was that peace would soon be concluded. ¶win ***golden*** *opinions* from all classes あらゆる階級から大評判を取る. ¶have a ***good*** (poor) *opinion* of the market 市場を楽(悲)観する. 【類】lose the ***good*** *opinion* of the world ‖ You have a ***good*** *opinion* of yourself. 君はうぬぼれている. ¶a ***hackneyed*** *opinion* 陳腐な意見. ¶a ***hastily-formed*** *opinion* 軽卒な意見. ¶He has an unutterably ***high*** *opinion* of himself. 彼は非常に自分をえらく思っている. 【類】I have a ***high*** *opinion* of his works. / express a ***high*** *opinion* of ... ¶give one's ***honest*** *opinion* その正直な意見を述べる. ¶Let me offer my ***humble*** *opinion*. 愚見を述べさして下さい. ¶public *opinion* would be ***indignant*** at ... ...に対し世論が沸騰するだろう. ¶This, of course, is simply an ***individual*** *opinion*. もちろんこれは一家言に過ぎない. 【類】I was untrained to take such an important step on an ***individ-***

ual opinion. ¶ ***influential*** *opinion* 有力な説. ¶The last disease on which a priest can form an ***intelligent*** *opinion* is insanity. 精神錯乱について正しい判断を下すには坊さんが一番不適当だ. ¶ ***journalistic*** *opinion* 新聞記者の説. ¶a ***judicial*** *opinion* 裁判所の見解. ¶It is no easy matter to form a ***just*** *opinion* on him. 彼を正しく判断することは容易なことではない. ¶The ***legal*** *opinion* is favorable (unfavorable). 法律上の説は有(不)利です. 【類】The ***legal*** *opinion* is against us. ¶He is of the ***like*** *opinion.* 彼も同じ説だ. ¶he has a ***low*** *opinion* of ... 彼は...を軽べつしている. 【類】convey one's excessively ***low*** *opinion* of ... ¶He had always had rather a ***mean*** *opinion* of his master. 彼は主人をいつも少し安っぽく思っていた. ¶ ***medical*** *opinion* seems to be agreed that ... ...ということには医家の説が一致しているようだ. 【類】Let us see what ***medical*** *opinion* is on this question. ¶a matter of ***mere personal*** *opinion* ほんの一個人の考え. ¶a man of ***moderate*** *opinions* 穏健な考えの人. ¶This is merely ***my own*** *opinion.* これは私一個人の考えに過ぎない. ¶The ***old*** *opinion* that ... is dead. ...という昔からの説はもうすたれている. ¶There was but ***one*** *opinion* in Court. 朝廷では衆議が一致していた. ¶arouse widely ***opposing*** *opinions* 広く反対説を喚起する. ¶hold quite an ***opposite*** *opinion* 全然反対の意見を持つ. ¶in ***outworn*** *opinion* 古い考えで. ¶ ***orthodox*** *opinions* 正統派の説. ¶prohibit the circulation of ***pernicious*** *opinions* 危険思想の普及を禁じる. ¶be unable to form a ***personal*** *opinion* in regard to ... ...に関し私見を立てることができない ‖ make a statement simply as an expression of ***personal*** *opinion* 単に一個人の意見発表として説をなす. ¶in the face of ***pessimistic*** *opinions* 悲観論が唱えられるにもかかわらず. ¶His views molded ***political*** *opinion* in England. 彼の考えが英国の政見をまとめた. ¶I have a ***poor*** *opinion* of him. 私はあの人を感心しない. ‖ he has a ***poor*** *opinion* upon ... 彼は...に不賛成である. ¶study postwar ***public*** *opinion* 戦後の世論を研究する. ¶His ideas on the subject are distorted by ***preconceived*** *opinions* and auto-suggestions. その問題に関する彼の考えは先入思想や自己暗示でゆがんでいる. ¶a ***premature*** *opinion* 未熟な意見. ¶the ***prevailing*** *opinion* 世上流布の説. ¶the *opinion* was ***prevalent*** among ... that ... ...という説が...の間にはやっていた. ¶ ***pro-Japanese*** *opinions* 親日的な意見. ¶moulders of ***public*** *opinion* 世論を作る人人 ‖ a reversal of ***public*** *opinion* 世論の逆転 ‖ an informed ***public*** *opinion* 知識階級の世論 ‖ poll ***public*** *opinion* [紙上で]世論調査をやる. ¶They have ***public*** *opinion* behind it. その背後に世論がある. 【類】a powerful ***public*** *opinion* in favor of ... / ***public*** *opinion* has not yet been sufficiently aroused to demand it. / ***Public*** *opinion* is divided on the question. / the final vote of ***public*** *opinion* was given against ... / offend ***public*** *opinion.* ¶it is a commonly ***received*** *opinion* that ... ...ということは一般に受入れられている説である. ¶his ***religious*** *opinions* 彼の宗教上の意見. ¶Are you of the ***same*** *opinion*? あなたも同じお考えですか. ¶ ***scientific*** *opinion* is far from being unanimous as to ... ...について科学者の説が決して一致していない. 【類】***scientific*** *opinion* seems to regard it as ... ¶a ***second-hand*** *opinion* 受け売り説. ¶a ***sensible*** *opinion* 賢明な説. ¶I have no ***settled*** *opinion* about it. 私はそれについて定説がない. ‖ form ***settled*** *opinions* 定説を立てる. ¶ ***social*** *opinion* 世人の考え. ¶People are gradually learning to form ***sound*** *opinions* about these matters. 世人はこれらのことについて漸次しっかりした説を立てるようになって来た. 【類】form a ***sound*** *opinion* on public questions. ¶ ***superficial popular*** *opinion* 皮相的な一般人の説. ¶to form a ***true*** *opinion* on this question it is necessary to ... この問題について本当の説を立てるには...することが必要だ. ¶there can be no ***two*** *opinions* as to ... ...について異論のありようはずはない. ¶his ***unbiased*** *opinion* 中正な意見. ¶Those who see the Englishman only in town are apt to form an ***unfavorable*** *opinion* of his social character. 英国人を都会でしか見ていない人は彼の社交的性格に付て香しくない考えをいだく傾向がある. ¶lack of a ***unified public*** *opinion* 世論の不一致. ¶a ***vague*** and ***wavering*** *opinion* ばく然としてまとまらない意見. ¶expert *opinion* is very ***variable*** as to ... ...に関する専門家の説は実にまちまちである. ¶people of ***various*** *opinions* 意見のまちまちの人たち. ¶form a ***well-grounded*** *opinion* しっかりした根拠のある説を立てる. ¶form and sustain a ***wholesome public*** *opinion* 健全な世論を作りこれを支持する. ¶there is a ***wide-spread*** *opinion* that ... ...という説が広く世に行われている. ¶the creation of a ***wide spread healthy public*** *opinion* 広はんにして健全な世論の喚起. ¶form a ***wrong*** *opinion* of ... ...について間違った考え方をする.

Q² in an ***eight-page*** *opinion* 八ページにわたる意見の発表において. ¶give ***expert*** *opinion* on ... ...について専門的意見を述べる ‖ a written ***expert*** *opinion* 鑑定書. 【類】obtain their ***expert*** *opinion* / Such an ***expert*** *opinion* will settle the matter. ¶represent ***majority*** *opinion* 多数意見を示す. ¶ ***mass*** *opinion* 大衆の意見. ¶ ***press*** *opinions* on the problem その問題に関する新聞の社説. ¶ ***student*** *opinion* 学生の考え. ¶in ***world*** *opinion* 世界の世論において. ¶rally ***world*** *opinion* against ... ...反対の世界の世論を喚起する. 【類】***World*** *opinion* is friendly to us. ‖ ***world public*** *opinion* 世界の公論.

P ***according to*** my *opinion* 私の意見では. ¶he gives it ***as*** his *opinion* that ... 彼は...を自分の考えとして述べている. ¶He halted for a time ***between*** the two *opinions.* 彼はしばらくその二説の中間に立っていた. ¶ ***in*** my *opinion* 私の考えでは ‖ ***in*** the *opinion* of some persons ある人々の考えでは ‖ ***in*** the *opinion* of those best able to judge 最もよく判断しうる人々の考えでは ‖ differ (=vary) ***in*** *opinion* 意見が相違する. ¶I am ***of*** *opinion* that ... 私は...という意見だ ‖ I am not ***of*** their *opinion.* 私はあの人たちには賛成していない. 【類】I personally am ***of*** the *opinion* that ... / we are very decidedly ***of*** the *opinion* that ... / he is strongly ***of*** the *opinion* that ... / he is, rightly (それは正しいのであるが), of *opinion* that ... / they almost unanimously (ほとんど全部が) ***of*** *opinion* that ... ‖ a matter concerning which there is no unanimity ***of*** *opinion* 少しも意見の一致が見られない事柄 ‖ men and women of all shades ***of*** *opinion* 色々と考えを異にしている男女 ‖ A variety ***of*** *opinions* have been expressed. 色々な意見が述べられた. 【類】there is much diversity (多種多様) ***of*** *opinion* as to ... / there were differences ***of*** *opinion* among ... / there is a consensus (一致) ***of*** *opinion* as regards ... / The consensus ***of*** *opinion* seems to tend that way. / That is not a matter ***of*** *opinion*, but of recorded fact. / it is the *opinion* ***of*** the writer that ... ¶stick ***to*** one's *opinion* その説を固持する ‖ act up ***to*** one's opinion 自分の意見通りに行動する.

P² an *opinion* ***about*** a matter or person 事柄または人についての意見. ¶Such was the trend of public *opinion* ***at*** the time. 当時の世論はこういった傾向のものであった. ¶ *opinions* ***from*** prominent business men on our trade opportunity わが国の商機に関する有名な実業家たちの意見. ¶in the *opinion* ***of*** the world 世間の評判では. ¶a history of *opinions* ***on*** the question その問題に関する批判史. ¶an *opinion* ***to*** the contrary=a contrary opinion 反対意見. 【類】in spite of popular *opinion* ***to*** the contrary.

opium, *n.* アヘン. 「吸う.

V ***eat*** *opium* アヘンを飲む(液体). ¶ ***smoke*** *opium* アヘンを

O an *opium* eater (smoker) アヘン常用者 ‖ an *opium* den アヘンくつ.

opponent, *n.* 反対者, 敵手, 相手.

V ***attack*** an *opponent* instead of his argument 反対者の議論でなくその人を攻撃する. ¶ ***beat*** an *opponent* at an election 選挙で対抗馬を負かす. 【類】He was elected to the Sixty-eighth Congress having ***beaten*** his *opponent*, H.W.I. McCormick, with a majority of 9,900 votes. ¶ ***condemn*** one's *opponent* 反対者を非難する. ¶ ***corner*** an *opponent* in an argument 反対者をやりこめる. ¶In size and appearance he ***dwarfed*** his *opponents.* 彼は風さい堂々としていて相手を圧倒した. ¶ ***floor*** (=***defeat***) an *opponent* in an argument 議論で相手をやっつける. ¶They easily ***outstripped*** their *opponents.* 彼らは容易にその敵手を抜いた. ¶ ***pulverize*** (=***demolish***) an *opponent* 敵手を粉砕する. ¶ ***refute*** one's *opponent* 相手を論ばくする. ¶ ***score*** an *opponent* in a debate 討論で相手に勝つ. ¶ ***talk*** an *opponent* ***down*** 弁舌で敵手をへこます. ¶He ***tore*** the *opponent's* argument to pieces (=tatters). 彼は完膚なきまでに相手の議論を粉砕した. ¶ ***treat*** one's *opponents* with perfect fairness and respect 競争相手を全く公平に敬意をもって遇する.

Q a better opponent 一層好い敵手. ¶a bitter opponent 骨の折れる相手. ¶be a determined opponent of … …のがん強な敵手である. ¶a fearless opponent 大胆な敵手. ¶a firm opponent of the view その見解をあくまで論難する人. ¶a formidable opponent 恐ろしい敵手. ¶his great opponent 彼の大敵. ¶ostensible opponents 表面だけの敵手. ¶a political opponent 政敵. ¶a most powerful opponent きわめて強力な相手. ¶a stout opponent がん強な相手. ¶a strenuous opponent of the Bill その議案のがん強な反対者. ¶an undesirable opponent in a contest 競争の苦手. ¶a vigorous opponent 威勢のよい相手. ¶He had a worthy opponent. 相手に不足はなかった.

P it is argued by the opponents of the innovation that … この革新に反対する者は…と論じている. ¶an opponent in a fight 闘争の相手.

opportune, *a.* 都合のよい, 好時機の.

P particularly opportune at this time when … …なるこの時に際しことに時宜に適した. ¶the present is most opportune for … 今は…に最も都合がよい. 【類】Time was opportune for making a start.

opportunity, *n.* 機会, 時機, 時宜.

V accept opportunities 機会に乗じる. ¶afford an opportunity for … …に対して機会を与える. 【類】afford (=give) an opportunity of … / afford the foreign tourist an opportunity to see some of Japan's rural life. ¶allow an opportunity to pass=let an opportunity slip 機会を逸する. ¶I appreciate this opportunity to voice my best wishes and greetings to all of you. 私は今あなた方皆様に私の心をこめた厚意とごあいさつを申述べる機会を得たことをうれしく存じます. ¶I await with pleasure an opportunity to reciprocate. 私は喜んでそれに報いる機会を待っています. ¶balk an opportunity 機会をむだにする. ¶choose a good opportunity 好機をとらえる. ¶cultivate an opportunity 機会を作る. ¶seriously curtail the opportunities of … 余ほど…の機会を少なくする. ¶dally away one's opportunities ぐずぐずして機会を失う. ¶demand equal opportunities 機会均等を要求する. ¶those who have been denied college opportunities 大学に入る機会を与えられなかった人人. ¶embrace an opportunity 機会に乗じる. ¶enlarge one's opportunities 機会を大ならしむ. ¶equalize educational opportunities 教育上の機会の範囲を広げる. ¶find ample opportunity in … …するに十分な機会を見出す. 【類】whenever he found the opportunity. ¶forgo an opportunity of … …する機会を捨てる. ¶it forms a fitting opportunity for … それは…に適する機会になる. ¶furnish an excellent opportunity for … …に好機会を与える. ¶give college graduates an opportunity to review the studies of earlier years 大学卒業生に既往の研究を復習する機会を与える ‖ give greater opportunity for advancement to commercial employees 商店員にもっと昇進の機会を与える ‖ without giving any opportunities for complaints 何ら苦情を持出す機会を与えないで ‖ give rare opportunity to … …にめったにない好機会を与える. ¶The association is grasping this opportunity. 同協会はこの機会をとらえつつある. 【類】combine a Frenchwoman's talent for business with the American ability to grasp an opportunity. ¶have an opportunity of studying (=to study) … …を研究する機会をもつ. 【類】He had no opportunity of displaying his genius. / I did see him, but I had not the opportunity to speak with him. ¶improve the opportunity of … to … …の機会を利用して…する. ¶I cannot let the opportunity pass to make an ironical comment on … 私はこの機会を利用して…に対して皮肉な批評を加えることにする. 【類】let no opportunity pass of doing … …する機会を逃がすな. ¶let slip (=let go) a golden opportunity 絶好の機会を逃す. ¶His opportunities for … were extremely limited. 彼の…する機会はきわめて少なかった. ¶I never lose an opportunity of doing … 私は…する機会を決してのがさない. 【類】I lost no opportunity to … / He loses no opportunity of expressing his antagonism. ‖ an opportunity not to be lost 失うべからざる機会. ¶She never missed an opportunity of being kind to him. 彼女は機会あるごとに彼に親切にした. 【類】Would it not be a pity to miss the opportunity? / miss a great opportunity. ¶muddle away one's opportunities その機会を空しく逃す. ¶neglect no opportunity of … …の機会を少しも等閑にしない. 【類】they should neglect no opportunity to … ¶offer golden opportunities 絶好の機会を与える. 【類】offer great opportunities for … ¶omit no opportunity of social service 機会を逸せず社会奉仕をやる. ¶open an unequalled opportunity to … …のまたとない機会を与える. ¶overlook the opportunity of … …の機会を逃す. ¶The River Thames presents to Londoners endless opportunities for day and week-end trips. テムズ河はロンドン人に日帰り遠足や週末旅行の機会を無限に与える. ¶provide an opportunity for … to … …に…する機会を与える. 【類】Leisure merely provides an opportunity for free choice. / provide a splendid opportunity for … ¶in this he saw his opportunity to … 彼は機至れりとして…した. ¶seek a favorable opportunity for … …に対する好機会を求める. ¶immediately seize the opportunity of doing (=to do) … 直ちに…する機会をとらえる. 【類】seize an opportunity of … / eagerly seize an opportunity / seize the excellent opportunity afforded by … ¶take this opportunity of thanking … for … この機会において…に…を感謝する. 【類】I may take this opportunity of stating that … / taking every opportunity available. ¶The student used his time and opportunity wisely. その学生はその時と機会を賢明に使用した. ¶utilize the opportunity その機会を利用する. ¶wait opportunity to … …する機会を待つ. ¶The opportunity must not be wasted in idleness. いたずらにこの機会を逸してはならない. ¶watch one's opportunity to … …する機会をねらう. ¶we welcome this opportunity to state that … われわれはこの機会を幸い…と述べたい.

V² as often as opportunity allows 機会の許す限りひん繁に. ¶whenever the opportunity arises (=presents itself) その機会あるごとに. ¶The opportunity has not yet arrived. 時節がまだ到来しない. ¶I think the opportunity has gone. 機会は去ったと思う. ¶Act promptly, or the opportunity will be gone. 敏活にしなければ機会は去ってしまう. ¶if opportunity occurs 機会があれば ‖ should an opportunity occur 機会があったら. 【類】whenever opportunity occurs (=offers). ¶The opportunity has passed away. その機会は過ぎてしまった. ¶The opportunities to do so are not wanting. そうする機会はないことはない. ¶Once an opportunity slips away, it is gone for good and ever. 好機一度逸すれば永久に去って帰らない.

Q he has abundant opportunity for … 彼は…する機会が多い ‖ have abundant opportunities to do so そうする機会は幾らでもある. ¶an ample opportunity was afforded for … …する機会が十分与えられた. 【類】the writer has had ample opportunity to observe … / there is ample opportunity for … ¶miss the best opportunity 最善の機会を失う. ¶offer boundless opportunities 限りない機会を与える. ¶Trade opportunities are bright. 商売は好況である. ¶a capital opportunity 絶好の機会. ¶find a convenient opportunity 好機を見つける. ¶at the earliest opportunity機会のあり次第. ¶equal commercial opportunities 商業上の機会均等. ¶seize every opportunity to … あらゆる機会をとらえて…する. ¶offer excellent opportunities for … …に好機会を与える. ¶Every man shall have a fair opportunity to make the best of himself. だれでも自己を最も向上させる公平な機会を与えられるべきである. ¶seize a favorable opportunity for pleading with a person for … 好機をとらえて…を人に嘆願する ‖ if a favorable opportunity presents itself まがよければ. 【類】deem this a favorable opportunity for … / seek a favorable opportunity for … ¶at the first opportunity 機会のあり次第. ¶a fit opportunity for … …に対する適切な機会. ¶he will have the fullest opportunity of … 彼は…の十分な機会があるだろう. ¶a glorious opportunity 絶好の機会. ¶this seems to be a golden opportunity for … これは…の好機会らしく思われる. 【類】thinking this a golden opportunity to … / miss a golden opportunity. ¶there is a good opportunity to … …する好機がある. 【類】when a good opportunity arises. ¶a grand opportunity すばらしい機会. ¶The opportunities are great. 機会は多い. ¶He has had intimate opportunities to acquaint himself with foreigners. 彼は外国人に親しく接する機会があった. ¶They have

little opportunity for obtaining education. 彼らは教育を受ける機会がほとんどない. ¶the ***looked-for opportunity*** その待ちに待った機会. ¶a ***lost opportunity*** 失った機会. ¶he had not ***much opportunity*** of doing ... 彼は...する機会があまりなかった. ¶a ***past opportunity*** 過ぎ去った機会. ¶He has had very ***poor opportunity*** for education. 彼は教育を受ける機会がはなはだ乏しかった. ¶a ***precious opportunity*** 貴重な機会. ¶This is a ***rare opportunity***. これは千載一遇である. 【類】have the ***rare*** and ***precious opportunity*** to ... ¶a ***real*** money-making ***opportunity*** 本当に金もうけになる機会. ¶persons to whom ***regular educational opportunities*** are denied 正規の教育を受ける機会のない人人. ¶a ***rich opportunity*** 豊富な機会. ¶there are ***scanty opportunities*** for ... ...する機会が乏しい. ¶a ***singular opportunity*** まれな機会. ¶***social opportunities*** 社交の機会. ¶He determined to have his revenge at ***some convenient opportunity***. 彼はいつか折を見てかたきを討とうと決心した. ¶These ***splendid opportunities*** are in the hand of the young men of America. これらのすばらしい機会は米国青年の手中にある. ¶diminish the ***strategical opportunity*** of ... 戦略的機会を低減する. ¶***sufficient opportunities*** 十分な機会. ¶a ***unique opportunity*** 無二の機会 ‖ utilize that ***unique opportunity*** for ... ...するためにその唯一無二の機会を利用する. 【類】have ***unique opportunities*** of ... ¶I had ***unusual opportunities*** to study ... 私は...を研究するという滅多にない機会を得た. ¶***valuable opportunities*** which fate threw in his way 運命が彼の手に授けた貴い機会. ¶***vocational opportunities*** for foreign language students 外国語学生に対する就職上の機会. ¶there are ***wide opportunities*** for the application of ... ...を応用する機会は多方面である. 【類】much ***wider opportunities*** are now open to ...

Q² a ***business opportunity*** 商機. ¶generous ***education opportunities*** 豊富な教育上の機会. ¶an ***employment opportunity*** 就職の機会.【類】widen ***employment opportunities*** for ... ¶at some ***future opportunity*** いつか将来の機会に. ¶spurn a ***job opportunity*** 就職の機会をける ‖ in these days of diminishing ***job opportunities*** 就職機会が漸減する当今において. ¶***learning opportunities*** 就学の機会. ¶a ***money-making opportunity*** 金もうけの機会. ¶enjoy the ***sight-seeing opportunities*** thus made possible かくして可能となった観光の機会を享有する. ¶one of the most attractive ***trading opportunities*** to American business アメリカ商人の最善の貿易機会の一つ.

P ***At*** the first ***opportunity*** I will write further regarding this country. 機会あり次第私はこの国についてさらに書こう. ‖ ***at*** the first ***opportunity*** that offers (=presents itself) 機会のあり次第. 【類】buy ***at*** first ***opportunity*** / ***at*** every ***opportunity***. ¶I am on the watch ***for*** an ***opportunity*** of ... 私は...の機会をねらっている. ¶equality ***of opportunity*** 機会均等 ‖ taking advantage ***of*** this rare ***opportunity*** この好機を利用して. ¶***on*** (=***upon***) the first ***opportunity*** 機会があり次第.

P² an ***opportunity for*** national aggrandizement 国家の勢力扶植の機会 ‖ ***Opportunity for*** ... was lacking. ...の機会がなかった. ‖ ***opportunity for*** actual training 実際的訓練の機会. ¶have ***opportunity of*** studying ... ...を研究する機会がある ‖ ***opportunity of*** selling 売れ口. ¶"***Opportunities with*** the Western Electric Company." [書名]「西部電気会社に入社希望者への注意」.

Q Time is ***opportunity*** to do things. 時はことをなす機会である(時のある所に機会がある).

oppose, *v*. 反対する, 反抗する, 反ばくする.

M ***bitterly opposed*** him はげしく彼に反対した. ¶His character is ***diametrically opposed*** to mine. 彼と私とは性格が全然反対だ. ¶***heartily oppose*** to ... 心から...に反対する. ¶***hotly oppose*** ... 猛烈に...に反対する. ¶***inevitably oppose*** やむなく反対する. ¶be ***much opposed*** to the proposition その提案に非常に反対している. ¶He ***rigorously opposed*** the scheme. 彼は手厳しくその計画に反対した. ¶***stoutly oppose*** がん強に反対する. ¶***strenuously oppose*** 強硬に反対する. ¶***strongly oppose*** 強く反対する. ¶***tenaciously oppose*** ねばり強く反対する. ¶be ***totally opposed*** to facts 全く事実に反している. ¶be ***unequivocably opposed*** to ... ...に明らかに反対している. ¶***vehemently oppose*** やっきとなって反対する. ¶***vigorously oppose*** 盛んに反対する. ¶***violently oppose*** 猛烈に反対する.

P words ***opposed in*** meaning 意見の反する語. ¶***oppose*** [***to***] a person 人に反対する ‖ ***opposed to*** the interests of ... ...のためにならない ‖ ***oppose to*** woman suffrage 婦人参政権に反対する. 【類】I have nothing to ***oppose to*** the marriage. ‖ ***oppose*** white ***to*** black 白を黒に対比させる. 【類】Good ***opposes*** bad. / international patriotism as ***opposed*** (=in contradistinction) ***to*** national patrotism.

opposite, *n*. 反対の物・人・事実など.

V ***say*** the ***opposite*** to what one intends 思っていることと反対のことを言う. ¶I ***thought*** quite the ***opposite***. 私は正反対のことを考えていた.

Q my ***direct opposite*** 私と全く反対の性格の人. ¶his ***exact opposite*** in these respects これらの点で彼と正反対の人. ¶the ***perfect opposite*** of himself 彼と正反対の人.

P² That is the very ***opposite of*** what I meant. それは私の考えと丁度反対です. 【類】Black is the ***opposite of*** white. / Vice is the ***opposite of*** virtue.

O The fact is just the ***opposite***. 事実は全く反対です.

opposite, *a*. 正反対の, 逆の.

M ***diagonally opposite*** to ... 対蹠(せき)的に...に反対の. ¶be ***directly opposite*** to this case これとは正反対である. ¶the house ***right opposite*** 真向いの家.

P I took a seat ***opposite to*** him. 私は彼と向い合って座を占めた. ‖ opinions ***opposite to*** each other 相反した意見.

O He played ***opposite*** her. 彼は彼女の相手役をやった.

opposition, *n*. 反対, 逆, 対比; 邪魔物.

V ***arouse*** the ***opposition*** of ... ...の反対を引起す. 【類】The appointment ***aroused*** no ***opposition***. ¶***beat opposition*** 反対者をたたく. ¶***break down opposition*** 障害を打破する. ¶***counter*** his ***opposition*** with my own 彼の反対意見に対抗する. ¶***create*** great ***opposition*** 大なる反対をかもす. ¶***develop*** much ***opposition*** 大いに反対を受ける. ¶***disarm*** the ***opposition*** of ... ...の反対を静める. ¶***opposition*** is ***displayed*** towards ... ...に対して反対の意向が示されている. ¶This will necessarily ***evoke opposition*** in many quarters. きっと各方面からこれに対して反対が起きるだろう. 【類】Considerable ***opposition*** was ***evoked***. ¶***excite*** considerable ***opposition*** 著しい反対を引起す. ¶***express opposition*** to ... ...への反対を表明する. ¶***give*** unqualified ***opposition*** to ... ...にあくまで反対する. ¶He ***has*** an ***opposition*** to my doing so. 彼は私がそうすることに反対している. ¶It will ***lessen opposition***. そうすると反対が減るだろう. ¶***make*** strenuous ***opposition*** 強硬に反対する. ¶***meet opposition*** 反対を受ける. 【類】without ***meeting opposition***. ¶***offer opposition*** to ... ...に反対する. 【類】***offer*** no ***opposition***. ¶***overcome*** all ***opposition*** あらゆる障害に打勝つ ‖ ***overcome*** all the ***opposition*** made to it それに対するすべての反対を圧倒する. ¶***raise*** a strong ***opposition*** against ... ...に対し強硬に反対する. ¶***set up*** an ***opposition*** to ... ...に反対する. ¶***show*** the most determined ***opposition*** 断固として反対する ‖ ***show*** sturdy ***opposition*** to the scheme その計画に対して強硬に反対する. ¶***stem opposition*** 反対を食い止める. ¶***stir up*** much ***opposition*** 盛んに反対運動を起す. ¶***Opposition*** to the plan is being ***voiced*** (=***aired***). この計画への反対論が行われている. ¶***withdraw opposition*** 反対を撤回する.

Q ***armed opposition*** 武力抵抗. ¶They aroused the ***bitterest opposition*** in the colonies. それは植民地に劇烈な反対を喚起した. ¶a ***determined opposition*** 断固たる反対. ¶in ***direct opposition*** to ... ...と正反対に. ¶in ***fierce opposition*** 猛烈に反対して. ¶***interested opposition*** 打算的な反対. ¶arouse ***keen opposition*** 激しい反対を喚起する ‖ I have ***keen opposition*** with ... 私は...と激しい競争をしている. ¶***persistent opposition*** 執ような反対. ¶***short-sighted opposition*** 近眼者流の反対. ¶***sly*** and ***mysterious opposition*** ずるいかげの反対. ¶meet with ***strenuous opposition*** がん強な反対に出会う. ¶write in ***strong opposition*** to ... ...に痛烈な反対の文を草する. ¶stand in ***unequivocal opposition*** はっきり対立状態になる. ¶***unreasonable opposition*** 不条理な反対.

P I will do as I please ***for*** all your ***opposition***. いかに君が反対しても僕は自分の好きなようにやる. ¶rise ***in opposition*** to ... 立って...に反対する ‖ whether in office or ***in opposition*** 朝にあると野にあるとを問わず. ¶the leader ***of*** the ***Opposition*** [party] 反対党の党首. ¶meet ***with opposi-***

tion 反対に会う. ¶He was re-elected ***without opposition.*** 彼は競争者なしに再選された. 【類】The scheme has passed ***without opposition.***

P² however great the *opposition* they arouse ***among*** the unthinking 彼らが思慮なきやからの間に喚起する反対がいかに大きかろうと. ¶He was elected without *opposition* ***to*** Congress. 彼は無競争で米国国会議員に選挙された. ‖ *opposition* ***to*** a person (view, party, movement) 人(など)に対する反対.

oppress, *v.* 圧迫する, しいたげる, 苦労させる.

P *oppressed* ***by*** disease 病苦に悩んで. ¶It seemed that the realization of his life's dream *oppressed* him ***with*** over-joy. 彼が一生の希望を実現したことがあまりにうれしいのでかえって彼の心を悩ましたようであった. ¶*oppressed* ***with*** anxiety 心配に心を悩まされて ‖ feel *oppressed* ***with*** the heat 暑熱で苦しい.

P² stand up ***for*** the *oppressed* しいたげられた者の味方をする.

oppression, *n.* 圧制, 圧迫, 抑圧; 虐待.

V ***bear*** the *oppression* of ... ...の圧迫にたえる. 【類】The weak have ***borne*** *oppression* in all ages. ¶Tears ***relieved*** the *oppression* of my heart. 私は涙で心の苦悩が除かれた.

Q under ***official*** *oppression* 官憲の圧迫の下に.

P struggle ***against*** *oppression* 圧制と戦う. ¶victims ***of*** *oppression* 圧制の犠牲者(圧制に苦しむ人民). ¶groan ***under*** *oppression* 圧迫の下にしんぎんする.

P² the *oppression* ***of*** the weak 弱いものいじめ.

oppressive, *a.* 圧制的な.

M The air is ***very*** *oppressive.* むっとする.

opprobrium, *n.* 不名誉, 悪口, 汚名.

Q level ***unmerited*** *opprobrium* at ... ...に対して無実な汚名を与える.

optimism, *n.* 楽観主義, 楽天主義.

V ***cultivate*** *optimism* 楽観的気分を養成する. ¶***express*** *optimism* 楽観する. ¶***recommend*** *optimism* 楽観的態度を勧める.

Q ***blind*** *optimism* 盲目的楽観. ¶a tone of ***breezy*** *optimism* 明朗な楽観的調子. ¶with his usual ***cheery*** *optimism* 彼のいつもの快活な楽観主義で. ¶***dangerous*** *optimism* 危険な楽観主義.

P ***with*** all the *optimism* of youth 若いものが持つ楽観に満ちて.

optimist, *n.* 楽観主義者, 楽天主義者.

Q an ***amiable*** *optimist* 愛すべき楽天主義者. ¶a ***born*** *optimist* 生れながらの楽天主義者. ¶a ***light-hearted*** *optimist* 気軽な楽天主義者.

Q² a ***poet*** *optimist* 楽天詩人.

O Let us be *optimists* enough to hope that all will end well. われわれにはよろしく楽天的に万事上首尾に終るものと考えよう.

optimistic, *a.* 楽天主義の, 楽観主義の.

M He was ***less*** *optimistic* about the result than others. その結果についてみんなほど楽観していなかった. ¶be ***too*** *optimistic* 考えがあま過ぎる.

P He is professedly *optimistic* ***regarding*** a solution of the difficulty. 彼はその難事の解決に関して表面では楽観的である.

option, *n.* 取捨, 選択, 随意, 任意.

V will ***allow*** the *option* upon consideration of ... ...を考慮してその選択を許すだろう. ¶***concede*** the *option* if ... ...ならばその選択を譲歩する. ¶***give*** *option* to cancel if ... ...ならば取消をする自由を許す. ¶***grant*** an *option* 選択を許す. ¶We ***have*** the *option* of going or not. われわれは行くも行かないも随意である. ‖ From there the traveller ***has*** the *option* of several routes. そこからは旅行者は五六の経路の中から適当に選ぶことができる. 【類】They ***had*** no *option* left them. / I ***have*** no *option* but to ... ¶***waive*** an *option* 選択を棄権する.

P ***at*** the *option* of the passenger 乗客の随意で ‖ It is ***at*** their *option* to do so. そうすることは彼らの勝手だ. ‖ Contracts are voidable ***at*** the *option* of the contracting parties. 当事者の考えで契約は取消すことができる. ¶That is left ***in*** my *option*. それは私の随意にできる. ¶Leave it ***to*** his *option*. それは彼の自由に任しておけ.

P² The *option* ***for*** a second language is between French and German. 第二外国語の選択はフランス語かドイツ語である. ¶There is no *option* ***in*** the matter. このことは選択ができない.

optional, *a.* 選択の, 随意の, 勝手次第の.

P It is *optional* ***with*** you. それは君の随意だ. ‖ It is *optional* ***with*** the writer or speaker either to express the "that" or to leave it out. その "that" を略すか略さないかは作者または話者の随意だ.

oracle, *n.* 神託, 託宣, 神のお告; 大聖, 賢人.

V ***consult*** the *oracle* about ... ...について神のお告を聞いて見る. ¶The fortune-teller ***delivered*** the *oracle*. その予言者が託宣を下した. ¶***fulfil*** an *oracle* 神託を実行する ‖ The *oracle* has been ***fulfilled.*** その神託が実際となって現われた. ¶***receive*** an *oracle* 神託を受ける.

Q a ***great*** *oracle* on ... ...の大聖.

Q² a ***family*** *oracle* 家族全体の意向.

P² the *oracles* ***of*** God 神託.

orange, *n.* かんきつ類.

V ***peel*** *oranges* みかんの皮をむく. ¶***slice*** an *orange* みかんを薄く切る.

Q the ***bitter*** (=***sour***) *orange* だいだい. ¶the ***navel*** *orange* ネーブル. ¶***sweet*** and ***juicy*** *oranges* 甘くて汁の多いみかん.

orange, *a.* だいだい色の.

P Carrots are *orange* ***in*** color (=reddish yellow). 人じんはオレンジ色だ.

oration, *n.* 演説, 式辞.

V ***make*** an *oration* 演説をする.

Q ***direct*** (***indirect***) *oration* (=speech)〚文法〛直(間)接話法. ¶a ***funeral*** *oration* 弔辞. ¶an ***outspoken*** *oration* 率直な演説. ¶a ***public*** *oration* 公開演説.

Q² a ***Fourth-of-July*** *oration* 独立祭演説(米国の). ¶***student*** *orations* 学生の演説.

orator, *n.* 演説者, 弁士.

V The *orator* was ***cheered.*** 弁士はかっさいをもって迎えられた. ¶***hear*** a good *orator* 雄弁家の演説を聞く.

Q a ***blazing*** *orator* まくし立てる弁士. ¶a ***budding*** *orator* 新参の弁士. ¶a ***dramatic*** *orator* 芝居がかりの弁士. ¶an ***eloquent*** *orator* 雄弁家. ¶the ***gold-digging*** *orators* without professional qualifications 金もうけが目的のしろうと弁士. ¶A ***good*** *orator* draws. うまい弁士は人を引付ける. ¶a ***great*** *orator* 大雄弁家. ¶an ***impressive*** *orator* 聴者を感動させる弁士. ¶a ***long-winded*** *orator* 長々と回りくどい弁士. ¶a ***matchless*** *orator* 天下一品の弁士. ¶***newly-fledged*** *orators* ぽっと出の弁士. ¶a ***picturesque*** *orator* 風さいの美しい弁士. ¶a fervent ***political*** *orator* 熱のある政治演説家. ¶a ***public*** *orator* 公開演説の弁士. ¶a ***ready*** *orator* 即席雄弁家. ¶a ***silver-tongued*** *orator* 雄弁家.

Q² a ***boy*** *orator* 少年雄弁家. ¶a ***Fourth-of-July*** *orator* (米国の)独立祭雄弁家. ¶a ***mob*** *orator* 扇動的雄弁家. ¶a ***pulpit*** *orator* 説教の名人. ¶a ***radio*** *orator* ラジオの雄弁家. ¶a ***sand-lot*** *orator* 砂地演説家(公園の). ¶a ***soap-box*** (=***packing-case***) *orator* 《米》街頭演説家(石けん箱に上ることから). ¶a ***spread-eagle*** *orator* 《米》愛国演説家(米国の紋章はわしが翼を拡げた形であるから). ¶a ***street-corner*** *orator* 街頭演説家. ¶a ***stump*** *orator* 《米》街頭演説家.

oratory, *n.* 雄弁術; 雄弁, 演説.

V ***attempt*** *oratory* 雄弁を試みる.

Q people who are susceptible to ***emotional*** *oratory* 感情に訴える弁舌に共鳴しやすい人々. ¶the ***old-fashioned florid*** *oratory* 昔風の花やかな雄弁. ¶***post-prandial*** *oratory* 食後の演説. ¶***stereotyped*** *oratory* 紋切型の演説. ¶***swelling*** *oratory* 誇張的な能弁. ¶it is mere ***thoughtless*** *oratory* to cry aloud that ... ...と壮語するのは全く考えの足りない演説家のすることである.

Q² ***after-dinner*** *oratory* 食後のテーブルスピーチ. ¶mere ***campaign*** *oratory* ただの選挙戦演説 ‖ the floods of ***campaign*** *oratory* 選挙演説のはんらん. ¶***highway*** *oratory* 大道演説.

orb, *n.* 球.

Q the flag of the ***blazing*** *orb* 日の丸.

P² the *orb* ***of*** the day 日輪, 太陽.

orbit, *n.* 軌道.

Q the ***earth's*** *orbit* round the sun 地球の軌道. ¶the ***lunar*** *orbit* 月の軌道.

Q² countries within the ***Soviet*** *orbit* ソ連圏内の国々. 【類】Poland is generally considered within the *Soviet orbit*.

P a planet's motion ***in*** its *orbit* 軌道上の遊星の運行. ¶the axis ***of*** an *orbit* 軌道の中軸.

orchard, *n.* 果樹園, 果物畑.

V ***plant*** an *orchard* 果樹園を作る. ¶***set out*** an *orchard* 果樹園を設計する.

Q² a ***citrus*** *orchard* かんきつ園. ¶a ***plum*** (an ***apple***) *orchard* あんず(など)果園.

P oranges ***from*** one's *orchard* その果樹園でできたみかん.

orchestra, *n.* 管弦楽団.

Q The music is scored for a ***small*** *orchestra*. この曲は小管弦楽団のためのものである.

Q² a *dance orchestra* 舞踏管弦楽団. ¶a *jazz orchestra* ジャズ管弦楽団. ¶a *symphony orchestra* 交響管弦楽団.

ordain, *v.* 命じる, 任命する.

P *ordained by* fate to be ... ...なるべく運命づけられた. ¶*ordain ... for* (=*to*) some office ...をある官職に任命する.

O what the law *ordains* 法の定めるところ.

ordeal, *n.* きびしい試練, かしゃく.

V ***escape*** (=***avoid***) the *ordeal* of being photographed by a great number of reporters 大勢の探訪記者に写真を取られるという苦難を免れる. ¶***evade*** this trying *ordeal* この苦しい試練を避ける. ¶***face*** the *ordeal* of being the laughing-stock of the Japanese 日本人の笑いものになる苦難に直面する. ¶***get*** an *ordeal* ***over*** 難関を突破する. ¶***stand*** the *ordeal* そのかしゃくにたえる. ¶***undergo*** the *ordeal* of the flames 火難に会う ‖ ***undergo*** the *ordeal* of questioning 質問攻めに会う.

Q undergo the ***dreaded*** *ordeal* of ... ...の恐ろしい責苦を受ける. ¶a ***formidable*** *ordeal* 恐ろしい責苦. ¶a very ***severe*** *ordeal* はなはだきびしい試練. ¶a ***terrible*** *ordeal* 恐ろしい試練. ¶***trying*** *ordeals* 辛い試練.

P go ***through*** those *ordeals* それらのきびしい試練を経る.

P² an *ordeal* ***by*** boiling water 湯責め, くがだち. ¶an *ordeal* ***of*** cross-questioning 詰問責め. ¶It was an *ordeal* ***to*** me. それは私に取って苦しい試練であった.

order, *n.* (**1**) 命令, 指揮; 注文.

V ***accept*** an *order* 注文に応じる. 【類】You had better not ***accept*** further *orders* at present. / ***accept*** *orders* for prompt delivery. ¶A remittance must ***accompany*** all *orders*. 御注文の節は必ず御送金を願います. ¶***bag*** a lot of *orders* どっさり注文を取る. ¶***book*** an *order* from ... ...からの注文を帳簿に記入する. ¶***cancel*** (=***annul***) an *order* 注文を取消す. ¶***carry out*** *orders* 命令を実行する ‖ forget to ***carry out*** one's wife's shopping *orders* 妻に頼まれた買物を忘れる. ¶***complete*** an *order* 受けた注文をまとめる. ¶***countermand*** one's *order* その命令を取消す. ¶***despatch*** *orders* 命令を発する. 【類】*Orders* will be ***despatched*** the same day as they are received. ¶***disobey*** a superior officer's *orders* 上官の命令にそむく. ¶***distribute*** an *order* over several makers 一つの注文を数人の製造者へ配分する. ¶The *order* will be ***enforced***. その命令は励行されるだろう. ¶please ***enter*** my *order* for ... ...私の...の注文をどうぞ御記帳下さい. ¶Prices having advanced, we cannot ***execute*** *orders* at your limits. 物価が騰貴したのでお指値では貴命に応じかねます. 【類】***execute*** an *order* given / We shall be glad to ***execute*** your *order* for a copy. / We cannot ***execute*** the *order* in the time mentioned. / All *orders* will be ***executed*** in rotation (順番に). ¶***fill*** an *order* exactly as per sample 見本通り正確に注文を果す ‖ Promptness in ***filling*** an *order* is always a feature of our business. すべてじん速に御注文に応じるのが私どもの店の特色で御座います. 【類】***fill*** carefully any *orders* committed to them / ***fill*** *orders* promptly / Large *orders* have recently been ***filled*** by us for the U.S. Navy. ¶***fix*** the *order* of call 召集の順序をきめる. ¶we expect to ***finish*** the *order* about ... 御注文は...ころできる見込です. ¶***fling*** one's *orders* to ... ...に命令を投げつける. ¶if he fails to ***follow*** *orders* もし彼が命令に従わなければ. ¶***fulfil*** an *order* 注文品を調達する. ¶***get*** *orders* from all directions 諸方面から注文を受ける. ¶***give*** *orders* 命令を下す, 注文を発する ‖ ***give*** an *order* to a boy for tea (coffee, beer) ボーイに紅茶(など)を注文する ‖ ***give*** strict *orders* to ... not to ... ...に...してはならないと厳命する. 【類】***give*** a marching *order*. ¶***give out*** an *order* for ... ...の注文を発する. ¶The firm ***has*** so many *orders* in hand. 店は沢山の注文を受けている. 【類】There is a constant demand for airships in this country and Europe, and most of factories ***have*** *orders* a year or two ahead. ‖ We ***have*** so many *orders* in hand. 当方手もとに注文が重なっています. ¶The *orders* are being ***ignored***. 命令が行われない. ¶***issue*** *orders* forbidding ... ...禁止の命令を発する. 【類】***issue*** an *order* giving power to local authorities to ... ¶***leave*** *orders* that ... ...と言いおく. ¶***lose*** an *order* 注文を取損ねる. ¶***make up*** (=***out***) *orders* 注文書を作成する. ¶***obey*** an *order* without remonstrance 文句なしに命令に従う ‖ The servant gradually got too stuck-up to ***obey*** my *orders*. 召使が段々増長して私の言うことをきかなくなった. 【類】refuse to ***obey*** *orders*. ¶***obtain*** *orders* for goods 商品の注文を受ける. ¶***overlook*** an *order* 命令を看過する. ¶***pass*** an *order* to ... ...に発注する. ¶***phrase*** *orders* pleasantly 命令を気持よく表現する. ¶***place*** an *order* with a firm ある商会へ注文する ‖ ***place*** an *order* for ... with ... ...に...の品の注文をする. 【類】*orders* may be ***placed*** direct with ... / To avoid disappointment please ***place*** your *orders* early. ¶we have ***put*** the *order* into work. 私どもは注文の品を製作する手はずをしました. ¶***receive*** *orders* by wire 電報で注文を受ける ‖ ***receive*** an *order* from ... ...から注文を受ける. ¶***refuse*** *orders* 注文を断る. ¶***remove*** previous *orders* relating to ... ...に関する前の訓令を取消す. ¶***renew*** an *order* 再注を出す. ¶***repeat*** an *order* 命令を復唱する; 再発注する. ¶***rescind*** an *order* 注文を取消す. ¶***reserve*** the *order* 注文を保留する. ¶The *order* was ***revoked***. 注文は取消された. ¶***secure*** good *orders* 結構な注文を入手する. ¶***seek*** *orders* 注文を求める. ¶***send*** an *order* to ... ...に発注する. ¶***send in*** *orders* for ... ...の注文を出す. ¶***shout*** *orders* どなって命令する. ¶***solicit*** your liberal *orders* どしどし御用命下さい. ¶***sound*** *orders* by bugle call らっぱを鳴らして命令する. ¶***supply*** *orders* 注文を調達する. ¶***take*** *orders* 注文を取る; 僧職につく. 【類】We can not ***take*** the *order* on terms quoted. / I have ***taken*** the *order* at an advanced price. ¶***transmit*** *orders* to ... ...に注文を回す. ¶***turn over*** an *order* to ... 注文を...に回す.

V² *Orders* are ***falling off***. 注文がだんだん減って来ている. ¶***wire*** an *order* 注文を打電する. ¶***withdraw*** an *order* 注文を撤回する.

Q a ***big*** *order* 大きな注文. ¶a ***domestic*** *order* 国内の注文. ¶send in ***duplicate*** *orders* 正副二通の注文書を送る. ¶an ***extensive*** *order* 大口の注文. ¶by the ***express*** *order* of ... 特に...の命令によって. ¶on ***foreign*** *orders* 外国からの注文により. ¶We cannot accept ***further*** *orders* at previous prices. 以前の値段では今後の御注文に応じ兼ねます. 【類】until ***further*** *orders*. ¶***imperative*** *orders* 厳命. ¶an ***Imperial*** *order* 勅命. ¶American toys for American children is the ***new*** *order* of things. アメリカの子供にアメリカ製(以前はドイツから輸入したもの)のおもちゃを与えるのは新しい事象である. ¶a conflict between the ***new*** and the ***old*** *order* of ideas 新旧思想の衝突. ¶***official*** (=government) *orders* 官命. ¶the price at which you can duplicate the ***previous*** *order* 前注文の品を重ねて引受けて下さる直段. 【類】remove ***previous*** *orders* relating to ... ¶***Rush*** *orders* made in 24 hours. [掲示]お急ぎの注文は二十四時間で仕上げます. ¶a ***sample*** *order* 見本注文. ¶***sealed*** *orders* 厳封命令. ¶***secret*** *orders* 秘密命令. ¶place a ***standing*** *order* for ... with your grocer あなたの乾物屋に...をきまって届けるよう注文をする. ¶by his ***strict*** *orders* 彼の厳命により. ¶we had the most ***stringent*** *orders* not to ... われわれは...しないようにとの厳命を受けた. ¶***summary*** *order* 略式命令. ¶a ***tall*** *order*=a difficult task むずかしい注文. ¶an ***urgent*** *order* 急ぎの注文. ¶***Your*** *order*? 御注文は(給仕人の問い).

Q² ***advance*** *orders* 進軍命令. ¶an ***Army*** *Order* issued in Oct., 1920 千九百二十年十月発令された陸軍命令. ¶a ***back-to-work*** *order* (ストライキの場合)職場に戻る命令. ¶a ***battle*** *order* 戦闘命令. ¶a ***Cabinet*** *Order* 閣令. ¶issue a ***cease-fire*** *order* 戦闘中止命令を発する. ¶a "***ceasework***" *order* 操業中止命令. ¶disregard a ***court*** *order* 裁判所の命令を無視する. ¶The soldier was waiting for his ***discharge*** *order*. 兵士は兵役解除命令を待っていた. ¶withdrawal of the ***dismissal*** *orders* against 66 workers 六十六人の従業員に対して発せられた解職の命令撤回. ¶an ***eleventh-hour*** *order* forbidding a general strike 総罷業を禁じる実行間際の命令. ¶stay ***eviction*** *orders* served the tenants 小作人に出された立退中止の命令. ¶On November 28,1913, the President issued the following ***Executive*** *order*: 千九百十三年十一月二十八日大統領は次の行政命令を発した. 【類】by the ***Executive*** *order* of December 3,1918. ¶flaunt the ***government*** *orders* 政府の命令を振り回す. ¶The British issued a ***housing eviction*** *order* to make room for a new Military Government Headquarters. 英国では新陸軍本営に敷地を譲るため強制疎開令を発した. ¶a ***large-quantity*** *order* 大量注文. ¶issue a ***mobilization*** *order* 動員令を発する. ¶a ***money*** *order* 為替, 郵便為替. ¶the

Organizations Control Order 団体等規正令. ¶the ***purge*** *order*, signed Jan. 4,1946. 千九百四十六年一月四日署名された追放令. ¶a ***quantity*** *order* 大量注文. ¶a ***repeat*** *order* 再度の注文. ¶The ship is under ***sailing orders***. 船は出帆命令を受けている. ¶under ***SCAP*** (Supreme Commander of Allied Powers) *order* 連合軍最高司令部の命令の下に. ¶a ***scarce order*** 微々たる注文. ¶ships under the ***scrap*** *order* 廃棄命令を受けている船舶. ¶a ***sealing order*** 封かん命令(開封時を指定した). ¶The ***strike order*** was given the workers at 3 a.m. yesterday. その罷業命令はきのう午前三時労務者に与えられた. ¶***supply*** *orders* 給与命令. ¶transmit ***surrender*** *orders* to one's troops その兵士に降伏命令を伝える. ¶place a ***trial*** *order* with ... ...へ試験的注文を出す. 【類】if you can place a ***trial*** *order* with us.

P You can't do anything of the sort; it is ***against*** *orders*. 君はそんなことはできない, それは命令違犯だ. ¶The soldier was ready to die ***at*** the *order* from his King. その兵は王の命令であればいつでも死ぬ覚悟であった. ¶***by*** *order* of the governor 知事の命によって. 【類】***by*** *order* of the C.O. (部隊長). ¶I believe I am ***in*** *order* in raising this question. 私はこの質問をしても反則でないと信じます. ¶the completion ***of*** an *order* 命令の完全実行 ‖ the execution ***of*** an *order* 命令の遂行. ¶It is rare that Scribner's purchases an article ***on*** *order*. スクリブナー誌が寄稿を依頼することは滅多にない. ‖ It can be secured ***on*** *order*. それは注文すれば得られる. ‖ It was bought ***on*** his *orders*. それは彼の命令で買った. 【類】The drug is not sold except ***on*** the *order* of a physician. ¶Swinburne could never write ***to*** *order*. スウィンバーンは注文によって執筆するということは決してできなかった. ‖ clothes (shoes) made ***to*** *order* 注文服(など) ‖ Any not in stock imported to *order* ***in*** three weeks. 〔掲示〕在庫しない品は御注文があれば三週間で輸入します. 【類】Some books are written "***to*** *order*." / manufacture ***to*** the *order* of ... / have it made ***to*** *order*. ¶The firm has a large number of aeroplanes ***under*** *order*. その会社は多数の飛行機の注文を受けている. ‖ translated ***under*** imperial *orders* by ... 勅命によって...が翻訳した ‖ men ***under*** one's *orders* その部下の者 ‖ put them all ***under*** his *orders* 彼らを皆彼の配下にする. 【類】These expeditions were made ***under*** the *orders* of the Russian Government. / ***under*** the *orders* of the Government / The regiment is now ***under*** *orders* for the front. / the warships are ***under*** *orders* to proceed to ... ¶***upon*** *order* of ... ...の指令によって.

P^2 issue an *order* ***against*** ... ...に禁止令を出す. ¶place an *order* ***at*** Genoa, Italy, for ... イタリアのジェノアに...の注文をする ‖ fill *orders* ***at*** $1.00 each 各々一ドルで注文に応じる. ¶Cheque should accompany *orders* ***by*** post. 小切手は郵便での注文書と同封で送るべきである. ¶*Orders* ***for*** two battleship-cruisers have just been placed on the Clyde by the British Government. 英国政府は戦闘巡洋艦二隻をクライドに丁度注文したところだ. 【類】a Japanese Government *order* ***for*** England / The *order* ***for*** the engines for the government railway has been given to Great Britain. ‖ *orders* ***for*** the advance of one's troops その軍隊の前進命令 ‖ an *order* ***for*** payment 支払命令. ¶under *orders* ***from*** higher up 上からの命令で. 【類】*orders* ***from*** the head office. ¶an *order* ***of*** assignment 譲渡命令. ¶an *order* ***on*** a bank for payment 銀行に対する支払命令 ‖ an *order* ***on*** the authorization by law 委任命令. ¶an *order* ***with*** a printer 印刷屋への注文.

(**2**) 秩序, 規律, 順序.

V ***bring order*** out of chaos 混とんから秩序を作り出す. 【類】***bring*** (=***gain***) *order* out of a chaotic state of affairs. ¶***bring about*** a new social *order* 新しい社会的秩序を立てる. ¶***disintegrate*** (=***break up***) the established *order* 確立している秩序を乱す. ¶***disturb*** the *order* 順序を乱す. 【類】***disturb*** the existing *order* of things / without seriously ***disturbing*** the social *order*. ¶***enforce*** strict *order* 規律を励行する. ¶***establish*** a new *order* of things 従来の慣例を一新する. ¶***improvise*** *order* out of chaos にわかに混乱を整理する. ¶***introduce*** *order* 秩序を立てる. ¶***invert*** the *order* of merit 価値の順位を転倒する ‖ ***invert*** this natural *order* of things この自然の順序を逆にする. ¶The class ***keeps*** good *order*. そのクラスは規律が正しい. 【類】The policeman ***keeps*** *order*. ‖ ask another to ***keep*** one's *order* in a waiting queue 行列に自分の番を取っておいてもらう. ¶***maintain*** [good] *order* 秩序を維持する. ¶***move up*** the *order* of ... ...の順を繰上げる. ¶so long as they ***observe*** *order* 彼らが秩序を乱さない限り ‖ ***observe*** no *order* 無遠慮にする. ¶***preserve*** *order* 静粛にしている ‖ ***preserve*** public *order* 社会の秩序を保つ. ¶***re-establish*** *order* 秩序を回復する. 【類】***re-establish*** the old *order*. ¶***respect*** *order* and authority 秩序と権力を尊重する. ¶***restore*** *order* out of chaos 混とんたる状態から秩序を回復する ‖ ***restore*** the old *order* 旧体制に復する. ¶***reverse*** the usual *order* いつもの順序を逆にする ‖ The *order* of their sequence is ***reversed***. その連続の順序が逆にされた. ¶***set aside*** the old *order* of things 旧慣を捨てる. ¶***usher in*** a new *order* 局面を一新する. ¶They ***wrought*** *order* from chaos. 混とん状態から秩序を回復した.

V^2 Now, however, the old *order* has ***changed***. しかし今は昔とは違う. ¶The old *order* ***returned***. 昔に帰った.

Q arranged in ***alphabetical*** (=ABC) *order* いろは順に並べた. ¶reduce them to ***alphabetical*** *order* それをABC順に分類する. ¶in an ***ascending*** *order* of importance 後になるほど漸次重要さを増して. ¶be in ***bad*** *order* 無秩序である. ¶be arranged in ***chronological*** *order* 年代順に整理してある. ¶in face of difficulties of no ***common*** *order* 並大抵でない困難に直面して. ¶put a grave in ***decent*** *order* 墓を修理する. ¶in ***decreasing*** *order* are ... 漸次減少の順序に並べると...となる. ¶in the ***exact*** *order* 正確な順序に. ¶Any person under the age of thirty, who, having any knowledge of the ***existing social*** *order*, is not a revolutionist, is an inferior.—G. B. Shaw. 三十歳以下の者で現時の社会状態を少しでも知っていながら革命家でない者は劣等者である. ¶The old watch is still in ***going*** (=working) *order*. その古い懐中時計はまだ動く. ¶keep a room in ***good*** *order* 室を整理しておく. ¶a disturbance of social tranquillity and ***good*** *order* 社会の安寧と秩序のかく乱. ¶rank them in a ***hierarchical*** *order* その番付をつくる. ¶in ***historical*** *order* 歴史的の順序で. ¶in ***lexicological*** *order* 辞書式に配列して. ¶the ***literal*** *order* (文の)文字的順序. ¶the ***logical*** *order* (文の)論理的順序. ¶soldiers in ***marching*** *order* 行進中の軍人. ¶do everything almost in ***military*** *order* 万事軍隊式にやる. ¶the maintenance of ***moral*** *order* 風紀の維持. ¶It is in the ***natural*** *order* of things. それは自然そういうことになる. ¶a ***new*** *order* 新体制 ‖ sufferers of a ***new*** *order* of things in a transitory condition 過渡期における変遷の犠牲者[士族の商法などの場合]. ¶be in the ***normal*** *order* 平常と変りはない. ¶the ***numerical*** *order* 数の大から小に移る順序. 【類】arrange in ***numerical*** *order*. ¶quite content with the ***old*** *order* of things 旧態に全く満足して ‖ passing away of the ***old*** *order* and its suppression by a new 新制と旧制の交代. ¶His accounts were not in ***perfect*** *order*. 彼の会計はよく整理されてなかった. ¶Everything is kept in ***proper*** *order*. 万事整然としている. ¶bundle them out in ***rapid*** (=***quick or short***) *order* 大急ぎでそれらをはこび出す. ¶On they came in fairly ***regular*** *order*, four or five abreast. 彼ら(兵士ら)はかなり整然と四五人並んでやって来た. ¶in the ***regular chronological*** *order* 整然と年代順に. ¶be in the ***right*** *order* 正しい順になっている. ¶a Japanese full name written in ***reverse*** *order* 順を逆にした日本人の姓名(名が先で姓が後). ¶They place themselves round the board in no ***set*** *order*. 彼らは勝手に卓席につく. ¶***social*** *order* 社会の秩序. ¶Other dishes on ***special*** *order*. 特別御注文によってその他の品もできます[料店理の掲示]. ¶beings of a ***superior*** *order* 人間以上のもの. ¶in a ***systematic*** *order* 整然たる秩序で. ¶the Cow Year according to the ***time-honored zodiac*** *order* 昔から行われている十二支の丑歳. ¶reverse the ***usual*** *order* of things 従来の順序を変える.

Q^2 the ***batting*** *order* of a team 野球チームの打順. ¶the ***rowing*** *order* of a crew ボート乗組員の席順. ¶The machine is in ***running*** *order*. 機械は運転可能の状態にある. ‖ The electric tram-cars will soon be in ***running*** *order*. 電車は直ちに運転するでしょう ‖ send a skilled machinist to see that it was properly set up and put in good ***running*** *order* 熟練な機械技師を派遣してそれがよく据付けられてうまく運転できるようにさせる. ¶machinery in ***smooth working*** *order* 好調子の機械. ¶a vessel in complete

steaming order 完全な運転可能状態にある船. ¶***subscription order*** 申込順. ¶The machinery is now erected and in capital ***working order*** 機械が今組立てられ運転きわめて良好である ‖ be expected to be in ***working order*** in a day or two 一日か二日で運転ができる予定である ‖ keep the system of digestion in proper ***working order*** 消化器を良い状態にしておく. 【類】The machines are in thorough ***working order***. / The railway is now in full ***working order***. ¶a ***world order*** based on justice 正義を基礎とした世界体制. 【類】construct a new ***world order*** / the old ***world order*** / establish a more rational and more desirable ***world order*** / lay the foundations of a stable and peaceful ***world order***.

P ***by*** *order* of receipt 先着順で. ¶accepted ***in*** the *order* of application 申込順に受付けた. 【類】The seats in the theatre, of which only a limited number are available, will be allotted ***in*** *order* of application. ‖ ***in*** *order* of time 時の後先からいうと ‖ ***in*** the order of arrival 到着順に ‖ buildings arranged ***in*** *order* of date その建築年代順に配列した建物 ‖ ***in*** *order* of mention 挙示した順に. 【類】They are arranged ***in*** *order* of increasing difficulty or importance. / ***In*** the *order* of our sitting, it is your turn to go on. / The largest bell in England is Big Ben of Westminster, which, reckoning up all the bells of the world, comes in as only eleventh ***in*** *order* of size. / ***in*** *order* of size of production ‖ next ***in*** [the] *order* of importance comes ... 重要さの順で次に来るのは... 【類】***in*** [the] *order* of their importance, they are :— / ***in*** *order* of age(年齢) / a list ***in*** [the] *order* of merit (成績) / arrange them ***in*** *order* of intensity, beginning with the strongest. / ***in*** the *order* of purchase (買入). / The name of applicant is enrolled ***in*** the *order* in which it is received. / The winners are listed ***in*** *order* of their scores (得点). / These numbers are ***in*** *order* (12345 のように). ‖ Save where formality is ***in*** *order*, written English has approached the conversational manner. 正式をむねとする場合を除いては英語の文語体は口語体に接近した. ‖ trusting this will be ***in*** *order* これで貴意に添う事と信じまして(商用文の結尾) ‖ Considering the circumstance fault-finding with him does not seem exactly ***in*** *order*. 事情を考えて見ると彼のあら捜しは全く当を得てないようだ. 【類】Is this correct and all ***in*** *order?* / The agreement appears all ***in*** *order*. ‖ I hope you will find ... ***in*** *order*. ...がお気に召すことと存じます. 【類】According to Chinese etiquette it is quite proper and ***in*** *order*. / Therefore the following suggestions may be ***in*** *order*. / Little now remains to be done but the final inspection to see that everything is ***in*** *order*. / satisfy Government officials that things are ***in*** *order* / The security is all ***in*** *order*. ‖ We will explain each of these, briefly, ***in*** *order*. / The chief reasons for life insurance rejection, ***in*** *order*, are : overweight, heart disease, high blood pressure, underweight, tuberculosis. ‖ ***in*** *order* that he may be put on trial 彼の審理のため ‖ at this point it may be ***in*** *order* to consider the question of ... この所で...の問題を考察するのが適当であろう. ¶The line is ***out of*** *order*. [電話など]混線している. ‖ it is considered ***out of*** *order* in the case of ... それは...の場合には不穏当と考えられている ‖ We found the electric lights ***out of*** *order*. 電灯が故障を生じているのがわれわれに分かった. ‖ The room is ***out of*** *order*. へやは乱雑になっている. ‖ The machine gets ***out of*** *order* again very soon. その機械はじきにまた狂う. ‖ Bell ***out of*** *order*. Please knock. [掲示] ベルが故障しています. ノックして下さい. 【類】The railway traffic is ***out of*** *order* owing to floods. ¶the first session of the meeting was called ***to*** *order* by President ... in ...その最初の会議が議長...によって...で正式に開かれた.

P² During the winter season, indoor hospitality is the *order* ***of*** the day. 冬季中は戸内の饗(きょう)応が毎日のことである. ‖ Books and games are the *order* ***of*** the day. 読書と競技が毎日の行事である. ‖ Anecdotes of Count ... are the *order* ***of*** the day in Germany. ドイツは...伯の逸話で持切りである. ‖ Fires seem to be the *order* ***of*** the day just now. 火事は目下の流行のようだ. ‖ when the silent pictures were the *order* ***of*** the day 無声映画だけの時代に ‖ Conditions have changed with the new *order* ***of*** things. 時代の変化新と共に事情が変った. ‖ an inversion of the *order* ***of*** heaven 天道の逆転 ‖ the *order* ***of*** business 議事手続 ‖ in the *order* ***of*** the alphabet = in alphabetical order.

(3) 僧団; 階級; 種類.

V ***serve*** one's *order* 司祭を勤める. ¶***suppress*** an *order* ある宗派を圧迫する. ¶***take*** *orders* 僧職につく ‖ ***take*** holy *orders* 聖職につく.

Q The music that you hear is rarely of the ***convivial*** *order*. 聞く音楽が娯楽的なものであることは滅多にない. ¶missionaries of the ***different*** *orders* 各派の宣教師. ¶a beauty of the ***first*** *order* 一流の美人 ‖ pamphlets written by military and naval authorities of the ***first*** *order* (= rank) 一流の陸海軍軍人によって書かれた小冊子. ¶an artist of ***high*** *order* すぐれた芸術家 ‖ It requires fortitude of a ***high*** *order* to stand under a rain of shells. 砲弾の雨の下に立つのにはりっぱな剛毅(き)の精神がなくてはならない. 【類】a novel of the ***highest*** *order* / a stage manager of the ***highest*** *order* / a general understanding of the ***high*** *order* of the work (作品内容の高尚さ). ¶be in ***holy*** *orders* 僧職にある. ¶the ***lower*** *orders* of London ロンドンの下層社会. ¶It requires technical knowledge of ***no mean*** *order*. それは非凡な専門的知識を必要とする. ‖ a journal of ***no mean*** *order* 高級な新聞. ¶belong to the ***military*** *order* 軍人である. ¶the members of the ***noble*** *order* of St. Jonas 聖ヨナス会の会員. ¶maladies of the ***physical*** *order* 肉体の方の諸病. ¶***rival religious*** *orders* 対立する宗派. ¶a journalist of the ***third*** *order* 三流の新聞記者.

Q² the existing ***capitalist*** *order* of the United States 合衆国の既存資本主義制度.

P go ***into*** *orders* 僧職につく. ¶persons ***of*** a certain *order* of mind ある種の考え方をしている人々 ‖ Support is ***of*** two *orders*, mental and financial. 援助にも精神的と財政的との二種ある.

P² an *order* ***of*** priests 僧職.

(4) 為替.

V ***cash*** a postal *order* 郵便為替を現金に替える. ¶***draw*** a money *order* 為替を組む. ¶***enclose*** an *order* 為替を封入する. 【類】I ***enclose*** a P.O. (=post office) money *order* which will cover the price of the books and the postage. ¶Do you ***issue*** telegraphic money *orders?* 電報為替の発送ができますか. ¶***send*** a money *order* for 100 yen 百円の為替を送る. 【類】***send*** a postal *order* in payment.

P remit ***by*** postal *order* 為替で送金する.

(5) 勲章.

V ***confer*** an *order* of merit on ... 勲章を...に授与する. ¶***receive*** *orders* 勲章を授けられる. ¶***wear*** *orders* 勲章をはい用する.

Q² a ***Distinguished Service Order*** 〚英軍〛 殊勲章 (*D.S.O.* と略す). ☞ 米軍では D.S.M. (Distinguished Service Medal) という.

P ***with*** many *orders* upon his breast むねに沢山の勲章を下げて.

P² the *Orders* ***of*** the Golden Kite, the Rising Sun, and the Sacred Treasure 金鵄(し)・旭日・瑞(ずい)宝勲章.

order, *v.* 命ずる; 注文する; 任命する.

M He has been *ordered* ***abroad***. 彼は洋行を命じられた. ¶*order* a person ***away*** for health 人を保養に行かせる. ¶He was *ordered* ***back*** to Japan. 彼は日本へ帰朝を命じられた. ¶*order* ***direct[ly]*** from the publishers 出版者へ直接に注文する. ¶They *order* these things ***differently*** in some other countries. これらのことは他国では事情を異にするものもある. ¶The minister has been *ordered* ***home***. 公使は帰朝を命じられた. ¶***judicially*** *order* 司法的に命じる. ¶He has been *ordered* ***out*** to the front. 彼は出征を命じられた. ‖ *order* lights ***out*** 消灯を命じる ‖ The army unit was *ordered* ***out*** to reinforce the police. 一部隊が警察を援護するため出張を命じられた.

M² *order* a person ***about*** 駆使する ‖ be *ordered* ***about*** 使い回される. ¶the plane was *ordered* ***down***. 機は着陸を命じられた. ¶He was *ordered* ***off*** (=***away***). 彼は去れと命じられた.

P *order* a copy of a magazine ***at*** the news stand or bookstore 新聞売場か本屋で雑誌を一冊注文する. ¶*order* ***by*** number 番号で注文する. 【類】Housewives in America often *order* their meat and groceries ***by*** telephone from the meat-markets and grocery stores. ¶I *ordered* lunch ***for*** $1.50. 私は一ドル半の昼食を注文した. 【類】

What shall I *order* ***for*** you, miss? ¶*order* them ***from*** Yokohama それを横浜から取寄せる. ‖ *order* ***from*** the hatter's 帽子屋へ注文する ‖ It was *ordered* ***from*** an English firm by the company. それは同会社が英国商会へ注文した. 【類】*order* a garment (suit) ***from*** a tailor / the merchandise you *order* ***from*** this catalogue ‖ It is even *ordered* ***from*** abroad. それは外国からも注文が来る. ‖ *order* a person ***from*** a room (one's presence) 人をへや(など)から退出を命じる. ¶All the ships will be *ordered* ***in*** England. それらの船は全部英国で注文される. ¶They were *ordered* ***into*** action. 彼らは実行を命じられた. ¶a statue *ordered* ***of*** Lorado Talft, the sculptor 彫刻家のロラード・タルフトに製作を依頼した立像 ‖ It was *ordered* ***of*** a company in New York. それはニューヨークの会社に注文した. ¶*order* a person ***out of*** a place (house, room) 人をある場所(など)から去るように命じる. ¶It may be *ordered* ***through*** (=from) Maruzen. それは丸善を通じて注文ができる. ¶He has been *ordered* ***to*** the front. 彼は出征命令に接した. 【類】*order* soldiers ***to*** a place (=country) / *order* children ***to*** bed / Sixteen battleships have been *ordered* ***to*** the Pacific.

O They *ordered* him to be punished. 彼を罰せよとの命が下った.

orderly, *n.* 番人.

Q² a ***street*** *orderly* 《米》道路清掃人.

ordinance, *n.* 訓令, 条例.

V ***repeal*** an *ordinance* 法令を廃止する.

Q an ***Imperial*** *ordinance* 勅令. ¶its ***implementing*** *ordinances* その実施法令. ¶a ***Ministerial*** *Ordinance* 省令.

Q² organizations included in Table 2, ***Cabinet*** and ***Home Ministry*** *Ordinance* of 1947 昭和二十三年閣令内務省令第二号表記載の団体. ¶an ***emergency*** *ordinance* 緊急令. ¶an ***enforcement*** *ordinance* 施行令. ¶a Temporary ***Investigation*** *Ordinance* 臨時調査令. ¶a ***purge*** *ordinance* 追放令.

P ***by*** *Ordinance* 法令により.

ordinary, *n.* 通常物, 常例, 常事, 常態, 定食.

Q² eat at a three ***penny*** *ordinary* 三ペニー規定食を食べる.

P He has brains ***above*** the *ordinary*. 彼は普通以上の頭脳の持主だ. ¶time, a great comforter ***in*** *ordinary* 通常大なる慰安者たる時[というもの]. ¶a physician ***in*** *ordinary* お抱えの医師 ‖ M. Zola's translator ***in*** *ordinary*, Ernest Vizetelly ゾラ氏の特定翻訳者アーネスト・ヴイゼトリー. ¶***out of*** the *ordinary* 並はずれた.

P² George Stanhope, D.D., Chaplain in *ordinary* ***to*** His Majesty 陛下御常任の礼拝堂牧師神学博士ジョージ・スタンホープ.

ore, *n.* 鉱石.

V ***melt*** *ores* 鉱石を溶解する. ¶***treat*** *ore* 鉱石を処理する. ¶Iron *ore* ***occurs*** there in abundance. そこは鉄鉱に富む.

Q ***lean*** *ores* 貧鉱. ¶***spent*** *ore* 使用済の鉱石.

Q² ***aluminum*** *ore* アルミニウム鉱. ¶dress ***gold*** *ore* 金鉱石を処理する. ¶***silver-lead*** *ore* 銀鉛鉱.

P a piece ***of*** *ore* 一片の鉱石. ¶*ore* ***of*** gold 金鉱.

organ, *n.* 機関; 器官; オルガン(風琴); 機関雑誌.

V If your *organs* were not regularly ***exercised,*** they would become atrophical. 諸器官を規則正しく用いないとい縮してしまいます. ¶***grind*** an *organ* 手回しオルガン鳴をらす. ¶the Association ***has*** a monthly *organ* entitled ... その協会は…という月刊の機関雑誌を持っている. ¶Singers, orators and teachers constantly ***overtax*** their vocal *organs*. 歌手や弁士や教師は絶えず発声器官を使い過ぎる. ¶***sound*** an *organ* オルガンを鳴らす.

V² An *organ* ***atrophies*** when not used. 器官は使用しないとい縮する.

Q an ***advisory*** *organ* 諮問機関. ¶the ***auditory*** *organ* 聴覚器官. ¶It is the most ***authoritative*** *organ* of the art. その雑誌はその芸術に関する最高権威である. ¶a ***cathedral*** *organ* 大会堂のオルガン. ¶***deeply-seated*** and ***vital*** *organs* 体内深く蔵されている大切な器官. ¶attack the ***digestive*** *organs* 消化器を冒す. ¶an ***important*** *organ* of French opinion フランスの世論を発表する重要な機関紙. ¶the ***internal*** *organs* 内臓. ¶The flagellum of the tadpole is a ***locomotive*** *organ*. おたまじゃくしの尾は運動の器官である. ¶The ear is the ***natural*** *organ*, the first organ, the most immediate organ of language. 耳は言語を修得する自然の器官であり最初の器官でありかつ最も直接な器官である. ¶the ***official*** *organ* of the association その会の正式機関 ‖ ***official*** *organs* for the promotion of the tourist traffic 観光業振興の公式機関雑誌. 【類】The Norddeutsche Allgemeine Zeitung, the ***official*** *organ* of the German Government. ¶a ***pro-British*** *organ* 英国びいきの機関紙. ¶the ***respiratory*** *organs* 呼吸器. ¶a ***vital*** *organ*, one necessary to the existence of life 生命を維持する必要な重要器官.

Q² a ***cabinet*** *organ* 室内用小型オルガン. ¶a ***cell*** *organ* 細胞紙(共産党などの). ¶a ***Communist*** *organ* 共産党機関紙. ¶a ***government*** *organ* 政府の機関紙. ¶a ***grievance*** *organ* 苦情陳述機関. ¶a ***house*** *organ* 会社の機関紙. ¶the sole ***law-making*** *organ* of the State 国のただ一つの立法機関. ¶the ***male*** (***female***) ***sex*** *organ* 雄(雌)生殖器. ¶a ***mouth*** *organ* ハーモニカ. ¶the ***party*** *organ* of ... …党の機関. ¶The *shichiriki* is a sort of pocket edition of a ***pipe*** *organ*. シチリキは携帯用の一種のパイプオルガンである. ¶a ***Red*** *organ* 共産党の機関紙.

P Mrs. ... ***at*** the *organ* played delightful improvisations. …夫人はオルガンで愉快な即興演奏をやった.

P² The machinery is the most important *organ* ***in*** the whole ship's system. 機関部は船の全構造中最も重要な部分である. ¶an *organ* ***of*** propaganda 宣伝機関. ¶play ***on*** the *organ* オルガンをひく ‖ The nose is the *organ* ***of*** the sense of smell. 鼻は嗅(きゅう)覚器官である.

organism, *n.* 有機体, 組織体, 組織.

V Germs ***invade*** the *organism*. 病菌は組織体を侵す.

Q Man is a ***complicate*** *organism*—the product of all past evolutionary processes. 人間は複雑な組織体即ち過去のあらゆる進化的過程の産物である. ¶a ***living*** *organism* 生物. ¶***microscopic*** *organisms* 微生物. ¶***pathogenic*** *organisms* 病原体.

organization, *n.* 組織, 構造, 機構, 団体.

V He is head of an *organization* ***created*** for that purpose. 彼はその目的で作られた団体の長である. ¶***dissolve*** an *organization* 団体を解散する. ¶an *organization* ***entitled*** "..." …という名称の団体. ¶an *organization* has been ***formed,*** called "..."「…」と呼ぶ団体が組織された.

Q its ***affiliated*** *organizations* その分会(支部). ¶the Communist Party and its ***auxiliary*** *organizations* 共産党及びその付属機関. ¶The carrying out of a work of this magnitude in such a few hours could only be accomplished with a great deal of ***careful*** *organization*. こんな大掛りな仕事をそんな短時間で遂行するには非常に注意深い企画によって初めて完成しうるだろう. ¶a ***central*** *organization* 中央機関. ¶***commercial*** *organizations* 商業上の団体. ¶the ***financial*** *organization* of society 社会の財政組織. ¶given ***good*** *organization* and sound management, it is almost always possible to ... 組織と管理のよろしきを得れば必ずといってよい位…することができる. ¶***industrial*** *organization* 産業組織. ¶an ***infant*** *organization* 創業初期の団体. ¶an ***intermediate*** *organization* 中間機構. ¶a ***kindred*** *organization* 類似の団体. ¶a ***lower*** *organization* 下部団体. ¶The Japan Tourist Bureau is a ***non-commercial*** *organization*. 日本旅行協会は非商業的団体である. ¶It is a ***non-profit-making*** (=not a profit-making) *organization*. それは非営利的団体である. ¶This can only be carried out by ***perfect*** *organization*. 組織が完備して始めてこれが実行される. ¶***philanthropic*** *organizations* 慈善団体. ¶a ***political*** *organization* 政治結社. ¶***private*** *organizations* 民間の団体. ¶a ***religious*** *organization* 宗教団体. ¶any ***representative*** *organization* recognized 承認せられる代表団体. ¶a ***secret*** *organization* of conspirators 謀反者の秘密結社. ¶***secular*** and ***religious*** *organizations* 俗界及び宗教界の団体. ¶The B.B.C. is a ***semi-public*** *organization*. 英国放送局は半官半民の団体である. ¶bring about a ***smooth*** and ***well-oiled*** *organization* 団体として円滑に活動するものを造り出す. ¶build up a ***social*** *organization* 社会組織を編成する ‖ the beginnings of ***social*** *organization* 社会組織の原始形態. 【類】In the majority of instances the offenders are driven into crime more by the defects of the ***social*** *organization* than by any innate tendencies of their own. ¶a ***subordinate*** (=***subsidiary***) *organization* 下部組織. ¶a ***younger*** *organization* than ... …より後にできた団体.

Q² a ***charity*** *organization* 慈善団体. ¶a ***communist*** *organization* 共産党組織. ¶an ***espionage*** *organization* 偵察団. ¶an ***extremist*** *organization* 過激派の団体. ¶a ***farm*** *organization* 農業組合. ¶a ***fighting*** (***peace***) *organization*

戦(平)時編制. ¶a communist-led *labor organization* 共産党指導下の労働団体. ¶a ***news-gathering*** *organization* 報道収集団体. ¶a ***non-profit*** *organization* 非営利団体. ¶a ***parent-teacher*** *organization* 父兄会. ¶a secret ***police*** *organization* 秘密警察団 ‖ secret military and naval ***police*** *organizations* 陸海軍秘密警察隊. ¶a ***publicity*** *organization* 宣伝機関 ‖ throw ***publicity*** *organizations* into high gear 広報団体を活発に運用させる. ¶a big ***radio*** *organization* in America アメリカの大ラジオ団体. ¶a ***research*** and ***study*** *organization* 調査研究団体. ¶a ***sister*** *organization* 姉妹団体. ¶a ***skeleton*** *organization* 定員不足の団体. ¶The ***slave-State*** *organization* of Europe was Hitler's ideal. ヨーロッパを隷属国家に組織することがヒトラーの理想であった. ¶***staff*** *organizations* 職制. ¶***student*** *organization* and activities 学生の団体とその活動 ‖ a leftist-dominated ***student*** *organization* 左派に牛耳られる学生団. ¶a ***terrorist*** *organization* テロ団. ¶***tourist-promoting*** *organizations* 観光奨励団体. ¶an ***underground*** *organization* 地下団体. ¶a ***utilities*** *organization* 公益団体. ¶a ***wartime*** *organization* 戦時の団体. ¶a ***welfare*** *organization* 福祉増進団体. ¶a ***world*** *organization* for peace [国際連合のような]平和のための世界的団体. ¶the framework of ***world*** *organization* 世界組織の輪郭. ¶a ***youth*** *organization* 青年団. ¶***Zaibatsu*** *organizations* 財閥団体.

P Laborers are going to form themselves ***into*** an *organization*. 労働者は団体を組織しようとしている. ¶***under*** a better social *organization* もっと善い社会組織の下に.

P^2 the *organization* ***of*** a company 会社の機構.

organize, *v.* 組織する, 編制する.

P a whole world *organized* ***for*** peace 平和を理想として組織された全世界. ¶officers and men *organized* ***into*** two regiments 二連隊に編制した将兵 ‖ *organize* themselves ***into*** a society (club) 会(など)を組織する. ¶*organize* a company ***with*** a capital of ... の資本金で会社を組織する.

organizer, *n.* 組織者, 〖労〗オルグ.

Q a ***good*** *organizer* 編制に巧みな人. ¶a ***topnotch*** *organizer* 《米》第一級のオルグ.

Q^2 a ***Communist fraction*** *organizer* 共産党フラクのオルグ. ¶a ***conference*** *organizer* 会議企画者. ¶a ***labor*** [***union***] *organizer* 労組のオルグ. ¶a ***price-cutting*** *organizer* 物価低減運動の組織者. ¶a ***travel*** *organizer* 旅行計画者(団体旅行など).

orgy, orgie, *n.* 乱飲乱舞, 底抜け騒ぎ.

Q a ***drunken*** *orgy* 乱ちき騒ぎ. ¶a ***musical*** *orgie* 大騒ぎの音楽会.

P^2 an *orgy* ***of*** parties 団体の大騒ぎの宴会.

orient, *n.* [しばしば O-] 東洋.

Q the ***Christian*** *Orient* キリスト教を奉るじ東洋. ¶the ***colorful*** *Orient* 色彩の豊かな東洋. ¶the ***extreme*** *Orient* 極東. ¶the ***Greek*** *Orient* 東方ギリシア. ¶the poetical charm of the still ***oriental*** *Orient* いまだに(西洋かぶれのしない)東洋的な東洋の詩的魅力.

P ***in*** the *Orient* 東洋に. ¶the peace ***of*** the *Orient* 東洋の平和.

Oriental, *n.* 東洋人.

V ***employ*** low-paid *Orientals* 薄給の東洋人を使う.

Q the "***backward***" *Orientals* いわゆる後進東洋人たち.

orientation, *n.* 東方位; 方向定め, 定位, 指導; 〖病〗見当識.

V aid the world to ***find*** its true *orientation* 世界をしてその真に向う所を定めさせる. ¶***give*** the right *orientation* to ... ...に正しい見方をさせる. ¶***preserve*** (***lose***) the *orientation* of time and place 時と場所の正しい観念を保持(喪失)する.

Q the ***patient's*** *orientation* of time [精神病]患者の時の観念.

P^2 give an *orientation* ***in*** the field of books 読書の方針を立てさせる ‖ complete loss of *orientation* ***of*** time and place in psychosis 精神病における時と場所の観念の全的喪失.

origin, *n.* 起原, 根源, 出所.

V ***assign*** its *origin* to Greece その起原をギリシアに帰する. ¶the race ***claims*** *origin* from ... その民族は...から起ったのであると主張する. ¶the sect ***derives*** its *origin* from ... その宗派は...が開いたものだ. ¶The best dictionary to consult for ***determining*** the *origin* of an English word is the OED. 英語の語原を知る最良の辞書は The Oxford English Dictionary である. ¶***explain*** the *origin* of a word ある語の語原を説明する. ¶This has ***given*** *origin* to the institution. その会が設置されたのはそのためであった. ¶It ***has*** the same *origin*. その原因は同じだ. ‖ ***have*** an *origin* distinct from ... ...と起原が違っている ‖ It ***has*** an *origin* lost in [the mists of] antiquity. その源は遠く古代にさかのぼりぼうばくとして知る由がない. ‖ The practice ***owes*** its *origin* to the Chinese. その慣習は中国に起原している. ‖ the order ***owes*** its *origin* to the learned ... その宗派の開基は学識深い...である. 【類】 words and meanings that ***have*** their *origin* or principal use in the United States / All human life and being ***has*** its *origin* in sexual relations. / All imitation ***has*** its *origin* in vanity.—Ruskin. / it ***has*** its *origin* in the desire to ... / Anarchism and nihilism ***owe*** their *origin* to Russia. / People say that the earthquake ***owes*** the *origin* to volcanoes. / Half the lies that are current in the world ***owe*** their *origin* to a misplaced confidence in memory, rather than to intentional falsehood. ¶He ***supports*** a European *origin* of the so-called Hindu-Arabic numerals. 彼はいわゆるインドアラビア数字はヨーロッパから起ったものであるという説を支持している. ¶***take*** their *origin* from ... ...から起る. ¶***trace*** the *origin* of some favorite quotation ある常用引用句の起原を調べる. 【類】 ***trace*** its *origin* back to the time of ...

V^2 The *origin* of spectacles ***dates*** from the end of the thirteenth century. 眼鏡の起原は第十三世紀の末に発する.

Q a game of very ***ancient*** *origin* 起原のきわめて古い競技. ¶of ***aristocratic*** *origin* 貴族出の. ¶a pastime of ***Chinese*** *origin* 中国伝来の娯楽. ¶a ***common*** *origin* of ... ...共通の起源. 【類】 The book is an attempt to show that the languages of Europe and Asia have a ***common*** *origin*. ¶The two are of ***contemporary*** *origin*. その二者は同時代に起ったものである. ¶his ***divine*** *origin* 彼の神性. ¶Playing-cards are known to be of ***Eastern*** *origin*. カルタ遊びの起原は東洋であるとされている. ¶The pictures were of the ***following*** *origin*:— その映画の製作国は次の通りである. ¶words of ***foreign*** *origin* 外来語. 【類】 musical terms of ***foreign*** *origin* / The art is of ***foreign*** *origin*. ¶The invention is of ***German*** *origin*. その発明はドイツから起ったものである. ¶spring from a ***humble*** *origin* 下層階級から身を起す. 【類】 a man of ***humble*** *origin* and station in life. ¶an ***independent*** *origin* それだけ独立して起ったもの. ¶be of ***Jewish*** *origin* ユダヤ系である. ¶although of ***low, vulgar*** *origin* 低俗な所から起ったのだが. ¶In April, 1926, the German Board of Censors passed 168 pictures, of which 108 were German, 50 American and 10 of ***miscellaneous*** *origin*. 一九二六年四月にドイツの検閲局は百六十八の映画の上映許可を与えた, その中百八はドイツのもの五十は米国のもの残りの十は他の諸国のものであった. ¶of comparatively ***modern*** *origin* 比較的近世に始まった. ¶***monastic*** *origin* of the potter's wheel 陶工のろくろの起原が僧院にあること. ¶It is of ***native*** *origin*. それはその国に起ったものである. ¶of ***obscure*** *origin* 起原の分からない. ¶the theory of the ***pictorial*** *origin* of written speech 文字は絵画が起原であるという説. ¶His face plainly indicates that he is of ***plebeian*** *origin*. 彼の顔は平民出身なることを明かに示している. ¶His pains have a ***psychic*** *origin*. 彼の痛みを感じるのは気のせいである. ¶It is comparatively of ***recent*** *origin*. それは比較的近代になって起ったものである. ¶It is of more ***remote*** *origin*. それはもっと遠い昔に起ったものである. ¶words of ***reputable*** *origin* 筋のいい言葉. ¶***single*** or ***multiple*** *origin* of inventions 発明の一元的または多元的起原. ¶The fire is supposed to be of ***suspicious*** *origin*. その火事の火元は不審と思われている. ¶Etruscan is of ***unknown*** *origin*. エトルリア語の起原は分からない. ‖ a fire of ***unknown*** *origin* 原因不明の火事.

Q^2 cosmetics of ***animal*** (***vegetable***) *origin* 動(植)物性のポマード. ¶a word of ***dialect*** *origin* 方言から起った語. ¶***personal-name*** *origins* proposed for many of the hitherto unsolved problems of etymology 従来語原不明だった多くの語は人名から起ったのだという説. ¶be of ***Western Pennsylvania*** *origin* 西部ペンシルヴァニア出身である.

P He is a Frenchman ***by*** *origin*. 彼は先祖はフランス人だ. ‖ He belonged ***by*** *origin* to the rural gentry. 彼は地方の素封家の出である. ¶American ***in*** *origin* アメリカ出の ‖ modern ***in*** *origin* 近代に発生した ‖ mysterious ***in*** *origin* 起原が不可思議な. ¶inquire ***into*** the *origin* of a thing 物

の起原を調査する. ¶the people ***of*** Latin *origin* ラテン系の国民. ¶***on account of*** its low *origin* その起原が卑しいので(タンゴ・ダンスなど). ¶trace a matter ***to*** its *origin* ある事柄をその起原までさかのぼる.

P^2 the *origin **of*** the present foundation 現在の財団の起原.

original, *n*. 原物; 原文, 原書.

V The translation ***follows*** closely the *original*. その訳は原文に忠実である. ¶Bad translation ***mutilates*** the *original*. へたな翻訳は原文を台なしにする. ¶The imitator may ***outshine*** his *original*. 似せものが本物以上に出ることもある. ¶a letter of which I ***possess*** the *original* 私が原物を持っている一通の手紙の写し.

P ***after*** the *original* 原本にならって. ¶illustrations reproduced ***from*** priceless *originals* 非常に貴重な原本から複製したさし絵. ¶Translations often stimulate purchases ***in*** the *original*. 翻訳書は往々原書の購読欲をそそる. ‖ read Homer ***in*** the *original* ホーマーを原本で読む. 【類】read Greek authors ***in*** the *original*. ¶refer ***to*** the *original* 原書を参照する. ¶See that the copy exactly corresponds ***with*** the *original*. 写しが原本と少しも違わないように注意せよ.

original, *a*. 本原の, 原物の; 独創的な.

M the teaching is not ***altogether*** *original* with ... その教えは全然...の創見という訳ではない. ¶It is ***entirely*** *original* with him. それは全く彼の創意に出たものである. ¶It is ***quite*** *original* with him[self]. それは全く彼の創意になったものである.

P *original **in*** plan 計画が独創的な ‖ a work *original **in*** its design その意匠が独創的な作. ¶The plan of the work is *original **with*** the author. その作の趣向は作者の創意に出ている. 【類】In many respects the plan is *original **with*** him.

originality, *n*. 創意, 独創; 本原.

V ***develop*** *originality* 独創力をかん養する. ¶***display*** *originality* 独創力を示す. ¶***encourage*** *originality* of thought 独創的な思想を奨励する. ¶***preserve*** one's *originality* その独創性を保存する. ¶***show*** much *originality* in ... ...において大いに独創力を示す. ¶***stunt*** *originality* 独創力をい縮させる.

P There is no attempt ***at*** *originality*. 何ら新機軸を出そうという試みがない.

P^2 *originality **of*** expression 表現の新奇.

originate, *v*. 始める, 発する, 起る.

P Eau de Cologne appears to have been *originated **by*** an Italian, named in France, and made in Germany. オードコロンはイタリア人が発明しフランスで名を付けドイツで製造されたようである. ¶it *originated **from*** a suggestion of ... それは...の示唆で創始された. ‖ *originate **from*** some cause ある原因から起る. 【類】It *originated **from*** a single centre. ¶the warehouse ***in*** which the fire *originated* 火元である倉庫 ‖ It *originated **in*** such a circumstance. それはこうした事情があって起った. ‖ the [earthquake] shock *originated* 4,000 miles away, either ***in*** ... or ... その地震の震源地は四千マイル離れた...かまたは...であった ‖ The Chinese have a saying: "Everything new *originates **in*** Canton." 中国には「何でも新しいことは広東から発生する」ということわざがある. 【類】The idea of ... *originated **in*** Britain. / the idea *originated **in*** the fact that ... / Many cases of sea-sickness *originate **in*** indigestion. / This *originated **in*** jealousy. / The war *originated **in*** ideological conflicts. / The Oxford English Dictionary *originated **in*** a resolusion (決議) of the English Philological Society, passed in 1857. / the book *originated **in*** a course of lectures delivered to the students of ... ¶It *originated **on*** American soil. それは米国で生れたものである. ¶It *originated **with*** the Japanese. それは日本人の発明にかかる. ‖ the idea (=notion) of this memorial *originated **with*** Mr. ... この記念物の思付は...氏の発案にかかる. 【類】The scheme *originated **with*** the King himself. / The theory *originated **with*** Dr. Einstein. ‖ The plan of the art exhibition was *originated **with*** several prominent artists and critics.

originator, *n*. 創作者, 発起者, 元祖.

P^2 the *originator **of*** a scheme (an idea) ある計画(など)の発起者 ‖ Dr. Horace Fletcher, the *originator **of*** "Fletcherism." [食物を十分にかめという]フレッチャー主義の元祖ホレース・フレッチャー博士.

ornament, *n*. 装飾, 装飾美, 文飾; 誇り.

Q ***adventitious*** *ornaments* 外面的な装飾. ¶***architectural*** *ornaments* of a city 都会の建築美. ¶a ***bright*** *ornament* to ... ...の誇り(となる人または物). ¶a ***charming*** *ornament* for ... ...の美しい飾り. ¶one of the ***chief*** *ornaments* of the university 同大学の主な誇りの一つ(名声ある教授など). ¶Marx's Capital was a ***delightful scientific*** *ornament* for a political movement of the déclassé sons of the lower middle classes. マルクスの資本論は下層没落中産階級の子弟の政治運動に対する快い科学的装飾として愛用された. ¶a ***fussy*** *ornament* こってりした装飾. ¶a ***garish*** *ornament* 華美に過ぎた装飾. ¶a ***gay*** *ornament* 華美な飾りもの. ¶entirely devoid of ***literary*** *ornament* 全く文飾のない. ¶a man who is a ***mere*** *ornament* to the board of directors 重役会の飾りに過ぎない人. ¶***meretricious*** *ornament* けばけばしい装飾. ¶a ***personal*** *ornament* 飾身具. ¶the ***prime*** *ornament* 主な誇り.

Q^2 ***dress*** *ornaments* 衣服のアクセサリ. ¶***church*** *ornaments* 教会の付属品(オルガン・鐘・銀器など). ¶a ***garden*** *ornament* 庭の飾り. ¶a ***mantel*** *ornament* 炉だなの装飾物.

P It is used ***as*** an *ornament*. それは装飾として用いられる. ¶***for*** mere *ornament* ほんの飾りに. 【類】raise a peacock ***for*** *ornament* ‖ Fifty years ago tomatoes were scarce and called "Love Apples," being principally cultivated ***for*** *ornament*. 五十年前はトマトは少なかったそして主として装飾用として栽培されて「愛のりんご」と呼ばれていた. ¶There was much elaboration ***of*** *ornament*. 大層手の込んだ飾りつけがあった. ¶***without*** *ornaments* 装飾なしに, アクセサリをつけないで.

P^2 an *ornament **for*** the ear (head) 耳(頭)の飾り. ¶It will be an *ornament **to*** your family. それはあなたの家の誇りとなるだろう. ‖ The building, when finished, will be an *ornament **to*** the city. その建物はでき上ると市の誇りになるだろう.

ornament, *v*. 飾る, 装飾する, 文飾する.

P highly *ornamented **with*** paintings and inlays 絵画や象眼でりっぱに装飾してある. 【類】*ornament* a dress ***with*** lace / be *ornamented **with*** sculpture / *ornamented **with*** fresco paintings (壁画).

ornamentation, *n*. 装飾, 修飾, 文飾.

Q be used for ***indoor*** *ornamentation* 家内の装飾に用いられる. ¶***Romanesque*** *ornamentation* ローマ風の装飾. ¶without ***silly*** *ornamentation* ばかげた装飾抜きで.

Q^2 ***wall*** *ornamentations* 壁面装飾品.

orphan, *n*. 孤児.

Q^2 an ***infant*** *orphan* 幼い孤児. ¶a ***raid*** *orphan* 戦災孤児. ¶a ***war*** *orphan* 戦災孤児.

P^2 He was left an *orphan **of*** an early age. 彼は幼い時孤児となった. ¶They were made *orphans **in*** the recent earthquake. 彼らはさきごろの地震で孤児になった.

O An *orphan* is a child whose parents are dead or who has lost one parent. orphan というのは両親または片親を失った子供である.

orphan, *v*. 孤児にする.

M ***newly*** *orphaned* 孤児となったばかりの.

P be *orphaned **at*** an early age 幼い時孤児となる.

orphanage, *n*. 孤児院.

Q^2 a ***church*** *orphanage* 教会付属の孤児院.

orthography, *n*. 正字法, つづり字法.

Q ***capricious*** *orthography* (英語のように)気まぐれ(不規則)なつづり. ¶adopt ***modern*** *orthography* 近代式つづり字法を採用する.

oscillate, *v*. 動揺する.

P *oscillate **between*** ... and ... (値段などが)...と...の間を動揺(上下)する.

oscillation, *n*. 動揺, 振動, 昇降.

Q ***violent*** *oscillations* in price 値段の劇変.

ossify, *v*. 骨化する, 堅くなる.

P The bones of a baby begin to *ossify **in*** the fourth month after birth. 赤児の骨は生後四カ月たってから堅くなり始める.

ostentation, *n*. 外飾, 虚飾.

V He ***detested*** *ostentation* in any form. 彼はあらゆる虚飾をきらった.

Q ***studied*** *ostentations* of learning はなはだしいげん学.

P^2 the *ostentation **of*** the newly-rich 成金[ども]の見せびらかし.

ostentacious, *a*. 見えを張った.

P It was thought *ostentacious **of*** him. それは彼の見え坊と思われた.

ostracism, *n*. [社会の]排撃, 疎外.

V ***brave*** social *ostracism* 社会の非難を忍ぶ. ¶***invite*** social *ostracism* 社会の排斥を招く.

Q the hardening and depraving influences of ***social*** *ostracism* 人をがん迷偏屈にさせる社会的疎外の力.

ostrich, *n.* だちょう.
V *pluck* an *ostrich* だちょうの羽をむしる.
Q the *so-called human ostrich* いわゆる人間のだちょう(美々しく飾り立てた婦人).
P bury one's head in the sand *like* an *ostrich* 頭隠してしり隠さず. ¶have the digestion *of* an *ostrich* 馬みたいな胃袋をもっている(大食する).

other, *n.* 他のもの.
Q and not a *few others* そして少なからぬ他のもの. ¶a *good many others* その他沢山. ¶It is *no other* than this. 余の儀にあらず. ¶*no other* than the president himself だれあろう大統領自身. ¶Show me *some others* of this kind. この手をもう少し見せて下さい.
P *among others* とりわけ. ¶He has no regard *for others*. 彼は他人のことは考えない. ¶suggestions *from others* はたからの注意. ¶Don't speak ill *of others* behind them. 人のかげ口をきくな.
P² it was no *other than* ... それはだれあろう…であった. ¶Do good *to others*. 人に親切にせよ. 【類】Do *to others* as you wish to have them do to you.

otherwise, *a.* 別な, 違った.
M It is *quite otherwise* with him. 彼の場合は全く別だ.

ounce, *n.* オンス.
Q *fluid ounces* (drachms) 液量オンス(ドラム).
P It is sold *by* the *ounce*. それはオンス売りをする.
P² an *ounce of* gold 一オンスの金 ‖ He's got not an *ounce of* humanity (charity, common sense, courage). 彼には人情味(など)はこれっぱかりもない.

oust, *v.* 追出す, 放逐する.
P *oust* a person *from* a place (school, firm) 人を場所(など)から放逐する. 【類】a person *ousted from* public office (公職).

out, *n.* 〖競技〗負け(アウト); ぱっとしないこと.
Q There was a *graceful* "*out*". [りっぱな負け方をして]負けても面目を失わずにすんだ. ¶make a *poor out* (＝show) ぱっとしない.
P She is *at outs* (＝on the outs) with her in-laws. ((米)) 彼女はこじゅうとたちと仲が悪い.

out, *ad.* 誤って, 間違って; 外に出て.
M when she was *a few days out* 船が出帆してから二三日目に. ¶It is *dangerously out* of the true reckoning. それははなはだしい誤算だ. ¶You are *quite out*. 君は全く見当違いをしている. ‖ I am *quite out* of ... 当店では…はすっかり品を切らしました.
P He is *out for* reputation (wealth, honor, success). 彼は名声(など)を得ようときゅうきゅうとしている. ¶a clerk *out of* a berth 失業中の元の店員. ¶The money is *out on* loan. その金は貸出してある. ¶I am a little *out with* him. 僕は彼と少しく折合が悪い. ‖ I am *out with* my anxiety (trouble). 私は心配(など)で途方に暮れている.
O He went *out* the door. ((米)) 彼は出て行った. 【類】look *out* the window. ¶drive *out* Main Street 大通りをドライブする.

outbreak, *n.* 発生, ぼっ発.
V an *outbreak* of typhoid *followed* ... …に続いてチブスが発生した. ¶the house where the *outbreak started* 火元の家.
Q owing to the *reported outbreak* of hostilities between ... …間に戦争がぼっ発したと報ぜられたので. ¶a *revolutionary outbreak* 革命のぼっ発. ¶Berlin was suffering then from a *severe outbreak* of duelling fever. ベルリンは当時決闘熱が大流行で困っていた. ¶a *spontaneous outbreak* of national feeling against ... …に対する国民的反感の自然的発生. ¶*sporadic outbreaks* of the same sort 同種類のものがまばらに発生すること. ¶a *threatened outbreak* of civil war 起りそうに思われる内乱のぼっ発. ¶*volcanic outbreaks* 火山の爆発.
Q² a *food-poisoning outbreak* 中毒発生. ¶*pre-Korean war outbreak* 朝鮮戦争ぼっ発前.
P *at* the *outbreak* of the European war (＝hostilities) ヨーロッパ戦争のぼっ発当時. ¶just *before* the *outbreak* of hostilities 戦争の始まるちょっと前に. ¶*on* the *outbreak* of war 戦端が開かれたときに.
P² an *outbreak of* peasants against land owners 地主に反抗する百姓一き ‖ an *outbreak of* fever 熱病の突発. 【類】an *outbreak of* fire (war) / an *outbreak of* rebellion.

outburst, *n.* ぼっ発.
Q *occasional outbursts* of license 折々の底抜け騒ぎ. ¶his *volcanic outbursts* against the ideas not in sympathy with his own 自分が共鳴しない思想に対する彼の猛烈な反抗. ¶many a *warm outburst* of "Viva Italia" なんども繰返される「イタリア万歳」の熱心な叫び.
P² an *outburst of* temper かんしゃく玉の破裂. 【類】an *outburst of* steam (anger, laughter).

outcast, *n.* 追放された人, 浪人, 無宿者.
V *rehabilitate* a social *outcast* 社会的制裁を受けた者を元の地位に復帰させる.
Q brand a harlot as a *social outcast* 売笑婦を社会ののけ者にする. ¶a *legal outcast* 法律上の罪人. ¶*tattered outcasts* ぼろを着た浮浪者.
P² an *outcast from* civilization 文明から除外された者 ‖ an *outcast from* society＝a social outcast.

outcome, *n.* 結果, 成果.
V *decide* the *outcome* of a war 戦争の勝敗を決定する. ¶But it would be premature to *forecast* the *outcome*. しかし結果を予想するのは尚早であろう. ¶*watch* the *outcome* of an affair 事件の結果を見守る.
Q the *direct outcome* of ... …の直接の結果. ¶as the *final outcome* あげくの果てに. ¶the *inevitable outcome* of ... …の不可避的結果. ¶Prostitution is the *logical outcome* of nymphomania. 売春は乱いん症の論理的帰着である. ¶*natural outcome* 自然の結果. ¶the *ultimate outcome* of ... …の究極の結果.
P *as* an *outcome* of this tendency この傾向の結果として.
P² The tragedy is the *outcome of* jealousy. その悲劇はしっとの結果である. ‖ the new organization is the *outcome of* a meeting held at ... その新団体は…で開かれた会合の結果成立したものである. 【類】The *outcome of* the war was involved in doubt.

outcry, *n.* 叫び; 騒ぎ.
V The robber warned him to *make* no *outcry*. 賊は声を立てるなと彼に警告を与えた. ‖ *make* an *outcry* for nothing なんでもないことに大騒ぎする. ¶The appearance of this work *occasioned* a great *outcry* (＝sensation) at Rome. この著作が出版されてローマに一大波紋を起した. ¶*raise* an *outcry* against ... 盛んに…を攻撃する.
Q there has been *continual outcry* against ... …非難の声が絶えない. ¶a *fierce outcry* is raised against ... …攻撃の猛烈な叫声があがっている. ¶I have no sympathy with a *jingo outcry*. 私は開戦論者の叫びには共鳴しない. ¶the *popular outcry* against ... …に反抗する民衆の叫声 ‖ *popular outcry* was raised against ... …に反対する民衆の叫び声があげられた. ¶a *public outcry* 世人の叫び.
P² spasmodic *outcries against* foreign competition 外国の競争に対抗して時々あげる叫び声.

outdistance, *v.* 追い越す, 抜く.
P *outdistanced by* their rivals 彼らの競争者に追い越されて.

outdo, *v.* りょうがする.
P be *outdone in* patience (fighting spirit) 根負け(など)がする.
O Not *outdone*, he tried it again. 気おちしないで再びやった.

outfit, *n.* 支度, 身支度.
V This *completed* the *outfit*. これで支度が全部調った. ¶The laboratory *demands* costly and elaborate *outfit*. その研究所は金のかかる手の込んだ設備を要する.
Q a *bride's outfit*. 花嫁の衣装一式. ¶a *complete outfit* of stores 用品一切. ¶a *good outfit* of underclothing and linen 下着やリンネルの十分の用意. ¶*infants' outfit* 幼児の身支度. ¶a *meager outfit* 貧弱な調度. ¶articles of *tourists' outfits* 観光者用品.
Q² an officer in the *Army outfit* 陸軍の軍服をつけた将校. ¶a *bath outfit* 入浴用品. ¶a *camping outfit* 野営装備. ¶a *cooking outfit* 割ぽう用具. ¶a *radio* (*TV*) *outfit* ラジオ(テレビ)セット. ¶a *ski outfit* スキー用具. ¶a *travel*[*ing*] *outfit* 旅行装具. ¶an *X-ray outfit* エックス線器具.
P² an *outfit for* a skiing trip スキー旅行のための装具 ‖ the *outfit of* a lady on her marriage 婦人の結婚衣装.

outfitter, *n.* 用度屋.
Q one of the most famous firms of *gentlemen's outfitters* 紳士装身具を商う有名な商会の一つ.

outgo, *n.* 出費.
Q *all outgo* and no income 出るばかりで入る金がない.

outgoing, *n.* 出発, 出立.
V *celebrate* the *outgoing* of the old year 忘年会をやる.

outgrow, *v.* より大きくなる; [悪い癖などを]捨てる.
O The child has *outgrown* his clothes. 子供が大きくなっ

てきものが小さくなった. ‖ One's family has *outgrown* one's house. 家族がふえて家が手ぜまになった. ‖ *outgrow* one's bad habits 悪い癖が抜ける.

outgrowth, *n.* 結果.

Q the ***direct*** *outgrowth* of ... ...の直接の結果.

P² the *outgrowth* ***of*** nine years' experience in the teaching of high school and college students 九年間の中学生及び大学生を教えた経験の結果 ‖ The Graduate School of Education at Cornell University is an *outgrowth* ***of*** the University Division of Education. コーネル大学の教育研究科は同大学教育部発展の結果である. ‖ the *outgrowth* ***of*** leaves on a tree 木の若葉.

outing, *n.* 郊外散策, 外出.

V ***have*** an *outing* 郊外散策をやる. ¶***plan*** an *outing* for the next day 翌日のハイキングを計画する. ¶***take*** one's *outing* with a pleasant companion 愉快な友人と一しょに散歩をする.

Q one of the ***annual*** *outings* of the Company's employees 同会社雇人の年一度の遠足. ¶To many any *outing* is ***insupportable*** unless accompanied by eating and drinking. 遠足をしても食物や飲む物がなくてはつまらないという人が多い.

Q² an ***auto*** (a ***bicycle***) *outing* 自動(転)車旅行. ¶a ***holiday*** *outing* 休日行楽. ¶a ***summer*** *outing* 夏の行楽.

outlaw, *n.* 無頼漢, 無法者.

Q the ***Littlest*** *Outlaw* 〘映画〙 少さな無法者.

outlaw, *v.* 《米》 禁止する.

P Genocidal weapons, such as H-bombs, ought to be *outlawed* ***for*** good and all. 大量殺人兵器例えば水爆などは永久に禁止すべきだ.

outlawry, *n.* 不法行為.

Q ***international*** *outlawry* 国際的暴行.

outlay, *n.* 出費, 費用, 入費.

V I cannot ***afford*** such an *outlay*. そんな出費にはたえられない. ¶This will not ***cover*** my original *outlay*. これでは私の元が取れないだろう. ¶***entail*** heavy *outlays* 多額の出費を余儀なくする. ¶***exceed*** a total *outlay* of ... ...の全出費を超過する. ¶The nation has never shown any inclination to ***grudge*** its *outlay* for educational purposes. その国民には教育のために出費を惜しむような傾向はいまだかつてなかった. ¶It ***involves*** a large *outlay* of money. それはばく大な支出を要する. ¶It does not ***justify*** the *outlay*. そのためにそれだけ出費をするのは当を得ない. ‖ The machine has several advantages which ***justify*** such a huge *outlay*. その機械にはそれだけの巨費を投じるだけの種々な利益がある. ¶considerable *outlay* has been ***made*** for ... ...のために巨額の費用が支出された. ¶***necessitate*** an *outlay* of ... ...の出費を必要とする. ¶***recoup*** the *outlay* 支出を回収する. ¶***reimburse*** an *outlay* 費用を弁償する. ¶it ***represents*** an *outlay* of ... その費用は...である. ¶***require*** a heavy *outlay* 巨大な出費を必要とする.

Q an ***additional*** *outlay* その上の費用. ¶owing to the heavy amount of ***capital*** *outlay* for ... ...の多額の出資のため. ¶The establishment of a sound film production requires an ***enormous*** *outlay* of capital. 録音フィルム製作所の設立には巨額の資本金がいる. ¶involve an ***estimated*** *outlay* of ... 概算...の出費を要する. ¶lead to a ***heavy*** *outlay* その結果巨額の出費となる. ¶***initial*** *outlay* 最初の出費. ¶a ***modest*** *outlay* 小額の出費. ¶with a ***small*** *outlay* わずかな費用で. ¶a ***trifling*** *outlay* ささいな費用. ¶entail ***vast*** *outlays* 巨額の出費を必要とする.

P ***at*** a heavy *outlay* 巨額の費用で. ¶***for*** an *outlay* of ... yen, you can obtain ... ...円出すと...が得られる. ¶form a collection ***on*** a comparatively small *outlay* 比較的わずかの費用で収集をやる. ¶There are few pleasures to be had ***with*** such a very little *outlay* of time and money as this. こんなきわめて零細な時間と金で買える楽しみはまずないといってよい.

P² That means an *outlay* ***of*** large capital. それは巨額の資本金を要するということになる.

outlet, *n.* 出口, はけ口; 販路.

V ***find*** an *outlet* for one's emotions その感情のはけ口を見出だす ‖ ***find*** an *outlet* for the energy of its people その国民の元気のはけ口を見出だす. 【類】***find*** *outlets* abroad. ¶***get*** an *outlet* for her surplus population その余剰人口のはけ口を求める. ¶***give*** wise *outlets* to the nation's resistless energies その国民のやむにやまれない元気に対して賢明なはけ口を与える. ¶***seek*** an *outlet* for their bored, restless existence 彼らの退屈な落着きのない生活に対して活路を求める. 【類】***seek*** an *outlet* for her increasing population and expanding trade / ***seek*** an *outlet* for her products / ***seek*** new *outlets* for these products / The child's pent-up energy (うっ積した元気) ***seeks*** its own *outlet*.

Q an ***emotional*** *outlet* 気晴し.

Q² give her a ***trade*** *outlet* to the Nile from her Congo possessions その国のコンゴーの領地からナイル川まで貿易の出口を与える. ¶a ***warm-water*** *outlet* 暖い海(不凍港)の出口. ¶Folly which is second nature to man and seems to be inborn must have a ***free*** *outlet* at least once a year. 人間の第二の天性でありかつ先天的と思われる愚行は少くとも一年に一度はこれを十分発揮させなくてはいけない.

P² an *outlet* ***for*** expression of one's inner feelings その心底にある感情表現のはけ口 ‖ an *outlet* ***for*** her overflowing population その国の過剰人口のはけ口 ‖ an *outlet* ***for*** internal trade 内国商業の販路. ¶the *outlet* ***of*** a lake 湖水の出口 ‖ find an *outlet* ***of*** (=for) expression 発表の機縁を見出だす.

outline, *n.* 輪郭, こう概, 概略, 綱領.

V the *outlines* of the subject may be ***followed*** in the works of ... その問題のこう概は...の著書においてうかがい見ることができる. ¶***give*** the *outline* of ... ...のこう概を述べる. 【類】***give*** a very brief and bold *outline* of the story of ... ¶***indicate*** its barest *outline* そのほんの輪郭だけを示す. ¶One good way to master the ideas of an article is to ***make*** an *outline* of it. 一文の内容をよく理解するよい方法はそれのこう概を作ることだ. ¶***sketch*** its *outlines* その概略を記す. ¶***trace*** the *outlines* of the history of ... ...史のこう概をたどる.

Q the ***bare*** *outlines* of his life 彼の伝記のほんの輪郭. 【類】The story, reduced to the ***barest*** *outline* (せんじ詰めると), is that of the relations of Trafford to his wife. / It is more than this short paper can sketch, even in ***bare*** *outline*. / a ***bare*** *outline* of the subject / the ***barest*** *outline* of the essential features of a proposal. ¶a ***biographical*** *outline* 小伝. ¶The mountains printed their ***bold*** *outlines* on the clear evening sky. 山々は晴れた夕空にそのくっきりした輪郭を染めつけた. 【類】stand in ***bold*** *outline* against the sky. ¶Such is a ***brief*** *outline* of the nature and contents of the present work. 以上が今の仕事の性質及び内容の簡単なこう概である. 【類】in ***brief*** *outline*. ¶in ***broad*** *outlines* 大体から見て ‖ a ***broad*** *outline* of ... ...の大意. 【類】It can only be described in its ***broadest*** *outline* here. ¶see in ***clearer*** *outline* ... 一層明確に...を認める. ¶a ***concise*** *outline* of Chinese history 中国歴史のこう概. ¶an ***elementary*** *outline* of ... ...の初歩的概略. ¶give in a ***few hasty*** *outlines* 二三の輪郭だけを略述する. ¶in the distance the ***hazy*** *outline* of Mt. Fuji 遠方には富士山のかすんだ輪郭. ¶a ***historical*** *outline* of French literature フランス文学史の大綱. ¶pyramidal in ***general*** *outline* 大体ピラミッド形の. ¶the ***main*** *outline* of a scheme 計画の概要. ¶try to build up a ***mental*** *outline* of その輪郭を思い浮べようと努める. ¶a ***rough*** *outline* 荒筋. ¶a ***shadowy*** *outline* of a church tower 教会塔の薄暗い輪郭. ¶with its ***sharp*** *outlines* rounded その鋭い輪郭のかどが取れて.

Q² ***plot*** *outlines* of famous novels 有名な小説の荒筋. ¶a ***skeleton*** *outline* 大要.

P treat a subject ***in*** *outline* ある問題を概説する ‖ a girl masculine ***in*** *outline* 男のような体つきの少女 ‖ give ***in*** bare *outline* a description of ... ...のほんの大体を記述する ‖ ***in*** its main *outlines*, though not in details 詳細にわたるものではないがその重大な点において. 【類】***in*** the briefest *outline*.

P² *outlines* ***of*** a case ある事件のこう概 ‖ an *outline* ***of*** a lecture 講演の大要 ‖ see the *outline* ***of*** the mountains ***against*** the evening sky 山々の姿が夕空にくっきり見える.

outline, *v.* 輪郭を描く, 概略を記す.

M ***briefly*** *outlined* 簡単に概説した.

P Mt. Fuji *outlined* ***against*** the morning sky 朝空に輪郭を描いた富士.

outlook, *n.* 眺望, 景色, 光景; ...観, 見方.

V The tower ***affords*** a magnificent *outlook*. その塔は壮大な光景を示している. ¶***broaden*** (***narrow***) one's *outlook* その視野を拡大(狭く)する ‖ ***broaden*** one's *outlook* on life もっと広く人生を観察する. 【類】those who have had opportunities of ***broadening*** their *outlook*. ¶his *outlook* on life is ***colored*** by ... 彼の人生観は...の影響を受けている. ¶profoundly ***effect*** one's *outlook* on life その人生観に深い影響を与える. ¶***give*** us an unexpected or wider *outlook* upon life われわれをして人生に対し予期しないまたは一層広い観察をなさしめる. ¶It ***has*** a fine *outlook* on Fujisan. そこから富士山がよく見える.【類】It ***has*** a wide *outlook*. ¶***improve*** the *outlook* 眺望をよくする. ¶***show*** a favorable *outlook* 好都合な形勢を示す. ¶***widen*** one's intellectual *outlook* その知的展望を拡大する.

V² The European *outlook* then ***looked black*** indeed. 当時欧州の前途は実に暗たんたるものであった.

Q The *outlook* is ***black*** indeed. 前途はなはだ暗たんである. ¶a ***bright*** *outlook* 晴れやかな前途. ¶with a ***brighter, happier***, and more ***hopeful*** *outlook* on life 一層朗らかに一層幸福にまた一層有望に人生を観じて. ¶a ***broad*** *outlook* 広い見晴し. ¶the constantly ***broadening*** *outlook* of farm folks 農民の絶えず拡大し行く前途. ¶a ***broad intellectual*** *outlook* 広い知的見解. ¶mountains viewed from a ***distant*** *outlook* 遠くからながめた山々. ¶The *outlook* is ***encouraging***. 前途有望である. ¶a ***favorable*** *outlook* 好調な前途. ¶a ***general*** *outlook* upon the world and life 世界と人生に対する概観. ¶a ***gloomy*** *outlook* 暗たんたる前途. ¶The hotel has a ***good*** *outlook*. そのホテルは展望がよい. ¶a ***grievous*** *outlook* 悲しい前途. ¶a ***grim*** *outlook* 不吉な前途. ¶a ***hopeful*** *outlook* 有望な前途. ¶widen the ***mental*** *outlook* 知的展望を拡大する. ¶superior in ***moral*** *outlook* 道徳的見解のすぐれた. ¶show a ***narrow*** *outlook* 視野が狭いことを示す. ¶It has given me a ***new*** *outlook* upon life. それで私の人生観が変った. ¶***optimistic*** *outlook* and mental buoyancy 楽観的な見解と精神的快活. ¶a ***pleasant*** *outlook* over mountains and valleys 山や谷のよいながめ. ¶the ***political*** *outlook* 政治上の前途. ¶In spite of these defects his *outlook* seems to me fundamentally ***sound***. これらの欠点があるにも拘らず彼の観察は根本的には健全のように私には思われる. ¶the *outlook* became so ***threatening*** that ... 形勢が非常に不穏になって来たので... ¶a ***wide*** *outlook* on life 大局から見た人生観.

Q² one's ***business*** (=***commercial***) *outlook* 事業の見通し. ¶the ***crop*** (=***harvest***) *outlook* 収穫の見込. ¶The ***job*** *outlook* is the poorest since the war. 就職の形勢は戦後最も面白くない形相を示している. ¶his ***world*** *outlook* 彼の世界観.

P a room ***with*** a sunny *outlook* 日当りが良くてながめの良いへや.

P² a bright *outlook* ***for*** the petroleum industry 石油工業に対する有望な前途. ¶the *outlook* ***from*** the drawingroom 応接室からのながめ. ¶a stormy *outlook* ***in*** the Far East 極東における暗たんたる風雲. ¶the English *outlook* ***on*** life 英国人の人生観 ‖ their *outlook* ***on*** the world 彼らの世界観.【類】His *outlook* ***on*** life was the same at fifty as at thirty. / the *outlook* ***on*** foreign affairs. ¶Its situation gives it a wonderful *outlook* ***over*** the sea. その位置からは海の見晴しがすばらしい. ‖ his *outlook* ***over*** life 彼の人生観. ¶His creed is optimism always with a bright *outlook* ***to*** the future. 彼の信条は楽観主義でありいつも未来に対して明るい考えを持っている. ¶youth with its fresh *outlook* ***upon*** life 人生に対して新しい見方をする青年.【類】Tennyson's *outlook* ***upon*** nature.

outmatch, *v.* よりまさる.

P though *outmatched* ***in*** skill (art) 手腕(など)ではかなわないが.

outnumber, *v.* 数においてまさる, ...より多い.

M although ***greatly*** *outnumbered* 数こそ余ほど少ないが.

P A is *outnumbered* ***by*** B. A より B の方が数が多い.

O The former *outnumbers* the latter. 前者は後者よりも数が多い.

outpost, *n.* 前しょう地点, 辺境.

V ***visit*** the *outposts* of the Empire 同帝国の辺境を訪れる.

Q the ***farthest*** *outpost* of Western civilization in the Far East 極東における西洋文明の一番遠い地点(すなわち日本).

Q² ***Communist*** *outposts* in every country. 各国における共産党の前しょう. ¶The plane is machine-gunning the ***enemy*** *outposts*. 飛行機は敵の前しょうに銃撃をしつつある.

P far away ***at*** the *outposts* of the Empire 遠く離れた帝国の辺境において.

output, *n.* 産出高, 生産高.

V ***curtail*** the *output* 生産高を切詰める. ¶***extend*** its *output* その産出高を拡大する. ¶The factory ***has*** an *output* of 9,000,000 cigarettes daily (=a day). 同工場は日々九百万本の紙巻タバコを生産する. ¶***increase*** the *output* to ... 生産高を...に増加する ‖ the country ***increased*** her *output* of ... by ... その国は...の生産高が...だけ増した. ¶***limit*** an *output* to ... 生産高を...に制限する. ¶***market*** the *output* into San Francisco 生産品をサンフランシスコ市場に送り出す. ¶***reduce*** the *output* to ... 生産高を...に減じる. ¶***secure*** larger *outputs* さらに多額の生産をやる.

Q an ***annual*** *output* of ... ...の年産額. ¶the ***average*** *output* of eggs from the farm その農園の平均鶏卵産出額. ¶the ***coal*** *output* at the mines of Great Britain 大英国の鉱山における石炭の産出高. ¶Books by the ton are the ***daily*** *output* of our publishers. わが出版業者は日々幾トンの書籍を産出している. ¶It resulted in a ***diminished*** *output*. その結果生産高が減少するに至った. ¶the ***entire*** *output* 全生産高. ¶The result is an ***increased*** *output* and a decreased cost. その結果生産高は増し工費は減じた. ¶the ***literary*** *output* of the year その年の文学作品の出版総数(著作量).【類】the ***literary*** *outputs* of the world, exclusive of newspapers and periodicals / During these years his ***literary*** *output* was small. ¶the recent increase in the ***monthly*** *output* of periodicals 新聞雑誌の月産額における最近の増加. ¶***potential*** *output* 可能な生産高. ¶the ***vast*** *output* of new novels 新しい小説のばく大な生産高. ¶London's ***wonderful diurnal*** and ***weekly*** *output*, from The Times downwards タイムズを初めとしロンドンの驚くべき生産高を示す日刊及び週刊. ¶add to the ***world's*** *output* 大いに世界の生産高を増す.

Q² ***capacity*** *output* 全能力の産出. ¶***hard-coal*** *output* 硬石炭の産額. ¶***lagging*** *output* にぶる産出高. ¶Production is topping the ***prewar*** *output*. 産額は戦前を超過している. ¶a ***production*** *output* 生産額. ¶The ***steel*** *output* of Russia in 1904 was for the largest in the history of the country. 千九百四年ロシアの鋼鉄産額は優に同国歴史中最大なものであった. ¶Canada produced 102,600 tons of nickel in 1939 out of a total ***world*** *output* of 121,000. 千九百三十九年カナダは全世界のニッケル産額 121,000 トン中 102,600 トンを産出した.

P² the total *output* ***for*** six years was under ... 六年間の全生産高は...以下であった. ¶the *output* ***of*** coal from the Naval Collieries 海軍採炭所の石炭採掘高.

outrage, *n.* 乱暴, 暴行, ろうぜき.

V ***cause*** an *outrage* to ... ...に暴行を加える. ¶***commit*** an *outrage* on the British flag 英国旗に対して暴行を加える ‖ ***commit*** an *outrage* on justice 正義を踏みにじる ‖ ***commit*** *outrages* upon ... ...に暴行を加える. ¶***perpetrate*** an *outrage* 暴行を働く. ¶***trace*** the *outrage* home to its perpetrator 暴行の下手人を調べ上げる.

Q an ***abominable*** *outrage* 忌まわしい暴行. ¶***another*** *outrage* on a foreigner 再び外人に対する暴行. ¶a ***gross*** *outrage* on good taste and manners 上品な趣味風習を無視したひどい乱暴. ¶commit a ***sacrilegious*** *outrage* 不敬の暴行を加える. ¶a ***serious*** *outrage* ひどい乱暴. ¶***terrible*** *outrage* 恐ろしい暴行.

Q² a ***bomb*** *outrage* 乱暴な爆撃.

P an art ***of*** *outrage* 乱暴な一行為. ¶never to be safe ***from*** *outrage* 暴力の不安からまぬかれないで.

P² an *outrage* ***against*** a person (country) 人(など)に対する暴行 ‖ *outrages* ***against*** public decency 風俗壊乱.【類】an *outrage* ***against*** (=on) humanity. ¶*outrages* ***on*** innocent individuals 何の罪もない人々に対する暴行.【類】an *outrage* ***on*** a woman.

outreach, *n.* 発展.

Q Japan's ***commercial*** *outreach* 日本の商業的海外発展.

outset, *n.* 手始め, 最初, 起首.

P Do not trouble yourself much about this matter ***at*** the *outset*. この件については最初あまり気をもんではいけない. ‖ The folly of the thing has been demonstrated ***at*** the very *outset*. そのことの愚かなことは最初から明確に分かっていた. ‖ as intended ***at*** the *outset* 予定通り.【類】***at*** the *outset* it should be stated that ... / ***at*** the *outset* of the proceedings (議事) / ***at*** the *outset* of one's career / ***at*** the *outset* of parturition (分べん徴候). ¶It fascinates the reader ***from*** the *outset*. それは読み始めから読者を魅了する.【類】***from*** the *outset* of the war beween Russia and Japan.

outside, *n.* 外側, 外部.

V ***criticize*** the *outside* of one's life 人の生活の表面に表われたところを批評する.

P He is some two and twenty ***at*** the *outside*. 彼はせいぜい二十二歳位だ. ‖ ***at*** the very *outside* いくら多くふんでも. 【類】$ 10 or $ 12 ***at*** the *outside*. ¶look ***from*** the *outside* very like ... 外部からは丁度...のように見える. ¶***on*** the *outside* of the gate 門の外側に.

P^2 The measurement is ***on*** the *outside*. 寸法は外法だ.

outside, *ad.* 外に, 外部に.

P Zeal without knowledge has done a vast amount of harm in the world, even *outside* ***of*** religion. 知識を伴わない熱心は宗教以外でも随分多くの害毒を流した. 【類】*Outside* ***of*** his secretary, no one knew his views.

outsider, *n.* 門外漢, しろうと.

V ***repel*** *outsiders* 門外漢を寄せつけない.

Q a rather ***inexperienced*** *outsider* いく分経験に乏しい門外漢 ‖ the ***inexperienced*** *outsider* may jump to the conclusion that ... 未経験のしろうとは...と早合点するかも知れない. ¶a ***mere*** *outsider* 全くの門外漢.

P ***to*** the *outsiders* はたで見ていると.

outskirt, *n.* 外辺, 辺境; [主に *pl.*] 郊外.

V streets ***fringing*** the *outskirts* of London ロンドンの周辺をふちどる街々.

Q on the ***eastern*** *outskirts* of Tokyo 東京の東郊に. 【類】On the ***extreme northwestern*** *outskirts* of the city stands the Buddhist temple of Gokokuji, now used as the headquarters of the Shingon sect.

P ***at*** the *outskirts* of a town 町外れに ‖ the Gobi Desert, just ***at*** the *outskirts* of China proper 中国本部の丁度外辺にあるゴビのさばく. ¶start a small plant ***in*** the *outskirts* of the city 同市の郊外に小工場を起す. ¶***on*** the *outskirts* of a town 町外れに. 【類】The children have been out for the day to some green spot ***on*** the *outskirts*—perhaps Richmond. / Maruyama is one of a range of hills rising ***on*** the *outskirts* of the ancient city of Kyoto. / ***on*** the *outskirts* (回りに) of the crowd.

outspoken, *a.* 率直な.

P He is *outspoken* ***in*** his remarks. 彼は言葉を飾らない.

outspokenness, *n.* 率直.

V ***admire*** his *outspokenness* 彼の率直を賞賛する.

outspread, *a.* 広げて.

O with wings *outspread* 翼をぐっとひろげて.

outstrip, *v.* 走り越す, 追い抜く; [力で]まさる.

P He was *outstripped* ***by*** his rivals. 彼はその競争者に追い越された. ¶*outstrip* the West ***in*** ... ...において西洋をしのぐ.

outvie, *v.* 競い勝つ.

P *outvying* each other ***in*** ... ...を互いに競いつつ.

outweigh, *v.* より重い.

P The gain is *outweighed* ***by*** the loss. 失う所多く得る所が少い.

O The advantages *outweigh* the drawbacks. 長所の方が欠点より多い.

outwit, *v.* 機知においてまさる, 知恵で勝つ.

P be *outwitted* ***by*** ... 機知では...に及ばない.

O The thief *outwitted* the police and beat it. その盗賊はうまく警官をごま化して逃げた.

ovation, *n.* 歓迎, 大かっさい.

V A great multitude of people ***gave*** him a tremendous *ovation*. 大群衆が盛んに彼を歓迎した. ¶He ***received*** a tremendous *ovation* on his initial appearance at the opera-house. 彼はオペラに初出演したとき大かっさいを受けた. ¶They ***rendered*** an *ovation* to the hero of Port Arthur. 彼らは旅順の勇士を歓迎した.

Q receive a ***great*** *ovation* 大歓迎を受ける. ¶receive ***tremendous*** *ovations* 大歓迎を受ける.

Q^2 draw a ***record*** *ovation* from ... ...から未曽有のかっさいを博する.

P He was received ***with*** a thunderous *ovation*. 彼は大かっさいをもって迎えられた.

P^2 He received an *ovation* ***from*** the throng. 彼は群衆から歓迎を受けた.

over, *ad.* 越えて, 終って.

M ***all*** *over* 到るところに, 一面. 【類】travel ***all*** *over* / get wet ***all*** *over* ‖ It's ***all*** *over* now. もう万事休すだ. ¶a person ***just*** *over* (外国から)来たての人. ¶The subscription was covered ***twice*** *over*. 応募者は二倍あった.

P *over* ***against*** the school 学校の向い側に. ¶It is all *over* ***with*** him. もう彼もだめだ.

O It's all *over*. もうだめだ, 万事休す.

overage, *a.* 年齢超過の.

P be *overage* ***for*** the draft 兵役適齢期を過ぎている.

overall, *n. pl.* [職工などの]仕事ズボン(オーバロール).

Q dock workers in ***white*** *overalls* 白いオーバロールを着たドック労務者たち.

Q^2 in ***denim*** *overalls* デニムのオーバロールを着て.

overawe, *v.* 威圧する, 感服させる, おどす.

P I was *overawed* ***by*** his grandeur. 私は彼の威光に打たれた. ¶He was *overawed* ***into*** submission (fear, respect). 彼はおどされて服従(など)した.

overbalance, *v.* まさる, (重さなどで)勝つ.

M ***overwhelmingly*** *overbalance* ... 圧倒的に...にまさる.

overburden, *v.* [責任など]負わせすぎる.

P be *overburdened* ***with*** work (grief) 仕事(など)が多過ぎる.

overcast, *a.* [空一面に]曇った.

P The sky was getting *overcast* ***before*** the storm. あらしの前に空が曇って来た.

overcharge, *n.* 掛値, 取りすぎ.

Q a ***monstrous*** *overcharge* ひどい掛値. ¶***greedy tradesmen's*** or ***innkeepers'*** *overcharges* 欲の深い商人や旅館主の吹掛け値.

overcharge, *v.* 掛値をする, 積み過ぎる.

M ***grossly*** *overcharge* foreigners 外人に対して大いにぼる.

P words of thanks gushing from hearts *overcharged* ***with*** gratitude 感謝にあふれる心からほとばしり出る礼の言葉.

overcoat, *n.* 外とう(オーバー).

V ***have on*** one's *overcoat* オーバーを着ている. ¶***keep on*** one's *overcoat* オーバーを着たままでいる. ¶***put*** (***throw***) ***on*** one's *overcoat* オーバーを(さっと)ひっかける. ¶***take*** (***slip***) ***off*** one's *overcoat* オーバーを(急いで)脱ぐ. ¶He ***threw*** his *overcoat* across his shoulders. 彼はオーバーを肩にひっかけた.

Q a ***dual*** *overcoat* 晴雨兼用オーバー.

Q^2 a ***cape*** *overcoat* カッパ型外とう.

P ***in*** *overcoat* オーバーを着て. ¶I helped her on (off) ***with*** her *overcoat*. 彼女にオーバーを着せて(ぬがして)やった.

overcome, *v.* 勝つ, 破る, 負かす.

M The fire was ***completely*** *overcome* by daybreak. 火は夜明けまでに全く消し止めた. ¶He was ***quite*** *overcome* with grief. 彼は全く悲嘆に暮れていた.

P *overcome* ***by*** despair 絶望のあまり ‖ He was *overcome* ***by*** their entreaties. 彼はその手合に拝み倒されてしまった. 【類】*overcome* ***by*** jealousy / He was *overcome* ***by*** numbers. 彼は数においては敵し得なかった. ¶He was *overcome* ***with*** astonishment. 彼は驚がくのあまり身のおく所を知らなかった. ‖ *overcome* ***with*** emotion 感きわまって. 【類】He is *overcome* ***with*** homesickness.

overdose, *n.* 薬の盛り過ぎ, 過量.

P^2 an *overdose* ***of*** cocaine コカインの分量過多.

overdue, *a.* 期間過ぎの.

P be *overdue* ***for*** repair 修理が手遅れになっている.

overemphasis, *n.* 過度の強調.

V ***put*** an *overemphasis* on ... ...を余り重く見過ぎる.

over-fatigue, *n.* 過労.

V It is apt to ***produce*** *over-fatigue*. それは過労をきたしやすい.

overflow, *n.* はんらん, 過多.

P^2 an *overflow* ***of*** population 人口の過剰. 【類】According to Herbert Spencer, the singing of birds is due to "*overflow* ***of*** energy."

overflow, *v.* はんらんする, あふれる.

P The crowd *overflowed* ***into*** the street. 群集はあふれて道路にはみ出した. ¶Banks are *overflowing* ***with*** deposits. 銀行は預金であふれている. ‖ hearts *overflowing* ***with*** sympathy (gratitude, grief) 同情(など)で一杯の胸 ‖ the bank *overflowing* ***with*** water はんらんする河畔.

O The river is *overflowing* its banks. 水が両岸からあふれている.

overflowing, *n.* あふれること.

P a glass filled ***to*** *overflowing*. [酒など]こぼれそうになったグラス.

overgrow, *v.* 一面に生える, はびこる.

M The recess of the mountain is ***beautifully*** *overgrown* with vegetation. その山のくぼみには美しく樹木が繁茂している.

P an open space *overgrown* ***with*** weeds (grass, wild flowers) 雑草(など)の一面に生えている空地. 【類】a tomb *overgrown* ***with*** thorns and briars.

overhaul, *v.* [機械を]精密検査する, 分解検査(オーバホール)する.

P a person to be *overhauled* ***by*** a doctor 人間ドックにはいる人.

O an engine (a motor) to be *overhauled* オーバーホール

するはずのエンジン(など).

overhaul[ing], *n.* [機械の]分解(精密)検査(オーバーホール).

V ***give*** their business a thorough *overhauling* 彼らの商売を十分に点検する. ¶an old plane (engine) that ***requires*** *overhauling* オーバーホールの必要ある古飛行機(など).

Q after a ***thorough overhaul*** 精密検査の後. 【類】have a ***thorough overhauling*** of the accounts (会計).

overhead, *n.*〘商〙諸掛り.

V ***reduce overheads*** 諸掛りを削減する.

overindulgence, *n.* たんでき.

Q ***sexual overindulgence*** 性のたんでき.

P² *overindulgence* ***in*** alcohol アルコールのたんでき.

overjoy, *v.* 大いに喜ばす.

P He was *overjoyed* ***with*** (=***at***) the news. 彼はその知らせを聞いて非常に喜んだ.

overlay, *v.* めっきする.

P *overlaid* ***with*** gold 金めっきをした.

overload, *v.* 積み過ぎる, 載せ過ぎる.

P *overloaded* ***with*** duties (=work) 仕事が多過ぎて ‖ be *overloaded* ***with*** notes 注をやたらに付けてある.

overneatness, *n.* 過度の簡素.

P² *overneatness* ***of*** style 文体の過度な簡素.

overnight, *ad.* 夜通し.

P It is just *overnight* ***from*** Tokyo by rail or boat. 東京から汽車か船でわずか一晩でそこに行かれる.

overpower, *v.* 威圧する, 屈服させる.

P *overpowered* ***by*** a person (the enemy) 人(など)によって威圧されて. ¶*overpowered* ***with*** her beauty 彼女の美ぼうに魅了されて.

overrank, *v.* 上位にある.

P The comma is ordinarily *overranked* ***by*** the dash. [句切りの軽重において]コンマは通常ダッシュの下位にある.

over-refineness, *n.* 過度の精練.

P² *over-refineness* ***of*** analysis 分析の過度の精密さ.

overrun, *v.* 漫延する, 繁茂する.

P *overrun* ***with*** weeds (grass) 雑草(など)のはびこった.

overscrupulous, *a.* 用心過ぎる.

P be *overscrupulous* ***about*** one's work 仕事に細心であり過ぎる. ¶young men who are not *overscrupulous* ***in*** the selection of topics for conversation 会話の話題選択に余り心を用いない青年.

overshadow, *v.* …の光りを奪う.

M *overshadow* a person ***entirely*** 人をして全く顔色なからしめる.

P The whole town was *overshadowed* ***by*** the sad news. その悲報で全市が憂色につつまれた.

overshoot, *v.* 射越す, 射はずす.

P *overshoot* oneself ***in*** making an estimate 失当の見積りをする.

oversight, *n.* 見落し, 遺脱; 失策; 取締り.

V It is incredible that he should have ***committed*** this *oversight*. 彼がこの失策をやったとは信じられない. ¶***exercise*** too severe an *oversight* あまり厳重な取締りをやる.

Q by ***extraordinary*** *oversight* 非常な失策で. ¶a ***regrettable*** *oversight* 遺憾な手抜かり. ¶an ***unintentional*** *oversight* うっかりやった手落ち.

P ***by*** (=through) an *oversight* 手落で. ¶***owing to*** some *oversight* ある手抜かりのため. ¶He did it ***through*** an *oversight*. 彼はうっかりそれをやった. ¶practice work ***under*** *oversight* 監督の下に仕事をする. 【類】The dictionary was compiled ***under*** his *oversight*. / work ***under*** the *oversight* of a foreman / be ***under*** the *oversight* and direction of …

overspread, *v.* 広がる; 広げる, 一面に塗る.

P slices of bread *overspread* ***with*** butter バターを一面に塗った数片のパン ‖ The sky is *overspreading* ***with*** black clouds. 空は黒雲で一面におおわれている.

overtake, *v.* 追い付く, 追及する.

P *overtaken* ***by*** misfortune 不幸に出会って ‖ *overtaken* ***by*** a storm (the darkness) 暴風雨(など)に襲われて.

overtax, *v.* 過労させる.

P a throat *overtaxed* ***by*** singing 歌で使い過ぎたのど.

overthrow, *n.* 転倒, 転覆.

Q the ***final*** *overthrow* of exclusivism 排他主義の最後の転覆.

P ***on*** the *overthrow* of that dynasty その王朝が亡びて.

overthrow, *v.* 転覆する.

P The government was *overthrown* ***by*** the hands of Communists その政府は共産党の手で転覆された.

overtime, *n.* 時間外労働.

V ***ban*** *overtime* 時間外勤務を禁じる.

overtone, *n. pl.* 暗示, 含蓄, 余波.

Q ***political*** *overtones* 政治的なふくみ.

P a reply full ***of*** *overtones* 含蓄の多い返事.

overture, *n.* 申出, 申込, 提案.

Q² make a ***peace*** *overture* 平和の提案をする.

P² an *overture* ***for*** peace 平和の申出.

overweight, *a.* 重量超過の.

O You have 50 yen *overweight*. あなたの荷物は五十円だけ規定の無料限度を超過しています.

overwhelm, *v.* 圧倒する; がっかりさせる.

M I am ***really*** *overwhelmed* by the sad news. 私はその悲報に接して本当にがっかりした.

P *overwhelm* a person ***by*** numbers 人を数で圧倒する. ¶a country *overwhelmed* ***with*** debt 負債で財政難に陥った国 ‖ *overwhelmed* ***with*** work (grief, gratitude) 仕事(など)のために閉口して ‖ be *overwhelmed* ***with*** orders 注文に追いまくられる.

overwork, *n.* 余分の仕事, 過労.

Q ***mental*** *overwork* 精神過労.

P get ill ***by*** *overwork* 過労で病気になる. 【類】He brought on an illness ***by*** *overwork*. ¶***from*** constant *overwork* 不断の過労のため. ¶The servant is always complaining ***of*** *overwork*. 召使は仕事が多過ぎるといつもこぼしている. ¶broken down ***through*** *overwork* 過労のため健康を害して.

P² *overwork* ***at*** school or college 学校や大学での過度の勉強.

overwork, *v.* 使い過ぎる, 過労させる.

M ***atrociously*** *overworked* and underpaid 酷使されそしてもらう給料も少く.

ovum, *n.* 卵子.

Q an ***impregnated*** *ovum* 受胎した卵子.

owe, *v.* 金を借りている, 負う.

P He *owes* (=is in debt) ***for*** his house. 彼は自分の家を建てたために借金している. ¶a debt *owed* ***to*** … …に借りた金 ‖ I *owe* much ***to*** him. 私は彼に負う所が多い. 【類】I *owe* my success ***to*** you. ‖ the book which we *owe* ***to*** the labors of … …の努力になる本. 【類】improvements which *owe* ***to*** the influence of the West.

owing, *a.* [に]よって.

P Oil stoves are convenient *owing* ***to*** their portability. 石油ストーブは持運びが便利だ. 【類】*owing* ***to*** the scantiness of … / the demand is *owing* ***to*** … / Business is neglected *owing* ***to*** the excitement caused by the election.

owl, *n.* ふくろう.

V The *owl* ***hoots***. ふくろうはほーほー鳴く. 【類】An *owl* softly ***hooted***. ¶The *owl* ***screams***. ふくろうは高い声で鳴く.

P The hooting ***of*** an *owl* broke the silence now and again. ふくろうの鳴声がときどき静けさを破った.

own, *n.* 自分のもの.

V will ***hold*** his *own* against … …に対抗できよう ‖ The patient is ***holding*** his *own*. 病人はまだしっかりしている.

P He can speak six languages ***besides*** his *own*. 彼は自分の国語の外に六カ国の国語を話すことができる. 【類】English is the only language he can speak ***besides*** his *own*. ¶a house ***of*** one's *own* 自分の家. 【類】property ***of*** one's *own*. ¶***on*** his *own* 自分の発意で ‖ stand ***on*** one's *own* 一本立ちになる. ¶I can do whatever I will ***with*** my *own*. 自分のものはどうしようと勝手だ.

own, *a.* 自身の, 独特の.

M features that are ***all*** his *own* 彼一流の特徴 ‖ The book has a value ***all*** its *own*. 同書には独特の価値がある. 【類】The orange has a scent ***all*** its *own*.

own, *v.* 所有する; 認める; 白状する.

M *own* ***ingenuously*** that … 自分から率直に…という. ¶the habit of reading a good ***personally*** *owned* book by the home fireplace 自分所蔵の良書をわが家の炉辺で読む習慣. ¶***privately*** *owned* property 私有財産.

M² *Own up* all you know about it. 知ってることは全部白状しろ. ‖ Nobody *owned up*. だれも自白しなかった.

P *own* a boy ***as*** one's child 子供をわが子と認定する. ¶*own* oneself ***in*** the wrong 自分が悪いと認める. ¶*own* ***to*** a fault 過失を認める ‖ He *owns* ***to*** the hobby of book collecting. 彼は書籍収集が趣味だと自分で言っている. ‖ It is his own money, though he will not *own* ***to*** it. 彼はそれを自分の金だとは言わないが事実彼のものだ.

O It is scarce worth *owning*. それは所有する価値がほとんどない.

owner, *n*. 所有者, 持主.

Q an ***extensive*** property *owner* 大地主. ¶the ***joint*** *owners* of the object possessed 所有物の共同所有者. ¶the ***largest*** *owner* of the surface of the globe 地球上最大の領土を有する国[すなわち英国]. ¶a ***new*** *owner* of the house 家屋の新しい所有者.【類】The bird was deftly put into a paper bag, with the corners twisted up, and so carried off by its ***new owner***. ¶coals mining properties leased by ***non-operating*** *owners* 自己経営でなく他人に貸与してある石炭鉱区. ¶the ***onetime*** *owners* of dead dogs 死んだ犬のもとの飼主. ¶a ***part*** *owner* of a spinning mill 紡績工場の共同所有者の一人. ¶its ***proper*** *owner* その正当所有主. ¶a ***proud*** *owner* of ... ...を自慢にしている持主. ¶a ***registered*** *owner* 登記済の所有主. ¶deliver it to the ***rightful*** *owner* それを当然の所有主に引渡す. ¶a ***sole*** *owner* (共同でない)単独の所有者.

Q² a ***colliery*** *owner* 炭鉱所有主. ¶a ***forest land*** *owner* 山林所有者. ¶a ***home*** *owner* 世帯主. ¶a ***land*** and ***house*** *owner* 土地及び家屋所有者. ¶a ***part*** *owner* (他と共同の)一部所有者. ¶a ***pet*** *owner* 犬ねこの飼主. ¶a ***property*** *owner* 財産所有人. ¶a ***restaurant*** (hotel) *owner* 料理店(など)所有者. ¶a ***slave*** *owner* どれい所有主. ¶a ***theatre*** *owner* 劇場所有者. ¶a ***used car*** *owner* 中古自動車持主. ¶a ***vehicle*** *owner* 乗物所有者.

P The firm has seen many changes ***of*** *owner* since then. その後その社は持主が数回変った.

P² the *owner* ***of*** a shop (proball team). 店(など)の持主.

ownership, *n*. 所有, 所有権.

V ***change*** *ownership* 所有権を変更する. ¶***prevent*** Japanese *ownership* of land in Canada カナダにおける日本人の土地所有を防止する. ¶the *ownership* of ... was ***transferred*** to ... ...の所有権は...の手に移った.

Q ***alien*** *ownership* 外人所有. ¶a ***fiduciary*** *ownership* 付たくされた所有. ¶He has a fanciful notion to abolish ***individual*** *ownership* of umbrellas. 彼はかさの個人所有を廃するという変った考えを持っている. ¶a ***joint*** *ownership* 共同所有. ¶***legal*** *ownership* 法律上の所有. ¶the ***new*** *ownership* of the Parker House パーカー・ハウス店の買収者. ¶***private*** *ownership* of land 土地私有. ¶***public*** *ownership* of the liquor trade 売酒業の公有. ¶***temporary*** and ***transient*** *ownership* 一時的所有.

Q² limitation of ***land*** *ownership* 土地所有の限界. ¶have ***part*** *ownership* in a business 事業の一部所有権をもっている. ¶bring the Bank of England under ***state*** *ownership* イングランド銀行を国有にする.

P the right ***of*** *ownership* in land 土地所有権. ¶stores ***under*** the same *ownership* 同一所有権下にある店.

P² *ownership* ***in*** literary work 文芸作品の所有権.

ox, *n*. 雄牛.

V ***drive*** an *ox* 牛を駆る.

V² *Oxen* ***low***. 雄牛はもーと鳴く.

P a herd ***of*** *oxen* 牛の群 ‖ a pair ***of*** *oxen* 一対の雄牛 ‖ a yoke ***of*** *oxen* 一連の雄牛.

oxidation, *n*. 酸化.

P produced ***by*** the *oxidation* of ... ...の酸化によって生じた.

oxide, *n*. 〘化〙酸化物.

Q² ***deuterium*** *oxide* 重水.

oyster, *n*. かき.

V "***lay down***" embryo *oysters* かきの稚貝を植え付ける[養殖などで].

Q ***shelled*** *oysters* かきのむきみ.

P

pace, *n*. 歩調, 足取; 速度.

V ***force*** the *pace* of one's rival [競走・競技などで]相手のペースを乱す ‖ ***force*** the *pace* of life がむしゃらに人生のコースを進む. ¶***go*** the *pace* 大速力で歩く; 大金を費消する. ¶***keep*** *pace* to those who are coming behind [行進などで]後から来る人々と歩調を合わせる ‖ ***keep*** *pace* with the advance of German investigation ドイツの研究の進歩と併行する.【類】The supply can hardly ***keep*** *pace* with the demand. / ***keep*** *pace* with the time / ***keep*** *pace* with the progress made / ***keep*** *pace* with all the latest developments / ***keep*** *pace* with the march of events (事件の進行) / ***keep*** *pace* with the needs of the changing world / ***keep*** pace with the discoveries of modern research / ***keep*** *pace* with the spirit and tendencies of the present day. ¶***mend*** one's *pace* 歩調を正す. ¶***quicken*** the *pace* 歩調を早める. ¶***show*** one's *pace* (=ability) 腕前を見せる ‖ ***show*** the donkey's *paces* ろばのような歩き振りをする. ¶***slacken*** one's *pace* 歩調を緩める.

V² The *pace* ***flagged***. 歩みがのろくなった. ¶The *pace* was ***getting faster*** and ***faster***. [自動車などの]速力がますます加わってきた. ¶His *pace* ***lengthened*** almost to a run. 彼は大またになり, ほとんど走るようにして行った.

Q He stepped backward ***a*** *pace* or ***two***. 一足二足後へ引いた. ¶at an ***accelerated*** *pace* 速度を早めて. ¶at a ***breakneck*** *pace* 危険千万な足取で. ¶move at an ***easy*** *pace* すらすら動く. ¶at an ***extraordinary*** *pace* 非常な速度で. ¶at a ***faster*** *pace* 一層 歩調を早めて. ¶rush through one's work at a ***feverish*** *pace* 猛烈に早く仕事をやってのける. ¶proceed at a ***funereal*** *pace* [馬車など]静々と進む. ¶walk at a ***good*** *pace* かなりの速度で歩く. ¶He strode along at a ***great*** *pace*. 彼は足早に大またに歩いて行った. ¶***at*** fifteen *paces* 十五歩の所で. ¶amble along at a ***leisurely*** *pace* ぶらぶら歩いて行く. ¶run at a ***lively*** *pace* 元気な足取で走る. ¶He walks at a ***quick*** *pace*. 彼は早足に歩く. ¶march forward at a ***rapid*** *pace* 早足で前進する. ¶at a ***round*** *pace* てきぱきと, 活発に.【類】He went a good ***round*** *pace* (さっそうと). ¶keep the ***same*** *pace* 同じ歩調を保つ. ¶with ***slacked*** *pace* 足どりを緩めて. ¶The funeral moved on at a ***slow*** *pace*. 葬列はゆっくりと進んだ. ¶***sluggish*** *pace* [汽車などの]緩漫な速度. ¶travel (proceed) at a ***snail's*** *pace* ゆるゆると旅をする(進む). ¶the ***snail-like*** *pace* of the omnibuses バスの牛の歩みののろさ. ¶a ***swaggering*** *pace* かっ歩. ¶proceed at a ***walking*** *pace* [馬車など]並足の速度で進む.

Q² at the old ***jog-trot*** *pace* 従来の牛の歩みで(スローモーで).

P ***At*** this *pace* we shall not be in time. この歩き方では間に合わない. ¶put a person ***through*** his *paces* 人の真価(力量)を試す. ¶He stood ***within*** ten *paces* of me. 彼は私から十歩以内のところに立っていた.

pace, *v*. ゆっくり歩く.

M He *paced* ***away*** the pleasant hours of ease. 彼は楽しい数時間をぶらついて過した. ¶*pace* ***out*** (=***off***) a distance of 40 miles 四十マイルの距離を歩き通す.

M² *pace* ***up*** and ***down*** 行きつ戻りつ歩く(考えごとなどして).

pacific, *a*. 平和的な.

M The Japanese people today are ***intensely*** *pacific*. 今日の日本人はきわめて平和的である.

pack, *n*. 一団, 一群; 一組のカルタ札; 小さい包み; 〘医〙湿布.

V ***give*** the *pack* a good shuffle トランプを十分切る. ¶***join*** a *pack* of knaves 悪漢の仲間入をする. ¶Four sets of cards ***make*** a *pack*. カルタ(トランプ)札四つぞろいで一組になる.

Q a ***regular*** *pack* of spectators 常連の見物人. ¶a ***wet hot*** (***cold***) *pack* 温(冷)水湿布.

P hunt ***in*** large *packs* 沢山群をなしてあさり歩く.

P² a *pack* ***of*** cards 一組のトランプ(通例 52 枚) ‖ a *pack* ***of*** wolves (hounds, thieves) 一群のおおかみ(など) ‖ It is all a *pack* ***of*** lies. それはどれもこれもうそだ. ‖ a *pack* (=package) ***of*** cigarettes シガレット一個 ‖ a *pack* ***of*** matches マッチの小箱.

pack, *v*. 荷造りする; 荷物を負わす; 《米》かん詰にする; 詰込む; 追払う.

M *pack* ***away*** things 荷造りをする. ¶The room is ***closely*** *packed*. 室内は立すいの余地もない. ¶The hall was *literally packed* with people. 講堂はほんとに人で一杯だった. ¶*pack out* a cargo of fish 魚の荷を解く. ¶Things are ***securely packed***. 丈夫に荷造りしてある. ¶People were *packed **together*** in a room. 一室内に人がぎっしり詰めてあった.

M[2] *pack **in*** cotton waste 綿くずを詰物にする. ¶*pack* a man ***off*** (=***away***) from ... ...から人を追い立てる. 【類】I *packed* him ***off*** to his home (school). ‖ *pack **off*** a servant 雇人に暇を出す. ¶*pack **up*** 荷造りする. 【類】*pack **up*** one's clothes / He is *packing **up*** his goods, preparatory to removal.

P All the salmon was *packed **for*** the market. さけは全部かん詰にされた. ¶a perfume *packed **in*** an elegant container 優美な容器に詰めた香水 ‖ *packed **in*** bales (a box, basket) こうり(など)詰にした ‖ It can be *packed **in*** a trunk when traveleing. それは旅行の際はトランクに詰められる. ‖ meat (fish, vegetables) *packed **in*** cans=canned meat (fish, vegetables) 《米》肉(など)のかん詰. ¶*pack* clothes ***into*** (=***in***) one's trunk 衣服をそのトランクに詰込む. 【類】*pack* her ***into*** a motor-car 彼女を自動車に押込む ‖ The leading facts of his career can easily be *packed **into*** a few sentences. 彼の経歴の主なる点は二三のセンテンスで楽に述べられる. ‖ The introduction *packs* a greal deal of information ***into*** a small space. その序文にはわずかのページに盛りたくさんの解説を詰め込んである. 【類】useful information *packed **into*** one volume. ¶They *packed* their goods ***on*** horses. 彼らは馬に貨物をつけた. ¶The movie-house was *packed **to*** capacity. 映画館は満員だった. ¶goods *packed **with*** iron bands 鉄輪でしめた商品 ‖ The car was *packed **with*** passengers. 電車は満員だった. ‖ His mind is *packed **with*** information. 彼は博識だ. ‖ an article *packed **with*** interesting facts 興味ある事実に富む記事.

P[2] *packed **like*** sardines すし詰になって.

package, *n.* 包, 小包み.

V ***express*** a *package* to ... 《米》...に小包を急送する(郵送でなく). ¶He ***took out*** a *package* of cigarettes and lighted one to puff at. 彼はシガレットを一箱取出して一本に火をつけて吸った. ¶***undo*** a *package* 包みをとく.

Q a ***bulky*** *package* かさ張った包み. ¶tie it up in ***neat*** *package* それをきちんとした包みにくくり上げる. ¶a ***small*** *package* 小包み.

Q[2] a ***candy*** *package* キャンデーの(入った)包み. ¶a ***paper*** *package* 紙包み. ¶a ***parcel post*** *package* 郵便の小包. ¶a ***surprise*** *package* (=packet) [子供のおみやげの]びっくり包み.

P do them up ***in*** a *package* それを小包にこしらえる.

packer, *n.* 包装する人; 《米》かん詰業者.

Q[2] He is a ***Chicago*** *packer*, doing big business. 彼はシカゴの大かん詰業者だ. ¶a ***meat*** *packer* 食肉かん詰業者.

packet, *n.* 小包.

P[2] a *packet **of*** medicine 薬一包み. 【類】a *packet* (=package) ***of*** cigarettes.

packing, *n.* 荷造り, 包装; 〖機〗パッキン; 《米》かん詰業.

V ***do*** some *packing* 荷造りをする ‖ ***do*** the *packing* free 包装は無料でする. 【類】***do*** the *packing* at cost (実費で). ¶***include*** the *packing* in the price 価格に包装料を含める.

Q very ***careful*** *packing* 非常に念入りな包装. ¶***slight*** *packing* 簡易な包装. ¶***strong*** *packing* 丈夫な包装.

Q[2] ***asbestos*** and ***cotton*** *packing* 石綿及び綿の詰物(パッキン). ¶***cotton*** and ***tallow*** *packing* 綿やろうのパッキン. ¶***india-rubber*** *packing* 弾性ゴムのパッキン. ¶***hemp*** *packing* 麻のパッキン. ¶***meat*** *packing* 食肉かん詰業.

pact, *n.* 条約.

V ***denounce*** the Washington *pact* ワシントン条約を廃棄する.

Q a ***tripartite*** *pact* 三国条約. ¶a ***tri-zonal*** *pact* ドイツ占領の条約.

Q[2] form a ***defense*** *pact* 国防条約を結ぶ. ¶a ***military mutual assistance*** *pact* 軍事相互援助条約. ¶a ***trade*** *pact* (=agreement) 通商協定.

pad, *n.* あて物; 詰め物; はぎとり帳.

Q[2] a ***blotting*** *pad*=a blotter 吸とりはさみ器(ブロッター). ¶a ***breast*** *pad* 〖服飾〗胸当て(ブレストパッド). ¶a ***desk*** *pad* はぎとり紙(つづり), メモ帳. ¶a ***drawing*** *pad* 画帳. ¶a ***heating*** *pad* 電気ぶとん. ¶a ***shoulder*** *pad* 〖服飾〗肩あて(ショールダーパッド). ¶a ***writing*** *pad* 便せん[つづり].

padding, *n.* 詰めもの.

V ***supply*** *padding* to make up a respectable volume 大きく見せるために詰めものをする.

paddle, *n.* [カヌー用の]平たいかい.

P propel a canoe ***with*** *paddles*=paddle a canoe カヌーをかいで進める.

paddle, *v.* ぱしゃぱしゃやる; 《米》[かい形の平たい板で]なぐる.

M *paddle **about*** in muddy water 泥水を歩き回る. ¶An escaped Negress was ***severely*** *paddled*. 逃亡した黒人の女がひどくなぐられた.

P *paddle **on*** the breasts 腹ばいになって水をばちゃぱちゃやる.

paddy, *n.* 田.

Q[2] a ***rice*** *paddy* 稲田.

page, *n.* ページ; 記録, 文書.

V ***add*** a new *page* to one's travel experiences その旅行の経験に新らしい一ページを加える ‖ The transpacific flight has ***added*** another brilliant *page* to the history of human communications. その太平洋横断飛行は人類の交通史にさらに光輝ある一ページを加えた. ¶characters that have ***adorned*** or ***defiled*** the *pages* of history 歴史のページを飾りまたは汚した人物. ¶... ***brighten*** the *pages* of ... ...が...本に光輝を添えている. ¶The magazine ***carries*** more *pages* in this number than in the last. その雑誌は前号よりページ数が多い. ¶the instances already ***cited*** some *pages* back すでに数ページ前に引いた例. ¶I advise you to ***consult*** its *pages*. その本を参照なさい. ¶It ***contains*** 120 *pages* of text and 20 of explanatory notes. その本には本文が百二十ページ注釈が二十ページある. ¶The article ***covers*** three *pages*. その記事は三ページになっている. 【類】the matter devoted to ... will ***cover*** about 150 *pages*. ¶many illustrious deeds which ***decorate*** the *pages* of the Russo-Japanese war history 日露戦史を飾る幾多の美談. ¶***devote*** 9 *pages* of his book to ... 彼の書物の九ページを...に当てる. ¶***disfigure*** his *pages* with much misinformation 事実と違った記事を沢山載せて彼の著わした本の値打を下げる. ¶***disgrace*** his *pages* of ... with a frequent use of slang 俗語をひん繁に使ってその文を下品にする. ¶I am anxious to ***embellish*** the *pages* of my magazine with an article from you. ぜひ私の雑誌に一文を寄稿していただいて光彩を添えたいと思います. ¶***enrich*** the *pages* of ... by contributions embodying his views on ... ...に対する氏の意見を寄稿することによって...の紙面飾をる. ¶***explore*** the *pages* of... [文献など]をあさる. ¶the picture ***facing*** the *page* このページと相対するさし絵. 【類】See map ***facing*** *page* 97. ¶many *pages* could be ***filled*** with ... そうしようと思えば...で沢山のページをふさぐことができる. ¶***Find*** *page* sixty-seven. 六十七ページの所をあけなさい. ‖ They will ***find*** these *pages* interesting. 彼らはこの本をおもしろく思うだろう. ¶Surely no more ingenious hero has ever ***graced*** the *pages* of a novel than Denry Michian. デンリー・ミシアン位に着想の巧妙な主人公は断じて小説には現われなかった. ¶***interlard*** his *pages* with anecdotes 逸話をはさんでその記述を飾る. ¶***mark*** a *page* ページに印(しるし)をつける. ¶The volume ***numbers*** some 250 *pages*. その本は約二百五十ページに上る. ¶The chapter ***occupies*** ten *pages*. その章は十ページある. ¶***photograph down*** the *pages* of a book to produce a cheap edition 廉価版を出すために書物の版面を写真縮刷にする. ¶since these *pages* were ***printed off*** この本の印刷が済んでから. ¶the episode ***quoted*** a few *pages* back 数ページ前に引いたそう話. ¶If you don't make a good wife, I've never ***read*** a *page* of woman.—George Meredith. あなたがりっぱな細君になれなかったとすると私にはよくよく女を見る目がないのだ. 【類】***read*** four *pages* of history / Its *pages* are now rarely ***read***. ¶it would ***require*** several *pages* to ... ...するには数ページを要するだろう. ¶***rip out*** *pages* 幾ページか切り取る. ¶***scan*** the *pages* of history 歴史に目を通す. ¶For description ***see*** *page* 424. 説明は四百二十四ページを見よ. ¶the names of well-known people ***star*** his *pages* 彼の本には著名人の名がいくつか出て来る. ¶It would ***take*** *pages* to give them in any detail. これは詳細に記述するには数ページを要する. 【類】It ***takes*** about five *pages* of typewriting to make a news-column. ¶***tear*** a *page* of a book 書物から一ページ引裂く. ¶***tear out*** several *pages* 数ページ抜取る. ¶***thumb*** the *pages* 書物に指あとをつける. ¶***turn*** the *pages* ページをめくる. 【類】you have but to ***turn*** a few *pages* to find that ... ¶There was a *page* ***turned down*** in the book. 本の中の一ページが折られてあった. ¶***turn over*** the *pages* of one's stamp album 切手帳のページをめくる.

Q How this was accomplished is told in the ***accompanying pages***. いかにしてこれが完成を見るに至ったかは本書に述べてある(序文の言葉). ¶see an announcement in ***advertising pages*** 広告欄に発表を見る. ¶***alluring pages*** 魅力のあるページ. ¶on ***another page*** we print ... 別ページに...を掲げる. ¶Details are given on the ***back page*** of this circular. 詳細はこの回状の裏面に載っている. ¶his ***best pages*** 書中最もよく書かれた部分. ¶***blank pages*** 余白ページ. ¶despite its many ***bright pages*** その輝かしいページで満ちてはいるが. ¶a ***colorful page*** in his life 花やかな彼の人生の一ページ. ¶four ***consecutive pages*** 続いた四ページ. ¶***choice pages*** from ... ...からの選り抜きのページ. ¶There is not a ***dull page*** in the book. その本にはおもしろくないページは一つもない. ¶The book occupies almost five hundred ***double-column pages*** 同書は二段組で約五百ページある. ¶***Every page*** is enthralling. どのページも実におもしろい. ¶The ***even page*** is the ***left-handed page*** of a printed book. 偶数ページは印刷した書物の左側のページである. ¶the story is told in the ***fascinating pages*** of ... ...その物語は興味深く...の本に書いてある. ¶a ***fat page*** [組むに楽な]余白の多いページ. ¶a ***few pages*** further 二三ページ先に. ¶on the ***first page*** 第一ページに. ¶the ***following pages*** [序文で指していう]本の本文 ‖ the writer of the ***following pages*** 本著者. ¶thumbing through ***frayed pages*** ぼろぼろのページをめくりながら. ¶the ***front page*** [本の]とびら. 【類】We are indebted to the ... Association for the use of the picture which is reproduced on the ***front page*** of the cover of this issue. ¶cover thirty ***full pages*** 三十ページぎっしりつまっている. ¶a ***glorious page*** in American history 米国史の輝やかしい一ページ. ¶in his ***graphic*** and ***eolquent pages*** 彼の鮮明にして雄弁な記録において. ¶These names never appear on ***his tory's page***. これらの人の名は歴史のページには決して載らない. ¶an advertisement on ***inside page*** of cover 表紙裏の広告. ¶opposite the ***last page*** in the present number 本月号の最後のページと向き合って ‖ keep the reader alert to the ***last page*** 最後のページまで読者を引きつける. ¶***literary*** and ***advertising pages*** of a magazine 雑誌の文芸欄と広告欄. ¶the information we gather from these ***lively pages*** このいきいきした内容の本からわれわれの得る知識. ¶***loose pages*** [とじてない]ばらのページ. ¶The fable is given on the ***next page***. その童話は次のページに載っている. ¶three hundred and ***odd pages*** 三百余ページ. ¶an ***opposite page*** 反対のページ. ¶Tickets consist of ***perforated pages***. 切符は切取るようにできている. ¶in the ***printed page*** 印刷に付した[書物など]. ¶a ***right*** (***left***)***-hand page*** [本の]右(左)側のページ. ¶in the ***scholarly pages*** of the review その学究的な誌上に. ¶without boring us on a ***single page*** 一ページでもわれわれを退屈させる所なく ‖ He is unable to write a ***single page*** without dropping into vulgar slang. 彼は下品な言葉使いをしないではただの一ページでも書けない. ¶in 160 ***small pages*** 百六十ページの小形の本に. ¶the editor of ***page three*** 三面担当の記者(社会部長など). ¶***time stained pages*** 古びた書物. ¶***uncut pages*** [へりの切ってない]アンカットのページ. ¶closely ***written pages*** ぎっしり書いた(印刷した)ページ. ¶***yellow pages*** 黄色紙のページ; [大昔の本の]黄ばんだページ. ¶the ***2nd*** (***3rd***) paper ***page*** of cover 表紙の表(裏)見返し.

Q[2] glance at the ***advertising pages*** of our periodicals わが国の雑誌の広告欄を一べつする. ¶***checking pages*** 印をつけたページ(広告主に送る広告を出したページ). ¶second (third, fourth) ***cover page*** 表紙二(三, 四)ページ. ¶350 ***foolscap pages*** of its manuscript 三百五十ページにわたるそのフールスキャップの草稿. ¶the first (last) ***inside cover page*** 表紙(裏表紙)の見返し. ¶the ***last back cover page*** 裏表紙面. ¶The story will cover ten ***magazine pages***. その物語は雑誌十ページ分位ある. ¶the ***news pages*** of a paper 新聞のニュース欄. ¶The big banner headlines that run across all eight columns at the top of the ***newspaper page*** are usually set in 72-point type. 新聞のトップに八段ぶっ通しで出る大見出しは通例七十二ポイント活字である. ¶over 10,000 ***royal octavo pages*** 一千ページを越える大形八ツ折判のページ. ¶***specimen pages*** from a dictionary 辞書の見本ページ. ¶be reported on the ***sports pages*** (=columns) スポーツ欄で報道されている. ¶the ***stock-exchange page*** of a morning paper 朝刊紙の株式取引のページ. ¶a ***three-column page*** 三段組のページ. ¶be undated on ***title page*** とびらに日付がない.

P It is found ***at pages*** 1280 to 1300 of this volume. それはこの本の千二百八十ページから千三百ページにわたって載っている. 【類】The description is given ***at page*** 80. / we read ***at page*** 348 that ... / the photographs ***at pages*** 18, 19 and 20 / ***at*** the tenth ***page***. ¶sit in a street-car ***behind*** the ***pages*** of a newspaper 新聞紙で顔を隠して電車に腰をかけている. ¶The book lay open on the floor ***between*** the 149th and 150th ***pages***. その本は149ページと150ページの間のところが開いて床の上においてあった. ¶continued ***from*** the previous ***page*** 前ページから続く. ¶***in*** these pages 本書(誌)上に ‖ as mentioned ***in page*** ... ...ページに挙げてあるように ‖ It was originally published ***in*** the ***pages*** of a magazine. それは元来ある雑誌に掲載されたものだ. ¶The whole tale seems to read ***like*** a ***page*** from real life. その物語はそっくりそのまま実生活の一部のような感がある. ¶the margin (=edge) ***of*** a ***page*** 欄外 ‖ at the top (bottom) ***of*** a ***page*** ページの上部(下部)に. ¶Webster's Academic Dictionary contains about 28,000 words ***on*** 648 ***pages***. ウェブスターのアカデミック辞典は六百四十八ページに約二万八千語を採録してある. ‖ Continued ***on page*** 218. 二百十八ページに続く(新聞・雑誌などの注意). ‖ the problems treated ***on*** (=in) these ***pages*** これらのページ中に取扱った問題 ‖ the book which we review ***on*** another ***page*** 別のページにその批評がのっている本. ¶Such a character is rarely to be met with ***outside*** the ***pages*** of "Pickwick." こうした人物は「ピックウィック」に載っている以外に滅多に出会わすものでない. ¶peep ***through pages*** [本など]ページをちらちらのぞき見する ‖ He sat there, ***going through*** the pages of a magazine. 彼はすわったまま, 雑誌をぱらぱらめくっていた. ¶the number of words ***to*** a ***page*** 一ページ当りの語数 ‖ turn back ***to page*** three 三ページにもどる. ¶So much information is found ***within*** the ***pages*** of a single book. 一巻の書中にそれほど色々な事項が載せてある.

P[2] read ***page after*** page 一ページ一ページと読み進む. ¶a ***page from*** the story of Protestant missions in China 中国における新教布教師の物語からの一ページ(の抜粋). ¶It seemed like a ***page from*** Gulliver. それはガリヴァーの旅行記に書いてあることのように感じられた. ¶a ***page in*** a ledger 台帳の一ページ. ¶characters familiar in the ***pages of*** fiction 小説によく出て来る人物.

page, *n.* 小姓; [ホテルの]ボーイ.

V ***call*** a *page* ボーイを呼ぶ.

Q[2] a ***hotel*** *page* 《英》ホテルのボーイ. ☞米語は bellboy 「とか bellhop.

P wait on the lady ***as page*** 婦人の給仕をする.

pageant, *n.* 美事な行列; 野外劇.

Q ***colorful*** *pageant* of people 色彩に富む人の流れ. ¶see the ***ever-changing pageant*** of passers-by strolling up and down the pavement 歩道をあちこちぶらつく絶えず変る行人の流れを見る. ¶a ***historical pageant*** 史実にちなんだ野外劇. ¶The Coronation of the new king was a ***splendid pageant***. 新王の戴冠式は全く壮観だった.

Q[2] display an ***air pageant*** 空のページェントを繰り広げる. ‖ a ***flag pageant*** 旗行列.

pagoda, *n.* 塔.

Q a ***big, top-heavy*** *pagoda* 大きくて上部の重い塔.

pail, *n.* バケツ, おけ.

Q[2] a ***garbage*** *pail* 料理くず入れバケツ.

pain, *n.* 苦痛, とう痛; 心痛; 骨折, 労; 刑罰.

V ***allay*** the *pain* of toothache 歯痛を静める. ¶***alleviate*** *pain* 苦痛を緩和する. ¶***banish*** *pain* 痛みを除く. ¶***bear*** the *pain* with fortitude じっと苦痛を忍ぶ. 【類】a willingness to ***bear*** present *pain* for the sake of future joy / ***bear up*** the *pain*. ¶great *pains* have been ***bestowed*** on ... 大いに...に骨を折った. ¶***cause*** intolerable *pain* to ... ...にたえ難い苦痛を与える. ¶***commute*** *pain* for pleasure 苦痛を楽しみに換える, 苦痛も楽しみと感じる. ¶***deaden*** one's *pain* その苦痛を静める. ¶This ***eased*** his *pain* slightly. これで彼の苦痛が少し楽になった. ¶***endure*** *pain* stoically 平然として苦痛を忍ぶ. ¶***experience*** sore *pains* 激しい痛みを感じる ‖ ***experience*** the *pain* or discomfort that comes of ... ...から来る心痛または不安を経験する. ¶I ***feel*** a *pain* in my side. 私は横っ腹が痛む.

【類】I do not *feel* any *pain*. ¶it *gives* me *pain* to ... 私は…するのは苦痛だ. ¶I *have* a *pain* in my back. 私は背中が痛い. ‖ *have* a *pain* from being burned やけどのあとが痛む. ¶*inflict pain* on ... …に苦痛を与える. ¶*kill pain* 痛みを止める. ¶*lull* (=*mitigate*, *mollify* or *palliate*) a *pain* 苦痛を静める. ¶*reduce* the *pain* to a minimum 苦痛を最小限度に軽減する. ¶*register* (=*show*) *pain* 痛みを表にあらわす. ¶*remove pain* 苦痛を除く. ¶*relieve pain* 苦痛を緩める. ¶This will *soothe* his *pain*. こうすれば彼の苦痛も和らぐだろう. ¶*suffer pain* 苦痛を感じる. ¶*undergo pain* 苦しい目に会う ‖ *undergo* the *pains* of child-bearing with ease and safety 陣痛の苦しみが軽く無事にすむ.

V² The *pain* has *abated* (*increased*). 苦痛が減じた(増した). ¶*Pain stopped* almost magically. 痛みが不思議に止まった.

Q cause *acute pain* 鋭い痛みを与える. 【類】The *pain* was so *acute* that it seemed like having cut with a knife. ¶*another pain* in the pocketbook また一つの財布の苦痛(出費). ¶*assiduous pains* have been taken to ... …するのに骨を折った. ¶I have a *bad pain* here. 私はここがひどく痛む. ¶inflict *bodily pain* on ... …に肉体的苦痛を与える. ¶a *burning pain* ぴりつくような痛み. ¶a *dull pain* 鈍痛. ¶an *excruciating pain* 劇痛. ¶a *gnawing pain* かまれるような痛み. ¶I have a *good pain* in my tooth. 私は大分歯が痛む. ¶feel a *gripping pain* [腸など]しくしく痛む. ¶an *intolerable pain* たえ難い痛み. ¶a *killing pain* 死ぬような痛み. ¶a *local pain* 局部の痛み. ¶*mental pain* 精神的苦痛. ¶have *much pain* in childbirth. お産が重い. ¶*physical pain* 肉体の苦痛. ¶a *poignant pain* 激しい痛み. ¶a *pricking pain* ひりひりする痛み. ¶a *self-inflicted pain* 自分で自分に与えた苦痛. ¶a *severe pain* 激しい痛み. ¶*severe abdominal pains* 激しい腹痛. ¶The sting caused a *sharp pain*. 虫に刺されたので激しい痛みを感じた. ¶a *sharp* and *cutting pain* 激しい身を切るような苦痛. ¶a *slight pain* ちょっとした痛み. ¶allay the *smarting pain* ずきずきする痛みを緩和する. ¶take *special pains* to ... …のために特に骨を折る. ¶a *stabbing pain* [刃物で]突きさすような痛み. ¶I have a *terrific pain* in the back of my head. 後頭部が割れるように痛む. ¶have a *throbbing pain* in my eye 目がちくちく痛む. ¶feel a *violent pain* in the head 頭部に劇痛を覚える.

Q² *joint pains* 節々の痛み. ¶*labor pains* 産の苦しみ.

P He is *in pain*. 彼は痛がっている. 【類】A cruel man likes to see others *in pain*. / He shrieked *in* his *pain*. ¶feel a pang *of pain* 激しい痛みを感じる ‖ a twinge *of pain* 刺されるような痛み. ¶It is forbidden to ... *on pain* of instant death. …を犯すものは直ちに死刑に処せられる. ‖ one must ... *on pain* of hell …しなくてはならない, 万一そうしないと地獄へ落ちる. ¶*under* (=on) *pain* of death 違反すれば死刑に処すという条件で ‖ They are strictly forbidden to ... *under pain* of losing their licenses. 厳禁を犯して…すれば免許状を取上げられる. 【類】*under pain* of imprisonment for refusal / *under pain* of forfeiting the goods so imported / forbid them, *under pain* of heavy penalties, to ...

P² take *pains about* one's meals 食事のことに苦心する. ¶a *pain in* the ear (nose, mouth) 耳(など)の痛み. 【類】*pains in* the limbs. ¶Hot-spring baths will often cure you of the *pain of* rheumatism. 温泉に入るとリューマチの痛みがとれることがよくある.

(**2**) *pl.* 苦心, 労苦.

V *repay* the *pains* 労苦に報いる. ¶My *pains* have been *rewarded*. 私の苦心は報いられた. ¶*share* pleasures and *pains* 苦楽をともにする. ¶He *spares* no *pains* to apologize. 彼はしきりに弁解に努めている. 【類】He is *sparing* no *pains* to benefit himself (自己の利益に). ¶*spend* endless *pains* on polishing the style of his narrative 彼の物語の文体の洗練に絶えず苦心する. ¶*take* the *pains* to learn Spanish スペイン語のけいこに骨折る ‖ by *taking pains* 骨を折って. 【類】He *takes* great *pains* in educating his children. ‖ The practiced man has learned to *take pains*. 熟練家は苦心の効を知っている.

Q He is a good teacher and takes *great pains* with his pupils. 彼は良い教師でよく生徒の世話をする. ¶take *considerable pains* to ... …しようと大いに努力する. ¶experience "*growing pains*" いわゆる「青年期の悩み」を経験する. ¶He discovered it by taking *incredible pains*. 彼は大変な努力を払ってその発見をなし遂げた. ¶collate books with *infinite pains* 非常に苦心して書物を校合する. ¶*Much pains*, no gains. 骨折損のくたびれもうけ. ¶*unremitting pains* 間断ない労苦. ¶take the *utmost pains* to ... …しようと精々骨を折る.

P historical materials he has been *at pains* to collect 彼が折角集めた史料 ‖ He is *at* great *pains* to do this work well. 彼はこの仕事をよくやろうと大層骨を折っている. ‖ I have been *at* some *pains* to investigate the matter. 私はその問題の研究を多少やって見た. ¶thank *for* his *pains* 彼の骨折りには感謝する ‖ I have got a thrashing *for* my *pains*. 私は骨を折ってかえって打たれた. ¶He has written it *with* great *pains*. 彼は大層苦心してそれを書いた. ‖ He cried *with pain*. 彼は痛がって泣いた. ¶Expect no gains *without pains*. 骨を折らずに得を取ろうと思うな.

P² He takes great *pains with* his task. 彼は仕事に大層骨を折る.

pain, *v.* 心痛させる.

M It *pains* me *deeply*. 私はそれが非常に心配だ.

P The father is *pained by* his boy's conduct. 父親は子供の行跡で心痛している.

painful, *a.* 骨の折れる, 難儀な.

P The task is *painful to* me. 私はその仕事がつらい. ‖ The region was *painful to* the touch. そこをさわると痛みを感じた.

paint, *n.* 塗料, ペンキ.

V *chip paint* from ... …からペンキを除く. ¶*get paint* on one's book (suit) 本(上着)にペンキをつける. ¶*lay paint* upon canvas 画布に油絵具を塗る. ¶The *paint* is carefully *laid on*. ペンキが丁寧に塗ってある. ¶The *paint* is *rubbed off*. ペンキがはげている. ¶*scrub off paint* ペンキをごしごしこすっておとす.

V² The *paint* easily *comes off*. ペンキがじきにはげる. ¶The *paint* is *peering off*. ペンキがはげかかっている. ¶The *paint* has *worn off*. ペンキが古くなってはげた.

Q *luminous paint* 発光塗料. ¶*Wet* (=*Fresh*) *paint!* ペンキ塗立て[御用心].

Q² *upstick-proof paint* はげない口紅化粧.

P It is used *as* a *paint*. それは塗料に使われる.

paint, *v.* ペンキを塗る; 描く; 化粧する.

M The wall is *freshly painted*. 壁は塗り立てだ. ¶He *paints nicely* in water colors. 彼は水彩画を巧に描く. ¶*paint realistically* 写実的に描く. ¶She *painted* her face *thickly*. 彼女はこってりお化粧をした. ‖ a girl with lips *thickly painted* 口べにを真赤に塗った娘. ¶The house has been *painted throughout*. 家は全部ペンキで塗られた. ¶The box was *painted within* and *without*. 箱は内外とも塗ってあった.

P The picture was *painted after* an original. この絵は原画を写したものだ. ‖ The ship has been *painted* in white and red *after* the Red Cross colors. その船を赤十字の旗にちなんで紅白に塗った. ¶*paint from* nature (life) 天然物(生物)を写生する. ¶He *paints* the situation *in* glowing colors (=roseate hues). 彼は時局に対して楽観的な見方をしている. ‖ *paint in* oils (water-colors) 油絵(水彩画)を描く. ¶*paint on* paper (silk, china) 紙(など)に描く. 【類】*paint* a landscape *on* a wall. ¶a portrait *painted to* the life 生写しの肖像 ‖ *painted to* order 依頼によって描いた.

painter, *n.* 画家.

Q an *accomplished painter* in water-colors 水彩画の名人. ¶a *marine painter* 海洋画家. ¶a *military painter* 従軍画家. ¶one of the most *original* and *powerful painters* 最も独創的で筆力のある画家の一人. ¶He has long been acknowledged as the most *popular painter* of the day. 彼は現代の最も人気ある画家として長い間認められている.

Q² a *futurist painter* 未来派の画家. ¶a *house painter* [家を塗装する]ペンキ屋. ¶a *landscape painter* 風景画家. ¶a *miniature painter* 細密画々家. ¶an *oil painter* 油彩画家. ¶a *portrait painter* 肖像画家. ¶a *sign painter* 看板屋.

P a *painter in* a cradle [建物などの側面に下げた]つり台に乗った塗装工. ¶a famous *painter of* the Kano school 狩野派の大家.

painting, *n.* 絵画; 絵をかくこと, 画法.

V *fake paintings* 絵画に手を入れてごまかす. ¶*take up painting* as a profession (hobby) 絵かきを職業(道楽)にする.

Q *mural paintings* by world-famous masters 世界的大家の筆になる壁画. ¶a *sensuous painting* 感覚派の絵画.
Q² *blast painting* 吹付塗装. ¶a *ceiling painting* 天井絵. ¶a *nude painting* 裸体画. ¶*polychrome painting* 着色絵画. ¶a *Rembrandt painting* レンブランの絵. ¶*sign painting* 看板画[法]. ¶*tempera painting* テンペラ画. ¶a *water-color painting*＝a painting in water colors 水彩画.
P it was engraved by ... *after* a *painting* by ... それは...の絵にならって...の彫刻したものだ. ¶He had a talent *for painting*. 彼は画才があった. ¶colored plate *from paintings* specially executed for this work 特にこの作品のために執筆した絵画から作成した彩色図版. ¶a gallery *of paintings* 画廊.
P² a *painting from* (＝after) nature 写生画. ¶a *painting in* oils (water-colors) 油絵(水彩画). ¶a *painting on* the wall 壁画.

pair, *n.* 一対, 一双, 一組; 一組の夫婦, 一番(つがい); 一組の片方.
V It tends to *drive* the *pair* further apart. それは二人の仲をさらに疎遠にするおそれがある. ¶the mother of 25 children *including* five *pairs* of twins 五組の双生児を入れて二十五人の子供らの母. ¶*wear* two or three *pairs* of woolen socks 毛糸のくつ下を二足もしくは三足はく.
Q I'll get you *another pair* of shoes. くつをもう一足買ってやるよ. ¶The *bridal pair* started for their honeymoon after the reception. 新婚の夫婦はひ露会を済ましてから蜜月旅行に出かけた. ¶show them a *clean pair* of heels 彼らをおきざりにしてすたこら逃げて行く. ¶a *complementary pair* [車の両輪のように]両々相まって有効な一対. ¶a *fine pair* of snowshoes 上等の雪ぐつ. ¶the *fugitive pair* かけ落の男女. ¶the *happy pair* 幸福な夫婦. ¶an *ill-assorted pair* 不つり合の夫婦. ¶a *large pair* of scissors 大きなはさみ. ¶a *lovely pair* かわいらしい夫婦. ¶*many pairs* of boots 沢山のくつ. ¶a newly *married pair* 新婚夫婦. ¶a *misfit pair* of shoes 足に合わないくつ. ¶I want a *new pair* of gloves. 私は新らしい手袋がほしい. ¶a *well-matched pair* 似合いの夫婦.
P On all orders *for* six *pairs* or more, we will allow 25 cents *per pair*. 六足以上の御注文に対してはすべて一足につき二十五セントの割引を致します. ¶stroll *in pairs* [アベック組などが]二人でする散歩. 【類】The company then went off *in pairs*. ‖ Musk deer are usually found *in pairs*, never congregating in herds. じゃこうじかは普通二匹ずつになっていて決して群をなさない.
P² a *pair of* ducks 一番(つがい)のかも ‖ a *pair of* horses 二頭立の馬. 【類】a *pair of* screens (spectacles, vases) ‖ a *pair of* compasses コンパス一本 ‖ Not one *pair of* eyes in this town can read what I write. 私の書いたものを読めるものはこの町に一人もいない. 【類】two (three) *pair of* spectacles (scissors, slacks, trousers, socks, etc.). ☞ a pair of ..., two pair of ... となり -s をつけない. ただし, 商業英語や口語では複数形にして -s をつけることがある. 例: How many *pairs* of socks do you have? / Show me a couple more *pairs*. ¶I have lost the *pair to* this glove この手袋の片方をなくした. 【類】Where is the *pair to* this sock?

pair, *v.* 夫婦になる.
M *pair off* [パーテなどで]二人づつになる(出かける); 二枚(個)づつ列べる ‖ *pair off* with some one《俗》ある人と結婚するとかをつきとめる.
P *pair* the man *with* his statement それはだれが言ったことかをつきとめる.

pal, *n.* 新しい友.
Q² girls who had been "*pen pals*" of the GI's 兵隊さんのいわゆるペンフレンドだった娘たち.

palace, *n.* 宮殿; りっぱな建物.
V The *palace* has been *thrown open*. 宮中の拝観を許されている.
Q *gayly gilded palaces* of pleasure 豪華な遊女屋. ¶*floating palaces* 浮城(船). ¶the *Imperial palace* 宮城. ¶the *luxurious palaces* of the rich 富豪のぜいたくな住宅. ¶a *veritable palace* of art 真の芸術の殿堂.
Q² an *exhibit palace* (exposition) 博覧会の陳列館. ¶a *gin palace* 豪華な飲屋. ¶a "million dollar" *moving picture palace* 百万ドルの(豪華な)映画の殿堂. ¶*picture* (＝*cinema*) *palace*《英》映画館.
P go (＝proceed *or* repair) *to* the *Palace* 参内する.

palatable, *a.* 美味な; 気に入る.
P food *palatable to* the foreign taste 外人の口に合う食物. ‖ make the book *palatable to* English readers by rigorous expurgation 厳密な削除を加えてその書を英国の読者の趣味に合うようにする.

palate, *n.* 味覚, 好み.
V *pall on* the *palate* 無味となる, うんざりする. ¶*please* one's *palate* その味覚を喜ばせる. 【類】The flavor *pleased* his *palate*. ¶so as to *suit* one's *palate* その口に合うように ‖ the choicest seasonable delicacies to *suit* all *palates* だれの口にも合う季節の選り抜きのごちそう. ¶*tickle* the *palate* 食欲をそそる.
Q have a *delicate palate* 好みがうるさい.
P It is pleasant *to* the *palate*. それはおいしい. ‖ *to* some *palate* [食物が]人によっては.

pale, *n.* くい, 境界, 範囲.
P *beyond* the *pale* of ... ...の範囲外. ¶To say ... is to place oneself almost *outside* the *pale* of serious discussion. ...などと言ってはまじめな討論からほとんど逸脱してしまうことになる. ¶*within* (*out of*) the *pale* of ... ...のさく内(外)で. ¶He is *within* the *pale* of good society. 彼は上流社会の人だ.

pale, *a.* そう白な.
M He turned *as pale* as death. 彼は死人のように真青になった. ¶*deadly pale* 真青な. ¶Her face was *ghastly pale*. 彼女は真青な顔をしていた.
P turn *pale to* the lips くちびるまで青くなる. 【類】turn *pale with* fright. ¶He turned *pale with* fright (apprehension, indignation). 彼は驚いて(心配などで)青くなった.

pale, *v.* 青ざめる, 色を失う.
P *pale before* (＝*beside or by the side of*) the splendor of ... ...の余りの壮麗さに比して顔色ない. ¶*pale into* insignificance beside ... ...に比べると顔色がなくなる(はなはだしく見劣りがする).

paleness, *n.* そう白なこと.
Q a face of *ashy paleness* 土のような(真青な)顔.

palette, *n.* 絵具板(パレット).
V *abandon* the *palette* 画家をやめる. ¶*set* the *palette* 絵具板に各種の絵具を配置する.

palisade, *n.* さく.
P fence in *with* a *palisade* さくで囲う.

pall, *n.* 幕, おおい.
P² a *pall of* darkness (fog, snow) やみ(など)の幕 ‖ A *pall of* smoke shut out the sun from the city. その市では煙りの幕で太陽が見えなくなった.

pall, *v.* 味を失う; 興がさめる.
P The world and its futile pleasures *palled on* me. 私は世の中とその無益な快楽がいやになった. ‖ The delights of the roundabouts never *pall on* the children. 回転木馬の楽しみは決して子供らを飽きさせない. ‖ *pall on* one's taste 興味がなくなる, まずくなる.

palm, *n.* 優勝の記号, 優勝, 勝利.
V *adjudge* (＝award) the *palm* to ... ...に軍配をあげる. ¶for ... the *palm* must be *awarded* to ... ...は...にとどめを刺す. ¶*bear* the *palm* 勝を奏する, 賞を獲得する. 【類】He *bore off* the *palm* in the contest. ¶He will *carry away* (＝*off*) the *palm* from all his rivals. 彼はあらゆる競争者に勝つだろう. ¶*deserve* the *palm* 優勝に値する. ¶With ... it *disputes* the *palm* for beauty. [風景など]...とその美を競う. ¶cheerfully *give* the *palm* to ... in ... ...の点で進んで...に軍配をあげる ‖ in point of excellence the *palm* must be *given* to ... 秀逸の点では...に軍配をあげねばならない. ¶*hold* the *palm* among ... ...の中で首位を占めている. 【類】Among the electrical achievements of the British Empire, Canada now *holds* the *palm*. ¶*give* the *palm* to ... ...に軍配をあげる. ¶*win* the *palm* 勝利を得る. ¶*yield* (＝give) the *palm* to ... ...に勝を譲る; ...の優秀を認める.
V² the *palm belongs* to ... ...が勝ち.
P He bore the *palm over* all competitors. 彼はあらゆる競争者中第一位を占めた.

palm, *n.* てのひら.
V *anoint* (＝*grease*) the *palm* of ...《俗》...にわいろを使う(つかませる). ¶*gild* (＝*grease or tickle*) one's *palm*《俗》金をつかませる, わいろをやる. ¶know it as one *knows* the *palm* of one's hand それを手のひらを指すように(よく)知っている. ¶*read* one's *palm* 手相をみる. ¶*rub* one's *palms* together もみ手をする. ¶*slap palms* [together] かしわ手をうつ. ¶*tickle* the *palm*《俗》心付けをやる.
Q with *folded palms* 合掌して. ¶He has an *itching*

palm (=is greedy of gain). 彼は欲張りだ.

palm, *v.* おっかぶせる; ごまかす.

M² *palm off* bad dollars on ... ...ににせドルをつかませる. 【類】 *palm off* fake money on ...

palpable, *a.* 触知できる.

P *palpable to* the touch さわるとわかる.

palpitate, *v.* 動悸(ᵏ)がする.

P Her heart *palpitated at* the sight. それを見ると彼女の胸がわくわくした. ¶*palpitate with* fear (interest, fright, excitement) こわがっておどおどして(など).

palpitation, *n.* 動悸(ᵏ).

V² *Palpitation* of the heart *comes on.* 心臓が動き出す.

Q He complained of *severe palpitation.* 彼は動きが激しかった.

P *with palpitation* 動きして, わくわくして.

palter, *v.* いい加減にごまかす.

P *palter with* one's pledge word 言質を与えて実行しない ‖ *palter with* a person about ... 人と...についてかけ引する.

pamphlet, *n.* 小冊子(パンフレット).

V *disseminate* Neo-Malthusian *pamphlets* 新マルサス主義(産児制限主義)の小冊子を分布する. ¶*distribute pamphlets* among ... ...にパンフレットを配布する. ¶*prepare* a *pamphlet* 小冊子をこしらえる.

Q a *descriptive pamphlet* 説明した小冊子. ¶an alarmist *quack pamphlet* 人騒がせなパンフレット. ¶a *vigorous pamphlet* 迫力のある小冊子.

Q² a *propagandist pamphlet* 宣伝者のパンフレット. ¶B.B.C. *talks pamphlets* [英国の] BBC 放送を印刷した小冊子.

P The lecture has since been republished by him *as* a *pamphlet* under the title of "...". その講義はその後「...」の表題で彼が出版している.

P² a *pamphlet on* universal suffrage 普通選挙に関するパンフレット.

pamphleteer, *n.* 小冊子(パンフレット)作者.

Q a *political pamphleteer* 政治問題のパンフレット記者.

pan, *n.* 平なべ.

Q² an *amalgamating pan* アマルガム化合なべ. ¶a *dust pan* ちり取り. ¶a *frying pan* フライパン. ¶a *stew pan* シチューなべ. ¶a *vulcanizing pan* ゴム製造のなべ. ¶a *warming pan* [一種の]湯たんぽ.

P bake *in* a *pan* なべで焼く. ¶boil in a *pan over* the fire 火に掛けたなべの中で煮る.

pan, *v.* 結果が出る.

M *pan out* well (badly) うまく(まずく)行く ‖ I mean to wait and see how things *pan out* before I invest more capital. 私は投資前に成行を見きわめる積りだ.

panacea, *n.* 万能薬.

V *seek* a *panacea* in serum therapy 血清療法で万病の治療を図る.

Q a *universal panacea* 万能薬.

P² a *panacea for* all the ills flesh is heir to 万病にきく薬. 【類】 Many teachers seem to regard the phonetic script as a *panacea for* all ills of pronunciation.

pancake, *n.* パンケーキ; うすい氷片.

V *fry pancakes* パンケーキをあげる.

Q *pancakes afloat,* large and small 大小の浮ぶ氷片.

pander, *v.* 悪事に誘導する.

P *pander to* vicious tastes 悪趣味に迎合する. 【類】 *pander to* the vulgar taste. / The yellow papers (黄色新聞) *pander to* vice and crime. / *pander to* one's folly / films which *pander to* the lower instincts (劣情) of mankind ‖ *pander* (=play) *to* the gallery 場当りをやる ‖ *pander to* a feeling of curiosity 好奇心をあおる.

pane, *n.* ガラス板.

V the joy of a school boy by *breaking* window *panes* 学童が窓ガラスをこわして喜ぶこと. ¶*put in* a *pane* of glass ガラス板を一枚入れる.

Q an oak-beamed ceiling and *leaded window panes* オークのはりで造った天井と鉛でついだ(着色)窓ガラス.

Q² Fine snow ticks the *window panes* behind drawn curtains. カーテンを引いた窓に細雪が音を立ててあたる.

panel, *n.* 飾り板, 鏡板, 羽目板; 委員会; 《英》保険医名簿.

Q² the chairman of a government *fact-finding panel* 政府実情調査委員会の委員長. ¶a *glass observation panel* [手術室など]ガラス張りの展望室. ¶a *low-tension panel* 低圧盤. ¶an *upright panel* たて羽目.

P be *on* the *panel* 保険医である.

P² a *panel of* educators 教育委員会.

panel, *v.* 鏡板を張る.

P *paneled in* oak オークの鏡板を張った(戸・障子など).

pang, *n.* 精神的苦痛, 悲痛.

V *endure* the *pangs* of martyrdom 殉難の苦痛を忍ぶ. ¶*experience* the *pangs* of hunger 飢渇に迫る. ¶he *felt* a *pang* at the thought of ... 彼は...を思出して苦もんした ‖ *feel* a *pang* of remorse 悔恨の苦しみを覚える. ¶jealous *pangs gnawing* at her heart 彼女の胸に食入る苦もんのしっと心.

Q *remorseful pangs* 悔恨の苦痛.

P² the *pangs of* conscience 良心のかしゃく ‖ the *pang of* death 死の苦しみ. 【類】 the *pangs of* hunger (toothache).

panic, *n.* 恐慌, ろうばい.

V *Panic* has been *averted* for a time. 恐慌は一時避けられた. ¶Efforts are being made to *avoid* a *panic*. 恐慌を避けようと骨折っている. ¶War rumors have *caused* a *panic*. 戦争のうわさが恐慌(状態)を起した. ¶This will *create* a *panic*. このために恐慌が起るだろう. ¶*get up* (=*start*) a *panic* 恐慌を引起す. ¶A *panic* is *feared* (=*expected*). 恐怖を来すおそれがある. ¶*generate* (=*produce*) a *panic* 恐慌を来す. ¶*start* a general *panic* in London [大会社の破産などで]ロンドンに大恐慌を起す.

V² a *panic prevails* in ... 恐慌が...に起っている. ¶The *panic* is *subsiding*. 恐慌は静まりつつある.

Q A *commercial panic* has commenced. 商業恐慌が始まった. ¶a *financial panic* 財政上の恐慌. ¶There is a *general panic* and market is going to pieces. 一般的恐慌のため市場は正に崩壊しようとしている. ¶a *vague panic* ばく然とした恐慌.

Q² a *fire panic* 火事騒ぎ. ¶a *money* (=monetary) *panic* 金融恐慌. ¶a *stock-exchange panic* 株式恐慌.

P financial straits *after* the *panic* of ... ...の恐慌後の財政難. ¶fly *in* a *panic* ろうばいして逃げ出す. 【類】 The crowd *in* a *panic* fled in all directions. ¶throw *into* a *panic* ろうばいさせる ‖ fall *into* a *panic* ろうばいする. ¶rumors *of* a *panic* 恐慌のうわさ. ¶The crowd was seized *with* a *panic*. 群衆はあわて出した.

panorama, *n.* 全景, パノラマ.

V The hill *commands* a fine *panorama* of the city and surrounding country. 山からその市と近在が見事なパノラマになって見える. 【類】 The summit *commands* an extensive *panorama*. ¶The whole coast *forms* a *panorama* of constant interest. その全海岸は興味の尽きないパノラマをなしている. ¶*obtain* a *panorama* of its gradual historical development その漸次の歴史的発展の姿を大観することができる. ¶This point *opens* an unobstructed *panorama* north, south, and west. この地点からは北も南も西もくまなく見渡せる. ¶*present* a moving *panorama* of society 社会の走馬灯を現出する. ¶a *panorama seen* from the windows of Hotel Green グリーンホテルの窓から見た全景. ¶If you would *watch* the great *panorama* of London life unfolding itself there is no better standpoint than a busy street corner. ロンドン生活の大走馬灯の動きを見るのにはにぎやかな街頭の一角に越した地点はない.

Q command a *magnificent panorama* of ... ...の壮麗な全景を見下ろす. ¶a *never-ending panorama* of happy faces 限りなく続くうれしそうな顔. ¶command from it an *unrivaled panorama* of ... そこから...の絶景を見下ろす.

P The surrounding country spreads *in* a *panorama* before us. 周囲の土地一帯がわれわれの前にパノラマのように展開する.

pant, *v.* あえぐ; 渇望する.

M The train came *panting fussily*. 列車が盛んにあえぎながらはいってきた. ¶*pant out* あえぎあえぎ言う. 【類】 *pant out* (=*forth*) a few words / His breath was almost gone, but enough left to *pant out* hurriedly.

P *pant after* (=for) liberty 自由を渇望する. ¶*pant for* breath あえぐ.

pants, *n.* 《俗》ずぼん.

Q *tailored pants* for women 婦人用仕立ずぼん.

Q² *army tan pants* [チョコレート色の]軍隊ずぼん. ¶*corduroy pants* コージュロイ(コール天)地のずぼん. ¶*knee pants* 半ずぼん.

paper, *n.* (1) [物質名詞] 紙.

V *fold* the *paper* so that the edge will be even 端がそろうように紙をたたむ. ¶I *have* some *paper*. 紙をいくらか持っている. ¶*make paper* 紙をつくる. ¶*roll* [*up*] *paper* 紙をまく.

Q *anti-rust paper* さび止めになる包紙. ¶*blank paper* 白

紙. ¶*brown paper* かっ色の包紙. ¶*corrugated paper* 段ボール紙. ¶printed on *English deckle-edged paper* 英国製の端を切ってない紙に印刷した. ¶*coated paper* アート紙 ¶a book printed on the *finest paper* and in elegant binding 上質紙に印刷し装てい優美な本. ¶*foreign paper* 外国製の紙. ¶*glossy paper* グラシ・ペーパー(光沢のある紙). ¶a small edition on *hand-made paper* limited to 50 copies 五十部を限る手すき紙のしゅう珍版. ¶*highly-glazed papar* つや出し紙. ¶*Japanese paper* 日本紙. ¶*laid paper* すき込みの紙. ¶*lined* (=*ruled*) *paper* けい紙. ¶*oiled paper* 油紙. ¶*plain paper* 無けい紙. ¶*privy paper* 落し紙. ¶*rough paper* ざら紙. ¶*simular Japanese paper* まがい日本紙. ¶*slick* (=*sleek*) *paper* 光沢のある上紙. ¶*smooth paper* [ロールのよくきいた]なめらかな紙. ¶*thin* (*thick*) *paper* うす(厚)手の紙. ¶very *thin soft paper* 非常にうす手の柔かい紙. ¶*time-yellowed paper* 古びて黄色になった紙. ¶*toned paper* うす色紙. ¶*waste paper* ほご, 紙くず. ¶They are not *worth* the *paper* they are written on. それらはその記述に使った紙代ほどの価値もない.

Q² *bank-note paper* 紙幣及び政府発行の証券用紙. ¶*copy paper* 原稿紙. ¶*end paper* 〖製本〗見返し. ¶*glass paper* やすり紙. ¶*India paper* インデヤン紙. ¶*letter paper* 便せん. ¶*Manila paper* マニラ紙. ¶*moisture-proof paper* 防湿紙. ¶*parchment paper* 羊皮紙. ¶a reel of *printing paper* 一巻きの印刷用紙. ¶be printed on *quality paper* 上質紙に印刷してある. ¶*rag paper* ぼろくず製の紙. ¶a good quality of *roofing paper* 良質の屋根ふき紙. ¶*safety paper* 安全紙(ぬり消し不能の). ¶*sand paper*=sandpaper 紙やすり. ¶*satin paper* 筆写用光沢紙. ¶*scrap paper* くず紙. ¶*scented toilet paper* 香入便所用紙. ¶*tarpaulin paper* 防水紙. ¶*tissue paper* 薄葉紙. ¶*tracing paper* 謄写紙. ¶*typewriter paper* タイプライター用紙. ¶*wrapping paper* 包装紙.

P It is made *from paper*. それは紙で造る. ¶do up *in paper* 紙に包む ‖ cut it out *in paper* それを紙で切る. ¶a bit (=piece) *of paper* 紙きれ一枚 ‖ a slip (=strip) *of paper* 細長い紙片 ‖ a sheet *of paper* 一枚の紙 ‖ fold up a piece *of paper* 紙片を折畳む. ¶put it down *on paper* それを紙に記す ‖ a book printed *on* tough *paper* 丈夫な紙に印刷した本 ‖ a prospectus *on paper* [筆記または印刷した]趣意書 ‖ Problems of any sort are easily worked out *on paper*. どんな問題でも紙上では容易に解決される. ¶I am *out of paper* and pens. 私は紙やペンが切れている.

(**2**) *pl.* 文書, 書類; *pl.* 証明書; 手形; 新聞, 新聞紙; 試験問題紙; 試験問題; 論文.

V a *paper* of questions was *addressed* to ... …に質問書を提出した. ¶regularly *buy* one *paper* きめて一つの新聞を買う. ¶*clip papers* 書類をクリップでとめる. ¶*collect* the *papers* 答案を寄せ集める. ¶before *commencing* one's *paper* その答案を書き出す前に. ¶*contribute* two *papers* on the subject その問題に関する二論文を寄稿する. ¶*distribute* examination *papers* 試験問題を配る. ¶*edit* a local *paper* 地方紙を編集する. ¶*exchange papers* for corrections [生徒が]訂正のため答案を交換する. ¶*papers* to be *filed* with an application 申込とともに差出すべき書類. ¶*floor* (=*clear*) a *paper* 《俗》試験問題をことごとくやってのける. ¶*give* a *paper* on current events 時事問題の朗読演説をする. ¶*grade* students' *papers* 学生の答案に点数をつける. 【類】If your *papers* were *graded* average less than 70 percent, your application would be rejected. ¶*papers* of naturalization were *granted* to ... 帰化証明書が…に下りた. ¶*hand in papers* 答案(書類)を出す. ¶*jab papers* on a file 書類を書類刺に通す. ¶*join* a *paper* 新聞社に入社する. ¶*keep papers* in order 書類を整理しておく. ¶*Let* my *papers alone*. 私の書類は(手をつけずに)そのままにしておけ. ¶*mark papers* liberally (bitterly) 点数をごく甘(辛)くつける. ¶*negotiate papers* 証券(手形)を金に換える. 【類】There are not many banks in the interior where foreign *paper* can be *negotiated*. ¶The contributors have *offered* their *papers* without remuneration. 寄稿者は無報酬で論文を提供した. ¶*present* a *paper* on this subject この問題に関する論文を提出する. ¶*produce* a new monthly *paper* 新規の月刊新聞を発行する. ¶*rate* exam *papers* 《米》答案を採点する. ¶*read* a *paper* before the Society on his exploration of ... その協会で彼の…探検に関する論文を朗読する. 【類】*read* a *paper* on the subject to the ... Society / *papers read* at the convention. ¶Vima Banky has *received papers* as (=for) a citizen of the U.S.A. ヴィーマ・バンキーは北米合衆国の公民としての証明書を受取った(すなわち米国への帰化が許された). ¶a *paper run* as a luxury or for a mission 道楽にまたはある伝道のために経営している新聞. ¶*scan* the evening *paper* 夕刊新聞に目を通す. ¶*scrape* their *papers* together 書類をかき集める. ¶*send in* (=*give*) one's *papers* その書類を出す. ¶English *papers set* at the examination その試験に出た英語の問題 ‖ *set* one's *papers* on order 書類を整理する. ¶*sign* a *paper* 文書に署名する. ¶*stamp* a *paper* 文書に判を押す. ¶*start* a *paper* 新聞を始める(起す). ¶*take out papers* of naturalization 帰化の手続をとる ‖ *take out* the first *papers* [帰化について](意志表示の)手続をする. ¶*turn over papers* 書類をめくる. ¶*write* a *paper* on ... …に関する論文を書く.

V² Here the *paper says*. ほら新聞に出ている.

Q *all* the *papers* bearing on the affair その事件関係一の切の書類. ¶an *Anglo-vernacular paper* 英語と自国語の新聞. ¶a *comic paper* 漫画新聞. ¶rediscount a *commercial paper* 商業手形を再割引する. ¶a *convertible paper* 兌(だ)換紙幣. ¶*daily papers* 日刊新聞 ‖ There is a *daily paper* gracing the breakfast table. 朝の食ぜんを飾る日刊新聞がある. ¶*elaborate papers* in physical science 自然科学における念入りな論文. ¶an *endowed paper* 補助金を受けている新聞. ¶*fragmentary papers* on science and other subjects 科学その他の問題に関する断片的論文. ¶a *gilt-edged paper* (=bill) 〖商〗一流手形. ¶*illustrated papers* 絵入新聞. ¶an *influential paper* 有力新聞. ¶his *learned paper* on the subject その問題に関する氏の博識なる論文. ¶*metropolitan papers* 首都発行の新聞. ¶*negotiable paper* 流通証書(手形). ¶a strictly *neutral, independent paper* 厳正中立の独立新聞. ¶an *old-established paper* 創立の古い新聞. ¶*posthumous papers* 遺稿. ¶the *private papers* of ... …の私文書. ¶in consequence of not having the *proper papers* 当然必要な書類を欠いているので. ¶*provincial* (=*local*) *papers* 地方新聞. ¶a *reputable paper* 評判のよい新聞. ¶*Russophile papers* ロシアびいきの新聞. ¶a *sensational paper* is one which pays more attention to what is startling than to what is important. 扇情的新聞とは事件の重要性よりは人騒がせの記事に重点をおく新聞をいう. ¶I saw your advertisement in *today's paper*. 本日の新聞で貴店の広告を拝見しました. ¶*typewritten papers* タイプ印書の書類. ¶*valuable papers* 重要書類. ¶a *vernacular paper* 自国語の新聞. ¶a *white paper* on economics 経済白書.

Q² an *accommodation* (*bank*) *paper* 融通(銀行)手形. ¶an *Army paper* 陸軍新聞(兵隊向け). ¶a *ballot paper* 投票用紙. ¶*birth papers* 出生届(書類). ¶*business* (=commercial) *paper* 商業手形. ¶fill in the *census paper* 国勢調査書に記入する. ¶a *college*[*-students*] *paper* 大学新聞. ¶*exam papers* 《米口語》試験問題(答案)用紙. ¶an *examination paper* of W.E. Gladstone グラドストーンの答案. 【類】*examination papers* in English composition / The *examination papers* (試験課目) include the classics, arithmetic, algebra, and geometry. ¶*foreign-language papers* 外国語の諸新聞. ¶a *home paper* 自国の新聞. ¶*identity papers* 身もと証明書類. ¶*legal-tender paper* 法定紙幣. ¶a *morning* (an *evening*) *paper* 朝(夕)刊. ¶file one's first *naturalization papers* [手続の第一歩として]その帰化志望の第一書類を呈出する. ¶a *one-man paper* 一人の経営の新聞. ¶the *opposition papers* 野党の諸機関紙. ¶bring out a miniature edition, on *Oxford India paper* オクスフォード特製のインディアンペーパーで小型版を出す. ¶a candidate's *qualifying papers* 候補者の資格証明書類. ¶a *question paper* 印刷した試験問題. ¶a *research paper* 研究報告書. ¶a *seminar paper* ゼミナールのレポート. ¶*state papers* 公文書. ¶a *student paper* 学生新聞. ¶a *subscription paper* 寄付金募集文書. ¶a *term paper* 〖教育〗学期末のレポート. ¶a *trade paper* 同業機関紙. 【類】"Le Cinema Belge," a *trade paper* covering Belgium (ベルギー関係同業機関紙). ¶*voting paper* 投票用紙. ¶*wall paper* 壁紙. ¶*work*[*ing*] *papers* 〖労〗就労書類.

P *according to* the *papers* 新聞の報じる所によれば. ¶I see *by* the *papers* that your husband is undergoing the cure at Karlsbad. 新聞で見ると御主人はカールスバートで

治療を受けていらっしゃるのですね. ¶one whose name is continually *in* the *papers* その名が絶えず新聞に出る人. 【類】Is there any interesting news *in* the *paper?* / I read *in* the *papers* that ... / here it says *in* the *paper* that ... / His name continually appears *in* the *papers.* / a writer *in* an American *paper* has said that ... ¶an extremely interesting series *of papers* on ... ...に関する非常におもしろい続きものの論文. ¶*on paper* 紙上では; 書いた物[印刷物]では; 理論的には ‖ It is all right *on paper.* 理論上は申し分ない. ‖ He is *on* a *paper.* 彼は新聞記者だ. ‖ figure out *on paper* the cost of ... ...の費用の概算書を作る. ¶Keep it *out of* the *papers.* それを新聞に出されないようにせよ. ¶go *through* the *papers* 新聞に目を通す ‖ ...gain publicity *through* the *papers* 新聞に出て世間に知られる.

P² a *paper about* ... ...に関する論文. ¶a good *paper for* young people to read 少年の読むに適した新聞 ‖ He is accused of buying proofs of the *papers for* forthcoming examinations. 彼は期日の近くなった試験問題の校正刷を買ったという非難を受けた. ¶a *paper of* high position 高級な新聞. ¶read a *paper on* a subject ある問題に関する論文を読む. ¶read a long *paper to* the Conference on the subject of "..."「...」問題の協議会で長論文を朗読する. ¶read a *paper upon* the value of ... ...の価値に関する論文を読む.

paper, *v.* 紙でおおう.
M *paper out* the cold wind 紙で目張りして寒気を防ぐ.
M² *paper up* book covers 本の表紙に紙をかぶせる.

par, *n.* 平価, 額面価格; 同等, 同格; 平均額.
Q² *issue par* 発行価額.
P The rate of exchange for dollars is *above par.* ドルの為替相場は平価以上だ. ‖ This stock is *above par.* この株は額面以上だ. ¶The stock is *at par.* この株は額面通りだ. 【類】buy *at par* / Foreign coins do not pass *at par.* ¶*at* or *under par* [株など]額面または額面以下で. ¶Shares have fallen *below par.* 株が額面以下に下落した. ‖ His health is *below par.* 彼は健康がすぐれない. 【類】feel *below par* / He is mentally (=intellectually) *below par* (コンマ). ¶sell at ... per cent *of par* 平価の...パーセントで売る. ¶put him *on* a *par* with ... 彼を...と同格におく ‖ Japan now stands *on* a *par* with European nations in ... 今日の日本は...の点では欧州諸国民と同等の地位を占めている. 【類】He is quite *on* a *par* with his brother in brains. / His knowledge on the subject seems to be *on* a *par* with my own. / The gains and losses are about *on* a *par.* ¶*over* (*under*) *par* 平価以上(以下)で. ¶The stock has risen *to par.* その株は値が出て額面通りになった. ¶The crops are *up to par.* 作物は平作に達した.

parachute, *n.* 落下さん.
V *discard* a *parachute* 落下さんを振り捨てる. ¶*release* a *parachute* 落下さんをはずす.
V² A *parachute flares.* 落下さんがパッと開く.

parade, *n.* 観兵式; 見せびらかし; 行列.
V *hold* a *parade* 観兵式を行う. ¶*inspect* the *parade* of rank and fashion 上流社会と流行のオン・パレードを見る. ¶*make* a great (=much) *parade* of one's learning (charity) 盛んに学問(など)を見せびらかす ‖ *make* a *parade* of unusual epithets 変った形容語を並べたてる. ¶the Emperor *ordered* a grand *parade* of his armies on the day of ... 天皇は...の日に陸軍観兵式挙行を命ぜられた.
Q hold a *barefoot parade* 素足行進をやる. ¶a *funeral parade* 葬儀の行列. ¶a *political parade* 政治デモ行進.
Q² a *dress* (an *undress*) *parade* 正式(略式)観兵式. ¶the *Emperor's Birthday parade* 天長節観兵式. ¶a *fashion parade* ファッション・モデルのショー. ¶a *hit parade* ヒット・ソングの大会. ¶a *labor parade* 労働者のデモ行進. 【類】a *Labor Day parade.* ¶a *nude parade* 裸体行列. ¶a *street parade* 街頭行進; ((米)) 分列行進. ¶a *victory parade* 勝利の行進. ¶a *woman suffrage parade* 婦人参政権デモ行進.
P march *in parade* [行列を作って]練り歩く. ¶*on parade* 行列を作って ‖ a contingent of lady marines *on parade* 行進中の女子陸戦隊.
P² a *parade of* wealth 富の誇示.

parade, *v.* ねり歩く.
M *cleverly parade* a barrage of queries 巧みに連続質問を浴びせる.
P *parade in* print 盛んに印刷されて出る. ¶*parade* [*through*] the streets 街々を練り歩く ‖ send sandwich-men *parading through* streets サンドイッチマンに街路をねって歩かせる.

paradise, *n.* 楽園, 極楽.
Q an *earthly paradise* 地上楽園. ¶The Inland Revenue Office is the *grumblers' paradise.* 英国内国税務署は所得税の不平をいう納税者の天国である. ¶keep one in a *fool's paradise* 人を幸福の夢にふけらせる. ¶*holiday-makers' paradise* 遊覧者の楽園. ¶Just now Japan is certainly a *shopper's paradise.* 目下日本はまさに買物をする人の楽園である(為替などの関係で観光外人などにとって費用が安くつくから). ¶a *terrestrial paradise* この世ながらの極楽.
Q² The *Buddhist Paradise* that lies in a region on trillion miles from the earth 十万億土. ¶a *holiday paradise* 行楽の楽天地. ¶the *sportsman paradise* スポーツマンの楽園.
P² The city is a *paradise for* cyclists. その市は自転車乗りに取っての楽園である. 【類】a *paradise for* tourists. ¶a *paradise on* earth 地上の楽園. ¶the life of a laborer is a *paradise to* that of ... 労働者の生活は...のそれに比すれば極楽だ.

paradox, *n.* 逆説, 奇言.
Q an *ironical paradox* 皮肉. ¶a *puzzling paradox* なぞのような奇言. ¶a *ridiculous paradox* 笑うべき逆説. ¶a *startling paradox* 驚くべき逆説.

paradoxical, *a.* 逆説的な.
O it may sound *paradoxical,* but ... 皮肉に聞えるかも知れんが...

paragon, *n.* 模範.
P² a *paragon among* reviewers 評論家中の模範人物. ¶She is considered a *paragon of* virtue. 彼女は淑女の手本とされている. ‖ a *paragon of* fashion 流行の典型.

paragraph, *n.* 節, 段; [新聞の]記事, 短評.
V not long ago the papers *contained* a little *paragraph* stating that ... ついこの間諸新聞に...のことを報じる短い記事が載っていた. ¶The *paragraph* was *headed* "A Deplorable Accident," and it ran in this way:— その記事は「惨たんたる事故」という見出しでこんな風に書いてあった. ¶*skip* the next *paragraph* 次の段を飛ばして先を読む.
Q the *concluding paragraph* 末項. ¶an *editorial paragraph* 短い社説. ¶*foregoing paragraphs* 前諸項目. ¶the art of constructing *good paragraphs* りっぱな文段を作る法. ¶*miscellaneous paragraphs* 雑報. ¶the *opening paragraph* of this article この論文の冒頭の段 ‖ in my *opening paragraph* この本の始めに. ¶*pointed paragraphs* [新聞などの]辛らつな短評. ¶the unity of a *well-built paragraph* 組立の巧妙な段の統一性. 【類】A *well-built paragraph* is ultimately the result of clear thinking.
P *under* the *paragraph* ... of the Constitution of Japan 日本国憲法第...条の下に.
P² this *paragraph from* the report 報告書のこの一段.

paragrapher, *n.*
Q² a *newspaper paragrapher* 新聞の(見出しのない)雑報記者.

parallel, *n.* 平行線; 類似の例; 相似点; 比較.
V Japan *affords* a close *parallel.* 日本にもそれに酷似した例がある. ¶*bear* a close *parallel* to ... ...にきわめて類似している. ¶*draw* a *parallel* between ... and ... ...と...との相似点を比較する. ¶a *parallel* can hardly be *found* for ... ...の比類は容易に見当らない ‖ *find* the nearest *parallels* to ... ...に最も近似した例を見出す. ¶*form* an apt *parallel* of ... ...と好一対をなす. ¶*have* no *parallel* in ... ...において匹敵するものがない ‖ it *has* a modern *parallel* in ... それは昔の...を今に見るのだ. ¶history *supplies* no trustworthy *parallel* for ... 歴史上...に匹敵する確実な例はない.
Q a *closer parallel* 一層似通った点. ¶*historic parallels* to ... ...の歴史的類例. ¶presenting a *remarkable parallel* そろいもそろって.
P *in parallel* with ... ...と平行して. ¶be *without* a *parallel* in the history of the world 世界歴史に類がない. ¶absolutely *without parallel* 全然比類のない ‖ *without parallel* east of Suez スエズ運河以東第一の. 【類】perhaps *without parallel* in the world / The complete success of Helen Keller's life is *without parallel* in history. / *without* a *parallel* in the annals of ... / *without* any contemporaneous (同時代の) *parallel* in the West.
P² a *parallel between* the careers *of* ... and ... ...と...との経歴の相似点.

parallel, *a.* 平行の.
P The railway line in this part is *parallel to* the river.

この辺の鉄道線路は川と平行している. ‖ offer courses which are *parallel* or equivalent *to* freshman and sophomore courses 大学の一年及び二年の課程に平行するあるいは同等の課程を設ける. ¶navigate *parallel with* the coast 海岸に平行して航行する. 【類】The river runs *parallel with* the main street.

parallel, *v.* 平行する; 比較する.

P You can *parallel* nobody *in* strength *to* him. 力では彼に匹敵する者はない. 「河.

O A canal that *parallels* the railroad 鉄道に添うている運

parallelism, *n.* 相似.

Q It may be doubted whether there is any *exact parallelism* between muscular strength and hairiness. 体力と多毛ということは何か正確な相関性があるかどうか疑わしい. ¶*striking parallelism* between ... and ... ...と...との著しい相似.

P² There is no *parallelism between* the two languages. その二国語間には何らの相似点がない.

paralysis, *n.* 麻ひ, 中風.

Q *cerebral paralysis* 卒中. ¶*facial paralysis* 顔面麻ひ. ¶*general paralysis* 全身麻ひ. ¶*moral paralysis* 道義心の麻ひ. 「かった.

P He had a stroke (=shock) *of paralysis.* 彼は中風にか

P² *paralysis of* the heart 心臓麻ひ. ¶the *paralysis of* fear 恐怖による麻ひ.

paralyze, *v.* 麻ひさせる.

M *practically paralyze* one's effort 事実上努力を不可能にする. ¶Business is *totally paralyzed.* 商売は全然休止状態だ. 「た.

P He was *paralyzed with* terror. 彼は恐怖で腰を抜かし

paramount, *a.* 卓絶した.

P be *paramount as* a dollar-earner ドルかせぎには最重要である(米国輸出品など). 【類】London is still *paramount as* a headquarter of exchange and banking. ¶Loyalty is a duty *paramount to* all others. 忠義はあらゆる他の義務に卓絶した義務である. 【類】This duty is *paramount to* all the others.

paramour, *n.* 情夫(婦). 「リー情婦.

Q a *jealous, hysterical paramour* やきもちやきのヒステ

P *as* her *paramour* 彼女の情夫として.

paraphernalia, *n.* 付属品, 七つ道具.

Q other *necessary paraphernalia* その他必要な雑品.

Q² *baseball paraphernalia* 野球の設備(道具など). ¶the leading maker of *croquet paraphernalia* クロッケー用付属品の一流製造人.

paraphrase, *n.* 意訳, 義解.

Q² *prose paraphrase* of a song 歌の散文訳.

paraphrase, *v.* 意訳する, 義解する.

P it was *paraphrased from* the Italian [original] *by* ... それは...によってイタリア語から義解したものだ. ¶*paraphrase* poetry *into* prose 詩を散文に意訳する.

parasite, *n.* 寄生虫.

P² a *parasite on* (=*upon*) the community (person, tree) 社会(など)の寄生虫.

parasitic, *a.* 寄生した.

P insects *parasitic on* plants 植物の寄生虫.

parasol, *n.* 日がさ.

V *put up* one's *parasol* 日がさをさす.

paratroops, *n.* 落下さん部隊.

V *land paratroops* 落下さん部隊を着陸させる.

parcel, *n.* 小包, 小荷物.

V Will you *carry* this *parcel* for me? この小包を持ってくれませんか. ¶*express* a *parcel* to ... ...に小包を速達便で送る. ¶*forward* one a *parcel* 人に小包を発送する. ¶*roll up* a *parcel* 小荷物を包む. ¶*send* a *parcel* posthaste 至急小包を発送する. ¶*send off* (=*away*) a *parcel* 小包を出す. ¶*sew up* a *parcel* in canvas 小包をズックに入れて縫付ける. ¶*undo* (=*untie*) a *parcel* 小包を解く. ¶*wrap up* a *parcel* in paper (cloth) 小荷物を紙(など)包にする.

Q² a *gift percel*=《米》a gift package 賜り物. ¶heavy *hand parcel* 重い手荷物.

P *by parcel* [post] 小包郵便で. ¶a label tied on *to* a *parcel* 小包につけてある荷札.

P² a *parcel of* rubbish 一包のくず物.

parcel, *v.* 分派する; 割当てる; 分かつ.

M *parcel* the men *off* to different places 人々を諸所に分派する. ¶The expenses were *parceled out* to individuals. 入費は個人個人に割当てた. 【類】*parcel out* the land to peasants (小作人) / The captain *parceled out* the spoils (分捕品) among his crew.

P *parcel* [out] the land *into* 10 divisions 土地を十区に分かつ.

parch, *v.* からからにする.

M² The road *parched up* with dry weather. 道路は日照りでからからになった.

P I am *parched with* thirst. 僕はのどがかわいてからからだ. 【類】The plant was *parched with* heat.

parchment, *n.* 羊皮紙.

P write *on parchment* 羊皮紙に書く.

pardon, *n.* 赦免, 容赦.

V *ask pardon* of ... ...の許しをこう ‖ *ask* his *pardon* 彼の許しをこう. ¶I *beg* your *pardon,* but ... 失礼ですが... ‖ *begging pardon* for my saying so はばかりながら ‖ I humbly *beg pardon.* 幾重にもお許しを願います. 【類】I *beg* [you] a thousand *pardons.* ¶We humbly *crave* your *pardon* for our default. われわれの怠慢については幾重にも御容赦を願います. ‖ *craving pardon* for this digression, I return to ... 脱線の儀は御容赦を願って話をもとへ戻して...します. ¶*entreat* (=*implore*) the *pardon* of ... 切に...のお許しをこう. ¶*grant pardons* to convicts 囚徒を赦免する ‖ *grant* general *pardon* 大赦を行う. ¶*obtain* one's *pardon* その許しを得る. ¶*seek pardon* for ... ...に対し許しを求める.

P² A thousand *pardons for* stepping (=treading) on your foot! お足を踏んで誠に相済みません. ¶a *pardon of* (=*to or for*) offenders 犯罪人の赦免.

pardon, *v.* 容赦する.

P I hope you will *pardon* me *for* doing so. 私がそう致したことは御勘弁を願います.

pare, *v.* 皮をむく; 削り取る.

M² *pare down* expenses 経費を削減する. 【類】*pare down* the Government personnel. ¶*pare off* potatoes (pears) じゃが芋(など)の皮をむく.

parent, *n.* 親; 本(もと), 本源.

V *disobey* one's *parents* 両親に逆らう. ¶He *lost* his *parent* early in life. 彼は早く片親を失った. ¶The *parents* are *mortified* by the child's rudeness. 子供の行儀が悪いので両親はそれを苦にしている. ¶*obey* one's *parents* 両親に従う. ¶*Parents* are earnestly *requested* to see that their daughters' wardrobe is simply furnished, as befitting school girls. お嬢さん方の衣類は女学生にふさわしく質素になされるよう御両親に懇望致します. ¶*respect* one's *parents* 両親を尊敬する. ¶*support* one's *parents* 両親を扶養する. ¶*tease* one's *parents* for ... 両親に...とせがむ.

Q The fall of our *first parents,* Adam and Eve 人間最初の両親アダムとイブの堕落. ¶The two languages have a *common linguistic parent.* この二国語は言語上その起原を同じにしている. ¶*fond parents* 子ぼんのうの親. ¶He was born of *good* but *humble parents.* 彼は善良で身分のいやしい両親から出た. ¶an *indulgent* (=*devoted*) *parent* 子に甘い親. ¶*one* or *both parents* 片親または両親. ¶He was born (=comes) of *poor parents.* 彼は貧家に生れた. ¶a child of *separated parents* 別れた両親の子. ¶*unnatural parents* 子を愛さない親.

P He is living *on* his *parents.* 彼は親のすねをかじっている. ¶You should be respectful *towards parents.* 親に孝行でなければならない.

P² Ignorance is the *parent of* many evils. 《諺》無知は罪悪の本. ¶Astrology is the *parent of* modern astronomy as alchemy is of chemistry. 錬金術が化学の本源であるように占星術は現代天文学の本源である. ¶The Pan-Pacific Union is *parent to* many clubs and organizations throughout the Pacific. 汎(はん)太平洋同盟は太平洋上至るところに存在する幾多のクラブや団体の親である.

parentage, *n.* 血統, 家柄; 門地.

Q He is a Colonial born or of *Colonial parentage.* 彼は植民地生れかまたは植民地の親にできた子だ. ¶of *doubtful parentage* いかがわしい血筋の(人など). ¶of *European* (*German*) *parentage* ヨーロッパ(ドイツ)系統の. ¶He is American born, but of *foreign parentage.* 彼はアメリカ生れだが外人系統だ. ¶pupils of *good parentage* 親の良い生徒たち. ¶of *humble* (=*base or mean*) *parentage* いやしい血筋の. ¶Americans of *Japanese parentage* 米国第

二世日本人. ¶He was born of ***mixed parentage.*** 彼は合の子だ. ‖a lady of ***mixed*** Spanish and English *parentage* スペイン人と英国人の両親から出た混血の婦人. ¶a man of ***noble*** (=***high or great***) *parentage* 高貴な家柄の人. ¶His *parentage* is ***unknown.*** 彼はだれの子だか分からない. ¶a young boy of exceedingly ***wealthy*** *parentage* 富貴な家柄の少年.

P He comes ***of*** good *parentage.* 彼は名門の出だ.

parenthesis, *n.* そう句; 括弧.

P ***between*** *parentheses* 括弧に入れて. ¶English equivalents are given ***in*** *parentheses* after Japanese words. 英訳は日本語の後に括弧に入れてある. ‖words ***in*** *parentheses* 括弧内の語 ‖I note ***in*** *parentheses* (=passing) that ... ちなみに記す. ‖put (=inclose) a word ***in*** *parentheses* 語を括弧に入れる ‖a clause printed ***in*** a *parenthesis* (=parentheses) そう句中(括弧内)に印刷した句. ¶it might also be remarked ***in*** *parentheses* that ... ちなみに記す... ¶It is added ***within*** *parentheses* (=a parenthesis). それは括弧内につけ加えてある.

parenthood, *n.* 親たること.

V ***attain*** *parenthood* 親となる(子を生む). ¶***prevent*** *parenthood* 産児を阻止する.

parer, *n.* 皮むき.

Q² an ***apple*** *parer* りんごむき(器具).

parity, *n.* 同等, 同格; 同価; 類似.

P ***by*** *parity* of reasoning 類推によって.

P² There is no *parity* ***between*** the two. 両者間に何ら類似の所はない. ¶*parity* ***of*** silver 銀平価 ‖The present gold *parity* ***of*** the dollar is about $5.36 in relation to the pound. 現在ドルの金平価は一ポンドに対しおよそ五ドル三十六セントである. ‖*parity* ***of*** treatment 待遇均等. ¶the establishment of music as a major subject on a *parity* ***with*** other studies 音楽を他の学科同様主要課目と定めること.

park, *n.* 公園; [兵器などの]廠(しょう); 《米》駐車場.

V ***lay out*** a *park* 公園を設計する. ¶The *park* has been ***thrown open.*** その公園は公開された.

Q Golden Gate Park is the largest ***artificial*** *park* in the world, containing 1,013 acres. 金門公園は千十三エーカーを有する世界最大の人工公園である. ¶a beautifully ***landscaped*** *park* 美しい風景園. ¶It forms a veritable ***large*** *park.* それは実に大きな公園となっている. ¶a ***private*** *park* 私設遊園. ¶a ***public*** *park* [市などの]公園. ¶a ***tree-embowered*** *park* 樹木に囲まれた公園. ¶a ***well-wooded*** *park* 樹木の多い公園. ¶a ***zoological*** *park* 動物園.

Q² a popular ***amusement*** *park* 公開遊園地. ¶an ***artillery*** *park* 砲兵廠. ¶a ***ball*** *park*=a ballpark 《米》野球場. ¶a ***car*** *park*=a parking place 駐車場. ¶a ***cemetery*** *park* 霊園. ¶a ***city*** *park* 市立公園. ¶a ***deer*** *park* しか猟の地. 【類】the great ***deer*** *park* of ancient Nara. ¶an ***engineer*** *park* 工兵廠. ¶a ***pleasure*** *park* 遊園地.

P take a walk ***in*** a *park* 公園を散歩する.

park, *v.* 《米》駐車させる; 造園する.

M² *park* ***about*** 林園をめぐらす.

P *park* a car ***along*** the side of a street 街路の片側に駐車をする.

parking, *n.* 《米》駐車.

Q ***live*** (***dead***) *parking* 運転手のいる(いない)車の駐車. ¶***No*** *parking* here. 〚掲示〛当所に自動車おくべからず.

Q² ***angle*** *parking* 斜列駐車. ¶***car*** *parking* 駐車.

parlance, *n.* 言い方.

Q in ***common*** *parlance* 俗にいう. ¶in ***legal*** (=law) *parlance* 法律語でいうと. ¶in ***military*** *parlance* 兵語にいわゆる. ¶in more ***modern*** *parlance* 現代風にいえば. ¶called, in ***nautical*** *parlance,* "..." 海語のいわゆる「...」. ¶in ***ordinary*** (=common) *parlance* くだけて言うと. ¶in ***popular*** *parlance* 平ったくいうと. ¶in ***scientific*** *parlance* 学術的にいえば. ¶in ***theatrical*** *parlance* 芝居道のいわゆる. ¶In ***vulgar*** *parlance* Sunday is called Dontaku, a corruption of the Dutch "Zon dag." 俗に日曜日をドンタクというのはオランダ語のゾンダクのなまったものだ.

Q² In ***Nazi*** *parlance,* the democracy of Western Europe is pluto-democracy ナチの言葉を借りると西欧民主々義とは貴族的民主々義だ. ¶in ***sailor*** *parlance* 海員語でいえば.

parley, *n.* 談判.

V ***hold*** *parley* with ... ...と談判する. 【類】The Government is ready to ***hold*** a *parley* at any moment.

Q² a ***Big 3*** *parley* 三巨頭会談. ¶a ***four-hour*** *parley* 四時間にわたる会談. ¶***Peace*** *parleys* had collapsed. 平和交渉は失敗した.

P ***without*** further *parley* その上談判をせずに.

parley, *v.* 談判する.

P *parley* ***with*** the enemy 敵と談判する.

Parliament, *n.* [英国]国会, 議会.

V ***adjourn*** *Parliament* 国会を停会する. ¶***convoke*** (=***convene or summon***) a *Parliament* 国会を召集する. ¶***dissolve*** *Parliament* 国会を解散する. ¶He first ***entered*** *Parliament* in 1911 as Conservative member for South Birmingham. 彼はサウス・バーミンガム選出の保守党議員として一九一一年初めて国会にはいった. ¶*Parliament* was ***opened*** by the King. 王が国会を開会した. ¶***pack*** a *parliament* 自己の都合いいような議員を集めて議会を作る. ¶***prorogue*** a *Parliament* 国会を停会する.

V² *Parliament* ***dissolves.*** 国会が解散する. ¶*Parliament* ***meets*** tomorrow. 議会は明日開会される. ¶*Parliament* is ***sitting.*** 国会は開会中だ.

Q the ***British*** *Parliament* 英国々会.

P The Bill is now ***before*** *Parliament.* その法案は今国会で審議中だ. ¶stand ***for*** *Parliament*=《米》run for Congress 国会議員候補に立つ. ¶He represents this town ***in*** *Parliament.* 彼は当市選出の国会議員だ. ¶an act ***of*** *Parliament* 法令, 条例 ‖a member ***of*** *Parliament*=an M.P. 国会議員 ‖the Houses ***of*** *Parliament* 上下両院. ¶He has been returned ***to*** *Parliament.* 彼は国会議員に選挙された. ¶The Admiralty is a department of the British government in which is vested ***under*** *Parliament,* the supreme charge of naval affairs. 海軍省は英国政府の一省で国会の下に海事の最高監督権を与えられている.

O *Parliament* is up at last. 国会は遂に閉会となった.

parlo[u]r, *n.* 客間; 営業室, 治療室.

Q a ***dental*** *parlor* 歯科診療室. ¶a ***hair-dresser's*** *parlor*=a barber shop 床屋.

Q² a ***beauty*** *parlor* 美容室. ¶a ***billiard*** (***pinball***) *parlor* 玉突場(パチンコ屋). ¶an ***ice-cream*** *parlor* アイスクリーム店. ¶a ***massage*** *parlor* [ぜい肉をとる]マッサージ治療所. ¶a ***shoe shine*** *parlor* くつみがき所. ¶a ***sun*** *parlor* サンルーム. ¶a ***tea*** *parlor* 喫茶店.

parody, *n.* 作り替え.

Q clad in ***hideous*** *parodies* of foreign dress 見苦しい洋服を着て.

P² a *parody* ***of*** (=***on***) a poem 詩の滑けいな作り替え, 替え歌.

parole, *n.* 宣誓.

V ***break*** *parole* [仮出所者など]宣誓を破る. ¶***grant*** a *parole* to a prisoner 囚人に仮出所を許可する. ¶put a person ***on*** *parole* 人を仮釈放する.

P ***by*** *parole* 〚法〛口頭で. ¶The prisoner was released ***on*** *parole.* 捕虜は宣誓の上釈放された. ‖a prisoner ***on*** *parole* 宣誓釈放捕虜.

parole, *v.* 宣誓釈放する.

M be ***temporarily*** *paroled* 仮出所を許される.

P He was *paroled* ***from*** the prison (penitentiary). 彼は宣誓の上刑務所(など)から釈放された.

parrot, *n.* おうむ.

V ***play*** the *parrot* 口まねをする.

V² The *parrot* ***talks.*** おうむは物を言う. ¶The *parrot* ***whistles.*** おうむは鳴く.

P learn ... ***like*** a *parrot* 機械的に...を覚える.

part, *n.* (1) 部分; 器官; 主要部; 分(ぶ), 割; 一半; 地方; 方, 側(がわ); *pl.* 才能.

V ***acquire*** the theoretical *part* of a branch of learning ある学科の理論的方面を修める. ¶***constitute*** a *part* of ... ...の一部分を成す. ¶***devote*** a *part* or all of one's time to ... 自分の時間の一部または全部を...に捧げる. ¶English ***forms part*** of the regular curriculum. 英語は正課の一部となっている. ‖it ***forms*** no *part* of my purpose to ... ...することは私の目的ではない. 【類】Speeches ***form*** *part* of the program. / It ***forms*** [a] *part* of the equipment (携帯品) of the expedition. / ***form*** *part* of the agenda (会議事項, 日程) ‖Luxemburg ***formed*** *part* of the Holy Roman Empire. / It is to ***form*** *part* of Mr. Heineman's series entitled "Literature of the world." / It ***forms*** *part* of His Majesty's prerogatives (大権). / It ***forms*** a large *part* of the collection (収集). / Students ***formed*** the chief *part* of the audience. / It ***forms*** *part* of the business of comic papers. / such technical terms as ***form*** *part* of the ordinary vocabulary / ***form*** but a *part* of ... / words which ***form*** no ***part*** of daily speech. ¶***make part*** of a journey on foot 旅行の一部を徒歩で行く. ¶The thought ***occupies*** a greater ***part*** of his reflections. その思想が彼の思索の大部分を占める. 【類】The trip will ***occupy*** the better ***part*** (大部分) of one year. ¶He ***received part*** of his education in England. 彼は教育を一部英国で受けた. ¶***show*** one's ***parts*** upon the public その腕前を公開する. ¶He has ***spent*** the major ***part*** of his career. 彼は人生の大部分を過ぎた.

Q cut out the ***affected parts*** 患部を切開する. ¶the ***annoying part*** of the matter is ... 困ったことは...だ. ¶the ***back part*** of ... ...の後部. ¶Trousers shortly become wrinkled at all ***bending parts*** of the leg. ズボンは曲り目の所がじきにしわくちゃになる. ¶the ***best part*** of a week 一週間の大部分. 【類】I rode (馬で行った) the ***best part*** of the way. ¶realizing that discretion is the ***better part*** of valor 三十六計逃ぐるにしかずと悟って ‖ for the ***better part*** of their time 彼らの時間の大部分は. ¶a ***better-paying part*** of the business 給料の高い方の仕事. ¶radio instruments and ***component parts*** ラジオ器械と組成部分 ‖ Blade and handle are the ***component part*** of a knife. ナイフは刃と柄でできている. ¶form a ***constituent part*** of ... ...の成分をなす. ‖ the ***constituent parts*** of the United Nations 国際連合機構. ¶a ***corporate part*** of our own lives われわれ生命の肉体的部分. ¶in the ***darkest part*** of the dark night of adversity 逆境のどん底にあって. ¶depth at the ***deepest part*** 最深部の深さ. ¶a ***defective part*** 不完全な部分. ¶That is the most ***difficult part*** of it. それが一番むずかしい所だ. ¶during the ***early part*** of the war 戦争の初めの中は. 【類】in the ***early part*** of the current year (present century) / in the ***early part*** of next week / in the ***earlier part*** of the sixteenth century. ¶take ***equal parts*** of ... ...を等分に取る(物を交ぜる時など). 【類】consisting of ***equal parts*** of ... ¶form an ***essential part*** of female education 女子教育の主要部分をなしている. ¶take it in ***excellent part*** それを気持よく受け入れる. ¶from a very ***far part*** of the world 遠い遠い国から. ¶One bullet passed through the ***fleshy part*** of the forearm. 一弾は上腕の肉を貫通した. ¶before sailing for ***foreign parts*** 外国へ向け出帆する前に. 【類】He spent most of his life in ***foreign parts***. ¶the ***former*** (***latter***) ***part*** of a statement 声明書の前(後)段. ¶The charge is one hundred yen for the first hour and thirty yen for each succeeding hour or ***fractional part*** thereof. 料金は最初の一時間は百円それから一時間またはその端数ごとに三十円. ¶He took my advice in ***good*** (***bad***) ***part***. 彼は快く私の忠告を容れた(悪く取った). ¶for a ***great part*** of the year 一年中の大半は. 【類】it consists in ***great part*** of ... / during the ***greater part*** of the season. ¶the ***hardest part*** of the work 作業のもっとも困難な部分. ¶***historical*** and ***descriptive parts*** of a work 著作の歴史的及び叙述的部分. ¶in the ***hot part*** of the day 暑い盛りに. ¶form an ***important part*** of ... ...の重要部分をなす. ¶the ***injured parts*** 負傷の部分. ¶the ***inner parts*** of a human body 人体の内臓. ¶The public library is an ***integral part*** of public education. 公立図書館は社会教育の完備に不可欠なものだ. 【類】Steel is an ***integral part*** of a modern building. / It has become an ***integral part*** of the life of the Metropolis. ‖ The University of Chicago Press is an ***integral part*** of the University. シカゴ大学出版部は同大学の一部である. ‖ the ***integral parts*** of a machine 機械の主要部分. ¶There comes an ***interesting part*** of the ceremony. 式の興味ある部分はこれからだ. ¶the ***inward parts*** of the body 肉体の内部. ¶a rod with ***jointed parts*** 継ぎざお. ¶the most ***laborious part*** of the undertaking その仕事の一番困難な部分. ¶His failure was due in ***large part*** to his carelessness. 彼の失敗は多くは不注意に基因した. ‖ he has a ***large part*** in ... 彼は...にあずかって力がある. ¶in the ***late*** (=***last***) ***part*** of the nineteenth century 十九世紀の末葉に. ¶the ***latter part*** of one's life 晩年 ‖ in the ***latter part*** of September or early October 九月の末か十月の初めに. ¶By the ancients courage was regarded as the ***main part*** of virtue. 昔の人は勇気を美徳の主要部と思った. ¶***malaria-stricken parts*** of the country その国のマラリア熱に襲われた地方. ¶in ***many parts*** of the world 世界諸国で. ¶The compass is a ***necessary part*** of sailor's outfit. ら針盤は船員に必要な品である. 【類】Women are a ***necessary part*** of men's society. ¶The ***negative*** part of a conversation is often as important as its positive. 会話の否定の部分は肯定の部分と同様重要なことが往々ある. ¶***nine parts*** in 10,000 by volume 量で一万分の九. ¶an ***obscure part*** of the town その町の(目抜の場所に対する)人目につかない部分. ¶They went prospecting in ***other parts*** of the district. 彼らはその地方の他の方面へ瀬ぶみに出かけた(探鉱家など). ¶an ***outlying part*** 遠隔の地方. ¶living in an ***out-of-the-way part*** of England 英国の片いなかに住んでいるので. ¶I have a ***personal part*** in it. 私はそれに直接関係がある. ¶the most densely ***populated*** and ***poverty-stricken part*** of London ロンドンの最も人口ちゅう密で貧民の住む区域. ¶the ***private*** (=***privy***) ***parts*** 陰部. ¶the last of ***six parts*** 六回連続物の最後の部分. ¶***quick parts*** 縦横の才. ¶in ***remote parts*** of the country その国の辺境に. 【類】go on trips to ***remote parts*** of the world. ¶He was born in a ***retired part*** of New England. 彼はニューイングランドの辺境に生れた. ¶a ***seventh part***=one-seventh 七分の一. ¶the ***sexual parts*** 生殖器. ¶a young man of ***promising parts*** 才能の延びる見込みのある青年. ¶form only a ***small part*** わずかに小部分をなす. ¶in ***some parts*** of America アメリカのある地方に. ¶the ***spectacular part*** of the celebration consisted of ... 祭典の中で一番観物は...であった. ¶a ***substantial part*** 大部分. ¶the ***terrestrial parts*** of the world 世界の陸地の部分(海に対して). ¶I am a stranger in ***these parts***. 私はこの辺は不案内だ. 【類】when you come into ***these parts***. ¶a ***thickly peopled part*** of the country その国の人口ちゅう密な地方. ¶in ***this part*** of the country この地方では. ¶the ***unthinking, emotional part*** of the population 思慮なく感情的な一部の住民. ¶in ***various parts*** of the country その国の諸方に. ¶***vital parts*** 急所. ¶***wearing parts*** 消耗する部分.

Q[2] the ***bellows part*** of an accordion アコーディオンのじゃ腹の部分. ¶***body parts*** 身体の部分. ¶the ***desert parts*** of southern Palestine 南部パレスチナのさばく地域. ¶the ***end parts*** of a foot 足のつま先. ¶These originally technical words have now become an ***everyday part*** of the language. これらは元来技術用語であったが今日では日常の言葉の中に取入れられている. ¶The dictionary appeared originally in ***shilling parts***. その辞書は始め一シリングづつの分冊で出たものだ.

P the cinema ***as part*** of school equipment 学校設備の一部としての映画. 【類】*karuta* (=card) playing ***as part*** of New Year celebrations / pursue zoology ***as part*** of a liberal education (高等教育) / the importance of the subject ***as part*** of elementary education (初等教育) / It is to be recognized ***as*** a ***part*** of the regular curriculum (正課). ‖ include it ***as part*** of the expenses of ... それを...の経費中に編入する. ¶***during*** the greater ***part*** of the summer 夏中大半は. ¶They rely on ... ***for*** a ***part*** of their support 彼らは...を生活のたしにしている. ‖ I ***for*** my ***part*** am unable to see the point. 私には要点が分からない. 【類】Of Latin prose, ***for*** my own ***part***, I value most the soldierly simplicity of Caesar. / ***for*** our ***part*** we think that ... / The Japanese, ***for*** their ***part***, consider themselves affronted and humiliated by the use of the word "Jap." ¶***from*** all ***parts*** of the earth 世界の各所から ‖ ***for*** the most ***part*** 大部分は. ¶***in parts*** 所々. ¶it reads (=runs) ***in part*** as follows:— それは大体次のように書いてある. 【類】His success is ***in part*** owing to luck. / it is ***in part*** cause and ***in part*** effect of ... ‖ The story appeared ***in parts***. その物語は数回に分載された. ‖ ***in*** greater ***part*** 大部分 ‖ ***in*** this (that) ***part*** of the world 世界のこの(その)地方では. 【類】***in*** that ***part*** of Asia / ***in*** many ***parts*** of the country / ***in*** all ***parts*** of the civilized world ‖ How much snow do you have ***in*** your ***part***? お国ではどの位雪が降りますか. ‖ ***in*** this ***part*** of the present treaty 現条約のこの部分に. ¶separate ***into parts*** いくつかに分割する. ¶a man ***of parts*** 有能の人. ¶That is due to carelessness ***on*** your ***part***. それは君の方の不注意からだ. 【類】We have done nothing wrong ***on*** our ***part***. / There is no neglect ***on*** our ***part***. ‖ the next (=second) cousin ***on*** the ***part*** of the father 父方のまたいとこ.

P[2] The control of procreation by the prevention of conception has become a ***part of*** the morality of civilized peoples. 避妊による出産の制限は文明国民の道徳の一部分となった. ‖ You are a *part of* myself. 貴女は私にとっては無くてはならない人だ. ‖ it is a *part of* the work of a university to ... ...するのは大学の仕事の一部分だ ‖ it is [a] *part of* her job to ... ...することも彼女の務めになっている ‖ make it a *part of* the union それを組合の中に併合する. 【類】 The gratuity called "hat-money," formerly paid to the captain for taking care of the cargo, is now *part* and parcel *of* the freight (運賃). ‖ *parts of* the body 身体の各部分. 【類】 *part of* the ceremonial of ... / a *part of* a fortification / *part of* the goods / It is a *part of* the Constitution. / *Part of* the crew is saved (lost, missing). / foreign words that are now *part of* the English language / I made *part of* the journey on foot. / You have omitted to reply to that *part of* my letter referring to ... ‖ *part of* the way 半途(途中). 【類】 May I follow (=accompany) you *part of* the way? ‖ the ordering of the *parts of* a sentence 〖文法〗文における品詞の配列. ¶ England has taken *part with* Japan. 英国は日本の肩を持った. ¶ a woman *without parts* 能なしの女.

(**2**) 役割.

V They ***acted*** their *parts* admirably. 彼らは見事に役割を果した. ‖ ***act*** the *part* of women 女形になる. 【類】 She ***acted*** her *part* with rare talent (非常にうまく). / ***act*** the *part* of a clown (道化師) ‖ ***act*** well one's *part* よくその本分を尽す. ¶ ***assign*** a *part* to each 銘々に役を割当てる. ¶ ***bear*** a *part* in the history of great events 歴史的大事件に参加する. 【類】 Conversation is like an orchestra, in which each one should ***bear*** a *part*.—Calton. ¶ ***cast*** *parts* to actors 俳優に役を振当てる. ¶ ***choose*** the *part* of attentive listener [弁じる方ではなく]聴いている方の役にまわる. ¶ ***do*** one's *part* wisely and well 自分の持役をりっぱに果す. 【類】 The illustrations (図解), too, generally speaking, ***do*** their *parts* well. / I will try to ***do*** my *part* in life to make the world a little better than we found it. / I'll ***do*** my *part*, if you do yours. / ***do*** one's *part* for world peace (a great cause). ¶ ***double*** the *parts* of ... ...の役を兼ねる. ¶ He ***filled*** the *part* with great success. 彼はりっぱにその役目を果した. ¶ He has ***found*** the *part* which nature has fitted him to play. 彼は自分の天職を見出した. ¶ He ***has*** a most difficult *part* to fill. 彼はなかなかむずかしい役割を引受けている. ‖ we have ***had*** our small *part* in ... われわれはいささか...に干与した. ¶ ***live*** one's *part* その役に成り切る. ¶ fail to ***perform*** one's *part* of a contract 契約における自分の責務を果さない. 【類】 ***perform*** one's *part* well. ¶ ***play*** one's *part* 役割を演じる ‖ ***play*** the *part* of ... ...の役をやる; ...の代りを勤める, ...の肩をもつ ‖ ***play*** a *part* in the evolution of civilization 文明の発達に干与する. 【類】 foreigners who have ***played*** a *part* in the country's history / events in which he ***played*** a *part* / the *part* he ***played*** in history / I ***played*** some little *part* in ... / ***play*** a great *part* in education / I am willing to ***play*** my *part* in joint action. / He ***played*** the *part* of Hamlet. / Donald Crish, who ***played*** [the *part* of] Battling Burrows in "Broken Blossom." / ***play*** the *part* of informer at the expense of one's fellow-clansmen / fully ***play*** one's *part* / ***play*** one's *part* worthily / the *part* woman now ***plays*** in our commercial life. ¶ ***re-act*** the *part* of ... ...の役を再演する. ¶ ***study*** one's *part* [俳優など]自分の役割を研究する. ¶ He actually ***took part*** in the South African Campaign. 彼は実際に南阿戦役に参加した. ‖ the states which ***took part*** at the conference 会議に参加した諸国 ‖ ***take part*** in a meeting 会に出席する. 【類】 Will she ***take part*** in the concert? / ***take part*** in an enterprise (undertaking) / The students ***took part*** in the demonstration at our departure. / ***take part*** in military service against one's own country ‖ He ***took*** my *part* in quarrel. 彼はけんかで僕の加勢をした. 【類】 ***take part*** in the proceedings of the congress (国会の議事). / Well done, Frank. You are a brave boy to ***take*** the *part* of a little fellow.

Q He himself took an ***active*** *part* in the movement. 彼自らその運動に参加した. 【類】 take an ***active*** *part* in the management (=business). ¶ the ***best*** *part* of his book is that which deals with ... 彼の著者の最も価値のある所は...に関する部分である. ¶ the youthful ***blooming*** *part* of our species 若い男女. ¶ in ***chief*** *part* 主として ‖ form a ***chief*** *part* of the plot その筋の主要部分をなしている. ¶ play a ***considerable*** *part* 重要な役を勤める. 【類】 The influence of suggestion plays a ***considerable*** *part* here. ¶ He played a ***conspicuous*** *part* in the history of New Japan. 彼は日本維新史において重要な役割を勤めた. ¶ play no ***decisive*** *part* 決定的(主要)な役割を演じない. ¶ take a ***distinguished*** *part* in ... ...にあずかって大いに力がある. ¶ Life is a great lottery, in which chance and opportunity play an ***enormous*** *part*. 人生は大仕掛けな福引のようなもので運や機会が重大な役を勤める. ¶ play an ***essential*** *part* in ... ...で重要な役割を演じる. ¶ play ***extra*** *parts* in pictures 映画でエキストラをやる. ¶ play ***featured*** *parts* (劇で)主役を勤める. ¶ In the plays of old Japan ***female*** *parts* are taken by men. 日本の旧劇では男が女の役をする. ¶ play a ***great*** *part* in politics 政界で大役を勤める. 【類】 Expressions play a ***great*** *part* in ordinary intercourse. ¶ take a ***humble*** *part* in the movement その運動で下っぱの仕事をする. ¶ There can be no doubt that the principle of economy plays the ***important*** *part* in the sound changes of language. 経済の原則が言語の音韻変化に重要な役目を果すということはいささかの疑もない. 【類】 Japan has played, and is destined to play, an ***important*** *part* in the Extreme Eastern question. / Diet (食餌) plays an ***important*** *part* in the treatment. ¶ Seismology undoubtedly plays a ***large*** *part* in the formation of the landscapes of Japan. 地震現象は日本の風景を形成する上においてたしかに重要な役割を持っている. ¶ he played (=took) a ***leading*** *part* in the movement for the reformation of ... 彼は...の改革運動で主役を勤めた. ¶ a building that plays ***many*** *parts* 色々な目的に使用される建物. ¶ play a ***noble*** *part* りっぱな役割を勤める. ¶ play ***odd*** *parts* 端(は)役を勤める. ¶ play the ***passive*** *part* in flagellation べんたつの受身になる(打たれる方になる). 【類】 play a more ***passive*** *part*. ¶ He played a very ***prominent*** *part* on the stage of life. 彼は人生の舞台で花形役を勤めた. ‖ Love in which the senses play too ***prominent*** a *part* can never be a true and lasting love. 余りに官能的な愛情は決して永続する真の愛情となり得ない. ¶ play one's ***right*** *part* in the world 社会に立って自分の本分を尽す. ¶ a ***secondary*** *part* 二次的の役目. ¶ Soon they gave her bits; then ***small*** *parts*. 間もなく彼女に端役が振当てられ, そして小役をつけるということになった. ‖ She played ***small*** *parts* in a travelling company. 彼女は旅行会社の下っぱだった. ‖ he played no ***small*** *part* in ... 彼は...に相当に力があった. 【類】 her first ***small*** *part* as a maid. ¶ act a ***studied*** *part* 考えた上の狂言をやる. ¶ play the ***thankless*** *part* of ... ...というありがたくない役割を勤める. ¶ act an ***undistinguished*** *part* in ... ...で栄(は)えない役をする. ¶ play an ***unfamiliar*** *part* 慣れないことをする. ¶ play a ***useful*** *part* in ... ...において有益な役を勤める(役に立つ). ¶ a ***weighty*** *part* 重い役. ¶ play a ***worthy*** (=an ***unworthy***) *part* りっぱな(見苦しい)振舞いをする.

Q[2] play a small ***chambermaid walk-on*** *part* 小女のただ立って歩くという端役を演じる. ¶ England played a ***pioneering*** *part* in the control of procreation. 英国は産児制限のさきがけをやった. ¶ a ***star*** *part* 主役. ¶ a ***star juvenile*** *part* スター級の子役.

P she was specially successful ***in*** the *part* of ... 彼女は...の役で特に評判がよかった. 【類】 Ennosuke ***in*** the *part* of (=as) Hamlet.

(**3**) *pl.* 〖機〗部分品, 部品.

V ***assemble*** *parts* into a complete unit 部品を組立てて完成品を作る. 【類】 ***assemble*** the *parts* of a machine.

Q[2] ***auto***[***mobile***] accessories and *parts* 自動車の付属品と部品. ¶ ***machine*** *parts* 機械の部品. ¶ ***spare*** *parts* of a machine 機械の予備部品. ¶ All the ***working*** *parts* are replaceable. すべて部品はとりかえがきく.

O a radio outfit and its *parts* ラジオセットとその部品.

part, *v.* 分配する; 別れる, 離れる; 手離す.

M *part* ***tearfully*** from ... ...と涙で別れる. ¶ The crowd *parted* ***right and left*** to make way for the party. 群衆は左右に分かれて一行を通した.

P *part* rice ***among*** the poor 貧民の間に米を分配する. ¶ We *parted* [***as***] friends. われわれは仲よく別れた. ¶ I *parted* ***from*** him at Tokyo Station. 私は東京駅で彼と別れた. 【類】 I *parted* ***from*** him reluctantly (いやいや). / It is hard to *part from* a good friend. / *part from* it with great regret / *part from* ... in displeasure (不快な気持で) ¶*part from* one's native shore 故国を出帆する ‖ *part from* the moorings (buoy) 繋留所(など)から離れる ‖ Bering Strait *parts* North America *from* Asia. ベーリング海峡は北米とアジアとを分かつ. ¶His hair was *parted* exactly *in* the middle. 彼の頭髪は丁度真中で分けてあった. ¶*part into* small fragments 小さく砕ける. ¶*part with* ... ...を手離す, ...と別れを惜しむ. 【類】I *parted with* him there yesterday. / I would not *part with* him for anything (どうしても). ‖ *part with* one's house (property) その家屋(など)を売払う. 【類】I would not *part with* it for the world (私はどんなことがあっても). / *part with* one's interest in ... ‖ Sell it? I'd *part with* my right arm first. 売る? それくらいなら右の腕を取られた方がいい位だ. ¶I'm afraid I must *part* company *with* you. 残念だが君と手を切らねばなるまい.

partake, *v.* あずかる, ...の性質を帯びる.

M He *partakes* ***equally*** of the poet and of the philosopher. 彼は詩人らしい所もあり哲学者らしい所もある. ¶*partake* ***greatly*** of the properties of both 両者の性質を多分に受けついでいる. ¶He ***largely*** *partakes* of the character of his father. 彼は父の性格を多分に受けている. ¶It *partakes* ***somewhat*** of a fairy tale. それはいく分おとぎ話めいた所がある.

P Let us *partake* ***of*** a meal before we part. お別れする前に御一緒に食事をしましょう. ‖ *partake* ***of*** the Lord's Supper (=Holy Sacrament)=take the Holy Communion 聖さんにあずかる ‖ *partake* ***of*** luncheon at the Imperial table 陪食を仰せ付けられる. 【類】*partake* ***of*** tea and cake ‖ *partake* ***of*** the hospitalities of ... ...の歓待を受ける. 【類】He was invited to *partake* ***of*** his friend's hospitality. ‖ *partake* ***of*** the nature of ... ...の性質を帯びる. 【類】He *partakes* ***of*** his father's character.

partaker, *n.* あずかる人.

P² a *partaker* ***in*** guilt 共犯者. ¶a *partaker* ***of*** his joys and sorrows 彼と苦楽を共にする者.

partial, *a.* 特に好きな.

P He is not *partial* ***to*** canary birds. 彼はカナリヤをあまり好かない. ‖ He is *partial* ***to*** sports. 彼は特にスポーツが好きだ.

partiality, *n.* 偏頗(へんぱ), えこひいき, 偏愛.

V He ***has*** a *partiality* for the Kano school. 彼は狩野派[の絵]が特に好きだ. 【類】He ***has*** a *partiality* for European diet. / ***have*** a *partiality* for moonlight walks (月下の散歩). ¶He ***shows*** *partiality* to his employees. 彼は使用人に不公平なことをする.

Q ***sectarian*** *partiality* 宗派特有のえこひいき. ¶his ***strong*** *partiality* for the Japanese 彼の大の日本びいき. ¶have an ***undue*** *partiality* for ... ...に対するえこひいき.

P He was swayed ***by*** *partiality*. 彼はへんぱ心に支配された. ¶***with*** a *partiality* for ... どっちかといえば...が好きで. ¶***without*** *partiality* (=prejudice)=with no partiality 公平に, へんぱなく.

P² I have no *partiality* ***for*** the race. 私には人種の好ききらいはない.

participant, *n.* 参加者.

Q ***active*** *participants* in the Olympic Games オリンピック大会参加競技者. ¶***useful*** *participants* 役に立つ参加者.

Q² ***treaty*** *participants* 条約参加国.

participate, *v.* あずかる, 加わる, 共にする.

M ***actively*** *participate* in ... ...に積極的に参加する.

P *participate* ***in*** a conference (business, discussion, war, game, work) 会議(など)にあずかる ‖ invite the world to *participate* ***in*** an international exposition 万国博覧会に参加するよう各国に勧誘する ‖ *participate* ***in*** a person's feelings 感情を共にする. 【類】*participate* ***in*** the profits. ¶He *participated* ***with*** his friend ***in*** his sufferings. 彼は友人と苦しみを共にした.

participation, *n.* 参加, 干与.

V The country has ***withdrawn*** her *participation* in the Exposition. その国は博覧会参加を取消した.

Q Japan's *participation* in the Fair is deplorably ***feeble***. その博覧会に対する日本の協力が微弱であることはなげかわしい次第である. ¶***students'*** *participation* in administration 学生の学校行政への参加.

Q² ***group*** *participation* 集団参加. ¶oppose ***Negro*** *participation* in the political life of the country 国の政治方面への黒人参加に反対する.

P² woman's ever-increasing *participation* ***in*** public life 日に日に増加する女子の公生活への参加 ‖ He shrunk from any direct *participation* ***in*** politics. 彼は政治に直接干与することを一切控えた. ‖ *participation* ***in*** management 経営参加.

participle, *n.* 〖文法〗分詞.

Q a ***present*** (***past***) *participle* 現在(過去)分詞. ¶an ***unrelated*** (=***dangling***) *participle* 〖文法〗懸垂独立分詞(文の主語と関係なく用いられる分詞).

particle, *n.* 微分子.

Q break into ***small*** *particles* 粉々に砕ける.

Q² ***rock*** *particles* 岩の砕片. ¶***soil*** *particles* こまかい土くれ.

P ***with*** a *particle* of dust in one's eye 目に小さいごみがはいって.

P² a *particle* ***of*** dust ごみの一片. 【類】a *particle* ***of*** food (極少量) ‖ She has not a *particle* ***of*** virtue. 彼女には貞操観念などみじんもない.

particular, *n.* 細目, てん末; *pl.* 詳細.

V Full *particulars* will be ***announced*** later. 詳細は追って発表されるだろう. ¶We cannot ***ascertain*** *particulars*. 詳細は確かめ兼ねる. ¶***detail*** the *particulars* 詳細事項を述べる. ¶***fill in*** *particulars* on a form 書式に細目を書入れる. ¶***fill up*** the *particulars* below 下に詳細を記入する. ¶***give*** *particulars* 詳細を述べる. 【類】***give*** full *particulars* of ... / I cannot ***give*** any *particulars*. ¶An awful accident has happened, but we ***have*** no *particulars* yet. 恐ろしいちん事があったが詳細はまだ分からない. ¶persons interested may ***obtain*** full (further) *particulars* from ... 関係者は...に申しでれば詳報が得られる. ¶***quote*** *particulars* by mail 詳細は手紙で申送る. ¶***secure*** the *particulars* of ... from ... ...から...の詳報を得る. ¶***send*** full *particulars* of ... by letter 書面で...を細かに申し送る. ¶***Telegraph*** (=***Wire***) full *particulars*. 委細打電せよ. ¶***write*** the *particulars* of the case 事件のてん末をくわしく書く.

Q ***additional*** (=***further***) *particulars* 続報. ¶***brief*** *particulars* 摘要. ¶***detailed*** *particulars* 詳細. ¶an ***essential*** *particular* 主要の項目. ¶The statement is correct in ***every*** *particular*. その陳述はあらゆる点において間違いがない. 【類】be superior in ***every*** *particular* to ... ¶for ***further*** *particulars* apply to ... 詳細は...に照会されたい. ¶It may not be strictly authentic in ***minor*** *particulars*, but is essentially true. 枝葉の細目にわたってどこまでも確実とはいわれないかも知れないが大体から言って間違いはない. ¶***minute*** *particulars* 委曲. ¶***one*** *particular* 一つの点.

P He talked about things in general, and his travels ***in*** *particular*. 彼は特にその旅行談をしたがその他色々のことを話した. ‖ I am going nowhere ***in*** *particular*. 私は別にどこへも行きはしません. 【類】I do not allude to any one ***in*** *particular*. ¶enter (=get *or* go) ***into*** *particulars* 詳細にわたる. 【類】You need not go ***into*** *particulars*. ¶a bill ***of*** *particulars* 明細書 ‖ an arrangement ***of*** *particulars* 細目協定. ¶descend ***to*** *particulars* 詳細にわたる ‖ ***with*** the minutest *particular* きわめて詳細に.

P² *particulars* ***about*** ... ...についての詳細. ¶Give me further *particulars* ***of*** the accident as soon as possible. 事件のてん末をできるだけ早くもっとくわしく話して下さい.

particular, *a.* 気むずかしい, きちょうめんな.

M You ought to be ***more*** *particular* as to whom you trust. もっとしっかり確かめてから人を信用するがよい. ¶You should not be ***too*** *particular*. 余り小やかましいことを言ってはいけない. 【類】He is ***too*** *particular* about (=as to) money matters.

P He is very *particular* ***about*** cleanliness. 彼はばかに潔癖だ. 【類】Father was very *particular* ***about*** manners (行儀). / It looks as if you were a stranger when you are so *particular* ***about*** forms. / He is very *particular* ***about*** food (appearance). ¶one cannot be too *particular* ***with*** ... ...はどんなに吟味してもし過ぎるということはない.

parting, *n.* 別離, けつ別; 分岐点.

V I couldn't ***stand*** *parting* from her. 私は彼女と別れるに忍びなかった.

Q a ***life-long*** *parting* 一生の別れ. ¶a ***sad*** *parting* 悲しい別れ.

P They shook hands with me ***at*** *parting*, and expressed regret. 彼らは別れに臨んで私と握手して哀惜の意を表した. ‖ Japan stood ***at*** the *parting* of the ways (=crossroads) 日本は岐路に立っていた. ¶the sorrow ***of*** *parting* 別離の悲

哀. ¶drink a glass of beer ***on parting*** 別れに臨んで一杯のビールを飲む.

partisan, partizan, *n.* 与党; 支持者.

Q ***blind*** (=***devoted***) *partisans* 盲目的な支持者. ¶***enthusiastic*** *partisans* of their government その政府に対する熱心な支持者たち. ¶betrayed by their ***own*** *partisans* 彼らの仲間に裏切られて. ¶***staunch*** *partisans* of ... ...のこりし屋.

P² a *partisan* ***of*** despotism 専制主義の主張者.

partition, *n.* 仕切.

Q ***sliding*** *partitions* ふすま.

Q² a ***pine board*** *partition* 杉の中戸.

P² a *partition* ***between*** two rooms 二室間の中仕切.

partition, *v.* 仕切る; 分割する.

M *partition* ***off*** [a] part of the room 室の一部分を仕切る.

P *partition* a country ***among*** themselves 一国を自分たちの間で分割する. ¶*partition* a room ***into*** three parts 一室を三つに仕切る. ¶*partition* a room ***with*** (=***by***) a screen スクリーンでへやを仕切る.

partner, *n.* 仲間; 組合員, [合資会社などの]役員; 配偶者; 「舞踏の相手.

V I must ***choose*** a life *partner* in the near future. 私は近い将来に終生の配偶者(妻または夫)を選ばねばならない. ¶I fear I ***make*** but a poor *partner*. (舞踏などで)どうも私にはお相手はむずかしいと思う. ¶***seek*** a life *partner* 終生の配偶者を求める. ¶He has ***sued*** his *partner*. 彼は自分の仲間を相手取って訴えた.

Q an ***active*** *partner* 業務担当社員. ¶a woman hired only for one's ***bed*** *partner* 二号. ¶her ***dancing*** *partner* 彼女のダンスの相手. ¶a ***desirable*** *partner* for marriage 好ましい結婚相手. ¶a ***general*** (***limited***) *partner* 無限(有限)責任社員. ¶a ***managing*** *partner* 専務社員. ¶a ***nominal*** *partner* 名目上の社員. ¶a ***salaried*** *partner* 有給社員. ¶a ***senior*** (***junior***) *partner* 代表(一般)社員. ¶a ***sleeping*** (=***dormant***) *partner* 匿名社員. ¶a ***special*** *partner* 《米》特別有限責任社員. ¶an ***undesirable*** *partner* in a contest コンクール(競技)における好ましからざる相手. ¶a ***working*** *partner* 労務出資社員.

Q² the two totalitarian ***axis*** *partners* 二つの全体主義枢軸国. ¶a ***business*** *partner* 事業の協力者(共同経営者). ¶a ***card*** *partner* トランプの相手. ¶the ***head*** *partner* in the publishing house 出版社の代表社員. ¶one's ***life*** *partner* その配偶者. ¶a ***side*** *partner* 同僚; 交代者(特に警官にいう).

P enter a company ***as*** a special *partner* 特別社員として入社する. ¶We have him ***for*** a *partner*. 彼はわが社の社員だ. ‖ Miss Sharp, I am quite proud of having you ***for*** a *partner*. シャープさん, あなたのお相手になるのは光栄です[舞踏などで].

P² a *partner* ***for*** life 終身社員 ‖ *partners* ***for*** parenthood =man and wife 夫婦. ¶Employers and employees are practically *partners* ***in*** business. 雇主と雇人は事実上商売の組合員も同然だ. ‖ He has become a *partner* ***in*** my business. 彼は私の商売の組合員となった. ‖ They are *partners* ***in*** trade. 彼らは組合で商売をしている. ¶his *partner* ***of*** the night 彼の相方(売春婦など). ¶a *partner* ***on*** limited liability 有限責任社員. ¶a *partner* ***with*** unlimited liability 無限責任社員.

partnership, *n.* 組合; 共有; 合資または合名組織.

V ***dissolve*** *partnership* 合名組織を解体する. 【類】The *partnership* which has existed between them has today been ***dissolved***. ¶We have ***formed*** a *partnership* with Mr. Smith under the title of ... Co. われわれは...会社の商号でスミス氏と合名会社を組織した. ¶***leave*** a *partnership* 協同経営から手を引く. ¶***wind up*** one's *partnership* in ... and retire one's share ...の組合関係を清算し株をもらって退社する.

Q a ***general*** *partnership* 合名会社. ¶a ***limited*** *partnership* 合資会社. ¶a ***particular*** *partnership* 《米》特殊組合. ¶a ***private*** *partnership* 私設の組合. ¶an ***unlimited*** *partnership* 合名会社.

P do business ***in*** *partnership* with ... ...と共同で商売する. ‖ organize a firm ***in*** *partnership* 合資で会社を作る ‖ own ... ***in*** *partnership* 共同で...を所有する. ¶enter ***into*** *partnership* with ... と合資組織(協同経営)にする. ¶admit a person ***into*** *partnership* 人を組合に入れる. ¶articles ***of*** *partnership* 合資(合名)会社定款. ¶He has entered into *partnership* ***with*** us. 彼はわれわれの組合に加入した.

party, *n.* 党派, 政党; 連中, 団体; 会合; 相手方; 関係人, 参加人, 仲間; 人, 者.

V ***arrange*** a *party* 会の準備をする. 【類】***arrange*** an excursion *party* for tomorrow. ¶***attend*** one's *party* その会に出る. ¶***change*** one's *party* 主義を変える. ¶***circularize*** all the *parties* concerned 関係者に回状を回す. ¶He ***conducted*** a *party* of educated persons round his cathedral. 彼は教育ある人々の団体を案内して彼の管理している本山を見学させた. ¶***crash*** a *party* 《口語》招待されない会に来る. ¶Here our tour ended and the *party* ***disbanded***. ここでわれわれの旅行は終り一行は解散した. ¶***dislike*** *parties* 人中に出るのをきらう. ¶***enter*** the *party* 入党する. ¶***form*** a *party* 団体をつくる ‖ ***form*** a *party* to go to China 中国行団体旅行を組織する. ¶***give*** a *party* 宴会を開く. ¶He ***had*** a *party* of friends at his home. 彼は自宅で友人たちの会合を催した. ¶***join*** a *party* 入党する. ¶***leave*** a *party* 脱党する. ¶***maintain*** a *party* in opposition to ... ...に対抗して党を維持する. ¶to ***make*** the *party* a success その会を盛会にさせるために. ¶***organize*** search *parties* 捜索隊を編成する ‖ ***organize*** a *party* for the theatre 観劇団体を組織する. ¶He ***rescued*** all *parties* from the dilemma by saying something which resulted in a hearty laugh. 彼は皆を心から笑わすようなことを言って一同を窮地から救った. ¶***take*** someone's *party* ある人に味方する ‖ ***take*** a large *party* on one's trip (picnic) 大勢を引連れて旅行(など)する.

V² The *party* did not ***break up*** until two in the morning. 宴会は朝の二時までずっと続いた. ¶The *party* ***ended up*** with a dance. 会は舞踏で終りを告げた. ¶The *party* ***went off*** well. 会は成功だった. ¶The *party* ***passed off*** well. 会は首尾よく済んだ. ¶When does the *party* ***take place***? 会はいつ催されるか.

Q by ***another*** *party* 別の人によって. ¶***both*** *parties* 双方. ¶the arrival of a ***bridal*** *party* at a fashionable church 上流社会の教会に花嫁一行の到着. ¶one's ***called*** *party* [電話の]相手方. ¶a ***certain*** *party* wants me to ... ある人が私に ...することを望んでいる. ¶the *party* ***concerned*** 関係者, 当事者. ¶the ***contending*** *parties* 双方の争議当事者. ¶the ***contracting*** *parties* in a marriage 結婚当事者(新郎新婦). ¶a ***defeated*** *party* [訴訟などで]敗訴した側. ¶the ***Democratic*** *Party* 民主党. ¶the ***disinterested*** *party* [利害関係のない]第三者. ¶the ***dominant*** *party* 第一党. ¶***duet*** *parties* of pleasure 恋を楽しむ男女の群れ. ¶We had a ***dull*** *party* yesterday. きのうの会はつまらなかった. ¶He was present at the ***farewell*** *party*. 彼はその送別会に出席した. ¶the ***feminine*** *party* to the contract 婚約の相手方たる婦人. ¶The shop assistants in most great emporiums take meals in ***five*** *parties*. 大抵の大きな商店では店員は五組に別れて食事をする. ¶a ***friendly*** *party* 与党(及び友好団体). ¶a ***gay*** *party* 陽気な連中. ¶a ***homely little*** *party* 質素な小集. ¶the ***injured*** *party* 被害者. ¶***interested*** *parties* 利害関係者. ¶***Large*** and ***small*** *parties* catered for. 大小御宴会御用命をたまわりたし[ホテルなど]. ¶I will be ***no*** *party* to such a quarrel. そんなけんかのお相手は真っ平だ. ¶an ***offended*** *party* 精神的被害者. ¶the ***opposite*** *party* 相手方. ¶trips in ***organized*** *parties* 団体旅行. ¶the ***other*** *party* 先方. ¶***participating*** *parties* 参加団体. ¶a ***political*** *party* 政党. ¶a ***reading*** *party* 読書会. ¶I must have a guarantee from a ***responsible*** *party*. 責任者からの保証をぜひ得たい. ¶a ***subpoenaed*** *party* 〖法〗召喚人. ¶a ***third*** *party* 第三者. ¶a ***visiting*** *party* 訪問団. ¶a ***winning*** *party* 〖法〗勝訴の当事者. ¶He is a ***worthy*** *party* in a conversation. あの男は話がおもしろい.

Q² an ***advance*** *party* 先発隊. ¶the ***anti-administration*** *party* 反対党(野党). ¶a blind date for a ***beach*** *party* 某月某日海岸の会. ¶give a ***birthday*** *party* 誕生日のパーティーを開く. ¶a ***boating*** *party* 舟遊びの集まり. ¶a ***breakfast*** *party* 朝さん会. ¶a ***card*** *party* トランプ(かるた)会. ¶a ***climbing*** *party* 登山者の一行. ¶He called off a ***cocktail*** *party* he had planned. 彼は企画していたカクテルパーティーを中止した. ¶a ***coming-out*** *party* 始めて社交界(初舞台)に出る若人の会. 【類】one's daughter's ***coming-out*** *party*. ¶***contending*** *parties* 競技参加者. ¶a ***costume*** *party* 仮装会. ¶give a ***dinner*** *party* in his honor 彼のために晩さん会を開く. 【類】prepare for a ***dinner*** *party*. ¶a ***donation*** *party* 寄進講(各自贈物を持参して牧師などの

家に集まる会). ¶a *drinking party* 宴会. ¶an *evening party* 夜会. ¶arrange an *excursion party* for next Sunday 次の日曜にピクニックをやる用意をする. ¶an *exploring party* 探検隊. ¶a *fishing party* つり仲間の集り. ¶a *garden party* 園遊会. ¶a luxurious *geisha party* ぜいたくなしゃみせんの入る宴会. ¶arrange a *good-bye party* for ... ...のため送別会を催す. ¶the *government* (*opposition*) *party* 与(野)党. ¶a *Halloween party* ハロイン(万聖節)の会. ¶when the *Hitler party* came into power ヒットラーの一党が政権を握ったとき. ¶a *holiday party* 休日行楽会. ¶a new *labor-farmer party* 新生労農党. ¶a *lawn-tennis party* 庭球大会. ¶the *Liberal Party* 自由党. ¶a *lunch party* 昼さん会. ¶the *majority party* in the House 議院の多数党. ¶a *picnic party* ピクニックの集い. ¶a *pleasure party* 慰安会. ¶a *plurality party* [議会で majority を制している]多数党. ¶a *preview party* [映画の]試写会. ¶a *reconnoitring party* 偵察隊. ¶a *rescue party* 救助隊. ¶a *pro forma charter party* 〘海運〙仮傭船契約. ¶*right-wing* (*left-wing*) *parties* 右(左)翼諸派. ¶a national *salvation party* 救国隊. ¶a *searching party* 捜索隊. ¶a *second-place party* 第二党. ¶a *send-off party* 送別会. ¶a *sewing party* お裁縫の集まり. ¶a "*shadow party*" 潜行派. ¶a *Socialist party* 社会党. ¶a *splinter party* [政党の]分離派. ¶a *storming party* 〘軍〙突撃隊. ¶have a *surprise party* 《米語》不意に押しかけてパーティーを開く. ¶a *survey party* 測量隊. ¶a *tea party* お茶の会. ¶a *tour party* 旅行会. ¶a *theatre party* 観劇会. ¶a *walking party* ハイキング会. ¶The *war party* is apparently getting stronger. 好戦政党は明かに強力になりつつある. ¶the *wartime* single *party* 戦時単一政党. ¶a *wedding party* 結婚祝賀会. ¶plan for a *week-end party* 週末パーティーのプランを立てる. ¶a *weekend beach party* 週末海水浴団体.

P I met him ***at*** a *party*. 私は会で彼に会った. ¶Please name a day ***for*** the *party*. どうぞ会の日をきめて下さい. ¶secede ***from*** the *party* 脱党する ‖ the *party* ***from*** whom it was purchased その品を買取った先(個人または団体). ¶when children are ***of*** the *party* 子供が一緒だと. ¶He is true ***to*** his *party*. 彼は自分の党派に忠実だ. ‖ I was asked ***to*** a *party*. 私は会に招かれた.

P² a literary *party* ***at*** Sir Joshua Reynolds' ジョシュア・レノルズ卿邸における文学者たちの集り. ¶the *party* ***in*** (***out of***) office 政府(在野)党 ‖ the *party* ***in*** power 政権を握っている党派 ‖ a *party* ***in*** the French Revolution フランス革命のときの一党派. ¶a *party* ***in*** a cause ある共同目的をもつ団体. ¶a *party* ***of*** students 学生の一行. ¶become a *party* ***to***... ...に加入(加盟)する ‖ one not a *party* ***to*** the course of action その行為に参加しない人 ‖ *parties* ***to*** a dispute 紛争当事者. 【類】He was a *party* ***to*** the affair. / both *parties* ***to*** the acts / He was accused of being *party* ***to*** the crime. / Sixty countries are now *parties* ***to*** the treaty. ‖ the companies, *parties* ***to*** the Railway Clearing System (鉄道切符清算制に加盟している).

pass, *n.* (**1**) 山路, 山道; ...越え.

V ***climb*** a *pass* 山路をよじ登る.

Q a ***mountain*** *pass* 山路. ¶go through a ***rugged*** *pass* でこぼこの山路を通って行く.

P a tea-house ***on*** a *pass* 峠の茶屋.

P a *pass* ***over*** the Andes between ... and ... ...間のアンデス越え.

「権利.

(**2**) 通行券, 無料乗車券; 〘野球〙[四球を得て]一塁に進む

V Only 33% of marks are necessary to ***give*** (=***get***) a *pass*. 三十三点とれば合格する. ‖ He ***got*** a *pass* (=walk) 〘野球〙四球を得て一塁に進んだ. 【類】He was ***given*** a *pass*. ¶***grant*** him a free *pass* on the railway 彼に鉄道無料乗車券を下付する. ¶He ***has*** a free *pass* over two of the great English railways. 彼は英国二大鉄道の無料乗車券を持っている. ¶free riders on railway trains ***holding*** complimentary *passes* as employees 従業員として優待乗車券を所持する鉄道無料乗用者.

Q have a ***free*** *pass* to a show ショーへの無料入場券を持っている ‖ a ***free*** *pass* for the stalls 〘劇〙平土間一等席の無料入場券. ¶***periodical*** *passes* over all the lines of the Imperial Government railways 国有鉄道全線にわたる定期乗車券.

Q² an ***admission*** *pass* 入場パス. ¶an ***Olympic Stadium*** *pass* オリンピック会場の無料パス. ¶a ***picket*** *pass* 監視通過証. ¶a ***season*** *pass* to a theatre 劇場の定期入場券.

P A railway worker is allowed to travel on Japanese railways ***on*** a [free] *pass*. 鉄道従業員はパスで日本国中の鉄道旅行を許されている.

P² a *pass* ***on*** (=***over***) a railway 鉄道無料乗車券.

(**3**) 羽目, 危期.

Q bring the matter to a ***pitiable*** *pass* 悲惨な事態を引起す. ¶The World War brought Germany to her ***present*** *pass*. 世界大戦がドイツを現在の(悲惨な)状態に至らしめた. ¶Things have come to a ***pretty*** (***strange, serious***) *pass*. 困った(妙な, 大変な)ことになった. ¶That things should have come to ***this*** *pass*! こういうことになろうとは.

pass, *v.* 通過する; 看過する; [時日を]過す, 暮らす; 通す, 通過させる; 検閲する; [判決など]下す; 渡す; 通る, 移る, 通行する; 及第する; 伝わる; 無事に済む.

M *pass* ... ***ahead*** [自動車などを]追越す. ¶*pass* ***away*** one's time 時間を過す ‖ The event is now *passing* ***away*** into history. その事件はもはや歴史的なものになりつつある. ‖ a generation now beginning to *pass* ***away*** 今や過ぎ去ろうとしている世代 ‖ Magazine reading helps *pass* ***away*** the time. 雑誌を読んでいると時の立つのを忘れる. 【類】*pass* ***away*** the time merrily and pleasantly in drinking, singing and dancing ‖ His illness will soon *pass* ***away***. 彼の病気はじきに直るだろう. ‖ He *passed* ***away*** at six o'clock this morning. 彼はけさ六時に息を引取った. ¶It ***commonly*** *passes* for genuine. それは普通本物で通用している. ¶This coin will *pass* ***current*** here. この貨幣はここでは通用する. ¶My advice *passed* ***entirely*** over his head. 私の忠告は彼には全然ぬかにくぎであった. ¶He *passed* ***first*** in the examination. 彼は一番で及第した. ¶The succession does not ***necessarily*** *pass* to a member of the same family. 相続権は必ずしも同家族の者に譲られるとは限らない. ¶*pass* ***peacefully away*** 大往生を遂げる. ¶The time *passed* ***pleasantly*** for me. 私は面白く暮した. ¶*pass* a few hours ***profitably*** 二三時間を有意義に過す. ¶Several days *passed* ***rapidly***. 数日がたちまちたった. ¶Let us *pass* ***round*** the hat for him. 彼のために寄付を集めようではないか. ¶I had never known time to *pass* so ***slowly***. 時間のたつのをあんなに待ち遠しく思ったことはそれまでになかった. ¶***successfully*** *pass* an examination 首尾よく試験に合格する. ¶The weather *passed* ***suddenly*** from cold to hot. 陽気が急に寒さから暑さに変った. ¶*pass* ***to and fro*** 往来する. ¶The resolution was ***unanimously*** *passed*. その決議案は満場一致で通過した. ¶This should not be *passed* ***unmentioned***. このことは不問に付すべきでない.

M² Hours *passed* ***by***. 数時間が過ぎ去った. 【類】The years quickly *passed* ***by***. / generations had *passed* ***by*** before ... ‖ I cannot *pass* ***by*** the remark in silence. その言葉は聞き捨てならん. 【類】They merely let the opportunity *pass* ***by*** untouched. / be too remarkable to be lightly *passed* ***by***. ¶The door-keeper *passed* us ***in***. 守衛はわれわれの入場を許してくれた. ¶*pass* ***in*** and ***out*** はいったり出たりする. ¶The day *passed* ***off*** calmly. その日は平穏に過ぎた. ‖ Everything *passed* ***off*** in perfect order. 万事順調に行った. 【類】The meeting *passed* ***off*** with success. / *pass* ***off*** without mischance (故障なく) / The storm *passed* ***off*** without doing much damage. / May Day *passed* ***off*** quietly. / Headache soon *passed* ***off***. ‖ *pass* ***off*** as genuine 本もので通っている ‖ She *passes* ***off*** as [a] white. 彼女は白人として通っている(混血の黒人など). 【類】He is *passing* ***off*** as a bachelor (独身者). / He *passed* himself ***off*** as a poet. ‖ *pass* himself ***off*** for a nobleman 貴族とふれこむ ‖ Public sales have *passed* ***off*** at firm prices. 公売は上値で行われた. ‖ The perspiration *passes* ***off*** through the skin. 汗は皮膚からにじみ出る. ‖ The attack *passed* ***off***. その急病が直った. ¶*pass* ***off*** a bad coin upon a person 人ににせ金をつかませる. ¶Please *pass* ***on***. [立止まらないで]どんどん通って行って下さい. 【類】I made my bow and *passed* ***on***. ‖ Read the paper and *pass* it ***on***. 新聞を読んだら順繰りに先へまわせ. ¶*pass* ***over*** three winters 三冬を越す ‖ *pass* ***over*** to the other side 向側へ渡る ‖ *pass* ***over*** one's fault その誤りを見逃す ‖ I can not *pass* it ***over*** in silence. それは聞き捨てにならない. ‖ A few items in the programme were *passed* ***over*** for lack of time. 時間が足りなかったのでプログラム中の項目を二三省いた. ‖ The rain has now *passed* ***over*** (=away). 雨はもう止んだ. 【類】The storm has *passed* ***over.*** ‖ A change *passed* ***over*** his face. 彼の顔色が変った. ‖ As for the rest of my life, I shall *pass* it ***over*** at Vienna. 後半生はウインで過そうと思う. ‖ *pass* ***over*** to (=join) the majority=die. ¶pass ***up*** a request (demand) 《米口》要求(など)を拒絶する. 【類】*pass* ***up*** (=let slip) the opportunity of ... / *pass* ***up*** (=decline) an invitation.

P *pass* a belt ***about*** the waist 腰のまわりに帯をしめる. ¶*pass* ***across*** a street 街路を横断する ‖ The blush *passed* ***across*** her face. 彼女は顔をぽっと赤くした. ¶*pass* ***along*** a street 街を行く(通る). ¶word is *passing* ***around*** that ... ...というううわさが飛んでいる. ¶He *passed* ***as*** A on his physical examination. 彼は体格検査で甲種合格になった. ‖ articles which would *pass* ***as*** relics from Pompeii ポムペイ廃虚の遺物として通用するような品物. ¶I intend to *pass* the winter ***at*** Paris. 私はパリでこの冬を越す積りだ. ¶Many letters *passed* ***between*** the lovers. その愛人間にはいくたびも手紙が取交わされた. ‖ Sharp words *passed* ***between*** them. その間に激しい言葉のやりとりがあった. 【類】Many whispers *passed* ***between*** them. / I do not know what has *passed* ***between*** the two. ¶*pass* ***beyond*** the bounds of ... ...の範囲を越える. ¶*pass* ***by*** the door ドアの前を通る ‖ His name is White, but he *passes* ***by*** the name of Black. 彼の名は White というのだが Black で通っている. ‖ He *passed* ***by*** her. 彼は彼女のそばを通って行った. ‖ plays *passed* ***by*** the censor 検閲に合格した演劇. 【類】films *passed* ***by*** the Board of Censors (検閲委員). ‖ The measure *passed* the Commons ***by*** 347 votes against 304. その案は三百四十七票対三百四票で議会を通過した. ‖ a scheme of arrangement *passed* ***by*** the shareholders 株主の承認した整理案. ¶as I was *passing* ***down*** the street 私が町を通って行ったとき. ¶It *passes* ***for*** slang. それは俗語とされている. ‖ Many a coward *passes* ***for*** a hero. 勇者で通っているおく病者がたくさんある. 【類】The world and life's too big to *pass* ***for*** a dream.—Browning. / They could have *passed* ***for*** sisters. / It might *pass* ***for*** silk. / He might *pass* ***for*** the chairman of a board of directors (理事長). / A coward often *passes* [off] ***for*** a hero. / It is strange that such a man should *pass* ***for*** a great scholar. ‖ He would *pass* ***for*** twelve on a railway. 彼は鉄道では十二歳で通るだろう. ¶*pass* ***from*** among us 世を去る, 死ぬ ‖ This recalls a fact which has nearly *passed* ***from*** my memory. これで私がほとんど忘れてしまった事実を思い起す. ‖ *pass* ***from*** one's mind 忘れてしまう ‖ *pass* ***from*** use with the spread of ... ...の普及と共に使われなくなる. ¶*pass* ***from*** a state of liquidity ***into*** a state of solidity 液体から固体に変る. ¶*pass* ***from*** thought ***to*** action 思想から行動に移る ‖ *pass* ***from*** triumph ***to*** triumph 勝利に勝利を重ねる ‖ *pass* ***from*** mouth ***to*** mouth 口から口へと伝わる. 【類】*pass* ***from*** high words ***to*** blows. ¶*pass* ***in*** the mind 心に浮ぶ ‖ The committee *passed* (=sent) ***in*** their report. 委員会はその報告書を提出した. ‖ *pass* an army ***in*** review 軍隊を検閲する ‖ We will *pass* ***in*** review these conditions. これらの条件を検討しよう. ‖ *pass* one's time ***in*** idleness なまけて時を過ごす. ¶*pass* ***into*** others' hands 人手に渡る. 【類】the responsibilities of editorship *passed* ***into*** the hands of ... / thence it *passed* ***into*** the possession of ... ‖ These measures have *passed* ***into*** law. これらの議案は法律となった. ‖ The expression *passed* ***into*** a proverb. その言葉はことわざになった. 【類】It has *passed* ***into*** an axiom (公理). ‖ One meaning *passed* ***into*** another. 甲の意味がいつか乙の意味に変った. ‖ Most of these names have by now *passed* ***into*** a deserved oblivion. これらの名は今日では大ていは忘れられているがそれも当然である. ‖ *pass* ***into*** coma 人事不省に陥る ‖ The poison has *passed* ***into*** his system. 毒が全身にまわった. ‖ *pass* ***into*** the shape of a river-salmon 川さけの形になる ‖ the people whose names have *passed* ***into*** our language その名前がわが国語の中に取入れられている人々(固有名詞が普通名詞化せられた場合に) ‖ The youth is now *passing* ***into*** adolescence. あの青年はもう年ごろになり掛けている. ‖ The disorder *passed* more or less ***into*** abeyance. 騒動は多少静まった. 【類】The science has *passed* ***into*** a new phase / His disease has *passed* ***into*** a chronic state (慢性). ‖ *pass* (=fall) ***into*** disuse=pass out of use 使用されなくなる ‖ This technical term has *passed* ***into*** general circulation (=use). この術語は一般に用いられるようになった. ‖ *pass* ***into*** the reserve 予備になる ‖ *pass* ***into*** the realm of history [時代など次第に経過して]歴史の領分にはいる. 【類】The days were *passing* ***into*** weeks, the weeks into months. ‖ *pass* a person ***into*** a theatre 人を劇場に入れる. ¶He has *passed* ***on*** me all the material which he had got together. 彼は集めたすべての材料を私に引渡した. ¶The company has *passed* ***out of*** existence. その会社はつぶれた. ‖ words that have *passed* ***out of*** current use 廃語 ‖ *pass* ***out of*** style very quickly 非常に早く型おくれとなる. 【類】soon *pass* ***out of*** our memory / *pass* ***out of*** print (絶版) / *pass* ***out of*** sight (hearing). ¶A dark cloud *passes* ***over*** the sky. 黒雲が空を通り過ぎる. 【類】The train *passes* ***over*** a bridge. ‖ There is no mass of technicality that will *pass* ***over*** the heads of readers. 読者の理解できないような沢山な専門的記事はない. ‖ *pass* ***over*** (=overlook) details 細かい点を見のがす ‖ *pass* one's eye ***over*** a letter 手紙に目を通す ‖ *pass* ***over*** a course 課程をふむ ‖ He will die before another night has *passed* ***over*** his head. 彼は夜明けを待たず死んで行くでしょう. ‖ a clerk ***over*** whose unlucky head juniors have *passed* 不幸にも後輩に追越された店員 ‖ *pass* the sweeper ***over*** a floor ほうきで床の上をはく ‖ All the people were *passed* ***over*** the river. 残らずの人が川を渡った. ¶*pass* ***through*** a town (street, strait, gate) 町(など)を通り抜ける. 【類】*pass* ***through*** lines formed by hundreds of children / She *passed* ***through*** the canal eastwards (westwards). ‖ *pass* ***through*** a college 大学の課程を経る. ‖ *pass* ***through*** life in a rather inert or dreamy state 酔生夢死の一生を送る ‖ after *passing* ***through*** various hands 大勢の手をくぐって ‖ after *passing* ***through*** the hands of one or two possessors, it was held by ... 一二所有者の手を経てそれは...の所有に帰した ‖ passengers *passing* ***through*** our hands on their way to ... ...へおもむく途中われわれの手に掛る旅客 ‖ He has *passed* ***through*** various adventures. 彼は色々な目にあった. 【類】*pass* ***through*** many changes / *pass* ***through*** many vicissitudes / *pass* ***through*** dangers or hardships (troubles) / The nation has *passed* ***through*** a period of great anxiety. / *pass* ***through*** an ordeal (試練). 【類】*pass* ***through*** a variety of fortunes (色々数奇な運命) ‖ This book has *passed* ***through*** many editions. 本書は幾版も重ねた. ‖ *pass* a rope ***through*** a hole なわを穴に通す ‖ *pass* it ***through*** a fine sieve それを目の細かいふるいにかける. 【類】see from a train the country ***through*** which one is *passing* ‖ He *passed* the measure ***through*** the committee. 彼はその案を委員会を通過させた. ¶*pass* ***to*** one's heirs [財産など]相続人に伝わる ‖ *pass* ***to*** other hands (=owners) 人手に渡る ‖ *pass* (=place) ***to*** the credit of our account 当方の貸方へ記帳する ‖ The measure *passed* ***to*** the second reading. 議案は第二読会に移った. ‖ *passing* now ***to*** ... 今度は...に話題を変えて ‖ Please *pass* the bottle ***to*** me. どうぞそのとっくりを私の方へおまわし下さい. ¶*pass* ***under*** an arch of a bridge 橋のアーチの下を通る ‖ *pass* ***under*** the name of ... ...の名で通る ‖ Formosa *passed* ***under*** Japanese rule. 台湾は日本の支配下に属した(属領だった). 【類】*pass* ***under*** the sway of some power. ¶The court dismissed the case without *passing* ***upon*** the merits. 裁判所は判決を下さずにその事件を却下した. ¶*pass* a night ***with*** a person 人と一夜を過ごす ‖ He has *passed* the examination ***with*** flying colors. 彼は堂々と試験に及第した. ‖ *pass* ***with*** the barest allusion ちょっぴり書いてあっさりと片付ける. ¶I never *pass* the spot ***without*** thinking of him. 私はここを通るときっと彼のことを思い出す. ‖ He will very likely have *passed* ***without*** notice. 彼はおそらく人目につかないで通過したであろう.

O *Pass* me the salt please. その食塩をとってください(食卓で). ¶Let's *pass* these pages. このページはとばそう.

passage, *n.* (**1**) 通行, 通過; 推移; 通行権; 航海, 渡航; 船賃; 通路; 打合, 仕合; 〖野球〗四球.

V The *passage* from Yokohama to Honolulu was ***accomplished*** in twelve days. 横浜からホノルルへの渡航は十二日でできた. ¶to ***afford*** *passage* through their territory to the forces 軍隊の領内通過を許可する. ¶***block*** [***up***] a *passage* 道路をふさぐ. ¶***book*** one's *passage* on a steamer 乗船切符を買う ‖ ***book*** *passages* through to the United

Kingdom 英本国行き通し切符を買う.【類】***book*** two *passages*. ¶collect enough money to ***buy*** a steerage *passage* to America 米国行の三等切符を買うだけの金を集める.【類】***buy*** *passage* for the steerage (三等). ¶***cancel*** one's *passage* on the China チヤイナ号での渡航を取消す.【類】He has been compelled to ***cancel*** his *passage* on the Shunyo-Maru, sailing on June 10. ¶***engage*** *passage* 乗船(乗車)切符を買う. ¶***expedite*** the *passage* of a bill 議案の通過を促進させる. ¶***fight*** a *passage* through the increasing throng on to ... ...を目指してだんだんふえる群衆の中をかき分けて進む. ¶***force*** the *passage* of a bill through the Diet 議案を無理やり議会を通過させる ‖ ***force*** the *passage* of a river against an enemy 敵前渡河をする.【類】***force*** a *passage* through a crowd. ¶***give*** a *passage* through the country 国内通行の権利を与える ‖ They ***gave*** me a free *passage*. 彼らは私に自由通行の権利を与えた. ‖ ***give*** *passage* to air 空気を取入れる. ¶We shall ***have*** a splendid *passage*. われわれはすばらしい航海ができるでしょう. ‖ The firm has ***had*** a rough *passage* during the war. 同商会は戦争中大打撃をこうむった. ¶The police ***keep*** a clear *passage* for the traffic. 警官が交通のために通路の障害の無いようにする. ¶***make*** *passage* 往航(または帰航)する.【類】We have ***made*** an excellent *passage*. / The distance from Dover to Ostend is 68 miles and the *passage* (thrice daily) is ***made*** in about 4 hours. ¶***obstruct*** the *passage* of ... ...の通行を妨げる. ¶He ***obtained*** a *passage* home. 彼は帰航の便乗ができた. ¶***occlude*** the *passage* of ... ...の通路を閉じる. ¶he had money enough left to ***pay*** a deck *passage* on a steamer to ... 彼には...行汽船の甲板乗船賃を払えるだけの金が残っていた. ¶***procure*** the *passage* of an act 法案を通過させる. ¶***secure*** *passage* 船室を取る ‖ ***secure*** the *passage* of a bill through the Diet 議案を議会に通過させる. ¶***take*** *passage* in the second cabin of a large steamer 大汽船の二等で旅行する.【類】he ***took*** *passage* on the Rotterdam for ... / I ***took*** *passage* on board (=in) a local small steamer, in preference to going by land. / ***take*** *passage* on a train / ***take*** one's *passage* to ... ¶***work*** one's *passage* as a cabin boy 船賃代りに船室ボーイになる ‖ ***work*** a *passage* through ... ...に穴を明ける.

v^2 The *passage* ***occupies*** three hours. その渡航は三時間かかる.

Q The temperature is sometimes taken in the bowels by an inch or so of the thermometer (oiled first) being passed into the ***back*** *passage*. 検温器に最初油を塗りこう門に一インチ位差込んで腸内体温を取ることがある. ¶a ***fair*** *passage* 順当な航海. ¶a ***free*** *passage* 無料旅行 ‖ give a batter ***free*** *passage* 〖野球〗打者に四球を与える. ¶The bill had a ***narrow*** *passage*. 議案はやっと通過した. ¶***nasal*** *passages* 鼻こう. ¶***No*** *passage* this way! この所通行無用. ¶after a ***protracted*** and ***stormy*** *passage* 長びいた難航の後. ¶a ***quick*** *passage* 早い航行. ¶The ship makes ***regular*** *passages*. その船は定期航海をする. ¶have a ***rough*** (=***stormy***) *passage* 航海中暴風雨に会う. ¶a ***slow*** *passage* のろい(時間のかかる)航海. ¶a ***smooth*** (=***quiet***) *passage* おだやかな航海. ¶the ***swift*** *passage* of time じん速な時の経過. ¶a ***transoceanic*** *passage* 大洋横断航海. ¶after ***two days'*** *passage* 二日間の航海の後. ¶tochkas connected by ***underground*** *passages* 地下道で連絡のとれているトーチカ.

Q^2 the ***day*** (***night***) *passage* 日中(夜間)の航行. ¶a ***first-class steamer*** *passage* 一等船室での航海. ¶an ***ocean*** *passage* 海洋航海.

P He arrived here ***after*** a safe *passage*. 彼は航海無事当地に到着した.【類】***after*** a *passage* of ... days. ¶***during*** (=on) the *passage* 渡航中. ¶a bird ***of*** *passage* 渡り鳥; 渡り者. ¶a liner ***on*** a *passage* from ... to ... ...から...へ航海中の定期船. ¶His affection for his wife increased ***with*** the *passage* of years (=time). 彼の妻に対する愛情は歳月とともに増した.

P^2 a *passage* ***across*** the Pacific 太平洋横断航海. ¶a *passage* ***in*** a building 屋内の通路. ¶take an easy *passage* ***into*** eternity 極楽往生を遂げる. ¶*passage* (=passing) ***of*** a bill《主に米》議案の通過 ‖ the *passage* ***of*** life to death 生から死への転換. ¶He worked his *passage* ***to*** England as a cook. 彼は英国へ行く船賃代りにコックとして働いた. ¶a *passage* ***under*** trees 木の下の通り. ¶a *passage* ***with*** swords 太刀打, 果し合い.

(**2**) 節, 句; できごと.

v ***delete*** the objectionable *passages* いかがわしい節を削除する. ¶Kindly ***explain*** this *passage*. どうぞこの所を説明して下さい. ¶***extract*** quotable *passages* from his work 引用に適した句を彼の作から抜く. ¶***quote*** apt *passages* from ... ...の中から適当な句を引用する.【類】***quote*** a *passage* from The Tempest.

v^2 In a letter received by me from ... the following remarkable and interesting *passages* ***occur***. ...から私が受取った手紙の中に次の注目すべき興味ある文句が載っている. ¶the *passage* ***runs*** thus: その句は次の通りだ.

Q exchange ***angry*** *passages* in a debate 議論を戦わす. ¶***beautiful*** and ***striking*** *passages* 流麗奇抜な句. ¶***choice*** *passages* より抜きの文句. ¶***difficult*** and ***subtle*** *passages* 難解で玄妙な句. ¶***expunge*** various *passages* 色々な個所を削除する. ¶***illustrative*** *passages* from literature 文献から抜粋した説明的文句. ¶an ***italicized*** *passage* 斜字体(イタリック)の個所. ¶***licentious*** *passages* みだらな文句. ¶***literary*** *passages* quoted in the Dictionary その辞書に引用してある文学的章句. ¶Excision of an ***obnoxious*** *passage* was required. 不当な個所は削除しなければならなかった. ¶interpretation of ***obscure*** *passages* in the book 同書の不明個所の説明. ¶an ***oft-quoted*** *passage* しばしば引用される文句. ¶***pathetic*** *passages* 悲そうな句. ¶***puzzling*** *passages* 難解な句. ¶the ***relevant*** *passage* [本など]それと関連した個所. ¶relate some ***striking*** *passages* of individual heart-history 変った霊的の経験を語る.

P^2 a *passage* ***from*** Shakespeare シェイクスピーアの句. ¶a *passage* ***in*** (=***of***) the Bible 聖書中の句 ‖ *passages* ***in*** the Life of Dr. Johnson ジョンソン博士伝の一節.

passenger, *n.* [汽車・汽船などの]旅客; 乗客; 旅人.

v *Passengers* can be ***booked*** through to Boston on the same terms as to New York. 乗客はニューヨーク行と同じ料金でボストン行の切符が買える. ‖ No *passengers* will be ***booked***. [汽船など]船客は乗せない. ‖ ***book*** *passengers* to any part of the world 旅客に世界各国への切符を売る. ¶***carry*** 1st and 3rd class *passengers* [汽船など]一等と三等の旅客を輸送する ‖ That steamer can ***carry*** 2,500 *passengers*. その汽船は乗客定員二千五百名だ. ‖ This motorcar ***carries*** four *passengers*. この自動車は四人乗だ. ¶***disembark*** her *passengers* on the other side 到着地で船客を降ろす. ¶***drop*** *passengers* at ... [汽船など]...で乗客を降ろす. ¶call at ... to ***embark*** *passengers* 船客を乗せるために...に寄港する.【類】All steamers ***embark*** *passengers* from quay at Yokohama. ¶***engage*** sufficient *passengers* and cargo for ... ...への船客と船荷を十分予約する. ¶***help*** *passengers* into a car 乗客の乗車に手を貸す. ¶Steamers ***land*** *passengers*. 汽船が乗客を上陸させる. ¶***let*** *passengers* ***off*** and ***on*** 船客を乗降させる. ¶***pick up*** *passengers* at ... [船・汽車・バスなど]...で乗客を収容して行く. ¶stop to ***take*** or ***leave*** *passengers* [汽車など]旅客乗降のために停車する. ¶stop to ***take in*** *passengers* [電車など]乗客を乗せるために停車する. ¶***take on*** *passengers* 乗客を乗せる. ¶***tranship*** *passengers* to ... 客を他船(車)に乗換えさせる.

v^2 *passengers* for ... ***alight*** at ... [汽車で]...行の旅客は...で下車する. ¶*passengers* for ... ***disembark*** at ... (汽船で)...行の船客は...で上陸する. ¶*Passengers* by this line ***transfer*** at Hongkong to Manila steamers. この航路による船客は香港でマニラ行の汽船に乗換える.

Q ***deckbound*** *passengers* 甲板乗客. ¶The through express train carries ***first-class*** *passengers* only. 直通急行列車は一等乗客だけを輸送する. ¶a ***seatless*** *passenger* 座席のない乗客. ¶the ***ship's*** *passengers* 船客. ¶a ***solitary*** *passenger* 話相手のない乗客. ¶***southward-bound*** (***westward-bound***) *passengers* 南行(西行)の乗客.

Q^2 an ***air*** *passenger* 空の旅行客. ¶a ***cabin*** *passenger* 特等船客. ¶a ***deck*** *passenger* 甲板客(移民・労働者など). ¶***fellow*** *passengers* [汽車などの]相客など. ¶a ***ferryboat*** *passenger* 渡し舟(連絡船)の船客. ¶***first-class*** (***second-class***) *passengers* 一(二)等乗客. ¶a ***foot*** *passenger*=a pedestrian 歩行者, 徒歩通行人. ¶"***long-distance***" *passengers* 長距離旅客. ¶a ***plane*** *passenger* 航空旅客. ¶a ***saloon*** *passenger*=《米》a parlorcar passenger [鉄道]特等乗客. ¶a ***steerage*** *passenger* 三等船客. ¶a ***train*** (=***railway*** *or* ***railroad***) *passenger* 列車乗客.

P he is ***among*** the *passengers* of ... 彼は...に乗船している.

P² *passengers* ***by*** the Peninsular & Oriental Steam Navigation Company from Hongkong to Brindisi ピー・オー汽船会社による香港よりブリンディージーへの船客. ¶ *Passengers* ***for*** and ***beyond*** New Jersey are requested to transfer at Trenton. ニュー・ジャージーまたはその先にお出での方はトレントンでお乗り換え下さい. ¶ a *passenger* ***in*** a railway carriage 汽車の乗客. 【類】 *passengers* ***in*** motor vehicles. ¶ a *passenger* ***on*** [board] the Empress of Japan エムプレス・オヴ・ジャパン号の船客. 【類】 a *passenger* ***on*** foot=foot passengers. ¶ *passengers* ***to*** the north 北行の乗客.

passer, *n.* 運ぶ人.

Q² Hundreds of ***coal*** *passers* were busy transferring thousands of tons of coal from barge to bunkers. 何百という石炭人夫は何千トンという石炭をはしけから石炭庫に忙しく運んでいた.

passer-by, *n.* 通行人.

Q There were seen very ***few*** *passers-by.* 人通りがいたって少なかった. ¶ ***hurried*** *passers-by.* 急ぎ足の通行人.

passing, *n.* 経過; [議案などの]通過.

V ***urge*** the *passing* during this session of the Bill その案を本会期中に通過させるように努力する.

Q the ***definite*** *passing* of the jinrikisha 人力車が明かに過去のものとなったこと.

P ***before*** *passing* ***to*** the consideration of ... ...に論及する前に. ¶ ***in*** *passing,* I may point out that ... ついでに...をあげてみたい. 【類】 I may note, ***in*** *passing,* that ...

P² the *passing* ***from*** the Old China ***to*** the New 旧中国から新中国への転換.

passion, *n.* 情; 熱情; 立腹; 色情, 情欲; 熱望.

V ***arouse*** the *passion* of a mob 暴民の激情を呼び起す. ¶ From his youth he ***cherished*** a *passion* for the sea. 青年時代から彼は海上生活の望みを抱いていた. ¶ ***confess*** one's *passion* 思想(熱情)をひ歴する. ¶ He ***contracted*** quite a *passion* for music. 彼は音楽が全く好きになった. ¶ ***control*** one's *passions* 情欲を制する. ¶ ***create*** in him the *passion* for research 彼に研究欲を起させる. 【類】 ***create*** in the minds of their pupils a real *passion* for learning (真の知識欲). ¶ it ***developed*** a *passion* to ... それが...しようとする熱情をさかんにした. ¶ ***excite*** (=***urge*** or ***stimulate***) the sexual *passions* 色情を起させる. ¶ He walked from one end of the room to the other to ***exhaust*** his *passion.* 彼は怒りを静めようとして室の端から端へ歩いた. ¶ He could not ***govern*** his *passion.* 彼は自分の怒りをおさえることができなかった. ¶ ***gratify*** one's *passion* 欲情を満足させる. ¶ She ***has*** a *passion* for music (studying, gambling). 彼女は音楽(など)にこっている. ‖ He ***has*** a *passion* for his pipe. 彼はタバコが大好きだ; 自分のパイプに非常な愛着を持っている(手離さない). ‖ She ***has*** a *passion* for society. 彼女は無性に人中へ出たがる. 【類】 He ***has*** a *passion* for "writing to the papers." ¶ ***hold*** the *passion* in check 激情をおさえる. ¶ ***indulge*** one's *passion* 情欲をほしいままにする. ¶ ***inflame*** one's *passions* 情欲をあおる ‖ ***inflame*** the *passion* of the ignorant (mob) 衆愚(など)を扇動する. ¶ ***irritate*** the *passions* 情熱を刺激する. ¶ ***kindle*** the *passions* 情火を燃やす. ¶ ***restrain*** our *passion* われわれの激情をおさえる. ¶ ***rouse*** (=***stir up***) one's low *passions* 劣情を起させる. ¶ ***satisfy*** one's brutal *passions* 獣欲を満足させる. ¶ ***set*** our base *passion* ***aflame*** われわれの劣情をたきつける. ¶ ***subdue*** one's *passion* 怒りを制する. ¶ ***subordinate*** *passions* to reason 感情をおさえて道理を立たせる. ¶ The *passions* of a mob can soon be ***worked up.*** 暴民はすぐ扇動にのる.

V² His *passions* ***overcame*** his reason. 感情が理性に勝った. ¶ *Passions* ***ran high.*** 感情が高まった.

Q He has an ***ardent*** (=burning) *passion* for fame. 名誉欲に燃えている. ¶ freedom from ***earthly*** *passion* 煩悩からの解放. ¶ inflame ***evil*** *passions* 劣情をあおり立てる. ¶ a ***foolish*** *passion* 痴情. ¶ his ***growing*** *passion* for ... 次第に募る...欲. ¶ the ***passionless modern*** *passion* for impartiality and original documents 不偏と根本史料に対する近代研究家の冷やかな熱情. ¶ He has ***philanthropic*** *passion.* 彼には博愛的情熱がある. ¶ one's ***predominant*** (=ruling) *passion* 主情. ¶ his ***present*** *passion* for wealth 彼の目下の富貴欲. ¶ It is one of the ***ruling*** *passions* of his life (=soul). それは彼の道楽の一つだ. ¶ ***sexual*** *passion* 性欲. ¶ the ***seven*** *passions* 七情. ¶ a ***strong*** *passion* for the other sex 異性に対する熱烈な愛慕. 【類】 He was seized with a ***strong*** *passion* for her. ¶ He had a ***temporary*** *passion* for a woman of thirty. 彼は三十女に一時うつつを抜かした. ¶ the ***tender*** *passion* 愛情. ¶ ***unbridled*** (=***unruly***) *passions* 始末に終えない情欲. ¶ excite ***unholy*** *passions* 劣情を起させる. ¶ He fell into a ***violent*** *passion.* 彼は激しく怒った. ¶ love another's child with the ***warmest*** *passion* of her soul 人の子を彼女の暖かい情熱でかわいがる.

Q² ***animal*** *passions* 獣欲, 劣情. ¶ the ***master*** (=ruling) *passion* of ... ...が一筋に思込んでいるもの ‖ Collecting of curios is a ***master*** *passion* with him. 骨とう収集は彼の道楽だ. ¶ a ***mutual love*** *passion* 相思相愛. ¶ ***queen*** *passion* =love 愛.

P He struck me ***in*** a *passion.* 彼はひどく怒って私を打った. 【類】 That child stamps her feet when she is ***in*** a *passion.* / ***In*** his *passion,* he killed a friend. ‖ ***in*** a *passion* at disappointment 失望のあまりやけになって ‖ put him ***in*** a *passion* 彼を怒らせる ‖ ***in*** a *passion* of grief 悲しさの余り. ¶ He flew (=got) ***into*** a *passion* at trifles. 彼は詰らないことにかんしゃくを起した. 【類】 work oneself up ***into*** a *passion* ‖ burst ***into*** a *passion* of crying わっと泣き出す. ¶ a violent burst ***of*** *passion* 激怒 ‖ in a fit ***of*** *passion.* かっと怒って. ¶ He is a slave ***to*** his *passions.* 彼は情欲のどれいだ(恋のやっこなど). ¶ He trembles ***with*** *passion.* 彼は怒りで震えている. ‖ a man ***with*** a *passion* for bric-a-brac 骨とう品の愛好者.

P² His *passion* ***for*** angling was greater than his discretions. 彼は釣魚にこって(私有地に侵入するなどの)無分別なことをやった. ‖ a *passion* ***for*** book-collecting 書籍収集欲 ‖ the *passion* ***for*** ease and comfort 安楽への欲望. 【類】 a *passion* ***for*** fame / a *passion* ***for*** novelty / his *passion* ***for*** original investigation ‖ a *passion* ***for*** the stage 俳優希望熱. ¶ Golf has become a *passion* ***with*** him. 彼はゴルフに凝りだした.

passivity, *n.* 受動.

Q stand by in ***complete*** *passivity* ふところ手で傍観する.

passkey, *n.* 《米》 合い鍵.

V ***use*** a *passkey* to open locks 合い鍵で錠をあける.

pass-mark, *n.* 及第点.

V ***raise*** the *pass-mark* from 60 to 70 及第点を六十点から七十点に引上げる.

passport, *n.* 旅行免状, 旅券, 通券.

V ***carry*** a *passport* 旅行免状を持っている. ¶ ***get*** one's *passport* 旅行免状を取る. ¶ ***grant*** a *passport* 旅行免状を下付する. ¶ ***issue*** *passports* to French citizens desirous of travelling abroad 海外旅行を希望するフランス人に旅行免状を発行する ‖ ***issue*** *passports* for women and children 女子及び小児のために旅行免状を発行する. ¶ ***procure*** (=***obtain***) a *passport* 旅行免状を取る. ¶ Tourists entering Canada do not ***require*** *passports.* 観光客がカナダにはいるには旅行免状はいらない. ¶ ***vise*** a *passport* 旅券に裏書する ‖ a *passport* ***vised*** by a consular officer 領事館員の証明した旅行免状. ¶ ***withhold*** *passports* 旅券下付を抑える. 【類】 the famous "Gentlemen's Agreement," providing that Japan should ***withhold*** *passports* from all laborers and prevent migration of that class of her subjects to the United States.

Q an ***expired*** *passport* 期限の切れた旅行免状.

Q² take out a ***Soviet*** *passport* ソ連への旅行免状をとる.

P apply to the authorities ***for*** *passport* 当局に旅券下付を出願する. ¶ provide oneself ***with*** a *passport* 旅行免状を持つ.

P² a *passport* ***for*** France フランス行の旅券. ¶ His virgin work was a *passport* ***into*** the world of letters. 氏の処女作は文壇への通行券であった. ¶ Flattery is the only *passport* ***to*** his favor. あの人に取入るにはおべっかを使うより外に道はない. 【類】 Politeness is a sure *passport* ***to*** any society. ‖ a *passport* ***to*** success 成功の手段. 【類】 a *passport* ***to*** lucrative employment in the profession or industry.

pass-word, *n.* 合言葉.

V ***demand*** a *pass-word* from every comer 来る者はだれにでも合言葉を言わせる.

past, *n.* 過去; 既往の歴史.

V ***bring*** the *past* to judgment 過去の行動に対して審判を下す(ドイツなどの). ¶ ***bury*** one's *past* 過去を葬る. ¶ ***forget*** the sad *past* 悲しい過去を忘れる. ¶ ***glorify*** the *past* 過去を賛美する. ¶ Punch has ***had*** a great *past.* ポンチ画報

は実に輝かしい歴史を持っている. ¶recall the past 昔をしのぶ. ¶his ability to recreate (=reconstruct) the past 彼の過去を再生する能力(歴史家としての手腕). ¶The past cannot be remedied. すんでしまったことはなんともしかたがない. ¶repair the past and start life again 過去を清算して生れかわる. ¶One cannot undo the past. 過去のことは取返しがつかない.

V^2 The past lives in the present. 過去は現在の中に生きている(存続している).

Q a nun who has had an adventurous past 多難の過去を持つ尼僧. ¶a dead past 消滅した過去. ¶in the dim past ぼうばくたる過去に. ¶in a dim and legendary past はっきりしない伝説的な昔に. ¶a lady with a dubious past いかがわしい経歴の婦人. ¶monuments of a glorious past 光栄ある過去の記念物. ¶from the hoary past (=antiquity) 悠遠の昔から. ¶inherited from an ignorant past 未開の過去から伝わった. ¶from the immemorial past =from time immemorial 太古から. ¶the irrevocable past and the uncertain future 取返しのつかない過去と不安な将来. ¶in the nearer past [時代が]さらにくだって. ¶in the recent past 最近の ‖ experiences of the recent past 余り古くない経験. ¶the remote past 往古. 【類】from a vastly remote past. ¶a man without a shadowy past 過去に暗い影を持たない人. ¶the traditions of a splendid past 輝かしい過去の伝統.

P during the immediate past つい近ごろまで. ¶a legend handed down from the long past 長い間伝わった伝説. ¶as it always has been in the past これまで通りに ‖ for three weeks in the past この三週間. ¶He is rather of the past than of the present. 彼は生きてはいるがもう過去の人である. ‖ actual facts of the past and the probabilities of the future 過去の事実と将来の見込. ¶a man with a long past 長い閲歴の人 ‖ a woman with a past いわくつきの女.

past, *a.* 過ぎ去った.

M The days are now irretrievably past. もはやその時代には帰れない. 【類】It recalls the memory of the day now irretrievably past. ¶in times long past ずーっと昔 ‖ It is long past midnight. もう大分真夜中を過ぎている.

paste, *n.* のり.

Q "grainy" paste 継粉(ままこ)の多いのり. ¶smooth paste 継粉のないのり. ¶thin (thick) paste 薄い(濃い)のり.

Q^2 polishing paste 練りみがき粉.

paste, *v.* はる.

M^2 paste up on a wall 壁にはり付ける ‖ paste up posters ポスターをはり付ける.

P paste a bulletin on the walls へいに告示をはる ‖ with the "certified" paper pasted on them 証紙を…にはり付けて.

pastel, *n.* パステル.

P^2 Pastels from Spain. 『書名』スペイン雑記.

pastime, *n.* 娯楽, 慰み, 遊戯.

V Hunting and fishing are pastimes ardently followed in the vicinity by devotees of those sports. 狩猟や魚釣りはその付近でその道の熱心家が盛んにやる娯楽だ.

Q In medieval days hawking was an aristocratic pastime. 中世ではたか狩は貴族の娯楽であった. ¶a childish pastime 子供っぽい慰み. ¶Literature should be more than an artificially elegant pastime. 文学は人工的に優雅な慰み以上のものであるべきだ. ¶an exciting pastime 興奮を誘う遊戯. ¶a fascinating pastime 魅力のある遊戯. ¶a favorite pastime of children 子供らの好きな遊戯. ¶manly pastimes 男らしい遊戯. ¶a national pastime 国民の娯楽. ¶Automobilism (=motoring) used to be a rich man's pastime. 自動車乗用は以前は金持の娯楽であった.

Q^2 an all-year pastime 年中できる遊戯. ¶a holiday pastime 休日の娯楽. ¶open-air (=outdoor) pastimes 戸外遊戯.

P the most alluring of pastimes 娯楽の中で最も魅惑的なもの.

P^2 Swimming has become in England a favorite pastime for women. 英国では水泳が女子の好む娯楽となった.

past-master, *n.* 名人.

P^2 He is a past-master at chess. 彼は将棋の名人だ.

pastry, *n.* パン菓子.

Q cheap but indigestible pastry 安いが消化の悪いパン菓子.

pasture, *n.* 牧場.

Q green pastures 青々した牧場. ¶permanent pastures 永久的の牧場. ¶a rich pasture 草の茂った牧場. ¶a wet, blossomy pasture 水気のある花の咲き乱れた牧場.

P Horses are grazing in the pasture. 馬が牧場で草を食っている.

pat, *n.* 軽打; 一塊.

V give it an affectionate little pat それをちょっと軽く打つ (pocket に物を入れた後などで).

P^2 a pat of butter 一かたまりのバター. ¶a pat on the head 頭を軽くたたくこと.

pat, *v.* 軽くたたく.

M He patted me gently on the back. [うまくやったなと]僕の背中を軽くたたいた.

V pat the dough into a flat cake こね粉をぺたぺた打って平たいパンにする. ¶pat a person on the shoulder (head) 人の肩(など)を軽くたたく ‖ He patted me on the back. [ほめて, 賛成して]背中をたたいた.

patch, *n.* 小地面, 畑.

V harrow a patch 草をまぐわでならす. ¶rake a patch 畑をくま手でかく.

Q golden patches of ripe grain 点在する黄金色に実った穀物の畑. ¶a grassy patch 一区の草地. ¶a great patch of floating pieces of ice 大きな浮氷のかたまり. ¶an open patch 囲いのない小地区. ¶The dog is of dark-brown color with a white patch on chest. その犬は茶かつ色で胸に一つ白い所がある.

Q^2 a cabbage patch キャベツ畑. ¶a farmer's melon patch 農家のメロン畑. ¶a shoulder patch 肩の記章(下士官兵の兵科を示すものなど). ¶a strawberry (tomato, turnip) patch いちご(など)畑.

P Flowers grow in patches. 草花がぽつぽつかたまって生えている.

P^2 a patch of beans 豆畑 ‖ patches of wood here and there あちこちに点在する森.

patch, *v.* 縫う, びほうする; てんてつする.

M patch bits of cloth together 小ぎれをつづり合わせる.

M^2 My old coat must be patched up. 私の古い上衣はつくろわなければならない. ‖ patch up a business 間に合わせ仕事をする ‖ patch up one's quarrels with … …のけんかをなんとか収める ‖ patch things up for the moment その場をとりつくろう. 【類】patch up the present factions for a brief time.

P rocks patched with moss こけのてんてつした岩.

patchwork, *n.* 寄せ物細工; つぎはぎ.

Q crazy patchwork [大小さまざまな布切れの]つづり合わせ.

V do patchwork つぎ当てをする.

P^2 a patchwork of quotations 引用句をつなぎ合わせた文 ‖ see a patchwork of fields, woods and buildings [上空から]色とりどりの畑, 森, 建物などのつぎ合わせを見る.

pate, *n.* 頭; 頭脳.

Q a bald pate はげ頭. ¶an empty pate 空な頭, 愚鈍. ¶a man with a shaven pate 坊主頭の人. ¶a shallow pate 浅薄な頭. ¶a shiny pate やかん頭.

patent, *n.* 特許, 専売特許; 特権, 特典.

V He got (=took out) his English patent. 彼は英国の特許を受けた. ¶give a patent 特許を与える. ¶A thousand patents a week are granted by the Patent Office at Washington. ワシントンの特許局では毎週一千の特許が下付される. ¶hold a patent 特許を持っている. ¶infringe the patent 特許権を侵害する. ¶issue a patent to … …に特許を下付する. ¶obtain (=secure) a patent for an invention 発明の特許を取る. ¶receive a patent of nobility for distinguished services 特殊の功労により授爵の恩典に浴する. ¶sell a patent 特許[権]を譲渡する. ¶a patent has been recently taken out in Australia for … 近ごろオーストラリアで…の特許を受けた. 【類】He took his patents out in all countries of Europe and America.

Q Patent pending. 特許出願中.

P an applicant for a patent 特許出願者. 【類】apply for a patent. ¶machines made under patent 特許によって製作された機械.

P^2 He has a patent of nobility in his face. 彼の顔には名門独特の特徴がある. ¶get a patent on an invention 発明品に特許を受ける.

patent, *a.* 明白な.

P^2 It is a fact patent to all the world. それは全世界に知れ渡った事実だ.

paternalism, *n.* 親心.

Q^2 government paternalism 政府の親心.

path, *n.* 小径; 通路; 人生の行路.

V bar the path 路をふさぐ. ¶beat a path 道を踏みならす. ¶the perils that beset his path 彼の進路に立ちふさがる危難. 【類】accidents (obstacles) which much beset our path in … / common pitfalls (おとし穴) that beset the path of the writer of Enghish. ¶***break*** a *path* 障害困難などを排して進む. ¶***clear*** a *path* for ... ...のために道の障害物を除く ‖ the pioneers who ***cleared*** the *path* of progress 進歩の路を開いた先駆者. ¶***cross*** one's *path* その前途を横切る ‖ They ***crossed*** each other's *path* one day at Shiba. 二人はある日芝で出あわした. ¶***follow*** the *path* (＝line) of least resistance 最少抵抗線をたどる(最も容易な方法をとる) ‖ ***follow*** the *path* opened up by ... ...の開いた道をたどる. 【類】 ***follow*** the *path* of virtue (正道). ¶***follow up*** a zigzag *path* がん木形の路をたどって行く. ¶***leave*** the *path* of righteousness (virtue) 正道を離れる. ¶***miss*** one's *path* 道を踏み違える. ¶The *path* to fortune is ***paved*** with good inventions. 好運への路はりっぱな発明品で舗装してある(発明の才があれば好運の道が開ける). ¶***scorn*** the beaten *paths* in advertising 広告の陳腐なやり方を笑う. ¶He aimed at ***smoothing*** the *path* for his successors by dictionary compiling. 彼は今後彼と同じ道を行く者(後輩)の助けになるように辞書編集を企てた. 【類】 a book designed to ***smooth*** the *path* of the beginner in Latin / ***smooth*** the *path* of international relations. ¶Their *path* was not always ***strewn*** with roses. 彼らの一生はいつも幸福であったという訳ではなかった. ¶young writers who are intent on ***striking out*** for themselves new *paths* in literature 文学において新天地を開拓しようと熱望している青年文士たち. 【類】 ***strike out*** a *path* of one's own. ¶***travel*** a rosy *path* to success 楽々と成功する. ¶***tread*** a *path* through the grass 草を踏み分けて道をつくる ‖ ***tread*** the *path* of knowledge 学問の道を歩む ‖ ***tread*** the primrose *path* of dalliance 逸楽を求め堕落への路を踏む.

V² The *path* now ***enters*** a narrow gorge in the mountains and almost immediately commences to rise steeply. 小径は今や山間の峡谷に入り間もなく急こう配の坂路になりかける. ¶The *path* ***runs*** by (＝along) the river. 道は川に沿うている. ¶A narrow *path* ***zigzagged*** up the steep hillside. 一筋の狭路が急な山腹を上ってジグザグに屈折していた.

Q go by ***another*** *path* 別の道を行く. ¶a ***beaten*** *path* (＝track) 踏みならした道 ‖ leave the ***beaten*** *path* (＝track) [旅行・研究など]少し変った方面に行く ‖ depart from ***beaten*** *paths* 常道からはずれる; 新機軸を出す. ¶The place is accessible by a ***concealed*** *path*. そこには間道を通って行ける. ¶***converging*** *paths* 一所に合する小径. ¶an ***easier*** *path* もっと楽な道. ¶an ***eightfold*** *path* 八つの道. ¶***narrow tortuous*** *paths* せまくて窮屈な曲り道. ¶strike out a ***new*** *path* for success 成功への新らしい道を発見する. ¶an ***old well-trodden*** *paths* 踏みならした古い道. ¶a ***paved*** *path* 舗装した小道. ¶draw one from sin to the ***right*** *path* 罪悪から正道へ人を引戻す. ¶take the ***river-side*** *path* 川沿の道をたどる. ¶***rough*** and ***rugged*** *paths* of life 困難な世路. ¶a ***rough*** and ***thorny*** *path* けわしいいばらの多い路. ¶a ***shady*** *path* [木かげなどの]薄暗い小道 ‖ the ***shady*** *paths* of life 人生の裏道. ¶the *path* ***soppy*** with the rain 雨でじめじめした道路. ¶a ***stony*** *path* 石ころ道. ¶the ***thorny*** *path* of life 人生の難路. ¶a ***wild*** and ***unfrequented*** *path* 人通りの少いひどい道. ¶a ***winding*** *path* 曲りくねった道. ¶take the ***wrong*** *path* 道を取違える. ¶a ***zigzag*** *path* ジグザグの小道.

Q² raised ***board*** *paths* [しょうぶ園などの]橋道. ¶a ***bridle*** *path* for equestrians 乗馬道. ¶a ***garden*** *path* 庭の小道. ¶a ***primrose*** *path* 桜草の多い道; 楽しい道 (a path of pleasure). ¶if Japan ever went on the ***war*** *path* again 万一日本が戦争街道を進むなら.

P ***along*** a *path* 道に沿うて. ¶err ***from*** the *path* of duty 本分にもとる. ¶walk ***in*** the *path* of righteousness 正道をふむ. ¶Prices are ***on*** the downward *path*. 物価は下り坂である. ¶come ***up*** the *path* 坂道を登って来る.

P² a *path* ***for*** passengers on foot 徒歩者の通る道. ¶a *path* ***from*** ... to ... ...から...に通じる道. ¶the *path* ***of*** development it has travelled in the past それが過去にたどった発達の道筋 ‖ the *path* ***of*** success (truth) 成功(など)の大道. 【類】 the *path* ***of*** duty (loyalty) / a *path* ***of*** pleasure / the *path* ***of*** an earth satellite (a comet, meteor) / a short and certain *path* ***to*** riches and honor.

pathos, *n.* 悲哀[感], ペーソス.

Q there is ***abundant*** *pathos* in the fact that ... ...ということは痛ましい限りである. ¶Her words were of almost ***heart-breaking*** *pathos*. 彼女の言葉は胸が張り裂けるばかりに悲そうなものであった.

P *pathos* ***in*** a play 劇の中のペーソス. ¶full ***of*** *pathos* 悲哀に満ちた(言葉など). ¶speak ***with*** *pathos* 哀感をこめて話す.

pathway, *n.* 径路, 道路.

V ***hew*** a *pathway* of one's own 独自の進路を切り開く. ¶The police were busy ***keeping*** a *pathway* for us. 警官たちはわれわれの通行のために交通整理に忙殺されていた.

patience, *n.* 忍耐, 辛抱; 勘弁, 勘忍.

V I will not long ***abuse*** your *patience*. 私は貴方に長く辛抱させるようなことはしない. ¶***cultivate*** *patience* 忍耐力を養う. ¶***exercise*** one's *patience* 辛抱する. ¶***exhaust*** one's *patience* 勘忍袋の緒を切る. ¶***Have*** *patience* for another day or two. もう一日二日辛抱してくれ給え. ‖ ***have*** no *patience* with ... ...には我慢ならない ‖ ***have*** the *patience* to ... 我慢強くも...する. ¶***implore*** *patience* 辛抱をこう. ¶***keep*** *patience* 辛抱する. ¶***lose*** one's *patience* かんしゃくを起す ‖ I have ***lost*** *patience* with you. お前には勘忍袋の緒が切れた. ¶it ***needs*** much *patience* to ... ...するには大いに忍耐を要する ‖ She ***needed*** all her *patience* not to cry out. 彼女は我慢してやっと泣かずにいた. ¶***practice*** *patience* 辛抱する. ¶it would ***require*** the utmost *patience* to ... ...するには最大の忍耐を要する. 【類】 It ***requires*** some *patience* to knit a sweater. ¶***show*** much *patience* 非常な我慢強さを見せる. ¶***take*** (＝have) *patience* 辛抱する. ¶***tax*** one's *patience* 人につらい辛抱をさせる. ¶I waited till I had ***tired*** my *patience* for his return. 私は彼の帰りを待ちあぐんだ. ¶I ***tired out*** my *patience*. それには私はもう我慢しきれなくなった. ¶Such a thing ***tries*** one's *patience* very severely. そうしたことは実にしゃくにさわるものだ. ¶***use*** *patience* 気長にやる. ¶My *patience* is quite ***worn out***. 私はどうしても我慢しきれない.

V² My *patience* ***has*** its limit (＝exhausted). もう勘弁ならん.

Q ***angelic*** *patience* 天使のような(非常な)忍耐. ¶with ***exemplary*** *patience* 感心するほど辛抱して. ¶He had a ***fisherman's*** *patience*. 彼はつり師のように辛抱強かった. ¶I have ***no*** *patience* with the man who ... ...するような人には我慢ができない. ¶wait in ***quiet*** *patience* for ... ...をじっと辛抱強く待つ. ¶***unfailing*** *patience* 続く忍耐. ¶***unwearied*** (＝***unyielding***) *patience* うまざる忍耐. ¶a man of ***wonderful*** *patience* 非常に辛抱強い人.

P It was too much for him and he was evidently ***beside*** his *patience*. それは彼にとってはあまりひど過ぎたしまた明かに腹を立てていた. ¶Such nonsense is ***beyond*** my *patience*. そんなばかげたことは私には我慢できない. 【類】 I have detained you ***beyond*** your *patience*, but one word and I shall have finished—and that is,... ¶learn ***in*** *patience* 根気よく習う ‖ be outdone ***in*** *patience* 根負けする. ¶I am ***out of*** *patience* with him. 私はあの男には勘忍袋の緒が切れた. ‖ put a person ***out of*** *patience* 人を怒らせる. ¶await ***with*** *patience* 気長に待つ. 【類】 He bears his misfortune ***with*** *patience*. / cannot hear ***with*** *patience* ‖ suffer ***with*** *patience* [苦しみなど]じっと堪えしのぶ.

P² the *patience* ***of*** Job ヨブのような非常な忍耐 ‖ the *patience* ***of*** hunger (toil) 飢餓(など)の我慢. ¶*patience* ***under*** afflictions 不幸に対する忍耐.

O Genius is *patience*. 〚諺〛 天才は忍耐である.

patient, *n.* 患者, 病人.

V ***attend*** a *patient* 看病する. ¶***commit*** or ***isolate*** an insane *patient* 精神病者を監禁しまたは隔離する. ¶***cure*** a *patient* of rheumatism 患者のリウマチスを直す. 【類】 try to ***cure*** a *patient* by psychic treatment alone (精神療法). ¶***dose*** a *patient* with bromides 患者に臭化物(睡眠剤)を服用させる. ¶***examine*** a *patient* 患者を診察する. ¶Our doctor ***has*** a great many *patients*. うちのかかりつけの医者は患者が沢山ある. ¶The hospital ***holds*** (＝can ***accommodate***) one hundred *patients*. あの病院は百人の患者を収容することができる. ¶***keep up*** a *patient* with plenty of nourishing food 滋養物を沢山やって病人の精分をつける. ¶***receive*** a *patient* into hospital 患者を入院させる. ¶go out to ***see*** a *patient* 往診に出かける. ¶***take*** a *patient* for treatment 病人の治療を引受ける. ¶***tend*** a *patient* 患者に付添う. ¶***treat*** a *patient* 患者を治療する.

V² The *patient* has ***improved*** slightly since the operation. 手術後患者は少し良くなった.

Q　a *chronic patient* 慢性患者. ¶a *consumptive patient* 肺病患者. ¶a *debilitated patient* 衰弱している病人. ¶He has a good many *free patients*. あの先生には施療患者が沢山ある. ¶It had been given to the physician by a *grateful patient*. それは謝恩の意味で患者から医師に贈ったものだ. ¶a *leprous patient* らい病患者. ¶a *paying patient* 有料患者. ¶*single patients* 独房(監禁の)患者(狂人など). ¶a *schizophrenic patient* 精神分裂症患者.

Q² a *cancer patient* がんの患者. ¶a *hospital patient* 病院の患者. ☞ hospital patients には inpatient (入院), outpatient (外来)がある. ¶a *leprosy patient* らい病患者.

P　operate *on* a *patient* 患者の手術をする. ¶sit up *with* a *patient* 病人に徹夜して付添う.

P² a *patient at* the Clermont Asylum クレルモン精神病院の患者. ¶*patients with* measles はしか患者.

patient, *a*. 辛抱強い; 勘忍強い.

M　*more patient* than Job ヨブより辛抱強い(非常に辛抱強い).

P　*patient of* hunger (cold, sufferings) 飢きん(など)に耐える. 【類】Sailors are *patient of* hardships. ¶He is *patient to* (=*toward*) others. 彼は他人に対して我慢強い. ¶He is *patient under* adversity (suffering, difficulties). 彼は不幸(など)に耐える. ¶He is *patient with* others. 彼は他人に対して我慢強い(人に対して寛容である).

patina, *n*. 青さび; 〖美術〗[古雅な]さび.

V　*gather patina* 青さびがつく.

patriot, *n*. 愛国者, 志士.

Q　an *ardent patriot* 熱烈な志士. ¶a *high-souled patriot* 気高い志士. ¶*noisy patriots* けんけんごうごうの志士. ¶*sincere patriot* 誠実な愛国者. ¶the *staunchest patriot* きわめて強固な愛国者. ¶a *zealous patriot* 熱誠な志士.

Q² a *feather-bed patriot* 苦労知らずの愛国者. ¶a *world patriot* 世界を愛する人.

patriotic, *a*. 愛国的.

M　people *fervidly patriotic* 熱烈に愛国的な人々. ¶*staunchly patriotic* 真に国を憂える. ¶be *truly patriotic* 真に愛国的である.

patriotism, *n*. 愛国心.

V　*arouse patriotism* 愛国心を呼び起す. ¶*extinguish patriotism* 愛国心を失わせる. ¶*foster patriotism* 愛国心を養成する. ¶We *glorify patriotism* because the patriot thinks first of his country and later of himself. われわれが愛国心を賛美するのは愛国の人はまずその国を思い然る後にその身を思うからである. ¶*inculcate patriotism* 愛国心を深く教え込む. ¶we cannot *show* greater *patriotism* or loyalty to our country than by ... われわれは...するのが何よりの愛国であり忠義である.

Q　*ardent patriotism* 熱烈な愛国心. ¶*emotional patriotism* 感情的愛国心. ¶*fanatic patriotism* 熱狂的な愛国心. ¶a *level-headed patriotism* 分別ある愛国心. ¶*local patriotism* 愛郷心. ¶*lofty patriotism* 気高い愛国心. ¶*misguided patriotism* 誤った愛国心. ¶excrescence of a *passionate patriotism* 熱烈な愛国心の結果. ¶it is *true patriotism* to ... ...するのが真の愛国心である. ¶the *vaunted patriotism* of the Japanese 日本人自慢の愛国心. ¶*vibrant patriotism* はつらつたる愛国心. ¶a *white-hot patriotism* 熱烈な愛国心.

P　an outburst *of patriotism* 愛国心の激発 ‖ a fire *of patriotism* 憂国の熱情. ¶*out of patriotism* 愛国の至情から. ¶Their hearts glow *with* genuine *patriotism*. 彼らの胸の中には真の愛国心が燃えている.

Q² "*carpet-bag*" *patriotism* 政治屋の愛国心. ¶*world patriotism* 世界愛.

patrol, *n*. 巡回, 巡視; [団]巡回する人(警官など).

V　*change* (=*shift*) the *patrol* at midnight 夜半に巡回を交替する.

Q² establish a Balkan *border patrol* バルカン国境巡視隊を組織する. ¶a *day* and *night patrol* 昼・夜間巡回. ¶a *foot patrol* 徒歩の巡回. ¶Police were on a *twenty-four-hour patrol*. 警官たちは二十四時間巡回をやっていた.

P　a policeman *on patrol* 巡回中の警官.

patrol, *v*. 巡視する.

P　The exhibition is *patrolled* at night *by* policemen and watchmen. 博覧会場は夜間は警官と夜警手が巡視する.

patrolman, *n*. 《米》警官, お巡りさん.

Q² a highway *patrolman* 交通巡査. ¶a *morals patrolman* 風俗取締りの警官. ¶a *radio patrolman* ラジオ巡回班員. ¶a *motor-cycle patrolman* オートバイで巡回中の警官.

P² a *patrolman in* uniform 制服の警官. ¶a *patrolman on* the beat 巡回中の警官. ☞ 英語は a constable on the beat.

patron, *n*. 保護者, 後援者, 顧客.

Q　a *munificent patron* of art おし気なく助成する芸術の保護者. ¶an *old-time patron* of the firm 同商会の古なじみ. ¶the artists of the Tokugawa period and their *princely patrons* 徳川時代の芸術家とその大名の保護者.

Q² a *cab patron* タクシーの乗客. ¶a *kinema patron* 映画ファン. ¶a *theatre patron*=a theatregoer [映画・演劇の]観客.

P　I hope that you will also become one *of* my *patrons*. あなたも私の後援者の一人となっていただきたい.

patronage, *n*. 保護, 愛顧; 得意, ひいき.

V　*get* good *patronage* 多くの得意先を作る. ¶That hotel *enjoys* a large *patronage*. あのホテルはひいき客が多い. ¶he *found* warm *patronage* among ... 彼は...から大いにひいきにされた. ¶*give* one's *patronage* to a shop 店をひいきにする. ¶*have patronage* of ... ...の引立を受ける. ¶*receive patronage* ひいきにされる. ¶*secure* the *patronage* of ... [商店などが]...にひいきにされる ‖ The physician has succeeded in *securing* a large *patronage*. その医者は大いにはやってきた. ¶humbly *seek* the *patronage* of ... うやうやしく...の引立をお願いする. ¶*solicit patronage* ひいきを懇願する. ¶*win* one's *patronage* その愛顧を受ける.

Q　*generous patronage* 多分の愛顧. ¶by the *kind patronage* of our customers お得意様のおかげで. ¶*misdirected* (=*unwise*) *patronage* ひいきの引き倒し.

P　We request a continuance *of* your *patronage*. 相変らずお引立のほどお願いします. ‖ Twenty per cent *of* his *patronage* comes from women. 彼のひいき筋の二割は婦人だ. ¶merchants *under patronage* お出入りの商人. 【類】It is *under* the *patronage* of the Imperial Household (宮内省御用). / flourish *under* the special *patronage* of ... ‖ *under* the *patronage* (=auspices) of ... ...主催の.

patronize, *v*. ひいきにする; 後援する.

M　The reading-room is always *well patronized*. 閲覧室はいつも大入りだ.

P　*patronized by* the Imperial Household 宮内省御用. ¶People do not *patronize* it *for* speed, but *for* economy. [船など]速力のためでなく経済だから人が乗る.

patter, *n*. ぱらぱら.

P² the *patter of* rain 雨のぱらぱら降る音.

patter, *v*. [雨などが]ぱらぱら降る, ぱたぱた音をたてる.

P　Rain came *pattering on* the ground. 雨がぱらぱらやってきた. ‖ A maid walked with short steps *pattering on* the floor. 女中が床をぱたぱた小走りに歩いた. 【類】hear steps *pattering on* the pavement.

pattern, *n*. 手本, 模範, 式; 型(㋕), 柄(㋒), 模様.

V　*cut* [*out*] a *pattern* for one's coat 上衣の型を裁(た)つ. ¶*follow* the *pattern* of their parents 彼らの両親を手本にする. ¶This carpet *has* a pretty *pattern*. このじゅうたんの模様は美しい. ¶*print* a *pattern* 型を押す. ¶*set* the *pattern* 範を垂れる. 【類】The *pattern* these men's lives have *set* will prove the inspiration that finally shall achieve the end for which they died. ¶Please *show* me some *patterns* of cloth. 布の見本を見せて下さい. ¶*take pattern* by him 彼を手本にする. 【類】I'd like to *take* a *pattern* of it.

Q　of *ancient pattern* 古式の. ¶an *archaic pattern* 旧式の型. ¶a *beautiful pattern* of raised flowers 美しい花の浮かし模様. ¶follow no *fixed patterns* 一定の型を追わない. ¶*flowered patterns* in gold thread 金糸の花模様. ¶a *flowery pattern* 花やかな模様. ¶an *irregular pattern* 不ぞろいの模様. ¶of the *latest pattern* 新型の. ¶a *living pattern* 生きた手本. ¶a machine of a *new pattern* 新式の機械 ‖ *newest patterns* of ... 最新式の... ¶break down the *old patterns* 古い型を破る. ¶an *ornamental pattern* in relief 浮彫り細工の飾模様. ¶a *plain pattern* あっさりした模様. ¶a silk fabric with a *raised pattern* 浮織り模様の絹布. ¶a chimney of a *square pattern* 四角形の煙突. ¶the *shepherd's plaid pattern* 弁慶じま. ¶a *stereotyped pattern* 紋切型. ¶*striped pattern* しま.

Q² a *behavior pattern* やり口. ¶In the old-time rural *family pattern*, parental authority centered in the father. 典型的な旧型の家庭では親権は父が中心であった. ¶a *hairdo pattern* 髪型. ¶a *hawthorne pattern* さんざし模様. ¶a *honeycomb pattern* 亀甲模様. ¶a *paper pattern*

(洋裁などの)紙型. ¶the *post-World War I pattern* (出産率異動の)第一次世界大戦戦後型. ¶after the ***Soviet*** *pattern* ソ連式をまねて.

P ***according to*** *pattern* 見本通りに. ¶an army trained ***after*** Western *pattern* 洋式に訓練された軍隊. ¶Girdles ***of*** that *pattern* are becoming fashionable now. あの模様の帯が近ごろはやってきた. ¶construct ***on*** the *pattern* of ... ...にならって組立てる ‖ Schools make persons all ***on*** one *pattern*. 学校は人を同じ型に入れてしまう. ¶adorn ***with*** a *pattern* 模様で飾る.

P^2 a *pattern* ***in*** several colors 様々の色の模様. ¶He is a *pattern* ***of*** propriety. 彼は礼儀のお手本だ. 【類】She is a *pattern* ***of*** female honor (淑徳). ‖ *patterns* ***of*** frost on the window 窓ガラスに凍りついてる霜の模様. ¶*patterns* ***on*** fabrics (china, wallpaper) 織物(など)の図柄. ¶She has become an example and a *pattern* ***to*** all nations. その国はすべての国民の模範となった.

pattern, *v.* 型を付ける; ならって作る.

M ***modernistically*** *patterned* [ゆかた地など]現代式の型を付けた.

P it is *patterned* ***after*** that of ... それは...にならって作ってある. ¶the statue was *patterned* ***from*** photographs of ... あの彫像は...の写真から模作したのだ. ¶*pattern* ***on*** (=after) a design 図柄をまねて作る.

paucity, *n.* きん少.

P ***owing to*** *paucity* of ... ...が少ないために.

P^2 the *paucity* ***of*** literature on the subject その題目に関する文献の欠乏.

pauper, *n.* 貧民, 細民.

Q ***old*** and ***bootless*** *paupers* くつもはかない老ぼれた貧民. ¶***propertyless*** *paupers* 無産の細民.

pauperism, *n.* 貧窮.

Q *Pauperism* was practically ***unknown*** in the country. その国は事実上貧乏知らずであった.

P He is exposed ***to*** *pauperism*. 彼は路頭に迷っている.

pause, *n.* 途切れ, 中止; ためらい.

V ***give*** (=***put***) a *pause* to some action ある行動を中止させる. ¶***make*** a *pause* 一息つく ‖ ***make*** a *pause* on the brink of a precipice 懸がいの絶端に立止まる.

Q a ***slight*** *pause* ちょっとした途切れ.

P ***in*** *pause* of the conversation 話の切れ目に ‖ He used such mannerisms as "er," "uh," and "and uh" to fill ***in*** a *pause*. 彼は話の合間合間に紋切形の「あー」とか「えー」とか「そしてあー」とかいう文句を使った. ¶pursue one's study ***without*** *pause* 絶えず研究を続ける. 【類】***without*** a single *pause*.

P^2 "Well," said he and there was a *pause* ***for*** some moments. 「そうだね」といってそこでちょっと口ごもった. ¶the *pause* (=lull) ***of*** the wind 風の小止み.

pause, *v.* 一時休む.

M *pause* ***awhile*** ちょっと休む.

P *pause* ***for*** breath 一息つく. 【類】*pause* ***for*** a reply.

pave, *v.* 舗装する.

P *pave* the way ***for*** an agreement (a contract, a peace, success) 協定(など)の準備をする, 道を開く. ¶*pave* a road ***with*** asphalt (brick, concrete, stone, wood) 道路をアスファルト(など)で舗装する.

pavement, *n.* 舗道; 《米》車道.

V ***lay*** asphalt *pavement* アスファルトの舗道を敷く. ¶***pound*** the *pavement* 舗道をこつこつと音を立てて行く. ¶***take up*** the *pavement* 舗道を(道路工事のため)掘上げる. ¶***tear up*** the *pavement* 舗道を引きはぐ(こわす).

Q fall on an ***icy*** *pavement* 凍った舗道ですべってころぶ. ¶***treeshaded*** *pavements* 木かげのある舗道. ¶the dark ***wooden*** pavement of a street 《米》木れんがの車道.

Q^2 ***brick*** (***tile, or concrete***) *pavement* れんが(など)の舗装(舗道). ¶***wood[-block]*** *pavement* 木れんが舗装.

P He was driven off ***into*** the *pavement*. 彼は車道に押し出された. ☞ "pavement" には「舗装・舗道」の他に《英》舗装した人道(歩道), 《米》車道の意がある. 《英》の車道は roadway, 《米》の人道は sidewalk という. ¶drop a watch ***on*** the *pavement* 舗道の上に時計を落す.

pavilion, *n.* 大天幕.

Q the Aoyama ***Funeral*** *Pavilion* 青山葬儀所.

paving, *n.* 舗装.

Q^2 ***street*** *paving* 街路の舗装. ¶***wooden-block*** *paving* 木れんが舗装.

paw, *n.* 手足.

V He will ***make*** a cat's *paw* of you. 彼は君を手先に使うだろう.

Q^2 a pussy with ***velvet*** *paws* すべすべした足裏の小ねこ.

paw, *v.* 前足で掘る(捕える).

O *paw* the ground 前足で土を掘る. ¶The cat *pawed* a mouse. ねこがねずみを捕えた.

pawn, *n.* 『将棋』歩(ふ).

V ***advance*** a *pawn* (将棋で)歩を進ませる. ¶***queen*** (***crown***) a *pawn* (将棋で)歩を成らしてクィーン(王)にする.

pawn, *n.* 質, 入質.

V ***redeem*** a *pawn* 質受けをする.

P My watch is ***in*** (=*at*) *pawn*. 時計は質にはいっている. ‖ He gave his ring ***in*** *pawn*. 彼は指環を質に入れた. 【類】put a watch ***in*** *pawn* ‖ take it ***in*** *pawn*. それを質に取る. ¶take it ***out of*** *pawn* その質受をする.

pawn, *v.* 入質する.

O *pawn* a watch to raise money 金を作るに時計を入質する.

pawning, *n.* 質入.

P an article ***for*** *pawning* 質草.

P^2 *pawning* ***without*** redeeming 質流し.

pay, *n.* 支払, 給料, 賃銭; 報酬.

V ***claim*** *pay* 支払を要求する. ¶***draw*** full *pay* 俸給全額の支給を受ける ‖ ***draw*** one's *pay* 給料をもらう ‖ ***draw*** *pay* equal to £500 a year 一年五百ポンドに相当する給料を受ける. ¶What *pay* does he ***get***? 彼の給料はいくらか. ¶***forfeit*** their *pay* 彼らの給料を取上げられる. ¶The tailor has called on you to ***get*** his *pay*. 仕立屋が賃銀をもらいに君を訪ねてきた. ‖ ***get*** the pay for ... ...の報酬をもらう, ...のむくいを受ける. ¶They ***grudge*** me my *pay*. 彼らは僕の給料を出し惜しんでいる. ¶***increase*** (=***raise***) one's *pay* 増給する. ¶***receive*** *pay* 給料を受取る. 【類】They expect to ***receive*** *pay*. ¶***refuse*** one's *pay* 報酬をことわる.

Q ***back*** *pay*=arrears of pay 《米》未払給料. 【類】He has not yet received his ***back pay***. ¶the ***basic*** *pays* of employees 職員基本給. ¶at ***beggarly*** *pay* なさけない報酬で. ¶one's ***daily*** *pay* 日給. ¶give ***double*** *pay* for double work 二倍の仕事に二倍の賃金を支払う. ¶***fixed*** (=***regular***) *pay* 固定給. ¶The officer is on ***full*** *pay*. その士官は本俸を受けている(現役だ). 【類】The naval officer was allowed to study abroad ***on*** full *pay*. / grant a leave of absence on captain's ***full*** *pay*. ¶He is ***good*** (***bad***) *pay*. 彼は払いがよい(悪い). ‖ He is a ***good*** *pay*. 彼は雇いがいがある. ‖ The *pay* is ***good***. 給料はよい. ¶an officer on ***half*** *pay* 休職士官. ¶***high*** (***low***) *pay* 高(薄)給. ¶***incentive*** *pay* 奨励金. ¶No cure ***no*** *pay*. [比ゆ的]支払は全快してから. ¶He is a ***poor*** (=***bad***) *pay*. 彼は給金ほどの仕事ができない(雇いがいのない人物だ). ¶***sundry*** *pays* 雑給与. ¶***twenty*** *pays* 二十回支払い. ¶***weekly*** *pay* 週給.

Q^2 a monthly ***base*** *pay* 基本月給. ¶***call*** *pay* 呼出し賃金. ¶***efficiency*** *pay* 能率給. ¶***overtime*** *pay* 時間外勤務手当. ¶***portal to portal*** *pay* 拘束時間払賃金. ¶Most laid-offs were given ***severance*** *pay*. [臨時]かく首者の多くは退職金をもらった. ¶***starting*** *pay* 初任給. ¶***take-home*** *pay* 手取りの給料(賃金). ¶a general rise in ***teacher*** *pay* 教師の給与の一般的向上. ¶give ***terminal leave*** *pay* to enlisted men 兵(下士官)に期末休暇手当てを出す. ¶***travel*** *pay* 旅費. ¶***waiting orders*** *pay* 待命給与.

P ***at*** full *pay* 本俸で. ¶***for*** liberal *pay* 十分の代価を得れば ‖ ***for*** *pay* 報酬をもらって. ¶He was reduced ***in*** *pay* from 250 yen to 200 yen. 彼は二百五十円から二百円に減俸された. ‖ He has six men ***in*** his *pay*. 彼は給料を払って六人雇っている. ‖ He was ***in*** the *pay* (=employment) of the company for many years. 彼は多年その会社に雇われていた. ‖ a samurai ***in*** the *pay* of the Prince of Mito 水戸公に抱えられている武士. ¶He is ***under*** the *pay* of the British Government. 彼は英国政府から給料を受けている. ¶vacation ***with*** *pay* 有給休暇. 【類】A professor is granted one year off ***with*** half *pay* after each ten years of service for purposes of study or travel. ¶work ***without*** *pay* 無給で働く. 【類】a party executive (党の総務) ***without*** *pay*.

P^2 *pay* ***for*** week-end work 週末作業手当.

pay, *v.* 報酬する; 支払う, 償却する.

M He is *paid* ***advantageously***. 彼は割のよい報酬を受けている. ¶He was ***amply*** *paid*. 彼は十分報酬をもらった. ¶*pay* ***away*** money 金を支払う. ¶*pay* ***back*** a debt 負債を償却する ‖ I will *pay* you ***back*** the money you lent me. 拝借の金をお返しします. ‖ He *paid* me ***back*** in kind. 彼は

私の貸金を品物で支払った. 【類】*pay* ***back*** money borrowed / *pay* ***back*** the cost of … ‖ *pay* her ***back*** her kiss 彼女のキッスのお返しをする ‖ *pay* ***back*** an injury by … …から受けた傷の仕返しをする. ¶*pay* ***dear*** for one's insolence 無礼なことをして非常な損をする. ¶You shall *pay* ***dearly*** for your idleness. なまけるとひどい目にあわしてやるぞ. 【類】*pay* ***dearly*** for what one has done ‖ You shall ***dearly*** *pay* for it. あとのたたりが恐ろしいぞ. ¶*pay* ***extra*** for … …に対して余分に手当を出す. ¶*pay* ***better*** than … …の方が利益がある. ¶They are now ***bitterly*** *paying* for their lack of vision. 先見の明がなかったのでひどい目にあっている. ¶*pay* ***cash*** 現金で支払う. ¶They ***fabulously*** *pay* professionals in baseball. 職業野球選手はすばらしく高給を取る. ¶The mine is *paying* ***fairly***. その鉱山は十分引合っている. ¶*pay* ***handsomely*** 割よく支払う. ¶He *paid* ***heavily*** for it. 彼はそれに対して高い代価を払った. ¶***highly*** *paid* employees 高給をもらっている使用人. ¶***How much*** did you *pay* for each of those dishes? そのさらは一枚いくらで買ったか. ¶*pay* ***inadequately*** 不十分な支払をする. ¶*pay* one's staff ***liberally*** その部員を優遇する. ¶*pay* as ***much*** as … …はずむ, 奮発する. ¶I'll *pay* you ***out*** some day. いつかかたきをとってやるぞ. ‖ cash received or *paid* ***out*** 受領したまたは支払った現金. ¶***poorly*** *paid* officials 薄給の官吏. ¶he *paid* me ***profusely*** for … 彼は…に対して私に手厚い支払をした. ¶*pay* ***promptly*** 即金で支払う. ¶*pay* [in] ***ready cash*** 現金で支払う. ¶Honesty ***surely*** *pays*. 正直にすれば必ずその報いがある. ¶I *paid* ***too much*** by two dollars. 私は二ドルだけ買かぶった. 【類】*pay* ***too much*** for a cheap article. ¶You shall have to *pay* ***up***. 君は残らず払わなくてはいけない. ¶He *pays* ***well***. 彼は払いがよい. ‖ It would *pay* ***well*** to start a hotel there. そこにホテルを開くともうかるだろう. 【類】This business *pays* ***well***. ‖ He is not *paying* ***well*** for our labor. われわれの仕事に対する彼の給与はあまりよくない.

M[2] The money is to be *paid* ***down***. 金は即金払いのこと. ‖ *pay* ***down*** … as compensation to the relative of … …の縁者へ弁償として…を即金で払う. 【類】*pay* ***down*** part of the price and the rest, later / They made him *pay* ***down*** his debt to the last farthing (借金の全額). ¶*pay* ***in*** for the subscription 寄付を払込む ‖ ¶*pay* ***in*** to his accounts in banks 銀行の彼の勘定口座に払込む. ¶*pay* ***off*** the crew 乗組員を給料を支払って解雇する. 【類】They *paid* me ***off*** without previous notice (前ぶれもなく). / *pay* ***off*** the striking employes (スト中の雇人) / *pay* ***off*** a portion of the debt I owe to … ‖ *pay* ***off*** a transport 運送船に支払をして契約を解除する. 【類】*pay* ***off*** a ship ‖ *pay* [***off***] old scores 旧債を償う, 旧恨を償う ‖ Honey *pays* ***off***. 養蜂は引合う. ¶*pay* it ***over*** to … …にそれを支払う ‖ be *paid* ***over*** if work is satisfactory 仕事がよくできていれば金が仕払われる ‖ *pay* ***over*** on cheque 小切手で支払う. ¶*pay* ***up*** one's stocks (debts) 株の全額払込みをすます(借金を皆済する).

P *pay* ***at*** the turnstile in the doorway 出入口の回転木戸で払う ‖ *pay* ***at*** sight 一覧払いをする ‖ *pay* ***at*** the rate of a yen a *ri* 一里一円の割で払う. ¶freight to be *paid* ***before*** departure 発送前に支払うべき運賃. ¶***Jinrikishamen*** are generally *paid* ***by*** the distance and not ***by*** the time. 人力車夫には普通時間でなく距離で車賃を払う. ‖ interest *paid* ***by*** a government on public loans 政府が公債に支払う利子 ‖ I am *paying* my debts ***by*** (=in) instalments. 私は負債をなしくずしにしている. ‖ be *paid* ***by*** the line 一行いくらで支払われる ‖ He is *paid* ***by*** the year. 彼は年俸だ. ¶I *pay* ***for*** my rooms by the day. へや代を日割で払う. ‖ With beautiful generosity, he offered to *pay* ***for*** my education. 美しい志から彼は私の教育費を出してやろうと言いだした. ‖ *pay* ***for*** one's account その勘定の支払をする ‖ The work has been *paid* ***for***. その仕事は支払ができている. ‖ *pay*, ***for*** A, £ … on insurance policies for B, deceased 死亡者 B 氏に対する保険金…ポンドを A 氏に支払う. 【類】Will you *pay* the jinrikisha-man ***for*** me? (立替え) / In China everything is *paid* ***for*** in silver (銀貨で). / He is *paid* ***for*** his work at a high rate. / *pay* ***for*** the discharge (解雇手当) / I wish to *pay* you ***for*** your trouble. / He *paid* me five dollars per hour (時間給で) ***for*** my service. / I *paid* ***for*** his education. / What (=How much) did you *pay* ***for*** it? ‖ He *paid* ***for*** his negligence by losing his situation. 彼はなまけた罰に地位を失った. ‖ *pay* ***for*** it with one's head (=life) 生命をもってそれをあがなう ‖ One dollar *pays* ***for*** a year's subscription. 一ドルで一年間購読ができる. ‖ They had to *pay* ***for*** it with their heads 彼らは斬罪に処すべきものであった. ¶*pay* ***in*** advance 前払いする, 立替える ‖ *pay* ***in*** cash 現金で払う ‖ They *paid* their taxes ***in*** kind. 彼らは現物で納税した. ‖ *pay* ***in*** full=pay up 皆済する; 〘株式〙全額払込みをする ‖ He *paid* me ***in*** kind for my service. 彼は私の仕事に対し品物で払った. 【類】*pay* ***in*** money instead of ***in*** kind (品物で) ‖ *pay* ***in*** monthly instalments 月賦で払う ‖ He *paid* part of the sum ***in*** bills and the rest in silver 彼は一部は紙幣で残額は銀貨で支払った. ¶*pay* ***into*** account 勘定に払込む ‖ *pay* money ***into*** a bank 銀行に金を払込む ‖ *pay* taxes ***into*** the treasury 国庫に租税を払込む. ¶*pay* custom-duties ***on*** imported articles 輸入品の関税を払う ‖ to be *paid* ***on*** delivery 現物引換払の ‖ This will be *paid* ***on*** demand. これは要求払です ‖ *pay* ***on*** your own account 貴下の勘定で支払って下さい ‖ The cotton mill *paid* 20 per cent ***on*** the ordinary shares. その紡績工場は通常株に対して二割の配当をした. ¶*pay* ***out of*** one's own pocket 自腹を切る ‖ be *paid* ***out of*** the public money その公金の中から支払われる. ¶*pay* one's way ***through*** college 苦学して大学を卒業する. ¶*pay* interest ***to*** a creditor 債権者に利子を払う ‖ My subscription to the magazine is *paid* ***to*** January lst, 1938. その雑誌購読費の払込は一九三八年一月一日まで済んでいる. ‖ *pay* ***to*** order (bearer) 指図人(持参人)に払う ‖ *pay* ***to*** one's bankers その銀行名当てで払う ‖ *pay* attention ***to*** … …に注目する ‖ *pay* court ***to*** a woman 女に言い寄る ‖ *pay* due respect ***to*** … …に然るべき尊敬を払う ‖ *pay* a visit ***to*** … …を訪問する. ¶Those who wish to attend the meeting are requested to *pay* ¥3 ***as*** expenses for the evening. 晩の会に御出席御希望の方は会費三円を御支払下さい. ¶*pay* a debt ***with*** interest 利子を付けて返金する.

O It *pays* to be careful. 用心深いのは得だ. 【類】It *pays* to buy good things. / This business doesn't *pay*. ¶The stock *pays* four percent. その株は四分の配当だ.

payable, *a.* 支払うべき.

P The bill is *payable* a week ***after*** sight. この手形は一覧後一週間払になっている. ¶*payable* ***at*** sight [手形の]一覧払. ¶a money-order made *payable* ***at*** the … post office …郵便局払の為替 ‖ a cheque *payable* ***at*** a local bank 地方銀行払の小切手 ‖ a bill *payable* ***at*** sight 一覧払手形. ¶The price is *payable* ***in*** monthly instalments. 代金は月賦払. ‖ *payable* ***in*** cash (dollar, gold, note) 現金(など)払 ‖ *payable* ***in*** London ロンドン払 ‖ *payable* ***in*** sterling ポンド貨支払いの. ¶The note is *payable* ***on*** demand. 手形は要求払になっている. 【類】It is *payable* ***on*** application. ‖ *payable* ***on*** delivery 現物引換払. ¶make it *payable* ***to*** bearer (order) [小切手などを]持参(指図)人払にする. 【類】make the check *payable* ***to*** Mr. … ¶*payable* ***with*** the Hongkong and Shanghai Banking Corporation ホンコン上海銀行払い.

pay-cut, *n.* 減給.

Q *Pay-cut* will be ***inevitable*** in near future. 近い中に減給は必ずあるだろう. ¶according to the ***recent*** *pay-cut* この間の減給制によると.

payday, *n.* 《米》給料日.

P[2] Today is *payday* ***for*** our company. きょうは当社の給料日だ.

pay-envelope, *n.* 給料袋.

Q her ***meager*** *pay-envelope* 彼女のわずかな給料.

payment, *n.* 支払; 払込; 支払金額.

V ***charge*** extra *payments* 余分の支払を請求する. ¶***complete*** *payment* of … …の支払を済ませる. ¶***delay*** *payment* as much as possible できるだけ支払を延ばす. 【類】***delay*** *payment* of the bill as long as three months. ¶***demand*** *payment* with importunity 支払を強要する. ¶***enforce*** *payment* 支払をしいる. ¶***get*** *payment* of … …の支払を受ける. ¶***give*** a rich *payment* to 厚い報酬をする. ¶***guarantee*** *payment* 支払を保証する. ¶I want to ***have*** partial (=part) *payment*. 内金をいただきたい. ¶***make*** (=***render***) *payment* 支払をする ‖ No *payment* is ***made***. 無報酬である. ‖ ***make*** a first *payment* of ¥500 第一回分五百円の払込をする. ¶***receive*** part *payment* of an account 勘定の内金を受取る ‖ *payment* ***received*** 受取りずみ. ¶***refuse*** *payment* 支払を拒絶する. ¶***repudiate*** *payment* 支払

を拒絶する. ¶*secure* the *payment* of ... ...の支払を受ける. ¶*shirk payment* of ... ...を踏み倒す. ¶The firm mentioned *stopped payment* some time ago. 例の商会は少し前に支払を停止した. ¶*suspend* (=*stop*) *payment* 支払を停止する. ¶*urge* the *payment* of overdue accounts 期限の切れた勘定の支払を催促する.

Q to be returned in *annual payments* 年賦償却のこと. ¶*daily* (*monthly, yearly*) *payment* 日(月, 年)払. ¶*down payment* 即金. ¶on *easy payments* 分割払いで. ¶*fair payment* 相当の報酬(雑誌など). ¶You can acquire the volumes on a *first payment* of 5/-. 最初五シリングを支払えば全巻が手に入れられる. ¶*immediate payment* 即時払い. ¶*initial payment* 頭金. ¶His *payments* have been very *irregular* for some time past. 彼の支払はここしばらくはなはだ不規則であった. ¶18 *monthly payments* of one guinea each 毎月一ギニーずつ十八カ月の月賦. 【類】by making *monthly payments* / by *monthly payments* of $6.30, and up / *monthly payments* to various tradesmen. ¶a *preliminary payment* 手付け金. ¶*punctual payment* 日限通りの支払. ¶a *quarterly payment* 四季払い. ¶a *ready payment* 即金. ¶a *single payment* of ten guineas 十ギニーの一時払. ¶for a *small payment* わずかな額を支払えば. ¶a *special low* $4.75 *down payment* and very easy terms 特別割引の四ドル七十五セント即金払残高はきわめて楽な分納.

Q² *advance payment* 前払い. ¶a *barter payment* [バーター制による]物品交易支払い(貿易交換支払い). ¶*benefi payments* to former employee's families [失業手当など]退職者家族に対する給付. ¶have *cash payment* 現金で支払を受ける. ¶a *dividend payment* 配当金支払い. ¶*emergency payment* 非常時払い. ¶an *income tax payment* 所得税納金. ¶suspend *interest payment* on wartime bonds 戦時公債の利息支払を停止する. ¶"*little-at-a-time*" *payment* 小額分割払い. ¶by *money payment* 金を払って. ¶*no-change payment* 精算払い. ¶in *part payment* of ... ...の内金として. 【類】as *part payment* / give an old watch in *part payment* for a new one ¶a *pension payment* 年金支払い. ¶*piecework payment* でき高払い. ¶*royalty payment* 印税払い. ¶spot delivery with monthly *instalment payment* 即納月賦払い. ¶suspension of *specie payments* 正金支払いの中止. ¶a *tax payment* 税納金. ¶a *time payment* 賦払い. ¶cases of delayed or skipped *wage payment* 遅給または欠給の例. ¶a *war indemnity payment* 戦時補償支払い. ¶make *yen* (*dollar*) *payment* 円(ドル)貨で支払う.

P deliver a bill of lading to ... *against payment* of ... ...の支払に対し貨物引換証を渡す. ¶*as* part *payment* 内金として. ¶*by* monthly (yearly) *payments* 月(年)賦で. ¶*for* a small *payment* 少額の払込で ‖ time *for* the *payment* of the purchase-money 代金支払期日. ¶*in payment* of the accompanying bill 同封勘定書の支払として. ¶sell *on* small *payments* 少額の分納で売る ‖ for sale *on* easy *payments* なしくずしの売物 ‖ *on payment* of an additional sum (=extra) of ... ...の追加額を支払って ‖ *on* the *payment* of a subscription (購読料, 予約金) of ... ¶Anyone can become a member *upon payment* of $10.00 annual dues. 年十ドルの会費を払えばだれでも会員になれる. ¶He is always behindhand *with* his *payment*. 彼はいつも払いが滞る. ¶receive a liberal education *without payment* of tuition 授業料なしで高等教育を受ける.

P² *payment by* bank 銀行払 ‖ *payment by* bill (cash) 手形(現金)払 ‖ *payment by* results でき高払い ‖ *payment by* the piece=peacework payment. ¶*payment for* one's time 手間賃 ‖ Perhaps ... would be a fair *payment for* the entire property. 恐らく...は財産全部に対して至当の支払金額だろう. ¶*payment in* full 全額支払 ‖ *payment in* advance 前納 ‖ *payment in* kind 物納. ¶*payment into* and withdrawal of money from a bank 銀行への金の出し入れ. ¶the *payment of* an annual subcription of one guinea 購読料年額一ギニーの払込. ¶*payment on* account 内金 ‖ Here's the receipt for half *payment on* goods. 品物の半額支払領収証を差上げます.

pay-roll, *n.* 俸給支払簿.

Q Their names appear on the *official pay-roll* of the office. 彼らの姓名は職員名簿に載っている. ¶be on the *regular pay-roll* 正社員である.

Q² slash *government payrolls* by one-third 公務員を三分の一減らす ‖ be on the *government pay-roll* 公務員である.

P We have over 1,200 people *on* our *pay-roll*. 当会社は千二百人以上の使用人に俸給を払っている. ‖ keep him *on* the *pay-roll* 彼に対して給料の支払を継続する.

pea, *n.* えんどう.

V *shell peas* えんどうのさやをむく.

Q *green peas* 青えんどう. ¶There are *many peas* in a pod. さやの中にえんどう豆が沢山ある.

Q² *garden peas* 白えんどう. 「姉妹はうり二つだ.

P The sisters resemble each other *like* [two] *peas*. あの

peace, *n.* 平和, 和親; 講和[条約]; 安心.

V *advocate peace* with ... ...との和親を唱道する. ¶*break* the *peace* 平和を破る. ¶*bring peace* to ... ...に平和をもたらす. ¶*bring about* [a] *peace* between ... ...を和ぼくさせる. ¶*cloud* one's inward *peace* 心の平和を曇らせる. ¶*conclude* a *peace* 平和条約を結ぶ ‖ *conclude* a separate *peace* 単独講和を結ぶ. 【類】*Peace* has been *concluded*. ¶*covet peace* 平和を愛する. ¶after *peace* is *declared* 平和が宣言されてから. ¶*desire peace* 平和を希望する. ¶*destroy* domestic *peace* 家庭の平和を破る. ¶end the power of an individual nation to *disturb* the *peace* of the world それぞれの国民の世界の平和かく乱の力を除去する ‖ *disturb* the public *peace* 公安をかく乱する. 【類】It threatens to *disturb* international *peace*. ¶*endanger* the *peace* of Europe 欧州の平和を危くする. ¶*enjoy peace* of mind 心の平和を得る. 【類】During nearly the whole of the Tokugawa age the nation *enjoyed* unbroken *peace*. ¶*ensure peace* by preparing for war 軍備によって平和を確保する. ¶*establish peace* on a sure and sound foundation 確実な基礎の上に平和を樹立する. ¶Nobody *expected peace* so soon. だれもそう早く平和になろうとは思っていなかった. ¶*forward* universal *peace* 世界の平和を助長する. ¶*give* no *peace* to ... ...の心を休ませない. ¶It will go a long way toward *guaranteeing* the *peace* of the world in the future. それは将来世界の平和を確保する上に大なる効果を有するであろう. ¶He *has* no *peace* of mind. 彼には心の平和というものがない. ¶*hold* one's *peace*=be silent 沈黙を守る. ¶*insure peace* through the world 全世界に平和を保証する. ¶*keep* the *peace* of the world 世界の平和を維持する. ¶I *lost* my *peace* of mind. 私は不安になった. ¶*love peace* 平和を愛好する. ¶*maintain* public *peace* 公安を維持する. 【類】a great help towards *maintaining* the *peace* of the world. ¶*make* one's *peace* 仲直りをする ‖ *make peace* with ... ...と和解する ‖ persuade the combatants to *make peace* 争闘者に和ぼくを勧める. 【類】I soon *made peace* between the two belligerents. ¶*menace* the *peace* of the world 世界の平和をおびやかす. ¶A *peace* was *patched up* between Russia and Turkey in the conference at Berlin. ベルリン会議でロシア・トルコ間にやっと講和が成立した. *perpetuate* the world's *peace* 世界平和を恒久化する. ¶*preach peace* 平和を唱道する. ¶*preserve* public *peace* and good order 社会の安寧秩序を維持する ‖ *preserve* the *peace* and health of the community 社会の平和と健康を維持させる. ¶*proclaim peace* 平和を宣言する. ¶increase the amity of all nations and *promote* the *peace* of the universe (=world) すべての国民の親善を増進し世界平和を助成する. ¶*purchase peace* by concessions 譲歩によって平和を獲得する. ¶*restore peace* 平和を克復する. ¶*ruin peace* 平和を破る. ¶take measures to *secure peace* 平和を得る手段を講じる. ¶*seek peace* 平和を求める. ¶*safeguard* the *peace* of nations 国際の平和を擁護する. ¶*shake* industrial *peace* 産業界の平和を乱す. ¶the issues which now *threaten* the *peace* of the world 世界平和をおびやかす諸問題. ¶threaten to *wreck peace* of Europe 今にも欧州の平和を破壊するおそれがある.

V² when *peace reigns* once more 平和克復の暁に.

Q an *armed peace* 武装せる平和. ¶After a *brief peace*, war broke out again. ちょっと休戦になり, 戦争は再開された. ¶It is a rock on which *domestic peace* is often wrecked. それは往々家庭の平和を破る暗礁になる. ¶elements of a *durable peace* 永続的平和の要素. ¶*enduring peace* 恒久の平和. ¶a disturbance of *European peace* 欧州平和のかく乱. ¶establish *everlasting peace* 恒久平和をうちたてる. ¶a *firm, just,* and *durable peace* 強固公正か

つ恒久の平和. ¶an ***honorable*** peace 光栄ある平和. ¶an ***ignoble*** peace 屈辱の平和. ¶an ***inconclusive*** peace 不徹底な平和. ¶***industrial*** peace 産業界の平和. ¶Tourism is conducive to ***international*** peace. 観光は国際平和を助長する. ¶***inward*** peace 心の平和. ¶a ***lasting*** peace 永続的平和. ¶a ***mailed-fist*** peace 武装平和. ¶an ***over-all*** peace 全面講和. ¶a ***permanent*** peace 恒久的平和. ¶a ***perpetual*** peace 永遠の平和. ¶noises of a nature (=kind) to disturb the ***public*** peace 安眠を妨害するような音響. ¶the maintenance of ***stable*** and ***durable*** peace 動かない永続的な平和の保持. ¶an advocate of ***universal*** peace 世界平和の唱道者.

Q² a threat to ***world*** peace 世界平和に対する脅威 ‖ contribute to ***world*** peace 世界平和に貢献する. 【類】endanger ***world*** peace / guard ***world*** peace / the cause of ***world*** peace / a pillar (柱石) of ***world*** peace / promote ***world*** peace and understanding.

P We are fortunately ***at*** peace with all the world today. われらは今日幸に世界各国と和親の状態にある. 【類】a Power with which we are nominally (表面上) ***at*** peace / a world ***at*** peace. ¶stand ***for*** peace 平和を支持する ‖ seek ***for*** peace 平和を求める. 【類】We are unanimous in our wish ***for*** peace. ¶***in*** peace as in war 戦時においても平時においても ‖ die ***in*** peace 安らかに死ぬ ‖ May his soul rest ***in*** peace!=Rest his soul! 彼の霊の休まらんことを. ‖ Leave me ***in*** peace. 私に構ってくれるな. ‖ live ***in*** peace and comfort 平和に安楽に暮す. ¶enjoy a life ***of*** peace 平和に暮す ‖ knit the whole world in bonds ***of*** cultured peace 全世界を教養ある平和のきずなで結びつける.

P² promote peace ***among*** the nations 国民間の平和を増進する. ¶peace ***at*** any price 絶対平和論. ¶peace ***in*** the Orient 東洋の平和. ¶the peace ***of*** society 社会の安寧 ‖ interfere with the general peace ***of*** the public 公衆の全般的平和と抵触する. ¶*Peace* ***to*** his ashes, brave son! 彼の勇魂安らかに眠れ! ¶peace ***with*** honor 光栄ある平和. 【類】We are in a state of peace ***with*** all nations.

O *Peace* be with you. どうぞ御無事に.

peacemaker, *n.* 調停者.

P act ***as*** peacemaker between ... and ... ...間の調停者となる.

peach, *n.* ももの実.

V ***do*** peaches ももの砂糖づけを造る.

Q a ***freestone*** peach 種ばなれのよいもも. ¶***newly gathered*** peaches, with the bloom on them 粉のふいている取り立てのももの実.

peacock, *n.* くじゃく.

P a muster ***of*** peacocks 一群のくじゃく.

peak, *n.* 峰, 山頂; 絶頂(ピーク).

V ***ascend*** the topmost peak 山頂をきわめる. ¶***pass*** its peak [比ゆ] その峠を越す ‖ She has ***passed*** the peak. 彼女は盛りが過ぎた. ¶The number ***reached*** a peak of ... in 1929. その数は一九二九年に...という最高位に達した. ¶***scale*** (=go up to) a mountain peak 山頂に登る. ¶He was the first to ***top*** the mountain peak. 彼はその山頂をきわめた最初の人であった.

V² This peak ***towers*** above all the others. この峰は他のすべての群峰をしのいでいる.

Q ***ever-snow-clad*** peaks 四季雪をいただく峰. ¶The ***highest*** peak of the Hakone mountains is Kamiyama, which is 4,700 ft. high. 箱根山の最高峰は神山で高さ四千七百フィートある. ¶the ***trifurcated*** peak of Fuji 三つまたになっている富士山頂.

Q² The ***export*** peak has been reached. 輸出は頭を突いた. ¶a ***mountain*** peak 山の峰. ¶the ***1943*** peak of aircraft production 一九四九年度の航空機生産最高量. ¶the ***wartime*** peak 戦争の最盛期.

P ***at*** peak 最高点で(生産など) ‖ ***at*** the peak of the boom (Roosevelt prosperity) その好景気(ルーズベルト景気)の絶頂で. ¶The necessary costs of living are now 25 per cent ***below*** the peak of July, 1920. 生活必需品の現在値段は一九二〇年七月の峠から二割五分の低落を示している. ¶***upon*** the topmost peak of ... ...の絶頂に.

P² the peak ***of*** the roof 屋根のせん端 ‖ the peak ***of*** war industry 戦争産業のピーク.

peal, *n.* [鳴り]響き.

V The bells ***rang*** a merry peal. 鐘が陽気に鳴り響いた.

Q The bells of the parish rang out a ***joyful*** peal. 教区の鐘は楽しげに鳴り渡った. ¶The church bells rang out a ***merry*** peal. 教会の鐘が陽気に鳴り響いた.

P ***amid*** peals of laughter 笑声の内に.

P² a peal ***of*** bells 鐘の響き ‖ There was a peal ***of*** laughter. 笑声がした. ‖ a peal ***of*** thunder 雷鳴.

peal, *v.* 響く.

M The bells *pealed* ***forth*** their message in a deep bass tone. 鐘が重々しいベースで(時などを)告げた.

pear, *n.* なし.

Q the russet-brown of ***ripe*** pears 熟したなしの赤かっ色.

pearl, *n.* 真珠.

V ***cast*** (=***throw***) pearls before swine 豚に真珠を与える(ねこに小判).

Q an ***artificial*** (=***imitation***) pearl 人造真珠. ¶a ***black*** pearl 黒真珠. ¶a ***culture[d]*** pearl 養殖真珠. ¶a ***genuine*** pearl ほんものの真珠. ¶a ***sham*** pearl にせ真珠.

P Her teeth are ***like*** pearls. 彼女の歯は真珠のようだ. ¶the culture ***of*** pearls=pearl culture 真珠養殖. ¶a ring set ***with*** pearls 真珠をちりばめた指輪.

peasant, *n.* 農夫, 百姓.

Q ***craven-hearted*** peasants 意気地のない農夫. ¶***landless*** peasants 土地を持たない百姓(小作人). ¶a ***rough*** peasant 礼儀を知らない(粗暴な)百姓.

P a group ***of*** peasants 一群の農夫.

peasantry, *n.* [団] 百姓.

Q ***landless*** peasantry 土地のない百姓. ¶a ***submissive*** peasantry 従順な百姓.

pebble, *n.* 小石.

V ***throw*** pebbles at ... ...をめがけて小石を投げる.

Q ***stream-(wave-)worn*** pebbles 流れ(波)にもまれて丸くなった小石.

peck, *v.* [くちばしで]つつく.

P *peck* ***at*** ... ...をくちばしでつつく. 【類】The painter drew and colored his grapes with such fidelity that (...ほど真に迫って) the birds *pecked* ***at*** the painting.

peculiar, *a.* 独特の, 特有の.

M The practice is ***quite*** *peculiar* to this country. その習慣は全くこの国特有のものである.

P The style is *peculiar* ***to*** him. その文体は彼独特のものだ. ‖ a table of terms *peculiar* ***to*** carpentry 大工特有の言葉の一覧表. 【類】diseases *peculiar* ***to*** man alone.

peculiarity, *n.* 特性, 特色, 性癖.

V He ***affects*** peculiarity in appearance. 彼は風さいの奇をてらう. ¶Celebrated men ***have*** all their individual peculiarities. 名高い人々には皆それぞれ独特の性癖がある. ¶I ***know*** his peculiarities. 私は彼の癖を知っている.

Q ***idiomatic*** peculiarities 慣用的語法の特性. ¶***individual*** peculiarities 個人的特性. ¶***national*** peculiarities 国民的特色. ¶***racial*** peculiarities 民族的特色. ¶a ***striking*** peculiarity 著しい特性.

P² peculiarities ***of*** Dr. Johnson ジョンソン博士の性癖 ‖ a peculiarity ***of*** mind 精神的特性 ‖ peculiarities ***of*** American speech 米語の特異性.

pedagogy, *n.* 教育.

Q² ***language*** pedagogy 語学教育.

pedal, *n.* ペダル, 踏子.

V ***work*** the pedals [自転車など]ペダルをふんで運転する.

pedantry, *n.* げん学.

P His language has a tinge (=savors) ***of*** pedantry. 彼の言葉には学者ぶった所がある.

peddle, *v.* 行商する.

P *peddle* goods ***about*** the country いなかを行商する.

ped[d]ler, pedlar, *n.* 行商人.

Q² a ***candy*** (***peanut***) peddler キャンデー(など)売り. ¶a ***gossip*** peddler=a gossiper ゴシップ屋. ¶a ***push-cart*** peddler 押し車の物売. ¶a ***street*** peddler 街頭の物売り.

P He is a peddler ***by*** occupation. 彼の職業は行商人.

pedestal, *n.* 台, 台座.

Q ***convenient*** pedestals for the feet [くつみがき屋などの用いる]便利な足台. ¶He stands upon a ***lofty*** pedestal. 彼はお高くとまっている.

P a statue ***on*** a granite pedestal 花こう岩の台座に据えた像.

pedestal, *v.* 台座に据える.

P He is *pedestal[l]ed* ***for*** a genius. 彼は天才として祭り上げられている.

pedigree, *n.* 系図; 出(ᵉ), 身元; 由来, 出所.

V These words ***have*** the same pedigree. これらの語の出所は同じだ. ¶***trace back*** the pedigree of the Hayashis 林家の系図をさかのぼって調べる.

Q a man of ***doubtful*** pedigree どこの馬の骨かわからない人. ¶his ***literary*** pedigree 彼の文学上の経歴 ‖ The words have a good ***literary pedigree*** extending several centuries back. それらの言葉は過去数世紀にわたるりっぱな文学的由来がある.

P He is ***by pedigree*** a nobleman. 彼の出は貴族だ.

peel, *n.* [くだものなどの]皮.

Q an orange with a very ***loose peel*** 皮のよくむけるオレンジ.

peel, *v.* 皮をむく(むける).

M^2 The skin of my back ***peeled off*** with too much exposure to the sun. 盛んに日に当ったので背の皮がむけた. ‖ The paint is ***peeling off.*** ペンキが段々はげてくる. ‖ The roof was ***peeling off*** with the wind. 風で屋根がはげかかっていた.

P *peel* the bark ***from*** a tree 木の皮をむく.

O The skin *peels* when sunburnt. 日にやけると皮がむける.

peeler, *n.* 皮むき.

Q^2 a ***potato peeler*** じゃが芋むき.

peep, *n.* のぞき見; 一見, べつ見; 出現; せん光.

V ***gain*** a strange *peep* through a crevice すき間からのぞいてみると不思議な光景が目にうつる. ¶***get*** a *peep* of life at a bathing resort 海水浴場で人生の一端をうかがう. 【類】***get*** a *peep* of the world. ¶***have*** a *peep* at ... …をちょっと見る. ¶let us ***take*** a *peep* at ... …をのぞいて見よう. 【類】***take*** a *peep* into a room.

Q a ***hurried*** (=***hasty***) *peep* into ... …に急いで目を通すこと.

P ***at peep*** of day=at dawn 夜明けに.

P^2 a *peep* ***at*** a theatre 劇場のぞき ‖ What do you say to a *peep* ***at*** pictures? 映画にちょっとはいって見ませんか. ‖ These cheap reprints enable the masses to have *peeps* ***at*** great books. これらの廉価版で大衆は大著作のべっ見ができる. ¶a *peep* ***of*** a lamp ちらと見えるラムプの光. ¶with a *peep* ***under*** the table テーブルの下をちょっとのぞいて.

peep, *v.* のぞく; 芽を出す.

M ***coyly*** (=***shyly***) *peep* through ... [少女などが]こわごわ…からのぞく. ¶go to the window to *peep* ***out*** at the weather 天気をのぞいて見るため窓へ行く.

M^2 ***peep in*** at the door 戸の所からのぞき込む. 【類】***peep in*** through a crack (keyhole). ¶***peep over*** a brink がけっぷちからのぞく.

P ***peep at*** a person through ... …から人をのぞき見する. 【類】***peep at*** oneself in a mirror / ***peep at*** the future. ¶***peep from*** the ground [植物・種子などが]地から芽を出す. ¶***peep into*** the room (basket, darkness, all the corners) へや(など)をのぞき込む. 【類】The morning sun ***peeped into*** the garret (中二階). ‖ ***peep into*** the future 未来を洞察する. ¶***peep out of*** a window 窓からのぞく. ¶***peep over*** one's shoulder 肩越しにのぞく ‖ The top ***peeps over*** a hillside. [せん塔・山などの]いただきが丘腹からのぞいている. ¶***peep through*** a keyhole かぎ穴からのぞく. 【類】***peep through*** chinks (すき間) of a palisade around a bathing-place. / A suspicious fellow (怪しいやつ) is ***peeping through*** the fence at us.

peer, *n.* 貴族; 匹敵するもの.

V It ***has*** no *peer.* それは二つとない.

Q ***busted*** *peers* 《米俗》斜陽族. ¶regard them as their ***intellectual*** *peers* 彼らを自分などと同等知識の人と見なす.

Q^2 a ***life*** *peer* 一代貴族.

P It is ***without*** a *peer* in the world. それは天下一品だ. 【類】be ***without*** *peer* in the entire history of the American West.

O He was created (=made) a *peer.* 彼は華族に列せられた.

peer, *v.* じっと見る, うかがう; ほのかに見える.

M^2 ***peer in*** (***out***) 中(外)をうかがう. 【類】They crept cautiously up to the windows and ***peered in.***

P The moon *peers* ***above*** the sea. 月が海上に昇って来る. ¶***peer at*** a person 人をじっと見る. ¶***peer into*** a forest 森をすかして見る. 【類】***peer into*** space (空間) / ***peer into*** the black darkness in a vain effort to discover ... ‖ ***peer*** eagerly ***into*** glass cases at autographs ガラスわくをのぞいて親筆をじっと見る. ¶***peer through*** a telescope 望遠鏡をのぞく. 【類】***peer through*** the darkness (cracks in the door) / The moon ***peers through*** the clouds.

peerage, *n.* 貴族の爵位.

V They ***earned*** their *peerages.* 彼らは貴族の爵位を賜わった. ¶Some argue that the *peerage* should be ***made durable*** only for the lifetime of the persons honored. 一代華族の説を唱える人がある.

P his promotion ***in*** the *peerage* 氏の爵位の昇叙. ¶He was suspended from the privileges ***of*** the *peerage.* 氏は華族の礼遇を停止された. 【類】members ***of*** the Japanese *peerage.* ¶He was raised (=elevated) ***to*** the *peerage* with the title of Baron in recognition of his services. 氏はその功労により華族に列し男爵を授けられた.

peevish, *a.* 気むずかしの.

P She looked vexed and *peevish* ***at*** the news. そのニュースにこまったというようないやな顔をした.

peg, *n.* 木くぎ, 金くぎ; [議論などの]口実.

V I ***have*** not a *peg* upon which safely to hang such a theory, yet ... こんな理屈を持出す筋合ではないが…

Q They are ***square*** *pegs* in round holes (=round pegs in square holes). 彼は円穴に四角なくぎだ(適材適所でない).

P use it ***as*** the *peg* for ... それを…の手段に用いる. ¶hang a coat ***on*** a *peg* 上衣を木くぎに掛ける ‖ Just fetch me the hat ***on*** the *peg,* there is a good boy. いい子だからちょっと帽子を取っておいで.

peg, *v.* せっせと働く; くぎで止める, [値段を]くぎづけにする.

M *peg* ***away*** at one's routine work 自分の毎日の仕事に精を出す.

M^2 The price is *pegged* ***down*** at $1.25 per bale. 値段は一俵一ドル二十五セントにおさえられている. ‖ be *pegged* ***down*** to slavish work どれい的な仕事にくぎづけされている.

P *peg* the price ***at*** ... 値を…で抑える.

O *peg* the market 市価を安定させる(法令などで).

pegging, *n.* くい打ち.

Q^2 ***tent*** *pegging* テントのくい打ち.

pelt, *v.* ひどく打つ.

M^2 Rain and sleet *pelted* ***down.*** みぞれ混りの冷雨がひどく降った.

P *pelt* one another ***with*** snowballs 雪合戦をする.

pen, *n.* がペン, ペン; 文筆, 著作; 文体, 筆力.

V ***bite*** one's *pen* and scowl [文が思うように書けないので]筆をくわえてまゆをしかめる. ¶This ***blunted*** his *pen.* このために彼の筆力は鈍った. ¶This ***demands*** the *pen* of a Russell or a Forbes. これはラッセルかフォーブスほどの文筆がなくては書けない. ¶***dip*** one's *pen* in [the] ink インキにペンを浸す ‖ ***dip*** one's *pen* in gall 〖比ゆ〗毒筆をふるう. ¶***draw*** one's *pen* against ... …を筆をもって攻撃する. ¶***drive*** a *pen* 筆を駆る. ¶***fling*** one's *pen* ***down*** ペンを投げ棄てる. ¶be written with the simplicity of one who knows how to ***handle*** his *pen* 達筆家の簡潔さをもって書かれて. ¶He ***has*** a sharp *pen.* 彼の筆力は鋭利だ(批評などの辛らつなこと). ¶***lay down*** one's *pen* 筆をおく. ¶***make*** a *pen* [小刀で]がペンを作る. ¶***mend*** a *pen* [小刀で]がペンの先を削り直す. ¶The subject has ***occupied*** the *pens* of hundreds of writers. その問題は数百の文士が取扱ったものだ. ¶***prostitute*** one's *pen* 売文を業とする. ¶Sometimes for six months he never ***put*** *pen* to paper. 彼はときには半年も筆をとらない. ¶***put down*** one's *pen* ペンをおく. ¶He has never ***set*** *pen* to paper. 彼は筆をとったことがない. ¶***sully*** our *pens* われわれの筆(文名)を汚す. ¶***supplement*** the *pen* with the scissors [他書を切抜きなどして]はさみで筆を補う. ¶***take*** one's *pen* in hand 筆をとる. ¶***take up*** one's *pen* to describe it ペンをとってそのことを書く. ¶***try*** one's *pen* in some translations 翻訳ものをやってみようとする. ¶he ***wields*** his *pen* so well that ... 彼は…なほど達者に筆を揮う. 【類】***wield*** a *pen* with the hand of a master.

V^2 my *pen* ***drops*** from me here in an attempt to describe ... …を記述しようとしても私の筆はこれ以上進まない. ¶The *pen* ***falters*** in my enfeebled, emaciated fingers. 私は支える指もやせて力なくペンは行悩む. ¶His *pen* ***glides*** over the paper. 彼のペンは紙の上をすべる(文句がすらすら出て来る). ¶More able *pens* than mine have ***written,*** and will ***write,*** of his great achievements. 氏の功績は私より更に達者な筆で書かれもしたしまた今後も書かれるだろう.

Q write with ***agile*** *pen* 軽妙な筆致で書く. ¶wield a ***bright*** and ***ready*** *pen* 才気ある達筆を揮う. ¶write with a ***caustic*** *pen* 痛烈な文を書く. ¶Other ***contemporary*** *pens* were active in its attack. その他同時代の論客は盛んにこれを攻撃した. ¶the ***eloquent*** *pen* of ... …の達筆. ¶a novelist with a ***facile*** *pen* 筆の立つ小説家. ¶Edinburgh has been praised by many ***famous*** *pens.* エジンバラは幾多知名の士の筆によって賞揚された. ¶He has a ***fluent*** *pen* to record. 彼の記録は達筆である. ¶wield a ***formidable*** *pen* 恐るべき筆を揮う. ¶a ***friendly*** (***hostile***) *pen*, that of ..., thus writes about ... ...に同情ある(反対した)人は...についてこんな風に書いている. ¶be written down by the ***glib pen*** of the ignorant but ready writer 頭はないが筆まめの人によって冗慢に書かれる. ¶a ***graceful pen*** 優美な書き方(文章). ¶written with a ***graphic pen*** 目で見るような(写実的)文章で書いた. ¶her *pen* has been ***idle*** since ... ...以来彼女は執筆しなかった. ¶his keen wit and ***inimitable pen*** 氏の明敏な機知と他の追随をゆるさない筆致. ¶No ***mean pens*** have dealt with the subject. 平凡な文士が書いたのではない(りっぱな文士がその問題を取扱ったのだ). ¶The *pen* is ***mightier*** than the sword. 文は武よりも力がある. ¶a ***pointed pen*** 痛烈な筆. ¶one of the most ***powerful journalistic pens*** in Germany ドイツにおける最も有力なる新聞記者の一人. ¶a ***practised pen*** 老練な筆. ¶from the ***prolific pen*** of Mr. S 多作家であるS氏の筆になる. ¶be sketched with a ***rapid pen*** 走り筆で描写される. ¶some day someone with a more ***ready pen*** than mine will write the epic of ... 私よりもっと達筆な人がいつか...の叙事詩を書くであろう. ¶a ***vivacious pen*** 健筆.

Q² a ***ball-point pen*** ボールペン. ¶a ***double-line pen*** 複線筆. ¶an ink sack of a ***fountain pen*** 万年筆のインキ袋 ‖ a 14-karat gold nib ***fountain pen*** 万年筆の十四金ペン先. ¶a ***goose-quill pen*** がペン. ¶a ***steel*** (***gold***) ***pen*** 鉄(金)ペン.

P live ***by*** one's *pen* 文筆で生計を立てる. 【類】He is making £5,000 a year ***by*** his *pen*. ¶a piece of writing ***from*** a Japanese *pen* 日本人の筆になる一編の文章 ‖ the translation appeared ***from*** the *pen* of ... その翻訳は...の手でなされた. 【類】a book ***from*** the *pen* of an eminent jurist (法学者). / a preface ***from*** the *pen* of ... / ***from*** the *pen* of S. comes an excellent paper (論文) on ... ¶a letter written ***in*** *pen* and ink ペン書きの手紙. ¶a portrait of Daruma by a mere stroke ***of*** the *pen* 一筆で描いた達磨の絵. ¶These expressions find their way ***to*** his *pen*. これらの文句は彼が使っている. ¶write ***with*** a *pen* ペンで書く ‖ write ***with*** a *pen* and ink ペンとインキで書く ‖ He is clever ***with*** his *pen*. 彼は筆の器用(達者)な人だ. ‖ defend the principle ***with*** his *pen* 文筆でその主義を弁護(支持)する. 【類】handle the subject ***with*** the *pen* of a master (達筆で) / be drawn ***with*** the *pen* of a master of literary portraiture (人物描写の名手).

pen, *v.* 書く.

P I *penned* a few lines ***to*** him. 彼に一筆書いてやった.

pen, *n.* おり; [潜水艦修理用]ドック.

Q² He was detained in a ***police pen*** (=cell). 彼は警察のぶた箱に入っていた. ¶a ***submarine pen*** 潜水艦ドック.

P² a *pen* ***for*** sheep (pigs) 羊(など)を入れるおり.

pen, *n.* =penitentiary《米俗》刑務所.

Q² move the criminal from the city jail to the ***State pen*** 犯人を市の刑務所から州の刑務所に移す.

pen, *v.* おりに入れる, 囲う.

M² hogs *penned* ***up*** in part of a yard 庭のすみに囲ってある豚.

penalize, *v.* 罰する.

M *penalize* ***heavily*** 重く罰する.

penalty, *n.* 刑罰; 罰金; 報い, 罰.

V ***assign*** a *penalty* 刑に処する. ¶***augment*** a *penalty* by one degree 本刑に一等を加える. ¶***endure*** a *penalty* 刑に服する. ¶***escape*** the *penalties* of their crimes 彼らの罪が罰せられずに済む. ¶***impose*** a *penalty* of from one to five years' imprisonment on ... 一年ないし五年の禁固の刑を...に課す. ¶One who acts against the regulations shall ***incur*** a *penalty* not exceeding one hundred pounds. 規則違犯者は百ポンド以下の罰金に処せらる. ¶***inflict*** a *penalty* upon an offender その罪を犯す者を罰する. ¶***issue*** *penalties* against offenders 違犯者に罰金を申渡す. ¶In our country a heavy *penalty* is ***laid*** on opium smoking. わが国ではアヘンを吸うと厳刑に処せられる. ¶***pay*** *penalty* for (=expiate) sin 罪をあがなう ‖ In that case they had to ***pay*** the *penalty* with their heads, or rather with their bowels. その場合には罰として首を差出すかあるいはむしろ(この方が多いのであるが)切腹をしなければならなかった. 【類】The bee stings and ***pays*** the *penalty* with its own life. / She ***paid*** the *penalty* of death for standing in the way of his designs. ¶***pronounce*** a *penalty* upon ... ...に刑を宣告する. ¶***reduce*** a *penalty* [by] one degree 刑一等を減じる. ¶***suffer*** a *penalty* 罰を受ける. ¶***visit*** a *penalty* upon ... ...を罰する.

Q an ***accessory*** *penalty* 付加刑. ¶a ***grave*** *penalty* 重刑. ¶pay a very ***grievous*** *penalty* 非常に重い罰金を納める. ¶impose ***heavy*** *penalties* on ... for any infringement of the right その権利侵害はすべて...に重刑を課する. ¶a ***high*** *penalty* 重い刑罰. ¶pay the ***inevitable*** *penalty* of ... ...ののっぴきならない罰金を納める. ¶***Maximum*** *penalties* for contempt are a year in jail and $1,000 fine. 侮辱罪の最高は一年の禁固または一千ドルの罰金である. ¶a ***monetary*** (=***pecuniary***) *penalty* 罰金刑. ¶the ***principal*** *penalty* 主刑. ¶***sharp*** (=***severe***) *penalties* 重刑.

Q² suffer the ***death penalty*** 死刑を受ける ‖ imposition of the ***death penalty*** 死刑の処分. 【類】face the ***death penalty*** / The ***death penalty*** has been recognized by the most learned and scientific men of all ages to be brutal and inefficient in its purposes (その目的が残酷でしかも効果がないと).

P ***as*** a *penalty* for ... ...の罰として. ¶the remission ***of*** a *penalty* 免刑. ¶***on*** (=under) *penalty* of ... ...の罰を受けてもよいとの条件で ‖ ***on*** (=***upon***) *penalty* of death 死をとして ‖ it is forbidden, ***on*** *penalty* of the law, to ... ...を犯す者は法律の罪に問われる. ¶An offender is subject ***to*** heavy *penalties*. 犯人は重刑に処せられる. ¶***under*** a *penalty* of £100 for default 違約に対しては金百ポンドを支払うべき条件で ‖ ***under*** *penalty* of death 死をとして ‖ they are responsible, ***under*** *penalty* of losing their positions, for ... ...の責任を果さないものは免職になる ‖ contract with a person to ... ***under*** a *penalty* 罰の条件づきで...することを人と契約する ‖ place (do) the work ***under*** *penalty* 不履行の場合は処刑という条件で仕事をさせる(する). 【類】Carrying fire-arms (火器) is forbidden ***under*** a heavy *penalty*. / order ... ***under*** a *penalty* of two years' imprisonment, to ... (二年の禁固) / Manufacturers will not accept ***under*** *penalty* / ***under*** the *penalties* of law / ***under*** a *penalty* of eighty strokes of the bamboo (むち刑).

P² *Penalties* ***for*** misconduct are severe. 不正行為に対する罰は重い. ‖ there is a heavy *penalty* ***for*** failing to ... ...を実行しない場合の罰は重い. ¶the *penalty* ***of*** beauty 美人の悩み ‖ the *penalty* ***of*** greatness 知名人の悩み(人からかつがれたりするので). 【類】Such are the *penalties* ***of*** greatness!

penance, *n.* 悔悟; 苦行, 難行.

V ***do*** *penance* by fasting 断食苦行する. ¶***impose*** *penance* on ... ...に代償を課す.

Q an ***ascetic*** *penance* 苦行.

P He mortified the flesh ***by*** a seven days' *penance*. 彼は七日間苦行して肉欲を制した.

P² do sincere *penance* ***for*** one's crime 心からその罪をざんげする. ¶in *penance* ***of*** one's sins その罪を悔悟して.

penchant, *n. F.* し好, し癖.

V He ***has*** a *penchant* for cats. 彼はねこが好きだ. 【類】Browning and some other noted writers ***have*** a *penchant* for obsolete words, using them as a kind of novelty. 「味を持っている人々.

P people ***with*** a *penchant* for chemistry 化学に対して趣

pencil, *n.* 鉛筆.

V ***escape*** the blue *pencil* and appear in print [投稿など] 没書を免れて印刷される. ¶***point*** a lead *pencil* 鉛筆の先をとがらす. ¶***put*** one's *pencil* on ... ...に鉛筆で印をつける. ¶***sharpen*** a *pencil* 鉛筆を削る.

Q an ***artist's*** *pencil* 画筆. ¶a newspaper editor's ***blue*** *pencil* 新聞編集長の青鉛筆. ¶a ***colored*** *pencil* 色鉛筆. ¶a ***cut-and-come-again*** *pencil* 製図用の長い鉛筆. ¶an ***indelible*** *pencil* 消えない鉛筆. ¶the ***masterly*** *pencil* of ... ...の偉大な筆[致]. ¶a ***metallic*** *pencil* 鉄筆. ¶a ***sharpened*** *pencil* とがらした鉛筆.

Q² a ***color pencil*** 色鉛筆. ¶a ***drawing pencil*** 図画用鉛筆. ¶an ***eyebrow pencil*** まゆ墨. ¶a ***flying pencil*** 空飛ぶ鉛筆(ロケット機). ¶a ***hair pencil*** 毛筆. ¶a ***lead pencil*** [普通の]鉛筆. ¶a ***lip pencil*** 棒べに. ¶a "***note-book***" ***pencil*** 手帳鉛筆. ¶a ***slate pencil*** 石筆.

P Excuse my writing to you ***in*** *pencil*. 鉛筆書きお許し下さい. 【類】make a record ***in*** *pencil* / On a fly-leaf (見返し) is this memorandum ***in*** *pencil*. ¶"stubs" ***of*** lead *pencils* 鉛筆の残部. ¶write ***with*** a lead *pencil* 鉛筆で書く. ‖ touch up one's eyebrows ***with*** a *pencil* きれいにまゆを引く.

pencil, *v.* 鉛筆で書く.

M² *Pencil down* what I am telling you. 私のいうことを鉛筆で書きとりなさい.

O *pencil* one's eyebrows まゆを書く.

pendant, *n.* 〖服飾〗ペンダント(首輪・耳輪・腕輪など).

V *pendants worn* round her neck and arms 彼女の首輪や腕輪.

pendent, *a.* たれ下がっている.

P The lamp is *pendent from* the ceiling. ランプが天井から下がっている. ¶The roofs are *pendent with* icicles. 屋根から氷柱が下がっている.

pending, *a.* 未決の.

P Application *pending at* Los Angeles, California, for entrance as Second-Class Matter under Act of Congress, July 16, 1894. 一八九四年七月十六日の法令により第二種郵便物として認可をカリフォルニア州ロスアンゼルスに出願中. ¶a question *pending between* Japan and America 日米間の懸案.

O while the agreement was *pending*＝pending the agreement 協定が解決しない中は.

pendulum, *n.* 振子.

V *attach* a *pendulum* to a timepiece 時計に振子をつける.

V² The *pendulum swang* back. 振子がゆれてもとへ戻った. ‖The *pendulum* is *swinging* in a more rational direction. 世論は一層合理的な動向を示している.

P swing back and forth *like* a *pendulum* 振子のように前後にゆれる.

penetrable, *a.* はいりうる, 浸透しうる.

P *penetrable to* light (reason) 光線(など)の通る.

penetrate, *v.* 入り込む; 洞察する.

M Western ideas had *slowly penetrated* through the East. 西欧思想が次第に東洋に浸透してきていた. ¶He is *thoroughly penetrated* with communism. 彼は骨まで共産主義が浸み込んでいる.

P It is very hard for foreigners to *penetrate below* the surface of Japanese affairs. 日本の事物の真相を察するのは外人には非常に困難だ. ¶*penetrate into* a country 国内に入り込む‖*penetrate into* a secret 秘密をどう察する‖*penetrate into* the holy of holies 奥の院にはいり込む. ¶The regret that ... *penetrated to* the marrow. ...というららみが骨髄に徹した. 【類】*penetrate to* the skin.

penetration, *n.* 眼識, 洞察; 浸透.

Q Japan's *commercial penetration* of Latin America ラテン・アメリカへの日本の商業発展. ¶economic penetration 経済浸透. ¶a thinker of *much penetration* どう察力に富む思想家. ¶*peaceful penetration* 平和的侵入[商業発展など].

Q² tactics of Communist *penetration* 共産党の浸透作戦.

P a man *of* great *penetration* 卓見の人.

P² *penetration into* ... ...のどう察. ¶the alleged imperialistic Japanese *penetration on* the continent of Asia いわゆる日本のアジア大陸への帝国主義的発展.

penicillin, *n.* ペニシリン.

Q a *fake penicillin* いんちきペニシリン.

peninsula, *n.* 半島.

V² A little *peninsula runs out* to the middle of the lake. 小さな半島が湖の中央部まで突出している. ¶a *peninsula jutting out* into the sea 海に突きでている半島.

Q the *Korean peninsula* 朝鮮半島.

P Ohito is a small town *to* (＝*on*) the Izu *peninsula*. 大仁は伊豆半島上の小都会だ.

P² The Surrey Commercial Docks are situated on a *peninsula in* the Thames. サリー商用ドックはテームズ河中の一半島にある.

penitence, *n.* 後悔.

P *with penitence* 後悔して.

P² *penitence for* a fault 過失の後悔.

penitent, *a.* 後悔している.

P He is *penitent for* his faults. 彼は過失を悔いている.

penitentiary, *n.* 刑務所.

Q² a *State penitentiary* 《米》州の刑務所 (a State pen と略す).

P² a *penitentiary for* prostitutes やみの女などの収容所.

penman, *n.* 書家.

Q a *nimble penman* 達筆家. ¶a *poor penman* 字のまずい人.

pen-name, *n.* 雅号.

P write *under* the *pen-name* of ... ...の雅号で書く.

pennant, *n.* 三角旗.

Q² a *college pennant* 大学の三角旗. ¶a *Yale pennant* エール大学の三角旗.

penny, *n.* ペニー, 金銭.

V It *cost* me a pretty *penny*. 私はそれに随分金をかけた. ¶*drop* a *penny* into the slot [自動販売機の]穴に一ペニー入れる. ¶*earn* the "nimble *penny*" 薄利多売主義で金をもうける. ¶*gather in* the humble *pennies* 薄利多売で金をもうける. ¶He *has* not a *penny*. 彼は一文なしだ. ¶The lightning-artist lives by the *pennies harvested* (＝earned) on the pavement. そのスケッチ画家は舗道で集めた金で暮している. ¶Who can't *keep* a *penny*, will never have many. 一文を持てない者は百文も持てない. ¶*make* an honest *penny* 働いて金をもうける. ¶*toss* a *penny* to a beggar こじきに一ペニー投げてやる. ¶*turn* (＝earn) an honest *penny* 正直に(働いて)金をもうける.

Q a *penny dreadful* 《英口》三文小説. ¶*Every penny* of profit is devoted to benevolent purposes. 利益は全部慈善のために使用する. 【類】many an *honest penny* is turned by the sale of ... ¶the principle of *nimble pennies* 薄利多売主義. ¶*odd pence* はしたの小銭. ¶It's a *pretty penny*. 《口語》そりゃ大した金額だ. ¶I have not a *single penny* left. 私の手もとに一文も残っていない. ¶It is not *worth* a *penny*. それは一文の価値もない.

P sell them in the streets *at* a *penny* each それを一個一ペニーで街で売る. ¶Give me my change *in pennies*. 銅銭でおつりを下さい. ¶I was left *without* a *penny*. 私は一文なしにされた.

P² A *penny for* your thoughts! 《俗》何を考えてるのか.

pennyworth, *n.* 一ペニー相当の物; 買物.

Q You will not find it a *dear pennyworth*. お買いになって御損なことはありますまい. ¶a *full pennyworth* たっぷり値段だけの値打のある品. ¶a *marvelous pennyworth* ばかに安い品.

pension, *n.* 年金, 恩給.

V go to the city to *draw* one's *pension* 年金を受取りに市へ出掛ける. ¶*enjoy* a *pension* from the King 国王から年金をもらう. ¶*grant* a *pension* to ... ...に年金を下賜する. ¶He was *offered* a *pension*. 彼は年金を与えようと言われた. ¶*receive* a *pension* of ... yen ...円の年金を受ける. ¶*relinquish* a *pension* 年金を撤回する.

Q live in a cottage on a *small pension* わずかな恩給で小さな家に住む.

Q² receive *civil list pension* 文官年金を受ける. ¶an *old age pension* 養老年金. ¶He was presented with the *one-million-yen merit pension* for his 50 years' service. 彼は五十年勤続に対し功労金として百万円の年金を受けることになった.

P an old ex-official *on pension* 年金を受けている年老いた元官吏‖He lives *on* a *pension*. 彼は恩給で暮している.‖retire *on* a *pension* 恩給をもらって引退する. 【類】retirement *on pension*.

pension, *v.* 年金を与える.

M He was *pensioned off* at the age limit. 彼は停年で年金退職になった.

pent, *pa.* とじ込められて.

M be *pent up* (＝confined) in a room へやに閉じこもっている. 【類】It is trying to be *pent up* in a large city, in hot weather.

penury, *n.* 貧乏.

V *eke out* his *penury* やりくり算段で暮す.

Q a *miserable penury* みじめな貧乏.

people, *n.* [単数に用いて]国民, 民族; [集合的に]人々; 世間; 家族.

V *accost people* in the street 街で人に呼びかける. ¶*appease* the *people* 人民を静める. ¶*arouse* the *people* to the importance of ... 国民を啓もうして...の重要性を認めさせる. ¶*bring* more closely *together* the *peoples* of two great nations 二大国民を一層密接に結合させる. 【類】*bring* the *peoples* of the Pacific *together* into better understanding and co-operative effort (協力). ¶*draw* the *peoples* of the world closer *together* 世界諸民族を一層親密にさせる. ¶He goes *frightening people* with his stories. 彼はよく話をして人をこわがらせる. ¶the art of *handling people* 人を使うこつ. ¶*help* the *people* to help themselves [結局]自らを助けるために人を助ける. ¶The hall *holds* two thousand *people*. その会館は二千人の収容力がある. ¶*interest people* in France and Germany in the scheme フランス及びドイツの人々をしてその計画に興味を持たせる. ¶*interpret* the *people* to the President 大統領に民意のある所を通じさせる. ¶*lead* his *people* into independence その民を指導して独立させる. ¶There is absolutely no doubt about the fact that a language does more to *link people together* than anything else in the world. およそ国語にはなにものにもまさって人民を結合する力があるこ

とは断じて疑いを容れない. ¶his inability to ***look people*** in the eye 彼がじっと人の目を見ることができないこと. ¶The church is ***losing people.*** あの教会は会員が減ってゆく. ¶the Teutonic ideal of ***making*** the ***people*** of one model 同型の人物を造ろうとするチュートン人種の理想. ¶***misgovern*** the ***people*** 国民の統治を誤る. ¶The theatre ***seats*** nearly five thousand ***people.*** その劇場には約五千人の座席がある. ¶Wednesday is her day for ***seeing people.*** 水曜日は彼女の面会日だ. ¶***serve*** the ***people*** 人民に奉仕する.

V[2] as ***people go*** 世間並からいうと. ¶***people say*** that ... ... だそうだ. ¶***People streamed in.*** 人々は流れ込んで来た. 【類】 ***people streamed*** into ...

Q ***advanced*** and ***backward peoples*** 進歩した国民と遅れている国民. ¶***agricultural people*** 農民. ¶the moral, educational and cultural development of ***all people*** 全国民の道徳的・教育的・ならびに文化的発展. ¶To me, of ***all people!*** 人もあろうに私にとは! ¶the ***ancient people*** of Germany 古代ドイツ人. ¶***average people*** 並の人. ¶one of the ***Basic people*** ベーシック語賛成者の一人. ¶the ***British peoples*** ブリトン族の諸民族. ¶the ***chosen people*** 選ばれた人々. 【類】 Some Westerners have the fond idea that the whites are the favorites of the gods, the ***chosen people.*** ¶***city people***=《英》 townspeople 都会人. ¶***city-bred people*** 都会育ちの人々. ¶a highly ***civilized people*** 非常に文化の進んだ国民. ¶a ***commercial people*** 商業国民. ¶***common people***=commoners 一般人. ¶***commonplace people*** 平々凡々の人々. ¶The English are a ***conservative people.*** 英国人は保守的な国民だ. ¶***countless people*** 無数の人々. ¶The ***people*** at the hotel were very ***courteous.*** ホテルの人たちは非常に丁寧だった. ¶***cultured people*** 教養ある人々. ¶They have a distinct appeal to ***discerning people.*** 目のある人たちはそれらの品を喜ぶ. ¶***distinguished people*** 名士連. ¶We are becoming a better ***educated*** and more ***competent people.*** われわれはもっと教育のあるもっと有能な国民になりつつある. ¶the ***English people*** 英国人. ¶***English-speaking peoples*** 英語国民. ¶an ***entire people*** 全国民. ¶an ***extinct people*** 絶滅した民族. ¶***fashionable people*** 上流人士. ¶***fastidious people*** きげんのとりにくい人々. ¶***forward looking people*** 将来を考える人々. ¶Both the Chinese and Japanese have been a ***frugal people.*** 中国人及び日本人は共に節約の国民だ. ¶***good-natured (ill-natured) people*** 温良(意地悪)な人々. ¶a ***great many people*** 大多数の人々. ¶***grown-up people***=grownups 成人. ¶***high-class people*** 上流の人々. ¶a ***home-loving people*** 家庭を愛する国民. ¶***How many people*** do you suppose there are in the city? その市の人口はどの位だと思いますか. ¶***illustrious people*** 名士連. ¶the ***imaginary people*** of his plot 彼の話の筋に現われた仮想人物. ¶***impressionable people*** 感受性の強い人々. ¶an ***inquiring people*** 研究心の強い国民. ¶***intelligent people*** 賢明な人々. ¶the ***laboring people***=laborers 労働者. ¶a ***law-abiding people*** 法律を遵守する国民. ¶***like-minded people*** 同志. ¶The Chinese are above all a ***literary people.*** 中国人は殊に文学的国民である. ‖ a club where ***literary people*** for[e]gather 文士連の会合するクラブ. ¶***low-down people*** 野卑な人々. ¶***mediocre people*** 並の人々. ¶***moneyed people*** 金持連. ¶***Most people*** think so. 大ていの人はそう思う. ¶a less ***narrow*** and less ***selfish people*** それほど偏狭でも利己的でもない国民. ¶***necessitous people*** 貧民. ¶***needy people***=the needy 貧困者たち. ¶***organized peoples*** 組織ある諸国民. ¶I don't care a damn what ***other people*** would say about it. 人がなんと言おうと私はちっとも構わない. ¶a school for ***out-of-school people*** 通信教授学校. ¶a man of her ***own people*** 彼女の仲間の男の人. ¶a ***peaceful people*** 平和な人民. ¶a ***peace-loving people*** 平和愛好国民. ¶The ***people present*** numbered a thousand. 出席者は千に達した. ¶a ***progressive*** and ***energetic people*** 進歩的で元気な国民. ¶***quiet people*** living in quiet corners of the earth 静かな世界のすみに住む静かな人々. ¶***rascally people***=rascals 悪いやつら. ¶We are a ***reading people.*** われわれは読書好きの国民である. ¶***religious people*** 善男善女. ¶Though poor, they are ***respectable people.*** 貧乏だが正直でいい人たちだ. ¶The Japanese are a ***reticent people.*** 日本人は寡黙な国民だ. ¶***salaried people*** 月給取り. ¶The British people have generally been a ***scholarly people.*** 英国人は概して学者的国民であった. ¶the ***Scotch people*** スコットランド国民. ¶The Japanese were a ***self-excluded people.*** 日本は鎖国をしていた. ¶***sensible people*** 良識ある人々. 【類】 ***Sensible people*** understand it as soon as [it is] said. With fools it is not worth while to argue. ¶***sharp (slow)-witted people*** 頭の鋭(鈍)い人々. ¶***serious, demure people*** まじめ一方の人々. ¶***sick people***=the sick 病人. ¶The Japanese are a ***splendid people*** when you get to know them. 日本人はよくわかって見るとすばらしい国民だ. ¶***squalid people*** 見すぼらしい人々. ¶***stupid people*** おろかな連中. ¶***Superstitious people*** believe that the harsh cry of a crow forebodes evil. 迷信家はからす鳴きが悪いと凶だと信じている. ¶***thinking people*** 思想家たち, 思慮深い人々. ¶***thoughtful, conservative people*** 思慮深い控え目な人々. ¶***time-serving worldly people*** 時勢に迎合する世なれた人々. ¶an ***undersized people*** 並外れて小さい民族. ¶***unliterary people*** 文字のない(文盲な)連中. ¶***unreflecting*** and ***uncritical peoples*** 無分別で鑑識力のない諸国民. ¶***unschooled*** and ***unlettered people*** 無学文盲の輩. ¶a ***vain people*** 虚栄的な国民. ¶The Saxons were a ***warlike people,*** who minded fighting more than writing. サクソン人は文よりも武を重んじた好戦的民族であった. ¶***wellbred people*** 育ちの良い人々. ¶***well-educated people*** 教育の高い人々. ¶***well-intentioned people*** 善意のある人々. ¶***white people*** 白人. ¶The southerners are the most ***wide-awake people*** in China. 中国では南部の人々が一番目ざめている. ¶***working people*** 労働者. ¶The Caucasians are the ***world's dominant people.*** 白人は世界で最優勢の人種だ. ¶curfews on ***young people*** 若者の夜間外出禁止.

Q[2] British ***Army people*** remaining in India インド駐在の英陸軍関係者. ¶***city people*** 都会人. ¶***church people*** 教会人. ¶***country people*** 地方人. ¶***custom-house people*** 税関吏. ¶***front-page people*** [新聞の一面に出る]一流の人々. ¶the "***have not***" ***peoples*** (="have-nots") of the world 世界の持たざる国民. ¶urban ***middle-class people*** 都会の中産階級[の人々]. ¶***non-Communist peoples*** 非共産諸国民. ¶***picture people*** 映画人. ¶***poultry people*** 養鶏家. ¶***second-rate people*** 二流の人々. ¶***summer people*** 避暑客. ¶***trade people*** 商人; 職人. ¶***upper-class people*** 上流階級の人々.

P ***among*** educated ***people*** 識者間に. 【類】 ***Among*** the ***people*** at the party, I did not know a single person. ‖ It stimulated the spirit of gambling ***among*** the ***people*** at large. それが一般国民の射幸心を刺激した. ¶***As*** a ***people*** the Chinese cling strongly to tradition. 国民としての中国人は強く伝統に執着する. ¶Unfortunately there is no court of appeal in affairs ***between peoples.*** 不幸にして国民間の事件にはこれを裁く上告裁判所というものがない. ¶Proverbs, like ballads, are the voice ***of*** a ***people,*** not of an individual person. 俗謡と同様ことわざは個人の声ではなくて国民の声である. ‖ the general (common) run ***of people*** 並の人. ¶government ***of*** the ***people, by*** the ***people,*** and ***for*** the ***people*** 人民の, 人民による, 人民のための政治 (Lincoln の Gettysburg Address の中の句). ¶He is always mild-spoken ***to*** his ***people.*** 彼はいつも配下には口のきき方がやさしい.

P[2] all the ***peoples of*** the earth 地球上のすべての民族 ‖ the ***peoples of*** Europe 欧州の諸民族 ‖ ***people of*** means 資産家 ‖ ***people of*** quality 高貴(位)の人々 ‖ a ***people of*** water-drinkers 禁酒国民.

O his ***people*** 彼をひいきにする人々; 彼の部下; 彼の家族. 【類】 My ***people*** live in the country. ¶Hawaiians are a ***people,*** not a nation. ハワイ人は民族で国民じゃない.

people, *v.* 在存させる.

M be ***densely (sparsely) peopled*** 人口ちゅう密(稀薄)である. 【類】 South America is ***sparsely peopled.*** ¶be ***thickly (thinly) peopled*** 人口ちゅう密(稀薄)である.

P The asylums are ***peopled with*** something like 100,000. それらの精神病院にはおよそ十万の人がはいっている.

pepper, *v.* こしょうをふり掛ける.

P ***peppered with*** technical terms and phrases [文章・演説など]専門的の語句の盛んに出てくる ‖ The speaker was ***peppered with*** awkward questions 弁士はやっかいな質問をあびせかけられた.

perceivable, *a.* 感知できる.

P things ***perceivable by*** the senses 感覚で分かる物.

perceive, *v.* 感知する, 看取する.

M It appears that he ***dimly perceived*** that his time to go (=die) had come. 彼は死期が来たということを薄々悟ったと見える. ¶ ***easily perceive*** 容易に見てとる.

P *perceive* ***by*** the ear (nose, eye) 耳(など)で感知する.

per cent, percent, *n.* 百每, 分, パーセント;《口語》パーセンテージ.

V Twenty *per cent* were ***dropped*** in the examination. 試験で二割不合格になった. ¶ The company is ***earning*** a bare one *per cent* on its stock. 会社はその株に対しようよう一分の利益を収めている. ¶ ***pay*** 10 *per cent.* on the capital 資本に対して一割の配当をする. ¶ Michigan ***provides*** 75 *per cent* of the annual output of motor vehicles in the U.S.A. ミシガン州では合衆国における毎年の自動車産出高の七割五分を供給する. ¶ ***return*** at least 25% on the investment 少くとも投資の二割五分の利がつく. ¶ ***save*** 20% on ... ...に対して二割節約する. ☞ per cent. (=per centum) は公文書以外は per cent, percent とする方が普通.

O Only a ***small percent*** (=percentage) of the class was (*or* were) there.—Writer's Guide.《口語》クラスには少数しかいなかった.

P In the case of rain fares are increased ***by*** about forty-five *percent.* 雨天の際は賃銀は約四割五分増しになる.

P² 200 *percent* ***above*** prewar rates 戦前の二倍. ¶ amount to some twenty or thirty *percent* ***of*** the whole 全体の約二三割に上る. ¶ Ten *percent* ***on*** the retail price is the most common figure. 小売値段の一割がごく普通だ.

percentage, *n.* 百分率(パーセンテージ); 割合; 一部分.

V ***comprise*** a large *percentage* of ... ...の大部分を包含する. ¶ ***constitute*** a large *percentage* of ... ...の大部分を成す. ¶ The liquor ***contains*** a small (high) *percentage* of alcohol. その酒はアルコール分が少な(多)い. ¶ ***form*** a large *percentage* of ... ...の大部分を成す. ¶ War is not an occupation in which death is certain, but only one in which the *percentage* of risk is greatly ***raised.*** 戦争という仕事は出れば必ず死ぬとは限らないがただ危険率は非常に高まる. ¶ ***reach*** the high *percentage* of 63 六割三分の高率に達する. ¶ He ***received*** a large *percentage.* 彼は沢山の歩合をもらった. ¶ ***retain*** the higher *percentage* of volatile matter 高率の揮発物を保留する. ¶ Of all ... ***shows*** the greatest *percentage.* 全部の中で ... が最高率を示している. 【類】a chart (図表) ***showing*** *percentage* among the 1,530 students using the library.

Q an ***appreciable*** *percentage* of ... ...のかなりの歩合. ¶ a ***fixed annual*** *percentage* on their capital 彼らの資本に対する一定した年歩. ¶ a ***good*** *percentage* of ... ...のかなりの数(量). 【類】A ***good*** *percentage* of the immigrants coming to America have never left the neighborhood of the City of New York. ¶ A ***great*** *percentage* of the automobiles produced in Japan are intended for export. 国産自動車の大半は輸出向である. 【類】the *percentage* is ***greater*** in ... than ... ¶ a ***heavy*** *percentage* of ... ...の著しい割合. ¶ He has succeeded in achieving a ***high*** *percentage* of cures. 彼の手で全治した患者の数は高率を示している. ¶ in a ***large*** (***small***) *percentage* of cases 大部分(少数)の場合に. 【類】A ***large*** *percentage* of the people are illiterate. ¶ reduce to a ***low*** *percentage* 低率に引下げる. ¶ a ***negligible*** *percentage* of the total 全体のほんの小部分. ¶ Those are ***remarkable*** *percentages.* それはすばらしい率だ. ¶ a pitifully ***small*** *percentage* なさけないほどの低率. ¶ ***What*** *percentage* of children of school age attend school in Japan? 日本では学齢児童の何割が就学しているか.

Q² a ***decimal point*** *percentage* of the total 合計の小数点以上の率. ¶ high ***literacy*** *percentage* 読み書きの能力の高率. ¶ ***mortality*** *percentage* 死亡率. ¶ ***Unemployment*** *percentage* rises. 未就業率が上る.

P figures shown ***in*** *percentages* (グラフなどで)割合を示した数字. ¶ ***on account of*** the high *percentage* of alcohol they contain それらはアルコールの含有率が高いので. ¶ He won the prize ***with*** the highest *percentage* of marks. 彼は最高点で受賞した.

P² a *percentage* ***of*** profit 利得の歩合. ¶ *percentage* ***of*** expenses ***to*** gross receipts 経費と総収入との割合. ¶ a *percentage* or commission ***on*** the turnover 総売上高の歩合.

perception, *n.* 感知; 知覚力.

V ***have*** an intuitive *perception* of ... ...を直覚する.

V² His *perception* of ... ***came*** in a flash. 彼は...の直感がひらめいた.

Q the ***intuitive*** *perception* of the poet 詩人の直覚. ¶ ***keen*** *perception* 鋭敏な知覚力. ¶ a ***lightning-like*** *perception* ひらめく知覚. ¶ a man of ***quick*** *perception* わかりの早い人.

P things ***beyond*** (=***above***) human *perception* 人知の及ばないこと.

perch, *v.* 止まる; 高所に据える.

P A bird *perched* ***on*** a tree. 鳥が木に止まった. 【類】A number of birds are *perching* ***on*** the telegraph wires. ‖ *perch* ***on*** a stool 丸いすに腰をおろす. ¶ The fortress is *perched* ***upon*** a mountain difficult of access. そのとりでは登り難い山の上にある.

percolate, *v.* こす, ふるう.

P *percolate* powder ***through*** a sieve 粉をふるいにかける. 【類】*percolate* water ***through*** sand.

O *percolate* coffee コーヒーをたてる.

percolator, *n.* [コーヒーの]パーコレーター.

O use a *percolator* to brew coffee コーヒーをたてるためにパーコレーターを使う.

perdition, *n.* 地獄.

Q ***bottomless*** *perdition* 底知らずの地獄.

P Go ***to*** *perdition* (=hell)! くたばりぞこないめ.

peregrination, *n.* 遊歴, 漫遊.

P² *peregrinations* ***in*** Eastern lands 東洋諸国の遊歴.

perennial, *a.* 不断の.

P be *perennial* ***in*** its interest 興味は尽きない.

perfect, *a.* 完全な, 円満な, 申分のない.

M ***fairly*** *perfect* かなり完全な. ¶ ***100 per cent*** *perfect* 全く申し分のない. ¶ He is a ***quite*** *perfect* gentleman. 彼は全くりっぱな紳士だ. ¶ ***relatively*** the most *perfect* 比較的最も完全な(もの).

P *perfect* ***in*** form 形の申分のない.

O You're *perfect* fool.《口語》お前は救いがたいばかだ.

perfect, *v.* 完全にする.

P He has *perfected* himself ***in*** the German language. 彼はドイツ語を完全にものにした.

perfection, *n.* 完全, 完備; 至極.

V most nearly ***approach*** *perfection* 一番完全の域に近づく. ¶ ***attain*** *perfection* 完全の域に達する. 【類】It ***attained*** its greatest (=highest) *perfection.* ¶ Don't ***expect*** *perfection* in a servant. 召使のものに完全を期待するな. ¶ You will ***find*** *perfection* of accommodation, service, and cuisine at the hotel. あのホテルへ行けば設備やサービスや料理の申分のないことが分かる. ¶ It ***makes*** *perfection* more perfect. そうすれば錦上さらに花を添える. ¶ ***reach*** *perfection* 完全の域に達する. ¶ ***touch*** *perfection* 完全の域に達する.

Q attain ***considerable*** *perfection* かなり完備する. ¶ arrive at a ***high*** *perfection* 大いに完備する ‖ can reach no ***higher*** *perfection* これ以上の完全は望まれない ‖ attain its ***highest*** *perfection* この上もなく完備する.

P The blossoms are ***at*** their full *perfection.* 花は真っ盛りだ. ¶ The flowers are now ***in*** *perfection.* 花は今盛りだ. ¶ be as ***near*** *perfection* as possible できるだけ完全に近い. ¶ the highest pitch ***of*** *perfection* この上もない完全 ‖ the present wonderful state ***of*** *perfection* 現在の驚くべき完備の状態. ¶ She cooks ***to*** *perfection.* 彼女はりっぱに料理ができる. ‖ The parrot imitates the sound ***to*** *perfection.* おおむはその音声を完全にまねる. ‖ attain ***to*** *perfection* 完全の域に達する. 【類】bring it ***to*** *perfection* / can do it ***to*** *perfection* / It fitted her ***to*** *perfection.* / Your habit (乗馬服) shows off your figure ***to*** *perfection.*

perfidious, *a.* 不誠実な.

M That a brother should be ***so*** *perfidious*! こんな信実のない兄弟があるだろうか.

P *perfidious* ***to*** a person 人に対して不信実な.

perforation, *n.* 切取線.

P tear off ***at*** *perforation* 穴線の個所を切取る. ¶ The ticket is divided into three portions ***by*** *perforation.* 切符は切取線で三つに切り離される.

perform, *v.* 行う, 果たす; 演じる.

M He always *performs* his duties ***faithfully***. 彼はいつも自分の職分を忠実に果たす. ¶ It has been *performed* ***inimitably***. まねのできないようなでき栄である. ¶ ***mechanically*** *perform* it それをお役目的にやる. ¶ *perform* one's

part skilfully (=well) 自分の役を達者に勤める. ¶perform one's work ungrudgingly 自分の仕事を快くやる.
P perform a part on the stage 舞台で役を勤める. ¶a dance performed to music 音楽につれての舞踊.

performance, *n.* 履行; 演奏, 興行; 所業.
V attend a theatrical performance 芝居見物に行く ‖ attend the performances in a body 団体で見物する. ¶exhibit various, curious performances 色々変った芸を見せる. ¶give a performance of "Othello" オセロを上演する ‖ The musician gave her first Japanese performance. 彼女は日本での初演奏をやった. ‖ A second performance was given to accommodate the overflow. 満員で入場できなかった客のために第二回の興行を催した. ¶have a trial performance with the new play 新劇の試演をやる. ¶license the performance of a play 劇の上演を認可する.
Q give acrobatic performances 曲芸をやる. ¶a continuous performance 連続興行. ¶The translation is a very creditable performance. その翻訳は上できだ. ¶give two distinct performances a day 一日二回興行をやる. ¶A security must be obtained for the due performance of the contract. 契約の適正履行のための保証を得なければならない. ¶an entirely fake performance 全くのいんちき興行. ¶Richard Wagner festival performances ワグナー祭興行. ¶a fetching performance 人気を引く興行. ¶give free performances 無料興行を催す. ¶a gala performance お祭り興行. ¶The paper of Mr. ... is quite a good performance. ...氏の論文は全くりっぱなできだ. ¶a gymnastic performance 機械体操. ¶an inaugural performance 初日興行. ¶the joint performance of several artists 画家数名の合作. ¶a lifeless performance 気の抜けた芸. ¶a musical performance [音楽]演奏(独唱を含む). ¶poor performance 不成績. ¶a senseless performance ばか気た演芸. ¶skilful performance 巧みな演芸. ¶great promise and small performance 大きな約束に小さい実行. ¶the successful and expeditious performance of the many activities of ... ...という色々な活動の上首尾でじん速な遂行. ¶superb performance 至高の芸. ¶theatrical performance 演劇. ¶a vocal performance 声楽演奏.
Q² an afternoon (evening) performance 午後(夕べ)の興行. ¶a band performance バンドの演奏. ¶a committee formed to aid ticket sales for the benefit performance 慈善興行の入場券販売助成委員. ¶the Eightieth Congress performance 第八十議会の成績. ¶a concert (=symphony) performance 音楽会の演奏. ¶a farewell performance おなごり興行. ¶a first-night performance [興行の]初日. ¶give a free matinee performance for ... ...のため無料昼間興行をやる. ¶a motion picture performance 一回の映画上映. ¶a press performance [新聞記者招待の]紹介興行. ¶a royal command performance 天覧興行. ¶a two-picture performance 二本立興行.
P They had crowded houses at every performance. 興行ごとに大入であった. ¶security to be given for the performance of a contract 契約履行のために与えられるべき保証. ¶interfere with an officer in the performance of his duty 官吏の執務に干渉する.
P² interesting performances in the circus サーカスでの面白い演技 ‖ his performances in high school 彼の高校の成績. ¶the performance of one's trust 使命遂行.

performer, *n.* 演技者, 演奏者.
Q In a strip show female performers reduce the amount of clothing to the vanishing point. ストリップショーでは女の演技者が最後の一点まで衣服をぬぐ. ¶He is a good performer on the flute. 彼は笛がうまい. ¶a musical performer 演奏者. ¶a professional performer 芸人. ¶a sleight-of-hand performer 手品師. ¶a vocal performer 声楽家.
Q² stage, motion-picture, and radio performers 劇, 映画及び放送芸能人. ¶a street performer 大道芸人.
P² aerial performers at the circus サーカスの空中曲芸師. ¶a skilful performer on the violin ヴァイオリンの名人.

perfume, *n.* 香; 香料, 香水.
V exhale a pleasant perfume 芳香を発散する. ¶give a subtle alluring perfume to clothing [香料などが]衣服に淡いほれぼれするような香をつける. ¶give off (=emit) a pleasing perfume 芳香を放つ. ¶It has the perfume of violets. それはすみれの香がする. ¶The toothpowder imparts a most pleasant perfume to the breath. その歯みが粉は息(いき)を大へん芳ばしくする. ¶She inhaled the violet perfume, saying "How sweet!" 彼女はすみれの香を吸いこみながら「まあいい香り」と言った. ¶possess an agreeable perfume 芳香を持っている. ¶spray perfume over ... ...に香水をふりかける. ¶use perfume 香水を用いる.
Q floral perfume 花から採った香料. ¶liquid perfume 香水. ¶It has the pleasant perfume of the ume blossom それは芳ばしい梅の花の香がする. ¶send forth their sweet and radiant perfume そのすばらしいにおいを発散する. ¶synthetic perfumes 人工香料.
P It is used in perfumes. それは香料の製造に使う. ¶It was mixed with perfume of the flowers. それに花の香を混ぜた.

perfume, *v.* 香をつける, かおらせる.
M delicately perfumed 芳ばしい香を付けた. ¶violently perfumed 強い香を付けた.
P perfume oneself with musk じゃ香で身をかおらせる. 【類】perfume one's garment (handherchief) with eau-de-Cologne (オードコロン).

peril, *n.* 危険.
V How can the peril be averted? どうすれば危険が避けられるか. ¶avoid the peril of ... ...の危険を避ける. ¶dare the perils of arctic travel 北極旅行の危険をおかす. ¶escape an impending peril 危い所を免れる. ¶face the frosty peril of the high Himalayas ヒマラヤ高山の厳寒の危険をおかす.
Q a deadly peril 恐ろしい危険. ¶there is great peril in ... ...するのは大危険がある. ¶The ship was in imminent peril of being wrecked. 船は今にも難破しようとしていた. ¶a marine peril 海上の危険. ¶a national peril 亡国論. ¶a threatening peril 降りかかっている危険. ¶It involves untold peril to all concerned. それは関係者一同に無限の危険をもたらすことになる. ¶the yellow peril 黄禍.
P Do it at your peril. すると危いぞ(危いからよせ). ‖ Keep off at your peril. 危いから離れていろ. ‖ Resist at your peril. 手向いすると危いぞ. ‖ at the peril of his life=at the penalty of death 彼の生命をとして. 【類】Approach a step nearer at the peril of your life. ¶His life is in peril.=He is in peril of his life. 彼は生命が危い. 【類】He was constantly in peril of death from hunger. ¶A seafaring life is full of perils. 海上生活は危険が多い. ¶on peril of their lives 彼らの生命をとして.

perimeter, *n.* 周囲.
Q² the chest perimeter 胸囲.

period, *n.* 時期, 時代; 時間; 終止; *pl.* 月経.
V The report covers a period of 12 months. その報告書は十二カ月の期間にわたっている. 【類】covering (にわたって) the period from ... to ... / His experience of teaching English covers a period of over (=extends over more than) thirty years. ¶extend the period of availability (切符などの)有効期間を延長する. ¶We have four periods before noon today. きょうは午前中四時間(学業が)あります. ¶She has her periods (=is unwell). 彼女は月経中だ. ¶overstay one's period of furlough 賜暇の期限を過ごす. ¶prolong the period その期間を延長する. ¶put a period (=stop) to a letter かく筆する ‖ I mean to put a period to this prodigality. 私はこんなむだ使いは止めにしようと思う. 【類】Gold from sea-water will have the effect of putting a period to ordinary gold mining. ¶shorten the period of convalescence 回復期を短縮する(早く回復する). ¶tide over a highly critical period 非常な危期を乗越す.
V² as her periods did not appear 彼女の月経がなかったので.
Q during the acute period of the disease 病気の募っている間は. ¶at all periods of our history わが国の歴史のいつの時代にも. ¶in a brief period later その後しばらくして ‖ in a brief period of time 短期に. ¶a brilliant period of Chinese history 中国歴史の花々しい時代. ¶during a certain period 一定の期間. ¶at the climacteric period 厄年に, 危機に. ¶during a considerable period 相当長期間. ¶He is now in a constructive period of his life. 彼は今一生の建設期にある. ¶The figure shows an increase in production of about one third above that of the corresponding period of last year. その数字は昨年同期の産出高の約三分の一増加を示している. ¶the most critical period of our relations with ... ...とのわれわれの関係の最危期. ¶at

this ***crucial period*** この重大な時期に際して. ¶Japanese costume at ***different periods*** 色々の時代における日本の服装 ‖ It is composed of many parts, erected at ***different periods***. それは色々の時代に建てた多くの部分から成っている. 【類】This edition contains three portraits of Mr. Browning at ***different periods*** of life. ¶the ***dry*** (***wet***) ***period*** of the year 一年中の雨のない(多い)季節. ¶an ***early period*** in history 歴史の初期. 【類】at an ***earlier period*** / at the ***earliest period*** (太古). ¶at the ***eighth period*** (授業の)第八時限に. ¶occur at ***fixed periods*** 一定期間をおいて起る. ¶the most ***fruitful period*** of his literary career 氏の文学的生がいの中で最も多作の時代. ¶after a ***further period*** of three years それから三年たって. ¶the most ***glorious period*** of ... ...の最も光輝ある時期. ¶a ***happy period*** 幸福な時期. ¶the ***hostile period*** [主義などに対する]反抗の時代. ¶***impressionable period*** of life 一生の最も印象を受けやすい時期. ¶for an ***incalculable period*** of time 数字では表わせないような長い期間. ¶an ***indefinite period*** of time 無期限. ¶the ***indifferent*** and ***apathetic period*** [主義などに対する]無関心無とん着の時代. ¶unsuitable alimentation during the ***lactational period*** ほ乳期間の不適当な栄養方法. ¶the ***latent*** (=incubation) ***period*** 病の潜伏期. ¶in a ***later period*** その後に. 【類】the very ***latest period*** of ... ¶the ***legendary period*** 伝説時代. ¶for a ***lengthy period*** of time 長い間. ¶stretch over the ***long*** and ***eventful period*** from ... ...以来の長い多事な時代にわたる. ¶***main periods*** and sub-periods 主なる時期と二次的の時期. ¶the ***majestic periods*** of Burke and Johnson バークやジョンソンの威風堂々たる時代. ¶a ***momentous period*** of their lives 彼らの生がいの大切な時代. ¶in an ***older period*** of the language 同国語のさらに古い時代には. ¶at ***one period*** ある時期に. ¶in the early ***postwar period*** 戦後間もなく. 【類】during the war years and the ***postwar period***. ¶the ***pre-Confucian period*** 孔子以前の時代. ¶the ***pre-adolescent period*** 未成年時代. ¶the ***prehistoric***, ***ancient*** and ***medieval periods*** 有史以前と古代と中世の時代. ¶the ***pre-harvest period*** 端境期. ¶the ***pre-school period*** 学齢前. ¶at the ***present period*** 現時において. 【類】in the ***present period*** of the English language. ¶He will receive £7 a week for his ***probationary period;*** afterwards, if proficient, rising to £30 a week. 見習期間中は彼に一週七ポンドを給し熟練の上は一週三十ポンドまで給する(工場などの規約). ¶enter into a more ***prosperous period*** 一層隆盛な時代にはいる. ¶at a very ***remote period*** 非常に遠い昔に. 【類】Scientists have lately proven that at some ***remote period*** Australia, America, and Africa were all one continent. ¶at the ***same period*** of time 同じ時期に. ¶Against the above record what has the ***second period*** to show? 第一期の以上の成績に対し第二期はどんなことになるだろうか. ¶the ***short period*** of the life of man 人類の短い生がい ‖ The wind lulled for a ***short period***. 風はちょっとの間やんだ. ¶the ***Socratic period*** ソクラテス時代. ¶at ***some period*** or other いつか一度は. ¶at ***some early period*** ある古い時代に. ¶at ***some unknown period*** いずれの時にか. ¶at ***stated periods*** 一定の時期に. ¶during the ***stormy period*** of the French Revolution フランス革命の波らん重畳の間. ¶during the ***stressful period*** of the Taiping Rebellion 太平賊(長髪賊)の乱の緊張した期間に. ¶a ***turbulent period*** of our history わが歴史中の動乱時代. ¶at ***various periods*** 様々の時代に. ¶Vermeer began to paint when he was young, and painted till the end, and had a ***working period*** of, say, twenty-four years. ヴェルメーアは若いときに絵を描き始め生がい丹青に親しみまず二十四年の活動期間があった. ¶the ***youthful period*** of Lincoln リンカンの青年時代.

Q² in "***boom***" ***periods*** when labor is scarce 労働者の払底しているにわか景気の時期に. ¶the ***border-line period*** 端境期. ¶The maximum ***child-bearing period*** of a woman is about thirty years. 婦人の最長産児期間は約三十年である. ¶the ***cooling period*** 〘労〙冷却期間. ¶provide for a sixty day ***cooling-off period*** before strikes スト前に六十日の冷却期間をおく. ¶be inspired with the spirit of the ***emergency period*** 非常時精神を鼓吹されている. ¶an ***examination period*** 試験施行期. ¶at a ***future period*** 将来のある時機において. ¶the ***gestation period*** 妊娠期間. ¶A ***grace period*** of thirty-one days is allowed after the due date of payment 支払期限後三十一日間の猶予期間を許される. ¶the ***growing period*** 成長期. ¶during the ***harvest period*** とり入れの期間に. ¶the Christmas ***holiday period*** クリスマス休暇[期間]. ¶the ***incubation*** (=latent) ***period of*** a disease 病気の潜伏期. ¶in (during) the ***interim period*** その中間期に. ¶Pay is furnished during the ***learning period*** 見習期間中給与を支給される. ¶the ***lying-in period*** [妊婦の]とこづきの期間. ¶a ***meal period*** 食事時間. ¶as the ***occupation period*** ends 占領期間が終ると. ¶during the ***off-season period*** 季節はずれの間. ¶extend a ***payment period*** 支払期限を延ばす. ¶a ***pioneer period*** 開拓時代. ¶a ***probation period*** 試届(見習)期間. ¶the ***reconstruction period*** 再建時代. ¶through the war years and ***reconversion period*** 戦時及び復旧の期間を通じて. ¶a ***rest period*** 休憩時間. ¶come to the ***ripening period*** 円熟期にはいる. ¶a ***school period*** [授業の]一校時. ¶most favorable ***selling period*** 販売にもっとも都合のよい時期. ¶during the ***five-year period***, 1920-24 一九二〇年から二四年までの五カ年間に. 【類】over a ***four-month period***. ¶a ***settlement period*** 出納整理期. ¶in the ***thirty-seven-month period*** between May, 1943, and June, 1946 一九四三年の五月から一九四六年六月の三十七カ月間に. ¶be still in the ***transition period*** toward a peacetime economy 今なお平和経済への過渡期である. ¶set the ***turning period*** as February of 1936 転換期を一九三六年二月と定める. ¶a ***vacation period*** 休暇期間. ¶during the ***war period***, 1914-18 一九一四年から十八年の戦時中. ¶the "***Warring Country***" ***period*** 戦国時代. ¶a ***work period*** 勤務期間. ¶during the ***World War period*** 世界大戦中. ¶We have four ***40-minute periods*** of lessons before noon. 午前中は四十分授業が四時限ある. ¶the ***12 month period*** ending June 30 六月三十日までの十二カ月間.

P ***at*** the ***period*** of their entrance upon the stage of history 彼らが歴史の舞台に登場した時代に ‖ ***at*** the ***period*** of menstruation 月経時に ‖ ***at*** the ***period*** of adolescence 青春期に ‖ ***at*** this ***period*** of life 人生のこの時期に. 【類】***at*** this ***period*** in modern history. ¶***before*** the written ***period*** 有史以前に. ¶***during*** the last ten-year ***period*** 最近十年間. 【類】***during*** the first ***period*** of the progress of Christianity in Japan / ***during*** the first ***period*** of his authorship. ¶***for*** the ***period*** of the war その戦争中 ‖ ***for*** the ***period*** (=space) of one year 一年間. ¶***from*** a ***period*** of great antiquity 大昔から. ¶***in*** a brief ***period*** of two or three days わずか二三日にして ‖ ***in*** the ***period*** of the Tokugawa Shogunate 徳川幕府の時代に. 【類】***In*** the classic ***period*** of the Tang dynasty (唐朝) China was at its greatest, perhaps the most civilized, power in the world. ¶from a contemporary print ***of*** the ***period*** by ... ...の筆になるその時代の絵草紙で見ると. ¶***with periods*** of ebb and flow 浮沈を経て. ¶***within*** the ***period*** covered by the ticket 切符の有効期限内に.

P² a transition ***period between*** the old day and the new 新旧時代の過渡期. ¶at one of the most critical ***periods in*** our annals わが歴史中最も危急な一時期に. ¶when the ***period of*** his apprenticeship was over 彼の年季が終った時に ‖ the ***period of*** incubation (=latency) [病気の]潜伏期 ‖ The ***period of*** instruction will cover about four months. 教授期間は約四カ月にわたる. ‖ the ***period of*** beginnings 初期. 【類】a ***period of*** adversity (失意の時代), extending over nearly twenty years / The ***period of*** his literary activity covers ... years. ‖ the ***period of*** incarceration 入所(監察)期間 ‖ the ***period of*** office 任期 ‖ a ***period of*** repression (resistance) 圧迫(など)の期間.

periodical, *n*. 定期刊行物. 「期刊行物を出す.

V ***issue periodicals***, weekly and monthly 週刊と月刊の定

Q ***current periodicals*** 今月号の雑誌類. ¶sixpenny and threepenny ***illustrated periodicals*** 六ペンスと三ペンスのさし絵入雑誌. ¶a ***technical periodical*** 工業雑誌. ¶a ***weekly periodical*** 週刊雑誌.

P subscribe ***for*** a ***periodical*** 雑誌の予約をする. ¶send (obtain) a subscription ***to*** a ***periodical*** 雑誌の購読を申込 └む(予約する).

periphrasis, *n*. 言回し; 遠回しの語.

V ***use*** a ***periphrasis*** 遠回しに言う.

Q a ***cumbrous periphrasis*** わずらわしい言回し. ¶a favorite *journalistic periphrasis* 新聞でよく使う間接表現法. ¶a *vague periphrasis* あいまいな言回し.

perish, *v*. 死ぬ; 滅亡する.

M He ***miserably perished***. 彼は悲惨な最後を遂げた.

P He *perished* ***by*** the sword. 彼は刃にかかってたおれた. ‖ *perish* ***by*** (=with) famine ききんで死ぬ. ¶A large number of his men *perished* ***from*** hunger and thirst. 多数の彼の部下が飢渇のためにたおれた. ¶He *perished* ***in*** the flames. 彼は焼け死んだ. ‖ he *perished* ***in*** the battle of ... 彼は...の戦で戦死した. ¶*perish* ***of*** hunger (cold) 餓(凍)死する ‖ *perish* ***of*** inaction 使用しないためにしなびる ‖ An art *perishes* ***of*** stagnation. 芸術は沈滞によって滅亡する. ¶He preserved your seed in the ark of Noah, that your race might not *perish* ***out of*** the world. 彼はノアの箱舟に人間の種を保存し人類が世界から絶えないようにした. ¶The force *perished* ***to*** a man in the battle. その部隊はその戦闘で一人残らず戦死した. ¶*perish* ***with*** a disease 病気で死ぬ. 【類】*perish* ***with*** heat / *perish* ***with*** cold and dry weather.

perjury, *n*. 偽証罪.

V ***commit*** [a] *perjury* 偽証罪を犯す.

perk, *v*. 元気づく.

M be *perked* ***out*** in her best 晴衣で着飾っている.

M[2] Business is *perking* ***up***. 商売は上向きだ. ‖ You will soon *perk* ***up***, quite ready to start again. すぐ元気がついて結構また仕事が始められるよ.

perm, *v*. 《米口》パーマをかける.

M have [got] her hair ***beautifully*** *permed* 頭に美しくパーマをかける.

O with *permed* hair パーマをかけて.

perm[anent], *n*. 《口語》パーマ.

Q I got a ***darling*** *perm[anent]*. 自分の気に入ったようにパーマをかけてもらったわ.

permeate, *v*. しみ通る.

P The whole is *permeated* ***by*** an atmosphere of refinement and cheerfulness. 優雅と快活の空気が全体にみなぎっている. ¶The air is *permeated* ***with*** smoke. 煙が空中に充満している. ‖ be *permeated* ***with*** this complex このコンプレックス(複合観念)に支配されている.

permissible, *a*. 許さるべき.

P Provincialisms and colloquialisms are *permissible* ***in*** conversation. 会話では地方語やくだけた表現が許されている.

permission, *n*. 許可, 免許; 免許証.

V *permission* has been ***accorded*** the members of the club to ... そのクラブ員は...の許可を得た. ¶***ask*** the *permission* of ... to ... ...に...の許可を願う. 【類】***Ask*** *permission* of your parents. / on ***asking*** *permission* / without ***asking*** my *permission*. ¶***get*** *permission* to ... ...する許可を得る. ¶***give*** *permission* to ... for ... ...に...の許可を与える. 【類】He has ***given*** me *permission* to use his library. ¶***grant*** *permission* 許可する. ¶I ***have*** *permission* to see the Imperial Palace. 私は宮城拝観の許しを得ている. ‖ You ***have*** my *permission*. 許してあげる. ¶***obtain*** (=***procure***) *permission* for ... ...の許可を得る. 【類】***obtain*** *permission* to do something. ¶Can you ***procure*** *permission* for me to photograph it? それを撮影する許可を得るようにしていただけないでしょうか. ¶***receive*** *permission* to ... ...すべき許可を受ける. ¶***secure*** *permission* 許可を得る. ¶***withdraw*** a *permission* 許可を撤回する.

Q by the ***courteous*** *permission* of ... ...の懇篤な許可得をて. ¶by ***kind*** *permission* of the proprietors of "Whitaker's Almanac"「ウィテーカー年鑑」社の厚意ある許可を得て. ¶The article is reproduced here by his ***obliging*** *permission*. その論文は氏の懇篤な許可を得てここに転載したものである. ¶a ***personal*** *permission* [著者から編集者への]直接の許可. ¶an article reproduced by the ***special*** *permission* of ... ...の特別の許可を得て転載した文. ¶by ***tacit*** *permission* 黙許で. ¶a ***written*** *permission* 許可書.

P ***by*** *permission* 許しを得て ‖ ***by*** your *permission* (=allowance) 失礼ですが. 【類】***by*** *permission* of the Government. ¶ask ***for*** *permission* 許可を願う. ¶***on*** special *permission* 特許の上で. ¶I should prefer—***with*** your *permission*—to do that myself. お差支えなければ私は自分で致したいのです. 【類】the book is dedicated, ***with*** *permission*, to ... ¶***without*** *permission* from ... ...からの許可なしに. 【類】***without*** Government *permission*.

P[2] *permission* ***for*** exportation 輸出の許可. ¶He could not obtain *permission* ***from*** the authorities. 彼はその筋から許可を得られなかった. ¶obtain *permission* ***of*** the authorities 当局の認可を得る.

permit, *n*. 許可, 免許; 免許証.

V ***get*** a *permit* 許可を得る. 【類】***get*** a police *permit*. ¶those ***holding*** a special *permit* from the Governor are allowed to ... 知事の特許状を所持するものは...することができる. ¶a *permit* for trading ***issued*** by the Japanese Shogun Iyeyasu in the year 1609 to the Dutch J. Grovenewegen 一六〇九年日本の将軍家康によってオランダの J. グルヴェネウェーヘンに対して発行された貿易免許状. ¶***obtain*** *permits* to copy or photograph objects in the collections [博物館などの]収集品を謄写しまたは撮影する許可を得る. ¶***receive*** a *permit* 免許を受ける. ¶Special *permit* ***required***. [注意書]特別の許可を要す. ¶***secure*** a *permit* 許可を得る.

Q obtain an ***angler's*** *permit* 魚つりの免許を得る. ¶obtain a ***special*** *permit* to ... ...する特別許可を得る.

Q[2] ***Building*** *permits* are granted by the City Building Department. 建築許可は都の建設局からおりる. ¶a ***driving*** *permit* 運転免許証. ¶an ***exit*** *permit* 外出許可書. ¶on a special ***government*** *permit* 政府からの特別許可によって. ¶an application for a ***reconstruction*** *permit* 再建設許可願い. ¶a ***residence*** *permit* 住居認可証. ¶a ***weekend outing*** *permit* 〚軍〛週末旅行許可証. ¶a ***work*** *permit* 作業許可.

P liquor-selling is prohibited unless ***by*** special *permit* from ... 酒類販売は...からの特別の許可がなくてはできない.

P[2] a *permit* ***for*** street speakers 大道演説者への許可. 【類】a *permit* ***for*** the weekend outing=a weekend outing permit. ¶a *permit* ***from*** the authorities 当局の許可.

permit, *v*. 許す; 放任する.

M ***gradually*** *permit* himself to ... 次第に自分でも...するようになる.

P Do not *permit* yourself ***in*** dissipation. 身を持くずすな. ¶The situation *permits* ***of*** no delay. 事態はいささかの猶予も許さない. ‖ the regulations do not *permit* ***of*** ... 規則が...を許さない ‖ a tool *permitting* ***of*** a variety of use 色色に使える道具 ‖ Nature *permits* ***of*** no alternative. 自然は他の方法を許さない. 【類】*permit* ***of*** no doubt / *permit* ***of*** no excuse / Your conduct *permits* ***of*** no further explanation.

O *Permit* (=Allow) me to explain. ¶so far as health *permits* 健康さえ許せば. 【類】when time *permits* / weather *permitting*.

pernicious, *a*. 有害な.

P *pernicious* ***to*** a person 人に有害な. 【類】a climate *pernicious* ***to*** health / an ideology *pernicious* ***to*** young minds.

perpendicular, *n*. 垂直線.

P ***out of*** the *perpendicular* 傾斜して.

perpendicular, *a*. 垂直の.

P Draw a line *perpendicular* ***to*** the given line. 与えられたる線に垂直の線を引け.

perpetrator, *n*. 下手人.

P[2] a *perpetrator* ***of*** an outrage 暴行の下手人.

perpetuate, *v*. 不朽に伝える.

P *perpetuate* ***in*** postage stamps the centenary of her political independence 郵便切手でその国の政治的独立の百年祭を永久に伝える. 【類】*perpetuate* one's name ***in*** history.

perpetuity, *n*. 永代.

P a lease ***in*** *perpetuity*=a perpetual lease 永代租借権 ‖ cede a territory ***in*** (=***to*** *or* ***for***) *perpetuity* 永久に領土を割譲する.

perplex, *v*. 当惑させる.

M I was ***sorely*** *perplexed* as to his intention. 私には彼の考えが一向分からなかった. ‖ be ***sorely*** *perplexed* to account for ... ...をどう説明してよいかひどく困っている.

P I was *perplexed* ***at*** ... 私は...に当惑した. ¶I was *perplexed* ***for*** an answer. 私は何と答えてよいか分からなかった. ¶He was *perplexed* ***over*** the situation. 彼はその事態に当惑した. ¶be *perplexed* ***with*** problems of ... ...の問題に悩んでいる.

perplexity, *n*. 紛糾, めんどう; めんどうな事項.

V ***clear up*** *perplexities* 紛糾を一掃する. ¶***face*** *perplexities* めんどうなことにぶつかって行く. ¶a man ***saw*** my *perplexity* and said ... ある人が私の当惑を見てとって...と言った.

V[2] The *perplexity* ***increases***. 事態がますます紛糾する.

Q the most ***discouraging*** *perplexities* ほんとにがっかりさせるような紛糾状態.

P He scratched his head ***in*** *perplexity*. 彼は当惑して頭を

かいた.【類】***In*** *perplexity* he was accustomed to say "Nuts!"

P² a matter ***of*** *perplexity* めんどうなこと.

persecute, *v.* 悩ます, 迫害する.

P be *persecuted* ***by*** his creditors 債鬼にせめ立てられる.【類】be *persecuted* ***by*** silly questions. ¶*persecute* a person ***with*** questions 質問して人を困らせる.

persecution, *n.* 迫害.

V ***institute*** a vigorous *persecution* 強硬な迫害を始める. ¶They ***suffered*** terrible *persecution.* 彼らは恐るべき迫害を受けた.

V² *Persecution* ***arose.*** 迫害が起った.

Q a most ***bloody*** *persecution* きわめて残忍な迫害. ¶***dire*** *persecutions* 恐ろしい迫害. ¶***political*** *persecution* 政治上の迫害. ¶***relentless*** *persecution* 非道な迫害. ¶***religious*** *persecution* 宗教上の迫害.

Q² the ***Jesuit*** *persecution* of Buddhism ジェスイト派の仏教に対する迫害.

P They were subjected ***to*** the worst *persecution.* 彼らは最も恐ろしい迫害を受けた.

P² the ten *persecutions* ***of*** Christians under the Roman emperors ローマ帝の支配下におけるキリスト教徒の十迫害.

perseverance, *n.* 根気, 辛抱.

V It ***requires*** a considerable amount of *perseverance* of industry. それは多大の根気と勤勉とを要する.

V² *Perseverance* was ***lacking*** (=***wanting***). 根気が足りなかった.

Q the ***indomitable*** *perseverance* 不屈不とうの根気. ¶***inexhaustible*** *perseverance* 不とう不屈の根気. ¶***patient plodding*** *perseverance* 我慢強くこつこつ働く根気. ¶by his ***pertinacious*** *perseverance* 氏のたゆまぬ根気で. ¶by ***sheer*** *perseverance* 根気一つで. ¶***untiring*** (=***unwearing***) *perseverance* たゆまぬ根気. ¶***unyielding*** (=***unflinching***) *perseverance* ひるまぬ根気.

P Difficult as this may be at first it can be done ***by*** *perseverance.* 初めは困難でもそれは根気でやれる. ‖ He has made a fortune ***by means*** (=***dint***) ***of*** *perseverance.* 彼は辛抱一つで財産を作った. ¶***with*** *perseverance* and industry 根気と勤勉とで.

P² *perseverance* ***in*** an attempt 根気よくやって見ること.

persevere, *v.* 忍耐する, 辛抱する; 固守する.

M He *persevered* ***day and night.*** 彼は日夜たゆまず精励した. ¶He ***obstinately*** *persevered* in his design. 彼は我慢強くその計画に精励した. ¶he *persevered* so ***steadily*** that ... 彼は...するほどしっかり辛抱した.

P He *persevered* ***amidst*** all these difficulties. 彼はかかる困難の中にあって始終たゆまず精励した. ¶*persevere* ***in*** one's efforts たゆまず努力する ‖ *persevere* ***in*** the right against all opposition あらゆる反対にもかかわらず正義を固執する. ¶*persevere* ***with*** one's task たゆまず仕事に精励する ‖ *persevere* ***with*** a good courage 雄々しくもがん張る.

persist, *v.* がん張る; 固執する.

M The tendency ***still*** *persists.* その傾向はなお根強い.

P *persist* ***against*** remonstrance あくまで忠告を入れない. ¶He *persisted* ***in*** his project (purpose, belief, opinion, resolution). 彼は計画(など)を固執した. ‖ *persist* ***in*** a refusal あくまで断る.【類】*persist* ***in*** continuing war. / He *persists* ***in*** denying his knowledge of it. / if the habit has been *persisted* ***in*** for a long time / He *persists* ***in*** talking when others want to be quiet.

persistence, *n.* 固執.

V² *persistence* ***won,*** as it usually does, and ... いつもながら熱心は恐ろしいもので...

Q with ***dogged*** *persistence* あくまで忍耐して. ¶***obstinate*** *persistence* (がん強な)固執.

P entice ... ***with*** *persistence* [悪女など]しつっこく...を誘惑する.

P² *persistence* ***in*** an attempt 計画の固執. ¶Those who have experience with type are aware of its satanic *persistence* ***towards*** error. 活字をいじったことのある人は誤植にかけては悪魔のような根強さがあることを知っている.

persistency, *n.* 不とう不屈.

P He devoted himself to it ***with*** slow *persistency.* 彼は徐徐にたゆまずそのことに当った.

person, *n.* 人; 人格; 身体; 容姿, 人品; 人物.

V ***abhor*** a *person* 人をきらう. ¶***adorn*** one's *person* 身を飾る. ¶the only woman in the world she would ***change*** *persons* with. 彼女がからだの替えっこをしてもいいと思うたった一人の女. ¶***commend*** (=***praise***) a *person* 人をほめる. ¶a delegation ***comprising*** notable *persons* from ... ...からの著名人を含む代表団. ¶***defraud*** a *person* of his estate 人の財産を詐取する. ¶***describe*** a *person* accurately 人の人相を正確に書く ‖ ***describe*** a *person* as a scoundrel 人を評して悪漢という. ¶***detest*** a *person* 人を憎む. ¶***emulate*** a *person* 人と競争する. ¶***expose*** one's *person* in public 人中で肉体を露出する. ¶***favor*** some *persons* above others えこひいきをする. ¶***give*** a *person* the jumps《口語》人をぎょっとするほど驚かせる. ¶The railroad service can ***handle*** 50,000 *persons* per hour. その鉄道は一時間五万人の旅客を取扱うことができる. ¶***harangue*** 20,000 *persons* 二万人の人を前に大演説する. ¶He ***has*** a fine *person* (=personality). 彼はりっぱな品格を備えている. ¶Three *persons* were ***killed*** and ten ***injured.*** 三人は死に十人は負傷した. ¶***license*** a *person* to do ... 人に...することを許す. ¶***miss*** a *person* 人の不在をさびしがる. ¶***mistrust*** a *person* 人を疑う. ¶***nominate*** a competent *person* 適任者を指名する. ¶not long ago I ***overheard*** two *persons* talking in a street car, and one said, "..." こないだ私は電車で二人の人の話をそばで聞いたが一人は「...」と言った. ¶***pamper*** a sick *person* 病人をわがままにさせる. ¶*persons* ***pressed*** for time [観光客など]時間に制限のある人々. ¶***respect*** the *persons* of ... ...の人物を尊重する. ¶The hall ***seats*** 474 *persons.* その会館には四百七十四人の座席がある. ¶***sell*** one's *person* 身を売る. ¶***sue*** a *person* 人を訴える. ¶He was absorbed in ***surveying*** the *persons.* 彼は人を見回わすことに気を取られていた. ¶***take*** a *person* ***off*** 人のまねをする. ¶the practice of attempting to ***torture*** or ***destroy*** a *person* by sticking pins into an image わら人形にのろいの針を打つ風習. ¶***trace*** missing *persons* ゆくえ不明の人々を捜索する. ¶***uncover*** one's *person* はだを見せる.

Q an ***abandoned*** *person* 堕落した人. ¶an ***able*** *person* 手腕家. ¶an ***able-bodied*** (=a ***robust***) *person* 屈強な人. ¶an ***able-minded*** (=a ***capable***) *person* 才幹ある人. ¶the old fashioned superstition of summoning an ***absent*** *person* 人寄せという旧式な迷信. ¶an ***accommodating*** *person* 親切な人. ¶There is enough evidence against the ***accused*** *person.* その被告には不利な証拠がそろっている. ¶an ***active*** *person* 活動家. ¶an ***admirable*** *person* 賞賛すべき人. ¶an ***adult*** *person* 大人. ¶an ***amusing*** *person* 面白い人. ¶an ***attractive*** *person* 愛きょうのある人. ¶an ***average-sized*** *person* 並の大きさの人. ¶a ***bashful*** *person* はにかみ屋. ¶a ***bookish*** *person* 本好きの人. ¶a ***brilliant*** *person* 出色の人. ¶A ***certain*** *person,* whom I will not name, told me the story. 名は言わないがある人がその話をした. ¶oblige ***civil*** *persons* 丁寧に出ればしてやる. ¶a ***collected*** *person* 落着いた人. ¶a ***competent*** *person* 有資格者, 適任者 ‖ send a ***competent*** *person* to take charge 担当のできる人を送る.【類】send a ***competent*** and ***responsible*** *person* immediately. ¶a ***compliant*** *person* よく人の言うことをきく(妥協的な)人. ¶the three ***distinct*** *Persons* in the Godhead 三位一体. ¶a ***democratic*** *person* ちょくな人. ¶think one an ***easy*** *person* to deal with 人を甘く見る. ¶a ***cool*** *person* 冷静な人. ¶a ***courageous*** *person* 勇敢な人. ¶a ***courteous*** *person* 丁寧な人. ¶a ***crafty*** *person* ずるい人. ¶a ***credible*** *person* 信ずべき人. ¶an ***emaciated*** *person* やせた人. ¶an ***employed*** *person*=an employé 雇人. ¶an ***energetic*** *person* 精力おお盛な人. ¶an ***enlightened*** *person* 開けた人. ¶an ***evil-minded*** *person* 心の曲った人. ¶an ***excellent*** *person* すぐれた人. ¶a ***faultless*** *person* 申し分のない人. ¶a ***fictitious*** or ***non-existing*** *person* 仮作のまたは実在しない人. ¶the ***first*** *persons* of the age in which they lived その当時の第一人者たち ‖ a story which is told in the ***first*** *person* 私小説. ¶a ***forlorn*** and ***friendless*** *person* 孤独の寄るべない人. ¶a ***frank*** *person* 飾り気のない人. ¶a ***gentle*** *person* おとなしい人. ¶a ***good-humored*** *person* 好人物. ¶a ***good-natured*** *person* 温良な人. ¶a ***grown*** [***up***] *person*=a grown-up 成年者. ¶a ***handy*** *person* 調法な人. ¶a ***hard-headed*** and ***successful*** *person* of the world 着実で世に成功した人. ¶a ***harmless*** *person* 無害な人. ¶a ***highly-gifted*** *person* 天資英明な人. ¶a ***historical*** *person* 歴史上の人物. ¶a ***horrible-looking*** *person* 人相の恐ろしい人. ¶a ***hot-headed*** *person* 性急な人. ¶a ***human*** *person* with many faults 欠点の多い人間らしい人. ¶a ***hypercritical*** *person* 酷評家. ¶an ***illiterate*** *person* 無学者. ¶an ***imaginary*** *person* 仮想人物. ¶a *person* least ***informed*** 一向物を知らない人. ¶an ***ingenious*** *person* 発明の才のある人. ¶charge ***innocent*** *per-*

sons with … 罪のない人に…の罪をきせる. ¶an ***insured** person* 被保険者. ¶an ***intellectual** person* 知識人, インテリ. ¶a meeting of ***interested** persons* 関係者の会合. ¶a ***juridical** person* 法人. ¶a ***keen** person* 鋭敏な人. 【類】He is the ***last** person* ever to do that. 彼はそんなことをする人間じゃない. 【類】he would be the ***last** person* in the world to … ¶a table of ***legal** persons* as to capital 資本別法人数表. ¶a ***live** person* 活動家. ¶a ***matter-of-fact** (=practical or business-like) person* 実際的な人. ¶a ***mild-eyed** person* 柔和な目をした人. ¶a ***misdirected** person* 不心得者. ¶***namby-pamby** persons* にやけた人々. ¶***necessitous** persons* of the laboring classes 労働階級の貧困な人々. ¶an ***obliging** person* 親切な人. ¶an ***obnoxious** person* いやな人. ¶an ***obstinate** person* がん固な人. ¶an ***old-fashioned** persons* 時代おくれの人たち. ¶an ***older** person* 年上の人. ¶A ***perfect** person* keeps off danger. 君子は危きに近よらず. ¶a ***pleasant** person* 面白い人. ¶a ***practical-minded** person* 実際家. ¶a ***praiseworthy** person* 感心な人. ¶a ***pretentious** person* 見掛倒しの人. ¶a ***professional** person* 専門家. ¶appoint a ***proper** person* to superintend the work その作業監督に適当な人を任命する. ¶a ***public** person* 公人. ¶examined and tested by a ***qualified** person* 専門家が検査しかつ試験した. ¶a ***quasi-incompetent** person* 準禁治産者. ¶a ***raw-boned** person* やせて骨ばかりの人. ¶leave a ***responsible** person* in charge 責任ある人に任せる. ¶a ***right-minded** person* 心の正しい人. ¶a ***rude** person* 不作法な人. ¶a ***seedy** person* 見すぼらしい身なりの人. ¶***self-possessed** person* 沈着な人. ¶no ***sensible** person* would … いやしくも利口な人は…しないだろう. 【類】every ***sensible** person* knows that … ¶a ***self-respecting** person* 自尊心のある人. ¶Write a curriculum vitae in the ***sightless** person* singular. 履歴書は一人称の I を省略し単数の動詞で書け. ¶Among the people at the meeting, I did not know a ***single** person*. 集会に出ていた人の中で一人も知った人がなかった. ¶a ***slender-figured** person* 姿のすらっとした人. ¶a ***sober** person* まじめな人. ¶a ***staggering** person* 千鳥足でよろめく人. ¶a ***stately** person* 堂々とした人物. ¶a ***stout** person* 肥った人. ¶a ***stupid** person* 鈍物. ¶a ***suave** person* 温和な人. ¶a ***suspected** person* 容疑者. ¶a ***suspicious** person* うろんなもの. ¶a ***taking** person* 人好きのする人. ¶a ***talented** person* 有能の士. ¶a ***talkative** person* 口数の多い人. ¶every ***third** person* いかなる第三者も. ¶She recovered into a calmer composure by the coming in of a ***third** person*. 彼女は二人の所へ別の一人がはいってきたので気が落着いて来た. ¶turn from one as a ***tiresome** person* 退屈な人として避ける. ¶a ***trusty** person* 信ずべき人. ¶no ***unbiased** person* will deny that … 公平な人ならだれでも…を否定しないだろう. ¶an ***undesirable** person* 好ましくない人物. ¶an ***unidentified** person* 素姓の知れない人. ¶***unthinking** persons* 思慮の足りない人々. ¶a ***venerable** person* 高齢な尊敬すべき人. ¶a ***warm-hearted** person* 情の深い人. ¶a ***weak** person* 身体または意思の弱い人. ¶***unauthorized** persons* 無許可の人々. ¶Dignity is one of the characteristics of a ***well-bred** person*. 威厳は育ちのよい人の特性である. ¶according to the opinion of ***well-informed** persons* 消息通の意見では. ¶a ***well-intentioned** person* 気だてのよい人. ¶a ***worthy, ambitious** person* りっぱな大望のある人. ¶a ***young** person* 若い人(主に娘, 若い女).

Q² a ***high-vocabulary** person* 語いの豊富な人.

P ***about** the person* 身のまわりに. ¶property in Britain held ***by** British persons* 英国人の所有する英国内の地所. ¶present it ***in** person* 親しく(手ずから)それを捧呈する ‖ You had better go and speak to him ***in** person*. 行ってじかにあの人に話した方がよい. 【類】She looks younger ***in** person* than on the screen. / I never had the pleasure of meeting him ***in** person*. / The Emperor opens the Diet ***in** person*. / offer his gifts ***in** person* at the throne ‖ ***In** person* he was handsome, strong, and healthy. 彼の容姿はりっぱで強壮だった. 【類】He was fifty or thereabouts and was corpulent and tall ***in** person*. ‖ A new hero of his race appeared ***in** the person* of Mohammed Ahmed. 彼の民族の新英雄モハメッド・アーメッドという人が現われた. 【類】America has produced a great inventor ***in** the person* of Mr. Edison. / The name is now in the third generation ***in** the person* of Louis H.E. Morequin. / a great scholar passed away ***in** the person* of … ¶an advisory committee ***of** twenty-five persons* 二十五名から成る顧問会. ¶The key of that cabinet she wears always ***on** her person*. 用だんすのかぎを彼女はいつもはだ身につけている. 【類】He had a chisel ***on** his person* at the time of arrest. / have a license ***on** the person* ‖ The physician failed to observe any symptom of disease ***on** his person*. 医師は彼の体になんら病気の徴候を認めなかった. ¶***per** person* 一人につき. ¶***through** a third person* 第三者の手を経て. ¶It cannot be carried away ***upon** the person*. それは身に付けては行かれない. ¶***with** two other persons* 三人づれで.

P² *persons **of*** influence 勢力家 ‖ a *person **of*** importance 重要人物 ‖ the *persons **of*** the time (month, week) 時(など)の人々 ‖ *persons **of*** all ranks and ages あらゆる階級及び年齢の人々. 【類】a *person **of*** rare loveliness of character / a *person **of*** understanding. ¶a *person **under*** disability 無能力者. ¶nice, orderly *persons **with*** normal ideas and habits 正常な考えと性癖を備えた善良で規律正しい人.

personage, *n.* 人, 人物; 貴人.

Q ***distinguished** personages* 名士連. ¶an ***elderly** personage* 中老の人. ¶***eminent** personages* 名士たち. ¶***exalted** personages* 貴人. ¶the most ***fascinating** personage* 一番魅力のある人. ¶He is probably not a ***historical** personage*. 彼は多分歴史上の人物ではない(仮想的人物). ¶an ***important** personage* 重要人物. ¶he was no ***less** a personage* than … 彼は…という偉い人であった. ¶a ***mythical** personage* 神話の人物. ¶Their Majesties and lesser ***Royal** personages* 両陛下以下皇族方. ¶***theatrical** personages* of importance 高級の男女俳優たち. ¶***titled** personages* 有爵者. ¶I was looked upon as a ***traveled** personage*. 私は大分旅行をやった人と見られていた. ¶He is to the majority an ***unknown** personage*. 多くの人にとって彼は未知の人物である.

personal, *a.* 私的な.

M It is said that his visit is ***purely** personal*. 彼の訪問は全く(政治的意味のない)私的なものと言われている.

personality, *n.* 人格; 個性; *pl.* 人身攻撃; 人, 人品.

V ***adjust** one's personality* to another's 自分の個性を人の個性と調和させる. ¶***admire** the personality* of … …の人物に敬服する. ¶Many ***ascribe** personality* to nature. 人格を天性に帰するものが多数ある. ¶a very well-known Japanese philologist, Mr…, but, no, we wish to ***avoid** personalities* 有名な日本の言語学者の…氏, いやしかしわれわれは人身攻撃は避けたい. ¶Every chair, drapery or decoration ***bespeaks** the owner's personality*. いす・掛布類または装飾まで何もかも持主の個性を表わす. ¶***develop** personality* 個性を発揮する. ¶Sharp *personalities* were ***exchanged*** on both sides. 激しい人身攻撃を双方でやった. ¶He ***has*** a very forceful *personality*. 彼は非常に強い個性を持っている. ¶***impart** one's personality* to one's writing 文章に自己の個性を移す. ¶He ***impressed** his personality* on the institution. 彼はその組織に彼の個性を植え付けた. ¶***incorporate** one's own personality* into … …に自己の個性を織込む. ¶***mobilize** the whole personality* 全人格を発揮させる. ¶He ***stamps** his personality* into his pupils. 彼は生徒にその個性を打込む. ¶I ***suspect** the personality* of Homer. 私は人間としてのホーマーの存在を疑っている. ¶He has ***taken** a new personality*. 彼は別人になった. ¶***talk** personalities* 個人の批評にわたることを語る. ¶***unfold** personality* 個性を発揮する. ¶***veil** her personality* 彼女の人柄を隠す. ¶His whole *personality* is ***warped*** out of shape. 彼の全人格がひねくれてしまった. ¶***write** personalities* 人物評を書く.

Q ***beautiful** personality* りっぱな人物. ¶his ***captivating** personality* 彼の魅力ある人品. ¶a ***cheery** and **genial** personality* 朗かなにこやかな人格. ¶a ***dignified** personality* 威儀堂々たる人物. ¶his ***dominating** and almost **overbearing** personality* 堂々人を威圧する人柄. ¶the primary and the second state of ***double** (=**dual**) personality* 二重人格の第一状態と第二状態. ¶a ***dynamic** personality* 活動家. ¶an ***eccentric** but **interesting** and, indeed, **lovable** personality* 変り者だが面白いそして全く愛すべき人物. ¶a woman of ***engaging** personality* 愛きょうのある婦人. ¶a ***fascinating** (=**captivating**) personality* 人を魅惑する人柄. ¶***forceful** personality* 力強い人格. ¶a dissector of ***historical** personalities* 史上の人物の解剖者. ¶an ***irre-***

sistible personality 人を魅惑する人柄. ¶a ***magnetic*** and ***active*** *personality* 人を引きつける活発な人物. ¶a ***many-sided*** *personality* 多面的な人格. ¶a ***memorable*** *personality* 記憶すべき人物. ¶a case of ***multiple*** *personality* 多重人格の一例. ¶***noted literary*** *personalities* 知名の文士連. ¶***offensive*** *personalities* 人身攻撃. ¶***outstanding*** *personalities* 知名の人々. ¶***Perfect*** *personality* is in God alone. 完全な人格は神にのみ存する. ¶A ***pleasing*** *personality* helps to sell goods. [看板娘など]人好きのするものがいると物がよく売れる. ¶***polished*** *personality* 洗練された人格. ¶a ***remarkable*** *personality* 非凡な人物. ¶a ***split-off*** *personality* [二重人格などの]分離した人格. ¶a ***striking*** *personality* 目に立つ人物. ¶a man of ***strong*** *personality* 線の太い人物. ¶a ***sympathetic*** *personality* 同情心に富む人物. ¶***tiresome*** *personalities* うるさい人の悪口. ¶***towering*** *personalities* そびえ立つ人物. ¶God's ***three-fold*** *Personality* 神の三位一体. ¶***violent*** *personalities* 猛烈な人身攻撃. ¶***winning*** *personality* 魅力ある人柄.

Q² important ***film*** *personalities* 映画関係重要人物. ¶sparkling ***Broadway Stage*** *personalities* ブロードウェーの劇界の花.

P indulge ***in*** *personalities* 人身攻撃に陥る. ¶a man ***of*** fine (strong) *personality* りっぱな(など)人物. ¶a man ***with*** *personality* 人格のりっぱな人.

P² one of the best-known *personalities* ***in*** journalism in the Far East 極東における新聞界の名士の一人. ¶geat *personalities* ***of*** history 史上の大人物.

personification, *n.* 人格化, 擬人; 権化.

Q give it a ***masculine*** *personification* それを男性として表わす.

P² He is the *personification* ***of*** poverty at its worst. 彼はどん底の貧乏の化身だ. 【類】He is the *personification* ***of*** patriotism. / the *personification* ***of*** energy ‖ Satan is the *personification* ***of*** evil. 魔王は悪の擬人化である.

personify, *v.* 擬人化する.

P Artists *personify* beauty ***in*** their works. 芸術家は美を作品に表現する.

personnel, *n.* [団]人員.

V ***reduce*** the *personnel* of an office 事務所の使用人員を減らす. ¶***increase*** *personnel* 増員する. ¶a campaign for ***recruiting*** *personnel* for his section 彼の部(課)に要員を補充するための募集.

Q ***allied military*** *personnel* 連合軍関係者. ¶These made up the ***entire*** *personnel*. これで従業員全部であった. ¶a better ***trained*** and more ***efficient*** *personnel* 一層よく訓練されて一層能率的な人員. ¶***managing*** *personnel* 経営者側. ¶living quarters for a community of 3,000 ***military*** and ***civilian*** *personnel* 三千の軍人及び軍属の共同生活のための住宅地域. ¶compensations of employees other than ***regular*** *personnel* 臨時職員給. ¶***subordinate*** *personnel* 属僚. ¶off limits to ***unauthorized*** *personnel* 許可を受けた者以外の者出入禁止.

Q² ***Allied Forces*** *personnel* 連合軍関係の人々. ¶***consular service*** *personnel* 領事館員. ¶reduce ***excess*** *personnel* 過剰人員を整理する. ¶***food-service*** *personnel* 食料関係の人員. ¶pare down the ***government*** *personnel* 政府役人の人員を削減する. ¶***gound*** *personnel* 地上部隊. ¶***intelligence*** *personnel* 情報係員. ¶***key*** *personnel* 主要役員. ¶109 ***merchant marine*** *personnel* 百九名の船員. ¶***Navy*** (***Army***) *personnel* 海(陸)軍関係者. ¶***occupation*** *personnel*, military or civilian 軍人もしくは軍属の占領軍要員. ¶***occupation force*** *personnel* 占領軍要員. ¶changes in ***organization*** *personnel* 機構要員の人事移動. ¶***school*** *personnel* 学校教職員. ¶***secretariat*** *personnel* and clerks 秘書課(官房)職員. ¶***surrender*** *personnel* 降服人員.

P ***with*** a *personnel* of about 300 約三百名の人員で.

P² the *personnel* ***of*** the new Cabinet 新内閣の顔ぶれ.

perspective, *n.* 配景画法, 透視画; 前途, 展望.

V ***draw*** a *perspective* of a place ある所の遠景画を描く. ¶to ***gain*** a clear *perspective* of the world's thought and achievement 世界の思想お及業績を明かに展望せんがために. ¶***get*** the right *perspective* 大局からの正しい見方をする. ¶Though all these views are enlightening they ***lack*** *perspective*. これらの意見はどれも卓見であるが見方が狭い. ¶A literary work, like sculpture, ***needs*** a proper *perspective*. 文学の作品は彫刻と同様適当に時をへだてて見ることが必要だ.

Q lose sight of ***historical*** *perspective* 歴史的背景を忘れる. ¶an ***isometric*** *perspective* for ... ...の上のぞき図(大和絵などの). ¶Few things are more difficult to attain than a ***just*** *perspective* in history. 歴史上の見通しで正鵠(せい)を得ることくらい困難なことは他にほとんど類がない. ¶a ***long*** *perspective* of ... [長く列をなした物などの]全ぼう. ¶appear in ***natural*** *perspective* [配景法にかなって]実際の通りに見える. ¶see a thing in a ***new*** *perspective* 新しい見通しで物を見る. 【類】The light thrown upon these events of past by recent investigators has revealed them in a ***new*** *perspective*. ¶see the subject in its ***proper*** (=true) *perspective* 正しい見方で問題を見る. ¶view them in their ***proper historic*** *perspective* それらを適当な歴史的配景において見る. ¶see it in the ***right*** *perspective* 正しい距離でそれを見る. ¶see things in their ***true*** *perspective* 物事を真に釣合のとれた見方をする.

Q² the American business man, as I see him from the advantage of a ***3,000 mile*** *perspective* 三千マイルの遠景という有利な地から見た米国の実業家.

P ***in*** (***out of***) *perspective* 遠近法にかなって(はずれて). 【類】Those events are less important to us when viewed ***in*** *perspective* (長い目で見れば). ¶the law ***of*** *perspective* 遠近法. ¶when seen ***through*** the *perspective* of years 歳月をへだてて見ると.

perspiration, *n.* 発汗; [人間の]汗.

V until a sufficient *perspiration* has been ***attained*** 汗を十分出してしまうまで. ¶***exude*** *perspiration* 汗をかく. ¶***induce*** *perspiration* 発汗させる. ¶***promote*** *perspiration* 発汗を促す. ¶***wipe*** *perspiration* 汗をぬぐう.

V² The *perspiration* ***came out*** in beads. 玉の汗が流れ出た. ¶The *perspiration* will easily ***escape*** through it. 汗はいくらでもそれからしみ出る. ¶*Perspiration* ***oozes out*** of him in great beads. 汗が玉になって彼の体から流れ出る. ‖ *Perspiration* ***oozes*** through the skin. 汗が皮膚からにじみ出る. ¶*perspiration* ***pours*** from ... 汗が...から流れ出る. ¶The *perspiration* ***rose*** on his brow. 彼は額に汗をかいた. ¶The *perspiration* was ***running*** down my back. 汗が背中を流れ落ちていた. ¶*Perspiration* ***streamed*** from his face. 汗が彼の顔から流れた.

Q A ***cold*** *perspiration* started out upon his brow. 額に冷たい汗が出てきた. ¶A ***copious*** *perspiration* streams from every pore. おびただしい汗が体中の気孔から流れる. ¶***Profuse*** *perspiration* streams down. 流汗りんりである.

P His brow is clammy ***with*** *perspiration*. 彼の額は汗でじとじとしている. ‖ My clothes are wet ***with*** *perspiration*. 服が汗で湿っている. 【類】be wet and slippery ***with*** *perspiration*.

perspire, *v.* 発汗する.

M *perspire* ***copiously*** (=***profusely***) おびただしく発汗する.

persuade, *v.* 説き付ける; 思い込ませる.

M be ***artfully*** *persuaded* to do ... 巧みに...するよう説きつけられる. ¶I am ***firmly*** *persuaded* of the man's innocence. 私はその人の無罪なことを堅く信じている. ¶I was ***fully*** *persuaded*. 私は全くそう思い込んでしまっていた.

P He was *persuaded* ***into*** doing it against his own wish. 彼は心ならずもそれをするように説き付けられた. 【類】I was *persuaded* ***into*** it (=to do it). / be *persuaded* ***into*** submission. ¶I *persuaded* him ***of*** the advantage of ... 私は彼に...するのがよいということを説き付けた. 【類】He has *persuaded* me ***of*** its truth (その真実なること). ¶I was *persuaded* ***out of*** it. 私はそれを止(や)すように勧められた. 【類】*persuade* a person ***out of*** these notions (=ideas).

O I am *persuaded* (=convinced) that death does not end all. 死が全てを終らせるものじゃないと信じている. ¶I was *persuaded* to give up the attempt. 私はその試みを止めるように説き伏せられた.

persuasion, *n.* 説服; 教派; ...に属する人.

V ***bring*** friendly *persuasion* to bear upon ... 友人として...を説きすかした.

Q a politician of the ***Hibernian*** *persuasion* アイルランド系の政治家. ¶my young hearers of the ***male*** *persuasion* 私の講演を聞かれる若い男子の方々. ¶***rational*** *persuasion* 合理的説服. ¶one's ***religious*** *persuasion* 宗教的信念・信仰.

Q² Englishmen of the ***Anarchist*** *persuasion* 無政府主義派の英人.

P ***after*** much *persuasion* he confessed that ... 色々と説得されて彼は...を自白した. 【類】***after*** much *persuasion* I induced him to ... ¶obtain another's consent ***by per-***

suasion 説きつけて承諾を得る. 【類】I obtained his consent *by persuasion*. ¶He knows how to act *with* gentle *persuasion*. 彼はやんわりと説き付ける手心を心得ている.

pertain, *v.* 付随する；関する.

P the enthusiasm *pertaining to* youth 若さから来る熱意 ‖ It does not *pertain to* the essentials of the subject. それはその問題の核心に触れない. ‖ all matters *pertaining to* …に関する一切の事項. 【類】give reliable information *pertaining to* … / regulations *pertaining to* … / information *pertaining to* … / Western students of matters *pertaining to* Japan generally.

pertinent, *a.* 適切な.

P Your remarks are *pertinent to* the subject. 君の言うことはこの問題に適切だ. 【類】*pertinent to* the time (case).

perturb, *v.* 心を乱す.

M She was *much perturbed* by her son's illness. 彼女は息子の病気を大いに心配した.

perturbation, *n.* ろうばい.

V *feel perturbation* concerning … …に関してろうばいを感じる.

perusal, *n.* 精読, 熟読.

V It well *deserves perusal*. それは大いに精読に値する. ¶*recommend* its *perusal* to … …にその精読を勧める. ¶a work which will *repay* a careful *perusal* 熟読する価値がある本.

Q recommend it to the *attentive perusal* of the public その熟読を一般に勧める. ¶The article is well worth *careful perusal* at the present time. その論文は刻下熟読する価値が十分ある. ¶a *diligent perusal* 精読. ¶It is worth *serious perusal*. それはまじめに熟読する価値がある.

P fling it aside *after* a single *perusal* 一読の後それを放棄する.

P^2 the *perusal of* the Bible 聖書の精読.

pervade, *v.* 広がる, 充満する.

P The station is *pervaded with* the scent of tar and new rope. 停車場にはタールと新らしいなわのにおいがぷんぷんしている. 【類】The air was *pervaded with* the strong odor of the pines.

perverse, *a.* ねじけた.

P *perverse in* temper (form) 性質のねじけた(変形の).

perversion, *n.* ねじくれ.

Q *vicious perversions* 邪悪なひねくれ.

Q^2 a *sex* (=sexual) *perversion* 変態性欲.

P^2 a *perversion of* judgment 判断のわい曲 ‖ It is a *perversion of* the term. それはその語の誤用(曲解)である.

pervert, *v.* 曲解する.

M He *purposefully perverted* my words. 彼は故意に私の言葉を曲解した.

P *pervert from* good to evil intent 善意から悪意へ転向する.

pervious, *a.* 通す；理解をもつ.

P Glass is *pervious to* light and heat, but not *to* air and water. ガラスは光線や熱を通すが空気や水は通さない. ‖ His mind is *pervious to* new ideas. 彼には新思想を受入れる能力がある.

pessary, *n.* ペッサリー(避妊用具).

V *use* (=*wear*) a *pessary* for contraception 避妊のためペッサリーを使う.

Q a *Dutch pessary* ダッチ・ペッサリー.

pessimism, *n.* 悲観, 悲観説.

Q *constructive pessimism* 建設的悲観説.

P There is no reason whatever *for pessimism*. 何も悲観すべきことはない.

pessimist, *n.* 悲観者.

Q a *sullen pessimist* 憂うつな悲観者.

Q^2 a *weak-kneed pessimist* 弱腰の悲観論者.

P^2 I was a *pessimist on* the question of … …については私は悲観論者だった.

pessimistic, *a.* 悲観的な.

M opinions *more or less pessimistic* いく分悲観的な意見. ¶That point of view sounds *rather pessimistic*. その見解はばかに悲観的な感じがする.

P There is no reason to be *pessimistic about* (=*of*) the future. 将来について悲観すべき理由は少しもない.

pest, *n.* 黒死病, ペスト；有害物.

V^2 The *pest* has *broken out* in Shanghai. 上海にペストが発生した. ¶the *pest* is *spreading* in … ペストが…で広がりつつある.

Q He is a *regular pest*. あれはほんとに困り者だ. ¶Prostitution is a *social pest*. 売春は社会的ペストである.

Q^2 The severe frost killed off most of the *insect pests*. ひどい霜で大半の害虫は死滅した.

P He is infected *with pest*. 彼はペストにかかっている.

P^2 a veritable *pest to* society 社会に取っての真の有害物.

pester, *v.* 悩ます.

P The house is *pestered by* rats. その家はねずみに悩まされている. 【類】*pestered by* hoodlums (よた者たち). ¶*pester* a person *with* complaints (requests) 不平(など)を言って人を困らせる. 【類】he is occasionally *pestered* by me *with* inquiries as to …

pestilence, *n.* 伝染病, 疫病.

V *avert pestilence* 疫病を除ける.

V^2 A *pestilence broke out*. 伝染病が発生した. ¶the *pestilence* is *raging* in … 伝染病が…で流行をきわめている.

pet, *n.* (**1**) 愛がん動物(鳥, 犬, ねこなど).

V "*deflea*" *pets* 手飼もののノミを取ってやる. ¶*make* a *pet* of a tiger とらをちょう愛する. 【類】The queen had a lion cub of which she *made* a great *pet*.

Q our native *feathered pets* わが本土の愛がん鳥類. ¶These are his special *floral pets*. これらの花を彼は特に愛している. ¶an *indoor pet* 室内の手飼もの. ¶He's *mother's pet*. あれはお母さん子だ.

Q^2 The *uguisu* is the favorite *bird pet* of the Japanse. うぐいすは日本人の愛好する飼鳥である. ¶*home pets*, furred and feathered 手飼の鳥獣. ¶a *household pet* 家中の人気もの.

P^2 a *pet among* the sailors 船員たちの人気もの. ¶be the *pet of* the family 一家の人気ものである. ¶The dog was a great *pet with* the boys. その犬は子供などのよいお相手であった.

(**2**) 不気げん.

P He is *in* a *pet*. 彼は気げんが悪い.

peter, *v.* 《米》次第に細(薄)くなる.

M The gas *peters out*. ガスの出が細くなる. ¶His business was promising at first, but has *petered out*. 彼の商売は最初は有望であったがしりつぼみになった.

petition, *n.* 祈願, 請願, 申請；請願書.

V *deny* a *petition* 請願書を却下する. ¶The company has *filed* a *petition* for liquidation. 会社は清算の申請書を提出した. ¶*forward* a *petition* 請願書を送達する. ¶*grant* a *petition* 請願を許可する. ¶*lodge* (=*hand in or send in*) one's *petition* to … …に嘆願する. ¶*make petition* 請願する. ¶*oppose* a *petition* 請願に反対する. ¶*present* a *petition* in this sense to … この意味の請願書を…に差出す. 【類】*present* a *petition* to … to ask permission for … ¶*put up* a *petition* to heaven 天に祈願をこめる. ¶*refuse* a *petition* 請願書を拒絶する. ¶*reject* a *petition* 請願を却下する. ¶People *signed* the *petition* asking the City Council for a new street. 市民は市会に対し新街路建設の請願書に署名した. ¶They are now working to *submit* a *petition* to the Government for the immunity of beans. 彼らは豆類免税の陳情書を政府に提出しようと目下奔走中. ¶*support* a *petition* 請願を支持する. ¶*throw out* a *petition* 請願を却下する.

Q a *direct petition* to the Sovereign 君主への直訴状. ¶an *earnest petition* 哀願.

P He was released *on* the *petition* of his wife. 彼は妻の嘆願で釈放された.

P^2 a *petition for* divorce 離婚請願書. 【類】a *petition for* naturalization (帰化). ¶a *petition from* the people 人民からの請願書. ¶a *petition of* bankruptcy 破産申請 ‖ a *petition of* appeal 控訴状. ¶a *petition to* the authorities その筋への請願書.

petition, *v.* 請願する.

P *petition* His Majesty *for* sanction 陛下の御裁可を仰ぐ ‖ *petition for* pardon (mercy) ゆるし(など)を請う. ¶*petition in* writing for permission to … …の許可を書面で願い出る.

petrify, *v.* 石化する.

P He was *petrified with* terror (fright, astonishment). 彼はびっくり(など)して身動きできなかった.

petticoat, *n.* 〖服飾〗ペチコート.

P She was then *in* her *petticoat*. 彼女は当時はまだ子供だった. 【類】I have known him ever since he was *in petticoats* (幼少). ‖ a Cromwell *in petticoats* 女武蔵.

petticoat-government, *n.* かかあ天下.

P He is *under petticoat-government*. 彼のうちはかかあ天下だ.

pew, *n.* [教会の]座席.

Q *cushioned pews* クッション付の席.

pharmacist, *n.* 薬剤師.

Q^2 a *graduate pharmacist* 薬剤師(大学出の).

phantom, *n.* まぼろし, 幻影.

P^2 *phantoms of* a dream 夢に現われるまぼろし ‖ He is only a *phantom of* a king. 彼は実権のない王様(ロボット)にすぎない.

phase, *n.* 状態, 形勢；局面, 方面.

V The question has ***assumed*** an acute *phase*. この問題はせん鋭化してきた. ¶***bring*** a new *phase* in ... ...に新生面を開く. ¶***enter*** another *phase* 新生面を開く. ¶The problem ***has*** many *phases*. この問題は多方面にわたっている. ¶***master*** all the *phases* of the subject その問題のあらゆる方面を会得する. ¶He ***studied*** the highest *phase* of art. 彼は芸術の最高方面を研究した.

Q a student of human nature in ***all its phases*** 人間性の各方面の研究者. ¶He adapted himself to the ***changing*** *phases* of society. 彼は変化する社会情勢に順応した. ¶an ***essential*** *phase* of the problem 問題の肝じんな方面. ¶He made himself proficient in nearly ***every*** *phase* of art. 彼は美術のほとんどあらゆる方面に上達した. ¶this ***final*** *phase* of the campaign その戦争の最終の情勢. ¶the most ***interesting*** *phase* of the affair その事件の最も興味ある方面. ¶***manifold*** *phases* of life 人生の各方面. ¶the ***multifarious*** *phases* of women's work and interests 婦人の仕事及び興味の種々雑多な面. ¶the development of each ***new*** *phase* of the plot その話の筋の各自新方面を発展させること. ¶but a ***passing*** *phase* in the development of society 社会の発達における単に一時的現象. ¶enter upon the ***second*** *phase* of the research その研究の第二段階にはいる. ¶a ***special*** *phase* of a larger subject 一層大きな問題の特殊な方面. ¶the ***theoretical*** *phases* of the problem その問題の理論的方面. ¶a realization of ***unexpected*** *phases* of American life アメリカ生活の思いがけない諸相の理解. ¶the ***various*** *phases* of their life history その生態の種々相.

P ***in*** every *phase* of national existence 国民生活のあらゆる面において ‖ Christianity ***in*** its first *phases* was utterly opposed to the military spirit. 創始期のキリスト教は軍事精神とは全然反対のものであった. ¶Women are increasingly entering ***into*** all *phases* of industrial, commercial, and administrative activities. 婦人は商工業及び行政の各方面にますます進出しつつある. ¶an inevitable *phase* ***in*** the development of new China 新中国の発達にともない必然的に生じる状態. ¶***on*** all *phases* of poultry (culture) 養鶏(など)のあらゆる面について. ¶pass ***through*** three *phases* (=stages) 三段階を経る. 【類】John has no use for girls; that is a *phase* most boys go ***through***.

P² two *phases* (=aspects) ***of*** single problem 一つの問題の二方面 ‖ that *phase* ***of*** the subject 問題のその面. 【類】*phases* ***of*** Japanese education.

pheasant, *n.* きじ.

Q We had ***roasted*** *pheasant* for dinner. 晩さんにきじの「むし焼を食べた.

P three brace ***of*** *pheasants* 六羽のきじ.

phenomenon, *n.* 現象; 非常のもの.

V ***interpret*** these complex *phenomena* これら複雑な現象を解釈する. ¶***investigate*** the *phenomena* of languages from its psychological side 心理学の方面から言語現象を研究する. ¶The same *phenomenon* is ***noted.*** 同一現象が認められる. ¶The same *phenomenon* has been ***observed.*** 同一現象が認められた.

Q Among ... ***analogous*** *phenomena* are observed. ...間に類似の現象が認められる. ¶Lightning is an ***electrical*** *phenomenon.* 稲光りは電気の一現象である. ¶It is a ***frequent*** *phenomenon* in chemical analysis. それは化学分析においてしばしば認められる現象だ. ¶an ***infant*** *phenomenon* 神童. ¶an ***isolated*** *phenomenon* 孤立現象. ¶a ***natural*** *phenomenon* 自然の現象. ¶a ***passing*** *phenomenon* 一時的現象. ¶a ***postwar*** *phenomenon* 戦後の現象. ¶***sensible*** *phenomena* 〘心理〙知覚諸現象. ¶observe a ***similar*** *phenomenon* 同じような諸現象を見る. ¶Prostitution is an ***urban*** *phenomenon.* 売春は都市の現象である.

Q² a wonderful ***fire-proof*** *phenomenon* [見せ物などで口から火を吹いたりなどする]火に耐える怪物.

P the vanity ***of*** all *phenomena* 色即是空.

P² a rare *phenomenon* ***in*** history 史上まれに見る現象. ¶*phenomena* ***of*** China culture 中国文化の諸相. 【類】a *phenomenon* ***of*** civilization / Fever and inflammation (炎症) are *phenomena* ***of*** disease.

philanthropist, *n.* 慈善家.

Q An ***anonymous*** *philanthropist* has given ... for the purpose. 匿名の慈善家がその用途に...を贈った. ¶an ***ardent*** and ***unwearying*** *philanthropist* 熱心で, たゆむことのない慈善家. ¶an ***eager*** *philanthropist* 熱心な慈善家. ¶an ***unassuming*** *philanthropist* 自家広告を好まない慈善家.

philanthropy, *n.* 博愛事業.

Q a ***far-sighted*** *philanthropy* 先見の明ある博愛事業. ¶an ***organized*** *philanthropy* 組織化された博愛事業. ¶A hospital is a ***useful*** *philanthropy.* 病院は有用な博愛事業であ「る.

philatelist, *n.* 郵趣家.

Q² one of the most ardent of ***lady*** *philatelists* in England. 英国の婦人郵趣家中でも最も熱心な一人.

philology, *n.* 言語学.

Q He belongs to the old school of ***comparative*** *philology.* 彼は古い比較言語学派に属する. ¶utilize the findings made in the field of ***scientific*** *philology* 科学的言語学の分野でなされた発見を利用する.

philosopher, *n.* 哲学者.

V ***play*** the *philosopher* 哲学者を気取る.

V² The *philosopher* ***flourished*** a century ago. その哲学者は百年前に盛名をうたわれた人だ.

Q a ***Chinese*** *philosopher* 儒者. ¶a ***dilettante*** *philosopher* 生(なま)半可な哲学者. ¶a ***homegrown*** *philosopher* 世間知らずの学者. ¶a ***pessimistic*** *philosopher* 悲観説の哲学者. ¶a ***popular*** *philosopher* 通俗哲学者. ¶a ***profound*** *philosopher* 深遠な哲学者.

Q² an ***attic*** *philosopher* 屋根裏の哲人. ¶a ***closet*** *philosopher* 世間を知らない学者. ¶a ***stay-at-home*** *philosopher* 出無精な(世事にうとい)哲学者.

P a school ***of*** *philosophers* 哲学者の一派.

philosophical, *a.* 哲学に通じている.

M ***profoundly*** *philosophical* 深く哲学に通じている.

philosophize, *v.* 哲理を究める; 哲学的に説明する.

P *philosophize* ***about*** ... ...について哲理を説く. ¶*philosophize* ***on*** ... ...に関する哲理を説く. ¶It is easy to *philosophize* ***over*** the wastefulness of money spent on elaborate funerals. 念入りな葬儀に費した金銭のむだなことを哲学的に説明するのはたやすい.

philosophy, *n.* 哲学; 哲理; 悟道.

V ***build up*** a *philosophy* that ... ...という哲学を建設する. ¶***carry*** one's *philosophy* into action 哲理を実行する. ¶***erect*** a new *philosophy* 新派の哲学を起す. ¶***establish*** a *philosophy* 哲学説を立てる. ¶***humanize*** *philosophy* 哲学を人間の要求に適合したものにする. ¶***ruffle*** his *philosophy* 彼の悟道をかく乱する. ¶***set forth*** a dangerous anarchistic *philosophy* 危険な無政府主義の哲学を公にする. ¶***use*** *philosophy* 悟りを開く; 我慢する.

Q the ***a priori*** *philosophy* of Kant カントの先験的哲学. ¶the ***Aristotelian*** *philosophy* アリストテレスの哲学. ¶***atomic*** *philosophy* 原子論. ¶His *philosophy* was ***gay*** and ***shallow.*** 彼の哲学は浮華で浅薄であった. ¶the nature of the ***Kantian*** *philosophy* カント哲学の性質. ¶the ***materialistic*** *philosophy* of Locke ロックの唯物論. ¶***modern*** *philosophy* 近世哲学. ¶***natural*** *philosophy* 自然哲学, 物理学. ¶an ***optimistic*** *philosophy* 楽観主義の哲学. ¶***personal*** *philosophies* 諸種の個人哲学. ¶***practical*** *philosophy* 実践哲学. ¶a work of ***pure*** *philosophy* 純正哲学の著作. ¶lead him to a ***sound*** *philosophy* of life 彼を指導して健全な人生観を持たせるようにする. ¶a ***spurious*** *philosophy* にせ哲学. ¶he is the possessor of a ***wholesome*** *philosophy* which consists in ... 彼は...という健全な哲学の持主である.

Q² an ***armaments*** *philosophy* of force 力の軍備論. ¶accept the ***Communist*** *philosophy* 共産党の理論を受入れる. ‖ the ***Communist*** economic *philosophy* 共産党の経済理論. ¶a ***middle-of-the-road*** *philosophy* of liberalism 自由主義の中道理論. ¶the "***New Deal***" *philosophy* of government 「新政策」政治論. ¶the Japanese ***samurai*** *philosophy* 日本の武士道精神. ¶***world*** *philosophy* 世界観.

P ***under*** the *philosophy* of "every man for himself and devil take the hindmost" 「銘々自己本位のこと後に残る者こそ災難」という主義で. ¶a man ***without*** a *philosophy* はっきりした人生観のない人.

P² a *philosophy* ***of*** life 人生哲学 ‖ one's *philosophy* ***of*** living その処生哲学 ‖ the *philosophy* ***of*** history (grammar) 歴史(文法)哲学.

phlegm, *n.* たん.

V ***bring up*** *phlegm* たんを吐く. ¶***loosen*** the *phlegm* たんを切る.

Q ***bloody*** *phlegm* 血の混じったたん.

P clear the throat ***of*** the *phlegm* せき払いしてたんを切る.

phobia, *n.* 恐怖症.

V *dissipate* a *phobia* 恐怖症をなくす.

phone, *n.* 《口語》 電話(器).

V He struck out to ***answer*** the *phone.* 彼は電話がかかるととびついて行った. ¶***pick up*** the *phone* 受話器を取上げる. ¶Who can that be, ***ringing*** our *phone* at this hour of the morning? だれでしょう, 朝こんなに早く電話をかけるなんて.

Q² a "***candlestick***" *phone* 「ろうそく立て式」受話器.

P call one ***at*** (=***on or to***) the *phone* 人を電話口へ呼出す ¶He is ***on*** the *phone.* 彼は電話を掛けている(電話に出ている). ‖ I was called up ***on*** the *phone.* 私に電話が掛ってきた. ‖ You are wanted ***on*** the (=by) *phone.* あなたにお電話です. ‖ Get him ***on*** the *phone,* won't you? 彼を電話に出してくれませんか. 【類】 Call the office and get him ***on*** the *phone.* / Mr. S wants to speak to you ***on*** the *phone.* / I failed to get him ***on*** the *phone.* ‖ We are ***on*** the *phone* now—our number is ... 電話を引いた, 番号は...です. ¶*Phone* ***to*** you, sir. お電話です.

phone, *v.* 《口語》 電話をかける.

P I'll *phone* [***to***] you later and tell you all about it. あとで電話で万事お話しします.

phonograph, *n.* 蓄音器.

P make a speech ***into*** a *phonograph* 蓄音器に演説を吹込む. ¶turn ***on*** a *phonograph* 蓄音器をかける ‖ Music will be played ***on*** a *phonograph.* レコード音楽が始まります.

phosphorus, *n.* 燐(りん).

Q ***white*** *phosphorus* 黄燐.

photo, *n.* 《口語》 写真.

V ***enlarge*** a *photo* 写真を引伸ばす. ¶***have*** one's *photo* ***taken*** 自分の写真をとる(とってもらう). ¶***print*** (***reprint***) a *photo* 写真を焼く(焼増しする). ¶***take*** a *photo* of ... ...の写真をとる.

Q² a ***color*** *photo* 色彩写真. ¶an ***examination*** *photo* 受験用写真. ¶a ***passport*** *photo* 旅券用写真.

P² *photo* ***by*** ... ...撮影.

photodrama, *n.* 映画劇.

V ***film*** a *photodrama* 映画劇を撮影する.

photograph, *n.* 写真.

V an album ***containing*** the *photographs* of ... ...の写真を収めたアルバム. ¶***enlarge*** *photographs* 写真を引伸ばす. ¶"***fake***" a *photograph* 変り写真をこしらえる. ¶I desire to ***have*** a *photograph* of yourself. あなたの写真を一枚いただきたい. ¶I wish to ***have*** my *photograph* ***taken.*** 写真をとってもらいたい. ‖ ***have*** a *photograph* ***taken*** of it その写真をとって下さい. ¶this *photograph* was ***made*** at ... この写真は...でとった. ¶***mount*** *photographs* 写真を台紙にはる. ¶***obtain*** a *photograph* of ... ...の写真を得る. ¶the author ***presents*** many *photographs* of ... in his book 著者は...の写真をその本に沢山載せている. ¶***print*** a *photograph* 写真を焼付ける. ¶***retouch*** a *photograph* 写真を修正する. ¶***take*** a *photograph* of ... ...の写真をとる. 【類】 The *photographs* you ***took*** of us the other day are not at all satisfactory. ¶***throw*** *photographs* upon the screen 写真を映写幕に映す.

V² a *photograph* ***showing*** ... ...の写真.

Q an ***autographed*** *photograph* of yourself 自筆入りの貴方の写真. ¶a ***composite*** *photograph* 重ね写真. ¶The illustrations are so good that they almost look like ***direct*** *photographs.* さし絵が非常に見事なのでどれも直接にとった写真のように見える. ¶I do not like to have my picture taken, because I never take a ***good*** *photograph.* 私は写真がうまくとれたことがないから自分の写真をとらせるのはいやだ. ¶You will take a ***handsome*** *photograph* today. きょうはりっぱに写真がとれるでしょう. ¶take an ***instantaneous*** *photograph* (=a snapshot) 早取写真をとる. ¶a ***life-like*** *photograph* 生写しの写真. ¶a ***permanent*** *photograph* 不変色写真. ¶a ***signed*** *photograph* 署名入りの写真. ¶a sort of ***verbal*** *photograph* 一種の言葉の写真(蓄音器など).

Q² a ***family*** *photograph* 家族一同の写真. ¶a ***flashlight*** *photograph* せん光撮影写真. ¶a ***four-color*** *photograph* 四色写真. ¶a ***natural color*** *photograph* 天然色写真. ¶a ***nude*** *photograph* 裸体(ヌード)写真. ¶a ***pin-up*** *photograph* ピンナップ(壁にピンでとめておく美人の写真). ¶take a ***snapshot*** [*photograph*] of ... ...のスナップをとる.

P pose ***for*** a *photograph* 写真をとるためにあるポーズを作る ‖ sit ***for*** a *photograph* 写真を写させる. ¶The volume is excellently illustrated ***from*** *photographs* by the author. その本は著者の撮影した写真が見事なさし絵になっている. ‖ Is this portrait copied ***from*** *a photogragh?* この肖像は写真から描いたのか. ‖ illustrations ***from*** *photographs* from nature 自然を写した写真のさし絵. ¶She looks better in the *photograph.*=She is photogenic. 彼女は写真顔がいい. ¶a copy ***of*** his *photograph* 彼の写真一葉.

P² a *photograph* ***in*** natural colors 天然色写真. ¶a *photograph* ***of*** himself 彼自身の写真.

photograph, *v.* 写真に写す; 写真に写る.

M I always *photograph* ***well*** (***badly***). 私はいつもうまく(まずく)写真に写る. 【類】 She doesn't *photograph* ***well.***

P The illustration has been *photographed* ***from*** a rare old print. そのさし絵は珍らしい古い版画からとったものである. ¶*photograph* ***under*** the X rays エックス光で撮影する.

photographer, *n.* 写真技師, カメラマン.

Q² a ***kinema*** *photographer*=a cinematographer 撮映技師(カメラマン). ¶a ***movie*** and ***still*** *photographer* 映画及びスチール(普通の)写真の写真技師. ¶a ***news*** *photographer* 新聞社のカメラマン. ¶a ***pavement*** *photographer* 街頭写真家. ¶a ***staff*** *photographer* [正式社員の]カメラマン.

photography, *n.* 写真術.

V ***encourage*** *photography* 写真熱を盛んにする.

Q an exhibition of ***amateur*** *photography* was held at ... アマチュア写真の展覧会が...で催された. ¶***pictorial*** *photography* 絵画的写真術.

Q² ***color*** *photography* 色彩写真術.

photogravure, *n.* 写真凹版(グラビヤ), 写真版.

P frontispiece ***in*** *photogravure* グラビヤ版の口絵 ‖ 30 plates ***in*** *photogravure* 三十枚の写真図版 ‖ reproduce it ***in*** *photogravure* それを複製にする ‖ a reproduction ***in*** *photogravure* グラビア(写真)による複製.

P² *photogravures* ***from*** pictures 絵画の写真版.

photoplay, *n.* 映画劇.

Q a ***novelized*** *photoplay* 小説化した映画劇.

phrase, *n.* 句; 辞句, 文句; 語法.

V ***abbreviate*** (=***contract***) a *phrase* 語句を短縮する. ¶to ***adopt*** Shakespeare's *phrase* シェークスピアの句を借りて言えば. ¶***avoid*** trite and hackneyed *phrases* 陳腐な文句を避ける. ¶to ***borrow*** the *phrase* of the delegate who has just sat down 今意見を述べた委員の言葉を借りて言えば. ¶***coin*** a *phrase* 句を新造する. ¶***employ*** a happy *phrase* 妙句を用いる. ¶***expand*** a *phrase* into a clause 句を節に言い替える. ¶***form*** some *phrases* with a verb ある動詞を使って何か句を作ってみる. ¶***mutter*** broken *phrases* 何か途切れ途切れにつぶやく. ¶to ***quote*** the official *phrase* お役所風の言い方をすれば. ¶***round*** one's *phrases* well 辞句を洗錬する. ¶***steal*** a *phrase* 文句を盗用する. ¶***use*** happy *phrases* うまい文句を使う. ¶***work*** *phrases* into a sentence 語句を文にまとめる. ¶***work up*** a new *phrase* 新しい句を作り出す.

Q an ***apologetical*** *phrase* 弁解の文句. ¶an ***awkward, ugly*** *phrase* 拙劣ないやな文句. ¶***big*** *phrases* 大げさな文句. ¶a ***cacophonous*** *phrase* 語ろの悪い句. ¶a ***common*** *phrase* 普通の文句. ¶***conventional*** *phrases* きまり文句. ¶a ***cumbersome*** *phrase* 煩雑な文句. ¶It is indeed a ***dead*** *phrase.* その文句はたしかに今日は通用しない. ¶utter ***disjointed*** *phrases* つじつまの合わないことを言う. ¶***easy*** and ***colloquial*** *phrases* やさしい口語体の文句. ¶an ***elastic*** *phrase* 融通のきく文句. ¶an ***empty*** *phrase* 無意味な文句. ¶a ***euphemistic*** *phrase* 遠曲な言い回し. ¶an ***exclamatory*** *phrase* 感嘆句. ¶to use an ***expressive Japanese*** *phrase* 含蓄のある日本語で言えば. ¶an ***extravagant*** *phrase* 突飛な文句. ¶***familiar*** *phrases* in the Bible 人口にかいしゃする聖書の句. ¶That's his ***favorite*** *phrase.* それは彼の口ぐせだ. ¶a ***felicitous*** *phrase* 妙句. ¶a ***fiery*** *phrase* 奇矯な言. ¶a ***foreign*** *phrase* 外国語の語句. ¶He is a gentleman and a scholar, in the ***good old*** *phrase.* 彼は昔からいういわゆる「紳士で学者」である. ¶***gorgeous*** *phrases* けんらんな辞句. ¶to use a ***grandiloquent*** *phrase* 大げさに言えば. ¶It is a ***hackneyed*** *phrase* that Japan is a paradise of the children. 日本は子供らの楽園だというのは古臭い文句だ. ¶hit upon a ***happy*** *phrase* うまい文句を思いつく ‖ His speech was gilded with ***happy*** *phrases.* 彼の演説は名文句で飾られていた. 【類】 in Plato's

happy** phrases.* ¶a ***hideous** phrase* ひどい文句. ¶He is fond of using ***high-sounding** phrases.* 彼は業々しい文句を使うのが好きだ. ¶a ***homely** phrase* 卑近な文句. ¶an ***idiomatic** phrase* 慣用句. ¶in the ***immortal** phrase* of … …の千古不磨の言を借りて言えば. ¶an ***illustrative** phrase* [語の用法など]説明のための句. ¶an ***indelicate** phrase* 下品な文句. ¶a ***large** phrase* 大げさな文句. ¶a ***long roundabout** phrase* 遠まわしな長い語句. ¶It is no ***mere** phrase* to speak of his "services to art and literature." 彼の「芸術と文学への奉仕」というのは口先だけの文句じゃない. ¶a ***metaphorical** phrase* 比ゆ的な言い回し. ¶an ***oft-quoted** phrase* しばしば引用される句. ¶his comment was confined to ***one curt** phrase* "…" 彼は「…」と一言いっただけであった. ¶a ***parallel** phrase* in a foreign language 外国語のそれに相当する句. ¶in ***Parliamentary** phrase* 議会で使う言葉で言えば. ¶a ***plain-sounding** phrase* 率直な文句. ¶a ***poetical** phrase* 詩的な言い回し. ¶a ***polished** phrase* 洗錬された辞句. ¶"Shikataganai" is a ***prevalent** phrase* used by the Japanese. 日本人はよく「仕方がない」という文句を使う. ¶to use the more ***recent** phrase* もっと新しい言葉で言えば. ¶a ***set** phrase* 紋切形の句. ¶speak in ***simple** phrases* 平易な言葉で話す. ¶a ***standing** phrase* 成句, 熟語. ¶a ***stereotyped** phrase* きまり文句. ¶a ***stilted** phrase* 大げさな文句. ¶use a ***stock** phrase* 陳腐な文句を使う. 【類】one of the ***stock** phrases* of the opponents of … ¶stopgap** phrases* 間に合わせの文句. ¶***telling** phrases* 迫力ある文句. ¶a ***terse** and **pregnant** phrase* 簡潔で含蓄のある文句. ¶***time-worn** phrases* 古臭い文句. ¶an ***un-English** phrase* 英語らしくない文句. ¶a ***usable** phrase* 役に立つ(調法な)句. ¶***weighty** and **polysyllabic** phrases* 重苦しい長たらしい文句. ¶a ***well-known** phrase* 名高い句. ¶a ***well-turned** phrase* うまい言回しの句.

Q² a ***cant** phrase* 通り言葉; [ギャングなどの]隠語. ¶a ***catch** phrase* 警句的文句. ¶***everyday** phrases* 日用語句. ¶a ***law** phrase* 法律用語. ¶a ***slang** phrase* 俗語. ¶a ***sporting** phrase* スポーツ用語. ¶a ***twonoun** phrase* 名詞プラス名詞句.

P ***in** a phrase* 一口に言えば ‖ ***in** such a phrase* こうした句で ‖ ***in** the phrase* of … …の言葉を引用して言えば ‖ summarized ***in** …'s phrase*, it is … それは…の句を借りて概括すれば…である.

phrase, *v.* 言葉に言表わす.

M as he ***picturesquely** phrased* it 彼が美しい文句でそれを述べているように. ¶*phrase* one's excuse ***politely*** 言いわけをうまく言う.

P an essay *phrased* (=written) ***in*** concise and lucid English 簡潔明確な英語で書いた論文.

phrase-making, *n.* 造語.

Q ***laborious** phrase-making* 苦心の造語.

phraseology, *n.* 言い方, 言葉使い, 語法.

V ***alter** phraseology* 言い方を変える. ¶***use*** rather stereotyped *phraseology* 古い言い方をする.

Q in ***dexterous** and **pungent** phraseology* 巧妙なぴりっと来る語句で. ¶***elegant** phraseology* 優雅な言回し. ¶***idiomatic** phraseology* 慣用的な言い方. ¶an ***inelegant** phraseology* 下品な言い回し. ¶in ***legal** phraseology* 法律上の用語で言えば. ¶the letter was in the ***same** phraseology* as … その書状は…と同文であった. ¶the use of ***technical** phraseology* 専門用語の使用. ¶in ***theatrical** phraseology* 芝居の方の言葉でいうと. ¶***trenchant** phraseology* 痛烈な言い方.

P changes ***in** phraseology* 語句の変更.

phrasing, *n.* 言葉使い.

Q an example of a sentence whose rhythm has been destroyed by ***bad** phrasing* 言葉の使い方でリズムが破壊された文の例. ¶a ***clumsy** phrasing* へたな言い回し.

physician, *n.* 内科医, 医師.

V A *physician* was ***called in.*** 医者に来てもらった. ¶***consult*** a *physician* 医者に診察してもらう. ¶***see*** a *physician* 医者のところへ行く.

Q an ***American missionary** physician* 伝道のために派遣された米国医師. ¶an ***attending** physician* その病人係の医師, 侍医. ¶his head ***consulting** physician* 彼の主治医. ¶an ***examining** physician* of an insurance company [生命]保険会社の保険医. ¶***his own** physician* 彼のかかりつけの医者. ¶I have in mind a ***noted** physician* who … …という有名な内科医のことを考えている. ¶a ***practicing** physician* 開業医. ¶a ***quack** physician* やぶ医者. ¶one's ***regular** physician* かかりつけの医者. ¶a ***visiting** physician* 出張医, 往診医.

Q² an ***Army** (a **Navy**) physician* 陸(海)軍医. ¶a ***brain** physician* 精神科医. ¶a ***city** physician* 町医者. ¶a ***court** physician* 侍医. ¶one's ***family** physician* かかりつけの医者. ¶He served a term as ***house** physician* to the U.S. Marine Hospital at Detroit, Michigan. 彼はミシガン州のデトロイトにある米海兵隊病院の住込み医として任期を勤めた. ¶a ***resident** physician* of village 村医. ¶a ***woman** physician* 婦人医.

P I have had myself carefully examined ***by** physicians.* 私は色々の医者に丁寧に見てもらった. ¶He is under the care ***of** a physician.* 彼は医者にかかっている.

P² He is a *physician* ***by*** profession. 彼の職業は医者だ. ¶the *physician* ***in*** charge 主治医 ‖ a *physician* ***in*** ordinary ***to*** His Majesty 陛下の侍医. ¶a *physician* ***of*** the Chinese school 漢法医 ‖ a *physician* ***of*** souls 霊魂の医者(牧師). ¶He was *physician* ***to*** the King. 彼は国王の侍医だった. 【類】Dr. Dukes, the *physician* ***to*** Rugby School. ¶a *physician* ***with*** a large practice. 患者の多い医者.

physicist, *n.* 物理学者.

Q a ***nuclear** physicist* 〖物理〗核物理学者.

Q² a ***Nobel Prize** physicist* ノーベル賞受賞物理学者.

physics, *n.* 物理学.

Q ***applied** physics* 応用物理学. ¶***experimental** physics* 実験物理学. ¶***nuclear** physics* 核物理学. ¶***theoretical** physics* 理論物理学.

physiologist, *n.* 生理学者.

Q² a ***research** physiologist* 生理学研究家.

physique, *n.* 体格, 骨格.

V ***build up*** the *physique* of young England 英国青年の体格を造り上げる. ¶Urban life is profoundly ***harming*** British *physique.* 都市生活は非常に英人の体格を害しつつある. ¶He ***has*** a magnificent *physique.* 彼はすばらしい体格を持っている. ¶***improve*** the *physique* 体位を向上させる. ¶***strengthen*** their *physique* 彼らの体格を強くする. ¶***weaken*** the *physique* 体格を弱くする.

Q a man of ***burly** physique* たくましい骨格の人. ¶a ***deteriorated** physique* 低下した体格. ¶young men of very ***fine** physique* 非常にりっぱな体格の青年. ¶of ***good** physique* 良い体格の. ¶deterioration in the ***national** physique* 国民体位の低下. ¶of ***perfect** physique* 申分のない体格の. ¶a man of ***powerful** physique* 体格のたくましい人. 【類】He is gifted with a ***powerful** physique.*

P He is magnificent ***in** physique.* 彼は体格がすばらしい. ¶The *physique* ***of*** the boys of Japan is steadily improving. 日本の少年の体格は着々改良されつつある.

piano, *n.* ピアノ.

V ***play*** the *piano* ピアノをひく. ¶she ***studied*** the *piano* under … 彼女は…についてピアノをけいこした. ¶the charge for ***tuning*** a *piano* ピアノの調律料.

Q an ***electric** piano* 電気ピアノ. ¶a ***grand** piano* 大型ピアノ. ¶The *piano* is ***in** (**out of**) **tune.*** そのピアノは調子が合って(はずれて)いる. ¶The *piano* is ***sharp** (**flat**).* そのピアノは調子が高(低)い.

Q² a ***cabinet** piano* [小型の]たて型ピアノ. ¶a ***cottage** piano* 小型ピアノ. ¶a ***dumb** piano* 装飾用のピアノ.

P ***at*** the *piano* will be … ピアノの演奏は…がやるでしょう. ¶He accompanied her ***on*** the *piano.* 彼はピアノで彼女の伴奏をした. ‖ play ***on*** the *piano* ピアノをひく ‖ She plays some tunes ***on*** the *piano.* 彼女はピアノを少しひく. ¶sing ***to*** the *piano* ピアノに合わせて歌う.

pick, *n.* 選択; 精鋭.

V I was the first to arrive at the inn and ***got*** the *pick* of rooms. 私が真先に旅館に着いたのでへやの選択ができた. ¶***have*** one's *pick* 選択することができる ‖ ***have*** the *pick* of the place 一番良い場所が取れる. ¶We ***offer*** you the *pick* of the bunch for six pence. 花より取り一束六ペンス. ¶***take*** one's *pick* from … …から勝手に選ぶ.

P The *pick* ***of*** the aviators of the world contested the passage of the Alps. 世界飛行家の精鋭が競ってアルプス山脈を越そうとした. 【類】the *pick* ***of*** music hall and variety talent (寄せ芸人) / the men who are, intellectually as well as physically, the *pick* ***of*** their generation.

pick, pickax, *n.* 〖工具〗つるはし.

P break up strong ground ***with*** a *pick[ax]* つるはしで石ころ地面をくだく. 【類】pick a road ***with*** a *pickax.*

pick, *v.* つつき掘る；ほじり出す；むしる；つみ取る；拾う；すり取る.

M *pick out* the best book 一番良い本を選り出す ‖ They were *picked out* for promotions. 彼らは抜てき昇進させられた. ‖ *pick out* the sense of a passage 章句の意味をつかむ ‖ *pick out* a scent においをかぎ出す ‖ an eye accustomed to *pick out* objects in the dark 所要の物が取れるようにくらやみで慣らされた目 ‖ *pick out* a successor to ... …の後継者を求める.【類】some modern maxims (格言) *picked out* at random.

M² *pick up* a purse on the street 通りで財布を拾う ‖ *pick up* passengers [タクシーが]客を拾う ‖ I'll *pick* you *up* at your home. [車で]君の家まで迎えに行く. ‖ *pick up* one by one 片っぱしから拾い上げる ‖ be *picked up* in a lifeboat 救助艇に収容される.【類】be *picked up* in a dramatic rescue (劇的な救助作業で) ‖ *pick up* offenders 犯罪人をつかまえる.【類】be *picked up* on a charge of ... …(のけん疑で) ‖ *pick up* a bus at ... …でバスに乗る ‖ There the train *picked up* two more cars. そこで列車は二両増結した. ‖ The party *picked up* fifty-two seats in the House. その党は議院に五十二席を獲得した. ‖ help a mother *pick up* a fallen tot お母さんを手伝ってころんだ子供を起してやる ‖ *pick up* a broadcast from ... …からの放送を傍受する ‖ *pick up* wheat and make a stack [刈取った]小麦を積重ねて山を造る ‖ The ship was *picked up* abandoned. 同船は放棄されたまま発見された. ‖ The firm is *picking up* now. あの商会は昨今見直しつつある.【類】The invalid (病人) is *picking up* (=improving). / Tourist travel to Japan is again *picking up*. / I lost thirty pounds through sickness, but am now *picking up* (回復しつつある). ‖ I have *picked up* with him. 私は彼と偶然懇意になった. ‖ I managed to *pick up* an acquaintance with him. とにかく彼と知合いになるようにした. ‖ *pick up* a quarrel with ... …にけんかを吹っかける ‖ *pick up* a few words or phrases 少しの言葉や文句を聞き覚える ‖ *pick up* a livelihood 生計の道を見付ける.【類】*pick up* a word for memory / *pick up* a precarious livelihood (不安な生活) ‖ *pick* oneself *up* [転倒した時]はね起きる.

P She had no appetite and only *picked* at the food. 彼女は食欲がなかったので料理をちょっぴり食べただけだった. ¶ *pick* apples *from* a tree 木からりんごをもぐ. ¶ *pick* one's way *into* a park 公園に足を運ぶ. ¶ *pick* one's pocket *of* one's purse 人のポケットから財布をする. ¶ *pick* the meat *off* a bone 骨から肉をむしり取る. ¶ *pick* a good one *out of* the lot 一山の中から良いのをより取る. ¶ The coat was *picked to* pieces. 上衣はずたずたに裂かれた. ‖ *pick* neighbors *to* pieces 近所の人を酷評する. ¶ *pick* a quarrel *with* a person 人にけんかを売る.

picker, *n.* 拾う人(もの).

Q² a *rag picker* [ぼろなど]拾い屋, くず屋.

picket, *n.* 見張り(ピケ).

V *post* (=*station*) a strong *picket* 見張りの者を多数配置する.

picketing, *n.* 〖労〗スト破り監視(ピケ).

Q² *cross picketing* [対立する二つ以上の組合の]交互スト監視. ¶ *mass picketing* 集団ピケ.

picking, *n.* とること.

Q² *pocket picking* すり行為.

pickpocket, *n.* すり.

Q an *expert pickpocket* 巧妙なすり.

P The public are cautioned *against pickpockets*. すりに御注意下さい. ¶ Beware *of* (=Look out *for*) *pickpockets*. すり御用心.

pickup, *n.* 〖ラジオ〗中継.

Q² *Short-wave pickups* carried the speech around the world. その演説は短波放送で世界中に中継された.

picnic, *n.* 遠足(ピクニック).

V *get up* a *picnic* 遠足を催す ‖ A *picnic* was *got up* in his honor. 彼を主客としてピクニックが催された. ¶ *have* a *picnic* 野外散策をする. ¶ *miss* a *picnic* ピクニックに行き損う. ¶ *organize* a scientific *picnic* to ... …へ「科学する遠足」の会を企てる. ¶ *plan* a *picnic* 遠足を企てる.

Q² a *bathing-dress picnic* 水泳着のピクニック. ¶ a *school picnic* 学校の遠足.

P We had capital fun *at* the *picnic*. 遠足はすてきにおもしろかった. ¶ go *on* a *picnic* ピクニックに出かける.

pictorial, *n.* 絵入雑誌.

Q a *beautiful pictorial* offered free every Sunday 日曜ごとに無代進呈の美しい絵入雑誌.

pictorial, *a.* 絵のように描写した.

P a novel *pictorial of* (=depicting) rural life 田園生活を詳細に描写した小説.

picture, *n.* 絵画；画像；写真, 生写し；化身；映画.

V The stamp *bears* the *picture* of George Washington. その切手にはワシントンの肖像が付いている. ¶ *collect pictures* 絵画を収集する. ¶ These features in the scenery *complete* an exquisite *picture*. 風景のこれらの美が絶妙の画面を造り上げている. ‖ But why can we have to *complete* a *picture* with which all are familiar? 一般によく知れていることを一層くわしく説く必要があろうか. ¶ Your letter *conjures up* mental *picture* of sylvan meadows and lowing herds. あなたの手紙で野趣ある草原や鳴く牛の群を想い起します.【類】He did his best to *conjure up* a *picture* of the scene. ¶ Once there was a panorama there which *contained* a *picture* of the Restoration War. 以前そこに戊辰(ぼしん)の役のパノラマがあった. ¶ *deface* a *picture* 絵画を汚損する. ¶ *develop pictures* 写真を現像する. ¶ *distort* a *picture* 真相をゆがめる. ¶ *draw* a *picture* [ペンや鉛筆で]絵を描く. ¶ *form* a clear *picture* (=idea) of ... …をはっきり頭に思い浮べる. ¶ *frame* a *picture* 絵に額ぶちを付ける.【類】Can you *frame* this *picture* for me? ¶ *give* a faithful *picture* ... …を忠実に描出する. ¶ *hang* a *picture* on the wall 絵を壁にかける. ¶ *hang up* a *picture* 絵をかける. ¶ I *had* my *picture taken* yesterday. 僕はきのう写真を取った. ¶ The *picture* was *knocked down* to me at a sale by auction. 絵は競売で私に落ちた. ¶ *knock off* a *picture* 絵を描きなぐる. ¶ *magnify* and *project pictures* on a screen 絵を拡大してスクリーンに映す. ¶ *make* a *picture* of an elephant 象の絵を描く ‖ These *made* a *picture* not soon to be forgotten. これらが総合して容易に忘れられない一つの場面を現出した. ‖ The frost on the window *made* a *picture*. 窓ガラスに霜が絵を描いた. ‖ ... unite to *make* a *picture unrivalled* in its loveliness …が総合的に類のないほど美しい風景を造り出す. ¶ all go to *make up* a *picture* which indicates that ... 全部が相集まって…を示す一幅の画面を作り上げている. ¶ *mount pictures* 絵を額にはめる；写真を台紙に張る. ¶ *paint* a *picture* worth selling 売物になるような絵を描く ‖ Music *paints* a *picture* in tone. 音楽は音色で絵を描く(有声の絵だ). ¶ I have *picked up* a good *picture*. 私はいい絵を一つ手に入れた. ¶ *pin* a *picture* of her lover to a wall 彼氏の写真を壁にピンでとめる.【類】a *picture pinned up* on the wall. ¶ The patient *presented* the *picture* of sadness, anxiety, and hopelessness. 患者はひどく悲哀・憂慮・絶望の相を呈した(満身悲哀の観があった). ¶ a *picture printed* in colors 色ずりの絵. ¶ ... *pull* the whole *picture* together …が全体の絵を引締めている. ¶ the *picture* has been *remade* as a talkie under the title of ... その映画は…という題名でトーキーに再製された. ¶ No [picture] theater with any respect for the intelligence of its patrons would *run* such a *picture*. こんな映画を上映するのは観客をばかにしたものだ. ¶ The frame *sets off* *picture*. その額ぶちは絵を引立たせる. ¶ *shade* a *picture* 絵を隈(くま)どる. ¶ Camera men are *shooting* their *pictures*. 撮影技師が映画をとっている. ¶ a theatre *showing* moving *pictures*=a movie house 映画館. ¶ *sign* one's *picture* 自分の写真に署名する. ¶ *submit* their *pictures* to the Academy 彼らの絵を美術院に提出する. ¶ *take* a *picture* [with a camera] 撮影する. ¶ *take down* a *picture* [掛っている]絵を取下ろす. ¶ *throw* a *picture* on to a screen 絵をスクリーンに映す. ¶ *title* a *picture* 絵に題をつける. ¶ *touch up* a *picture*=finish the last touch 絵の仕上げをする. ¶ *trample* the *picture* under foot 写真を踏みつける. ¶ *unveil* a *picture* of Russia ロシアの一風景を示す. ¶ *work pictures* 絵を描き上げる.

V² The *picture represents* their farewell. 絵は彼らの別れの場面を示す.

Q an *accurate picture* 精密な絵. ¶ a *brilliant* and *entrancing picture* さん然として人をこうこつたらしめる絵. ¶ a *careful picture* of Indian manners インディアンの習性の細かな描写. ¶ a *celebrated picture* 名画. ¶ a high-toned *classic picture* 調子の高い古典画. ¶ be given a *clear picture* of the problem その問題の全ぼうをはっきり分からせる. ¶ gain a *clear* and *concise picture* of how it functions その機能が簡明に分かる. ¶ *comic pictures*=funnies 続き漫画. ¶ She gave me the most *complete picture* of the beginning of pregnancy. 容体を聞いて彼女はてっきり妊娠の初期であることを知った. ¶take a ***composite picture*** of ... …の重ね写真を取る. ¶Many Chinese characters are ***conventionalized pictures***. 漢字中には象形文字が多い. ¶a ***dark picture*** of Europe's situation ヨーロッパ形勢の暗たんたる様相. ¶a ***delightful*** and ***piquant picture*** of German social life ドイツの社会生活の愉快な風刺的な描写. ¶paint much too ***dismal*** a ***picture*** of the fate of ... …の運命をあまりにも悲観的に描写する. ¶This will give an ***exact picture*** of the situation of the day. これを見ると当時の情況の一面がよく分かるだろう. ¶an ***exaggerated*** or ***overdrawn picture*** 誇張したすなわち大げさな描写. 【類】an ***excellent picture*** of English life. ¶give a ***faithful picture*** of ... …を忠実に描写する. ¶the fabrication of ***faked pictures*** 映画のトリック製作. ¶draw a ***fine picture*** of one's future その将来を有望と見る. ¶a ***funny picture*** 漫画. ¶a ***genuine picture*** by Rubens 本もののルーベンスの絵画. ¶This is too ***gloomy*** a ***picture***. これはあまりにも悲観的過ぎる. ¶take ***good pictures*** with one's new camera 新しいカメラでよい写真をとる. ¶a ***graphic picture*** 絵を見るような(躍如たる)描写. ¶They paint a ***heroic picture*** of themselves as the savior of "progressive elements" いわゆる進歩派の救世主と自画自賛する. ¶a ***high-colored picture*** 色彩の強い絵. ¶an ***illustrative picture*** さし絵. ¶It gives us an ***incidental picture*** of English life at the period. それによってわれらはその時代における英国人の生活をその副産物として知ることができる. ¶***instructional pictures***＝educational films 教育映画. ¶The ***industrial picture*** seems bright. 産業の現状は好況らしく見える. ¶That is not too ***lurid*** a ***picture*** of the situation. こう述べたからといってその無残な局面をはなはだしく誇張したものではない. ¶***masterly pictures*** of famous writers 文豪の雄大な描写. ¶draw a ***melancholy picture*** from the failure of ... …の失敗について悲観的観察を下す. ¶a sort of ***microcosmic picture*** of ... …の一種の縮図. ¶We see the ***moving picture*** on a screen. 映画はスクリーンで見る. ¶a ***naughty picture*** わい画. ¶***No picture*** of the City of London may neglect St. Paul's Churchyard. ロンドンを語る場合聖ポーロの教会境内を除外することはできない. ¶***objectionable pictures*** けしからぬ絵. ¶the suppression of ***obscene pictures*** and publications (＝literature) エロな絵画や発行物の発売禁止. ¶a ***perfect picture*** of a thriving, contented, liberal-hearted farmer 繁栄し満足している大まかな農夫の如実の姿. ¶as shown in the ***photographic picture*** above 上掲の写真に示す通り. ¶***profane pictures*** snapped by the staff photographer 写真班員が取った冒とく的な写真. ¶a ***realistic picture*** of the home-life of a great thinker 大思想家の私生活の写実的描写. ¶a ***rich-colored picture*** 色彩の豊かな絵. ¶a ***silent*** (***sound***) ***picture*** 無(発)声映画. ¶***still pictures*** [活動写真に対し]普通の写真. ¶draw a ***somber picture*** of ... …を悲観する. ¶a ***suggestive picture*** エロがかった絵. ¶***tawdry-framed pictures*** of actresses けばけばしい額縁を付けた女優の写真. ¶a ***true picture*** of English society 英国社会のありのままの描写. ¶an ***undistorted picture*** of ... …の(筆を曲げてない)正しい描写. ¶a ***very picture*** of health 健康そのもの. ¶***give*** a vivid ***picture*** of ... …を生々と描写する. ¶***vivid*** and ***realistic pictures*** of life in feudal Japan 封建時代の日本の生々しい現実的な描写. ¶early ***Western pictures*** 〖映画〗初期の西部もの.

Q² an ***animal picture*** 動物の絵. ¶an ***art picture*** 芸術的絵画. ¶a ***cloud picture*** 雲の模様. ¶The curious medley of things piled up almost suggests a ***cubist picture***. 種々雑多の珍奇なものの集りはまるで立体派の絵を見るようだ. ¶a 1950 ***food picture*** 一九五〇年の食料事情. ¶a ***frost picture*** [窓ガラスなどの]霜の花. ¶***pictures***, both "inset" and ***full page*** さし込み絵と一ページ大の絵. ¶a ***full-page colored picture*** 全ページ大の色彩画. ¶a ***full-size*** (＝***full-length***) ***picture*** 全身像. ¶a ***group picture*** 集団写真 ‖ take a ***group picture*** of the assembled family 家族集団の写真を取る. ¶a ***half-length picture*** 半身像. ¶a ***Hollywood picture*** ハリウッド映画. ¶a ***human nature picture*** 人間性のあらわれ. ¶an ***impression picture*** 写し絵. ¶a ***landscape picture*** 風景画. ¶a ***lantern picture*** 幻灯. ¶a ***life picture*** 実物大の絵. ¶a ***light picture***＝pictorial photograph 光線画. ¶a ***living picture*** 活人画. ¶a ***marine picture***＝a seapiece, a seascape 海景画. ¶a ***million-dollar picture*** 百万ドル映画. ¶a ***nude picture*** 裸体画. ¶an old ***print picture*** 古い版画. ¶an ***on-the-spot news picture*** 実況ニュース映画. ¶a ***Paramount*** (an ***M-G-M***) ***picture*** パラマウント(メトロ・ゴールドウイン)社映画. ¶a ***pen picture*** ペン画. ¶a ***pen-and-ink picture*** ペン画. ¶a ***photograph picture*** 写真画. ¶a "***pin-up girl***" ***picture*** [壁にピンで留めて見る]美人写真. ☞ 《米》 a pin-up picture (girl), a pin-up ともいう. ¶a ***program picture*** 〖映〗短編添付映画. ¶his ***Salon picture*** of 1904 彼の一九〇四年度サロン出品画. ¶a ***sea picture*** 海の絵. ¶a ***slow-motion picture*** of a race process 競馬の高速度映画(決勝点などを示す). ¶***sound pictures***＝talkies. ¶***talking pictures***＝talkies. ¶a ***theatrical*** motion ***picture***＝a photoplay 映画. ¶a ***three-dimensional motion picture***＝a 3-D picture 立体映画. ¶a ***travel picture*** 旅行宣伝映画. ¶a ***wide-screen picture*** ワイドスクリーン(シネマスコープなど). ¶a ***word picture*** 象形文字. ¶give (＝paint) a ***word picture*** of ... 言葉で…を描写する. ¶an ***X-ray*** (＝Roentgen) ***picture*** レントゲン写真.

P I have seen you so many times ***in*** the ***pictures***. 映画面(スクリーン)で度々あなたにお目に掛りました. ‖ news ***in pictures*** 時事画報 ‖ Tokyo news ***in pictures*** 東京写真だより ‖ ***in*** this ***picture*** he is seen ... ing ... この写真では彼は…している所がとってある. ¶You look good (＝nice) ***in*** this ***picture***. 君のこの写真はよく取れているね. ¶point to various objects ***on*** the ***picture*** 絵にでている色々な物を指し示す.

P² a ***picture by*** a famous artist 巨匠の絵. ¶a ***picture of*** a girl 少女の写っている写真 ‖ She was a ***picture of*** beauty. 彼女は絵に描いたような美人だった. ¶A gentleman by his bearing, debonair and graceful, he looks the very ***picture of*** an impecunious count. 態度は紳士的で上品で優雅で貧乏伯爵というのは彼のような人をいうのである. 【類】His face is a ***picture of*** sadness. / She is the ***picture*** (化身) ***of*** health and sweetness. / He became the ***picture of*** despair. / She became the ***picture of*** astonishment at seeing him. / a ***picture of*** a battle / a ***picture of*** landscape＝a landscape ‖ a ***picture of*** memory 記憶の一こま ‖ a ***picture of*** portraiture 肖像画 ‖ The child is the very ***picture of*** his father. あの子はお父さんそっくりだ. ¶a clear, sharp ***picture on*** the screen 映写幕に写った明りょうなはっきりした絵. ¶paint vivid ***pictures with*** the fewest possible strokes of the brush なるたけ筆数を少くして真に迫った絵を描く.

O It's quite a ***picture***, isn't it? それは丸で絵のようではありませんか.

picture, *v*. 描く; 心に描く.

P I can ***picture*** (＝gather) ***from*** this that ... このことから…と想像できる. ¶***picture*** (＝make a picture) ***in*** one's mind 心に描く. ¶just ***picture to*** yourselves the horror with which ... …する恐ろしさをちょっと想像して御覧なさい.

O ***picture*** the sufferings of the poor 貧民の苦労を想像する.

picturedom, *n*. 映画界.

Q² ***moving picturedom*** 映画界.

picturesqueness, *n*. 雅致.

V ***give*** great ***picturesqueness*** to the scene 景色に非常な雅趣を添える.

piddle, *v*. 徒費する.

M a house where she used to ***piddle*** (＝trifle) ***away*** her leisure hours 彼女が以前のんきに暮した家.

pie, *n*. パイ.

Q a ***whole pie*** cut into five pieces 五つに切った一つのパイ.

Q² a slice of ***apple pie*** アップルパイの一切れ. ¶a ***mud pie*** 泥だんご. ¶a ***mince pie*** ミンスパイ. ¶a slice of ***pumpkin pie*** パンプキンパイの一切れ. ¶a ***resurrection pie*** 残肉パイ. ¶a ***squash pie*** 夏かぼちゃのパイ.

piece, *n*. 肉片, 一個, 一枚; (詩歌などの)一篇; 部分品; 貨幣; [文芸上の]作品.

V I ***gave*** him a ***piece*** of my mind. 私は打つけにあの男に小言をいった. ¶***play*** (＝***act or represent***) a ***piece*** 劇を演じる. ¶***set*** a ***piece*** to music 作曲する. ¶***tear*** a ***piece*** from the loaf 一塊のパンからひと切れむしる.

Q put ***another piece*** of wood on the fire まきをもう一本くべる. ¶a ***brilliant piece*** of work すばらしい作品の一つ. ¶a very ***clever piece*** of work きわめて巧妙な作品. ¶a ***clever*** and ***interesting piece*** of work 巧妙で興味ある作品. ¶a ***copyrighted piece*** 版権のある作品. ¶This is an ***elabo-***

rate piece of job. これは仲々手のこんだ仕事だ. ¶a delicate piece of mechanism 一個の微妙な機構. ¶one of the most effective pieces of character-drawing in the novel 小説でもっとも効果的に性格を描写した一つ. ¶a very exacting piece of work 非常に骨の折れる一つの仕事. ¶the finest and most interesting pieces of literature 興味深い最高の文学作品. ¶She is a forward piece. 彼女は生意気な女だ. ¶Tulipmania in the Netherlands was a frantic piece of folly. オランダのチューリップの熱狂的流行は愚の骨頂だった. ¶an intricate piece of machinery 複雑な一個の機械. ¶A little piece of business fell to his lot. ちょっとした仕事が彼の手にはいった. ¶a long, thin, narrow piece of wood=a slat 小割板. ¶a less mature piece of work それほどに完成していない作. ¶middle pieces 中位の大きさのもの. ¶a neat piece of work 見事なでき栄えの仕事. ¶a nickel piece of ten sen 拾銭の白銅貨. ¶an overacted piece of movie love-making 芝居をやり過ぎるラブシーン映画. ¶scattered pieces 雑篇. ¶a few lonely silver pieces in my pocket ポケットにある少しばかりの銀貨. ¶a sixpenny piece 六ペンスの貨幣. ¶a spotty piece of work できの悪い仕事. ¶It's a pretty stiff piece of work. 仲々骨だ. ¶The writer is to be congratulated on a highly suggestive and stimulative piece of work. このきわめて示唆と刺激に富む著作を世に送った著者に敬意を表すべきだ. ¶The book is a thorough piece of work. 同書は行き届いた本である. ¶a collection of more than two hundred pieces 二百点以上に達する収集.

Q² an animal piece (=painting) 動物画. ¶an artillery piece 一門の銃砲. ¶Chopin, Mozart and Beethoven pieces ショパン, モーツアルト, ベートーベンの曲. ¶a companion piece to ... …の姉妹篇. ¶a gold piece 金貨. ¶They are truly museum pieces. それは博物館に陳列のできるものだ. ¶Rocking chairs have become museum pieces in Britain. ゆりいすは英国では博物館にでも行かなければ見られないほどになった. ¶Sung dynasty pieces 宋(ソ)物(陶磁器など).

P undertake the work by the piece 仕事をでき高計算で引受ける. 【類】The workers are paid by the piece. ‖ by a piece (=stroke) of good luck 幸運にも. ¶meat in small pieces 細かに切った肉 ‖ break in (=into or to) pieces 粉みじんにくだける ‖ tear it in pieces それをずたずたに裂く ‖ paper in (=of) one piece 継目なしの紙 ‖ cut it in two pieces それを二つに切る. ¶The glass fell and was smashed into pieces. コップが落ちてみじんにくだけた. 【類】break into pieces. ¶a set of dishes of six pieces 六枚一組のさら ‖ it is of a piece with ... それは…と同類だ ‖ It is all of a piece with his previous conduct. それは前と同じ手口の仕打ちである. ‖ All things in the universe are evidently of a piece.—Hume. 宇宙間のあらゆる物は明かに全一体をなしている. ¶work on piece 仕事の分量で支払を受ける仕事(をする) ‖ The parley has gone to pieces. 談判が破裂した. ‖ The carriage was dashed to pieces. 馬車がばらばらにこわれた. 【類】The glass has fallen (=dropped) to pieces. / My old boat has gone to pieces on the rocks (岩に当って). ‖ The watch will have to be taken all to pieces and thoroughly cleaned. その時計はすっかり分解して掃除をしなけりゃいけないでしょう. ¶I'm fed up with that piece of junk. そんながらくたにはあきあきだ.

P² A knight is a piece in the game of chess. 騎士は将棋のこまである. ¶a piece of bread (sugar, wood) 一片のパン(など). ‖ pieces of broken glass ガラスの破片 ‖ a piece of gold (silver) 金(銀)貨 ‖ I enjoyed myself most in this piece (=part) of my journey. 私の旅行でここの所が一番面白かった. ‖ a piece of land 一区の土地 ‖ a piece of machinery 一個の機械 ‖ two pieces (=sheets) of paper 二枚の紙 ‖ one hundred pieces of mail matter 百点の郵便物 ‖ a piece of news (information, advice) 一片の報道(など) ‖ a piece of poetry 一首の詩 ‖ perform a piece of music 一曲を演奏する. 【類】a piece of evidence / It is a piece of conduct unworthy of a student. ‖ He is a piece of surgeon. 彼も外科医のはしくれだ. ‖ There is quite a piece of labor in it. [絵など]相当の労作だ. ¶it is not all of a piece with ... それは…と全然同一というのではない.

piece, *v.* つなぎ合わせる.

M piece together a story 物語(小説)にまとめあげる ‖ piece evidence together 証拠を総合する ‖ piece together odds and ends of cloth to make a quilt 切れっぱしを縫い合わせて布とんを作る.

M² piece up a story with data gathered from various sources いろんな材料をまとめて小説を作り上げる.

pier, *n.* 桟橋, 波止場.

V The pier was washed away by the waves. 桟橋が波で流されて仕舞った. 「函(ｶﾝ)(ケーソン).

Q² a caisson for sinking bridge piers 橋台を沈下させる潜

P steamers go alongside a pier at ... …では汽船が桟橋に横付けになる. ¶The steamer lies at (=alongside) the pier. その汽船は桟橋に横付けになっている. ‖ Our representative will meet you at the pier in New York [旅館などの]手代がニューヨークの波止場まで御出迎えを致します. ¶I waited on the pier. 私は波止場で待っていた.

pierce, *v.* 突き通す; うがつ; 透徹する. 「突かれた.

M He was pierced through and through. 彼は滅多突きに

P pierce beneath the shows of things 事物の真相をうがつ. ¶a mountain pierced by a tunnel トンネルで抜いた山 ‖ a wound pierced by a bullet 貫通銃創. ¶The cold pierces me to the bone. 寒気が骨にしみる. ‖ I felt as if he had pierced me to the heart. 私は彼に心臓を突かれたように感じた. ¶He was pierced with a lance. 彼はやりで突刺された. ‖ They pierced the still air with their cries. 彼らの叫声が静寂を破った.

piety, *n.* 敬けん; 孝順. 「る.

V practice filial piety towards one's parents 親孝行をす

Q the fervent piety and humanity of Charles Kingsley チャールズ・キングスレイの熱烈な信仰心と人間性. ¶a man of marked piety 非常に敬けんな人.

P² piety towards God 敬神.

pig, *n.* 豚; (米) 子豚; 銑鉄. 「pen 豚の飼養場.

V keep pigs 豚を飼う ‖ a pen to keep the pig in=a pig

V² Pigs grunt. 豚がぶーぶーいう. 「丸と太った子豚.

Q You dirty old pig! この古豚め. ¶a plump little pig 丸

Q² a baby pig 子豚. ¶Japan is a guinea pig in the laboratory of democracy. 日本は民主々義実験室のモルモットである. ¶iron pig=pig iron 銑鉄.

P a drove of pigs 一群の豚 ‖ a litter of pigs 豚の一腹子.

pigeon, *n.* はと.

V liberate (=release) pigeons はとを放つ. ¶let loose (=toss) pigeons はとを放つ.

V² Pigeons coo. はとがくーくー鳴く.

Q a Belgian homing pigeon=a Belgian homer ベルギーの伝書ばと. ¶blue pigeon (俗) 測鉛. ¶a homing pigeon 伝書ばと. ¶a pet pigeon 子飼いのはと.

Q² a carrier pigeon 伝書ばと.

P² pigeons on war services 軍用ばと.

pigeonhole, *v.* 棚上げする. 「を放たらかす.

P pigeonhole the request for a new park 公園新設の請願

pigeon-message, *n.* はと通信.

V receive a pigeon-message dated ... …日付のはと通信を

pigtail, *n.* 豚尾; 弁髪; おさげ. 」受取る.

V wear a pigtail 弁髪を着ける.

P a girl wearing her hair hanging down in a pigtail [fashion] おさげの少女.

pike, *n.* [やりなどの]穂先.

P be finished by a stab with one's pike 止めを刺される.

pike, *n.* 〖魚〗 かます.

Q² early mackerel pikes さんまの走り.

pile, *n.* 堆(ﾀｲ)積, 山; 多量, 多額; 電気炉.

V Her fan mail forms a huge pile. 彼女のファンからの来状は大きな山を成す. ¶have a pile of good sense 分別に富む. ¶The dead bodies lay in piles on the field. 死体は戦場にるいるいとしていた. ¶make a pile (=fortune) (米) 財産を作る. 【類】They made their mark (名をあげ) and "their piles."

Q make a small pile [ごみなど]小山をなす. ¶an atomic pile 〖物理〗 原子炉. ¶a mountainous pile of mail 山なす郵便物. ¶send it to the rubbish pile それを掃きだめに捨てる. ¶a huge pile (物資などの)大山.

Q² discard it on a dump pile それをごみためにに捨てる. ¶a leaf pile 木の葉のたい積.

P² piles of books 山積の本 ‖ a pile of hay (ruins, stone, rubbish) 一山のほし草(など). ¶a pile (=piles) of money 巨額の金.

pile, *v.* 積上げる, 重ねる. 「たさら.

M a dish piled high and thick with meat 肉を沢山盛っ

M^2 *pile* more coal ***on*** 石炭をさらに積み上げる. ¶plates and dishes ***piled up*** on a table テーブルに積重っているさら類 ‖ ***pile up*** debts 借金をためる ‖ ***pile up*** wealth 資産を作る ‖ ***pile up*** government indebtedness to the tune of … …の金額に達するまで政府の負債を増大させる. 【類】a chance to ***pile up*** a fortune / be ***piled up*** into a total result that … ‖ The plane shot off the end of a runaway without taking to the air and ***piled up*** in flames in a bog. 機は離陸しないで滑走路をとび越え泥沼の中に火炎となって積重なった. ‖ the freight ***piled up*** on the wharf 波止場に積上げた貨物.

P *pile* one ***above*** (=***on***) another 積上げる. 【類】*pile* logs ***on*** each other ‖ dangerous as eggs *piled* one ***on*** the other 〘比喩〙累卵のようにあやうい ‖ hills *piled* ***on*** hills 重畳した丘. ¶a table *piled* high ***with*** paper 紙をうず高く積上げた卓. 【類】The counter (売場の台) was *piled* high ⌊***with*** goods.

pilgrim, *n.* 巡礼者; 遊歴者.

V He has ***made*** a golfing *pilgrim* to many links. 彼はあちらこちらとゴルフ場めぐりをした(ゴルフの練習をして回った). 「*pilgrims* 文学修行遍路.

Q *pilgrims* ***bound*** for Minobu 身延まいりの人. ¶***literary***

P^2 a *pilgrim* ***from*** the Holy Land 聖地戻りの巡礼者. ¶a *pilgrim* ***to*** the Ise Shrines 伊勢まいりの人.

pilgrimage, *n.* 巡礼, 回国; 現世の旅路.

V ***begin*** one's *pilgrimage* to temples 諸寺巡礼を始める. ¶In that retreat, in the odor of sanctity, she ***closed*** her earthly *pilgrimage*. あの幽居で清浄の香りに包まれて彼女は現世の巡礼を終った(他界した). ¶one who visits … should ***extend*** his *pilgrimage* to … …を見物に行く人は…まで行って見るべきだ. ¶***make*** one's *pilgrimage* to … …へ参けいする. 【類】The custom of ***making*** *pilgrimages* to sacred peaks (お山まいり) is an ancient one in Japan.

Q Lourdes has become the place of the most ***frequent*** *pilgrimages*. ルールドは参けいの絶えない霊場となった. 【類】I made ***frequent*** *pilgrimages* to the house of that great man. ¶Some of the colonists make ***homeward*** *pilgrimages* annually. 「ける.

Q^2 go on ***flower*** *pilgrimages* あっちこっちの花見旅行に出か

P a place ***of*** weekly *pilgrimage* 毎週でかける場所. ¶go ***on*** *pilgrimages* あんぎゃにでかける. 【類】devotees (信徒) who come ***on*** *pilgrimage* to the shrine / go ***on*** *pilgrimage* to Ise (=the Ise Shrines).

P^2 make a *pilgrimage* ***through*** various provinces 諸国を巡礼する. ¶a *pilgrimage* ***to*** the grave of dear one gone before 先立って死んだ愛人の墓参り. 【類】*pilgrimage* ***to*** Ise / *pilgrimages* ***to*** temples.

pill, *n.* 丸薬; いやなこと.

V ***compound*** *pills* of immortality 不死の薬を調合する. ¶***gild*** a *pill* 丸薬に金ぱくをかける ‖ ***gild*** (=***sugar***) the *pill* いやなことを気持よくやれるように仕向ける ‖ ***gild*** the *pill* with deceptive euphemisms 辞令巧みに事実をおおう. ¶***sugar-coat*** a *pill* (飲みよいように)丸薬に糖衣を施す.

Q a ***bitter*** *pill* にがい丸薬; いやなこと. ¶***sugar-coated*** *pills* 糖衣丸薬.

Q^2 take ***sleeping*** *pills* 催眠薬(丸薬)を飲む ‖ an overdose of ***sleeping*** *pills* 催眠薬の飲み過ぎ.

pillage, *v.* 略奪する.

P Pirates *pillaged* the town ***along*** the coast. 海賊が海岸⌊の都市を略奪した.

pillar, *n.* 柱, 柱石.

V ***plane*** a *pillar* 柱を削る.

Q a ***massive*** *pillar* 太い柱.

Q^2 a ***gingerbread*** *pillar* 安っぽい飾りの柱.

P Drifting ***from*** *pillar* to post, she had come to Munich. 旅から旅へ渡ってそのとき彼女はムューニッヒへ来ていた. ¶a groove ***in*** a *pillar* 柱のみぞ.

P^2 a *pillar* ***of*** fire 火柱 ‖ a *pillar* ***of*** the state 国家の柱石. 【類】a *pillar* of society.

pillory, *n.* さらし台.

P ***in*** the *pillory* (公衆の)笑い物となって ‖ a criminal ***in*** the *pillory* さらし台にかかっている罪人. 【類】He deserves to be put ***in*** the *pillory*.

pillow, *n.* まくら.

V ***smooth*** the *pillows* of a dying man 死に水を取る. ¶The child went to sleep as soon as it ***touched*** the *pillow*. 子供は床につくとすぐ寝付いた. 「たまくら.

Q^2 an ***air*** *pillow* 空気まくら. ¶a ***stuff*** *pillow* 詰め物をし

P place one's revolver ***beneath*** (=***under***) one's *pillow* 連発銃をまくらの下におく. ¶bury one's tired head ***in*** a *pillow* 疲れた頭をまくらに埋める. ¶rest one's head ***on*** a *pillow* 頭をまくらに載せる. ¶He laid down his head ***upon*** his *pillow* to rest. 彼は寝ころんで頭をまくらにおいた. ¶Consult ***with*** your *pillow*. 一晩寝てとっくり考え給⌊え.

pillow, *v.* まくらする.

P with my head *pillowed* (=rested) ***on*** her laps 私は彼女のひざをまくらにして. ¶*pillow* one's head ***upon*** one's arm 腕をまくらする.

pilot, *n.* 水先案内者; 指導者; 航空士. 「内を雇う.

V ***drop*** the *pilot* 指導者を退ける. ¶***take on*** a *pilot* 水先案

Q a ***chief*** *pilot* 〘航空〙機長. ¶a ***grounded*** *pilot* 墜落した操縦士. ¶a ***licensed*** *pilot* 有資格の操縦士.

Q^2 an ***air-mail*** *pilot* 郵便輸送機操縦士. ¶an ***airline*** *pilot* 定期航空操縦者. ¶a ***fighter*** *pilot* 戦闘機操縦士. ¶a former ***Kamikaze*** *pilot* 元神風隊操縦士. ¶a ***sky*** *pilot* 空のパイロット(海に対して), 操縦士. ¶a venturesome ***test*** *pilot* 危険なテストパイロット.

pilot, *v.* 案内する.

P *pilot* ***across*** the street an elderly lady from the country 年長ないなか出の婦人を案内して通路を横断させる. ¶I was *piloted* (=guided) ***through*** the park. 私は公園の中を⌊案内してもらった.

pilotage, *n.* 操縦.

P ***under*** the *pilotage* of … …の操縦の下に.

pimple, *n.* にきび.

V^2 *Pimples* began to ***break out*** on my chin. 私のあごににきびが出だした. ¶*Pimples* have ***come out*** in his face. 彼は顔ににきびがで出た.

P^2 a *pimple* ***on*** the nose 鼻の上の吹で物.

pin, *n.* 留針, ピン; [九柱戯の]柱.

V ***have*** *pins* and needles in one's legs 足にしびれがきれる. ¶***put*** (=stick) ***in*** a *pin* ピンを差込む. ¶***stick*** a *pin* 針を刺す ‖ ***Stick*** a *pin* there. 《俗》忘れいようにそれを書留めておき給え. ¶***straighten*** a bent *pin* 曲ったピンを伸ばす. ¶***take out*** a *pin* ピンを抜き取る.

Q an ***ornamental*** *pin* [ネクタイの]飾りピン. ¶stump through life on the ***wooden*** *pin* 一生を義足に助けられて送る ‖ hurl a heavy ball at a set of ***wooden*** *pins* [九柱戯などで]一組の木柱に重い球を投げつける.

Q^2 a ***breast*** *pin* = a breastpin 《米》ブローチ. ☞英語の breast pin はネクタイどめ. なお米語の stickpin はネクタイどめ, バッジの意に用いる. ¶a ***hair*** *pin* ヘヤピン. ¶an ***office*** *pin* 会社のマークのついたえりピン. ¶a ***scarf*** *pin* スカーフピン. ¶a ***school*** *pin* 学校の記章.

P I was ***on*** *pins* and needles. 私は針のむしろにすわる心地がした; しびれがきれてちくちくした.

pin, *v.* ピンで留める; 押しつける.

M He was *pinned* ***down*** to the ground under a heavy fallen tree. 彼は重い倒木の下じきになり身動きもできなかった. ‖ You can never *pin* him ***down*** to any job. あいつときたら一つの仕事に精を出す男じゃないからね. ‖ *pin* a person ***down*** to a promise (an admission) その言質をとる(いや応なしに承認させる).

M^2 *pin* ***up*** a dress 着物をピンで留める ‖ *pin* ***up*** a picture on the wall 写真(絵)を壁にピンで留める. 【類】*pin* ***up*** a notice (poster).

P I was *pinned* ***against*** the wall. 私は壁に押しつけられた. ¶He was *pinned* ***beneath*** (=***under***) the overturned automobile. 彼は転覆した自動車の下敷になった. ¶*pin* … ***on*** one's coat (cap) 上衣(など)に…をピンで留める ‖ *pin* my hopes ***on*** a meeting at … …で会合ができるという私の希望をつなぐ. ¶it is *pinned* ***to*** … それは…に留針で留めてある ‖ *pin* a person ***to*** an agreement (promise) 協定(など)を忠実に守らせる ‖ *pin* a person's arms ***to*** his sides 人の両腕をその両わきへ締めつける.

pinch, *n.* つねり, つまみ; 困苦, 苦痛; 危機.

V ***feel*** the *pinch* of hard times (foreign competition) 不景気(外国の競争)のあおりを食う. ¶***give*** one a sharp *pinch* きつくつねる. ***stand*** (=***endure***) the *pinch* of poverty 困窮にたえる. 「た.

V^2 At last ***came*** the *pinch*. いよいよのっぴきならなくなっ

Q They do not feel the ***real*** *pinch* of want. 彼らは真の貧苦を感じていない.

P They'll stand by me ***at a*** *pinch*. 彼らはまさかの時には私を助けてくれるだろう. ‖ do it ***at a*** *pinch* せっぱつまってそ

れをやる ‖ ***at*** a *pinch* for money 金に詰ったときに. ¶if it comes ***to*** a *pinch* まさかのときになれば. ¶They are ***under*** the *pinch* of want. 彼らは生活に困っている.

P² the *pinch **of*** hunger 飢餓の切迫 ‖ a *pinch **of*** salt 一つまみの塩.

pinch, *v*. つねる, つまむ, はさむ; 困窮させる.

M *pinch* a child ***black and blue*** 子供を青あざのできるほどつねる. ¶*pinch **out*** side-growths わき生えをつみとる.

P The shoe *pinches* me ***at*** the toes. くつの指の所が痛い. ¶a face *pinched **by*** hunger 飢餓でやつれた顔. ¶be *pinched **for*** money (food) 金(など)に困っている. 【類】be *pinched **for*** housing. ¶The fingers were *pinched **under*** a hawser. 指がいかりつなの下にはさまった. ¶be *pinched **with*** cold (poverty) 寒さ(貧)でやつれる.

pinchbeck, *n*. にせ物.

V The idea that advertising was merely a method of ***puffing*** the *pinchbeck* and the catchpenny has long passed. 広告はにせ物や銭取主義の商品をほめ立てる方法に過ぎないという考えはとうの昔のことだ.

pine, pine-tree, *n*. 松.

V² The *pines **soughed*** when the wind blew. 風で松籟(らい)が起った.

Q the trail of the ***lonesome*** *pine* 一本松の山道. ¶a ***long-leaf*** *pine* 長葉の松. ¶a ***monster*** *pine-tree* 松の巨木. ¶a large forest of ***white*** *pines* 白松の大きな林.

P whisperings of the wind ***among*** *pine-trees* 松風の音.

pine, *v*. 嘆き暮す; やつれさせる; 恋いこがれる.

M *pine **away*** one's life 憂いの中に一生を送る ‖ *pine **away*** one's health 嘆きのあまり健康を損じる. ¶*pine **away*** to skin and bone やせて骨と皮になる. 【類】*pine **away*** with hunger and thirst.

P *pine **after*** him to see 彼に会おうと思いをこがす. ¶Day and night she *pined **for*** her departed mother. 日夜彼女は死んだ母親を思って悲嘆にくれた. 【類】She secretly *pined **for*** his affections (身をこがした).

pine-woods, *n*. 松林.

P ***among*** *pine-woods* 松林の中で.

pink, *n*. 精華, 極致.

P My children are all ***in*** the *pink* of health. 《俗》うちの子供らは皆びんぴんしています.

P² the *pink **of*** fashion 流行の粋. ¶She is the *pink **of*** girls. 彼女は女子のはなだ. ‖ He is the *pink* (=acme) ***of*** perfection. 彼は全く申分のない人だ.

pinnacle, *n*. 絶頂.

V ***reach*** the loftiest *pinnacle* of power and fame 権力と名誉の絶頂に達する.

Q It placed him on the ***highest*** *pinnacle* of literary fame. それで彼は文学界最高の名誉ある地位に立った.

P ***at*** the *pinnacle* of his fame 彼の黄金時代に. ¶once ***on*** the *pinnacle* of prosperity かつては繁栄をきわめた.

pioneer, *n*. 先駆者, 率先者; 始祖.

V They were sent out from home to ***reinforce*** the *pioneers*. 彼らは先駆者の増援に本国から派遣された.

Q Fukuzawa, the ***celebrated*** *pioneer* in Japanese education 日本教育の先覚者福沢. ¶***early*** *pioneers* in commercial education in Japan 日本商業教育の先駆者たち. 【類】these ***early*** *pioneers* of religion and civilization. ¶an ***energetic*** *pioneer* 精力おう盛な率先者. ¶a ***fearless*** *pioneer* 恐れるもののない先駆者. ¶the ***great*** *pioneers* of Westernization in Oriental countries 東洋諸国における西洋化の大先駆者たち. ¶***trail-blazing*** *pioneers* 先駆者たち.

Q² ***women*** *pioneers* in professions 高等職業における婦人の率先者たち.

P He acted ***as*** *pioneer* in introducing the method. 彼は率先してその方法を採用した.

P² *pioneers **among*** newspaper writers in ... ...において新聞記者仲間での先駆者. ¶Colonel Sir Henry Yule, a *pioneer **in*** the historical geography of Central Asia 中央アジアの歴史地理学の始祖たるユール大佐. 【類】the *pioneer **in*** Japanese archaeological resarch (日本の考古学研究) / a *pioneer **in*** the advocacy (唱道) of this system / Dr. J. Hall Edwards, a *pioneer **in*** the use of X-rays (エクス線使用) / a *pioneer **in*** the teaching of the English language in Japan / a *pioneer **in*** technical education(専門教育) / a *pioneer **in*** the launching of Esperanto / one of the *pioneers **in*** the work of ... ¶the *pioneer **of*** similar establishments in the country この国における類似施設の起り. 【類】a *pioneer **of*** the ... trade (...業) / the *pioneer **of*** a new era of English literature / He is the *pioneer* (草分け) ***of*** this village.

pioneering, *n*. 開発.

Q various individuals who took so conspicuous a part in the ***early*** *pioneering* of ... ...の開拓時代に花々しい役割を演じた色々の人物.

pipe, *n*. 管; キセル(パイプ).

V ***fill*** one's *pipe* パイプにタバコをつめる. ¶***have*** a *pipe* between one's lips (=teeth) パイプをくわえる. ¶***light*** one's *pipe* パイプに火をつける. ¶***relay*** *pipes* 導管を継ぐ. ¶***smoke*** a *pipe* 一服やる. ¶***whiff*** (=***puff***) a small *pipe* 細いキセルでタバコをふかす.

Q a ***metalic*** *pipe* 金属管. ¶a ***perforated*** *pipe* 多孔管. ¶a ***riveted*** *pipe* びょうで留めてある管. ¶a ***seamless*** *pipe* 継目なし管. ¶a ***steel hydraulic*** *pipe* 鋼鉄製の水道管. ¶a ***vertical*** *pipe* たて管. ¶a ***welded*** *pipe* 溶接管.

Q² his ***after-dinner*** *pipe* 彼の食後の一服. ¶a ***briar-root*** *pipe* ブライア(南欧産のいばら)の根で製したパイプ. ¶a ***cast-iron*** *pipe* 鋳鉄管. ¶smoke a ***clay*** *pipe* 粘土製のパイプでタバコを吸う. ¶Gen. Douglas MacArthur's famous campaign ***corn-cob*** *pipe* マッカーサー元帥の野戦で愛用したとうもろこしパイプ. ¶a ***drain*** *pipe* 排水管. ¶an ***earthenware*** *pipe* 土管. ¶a composition ***gas*** *pipe* 複合ガス管. ¶a ***gas main*** [*pipe*] ガスのメーンパイプ(本管). ¶a ***hydrant stand*** *pipe* たて管消火(給水)管. ¶a ***lead*** *pipe* 鉛管. ¶a ***rainwater*** *pipe* 雨どい. ¶a ***service*** *pipe* [水道など本線からの]引込管. ¶a ***socket*** *pipe* 受管. ¶a ***soil*** *pipe* ふん尿管. ¶a ***steam*** *pipe* 蒸気管. ¶a ***steel*** *pipe* 鋼鉄管. ¶a ***stove*** *pipe* ストーブの煙突. ¶a ***tobacco*** *pipe* タバコのパイプ. ¶a ***water*** *pipe* 水道管. ¶a ***water main*** [*pipe*] 水道本管. ¶a ***wrought-iron*** *pipe* 錬鉄管.

P He was puffing ***at*** his *pipe* furiously. 彼はさかんにパイプをすっていた. ¶He knocked the ashes ***out of*** his *pipe*. 彼はキセルをたたいて吸殻を出した. ¶***Over*** my *pipe* I fell into a reflexion vein. 私はタバコを吸いながら考え込んでしまった. ¶lead water ***through*** bamboo *pipes* 竹の管で水を引く. ¶***with*** a *pipe* in one's mouth パイプをくわえて.

pipe, *v*. 笛を吹く.

M *pipe* a child ***asleep*** 笛を吹いて子供を寝つかせる.

M² "*Pipe **down**!*" barked Jim. 《俗》「やかましいやい」とジムがどなった. ¶He *piped **up*** to a different air, a kind of country love-song. 彼は一種のいなかの恋愛歌である変った曲を歌い始めた. ‖ The wind *piped **up*** to quite a gale overnight. 風は次第に強くなり一晩中吹きすさんでいた.

P *pipe* them ***to*** work (a meal) 号笛で作業(食事)につかせる.

piper, *n*. 笛吹き.

V ***pay*** the *piper* 費用を負担する ‖ He who ***pays*** the *piper* may call the tune. 〘諺〙笛吹きに金を払うものが曲を注文する(費用を払うものに権利がある).

piping, *n*. 管.

Q² ***earthenware*** *piping* 土管.

pique, *n*. 立腹.

P go out ***in*** a [fit of] *pique* かっと腹を立てて出て行く. ¶He did it ***out of*** *pique*. 彼はそれを腹立ちまぎれにやった.

pique, *v*. 誇る; 刺激する, 腹を立てる.

P be *piqued **at*** a refusal 拒絶されて憤慨する. ¶His curiosity was *piqued **by*** the gadget.=The gadget piqued his curiosity. その器具に興味を感じた. ¶He *piques* himself ***on*** his family (good taste). 彼は家柄の良いの(など)を自慢する. ‖ Temperance reformers were wont to *pique **on*** the progress of the cause in the colonies. 禁酒論者たちはよく植民地におけるその運動の進歩を自慢しつけていた. ☞ *pique* oneself on の型が普通.

piracy, *n*. 海賊行為; 著作権侵害.

V ***commit*** (=***practice***) *piracies* on the coast of China 中国沿岸で海賊を働く.

Q ***literary*** *piracy* 著作権の侵害. ¶***rampant*** *piracy* 海賊の横行振り.

pirate, *n*. 海賊; 著作権侵害者.

Q ***fierce*** and ***bloodthirsty*** *pirates* どう猛で残忍な海賊. ¶a ***literary*** *pirate* ひょう窃者, 著作権侵害者.

Q² ferocious ***river*** *pirates* 恐ろしい河川荒し.

P a nest ***of*** *pirates* 海賊の巣くつ.

pistol, *n*. けん銃(ピストル).

V ***aim*** a *pistol* at ... ...にけん銃を向ける. ¶***carry*** a *pistol* けん銃を携帯する. ¶***conceal*** a *pistol* in one's hip-pocket しりのポケットにピストルを忍ばせる. ¶***draw*** a *pistol* けん銃を(さやから)抜く. 【類】***draw*** one's *pistol* from one's pocket. ¶***fire*** a *pistol* at ... ...を目がけてけん銃を放つ.

¶He ***fired off*** his *pistol*. 彼はけん銃を放った. ¶He ***had*** a *pistol* about him. 彼はけん銃を携えていた. ¶***level*** one's *pistol* and fire けん銃を向けて発射する. ¶***load*** a *pistol* けん銃に装てんする. ¶***point*** a *pistol* at ... ...にけん銃を向ける. ¶***pop*** (=***let off***) a *pistol* けん銃をどんと放つ. ¶***take*** (=carry) a *pistol* [with a person] けん銃を携える. ¶***turn*** the *pistol* on himself 彼自身にけん銃を向ける. ¶My *pistol* does not ***carry*** (=***reach***) far. 私のけん銃は遠くへは届かない.

Q² a ***Browning*** (***Colt***) *pistol* ブローニング(コルト)けん銃. ¶a ***toy*** *pistol* おもちゃのピストル. ¶a ***water*** *pistol* 水鉄砲.

P I heard the report ***of*** a *pistol*. 私はけん銃の音を聞いた. ¶He was shot ***with*** a *pistol*. 彼はけん銃でうたれた.

pistol-shot, *n.* けん銃弾, けん銃着弾距離.

V A *pistol-shot* was ***fired***. けん銃を一発発射した.

P He came ***within*** *pistol-shot*. 彼はけん銃の射程内にやって来た.

piston, *n.* 〖機〗 ピストン.

Q a ***counter*** *piston* 逆ピストン.

pit, *n.* 穴, 落し穴; 採掘場; (芝居の)土間.

V He who ***digs*** a *pit* for others falls in himself. 人を落し入れようとすると自分が落し穴に落ちる.

Q a ***bottomless*** *pit* 底なし地獄. ¶sink into a ***deep*** *pit* of degradation 堕落のふちに沈む.

Q² a ***gravel*** *pit* 砂利採掘場. ¶a ***stone*** *pit* 採石場. ¶a ***storage*** *pit* 貯蔵穴.

P a spectator ***in*** the *pit* of a theatre 土間の観客. ¶fall ***into*** a *pit* of one's own digging 自分の掘った穴に落ちる. ¶a *pit* ***in*** the earth 地面の穴.

pit, *v.* 対抗させる; 痘こんを残す.

P The armies were *pitted* ***against*** each other. 軍隊が相対抗していた. ‖ *pit* ... ***against*** the enemy ...を敵に対抗させる. 【類】They *pitted* two cocks ***against*** each other. ¶He is *pitted* ***with*** smallpox. 彼は痘こん(あばた)がある.

pit-a-pat, *ad.* =pitter-patter.

pitch, *n.* 最高点; 音の高度, 調子; 張場; 〖機〗 ピッチ(きざみ).

V ***select*** a *pitch* [大道商人などが]売場を選定する.

Q The voices rose to a ***deafening*** *pitch*. 声の調子が高くって耳をろうせんばかりであった. ¶Near a railway station is his ***favorite*** *pitch*. 彼の張場は駅の付近である. 【類】Trafalgar square is a ***favorite*** '*pitch*' of the tramps (ルンペン) of both sexes. ¶I cannot sing at so ***high*** a *pitch*. 私はそんな高い調子では歌えない. ‖ War fever is at ***high*** *pitch*. 戦争熱は高調に達している. ‖ the ***highest*** *pitch* of honor この上もない名誉. ¶at ***shouting*** *pitch* 大声で.

P cry out ***at*** the *pitch* (=top) of one's voice 声を限りに叫ぶ. ¶carry the art ***to*** the highest *pitch* 芸術を最高水準に達せさせる. 【類】All my feelings were excited ***to*** a high *pitch*.

P² the *pitch* ***of*** merriment 歓楽のきわみ ‖ the *pitch* ***of*** screws ねじの刻み(ピッチ) ‖ the *pitch* ***of*** a saw のこの歯.

pitch, *v.* 投げる; 上下動する; 陣営を張る; 取りきめる.

M He *pitched* ***headforemost*** downstairs. 彼は真っさかさまに階下に落ちた. ¶Our boat *pitched* ***heavily***. われわれの船はひどく上下動をした.

P *pitch* ***against*** each other 相対して陣営を張る. ¶He has *pitched* his ball ***into*** our house. 彼は球を僕の家へほうり込んだ. ¶get *pitched* ***off*** one's bicycle 自転車からほうり出される. ¶*pitch* ***on*** (=***upon***) a candidate 候補者を定める ‖ *pitch* ***on*** (=select) an expedient 便法を取る.

pitch, *n.* ピッチ(タールなど).

V One cannot ***touch*** *pitch* without being defiled. 朱に交われば赤くなる.

Q² ***coal-tar*** *pitch* コールター・ピッチ.

P He who plays ***with*** *pitch* must defile his fingers. 朱に交われば赤くなる.

pitcher, *n.* 水差し; 〖野球〗 投手.

V ***lick*** the *pitcher* 投手をノックアウトする.

Q a ***winning*** (***losing***) *pitcher* 勝利(敗戦)投手.

Q² a ***glass*** *pitcher* ガラスの水さし. ¶a "***go-through***" *pitcher* 「完投」投手. ¶a ***smokeball*** *pitcher* 快速投手. ¶a ***speedball*** *pitcher* 速球投手.

pitching, *n.* 〖野球〗 投球.

Q² ***horseshoe*** *pitching* 曲球投球.

pitfall, *n.* 落し穴.

V ***provide*** *pitfalls* for the unwary ぼんやり者をおとす穴を作る.

Q The use of the articles is a ***grammatical*** *pitfall* that catches many Japanese students of English. 冠詞の用法は日本の多くの英学生を陥れる文法上の落し穴である. ¶a ***hidden*** *pitfall* 隠れたおとし穴.

P² *pitfalls* ***for*** the unwary so cunningly designed 巧妙に仕組まれたうっかり者への落し穴. ¶It proves a constant *pitfall* ***to*** the unwary. それは不注意な人が絶えず落ちる落し穴だ.

pittance, *n.* わずかな手当, 薄給.

V ***earn*** a *pittance* 薄給を取る. ¶He ***receives*** a miserable *pittance*. 彼はみじめな手当を受けている.

Q a ***mere*** *pittance* 目腐れ金. ¶The minister of a little church receives the ***wretched*** *pittance* of 26s. a week. 小さい教会の牧師は一週二十六シリングというみじめな手当を受ける.

P ***for*** a *pittance* of ... ...というわずかな手当で.

pitter-patter, *ad.* ぱたぱたと.

P walk *pitter-patter* ***along*** the hallway (floor) 廊下(など)をぱたぱた歩く. ¶The rain was falling *pitter-patter* ***on*** the roofs and the pavements. 雨が屋根やほ道にばらばら音を立てて降っていた.

pitting, *n.* 対抗.

P It is the *pitting* ***of*** skill ***against*** skill. それは秘術を尽しての戦いである.

pity, *n.* れんびん, 同情; 遺憾なこと.

V ***arouse*** *pity* あわれみの情を呼び起す. ¶he ***enlisted*** the *pity* of ... 彼は...の同情を買った. ¶***feel*** *pity* for ... ...をふびんに思う. 【類】I ***felt*** *pity* stirring in my heart. ¶***have*** *pity* on ... ...をふびんに思う ‖ ***have*** no *pity* for ... ...に同情がない, ...をふびんとは思わない. 【類】Do ***have*** some *pity* on us. / ***Have*** *pity* on the poor old man. ¶***incur*** the *pity* of ... ...の同情を買う. ¶***put on*** a false *pity* 心にもない同情を装う. ¶***stir*** one's *pity* そくいんの情を動かす. ¶***take*** *pity* on ... ...をふびんに思う.

Q It's a ***great*** *pity*. 実に遺憾だ. ¶a ***real*** *pity* 真の同情. ¶look on him in ***silent*** *pity* 口には出さないが腹で気の毒に思って彼を見る. ¶it is a ***thousand*** *pities* that ... ...とは遺憾千万だ. ¶Oh! ***What*** a *pity* it was that he should have fared so badly. まーあの方がそんな目にお会いになったとは実にお気の毒なことだ.

P ***in*** *pity* of ... ...をふびんに思って. ¶He married her ***out of*** *pity*. 彼は彼女を気の毒に思って結婚した. ‖ I saved him ***out of*** *pity* for his children. 子供たちがかわいそうだから彼を救ってやった. ¶I was moved ***to*** (=with) *pity*. 私はかわいそうになった. ¶My heart swelled ***with*** *pity*. 私はかわいそうで胸が一杯になった. ¶No one could look at it ***without*** *pity*. それを見てかわいそうだと思わないものはなかった.

P² feel a rush of *pity* ***at*** ... ...に対するあわれみの情がこみ上げて来る. ¶He was touched with *pity* ***for*** the poor. 彼は貧乏人をふびんに思った.

O It is a *pity* that he has failed in it. 彼がそれに失敗したのは気の毒だ.

pity, *v.* あわれむ, ふびんに思う.

M He is ***much*** to be *pitied*. 彼は実にかわいそうだ. ¶*pity* ***needlessly*** 訳もなくあわれむ. ¶I ***sincerely*** *pity* these unfortunate beings. 私は衷心からこれら不幸の人々をふびんに思う.

O I cannot but *pity* him. 私は彼をあわれまざるを得ない.

pivot, *n.* 枢軸.

P turn ***on*** a *pivot* 枢軸の上で回転する. ¶the very *pivot* ***round*** which the intrigue revolved その陰謀策動の中枢.

placard, *n.* 張札, ビラ; プラカード.

V ***hang up*** a *placard* in the window 窓に張札を下げる. ¶***post*** huge *placards* reading ... ...と書いてある大きなビラを張出す. ¶***post up*** a *placard* 張札を出す. ¶The rebels ***set*** (=***put or stick***) ***up*** *placards* everywhere. 反乱者は至る所に張札をした.

Q The workers paraded, ***vari-sized*** *placards* put up. 労働者は大小さまざまのプラカードかかげて行進した.

placard, *v.* 張札を張る.

P They *placarded* all ***over*** the country. 国内至る所に張札が出された. ¶in the London area every district is *placarded* ***with*** notices indicating ... ロンドン市内では各区ともに...という掲示を張出した. 【類】The circus *placarded* the whole city ***with*** ad bills (広告ビラ).

place, *n.* 所, 場所; 個所; 住宅; 館; 室; 座席; 空位; 余地; 地位, 職, 身分, 分限.

V ***assign*** *places* (=seats) to ... ...に座席を指定する. ¶***assume*** a leading *place* among ... ...間に主要な位置を占める. ¶The simple-hearted people believed that a conscientious observance of these forms would ***assure*** them a *place* in Heaven. 考えの単純な人々はこれらの儀式を正直に守れば確実に天国に行けるものと信じた. ¶Tourists ***benefit*** the *place* to the extent of … a year. 観光客は一年に…の金を同地に落す. ¶***book places*** at the theatre 劇場の座席を予約する. ¶***change places*** with a person 人と席(地位)を交換する.【類】I would not ***change places*** with anyone in the world. ¶***chuck up*** a *place* 職をやめる. ¶He may fairly ***claim*** a *place* in literature. 彼にはりっぱに文壇人と認められる資格がある. ‖ It may justly ***claim*** the first *place*. それは当然首位を占める資格がある. ¶***clear*** a *place* of people 人払をする. ¶***deserve*** a *place* in the records of contemporary literature 現代文学史に名を留める価値がある. ¶***determine*** one's social *place* その社会上の地位を確定する. ¶***disfigure*** a *place* 場所を見苦しくする. ¶He ***earned*** a *place* among the prophets. 彼は予言者たるの資格を造った. ‖ ***earn*** a *place* in the sun 生きがいある身となる ‖ ***earn*** one's *place* in history 後世に伝えられる資格を造る. ¶This work has firmly ***established*** its *place* in the literature of banking. この書は銀行業の文献中に確実にその地位を占めている. ¶***fill*** the *place* of the late … 故…の後継者になる ‖ The servant ***filled*** his *place* well. その召使はよく勤めた.【類】He bravely ***filled*** a *place* in the ranks during the last War. ¶His book should ***find*** a *place* certainly in every library. 彼の著作はどこの図書館でも備えておくべきだ. ‖ The words ***find*** their *places* in the following pages. その語句は次の各ページに説明してある. ¶He ***gained*** the second *place* in the competition. 彼はその競技で第二位をかち得た.【類】***gain*** a high *place* in business [circles]. ¶***get*** a good *place* in a bank 銀行で好い地位を得る ‖ She ***got*** a *place* with a false character. 彼は人物証明書を偽造して職を得た. ‖ ***get*** front *places* 正面の座席を得る. ¶***give place*** to … …に席(地位)を譲る ‖ This has ***given*** her a *place* prominent among the nations of the world. このためにこの国は世界列国間に卓越した地位を得た.【類】***give*** the *place* of honor (上席) to … ‖ A steamer always ***gives place*** to a sailing ship. 汽船はいつでも帆船に路を譲る. ‖ Wonder ***gave place*** to admiration. 驚異が感嘆に変った ‖ From that time he has never ceased to ***give*** the Japanese Alps the first *place* in his affections. その時から引続き彼は日本アルプスを一番好むようになった. ¶He ***gave up*** his *place* on account of his failing health. 彼は健康がすぐれないのでその職を辞した. ¶You ***have*** a *place* in the country, I think? あなたはいなかに住宅をお持ちでしたね. ‖ They ***have*** a *place* in my heart. 私は彼らが好きだ(忘れられない). ‖ You shall ***have*** a *place* in my office. 私のところで使ってやろう. ‖ Vague assertions ***have*** no *place* in a scientific discussion. ばく然とした言説は科学上の議論には無用である. ‖ the world ***has*** no *place* for … 世間は…を入れる余地がない.【類】Such desires can ***have*** no *place* in a good heart. / But discouragement ***had*** no *place* in his vocabulary. ‖ A mitten ***has*** a *place* for the thumb, but not for each of the fingers. ミットは親指はあるが一本一本の指はない. ‖ ***have*** a *place* in Westminster Abbey ウエストミンスター寺院に葬埋されている(名士が). ¶the *place* the country ***holds*** in the world その国が世界に占めている地位 ‖ it ***held*** an honorable *place* for nearly two centuries among … それは二百年近くの間…に光栄ある位地を占めていた.【類】Pennsylvania has long ***held*** the first *place* as a glass manufacturing state. / In the manufacture of cutlery, Sheffield ***holds*** the first *place*. ¶The *place* was ***jammed*** with spectators. 場所は見物人ですし詰の状態だった. ¶I wish to go out; will you have the goodness to ***keep*** my *place?* 私は席を立つから君とっておいてくれ(人が来てもすわらせないように). ‖ fight hard to ***keep*** its *place* against industrial and commercial rivals 商工業の競争者に対してその地位を維持しようと奮闘する.【類】***keep*** one's *place* at the head of one's class / ***keep places*** for one's companions (つれの席). ¶***know*** one's *place* その分を知る. ¶He has ***left*** his *place* and is looking for work. 彼は前の所はやめて今仕事を捜している. ‖ ***leave*** the *place* clear for a person to come in 人が来たらすわれるように席をあけておく. ¶***locate*** on a map the *places* about which one read in a book 地図を見て本で読んだ地名を捜し出す. ¶***lose*** one's *place* その職を失う.【類】You must work hard, or you will ***lose*** your *place* in the class (席次が下がる). ‖ stay on fearful of ***losing*** their *places* 席を取られると困るのですわっている. ¶***maintain*** her high *place* among nations 諸国民の間にその国の高地位を維持する. ¶The work has evidently ***made*** a *place* for itself. その本はたしかに独特の地位を占めるに至った. ¶***merit*** a *place* therein その地位に値する.【類】it ***merits*** an honorable *place* after (=next) … ¶The country is overcrowded and ***needs*** a *place* in the sun. その国は人口がちゅう密で発展の場所を求めている. ¶He ***occupies*** a very high *place* in our literature (the world of letters). 彼はわが文学界(など)できわめて高い地位を占めている.【類】His house ***occupies*** a good *place*. ¶The dentist ***opened*** his *place* on the second floor. 歯科医は二階で開業した. ¶The watering *place* is ***patronized*** by excursionists from the neighboring cities. その海水浴場へは付近の都市から人が出る. ¶***provide*** a *place* for everything それぞれおく場所を設ける. ¶***reassume*** her *place* among the sovereign countries 再び主権国家の仲間入りをする. ¶***resign*** one's *place* on the committee 委員を辞する. ¶***secure*** a good *place* in a coach 客車内の良い座席を取る. ¶The products are ***seeking*** a *place* in the markets of the world. これらの産物は世界市場に進出しようとしている. ¶He ***showed*** us *places* of interest. 彼はわれわれにおもしろい場所を見物させてくれた. ¶Who will ***supply*** her *place?* 彼女のあとへだれがすわるでしょうか. ‖ It ***supplies*** the *place* of a dictionary. それは辞書の代用になる. ¶the exhibition ***takes place*** from … to … 博覧会は…から…まで催される. ‖ They have ***taken*** their *places*. それぞれ席についた. ‖ ***take*** its *place* beside … …と相並んでいる, …に劣らない ‖ The wedding cake ***takes*** the *place* of honor. 結婚ひ露の席で祝いの菓子は上席に据える. ‖ Of these it easily ***takes*** the first *place*. これらの中でそれが優に第一位を占める. ‖ it is sufficiently good to ***take a place*** beside … それは…と比肩する位優良だ.【類】… is worthy to ***take*** its *place* beside … ‖ ***take places*** for the concert 音楽会の座席を取る ‖ They ***take*** their *places* on the dais (right side). 彼らは一段高い席(など)に席を取る.【類】he ***takes*** the first *place* amid … ¶Mr. X ***took*** [***up***] his *place* as umpire. X氏が審判としてその持場についた.【類】She has not sufficient strength to ***take*** her *place* as the mother of her family. / She ***took*** a *place* as a servant (女中に雇われた). ‖ I ***took*** his *place* as judge. 私が審判者として彼に代った. ‖ Owing to her indisposition her place was ***taken*** by … 彼女が病気で…が代役を勤めた. ‖ Some of the slang words ***take*** their *places* in the colloquial language of the whole people. 俗語の中には全国民の使う口語体の中に取り入れられたものがある. ‖ It has ***taken place*** amongst the classics of French literature. それはフランス文学の一古典となった.【類】it easily ***takes*** a front *place* among current literature as … / ***take*** their *place* among the great self-governing nations of the world / She ***takes*** her *place* among the women whose eyes have been the doom of kings (傾国の美人). / ***take*** their *places* in the procession (行列に) / ***take*** one's *place* in the ranks / Japan ***takes*** her *place* in the sisterhood of nations (列国). / He never ***took*** a high *place* in his classes. / ***take*** a high *place* in the literary world / ***take*** its *place* in the very first line of Powers of the world / women are more and more ***taking*** *places* in the business world ‖ A *torii* ***takes*** the *place* of an arch in Japan. 日本では鳥居がアーチの代りになる. ‖ the new ***taking*** the *place* of the old 新陳代謝.【類】Remember always that nothing, not even the highest natural ability, will ***take*** the *place* of persistent hard work (不断の努力). ¶***win*** the leading *place* in … …の首位をかち得る ‖ He has ***won*** a *place* in the red book of *Who's Who*. 彼は赤表紙の Who's Who (紳士録の)中に名をつらねられるようになった. ‖ The party has ***won*** 79 *places* in the election. その党は選挙で七十九議席を得た.

v² the first *place* ***belongs*** unquestionably to … 第一に指を…に屈しなければならない. ¶The first *place* ought to ***go*** to … 第一席は…のものだ.

Q It is an ***admirable*** *place* to come to for a holiday and rest. それは休日や静養にやって来るには好い所だ. ¶Hang it in an ***airy*** *place*. 風通の好い所にそれを下げておけ. ¶of ***all*** *places* 所もあろうに. ¶sit down in their ***allotted*** *places* それぞれ指定の席に着く. ¶be arranged in their respective ***alphabetical** places* それぞれアルファベット順に並べてある. ¶It is discussed in ***another** places.* それは章を改めて論じてある. ¶put oneself in ***another's** place* 人の身になって見る. ¶The names of ... have an ***assured** place* in the hall of fame. ...の名は名誉の殿堂に確実な地位を占めている(その名が後世に伝わる).【類】It has an ***assured** place* in the literature of England. / He will always enjoy a permanent and ***assured** place* in English literature. ¶a ***bad** place* in the path 道のわるい箇所. ¶a ***brisk** place* such as a post-office 郵便局のような忙しい所. ¶a ***bustling** place* 雑とうする場所, 盛り場. ¶***central** places* as Wall Street in New York ニューヨークのウォール街のような中心地 ‖ hold the ***central** place* in ... ...の中心になる. ¶hold the ***chief** place* 首位を占める. ¶frame the portrait and hang it in a ***conspicuous** place* 肖像画に額ぶちをはめて目につく所にかける.【類】a bill posted in a ***conspicuous** place.* ¶a ***convenient** place* to see games 競技を見るに都合のよい所. ¶the ***cosiest** place* in the house 家中で一番居心地のよい所. ¶in a ***country** place* いなかで. ¶a ***cozy little** place* in one's home 家庭の安楽な小さい場所. ¶if the country is to maintain a ***creditable** place* among the civilized communities その国が文明諸国の間にりっぱな地位を維持して行こうとすれば. ¶take one's ***customary** place* at the breakfast table 朝食の食卓でいつもの席に着く. ¶keep it in a ***damp** place* それを湿気のある場所に置く. ¶the ***dearest** place* on earth 地球上一番なつかしい場所. ¶***disreputable** places* いかがわしい場所(悪所). ¶A dancing-master holds no ***distinguished** place* in the eye of exclusive society. 舞踏教師などは上流社会からは重く見られていない. ¶***eligible** places* in trains 汽車の(車室の)居心地のよい座席. ¶rise to an ***eminent** place* 高位に昇る. ¶take an ***equal** place* amongst the foremost nations of the world 世界の先進国民の間に列する. ¶hold an ***established** place* among ... ...間に確実な地位を占める. ¶He knows the ***exact** place* where it is concealed. 彼はそれが隠されている場所を正確に知っている. ¶occupy an ***exceptional** place* among ... ...間に独特の位置を占める. ¶the most ***famous** place* for ... ...の名所. ¶a ***favorite** place* of pilgrimage for ... ...のよく行く巡礼地. ¶get the ***fifth** place* 第五位になる. ¶live in an abominably ***filthy** place* ひどく不潔な場所に住む. ¶hold ***first** place* among ... in ... ...において...間に第一位を占める ‖ assign the ***first** place* to ... 第一位を...に与える ‖ win ***first** place* 等をとる, 優勝する ‖ be in ***first** place* 第一位である.【類】English is given ***first** place* in the secondary schools of Japan. ‖ in the ***first** (**second, third**) place* [列挙する場合]第一(第二・第三)に.【類】in the ***first** place,* it should be said that ... ¶a ***fit** place* to live in 住むによい所. ¶The premier occupies the ***foremost** place* in the world of politics. 首相は政治界で首位を占める. ¶take ***fourth** place* 第四位に立つ. ¶arrive too late to get ***front** places* in their waiting lines おそくきたので待っている人の列の先になれない. ‖ We have always held the ***front** place* in point of quality. 手前どもでは品質の点ではこれまで引けを取ったことはありません. ¶raise the Japanese fleet to a ***glorious** place* among the fleets of the world 日本艦隊を改善して世界の艦隊間において栄誉ある地位を得させる. ¶a ***good** place* for luncheon ランチにはよい場所 ‖ the ***best** place* for sight-seeing headquarters (諸方へ遊覧するに便利な)遊覧根拠地. ¶She took her ***habitual** place* at the table. 食卓のいつもの席についた. ¶He never took a ***high** place* in his class. 彼はクラスで上位になったことがない. ¶the meanness and crime which he saw about him in ***high** places* 彼が上流社会の中に目撃した卑劣と罪悪.【類】the corruption that is rampant in ***high** places* (上流社会にはびこる) ‖ take a ***high** place* in these questions これら諸問題において重要な地位を占める.【類】The book will take ***high** place* among the great imaginative biographies (伝記小説) of our time. ‖ This endorsement in ***high** places* greatly added to my reputation as a physician. 有力な方面からかく折紙をつけられたので私の医師としての名声が大いに高まった. ¶a ***historical** place* 史跡. ¶Let me congratulate you on having taken an ***honorable** place* among the cultivators of the English language. 英語研究者として光栄ある位置を占められたことに対して貴下にお祝を申上げます. ¶hold an ***honored** place* in the ranks of ... の階級において栄誉ある地位を占める. ¶hold an ***important** place* among the countries of the world 世界列国間に重要な地位を占める. ¶in ***inconspicuous** places* 目立たない場所で. ¶It has an ***insignificant** place* in the national system of education. それは国民の教育組織中に微々たる地位を占めている. ¶enable a ship to reach her ***intended** place* of discharge 船がその荷卸しをする目的地に着くようにする. ¶occupy an ***intermediate** place* between ... and ... ...と...との中間の地位を占める. ¶a very ***jolly** place* 実に愉快な場所. ¶in the ***last** place* [列挙などの場合]最後に. ☞ in the first (second ...) place に対する語句. ¶the ***last resting** place* of the dead 死者の墓地.【類】It was chosen as the site for a ***last resting** place* because he loved it. ¶take a ***leading** place* in the supply of ... ...の供給において重要な地位を占める.【類】take a ***leading** place* in the march of civilization (文明の進歩) / maintain its ***leading** place.* ¶I went to the room and hunted in all the ***likely** places,* but didn't discover the missing article. 私はへやへ行ってここぞと思う場所を残らず捜したが紛失した物は見当らなかった. ¶occupy a ***middle** place* between ... ...の中位を占める. ¶one's ***native** place* 生地. ¶arrange for picnics and excursions to ***neighboring** places* of interest 付近の遊覧地へ野遊びや遠足を催す手はずをする. ¶This is ***no** place* for a young man. ここは若い者の来る所ではない. ‖ ***No** place* could be worse. こんなひどい所はない. ¶He undoubtedly deserves ***no mean** place* among English poets 彼は英詩人としては疑いもなく相当の価値をもっている. ¶an ***objectionable** place* いかがわしい場所. ¶at some ***out-of-the-way** place* どこか辺ぴな所で. ¶Freud and his school have tended to give sex the ***paramount** place* among human motives. フロイド及びその一派の人は性欲を人間の動機中最も重要性のあるものとする傾向がある. ¶deserve a ***permanent** place* in literature 文学の中に永遠の地位を占めるだけの価値がある.【類】He takes a ***permanent** place* among the very best books of travel (最高の旅行記). ¶a ***pleasure-loving** place* 行楽地. ¶a ***poky** place* むさくるしい場所. ¶a ***popular** place* for picnic parties よく人の行く遊山場. ¶win a ***pre-eminent** place* in literature 文学の卓越した地歩を占める. ¶The paper has gained the ***premier** place* in New York journalism. その新聞はニューヨークの新聞界において首位を占めている. ¶His university diploma is framed and given a ***prominent** place* on the wall of his study. 彼の大学卒業証は額ぶちに入れて書斉の壁の人目につく場所に掛けてある.【類】He holds such a ***prominent** place* among our great artists. ¶I found everything in its ***proper** place.* 私は万事整とんしていると思った. ‖ be in the ***proper** (=**right**) places* 所を得ている.【類】Examinations in their ***proper** place* have their value. ‖ Some forceful and expressive slang words have their ***proper** place* in your speech. 力強く表現豊かな俗語は言葉の中に使って差支えない. ¶ignorant and incompetent men in important ***public** places* 要職にあって無知で無能な人たち ‖ The [dead] body was exposed to view in a ***public** place* for some days. 死がいは数日間さらし物にしてあった.【類】Boston has many beautiful ***public** places* (民衆娯楽の場所). / The unguarded sneeze or cough (口をおおわずにくしゃみやせきをすること) in the ***public** place* is objectionable. ¶a quiet, ***secluded** place* 閑散で奥まった場所. ¶a letter addressed to him at his ***registered** place* of abode 帳簿に登録してある彼の住宅へあてた書簡. ¶in ***remote little** places* 辺ぴな所に. ¶the right man in the ***right** place* 適材適所 ‖ I admit that his heart is in the ***right** place.* 彼の心掛けの正しいのは認める. ‖ One's heart is not in the ***right** place.* 虫の居所が悪い. ¶To be removed to a ***safe** place* in emergency 非常持出しのこと. ¶occupy ***second** place* 第二位を占める. ¶have a ***secure** place* in ... ...において確実な地位を占める. ¶He was wounded in ***several** places.* 彼は所々負傷した. ¶***smart** places* to dine 気のきいた食事をする所. ¶a ***sore** place* on the arm (leg) 腕(など)の痛み箇所 ‖ touch a person on a ***sore** place* [比ゆ的に]人の痛いところに触れる. ¶a ***special** place* of prominence 一際目に立つ場所. ¶take a ***subordinate** place* 次位を占める. ¶a ***sunless** place* 日の当らない場所. ¶he has held a ***supreme** place* as ... 彼は...として最高の地位を占めている. ¶take ***third** place* among the nations of the world 世界の国民中

第三位に立つ ‖ ***third place*** in the contest went to ... 競技(コンクール)の第三等は…に与えられた. ¶I am in a ***tight place*** and have no other resources. 私は動きが取れない立場で他に採るべき方法がない. ¶take the ***top place*** in competition with others 競争で首位を占める. ¶Harvard and Yale have long held an ***unchallenged place*** in American education. ハーヴァードとエールは永く米国の教育界で押しも押されもしない地位を占めて来た. ¶He earned an ***undisputed place*** in baseball. 彼は野球界でそうそうたる者となった. ¶in an ***unexpected place*** 飛んでもない所に. ¶some ***unheard-of*** (=***unknown***) ***place*** ある聞いたことのない場所. ¶they gave him a ***unique place*** among ... 彼らは彼に…中ならびない地位を与えた. 【類】He held a ***unique place*** in the scientific world. ¶There really is no such ***unpleasant place*** north of the Arctic Circle. 全く北極圏内ではそのような不愉快という場所はない. ¶She occupies a very ***warm place*** in his heart. 彼女は彼に非常に愛されている. ¶a ***wholesome*** (an ***unwholesome***) ***place*** [不]健康地. ¶"London is a very ***wicked, vile place***"—so she thought. 「ロンドンは実に恐ろしい所だ」彼女はそう思った.

Q² an ***amusement place*** 遊戯場. ¶an ***angling place*** つり場. ¶a ***balloting place*** 投票場. ¶a ***bathing place*** 海水浴場. ¶Cholera suddenly spread from India, its ***breeding place***, in 1883. コレラは一八八三年その温床であるインドから突然が広まった. ‖ Slums are often ***breeding places*** for criminals. 貧民くつはしばしば犯人の温床となる. ¶a ***burial place*** 埋葬地. ¶***business places*** of the company 会社の営業所 ‖ Our homes and ***business places*** are far apart. われわれの自宅と勤め場所(会社)はずっと離れている. ¶***business*** and ***dwelling places*** 営業所と住宅. ¶a cheap ***catchpenny place*** 低俗な見せ物などの興行所. ¶a great ***cherry-blossom place*** 桜の名所. ¶small towns and ***country places*** 小都会と村. 【類】out in the ***country places*** / trips to nearby ***country places***. ¶a ***crossing place*** 横断場所; 踏切. ¶a ***dumping place*** for ... …のはきだめ. ¶clean up the city's ***eating places*** 市の食堂を清潔にする. ¶an ***eating*** and ***drinking place*** 飲食店. ¶a safe, ***fire-proof place*** 安全な耐火建物. ¶This is a ***gathering place*** for the free thinkers. ここは自由思想家の集合所だ. ‖ a public ***gathering place*** 人のよく集まる場所(公園など). ¶a ***hiding place*** 隠し場所. ¶some ***inland place*** ある海から離れた場所. ¶The ***landing place*** of the immigrants is on this island. 移民の上陸地点はこの島にある. ¶a ***loafing place*** of the idle なまけ者のぶらぶらしている場所. ¶a cheap ***lunch place*** 安く中食のできる場所. ¶a ***manufacturing place*** 製造工業地. ¶a ***market place*** 市場. ¶a ***meeting place*** for ... 会合の場所 ‖ the ***meeting place*** of the United Nations General Assembly 国際連合総会の会場. 【類】Paris was chosen as the ***meeting place*** of the Big Four Foreign Ministers. ¶his ***old home place*** 彼の故郷. ¶an ***opium place*** あへんくつ. ¶a ***parting place*** 分かれの場所. ¶a favorite ***picnic place*** よくピクニックに行く場所. ¶a ***polling place*** 投票所. ¶one's ***resting place*** その休息所 ‖ their final ***resting places*** 彼らの老後の安住地. ¶hotels or ***rooming places*** ホテルまたはアパート. ¶a ***roosting place*** ねぐら. ¶a nice quiet little ***seaside place*** ちょっとした静かな海辺地. ¶a nice ***shopping place*** いい買物地. ¶a ***show place*** 遊覧地; [劇など]見せ場 ‖ As a ***show place***, it is full of historic interest. それは遊覧地として歴史的興味に富んでいる. 【類】Sankei-en is one of the ***show places*** of Yokohama. / Miyajima is one of the three famous ***show places*** of Japan. / one of the ***show places*** (名所) in Tokyo. ¶a good ***starting place*** よい出発点(山登りなど) ‖ the ***starting place*** of the Hampstead coach ハンプステッド行の馬車の出発点(発駅). ¶a ***storage place*** 貯蔵所(倉庫). ¶a ***summer place*** 夏の別荘. ¶a ***tourist show place*** 観光地. ¶a ***vacation place*** 休暇旅行地. ¶These words are defined in their ***vocabulary places***. それらの語は字引きのそれぞれの見出語の所に説明されてある. ¶their ***wartime place*** of safekeeping 彼らの戦時中の保管場所. ¶a ***watering place*** 《英》海水浴場; 《英》温泉場. ¶a ***work***[***ing***] ***place*** 職場 ‖ safeguarding of machinery and dangerous ***working places*** 機械の安全装置と危険な職場の安全施設.

P he says ***at*** one ***place*** that ... 彼はある所で…と言っている ‖ ***at*** a ***place*** called ... …という所で ‖ ***at*** such hour and ***place*** as it may designate 指定の時間と場所で. ¶He is looking ***for*** a ***place*** with a good tailor. 彼はしっかりした仕立屋の店に勤め口を捜している. ‖ look ***for*** a more comfortable ***place*** もっとよいいこいの場所を求める. 【類】look around ***for*** one's ***place***. ¶drag a dead body ***from*** the ***place*** of its repose 墓から死体をひきずり出す. ¶wander ***from place to place*** 所々をさまよい歩く. ¶Everything was ***in place***. 万事整とんしていた; 好都合であった. 【類】keep everything ***in*** its ***place*** ‖ Your suggestion is quite ***in place***. 君の注意は全く当を得ている. ‖ it seems ***in place*** to inform ... …を御通知申上げるべきだと思う. 【類】A word or two on (=about) that point seems ***in place*** here. ‖ ***in places*** 所によっては, 諸所に. 【類】The story retains our interest from beginning to end, and ***in places*** even awakens our emotions. ‖ be interesting ***in places*** ところどころおもしろい(本など) ‖ substitute ... ***in place*** of ... …を…の代りにする ‖ were I ***in*** your ***place*** 私だったら ‖ he was elected president of the society ***in*** [the] ***place*** (=room *or* lieu) of ... 彼は…の後継者としてその会の会長に選ばれた. 【類】A new house stands ***in place*** of the old one. / Plant a willow tree ***in*** the ***place*** of this dead pine. / Put yourself ***in*** my ***place***. / Were I ***in*** your ***place***, I would act differently. / Mr. A is sick and Mr. B teaches ***in*** his ***place*** today. ‖ The wheel is not ***in*** its ***place***. 車がはずれている. 【類】Signature must be ***in*** the ***place*** indicated. / I like everything to be ***in*** [its] ***place***. ¶domestic servants ***out of place*** 勤め口のない召使 ‖ it may not be altogether ***out of place*** to say that ... 余談ではあるが. 【類】Here a remark regarding it may not be ***out of place***. ‖ Your conduct is quite ***out of place***. 君の行為は時宜を得ない. ¶We will send the goods ***to*** any ***place*** in the United States which you designate. 米国内はどこでも御指定の場所へその品物を発送致します. ‖ entitle him ***to*** a ***place*** among poets of the first rank [作品などが]彼に一流詩人に数えられる資格を与える ‖ fall ***to*** third ***place*** 第三位に下る.

P² Waseda is no ***place for*** them. 早稲田は彼らの来るべき所でない. ‖ There is no ***place for*** doubt. 疑いを容れる余地がない. ‖ a ***place for*** dining 食堂. ¶those writers whose ***place in*** literature has been achieved in the past decade 過去十年間に文壇に地位を得た文士たち ‖ He is ambitious for a ***place in*** the sun. 彼は表面(優位)に立つことを熱望している. ‖ It will be found worthy of a ***place in*** every household. それはどこの家庭にも一品を備うべきものであるということが認められるだろう. ‖ make for oneself a ***place in*** the sun 自分のために有利な地位を作る. 【類】Mendel was an abbot of a monastery, but his ***place in*** the sun is due to his contributions to genetics (発生学) ‖ prehistoric Scotland and its ***place in*** European civilization 有史前のスコットランドとその欧州文明における地位. ¶There is no ***place like*** home. 家庭にまさる場所はない. ¶the jeweller's ***place of*** business その宝石業者の営業所 ‖ his ***place of*** abode 彼の住所 ‖ ***places of*** doubtful reputation いかがわしい場所 ‖ ***places of*** beauty and interest 景色がよく興味のある地点. 【類】***places of*** interest and amusement. / the ***place of*** meeting ‖ a ***place of*** pilgrimage 巡礼地 ‖ a ***place of*** exile 配所 ‖ a ***place of*** residence 住居 ‖ a ***place of*** voting=a voting place 投票所 ‖ one's ***place of*** work=one's working place その勤め先(職場) ‖ a ***place of*** reverence and worship 礼拝の場所(神社仏閣など). 【類】Lourdes has become the ***place of*** the most frequent pilgrimages. ‖ a ***place of*** refuge 隠れ場所. 【類】a ***place of*** business=a business place / a ***place of*** amusement=an amusement place / a ***place of*** offense (犯罪) / a ***place of*** strategic and military importance. ¶in a conspicuous ***place on*** his premises 彼の屋敷の目につきやすい所に.

O but this is not the ***place*** to consider them in detail しかしここではその詳論は避ける.

place, *v.* おく; 配置する, 就任させる.

M ***place*** it ***ahead*** of ... それを…の上位におく. ¶a hotel ***charmingly placed*** 風光明美の地を占めたホテル. ¶If the bottles manufactured in the United States annually were ***placed end to end***, they would girdle the globe nearly 25 times. 毎年米国で製造されるびんを縦に列べると地球をほとんど二十五回巻くことができる. ¶might ***fair-***

ly be *placed* among ... 当然...におかれてよいだろう. ¶be *placed* ***first*** 第一に出す. ¶***How*** is he *placed* in the firm? 彼は会社ではどういう待遇ですか. ¶be *placed* ***out*** in life 世に送り出す. ¶*place* one's words ***properly*** 語を適当に配列する. ¶*place* books ***respectfully*** on the shelf 本をうやうやしくたなに積んでおく. ¶*place* oneself ***squarely*** in opposition to ... 堂々と...に反対の立場を示す. ¶He *placed* ***unreservedly*** all the data he has collected at the disposal of a friend. 彼はその収集した材料を全部進んである友人の使用に供した.

P *place* health ***above*** every other consideration 健康を第一におく‖*place* campus activities and honors ***above*** achievements in scholarship 学内の諸活動量と栄誉を学科の成績より重く見る. ¶*place* it ***against*** the wall (window, door) それを壁(など)に立てかける. ¶*place* one's son ***as*** a pupil with ... 息子を...に弟子入りさせる. 【類】The boy was *placed* ***at*** a school in England.‖*place* him ***as*** minister of a church 彼を教会の牧師に任じる‖The author *places* the maximum child-bearing period of a woman ***as*** perhaps thirty-five years. その著者は婦人の出産期間を最長およそ三十五年としている. ¶Economically, parentage is *placed* ***at*** a great disadvantage in the battle of life. 経済上子を持つことは生活戦線に立って非常に不利益だ.‖*place* ***at*** the service of humanity knowledge gained through long research 多年の研究によって得た知識を人類の用に供する. 【類】I will *place* anything ***at*** your service.‖I will *place* ***at*** your disposal any sum you may need. 金は御入用だけ御用立てしましょう.‖*place* the height of the mountain ***at*** 20,500 ft. その山の高さを二万五百フィートとする. 【類】*place* the time necessary ***at*** twenty-four hours. / The California Japanese population is *placed* ***at*** 96,000 in an estimate made by L.E. Ross, Register of the State Board of Health, from birth and population statistics completed for 1919. ¶*place* the second edition ***before*** the public 第二版を公にする‖The loan will shortly be *placed* ***before*** the public for subscription. 公債は近々募集の運びになるだろう.‖*place* information ***before*** the traveling public 一般旅行者に参考事項を提供する. ¶their lives were *placed* in great danger ***by*** ... 彼らの生命は...によって非常に危険な状態にあった‖What have we in Japan to *place* ***by*** the side of this? 日本でこれに対抗するものがあるだろうか. ¶*place* it ***for*** security それを抵当にする. ¶*place* a pot-plant ***in*** the sun 盆栽を日なたに出しておく‖*place* them ***in*** right order 置くべき場所に置く(きちんとして置く)‖*place* them ***in*** a heap それを山積みにする‖*place* it ***in*** the class of ... それを...の部に入れる‖*place* him ***in*** confinement 彼を留置する‖*place* them ***in*** employment この手合を職につかせる‖He has *placed* not only the Empire but the world ***in*** his debt. 彼は単に帝国のみならず全世界の恩人である.‖be *placed* ***in*** that category その部に入れる‖*place* the matter ***in*** the hands of ... その事件を...にゆだねる‖be *placed* ***in*** the position of being able to enter into the workings of his mind 彼の精神活動がのみ込めるような立場におかれている‖He was *placed* ***in*** a boarding school. 彼は塾に入れられた.‖*place* confidence ***in*** (=on) a man 人を信用する‖*place* hope or trust ***in God*** 神に信頼する‖The memorial tablet was *placed* ***in*** position. 記念板が取付けられた.‖*place* him ***in*** the company's service 彼をその会社に就職させる‖He was highly *placed* ***in*** the English Government service. 彼は英国政府に重用された.‖*place* others ***in*** subjection 他人を隷属状態におく‖the ship was *placed* ***in*** command of Captain ... その船は...船長が指揮することとなった. 【類】*place* an ad (広告) ***in*** a publication. ¶an admirable book to *place* ***into*** the hands of English students 英学生の持つべきすばらしい本. ¶be *placed* ***off*** limits オフリミッツ(出入禁止)になる. ¶*place* it ***on*** exhibition (=view) それを展覧に供する‖*place* it ***on*** sale (=the market) それを売出す‖be *placed* ***on*** record 記録にとどめられる‖on the occasion of your departure from ..., the undersigned desire to *place* ***on*** record their appreciation of ... あなたが...を去るに当って下記の一同は...に対して感謝の意を表する[頌徳表]. 【類】we, the undersigned, members of ..., wish to *place* ***on*** record our thanks for ... / *place* ... ***on*** the list (program)‖be *placed* ***on*** (=***upon***) the tapis 〘比ゆ〙審議される‖*place* it ***on*** the market 市販する‖*place* a stone ***on*** one's grave その墓の上に石をおく‖*place* reliance ***on*** others 人を信頼する. ¶He is *placed* ***over*** me. 彼は私の上役だ. ¶*place* one's ear ***to*** the door 戸に耳を当てる‖*place* it ***to*** one's account それをその勘定につける‖*place* a sum ***to*** one's credit (debit) 金額をその貸方(借方)につける‖The sum was *placed* ***to*** reserve. その金額は積立金に繰入れた. ¶*place* the capital ***under*** martial law 首府に戒厳令を布く‖*place* each department ***under*** a state minister 各省に大臣をおく. 【類】be *placed* ***under*** the direction of ... (...の指揮下に) / *place* a boy ***under*** the care of a teacher / *place* oneself ***under*** the protection of ... ¶*place* an order for ... ***with*** the firm ...の注文をその店に出す.

placement, *n.* 配置.

Q^2 ***employment** placement* 職配置. ¶***inter-area** placement* 区域間配置. ¶verification of ***job** placement* 職業配置の確定.

placidity, *n.* 平静.

V ***preserve*** an imperturbable *placidity* of countenance 顔色を変えずにいる.

placing, *n.* 授与.

P^2 a dispute about the *placing* ***of*** awards 賞の授与についての論議.

plagiarize, *v.* [文・思想など]盗用する.

P *plagiarize* ***from*** ... ...から思考(アイディア)を盗む.

plague, *n.* 害物; 疫病; 災害.

V ***catch*** the *plague* 疫病にかかる. ¶***exterminate*** the bubonic *plague* 腺ペストを撲滅する. ¶The *plague* was ***imported*** into this city by rats brought in steamers and trains from Bombay. ペストは汽船や汽車でボムベイから運ばれたねずみのためにこの市に輸入された. ¶***stamp out*** the great white *plague* (=consumption) 白魔(肺病)を撲滅する.

V^2 The *plague* has ***broken out***. ペストが発生した. ¶the *plague* is now ***prevailing*** in ... ペストは目下...で流行している. ¶A great *plague* was then ***raging*** in the city. 一大疫病が当時その市で流行をきわめていた.

Q the ***black** plague* 黒死病. ¶***bubonic** plague* 腺ペスト. ¶the ***minor** plagues*, such as scarlet fever, [w]hooping-cough and measles, or the major ones, such as influenza, pneumonia and tuberculosis しょう紅熱・百日ぜき・麻しんなどの軽症伝染病または流行性感冒・肺炎・肺結核などの重症伝染病. ¶***pneumonic** plague* 肺ペスト.

Q^2 ***cattle** plague* 牛疫. ¶***insect** plague* こん虫の被害. ¶the ***locust** plague* いなごの大被害.

P A great many people have been swept away ***by*** the *plague*. ペストで沢山の人が死んだ. ¶We are suffering ***from*** a *plague* of flies. われわれははえがうるさくって閉口している. ¶He has been smitten ***with*** the *plague*. 彼はペストにかかった.

P^2 a *plague* ***of*** rats ねずみの害. 【類】*plagues* ***of*** lice, grasshoppers, ants, and mice‖That child is the *plague* ***of*** our lives. あの子はわれわれの厄介者だ. ¶*Plague* ***on*** it! ええいまいましい. ¶be a *plague* ***to*** ... ...の厄介者だ.

plague, *v.* 悩ます.

P be *plagued* ***by*** poor health 身体が弱くて困る. ¶*plague* a person ***into*** doing something 人にうるさく言ってあることをさせる. ¶I am *plagued* ***to*** death by it. 私はそれには実に弱り切っている. ¶be *plagued* ***to*** death by his everlasting begging 彼にしょっちゅう無心をいわれるので弱りきる. ¶be *plagued* ***with*** the thought of ... ...を気に病む‖*plague* a man ***with*** questions 人にうるさく質問する.

plain, *n.* 平原, 平野, 広野.

Q an ***arid** plain* 不毛の平原. ¶a ***bare** plain* 落ばくたる平原. ¶the *plain* ***below*** すそ野. ¶a ***bleak** plain* 荒涼たる平野. ¶the ***burning** plains* of the desert 焼けつくようなさばくの原野. ¶a ***cultivated** plain* 耕作した平野. ¶the course of the river across the ***level** plains* 平原を流れる川筋. ¶a ***flat*** (=***level***) *plain* 平野. ¶a ***grassy** plain* 草原. ¶a ***hill*** (***mountain***)***-girt** plain* 丘(山)に囲まれた平野. ¶overlook a ***rich*** and ***varied*** *plain* 肥よくな変化のある原野を見おろす. ¶a ***treeless** plain* 木のない原野. ¶an ***undulating** plain* 起伏する広野. ¶a ***vast fertile** plain* 広ばくたるよく野.

P The mountain rises ***above*** the *plain*. その山は平野にそびえている. ¶They are found ***in*** the *plain* of India. それはインドの平野にある. ¶winter ***on*** the *plains* of Manchuria 満州の平野で越冬する. ¶The mountain towers ***over*** the *plain*. その山は平野にそびえ立っている.

plain, *a.* 平易な，単純な，明確な；質素な；[容色の]すぐれない．

M ***as plain*** as print (＝a pikestaff) きわめて明確な．¶it is *plain* ***enough*** that … …は分かり切っている．¶it is ***perfectly*** *plain* that … …は明々白々だ．¶The matter is ***quite*** *plain*. そのことはよく分かっている．【類】It is ***quite*** *plain* that he will fail. ¶Her dress is ***severely*** *plain*. 彼女の服装はあくまで質素だ．

P *plain* ***in*** language (speech, words) 言葉(など)の平易な ‖ *plain* ***in*** taste (habit) 趣味(など)の単純な．【類】dishes *plain* ***in*** design. ¶I will try to make it *plain* ***to*** you. 君に分かるように僕が説明しましょう．‖ be *plain* ***to*** one who reads as he runs 走り読みをする人にもよく分かる．¶to be *plain* ***with*** you あからさまに言えば．【類】I will be perfectly *plain* ***with*** you.

O I'm a tall woman, *plain* and skinny. 私はのっぽでみにくいほどやせこけている．

plaintiff, *n.* 原告人．

P Mr. A was counsel ***for*** the *plaintiff*, and Mr. B for the defendant. A 氏は原告人の，B 氏は被告人の弁護士であった．

plait, *v.* 編む．

P *plait* hair ***into*** a pigtail 髪を弁髪に編む．

plan, *n.* 考案，設計，計画；やり方，式．

V The *plan* was ***abandoned*** as impracticable. その計画は実行不能として捨てられた．¶***abolish*** the old *plan* of … …の旧計画をやめにする．¶***act out*** one's dastardly *plans* 卑劣な計画を実行する．¶***adopt*** the same *plan* 同じ計画を採用する．¶***advocate*** a *plan* 計画を支持する．¶The *plan* was ***approved***. その案は承認された ‖ ***approve*** the *plan* to … …する計画を是認する．¶***back up*** a *plan* 計画を後援する．¶***cancel*** one's *plan* その案を取消す．¶***carry*** a *plan* to completion 計画を完成する ‖ ***carry*** the *plan* into execution その計画を実行する．¶resolutely ***carry out*** a *plan* 計画を敢行する．¶***carry through*** a *plan* 計画を完成させる．¶***change*** one's *plans* 計画を変更する．¶***conceive*** a *plan* 案をめぐらす，考案する．¶***consider*** our *plan* of campaign わが作戦計画を練る．¶make every effort to ***controvert*** his *plans* 彼の計画の裏をかくようにあらゆる努力をする．¶***cripple*** a *plan* 案を骨抜きにする．¶***defeat*** a *plan* 計画を破る．¶***design*** a *plan* 計画を立てる．¶***devise*** a *plan* 考案する．¶***disconcert*** (＝spoil) the whole *plan* 計画全体をぶちこわす．¶***discuss*** *plans* and prospects 計画や予想を討議する．¶***draft*** *plans* for international projects 国際的事業の計画を起草する．¶***draw*** the *plans* for … …の図面を引く．¶***draw up*** a *plan* of campaign 作戦計画を立てる．【類】***draw up*** a *plan* of progress. ¶The *plan* has been ***dropped***. その計画はさた止みとなった．¶***execute*** a *plan* 計画を決行する．¶***favor*** the *plan* その案に賛成する．¶***foil*** one's *plan* その計画を破る．¶***follow*** a fixed *plan* in reading 予定の計画通りに読書する．【類】***follow*** a *plan* as laid out / His father's death left him free to ***follow*** his own *plans*. ¶***follow out*** a uniform *plan* throughout 終始一貫したやり方をする．¶***forestall*** the enemy's *plan* 敵の計画の裏をかく．¶***form*** a *plan* for … …の計画を立てる．¶***formulate*** a definite *plan* はっきりした案を立てる．¶***frame*** one's *plans* in complete disregard of … …に一切かまわず立案する．¶The rain ***frustrated*** the *plan*. 雨で計画がお流れになった．【類】This ***frustrated*** his *plan* of escape. ¶***further*** a *plan* 計画を推進する．¶***get up*** (＝make) a *plan* 計画をたてる．¶***hang up*** a *plan* 地図を掛ける．¶I ***have*** *plans* on hand for … 私は…を計画中である．¶***hold up*** *plans* for … …の計画を中止する．¶***initiate*** (＝***introduce***) a *plan* 案を提出する．¶***lay*** one's *plans* before … …に献策する ‖ ***lay*** one's *plans* of escaping from the country 国外逃亡の策をたてる．¶It has been conducted according to a *plan* previously ***laid out***. それは予定通りに進行した．‖ ***lay*** [***out***] a *plan* of … …の案を立てる．【類】***lay*** [***out***] a *plan* for the future. ¶I beg leave to ***propose*** a *plan* for … はばかりながら…に対し献策を致します．¶He died in midcareer, and ***left*** his *plan* only half executed. 彼は中途で死んでその計画を未完成のまま後に残した．¶***make plans*** for the holiday 休日利用の案を立てる ‖ He ***made plans*** for the future in that conviction. 彼はその信念で将来の案を立てた．‖ ***make plans*** of revenge in one's mind 心に報復の計画を立てる．¶***map out*** a general *plan* 大体の計画を立てる．¶It is considered almost certain that the *plan* will be ***matured*** and carried into effect sooner or later. その計画が熟して早晩実行の運びに至ることはほとんど疑いの余地がないものと考えられている．¶His *plan* was ***miscarried***. 彼の計画は失敗した．¶The *plan* was ***nipped*** in the bud. その計画は実行の運びに至らなかった．¶***organize plans*** for their relief 彼らの救済案を立てる．¶***originate*** the *plan* for the trip 遠足の発案をする．¶***outline*** a *plan* 計画の荒筋を示す ‖ ***outline*** a general *plan* 大体の計画を示す．¶***postpone*** one's *plan* of …ing …の計画を延ばす．¶***prepare*** a *plan* 計画の準備をする．¶***propose*** a daring *plan* 冒険的な計画をもくろむ．¶seriously and honestly ***prosecute*** a *plan* まじめに正直に計画を実行する．¶***provide*** a special *plan* 特別の計画を立てる．¶***pursue*** a *plan* 計画を進める．¶***put*** a *plan* into action 計画を実行する．【類】After a quarter of a century of talk, the *plan* was finally ***put*** into execution. ¶***realize*** a long-cherished *plan* 多年の懸案を実現する．¶***reframe*** a *plan* 案を練直す．¶***relinquish*** a *plan* 案を撤回する．¶***revise*** a *plan* of … …の計画を練り直す．¶***ruin*** one's *plans* 計画をばらす．¶The *plan* was much ***scouted*** in many quarters when first announced. その案が初めて発表された時には諸方面から一笑に付せられた．¶***select*** the most fitting *plan* 最も適当な計画を選ぶ．¶***set forth*** a *plan* 計画を発表する(始める)．¶a *plan* was ***set on foot*** to … …の計画が始まった．¶***shape*** one's *plans* 計画を立てる．¶Sleep over it! Time will ***show*** a *plan*. 一晩おいてみろ，時が解決するよ．¶***spoil*** the *plan* to … …しようとする計画をぶちこわす．¶***sponsor*** a *plan* for … …の計画を起す．¶This difficulty ***stalled*** (＝blocked) the whole *plan* of ours. この難関でわれわれの計画は全部ストップした．¶***start*** a new *plan* 新計画を始める．¶***submit*** a *plan* to … …に献策する．¶***suggest*** a new *plan* 新計画を提案する．¶***think out*** (＝devise) a *plan* 計画を立てる．¶These best laid *plans* were ***thrown*** temporarily out of gear. これらの上々策も一時は何の効果も奏しなかった．¶***thwart*** the *plan* of … …の計画を妨げる．¶***try*** a *plan* with … その計画を…にやって見る ‖ I ***tried*** your *plan*, but it would not work. 僕は君の案を試みたがうまく行かない．¶***unfold*** one's *plans* その計画を発表する．¶This ***upset*** all his *plans*. これで彼の計画も丸で狂ってしまった．¶***urge*** a *plan* 一策を力説する．¶***view*** a *plan* with approbation 計画に賛成する．¶***work out*** a *plan* 計画を立てる．¶The *plan* was ***wrecked***. その計画は失敗した．

V² The *plan* has ***bogged down***. 計画がストップした．¶Even the wisest *plan* often ***fails***. 最上の計画でも失敗することがよくある．¶My *plans* ***fell through***. 私の計画が思うように行かなかった．¶The *plan* has ***miscarried*** (＝***failed***＝***broken down***). その計画は失敗だった．‖ if the present *plan* does not ***miscarry*** この計画通りに行けば．¶The *plan* ***ripened***. その計画は熟した．¶This *plan* has ***worked*** exceptionally well. この案が殊にうまく行った．【類】The *plan* in all its details ***worked*** without a hitch (滞りなく)．

Q an ***aeroscopic*** *plan* 露腸図(土佐絵などのように天井抜に室内または間取を現わした)．¶make ***ambitious*** *plans* for the future 将来の大計画を立てる．¶a hotel operated (＝run) on the ***American*** (***European***) *plan* 宿泊料に食費を含む(宿泊料・食費別勘定)方式のホテル．【類】All hotels in Japan are conducted on the ***American*** *plan*. / Some American hotels are run on the ***European*** *plan*. ¶it is a ***bad*** *plan* to … …するのはよくないやり方だ．¶This seems the ***better*** *plan*. この方がよい方法のようだ．【類】The ***better*** *plan* is to peel them after boiling (煮てから皮をむく)．¶a ***blue printed*** *plan* 青写真図面．¶That is a ***capital*** *plan*. それは名案だ．¶according to a ***clearly-formed*** *plan* ちゃんと案を立てて．¶a ***clever*** *plan* 巧妙な計画．¶a ***concrete*** *plan* 具体案．¶Payments may be arranged on the ***convenient monthly*** *plan*. 支払は便利な月賦制にもできる．¶a ***deep***[***-laid***] *plan* 深い魂胆のある計画．¶form a ***detailed*** *plan* for this purpose この目的で細かい案を作る．¶It was organized on a ***different*** *plan*. それは別の方法で組織された．¶an ***effectual*** *plan* 効果的な方法．¶an ***excellent*** *plan* 妙案．¶a more ***feasible*** *plan* 一層実行性のある計画．¶lay down a ***general*** *plan* 大体の計画を立てる．¶it is a ***good*** *plan* to … …はいい方法だ．【類】a ***good*** *plan* [to follow] is … / you will find it a ***good*** *plan* to … ¶the ***great*** *plan* of the Creator 造物主の偉大な摂理．【類】I have ***great*** *plans* for his future. ¶upset an ***important plan*** 重要計画をくつがえす. ¶fantastic hopes and ***impractical plans*** 突飛な希望や実行性のない計画(机上論). ¶hit on an ***ingenious plan*** for making money 金をこしらえる名案を思い付く. ¶a ***nation-wide plan*** 国家的計画. ¶That seems to be ***Nature's plan***. それは天の配剤らしい. ¶be devised on an entirely ***new plan*** 全く新しい企画で考案されている. ¶a ***novel plan*** 目新しい仕組. ¶changes in their ***operational plans*** 作戦計画の変更. ¶an ***organized plan*** of selling 組織的な販売法. ¶give up the ***original plan*** 初志を翻えす. ¶a dictionary compiled on an ***original plan*** ざん新な方法で編まれた辞書. 【類】be constructed on an ***original plan***. ¶a ***permanent plan*** 永久の計画. ¶a ***preconceived plan*** 前から考えておいた案(腹案). ¶a ***premeditated plan*** 予謀計画. ¶according to the ***previous plans*** この前の計画によれば. ¶***provisional plans*** 暫定案. ¶classes set upon a ***rational plan*** 合理的編成のクラス. ¶a ***rough plan*** 大体の計画 ‖ The letter "H" forms the ***rough plan*** of the entire system of the underground railways. 地下鉄全線の系統はほぼH形になっている. ¶the ***safe plan***, therefore, is to ... したがって安全な方法は…することである. ¶on the ***same plan*** as ... …と同じ仕組で. 【類】be conducted on the ***same plan*** as ... ¶a ***similar plan*** 類似の計画. ¶a ***specious plan*** もっともらしい計画. ¶Business letters are constructed on a ***stereotyped plan***. 商業通信文は紋切型でつづられている. ¶a ***ten-year plan*** 十年計画. ¶a carefully ***thought-out plan*** 万全の策. ¶on a ***uniform plan*** 画一案によって. ¶a ***well-laid plan*** 十分練られた案. ¶It is not a ***wise plan***. それは賢明な策ではない. ¶the ***wisest*** and ***safest plan*** 万全の策. ¶a ***workable plan*** for the way out 実行性のある打開策.

Q² an ***afforestation plan*** 植林計画. ¶an ***arms reduction plan*** 兵器縮小案. ¶a ***city plan*** 都市計画. ¶present a ***compromise plan*** 妥協案を出す. ¶an ***easy payment plan*** 分割払い. ¶the veteran's ***education plan*** 退役軍人教育案. ¶an ***exit plan*** [劇場などの]非常退出案内図. ¶the ***five-year*** trusteeship ***plan*** 五カ年信託統治案. ¶a ***future plan*** 将来の計画. ¶a ***ground floor plan*** [建物の]地取図. ¶a ***happy-go-lucky plan*** 行き当りばったりの計画. ¶a ***hush-hush plan*** 秘密の計画. ¶It is to be paid for on the ***installment plan***. それは分納法で支払うことになっている. 【類】buy things on the ***installment plan***. ¶the ***Japan Control Plan*** approved at Moscow モスコーで定められた日本監理案. ¶prepare and carry out ***lesson plans*** 教案を作り実行する. ¶a ***long-range*** industrial ***plan*** 長期産業計画. ¶a ***long-term plan*** 長期計画. ¶The ***majority-approved control plan*** of atomic energy was vetoed by Russia. 多数で定められた原子力監理案にロシアは拒否権を行使した. ¶a ***makeshift plan*** 暫定案. ¶block the ***Marshall Plan*** and American aid to Europe マーシャルプランと対欧アメリカ援助を封じる. ¶a ***master plan*** 最善策. ¶a convenient ***monthly payment plan*** 便利な月賦支払制度. ¶a five-year ***national defense plan*** 五カ年国防計画. ¶a ***no-tipping plan*** チップなし制サービス. ¶an ***obligation plan*** 支出負担行為計画. ¶a ***paper plan*** 紙上案. ¶The street-cars are operated on the ***pay-as-you-enter plan***. 電車は乗る時払い式で運転している. 【類】the "***pay-as-you-go***" ***plan***. ¶***peace*** and ***war plans*** 平和と戦争の計画. ¶institute a ***profit-sharing plan*** 利益配分の計画をたてる. 【類】factories conducted on the ***profitsharing plan***. ¶a ***short-range plan*** 短期計画. ¶a ***shortrange, interim plan*** 短期の中間案. ¶an effective ***sales plan*** 効果的な販売方法. ¶a ***seven-point plan*** of physical education 体育の七カ条案. ¶form a ***sightseeing plan*** 遊覧の計画を立てる. ¶a ***skeleton plan*** 概案. ¶the arrangement of a ***table plan*** 食卓の座席配列. ¶a ***traffic relief plan*** 交通緩和案. ¶a ***working plan*** 工作図.

P work ***according to*** a *plan* 計画を立てて仕事をする. 【類】Handel, ***according to*** his father's *plans*, was to be a lawyer. ¶prepared ***after*** a definite *plan* 一定の方法に従って調製した ‖ a building erected ***after*** the *plans* of an eminent architect 有名な建築家の設計でできた建物. 【類】The building was completed ***after*** the *plans* of ..., ..., and ..., architects. ¶He was crossed ***in*** his *plans* 彼は計画の邪魔をされた. ¶a man full ***of*** *plans* for the future 将来の計画をうんと持っている人. ¶education ***on*** the Dalton *plan* ドールトン式の教育 ‖ if ever I am able to finish this work ***on*** the *plan* I have commenced 始めの計画通りにこの著作を完成することができるとしたら. 【類】English teaching conducted ***on*** that *plan* / The money has been donated as a fund for the establishment of a lectureship ***on*** a *plan* somewhat similar to that of the ... lecture. ¶***under*** the *plan* その案によって. 【類】The work will be more fruitful ***under*** this *plan*. ¶hit ***upon*** a good *plan* いい案を思いつく.

P² lay one's *plans* ***for*** an attack on ... …攻撃の作戦をする ‖ *plans* ***for*** eliminating unnecessary expenses 冗費節減法 ‖ think of a *plan* ***for*** revenge 復しゅうを計画する ‖ *plans* ***for*** this hotel were drawn by one of the most outstanding architectural firms in New York. このホテルの設計はニューヨーク一流の建築会社の手になった. ¶the *plan* ***of*** Nature 天の配剤 ‖ formulate a *plan* ***of*** study 勉強の方法を立てる.

O The *plan* is now on foot (=under way). その案は着々進行中だ.

plan, *v.* 計画する.

M ***deliberately plan*** a revenge 徐々に復しゅうを企てる. ¶***intelligently plan*** 理知的に計画する. ¶as ***originally planned*** 始めの設計通り. ¶***plan realistically*** 現実に即して計画を立てる.

P I am *planning* ***on*** spending the coming holidays at Kyoto and Nara. 私は京都と奈良で今度の休暇を過す積りだ.

plane, *n.* 水平面; 地位, 程度; (米) 飛行機.

V ***board*** a *plane* for ... …行きの飛行機に乗る. ¶The *plane* lost its control and was ***ditched*** on the lake. 同機は機能を喪失して湖水に不時着した. ¶***fly*** a *plane* 飛行機を操縦する. ¶***guide*** a *plane* for safe landing 安全着陸させるよう機を導く. ¶***land*** a *plane* 飛行機を着陸させる. ¶***operate*** five *planes* on the Atlantic route 大西洋航空路に五機を運航させる. ¶***pilot*** a *plane* 飛行機を操縦する.

V² The *plane* successfully ***hopped off***. その機はうまく離陸した. ¶The *plane* was ***swooping down*** on the enemy troopers. その機は敵の輸送船に急降下で襲いかかった. ¶The *plane* ***took off*** for North Africa. 飛行機は北アフリカ向け出航した. ¶The *plane* ***zoomed up*** almost vertically 機はほとんど垂直に空中に飛上った.

Q The *Divine Wind* is an ***all-Japanese plane***. 神風号は全部国産である. ¶an ***amphibious plane*** 空陸両用飛行機. ¶be on ***another plane*** これと選を異にする. ¶The whirring heard over the metropolis is that of a ***friendly plane***. 帝都上空にある爆音は友軍機のものだ. ¶a ***high plane*** of civilization 高度の文明 ‖ put a man on a ***higher plane*** 人を一層高い地位におく. 【類】look at things from a ***higher plane***. ¶a railway engine trying to draw a long train of cars up an ***inclined plane*** 長い列車を引いてこう配を上ろうとする機関車. ¶There was a ***lofty plane*** of discussion in the conference. その会議での議論は高級のものであった. ¶a ***low plane*** of life 程度の低い生活 ‖ a writer on a much ***lower plane*** はるかに低級の文士. ¶a ***radio-controlled, pilotless plane*** 無電操縦の無人機. ¶be placed on the ***same plane*** as ... …と同列(同格)におかれる. 【類】admit women students on the ***same plane*** (=level) with men. ¶a ***twin-motored plane*** 双発機. ¶in a ***vertical plane*** 垂直面に.

Q² an ***air-force plane*** 空軍機. ¶an ***army transport plane*** 陸軍輸送機. ¶an ***Army C-54*** transport ***plane*** 陸軍C-54輸送機. ¶an ***atom plane*** 原子飛行機. ¶a ***combat plane*** 戦闘機. ¶a ***fighter*** [*plane*] 戦闘機. ¶*Kamikaze* (Divine Wind) was the term given to the ***Japanese suicide planes*** used in the Pacific. 「神風」は太平洋上で用いられた日本決死空軍機に与えられた名前であった. ¶a ***jet plane*** ジェット機. ¶the ***lead plane*** of a flight of four Army bombers 四陸軍爆撃機運航の先導機. ¶a ***liaison plane*** 連絡機. ¶aboard a ***Pan-American Airways plane*** パンアメリカン航空会社旅客機に乗って. ¶a ***parachute plane*** carrying armed troops 武装落下さん部隊を運ぶ空輸機. ¶a ***passenger plane*** 旅客機. 【類】a long-distance ***passenger plane*** / a ***passenger-carrying plane***. ¶a ***photo-reconnaissance plane*** 空中撮影機. ¶a ***pursuit plane***=a pursuiter 追撃機. ¶dispatch a ***rescue plane*** 救助機を派遣する. ¶a ***torpedo plane*** 空雷飛行機. ¶a series of disasters that have struck ***transport planes*** recently 最近ひんぴんと起る輸送機事故. ¶a ***two-seater plane*** 両座式飛行機. ¶a U.S. ***war plane***

(=warplane) 米軍機.

P travel *by plane* 空路旅行する. ¶set it *on* the *plane* of highest art 最高芸術の水準にそれをおく ‖ It is *on* another *plane*. それは選を異にしている.

plane, *v.* かんなで削る.

M *plane away* (=*down or off*) 削り取る；平にする. ¶*plane* a board *smooth* 板にかんなをかけて滑らかにする.

planet, *n.* 遊星.

Q the *major planets* 大遊星. ¶a *minor planet* 小遊星. ¶the *superior* (*inferior*) *planets* 外(内)遊星(地球を中心に).

P The night *on* the *planet* Mars must be intensely cold, owing to the thinness and clearness of the air. 空気が希薄で清澄であるから火星の夜は寒さが激しいに違いない.

plank, *n.* 厚板；項目.

V *walk* the *plank* げん側から突き出した板を目かくしして歩かせる(昔捕虜を殺すに用いた方法).

Q² a *tariff plank* 関税政策.

P² a *plank in* a platform 政綱の一項目.

plank, *v.* 支払う.

M² *plank down* (=out) one's money 《口語》即金で支払う.

planner, *n.* 立案者.

Q² a *city planner* 都市計画立案者. ¶a *Communist planner* 共産党政策立案者. ¶a *program planner* 計画立案者.

planning, *n.* 企画.

Q with *no planning* 行当りばったりで. ¶through *organized intelligent planning* 組織的で賢明な企画によって. ¶*skilful planning* 巧みな計画.

Q² *lesson planning* 教案作製. ¶*long-range planning* for ... ...に対する遠大な計画. ¶*long-time planning* 長期計画. ¶the Minister of *Town and Country Planning* 建設大臣.

P spending *without planning* 無計画な支出.

plant, *n.* (**1**) 植物；植木, 苗木；生長.

V *bed out* young rice *plants* 早苗を植え付ける. ¶*breed* a *plant* downward 植物を小さくする. ¶*force plants* [温室などに入れて]植物を促成させる. ¶Roots *help plants* get food and water from the ground. 根によって植木は地下から養分と水を吸収する. ¶Are you sure that frost won't *kill* those *plants?* これらの植物は霜に強いというのはたしかですか. ¶The ship's gardener *re-bedded* the *plants* all through. 船の園丁は植木をすっかり植替えた. ¶*top* a *plant* 木のうらを止める. ¶*train* a *plant* 植木を仕立てる. ¶*plants used* for food 食用植物.

V² The *plant died.* その植物が枯れた. ¶The *plant dies down* in winter. その植物は冬枯れる. ¶The *plant* has *drooped.* その植物がしおれた. ¶The *plants* are beginning to *shoot.* 草木が芽ぐんで来た. ¶This *plant thrives* in this climate. この植物にはこの気候がよく適して繁茂する.

Q a *creeping evergreen plant* 常緑のつる木. ¶a *deciduous plant* 落葉植物. ¶a *decorative plant* 賞がん植物. ¶*economic plants* 実用植物. ¶cut the *evil plant* in the roots 悪草を根絶する. ¶*exotic plants* 外来の植物. ¶*faded plants* しおれた植物. ¶*Few plants* grow in a desert. さばくではあまり植物は生えない. ¶*flowering plants* 顕花植物. ¶a *flowerless plant* 隠花植物. ¶*hardy plants* 容易に枯れない強い草木. ¶*medical* (=*drug*) *plants* 薬用植物. ¶a *poisonous plant* 有毒植物. ¶place a *potted plant* in the sun 盆栽を日なたに出す. ¶a *rare plant* 珍らしい植木. ¶a *tropical plant* 熱帯植物.

Q² an *air plant* 〖植〗空気植物. ¶a *bedding plant* 花壇の草木. ¶a *climbing plant* つる木. ¶a *desert plant* さばくの植物. ¶a *forest plant* 森林の植物. ¶a *garden plant* 庭木. ¶a *greenhouse* (=*glasshouse*) *plant* 温室植物. ¶a *hothouse plant* 温室植物. ¶a *house plant* 室内植物. ¶a *leaf plant* 葉だけの植物. ¶a *mountain plant* 山地植物. ¶a *pot plant* はち植え(盆栽). ¶planting of young *rice plants* 田植え. ¶*running plants* つる木. ¶a *seaside plant* 海辺植物. ¶a *seed plant* 苗木. ¶a young *seedling plant* 苗木. ¶a *vine plant* つる植物(つた). ¶a *water plant* 水生植物.

P a disease *of plants* 植物の病気. ¶a disease *on plants* (葉面・樹皮などの)植物の病. ¶a *plant of* this order この科の植物. ¶Nine out of every ten *plants on* earth are grasses. 地球上の各植物の内九割までは草である. ¶a *plant with* aromatic seeds 芳香ある種子を有する植物.

P² a *plant in* a jar はち植えの植木.

(**2**) 機械装置, 工場設備；工場.

V *drive* a *plant* 工場を経営する. ¶*erect* a *plant* 工場を建設する. ¶*establish plants* for producing ... ...の製作所を設ける. ¶The dance-hall, the café, and the assignation house, closely adjoining one another, *form* a *plant* under one management. 相隣接しているダンスホールとカフェーと待合が一つの建物になっていてその経営者が同じである. ¶*install* a new *plant* 新規の機械を据え付ける. ¶*lay down* a *plant* of sufficient capacity 十分の性能を有する機械を据え付ける. ¶The *plant* is *operated* by an electric motor of 120 horse-power. その機械は百二十馬力のモーターで運転されている. ¶*put up* a *plant* 工場を建てる. ¶Ironworks *require* a large *plant*. 鉄工場は大規模の設備を要する. ¶*run* its *plants* day and night to meet a rush of orders 注文殺到のため昼夜兼行で機械を運転する.

Q Michigan's *athletic plant* is the most complete in America. ミシガン大学の運動設備は米国中で一番完備したものだ. ¶an *automated plant* オートメーション化した工場. ¶a *fixed plant* 固定工場. ¶one of the largest *industrial plants* in the world 世界の最大工場の一つ. ¶a secrecy-shrouded *plant* 秘密工場. ¶a *self-contained plant* 自給自足工場. ¶a *small plant* of machinery for ... ...の小機械工場. ¶a *wireless* (=radio) *plant* 無線電信局.

Q² an *assembly plant* 組立(仕上げ)工場. ¶an *atomic fission plant* on a laboratory scale 実験段階の原子工場. ¶an *automobile plant* 自動車工場. ¶an *automobile assembly plant* 自動車組立工場. ¶a *beetroot-sugar plant* ビート糖工場. ¶a *Bessemer plant* for steel-making ベッセマー式製鋼工場. ¶a *bleaching plant* 漂白工場. ¶a *boot and shoe making plant* 製靴(〃)工場. ¶a *brick* and *tile making plant* レンガ及びタイル工場. ¶a *calico-printing plant* さらさ(プリントもの)生産工場. ¶a *canning plant* かん詰工場. ¶a *candle-making plant* ろうそく工場. ¶a *castor-oil* (*hemp oil, cotton-seed oil*) *plant* ひまし油(など)工場. ¶a *cloth-finishing plant* 織物仕上工場. ¶a *cloth-manufacturing plant* 織物工場. ¶a *coffee plant* コーヒー工場. ¶a *coaling plant* 給炭所. ¶a *coke* and *cement plant* コークス及びセメント工場. ¶a *college plant* 大学の建物及び施設. ¶a *confectionery plant* 製菓工場. ¶a *distilling plant* for whisky ウイスキー醸造工場. ¶a *dry cleaning plant* ドライクリーニング工場. ¶an *electric-lighting plant* 照明配電所. ¶an *electric-power plant* 発電所. ¶a *farming plant* 農場. ¶a *filtration plant* ろ過工場. ¶a *food plant* 食料品会社. ¶a central *heating plant* 中央分送式暖房装置. ¶a *fueling plant* 燃料工場. ¶a *gas-making plant* ガス工場. ¶a *generating plant* 発電所. ¶a *glass-making plant* ガラス工場. ¶a *hemp-manufacturing plant* 製麻工場. ¶a *hydro-power* (=water-power) *plant* 水力発電所. ¶an *ice plant* 製氷工場. ¶an *india-rubber manufacturing plant* 弾性ゴム製造工場. ¶an *iron-foundry plant* 製鉄工場. ¶the great *Krupp plant,* at Essen エッセンのクルップ大工場. ¶a *laundry plant* 洗たく工場. ¶a *lighting plant* 照明用配電所. ¶a *machinery plant* 機械工場. ¶a *manufacturing plant* 生産工場, 製作所. ¶a *marine manufacturing plant* 海産物生産工場. ¶a *metal-products plant* 金属部品工場. ¶build a *munition plant* 兵器工場を建設する. 【類】a $30,000,000 *munitions plant.* ¶take pupils through (=over) a *newspaper plant* 生徒を連れて新聞社を見学させる. ¶an *ordnance plant* 兵器工場. ¶an *ore-dressing plant* 鉱石処理工場. ¶a *paper-making plant* 製紙工場. ¶a *parent plant* 親工場. ¶a *parts plant* 部品工場. ¶a *patent fuel plant* 専売燃料工場. ¶a *power*[*-producing*] *plant* 発電所. ¶an electric light and *power plant* 配電及び水力発電所. ¶a *poultry plant* 養鶏場. ¶a *printing plant* 印刷工場. ¶a *production plant* 生産工場. ¶a *prospecting plant* 探鉱用機械その他用具. ¶a *purification plant* 浄水所(水道の). ¶a *repair plant* 修理工場. ¶a wider use of the *school plant* 学校の施設のより広い利用. ¶a *sewage disposal plant* 下水処理所. ¶a *shipbuilding plant* 造船所. ¶a *small arms plant* 小型兵器工場. ¶a *soap-making plant* 石けん工場. ¶a *starch-manufacturing plant* でん粉工場. ¶a *steel plant* 製鋼所. ¶a *steam-power plant* 火力発電所. ¶a *storage plant* 倉庫. ¶a *sugar* [*refinery*] *plant* 精糖工場. ¶a *thrashing plant* 脱穀工場. ¶a *thread-manufacturing plant* 製糸工場. ¶can factories and other *tin plants* 製かん工場及びブリキ工場など. ¶a *tobacco-manufacturing plant* タバコ工場. ¶*war plants* owned or financed by the Government during the war 戦時中の政府所有または監理の軍需品諸工場.

plant, *v.* 植える, 栽培する；据え付ける；立てる.

M *plant on* [装飾など]取付ける. ¶Rice is *planted out* in June. 稲は六月に植え付ける.

P a X'mas tree *planted* (=set up) ***at*** the door ドアーのところにたてたクリスマス・ツリー. ¶a pine-tree which was *planted* ***by*** the Emperor's own hand 陛下御手植の松. ¶They are *planted* ***for*** hedges (ornament). それを生垣(など)用に植える. ¶The trees are *planted* ***in*** the garden (earth, ground, streets). その樹が庭(など)に植えてある. ‖ I have my ground mostly *planted* ***in*** fruit trees. 私の邸内には大抵果樹を植えさせてある. ‖ *plant* a stake ***in*** the ground 地面にくいを打ち込む. ¶*plant* a flag ***on*** a building (an island) 建物(など)の上に旗を立てる. 【類】The trees are *planted* ***on*** the banks. ¶The field is *planted* ***to*** wheat (rice). 畑には小麦(など)が作ってある. ¶*plant* a churchyard ***with*** yew trees 墓地にいちいを植える. 【類】The gardens are tastefully *planted* ***with*** fruit and other trees, bounded with green hedges, and enlivened with beds of flowers. / *plant* a garden ***with*** roses.

plantation, *n.* 耕地, 農園.

V ***establish*** *plantations* 耕地を設ける.

Q^{2} a ***coffee*** *plantation* コーヒー園. ¶a ***cotton*** *plantation* 綿花耕地. ¶a ***mulberry*** *plantation* 桑畑. ¶a ***rubber*** *plantation* ゴム園. ¶a ***sugar*** *plantation* 砂糖園. ¶a ***tea*** *plantation* 茶畑.

P a strike of Indians ***on*** the *plantations* 耕地における米国土人の罷業.

planter, *n.* 栽培者；《米》農園経営者.

Q He was one of the ***richest*** *planters* in Virginia. 彼はヴァージニアでは最も富裕な農場主の一人だった.

Q^{2} a ***cotton*** (***coffee, sugar***) *planter* 綿花(など)農場主.

planting, *n.* 植樹；植えつけ.

V ***do*** the *planting* 植込をする.

Q encourage ***civic*** *planting* 都市の植樹を奨励する.

Q^{2} ***Crop*** *plantings* were ruined in many places. 作物がめちゃめちゃになった所が多い. ¶***succession*** *planting* 連作.

plaque, *n.* 飾り板.

Q^{2} there is a ***brass*** *plaque* on the gate: "…" 門に「…」と書いた真ちゅうの門標が出ている. ¶a ***bronze metal*** *plaque* 青銅の飾り板. ¶a meritorious ***service*** *plaque* 勲功章.

plaster, *n.* こう薬.

V ***put on*** (=***apply***) a *plaster* こう薬を張る. ¶***remove*** a *plaster* こう薬をはぐ.

plaster, *v.* 塗る.

M^{2} Her hair was *plastered* ***down*** with rain. 彼女の髪は雨でぺったりくっついてしまった.

P *plaster* one's face ***with*** powder 顔におしろいを塗る.

plate, *n.* 板；鉛板；料理の一さら；〖野球〗プレート.

V The *plate* was ***destroyed*** by Méryon after ten impressions had been taken. メルヨンは(エッチング)版図を十枚刷ってからその金属版をつぶしてしまった. ¶*Plates* were ***laid*** for 50 persons. 食卓に五十人分の食事が用意された. ‖ the ceremony of ***laying*** the first *plate* 造船の始工式. ¶***put up*** one's *plate* 門札を出す. ¶***remove*** (=***put away***) the *plates* さらを片づける. ¶***scrape*** one's *plate* さらの物を食尽す. ¶***set*** the *plates* for three 食卓に三人分の用意をする. ¶***share*** a *plate* of strawberries いちごのごちそうにあずかる.

Q a ***clean*** *plate* [ふいて]きれいなさら. ¶a ***colored*** *plate* 着色ざら. ¶a ***terminal*** *plate* 端っこ板. ¶a ***dry*** *plate* かわいたさら.

Q^{2} a notice on a ***brass*** *plate* announcing that … …と記した真ちゅう板の掲示. ¶***bread*** *plates* パンざら. ¶a ***ceiling*** *plate* 天井座金. ¶a ***church*** *plate* 教会の献金ざら. ¶a ***collection*** *plate* 集金のぼん. ¶a ***dessert*** *plate* 食後(の果物など)を出すさら. ¶a ***dinner*** *plate* 料理をだすさら. ¶a ***door*** *plate*=a doorplate 門標. ¶a ***double-page*** *plate* 二ページで一つの図版. ¶the ***home*** *plate* 〖野球〗本塁. ¶a ***metal license*** *plate* [自動車などの]金属製の許可札. ¶***New License*** *Plates* Issued Here. 〖掲示〗新しい許可札はここで発行します. ¶a ***full-page*** (***part-page***) *plate* 一ページ大(など)の図版. ¶a galvanized ***steel*** *plate* 鋼鉄のトタン板. ¶a ***tin*** *plate* ブリキ板.

P stand ***at*** the *plate* 〖野球〗[打者が]プレートに立つ.

P^{2} a *plate* ***of*** fish 一さらの魚肉.

plate, *v.* 被(き)せる.

P It is *plated* ***with*** gold. それは金被せになっている. 【類】*plate* copper ***with*** silver.

platform, *n.* 昇降場(ホーム)；演壇；主義；《米》[政党の]政綱, 綱領.

V ***adopt*** the Socialist *platform* 社会党の政綱を採用する. ¶***enter*** the *platform* ホームにはいる. ¶He ***paced*** the *platform* back and forth. ホームをあっちへ行ったりこっちへ来たりした. 【類】He ***paced*** the *platform* of the railway station for two hours before her train was due. ¶Each speaker was greeted with applause on ***taking*** the *platform*. 弁士が登壇するたびにかっさいをもって迎えられた.

Q the ***candidate's*** *platform* 候補者の政見. ¶a ***draughty*** *platform* 吹きさらしのホーム. ¶make a speech from a ***public*** *platform* 演壇から公衆に向って演説をする. ¶a ***raised*** *platform* 一段高い壇. ¶a ***rear*** *platform* of a car 電車の後部昇降段.

Q^{2} a ***departure*** (an ***arrival***) *platform* 発車(到着)ホーム. ¶a ***lecture*** *platform* 講壇. ¶an "***L***" *platform* 高架鉄道のホーム. ¶a ***party*** *platform* 党の政綱. ¶the ***reviewing*** *platform* 観兵式の壇. ¶a ***revolving*** *platform* 回り舞台. ¶one of the chief planks of the Republican *platform* 共和党の主要綱領の一つ.

P adopt it ***as*** a *platform* それを標傍する. ¶the chief plank ***in*** the society's *platform* その協会の綱領の眼目. ¶meet a person ***on*** the *platform* ホームに人を迎える.

platitude, *n.* 平凡さ, 単調さ.

V ***talk*** *platitudes* お座なりを言う.

Q To say that … is but a very ***mild*** *platitude* indeed. …というのは実際体裁のよい愚説に過ぎない.

Q^{2} ***milk-and-water*** *platitudes* 水を混ぜた牛乳のような底力のない言葉.

platoon, *n.* 小隊.

Q^{2} a ***fire-fighting*** *platoon* 消防小隊.

plaudit, *n.* 賞賛, かっさい.

V He ***acknowledged*** the *plaudits* of the crowd that greeted him as a hero. 彼は勇者として彼を迎えた群衆のかっさいに答礼した. ¶That course would have ***received*** the *plaudits* of the multitude. そのやり口なら民衆の賞賛を博したであろう.

Q the ***enthusiastic*** *plaudits* of the people 人民の熱心なかっさい.

P ***amid*** the united *plaudits* of the company 一同のかっさいのうちに. ¶***with*** hearty *plaudits* 心から賞賛して.

plausibility, *n.* もっともらしいこと.

P he tells ***with*** much *plausibility* that … 彼は…と言っているがこれは誠にもっともらしく思われる. 【類】infer (推論する) ***with*** great *plausibility* that …

plausible, *a.* もっともらしい.

M Such a conclusion is ***extremely*** *plausible*. そのような決論は至当である.

O make it sound as *plausible* as possible それを出来るだけ本当らしくする.

play, *n.* (1) 演劇, 脚本.

V ***act*** a *play* 劇を演じる. ¶***cast*** a *play* 劇の役割を決める ‖ go beyond the limits of his own company in ***casting*** the *play* 座以外の人にも役を頼む. ¶***do*** a *play* 芝居をやる. ¶Have you been ***following*** the *play*? この競技を続けて見ておいででしたか. ‖ ***follow*** a *play* with a play book 脚本と照らし合わせながら劇を見る. ¶We are ***giving*** a *play*. 劇をやるところだ. ¶The *play* has been ***interdicted*** by the Government on account of its "dangerous revolutionary tendencies." その劇は危険な革命的色彩を帯びているというので政府から上演を禁止された. ¶***license*** the *play* to be performed その劇の興行を許可する. ¶***novelize*** a *play* 劇を小説化する. ¶The *play* is ***played***. その芝居は済んだ. ¶***present*** a *play* 芝居を打つ. ¶***produce*** a *play* 劇を上演する. 【類】This *play* was ***produced*** by … at the … Theatre in 1916 with great success. ¶***put*** a *play* on a stage 脚本を舞台にかける ‖ ***put*** the *play* on the air 劇を放送する. ¶***rehearse*** a *play* in ordinary dress 平常服で劇の試演をやる. ¶***render*** a *play* 劇を演出する. ¶***see*** a *play* 劇を見る. ¶The *play* will be ***shown*** in the … Theatre, September 25. その劇は九月二十五日…劇場で上演される. ¶***sit out*** the whole *play* 芝居を大詰まで見る. ¶The *play* has been ***staged*** with financial success. その劇は大入を取って上演された. ¶***telecast*** a *play* 劇をテレビ放送する.

V^{2} The *play* ***caught on*** well. その芝居は当った. ¶The *play* ***draws well***. その芝居は大入りだ. ¶The *play* ***fell***

flat. 芝居は受けなかった. ¶The *play* ***ran*** 100 nights (for two weeks). その芝居は百晩(など)続いた.

Q a ***historical*** *play* 史劇. ¶a ***musical*** *play* 音楽劇. ¶The ***new*** *play* is a great draw. 今度の芝居は大当りだ. ¶an author of ***numerous, well-received*** *plays* 多数の評判のよい劇の作者. ¶This *play* is ***rubbish.*** この劇はだ作だ. ¶a ***Shakespearean*** *play* シェークスピア劇. ¶a ***successful*** *play* 当り狂言.

Q² an ***action*** *play* 活劇, ちゃんばらもの. ¶a ***benefit*** *play* 寄付演劇, 慈善興行. ¶a ***broadcast*** *play* ラジオドラマ. ¶a ***dream*** *play* 夢幻劇. ¶the ***gun*** *play* of gangsters ギャングもの. ¶a ***miracle*** *play* 奇跡劇. ¶a ***morality*** *play* 道徳劇, 教訓もの. ¶a ***motion picture*** *play* 映画劇. ¶It is obviously a ***propagandist*** *play* それは明らかに宣伝劇だ. ¶a ***reading*** *play* 読む劇(上演には適しない). ¶***screen*** (=***shadow***) *play* 映画. ¶a ***society*** *play* 社会劇. ¶a ***stage*** *play* 舞台劇. ¶***stand*** *play* 場当りをねらうこと. ¶a ***sword[-rattling]*** *play* 剣劇. ¶a ***two-act*** *play* 二幕もの. ¶a ***two-character*** *play* 役者が二人の(簡単な)劇.

P ***after*** the *play* 芝居がはねてから. ¶I saw you in the distance ***at*** the *play* last night. 僕は昨夜芝居で遠くから君を見た. 【類】spend the evening ***at*** the *play*. ¶actors who play the rôles of women ***in*** the old *play* of Japan 日本の旧劇の女形. ¶Let us go ***to*** the *play*. 芝居に行こう.

P² a *play* ***of*** Shakespeare シェークスピア劇.

(**2**) 遊戯; 競技; と博; 仕打; 活動; 余裕.

V ***allow*** full *play* to curiosity 好奇心をほしいままにさせる. ¶No one who has not been working can truly ***enjoy*** *play*. 働いたことのない人には本当に遊びの味は分からない. ¶***give*** free *play* to one's ability その手腕を十分に発揮させる ‖ ***give*** *play* to imagination 気を回す. 【類】***give*** full *play* to one's imagination. ¶***have*** full *play* 十分活動している. ¶Come, ***leave*** your *play!* さーやめろ(競技などしている時の用語). ¶There were some good *plays* ***made*** in the game. …その競技には妙技が二三あった. ‖ ***make*** *play* with … …をもてあそぶ. ¶***secure*** fair *play* for … …に対して公平な取扱いを受けるようにする. ¶***suspect*** foul *play* 卑劣な行為がありそうに思う. ¶***use*** fair *play* to gain one's ends 目的達成に公明正大な行動を取る.

V² *Play* ***begins*** at 2 p.m. [野球など]午後二時開始. ¶*Play* will ***commence*** at 4.30 o'clock sharp. (野球など)正四時半開始.

Q it is ***child's*** *play* to … …するのは朝飯前の仕事だ. 【類】It is mere ***child's*** *play*. ¶a ***double*** *play* 〚野球〛併殺. ¶***fair*** *play* 公明正大の行動 ‖ for ***fair*** *play* 恨みっこのないように ‖ to see that ***fair*** *play* is observed ずるいことをしないように. ¶a ***fine*** *play* 〚競技〛美技. ¶a ***foul*** *play* 〚競技〛反則; 不正行為 ‖ When a dead body is found, ***foul*** *play* is often suspected. 死体が見つかると他殺じゃないかと疑われることがよくある. ¶a ***rough*** *play* 荒わざ. ¶Compared with yours my present work is ***sheer*** *play*. 君のと比べると私の今の仕事などはほんの遊びごとだ. ¶a ***triple*** *play* 〚野球〛三重殺.

Q² No ***baby*** *play*, mind you. ままごとじゃないんだぜ君. ¶a ***bonehead*** *play* 〚野球〛拙技. ¶***outdoor*** (***indoor***) *play* 戸外(室内)の遊び.

P He was ***at*** *play* while the rest were at work. 彼は他の人が皆仕事しているときに遊んでいた. ‖ a tiger gamboling ***at*** *play* 戯れてはね回っているとら ‖ the noise of children ***at*** *play* 遊んでいる子供らの声. ¶***by*** a *play* of the imagination 想像の働きで. ¶I am not in the humor (=mood) ***for*** *play*. 僕には遊ぼうという気がない. ¶I said it ***in*** *play* (=for fun). 私はそれを冗談に言ったのだ. ¶bring it ***into*** *play* それを働かせる ‖ come ***into*** *play* 活動するようになる. ¶a proverb turning ***on*** a *play* of words 地口になっていることわざ.

P² *play* ***of*** wit 才気の発動. ¶a *play* ***of*** words き弁. ¶give *play* ***to*** one's imagination 想像をたくましくする. ¶I may be allowed so poor a *play* ***upon*** words. まずいしゃれで恐縮ですが. ¶his *play* ***with*** the instrument その楽器での彼の演奏.

play, *v.* 遊戯をする; 演技する, 演奏する; 浴せかける, 勝負ごとをする; 振舞う.

M ***Play away!*** It is your lead. さーやれ君が鼻番だ(カードなどの遊戯で). ‖ *play* ***away*** one's fortune 遊んで身代をつぶす. 【類】*play* ***away*** one's time / *play* ***away*** one's youth (money) 若さ(金)を徒費する / *play* ***away*** the summer. ¶Why, hang it, I could *play* it ***better*** myself. (へたな音楽を聞いて)へたくそだ! 僕ならもっとうまくやる. ¶*play* ***by turns*** (=***in turn***) 順番にやる. ¶*play* ***double*** ふたまたをかける. ¶*play* ***fair*** 正直に勝負をする, 公明正大に行動する. ¶He *played* ***false*** with us.=He *played* us ***false.*** 彼はわれわれをだました. ‖ His memory *played* him ***false*** in this matter. それはあの人の覚え違いだ. ¶She *played* ***fast and loose*** with him. 彼女は彼に対して誠意がなかった. ¶*play* ***high*** 荒いかけごとをする. ¶The band *played* ***magnificently.*** 楽隊がすばらしい演奏をした. ¶*play* ***poorly*** へたなプレーをやる, へまをやる. ¶*play* ***out*** 劇(競技)を終了する. 【類】The game was *played* ***out*** at the end of the day (日暮れに). ‖ My good luck is *played* ***out.*** 僕の運の尽きだ. ‖ He is *played* ***out*** by overwork and worry. 彼は過労と悩みとで疲れ切っている. ¶*play* music ***softly*** and ***delicately*** 曲を静かにしかもせん細に奏する. ¶*play* ***square*** with … …に対して正々堂々とやる. ¶***successfully*** *play* to the gallery 大向うをうならせる. ¶He has *played* ***truant*** from school. 彼は学校をずるけた. ☞ 米語用法は play hooky.

M² *play* ***down*** 軽視する; 〚新聞〛[記事を]小さく扱う ‖ He *played* ***down*** on (=doublecrossed) me alright. あいつに一杯くわされた. ¶*play* ***off*** A against B AとBを張り合わせてうまい汁を吸う. 【類】Russia was trying to *play* ***off*** the other powers against Japan. ‖ He is not ill really; he is just *playing* ***off.*** 彼は病気なもんか. 病気のふりをしてるだけだ. ‖ a fraud *played* ***off*** as a jest (=a hoax) 冗談に紛らした詐欺. ¶*Play* ***up!*** It's your turn. しっかりやれ. 君の番だ. ‖ *play* ***up*** [a piece of news] in bold type 〚新聞〛ニュースを大見出しで出す ‖ *play* ***up*** to one's superiors 上役のごまをする.

P *play* ***at*** baseball (billiards, cricket, football) 野球(など)をする. 【類】groups *playing* ***at*** battledore and shuttlecock (追羽根) / *play* ***at*** some game of chance (一か八かの勝負ごと) / *play* ***at*** games for stakes (かけごと) / *play* ***at*** heads or tails (勝負をきめる時の表か裏か) / He *plays* ***at*** cards for high stakes (沢山かけて). / *play* ***at*** hide-and-seek (かくれんぼ) / *play* ***at*** marbles (石はじき) / A party of boys *played* [***at***] soldiers and mounted on a row of upright tombstones for horses. / *play* ***at*** soldiering (snowballing) ‖ *play* ***at*** peril [山登りなど]危険な遊びをする ‖ *play* ***at*** love 恋愛遊戯をする. 【類】*play* ***at*** love-relationships with … ‖ *play* ***at*** concerts 音楽会で演奏する. ¶*play* ***by*** ear 楽譜を見ずに演奏する ‖ Western children *playing* Japanese ***by*** wearing ***kimono*** きものを着て日本人ごっこをやる西洋の子供. ¶*play* ***for*** pleasure, not for money もうけるためでなく遊楽にやる ‖ *play* ***for*** heavy stakes 大ばくちをやる ‖ *play* ***for*** kingdom (=empire) 天下取りのばくちをうつ ‖ *play* ***for*** love (=pleasure) 金をかけずに勝負ごとをする ‖ *play* ***for*** money 金をかけて勝負ごとをする ‖ The World Championship in tennis is *played* ***for*** at Wimbledon. 世界庭球選手権獲得競技はウィンブルドンで行われる. ¶*play* ***in*** the water 水中で遊ぶ. 【類】*play* ***in*** the sand on the beach ‖ A fountain was *playing* ***in*** the sunlight. 泉水が日光に当ってきらきら輝いていた. ¶He has been a football coach for 16 years, but has never *played* ***in*** a game. 彼は十六年もしゅう球のコーチをやっていたが一度も競技に参加したことはない. ‖ *play* ***in*** theatricals しろうと芝居に出演する ‖ The glitter of her diamond ring *played* ***in*** my eyes, as she waved her hand in talking. 彼女が話しながら手を振るとダイヤの光が私の目を射た. ¶*play* ***inside*** the yard 庭内で遊ぶ. ¶*play* ***into*** the hands of … …の思うつぼにはまる ‖ *play* the people ***into*** the dining-room 音楽を奏して人々を食堂に送り込む. ¶*play* well ***on*** the flute 笛をうまく吹く. 【類】She can *play* ***on*** many an instrument. / *play* ***on*** a mouth organ (ハーモニカ) / *play* [***on***] the piano / *play* a nice tune ***on*** a flute ‖ *play* ***on*** (=***upon***) one's feeling 人の感情をもてあそぶ ‖ as the first rays of the rising sun began to *play* on the summit 朝日の初光が山頂に射(さ)し初めた時 ‖ The moonshine *plays* ***on*** the waters. 月光が水面にちらちらする. ‖ Wind *plays* ***on*** water. 風が水面をかすめる. ¶The fire brigade *played* a stream of water ***on*** flames. 消防隊が火炎に水を浴せかけた. 【類】The fire-engine *played* ***on*** the flames. / *play* the hose ***on*** a burning house ‖ *play*

on (=upon) a word しゃれを言う.【類】if I may *play* ***on*** words. ‖ *play* ***on*** (=***with***) both hands 表裏のある行動をする ‖ *play* ***on*** the stage 舞台で演じる. ¶He *played* ***opposite*** her. 彼は彼女の相手役(二枚目)を勤めた[映画などで].【類】There is a saying in Hollywood that it is lucky to *play* ***opposite*** Richard Dix. ¶*play* ***to*** the gallery スタンドプレーをやる, 大衆に迎合する ‖ The troupe *played* ***to*** empty houses. 一座は入りがなかった. ‖ *play* ***to*** the singing of ... ...の歌に合わせてひく. ¶*play* ***upon*** the violin ヴァイオリンをひく ‖ The wind *played* ***upon*** the surface of the water. 風が水面をかすめた. ‖ I *played* ***upon*** his love of flattery. 私は彼のおべっか好きを利用した.【類】*play* ***upon*** ignorant people's superstitions. ¶*play* ***with*** his sisters ***at*** hide-and-seek 彼の姉妹たちとかくれんぼをして遊ぶ.【類】*play* ***with*** toys / *play* ***with*** love (chastity, women's honor) / *play* ***with*** fire (sand, water) ‖ *play* ***with*** words [詩人など]言葉をもてあそぶ.

playboy, *n.* 《米》[金持ちの]道楽息子.
Q² ***Hollywood*** *playboy* 色事で鳴る映画俳優.

player, *n.* 俳優; 演技者; 競技者.
V ***assign*** *players* to parts 役者の配役をする. ¶***put*** a *player* ***out*** [野球で]打者または走者をアウトにする. ¶***rank*** *players* [庭球などで]競技者を等級別にする(第何位などに). ¶***seed*** *players* [テニスなどで]選手をシードする(組み合わせで階級をつける).
Q a ***good chess*** *player* 将棋のじょうず. ¶***featured*** *players* 主演俳優. ¶a ***representative*** *player* 代表選手. ¶quite ***respectable*** *players* なかなかりっぱな演技者. ¶***seeded*** *players* 〖テニス〗シードされた選手. ¶very ***skilful*** *player* on a *biwa* びわの名手.
Q² a University of Michigan ***baseball*** *player* ミシガン大学の野球選手. ¶a famous ***billiard*** *player* 有名などう球選手. ¶The Greeks are a nation of "***grand stand*** *players*". ギリシア人はスタンドプレーをやる国民である. ¶a ***guitar*** *player* ギター演奏者. ¶a ***jazz band*** *player* [ジャズ]バンドマン. ¶a ***losing*** (***winning***) *player* 敗戦(勝利)選手. ¶a ***moving-picture*** (=***screen***) *player* 映画俳優. ¶a ***pro-ball*** *player* 職業野球選手. ¶a ***rank*** *player* 有段者. ¶a ***screen*** *player* 映画俳優. ¶a ***stage*** *player* 舞台俳優. ¶a ***star*** *player* 花形選手. ¶a ***tennis*** *player* 庭球選手.
P² *players* ***at*** cricket クリケットをやる人々. ¶*players* ***from*** the stage 舞台から映画に転向した俳優. ¶a *player* ***on*** a piano (flute) ピアノ(など)演奏者 ‖ *players* ***on*** the stage 舞台俳優.

playground, *n.* 遊び場, 運動場.
Q ***favorite*** summer *playgrounds* 有名な夏の遊び場所. ¶Takarazuka, a ***popular*** *playground* for Osaka folks 大阪人に人気のある歓楽境宝塚.
P ***in*** the *playground* 運動場で.
P² *playgrounds* ***for*** the idle rich 有閑富豪の遊び場. ¶the *playground* ***of*** Europe 欧州の遊び場.

playing, *n.* 遊戯.
V ***encourage*** the *playing* of football しゅう球を奨励する. ¶***make*** the *playing* of illusions 錯覚を起させる.

playlet, *n.* 小ドラマ.
Q² a ***radio*** *playlet* ラジオドラマ.

plaza, *n.* 広場.
Q² the ***Imperial Palace*** *plaza* 皇居前広場.

plea, *n.* 弁疏(そ), 弁解, 口実; 懇望.
V ***enter*** a strong *plea* for ... ...のために熱心な弁解をする. ¶***make*** a *plea* 弁解する. ¶***put forward*** a *plea* for ... ...を弁疏する. ¶***raise*** a *plea* against ... ...に対して弁解する. ¶No *plea* can be ***set up*** on the ground of ignorance. 知らないということは何ら弁解にならない.
Q a ***dilatory*** *plea* だらだらした答弁. ¶a ***forceful*** *plea* for ... ...のための有力な口実. ¶a ***special*** *plea* in bar 〖法〗特殊弁論(新事実に基いて無罪を主張する).
P ***on*** the *plea* of illness 病気を口実に.【類】***on*** the *plea* of political expediency. ¶resort ***to*** the *plea* of ... ...を口実にする. ¶He resigned ***under*** the *plea* of ill-health. 氏は病気を口実に辞職した.【類】***under*** *plea* of infancy (年少).
P² a *plea* ***for*** Government action 政府の処置に対する懇望 ‖ a *plea* ***for*** pity (mercy) れんびん(慈悲)の懇願 ‖ To our Readers. This is a *plea* ***for*** counsel. 読者諸君, 諸君のお知恵を拝借したい. ¶a *plea* ***of*** guilt 有罪答弁 ‖ a *plea* ***of*** "Not Guilty" 無罪の申立て.

plead, *v.* 訴願する; 弁護する.
M *plead* ***eloquently*** in favor of ... ...のためにとうとうと弁護する.
P *plead* ***against*** the oppression 圧迫に対して抗弁する. ¶*plead* ***at*** the bar 法廷で弁論する. ¶*plead* ***before*** the court 法廷で弁論する. ¶*plead* ***for*** the accused (=defendant) 被告の弁護をする ‖ I *pleaded* ***for*** him in vain. 私は彼のために弁じたがむだだった. ‖ His youth *pleads* ***for*** him. 彼が若いということが彼の弁護になる. ‖ *plead* ***for*** the life of ... ...の命ごいをする.【類】*plead* ***for*** mercy for a person / *plead* ***for*** the release (釈放) of ... ¶*plead* ***of favor of*** ... ...のために弁護する. ¶*plead* ***to*** the indictment 起訴に対して弁護する. ¶The defense attorney *pleads* ***with*** the jury. 弁護人が陪審団に抗弁する. ¶*plead* ***with*** a creditor ***for*** a longer time 債権者に延期を頼む.【類】*plead* ***with*** the tyrant ***for*** the captive.

pleasant, *a.* 楽しい, 喜ばしい.
P it is *pleasant* ***for*** us to ... ...するのは愉快なことだ. ¶*pleasant* ***to*** the ear (eye) 耳(など)に快い ‖ It is *pleasant* ***to*** the taste (=palate). それは食べてうまい.

pleasantry, *n.* かいぎゃく.
Q indulge in ***gross*** *pleasantries* 下品な冗談を言う.

please, *v.* 喜ばす; (命令的に)どうぞ.
M What *pleases* you ***best***? 何が一番お気に召しますか. ‖ What poet's works *please* you ***best***? どの詩人の作が一番お気に召しますか.
O No noise, *please*. お静かに. ¶One cannot *please* everybody. 万人を満足させることはできない.【類】a picture that *pleases* the eye. ¶Do what you *please*. 勝手に.

pleased, *pa.* 喜んでいる, 満足している.
M He was ***distinctly*** *pleased*. 彼は大喜びでした. ¶They are ***exceedingly*** *pleased*. 彼らは非常に喜んでいる. ¶His Majesty was ***graciously*** *pleased* to pay a visit. 陛下はかしこくも行幸遊ばされた. ¶He was ***highly*** *pleased*. 彼は非常に喜んでいた. ¶I am ***immensely*** *pleased* with it. 私はそれが非常に気に入った. ¶he is ***much*** *pleased* with ... 彼は...が大層気に入った ‖ so ***much*** *pleased* that ... 喜びのあまり... ¶I am ***very*** *pleased* to inform you that ... ...をお通知申上げます. ¶***well*** *pleased* 大いに満足して.
P be *pleased* ***about*** something ある件について満足する. ¶I am *pleased* ***at*** your coming. 私はあなたがいらしって下さったのを喜んでおります.【類】He is *pleased* ***at*** his success (good fortune). ¶be *pleased* ***with*** oneself 自分に対して満足を感じる.【類】I am *pleased* ***with*** my new servant (house). / They are *pleased* ***with*** the visit of the warship.
O Do as you *please*. 好きなようになさい. ¶You may have it if you *please*. 何ならさしあげましょう. ¶This was done just to *please* him. あいつをよろこばしてやろうとしてやったことだ.

pleasing, *a.* 快い.
M The expression has a certain rotundity of sound which is ***quite*** *pleasing* to the ear. その言葉には玉をころばすような感じがし聞いていていかにも気持がいい.
P *pleasing* ***in*** appearance 容姿のよい. ¶objects *pleasing* ***to*** the eye (ear, mind) 目(など)に快適の物 ‖ things *pleasing* ***to*** women 女の喜ぶもの ‖ abstain from foods that are prohibited, though *pleasing* ***to*** the palate 禁ぜられている食物はいかに美味であってもこれを避ける.

pleasure, *n.* 愉快, 楽しみごと; 意向, 希望.
V ***abandon*** *pleasure* 娯楽を断つ. ¶It ***afforded*** him *pleasure*. 彼はそれを喜んだ ‖ ***afford*** *pleasure* to the eye 目を喜ばせる. ¶***alloy*** *pleasure* 愉快を減殺する. ¶***appreciate*** the *pleasure* of ... ...の楽しい味がわかる. ¶The captain left the deck in order to ***ascertain*** his superior's *pleasure* (=will). 艦長は上官の意向を確かめるために甲板を去った. ¶***await*** his *pleasure* その気の向くのを待つ. ¶The *pleasure* cannot be ***bought***. その楽しみは金では買えない. ¶***cloud*** one's *pleasure* 人の機げんを損じる. ¶***combine*** the *pleasure* of ... with that of ... ...の快楽と...の快楽とを併有する. ¶***consult*** a person's *pleasure* 人の都合を聞く. ¶***dampen*** *pleasure* 興をさます. ¶Do not ***deny*** me the *pleasure* of seeing you. どうか私に会って下さい. ¶***derive*** much *pleasure* from books 読書を非常におもしろく思う ‖ He seems to ***derive*** (=***obtain***) little *pleasure* from seeing the pictures. 彼は映画を余り面白いとは思わないらしい. ¶***diminish*** the *pleasure* 感興を殺(そ)ぐ. ¶***disturb*** one's *pleasures* その楽しみの邪魔をする. ¶Will you ***do*** me the

pleasure of dining with me on Friday next week? 来週金曜日に晩さんを差上げ度いのですがお出で下さいませんか. ¶***enhance*** the *pleasure* of ... ...の快楽を増す. ¶***enjoy*** *pleasure* 快楽を享有する ‖ ***enjoy*** the double *pleasure* of ... and ... ...と...との二重の快楽を味わう. ¶***exalt*** one's *pleasure* 快楽を高める. ¶***expand*** the *pleasure* of ... ...の快楽を増す. ¶***experience*** little or no *pleasure* ほとんどあるいは全く快感を感じない. ¶***express*** one's *pleasure* at [hearing of]... ...の報を得て喜ぶ. ¶***extract*** *pleasure* from daily toil 日常の労働を楽しむ. ¶***feel*** more *pleasure* in it than in ... ...よりもそれの方を愉快に感じる. ¶He always ***finds*** *pleasure* in traveling. 彼はいつも愉快に旅行をする.【類】He ***finds*** *pleasure* in reading (looking at a crowd, a country walk). / ***find*** *pleasure* in another's misfortune. ¶***forgo*** *pleasures* and comforts in life 人生の快楽を断つ. ‖ I cannot ***forgo*** the *pleasure* of quoting the magnificent peroration of ... 私は...の堂々たる名文を引用せずにはいられない. ¶it ***gives*** me *pleasure* to say that ... 私は...と言うことを喜ばしく感じる ‖ It ***gives*** me *pleasure* to enclose you here with a copy of my latest picture with my compliments. 小生最近の写真一葉同封貴覧に供します. ¶***gratify*** one's *pleasure* その喜びを満足させる. ¶we ***have*** *pleasure* in advising (informing) you that ... ...を喜んでお知らせする ‖ May I ***have*** the *pleasure* of taking a glass of wine with you? 一杯お付合下さいませんか.【類】I once ***had*** the *pleasure* of being introduced to you. / I am sorry I cannot ***have*** the *pleasure* of accompanying you today. / When may I ***have*** the *pleasure* of seeing you again? ¶***increase*** the *pleasure* of the table 食生活をより楽しくする. ¶***make*** it a *pleasure* to ... ...することを一つの楽しみにする ‖ ***make*** *pleasure* instructive and knowledge attractive 娯楽を教訓的に知識を興味あるものにする. ¶***mar*** our *pleasure* われわれの楽しみをだめにする. ¶***purchase*** the *pleasure* at the cost of ... ...を費してこの快楽を買う. ¶ardently ***pursue*** *pleasures* 熱心に快楽を求める. ¶***receive*** (=derive) no *pleasure* from ... ...は少しも愉快でない. ¶***renounce*** the *pleasure* of ... ...を断念する. ¶I ***request*** the *pleasure* of your company. 御同伴の栄をお願いします. ¶I cannot ***resist*** the *pleasure* of writing to you to say how much I enjoyed the perusal of your book "...". 貴著「...」面白く拝見したことを是非一筆申上げたい. ¶***sacrifice*** ordinary social *pleasures* 日常の社交的快楽を犠牲にする. ¶The crowd was so appreciative, it ***screamed*** its *pleasure*. 群集は敏感で声を立てて面白がった. ¶***seek*** *pleasure* 快楽を求める. ¶a kind and loving wife, who will ***share*** his *pleasures* and pains 彼と苦楽を共にする親切な良人思いの妻. ¶***show*** *pleasure* うれしがる. ¶***spoil*** one's *pleasure* その楽しみをそこなう ‖ The *pleasure* of the company was ***spoiled***. 座が白けた. ¶***study*** the *pleasure* of others 他人を喜ばせるようにする. ¶people who ***take*** a *pleasure* in cock fighting 闘鶏好きな人 ‖ I ***take*** *pleasure* in the thought that ... 私は...と思うとうれしい.【類】He ***takes*** *pleasure* in doing good. / ***take*** a great *pleasure* in ... / He ***took*** *pleasure* in showing it to friends who call on him. / Children ***take*** *pleasure* in making and breaking toys. / He is a devotee of sports ***taking*** especial *pleasure* in cantering about on the bridle path (乗馬道). ‖ ***take*** His Majesty's *pleasure* regarding ... ...の件を奏上する. ¶***Use*** your *pleasure*=Please yourself. 好きなようになさい.

V² my chief *pleasure* ***lay*** in ... 私の主なる快楽は...にあった. ¶The *pleasure* of success ***overpaid*** me for all my sufferings. 成功の喜びが私の受けたすべての苦しみを償って余りあった.

Q with ***beaming*** *pleasure* 欣然として. ¶***diabolic*** *pleasure* 悪魔の快楽. ¶experience the ***divine*** *pleasure* of creation 創造の法悦を体験する. ¶an ***ecstatic*** *pleasure* 有頂天の快楽. ¶***fleeting*** *pleasure* はかない快楽. ¶a ***forbidden*** *pleasure* 禁ぜられた遊び. ¶it is a ***genuine*** *pleasure* to ... ...するのは真に愉快だ. ¶take a ***gentleman's*** *pleasure* in being helpful to ... 紳士的に...を後援する. ¶It gives me a ***great*** *pleasure* to do something on this occasion. この機会になにかをさせていただくことは大変うれしい. ‖ one of his ***greatest*** *pleasures* その最大の楽しみの一つ. ¶***high*** (=***great***) *pleasure* 非常な愉快. ¶***homely*** (=domestic) *pleasures* 色々な家庭的の楽しみ. ¶it is my ***imperial*** *pleasure* that ... ...は私に取って上々の喜びだ. ¶***infinite*** *pleasure* 無限の快楽. ¶***innocent*** *pleasure* 罪のない快楽. ¶I felt with a sense of ***inward*** *pleasure* that ... 私は心ひそかに喜んで...ということを感じた. ¶experience a ***keen*** *pleasure* 強烈な愉快を感じる ‖ enjoy some of the ***keenest*** *pleasure* the theatre can afford 観劇の与えるもっとも強烈な快感を楽しむ. ¶take a ***lascivious*** *pleasure* in ...ing ... ...のいん楽にふける. ¶***licentious*** *pleasures* いんとうな快楽. ¶It is not necessary to be a specialist in order to read them with a ***lively*** *pleasure*. それらを読んで生々した喜びを感じるにはなにも専門家になる必要はない. ¶the ***major*** or ***minor*** *pleasures* of life 一生の大きなまたは小さな楽しみ. ¶He seems to take a ***malicious*** *pleasure* in giving them trouble! 彼は彼らに迷惑を掛けて意地悪く喜んでいるらしい. ¶He often turns to carpentering for the ***mere*** *pleasure* of it. 彼は時々道楽に大工仕事をやる. ¶find ***much*** *pleasure* in ... ...を非常に愉快に思う. ¶He took ***particular*** *pleasure* in deer-stalking. 彼はしか狩がとりわけ好きであった. ¶***passing*** *pleasure* つかの間の快楽. ¶***plain*** *pleasures* 清遊. ¶the saving of money—the forgoing of a ***present*** *pleasure* for a future security 貯金すなわち将来の安全のために現在の快楽を抑制すること. ¶a ***prospective*** *pleasure* 将来得られる快楽. ¶It is a ***real*** *pleasure* to meet you. お目に掛るのは本当にうれしい. ¶a ***refined intellectual*** *pleasure* 高雅な知的快楽. ¶***sane*** *pleasures* まじめな快楽. ¶***selfish*** *pleasure* 利己的な快楽. ¶take a ***supreme*** *pleasure* in ... ...に無上の楽しみを感じる. ¶the pursuit of ***sensual*** *pleasures* 肉欲にふけること. ¶value the ***sexual*** (=***carnal***) *pleasure* above all else 房事をなによりも好む.【類】indulge in ***sensual*** *pleasure*. ¶make the "burdens of life" ***veritable*** *pleasure* 人生の重荷を真の楽しみにする(苦しみを楽しみと感じる). ¶have a ***sweet*** *pleasure* in ...ing ... ...を痛快に感じる. ¶***unalloyed*** *pleasure* 本当の快楽. ¶an ***uninterrupted*** *pleasure* 妨げられずに続く快楽. ¶feel a more ***vivid*** *pleasure* さらにはっきりした喜びを感じる. ¶He had his natural share of ***worldly*** *pleasures* and life's enjoyments. 彼も人として現世の快楽や生の喜びを当然享有したのである. ¶Travel gives us a ***worthy*** and ***improving*** *pleasure*. 旅行は人を向上させるりっぱな快楽である.

Q² ***animal*** *pleasures* 色々な動物的快楽. ¶***smoking*** *pleasure* 喫煙の楽しみ.

P I can make my horse go fast or slow ***at*** *pleasure* (=will). 馬を速くも遅くも意のままに御せられる. ‖ You may come or go ***at*** *pleasure*. 来るも行くもご随意だ. ‖ a table that can be lengthened ***at*** *pleasure* 随意に引き延ばしのできる食卓. ¶read half ***for*** *pleasure* 慰み半分に読書する ‖ passengers travelling ***for*** *pleasure* 観光の乗客 ‖ bird-keeping ***for*** *pleasure* 趣味の飼鳥. ¶rush ***into*** *pleasures* 快楽をほしいままにする. ¶in the midst ***of*** *pleasures* 歓楽の最中に ‖ a man ***of*** *pleasure* 道楽者 ‖ the pursuit ***of*** *pleasure* 道楽三昧. ¶visit the country ***on*** *pleasure* 慰みにその国へ行く ‖ when ***on*** *pleasure* bent 気が向くと. ¶give oneself up ***to*** *pleasure* 快楽にふける.【類】a life given up ***to*** *pleasure*. ¶I will do it ***with*** *pleasure*. 私はそれを喜んで致します. ‖ acknowledge ***with*** *pleasure* the co-operation of ... ...の協力を感謝する ‖ looking forward ***with*** *pleasure* to ... ...を楽しみにして待つ.

P² It was a rare *pleasure* ***for*** (=to) me. それは私に取っては絶好の快楽だった. ¶I received a great deal of *pleasure* ***from*** that novel. 私はその小説を面白く読んだ. ¶man's *pleasure* ***in*** his handiwork 細工仕事をやる人間の楽しみ. ¶the *pleasure* ***of*** the senses 五官(全身)の快感. ¶I have not the *pleasure* ***of*** his acquaintance. 私はまだあの方は存じません. ‖ the *pleasures* ***of*** the table 食道楽. ¶Work is a *pleasure* ***to*** him. 仕事は彼に取っては一つの楽しみだ.

O those whose *pleasure* it is to call America "God's own country" アメリカを「神の国」と呼んで喜んでいる人たち. ¶it is a *pleasure* to recall the fact that ... ...の事実を想起するのは一快事だ.【類】It is a *pleasure*, not a duty, to work for a man like him.

pleat, *n.* 〖服飾〗プリーツ.

Q² a skirt with ***accordion*** (=***permanent***) *pleats* 〖服飾〗パーマネント・プリーツのついているスカート.

P² *pleats* ***on*** a skirt スカートのひだ.

plebiscite, *n.* 国民投票, 一般投票.

V ***demand*** (=call for) a *plebiscite* on the continuation of the war 戦争の継続いかんの問題に関して国民投票を行うべしと主張する. ¶*take* a *plebiscite* in respect of ... …に関して民衆投票を行う.

Q² *postcard plebiscites* [新聞などの]はがき投票.

P solve a question *by* a *plebiscite* 民衆投票によって問題を解決する. ¶have the right to vote *in* the *plebiscite* その民衆投票に参加すべき権利を有する. ¶decide *through* a *plebiscite* 国民投票によって決定する.

pledge, *n.* 担保, 保証; 誓約; 質, 質物.

V *break* one's *pledge* to ... …するというその誓約を破る. ¶*carry out* a *pledge* 誓約を実行する. ¶*exact* the *pledge* of secrecy 秘密を誓わせる. ¶*give* a *pledge* to ... …に約束する ‖ they *gave* a *pledge* at the last election that ... 彼らはこの前の選挙で…と公約した. 【類】Will you *give* me your *pledge*—that you will never tell it to anyone? ¶He bravely *kept* his *pledge*. 彼は勇敢にその誓を守った. ¶*make* a *pledge* of allegiance 忠誠を誓う. ¶*redeem pledges* 質物を受け出す ‖ *redeem* one's *pledge* [比ゆ的に]責をふさぐ. ¶we *secured* from him a *pledge* that ... われわれは彼から…の保証を得た. ¶*sign* a *pledge* never to ... 決して…しないという誓約に署名する. ¶*take* (=sign) the *pledge* 禁酒を誓う. ¶a *pledge taken in* at the shop 店で取った質物. ¶*violate* one's *pledge* 誓言をほごにする. ⌈てしまった.

V² The *pledge* has long since *run out*. 質はとうの昔流れ

Q She miscarried of (=failed to carry out) the *dear pledge* of his love. 彼女は彼氏の子を宿していたが流産をした. ¶give a *solemn pledge* おごそかに誓約する. ¶this *tiny pledge* of their mutual affection 相思のかすがいであるこの愛児. ¶*unredeemed pledges* 質流れ.

Q² make good (=carry out) a *campaign pledge* 選挙の公約を実行する. ¶carry out *Democratic platform pledges* 民主党政綱の公約を実行する. ¶the value of *election pledges* 選挙公約の価値.

P *as* a *pledge* for ... …の担保として. 【類】leave a watch *as pledge* for borrowed money. ¶It is *in pledge*. それは質に入れてある. ‖ hold it *in pledge* それを担保にとっておく. 【類】put it *in pledge*. ¶a loan *on pledges* of personal property 動産抵当の貸金 ‖ *on* one's *pledge* of honor その名誉にかけて. ¶take it *out of pledge* それを質受する. ¶conform *to* the *pledge* given 誓約を履行する. ¶he is *under* no *pledge* to ... 彼は…という約束はしていない.

P² a *pledge of* friendship 友情の保証 ‖ a gambler's *pledge of* reformation 博徒改心の誓 ‖ A child is a *pledge of* love. 子は愛のかすがい.

pledge, *v.* 質におく; 誓約する.

P it is *pledged as* security for ... それは…の担保にはいっている. ¶*pledge before* Gods 神明に誓う. ¶*pledge* an article *for* ... yen 物品を…円で質に入れる. ¶*pledge to* a person 人に誓う ‖ They *pledged* themselves *to* each other. 彼らは互に誓った. ‖ He is *pledged to* many reforms—the education of the masses; the development of agriculture; etc. 彼は大衆の教育・農業の発展などいく多の改良を断行することを誓っている.

plenteous, *a.* 沢山な.

P *plenteous in* natural resources 天然資源の豊富な.

plentiful, *a.* 沢山な.

P a speech *plentiful in* humor ユーモアたっぷりの演説.

O as *plentiful* as blackberries on a September hedgerow

plenty, *n.* 沢山; 豊富. ⌊ざらにある.

V *drink plenty* of plain water 真水を沢山飲む. ¶*give plenty* of evidence for suspicion 疑うべき多くの証拠を提供する. ¶We *had plenty* of amusement. 大変面白かった. ‖ I've *had plenty* (=enough). もう十分いただきました. 【類】The rooms *have plenty* of ventilation (空気の流通がよい). / America *has plenty* of good small colleges. / He *has plenty* of animal spirits (血気). / He *has plenty* of money to spare. / I *had plenty* to do. / We *have plenty* of time before the train comes in. / We *have plenty* of sunlight. / I've got to *have plenty* of practice (練習). / The firm *has plenty* of means, but its character is unsatisfactory. ¶The business *offers plenty* of scope for expansion. その事業は発展の余地が十分ある. ¶*take plenty* of outdoor exercise 盛に戸外運動をやる.

Q in *great plenty*=in abundance ふんだんに ‖ Of these there is *great plenty* to be found. これらのものは豊富にある.

P He lived *in plenty* the rest of his days. 彼は裕福に余生を送った. 【類】possess money *in plenty* / They are found there *in plenty*. / You can reply by post *in plenty* of time. ¶The occasion was celebrated *with plenty* of festivities. その折はにぎやかな祝典があった. 【類】people *with plenty* of money and more or less leisure / School books should have large, clear type and good margins, *with plenty* of space between lines (行間を十分あけて). ‖ You must keep up the patient *with plenty* of good food. 病人には十分滋養物を取らせなくてはならない.

P² there are *plenty of* signs that ... …の徴候が明かにある. 【類】there is *plenly of* evidence to prove that ... / There is *plenty of* airspace (空地) around the houses. / In spite of repeated defeats, they still had *plenty of* ⌊fight.

pleonasm, *n.* 冗語.

V You *commit* a *pleonasm* when you say Honganji temple. 本願寺のお寺といっては言葉が重複する.

plethora, *n.* 過剰.

P² a *plethora of* energy 精力の過剰.

pliable, *a.* しなやかな, 融通のきく.

M He is *too pliable* to be a good leader. 彼は人がよすぎていい指導者にはなれない.

pliers, *n.* ペンチ.

Q² *cutting pliers* 針金切り(ペンチ).

plight, *n.* 状態, 有様.

Q a *hopeless plight* 絶望の状態. ¶be in a *pitiable plight* 哀れな境遇にある. ¶reduce the situation to a *pitiful plight* 局面をなさけない状態に陥れる. ¶a *sad plight* 悲惨な状態. ¶He was wounded and in a *serious plight*. 彼は負傷して重態だった. ¶It is in a very *sorry plight*. それはなさけない状態になっている. ¶It is in a far *worse plight*. はるかに悪化した状態にある. ¶He found himself in a *wretched plight*. 彼は自分がみじめな境がいにあることを ⌊知った.

plod, *v.* のそのそと歩く.

M *plod away*=work hard 一生懸命に働く. 【類】*plod away* day and night.

M² The old man *plodded along*. 老人はとぼとぼと足を運んで行った. ‖ *plod* slowly *along* 牛の歩みを続ける. ¶*plod* ⌊*on* とぼとぼ歩く.

plop, *n.* どぶん.

P fall *with* a *plop* どぶんと落ちる.

plop, *ad.* ぼちゃんと.

P fall *plop into* the water 水にぼちゃんと落ちる.

plop, *v.* ふつふつ音をたてる.

M *plop out* ふつふつと音をたてて昇る(あわのように).

plot, *n.* 陰謀; 脚色, 筋.

V *abet* a *plot* 陰謀をほう助する. ¶What *plot* are you *brewing*? 君はどんなことをもくろんでいるのか. ¶to *complicate* the *plot* 問題をますます複雑にして. ¶*defeat* a *plot* 謀略をだめにする. ¶*draw* his *plot* from ... …からその話の種を取る. ¶*expose* a *plot* 陰謀をあばく. ¶*fail* an assassination *plot* 暗殺の陰謀をくじく. ¶The *plot* is somewhat *forced*. その筋には少し無理がある. ¶*frame* a *plot* 陰謀を企てる. ¶*hatch* a *plot* 陰謀を企てる. ¶the *plot* will be *laid* about the time of Charles II. 場面をチャールズ二世時代のころにとる. ¶He managed to *lay bare* (=expose) their *plots*. 彼はようやく彼らの陰謀をあばいた. ¶briefly *sketch* the *plot* その荒筋を書く. ¶*sketch out* a *plot* 荒筋を立てる. ¶*take plots* from ... [小説など]筋を…から取る. ¶*weave* a *plot* to ... …の密計を回らす. 【類】I was well-nigh certain that some foul *plots* had been *woven* round him. ¶*work on* (=*develop*) the *plot* of a novel 小説の筋を進行させる.

V² the *plot ends* with the death of ... 筋は…が死んだところで終りを告げる. ¶Then the *plot thickens*. それから筋が込みいって来る.

Q a *counter plot* 敵の計略の裏をかく計略. ¶a *deep-laid plot* 深く企んだ陰謀. ¶a *far-reaching plot* 遠大な計略. ¶an *enthralling plot* 思わず引き入れられる話の筋. ¶an *impenetrable plot* 不可解なからくり. ¶an *ingenious plot* 独創的な構想. ¶an *iniquitous plot* かん計. ¶*intricate plots* [小説など)入りくんだ筋. ¶a *novel plot* 新しい構想. ¶a *political plot* 政治的謀略. ¶discover the *whole plot* からくりを見破る. ¶*stupid plots* of photoplays 映画劇の愚にもつかない筋. ¶a *threadbare plot* ありふれた筋. ¶a *time-honored plot* 古くからある筋. ¶a *trite plot* 陳腐な脚色. ¶an *out-worn plot* 使い古した筋. ¶an intricately *woven* plot 入りくんだ筋.

Q² an ***assassination plot*** against ... ...暗殺の陰謀. ¶a ***bolshevization plot*** 赤化謀略. ¶a ***Communist plot*** 共産党の謀略. ¶a ***movie plot*** 映画の筋書.

P one of the chief agents ***in*** a *plot* against ... ...に対する陰謀の主謀者の一人. ¶privy ***to*** the *plot* 密謀に干与している ‖ I will not be a party ***to*** a *plot*. 私は陰謀などにかかわらない.

P² Do you think there are *plots* ***against*** any of the Cabinet members? 閣員のだれかを目ざした陰謀でもあるのでしょうか. ¶the *plot* ***of*** the story 物語の筋.

plot, *v*. 陰謀を企てる; 地取りをする.

M *plot* ***together*** to ... ...しようと共謀する. ¶*plot* ***out*** a farm into house lots 農地を宅地に分割する.

P *plot* ***against*** one's life その生命を奪おうと企てる ‖ *plot* ***against*** the Government 政府に対して陰謀を企てる.【類】an anarchist leader grown gray in *plotting* ***against*** social order. ¶*plot* ***for*** one's assassination その暗殺を企てる. ¶They were *plotting* ***with*** him ***against*** his king. 彼らは彼とともに国王に対して陰謀を企てていた.

plot, *n*. 一区画の小地面.

V *Plots* may be ***bought*** or ***leased*** on moderate terms. 格安に土地を買ったり借りたりすることができる.

Q² a ***breeding plot*** 試験用農園. ¶***garden plots*** of from 20 to 40 roods in area 二十ルードから四十ルードの庭園. ¶a ***seventeen acre plot*** of land 十七エーカーの土地.

P it was built ***on*** the *plot* formerly occupied by ... それはもと...があった敷地に建てられた.

P² a *plot* ***of*** land＝a lot 一区画の土地 ‖ a *plot* ***of*** two acres 二エーカーの地面 ‖ a *plot* ***of*** medicinal herbs 薬草園床.

plotting, *n*. [筋の]構想.

Q ***fresh plotting*** 生新の作風.

plow,《英》**plough,** *n*.〖農〗すき.

V ***follow*** the *plow* 農耕に従事する.

P be ***at*** the *plow* 農業をやっている. ¶land ***under*** the *plow* 耕作された土地.

plow,《英》**plough,** *v*. すく; 刻苦する.

M This land *plows* ***hard***. この土地は耕作しにくい. ¶*plow* ***out*** weeds 雑草をすき取る.

M² *plow* ***up*** the ground 耕作する.【類】*plow* ***up*** roots.

P wrinkles *plowed* ***in*** one's forehead by time 年のせいで額に寄ったしわ ‖ *plow* ***in*** a home garden 自家農園を耕す. ¶wrinkles *plowed* ***in*** his face ***by*** time and labor 長い年月と労働で顔によったしわ. ¶*plow* ***into*** ridges すいてうねを作る ‖ a truck which *plowed* ***into*** a road-roller ロードローラーに衝突したトラック. ¶*plow* ***through*** a bulky volume 骨を折ってこうかんな書を読む.【類】as the engine *plowed* ***through*** the streets. ¶a face *plowed* ***with*** wrisnkles しわの寄った顔.

pluck, *n*. 勇気, 胆力.

V ***show*** *pluck* 勇気を示す.

Q² ***dare-devil*** *pluck* 向う見ずの勇気.

P An ounce ***of*** *pluck* is worth a pound of luck. 一オンスの勇気は一ポンドの好運の価値がある. ‖ He is full ***of*** *pluck*. 彼は勇気が満ちている.

pluck, *v*. むしる; 引っ張る.

M *pluck* (＝tear) ***away*** もぎとる, 引きちぎる.

M² *pluck* ***down*** a building 建物を取りこわす. ¶*pluck* (＝tear) ***off*** 裂き取る. ¶*Pluck* ***up***! You aren't hurt badly. 大丈夫元気を出せ, 傷は大したことはない. ‖ *pluck* ***up*** courage to ... 元気を出して...する.【類】*pluck* ***up*** spirits (＝heart) ‖ *pluck* ***up*** weeds from the garden 庭の雑草を抜きとる ‖ Political dishonesty ought to be *plucked* ***up*** by the roots. 政治的不正は根こそぎすべきだ.

P A drowning man *plucks* ***at*** a straw おぼれんとする者はわらをもつかむ. ¶*pluck* a flower ***by*** the stem (root) 花をくきからちぎる(根こそぎする) ‖ *pluck* a person ***by*** the sleeve 人のそでを引っ張る. ¶*pluck* [feather ***out*** ***of***] a chicken にわとりの羽をむしる.

plug, *n*. せん; [電気などの]差込み(プラグ).

V ***put in*** a *plug* せんをする; [ラジオなどの]スイッチを入れる.

Q an ***attaching*** *plug* さし込み(電気の). ¶***old plugs***《米口》売残り品, たなざらし品.

Q² a ***basin*** *plug* 手洗いばち排水せん. ¶a ***fire plug*** 消火せん. ¶a ***spark plug***＝a sparkplug [自動車の]発火せん(スパーク・プラグ) ‖ its ideological ***spark plug***《米》そのイデオロギー的指導者.

plug, *v*. せんをする; ふさぐ.

M² Just *plug* ***in***, and you'll get hot water.〖広告〗さし込みをしさえすればお湯が出て来ます. ¶*plug* ***up*** a hole 穴をふさぐ ‖ *plug* ***up*** shortcomings 欠点を補う.

P *plug* wounds (mouth, anus) ***with*** cotton 綿で切り傷(など)をふさぐ.

plum, *n*. 西洋すもも; 特別配当, 利益.

V ***get*** *plums* in the settlement その取りきめでうまいことをする.

Q office-hunters after ***political plums*** うまいしるにありつこうとする猟官連.

plumage, *n*. 羽.

V ***prune*** and ***trim*** its *plumage* [鳥が]その羽をつついて整える.

Q in ***borrowed*** *plumage* 借着で. ¶A peacock has ***brilliant*** *plumage*. くじゃくは羽がすてきだ.

P a bird ***with*** glossy black *plumage* 黒いつやのある羽の鳥.

plumb, *n*. おもり, 測鉛.

P be ***off*** (＝***out of***) *plumb* ゆがんでいる.

plumb, *v*. [水深を]はかる.

O *plumb* the depth of a lake 湖水の深度をはかる. ¶*plumb* the mystery その神秘をとく.

plumber, *n*. 鉛管屋.

V ***call in*** a *plumber* 鉛管屋を呼ぶ.

plumbing, *n*. 鉛管工事.

Q² ***bathroom*** *plumbing* 風呂場の鉛管工事.

plume, *n*. 羽毛.

V Chimneys ***pour out*** (＝***give out***) smoke *plumes*. 煙突が羽毛状の煙をはき出す.

Q a writing decked with ***borrowed*** *plumes* 引用句で飾り立てた文章. ¶the horses with their ***nodding*** *plumes* [葬式の]飾り毛を振る馬.

plume, *v*. 自慢する.

P *plume* ourselves ***as*** being in advance of other nations 自分らの国が他国よりすぐれているものと自慢する. ¶*plume* oneself ***on*** one's ability (appearance, dress) 自分の手腕(など)を自慢する.

plunder, *n*. 分捕品, ひょうせつ.

V² Much *plunder* from Europe ***reached*** America after the war. 戦後分捕品が沢山アメリカに着いた.

Q ***lawful*** *plunder* 合法的ひょうせつ(辞書編集など).

plunder, *v*. 略奪する.

P be *plundered* ***by*** pirates 海賊に略奪される. ¶They *plundered* Italy ***of*** many works of art. [戦争などで]イタリアから多数の美術品を略奪した. ‖ *plunder* a moored barge ***of*** its coal けい留中の荷船から石炭を奪う.

plunge, *n*. 飛び込み; 思い切った手段.

V ***take*** a *plunge* 思い切った手段をとる.

Q² take a ***salt-water*** *plunge* 海水に飛込む.

P ***With*** a wild *plunge* the mule went tearing down the street. いきなり飛出してらばは通りをひた走りに走って行った.

plunge, *v*. 飛び込む, 突入する.

M *plunge* ***at once*** into business 直ちに用件に入る. ¶*plunge* ***boldly*** into the unknown waters 無謀にも未知の水域に突進する. ¶*plunge* ***head over heels*** into the river まさかさまに川の中に飛び込む.

M² *plunge* ***off*** (＝jump) the tracks 脱線する.

P He is *plunged* ***in*** grief. 彼は悲嘆にかき暮れている. ‖ He was *plunged* ***in*** a deep sleep produced by fatigue. 彼は疲れて深い眠りに落ちた. ‖ He was *plunged* ***in*** debt. 彼は借金のふちにはまっていた. ‖ become *plunged* ***in*** despair 絶望する ‖ *plunge* ***into*** action 早速行動にうつる.【類】The discovery would *plunge* both you and me ***in*** ruin. ¶be *plunged* ***into*** darkness 急に暗くなる(停電などで).【類】The city *plunged* ***into*** darkness through the failure of electric light. / Suddenly we *plunged* ***into*** a longer tunnel than before. / Those individuals who *plunge* ***into*** action at every suggested stimulus are popularly called "suggestible." (気の早い人) / The market will be *plunged* ***into*** confusion. / He was *plunged* ***into*** the depth of (＝deepest) despair (失望のふち). ‖ *plunge* ***into*** luxury ぜいたくをやり出す ‖ he *plunged* ***into*** an appreciation of ... 彼は...を盛んにほめ出した ‖ *plunge* ***into*** the work direct from the common school 小学校からすぐ実務に入る ‖ *plunge* a dagger ***into*** the breast 胸に短刀を突きさす. ¶He *plunged* ***out of*** the beaten path in selecting his occupation. 彼は一風変った職業の選び方をした. ¶*plunge* ***over*** an embankment [自動車など]土手越しに突入する. ¶His automobile *plunged* ***through*** a fence. 彼の自動車はかきねを突破した. ¶*plunge* ***under*** fire 砲火の中に飛び込む.

plural, *n*.〖文法〗複数.

V In such a case the verb does not ***take a plural***. こうした場合には動詞は複数形を取らない.

Q ***irregular plurals*** 不規則複数.

P It is here used *as* a *plural*. それはここでは複数として使ってある. ¶The same form is used *in* the *plural*. 同形を複数で使う.

P^{2} the *plural of* the word その語の複数.

plurality, *n*. 多数; 過半数; 《米》投票数の開き(特に最高得点と次点との).

V the *plurality given* for that electoral district was ... その選挙区最高の投票数は...であった. ¶*have* a *plurality* of votes 投票で多数になる.

P^{2} a *plurality of* wives 多妻制. ¶*plurality over* one's rival candidates 《米》その得票の競争者の得票に対する超過.

ply, *v*. 往復する, 通う; 通る.

P a trader *plying among* the islands of the Pacific 太平洋の諸島間を往復する貿易船. ¶[omni]buses *plying between* hotels and stations ホテルと駅との間を往復するバス. ¶boats *plying on* (=*along*) the Thames テムズ川を通う船. ¶He was *plied with* questions. 彼は質問攻めに会った.

pneumonia, *n*. 肺炎.

V *develop pneumonia* 肺炎を起す.

Q *acute pneumonia* 急性肺炎. ¶*bronchial pneumonia* 気管支肺炎.

poach, *v*. 密猟する; 侵入する.

P *poach for* salmon (seals) さけ(など)の密漁をやる ‖ *poach for* fresh ideas 新しい思想をあさる(人の著書などから). ¶*poach on* ...'s ground ...の地方に侵入する; [比ゆ的に]...のなわ張を犯す.

pocket, *n*. ポケット; 懐中.

V *cram* one's *pocket* with ... そのポケットへ...を詰込む. ¶*enrich* the *pocket* ふところ勘定をよくする. ¶*fill* one's own *pockets* 自分のふところを肥やす. ¶*have* one's *pocket picked* すられる. ¶He *lightened* his *pocket* of some gold pieces. 彼は金貨をポケットから出してやった. ¶*line* one's own *pocket* 私腹を肥やす. 【類】fool the public and *line* their own *pockets*. ¶*pick* a [man's] *pocket* する. ¶*search* one's *pocket* ポケットの中をさがす. ¶lower the price to *suit* the *pockets* of these people 値下げをしてこれらの人人の購買力に合うようにする. 【類】choose accommodation to *suit* one's *pocket*.

V^{2} His *pockets bulged* with apples and candy. 彼のポケットはりんごやキャンデーでふくらんでいた.

Q a *deep pocket* 富. ¶an *empty pocket* からの財布. ¶his *pockets* are *fat* with ... 彼の懐中は...で肥えている. ¶the traditionally *improvident pocket* of newswriters 新聞記者の伝統的によい越の金を持たないこと. ¶the *inside pocket* 内かくし. ¶*light pockets* 軽い財布, さびしい懐中. ¶globetrotters with *well-filled pockets* 懐中の豊かな世界漫遊者たち.

Q^{2} an *air pocket* 〖航空〗風洞(エアポケット). ¶an *apron pocket* エプロンのポケット. ¶the inside *breast pocket* of a coat 上着の内ポケット ‖ an outside *breast pocket* for a handkerchief ハンケチ用の胸のポケット. ¶a *change pocket* 小銭用の小ポケット(上衣の side pocket の中にある). ¶a *fob pocket* ずぼんの(時計用の)小ポケット. ¶I have it in one of my *coat pockets*. それらは私の上衣のポケットに入っている. ¶the right-hand *hip pocket* [ずぼんの]右側のヒップポケット. ¶a *trousers pocket* ずぼんのポケット.

P draw a newspaper *from* one's *pocket* ポケットから新聞を取出す. ¶have ten shillings *in pocket* 十シリング持っている ‖ with his hands buried *in* his *pockets* 両手をポケットに入れて. 【類】put one's hand *in* one's *pocket*. / fumble *in* one's *pocket* for ... ¶Whenever he goes out for his daily constitutional, he never fails to drop a volume *into* his *pocket*. 毎日の散歩に出かける時にはいつも彼は必ず本を一冊ポケットに入れる. ¶the depth *of* one's *pocket* =one's financial circumstances そのふところ具合. ¶He took a handkerchief *out of* his *pocket*. 彼はポケットからハンカチを取出した. ‖ pay for it *out of* one's own *pocket* 身銭を切る ‖ I've just taken a hundred yen *out of pocket* by that transaction. 私はその取引でちょうど百円損をした. ¶It depends *upon* the *pocket* of the hostess. それは(ぜいたくにしようと安く上るようにしようと)お客をする主婦の資力できまることだ. ¶persons *with* limited *pockets* ふところの豊かでない人々.

pocketbook, *n*. 懐中物; 資力.

V *fatten* one's *pocketbook* 私腹を肥やす ‖ He starves his body and *fattens* his *pocketbook*. 彼は食うものも食わないで金をためる. ¶They are sold at prices which will *meet* every *pocketbook*. それをだれにも買える値段で売っている. ¶What an embarrassment! I've forgotten to *take* my *pocketbook* with me. さあ大変, 紙入を持って来るのを忘れた.

pocket-change, *n*. 小使銭.

Q *mere pocket-change* ほんの小使銭.

pocket-money, *n*. 小使銭.

V to *earn pocket-money* 小使い取りに.

pod, *n*. [豆の]さや.

P beans *in* (*without*) the *pods* さや入り(なし)の豆.

poem, *n*. 詩, 韻文.

V He long *carried* the *poem about* with him in thought. 彼は長い間その詩を腹案として持っていた. ¶*compose* (=*indite*) a *poem* 詩を作る ‖ Many *poems* have been *composed* to Bacchus, god of wine. 酒神に寄せた詩は多数ある. ¶How do you *like* this *poem*? この詩はどうです. ¶*parody* a *poem* 詩をもじる(替え歌など). ¶*recite* a *poem* 詩を吟じる. ¶*set* a *poem* to music 詩を音楽に合わせる. ¶*touch up* a *poem* 詩句を練る. ¶*write* a *poem* 詩を作る.

Q a *ceremonial poem* 儀式の詩. ¶a *dramatic poem* 劇的な詩. ¶a *Chinese poem* 漢詩, 中国の詩. ¶Longfellow wrote many *popular poems*. ロングフェローは数多くの通俗詩を書いた. ¶*rubbish poems* だ作の詩. ¶elect to write *short poems* 好んで短詩を作る. ¶a very *suggestive poem* きわめて暗示に富んだ詩.

Q^{2} R.L. Stevenson's pretty *child poems* スチーブンソンの美しい子供の読む詩. ¶an *epic poem* 叙事詩. ¶a *love poem* 恋愛詩. ¶a *narrative poem* 物語詩. ¶a superb *prose poem* すばらしい散文詩. ¶the *sea poems* of John Masefield メースフィールドの海の詩.

P^{2} *poems by* ... ...作詩. ¶the *poems of* Shakespeare シェークスピアの詩. 【類】a *poem of* nature. ¶a beautiful *poem on* peace 平和をうたった美しい詩.

poet, *n*. 詩人.

V *decry* a *poet* 詩人をけなす. ¶*quote* a *poet* 詩人の句を引用する. ¶Many a love scene in the London parks is as idyllic, as tender, and as true as any that ever *poets sang*. ロンドンの公園における男女恋愛の情景は従来の詩人の作ったいずれの詩にも劣らず牧歌的でやさしく純真なものがある. ¶*seek after* new poets 新詩人を求める. 【類】A new *poet* is much *sought after*.

V^{2} A new *poet* has *sprung up*. 新詩人が出た.

Q the *amatory poet* 恋愛詩人. ¶the *best read poets* 一番よく読まれる詩人. ¶one of the *clearest poets* もっとも明からな詩人の一人. ¶a *creative poet* 独創的な詩人. ¶Chaucre, the first great *English poet* 英国最初の大詩人チョーサー. ¶the *poet laureate* けい冠詩人. ¶a *living poet* 現存の詩人. ¶a *martial poet* 戦争詩人. ¶a *minor poet* 二流詩人. ¶Shelley was a *romantic poet*. シェリーはロマン派の詩人だった.

Q^{2} a *court poet* 宮庭詩人. ¶a *lyric poet* 叙情詩人. ¶a *prose poet* 散文詩人. ¶a *worker poet* 労働詩人.

P^{2} He is the *poet of* the age. 彼は当代の最もすぐれた詩人だ. ‖ a *poet of* the nursery 童謡作家.

poetic, *a*. 詩的な.

O There is something *poetic* in the story. この物語は詩的なおかりがする. ¶That sounds *poetic*. それは詩的だ.

poetry, *n*. 詩, 詩趣.

V *compose* (=*indite*) *poetry*=poetize 詩を作る. ¶*make* (=*write*) *poetry* 詩を書く. ¶You can write a poem on any subject if you can *see poetry* in it. その詩趣がつかめればどんな題目でも詩は作れる. ¶*spoil* the *poetry* of ... ...の詩趣(美)を損じる.

Q *beautiful poetry* 美しい詩. ¶*bucolic poetry* 田園詩. ¶the *classical poetry* of Old Japan 古代日本の古典詩. ¶*didactic poetry* 教訓詩. ¶*great poetry* 偉大な詩. ¶*lofty poetry* 高尚な詩. ¶*martial* and *patriotic poetry* 尚武的愛国的な詩. ¶*rich poetry* 光彩に富む詩. ¶distinguish true poetry from *sham poetry* 真の詩とまねごとの詩とを区別する. ¶Scottish *post-Burnsian poetry* スコットランドのバーンズ以後の詩. ¶Sport is *speechless poetry*.—G.K. Chesterton. スポーツは無声の詩である. ¶*suggestive poetry* 暗示に富む詩. ¶*thoughtful poetry* 思想の深い詩.

Q^{2} *dilettante poetry* 好事家の詩. ¶*narrative poetry* 物語詩. ¶*tree poetry* 木の姿の詩的な美しさ(詩趣). ¶*war poetry* 戦争詩. ¶*winter poetry* 冬の詩情.

P represent the scene *in poetry* その場面を詩にする. ¶the charm *of* his *poetry* 彼の詩の魅力 ‖ a piece *of poet-*

ry =a poem 一編の詩.

P² the *poetry in* nature 自然の詩情.【類】There is some *poetry in* a snow scene. ¶the *poetry of* rhythmical movement 詩的な律動美 ‖ the *poetry of* life suffers from such a treatment. そんな扱い方をすると人生もつや消しだ.

poignancy, *n.* 痛烈さ.

P² *poignancy of* effect ぴりっとした味.

poignant, *a.* 痛烈な. 「葉.

M remarks that sounds *rather poignant* しんらつに響く言

point, *n.* せん端; 先端, みさき; 点, 評点; 地点, 目的点; 主点, 要領; 長所; ささいな事項; 〖教育〗単位.

V ***accentuate*** the *point* of a story 話の山を強調する. ¶***adjust*** the *point* その点を片づける. ¶To ***argue*** this *point* would carry me too far away from the purpose I have had in view. 当面の目的と余りかけ離れることになるから私はこの点は論じないことにする.【類】The *point* might be ***argued*** pro or con (賛否). / The *point* was ***argued*** with great warmth and eagerness on both sides. ¶to ***attain*** this *point*, I have sometimes found it necessary to ... この目的を達するため私は時折...の必要を感じた. ¶***award*** *points* [考査などで]点を与える. ¶***bring out*** one's strong *points* その長所を発揮させる ‖ vividly ***bring out*** the *point* of a satirical story 風刺物語の要点を明確にする.【類】***bring out*** the best *points* / The diagrams (図表) ***bring out*** his *points* with striking clearness. / ***bring out*** several *points* of difference between ... ¶***bring up*** a *point* 一つの要点を(討議のために)持出す. ¶***calculate*** *points* 得点を計算する. ¶She ***carried*** her *point* with her husband. 彼女は夫に対して自分の言分を通した.【類】At last I ***carried*** my *point*. ¶***catch*** the *point* of a speech 演説の要点をつかむ. ¶I advised him to ***choose*** this *point* for building his home. 私はこの地点を住宅地に選定するように彼に勧めた. ¶***clear up*** the *point* その点を明白にする.【類】***clear up*** *points* of difficulty. ¶***concede*** a *point* ある点を譲歩する. ¶And now let us ***consider*** another *point*. そこで少し方面を変えて論じてみよう. ‖ *points* ***considered*** in the award 審査で考慮された諸点. ¶***count*** 10 *points* againt ... ...の得点を一10 とする. ¶***cover*** all *points* on which information is usually desired 知りたいと思われる点を網らする. ¶***decide*** disputed *points* 論点を解決する. ¶the theory ***derives*** further *points* by the fact that ... その学説は...という事実によってさらに有力となる. ¶Do not ***despise*** little *points* 細かい点を軽視するな. ¶apply to him to ***determine*** the *point* その点で彼の裁断を仰ぐ.【類】Further investigation will be necessary before the *point* is definitely ***determined.*** ¶He ***developed*** these *points* more in detail in an article in the Chuo Koron. 彼は中央公論の論文でこれらの点を一層詳細に説いた. ¶***discuss*** several nice *points* of law 法律の種々の細微な問題を論議する.【類】***discuss*** a *point* with ... ¶***dispute*** the *point* with ... ...と論じ合う. ¶His article ***drives home*** the *point* I am going to make. 彼の論文は私が説明しようとする点を徹底させた. ¶***dull*** the *point* of pleasure 快楽をそぐ. ¶***earn*** ... *points* [勝負などで]...点を得る. ¶***elaborate*** needlessly so plain a *point* そんなに明確な点をいたずらに力説する. ¶***elect*** nine *points* 〖教育〗九単位を選ぶ. ¶***elucidate*** a *point* of importance 肝心の点を明らかにする. ¶***emphasize*** a *point* ある点を強調する.【類】The speaker ***emphasized*** his *points* by knocking on the table. ¶That *point* I will now ***enlarge.*** その点を今私が詳説します. ¶***examine*** *points* of contrast and resemblance 対照と相似の点を吟味する. ¶***exemplify*** the *point* その点を例示する. ¶***explain*** the *point* その点を説明する. ¶The two ***find*** no *points* of agreement. その二人は気が合わない. ‖ He is clever at ***finding*** weak *points*. 彼は他人の穴捜しがうまい. ‖ ***find*** new *points* of view for old and familiar objects 古い見なれた物に対して新しい見方をする. ¶The tramway car ***fouled*** the *points*. 電車がスイッチを入れそこねた. ¶***gain*** a *point* 一点を得る ‖ ***gain*** one's *point* 目的を遂げる ‖ Thus one very important *point* was ***gained.*** かくして一つのきわめて重要な論旨が通った. ¶***give point*** to ... ...に先をつける(とがらす); ...に力点をおく(強める).【類】***give point*** to a tool. ¶***give points*** to ... ...にハンデをつける.【類】He can ***give points*** in the game to any opponent. ‖ A ***gives*** B three *points*. A は B に三点を与える; A はハンデキャップとして B に三点を許す. ¶***grasp*** the *point* at issue 論争の要点をつかむ ‖ ***grasp*** the main *points* 要領を得る. ¶***hammer home*** each *point* of one's message with telling strokes その使命の各要点を有効にたたき込む. ¶***have*** this *point* always in mind この点を心に留めておく ‖ it ***has*** *points* of contact with ... それは...との接触点をもつ ‖ It ***has*** more *points* of excellence than any other machine on the market. それは市場にある他の機械のどれよりも長所が多い. ‖ as often as we ***have*** a *point* to gain 得点の機会がある度に.【類】They ***have*** *points* of resemblance (相似点). ¶Here is a story which serves to ***illustrate*** this *point*. この点の説明として役立つ一つの話がある. ‖ The example ***illustrates*** this *point* neatly. その例がこの点を美事に説明している.【類】the *point* is perhaps most vividly ***illustrated*** by ... ¶***impress*** that particular *point* その特殊の点を感銘させる. ¶he ***indicates*** the vital *point* when he says that ... 彼は...と言って急所を突いている. ¶***labor*** the *point* その論点を詳説する. ¶He could ***level*** the most abstruse *points* to the meanest capacities. 彼は最も奥妙な点をどんな頭の悪い人にも分かるようにこなすことができた. ¶It ***loses*** its *point*. それは要領を得ないものになる. ¶***make*** a *point* that ...を主張する(強調する) ‖ ***make*** a *point* of ...ing 必ず...することにしている.【類】He ***makes*** a *point* of attending such meetings. / Well, then, I'll ***make*** a *point* of looking you up on the 10th. / ***make*** a *point* of succeeding at all hazards (=any cost) / ***make*** a *point* of investigating the industrial conditions of Japan ‖ I ***make*** a *point* of putting the sentences right in my head before writing them down. ‖ ***make*** it a *point* of honor to ... ...することを光栄に思う.【類】***make*** it a main *point* to ... ¶He will undertake to ***manage*** this nice *point* for me. 彼は私のためにこの微妙な点の処理に当ってくれるでしょう. ¶***mark*** another *point* 別の点に注意する. ¶***master*** all the nice *points* 細微な点に通暁する. ¶***miss*** the *point* はき違える, 意味を取違える.【類】I ***missed*** the *point* of the joke. ‖ But this ***misses*** the whole *point*. しかしそれは全然見当違いだ.【類】He quite ***missed*** the main *points*. ¶He ***misunderstood*** the *point* originally raised. 彼は初めに意図された要点をはき違えた. ¶***modify*** his *point* of view 彼の観点を変更する. ¶***obtain*** one's *point* 論旨を徹底さす, 目的を達する ‖ ***obtain*** 75 *points* out of 100 百点満点で七十五点をとる. ¶a little ***overstate*** the *point* その点をいささか誇張する. ¶***pass*** the danger *point* 危険を通り越す. ¶He is quick to ***perceive*** the good *points* possessed by his inferiors. 彼はたちまち部下の長所を見抜く頭を持っている. ¶I have heard that this castle ***possesses*** many *points* of interest. この城には興味ある点が多いと聞いている. ¶***prefer*** a *point* of pleasure to a point of pride 見栄を棄てて快味の多い方を採る. ¶It ***presents*** *points* of exceptional interest. それには格別興味ある点がある. ¶I do not ***press*** that *point*. 僕はその点を言い張ろうとはしない. ¶Taking it for granted, can you ***prove*** the *point?* それはそれとしてこれを証明ができますか. ¶The *point* you have ***put*** is one I must consider. 君のあげた点は一考してみなければならない ‖ He ***puts*** the *point* admirably. 彼はその点を巧く説いている. ¶***raise*** a *point* for discussion 論題を持出す ‖ ***raise*** no *point* about ... ...を問題にしない. ¶He ***reached*** that *point* where he was mentally and physically dead. 彼は精神的にも肉体的にも死んでいるというあの状態に達した. ¶Don't forget to ***recognize*** the other man's *point* of view. 先方の見方を認識する(人の身になって物を見る)ことを忘れるな. ¶This *point* will be ***referred to*** again later. この点は後章において再説することにする. ¶***sail round*** the extreme *point* of ... ...みさきを回航する. ¶He ***scored*** 300 *points* in 8 breaks. 彼は(玉突で)八回連続で三百点を得た. ¶***see*** the *point* 要点を見てとる.【類】***see*** the *point* of the joke. ¶***seize*** (=grasp) the main *point* 要点をつかむ. ¶***set out*** these *points* これらの点を述べる. ¶***settle*** a disputed *point* 争点を解決する.【類】Further investigation seems necessary to ***settle*** this *point*. ¶***sharpen*** the *point* of a pencil 鉛筆の先をとがらす. ¶***show off*** all his good *points* あらゆる彼の長所を発揮する. ¶***strain*** a *point* 一点を強調しすぎる. ¶***stress*** the *point* that ... ...という点を強調する. ¶he seemed to have ***stretched*** a *point* or two in favor of ... 彼は...に有利になるように一二事実を曲げたらしい.【類】He ***stretched*** some *points* in order to arrive at the conclusion.

¶***summarize*** the prominent *points* embraced in the agreement 契約中の要点を一括する.【類】the main *points* may be ***summarized*** as follows. ¶***sum up*** the main *points* brought out in the foregoing discussion 以上論じた主な諸点を要約する. ¶***take*** a stronger *point* of view 一歩進んで論じる ‖ ***take*** a second *point* 次の議論に移る. ¶Can you ***tell*** the *point* of the following story? 次の話の落ちが分かりますか. ¶***touch*** the *point* 要点に触れる.【類】In subtle grace, perfection of curve, refinement of composition, this structure ***touches*** the higest *point* in Japanese architecture. ¶***treat*** the *point* fully その点を詳説する. ¶I cannot ***understand*** that *point* of view. 私にはその見方が解(ゲ)せない. ¶***visit*** *points* of interest 名所を見物する. ¶I do not ***waive*** this *point*. 私はこの説を譲歩しない. ¶***win*** the largest *points* 最大の点数を得る. ¶***yield*** a *point* in debate 議論で一つの点を譲る ‖ ***yield*** a *point* at issue 係争の一点を容認する.

v² Here ***lies*** the *point*. そこが問題だ.

Q There is an ***additional*** *point* to be considered in connection with this question. この問題とあわせて考うべき点がもう一つある. ¶from an ***aesthetic*** *point* of view 審美的見地からして. ¶arrive from ***all*** *points* of the compass 四方八方から集まる. ¶***altered*** *points* of view 変更した観点. ¶an ***agreeable*** *point* 妥協の余地ある点. ¶from the purely ***artistic*** *point* of view 純芸術的見地からして. ¶***basic*** *points* of discussion 議論の基点. ¶The ***boiling*** *point* of water is 212°F. 水の沸騰点は華氏二百十二度である. ¶the ***breaking*** *point* 切断点(切断するまで牽引された状態).【類】The relations between the two countries were strained to the ***breaking*** *point*. / The war strained her resources to the ***breaking*** *point*. / The strain between the two reached the ***breaking*** *point*. ¶from the ***broadest*** *point* of view 最も大局的な見地から言って.【類】look at it from a ***broader*** *point* of view. ¶a ***cardinal*** *point* in home management 家政上枢要な一つの点. ¶He was the ***central*** *point* of attack. 彼が攻撃の中心人物であった. ¶it has ***certain*** *points* of likeness to … それは…に似通った所がある ‖ to a ***certain*** *point* (=extent) ある点までは. ¶the ***chief*** *points* of controversy 主な論点.【類】the ***chief*** *points* to be observed. ¶the most ***commanding*** *point* of view is the eminence called … 一番展望の広い地点は…という高地だ. ¶from a ***commercial*** *point* of view 商業上の見地から. ¶They have their ***common*** *points* 彼らには共通点がある. ¶It is a ***considerable*** *point* ***in*** his favor. それは彼にとって余程有利な点である. ¶a ***controversial*** *point* 論点. ¶the ***cosmopolitan*** *point* of view 世界主義的な見解. ¶the ***crowning*** *point* of a man's ambition 人間の功名心の絶頂. ¶the ***crucial*** *point* is that … 重要な点は…である. ¶an able defense of the humanities from the ***cultural*** *point* of view 文化的見地から古典文学を必要とした有力な議論. ¶You see everything from a ***dark*** *point* of view. 君は悲観論者だ. ¶a ***debatable*** *point* 議論の余地のある点. ¶a much ***debated*** *point* 大に議論のある点. ¶a ***deciding*** *point* 決定点. ¶a ***decimal*** *point* 〚数〛小数点. ¶progress constantly forward toward some ***definite objective*** *point* ある一定の目標に向って絶えず前進する. ¶We await information from you on these ***different*** *points*. われわれはこれら種々の点について君の通報を待っている. ¶***different-angled*** *points* of view 角度の異った観察点. ¶a ***difficult*** *point* in grammar 文法の難点. ¶these two ***diverse*** *points* of view これら二つの異なった観察点. ¶a ***doubtful*** *point* 疑わしい点.【類】make clear the ***doubtful*** *point*. ¶a ***dull*** *point* 鈍い先端. ¶in the ***economic*** *point* of view 経済上の見解では.【類】from an ***economical*** *point* of view ¶from the ***economist's*** *point* of view 経済学者の見地から. ¶from the ***educational*** *point* of view 教育上の見地から. ¶bring out the ***essential*** *points* 要点を明かにする. ¶treat a subject from the ***evangelical*** *point* of view 問題を伝道の見地から取扱う. ¶consult him on ***every*** *point* 万事彼に相談する. ¶The view has not been taken from the most ***favorable*** *point*. その景色(の写真)は一番よい場所からとってない. ¶a ***few*** *points* on make-up hints メーキャップに関する二三の注意. ¶It did not prove successful from a ***financial*** *point* of view. それは経済的には成功とはいえなかった. ¶a ***fine*** *point* (針・刺などの)せん端 ‖ That is a very ***fine*** *point*. それは非常にむずかしい点だ. ‖ This is one of the ***finest*** *points* of view in the neighorhood. これがこの付近での一番りっぱな見晴らしだ. ¶the ***first*** *points* of consideration in value of … …を評価する場合の要点. ¶the ***focal*** *point* of all the railway lines of the Empire 帝国のあらゆる鉄道線路の焦点 ‖ the ***focal*** *point* of the celebration 祝典の中心点. ¶in …ing the ***following*** *points* should be observed. …するには次の点に注意すべきである. ¶consuls at ***foreign*** *points* 外国在勤の領事. ¶from a ***French*** *point* of view フランス人の見地から. ¶a ***good*** *point* of view 眺望のよい地点 ‖ tell the ***good*** *points* of their machines その機械の長所を述べる.【類】Though made in Japan, it has all the ***good*** *points* of a foreign make. ¶The conference has to settle many ***grave*** *points*. その会議はいく多重大な問題を解決しなくてはならない. ¶This is one of its ***great*** *points* of merit. これがその主な長所の一つだ. ‖ I hold it a ***great*** *point* in self-education that … 自学自習には…が大事な点だと思う. ¶The book marks the ***high*** *point* now reached in English studies in France. その本はフランスにおける英語研究が現在達したその高い位置を示している. ‖ a ***high*** or ***mountainous*** *point* of land 高いもしくは山岳地点. ¶From a ***historical*** and ***archaeological*** *point* of view the value of the antique is of quite priceless. 歴史的見地からすればその古物の価値はほとんど計り知れないほどだ. ¶from a ***hygienic*** *points* of view 衛生上の見地から. ¶look at it from an ***impersonal*** *point* of view それを自分を離れて考慮する. ¶mark an ***important*** *point* in the history of … …の歴史に重要な一点を記す. ¶a very ***important strategic*** *point* 軍事上きわめて重要な地点. ¶***interesting*** *points* of contrast and similarity in the histories and developments of … …の歴史と発達における対照及び相似の興味ある点 ‖ an ***interesting objective*** *point* for a motor-car drive 自動車ででかけるちょうどよい地点. ¶destination or an ***intermediate*** *point* 目的地または中間の一地点 ‖ the Pacific coast and ***intermediate*** *points* 太平洋沿岸並にその方面の地点. ¶from the ***international*** *point* of view 国際的見地から. ¶a ***knotty*** *point* むずかしい込入った点. ¶from the ***jevenile*** (***adult***) *point* of view 年少者(成人)の観点からは. ¶Of this more will be said at a ***later*** *point*. その詳細はなお後に述べる. ¶from a ***legal*** *point* of view 法律上の見地から.【類】clearly irresponsible from the ***legal*** *point* of view. ¶there is ***little*** *point* in … …にはほとんど意味がない. ¶from a strictly ***logical*** *point* of view 厳格に論理学上の見地から. ¶the ***lowest*** *point* 最低限度. ¶a ***luminous*** *point* in my memory 私の記憶にはっきり残っている一つのこと. ¶***main*** *points* of a lecture 講義の要点. ¶a ***major*** (***minor***) *point* 主旨(細かい点). ¶there are ***many*** *points* of similarity between … …間には多くの類似点がある.【類】We are united in so ***many*** *points* and divided in so few. ¶from the ***medical*** *point* of view 医学上の見地から. ¶the ***melting*** *point* 溶解点. ¶It is a ***mere*** *point*. 何でもないことだ. ¶from a ***military*** *point* of view 軍事上の見地から. ¶The most ***noticeable*** *point* in the report is the fact that … 同報告書のもっとも注目すべき点は…というにある. ¶The year 1615 is a ***momentous*** *point* in the history of English glass-making. 一六一五年は英国ガラス製造史における重要な一時期であった. ¶from the ***monetary*** *point* of view 金銭上の見地から. ¶a very ***moot*** *point* 非常にやかましい論点.【類】it is still a ***moot*** *point* whether … ¶examine a question from a ***moral*** *point* of view 道徳上の見地から問題を調査する. ¶from a ***national*** *point* of view 国家的見地から. ¶He was called upon to decide a ***nice*** *point* of dispute in the game. 彼は競技における論争の微妙な点の裁決を委任された. ¶a very ***minute*** *point* すこぶる細い点. ¶an ***obscure*** *point* あいまいな点. ¶***one-day-distant*** *points* 日帰り諸地点. ¶***original*** *points* [書物などの]独創的な点. ¶from a ***pecuniary*** *point* of view 金銭上の見地から. ¶in a ***physiological*** *point* of view 生理学上の見地から見て. ¶San Francisco is the ***pivotal*** *point* of the Western market. サンフランシスコは西部市場の枢要な地点である. ¶from an economic as distinguished from a ***political*** *point* of view 政治上の見地からでなく経済上の見地から. ¶It is erroneous in principle and unwise from a ***practical*** *point* of view. それは原則が誤っていて実際的見地から見れば愚かなことである. ¶the ***principal*** *point* is that …主要な点は…だ.【類】It is the ***principal point*** of interest. ¶study suicide elaborately from the ***psychological point*** of view 心理学上の見地から苦心して自殺を研究する. ¶regarded from the ***racial point*** of view 人種的見地から見て. ¶the ***salient points*** in a speech 演説の要点. ¶from the ***scientific point*** of view 科学的見地から. ¶my ***second point*** is that ... 第二の点は ...ということである. ¶It has ***several points*** in its favor. それには長所がいくつかある. ¶a ***sharp point*** [刃物やきりなど] とがった先. ¶This was the ***shrewdest point*** in his lecture. これが氏の講演中最も痛烈な点であった. ¶be strained to a ***snapping point*** 切れるほど張り切っている ‖ The chain seemed stretched to ***snapping point***. 鎖が切れる位に引締めてあるように思われた. ¶On December 21 the sun reaches its most ***southern point***. 十二月二十一日には太陽は最南端に達する. ¶make a ***special point*** of ... 特に...に注意する. ¶from the ***standard point*** of view 一般の標準から見れば. ¶until he comes to a natural ***stopping point*** 仕事の切れ目になるまで. ¶a ***strategic point*** 戦略的要衝. ¶Mathematics is not her ***strong point***. 数学は彼女の得意でない. 【類】Accuracy (正確) is not his ***strong point***. / One of her ***strong points*** of learning was the history of costume. / it is a ***strong point*** in his favor that ... ¶***subtler points*** of English grammar 英文法のさらに細微な点. ¶a ***suggestive point*** 暗示に富んだ点. ¶a ***talking point*** 話の題目. ¶***technical points*** 技術的な諸点. ¶from a ***technological point*** of view 技術的な見地から言えば. ¶a ***telling point*** 手応えのある点. ¶from a ***theoretical point*** of view 学理上の見地から. ¶from a ***triple point*** of view—the psychic, the intellectual, and the moral 心理的·知的·道徳的の三重の見地から. ¶from this ***twofold point*** of view この二重の見地から. ¶the ***vital point*** is ... 要点は...にある. ¶He was struck at his most ***vulnerable point***. 彼は最弱点を突かれた. ¶the ***weak point*** of that argument is that ... その議論の弱味は...にある ‖ The rope snapped at the ***weakest point***. ロープは弱い点でぽつんと切れた. ¶Land's End is a cape in Cornwall, the most ***westerly point*** of England. ランズ·エンドはイングランドの西端にあるコーンウォール州のみさきだ. ¶from the ***Westerner's point*** of view 西洋人の見地から. ¶That's the ***whole point!*** それが大事な点だ. ¶from a ***wider point*** of view さらに大局から見て.

Q² pass an ***Army check point*** 陸軍の検問所を通過する. ¶the ***boiling point*** of water 水の沸騰点. 【類】reach the ***boiling point***. ¶Let us attack our problem from a ***commonsense point*** of view. 常識の見地からわれらの問題を検討しよう. ¶a ***concentration point*** 捕虜収容所. ¶pass the ***danger point*** 危険地点を通り抜ける. 【類】be at the ***danger point*** / to the ***danger point***. ¶a ***delivery point*** 荷渡地. ¶a ***departure point*** for the climb up Mt. Asama 浅間山登山口. ¶a ***destination point*** 目的地点. ¶a ***discharge point*** 〘軍〙解任点数. ¶a ***distributing point*** 配給地点. ¶a ***division point*** 意見の分岐点. ¶an ***exclamation point*** 《米》感嘆符. ☞英語では a note of exclamation とか an exclamation mark という. ¶set the basic ***exemption point*** at ¥24,000 基本免税点を二万四千円におく. ¶combine both ***fancy*** and ***utility points*** 趣味と実益を合せる. ¶a ***flash[ing] point*** 油の引火点. ¶the ***freezing point*** 氷点, 凍結点. ¶the comma, a ***general-utility point*** 一般に利用される句とう点のコンマ. ¶an ***interrogation point*** 《米》疑問符. ¶put an ***interrogation point*** after it その後に疑問点を付ける. ☞英語では a question mark とか an interrogation mark という. ¶a railroad ***junction point*** 鉄道の接続点. ¶a ***key point*** 重要点, 肝心な点 ‖ make these two items the ***key points*** この二点を骨子とする. ¶a ***launching point*** for an attack on ... ...攻撃の拠点. ¶***maximum points*** 満点. ¶the ***melting point*** of ice 氷の溶解点. ¶reach the ***midway point*** [道の]半ばに達する. ¶The cold weather greatly reduced the usual amount of coal sent to ***New England points*** by water. 寒さのため海路ニューイングランドの諸地点に送り込まれる従来の石炭の量は著しく減少した. ¶a beautiful ***outlook point*** 見晴しのよい地点. ¶be now at its ***peak personnel point*** 今や人員は最大限に達している. ¶a ***pen point*** 《米》ペン先. ☞英語は nib. ‖ submerge the ***pen point*** in the ink ペン先をインキに浸す ‖ They are at ***pen points***. 彼らは筆戦をやっている. ¶the sudden dropping of a ***percentage point*** in the popularity rating of President 大統領の人気(投票)の率の突然の下降. ¶The rascal forced her at ***pistol point*** to hand over her savings. 悪漢は彼女にピストルをつきつけて無理に貯金を渡させた. ¶a ***rallying point*** 集合地点. ¶a ***rationing point*** 配給所 ¶a ***receiving*** and ***distributing point*** for grain 穀物の一集散地. ¶That is a ***redeeming point***. それが取柄だ. ¶reach the ***saturation point*** 飽和点に達する ‖ the ***saturation point*** of a hot liquid 高温の液体の飽和点. ¶This pen has a ***scratch point*** (=《英》a scratchy nib). このペン先はひっかかる. ¶a ***selling point*** 販売に有利な点. 【類】big ***selling points***. ¶***service points*** 〘軍〙従軍点数. ¶a ***shipping point*** for grain 穀物の発送地点. ¶an important ***shipping point*** for coal 貯炭所. ¶a ***silver point*** 銀筆(以前下図などを描くに用いた). ¶form a suitable ***starting point*** 適切な起点となる. 【類】the natural ***starting point*** for such a study is ... ¶a ***storage point*** 貯蔵所. ¶***talking points*** on Australia 豪州についての話題. 【類】use it simply as a ***talking point*** / give them a strong ***talking point*** for demanding ... ¶a ***tourist point*** 遊覧地. ¶a ***trading point*** 交易地. ¶a ***transfer point*** [電車などの]乗換場. ¶a great ***transshipment point*** for ... ...の大積換え地(香港など中継地). ¶at a ***transition point*** from the old to the new 旧から新に移る転換期に際し. ¶Bismarck's marriage was the ***turning point*** in his life. ビスマークの結婚は氏の生がいの一転期であった. 【類】the ***turning points*** in the life of the nation / This was the ***turning point*** of my career. / this event marks a ***turning point*** in the history of ... / at the ***turning points*** of the thoughts. ¶***utility points*** 養鶏など実益になる点. ¶Opportunities are reduced to the ***vanishing point***. 機会は減じてほとんど絶無となっている. ¶attack a problem from a ***vantage point*** 有利な地点に立って問題を研究する. ¶a ***world point*** of view 世界的見地. ¶keep one's losses as near the ***zero point*** as possible その損害をできるだけ少く食い止める. ¶a ***14-karat solid gold point*** tipped with iridium イリジューム付の十四金ペン先.

P The heat is ***above*** the boiling ***point***. 熱は沸騰点以上だ. ¶***at*** a ***point*** near the island その島付近のみさきで ‖ rob a bank ***at*** the ***point*** of a gun 銃を用いて銀行強盗をやる ‖ sharp ***at*** the ***point*** 先のとがった ‖ The fort was taken ***at*** the ***point*** of the bayonet. その要さいを突貫して占領した. ‖ It is forced on the country ***at*** the ***point*** of the sword by an outside power. それは外部の強国が武力をもって強請したものである. ‖ They are ***at*** swords' ***points*** with each other 彼らはお互につのつき合をしている. ‖ ***at*** the ***point*** west of ... ...の西の地点で. 【類】***at points*** of strategic importance / He is ***at*** the ***point*** of his highest efficiency (働き盛り). ‖ It resembles ... ***at*** three ***points***. それは三つの点で...に似ている. ‖ adhere to the mediaeval formula which puts the merchant ***at*** the lowest ***point*** in the social scale 社会階級の最下層に商人をおく中世の慣例に執着する ‖ ***at*** this ***point*** in the evolution of civilization 文化発達のこの段階に ‖ ***at*** no ***point*** of human history 人類の歴史のいかなる段階においても(...しない) ‖ ***at*** the ***point*** of death 死にひんして. 【類】***At*** the ***point*** of his death all the events of his life passed through his mind as of mnemonic panorama (記憶のパノラマ). ¶The thermometer has gone ***below*** the freezing ***point*** but once. 寒暖計はたった一回だけ氷点下に降った. ¶argue ***beside*** the ***point*** 要点を外れた議論をする ‖ All that is ***beside*** the ***point***. それはまるきり不得要領だ. 【類】What is said of it is ***beside*** the ***point***. ¶His research is dominated ***by*** the scientific ***point*** of view. 彼の研究は科学的見地に立脚している ‖ ask questions point ***by point*** 一つ一つ細かに質問する. ¶passengers ***for points*** beyond Chicago 《米》シカゴより先に行く乗客. ¶***from*** this ***point on*** ... この地点から先は ‖ congregate ***from*** all ***points*** of the compass 四方八方から寄って来る ‖ ***from*** the ***point*** of view of an engineer 技師の見地から ‖ ***from*** the ***point*** of view we now occupy 現在の観点から論じて ‖ regarded ***from*** this ***point*** of view この見地から考えて. 【類】***from*** a woman's ***point*** of view / consider ***from*** a ...'s ***point*** of view ... / ***from*** the ***point*** of view of health. ¶meet ***in*** a ***point*** 一点に会合する ‖ resemble ***in*** many ***points*** 色々の点で似ている ‖ ***in point*** of sheer numbers 数だけは. 【類】the largest ***in point*** of numbers ‖ ***in point*** of fact 実際の所 ‖ ***in point*** of time 時間の点で.【類】*In point* of ability, learning, culture my friend is superior. ‖ a case *in point* 適例.【類】an instance *in point* ‖ *in* an economical *point* of view 経済という見地では ‖ with four sides that come together *in* a *point* at the top like a pyramid ピラミッドのように四辺が頂点で集まるようになっていて. ¶ taper *into* a sharp *point* 先へ行ってとがる. ¶ be *off* the *point* 要領を得ない. ¶ In that book there are some interesting remarks *on* this *point*. その本にこのことに関してあるおもしろいことが書いてある. ‖ *On* this *point* no fixed rule can be given. この点では一定の規則は立てられない.【類】I am uncertain *on* that point. / I'm with you *on* that *point*. / Do not trouble yourself *on* that *point*. / Then *on* that *point* we are agreed. / I was reassured *on* this *point*. ‖ What you say has no bearing *on* the *point*. 君の言うことは一向要点に触れていない ‖ She was *on* the *point* of swooning. 彼女は卒倒しそうであった.【類】He is *on* the *point* of breathing his last (息を引取る). / He is *on* the *point* of going out (出掛ける). ‖ when *on* the *point* of death 死に臨んで ‖ Controversy has raged *round* this *point*. この点は大分議論がやかましかった. ¶ *to* a [certain] *point* ある程度, いく分.【類】He was a pessimist *to* a *point*. ¶ His talk was crude enough almost *to* a *point* of indecency. 彼の話はほとんど尾ろうというべきほどに下品なものであった. ‖ He is modest *to* the *point* of ridicule. 彼はおかしい位腰がひくい.【類】It is exaggerated *to* the *point* of absurdity (ばからしいまでに). / The author's style is individual *to* the *point* of eccentricity (奇矯). / a poison weakened *to* the *point* of uselessness ‖ be more *to* the *point* 一層要領を得ている.【類】His remarks on the subject are much *to* the *point*. / describe it tersely but *to* the *point* / He speaks *to* the *point*. / keep *to* the *point* / come *to* the *point* in an interview / Your objection is nothing *to* the *point* / an answer *to* the *point* / the *point to* which I have been making is this—that ... ‖ frankness *to* the *point* of insult ぶじょくともとられるほどの率直さ. ¶ A score *under* 60 *points* is poor. 六十点以下は不可. ¶ *up to* a certain *point* ある点まで ‖ all had gone well *up to* this *point*, when ... ここまでは万事うまく行った, すると... ¶ No one, we think, will contradict us *upon* this *point*. 何人もこの点についてはわれわれに反対はすまいと思う. ¶ *with* this *point* in view この点を考慮して ‖ The college acredited him *with* 5 *points* for his seminar work. 大学は彼のゼミの成績に対し五単位を与えた.

P² a *point at* issue 論点.【類】This is not the *point at* issue. ¶ correspond *point for* point 一々符合する ‖ a shipping *point for* lumber 木材積出し場. ¶ the *point in* dispute 論争点 ‖ a *point in* doubt 疑わしい点 ‖ a *point in* grammar 文法の一問題.【類】The *point in* question is simple. ¶ *points of* goodness 長所 ‖ a *point of* intersection 交差点 ‖ his *points of* delivery 彼に品物を引渡す場所 ‖ *points of* historical interest 史的興味ある場点(史跡など) ‖ Precisely here is the *point of* my argument. 私の議論の要点は全くここにある.【類】*points of* attraction / It is a *point of* conscience. ‖ the *point of* production 産地 ‖ The *point of* departure is false. 出発点が間違っている. ‖ *points of* style スタイル(型)の問題 ‖ the *points of* contact between poetry and music 詩と音楽との接触点.【類】Nagasaki was then the only *point of* contact between the then secluded land of Japan and the commerce and civilization of the West. ‖ *points of* difference 相違点 ‖ *points of* detail 細かな点.【類】a *point of* vision / *points of* resemblance / a *point of* dispute / many *points of* uncertainty remain / the *point of* one's remarks. ¶ the *point under* discussion 論点.

O The *point* is this. 要点はこうだ.

point, *v*. 指し向ける; 指示する, 指摘する.

M *point conclusively* to ... 判然...を示す. ¶ The hand *points north* その手は北を指している. ¶ He expressly *pointed out* the mistake. 彼は特にその誤びゅうを指摘した. ‖ he delivered an address, in which he *pointed out* that ... 彼は演説をやったがその中で...と指摘した ‖ It *points out* the lines for further investigation. それは今後の調査に対する方面を示している.【類】as he has truly *pointed out* / *point out* deficiencies / *point out* errors (=mistakes) / may I be allowed to *point out* certain errors in ...? / I wish to *point out* that ... / to be just to him it must be *pointed out*, however, that ... / as history would seem to *point out* / I had occasion to *point out* that ... / economists have long pointed *out* that ...

M² *point off* figures 数字の間をコンマで切る. ¶ be *pointed up* sharply 著しく目立つようになる ‖ *point up* a contrast 対照を著しくする ‖ *point up* a debate 討論を活発にする.

P *point after* him 彼に後指をさす. ¶ It's rude to *point at* another. 人を指さすのは失礼である.【類】*point at* a person with a scorn (侮べつして) / *point* the finger of scorn *at* a person ‖ *point* a revolver *at* a person 人にけん銃を向ける. ¶ *point in* the same direction 同じ方向を指す. ¶ *point to* the west 西を指す ‖ *point* a person *to* a place すわれと人に場所を示す.【類】Everything *points to* (=indicates) the ultimate predominance of English. / The cause is so obscure that one may not be able to *point to* it definitely.

pointer, *n*. 指す人(物); 《口語》ヒント; 《米》従軍点をとった兵士.

V Let me *give* you a *pointer* ちょっと知恵を貸そう.

Q the *highest pointer* 最高点をとった人.

Q² a *lecture-hall pointer* [講演のとき図などに用いる]指し棒. ¶ a *West Pointer* 《米》陸大出身の士官.

poise, *n*. つり合い.

V without *losing* one's *poise* 姿勢をくずさずに.

Q He has *perfect poise* of both mind and body. 精神と肉体が完全な平衡を示している.【類】He has *perfect poise* and never seems to lose his composure.

poise, *v*. つり合を保つ; つり合を保たせる.

M a little bird *poising cleverly* on a wire 針金に止っている小鳥. ¶ *poise* oneself *gracefully* upon ... ...の上で美しく身体のバランスをとる(体操など).

P *poise* a bucket of water *on* the head 頭上に水入りバケツをのせる ‖ *poise* oneself *on* one's toes つま先で立つ.

poison, *n*. 毒.

V *put poison* in ... ...に毒を入れる. ¶ *take poison* instead of medicine 薬ではなく毒を飲む.

V² The *poison got* into circulation. その毒が回った.

Q It is a *deadly poison* if drunk. それを飲むと恐ろしい毒になる.【類】strophanthus, a *deadly poison* from Africa / a *deadly poison* to ... ¶ a *death-dealing poison* 生命を奪う毒. ¶ a *devilish poison* 猛毒. ¶ a *powerful* (=*strong*) *poison* 激しい毒. ¶ It is a *rank poison*. それは猛毒だ. ¶ a *slow poison* きき目のおそい毒. ¶ a *violent poison* ⌊激しい毒.

Q² a *rat poison* ねずみとり(劇薬).

P proof *against poison* 毒の害を受けない(防毒の). ¶ Alcoholic drinks act *as* a *poison* to a child. 酒精飲料は子供には毒になる. ¶ kill oneself *by poison* 毒薬で自殺する. ¶ an antidote *for* (=*to*) *poison* 解毒剤. ¶ It acts *like poison*. それは毒にに似た作用がある.

P² a *poison to* morals 道徳を乱すもの.

poison, *v*. 毒する.

P I got *poisoned by* eating ... 私は...を食べて中毒した. ‖ I am easily *poisoned by* lacquer. 私はじきにうるしにかぶれる. ¶ His dog has been *poisoned to* death. 彼の犬は毒殺された. ¶ *poisoned with* one's own breath 自分の息で中毒(窒息)して.

poisoning, *n*. 中毒. 「毒.

Q² *food poisoning* 食あたり(中毒). ¶ *lead poisoning* 鉛中

P² *poisoning by* strychnin(e) ストリキニーネ中毒. ¶ *poisoning from* eating 食傷.

poisonous, *a*. 有毒な.

M a *deadly poisonous* plant 致命的な毒草. ¶ *highly poisonous* 非常に有毒な.

poke, *v*. 差出る; ぐずぐずする; つっつく.

M² *poke about* 差出る; おせっかいに奔走する. ¶ *poke up* a fire 火をかきたてる.

P *poke about* work 仕事をなまける. ¶ *poke* fun *at* a person 人をからかう. ¶ He *poked* me *in* the ribs *with* his elbow. 彼はひじで僕のあばらを突いた. ¶ *poke* one's nose *into* everything 何ごとにも口を出す.【類】Don't *poke* your nose *into* another's business. ¶ *poke* one's head *out of* the window 窓から頭を出す.

pole, *n*. 棒, さお.

V *shin* (=*climb*) *up* a *pole* 棒に手足をかけてよじ上る.

Q² a *flag pole* 旗ざお. ¶ a *telephone pole* 電[話]柱.

P propel a boat *by* a *pole* さおで舟を進める. ¶jumping *with* a *pole* 棒[高]とび.

pole, *v.* 打つ.

M *pole out* three homers〘野球〙三ホーマをかっ飛ばす.

pole, *n.* 極.

Q at the ***opposite social** pole* 社会的地位から見てそれとは対照的な.

P the two groups of thinkers who are ***at*** opposite *poles* 対照的になっている二つの思想家の群.

O Their views are *poles* apart (=asunder). 彼らの意見は天地の相違がある.

police, *n.* 警察; [団]警官.

V ***call*** the *police* 警官を呼ぶ(電話で). ¶At this point the *police* was ***called in.*** この時警察の人に来てもらった. ¶***disband*** the secret *police* 秘密警察を解散する. ¶***dispatch*** the *police* to the scene 警官を現場に急派する. ¶***hail*** the *police* 警官を(声をあげて)呼ぶ. ¶I ***informed*** (=***instructed***) the *police* of the fact. 私はその事実を警察に知らせた. ¶***mobilize*** the *police* 警官を動員する. ¶***notify*** the *police* 警官に通告する. ¶***phone*** [the] *police* 警察に電話する. ¶***put*** the *police* on her track 警官に彼女の跡をつけさせる. ¶***resist*** the *police* 警察に抵抗する. ¶***tell*** *police* 警察に密告する.

V² The *police* ***interfered.*** 警官が干渉した.

Q the chief of the ***parliamentary*** *police* 議会の守衛長. ¶a carload of ***secret*** *police* トラックに乗込んだ秘密警察の一隊. ¶The *police* cannot of course be ***ubiquitous.*** 警察官がどこにでもいるということはもちろん望めない.

Q² the ***city*** *police* 市警(察署). ¶a ***fire*** *police* 消防署. ¶***morals*** *police* (=Sitterpolizei) 道徳警察. ¶He serves the 800 citizens as a ***one-man*** *police.* 彼は八百の集団のためにワン・マン警察として勤務した. ¶***plain-clothes*** *police* 捜査係(の警官). ¶***plain-clothes*** moral *police* 平服の補導係. ¶the ***river*** *police* 河川警察. ¶***safety, health,*** and ***morals*** *police* 保安, 保健及び風俗取締警察. ¶***security*** *police* 保安警察. ¶"***thought*** *police*" 思想警察. ¶***women*** *police* [集団]婦人警官.

P The thief has been caught ***by*** the *police.* 賊は警官に逮捕された. 【類】men wanted ***by*** the *police* for various offenses. ¶It is a case ***for*** the *police.* それは警察で扱うべきものだ. ¶A strong body ***of*** *police* arrived and arrested a score of the rioters. 優勢の警官隊が到着して多数の暴徒を捕縛した. ‖ put the matter in the hands ***of*** the *police* その事件を警察に届ける. ¶give oneself up ***to*** the *police* 警察へ自首する ‖ complain ***to*** the *police* 警察に訴える ‖ report the matter ***to*** the *police*=report to the police of the matter その件を警察に届ける. 【類】deliver (=hand over) a criminal suspect ***to*** the *police.* ¶communicate ***with*** the *police* 警察に届ける ‖ The street was lined ***with*** *police.* その通りは警官の列で固められた.

policeman, *n.* 警官, 巡査.

V The *policeman* must be ***liked*** (=***loved***). 警官は人民に愛されなくてはいけない. ¶***summon*** a *policeman* 警官を呼ぶ. ¶The *policeman* ***goes*** round the town. 警官が町を巡回する.

Q a ***big plump*** *policeman* 大柄な丸々と太った巡査. ¶a ***burly[-looking]*** *policeman* [いなか出の]がん丈な巡査. ¶an ***ignorant*** or ***over-officious*** *policeman* 無学なまたはおせっかいな巡査. ¶a ***mounted*** *policeman* 騎馬巡査. ¶a ***stalwart*** *policeman* 筋肉たくましい巡査.

Q² a ***fire*** *policeman* 消防官. ¶a ***motorcycle*** *policeman* 白バイ警官. ¶a ***special-duty*** *policeman* 特務巡査. ¶a ***traffic*** *policeman* 交通巡査.

P send ***for*** a policeman 警官を呼びにやる.

P² a *policeman* ***in*** plain clothes 角そで(私服)巡査. ¶a *policeman* ***off*** duty 非番巡査. ¶a *policeman* ***on*** duty 当直巡査 ‖ a *policeman* ***on*** guards 護衛(または当直)巡査 ‖ a *policeman* ***on*** the beat 巡回中の巡査. 【類】a *policeman* ***on*** special mission.

police-officer, *n.* 警官.

Q² a ***plain-clothes*** *police-officer* 平服の警官.

policy, *n.* (**1**) 政策, 政略, 方針; 策.

V He was convinced that the time had arrived when Japan must ***abandon*** her exclusive *policy.* 彼は日本の排外政策を棄却すべき時が到来したと確信した. ¶***adopt*** a selfish *policy* 利己的な方針を採る. 【類】they have ***adopted*** the wise *policy* of ... ¶***advocate*** a "Fabian" *policy* 持久策を主張する. ¶***alter*** one's *policy* 方針を変える. ¶***apply*** the worst *policy* 最悪の策を充当する. ¶***buck*** a *policy* 政策に反対する. ¶His *policy* is much ***canvassed.*** 彼の政策は盛んに宣伝されている. ¶***carry out*** (=***execute***) a *policy* 方針を実行する. ¶***change*** their *policy* 彼らの方針を変更する. ¶***continue*** a *policy* 方針を継続する. ¶***direct*** the *policy* 政策を指導する. ¶***employ*** a *policy* 政策を採る. ¶***enforce*** her *policy* 方針を実行する. ¶A definite *policy* of ... has already been ***entered on.*** ...の一定方針はすでに着手された. ¶***espouse*** an anti-tradeunion *policy* 労働組合反対政策を擁護する. ¶***establish*** a definite and unchanging *policy* 一定不変の方針を確立する. ¶consistently ***follow*** a *policy* 一貫して方針を守る. 【類】***follow*** the *policy* of the open door (門戸開放政策) / the *policy* we have ***followed*** in the past / ***follow*** a *policy* of national isolation. ¶***formulate*** a *policy* of ... ...の方策を立てる. ¶***frame*** one's *policy* accordingly それに基づいてその方針を立てる. ¶***further*** one's *policy* の方針を進める. ¶***guide*** the *policy* of ... ...の政策を指導する. ¶***materialize*** a *policy* 政策を実現する. ¶***modify*** a *policy* 方針を一部変更する. ¶***pursue*** the same *policy* 同一方針を続行する. ¶***scrap*** a *policy* 政策を廃棄する. ¶***shape*** the *policy* accordingly これに準じて方針を定める. ¶***support*** a *policy* 政策を支持する. ¶The idea ***swayed*** German *policy* throughout. その観念が全体にわたってドイツの政策を左右した.

Q an ***aggressive*** *policy* 侵略的政策. ¶***Allied*** *policy* in Germany ドイツにおける国連の政策. ¶it is ***bad*** *policy* to ... ...するのは愚策だ. ¶Precaution is the ***best*** *policy.* 用心にしくはなし. ¶a ***broad*** *policy* 大方針. ¶pursue a ***cautious*** *policy* 慎重に政策を行う. ¶a ***cheese-paring*** *policy* けちなやり方. ¶adopt a ***conciliatory*** *policy* towards ... ...に対して譲歩的方策を採る. ¶a ***conservative*** *policy* 保守政策. ¶a ***constant*** *policy* 一貫した方針. ¶a ***constructive*** *policy* 建設的政策. ¶adopt the ***contrary*** *policy* 反対の方針を採る. ¶pursue the ***defensive*** *policy* 守勢的方針を続ける. ¶A very ***definite*** *policy* is pursued. 確立した方針で進んでいる. ¶a ***destructive*** *policy* 破壊的方針. ¶a ***diplomatic*** *policy* 外交政策. ¶a ***domestic*** *policy* 国内方針. ¶an ***editorial*** *policy* 編集方針. ¶enforce her ***enlightened-beneficent*** *policy* その進歩した厚生策を実行する. ¶a ***far-reaching*** (***far-sighted***) *policy* 遠大な政策. ¶a ***fatal*** *policy* 致命的政策. ¶a ***financial*** (an ***economic***) *policy* 金融(経済)政策. ¶a ***firm*** *policy* 不動の方針. ¶a ***fiscal*** *policy* 財政政策. ¶***foreign*** (=***diplomatic***) *policies* 外交政策. 【類】a long-range ***foreign*** *policy.* ¶a ***forward*** *policy* 進取的方針. ¶control ***general*** *policy* 一般政策を監理する. ¶a ***global*** *policy* 世界政策. ¶it is ***good*** *policy* to ... ...するのは策の得たものだ. 【類】I thought it ***good*** *policy* not to let him ... ¶a ***high-handed*** *policy* 高圧政策. ¶the final word in all matters of ***higher*** *policy* rests with ... 一切高等政策の決定は...の掌中にある. ¶pursue an ***imperialistic*** *policy* 帝国主義的政策で進む. ¶a ***judicious*** *policy* 思慮ある方針. ¶a ***just*** *policy* 正しい方針. ¶a more ***lenient*** *policy* 一層寛大な政策. ¶a ***liberal*** *policy* 自由政策. ¶a ***long-range*** *policy*=a far reaching policy. ¶a ***middle*** and ***temperate*** *policy* 中庸で穏当な方針. ¶follow a ***militalistic*** *policy* in Manchuria 満州において武断政略を取る. ¶a ***mistaken*** *policy* 間違った方針. ¶an extremely ***narrow-minded*** *policy* 極端に偏狭な政策. ¶follow a ***national*** *policy* 国策に副う. ¶the ***nationalizing*** *policy* adopted in German Poland ドイツ領ポーランドで採用した国有政策. ¶Japan's ***naval*** *policy,* based on the principles of non-menace and non-aggression 不脅威不侵略主義の日本海軍政策. ¶a ***new*** *policy* of ... has come to light ...の新政策が発表になった. ¶pursue a ***pacific*** *policy* 平和的政策を取る. ¶a ***party*** *policy* 政党政策. ¶a ***passive*** *policy* 消極的政策. ¶form a ***permanent*** *policy* 百年の計を立てる. ¶a ***poor*** *policy* 貧弱な政策. ¶a ***praise-all*** *policy* 八方美人のやり口. ¶a ***progressive*** *policy* 進取的政策. ¶a ***public*** *policy* 公政策, 国是. ¶the ***safest*** *policy* to follow 最も安全に取れる方策. ¶a ***sagacious*** *policy* 賢明な政略. ¶follow a ***selfish*** *policy* in the interests of their own class 彼ら自身の階級のために利己的政策を取る. ¶the result of a ***settled*** and ***constructive*** *policy* 確固たる建設的政策の成果. ¶a ***short-sighted*** *policy* 近視眼的な政策. ¶a ***sound*** *policy* 健全な方針. ¶a '***spirited***' ***foreign*** *policy* 活気ある外交政策. ¶a ***straightforward*** and ***truthful*** *policy* 直さい誠実な方針. ¶a ***successful*** *policy* 成功した政策. ¶a ***suicidal*** *policy* 自

殺的政策. ¶a *sweeping policy* 概括的な方針. ¶a *tentative policy* 試験的方策. ¶it was the *uniform policy* of ... to ... ...するのが...の一貫した方針だった. ¶a *vacillating* and *inconsistent policy* ぐらつきやすい無定な政策. ¶a *weak-kneed policy* 腰抜け政策. ¶a *wise policy* 賢い政策 ‖ it is *wiser policy* to ... ...するのが一層賢明な政策だ. ¶a *wrong policy* 間違った方針.

Q² an *anti-inflation policy* 反インフレ政策. ¶*anti-Soviet policies* of the United States 米国の反ソ政策. ¶an *appeasement policy* 緩和政策. ¶the "*blood and iron policy* of the Iron Chancellor" 鉄血宰相(ビスマーク)の血と鉄の政策. ¶*business policy* 営業方針. ¶a *dog-in-the-manger policy* 意地悪政略. ¶a *food policy* 食料対策. ¶abandon her *free-trade policy* その国の自由貿易方針を放棄する. ¶a "*get tough*" *policy* 強硬策. ¶the Roosevelt "*good neighbor*" *policy* ルーズベルトの善隣方策. ¶its *governing policy* その管理方針. ¶the *Government policy* against inflation 政府のインフレ対策. ¶the *guiding policy* of a party 党の指導方針. ¶its "*hand-off*" *policy* toward China その中国に対する不干渉政策. ¶the British *imperialist policy* 英国の帝国主義政策. ¶an *intervention policy* 干渉政策. ¶follow a *laissez-faire policy* 自由放任策を採る. ¶a *long-range policy* 長期政策. ¶pursue a *middle-of-the-road policy* 中道政策を採る. ¶a *cheap money policy* 低金利政策. ¶a *must policy* for ... ...に対してぜひ採用しなければならない方針. ¶a *no tipping policy* ノー・チップ制. ¶a mild *occupation policy* 穏健な占領政策. ¶the *open-door policy* 門戸解放政策. ¶Russia's *obstructionist policy* ロシアの妨害政策. ¶a *party policy* 党の方針. ¶This is a most "*penny-wise and pound-foolish*" *policy* これは極端な一文惜しみの百知らず式方針である. ¶follow the *praise-all policy* 八方美人主義を取る. ¶follow the general line of *policy* developed by his *predecessor* 彼の先任者の採って来た方針の大綱を踏襲する. ¶*price policies* 物価諸政策. ¶*procrastination policy* to maneuver the negotiation on Britain's advantage 英国側の有利に交渉を動かす牛歩政策. ¶a *running policy* 継続政策. ¶the "*scorched earth*" *policy* of the Nationalist Government 国民政府の焦土政策. ¶a *shake-hand policy* toward ... ...に対する握手(親善)政策. ¶our *trade policy* toward China わが国の対中国貿易政策. ¶an "*unpartisan*" *foreign policy* 超党派的外交政策. ¶a "*wait and see*" *policy* 静観政策.

P it is *against* our *policy* to ... ...するのはわれわれの方針にもとる. ¶*from policy* 政策上.

P² the proper *policy for* Japan to pursue 日本が採るべき適当の政策 ‖ a *policy for* the regulation of prices 物価調節策. ¶the *policy of* fair play towards ... ...に対する公平な政策 ‖ the *policy of* segregation《米》黒人などに対する差別待遇 ‖ the *policy of* congregation《米》白・黒人の融合政策. ¶Japan's *policy towards* China 日本の中国政策.

(2) 保険証券, 保険契約.

V *effect* a life *policy* 生命保険をつける ‖ ¶*effect* a *policy* of insurance against all sea risk upon goods 全体の海損保険をつける. ¶*grant policy* at low rates 低率で保険証券を交付する(保険契約に応じる). ¶He *has* a *policy* in a life insurance company. 彼は生命保険にはいっている. ¶*issue policies* for educational purposes (marriage settlements) 教育(など)の保険証券を発行する. ¶*protect* one's *policy* by paying an extra premium 割増保険料を払って保険証券を保護する. ¶*surrender* one's *policy* for cash 生命保険で会社から金を借りる. ¶*take* a *policy* 保険を付ける. ¶*take out* a life-insurance *policy* in a company ある会社の生命保険にはいる. ¶*vitiate* a *policy* 保険証券を無効にする.

Q an *extended policy* 払込延期証券. ¶renew an *open policy*〘保険〙継続予定契約を更新する.【類】have an *open policy* of insurance. ¶a *paid-up policy* 払込済証券. ¶a *valued policy*〘保険〙確定保険証券.

Q² a *blanket policy* 総括保険証券. ¶an *endowment* [*insurance*] *policy* 養老保険証券. ¶a *fire policy* 火災保険証券. ¶a *floating policy*〘保険〙船名不詳保険証券. ¶an *instalment policy* 賦払証券. ¶sell a person an *insurance policy* その人を保険に加入させる ‖ take out an *insurance policy* on one's life 生命保険に加入する. ¶a *marine policy* 水上保険証. ¶a *time policy* 定期保険証券. ¶a *voyage policy*〘海保〙航行保険証券.

P *under* an insurance *policy* 保険証券により.

P² a *policy on* one's life (freights) 生命(など)保険証券.

policy-holder, *n.* 証券所有者.

Q² an *insurance policy-holder* 保険証所持者.

policy-maker, *n.* 政策立案者.

Q² a *wartime policy-maker* 戦時政策立案者.

polish, *n.* みがき; つや, 光沢.

V *admit* a good *polish* みがくとよいつやが出る. ¶*give* a good *polish* to ... ...によいつやをつける. ¶*put* a *polish* on ... ...のつやを出す. ¶The *polish* is *rubbed off*. つやがすれてなくなっている.

V² The *polish* has *worn out*. つやがすれてなくなった.

Q the *exquisite polish* of Stevenson's style スチーブンソンの文体の凝った洗練さ. ¶the *final polish* 仕上げのみがき.

Q² *boot* (=*shoe*) *polish* くつ墨. ¶*floor* (*stove*) *polish* 床(ストーブ)みがき. ¶*furniture polish* 家具用のつや出し. ¶*red fingernail polish* 紅入りつめみがきクリーム.

polish, *v.* みがく.

M² *polish off* one's work 仕事を仕上げる. ¶*polish* (=brush) *up* one's French 習得したフランス語にみがきをかける.【類】*polish up* the style (文体).

polished, *pa.* 優雅な.

M shoes *freshly polished* つやつやとみがかれたくつ.

P *polished in* manners あかぬけのした.

polisher, *n.* みがく人.

Q² a *diamond polisher* ダイヤみがき人.

polishing, *n.* 練磨.

V *do* much *polishing* of the ship's brass-work 船の真ちゅう金具を盛んにみがく. ¶he *received* his final *polishing* at the hands of ... 彼は...の手でその最後のみがきをかけられた.

polite, *a.* 優雅な, いんぎんな.

M be *prodigiously polite* to young ladies 若い婦人にはばかばかしく丁寧である. ¶*steely polite* 冷やかに丁重な.

P *polite in* one's manners 挙動の優雅な. ¶*polite to* the ladies 婦人にいんぎんな ‖ be *polite to* a fault いんぎんに過ぎる.

politeness, *n.* 礼儀, いんぎん.

V I *acknowledged* his *politeness* with a bow. 私はあの人の丁寧さに頭を下げた. ¶*Have* you no more *politeness* than that? そんなことをして失礼じゃないか. ‖ He *had* not the *politeness* to stand aside. 彼は無礼にもそばへ寄ってきた.

Q *excessive politeness* ばか丁寧. ¶They have only *formal politeness*. 彼らの丁寧は単に形式的だ. ¶a *frigid politeness* 冷やかな(義務一遍の)礼儀. ¶*hollow politeness* 真心のこもらない礼儀, 虚礼. ¶*meretricious politeness* いやに作った礼儀. ¶with *studied politeness* つとめていんぎんに. ¶*studious politeness* 念の入った礼儀.

P He said so, *for politeness*. 彼はお世辞にそう言った.【類】I lifted the *sake* cup to my lips *for politeness* (おつきあいに). ¶He is wanting *in politeness*. 彼は礼儀を欠いている. ¶After this exchange *of politenesses*, they conversed on various subjects. こんな風に一応あいさつが済んでから一同は色々な問題について話した. ‖ He is the pink *of politeness*. 彼はいんぎんの精華とも称すべきだ. ¶He says so *out of politeness*. 彼は礼儀上そう言うのだ. ¶treat one *with* studious *politeness* 念の入った丁寧さで(きわめていんぎんに)人を取扱う.

politician, *n.* 政治家, 政治屋.

Q an *adroit politician* 抜目のない政治家. ¶*amateur politicians* しろうと政治家. ¶a *budding politician* 売だしたばかりの政客. ¶a *cheap politician* くだらない政治屋. ¶an *eager politician* [ある目的に]熱心な政治家. ¶an *incorruptible politician* 廉潔の政治家. ¶a *keen politician* 頭の鋭い政治家. ¶*minor politicians* [政治界の]陣笠連. ¶a *professional politician* 職業政治家. ¶a *self-seeking politician* 利己主義の政治屋. ¶a *small politician* 小政治家. ¶a *time-serving politician* 日より見主義(御都合主義)の政治家. ¶an *unprincipled politician*=a demagogue 無主義の政治家. ¶a *wary politician* 抜目のない政治家.

Q² a *coffee-house* (=*pot-house*) *politician* 政界の陣笠; ごろつき政治屋. ¶a *middle-of-the-road politician* 中道政治家. ¶an *obscurantist politician* 反啓もう主義的政治家. ¶an *old-style politician* 旧式の政治家. ¶*parasite politicians* [...派の]小もの連.

P a knot *of politicians* 一群の政治家.

P² *politicians of* different schools 各派の政治家.

politics, *n.* [単·複同形] 政治, 政治問題; 政争; 政治論.
V *discuss politics* 政治を談じる. ¶He did not *enter politics* until he was forty-five. 彼は四十五歳までは政界にはいらなかった. ¶*leave* (=*let*) *politics* alone 政治に関係しない. ¶*play politics* 政治をもてあそぶ. ¶He has *taken up politics*. 彼は政治に関係し出した. ¶He likes to *talk politics*. 彼は好んで政治を談じる.
Q *clean politics* 明朗な政治. ¶*constructive politics* 建設的政治. ¶*dirty politics* 汚濁の政治. ¶the present entanglements of *European politics* 欧州政界現在の紛糾. ¶it is *good politics* for the party leader to ... 党指導者にとって...することは賢明な政治である. ¶*practical politics* 実際政治. ¶*realistic politics* 現実政治.
Q² *Diet politics* 議会政治. ¶a policy of "*hands off politics*"「無干渉政治」の政策. ¶*party politics* 政党政治. ¶modern *power politics* 現代の力の政治 ‖ in our world of *power politics* 力の政治のこの世界で ‖ the zone of conflicting *power politics* 力の衝突する地帯. ¶Russia's *pressure politics* ロシアの高圧政策. ¶*school politics* 学校の政策. ☞ politics の用法は次例による: (1) Politics *is* a good topic for discussion. (2) His politics (政治論) *were* a matter for great concern to his friends.
P the young men *in politics* 政治界に立つ青年たち ‖ engage *in politics* 政治に関係する ‖ go *in politics* 政界に入る ‖ meddle *in politics* 政治に干渉する.

polity, *n.* 国体.
Q the *national polity* of a country 一国の国体.

poll, *n.* 投票; 投票数; 投票所.
V *close polls* 投票を終る. ¶*conduct* a *poll* 世論調査を行う. ¶*take* a *poll* of members 全員の票決を取る ‖ The *poll* will be *taken* on Sunday. 投票は月曜に行われる. 【類】*take* a *poll* with reference to ...
Q a *heavy poll* おびただしい投票数. ¶a *nation-wide poll* 一般投票.
Q² a *Gallup poll* ギャラップ世論調査. ¶a nation-wide *public opinion poll* 全国世論調査. 【類】local *public opinion poll* / the *public opinion poll* conducted by the Jiji Press. ¶a *straw poll* 紙上投票(人気投票). ¶There was a *100 per cent poll*. 百パーセントの投票率だった.
P the exclusion of women *from* the *poll* 婦人の投票除外. ¶He was returned at the head *of* the *poll*. 彼は最高得票で選挙された. ‖ the closing *of* the *polls* 投票の締切. ¶go *to* the *poll* 投票所へ出かける.

poll, *v.* 投票する.
P *poll* (=vote) *for* (*against*) ... ...に賛成(反対)投票をする.

pollute, *v.* 汚染する.
P The water there was *polluted by* refuse from the factory. その辺の水は工場のかすで大いに汚染していた. 【類】The air frightfully *polluted by* radio-active fallouts (放射能ちり).

pollution, *n.* 汚染.
Q² *air pollution* by smoke and gases, dust and other impurities ばい煙, ガス, ほこり及びその他の不純物による空気の汚染. ¶*stream pollution* 流れの汚染.

polygamy, *n.* 一夫多妻.
P women *under polygamy* 一夫多妻制の下にある婦人.

polypus, *n.* 〖病理〗鼻たけ.
Q a *nasal polypus* 鼻たけ.

pomp, *n.* 偉観, 盛観.
P *in* great *pomp* 威儀堂々と. ¶*with* much (=great) *pomp* 堂々と, 花々しく. 【類】*with pomp* and splendor (けんらん).

pond, *n.* 池, 水たまり.
V *drain* (=*dry up or pump out*) a *pond* 池の排水をする. ¶The *pond* was *frozen* a foot thick. 池は一フィートの厚さに凍った. ¶*pump* a *pond dry* 池の水をポンプでくみ出す. ¶The *pond* was *walled* (=*hedged*) *in* by low hills. その池は低い丘に囲まれていた.
Q the sacred lotus flowers on the *great pond* near Ueno Park 上野公園付近の大池の神聖なはすの花.
Q² a *culture pond* 養魚池. ¶a *farm pond* 農園池. ¶a *preserve pond* 貯水池. ¶a *safe pond* 生洲(いけす). ¶a *winter pond* 囲い池(冬期).
P swim *in* a *pond* 池の中で泳ぐ. ¶The ice was thick *on* the *pond*. 池には厚く氷が張っていた. ‖ There were ducks and geese *on* the *pond*. 池にはあひるとが鳥がいた. ‖ skate *on* a *pond* 池でスケートする.

ponder, *v.* 考える.
M *ponder long* and *deeply* over it それを長時間とくと考える. ¶*ponder* this *well* このことをよく考える.
P *ponder on* reasons why ... ...の理由を熟考する. 【類】*ponder* deeply *on* some of the most spiritual aspects of religion. ¶*ponder over* a matter (question) 問題(など)を熟考する. 【類】*ponder over* the words. ¶*ponder upon* (=*on*) a momentous issue 重要問題を慎重に考える.

pontificate, *n.* 法王の在職期.
P *during* the *pontificate* of Sixtus IV シクスタス四世の在職期中.

pony, *n.* 小馬.
Q a *razor-backed pony* [やせて]背中のとがった小馬. ¶a *shaggy pony* 毛のもじゃもじゃした小馬.

pony, *v.* 清算する; 《米》とらの巻を使う.
M² It is time to *pony up* on that bill. その勘定を片づけてもいいころだ.
P² *pony for* the examination とらの巻で試験準備をする.

poodle, *n.* プードル, むく犬.
V *trim* [up] one's *poodle* むく犬の毛をきれいに刈る.
Q a *full-grown poodle* 成長したプードル(むく犬). ¶her *pet poodle* 彼女の愛犬プードル.

pooh-pooh, *v.* 軽べつする.
P *pooh-pooh at* ... ...を軽べつする, ...をやじる.

pool, *n.* 数人共同して出したかけ金.
V *take* the *pool* 出し合ったかけ金全部をかち得る.

pool, *n.* 水たまり; プール; 共同計算制; 自動車置場.
Q an *international pool* of atomic power 原子力の国際共同保有. ¶a *landscaped pool* 風景園内に造ったプール. ¶There were lots of tiny *muddy pools* found all over after the rain. 雨後あちこちに水たまりができた. ¶a *stagnant pool* よどんだ水たまり. ¶a *sylvan pool* 森の中の池.
Q² a *bathing pool* 水泳場(プール). ¶the *dollar pool* 〖商〗ドル共同計算制. ¶a *motor* (*truck*) *pool* 自動車(トラック)置場. ¶a *vehicle pool* 車両置場. ¶a *pyramid pool* 金字塔球戯(米国). ¶He has a *swimming pool* on his estate 彼の屋敷内にプールがある. ¶a *wading pool* [公園などにある]子供の水遊び場.

pooling, *n.* 貯水池.
Q A large dictionary represents a *progidious pooling* of erudition. 大きな辞書は巨大な知識の大成である.

poor, *n.* 貧者, 貧民.
V *relieve* the *poor* 貧民を救助する.
Q Dublin's *hungry poor* ダブリン市の飢えた貧民. ¶the *needy poor* 貧民. ¶the *newly poor* 新たに貧困に陥った人々. ¶the *worthy poor* 清貧に甘んじるりっぱな人たち.
P He was touched with pity *for* the *poor*. 彼は貧民をかわいそうだと思った. ‖ A bazaar was held *for* the *poor*. 貧民のために慈善市を催した. ¶for the benefit *of* the *poor* 貧民のために. ¶He ministers *to* the *poor*. 彼は貧民の世話をする.

poor, *a.* 貧乏な; あわれな.
M He is *as poor as a church mouse*. 彼は赤貧洗うがごとしだ. ¶be *notably poor* in ... ...はたしかにへただ.
P You will be *poorer by* that amount. 君はそれだけの金額を損するだろう. ¶Japan will be *poorer for* his death. 彼の死は日本の損失となるであろう. ¶*poor in* minerals 鉱物に乏しい ‖ He is *poor in* money, but rich in knowledge. 彼は金はないが知識は豊富だ. ‖ be *poor in* execution 不首尾である. 【類】*poor in* thought (language) / a conference *poor in* results=an unfruitful conference.
O become *poor* 貧乏になる. ¶a *poor* widow あわれな未亡人. 【類】The dog has sunk into the water in a moment. *Poor* thing!

pop, *n.* ぽん, ぱちっ[音].
V I have never tried before, but I'll *have* a *pop* ([colloq.]=an attempt) at it. やったことはないがやって見よう.
P *with* a *pop* ぽんと, ぱちっと. 【類】uncork a champagne bottle *with* a *pop* / The cork (コルク) came out *with* a *pop*.

pop, *v.* 不意に出す, または入れる.
M *pop out* a remark 突然口を出す ‖ his face *popped out*, very red, bellowing "..." 彼の顔がぬっと出て, 真赤な顔で「...」とどなった ‖ The surprise made her eyes *pop out*. 彼女は驚いて目をむいた.
M² He *popped* his head *in* at the door. 彼はひょっくり入口に頭を出した. ‖ the maidservant *popped in* on them with ... 下女が彼らのもとへひょっくり頭を出して ... と言った. ¶The children are always *popping in* and *out*. 子供らが始終出たりはいったりしている. ¶*pop off* 《俗》急に去る; 死ぬ. ¶*pop up* from nowhere どこからともなく現われる ‖

pop up and ***down*** every moment しょっちゅう出たり引込んだりする.

P *pop* ... ***into*** a box (pocket) ...を箱(など)にひょいと入れる.【類】*pop* a cherry ***into*** the mouth. ¶*pop* one's head ***out of*** the window 頭を窓からひょいと出す. ¶He *popped* the question ***to*** her. 彼は彼女に結婚を申込んだ. ¶*pop* a piece of paper ***under*** the tablecloth 食卓布の下に紙をそっと差込む.

pope, *n.* 法王.

Q He is a "***financial pope***". 彼はいわゆる金融界の法王だ.

pop-eyed, *pa.* 《米》出目の.

P He was *pop-eyed* ***with*** alarm. 彼はびっくり仰天した.【類】The professor was really *pop-eyed* ***with*** wonder.

populace, *n.* [団] 民衆, 大衆.

V ***benefit*** the *populace* 民衆を益する. ¶***excite*** the *populace* to riot and violence 民衆を扇動して乱暴を働かせる. ¶a quack-doctor ***haranguing*** the *populace* 大衆に向って熱弁をふるうやぶ医者.

Q the ***superstitious*** *populace* 迷信深い民衆.

P dramas ***of*** the *populace* 大衆向の劇.

popular, *a.* 人望のある, 人気のある.

M He is ***deservedly*** *popular*. 彼は評判だけのことはある. ¶become ***immensely*** *popular* with ... ...に非常に人気が出る. ¶be ***less*** *popular* at home than abroad 国内より国外で人気がある. ¶He is becoming ***more*** *popular* with the public than ever before. 彼は以前にも増して一般大衆の気受けがよくなって来た. ¶The book is becoming ***widely*** *popular*. その本はますます好評を得つつある.

P He is *popular* ***among*** the students. 彼は学生間に受けがよい.【類】He is *popular* ***among*** men, though not, perhaps, with ladies. ¶He is *popular* ***for*** his kindness. 彼は親切なので人望がある. ¶He is *popular* ***in*** the office. 彼は職場で人望がある. ¶He is very *popular* ***with*** the ladies. 彼は婦人に大層受けがよい.

popularity, *n.* 人気, 人望.

V ***achieve*** [a] *popularity* 人望を得る. ¶***acquire*** (=***attain***) [a] *popularity* 人望を得る.【類】***acquire*** great *popularity*. ¶***command*** *popularity* 人気を博する. ¶***court*** *popularity* 人望を得ようとする. ¶***deserve*** *popularity* 好評だけのことはある.【類】It will ***deserve*** the *popularity* which it speedily attained. ¶***destroy*** *popularity* 人望をめちゃめちゃにする. ¶***earn*** a *popularity* with boys 子供らに評判がよくなる. ¶***enhance*** the *popularity* of ... ...の人気を増す. ¶The book ***enjoyed*** great *popularity*. その本は大評判を取った. ¶***establish*** one's *popularity* その人気を樹立させる. ¶***forfeit*** one's *popularity* 人望を失う. ¶***gain*** much *popularity* [本など]大評判を取る.【類】***gain*** a general *popularity*. ¶***gauge*** the *popularity* from bald figures 数字だけでその評判(人気)を測定する. ¶The textbook ***had*** great *popularity*. その教科書は大評判を取った. ¶***heighten*** one's *popularity* その人気を高める. ¶***hurt*** one's *popularity* その人望を傷つける. ¶***increase*** one's *popularity* その人気を増す. ¶***keep*** one's personal *popularity* その人気を失わないようにする. ¶***lose*** its *popularity* その人気をなくする.【類】Dickens has not ***lost*** his *popularity* among the book collectors. ‖ It is fast ***losing*** *popularity* それは急速に人気を失いつつある. ¶***maintain*** its *popularity* until ... ...までその人気をもち続ける. ¶***monopolize*** *popularity* 人気をさらう. ¶The book ***obtained*** great *popularity*. その本は大評判を取った. ¶it ***owes*** its *popularity* to the fact that ... その人気は...の事実に帰すべきである. ¶***receive*** the *popularity* of ... ...の人望を盛り返す. ¶***regain*** *popularity* 人気を回復する. ¶Do you think the historical novel will ***retain*** its *popularity?* その歴史小説は長く愛読されるでしょうか. ¶can not ***rival*** the *popularity* of ... ...の人気にはかなわない. ¶***secure*** *popularity* 人望を得る. ¶he has somewhat ***worn out*** his *popularity* by ... 彼は...によってやや人気をなくした. ¶***win*** *popularity* 好評を博す.【類】He ***won*** great *popularity* in his art.

V² His *popularity* is ***descending*** rapidly. 彼の人気は急速に減退している. ¶Her *popularity* steadily ***drooped.*** 彼女の人気はますます落ちた. ¶His *popularity* with the students has been ***increasing*** year by year. 彼の学生間の人気は年一年と加わりつつある. ¶Its *popularity* is ***waning*** (=***declining***). その人気は落ちつつある.

Q Smiles' Self-Help achieved ***amazing*** *popularity* all over the world. スマイルズの自助論は世界中いたる所で驚くべき評判を取った. ¶a ***brief*** *popularity* 暫時の人気. ¶***cheap*** *popularity* 安っぽい人気, 場当り. ¶enjoy ***considerable*** *popularity* 非常な人気を取る. ¶He enjoys a greatly ***enhanced*** *popularity*. 彼は非常に人望が高まった. ¶***enormous*** *popularity* 大評判. ¶an ***ephemeral*** *popularity* 暫時の(はかない)人気. ¶It had an ***extensive*** *popularity* among American readers. それは米国の読者に広く人気があった. ¶He has been acquiring ***extraordinary*** *popularity*. 彼は非常な人気を博しつつあった. ¶a ***fair,*** and not a ***meretricious*** *popularity* 俗悪な人気ではなく着実な人望. ¶win ***general*** *popularity* 一般の人気を取る. ¶It helps to increase his already ***great*** *popularity*. それは今までの高い名声をさらに高めるのに役立つ. ¶The author is still in ***high*** *popularity*. その著作家は依然人気が高い. ¶The music hall enjoys an ***immense*** *popularity*. その寄席は大評判を取っている.【類】The story achieved ***immense*** *popularity*. ¶These books achieved ***much*** *popularity*. これらの作品はすこぶる好評だった. ¶win a ***nation-wide*** *popularity* 全国的人気を得る. ¶No wonder it has won such an ***overwhelming*** *popularity*. かく圧倒的な人気を取ったのももっともなことだ. ¶he enjoyed ***such*** a *popularity* that ... 彼は...ほどの人望を得た. ¶A ***tremendous*** *popularity* has been earned by this machine. この機械は恐ろしい人気を取った. ¶It enjoyed ***unbroken*** *popularity* for many years. それは多年続いて人気があった. ¶show signs of ***waning*** *popularity* 人気の傾きかけた徴候を示す. ¶achieve ***wide[-spread]*** *popularity* as ... ...として一般に好評を博する. ¶the ***world-wide*** *popularity* of the motion picture 映画の世界的人気.

Q² enjoy a mere ***mushroom*** *popularity* ほんの一時の人気があるに過ぎない.

P decline ***in*** *popularity* 人気が衰える ‖ It will probably go on forever undiminished ***in*** *popularity*. 恐らくその人気はこのまま落ちずに永久に続くだろう. ¶the secret ***of*** his *popularity* 彼の人気の秘訣.

P² it has lost none of its *popularity* ***as*** ... それは...としての名声を少しも落していない.

populate, *v.* 民を住まわせる, 植民する.

M a ***densely*** (***sparsely***) *populated* district 人口ちゅう密(希薄)な地方.【類】Japan is ***densely*** *populated* in a limited space of land. ¶***thinly*** (***thickly***) *populated* 人口希薄(ちゅう密)な.

P *populated* ***by*** some 150,000 people 約十五万の住民がある. ¶*populated* ***with*** immigrants 移入民が住んでいる.

population, *n.* 人口, 住民数; [団] ある土地の住民.

V ***arouse*** the *population* against ... 民衆の...反対を激成する. ¶it ***comprises*** a *population* of ... そこには...の人口がある. ¶New York City ***contains*** 7,000,000 *population*. ニューヨーク市は七百万の人口を有する.【類】Chicago city ***contains*** (=has) a *population* of ... ¶***deplete*** a *population* 人口を減少させる. ¶***disperse*** the *population* 人口を疎開させる. ¶***gain*** *population* (都市など)人口がふえる. ¶Honolulu ***has*** a *population* of 60,000 souls. ホノルルは六万の人口を有する.【類】The City of London ***has*** a small night *population* (夜間人口). ¶The country is ***losing*** *population*. その国の人口は段々減る. ¶the heterogeneous mass of human beings who ***make up*** the *population* of London ロンドンの人口を組成している種々雑多な人間の集団. ¶the city ***reached*** a *population* of ... 同市の人口は...に達した. ¶vegetable gardens to ***supply*** the neighboring *population* 付近の住民に供給する野菜畑. ¶***swell*** the *population* of ... ...の人口を膨張させる.

V² The *population* will ***dwindle*** dangerously. 人口が危険な程度まで減少するであろう. ¶The *population* ***grows.*** 人口が増加する. ¶The *population* ***poured out*** to welcome him. 彼を歓迎する人が押し寄せた. ¶*Population* ***remains*** stationary (=unchanged). 人口は動かない(変らない). ¶*Population* ***sinks*** rapidly. 人口がじん速に減る.

Q the ***agrarian*** *population* of Ireland アイルランドの農民人口. ¶***British*** *population* 英国の人口. ¶Shanghai has a ***cosmopolitan*** *population*. 上海の住民は全世界の人からなっている. ¶a ***cultured*** *population* インテリ階級. ¶the ***educated*** *populations* of Japan and China 日本及び中国の知識階級. ¶send its ***excess*** *population* to ... その過剰人口を...に送り出す. ¶***fallible rustic*** *populations* だまされ

やすいいなかの人々. ¶the *farming population* [集団的に]農民. ¶the *feminine* (＝female) *population* 女の住民. ¶the *foreign population* of New York ニューヨーク在住の外国人. 【類】San Francisco has a fairly large *foreign population*. ¶The United States has the largest proportions of *foreign-born population*. 米国は最大の外国生れの人口を擁している. ¶a *huge population* ばく大な人口. ¶*indigenous population* 土着の人民. ¶a *laboring population* 労働者. ¶It has a large proportion of *foreign born population* そこには外国系の人が大分いる. ¶The resort this year has a *larger population* than any previous year. その(軽井沢などの)行楽地は今年は例年よりは人の入りが多い. ¶the *male* (*female*) *population* 男(女)子の人口. ¶*motoring population* 自動車利用人口. ¶an outlet for her *overflowing population* その国の過剰人口のはけ口. ¶the town has a *permanent population* of ... その町の常住者人口は...である. ¶the *reading population* 読者層. ¶*redundant population* of a large city 大都市の過剰人口. ¶the *registered population* 登録した人口. ¶the *resident population* of a city 都市の居住人口. ¶the migration of the *rural population* 地方人の移住. ¶maintain a *stationary population* 固定人口を持っている. ¶*surplus population* 過剰人口. ¶a *teeming population* ちゅう密な人口. ¶a *thin population* 希薄な人口. ¶a *thinning* (*thickening*) *population* 減少(増加)しつつある人口. ¶a great city of *three million population* 人口三百万の大都市. ¶concentrate *urban population* 人を都市に集中する. ¶the *vast population* of China 中国のばく大な人口. ¶*visiting population* 一時的在住者たち. ¶the *whole population* came out to see ... 町中の人が...を見に出た. ¶American cities of *60* to *70 thousand population*. 六万から七万の人口を有するアメリカの諸都市.

Q² Veterans represent about half the *campus population* (＝a student body) 帰還軍人が全学生数の約半分を占める. ¶the remarkable growth of *city population* 都市人口の驚くべき増加. ¶the *day* (*night*) *population* of a metropolis 首都の昼(夜)間人口. ¶most of the *elementary school population* from six to twelve of age 六歳から十二歳の小学児童の大部分. ¶the *farm* (＝*farming*) *population* 農民人口. ¶a *floating population* 浮動人口. 【類】a huge *floating population* in London in search of trade, excitement or amusement. ¶the *horse population* 馬匹の数. ¶a *hospital population* 入院患者[数]. ¶the *mass population* 一般大衆. ¶*non-farm population* 非農民人口. ¶*overflow population* from a crowded country 人口の多い国からあふれ出た人口. ¶a *polyglot population* 色々な言語の混交した人々. ¶the *prison population* 囚人の総数. ¶a *producing* (*consuming*) *population* 生産(消費)人口. ¶the *student population* of the urban district 市区の学生人口. ¶the *working population* of Japan 日本の労働者. 【類】the density of the *working population* in the heart of the city.

P growth *in population* 人口の増加. 【類】diminish (increase) *in population*. ¶congestion *of population* 人口過剰. 【類】minute towns *of* less than two thousand *population* / a city *of* 50,000 or more *population* / places *of* 5,000 *population* ‖ the number *of* the *population* 住民数 ‖ per head *of population* 人口一人当り. ¶America, *with* a *population* of 160,000,000 一億六千万の人口を有するアメリカ. 【類】the British Empire *with* its huge *population* of 450,000,000 / New York City *with* its 8,000,000 *population*.

P² the *population of* asylums 養育院在住者.

porch, *n*. 玄関; ((米)) ベランダ.

V He *paced* the back *porch* slowly. 彼は裏手の入口をゆっくり歩いた.

Q a *front* (*side*) *porch* 表(横)玄関.

Q² a *sun* (＝*sunny*) *porch* ((米)) 日のよく当る縁側(ベランダ).

porcelain, *n*. 磁器.

Q² *egg-shell porcelain* 薄手の磁器. ¶the *Kutani porcelain* 九谷焼.

pore, *v*. たん読する; 沈思する.

P *pore over* (＝*on*) a book 本を読みふける. 【類】a tradesman *poring over* his accounts. ¶*pore upon* (＝*at*) one's new scheme その新企画をじっと考える.

pork, *n*. 豚肉.

Q *pickled pork* 塩豚. ¶*smoke-cured pork* くん製豚.

Q² *mess pork* 極上豚肉(軍艦納入用の豚肉). ¶*roast pork* 焼豚.

porker, *n*. 食用豚.

Q *sleek unwieldy porkers* すべすべして扱いにくい食用豚.

porpoise, *n*. いるか.

P a school *of porpoises* 一群のいるか.

porridge, *n*. かゆ.

P The peasant thrives *on porridge*. 百姓はかゆ食で結構丈夫だ.

port, *n*. 港.

V *close* the *ports* 鎖港する. ¶*clear* a *port* 出港する. ¶*enter* [a] *port* 入港する. ¶*frequent* a *port* 港をしばしば訪れる. ¶Turning your back on this mountain, you *have* a *port* before you. この山に背を向けると港が目の前にある. ¶*leave* [a] *port* 出港する. ¶*make* [a] *port* 入港する; 寄港する ‖ the ship has no *port* to *make* between ... その船は...間は寄港しない. ¶*open* a *port* 開港する. ¶*reach port* 着港する. ¶*shut* the *ports* of the country against the commerce of nearly all the civilized world ほとんどすべての文明国の通商に反対してその国の諸港を閉鎖する.

Q a *central port* 主要港. ¶a *closed* (an *open*) *port* 不開(開)港場. ¶a *commercial port* 商業港. ¶a *domestic port* 国内港. ¶an *ice-free* (＝a *non-freezing*) *port* 不凍港. ¶an *infected port* 伝染病流行港. ¶the *intended port* of destination 到着目的港, 仕向港. ¶an *intermediate port* 中継港. ¶a *mercantile port* 商港. ¶a *military port* 軍港. ¶*naval port* 軍港. ¶an *open port* 開港場. ¶the *premier port* in the world for the shipment of coal 石炭積出し港として世界第一の港. ¶It is a *safe port* for vessels of any size. それはどんな大きさの船にも安全な港である. ¶a well *sheltered port* 十分風波がしのげる港.

Q² a *coaling port* 石炭積込港. ¶an unannounced (＝undisclosed *or* unnamed) West *Coast port* 西海岸の○○港. ¶an Atlantic *cotton port* 大西洋岸の綿花積出し港. ¶a *deep-water port* 深海港. ¶at the *departing port* 出帆港で. ¶an *export* (*import*) 輸出(入)港. ¶at *home port* 本籍港で. 【類】her *English home port* / her *home port* of Southampton ‖ The captain made his last *home port*. [引退する]船長は最後の帰港をした. ¶a *loading port* 積出し港. ¶Baku, the great *naphtha port* 大石油港バクー. ¶*Pacific ports* 太平洋岸諸港. ¶a *rice port* 米積込港. ¶New Castle is a *river port*. ニューカッスルは河港である. ¶a *salt-water port* 塩水港. ¶a *shipping port* 船積港. ¶a *trading port* 商港. ¶a *transshipment port* 貨物積換港. ¶Hakodate is the most northerly of the old *treaty ports* of Japan. 函館は日本の最北部にある旧条約港の一つである. ¶a *warm-water port* on the Pacific 太平洋岸の不凍港. ¶a *winter port* for the fleet. その艦隊の越冬避難港.

P *at* the Japanese *port* of Yokohama 日本の横浜港で ‖ *at* home *ports* 母港で ‖ *at ports* of discharge 荷揚港で. 【類】enter the country *at ports* of the eastern seaboard ‖ make a call *at* a *port* 寄港する. ¶vessels *in port* 入港中の船舶 ‖ The steamer has arrived *in port*. その汽船が入港した. ¶The ship is coming *into port*. 船が入港する所だ. ‖ get *into port* 入港する ‖ put *into port* 入港する, 寄港する ‖ return *into port* 帰港する.

P² a *port for* foreign trade 外国貿易港. ¶a *port of* arrival 到着港 ‖ a *port of* call 寄港地 ‖ a *port of* coaling 石炭積込港 ‖ a *port of* delivery (＝discharge) 荷卸港 ‖ a *port of* departure 発航地 ‖ a *port of* destination 仕向け港 ‖ a *port of* refuge (＝distress) 避難港 ‖ a *port of* entry 通関港 ‖ a *port of* sailing 発航地 ‖ a *port of* loading (unloading) 積込(荷卸)港 ‖ a *port of* registry 船籍港. 【類】The ship is at her *port of* registry.

port, *n*. 左げん.

Q² a *bow* (*stern*) *port* 船首(船尾)荷役口.

P list *to port* 左げんに傾く.

portal, *n*. 戸口, 正門.

P stand *at* the *portals* of a palace 宮殿の門に立つ ‖ perish *at* the *portals* of safety もう一息で安全という所で死ぬ.

porter, *n*. 門番; 荷物運搬人(ポーター).

Q² a *door porter* ドアマン, 門番. ¶a *hotel porter* ホテルのポーター. ¶a [*railway*] *station porter* 赤帽.

portfolio, *n*. 折かばん; 国務大臣の職.

V *accept* an important *portfolio* in the Chinese Government 中国政府で重要な職につく. ¶*enrich* one's *portfolio* with ... ...で自分の懐中を肥やす. ¶*hold* the additional *portfolio* of Foreign Affairs 外務大臣を兼ねる ‖ the Minister *holding* the single *portfolio* of Home Affairs 専任内務大臣. ¶He has *received* the *portfolio* of war. 彼は陸軍

大臣に就任した. ¶He has *resigned* the *portfolio* of education. 彼は文部大臣の職を辞した.

Q² hold a ***Cabinet portfolio*** 閣僚の地位にある. ¶assume the ***Home*** (***Foreign***) ***Affairs portfolio*** 内(外)務大臣に就任する.

P a minister ***without portfolio*** 無任所大臣.

P² the *portfolio* ***of*** Justice 司法大臣の職.

portion, *n.* 部分; 若干; 配当分.

V If slavery is a disgrace, then the slave-holder must ***bear*** his full *portion* of obloquy. どれいの身分が恥とすればどれい所有者もその恥を多分に分担しなければならない. ¶We've ***had*** two *portions* of beefsteak and curry and rice. 僕らはビフテキとライスカレーを二人前食べた. ¶she ***left*** the major *portion* of her estate to ... 彼女は財産の大部分を...に残した.

Q a ***considerable portion*** of his estate 彼の財産の相当部分. ¶the ***damaged portion*** of ... ...の破損部分. ¶***edible portion*** 食べられる部分. ¶in ***equal portions*** 同じ分量で. ¶the ***fairer portion*** of the spectators 婦人の見物人たち. ¶the ***feminine portion*** of the community その社会の一部分たる女性たち. ¶a ***goodly portion*** 相当の部分. ¶A ***great portion*** of the crop has been destroyed by storms. 大量の作物はあらしで被害を受けた. ¶***habitable portions*** of the globe 地球上の居住できる部分. ¶a ***half portion*** 半量. ¶*Portions* are ***large***. [食物など]もりが良い. ‖a ***large portion*** of the population 住民の大部分. ¶the ***major portion*** of these writers are ... この執筆者の大部分は...である. ¶***one portion*** of roast beef 一人前のロースト・ビーフ. ¶at a ***previous portion*** of our essay, we stated that ... この論文の前段でわれわれは...と述べた. ¶the ***profound portion*** of a record 奥書. ¶the ***residential portions*** of London ロンドンの住宅区域. ¶the ***serious portion*** of French youth まじめなフランス青年たち. ¶a ***single portion*** of a liquid (=drink) 飲物一回分. ¶deal out in ***small portions*** 小わけして分配する ‖during a very ***small portion*** of the year 一年のごくわずかの期間中. ¶the ***sound portion*** 完全な部分. ¶the ***thinking portion*** of the community 社会の思慮ある階層. ¶the ***tidal portion*** of the Thames テムズ河の中で潮の干満する部分. ¶the ***undocumented portion*** of a national history 国民歴史の文献を欠く部分. ¶The ***unexecuted portion*** of the order is now cancelled. 注文の不調達の分は取消しになった.

Q² a ***marriage portion*** 持参財産, 持参金.

P He lived in the Orient ***for*** a great *portion* of his life. 彼は生がいの大半を東洋で暮した. ¶deal out ***in*** equal *portions* 同じ分量に分ける ‖***in*** small *portions* 少しずつ ‖The book is to be sold ***in*** two *portions*. その本は二冊一組にして売る. ¶They may be roughly divided ***into*** three *portions*. それは大体三分することができる.

P² A *portion* ***of*** the cargo was jettisoned. 船荷の一部は投荷された(暴風雨などのため).

portion, *v.* 分配する.

P they were *portioned* ***by*** lot among ... それは...の間にくじで分けた.

portrait, *n.* 肖像, 画像; 描写.

V I am going to ***have*** my *portrait* ***taken***. 僕の肖像を描いてもらおうと思っている. ¶***make*** a *portrait* with crayon クレヨンで肖像画を描く. ¶These biographies are *portraits* ***sketched*** with the deft assured hand of the practised artist. これらの伝記はあのしっかりした腕のある達筆家が書いた人物評である. ¶He ***takes*** *portraits* correctly. 彼は肖像を正確に描く.

V² An excellent *portrait* of ... ***hangs*** upon the walls of his study. ...の見事な肖像が彼の書斎の壁上にかけてある.

Q ***autographed portraits*** 自筆署名のある(写真などの)肖像画. ¶a ***detailed portrait*** 細密人物画. ¶one of the very ***latest portraits*** taken of ... ...の最近の肖像の一つ. ¶a ***life-like portrait*** 実物そのままの肖像. ¶a ***photographic portrait*** 肖像写真. ¶a ***self portrait*** 自画像. ¶an ***unretouched portrait*** 手加減のしてない肖像画; 赤裸々な人物評.

Q² ***bas-relief portraits*** 薄肉彫(ﾚﾘｰﾌ)の肖像. ¶a ***full-length portrait*** 全身像. ¶a ***life-size portrait*** 等身大の肖像. ¶An ***oil portrait*** of Queen Victoria adorns the wall. ビクトリア女王の肖像画が壁を飾っている.

P I am sitting ***for*** my *portrait*. 私は肖像を描いてもらっているところだ. ¶This is a *portrait* ***from*** life. これは人物の写生だ.

P² a fine *portrait* ***in*** oils りっぱな油絵. ¶She is the very *portrait* (=picture) ***of*** her mother. 彼女はお母さんそっくりだ.

portraiture, *n.* 描写.

Q a ***vivid*** and ***life-like portraiture*** of ... ...の生けるがごとき躍如たる描写.

portray, *v.* 描く, 描写する; 《米》【劇】演じる.

M ***faithfully portray*** our thoughts われわれの思想を忠実に描く. ¶portray a character ***poorly*** (***brilliantly***) 役をへたに(すばらしく)演じる.

P To *portray* the scene ***in*** words is impossible. この風景を言葉で述べることは不可能だ. ‖*portray* ... ***in*** the forthcoming film "..." ...という近々上映の映画で...の役を勤める. ¶The author *portrays* his characters ***to*** the life. 作者はその人物を如実に描いている.

portrayal, *n.* 描写.

Q² be skill in ***character portrayal*** 性格描写に巧みである.

P be not intended ***as*** a *portrayal* of factual events 実際の事件を取扱うのがその目的ではない.

pose, *n.* 姿勢.

V ***make*** a *pose* しなを作る.

Q make an ***affected pose*** 気取る. ¶His liberalism is a ***mere pose***. 彼の自由主義は見せかけだ.

pose, *v.* 姿勢を作る, ポーズをする, らしく見せる; [問題を]提起する.

P *pose* a serious question ***among*** ... ...の間に重要問題を投げる. ¶*pose* ***as*** a model for ... ...のモデルとしてポーズする ‖*pose* ***as*** a critic (reformer, sentimentalist, authority) 批評家(など)らしく構える ‖*pose* ***as*** a millionaire 大尽風を吹かせる ‖*pose* ***as*** a benefactor to ... ...に恩をきせる. 【類】*posing* ***as*** (=pretend to be) a gas-meter inspector (ガスメートルの検査員), a thief gained access to the home of ... ¶He kindly *posed* ***for*** the photographs which illustrate this article. 彼はこの文のさし絵になっている彼の写真をとらして下さった. 【類】*pose* ***for*** an artist / *pose* ***for*** the motion pictures / *pose* an hour ***for*** one's portrait.

O *pose* as if he were a great man えらそうに構える.

position, *n.* 位置; 姿勢, 態度; 陣地; 地位; 立場.

V ***abuse*** one's *position* その地位(職権)を濫用する. ¶***accept*** the *position* of ... ...のいすを引受ける. 【類】Much against his will (しぶしぶ) he ***accepted*** the *position*. / He ***accepted*** the *position* under President McKinley as Secretary of War. 【類】She ***accepted*** her *position* (=the situation) gaily enough. ¶***achieve*** a *position* of primacy for ... ...に対して首位を占める. ¶***acquire*** a *position* as a poet 詩人としての地位を獲得する. ¶***aggrandize*** the political *position* of a country 一国の政治上の地位を強大にする. ¶It quite ***altered*** the *position* of Japan in international affairs. そのために国際的関係における日本の地位が全然一変した. ¶***arrange*** the *position* of her hat 彼女の帽子の位置を整える. ¶***assume*** *positions* of leadership and of command 指導者の地位につく. 【類】***assume*** the *position* of "Attention" (不動の姿勢). ¶***attain positions*** of consequence 重要な地位を獲得する. 【類】She has ***attained*** a *position* of equality with other nations. ¶***better*** (=improve) one's *position* その地位を向上させる. ¶***capture*** enemy *positions* 敵の陣地を攻略する. ¶They ***carried*** the *position* by assault. 彼らは強襲によって陣地を占領した. ¶***change positions*** 主客転倒する. ¶Wealth ***commands position***. 金で地位が自由になる. ¶hold a conference to ***consider*** the *position* 時局討議のために会議を開く. ¶England has ***consolidated*** her *position* in the eyes of the world. 英国は世界の目から見てその地位が強固になった. ¶***create*** for oneself a lofty *position* 独力で高い地位を築き上げる. ¶***defend*** one's *position* against ... ...に対して自己の立場を弁護する. 【類】trying to ***defend*** his *position*, he said that ... / excitedly ***defend*** one's country's *position*. ¶***define*** one's *position* 自己の立場を明確にする. ¶***determine*** its true *position* その真の立場を定める. ¶***elucidate*** the *position* その立場をはきっりさせる. ¶It will ***enhance*** the *position* which he already holds in the eyes of the world. それが社会からすでに認められている彼の地位を一そう高めることになろう. ¶***explain*** the *position* その立場を説明する. ¶***fill*** a *position* honestly and well 職を正直にりっぱに勤める. 【類】He worthily ***filled*** the *position*. / ***fill positions*** of trust (=responsibility) (責任ある地位). ¶***find*** good *positions* 好い勤め口

を捜す. ¶***gain*** a *position* of influence 有力な地位を得る. ¶I ***got*** a *position* at $8 a week. 一週八ドルの職を得た. ¶It has ***given*** the company a leading *position* among the steel workers of the world. そのために同会社は世界製鋼業者間に重要な地位をかち得た. ¶He ***has*** wealth and social *position.* 彼には富と社会的地位がある. ¶He ***holds*** a high official *position.* あの方は顕職についている. ‖ ***hold*** a *position* with a company 会社に務める. 【類】***hold*** a government *position* / It ***holds*** a high *position* among authoritative works. / She ***held*** a *position* as governess. / He ***held*** the *position* for a quarter of a century. / he formerly ***held*** the *position* of ... / That *position* he now very ably ***holds.*** / The Almanach Hachette ***holds*** in France the *position* that "Whitaker's Almanac" holds in England. ‖ The word has recently been revived and seems likely to ***hold*** its *position.* その語は最近復活したがおそらく引続き長く使用されるであろう. ¶***imperil*** our industrial *position* わが工業界を危地に陥れる. ¶***improve*** the *position* of the staff by increase of salary 増給によって部員の地位を向上させる. ¶***keep*** one's *position* やめさせられないでいる. ¶***look*** the *position* steadily in the face 形勢をじっと正面から見る. ¶***lose*** one's *position* 職(立場)を失う. 【類】Otherwise you will ***lose*** the *position* you now hold. ¶***maintain*** a *position* of impartiality 公平の立場を持続する. 【類】the *position* Waseda ***maintains*** among universities of this country. ¶an author who has ***made*** a *position* and can count on a public 地位を確立し読者層の支持を当てにすることができる作家. ¶***obtain*** a *position* in the postal service 郵便局に就職する. ¶***occupy*** a good *position* in society 社会にりっぱな地位を占める. 【類】He ***occupied*** the *position* in a worthy manner. / It ***occupies*** a high *position* among like institutions in that country. / Her husband ***occupies*** a good social *position.* / ***occupy*** a responsible *position* in a business house (商館) / ***occupy*** a prominent *position* in the public eye (公衆の目から見て) / He ***occupied*** a high *position* in the civil service (文官勤務) / the *position* which the book ***occupies*** in public esteem. ¶***possess*** education and social *position* 学歴と社会的地位とをもっている. ¶***preserve*** a proud *position* 光栄ある地位を維持する. ¶***procure*** a *position* for ... ...のためにある位置に世話をする. ¶***raise*** one's *position* その地位を向上させる. 【類】distinctly ***raised*** the *position* of the author among the poets of the day. ¶***realizing*** the dreadful *position* in which I was placed 私のおった恐ろしい地位を自覚して. ¶completely ***recast*** its *position* その根本的改造をやる. ¶He ***receives*** a small salaried *position* in the firm. 彼はその商会で少しばかりの俸給をもらっている. ¶He ***recovered*** the *position* he had lost. 彼は前に失った地位を回復した. ¶***regain*** the *position* in public favor 好評を取り戻す. ¶***relinquish*** the *position* of general manager of ... ...の総支配人の職を辞する. 【類】***relinquish*** his *position* as ... ¶***resign*** one's *position* in a firm 商会の職を辞する. 【類】***resign*** the *position* of ... to take up Red Cross work (赤十字の事業) / ***resign*** one's *position* after a tenure (在職) of two years / ***resign*** [from] his *position* on the board of directors (理事の職). ¶***resume*** its original *position* 旧態に復する. ¶He ***retained*** that *position* till his death. 彼は死ぬまでその職についていた. ¶Now the *position* is ***reversed.*** 今ではその地位が転倒した. ¶***secure*** the *position* one holds 現在の地位を安全にする. 【類】His discoveries were of such a nature as to ***secure*** for him an enviable *position* in "Who's Who in archaeology" (考古学者名簿). ¶***see*** the *position* as it really stands 局面の真相を見て取る. ¶***seek*** a responsible *position* 責任ある地位を求める. ¶***shift*** one's *position* to ... ...に席を移す. ¶he ***took*** the *position* that ... 彼は...という立場を取った. 【類】***take*** the *position* of chairman of the Board of Directors of the company (取締役会長) / ***take*** a *position* as a barmaid (バーの女給) / Women have not often ***taken*** a very high *position* on Parnassus. ‖ ***take up*** their *positions* それぞれ位置につく ‖ tree-frogs scarcely to be distinguished from the leaves on which they have ***taken up*** their *position* 止っている葉っぱとほとんど区別のつかない雨がえる. 【類】There a large mass of troops are to be seen ***taking up*** *position.* / He ***took up*** his *position* on the rostrum amidst a round of applause (かっさいを浴びて). / ***take up*** a *position* of hostility (反抗的態度). ¶He ***threw up*** a good *position* in the office. 彼は勤めていた社の好地位を放棄した. ¶***weaken*** the *position* of the great journal その大新聞の地位を弱める. ¶He ***won*** high *position* at the bar. 彼は弁護士社会で高い地位を占めた. 【類】They ***won*** high *positions* in the Government. ¶***wrestle*** from ... the premier *position* ...から首位の栄冠を奪う. 「しない.

v² The *position* of affairs has not ***improved.*** 局面が好転

Q He is in a more ***advantageous*** *position* for it. 彼はそれには一層有利な地位にある. ¶an ***allotted*** *position* 割当てられた地位. ¶be left in an ***ambiguous*** *position* あいまいな立場におかれる. ¶assume an ***antagonistic*** or ***hostile*** *position* towards ... ...に対して反抗または敵対的態度を取る. ¶an ***attractive*** *position* 魅力のある職場. ¶He occupies an ***authoritative*** *position* as critic. 彼は批評家としての権威ある地位を占めている. ¶He is placed in a very ***awkward*** *position.* 彼はきわめて苦しい立場にある. ¶The wreck is now in a ***bad*** *position* その難破船は今悪い状態におかれている. ¶***better paying*** *positions* もっと給料の高い地位. ¶the ***biped*** (=***erect***) *position* 両足直立の姿勢. ¶occupy a ***central*** *position* 中央の位置を占める. ¶"***classified***" *positions* 各種分類職場. ¶take a ***commanding*** *position* in international commerce 国際貿易の牛耳をとる ‖ be in a ***commanding*** *position* 指導の地位にある. 【類】raise the empire to a ***commanding*** *position* among other nations. ¶ruin one's ***commercial*** *position* その商人としての地位を棒に振る. ¶***corporate*** *positions* 法人その他の団体における地位. ¶The *position* is very ***critical.*** 形勢はきわめて重大だ. ¶be in a ***corresponding*** *position* to ... ...に相当する地位にある. ¶Women occupy a ***degraded*** *position* among the Turks. トルコ人の間では婦人は劣等な地位を占めている. ¶He is in a ***delicate*** *position.* 彼はやりにくい立場にある. ¶a ***difficult*** *position* 難局. ¶occupy a ***distinguished*** *position* in society 社会で高い地位を占める. ¶hold a ***dominant*** *position* in the world 社会で優位を占める. 【類】It occupies a ***dominant*** *position* in the industry (産業). ¶a ***dominating*** *position* 要害の地; 優位. ¶an ***elevated*** *position* 高台; 高位. ¶an ***embarrassing*** *position* やっかいな立場. ¶an ***entrenched*** *position* ざんごう線で固めた陣地. ¶hold an ***enviable*** *position* in ... ...にうらやむべき地位を占めている. 【類】place a person in an ***enviable*** *position* of being ... ¶those who occupy these ***exalted*** *positions* これらの高貴な地位を占める人々. ¶an ***excellent*** *position* 絶好の地位. ¶hold an ***executive*** *position* 執行部(経営者)の地位にある ‖ He is on the ***executive*** *position.* 彼は幹部(部長級)である. ¶a ***favorable*** *position* 有利な地位. ¶***Federal*** (***State***) *positions* 《米》連邦(州)政府の官吏の地位. ¶***fiduciary*** *positions* 責任ある地位. ¶The ***financial*** *position* of the company is improving. 会社の財政状態は良い方に向いている. 【類】improve the ***financial*** *position* of ... / be in better ***financial*** *positions* / The firm was then in a weak ***financial*** *position.* ¶a ***first-class*** *position* 一等の地位. ¶occupy the ***foremost*** *position* in its class その部類中で首位を占める. 【類】maintain the ***foremost*** *position* amongst ... ¶a ***forlorn*** *position* 孤立状態. ¶owing to her geographical *position* その国の地理的状態のために. ¶hold a ***good*** *position* 良い地位を占める. 【類】a merchant (young man) in a ***good*** *position.* ¶of ***good social*** *position* 社会的に地位のある. ¶a ***good strategic*** *position* 要害堅固な地点. ¶its ***governmental*** *position* その政府の事業という立場. ¶a ***graceful*** *position* 端正な姿勢. ¶a person of ***high*** *position* 高位の人 ‖ a paper of ***high*** *position* 一流の新聞. 【類】They attained ***high*** *position* at an early age. / Such a person will never attain a ***higher*** *position* in life than that of a clerk or book-keeper. / Hoffmann occupied a ***high*** *position* in the German literature of his time. ¶They filled ***honorable*** *positions* with credit to themselves and advantage to their country. 彼らは名誉ある地位を占めて自分らの信用を得ると同時に国家をも益する所があった. ¶in a ***horizontal*** *position* 水平に. ¶a ***humiliating*** *position* 屈辱的な地位. ¶the ***ignominious social*** *position* to which his reverses had driven him to descend 彼が逆運に駆られて零落した不名誉な社会的地位. ¶Otherwise their *position* becomes wholly ***illogical.*** さもなければ彼らの地位は全然不条理なものとなる. ¶take an ***impartial position*** 公平な態度を取る. ¶occupy an ***important position*** 要路に立つ. 【類】hold an ***important position*** in the manufacturing industry / hold an ***important position*** in the history of ... / He occupied an ***important position*** with the Mitsui firm. ¶an ***impregnable position*** 難攻不落の陣地. ¶The aeroplane has gained an ***indisputable position*** as a necessary arm in warfare. 飛行機は戦闘における必要な武器として押しも押されもしない地位を占めるに至った. ¶officials of ***inferior position*** 下っぱの役人たち. ¶hold an ***influential position*** 有力な地位を占める. ¶her ***insular position*** その島国たること. ¶occupy an ***intermediate position*** between ... ...の中間に位する. ¶an ***invidious position*** 恨みを買いそうな立場. ¶by our geographically ***isolated position*** 地理的に孤立しているために. ¶His ***just position*** in the world of letters became assured. 作家としての彼の正しい地位は確立された. ¶a ***key position*** 要害の地; 要職. 【類】an officer in a ***key position*** / officers in ***key positions*** of command (司令部) / hold ***key positions*** in the Government. ¶maintain the ***leading position*** among ... ...の間に首位を維持する. 【類】In Switzerland the hotel industry occupies a ***leading position*** among the national economic activities (活動). / It puts the country in a ***leading position*** in athletics. ¶It got him into a ***ludicrous position***. そのために彼は人の笑いものになった. ¶hold a ***middle position*** between the two parties 二者の中間に立つ. ¶It was relegated to a ***minor position***, if not discarded altogether. それは全然放棄されないまでも第二位に落された. ‖ He has a ***minor position*** in the bank. 彼は銀行の下っぱである. ¶a ***municipal position*** 市吏の職. ¶He holds an ***official position***. 彼は役付である. ¶be in a ***perilous position*** 危険状態にある. ¶a ***permanent position*** 永久的の地位; [臨時でなく]定職. ¶What ***position*** are you on the team?—[I'm] on the ***pitcher's positions***. 君はチームで何をやってるの.—投手だよ. ¶Adam Smith's The Wealth of Nations occupies a ***pivotal position*** in modern economic thought. アダム・スミスの富国論は近代経済思想において枢要な地位を占めている. ¶He is in a ***precarious position***. 彼は不安な立場にある. ¶his ***preeminent position*** 彼のきわめて顕著な地位. ¶continue to hold the ***premier position*** (=first place) 依然王者の地位を占めている. ¶restore the ***prewar position*** in mechanical industry 機械産業では戦前の状態に復帰する. ¶restore the ***pre-1914 position*** 一九一四年前の状態に復帰する. ¶give a ***privileged position*** with a Government 権力ある官位につかせる. 【類】occupy a ***privileged position***. ¶take up ***professional positions*** in America 米国で知的職業につく. ¶hang it in a ***prominent position*** それを目に立つ位置に掛ける. 【類】He occupies a ***prominent position*** in business circles. / occupy a ***prominent position*** in commercial circles / the subject holds a ***prominent position*** in the discussion of ... ¶be offered a ***promising position*** 有望な地位を与えようと言われる. ¶Great Britain's ***proud position*** 大ブリテンの誇るべき地位. 【類】She will lose her ***proud position*** as the greatest nation in the world. ¶after holding many ***public positions*** 多くの公職についた後に. 【類】hold a ***public position*** of distinction. ¶a person of ***recognized position*** 相当の地位にある人. ¶a plan showing the ***relative positions*** of these points これらの地点の位置の関係を示した図. ¶a ***remunerative position*** 報酬のよい地位. ¶attain a ***responsible position*** 責任ある地位につく. 【類】hold a ***responsible position*** as newspaper correspondent (特派員) / filling successfully a very ***responsible position***. ¶a ***salaried position*** 有給の地位. ¶reduce it to a ***secondary position*** それを二位に落す(第二義的にする). ¶a ***secure position*** 安全な地位. ¶a very ***serious position*** 非常に重大な地位. ¶hold a ***similar position*** 類似の地位を占める. ¶of high ***social position*** 社会的地位の高い. 【類】penniless and without ***social position*** / some lady of or above my ***social position***. ¶hold a ***stable position*** 安定した地位にある. ¶in a ***standing position*** 立姿で. ¶a ***strategic position*** 要害の地点. ¶a ***strong position*** 堅固な陣地. ¶accept a ***subordinate position*** 従属的な地位を甘受する. ¶in the ***supine*** (***prone***) ***position*** あお向け(うつむき)にふして. ¶a ***temporary position*** 仮設陣地; 臨時の地位. ¶It served to place matters in their ***true position***. それで真相が明かになった.

¶an ***undisputed position*** 押しも押されもしない地位. ¶an ***uneasy position*** 不安な状態. ¶It fills a ***unique position***. それは無比の地位を占めている. 【類】The junior college occupies a ***unique position*** in American education. / London now occupies her ***unique position*** owing to her money power. / maintain a ***unique position*** in the annals of ... ¶an ***unsafe position*** 不安な地位. ¶owing to the ***unstable position*** of the exchanges 為替相場の変動が激しいので. ¶an ***untenable position*** 不安定な地位. 【類】be in an extremely ***untenable position***. ¶in an ***upright position*** 直立して. ¶hair in the ***usual positions*** あるべき所にある毛. ¶fill ***vacant positions*** 空位を補充する ‖ apply for a ***vacant position*** 欠員に対する採用申込みをする. ¶be in a ***vertical position*** 直立の姿勢になっている. ¶a ***weak position*** 薄弱な地位. ¶***well-paid positions*** 高給の地位. ¶***What position*** would the country be placed in, I wonder? 同国はどんな立場に追いこまれるだろう.

Q[2] hold an ***advance position*** 上位を占める. ¶blast an ***artillery position*** 砲兵陣地を爆破する. ¶hold a ***Cabinet position*** 閣僚のいすを占める. ¶an applicant for a ***civil service position*** 文官の志願者. ¶our ***food position*** わが食糧事情. ¶improve the ***foreign exchange position*** of the Japanese 日本の外国為替事情を改善する. ¶take a ***front-rank position*** among nations 世界各国中主要な地位を占める. ¶a ***full-(part-)time position*** 専任(嘱託). ¶serve in a ***government position*** 公務員になる ‖ with no ***government position*** 官職はなく. 【類】fill a ***government position*** by appointment / hold a high ***government position***. ¶a ***leadership position*** 指導者の地位. ¶a ***life position*** 終身的地位. ¶***newspaper*** and ***magazine positions*** 新聞雑誌関係の地位. ¶***office positions*** 官職. ¶the ***opposition position*** with regard to it was ... それに関する反対党の立場は...であった. ¶a typewriter in the "***shift***" *or* "***unshift***" ***position*** シフト・キーが動いているかもとのままの状態にあるタイプライター. ☞シフトキーを下げると small letters が capital letters に変わる. ¶a "***small pay***" ***position*** 低給の地位. ¶hold a ***state position*** 官についている. ¶be approached with an offer of a ***teaching position*** 教師に招へいしたいという申出に接する. ¶jeopardize America's ***world position*** 米国の世界的地位を危機に落し入れる. 【類】enhance her general ***world position***.

P She will marry ***for*** a good *position*. 彼女は地位の良い人となら結婚するだろう. 【類】apply ***for*** a *position*. ¶sit ***in*** the *position* of the Red Indians, namely, squatting on the heels [米国の]インディアンのすわり方すなわちかかとの上にしりを乗せたすわり方をする ‖ two front rooms ***in*** prominent *position* in Main Street 本通り目抜の場所にある正面の二室 ‖ men ***in*** *positions* of trust=men of responsible position 責任の地位にある人々 ‖ people ***in*** high *position* 身分の高い人々 ‖ I am not ***in*** a *position* to make any promises. 私としては約束は今致しかねる. ‖ one who is ***in*** a *position* to know the circumstances 消息に通じた人. 【類】According to the statement of those who are ***in*** the *position* to know ... / it is emphatically and positively asserted by persons who are ***in*** the *position* to be well informed, that ... / I am sorry not to be ***in*** a *position* to give you a definite answer at this moment. / I am ***in*** no *position* to talk to you on the question. ¶a man ***of*** *position* 地位のある人 ‖ a church dignitary ***of*** high *position* 高僧 ‖ a lady ***of*** some *position* 多少身分のある婦人. ¶a gun ***on*** *position* 砲座についた砲. ¶be ***out of*** *position* 所を得ない, 適所にない.

P[2] His *position* ***among*** the seats of the mighty is assured. 彼の有力な人々の中における地位は確立されている. ¶the bettering of women's *position* ***in*** Japan 日本における婦人の地位向上. ¶What is the *position* ***of*** affairs? 形勢はどうだ. ‖ the social *position* ***of*** the Indian potter インドの製陶家の社会的地位 ‖ a *position* ***of*** responsibility (=trust) 責任ある地位 【類】I feel that this *position* (=state) ***of*** affairs constitutes a national danger.

positive, *a.* 確信している, 独断的な.

P He is very *positive* ***about*** it. 彼はそうだと堅く信じている. ¶He is *positive* ***as to*** the being of God. 彼は神の存在を確信している.

O I am *positive* (=quite certain) that ... 私は...を確信している. 【類】I am *positive* somebody has told it.

possess, *v.* 所有する；[悪魔など]取りつく，つく．

M He has ***recently*** *possessed* himself of the splendid library of Retana. 最近レタナのすばらしい集書を手に入れた．¶It is ***scarcely*** *possessed* of any particular literary merit. それは文学的価値はほとんどない．

P They *possess* property ***between*** them. 彼らは財産を共有している．¶be *possessed* ***by*** a feeling of danger 不安の念にかられる．【類】*possessed* ***by*** a fancy idea (変った考え) / These assassins (刺客) are *possessed* ***by*** a hatred of society and Government as at present constituted. ‖ people *possessed* ***by*** foxes and cats きつねやねこにつかれた人々 ‖ be *possessed* ***by*** (=***with***) a demon (devil) 悪魔にとりつかれる．¶*possess* oneself ***in*** patience じっと辛抱している．¶be *possessed* ***of*** absolute power 絶対権力をもっている ‖ be *possessed* ***of*** "souls so dead" as never to ... …は絶対できないような死んだたましいをもっている．【類】At the end of the sixteenth century England was not yet *possessed* ***of*** a single foreign settlement. ‖ *possess* oneself ***of*** lands 土地を手に入れる ‖ He is *possessed* ***of*** a copious vocabulary. 彼は語いが豊富だ．【類】She was *possessed* ***of*** a rare and delicate beauty of person. / those who, although *possessed* ***of*** great scholarship, are nevertheless destitute of experience / an aggressor (侵略国) *possessed* ***of*** great military strength ‖ He was like a man *possessed* ***of*** devils. 彼は悪魔に取りつかれた人のようであった．¶*possess* oneself ***under*** all trials あらゆる苦難にたえる．¶he is *possessed* ***with*** the delusion that ... 彼は…の錯覚にとらわれている．【類】He is *possessed* ***with*** a sense of being in danger. ‖ At times she appeared to be *possessed* ***with*** an evil spirit. 彼女は悪鬼に取りつかれているのではないかと思われることがあった．¶*possess* ***without*** utility 死蔵する．

O *possess* a woman 女を自由にする．¶What's *possessed* you to do that? 君は一体正気でやったのか．¶He fought like one *possessed*. 《米》彼は(ものにとりつかれたように)無我夢中で戦った．

possession, *n.* 所有，占有；所有物；[*pl.*] 財産，富；領土．

V Under the Hay-Bunau-Varilla treaty the United States ***acquired*** *possession* of the strip of land as the Canal Zone. ヘイ・ビューノー・ヴァリーヤ条約で合衆国は運河地帯としての一小地帯を獲得した．¶a race held annually to ***decide*** the *possession* of the trophy given by ... …贈与の賞杯獲得を決定するために毎年挙行される競技．¶***demand*** immediate *possession* 即時の引渡を要求する．¶A copy of the Chinese encyclopedia, secured in 1877, ***forms*** a prized *possession* of the British Museum. 一八七七年に手に入れた一部の中国百科辞典は大英博物館の貴重書になっている．¶***gain*** *possession* of ... …を手に入れる．¶***get*** *possession* of property 資産を手に入れる ‖ For a few shillings I ***got*** *possession* of a good one. 私は二三シリングで良いのを手に入れた．¶refuse to ***give*** *possession* 引渡を拒絶する．¶***give up*** *possession* 引渡す，譲る．¶they ***had*** undisputed *possession* of ... 彼らは…を確実に占有した．¶***hoard*** their *possessions* 彼らの所有物を死蔵する．¶***hold*** *possession* of the land for ... years …年間その土地を領有する．¶In 1839 the British ***obtained*** *possession* of Aden. 一八三九年に英人はアーデンを占有した．¶***preserve*** *possession* 所有権を継続する．¶***recover*** *possession* 所有権を取り戻す ‖ ***recover*** the former *possessions* in Central Asia 中央アジヤの以前の領土を取り返す．¶***relinquish*** *possession* 所有権を放棄する．¶***resume*** *possession* at all hazards あらゆる危険を冒してその所有を回復する．¶***retain*** *possession* of one's effects その所有品を渡さないでいる ‖ ***retain*** *possession* of a trophy by a second victory 連勝によって優勝カップ(など)を守り続ける．¶***secure*** full *possession* of ... …を完全に占有する．¶***seize*** the *possession* of ... …を手に入れる．¶***take*** *possession* of the new property 新たに財産を取得する ‖ ***take*** *possession* of one's new house 新居に引越す．【類】He ***took*** *possession* of the islands in the name of the King of Spain. ¶***value*** one's *possessions* 所有品を大切にする．¶I ***want*** entire *possession*. (愛人などを)私一人のものにしたい．¶***win*** *possession* of a mate 配偶をかち得る．

Q The Philippine Islands became an ***American*** *possession* in 1898. フィリッピン諸島は一八九八年に米国の領地となった．¶The piano was the ***cherished*** *possession* of her father's mother. ピアノは彼女の父方の祖母愛蔵品であった．¶facts which should be the ***common*** *possession* of every educated person 教育ある人士の等しく知っておるべき事実．¶***earthly*** *possessions* 現世の財宝．¶an ***embarrassing*** *possession* 邪魔になる所有物．¶$500—his ***entire worldly*** *possessions* 彼の財産全部である五百ドル．¶the ***exclusive*** *possession* of ... …の専有．¶take ***forcible*** *possession* of Java ジャヴァを強行的に占領する．¶The old man remained in ***full*** *possession* of his faculties. その老人は知力が確かであった．‖ Though ninety years of age, she is in ***full*** *possession* of her senses. 九十でも彼女はまだしっかりしている．¶Virtue is a ***greater*** *possession* than learning. 身につけた徳は学問よりも偉大なものだ．¶The law makers have not been in ***full*** *possession* of facts. 法制定者たちは事実を十分に調べていなかった．¶Mt. Fuji is a ***great national*** *possession*. 富士山は一大国宝である．【類】Life is incomparably man's ***greatest*** *possession*. ¶a house to let, with ***immediate*** *possession* (現住者がなく)即時引越せる貸家．¶take ***illegal*** *possession* of = misappropriate 横領する，ねこばばをきめる．¶***insular*** *possessions* 島しょの領土．¶the land is in the ***joint*** *possession* between ... その土地は…間の共有になっている．¶owners ignorant of the value of their ***literary*** *possessions* 自己所蔵の文献の価値をわきまえない持主．¶the ***long*** *possession* of the shogunate by the Tokugawa family 徳川家による将軍制の長期にわたる占有．¶***material*** *possessions* 物質上の富．¶the ***nation's proudest*** *possession* その国民の最も大きな自慢になる所有物．¶gain ***permanent*** *possession* of ... …を永久に自分のものにする．¶a ***personal*** *possession* 一私人の所有物．¶a ***precious national*** *possession* 貴重な国宝．¶one's ***prized*** *possession* 珍蔵品．¶The park is the ***proud*** *possession* of us all. その公園はわれらすべての誇りとするものである．¶We must pay for knowledge with our effort if it is to become a ***real*** *possession*. 知識が身につくようにするには努力を払わなくてはならない．¶the groups of men who are in ***temporary*** *possession* of power 一時権力を握っている人々の群．¶a ***treasured*** *possession* 珍蔵品．¶he remains in ***undisputed*** *possession* of ... 彼は確実に…所有権を握っている．¶***undisturbed*** *possession* of ... 安全確実な…の占有．¶take ***unjustified*** *possession* of ... …を不当に所有物とする．¶***unlawful*** *possession* 不法占有．¶knowledge is a ***valuable*** *possession*. 知識は価値のある所有物である．¶her only ***worldly*** *possession* 彼女の唯一の財産．¶***wrongful*** *possession* 不当所有．

Q² a ***family*** *possession* 家族の所有物．¶be in ***Government*** *possession* 政府の所有である．¶I treasure as a ***life*** *possession* the memory of his true and loyal friendship. 彼の真実で忠実な友情は一生の宝として忘れない．¶***overseas*** *possessions* 海外領土．¶Guam is a ***United States*** *possession*. グァム島は米国の領土である．

P have it ***in*** *possession* それを持っている ‖ put him ***in*** *possession* of it = give it to him それを彼に与える ‖ if not ***in*** your *possession* お持ちになっていないなら ‖ He was ***in*** *possession* of his room. [ホテルで]彼はへやに通されていた．【類】Washington Irving was born in New York on April 3, 1783, while the city was still ***in*** the *possession* of the British troops (英軍占領下の). ‖ I am ***in*** *possession* of new information. 私は新しい情報を手に入れている．‖ The police is ***in*** *possession* of evidence. 証拠があがっている．¶it came ***into*** *possession* of ... それは…の手にはいった ‖ the land passed ***into*** the *possession* of ... その土地は…の手に渡った．

P² *possessions* ***by*** demons 悪魔につかれること．

possessive, *a.* 所有欲のある，所有[上]の．

O A *possessive* (=devoted) mother doesn't want her son to go too far off. 子供第一の母は息子が遠く離れるのを喜ばない．‖ his *possessive* nature 彼の所有欲．

possessor, *n.* 所有者．

Q the ***dear*** *possessor* of my virgin heart 私の初恋を勝ち得た男．¶the ***latest*** *possessor* 最近の所有者．¶he is the ***proud*** *possessor* of a medal given for distinguished service in ... by ... 彼は…に対する殊勲によって光栄にも…から勲賞をいただいている．‖ Oxford men who are ***proud*** *possessors* of pass degrees 普通学位を取ったりっぱなオックスフォード出身者．

P² the *possessor* ***of*** a grim power 恐るべき力の持主．¶I am the proud *possessor* ***of*** a copy sent to me by the author. 私は著者から寄贈された自慢の本を一部持っている．‖

become the *possessor of* … …を手に入れる.

possibility, *n.* 可能性;可能事.

V Lacking this, aviation cannot ***achieve*** its fullest *possibilities.* これを欠いては航空術もその最高度の発展はとげられない. ¶to ***avoid*** the *possibility* of being "short changed" つり銭を少なく出すという間違いのないように. ¶The Dictionary found an editor capable of ***converting*** its latent *possibilities* into a great reality. この辞書はその潜在的可能性を偉大なる実在たらしめうる編集者を見出した. ¶***deny*** the *possibility* of … …を不可能と断定する. ¶The compiler has striven to ***develop*** the *possibilities* of the pocket English dictionary to a degree not heretofore attained. 編集者はポケット型英語辞典の従来不可能と思われた程度までやってみようと努力した. ¶***eliminate*** (=remove) the *possibility* of … …の可能性を取去る. ¶it cannot ***exclude*** the *possibility* that … それでも…がないとも限らない. ¶***exhaust*** the *possibilities* of wise action in reference to … …に関して人事を尽す ‖ We have just about ***exhausted*** the *possibilities* of the ordinary black-and-white screen. 普通の白黒映画はほとんど行詰りになっている. ¶***explore*** the *possibilities* of … …の将来性を調査する. ¶***foresee*** the *possibilities* of … …の可能性を予想する. ¶***further*** the *possibility* of … …の実現を助成する. ¶It ***has*** in it the *possibilities* of a great future. それには大なる将来性がある. ¶Unfortunately, each of these *possibilities* is ***hedged*** with practical difficulties. 不幸にしてこれらの可能性には実際上の困難が伴っている. ¶we ***incur*** *possibility* of … …の恐れがある. ¶***open up*** the *possibilities* of … …の可能性を開拓する. ¶***preclude*** the *possibility* of … …を不可能ならしめる. 【類】 definitely ***preclude*** any *possibility* of … ¶***prevent*** the *possibility* of … …の可能を妨げる. ¶***prove*** the *possibility* of … …の可能を立証する. ¶I ***question*** the *possibility* of … 私は…の可能性を疑う. ¶***realize*** the commercial *possibilities* of the city 同市の商業上の将来性を認識する. ¶I ***see*** a *possibility* of … 私は…の可能性を認める. 【類】 Nobody could then ***see*** the commercial *possibilities* of this invention.

V² The *possibility* will ***diminish.*** その可能性は薄らぐだろう. ¶The *possibility* is ***getting smaller.*** 可能性はうすれつつある.

Q I could not in ***all possibility*** suspect it. よもやそんなことがあろうとは知らなかった. ¶Is there ***any possibility*** of your knowing him? もしや君はあの人をお知りではないでしょうか. ¶a ***bare possibility*** 万一のこと. ¶the ***chemical*** *possibilities* of coal 石炭の化学的発展性. ¶The story is full of ***dramatic*** *possibilities.* その話は十分芝居になる. ¶there is a very ***fair*** *possibility* of his …ing … 彼が…することの可能性はかなりある. ¶open up ***fresh*** *possibilities* for … …にとって新生面を切り開く. ¶open ***great*** *possibilities* to us in this direction この方面に大きな発展性がある. ¶This process is said to have ***great industrial*** *possibilities.* この工作は産業上大いに将来性があると言われている. ¶develop their ***highest*** *possibilities* 彼らの最大の可能性を発揮させる. ¶There is no ***industrial*** *possibility* of the new invention. その新発明品には工業生産化の可能性はない. ¶convert the ***latent*** *possibilities* into a great reality 内蔵する可能性を偉大な現実に変える. ¶It has ***limited*** *possibilities.* それには余り将来性がない. ¶there is ***little*** *possibility* of … …はありそうもない. ¶He is talked of as a ***presidential*** *possibility.* 彼は将来の大統領をもって目せられている. ¶a ***realizable*** *possibility* 実現しうべき可能性. ¶In this case there is not ***remote*** *possibility* of improvement. この場合改善される見込が立たない. 【類】 There is a ***remote*** *possibility.* ¶be a very ***strong*** *possibility* 大いに可能性がある. ¶an ***uncomfortable*** *possibility* そうなったら困ること. ¶The atomic studies have ***wonderful*** *possibilities.* 原子研究にはすばらしい将来性がある.

Q² ***employment*** *possibilities* 就職の見込み. ¶He has ***future*** *possibilities.* 彼は将来見込がある. ¶study ***trade*** *possibilities* between the two nations 両国間における貿易の将来性を研究する.

P ***beyond*** any *possibility* of expression in words 到底言葉に表わし得ない ‖ It is a task ***beyond*** the *possibilities* of one human life. それは一生を費してもできない仕事だ. 【類】 prove ***beyond*** a *possibility* of doubt. ¶***by*** any *possibility* ひょっとして. ¶it is out of the bounds ***of*** *possibility* that … …は到底有り得ない. 【類】 it is quite within the bounds (=range) ***of*** *possibility* that …

P² *possibilities* ***for*** women's work in civic life 市民生活における女子従業の可能性. ¶a *possibility* ***of*** the future 将来有りうべきこと. 【類】 There is no *possibility* ***of*** success. / The *possibilities* ***of*** the motion picture in the preservation of peace, in the creation of international good-will, otherwise, are immeasurable.

possible, *n.* 可能性.

V ***do*** one's *possible* (=utmost) 全力を尽す. ¶He ***scored*** a *possible* at 200 yards. 彼は 200 ヤードで最高点を得た.

P It is hard to see the limit ***of*** the *possible* in modern science. 近代科学における可能性の限界は見きわめがたい.

possible, *a.* 有りうべき, できうべき.

M That is ***conceivably*** *possible.* それは有りうるように考えられる. ¶That is ***hardly*** *possible.* よもやそんなことはあるまい. ¶so far as is ***humanly*** *possible* 人力の及ぶ限り. 【類】 as accurately and impartially as is ***humanly*** *possible* / as nearly impartial as is ***humanly*** *possible* / make it as certain as ***humanly*** *possible* that … ¶it would, of course, have been ***perfectly*** *possible* to … もちろん…するのは完全にできうることであったろう. ¶That is ***quite*** *possible.* それは全くありうることだ. ¶it is ***scarcely*** *possible* to say … …と言うことはほとんどできない.

P It is *possible* ***for*** me to do so. 僕にはそうすることができる. ¶Frost is *possible* ***in*** early summer. 初夏にも霜がおりることはありうる. ¶*possible* ***of*** realization 実現のできる. ¶All things are *possible* ***to*** God. 神は万能である. ¶No career is *possible* ***in*** this small village. この小さな村にいては生がい発展の見込みがない. ¶It is *possible* ***with*** a man of his talent. それはあの人の腕ならできうることだ.

possum, *n.* 《米》とぼけること. 「病を使う.

V ***play*** (=***act***) *possum* 気を失った振りをする; とぼける, け

post, *n.* (1) 地位, 官職; 《米》駐とん地(部隊).

V ***abandon*** one's *post* 職を辞する. 【類】 ***abandon*** a *post* in the face of danger (difficulty). ¶He ***accepted*** the *post* of English teacher at a middle school. 彼は中学校の英語教師に就任した. 【類】 ***accept*** a *post* as dean of the law school (法学部長). ¶*posts* of responsibility are frequently ***allotted*** to … 責任ある地位はしばしば…に割当てられる. ¶***decline*** a *post* 就任を辞退する. ¶***desert*** (=***forsake***) one's *post* その地位を捨てる. ¶***fill*** a *post* 職につく ‖ For eighteen years he has ***filled*** the *post* of librarian in the library. 十八年間彼は図書館で司書の職にあった. 【類】 Someone is wanted to ***fill*** the *post.* / ***fill*** successively the *posts* (歴任) of … / ***fill*** a *post* with credit (りっぱに). ¶I ***got*** a *post* through my friend's good offices. 私は友人のつてで職を得た. ‖ He has ***got*** a most difficult *post* to fill. 彼は非常に困難な職についた. 【類】 He has ***got*** a good *post* in the civil service. ¶***give up*** a lucrative *post* 有利な職を捨てる. 【類】 ***give up*** a *post* for a better one. ¶He ***held*** a *post* at Seoul. 彼は京城で, ある役についていた. 【類】 He ***holds*** the *post* of consul general for the United States at Shanghai. / Since 1918 he has ***held*** various *posts* in the Cabinet. / ***hold*** a *post* at one of the great London hospitals. ¶He has ***obtained*** a *post* in the National Library. 彼は国立図書館で職を得た. 【類】 he has ***obtained*** the *post* of … ¶Later he ***occupied*** a *post* of some kind under the Government of the Bombay Presidency. その後彼はボムベイ省政府部内で何か職についた. 【類】 ***occupy*** the *post* of parish clerk / those who ***occupy***, or who aspire to occupy, the *post* of … / ***occupy*** a *post* of authority. ¶he was ***offered*** the *post* of … 彼は…の職を持ち込まれた. ¶he ***quit*** the *post* to become … 彼は…になるためにその職を去った. ‖ the notion that there is something base in ***quitting*** one's *post* 自分の持場を捨てるのは何だか卑劣だという考え. ¶***relinquish*** one's *post* 職をなげうつ. ¶He has ***resigned*** his *post* in favor of his son. 彼は子息のためにその職を辞した. 【類】 ***resign*** one's *post* on account of old age. ¶***secure*** a good *post* in business circles 商業界で良い職を得る. ¶There are many teachers who are ***seeking*** *posts.* 職を求めている教師が多い. ¶***take*** the *post* of … …の職につく. ¶***take up*** one's fresh *post* 新任の職につく. ¶He ***threw away*** his *post* as one casts off a worn-out shoe. 彼は自分の地位を弊履のごとく捨てた. ¶***vacate*** one's *post* 退職する. 【類】 The *post* was left *vacated* (=*unoccupied*) for long.

Q go to one's *appointed post* 赴任する. ¶a *diplomatic post* 一つの外交官職. ¶fill some *educational post* 何か教職につく. ¶a *good post* in the public service 公職の好地位. ¶occupy a *high post* 高い地位についている. ¶an *important post* 要職. ¶hold a *key post* in the Government 政府の要職を占める. ¶the *loftiest post* of honor 最高名誉の地位. ¶a *ministerial post* 閣僚のいす. ¶he occupies the *responsible post* of Minister of ... 彼は...大臣という責任ある官職にある. ¶He took a *small clerical post* in a Government office. 彼は官庁で微々たる書記の職についた. ¶*subordinate posts* 下級の地位. ¶a *vacant post* 欠員になっている地位. ¶after filling *various posts* 様々の職についた後.

Q² He left an *Army post* in Japan in early 1948. 彼は一九四八年の初めに日本の陸軍を退いた. ¶hold a *cabinet post* 閣僚のいすを占める ‖ The Postmaster General is a *cabinet post*. 郵政長官は閣員である. ¶a high *Government post* 政府の要職. ¶leave one's *guard post* その守衛の持場を離れる. ¶a *party post* 党の役. ¶the *vice-presidency post* 副大統領(副社長)の職.

P He was accused of sleeping *at* his *post*. 彼は持場で居眠りしたという問責を受けた. ‖ He died *at* his *post*. 彼はその持場(任地)でたおれた. 【類】They are *at* their *posts*. / The consul is *at* his *post* at Vladivostok. ¶*At* some *posts* the desertions have reached as high as 30 per cent. 〘軍〙駐とん部隊の中には逃亡兵が三十パーセントに達したものもあった. ¶He went *for* his *post*. 彼は赴任した. ‖ He is fitted *for* the *post*. 彼は適任だ. ‖ He is prominently named *for* the *post*. その職の候補として彼の呼び声が高い. 【類】He is the very man *for* the *post*. ¶*from* this *post* he was promoted to be ... この地位から彼は...に昇叙された. 【類】rise *from* small *posts* to places of high emolument and power. ¶The canteen kept *in* the *post* is called Post Exchange (PX). 《米》駐とん所にある酒保は PX と呼ばれる. ¶a policeman *on post* 巡回中の警官. ¶proceed *to* one's *post* 赴任する ‖ stick *to* one's *post* その地位にかじりつく. ¶a *post as* a professor 教授の地位. 【類】his *post as* Keeper of Printed Books at the British Museum. ¶He has got a good *post* in the navy. 彼は海軍に好地位を得た. ¶the *post of* Secretary of State 《米》国務長官のいす. ¶He accepted a *post under* the Japanese Government. 彼は日本政府に仕えた.

(**2**) 《米》mail; 《英》郵便, 郵書; 《英》ポスト, 郵便局.

V Those letters *caught* the *post*. それらの手紙は郵便時間に間に合った(いなかの便少い所で). ¶I *had* a heavy *post* today. きょう私の所に郵便が沢山来た. ‖ How many *posts have* you in a day here? ここでは郵便は一日になん回集配しますか. ¶I *missed* the morning *post*. 私は朝の郵便に出しそこなった. ¶When does the next *post come in* (*go out*)? 次の郵便はいつ来るか(出るか).

Q *aerial post*=《米》air mail 航空郵便. ¶send cheque [by] *first post* 第一便で小切手を郵送する. 【類】The answers must reach the office not later than *first post* on Wednesday morning. ¶by a *later post* 後便で. ¶the *outermost post* of south-advancing Japan 南進の最先陣. ¶by *registered post* 書留郵便で. ¶per *separate post*= under another cover 別便で. ¶It will be sent to you by *tonight's post*. それはきょうの郵便でお送りします.

Q² What will this cost by *book post?* 《英》これは書籍郵便だと送料はいくらしますか. ¶*field post* 野戦郵便. ¶a *money-order post* [米国の] 郵便為替取扱局. ¶I missed the *morning* (*evening*) *post*. 《英》朝(晩)の集配に間に合わなかった. ¶send a book by *parcel post* 本を小包郵便で送る. ¶*penny post* [英国]一ペニー郵便制.

P notify ... *by post* ...郵便で通知する ‖ send a package *by post* 小包を郵送する. 【類】The message of congratulation *by post* and telegraph poured in upon him from home and abroad. ¶The letter has been lost *in* [the] *post*. その手紙は郵送中に紛失した. ‖ Then the letter must have been thirty days *in* the *post*. そうするとその手紙は三十日かかって届いたに違いない. ¶the director *of posts* and telegraphs 郵便電信局長 ‖ Please send me an answer by return *of post* (=return post). 折返し御返事をこう. ¶verbally (=orally) or *through* the *post* 口頭または郵便で. 【類】inquiries received *through* the *post* / circulate (send) ... *through* the *post* / supply *through* the *post* to customers. ¶Take this letter *to* [the] *post*. この手紙を郵便局(またはポスト)に持って行きなさい.

post, *n.* 駐とん所, 番所.

Q cigarettes sold at *overseas posts* 海外駐とん所で売られるタバコ.

Q² a *marine post* 海兵隊駐とん地. ¶a *police post* 交番.

post, *n.* 柱.

V *fix* a *post* in the ground 柱を地につきさす.

Q an *upright post* 直立した柱.

Q² a *clearance post* 〘鉄〙接触限界標. ¶the installation of *direction* and *distance sign posts* 方向及び距離の指標設置. ¶a *finger post* 道しるべ ‖ a historical *finger post* 歴史上の参考, 史跡. ¶a *lamp post* 街灯柱.

post, *v.* 《英》郵便に出す, 郵送する; 転記する; 消息に通じさせる; 掲示する, はりだす.

M keep one *fully posted* up to the times in matters concerning ... ...に関する問題では十分新時代に遅れないようにさせる. ¶I want the newspaper *regularly posted*. 新聞をきまって郵送してもらいたい. ¶He is *thoroughly posted* on that subject. 彼はそのことをよく知っている. ¶be *well posted* up in current politics 政界の現状に通じている.

M² *post off* at once 直ちに急行する. ¶a wall *posted over* with notices 掲示がべたべたはってある壁. ¶*post up* a sign はり紙を出す. 【類】*post up* bills / *post up* a notice at the stations to indicate that ... / notices *posted up* at street-corners.

P Tariff of charges for telegraphs is *posted at* all telegraph offices. 電報料金表はどの電信局にもはり出してある. ¶*post* a letter *by* special delivery 書状を特別配達で出す. 【類】*post* a letter *by* registered post (書留で). ¶He is well *posted in* European politics. 彼は欧州政界の消息に通じている. ¶*post* it *on* the school bulletin board それを学校の掲示板にはり出す. 【類】an announcement *posted* [up] *on* a wall ‖ the opinion of the best *posted on* the situation is that ... 時局に関する消息通の意見は...だ ‖ Reading of these papers will keep one *posted on* the latest happenings in the world. これらの新聞を読むと最近のでき事に通じるようになる. ¶*post* a proclamation *upon* the front gate 布告を正門にはり出す.

postage, *n.* 郵税.

V a letter *bearing* the full *postage* 不足なく郵券のはってある書状. ¶I enclose 10c. stamp which I think will *cover postage*. 郵税として十セント切手を封入いたします. ¶*enclose* return *postage* 返信料を封入する. ¶See that the right *postage* is *paid*. 郵税不足にならないようご注意. 【類】Do you *pay* the *postage* on all your letters? / send 10 cents to *pay postage*.

Q The letter was submitted on delivery to the payment of double the *deficient postage* required. その手紙は配達先で二倍の不足を取られた. ¶*postage due* 郵税不足. ¶*extra postage* 付加郵税. ¶*postage free* 郵税無料. ¶*short postage* 郵税不足. ¶New Zealand has *universal penny postage*. ニュージーランドには万国郵便法による一ペニー均一郵便制が布かれている.

P² What is the *postage for* this? この郵税はいくらですか. ¶rates of *postage on* parcels 小包郵便料 ‖ What is the *postage on* the letter? 書状の郵税はいくらですか? 【類】How much will the *postage* cost *on* these letters? / *postage* to the United States *on* ...

postal [card], *n.* 《米》郵便はがき.

V *drop* a *postal* to ... ...へはがきを出す. ¶I *got* a *postal* from him stating that ... 彼から...というはがきを受取った.

post-card, post card, *n.* 《英》郵便はがき; 《米》私製はがき.

V *Drop* me a *post-card* if you can come. 来られるならはがきをください. 【類】*drop* a *post-card* to ... ¶I *received* a *post-card* from him stating that ... 私は彼から...の旨のはがきを受取った. ¶*send post-cards* broadcast among ... ...間にはがきをばらまく. ¶*write* a *post-card* to him 彼にはがきを出す.

Q *illustrated post-cards* 絵はがき. ¶*pictorial* (=picture) *post-cards* 絵はがき. ¶a *scenic post-card* 《米》風景絵はがき.

Q² the *reply post-card* 返信用はがき. ¶a *return post-card* 往復はがき. ¶a *picture post card* 《米》絵はがき. ¶*souvenir post-cards* of scenes 《米》記念風景絵はがき. ☞ post card は《英》郵便はがき,《米》私製はがき. また《米》の官製はがきは postal[card], 英は官私製とも post card という [post card, post-card, postcard と三様のつづり方がある].

P on application ***on*** a *post-card* to ... はがきで...へ申込めば ‖ I wrote ***on*** a *post-card* that ... 私ははがきに...と書い ⌊た.

poster, *n.* はり札(ビラ), ポスター; ビラ張り(人).

V ***display*** *posters* ポスターを陳列する. ¶ ***hang*** a *poster* in the window 窓にポスターを下げる. ¶ ***put up*** a *poster* ポスターを掲げる.

Q ***garish*** *posters* けばけばしいポスター. ¶ ***pictorial*** *posters* 絵入ポスター. ¶ *posters,* ***plain*** and ***pictorial, artistic*** and the reverse 文字だけと絵入, 芸術的と非芸術的のポスター.

Q^2 a ***bill*** *poster* ビラ張り. ¶ a ***campaign*** *poster* 選挙ポスター(ビラ). ¶ There each side tears down the opponent's ***election*** *posters* almost as fast as the workers can put them up. そこで両側から敵方の候補者の選挙ポスターを運動員が張るが早いか引き裂く. ¶ a ***letter-press*** *poster* 文字印刷のポスター. ¶ paste up ***movie*** *posters* on the walls of the city 市街の壁に映画ポスターをはりつける. ¶ a ***publicity*** *poster* 宣伝ポスター. ¶ a gigantic ***24-sheet*** *poster* 大大的二十四枚張りのポスター.

posterior, *n.* しり.

V He ***slapped*** her *posterior*, saying, "This for you!" 彼は「そらやるよ」と言って彼女のしりを平手打した.

posterior, *a.* 後の.

P *posterior* ***to*** the year 1893 一八九三年後の.

posterity, *n.* [団]子孫. 「男(女)系の子孫.

Q ***distant*** *posterity* 遠い後代. ¶ ***male (female)*** *posterity*

P deserve the gratitude ***of*** *posterity* 後世の感謝に値する. ¶ go down ***to*** *posterity* 子孫に伝わる ‖ He left [behind] an immortal example ***to*** all *posterity*. 彼は後世に不滅の手本 ⌊を残した.

postman, *n.* 《英》郵便配達夫.

V^2 The *postman* ***carries*** and ***delivers mail***. 郵便屋さんは郵便を運んで配達する.

postmark, *n.* 郵便消印. 「手紙.

V a letter ***bearing*** the Kyoto *postmark* 京都の消印のある

P You can generally tell ***by*** the *postmark* where and when a letter was posted. いつどこで手紙を出したのか大抵消印を見れば分かる.

postmark, *v.* 消印する. 「手紙.

P a letter *postmarked* ***from*** London ロンドンの消印のある

post office, 《英》**post-office,** 郵便局. 「便局.

Q a ***general*** *post office* 本局. ¶ ***special*** *post office* 特定郵

Q^2 an ***army*** *post office* 軍事郵便局 (APO と略す). ¶ a ***field*** *post office* 野戦郵便局. ¶ a ***branch*** *post office* 郵便支局. ☞《米》post office,《英》post-office とつづるのが通例. ただし米・英共 *post-office* order, a *post-office* car.

postpone, *v.* 延期する; 後回しにする.

M The party was *postponed* ***a few days***. 会が数日延期になった. ¶ The meeting has been *postponed* ***indefinitely*** (=***sine die***). 集会は無期延期になった. ¶ be ***infinitely*** *postponed* 無期延期となる.

P It was *postponed* ***for*** five months. それは五カ月間延期になった. ¶ it was *postponed* ***from*** the evening of ... それは...の夕刻から延期されたのであった. ¶ The meeting was *postponed* ***on account of*** rain. 集会は雨で延期になった. ¶ the meeting has been *postponed* ***to*** (=***till***) ... 会は...まで延期になった ‖ *postpone* the public interest ***to*** one's own 私利を先にして公益を後回しにする.

postponement, *n.* 延期, 延引.

V ***demand*** (=***ask for***) a *postponement* of five days 五日間の延期を要求する.

Q Any ***further*** *postponement* would be dangerous. これ以上少しでも延引するのは危険だろう. ¶ an ***indefinite*** *postponement* 無期延期.

Q^2 a ***five-day*** *postponement* 五日間の延期.

P ***after*** several *postponements* because of bad weather and other interruptions 天候不良その他の故障で数回延期の後. ¶ ***owing to*** the *postponement* of ... ...の延期のため.

postscript, *n.* 追書.

V ***add*** a *postscript* to a letter 手紙に追書を添える.

P It was added ***in*** a *postscript*. それは追書として添えてあった.

P^2 the *postscript* ***of*** (=***to***) a letter 手紙の追書. ¶ a *postscript* ***to*** the tragic story of ... ...の悲劇の後日ばなし.

posture, *n.* 姿勢.

V ***assume*** a *posture* of defense 防御の姿勢を取る.

Q in an ***erect*** *posture* 直立の姿勢で. ¶ in a ***kneeling*** *posture* ひざまずいている姿勢で. ¶ in a ***reclining*** *posture* [長いすに]横になった姿勢で. ¶ in the ***recumbent*** *posture* もたれている姿勢で. ¶ in a ***seated*** (=***sitting***) *posture* すわった姿で. ¶ in a ***squatting*** *posture* しゃがんで(いる姿勢で). ¶ in a ***standing*** *posture* 立っている姿勢で. ¶ ***supine*** *posture* 仰臥(ぎょう)位.

Q^2 ***hand*** *postures* in dancing 舞踊(ダンス)の手振り.

P ***in*** a *posture* of repose 休息の姿勢で ‖ be unsightly ***in*** one's *posture* when sleeping 寝相が悪い.

P^2 the best *posture* ***for*** writing 字を書くに最も適した姿 ⌊勢.

pot, *n.* なべ; はち; るつぼ; 一杯.

V *pots* ***fashioned*** by hand 手作りのつぼ. ¶ ***keep*** the *pot* ***boiling*** 暮しを立てて行く. ¶ ***make*** the *pot* ***boil*** 生活する.

Q^2 an ***earthenware*** *pot* 土器のつぼ. ¶ a ***flower*** *pot* 花生けばち. ¶ a ***frying*** *pot* フライなべ. ¶ a ***kitchen*** *pot* 料理用深なべ. ¶ a racial ***melting*** *pot* 人種のるつぼ(ニューヨーク市など). ¶ use shears and a ***mucilage*** *pot* はさみとのり入れを使う(切抜張りなどに). ¶ a ***pharmacy*** *pot* 調剤用つぼ. ¶ a ***tea*** *pot* 茶つぼ.

P cook it ***in*** a *pot* なべでそれを煮る ‖ plant a tree ***in*** a *pot* はちに木を植える. ¶ go ***to*** *pot* おちぶれる, 破滅する.

P^2 a *pot* ***for*** melting ores 鉱石を溶かすつぼ. ¶ a *pot* (=potful) ***of*** ale (tea) ビール(など)一杯.

potato, *n.* じゃがいも.

V ***dig out*** (=***up***) *potatoes* じゃがいもを掘る. ¶ ***grow*** *potatoes* じゃがいもを作る. ¶ ***peel*** (=***pare***) *potatoes* じゃがいもの皮をむく.

Q ***chipped*** *potatoes* 薄切りのじゃがいも. ¶ ***Irish*** *potatoes* じゃがいも. ¶ ***mashed*** *potatoes* [料理用]すりつぶしたじゃがいも. ¶ a ***sweet*** *potato* さつまいも. ¶ a ***white*** *potato* じゃがいも. 「も.

Q^2 the ***Canada*** *potato* カナダじゃが. ¶ a ***taro*** *potato* 里い

P They thrive ***on*** *potatoes*. 彼らはじゃがいもを食って結構生活している.

pot-boiling, *n.* 《口語》生活のかてとしての文筆.

P ***for*** *pot-boiling* 単なる原稿料欲しさから.

potency, *n.* 能力.

Q^2 ***sex*** *potency* 性交能力. ¶ ***vitamin*** *potency*, 60 milligrams 六十ミリグラムのビタミンの価.

P^2 the *potency* ***of*** a drug 薬の効力 ‖ the *potency* ***of*** an argument 論拠の価値.

potent, *a.* 効験のある.

P *potent* ***over*** ... ...に効験のある.

potentate, *n.* 有力者.

Q a ***literary*** *potentate* 文豪.

potential, *a., n.* 可能な; 可能度.

Q the ***democratic*** *potential* of the Japanese people 日本人の民主々義的素質.

Q^2 be stripped of her industrial ***war*** *potential* その国の産業的潜在戦力を取去る ‖ complete removal of Japan's ***war*** *potential* 日本の潜在戦力の完全な除去. 【類】 destruction of the German ***war*** *potential* / curb (抑える) the ***war*** *potential* of Japan / Japan lacked ***war*** *potential* to stand up against (に対し立ち向うべき) the power of the United States. / Germany's ***war***[***-making***] *potential*.

P It means dollars ***in*** *potential*. それはかねになる.

O the *potential* child in her womb その胎内に宿る子.

potentiality, *n.* 可能性. ⌊【類】 a *potential* genius.

V I ***discerned*** the *potentialities* of great things in him. あの人は将来偉くなると私は見て取った. ¶ ***have*** enormous *potentialities* 大いに可能性がある. ¶ ***work out*** its *potentialities* その能力を発展させる. 「る.

Q has ***enormous*** *potentialities* 将来大いに発展の見込があ

Q^2 Japan's ***comeback*** *potentiality* 日本の復興潜在力. ¶ investigate Japan's ***trade*** *potentialities* 日本の通商能力 ⌊の将来性を調べる.

potter, *n.* 陶器師.

V^2 A *potter* ***makes*** pots and dishes out of clay. 陶工は粘土からつぼやさらを作る.

potter, *v.* [仕事など]ぐずぐずする.

M^2 *potter* ***about*** ぶらつく; 働くふりをする ‖ What are those coolies *pottering* ***about*** there? あの苦力たちはあすこでなにをうろうろしているのか.

pottery, *n.* 陶器.

Q ***prehistoric*** *pottery* from China 中国から渡来した有史以前の陶器. ¶ ***unfired*** *pottery* 土器. ¶ ***unglazed*** *pottery*

素焼.

Q² *acid-proof pottery* and porcelain 耐酸陶磁器. ¶*straw-rope pattern pottery* 縄(じょう)紋式土器.

pouch, *n.* 小袋, 紙入.

Q a *postman's pouch* 郵便屋のかばん.

Q² a *handbag pouch* ハンドバックの紙入. ¶a silken *tobacco pouch* 絹製のたばこ入れ.

poultice, *n.* はっぷ, 湿布.

V *apply* a *poultice* はっぷを当てる.

poultry, *n.* [団] 家きん.

V *breed poultry* 養鶏をやる. ¶*draw poultry* 家きんのはらわたを抜く. ¶*handle poultry* for pleasure 道楽に養鶏をやる. ¶worms *infesting poultry* 鶏の寄生虫. ¶*keep poultry* 家きんを飼う. ¶*pick poultry* 家きんの羽毛をむしり取る. ¶*prepare poultry* for show (=exhibition) or sale (=for the market) 共進会出品または販売のために家きんを仕立てる.

Q *commercial poultry*=poultry for profit 養鶏業. ¶*live poultry* 生きている鶏(鶏肉に対して).

poultryman, *n.* 養鶏業者.

Q² a *town poultryman* 町の養鶏業者.

pounce, *n.* とびかかること.

V *make* a *pounce* upon … …に襲いかかる.

P be *on* the *pounce* 飛びかかろうとしている.

pounce, *v.* 飛付く, 襲う.

M *pounce away* さらって行く.

P *pounce on* (=*upon*) a person 人に飛びつく. ¶He would *pounce on* any mistake of grammar. 彼はよく文法の誤りをのがさず指摘した. 【類】The cat *pounced upon* a rat. / The police *pounced upon* the thief.

pound, *n.* ポンド(目方); ポンド(英貨).

V It *costs* five *pounds*. それは五ポンドかかる. ¶He *gained* twenty-eight *pounds* in weight. 彼は体量が二十八ポンド増した. ¶I *have* a *pound* in my purse. 私は財布に一ポンドある. ¶He can *lift* three hundred *pounds*. 彼は三百ポンドの重量物をあげることができる. ¶She *lost* about twenty-five *pounds* in the space of a few months. 彼女は二三カ月間に二十五ポンドばかり体重が減った. 【類】I've *lost* 10 *pounds* since over here. ¶*regain* one's lost *pounds* その減っていた体重が元通りになる. ¶*weigh* 200 *pounds* 目方が二百ポンドある. 【類】How many *pounds* do you *weigh*?

P He weighs *above* 200 *pounds*. 彼は目方が二百ポンド以上ある. ¶The house lets *at* a hundred *pounds* a year. その家は家賃年百ポンドだ. ¶Tea is sold *by* the *pound*. 茶は一ポンドいくらで売る. ¶He sold his horse *for* forty *pounds*. 彼は四十ポンドで馬を売った. ¶discount 5s. *in* the *pound* 一ポンドに付五シリング割引する. ¶He lives *on* a *pound* a week. 彼は一週一ポンドで暮している. ¶His bill comes *to* £30. 彼の勘定は三十ポンドになる.

P² six *pounds of* sugar 六ポンドの砂糖.

pound, *v.* つき砕く; たたく.

M *pound away* (=work hard) at one's work せっせと仕事をやる. ¶Her heart was *pounding* (=hammering) *furiously*. 彼女の心臓はものすごくどきんどきんしていた.

M² He *pounded along* a rough road. でこぼこ道をどしんどしんと歩いて行った. ¶*pound off* 小さく仕切る.

P The chairman *pounded for* order. 議長は静しゅくにせよと(木づちで)こつこつたたいた. ¶*pound* rice *in* a mortar うすで米をつく. ¶I was awakened by some one *pounding on* the door. 私はだれかが戸をたたいたので目を覚ました. ‖*pound on* drums 太鼓をたたく. ¶*pound* the fish *to* a jelly 魚肉をつきつぶす. ¶*pound with* a hammer ハンマーで打つ.

poundage, *n.* 目方.

Q fight off *superfluous poundage* 運動で過剰体重を下げる(けん闘選手など).

pour, *v.* 注(つ)ぐ; そそぐ; 吐露する; どしゃ降りする.

M novels *poured forth* from the press 続々出版される小説 ‖*pour forth* one's feelings in a torrent of eloquence 懸河の弁で所感をひれきする. ¶He *poured out* his heart of her. 彼女に思いのたけを打明けた. 【類】Birds *poured out* their songs. / Passengers *poured out* on to the platform. ‖*pour out* the tea 茶をつぐ. 【類】We *poured out* into the welcome air of the street.

M² The cold blasts *pour down* from mountains. 寒い木枯しが山から吹き下ろして来る. ‖The stream was *pouring down* over the rocks. 川は岩を越して滝のように流れた. ¶Orders for … *poured in*. …の注文が殺到した. ‖*pour in* water 水を注ぐ. 【類】Letters (Intelligence) *pour in* from all quarters. / Sunlight *poured in* through the windows. / Mail is *pouring in*. / applications are *pouring in* from all quarters for … / Support of their action *poured in* from all parts of the country. / Commissions *poured in* upon him from all sides. ¶*pour* it *into* a mould それを型に注ぎ込む.

P tears *pouring down* her cheeks とめどもなくほおを流れる涙. ¶*pour* milk *from* a pitcher つぼからミルクを注ぎ出す ‖Blood *poured from* the main artery of the thigh. 血がまたの大動脈からこんこんと流れ出た. 【類】Books of this kind has *poured fom* the press in recent years. ¶It *poured in* torrents. どしゃ降りだった. ¶*pour* water *into* a vessel 器に水を注ぐ ‖*pour* one's songs *into* the recording instrument 歌を録音器に吹込む ‖People *pour into* a big city. 人々は大都会に流れ込む. ¶*pour* coal *on* [the] fire 火に石炭をつぐ ‖*pour* oil *on* [the] troubled waters 荒海に油を注いで波を静める; 調停する ‖*Pour* some tea *on* my rice. 御飯にお茶をかけて下さい. ¶*pour* water *out of* a vessel 器から水を注ぎ出す. ¶*pour* hot water *over* it それに熱湯を浴せかける ‖*pour* sauce *over* food 食品にソースをかける. ¶It has *poured with* rain—not stopping for a single moment—since he arrived here last night. 昨夜彼が当地へ到着してから雨は少しもやまず盛んに降っていた.

pouring, *a.* どしゃ降りの.

P² It was *pouring of* rain when we reached the steamer. 汽船に着いたときは雨がひどく降っていた.

poverty, *n.* 貧乏; 貧弱.

V *conceal* the *poverty* of thought by an eccentric diction 奇矯な語法で思想の貧弱を隠す. ¶*plead poverty* as one's excuse 貧乏を口実にする. ¶He *showed* a striking *poverty* in his knowledge of Japan. 彼は日本に対する認識が著しく欠けていることを示した. ¶*suffer* the bitterest *poverty* どん底の貧に苦しむ.

V² *Poverty brings* stupidity. 貧すれば鈍する. ¶*Poverty stared* him in the face. 彼は貧乏に身を責められていた.

Q He died in *abject poverty*. 彼は極貧の中に死んだ. 【類】live in the most *abject poverty* / He has been reduced to *abject poverty*. ‖steeped in the most *abject poverty* 赤貧洗うがごとき状態に陥って ‖from *abject poverty* to affluence 極貧から富裕へ. ¶*acute poverty* 身にこたえる貧乏. ¶his *chronic poverty* 彼の慢性的貧困. ¶*dire poverty* 悲惨な貧乏. ¶*downright poverty* 全くの貧乏. ¶He is reduced to *extreme poverty*. 彼は貧乏のどん底にある. ¶By the law of compensation, *financial poverty* is often a blessing in disguise. ありがたいことに財政上の貧乏は不幸のように見えてもその実は幸福なことが往々ある. ¶*frank poverty* decently disguised 体裁よく隠されている赤貧. ¶live in *genteel poverty* 貧乏だがなんとか世間体をつくろって暮す. 【類】*Genteel poverty* is one of the tragedies of modern society. ¶*grinding poverty* 身を削る貧乏. ¶*holy poverty* 清貧. ¶*honest poverty* 清貧. ¶*noble poverty* 清貧. ¶*pinching poverty* 貧苦. ¶live in *sad poverty* 哀れな貧乏暮しをする.

P He was tempted *by poverty* to commit a crime. 彼は貧に迫られて罪を犯した. ¶emerge *from poverty* 貧苦を脱する. ¶He was fed *in poverty*. 彼は貧乏の中で育った. 【類】He was born *in poverty*. / die *in poverty*. / He is *in poverty*. ¶He was born *to poverty*. 彼は貧乏の家に生れた. ‖He has brought himself *to poverty*. 彼は自業自得で貧乏になった. ¶sink *into poverty* 貧する.

P² Japan's *poverty in* iron ore and *in* coal 日本における鉄鉱及び石炭の不足. ¶*poverty of* the blood=anemia 〚医〛貧血 ‖*poverty of* thought 思想の貧困 ‖*poverty of* invention 創意の貧困(欠乏).

powder, *n.* 白粉(おしろい); 火薬.

V *apply powder* to the face=*put powder* on one's face 顔におしろいを塗る. ¶*use powder* おしろいをつける. ¶*waste* one's *powder* and shot 弾薬を浪費する. 「煙火薬.

Q a *smokeless powder* for sporting purposes 狩猟用の無

Q² *beverage powder* 飲料水の粉末素. ¶*bouillon powder* ブイヨン・パウダー(スープの素). ¶*bursting powder* 爆薬. ¶*cocoa beverage powder* ココア飲料を製する粉末. ¶*compound powder* 合成火薬. ¶*detonating powder* 爆発薬.

¶reconstitute ***dried egg** powder* to normal fresh egg consistency 乾燥卵の粉末を普通の生卵の成分に還元する. ¶***dried whole-egg** powder* 生卵そのままの乾燥鶏卵の粉末. ¶***face** powder* おしろい. ¶***flea** powder* のみ取粉. ¶***foot** powder* 足につける粉. ¶***fulminating** powder* 爆発火薬. ¶***insect** powder*＝insecticide 駆虫剤. ¶***liquid** powder* 水おしろい. ¶***orangeade** powder* オレンジエードを製する粉末. ¶***polishing** powder* みがき粉. ¶***service** powder* 軍用火薬. ¶***soap** powder* 粉石けん. ¶***sporting** powder* 猟銃の火薬. ¶***tobacco** powder* 粉たばこ. ¶a ***toilet** powder* for the complexion 美顔おしろい. ¶***tooth** powder*＝dentifrice 歯みがき粉. ¶***washing** powder* 粉石けん.

P grind it ***into** powder* それをひいて粉にする. ¶reduce it ***to** powder* それを粉にする. ¶plaster a face ***with** powder* 顔におしろいを塗る. ¶There was no *powder* ***on*** her face. 彼女の顔にはおしろい気がなかった.

P^2 *powder* ***for*** bleaching さらし粉.

powder, *v.* 白粉を付ける; なし地に装飾する.

M She is ***much** powdered.* 彼女はこってりおしろいを塗っている. ¶She is ***thickly** (**thinly**) powdered* 彼女は厚(薄)化粧をしている.

P She was *powdered* and rouged ***for*** a holiday outing. 彼女は祭日ででかけるのでおしろいを塗り口紅を付けていた. ¶The sky is *powdered* ***with*** stars. 空は星でなし地に飾られている.

power, *n.* (**1**) 力; [通例 *pl.*] 才能, 能力; 権力; 強固; 国, 強国.

V *Power* can always be ***abused.*** 力はいつでも濫用できる. ¶He ***acquired*** the *power* of reading in eleven languages. 彼は十一カ国の国語を読める力をつけた. ¶A few drops of carbolic acid will greatly ***aid*** the preserving *powers* of spirit. 石炭酸を数滴加えると酒精の保存力を大いに増す. ¶The ideas ***aroused*** the slumbering *powers* of his real self. その思想が彼の真の自我が持つ眠れる力を喚起した. ¶The country ***asserted*** her *power.* その国は自国の権力を主張した. ¶He ***assumed*** the *power* of the sword. 彼は兵馬の権を握った. ¶***attain** power* 政権を握る ‖ ***attain*** its full *power* その全機能を獲得する. 【類】Iyeyasu ***attained*** supreme *power* after the decisive battle of Sekigahara. ¶***augment*** our *power* over the forces of nature 自然力を支配す人間の力を増す. ¶***call for*** much *power* of the will 多大なる意志の力を要する. ¶***communicate*** their full *powers* その全権委任の旨を通達する. ¶***confer** power* upon ... ...に権力を付与する. ¶those who ***control** power*＝those in power 権力者. ¶***cripple*** the sea *power* of ... ...の海軍力を無能にする. 【類】***cripple*** one's *power* of locomotion (機動力). ¶***cultivate*** the *power* of observation 観察力を養う ‖ ***cultivate*** a *power* of original expression 独創的な表現力を養う. ¶***curb*** one's *power* その権力を抑制する. ¶***curtail*** the *powers* of the committee 委員会の権能を削る. ¶***define*** one's *powers* その権限を明らかにする. ¶The motive *power* in ... is ***derived*** from water power. ...の原動力は水力から得ている. ¶***develop** powers* of accurate thought and expression 正確な思考及び表現の力を発達させる. 【類】***develop*** one's *powers* of observation and appreciation (観察及び鑑識の力) / ***develop*** the *powers* latent within one (潜在力). ¶***devote*** one's intellectual and spiritual *powers* to the service of society その知力と精神力を社会の奉仕にささげる. ¶***diminish*** its *power* of destruction その破壊力を減退させる. ¶***distrust*** one's *power* その力を危ぶむ. ¶***do*** (＝***make***) one's *power* 全力を尽す. ¶***double*** or ***treble*** one's earning *power* [技術の修得など]所得の能力を二倍または三倍にする. ¶***draw*** its *power* from ... ...からその力を引出す. ¶***dwarf*** the intellectual *powers* 知力の発達を減退させる. ¶The subject arrested the attention and ***employed*** the *powers* of great talents. その問題は敏腕家の注意を引きまたその頭をこれに使わせた. ¶***encourage*** and ***train*** the *power* of guessing 推察力を奨励しかつ訓練する. ¶The rate of exchange favorable to America has ***enhanced*** the purchasing *power* of the dollar. 米国に有利な為替相場でドルの購買力が高まった. ¶***enjoy*** peculiar *powers* of intuition 特殊の直覚力を有している. ¶***exceed*** one's *powers* 越権に及ぶ. ¶***exercise*** one's *power* for good その力を善用する ‖ ***exercise** powers* of inspection 監察権を行使する ‖ Embryo orators ***exercise*** their *powers* of speech at the "practice" debates. 雄弁家の卵は討論実習会で弁論の力を練る. ‖ the *powers* ***exercised*** by the police in respect to ... are derived from ... ...に関する警察権は...から由来したものである. ¶***exert*** all one's *powers* その全力を尽す. ¶***exhibit*** the splendid *power* of organization 鮮かな統制力を示す. ¶***extend*** one's *power* その権限を拡張する. ¶***foster*** one's *powers* of observation 観察力を養う. ¶Temptation ***gained** power* over her. 彼女は誘惑にかかった. 【類】The lion-tamer ***gained*** wonderful *power* over animals. ‖ ***gain** power* directly from the sun 太陽から直接にエネルギーをとる. 【類】As the sun ***gains** power* roses in pots will require a more liberal supply of water. ‖ when the Bolsheviks ***gained** power* ボルシェヴィキが権力を得たとき. ¶***generate** power* 動力を発生する. ¶***give** power* of attorney to ... ...に代理権を与える. ¶***hand over*** one's *power* to ... 政権を...に譲る. ¶He ***has** power* to sign. 彼には署名の権能がある. ‖ I ***have*** the *power* of the law behind me. 私の背後には法律の力が控えている. ‖ The fish seems to ***have*** no *power* to live on. その魚はもう生きる力がないようだ. ‖ I ***have*** no *power* to act as you desire. 御希望通りには取計らい兼ねます. ¶***hold** power* of attorney 代理権を持っている ‖ ***hold** power* over ... ...の支配権を握っている. 【類】***hold*** the *power* of life and death over ... ¶***improve*** one's *powers* of expression その表現力を増進させる. ¶***increase*** the *power* of reading (language) 読書(などの)力を増す. ¶***invoke*** the *power* of the press 新聞雑誌の力に訴える ‖ The *power* of the Church was ***invoked*** against him. 教会の力をもって彼に対することとなった. ¶***lessen*** the *power* of work 活動力を減じる. ¶***lose*** the *power* of walking 歩行の自由を失う. ¶***lower*** the resisting *powers* of the organism その有機体の抵抗力を弱める. ¶***obtain** power* from waves 波を利用して動力を得る. ¶In the year 1758, Wolfe, by capture of Quebec, ***overthrew*** the whole French *power* in North America. 一七五九年ウルフはケベックを陥れて北米におけるフランスの全勢力を一掃した. ¶***possess*** all *power* 全権を有する. ¶***proclaim*** their *power* from the house-top 彼らの権力を吹聴する. ¶***produce*** electric *power* 発電する. 【類】Running water ***produces** power* to run mills. ¶sacrifices, even human sacrifices, were ***offered*** to propitiate the *powers* of evil いけにえ, それは人間のいけにえすらも悪神の威力を和げるためにささげられた. ¶***put out*** one's full *powers* その全力量を発揮する. ¶I ***question*** the *power* of his personality. 私は彼が人格の力を具えているかを疑う. ¶***reduce*** the *powers* of intellectual activity 知的活動力を減殺する. ¶He has ***regained*** his *power* to work. 彼は再び仕事ができるようになった. ¶***require*** all one's *power* 満身の力を要する. 【類】***require** power* of attorney (委任権). ¶***reserve*** the *power* to ... ...すべき権力を保留しておく. ¶***resign*** one's *power* [皇帝など]権力の地位から去る. ¶He ***retained*** his *power* until his death. 彼は最後までその権力を確保した. ¶***secure*** the *power* in their own hands 権力を自分たちの手に収める. ¶***seize** power* 権力を握る. ¶***show*** great *power* in that line 大いにその方面の技量を示す. ¶***stimulate*** the reasoning *powers* 推理力を刺激する. ¶***strengthen*** one's *power* of thought その思考力を強める. 【類】***strengthen*** the *powers* of the will / ***Strengthen*** your *power* of inhibition (制止力) by constant practice. ¶***squander*** one's *powers* in dissipation 遊とうに精力を消耗する. ¶It ***surpasses*** the *power* of Westerners' comprehension. それは西洋人には理解できない. ¶***tax*** one's *powers* to the utmost 精一杯の力を出させる. ¶***undervalue*** (***underestimate** or **belittle***) one's *powers* 人の力を見くびる. ¶***use*** one's *power* in the interest of ... ...のために尽力する. 【類】***use*** one's *powers* arbitrarily (勝手に) / legitimately (合法的に) ***use*** the *power* / cleverly ***use*** the mighty *power* of the press (新聞雑誌の偉力). ¶***utilize** power* from the sun 日光力を利用する. ¶***vest** power* in ... ...に権力を付与する. ¶***weaken*** one's working *power* その作業能率を弱める. 【類】The development of feudalism ***weakened*** the *power* of the shoguns. ¶***wield** power* 権力を揮う.

V^2 The purchasing *power* of money ***declined*** one-third. 通貨の購買力が三分の一低下した. ¶The *power* of man over nature has ***increased.*** 自然を支配する人間の力が増加した. ¶His *power* ***lies*** elsewhere. 彼の長所は別にある. ¶The *power* of ... ***waned.*** ...の勢力は衰えた.

Q wield the ***absolute power*** over ... ...に絶対権力を揮う. ¶***Allied powers*** 連合国. ¶***artificial power*** 人為の力. ¶an ***Asiatic Power*** アジアの一強国. ¶***bodily powers*** 体力. ¶***brutal power*** 暴力. ¶***civil power*** 民力. ¶the ***civilized Powers*** of the world 世界の文明国. ¶a ***colonial power*** 植民国. ¶Great Britain has become the greatest ***colonizing power*** in the world. 大英国は世界最大の植民国になった. ¶wield a ***considerable power*** かなりの権力を揮う. ¶He lacks ***constitutional power*** for recovery. 彼には回復するだけの体力が欠けている. ¶***contractual power*** 契約(の拘束)力. ¶develop ***conversational powers*** 会話の力を養う. ¶develop one's ***creative powers*** 創作力を延ばす. ¶with ***deficient powers*** of resistance 不十分な抵抗力で. ¶He has no ***discretionary power***. 彼には自由裁量の権限がない. ¶the ***disinfective power*** of sunshine 日光の消毒力. ¶a preacher of ***distinguished power*** 卓越した力をもつ説教師. ¶a ***dominant Power*** in Europe 欧州における優勢な強国. 【類】Japan's position as the ***dominant power*** in East Asia. ¶Capital is the ***dominating power*** in modern society. 資本は現代の社会における優勢な権力である. ¶Chevalier's ***drawing power*** シュヴァリエの魅力. ¶eliminate those concentrations of ***economic power*** which are in derogation of the public interest 大衆の利益に反する経済力の集中を排除する. ¶the ***educational*** "***powers*** that be" 教育当局者. ¶***Electric power*** is cut off. 配電が中断されている. ‖ the source of ***electric power*** 電源 ‖ a dam for the production of ***electric power*** 発電ダム. ¶be possessed of marked ***elocutionary powers*** すぐれた弁舌の才を有する. ¶wield ***enormous power*** 偉大な権力を揮う. ¶its ***enormous productive powers*** そのばく大な生産力. ¶The ***fatal power*** of beauty is responssible for it. それは美人薄命というものだ. ¶a ***first-rate Power*** 一等国. ¶the ***five Powers*** of the first magnitude 五大強国. ¶a ***friendly power*** 友邦. ¶he has ***full power*** to act for ... 彼は...の全権を持っている. 【類】in the ***full powers*** of maturity (円熟した能力) / the recovery of ***full power*** by the Emperor (王政復古) / possess ***full power*** over (対して)... / have a ***full power*** of decision (決定) / I have ***full power*** to enter into arrangements on his behalf (彼に代って). ¶***germicidal power*** 殺菌力. ¶***good powers*** of observation りっぱな観察力. ¶the ***generative power*** 発電力. ¶the ***Great Powers*** of Europe 欧州の列強. ¶The industrial classes are the ***growing power*** in the country. 産業階級はその国の新興勢力である. ¶engines of ***high power*** and low weight 強力軽量な機関. ¶men of ***high intellectual power*** 知能優秀の人々. ¶***histrionic powers*** 俳優の腕前(演技). ¶the utilization of ***hydroelectric power*** 水力電気の利用. 【類】streams and waterfalls suitable for the development of ***hydroelectric power***. ¶***imitative power*** 模倣力. ¶by the exercise of his ***intellectual power*** 知力の運用によって. 【類】train the creative power, the highest of ***intellectual powers*** / the fruits of his ***intellectual power*** / a child's ***intellectual power*** / He devoted his immense ***intellectual power*** to it with brilliant success. ¶***inventive*** and ***plot-devising power*** 創意と企画の力. ¶his ***irresistible persuasive powers*** 彼の否応なしに人を動かす力. ¶***keen powers*** of observation 鋭利な観察力. ¶the unfolding of ***latent powers*** 潜勢力の展開. ¶the ***Lesser Powers*** of Europe 欧州の弱小国. ¶He has no pretensions to ***literary power***. 彼は文才があるなどと自負していない. ¶Bells were thought to have a ***power magic*** over the forces of nature. 鐘は自然力を支配する魔力のあるものと思われていた. 【類】It was supposed he had some ***magic powers***. ¶the ***magnetic power*** of her beauty (charm) 彼女の男を引きつける力. ¶a ***mandatory power*** 委任統治国. ¶the rise of England as a ***maritime power*** 海国としての英国の興起. ¶The country showed a ***marvelous power*** of recuperation. その国は驚異的な回復力を示した. ¶use ***mechanical power*** 機械力を使用する. ¶develop ***mental powers*** 知能をみがく. ¶Buddhism was then a ***mighty power*** in the land. 当時仏教はその国における偉大な勢力であった. ¶***military power*** 武力 ‖ the most ***military powers*** of the world 世界最強陸軍国. ¶It is believed to possess ***miraculous powers***. それは不思議な力があると信じられている. ¶***misused power*** 濫用された力. ¶***motive power*** 原動力. ¶a great ***naval*** and ***military power*** 一大陸海軍国. ¶the cinema, a ***new educational power*** 新教育機関たる映画. ¶show ***no mean dramatic power*** りっぱな演技を見せる. ¶***occult power*** 神秘的な力(天眼通などの). ¶the ***occupying powers*** 占領国群. ¶***political power*** 政権 ‖ The Arabs were once an outstanding ***political power*** in the world. アラビア人は世界における傑出した政治国であったことがある. ¶France was then the ***predominating power*** in continental Europe. フランスは当時ヨーロッパ大陸において卓絶した強国であった. ¶The problem is evidently beyond our ***present powers*** of solution. その問題は現在のわれわれの力ではとても解決されないことは明らかだ. ¶His ***power*** to work was ***prodigious***. 彼の仕事の能率はすばらしかった. ¶***ratiocinative powers*** 推理力. ¶evidence of ***real power*** 真に力ある証拠. ¶his ***remarkable*** story-telling ***powers*** 彼の非凡な話術の腕前. ¶the ***reparative power*** of nature 自然治ゆ力. ¶***sexual powers*** 生殖力. ¶through ***sheer mass power*** 数量の力だけで. ¶***signatory powers*** 加盟国. ¶***sovereign power*** 主権. ¶He has ***supreme power***. 彼は最高の権力を握っている. ‖ a usurpation of ***supreme power*** 主権略奪. ¶possess ***talismanic powers*** 不思議な力を有する. ¶a ***terrible power*** of money《俗》非常に多額の金. ¶***tyrannical power*** 暴力. ¶he has an ***unlimited power*** of ... 彼は...する無限の力を有している. ¶a manager with ***unusual powers*** 非凡の手腕のある支配人. ¶a man of ***varied powers*** 多能の人. ¶He dissipated the greater part of his ***virile power*** before entering upon marriage. 彼は結婚前に生殖力の大部分を消耗した. ¶***vital power***=vitality 生命力, 活力. ¶persons with ***weak resisting powers*** 抵抗力の弱い人. ¶The hot spring has ***wonderful recuperative powers***. その温泉は不思議な回復力をもっている.

Q² ***air power*** 空軍力. ¶the employment of ***animal power*** 動物力(馬など)の利用. ¶the ***axis powers*** 枢軸国群. ¶Since the days of Waterloo England has been the ***balancing power*** of the world, not only in arms, but in literature, art, learning and the sciences. ウォタルーの戦の当時から英国は軍事においてのみならず文学・芸術・学問ならびに諸科学において世界の均勢を保つ勢力であった. ¶the union's ***bargaining power*** 労組の団体交渉権. ¶pictures of proven ***box office power*** 興行価値百パーセントの諸映画. ¶***brain power*** 知力. ¶***Buying power*** is growing. 購買力は増大しつつある. 【類】the expansion of ***buying power*** / shrink still further the ***buying power*** of the consumer's dollar / be long inured to the squeeze of rising costs and diminishing ***buying power*** for his dollar. 【類】The ***buying power*** of money is in the United States about 70 per cent less than in Great Britain. / The ***buying power*** of agriculture (農業者) is below that of industry. ¶***cementing power*** 接合力. ¶***compelling power*** 強制力. ¶By "love's ***constraining power***," he gained a hold upon her. 愛の拘束力で彼は彼女を抑えつけた. ¶***consumer buying power*** 消費者の購買力. ¶for lack of an official head with ***disbursing powers*** 金銭支払の権力を持つ長官がいないので. ¶***discriminating power*** 識別力. ¶increase one's ***earning power*** 生活力を延ばす. ¶the assumption of ***emergency powers*** 非常時権力の横領 ‖ bestow ***emergency power*** upon ... ...に非常権力を与える ‖ be given vast temporary ***emergency powers*** 特別非常大権を与えられる. 【類】government by ***emergency powers***. ¶***fertilizing power***〘生物〙受精能力. ¶a ***first-class power*** 一等国. ¶a ***first-rank power*** 一流国. ¶use all the ***Government powers*** 官権を総動員する. ¶by ***hand power*** 手動で. ¶the ***hauling power*** けん引力. ¶the ***healing power*** of drugs 薬剤の治療力. ¶cultivation by ***horse power*** 馬力による耕作 ‖ a lawn mower for ***horse power*** 馬力による芝刈器 ‖ nominal ***horse power*** 公称馬力. ¶his ***hurling power*** 投てき力. ¶the ***invigorating*** and ***stimulating power*** of exercise 活力を与え刺激を与える運動の力. ¶an ***island power*** 島国. ¶He had ***life and death powers*** over his subjects. 彼は人民に対し生殺与奪の権力を持った. ¶***life-saving power*** 救命力. ¶***man power*** 労働力 ‖ measures for conserving ***man power*** 労働力保存の方策. ¶***man-killing power*** 男子を悩殺する力. ¶***mandate power*** 委任統治権. ¶Canada, a ***mediating power*** in world affairs. 世界政治における調停勢力たるカナダ. ¶Italy as a

Mediterranean sea power 地中海の海軍国としてのイタリア. ¶***memory powers*** 記憶力. ¶a ***number two power*** in the country 大統領の次に位置する要人(米国では国務長官). ¶the four ***occupation powers*** 四つの占領国. ¶***organizing power*** 構成力. ¶the great ***Pacific Powers***, Japan and America 太平洋の大国日本とアメリカ. ¶with enormous ***penetrating power*** 非凡な洞察力のある. ¶take ovr ***police powers*** [反乱軍などが]警察権を握る‖through exercise of ***police power*** 警察権の発動により. ¶***producing power***=productivity 生産力. ¶absorption of surplus ***purchasing power*** 浮遊購買力の吸収. 【類】The ***purchasing power*** of the public is falling. / augmented public ***purchasing power*** / her foreign ***purchasing power***. ¶***reasoning powers*** 説得力. ¶exercise the ***ruling power*** 統治権を行使する. ¶***satellite powers*** 衛星国. ¶***sea power*** 海軍力. 【類】the rise of Japan's ***sea power***. ¶***sea-air power*** 海空軍力. ¶***staying power*** 維持力. ¶***steam power*** 蒸気力(火力). 【類】the application of ***steam power***. ¶***teaching power*** 教授能力. ¶a person of ***loose thinking powers*** 思考力の緩漫な人. ¶the development of the ***thinking powers*** 思考力の発達. ¶***transit*** (=***carrying***) ***power*** 輸送力. ¶***treaty powers*** 条約[加盟]諸国. ¶exercise (=use) the ***veto power*** 拒否権を行使する. 【類】hold ***veto power*** / has absolute ***veto power*** on ... ¶one's ***vocabulary power*** その使用し得る語彙(ごい). ¶his ***vote-getting power*** 彼の得票力. ¶***voting power*** 投票権. ¶President Truman asked the cut of most ***war powers*** last week. トルーマン大統領は先週軍事力の大半を削除することを求めた. ¶destruction of the industrial basis of Japan's ***war-making power*** (=war potential) 日本軍事遂行能力の産業基盤の破壊. ¶***water power*** 水力. ¶the ***water-retaining power*** of the soil 土壌の含水力. ¶have much ***will power*** 強い意志の力を持つ. 【類】his wavering ***will power***. ¶***wind power*** 風力. ¶increase the ***word power*** 語彙(ごい)の使用力を増大させる. ¶***world powers*** 世界の国々, 列強. 【類】a new ***world power*** / the growth of the United States to the status of a great ***world Power***.

P the emergence of Japan ***as*** a great *Power* in the Far East 極東の一強国としての日本の出現. ¶a situation ***beyond*** our *power* to control 拾収すべからざる局面. ¶painful (beautiful) ***beyond*** any *power* of language to express (=words to tell) 言語に絶して苦しい(など). 【類】it is ***beyond*** my *power* to ... / It is ***beyond*** the *power* of thought to conceive it. / technical matters (専門のこと) ***beyond*** his *power* to understand / ***beyond*** the *power* of the mind to grasp / for reasons ***beyond*** our *powers* of perception. ¶a struggle ***for*** *power* 勢力争い‖the desire ***for*** *power* 権力欲. ¶decline ***in*** *power* 権力が衰える‖the men ***in*** *power* 権力の座にある人々. 【類】the Democrats then ***in*** *power* / the politicians ***in*** *power* / the party that was yesterday ***in*** *power* / The Government continues ***in*** *power* until the present time. / The present cabinet has been ***in*** *power* for four years. / It became an instrument of political propaganda by the party ***in*** *power*. / the Shogun was ***in*** *power* from ... to ...‖It is ***in*** your *power* to refuse or accept the proposal. その申出を拒否しようと受諾しようと君の勝手だ. 【類】I am sorry to say it is not ***in*** my *power* to do as you desire. / do all ***in*** one's *power*. / he has it ***in*** his *power* to ... ¶come ***into*** *power* 権力を握る. ¶a man ***of*** *power* 力の強い人‖The great Ming dynasty came to a close in 1644, after three hundred years ***of*** *power*. 大明朝は政権を握ること三百年にして一六四四年に終結を告げた.‖the advance ***of*** Russian *power* in Asia アジアにおけるロシア勢力の浸透. ¶The party went ***out of*** *power*. その党は政権から離れた.‖it is ***out of*** my *power* to ... ...は私の力に及ばない. ¶smirking subserviency ***to*** the *powers* that be 笑顔つくって当局に屈従すること. ¶***under*** the *powers* of the warm rains 暖かな雨の力で‖With only the bow tug in attendance the liner moved off ***under*** her own *power*. 引き船がともにつないであっただけでその定期船は自力で進航した.‖***under*** a *power* conferred by the law 法が与えた権力のもとに‖bring it ***under*** the *power* of ... それを...に従わせる. ¶The sun rose ***with*** *power*. 太陽は威勢よく昇った.‖He yelled ***with*** all the *power* of his voice. 彼はあらん限りの声で叫んだ. ¶This is not ***within*** (=beyond) my *power*. これは私の力に及ばない.‖A man has it ***within*** his will *power* to govern the passions. 人は情欲を支配するだけの意志の力を持っている. ¶***without*** further *power* of speech それ以上は物が言えなくて.

P[2] He had remarkable *powers* ***as*** a guesser. 彼には非凡の推察力があった.‖for the advancement of one's *powers* ***as*** a teacher 教師としての手腕を養うために. ¶The Russian Ambassador at Constantinople has been the *power* ***behind*** the Throne. コンスタンチノーブル駐さつの露国大使は国王の黒幕であった. ¶*power* ***for*** evil 悪に走る力‖a *power* ***for*** good 善に導く力‖use of *power* ***for*** cruel and selfish ends 残忍で利己的な目的への力の用い方. ¶He became a *power* ***in*** the industry. 彼はその産業における大立者となった. ¶the *power* ***of*** generation 生殖力‖have good *powers* ***of*** mental digestion すぐれた理解力がある‖his *power* ***of*** word-painting 彼の言語表現力‖In geisha *powers* ***of*** the tongue ripen fully only when her physical charms decline. 芸者はその美ぼうが衰えるころになってようやくその口の力が十分に成熟する.‖a *power* ***of*** eloquence 弁舌の才‖a *power* ***of*** people (work) 沢山の人(など). 【類】they have the *power* ***of*** numbers, but not the *power* ***of*** ability‖*powers* ***of*** darkness (=evil) 悪魔たち‖the *power* ***of*** a lens レンズの強度. ¶*power* ***over*** men 人を支配する力. 【類】The Austrian house held *power* ***over*** the Netherlanders for eighty-six years. ¶the *power* of books ***to*** interest 人に興味を与える書物の力. ¶I have no *power* ***with*** the trustees. 私は維持員に対しては何らの権力もない.

O the *powers* that be=those who are in authority 当局者, 幹部. 【類】I recommended him to the *powers* that be. ¶the *power* to read English 英語の読書力‖I had not *power* to sit up. 私には起きているだけの気力がなかった.‖the *power* to write good English りっぱな英文を書く力.

(2) 〖数学〗...乗, べき.

Q raise ... to ***2nd*** (***3rd, 4th***) *power* ...を 2 (3, 4) 乗する‖32 is the ***5th*** *power* of 2 三十二は二の五乗である. 【類】16 is the ***4th*** *power* of 2.

powerful, *a.* 有力な.

P *powerful* ***over*** his men 彼の部下に対して勢力のある.

powerless, *a.* 力のない.

P All the resources of medical science are *powerless* ***in*** that disease. 医学のあらゆる手段もその病気には手の施しようがない.

practicability, *n.* 実行性.

V ***consider*** the *practicability* of ... ...の実行性を考える. ¶***demonstrate*** its *practicability* その実行性を証明する. ¶***question*** its *practicability* その実行性を疑う.

P[2] the *practicability* ***of*** this proposal depends upon the attitude of ... この提議の成否は...の態度いかんによる.

practicable, *a.* 実行できる; 通れる.

M While possible, it is not ***commercially*** *practicable*. やれはするが採算が立たない. ¶The road is ***partly*** *practicable* for automobiles. その道路の一部は自動車が通れる.

practical, *a.* 実際的な.

M ***eminently*** *practical* きわめて実際的な. ¶***severely*** *practical* あくまで実際的な.

practice, *n.* 習慣, 常習, 癖; 慣例; 実行, 実習; 演習; 手腕; [医師などの]開業.

V ***abandon*** the *practice* その習慣を捨てる. ¶***abjure*** a wrong *practice* 悪癖を誓って絶つ. ¶It ***affords*** good *practice* in English composition. それは英作文のよい練習になる. ¶***begin*** (=***enter***) *practice* of [the] law 弁護士を開業する. ¶It takes years for a new dentist to ***build up*** a paying *practice*. 新しい歯科医が自分の商売をものにするには数年かかる. ¶***commence*** the *practice* of dentistry 歯科医を開業する. ¶***continue*** the barbarous *practice* of ... ...の蛮行を続ける. ¶***defend*** the *practice* on the ground that ... ...という根拠でそのやり方を弁護する. ¶to ***discourage*** such a *practice* そのようなやり方をやめさせるために. ¶*Practice* is ***divided*** on that point. [言葉など]慣用はその点ではまちまちである. ¶***do*** *practice* in the art of fencing フェンシングの練習をする. ¶The *practice* of ... is to be much ***deprecated***. ...の習慣は大いに排斥すべきものだ. ¶***do*** rifle shooting *practice* 射撃の演習をやる. ¶The doctor has ***established*** a large *practice*. あの医者は大分はやっている. ¶***follow*** the *practice* 医者(または弁護士)をやる‖***follow*** the *practice* of ... ...という風にする‖To assume a pen name is a *practice* widely ***followed*** in Russia. 雅名

をつけることはロシアで広く行われている習慣である. ¶***forbid*** a *practice* 一つの習慣を禁じる. ¶The doctor (lawyer) ***has*** an extensive *practice.* あの医者(弁護士)は手広くやっている. ¶***introduce*** an entirely new *practice* in the conduct of a journal 新聞経営の上に新機軸を出す. ¶***make*** a *practice* of travelling abroad よく海外旅行をする ‖ ***make*** a *practice* of overcharging いつも過当料金を取る. 【類】 ***make*** a *practice* of using words without understanding them. ¶***obtain practice*** in ... ...を練習する. ¶***open practice*** of vice 邪道にはいる. ¶***popularize*** the *practice* of cremation 火葬の風習を一般に普及させる. ¶***practice*** this heinous *practice* このけしからんことを実行する. ¶***put down*** this *practice* この習慣をやめる. ¶***relinquish*** one's *practice* 医者(弁護士)を廃業する. ¶It ***requires*** much *practice.* それは大いに熟練を要する. ‖ It is a feat that ***requires*** long *practice.* それはちょっとやそっとではできない芸当だ. ¶***sell*** one's *practice* [医者・弁護士などの]商売の株を売る. ¶***set up*** a *practice* [医師などが]開業する. ¶***stamp out*** the *practice* of ... ...の習慣を絶滅する. ¶***start*** the *practice* under the impression that ... ...と思ってこれを実行する. ¶***taboo*** a *practice* 習慣を禁制する. ¶The *practice* is being ***taken up*** in other large towns. 他の大都市でもこれにならっている.

V[2] the *practice* ***broke down*** because of objections from ... ...からの反対に会ってその実行は腰くだけとなった. ¶The *practice* appears to have ***died out*** entirely. その習慣は全然すたれたらしい. ¶The *practice* especially ***flourishes*** in the United States. その習慣は特に合衆国に盛んに行われている. ¶My *practice* has steadily ***increased.*** 私の患者がだんだんふえて来た. ¶The *practice* still ***prevails.*** その習慣は今なお行われている. ‖ The old *practice* of ... no longer ***prevails*** (=***obtains***). ...の旧習はもう行われていない.

Q in ***actual*** *practice* 実際行われている所では ‖ carry the story into ***actual*** *practice* その話を地で行く. ¶the ***ancient*** *practice* of a fortune-teller 占者の古臭いやり方. ¶an ***artful*** *practice* ずるいやり方(策略). ¶He was in high repute for his ***ascetic*** *practices.* 彼は苦行で評判が高かった. ¶It is a ***bad*** *practice* to allow a boy much pocket-money. 子供に小使を沢山持たせるのは悪いことだ. ¶a ***baneful*** *practice* 有害なこと. ¶a far more ***better*** *practice,* to my mind, than ... 私の考えでは...よりははるかによい習慣. ¶it is a ***common*** *practice* for ... to ... ...に取っては...するのが普通の習わしだ. 【類】 a ***common*** *practice* among students. ¶do ***considerable*** *practice* 大いに練習をやる. ¶The first requisite in the study of a language is ***constant*** *practice.* 言語の研究の第一要件は絶えず練習することである. ¶birth control through ***contraceptive*** *practices* 避妊法による産児制限. ¶***conventional*** *practice* しきたり. ¶***corrupt*** *practices* 悪習慣. ¶***customary*** *practice* 慣行. ¶a matter of ***daily*** *practice* 日常の習わし, 常習. ¶a ***depraved*** *practice* 醜行. ¶a ***diabolical*** *practice* 非道なやり方. ¶give ***diligent*** *practice* to the rules その規則を熱心に実行する. ¶***dishonest*** *practice* 不正直なやり方. ¶a ***disreputable*** *practice* 失行. ¶According to ***European*** *practice,* the day precedes the month in letter headings; as 12 May, 1928. [米国と違って]ヨーロッパの習慣では手紙の書出しは 12 May, 1928 のように日の方を先にして月を後にする. ¶Correct spelling will only come from ***extensive*** *practice.* 正確なスペリングは盛んに練習するに限る. ¶give ***faithful*** (=diligent) *practice* to the following rules 次の規則を必ず実行する. ¶observe the ***following*** *practices* 次にあげてある慣行に従う(通りにする). ¶***fraudulent*** *practices* 詐欺行為. ¶it would be ***good*** *practice* to ... ...するのはよいことだ. 【類】 Translation from Japanese is ***good*** *practice* in English. ¶a ***habitual*** *practice* 常習. ¶a ***hackneyed*** *practice* 常とう手段. ¶***honest commercial*** *practice* 正直な商業的取引. ¶the kissing of pictures, reliance on the images of saints, and other ***idolatrous*** *practices* 写真に接ぷんすること聖像に頼ること及びその他の偶像礼拝的習慣. ¶an ***immemorial*** *practice* 太古の風習. ¶queer ***Indian*** *practice* 変ったインデアンの風習. ¶***intelligent*** *practice* 知力の練習. ¶an ***international*** *practice* 国際的慣行. ¶The physician has a ***large*** *practice.* あの医者は大いにはやる. ¶handle it with the quickness and dexterity of ***long*** *practice* 長い経験で手早くかつ手際よくそれを取扱う. ¶***Malthusian*** *practice* 産児制限の方法. ¶contrary to ***modern*** *practice* 現代風に反して. ¶modern ***medical*** *practice* 現代医術の実際. ¶a young doctor looking for a ***new*** *practice* 開業を目指している若い医師. ¶an ***orthodox*** *practice* 昔からのきまったやり方. ¶a ***preliminary*** *practice* 予行演習. ¶The ***present*** *practice* is to place a hydrant at the corner of every street. 現在では町々の角に消火せんが設けられている. ¶enter into ***private*** *practice* [病院などをやめて]自分で開業する. ¶a ***recognized*** *practice* 認められた慣習. ¶a matter of ***regular*** (***common***) *practice* きまりきった(ありふれたこと) ‖ do ***regular*** *practice* in fencing フェンシングのけいこをかかさずやる. ¶It is a ***reprehensible*** *practice* to keep a child up till nine or ten o'clock at night. 子供を夜分九時か十時までも寝させないでいるのはよくないことだ. ¶Smoking in bed is a ***risky*** *practice.* 床中で喫煙するのは危険なことだ. ¶it is a ***safe*** *practice* to ... ...するのが安全なやり方だ. ¶***scandalous*** *practices* of a trust トラスト企業組合の醜行為. ¶***sharp*** *practices* 抜け目のないやり方. ¶The Oxford crew are having some ***smart*** *practice.* オックスフォードのクルーは猛練習をやっている. ¶a ***sounder educational*** *practice* 一層堅実な教育上の慣行. ¶depart from ***standard*** *practice* 標準的行為から離れる. ¶a ***superstitious*** *practice* 迷信的慣行. ¶the ***timehonored*** *practice* 古くからの習慣. ¶***traditional*** *practice* 伝統的慣行, しきたり. ¶an attempt to codify the best ***typographical*** *practices* of the present day 今日における最良の印刷技術の集大成的試み. ¶a series of ***unfair*** *practices* 一連の不公平なやり方. ¶an ***unhealthy*** *practice* 非衛生的な習慣. ¶a ***universal*** *practice* 広く世の中に行われている慣行. ¶The *practice* of ... was ***unknown*** in his day. その時代には...ということはなかった. ¶a ***usual*** *practice* 恒例. ¶an ***unwholesome*** *practice* 有害なやり方. ¶***weird*** *practices* of ascetic devotees 行者の物すごい荒業. ¶the ***wide-spread*** *practice* among ... of ... ...間に広く行われている...の慣習.

Q[2] ***blackmarket*** *practices* 色々のやみ取引. ¶***charlatan*** *practices* いんちき. ¶***classroom*** *practice* 実地教授. ¶a ***firing*** *practice* 発火演習. ¶***gun*** (=shooting) *practice* 射撃の練習. ¶unfair ***labor*** *practice* 不当労働慣行. ¶establish a ***law*** *practice* 弁護士を開業する. ¶the weight of ***majority*** *practice* 多数の者がやっている場合の強み. ¶***music*** *practice* 音楽の練習. ¶***present-day*** *practices* 現代の慣行. ¶***rifle*** *practice* ライフル銃の射撃の練習. ¶distortion of the normal clean ***sex*** *practices* 通常の清潔な性行為をゆがめること. ¶***target*** *practice* 射的. ¶unfair ***trade*** *practices* 不正な商取引. ¶***wartime*** *practice* 戦時中の慣行.

P ***according to*** the established *practice* 慣例によって. ¶This disease is ***beyond*** my *practice.* この病気は私の手に負えない. ¶show ***by*** *practice* rather than by precept 教訓よりも実行で示す. ¶***by way of*** *practice* 練習のため. ¶opportunities ***for*** *practice* in a language ある言語を練習する機会. ¶depart from the usual *practice* 常例に反する ‖ retire ***from*** *practice* [医者・弁護士など]廃業する. ¶an example of this principle ***in*** *practice* その主義履行の実例 ‖ a physician ***in*** *practice* 開業医 ‖ spend time ***in*** the *practice* of arms 武道の修業にときを費す. 【類】 It is not so easy ***in*** *practice* as in theory. ‖ an idea that will hardly work ***in*** *practice* ものになりそうもない考え ‖ keep ***in*** *practice* へたにならないように練習する. 【類】 In France, especially in Paris, there has been a great increase during recent years ***in*** the *practice* of abortion (堕胎). ¶carry (=bring *or* ***put***) ... ***into*** *practice* ...を実行する ‖ put an idea ***into*** *practice* 考えを実行する. ¶I can't speak English fluently as I am ***out of*** *practice.* 私はやらずにいるから英語はすらすら話せない. ‖ get ***out of*** *practice* [しばらくやらないので]へたになる. 【類】 He has long been ***out of*** *practice* at golfing. ¶***with*** *practice* 練習するにつれて. ¶***without*** considerable *practice* 大して練習しないでも.

P[2] a *practice* ***at*** war in maneuvers and mock battles 演習及び模擬戦における戦争の実習 ‖ a *practice* ***at*** ... m. distance ...マイル距離射撃実習. ¶a *practice* ***in*** writing English 英作文の練習 ‖ a *practice* ***in*** music 音楽の練習. ¶the *practice* ***of*** rising early 早起の習慣 ‖ the *practice* ***of*** a lawyer 弁護士業 ‖ the *practice* ***of*** polygamy 一夫多妻主義の実行. 【類】 the *practice* ***of*** writing (shaking hands).

¶have a *practice* ***upon*** (=***on***) a music instrument 楽器で(音楽の)練習をする. ¶a *practice* ***with*** full charge 実弾射撃.
O make it a *practice* to ... ...を常習とする.

practice, practise, *v.* 練習する, 実行する.
M ***assiduously*** *practice* the game その競技を熱心に練習する. ¶*practice* ***faithfully*** まじめに練習する. ¶He *practices* medicine ***largely.*** 彼は手広く医業をやっている. ¶do not *practice* it ***professionally*** それを商売でやるのではない. ¶*practice* ***regularly*** 規則的に練習する. ¶The wise man not only speaks, but *practices,* ***wisely.*** 賢者は言うことが賢い計りでなく行うことも賢い.
M^2 I'm *practicing* ***up*** on the art of self-defence. 僕は自衛術(柔道)を練習している.
P He *practices* ***as*** a physician (lawyer). 彼は開業医(など)だ. ‖ certificates to *practice* ***as*** certified public accountant 公認会計士免許状. ¶He previously *practiced* ***at*** the Bar. 彼は以前弁護士をしていた. ¶*practice* ***at*** typing タイプの練習をする. 【類】a young lady *practicing* ***at*** the piano. ¶*practice* pupils ***in*** English 生徒に英語を練習させる. ¶*practice* ***in*** an art 技術を練習する. ¶*practice* ***on*** the typewriter (piano) タイプライター(など)を練習する. ¶She *practiced* music ***upon*** Prof. Stokowski. 彼女はストコフスキー先生のもとで音楽を練習した. ¶He has *practiced* ***upon*** (=***on***) my credulity. 彼は私の信じやすいのに付込んだ. ¶*practice* ***with*** the rifle 射的を練習する.

practitioner, *n.* [医者・弁護士の]開業者.
Q a ***general*** *practitioner* 一般医 (specialist に対し). ¶a ***medical*** *practitioner* 開業医. ¶a duly ***qualified medical*** *practitioner* ちゃんと免許を取った医師. ¶an ***unethical*** *practitioners* in the profession 不徳義な医者弁護士たち. ¶an ***unqualified*** *practitioner* 無免許医師または弁護士.
P^2 a *practitioner* ***in*** the law 弁護士.

prairie, *n.* 《米》大草原(プレーリー).
Q coyotes of the ***Western*** *prairies* 西部大草原のコヨーテ(おおかみ).

praise, *n.* 称賛, 賞賛; 賛美.
V ***accord*** *praise* to God 神を賛美する. ¶***adjudge*** *praise* or blame to ... 審判の上...の賞罰を決める. ¶***allot*** one's *praise* and blame impartially 公平に賞罰を行う. ¶***award*** *praise* and blame ほめたりけなしたりする. ¶***bestow*** our unqualified *praise* on ... ...を絶賛する. 【類】the highest *praise* that can be ***bestowed*** upon him is that ... / It is worthy of all the *praises* ***bestowed*** on it. ¶***bring forth*** *praise* from ... ...からの称賛にあずかる. ¶***chant*** the *praises* of ... ...を賞揚する. ¶***deserve*** (=***merit***) *praise* 称賛に価する. ¶He ***earned*** unstinted *praise* from the critics. 彼は批評家たちから惜気もなくほめられた. ¶***enjoy*** unmitigated *praise* 盛んに称賛される. ¶***express*** *praise* 称賛する. ¶***extort*** the reluctant *praise* of ... 無理強いに...にほめさせる. ¶***give*** unstinted *praise* to ... ...に対して賛辞を惜しまない ‖ ***give*** *praises* unto God 神に賛辞を呈する(神様のおかげでなど). ¶we ***have*** high *praise* to bestow upon ... われわれは...に大いに賛辞を呈するものである. ¶***heap*** *praises* on him 彼をほめ抜く. ¶***lavish*** *praise* on a person 人をやたらにほめ立てる. ¶***receive*** his *praise* 彼にほめられる. 【類】He ***received*** great *praise* from critics. ¶***sing*** its *praises* それをほめちぎる. 【類】His *praises* were ***sung*** by poets. / ***sing*** his *praises* highly (盛んに). ¶***sound*** his *praises* 彼をほめ立てる. ¶***sound forth*** the *praises* of a hero (a great man) 英雄(など)を盛んにほめ称える. ¶loudly ***trumpet*** the *praises* of ... 盛んに...をほめ立てる. ¶***win*** high *praise* 非常な賞賛を博する. 【類】he ***won*** the *praise* of ...
V^2 unstinted *praise* ***belongs*** to ... for ... ...は...で大いに賞賛すべきだ.
Q His conduct is deserving (=worthy) of ***all*** *praise.* 彼の行為はあらゆる賞賛に値している. ¶the poor ambition of titles, honors, and ***contemporary*** *praise* 肩書や名誉や当代の賞賛を求めるつまらない野心. ¶earn ***discriminating*** *praise* 具眼者の賞賛を博する. ¶*praise* is ***due*** to him for ... 彼は...でほめられるのが当然だ. 【類】every *praise* is ***due*** to the wisdom of ... in ... ¶give ***enthusiastic*** *praise* to ... ...を熱心に賞揚する. ¶rather ***exaggerated*** *praise* むしろ過当の賛辞. ¶***excessive*** *praise* 過当の賛辞. ¶to say ... would be but ***faint*** *praise* ...と言うのは心にもない賛辞に過ぎない. ¶with ***fervent*** *praise* 熱烈な賛辞を呈して. ¶***fulsome*** *praise* うんざりする賛辞. ¶***Great*** *praise* is due to him. 彼は大いに賞賛すべきだ. ¶That is ***high*** *praise.* それは思い切ったほめ方だ. ‖ in terms of ***high*** *praise* 絶賛の言葉で. 【類】He deserves ***high*** *praise.* / the ***highest*** *praise* for ... / accord ***high*** *praise* to ... / the ***highest*** *praise* that can be given to them is to say that ... / my ***highest*** *praise* goes to ... ¶his ***merited*** *praise* 当然彼に呈すべき賞賛. ¶***ink-spilling*** *praises* 惜気ない賛辞. ¶it is ***no small*** *praise* to say that ... ...と言うのは中々の賛辞である. ¶He has received so much ***public*** *praise.* 彼は公衆の多大の賞賛を博した. ¶I have the ***strongest*** *praise* for ... 私は...に対して最大の賛辞を呈する. ¶bespatter him with flattery or ***undue*** *praise* 彼におついしょう即ち不当なほめ言葉を浴せかける. ¶enjoy ***unmitigated*** *praise* 絶賛を博する. ¶it brought to him the ***unstinted*** *praise* from ... そのために...から彼に惜しみない賛辞をおくられた.
P I felt myself color ***at*** this *praise.* 私はこの称賛には赤面した. ¶His magnificent conduct is ***beyond*** all *praise.* 彼の堂々たる行為はこれを賞賛する言葉がない. ¶he is generous ***in*** *praise* of ... 彼は...に賛辞を惜しまない ‖ sing ***in*** *praise* of ... ...をおう歌する ‖ He is loud (=profuse) ***in*** *praise* of his wares. 彼はしきりに自分の商品をほめ立てている. ‖ they were warm ***in*** their *praise* of ... 彼らは熱心に...をほめた. 【類】Much was said (written) ***in*** *praise* of him. / We can not speak ***in*** too high *praise* of its efforts. ¶*praise* a person ***to*** the skies 人を絶賛する. ¶He is entitled ***to*** high *praise.* 彼は大いにほめてやってよい. ‖ sing ***to*** the *praise* of God 神を賛美して歌う. ¶***with*** unstinted *praise* 賛辞を惜しまずに.
P^2 I have a word of *praise* ***for*** him. 私は彼に対して賛辞を呈する. ¶sing the *praises* ***of*** Him 神を賛美する. ¶sing *praises* ***to*** God 神に賛美をささげる.

praise, *v.* 賞賛する, 称揚する.
M He was ***highly praised*** for his honesty. 彼は正直なのを非常にほめられた. ‖ He can be *praised* ***highly*** without any qualifications. 彼は無条件でほめ称えてよい(絶賛に価する). ¶He was *praised* ***sky-high.*** 彼は非常にほめられた. ¶He was ***warmly*** *praised.* 彼は熱烈に賞揚された.
P I *praised* him ***for*** his diligence (frugality). 私は彼の勤勉(など)なのをほめた. 【類】Men *praise* Nikko ***for*** its scenery. / The Japanese are *praised* ***for*** bravery. / We have nothing but *praise* ***for*** him. ¶*praise* ***in*** song (speech, words) 歌(など)でほめる. ¶They *praised* him ***to*** his face. 彼らは面と向って彼をほめた. ¶He *praised* his friend [***up***] ***to*** the skies. 彼は口を極めて友人をほめた. ¶They *praised* him ***with*** one accord. 彼らは彼を異口同音に賞賛した.

praiseworthy, *a.* ほむべき.
P what is *praiseworthy* ***of*** him is that ... 奇特にも...

prance, *v.* [馬が]はねて進む; [比ゆ的に]いばって歩く.
M^2 *prance* ***about*** はね回る; いばって歩く.

prank, *n.* いたずら.
V They ***acted*** their wanton *pranks* with undoubted licentiousness. 彼らは底抜けのいたずらをした. ¶nature ***plays*** a *prank* on ... 自然は...にいたずらをする. 【類】The boys are fond of ***playing*** *pranks.*
Q ***boyish*** *pranks* 子供らしいいたずら. ¶play ***foolish*** *pranks* on ... ...にばかげたいたずらをする. ¶a ***harmless*** *prank* 害にならないいたずら. ¶***mischievous*** *pranks* [子供の]たちの悪いいたずら.

prattle, *n.* おしゃべり.
Q ***mere*** *prattle,* without practice 口だけで実行の伴わないこと.

pray, *v.* 祈る, 祈とうする.
M ***devoutly*** *pray* that he may ... 彼が...せんことをひとえに祈る. ¶She *prayed* ***earnestly*** to the gods. 彼女は熱心に神々に祈った. ‖ ***earnestly*** *pray* for your pardon (=leniency) 平に御容赦を願う. ¶*pray* ***fervently*** for a sign 熱心に御利益のあるように祈る. 【類】She ***fervently*** *prayed* to Heaven. ¶*pray* ***out*** しるしの見えるまで祈る. ¶***secretly*** *praying* he may not be seen by anybody who knows him 彼は自分を知っている人に見られないようにと心ひそかに祈って.
M^2 *pray* ***down*** enemies 敵を調伏する.
P They *prayed* ***against*** the coming of that fatal day. 彼らはあの凶日の来ないようにと祈った. ¶*pray* ***at*** their mothers' knee 母のひざもとで祈る. ¶*pray* ***before*** a shrine 神前に祈る. ¶*pray* ***for*** the success of ... ...の成功を祈る. ¶*pray* ***in*** a church 教会で祈とうする. ¶*pray* ***to*** God 神に祈る ‖ *pray* ***to*** the gods for mercy 神々の恵みを祈る.

prayer, *n.* 祈とう; 祈願; とう詞.
V God ***answered*** his *prayers.* 神は彼の祈願にこたえた. ‖ Her *prayer* was ***answered*** (=***granted***). 彼女の祈りがかなった. ‖ At last his *prayers* were ***answered*** by a vision of the god. 遂に彼の祈りがかなって神が夢まくらに立った. 【類】 *Prayers* to the Goddess in seasons of drought are said to be invariably ***answered*** (御利益がある). ¶ ***breathe*** a *prayer* to ... 低声で...に祈願する. ¶ ***chant*** *prayers* 祈とうを唱える. ¶ dully, mechanically ***intone*** their *prayers* and liturgy 祈とうや祈とう書をものうげにお役目的に唱える. ¶ ***mutter*** a *prayer* of thanks to God 低声で神に感謝の祈りをする. ¶ ***offer*** *prayer* お祈りを上げる. 【類】 ***offer*** a *prayer* of thankfulness / The minister commenced the service by ***offering*** a short *prayer.* / ***offer*** *prayers* in the temple for the recovery of ... ¶ ***offer up*** a *prayer* お祈りをする. ¶ ***perform*** a *prayer* 祈る. ¶ She ***prayed*** an earnest *prayer.* 彼女は熱心に祈った. ¶ ***raise*** *prayer* to God 神に祈りをささげる. ¶ ***read*** *prayers* 祈とう文を読み上げる. ¶ ***recite*** *prayers* for the dead 死者のためにとう詞を朗読する. 【類】 ***recite*** a certain number of *prayers* for the repose of his soul (慰霊). ¶ tell one's beads and ***repeat*** one's *prayer* じゅずをつま繰ってお祈りを繰返す. ¶ ***say*** (=offer up) a *prayer* お祈りをする. ¶ ***utter*** one's *prayer* お祈りを上げる.
V² *Prayers* ***go on*** night and day 夜となく昼となく祈とうが続く. 【類】 Night after night the loving women's *prayers* ***went up*** to the darling of the house, the brave brother, the noble son fighting for England at the front.
Q an ***earnest*** *prayer* 悲願. ¶ a ***fervent*** *prayer* 熱心なお祈り. ¶ shout an ***impressioned*** *prayer* with his face turned heavenward 天を仰いで熱誠な祈願を叫ぶ. ¶ his ***one*** *prayer* was ... 彼の一つの念願は...であった. ¶ a ***short*** *prayer* 簡単なお祈り. ¶ offer up a ***silent*** *prayer* 黙とうをささげる. 【類】 a one-minute ***silent*** *prayer.* ¶ The *prayer* has become ***stereotyped.*** 祈とうが紋切型になった. ¶ His *prayers* were ***unanswered.*** 彼の祈願は届かなかった.
Q² a ***family*** *prayer* 家庭のお祈り. ¶ a ***morning*** (an ***evening***) *prayer* 朝(夕)の祈り.
P They were ***at*** *prayer* in the chapel. 彼らは礼拝堂でお祈りをしていた. ¶ The portrait is represented as kneeling ***in*** *prayer.* その画像はつまずいて祈とうをしている所が描いてある. ‖ I found her ***in*** *prayer.* 彼女がお祈りを上げているのを見た. ‖ with his hands clasped ***in*** *prayer* 合掌して.
P² a *prayer* ***against*** ... ...よけの祈とう. ¶ offer a short *prayer* ***at*** meal=say grace 食前のお祈りをする. ¶ a *prayer* ***for*** rain 雨ごい ‖ *prayers* ***for*** victory 戦勝祈願. 【類】 a *prayer* ***for*** the happiness of the soul of the deceased. ¶ a *prayer* ***to*** Buddha 念仏 ‖ a *prayer* ***to*** the Rising Sun 日の出の礼拝.

preach, *v.* 説教する; 講話する; 宣伝する.
M He *preached* himself ***hoarse.*** 彼は説教して声をからした.
M² *preach* ***down*** こきおろす; 説伏する. ¶ *preach* ***up*** ほめ立てる.
P *preach* ***against*** drinking (intemperance) 飲酒(など)の害を説く. ¶ a sermon *preached* ***by*** Father ...... 神父の説教. ¶ *preach* a funeral ***from*** the pulpit 教壇から葬式の説教をする. ¶ *preach* ***in*** the streets 街頭で説教する. ¶ *preach* ***on*** a subject (text) ある問題(など)について講話する. ¶ *preach* temperance ***to*** people 人々に禁酒を説く.

preacher, *n.* 説教師.
Q a ***lay*** *preacher* 説教する平信徒.
Q² a ***soap-box*** *preacher* 《米》つじ説法者.

preaching, *n.* 説教.
V ***Adapt*** your *preaching* to the audience. 人を見て法を説け. ¶ They ***hear*** no *preaching* of birth control. 彼らは産児制限の宣伝を聞き入れない. ¶ ***practice*** one's *preaching* その説く教えを実行する.

preamble, *n.* 前置, 前文; 前兆.
Q a ***good*** *preamble* to ... ...に取っての吉兆.
P we may conclude ***without*** further *preamble* that ... これだけの前置で...と結論して差支えないだろう.

pre-arrangement, *n.* 打合わせ.
P ***by*** *pre-arrangement* with ... ...との前もっての打合わせで.

precarious, *a.* 不安な.
M Living in those days was ***very*** *precarious.* 当時の生活はすこぶる不安だった.
O a *precarious* foothold 危険な足場. 【類】 a *precarious* life.

precaution, *n.* 警戒; 予防, 予防策.
V ***exercise*** *precautions* 用心する. ¶ ***neglect*** no *precaution* 警戒を怠らない. ¶ ***omit*** *precautions* 警戒を怠る. ¶ ***prescribe*** suitable hygienic *precautions* 適当な衛生上の予防法を規定する. ¶ ***take*** *precautions* against ... ...に対して用心をする. 【類】 ***take*** *precaution* against fires (burglars, accidents) / *Precautions* will be ***taken*** to guard against the recurrence of such incidents. / the *precaution* should be ***taken*** of ... / having ***taken*** the *precautions* to ... ¶ ***throw*** all *precautions* to the winds 一向警戒しないでいる. ¶ ***use*** due *precaution* for ... ...に対して適当な予防策を講じる. 【類】 ***use*** the proper *precaution* against danger.
Q take ***elaborate*** *precautions* 手を尽して予防する. ¶ ***every business-like*** *precaution* あらゆる実際的な予防策. ¶ take ***every possible*** *precaution* 万遺憾なきを期する. ¶ ***minute*** *precaution* 細心な警戒. ¶ take the ***necessary*** *precautions* to ... ...するのに必要な用意をしておく. ¶ take ***proper*** *precautions* 適当な用心をする. ¶ if proper ***sanitary*** *precautions* were taken 適当な衛生上の予防策を講じれば. ¶ take ***sensible*** *precautions* to ... 気をきかして...の用意をしておく. ¶ take ***special*** *precautions* to prevent fire 特に火災防止に注意する. ¶ That is certainly a very ***wise*** *precaution.* それはたしかに至極賢明な用心だ.
Q² ***air-raid*** *precautions* 空襲警戒警報.
P ***as*** a *precaution* against delay 遅れない用心に. 【類】 take an umbrella along ***as*** a *precaution.* ¶ ***by way of*** *precaution* against a bad year 凶年の用意に.

precede, *v.* 先立つ; 先導する.
M ***immediately*** *preceding* this paragraph 本節の直前に(前項の).
P It is *preceded* ***by*** two vowels. 前に二つの母音がある. ‖ This measure must be *preceded* ***by*** milder ones. この手段に出る前にもっと穏和な手段を採らなければならない. ‖ *preceded* ***by*** our guide 案内者に先導されて. ¶ apologize for *preceding* one's parents ***in*** death 親に先立つ不幸をわびる. ¶ *precede* a person ***to*** the grave 人に先立つ.

precedence, -cy, *n.* 先行, 上位, 上席; 席次.
V Neither discoverer could ***claim*** *precedence.* どちらの発見者も自分の方が先だと主張することができなかった. ‖ It ***claims***—and rightly—*precedence* of all the neighboring places of the sort. それはこれに隣接したその種の場所の当然先駆者である. ¶ The *precedence* to be ***given*** to the guests at such a reception is a difficult matter. こんな招待会で来客の席次を定めるのは困難なことだ. ¶ ***have*** the *precedence* of (=over) ... ...より優位に立つ. ¶ *Precedence* is strictly ***observed.*** 席次が厳重に守られている. ¶ ***take*** the *precedence* of... ...の上位に立つ(優先する) ‖ The question of expense ***takes*** *precedence* of all others. 費用の問題が何より先きだ. 【類】 The welfare of the country ***takes*** *precedence* of parties. / Social claims should ***take*** *precedence* of personal claims. / Play ***takes*** *precedence* over work. / The "S.O.S." call ***takes*** *precedence* over all other signals. / Government messages ***take*** *precedence* over all others. ¶ ***yield*** *precedence* to ... 優先権を...に譲る.
P a table ***of*** *precedence* 上席の食卓.

precedent, *n.* 先例, 例.
V In 1916 Hu Shih ***broke*** all *precedent* by writing a poem in the spoken tongue. 一九一六年に胡適は先例を破って口語で詩を作った. ¶ the *precedent* set was ***caught up*** by ... そのお手本の先例を...が採り上げた. ¶ ***create*** a *precedent* 先例を作る. ¶ ***follow*** a *precedent* 先例にならう. 【類】 ***following*** the *precedent* established in the dim and misty past (ぼうばくたる太古). ¶ ***form*** a *precedent* for future occasions 将来の場合のために先例を作る. ¶ this ***gives*** *precedent* for ... これが...の先例となる. ¶ ***have*** *precedents* in the history of ... ...の歴史に先例が沢山ある. ¶ ***quote*** *precedents* 先例を引用する. ¶ ***set*** a *precedent* 先例を作る. 【類】 conform to the *precedent* ***set*** by ... ¶ ***set up*** a new *precedent* 新例を作る. ¶ ***violate*** *precedents* 先例を破る.
Q set a ***bad*** *precedent* 悪例を作る. ¶ a ***dangerous*** *precedent* 危険な先例. ¶ faithfully follow an ***established*** *precedent* 確立した先例を忠実に守る. ¶ a ***historic*** *precedent* 歴史上の先例. ¶ it established an ***interesting*** *precedent* in ... それは...におけるおもしろい先例となった. ¶ establish an ***inviolable*** *precedent* 犯すべからざる先例となる. ¶ a ***long-established*** *precedent* 長い間行われた先例. ¶ ***neces-***

sary precedents to … …に必要な前提. ¶establish a ***new*** *precedent* 新例を開く. ¶There is ***no precedent*** for this. これには一つも先例がない. ¶a ***time-honored precedent*** 古来の慣例(しきたり).

P *according* ***to*** *precedent* 先例によって. ¶copy ***after*** bad *precedents* 悪例をまねる. ¶***against*** all *precedents* 先例にそむいて. ¶Do not take this ***as*** a *precedent*. これを先例とするな. ¶It is ***beyond*** all *precedents*. それは先例がない. ¶be governed ***by*** *precedent* 先例によって支配される. ¶depart ***from*** *precedent* 先例にそむく. ¶It is contrary ***to*** all *precedents*. それは先例に反する. ¶It is ***without*** *precedent* in history. それは歴史に先例がない.

O become a *precedent* 先例になる.

precept, *n.* 教訓, 戒律.

V ***carry*** these *precepts* into practice これらの教訓を実行する. ¶***instill*** the *precepts* of Christianity into one's mind キリスト教の教えを教え込む. ¶These *precepts* he both ***preached*** and ***practiced***. 彼はこの教訓を説きかつ実行した. ¶***violate*** the *precepts* of Christianity キリストの教えにそむく.

Q ***practical*** *precepts* 実行できる教訓.

precinct, *n.* 《英》境内; 《米》行政区域, 選挙区.

V ***enter*** the charmed *precincts* of the Tower ロンドン塔の神秘な感じの境内にはいる.

Q the ***sacred*** *precincts* of the Great Shrines of Ise 伊勢大神宮の聖域.

Q[2] within the ***city*** *precincts* (=limits) 市内の行政区画内に. ¶an ***election*** *precinct* 選挙区. ¶leave the ***school*** *precincts* during school hours 授業時間内に学校から外に出る. ¶a ***voting*** *precinct* 選挙区.

P The wrestling tournament was held ***in*** the *precincts* of the shrine. 相撲は神社の境内で催された. ¶***within*** the *precinct* of Parliament (a temple) 《英》議院(など)の構内に. ¶the non-resident voters ***of*** the *precinct* その選挙区の住居を持たない選挙人.

precious, *a.* 貴重な, 大切な.

M ***as*** *precious* as gold 金のように貴い.

P Time is *precious* ***to*** me. 時間は僕には貴重だ.

precipice, *n.* がけ, 懸がい.

Q ***beetling*** *precipices* 突出した懸がい. ¶a ***sheer*** *precipice* 絶壁.

P fall (stumble) ***down*** a *precipice* がけから落ちる(がけを踏み外す). ¶Keep ***off from*** the *precipice*. がけふちに寄るな. ¶fall ***off*** a *precipice* がけから落ちる. ¶walk ***on*** a *precipice* がけの上を歩く. ¶go ***over*** a *precipice* がけをよじ上る.

precipitate, *v.* 投げ落す; 真さかさまに墜落する; 促進させる.

P A cold wave *precipitates* a drop ***in*** temperature. = A cold wave causes a precipitate drop in temperature. 寒波が来ると温度が急下降する. ¶*precipitate* oneself ***over*** the precipice into the whirlpool がけから渦流へ真さかさまに墜落する. ¶He lost his footing and was *precipitated* ***to*** the ground. 彼は足を踏み外して地上へ真っさかさまにほうりつけられた. ¶*precipitate* oneself ***upon*** another 他人の上に真っさかさまに墜落する.

précis, *n. F.* 要略, 大意.

V ***draw up*** a *précis* of … …の要略を作製する. ¶***make*** a *précis* of … …の大意を書く.

precise, *a.* 正確な.

M at this period, to be ***more*** *precise* (=that is), during the several post-war years この時代に, つまり戦後の数年間に. ¶be ***very*** *precise* in following instructions 指命通り正確に実行している.

P be prim and *precise* ***in*** manner. 態度がきちんとしてかたくるしい.

precision, *n.* 正確, 精確.

V ***give*** *precision* to the report 報告を正確にする. ¶The information ***lacks*** *precision*. その情報は正確を欠く.

Q a ***fastidious*** *precision* in language 言語のやかましく正確な使用. ¶***mathematical*** *precision* 数学的正確. ¶a ***meticulous*** and ***scientific*** *precision* 細密で科学的な精確. ¶the system with ***military*** *precision* 軍隊式に正確な方法. ¶relate with ***surprising*** *precision* 驚くほど正確に話す. ¶with ***unerring*** *precision* 間違いのない正確さで.

Q[2] with ***clockwork*** *precision* 時計のように正確に. ¶Planes fly daily over regular routes with ***time-table*** *precision*. 飛行機は毎日時刻表通り正確に正規空路を飛んでいる.

P define a word ***with*** *precision* 正確に語の定義を下す‖ ***with*** the *precision* of machinery 機械のように正確に. 【類】 ***with*** the *precision* of an artist.

preclude, *v.* 防止する.

P *preclude* it ***from*** entering はいらないように防止する‖it is *precluded* ***from*** … それは…にはいる余地がない. 【類】 He was *precluded* ***from*** the membership.

precocious, *a.* ませた.

M Those children were found ***frightfully*** *precocious*. これらの子供たちは恐ろしいほどませていることが分かった. ¶There is something ***unpleasantly*** *precocious* about her. 彼女はいやにませたところがある.

precocity, *n.* 早熟.

V He ***displayed*** a singular *precocity* in regard to calculation. 彼は計算にかけては特に年齢以上の能力を示した.

predecessor, *n.* 前任者; 前身.

V endeavor to ***go*** (=***excel***) his *predecessors* one better 前任者を一段とりょうがしようと努力する. ¶It ***surpasses*** its *predecessors* in the same field. それは同じ分野で今まで出たものよりはるかによい.

Q the astrolabe, the ***clumsy*** *predecessor* of the modern sextant 現代の六分儀の不細工な前身とも言うべき天体観測儀. ¶his ***immediate*** *predecessor* 彼の直前の前任者. 【類】 The present Cliff House is the third of a series, and was erected in 1909, its ***immediate*** *predecessor* (すぐ前の建物) having burned in 1907. ¶The machine he originated and perfected has no ***modern*** *predecessor* or ancient prototype. 彼が創案しかつ完成した機械は古今独歩だ. ¶***Wilson's*** *predecessor* ウィルソンの前任者.

P This work, ***like*** its *predecessors* in the series, will find a wide circle of readers. 本書はその双書の既刊のもの同様に広く愛読されるであろう.

P[2] The harquebus is the *predecessor* ***of*** the musket. 火なわ銃は小銃の前身だ.

O open the door of a consulting-room while one's *predecessor* is still present 先に来た人がまだいるのに診察室のとびらをあける.

predestination, *n.* 運命.

P[2] *predestination* ***of*** believers ***to*** eternal life 信者たちが永遠の生命を与えられる運命.

predicament, *n.* 苦境, 窮地.

V I ***realized*** my *predicament*. 私は本当に困った.

Q I was placed in an ***awkward*** *predicament*. 私はどうにも困ってしまった. ¶He was in a ***cruel*** *predicament*. 彼はえらく困っていた. ¶I was in a ***dreadful*** *predicament*. 私は非常に困った. ¶our ***financial*** *predicament* われわれの財政的困難. ¶I am in the ***identical*** *predicament* with yourself. 私は君と同じ苦境に立っている. ¶stand in a ***serious*** *predicament* 深刻な苦境に立つ. ¶a ***woeful*** *predicament* ひどい難局.

P He found himself ***in*** a strange *predicament*. 彼は自分が不思議な窮地にあるのを知った.

predication, *n.* 〘文法〙述語部.

V ***complete*** a *predication* 〘文法〙述語部を完成させる.

predict, *v.* 予言する.

M we ***confidently*** *predict* success for … われわれは…の成功を信じて疑わない. ¶one may ***safely*** *predict* that … …と予言して差支えない. ¶***truly*** *predict* 正しく予言する.

P *predict* ***for*** it a similar fate それが同様の運命に終ることを予言する. ¶*predict* ***from*** pure conjecture 全くの推測によって予言する.

O *predict* good harvest 豊作を予言する.

prediction, *n.* 予言.

V This *prediction* was ***fulfilled***. この予言は実現された. ¶many dire *predictions* have been ***made*** as to … …に関して色々恐るべき予言があった. ¶***utter*** a *prediction* 予言する. ¶This *prediction* was ***verified*** shortly afterward. この予言は間もなく事実となって現われた.

V[2] My *prediction* has ***come*** true. 僕の予言が的中した.

Q ***bold*** *predictions* 大胆な予言. ¶***gloomy*** *prediction* 悲観的な予言. ¶***ominous*** *predictions* 不吉な予言. ¶***optimistic*** *predictions* 楽観的な予言. ¶***wild*** *predictions* 途方もない予言.

Q[2] ***weather*** *prediction* 天気予報.

P[2] one's *prediction* ***as to*** … …に関するその予言.

predilection, *n.* 偏愛, より好み.

V He ***has*** a *predilection* for mathematics. 彼は殊に数学が好きだ. ‖those who ***have*** *predilections* towards theft 盗癖のある人々. ¶***manifest*** a *predilection* for town life 殊に都会生活を好む. ¶From the first he ***showed*** a *predilec-*

tion for it. 最初から彼は特にそれが好きだった.

P^2 a predilection for history 歴史好き.

predispose, *v.* あらかじめ傾向を与える; 病気にかかりやすくさせる.

M He is hereditarily predisposed to consumption. 彼は遺伝的に肺病にかかりやすくなっている.

P Some constitutions are predisposed to consumption. 体質によっては肺病にかかりやすいのがある. 【類】A cold (感冒) predisposes us to other diseases. ¶if a nature is predisposed towards it 天性がその方に向いてると(素質があれば).

predisposition, *n.* 性癖; 素質.

V excite the latent predisposition 隠れた素質を引出す.

Q a congenial predisposition 先天的傾向. ¶inborn predisposition 生れついての素質(天性).

P^2 He has a hereditary predisposition to a disease. 彼には遺伝的に病気にかかりやすい素質がある. 【類】their predisposition to disease.

predominance, *n.* 優勢, 卓越.

P^2 the predominance of the money influnce 金力の優勢 ‖ the predominance of the military over the civil power 文政に対する軍事力の優勢. ¶predominance over … …に対する卓越.

predominate, *v.* まさっている; 勢力を揮う.

M Knowledge will always predominate over ignorance. 有識は常に無知にまさる.

P Red and scarlet predominate in the flowers. その花は赤と深紅色が多い. 【類】Pine-trees predominate in the forest. / He soon began to predominate over them.

pre-eminence, *n.* 優位, 優越.

V win a great pre-eminence in the building of dirigibles 飛行船などの建造において優位を占める.

P by pre-eminence 優に.

pre-eminent, *a.* 卓絶している.

P he is pre-eminent above the rest for … 彼は…にかけては抜群だ. ¶He is pre-eminent in cleverness. 彼は非常にりこうだ.

prefab, *n.* 《米》組立住宅.

V crest (=plant) a prefab 組立住宅を建てる.

Q^2 metropolis prefabs 都市の組立諸住宅.

prefabricator, *n.* 《米》組立住宅建築業者.

Q^2 a housing prefabricator 組立住宅の建築業者.

preface, *n.* 序文.

V contribute a preface to the volume その書に序文を寄せる. ¶write a preface to … …に序文を書く.

P for a preface 序文として. ¶in the preface to this book 本書の序文に. ¶with a preface by Prof.… …教授の序文付きで.

P^2 in his preface to the work その書の序文に. 【類】the author's preface to the first edition.

prefer, *v.* むしろ…を取る.

M I would immeasurably prefer to … …の方がどの位よいか知れない.

P I prefer it above all others. なによりそれが好い. ¶prefer a charge against a motorist 運転していた人を告発する. ¶I prefer … over others in its class. 私はその中では一番…が好いと思う. ¶I prefer death to surrender (dishonor). 私は降参する(恥をかく)より死んだ方がよい. 【類】prefer beer to wine / I prefer paper money to [small] change (小銭). / prefer silence to speech / The Englishman prefers doing to talking.

O For the time being the captain is the king, or president, as you prefer, of all on board ship. さしずめ船長は船上では王または(そういった方がよければ)大統領である.

preferable, *a.* むしろ好ましい.

P Death is preferable to dishonor. 生きて恥辱を受けるよりも死んだ方がました.

preference, *n.* 選み, えり好み; 優先権.

V exhibit (=express) a preference for … …の方を好く. ¶give a preference to … …の方を取る ‖ preference is given to … over … …を捨てて…を取る ‖ Give him his preference. 彼に選ばせよ. ‖ I will give you the preference. 君に選ばせよう. ¶motives that guide the preference 選択を指導する精神. ¶I have a preference for town life. 僕は都会生活の方が好きだ. 【類】he has preference to … = he prefers … ‖ You have your preference (=choice) of seats. 座席は御自由に選べます. ¶show a preference for … …の方を好む.

Q my decided preference is for … 私は断然…することの方が好きだ ‖ I have no decided preference among several dances. 僕はどの舞踊といって別段えり好みはない. ¶with an expressed preference for … …の方がはっきり好きなので. ¶That is a matter of individual preference. それは人の好き好きだ. ¶show a marked preference for … …の方を非常に好む. ¶It is merely a matter of personal preference. それは全く人の好き好きだ.

Q^2 color preference [はえなどの]色彩偏好.

P select according to one's preference 自分の好みによって選ぶ. ¶by preference 好んで, 先ず. 【類】In science, read by preference the newest works; in literature, the oldest.—Bulwer-Lytton. ¶by electric light or gas light—gas light for preference 電灯またはガス灯で—なるべくガス灯で ‖ associate for preference (好んで) with … / learn a foreign language, English for preference (第一に). ¶choose … in preference to … …よりも…を選ぶ. 【類】It was chosen in preference to several others. / wear flowers in preference to jewels. ¶through preference 好きで.

P^2 preference for learning to wealth 富よりも学問を好むこと ‖ preference for … over … …より…の方を採ること ‖ give one creditor a preference over the others 一債権者に優先権を与える.

prefix, *n.* 接頭語; 人名に冠する敬称語.

P^2 a prefix in English names [Sir, Mr., Dr. など]英語の姓名の前につける敬称語. ¶a prefix to … …の接頭語.

prefix, *v.* 前におく.

P prefix a syllable to a word 語の前に一シラブル付ける ‖ prefix an introduction to … …に序文をつける.

pregnancy, *n.* 妊娠.

V avoid pregnancy 避妊する. ¶cause pregnancy 妊娠させる. ¶She underwent another pregnancy. 彼女はまた身ごもった.

V^2 In the third year of her marriage a second pregnancy took place. 彼女は結婚後三年目に二度目の妊娠をした. ¶terminate a pregnancy by abortion 流産によって妊娠を終える.

Q a beginning pregnancy 妊娠の初期. ¶secret pregnancy 秘密の妊娠. ¶rapidly successive pregnancies 矢つぎばやの妊娠.

Q^2 a twin pregnancy 双生児の妊娠.

P during pregnancy 妊娠中.

pregnant, *a.* 妊娠して, はらんで.

P She is pregnant by the former husband. 彼女は先夫のたねを宿している. ¶words pregnant in (=with) meaning 意味深長な言葉. ¶His writings are pregnant of (=with) poetry. 彼の文章は詩趣に富んでいる. ¶She is pregnant with her first child. 彼女は始めての妊娠をしている. ‖ an enterprise pregnant with dangerous consequences 危険な結果をはらんでいる計画 ‖ pregnant with greater results さらに重大な結果をはらんで.

O become pregnant 妊娠する.

prejudice, *n.* 偏見; 毛ぎらい; 偏見から起る損害.

V banish prejudice from one's mind 心から偏見を一掃する. ¶break down racial prejudices 人種的偏見を打破する. ¶cast prejudice aside 偏見をすてる. ¶Let us cast away all prejudices. 偏見は一切捨てよう. ¶combat any prejudices that may exist against … …に対するあらゆる偏見と闘う. ¶counteract the existing prejudice against the Japanese 日本人に対する現下の偏見に抗する. ¶create prejudice against … …に対して偏見を持たせる. ¶disarm prejudices 偏見を解く. ¶dispell prejudices 偏見を一掃する. ¶dissipate prejudices 偏見を解消させる. ¶Divest prejudice from your mind. 偏見を去れ. ¶eradicate the ingrained prejudice 根深い偏見を一掃する. ¶excite some prejudice against … …に反対する偏見をかきたてる. ¶exclude prejudice 偏見をしりぞける. ¶fight down prejudices 偏見を打倒する. ¶get over one's prejudice 偏見を抑制する. ¶harbor European prejudice 西洋かぶれがしている. ¶have a prejudice against … …に対して偏見をいだく. ¶hold no national prejudice なんら国家的偏見をいだかない. ¶imbibe the prejudices of the English 英人の偏見が浸み込む. ¶A man may easily mistake his prejudice for principle. 人はとかく主義と偏見をはき違えがちのものだ. ¶offend the prejudices of … …の感情を害して毛ぎらいされる. ¶but once you have overcome your first prejudices しかし人は一度最初の偏見に打勝つと. ¶put one's prejudices in one's pocket その偏見を表に出さない. ¶put

(=cast) *away* all *prejudice* あらゆる偏見を捨てる. ¶*remove prejudice* 偏見を除く. ¶*shock* the *prejudices* of … …の持つ偏見と衝突する. ¶*Throw aside* your *prejudices.* なんじの偏見を去れ. ¶*weaken* and *dispel* the *prejudices* against … …に対する偏見を弱めかつ打破する.

Q abate ***confirmed*** *prejudice* 動かし難い偏見を和げる. ¶shock ***conventional*** *prejudice* 因襲的な偏見に衝撃を与える. ¶the ***critical*** *prejudice* of the man 一個人が持つ批評上の偏見. ¶***deeply-rooted*** *prejudices* 根深い偏見. ¶there is ***great*** *prejudice* against … …に反対する大きな偏見がある. ¶a ***historical*** *prejudice* 歴史上の偏見. ¶an ***insular*** *prejudice* and conceit 島国民の(井の中のかえる的)偏見とうぬぼれ. ¶an ***inveterate*** *prejudice* 抜くべからざる偏見. ¶there is an ***invincible*** *prejudice* against … …に対するいかんともし難い偏見がある. ¶***irrational*** *prejudice* 不合理な偏見. ¶This is ***mere*** *prejudice.* これは偏見に過ぎない. ¶the most ***obstinate*** *prejudice* 最もがん迷な偏見. ¶The ***oldfashioned*** *prejudice* against acting or singing as a profession no longer exists. 職業としての演劇または歌謡に対する時代遅れの偏見はもうなくなった. ¶a ***popular*** *prejudice* 一般民衆の偏見. ¶a ***preconceived*** *prejudice* against the method その方法に対する先入的偏見. ¶a ***ridiculous*** *prejudice* ばかばかしい偏見. ¶***social*** *prejudices* 社会的偏見. ¶the wholly ***undeserved*** *prejudice* 全然いわれのない偏見.

Q² natural ***party*** *prejudice* もっともな党の偏見.

P It is deeply rooted ***in*** *prejudice.* それは偏見に深く根ざしている. ¶an opinion with a strong tincture ***of*** *prejudice* 大いに偏見が加味された意見 ‖ a person ***of*** strong *prejudices* 偏見の強い人. ¶even ***to*** the *prejudice* of others 人の迷惑すらかえりみないで ‖ it is greatly ***to*** the *prejudice* of the State that … …は大いに国家の害になる ‖ talk ***to*** the *prejudice* of Mr. … …君を傷つけるようなことを言う. 【類】words which tend ***to*** the *prejudice* of the reputation of … ¶views strongly tinctured ***with*** party *prejudice* 党派的偏見を強く加味された意見. ¶***without*** *prejudice* 権利を侵害せずに, 既得権を犯さずに ‖ ***without*** *prejudice* to health 健康に害なく. 【類】He was relieved of his duty ***without*** *prejudice.*

P² *prejudice* ***against*** color (country, person, idea) 人種(など)に対する偏見 ‖ *Prejudice* ***against*** any novel form of street traffic dies hard. [右側通行など]街路交通の新方式に対する偏見はなかなか抜けない. 【類】have a *prejudice* ***against*** foreigners. ¶He has a *prejudice* ***in*** our favor. 彼はわれわれをひいき目に見てくれる.

prejudice, *v.* …に偏見をいだかせる.

M He is ***strongly*** *prejudiced* against me. 彼は僕のことをえらく悪く思っている. ¶He was ***unfairly*** *prejudiced.* 彼は色めがねで見ていた.

P become *prejudiced* ***against*** the profession of guides ガイドというものはいけないものだと思い込む. 【類】*prejudice* ***against*** the government ‖ His conduct has *prejudiced* the public ***against*** him. 彼の行動を世間は悪く解している. / *prejudice* graduates ***against*** wifehood and motherhood / They tried to *prejudice* the public ***against*** me. ¶These facts have *prejudiced* us ***in*** his favor. こんなことでわれわれは彼をひいき目に見るようになった. ‖ *prejudice* ***in favor of*** … …への偏好.

prejudicial, *a.* 有害な, 不利な.

M The climate is ***gravely*** *prejudicial* to his health. その気候は彼の健康に非常に有害だ.

P Smoking to excess is *prejudicial* ***to*** health. 過度の喫煙は健康に有害だ. 【類】*prejudicial* ***to*** one's interests (利益) / *prejudicial* ***to*** the public safety (公安) / *prejudicial* ***to*** the spirit of the law / *prejudicial* ***to*** one's dignity (威厳).

preliminary, *n.* 予備工作, 手始め.

V ***arrange*** all the *preliminaries* for … …に対するすべての手はずをする. ¶***Cut*** all these wearisome *preliminaries.* こんなおもしろくもない前置はみんな除いてしまえ. ¶unless this indispensable *preliminary* is ***fulfilled*** このぜひ必要な予備工作を済まさなければ.

Q After a few ***complimentary*** and ***commonplace*** *preliminaries,* the business they had come about began. 二三型のごとき普通のあいさつがあってから彼らがそのためにやってきた仕事が始まった. ¶an ***indispensable*** *preliminary* to … …に取って欠くべからざる予備行為. ¶the ***never-failing*** *preliminary* 必ずやる予備工作.

P ***as*** a *preliminary* 第一歩として, まず. ¶***without*** *preliminaries*=abruptly やぶから棒に.

preliminary, *a.* 準備の.

M ***as*** *preliminary* to this この手始めとして.

prelude, *n.* 前奏曲; 序幕.

Q the settlement of the difficulty was a ***necessary*** *prelude* to … そのもん着の解決が…に至る必要な準備だった.

P² The Shimabara insurrection was the *prelude* ***to*** the extinction of Christianity in Japan. 島原の乱は日本におけるキリスト教絶滅の序幕だった.

premier, *n.* 首相.

Q² the ***Christian Socialist*** *Premier* キリスト教社会党首相.

P² the *premier* ***of*** a British Dominion 英領首相. 【類】the *Premier* ***of*** the Dominion of India.

première, *n. F.* 初興行, プレミヤ.

Q² The film had its ***midnight*** *première* last week. その映画は先週深夜興行として封切された. ¶The film star is to appear at the ***trade*** *première* of his new film. 映画スターはその新映画の招待試写会に姿を見せることになっている. ¶The play was given the ***world*** *première.* その劇は世界のひのき舞台に始めて上演された.

premiership, *n.* 首相の職.

V the first commoner that ***hold*** *premiership* 最初の平民宰相. ¶***reach*** the *premiership* 首相の位に上る.

premise, *n.* **(1)** 前提; 上述の次第.

Q an ***assumed*** *premise* 仮定の前提. ¶wrong conclusions based on ***false*** *premises* 誤った前提に基づく間違った結論. ¶a ***major*** (***minor***) *premise* 大(小)前提. ¶proceed from the ***wrong*** *premises* that … …という誤った前提から議論を進める.

P ***in*** the (=these) *premises* 前述の次第によって. ¶in the consideration ***of*** the *premises* 上述の次第によって. ¶***on*** the *premise* that … …ということを前提にして. 【類】start off ***on*** false *premises.* ¶criticisms based ***upon*** false *premises* 誤った前提に基づいた批評.

(2) *pl.* 邸宅, 家宅, 店舗.

V The tenant refused to ***deliver up*** the *premises.* 借家人が移転を拒んだ. ¶Street cars ***enter*** these *premises* 市街電車がこの構内にはいっている. ¶We have ***had*** our *premises* on fire. われわれの建物は火事に会った. ¶comparatively ***humble*** *premises* 比較的粗末な家. ¶***insure*** its *premises* against fire その家宅に火災保険を付ける. ¶***lease*** *premises* 邸宅を賃貸借する. ¶***light*** their *premises* at day (=in the daytime) 日中彼らの邸宅に灯火を用いる. ¶jointly ***occupy*** *premises* 建物を共同で使用する. ¶The *premises* were ***raided*** by the police. その邸宅は警官に襲われた. ¶***search*** the *premises* 家宅捜索をする. ¶***vacate*** the *premises* その家をあけ渡す.

Q ***adjoining*** *premises* 隣りの建物. ¶move to more ***commodious*** *premises* もっと手広い店に移転する. 【類】the firm was transferred to more ***commodious*** *premises* in … ¶the *premises* ***insured*** 保険のついている屋敷. ¶the Baron's ***magnificent*** *premises* 男爵の豪華な屋敷. ¶the ***palatial*** *premises* of Messrs. … …社の壮麗な建物.

Q² ***banking*** *premises* 銀行営業所. ¶one's ***business*** *premises* その営業用の家屋土地. 【類】clerks employed in the surrounding ***business*** *premises.* ¶except on the ***college*** *premises* 校内を除いては. ¶keep ***poultry*** *premises* in a sanitary condition 鶏舎を清潔にしておく.

P He lingered ***about*** the *premises.* 彼はその邸宅の付近をぐずついていた. ¶the new library ***at*** the new *premises* of the Oxford University Press オックスフォード大学出版部の新構内にある新図書館. 【類】The Rotary Club, an international system of service clubs, was formed by P.P. Harris of Chicago in 1905 and met ***at*** the *premises* of each member in turn, hence the name. ¶live ***on*** the *premises* of one's employer 主人の屋敷に住込む. 【類】Everyone ***on*** the *premises* was arrested and taken to the police station. / A disastrous fire broke out ***on*** (=***upon***) the *premises.*

premium, *n.* 賞与; 打歩, 割増(プレミアム); 保険料.

V ***command*** *premium* [株券など]額面価格以上に取引される. ¶Prescribed questions in text-books ***offer*** a *premium* to sloth and ignorance on the part of an instructor. 教科書に質問を設けておくと教師の怠慢と無知を奨励することになる. ‖ That would be ***offering*** a *premium* to fraud. それ

では詐欺を奨励するようなものじゃないか. ¶*pay premiums* on one's life insurance 生命保険料を払う. ¶*place* (=*put*) a *premium* on ... ...にプレミアムを付ける; 奨励する. 【類】Mere giving money will *put* a *premium* on idleness.

Q *deferred premium* 延滞料金. ¶*extra premium* 特別賞与; 〘保険〙[年齢ごとに加わる]割増料金. ¶You may for *small premium* insure your baggage for loss. 少額の料金で手荷物に保険をつけられる. ¶The shares stand at an extremely *high premium*. その株ははるかに額面以上になっている.

Q² *exchange premium* 為替相場のプレミアム. ¶*instalment premium* 賦払保険料金. ¶*insurance premium* 保険料.

P *at a premium* 打歩で, 割増金(プレミアム)付きで; 〘転義〙需要があって, 珍重されて. 【類】The goods will be *at* a *premium* (=in great demand). / Tickets are *at* a *premium*. / sell *at* a *premium* of 5 per cent / These shares are *at* a *premium*. / gold is now *at* a *premium* of ... ‖ When folly is *at* a *premium*, reason is at a discount. 無理が通れば道理引っこむ. ‖ In a ship every inch of space is *at* a *premium*. 船ではわずかの面積も貴い. ¶*with* a *premium* プレミアム付で.

P² The *premium of* insurance on ... ...に対する保険料. ¶*premium on* endowment policy 養老保険証券に対する保険料 ‖ *premium on* a draft 為替手形の打歩.

premonition, *n.* 予感; 前兆.

V we *experienced* no *premonition* of ... ...の前兆は少しもなかった. ¶I *had* a strange *premonition* that ... 私は...という不思議な予感を持った. ‖ as if he *had* a *premonition* of evil 虫が知らせたのか.

P² a *premonition of* failure 失敗のきざし.

preoccupation, *n.* 先入主. 屈託.

Q The question of ... was my *constant preoccupation*. ...の問題は始終私の気にかかっていたことだ. 【類】To get not enough to eat, but enough to prevent them from dying of starvation was their *constant preoccupation*.

Q² a life where *self preoccupations* are dominant 自己本位の生がい.

preoccupy, *v.* 心を奪う, 屈託させる.

M *anxiously preoccupied* 気が気でなく.

P She is always *preoccupied with* her own well-being. 彼女はいつも自分のことにばかり屈託している. ‖ One finds her continually *preoccupied with* herself. 彼女はいつも考えごとをしている. 【類】My mind is *preoccupied with* domestic cares.

prepaid, *a.* 前払いの.

O a telegram with reply *prepaid* 返信料付き電報.

preparation, *n.* 準備, 食品; 薬剤.

V I *have* no adequate *preparation*. 私は十分準備ができていない. ¶*make preparations* for ... ...の準備をする ‖ be thoroughgoing in *making preparations* 用意周到である. ¶*Preparations* for a general war are being quietly but vigorously *pushed forward*. 大戦の準備が静粛にかつ活発に進められている. ¶*undertake* the *preparation* of a book 書物の下ごしらえをする.

Q We are in *active preparation*. われわれは準備に忙しい. ¶make *ample preparations* for war 十分な戦備をする. ¶*chemical preparations* 化学薬品. ¶The *preparation* is *complete*. 準備は整った. 【類】*preparations* are practically *complete* for the entertainment of ... ¶*extensive preparations* were made for the reception of ... ...の歓迎に大々的な準備をした. ¶a nation in *good preparation* for war 軍備のよく整っている国. ¶He has *little preparation* for any particular vocation. 彼には何ら特定の職業に対する準備がほとんどない. ¶*medical preparations* 調合薬剤. ¶make all *necessary preparations* for ... ...の万端必要な準備をする. ¶a *new preparation* for the hair (skin) 毛髪(皮膚)の新薬. ¶This drug is widely used in *pleasant-tasting preparations*. この薬品は口当りをよくした薬品の調剤には広く用いられている. ¶*purgative preparations* 下剤. ¶The book is in *rapid preparation*. その本は早急に編集の準備中だ. ¶make *rough preparations* 大体の準備をする. ¶make *thoroughgoing preparations* 周到な用意をする. ¶make a *thousand preparations* beforehand 前もって万端の準備をする. ¶*Warlike preparations* are underway (=in progress). 戦争準備が進行中だ.

Q² *beauty preparations* 美容料. ¶*boot preparations* くつみがきの道具. ¶*face preparations*=beauty aids 美顔料. ¶assign for *home preparation* 宿題として課す. ¶*war preparation* 戦争準備.

P What time will be required *for preparation?* 準備にどの位かかるか. ¶*in preparation* for ... ...の準備に ‖ The book is *in preparation*. その本は今編集中だ. 【類】*in* the *preparation* of the book I have been amply assisted by ... ‖ *in preparation* at the Clarendon Press クラレンドン出版社で編集中. ¶*without preparation* 即席に.

P² *preparation for* examinations (lessons) 試験(など)の準備. 【類】*preparations for* war (a journey) ‖ a *preparation for* the hair (tooth, skin) 毛髪(など)用の薬剤. ¶the *preparation of* troops *for* battle 軍隊の戦闘準備 ‖ Chocolate is a *preparation of* cocoa. チョコレートはココアの調製品だ. ‖ *preparation of* drugs 調剤 ‖ the *preparation of* documents 書類作成 ‖ *preparation of* the soil 整土.

preparatory, *a.* 準備の, 予備の.

P *preparatory for* the next stage of education 次の教育段階の準備に. ¶*preparatory to* ... ...の準備として, ...に先んじて. 【類】He arrived in Yokohama *preparatory to* sailing for the United States on the Korea. / I am packing it up *preparatory to* my journey. / study it *preparatory to* learning ...

prepare, *v.* 準備する; 調製する; 覚悟させる.

M be *prepared beforehand* 手回しがいい. ¶I am *busily preparing* for ... 私は...の準備にいそがしい. ¶*calmly prepare* for death 心静かに死ぬ覚悟をする. ¶*expressly prepared* for ... 特に...のためにこしらえた. ¶he is *feverishly preparing* to ... 彼は...の準備に熱狂している. ¶The soil is *fully prepared* for the development of mental disorder. 精神病にかかる下地が十分にできている. 【類】be *fully prepared* for war. ¶I am *quite prepared* to do it. 私は喜んで致します. ¶a very *tastily prepared* dish おいしく調理した品. ¶*prepare* a table *tentatively* 試験的に表を作製する. ¶*prepare thoroughly* for the examination for a certificate of competency 資格試験の準備を徹底的にやる. ¶leave school *well prepared* for the work of life, whatever that work may be 仕事の何たるを問わず人生の仕事にりっぱに当り得るよう用意して学校を出る.

P *prepare against* disaster 災害に備える. ¶*prepare* oneself *as* a specialist 専門家としての素養を作る. ¶*prepare for* an emergency 万一の用意をする ‖ *prepare for* the worst 最悪に備える ‖ I am busy *preparing for* the next examination. 今度の試験準備でいそがしい. 【類】memorize ... in *preparing for* examinations / The school is intended for students *preparing for* such examinations. / be *prepared for* future contingencies (将来) / *prepare* it *for* publication / be *prepared for* what is to come / be *prepared for* the worst / *prepare* himself *for* the examination for Harvard / *prepare* a boy *for* college ‖ *prepare* students *for* citizenship 学生を一人前の公民に仕立てる / He *prepared for* a feast (journey). ‖ *prepare* ground *for* seed 種子のまけるよう土地の下ごしらえをする ‖ They *prepared* her *for* the mournful news. 彼らは彼女に凶報のあることを覚悟させた. ‖ The coins were "duffers," artfully *prepared for* the cheat's market. その貨幣はいんちき屋に売るために巧みに製造した偽物であった ‖ We were not *prepared for* rain. まさか雨になろうとは思わなかった. 【類】We must be *prepared for* the expenditure of a sum not less than thousands. / The country was not yet *prepared for* such a work. ¶a food *prepared from* the best materials 極上の材料で製した食物 ‖ *prepared from* flour =farinaceous 小麦粉で造った. 【類】photos *prepared from* negatives taken by ... ‖ diagrams *prepared from* figures supplied by ... ...の供給した図で調製した図表.

O I'm *prepared* to admit my fault. 私の誤ちはいさぎよく認める.

preparedness, *n.* 準備; 《米》軍備充実.

Q President Wilson's policy of *military preparedness* ウイルスン大統領の軍備充実政策.

P *for lack of preparedness* 軍備不十分のため. ¶*in preparedness* for possible hostilities 将来の戦争に備えて.

P² *preparedness for* war 戦備.

preponderance, *n.* 優位.

V *acquire* a stupendous *preponderance* 絶大の優位に立つ. ¶Human society *has* a great *preponderance* of women members. 人間社会は婦人の数が非常に多くなっている. ¶*show* a *preponderance* of ... ...の優勢を示す.

Q *numerical preponderance* 数の優勢.

P² the great *preponderance of* numbers 数の著しい優勢 ‖ the *preponderance of* evidence seems to favor the view that … …という見解を支持する証拠が優勢のようだ.

preponderate, *v.* まさる.

P Boys *preponderate in* number. 男子の方が数がまさっている. ¶a world where pain overwhelmingly *preponderates over* pleasure 苦が圧倒的に楽にまさっている世の中.

prepossess, *v.* あらかじめ思い込ませる, 初めから感心させる.

M His manners ***strongly*** *prepossessed* them in his favor. 彼の態度は初めから著しく好印象を彼らに与えた.

P he was *prepossessed* ***against*** (***for***) … 彼は前から…を悪く(善く)思っていた. ¶I'm *prepossessed* ***by*** her manners. 彼女の態度に好感を持っている. ¶His appearance *prepossessed* me ***in*** his favor. 彼の容ぼうは初めから私に好感を持たせた. ¶He is *prepossessed* ***with*** some idea. 彼は初めからある考えにとらわれている.

prepossession, *n.* 先入主.

Q after making all the allowance that I can for my own ***personal*** *prepossessions* 私の先入感をできるだけ割引しても.

P ***in*** his *prepossession* of everything Western, he is of opinion that … 西洋の物はなんでも良いと思い込んでいるので彼は…という考えを持っている.

prerequisite, *n.* 必要条件.

Q an ***essential*** *prerequisite* to a successful work 事業の成功に欠くべからざる必要条件. ¶***indispensable*** *prerequisites* of … …の必須条件. ¶a ***necessary*** *prerequisite* to freedom 自由を得るための必要条件. 【類】A command of information is the ***necessary*** *prerequisite* to the scientific consideration of any subject.

P² Latin and Greek are the only *prerequisites* ***for*** admission to the college. その大学の入学考査科目はラテン語とギリシア語だけだ. ¶a *prerequisite* ***to*** membership 入会(資格)としての一つの条件.

prerequisite, *a.* あらかじめ必要な.

M² ***as*** *prerequisite* to the act その行動の前提条件として.

P A congenial climate is *prerequisite* ***to*** social development. 快適な気候というものは社会の発達にはあらかじめ必要なものだ.

prerogative, *n.* 特権.

V ***enjoy*** an exclusive *prerogative* of … …の専有の特権を享有する. ¶***exercise*** the parental *prerogative* 親権を行使する. ¶we ***have*** the *prerogative* of … われわれは…の特権を有する.

Q the ***royal*** *prerogative* 王の大権.

P² the *prerogative* ***of*** legislature 立法部の特権.

presage, *n.* 予感.

V² her *presage* ***suggested*** to her that … 彼女に…と虫が知らせた.

P² a *presage* ***of*** the death of … …の死の前兆.

presage, *v.* 前兆する; 予知する.

P *presage* well ***for*** the future 将来の有望を示す. ¶*presage* ***from*** something あることから予知する.

prescience, *n.* 先見.

Q² a man of remarkable ***business*** *prescience* すぐれた先見の明ある実業家.

prescribe, *v.* 指図する; 処方する.

M prepare medicine ***as*** *prescribed* 処方せん通り調剤する. ¶Silence is "***sternly***" *prescribed*.「断然」他言してはならないと言いきかされている.

P as may be *prescribed* ***by*** … …の指図がある場合はそれに従って. ¶*prescribe* ***for*** a disease 病気の処方せんを書く. ¶Do not *prescribe* ***to*** me what I am going to do. 私のなすべきことを私に指図するな. ‖ *prescribe* medicine ***to*** a person 人に薬剤を処方する.

O do what the rules *prescribe* ルールの示す通りやる.

prescription, *n.* 処方; 処方せん, 処方薬; 訓令; 時効.

V The *prescription* has been ***acquired***. 時効は完成した. ¶***compound*** medical *prescriptions* 処方剤を調合する. ¶*prescriptions* ***dispensed*** only by registered pharmacists 登録薬剤師のみ投薬しうる処方. ¶***fill*** *prescriptions* [薬剤師など]処方薬を調合する ‖ "*Prescription* ***Filled***."〘掲示〙処方調剤. ¶***have*** this *prescription* ***made*** at the chemistry この処方を薬屋で調剤してもらう. ¶The physician ***made*** no *prescription* of diet. 医者は食物については別に制限しなかった. ¶***make up*** (＝dispense) a *prescription* 処方通りに調剤する. ¶***prepare*** a *prescription* 処方の調剤をする. ¶***write*** a *prescription* to be filled by some druggist 薬剤師の調剤すべき処方を書く. ¶***write*** (＝***make***) ***out*** a *prescription* 処方せんを書く.

Q ***acquisitive*** *prescription* 取得時効. ¶***extinctive*** *prescription* 消滅時効. ¶a ***medical*** *prescription* 処方せん.

P *prescription* ***against*** public action 公訴の時効. ¶This medicine is obtainable only ***on*** a physician's *prescription*. この薬剤は医師の処方でなくては手に入らない. ¶The druggist objected to giving morphine ***without*** a *prescription*. その薬剤師は処方せんがなくてはモルヒネは渡されないと言った.

P² a *prescription* ***against*** sea-sickness 船酔い予防の処方薬. ¶a *prescription* ***for*** a disease 病気の処方せん.

O my *prescription* is … 私の忠告は…だ.

presence, *n.* 現存; 出席, 列席; 面前; 謁見; 風さい; 貴人; 幽鬼.

V ***conceal*** the *presence* of … …の所在を隠す. ¶The *presence* of fever was ***detected***. 熱のあることが分かった. ¶***enter*** the *presence* of … …の前に出る, …に面会する. ¶He ***has*** no *presence*. 彼は風さいが上がらない. ‖ he ***had*** the *presence* of mind to … 彼は落着いて…した. 【類】I ***had*** scarcely *presence* of mind enough to return a courtesy to his bow. ¶The ghost ***indicated*** its *presence* by the ringing of the bells in the house and other alarming signs. 化物は家の中の鐘を鳴らしまたは他の恐ろしい合図をしてその存在を示した. ¶***leave*** a king's *presence* 王の御前を辞去する. ¶***lose*** one's *presence* of mind あわてる. ¶The drunken fellow ***made*** his *presence* ***felt*** in various ways. その飲んだくれは様々なことをして自分の存在を感じさせた. ¶Your *presence* is ***requested***. 貴下の御出席をお願いします. ¶dare not to ***reveal*** one's *presence* [隠れている人など]自ら名乗って出ようとしない. ¶***saving*** your *presence* 貴方の前でこう言うのはなんですけれど. ¶***seek*** his *presence* 彼に会見を求める. ¶***suspect*** the *presence* of danger 危険があるような気がする.

Q in the ***actual*** *presence* of danger 実際危険に直面して. ¶his ***commanding*** *presence* 彼の堂々たる風さい. ¶be of ***dignified*** *presence* 押し出しがきく. ¶a man of ***fine*** *presence* 風さいのよい人. ¶of ***good*** *presence* 風さいのよい. ¶in the ***grand, majestic*** *presence* of death 雄大荘厳な死に臨んで. ¶a young man of ***handsome*** *presence* 美ぼうの青年. ¶his ***invisible*** *presence* 彼(死人など)の死霊. ¶a stately lady of ***imposing*** *presence* and dignified manner 堂々たる風さいと威厳ある態度のりっぱな貴婦人. ¶a ***pleading*** *presence* 嘆願的なようす. ¶His ***quiet, unobtrusive*** *presence* was hardly observed. 彼は動作が静かで目立たないのでその存在がほとんど気付かれなかった. ¶a man of ***remarkable*** *presence* 風さいの目立つ人物. ¶He was admitted to the ***royal*** *presence*. 彼は王に拝謁を許された. ¶his ***silent*** *presence* 彼の無言の在席(死者など). ¶a pleasant manner and ***vigorous*** *presence* 態度の気持のよさと風さいの線の太さ.

Q² a man of fine ***platform*** *presence* 演説振りのりっぱな人. ¶She has a ***stage*** *presence*. 彼女は舞台度胸がある. ‖ He has an easy ***stage*** *presence*. 彼にはゆったりとした舞台度胸がある.

P ***before*** the *presence* of … …の面前で. ¶***during*** his *presence* in the room 彼が室内にいる間. ¶Get [away] ***from*** my *presence*! 下がれ! 【類】retire ***from*** his *presence* / retire ***from*** the Imperial *presence* ‖ He was banished ***from*** the *presence*. 彼は退場を命ぜられた. ¶***in*** the *presence* of others 人前で ‖ ***in*** [the] *presence* of a large assembly of spectators (distinguished assemblage, large company) 見物(など)の大勢集っている前で ‖ feel shy (＝bashful) ***in*** the *presence* of the opposite sex 異性の面前で恥かしがる ‖ discouraged ***in*** the *presence* of failure 失敗で落胆して ‖ The accident happened ***in*** my *presence*. その事件は私の目の前で起った. ‖ if you were ***in*** her *presence* for a few munites 二三分でも彼女と一しょにいたら. 【類】lecture ***in*** the Imperial *presence*. ¶***in spite of*** the *presence* of others 人前もはばからず. ¶go ***into*** one's *presence* その前に進み出る. ¶I was admitted ***to*** his *presence*. 私は彼に目通りを許された. ¶act ***with*** great *presence* of mind and courage in the face of … …に直面して非常な沈着と勇気とをもって働く. 【類】***with*** his *presence* at the meeting.

present, *n.* 贈物(プレゼント).

V I would be very much pleased if you would ***accept*** the trifling *present* from me. 粗品を御受納いただければ幸

いです. ¶***accompany*** a *present* by a letter 贈物に手紙を添える. ¶***bring*** her a *present* 彼女への贈物を持って来る. ¶***deliver*** one's *present* 贈物を届ける. ¶***distribute presents*** as a sign of rejoicing 祝いの印に贈物を配る. ¶***exchange*** *presents* with each other 互いに贈りものを交換する. ¶They will ***form*** ideal *presents*. それは理想的な贈物になる. ¶He kindly ***gave*** me a *present* of some fruit. 彼は親切にも私に果物を贈ってくれた. ¶The *present* is not ***intended*** for him. この贈物は彼にやるのではない. ¶***make*** a small *present* ちょっとした贈物をする. 【類】***make*** him *presents* of various kinds / ***make*** them a *present* of a gold watch (a diamond ring). ¶formally ***present*** a *present* 贈呈の式を行う. ¶He was ***promised*** a *present*. 彼は贈物をやると言われた. ¶***receive*** a *present* of ... from ... ...から...のプレゼントを受ける. ¶***send*** a *present* of a plum tree in full bloom 満開の梅の木を贈る.

Q an ***acceptable*** *present* 気のきいた贈物. ¶It would make an ***admirable*** *present* to an English student. それは英学生への絶好の贈物になるだろう. ¶a ***bridal*** (=***wedding or nuptial***) *present* (=gift) 結婚の贈答品. ¶Some ***choice*** *presents* were given him. 彼にすばらしい贈物をした. ¶The book would make an ***excellent*** *present* for Christmas. その本は見事なクリスマスの贈答品になるだろう. ¶a ***handsome*** *present* 結構な贈物. ¶a ***humble*** *present* 粗末な品. ¶the ***Imperial*** *presents* to ... ...への御下賜品. ¶Happy birthday, Teddy. Here's a ***little*** *present* from your father and me. 誕生日おめでとうテディーちゃん. これお父さんとお母さんからのプレゼントよ. ¶Oh, what a ***lovely*** *present!* まあ, すてきなプレゼントよ. ¶a ***popular*** *present* 好評のある贈答品. ¶send a ***rich*** *present* of jewels りっぱな宝石の贈物をする. ¶***useful*** *presents* 重宝な贈物. ¶a very ***welcome*** *present* for the New Year 非常に喜ばれる新年の贈物.

Q² exchange customary ***betrothal*** *presents* 慣例の結納を取交わす. ¶a ***birthday*** *present* 誕生日の贈物. ¶a free ***bonus*** *present* 景品. ¶as a ***Christmas*** *present* クリスマス・プレゼントとして. ¶a ***farewell*** *present* せん別の贈物. ¶This is my uncle's ***home-coming*** *present*. これはおじの帰郷みやげです. ¶a ***money*** *present* 金銭の贈物. ¶***obituary*** *presents* 死者への贈物. ¶a ***parting*** *present* せん別の贈物. ¶he sent me a ***return*** *present* of ... 彼は返礼に...を私に贈ってくれた. ¶take home as ***souvenir*** *presents* for their friends 友人たちへのみやげものとして持ち帰る. ¶a "***welcome home***" *present*「無事帰郷」を祝う贈物. ¶a ***year-end*** *present* 歳暮贈答品.

P accept a thing ***as*** a *present* 進物として物を受納する.

P² a *present* ***for*** a lady 婦人に贈る進物 ‖ Here's a little *present* ***for*** tea-money. 軽少ですがここに茶代をおきます. ¶an official *present* ***from*** the university 大学からの正式の贈物. ¶a *present* ***of*** a pair of porcelain vases was sent to ... 磁器製の花びん一対が...に贈られた ‖ Will you make me a *present* ***of*** your photograph? お写真を下さいませんか.

present, *n.* 現今, 現時;〖文法〗現在.

V ***represent*** the *present* as well as the past〖文法〗過去はもちろん現在をも表わす. ¶***sacrifice*** the *present* to the future 現在を将来のために犠牲にする.

Q the ***historic***[***al***] *present*〖文法〗歴史的現在. ¶work for the ***immediate*** *present* 目前のために働く. ¶***that*** *present* その当時. ¶***this*** *present* 現今.

P He is ***at*** *present* in London. 彼は今ロンドンにいる. ‖ I do not want any more ***at*** *present*. 今の所それ以上は要(ᵛ)らない. ‖ I have no money to spare ***at*** *present*. 今の所私は少しも余分の金はない. ‖ just ***at*** *present* 丁度今 ‖ same as ***at*** *present* 現行通り. 【類】We cannot accept new orders just ***at*** *present*. ¶just ***for*** the *present* ちょっとここんところ ‖ leave the matter as it is ***for*** the *present* 当分そのままにしておく ‖ call it "..." ***for*** the *present* それを仮に「...」と呼ぶ. 【類】I've forgotten the name ***for*** the *present*. / That will do ***for*** the *present*. / stop selling ***for*** the *present* / ***for*** the *present* it is sufficient to note that ... / The work is suspended ***for*** the *present* (当分中止). / ***For*** the *present* there is no prospect of improvement. ‖ Athens as it was in the glorious past and as it is ***in*** the *present*. 過去の全盛時代のアテネと現在のアテネ. ‖ The verb is ***in*** the *present*.〖文法〗その動詞は現在だ. ¶No time ***like*** the *present*. 現在のようなときはまたとない. ¶***up to*** the *present* 今に至るまで.

present, *a.* 居合わしている; 現存する.

M He will be *present* ***here*** this evening. 彼は今晩ここへ来ます.

P He was *present* ***at*** the ceremony (meeting). 彼はその式(など)に列席していた. ‖ be not *present* ***at*** the death-bed of one's parent 親の死に目に会わない. 【類】I invite you to be *present* ***at*** ... ¶the metal *present* ***in*** chalk 白亜中に存在する金属 ‖ He was *present* ***in*** many battles. 彼は数回の戦闘に参加した. ¶I will be *present* ***on*** the occasion. 私はその折出席します. ¶They were ever present ***to*** my mind. 彼らのことは始終私の心を離れなかった. ‖ in one case *present* ***to*** my mind 私の頭に浮ぶ一つの場合では. 【類】Her face is ever *present* ***to*** my eye. / the sound of a voice, ever *present* ***to*** my heart.

present, *v.* 紹介する; 贈る, 捧呈する; 呈する, 示す; 述べる; 向ける.

M The novel was *presented* ***dramatically*** in the ... theatre. その小説は劇化され...座で上場された. ¶Samples are *presented* ***free***. 見本は無料で進呈します. ¶the art of *presenting* his characters ***impersonally***, allowing them to make their own impression without asides and comments その登場人物を非人格的に表現する術, 即ちそれらの人物がなんらのわきぜりふも文句もなく自分自身を印象づけさせる術. ¶two questions which ***naturally*** *present* themselves to the mind are, first ..., and second ... 当然心に起る二つの疑問は第一...第二...である. 【類】The question ***naturally*** *presents* itself: How then ...? ¶The characters in the book are ***vividly*** *presented*. 同書の登場人物は生き生きと描かれている. ¶***voluntarily*** *present* oneself at ... 自分から...に出頭する.

P *present* it ***as*** a Christmas gift それをクリスマスの贈物として贈る. ¶*present* a card ***at*** the entrance 入口で(招待などの)カードを出す ‖ He was *presented* (=He presented himself) ***at*** court. 彼は宮中に伺候した. ‖ the report *presented* ***at*** the meeting その会でなされた報告 ‖ *present* a revolver ***at*** a person 人にピストルをつきつける. ¶He *presented* himself ***before*** me. 彼は僕の所へ来た. ¶The paper was *presented* ***by*** the author as a dissertation for the degree of Ph. D. at Columbia University. その論文は著者が哲学博士の博士論文としてコロムビア大学に提出したものだ. ‖ After six years of married childlessness, the father was suddenly *presented* ***by*** his wife ***with*** a pair of twins. 結婚後六年も子がなくていた親父(おや)さんのところに突然ふた子が生れた. ¶He *presented* himself ***for*** an examination. 彼は試験に出た. ‖ The matter was *presented* ***for*** consideration. その問題が審議のために提出された. 【類】The problem *presented* itself ***for*** our solution (解決). ¶The picture *presents* him ***in*** his prime. その写真は彼の年盛りのときのものだ. ‖ *present* ***in*** array all sorts of lie うそ八百を並べる. ¶Material objects are *presented* ***through*** the senses. 物質は五官を通じて知覚される. ¶*present* a book ***to*** her=present her with a book 彼女に書物を贈る. 【類】*present* a card (名刺) ***to*** a person / *present* the book ***to*** the public=publish the book / This was *presented* ***to*** me ***as*** a gift for my birthday. / The work is now *presented* ***to*** the English reader in an improved form. ‖ He has *presented* a petition ***to*** the authorities. 彼は当局に嘆願書を出した. ‖ A sad picture was *presented* ***to*** our sight. 惨たんたる光景がわれわれの目に映じた. ‖ be *presented* ***to*** the mind (view) 心(目)に映る ‖ *present* a person ***to*** another person 人を他の人に紹介する. 【類】He *presented* me ***to*** his wife. / He was *presented* ***to*** the queen. ‖ He was *presented* ***to*** society. 彼は交際社会に出た. ‖ faithfully and sympathetically *present* the East ***to*** the West 忠実にかつ同情をもって東洋を西洋に紹介する. ‖ *present* one's face ***to*** the foe 敵に顔を向ける ‖ She *presents* a smiling face ***to*** the rest of the world. 同国は(八方美人的に)世界各国に微笑を振りまく. ‖ Motion pictures *present* ***to*** the eye twenty pictures a second. 映画は一秒二十枚の絵をスクリーンに映写する. ¶*present* her ***with*** a bouquet of flowers 彼女に花束を贈る. 【類】They *presented* the Queen ***with*** a bouquet on behalf of the women students. / His wife was not able to *present* him ***with*** the heir (嗣子) he so much desired. / He was *presented* ***with*** ... from friends. / He was *presented* ***with*** an address of welcome contained in a gold casket (金箱に納めた歓迎の辞).

presentable, *a.* 服装のととのった, 体裁のよい.
M I hope I look *presentable* **enough** among them. みんなと一緒になっても(服装などが)おかしくないでしょうね. ¶a **really** *presentable* young man 一分のすきもない青年.
O make *presentable* what one has on 服装などをきちんと

presentation, *n.* 呈示, 授与(式); 謁見; 表現. ⌊する.
V **make** the *presentation* of the trophy to ... そのトロフィーを...に贈与する.
Q **auditory** *presentation* 聴覚に訴えること. ¶a **complete** *presentation* of the present status of human knowledge of the science. その科学に対する現段階における人間知識の完全な解説. ¶a **demonstrative** *presentation* 実演. ¶**dramatic** *presentations* 劇の演出. ¶an **elaborate tabular** *presentation* of facts 事実を細かに表で示すこと. ¶give a **fair** *presentation* of both sides 双方を公平に示す. ¶**fair** and **impartial** *presentation* of actual conditions 公平無私の実情陳述. ¶her **first** *presentation* at Court 彼女の最初の参内. ¶the **graphic** *presentation* of facts in the form of charts and diagrams 表やダイヤによる事実の図的表示. ¶a **handsome** *presentation* was made to ... ...に見事な記念品が贈られた. ¶a **masterly** *presentation* あっぱれな演技. ¶an **objective, scientific** *presentation* of facts 事実の客観的科学的表示. ¶**sensational** *presentation* 扇情的表現. ¶a **successful** *presentation* of a play 成功を収めた劇の演出. ¶give a **systematic** *presentation* of ... ...の組織だった説明をする. ¶**visual** *presentation* 視覚への訴え.
P **at** (=on) *presentation* (書類など)呈示次第. ¶the ceremony **of** the *presentation* of ... ...の贈呈式. ¶**on** *presentation* of visiting cards 名刺を出すと ‖ Your draft will be paid **on** *presentation*. あなたの手形は御提出の際お支払します.
P² *presentation* **of** colours 軍旗授与式 ‖ *presentation* **of** credentials 国書捧呈 ‖ the *presentation* **of** one's thesis 論文提出 ‖ the *presentation* **of** a new play 新しい劇の上演.【類】The *presentation* **of** the medal was made by the President of the Association. / there was a *presentation* ⌊**of** gifts to ...

presentiment, *n.* 予感.
V I **felt** a strange *presentiment* from the very first that ... 最初から不思議に...と虫が知らせた. ¶**have** a *presentiment* that ... ...と虫が知らせる.【類】I **have** a *presentiment* of ⌊...
Q an **ominous** *presentiment* 不吉な予感.
P as if **by** *presentiment* 虫が知らせたか. ¶a **strong** *presentiment* that my belief would finally give way 自分の信念もくずれはしないかという強い疑念.
P² We have a *presentiment* **of** evil. 凶事が起りそうな気が

presentment, *n.* 叙述. ⌊する.
V we doubt of any fairer *presentment* has ever been **made** of ... ...についてこれまでにこれ以上公平な叙述があっ⌊たかどうかを疑う.

preservation, *n.* 保存, 保全.
V **secure** the *preservation* of ... ...を確実に保存する.
Q a picture in **fair** (**poor**) *preservation*. 保存のよい(悪い)絵. ¶It is in **fine** (=a fine state of) *preservation*. それは保存状態がよい. ¶a sculpture in **good** *preservation* 好く保存された彫刻物. ¶The book is in **splendid** *preservation*. 同書はりっぱに保存されている.
Q² **forestry** *preservation* 森林保存.
P **for** the *preservation* of peace 平和を維持するために. ¶eggs in a good (bad) state **of** *preservation* 保存のよい(悪い)卵.
P² *preservation* **from** decay 防腐. ¶the *preservation* **of** life 生命の保全 ‖ the *preservation* **of** order 秩序の保持 ‖ *preservation* **of** evidence 証拠保全. ‖ the *preservation* **of** timber **against** decay 木材の防腐保存.【類】the *preservation* **of** the English language in its purity (英語としての純正さ).

preservative, *n.* 防腐剤; 予防薬; 保全手段.
Q the **best** *preservative* of health 最良の保健剤.
Q² a **wood** *preservative* 木材防腐剤.
P It is used **as** a *preservative*. それは防腐剤に用いる. ¶The possession of a caul is believed to be a *preservative* **against** drowning. [産児の]大網膜を持っているとでき死しないという信仰がある. ‖ Salt is the best *preservative* **against** putrefaction. 塩は最上の防腐剤である.

preserve, *n.* [通例 *pl.*] 貯蔵食料(砂糖煮・ジャム・塩づけな
Q² **plum** (**apricot**) *preserves* すもも(など)の砂糖づけ. ⌊ど).
P a store **of** *preserves* 保存食料.

preserve, *v.* 保存する; つけ物にしておく.
M I flatter myself I am very **well** *preserved* and don't look half my age. 私は非常に若々しくて年の半分にも見えないとうぬぼれている.
P omens *preserved* **by** history 歴史に現われた前兆. ¶*preserve* the building and its interesting associations **from** oblivion その建物とそれにまつわる興味ある連想を忘れさせないようにする ‖ Salt *preserves* vegetables **from** decay. 塩は野菜の腐敗を防ぐ. ¶*preserve* ...**in** (=**with**) alcohol (salt) ...をアルコール(など)づけにする ‖ *preserve* the scene **in** motion pictures その光景を映画にして保存する.【類】The story has been *preserved* **in** various European languages. ¶*preserve* a seat **on** a train **for** ... ...のために列車の座席をとっておく.

preside, *v.* 司会する; 主宰する.
P *preside* **as** master of ceremonies (chairman) 式場係(など)として司会する. ¶*preside* **at** a meeting (ceremony) 会(など)を司会する.【類】*preside* **at** a trial (裁判長を勤める) ‖ *preside* **at** the organ (piano) オルガン(など)弾奏の役を勤める ‖ *preside* **at** a family dinner 家族の正さんの主人役を勤める. ¶*preside* **over** a conference on ... ...会議の議長となる ‖ the ceremony was *presided* **over** by ... その式典は...が司会した.【類】A Governor *presides* **over** a State. / Nymphs (水神) are goddesses who *preside* **over** streams. / *preside* **over** man's destiny (運命).

presidency, *n.* 大統領・総理などの職; 主宰.
V **assume** the *Presidency* of Cornell コーネル大学の総長に就任する.
P **during** the *presidency* of Madison マディスン大統領の時代に. ¶a committee **under** the *presidency* of a Government official 官吏の主宰する委員会.【類】**under** Mr. Cleveland's *presidency*.

president, *n.* [P-] 大統領; 総長, 会長.
V quadrennially **elect** a *President* 四年ごとに大統領を選挙する.
Q There goes the *President* **designate** of the United States. あれがこの次の大統領だ. ☞〘米国〙大統領候補者 (Presidential candidate) が選挙委員団 (electoral college) によって選ばれ, 実際に就任するまでを "President-elect" という. President designate はその選挙委員選挙によって決定した次期の大統領をいう. ¶Dr. ..., **former** *President* of the State University at Berkeley バークレーの州立大学(カリフォルニア)の前学長...博士. ¶the **incoming** (**outgoing**) *president* 新任(前)会長. ¶the **newly-elected** (=**-nominated**) *president* 今度の会長. ¶Every American boy is a **possible** *President* of the United States. どのアメリカの少年も将来米国大統領になり得るという可能性はある.
Q² a **commission** *president* 審査会々長. ¶a **company** *president* 会社々長. ¶the Lord *President* of the Council 〘英〙枢密院議長. ¶a **party** *president* 党の総裁. ¶a **puppet** *President* かいらい大統領. ¶a **union** *president* 組合長.
P **as** *president* of that learned body その学会の会長として. ¶The Philological Society has ... **for** *president*. 言語学会は...を会長にいただいている.
P² the *president* **of** a court 裁判所長.

presidium, *n.* 〘ソ連〙最高会議.
Q² a **Soviet-type** *Presidium* ソ連型最高幹部会.

press, *n.* 印刷機; 圧搾器(プレス); 印刷所; 印刷, 出版; [団] 出版物, 新聞雑誌; 新聞雑誌の評論.
V **correct** the *press* 印刷物を校正する. ¶war news with which the daily *press* is **flooded** 日刊新聞に満載してある戦況ニュース. ¶The government **muzzled** the *press*. 政府が新聞紙を抑圧した. ¶**silence** the *press* 新聞紙を沈黙させる. ¶**subsidize** the *press* 新聞に助成金を与える. ¶News agencies **supply** the *press* with news. 通信社は諸新聞にニュースを供給する.
Q the **Associated** *Press* [米国の]連合通信社. ¶receive "a **bad** *press*" 新聞によく言われない. ¶a **bookbinder's** *press* 製本用圧搾機. ¶the **cheap** *press* 三流新聞. ¶appear in the **daily** *press* 日刊新聞に出る. ¶the **foreign** *press* 外字諸新聞. ¶the **free** and **honest** *press* 自由で公明な諸新聞. ¶It was given a **good** *press*. それは新聞の好評を博した. ¶a **hydraulic** baling *press* 水力荷造り機. ¶appear in the **periodical** *press* 定期刊行物に出る.【類】Practically all the best essays in the language have first seen the light in the **periodical** *press*. ¶pamphlets printed on a **private**

press 私設の印刷所で印刷した小冊子. ¶he was attacked in the ***public*** *press* because of ... 彼は...の理由で新聞雑誌から攻撃された. ¶a ***rotary*** *press* 輪転機. ¶the ***United*** *Press* [米国の]合同通信社. ¶the ***vernacular*** *press* 邦字諸新聞. ¶the ***weekly*** (***monthly***) *press* 週(月)刊雑誌.

Q² the officials of the ***Clarendon*** *Press* クラレンドン印刷所の役員たち. ¶a ***copying*** *press* 謄写器. ¶a ***cotton*** *press* 綿花圧搾機. ¶a ***finishing*** *press* 仕上げプレス. ¶a high speed rotary or ***flat bed*** *press* 高速度輪転または平盤印刷機. ¶a modern ***high speed*** *press* 新型高速度印刷機. ¶a ***hydraulic*** *press* 水力圧搾機. ¶the ***jingo*** *press* 主戦派の新聞. ¶the South American ***newspaper*** *press* 南米の諸新聞. 【類】He is to discourse upon the ***Newspaper*** *Press* of the last sixty years. ¶a ***paper*** *press* 〚製本〛紙圧機. ¶***Printing*** *press* is one of the potent and indispensable agencies in our modern civilization. 印刷機は現代文明の有力不可欠の利器の一つだ. ¶Everitt's patent ***trousers*** *press* エバリット式特許ずぼんプレス機. ¶a ***screw*** *press* 旋動圧搾機.

P ***according to*** the *press* 諸新聞によれば. ¶The first impression (60,000 copies) has been at once exhausted, and a second is now ***at*** *press*. 第一版(六万部)はすぐ品切れ第二版印刷中. ‖ pamphlets printed ***at*** the Merrymount *Press* メリマウント印刷所で印刷した小冊子. ¶The book was favorably noticed ***by*** the *press*. その本は諸新聞で好評を受けた. ¶The book is now ***in*** [the] *press*. 書物は目下印刷中だ. 【類】A new novel by ... is announced by Messrs. ... as being ***in*** the *press*. / This wane of the interest (興味の減退) in China may be seen everywhere, ***in*** the *press* (新聞) and in conversation. ¶the assaults ***of*** the *press* 諸新聞の攻撃 ‖ the power ***of*** the *press* 新聞雑誌の力 ‖ members ***of*** the *Press* were privileged to witness ... 新聞社員は...観覧の栄を得た ‖ freedom ***of*** the *press* 出版の自由. ¶as soon as it is ***off*** the *press* (=ready) 印刷でき上り次第. 【類】The book is just ***off*** the *press*. ¶men ***on*** the *Press* 新聞記者 ‖ The book is now ***on*** the *press* and will be ready at the end of this month. 書籍は目下印刷中だから月末にはでき上がります. 【類】the printing has been done ***on*** the *press* of ... ¶as it goes ***through*** the *press* 印刷中に. 【類】The new book is passing ***through*** the *press*. ¶go (come) ***to*** the *press* 印刷に付せられる. 【類】send (=put) it ***to*** the *press*.

P² the *press* ***of*** France and England 仏英の諸新聞.

(**2**) 群衆; 切迫, 繁忙; 開き戸だな, 本だな.

P ***due to*** the *press* (=pressure) of business 多用のため. ¶I keep some of my books ***in*** the *press*. 書物は幾らか書だなに入れてある. ‖ The child was lost ***in*** the *press* [of people]. その子は人ごみで見えなくなった.

P² in the *press* ***of*** business 業務の繁忙のため ‖ the *press* ***of*** modern life 近代生活の忙しさ.

press, *v.* 押す, 押しつける; しぼる; 圧迫する; しいる; 押しかける; 影響する.

M *press* a crowd ***back*** 群衆を押返す. ¶*press* a fugitive ***close*** 逃走者に肉迫する. ¶*press* ***forward*** 道を急ぐ; [群集が]押し合って前に出る. ¶*press* ***forward*** confidently 断固として進む. 【類】The crowd *pressed* ***forward***. / He *pressed* the troops ***forward***. ¶upon being *pressed* ***further*** それ以上しいられたので. ¶when ***hard*** *pressed* いよいよというときは, ピンチの際は. ¶*press* ***hard*** with questions 詰問する ‖ so ***hard*** *pressed* for food that ... 食う物に困ったので... 【類】Although ***hard*** *pressed* at first, the force eventually gained a victory. / The banks there are ***hard*** *pressed* for funds. ¶Taxes *press* ***heavily*** upon us. 税に悩まされている. ¶*press* ***lightly*** under damp cloth ぬれた布で軽く押える. ¶He is very ***much*** *pressed* for money. 彼は非常に金に窮している. ¶be *pressed* ***out*** はみ出る. ¶***warmly*** *press* 切に勧告する. ¶*press* ***westward*** 西方に押し進む.

M² *press* ***down*** keys (linotype などの) 鍵(キー)を押す. ‖ *press* ***down*** 押しつける. ¶*press* ***in*** upon one's consciousness as reminders of ... ...の想い出としてその意識に迫って来る. ¶*press* ***on*** unfalteringly and unheedingly more and more toward socialism ためらわず余念なく社会主義の方向に急ぐ.

P *press* one's ear ***against*** the door 戸に耳を押当てる ‖ He *pressed* his hands ***against*** his forehead. 彼は額に手を押当てた. ‖ Crowds *pressing* ***against*** a barrier 障壁に押し寄せる群集. 【類】I was *pressed* ***against*** the wall. ¶He was *pressed* ***by*** hunger. 彼は飢えに迫られた. ‖ *pressed* ***by*** necessity 必要に迫られて. ¶I must *press* ***for*** an answer. 至急御返事をいただきたい. 【類】If *pressed* ***for*** an answer, it must be in the negative (affirmative). ‖ the question *pressing* ***for*** serious consideration 慎重な考慮を促す問題. 【類】problems *pressing* ***for*** solution ‖ I am *pressed* ***for*** funds (=money). 私は金に差支えている. ‖ *press* ***for*** a remittance (payment of money) 送金(など)を催促する ‖ be *pressed* ***for*** orders 注文に追われて ‖ when *pressed* ***for*** reason, he explained ... 理由をしいて聞かれたので彼は...と説明した ‖ I am rather *pressed* ***for*** time today. きょうはちと忙しくって暇がない. ¶*press* the juice ***from*** grapes ぶどうから汁をしぼる. ¶I was *pressed* ***in*** a crowd. 私は人込みの中で押された. ¶*press* ... ***into*** folds (wrinkles) 押してひだ(など)を作る ‖ *press* ***into*** service an usually unused room 日常使わない室で間に合わせる ‖ *press* science ***into*** its service 科学をこれに応用する. ¶School duties did not *press* heavily ***on*** his time or application. 学校の仕事は彼の時間とか勉強とかに大した影響はなかった. ‖ *press* ***on*** (=push) the call button ベルを押す ‖ *press* a sticker (=label) ***on*** a trunk トランクにレッテルを押して張る ‖ what I should like to *press* ***on*** the consideration of ... ぜひ...に考えてもらいたいことは ‖ *press* wine and food ***on*** a guest 客に酒食をしいる ‖ *press* ***on*** the notice of the public such facts as ... ...のような事実に対して公衆の注意を呼び起す. ¶an oil *pressed* ***out of*** the seeds of ... ...の種子からしぼった油. ¶The noise *presses* ***round*** us. 騒音がまわりに迫る. ¶*press* the baby ***to*** the bosom 赤ん坊を抱きしめる ‖ if *pressed* ***to*** the vote しいて票決にすることになれば. ¶*press* ***toward*** a place ある場所へ押寄せる. ¶*press* it ***under*** a stone その上に石を載せて重しをする. ¶The troop *pressed* ***upon*** the enemy's right flank. 軍隊は敵の右翼を突いた. ‖ famine *pressing* close ***upon*** his heels 彼に肉迫する飢餓 ‖ The argument *pressed* ***upon*** the judgment. その議論の結果その判決が下されることになった. ‖ I *pressed* the money ***upon*** him, but he would not take it. 私は金を彼に無理に取らせようとしたが彼は取ろうとしなかった. ¶*press* a button ***with*** one's finger 指でボタンを押す ‖ *press* one ***with*** questions 質問で人を苦しめる ‖ I am *pressed* ***with*** sorrows. 心配で気がふさいでいる. ‖ *pressed* ***with*** business 仕事に追われて. 【類】I have been too *pressed* ***with*** work to do so. / *pressed* ***with*** hunger.

O Don't *press* me, you all. おい押すな(満員電車などで).

pressure, *n.* 圧力; 圧迫; 繁忙; 苦痛.

V ***apply*** *pressure* on ... ...に圧迫を加える. ¶great *pressure* was ***brought*** to bear on him to ... 彼に...させるように大いに圧迫が加えられた. 【類】*Pressure* is ***brought*** to bear on those responsible to see that a settlement is arrived at. ¶***correct*** one's blood *pressure* 血圧を整える. ¶***exert*** *pressure* on ... ...に迫る. ¶They ***exchanged*** a *pressure* of hands. 彼らは握手を交した. ¶I ***felt*** a *pressure* on the right shoulder. 私は右の肩が凝った. 【類】I ***feel*** the *pressure* of the shoes on my feet (くつがきつい). ¶The garrison began to ***feel*** the *pressure* of hunger. 守備隊は飢餓に迫られた. ¶I ***have*** a *pressure* of business. 用が重なる(忙しい). 【類】***have*** a great *pressure* of work. ¶***lighten*** the *pressure* of ... ...の圧力を弱める. ¶increase salaries to ***meet*** the *pressure* of the high cost of living 生活費上昇の重圧に応じるよう俸給を上げる. ¶***put*** *pressure* on the government 政府に迫る. 【類】*pressure* should not be ***put*** on them to ... ¶***relieve*** the *pressure* of pecuniary need 金銭上のひっ迫を救う. ¶***use*** all *pressure* in enforcing ... ...を励行するためにあらゆる高圧手段を用いる.

Q ***atmospheric*** *pressure* 気圧. 【類】high (low) ***atmospheric*** *pressure*. ¶wring from the country by ***diplomatic*** *pressure* ... その国から外交手段によって...を無理やりに奪取する. ¶She was forced into a vicious life by ***economic*** *pressure*. 彼女は困窮してやむなく邪悪の生活にはいった. ¶***financial*** *pressure* 財政のひっ迫. ¶During that period there is the ***greatest*** *pressure* for accommodation on all passenger steamers. その期間中はどの客船も乗客が一番多い. ¶by reason of very ***heavy*** *pressure* of the Christmas season クリスマス季節は非常に繁忙なので. ¶a ***high*** *pressure* boiler 高圧ボイラー ‖ work at ***high*** *pressure* 大車輪で働く. ¶***hydraulic*** *pressure* 水圧. ¶the continuously ***increasing*** *pressure* of foreign competition 絶えず増大する

外国の競争という圧力. ¶succumb to *international pressures* 国際的圧力に屈する. ¶a *long lingering pressure* of hands 長い間握ったままにした握手. ¶*mental pressure* 精神的苦痛. ¶exert direct *military pressure* upon ... 直接軍事的圧力を...に加える. ¶bring *opportune pressure* to bear upon ... to ... ...に...させるよう時機を得た圧迫を加える. ¶*outside pressure* 外部からの圧迫. ¶He took up business under *parental pressure*. 彼は親からしいられて仕事に取掛った. ¶yield to *popular pressure* まげて民衆の希望に添う. ¶under *strong pressure* 切羽詰って. ¶*unswerving pressure* ひるまない圧迫.

Q² *air* (*steam, water*) *pressure* 気(蒸気・水)圧. ¶correct one's *blood pressure* 血圧を調整する. 【類】elevation (上昇) of the *blood pressure*. ¶high *blood pressure* 高血圧. ¶low *gas pressure* 低いガス圧. ¶relieve *inflation pressure* インフレの圧迫を緩和する. ¶*population pressure* 人口過剰. ¶use *propaganda pressure* against ... ...に対し宣伝の圧力を加える. ¶Those air bases were built hurriedly under *wartime pressure*. これらの空軍基地は戦時の要求に迫られて急造されたのであった. ¶to meet the *war pressure* 戦時の要求に応じるため.

P *at* full *pressure* 非常に忙しく, 大車輪に. ¶*but for* the *pressure* of his work at the school 学校の事仕が多忙でなかったら. ¶*by pressure* of official business 公務多忙のため ‖ *by pressure* from ... ...にしいられて. ¶*despite* the *pressure* of his war duties, he has found time to ... 軍務多忙中暇を作って...した. ¶due to the *pressure of* business 事務繁忙のため. ¶*in* the *pressure* of modern life 現代生活の繁忙中に. ¶*on pressure* of the button ボタンを押すと ‖ There is pitting *on pressure*. 押すと穴があく(脚気患者の足など). ‖ painful *on pressure* 押すと痛む. ¶*owing to* the *pressure* on our space [雑誌など]余白がないので. ¶*through pressure* of other work 他の仕事が忙しいので ‖ *through* the *pressure* of public opinion 世論の力で. ¶yielding *to* the *pressure* of public opinion 世論の圧迫に屈服して. ¶A newspaper man must have the ability to work *under pressure*. 新聞記者は時間を制限されて働く腕がなくてはいけない. ‖ They felt constantly harried *under pressure* from outside. 外部からの圧迫に絶えず悩まされていた. ‖ *under* the *pressure* of necessity 苦しまぎれに ‖ The experiments were abandoned *under pressure* of losses. 損失に耐えずその試みは放棄することになった ‖ *under* the *pressure* of poverty 貧にかられて. 【類】*under* [the] *pressure* of circumstances (necessity, public opinion, adverse public sentiment) / *under* the very *pressure* of the times through which we are passing. ¶handshakes *with* a friendly *pressure* 友情をこめた握手.

P² These schools are very popular and there is always great *pressure for* admittance to them. これらの学校は非常に評判がよいのでいつでも入学希望者が押しかける. ‖ *pressure for* money 金銭ひっ迫. ¶No *pressure from* without can compel a man to open his lips, if he is determined to keep them closed. もし自分が沈黙を守ろうと決心しておれば外部からの圧迫では人の口を開かせることはできない. 【類】*pressure from* the society in which one lives. ¶the *pressure of* taxation 税の重荷. ¶the *pressure on* the money market 金融市場のひっ迫.

prestige, *n.* 威信, 威光, 勢望.

V The firm has *acquired* an increased *prestige*. その社は威信を増した. ¶*add prestige* to ... ...に威信を添える. ¶*advance* the *prestige* of his country その国家の威光を増す. ¶The question *affects* our national *prestige*. その問題はわが国家の威信にかかわる. ¶*damage* Japanese *prestige* in China 中国における日本の勢望を傷つける. ¶*dim* the *prestige* of ... ...の威信を落す. ¶*discount* national *prestige* 国威を減殺する. ¶*earn* much *prestige* 多大の信望を得る. ¶*enhance* national *prestige* 国威を宣揚する. ¶The reformers now *enjoy* the *prestige* their efforts have earned for them. 革新家は今や彼らが努力してかち得た信望を享有している. ¶*hurt* the *prestige* of ... ...の威信を損じる. ¶*injure* British *prestige* in the Far East 極東における英国の威信を傷つける. ¶*keep up* its *prestige* in the eyes of ... ...に対してその威信を落さない. ¶The city has *lost* its *prestige*. その都市はその名声を失った. ¶*lower* Japanese *prestige* in the eyes of other nations 他国民に対して日本の威信を落す. ¶*maintain* her national *prestige* in the world competition 世界の競争においてその国威を維持する. ¶*recover* lost *prestige* 失った信望を回復する. ¶*safeguard* Japanese *prestige* 日本の威信を擁護する. ¶*secure* such *prestige* for his journal that ... 氏の新聞に...ほどの信望をかち得る. ¶seriously *shake* the *prestige* of ... 大いに...の威信を落す. ¶*shatter* his *prestige* at home and among nations 彼の国内及び国際間の信用をめちゃめちゃにする. ¶*uphold* the *prestige* of German science ドイツ科学の威信を維持する.

Q *high prestige* 高い信望. ¶authors of *international prestige* 国際的勢望のある著作家. ¶recovery of our *lost athletic prestige* わが国の失墜した運動上の威信回復. ¶a gain in *national prestige* 国家の信望を増す一事例. ¶Gradually Greek art lost its *solitary prestige*. 次第にギリシアの美術はその独占の栄光を失った. ¶recover some of their *vanished prestige* 彼らの失った信望のいく分を回復する.

P *With* the *prestige* of the Metropolitan Museum behind it, the experiment is bound to be a great stimulus to the other Museums of the country. 信望あるメトロポリタン・ミュージアムの試みであるからそれは国内における他の博物館に必ず大なる刺激を与えることとなるであろう. ¶the rise *of* national *prestige* 国力の発展.

P² it will do the *prestige of* Japan more substantial good than ... それは...よりもはるかに実質的に日本の国威を増すであろう.

presume, *v.* 見なす; 甘える, つけ上がる; 鼻にかける; たのむ.

M *presume* a person *dead* その人を死んだものと見なす. ¶it may *fairly* be *presumed* that ... ...と思うのが至当だ. ¶He *presumes too much* on his strength. 彼は自分の力をたのみ過ぎる.

P I *presume* (=gather) *from* your words that ... 君の言葉から察すると... ¶*presume on* (=upon) kindness (friendship, favor, good nature) 人の親切(など)に甘える ‖ You *presume on* your high position. 君は地位の高いのを鼻にかけている. 【類】*presuming on* one's position as a guest. ¶*presume upon* (=on) one's patience がまんしているのにつけ上がる.

O he *presumes* to think that ... 彼は...と思うほどにうぬぼれている. ‖ I won't *presume* to disturb you. おじゃまをするつもりはない. ¶Mr. Henderson, I *presume?* ヘンダソンさんじゃありませんか.

presumption, *n.* せん越; 推測; 推測の理由.

V Please *pardon* my *presumption* in writing you. お手紙を差上げる失礼をお許し下さい.

Q a *mere presumption* 単なる推測.

P *on* the *presumption* that ... ...と仮定して.

P² There is a strong *presumption against* its truth. それが本当でないと思われる強い理由がある.

presumptuous, *a.* せん越な, 生意気な.

M he is *presumptuous enough* to think that ... 彼は生意気にも...と思った.

P it is *presumptuous of* me to ... ...するのは私としてせん越だ.

pretend, *v.* みせびらかす; いつわる; 主張する.

P He *pretends to* great learning. 彼はえらく物知り顔をする. ‖ *pretend to* genius 天才ぶる ‖ *pretend to* the throne 王位をねらう.

O He *pretends* to admire me, though privately he hates me. 彼は心では私を憎んでいるがうわべでは私をほめている. 【類】He *pretends* to be deaf, but hears all we are saying. / He *pretended* to be a doctor. / She *pretended* that she was a princess.

pretender, *n.* 見せかける人.

Q *mere pretenders* to learning 学者振る人々.

pretense, 《英》 **pretence,** *n.* 口実; まね, ふり; 主張.

V He *disclaims* all *pretense* to military skill. 彼は軍事上の手腕は一向持っていないと言っている. ‖ modestly *disclaim* all *pretense* to originality 謙そんして新味は少しもないという. ¶*make* a *pretense* to knowledge 知った風をする ‖ *make* but a *pretense* of eating ほんの食べるまねをする ‖ The book *makes* no *pretense* at being exhaustive. [著者は]その本に遺漏がないなどとは言っていない. ¶*throw off* the *pretense* of allegiance to ... ...への忠誠という仮面をかなぐり捨てる.

Q with *elaborate pretense* of ... どこまでも...と見せかけ

て. ¶He obtained money under ***false pretenses.*** 彼は金を詐取した. 【類】He was cheated of ¥... by ***false pretenses.*** ¶***hocus-pocus*** *pretenses* ごまかしの口実. ¶His religion is a ***mere*** *pretense.* 彼の信心はほんの見せかけだ. ¶a ***ridiculous*** *pretense* ばかげた口実. ¶on the ***slightest*** *pretense* ほんのちょっとした口実で. ¶a ***specious*** *pretense* もっともらしい口実.

P obtain goods ***by*** (=under) false *pretenses* 財物を詐取する. ¶He is devoid ***of*** all *pretense.* 彼はちっとも気どらない. ¶***on*** *pretense* of patriotism (religion, ill health) 愛国心(など)にことよせて. 【類】***on*** some *pretense* or other. ¶He declined ***under*** *pretense* of an important engagement. 彼は大事な約束があると言って断った. 【類】He cheated me ***under*** [the] *pretense* of friendship. / ***under*** the *pretense* of helping. ¶***Upon*** no *pretense* whatever may any outsider gain admission. いかなる理由があっても外来者の入場を拒絶する. ¶***with*** a *pretense* of seeking health 保養にこと寄せて. ¶a man ***without*** *pretense* ぶらない人.

P^2 *pretense* ***of*** illness 仮病.

pretension, *n.* 主張; 権利, 言分; てらうこと; 抱負.

V It ***has*** some *pretensions* to be chosen as the site. それはその敷地として選定せられるべきいく分の資格がある. ‖ He ***has*** no *pretension* to scholarship. 彼は学者とは言えない. ‖ What *pretension* ***has*** he? 彼になんの言分があるか. ¶***lay*** *pretension* to a right 権利を主張する. ¶She ***makes*** no *pretensions* to beauty. 彼女は美人ぶらない. 【類】***make*** no *pretension* to completeness / The present work ***makes*** no *pretensions* to originality.

Q a very ***absurd*** *pretension* きわめてばかげた言分. ¶buildings of no ***architectural*** *pretensions* 建築学上これといって誇るべき点のない建物. ¶the ***artistic*** *pretensions* of players 演技者の切る芸道の見栄(舞台の誇張した演技). ¶a person of ***great*** *pretension* 大抱負を持っている人. ¶a composition of some ***literary*** *pretensions* 多少文学的趣味のある文. ¶houses of the most ***modest*** *pretensions* 至極地味な家.

P^2 *pretension* ***to*** learning (greatness) 学識(など)をてらうこと. 【類】*pretentions* ***to*** the throne 王位継承権.

pretext, *n.* 口実, 言いわけ.

V if he could ***find*** a good *pretext* for doing so もし彼にそうする好い口実が見付かれば. ¶***form*** a good *pretext* for ... ...の好い口実になる. ¶a *pretext* ***put forward*** by ... ...の申立てた理くつ. ¶***use*** one *pretext* or another 言を左右に託する.

Q on ***any*** *pretext* いかなる口実を設けても. ¶find a ***fair*** *pretext* for ... ...のうまい口実を見つける. ¶on some ***flimsy*** *pretext* or other 何か薄弱な口実で. ¶He was condemned to death on ***frivolous*** *pretext.* 彼はくだらない理由で死刑の宣告を受けた. ¶on some ***idle*** *pretext* 何とかくだらない口実を設けて. ¶on the most ***ridiculous*** *pretext* 最もばかげた理由で.

P Anything serves him ***as*** a *pretext* for idleness. どんなことでも彼にはなまける口実になる. ¶***on*** (=under) the *pretext* of ill health 病気を口実に ‖ ***on*** one *pretext* or another 何とか口実を設けて. 【類】***on*** some *pretext* / ***on*** the *pretext* that ... ¶***under*** (=with) the *pretext* that ... ...の口実(理由)で. 【類】He cheated me ***under*** [the] *pretext* of friendship. ¶***upon*** some *pretext* or other 何かの口実で. ¶it furnished him ***with*** a *pretext* for ... それが...の口実を彼に与えた.

P^2 a *pretext* ***for*** playing truant 学校をさぼる口実.

pretty, *a.* 美しい, きれいな.

M be ***placidly*** *pretty* 静かで美しい. ¶She is ***rather*** *pretty.* 彼女は中々きれいだ. ¶be ***vastly*** *pretty* すごく美しい.

prevail, *v.* 打勝つ; 説きつける; 優勢を占める, 流行する.

M he is not ***easily*** *prevailed* upon to ... 彼は容易に...させられない. ¶the opinion ***generally*** *prevails* here that ... 当地では...という意見が一般に行われている. ¶the practice ***still*** *prevails* locally in parts of Japan その慣習は今なお日本の所どころで行われている.

P *prevail* ***against*** a person (truth, principle) 人(など)に勝つ. ¶Dark eyes *prevail* ***among*** the races who live in the glare of a tropical sun. 黒い目は熱帯の太陽のまばゆい中に住んでいる人に多い. ¶Such ideas *prevail* ***in*** this age. こんな考えが今日持てはやされている. ‖ *prevail* ***in*** a struggle 闘争に打勝つ. ¶*prevail* ***on*** (=upon) government 政府を説きつける ‖ I tried to *prevail* ***on*** (=upon) him to stay. 彼に留まるよう説きつけようとした. 【類】I could not *prevail* ***on*** him to marry the girl. ¶We have *prevailed* ***over*** our enemies. われわれは敵に打勝った. 【類】[The] Good must ultimately *prevail* ***over*** the vile. / As in the arts, so in politics, the new must always *prevail* ***over*** the old. ¶Buddhism *prevails* ***throughout*** the country. 仏教は全国を通じて優勢を占めている. ¶Such practice *prevails* ***to this day.*** かかる風習が今日まで行われている. ¶he could not be *pravailed* ***upon*** to ... 彼は中々...すると言わなかった ‖ *prevail* ***upon*** a person by argument 人を説き伏せる. 【類】He was *prevailed* ***upon*** to stay. ¶I tried but could not *prevail* ***with*** (=on) him. 彼を説き伏せようとしたがだめだった. ‖ My mother, with much reluctance, *prevailed* ***with*** herself to go without me. 母は不承不承に私を連れずに行く気になった.

prevalence, *n.* 流行.

Q the ***overwhelming*** *prevalence* of crime in ... compared with other countries 他国に比して...に犯罪が圧倒的に多いこと. ¶None expected the ***present*** *prevalence* of television ten years ago. 十年前今日のテレビの流行を予期したものはなかった. ¶Bribery is of very ***wide*** *prevalence.* わいろは非常に広く行われている. 【類】the ***wide*** *prevalence* ***of*** serious crime (凶悪犯罪) のため.

P ***owing to*** the *prevalence* of scarlet fever しょう紅熱流行

P^2 the general *prevalence* ***among*** the upper classes ***of*** luxury 上流社会に広くぜいたくの行われていること ‖ the *prevalence* ***of*** bribery わいろの流行.

prevalent, *a.* 優勢な, 一般に流行する.

M ***exceedingly*** (=***extremely***) *prevalent* 非常に優勢な. ¶become ***more and more*** *prevalent* ますます流行して来る. ¶The ***most*** *prevalent* winds in this district are the N.E. この地方で一番多い風は北東風だ. ¶***universally*** *prevalent* 一般に流行する. ¶Burglaries seem to be ***very*** *prevalent* these times. このごろ夜盗事件がとても多いようだ.

P The plague is now *prevalent* ***in*** India. ペストが目下インドに流行している. ‖ The cholera was *prevalent* ***in*** that year. コレラがあの年流行した. ¶Flu is *prevalent* ***throughout*** the country. 流感が全国に流行している.

prevent, *v.* 妨げる, 邪魔する; 予防する.

M Do not await a moment after your dinner hour, please, as that affair will ***probably*** *prevent* my (=me from) coming. どうぞお食事の時間がちょっとでも過ぎたらお待ち下さいますな, あの件で多分私は参られますまい. ¶I have been ***unavoidably*** *prevented* from coming. 私は余儀ない用事で来られなかった.

P On that day he was *prevented* ***by*** illness ***from*** attending. その日彼は病気で出られなかった. 【類】I was *prevented* ***by*** the rain ***from*** taking any outdoor exercise. ¶*prevent* a prisoner ***from*** escaping 囚人が逃げられないようにする. 【類】Bad weather *prevented* me ***from*** starting. / He was *prevented* ***from*** doing so by urgent business. ☞ from を省くことがある: What *prevented* you ***from*** coming (=*prevented* you coming *or prevented* your coming)?

prevention, *n.* 予防, 防止.

Q Education would be the ***best*** and ***final*** *prevention* against social evils. 教育が社会悪の最善かつ最終的防止法であろう.

Q^2 ***accident*** *prevention* 事故防止. ¶***fire*** *prevention* at sea 海上火災防止.

P^2 *prevention* ***of*** unemployment 失業の防止 ‖ the *prevention* ***of*** juvenile crimes 少年犯罪の防止.

preventive, *n.* 予防薬, 予防策.

Q the ***best*** *preventive* of disease 一番よい病気の予防法.

P It is impotent ***as*** a *preventive* of war. それは戦争の予防策としては無力だ.

P^2 Europeans take melons for a *preventive* ***against*** seasickness. 欧州人は船酔の予防にメロンを食べる. 【類】Vaccination (種痘) is a *preventive* ***against*** smallpox. ¶a *preventive* ***of*** (=***for***) fever (disease, crime) 熱病(など)の予防薬.

previous, *a.* 前の; 《口語》早過ぎる.

M You have been a little ***too*** *previous.* 君は少し早まり過ぎた. ‖ Summer is a trifle ***too*** *previous.* 《俗》夏の来かたが少し早過ぎる.

P about a year *previous* ***to*** the time of which I am now writing 私が今書いている時より約一年前. 【類】His mother died two days *previous* ***to*** his arrival.

previously, *ad.* 前に, 先に.

P *previously* ***to*** my arrival 私の到着に先立って. 【類】The ground must be well dug *previously* ***to*** the sowing of the seed.

prey, *n.* 餌食(えじき), 食い物; 犠牲.

V ***capture*** one's *prey* そのえじきを捕える. ¶The wolf ***devoured*** its *prey* ravenously. おおかみはそのえじきをむさぼり食った. ¶***find*** an easy *prey* in him 彼こそだましやすいと見る. ¶The detective ***discovered*** among them his long-sought *prey*. 探偵は彼らの中に自分の長い間捜していた捕物(えもの)のいるのを発見した. ¶he is ***made*** the easy *prey* of ... 彼は...にだまされやすい.

Q a ***desirable*** *prey* いいかも. ¶I found them an ***easy*** *prey*. 私は彼らを容易にだませた. ‖ fall an ***easy*** *prey* to deception まんまとだまされる. 【類】fall an ***easy*** *prey* to a vulgar French adventuress. ¶It was in these circumstances that the Devil found him a ***ready*** *prey*. こうした事情で彼は訳なく邪道にはいった.

P a bird (beast) ***of*** *prey* 肉食鳥(獣). ¶become the *prey* ***of*** a lion ししのえじきになる ‖ He was left alone with himself, the *prey* ***of*** his own and thoughts. 彼は独り後に残されて悲嘆に暮れた. ‖ He has for a long time been the *prey* ***of*** fears concerning his heart. 彼は長らく心臓の悪いのを苦に病んでいた. ‖ be the *prey* ***of*** a malady 病気にかかる ‖ remain a *prey* ***of*** conflicting emotions (nightmare, fearful fancies) 矛盾する感情(など)の犠牲になっている. 【類】He has hitherto been the *prey* ***of*** gamester (とばく師). ¶be a *prey* ***to*** fear (an undefinable terror, anxiety, anger, sorrow, remorse). 彼は恐怖(など)にとらわれている. ‖ fall a *prey* ***to*** stronger powers 一層強い力のえじきになる. 【類】fall a *prey* ***to*** melancholy (lovesickness).

prey, *v.* 捕食する; 食い込む; 悩ます.

P *prey* ***on*** (=upon) living animals (small birds) 生物(など)を捕えて食う ‖ His misfortune *preys* ***on*** (=upon) his mind. 不幸が彼の心に食い込む. ¶*prey* ***upon*** the beginner 初心者を食い物にする ‖ burglars *preying* ***upon*** society 世間を騒がす夜盗. 【類】*prey* ***upon*** the weakness and vices of immature youths / *prey* ***upon*** defenseless people (うっかりもの) / Remorse *preyed* ***upon*** his mind. 彼は後悔の念に心をくさらした.

price, *n.* 代価, 値段; 犠牲.

V ***abate*** the *price* 値引する. ¶He ***accepted*** (=***agreed to***) my *price*. 彼は私の言値を承諾した. ¶***advance*** (=raise) *prices* from ... to ... 値段を...から...に上げる. ¶***affect*** the *price* of ... ...の値段に影響する. ¶After long haggling, a *price* was ***agreed upon***. 長い間押問答をしたあげくに値段がまとまった. ¶***ask*** (=***demand***) an exorbitant *price* 法外な値段を請求する ‖ We never ***ask*** two *prices*. 手前どもではかけ値はしません. 【類】***ask*** a high *price* for an antique. ¶***assess*** a *price* 値を決める. ¶***assign*** (=***fix***) a *price* to ... ...の値をきめる. ¶They ***bear*** large *prices*. それは値が高い. ¶***beat down*** the *price* 値切る. ¶***bid*** a better *price* もっとよい値をつける. ¶***bid up*** the *price* 値段をせり上げる. ¶***boost*** *prices* 値段をつり上げる. 【類】*Prices* are being ***boosted*** to the sky (天井知らずに). ¶The picture promises to ***bring*** the largest *price*. その絵は一番よい値がつきそうだ. ‖ It ***brought*** the record *price* of ... at the sale. れはその売立てで...という記録的な値段が出た. ‖ It ***brought*** a smaller *price* on account of the defect. それはその欠点があるのでそれほど高く売れなかった. ¶***bully*** the *price* of another drink out of her 彼女からもう一杯飲む金をゆする. ¶***calculate*** a *price* 値段を計算する. ¶***charge*** double *prices* 二倍の値段を取る. 【類】He ***charged*** me a higher *price* than he charged you. ‖ a small *price* is usually ***charged*** for ... ¶Wheat ***commands*** a good *price*. 小麦はよい値に売れる. 【類】***command*** exceedingly high *prices* (非常な高価). ¶***cut*** *prices* 値を下げる ‖ try to ***cut*** the other *prices* 他店の値段と競争する. ¶***cut down*** *prices* 値切る. ¶***drop*** *prices* 値段を下げる. ¶***enclose*** the *price* for ... ...の代価を同封する. ¶***enhance*** (=rise) *prices* 値段を上げる. ¶***establish*** the *price* of his liberty [囚人などの]身もと引受けの保証金(身のしろ金)を設定する. ¶***fetch*** (=bring) a good *price* in the market 市場で値が出る. ¶***figure out*** the printer's *price* for booklets 小冊子の印刷代を計算する. ¶Be careful to ***fix*** the *price* in advance. [タクシーを雇う時など]先に値段をきめるようになさい. ‖ ***fix*** *prices* at the lowest possible scale できるだけ安く値段をつける. ¶***force*** *prices* ***higher*** 値をつり上げる. ¶***force up*** (***down***) *prices* 値をつり上げる(無理に下げる). ¶I ***got*** a good *price* for ... 私は...を好い値に売った. 【類】What *price* can you ***get*** for it? ¶***give*** the current *price* of ... ...の時価を示す ‖ I can ***give*** a good *price* for this. これはふめる. ¶***harden*** *prices* 値段を上げる. ¶Everything in my store ***has*** a fixed *price*. 手前の店ではすべて定価がついています. ‖ All goods ***have*** one *price*, printed in plain figrues. 品はすべて明りょうな数字で正札値段がついている. ‖ They ***have*** two *prices*. そこの店では掛値をいう. ‖ Every man ***has*** his *price*. だれでもわいろはきくものだ. ¶Wheat has ***hit*** its lowest *price* in seventy years. 小麦は七十年の安値を示した. ¶try to ***improve*** *prices* 価格を高くしようとする. ¶***keep down*** the *prices* 物価を(上がらないよう)押えておく. ¶***keep up*** the *prices* 物価を維持する. ¶***knock*** the *price* ***down*** 値切る. ¶Let me ***know*** at once your last *price*. 最近の値段をすぐお知らせ下さい. ¶If I take many, will you ***lessen*** the *price*? 沢山買えば値を引くか. ¶***lower*** (=abate) the *prices* 値を引く. ¶***maintain*** old *prices* もとの値に据えおく. 【類】***maintain*** *prices* at a figure that leaves a reasonable profit (適当にさやを見込んだ値に). ¶***mark*** the *price* on every article 商品に残らず値段をつける ‖ He has ***marked*** his *prices* way down to start with. 彼はまず手始に値段をぐっと安く付けた. 【類】The *prices* are ***marked*** (=set in plain figures). ¶***name*** a *price* 値を言う ‖ at the *prices* you ***name*** 言値で ‖ ***Name*** your *price*. いくらあげたらいいか. ¶high *prices* are asked and ***obtained*** for ... ...に対して高値を言いまたそれで売れている. ¶***offer*** reasonable *prices* 相当な値をつける. 【類】He ***offered*** me a good *price*. / What *price* can you ***offer***? / ***offer*** lower *prices* for ... / We can ***offer*** a reasonable *price* (適正価格). ¶***pay*** the *price* for ... ...の代を払う ‖ He ***paid*** the *price* of ... with his life-blood. 彼は...のために命を取られた. ‖ He will ***pay*** almost any *price* to obtain it. 彼は値段に構わずそれを手に入れようとしている. ¶***put*** *prices* on goods 商品に値段をつける. 【類】He refuses to ***put*** a *price* on his collection. ‖ ***put*** (=set) a *price* on his head 彼の逮捕または首に賞を懸ける. ¶***put up*** the *price* 値段を上げる. ¶***quote*** *prices* 値段を知らせる ‖ Competitors are ***quoting*** lower *prices*. 競争者がもっと安値を言っている. ¶temporarily ***raise*** a *price* 一時的に値段を上げる. ¶sacrifice the quality of goods in order to ***reach*** low *price* 値段を安くするために品質を落す. ¶The goods have ***realized*** good (poor) *prices*. その品はよい(安い)値で売れた. 【類】The land sold ***realized*** a fair *price*. ¶What *price* would you ***recommend***? いくらならよろしゅうございますか. ¶***reduce*** one's *prices* 言値を引下げる(値引きする). 【類】***reduce*** the *price* by ... yen / ***reduce*** *prices* to prewar levels. ¶***refund*** the *price* paid 支払代金を払戻す. ¶***regulate*** *prices* 物価を調節する. ¶I will ***remit*** the *price* upon receipt of bill 勘定書受取次第代金をお送りします. ¶***renew*** a *price* 値段を付けかえる. ¶***revise*** *prices* 価格を改訂する. ¶All *prices* are ***scaled*** ten per cent. 品物はすべて一割引になっている. ¶***send*** him the *price* 彼に代金を送る. ¶***set*** a *price* upon a thing 物に値をつける ‖ A *price* was ***set*** on the head of every Jesuit. だれのでもジェスイト教徒の首を取ったものには賞を与えた. ¶***settle*** the *price* 値段を決める. ¶***slash*** *prices* 物価を下げる. 【類】The *price* of newspapers was ***slashed*** so that all could buy. ¶***stabilize*** the *prices* of food 食料品の値段を安定させる. ¶Is this the lowest *price* you can ***take***? これより引けませんか. ¶***undercut*** our *prices* 当方の値を切下げる. 【類】***undercut*** the market *price* of ... ¶*Prices* are strongly ***upheld***. 値段は動かない.

V² *Prices* ***advanced*** over 50 per cent. 物価は五割以上騰貴した. ¶a *price* that ***covers*** 引合う値段. ¶*Prices* are ***declining***. 物価は下落しつつある. ¶The *price* has ***dropped***. 物価が下落した. ¶In 1932 *price* of cork ***fell*** to the lowest point in the history of the industry. 一九三二年にはコルクの値段は同工業史上最低価に下落した. ¶*Prices* have ***gone down*** (***up***) all round. 物価は一体に下(上)がった. ¶Wait until the *price* ***improves***. 値が出るまで待て. 【類】Supplies will increase as soon as *prices* ***improve***. ¶*Prices* ***jump up*** madly. 物価がむやみに飛上る. ¶Supply is short and *prices* are ***mounting*** accordingly. 供給が不足なので物価は騰貴しつつある. ¶*prices* ***obtaining*** in Europe 欧州

における通り相場. ¶Better *prices* now ***prevail***. 値が出た. ¶*Prices* have not ***rallied*** since the panic. 恐こう以来物価は持直さない. ¶*Prices* are ***rising*** (***declining***). 物価は上(下)っている.【類】*Prices* ***rose*** to preposterous heights. (途方もない高価). ¶*Prices* ***rule*** high (low). 相場は高値(安値)を唱えている. ¶*Prices* ***shoot up*** (=rise suddenly). 物価が急に上がる. ¶*Prices* ***shrank*** very low. 物価は非常に低く引締った. ¶*Prices* are ***skyrocketing*** (***tobogganing***). 《米口語》物価は急騰(落)している. ¶After American Pewter was published *prices* for pewter ***soared***. 米国製白ろうが出てから白ろうの値段が奔騰した. ¶The *price* ***varies*** according to the quality. 値段は質によって違う.

Q on the ***advertised*** *price* 広告した価段で. ¶at ***agreed*** *prices* 折合った値段で. ¶***all-round*** *price* 込みの値段. ¶cannot be attained at ***any*** *price* いくら金を出しても手に入らない. ¶quote an ***approximate*** *price* 見積価格を申し送る. ¶*price* ***asked***=asked price 言い値. ¶his ***asking*** *price* for it 彼の言い値. ¶***average*** *prices* 平均値. ¶an ***awful big*** *price* 恐ろしい高値. ¶the ***best*** *price* ***obtainable*** この上なしの高値. ¶They are produced to meet a ***certain*** *price* 一定の価格で引合うように生産している. ¶sell at ***competitive*** *prices* 競争値段で売る. ¶fetch a ***considerable*** *price* 余ほどの値で売れる. ¶The book is issued at ***cost*** *price*. その本は原価発行である.【類】sell at ***cost*** *price*. ¶*prices* ***current*** 時価. ¶name a ***dear*** *price* 高値をいう ‖ supply at the lowest ***current*** *price* 時価の最低で(品物を)出す. ¶at ***decreased*** *prices* 値下げをした. ¶a ***definite*** *price* 定価. ¶the *price* ***delivered*** 引渡し価格. ¶The *price* is ***elastic***. その値段は多少融通がつく. ¶The prospect of a war is causing ***enhanced*** *prices*. 戦争を見越して物価が上っている. ¶at an ***exceptional*** *price* 特価で. ¶Command more ***exceptional*** *prices* than ... …よりは特別高く売る. ¶an ***excessive*** *price* 掛値. ¶He charged me an ***exorbitant*** *price* for it. 彼はそれに対しとっぴょうしもない値を吹っかけた. ¶***extortionate*** *prices* 法外な値段. ¶an ***extra*** *price* 割増値段. ¶name an ***extravagant*** *price* 法外な値段を吹きかける. ¶At war times its *price* is ***fabulous***. 戦時はそれはばか値だ.【類】In the seventeenth century rare varieties of tulip (チューリップの珍種) were sold at ***fabulous*** *prices*. ¶a ***fair*** *price* 公正値段. ¶***fancy*** *prices* 掛値. ¶a ***firm*** *price*〖相場〗期限付売買価格 ‖ *Prices* are very ***firm*** with a tendency to rise (=advance). 相場上向きでしっかりだ. ‖ *Prices* are ***firmer***. 相場は一層手堅い. ¶give the ***first*** *price* asked for ... …を言い値で買う. ¶sell goods at ***fixed*** *prices* 品物を定価で売る. ¶a ***forward*** *price* 先物相場. ¶a ***frightful*** *price* 恐ろしい値段. ¶Sellers are only willing to sell small parcel at ***full*** *prices*. 売手は小量を割引なしでなければ売ってくれない. ¶the "***going*** *price*" 通り相場. ¶sell at ***good*** (***bad***) *price* よい(安)値で売る.【類】That will bring (=get) you a good *price*. ¶at ***half*** *price* 半値で. ¶The book is now sold at ***half published*** *price*. その本は定価の半値で売っている. ¶at ***heavy*** *prices* 高価で. ¶sell at ***high*** *prices* 高価に売る ‖ marketable at a ***high*** *price* 高価で売れる.【類】offer it at absurdly ***high*** *prices* and sell it at absurdly ***low*** *prices* / the ***highest possible*** *price* we can sell at is ... ¶purchased at ***immense*** *prices* ばく大の代価をもって買い上げられた. ¶at ***increased*** *prices* 割増値段で. ¶an ***incredible*** *price* 法外な値段. ¶sell at greatly ***inflated*** *prices* 暴騰値段で売る. ¶***inside*** *prices* 仲間値段. ¶pay a ***just*** *price* for ... …に適正な代価を払う. ¶bear ***large*** *prices* 高い値が付いている. ¶The market opened at ***last*** *prices*, but declined towards the close. 市場は最高値で開始されたが大引け近くには下った. ¶pay ***liberal*** *prices* 気前よく十分の代を払う. ¶It is a ***long*** *price* to pay. それは中中いい値だ. ¶at the astonishingly (ruinously, ridiculously) ***low*** *price* of ... …という驚くべき(など)廉価で ‖ my opponents are quoting ***lower*** *prices* 同業者はもっと安値で売り出している ‖ the ***lowest*** *price* ***possible*** ぎりぎり決着の値段.【類】at the ***lowest*** possible *prices*. ¶at the ***lowest current*** *price* 最低の時価で. ¶the ***minimum*** (=floor) *price* 最低価. ¶at ***moderate*** *prices* 廉価で.【類】There is good eating and drinking at ***moderate*** *prices*. / at *prices* strictly ***moderate***. ¶fix a ***modest*** *price* at the start 初めに廉価をつける. ¶a ***net*** *price* (掛値なしの)正価. ¶at the ***nominal*** *price* of ... …の名目値段で. ¶a ***normal*** *price* 平時相場. ¶an ***offered*** *price* 申込値段. ¶an ***official*** *price* 公定値段. ¶***opening*** *prices* 寄付相場. ¶five times the ***ordinary*** *price* 普通の値段の五倍. ¶at the ***original*** *price* 最初の値で. ¶50% less than ***original*** *prices* 原価の五割引. ¶It realized a ***poor*** *price*. それは高く売れなかった. ¶available at a ***popular*** *price* 格安の値段で買える.【類】Luncheons and dinners served at ***popular*** *prices*. / the best of fiction at a ***popular*** *price*. ¶a ***present*** *price* 現在価格. ¶What is the ***present*** buying (selling) *price* per share? 一株につき現在の買(売)相場はいくらか. ¶at ***prevailing*** *prices* 時価で. ¶sell it at a ***prewar*** *price* それを戦前の値で売る. ¶a ***probable*** *price* [近刊書の]予定定価. ¶a ***prohibitive*** *price* 禁止的値段(けたはずれな高値).【類】hitherto unattainable except at ***prohibitive*** *prices*. ¶the ***proper*** *price* is ..., but I'll let you have it for ... 本当なら値段は…だが…でお分けしましょう. ¶a ***published*** *price* [出版物の]定価 ‖ allow one-third off the ***published*** *price* 定価の三分の一にまける. ¶We'll repay you back full ***purchase*** *price*. 買値を全部お返しします. ¶***quoted*** *price* 言ってやった値. ¶purchase at ***reasonable*** *prices* 相当の値段で買う. ¶offer at ***reduced*** *prices* 値引で提供する. ¶at about half the ***regular*** *price* 普通値段の半分で. ¶***ruling*** *prices* 時価. ¶I can offer you very ***satisfactory*** *prices*. 当方は御満足の行く値を申上げられます.【類】if the *price* is ***satisfactory***. ¶Needless to say ***scarcity*** *prices* obtained. もちろん品払底で相場が上った. ¶We have no ***second*** (=fancy) *price*. 掛値は致しません. ¶***sensational*** *prices* [名物茶器などの]けた外れの値段. ¶a ***set*** *price* 定価. ¶He paid a ***severe*** *price* for it. 彼はその罰が当ってひどい目に会った. ¶***skyrocketing*** *prices* 急騰している物価. ¶a ridiculously ***small*** (=low) *price* ばかげた廉価.【類】at ***small*** *prices* of admission (入場料) / Some of these bulletins have a ***small*** *price* attached, though many are free. ¶the ***soaring*** *price* of rice 天井知らずの米価. ¶at a ***staggering*** *price* ぎょっとするような値で. ¶at ***steady*** *prices* 安定した(動かない)値で. ¶a ***steep*** *price*《俗》不当な値段. ¶*Prices* are rather ***stiff***.《俗》物価は少し高い.【類】This was a ***stiff*** *price* to pay for what was an admitted forgery (疑いないにせ物). ¶at most ***tempting*** *prices* 飛付きたいほど(安い)値段で. ¶the *price* ***tendered*** 入札代価. ¶at a ***thrifty*** *price* 経済的な値段で. ¶The *price* was ***trifling***. 値段はわずかだった.【類】it is too ***trifling*** a *price* to pay for ... ¶No ***two*** *prices*. 掛値なし. ¶The market is firm at ***unchanged*** *prices*. 市場は安定した相場で手堅い. ¶at a ***uniform*** *price* of 15 cents each 十五セント均一で.【類】at the ***uniform*** *price* of 3s. 6d. per volume. ¶That is certainly an ***unreasonable*** *price* to ask. そんな値ってありゃしない. ¶at the ***upset*** *price* of ... …の売唱え価格で(競売の) ‖ an ***upset*** *price* [競売の]差値. ¶the ***usual*** *price* for ... …の通常値段. ¶the ***upmost*** *price* [要求できる]最高の価格. ¶***varying*** *prices* [高低]まちまちの価格. ¶offer at the ***wholesale*** *price* of ... …の卸値で提供する. ¶It is well ***worth*** the *price* of admission. りっぱに入場料だけの価値はある. ¶I will buy it at ***your own*** *price*. それを言い値で買いましょう.

Q^2 charge ***above-ceiling*** *prices* やみ値を要求する. ¶the special ***advance-of-publication*** *price* [本の]特売価格. ¶Clothing can be purchased at ***Army*** *prices*. 衣類は陸軍価格で買える. ¶sell at ***bargain*** *prices* 見切値で売る. ¶***before-publication*** *price* [本など]出版以前の予定価. ¶at ***below-cost*** *prices* 原価を割る値で(出血価格で). ¶a ***bid*** *price*〖競売〗つけ値. ¶sell at ***blackmarket*** *prices* やみ値で売る ‖ command the ***black-market*** *price* of ... …というやみ値で売れる.【類】They will bring $500,000 at present ***black-market*** *prices*. ¶***buying*** *prices* 買い相場. ¶a ***cash*** *price* 現金値. ¶a ***catalogue*** *price* カタログ記載の価格. ¶the ***ceiling*** (***floor***) *price*《米》最高(低)価格.【類】purchase at ***ceiling*** *prices* / violate ***ceiling*** *prices* on housing / impose ***ceiling*** *prices* on the sale of new houses / end the ***ceiling*** *price* on meat. ¶bargains at ***clearance*** *prices* 見切値(赤札付)の掘出しもの色々. ¶***closing*** *prices* 大引け相場. ¶***clothing*** *prices* 衣類の価格. ¶***commodity*** *prices* in the United States 米国の諸物価. ¶the ***consumer*** *price* 消費者価格. ¶the ***contract*** *price* 消費値段. ¶at ***cost*** *price* 原価で, 仕入値で.【類】goods sold below ***cost*** *price* (コストを割って) ‖ a sale of salvage goods at fifty per cent under *cost price* 原価半額の難船引上げ品売出し. ¶a *dozen* (*gross*) *price* ダース(グロス)値. ¶*famine prices* ききん相場(払底に因る法外の高値). ¶protect *farm prices* 農産物価を保護する. ¶*Farm product prices* shot up by 11 per cent. 農産物価格が一割一分急騰した. ¶high *feed-grain prices* [馬料などの]高い穀類相場. ¶rising *food prices* 騰貴する食料価格. ¶The following are *going-to-press Stock Exchange prices*. 最新の株式相場一覧表(新聞用語). ¶the *home market price* 国内相場. ¶provide delicious food at *honest-value prices* 正当の値段でうまい食物を供給する. ¶the *issue price* of a loan 公債の発行価格. ¶a *list price* 表記価格, 定価表値段. ¶*Livestock prices* zoomed to highest levels since 1919. 家畜の相場は一九一九年以来最高にはね上った. ¶the *mailing price* of a book 郵送料込みの本の値段. ¶at *market price* 市価で. ¶sell at the current *market price* きょうの相場で売る. ¶save one 40 cents under the *newsstand price*. 新聞売場の値段より 40 セントやすくつく(予約した場合など). ¶a *non-profit price* 非営利的価格, 実費値段. ¶"*Parlor prices* charged in this department" このへやでは室料を頂戴致します(料理屋など). ¶Ups and downs of *picture prices* 絵画相場の変動. ¶full refund of the *purchase price* 代金の全額返金. ¶return the *purchasing price* 代金を返す. ¶*real estates prices* 家屋土地の相場. ¶a *record price* [最高]記録値. ¶at low *ready-money prices* 安い現金値で. ¶These curios are often offered for sale not at fair *reproduction prices* but much higher. この種の骨とう品が複製物相当の値段ではなく非常な高値でよく売りに出る. ¶a *reserve price* 〘競売〙売主がその品に対して定めておく最低値段. 【類】put a *reserve price* on the house. ¶*rock-bottom prices* 《米》ぎりぎり決着の値段. ¶a *regular price* 正規の値段. ¶*retail prices* 小売値段. ¶a *runaway price* 〘商〙天井知らずの上り相場. ¶at *sacrifice prices* [コストを割る]犠牲値段で. ¶a *sale price* 売値. ¶the *selling price* ruling at the time 時価 ‖ What is the present *selling* (*buying*) *price* per share? 今一株の売(買)相場はいくらですか. 【類】They have no settled *selling prices* (定った売価) for goods. / the difference between the appraised value (査定価格) and the actual *selling price*. ¶*speak-easy prices* 《米》やみ値の値段. ¶the *spot price* 現場渡し値. ¶the *subscription price* of a magazine 雑誌の予約値(購読料). ¶*Subscription price*, $5.00 a year; single copy, 50 cents; foreign postage, 24 cents. 予約購読年五ドル; 一部売り五十セント; 海外郵送料二十四セント. ¶*super-ceiling* (=above-ceiling) *prices* 限界の高値を上回った値. ¶a *trade price* 仲間相場. ¶a *unit price* 単価. ¶*war*[*time*] *prices* 戦時相場. ¶*World prices* mounted. 世界相場は上った.

P *above* (=*beyond or without*) *price* 評価すべからざるほど高価の. 【類】jewels *avove price*=priceless jewels ‖ be *above* (*below*) the market *price* 市価より高(安)い. ¶dispose of it *at* a *price* 代金を取って売る. 【類】it was purchased for the British Museum *at* the (=a) *price* of ... / It is supplied *at* a *price* much lower than the market price. / I will let you have it *at* that *price*. ‖ Experience is cheap *at* any *price*. 経験というものはどんな犠牲を払っても安いものだ. 【類】I will do it *at* any *price*. ‖ take it *at* one's *price* 言い値でそれを買う. ¶He offered it to me *for* a low *price*. 彼はそれを廉価で私に提供した. ‖ not to be had *for* any *price* 金をいくらだしても手に入らない. 【類】sell *for* small *prices*. / sell *for* a still smaller *price*. ¶in consequence of decline *in prices* 物価下落の結果 ‖ a fall *in price* 値段の下落 ‖ a big jump *in prices* 相場の暴騰 ‖ It improved *in price*. 値が出た. ‖ They have become prohibitive *in price*. 値段が手が出ないほど高くなった. ¶*of* great *price* はなはだ貴重な ‖ a general stiffening *of prices* 一般に物価の引締ること ‖ They are all *of* a *price*. 皆同値段だ. ¶at a discount of 15 or 20 per cent *off* the *prices* marked 値札の一割五分ないし二割引で. 【類】at from 25% to 40% *off* regular *prices*. ¶It is *under* the original *price*. それは原価以下になっている. ¶*with prices* shooting (=soaring) skyward 物価は暴騰して ‖ an outlaw *with* a *price* upon his head 首に懸賞付のお尋ねもの. ¶be not *worth* the *price*. その値段だけの価値がない.

P² at a *price* considerably *below* the market value 市価よりもずっと低い値段で. ¶*prices for* goods 商品の値段. ¶The *price of* admission is low. 入場料は安い. ‖ This is the *price of* success. この代価を払って成功が買われるのだ. ‖ hand over a shilling as the *price of* peace (物もらいなど)うるさいから一シリング渡す. 【類】Alsace Lorraine was accorded to France as a part of the *price of* peace (和平の代償). ¶*Prices on* some items are slightly higher in Canada. カナダでは品によっては物価が少し高い.

price, *v*. 値段づけをする.

M *priced high* (*low*) 高(安)値の. ¶goods *moderately priced* 廉価な商品. ¶*sensibly* (=*reasonably*) *priced* 無理でない値を付けた. ¶*priced $12.50* 十二ドル五十セントの値の付いた.

P *price* it *at* 10 yen それに十円と値をつける. 【類】it is priced *at* ... / goods *priced at* a figure which strikes the happy medium (中を取った). ¶*price* a person (goods) *out of* the market 人(物)を市場から閉め出す.

prick, *n*. とげ; さした痛み; 苦しみ.

V I *feel* the *prick* of conscience. 私は良心がとがめる. ‖ I *feel* no *prick* of conscience whatever. 少しも心にやましい所はない. ¶I've *got* a *prick* in my finger 指にとげがささった. ¶a *prick made* by a needle ちくりと針の一刺.

Q feel a *slight prick* 少しちくちくする. ¶stony in sensibility to the *small pricks* and frictions of daily life 日常生活の小さな苦悩やあつれきに対する全くの無とん着.

Q² a *pin prick* ピンで刺した跡.

P² the *prick of* a needle (thorn) 針(など)の一突き.

prick, *v*. そばだてる; 刺す; うがつ.

M The dog *pricked up* its ears. 犬が耳をそばだてた ‖ *prick up* oneself めかす, 見せびらかす.

P *prick beneath* the surface of Tokyo life 東京生活の裏面をのぞく. ¶some who are *pricked for* sheriffs 州保安吏に選抜された人々. ¶*prick* a hole *in* it *with* a pin 留針でそれに穴を突きあける. ¶*prick* a picture *on* a wall [ピンなどで)壁に絵を止める. ¶*prick* one's finger *with* a needle (thorn) 針(など)で指を刺す.

pricking, *n*. 刺すこと.

V *experience* a *pricking* of conscience 良心のかしゃくを受ける.

pride, *n*. 自慢; 誇り; 自尊; 最盛期.

V *appeal to* one's *pride* 自尊心に訴える. ¶*bend* one's *pride* 高慢の鼻をくじく. ¶*crush* the *pride* of ... ...の面目をつぶす. ¶*display pride* 高慢な風をする. ¶*feel* a noble *pride* 気高い誇りを感じる ‖ *feel pride* at one's success その成功を誇る. ¶*flinging* her *pride* to the four winds 彼女は女としての誇りをかなぐりすてて. ¶*gratify* her *pride* 彼女の自尊心を満足させる. 【類】*gratify* French national *pride* (フランス人の国民的自尊心). ¶*have* a *pride* in one's ability (birth, wealth) 己が手腕(など)を誇る. 【類】Jingoro *had* a *pride* in his skill. / They *have* each a *pride* of their own. ¶*heal* a wounded *pride* 自尊心の痛手をいやす. ¶*humble* the *pride* of ... in the dust ...のごう慢の鼻を折る. ¶His *pride* was *hurt* (=*wounded*). 彼の自尊心が傷つけられた. ¶*inflate* the *pride* of ... ...を得意がらせる. ¶*pamper pride* わがままをほしいままにする. ¶*pocket* one's *pride* その自尊心を抑える, 雌伏する. ¶*put* the *pride* in one's pocket 自尊心を忘れる(外聞をかまわない). ¶*recall* one's *pride* その自尊心を喚起する. ¶*satisfy* one's *pride* その自負心を満足させる. ¶*shock* one's *pride* 大いにその自負心を傷つける. ¶A man has a right to *show pride* in his library. 人は自分の書斎を誇る権利がある. 【類】*show* more *pride* in ... than in ... ¶That will *sink* their *pride*. それで彼らの鼻もぺちゃんこだ. ¶*subdue* his *pride* 彼の高慢の鼻を折る. ¶*swallow* one's *pride* 自負心を抑える. ¶*take pride* in one's work 自分の仕事を誇りとする. 【類】we may *take* a little *pride* in the fact that ... / very naturally *take* great *pride* in ... / *take pride* in splendid isolation (栄光の孤立) / She *takes* great *pride* in her beauty. ¶*wound* one's *pride* 鼻柱を折る. ¶He will not *yield pride* of place to his rival without a fight. 彼は一戦なくしては(むざむざ)勝ちをゆずるようなことはないだろう.

P *civic pride* 市民の誇り. ¶*false pride* から威張り. ¶one of Japan's *greatest prides* 日本の最も誇りとするものの一つ. ¶in *high pride* 大得意で. ¶*honest pride* 自重心. ¶an *honorable pride* in labor 労働者の貴い誇り. ¶with *humble pride* 心ひそかに得意で. ¶lead to the collapse of an *inflated pride* 高慢の鼻を折られることになる. ¶take *intense pride* in ... ひどく...を自慢する. ¶*local pride* 郷土

の誇り. ¶*maidenly pride* 娘の誇り. ¶*modest pride* 卑下自慢. ¶She is her *mother's pride.* 彼女は母親の自慢娘だ. ¶His college takes *much pride* in his success. 氏の大学では氏の成功を大いに誇っている. ¶an hour of *national pride* 国民が得意のとき ‖ with *national pride* 国民的誇りをもって ‖ None can speak of it without a swelling of *national pride.* それを語ると国民としての誇りを感ぜずにはおられない. ¶with an air of *ostentatious pride* これ見よがしに. ¶*overweening pride* ごう慢. ¶My heart glowed with *paternal pride.* わが胸は父たるの誇りに燃えた. ¶*patriotic pride* お国自慢. ¶*professional pride* 職業の誇り. ¶*proper pride* 自重心. ¶take a *special pride* in ... 特に...を誇る. ¶the *stanch pride* they hold of ... 彼らが...について持っている強い誇り. ¶*summer's pride* 夏の誇り(風物). ¶her heart hot with anger and *wounded pride* 怒りと自尊心を傷つけられた悔しさで熱した彼女の胸.

Q² He is a *family pride* of ours 彼はうちの自慢息子だ. ‖ hurt the *family pride* 家名を汚す. ¶a *London pride* ロンドンの誇り. ¶*race pride* 民族の誇り.

P a peacock *in* his *pride* 尾を広げた得意姿のくじゃく ‖ the city *in* all her *pride* of prosperity 全盛時のその都市 ‖ *in* the *pride* of his heart 得意の余り ‖ die *in* the *pride* of one's life 若盛りに死ぬ. 【類】 *in* the *pride* of manhood / *in* the full *pride* of youth ‖ be *in pride* (=prime) of grease 〚狩〛 脂がのり切っている(今が打ちごろ). ¶I felt a thrill *of pride* when I heard ... ...と聞いたときは胸もときめく誇りを感じた. ‖ take a sort *of pride* in ... ...に一種の誇りを感じる ‖ His nostrils were dilated *with pride.* 彼は鼻をうごめかしていた. ‖ we point *with pride* to ... われわれは誇りをもって...を指摘する ‖ be inflated *with pride* 慢心している. 【類】 He is puffed up (=swells) *with pride.*

P² He is the *pride of* his school. 彼は学校の誇りだ. ‖ the *pride of* his collection 氏の収集品中の白眉(はくび) ‖ the *pride of* literary America アメリカ文学界の誇り ‖ the *pride of* France will be satisfied with nothing but ... ...がなくてはフランスの誇りは十分でない.

pride, *v.* 自慢する.

P *pride* oneself *on* (=*upon*) one's success (wealth, ability) その成功(など)を自慢する. 【類】 He *prides* himself *on* being a self-made man.

priest, *n.* 僧りょ, 牧師.

V *Hate* a *priest,* and you will hate his very hood. 〚諺〛 坊主憎けりゃけさまで憎い.

Q a *begging priest* こじき坊主. ¶a *mendicant priest* たくはつ僧. ¶the chief *officiating priest* 司祭.

O become a *priest* 牧師になる.

priesthood, *n.* 僧職.

V *enter* the *priesthood* 僧籍に入る ‖ He *entered* the Buddhist *priesthood,* but returned to civil life. 彼は仏門に入ったが還俗(げんぞく)した. ¶*quit* the *priesthood* 還俗する.

P He was educated *for* the *priesthood.* 彼は聖職の教育を受けた.

primacy, *n.* 首位.

V *forfeit* its *primacy* 首位から転落する.

P² The *primacy among* the nations, economic and political, is destined to go to the United States. 列国間における経済上及び政治上の首位は米国のものとなる運命を持っている.

prim, *a.* きちんとした.

P *prim* and proper *in* manner 態度のきちんとした.

prime, *n.* 真盛り.

V Women *attain* the *prime* of the beauty usually somewhere about the age of twenty. 婦人は通例二十歳前後が美しい盛りだ. ¶*pass* its *prime* 盛りを過ぎる. 【類】 *pass* one's *prime* and get on the wrong side of thirty 若盛りを過ぎて三十の坂を越す.

P a woman *at* her *prime* 若盛りの婦人. ¶*during* his *prime* 彼の全盛時に. ¶Grapes are just now *in* their *prime.* ぶどうは今が丁度盛りだ. ‖ die *in* the *prime* of life 人生の盛りに死ぬ ‖ be *in prime* of grease [猟鳥など]脂肪が乗切っている. 【類】 be *in* the *prime* of health.

P² the *prime of* manhood 男盛り. 【類】 the *prime of* youth.

prime, *v.* 前もって知らせる; たらふく食う(飲む).

M be *fully primed* with the latest news 最近の事情に精通している. ¶*well primed* たらふく食って; 酔っぱらって.

primer, *n.* 初学書, 入門.

P² a *primer of* geography 地理学手引き. ¶a *primer on* Browning ブラウニング入門書.

prince, *n.* 王子; 皇子; 巨頭.

Q a *financial prince* 財政王. ¶the *Prince Imperial* 皇太子. ¶India's *native princes* インド土侯. ¶one of the *petty princes* of the empire 小さな大名の一人. ¶the *Prince Regent* 摂政の宮. ¶the *Prince Royal* 王世子.

Q² a *banking prince* 銀行王. ¶an *infant prince* 幼君. ¶a *merchant prince* 豪商.

P² the *prince among* American educators 米国教育界の大立物. ¶a *prince in* disguise おしのびの王子. ¶Japanese *princes of* the blood 日本の皇族方 ‖ the *princes of* India インドの諸王 ‖ the *Prince of* Wales ウェールス公(英国の皇太子) ‖ photography—the *prince of* hobbies 道楽の王(大関)たる写真術. 【類】 Lord Kutsford, that *prince of* beggars (例の慈善のために寄付を仰ぐ人).

principal, *n.* 本人; 〚法〛 主犯者; 校長.

V I must *consult* my *principal.* 本人に相談しなければならない[代人の言]. ¶It *took* the *principal* to quiet us. 校長が仲へはいってやっと静まった.

Q² a *school principal* 学校長. ☞英国では head master とか the head of a school という.

P He commits the offense *as* a *principal.* 彼は主犯者だ.

P² the *principal of* the troupe 座頭, 団長.

principle, *n.* 主義; 原理; 本元; 道義.

V *abandon* one's *principles* その主義を捨てる. ¶*accept* the *principle* その原則を承認する. ¶*advocate* a *principle* 主義を唱道する. ¶*apply* a *principle* to ... ...に原則を適用する. 【類】 general *principles* that cannot be *applied* rigidly / *apply* the *principles* of science for the good of mankind. ¶*carry out* the *principle* one professes 自分が表明する主義を実行する. ¶*contravene* the fundamental *principle* of ... ...の根本原則に抵触する. ¶*desert* a *principle* 主義を捨てる. ¶*establish* the fundamental *principles* 根本原則を確定する. ¶*follow* the *principle* of ... ...の主義を奉じる. 【類】 The *principle* which I have *followed* is practical rather than theoretical. ¶*formulate* a *principle* 主義を立てる. ¶*forsake principles* 主義を捨てる. ¶*further* the *principle* of ... ...の主義を助長する. ¶He *has* no *principles.* 彼には主義(節操)がない. ¶*hold* the same *principles* 同じ主義を抱く. ¶*illustrate* the same *principle* from different standpoints 異った見地から同一の原理を説明する. ¶*instill* these *principles* into those who ... これらの主義を...の人々に注入する. ¶*lay down* a *principle* 原則を立てる. 【類】 Early in his work he *laid down* two or three *principles.* ¶loyally *maintain principles* 忠実に主義を固執する. 【類】 *maintain* the *principle* of academic freedom (学の独立). ¶*master* the *principles* of ... ...の法則に通暁する. ¶*observe* the *principle* of ... ...の主義を守る. ¶a real party representing *principles placed* above personalities 個人関係を超越した主義を代表する真の政党. ¶*put* one's *principles* into practice その主義を実行に移す. ¶*renounce* (one's) *principles* 主義を放棄する. ¶Left *represents* (=is) the male *principle.* 左は陽だ. ¶*sacrifice principle* for the sake of a mistaken loyalty はき違えた忠節のために主義を犠牲にする. ¶*uphold* the *principles* of the party 党の主義を高揚する. ¶*utilize* the *principles* of the lever and fulcrum てこ[とてこ台]の原理を利用する. ¶*violate* the *principles* of the open door and equal opportunities for all nations in China 中国における門戸開放機会均等の原則を破る. 【類】 *violate* the *principle* of unity (統一).

V² the *principle,* generally stated, *consists* in ... その原則を概説すると...ということになる. ¶the *principles governing* ... ...を支配する法則. ¶The same *principle holds.* 同一原理が当てはまる. ¶the *principles underlying* beauty 美の根底をなす原則. 【類】 *principles underlying* teaching methods.

Q *abstract principles* of personal liberty 個人の自由という抽象論. ¶it is an *accepted principle* that ... ...は動かすべからざる原則である ‖ the reorganization of business methods on the most recently *accepted principle* 最新の原則に基づいた営業法の改正. ¶an *all-pervading principle* 普遍的に行きわたっている原則. ¶on *analogous principles* 類似の原則によって. ¶It is organized on too *bad* a *principle.* それは余りにも誤った原則に基づいて編制されてある.

¶act on a ***barbarous*** and ***savage principle*** 野蛮的な主義に基づいて行動する. ¶a ***basic principle*** 根本原則 ‖ the ***basic principles*** of grammar 文法の基本原則. ¶three ***broad principles*** 三大原則. ¶a ***cardinal principle*** 根本原則. ¶the ***Christian principle*** of full equality for male and female 完全なる男女平等を主張するキリスト教の主義. ¶the ***Confucian principle*** of "benevolence" 孔子の仁の道. ¶a ***constituting principle*** 構成原理. ¶a ***dangerous principle*** 危険な主義. ¶the ***dominant principle*** 大方針. ¶the ***elemental principle*** of … …の第一原理. ¶***essential principles*** 基本原則. ¶a ***fine principle*** りっぱな原理. ¶the ***first principle*** of all things 万物の本元. ¶it is opposed to the ***first principles*** of … それは…の第一原理に反する. 【類】be ignorant of the ***first principles*** of politics. ¶the ***fundamental principles*** of architectural beauty 建築美の根本原則. ¶establish a ***general principle*** 通則を設ける. 【類】It is a ***general principle*** that may safely be followed. ¶the ***governing principle*** 原則. ¶the ***guiding principle*** of … …の指導精神. ¶a man of ***high principle*** りっぱな主義を持つ人. ¶a new English dictionary on ***historical principles*** 歴史的原則に基づいて編集した新英語辞典. ¶an ***invariable principle*** 不変の原理. ¶one of its ***main principles*** その主要原則の一つ. ¶administer on ***military principles*** 軍隊主義で処理する. ¶***minor principles*** 小原則. ¶ships designed upon the most ***modern principles*** 最新式に従って設計した船. ¶***moral principles*** 道義. ¶The entries are arranged on a ***new principle***. 事項が新しい原則によって配列されている. ¶a platform of ***political principles*** 政綱, 綱領. ¶a man of his ***own principle*** 独自の主義を持つ人. ¶a man of ***no principle*** 主義のない人. ¶***practical*** and ***sound economic principles*** 実際的で確実な経済原理. ¶the ***ruling principle*** of life 生活の指導原理. ¶the ***same principle*** applies to … 同じ原理が…に適用される. 【類】The two machines work on the ***same principle***. ¶apply ***scientific principles*** 科学の原理を応用する. 【類】Only since the middle of the 19th century has beer been brewed on ***scientific principles***. ¶it is constructed on a ***similar principle*** to that used in … それは…に応用したのと同様の原理に基づいて構成してある. ¶proceed on ***sound principles*** 健実な主義に基づいて進む. 【類】acting on a ***sound principle*** / a civilization built on the ***soundest principles*** of self-goverment. ¶prudish women of ***strong moral principle*** 道義心の強い小やかましい婦人. ¶***tested principles*** 試験済みの原理. ¶well-established ***theoretical principles*** 基礎の固い原理. ¶***tried, proved, sound, sensible rinciples*** 試験済で証明された堅実賢明の原理. ¶the ***true principles*** on which charity may be usefully administered 博愛を有効に行うための正しい原則. 【類】supply ***true principles*** to popular enthusiasm. ¶design on ***true mechanical principles*** 真の機械学の原理に基づいて設計する. ¶the ***underlying principles*** of … …の根本原理. ¶establish ***universal principles*** 普遍的原則を立てる. ¶the ***vital principle*** 活力, 精気. ¶***warring principles*** 両立しない主義. ¶a ***well-established linguistic principle*** 基礎の確実な言語学上の原理.

Q² a ***bed-rock*** (=rock-bottom) ***principle*** 根本義. ¶The eating-house is run on the ***cafeteria principle*** その飲食店はカフェテリヤ(客自身給仕する)方式で経営されている. ¶retail stores conducted on the ***chain-store principle*** 連鎖式小売店. ¶Church of ***England principles*** 英国々教教会主義. ¶the "***Family-head First***" ***principle*** 戸主第一の原則. ¶the ***foundation principles*** underlying … …の根底をなす原則. ¶the ***ground principle*** 根本原則. ¶the ***guiding principle*** 指導原理. ¶on the "***nationality***" ***principle*** [国籍など]属人主義で. ¶the ***root principles*** of investment 投資の基本原則. ¶the ***short-haul principle*** 距離比例法(貨物運賃測定法の一). ¶a full economiser on the ***smoke-consuming principle*** 吸煙(完全燃焼)方式による燃料節約器. ¶on the ***stitch-in-time principle*** ちょいちょい手入れをする主義で. ¶on the "***territory***" ***principle*** 〘法〙属地主義で. ¶the "***three-peoples***" ***principles*** 三民主義. ¶***working principles*** 経営(営業)方針.

P It is ***against*** my ***principles***. それは私の主義に反する. ¶act ***from principle*** 主義で行動する. ¶same ***in principle*** 原則は同様な ‖ he has admitted ***in principle*** liability for … 彼は原則として…に対する責任を承認した. ¶a man ***of*** (no) ***principle*** 主義(無節操)の人. 【類】as a matter ***of principle***. ¶get up early ***on principle*** 主義で早起する ‖ ***on*** the ***principle*** of "making hay while the sun shines" 好機を逃さない主義で. 【類】those who oppose contraception (避妊) either ***on principle*** or from prejudice / To this he objected ***on principle***. / I take my stand ***on principle***. / act ***on*** this ***principle*** / carry on foreign trade ***on*** the ***principles*** of protection (保護主義) / ***on*** the ***principle*** of giving the devil his due (どんな者も公平に認めるという) / He was one of those moralizing nuisances who always do things ***on principles***. ‖ be built ***on*** the ***principle*** that … …という原理の上に建てられている ‖ The monotype machine is a device working ***on*** the ***principle*** of the linotype. モノタイプは鋳込植字機「ライノタイプ」と同原理で動く装置だ. 【類】work ***on*** the ***principle*** of you-press-the-button-we-do-the-rest (簡便主義) / a machine made ***on*** a new ***principle*** ‖ The information contained in this book is arranged ***on*** the A B C ***principle*** throughout. この本の内容はすべてＡＢＣ順に排列してある. 【類】icecream-soda fountains ***on*** the American ***principle*** 米国式のアイスクリーム・ソーダ水容器. ¶He is always true ***to*** his ***principles***. 彼はいつも自己の主義に忠実だ. ‖ live up ***to*** one's ***principles*** 自分の主義を遵守する. ¶***upon*** this ***principle*** この原則に基づいて ‖ go ***upon*** the ***principe*** of … …の原理による. 【類】the ***principle upon*** which it is based. ¶The barbarian lives ***without principle***. 野蛮人は定見なしに暮して行く.

P² The ***principle in*** both machines is the same. 機械は双方共原理は同じだ. ‖ a guiding ***principle in*** one's life 生活の指針 ‖ I have always made it a ***principle in*** life never to borrow or to lend money. 私は常に金銭の貸借をしないということを処世の主義として来た. ¶the great ***principle of*** evolution 進化の大原則 ‖ a ***principle of*** human nature 人間性の一原則 ‖ the ***principle of*** natural selection 自然とうたの原則.

print, *n.* 印刷; 印刷物; 版画; 〘写真〙印画(プリント); 《米》新聞.

V ***read*** small ***prints*** 細字の印刷物を読む.

V² The ***prints*** of her love-bites did not ***wear out*** for some days after. 彼女のかわいさの余りかんだ跡が数日間消えずにいた.

Q ***blue print*** 青写真. ¶The ***print*** is ***clear***. 印刷は鮮明だ. ¶read it in ***cold print*** それを(冷い)印刷物で読む. ¶***daily prints*** 《米》日刊新聞. ¶get ***extra prints*** of one's favorite snapshots その得意のスナップを複写させる. ¶***Fine print*** is trying to one's eyes. 細かい字体は見るのに骨が折れる. ¶***good print*** りっぱな印刷. ¶The ***print*** is ***illegible***. 版が(不鮮明で)読みにくい. ¶write on the box in ***large print*** 大きな活字体の文字で箱に書く. ¶in ***large bold print*** 大きな肉太の活字に印刷した. ¶***microscopic print*** ごく細字の印刷. ¶an ***old print*** of London Bridge ロンドン橋の古い版画 ‖ an ***old print*** depicting … …の古版画. ¶I have read it in the ***public prints***. 私は新聞でそれを読んだ. ¶a ***scurrilous half-penny print*** 野卑な一文版画. ¶***separate prints*** from the Journal その雑誌の別冊(付録). ¶***weekly prints*** 《米》週刊紙(誌).

Q² ***finger prints*** 指紋. ¶***news print***=newsprint 新聞印刷用紙. ¶a ***silver print*** 硝酸銀写真.

P The book is now ***in print***. その本は目下印刷中だ. ‖ the best picture ***in print*** of … 活字になった…の最上の伝記. 【類】Those numbers which are ***in print*** can be supplied. / These books are still ***in print*** and available. / The essay appeared ***in print*** for the first time in the year 1650. / It appeared ***in print*** in magazines or otherwise. / come out ***in print*** ‖ be attacked ***in print*** 紙上で攻撃される ‖ be undesirable ***in print*** in full 全文印刷は好ましくない. ¶put it ***into print*** それを印刷に付する ‖ rush it ***into print*** それを大急ぎで印刷する. ¶two solid tomes twelve hundred pages ***of print*** 千二百ページの大冊二巻. ¶It has been debated ***on*** the public ***prints***. それは新聞紙上で論議された. ¶a book ***out of print*** 絶版の本. 【類】It's impossible to get one, for the book is ***out of print***.

P² a ***print from*** stone 石ずり.

print, *v.* 印刷する; 刊行する; 〘写真〙焼つける(プリントする).

M ***beautifully printed*** and artistically bound 印刷美麗装本高雅. ¶It is ***clearly printed*** in a type especially founded for the series. それは特にその双書のための特鋳活字で鮮明に印刷してある. ¶ *exquisitely printed* 精巧に印刷した. ¶ be *handsomely printed* 鮮明に印刷してある. ¶ be *legibly printed* on specially made paper 特製紙に読みやすいように印刷してある. ¶ be *lightly printed* 薄色で印刷してある. ¶ *neatly printed* 印刷のきれいな. ¶ *Printing neatly* and *quickly* done here. 〚広告〛印刷は美麗じん速に仕上げます. ¶ *poorly printed* 印刷の悪い. ¶ It was *printed privately* for presentation only. それは寄贈用私版として印刷された. ¶ a book *printed surreptitiously* 秘密出版の書物.

M² *print off* (=*out*) 〚写真〛焼付ける ‖ *print off* 3000 copies a day 一日に三千部を刷り上げる ‖ footmarks *printed off* distinctly in the snow 雪にはっきり残した足跡.

P *Printed at* the Clarendon Press *by* Henry Smith クラレンドン印刷所内ヘンリー・スミス印刷 (本のとびらの裏面などに). ¶ a publication privately *printed for* subscribers only 予約者だけに配布した私版本. ¶ be *printed from* type 活字印刷である ‖ a picture *printed from* an engraved plate 彫刻版で刷った絵 ‖ old books *printed from* blocks on Japanese paper 日本紙に版木で刷った古書. 【類】 *printed* partly *from* wooden blocks and partly *from* movable types (活字). ¶ *print in* italics イタリック体の活字で印刷する ‖ a newspaper *printed in* English=an English [language] newspaper 英字新聞. 【類】 The text is *printed in* large type. / capital letters *printed in* colors (色刷り). / novels *printed in* the English language ‖ It is so *printed in* the Revised Version. 改正訳聖書にはそうなっている. ¶ books *printed on* good paper 良質紙に刷った本 ‖ *printed on* one side 片面刷. ¶ *print with* capital letters 頭文字で印刷する ‖ *print with* stereotypes ステロ版で刷る.

printer, *n.* 印刷職工; 印刷業者.

V *employ* over a hundred *printers* 百人以上の印刷工を使う.

P² a *printer at* the case=a compositor 植字工.

O Houghton & Co, *printers* and binders ヒュートン印刷製本会社.

printing, *n.* 印刷; 印刷物.

V The publisher usually *makes* a first *printing* of from 2500 to 3000 copies. 出版者は通例初版は二千五百ないし三千部印刷する.

Q an *advance printing* of a portion of a work 著書の一部分の見本刷. ¶ *colored* (*three-colored*) *printing* 色(三色)刷り. ¶ *unlicensed printing* 無許可印刷.

Q² *job printing* 端もの印刷. ¶ *plate printing* 電気(ステロ)盤印刷. ¶ *transfer printing* 転写印刷. ¶ *wood-cut* (=*block*) *printing* 木版印刷.

P² In the art of *printing in* color from wood-blocks, Japan has been absolutely unparalleled among the nations. 木版色刷の術にかけては日本は断然世界無比だ.

prior, *n.* 寺院の院長.

Q² a *Buddhist prior* 寺の住職.

prior, *a.* 先の, 前の.

P The will was made two days *prior to* his death. 遺書は彼の死ぬ二日前に作られたものだ. ‖ I called on him *prior to* my departure. 私は出発前に彼を訪ねた.

priority, *n.* 先, 前; 優先権.

V *acquire* a *priority* 優先権を得る. ¶ *dispute priority* 本家(元祖)争いをする. ¶ *give priority* over ... ...に対して優先権を与える ‖ be *given priority* of place 上席を与えられる, 先に出してもらう. 【類】 *priority* is *given* to war industry. ¶ *have priority* over ... ...に優先する. ¶ *hold priority* 優位に立つ. ¶ *receive priority* for ... 優先的に...させてもらう.

Q The Government proposed to give housing the *highest priority*. 政府は住宅問題に最重点をおくことを申入れた. ¶ give *special priority* for materials and labor to industries engaged in production for export 輸出品生産工場に資材や労力の優先権を与える.

P *according to priority* 順ぐりに. ¶ *by priority* 優先的に ‖ *by priority* of age comes ... 年齢順で言うと...

P² *priority in* time 時の順序が先き. ¶ *priority of* mention is due to ... 筆頭に...を書かなくってはならない(先ず第一に指を...に屈せざるを得ない) ‖ in the order of *priority of* appointment 任命順に. ¶ the *priority of* ... *as to* this honor この光栄に関する...の優先権. ¶ *priority of* one event *to* another 一事件の他の事件に先立つこと. 【類】 the *priority of* social regeneration *to* political reform / *priority of* one's rank *to* another's.

prison, *n.* 刑務所, ろう屋; 監禁.

Q the chief of a *juvenile prison* 少年院院長. ¶ a *murky prison* 陰気な刑務所.

Q² a *convict prison* [既決囚の]刑務所.

V *break prison* 破獄する. ¶ He *found prison* at last. 彼は遂に収監された.

P He was hanged *at* the *prison*. 彼は刑務所で絞刑に処せられた. ¶ run away *from prison* 脱獄する. ¶ He was confined (=put) *in prison*. 彼は刑務所に監禁された. 【類】 He died *in prison*. ¶ cast (=throw) one *into prison* 人を投獄する. ¶ He was let *out of prison*. 彼は出所を許された. ‖ come *out of prison* 出所する. ¶ He was committed *to prison*. 刑務所に入れられた. 【類】 He was sent *to prison* for theft. 「prisoners 男囚刑務所.

P² a *prison for* confinement 留置所 ‖ a *prison for* male

prisoner, *n.* 囚人; 捕虜; 刑事被告.

V *admit prisoners* to bail 囚人の保釈を許す. ¶ *capture prisoners* 捕虜を捕える. ¶ *commit* the discharged *prisoner* to a workhouse, or a protectory, or a house of correction, or other asylum 免囚を養育院か保護所か矯正院かまたはその他の収容所へ引渡す. ¶ The German *prisoners* were *detained* there. ドイツ人の捕虜がそこに留置されていた. ¶ *discharge* (=*let off*) a *prisoner* 囚人を放免する. ¶ *free* a *prisoner* 囚人を放免する. ¶ *hang* a *prisoner* 囚人を絞首刑に処する. ¶ *prisoners incarcerated* in prison 監禁の囚人. ¶ *keep prisoners* in order 囚人たちに規律を守らせる. ¶ They were *kept prisoners* by typhoon for nearly three days in a mountain hut. 彼らは台風のために山小屋に約三日間ろう城した. 【類】 Flu *kept* me a *prisoner* in my room. ¶ *let* a *prisoner out* on bail 囚人を保釈する. ¶ *liberate* (=*release*) *prisoners* 囚人を放免する. ¶ They were *made* (=*taken*) *prisoner*. 彼らはとりこになった. ¶ *parole* a *prisoner* 囚人を仮出所させる. ¶ *remand* a *prisoner* 捕虜を召喚する. ¶ The *prisoner* has been *set free*. 囚人は放免された. ¶ The *prisoner* was *tried* by a judge. 被告が判事に調べられた.

Q *civil prisoners* 収容された人々 (war prisoners に対して). ¶ keep a person a *close prisoner* 人を厳重に監禁しておく. ¶ sentence a *convicted prisoner* to a term of five to ten years in the state *prison* 犯人に州刑務所で五年ないし十年の刑を宣告する. ¶ *convicted* and *non-convicted prisoners* 未既決囚人. ¶ *discharged prisoners* 出所者. ¶ an *escaped prisoner* 脱獄囚. ¶ a prison for *female prisoners* 女囚刑務所. ¶ a *political prisoner* 政治犯人. ¶ a *released prisoner* 出所者. ¶ *rioting prisoners* 暴徒化した囚人たち. ¶ an *unconvicted prisoner* 未決囚.

Q² *enemy prisoners* 敵方の捕虜たち. ¶ a *life-term prisoner* 終身囚. ¶ a *State prisoner* 国事犯人. ¶ a *war prisoner* 捕虜 ‖ Communist indoctrinated *war prisoners* 共産党筋金入りの捕虜たち.

P *among* the *prisoners* taken 捕虜の中に. ¶ He is held *as prisoner* of war. 彼は捕虜になっている. ¶ The evidence tells *in favor of* the *prisoner*. その証拠は被告の有利になる. ¶ The judge has passed a sentence *on* the *prisoner*. 判事が被告に判決を与えた.

P² a *prisoner at* the bar 刑事被告. ¶ a *prisoner in* chains (=jail) 鎖につながれた(在監)囚人. ¶ a *prisoner of* State =a State prisoner ‖ *prisoners of* war=war prisoners ‖ He is to some extent the *prisoner of* his former speeches on the subject of the land annuities. 氏は土地代金年賦払の問題に関して彼の以前の演説にいく分自じょう自縛の形である. ¶ He is a *prisoner to* his room. 彼はへやにこもりきりだ. ‖ a *prisoner to* his bed 床についた病人.

O He made her hand a *prisoner*. 彼は彼女の手をとらえた.

privacy, *n.* 隠とん, ちっ居; 秘密, 内証.

V *disturb* one's *privacy* ひとり居を妨害する. 【類】 I don't want my *privacy* to be *disturbed*. ¶ to *ensure privacy* 秘密を確保するため. ¶ Instead of doors there are little cotton curtains, which can at night *secure privacy*. ドアはなく木綿地の小さな幕があってこれを引けば夜は人目を避けることができる. ¶ *violate* one's *privacy* 人のへやにみだりにはいり込む.

Q live in *absolute privacy* 完全な隠とん生活を送る. ¶ In such matters *privacy* is *impossible*. こういったことの秘密を保つことは不可能なものだ. ¶ *personal privacies* 一身の

秘密. ¶There is *quite privacy* as regards sound. 声は一切外へもれない.

P She wept *in* the *privacy* of her own room. 彼女は自分のへやに一人かくれて泣いた. ¶intrude *on* one's *privacy* 人の私事に立ち入る. ¶The plan is being carried out *with* the utmost *privacy*. その計画は極秘で実行されつつある.

private, *n.* 秘密; 兵隊.

Q a *first-class private* 一等兵 (Pfc. と略す).

P I wish to speak to you *in private*. 内々でお話したい.

private, *a.* 秘密な.

M This telegram is *strictly private*. この電報は極秘です.

O a letter marked "*Private*"「親展」と表記した手紙.

privation, *n.* 窮乏, 難渋.

V ***bear*** *privations* 不便を忍ぶ. ¶He ***suffered*** many *privations* that injured his health. 彼は色々難渋して健康を害した. ¶***undergo*** endless *privations* 引続き難渋する.

Q suffer ***bitter*** *privation* ひどく難渋する.

P He died *of privation*. 彼は困窮のために死んだ. ¶I am unused *to privation*. 私はかん難には慣れていない. ¶live on *without privation* 困らないで暮す.

privilege, *n.* 特典, 特権; [個人の]恩典.

V ***accord*** the *privileges* of ... to ... ...に...の特権を与える. ¶***allow*** stop-over *privileges* at several points 数カ所で途中下車を許す. ¶***attain*** the *privilege* その特権を得る. ¶***concede*** *privileges* to ... ...に特権を与える. ¶***confer*** *privileges* of ... on ... ...に...の特権を与える. ¶***curtail*** *privileges* 特権をそぐ. ¶He was ***denied*** the *privileges* of a library. 彼は図書室出入の特典を拒絶された. ¶***enjoy*** *privileges* without burdens 負担なしに特権を享有する ‖ Beauties so excessive could not but ***enjoy*** the *privileges* of eternal novelty. かかる優秀の美は永久に新鮮味を失うようなことは断じてない. ¶***enlarge*** *privileges* 特権を伸ばす. ¶***exercise*** the *privilege* of free admission to ... ...へ無料入場の特権を行使する. 【類】***exercise*** one's *privilege* lamely / ***exercise*** thc *priviledge* of voting. ¶***extend*** thc *privilege* to ... その特権を...に及ぼす. ¶he was ***given*** the rare *privilege* of ... 彼は...のまれな特典を与えられた. ¶The steamship company ***grants*** stop-over *privileges*. その汽船には途中下船の便がある. ‖ ***grant*** the *privilege* of a one-year volunteer 一年志願兵の特権を与える. ¶I ***have*** the *privilege* of his friendship. 私は彼の親交をかたじけなくしている. ¶***obtain*** *privileges* 特権を得る. ¶***offer*** special *privileges* with regard to ... ...に関して特権を提供する. ¶the ticket ***prints*** stop-over *privileges* at ... その切符には...で途中下車ができる旨記してある. ¶the *privilege* was ***reserved*** for ... その特権を...のために保留した. ¶***revoke*** the *privilege* of ... ...の特典を取消す. ¶***secure*** that *privilege* その特権を確保する.

Q claim one's ***constitutional*** *privilege* in refusing to ... その憲法上の特権を主張して...を拒絶する. ¶obtain the ***exclusive*** *privilege* of ... ...の特権を得る. ¶I consider it a ***great*** *privilege* to be allowed to make a speech today. 私に演説をしろと仰しゃって下さるのは実に名誉なことと存じます. ¶a ***high*** *privilege* 貴重な特典. ¶one's ***parliamentary*** *priviledge* その議員の特権. ¶***personal*** *privilege* 一個人の特権. ¶the ***precious*** *privilege* of seeing things as they are 事物をありのままに見るという貴重な能力. ¶***professional*** *privileges* 役得. ¶he was given the ***rare*** *privilege* of ... 彼は...というまれな特権を与えられた. ¶***treaty-secured*** *privileges* 条約で保証された特権.

Q² ***class*** *privileges* 階級特権. ¶unlimited ***stop-over*** *privileges* 無制限の途中下車の便. 【類】several ***stop-over*** *privileges*.

P he was allowed, *as* a special *privilege*, to ... 彼は特に...を許可された. ¶*by* special *privilege* 特権によって. ¶Goods cannot be sent C.O.D. *with privilege* of examination. 代金引換でお送りした品は気に入らなくとも返品ができないことになっています.

P² the *privilege of* exemption from conscription 徴兵免除の特典 ‖ the *privileges of* birth 生れついている特権(王・貴族など). ¶*privileges to* members 会員の特権.

O I count it a *privilege* to ... 私は...することを恩典(ありがたい事だ)と思う.

privy, *n.* 便所.

Q an ***outdoor*** *privy* 屋外便所.

privy, *a.* ひそかに関係した.

P Many persons were *privy to* the plot. 多くの人がこの陰謀にあずかっていた. ‖ He must be *privy to* the secret. 彼はその秘密を知っているに相違ない.

prize, *n.*賞品, 賞与, 懸賞金; 分捕品, 獲物.

V ***award*** a *prize* to ... ...に賞品を与える ‖ *prize* being ***awarded*** to the most expert 優等賞. ¶***beat off*** the *prize* 賞を獲得する. ¶***bestow*** the grand *prize* upon ... for ... ...に...の優等賞を与える. ¶***carry*** (=***bear***) ***away*** a *prize* 賞を取る. ¶***carry off*** the *prize* for ... ...の賞を取る. 【類】He ***carried off*** every *prize* that was open to him. ¶***contest*** a *prize* 懸賞を得んと争う. ¶***create*** a *prize* to encourage research in that line その方面の研究を奨励するために賞を設ける. ¶***dispute*** the *prize* with one's rivals 競争者と賞を争う. ¶***distribute*** *prizes* to the victors 勝利者に賞を分配する. ¶the *prize* was ***divided*** between ... ...とで分捕品を分けた. ¶***draw*** a *prize* in a lottery 福引で賞品を引き当てる. 【類】The ticket has ***drawn*** no *prize*. ¶***established*** the ... *Prize* by the will of ... ...の遺言によって...賞を設定した. ¶***forfeit*** one's *prize* その賞を失う. ¶***found*** a small *prize* for the encouragement of English literature 英文学奨励のために少額の賞を設ける. ¶***furnish*** *prizes* 賞品を給与する. ¶He ***gained*** a *prize* last year; but he failed to gain one this year. 彼は去年は賞品を取ったが今年はもらいそこなった. ¶***get*** the first *prize* 一等賞を得る. ¶***hand out*** *prizes* to ... 賞を...に授与する. ¶***hang up*** a *prize* 懸賞をする. ¶the *prize* was ***instituted*** in memory of his son ... その賞金は氏の令息...の記念に設定されたものだ ‖ ***institute*** a *prize* ほう賞制を設ける. ¶***make*** *prize* of ... [敵船などを]だ捕する. 【類】the ship was ***made*** *prize* of by ... ¶***obtain*** a *prize* offered by ... ...提供の懸賞を獲得する. ¶***offer*** *prizes* for... ...に賞をかける. ¶***pick up*** a *prize* at the bargain sale 特売場ですばらしいものを見つける. ¶***present*** a *prize* to... ...に賞品を贈る. ¶***provide*** two yearly *prizes* for literature, one for the best novel and the other for the best biography 一つは最良の小説に他は最良の伝記に対して毎年二種の文学賞金を授与する. ¶he ***received*** the first *prize* of $750 for a paper dealing with ... 彼は...に関する論文の一等賞金七百五十ドルを得た. ¶***run*** *prizes* 賞を得んと競走する. ¶***secure*** a *prize* 懸賞を取る. ¶***take*** first (second) *prize* 一等賞を取る. 【類】His design for the school (校舎の設計) ***took*** the second *prize*. ¶***win*** a *prize* with a machine [出品の]機械で賞を得る. 【類】***win*** a *prize* in penmanship (習字) / He failed to ***win*** a *prize* at all. / ***win*** a *prize* for writing the best story / ***win*** a *prize* offered for an essay (懸賞論文) on "...".

V² the *prize* ***fell*** to ... 賞は...の手に落ちた.

Q draw a ***big*** *prize* [くじで]大当りとなる. ¶obtain a ***coveted*** *prize* ねらっていた賞を獲得する. ¶the ***first*** *prize* of £500 was awarded ... 五百ポンドの一等賞は...に与えられた. ¶He won the ***grand*** *prize* at the exhibition. 彼はその博覧会で大賞を獲得した. ¶carry off the ***highest*** *prize* 最高賞を取る. ¶Health is an ***inestimable*** *prize*. 健康は評価できない宝である. ¶a ***maritime*** *prize* 海上だ捕品. ¶a ***piscatorial*** *prize* 釣魚の賞. ¶award a ***substantial*** *prize* 多大の賞を与える. ¶a ***supplementary*** *prize* 副賞. ¶a ***worth-while*** *prize* 骨折りがいのある賞.

Q² a ***beauty*** *prize* 美人コンクール賞. ¶award ***cash*** *prizes* 賞金を与える. ¶a ***consolation*** *prize* 残念賞. ¶***exhibition*** *prizes* 博覧会諸賞. ¶The ***gold*** *prize* was a ten dollar gold piece. 金賞は十ドル金貨一枚だった. ¶a ***money*** *prize* 賞金. ¶He was awarded the ***Nobel*** *Prize* for physics. 彼はノーベル物理学賞をもらった. 【類】won the ***Nobel*** *prize* for literature / The ***Nobel*** *prizes* are paid from the income from a large fund established by A.B. Nobel. ¶this year's ***Nobel Peace*** *Prize* 今年度のノーベル平和賞.

P compete *for* a *prize* 賞品を争う ‖ Many competitors have entered *for* the *prize*. 多数の人々が懸賞に応じた.

P² take first *prize at* a dog show 犬の展覧会で一等賞を取る ‖ Who'll get the *prize for* drawing? だれが製図で賞金を取るでしょう. ¶He carried off the *prize from* over sixteen hundred competitors. 彼は千六百人以上の競争者と競って賞を得た. ¶found a *prize in* mathematics 数学賞を設ける. ¶offer a special *prize of* two guineas for the best tale of not more than 1,200 words 千二百字以下の優良な物語に二ギニーの特別賞を出す ‖ the great *prizes of* life [富貴栄達など]人生の大目的物 ‖ the *prizes of* the profession [学位名誉など]専門職業の目的物. ¶award *prizes to* the winners of each contest 各競技の勝利者に賞品を授与する.

prize, *v*. 尊重する, 珍重する.

M *prize* very ***highly*** 非常に尊重する.【類】The turkey is the most ***highly prized*** bird for food. ¶*prize* liberty ***more*** than life 生命よりも自由を尊ぶ.

P *prize* honor ***above*** money 金銭以上に名誉を尊重する ‖ *prize* it ***above*** measure それを非常に大切にする. ¶*prize* it ***as*** a keepsake (rarity) それを記念物(珍物)として大切にする. ¶The library for the blind is greatly ***prized by*** those for whom it is intended. その盲人図書館はその目的とする人々に便利がられている.

probability, *n*. ありそうなこと.

V ***add probability*** to the tradition その伝説の真実性を増す. ¶I ***concede*** the *probability* of the theory. 私は譲歩してその学説が確立されるだろうということを認める. ¶***give*** some *probability* to this view この見解を幾分もっともらしくする. ¶The country is ready to take any measure likely to ***lessen*** the *probability* of war. その国は戦争を避けるためにはいかなる手段をも講ずる考えでいる.

Q In ***all probability*** the money will not be paid. 多分金は払ってくれまい. ¶in ***all human probability*** 大概, 八九分通り. ¶there is no longer ***any probability*** that ... ...のようなことはもうなさそうだ. ¶there is ***every probability*** that (of) ... どう見ても...しそうだ. ¶There is a ***heavy probability*** against it. そんなことはまずなさそうだ. ¶there is ***little probability*** that ... ...しそうもない. ¶There is ***no probability*** of his coming. 彼はどうも来そうもない.【類】there is ***no probability*** of obtaining security. ¶there is a ***strong probability*** that ... どうも...らしい.

P² There is every ***probability of*** his being arrested. どうも彼は逮捕されるらしい.

O *Probability* is that he will come. おそらく彼は来るだろう.【類】His visit is a *probability*. ¶The *probabilities* are against us (in our favor). われわれには勝算がない(ある). ¶it is possible but not *probable* that ... 可能性はあるがおそらく...とはなるまい.

probable, *a*. ありそうな.

M it is ***extremely probable*** that ... ...は至極ありそうなことだ. ¶It is ***hardly probable*** that he will succeed. 彼はどうも成功しそうもない. ¶it is ***highly*** (=***very***) ***probable*** that ... 多分... ¶***most probable*** 至極そうありそうな.

probably, *ad*. 多分.

M I shall come ***most probably***. 僕は大てい来ます. ¶He will go ***very probably***. 彼は大てい行くだろう.

probation, *n*. 試験; 見習; 《米》仮及第(仮進学期間).

V ***break*** their *probation* 刑の執行猶予中に再び犯罪を犯す. ¶***pass*** one's *probation* 本採用にきまる.

Q² be on ***three-month probation*** 三カ月の見習期間中である ‖ place professors on ***two-year probation*** 教授連を二カ年の仮採用とする.

P ***during*** a *probation* 見習期間中. ¶He is engaged ***on probation***. 彼は仮採用だ. ‖ an officer ***on probation***=a probation officer 《英》少年保護司; 《米》執行猶予中の犯人の保護監視官 ‖ a hired man ***on probation*** 仮採用者 ‖ admitted to college ***on probation*** 仮入学を許される ‖ a student ***on probation***=a probation (=conditioned) student 《米》仮及第(仮進学)期間中の学生.

probe, *v*. 精査する.

P *probe* deeply ***into*** human nature 人間性を深く掘下げて研究する. ¶The matter must be ***probed to*** the bottom. その事件は徹底的に調べなければならない.

probity, *n*. 節操.

V one does not ***want probity*** in not ... ...しないからといって正直を欠くことはない.

Q ***commercial probity*** 商業上の道徳.

problem, *n*. 問題; 疑問; 悩み.

V ***approach*** a *problem* with preconceived notions 予め意見をいだいて問題に接する. ¶The *problem* is being scientifically ***attacked***. その問題は科学的に研究されている. ¶***clear up problems*** 問題を釈明する. ¶the discussions are likely to ***cover*** the *problem* of ... 議論は...の問題にわたるらしい. ¶This is not the place to ***discuss*** such a many-sided *problem*. ここではこんな多方面の問題を論議すべきではない. ¶***do problems*** 問題をやる. ¶***encounter problems*** 問題に遭遇する. ¶The *problems* of existence are ***grasped*** and ***handled*** firmly. 生活問題をしっかりとつかまえて論究している. ¶I ***have*** many *problems* to solve. 私は解決すべき問題が沢山ある. ¶ways of ***meeting*** a *problem* 問題に対処する方法.【類】one of the greatest *problems* which a teacher ***meets*** (=faces) is ... ¶It ***offers*** no *problem*. それは問題にならない(わかりきっている). ¶***open*** a *problem* 問題を提出する. ¶***point up*** the *problem* confronting ... ...が当面している問題をせん鋭化する. ¶***pose*** a serious *problem* 重要問題を提起する. ¶***present*** some knotty *problems* ある難解の問題を提出する. ¶***settle*** this *problem* definitely 明確にこの問題を解決する. ¶***simplify*** a *problem* ある問題を単純化する. ¶completely ***solve*** the *problem* of ... 完全に...の問題を解決する ‖ ***solve*** the economic *problems* pending between the United States and Japan 日米両国間に懸案中の経済問題を解決する.【類】***solve*** the *problem* of aerial navigation (航空問題) / ***solve*** the *problem* how to exist (生活問題). ¶practically all those who have ***studied*** the *problem* agree that ... その問題を研究した者はほとんど全部が...に一致している. ¶carefully ***study*** and ***discuss*** the *problem* in all its bearings 各方面からその問題を慎重に研究かつ論議する. ¶***tackle*** the *problem*, not blindly, but intelligently 盲目的でなく賢明に問題の解決に努める.【類】seriously (まじめに) ***tackle*** a *problem* / The *problem* is now being ***tackled*** in earnest (真剣に). ¶***treat*** the *problem* from an entirely new angle 全然新しい角度からその問題を取扱う. ¶***unlock*** a *problem* ある問題を解決する. ¶I'm at a loss how to ***unravel*** the *problem*. 私はどうしてその事件を解決すべきか迷っている. ¶***untangle*** (=***undo***) a difficult *problem* 難問題を解く. ¶***view*** the *problem* in its right prospective その正しい見方でその問題を考察する. ¶correctly ***work out*** a *problem* in mathematics 数学の問題を正しく解く.

V² With them the ***problem becomes*** an intensely personal one. 彼らに取ってその問題ははなはだしく個人的なものとなる. ¶***problems*** that ***confront*** us today 今日われわれに直面する諸問題.【類】one of the most serious *problems* that ***confront*** employees of labor today / ***problems confronting*** the Soviet Union.

Q an ***academic*** *problem* 学問上の問題. ¶The *problem* is ***acute***. その問題はせん鋭化している. ¶an ***aesthetic problem*** [ばい煙など]美観に関する問題. ¶an ***arduous problem*** 難問題. ¶Your ***big problem*** here is ... ここで大事なことは...である. ¶the ***burning problem*** of America's future 米国の将来に取っての緊急問題. ¶Sex is the ***central problem*** of life. 性は人生の中心問題である. ¶a ***civic problem*** 市政の問題. ¶There are ***complex problems*** ahead of us. 複雑な問題が前途に横たわる.【類】Business tomorrow will be a far more ***complex plobl̲em*** than it is today. ¶***current social problems*** 現下の社会問題. ¶a ***debatable problem*** 議論の余地のある問題. ¶***deeper problems*** of life 人生のもっと深い問題. ¶the solution of the ***delicate problem*** 微妙な問題の解決. ¶work out ***difficult problems*** that confront them 彼らの面前に横たわる難問題を解決する.【類】face a ***difficult problem***. ¶more ***dignified problems*** 一層重要な諸問題. ¶solve the ***domestic service problem*** 召使の問題を解決する. ¶He is an ***educational problem***. 彼は教育上研究を要する人物だ. ¶the ***essential problem*** 主要問題. ¶the ***fundamental problem*** of education is to get the right teachers teaching the right things to the right pupils. 教育の根本問題は適当なことを適当な生徒に教える適当な先生を得るということである. ¶***gigantic problems*** 大問題. ¶a ***good problem*** for them to study 彼らにとって研究すべき好問題. ¶the ***grave problems*** of the day 今日の重大問題. ¶It is a ***hard problems*** to solve. それは解決困難な問題だ. ‖ the ***hardest problem*** in it, therefore, is to ... だからそれについてもっとも難問題は...することである. ¶The selection of a school is an ***important problem***. 学校の選択は重要な問題だ.【類】This is probably the most ***important problem*** of all. ¶the ***inscrutable*** and ***awful problems*** of existence 不可思議にして恐るべき生存の問題. ¶an attempt to solve an ***insoluble problem*** 難解の問題を解こうとする試み. ¶It opens up some very ***interesting problems***. それは非常に興味ある諸問題を展開する. ¶***intricate problems*** 複雑な問題. ¶handle a ***knotty problem*** 困難な問題を扱う. ¶the ***long-pending problem*** of repatriation of Japanese prisoners 日本

捕虜を帰還させるという長い間の懸案. ¶one of the ***major*** *problems* of society 大きな社会問題の一つ. 【類】***major*** *problems* in diplomacy. ¶a ***matrimonial*** *problem* 結婚問題. ¶the ***mightiest*** *problem* of the world 世界で最も重大な問題. ¶a ***minor*** *problem* 枝葉の問題. ¶a ***momentous social*** *problem* 重大な社会問題. ¶***national*** *problems* 国家の問題. ¶***old*** *problems* and new theories 古い問題と新しい理論. ¶the ***paramount*** *problem* of the time 現代の主要問題. ¶a ***perennial*** *problem* 多年にわたる問題, 宿題. ¶a ***perplexing*** *problem* 頭を悩ます問題. ¶a ***practical*** *problem* 実際問題. ¶one of the ***pressing*** *problems* of the day (moment) 今日(刻下)の緊急問題の一つ. ¶a ***profound*** *problem* 深奥な問題. ¶a ***puzzling*** *problem* 難解な問題. ¶a ***serious*** *problem* 重大問題. ¶Unemployment poses a serious ***social*** *problem*. 失業は重要な社会問題を提起する. 【類】sex, a vital ***social*** *problem*. ¶a ***tangled*** *problem* 紛糾した問題. ¶a ***theoretical*** *problem* 理論の問題. ¶***thorny*** *problems* 難問題. ¶a ***tough financial*** *problem* 財政上の難問題. ¶Sex is a ***tremendous*** *problem*. 性は一大問題である. ¶a ***triangular*** *problem* 三角関係の問題. ¶***tricky*** *problems* in mathematics 数学の誤りやすい諸問題. ¶Tied to the price question is the ***twin*** *problem* of wages. 物価問題と関連して賃金問題がある. ¶It remains an ***unsolved*** *problem*. それは依然未解決の問題となっている. 【類】there are, as yet, many ***unsolved*** *problems* concerning ... ¶***vital*** *problems* of university and student concern 大学及び学生のきわめて重要な諸問題. 【類】***vital international*** *problems* / *problems* ***vital*** to daily life. ¶***weighty*** *problems* confronting Japan 日本に直面している重大問題. ¶***worldwide*** *problems* 世界的問題.

Q² touching ***after-the-war*** *problems* he said that ... 戦争後の諸問題に触れて彼は…と言った. ¶***boy*** *problems* 少年の諸問題. ¶the ***bread-winning*** *problem* 生活問題. ¶a ***checker*** *problem* 詰碁. ¶a ***chess*** *problem* 将棋の一研究題目. ¶a ***crime*** *problem* 犯罪事件. ¶minor ***day by day*** *problems* 日々の小さい問題. ¶face serious ***employment*** *problems* 深刻な雇用問題に直面する. ¶***farm power*** *problems* 農村動力問題. ¶solution of the ***food*** *problem* 食料問題の解決. ¶master the ***house-heating*** *problem* 暖房問題を解決する. ¶***household*** *problems* 家庭の諸問題. ¶The ***housing*** *problem* is as acute as ever. 住宅問題は相変らず深刻だ. ¶the ***housing shortage*** *problem* 住宅不足問題. ¶***job*** *problems* 職業問題. ¶study ***labor*** *problems* 労働問題を研究する. 【類】a complicated ***labor*** *problem*. ¶a student of ***social*** and ***labor*** *problems* 社会問題及び労働問題研究の学徒. ¶a ***life*** *problem* 一生の問題. ¶solve ***livelihood*** (=***living***) *problems* 生活問題を解決する. ¶a ***long-range*** *problem* 将来にわたる問題. ¶the ***low-range teacher-salary*** *problem* 教師の薄給問題. ¶the nation's ***number one*** *problem* 国家第一の問題. ¶***out-of-class*** *problems* 教場外の問題. ¶counsel students on ***personal adjustment*** *problems* 個人的な処理を要する問題について学生に助言をする. ¶***present day*** *problems* 今日の問題. ¶a ***rapid transit*** *problem* 高速度輸送の問題. ¶a ***reconstruction*** (***rehabilitation***) *problem* 再建(復興)問題. ¶Asia's ***Red*** *problem* アジアの赤化問題. ¶the German ***revival*** *problem* ドイツ復活問題. ¶the ***servant*** *problem* is more acute than ever 女中問題は相変らず深刻だ. ¶the ***sex*** *problem* 性の問題. 【類】the ***sex*** *problem* of boyhood. ¶a ***short-range*** *problem* 目前の問題. ¶London and its ***traffic*** *problem* ロンドンとその交通問題. ¶the ***unemployment*** *problem* 失業問題. ¶***vice*** *problems* 悪徳(不道徳)諸問題. ¶vexing ***world*** *problems* やっかいな世界の諸問題. 【類】solve ***world*** *problems* / They pose new ***world*** *problems* for the United States.

P I regard sex ***as*** the central *problem* of life. 私は性を人生の中心問題と見なす. ¶the *problems* ***by*** which the country is confronted 国民当面の問題. ¶grapple ***with*** a vital *problem* 重要問題と取組む. 【類】wrestle ***with*** complex *problems*.

P² the *problem* ***before*** us is ... われわれの直面する問題は…である. ¶*problems* ***for*** solution 解決すべき問題. ¶Tuberculosis is a disease of defective society, and to eradicate it is a *problem* ***in*** sociology.—M. J. Rosenan. 結核病は欠陥ある社会の疾病でこれを撲滅するのが社会学における一問題である. ¶the *problem* ***of*** unemployment 失業問題. ‖ *problems* ***of*** youth 青春の悩み. ¶His whole conduct is a *problem* ***to*** me. 彼の行為は私には一向合点が行かない.

problematical, *a.* 疑問のある.

M it is ***highly*** *problematical* whether ... …かどうかは大きな疑問である.

procedure, *n.* 方法, 手続; 処置, 処理.

V ***follow*** the same *procedure* 同じ手続を取る. ¶***reverse*** the usual *procedure* 普通の手順を逆に行く. ¶***vary*** the *procedure* 手を変える.

Q ***accusatorial*** *procedure* 告訴手続. ¶a ***business-like*** *procedure* 事務的な処置. ¶a more ***concise*** *procedure* 一層簡単な方法. ¶the code of ***criminal*** *procedure* 刑事訴訟法. ¶***democratic*** *procedure* 民主的手続. ¶***illegal*** *procedure* 不法な手続. ¶***interim*** *procedures* 暫定処理. ¶without ***legal*** *procedures* 法律の手続を取らずに. ¶Otherwise it will become a matter of ***legal*** and ***unpleasant*** *procedure*. そうでないとそれは法律問題になっておもしろくない手続をふむことになるだろう. ¶It has degenerated into a ***mere*** *procedure*. それは単なる手続となって仕舞った. ¶the ***next*** *procedure*, called "...," consists of ...ing …と称する次の工作は…することだ. ¶conclusion of ***oral*** *procedure* 口頭弁論の終結. ¶a ***pre-arranged*** *procedure* 予定の行動. ¶follow the ***regular*** *procedure* 正規の手続きをふむ. ¶a ***safe*** *procedure* 安全な方法. ¶carry out ***sanitary*** *procedures* 衛生上の手続をふむ. ¶a very ***simple*** *procedure* 至極簡単な方法. ¶***summary*** *procedure* 略式手続.

Q² steps in ***admission*** *procedure* 入会(など)の手続を踏む. ¶***arbitration*** *procedures* [争議などの]仲裁々判手続. ¶simplify ***office*** *procedure* 役所の手続を簡素化する. ¶***public summons*** *procedure* 公示催告手続. ¶***research*** *procedure* 調査手続. ¶a change in ***routine*** *procedure* 慣行的な手順の変化. ¶***teaching-learning*** *procedures* 授業及び学習の方法. ¶***trial*** *procedure* 諮問手続. ¶The ***voting*** *procedure* will be controlled by the Government. 投票事務は政府がさい配を振るだろう.

P the mode ***of*** *procedure* 手続の仕方. ¶He is familiar ***with*** export *procedure*. 彼は輸出手続に明るい.

P² *procedure* ***for*** a comparison 照査手続. ¶*procedure* ***in*** public trial 公判手続.

proceed, *v.* 進む; 仕続ける; 取掛る; 発する, 来る; 手続をする.

M tourists *proceeding* ***abroad*** 海外への観光客. ¶*proceed* ***advisedly*** 慎重に進行する. ¶*proceed* ***afoot*** to ... …へ歩いて行く. ¶The preparations are *proceeding* ***apace***. 準備はずんずん進行している. ¶*proceed* ***at once*** to business 直ちに仕事に取りかかる. ¶Work is *proceeding* ***briskly*** (=***actively***). 仕事は盛んに進行している. ¶*proceed* ***further*** with work さらに仕事を仕続ける. ¶*proceed* ***instantly*** to essentials 早速肝じんのことに取掛る. ¶The play will ***now*** *proceed*. 芝居は今始まります. ¶Preparations for ... are *proceeding* ***rapidly***. …の準備はじん速に進行している. ¶The work is *proceeding* ***slowly***. 仕事ははかばかしくない.

M² The speaker *proceeded* **[*on*]** to say that ... 弁士はさらに…と言った.

P *proceed* ***against*** him for trespass 侵害罪で彼を訴える. 【類】He *proceeded* ***against*** the man for the usurpation of his property (財産横領). ¶*proceed* ***at*** reduced speed (自動車など)徐行する. ¶*proceed* ***for*** destination (a port) 目的地(など)へ向って行く. ¶the river which *proceeds* ***from*** the lake 湖から流れ出る川 ‖ ***From*** where did the shot *proceed*? 弾丸はどこからとんで来たか. 【類】Light *proceeds* ***from*** the sun. / Sobs were heard to *proceed* ***from*** the nex room. / *proceed* ***from*** fact ***to*** theory / the book that *proceeded* ***from*** the pen of ... / This *proceeds* ***from*** ignorance. ¶*proceed* ***into*** the hall 大広間にはいって行く. ¶The airman *proceeded* ***on*** his flight. 飛行家が飛行の途についた. 【類】*proceed* ***on*** a journey / The steamer *proceeded* ***on*** her voyage. ‖ *proceed* ***on*** this line これと同筆法を取る ‖ We must *proceed* ***on*** sound principles. われわれは健全な主義でやらねばならない. ¶***Out of*** the same mouth *proceeded* blessing and curse. 祝福をする口からのろいの言葉が出た. ¶*proceed* ***to*** business 仕事に取掛る ‖ *proceed* ***to*** one's post 就任する ‖ *proceed* ***to*** her destination [船など]目的地へ向って行く. 【類】In 1895 he *proceeded* ***to*** France. / *proceed* ***to*** the Imperial Palace / Let's *proceed* ***to*** the next question. / *proceed* ***to*** university (進

学する) / *proceed* ***to*** the degree of M.A. ¶*proceed* ***with*** one's argument (work) その議論(など)を続ける ‖ *proceed* ***with*** one's intention 意向を実行する. 【類】*proceed* ***with*** a game / *proceed* ***with*** the scheme / Please *proceed* ***with*** your story. / These points being settled, we can *proceed* ***with*** our problem.

O The statement *proceeds* as follows. その声明は次の通りである. 【類】*proceed* to tell the rest of the story.

proceeding, *n.* 所為, 処置; *pl.* 訴訟手続; *pl.* 議事.

V ***abandon*** *proceedings* [訴訟]手続を取りやめにする. ¶*proceedings* will be ***brought to bear*** against ... ...に対して民事訴訟手続を取ることになるだろう. ¶the impunity with which he ***carried on*** these shady *proceedings* 彼がまんまとこれらの後ろ暗い所為を続行したこと. ¶***commence*** *proceedings* against ... ...を起訴する. ¶The *proceedings* were ***conducted*** in three languages—English, French, and German. [会議など]議事に英仏独の三カ国語が用いられた. ¶***dismiss*** *proceedings* 議事を終了する. ¶***enliven*** the *proceedings* 会の進行に活気を与える. ¶***expedite*** *proceedings* 会の進行を助ける. ¶***institute*** legal *proceedings* against ... ...を起訴する ‖ ***institute*** penal *proceedings* 処罰の手続を取る ‖ ***institute*** exceptional *proceedings* against ... ...に対して例外的取扱方法を設ける. ¶The accident ***marred*** the whole *proceeding*. そのちん事で会はめちゃめちゃになった. ¶he ***opened*** *proceedings* by saying ... 彼は開会に当って...と述べた ‖ A vocal solo by Miss ... will ***open*** the *proceedings*. ...嬢の独唱が番組の第一にある. ¶The police ***ordered*** the *proceedings* to be stopped. 警官は会の中止を命じた. ¶***recommence*** the *proceedings* of a public trial 公判の弁論を再開する. ¶***record*** *proceedings* [in the House] 議事を記録する. ¶***reopen*** the *proceedings* 弁論を再開する. ¶***report*** the *proceedings* 経過を報告する. ¶***suspend*** *proceedings* in a lawsuit 訴訟手続を中止する. ¶threaten to ***take*** *proceedings* 訴えると言っておどかす. 【類】If the difficulty cannot be arranged, it only remains to ***take*** legal *proceedings* (起訴する). ¶***threaten*** legal *proceedings* if ... ...なら訴えると言っておどかす. ¶In the last resort we will ***undertake*** legal *proceedings*. 最後の手段として当方は起訴することにします. ¶***watch*** one's *proceedings* 相手のようすを見る. ¶***withdraw*** *proceedings* 手続を撤回する.

V^2 the *proceedings* ***began*** with ... 開会第一に...があった. ¶The *proceedings* then ***terminated***. これで散会となった.

Q She has instituted ***divorce*** *proceedings*. 彼女は離婚の訴訟を起した. ¶***gastronomic*** or ***spirituous*** *proceedings* 飲んだり食べたりすること. ¶a ***high-handed*** *proceeding* 高圧手段. ¶a ***hopeless*** *proceeding* 徒労. ¶a ***legal*** (an ***illegal***) *proceeding* 法的(不法)な処置. ¶***legislative*** *proceedings* 立法措置. ¶in ***legislative*** and other ***public*** *proceedings* 立法その他公けの手続において. ¶hold ***oral*** *proceedings* in public 口頭弁論を公開する. ¶the ***Parliamentary*** *proceedings* 議会の議事録. ¶***preliminary*** *proceedings* 予審手続. ¶Isn't it a ***queer*** *proceeding?* 変な仕打ではありませんか. ¶a ***rash*** *proceeding* 軽率な所為. ¶a ***risky*** *proceeding* 危険な所為. ¶***shady*** *proceedings* (=transactions) いんちきなやり方(やみ取引などの). ¶***summary*** *proceedings* 略式裁判. ¶an ***underhand*** *proceeding* 陰険な所為. ¶a very ***unjust*** *proceeding* きわめて不正な処置.

Q^2 a report of ***business*** *proceedings* 営業成績の報告. ¶The first ***court*** *proceedings* are expected to begin in February. 第一回公判は二月開始の予定. ¶***floor*** *proceedings* 議会の本会議(委員会の議事に対して). ¶a ***Rip van Winkle*** *proceeding* おそまき, 遅ればせ. ¶***transshipment*** *proceedings* 船荷積換手続.

P They are not satisfied ***with*** his *proceedings*. 彼らは彼の処置に満足していない.

P^2 take legal *proceedings* ***against*** ... ...を起訴する. ¶minutes of *proceedings* ***at*** the annual meeting of ... ...の年会における議事録控. ¶he took *proceedings* ***for*** publishing false statement about ... ...について無根の記事を掲げたので訴訟を起した ‖ take *proceedings* ***for*** divorce 離婚訴訟を起す.

proceeds, *n. pl.* 収益, 利益, 売上代金.

V The *proceeds* of the sale are to be ***devoted*** to the American Red Cross. 売上代金は米国赤十字へ献納することになっている. 【類】The *proceeds* are ***devoted*** to charity (charitable purposes). / The *proceeds* of the sales will be ***devoted*** to the assistance of hospitals (病院). ¶***donate*** the *proceeds* to ... 収益を...に寄付する. ¶***reserve*** the *proceeds* 収益を貯える. ¶The *proceeds* will be ***used*** for a spree. [罰金など]収益は懇親会費に当てる.

V^2 The total *proceeds* ***amounted*** to ... yen. 総収益...円に上った. ¶all the *proceeds* of the sales (play) will ***go*** to ... 売上(など)の収益は...に上るだろう.

Q the ***day's*** *proceeds* 当日の収益. ¶***gross*** *proceeds* 総手取り金. ¶***net*** *proceeds* 純収益. ¶The ***whole*** *proceeds* will go to charity work. 売上の総収入は慈善事業に寄付する.

P ***from*** the *proceeds* of the exhibition 展覧会の収益から. ¶live ***on*** the *proceeds* of their industry 彼らの勤労からの収入で生活する.

P^2 the *proceeds* ***from*** the sale of ... ...の売上代金 ‖ *proceeds* ***from*** benefit entertainments 慈善興行の収益. 【類】*proceeds* ***from*** prostitution / the *proceeds* ***from*** the sales of its products. ¶the *proceeds* ***of*** liquidation 精算残額 ‖ the *proceeds* ***of*** a business 営業成績 ‖ the *proceeds* ***of*** the sale amounted to ... 売上高は...に上った ‖ the *proceeds* ***of*** the sale of this book will be devoted to the fund for ... この本の売上代金は...の基金にあてる.

process, *n.* 方法, 作用; 過程; 加工; 裁判手続.

V they have ***commenced*** a *process*, the completion of which will ... 彼らはこんな工作をやり出したがそれは...という結果に終るだろう. ¶***devise*** a secret *process* in virtue of which ... その力で...するような秘法を案出する. ¶***explain*** the *process* of making ... ...の製法を説明する. ¶***facilitate*** the *process* 手順を簡易化する. ¶certain secret *processes* jealously ***guarded*** by glass manufacturers ガラス製造人が断じて他に漏らさないある秘法. ¶***hasten*** the *process* of decay 腐敗を早める. ¶***invent*** a *process* for making rubber from starch でん粉からゴムを製する方法を発明する. ¶***perfect*** a new *process* 新しい方法を完成する. ¶***reverse*** the *process* その手順を逆にする. ¶***shorten*** the *process* その工作過程を短縮する. ¶***simplify*** *processes* 方法を簡易にする. ¶***unravel*** many of the hidden *processes* of life 生命の神秘の数々を解明する. 「でいった.

V^2 The *process* of disrobing ***went on***. 着物を次々と脱い

Q by ***chemical*** *process* 化学操作によって. ¶Teaching and examination are ***complementary*** *processes*. 教授と試験は互に補足する方法だ. ¶a highly ***complicated*** *process* 非常に複雑なやり方. ¶the ***cumbersome*** *processes* of the law わずらわしい法律上の手続. ¶without ***due*** *process* of law 適当な法的手続を踏まないで. ¶the ***digestive*** *process* 消化作用. ¶the ***final*** *process* 〖法〗最終手続. ¶by a ***gradual*** *process* 漸次に. ¶by an ***imperceptible*** *process* 知らず知らずのうちに. ¶by ***industrial*** *processes* 加工して. ¶part of the ***inevitable*** *process* of the world's course 世界の必然的行程の一つ. ¶***judicial*** *process* 裁判手続. ¶by ***legal*** *process* 法律上の手続をふんで. ¶the regular ***legislative*** *process* 法律制定の手続. ¶quite a ***lengthy*** *process* 随分長たらしい経過. ¶Education is a ***lifelong*** *process*. 教育は一生の仕事だ. ¶The bargain was a ***long*** *process*. 取引は長いことかかった. 【類】Unloading the cargo was a ***long*** *process*. ¶by some ***magical*** *process* ある不思議な方法で. ¶an exact ***mathematical*** *process* 正確な数学的方法. ¶by merely a ***mechanical*** *process* 単に機械的に. ¶in one's ***mental*** *processes* その精神作用で. ¶by some ***mysterious*** *process* ある不可思議な方法で. ¶The building has succumbed to the ***natural*** *processes* of time and wear and tear. その建物は時がたてば磨損するという自然の作用に影響された. ¶under an entirely ***new*** *process* 全く新しい工程によって. ¶made by ***patented*** *process* 特許になった方法で製した. ¶go through the ***preliminary*** *process* of ... ...予備の過程を経る. ¶a ***psychological*** *process* 心理作用. ¶study by ***scientific*** *processes* 科学的研究. ¶a ***secret*** *process* 秘法. ¶the ***slow*** *process* of growth 遅々たる生長過程 ‖ It's a ***slow*** *process*. 気の長い話だ. ¶sterilized by a ***special*** *process* 特別の方法で滅菌した[牛乳など]. ¶The *process* of making lacquer is very ***tedious***. うるしの製造は非常に手がかかる. ¶Resorting to law is often a ***tedious*** and ***expensive*** *process*. 裁判ざたは往々長びくし費用がかかる. ¶***unhealthy*** *processes* 健康上有害な作業. ¶reverse the ***usual*** *process* いつものやり方を逆にする. ¶***vital*** *processes* 生存諸作用. ¶this ***weeding-out*** *process*

このとうた方法.

Q² by the ***amalgamating process*** アマルガム式加工によって. ¶ take a copy by the ***carbon process*** 複写で写しをとる. ¶ Evaporation is a ***cooling process*** 蒸発は一つの冷却法である. ¶ new techniques and ***cost-saving processes*** 新技術と経済的な作業. ¶ the ***cyanide process*** of extracting gold patented in 1890 一八九〇年に特許になった青化採金法. ¶ a ***germkilling process*** 殺菌法. ¶ stream-line the ***law-making process*** 立法手続きを流線型(円滑)にする. ¶ the ***learning process*** 学習会. ¶ the ***Manufacturing process*** of ... ...の製法. ¶ the ***orientation process*** 再教育方式. ¶ ***placement process*** 配置手続. ¶ He was benefited by the ***polishing-off process*** of European schooling. 彼はヨーロッパで教育を受けて得る所があった. ¶ the ***printing process*** 〖写真〗印画法. ¶ the ***reproduction process*** 再生(複製)法. ¶ a ***shifting process*** 交替作業. ¶ a ***sifting-out process*** とうた作用. ¶ the ***sinking process*** of caisson tube construction ケーソン式建築の沈下作業. ¶ prepared by a modern ***sterilizing process*** 新式の滅菌法によって調製された(乳製品など). ¶ the ***teaching process*** 授業方法. ¶ ***textile processes*** 織物の生産工程. ¶ ***thought processes*** 思想の動き. ¶ the ***three-color process*** 〖印刷〗三色印刷. ¶ ***trade processes*** 標準型製法.

P ***By*** what *process* is the cloth made? どういうやり方でその布が作られるか. ¶ goods ***in*** *process* 仕掛け品(加工中の製品) ‖ ***in*** *process* (=course) of time 時がたつに従って ‖ The work of construction is still ***in*** *process* (=progress). 建築工事は今なお進行中である. 【類】***in*** *process* of construction (=erection) / ***in*** *process* of negotiation (交渉) / The society is now ***in*** *process* of organization (=formation). ‖ The society is now being formed. / The project (企画) is ***in*** *process* of realization. / The street was ***in*** *process* of repair. ‖ The original passage has been impaired ***in*** the *process* of "transmutation." 原文の旬は旨く翻訳されていない. ‖ stages ***in*** the *process* of manufacture 製作の段階. ¶ It has passed ***through*** an interesting *process* of evolution. それは進化の興味ある過程を経て来た. ¶ manufacture newsprint from waste paper ***under*** an entirely new *process* 全然新しい方法で紙くずから新聞印刷用紙を製造する. ¶ The thoughts of men are widened ***with*** the *process* of the suns. 人間の思想は歳月と共に広められる. ‖ cloth dyed ***with*** the latest *processes* 最新の染色法によった織物.

P² a *process* ***for*** the recovery of taxes in arrear[s] 税金滞納処分. ¶ a *process* ***of*** manufacture 製法 ‖ *processes* ***of*** nature 自然の作用 ‖ a *process* ***of*** natural development 自然発達の過程 ‖ the *process* ***of*** colloquialization of words 語の口語化の過程 ‖ a *process* ***of*** reasoning 推理法. ¶ education as continuing *process* ***throughout*** life 終生にわたる教育.

processing, *n.* 加工.

Q ***industrial processing*** 生産加工.

Q² ***food processing*** 食品加工.

procession, *n.* 行列, 行進.

V ***form*** a *procession* 行列を作る. ¶ We ***had*** a torch-light *procession.* われわれはたいまつ行列をやった. ¶ ***heading*** the *procession* comes ... ...行列の先に立って…がやって来る. ¶ ***hold*** a lantern *procession* in welcome of ... ...の歓迎にちょうちん行列を催す. ¶ ***lead*** the grand *procession* of the nations 世界諸国の先頭に立って牛耳を執る. ¶ ***organize*** a torch-light *procession* to ... ...行のたいまつ行列を編成する.

V² the *procession* will ***assemble*** at ... その行列は...に集合するはず. ¶ Then the *procession* ***broke up.*** それから行列が解散した. ¶ the *procession* will ***disperse*** in ... 行列は...で解散する. ¶ A long *procession* ***marched*** past him amidst the sounds of music and the perfume of flowers and censers. 長い行列が楽の音(ね)と花や香炉の香との中に彼の前を行進した. ¶ *Processions* ***parade*** streets. 行列が街路を練り歩く. ¶ the *procession* ***proceeds*** by way of ... 行列は...を通って行く. ¶ the *procession* ***returns*** by ... 行列は...を通って帰る. ¶ The *procession* ***swept past.*** 行列がその前をさっと通り過ぎた.

Q The ***funeral procession*** was formed by 2 o'clock and numbered fully 20,000. 葬列は二時までに作られその数たっぷり二万人を算した. ¶ a ***historical procession*** 歴史にちなんだ行列. ¶ an ***imperial*** *procession* 行幸・行啓の列. ¶ a ***pompous procession*** 仰々しい行列. ¶ in ***solemn procession*** おごそかな行列で.

Q² a ***circus procession*** サーカスの行列(宣伝のための). ¶ a ***costume procession*** 仮装行列. ¶ a ***flag procession*** 旗行列. ¶ a ***funeral procession*** 葬儀の行列. ¶ a big ***lantern procession*** was organized at ... and proceeded along ... 大ちょうちん行列が...に作られ...に添うて行進した. ¶ have a ***torchlight procession*** たいまつ行列をやる. ¶ a ***wedding*** (=***marriage***) ***procession*** 婚礼の行列.

P a hymn sung ***during*** a *procession* 行進中に歌う賛[美]歌. ¶ march ***in*** *procession* 列を作って進む. 【類】walk ***in*** *procession* through the town to the strains of a band of music (楽隊の曲に合わせて). ¶ fall ***into*** *procession* 列を作る.

P² a *procession* ***of*** mourners 一列の会葬者.

processor, *n.* 加工業者.

Q² ***food processors*** and distributors 食料品加工業者及び配給業者たち. ¶ ***meat processors*** 食肉加工業者(ハムやソーセージなど).

proclaim, *v.* 宣言する, 布告する.

M ***loudly proclaim*** 声高らかに宣言する. ¶ ***proclaim prophetically*** 予言的に布告する. ¶ ***publicly proclaim*** 公言する.

P *proclaim* war ***against*** ... ...に対し宣戦を布告する. ¶ He was *proclaimed* king ***by*** them. 彼は王として推戴(たい)された.

O He was *proclaimed* [to be] a traitor. 彼は売国奴と宣言された.

proclamation, *n.* 布令, 布告.

V ***issue*** a *proclamation*, announcing that ... ...の布令を発する. 【類】***issue*** a *proclamation* warning the public that ... / A *proclamation* was ***issued*** against tobacco. ¶ an imperial *proclamation* ***decreed*** that ... 勅令で...を公布した.

Q a ***public proclamation*** 布告. 【類】by ***public proclamation.*** 「する.

Q² ancept the ***Potsdam Proclamation*** ポツダム宣言を受諾

P² issue a *proclamation* ***against*** tobacco タバコ禁止令を発布する. ¶ the *proclamation* ***of*** war (peace) 宣戦(など)の布告.

proclivity, *n.* 傾向, 性癖.

P have a *proclivity* ***to*** (=***towards***) vice (warlike activities) 悪(など)に走る傾向がある.

O a *proclivity* to catch cold 風を引きやすいこと. ¶ a *proclivity* to steal 盗癖.

procrastinate, *v.* 遅延する.

M *procrastinate* ***from week to week*** 翌週へ翌週へと延ばす.

procurable, *a.* 得られる.

M be not ***easily procurable*** 容易に手にはいらない. ¶ be *procurable* ***separately*** 分冊で手にはいる.

P it is *procurable* ***from*** ... それは...(の店)で売っている.

procuration, *n.* 代理.

P ***per*** *procuration* 代理で.

procurator, *n.* 検事.

Q an ***assistant chief public procurator*** [検事]次席. ¶ a ***supernumerary public procurator*** 予備検事.

procure, *v.* 手に入れる.

P it may be *procured* ***of*** ... それは...で売っている.

prodigal, *n.* 放とう息子.

P the return ***of*** the *prodigal* 放とう息子の帰宅.

prodigal, *a.* 浪費する.

P He is *prodigal* ***of*** expenditure. 彼は金使いが荒い. 【類】He is *prodigal* ***of*** time (labor). / The young are *prodigal* ***of*** life and health.

prodigality, *n.* 放とう.

P ***Through*** his *prodigality*, he soon came to the end of his inheritance. 彼は放とうの結果親の遺産をたちまちとう尽してしまった.

prodigious, *a.* ばく大な.

M The labor involved must ***obviously*** be *prodigious.* その労力はばく大なものに違いない.

prodigy, *n.* 非凡者, 異才, 鬼才.

Q an ***arithmetical prodigy*** 算術の鬼才. ¶ an ***infant prodigy*** 神童. 【類】Jackie Coogan, Baby Peggy, and other ***infant prodigies*** of the film world.

Q² a ***child prodigy*** 天才児.

P² a *prodigy* ***of*** learning 非凡の大学者 ‖ a *prodigy* ***of*** valor 抜群の勇者.

produce, *n.* 産物, 製作品.

V ***market*** one's *produce* その産物を市場に出す. ¶ ***turn out*** a *produce* 産物を造り出す.

Q the market for ***British produce*** 英国製品の市場. ¶ a ***finished produce*** 完製品.

Q² hlod back ***farm produce*** 農産物の出荷を控える. ¶ ***home***

produce and manufactures 国内産物と生産品. ¶*mineral produce* 鉱産物. ¶*raw produce* 原料生産物.

produce, *v.* 生じる；製作する；出す.

M England has *of late produced* great philosophers. 英国は近年大哲学者を出した. ¶an artist who *produces very little* 寡作の芸術家.

P *produced by* ...〘映〙製作... ‖ *produce by* electricity 電気で製作する. 【類】*produced by* chemical action. ¶an acid *produced from* coal-tar コールターから採った酸.【類】Alizarin is *produced from* madder (あかね草) or synthesized from coal-tar. / Resin (樹脂) is a substance *produced from* the sap of certain trees. ‖ *produce* it *from* (= *out of*) one's pocket それをポケットから取り出す. ¶It *produced* a profound impression *on* him. それは彼に深い印象を与えた. ¶*produce* it *with* labor 骨折ってそれを造り出す.

producer, *n.* 生産者；〘映〙製作者.

Q a *big theatrical producer* 芝居の大興行主. ¶an *executive producer*〘映〙製作責任者. ¶the world's *largest producer* 世界最大の生産者. ¶*professional producers* of films 映画の専門製作者. ¶a *prolific producer* 大量生産者.

Q² an *egg producer* 鶏卵生産業者. ¶a *film producer* 映画製作者. ¶a *hand producer* 手工業者. ¶a *journeyman producer* of thrillers 腕のあるスリルものの[職人的]作家. ¶a large *market producer* of eggs 市場向鶏卵の多量生産業者. ¶a *movie producer* 映画製作者. ¶a *poultry producer*＝《米》a chicken raiser 養鶏家. ¶coal as a *power producer* 動力生産用石炭. ¶a *radio show producer* 放送劇などのプロデューサー. ¶a *stage producer* 舞台演出者(監督).

P² *producers of* all things typographical 活版製造業者.

product, *n.* 産物；製作品；結果.

V *manufacture* their *products* 彼らの製品を製作する. ¶*market* a *product* 生産品を市場に出す. ¶*yield* a *product* 産物を出す.

Q Dickens was not an *academic product*. ディケンズは学校出ではなかった. ¶*agricultural products* 農産物. ¶*aquatic products* 諸水産物. ¶the *chief products* of ... ...の主要産物. ¶the *co-operative product* of several authors 数名の著者の共同作品. ¶not an *exotic*, but a *genuine product* of the soil of that country 外国産ではなくて純然たるその国の土地の産物. ¶one of the *fastest-growing products* in the country 国内で使用が最も増大しつつある製品の一つ. ¶a *finished product* [未製品などに対し]完製品. ¶a *human product* 人間の製作品. ¶*industrial products* 工業の産物. ¶*intellectual products* 知能の産物. ¶*last-minute products* of Chinese Impressionists 中国印象派の最近の作. ¶*literary products* 文芸作品. ¶*manufactured products* 製作品. ¶*marine products* 海産物. ¶a constant supply of *meritorious product* 価値ある作品を途切れずに供給すること. ¶*motorized products* 色々な動力製品(モーター・自動車・トラックなど). ¶a *native product* 国産品. ¶*natural products* 天産物. ¶a *product peculiar* to our soil わが国の特産物. ¶The egg is a *perishable product*. 卵は腐敗しやすい品だ. ¶the *principal products* in the peninsula その半島における主要産物. ¶*proud products* of ... ...の自慢の産物. ¶*raw products* 未製原料品. ¶*refined products* 精製品. ¶a *residual product* 副産物. ¶The book is one of the great *scientific products* of the nineteenth century. その本は十九世紀の偉大な科学的産物の一つである. ¶a *slovenly product* ずさんな製品. ¶regard language as a purely *social product* 国語を純然たる社会的産物と見なす. ¶the *staple products* of the earth—corn, wheat, rye, and other grains 主要農産物，すなわちとうもろこし，小麦，裸麦その他の穀類. ¶a *true product* of art 真の芸術品. ¶*wild products* of nature 野生の天然物.

Q² a new *coal-tar product* コールターからの新製品. ¶*coconut products* ココやし生産品(石けん，人造バターなど). ¶*dairy* and *farm products* 酪農生産物. ¶*factory products* 工場諸生産品. ¶*farm products* 諸種農産物. ¶*fish products* 魚加工品. ¶*fisheries* (fishery) *products* 漁業生産物. ¶an excellent *food product* 優良食品.【類】milk and other *food products*. ¶*forest products* 林産物. ¶*garden products* 花・野菜など. ¶a tax on *home* and *foreign products* 国産品及び外国品に対する課税. ¶the patriotic duty of buying *home products* first and *overseas products* next 国産品を先に外国品をあとという愛国的義務. ¶a *liquid* (*solid*) *food product* 液体(固形)食品. ¶*livestock products* 家畜生産品. ¶turn out *machine products* 機械製品を出す. ¶*meat products* 食肉製品(ハム，ソーセジなど). ¶*oven products* かまど焼きもの(パン，ホットケーキなど). ¶*petroleum products* 石油諸製品. ¶*poultry products* 鶏肉食品類. ¶*quality products* 諸種の高級品. ¶*rolling-mill products*〘機〙圧延工場諸製品. ¶*semi-finished steel products* 鋼鉄半製品. ¶a *staple food product* 主要食品. ¶*timber products* 木工製品. ¶*wheat products* 小麦製品. ¶*wood products* 木工品.

P² the *products of* American industry 米国工業の産物 ‖ the book is the *product of* ... その本は...の著作だ ‖ a *product of* coal-tar コールター系の一製品 ‖ the *products of* genius [文芸・芸術]作品.【類】the *product of* the factories / the *product of* one's labor. / the *product of* many men's minds. / He was the *product of* his period (時代の産物). / a *product of* the time / the *products of* the soil (農産物) / Man is not the *product of* his environment. / the *product* (成果) *of* an action / He is a *product* (出身) *of* high school.

production, *n.* 産出；産物，製品；〘映〙製作.

V *boost production* 増産を助長する. ¶The company *controls* all told (＝in all) about ... per cent of the electricity *production* of the nation. その会社はその国の発電力全量の約...パーセントを支配している. ¶*curtail productions* 生産額を切詰める. ¶*filmize* a *production* of Homer's "Odyssey" ホーマーのオデッセイを映画化する. ¶*give* a *production* of a play 劇を演出する. ¶*increase* (＝*raise*) *production* 生産を増大する. ¶the best motion picture *production released* in 1937 一九三七年に封切した内で一番良い映画作品. ¶*step up production* 増産を助成する.

V² among the multifarious *productions* which *came* from his pen was ... 氏の筆に成った多数の作品の中に...があった. ¶*Production* has *gone up* to all-time high. 生産力が最高記録に上った.

Q an *artistic production* 芸術的作品. ¶*choice productions* of Chelsea チェルシー磁器の上等品. ¶a student *dramatic production* 学生の劇作品. ¶the *economical production* of his goods and the disposal of these in the market 氏の商品の経済的製作と市場におけるその処分. ¶a *gigantic production* 非常な大作. ¶a great *imaginative production* 大なる想像上の産物[小説など]. ¶an *intentional production* of tiny plants or animals 微小動植物の人為的生産. ¶*literary productions* 著作物. ¶increase *literary* and *artistic production* 文芸上の製作を増大する. ¶*low production* 生産低下. ¶modern methods of *machine production* 近代機械製作法. ¶a *marvellous production* 驚嘆すべき製品. ¶*modern large-scale production* 近代の大規模製作. ¶a *monumental production* in literary history 文学史上記念すべき作品. ¶a *native production* 国産品. ¶the *natural productions* of earth or water 水陸の産物. ¶the *newest production* of a war plant 兵器工場の最新式生産品. ¶the cast of the *original production* of the play 初めての劇上演当時の配役. ¶the *principal productions* of his pen 氏の筆になる主な作品.

Q² skilled workers qualified for employment on *aircraft production* 飛行機生産の熟練工. ¶an *amateur production* of a play 劇のしろうと演出. ¶control all phases of *atomic energy production* あらゆる分野の原子力生産を統制する. ¶the rise of the system of *capitalist production* 資本家生産制度の発達. ¶*Coal production* dropped further. 石炭生産はさらに減退した. ‖ lagging *coal production* 低下する石炭生産 ‖ Forty-five days' *coal production* was lost. [ストライキの結果]四十五日分の石炭生産額を失った. ¶*crop production* 農作物の生産. ¶high (＝heavy) *egg production* 卵の高い生産力 ‖ the "flush" season of *egg production* 卵生産の増産期. ¶The novel is in the *process* of *film production*. その小説は映画化進行中である. ‖ finance British *film production* 英国映画製作に金を注ぎ込む. ¶*flesh* (＝*meat*) *production* 食肉生産. ¶increase *food production* 食料を増産する.【類】enlarge *frozen food* (冷凍食料) *production*. ¶*high-class production* 高級品生産. ¶encourage *high-volume production* 大量生産を奨励する. ¶the cost of *film* (＝*screen*) *production* 映画製作費. ¶*large-scale production* 大規模生産. ¶This is the age of *mass production*. 今日は大量生産の時代である.【類】

The machine is now in ***mass production.*** / ***mass production*** and standardization (規格化). ¶ ***M-G-M production*** [米国]メトロゴールドウイン提供(製作). ¶ the world's greatest ***motion picture*** *production* 世界最大の特作映画. ¶ 1929 the year of ***peak*** *production* 一九二九年, すなわち生産最高の年. ¶ ***play*** *production* 劇の演出. ¶ economic consequences of ***power*** *production* 動力生産の経済的結果. ¶ ***quality*** (***quantity***) *production* 質(量)の生産 ‖ He did not believe the Russians have an atomic bomb in "***quantity*** *production*." ¶ the ***record*** *production* of ... ...の記録的生産 ‖ an all-time ***record*** *production* 《米》前代未聞の記録的生産高. ¶ ***Rice*** *production* is the mainstay of one billion Asiatics. 米生産は十億アジア人民の大黒柱である. ¶ ***speed*** *production* of coal 石炭の高速度生産. ¶ its ***steel goal*** *production* of some 25,400,000 tons その鋼鉄目標額約二千五百四十万トンの生産. 【類】***Steel*** *production* is falling off. ¶ materials for ***war*** *production* 戦争の生産資材. 【類】activated American ***war*** *production*.

P Gas is now largely used ***for*** the *production* of heat. ガスは今では熱用として広く用いられている. ¶ efficient ***in*** *production* 生産に能率的な. ¶ It is ***of*** British *production*. それは英国製だ.

P^2 It is a *production* ***of*** his chisel. それは氏の彫刻したものだ. ‖ one of the highest *productions* ***of*** literature 文学の最高作品の一つ ‖ the *production* ***of*** scientific research 科学研究の成果. 【類】the *production* ***of*** films ***for*** foreign market (外国向けの). ¶ *production* ***per*** man 一人当り生産量.

productive, *a.* 生じる, 生む.

M be *productive* ***only*** of ... ...しか生産しない. ¶ be ***richly*** *productive* of ... 大いに...を生産する.

P *productive* ***of*** great inconvenience 大なる不便を生じる ‖ an age *productive* ***of*** atomic weapons 原子兵器生産の時代. 【類】*productive* ***of*** happiness / trees *productive* ***of*** nuts (堅果) / a method most *productive* ***of*** results (最も効果的な) / *productive* ***of*** ill (harmful) effects / *productive* ***of*** particularly valuable results.

productiveness, *n.* 生産力.

P^2 the waning health and *productiveness* ***of*** poultry 養鶏の不健康と産卵力の低下.

productivity, *n.* 生産力.

V ***increase*** the *productivity* of electric power 電力生産を増大させる.

Q ***literary*** *productivity* 文学作品の生産力. ¶ ***low*** (***high***) *productivity* 低(高)い生産力. ¶ ***racial*** *productivity* 種族の増加力.

P be highly efficient ***in*** *productivity* 増産は大いに効果的である. ¶ expansion ***of*** *productivity* 生産力拡充.

prof, 《米口》教授.

Q^2 He is a ***history*** (***physics***) *prof*. 彼は歴史(など)の教授だ.

profession, *n.* (**1**) [専門の]職業, 頭脳職業.

V ***adopt*** some *profession* ある職業につく. 【類】***adopt*** the *profession* of an expert in literature and art. ¶ ***choose*** a *profession* 職業を選ぶ. ¶ one of those booksellers who ***disgrace*** their *profession* 自己の職業をはずかしめる(仲間の顔に泥を塗る)書籍商の一人. ¶ ***embrace*** the *profession* of law 弁護士を開業する. ¶ ***enter*** a *profession* 職業を始める. 【類】***enter*** the *profession* of journalism (teaching profession). ¶ ***exercise*** the *profession* of journalism 新聞記者をやる. 【類】***follow*** a *profession*. ¶ Is it suprising that men of ability refuse to ***join*** a *profession* which offers such stipends as these? 敏腕家がこんな(安い)給料の仕事につくのを断ることに何の不思議があろうか. ¶ ***leave*** the *profession* to become ... その職をやめて...になる. ¶ a movement for ***opening*** the legal *profession* to women 婦人に(弁護士などの)法律業の道を開く運動. ¶ ***ply*** a disgraceful *profession* 恥ずべき職業をする. ¶ physicians ***practicing*** a *prefession* 開業医 ‖ qualify one to ***practice*** a *profession* 開業の資格を付与する. ¶ ***pursue*** a *profession* 職業に従事する. 【類】He was ambitious to ***pursue*** the *profession* of arms.

V^2 Today the *professions* ***include*** the functions of engineering, teaching, amusing, governing, advertising and many other types of service. 今日では自由職業の中には技術家, 教師, 芸能人, 経営者, 宣伝係その他色々の業務がはいる. ¶ This *profession* ***pays*** well. この職業は割がよい.

Q ***female*** *professions* 女子の(高等)職業. ¶ the ***honorable*** *profession* 教職. ¶ ***intellectual*** *professions* 知能の職業. ¶ enter the ***journalistic*** *profession* 新聞記者になる. ¶ the ***leading*** *professions* [牧師・医師・弁護士・教師など]主要職業. ¶ the three ***learned*** *professions*—law, medicine, and ministry 法・医及び神学の学問的三職業. ¶ enter the ***legal*** *profession* 法そう界にはいる. ¶ ***manual*** *professions* 筋肉の職業. ¶ representatives of the ***medical*** *profession* from all parts of the world 世界各国からの医師の代表者. 【類】men who stand highest in the ***medical*** *profession* / the best-known men of the ***medical*** *profession*. ¶ the ***military*** *profession* 軍職. ¶ members of the ***musical*** *profession* 音楽界の人々. ¶ of ***no*** *profession* 無職業の. ¶ The law is a very much ***overcrowded*** *profession*. 弁護士業は人が多過ぎる. ¶ members of the more ***reputable*** *profession* もっと体裁のよい職業に従事する人々. ¶ They are in the ***same*** *profession*. 彼らは職業が同じだ. ¶ the ***twin*** *professions* of shorthand and typewriting 速記術とタイプライター術という相関連した職業.

Q^2 the ***advertising*** *profession* 宣伝(広告)の業務. ¶ a "***cinch***" *profession* [講演のような]確実で楽な職業. ¶ select linguistics as a ***future life*** *profession* 言語学を将来一生の仕事として選ぶ. ¶ the ***nursing*** *profession* 看護婦(託児所)の仕事. ¶ the ***shorthand*** *profession* 速記の仕事. ¶ the ***teaching*** *profession* 教職.

P He is a carpenter ***by*** *profession* (=trade). 彼の職は大工だ. ‖ a man of letters ***by*** *profession* 職業文士. 【類】He was a writer, although not so ***by*** *profession* (本職ではないが). / He was ***by*** *profession* a doctor, but by nature a wanderer and sportsman. ¶ people ***in*** this *profession* この商売の人々 ‖ those who stand highest ***in*** the medical *profession* 医学界の泰斗. 【類】He is getting on well ***in*** his *profession*. ¶ humbler members ***of*** the *profession* その職業人の下っぱ ‖ give up the practice ***of*** one's *profession* 廃業する ‖ the ladies and gentlemen ***of*** the *profession* その職業に従事する男女[俳優など]. ¶ I hope you will live ***up to*** your *profession*. 君がその職をはずかしめないよう希望する. ¶ enter ***upon*** a *profession* 職につく. ¶ ***without*** *profession* 無職の.

P^2 teaching as a *profession* ***for*** women 女子の職業としての教師の道. ¶ the *profession* ***of*** an architect 建築業 ‖ the *profession* ***of*** arms 軍職.

(**2**) 言明, 告白; 信仰の告白.

V ***Accept*** my sincere *professions* of regard. 私の衷心よりの敬意をお受け下さい. ¶ ***make*** *profession* of one's faith in Christianity キリスト教の信仰を告白する. 【類】***make*** a *profession* of faith.

Q ***conciliatory*** *professions* of the Russian Government ロシア政府の妥協的言明. ¶ a ***personal*** *profession* of faith 自己の信仰告白. ¶ I believe his *professions* to be perfectly ***sincere***. 私は彼の告白は全く衷心から出たものと信じる. ¶ His *professions* are not ***trustworthy***. 彼の言うことは当てにならない.

P though democrats ***by*** *profession* 口では民主論者だが. ¶ He is a saint in practice if not ***in*** *profession*. 彼は言葉はそうでなくとも行いの方は聖人だ(りっぱな不言実行家).

P^2 the *profession* ***of*** one's faith 信仰の告白.

professionalism, *n.* 専門家気質.

Q too ***much*** *professionalism* どぎつい専門家気質.

professor, *n.* 教授.

V ***exchange*** *professors* 教授を交換する.

Q an ***adjunct*** *professor* 準教授. ¶ an ***associate*** *professor* of English literature 英文学科副教授. 【類】Mr. Blake has been ***associate*** *professor* of English and will be made full professor this term. ¶ ***dusty-minded*** *professors* 頭の古い教授連. ¶ an "***emeritus***" *professor* = a professor emeritus 名誉教授. 【類】***emeritus*** *professor* of French lieratture at King's College. ¶ an ***extraordinary*** *professor* 課外教授. ¶ a ***favorite*** *professor* 人気教授. ¶ a ***foreign*** *professor* 外人教授. ¶ ***foreign visiting*** *professors* 外来臨時教授. ¶ a ***non-resident*** *professor* 科外教授. ¶ ***ordinary*** *professor* 正教授. ¶ a ***senior*** *professor* 上席教授. ¶ ***shopworn*** *professors* 老朽教授. ¶ a ***stupid, dry-as-dust old*** *professor* 頭の鈍い無味乾燥な老教授.

Q^2 a ***biology*** *professor* 生物学教授. ¶ a ***college*** (***university***) *professor* 大学教授. ¶ an Amherst ***economics*** *professor* アムハース大学経済学教授. ¶ an ***English literature*** *professor* 英文学教授. ¶ an ***exchange*** *professor* 交換教授. ¶ crazy notions of a couple of "***fool professors***" 二人の

ばかな教授連の気狂いじみた考え. ¶a *full-time professor* 専任教授. ¶a *language professor* 語学教授. ¶a *law professor* 法学教授. ¶a *loan professor* [他大学からの]借りもの教授. ¶a *pedagogics professor* 教育学教授. ¶Dr. P, Ohio State University *physics* and *astronomy professor* オハイオ大学の物理学天文学教授 P 博士. ¶a *regius professor* 欽定講座担任教授.

P the whole faculty *of professors* 全教授団.

P^{2} Visiting *Professors at* the California College in China at Peiping 在北平駐支加州大学客員教授. ¶Walter B. Pitkin, *professor in* journalism *at* Columbia Uuiversity コロムビア大学新聞科教授ピッキン氏. 【類】*professor in* law and politics *at* Hamilton College / R.H.A. Pimmer, D. Sc., *professor of* chemistry *in* the University of London at St. Thomas's Hospital Medical School. / Dr. H.B. Allen, assistant *professor of* English, University of Minnesota. / Herbert A. Giles, *Professor of* Chinese language and literature at the University of Cambridge. / He is *professor of* painting *to* the Royal Academy.

professoriate, *n.* 教授陣.

Q formation of a *strong professoriate* 強力な教授陣の編成.

professorship, *n.* 教授の職または地位.

V He *accepted* the *prosessorship* in applied mathematics at the College. 彼は同大学の応用数学教授の職を拝命した. ¶*found* a *Professorship* of Anglo-Saxon アングロサクソン語の講座を設ける. ¶*hold* a *professorship* 講座を持っている. ¶The first *professorship* in archaeology was *instituted* at Cambridge about the middle of the 19th century. 考古学の最初の講座はケンブリッジ大学で十九世紀の中ごろに設けられた.

proffer, *v.* 述べる.

P He *proffered* regrets *at* having to leave so early. 彼はそんなに早く別れなければならないことを残念だと言った.

proficiency, *n.* 熟達, 上達.

V *acquire proficiency* in the use of language 言葉の使い方に熟達する. ¶*attain* great *proficiency* in ... ...では名人の域に入る. 【類】when a certain *proficiency* has been *attained*.

Q *English proficiency* 英語のたん能. ¶attain *linguistic proficiency* 言語に上達する. ¶He acquired a *reasonable proficiency* in the language. 彼はその国語が相当できるようになった. ¶attain a *special proficiency* 特に熟達する.

P^{2} *proficiency in* English 英語の熟達.

proficient, *a.* 熟達した, じょうずな.

M become *thoroughly proficient* in ... ...に十分熟達する.

P be *proficient at* repartee 当意即妙の返答ぶりである. ¶He is *proficient in* English (botany, algebra). 彼は英語(など)に熟達している. 【類】He is *proficient in* using (= the use of) the gun. ¶He became *proficient on* the organ. 彼はオルガンがじょうずになった.

profile, *n.* 輪郭; 横顔.

V *draw* a *profile* of ... ...の輪郭を描く.

Q She has a *beautiful profile*. 彼女は横顔がよい.

P a face *in profile* 横顔 ‖ draw ... *in profile* ...の輪郭を描く.

profit, *n.* 利益, 利得.

V *bring* a handsome *profit* to ... ...にかなりの利益をもたらす. ¶It *brought* them *in* large *profits*. それが彼らに大きな利益をもたらした. ¶*chase* a *profit* 利益を追う. ¶*clear* a *profit* of 25 per cent. 二割五分の純益を見る. ¶*cut profits* to narrow margin 利益を少くする. ¶the *profits derived* from the sale of the book この本の売上げから得た利益. ¶*devote* one's *profits* to the war fund そのもうけを戦争基金に充当する. ¶*diminish* (=*narrow down*) *profits* 利益を薄くする. ¶*divide profits* 利益を分配する. ¶the *profits* from ... will be *donated* to ... ...の収益は...へ寄付する. ¶*earn profits* of 100% a year 一年に十割の利益を得る. ¶The cost of living *eats up* all the *profit*. 利益は皆生活費に取られてしまう. ¶*expect* a large *profit* ばく大な利益を予期する. ¶This will *fetch* you a good *profit*. これで相当もうかる. ¶*gain* rich *profits* おびただしい利益を得る. ¶*get* a greater *profit* on them それらからより以上の利益を得る. ¶The paper *has* a clear *profit* of 1000 yen a day on advertisements alone. その新聞は広告だけでも日に千円の純益がある. 【類】Stealing as business *has* poor *profits*. / He *has* a *profit* on everything he sells. ¶*increase profits* 利益を増す. ¶maintain prices at a figure that *leaves* a reasonable *profit* 相当の利益が得られる程度に値段を維持する. 【類】it will *leave* a *profit* of at least ... dollars. / *leave* no *profit* whatever / It *leaves* little or no *profit*. ¶*make* a *profit* on the transaction その取引で一もうけする ‖ *make* a *profit* of one's hobby 道楽から利益を得る. ¶*net* (=yield) a *profit* to ... ...に利益をもたらす. ¶*obtain* a substantial *profit* 多大の利益を得る. ¶*prefer* one's own immediate *profit* to what will benefit us all in the future 将来われわれ全部を利するものよりも自己目前の利益となるものを取る. ¶the year's operations have *produced* a *profit* of ... その年の営業は...の利益を生んだ. ¶*realize* a *profit* of thirty per cent on his original outlay 彼の最初の出費で三割の利益を得る ‖ *profits* fairly and legitimately *realized* 正当に得た利益. ¶*reap* big *profits* ばく大な利益を収める. 【類】*reap* no *profit* / *reap* a *profit* from exertions. ¶*receive* handsome *profits* on their investments 彼らの投資でかなりの利益を得る. ¶*save* intermediate *profits* 中間者の利益を除く. ¶*share profits* with ... 利益を...とともに分ける. ¶*show* a *profit* of ... ...の利益を示す. ¶*swell* one's profits その利益を高める. 【類】*profits swollen* by war boom. ¶*turn out* a *profit* 利益を生む. ¶*yield* a *profit* of ... to ... ...に...のもうけとなる.

V^{2} No small *profits* will *accrue*. 少なからぬ利益を生じるだろう. ¶No *profits* will *come in*. もうけはないだろう.

Q make an *adequate profit* 十分もうける. ¶*all profits* from the sale of the book will be sent to ... 同書売上げのもうけはすべて...に贈られる. ¶produce an *annual profit* of ... 年々...の利益となる. ¶realize just a *bare profit* かろうじてもうけを見る. ¶It means a *better profit* to the produce. それは結局生産者がそれだけもうかるということになる. ¶make *big profits* 大もうけをする. ¶I made £2500 *clear profit*. 私は二千五百ポンドの利益を得た. ¶it yields a *comfortable profit* to ... それは...にかなりの利益となる. ¶He sold it at a *considerable profit*. 彼は余ほどもうけてそれを売った. ¶It will leave a *double profit*. 倍のもうけになる. ¶an enterprise of *doubtful profit* もうかりそうもない企業. ¶He sold it at *enormous profits*. 彼は法外にもうけてそれを売った. 【類】make *enormous profits*. ¶He gained an *enormous personal profit* in this transaction. 彼はこの取引でばく大の私利を得た. ¶*ex-officio profits* 役得. ¶an *exorbitant profit* ぼろいもうけ. ¶make an *exorbitant* and *unreasonable profit* 不法不当なもうけ方をする. ¶wipe out one's *expected profit* その期待したもうけをだめにする. ¶*extortionate profits* 法外な暴利. ¶sell at a *fair* (*great*) *profit* 相当(大いに)もうけて売る. 【類】The business will leave a *fair profit*. ¶*fat profits* 多大の利益. ¶at a *good profit* しっかりもうけて. ¶It is likely to show a very *great profit* それは大分もうかりそうだ. ¶*gross profits* 総利益. ¶at a *handsome profit* かなりの利益で. 【類】He has been making a *handsome profit* out of those sales. ¶make some very *heavy profits* 相当大きなもうけをする. ¶make a *huge profit* out of ... ...で大もうけをする. ¶In order to make an *immediate profit*, he will lose a lifelong and profitable customer. 彼は目前の利益のために一生有益なお得意を失うであろう. ¶make *immense profits* 巨利を博する. ¶make a *large profit* on it それで大もうけをする ‖ It will leave a very *large profit* 利ざやがばく大の見込み. ¶sell at a *large remunerative profit* 割に合うよう大いにもうけて売る. ¶I am contented with a *legitimate profit*. 私は地道の利益で満足している. ¶I am afraid there is very *little profit* in the transaction. その取引にあまりいい汁はなさそうだ. 【類】The business is sound, though it yields but *little profit*. ¶realize a good *monthly profit* 月々大分利益をあげる. ¶*moral, intellectual*, and *aesthetic profit* to be gained from acquaintance with good translations of Plato and Sophocles プラトーやソフォクレスのりっぱな翻訳に親しんで得らるべき道徳的・知的及び審美的利益. ¶That will turn a *neat profit*. それでひともうけできよう. ¶clear (=gain) a *net profit* of ... ...の純益を得る. 【類】three per cent on the *net profits* (純利益). ¶It brought *no profits*. それは少しの得にもならなかった. ¶not for *pecuniary profit* 金銭上の利得のためではなく. 【類】with the object of *pecuniary profit*. ¶work for *personal profit* 私利のために働く. ¶has *poor profit* 利が薄い. ¶schools conducted for *private profit* 私利のため

に経営している学校. ¶a ***reasonable profit*** 適正な利益. ¶The *profit* is ***small***, but he makes it up by the number he sells. 利益は薄いが数で補う. ‖ ***small profits*** and quick returns 薄利多売. ¶reap a ***special profit*** 特別(例外)の利益を得る. ¶make an ***unfair*** (=***unreasonable***) *profit* 不当の利を得る.

Q² make a ***monopoly profit*** 独占的にもうける. ¶the theory of ***nimble penny profit*** on large sales 薄利多売主義. ¶obtain not less than ***6d. per lb. profit*** 一ポンドにつき六ペンス以上の利益を得る.

P sell ***at*** a *profit* (=gain) of ... ...のもうけで売る. 【類】do it ***at*** a *profit* / He succeeded in disposing of (処分する) his wares ***at*** a large *profit*. ¶either ***for*** *profit* or for amusement 利益のためか娯楽のために. 【類】not ***for*** *profit* but as an advertisement of ... / ***for*** your own *profit* ‖ work ***for*** *profit* 利欲のために働く ‖ a school not conducted ***for*** *profit* 営利的でない学校. 【類】The college is not operated ***for*** *profit* / run a theatre ***for*** *profit* / writing ***for*** *profit*. ¶He has a share ***in*** the *profits*. 彼は利益の配分を受ける. ¶There is a fair margin ***of*** *profit*. 相当の利ざやがある. ¶live like a prince ***on*** the *profits* of his business 彼の商売の利益で王侯の生活をする. ¶I have done it ***to*** my *profit*. 私はそれをやってもうけた. ‖ turn anything ***to*** *profit* どんな物でも利用する. ¶bent solely ***upon*** *profit* 営利一方の. ¶I have read it ***with*** *profit*. 私はそれを読んで利益を得た. 【類】It can be read ***with*** *profit* as well as with pleasure. ¶The mine is working ***without*** *profit*. その鉱山は作業はやっているが利益はない. ‖ a transaction ***without*** *profit* ほんのお取次ぎ.

P² *profit* ***by*** experience 経験による利益. ¶a *profit* ***from*** business (transaction, sale) 商売(など)の利益. ¶a *profit* ***in*** business 商売の利. 【類】There is no *profit* ***in*** such pursuits. / the *profits* ***in*** poultry keeping (養鶏業). ¶the *profit* ***of*** labor 労働の収益. ¶*profit* ***on*** the goods sold 売上品に対するもうけ. 【類】the *profits* ***on*** the railways ‖ the *profit* ***on*** capital / *profit* ***on*** investment (利回り) / a *profit* ***on*** the sale. ¶an annual *profit* ***over*** expenditure of $... 経費差引...ドルの年収益 ‖ the *profit* ***over*** cost 原価を引いての利ざや. ¶a *profit* ***to*** the seller 売手の利益. ¶*profits* ***upon*** investments in shares 株の利回り.

profit, *v.* 利を得る, 利益する.

M I have *profited* ***greatly*** from ... 私は...で大いに利益を得た. ¶I have *profited* ***much*** by his explanation. 彼の説明が大いに参考になった.

P I hope to *profit* ***by*** your advice (criticism). 御忠告(など)にあずかりたい. 【類】I hope to *profit* ***by*** your friendship. / Future generations must *profft* ***by*** the mistakes that have been made in the past / *profit* ***by*** the lessons (教訓) of the past / One inventor *profits* ***by*** the work of others. / *profit* ***by*** the example of others (one's own experience) / It is better to *profit* ***by*** insults than to resent them. ¶in order that the rest of us may *profit* ***from*** your experience 他の者が君の経験から利益を得るように ‖ be *profited* ***from*** consulting ... [辞典など]...を調べて得るところがある. 【類】Let us *profit* ***from*** our costly lessons (失敗など) / *profit* ***from*** the sale of ...

profitable, *a.* 有利な, 有益な.

P The study of language is *profitable* ***for*** mental discipline. 語学の勉強は頭の鍛練に有利である. ¶*profitable* ***to*** the seller 売手に有利な.

profiteer, *n.* 不当利得者.

Q² a ***war*** *profiteer* 戦争利得者.

profiteer, *v.* 暴利をむさぼる.

P *profiteer* ***at*** the expense of public interest 世間に迷惑をかけて暴利をむさぼる. ¶*profiteer* ***in*** house rents 家賃で暴利をむさぼる.

profiteering, *n.* 不当利得.

Q² ***landlord*** *profiteering* 地主の搾取.

profuse, *a.* 大まかな, 大ざっぱな.

P He was *profuse* ***in*** thanks (praises, apologies). 彼はやたらに礼(など)を言った. 【類】He is very *profuse* ***in*** his expenditure. ¶be *profuse* ***in*** ideas. ¶He is *profuse* ***of*** (=***with***) his money. 彼は金銭に大ざっぱだ.

profusion, *n.* 豊富; 過多.

Q Bees cluster together in ***thick*** *profusion*. はちは盛んに密集する.

P flowers blooming ***in*** *profusion* 今を盛りと咲く花. ¶He is liberal ***to*** *profusion*. 彼は大まか過ぎる.

P² a *profusion* ***of*** promises 無暗に約束すること.

progenitor, *n.* 先祖.

Q the ***original*** *progenitor* of domestic fowls 家きんの先祖.

progeny, *n.* 子孫.

Q hens producing ***many*** and ***vigorous*** *progeny* 多数の元気よい子孫を作る雌鳥.

P² *progeny* ***from*** a stock 一つの根から出たもの.

program[me], *n.* 順序書, 番組, 段取り; 時間割, 日割; 計画.

V ***announce*** the ministerial *program* (首相など)施政方針を発表する. ¶***arrange*** a *program* 番組を作る. ¶***carry out*** a *program* 計画を実行する. ¶The picture house ***changes*** its *program* weekly—on Friday. その映画館は毎週金曜日にその番組を変える. ¶This ***concludes*** today's *program*. これできょうの番組を終ります. ¶***conduct*** a *program* プログラムを進行させる. ¶***devise*** and ***carry out*** an effective *program* 有効な段取りを案出して実行する. ¶***draw up*** a *program* of study 研究の予定書を作る. ¶***extend*** the naval *program* of a country 一国の海軍計画を拡張する. ¶***formulate*** (=draw up) a long and elaborate *program* 長い念入りな順序書を作成する. ¶He is to be congratulated on having ***got up*** such an interesting *program*. 彼がこんな面白い番組を作り上げたのはお手柄である. ¶At the reception a *program* of Japanese dances and music was ***given***. 招待会で数番の日本舞踊と音楽が催された. ¶***inaugurate*** a *program* of ... ...の計画に取かかる. ¶***lay out*** (=draw up) a *program* of naval and military expansion 陸海軍拡張計画を立てる. ¶***map out*** a *program* of development 発展の計画を立てる. 【類】***map out*** a new *program*. ¶***offer*** no *programme* at all 白紙でのぞむ. ¶***outline*** a *program* 計画の荒筋を立てる. ¶The band ***plays*** the following *program* of music. バンドは次のプログラム通り演奏する. ¶***prepare*** a tentative *program* 仮番組を作る. ¶***realize*** its *program* その目的(主義主張)を貫徹する. ¶The Toyama Military Band ***rendered*** a *program* of popular selections during the afternoon. 戸山軍楽隊が午後に選り抜きの通俗物を演奏した. ¶***sponsor*** a *program* 〘ラジオ〙番組を提供する. ¶***vary*** the usual *program* いつもの順序を変える ‖ ***vary*** the *program* of a magazine 雑誌の面目を改める. ¶***work out*** (=fulfil) a *program* 案を実行する.

V² the *program* ***consists*** of ... 番組は...から成る. ¶the *program* of the day ***included*** ... 当日の番組には...が載っていた.

Q one of the most ***alluring*** *programs* of the day 〘ラジオ〙きょうの聞きもの; 〘ショー〙きょうの見もの. ¶a somewhat ***ambitious*** *program* やや大仕掛な計画. ¶A most ***attractive*** *program* has been drawn up. 非常に人気を引く番組ができ上がった. ¶a ***commercial*** [*program*] 〘ラジオ〙商業番組. 【類】offer a 15-minute ***commercial*** [*program*]. ¶The tourist has a ***crowded*** *program*. その観光客(招待や見物などの)はなかなか忙しい. ¶a ***diversified*** *program* of entertainment 内容の多様な演芸番組. ¶a ***financial*** *program* 財政計画. ¶The meeting had a ***formidable*** *program* of business. その会は審議すべきことがばかに多かった. ¶an ***ideal*** *program* for the study of a foreign language 外国語研究の理想案. ¶***New*** *program* from today. きょうから新番組. ¶a ***non-commercial*** *program* 〘ラジオ〙自由番組. ¶a ***pleasing*** *program* 面白い番組. ¶the ***printed*** *program* at a play or entertainment 劇やショーなどの印刷したプログラム. ¶Is there any ***special*** *program* for the day? その日はなにか特別の行事があるんですか. ¶a ***sponsorless*** *program* 〘ラジオ〙スポンサーのない番組(自由番組). ¶a ***sponsored*** *program* 〘ラジオ〙スポンサー付番組(商業番組). ¶They kept to the ***stereotyped*** *programs* of their predecessors. 彼らは先人のきまりきった目論見を固執した. ¶one's ***traveling*** *program* その旅行の日割. ¶changing the ***usual*** *program* 趣を替える. ¶a ***varied*** and ***excellent*** *program* 変化に富む好番組. ¶a ***vote-catching*** *program* at election-time 選挙のときの投票獲得作戦.

Q² an ***agrarian-reform*** *program* 農地改革案. ¶an ***anti-inflation*** *program* of self-restraint and sacrifice 耐乏生活によるインフレ対策案. ¶***broadcast*** *programs* ラジオの番組. ¶a ***business*** *program* 事業計画. ¶the Party's ***campaign*** *program* その政党の選挙遊説計画. ¶a ***case-by-case*** *program* 事件毎処理案. ¶as one item of the *celebration program* 慶祝行事の一つとして. ¶a ***collegiate-level*** *program* 大学程度の講義要目. ¶A short ***concert*** *program* was gone through. 簡単な演奏会の番組が終った. ¶an ***eight-point*** *program* 八カ条計画. ¶an ***emergency aid*** *program* 非常時援助計画. ¶an ***emergency relief*** *program* 非常時救済案. ¶an ***entertainment*** *program* 余興番組. ¶the ***European Recovery*** *Program* 欧州復興計画(マーシャルプランともいう). ¶under a ***five-year*** *program* 五カ年計画によって. ¶the ***five-year " anti-illiteracy*** *program* " 識字(文盲追放)五カ年計画. ¶a ***Government*** *program* 政府案. ¶a ***give-away*** *program* 〖ラジオ〗懸賞付番組. ¶an ***industrial dismantling*** *program* 産業施設解体案. ¶a ***land-readjustment*** *program* 土地整理案. ¶an integrated ***long-range*** *program* 総合長期計画. ¶begin the spadework on a ***long-range*** *program* of ... ...長期計画の基礎工事を始める. 【類】be engaged in a ***long-range*** *program* to ... ¶a ***long-term*** *program* 長期計画. ¶the ***Marshall Plan aid*** *program* マーシャルプランによる援助計画. ¶a mixed ***music*** and ***film*** *program* 音楽映画の組合せ番組. ¶a ***naval expansion*** *program* 海軍拡張案. ¶The executive committee direct the ***party*** *programs*. 執行部が党の政綱を指導する. ¶Japan accepted the American offer of enriched uranium for ***peace*** *program*. 日本は平和産業向け濃縮ウランのアメリカ提供を受諾した. ¶the ***Point-four*** *Program* 後進地域開発計画(トルーマン大統領が 1949 年に発表した four-point policy の第四番目にあるもの). ¶a ***postwar*** *program* of social reforms 社会改革案の戦後案. ¶formulate a ***propaganda*** *program* on that basis それを骨子にして宣伝の計画を立てる. ¶an extensive ***public works*** *program* ぼう大な公共事業案. ¶the sponsor of a ***radio*** *program* ラジオ番組のスポンサー. ¶It will be broadcast in the B.B.C.'s ***oversea*** *programs* それは BBC の海外放送番組で放送される. ¶a ***rearmament*** *program* ... ...再軍備計画. ¶***Reconversion*** *program* is in progress there. 同地では産業再転換計画が進められている. ¶a ***relief*** *program* 救済案. ¶a ***reorientation*** *program* 再教育案. ¶organize a ***rest*** and ***recreation*** *program* 休養及びレクリエーションの番組を作る. ¶as a part of their ***retrenchment*** *program* 経費節約案の一環として. ¶a ***river development*** *program* 河川改修案. ¶a ***safety*** *program* 安全計画. ¶a new ***school*** *program* 新しい学校の企画. ¶a ***short-range*** *program* 短期計画. ¶a ***small-farms*** *program* 小農地計画. ¶complete a ***socialization*** *program* 社会主義化計画を完遂する. ¶a ***supporting*** *program* 〖映〗おまけ番組(主要映画に付加するもの). ¶a ***sustaining*** *program* 〖ラジオ〗非スポンサー番組(サスプロ). ¶a ***television*** *program* called " Robert Montgomery presents "「ロバート・モンゴメリー演出」と題するテレビ番組. ¶a ***theater*** *program* 劇の番組. ¶a ***two-picture*** *program* 二本立上映. ¶an efficient ***venereal disease control*** *program* 効果的な性病防止案. ¶a ***war*** *program* 戦争計画. ¶a ***year-by-year*** *program* 一年切換案. ¶a ***12-point administrative*** *program* 十二カ条施政方針.

P Many novel events figured ***in*** the *program*. 番組の中には大分珍趣向があった ‖ an item (=a number) ***in*** the *program* 番組中の一項. ¶depart from the order ***of*** the *program* 番組の順序を変える ‖ features ***of*** the *program* その番組の特徴. ¶the first number ***on*** the *program* 番組の第一番 ‖ What's the next number ***on*** the *program?* [音楽会で]次の曲目は何ですか. ‖ Items ***on*** the *program* are not few. 番組が盛り沢山だ. 【類】the best number (圧巻) ***on*** the *program* was the speech of ... / the last event (=item) ***on*** the *program* / what is the next thing ***on*** the *program?* / put it ***on*** the *program* ‖ It was found low down ***on*** the *program*. それは番組の終りのところにあった. ¶the ship to be built ***under*** this year's *program* 今年度の計画で建造せらるべき船. ¶a special student matinee ***with*** a shorter *program* 簡単な番組の学生(招待)特別マチネー.

P² a shipbuilding *program* ***for*** an expenditure of ... ...の経費での造船計画 ‖ a *program* ***for*** reception (meeting) 招待会(など)の順序書. ¶*program* ***of*** studies [授業など]時間割 ‖ *program* ***of*** sightseeing 遊覧日程.

progress, *n.* 進行; 進歩, 経過; 巡行.

V ***advance*** the *progress* of knowledge 知識の進歩を促す. ¶***affect*** the *progress* of the country 国の消長に関係する. ¶***bar*** *progress* 進歩を妨げる. ¶***blockade*** the *progress* of mankind 人類の進歩を阻止する. ¶***continue*** one's *progress* その進行を続ける. ¶***delay*** *progress* 進歩を遅らす. ¶***expedite*** *progress* 進歩を促進する. ¶***facilitate*** the *progress* of civilization 文化の進歩を助長する. 【類】His assistance greatly ***facilitated*** the *progress* of my researches (研究). ¶***further*** the *progress* of a natural evolution [人為をもって]自然の発展を助ける. ¶***gauge*** one's *progress* in studies その研究の進歩を測定する. ¶***hamper*** *progress* 進歩を妨げる. ¶***hinder*** the *progress* of the work 仕事の進行を妨げる. ¶***impede*** the *progress* of thought 思想の進歩を阻害する. ¶***maintain*** a steady *progress* 着々進歩を続ける. ¶The world's work of today would ***make*** but little *progress* without the labor of women. 今日の世界の事業は婦人の労力がなかったら幾らもはかどらないだろう. 【類】*progress* is being ***made*** at a gratifying pace on ... / This patient (病人) is ***making*** good *progress* toward restoration. / He is ***making*** rapid *progress* in his English. / He ***makes*** no *progress* in his studies (学業). ¶Every month has ***marked*** a good *progress*. 毎月りっぱな進歩の成績をあげた. ¶***obstruct*** the enemy's *progress* 敵の進撃を妨害する. ¶***report*** *progress* 経過を報告する. ¶***retard*** the *progress* of my labors 私の仕事の進行を妨げる. ¶***retrace*** the *progress* of civilization 文明進歩の跡を尋ねる. ¶***review*** the *progress* made in the past これまでの進歩を回顧する. ¶Ten years will ***show*** vast *progress*. 十年たてばばく大な進歩を見るだろう. ¶***speed*** *progress* 進歩を促進する. ¶***stay*** the *progress* of the devouring flames 猛火のまん延を防止する. ¶try to ***stem*** the *progress* of thought by persecuting men of letters 文士連を迫害して思想の進歩を抑えようとする. ¶***stimulate*** *progress* 進歩を激励する. ¶until perfection ***stops*** their *progress* and ends their labor 彼らの仕事が完成して仕事を終えるまで. ¶***stunt*** *progress* 進歩を妨げる. ¶***watch*** the *progress* of the work その仕事の進行を見守る.

Q The work of construction is in ***active*** *progress*. その工事は進行しつつある. ¶the ***amazing*** *progress* made by ... ...の遂げた驚くべき進歩. ¶show an ***astonishing*** *progress* in ... ...における驚異的な進歩を示す. ¶***civic*** *progress* 市の発展. ¶***considerable*** *progress* 著しい進歩. ¶His knowledge of English is making ***continued*** *progress*. 彼の英語は不断に進歩している. ¶The work of colonization has made ***decided*** *progress*. 開拓事業は顕然たる進歩を遂げた. ¶***economic*** and ***social*** *progress* 経済上及び社会上の進歩. ¶***encouraging*** *progress* is being made in ... ...は頼もしい進歩を見せている. ¶***enormous*** *progress* 著しい進歩. ¶***excellent*** *progress* すばらしい進歩. ¶Japan's marvellously ***expeditious*** *progress* 日本の驚くべき急速な進歩. ¶make ***fast*** *progress* in acquiring a foreign language 外国語修得においてじん速の進歩を遂げる. ¶The purchase of Christmas gifts is now in ***full*** *progress*. クリスマス贈答品の買ものは今が真最中だ. ¶he has made ***good*** *progress* in ... 彼は...が大分進んだ. 【類】The patient made ***good*** *progress*. ¶***great*** *progress* 大進歩. ¶the march of ***human*** *progress* 人類進歩の行進. ¶***immense*** *progress* has been made in regard to ... ...はすばらしく進歩した. ¶***intellectual*** *progress* 知力の進歩. ¶The new railway has been laid down, but ***little*** *progress* has been made with the work. 新しい鉄道が敷設され始めたが工事が余りはかばかしくない. 【類】The teacher makes ***little*** *progress* with his lectures. ¶***marked*** *progress* 著しい進歩. ¶England's ***marvelous*** *progress* 英国の驚くべき進歩. ¶***much*** *progress* has recently been made in ... 近ごろ...は大いに進歩した ‖ The work is not making as ***much*** *progress* as is desirable. 作業は期待ほどの進行はしていない. ¶he is making very ***poor*** *progress* in ... 彼は...が一向進歩しない. ¶a ***prodigious*** *progress* 驚くべき進歩. ¶he made ***rapid*** *progress* under the tuition of ... 彼は...について学んでぐんぐん進んだ. 【類】make ***rapid*** *progress* in the study of English. ¶He has made ***rapid*** and ***brilliant*** *progress* in his studies at the university. 彼の大学における学業はぐんぐんめざましく進歩した. ¶***remarkable*** *progress* 著しい進歩. ¶a ***royal*** *progress* 巡幸. ¶make ***satisfactory*** *progress* 満足に進歩する ‖ He is making ***satisfactory*** *progress* towards recovery. 彼はぐんぐん快方に向っている. ¶He who never investigates makes ***slow*** *progress*. 研究しない人は進歩がおそい. 【類】he makes but ***slow*** *progress* with ... ¶He is making ***slow*** but ***steady*** *progress* towards recovery. 彼は遅々ではあるが確実に回復に向っている. ¶ *social progress* 社会の進歩. ¶he is making ***solid*** (=***real***) *progress* in ... 彼の...は着々進歩している. ¶He has made ***some*** *progress* in English. 彼は英語がいくらか上達した. ¶ ***startling*** *progress* 驚くべき進歩. ¶ ***steady*** *progress* is being made with the scheme for ... ...の計画は着々進行している. ¶It has already made ***substantial*** *progress* in this direction. それはこの方面においてすでに堅実な進歩を見せている. ¶ ***tremendous*** *progress* 大進歩. ¶he is making ***undeniable*** *progress* towards ... 彼が...の方に進歩しつつあるのは争われない. ¶ ***vast*** (=immense) *progress* 大進歩.

Q² report the ***day-to-day*** *progress* 日々の進行を報告する. ¶ ***world*** prosperity and *progress* 世界の繁栄と進歩.

P ***during*** the *progress* of the meeting 開会中. ¶The inquiry is now ***in*** *progress*. その調査は目下進行中だ. ‖ ***in*** *progress* (=course) of manufacture 製作中 ‖ ***in progress*** (=course) of time (=years) 時のたつにつれて ‖ There are no auctions ***in*** *progress* at present. 今競売はどこもやっていない. ‖ The harvest is still ***in*** *progress*. 今なお収穫中だ. 【類】It has taken great strides ***in*** its *progress*. ¶hinder our own march ***of*** *progress* at least half a century 少くとも五十年はわれわれの進歩を妨げる. ¶ ***on account of*** the *progress* of events abroad 海外における事件の進展により. ¶a barrier ***to*** *progress* 進歩の障害 ‖ due ***to*** the *progress* in medical science 医学の進歩したために. ¶ ***with*** the *progress* of civilization 文明の進歩とともに.

P² We made slow *progress* ***against*** the current. われわれは水流に逆って行くのでらちがあかなかった. ¶rapid *progress* ***in*** the use of destructive mechanism [戦争などの]破壊的機械の使用におけるじん速の進歩. 【類】the *progress* ***in*** philology (言語学) has been so notable in recent years. ¶the *progress* ***of*** a disease 病気の経過 ‖ conduce to (=make for) the peace and *progress* ***of*** the world 世界の平和と進歩に資する. ¶negotiations have recently been in *progress* ***regarding*** ... ...に関する談判が昨今進行中であった. ¶ *progress* ***towards*** completion 完成に向って進むこと.

progress, *v*. 進む, 進行する, 進歩する.

M The work is *progressing* ***admirably***. その仕事はすこぶる順調に運ばれている. ¶He *progressed* ***brilliantly*** in his studies. 彼の学業は見事に進んだ. ¶They are *progressing* ***fairly*** with the work. 彼らの作業は順調に進んでいる. ¶The work is *progressing* very ***fast***. 仕事は急速に進んでいる. ¶The patient is *progressing* ***favorably***. 患者は経過がよい. 【類】Salvage (引揚作業) is *progressing* very ***favorably***. ¶ ***leisurely*** *progress* ゆうゆうと(急がずに)進む. ¶Thanks to the devoted services of the doctors, all the patients are *progressing* most ***satisfactorily***. 先生方の献身的な骨折のおかげで病人の経過は皆申分がない. ¶The sick are *progressing* very ***slowly***. 病人(の病勢)は除々に進んでいる. ¶We *progress* in learning ***step by step***. 勉学は除々に進歩する. ¶The controversy ***still*** *progresses*. その論争はいまだにやっている.

P *progress* ***at*** a snail's pace 牛歩で進む. ¶ *progress* ***from*** a lower state ***to*** a higher 低い段階から高い段階へ上昇する. ¶We *progress* ***in*** knowledge. われわれの知識は進む. ‖ Are the children *progressing* ***in*** their studies? 子供らの学業は進みますか. ¶The book *progresses* ***to*** its climax ***with*** the inevitableness of a Greek tragedy. その本はギリシア悲劇に見る必然性をもって一歩一歩土壇場に進んで行く.

progression, *n*. 進行; 〖数学〗級数.

Q growth with ***geometrical*** *progression* 幾何級数的な増加 ‖ According to Robert Malthus, whereas human beings tend to increase in ***geometrical*** *progression*, their means of subsistence increase only in ***arithmetical*** *progression*. ロバート・マルサスの説によると人口は幾何級数的にふえるが生活資財は算術級数的にしかふえない.

progressist, *n*. 進歩主義者.

P² *progressists* ***within*** the Conservatives 保守党内の進歩主義者.

progressive, *n*. [P-] 進歩党員.

V ***lead*** the *Progressives* back into the Republican fold 進歩派を脱退させて共和陣に復帰させる.

P² the *Progressives* then ***in*** power 当時の政権担当の進歩党.

prohibit, *v*. 禁止する.

M Smoking is ***absolutely*** (=strictly) *prohibited*. タバコは絶対禁止だ. ¶All alcoholic beverages should be ***rigidly*** *prohibited*. 酒精飲料はすべて厳禁すべきだ. ¶be ***strictly*** *prohibited* by law 法律で厳重に禁止されている.

P *prohibited* ***by*** law ***from*** doing ... 法律で...をなすことを禁じられている. 【類】Students are *prohibited* ***from*** smoking inside school. ¶It was *prohibited* ***on*** pain of death. それを犯すものは死刑に処せられた.

prohibition, *n*. 禁止, 禁制.

V ***ignore*** *prohibition* 禁制を無視する. ¶ *Prohibition* was ***laid*** on the export of coal. 石炭の輸出を禁止した. ¶ ***nullify*** a *prohibition* 禁制を取消す. ¶ ***withdraw*** the *prohibition* 禁制を撤回する.

Q ***Imperial*** *prohibition* of the opium trade 勅令によるアヘン取引の禁止.

Q² a ***police*** *prohibition* 警察の禁止.

P² the *prohibition* ***against*** smoking 禁煙. ¶ *prohibition* ***upon*** the marriage of ... ...の結婚禁止.

prohibitive, *a*. 禁止する.

M be ***almost*** *prohibitive* in price ほとんど禁止的値段である.

project, *n*. 計画, 設計, 案.

V ***abandon*** his *project* of ... 彼の...の計画をやめる. ¶ ***carry*** a *project* to completion 計画を完成する ‖ ***carry*** a *project* into execution 計画を実行する. ¶The *project* seems unable to be ***carried on*** through lack of capital. その計画は資金欠乏のため実行不可能らしい. ¶ ***carry out*** one's *project* その計画を遂行する. ¶ ***carry through*** a *project* 計画をやり通す. ¶ ***conceive*** the *project* of ... ...の計画を立てる. ¶ ***draw up*** a *project* 計画を立てる. ¶The *project* is now being ***embodied*** in a bill for presentation to the Diet next session. その計画は議案として次期議会に提出すべく具体化されつつある. ¶ ***entertain*** a *project* 計画をいだく. ¶ ***finance*** a *project* 計画に出資する. ¶ ***form*** a *project* in one's head 策を立てる. ¶ ***give up*** a *project* 計画をやめる. ¶The new *project* has been ***hung up***. その新計画は延期された. ¶He always ***has*** some *project* or other on the brain. 彼はいつも何かもくろんでいる. ¶ ***initiate*** a *project* to ... ...する計画を立てる. ¶energetically ***oppose*** the *project* 極力その計画に反対する. ¶ ***organize*** a *project* 計画を起す. ¶The *project* is now being ***pushed forward***. その計画は実行準備中. ¶I earnestly desire to see the *project* ***put*** into execution. 私はその計画が実行されることを熱望する. ¶For some reason the *project* was ***shelved***. 何かの理由でその案は握りつぶされた. ¶ ***start*** a new *project* 新規に計画を起す. ¶It is understood that the Government has ***subsidized*** the *project* for an experimental period. 政府は試験期間中その計画に補助金を与えたそうだ. ¶The *project* was ***tabled*** without being referred to committees or receiving any further consideration. 《米》同案は委員会にも付託せず再審もせずにたな上げされた. ¶ ***throw up*** a *project* 計画を放棄する. ¶ ***undertake*** an ambitious *project* 大計画を起す.

V² The *project* thus ***dropped***, and nothing further has since been done. かくしてその計画は取りやめとなりその後は何の手も打っていない. ¶The *project* will soon ***materialize***. その計画は近々実現するだろう. ¶The new *project* has ***miscarried***. 新計画は流産した.

Q a ***benevolent*** *project* 慈善的計画. ¶a ***colossal*** *project* 大計画. ¶a ***feasible*** *project* 実行のできる計画. ¶an ***impracticable*** *project* 実行し難い計画. ¶A ***new*** *project* has been set on foot. 新計画に着手した. ¶ ***visionary*** *projects* 架空的計画.

Q² a ***business*** *project* 事業の計画. ¶ ***Christmas goodwill*** *projects* クリスマス親善諸計画. ¶a ***construction*** *project* 建築案. ¶an ***engineering*** *project* 土木計画. ¶a ***home*** *project* 家庭実習. ¶an ***irrigation*** *project* かんがい計画. ¶ ***irrigation*** and ***reclamation*** *projects* かんがいと埋立計画. ¶a ***labor housing*** *project* 労働者住宅計画. ¶a ***labor supply*** *project* 労働供給事業. ¶a ***public works*** (=relief work) *project* 公共事業(救済事業). ¶a ***railway*** *project* 鉄道敷設計画.

P be energetically opposed ***to*** the *project* その案に大反対である. ¶ ***under*** this *project* この案によれば.

P² a *project* ***for*** building a house 家屋建築の計画. ¶the *project* ***of*** a new building 新築案.

O The new *project* is still in embryo. 新計画はまだ熟さない.

project, *v*. 突出する; 〖映〗映写する.

P *project* ***into*** the street 往来へ突き出ている. ¶a scene *projected* ***on*** the screen 銀幕に映じた一こま.

projectile, *n.* 発射物.

V *throw* a *projectile* 手りゅう弾(など)を投げる.

Q² an *artillery projectile* 砲弾(ロケット弾など).

projection, *n.* 突起; 突起物; 投射図法; 映写.

Q the *posterior projection* of the buttocks しりの出っぱり.

P The map is drawn ***on*** Mercator's *projection*. その地図はメルカトル式投射図法で描かれてある.

P² The skin is the *projection **of*** the nervous system. 皮膚は神経系統の延長である. ¶a *projection **on*** a bone 骨にある突起物 ‖ a *projection **on*** the screen 銀幕への映写.

projector, *n.* 映写機.

Q² a *motion-picture projector*=a cinematograph 映写機.

prolific, *a.* 多産の, 多作の.

P The 19th century was *prolific **in*** discoveries and inventions. 十九世紀には発見や発明が多かった. ‖ *prolific **in*** results 成績のあがった. ¶a couple *prolific **of*** children 子供の多い夫婦. 【類】a subject *prolific **of*** controversy ‖ a quarter dirty and *prolific **of*** disease 不潔で病気の多く出る区域.

prolixity, *n.* 冗長, 冗漫.

V *avoid prolixity* 冗長を避ける. ¶*dock prolixities* 冗漫を切りつめる.

prologue, *n.* 序口上.

P² the *prologue **to*** Chaucer's "Canterbury Tales" チョーサーのカンタベリ物語の序詩 ‖ The murder at Serajévo was the *prologue **to*** World War I. セラエヴォの暗殺が第一次大戦の発端だった.

prolong, *v.* 延ばす.

P² *prolong* life ***beyond*** the fixed limit 定命を延ばす.【類】*prolong* one's journey ***beyond*** a certain period. ¶The meeting was *prolonged **into*** the evening. 会合は夕刻までかかった.

prolongation, *n.* 延期.

Q *infinite prolongation* 無期延期.

P² the *prolongation **of*** one's life (agony) 寿命(苦痛)の延長.

promenade, *n.* 遊歩, 行進.

Q² the *Easter Promenade* 復活祭の僧りょの行列. ¶a military *promenade* 軍隊行進.

promenade, *v.* 遊歩する, 散歩する.

P *promenade **about*** the town 市をぶらつく. ¶*promenade **along*** the beach at … …の海岸を散歩する. ¶*promenade* [*in*] the street 通路をぶらつく. ¶*promenade **on*** the Ginza 銀ぶらをやる. ¶土手をぶらつく.

O *promenade* the Thames embankment テームズ河畔の

prominence, *n.* 傑出, 卓越; 突起(物).

V ***acquire*** new *prominence* and value 新たに重要性と価値が出る. ¶***assume*** greater *prominence* 台頭して来る. ¶***attain*** a *prominence* 傑出する. ¶***gain*** *prominence* ぬきんでる. ¶***give*** *prominence* to careless utterances by … …の不用意の発言を重視する ‖ printed in red to ***give*** it *prominence* 目に立つように赤色で印刷された ‖ due *prominence* has been ***given*** to … …を適当に重視する. 【類】***give*** special *prominence* to … ¶He ***has*** a *prominence* on the back. 彼は背に突起物がある. ¶He ***won*** some *prominence* as a fencer. 彼は剣客として多少名があった.

Q give ***greater*** *prominence* to … …を一層目に立たせる. ¶men of ***intellectual*** *prominence* 知能卓絶の人々. ¶give ***particular*** *prominence* to … …に特別重きをおく. ¶a woman of ***social*** *prominence* 社会的に地位のある婦人. ¶give an ***undue*** *prominence* to … …を過度に重要視する.

Q² of ***newspaper*** *prominence* ジャーナリズムで有名な.

P² a *prominence **on*** the landscape 景色中の特に目立った点.

prominent, *a.* 傑出した; 著名な.

P He is *prominent **among*** Osaka business men. 彼は大阪商人の間に傑出している. ‖ *prominent **among*** his pupils are … 門下にその人ありと知られた… ¶people *prominent **in*** science and letters 学術界及び文学界の名士 ‖ They are *prominent **in*** the public eye. 彼らは時の主役である. 【類】a man *prominent **in*** public life / a group of gentlemen *prominent **in*** the public and business affairs of Japan.

promiscuity, *n.* 無差別.

Q *sexual promiscuity* 性的混こう(無差別).

promise, *n.* **(1)** 約束.

V ***break*** (=***violate***) one's *promise* 約束を破る. ¶***carry out*** a *promise* 約束を履行する. ¶I ***claim*** your *promise*. 約束を履行してもらいたい. ¶***exact*** a *promise* that … …という言質を取る. ¶***exchange*** *promises* 約束を交わす. ¶We ***extracted*** from him a *promise* to return again soon. われわれはすぐまた帰るようしいて彼に約束させた. ¶***force*** a *promise* from … …から約束を強要する. ¶faithfully ***fulfil*** the *promise* 忠実に約束を果す. 【類】***fulfil*** the *promises* made at the beginning (最初に). ¶he ***gave*** me his *promise* (=promised me) to … 彼は私に…を約束した ‖ ***give*** a *promise* of subsequent payment 後での支払を約する. ¶I ***have*** his *promise* that he will not … 彼は…しないと私に約束している. ¶honorably ***keep promises*** りっぱに約束を守る. ¶***make*** a *promise* to … …の約束をする ‖ be very ready to ***make*** *promise* 安請合する ‖ ***make good*** one's *promise* その約束を果す. ¶fail to ***meet*** the *promises* made to … …に言いかわした約束を果さない. ¶We ***obtained*** a *promise* of his attendance. 同氏出席の約を得た. ¶***perform*** one's *promise* 約束を果す. ¶I ***received*** secret *promises* of support from … 私は…から援助の密約を得た. ¶***redeem*** one's *promise* 約束を履行する. ¶***respect*** one's *promise* 約束を重んじる. ¶***secure*** his *promise* to … 彼の…の約束を得る. ¶***withdraw*** (=***go back on***) one's *promise* 約束を取り消す.

Q a ***broken*** *promise* 破約. ¶an ***express*** *promise* 明示契約. ¶a ***false*** *promise* 口先だけの約束. 【類】girls who have been seduced by a ***false*** *promise* of marriage. ¶an ***implied*** *promise* 默約 ¶give an ***imprudent*** *promise* 安請合する. ¶an ***irresponsible*** *promise* 安請合. ¶He made ***large*** *promises* of reward. 彼は多大の報酬を約した. ¶try to put one off with ***mere*** *promise* 口先だけの約束でごまかそうとする. ¶He carried out his ***prodigious*** *promise*. 彼はすばらしい約束を果した. ¶make ***rash*** *promises* 安請合をする. ¶a ***solemn*** *promise* まじめな約束. ¶a ***verbal*** *promise* 口約束. ¶give a ***written*** *promise* 契約書を出す.

Q² carry out its ***campaign*** *promises* その選挙公約を実行する. ¶***parole*** *promise* 口頭契約, 無印の略式契約.

P ***according to*** one's *promise* その約束通り. ¶He is bound ***by*** his *promise*. 彼は約束でしばられている. ‖ abide ***by*** one's *promise* 約束を守る. ¶transfer of property ***on*** *promise* of future payment 後払の約束での財産譲渡 ‖ He told me ***on*** a *promise* of secrecy. 他言しない約束で彼は私に話した. 【類】The boy was allowed to accompany us ***on*** the *promise* that he would behave well. ¶***through*** verbal *promise* 口約で. ¶stand ***to*** one's *promise* 約束を守る ‖ true ***to*** one's *promise* 約束を守って ‖ act up ***to*** one's *promise* 約束を履行する. ¶I am ***under*** a *promise* to keep the secret. 私は他言しない約束をしている. ‖ He seduced her ***under*** *promise* of marriage. 彼は結婚する約束で彼女をだました.

P² a *promise **of*** help 援助の約束. ¶because of a *promise* ***to*** myself that I would … 私は…しようと心に誓ったので.

(2) 見込, 気合.

V ***give*** *promise* of ultimate success 結局成功の見込がある ‖ He early ***gave*** *promise* of his future greatness. 彼はとっくに将来を有望視された. 【類】The sky ***gives*** *promise* of fine weather. / ***give*** *promise* for the future / This ***gives*** *promise* of his future achievements. / The fields ***give*** *promise* of abundant harvest (豊作). ¶He ***had*** a high *promise* for the future. 彼は前途非常に有望であった. 【類】We ***have*** best *promise* of success. ¶It ***holds out*** considerable *promise* for the future. それは将来大いに有望だ. ¶***make*** that *promise* good その期待にそむかない. ¶***offer*** the best *promise* for the future 将来きわめて有望である. ¶We ***see*** *promise* of better things. もっとよくなりそうだ. ¶a writer that ***shows*** *promise* 前途有望な作家. 【類】***show*** great *promise* / The author ***shows*** *promise* of better things. ¶The *promise* of the first number has been fully ***sustained*** throughout its successors. [その双書の]第一巻が与えた前途の有望さが後続の諸巻によって十分に実現された.

Q with ***bright*** *promises* of success りっぱに成功の望みがあって. ¶The sky gave ***every*** *promise* of a storm. 空模様ではどうしてもあらしがありそうだった. ¶full of ***fair*** *promises* すこぶる有望な. ¶an artist of ***high*** *promise* 前途有望な芸術家. ¶Life became sweet and full of ***golden*** *promise*. 人生がおもしろく将来有望のものになった. ¶a youth of ***great*** *promise* 前途大いに有望な青年. ¶His planning gives ***reasonable*** *promise* of being successful. 彼の計画は相当成功の見込がありそうだ. ¶The day opened with a ***slight*** *promise* of rain, the heaven being hung with clouds. その日の朝になったが空には雲がかかっていてちょっと雨模様であった. ¶young men of ***unusual*** *promise*

きわめて有望な青年.

P a youth full *of promise* 有望な青年. 【類】a young portrait-painter (青年肖像画家) *of promise*. ¶Her future is bright *with* the *promise* of boundless development. その(都市などの)将来は無限の発展性で輝いている.

P² a *promise for* good crops 豊作の見込. 【類】Is there any *promise for* my English? ¶We found much of *promise in* the boy. われわれはその少年を大いにしょく望した. ¶those words and phrases of which there is a *promise of* permanency [一時的でなく]長く使用されそうな語や句. 【類】There is a *promise of* permanency of these slang words.

promise, *v.* 約束する; 見込がある.

M I cannot *promise certainly.* しかとお受合いはできない. ¶*promise faithfully* to ... ...と堅く約束する. ¶a youth who *promises highly*=a highly promising youth 非常に有望な少年. ¶I cannot *positively promise.* 私ははっきりと約束することはできない. ¶Each witness *promises solemnly,* or swears, to tell "the truth, the whole truth, and nothing but the truth." 各証人はおごそかに約束する, すなわち「真実を, 全くの真実を, 真実のみを」と言って誓う. ¶It *promises well* for the future. それは前途大いに有望だ.

P It *promises for* another fine day tomorrow. あしたも上天気らしい. ¶I *promise on* my honor not to ... 私の名誉に掛けて...しないことを約束する.

O Japan *promises* to become ... 日本は...となる望みがある. ¶he *promised* to try ... 彼は...を試みると約束した. ¶The weather *promises* a good harvest. この天候は豊作┘形だ.

promontory, みさき.

V² a *promontory jutting out* deep into the sea 海中深く突き出たみさき.

promote, *v.* 昇進させる, 進級させる; 発起する.

P *promote* one *from* one position *to* another 人を甲の地位から乙の地位に昇進させる. 【類】be *promoted from* a clerk *to* a manager. ¶*promote* a bill in the House 議案を提起する. ¶*promote* a pupil *into* (=to) the second year class 生徒を第二学年に進級させる. ¶He has been *promoted over* my head. 彼は僕を越して上になった. ¶persons appointed or *promoted through* the influence of the political boss 政治ボスの後だてで任命されたり昇進したりする人々. ¶*promote* a person *to* the peerage 人を華族に叙する. 【類】He has been *promoted to* a captaincy (陸軍大尉). / They have been *promoted to* more difficult books. / be *promoted to* the rank of heroine (女傑).

O *promote* a new company 新会社の発起人となる.

promoter, *n.* 発起人.

Q² *company promoters* 会社発起人たち. ¶*contest promoters* コンクール発起人たち. ¶*get-rich-quick promoters* 一かく千金を夢みる発起人たち. ¶*sports promoters* 競技会主催者側.

P² a *promoter at* work on the formation of a new company 新会社設立に携っている発起人.

promotion, *n.* 昇進, 昇級; 増進; 振興.

V Staying away so long from office will *affect promotion.* そう休んでは昇級にひびくだろう. ¶*attain* (=*get, obtain, receive or win*) *promotion* 昇進する.

Q *accelerated promotion* 抜てき進級. ¶*honorary promotion* 名誉進級. ¶*quick* (=*rapid*) *promotion* 早い昇進. ¶He has won *speedy promotion.* 彼はずんずん昇進した.

Q² *efficiency promotion* 能率増進. ¶*subject promotion* [進級の場合の]単位制度.

P an examination *for promotion* 昇級試験. ¶the avenue *of promotion* 昇進の道 ‖ chances *of promotion* 昇進の機会. ¶He is *on* his *promotion.* 彼は昇級の順が来ている.

P² He has got *promotion by* the aid of favoritism. 彼は引きで昇進した. 【類】*promotion by* merits (実力) / *promotion by* selection (抜てき). ¶one's *promotion in* the peerage 昇爵(しゃく). ¶the *promotion of* peace 平和増進 ‖ *promotion of* health 健康増進 ‖ a society for the *promotion of* science 学術振興会. ¶his *promotion to* the rank of rear admiral 彼の海軍少将への進級.

promotive, *a.* 増進する.

P Strenuous work after a hearty meal is certainly not *promotive of* health. 腹一杯の食事の後で激しい仕事をするのはたしかに健康によくない.

prompt, *a.* 敏速な.

P He is *prompt in* paying his rent. 彼は家賃の払いがよい.

prompt, *v.* 鼓舞する.

P *prompted by* the whim of the moment でき心で ‖ *prompted by* instinct 本能に鼓舞されて. 【類】*prompted by* the feeling that it was his duty / *prompted by* curiosity, he asked how ... ¶the chief reason which *prompts* me *to* this conclusion is, that ... 私をこの結論に達せさせる主な理由は...である.

prompter, *n.* 〖劇〗プロンプター.

V² A *prompter helped* him speak up his lines. プロンプターが彼のせりふを助けてやった.

prompting, *n.* 刺激.

P *under* the *promptings* of this very honorable sentiment このきわめて貴い感情に刺激されて ‖ *under* the *promptings* of his superiors 先輩に激励されて.

P² the *prompting of* appetites 食欲の刺激.

promulgation, *n.* 布告, 発布.

V *issue* a *promulgation* 布告を発する.

P² the *promulgation of* the law 法律の発布.

prone, *a.* うつむきの, ...の傾きある, ...し勝ちな.

P *prone on* the ground 地上にうつむきになる. 【類】an unhappy automobilist *prone on* his back on the road beneath his vehicle struggling with some obstinate adjustment. ¶He is *prone* by nature *to* superstition. 彼は天性迷信に落入りやすい. 【類】some are *prone to* the belief that ... / Our hearts are *prone to* evil. / He is *prone to* idleness.

O "the old man," as his fellow-workers were *prone* to call him, ...「大将」こういうように仲間が彼を呼ぶのであるが... 【類】We are *prone* to think that...

pronoun, *n.* 〖文法〗代名詞.

Q an *indefinite pronoun* 不定代名詞. ¶a *reflexive pronoun* 再帰代名詞.

pronounce, *v.* 発音する; 朗読する; 宣告する; 断言する.

M *pronounce clearly* (*nasally*) はっきり(鼻にかけて)発音する. He was *pronounced completely cured.* 彼は完全に治ったと言われた. ¶*pronounce* each word *correctly.* 一語一語正しく発音する. ¶*dogmatically pronounce* on ... ...について独断的な意見を述べる. ¶show *how* letters are *pronounced* in a word 単語の一字の発音法を示す. 【類】Tell me *how* to *pronounce* this word. ¶The child is *pronounced out of danger.* その子供はもう生命には別条はないそうです. ¶*pronounce oracularly* on Japanese politics. 日本の政治について神がかりな判断を下す. ¶*pronounce out* loud 大声に朗読する. ¶*rightly pronounce* a word 正しく語を発音する. ¶I *pronounce* the pears *unripe.* 私はそのなしは熟していないと断言する. ¶be *pronounced variously* 色々に発音される. ¶Many eminent philologists have *pronounced warmly* in favor of Esperanto. 知名の言語学者でエスペラントを賛称したものは多い.

P *pronounce after* me ... 私のやるように...と発音してごらん. ¶*pronounce against* him 彼には不利な宣告を下す. ¶It is *pronounced by* the lips. それは口びるで発音する. ¶*pronounce for* (=*in favor of*) ... ...に有利な宣告を下す. ¶*pronounce* judgment *on* one's conduct (work) その行為(など)に判断を下す. 【類】He is best qualified to *pronounce on* such a matter. ¶*pronounce through* the nose 鼻にかけて発音する. ¶It is *pronounced with* an accent on the second syllable. それは第二つづりにアクセントを付けて発音する.

O In English few words are *pronounced* as they are spelled. 英語ではつづりの通り発音される語はほとんどな┘い.

pronouncement, *n.* 声明, 宣言, 発表.

V *issue* a *pronouncement* 声明書を出す. ¶*make* a remarkable *pronouncement* 注意すべき声明をする.

Q In fact, it is indisputably the most *authoritative pronouncement* on the subject that has ever appeared. 実際それがこの問題に関するこれまでの声明の中で最も権威あるものであることは明白だ. ¶in his *recent pronouncement,* he ... 最近の声明中に氏は... ¶a *weighty pronouncement* 重大な声明. 「勇敢な宣言.

P a courageous *pronouncement concerning* ... ...に関する

P² *pronouncement of* "not guilty" 無罪の言渡し ‖ *pronouncement of* a judgment 宣告. ¶*pronouncements on* the subject その問題に関する発表. 【類】a *pronouncement on* modern American usage.

pronunciation, *n.* 発音.

V ***acquire*** a good *pronunciation* of French フランス語のよい発音を覚える. ¶***correct*** bad *pronunciation* 間違った発音を矯正する. ¶***cultivate*** clear *pronunciation* 明りょうな発音を養成する. ¶He ***has*** a good *pronunciation*. 彼は発音が良い. ¶***impart*** an accurate *pronunciation* to the pupils 生徒に正確な発音を授ける. ¶***indicate*** *pronunciations* 発音を示す. ¶***look up*** the *pronunciation* of a word in a dictionary ある語の発音を辞書で調べる. ¶***obtain*** a good *pronunciation* 正しい発音を覚える. ¶***practice*** the *pronunciation* 発音のけい古をする. ¶***record*** variant *pronunciations* [辞書などで]色々の発音を記録する. ¶the efforts to ***standardize*** *pronunciation* 発音を統一しようとする努力. ¶I could not ***understand*** his *pronunciation* of certain words. ある語の彼の発音は私には分からなかった.

Q an ***accurate*** *pronunciation* of English 英語の正確な発音. ¶an ***affected, highbrow*** *pronunciation* 気どったインテリらしい発音. ¶There are two ***acknowledged*** *pronunciations* of that word. その語の認められた発音が二つある. ¶English *pronunciation* is ***anarchical.*** 英語の発音は乱暴きわまる. ¶an ***antiquated*** *pronunciation* 旧式の発音. ¶an ***approved*** *pronunciation* 認められた発音. ¶an ***aristocratic*** *pronunciation* 上品な発音. ¶***artificial*** *pronunciations* 不自然な発音. ¶a ***barbarous*** *pronunciation* めちゃめちゃな発音. ¶***colloquial*** *pronunciations* 口語的な発音. ¶***conventionalized*** *pronunciation* 読癖. ¶a ***correct*** *pronunciation* 正しい発音. ¶a ***corrupt*** *pronunciation* くずれた発音. ¶the ***current*** *pronunciation* of the word その語の現代発音. ¶***disputed*** *pronunciations* 議論のある発音. ¶words of ***doubtful*** *pronunciation* 発音のはっきりしない諸語. ¶the ***established*** *pronunciation* of the language その語の標準発音. 【類】Words that are seldom spoken, or met with only in books, have no ***established*** *pronunciation.* ¶acquire ***false*** *pronunciations* 誤った発音の癖がつく. ¶a ***faulty*** *pronunciation* 間違った発音. ¶a ***finicking*** *pronunciation* こまか過ぎる発音. ¶***fixed*** *pronunciation* in standard English 標準英語による一定した発音. ¶His *pronunciation* is ***impeccable.*** 彼の発音は申し分がない. ¶***inarticulate*** *pronunciation* はっきりしない発音. ¶His *pronunciation* is ***meticulous.*** 彼の発音はこまかすぎる. ¶***natural*** *pronunciations* 自然の発音. ¶***ordinary, unpedantic*** *pronunciations* てらわない普通の発音. ¶a ***perfect*** *pronunciation* 申分のない発音. ¶a ***plebeian*** *pronunciation* 俗な発音. ¶acquire a ***practical working*** *pronunciation* of a foreign language 外国語の実際的な役に立つ発音を覚える. ¶pedantically ***precise*** *pronunciation* 学者ぶった固くるしい発音. ¶in ***rapid*** *pronunciation* 口早に言うと. ¶a ***regional*** *pronunciation* 地方の発音. ¶a ***second*** or ***variant*** *pronunciation* 第二の即ち別種の発音. ¶***slipshod*** *pronunciation* ぞんざいな発音. ¶***slovenly*** *pronunciation* だらしのない発音. ¶***studied*** *pronunciation* わざとらしく作った発音. ¶***theoretical*** *pronunciation* 理論的な発音. ¶an ***unobjectionable*** *pronunciation* 申分のない発音.

Q² the ***B.B.C.*** *pronunciation* 英国放送協会の標準発音. ¶a ***church*** *pronunciation* 牧師の発音. ¶acquire a standard ***English*** *pronunciation* 標準英語の発音を覚える.

P a purist ***in*** *pronunciation* 発音の純正をとうとぶ人. 【類】There is no distinction ***in*** *pronunciation.* ¶speak English ***with*** correct *pronunciation* 正しい発音で英語を話す.

P² The *pronunciation* ***of*** Japanese is comparatively easy. 日本語の発音は比較的容易だ.

proof, *n.* (**1**) 立証; 取調, 吟味; 証拠.

V ***accumulate*** *proofs* 証拠を集める. ¶***adduce*** *proofs* 証拠としてあげる. ¶***afford*** an irrefragable *proof* of ... ...の確実な証拠を提供する. ¶***furnish*** an irrefragable *proof* that ... ...という確実な証拠を示す. ¶***get*** positive *proof* of ... ...の確証を握る. ¶He has ***given*** *proof* of his honesty. 彼は自分の正直なことを証明した. ¶we ***have*** sufficient *proof* of ... ...の十分な証拠がある. 【類】***Have*** you any *proof* of it? ‖ ***have*** *proof* of shot 防弾になっている. ¶***hold*** *proofs* 証拠を握る. ¶***make*** *proof* of a person's courage (skill, talent) 人の勇気(など)をためして見る. 【類】he ***made*** *proof* of patriotism by ... ¶***offer*** *proof* 証明する. ¶***overlook*** the *proofs* of ... ...の証拠を看過する. ¶***produce*** *proof* on one's statement その陳述に対する証拠を提出する ‖ ***produce*** the most conclusive *proof* that ... ...の最も決定的な証拠を提出する. ¶***require*** further *proof* それ以上の証拠を要する. 【類】It is too evident to ***require*** *proof.* ¶***stand*** the *proof* その試験に耐える. 【類】***stand*** a severe *proof.* ¶He ***supplied*** an incontestable *proof* to the contrary. 彼は異論のない反証を示した. ¶I ***want*** some *proof* of what he says. 私は彼の言っていることの何か証拠を得たいと思う.

Q an ***absolute*** *proof* of ... ...の確証. ¶there is ***abundant*** *proof* of ... ...の証拠は沢山ある. ¶it is ***ample*** *proof* that ... それは...の十分な証拠だ. 【類】give ***ample*** *proof* of ... ¶There is no ***authentic*** *proof* for it. それには確実な証拠がない. ¶***clear*** *proof* 明白な証拠. ¶***clearest possible*** *proof* この上もなく明白な証拠. ¶a ***clinching*** *proof* of its excellence それがすぐれていることの決定的な証拠. ¶there is no ***conclusive*** *proof* as to ... ...に関しては決定的な証拠がない. ¶a ***conspicuous*** *proof* 歴然たる証拠. ¶give ***convincing*** *proofs* of ... ...の適確な証拠を与える. ¶a ***decisive*** *proof* 決定的な証拠. ¶***demonstrative*** *proofs* [決定的な]証拠. ¶satisfy us of this fact by ***documentary*** *proof* この事実については証拠書類によってわれわれを納得させる. ¶afford a ***fresh*** *proof* 別の新しい証拠を示す. ¶give ***full*** *proof* of the fact その事実を十分証明する. ¶***Full documentary*** *proof* has been adduced in support of the statement. その言明に対して十分の証拠書類があげられた. ¶represent miracles as the ***fundamental*** *proof* of religion 宗教の根本的な証明として奇跡を説明する. ¶for ***further*** *proof* thereof let the reader turn to the pages of ... それについてこの上の証拠を望まれる読者は...(書)を御覧下さい. 【類】we may note as a ***further*** *proof* that ... ¶an ***incontrovertible*** *proof* 争われない証拠. ¶***independent*** *proofs* [他と関連のない]それぞれ独立した証拠. ¶an ***irrefutable*** *proof* 反ばくを許さない証拠. ¶an ***irresistible*** *proof* 否認できない証拠. ¶Military victory is ***no*** *proof* that right is on the victor's side. 戦に勝ったからと言って勝利者の方が正しいという証拠にはならない. ¶***no small*** *proof* of ... ...の軽視できない証拠. ¶an ***obvious*** and ***incontestable*** *proof* 明白で争う余地のない証拠. ¶give you ***ocular*** *proof* of the value of ... ...の価値を示すはっきりした証拠を示す. ¶get ***positive*** *proof* of ... ...の確証を得る. 【類】this is ***positive*** *proof* that ... / We have no ***positive*** *proof.* / He has nothing in the shape of [a] ***positive*** *proof.* ¶a ***probable*** though not an ***irrefragable*** *proof* of ... ...の絶対確実というほどではないが, 幾分確からしく思われる典拠. ¶a ***signal*** *proof* すてきな根拠. ¶a ***silent*** and ***eloquent*** *proof* of the fact その事実の無言にして雄弁な証拠. ¶***solid*** *proof* of progress 進歩の確実な証拠. ¶a ***striking*** *proof* of ... ...のすばらしい証拠. ¶a ***strong*** *proof* 確かな証拠. ¶have ***sufficient*** (=***ample***) *proof* of ... ...の十分な証拠がある. 【類】The number of the editions (版数) is ***sufficient*** *proof* of the popularity of the work. ¶it is a ***sure*** *proof* that ... それは...という確証である. ¶a ***tangible*** *proof* 実質的な証拠. ¶the ***ultimate*** *proof* that ... ...の究極の証拠. ¶an ***uncontrovertible*** *proof* 異論のない証拠. ¶***unquestionable*** *proof* 疑いを入れない証拠. ¶a ***visible*** *proof* 歴然たる証拠.

P ***as*** a *proof* of gratitude to ... for ... ...に対して...への感謝の印(しるし)として. 【類】***as*** a *proof* of penitence (ざんげ) / keep bread upon one's shelf with one's fork stuck into it ***as*** *proof* of ownership. ¶***for*** *proof* of this, one has but to ... この証明には人は...すればよい. ¶an instance ***in*** *proof* 証明 ‖ ***in*** *proof* of this statement この陳述を立証するために. 【類】He produced papers ***in*** *proof* of the justice of his claims. ‖ put ***in*** *proof* 吟味する. ¶the burden ***of*** *proof* 挙証の責任. ¶Lost property is handed back to its owners ***on*** *proof* and payment of the necessary fees. 拾得品は所有主たる証拠と必要な手数料を払えばその持主に戻される. ¶I should like to put their loyalty ***to*** the *proof.* 彼らの忠誠をためして見たい. ¶***without*** convincing *proof* 的確な証拠なしに.

P² a *proof* ***against*** ... ...の反証. ¶The *proof* ***of*** the pudding is in the eating. 論より証拠だ. ¶It cannot be regarded as *proof* ***to*** the contrary. それを反対の証拠と見なすことはできない.

(**2**) 校正刷.

V ***correct*** (=***read or revise***) the *proof* 校正する. ¶drudgery of ***reading*** *proof* 校正といういやな仕事. 【類】He has already ***read proof*** on the 400 pages of the book. / The *proofs* of the books have been most carelessly ***read.*** ¶ ***submit proofs*** of contributions to their writers for revision 寄稿の筆者に訂正のため校正刷を送る.

Q *a **foul proof*** 沢山直しを要する校正刷. ¶ ***O'Kd proofs***＝proofs marked "O.K." 稿了になった校正. ¶ I overlooked the error in ***three proofs.*** 私は三校まで見たのにその間違いを見落した.

Q² in the ***galley proof*** ゲラ刷で.

P correct one's books ***in proof*** その著作の校正を見る ‖ be submitted to the writer ***in proof*** for verification or correction 検閲もしくは正誤のため校正刷のまま筆者に提出する.

P² a *proof **for*** correction 校正刷.

proof, *a.* 犯されない.

P He is ***proof against*** flattery. 彼はおべっかなどには乗らない. ‖ The building is ***proof against*** fire (earthquake, sound, the weather, water). それは耐火(など)家屋だ. ‖ She is ***proof against*** love. 彼女は恋愛には不感症だ. 【類】 He is quite ***proof against*** the temptations of the flesh (肉欲の誘惑). / He is ***proof against*** temptation (bribery).

prop, *n.* 支柱.

Q the ***main prop*** of a state 国家の柱石 ‖ the ***main prop*** and stay of the Far East 極東の安定勢力. ¶ He is the ***only prop*** of hers for her old age. 彼は彼女の老後のただ一つの柱だ.

P a round piece of board resting ***on*** three *props* 三本の支柱のある円形の板. ¶ It will not stand ***without*** a *prop.* それは支柱がなくては立っていまい.

P² Agriculture is the *prop **of*** the country. 農は国の本. 【類】 He is the *prop* and stay ***of*** the home.

prop, *v.* 支える.

M² *prop* the bicycle ***up*** against the wall 自転車を壁に立て掛ける ‖ This fence should be ***propped up.*** このかき根は支柱で補強しなければいけない. 【類】 ***prop up*** a bankrupt regime / dolls ***proped up*** in a row against the wall / ***prop up*** the weakened democracies (民主国) of Europe against communism. / The nation's economy has been ***propped up*** by U.S. aid.

propaganda, *n.* 宣伝.

V ***carry on*** an active *propaganda* 盛んに宣伝する. ¶ ***carry out** propaganda* on a large scale 大仕掛の宣伝をやる. ¶ ***conduct** propaganda* in the interests of Japan 日本のために宣伝をする. ¶ ***counteract*** the anti-Japanease *propaganda* 反日宣伝に対抗する. ¶ ***further*** the *propaganda* 宣伝を助ける. ¶ ***institute*** a *propaganda* which will work a change in public opinion 世論の変化を起すような宣伝を始める. ¶ ***launch** propaganda* against (in favor of)... ...を攻撃する(に有利な)宣伝を開始する. ¶ The magazine ***maintains*** costly *propaganda* to get new advertisers. 同雑誌は新規の広告を取るために費用のかかる宣伝を続行している. ¶ ***push*** a *propaganda* 宣伝を押し進める. ¶ ***set up*** a *propaganda* for ... ...のための宣伝機関を作る. ¶ Socialists ***urge*** their *propaganda* with energy and daring. 社会主義者は勢よく大胆にその主義を宣伝する.

Q ***anti-British** propaganda* 反英宣伝. ¶ ***anti(pro)-war** propaganda* 反(好)戦宣伝. ¶ ***destructive revolutionary** propaganda* 破壊的革命宣伝. ¶ ***dishonest** propaganda* でたらめな宣伝. ¶ ***effective** propaganda* 効果的宣伝. ¶ ***false** propaganda* 悪宣伝. ¶ counteract the ***false** propaganda* now current in ... 目下...に行われている虚偽の宣伝の裏をかく. ¶ ***harmful** propaganda* 悪宣伝. ¶ ***ideological** propaganda* イデオロギーの宣伝. ¶ ***intensive** propaganda* 猛烈な宣伝. ¶ During the war the cinema was widely used for ***patriotic** propaganda.* 戦時中映画が広く愛国的宣伝に用いられた. ¶ conduct ***vigorous** propaganda* 活発な宣伝をやる. ¶ be misled by ***pernicious** propaganda* 悪宣伝にまどわされる. ¶ vigorously ***urged** propaganda* 盛んにあおり立てた宣伝. ¶ ***vile** propaganda* 悪宣伝. ¶ a ***well-planned** propaganda* 巧みに企画した宣伝.

Q² handbills containing ***Communist** propaganda* 共産党の宣伝ビラ. ¶ broadcast ***enemy** propaganda* 敵の宣伝を放送する. ¶ ***film** propaganda* 映画の宣伝. ¶ ***love-of-country** propaganda* 愛国宣伝. ¶ ***Nazi** propaganda* ナチの宣伝. ¶ ***pacifist** propaganda* 平和主義者の宣伝. ¶ ***peace** propaganda* 平和の宣伝. ¶ ***Soviet** propaganda* ソ連の宣伝. ¶ printed matter and posters for ***tourist** propaganda* 観光宣伝の刷り物やポスター. ¶ carry on ***war** propaganda* 戦争宣伝をやる. 【類】 a third ***world war** propaganda* / the prevention and suppression of ***war** propaganda.*

P This will serve ***as*** good *propaganda.* これは宣伝になる. ¶ a war ***of*** *propaganda*＝a propaganda war 宣伝戦. ¶ ***through*** skilful *propaganda* 巧妙な宣伝で.

P² practicers of the "*propaganda **by*** deed" 行動宣伝の実行者.

propagandize, *v.* 宣伝する

P *propagandize ... **against*** (***in favor of***) ... ...に反対(賛成)して...の宣伝をやる. ¶ *propagandize* [***in***] Marxism マルクス主義を宣伝する.

propagate, *v.* 繁殖させる.

M The germs *propagate **rapidly.*** その菌は急速繁殖させる.

P *propagate **by*** means of cutting さし木にする. ¶ These plants can be *propagated **from*** cuttings. この植物はさし木で栽培ができる.

propagation, *n.* 繁殖.

V ***stop*** the *propagation* of the bacteria in ... ...における細菌の繁殖を防止する.

Q ***reckless** propagation* 乱殖.

P² the *propagation **of*** the species 種族の繁殖.

propagator, *n.* 伝播(ぱ)者.

P² *propagators **of*** ideas 思想の伝播者.

propel, *v.* 押進める, 推進する.

P *propel* a boat ***by*** a pole (oars) さお(など)で舟をやる ‖ The ship is ***propelled by*** steam (screws). その船は蒸気(など)の力で推進する. ‖ He was ***propelled by*** the desire of glory. 彼は名誉欲に駆られた. 【類】 be ***propelled by*** ambition / *propel ... **by*** force (横車).

propeller, *n.* 推進器(プロペラー).

V² The *propeller* began ***whirling.*** プロペラーがぶんぶん回転し出した.

Q² an ***airplane** propeller* 飛行機のプロペラー. ¶ a ***cast-steel*** (***forged-steel***) ***propeller*** 鋳鋼(鍛鋼)プロペラー. ¶ a ***screw** propeller* ねじプロペラー, 「スクリュー」. ¶ a ***three-blade metal** propeller* 三枚羽根の金属製プロペラー.

propensity, *n.* 偏向, 癖.

V He ***has*** a *propensity* for exaggeration. あの人は物事を大げさにいう癖がある. 【類】 ***have*** a *propensity* for drinking (gambling).

Q ***egocentric** propensities* 自己中心癖. ¶ the ***evil** propensities* of human nature 人間性にひそむ悪.

Q² ***fighting** propensities* 戦闘的性癖. ¶ women of ***thieving*** or ***drinking** propensities* 盗癖または飲酒癖のある女.

P² a *propensity **for*** heavy drinking 大酒のくせ. ¶ an ineradicable *propensity **to*** gambling と博の抜き難い癖.

proper, *a.* 適当な; 特有の, 固有の.

P *proper **for*** the occasion 機宜に適した. ¶ Cleanliness is *proper **to*** the Japanese. 清潔は日本人の習性だ.

property, *n.* (**1**) 財産, 資産; 所有地.

V ***assign** property* to ... ...に財産を譲渡する. ¶ ***buy*** a *property* (*properties*) 所有物を買う. ¶ ***communize** property* 土地家屋を共有にする. ¶ I ***confide*** my *property* to your care. あなたに財産の管理を託する. ¶ ***confiscate*** the *property* of ... ...の財産を没収する. 【類】 ***confiscate*** their *property* for the use of the State (公用に). ¶ ***convert*** another's *property* (money) to one's own use 人の財産(金)を私消する. ¶ ***convey*** one's *property* to ... ...に財産を譲る. ¶ Much valuable *property* was ***damaged*** by the fire. 貴重な財産がその火事で多大の損害を受けた. ¶ His *property* was ***destroyed*** by a flood. 彼の財産は洪水でめちゃくちゃになった. ¶ ***endanger** property* 財産を危くする. ¶ his family ***had** property* near ... 彼の家族は...の近くに不動産を持っていた. ¶ ***hold** property* 財産を所有する. ¶ He ***inherited*** a large *property.* 彼は大した財産を相続した. ¶ ***insure*** life and *property* 生命財産を保証する. ¶ ***property left*** in a car 電車内におき忘れた所有品. ¶ He has ***lost*** all his *property.* 彼は全財産を失った. ¶ ***mortgage** property* 財産を抵当にする. ¶ The ***property occupied*** by the College is in grave danger of passing into other hands. その大学の財産がどうやら人手に渡りそうだ. ¶ ***own*** considerable *property* かなりの財産を所有する. 【類】 There she ***owns*** a lot of *property.* ¶ ***possess*** a landed *property* 土地を所有する. ¶ ***protect** property* from fire 財産を火災からまもる. ¶ ***reclaim*** lost *property* 遺失品の取戻しを請求する. ¶ ***seize*** one's *property* 財産を没収する. ¶ ***transfer*** the *property* (＝ownership) in ... ...の所有権を譲渡する. ¶ He ***wasted*** his *property* in wild extravagance. 彼は放

とうで資産を浪費した. ¶*will* one's *property* 財産を遺贈する.

V² Whom does this *property* ***belong*** to? この財産はだれの所有か. ¶How many acres does this *property* ***contain***? この所有地は幾エーカーあるか. ¶All the *property* will ***go*** to ... その財産はすべて...のものになるだろう. ¶The *property* has ***fallen*** to the heir. 財産は相続者のものになった. ¶On the death of ..., the *property* ***passed*** to his widow. ...が死んだので財産は未亡人のものになった.

Q a really ***cheap*** *property* 本当に安い地所. ¶As soon as a man has had the misfortune to make himself a name, he becomes ***common*** *property*. 人が不幸にして名を成すと同時に彼は社会の共有財産となる. 【類】The idea has become the ***common*** *property* of thinking minds. / There are some facts and ideas that have become ***common*** *property*. ¶***damaged*** *property* 被害をこうむった財産. ¶the ***exclusive*** *property* of the intellectuals 知識人の専有財産 ‖ have ***exclusive*** *property* in ... ...という独占物がある. 【類】by no means the ***exclusive*** *property* of the privileged classes (特権階級). ¶***fixed*** *property* 固定財産. ¶He has a ***handsome*** *property*. 彼は相当の財産を持っている. ¶***hereditary*** *property* 世襲財産. ¶***individual*** *property* 私有財産. ¶a man of ***large*** (small) *property* 財産の沢山(少し)ある人. ¶***literary*** *property* 著作権; 文芸作品. 【類】those who make ***literary*** *property*. ¶***lost*** *property* found in cars 電車内の遺失物. ¶***movable*** (=***personal***) *property* 動産. ¶***national*** *property* 国有財産. ¶***private*** (***public***) *property* 私(公)有財産 ‖ respect ***private*** *property* 私有財産を認める ‖ The news of his contemplated step became ***public*** *property*. 彼の計画中の行動が一般に知れた. ¶***real*** (=***landed***) *property* 不動産(土地・家屋). ¶guard ***salvaged*** *property* from the attentions of light-fingered looters 焼残り品に対しかっさらいを予防する. ¶I have a ***small*** *property* in Kyoto. 私は京都に少しばかり地所を持っている. ¶descriptions of ***stolen*** *property* 盗まれた物の品書. ¶***subsidiary*** *property* 付属財産. ¶***suburban*** and ***country*** *properties* 郊外及びいなかの所有地. ¶***tangible*** *property* 有形財産.

Q² hold meetings on ***company*** *property* 会社の敷地で会合を開く. ¶***capitalist*** *property* 資本家の財産. ¶one's ***family*** *property* その家産. ¶sale of ***government*** *property* 国有物の払下げ. ¶***house*** and ***land*** *property* 土地家屋. ¶***inventory*** and ***catalogue*** *property* 明細書品目及び目録記載の財産. ¶***park*** *property* 公園の所有物. ¶a ***riverside*** *property* 河岸の所有地. ¶destroy ***school*** *property* 学校の所有物を破壊する. ¶sales of ***State*** *property* 国有財産の払下げ. ¶transfer of ***State*** *property* to private ownership 国有財産払下げ. ¶surplus ***war*** *property* 余剰戦争物資.

P a piece ***of*** *property* 一個の財産 ‖ a man ***of*** *property* 財産家 ‖ the care ***of*** one's *property* その財産の管理. ¶it is ***on*** the *property* of ... それは...の邸内にある ‖ A fire broke out ***on*** the *property* of the company. その会社に火事があった. ¶quarrel ***over*** one's *property* その財産を争う. ¶succeed ***to*** one's *property* その財産を相続する ‖ on his succession ***to*** his *property* 彼が財産を継ぐときに ‖ He has a right ***to*** some *property*. 彼には若干の財産を受ける権利がある. ¶a man ***with*** no *property* but his own body はだか一貫の人.

P² *property* ***in*** money 現金資産. ¶This book is the *property* ***of*** the Yokohama United Club. この本は横浜連合クラブのものだ. 【類】It became the *property* ***of*** the state. / Craigenputtock, a *property* ***of*** Mrs. Carlyle is in the wilds of Dumfries. / *property* ***of*** various kinds, real and personal, fixed and movable, material and immaterial.

(2) 性能, 特性.

V ***acquire*** the *property* of ... ...の性質を帯びる. ¶***diminish*** its dangerous *property* [毒薬など]その危険性を軽減する. ¶***have*** the *properties* of dissolving grease 脂肪を分解する特性がある. 【類】A prism ***has*** the *property* of decomposing light / a fountain whose waters ***have*** the *properties* of restoring youth to the aged who taste them (不老泉) / Soap ***has*** the *property* of removing dirt. ¶These hot springs are said to ***possess*** healing *properties*. この温泉は病気にきくそうだ.

Q have ***bactericidal*** *properties* 殺菌性がある. ¶***curative*** *properties* 治ゆ性. ¶The blood of living animals possesses extraordinary ***germicidal*** *properties*. 動物の生血には非常な殺菌性がある. ¶***health-giving*** *properties* of travel 旅行の健康増進性. ¶The serum of the blood has ***microbe-killing*** *properties*. 血清には殺菌性がある. ¶The food is destitute of ***nourishing*** *properties*. その食物は栄養分にとぼしい. ¶***physical*** *properties* 物理的性質.

P dispose ***of*** one's *property* by sale or otherwise 私財を売却とかその他の方法で始末をつける. ¶a medicine ***with*** this *property* この性質を備えた薬.

P² Sweetness is a *property* ***of*** sugar. 甘いのは砂糖の特性だ. ¶*property* ***of*** the verb 動詞の性質. 【類】Bitterness is a *property* ***of*** tea.

prophecy, *n.* 予言.

V The development of the situation ***baffles*** our *prophecies*. 時局の展開はわれわれの予想を許さない. ¶The *prophecy* was ***fulfilled***. その予言は実現した. ¶I will ***venture*** a *prophecy* as to ... 私は...につきあえて予言する.

V² The *prophecy* ***came*** to pass. その予言通りになった. ¶The *prophecy* ***came out*** true. その予言が当った. ¶The *prophecy* ***turned out*** (=proved) to be true. 予言が当った.

Q ***Dire*** were their *prophecies* of disaster. 彼らの災害の予言は恐ろしかった. ¶the ***gloomy*** *prophecies* of the pessimists 厭世家の憂うつな予言. ¶a ***rash*** *prophecy* 軽率な予言. ¶it is a ***safe*** *prophecy* that ... ...というのは間違いのない予言だ. ¶a ***startling*** *prophecy* 驚くべき予言.

P It is ***beyond*** *prophecy* それは予言の限りでない.

prophesy, *v.* 予言する.

M ***boldly*** *prophesy* 大胆に予言する.

P² *prophesy* [***of***] famine ききんを予言する. ¶*prophesy* ***to*** a nicety ... 正確に...を予言する.

O *prophesy* a severe earthquake 強震を予言する.

prophet, *n.* 予言者, 予告者.

V it ***requires*** a *prophet* to predict that ... 予言者ならでは...の予言はできない. ¶A *prophet* has ***sprung*** (=***risen***) ***up***. 一人の予言者が現われた.

Q a ***bad*** *prophet* 先見の明のない人. ¶a ***false*** *prophet* 偽予言者. ¶the ***Mormon*** *prophet* モルモン教主. ¶***No*** *prophet* is accepted in his own age. 自分の生きてる間は先覚者は世の中に受入れられない. ¶a ***sad-visaged*** *prophet* 悲しげな顔つき付きの予言者. ¶a ***self-appointed*** *prophet* 自称予言者. ¶a ***weak-kneed*** *prophet* 気の弱い予言者. ¶a ***wild*** *prophet* 途てつもない予言者.

Q² a ***weather*** *prophet*=(米) a weatherman 天気予報者.

P He sets up ***for*** a *prophet*. 彼は予言者だと自称している.

P² a *prophet* ***of*** evil 凶事を予言する人 ‖ a *prophet* ***of*** air power 空軍の先覚者.

prophetic, *a.* 予言する.

P a sign *prophetic* ***of*** good (evil) 吉(凶)兆.

prophylactic, *n.* 予防具.

Q² a ***rubber*** *prophylactic* [避妊用]ルーデサック.

propitiation, *n.* 慰め.

P ***as*** a *propitiation* of God 神の慰めとして.

propitious, *a.* 都合のよい.

P weather *propitious* ***for*** the trip 旅行に具合のよい天候. ¶*propitious* ***to*** the enterprise (undertaking) その計画(など)に都合のよい.

proponent, *n.* 提唱者.

Q² a ***birth control*** *proponent* 産児制限提唱者.

proportion, *n.* 比例, 割合; 釣合い; 部分; *pl.* 大きさ, 広さ.

V ***alter*** the *proportions* of ... ...の比率を変更する. ¶***assume*** *proportions* which seem to threaten danger 今にも危険になりそうな勢いを見せる ‖ ***assume*** unduly bulky *proportions* 不当に大きな容積となる, 余りに重要視されるようになる. ¶The industry has ***attained*** large *proportions*. その産業は盛んになった. ¶His reputation ***bore*** no *proportion* to his merit. 彼の名声は真価とは釣合わなかった. ¶The *proportion* of cost for wages was ***estimated*** at (=to be) £100 to £135 in 1913. 工費と労銀の割合は一九一三年には百ポンド対百三十五ポンドと概算された. ¶it ***forms*** but a small *proportion* of ... それは...の一小部分に過ぎない. 【類】***form*** a large *proportion* of the buyers. ¶***mix*** the proper *proportions* 適当の割合に混ぜる. ¶***monopolize*** a preponderating *proportion* of ... ...の優位を独占する. ¶***preserve*** due *proportion* 適当の均衡を保つ. ¶***reach*** such colossal *proportions* こんなにぼう大な割合になる. ¶We only ***realize*** a small *proportion* of powers inherent in coal. われわれは石炭に含まれたエネルギーのほんの一部を利用するに過ぎない. ¶The workmen *receive* a *proportion* of the profits. 労働者は利益の分前をもらう. ¶*recognize* the due *proportion* of things 適当な振合を看取する.

Q in *adjusted proportions* ちゃんとつり合って. ¶All is in *admirable proportion*. すべて非常にうまくつり合がとれている. ¶assume *alarming proportions* 驚くべき割合になる. ¶He is of *ample proportions*. でっぷり太っている. ¶a *big proportion* 大部分. ¶*compound proportion* 複比例. ¶in a *considerable proportion* of cases 相当多くの場合において. ¶... and water in *equal proportions* ...と等量の水. ¶increase in *exact proportion* to ... ...と正比例で増加する. ¶a *fair proportion* of people 相当多数の人々. ¶of *fair physical proportions* 相当体格のしっかりした. ¶The *proportions* of the building are *faulty*. その建物は均斉がとれていない. ¶in a *full proportion* 実物大に. ¶a lock-out of *gigantic proportions* 大規模の工場閉鎖. ¶a *goodly proportion* of ... ...のかなりの部分. ¶The *proportion* of ... to ... is surprisingly *high*. ...に対する...の比は驚くほど高い. ¶a building of *huge proportions* 大建築物. ¶The industry attained *important proportions*. 工業が大いに発展した. ¶it is of *insignificant proportion* as compared with ... それは...に比べるとお話にならない. ¶in *inverse proportion* to ... ...に反比例して. ¶a *large proportion* of the earth's surface 地球の表面の大部分. 【類】 a *large proportion* of the profit. ¶an athlete of *magnificent proportions* りっぱなからだの選手. ¶Unemployment assumed *menacing proportions*. 失業者が恐ろしくふえてきた. ¶*no small proportion* of ... ...の大部分. ¶be in *perfect proportion* to ... ...と完全に調和がとれている. ¶in the *proper proportion* 適当の割合で. ¶*reciprocal proportion* 反比例. ¶in *reverse proportion* 反比例して. ¶assume *ridiculous proportions* ばかばかしい割合になる. ¶it has the *right proportion* of ... それには...が適当に配合してある. ¶assume *serious proportions* 大事になる. ¶in *similar proportion* 同様の割合で. ¶*simple proportion* 単比例. ¶form a very *small proportion* of the large numbers その大きな数のほんの小部分を占める. ¶The business attained *stupendous proportions*. 商売が途方もなく発展した. ¶see things in their *true proportions* 物の軽重を正しく見る. 【類】 see his faults in their *true proportions*. ¶Farmers are holding out an *undue proportion* of their rice produce for their own tables. 農夫は自家用分としての保有米を多くとり過ぎている. ¶It is mixed with *various proportions* of water. それに種々の割合で水を混ぜる. ¶Bell-metal is a compound of copper and tin, in *varying proportions*. 鐘銅は色々の割合に銅とすずを混ぜ合わした物だ. ¶assume *vast proportions* 大きな数(量)に達する; 大事になる.

Q² The rice crop turned out to be one of *record proportions*. 米作は記録的なものとなった.

P He has a great taste for art, but his critical ability is not *in proportion*. 彼は美術には十分趣味を持っているが鑑識力は割合にない. ‖ *In proportion* as the structure of a government gives force to public opinion, it is essential that public opinion should be enlightened.—Washington. 政治組織が世論に勢力を与えれば与えるほど世論を啓発することが肝要になる. ‖ the addition to the water of lysol *in* the *proportion* of 1/4 to 1/2 per cent. リゾール水を四百倍ないし二百倍の水に薄めること. 【類】 *in* the *proportion* of three to one / The air becomes cooler *in proportion* to the height of the ground. ‖ *in proportion* to ... ...に準じて, ...に比例して. 【類】 Men's wants become greater *in proportion* to the increase in their possession. / He is cleverer than you [are] *in proportion* to his years. / His expenditure is not *in proportion* to his means (収入). / The camel possesses strength *in proportion* to its size. ¶grow up *into* quite formidable *proportions* [危険の程度まで]非常に恐ろしい割合になる. ¶The building is *out of proportion*. その建物はつり合が取れていない. ‖ exaggerate *out of* all *proportion* 途方もなく誇張する ‖ His extravagance is *out of proportion* to his means. 彼のぜいたくは収入につり合わない. 【類】 *out of* all *proportion* to ... / be utterly *out of proportion* to ... ‖ be *out of proportion* with ... ...と調和がとれていない. 【類】 entirely *out of proportion* with ... ¶ore *with* a small *proportion* of gold 少量の金を含んだ鉱物.

P² A *proportion of* the apples proved rotten. そのりんごの一部分は腐っていることが分った. ‖ the *proportion of* meat *to* bones in a fowl 鶏の肉と骨との比率. ¶the *proportion of* ... *for* every 100,000 inhabitants 住民十万ごとに...の割合 ‖ The *proportion of* women holds very low. 婦人の数の割合は非常に低い. ¶the *proportion of* births *to* the population 人口に対する出生の割合. 【類】 the *proportion* or percentage *of* deaths *to* the population for any given period / the *proportion of* iron *to* nickel in a meteorite (いん石) / The *proportion of* births *to* deaths is as 3 to 1. / The *proportion of* Chinese *to* Japanese residents in Manchukuo at present is ranging one hundred to one.

proportion, *v.* つり合はせる.

M The designs in the rug are *well proportioned*. その敷物の模様はしっくりしている.

P We must *proportion* the punishment *to* the crime. 犯罪に刑罰をつり合わせなければならない.

proportional, *n.* 〘数〙比例数.

Q a *mean proportional* 〘数〙比例中項.

proportional, *a.* 比例して.

M be *directly proportional* to ... ...に正比例する. ¶*inversely proportional* to ... ...に反比例して.

P be *proportional* (=in proportion) *to* ... ...につり合う. 【類】 The increase of wages *proportional to* the rise in price.

proportionate, *a.* 比例した.

M *directly* (*inversely*) *proportionate* to ... ...に正(反)比例した.

P The profit is *proportionate to* the amount spent. 利益は出費に準じる. 【類】 a sum of money *proportionate to* one's means (所得).

proportionately, *ad.* 比例して.

P *proportionately with* the increase of product 生産の増加に比例して.

proportioned, *a.* つり合った.

M *well* (*ill*) *proportioned* to ... ...によくつり合った(つり合わない).

proposal, *n.* 申込, 提案; 計画; 結婚申込.

V *accept* a *proposal* 申込を承諾する. ¶*adopt* a *proposal* 提案を採用する. ¶*advance* a *proposal* on ... ...に関して提案する. ¶*advocate* a *proposal* 提案を弁護する. ¶should the *proposal* be *approved* 提案が承認されれば. ¶The *proposal* was *carried* with acclamation. 提案は拍手喝采で通過した. 【類】 The *proposal* was *carried* by a considerable majority. ¶The *proposal* was never *carried out*. その提案は一向実行されなかった. ¶*confound* a *proposal* 提案をののしる. ¶He *countered* my *proposal* with one of his own. 彼は私の提案に対して自案を持ち出した. ¶*decline* a *proposal* 申込を謝絶する. ¶The *proposal* to ... was *defeated* by a large majority. ...すべき提案は大多数で否決になった. ¶The *proposal* was *dropped*. 提案は撤回された. ¶*encourage* a *proposal* 結婚の申込みをするように持ちかける. ¶*entertain* a *proposal* 申出を採用する. ¶*enunciate* a *proposal* 提案を陳述する. ¶I *have* a *proposal* to make to this meeting. 私にはこの会に提出すべき案がある. 【類】 You must *have* a more definite *proposal*. ‖ I have *had* a *proposal*. 私は結婚の申込を受けた. ¶*Hear* his *proposal*. 彼の案を聞き給え. ¶*make* a *proposal* to ... ...に申入れる(縁談など). ¶*offer* (=make) a *proposal* of marriage 結婚を申込む. ¶*put forward* definite *proposals* for ... ...に関する明確な案を提出する. ¶*receive* a *proposal* 縁談の申込を受ける. ¶*refuse* a *proposal* 申込を拒絶する. ¶be compelled to *reject* the *proposal* 余儀なくその申入を拒絶する. ¶*scout* a *proposal* 申込をはねつける. ¶*spurn* a *proposal* in cold blood すげなく申込をはねつける. ¶*start* a *proposal* 提議を起す. ¶*submit* a *proposal* 提案する. ¶The *proposal* was most enthusiastically *supported*. その提案はきわめて熱心に支持された. ¶*take up* a *proposal* 申出を採用する. ¶*turn down* a *proposal* 申込を拒絶する. ¶*withdraw* a *proposal* 申込を撤回する.

V² The *proposal came* to nothing. 提案は失敗に終った. ¶The *proposal fell through*. 提案は採用されなかった. ¶The *proposal* does not *suit*. その提案は不適当だ.

Q *concrete proposals* 具体的な提案. ¶make a *counter proposal* [先方の申出に対し]改めて申出をする. ¶a *fair* and *reasonable proposal* 公平でもっともな提議. ¶make *immoral proposals* to a woman 婦人に不義を持掛ける. ¶an *impracticable proposal* 実現性のない案. ¶make *indecent proposals* みだらなことを言掛ける. ¶*legislative proposals* which have been recommended to the consideration of the Congress by this Department 同省から議会に審議に付した立法案. ¶A fair and ***reasonable proposal*** will have attention. 公正で筋の通った提言は傾聴されよう. ¶a ***repugnant*** *proposal* 面白くない提案. ¶It is too ***ridiculous*** *proposal* to deserve discussion. それはあまりばかげていて論じるに足らない. ¶***sealed proposals*** 入札書. ¶Your *proposal* is not sufficiently ***tempting.*** 君の申込は飛びつきたいというほどのものではない. 【類】 decline a very ***tempting*** *proposal.* ¶We may venture upon one or two ***tentative*** *proposals.* 一, 二の案を試験的に提出してみよう.

Q² submit a ***compromise*** *proposal* 妥協案を出す. ¶a ***leap-year*** *proposal* うるう年の求婚(うるう年には婦人からの求婚が許される). ¶a ***paper*** *proposal* (＝plan) 机上案. ¶a ***reform*** *proposal* 改革案.

P He threw cold water ***on*** my *proposal.* 彼は私の提案にけちをつけた. ¶agree ***to*** one's *proposal* その提議に同意する ‖ respond ***to*** a *proposal* 申込みに応じる.

P² a *proposal* ***for*** its remedy その救済案. ¶a *proposal* ***of*** marriage ***to*** … …への結婚の申込. ¶a *proposal* ***to*** a meeting 会合の申込.

propose, *v.* 申込む; 推薦する.

P *propose* Mr.… ***as*** president …氏を会長に推薦する ‖ It was *proposed* ***as*** the place for the meeting. それが会の場所に提案された. ¶*propose* a person ***for*** membership 人を会員に推す. ¶the object I *propose* ***to*** myself 私の考えている目的 ‖ *propose* ***to*** oneself the question "…?"「…」の問題を自己の心に問う ‖ *propose* ***to*** a woman 求婚する.

O He *proposed* to pool part of what they had earned. もうけの一部を共託にしようと提議した.

proposition, *n.* 提案, 提議; ((米)) 仕事; ((米口)) しろもの, 手合.

V we decline to ***accept*** the *proposition* その提案は引受けられない. ¶the *proposition* ***carried*** by 20,000 majority 二万の多数で通過した建議案. ¶***champion*** the *proposition* that … …の提案を支持する. ¶***controvert*** a *proposition* 提案を論ばくする. ¶The *proposition* was ***defeated.*** その建議案は敗れた. ¶***enunciate*** a *proposition* 提案を陳述する. ¶***establish*** the *proposition* beyond dispute 進言を異議なきまでに解明する. ¶***make*** a *proposition* 建議する. 【類】 He ***made*** a *proposition* to buy out his rival's business. ¶The *proposition* ***strikes*** us as an exceedingly rash one to hazard. その提案を出して見るのは無謀に失するように思われる.

Q offer an ***attractive financial*** *proposition* 有利な財政上の条件を提供する. ¶Now the popular magazine is what we moderns call a ***commercial*** *proposition.* そもそも通俗雑誌というものは新しい言葉でいうと一つの営業である. ¶It's a ***different*** *proposition.* それは問題が別だ. ¶It is not an ***economic*** *proposition.* そろばんのとれない話だ. ¶not strictly an ***educational*** *proposition* 厳密の意味での教育課目ではない(中学校の野球のように). ¶It is an ***impossible*** *proposition.* それはできない相談である. ¶***incontrovertible*** *propositions* 議論の余地のない提議. ¶a ***money-making*** *proposition* 営利事業. ¶a ***paying commercial*** *proposition* 引き合う商売. ¶It is a ***practicable*** *proposition.* それはできない相談ではない. 【類】 as a ***practical*** *proposition.* ¶a reasonable *proposition* もっともな提案. ¶Englishmen regard lecturing as a free amateur entertainment rather than a ***serious economic*** *proposition.* 英国人は講演をまじめな経済的問題よりもむしろしろうとの無料娯楽といった風な考え方をしている. ¶a ***tough*** *proposition* やっかいな代物. ¶a ***workable*** (an ***unworkable***) *proposition* 実行できる(実行不能の)提案.

Q² a ***business*** *proposition* 商売上の提案. 【類】 a practical ***business*** *proposition* / City planning is a ***business*** *proposition* of the first importance. ¶***marketing*** *proposition* [食料品などの]購入計画. ¶a ***paying*** *proposition* 引合う仕事.

P It is a great pleasure to meet you ***on*** this *proposition.* このお申込に応じることのできるのは非常に愉快です.

proprietor, *n.* 所有者, 持主.

Q That store is now run by a successor of its ***former*** *proprietor.* あの店は代が替った. ¶a ***land[ed]*** *proprietor* 土地所有者, 地主.

Q² a ***business*** *proprietor* 事業者. ¶a ***colliery*** *proprietor* 炭鉱業者, 炭鉱主. ¶a ***hotel*** *proprietor* ホテル所有者(ホテルの主人). ¶a ***part*** *proprietor* 一部分だけの所有主. ¶a ***well-to-do peasant*** *proprietor* 裕福な小農(自作農).

P² the *proprietor* ***of*** a business 事業主 ‖ a *proprietor* ***of*** patent medicines 売薬業者 ‖ the *proprietor* ***of*** the establishment 社主.

propriety, *n.* 適当, 正確; 適否; 礼儀.

V ***attain*** *propriety* よろしきを得る. ¶***dispute*** the *propriety* of a construction 解釈の適否を問題にする ‖ Its *propriety* has been much ***disputed.*** その当否が大いに論じられた. ¶***doubt*** the *propriety* of … …の適否を疑う. ¶***know*** the *proprieties* 礼儀を知る. ¶***observe*** the *proprieties* 礼儀を守る. ¶***outrage*** *propriety* 礼儀を無視する. ¶I question the *propriety* (wisdom) of doing so. そうするのはどうかと思う. ¶***violate*** *propriety* 礼儀にはずれる.

Q a word or expression that is of ***doubtful*** *propriety* 適切かどうか疑わしい語句. ¶No rowdiness, no drunkenness, no discordant bawling of songs of ***dubious*** *propriety.* 粗暴な振舞をしたり, 酒びたりになったり, いかがわしい歌を調子はずれに怒鳴り立てたりする者は一人もない ¶***punctilious*** *propriety* やかましい作法. ¶conduct of ***questionable*** *propriety* いかがわしい行動.

P a breach ***of*** *propriety* 無礼 ‖ They had at least some sense ***of*** *propriety.* 彼らには少くとも多少礼儀の念があった. 【類】 He is lost to all sense (全く無感覚) ***of*** *propriety.* ¶it might ***with*** greater *propriety* be termed "…" それは「…」と称するのが一層適当かも知れない ‖ speak and write ***with*** *propriety* 正しく話しかつ書く. 【類】 words and expressions which could not ***with*** *propriety* be read in a family.

propulsion, *n.* 推進.

Q² ***jet*** *propulsion* 噴射推進.

pros and cons, *phr.* 可否の議論.

V carefully ***weigh*** the *pros and cons* of the bargain その取引の可否をとくと考える. 【類】 ***weigh*** without prejudice or preconceived notions all the *pros and cons.*

Q ***some*** *pros and cons* of theatrical life for women (Chinese dress) 女子俳優生活(など)の可否.

proscription, *n.* 禁止.

P the *proscription* ***against*** Christianity キリスト教の禁止.

prose, *n.* 散文.

V Not many people these days can ***read*** *prose* aloud acceptably. 今日満足に散文を朗読しうる者は沢山ない. ¶The barber ***tempers*** the *prose* of his occupation with the poetry of gossip. 理髪師はその職業の平凡さを世間話でいく分慰めている.

Q express oneself in ***graceful*** and ***correct English*** *prose* 優雅で正確な英文で自己を表現する. ¶speak ***plain English*** *prose* 平易な英語を話す. ¶***vigorous*** and ***flexible*** *prose* 力強く自由奔放な散文.

Q² ***non-fiction*** *prose* 小説以外の散文. ¶in ***twentieth century*** English *prose* 二十世紀の英国散文では. ¶the writer of ***workaday*** *prose* 日用文を書く人.

P write ***in*** good *prose* りっぱな散文で書く. ¶a writer ***of*** *prose*＝a prose writer 散文家.

prosecute, *v.* 起訴する.

P *prosecute* him ***for*** violation of the laws 法律違反で彼を起訴する ‖ be *prosecuted* ***for*** a breach of the Election Law (選挙法違反). 【類】 He was *prosecuted* ***for*** bigamy (重婚).

prosecution, *n.* 遂行; 起訴, 訴追.

V ***escape*** *prosecution* 訴追を免れる. ¶*Prosecution* will be ***instituted*** against the offending persons. 犯罪人は起訴される.

V² *Prosecution* will ***follow*** violation of the order. 秩序を乱す者は告発される.

Q ***criminal*** *prosecution* 犯罪の訴追.

P ***for*** the *prosecution* of studies 学術研究のため.

prospect, *n.* (**1**) 見晴し, 眺望; 風景; 向き.

V It ***affords*** an extensive *prospect* of the sea and distant hills. そこから海や遠い山々を広く見晴す. ¶***command*** a broad (＝wide) *prospect* of … …を広く見渡せる. ¶***enjoy*** the *prospect* with a telescope 望遠鏡でながめる. ¶The mountain ***gives*** a commanding *prospect.* あの山へ登れば見晴しはすてきだ. ¶The hotel ***has*** a good *prospect.* そのホテルは眺望がよい. ¶A tall building ***shuts out*** the *prospect* in that direction. 高い建物でその方向の眺望がさえぎられている. ¶one of the most superb *prospects* in all Japan may be ***viewed*** from … 全日本における最も絶佳

なる風景の一つは…からながめられる.「開している.

V² A fine *prospect* ***spreads around.*** 絶佳な眺望が周囲に展

Q a ***bleak*** *prospect* 荒涼たる眺め. ¶a ***delightful*** *prospect* 目を喜ばす風景. ¶a ***distant*** *prospect* of … …の遠景. ¶The *prospect* is ***entrancing.*** その風景は人をうっとりとさせるものがある. ¶It commands a ***fine*** *prospect* over some gardens. 庭園の見晴らしが好い. ¶The room has a ***southern*** *prospect.* そのへやは南向きになっている. 【類】There is not such another ***splendid*** *prospect* in all Japan. ¶an ***unpicturesque*** *prospect* 醜い景色.

P The *prospect* ***from*** my window is pleasant. 私の窓からの眺望は気持がよい.

(**2**) 将来の見込, 目あて, 予想; 《米》買気のある客.

V All *prospects* of an immediate war are ***abandoned.*** あらゆる即戦の可能性はなくなった. ¶everything ***betokened*** a fair *prospect* for a successful issue to … すべてが…にりっぱな結果をもたらすべき吉兆を示した. ¶***becloud*** the *prospect* of … …の前途を暗くする. ¶***blight*** one's *prospects* or hopes その前途の希望を曇らす. ¶***brighten*** the *prospects* 前途の望みを明るくする. ¶***carry*** *prospects* on free trips 《米》買いそうな客を無料で運ぶ. ¶***compromise*** its *prospect* その前途を危くする. ¶***face*** the *prospect* of … …となる予定である. ¶***Have*** you any *prospect* of improvement? いくらか改善の見込があるか. 【類】They ***have*** a good *prospect* opened before them. / They ***have*** no *prospects* of becoming rich. / We ***have*** (=There are) *prospects* of fine weather all through the season. ¶***hold out*** a *prospect* of … …の有望を示す ‖ It ***holds out*** *prospects* of a less gorgeous hue. その前途はそれほど有望でない. ¶My *prospects* have been ***nipped*** in the bud. 私の前途の望みは出端をくじかれた. ¶***offer*** a very promising *prospect* for … …は前途きわめて有望だ. ¶The *prospect* is ***regarded*** as illusory. その見込は架空的と見なされる. ¶I did not ***relish*** the *prospect* of standing the night in their company. 夜通し彼らと一緒に過したくなかった. ¶I ***see*** every *prospect* of success. どう見ても成功する. 【類】I ***see*** no *prospect* of promotion (昇進).

V² there ***appears*** no immediate *prospect* of … 差当り…の見込がないらしい. ¶The *prospects* of business have ***become*** more encouraging. 商売の前途はますます有望になった. ¶My *prospects* are ***looking up.*** 私の前途の望みは立ち直って来た.

Q Is there ***any*** *prospect* of success? 成功の望みがあるか. ¶a youth with ***bright*** *prospects* 前途洋々たる青年. ¶***brilliant*** *prospects* 輝かしい前途. 【類】*prospects* seem ***bright*** for … ¶*Prospects* are more ***cheering.*** 前途はますます頼もしい. ¶***commercial*** *prospects* 商売の将来性. ¶***cotton crop*** *prospects* in … …における綿花収穫予想. ¶*Prospects* are ***critical.*** 前途は危い. ¶The *prospects* are ***depressing.*** 前途の模様は暗たんたるものがある. ¶*Prospects* are very ***doubtful.*** 前途はおぼつかない. ¶The *prospects* are ***encouraging*** (***discouraging***). 前途は頼もしい(頼り少ない). ¶There is ***every*** *prospect* of the conclusion of the war. どう見ても戦争は終局を告げそうだ. 【類】There is ***every*** *prospect* of the rain continuing for some days. ¶He has ***excellent*** *prospects* before him. 彼の前途はすこぶる有望だ. ¶there is a very ***fair*** *prospect* that … …という見込が十分ある. ¶***favorable*** *prospects* 有望な前途. ¶a ***gloomy*** *prospect* 暗たんたる前途. 【類】when our *prospects* were ***gloomiest.*** ¶There is a very ***good*** *prospect* of cure. 大丈夫直りそうだ. 【類】He has a ***good*** *prospect.* / He has ***good*** *prospects* of being elected. / It has a ***good*** *prospect* of continuance. ‖ strike a ***good*** *prospect* よい鉱脈を見つける. ¶He has a ***great*** *prospect* before him. 彼は前途きわめて有望である. ¶There is no ***immediate*** *prospect* of improvement. さしあたり好転しそうもない. ¶There is ***little*** *prospect* of his recovery. 彼の回復はまず見込がない. 【類】There is ***little*** *prospect* of lower prices at present. / I have ***little*** *prospect* of success. / a man of small talent and ***little*** *prospects.* ¶There is ***no*** *prospect* of selling at your price. 君の値段では売れそうもない. 【類】there is ***no*** *prospect* yet of his success. ¶***pecuniary*** *prospects* 財政の前途. ¶*Prospects* are very ***remote.*** 前途りょう遠だ. ¶He has such ***shining*** *prospects.* 彼の前途はさん然としている. ¶with ***some reasonable*** *prospect* of success 成功の見込が相当あって. 【類】There is ***some*** *prospect* of improvement. ¶The *prospects* of the crop are ***splendid.*** 作柄の見込は上乗だ. ¶a man of a ***thousand*** *prospects* 多方面の人. ¶without ***visible*** *prospect* of a speedy change for the better 急に善くなるというはっきりした見込もなく. ¶***what*** *prospect* have you of …? …についての見込はいかが.

Q² ***Business*** *prospects* are fair (poor) 商売は有望(など)だ. 【類】improve one's ***business*** *prospects* / fair (=good) ***business*** *prospects* ‖ weigh fall ***business*** *prospect* 秋の景気を勘考する. 【類】forecasts of future ***business*** *prospects.* ¶lots of ***buying*** *prospects* 《米》多数の買いそうな客. ¶***crop*** *prospects* 作柄の予想. ¶the distant (immediate) ***future*** *prospect* 遠い(近い)将来の見込み. ¶***Employment*** *prospects* for this year's college graduates appear to be brighter than last year's. 今年度の大学卒業生の就職見込みは昨年度より明るい. ‖ ***future*** *prospcts* 将来の見込. ¶***harvest*** *prospects* 収穫予想. 【類】This year's ***harvest*** *prospects* are poor. ¶***Job*** *prospects* are bright. 就職予想は明るい. ¶***long-range*** *prospects* for … …に対する長期の予想. ¶there are poor ***trade*** *prospects* for … …の貿易は見込み薄 ‖ rosy ***trade*** *prospects* 明るい貿易の前途.

P Her heart had been breaking all day ***at*** the *prospect* of parting. 彼女は別離を控えて終日胸を痛めていた. ¶Men plough and sow ***in*** *prospect* of the coming harvest. 人は来る収穫を見込んですいたりまいたりする. ‖ I have nothing ***in*** *prospect* at present. 今の所見込は私には何もない. ‖ He has two new plays ***in*** *prospect.* 彼は二種の新しい劇を企画中. ‖ diplomatic changes achieved or ***in*** *prospect* 今までやったもしくは今後やるべき外交上の変化 ‖ Business in war risks at insurance offices has largely increased ***upon*** the *prospect* of a war. 保険会社における戦争保険の業務は戦争近しの予想に大繁忙を来している. ¶***with*** every *prospect* of … どう見ても…しそうで. ¶The work is ***without*** *prospect.* その仕事は見込がない.

P² a hopeful *prospect* ***for*** a distant future 遠い将来に対する有望な見込. 【類】The *prospects* ***for*** the crop are very disheartening. ¶a *prospect* ***of*** a good harvest 豊作の見込 ‖ a *prospect* ***of*** the future state 将来の状態の予想 ‖ There is no *prospect* ***of*** success. 成功の見込がない. 【類】The *prospects* ***of*** the rice crop are splendid. / the *prospects* ***of*** fruits next season / The *prospects* ***of*** grain next season are very good (poor). ‖ There is a *prospect* ***of*** the renewal of the war. 戦争再開のおそれがある.

prospective, *a.* 予期された.

O the *prospective* home-owner 家を持とうとしている人 ‖ a *prospective* bride 近々花嫁になる女.

prospect, *v.* 試掘する.

P *prospect* ***for*** gold (oil) 金(石油)の試掘をやる.

prospectus, *n.* 趣意書, 規則書.

V a *prospectus* of a proposed company is ***issued.*** 会社の設立趣意書が発行されている. ¶***See*** the *prospectus* for further detail. 詳細は(学校などの)案内を参照されたい.

Q a ***full explanatory*** *prospectus* 詳細な解説趣意書.

P² *Prospectus* ***on*** application. 申込次第規則書進呈.

prosper, *v.* 繁盛する, 成功する.

M Cheats ***never*** *prosper.* 詐欺は決して成功しない. ¶Wicked men ***often*** *prosper* in this world. 現世では悪人でも往々成功する. ¶His business has *prospered* ***well.*** 彼の商売は繁盛した.

P Nothing will ever *prosper* ***in*** his hands. 彼の手では何一つうまく行くまい. ¶Everything *prospers* ***with*** him. 彼はすることなすこと皆成功する.

prosperity, *n.* 繁栄, 隆盛.

V ***attain*** *prosperity* 繁栄する. ¶***benefit*** *prosperity* 繁栄に資する. ¶This ***bespeaks*** commercial *prosperity.* これで商業の隆盛なことが分かる. ¶***destroy*** *prosperity* 繁栄を破壊する. ¶***drink*** the *prosperity* of the cause 杯をあげてその公益事業の隆盛を祝う. ¶***enhance*** the *prosperity* of the country 国運の隆盛を助ける. ¶***gain*** (***enjoy***) *prosperity* 繁盛する. ¶Since that time it has ***had*** uninterrupted *prosperity.* それ以来引続き成功して来た. ¶***injure*** the *prosperity* of … …の繁栄を傷つける. ¶the city ***owes*** its *prosperity* most of all to … 市はその隆盛をなかんずく…に負うている. ¶***restore*** *prosperity* 繁栄を回復する. ¶***seek*** a material *prosperity* by industrial expansion 工業の拡張によって物質的の繁栄を求める. ¶***threaten*** seriously the *prosperity* of the town 大いに町の繁栄をおびやかす. ¶I *wish* you all *prosperity*. 御成功を祈る.

V^2 Britain's *prosperity* ***depends*** upon foreign trade. 英国の隆盛は外国貿易による. ¶The *prosperity* of the town is ***waning*** (=***declining***). その町は衰微しつつある.

Q a town of ***decreasing*** *prosperity* 衰え行く都市. ¶the ***highest*** *prosperity* 最盛. ¶a magazine devoted to the advancement of the ***industrial*** and ***commercial*** *prosperity* of Japan 日本商工業の発達を図る雑誌. ¶***material*** *prosperity* 物質的な繁栄. ¶foundations of ***national*** *prosperity* 国家隆盛の基礎 ‖ a constant brake on the wheel of ***national*** *prosperity* 絶えず国家の隆盛を阻害するもの. ¶There will be experienced a ***sounder*** and more ***permanent*** *prosperity* than ever before. 以前に増して一層堅実な一層永久性のある繁栄を見ることであろう.

Q^2 enjoy ***business*** *prosperity* 商売が繁盛する. ¶at the peak of the ***Coolidge*** *prosperity* クーリッジ景気の最盛期に. ¶***world*** *prosperity* 世界の好景気.

P decline ***in*** *prosperity* 衰微する.

P^2 the *prosperity* ***of*** the country 国家の隆盛. 【類】the *prosperity* ***of*** business.

prosperous, *a.* 富裕な; 好都合な.

M ***financially*** *prosperous* 財政的にゆたかな.

P it looks *prosperous* ***for*** … …は上首尾らしい. ¶the weather *prosperous* ***for*** growing wheat 麦まきによい天候.

prostitute, *n.* 売春婦, 娼婦.

Q a ***clandestine*** *prostitute* 私しょう. ¶a ***reformed*** *prostitute* 正業に復したしょう婦. ¶an ***inscribed*** *prostitute* 登録されたしょう婦. ¶a ***male*** *prostitute* 男しょう. ¶an ***open*** (***concealed***) *prostitute* 公(私)しょう. ¶a ***registered*** (***licensed***) *prostitute* 登録した(鑑札のある)しょう婦.

prostitute, *v.* 売春する, 節を売る.

P *prostitute* oneself ***for*** living 生活のために売春する. ¶*prostitute* oneself ***to*** the enemy 敵に通じる.

prostitution, *n.* 売春.

V ***banish*** *prostitution* out of the town 売春を町から追放する. ¶The public opinion ***condemns*** (***supports***) *prostitution*. 世論は売春を非とする(支持する). ¶***enter*** *prostitution* 苦界に身を沈める. 【類】their circumstances and reason which have caused them to ***enter*** *prostitution*. ¶***permit*** *prostitution* for the avoidance of greater evils 一層はなはだしい害悪を防ぐために売春を許す. ¶women who ***practice*** *prostitution* under cloak of other occupations 他の職業に偽装して売春をする女. 【類】***practice*** *prostitution* for money. ¶***repress*** *prostitution* by severe enactments きびしく売春を取締る. ¶vigorous attempts to ***uproot*** *prostitution* きびしい売春征伐.

Q ***clandestine*** (***professional***) *prostitution* 私(公)しょう制度. ¶the transformation of ***cloistered*** *prostitution* into free prostitution 制区しょう制度の散しょう制度への変更. ¶***commercialized*** *prostitution* 職業化した売春. ¶***interned*** (***scattered***) *prostitution* 制区(散)しょう制度. ¶***male*** *prostitution* 男しょう行為. ¶***private*** *prostitution* 私しょう[行為]. ¶***sacred*** (***secular***) *prostitution* 聖(俗)しょう. ¶***state-regulated*** *prostitution* 公しょう制度. ¶***unlicensed*** *prostitution* 私しょう行為.

Q^2 ***full-time*** (***part-time***) *prostitution* 本職(内職)の売春.

P^2 *prostitution* ***of*** learning 曲学阿世 ‖ the *prostitution* ***of*** one's genius (talent) 天才(才能)の悪用.

prostrate, *a.* 屈した.

P lie *prostrate* ***before*** … …の前に屈する(平伏する). ¶be *prostrate* ***beneath*** the tyranny of the oppressor 圧制者の暴虐に屈する.

prostrate, *n.* 平伏させる; 衰弱させる.

P They *prostrated* themselves ***before*** the emperor. 彼らは皇帝の前に平伏した. ‖ *prostrate* oneself ***before*** rank and wealth 位と富に屈する. ¶He was *prostrated* ***by*** heat (disease, overwork). 彼は熱(など)で参っていた. ‖ crops *prostrated* ***by*** a hurricane 暴風で吹倒された作物. ¶He is *prostrated* ***with*** sorrow (grief, failure). 彼は悲嘆(などに)暮れている.

prostration, *n.* 平伏; 衰弱.

Q ***nervous*** *prostration* (=break-down) 神経衰弱.

P ***with*** many *prostrations* 平身低頭して.

P^2 *prostration* ***before*** the altar 祭壇前の平伏. ¶*prostration* ***of*** mind and spirit 心神の衰弱.

protagonist, *n.* 大立物.

P^2 a *protagonist* ***for*** Calvinism カルヴィン派の大立物. ¶a *protagonist* ***of*** naturalism 自然主義の首唱者.

protect, *v.* 保護する, 防護する.

M It is ***effectively*** *protected* against the attacks of bacteria. それは細菌に犯されないよう有効に防護されている.

P *protect* oneself ***against*** the danger 危険に対して身を護る ‖ *protect* him ***against*** fraudulent imitation 不正な模倣をされないように彼を保護する. 【類】*protect* a tree ***against*** the frost / *protect* one's country ***against*** the invaders (aggression) / *protect* a person ***against*** a disease / *protect* the fair fame of our nation ***against*** shame and scandal. ¶The book is *protected* ***by*** copyright. その本は著作権の保護を受けている. 【類】This machine is *protected* ***by*** U.S. and foreign patents. ¶*protect* a person ***from*** harm (evil, danger) その害(など)を防ぐ. ¶*protect* oneself ***with*** a shield 盾で防ぐ.

protection, *n.* 保護, 防護; 保護物.

V It ***affords*** *protection* against weather. それが風雨を防いでくれる. ‖ ***afford*** little *protection* from theft 泥棒の用心が悪い. ¶***furnish*** them *protection* 彼らに保護を与える. ¶***give*** *protection* to … …に保護を与える. ¶The weak and the aged ***need*** the *protection* of the state. 弱者や高齢者は国の保護を要する. ¶***provide*** adequate *protection* from wind and weather 適当な風雨よけを準備する. ¶***receive*** *protection* 保護を受ける.

Q a ***capital*** *protection* against … りっぱな…よけ. ¶I owe my life to your ***kind*** *protection*. 私が今生きていられるのは君が保護してくれたおかげだ. ¶***mutual*** *protection* 相互の保護. ¶***various*** *protections* against moths 虫よけの色々な設備.

Q^2 ***fire*** *protection* 防火. ¶under ***government*** *protection* 政府の保護の下に. ¶***peace*** *protection* 保安. ¶apply for ***police*** *protection* 警察の保護を願い出る. ¶***rust*** *protection* さび止め.

P We live ***under*** the *protection* of the government. われわれは政府の保護の下に生活する.

P^2 a *protection* ***against*** the sun (fire, lightning, moths, frost) 日(など)よけ ‖ wear woollen clothing as a *protection* ***against*** cold 防寒に毛織の衣服を着る ‖ The dog is a *protection* ***against*** burglars. 犬は泥棒の用心になる. ‖ *protection* ***against*** eyestrain 視力[の過労の]保護. ¶a *protection* ***for*** the head 頭おおい. ¶a *protection* ***from*** the wind (cold, disease 風(など)よけ. ¶*protection* ***of*** the weak 弱者の保護. 【類】the *protection* ***of*** war industries ‖ *protection* ***of*** property (所有権).

protectionist, *n.* 保護貿易論者.

Q^2 a ***dyed-in-the-wool*** *protectionist* 生粋の保護貿易論者.

protective, *n.* 保護物.

P^2 a *protective* ***against*** the devil 魔よけ.

protector, *n.* 擁護者.

Q a ***fervent*** *protector* of peace 平和の熱心な擁護者.

Q^2 a ***chest*** *protector* 胸当て. ¶a ***plant*** *protector* 植物の風(雪)よけ. ¶a ***point*** *protector* 鉛筆(ペン)のキャップ.

protectorate, *n.* 保護権.

V ***establish*** a *protectorate* over … …に対する保護権を確立する.

P These islands are ***under*** the French *protectorate*. この諸島はフランスの保護下にある. 【類】It is ***under*** the *protectorate* of the British government.

P^2 Britain's *protectorate* ***over*** Malaya マライに対する英国の保護権.

protein, *n.* 〖生化学〗たん白質.

Q^2 ***animal*** and ***vegetable*** *protein* 動物質及び植物質たん白.

protest, *n.* 抗議, 異議申立; 抗議書.

V ***address*** a *protest* to … …に抗議を申込む. ¶it ***aroused*** a vehement *protest* on the part of … それが…の方の猛烈な抗議を呼び起した. ¶It ***caused*** some *protest* and indignation. それが多少の抗議と公憤の種となった. ¶***direct*** one's *protest* against … その抗議のほこを…に向ける. ¶the criticism ***drew*** a *protest* from … その批評が…からの抗議を招いた. ¶***draw forth*** a strong *protest* from … …から強硬な抗議を呼び起す. ¶I must ***enter*** a *protest* against the verdict. 私はその評決に対して異議を唱えなければならない. ¶***evoke*** some *protest* 多少の物議をかもす. ¶It ***excited*** bitter *protest* from many sources. それは各方面からの痛烈な抗議を呼び起した. ¶***extend*** *protest* to … 異議を…に申出る. ¶he had to ***face*** *protests* from … 彼は…からの抗議に直面しなければならなかった. ¶***file*** a vigorous *protest* against … …に対して強硬な抗議を提出する. 【類】***file*** a formal *protest* with the Government. ¶ *launch* a *protest* 異議を持出す. ¶ *lodge* a strong *protest* against ... …に強硬な異議を申込む. 【類】 *lodge* a *protest* with a person (committee). ¶ *make* a *protest* against ... …に異議を唱える. 【類】 when one sees ..., it is time to *make* a *protest*. ¶ *prepare* a *protest* against ... …の抗議の準備をする. ¶ *present* a *protest* against ... …に異議を申立てる. ¶ *put* a *protest* before the authorities 当局に異議を申立てる. ¶ *put* (=*send*) *in* a written *protest* against the proceeding of ... …の処置に対する抗議書を提出する. ¶ *raise* (=enter) a *protest* 抗議を申立てる. 【類】 He *raised* his *protest* in Parliament against some infringement (侵害) of workmen's rights. ¶ *register* a *protest* against ... …の抗議書に記名する. ¶ *sign* a *protest* against ... …の抗議書に署名する. ¶ *utter* their *protests* in vain いたずらに異議を唱える. ¶ *voice* a *protest* 異議を唱える.

V[2] the *protest seems* an idle one when we consider that ... その抗議は一方…を考えるとばからしく思われる.

Q make an *active protest* against ... …に盛んに異議を唱える. ¶ a *clamorous protest* ごうごうたる抗議. ¶ a most *earnest protest* 非常に熱心な抗議. ¶ an *emphatic protest* 熱心な抗議. ¶ a *feeble protest* 腰の弱い抗議. ¶ He made no *further protest*. 彼はそれ以上抗議はしなかった. ¶ a *futile protest* 無益な異議. ¶ a *mild protest* 穏当な抗議. 【類】 make a rather *mild protest*. ¶ enter an *official protest* against ... …に正式の抗議を申込む. ¶ a *scathing protest* きびしい抗議. ¶ arouse *sharp protests* 鋭い抗議を呼び起す. ¶ a *stern protest* 断固たる抗議. ¶ a *strong protest* 強硬な抗議. ¶ The suggestion was met with a chorus of *vehement protest*. その提議は一斉に猛烈な抗議を浴びせられた. 【類】 A *vehement protest* arose from ..., but to no avail. ¶ a *vigorous protest* 強硬な異議. ¶ a *violent protest* 猛烈な異議. ¶ a *wholesome protest* 有益な抗議.

P *in protest* against ... …に憤慨して, …に抗議して. ¶ She drummed the table softly with her fingers, as if *in protest* against the waste of time. ‖ He wrote to The Times *in protest*. 彼はタイムズ社へ抗議文を送った. ¶ a slight murmur *of protest* 不服のかすかなささやき. ¶ accept *under protest* 異議あることを保留して受入れる ‖ sign *under protest* 不承不承署名する. 【類】 pay the amount claimed *under protest* / give in (譲歩する) *under protest*. / sign a bill of lading (船荷証券) *under protest*.

P[2] a *protest against* ... …に対する抗議. ¶ a *protest for* nonpayment (nonacceptance) 〘商〙 支払(引受)拒絶証書. ¶ *With* that the *protests* subsided. それで不平も収まった.

protest, *v.* 言い張る; 抗議する.

M *emphatically protest* against ... …にきっぱりと不承知を言う. ¶ *protest strongly* against ... …に強硬に反対する. ¶ *timidly protest* こわごわ抗議する. ¶ I wish to *protest vehemently* against a certain paragraph in Mr. ...'s article. …氏の文中の一節に対して大いに異議を唱えたい. ¶ *protest vigorously* against a measure 政策に対して強硬に反対する. ¶ *protest warmly* やっきとなって抗議する.

P I must *protest against* ... 私は…に異議を唱えねばならない. 【類】 it is being *protested against* very strongly by ... / *protest against* the measure (政策).

protestation, *n.* 抗議.

P *protestation against* the ratification of the treaty 条約の批准に対する抗議. ¶ *amid* laughing *protestation* だめだと一笑に付せられて. ¶ He accepted this idea *without protestation*. 彼は異議なくこの意見を容れた.

P[2] a *protestation of* innocence (loyalty, faith) 無実(など)の申立て(確言).

protocol, *n.* 議定書, 協約書.

Q the *industrial protocol* of 1910 in the clothing trades of New York City ニューヨーク市の一九一〇年に締結した衣類貿易に関する産業暫定協定.

Q[2] the *London protocol* of 1852 〘外交〙 一八五二年のロンドン議定書.

P[2] a *protocol of* a conference 会議の議事録 ‖ a *protocol of* examination 尋問調書 ‖ a *protocol of* on-the-spot inspection 検証調書.

prototype, *n.* 原型; 模型, 手本.

Q almost a *tailored prototype* for ... …にほとんどうってつけの型.

P It has been moulded *on* the German *prototype*. それはドイツの原型にならって造ったものだ. ¶ *without* a *prototype* or a subsequent rival 古今独歩.

P[2] The life of the London art student is very much more prosaic than that of his *prototype at* Paris or Munich. ロンドンの美術学生の生活はパリやミュンヘンのそれよりははるかに没風流だ. ¶ his *prototype in* life 氏の(作中の)モデルとなった人物. ¶ the *prototype of* ... …の元祖. ¶ the *prototypes of* the characters [劇などの]登場人物のモデル ‖ the *prototype of* the school その学校の前身.

protract, *v.* 延ばす, 長引かせる.

P The war was *protracted during* (=*for or through*) four years. 戦争は四年間続いた. ¶ *protract* one's stay *for* ten days 滞在を十日間延ばす.

protracted, *a.* 長引いた.

M a *much protracted* disease ひどく長引いた病気.

protraction, *n.* 引延ばし.

Q a *purposeful protraction* of peace negotiation 平和交渉の故意の引延ばし.

P[2] the *protraction of* debate (negotiation) 論議(交渉)の引延ばし.

protrude, *v.* はみ出る.

M His eyes *somewhat protrude*. 彼は少し出目だ.

P *protrude from* one's pocket ポケットからはみ出る.

proud, *a.* 誇る; 気位の高い; 光栄に思う.

M she is *childishly proud* of ... 彼女は子供くさく…を誇っている. ¶ be *justifiably proud* of ... …を誇っているがそれはもっともである. ¶ Americans are *justly proud* of the West Point Military Academy. 米国人がウェスト・ポイント士官学校を誇るのはもっともなことだ. ¶ He is *too proud* to complain. 彼は気位が高くて中々ぐちをこぼさない. ‖ be *too proud* to beg こじきをするを潔しとしない. 【類】 She is *too proud* to do it. ¶ he might *well* be *proud* of ... 彼が…を誇るのももっともだ.

P people *proud in* mind 心のおごった人々. ¶ Some people are rather *proud of* being ignorant of punctuation. 句読法などを知らないのをむしろ得意がっている人もある. ‖ I am *proud of* your friendship. 貴下との親交を光栄とする. 【類】 England is *proud of* the fact that ... / These are poets *of* whom any country might be *proud*. / He is naturally very *proud of* the royal appreciation (認識).

O You do me *proud*. 光栄の至りです.

provable, *a.* 証明できる.

M a story *historically provable* 歴史的に証明のできる話.

prove, *v.* 証明する; …と判明する.

M be *amply proved* by ... …によって十分に証明されている. ¶ *amply* and *irrefutably prove* that ... …なることを反対できないように十分に証明する. ¶ *prove* oneself *capable* of doing it それをやりうる能力を示す. ¶ these figures perfectly *prove clearly* that ... これらの数字は…なることを十分明りょうに証明する. 【類】 go to *prove clearly* that ... ¶ *prove clearly* and *indisputably* 明りょうに異論のないように証明する. ¶ The pupil *proved* more *clever* than his teacher. 生徒の方が教師よりも利口だった. ¶ medical experience has *conclusively proved* that ... 医術の経験で…を決定的に証明した. ¶ He *proved faithful* to his master. 彼はその主人に忠実であることが分かった. ¶ The statement *proved false* (*incorrect*). その陳述は虚偽だった(間違っていた). ‖ *prove false* to his trust 彼の信頼にそむく. ¶ The wound *proved fatal*. それは致命傷だった. ¶ The plan *proved impossible*. その計画は不可能だった. ¶ *prove incontestably* 議論の余地なきまでに証明する. ¶ The union *proved infertile*. その結婚には子供ができなかった. ¶ "*not proven*" 「証拠不十分」. ¶ It *proved otherwise*. そうでないことが分かった. ¶ be *presumptively proved* by the fact that ... …という事実によって推定上証明される. ¶ It *proved* very *puzzling* to a foreigner. それは外国人には非常に不思議だった. ¶ The measure *proved salutary*. その方策は有益だと分かった. ¶ if the ownership can be *satisfactorily proved* その所有権が満足に証明できれば. ¶ *prove statistically* 統計的に証明する. ¶ The report *proved true*. 報告が本当だった. ¶ I generally find that if a thing is cheap, it *ultimately proves* to be a deception. 物が安ければ結局にせ物だと分かるのが普通だ. ¶ *undoubtedly prove* 確実に証明する. ¶ The venture *proved unsuccessful*. その試みは不成功だった. ¶ He *proved* very *useful*. 彼は非常に役に立った. ¶ He *proved* himself *worthy* of confidence. 彼は自己の信用するに足ることを示した.

P It has been *proved against* him. それは彼に不利益に証明された. ¶ *prove beyond* a possibility of doubt 疑を容れる余地のないように証明する. ¶ *prove* it *by* arithmetic 算術

的にそれを証明する ‖ It has been *proved by* evidence. それは証拠をあげて証明された. ¶That is yet to be *proven by* his further experiments. それは今後の彼の実験によって明かになるだろう. ☞ proven (*p.p.*) は英語では archaic だが米語では現代の用法である. 例: He has already *proven* himself a bold speaker. ¶It was *proved from* another fact. それは別の事実から証明された. ¶It will *prove of* little use. それは余り役に立たないだろう. ‖ *prove of* no avail 利用価値がないことが分かる. 【類】 *prove of* no use / it will *prove of* permanent value to ... / *prove of* service to ... / cannot but *prove of* immense advantage to ... / be sure to *prove of* interest to ... ¶It *proved to* his advantage. それは彼の利益だった.

O *prove* to be an imposter 詐欺師であることが分かる. 【類】 The rumor *proved* [to be] true.

provenance, *n.* 出所, 伝来.

V *settle* the *provenance* of an antique 古物の伝来を決定する.

Q a piece of pottery of *doubtful provenance* 伝来不明の陶器.

P It is *of* Chinese *provenance.* それは中国伝来だ.

proverb, *n.* ことわざ; 通りもの.

V the Japanese *have* a *proverb* which says in effect "..." 日本人間には「...」という意味のことわざがある. ¶there is a *proverb* which *runs* (=*goes*) "..."「...」ということわざがある. ¶as the *proverb says* ことわざにいわゆる.

Q *cheap proverbs* 安っぽいことわざ. ¶a *curious proverb* relating to mirrors 鏡に関する珍奇なことわざ. ¶a *homely proverb* よく人の口にのぼることわざ. ¶a *false proverb* 道理の間違ったことわざ. ¶a *sententious proverb* 奇警なことわざ. ¶a *vulgar proverb* 通俗なことわざ.

P speak *in* a *proverb* ことわざを混ぜて話す. ¶pass *into* a *proverb* ことわざになる, 評判になる. ¶He is punctual *to* a *proverb.* 彼が時間を厳守するのは有名なものだ. ‖ Women are hard-lived *to* a *proverb.* 女はことわざにも言うように命みょうがなものだ.

P^2 He is a *proverb for* punctuality.=His punctuality is proverbial. あの人は時間を守る点では有名だ. ‖ He is a *proverb for* inaccuracy (stinginess, inefficiency). 彼のずぼら(など)は有名なものだ. ¶a *proverb relating to* ... ...に関することわざ. ¶He was made a *proverb to* all the people. 彼は人の笑い草となった.

proverbial, *a.* ことわざのような, 有名な.

P he has become *proverbial for* ... 彼は...で有名になった. ‖ He is *proverbial for* his stupidity (inaccuracy, stinginess). 彼はぽんつく(など)で有名だ.

O sell for the *proverbial* song 二束三文で売る.

provide, *v.* 準備する; 支給する; 条件として規定する; 日用品を給与する.

M *provide adequately* for the support of one's wife after one's death 自分の死後妻の生活に十分備える. ¶except as otherwise *expressly provided* 別段の規定ある場合の外. ¶*provide handsomely* for wife and children 妻子がりっぱに暮せる用意をする. ¶*provide liberally* for one's family 家族をらくに暮させる. ¶They are *ill provided* with food. 彼らは食物が不十分だ. ¶He has *provided well* for his children (old age). 彼は子供たち(老後)に心配のないよう十分用意した. 【類】 They are *well provided* with clothing.

P *provide against* accidents (emergency, the evil day, unemployment) 不慮(など)の用意をしておく ‖ the law *provides against* ... その法律には...を罰する規定がある. 【類】 *provide against* a rainy day (困難のとき) / *provide against* the enemy's attack / *provide against* a time of necessity or distress. ¶it is *provided by* resolution that ... 決議で...ということが規定されている. ¶*provide for* their children livelihood 子供らの生計の方法を立てる ‖ *provide for* the future (one's old age) 将来(など)に備える. 【類】 *provide for* contingencies (万一) / cannot *provide for* all who want them / *provide* materials *for* carrying on an enterprise / *provide* special trains *for* the guests (来賓) ‖ It is *provided for* in the contract. そのことは契約書に書いてある. 【類】 The rules are *provided in* the law. / as *provided for* in Rule 221. ¶*provide* money *to* him=provide him with money 彼に金銭を支給する. ¶The rules are *provided under* the regulations. 規則は条例の下に規定されている. ¶*provide* a building *with* fire escapes 建物に非常はしごを付ける ‖ *provide* her *with* an allowance 彼女に仕送りをする. 【類】 regularly *provide* one's son *with* money / *provide* soldiers *with* employment on demobilization (除隊) / *provide* him *with* a work of compilation (編集の仕事) / *provide* the poor *with* work and wages / be *provided with* everything we need for living / *provide* a person *with* whatever he needs / travellers *provided with* (=holding) first-class tickets / be *provided with* weapons against the attacks of wild beasts.

providence, *n.* 神慮, 神わざ; [P-] 神.

V inwardly *bless Providence* for ... ...に対してひそかに神を賛美する. ¶To do a rash act is to *tempt Providence.* 軽率なことをするのは進んで神罰を受けようとするも同然だ.

V^2 *Providence decided* for him. 彼に天の助けがあった.

Q *Divine Providence* 天の配剤, 神慮. ¶The *wise providence* of Heaven. 天の摂理.

P *by* God's *providence* 天の配剤で ‖ *by* wise *Providence* よくしたもので. ¶This is *like Providence!* これはまるで神業だ. ¶trust *to* (=*in*) *providence* [運を]天に任せる. ¶*with* no *providence* for the rainy day あればありしたがいで. ¶a visitation *of Providence* 災難.

P^2 *providence of* God=Divine Providence 神の摂理.

provident, *a.* 用意深い, 勤倹な.

P He is *provident of* his money. 彼は金銭につましい. ‖ He is *provident of* the future. 彼は先きの用意が周到だ.

provider, *n.* 供給する人(もの).

Q a *good* (*poor*) *provider* 《米》 働きのある(ない)人. ¶a *universal provider* よろず屋 ‖ a *universal provider* of knowledge [百科辞典など]知識の宝庫.

providing, *n.* 備え付け.

Q in a motor-car of one's *own providing* 自家用車で.

province, *n.* 領分; 地方; 本領, 権限, 職掌.

V *discover* new *provinces* (=phases) of inquiry 研究の新方面を発見する. ¶Suggestion *enters* the *province* of medicine. 暗示は医術の領分にはいる. ¶a theatrical company *touring* the *provinces* 地方巡業中の役者の一座.

Q Where is your *native province?* お国はどちらですか. ¶But it is not *our province* to speak of these. しかしこの話をするのはわれわれの権限ではない. ¶the *proper province* 本領. ¶his *special province* 彼の独壇場. ¶its *true province* その本領. ¶*woman's province* 女子の本領.

P be *beyond* my *province* 私のはたけではない ‖ it is *beyond* the *province* of this article to ... ¶It is situated at a village called Takata, *in* the *province* of Kai. それは甲斐国の高田村にある. ‖ it is not *in* my *province* (=business) to ... ...するのは僕の職掌でない. ¶It lies *outside* the *province* of the police. それは警察の権限外だ. ¶That kind of work is not *within* my *province.* そういう仕事は僕の本領でない. 【類】 It is not *within* our *province* to inquire. / it does not come *within* the *province* of my subject to ... 域.

P^2 the *province of* chemistry (literature) 化学(など)の領域.

O a society whose *province* is to ... ...するのを本領とする協会.

provision, *n.* (**1**) 用意, 設備; [法律の]規定; 配剤.

V This *provision* has since *abolished.* この規定はその後廃止になった. ¶*carry out* the *provisions* of a law 法律上の規定を実行する. 【類】 *carry out* the *provisions* of the Potsdam Declaration (ポツダム宣言). ¶*enact* a *provision* 条項を規定する. 【類】 *provisions enacted* in these regulations (条例). ¶*follow out* the *provisions* of a will 遺言状の条項を実行する. ¶*make provision* for a system of ... ...の制度を設ける ‖ *make provision* against rainy days (accidents) 不慮の用意をしておく. 【類】 *make provision* for one's children (old age) / *provision* must be *made* for the future / He has made *little provision* for the future. ¶*respect* the *provision* of the treaty 条約の条項を尊重する. ¶Any person who shall *violate* any *provision* of this ... shall be punished by a fine of not more than ... or by imprisonment for not exceeding ... days. この...の条項のいずれかを犯す者は...以下の科料または...日を越えない禁固に処せられる.

Q *adequate provision* has been made for ... ...に対する適当な対策がたてられている. ¶make very *ample provision* for the maintenance of machinery 機械維持のために(積立などをして)十分の準備をする. ¶a most *desirable provision* 最も好ましい用意(設備). ¶there is no *direct provision* that ... [法律などに]...の直接の規定はない. ¶an *educational provision* 教育上の設備. ¶an *express provision* [法律の]明文. ¶*general provisions* 一般規定. ¶He made a *handsome provision* for her and hers. 彼は彼女ならびにその子供らのために手厚い生活上の用意をした. ¶there is no *legal provision* for ... ...に対する法律上の規定はない. ¶a *liberalized provision* [法律の]寛大な規定. ¶a *liberal provision* of seats in a park 公園における豊富な腰かけの設備. ¶a *merciful provision* of Nature 天の配剤. ¶*penal provisions* 罰則規定. ¶*punitive provisions* 罰則. ¶take for public use under *special provision* of the law 特別法の条項によって収用する. ¶a *sufficient provision* for the educational needs of Ireland アイルランドの教育上の必要を満たすに十分な設備. ¶*supplementary provisions* 付則.

Q^2 Under a *closed-shop provision*, union membership is a requirement for employment. クローズド・ショップ法により組合員の資格が就職の条件となっている. ¶the *key provision* of the pact その条約の主要条項. ¶*seniority provision* 年功規定. ¶*State provision* 国家的施設. ¶Under a *union-shop provision* an employe must join a union within a specified time after being employed. ユニオン・ショップ法によると雇用人は就職後一定期間内に組合に加入しなければならない.

P make charge *as* a *provision* for the cost of maintenance 経常費に当てるため料金を徴収する. ¶*in accordance with* (=*according to*) the *provisions* of Article I. 第一条の規定により. ¶*under* the existing *provision* 現行の規定で. 【類】*under* the *provisions* of paragraph III. of the Protocol of Brussels of October 20th, 1934.

P^2 *provision against* accidents (emergency, old age) 不慮(など)の用意. ¶*provision for* old age and injury 老年および廃疾に対する施設 ‖ the *provision for* out-of-door recreation 戸外娯楽の設備 ‖ *provision for* cleanliness 浄化施設. 【類】provision *for* merry-go-round, wooden horses, and other *provision for* children's amusements. ¶a *provision in* nature 自然の配剤. ¶the *provision of* God 神の配剤. 【類】the *provision of* facilities for the use of ... / the *provision of* national parks.

(2) 食料品, 食糧.

V *lay in provisions* 食糧を蓄える. ¶*lay up provisions* 糧食を貯蔵する. ¶I *require provisions* for the journey. 旅行用の食糧が要(い)る.

V^2 *Provisions fell* (−*ran*) *short*. 食糧が不足した. ¶The *provisions* will *suffice* for three weeks. 食糧は三週間は足りる.

Q *tinned* (=*canned*) *provisions* かん詰食料品.

Q^2 *food provisions* 食料品.

P a dealer *in provisions* 食料品商. ¶a shortage *of provisions* 糧食の欠乏 ‖ We ran short *of provisions*. われわれは食糧が不足した. ¶run *out of provisions* 食糧がなくなる.

provision, *v.* 糧食を供給する.

M *well provisioned* 糧食の供給の豊かな.

P The ship is *provisioned for* two months. その船は二カ月分の糧食を積込んでいる. ‖ The castle is *provisioned for* a siege. その城にはろう城用の糧食が貯えてある. ¶They are *provisioned with* seven days' rations. 彼らは七日の食糧を支給されている.

proviso, *n.* ただし書.

V *add* the *proviso* that ... ...というただし書を添える. ¶I must *make* it a *proviso* that I am absolutely free to ... 私が...して一向差支ないということをぜひ条件としたい.

provocation, *n.* ちょう発, 刺激.

V *give provocation* 怒らせるようなことをする ‖ *give provocation* to laughter 笑わせる.

Q a *gross* and *flagrant provocation* ひどいむき出しのちょう発. ¶without *real provocation* 実際腹を立てることもないのに. ¶She blushes on the *slightest provocation*. 彼女はすぐ赤くなる. ¶*wilful provocation* of disorder 悪意の秩序かく乱.

P be guilty *of provocation* 怒らせた罪がある. ¶resort to force (torture) *on* the least *provocation* 少しでも気にさわると暴力に訴える(拷問にかける). ¶commit a crime *under* great *provocation* 腹立ちまぎれに罪を犯す ‖ composure *under provocation* 気にさわることをされても動じないこと. ¶entirely *without provocation* from ... ...から全く何も気にさわることはされないのに.

P^2 There was no *provocation for* such an angry letter. こんなにまで腹を立てた手紙をよこすほどのこともなかった.

P^2 *provocation to* anger 立腹させること.

provocative, *a.* ちょう発的な.

M The book is *highly provocative*. 同書は示唆に富む.

P *provocative in* appearance 服装がちょう発的な. ¶a smile *provocative of* criticism 非難を招きやすい微笑の仕方 ‖ be *provocative of* sorrow (mirth) 悲しみ(喜び)の種となる. 【類】a scene *provocative of* a laughter (fright).

provoke, *v.* 怒らせる, そそる.

M *enough* to *provoke* a saint 聖人でも怒らせるほどの. ¶His father was *greatly provoked*. 彼の父は非常に怒っていた.

P I am *provoked at* his impudence. 彼の無礼には腹が立つ. ¶*provoked beyond* endurance かんにん袋の緒(お)を切って. ¶*provoke* a person *to* anger 人を怒らせる. 【類】Oppression *provoked* the people *to* rebellion. / *provoke* a person *to* a smile.

provoking, *a.* じれったい, 腹が立つ.

M *How provoking!* 本当に腹が立つ. ¶It is *most provoking*. 実にじれったい.

prowess, *n.* 勇気, 武勇.

Q *military prowess* 武勇. 【類】Japan owes her position as one of the great powers a good deal to her *military prowess*.

P crew and scullers *of* no mean *prowess* 非常に勇敢な乗組員とこぎ手.

prowl, *n.* はい回, 歩き回り.

V *take* a *prowl* うろつく.

P be *on* the *prowl* [盗人などが]うろついている.

prowl, *v.* はい回する.

M Wild animals *prowl here* at night. この辺は夜になると野獣が出没する.

P He *prowled about* his room. 彼は室内を歩き回った. ¶beasts *prowling after* their prey えさをあさって歩き回る野獣.

prowler, *n.* うろつく人.

Q a *cold-slough prowler* 《口語》あき巣ねらい.

proximity, *n.* 接近.

Q His house is in *close proximity* to a park. 彼の家は公園に隣接している. 【類】The ground lies in *close proximity* to the school. ¶The buildings are in *immediate proximity* to the sea. その建物は海のすぐ近くに建っている. ¶The house is in *no hazardous proximity*. その家屋は(火災保険の)危険区域内にはいっていない. ¶two taxis in *perilous proximity* 危険なほど接近した二台のタクシー.

P *in* the *proximity* of a town 町の近くに.

P^2 *proximity of* blood 近親 ‖ the *proximity of* war 戦争の切迫. ¶*proximity to* natural resources, such as coal and iron 石炭・鉄などの天然資源の産地への隣接. ¶bring ... into close *proximity with* ... ...を...のすぐそばへ持って来る.

proxy, *n.* 代理, 代理人.

V *send* one's *proxy* その代理を出す.

Q the *Emperor's proxy* 陛下のご名代.

P No member shall vote *by proxy*. 会員は代人で投票してはいけない. ‖ marriage *by proxy* 代理人結婚(米国で戦時中に行われたもの). 【類】The address was read *by proxy*.

P^2 be (=stand) *proxy for* ... =represent ... ...の代理をする.

prudence, *n.* 慎重, 思慮分別.

V He *combines prudence* with zeal. 彼は熱心であってしかも慎重である. ¶*exercise prudence* in dealing with ... ...を処置するに思慮分別を働かせる. ¶*Use* your *prudence* a bit more. もう少し慎重にやりたまえ.

Q a *short-sighted prudence* 短見的な思慮.

P a man *of prudence* 大事をとる人. ¶He acted *with prudence*. 彼は用心してやった.

prudent, *a.* 慎重な.

M He was *prudent enough* to keep away from the danger. 彼は用心深くその危険を避けた.

P be *prudent in* utterance 言葉を慎む.

prudery, *n.* おとなしぶり.

V America is *throwing off* the *prudery* of the past 米国は過去のおとなしぶりを振り棄てつつある.

prudish, *a.* 上品ぶった, すました.

P *prudish in* manner 気どった(すました)態度で. 【類】*prudish in* her gait (speech, dress).

prune, *v.* 刈り込む.

M *prune away* 刈り込む; むだをはぶく. 【類】*prune away* the adjectives (superfluities).

M^2 *prune off* (=*down*) dead branches 枯れ枝を切りとる.

pry, *v.* 目をつける, せんさくする.

M^2 *pry up* a stone with a pickax つるはしで石を掘り返す.

P *pry about* a house 家の中をじろじろ見る. ¶*pry into* one's personal affairs 人の私事をせんさくする.【類】*pry into* another's secrets (人の内幕) / *pry into* one's family affairs. ¶*pry* a secret *out of* a person ある人の秘密をさぐり出す.

prying, *n.* せんさく.

Q an *impertinent prying* into ... ...への失礼なせんさく.

psalm, *n.* 賛美歌.

V *sing* a *psalm together* 賛美歌を合唱する.

P² The *Psalm of* Life (ロングフェローの)人生賦.

pseudo-argument, *n.* こじつけのへりくつ.

Q *far-fetched pseudo-argument* へりくつ.

pseudonym, *n.* 変名, 仮名.

V *adopt* a masculine *pseudonym* [George Eliot など]男の変名を採用する. ¶*use pseudonyms* 色々な仮名を使用する.

Q under *various pseudonyms* 色々な仮名を使って.

P write *under* a *pseudonym* 変名で書く.【類】publish it *under* the *pseudonym* of "..."

psychologist, *n.* 心理学者.

Q an *industrial psychologist* 産業にをける心理専門家.

Q² a *speech psychologist* 言語心理学者.

psychology, *n.* 心理学; 心理.

V *analyse* the *psychology* of ... ...の心理を分析する.

Q *criminal psychology* 犯罪心理学. ¶*comparative psychology* 比較心理学. ¶*educational* (=*pedagogical*) *psychology* 教育心理学. ¶*experimental psychology* 実験心理学. ¶He has an unusual knowledge of *feminine psychology* 彼は女性の心理を非常によく知っている. ¶a problem in *human psychology* 人間心理の一つの不可解な点. ¶*juvenile* (=child) *psychology* 児童心理学. ¶understand *male* (*female*) *psychology* 男(女)性心理を理解する. ¶*social psychology* 社会心理学.

Q² *children psychology* 児童心理学. ¶*folk psychology* 民族心理. ¶*mob* (=*mass*) *psychology* 群衆心理(学).

P *in* the *psychology* of crowds 大衆心理で.

puberty, *n.* 妙齢, 思春期.

V *attain* (=*arrive at or reach*) *puberty* 年ごろになる.

P The venereal desire commences in man *at puberty*. 人間の色情は思春期に発動する. ¶the age *of puberty* 春機発動の年齢.

public, *n.* 公衆; 社会; 界, 連中.

V *address* a wider *public* もっと広い範囲の公衆に呼び掛ける. ¶the desire to *attract* an ignorant *public* 無知の公衆を引きつけようとする望み. ¶*benefit* the *public* 公衆を益する. ¶*cajole* the *public* 公衆をだまし込む. ¶A bus is a motor-car which *carries* the *public* on a small fare. バスはわずかな料金で公衆を運搬する自動車である. ¶*deceive* the *public* by selling them ... 公衆を欺いて...を売付ける. ¶*defraud* the *public* 公衆を欺く. ¶*educate* the *public* in ... ...の点で大衆を教育する.【類】high-class dramatic performances to *educate* the *public* to higher standards / the *public* at large must be *educated* to an understanding that ... ¶*enlighten* the *public* as to ... ...に関して公衆を啓発する. ¶*exclude* the *public* from a trial 公開をやめる. ¶*exploit* the *public* 大衆を搾取する. ¶*fool* the *public* 公衆を愚ろうする. ¶*impress* the *public* 公衆に感銘を与える. ¶*instruct* the *public* in ... 公衆に...を教える. ¶*interest* the Western *public* in Japanese travel 西洋国民の間に日本旅行の興味を持たせる. ¶*invite* the *public* to ... ...するように公衆を誘致する. ¶The newspaper *leads* the *public*. 新聞紙は公衆を指導する. ‖ it is liable to *lead* the *public* to think that ... そうするとややもすれば公衆に...と思わせる. ¶*misguide* the buying *public* 一般購買者を惑わす. ¶*mislead* the *public* 公衆を誤らす. ¶The newspaper enables its advertisers to *reach* as large a *public* as possible. その新聞に広告すると最大範囲の公衆に行き渡る. ¶The *public* are *requested* to enter their names in the book. どなたもこの帳簿に御記名を願います. ¶*serve* the *public* 公衆のために尽す. ¶Today a silent *picture strikes* the sound-educated *public* as more or less of an oddity. 今日では無声映画はトーキーになれた公衆には多少変に感じられる. ¶*take* the *public* into complete confidence concerning ... ...を腹蔵なく大衆に発表する ‖ *take* a new *public* 新方面の需要を作る ‖ The novel *took* the *public* by storm. その小説はたちまち一般の人気を博した. ¶The *public* are *warned* not to negotiate the draft. その手形を割引しないように一般の方々に御注意申上げる. ¶*win* one's *public* その聴衆(読者)の心を捕える.

Q an *author's public* 一作家の愛読者層. ¶The *British public* are much more alive than they were 20 years ago to the uses of education. 英人は二十年前よりも教育の価値にはるかに目覚めてきた. ¶a *car-hungry public* 自動車ファン. ¶the *charitable public* 慈善界. ¶the *discerning public* 眼識のある公衆. ¶the *discriminating public* 目のある人々. ¶the *English-speaking* and *English-reading public* 英語を話し英文を読む社会. ¶the *film-hungry public* 映画ファン. ¶meet the changing moods of a *fickle public* 気紛れの公衆の御機げんを取る. ¶the author's *favorite public* その作家の愛読者たち. ¶before the *foreign public* 外国の公衆の前で. ¶These meetings are secret as far as *general public* are concerned. これらの会は一般公衆からは秘密になっている. ¶the *ignorant emotional public* 無知で感情的大衆. ¶His novels appeal to an *immense public*. 彼の小説を愛読するものは非常に多い. ¶the *inquisitive public* せんさく好きな世間. ¶It was eagerly read by *interested public*. それは興味を持つ公衆に熱心に読まれた. ¶The book should appeal to a *large public*. その本は一般公衆がおもしろがるだろう. ¶the *lay public* しろうとの方々. ¶the *motoring public* 自動車に乗る連中. ¶the *musical public* 音楽愛好者たち. ¶a *small* but *kindly public* 少数だが親切な人々. ¶the *theatrical public* 芝居好きの連中. ¶The novelist has a *vast public*. その作家は広い支持層をもっている. ¶receive the attention of a *wide public* 広く世間から注目される.

Q² the *buying public* 消費者層 ‖ catch a *buying public* 買手を引きつける. ¶He mulcted the American *investment public* of \$... through dishonest methods of "bookkeeping." 彼はいわゆる帳簿上のからくりによってアメリカの一般投資者から...ドルの金をだまし取った. ¶the *listening public* [ラジオの]聴取者層. ¶the *movie-going public* 映画ファンたち. ¶the *music-loving public* 音楽愛好層. ¶the *novel-reading public* 小説愛読者たち. ¶the *playgoing* (=*theater-going*) *public* 好劇家連. ¶extension of the *reading public* 読者層の膨張.【類】appeal to the *reading public*. ¶the *restaurant-eating public* 料理屋の常連. ¶the *show-going public* レビューを見に行く連中. ¶the *sporting public* スポーツ界. ¶the *student public* 一般学生. ¶the *theater-going* (=*playgoing*) *public* 好劇家たち. ¶a guide for the *traveling public* 旅行家への指針. ¶the *tourist public* 観光界. ¶the *world public* 世界の大衆.

P appear *before* the *public* [文士など]世に出る ‖ be *before* the *public* as a lecturer 講演者として立っている ‖ The subject is now *before* the *public* and the pros and cons are in every one's mouth. その問題は今や公衆の前に提示され銘々可否の議論を戦わしている.【類】The translation has been put *before* the *public* for the first time. / The scheme has been *before* the *public* for some years. / The actor retired from the stage after having been *before* the *public* more than 40 years. / people who are much *before* the *public*. ¶Though praised *in public*, he was abused behind. 彼は人前で賞められて, かげでくさされた.【類】It is not to be said *in public*. / I am not used to speaking *in public*. / I don't want to be seen *in public*. / He is nervous (おじおじする) *in public*. / behave *in public* as if the public did not exist. ¶a large section *of* the *public* is ... 公衆の大部分は...だ. ¶It is open *to* the *public*. それは公開している.

P² the *public at* large 一般社会, 大衆.

publication, *n.* 公表; 出版; 出版物.

V *bear publication* 出版に値する. ¶The magazine *began* [its] *publication* in January, 1927. その雑誌は一九二七年一月に創刊された. ¶The magazine has *ceased publication*. その雑誌は廃刊した. ¶The manuscript is so good that it *deserves publication*. 原稿はよくできてるので出版する価値がある. ¶*finance* the *publication* of his book at his own expense 自費で出版する. ¶*hold up* the *publication* of a book 書籍の刊行を禁止する. ¶*license* the *publication* of a book ある本の出版を許可する. ¶I found it difficult to *obtain publication*. 私はそれを出版するのは困難であることを知った. ‖ it failed to *obtain publication* until ... それは...までは出版されなかった. ¶*suppress publications* 出版物の発売を禁止する.【類】*suppress* the *publication* of trash (だ本). ¶*suspend publication* 発行を停止する. ¶No publisher could be found to *undertake* the *publication*.

その発行を引受けてくれる出版者が見つからなかった.

Q an *annual publication* 年一回の刊行物. ¶ *catchpenny publications* くだらない刊行物. ¶ a *censorable publication* 検閲に引っかかりそうな出版物. ¶ one of the *choicest publications* of our time 現代の最も優良な刊行物の一つ. ¶ *free publication* of thoughts 思想の自由発表 ‖ *free publications* 無料の刊行物. ¶ a *frivolous publication* 浅薄な刊行物. ¶ *leading publications* 主なる刊行物. ¶ a *learned publication* 学究的な出版物. ¶ a *monthly publication* 月刊物. ¶ a list of *new publications* 新刊書目録. ¶ an entirely *new up-to-date publication* 全然新しいせん端的の刊行物. ¶ *obscene publications* いん書. ¶ a magazine issued as the *official publication* of ... ...の正式刊行物として発行した雑誌. ¶ the *only publication* of the kind in the English language その種の唯一の英文刊行物. ¶ a *peace-disturbing publication* 平和かく乱(危険思想)の出版物. ¶ a *periodical* [*publication*] 定期刊行物. ¶ a *post-mortem publication* 死後の(遺稿)出版物. ¶ *revived publication* 復刊. ¶ The American Angler, one of the best and most *sportsmanlike publications* devoted to the art of Izaak Walton つり魚術研究を目標とした刊行物中最善にしてかつ最もよくスポーツ精神を発揮した「アメリカン・アングラー」誌. ¶ a *suspended publication* 刊行停止中の出版物. ¶ a *timely publication* 時局もの. ¶ a *transient publication* きわもの.

Q² a *border-line publication* エロがかった出版物. ¶ The Sphere and its *sister publications* スフィァ誌とその姉妹(同系)出版物. ¶ a *semi-official publication* 半官半民の出版物. ¶ The story has been accepted by the Graphic for *serial publication*. その物語はグラフイック誌が連載を引受けた.

P good terms *of publication* 有利な出版条件 ‖ a report *of publication* 出版届. ¶ pay *on publication* [稿料など]出版直後に支払う. ¶ secure *through* the press *publication* of ... ...を新聞雑誌に発表してもらう.

P² *publication by* subscription 予約出版. ¶ *publication on* one's own account 自費出版 ‖ *publications on* religion 宗教に関する刊行物.

publicity, *n.* 周知; 発表, 公表; 宣伝.

V *accord publicity* to ... ...を発表する. ¶ *avoid* (=*burke*) *publicity* 人に知られないようにする. ¶ *court publicity* 売名に努める. ¶ *gain publicity* 名を売る(人に知られる). 【類】 It *gained publicity* through papers. ¶ *get publicity* for the enterprise その事業を宣伝する. ¶ *give publicity* to the fact that ... ...という事実を公表する ‖ *give* it the *publicity* it deserves 当然世間に知らるべきはずであるその物を宣伝する ‖ Due *publicity* will be *given* in the press before the changes are made. 変更前に然るべく新聞に発表されるだろう. ¶ The matter *received* wide *publicity* in the United States. そのことは合衆国に広く知られるようになった. ¶ *seek publicity* 自己宣伝する, 名を求める. ¶ a hermit who *shuns publicity* 人目をさける隠者.

Q the British press has given *considerable publicity* to ... 英国の諸新聞は...を盛んに書き立てて来た. ¶ glare in the *naked publicity* of type [間違など]活字になった文で目立つ. ¶ give *wider publicity* to ... ...をもっと広く知らせる. ¶ give *wider* and *authoritative publicity* 一層広くまた確実に知らせる.

Q² *film publicity* 映画による宣伝. ¶ *newspaper* (=*press*) *publicity* 新聞広告. ¶ All future sales will be preceded by adequate *press* and *radio publicity*. 今後の販売はすべて適当な新聞やラジオの宣伝をしてからなされるであろう.

P His head was drooping in shame *at* such painful *publicity*. こんな困ったことが世間に知れたので彼は恥かしそうにうなだれていた. ¶ be hungry (=thirsty) *for publicity* 自己宣伝(売名)に熱心である.

publish, *v.* 発表する; 出版する.

M *publish anonymously* 匿名で発表する. ¶ It was *first published* in 1899. それは一八九九年に初めて出版された. ¶ but *recently published* まだ刊行後間もない[書物など]. ¶ *When* will the book be *published?* 書物はいつ発行になりますか.

P It was *published at* the office of the Chronicle. それはクロニクル社の発行だった. 【類】 be *published at* the Review of Reviews office. ¶ The work will be *published by* the Clarendon Press. 同書はクラレンドン出版部から出版される. 【類】 *published by* The New American Library of World Literature, Inc. ¶ The firm *published for* Dryden, Addison and Steele. その書店はドライデン・アディソン及びスティールの著作を出版した. ¶ it has recently been *published from* the office ... それは近ごろ...社から出た ‖ a book *published from* the income of the ... Fund ...基金の補助金で公刊された書物. ¶ a book *published in* English 英文の書物. 【類】 newspapers *published in* foreign languages / It was *published in* a certain newspaper. ‖ be *published in* book form 単行本として出版される. ¶ the first *published on* the subject この問題では始めての出版物. ¶ *publish* a book *through* Messrs. Sonnenschein ゾンネンシャイン社から書物を出す. 【類】 *published through* the Boston firm of Small Maynard and Co. (Messrs. Scribner) / He will *publish through* Messrs. Longmans (ロングマンズ出版社) a volume of sermons entitled "...". ¶ *publish to* the world 天下に公表する. ¶ *publish under* one's real name (the pseudonym of ...) 本名(...の変名)で発表する. ¶ He has *published* many works *with* Messrs. Routledge during the past six or seven years. 氏は過去六七年間にラウトレッジ社から沢山著作を出した. 【類】 He will *publish* it *with* (=through) Mr. T. Fisher Unwin early next year.

publisher, *n.* 出版社.

V I was unable to *find* a *publisher* for it. それを引受けてくれる出版者が見つからなかった. ‖ The book *found* a *publisher* in Germany. その本はドイツで出版することになった. ¶ The manuscript *sought publishers* in vain. その原稿を出版しようとしたが引受けるものがなかった.

Q submit manuscripts to *likely publishers* 出してくれそうな出版屋に原稿を持込む. ¶ This dictionary is not published by the *original publishers* of Webster's Dictionary or by their successors. 本辞典は最初のウェブスター辞典の出版社あるいはその後継者によっての出版ではない. ¶ an *uncommercial publisher* 非営利的出版者. ¶ an *unscrupulous publisher* 良心的でない出版者. ¶ a *visiting publisher* from Germany ドイツから来訪した出版者.

Q² a *big* (*small*)-*time publisher* 《米》一(二)流の出版屋. ¶ a *law publisher* 法律書出版社. ¶ a *magazine publisher* 雑誌出版社. ¶ a *newspaper publisher* 新聞出版社.

P² The Clarendon Press is *publisher to* the University of Oxford. クラレンドン・プレスはオックスフォード大学御用の出版社だ.

pucker, *v.* [口を]すぼめる, [顔を]しかめる.

M² *pucker up* the face (one's brows) 顔をしかめる(まゆをひそめる) ‖ *pucker up* one's mouth 口をすぼめる, おちょぼ口をする.

pudding, *n.* プディング.

Q² *chocolate* (*cornstarch*) *pudding* チョコレート(など)プディング. ¶ a *Christmas pudding* クリスマス・プディング. ¶ *rice pudding* 米粉のプディング.

puddle, *n.* 水たまり, 水はね.

Q a *muddy puddle* 水たまり.

Q² wade in the *rain puddles* of the roadway 道路の水たまりを通る.

P splash *in* the *puddle* 水たまりでぱちゃぱちゃやる.

P² a *puddle of* rain-water (ink) 雨(インキ)のたまり.

puddle, *v.* 泥水をかきまわす; こね土を塗る.

M² He found a pig *puddling about*. 子豚が泥水の中を歩き回っているのを見かけた. ¶ *puddle up* a leakage [壁土で]水漏りをふさぐ.

puerility, *n.* 子供くさいこと.

Q the *utter puerility* of his conception 彼の考えのいかにも子供くさいこと.

puff, *n.* 一吹; 自賛的ほら.

V I *gave* two or three *puffs* to extinguish the candle. 私はろうそくを消そうと二三度吹いた. ‖ *giving* to the wind the *puffs* of smoke from their pipes きせるからぱっと出る煙を風になびかせて. ¶ *have* a *puff* [タバコを]一服やる. ¶ He *inserts* his *puffs* in the papers. 彼は新聞に自賛的の広告を出す.

Q² a *powder puff* おしろいのパッフ(はけ).

P a candle blown out *with* a *puff* of breath ぷっと一息で吹消したろうそく.

P² a few *puffs at* one's cigar 葉巻を二三服吹かすこと. ¶ a *puff of* wind (smoke, steam) 一陣の風(など).

puff, *v.* ぷっと吹く; ふくらます; 慢心させる; ほめ上げる.

M *puff away* at one's cigarette (pipe) 巻タバコ(など)をすぱすぱ吸う ‖ The north wind *puffed away* the cloud. 北風が雲を吹き払った. 【類】 *puff away* smoke. ¶ *puffing calmly* at his cigar ゆうゆうと葉巻を吹かしながら. ¶ *puff contentedly* at a clay-pipe 満足げに陶製のきせるを吹かす.

¶puff out one's cheeks ほおをぷっとふくらませる ‖ puff out a candle ろうそくを吹き消す ‖ The sails were puffed out with wind. 帆は風をはらんでいた. ¶puff prudishly 気取って口から息を吹く. ¶puff slowly at a cigar ゆっくり葉巻をくゆらす ‖ The engine puffed slowly away. 機関車はぱっぱっと煙を吐きながらゆっくり出ていった.

M^2 puff off the smoke of tobacco たばこの煙を吹き出す. ¶puff up one's own invention 自分の発明を自慢する ‖ puff up (=out) with self-importance もったいぶっている ‖ be puffed up with pride (vanity, conceit, praise, flattery) 慢心(など)で威張りくさっている ‖ puff up and down the stair 階段をはーはー言って上り下りする ‖ Smoke puffed up from his pipe. 彼のパイプからぱっと煙が立った.

P puff at his pipe furiously [タバコを]パイプで猛烈に吹かす. ¶puff smoke in (=into) one's face 顔に煙を吹きかける. ¶The train puffed out of the station. 列車はぽっぽっと(煙をはいて)発車した. ¶They puffed him to the skies. 彼をばかにもちあげた. ¶puffed with ambition 大望で得意になって.

puffy, *a.* ふくれて, 息切れがして.

M We were rather puffy after climbing. われわれは山登りでかなり息切れがしていた.

P be puffy under the eye 目の下がはれ上っている.

pugilist, *n.* けん闘家.

Q a Mexican pugilist メキシコのけん闘家.

P tough like a pugilist けん闘家のように不死身の.

pull, *n.* けん引; 《米口》ひき, 手づる(コネ); 一杯.

V give a pull at the bell 鐘の綱を引っ張る ‖ give a quick pull ぐいと引っ張る ‖ His wealth gives him a great pull. 金があるのが彼に非常な利益だ. ¶have a pull at the mug コップで一杯引かける ‖ These ads have a pull. この広告は人目を引く. ¶Take a pull at my flask. 僕のフラスコで一杯やり給え. 【類】take a pull at cigar.

Q I have no particular pull in that field. その方面には特別のコネもない. ¶It is quite a hard pull to get up the mountain. その山登りは相当骨だ. ¶have a short pull on the river 川で一こぎやる. ¶keep a steady pull on a rope 綱をぐんぐん引張り続ける. ¶A stiff pull brought us to the top. 一がん張りやって頂上に着いた. ¶with a strong, steady pull ぐっと引張って.

Q^2 drawer pulls 引出しの引手. ¶He came to the end of his eight-mile pull. 彼は八マイルの道を歩いて行先に着いた. ¶a razor "pull" かみそりの(切れが悪くての)引き.

P He secured office through his pull with the Governor. 彼は知事のひきで就職した. ‖ He went ahead through pull. あの男は引きで昇進した.

P^2 give a pull at the rope 綱を引張る ‖ All of a sudden there came a pull at my line. [つりで]不意に僕の糸にあたりがあった. ¶give a person a pull on the ear 人の耳を引張る.

O There are "pulls" everywhere. どこにもコネというものがある.

pull, *v.* 引っ張る; 引抜く; 船をこぐ.

M pull it apart それを引離す ‖ pull apart a doorknob ドアのハンドルをもぎとる. ¶pull asunder ばらばらにする. ¶pull away a tape from ... …からテープをもぎとる ‖ A train pulls away from a station. 列車は駅から出て行く. 【類】I was on the point of sitting down when somebody pulled away the chair and I fell on the floor. ¶pull back one's foot 足を引込める. ¶pull convulsively at one's mustache その口ひげをやけに引っぱる. ¶pull a door open (shut) ドアを引きあける(閉める). ¶I pulled out the dog from under the veranda. 私はえんの下から犬を引っ張り出した. ‖ pull out a tooth 歯を抜く. 【類】pull out hair ‖ pull out a book 本を抜き出す[書だなから] ‖ pull out a letter and read [ポケットから]手紙を出して読む ‖ pull out a gun (revolver) けん銃を引き抜く ‖ Help! Pull me out! 助けて! 引っぱり出して! [穴へ落ちた人などの言葉]. ‖ pull out to sea 海にこぎ出る ‖ pull out the stitching 縫目がほどける ‖ The drawer won't pull out. 引出しが抜けない. ‖ pull out a car 車を前に出す ‖ A train is pulling out. 列車が出て行く. ¶pull smartly towards ... 力一杯…の方へこぐ. ¶pull taut [綱など]強く引っ張る. ¶Pull yourself together. 落着け, しっかりしろ. ¶the new director and the professors are said not to pull together 新任理事と教授団は折合がうまく行かないようだ.

M^2 pull her about 彼女にモーションをかける. ¶It is difficult to pull along without a real friend. 本当の友だちなしでやって行くことはむつかしい. ¶pull down a tree 木を引き倒す ‖ pull down the window shade 窓の日除けを降ろす. 【類】pull down a flag / pull a curtain down (up). ‖ The old house has been pulled down. 古家屋は取り崩された. ‖ pull down a government 政府を打倒する ‖ He is pretty much pulled down by his illness. 病気で相当弱っている. ¶The train was (pulling) in right on time. 列車は時間通りに正確に入ってきた. ¶pull off a coat 上衣をぬぐ. 【類】pull off one's stockings (shoes). ¶pull on one's stockings (gloves) くつ下(など)をはく. ¶pull over a jersey (sweater) セーターを頭からかぶって着る ‖ pull one's boots (stockings) over 長ぐつ(など)をはく. ¶pull through [病気・困難など]切り抜ける ‖ I hope he will pull through. 病気が直ってほしいものです. ‖ Good nursing pulled him through. 看護がよかったので助かった. ‖ The plan looked difficult and risky at first, but finally we pulled it through. その計画は始めはむずかしそうだったが, 遂にそれをやり遂げた. ¶pull up a car 車を停める. 【類】pull up a horse / I told the driver to pull up there. / The train pulled up at a station. ‖ pull up one's shirt-sleeves ワイシャツのそでをたくし上げる ‖ pull up stakes くいを引き抜く ‖ pull up a window (shade, one's hood) ‖ pull up a tree by the roots 木を根こそぎにする. 【類】pull (=pluck) up wild flowers (weeds) ‖ pull up one's socks (stockings) [くつ下を引っぱりあげる意から]緊こん一番する ‖ pull bedclothes up under one's chin 夜着をあごの所まで引っぱる ‖ The boat pulled up alongside her. 小艇は同船に横づけとなった. ‖ He was pulled up for his error. 彼は間違いをやってしかられた.

P pull a passenger across a stream 船で通行人を川向うへ運ぶ. ¶pull at a wire 綱を引っぱる. ¶pull one by the hand (ear, sleeve) 人の手(など)を引っ張る. ¶pull for the beach 海浜にこぎ寄る ‖ pull for the goal 目的に向って努力する. ¶pull in pieces [機械など]ばらばらにする. ¶pull one into the room 室内に人を引っ張り込む ‖ We (=Our train) pulled into the station. われわれの乗った汽車が駅にはいった. ¶The fish pulls on the line. 魚がつり糸を引っ張る. ¶I pulled him out of the water. 彼を水から引き揚げた. ‖ The circus pulls out of Madison Square Garden tonight. そのサーカスは今晩マジソンスクエヤガーデンから引あげる(最終興行で). ‖ He may pull out of it (=pull it through). 彼はそれ(困難・病気)からうまく切り抜けるだろう. ‖ a train pulling out of the station 駅から発車する列車. ¶He pulled his hat over his eyes. 帽子を目深にかぶった. ‖ He pulled my hat down over my ears. 彼は僕の帽子をぐっと引っぱって耳が隠れるようにした(いたずらかまたは怒って). ‖ pull one's blanket over one's face 毛布を引っぱって顔を隠す. ¶You'll need every ounce of strength you have to pull through this. これを切り抜けるには大いにがんばらなきやだめですぞ. ¶pull it to pieces それをひっぱってばらばらにする. 【類】pull a toy to pieces. ¶pull a sled up the hill そりを小山に引っ張り上げる. ¶pull with a sudden jerk ぐいと引っ張る.

pulley, *n.* 〖機〗滑車.

Q a fixed pulley 定軸滑車.

Q^2 a driving pulley 主動滑車. ¶a belt pulley ベルト滑車. ¶a screw pulley ねじ込滑車. ¶a cast-iron pulley. 鋳鉄製割り滑車.

pulp, *n.* パルプ.

Q bleached (dry) pulp さらし(乾燥)パルプ. ¶chemical pulp 化学パルプ.

Q^2 kraft pulp クラフト[紙]パルプ. ¶soda (sulfite) pulp ソーダ(亜硫酸)パルプ. ¶wood pulp 木材パルプ.

P crush it into a pulp それをつぶして軟塊にする. ¶beat it to a pulp それを打って軟かい塊にする ‖ be reduced to pulp どろどろにとかす(パルプにする).

pulpit, *n.* [教会の]説教壇.

V ascend the pulpit 説教壇に登る. ¶fill the pulpit of a sick friend 病友に代って説教する. ¶occupy (=stand at) the pulpit 説教壇に立つ.

P be denounced alike by pulpit and platform 宗教界と言論界の両方面から非難される. ¶He is always dry in the pulpit. 彼の説教はいつも乾燥無味だ. ¶go into the pulpit 説教壇に登る.

P^2 He is successor of ... in the pulpit of the church. 彼はその教会で…の後継者として説教をしている.

pulsate, *v.* 鼓動する.

P a story *pulsating with* life 生気発らつたる物語 ‖ verses *pulsating with* the vigor of protest 感激悲憤の気当るべからざる詩.

pulse, *n.* 脈, 脈はく.

V ***count*** one's *pulse* その脈を数える. ¶***feel*** a patient's *pulse* 病人の脈をみる ‖ ***feel*** the *pulse* of the public 世論を打診する. ¶accurately ***gauge*** the *pulse* of ... ...の真相を打診する. ¶***have*** a weak *pulse* 脈が弱い. ¶***increase*** the *pulse* from ... to ... beats ...から...に脈はくを増す. ¶***quicken*** one's *pulse* 脈はくを早くする. 【類】Delivered with eloquence and power, the address was a message which stirred the heart and ***quickened*** the *pulse* of every one present. ¶***recover*** a normal *pulse* 平常脈に復する. ¶***reduce*** the *pulse* 脈はくを減じる. ¶***set*** the *pulses* ***beating***=make a riot in the blood 血をわかす. ¶***slow*** the *pulse* 脈はくを緩める. ¶***take*** his *pulse* 彼の脈を取る.

V² The *pulse* is still ***beating***. 脈はまだ打っている. ¶The *pulse* has ***ceased*** to beat! 脈が打たなくなった. ¶The *pulse* ***mounted*** (=***ran***) ***up*** to 120. 脈はくが百二十に上った. ¶The *pulse* ***quickens***. 脈はくが早くなる. ¶The *pulse* ***sank*** steadily 脈はくが段々弱くなった. ¶The *pulse* ***slowed*** down. 脈が低くなった. ¶my *pulse* still ***tingles*** as I realize ... 私が...を思い浮べると今でも胸がどきどきする.

Q quicken the ***failing*** *pulses* of national life 国家の退勢をばん回する. ¶The *pulse* is ***fast*** (***slow***, ***weak***). 脈はくが早い(など). ¶a ***hard*** *pulse* しっかりした脈はく. ¶a ***high*** *pulse* 高い脈はく. ¶an ***intermittent*** *pulse* 結滞性脈はく. ¶The *pulse* is ***irregular*** 脈はくが不整だ. ¶a ***long*** (=***slow***) *pulse* 遅脈. ¶The *pulse* is ***normal*** (=***regular***). 脈はくが順調だ. ¶a ***quick*** (=***rapid or short***) *pulse* 速脈. ¶With ***quickened*** *pulses* we watched the program of the struggle. われわれは胸をおどらせてその競技の進行を見詰めていた. ¶a ***sharp*** *pulse* 急脈. ¶a ***small*** *pulse* 弱い脈はく. ¶a ***thready*** *pulse* 微弱で急速な脈はく.

P increase the frequency ***of*** (=quicken) the *pulse* 脈はくを早くする.

pulse, *v.* 脈打つ.

P *pulse* ***with*** life 生々と脈打つ. 【類】His heart *pulsed* ***with*** excitement.

pulse-frequency, *n.* 脈はく数.

V² The *pulse-frequency* ***fell*** again to the normal. 脈はく数が順調に復した.

pulverizer, *n.* 粉砕機.

Q² a ***coal*** *pulverizer* 砕炭機.

pump, *n.* ポンプ.

P raise water ***with*** a *pump* ポンプで揚水する.

V ***prime*** the *pump* さそい水をやる. ¶***work*** a *pump* ポンプを動かす.

Q a ***centrifugal*** *pump* 遠心ポンプ. ¶a ***domestic*** *pump* 家庭用ポンプ. ¶a ***hydraulic*** *pump* 水圧ポンプ.

Q² an ***air*** *pump* 空気ポンプ. ¶a ***drainage*** *pump* 排水ポンプ. ¶a ***feed*** *pump* 給水ポンプ. ¶a ***force*** *pump* 押上げポンプ. ¶a ***hand*** *pump* 手押しポンプ. ¶a ***steam*** *pump* 蒸気ポンプ. ¶a ***spray*** *pump* 噴霧器. ¶a ***suction*** *pump* 吸水ポンプ. ¶a ***vacuum*** *pump* 真空ポンプ. ¶a ***water*** *pump* 水揚げポンプ.

pump, *v.* ポンプでかい出す; 浴びせかける; かまをかけて探り出す.

M *pump* a cistern ***dry*** ポンプで水そうの水をくみ出す. ¶*pump* ***out*** [water from] a well ポンプで井戸の水をかいだす ‖ *pump* ***out*** secrets かまをかけて秘密を聞き出す.

M² *pump* ***up*** water from a well 水を井戸からポンプで吸上げる ‖ *pump* ***up*** a tire タイヤに空気を入れてふくらませる ‖ *pump* ***up*** one's brains for an idea 考えを頭からしぼり出す.

P *pump* bullets ***at*** a foe 敵に弾丸を浴びせかける. ¶*pump* water ***into*** the reservoir 貯水池にポンプで水を注入する. ¶*pump* information ***out of*** a person かまをかけて人から情報を聞き出す. 【類】*pump* something ***out of*** the servant about the family.

pumps, *n.* 〚服飾〛パンプス型のくつ.

P a cabaret dancer ***in*** *pumps* パンプスをはいたキャバレーの踊り子.

pun, *n.* 地口, しゃれ.

V ***let off*** one's *puns* しゃれを言う. ¶***make*** *puns* しゃれを言う.

Q a ***clever*** *pun* 巧妙なしゃれ. ¶make an ***execrable*** *pun* へたなしゃれを言う. ¶Such a ***good*** *pun!* うまいしゃれだ. ¶a ***poor*** *pun* だじゃれ. ¶a ***quiet*** *pun* 上品なしゃれ. ¶a ***subtle*** *pun* 巧妙なしゃれ. ¶The little *pun* is ***unintentional***. そのちょっとしたしゃれは(しゃれを言う積りでなく)自然に出たものだ.

P² here is a *pun* ***on*** the word ... ここに...という言葉のしゃれがある ‖ *puns* ***on*** sacred texts 聖典の文句などをもじったしゃれ.

punch, *n.* 打印器; 穴あけ器(パンチ).

Q² a ***figure*** (***letter***) *punch* 数字(文字)打印器. ¶a ***hollow*** *punch* つぼのみ.

punch, *n.* 〚拳闘〛パンチ.

V ***get*** a *punch* on the head 頭をこつんと打たれる. ¶***give*** a *punch* on the nose 鼻にパンチを一発食らわせる. ¶***land*** a *punch* in the eye 目にパンチを食わせる.

punctilious, *a.* 末節にこだわる.

P *punctilious* ***about*** religious observances 宗教上の慣例に小むずかしい. ¶be *punctilious* ***in*** one's devotions 祈とうの儀式がやかましい.

punctual, *a.* 時間の正しい, 日限をたがえない.

P The teacher is *punctual* ***in*** attending class. その教師はクラスに出講の時間が正しい. 【類】He is *punctual* ***in*** paying his bills. ¶*punctual* ***like*** clockwork (=like a clock) 時計のように正確な. ¶*punctual* ***to*** the minute (=moment) 寸刻も時間をたがえない ‖ *punctual* ***to*** his promise 期日を約束通りにする. 【類】*Punctual* ***to*** his appointment he appeared [the] next morning.

punctuality, *n.* 時間厳守; 厳正.

V ***secure*** the *punctuality* of trains and boats 列車や汽船の発着を時間通りにする.

P These coast steamers do not sail ***with*** the *punctuality* of mail steamers. これらの沿岸航行船は郵船のように時間が正確でない.

P² *punctuality* ***in*** keeping appointments 約束時間の厳守.

punctuate, *v.* 句点を付ける; 句切る, 強調する.

M *punctuate* ***clearly***, ***economically***, and ***effectively*** 明りょうに経済的にかつ有効に句点を付ける. ¶sentences ***correctly*** *punctuated* 正確に句点を付けた文. ¶***decently*** *punctuated* 本格的に句点を付けた. ¶*punctuate* ***heavily*** 句読点を濫用する.

P Each word was *punctuated* ***by*** a blow. 一語一語卓をたたいて強調した. ‖ The audience *punctuated* the speech ***by*** outbursts of applause. 聴衆は演説の切れ目切れ目に拍手した. ¶*punctuated* his refusal ***with*** gestures その拒絶をゼスチュアで強調した(いやだと手を振るなど) ‖ She *punctuated* her tale ***with*** sobs.=Sobs punctuated her tale. 彼女の物語は時々涙でとぎれた.

punctuation, *n.* 句点.

V Usually no *punctuation* is ***used*** after the last word in a heading. 見出しは最後の語の後に句点を打たないのが普通だ.

Q ***close*** *punctuation* 正式句点法. ¶***heavy*** *punctuation* 句点の繁用. ¶***loose*** *punctuation* 略式句点法. ¶***open*** *punctuation* 省略句点法.

puncture, *v.* 破裂(パンク)する.

P *puncture* a hole ***in*** a bag 袋に穴をあける(とがったものを刺して). ¶We had one of the car tires *punctured* ***on*** the way. 途中でタイヤがパンクした. ¶*puncture* a rubber ball ***with*** a pin ピンでゴム球に穴をあける.

punish, *v.* 罰する, こらしめる.

M *punish* ***heavily*** 重く罰する. ¶be ***sadly*** *punished* for ... ...のためひどく罰を受ける. ¶*punish* ***severely*** 厳罰に処する. 【類】***severely*** *punish* the enemy by machine-gunning.

P He will be punished ***according to*** his deserts. 彼はその罪に応じて罰せられるだろう. ¶They *punished* the idle ***as*** criminals. 彼らはなまけ者を罪人として罰した. ¶*punish* ... ***by*** a fine ...を罰金刑に処する. 【類】He was *punished* ***by*** arrest (imprisonment, death). / Nuisances (妨害) can be *punished* ***by*** law. ¶*punish* him ***for*** his carelessness (misdeed) 彼の不注意(など)をこらしめる. ¶They were *punished* ***with*** death. 彼らは死刑に処せられた. 【類】An offender will be *punished* ***with*** imprisonment [for a period] not exceeding three years. / Any infringement of the law shall be *punished* ***with*** a fine (罰金) of from ... to ...

punishable, *a.* 罰すべき.

P an offense *punishable* ***by*** law 法律によって罰すべき罪. 【類】A neglect is *punishable* ***by*** a heavy penalty. / an offense *punishable* ***by*** imprisonment and hard labor / Conversation between the clerks was then *punishable* ***by*** discharge (解雇). / it is *punishable* ***by*** a fine of ... / The violation of the rule was *punishable* ***by*** death. ¶In those days when found to be a Christian he was *punishable* ***with*** death. 当時キリシタンだということが知れると死

刑に処せられたのだ. 【類】 ***punishable with*** death or imprisonment.

punishment, *n.* 罰, 懲罰; 刑罰.

V ***bear*** *punishment* 刑罰を受ける. ¶You will ***bring*** (=***incur***) the *punishment* of heaven on you. 天罰があたる. ‖ Such a crime ***brings*** its own *punishment* with it. こうした犯罪は自ずと酬いが来る. ¶***carry out*** a *punishment* 処罰する. ¶If there are extenuating circumstances, the *punishment* may be ***commuted*** to a fine. 酌量すべき事情がある場合には減刑して科料にすることができる. ¶***deal out*** *punishment* to offenders 犯罪人に罰を加える. ¶***defer*** a *punishment* 刑の執行を猶予する. ¶***deserve*** *punishment* 懲罰に値する. ¶***escape*** the *punishment* of crime 罰を免かれる. ¶***evade*** (=***elude***) *punishment* 罰を回避する. ¶***fix*** the *punishment* which it considers should be imposed その至当と認める刑罰を決定する. ¶***incur*** (=bring on oneself) a *punishment* 罰をこうむる ‖ ***incur*** the *punishment* of heaven 天罰をこうむる. ¶***inflict*** the severest *punishment* provided by the law 法の許す限り極刑に処する. ¶the *punishment* which nature ***metes out*** to ... 天の...に降す罰. ¶***merit*** heavy *punishment* 厳罰に値する. ¶***mitigate*** one's *punishment* その刑を減じる. ¶***receive*** *punishment* 罰を受ける. 【類】 ***receive*** the *punishment* of the knout (むち刑). ¶***remit*** a *punishment* 赦免する. ¶***suffer*** *punishment* 罰を受ける. 【類】 ***suffer*** a *punishment* / They will in the end ***suffer*** the natural *punishment* of their injustice (罪悪の報い). ¶***take*** one's *punishment* 罰に服する. ¶***transfer*** *punishment* from private hand to the state 懲罰を個人の手から国家の手に移す.

Q ***barbarous*** and ***degrading*** *punishments* 野蛮で不名誉な刑罰. ¶blow and ***brutal*** *punishment* 殴打や残忍な懲罰. ¶a ***capital*** *punishment* 極刑. ¶***certain*** *punishment* 必至の処罰. ¶inflict ***condign*** *punishment* on ... ...に当然の罰を加える. ¶a ***corporal*** *punishment* 体刑. ¶***cruel*** *punishments* 残忍な刑罰(はりつけのような). ¶a ***dire*** *punishment* (天罰・たたりなどの)恐ろしい罰. ¶a ***disciplinary*** *punishment* 懲戒 ‖ minor confinement in a ***disciplinary*** *punishment* 軟禁. ¶***drastic*** *punishments* 手荒い罰. ¶***dreadful*** *punishments* 恐ろしい刑罰. ¶an ***exemplary*** *punishment* みせしめの懲罰 ‖ by way of ***exemplary*** *punishment* みせしめに. ¶the ***heaviest*** *punishment* 極刑. ¶a ***lenient*** *punishment* 寛大な刑罰. ¶a ***mild*** (=***light***) *punishment* 軽い罰. ¶a ***pecuniary*** *punishment* 罰金刑. ¶inflict ***physical*** *punishment* 体刑を課する. ¶a ***severe*** *punishment* 厳罰. ¶a ***summary*** *punishment* [簡易裁判所の]即決刑. ¶a ***vicarious*** *punishment* 身代りに受ける罰.

P ***as*** a *punishment* for ... ...に対する罰として. ¶strike him ***in*** *punishment* 罰として彼を打つ. ¶a form ***of*** *punishment* 罰の一形式. ¶He will be visited ***with*** *punishment*. 彼は天罰を受けるだろう.

P^2 a *punishment* ***by*** blows 殴打の刑. ¶a *punishment* ***for*** a crime (misdeed) 犯罪(など)に対する刑罰. ¶the *punishment* ***of*** death=death penalty 死刑. ¶inflict *punishment* ***on*** his person 彼に体刑を課する.

pup, *n.* 小犬; [小生意気な]小僧.

Q a ***conceited*** *pup* 生意気な青二才. ¶an ***uppish*** *pup* 思い上った青二才. ¶a clever ***young*** *pup* 利口な小僧.

P That bitch seems to be ***in*** *pup*. その雌犬は子持らしい.

pupil, *n.* 生徒, 弟子.

V ***coach*** a *pupil* to pass an examination in a subject ある科目の試験準備に生徒を指導してやる. ¶***confuse*** a *pupil* by a perplexing question 難問を出して生徒を面くらわせる. ¶***cram*** *pupils* with knowledge 生徒に知識を詰め込む. ¶***enrol(l)*** *pupils* 生徒を学籍に登録する. ¶***fit*** a *pupil* for college 《米》生徒に大学入学の準備を施す ‖ ***fit*** the *pupil* for life 生徒に世の中に出る準備をさせる. ¶***initiate*** the *pupils* into ... 生徒に...を教え込む. ¶Teachers ***instruct*** *pupils*. 教師は生徒に教える. ¶a master ***lecturing*** an unruly *pupil* 乱暴な生徒をけん責する教師. ¶***let*** the *pupils* ***try*** to explain how ... 生徒に...の説明をやらして見る. ¶***push on*** dull *pupils* and ***hold back*** bright *pupils* 頭の悪い生徒を押し進め頭の良い生徒を押えておく. ¶***take*** *pupils* 弟子を取る.

Q his most ***appreciative*** *pupil* もっとも彼に敬服している生徒. ¶an ***apt*** *pupil* よく覚える生徒. ¶solicitors take ***articled*** *pupils* 事務弁護人は年季で書生を雇い入れる. ¶the ***best*** *pupil* of ... ...の高弟. ¶very ***bright*** *pupils* きわめて明敏な生徒. ¶***bright*** and ***responsive*** *pupils* 頭がよくって手応えのある生徒. ¶a ***docile*** *pupil* すなおな生徒. ¶an ***eager, humble, docile*** *pupil* 熱心で, 腰の低い, すなおな弟子. ¶his ***favorite*** *pupil* 彼の愛弟子. ¶weed out ***hopeless*** *pupils* from class 見込みのない生徒をクラスから除く. ¶***illustrious*** *pupils* りっぱな(あっぱれな)生徒. ¶***non-English-speaking*** *pupils* 英語国でない国の生徒たち. ¶***primary*** [***school***] *puplis* 小学校の生徒. ¶***promising*** *pupils* 有望な生徒. ¶a ***true*** *pupil* of ... ...に恥ないお弟子. ¶a ***sorry*** *pupil* はえない弟子. ¶***uneducable*** *pupils* 手におえない生徒. ¶***weaker*** *pupils* 力の足りない方の生徒. ¶one of his ***whilom*** (=***former***) *pupils* 氏の旧門弟の一人. ¶***willing*** *pupils* 進んで学ぶ生徒. ¶a ***zealous*** *pupil* 熱心な生徒.

Q^2 ***grade-school*** *pupils* 《米》小学生. ¶a ***high-school*** *pupil* 高校生. ¶a ***junior high*** *pupil* 中学生.

P take him ***as*** *pupil* 彼を弟子にする.

P^2 a *pupil* ***of*** ... in philosophy ...について哲学を学んだ人; ...派の哲学者 ‖ She is the *pupil* ***of*** his eye. 彼は彼女を目の中に入れても痛くないほど愛している. ¶he was a *pupil* ***to*** ... 彼は...の弟子だった.

O become one's *pupil* 弟子になる.

pupilage, *n.* 門弟たること.

V after ***serving*** his *pupilage* with ... ...の弟子となっていた後.

puppet, *n.* かいらい, あやつり人形.

V ***make*** a *puppet* of the king その王をあやつり人形にする. ¶the fingers ***manipulating*** the *puppets* 人形をあやつる指.

Q a ***complete*** *puppet* in the hands of the war party 全く主戦派の手中にあるあやつり人形. ¶***mere*** *puppets*, of which the strings are pulled from ... ...に操られる全くのかいらい. 【類】 ***mere*** *puppets* in the hands of others.

puppy, *n.* 小犬; [小生意気な]小僧.

V^2 A little *puppy* ***yaps***. 小犬はくんくん鳴く.

Q a ***cute*** *puppy* かわいい子犬. ¶an ***ill-bred, awkward*** *puppy* with a money bag under his arm 財布をかかえた育ちの悪い妙な格好の小僧. ¶fondle a ***pet*** *puppy* 小さい愛犬をなでまわす.

P ***with*** a *puppy* in her arms 小犬をだいて.

purchase, *n.* 買入, 買収; 買物.

V ***cancel*** a *purchase* 買物を取消す. ¶***close*** the *purchase* of ... ...の購買を完了する. ¶***commence*** a *purchase* 買物を始める. ¶***complete*** all *purchases* 買物を全部そろえる. ¶***conclude*** *purchase* of ... ...の買入れを終る. ¶***confirm*** a *purchase* 買入を確認する. ¶when ***contemplating*** the *purchase* of ... ...の買物をしようと考えている時に. ¶***effect*** a *purchase* 買物をする. 【類】 before you ***effect*** any *purchases*. ¶***finish*** a *purchase* 買物を済ます. ¶***hold off*** *purchases* 買物を控える. ¶***make*** a *purchase* 買物をする. 【類】 when ***making*** *purchases* / ***make*** a little *purchase* in a shop / *purchases* ***made*** through any responsible bookseller or from the publishers. ¶I will ***put off*** this *purchase* till another (=next) time. この買物はこの次まで延ばしましょう. ¶***return*** one's *purchase* 買物を返す. ¶Bulls are ***selling out*** their *purchases*. 『市場』 買方が売出している. ¶***transfer*** one's *purchases* その買入品を転送する.

Q make a ***considerable*** *purchase* of books 本を大分買い込む. ¶He made many ***costly*** *purchases*. 彼は沢山高価な買物をした. ¶This watch is a ***dear*** *purchase*. この時計は高い買物だ. ¶He made ***extensive*** *purchases* in Paris. 彼はパリーで色々の買物をした. ¶a ***fortunate*** *purchase* at an advantageous price 運好く得の行く値段で買った品. ¶make no ***fresh*** *purchases* 新規買入をしない. ¶It is a ***good*** (***bad***) *purchase*. それは安(高)い買物だ. 【類】 make a ***good*** (***bad***) *purchase*. ¶His life would not have been worth an ***hour's*** *purchase*. 彼の命は一時間と持ちそうになかった. ¶make a ***large*** *purchase* of ... ...を大量買入れる. ¶have no money to make ***necessary*** *purchases* 必要品を買うだけの金がない. ¶make ***numerous*** *purchases* 色々買物をする. ¶This is a ***recent*** *purchase* of mine. これは私がこのごろ買ったものだ. ¶a ***ridiculous*** *purchase* ばかげた買物. ¶make ***seasonal*** *purchases* at a fair 市で季節の買物をする. ¶make ***several*** *purchases* 色々買物をする. ¶Dealings consist principally of ***speculative*** *purchases*. 取引は主に思わく買いである. ¶make ***sundry*** *purchases* 色々買物をする. ¶I made some ***valuable*** *purchases* of jewelry. 私は貴重な宝石を若干買った. ¶That house is a ***wise*** *purchase*. その家はうまい買物だった.

Q^2 ***gift*** *purchases* 贈答品の買物. ¶***hire*** *purchase* 分割払の

買入れ.【類】hire purchase payment. ¶an open-market purchase 公開市場での買物. ¶ready-money purchase 現金買い.

P acquire by purchase 買受ける. 【類】nationalization (国有) of the mines by purchase. ¶make a number of purchases 沢山買物をする. ¶Exhibits may be removed on purchase. 陳列品はお買上げと同時に御持参ができます. ‖ We pay express charges on purchases of $500 or more. 五百ドル以上のお買物の速達運賃は弊店において負担いたします.

P^2 He went out to make some little purchases at the shops. 彼は数カ所の店へ少し買物に出掛けた. ¶make the purchase for ... ...で買う. ¶In 1876 America acquired Alaska by purchase from Russia. 一八七六年に米国はアラスカをロシアから買収した. ¶make some purchases in [the] Ginza 銀座で少し買物をする. ¶purchase of immovables 不動産の購入 ‖ the purchase of liberty at the risk of many lives 多くの生命をとしての自由の獲得.

purchase, v. 買う; 取得する.

P purchase ... at the store その店で...を買う. 【類】purchase ... at a public sale (競売で) / parchase it at ten yen / purchase ... at auction (競売で). ¶purchase peace by concessions 譲歩して平和の解決を得る. 【類】victory purchased by much blood and many tears. ¶purchase ... for cash 即金で...を買う. 【類】The portrait was purchased for 5,000 francs in 1863. ¶purchase ... from (=of) a person 人から...を買う ‖ It was purchased from the ... Fund. それは...基金の内から買った. ¶It can be purchased of the H. W. Wilson Company. それはウイルスン会社から買える.【類】any article purchased of us ... ¶purchase ... with money 金で...を買う. 【類】purchase favor with flattery (おべっか) / purchase freedom with blood / purchase ease (=comfort) with toil.

O purchase land and wait for rise in its value 土地を買って値の出るのを待つ.

purchaser, n. 買手.

V If he did not ask such an exorbitant price, he would easily find a purchaser. あんな法外な値を言わなければじきに買い手があるだろうに.

Q frequent purchasers of books 本をひん繁に買う人. ¶great purchasers of our silk わが国の絹糸の大口の買い手. ¶intending (=prospective) purchasers =《米》prospects 買いそうな客.

Q^2 a "dummy" purchaser 見掛けの買い手, さくら. ¶a retail purchaser 小売買いの人.

pure, a. 純粋な, 清い.

P He is pure in (=of) heart.=He has a pure heart. 彼は心が純真だ. ‖ Blessed are the pure in heart. 心の清き者は幸いなり. ¶a heart pure of (=from) evil (taint) 邪念(しみ)のない心.

purgative, n. 下剤.

Q active purgative 強い下剤. ¶a powerful purgative 強力な下剤.

purge, n. 追放(パージ).

Q The sweeping purge of radicalists 急進派のパージ旋風.

Q^2 the Nazi blood purge もとナチ党の血液(ユダヤ人の)追放. ¶a recent Red purge 最近の赤追放.

purge, v. 清める; 一掃する; 追放(パージ)する.

P purge the barley from the bran 大麦のふすまを取除く ‖ be purged from public life 公職から追放される ‖ purge from their souls the will to ... 彼らのたましいから...しようという意欲を除き去る. ¶purge a person of his office 人をその職から追放する ‖ purge the mind of (=from) false notions 心から間違った考えを一掃する ‖ He was purged of (=from) sin. 彼の罪は清められた. ‖ purge oneself of suspicion 身の明しを立てる ‖ The party was purged of its corrupt members その党は腐敗分子を一掃した. 【類】purge a country of undesirable foreigners.

purgee, n. 被追放者.

V release the purgees 被追放者を解放する.

Q an ex-purgee かって追放された人. ¶a prominent purgee 追放有名人.

Q^2 "memorandum cases" purgees メモランダム(覚書)ケースによる被追放者.

purging, n. 下痢.

Q violent purgings 激しい下痢.

purification, n. 浄化.

Q^2 Aeration is very useful in water purification. 空気にさらすことは水の浄化にはきわめて必要なことである.

purifier, n. 浄化器.

Q^2 an oil purifier 浄油器. ¶a water purifier 浄水器.

purify, v. 清める.

M The French tongue was much purified. フランス語は非常に純化された.

P He was purified from all sin. 彼はすべての罪を清められた. ¶purify a country of undesirable aliens 国内から不良外人を一掃する ‖ Shinto shrines were purified of Buddhist annexes. 神仏混こうの制が改まった.

puritan, n. 清教徒.

Q^2 a Confucianist puritans 厳格な儒学者.

purity, n. 純粋, 純潔; 純正.

V acquire a purity of sound in foreign languages 外国語の純正な発音を覚える. ¶corrupt the purity of the language その国語の純正をそこなう ‖ corrupt her native purity 彼女の生れついた純な心を毒する. ¶destroy the purity of the English language 英語の純正さを汚す. ¶those who have the purity of the language at heart その国語の純粋を心懸けている人々. ¶I know the purity of your motives. 私には君の動機の純なことは分かっている. ¶Only with woman can one lose purity, only with her can one preserve it. 男が純潔を失うのも女であるしそれを保つのも女である. ¶sully the purity of ... ...の純潔を汚す. ¶Public opinion is the only means of sustaining the purity of politics. 世論が政治の純潔を維持する唯一の手段である.

Q a man of moral purity 品行方正の人. ¶Sexual purity is a romantic dream to the youth. 性的純潔ということは青年に取ってはロマンチックな夢だ. ¶social purity 社交上の純潔.

Q^2 maintain proper air purity 適度の空気の純度を保つ. ¶silver (gold) purity 銀(金)の純度.

P The building represents a style in its purity. その建物はくずれていない一つの様式を示す. ‖ in all purity of intent 意図に少しの不純さもなく. ¶He speaks English and German with the same purity of diction. 彼は英独両語を同じように正しく話す.

P^2 purity of life 生活の清らかさ ‖ purity of thought, word, and deed 思想・言語及び行為の純潔 ‖ purity of motives (life) 正しい動機(純潔な生活).

purple, n. 紫衣; 王位, 高位.

V wear the purple 帝位につく.

P He is attired in purple. 彼は紫衣を着けている. ‖ those who were born in (=to) the purple 王公の家に生れた人人. ¶marry into the purple [氏なくして]玉のこしに乗る.

purple, a. 紫色の, [血で]赤い.

P He was purple with incredulity. 彼はそりゃうそだといった顔付をしていた. ‖ He looked purple with rage. 彼は怒りで顔色が真赤になっていた. 【類】turn purple with cold.

purport, n. 要旨.

V I do not understand the purport of your telegram. 貴電の意味が分からない.

Q the main purport of his speech 彼の演説の要旨.

P^2 What was the purport of his visit? 彼は何の用で来たんだ.

purpose, n. 目的; 意志; 用途; 趣旨.

V accomplish (=achieve) one's purpose その目的を達する. ¶The regulation failed to achieve its purpose. その取締規則が行われなかった. 【類】some other method of achieving one's purpose. / satisfactorily achieve the purpose. ¶answer the purpose 目的にかなう, 間に合う. 【類】Either will answer our purpose. / It answers the purpose intended very well. / answer the purpose equally well / answer the double purpose (二重の目的) of ... and ... ¶resort to other means of attaining one's purpose 他の目的達成手段に訴える. 【類】fail to attain (=miss) the purpose. ¶carry out the purpose その目的を果す. ¶conceal one's true purpose その本当の目的を隠す. ¶cover treacherous purposes with smiles 油断のならない底意を笑いに紛らす. ¶defeat its own purpose その本来の目的にそわない(逆効果となる). 【類】defeat the very purpose for which one is working. ¶manage to effect one's purpose どうにかしてその目的を達する. ¶execute a purpose 目的を遂げる. ¶Many find their life's real purpose by accident. 多数の者は自己の一生の真の目的を偶然に発見する. ¶make use of any tale that fits their purposes 彼らの目的に適する話は何んでも利用する. ¶forgo one's purpose 自己の目算を見合わせる. ¶It frustrated our purposes. それがわれわれの目論見を中止させた. ¶fulfil a useful purpose 有益な目的に適う. 【類】can best fulfil its purpose by ...ing ... ¶further the purposes of the association その協会の目的を

助長する. ¶***gain*** one's *purpose* その目的を達する. ¶***give*** *purpose* to one's work その仕事を意義あらしめる. ¶***harden*** one's *purpose* 意志を強固にする. ¶The book ***has*** a double *purpose.* その書には二重の目的がある. ¶the main *purpose* ***kept*** in view 眼中においた主な目的 ‖ ***keep*** our *purpose* sufficiently high われわれの目標を十分高い所におくようにする ‖ This *purpose* has been ***kept*** constantly in view in preparation of the present work. 本書編集に当ってこの点に絶えず留意して来た. ¶***meet*** the *purposes* of ... ...の目的にかなう. ¶***mold*** the *purpose* of the nation 国民の決意を結成する. ¶***outlive*** its *purpose* その目的を達成した後まで役に立つ. ¶***procure*** an illegal *purpose* 不法の目的を遂げる. ¶a committee formed to ***promote*** this *purpose* この目的助成のために組織した委員会. ¶***pursue*** these *purposes* これらの目的を追求する. ¶***realize*** one's *purpose* その目的を実現する. ¶***serve*** its *purpose* その目的に役立つ. 【類】It ***serves*** the *purpose* better. / would equally (同じように) well ***serve*** the *purpose* / This will help ***serve*** the *purpose.* / I wanted a knife, but scissors will ***serve*** my *purpose.* / it would ***serve*** little *purpose* to ... / no good *purpose* would be ***served*** by ... / I trust these will ***serve*** the *purpose* for which you desire them. / The capitalist press ***serves*** the *purposes* of capital. / make it ***serve*** the *purpose* / His death ***served*** no useful *purpose.* / it would not ***serve*** any (=subserve no) useful *purpose* to ... / the *purpose* is best ***served*** by ... ¶***set up*** a *purpose* 目的を定める. ¶I hope it will ***suit*** your *purpose.* お間に合えばよいが.

Q ¶apply it to a ***bad*** *purpose* それを悪い目的に使う. ¶use it to ***better*** *purpose* それをさらに有効に使う. ¶the ***central*** *purpose* 中心目的. ¶use the proceeds for ***charitable*** *purposes* 収益を慈善に使う. ¶one's ***chief*** *purpose* その主意. ¶a very ***commendable*** *purpose* 至極りっぱな目的. ¶English for ***commercial*** *purposes* 商売(貿易)のための英語. ¶ships for ***commercial*** *purposes* 商船. ¶it is at ***cross*** *purposes* with ... それは目的が...と食い違っている. ¶for ***culinary*** *purposes* 調理用として. ¶for ***curative*** *purposes* 医療のために. ¶with a ***deeper*** *purpose,* that of ... ...というもっと深い目的で. ¶It should be kept in mind as a distinctly ***defined*** *purpose.* それをはっきりした目的として頭に入れておくべきだ. ¶a ***definite*** *purpose* 一定の目的. ¶with a ***deliberate*** *purpose* ことさらに. ¶successfully achieve the ***desired*** *purpose* 初期の目的を達成する. ¶the ***didactic*** *purpose* 教訓の目的. ¶a ***dishonest*** *purpose* 不正な目的. ¶Its ***dominating*** (=main) *purpose* is practicalness. その主なる目的は実用にある. ¶*Tatami* serve the ***double*** (=***dual***) *purpose* of seats by day and beds by night. 畳は昼は座席に夜は寝床にという二重の用をする. ¶a trip for ***educational*** *purposes* 修学旅行. ¶the utilization of Niagara Falls for ***electric*** *purposes* ナイヤガラばく布を水力電気に利用すること. ¶He thinks that fiction should be the handmaid of an ***ethical*** *purpose.* 彼は小説は道徳的目的達成の道具であるべきだと考えている. ¶an ***evil*** *purpose* 悪い目的. ¶the society was founded for the ***express*** *purposes* of ... その協会は...という特殊の目的で設立したものである. ¶He has a ***firm*** *purpose* in life. 彼は人生に確固たる目的をもっている. 【類】with ***firm*** *purpose.* ¶It has no ***fixed*** *purpose.* それにはこれという目的はない. ¶for ***general*** *purposes* 一般用に ‖ a jeep—a car for ***general*** *purposes* 万能車ジープ. ¶serve a ***good*** *purpose* 結構役に立つ. ¶some ***hidden*** *purposes* ある隠れた目的. ¶Good habits serve a ***high*** *purpose* everywhere. よい習慣はどの方面でもりっぱに役に立つ. ¶utilize it for ***human*** *purposes* 人類の用途にそれを利用する. ¶an ***immovable*** *purpose* 不動の目的. ¶answer the ***intended*** *purpose* 企画した目的に適う. ¶with the ***laudable*** *purpose* of ... ...という奇特な意図で. ¶for some ***legitimate*** *purpose* なにか合理的な目的のために. ¶learn a foreign language for ***literary*** *purposes* 文学上の目的で外国語を学ぶ. ¶People sometimes work hard to ***little*** *purpose.* 人は往々懸命に働いても得る所がほとんどないことがある. ¶a ***lofty*** *purpose* 高尚な目的. ¶the ***main*** *purpose* of ... ...の主な目的. ¶to carry out this ***manifold*** *purpose* この多様な目的を貫徹するために. ¶It is used for ***medicinal*** *purposes.* それは薬用にする. ¶a high man with clean hands and ***moral*** *purpose* 清廉で道念の高い人. 【類】a work of art that has a ***moral*** *purpose.* ¶It is good enough for ***ordinary*** *purposes.* 普通のことにはそれで結構間に合って行く. ¶It is used for ***ornamental*** *purposes.* それを装飾に使う. ¶one's ***ostensible*** *purpose* その表面上の目的. ¶for ***pacific*** *purposes* 平和の目的. ¶a ***particular*** *purpose* 特別の目的. ¶for ***political*** and ***strategical*** *purposes* 政治上及び戦略上の目的. ¶for ***practical*** *purposes* 実用向きには. 【類】for more ***practical*** *purposes.* ¶for our ***present*** *purposes* it is sufficient to ... 差当り...すれば足りる ‖ a man whom for ***present*** *purposes* I will call Mr. Jones 仮に私がジョーンズ氏と呼ぶ人. ¶our ***prevailing*** *purpose* われわれの主なる目的. ¶The ***primary*** *purpose* of art is to pleasure. 芸術の根本の目的は心を楽しませせることにある. ¶bequeath for ***public*** *purposes* 公共のことに遺贈する. ¶devote the house to some ***public*** or ***national*** *purpose* その家をなにか公共的なまたは国家的な用途に当てる. ¶for ***recreative*** *purposes* 気晴らしに. ¶for ***religious*** *purposes* 宗教上のことに. ¶be not large enough for the ***required*** *purpose* そのときには小さ過ぎる. ¶It answers the ***same*** *purpose.* それでもよい. ¶Such statistics are a mockery for any ***scientific*** *purposes.* こうした統計は科学上の研究にはなんにもならないとだ. ¶for ***selfish*** *purposes* 利己的な目的に. ¶with a ***set*** *purpose* 断固として. ¶serve ***several*** *purposes* 様々の目的に適する. ¶with a ***single*** *purpose* ひたすら, 一筋に. ¶a ***singlehearted*** *purpose* to ... ...にしようとする一ずの目的. ¶a ***social*** *purpose* 社交上の目的. ¶the ***sole*** *purpose* 唯一の目的. 【類】the ***sole*** or the ***main*** *purpose* of ... ¶If I succeed in this undertaking, I shall have been born to ***some*** *purpose.* この事業に成功すれば私も生がいがあるというものだ. ¶for one ***special*** *purpose* ある特定の目的のために. ¶For ***statistical*** *purposes* ... have been classified under three classes. 統計のために...を三種に分類した. ¶a ***steady*** *purpose* 確固たる目的. ¶for some ***subsidiary*** *purposes* 補助的目的として. ¶serve a ***temporary*** *purpose* 一時の間に合う. ¶cover a ***treacherous*** *purpose* with smiles 笑い顔で腹黒さをごまかす. ¶it serves the ***triple*** *purpose* of ... それは...という三重の目的に役立つ. ¶its ***twofold*** (***threefold***) *purpose* その二(三)重の用途. ¶for the ***ulterior*** *purpose* of ... ...という先の目的に. 【類】He had an ***ulterior*** *purpose* in doing this. ¶an ***unlawful*** *purpose* 不法な意図. ¶It would serve no ***useful*** *purpose* to change the terminology. 用語を変えて見た所でなんの益にもならないだろう. 【類】serve no ***useful*** *purpose.* ¶fulfil ***valuable*** *purposes* 重要な目的を遂げる. ¶for ***warlike*** *purposes* 軍事上の目的に. ¶For ***what*** *purpose* is this instrument? この道具はなにに使うのか. ¶use it for a ***wrong*** *purpose* それを誤用する.

Q² for ***advertising*** *purposes* 広告の目的で. ¶Farmers withhold portions of rice crops for ***bartering*** *purposes.* 農夫は物々交換用として作米の一部を保有する. ¶The land was sold in lots for ***building*** *purposes.* その土地は宅地として売られた. 【類】The ground on which the old home stood was sold for ***building*** *purposes.* ¶for ***business*** *purpose* 営業用に. 【類】learn Spanish for ***business*** *purposes.* ¶for ***defense*** *purposes* 保安のために, 護身用として. ¶water supplies used for ***drinking*** and ***culinary*** *purposes* 飲料及び調理用の給水. ¶for ***emergency*** *purposes* 非常用として. ¶for ***examination*** *purposes* 試験のために. ¶be sold for ***exhibition*** *purposes* 見世物師に売られる. ¶those for ***export*** *purposes* 輸出向けの品物. ¶use for ***gift*** *purposes* 贈答用として用いる. ¶for ***fire fighting*** *purposes* 防火用に. ¶for ***household*** *purposes* 家庭用の. ¶be provided with wireless apparatus for ***liaison*** *purposes* 連絡用に無線施設がしてある. ¶a ***life*** *purpose* 一生の目的. ¶grow the squash on a large scale for ***market*** *purposes* 夏かぼちゃを市場向けに作る. ¶Many people visit the Alps for ***mountaineering*** *purposes* 登山のためアルプスを訪れるものが多い. ¶for ***peace*** (***war***) *purposes* 平和(戦争)のために. ¶a piece of land used by the public for ***pleasure*** *purposes* 遊園地に当てた一区画の土地. 【類】keep a horse for ***pleasure*** *purposes* (道楽に). ¶electricity for ***power*** and ***heating*** *purposes* 動力と熱に使う電気. ¶made for ***propaganda*** *purposes* 宣伝用に作られた. ¶Those who register will receive a badge which is to be worn for ***recognition*** *purposes.* 登録完了の諸君には会員証として着けるバッジをお渡しする. ¶regrouping of forces for *redeployment purposes* 兵力転進のための再編成. ¶use a book for *reference purposes* 本を参考用に使う. ¶contribute materials for *relief purposes* 救済のため資材を寄贈する. ¶a library for *research purposes* 研究用図書館. ¶peanuts for *seed purposes* 種子用(としての)ピーナッツ. ¶a smokeless powder for *starting purposes*〘競技〙スタート用の無煙火薬. ¶flintglass for *table purposes* 食卓用のフリントガラス. ¶for *toilet purposes* 化粧用に. ¶for *training purposes* 訓練用. ¶only for *utility purposes* 実用一点張りの. ¶ships for *war purposes* 軍用船. ¶for *writing purposes* 書きもの用の.

P This is ***beside*** our present *purpose*. これはわれわれの当面の目的に関係がない. ¶actuated ***by*** a high *purpose* 理想にもえて. 【類】a life characterized ***by*** high *purpose*. ¶set it aside ***for*** a *purpose* ある目的のためにそれをとっておく ‖ learn German ***for*** *purposes* of ... ...の目的のためにドイツ語を学ぶ ‖ impracticable ***for*** *purposes* of modern efficiency 現代の高能率をあげるには非実用的な. 【類】He would not sell them because he wanted to keep them ***for*** *purposes* of comparison (参考に取っておく). / serve ***for*** both *purposes* / He bought the land ***for*** the *purpose* of building on it. / ostensibly ***for*** the *purpose* of ... / unfit ***for*** the intended *purpose* ‖ I have sufficient cash ***for*** all *purposes*. 私にはどんな用途にも向けられる現金がある. ¶it is aside ***from*** the *purpose* of ... それは...の目的にかなわない ‖ Nothing will deter him ***from*** his *purpose*. なに物も彼の目的をさまたげることはできない. ¶firm ***in*** *purpose* 志の堅固な ‖ similar ***in*** *purpose* 目的が同じな ‖ waver ***in*** *purpose* 目的がふらつく ‖ He is wanting ***in*** *purpose*. 彼は決意が弱い. ¶He did it ***of*** set *purpose*. 彼は確固とした目当があって(故意に)それをやった. ¶You did it ***on*** *purpose*. 君はわざとやった. ‖ It is not likely that he did it ***on*** *purpose*. わざとそうしたとも思えない. 【類】When he was in America he made a journey of seven hundred miles ***on*** *purpose* to get a glimpse of the Niagara. / Pray don't trouble yourself to come ***on*** *purpose*. ¶He talked much ***to*** the *purpose*. 彼は大いに要領を得た話をした. ‖ It came off ***to*** no *purpose*. 結局なんにもならなかった. ¶It is not ***to*** my present *purpose*. それは差当り私の目的でない. ‖ those who live ***to*** no *purpose* 生きがいのない人々. 【類】An Italian proverb declares that a man has lived ***to*** no *purpose* unless he has either built a house, begotten a son, or written a book. ‖ We must live ***to*** some *purpose*. われわれはなにか意義ある生活をせねばならない. ‖ ***to*** the *purpose* (=effect) that ... ...という意味の. ¶a novel (story) ***with*** a *purpose*=a purpose novel (=story) [作者の意図を盛った]目的小説 ‖ ***with*** the *purpose* of ... ...の目的で ‖ ***with*** this *purpose* in mind (=view) この目的を眼中において. ¶it is not ***within*** the *purpose* of this volume to ... ...するのは本書の目的でない. ¶reading ***without*** *purpose* 目的なしの読書.

P² Such is the *purpose* ***of*** this document. よってくだんのごとし. 【類】the *purpose* ***of*** the foundation of a society.

purpose, *v*. 計画する.

M be ***fully*** *purposed* ねらいはしっかりしている.

O *purpose* a visit to America アメリカ行を計画する.

purr, *v*. [ねこが]ごろごろのどを鳴らす; 悦に入る. 「た.

M The cat *purred* ***softly***. ねこはごろごろとのどを鳴らし

M² a pussy *purring* ***on*** to her master 主人のもとにのどを鳴らしながら行く小ねこ.

P She was *purring* ***at*** her lover. 彼女は恋人に鼻声で甘えていた. ¶*purr* ***with*** delight (=pleasure) 喜んでのどを鳴らす; 悦に入る. 【類】*purr* ***with*** content (=satisfaction).

purse, *n*. 財布; 資財; 懸賞金; 寄金.

V ***abstract*** the *purse* from the pocket ポケットから財布をする. ¶***carry*** one's *purse* ***along*** 財布を持ち歩く. ¶***close*** one's *purse* 財布を締める. ¶***draw out*** one's *purse* 財布を取り出す. ¶***drop*** one's *purse* 財布を落す. ¶***empty*** one's *purse* to the last penny 財布の底をはたく. ¶***exhaust*** a nation's *purse* 国民の財源をからす. ¶***fill*** a *purse* [with money] 財布に銭を満たす. ¶***fit*** the buyer's *purse* 買手の懐勘定に合う. ¶***give*** (=***put up***) a *purse* [競技など]賞金を与える. ¶I ***have*** my *purse* with me. 私は財布を持っている. ¶Who ***holds*** the *purse* rules the house. 〘諺〙財布の主が家の主. ¶***let fall*** one's *purse* 財布を落す. ¶***make*** a *purse* 人のために寄付金を募る ‖ ***make*** a silk *purse* out of a sow's ear (=unpromising material) 一見望みのない人または材料をりっぱに利用する. ¶***make up*** a *purse* as a present 贈呈の目的で寄金する. 【類】They ***made up*** a *purse* for the poor widow. ¶I ***miss*** my *purse*. 私の財布が見付からない. ¶***open*** one's *purse* 財布を開ける. ¶***pick up*** a *purse* 財布を拾う. ¶***present*** him a *purse* containing ... ...の寄金を彼に贈る. ¶***raise*** a *purse* for the purpose そのために寄金する. ¶***recover*** one's *purse* [失った]財布をとり戻す. ¶***replenish*** one's *purse* 中味のなくなった財布へ新たに金を入れる. ¶***require*** a full *purse* 大分金がいる. ¶The hotel provides accommodations to ***suit*** every *purse*. そのホテルにはだれの懐都合にも適する宿泊設備がある. ¶***take out*** one's *purse* 財布を取出す. ¶***win*** the *purse* in a horse-race 競馬で懸賞金を得る.

V² My *purse* ***is gone!*** 私の財布が失くなった.

Q a patron with ***ample*** *purse* 金持の後援者. ¶a *purse* ***bulged*** with money お金でふくらんだ財布. ¶a ***cold*** (=an ***empty***) *purse* 乏しい所持金. ¶a ***common*** *purse* 共有金. ¶suited to both ***fat*** and ***lean*** *purses* 金持にも貧乏人にも適した. ¶A happy heart is better than a ***full*** *purse*. ふくれた財布より幸福な心の方がよい. ¶a ***heavy*** (=***long***) *purse* 重い財布; 富裕. 【類】have a ***heavy*** (=***long***) *purse*. ¶In the newsreel theatre I can enjoy a recreation my ***humble*** *purse* can afford. ニュース映画劇場で私相応の安い娯楽が得られる. ¶a ***light*** *purse* 軽い財布. ¶with ***limited*** *purse* 限りある資力で. ¶find a ***lost*** *purse* 失くした財布を見つける. ¶a ***missing*** *purse* 失くした財布. ¶for ***modest*** *purses* 余り金のないものには. ¶Your *purse* is ***normal***. 君の収入は並だ. ¶embryo millionaires with ***plethoric*** (=fat) *purses* 金のたんまりある小成金ども. ¶a ***plump*** *purse* ふくれた財布. ¶the ***public*** *purse* 公庫. ¶because of a ***restricted*** *purse* 支出に限りがあるので. ¶a student with a ***shallow*** *purse* 学費の不十分な学生. ¶a ***short*** (=***thin***) *purse* 中味の少ない財布. ¶a ***slender*** (=***slim***) *purse* 中味の少ない財布 ‖ They are within the reach of most ***slender*** *purses*. それらはどんな貧乏人にも買える. 【類】The terms of payment are so liberal that they present no obstacle even to the ***slenderest*** *purse*. ¶a ***sovereign*** *purse* 国家の財政. ¶a ***well-lined*** *purse* 中味の沢山ある財布.

Q² the ***city*** *purse* 市の財政. ¶a ***patent stocking*** *purse* for ladies くつ下にとりつける特許婦人用紙入れ.

P live ***according to*** one's *purse* 収入相応の暮しをする. ¶***beyond*** the *purse* of ... ...の資力の及ばない. ¶I have a pound ***in*** my *purse*. 私は財布に一ポンド持っている. ¶put it ***into*** a *purse* それを財布に入れる. ¶the power ***of*** the *purse* 金の力. ¶He is favored ***with*** a fat *purse*. 彼は裕福だ. ¶live ***within*** one's *purse* (=means) 収入以内で生活する.

P² I have not my *purse* ***with*** me. 私は財布を持っていない.

purse, *v*. つぼめる; 〘まれ〙財布に入れる.

M *purse* ***up*** one's lips (mouth) くちびる(口)をつぼめる ‖ *purse* ***up*** one's money 銭を財布に入れる.

purser, *n*. 事務長.

Q² a ***Cunard*** *purser* [英国]キューナード汽船の事務長.

purse-string, *n*. 財布のひも.

V ***hold*** the *purse-strings* 出納をつかさどる. ¶***loosen*** (***tighten***) one's *purse-strings* 気前よく金を出す(出さない). ¶***untie*** one's *purse-strings* 財布を解く, 金を出す.

pushcart, *n*. [行商人の]手押し車.

P buy fruit and vegetable from a *pushcart* (=pushcart pedler) [くだものや野菜を]行商人から買う.

pursuance, *n*. 追求, 遂行.

P ***in*** *pursuance* of Article ... 第...条により ‖ ***in*** *pursuance* of the terms of an obligation [契約上の]義務条件に従って. 【類】***in*** *pursuance* of an ancient custom which dates back over 300 years / ***in*** *pursuance* of your instructions (示教) / ***in*** *pursuance* of the orders (policy hitherto adopted) / ***in*** *pursuance* of a resolution of the Delegates to the Congress in London on July 5, 1912 / ***in*** *pursuance* of the resolution passed by ... / ***in*** *pursuance* of this aim.

pursuant, *a*. 従って, よって.

P *pursuant* ***to*** Article VIII. of the Articles of Association of the above-named Club 上記会の定款第八条により. 【類】*pursuant* ***to*** the Statute 22 and 23: C. 35 (第三十五章第二十二・三節) / *pursuant* ***to*** the agreement with ...

pursue, *v*. 追う, 追求する; 続行する.

M *closely pursue* the enemy すぐ敵の後を追う. ¶when *hotly pursued* 激しく追求されたときに. ¶He *prudently pursued* a plan. 彼は大事を取って計画を続行した.

P *pursue after* ... ...を追う. ¶*pursue* a remedy *at* law 救済を法律に求める. ¶*pursued by* the law 法律の手で追求されて. ¶*pursue* the study of English *for* five years 五年間英語をやる. ¶*pursue* a teacher *with* questions 先生を質問攻めにする.

O *pursue* a 4-year course of study at Lincoln High リンカン高校で四年間履習する.

pursuit, *n.* 追跡, 追求; 研究; 職業, 業務.

V *abandon* the *pursuit* of learning 学業を廃する. ¶*give up* (=*relinquish*) the *pursuit* [狩などで]追跡をあきらめる. ¶*take up* a *pursuit* with whole-hearted zest 専心研究を始める.

Q *agricultural* (*commercial*) *pursuits* 農(商)業. ¶*amorous pursuits* 女(男)道楽. ¶those who are engaged in *artistic pursuits* 芸術的な業務に従事している人々. ¶throw aside commercial for more *congenial pursuits* 一層適切な職業のために商業をやめる. ¶*daily pursuits* 日々の仕事. ¶the *endless persuit* of wealth 富の際限ない追求. ¶a *fascinating pursuit* 魅力ある職業. ¶a *favorite pursuit*= a ruling passion, a hobby 道楽.【類】Hawking (たか狩) was a *favorite pursuit* of the Japanese nobility in the middle ages. ¶*gentle* (=honorable) *pursuits* りっぱな仕事. ¶a *humble* but *honorable* (=*respectable*) *pursuit* 微せんではあるが恥かしくない職業. ¶*industrial pursuits* 工業. ¶acquire interest in some *intellectual pursuit* ある知的な仕事に興味を覚える. ¶Agriculture is the *leading pursuit* in Berkshire. 農業はバークシャにおける主な職業である. ¶adopt a *legitimate pursuit* 正業につく. ¶the *lifelong pursuit* of their chosen subject 彼らの選択科目の終生の研究. ¶devote oneself to *literary pursuits* 文筆に一身を委ねる. ¶*lucrative pursuits* 有利な職業. ¶*mercantile pursuits* 商売. ¶in the *peaceful pursuit* of learning のんびりした学問の研究に. ¶the *sabbathless pursuit* of wealth 安息日も守らずに富を追うこと. ¶*sedentary pursuits* 座業. ¶a profession the *successful pursuit* of which might lead to fortune うまく行けば一財産作れそうな職業. ¶a *thriving pursuit* 好況産業. ¶an *undignified pursuit* 下品な職業. ¶Fishing and hunting were their *universal pursuits*. 漁猟と狩猟が彼ら一般の職業であった. ¶a life wasted in the *vain pursuit* of pleasure 無益な快楽の追求に浪費した一生. ¶adults who wish to be trained for a *vocational pursuit* 職業の訓練を得たいと思う成年者. ¶a *worthy pursuit* りっぱな研究.

Q² be engaged in *business pursuit* 商売をやっている. ¶*peace-time pursuits* 平和時の職業.

P He is now *beyond* successful *pursuit*. 彼にはもうとても追付かれない. ¶indulge *in pursuit* 研究にふける ‖ *in pursuit* of health (pleasure) 健康(など)を求めて ‖ come (go) *in pursuit* of ... ...を追って来る(行く) ‖ send a person *in pursuit* 人にその跡を追わせる ‖ *in* the *pursuit* of this purpose=to attain this end この目的達成のために.【類】*in* the *pursuits* of wealth (=money making) / *in pursuit* of happiness (peace, pleasure) / I hope that it will meet with success *in* the *pusuit* of its object.

P² with ... in hot *pursuit after* him ...が彼の後を夢中に追ってきて. ¶the *pursuit of* an enemy 敵の追及 ‖ the *pursuit of* advanced study 高級の研究 ‖ the *pursuit of* a plan 計画の遂行 ‖ the *pursuit of* pleasure 快楽の追求.

purvey, *v.* 食料品を調達する.

P *purvey* meat *for* the army 陸軍に食肉をおさめる.【類】*purvey for* the Royal Household.

purveyor, *n.* 用達商人.

P *from* the *purveyor* to the consumer 用達商人から消費者へ.

P² *purveyors to* the Government (Imperial Household) 諸官省(など)御用達.

purview, *n.* 権限, 限界, 活動範囲.

V It *dominates* the *purview*. それは顕著な存在を示している.

P come *within* the *purview* of ... ...の権限内に入る.

pus, *n.* のう.

V It *discharges pus* うみを出す. ¶*Pus forms* (=*gathers*) in a wound. きずがのうを持つ.

Q *blue pus* うみ.

push, *n.* 押すこと; 奮進; 奮発; ひっ迫.

V I *gave* him a hard *push*. 私は彼を激しく押しのけた. ‖ *give* a *push* to the door ドアを押す / He *gave* me a good *push*. ¶*make* a *push* 奮進する, 奮発する ‖ *make* a *push* to get it done quickly 急いでやってもらうように催促する. ¶It *shows* no *push*. それは活動していない.

Q He gave me a *sudden push* backwards. 彼は突然私を押し返した. ¶a *vigorous push* まい進.

Q² a *bell push* ベル押し. ¶automatic alarms and "*break glass*" *pushes* 自動報知器と「ガラス割り」ボタン押し装置.

P *at* a *push* (=pinch) 危機に際して ‖ *at* one *push* 一押しに, 一気に. ¶come *to* the *push* せっぱ詰る. ¶He gave a *push at* the door. 彼は戸を一押し押した.

P² at a *push for* money 金に詰って.

push, *v.* 押す, 突く; 押し進める.

M Preparations are being *pushed actively*. 準備が盛んに進められている. ¶*push* oneself *ahead* 奮闘する. ¶*push apart* 押分ける. ¶*push aside* (=*away*) 推しのける. ¶*push back* 押返す ‖ *push back* the deadline 締切時間を延ばす. ¶She *pushed* the drawer *closed*. 彼女はぴしゃと引出しを閉めた. ¶The peninsula *pushes far* into the sea. その半島はずっと海に突き出ている. ¶vigorously *push forward* まい進する ‖ *push forward* a claim [損害賠償の]要求を推進する ‖ *push forward* the delivery 配達を速進させる.【類】*push forward* one's action / The work will be *pushed forward* with the utmost despatch (大至急). / vigorously *push forward* enterprises of productive significance (生産的な企業) / *push forward* the boundaries of science (科学の領域) / *push forward* to avoid delay. ¶*push* a door *open* (*shut*) ドアを押してあける(しめる). ¶*push out* new shoots 新芽を出す ‖ *push out* to sea [舟が]海に出る ‖ a cape *pushing out* a long way into the sea 長く海に突出しているみさき. ¶*push upward* the standards of living 生活水準を高める. ¶The work is now being *vigorously pushed* on. その仕事は目下猛烈に促進されている.

M² *push* the work *along* 仕事を進める. ¶*push* ... *down* ... を押し倒す. ¶*push off* in a boat 小舟でこぎ出す. ¶We must *push on* (=hurry up). われわれは急がねばならない. ‖ *push on* business 事業を発展させる.【類】The work is being *pushed on* as quickly as possible. ‖ *push on* at a rapid pace 急速に突進する ‖ *push on* to the front 前進する.【類】He studied very hard and soon *pushed on* to the front (首席). ‖ *push on* with one's work 仕事を押し進める. ¶*push* a bill *through* 議案を通過させる ‖ *push* the matter *through* その仕事をやり通す. ¶*push up* a shade (blind, window) 日よけ(など)をあげる ‖ *push up* production 生産をあげる ‖ pay well to *push up* a disagreeable affair いやな仕事をやってのけるようにいい報酬を出す.

P *push against* the fence へいに押しかかる ‖ Do not *push against* me. 私に寄りかかるな. ¶*push at* a doorbell ドアのベルを押す. ¶*push* a person *for* payment 支払いを人に迫る ‖ I am *pushed* (=pressed) *for* time (money). 私は時間(金)の余裕がない. ¶*push* money *in* the girl's hands, saying ... ...と言いながら少女の手に金を握らせる. ¶*push into* world market 世界市場に進出する ‖ *push* the war *into* the enemy's country 敵国に攻め入る. ¶*push* the table *nearer* [to] the window もっと窓の方へ食卓を寄せる. ¶*push* a person *off* a train (car) 列車(など)から人を押出す. ¶*push* a person *out of* a room 人を室外に押出す. ¶*push* a person *over* cliff がけから人を突き落す. ¶*push* one's way *through* a big crowd 人込みの中を押分けて行く. ¶*push to* the front 進出する ‖ *Push* it a little *to* the right. それを少し右の方へ寄せろ. ‖ *push* a horse *to* a greater speed 馬の速度をもっと早める ‖ asceticism *pushed to* the point of self-torture 苦行と称すべきほどの禁欲.【類】The series have not yet been *pushed to* completion. / *push* a person *to* the verge of exhaustion / It can develop a speed of ... when *pushed to* the utmost (最高速度). ‖ *pushed to* the last extremity せっぱ詰って. ‖ He *pushed* the door *to*. ドアを押してしめた. ¶*push with* all one's might. 力一杯に押す.

put, *v.* おく(など).

M *put apart* from the rest=segregate 他のものと分ける. ¶*Put aside* thy duty for no man. おのれのなすべき仕事を人に任すなかれ. ‖ *putting aside* an argument 議論はしばらくおき ‖ *put aside* rivalries 張り合うことはやめる.【類】*put aside* one's *pride* / *put aside* every other consideration / *put* ***aside*** the book one is reading. ¶*put* ***away*** a wife 妻を離婚する ‖ *put* it ***away*** それをしまい込む. 【類】 *put* ***away*** tea things (茶道具) in the cupboard / *put* ***away*** the tools / The last dish was now *put* ***away.*** / *put* ***away*** (貯える) a little money / *put* it ***away*** for use later / *put* ***away*** temptation (誘惑) ‖ *put* ***away*** all prejudices すべての偏見を除去する. ¶*put* them ***back*** in the closet もと通り戸だなにそれを入れておく.【類】*put* the manuscript ***back*** into the bookcase / *Put* it ***back*** on the shelf when you're through. / *Put* them ***back*** just as they were. ‖ *put* him ***back*** to bed (=sleep) ‖ *put* ***back*** the hands of a clock 時計の針をもどす.【類】All the clocks and watches were *put* ***back*** an hour on Saturday night. ‖ *put* the clock ***back***〖比ゆ〗時代に逆行する ‖ *put* ***back*** (=check) the efforts of reformers 改革派の努力を抑える ‖ the ship, seriously damaged, *put* ***back*** for repairs ひどくいたんだので修繕のため入きょさせた船 ‖ be *put* ***back*** in its progress [仕事などが]後戻りする ‖ *put* ***back*** the ship into active service 船を再び現役につかせる. ¶to *put* it ***boldly*** 露骨に言えば. ¶to *put* it ***bluntly*** 無遠慮に言えば.【類】To *put* ***bluntly,*** he is far from a gentleman. ¶to *put* it ***briefly*** 簡単に言うと.【類】to *put* it ***briefly,*** his idea is that ... ¶He *puts* it ***clearly*** and ***concisely*** when he says. 彼は言う時にははっきりと簡潔に言う. ¶as one writer ***cleverly*** *puts* it ある作家がうまいことを言っているが. ¶*put* the counsels more ***concretely*** この助言をもっと具体的に言う. ¶*put* the watch ***fast*** 時計を進める. ¶be hard *put* ***financially*** 財政難に陥っている. ¶The pronunciation preferred by the Editor is *put* ***first.*** (辞書などの)編者がよいと思う発音は第一においてある. ‖ *put* interest ***first*** and the truth second 興味を第一に事実を第二におく. ¶as he ***forcibly*** *put* it 彼が力強く言っている通り. ¶Trees *put* ***forth*** buds in spring. 木は春芽を出す.【類】*put* ***forth*** green leaves / *put* ***forth*** young *shoots* (若芽) / *put* ***forth*** flowers / Trees are beginning to *put* ***forth*** buds and leaves. / The tree *puts* ***forth*** its sprouts (芽). ‖ *put* ***forth*** the arm 腕をのばす ‖ *put* ***forth*** strength 力を揮う.【類】*put* ***forth*** a great deal of effort / *put* ***forth*** one's best effort / the efforts that are being *put* ***forth*** for the good of the community at large (社会全般の利益のため) / *put* ***forth*** energy=energize / *put* ***forth*** reasons (理由をあげる) ‖ *put* ***forth*** (=make known) opinions 意見を発表する ‖ *put* ***forth*** an argument 議論を持出す ‖ *put* ***forth*** a book 書籍を発行する ‖ *put* ***forth*** a prior claim さらに重要な要求を出す ‖ *put* ***forth*** one's hand against ... …に対して暴力を揮う；殺す. ¶*put* ***forward*** an amendment 修正案を出す.【類】*put* ***forward*** an argument / *put* ***forward*** a motion (動議) / *put* ***forward*** (発表する) a plan / *put* ***forward*** conditions (条件) / *put* ***forward*** facts or reasons (事実または理由) / *put* ***forward*** a proposal (提案) / *put* ***forward*** a proposition (計画案) / *put* ***forward*** criticisms and opinions (批判や意見) / *put* ***forward*** one suggestion (参考案) after another / various theories are *put* ***forward*** concerning ... / *put* ***forward*** a new theory / views *put* ***forward*** by ... / *put* ***forward*** the view which he has always held (持説) / humbly *put* ***forward*** the excuse that ... / has no desire to *put* ***forward*** a claim to exhaustiveness / *put* one's business ***forward*** / *put* ***forward*** a competition ‖ *put* an hour ***forward*** (***backward***) [時計の針を]一時間進ませる(遅らせる).【類】*put* the hands of a clock ***forward*** by five minutes ‖ a person who is *put* ***forward*** by others as an aspirant to an office ある地位の志望者として人から推薦された人. ¶be ***hard*** *put* to it to ... やむなく…する. ¶***How*** shall I *put* it? どう言ったらいいかしら. ¶To *put* it ***mildly,*** I don't care for him. ひかえめに言って, 私は彼を好かない.【類】To *put* ***mildly,*** he is not a gentleman. / To say that I was frightened is *putting* it ***mildly.*** ¶to *put* it ***plainly*** (=*frankly*) はっきり(率直に)言って. ¶*put* (=stick) ***out*** one's tongue 舌を出す ‖ *put* ***out*** one's head up out of water 水面に首を出す. ‖ *put* ***out*** (=stretch) an arm (arms) 片(両)腕を延ばす. ¶All trees *put* ***out*** (=forth) their green leaves in spring. 木々は春に青葉を出す ‖ *put* ***out*** advertising in papers 新聞に広告を出す ‖ *put* ***out*** to sea 出港する ‖ *put* ***out*** for ... …に向け舟を出す.【類】*put* ***out*** in a boat ‖ *put* ***out*** [articles] in a little booklet [論文を]小冊子として出す.【類】*put* ***out*** in a small boat upon a calm sea / *put* ***out*** a bulletin of ... ‖ *put* ***out*** (=spend) a good deal of money 相当の金を使う ‖ *put* ***out*** the lamp ランプを消す.【類】*Put* the light ***out.***=*Put* ***out*** the light. / try to *put* ***out*** the flames / *put* ***out*** a fire with water / just before lights were *put* ***out*** / *Put* it ***out,*** please (ラジオ・電灯など). / The fire department had to be called to *put* the fire ***out.*** ‖ the products *put* ***out*** by this firm 本会社の製品 ‖ *put* ***out*** the eyes of prisoners 捕虜の目を失明させる ‖ be quite *put* ***out*** すっかり度胆を抜かれる ‖ *put* ***out*** feelers さぐりを入れる.【類】*put* ***out*** its first cautious feeler to ... ‖ *put* oneself ***out*** 心配する ‖ He was very much *put* ***out*** because he heard his landlord would put him out. 家主が追出すと聞いて彼は困りに困った. ‖ *put* one's servant ***out*** 召使を出してしまう ‖ He had his ankle *put* ***out*** (=dislocated) during the game. 彼はその競技中足首をねんざした.【類】My arm was *put* ***out*** by accident. ‖ He is so good-tempered a man that he is not easily *put* ***out.*** 彼は人がいいので中々怒らない. ‖ *put* ***out*** (=place) money at interest [金を寝かしておかないで]利が付くようにする ‖ The batter was *put* ***out.***〖野球〗三振(凡打)した. ‖ The runner was *put* ***out*** an inch before the home plate.〖野球〗走者は本塁寸前で刺殺された. ‖ have one's light *put* ***out*** [比ゆ的に] 信用が地に落ちる ‖ be *put* ***out*** by a caught fly〖野球〗フライをあげてアウトになる. ¶to *put* it ***pithily*** 一口に言うと. ¶to *put* it ***plainly*** (=frankly) もっと分かりやすく言うと. ¶*put* the matter ***right*** (***wrong***) 事件を落着させる(荒立たせる). ¶*putting* it ***shortly,*** we can say that ... 簡単に言えば…となる. ¶to *put* it ***squarely*** はっきり言えば. ¶*put* the argument ***strong*** 議論を強く言い表わす. ¶to *put* it ***strongly*** 極言すれば. ¶He did not *put* it ***that way*** exactly. 彼ははっきりそうとは言わなかった. ¶He is most anxious that the plan should be *put* ***through.*** 彼はその計画の実行を熱望している. ¶*put* the poems ***together*** in a volume その詩を集めて一巻にする ‖ Some furniture is *put* ***together*** with glue. 家具にはにかわづけのもある. ‖ *put* ***together*** a large amount of learning in a book 多量の知識を一冊の本に集積する.【類】There are nearly as many medical schools in the United States as in all of the rest of the civilized world *put* ***together.*** ‖ *put* this and that ***together*** かれこれを総合して考える. ¶*put* a person ***wise*** (=inform a person) about ...〘口語〙…を人に知らせる. ¶to say ... would be *putting* it ***wrongly*** …と言うのは当らない.

M[2] *put* ***about*** (=change the course of) a ship 船の進路を変える. ¶*put* it ***across*** ...=get even with ... …に復しゅうする. ¶*put* ***by*** ... against a rainy day まさかの用意に…を貯えておく ‖ *put* money ***by*** 貯金する. ¶*put* a book ***down*** on the desk 本を机上におく ‖ *put* ***down*** one's pen 筆をおく；もう筆を執らない ‖ *Put* your hands ***down*** on your sides and stand erect. 両手を両わきにつけてちゃんと立ちなさい. ‖ *put* me ***down*** at ... …で降ろしてくれ(電車の乗客の言葉) ‖ *put* ***down*** boring [探鉱用の]ボーリングをおろす ‖ *Put* ***down*** here your name and address, please. ここにお名前と住所を記入して下さい. ‖ *put* ***down*** an idea in black and white 考えを文に書く.【類】*put* down every item of domestic expenses ‖ *Put* me ***down*** for $50. 私の分を五十ドルとしておいて下さい(寄付など). ‖ *Put* them ***down*** to me, please. 私の分として記帳しておいて下さい.【類】*Put* it ***down*** to my acconnt. ‖ The damage is *put* ***down*** at between $7,000 to $10,000. その損害は七千ドルから一万ドルと見積られる. ‖ *put* ***down*** a rebellion (riot, revolt, insurrection) 反乱(など)を静める.【類】*put* ***down*** a strike / *put* ***down*** threats to peace / *put* ***down*** an attack ‖ *Put* me ***down*** at the Jockey Club. ジョッキークラブで僕を降ろしてくれ. ‖ Sugar has *put* ***down*** the use of honey. 砂糖ができてはちみつがすたれた. ‖ *put* ***down*** one's expenditure 出費を切りつめる ‖ *put* ***down*** old *practices* 旧慣をやめる ‖ *put* ***down*** the nuisance 妨害を除く ‖ *put* it ***down*** to his neglect that ... …を彼の怠慢によるものとする ‖ If so we may safely *put* him ***down*** as a person with a small mind. もしそうならわれわれは彼を小人と見て間違いない.【類】Must we *put* all this ***down*** to mere chance? / you may *put* it ***down*** as a certainty that ... ‖ *put* a person ***down*** as a fool 人をばかだときめ込む ‖ I *put* him ***down*** for nine years old (=as nine). 私は彼を九歳と見当をつけた.【類】I *put* him ***down*** at 35. ‖ *put* ***down*** the price of ... …の値を下げる.【類】Can't you *put* it ***down*** to 500 yen? ¶*put* *in* one's answer 返事をする ‖ He has *put in* an appearance. 彼はやって来た. ‖ *put in* a claim for compensation 損害賠償の訴訟を起す ‖ *put in* a word 口をはさむ ‖ *put in* wedgewise 横合から口を出す ‖ *put in* a passage (clause) 一節(項)をはさむ ‖ *put in* a claim for the damage 損害に対し苦情を申入れる. 【類】*put in* a word of sympathy for ... ‖ The glazier has *put in* a new pane of glass. ガラス屋が新しいガラス板をはめた. ‖ *put* one's head *in* at the door 戸口からのぞき込む ‖ *put in* for a vacant position [欠員に対して]求職する. 【類】*put in* (=apply) for a job (an appointment) ‖ *put in* a petition 請願書を出す ‖ *put in* an appearance at ... …に姿を見せる(顔を出す). 【類】It was not long before he *put in* an appearance. / I haven't *put in* at the office all day. ‖ *put in* at an inn 投宿する. 【類】Could you *put* us *in* for the night? ‖ I had business in Kyoto, so I *put in* there. 京都に用事があったのでそこで降りた. ‖ have a telephone *put in* (=installed) 電話を引く ‖ *put in* another supply of ... …をさらに補給する ‖ *put in* a comma コンマを打つ ‖ *put in* hard work 勉強する ‖ *put in* at a port 寄港する. 【類】*put in* [at a port] for repairs / She has *put in* here from the stress of the weather. ‖ *put in* (=spend) time (money) 時(金)を費消する ‖ when the spring *puts* in 春が訪れたら. ¶*put in* at a port 港へ[船を]着ける ‖ *put in* at an airfield [飛行機を]着陸する. ¶*put off* one's apparel (coat) 着物(など)をぬぐ. 【類】*put off* one's winter encumbrances (冬の厄介もの) ‖ When a child asks such a question, it must not be *put off* with conventional lies and prevarications. 子供がこうした質問をした場合は従来のうそを言ったりごま化したりしてお茶を濁してはいけない. ‖ *put off* the light (radio, phonograph) 灯(など)を止める ‖ *put off* a boat into the stormy seas あらしの海に舟を出す. 【類】*put off* in a boat to ... ‖ *put off* on a long journey 長途の旅に立つ ‖ *put off* one's departure 出発を延ばす ‖ *put off* the evil hour そのいやな時を延ばす. 【類】*put* it *off* to a later date / Don't *put off* till tomorrow what should be done today. / The meeting was *put off* till Saturday. / *put off* what one has to do till the last moment (ぎりぎりまで) / As it has come on to rain, I think I will *put off* my walk. ‖ *put off* (=sell) the store of provisions at easy rates 食料品のストックを安く売払う ‖ *put off* (=get rid of) one's doubts and fears 疑問や恐怖を吹き飛ばす ‖ Conductor, *put* me *off* at Newhaven. 車掌さん, ニューヘブンで降して下さい. ‖ a boat at once *put off* from ... to ... 船は…から…に進路を変えた ‖ *put* a fleet *off* to sea 艦隊を出動させる ‖ *put off* a man with a good excuse 口先で人を言いくるめる. 【類】He tried to *put* me *off* with a mere promise. ‖ All modesty is *put off*. 恥も忘れてしまう. ‖ *put off* a counterfeit (fake money) on ... にせ札(など)を…に押しつける ‖ *put off* an application for promotion 昇給の願い出を(いずれその内にと言って)撃退する ‖ I was not to be *put off* so easily. 私はそんなことで閉口しなかった. ¶*put on* one's coat 上衣を着る ‖ *put on* earphones イヤフォーンを着ける. 【類】*put on* a dress suit ‖ I asked to be *put on* to ... 私は(電話を)何番へつないで下さいと言った. ‖ *put* a disk (=record) *on* レコードをかける. 【類】*put on* a radio program ‖ *put* "Hamlet" *on* ハムレットを上演する ‖ an opera *put on* the air 〘ラジオ〙 放送歌劇 ‖ One of the finest talks *put on* the air in recent years. 近年ラジオで聞いた中では一番いい話の一つ. ‖ *put on* more cars to accommodate the traffic 交通緩和に車両を増加する ‖ Plants *put on* fresh green colors. 植物は新緑の装いをした. ‖ *put on* a new airliner 新しい定期飛行機を就航させる ‖ *put on* a display of spring hats 春の帽子を陳列する ‖ *put on* (=gather) speed スピードを増す ‖ *put on* flesh (=weight) 肉がつく(太る). 【類】*put on* one's strength ‖ *put on* pressure 圧力をかける. 【類】*put on* pressure for a reconsideration of ... ‖ *put on* years 年をとる ‖ *put on* (=assume) a grave face むずかしい顔をする. 【類】*put on* a serious countenance (深刻な顔) / *put on* a solemn countenance (まじめくさった顔) / *put on* a grimace (しかめ顔) ‖ *put on* airs [of dignity] もったいぶる. 【類】*put on* airs of innocence (そ知らぬようす) / *put on* a serious air ‖ *put on* assumption of ignorance 知らん振りをする ‖ *put on* supposition 推察する ‖ *put on* a show of learning 学問があるように見せかける ‖ He *put on* as brave a look as he could. 彼はできるだけ弱気を見せまいとした. ‖ I won't be *put on* (=taken in) never. もう決してだまされないぞ. ‖ *put* the screw *on* (=*put on* the screw) a billiard ball 〘玉突〙 球に一ひねりくれる. ¶*put* them *over* to the other side of a river 川向うに渡らせる ‖ *put over* the doctrines of the "Right" 右翼の主義を周知させる ‖ *put* it *over* with success 《米口》 首尾よくやり遂げる. ¶*Put* me *through* to 67-4005 〘電話〙 局番六七の四〇〇五番につないで下さい. ¶*put up* one's hand 片手をあげる. 【類】*Put* your hands *up*. ‖ *put up* an umbrella かさをさす ‖ *put up* a notice 掲示する ‖ a tablet provided for *putting up* messages 告知板. 【類】*put up* a sign reading "..." / *put up* posters / *put up* a sheet of paper saying ... / Let's go to the theater before an SRO sign is *put up* (座席満員). / *put up* the sail 帆をあげる / *put up* a signal of distress (=an SOS sign) ‖ *put up* the curtain at the window 窓のカーテンをあげる / *put up* your windows at night to let in the air (換気のため) / He often *puts up* the window and lets in fresh air. ‖ *put up* a new house 新しい家を建てる ‖ *put up* markers to show the way to ... …の方角を示す道路標を立てる ‖ *put up* pickets against ... …に対しピケをしく ‖ *put* it *up* for sale それを売りに出す ‖ *put* a car *up* in a garage 車を車庫に入れる ‖ *put up* at a hotel ホテルに止宿する ‖ be *put up* for the night by the Red Cross 赤十字の世話で一晩泊めてもらう ‖ The hotel *put up* his retinue free of charge. ホテルでは彼の随員は無料サービスした. 【類】That inn can *put up* 300 guests. / Will you *put* us *up* for the night? ‖ *put up* a purse in the pocket 財布をポケットにしまう ‖ *put up* money for rainy days まさかの用心に貯金する. 【類】*put up* lots of money ‖ *put up* the camping outfit for the winter 冬になるのでキャンプ用具を片づける ‖ *put up* a good (=fine) fight against ... …と健闘する ‖ *put* (=do) *up* one's hair 髪を結う ‖ *put* it *up* as collateral それを見返り品にする ‖ I have nothing to *put up* as security. 担保にするものは何もない. ‖ be *put up* for ballot 票決に付される ‖ *put up* barricades of live wire around the concession その区域の回りに電流鉄条網を張り回らす ‖ have a telephone *put up* in one's room そのへやに電話を取付ける ‖ *put up* shutters at night 夜間雨戸を閉める ‖ *put up* one's clothes その着物をまくる ‖ *put up* shelves たなをつける(つる) ‖ *put up* swings ブランコを造る ‖ The machinery is now all *put up*. 機械を全部据えつけた ‖ have the fittings *put up* 造作を取りつける ‖ *put* a person *up* to some mischief (crime) 人をけしかけてわるさ(罪)をやらせる. 【類】He *put* them *up* to mischief. / Who *put* him *up* to this piece of mischief? ‖ *put up* with (=pocket *or* swallow) an affront 侮辱を我慢する ‖ can no longer *put up* with ... もう…は我慢できない ‖ *put up* with inconveniences 不便をしのぶ. 【類】I can't *put up* with your insolence any longer. ‖ *put* a person *up* to the ropes 人にこつを教える ‖ *put up* a sword 剣をさやに収める ‖ It was *put up* at auction at 3 s. 6 d. それは三シリング六ペンスで競売に付せられた ‖ be *put up* for public tender 公売に付する. 【類】*put up* for sale as delinquent tax property (税金滞納品として) / The property was *put up* for sale. ‖ He is *putting up* for Parliament. 彼は英国々会議員の候補に立っている ‖ I can not *put up* with simple fare (inconvenience, such rudeness). 私は粗食(など)にたえられない. ¶*vivaciously put* it 生き生きとした言葉で言う.

P *put* humanity *above* nationality 人間というものを国民以上に重んじる. ¶*put* a person *across* a river (railroad tracks) 川(など)を渡らせる. ¶*put* a × *against* the name of ... …の名に×符を付ける. ¶The men who figure have *put* the per cent of success *as* one out of twenty. 計算した人たちの話では成功率は二十対一である. ¶*put* the rent *at* ... yen 家賃を…とする ‖ it is roughly *put at* ¥... それは…円と概算される. 【類】the number is *put at* ... / the total height of ... is *put at* ... ‖ *put* him *at* his ease 彼の気持を楽にしてやる(緊張をほぐしてやる). 【類】Most pawnbrokers try to *put* their customers as much *at* ease as possible. ‖ He *put* me *at* home with plain, kind speeches. 彼は飾らない親切な言葉づかいで私をくつろがせた. ‖ He *put* his villa *at* my service. 彼は別荘を私に使わせてくれた. ‖ money *put at* interest 利息をかせぐ投

資 ‖ any doubt on this point can be very easily *put at* rest by ... この点についての疑いは...ですぐ晴れる. ¶*put* it *beween* ... それを...の間にはさむ. ¶*put* a bottle of beer *down* the well for cooling 冷すためにビールを一本井戸にさげる. ¶*put* confidence (=faith or trust) *in* him 彼を信頼する ‖ *put* many hours *in* it それに多くの時間をかける ‖ *put* the money *in* the bank その金を銀行に預ける ‖ *put* it *in* the catalogue それをカタログに載せる ‖ They *put* him *in* the chair. 彼らは彼を議長に選んだ. ‖ *put* a letter *in* a mail box=mail a letter 手紙を投かんする. 【類】*put* a letter *in* (=*into*) an envelope ‖ *put* a thing *in* one's hand 物を人に渡す ‖ *put* a child *in* (=*into*) his hands 子供を彼の手にたくする ‖ *put* goods *in* the market 品を市場に出す ‖ be *put in* gaol (=jail) for ... ...で投獄される ‖ *put* him *in* a madhouse 彼を精神病院に入れる ‖ *Put* yourself *in* his place. 彼と地位を換えて考えて御覧. ‖ *put* the name of a person *in* a table 人の名を表に載せる ‖ *put* all his pieces for children *in* one volume 彼の子供のための物語を全部一巻にまとめる ‖ *put* patriotism *in* front of (=before) self-love 自己愛よりも愛国心を重んじる ‖ *put* him *in* (=*into*) a funk 彼を驚かす ‖ *put* him *in* the publishing business 彼を出版業に従事させる ‖ If you *put* it *in* that light, I haven't a word to protest. そういわれては一言もない. ‖ it *puts* me *in* a cold perspiration to hear him remark that ... 彼に...と言われると冷あせが出る ‖ *put* a person *in* the shade しょげさせる ‖ to *put* it *in* another way 表現(言葉)を変えて言えば. 【類】Let us *put* this *in* another way. / Well, if you *put* it in that way, it certainly sounds reasonable. ‖ If you say so, you will *put* him *in* the wrong. 君がそういう言い方をすると彼が悪いように見える. ‖ Very few copies were *put in* circulation. 極少数の部数を発行した. ‖ The company will be *put in* (=*into*) liquidation. その会社は清算人の手に渡されるだろう. ‖ *put in* motion a piece of mechanism ingeniously contrived 巧妙な一個の機械を運転させる. 【類】*put* an engine *in* motion ‖ *put* it *in* (=carry it into) operation それを実施する ‖ *put* it *in* pledge それを質に入れる ‖ *put* a plan *in* (=*into*) practice 計画を実行する ‖ The ship sprang a leak, and the pumps were *put in* requisition. 船に漏水を生じたのでポンプが必要となった. ‖ For best results *put in* service before Nov. 1938. 一九三八年十一月前に使用しないと効力が薄い[電池などの使用期間指定]. ‖ *put* the piano *in* tune ピアノを調律する ‖ *put* his impressions *in* writing 彼の印象を書き留める ‖ *put* oneself *in* correspondence with ... ...と文通する ‖ I must *put* you *in* mind of your promise. 君の約束を思い出してもらわなければならない. ‖ *put* a person *in* touch with some German business house dealing in ... あるドイツの...商と渡りを付けさせる ‖ *put* the house *in* order 家の中を整とんする. 【類】*Put* them all *in* order and sweep the room clean / *put* manuscripts *in* order for publication ‖ Polite orders or requests are often *put in* question form. 丁重な命令や依頼はよく疑問形で表わされる. ‖ You will be *put in* funds before due. 期限前に金を手にすることができるだろう. ‖ *put* a law *in* force 法律を施行する ‖ be *put in* liquidation [会社など]清算される ‖ *put* it *in* print それを印刷に付する ‖ Titles of books are commonly *put in* italics. 本の題名は通例[文の中で]イタリックで印刷される ‖ be *put in* type 活字に組まれる ‖ *put* those specimens back *in* the cabinet それらの見本を陳列だなの中に片付けておく ‖ *put in* a word for one's friend 友人のため一言弁じる ‖ make a dictionary up-to-date by *putting in* quite a number of new words 新語を相当入れて辞書を新しくする ‖ *put* a person *in* possession of a debtor's house 人に債務者の家を入手させる. ¶*put* a ship *into* harbor 船を入港させる. 【類】*put into* port for shelter ‖ The offender has been apprehended and *put into* jail. 犯人は逮捕されて入所となった. ‖ *put* a book *into* circulation 本を配布する ‖ *put* ideas *into* action 考えを行動に移す ‖ *put* a plan *into* execution 計画を実行する ‖ *put* a reform *into* effect 改革を実行する ‖ *put* (=translate)Goethe *into* English ゲーテを英語に翻訳する ‖ *put* a law *into* operation 法令を実施する ‖ a law *put into* force against smuggling 密輸入禁止法 ‖ *put* an idea *into* practice 考えを実行する. 【類】It was *put* (=carried) *into* successful practice. ‖ A pair of scissors was *put into* immediate requisition. [必要な個所などに]早速はさみを用いた(切抜いた). ‖ The buses will be *put into* service on routes of the company. バスはその会社の線路に使用するはず. 【類】*put* new cars *into* service ‖ *put into* one's desire that ... ...という自己の念願を文面に認める ‖ *put* it *into* French それをフランス語に訳す. 【類】works of foreign authors *put into* Japanese dress ‖ *put* one's money *into* land 土地に投資する ‖ It has not yet been *put into* print. それはまだ印刷に付せられない. ‖ I had specimen pages *put into* type. 見本ページを組ませた. ‖ *put* a knife *into* his body 彼の身体へナイフを突刺す ‖ God *put* it *into* my heart. それは神様から授かった考えだ. ‖ Shakespeare has *put into* Antony's mouth some of his noblest verses. シェークスピアはその最も高尚な詩の若干をアントニーに言わせた. ‖ *put* a halfpenny *into* a slot 半ペニーを自動機に入れる ‖ *put* one's feeling *into* it それに感情をこめる ‖ Good actors and actresses know how to *put* emotion *into* their spoken words. ‖ the energy (work) that has been *put into* it それに注ぎ込んだ精(労)力 ‖ *Put* more nerve *into* it! もっとがん張れ! ‖ *put* them *into* a separate class それを別の部類に入れる ‖ *put* data *into* tabular form 材料を表に作る ‖ *put* a course of lectures *into* the form of a book 連続講演を単行本にする ‖ *put* figures *into* the form of diagrams 数字を図表に作る ‖ *put into* words effectively ideas which are interesting and valuable to others 他人にとって興味あり価値のある考えを効果的に表現する ‖ He *put* so much money *into* a mere hobby. 彼は多額の金をくだらない道楽に注ぎ込んだ ‖ He is soon *put into* a passion. 彼はすぐ怒る. ‖ *put* one *into* a state of hypnosis (=somnambulistic state) 人を催眠状態におく ‖ He *put* me *into* the way of obtaining my own livelihood. 彼は私に自活の道を与えてくれた. ‖ be *put into* the best condition 最良の状態(コンディション)にする ‖ The ship was *put into* water. 同船は進水した. ‖ *put* words *into* blanks 空所に言葉を入れる ‖ *put* the seeds *into* the ground 種子をまく ‖ be *put into* quarantine for several days 数日間検疫に付せられる ‖ *put* a word or two *into* another's ear about ... ...について一言二言人に耳打をする ‖ *put into* the field the troops from ... ...の軍隊を戦線に送り出す. ¶*put* the blame *on* some one else 人のせいにする ‖ *put* the crime *on* (=*upon*) him 彼に罪をきせる ‖ *put* an insult (scorn, censure) *on* (=*upon*) him 彼に侮辱(など)を加える ‖ I will *put* you *on* the right electric car. 貴方がお乗りになる電車に乗せてあげましょう. 【類】I will walk with you there and *put* you *on* the car. / *put* him *on* the right road ‖ *put* a ring *on* the finger 指に指輪をはめる ‖ *put* two socks *on* one foot 片足にくつ下を二つ重ねてはく ‖ *put* money *on* a horse 馬に金をかける ‖ I am afraid you forgot to *put* a stamp *on* your letter. 君手紙に切手をはるのを忘れゃしなかったか. ‖ *put* him *on* the list 彼の名を表に記入する ‖ *put* goods *on* the market 商品を市場に出す. ¶be *put on* sale 売出す ‖ *put* a play *on* the stage 劇を上場する ‖ He made inquiries which would *put* him *on* the track of the lost article. 彼は紛失品のゆくえを調べた. ‖ *put* heavy dues *on* (=*upon*) cattle 家畜に重税を課する ‖ *put* a kettle *on* the fire なべを火にかける ‖ *put* it *on* fire それを火にくべる ‖ *put* the patient *on* milk diet 患者に牛乳食をとらせる ‖ *put on* paper 紙に記す ‖ *put* it *on* exhibition それを展覧に供する ‖ *put* one *on* oath 誓わせる ‖ an incident sufficiently strange to merit (=deserve) being *put on* record 記録に値する不思議なできごと. 【類】I desire to *put on* record some appreciation of his personal worth (人物の価値). ‖ *put* one's conduct *on* (=*upon*) the custom その行動を習慣に従わせる ‖ be *put on* trial 審理に付せられる ‖ *put* all *on* (=*upon*) the issue ことの成否一切をその結果いかんによらせる ‖ *put* one *on* the wrong scent 感違いをさせる ‖ He was again *put on* the same treatment with the same good result. 彼は同じ治療を受けて結果は同様良好であった. ‖ *put* him *on* his good behavior 彼に謹慎を申付ける ‖ *put* a person *on* (*off*) one's guard 用心(油断)させる. ¶*put* it *on* its legs again それをばん回させる ‖ *put* her *on* the berth 船を停泊させる ‖ be *put on* earth to ... ...するために生れて来る ‖ be *put on* army payroll 俸給を軍の方から支出する ‖ He *put* the blame *on* me. 彼は私のせいにした ‖ Quote prices including *putting on* rail at your end. 貴駅着運賃込み価格を言ってよこして下さい. ‖ Embargo has been *put on* the ship and cargo. 同船及びその船荷は出(入)港禁止となった. ¶*put* a person *out of* business (employment) 人を失業させる ‖ *put* a person *out of* his life 人の生命を奪う(殺す) ‖ freight cars *put out of* operation due to old age 使用中止となった老朽貨車 ‖ *put* a warship *out of* action 軍艦を戦列外におく ‖ *put* a person *out of* countenance その顔(面目)をつぶす ‖ He was ludicrously *put out of* countenance when he tried to talk that language. 彼はその国語を話そうとしたときにおかしいほど面食った. ‖ a complexion to *put* the rose and lily *out of* countenance ばらやゆりも顔負けがするほどの容色 ‖ He was *put out of* the Court. 彼は朝廷の寵(ちょう)を失った. ‖ *put* one *out of* humor 人の機げんをそこなう ‖ *put* it *out of* one's mind それを忘れる ‖ *put* it *out of* sight それを隠す ‖ *put* one's nose *out of* joint 《口語》人の鼻をあかせる ‖ *put* a car *out of* service 廃車にする ‖ *put* it *out of* account それを計算外にする. ¶*put* a general *over* a division of an army 将官を師団長にすえる ‖ *put* a macron *over* a vowel 母字の上に長音符(-)をつける ‖ *put* one *over* the river 人を川向うへ渡す ‖ *put* a net *over* the lion ライオンに網をかぶせる ‖ *put* gold (silver, tin) leaf *over* ... ...に金(など)ばくをおく. ¶*put* a bullet *through* one's head 弾丸でその頭をぶち抜く ‖ *put* the rope *through* a wrong hole 綱を間違った穴へ通す ‖ *put* them *through* a course of English 彼らに英語科を履修させる ‖ *put* a person *through* a test 人を考査する ‖ *put* the book *through* (=*to*) the press 同書を印刷に付する. ¶*put* a horse *to* a cart 馬を荷車につなぐ ‖ *put* milk *to* (=*in*) tea 茶に牛乳を入れる ‖ *put* a person to trouble 人に迷惑をかける. 【類】Did I *put* you *to* inconvenience (=trouble)? / I am *putting* you *to* a good deal of trouble. ‖ *put* a hard question *to* him 彼に難問をかける ‖ I *put* it *to* you. お考えを願います. ‖ At what hour ought a child to be *put to* his bed in the evening? 子供は夜何時に寝かしたらよいものでしょうか. 【類】The physician *put* the patient *to* bed for six weeks. / *Put* the patient *to* bed at once, between blankets and in flannel night-shirt. ‖ *put* (=send) a girl *to* school 女児を学校に入れる ‖ *put to* sea in one's yacht 自用のヨットで出航する ‖ No ship *puts to* sea without an experienced pilot. 老練な水先案内を付けずに出帆する船はない. 【類】*put* a fleet *to* sea / *put to* sea braving stormy weather and rough sea / *put* him *to* the bayonet 彼を銃剣にかける ‖ *put* a person *to* the rack (=torture) ごう問にかける ‖ He was *put to* the sword. 彼はきり殺された. ‖ *put* it *to* a vote 決を採る. 【類】*put* the question *to* the vote / when the question was *put to* the vote, A found 446 supporters and B only 271 / The amendment (修正案) was *put to* the vote and lost. / *put* (=submit) a resolution (決議案) *to* a vote ‖ *put* it *to* the word それを言い表わす ‖ *put* a person *to* the blush 人を赤面させる ‖ *put* it *to* the proof (=test) それを考査する ‖ *put* (=place) it *to* the credit of ... それを...の貸方に記帳する ‖ *put* him *to* the worst 彼をやっつける ‖ *put* a person *to* death 人を死刑にする ‖ *put* a person *to* expense 人に散財をかける. 【類】It *puts* me *to* heavy expense. ‖ The enemy was *put to* flight. 敵が逃走した. 【類】*put* evil spirits *to* flight / *put* the enemy *to* rout (敗走) ‖ *put* a boy *to* prentice 少年を年期奉公にやる ‖ *put* all *to* rights in a jiffy 直ちに整とんさせる ‖ He *put* me *to* right on the error. 彼は私の誤りを正してくれた ‖ *put* goods (a house) *to* sale 商品(など)を売りに出す ‖ *put* a person *to* shame =shame a person 人をはずかしめる ‖ *put* a person *to* trial 人を審問する; 試験する ‖ It can be *put to* use. それは役に立つ. 【類】*put* it *to* practical use / the uses *to* which they can be *put* ‖ Knowledge and timber should be well seasoned (枯らす) before being *put to* use. / It is *put to* increasing use. / *put* it *to* a good use / *put* it *to* some other use / *To* what uses are they to be *put?* ‖ He *put* me *to* work at once. 彼は私にすぐ仕事をやらせてくれた. ‖ *put* a girl *to* domestic service 女の子を家事に使う ‖ *put* a child *to* sleep 子供を寝かしつける ‖ *put* one's hand *to* a new undertaking 新しい事業に着手する. ¶*put* him *under* arrest 彼を拘留する ‖ *put* ... *under* his care (protection) ...を彼の管理(など)の下におく ‖ *put* ... *under* his charge ...を彼に預ける ‖ The modern community *puts under* contribution for its food the remotest corners of the earth. 近代の社会はその食物の補給を世界の果ての国々にまで仰いでいる. ‖ *put* a criminal *under* the screw 犯人をきびしくきめつける ‖ *put* these customs *under* taboo これらの習慣を禁じる ‖ The paper has been *put under* ban. 同紙は発売禁止となった. ¶*put* the blame *upon* a person 人に責を負わせる ‖ *put* her *upon* my usual treatment 彼女に私の例の療法を施す ‖ *put* all *upon* a battle 万事を一戦にかける(背水の陣を布く) ‖ be *put upon* the stage [劇を]上場する ‖ *put* eau-de-cologne *upon* a pocket-handkerchief オー・ド・コロンをハンカチにかける ‖ This *puts* me *upon* the true lines of investigation. これで私の研究は真の軌道に乗った. ‖ *put upon* record one's impressions 印象を記録しておく.

puttee, *n.* 巻ゲートル.

V *wear puttees* 巻ゲートルを着ける.

P *in puttees* 巻ゲートルを着けて.

putter, *v.* ぶらぶらする, だらだら仕事をする. 「を売る.

M *putter away* one's time ぶらぶらして時間をつぶす, 油

M² *putter about* (=*along*) ぶらぶらする, うろつき回る.

P *putter over* a task ぐずぐずする.

putty, *v.* パテでふさぐ.

M² He *puttied up* the holes and cracks on the wall before painting it. 彼はペンキを塗る前に壁の穴やわれ目をパテでふさいだ. 【類】*putty up* window panes.

puzzle, *n.* なぞ; 難問.

V *construct* (=*solve or undo*) *puzzles* なぞを解く. ¶I have *found out* the *puzzle*. なぞが私に分かった ¶*produce puzzles* なぞを出す. ¶*strike* a *puzzle* 難題にぶっつかる. ¶*study out* a *puzzle* 難問を解く. ¶*work [out]* a *puzzle* なぞを解く.

Q A *hopeless puzzle!* 到底解けそうもないなぞ. ¶an *impenetrable puzzle* 解けないなぞ. ¶an *insoluble puzzle* 解けないなぞ. ¶there is *no puzzle* in ... ...にはなんの不思議もない. ¶the *perpetual puzzle* of human hife 人生という永久のなぞ. ¶a *standing puzzle* of the scientist いまだに解けない科学者のなぞ. ¶It remains an *unsolved puzzle*.=The puzzle still remains unsolved. それは依然解けないなぞとなっている.

Q² work [out] a *crossword puzzle* クロスワード・パズルを解く. ¶a complicated *jigsaw puzzle* 複雑なジグソー・パズル(寄せ絵パズル). ¶a *picture puzzle* 判じ絵.

P² a *puzzle in* words 言葉のなぞ. ¶The Ainu is the *puzzle of* the ethnologist. アイヌ人は人種学上の難問である. ¶It is a *puzzle to* me how he managed to do it. 彼がどうしてそれをやったのか私にはとんと分からない.

puzzle, *v.* 迷わす, 困らす; 判じる.

M The question has *always puzzled* me. その問題にはいつも私は困っている. ¶*puzzle out* a mystery 神秘を解く ‖ *puzzle out* a truth 真理を発見する. 【類】*puzzle* it *out*= decipher it ‖ *puzzle out* its meaning その意味を判じる. ¶I am *quite* (=*solely*) *puzzled*. 私は実に困った. ¶I'm *utterly puzzled* what to do with it. それをどう処置してよいかほとほと弱っている.

P *puzzle* one's brain *about* (=*over or upon*) a problem ある問題で頭を悩ます. ¶*puzzle in* one's pocket ポケットの中を捜し抜く. ¶*puzzle over* a question quite awhile 難問でしばらく頭をかかえる. ¶I was *puzzled with* the question=The question puzzled me. 私はその問題には閉口した.

pyjamas, *n.* パジャマ.

V *wear pyjamas* (=pajamas) パジャマを着る.

pyramid, *n.* ピラミッド, 金字塔; 〔数学〕角すい.

Q the *headless pyramid* of Fujiyama 尖頭のない金字塔富士山. ¶It rests on an *inverted pyramid*. それは累卵の危きにある. ¶a *regular pyramid* 正角すい. ¶Families are at the base of a *socioeconomic pyramid*. 家庭が社会経済組織の基底をなしている. ¶a *triangular pyramid* 三角すい.

Q² the *color pyramid* 〔写〕色彩調合.

pyre, *n.* [火葬用]積み薪.

Q a *funeral pyre* 火葬のための積み薪.

pyrotechnics, *n.* 煙火術.

Q *fancy pyrotechnics* 仕掛花火.

Q

quack, *n.* やぶ医者.

Q an ***advertising*** *quack* 自己宣伝のやぶ医者.

quack, *n.* [あひるなどの]があがあ.

Q the ***noisy*** *quack* of ducks あひるのやかましい鳴声.

quad, *n.* 〚印刷〛詰めもの.

Q^2 an ***em*** *quad* 全角詰めもの. ¶an ***en*** *quad* 二分の一詰めもの.

quail, *n.* うずら.

P a bevy ***of*** *quails* 一群のうずら.

quail, *v.* たじろぐ.

P His spirit *quailed* ***at*** the sight. 彼はそれを見て気がおじけた. ¶*quail* ***before*** the enemy 敵の前でたじろぐ.

quaint, *a.* 奇抜な.

P express in a phraseology *quaint* ***to*** our ears われわれの耳には変に聞える言葉で表現する.

quaintness, *n.* 珍奇.

P^2 *quaintness* ***of*** old-fashioned customs (manners, etc.) 古めかしい風習(など)の珍妙さ.

quake, *v.* 震える.

P *quake* ***at*** a threat 恐かつに震える. ¶*quake* ***with*** (=***for***) fear (cold) 恐怖(など)で震える. 【類】*quake* ***with*** fear ***at*** the threat.

Quaker, *n.* クエーカー教徒.

Q the ***narrow, upright, conscientious, unbending*** *Quaker* of the old school 昔風の狭量で正直で良心的でがん固なクエーカー教徒.

qualification, *n.* 資格, 資質; 条件, 制限.

V What ***constitutes*** his *qualification?* 彼にどういう資格があるか. ¶***determine*** their *qualifications* 彼らの資格を確定する. ¶***meet*** these *qualifications* これらの条件に合致する. ¶He ***has*** many *qualifications* for the task. 彼はその仕事には色々資格を備えている. ‖ His happiness ***had*** one *qualification* 彼の幸福にも一つ欠けるものがあった. ¶***obtain*** a *qualification* to practice medicine and surgery 内科外科医開業の資格を取る. ¶***possess*** all these *qualifications* すべてこれらの資格を具備している. ¶***prescribe*** *qualifications* あらかじめ資格を定める. ¶The statement ***requires*** some *qualification.* その陳述は多少の制限を要する. ¶***test*** their *qualifications* 彼らの資格を考査する.

Q a Liberal without any ***adjective*** *qualification* (Irish など)形容詞を伴わない自由党員. ¶He brought ***ample*** *qualifications* to the task he has undertaken. 十分の資格を持ってその仕事に当った. ¶He has many ***admirable*** *qualifications* for such a task. 彼はこうした仕事には色々りっぱな資格を備えている. ¶have the ***best*** *qualification* for … …に一番よい資格を備えている. ¶You may accept his statement with ***certain*** *qualifications.* 彼の言うことは多少割引きして聞いた方がいい. ¶the ***chief*** *qualification* for a teacher 教師に第一に必要な資格. ¶an ***educational*** *qualification* 教育上の資格. ¶He had ***every*** *qualification* for success. 彼には成功する資格が十分そろっていた. ¶an ***important*** *qualification* 重要な資質. ¶***intellectual*** *qualifications* 知力上の資格. ¶***muscular*** *qualifications* 体力上の資格. ¶a ***necessary*** *qualification* for … …に必要な資格. ¶the ***residential*** *qualification* for voters 投票者に対する住居の条件. ¶a most ***serviceable*** *qualification* for … …にきわめて有用な資格. ¶his ***strong*** *qualifications* for a work 仕事に対する彼の有力な資質.

Q^2 ***job*** *qualification* 仕事の資格. ¶throw away all ***property*** *qualifications* on the suffrage 選挙権に対する一切の財産資格を撤廃する.

P a statement ***with*** many *qualifications* 多くの制限または条件のついている声明. ¶promise ***without*** *qualification* 無条件(または無制限)で約束する. 【類】I am for you (=I agree) ***without*** *qualifications.*

P^2 his *qualifications* ***for*** a teacher (teaching) 彼の教員としての資格 ‖ *qualifications* ***for*** entering a higher school 高等学校入学資格 ‖ *qualifications* ***for*** franchise (examination) 選挙(など)の資格. 【類】*qualifications* ***for*** voting. ¶the *qualifications* ***of*** an elector 選挙人資格. ¶The *qualification* ***of*** his doctrine ***as*** heretical is unfair. 彼の説を異端と称するのは不当だ. ¶*qualifications* ***of*** the applicant =application requirements 申込者資格. 【類】the *qualification* ***of*** his policy ***as*** opportunist (日より見主義者).

qualify, *v.* 資格を付ける; 限定する.

M those ***best*** *qualified* to judge (=entitled to authoritative judgement) 最も権威ある説を立てうる人々 ‖ topics he is ***least*** *qualified* to handle 彼が取扱って最も不適任な問題. ¶He is ***eminently*** (=***highly***) *qualified* for (=to undertake) the task. その仕事に極めて適任である. ¶be ***especially*** *qualified* for the task 特にその仕事に適格だ. ¶a ***fully*** *qualified* person 十分資格のある人. ¶he is but ***imperfectly*** *qualified* to … 彼は…には余り適しない. ¶a person ***officially*** *qualified* to … 公けに…する資格のある人. ¶a ***properly*** *qualified* person 適格者. ¶He is ***well*** (***best***) *qualified* for the post. 彼はその地位によく(一番)適している. ‖ be peculiarly ***well*** *qualified* to … 特に…することに適している.

P *qualify* a person ***as*** a voter 選挙権を与える ‖ He is *qualified* ***as*** a solicitor (teacher). 彼には弁護士(など)の資格がある. ‖ They *qualified* him ***as*** a scoundrel. 彼らは彼に悪漢の銘を打った. 【類】*qualify* his opinions ***as*** erroneous. ¶he is *qualified* ***by*** training and natural gifts to undertake … 彼は修練と天賦で…に当る資格がある. 【類】he is eminently *qualified* ***by*** his natural characteristics for … ‖ It is *qualified* ***by*** an adjective. それは形容詞に限定されている. ¶He is eminently *qualified* ***for*** such a labor. 彼はこんな仕事には非常に適している. ‖ He is *qualified* ***for*** the lunatic asylum. 彼は精神病院ものだ. ‖ *qualify* oneself ***for*** an elector 自分の選挙資格を造る. 【類】He is *qualified* ***for*** teaching (=as a teacher). ¶He is fairly *qualified* ***in*** English composition. 彼は英作文にたん能だ.

O He is *qualified* to teach (=for teaching) English. 彼は英語教師の資格がある.

quality, *n.* 性質; 品質; 性格; 良質.

V ***affect*** mannish *qualities* [少女など]男らしい性格を装う. ¶***augment*** the *quality* of … …の品質を高める. ¶***check*** the *quality* and quantity of coal 石炭の質や量を吟味する. ¶***cultivate*** these *qualities* これらの徳性をかん養する. ¶***debase*** the *quality* of the goods they manufacture その製品の質を落す. ¶***deteriorate*** *quality* 質を下げる. ¶It is well calculated to ***develop*** the finer *qualities* of a man. それは人間の一層りっぱな性格を発達せしめるに好く適している. ¶***lower*** the *quality* of … …の質をおとす. ¶The stove ***embodies*** in the highest degree the *qualities* of an ideal heater. その暖炉は理想暖房器最高の特徴を具備している. ¶***enumerate*** the good moral *qualities* displayed by him in childhood 彼が幼年時代に発揮したりっぱな徳性を枚挙する. ¶***have*** the *quality* of … …の素質をもっている ‖ He ***has*** *qualities* of horsemanship, dancing, and fencing. 彼には騎馬・舞踊及び剣道の心得がある. ¶***improve*** the *quality* 品をよくする. ¶***increase*** its nutritive *qualities* その栄養分を増す. ¶***keep*** *quality* ***up*** and price down 質も落さず値段も上げずにおく. ¶***possess*** the *quality* of simplicity 単純という特性をもっている ‖ herbs ***possessing*** healing *qualities* 薬草. ¶***preserve*** their best national *qualities* intact その国粋を保存する. ¶***sacrifice*** *qualities* to quantity 粗製らん造.

V^2 Their *quality* is ***declining.*** 彼らの質が低下しつつある. ¶*Quality* ***matters*** more than quantity. 質は量よりも大切だ.

Q ***accidental*** *quality* 偶有性. ¶The goods are of ***average*** *quality.* その品質は並だ. ‖ be inferior to fair ***average*** *quality* 相当よい中級品より劣る ‖ of high ***average*** *quality* 中の上位の品の. ¶goods of ***bad*** *quality* 悪質の商品. ¶of the ***best*** *quality* 最良質の ‖ This is our ***best*** *quality.*

これが手前どもでは最上の品です. ¶of very ***best possible*** *quality* 無類飛切の. ¶***better*** (***lower***) *quality* than [the] last この前のより良い(劣った)質. ¶a man of ***commendable*** *qualities* りっぱな性格の人. ¶***common*** *quality* 普通の品質. ¶It is acknowledged to have the highest ***curative*** *qualities* in all cases of rheumatic diseases. それはレウマチ性のあらゆる疾患に特効があると認められている. ¶the ***disease-resistant*** *quality* 抗病の特性. ¶improve its ***economic*** *qualities* その経済的特質を改善する. ¶It has the ***elemental*** *qualities* of a song that is meant to be sung. それは歌わせるための歌としての基本的な音質をもっている. ¶Unity is an ***essential*** *quality* of a good sentence. 統一はよい文の本質である. ¶a man of ***excellent*** *qualities* 徳の高い人. ¶***extra best*** (=extra fine) *quality* 特上. ¶***extra superfine*** *quality* とび切り上等. ¶a hat of ***extra superior*** *quality* 特別上等の帽子. ¶of ***fair*** *quality* 相当質のよい. ¶sugar of ***fine*** (=excellent) *quality* 品質上等の砂糖.【類】The ***fine*** *quality* of the cloth justifies its high price. ¶***first-class*** *quality* 一等品. ¶the ***fundamental*** *qualities* in human nature 人間性の基本的性格. ¶He is possessed of the ***genial*** *qualities* which distinguish a gentleman. 彼は紳士の特徴と称すべき懇篤な性格を備えている. ¶***good*** *quality* 良質.【類】be printed on a ***good*** *quality* of paper ‖ The *quality* is too ***good*** (***low***) for this market. その品質は当市場向きには良(悪)過ぎる.【類】of undoubtedly ***good*** *quality*. ¶have ***good*** (***poor***) ***hunger-staying*** *quality* 腹持がい(わる)い. ¶those ***great*** or ***shining*** *qualities* that constitute a genius 天才の持つあの偉大なまたは光った資性. ¶It was the touchstone by means of which his ***hidden*** *qualities* were brought to light. それは潜在する彼の資性を明らかにさせる試金石であった. ¶her ***high*** *qualities* of mind and character 彼女の高潔な精神と性格 ‖ The present stock is chiefly of ***high*** (***low***, ***medium***) *qualities*. 現在の手持ちは上等(下級, 中級)品が主です. ¶***hot biting*** *qualities* ひどくひりひりする性質(こしょうなど). ¶the ***imitative*** *qualities* inherent in the Japanese 日本人固有の模倣性. ¶A genuine one has that ***indefinable*** *quality* which distinguishes it from a fake. 本物はにせ物に見るべからざる何とも名状し難い特徴を持っている. ¶***indispensable*** *quality* 欠くべからざる性質. ¶of ***inferior*** *quality* 品質劣等の. ¶***intellectual*** *qualities* 知的能力. ¶***lasting*** *quality*=durability 耐久性. ¶improve the ***keeping*** *qualities* [poultry を殺す前二十四時間絶食させると]もちがよくなる. ¶***legal*** *quality* 分限. ¶The book has no ***literary*** *qualities*. その本は全く文学的要素を欠いている. ¶The Cossacks are noted for their ***martial*** *qualities*. コサック人はその勇武で名高い. ¶her ***mental*** and ***bodily*** *qualities* 彼女の精神上並に肉体上の資性. ¶good sound ***merchantable*** *quality* しっかりした市販向きの品. ¶***middling*** *quality* かなりな品質. ¶***militant*** *qualities* 好戦的性質. ¶the high ***nutritive*** *quality* of the egg 鶏卵の高い栄養価.【類】have scarce ***nutritive*** *qualities*. ¶a medicine free from ***objectionable*** *qualities* 副作用を起さない薬. ¶***ordinary*** *quality* 普通の品質. ¶***poor*** *quality* 劣等の品質.【類】the ***poor*** *quality* of his work. ¶***potential*** *qualities* 可能性. ¶a ***prime*** *quality* of cloth 最上級の織物.【類】cloth of ***prime*** *quality*. ¶of ***rare*** *quality* [めったにないほど]すぐれた品質(性格)の. ¶the ***restorative*** *quality* of the Turkish bath トルコぶろの元気回復の効能. ¶Exaggeration is a ***salient*** *quality* of Yankee humor. 誇張は米人気質の特徴である. ¶This is of the ***same*** *quality* as of the last. それはこの前のと同じ質だ. ¶***second***(***third***)***-class*** *quality* 第二(三)の品位. ¶He lacks all ***soldier-like*** *qualities*. 彼には軍人らしい性質が全く欠けている. ¶***sterling*** *qualities* [本ものの]実力. ¶eggs of ***superior*** *quality* 極上の鶏卵. ¶the ***tonic*** *quality* of sea air 海風の健康増進性. ¶of ***unimpeachable*** *quality* 申分のない品質の. ¶***unrivaled*** *quality* 無類の品質. ¶of ***useful*** *qualities* 役に立つ(有用な). ¶***usual*** *quality* 普通の品質. ¶manufacture goods in ***various*** *qualities* 色々な等級の品を製作する. ¶specially of ***wearing*** *quality* ことに持ちがよい. ¶***welding*** *quality* of iron 鉄の鍛接性.

Q^2 ***first-class*** *quality* 一級の品質. ¶They have superior ***egg-laying*** *qualities*. 産卵能力ではあの鶏が一番です. ¶personality and ***leadership*** *qualities* 人格と指導者的素質. ¶***laying*** and ***table*** *qualities* of fowls 鶏の産卵能力と食肉としての価値(肉の味). ¶Sardines have now good ***table*** *quality*. いわしは今油が乗っている. ¶***tough*** (=ductile) *quality* of iron 鉄の展延性.

P ***according to*** *quality* 品質によって. ¶inferior ***in*** *quality* 品質劣等な ‖ a change ***in*** *quality* 質の変化 ‖ They differ much ***in*** *quality*. 彼らは質が大層違う. ‖ deterioration ***in*** *quality* 品質の低下.【類】superior (inferior) ***in*** *quality* ‖ ***in*** the *quality* of agent 代理人の資格で. ¶The goods are ***of*** poor *quality*. その品は質が悪い. ‖ goods ***of*** *quality* 高級品 ‖ people ***of*** *quality* 上流の人々 ‖ a magazine ***of*** *quality*=a quality magazine 《米》高級雑誌.【類】wine ***of*** *quality* / The article ***of*** this *quality* is sure to fetch the price of that.

P^2 *qualities* ***for*** a statesman 政治家たる資格. ¶Hardness is a *quality* ***of*** rock. 堅いのは岩石の性質だ. ‖ the *quality* ***of*** courage 勇気という素質 ‖ the *qualities* ***of*** a ruler 君主たるの徳.

qualm, *n.* はき気; 良心のかしゃく; 疑念.

V cause one to ***feel*** *qualms* in the stomach 人にはき気を覚えさせる. ¶He sometimes ***has*** (=***suffers***) the *qualms* of conscience. 彼は時々良心のかしゃくを受ける.

P try ***with*** some *qualms* いくつかの疑念をもってやる.

Q feel a ***sudden*** *qualm* ああ悪かったと気付く.

Q^2 *qualms* ***of*** seasickness 船酔い ‖ *qualms* ***of*** conscience 良心のとがめ.

quandary, *n.* 苦境.

P he is ***in*** a *quandary* because ... 彼は...で弱っている.

quantity, *n.* 量; 多量.

V ***allow*** a small *quantity* of stimulant, a pint of beer, or half-a-pint of wine 一パイントのビール・半パイントのぶどう酒など小量の刺激物を与える. ¶***double*** the *quantity* of ... ...の分量を二倍にする. ¶We ***had*** *quantities* of rain during the night. 夜通し沢山の雨が降った. ¶***order*** a large *quantity* of goods 品物を多量に注文する. ¶***produce*** huge *quantities* of ... 多量の...を産する. ¶What *quantity* can you ***ship***? どの位の量の出貨ができますか. ¶What *quantity* can you ***take***? どの位お買入れ下さいますか.

Q vomit an ***alarming*** *quantity* of blood 大かっ血をする. ¶a ***certain*** *quantity* 若干量. ¶They are found in ***considerable*** *quantities*. それは沢山にある. ‖ be taken in ***considerable*** *quantities* 相当大量に仕入れてある. ¶an ***enormous*** *quantity* of water 多量の水. ¶The ***exact*** *quantity* cannot be determined at present. 正確な量は今のところはっきり言えない. ¶a ***generous*** *quantity* of ... 相当豊富な量の... ¶a ***fixed*** *quantity* 一定量. ¶a ***great*** *quantity* 大量, 沢山.【類】***Great*** *quantities* of fish have recently been caught there. ¶***huge*** *quantities* of ... ...のものすごい量. ¶an ***immense*** *quantity* ばく大な分量. ¶we export an ***inconsiderable*** *quantity* of ... ...が少しばかりこの国から輸出される. ¶a ***large*** *quantity* 沢山 ‖ be printed in ***large*** *quantities* 大量印刷される.【類】in ***larger*** *quantity* than heretofore. ¶They are produced in ***limited*** *quantities*. その生産高は限られている. ¶Gold is produced in ***moderate*** *quantity* in Japan. 金は日本では余り多くとれない. ¶It is nowadays a ***neglected*** *quantity*. それは今日では問題にならないほどの量である. ¶a ***negligible*** *quantity* とるに足らない数量. ¶***prodigious*** *quantities* 法外に沢山. ¶in ***small*** *quantity* 小量で.【類】Few people can digest and assimilate cheese except in ***small*** *quantity*. / They are turned out in ***small*** *quantities*. / Only a ***small*** *quantity* can be had. ¶in ***sufficient*** *quantity* 十分に. ¶Such a thing as loss of time is an utterly ***unknown*** *quantity*. 時の損失といったようなものは全然未知量だ.【類】His bravery is an ***unknown*** *quantity* (未知数). / There being no working arrangements between the companies the through ticket would be an ***unknown*** *quantity*. ¶Gold is found there in ***workable*** *quantities*. 金はそこでものになる位取れる.

Q^2 The extent of its influence is as yet a ***speculation*** *quantity*. その影響はどの程度まであるか今の所雲をつかむようなものだ. ¶buy in ***wholesale*** *quantities* 大量に買入れる.

P English music is regarded throughout Europe ***as*** a *quantity* that does not exist. 全欧州では英国音楽というものはないものとなっている. ¶***in*** a *quantity* 幾らか ‖ It can be had ***in*** any *quantity*. それは幾らでも(欲しいだけ)得られる. ‖ diminish (gain) ***in*** *quantity* 量が減る(増す) ‖ an increase ***in*** *quantity* 量の増加 ‖ be tremendous ***in*** *quantity* おびただしい量である. 【類】There are blackberries ***in*** *quantity*. / Fish are caught ***in*** great *quantities*.

P^2 the *quantity* ***of*** heat in an animal body 動物体の熱量 ‖ *quantity* ***of*** matter (motion) 質(運動)量 ‖ a *quantity* ***of*** opiates 若干量のアヘン剤.

quarantine, *n.* 検疫; 検疫所; 交通しゃ断.

V ***declare*** a *quarantine* for all steamers coming from ... ...から来るすべての汽船に検疫を言渡す. ¶It is said that *quarantine* will be ***established*** at Kobe against all ships coming from China. 中国から来るすべての船舶を神戸で検疫することになるそうだ. ¶***institute*** a *quarantine* on cattle 家畜の検疫を始める. ¶***lift*** a *quarantine* 検疫実施を廃止する. ¶***pass*** a *quarantine* 検疫を通過する. ¶***perform*** *quarantine* 交通しゃ断を行う. 【類】***perform*** three days *quarantine*. ¶The *quarantine* has been ***re-established***. 検疫が再開された. ¶The *quarantine* is now ***removed***. 今は検疫は行われていない. ‖ ***remove*** (=***abolish***) the yellow-fever *quarantine* against ... ...に対する黄熱の検疫を廃する. ¶***serve*** a *quarantine* 検疫で留置される. ¶***withdraw*** *quarantine* 検疫を廃止する. 【類】Singapore has ***withdrawn*** the *quarantine* hitherto existing against Hongkong.

V^2 The *quarantine* will ***cease*** in a few days. 検疫は二三日中に廃される.

Q be subjected to a ***rigorous*** *quarantine* 厳重な検疫を受けさせる. ¶The ship is still in ***strict*** *quarantine*. 同船はまだ厳重な検疫中である.

Q^2 ***plant*** *quarantine* 植物の検疫.

P a vessel held ***at*** *quarantine* 検疫所留置の船. ¶passengers will be held ***in*** *quarantine* until ... 船客は...まで検疫で留置される ‖ A yellow flag means that the vessel is ***in*** *quarantine*. 黄旗はその船が検疫隔離中であることを示す. ‖ The ship is detained ***in*** *quarantine*. 同船は検疫のため停船している. ‖ put them ***in*** (***out of***) *quarantine* それらの検疫を始める(検疫から解除する) ¶be ***out of*** *quarantine* 検疫済になる. ¶houses placed ***under*** *quarantine* 目下検疫隔離中の家屋.

P^2 a *quarantine* ***against*** cholera (pest) コレラ(など)の検疫. 【類】The *quarantine* at Singapore ***against*** Hongkong has been abolished since the 4th inst.

quarrel, *n.* けんか, 争い; 言い分.

V ***avoid*** a *quarrel* けんかを避ける. ¶***bury*** the old *quarrels* 古いけんかを水に流す. ¶***cause*** a *quarrel* けんかを起す. ¶***compound*** a *quarrel* 双方歩み合う. ¶***espouse*** one's *quarrel* その言い分に肩を持つ. ¶***fasten*** (=***fix or force***) a *quarrel* on ... ...にけんかをしかける. ¶***ferment*** *quarrels* 争議の種をまく. ¶***fight*** another's *quarrel* for oneself 人のけんかを買って出る. ¶***fight out*** one's *quarrel* to a finish あくまで口論を戦わす. ¶***force*** a *quarrel* on ... ...にけんかを売る. ¶***have*** a *quarrel* with ... ...とけんかする ‖ I ***have*** no *quarrel* against him. 私は彼とけんかする理由は何もない. ¶***heal*** a *quarrel* born of misunderstanding 誤解から起った紛争を調停する. ¶A third person stepped in and ***made up*** (=settled) the *quarrel*. 人が間にはいってけんかを止めてくれた. ¶***patch up*** a *quarrel* けんかをまとめる. ¶***pick*** [***up***] (=***raise or seek***) a *quarrel* with ... ...にけんかを売る. ¶***promote*** international *quarrels* 国際間の紛争をかもす. ¶***provoke*** a *quarrel* けんかを起す. ¶the kind of *quarrel* you can ***see*** between man and wife 夫婦間で見るような争い. ¶***set aside*** a *quarrel* けんかをやめる. ¶***settle*** a *quarrel* amicably 争いを円満に解決する. ¶***start*** a *quarrel* with ... ...とけんかを始める. ¶***stir up*** a *quarrel* 紛争を引起す. ¶***take up*** a *quarrel* けんかの相手になる ‖ ***take up*** another's *quarrel* 人のけんかを買って出る. 【類】***take up*** no man's *quarrel* but his own.

V^2 A *quarrel* ***arose*** among them. 彼らの間にけんかが持ち上がった.

Q a ***deadly*** *quarrel* 命がけのけんか. ¶a ***futile*** *quarrel* 無益の争い. ¶a ***good*** *quarrel* 正義の争い. ¶an ***honest*** *quarrel* 本気の争い. ¶a ***little*** *quarrel* ちょっとしたけんか. ¶They had a ***lover's*** *quarrel*. 彼らは痴話げんかをやった. ¶a ***matrimonial*** (=***marital***) *quarrel*=a family jar 夫婦げんか. ¶a ***noisy*** *quarrel* やかましい争論. ¶They had a few ***occasional*** *quarrels*, but these were soon healed by kisses. 彼らは二三回けんかをしたことはしたがすぐにキッスで仲直りができた. ¶engage in a ***severe*** *quarrel* on the subject of ... ...の問題について猛烈な口論をする. ¶They didn't have a ***single*** *quarrel* in all that time. 彼らはその間ただの一度も争ったことがなかった. ¶a ***tremendous*** *quarrel* えらいけんか. ¶a ***violent*** *quarrel*=a brawl 猛烈なけんか.

Q^2 a ***family*** *quarrel* 家庭争議. ¶a ***love*** *quarrel* 痴話げんか.

P ***In*** *quarrels* both parties are equally criminal.=***In*** a *quarrel* both sides are to blame. けんか両成敗.

P^2 a *quarrel* ***about*** a matter ある件についての争い. ¶a *quarrel* ***between*** father and son 親子げんか. ¶a *quarrel* ***for*** possession resulting in the gain of a third party (=an outsider) 漁夫の利を得られるのがオチのけんか. ¶a *quarrel* ***of*** long standing 久しく持越のけんか. ¶a *quarrel* ***over*** a matter ある事に関する争い.

quarrel, *v.* けんかする.

M They are ***perpetually*** *quarreling*. 彼らは絶えずけんかをしている.

P *quarrel* ***about*** (=over) trifles つまらないことでけんかする. ¶Those three men *quarreled* ***among*** themselves. 彼ら三人は同士げんかをした. ¶*quarrel* ***between*** the two 互いにけんかをする. ¶*quarrel* ***for*** a trifle つまらないことでけんかをする. ¶They *quarreled* ***over*** such a trifling matter. 彼らはこんなささいなことでけんかした. ¶They *quarreled* ***with*** each other. 彼らは互いにけんかをした. 【類】*quarrel* ***with*** some one over some thing / *quarrel* ***with*** a person concerning ... ‖ *quarrel* ***with*** one's bread and butter われとわが身を詰める ‖ *quarrel* ***with*** one's lot その運命をかこつ ‖ *quarrel* ***with*** Providence 天を恨む ‖ A bad workman *quarrels* ***with*** his tools. へたな職人は道具にけちをつける.

quart, *n.* コート(一ガロンの四分の一).

P buy (sell) ***by*** the *quart* 一コートいくらで買う(売る).

quarter, *n.* (**1**) [通例 *pl.*] 特別地域; *pl.* 住居, 宿舎, とん所.

V ***find*** suitable *quarter*[*s*] (=lodgings) 適当な下宿を見つける. ¶***found*** *quarters* in ... ...に住居を占める(事務所など). ¶He ***frequents*** the gay *quarters*. 彼はよく花柳のちまたに足を入れる. ¶***furnish*** comfortable *quarters* for ... ...に居心地のよい宿所をあてがう. ¶***give*** comfortable *quarters* to 400 Leghorns 四百羽のレグホンに住み心地のよいねぐらを作ってやる. ¶London ***has*** no students' *quarter*. ロンドンには学生街というものがない. ¶***obtain*** *quarters* at a hotel ホテルに宿泊する. ¶The bank ***occupies*** very fine *quarters* at the corner of ... and ... streets. その銀行は...街と...街との角のりっぱな位置を占めている. ¶***procure*** suitable *quarters* 適当な居所を手に入れる. ¶***provide*** comfortable and economical living *quarters* 居心地のよい経済的な居所をあてがう. ¶The business prospered so rapidly that within a few months he was obliged to ***seek*** larger *quarters*. 商売が繁盛して二三カ月の中にもっと大きな店に引越す必要を生じた. ¶This *quarter* was ***swept away*** by the fire of 1906. この辺は一九〇六年の火災で一掃された. ¶He hired a large house, where he ***took up*** his *quarters*. 彼は大きな家を借りてそこに腰を据えた. 【類】***take up*** one's *quarters* in New York / ***take up*** one's *quarters* at a hotel / ***take up*** new *quarters* (新宅).

Q People gathered from ***all*** *quarters*. 各方面から人が集った. ¶in ***another*** *quarter*, also, I received valuable encouragement, namely from my friend ... 私はまた別の方面すなわち友人...から貴重な声援を受けた. ¶live in ***close*** *quarters* [狭いところに]ごちゃごちゃ住んでいる ‖ fight at ***close*** *quarters* 接戦する ‖ come to ***close*** *quarters* 肉薄する. ¶He has ***comfortable*** *quarters*. 彼は住み心地のよい所に落着いている. ¶in ***every*** *quarter* of the globe 地球のいたる所に. 【類】I hear the same complaint in ***every*** *quarter*. ¶a ***fashionable*** *quarter* 上流人士の出入する区域. ¶Wind blows from all ***four*** *quarters*. 風は四方から吹く. 【類】men and women from the ***four*** *quarters* of the globe. ¶***gay*** *quarters* [浅草・銀座のような]歓楽街. ¶I had the news from a ***good*** (=***high***) *quarter*. 私はそのニュースを確かな筋から聞いた. ¶in some ***influential*** *quarters* ある有力な方面に. ¶the ***Jew's*** *quarters* in Rome ローマのユダヤ人街. ¶***licensed*** *quarters* 遊郭. ¶it is thought (=held) in ***many*** *quarters* that time is not yet ripe for ... ...の時機がまだ熟していないという見方が諸方面でなされている. ¶the ***mercantile*** *quarter* 商業区. ¶the ***officers'*** *quarters* 士官とん所. 【類】the GHQ ***officers'*** *quarters*. ¶owing to ignorance and neglect in ***official*** *quarters* 官辺の無知と怠慢とで ‖ ***Official*** *quarters* have expressed their approval. 官辺は賛意を表した. ¶ the *old* (*new*) *quarter* of the city 市の旧(新)区域. 【類】the *poor quarters* 貧民くつ. 【類】the *poorer quarters* of the city. ¶ my *present quarters* 私の今の住所. ¶ Subscriptions should be forwarded to the *proper quarter*. 寄付はしかるべき向へ発送すること. ¶ *questionable quarters* いかがわしい方面. ¶ news from *reliable quarters* (=sources) 信ずべき筋からの報道. ¶ *residential quarters* 住宅地. ¶ the *servants' quarters* 小使控所. ¶ For the loan of scarce books my thanks are due in *several quarters*. 諸方面から珍書の借用を受けたことを感謝する. ¶ the question has arisen in *some quarters* whether ... ...という疑問がある方面に起った. ¶ The society is given *temporary quarters* in that building. 同協会はそのビルディング内に仮事務所がある. ¶ I have learned from *trustworthy quarters* that ... 確かな筋から聞く所によれば... ¶ reports reaching *unnamed quarters* here 某所に届いた報告. ¶ the *wealthy quarter* 富豪連の住宅地. ¶ *Well-informed quarters* do not judge favorably of the situation. 消息通は事態を楽観していない. ¶ *What quarter* is the wind in? 風はどの方角か.

Q[2] a popular *amusement quarter* 大衆的歓楽街. ¶ the populous and *business quarters* of a city 市の人口ちゅう密な商業区域. ¶ the *cinema quarters* 映画街. ¶ a *factory quarter* of London ロンドンの工場地区. ¶ *finance Ministry quarters* 大蔵省筋. ¶ in *Government quarters* 政府筋では. ¶ *Government office quarters* 官庁街. ¶ it is now stated in *labor quarters* that ... ...と労務者間に言われている. ¶ *licensed* [*prostitute*] *quarters* 遊郭. ¶ modern *living quarters* 文化住宅街 ‖ have difficulty in finding *living quarters* 住居を見つけることがむずかしい ‖ workers' *living quarters* 飯場. ¶ a *manufacturing quarter* 工業区. ¶ *office quarters* occupied by the bureau その局が占めている事務所. ¶ the *Chinese quarters* 南京街. ¶ the *port quarter* 〘航〙 左げんの船尾. ¶ the *prostitution quarters* 遊郭, 色町. ¶ *shopping quarters* 商店街. ¶ the *slum quarters* 貧民くつ. ¶ *vacation quarters* 休暇旅行によい場所. ¶ gather at the *waiting quarters* 待合所に集まる. ¶ *winter* (= *summer*) *quarters* 冬営地; 避寒(暑)地. 【類】The army went into *winter quarters*. ¶ the *workingclass quarters* 職工町.

P a message received *at* a certain *quarter* in Tokyo 東京のある方面で受取った情報. ¶ tourists *from* every *quarter* of the globe 世界各方面からの観光者 ‖ *from* many *quarters* 諸方面から. 【類】no matter *from* what *quarter* of the world he comes / The idle and curious throng thither *from* all *quarters* of the world. ¶ *in* this *quarter* of the globe 地球のこの方面に. 【類】*in* all *quarters* of the globe ‖ *in* some *quarters* it is suggested that ... ある方面には...という説がある.

P[2] my *quarters near* Hongo 本郷付近の私の下宿. ¶ I took up my *quarters with* my uncle. 私はおじの家に宿を取った.

(2) 四分の一; 四分の一マイル競争; 十五分.

V *cut up* the *quarters* 四つ割に切る. ¶ He has *done* the *quarter* (of a mile) in 50''. 彼は五十秒で四分の一マイルを走った. ¶ The clock *strikes* hours, half-hours, and *quarters*. この時計は時間と三十分と十五分を打つ. ¶ *win* the *quarter* 四分の一マイル競走に勝つ.

Q I pay my rent *every quarter*. 私は三月ごとに家賃を払う. 【類】The omnibus goes *every quarter* of an hour. ¶ the *first* (*second*) *quarter* of the moon 上弦(第二弦)の月. 【類】the *1st* (*2nd*) *quarter* [of the year] (四半期). ¶ the *fourth* (=*last*) *quarter* 下弦. ¶ I had a *nasty quarter* of an hour. 私は十五分位の間いやな思いをした. ¶ the *third quarter* of the century その世紀の第五十一年から七十五年まで.

P I can get it at the general stores *for* a *quarter* (of) the price. 雑貨店ではその価の四分の一で買える. ¶ cut an orange *in quarters* みかんを四切りにする. ¶ cut an apple *into quarters* りんごを四切りにする. ¶ He lets his house at two guineas *per quarter* 彼は三カ月二ギニーで家を貸す.

P[2] It's a *quarter after* three. 《米》三時十五分過ぎだ. ¶ a *quarter of* an hour (a century, a circle, a mile, an apple) 一時間(など)の四分の一. ¶ about a *quarter of* a century ago 約二十五年前. ¶ the product of his industry *over* a *quarter* of a century 四半世紀以上にわたる彼の努力の産物 ‖ a *quarter* (*of*) the price その価の四分の一 ‖ It's a *quarter of* three 《米》三時十五分前だ. ¶ this *quatrer of* the year 一年のこの四半期. ¶ a *quarter past* two 二時十五分過ぎ. ¶ a *quarter to* ten 十時十五分前.

quarter, *n*. 助命; 寛大.

V I *found* no *quarter* from ... 私は...に手荒く取り扱われた. ¶ *give* (=show) *quarter* to an enemy 敵を助命する; 敵に雅量を示す ‖ *Give* no *quarter*. 容赦するな ‖ To an enemy he shows no leniency and *gives* no *quarter*. 彼は敵を容赦なく攻めたてる. ¶ *grant quarter* 助命する. ¶ *receive quarter* from one's creditor 債権者からゆるしてもらう. ¶ *show* no *quarter* to ... ...に対してきびしくやる.

P ask *for quarter* 命ごいする.

quarter, *v*. 宿泊させる, 宿営させる; 四つ裂きにする.

M He was hanged and *quartered later*. 彼は絞首にされたあとで四つ裂きにされた(謀反人など).

P The troops *quartered at* Crimea. 軍隊はクリミヤに宿営した. ¶ be *quartered in* camps 野(露)営している ‖ We are *quartered in* a beautiful villa. われわれは美しい別荘に宿泊している.

quarter-century, *n*. 二十五年.

P during the *past quarter-century* 最近二十五カ年間に.

quarter-day, *n*. 四季の支払日.

V[2] as busy as all *quarter-days* have *come together* ぼんと正月が一緒に来たように.

quarterly, *n*. 年四回の定期刊行物.

Q[2] a *highbrow quarterly* [年四回発行の]高級雑誌.

quay, *n*. 波止場.

P be *alongside* the *quay* 波止場に横づけになっている. ¶ a berth *at* the *quay* 波止場の停船位置.

quayside, *n*. けい船所際.

P *along* the *quaysides* けい船所際に.

queen, *n*. 女皇, 女王.

Q an *abdicated* (=a *self-divested*) *queen* 位を譲った女王. ¶ a *dethroned queen* 位を奪われた女王.

Q[2] a *beauty queen* ミス...嬢(美人コンクールなどの). ¶ a *movie queen* 映画スター(女優). ¶ the 23,000-ton Malolo, *speed queen* of the Pacific, famed for spacious luxury 太平洋の速度の女王であり特に豪華船として有名な二万三千トンのマロロ号.

P pick out a girl *for* the *Queen* of the Fair そのお祭りに特に女王として一少女を選ぶ.

P[2] a *queen among* girls 少女の中で一番の美女. ¶ the *Queen of* England 英国女王 ‖ the *queen of* pleasure-grounds 遊園地中の随一 ‖ the *queen of* flowers=roses 花の女王(ばら) ‖ a *queen of* society 社交界の女王 ‖ the *queen of* queens 女王の中の女王 ‖ the *queen of* clubs (hearts, diamonds) 〘トランプ〙 クラブ(など)の女王 ‖ a *queen of* beauty=a beauty queen.

queer, *a*. 変った, 妙な.

M feel a *little queer* 少し気分が悪い.

P There is something *queer about* him. 彼はどこか変なところがある. ¶ be *queer in* the head 頭がどうかしている.

O it may sound *queer* when I say that ... 私が...と言ったら妙に聞えるかも知れない.

quench, *v*. 消す.

P The fire was *quenched* ([rhet.]=extinguished) *with* (= *by*) water. 火を水で消した.

O *quench* hatred (passion, desire) 恨み(など)をおさえる.

query, *n*. 質問, 疑問.

V I *have* a *query* about his sincerity. 私は彼の誠意については疑問がある. ¶ *put* this *query* to ... この質問を...にかける. ¶ *rouse* the *query* "why ...?" 「何故...か」という疑問を起させる. ¶ he *shot* a sarcastic *query* at ... 彼は...に皮肉な質問を放った. ¶ She was prepared to *suppress* all *queries*. 彼女はどんな質問もこれを撃退する覚悟でいた.

Q ... was the *first query* ...が第一の質問であった. ¶ *intelligent queries* そう明な質疑. ¶ a *natural query* 自然に起る不審. ¶ *pertinent queries* 適切な質問.

query, *v*. 質問する.

M *query querulously* ぷんぷん怒って尋ねる. ¶ *query softly* 穏やかに質問する.

P *query about* (=*as to*) a matter ある事柄について質問する.

quest, *n*. 捜索, 探求; 探索.

V *give up* the *quest* 根掘り葉掘り尋ねることを断念する.

Q set him upon a *healthful quest* for knowledge 彼に健全な知識の追求をやらせる. ¶ He is bent upon a *similar literary quest*. 彼は同じような文学上の研究に熱中している.

P They went out to Australia *in quest* of gold. 彼らは金を捜しに豪州へ出かけた. 【類】*in quest* of the missing child (迷子) / be *in quest* of something to amuse oneself ‖ *in quest* of the prizes which ambition offered 青雲の志を抱いて ‖ a woman much *in quest* as a wife 妻にもらい手の多い女. ¶He was ***upon*** a bootless *quest*. 彼は骨折り損をした.

P² his perpetual *quest* ***for*** a new experience 新しい経験への不断の追求. ¶the *quest* ***of*** truth 真理の探求.

question, *n.* (**1**) 疑問, 疑義.

V It ***admits*** [***of***] no *question*. それは疑いを容れない. ¶Only the future can ***answer*** this *question*. この疑問は時がたって始めて解決する. ¶***arouse*** a *question* in one's mind 心に疑義を起させる. ¶***make*** no *question* of ... ...について少しも疑いをはさまない. ¶sceptics will naturally ***raise*** the *question* whether ... 懐疑家は自然...の疑問を起すだろう. 【類】the *question* may be ***raised*** how (why) ...

Q an ***early*** *question* to arise is whether to ... or to ... 先ず起きる疑問は...かどうかということだ. ¶a ***hypothetical*** *question* 仮設の疑問. ¶There is ***no*** *question* about it. それには疑問の余地がない. 【類】there seem to be ***no*** *questions* that ... ¶We leave it an ***open*** *question* whether the supposition is true or not. われわれにはその推定の真偽は未解決のままになっている. ¶It is open to ***serious*** *question*. それは大いに疑問がある.

P it is ***beyond*** *question* that ... ...は論をまたない ‖ This much is ***beyond*** *question*. ここまではは っきりしている. 【類】***Beyond*** all *question* you are right. / ***beyond*** any *question*. ¶It is beyond the possibility ***of*** *question*. それには疑問の余地がない. ¶***past*** (=beyond) all *question* 疑いもなく, 無論. ¶It is open ***to*** *question*. それは大いに疑問の余地がある. ¶It is ***without*** *question* unparalleled. それはもちろん天下一品だ. 【類】it is, ***without*** *question*, desirable that ... / accept ***without*** *question* / You must obey orders ***without*** *question*.

(**2**) 質問.

V ***address*** a *question* to ... ...に問いかける. 【類】I don't know whom this *question* should be ***addressed*** (=put) to? ¶***answer*** *qusetions* 質問に答える. 【類】***Answer*** me this *question*. / ***Answer*** the *questions* given below. ¶He ***asked*** me a *question*=He ***asked*** a *question* of me. 彼は私に尋ねた. ‖ An interrogative pronoun ***asks*** a *question*. 疑問代名詞は質問に用いられる. 【類】***ask*** him *questions* of explanation. / If a man's mind ***asks*** *questions*, it has a healthy desire to grow. / the *question* ever ***asked*** and never ***answered*** is ... ¶I ***base*** my *question* on the lesson the pupils have learned. 私は学生が習った章について質問をする. 【類】***base*** *questions* on a story. ¶***direct*** a *question* to ... ...に質問を向ける. ¶try to ***evade*** the *question* その質問を避けようとする. ¶I ***fired*** a hundred *questions* at him about ... ...について彼に対して盛んに質問の矢を放った. 【類】*Question* after *question* was ***fired*** at him / ***fire*** [***off***] *questions* at ... ¶he suddenly ***flung*** this *question* at ... 彼は突然...にこの質問を放った. ¶***frame*** a *question* so as to ... ...するように質問をこしらえる. ¶***give out*** *questions* 質問を発する. ¶***hazard*** the *question* whether ... ...か否やの質問をかけて見る. ¶***hurl*** a *question* at ... ...に質問を発する. ¶diplomatically ***ignore*** the *question* 巧みにその質問をそらす. ¶***parry*** one's *question* その質問を受け流す. 【類】He ***parried*** the *question* by changing the subject. ¶He ***pondered*** my *question* for a moment. 彼は私の質問をちょっと考えていた. ¶***propound*** *questions* to ... ...に質問を発する. ¶***put*** a *question* to ...=interrogate ... ...に質問を発する ‖ I'll ***put*** you a *question*. 一つ質問をします. 【類】***put*** a *question* gently. ¶***rain*** (=***shower***) *questions* on ... ...に矢継早に質問する. ¶***resolve*** a *question* put 質問を解く. ¶***risk*** the *question* 聞いて見る. ¶***turn*** a *question* ***off*** 質問をそらす.

Q a ***blunt*** *question* 露骨な質問. ¶He asked one or two ***brusque*** *questions*. 彼は一二つっけんどんな質問をした. ¶a ***catch*** *question* かまをかける質問. ¶a ***disjunctive*** *question* イエスかノーで答えるように持ちかけた質問. ¶This is no ***easy*** *question* to answer. これは容易に答えられる質問ではない. ¶he waved off ***further*** *questions* with a remark that ... 彼は...と言ってそれ以上の質問には手を振って答えなかった. ¶put ***indiscreet*** *questions* to ... ...に不謹慎な問いを発する. ¶an ***inevitable*** *question* comes to mind—what ...?「...とは何ぞや」という必然の疑問が心に起る. ¶ask ***intelligent*** *questions* 気のきいた質問をする. ¶an ***irrelevant*** *question* 突飛な質問. ¶a ***leading*** *question* 誘導尋問 ‖ He asked her several ***leading*** *questions*, such as, "...?" "...?" "...?" and the like. 彼は「...」「...」「...」といったような下心のある問を彼女に発した. ¶Of this there can be ***no*** *question*. これについては少しも疑いがあろうはずがない. ¶a ***perplexing*** *question* 厄介な質問. ¶I did not know him well enough to ask ***personal*** *questions*. あの人と親しくなかったから(年齢など)身の上の質問はできなかった. ¶a ***pertinent*** *question* 適切な質問. ¶ask one ***plaguing*** *questions* 人にうるさい質問をする. ¶a ***pointed*** *question* 鋭い質問. ¶a ***point-blank*** *question* 率直な質問. ¶a ***puerile*** *question* 子供らしい質問. ¶a ***relevant*** *question* 適切な質問. ¶if it is not a ***rude*** *question* 失礼ですが(遠慮すべき質問の申し訳). ¶a ***searching*** *question* 突っ込んだ質問. ¶tease a person with ***sharp*** *questions* 人をつるしあげる. ¶***silly*** *questions* asked for the purpose of asking 問うために問うた愚問. 【類】He had to bear with people who ask him all sorts of ***silly*** *questions*. / I consider that a very ***silly*** *question*. ¶put a ***similar*** *question* to another, and it will be found that ... だれか別の人に同じような質問をすれば...ということが分かる. ¶a ***startling*** *question* 驚くべき質問. ¶a ***straightforward*** *question* 率直な質問. ¶***suggestive*** *questions* 暗示に富む質問. ¶a ***superfluous*** *question* なくもがなの質問. ¶ask a ***thousand*** *questions* 無数の質問をする. ¶sidestep ***tricky*** *questions* かまをかけた質問をはずす. ¶Children worry their elders with ***unanswerable*** *questions*. 子供たちは厄介な質問をして年上の者を困らす. ¶a ***vague*** *question* ばく然とした質問. ¶***well-directed*** *questions* 要領を得た質問.

Q² answers to the ***Gallup poll*** *question*, "...?" ギャラップ世論調査の「...」という質問に対する答え. ¶a ***selftest*** *question* [自問による]自己批判. ¶a ***sphinx*** *question* 不可解な質問.

P he was pestered to death ***by*** *questions* which were fired off at him incessantly from ... 彼は...から絶えず放たれる質問で非常に悩まされた. ¶pester one ***with*** vexatious *questions* 厄介な質問で人を悩ます.

P² *questions* ***on*** a picture 絵についての質問 ‖ *questions* and answers ***on*** commerce 貿易問答. ¶upon a *question* ***from*** his friend, he explained that ... 友人からの質問に彼は...と説明した.

(**3**) 問題.

V The long outstanding *questions* have thus been successfully ***adjusted***. その長い間未決のままであった問題もこんな具合にうまく片が付いた. ¶The *question* was ***allowed*** to slumber for 30 years. その問題は三十年来の懸案になっていた. ¶***argue out*** the *question* 問題を審議する. ¶***beg*** the *question* 未証明の事を論拠として論じる ‖ it is ***begging*** the *question* to say ... ...と言ったのでは堂々巡りにすぎない. ¶***blanket*** (=stifle) a *question* 《俗》問題をもみ消す. ¶***blink*** no ugly *questions* [歴史家など]どんな厄介な問題をも手控をしない. ¶***bring out*** (=***forth***) a *question* 問題を提起する. ¶***clear up*** this *question* この問題を片付ける. ¶***commit*** the *question* to his consideration その問題を彼に考慮してもらう. ¶the *question* is further ***complicated*** by the fact that ... その問題は...の事実によって一層紛糾して来た. ¶***comprehend*** the *question* その問題を理解する. ¶***consider*** the *question* in relation to various other departments 種々の他の部門と関連してその問題を考慮する ‖ this is not the place to ***consider*** the *question*, "...?" 今は...の問題を考慮すべき場合でない. 【類】***consider*** the *question* of the advisability of ... (...の可否). ¶The *question* was furiously ***debated***. その問題は猛烈に論議された. ¶***decide*** the *question* その問題を決する ‖ ***decide*** the *question* in the negative その問題を否決する. ¶***determine*** the *question* 問題を決定する. ¶***discuss*** at length the *question* of ... ...の問題を十分論じる ‖ The *question* is now being ***discussed***. その問題は目下論議中だ. ¶One cannot ***dismiss*** this *question* as simply as that. この問題はあの問題のようにそうあっさりとは片付けられない. ¶***evade*** the *question* by raising side issues 枝葉の問題を持出して本論を避ける. ¶***handle*** a *question* 問題を論議する. ¶His statement ***illuminated*** the entire *question* under discussion. 彼の陳述で論議中の問題全体がはっきりして来た. ¶an authority who has especially ***investigated*** this *question* 特にこの問題を研究した権威者. ¶as it ***involves*** the *question* of proportion with others 他との振合もあることだから. ¶***leave*** the other *question* of ... as much in the dark as ever ...の方の問題は依然として迷宮入りになっている ‖ ***leave*** the *question* untouched その問題は触れずにおく ‖ The discussion ***left*** the central *question* and ran into side issues. 討議が中心問題を離れて枝葉の問題に走った. ¶***meet*** the *question* half way 問題解決のため妥協する. ¶***moot*** a *question* 問題を論議する. ¶***move*** a previous *question* 先決問題を動議として提出する. ¶I cannot ***pass*** this *question* ***by*** in silence. この問題を不問に付することはできない. ¶***pop*** the *question* 《俗》女に求婚する. ¶***pose*** an important *question* 重要問題を持出す ‖ the *question* was ***posed*** when ... この問題の起りは...であった. ¶***propound*** (=bring out) a *question* 問題を提出する. 【類】his answers to a series of *questions* ***propounded*** by a report / when the *question* was ***propounded*** to him, he replied ... ¶***put*** a *question* before a person ある問題を人に持出す. ¶***putting aside*** the *question* as to ... ...の問題はしばらくおき. ¶A letter to the newspaper ***raised*** a *question* of urgency. 新聞への投書で緊急問題を起した. 【類】The *question* ***raised*** is an interesting one. ¶***regard*** the *question* from this point of view こうした観点からその問題を考察する. ¶it ***revived*** the old and much-disputed *question* as to ... それが...に関する古くから議論のやかましかった問題を復活させた. ¶***scan*** the *questions* その問題を精査する. ¶*questions* ***set*** at examinations 試験に出た問題. ¶attempt to ***settle*** *questions* of priority of discovery 発見者の順位問題を解決しようとする ‖ ***settle*** the question of 'hyphen or no hyphen' ハイフェンをつけるべきかどうかの問題を決定する. ¶properly ***solve*** a *question* 適当に問題を解決する. ¶***stifle*** a *question* 問題をもみ消す. ¶***submit*** *questions* as subjects for discussion at the conference 会議の議題として問題を提出する. ¶seriously ***tackle*** a *question* 本腰になって問題と取組む ‖ That is the *question* which they will need to ***tackle*** in no half-hearted manner. それは彼らが冷淡な態度で当ってはいけない問題だ. ¶***take*** the *question* seriously in hand 真剣にその問題に取りかかる. ¶***take up*** seriously the *question* of ... ...の問題に真剣に取りかかる. ¶it would seem that this *question* should have been ***threshed out*** long ago, but ... この問題はずっと前に研究し尽さるべきはずのように思われようが... ¶It does not ***touch*** the real *question*. それは本問題に触れていない. ¶He ***treated*** the *question* with scorn. 彼はその問題を鼻であしらった. ‖ the way in which the author ***treats*** the *question* 著者のその問題の取扱い方. ¶***try*** the *question* by law その問題を法律でさばく. ¶***turn*** a *question* ***off*** 問題をそらす. ¶The *question* has been ***withdrawn*** from the arena of public interes. その問題はもう早世人の注意を引かなくなった. ¶***work out*** the *question* その問題を解く.

V² The important *question* ***arises***. 重要な問題が持上がる. ‖ a *question* ***arose*** as to ... ...に関する問題が持上がった. 【類】the *question* will at once ***arise*** why ... / hence the *question* often ***arises*** whether ... ¶The *question* is now ***burning*** on the Continent. その問題は今大陸で火の手を揚げている. ¶The *question* of ... has ***come*** to the front. ...の問題が台頭して来た. ¶The *question* ***came up*** before the County Council on Tuesday. その問題は火曜日に郡会の議題にのぼった. ‖ now ***comes up*** the *question* of ... そこで...の問題が起って来る. ¶A second, and even graver, *question* now ***confronts*** us. 次に一層重大と見るべき問題が今われわれに直面している. ¶A *question* has ***cropped up***. 一問題が持上がった. ¶New and stirring *questions* are ***pressing*** upon us. 新規な耳目を刺激する問題がわれわれに迫っている. ¶the *question* still ***remains*** for solution whether ... ...の問題は依然未解決のままになっている.

Q an ***absorbing*** *question* 興味をそそる問題. ¶***affiliated*** *questions* 関係の諸問題. ¶an ***age-old*** *question* 多年の懸案. ¶an ***agrarian*** *question* 農地問題. ¶***another*** *question* 別個の問題. ¶an ***awkward*** (=***embarrassing***) *question* やっかいな問題. ¶a ***basic*** *question* 根本問題. ¶***bread-and-butter*** *questions* affecting the daily life and work of the people 国民の日常生活や仕事に影響を与えるパンの問題. ¶a ***broader*** *question* 一層広はんな問題. ¶some of the ***burning*** *questions* of university life 大学生活の緊急問題のあるもの. 【類】It is the ***burning*** *question* of the day to bring about a rapprochement (和解) between Japan and China. ¶a very ***complicated*** *question* きわめて複雑な問題. ¶***controverted*** *questions* 論議された問題. ¶these and ***countless other*** *questions* これらの問題及びその他無数の問題. ¶it is a ***debatable*** *question* whether ...かどうかは論議の余地のある問題だ. ¶It is still a hotly ***debated*** *question*. それは今なおお盛んに論議されている問題である. ¶a ***deeper*** *question* 一層深奥な問題. ¶the ***deepest*** *question* もっとも重大な問題. ¶a ***delicate*** *question* 微妙な問題. ¶a ***disputed*** *question* 論議された問題. ¶a ***distinct*** *question* from ... ...と別個の問題. ¶there remains the ***further*** *question* as to ... ...についてはなお問題が残る. ¶the ***Eastern*** *question* 東方問題. ¶a very ***fine*** *question* 仲々困難な問題. ¶the ***first*** *question* to be decided is ... 第一に決すべき問題は...だ. ¶settle the hitherto ***dubious*** *question* as to ... ...に関する今まで疑問になっていた問題を解決する. ¶Answer the ***following*** *questions*: 次の問題に答えよ. ¶a ***formidable*** *question* 難問題. ¶a ***fruitful*** (***fruitless***) *question* 効果のある(効果のない)問題. ¶***forcing*** *questions* 価格の維持に努めること(株式界用語). ¶a ***gigantic national*** *question* どえらい国家問題. ¶concern oneself with the ***grave*** *questions* of State 重大な国家問題に頭を使う. ¶an ***idle*** *question* くだらない問題. ¶a vitally ***important*** *question* 根本的に重要な問題. ¶raise an ***interesting*** *question* おもしろい問題を提起する. ¶an ***intricate*** (=***complicated***) *question* 入組んだ問題. ¶a ***knotty*** *question* of social reform 社会改良という困難な問題. ¶a very ***large*** *question* 非常に大きい問題. ¶the ***live*** *questions* of the day 刻下の死活問題. ¶some ***major*** *questions* at the present time 現時のある重要問題. ¶It is not a ***mere*** *question* of money. それは単なる金銭問題ではない. ¶the most ***momentous*** *questions* before England at the present day 今日英国が直面する最も重大な問題. ¶It has long been a ***moot***[***ed***] *question*. それは長い間未決の問題であった. ¶a ***much-debated*** *question* やかましかった問題. ¶a ***much-disputed*** *question* 非常に議論のあった問題. ¶a ***much-vexed*** *question* 非常に厄介な問題. ¶It raised an entirely ***new*** *question* in copyright law. それは著作権法に全く新らしい問題を投げた. ¶a ***nice*** *question* むずかしい問題. ¶***nice*** and ***puzzling*** *questions* むずかしいなぞのような問題. ¶raise once again the ***old*** *question* as to ... またもや...に関する古い問題を持出す. ¶an ***old*** and still ***debated*** *question* いまだに議論の絶えない古い問題. ¶It is an ***open*** *question*. それは未決の問題です. 【類】The *question* is still ***open***. ‖ leave it an ***open*** *question* それを研究問題として保留する. ¶confuse a pupil by a ***perplexing*** *question* やっかいな問題で生徒を混乱させる. ¶a ***personal*** (***private***) *question* 個人(私)的な問題. ¶a ***political*** *question* 政治問題. ¶a ***practical*** and ***fundamental*** *question* 実際的で根本的な問題. ¶the most ***pressing*** *question* of the moment 刻下の最も緊急な問題. ¶I move a ***previous*** *question*. 私は先決問題を提出します. ¶Some ***prior*** *questions* arise for settlement. 先決の問題が起る. ¶discussion of ***public*** *questions* 公共問題の論議. ¶Your reply to the teacher's ***puzzling*** *question* was really spirited. 先生の難問に対する君の答は実にきびきびしていた. ¶a ***serious*** *question* had to be faced in ... ...という重要問題に直面せざるを得なかった. ¶***sexual*** *questions* 性の諸問題. ¶a grave ***social*** *question* 由々しい社会問題. ¶purely ***technical*** *questions* 純然たる専門的な問題. ¶the ***thorny*** *question* of examinations 試験という取扱いにくい問題. ¶a ***ticklish*** *question* 困難な問題. ¶a ***touchy*** (=delicate) *question* 微妙な問題. ¶propound ***tough*** *questions* 困難な問題を提出する. ¶***trivial*** *questions* 微々たる問題. ¶a ***troublesome*** *question* 厄介な問題. ¶an ***unseen*** *question* [語学の]応用問題. ¶it remains an ***unsettled*** *question* whether ... or ... ...か...かは依然未解決の問題となっている. ¶a ***vexed*** *question* やっかいな問題. ¶a ***vexing*** *question* わずらわしい問題. ¶a ***vital*** *question* 死活問題. ¶a ***weighty*** *question* 重大問題. ¶The ***whole*** *question* is one of personality. それは全く人格の問題だ. ¶a ***wide*** *question* 大問題.

Q² the ***cost of living*** *question* 生活費の問題. ¶the ***drink*** *question* 飲酒問題. ¶***examination*** *questions* on grammar 文法試験問題. ¶the ***labor*** *question* 労働問題. ¶the ***land*** *question* 土地問題. ¶It was a ***life and death*** *question* to ... それは...にとって死活問題だった. ¶the ***liquor*** *question* 酒の問題. ¶a ***party*** *question* 党派問題. ¶discuss the various phases of the ***sex*** *question* 性問題の種々相を論議する. ¶a ***sphinx*** *question* 大難問. ¶the ***temperance*** *ques-*

tion 禁酒問題. ¶put the *wage question* to arbitration 賃金問題を仲裁々判に持ち出す. ¶a sociological study of the *woman question* 婦人問題の社会学的研究.

P Your answer is ***beside*** (=aside from) the *qnestion.* 君の答はピントを外れている. ¶Where were you on the afternoon ***in** question?* 君はその午後はどこにいましたか. 【類】the person (matter, point) ***in** question* ‖ It was called ***in** question.* それが問題となった ‖ the cause ***in** question* 〖法〗訴訟事実 ‖ the Government ***in** question* 当該国政府 ‖ the point ***in** question* 問題点. ¶come ***into** question* 問題になる. ¶another phase ***of*** the *question* その問題の今一つの面. ¶take advice ***on*** the *question* この問題で相談する ‖ What you say has no bearing ***on*** the *question.* 君の言うことは本問題には関係がない. ‖ essays ***on*** the Chinese *question* 中国問題に関する論文. ¶What you say is ***out of*** the *question.* 君の言うことは問題にならない. ¶the controversies that rage ***round*** the *question* その問題をめぐって猛烈に行われている論戦. ¶He does not speak ***to*** the *question.* 彼の言うことは適切でない.

P² a *question **about*** (=***as to***) a matter (person) ある事件(など)についての問題. ¶the *question **before*** the House [議会の]議題に上っている問題. ¶*questions* yet ***in*** debate なお議論中の問題 ‖ the *question **in*** hand 審議中の問題 ‖ a leading *question **in*** international diplomacy 国際間の外交における主なる問題. ¶The sick man will die soon; it is only a *question **of*** days. 病人は間もなく死ぬ, ただ時日の問題だ. ‖ a *question **of*** death or life 死活の問題 ‖ *questions **of*** larger issues もっと重大な問題 ‖ *questions **of*** the day (moment) 今日(刻下)の問題 ‖ *questions **of*** the times 時事問題. ‖ dispose of a *question **of*** long standing 長い間の懸案を解決する ‖ a *question **of*** sheer strength 実力の問題 ‖ a *question **of*** degree 程度問題 ‖ a *question **of*** precedence 席次の問題. 【類】That is a *question **of*** great interest and importance to the public. / It is only a *question **of*** time when a reaction will occur. / It is a *question **of*** disposition (気分). / Drama, like all art, is a *question* not ***of*** intellectual but of emotional content. / a *question **of*** loyalty / a *question **of*** taste / It is not at present a *question **of*** practical politics. ¶But it is a *question **upon*** which just at the present time there is much controversy. しかしそれは目下議論の多い問題だ.

O It is a *question* yet to be solved. その解決は今後の問題だ.

question, *v.* 質問する; 異論を唱える; 疑う.

M *question* a person ***closely*** 人に突込んで質問する. ¶He did not ***in the least*** *question* the accuracy of it. 彼はそれの正確さを少しも疑わなかった. ¶I very ***much*** *question* whether ... 僕は...かどうかを大いに疑う. ¶it has ***never*** been *questioned* that ... ...はだれも疑いをいれたことがない. ¶***openly*** *question* the truth of Christianity キリスト教の真理に公然異論を唱える. ¶*question* him ***persistently*** 彼をどこまでも追求する. ¶it may ***sometimes*** be *questioned* whether ... ...かどうかは時としては疑われる. ¶it may ***well*** be *questioned* whether it is worth while to ... ...する価値があるかどうかが疑われるのは無理もない.

P I *question **about*** this one's being gold too. 私はこれも金かどうかということに疑をいだいている. ‖ *question ... **on*** this point この点に関して...に質問する. ¶I beg that you *question* me ***upon*** any point which I do not make clear. はっきりしない点はどうぞ質問して下さい.

question-answerer, *n.* 質疑応答書.

Q a ***great*** "*question-answerer*" りっぱな参考書(どんなことでもわかる).

questioner, *n.* 質問者.

V ***enlighten*** one's *questioner* 質問者のもうを開く.

Q an ***inveterate*** *questioner* しつこい質問者.

questioning, *n.* 質問.

Q ***prolonged*** *questioning* 長々とやる質問. ¶***routine*** *questionings* きまりきった質問.

questionnaire, *n.* 質問状, アンケート.

V ***address*** a *questionnaire* to ... ...に質問状を出す. ¶***circulate*** a series of *questionnaires* among ... ...の間に数次の質問状をまわす. ¶***distribute*** *questionnaires* relating to their views on the China situation 中国の時局に関する彼らの意見を徴する質問状を配布する. ¶***fill out*** a *questionnaire* 質問状に書入れる. ¶***formulate*** a *questionnaire* 質問状を作成する. ¶***institute*** a *questionnaire* 質問状で意見を求めるようにする. ¶a *questionnaire* was ***issued*** by the society bearing the title "..." 「...」という表題の質問状が協会から発せられた. ¶***send out*** a *questionnaire* to a great many people asking them ... 大多数の人に...の質問状を発する. 【類】the results of the *questionnaire **sent out*** by ...

Q the results of his ***private*** *questionnaire* to over 100 medical practitioners 彼の個人として百余人の開業医に発した質問状の結果.

P the information was obtained ***through*** *questionnaires* sent to ... ...に送った質問状でその事実が得られた.

P² a *questionnaire **to*** Harvard freshmen on the choice of careers 職業の選択についてハーヴァード大学新入生に答えさせた質問状.

queue, *v.* 列を作る.

M² *queue **up*** at ... ...で(順番のための)列を作る. 【類】*queue **up*** before an eating-house / *queue **up*** for a show.

queue, *n.* 弁髪, おさげ; [人・馬・車の]列.

V ***braid*** *queues* 髪をおさげに編む. ¶***form*** a *queue* 列を作る. ¶***wear*** a *queue* 弁髪を着ける.

Q stand in a ***long*** *queue* 長い列を作って立つ.

Q² a ***food*** *queue* 食料(配給の)行列. ¶a ***movie*** *queue* 映画(観覧者の)行列. ¶a ***rush hour*** *queue* 混雑時の行列. ¶a ***theatre*** *queue* 観劇の行列.

P people standing (=drawn up) ***in** queues* awaiting their turn to ... ...する順番を待つために列を作った人たち.

quibble, *n.* 地口, しゃれ.

P² the *quibble **between*** "soles" and "souls" ソールズ(足裏)をソールズ(精神)に掛けたしゃれ.

Q despite ***verval*** *quibbles* 色々弁解はあるが.

quibble, *v.* へ理くつをつける.

P He was *quibbled **out of*** his right (property). 彼はへ理くつをつけられて権利(など)を奪われた. ¶I *quibble **over*** this, but I feel that you are right! 色々僕はへ理くつを付けて見るものの君が正しいようだ.

quibbling, *n.* 言いぬけ.

P Money will be returned ***without*** *quibbling* of any kind if found unsatisfactory. 気に入らなければ文句なしに返金します.

quick, *n.* なま身, つめの下の活身(いきみ); 急所.

P He was wounded ***to*** the *quick.* 彼は大けがをした. ‖ paint ***to*** the *quick* 真に迫るように描く ‖ He is a Tory ***to*** the *quick.* 彼は徹底的な保守党だ. ¶His words stung me ***to*** the *quick.* 彼の言葉は私に痛切に応(こた)えた. 【類】Their insult cut him ***to*** the *quick.*

quick, *a., ad.* 早い; さとい; 気の早い; いきいきした; じん速に.

M be not *quick **enough*** もどかしい.

M² ***as*** *quick* as (thought) lightning 電光石火のごとく(非常に早く) ‖ run ***as*** *quick* as one can 一所懸命に走る. ¶You speak ***too*** *quick.* 君の話は早過ぎる.

P Be *quick **about*** it. 早くやれ. ¶He is *quick **at*** arithmetic (figures, his work). 彼は計算(など)が早い. ‖ He is *quick **at*** promising. 彼は無暗に約束する. ‖ He is *quick **at*** taking (=to take) offense. 彼は怒りっぽい. 【類】a boy *quick **at*** learning. ¶He is *quick **in*** action (speech, answering questions). 彼は行動(など)がてきぱきしている. ‖ He is *quick **in*** temper. 彼は短気だ. ¶He is *quick **of*** hearing. 彼は耳が早い(さとい). ‖ *quick **of*** perception (apprehension, understanding) 悟り(など)の早い ‖ His temper is ***of*** the *quickest.* 彼はごく短気だ. ¶He is *quick **on*** his feet like a rabbit. 彼はうさぎのように足が早い. ¶*quick **with*** life 生気発らつたる.

O he replied *quick* as thought in the maxim of ... 即座に彼は...の格言で答えた. ¶*quicker* than thought たちまち. ¶He is *quick* to be glad (melancholy). 彼はすぐ喜ぶ(ふさぎこむ). ¶His ear is *quick* to hear. 彼は耳が早い.

quicken, *v.* 急がせる; 活気づかせる.

P *quicken* the hot ashes ***into*** flames 熱い灰をかき回して燃え立たせる.

O *quicken* one's imagination 色々想像をたくましくする. ¶Let's *quicken* our pace (=steps). 急ごうじゃないか.

quickie, *n.* 〘米〙急にやるもの; 〘映〙安ものの間に合わせ映画.

V Let's ***have*** a *quickie* 〘ラジオ〙一分ゲームをしましょう.

Q² We shall have to protect the industry against the ***quota*** *quickies.* 〘映〙われわれとしては割当本数を満たすための「割当用の(粗製)短編もの」から(映画)事業を守らねばならないであろう.

quicksand, *n.* 流砂.

P It is built ***on*** the *quicksand.* それは流砂の上に立っている(危険だ).

P² the "*quicksand **of*** debt" 借財の泥沼.

quickstep, *n.* 早足.

P They resumed their march ***at*** a *quickstep.* 彼らは早足でまた進行を起した.

quiet, *n.* 安静, 平穏.

V ***enjoy*** perfect *quiet* のうのうする. ¶Wind ***disturbs*** the *quiet* of the air. 風があたりの平穏をかく乱する. ¶***restore*** *quiet* 安静を回復する.

Q She disturbs the ***domestic*** *quiet* (=peace). 彼女は家庭の平和を乱す.【類】disturb the ***public*** *quiet* of the country. ¶the ***public*** *quiet* 公安.

P ***at*** *quiet* 静かに, 平穏に. ¶live ***in*** *quiet* 平穏に暮らす ‖ ***in*** the *quiet* of one's own home 家で静かに.【類】He settledd own there to end his days (余生) ***in*** *quiet.* ¶run ***on*** the *quiet* in violation of the law 法律を犯して秘密に営業している. ¶***out of*** *quiet* 落着かずに.

quiet, *a.* 静かな, おとなしい.

M be ***absolutely*** *quiet* 絶対安静である. ¶Oh, please go on with your story, I'll be ***quite*** *quiet.* どうぞ話の先をして下さい, ごく静かにしておりますから. ¶Be ***real*** *quiet.* ほんとに静かにしておいで.

M^{2} ***as*** *quiet* ***as*** a lamb 小羊のようにおとなしく.【類】people ***as*** *quiet* ***as*** mice.

P keep *quiet* ***for*** a while しばらくじっとしている. ¶He is *quiet* ***in*** his demeanor (movement). 彼は態度(動作)が静かだ.

quiet, *v.* 静まる.

M^{2} Everything *quieted* ***down.*** 四辺がひっそりとした.【類】after things (世間) *quieted* ***down*** / The disturbance *quieted* ***down*** at last under the touch of Sunday (日曜日の朝になって). / The excitement is *quieting* ***down.*** / The guns in North China seem to be *quieting* ***down*** in most places. / The storm *quieted* ***down.***

quietude, *n.* 安静.

V ***love*** the *quietude* of the study 書斉の安静を愛する.

quilt, *n.* ふとん.

V ***spread*** one's *quilts* ふとんを敷く.

Q^{2} ***down*** *quilts* 羽根ぶとん.

quint, *n.* 《米口》五つ児 (quintuplet).

Q^{2} the ***Dionne*** *quints* (Emilie, Marie, Yvonne, Annette, and Cecile) ディオンヌ家の五つ児.

quintessence, *n.* 真髄, 典型.

P^{2} the *quintessence* ***of*** virtue (beauty) 徳(美)の典型.【類】the *quintessence* ***of*** socialism (democracy).

quire, *n.* 一帖.

P Paper is sold ***in*** *quires.* 紙は帖で売る.

P^{2} several *quires* ***of*** paper 数帖の紙.

quit, *a.* まぬかれた.

P get *quit* ***of*** ... ...をまぬかれる ‖ He was glad to be *quit* ***of*** the trouble. 彼はやっかい払いをして喜んでいた.

quit, *v.* 去る; 捨てる, やめる.

M ***definitely*** *quit* smoking 断然禁煙する. ¶He *quit* smoking and drinking ***early*** in his life. 彼は早くから酒・タバコをやめた.

P He *quitted* (*quit*) Tokyo ***at*** midnight. 彼は真夜中に東京を去った. ¶She *quitted* (*quit*) him ***in*** anger. 彼女は怒って彼から去った(を捨てた). ☞ quit (*v.*) の無変化は主に米語用法.

quits, *a.* 互角の, あいこの.

P I will be *quits* ***with*** him. 彼に返報をしてやろう.

quiver, *n.* 震え.

P^{2} there was a tear in his eye and a *quiver* ***in*** his voice as he told of ... 彼が...を語ったときに目には涙を浮べその声はふるえていた.

quiver, *v.* 震える.

P A dry leaf was seen *quivering* ***in*** the air. 枯葉が一枚ぶるぶる震えていた.【類】dead leaves on a twig *quivering* ***in*** the wind. ¶the beams of the moon *quivering* ***on*** the water 水面にちらちらしている月光. ¶His lips *quivered* ***with*** rage (fright, cold, emotion). 彼は怒って(など)くちびるが震えた.【類】His voice *quivered* ***with*** *agitation* (激して).

quorum, *n.* 定員数.

V Eight members ***constitute*** a *quorum* at a meeting. 八名出席すれば会の定数になる. ¶Nine members shall ***form*** a *quorum* at any general meeting. 総会においては九名を定数とする. ¶***lack*** a *quorum* 定数を欠く. ¶***procure*** a *quorum* 定数を得る.

V^{2} A *quorum* ***consists*** of a majority of the members. 会員の過半数をもって定数とする.

quota, *n.* 分け前, 持分; 割当(額).

V ***add*** an important *quota* to ... ...に大いに貢献する. ¶***allot*** a *quota* of $... to ... ...に...ドルの割当をする. ¶***contribute*** one's *quota* 自分の割当を出資する ‖ Both Ireland and Scotland ***contribute*** their *quota* of musical talent. アイルランドもスコットランドもそれぞれ音楽の大家を出している.【類】There was a vast concourse of visitors from the surrounding villages and towns ***contributing*** that *quota.* ¶***cut*** the *quota* of foreign films that can be imported 輸入できる映画の割当を削減する. ¶***reach*** the ful *quota* 定員に達する.

Q the ***publisher's*** *quota* of free copies to an author 出版者がその著者に無料で供給する本の定数. ¶countries with ***small*** *quotas* of emigrants 小数移民割当の国々.

Q^{2} fail to fill the ***collection*** *quotas* by 25 per cent 供出割当に二十五パーセント不足する. ¶assign the staple ***food crops*** *quota* 主食を割当てる. ¶meet the ***grain-collection*** *quotas* 穀物の供出割当を出す. ¶increase the ***immigration*** *quota* from 1,500 to 2,500 a month 移民割当を千五百人から二千五百人に増加する. ¶suspend ***paper*** *quotas* to publishers 出版用紙の割当を中止する. ¶meet their required ***production*** *quotas* 必要な生産割当を満たす.

quotable, *a.* 引用しうる.

O passages (words) not to be *quotable* 引用にたえないような(下品な)句(語).

quotation, *n.* (**1**) 引例; 引用句.

V ***adduce*** a *quotation* from ... ...から語句を引用する. ¶***deserve*** *quotation* [文句など]引用する価値がある. ¶***identify*** the following *quotations* 次の引用句の出所を明かにする. ¶mutilated *quotations* ***made*** from my previous letter 私のこの前の書簡から所々勝手に引用した文句. ¶***miscredit*** a *quotation* 引用語を信用しない. ¶in this I ***recall*** the *quotation*: この点で私は...という引用句を想起する. ¶It has not always been possible to ***trace*** *quotations* to their original sources. 引用文の出典を明かにすることのできない場合もあった. ¶***use*** foreign *quotations* 外国の引用句を用いる. ¶***verify*** a *quotation* 引用句を原本について校合する.【類】***verify*** doubtful *quotations.*

Q an ***apposite*** (=***apt***) *quotation* 適切な引用句. ¶***dated*** *quotations* 年代を示した引用句(NED などのように). ¶the ***following*** *quotation* from ... will be of interest here 次にあげる...からの引用はここでは興味があろう. ¶an ***illustrative*** *quotation* 説明になる引用句. ¶***literary*** *quotations* 文学上の引用句. ¶a ***relevant*** *quotation* 適切な引用句. ¶a ***threadbare*** *quotation* 陳腐な引用句.

P^{2} *quotations* ***from*** the Bible 聖書からの引用句.

(**2**) 〖商〗相場, 直段, 時価表.

V ***give*** *quotations* for future deliveries 先渡しを見越して相場を示す ‖ The *quotations* are not ***given*** in the official list. その相場は公定の価格表に出ていない.【類】***give*** a *quotation* (見積り) for painting. ¶*Quotations* are barely ***maintained.*** 相場は弱保合(もちあい)だ. ¶Kindly ***send*** your *quotations* on wire screens. 金網の貴店相場をお知らせ下さい.

Q ***current*** *quotations* for ... ...の時価.【類】You are above ***current*** *quotations.* ¶After a very firm opening the Bourse became weak, and the ***final*** *quotations* were almost all below yesterday. 相場は始めは強気だったが取引所は弱気となり最後の相場はいずれもきのうより下回った. ¶***high*** (***low***) *quotation* 高(低)い言値. ¶***official*** *quotations* of a stock exchange 株式取引所の公定相場. ¶the ***present low*** *quotations* of the mark 現在の低いマルク相場值. ¶a ***nominal*** *quotation* 名目相場. ¶***public*** (=***official***) *quotation* 公定相場. ¶*Quotations* are ***unchanged*** since last. 相場はこの前と変りがない.

Q^{2} ***black-market*** *quotations* やみ相場. ¶a ***closing*** *quotation* 大引相場. ¶the ***daily market*** *quotation* 日々の市場相場. ¶the ***exchange*** *quotations* [外国]為替相場表. ¶***futures*** (***spot***) *quotations* 先もの(現物)相場. ¶an ***opening*** *quotation* 寄付相場.

P I will buy ***at*** your *quotations.* 私は貴店の指(さし)値で買います.

P^{2} a *quotation* ***for*** silk 蚕糸相場. ¶*quotations* ***in*** the dry goods (grocery, fruit) 呉服(など)の相場. ¶These papers print *quotations* ***on*** the stock, cotton, produce, coffee, sugar, and other exchanges. これらの新聞紙は株式・綿花・農産物・コーヒー・砂糖その他の商品取引所の相場を掲載する. ¶Special *quotations* (=rates) ***to*** clubs, public institutions, etc.〘広告〙クラブ・公共団体などへは特別割引を致します.

quote, *v.* 引用する; 相場を付ける.

M *freely quote* … 自由に…を引用する. ¶the sentence *just quoted* たった今引用した文. ¶*quote lower* than our opponents, if necessary 必要ならば競争者側より安く仕切る. ¶in order to illustrate this point we can very *profitably quote* from … この点を証明するには…から引証するのがきわめて有利だ.

P *quote* a few instances of battles *as* (being) more bloody ones 一層殺伐な例として二三戦役を例示する‖*quote* … *as* authorities 権威あるものとして…を引用する‖he was *quoted as* saying that … …という彼の言葉が出ていた(新聞などに). ¶It is *quoted at* $5. それは五ドルと相場が付いている.‖*quote at* second hand 孫引用をする. ¶Please *quote for* the articles named. 指示の品物に相場をつけて下さい.【類】be *quoted for* separately. ¶*quote* a passage *from* a book (speech, document) 書物(など)から文句を引用する.【類】a passage *quoted from* Milton. ¶*quote in* part (full) 一部(全部)引用する‖*quote in* total 全部引用する‖It is *quoted* earlier *in* this chapter. それはこの章の初めの方に引用してある.

O Let me *quote* you the words of Byron. バイロンの語を引用して君に示そう.

quotes, *n. pl.* 引用符.

Q *ending* (=*closing*) *quotes* 終りの方の引用符. ¶*opening* (=*beginning*) *quotes* 始めの方の引用符.

quotient, *n.* 商, 指数.

Q[2] *intelligence quotient*〘心理〙知能指数.

R

r, *n.* アール.

V *trill* the "*r*" ル(r) をひびかせて発音する.

Q art as a *fourth* "*R*" 第四のアールとしての芸術. ¶the *three R's* 三つのアール('riting と reading と 'rithmetic, 読み書き算術).

Q[2] the *consonant r* 子音のアール. ¶the *glide r*〘音声〙経過音のアール.

rabbit, *n.* うさぎ.

V *rabbits* that are *raised* in the warren (うさぎ飼場).

V[2] *Rabbits breed* quickly. うさぎはすぐ子を生む(ふえる).

Q an *albino rabbit* 白うさぎ. ¶raise *Angora rabbits* アンゴラうさぎを飼う.

P run *like* a *rabbit* 一目散に逃げる‖scared *like* (=*as*) a *rabbit* [うさぎのように]びくびくして.

rabble, *n.* わいわい連, う合の衆.

Q a *mere rabble* ほんのわいわい連.

rabies, *n.* 狂犬病.

V He's *got rabies.* 彼は狂犬病にかかった. ¶The dog might *have rabies.* 狂犬かもしれない.

P be seized *with rabies* 恐水病にかかる.

race, *n.* **(1)** 競走, 競馬; 人生の行路.

V The yacht team *race* was *cancelled* because of the continued bad weather. ヨット競走は続いた悪天候のため取消になった. ¶*carry off* a big *race* 大競馬に勝つ. ¶He *entered* the *race* for Congress against …, Democrat, incumbent. 彼は現在議員である民主党の…氏に対抗して議員候補に打って出た. ¶*fix up* a *race* between … …間の競走を決定する. ¶With this heavy rain, we cannot *have* any *races* tomorrow. この大雨ではあすは競走はできまい. ¶*have* a close *race* with … …と接戦をやる. ¶The yacht club *held* a *race* yesterday. そのヨットクラブはきのう競漕会を催した. ¶*lose* a *race* 競走に負ける. ¶*pay races*《米》競馬にかける. ¶*ride* a *race* 競馬に出る. ¶*row* a *race* 短艇競漕をする. ¶*run* a *race* 競走をやる‖He has *run* his *race.* 彼の命数は尽きた.【類】His *race* was *run.*‖*run* a *race* with Death 死と競争をやる[水におぼれようとする者を救う場合など]. ¶*sail* a *race* 帆船競走をやる. ¶*start* a *race* 競走を開始する. ¶*time* a *race* 競走時間を測定する. ¶*try* a *race* 競走を試みる. ¶*win* the *race* by a wide margin ゆうゆうと(大差で)競走に勝つ.

V[2] The first *race* on the turf will *start* at 1.00 p.m. each day. 最初の競馬は毎日午後一時に始まる.

Q a *blindfold race* 目隠し競走. ¶a keenly *contested race* 猛烈な競走. ¶There was an *exciting race* to the scene of the accident. 事件の現場へと手に汗を握らせるような競走が起った(救助船など). ¶a *go-as-you-please race* ルールのない自由競走. ¶a *visitors' race* 来賓競走.

Q[2] an *air race* 飛行競走. ¶an *armament race* between the United States and Russia 合衆国とロシア間の軍備競争. ¶enter into (=start) the *arms race* 軍備競争を始める. ¶have an *atomic bomb race* with … …と原子爆弾競争をする. ¶an *auto-cycle race*=a motor-cycle race《米》オートバイ競走. ¶a *bicycle race* 自転車競走. ¶row a *boat race* ボートレースをやる. ¶a *cross-country race* 林野横断競走. ¶a *ding-dong* (=neck-and-neck) *race* 五分五分の競走. ¶a *foot race* 徒歩競走. ¶a *hot-rod race*《米俗》自動車競走. ¶a *Marathon* [*race*] マラソン競争. ¶an *obstacle race* 障害物競走. ¶take to *running races* 競走をやり出す(その方に興味が移る). ¶a *short distance race* 短距離競走. ¶a *skipping race* なわとび競走. ¶a "*strangers*" *race*=a free-for-all race 飛入競走. ¶a *swimming race* 競泳. ¶the forthcoming *university boat race* 近く催される大学ボートレース. ¶a *world armament race* 世界軍備競争. ¶a *yacht race* ヨットレース.【類】international trophy *yacht races.*

P They are expected to be present *at* the *races.* 彼らはその競走に出席するはず. ¶train a man *for* a *race* 競走出場のため人を訓練する.【類】drill horses *for* a *race.* ¶competition *in* the *race* for wealth 金もうけの競争‖take part *in* a *race* 競走に参加する‖engage *in* a *race* 競走に加わる. ¶lose money *on* the *races* 競馬にかけて金を失う.

P[2] a *race between* … …間の競走. ¶a *race by* horses=a horserace 競馬. ¶the international *race for* increased armaments 国際間の軍拡競争. ¶the *race of* life 人生コース. ¶a *race on* foot 徒歩競走. ¶Let us have a *race to* the house. その家までかけっこしよう. ¶do a *race up* the stairs 階段上りの競走をやる.【類】Mrs. Rebecca Kissick, of Philadelphia, aged 104, is reported to have challenged any woman more than fifty years old to a *race up* the 320 steps of the City Hall tower. ¶a *race with* a person 人との競争.

(2) 人種, 民族.

V endeavor to *blend* the two *races* 二種類の雑種を作ろうと努める. ¶Only the healthiest in mind and body should undertake the responsibility of *continuing* the *race.* 身心の最も強健なるもののみが種族存続の責任を引受けるべきである. ¶the persons best adapted to *propagate* the *race* 人類を繁殖させるのに最も適した人たち. ¶*raise* a *race* of stubborn heroes がん強な勇士を造る.

Q *alien races* 外国の民族. ¶the *Anglo-Saxon race* アングロ・サクソン民族. ¶the *Barbarian races* around China 中国をめぐる諸蛮族. ¶*barbaric races* 野蛮人種. ¶the *brave race* of seamen [命知らずの] 勇敢な船員たち. ¶*colored races*—yellow, brown, black and red 黄・褐(かつ)・黒・赤の有色人種. ¶teachers, a *conservative race* as a rule 概して保守的な人物たる教師. ¶It controls the good of the *coming race.* それは人類将来の幸福にかかわる. ¶a *conquered race* 征服された民族. ¶a *diminutive race* of horses 小馬の一種. ¶The Americans are a *dyspeptic race.* 米人は胃病になりやすい民族である. ¶Artists are an *eccentric race* all the world over. 芸術家は世界いたるところ変った人間である. ¶the members of the *English-speaking race* 英語民族の仲間. ¶smaller members of the *equine race* 小馬の種属. ¶women of *European race* ヨーロッパ民族に属する女. ¶The Dutches are a *hardy race.* オランダ人は強健な民族である. ¶the *human race* 人類. ¶The British and Americans are two great nations *of* kindred race. 英米は同血族の二大国民である. ¶the Latin races ラテン民族. ¶the living races of mankind 地上に生存している諸民族. ¶the lost race of Tasmania 絶滅したタスマニヤ民族. ¶a martial race 尚武の民. ¶a meat-eating race 肉食人種. ¶aid an oppressed race しいたげられた民族を助ける. ¶a patriotic race 愛国的人種. ¶a proud and stiff-necked race 自尊心のあるがん固な人種. ¶a strong, robust race 強壮でがん丈な人種. ¶the last home of a vanishing race 消え行く人種の最後の居住地. ¶raise up a vigorous, intelligent, enterprising, self-reliant and healthy race 強く賢く有為で自信のある健全な民族を育成する. ¶the white races of Europe ヨーロッパの白色人種. ¶Punishment fell upon the whole race of the offender. 罪人一味の者全部が刑罰を受けた. 【類】They do more service to the country than the whole race of politicians put together. ¶the winged race 羽翼族(鳥類). ¶They are a worldly race. 彼らは後生を願わない俗人たちだ. ¶the yellow race 黄色人種.

P Among the lower races of mankind the female is merely a chattel. 下等人種の間では女は道具にすぎない. ¶The Japanese are, as a race, honest. 日本人は民族全体として見ると正直だ. ¶He is a German by race. 彼はドイツ民族に属する.

P[2] segregation between races 《米》人種間(特に・白・黒)の分離. ¶The Hindus, as a rule, are a race of vegetarians. インド人は概して菜食者だ.

race, *v.* 競走する, 競走させる.

M He raced all his money away. 競馬(競輪など)で金を全部すった.

P He raced his bicycle against a motorcar. 彼は自転車で自動車と競走した. ¶He races for a living. 彼は競馬騎手を職としている. ¶race a bill through Congress 議案を大急ぎで議会を通す. ¶I will race you to ... …まで君と競走しよう.

racer, *n.* レースの選手, 競馬馬.

Q[2] a mile racer=a miler 一マイル・レース選手. ¶a winning racer 勝った競馬馬.

racing, *n.* 競走.

Q[2] automobile racing 自動車競走.

rack, *n.* 架; ごう問, ごう問台; 荷物だな.

Q[2] luggage (=baggage) racks 荷物だな(車内の).

P He is on the rack. 彼は拷問にあっている; 責苦にあっている. ‖His brain is continually on the rack about the means of living. 彼は生計のために絶えず頭を悩ましている. ¶put a person to the rack 人を拷問にかける; 人をひどい目にあわせる.

rack, *n.* 荒廃.

P go to rack and ruin 荒廃する.

rack, *v.* 苦しめる, 悩ます.

P I racked my brain for a way of escape. 私は逃げる方法を考えて頭を悩ました. ¶rack heavy rents from sharecroppers 小作人から高い地代を搾り取る.

racket, *n.* ラケット.

P bat a ball back and forth with rackets ラケットでボールを打合う.

racket *v.* 浮かれ暮す.

M racket away one's life (time) 浮かれ暮す.

M[2] racket about 浮かれ暮す, 夜警に回る.

racketeer, *n.* 《米》ごろつき.

Q petty racketeers 下っぱのよた者たち.

Q[2] a blackmarket racketeer やみ市のよた者.

racy, *a.* 風味のある, きびきびした.

P The dialects have supplied to literature so much that is racy to the soil. 方言は文学に大いに郷土的風味あるものを提供した.

radiance, *n.* 光輝, 射光.

V a diadem of glittering gems cast its prismatic radiance over ... さん然たる宝石の王冠はその陸離たる光彩を…の上に投じた. ¶Hundreds of multicolored fairy lamps shed their soft radiance on the forms of beautiful women gloriously gowned. いく百の多彩なランプがその軟かな光を豪華な服装をした美人たちの姿に投げかけた.

Q glow with an incomparably brighter radiance 比較にならないほどきらきらした光で輝く. ¶At night these streets are brilliant with a pearly radiance of electricity. 夜になるとこれらの街路は真珠のような電気の光でさん然と輝く. ¶with prismatic radiance 五彩さんらんと.

radiant, *a.* 晴々した, 輝やかしい.

P faces radiant with smiles (hopes, happiness) 微笑(など)で晴々した顔.

radiate, *v.* ふく射する, 放散する.

M radiate fanwise from ... …から扇状を成して放射する.

P railways (steamer lines) radiating from ... …から放射する鉄道(など) ‖Light radiates from luminous bodies directly to our eyes. 光は発光体から直接にわれわれの目に放射する. 【類】Heat radiates from a gas heater (ガス・ストーブ). ¶roads radiating in all directions 八方に延びる道路. ¶About 1885, Volapuk conquered France, whence it radiated all over the world. 一八八五年ごろヴォラプュック語はフランスを征服しそこから世界に広まった. ¶Tramways radiate to outlying sections of the city from the business center. 電車線が市の商業中心区域から郊外へ放射状に広がる.

radiation, *n.* ふく射熱.

Q utilize solar radiation 太陽熱を利用する.

radiator, *n.* 放熱器, 暖房器.

Q a small three-pronged radiator 三尖頭の小さな放熱器.

radical, *n.* [漢字]扁(など).

P look up a character under its radical その扁などで字を引く.

radio, *n.* 無線通信(電話); ラジオ.

V own a radio ラジオを取付ける. ¶play the radio ラジオをかける. ¶put on (off) the radio ラジオをかける(切る). ¶tune one's radio in on to ... ラジオを…に合わせる. ¶turn on (off) the radio ラジオをかける(切る). 【類】switch on (off) the radio.

Q the ubiquitous radio どこにでもあるラジオ.

Q[2] an all-wave radio 全音波ラジオ. ¶an auto radio 自動車用ラジオ. ¶a midget radio 極小型ラジオ器.

P broadcasting by radio ラジオによる放送. ¶send a message by radio=radio a message 《米》無線電報を打つ. ☞英語用法は wireless. 【類】music broadcast by radio / speak from England by radio. ¶speak on the radio ラジオで話す ‖listen in on the radio ラジオを聴取する. 【類】listen in to symphonies and chamber music (室内楽) [on the radio]. ¶I heard it over the radio. 私はラジオでそれを聞いた. ‖the unseen audience over the radio ラジオで呼び掛ける目に見えない聴衆. 【類】talk over the radio / It was broadcasted over the radio. / hear news over the radio / It could be heard over the radio from ... by anybody who knows the correct wavelength. / A few nights ago I listened over the radio to his talk. ¶through (=over) the radio ラジオを通じて.

radiophone, *n.* 無線電話.

P talk to ... over the radiophone 無線電話で…に話す.

radish, *n.* 大根.

Q[2] grated horse radish おろし大根.

radius, *n.* 半径.

Q[2] an action radius 〖軍〗行動半径. ¶within a forty-mile radius of the city 市の四十マイル半径内に. ¶one's shopping radius ある人の買物範囲. ¶words and expressions deemed beyond the vocabulary radius of middle-school pupils 中学生の使う言葉の範囲外と考えられる単語や表現.

P for a radius of 75 miles from Chicago シカゴから半径七十五マイルの間. ¶The first shock of explosion was felt over a radius of twenty miles. 爆発最初の衝動は半径二十マイルの間で感じた. ¶within a radius of 30 miles from ... …から半径三十マイルの間. 【類】The forbidden zones (立入禁止地帯) cover all territory within a radius of six miles round the places mentioned. / within a short radius of ... (わずかに半径…) / within a 15-mile (=a 15 miles') radius of ...

raffle, *n.* 富くじ.

Q[2] I got it in the theater raffle. それは劇場の福引で当った.

raffle, *v.* 富くじで売る.

M[2] raffle off a washing machine (video set, radio outfit) 富くじ式で洗たく機械(など)を売る.

P raffle for an auto 《米》自動車の当る富くじを買う.

raft, *n.* いかだ.

Q a rudely fashioned raft 粗造ないかだ.

Q[2] a fire raft 火いかだ(敵船を焼くための).

P on a raft いかだに乗って(乗せて).

rag, *n. pl.* ぼろ; 《米》着物.

V pick up rags in the streets 町でぼろを拾う.

Q She went out in glad rags. 《米》彼女は一ちょうらを着てでかけた.

P clad in rags ぼろを着て ‖a beggar in rags ぼろを着たこじき ‖a dealer in rags ぼろを売買する人 ‖in rags that were hanging about in ribbons あらめの行列といった格好で(ルンペンなど). ¶worn to rags ぼろぼろになって.

rag, *v.* 着物を着る.

M *rag out* for a party《俗》パーティに出るため着飾る.

rage, *n.* 激怒, 激烈; 熱望; 流行.

V ***allay*** one's *rage* その怒りをなだめる. ¶he ***has*** a *rage* for ... 彼は…を熱望している. ¶***vent*** (=***wreak***) one's *rage* on ... …に対して激怒をもらす. ¶His *rage* was ***boiling*** over. 彼はかんかんになっていた.

Q It is now ***all*** the *rage* in America. それは米国では目下大流行である. ¶in a ***black*** *rage* 真赤に怒って. ¶with a look of ***desperate*** *rage* やけくそ気味の怒りを面に浮べて. ¶***divine*** *rage* 義憤. ¶in a ***humming*** *rage* ぷんぷん怒って. ¶***inarticulate*** *rage* 口もはっきりきけないほどの憤怒. ¶in a fit of ***jealous*** *rage* さい疑の怒りを激発して. ¶a ***noble*** *rage* 気高い憤激. ¶It is ***quite*** the *rage*. それは大流行だ. ¶throw one into a ***silent*** *rage* 腹を立たせて黙りこくらせる. ¶in a ***towering*** *rage* たけり立って. ¶an ***unbridled*** *rage* むきだしの怒り. ¶fall into a ***violent*** *rage* 激しく怒りだす.

P He left the room ***in*** a *rage*. 彼はかっとなって室を出て行った. 【類】***In*** his *rage*, he broke the vase. ¶fly (=get) ***into*** a *rage* (passion) かんしゃくを起す. ¶in a fit ***of*** *rage* かっとなって. ¶give vent ***to*** one's *rage* うっぷんを漏らす. ¶quivering ***with*** *rage* 怒りで震えて ‖ boil ***with*** *rage* 激怒で煮えくりかえる ‖ hot ***with*** *rage* 真赤になって怒って ‖ ***with*** *rage* in her heart むっとして. 【類】get red-hot ***with*** *rage*.

P^2 He is in a great *rage* ***about*** an article just published. 彼は公にされたばかりの記事について非常に立腹している. ¶*rage* (=fashion) ***for*** ivory 象牙(ゾウゲ)の流行. ¶a *rage* ***of*** grief 悲憤. ¶the *rage* ***of*** the sea 海の猛威. 【類】the *rage* ***of*** a storm (wild animal).

rage, *v.* 流行する; 激怒する; 荒狂う.

M Cholera is *raging* very ***badly***. コレラがひどく流行している. ¶The flu (=influenza epidemic) is *raging* very ***fiercely*** there. インフルエンザがその地で非常に流行している. ¶The great Tooley Street fire *raged* ***furiously*** for several weeks. トーレー街の大火は数週間猛威をふるった. ¶I went to see him *raging* ***inwardly***. 私は腹が治まらないで彼に会いに行った. ¶The fire is ***still*** *raging*. 火勢はまだ盛んだ. ¶For three days the tempest *raged* ***unceasingly***. 三日間続けてあらしが吹きまくった.

P *rage* ***against*** restraint 抑圧に猛烈な反対をする. ¶*rage* ***at*** a person 人に怒りつける. ¶*rage* ***with*** unabated fury 猛威をゆるめず荒狂う. 【類】The typhoon *raged* ***with*** great and everincreasing violence. / A gale was then *raging* ***with*** extreme violence. ‖ *raging* ***with*** anger かっと怒って.

O A storm (fire, flu) is *raging*. あらし(など)が猛威をふるっている.

raid, *n.* 侵入, 攻撃.

V ***carry out*** a *raid* on food shops 食料店を襲う. 【類】British aeroplanes ***carried out*** a very successful bombing *raid* this afternoon into German territory. ¶***make*** *raids* for booty 略奪のため侵入をする. ¶The police ***made*** a *raid* on the house. その家に警察の手がはいった. 【類】***make*** a *raid* into hostile territory (敵地) / ***make*** *raids* on the Spaniards.

Q^2 houses burned up in an ***air*** *raid* 空襲で焼けた家屋. ¶a ***B-29 air*** *raid* B-29 の空襲. ¶a ***bombing*** *raid* on London ロンドンに対する爆撃. 【類】the first ***bombing*** *raid* on Tokyo. ¶a ***daylight*** *raid* 白昼攻撃. ¶The police staged a series of ***early morning*** *raids*. 警察が引続き早朝手入れを行った. ¶a ***hit-and-run night*** *raid* 急撃急退夜襲. ¶an ***incendiary bomb*** *raid* 焼い弾爆撃. ¶a ***police*** *raid* 警察の手入れ. ¶a ***guerrilla*** *raid* 不正規兵の急襲. ¶a ***shuttle*** *raid* 反復爆撃. ¶a ***suicide*** *raid* 特攻隊爆撃. ¶the ***1944*** *raids* on Tokyo 一九四四年の東京空襲.

P^2 a *raid* ***on*** gamblers 博徒への手入れ.

raid, *v.* [警察が]手入れする.

O The police *raided* the gambling den. ばくち場に手入れがあった.

raider, *n.* 襲撃者, 爆撃機.

Q^2 intercept an ***air*** *raider* 敵機を食い止める. ¶an ***enemy*** *raider* 敵機.

rail, *n.* 軌条; 鉄道; 手すり.

V ***clear*** the *rails* 鉄道線路の障害物を除去する. ¶The engine of the train ***left*** the *rails* at a curve. 機関車がカーブの処で脱線した. ¶***move on*** *rails* 線路上を走る. ¶***rip up*** *rails* レールを撤去する. ¶***run off*** the *rails* (車両が)脱線する. ¶***take*** *rail* (=train) from ... to ... 汽車で…から…へ行く.

Q^2 a ***steel*** *rail* 鉄の手すり. ¶***tram*** *rails* 市電の線路.

P a *rail* ***around*** the porch 車寄せ(入口)の周囲の(木または鉄の)横木. ¶stand ***at*** the ship's *rail* 船の手すりの所に立つ. ¶It may be approached ***by*** *rail* (=by train). そこへは汽車で行かれる. ‖ travel (send) ***by*** *rail* 汽車で旅行する(など). ¶run ***off*** the *rail*=(leave the metals, *or* get derailed) 鉄道線路から脱線する. ¶move (=run) ***on*** *rails* 軌条を走る.

rail, *v.* 手すりで囲う.

M The choir is *railed* ***in***. 唱歌隊席は手すりで囲まれている. ‖ a yard *railed* ***in*** by stakes くいで囲ってある区域. ¶be *railed* ***off*** from the highway 公道との間を仕切ってある. 【類】The footpaths were *railed* ***off*** along the whole distance.

rail, *v.* ののしる, あざける.

M *rail* ***furiously*** 激しくののしる.

P *rail* ***against*** (=***at***) a person (matter, idea) 人(など)をののしる. 【類】*rail* ***at*** one's own lot (自分の運命). ☞ *rail* ***upon*** ... は古体.

railing, *n.* 手すり, 欄干.

V^2 A *railing* ***runs*** across the room. 棒仕切りが室を横切って作ってある.

Q^2 a ***cast-iron*** *railing* 鋳鉄の欄干. ¶The top of that tower has an ***iron*** *railing*. その塔の頂上に鉄の欄干がある. ¶an ***iron-bar*** *railing* 鉄棒の欄干.

P lean ***over*** a *railing* 欄干にもたれる.

railroad, *n.* 《米》鉄道.

V ***construct*** a *railroad* 鉄道を敷設する.

V^2 This *railroad* ***operates*** 20 trains an hour. この鉄道は一時間二十列車を運転している.

Q The opening of the ***first*** *railroad* in China was in 1896. 中国における最初の鉄道開始は千八百九十六年であった. ¶a ***transcontinental*** *railroad* 大陸横断鉄道.

Q^2 a ***horse*** *railroad* 馬車鉄道.

P He worked as a ticket-collector ***on*** a *railroad*. 彼は鉄道の集札係をやった.

railroad, *v.* 《米》議案を急いで通過させる.

P *railroad* a bill ***through*** Congress《米》国会で議案を強行突破で通過させる.

railroader, *n.* 《米》鉄道員.

M *Railroaders* ***walked out***. 鉄道従業員がストライキをした.

railway, *n.* 鉄道.

V here the *railway* may be ***availed*** of to ... ここで…行の鉄道を利用することができる. ¶***build*** (=***construct***) a *railway* 鉄道を敷設する. ¶***double-track*** a *railway* 鉄道を複線にする. ¶***electrify*** *railways* 鉄道を電化する. ¶***extend*** the *railway* from A to B 鉄道を A から B へ延長する. ¶***make*** a *railway* 鉄道を敷設する. ¶***manage*** (=***conduct*** ***or direct***) a *railway* 鉄道を経営する. ¶The *railway* was ***opened*** to traffic last year. その鉄道は去年開通した. ¶***rejoin*** the *railway* at ... …でその鉄道と再び連絡する. ¶***take*** the Siberian *railway* シベリア鉄道に乗る. ¶This position of the *railway* is ***worked*** with only a single pair of rails. その鉄道のこの区間は単線になっている.

V^2 *railways* ***extend*** from ... to ... 鉄道線路が…から…へ延びている.

Q ***inter-urban electric*** *railways* 都市連絡電気鉄道. ¶a ***light*** *railway* 軽便鉄道. ¶a ***military*** *railway* 軍用鉄道. ¶a ***portable*** *railway* 運搬のできる鉄道線路. ¶a ***private*** *railway* 私設鉄道. ¶a ***projected*** *railway* 計画中の鉄道. ¶There is not a ***single*** *railway* or other means of mechanical transportation. 一条の鉄道もなくその他機械による交通の便がない. ¶a ***state-owned*** (=government) *railway* 国有鉄道. ¶a ***strategic*** *railway* 軍用鉄道. ¶a ***suburban*** *railway* 郊外鉄道. ¶an ***underground electric*** *railway* 地下鉄道.

Q^2 a ***bicycle*** *railway* 双輪鉄道. ¶a ***broad*** (***narrow***)***-guage*** *railway* 広(狭)軌鉄道. ¶a ***cable*** *railway* ケーブル鉄道. ¶an ***electric street*** *railway* 電車(電気鉄道). ¶a ***ferry*** *railway* 連絡船鉄道. ¶place an ***iron*** *railway* 鉄道を敷設する. ¶the ***London, Brighton***, and ***South Coast*** *Railway* ロンドンブライトン南海岸鉄道. ¶a light ***narrow-gauge*** *railway* 軽狭軌鉄道. ¶Australia's "***Ocean to Ocean***" *railway* 豪州横断鉄道. ¶a ***rack*** and ***pinion*** *railway* アプト式登山鉄道. ¶a ***single***(***double***)***-track*** *railway* 単(複)線鉄道. ¶a ***steam*** *railway* 汽車鉄道(馬車鉄道などに対して). ¶a ***surface*** *railway* 路面鉄道. ¶a ***tube*** *railway* 地下鉄. ¶an ***underground*** *railway* (=《米》a subway)《英》地下鉄.

P rambles ***beyond*** *railways* 鉄道を離れての散策. ¶travel ***by*** *rail*[*way*] 鉄道旅行. ¶a line ***of*** *railway* 一条の鉄道.

¶since the opening *of railways in* Japan 日本に鉄道が開通して以来. ¶a workman *on* a *railway* 鉄道従業員 ‖ travel third class *on* the *railway* 鉄道の三等で旅行する ‖ an accident *on* the *railway* 鉄道の事故. 【類】travel *on* a *railway* (=by rail) / a trip *on* the ... *railway*. / Fares *on* the Trans-Siberian *Railway* reduced 50%. ¶a journey *over* the Siberian *railway* シベリア鉄道の旅. 【類】a 50-mile trip from ... *over* the ... *Railway*. ¶men employed *upon* a *railway* 鉄道の使用人. ¶The country is provided *with railways*. その国には鉄道の便がある.

P^2 a *railway across* ... ...横断の鉄道. ¶the *railway between* ... ...との間の鉄道.

railway-crossing, *n.* 鉄道踏切り.

P signs *at railway-crossings* 鉄道踏切の標識.

raiment, *n.* 着物, 衣服.

V *wear* gaudy *raiment* けばけばしい着物を着る.

Q be decked out in one's *best raiment* 最上の晴着で着飾っている. ¶office boys in *gorgeous raiment* りっぱな制服を着けた小店員(給仕). ¶*modern woman's scanty raiment* 現代婦人のはだもあらわの服.

rain, *n.* 雨, 降雨; [the -s] 雨季.

V *exclude rain* 雨を避ける. ¶We shall *have rain*. 雨が降るだろう. ‖ We *have* the *rains* in early summer. 初夏が雨期だ. ¶*ignoring* the soaking *rain* 雨でびしょぬれになるのを物ともせず. ¶The hut is barely able to *keep out* (=*off*) the rain. その小屋はようよう雨を防ぐだけだ. 【類】The umbrella *keeps* the *rain* off the user. / This coat will *keep off rain*. ¶*Rain* is much *needed*. 一雨ほしい. ¶*shut out* the *rain* 雨の降り込まないようにする.

V^2 The *rain* has *abated*. 雨がやんだ. ¶A sharp *rain* was *beating* against the window-panes. 猛烈な雨が窓ガラスを打っていた. ¶The *rain began* to fall. 雨が降り出した. ¶The *rain cleared off*. 雨が上った. ¶Here *comes* the *rain!* 雨だ! ¶The *rain* is *coming down* in sheets. しのつく雨だ. 【類】The *rain came down* in torrents. / A *rain* now *came on*, which continued for two or three hours, and made the road slippery and toilsome. ¶Unfortunately the *rain commenced* pouring violently down. 運悪く雨が猛烈に降り出した. ¶A cold *rain* was *drizzling down*. 冷たい雨がびしょびしょ降っていた. ¶A soft *rain fell* like tears. 静かな雨が涙のようにしとしとと降った. 【類】*Rain fell* in torrents(どしゃぶり). ¶Fortunately the *rain held off*. 幸い雨が降り出さなかった. ¶The *rain* has *left off*. 雨がやんだ. ¶The *rain* has *passed over* (=*off*). 雨が上った. ¶The *rain pelted* against the windows of my car. 雨が私の乗っていた自動車の窓を打った. ¶The *rain poured* [*down*] all day. 終日どしゃ降りだった. ¶The *rain* was *rushing down*. 大降りだった. ¶*Rain* has *set in*. 雨が降り出した. ¶The *rain down*, obscuring the country. しのつく雨であたりが見えなくなった. ¶The *rain shut* us *up* in the cabin. 雨で小屋にとじ込められた. ¶By this time the *rain* had *started*. このときにはもう雨が降り始めていた. 【類】*Rain started* to fall. ¶after the *rain stops* 雨がやんだ後. ¶The *rain* has *subsided*. 雨が小降りになった. ¶A heavy *rain visited* the city. その市に豪雨があった.

Q It was visited by *abundant rains*. そこは豪雨に襲われた. ¶in the *blinding rain* and driving wind 目もあけられないような雨と吹きまくる風の中に. ¶a *constant rain* 降り続く雨. ¶a *continuous rain* 降り続く雨. ¶a *copious rain* 大雨. ¶The crops are suffering from *deficient rain*. 雨不足で作物は弱っている. ¶a *drenching rain* びしょぬれになる雨. ¶a *driving rain* どしゃ降り. ¶a *drizzling rain* そぼ降る雨. ¶A *gentle rain* is falling on the grass. 静かな雨が草の上に降っている. ¶a *fine rain* 細雨. ¶a *hard slanting rain* 強い横降りの雨. ¶The river rises after *heavy rains*. その川は豪雨の後水かさが増す. ¶an *intermittent rain* 断続する雨. ¶When the sun shines through a *light rain*, it makes a rainbow. 陽光がきりあめを通るとにじが現われる. ¶a country of *little rain* 雨の少い国. 【類】*Little rain* falls in a desert. ¶in the *pelting rain* しのつく雨に. ¶a *pluvial rain* 大雨. ¶in a *pouring rain* 雨の最中. ¶Meet held in case of *slight rain*. 小雨決行(運動会など). ¶in a *streaming rain* ざあざあ降る雨の中で. ¶a *torrential rain* 滝なす雨. ¶a *welcome rain* いいおしめり.

Q^2 *monsoon rains* モンスーン(南アジアの定期風)に伴う雨.

¶a *silver rain* 銀雨(花火の一種). ¶a soft *spring rain* 春雨. ¶A *summer rain* often forms a rainbow. 夏の雨ではよくにじが出る.

P The coat is proof *against rain* (=rainproof). そのコートは防水になっている(雨にあたっても大丈夫だ). ¶*amidst* the drizzling *rain* びしょびしょ降る雨の中を. ¶a well fed *by rain* 雨水が水源になっている井戸. ¶take shelter *from rain* 雨宿りをする. ¶a mountain view *in rain* 雨中の山景 ‖ Vapor falls *in rain* from the sky. 水蒸気は雨になって天から降る. ‖ I was caught *in* [the] *rain*. 私は雨に会った. ¶Take an umbrella with you *in case of rain*. 雨が降るといけないからかさを持っておいで. ¶*in spite of* drenching *rain* どしゃ降りにもかかわらず. ¶go out *into* the *rain* 雨中を出掛ける. ¶It looks *like rain*. = It's likely to rain. 雨らしい. ¶We have had a great deal *of rain* this spring. この春は大分降雨があった. ¶The athletic meet was postponed *on account of* the *rain*. 運動会は雨のために延期された. ¶get in *out of* the *rain* 雨をよけて室内に入る. ¶tramp in the mud and slush of the roadway *through* the pouring *rain* どしゃ降りの最中ぬかるみ道をぴしゃぴしゃ歩く. ¶wet *with rain* 雨にぬれて. ¶We have been *without rain* for a long time. 久しく雨がなかった.

rain, *v.* 雨が降る.

M It *rained all day*. 終日雨が降った. ¶It has *rained all the week*. 一週間降り通した. ¶It is *raining cats and dogs* (=*pitchforks*). 雨が車軸を流すように降っている. ¶It is *raining* very *fast*. 雨がしきりに降り注いでいる. ¶It is *raining hard*. 激しく降っている. ¶It began to *rain heavily*. 盛んに降り出した. ¶*rain thick* and *fast* ざあざあ降る. ¶*rain uninterruptedly* 雨がひっきりなしに降る.

M^2 Incendiary bombs *rained down*. 焼い爆弾が雨と降った. ¶Letters *rained* (=snowed) *in* from all quarters. 手紙が諸方から舞い込んだ.

P It *rained for* ... days. ...日間雨が降った. ¶*rain in* torrents 滝なす雨が降る ‖ It began to *rain in* earnest. 本降りになって来た. ‖ *rain in* showers ざあざあ雨が降る. ¶*rain* blows *on* ... げん骨を...に雨と降らせる. ¶Shells were *rained on* (=*upon*) us. 砲弾がわれわれの頭上に雨と降った. 【類】They *rained* gifts *upon* the poor children.

O I will be there unless it *rains* such that I cannot reach the station. 雨が降って停車場に行けないようなことがなければ私はそこへ行きます. ¶if it comes on to *rain* 雨降りになったら.

rainbow, *n.* にじ.

V A *rainbow rose* against the dark sky. 真暗な空ににじが現われた. ¶*see* the *rainbow* in a sky 空ににじが見える.

Q A *beautiful rainbow* was formed. 美しいにじが現われた. ¶a *lunar rainbow* 月光のにじ. ¶a *perfect rainbow* 完全なにじ.

rainfall, *n.* 降雨.

Q the *annual rainfall* in London ロンドンにおける年々の雨量. ¶a *big rainfall* 大雨. ¶a *copious* and *well-distributed rainfall* よく行き渡った大雨. ¶*excessive rainfall* 過多な降雨. ¶a *heavy rainfall* 激しい雨. ¶a *light rainfall* 少雨. ¶*Rainfall* is *plentiful*. 雨量が多い. ¶*scanty rain fall* 少量の降雨. ¶*torrential rainfall* 滝なす雨.

P Frogs croak *with* a *rainfall*. かえるは雨が降ると鳴き出す.

rainshoe, *n.* 雨ぐつ.

V *wear rainshoes* 雨ぐつをはく.

P^2 *rainshoes for* boys and girls 少年少女用の雨ぐつ.

rain-storm, *n.* 暴風雨.

Q in a *blinding rain-storm* 目をあいていられないような暴風雨に.

raise, *n.* 上げること; 増加.

V *demand* a *raise* from a company 会社に昇給を要求する. ¶*get* a *raise* in salary 昇給される. ¶I'm going to *give* you a *raise*. 増給してあげる. ¶We have *had* a small *raise* in salary. 月給が少しあがった.

Q a *steep raise* in taxes 税の急激な増加. ¶a *three-fold raise* in salary 俸給の三倍増加.

Q^2 5 per cent *pay raise* 五分の昇給. 【類】demand a ¥1,000 *pay raise*. ¶win a *wage raise* of around 28 to 30 per cent 約二十八パーセントないし三十パーセントの賃銀引上げを獲得する.

P cry for (demand) a *raise* (=rise) *in* pay 昇給してくれと叫ぶ(など). ☞ a *raise* in salary (wages) は米語用法. 英語では a *rise* in salary (wages) が普通.

raise, *v.* 揚げる; 出す; 募集する; 《米》育てる, 飼養する, 栽培する.

M This *raised* me *considerably* in his estimation. これで

彼の目から見て著しく私の貫録が上った.

M² *raise up* forces 兵を集める, 師を起す.

P The building *raises* its tower ***above*** the city. その建物の塔が市街の上にそつ立している. ¶*raise* one's voice ***against*** a measure 方策反対の声をあげる. ¶*raise* funds ***as*** the nucleus of a benevolent fund for distressed members of the teaching profession 教職にある困窮者のための慈善資金の基金を募集する. ¶*raise* the price ***by*** 20 per cent. 二割だけ代価を上げる ‖ *raise* money ***by*** subscription 寄付で金を募る ‖ the amounts of money that are *raised* ***by*** taxation 税金でとりあげた金額. ¶*raise* one's hand ***for*** an answer 答をしようと手をあげる ‖ *raise* the fund ***for*** ... …の基金を募る. ¶plants *raised* ***from*** seed (cuttings) 種子(苗)から育てた植物 ‖ The firm was twice *raised* ***from*** its ashes. その社は二回火災にかかったが復興した. ‖ *raise* a person ***from*** the dead 人を生返らせる ‖ This work *raised* the author ***from*** obscurity to fame. この著作で作者は名をなした. ‖ *raise* the price ***from*** ... yen ***to*** ... yen 代価を…円から…円に上げる ‖ It *raised* Prussia ***from*** poverty and misery ***to*** the rank of a great European Power. それでプロシアを貧窮状態から欧州の大国にまで格上げした. ¶*raise* one's voice ***in*** defense 声をあげて弁護する ‖ We *raised* him ***in*** our arms. われわれは彼を胴上げにした. ‖ He was *raised* ***in*** rank (pay). 彼は位(など)が上がった. 【類】This *raised* Japan ***in*** the esteem of the world. ‖ He was born, *raised* and educated ***in*** California. 彼はカリフォルニアで生れ, 育ち, 教育を受けた. ☞米語用法の raise は grow (栽培する), breed (飼養する), bring up (育てる)の意がある. 例 My uncle *raises* chickens, hogs and cattle (牛). ¶This *raised* him ***into*** the seventh heaven of delight. これで彼は有頂天になった. ¶The baby was *raised* ***on*** cow's milk. この赤ん坊は牛乳で育った. ¶*raise* one ***out of*** sleep 人を眠りから覚ます. ¶Pagodas were originally *raised* ***over*** the relics of Buddha, bones of a saint, etc. 塔婆はもともと仏陀の遺物や聖者の遺骨などの上に建てられたものであった. ¶The legation was *raised* ***to*** the status of an embassy. その公使館は大使館に昇格した. ‖ *raise* dead persons ***to*** life 死者を生返らせる ‖ It has been *raised* ***to*** the level of a fine art. それは美術の一分科程度まで格が上った. ‖ this conjecture is *raised* almost ***to*** a certainty by ... この臆測は…のためにほとんど確実なものになった ‖ he was *raised* ***to*** the peerage (=ennobled) for his distinguished services in ... 彼は…における功績で貴族に列せられた. 【類】He was *raised* ***to*** the peerage with the title of Baron Avebury' / This *raised* him ***to*** the first rank among the writers of fiction. / This *raised* the University of Leyden ***to*** the summit of its fame. / He was *raised* ***to*** the honor of G.C.M.G. in 1897. / His wealth and not merit *raised* them ***to*** that dignity. ‖ a monument *raised* ***to*** the memory of ... …の記念塔 ‖ *raise* ***to*** the throne a son of ... …の一子を王座につける. ¶*raise* water ***with*** a pump ポンプで水を揚げる.

raiser, *n.* 《米》[家畜の]飼養者; 改ざん者(小切手など).

Q² a ***cattle*** *raiser* 牧牛者. ¶a professional ***check*** *raiser* 常習の(金高を多くする)小切手変造者. ¶a ***chicken*** *raiser* 養鶏業者. ¶a ***curtain*** *raiser* 序幕. ¶a ***hog*** *raiser* 養豚業者. ¶a ***poultry*** *raiser* 養鶏業者. 【類】a commercial ***poultry*** *raiser* / a woman ***poultry*** *raiser*.

raisin, *n.* 干ぶどう(レーズン).

Q ***chocolate-coated*** *raisins* チョコレーズン. ¶contain ***dried*** *raisins* 干ぶどう入りである.

P² *raisins* ***on*** cookies 菓子パンについている干ぶどう.

raising, *n.* あげること; 募集; 《米》飼養.

Q² ***cattle*** (***hog, poultry***) *raising* 牧牛(など)業. ¶***college fund*** *raising* 大学基金募集. ¶bring ***eyebrow*** *raising* from ... …から驚きの目で見られる. ¶***poultry*** *raising* 養鶏. ¶forced ***price*** *raising* 強制物価つり上げ. ¶***stock*** *raising* 畜産.

rake, *v.* くま手で集める, かき集める; 捜し回る.

M *rake* ***out*** the coal ashes 石炭がらを炉の火格子からかき出す ‖ Do not *rake* ***out*** grievances. 昔の不平を洗い立てるな.

M² *rake* ***off*** the leaves 葉をくま手でかき除ける. ¶*rake* ***up*** a little history 少し由来をほじくる ‖ *rake* ***up*** an old score (a forgotten quarrel) 昔のうらみ(忘れた争い)をかき立てる ‖ Gardeners *rake* ***up*** the flower-beds. 園丁が花床の土をくま手でかきならす.

P *rake* ***among*** (=***in***) old records 古い記録を調べる. ¶The speaker was *raked* ***by*** the eyes of the audience. 弁士は聴衆にじろじろ見られた. ¶He has *raked* all history ***for*** proofs. 彼は証拠を求めようと歴史をくまなく探った. ¶The newspaper man *rakes* ***into*** one's life. 新聞記者は人の(私)生活に立入って調べる. ¶He laboriously *raked* ***through*** his mind for something to say. 彼は何か言おうと思案していた.

rally, *n.* 盛返し; 《米俗》国民大会.

V It was a notable game, because in the ninth inning Waseda ***made*** a wonderful *rally*, and almost overcame Chicago's lead. それは注目に値する勝負であった, というのは第九回戦で早稲田がすばらしく盛返してシカゴのリードを逆転しかけたからであった.

Q ***Enthusiastic*** *rallies* were held at which he was appointed as their champion. 熱心な大会が催されその際彼はその首領として選任された. ¶an ***evangelistic*** *rally* 福音伝道大会. ¶a ***political*** *rally* 政治大会.

Q² a ***boy scout*** *rally* ボーイスカウト大会(政党などの). ¶hold a ***mass*** *rally* 民衆大会を開催する. 【類】a ***mass*** *rally* of students 学生大集会. ¶an International Christian *Youth Rally* 国際キリスト教青年大会.

P² a *rally* ***from*** sickness (depression) 病気(など)からの回復. ¶a *rally* ***in*** price 価格のもち直し.

rally, *v.* 盛り返す, 再び盛んになる.

M Rain *rallied* almost ***ceaselessly***. 雨がほとんど絶間なく降りしきっていた. ¶The market will ***soon*** *rally*. 相場はじきもち直すだろう. 【類】The sick child will ***soon*** *rally*, I hope.

P *rally* ***on*** (=***about***) one's failure その失敗を盛り返す. ¶*rally* ***to*** the support of ... …の援助にかけつける.

ram, *n.* 突き棒, かねつち; 〖機〗水圧機のピストン.

Q a ***hanging*** *ram* of timber しゅもく ☞西洋のは metal hammr. ¶a ***hydraulic*** *ram* 水撃ポンプ.

Q² a ***single*** (***double***)-***action*** *ram* 単(複)作用つち.

ram, *v.* 打ちこむ.

M² *ram* ***down*** a stake くいを打ち込む.

P *ram* clothes ***into*** a trunk 衣類をトランクに詰め込む.

ramble, *n.* 散歩, ぶらぶら歩き.

V Pleasant *rambles* may be ***taken*** in the vicinity. その付近で愉快な散歩ができる.

Q a ***literary*** *ramble* 文学書の漫読. ¶a ***romantic moonlight*** *ramble* ロマンチックな月夜の散歩.

Q² an ***after-supper*** *ramble* 夕食後の散歩. ¶a ***lunch-time*** *ramble* 昼休みの散歩.

P This is the best season ***for*** a *ramble* in the suburbs. 今は郊外をぶらつくに一番よい季節だ. ¶I came across this rare book ***on*** my *rambles* among second-hand bookstores. 私が古本屋を回っている時この珍本が目についた. ¶He spent much of his time in unaccompanied *rambles* ***through*** the streets. 彼は独りで町をぶらぶらして多くの時をすごした.

ramble, *v.* ぶらぶら歩く, 散歩する.

P *ramble* ***about*** the streets 街をぶらつく. ¶He is fond of *rambling* ***among*** the trees. 彼は樹間の散歩が好きだ. ¶*ramble* ***in*** the garden 庭の中をぶらつく ‖ He *rambles* ***in*** his talk. 彼はまとまりのつかない話をする. ¶Vines *rambled* ***over*** the wall. つたが壁にはっていた. ¶*ramble* ***round*** Shanghai 上海をぶらぶらする. ¶*ramble* ***through*** Japan without a guide 案内者なしに日本を遍歴する. 【類】*ramble* here and there ***through*** the woods.

ramification, *n.* 派出, 分岐.

Q in its ***diverse*** *ramifications* それがさまざまに分岐して ‖ the ***diverse*** and ***multitudinous*** *ramifications* of the English language 英語の種々雑多な相. ¶He learned English thoroughly in all its ***manifold*** *ramifications*. 彼は英語のあらゆる分野を徹底的に修得した. ¶It has ***many*** *ramifications* それは多方面に分岐している. ¶this subjects and its ***numerous*** *ramifications* この問題とそれから派生した種々の細かい問題.

P² a *ramification* ***of*** the Whig party 英国自由党内の分派. ¶The *ramifications* ***of*** the plot are said to have extended to other cities. その陰謀の手が他の都市にも伸びたということである.

ramify, *v.* 分派する, 分裂する, 分岐する.

P *ramify* ***from*** ... …から分裂する. ¶*ramify* ***into*** a labyrinth 分かれて迷宮に入る. ¶Railways have *ramified* ***over*** the country. 鉄道が国中に行渡った.

rampage, *n.* 暴行.

P He was *on* the (=a) *rampage.* 彼は暴れ回っていた.

rampart, *n.* 城壁.

Q a *huge rampart* of rock 岩の巨大な絶壁.

ranch, *n.* 《米》牧場.

V *own* a *ranch* 牧場(米国西部の)を所有する

Q² a *cattle ranch* 牛の牧場.

P live *on* the *ranch* 牧畜農場に住む.

rancher, *n.* 牧場経営者.

Q² a *cattle rancher* 牛の牧場経営者. ¶a *turkey rancher* 七面鳥飼育業者.

rancor, *n.* うらみ, 遺恨.

V he *had* no *rancor* at heart against ... 彼は...に対して胸中何ら恨みはなかった. ¶*nurse rancor* against ... ...に対して恨みをいだく. 「恨みをいだいている.

Q have *deep-rooted rancour* against ... ...に対して根強い

P a *rancor against* a person (government) 人(など)に対するうっ憤. ¶*rancor towards* ... ...に対する恨み.

random, *n.* 手当り次第, むやみ.

P He fired a shot *at random.* 彼はでたらめに発砲した. ‖ open a book *at random* 手当り次第に本を開く.【類】reading *at random*=random reading / guess *at randon.*

range, *n.* 列, 並び; 山脈; 範囲, 区域; [銃・砲の]射程; 射的場.

V It *answers* a wide *range* of requirements. それは種々の要求を満たす. ¶The vibrations *attained* a *range* of ... millimeters [地震の]震幅は...ミリメートルに達した. ¶*cover* a wide *range* 広範囲にわたる. ¶*increase* the *range* 戦闘距離を増大する. ¶The book *covers* a wide *range* of subjects (=topics). その本に取扱ってある題目は広範囲にわたる. ¶*enlarge* the *range* of our knowledge われわれの知識の範囲を拡大する. ¶Their shapes *exhibit* a wide *range* of variation. その形態は種々様々である. ¶*extend* one's *range* of languages, both dead and living 死語及び現代語ともにその知識を拡大する.【類】*extend* the *range* of one's vocabulary. ¶*find* the *range* 着弾距離を測定する. ¶His vocabulary *showed* a fairly wide *range.* 彼の語いはかなり広い.

Q the *Appalachian range* アパラチア山系. ¶may be viewed at *close range* 手近で観覧できる. ¶within *easy range* of one's eye 容易に肉眼で見られる範囲に. ¶Fowls have *free range* on the farm. 鶏は農園で自由行動ができる(放し飼になっている). ¶The *geographical range* of North America is such that almost any climate can be found there throughout the year by selection of locality. 北アメリカの地理的範囲が非常に広いので場所を選びさえすれば一年中どんな気候でもある. ¶The routes allow of a *large range* of choice. 路筋は種々あって自由に選択ができる. ¶at a very *long range* はなはだ遠い距離で ‖ What at *long range* is called ... proved on further knowledge to be ... 一口に...というがよく考えて見ると...ということになる. ¶a *narrow* (*wide*) *range* of choice せまい(広い)選択範囲. ¶a *new range* of price 新物価範囲. ¶It is regarded as within the *normal range* of variation. それは(変態的でない)普通の変化と見なされている. ¶a *select range* of hosiery, suspenders, links, studs, etc. 特選メリヤス・ズボンつり・夫婦ボタン・カフスボタンなど色々. ¶at a *short range* 近距離で. ¶a *vertical range* たてレンジ(こんろ). ¶in the *whole range* of human history 人類史の全般にわたって.【類】in the *whole range* of educational literature. ¶the *wide range* of information brought together within its covers その本の中に集めた広範囲の知識(百科全書など). ‖ the *wide range* of his interests.

Q² a *firing range* 射的場. ¶a *kitchen range* ガスレンジ. ¶at *point-blank range* 標点射程で. ¶within a *rifle range* 小銃射程内に.

P see *at* closer *range* もっと接近して見る ‖ Hitler *at* close *range* 近くで見たヒトラー ‖ shoot *at* a *range* of ... ...の距離で発射する. ¶aim *beyond* the *range* of one's ability 自分の力量以上のことをねらう.【類】be *beyond* the *range* of my conjecture. ¶*in* the whole *range* of English writings 英語の文献全般にわたって. ¶Her voice is one *of* wide *range* with the real soprano timbre. 本当のソプラノが出て彼女の声には幅がある. ¶*out of* the *range* of fire 射程外の.【類】The enemy is *out of range.* ¶*outside* the *range* of one's possibility そのなしうる範囲外に.【類】The word is *outside* the *range* of the middle school boy's vocabulary. ¶The ship came *within range* of guns. その船は砲火の届く範囲内に来た.【類】*within* the *range* of cannon-shot from the shore / *within* the *range* of the enemy's fire / It has come *within* the *range* of practical politics.

P² the *range of* the operation of his energies 彼の勢力の及ぶ範囲 ‖ The *range of* his interests may be seen from the subjects on which he has written books. 彼の趣味が広範囲にわたることは彼の書いた書物の主題からうかがわれる. ¶the *range of* ages 年齢の範囲 ‖ this *range of* goods この口の品.【類】the *range of* temperature between the hottest and coldest periods of the year / The *range of* his reading must be enormous. / the *range of* prices for a commodity ‖ This gun has a *range of* 4 miles. この砲の射程は四マイルだ. ‖ A *range of* hills rose on their left. 続いた丘がその左手でそびえていた.

range, *v.* 一列に並ぶ, 序列する; さまよう.

M Fowls *range free* on the farms. 鶏は放し飼にしてある. ¶mountains *ranging northward* and *southward* 南北に延びる山々. 「いるがけ.

M² the cliffs *ranging along* the coast 海岸線に切り立って

P the temperature *ranges between* ... and ... 温度は...と...の間を往来する. ¶*range* books *by* size 本を大きさの順に列べる. ¶The price *ranges from* ... cent up *to* several dollars. 値段は...セントから五六ドルにまで及んでいる.【類】Prices *range from* $16.00 *to* $125.00. / Ages *range from* 7 *to* 14. / the issues discussed *range from* ... *to* ... / the prices realized (決定価格) *range from* ... *to* ... ‖ *range from* very poor *to* very good きわめて貧弱なものからきわめて高級のものまで色々ある ‖ *range* the woods *in* search of game 獲物を求めて森を歩き回る. ¶*range* cards *in* alphabetical order カードをアルファベット順にする. ¶a considerable number of coins *ranging in* date *from* A.D. 139 *to* A.D. 337 紀元一三九年から三三七年にわたる間の非常に多数の貨幣. ¶Our thought *ranges over* past, present, and future. われわれの考えは過去・現在・未来の三世にわたる. ‖ The network of railroads *ranges over* the whole country 鉄道網は全国に及んでいる. ¶*range with* a person in ... ...では...と肩を並べる.

ranger, *n.* 監視人; 《米》遊撃兵.

Q² a *forest* (*park*) *ranger* 森林(公園)看守. ¶*U. S. Army Rangers* 米陸軍遊撃兵. ☞英軍の Commandos に当る.

rank, *n.* 列, 伍(ご)列; 位, 地位, 階級; 等級.

V San Francisco must be *accorded* high *rank* as a manufacturing city. サンフランシスコには製造工業都市として高い位置を与えねばならない. ¶*attain* a *rank* among the Great Powers 強国の間に列する. ¶*break* their *ranks* 列を乱す. ¶*close* (*up*) the *ranks* 列を詰める. ¶*confer* a posthumous *rank* 死後に位階を授ける. ¶*gain* the first *rank* 最高級に達する. ¶I am inclined to *give* premier *rank* to ... 私は...に第一の地位を与えたい気がする. ¶people *having rank* and wealth 身分と富を持っている人々.【類】*have* the *ranks* of petty officialdom (小役人) in Government colonial service. ¶*hold* first *rank* 第一位を占める.【類】*hold* high *rank* in the diplomatic services / men who *hold* high *rank* in the world of art / He *holds* the highest *rank* in the literature of the country. ¶*join* the *ranks* of non-smokers 禁煙家の仲間入をする. ¶*leave* the *ranks* of Mr. Gladstone's adherents グラッドストーン氏の味方をするのをやめる. ¶It is a fact pregnant with meaning that the nations which possess the most extensive libraries *maintain* the foremost *rank* in civilization. 最大の図書館を有する国民は最も文化が進んでいるということは意義の深い事実である. ¶The shots of the enemy *mowed down* our *ranks* with frightful rapidity. 敵の砲弾はあっという間にわが隊を倒した. ¶*occupy* the front *rank* 前列を占める. ¶*reach* the front *rank* among the world's film manufactures 世界の映画製作者間に優秀な地歩を占めるにいたる. ¶Scotland and Ireland largely *recruit* the *ranks* of the police force. スコットランドとアイルランドから主として警察官が出る. ¶Business depression *swells* the *ranks* of the unemployed. 不景気で失業者の数が多くなる. ¶*take* the first *rank* 第一位を占める.【類】*take* first *rank* as the cause of death (死因) ‖ *take rank* immediately after ...=rank next below ... ...の直後に位する(官位など) ‖ he can never *take rank* with ... 彼は...と肩を並べることはとうていできない.【類】*take rank* as the standard English edition / It *takes* high *rank* among modern railway stations. / Some say that Berlin can never *take rank* among those capitals of the world which we cannot afford not to see. / *take* high *rank* as writers / It *takes rank* as one of the best treatises on the subject yet published. / *take rank* as the third (第三位に) in ... / The aniline and soda works at Baden (ドイツの一連邦) *take rank* as the largest chemical factory in the world. / He *takes* high *rank* in his profession. ¶death has *thinned* the *ranks* of ... 死んで行くので...の人員が少なくなった. ¶They have *won* high *rank* in their specialities. 彼らはそれぞれの専門において高い地位を得た.

Q take *advanced rank* in ... ...に高位を占める. ¶people of *all ranks* and classes すべての階級地位の人々. ¶"The Playground of Europe" by Leslie Stephen won *classical rank* in Alpine literature. レスリー・スティーブン氏の「ヨーロッパの遊覧地」はアルプス文学において古典的地位を獲得した. ¶It is by matter and not by form that the poet takes his *final rank*.—J.A. Symonds. 詩人が最後の地歩を占めるのは形式によるのではなく本質によるのである. ¶stand in the *first* (=*foremost*) *rank* 第一位に立つ ‖ a university (nation) of *first rank* 一流の大学(など). ¶be in the *foremost rank* 一流である. 【類】a statesman of *foremost rank*. ¶The work has won for its author a place in the *front rank* of American novelists. その著作は作者に米国小説家中第一位を獲得せしめた. 【類】take *front rank* in ... / place him in the *front rank* of ... ¶English literature holds a very *high rank* among the literatures of the West. / *higher ranks* of society. ¶take a *leading rank* among ... ...の間に主要な地位を占める. ¶The Marquis is sociable and democratic in his association with individuals of *lesser rank*. 同侯爵は目下のものとの交際に当って平民的で四角張らない. ¶hold a very *low rank* compared with ... ...に比べてはなはだ低い地位を占めている ‖ belong to the *lower ranks* 下層階級に属する. ¶a man of *middle rank* 中流階級の人. ¶Love is of *no rank* and no degree. 恋に上下の隔てなし. ¶the *scholastic rank* of a student 学生の成績順.

Q² have *Cabinet rank* 閣僚である ‖ a Secretary with *Cabinet rank* 閣僚待遇の長官. ¶one with the *civil service rank* of *Chokunin* 勅任官の人 ¶names of cities arranged in order of *population rank* 人口の多少で排列した都市名. ¶institutions of *university rank* 大学級の学校.

P *above* (*below*) one's *rank* その身分以上(下)の ‖ be *above* (*below*) him in *rank* 彼より位が上(下)である. ¶The names are grouped, *according to* their *rank*. 姓名は彼らの身分に応じて分類してある. ¶a justice *by rank* and office 官職から言って一個の裁判官. ¶rise *from* a lowly *rank* of life 低い身分から身を起す. ¶He has risen *from* the *ranks*. 彼は下層階級から身を起した. ¶be higher (lower) *in rank* 位が一層高い(低い) ‖ It holds an honored place *in* the *ranks* of literature. それは文学上名誉ある地位を占めている. ¶*in* [*point of*] *rank* 階級の点で. ¶entomologists *of* the *rank* of Kirby and Spence カービー, スペンス級のこん虫学者 ‖ a neighbor's son *of* her own *rank* 彼女と社会的地位が同等の隣人の息子. ¶a man *of* [high] *rank* 地位の高い人. ¶he was raised *to* the *rank* of ... 彼は...の地位にまで上った. ¶No one *under Chokunin rank* was invited. 勅任官以下の官吏は招待されなかった. ¶a *rank between* ... and ... ...と...の間の階級. ¶rise to the *rank of* captain and admiral 艦長や提督の地位にまで昇進する.

rank, *v.* 列を占める, 位する, 列する; 《米》より上に位する.

M entitle him to *rank along* with ... 彼を...の間に列するようにさせる. ¶he *easily ranks* with ... 彼は優に...と肩を並べる. ¶*rank high* among ... ...の間に高い地位を占める. 【類】*rank high* in general scholarship / Manliness is a characteristic which *ranks* very *high* in our estimation. ¶*rank indisputably* with the masterpieces of contemporary fiction 疑いもなく現代小説中の傑作と肩を並べる. ¶*rank low* in the social scale 社会の低い地位にある. ¶*rank second* in the graduating class 卒業生中第二位にある ‖ *rank second* to none 何人にも譲らない. 【類】*rank second* only to ...

P *rank* Dante *above* Shakespeare ダンテをシェクスピアの上におく. ¶be *ranked according to* their merit 生徒が成績順に並んでいる. ¶He *ranks among* the best platform and Parliamentary speakers in the country. 彼は国内において最もすぐれた演壇及び議会の弁士中に位する. ‖ It rightly *ranks among* the greatest achievements in the potter's art. それは当然陶芸界における最大傑作であると言える. ‖ I am fortunate enough to *rank among* his acquaintance. 私は幸いあの人と知り合です. 【類】Captain Brinkley left his mark on his contemporaries and is entitled to *rank among* the greatest literary luminaries of the Far Eastern world.—The Japan Chronicle. / Low Savile *ranks among* the best shots (名射手) in England. / The colossal Buddha at Lung Mén (竜門) must be *ranked among* the world's masterpieces in stone. ¶*rank as* the oldest *in* ... ...では最古のものに属する. ‖ The chrysanthemum *ranks as* the national flower of Japan. 菊は日本の国華である. ‖ The book *ranks as* a classic in its own subject. その本はその主題において古典の地位を占めている. 【類】*rank as* the foremost of ... / Today Buffalo City *ranks as* the sixth commercial city of the world. / He *ranks as* standard authority (権威者) on the subject. / he deservedly *ranks as* one of the highest authorities on ... / *rank as* the second largest ..., coming after ... / The book undoubtedly *ranks as* one of the most valuable contributions to general geography which has appeared for many years. / The Art Institute now *ranks as* an art museum among the first three or four in the country. ¶it is worthy to *rank* little *below* ... それは...の塁を摩している. ¶*rank beside* ... ...と肩を並べる. ¶Glasgow *ranks in* size *as* the second city in Scotland. グラスゴーは大きさの点ではスコットランド第二の都会である. ¶Hamburg, the second city of the German Empire, *ranks in* commercial importance *before* any other town on the Continent of Europe. ドイツ第二の都会たるハンブルグは商業上ヨーロッパ大陸中他のどの都市にも譲らない. ¶*rank with* the Great Powers of the world 世界最大強国中に列する ‖ he *ranks*, in my estimation, *with* ... 彼は私の考えでは...と肩を比べる. 【類】The name of Togo will *rank in* history *with* that of Nelson. / He deserves (=is worthy) to *rank with* the foremost writers and thinkers of the time. / This name will *rank with* the foremost (=greatest).

O The Secretary of State *ranks* all other members of the Cabinet. 《米》国務長官は他の長官の上位にある.

rank, *a.* はびこった.

P an English garden *rank with* rose bushes ばらのはびこっている英国の庭園.

O weeds growing *rank*=rank growth of weeds 雑草のはびこり.

rank and file, 平党員, 陣がさ, 大衆.

P rise *from among rank and file* 卑賤(ㄚ)から身を起す. ¶listen to the voice *of rank and file* 大衆の声に耳を傾ける.

Q² the *Communist rank and file* 共産党の平党員たち.

ransack, *v.* くまなく捜す, 探索する.

M *thoroughly ransack* くまなく捜す.

P *ransack* a bureau drawer *for* jewelry 宝石を求めてたんすの引き出しをかき回す. 【類】*ransach* a house *for* ...

ransom, *v.* あがなう, 身受けする.

P *ransom* a person *at* a heavy price 大金を出して人をあがなう.

rap, *n.* たたき; たたく音.

V *give* several *raps* (=knocks) with the knocker ノッカー(ドアたたき)で数回たたく.

P emphasize by a *rap with* one's fan 扇子でたたいて強調する.

rap, *v.* たたく, 打つ.

M *rap out* a tune on the piano ピアノをたたくようにひく ‖ *rap out* one's opinion 意見をはき出す ‖ *rap out* an answer どなるように返事をする.

P *rap on* (=*at*) the door instead of ringing the bell ベルを鳴らさずに戸をたたく ‖ *rap on* (=*upon*) the desk for silence (order) 机をこつこつたたいて静粛(など)にさせる.

rapacity, *n.* どん欲, どん食.

Q *insatiable rapacity* あくことなきどん欲.

rape, *n.* 強かん.

V *commit* a *rape* on (=ravish) a woman 女に暴行する.

rape, *v.* [女に]暴行する.

P *rape* a girl *by* turns 輪かんする.

rapid, *n.* [通例 *pl.*] 急流, 奔流.

V *descend* the *rapids* of the river Katsura 桂川の急流を

下る. ¶The boatmen ***negotiate rapids*** in a boat with marvelous dexterity. 船頭が小舟を驚嘆するほど巧みにあやつって急流を下る. ¶***shoot*** the ***rapids*** 矢を射るように急流を下る.

P descend ***along*** the *rapids* 急流に沿うて下る. ¶shoot (=run) ***down rapids*** 急流を下る ‖ a trip ***down*** the Hozu *rapids* 保津川下り.

P² a *rapid* ***in*** a river 川の早瀬.

rapidity, *n.* じん速, 早さ, 速度.

Q the ***amazing rapidity*** of American progress 米国の驚くほどじん速な進歩. ¶with ***astonishing rapidity*** 驚くほどじん速に. ¶with a ***bewildering rapidity*** 目まぐるしいほどじん速に. ¶with such ***fearful rapidity*** そんなにも恐ろしく急速に. ¶follow one after another with ***startling rapidity*** 矢つぎ早に続く. ¶work with ***vertiginous rapidity*** 目が回るほど速かに働く.

Q² be handled with the ***lightning rapidity*** of a conjuring trick 奇術の電光石火の速さで取扱われる.

P ***with*** the *rapidity* of lightning 電光石火の速さで. 【類】 be carried away ***with*** the greatest *rapidity*.

rapprochement, *n. F.* 近づき, 和解, 和ぼく.

P a *rapprochement* ***between*** ... …間の和解. ¶a *rapprochement* ***with*** a country ある国との和ぼく.

rapt, *a.* 夢中の, 有頂天の, 熱心な.

P *rapt* ***in*** admiration ほとほと感嘆して. ¶*rapt* ***with*** joy うれしさに夢中になって.

rapture, *n.* 有頂天, うっとり, 大喜び.

P² listen to the sweet music, in a ***perfect rapture*** 全くうっとりとして美しい音楽に耳を傾ける. ¶in ***silent rapture*** うつとりとして声もなく.

P lost ***in*** the *rapture* of "Love's Young Dream" 「恋の若き夢」に陶酔して ‖ listen ***in*** *raptures* うっとりとして耳を傾ける. ¶fall ***into*** *raptures* 有頂天になる.

P² in *rapture* ***over*** something 何かに有頂天になって.

rare, *a.* まれな.

M paper ***commercially*** very *rare* 売物にはごく珍らしい「紙.

O It is *rare* to see a man over 100 years old=a man over 100 years old is a rarity. 百歳以上の人はまれだ.

rarefy, *v.* 希薄になる.

M The air was ***greatly rarefied*** on the summit of the mountain. 山頂では空気が非常に希薄だった.

rarity, *n.* 希有, 珍奇; 珍物.

Q an ***expensive rarity*** 高価な珍品. ¶one of the ***greatest rarities*** 最もまれな物の一つ.

P ***of*** great *rarity* 非常に珍しい.

P² a *rarity* ***in*** movieland 映画界の珍物.

O This year's snow is a *rarity*. 今年の雪は珍らしい.

rascal, *n.* 悪漢, 無頼漢; 《口語》やつ.

V I will ***teach*** the *rascal* to play a runaway knock on this door. このドアーをたたいて逃げて行くやつはどうするか見ていろ.

Q a rather ***eminent rascal*** かなり有名な悪漢. ¶What an ***impudent rascal!*** なんという無礼なやつだろう! ¶You ***little rascal***. [子供に]この茶目公! ¶a ***thorough rascal*** 全くの悪漢. ¶You ***young rascal***. おい若いの.

rascality, *n.* 悪事.

Q ***infamous rascality***. 破廉恥な悪事.

rash, *a.* 軽率な, 無鉄砲な.

O it would be *rash* to assert that ... …というならそれは軽率であろう. 【類】 it would be *rash* to say just yet whether ... ‖ Don't make *rash* promises. でたら目な約束はするな. 【類】 a *rash* act.

rashness, *n.* 軽率.

V ***regret*** the *rashness* of one's speech 己が言葉の軽率を後悔する.

Q ***honest rashness*** and manly straightforwardness 正直な向う見ずと男らしい単刀直入.

rat, *n.* ねずみ; 卑劣漢.

V ***catch*** a *rat* by the trap わなでねずみを捕える. ¶***exterminate*** *rats* by poison 毒でねずみを全滅させる. ¶He ***smelled*** a rat. 彼はうさん臭いと思った. ¶***worry*** a *rat* [ねこなどが]ねずみを悩ます.

V² A *rat* ***squeaks***. ねずみがちゅうと鳴く.

Q You ***dirty old rat!*** このどぶねずみめ(ののしり). ¶a ***plague-infested rat*** 保菌ねずみ.

Q² a ***sewer rat*** どぶねずみ.

P a trap ***for*** *rats* ねずみ取りのわな.

rate, *n.* (**1**) 割合, 率.

V ***decrease*** death *rate* 死亡率を減じる. ¶***intensify*** the *rate* of progress 進歩をはか取らせる. ¶***lower*** the birth *rate* 出産率を下げる. ¶***show*** a lower birth *rate* より低い出産率を示す.

Q at the ***average rate*** of ... …の平均率で. ¶***competitive rate*** 競争率. ¶the ***current rate*** of absenteeism 欠席者の現在率. ¶a ***current rate*** of exchange 現在の為替相場. ¶at ***cut rates*** 割引として. ¶pay an ***exorbitant rate*** of interest 法外な利息を払う. ¶***fair rates*** 公正な率(相場). ¶at a ***fixed rate*** of ... …の一定率で. ¶A good business has been done at ***full rates***. 割引なしでいい商売ができた. ¶a ***high rate*** of mortality in ... …の高い死亡率 ‖ Other buyers are offering ***higher rates***. 外の買手がもっと高い値を申込んでいる. ‖ the ***highest rate*** the sellers will accept 売手が承諾する最高率. ¶What is the ***lowest rate*** the buyers can give? 買手が承知する最低率は何ほどですか. ¶at the ***present rate*** of progress 今の程度の進歩で ‖ the ***present rates*** of freight 運賃の現行率. ¶at the ***prodigious rate*** 驚くべき割合で. ¶***prohibitory rates*** [輸入]禁止的高税率. ¶The city has grown at a very ***rapid rate***. その市は非常な速度で発展した. ¶at a ***reduced rate*** 割引して. ¶at a ***round rate*** まとまった率で(はしたのでない率で). ¶The ***ruling rates*** of wages are very low. 現行賃金率ははなはだ低い. ¶a ***slow rate*** of progress 遅々たる進歩. ¶go at a ***terrific rate*** 恐ろしい速度で進む. ¶I could feel my heart going at a ***tremendous rate***. 心臓がおそろしい早さで打つのが感じられた. ¶reach the ***top rates*** 最高率に達する. ¶at the ***uniform rate*** of ... …均一で ‖ at a ***uniform rate*** of speed 平均速度で. ¶lend money at the ***usurious rate*** of 60% per annum 年六割という高利で金を貸す.

Q² The ***accident rate*** is continually climbing. 事故がますます多くなりつつある. ¶the ***bank rate*** 銀行担保の貸利率; [手形など] 銀行割引率. ¶Their ***birth rate*** is low. 彼らの出産率は低い. ¶reopen an idle factory at ***capacity rate*** 全操業で休業工場を再開する. ¶at the ***conversion rate*** of ¥360 to the dollar 一ドル三百六十円の換算率で ‖ the military ***conversion rate*** 軍隊の換算率(軍票). ¶Its ***crime rate*** is low. その国の犯罪率は低い. 【類】 countries which have low ***crime rates***. ¶decrease ***death rate*** 死亡率を減じる. 【類】 the high ***death rates*** of children. ¶a ***discount rate*** 割引率. ¶the authorized ***dollar-yen conversion rate*** 公認ドル円換算率. ¶***exchange rates*** 為替相場. ¶***fertility rates*** 出産率. ¶lower the ***illiteracy rate*** 未就学者の率を低くする. ¶the ***import rate*** of duty 輸入税率. ¶***insurance rates*** 保険率. ¶***labor turn over rate*** 労働移動率. ¶advance ***loan interest rate*** 貸付金利子の率を増す. ¶It was paid for at the ***market rate***. それは市場相場で支払われた. ‖ at current ***market rates*** 現行の市場率で. ¶***mortality rates*** 死亡率. ¶improved ***overtime rates*** 超勤手当改善率. ¶Special ***pay rates*** 特別給与率. ¶***piece rate*** 請負率. ¶be paid on the ***piece-work rate*** (=basis) 請負率で支払われる. 【類】 pay at ***piece-work rates***. ¶the ***prewar rate*** 戦前の率. ¶an increase in the ***production rate*** 生産率の増加. ¶at ***quantity rates*** 大量(割引)率で. ¶a ***salary rate*** (including overseas differential) 俸給率(海外の特別手当も含めた). ¶The best contributions will be published and paid for at ***space rates***. 最も優秀な寄稿文はこれを出版した(雑誌などの)行数によって原稿料を支払う. 【類】 work at ***space rates*** on a metropolitan daily. ¶***transfer rates*** 転勤率. ¶the ***wage rate*** 賃金率 ‖ minimum ***wage rates*** 最低賃金制 ‖ occupational ***wage rate*** 職業別賃金率. ¶the decline in the ***yen rate*** 円為替レートの下落. ¶the ***yen exchange rate*** 円為替率.

P be ***above*** (***below***) the current *rate* 現行率以上(以下). ¶chatter ***at*** the (=a) *rate* of three hundred words a minute 一分間三百語の割でしゃべる ‖ if things go on ***at*** this *rate* この調子で行けば. 【類】 ***at*** the same *rate* ‖ cannot insure ***at*** your *rate* あなたの率では保険が付けられない ‖ ***at*** the *rate* of 1 lb. yeast per 100 lbs. flour 百ポンドの麦粉に一ポンドのイーストの割合で. 【類】 ***at*** the *rate* of sixteen miles an hour / in the event of non-payment interest is to accrue ***at*** the *rate* of ... ‖ I will come ***at*** any *rate*. とも角やって来ます. 【類】 lend money ***at*** the rate of four per cent. ¶This is made possible ***by*** the low *rate* of exchange. これは為替相場が安いのでできる. ¶Fluctuations

in rates of exchange effect the cost. 為替相場の動揺は値段に影響する。
P² the exchange *rate between* London and New York ロンドンとニューヨーク間の為替相場. ¶the death *rate from* tuberculosis 結核死亡率. ¶the *rate of* absenteeism 欠勤率 ‖ the *rate of* discount 割引率 ‖ the *rate of* usance 手形仕払の慣習期限の利率.
(2) 料金; 《英》地方税.
V *advance* (*lower*) the *rate* 料金を増す(下げる) ‖ This caused sellers to *advance rates* このため売手が代価を上げなければならなくなった.【類】Hotel *rates* will not be *advanced*. ¶*charge* the same *rate* 同じ割合で徴集する. ¶*grant* special *rates* lower than usual fares 普通の料金よりも安くする. ¶*levy* a *rate* 地方税を課する. ¶The line of steamers *makes* a *rate* of $1.50 for the round trip. その汽船会社は往復だと料金を一ドル五十セントにする. ¶*offer* cut *rates* 料金の割引をする. ¶I have to *pay* high *rates* to the boarding-house. 私は高い料金を下宿屋に払わねばならない. ¶*raise* the *rate* その料金を上げる. ¶*reduce* the telephone *rate* to five cents a call 電話料金を一通話五セントに引き下げる. ¶Freight will *resume* its normal *rates*. 運賃が普通料金に復するだろう.
Q The hotel makes *half rates* for children under eight years of age. そのホテルは八歳以下の子供は半額にする. ¶at *low rates* 低率の料金で.【類】Excellent food is to be obtained at very *low rates*. / Baggage can be insured at *low rates*. / offered at surprisingly *low rates*. ¶With a new low *minimum rate* of $1,750 the Franconia World Cruise becomes more attractive than ever before. 今度最低額千七百五十ドルでフランコニア世界一周旅行は以前よりも人気を呼ぶようになる. ¶It will be charged at the *new rates*. それは新税率で取られる. ¶rent at a *nominal rate* ほんの名目だけの料金で貸す. ¶*postal rates* on letters 手紙に対する郵税. ¶Reliable cars can be hired at *reasonable rates*. 信用のできる車が相当の料金で乗れる.【類】Board and room can be obtained at *reasonable rates*. ¶*reduced rates* for the holidays 休日の割引料金(汽車賃など). ¶at *regular rates* 一定の料金で. ¶at *revised rates* 改正料金で. ¶give *special rates* to … members …会員は特別料金にする. ¶at *specified rates* 特定料金で.
Q² *advertising* (=ad) *rates* 広告料. ¶*airmail rates* 航空郵便料金. ¶*bargain rates* 特価値段. ¶This will go at *book rate*. これは書籍(の料金)として送れる. ¶special *classroom rate* of magazines and newspapers 教材用新聞雑誌の特別料金. ¶*freight rates*=freightage 貨物運賃. ¶In Japan the *gas rate* is not very low. 日本ではガス料金はあまり安くはない. ¶*goods rates* 《英》貨物運賃.【類】*good rates* on railways. ¶reduce *passage rates* slightly 少し船賃を下げる. ¶*railway rates* 鉄道運賃. ¶They are remunerated at "*sweating*" *rates*. 彼らは搾取的な賃金で働かされている. ¶the *telephone rate* 電話料金. ¶The *ticket rates* include a berth, but not the meals. 切符料金はベッド料を含むが食事は含まない.
P² *rates at* inns 宿泊料.【類】The *rate at* the hotel is from $4.00 per day up. ¶a 15-yen *rate for* all rides on street-cars 市内電車はすべて十五円均一 ‖ *Rates for* this hostelry are moderate. この旅館の料金は手ごろだ. ‖ the *rate* of freight 運賃(率). ¶exchange *rates on* France 対仏為替換算率. ¶special *rates to* parties, tours, and conventions [ホテルなど] 団体・観光旅行・集会に対する特別料金.

rate, *v.* 評価する, 見積る, 見なす; ののしる; 《米》採点する.
M *rate* one's merits *high* (*low*) その功績を高(低)く評価する.【類】The merchants of Shanghai are not *rated* very *high* in the scale of commercial probity. ¶The author is *rated low* in originality. その著者は余り独創性がないと言われている. ¶well *rate* the *adjective* "historic" 「歴史的」という形容詞に値する.
M² *rate* him *up* [健康保険など] 彼のかけ金の率をあげる.
P those travellers who *rate* cheapness *above* time 時間よりも費用を重んじる旅行者. ¶be *rated among* the most influential men 最有力者の一人と見なされる. ¶*rated as* most efficient もっとも能率的と評価されて. ¶He is *rated as* an independent in politics. 彼は政治上中立と見なされている. ‖ an officer *rated as* colonel 大佐級の武官.【類】*rate* a house *as* worth $10,000. ¶*rate* it *at* its proper worth それをその本当の価値で評価する. ¶I *rated* him *for* his impertinence. 彼が生意気なのでしかりつけた. ‖ The radio is highly *rated for* education. ラジオは教育上高く評価されている.
O an exam paper *rated* A 《米》優の点をつけられた試験答「案.

ratification, *n.* 批准, 是認.
V *await ratification* 批准を待つ. ¶*exchange ratifications* of a treaty 条約の批准を交換する. ¶*extort ratification* of treaties by the foreign powers 外国諸邦の条約批准を強請する. ¶The *ratification* has been *given*. 批准済み.
Q *formal ratification* 正式批准.

rating, *n.* 採点; 格付け.
V *get ratings* for … …の格付けをする. ¶*win* high *ratings* in the examinations 試験に優の点をとる.
Q² *efficiency ratings* of each and every employe in the department 部内のあらゆる勤務員の能率. ¶For raw materials and finished products the firm is given a *good credit rating* by at least two banks. 原料及び仕上品に付いてその商社は少くとも二銀行によってりっぱな信用格付けを与えられている. ¶get a *fourteen per cent rating* 十四点を獲得する. ¶*pupil ratings* of teacher 生徒に対する教師の評価. ¶*scholarship ratings* 学力採点.
P² the *rating* (=marking) *of* candidates 候補者の採点.

ratio, *n.* 比, 比率, 割合.
V What *ratio* does the practice of writing *bear* to that of speaking in your life? 貴下の御生活では書くのと話すのとどんな割合になっていますか. ¶*have* the *ratio* of about … to … 約…対…の割合になる. ¶*show* a *ratio* of … to … …対…の比率を示す.
Q in an *arithmetical ratio* 算術級数で. ¶in *direct ratio* to (=with) … …に対する正比で. ¶according to a *fixed ratio* 一定の比率に従って. ¶increase in (a) *geometrical ratio* to … …に対して幾何級数で増加する.【類】vary in an almost *geometrical ratio* with … ¶in (an) *inverse ratio* to … …と逆比例に. ¶in the *same ratio as* … …と同じ割合で.
Q² the *one-to-ten exchange ratio* 十対一の交換比率.
P *at* the (=a) *ratio* of … to … …に対する…の比例で. ¶*by* a *ratio* of … …の割合で. ¶Such a man exists *in* a (=the) *ratio* of one to a thousand of ordinary mortals. こういう人は普通人の千人に対する一人の割で存在する. ¶increase *with* the *ratio* of … …の割合で増加する.
P² the *ratio between* … …間の比率. ¶the *ratio of* product *to* energy expended 動力消費に対する生産比率 ‖ a *ratio of* three *to* one 三対一の比率.【類】the *ratio of* births *to* deaths.

ration, *n.* 一日分の糧食, 配給量.
Q a 2.7 *go daily ration* 二・七合の日々配給. ¶*delayed* or *omitted rations* 遅配欠配. ¶get *extra rations* 増配を受ける. ¶be on *short rations* 配給が制限されている.
Q² *army rations* 軍隊の食物配給. ¶Their *basic food ration* is 1,550 calories a day. 彼らの基本食料配給は一日1,550カロリーである. ¶cut the *bread ration* further パンの配給を一層減らす. ¶increase the *calory ration* カロリー配給を増す. ¶the *candy ration* 糖菓配給. ¶Overseas, officers drew *liquor rations*, but enlisted men did not. 海外では士官は酒類の配給を得たが兵士はこれを受けなかった. ¶eat *maintenance ration* 自分の生命を維持するだけの割当を食う. ¶deduce one day's *rice ration* for two loaves of bread パン二塊(二斤)に対して一日分の米の配給を差引く. ¶the minimum *subsistence ration* 最小生活維持の食糧配給. ¶*sugar* and *match rations* 砂糖とマッチの配給.
P put a person *on rations* 一定の食糧を給する. ¶A dwelling was allotted to him, *with rations* of rice. 禄(ろく)とともに家屋敷が彼に与えられた.
P² a *ration of* food 食物の配給.

ration, *v.* 割当配給する.
M The Army is *well rationed*. 陸軍の食糧(配給)はよい.

rationing, *n.* 配給.
Q² *coffee rationing* ended in France in January, 1950. フランスではコーヒーの配給は1950年一月十五日で終った. ¶price controls and *food rationing* 物価統制と食物配給. ¶*wartime rationing* 戦時食料配給.

rattle, *n.* がらがら(音).
O the *rattle* of empty bottles あきびんのがらがら.

rattle, *v.* がらがら走る；べらべらしゃべる．

M *rattle away* がらがら(がたごと)過ぎ去る．¶Children's wagon *rattles* ***noisily*** down the hill. 子供たちの馬車はがたごと丘を下って行く．

M² Our wagon was *rattling* ***down*** the road. われわれの荷車はがたごとと道路を走って行った．¶*rattle* ***off*** (=***away***) ががら走り去る‖*rattle* ***off*** a story 話をぺらぺらしゃべる(読む)‖*rattle* ***off*** the numbers up to ten 数を十まで急いで数える‖*rattle* ***off*** the mimeograph machines 謄写版をぱたぱた動かす(コッピィをとる)．¶*rattle* ***on*** しゃべり続ける．¶*rattle* ***up*** (***down***) an anchor いかりをがらがら引上げる(おろす)．

P the hail *rattling* ***against*** the window pane 窓ガラスにぱらぱら当るあられ．¶The hail was *rattling* ***on*** the roofs and walls. あられが屋根や壁にぱらぱら当っていた．¶The train *rattled* ***over*** the points and crossings. 列車はポイントやクロシングをがたごと通った．

ravage, *n.* 荒廃；損害，惨害．

V The temple ***escaped*** the *ravages* of fire. その寺は火災をまぬかれた．¶The suicide mania was ***making*** great *ravages*. 自殺の流行が大なる惨害を与えていた．¶The building has ***survived*** the *ravages* of time. その建物は長年月の荒廃にたえて存続した．

Q² ***flood*** *ravages* 水害．

P² the *ravages* ***of*** time 時の(歳月の経過による)荒廃‖Many architectural treasures suffered from the *ravages* ***of*** war. 多数の貴重な建造物が戦争の惨禍をこうむった．

ravage, *v.* 荒す，荒廃させる．

M The fire *ravaged* the forests ***for miles around.*** その火事で森林が何マイル四方も焼けた．

P The land was *ravaged* ***with*** fire and sword. その土地は戦火に荒された．

rave, *v.* 熱狂して語る，怒号する．

M *rave* oneself ***hoarse*** 怒鳴り散らして声を枯らす．

P *rave* ***on*** … …のことをうわ言に言う．¶*rave* ***over*** one's good looks その美ぼうを夢中になってほめる．¶The wind *raved* ***over*** the fields and ***through*** the forests. 風が野や森を吹き荒れた．

ravel, *v.* 解く，ほぐれる．

M *ravel* ***out*** (=unravel) a frayed sweater ほつれたセーター(の毛糸)を解く‖A stocking *ravels* ***out.*** くつ下がほぐれる．

P The sweater *raveled* ***at*** the elbow. セーターはひじがすり切れた．

raven, *n.* 大がらす．

V² *Ravens* ***croak.*** 大がらすは鳴く．

ravenous, *a.* がつがつして．

P be *ravenous* ***for*** food 食物にがつがつしている．

raving, *n.* うわごと．

V ***utter*** *ravings* うわごとを言う．

Q the ***mere*** *ravings* of megalomaniacs 誇大もう想狂のほんのうわごと．

ravish, *v.* 夢中にする，有頂天にする．

M The money was *ravished* ***away*** from him. その金は彼から羽根が生えて飛んで行った．

P He was *ravished* ***with*** her beauty. 彼は彼女の美ぼうに夢中になった‖*ravish* a lover ***with*** kisses 愛人にキッスの雨を降らせる．

raw, *n.* 赤はだ．

P take a bath ***in*** the *raw* in a cold mountain stream 冷い山間の小川で素はだかになって水を浴びる．¶touch a person ***on*** the *raw* 人の痛いところに触れる．

raw, *a.* [さわると]痛い；なまの．

P a nose *raw* ***from*** rubbing こすって赤くなっている鼻‖a throat *raw* ***from*** shouting 叫んだため痛むのど．

O a *raw* spot 痛い部分‖*raw* hides (=rawhides) 生皮‖a *raw* deal《口語》不正な取引．

ray, *n.* 光線．

V ***concentrate*** the sun's *rays* at its focus 太陽の光線を焦点に集める．¶***emit*** *rays* 光線を発散する．¶My eyes were blinded by ***meeting*** the direct *rays* of light. 私は光の直射で目がくらんだ．¶The sun ***poured down*** its yellow *rays*. 太陽はその黄色い光を注いだ．¶***shed*** its *ray* その光線を注ぐ．¶The sun ***shoots*** its *rays*. 太陽はその光線を射る．¶***shut out*** the sun's *rays* 太陽の光線をさえぎる．¶The *rays* of the late sun ***slanted*** in streams through the cypress trees. 夕陽が糸杉の木の間から斜めに漏れて来た．

V² Not a *ray* of hope ***pierced*** our gloom. われわれには何らの希望の光もなく暗たんたるものだった．

Q ***cosmic*** *rays*, nature's mightiest force 自然の最大力である宇宙光線．¶***effulgent*** *rays* こうこうたる光．¶the last ***departing*** *rays* 入日の光．¶***invisible*** *rays* 不可視線(波長360ミリミクロン以下の紫外線)．¶the ***electric*** *ray* 電光．¶The candle threw its ***last flickering*** *rays*, and then went out. ろうそくは最後にぱっと輝いて消えた．¶London lay before us in the ***soft mellow*** *rays* of the moon. ロンドンは柔かい融けるような月光を浴びてわれわれの眼前に見えていた．¶the ***spreading*** *rays* 四方に広がる光．

Q² the ***heat*** *rays* from the sun 太陽からの熱線．¶when the western horizon is glowing with the ***last evening*** *rays* 西方の地平線が入日の光に照りはえるとき．¶***ultra-violet*** *rays* of light 紫外線．¶***X-*** (Röntgen) *rays* エックス線(レントゲン線)．

P The view of Mt. Fuji tawny red and orange ***in*** the *rays* of the declining sun, was truly magnificent. 入日の光を浴びてだいだい色に染められた富士山の景色は実に壮麗であった．¶photograph ***under*** the X-*rays* エックス光線でとった写真．

P² There was not a *ray* ***of*** hope before them. 彼らの前途には一道の希望の光もなかった．

raze, *v.* 全滅させる．

P The buildings were *razed* ***to*** the ground. 建物は全壊した．

razor, *n.* かみそり．

V ***hone*** a *razor* かみそりをとぐ．¶*razors* ***put*** in order 使えるようになっているかみそり．¶***sharpen*** a *razor* on a strop 皮とでかみそりをとぐ．¶***strop*** (=***set***) a *razor* かみそりをとぐ．¶Don't ***use*** the *razor* against the grain. かみそりでさかぞりをするな．【類】***use*** a *razor* twice a day, morning and evening.

Q ***dull*** *razors* 鈍いかみそり．¶a ***sharp*** (=***keen***) *razor* よく切れるかみそり．

Q² a ***safety*** *razor* 安全かみそり．

P remove hair ***by*** a *razor* かみそりで毛をそる．¶a pair ***of*** *razors* 二ちょうのかみそり．

reach, *n.* 区域，範囲；力量，力；知力．

Q within ***easy*** *reach* of water-carriage 水運に便利な区域内にある‖it is within ***easier*** *reach* of … それは…へ行くのに一層便利である．【類】The village is within ***easy*** *reach* of London. ¶the ***highest*** *reach* of oratory 雄弁術の極致．¶The business, now fairly launched, was carried to ***new*** *reaches* of success. すべり出した商売はさらに発展するようになった．¶water from the ***pure*** *reaches* of the Thames テムズ川の清い流域からの水．¶a ***shallow*** *reach* 瀬．¶the ***upper*** (***lower***) *reaches* of a river 川の上(下)流．¶the ***upper*** *reaches* of society 上流社会．

P The problem is ***beyond*** the *reach* of my understanding. その問題は僕には理解できない．【類】It is altogether ***beyond*** the *reach* of possibility. ¶***by*** a long *reach* ぐっと腕をさしのべて．¶It winds ***in*** its lower *reaches* through dense subtropical vegetation. それは下流に行って亜熱帯地方の密生植物の間をうねり曲る．¶He was ***out of*** *reach* of their arrows. 彼は彼らの矢の届かない所にいた．【類】His house and property are in his wife's name so as to be ***out of*** *reach* of any creditors (債権者)．¶at a price ***within*** your *reach* 格好な値段で‖bring … ***within*** the *reach* of the law …を法律の制裁を受けるようにする‖with the idea of bringing it ***within*** the *reach* of the thinnest pocketbook (=even the modest purses) それをだれにでも買えるようにしようという考えで．【類】the most useful dictionary ever placed ***within*** the *reach* of the public / bring the results of recent German research ***within*** the *reach* of English readers.

reach, *v.* 届く，達する，到着する．

M reach ***out*** one's hands 両手をさしのべる‖*reach* ***out*** for a new market 新販路を求める．¶The loss is estimated to *reach* ***upward*** of 3,000,000 yen, while the insurance is 60,000 yen. その損失は概算三百万円以上に達し一方保険は六万円である．¶words that have histories *reaching* ***well back*** into the past 相当古い歴史をもっている語．

P *reach* ***after*** (=***at***) … …に手をのばす．¶can be *reached* ***by*** a ladder はしごを登って行かれる．【類】It is easily *reached* ***by*** rail.‖It cannot be *reached* ***by*** telephone. そこには電話は通じない．‖The opinion should be *reached* ***by*** reason, not ***by*** force. 意見は道理で徹底させるもので無理押しすべきではない．¶*reach* ***for*** a book on the shelf たなの上の本を取ろうと手を延ばす．¶such is the conclusion he *reached* ***from*** the journey ***through*** the region これがその土地の旅行で彼が得た結論である‖Trousers *reach* ***from*** the waist ***to*** the ankle. ズボンは腰からくるぶしに達する. ¶We can *reach* the town ***in*** $4^1/_2$ miles. その町へは四マイル半ある. ¶*reach* ***into*** the millions 数百万に及ぶ ‖ The summer vacation *reaches* ***into*** September. 夏休は九月に掛る. ¶The understanding which was *reached* ***on*** the issue ***between*** ... and ... …と…との相互間の論争で達し得られた妥結. ¶A deadlock was *reached* ***over*** the problem. その問題は行詰りとなった. ¶*reach* ***to*** a great height of perfection 非常に完全な所まで達する. 【類】*raech* nearly ***to*** the ground / The plain *reaches* far ***to*** the sea. / *reach* ***to*** the top of the wall.

O Please *reach* me the newspaper. すみませんがその新聞「をとってください.

react, *v.* 反動する, 反作用する.

M *react* ***disastrously*** upon ... …に由々しい反動を与える. ¶Unkindness ***often reacts*** on an unkind person. 〘諺〙不親切は不親切な人に戻って行く. ¶An audience ***readily*** *reacts* to a good speaker. 聴衆は直ちにうまい演説に反応を示す(拍手するなど). ¶The dog *reacted* ***slowly*** to the kindness of his master. その犬はだんだん飼い主の親切に反応を見せてきた(始めての飼犬). ¶*react* ***splendidly*** to a drug 薬がよくきく.

P Prices *reacted* ***from*** an early advance. 値段は以前の騰貴の反動で下落した. ¶*react* ***on*** industry (commerce, market) 産業(など)に反動を及ぼす. ¶Dogs *react* ***to*** kindness. 犬は親切にすると甘える(尾を振るなど).

reaction, *n.* 反動, 反作用; 〘物理〙原子核反応.

V ***cause*** (=***occasion***) a *reaction* 反動を起す. ¶***induce*** no *reaction* 副作用を起さない. ¶***produce*** fierce *reactions* in the young men 青年に激しい反動を起させる. ¶***promote*** *reaction* 反動をそそる. ¶***represent*** a *reaction* against ... …反対運動を示す. ¶***show*** no *reactions* 反応を示さない.

V[2] the *reactions* ***consist*** of ... その反応は…だ. ¶A strong *reaction* ***followed.*** ついで強い反動が起った. ¶a *reaction* has ***set in*** against ... …に対して反動が起った.

Q Fever is a ***common*** *reaction* from a chill. かぜを引くと熱が出る. ¶an intoxication that is followed by no ***evil*** *reaction* 悪い副作用を伴わないめいてい. 【類】It was followed by no ***evil*** *reaction.* ¶a ***healthy*** *reaction* to ... …に対する健全な反動. ¶an ***inevitable*** *reaction* 必然の反動. ¶a ***natural*** *reaction* 自然の反動. ¶control the ***nuclear chain*** *reaction* 核連鎖反応を抑える. ¶the oddities of public interest and ***public*** *reactions* 世人の興味と世人の反動の変異性.

P a rise (decline) ***in*** *reaction* 反動の起り(衰退). ¶there are signs ***of*** a *reaction* against ... …に対する反動の徴候がある.

P[2] the idealistic *reaction* ***against*** science 科学に対抗する唯心派の反動. ¶a *reaction* ***from*** the old system 旧制度からの反動. ¶A *reaction* ***in*** its favor has set in. それに有利な反動が起り出した. ¶a patient's *reactions* ***to*** a medical test 医療テストに対する患者の反応. ¶a *reaction* ***toward*** the Christian faith against science accused of having been unable to explain life 人生を説明することができないと非難された科学に対する反動として起ったキリスト教への転向. ¶a careful study of the mutual *reaction* ***upon*** each other of character and environment 品性と環境の相互的反動に対する細心の研究.

reactionary, *n.* 反動政治家.

Q those ***stubborn*** (=***stiff-necked***) *reactionaries* これらがん固な反動政治家ども.

reactionary, *a.* 反動の.

M branded ***as*** *reactionary* 反動の焼印を押されて.

reactor, *n.* 原子炉.

Q a ***nuclear*** *reactor*=an atomic pile 原子炉.

read, *v.* 読む, 音読する, 朗読する.

M She *reads* me ***admirably.*** 彼女は私の心を巧みに読取る. ¶*read* ***all day*** (***long***) 終日読書する. ¶*read* ***aloud*** 声を出して読む ‖ *Reading* poetry ***aloud*** makes us understand it better. 詩は朗読することによって一層理解を深める. ‖ *read* ***aloud*** to the family 家族のものに声を出して読んで聞かせる. ¶*read* ***carefully*** 念入りに読む. ¶I cannot ***clearly*** *read* your telegram. あなたの電報ははっきり分からない. ¶***cleverly*** *read* another's heart (face) 人の心中(顔色)をよく察しる. ¶cultivate one's power to *read* ***closely*** and ***discriminately*** 綿密にかつ識別的に読む力を養成する. ¶*read* ***deeply*** in literature 深く文学書を読む. ¶*read* ***devoutly*** 熱心に読む. ¶*read* the newspapers ***diligently*** 新聞を丹念に読む. ¶*read* more ***distinctly*** もっとはっきり読む. ¶*read* ***down*** to the foot of a page ページの下まで読む. ¶Few will *read* it ***dry-eyed.*** それを読んで泣かないものはほとんどないだろう. ¶*read* it ***eagerly*** 熱心にそれを読む. ¶The book is more ***easily*** *read* than described. その本の内容は説明するより読んでもらった方がわかりが早い. ¶Have you ***ever*** *read* about the Eskimos? エスキモーのことに関して何か読んだことがあるか. ¶the art of *reading* music ***fluently*** 楽譜をすらすら読める能力. 【類】He cannot *read* English or German ***fluently.*** ¶the power to *read* ***fluently***, ***intelligently*** and ***sympathetically*** in a foreign language 外国語で流ちょうにかつ理解し同感して読む力. ¶***glibly*** *read* すらすら読む. ¶It will be ***greedily*** *read* by ... それは…によってむさぼるように読まれるだろう. ¶***hungrily*** *read* every word of it そのすべての言葉を読みふける. ¶*read* ***hurriedly*** 急いで読む. ¶*read* ***inexactly*** 不正確に読む. ¶*read* ***intensively*** rather than extensively 広く読むより深く読む. ¶It is ***largely*** *read* by young men. それは青年によって広く読まれている. ¶be ***little*** *read* nowadays 今ではあまり読まれていない. ¶We have been *reading* so ***much*** about the man lately. その人のことは最近よく新聞雑誌に出ている. ¶The passage *reads* ***oddly.*** この文は意味が変だ. ¶*read* ***out*** in full (U.S. を United States などと)全部読み上げる ‖ *read* ***out*** the result of a voting 投票の結果を報告する ‖ *read* it ***out*** to one's class それをクラスの生徒たちに読んで聞かせる. ¶*read* it ***over again*** それを繰り返し読む. 【類】*read* it ***over and over*** [***again***]. ¶*read* ***purposefully*** 目的をもって読む. ¶That sentence *reads* ***queerly.*** その文は読んで奇妙な感じがする. ¶read newspapers ***scantily*** (=***sparingly***) 新聞を控え目に読む. ¶*read* ***silently*** 黙読する. ¶the passage *reads* ***thus*** in the original ... その個所は原文では…となっている. ¶The passage has to be *read* ***twice*** before the meaning is grasped. その節は読み返さないと意味がつかめない. ¶*read* ***understandingly*** 理解して読む. ¶*read* ***vagariously*** 気まぐれに読む. ¶*read* ***voraciously*** むさぼるように読む. ¶The book *reads* ***well.*** その本はよく書いてある. ‖ He *reads* very ***well.*** 彼は実に読方がうまい. ‖ be ***well*** *read* in English literature 英文学の素養が深い. ¶a person ***widely*** *read* 多読の人. ¶*read* ***widely*** and ***miscellaneously*** 広く雑読する. 【類】*read* ***widely*** and ***wisely.*** ¶*read* ***word by word*** 一語一語読む.

M[2] *read* ***in*** a book 本を朗読する. ¶*read* ***on*** to the end of a story 物語を終りまで読み続ける. 【類】make us *read* ***on*** to the dénouement (結果). ¶*read* a book ***through*** 本を読み通す. ¶*read* ***up*** a proposed measure to the assembly 提案を会議で読上げる ‖ *read* ***up*** [on] a subject ある題目を文献で調べる ‖ begin at the bottom and *read* ***up*** 終りの方から読み出して始めの方に進む.

P *read* ***about*** a matter (affair, person) あることがら(など)について読む. ¶*read* ***at*** the page where he turned the leaf down 彼は本のページを折ったところから読む ‖ He learned to *read* a book ***at*** the age of three. 彼は三歳のときに読書することを覚えた. ¶*read* ***before*** the class クラスで読む. ¶know how to *read* ***between*** the [printed] lines 言外の意を読取ることを知る ‖ Diplomatic messages have to be *read* ***between*** the lines. 外交文書は言外の意を読まねばならない. ¶*read* ***by*** candle-light ろうそくの光で読む ‖ *read* ***by*** turns かわるがわる読む ‖ *read* a telegram ***by*** the A 1 Code. 電報を A 1 暗号簿で解読する. ¶*read* ***for*** an examination 試験のために読む ‖ *read* ***for*** the bar 弁護士になるために研究する ‖ *read* mainly ***for*** amusement or relaxation 主として娯楽または慰めのために読書する ‖ *read* ***for*** pleasure (profit, inspiration) 娯楽(など)のために読む. ¶*read* aloud ***from*** some magazine 雑誌を声出して読む ‖ *read* ***from*** one's favorite author その好きな作家の著作を読む ‖ *read* ***from*** curiosity 好奇心で読む. ¶He can *read* ***in*** a foreign language fairly well. 彼はかなり外国語が読める. ‖ The inscriptions on the cards *read* ***in*** English: カードの文字は英語に訳すと次のようになる. ‖ *read* it ***in*** the text それをテキストで読む. 【類】*read* an account ***in*** a newspaper / *read* the author ***in*** the original (原文) ‖ I *read* it ***in*** your face. 君の顔色でそれを読取った(君の顔に書いてある). 【類】She *read* his thought ***in*** his eyes. ‖ when *read* ***in*** print 印刷してあるのを読むと. ¶*read* (=interpret) it ***into*** ... それを…の意とさとる. ¶The story is *read like* a romance (page of Dante's Inferno, tale from the Arabian Nights). その物語は読んで見ると小説(など)のようだ. 【類】Japanese poems *read like* telegrams. / The book *reads like* a novel. / This does not *read like* a child's composition. / The story of his adventures *reads like* a wild dream. ¶I have *read* very little *of* him. 私は彼の著書をほとんど読んでいない. ¶be *read out of* a political party 政党から除名される. ¶I *read to* my mother while she nursed the baby. 私は赤ん坊をもりしている母に読んで聞かした. ‖ *read to* oneself 黙読する ‖ *read to* no purpose 漫然と読む ‖ *read* oneself *to* sleep 読みながら眠ってしまう ‖ This ticket *reads to* Boston via Providence. この切符はプロヴィデンス経由ボストン行になっている. ¶*read with* avidity むさぼるように読む ‖ *read with* the lips 音読する. 【類】*read* English poetry *with* intelligence, interest, and appreciation / *read with* critical intelligence (批判的に) / *read with* expression / *read with* so much pain (非常に骨折って).

O The telegram *reads* as follows. 電文は次のようだ ‖ His silence can be *read* as consent. 返事のないのを承諾と見なす. ¶The thermometer *reads* 70 degrees. 寒暖計は(華氏)七十度を示している. 「の]顧問.

reader, *n.* 読者; 読本(リーダー); 読書家; 校正者; [出版社

V *bewilder* the *reader* 読者をめんくらわせる. ¶*bother readers* 読者を悩ます. ¶The book *carries* the *reader* with a growing interest to the end. その本は読者の感興を高めつつ最後まで読み通させる. ¶The book *holds* the *reader* from the commencement. その本は初めから読者を引きつける. ‖ *hold* the *reader spellbound* 読者を魅了する. ¶*interest* the general *reader* 一般の読者に興味を与える. ¶*perplex* the *reader* 読者を迷わす. ¶*prejudice* a *reader* against ... ...に対して読者に偏見をいだかせる. ¶*refer* the *reader* to the eloquent pages of the book 読者に同書の十二分に書かれた記事を参考せられることをすすめる.

Q No *attentive reader* can fail to observe it. 注意して読む人は何人もそれに気付かずにはいない. ¶an *avid reader* 速読家. ¶a *close reader* of ... will have observed, doubtless, that ... ...を注意して読んだ人は疑もなく...を認めたことだろう. ¶a *cockney reader* ロンドンっ子の読者. ¶a *constant* (=*regular*) *reader* of a newspaper 常に新聞を読む人. ¶a *diligent reader* of doctors' dissertations 博士論文を熱心に研究する人. ¶an *English* (a *French*) *reader* 英語(など)のリーダー; 英(など)人の読者. ¶the *English-speaking reader*英語の話せる読者. ¶*esoteric readers* その道の専門の読者. ¶A *general reader* may prefer a different kind of books. 普通の読者は[これとは]違った種類の本をむしろ好むだろう. ¶a *gymnastic* (=*skipping*) *reader* とびとびに読む人. ¶a *healthy-minded reader* 健全な精神の読者. ¶an *indiscriminate reader* 乱読家. ¶an *inveterate reader* たん読家. ¶the praise of *judicious readers* 賢明な読者の賞賛. ¶*juvenile readers* 年少の読者. ¶a *keen reader* of the signs of the times and the drift of opinion 時代の徴候や思想の流れを鋭く読み取る人. ¶books intended for the *lay reader* 一般読者向きの本. ¶*non-scholastic readers* 非学者的な読者. ¶an *official reader* 公式朗読者. ¶an *omnivorous reader* 乱読家. ¶the *perceptive reader* will not require to be told that ... 敏感な読者には...と述べる必要はないであろう. ¶*popular readers* 一般の読者. ¶No author can write effectively on any topic without a mental image of his *prospective readers*. 自分の読者を予想しないではどんな問題に関してでも効果的に書けるものではない. ¶a *publisher's reader* 出版者の顧問. ¶The best readers are the most *rapid readers*. 最善の読者は最高速度の読者である. ¶a *rough reader* 初校の校正者. ¶*self-educating readers* 独学者. ¶He is a *shrewd reader* of human nature. 彼は人間性の機微をよく察知する男だ. ¶a *typical reader* 代表的な読者. ¶the *unscientific* (=lay) *reader* 科学の知識のない一般の読者. ¶a *voluminous reader* 多読家.

Q^2 a favorite book for *family* (=house) *readers* 家庭で愛読される本. ¶a good *mind reader* 察しのいい人. ¶a *lightning reader* who takes in the whole pages at a glance 全ページを一目に見て取る電光石火的な読者. ¶the *non-expert reader* [読書に不なれな]専門家でない読者. ¶a *Scripture reader* 聖典の読者; 聖書読本.

P^2 He was a great *reader in* French as well as in English literature. 彼は英文学並に仏文学を博く読んだ人であった. ‖ a *Reader in* Geography to the University of Oxford オクスフォード大学地理学講師. ¶a great *reader of* poetry 非常に詩を読む人 ‖ a *reader of* omens 前兆を解する人. ¶Mr. W.H. Swift, *reader to* the Cambridge University Press ケンブリッジ大学出版部の顧問 W.H. スウィフト氏.

readiness, *n.* 容易, 敏速; 快諾; 用意.

V he *expressed* his *readiness* to adopt ... 彼は直ちに...を採用しようとの意を示した.

Q his *constant readiness* to devote his time and energies to the advancement of these objects これらの目的を達成するために絶えず時と精力をささげようとの彼の心構え ‖ maintain a force in *constant readiness* for an emergency 軍隊を常備して非常時に応じる用意をする.

Q^2 *reading readiness* 読書の敏速.

P be *in readiness* for ... ...の用意をしている. 【類】Everything is *in readiness* for the arrival of the guests. / The motor(-car) is at the door *in readiness.* / everything now being *in readiness* / A boat is always moored *in readiness* to put off at any moment. / We had a carriage *in readiness* to meet them at the railway station. ¶*with readiness* 進んで. 【類】*readiness for* new friendships.

O those who have a *readiness* to place Japan first and self last 日本のことを先きにして自分を最後にするだけの用意のある人.

reading, *n.* (**1**) 読書; 読み方; [しばしば *pl.*] 読み物.

V They *afford* most satisfactory *reading*. それらの本は最も快適な読み物だ. ¶His chapter on the critics of the stage *contains* some good *reading*. 演劇批評家に関する彼の文中には読むに足るものがある. ¶Each actor gave the lines *different reading*. 俳優はそれぞれそのせりふを違った読み方をした(声いろを使って). ¶when you *finish reading* this 君がこれを読み終えたら. ¶*form* lively *reading* 生き生きした読み物になる. ¶It *makes* excellent *reading*, despite its defects of literary form. それは文体に欠点はあるがりっぱな読み物だ. ¶*practice reading* 読み方を練習する. ¶The "Personal" column of the London Times often *provides* interesting *reading*. ロンドン・タイムズの人事欄はしばしば興味ある読み物になる. ¶*record* accurate thermometrical *readings* for each of the days 毎日の正確な温度を記録する. ¶well (=abundantly) *repay* careful *reading* by ... ...が注意して読むだけの価値はある. 【類】The book is full of fine thoughts and will *repay* careful *reading*. ¶it *requires* but little *reading* between the lines to perceive that ... ちょっと頭を働かして読めば...と言うことが分る.

Q most *agreeable reading* きわめて愉快な読み物. ¶*attentive reading* 精読. ¶This makes the volumes very *attractive reading*. このためにその本が非常におもしろく読める. 【類】386 pages of *attractive reading*. ¶*captivating reading* 魅力ある読み物. ¶A *careful reading* of his article is commended. 彼の論文を精読することをお勧めする. ¶a collection of words and phrases made in the course of *catholic reading* ひろく読書する間に出来た語句の収集. ¶*collateral reading* 課外の読み物. 【類】supervised (教師指導の) *collateral reading* / helpful *collateral reading* for the high school. ¶*curious reading* 珍らしい読み物. ¶in his *daily reading* or writing 彼が日々読書あるいは執筆する時に. ¶*dangerous reading* 危険な読み物. ¶*delightful reading* 愉快な読み物. ¶*desultory reading* 乱読. ¶*dreary reading* 退屈な読み物. ¶Figures are often *dry reading*. 数字(統計)は往々にして無味乾燥な読み物である. ¶*easy reading* 容易な読み物. ¶*entertaining reading* おもしろい読み物. ¶make *excellent reading* 結構な読み物になる. ¶*extensive reading* 広い読書. ¶*fascinating reading* 魅力のある読み物. ¶*favorite reading* 気に入りの読み物. ¶It is not designed for *general reading*, but for the erudite few. それは一般の読み物に作ったのではなく学識ある少数者をねらったものである. ¶*hurtful reading* 有害な読み物. ¶a man of *immense reading* 広く読書した人. ¶*inspiring reading* 感奮させる読み物. ¶*intelligent* and *fluent reading* 理解のある流ちょうな読み方. ¶*interesting reading* 興味ある読み物. 【類】The book makes *interesting* and *instructive reading*. ¶*interpretative reading* of modern drama 近代劇の演出的朗読(劇中の人物になりきって). ¶his *keen-eyed reading* of the proofs 彼の正確な校

正ぶり. ¶give one's paper a *last reading* 自分で書いた文を最後に読み下して見る. ¶*light reading* 軽い読み物. ¶his *multifarious reading* 彼の乱読. ¶*omnivorous reading* 手当り次第の読書. ¶*oral reading* 音読. ¶*pleasant reading* 愉快な読み物. ¶do a little *preparatory reading* for a tour 旅行のために少し予備研究をやる. ¶*profitable reading* 有益な読み物. ¶*racy reading* きびきびした読み物. ¶*random reading* 手当り次第な読書. ¶*rapid, effortless reading* 大急ぎでなぐり書きをした読み物. ¶In modern life, as ever before, magazines and newspapers provide a large part of the *recreational reading* of both children and adults. 以前と同様現代生活において新聞雑誌は子供にとっても大人にとっても広く娯楽的な読み物となっている. ¶*required reading* [教師から]課せられた読み物. ¶It is worth a *second reading*. それは再読の価値がある. ¶*selected readings* in public finance 財政論文選集. ¶*side readings* 副読本的な読みもの. ¶*Silent reading* is the process of thought getting from a printed page. 默読は印刷したページから思想を得る方法である. ¶*sensational reading* 扇情的な読み物. ¶a habit of *slovenly reading* だらしのない読み方の習慣. ¶*solid* (=*serious*) *reading* かたい読みもの. ¶a man of *some reading* いくらか本を読んでいる人. ¶*spirited reading* 活気のある読み物. ¶*substantial reading* 実質的な読み物. ¶*suggested readings* 参考にせよと注意された読み物. ¶a man of extensive and not *superficial reading* ひろくしかも皮相的でない読書家. ¶*systematic reading* 系統立った読書. ¶*tedious reading* あきあきする読み物. ¶*thoughtful reading* 考え深い読書. ¶make his verse *welcome reading* 彼の詩がおもしろく読める. ¶a man of *wide reading* 博識の人. 【類】*wider* and more *attentive reading*.

Q² excellent *family reading* すぐれた家庭向き読み物. ¶too busy to do much *fiction reading* いそがしくて多くの小説を読む時間がない. ¶*finger reading* 点字指読. ¶books for *home reading* for children 家庭で子供が読む本. ¶There is plenty of *interesting reading* in the volume. その本にはおもしろい読み物が沢山ある. ¶*Manuscript reading* is one of the most trying of the editor's tasks. 原稿を読むのは編集者の仕事の中で一番つらいことの一つである. ¶*meter readings* メートルの指示. ¶*penny reading* しろうと演芸会(朗読・詩吟・音楽などを演じ一ペニーの入場料を取る). ¶books for *seaside* and *holiday reading* 海岸や休日の読み物. ¶*sight reading* 音譜を見てすらすら奏する(歌う)こと. ¶books for *summer reading* 夏の読み物. ¶"*work-type*," or *informative*, *reading* 研究すなわち知識的な読物.

P throw it away *after* a single *reading* ただ一度読んだ後それを捨てる. ¶*at* first *reading* 最初読んだ時. ¶master a book *in* one *reading* 一読して本をわがものとする. ¶have a desire *for reading* 読書欲を持っている. ¶facts gleaned *from* wide *reading* 広く読書して得た事実. ¶*on* my first *reading* 私が初めて読んだときに.

P² *reading for* pleasure 娯楽読み物. 【類】*reading for* thought. ¶*readings from* English history (great authors) 英国史(など)から抜粋した読み物 ‖ *readings from* Dickens ディッケンス精選集. ¶college *readings in* English prose 大学生のための散文英語. ¶The *reading of* the thermometer was 95 degrees. 温度計は 95 度を示した.

(**2**) 朗読; [国会の]読会.

V hear him *give* a *reading* from perhaps the best-known of his books, ... 彼が自著の中で多分最も有名なものの中から朗読するのを聞く. ¶*omit* the *reading* of the report 報告の朗読を省略する. ¶The Bill has *passed* its second *reading*. その法律案は第二読会を通過した. 【類】The Bill unanimously *passed* its second *reading* in the House of Commons. ¶The bill has now *reached* its second *reading*. その法律案は今や第二読会に回った.

Q *expressive reading* 表情朗読. ¶at *first reading* 最初読んだときは ‖ It appeared unreasonable on *first reading*. それは一読した時には不合理に思われた. ¶The bill passed the *second reading*. その議案は第二読会を通過した. 【類】attain a *second* (*third*) *reading*. ¶a meeting for *studied reading* of papers on subjects 研究発表会.

P² The Bill was thrown out *on* its second *reading*. その法律案は第二読会で葬られた. ¶The Bill passed *to* its second *reading*. 議案は第二読会に回った.

readjustment, *n*. 再整理, 再調節.

Q problems of *post-war readjustment* 戦後の後始末の問題.

ready, *a*. 用意している, 準備している.

M a bud *nearly ready* to burst 今にもほころびそうなつぼみ. ¶I am *perfectly ready* to assent to the arrangement. 私はその協定に大賛成だ. ¶I am only *too ready* to accept such a proposal. 私はこういった申出は自分から進んでお受けしたい. ¶He is *very ready* to argue about that subject. 彼はその問題をよく論議したがる.

P Let them be *ready against* the first of next month. 彼らに来月一日の用意をさせろ. ¶He is very *ready at* excuses. あの男は言訳がうまい. ‖ *ready at* reckoning 計算が早い. ¶He must be *ready by* then. 彼はそのときまでには準備ができているに違いない. ¶shoes *ready for* wear でき合いのくつ ‖ If so I stand *ready for* rebuke and correction. もしそうなら私は喜んで非難とおしかりを受ける. ‖ be *ready for* shipment 発送(船荷など)の用意ができている ‖ She will be *ready for* launching next spring. その船は来春進水ができるだろう. 【類】The guide will soon be *ready for* distribution. / guarantee to be *ready for* delivery by ... / The goods are now *ready for* packing. / The contract is *ready for* signature. / be *ready for* instant use / be now *ready for* publication / Troops are *ready for* mobilization (battle). ‖ He was *ready for* his fate. 彼はその運命を覚悟していた. ¶He is *ready in* helping his friends. 彼は進んで友人を助ける. ¶He was all *ready with* his answer. 彼は言下に答えた. ‖ He was wonderfully *ready with* retort and sarcasm. 彼はしっぺい返しや皮肉が驚くほどうまかった.

O *ready* to die rather than surrender 降参するよりむしろ死のうと覚悟して. 【類】*ready* to work for others.

real, *n*. 真.

V *tell* the *real* from the false 真偽を見分ける.

realism, *n*. 真実感, 現実主義.

V the noises that *lend realism* to radio drama ラジオ・ドラマに実感を与える擬音.

V² His *realism caused* him to give up the plan. 彼の現実主義がその計画を中止させることになった.

realistic, *a*. 現実的な.

M His view of life is *very realistic*. 彼の人生観は非常に現実的だ.

reality, *n*. 真実, 現実, 実際.

V *achieve* the *reality* of reform 改革の実をあげる. ¶*reconcile* the *realities* of life with the dreams of poetry 人生の実際と詩の夢想とを調和させる. ¶*verify* its *reality* その真実を確かめる. 【類】*verify* the *reality* of an event.

Q the *grim realities* of bombed areas 被爆地域のものすごい現実. ¶a *gruesome reality* ぞっとするような事実. ¶sensations which have no *objective reality* 客観的実在を伴わない感覚. ¶*sober reality* まじめな現実. ¶the *stern realities* of fire brigade life 消防隊生活の厳然たる実状. 【類】let the people know the *stern reality* of war / fight with the *stern realities* of poverty. ¶*superphenomenal realities* 超感覚的実在. ¶an *unhappy reality* 不幸な事実.

Q² The society is a *working reality*. その協会は実績をあげている.

P free *in reality* as well as in name 名実ともに自由な. 【類】He was *in reality* penniless. / *in reality*, though not in name. ¶when they returned *to realities*. 彼らが(夢などから)現実に返ったとき. ¶mere show *without reality* 実のないほんの見せかけ.

realization, *n*. 実現; 実感; 現実化.

V experience and maturity have *brought* me the poignant *realization* that ... 経験と年の功で私は...ということを痛切に実感するようになった. ¶Then *came* the glad *realization* of his cherished hopes. それから彼の宿望がうれしくも実現した.

Q I came to a *fuller realization* of ... 私は...を一層深く実感するようになった. ¶a *keen realization* of the fact that ... ...という事実の痛切な実感. ¶a *perfect realization* of all the stories of adventures one has ever read それまでに読んだあらゆる冒険物語の完全な実現. ¶a *quick realization* of essentials 要領のじん速な体得.

P The ideal has been brought *to realization*. その理想は実現されるにいたった. ¶*with* no *realization* of the nature of the occasion 場所柄もわきまえず.

P² a *realization of* Jules Verne's dreams ジュール・ヴェ

ルヌの夢想の実現.

realize, *v.* 実現する, 悟る; もうける.

M a project not ***actually realized*** 実現していない計画. ¶*realize* ***clearly*** that ... ...ということをはっきり会得する. ¶***dimly*** *realize* ぼんやり分かる. ¶I ***fully*** *realize* that ... ...とつくづく思う. ¶I can ***hardly realize*** how large was his loss. 彼の損失がいかに大きなものか想像できないほどだ. ¶Do you *realize* ***how*** time is flying? 時間がどんどん過ぎて行くことが君は本当によく分かるか. ¶one ***keenly*** *realizes* the change time has brought 今昔の感にたえない. ¶***now*** I *realize* that ... さては...であろう.

P I *realize* ¥3,000 ***from*** the sale of ... ...の売上から三千円私の手にはいった. ‖ I *realize* ***from*** his remarks that ... 彼の言葉からは...と察せられる.

O it must be *realized* that ... ...ということをよく悟らねばならない. ¶from the expressions on the faces of ..., I *realized* that ... ...の顔の表情から私は...ということが分かった.

realm, *n.* 国土, 領土, 領域.

V ***expand*** its *realm* その領域を広げる.

Q Japan is a ***powerful insular*** *realm*. 日本は強大な島国である. ¶the ***whole*** *realm* of science 科学の全範囲. ¶the ***world-wide*** *realm* 全世界にわたる領土.

P ***in*** the *realm* of sport 競技界で ‖ He traveled only ***in*** the *realms* of thought. 彼は思想界だけを旅行した(ただ読書思索にふけった). 【類】***in*** the other *realms* of human activity.

P² the *realm* ***of*** dreams 夢の国.

ream, *n.* [紙の]れん; 大量.

V ***write*** *reams* of verse 詩を沢山書く.

P² a *ream* (two reams) ***of*** paper 紙一(二)れん.

reap, *v.* 刈る, 刈り取る.

P *reap* ***from*** ... ...から刈り集める.

O *reap* a field of barley (beans) 大麦(など)を刈る ‖ *reap* the fruits of one's effort 労力の成果を得る.

reaper, *n.* 刈り手; 刈りとり機.

Q² a ***one(two)-horse*** *reaper* 一頭(二頭)引刈り取機.

P² a *reaper* ***in*** harvests 収穫時の刈り手.

rear, *n.* 後部, 背部.

V ***bring up*** the *rear* しんがりを勤める. 【類】A leads with sixteen, B following with fourteen and C ***bringing up*** the *rear* with eleven.

P ***at*** the *rear* of ... ...の後ろに. ¶We attacked the enemy ***in*** the *rear*. われわれは敵の背後を攻撃した. ‖ ***in*** (=at) the *rear* of her home 彼女の家の後ろに ‖ be far ***in*** the *rear* of Europe ヨーロッパよりずっと遅れている. ¶pressing ***on*** its *rear* その背後に迫って. ¶The hill ***to*** the *rear* of the temple is an excellent spot for observation. その寺の後ろの丘は見はらしがよい場所である.

rear, *v.* 育てる; あげる.

P be *reared* ***in*** an atmosphere of freedom 自由の空気の中で育つ. ¶The daughter was *reared* ***with*** the utmost care and affection. その娘はちょうよ花よと育てられた.

O *rear* its head [動物など]頭をもたげる.

rearm, *v.* 再武装する.

P *rearm* a country ***with*** newer and more improved weapons より新型の兵器で国を再武装する.

reason, *n.* 理由, 道理, 理論; 理性.

V ***adduce*** *reason* in support of one's opinion 自己の説を主張する理由をあげる. ¶for *reasons* which have been ***advanced*** in the preceding chapter 前章に述べた理由で. ¶***apply*** *reason* to instinct 本能に理性を加味する. ¶a very good *reason* which I feel sure you will ***appreciate*** あなたがきっと賛成して下さると私が信じるきわめて有力な理由. ¶***ascertain*** the *reason* その理由を確かめる. ¶without ***assigning*** a *reason* for ... ...の理由を示すことなく. 【類】They can ***assign*** no *reason* for his suicide. ¶he ***brings forward*** *reasons* in favor of the view that ... 彼は...の説に有利な理由を指示している. ¶***demand*** a *reason* 理由を詰問する. ¶for no *reason* that could be ***discovered*** どういう訳だか. ¶***disregard*** *reason* 理屈を無視する. ¶***explain*** the *reason* for ... ...の理由を説明する. 【類】for some *reason* which has not been adequately ***explained***. ¶the present volume ***finds*** its *reason* for existence in the fact that ... 本書は...という目的で刊行したものである. 【類】it is hard to ***find*** a valid *reason* for ... / ***furnish*** some *reason* for ... ¶***give*** a *reason* for ... ...を理由づける. 【類】***give*** an intelligent *reason* for ... ...に対して筋のたった理由を与える. ¶I ***have*** *reasons* for it. それにはわけがある. 【類】we ***have*** abundant *reason* to congratulate ourselves on ... / He ***had*** no *reason* sufficiently good to advance for the refusal of the post. / he ***has*** good *reason* to hope that ... / we ***have*** the best of *reasons* for believing that ... ¶Will you not ***hear*** *reason?* 君は物の道理を聞き分けないのか. ‖ He would not ***hear*** *reason*. 彼はどうにも聞き分けなかった. ¶***hold out*** a false *reason* 虚偽の理由を申し立てる. ¶on the *reason* being ***inquired***, he replied that ... 理由を求められたときに彼は...と答えた. ¶I do not ***know*** the *reason*. 私はその理由は知らない. ¶***list*** six *reasons* for ... 六カ条の...に対する理由を列記する. ¶Overwhelmed by his achievement, he ***lost*** his *reason*. 彼は自分の成功に有頂天になって気が変になった. 【類】She ***lost*** her *reason* after the execution of her husband. / ***lost*** his *reason* as a result for ... ¶***make*** him ***see*** *reason* 彼に道理をわきまえさせる. ¶***mention*** three *reasons* 三つの理由をあげる. ¶***offer*** a *reason* for (against) ... ...に有利な(不利な)理由を出す. ¶***put*** (=***set***) ***forth*** reasons why ... ...の理由を述べる. 【類】***put forth*** the most trivial *reasons*. ¶I ***see*** no *reason* why it should be ... なにゆえそれが...であるべきかの理由が私には分からない. 【類】I ***see*** no *reason* why this may not be true. / I never ***see*** *reason* to believe that ... ¶***seize*** the most trifling *reasons* to incite their readers against ... 最もつまらない理由をたてにして彼らの読者を刺激し...に反対させる. ¶for *reasons* already ***stated*** すでに述べた理由のために. ¶this fact ***supplies*** a *reason* for ... この事実が...に対する一つの理由になる. ¶***Tell*** the *reason* for your choice. 君の選択の理由を言ってみたまえ. ¶I cannot ***understand*** the *reason*. 私にはその理由を了解し兼ねる. ¶it is not necessary to ***urge*** further *reasons* why he should ... 彼がなぜ...すべきかの理由をこれ以上述べる必要はない.

V² for *reasons* which will ***appear*** hereafter 後になって述べる理由からして. ¶but with the morning ***came*** *reason*, and ... しかし朝になって物が分かって来て... ¶a sufficient *reason* ***exists*** for ... ...に対して十分の理由がある.

Q for the ***above*** *reason*=for the reason above 上記の理由で. ¶there is ***abundant*** *reason* why ... なぜ...であるかの十分な理由がある. ¶an ***adequate*** (***inadequate***) *reason* 十分(不十分)な理由. ¶there are ***ample*** *reasons* why ... なぜ...かに対しては十分の理由がある. ¶for not very ***apparent*** *reason* はなはだ明りょうならざる理由で. ¶the ***basic*** *reason* 根本の理由. ¶for ***certain*** *reasons* ある理由で. ¶it is not a very ***cogent*** (=***convincing***) *reason* for ... それは...に対して筋道の立った理由にはならない. 【類】There appears to be no ***cogent*** *reason* for ... ¶***competent*** *reasons* 有力な理由. ¶for *reasons* too ***complicated*** (=***complex***) to mention あまりにも複雑で述べ得ない理由で. ¶there is no ***conclusive*** *reason* to suppose that ... ...と想像する確固たる理由がない. ¶with ***considerable*** *reason* 誠にもっともな理由で. ¶for an exactly ***contrary*** *reason* 正反対の理由で. ¶a ***deeper*** *reason* さらに深い理由. ¶with little or no ***definite*** *reason* why ... なぜ...であるかの理由がほとんどまたは全然なく. ¶a lady, who for ***diplomatic*** *reasons* shall be nameless 差しさわりがあるのでここに名前を言うことのできないある婦人. ¶urge ***divers*** *reasons* for one's conduct その行為に対し様々の理由を述べる. ¶he saw no ***earthly*** *reasons* why he shouldn't ... 彼にはなぜ...してはいけないのか理由が皆目分からなかった. ¶for ***erotic*** *reasons* 恋愛上の理由で. ¶I have ***every*** *reason* to believe that ... 私には...と信ずべき十分の理由がある. ¶I don't know the ***exact*** *reason* why ... 私はなぜ...であるかの正確な理由を知らない. ¶unless there is ***excellent*** *reason* to the contrary それと反対のりっぱな理由がなければ. ¶for ***financial*** *reasons* 財政上の理由で. ¶***flippant*** *reasons* 薄弱な理由. ¶there is ***good*** *reason* for ... ...の十分な理由がある. 【類】assign (=point out) ***good*** *reasons* for delay ‖ for seemingly ***good*** *reason* 一見もっともな理由で. 【類】it is with ***good*** *reason*, therefore, that ... ¶have ***grave*** *reason* to complain 不平をいう重大な理由がある. ¶for some ***inexplicable*** *reason* ある説明し得ない理由で. ¶for some ***inscrutable*** *reason* どういう訳だか. ¶have an ***intelligent*** *reason* for one's own usage 自身の用語法についてはしっかりした理由がある. ¶for sound ***international*** *reasons* しっかりした国際上の理由で. ¶except for ***justifiable*** *reasons* 正当の理由がなければ. ¶a ***legitimate*** *reason* 正当の理由. ¶the ***main*** (=

chief*) *reason is that ... 主な理由は...である. ¶constitute the ***major reasons*** for the existence of ... ...の主な存在理由となっている. ¶this is one ***material reason*** why ... これはなぜ...であるかの重要な一つの理由である. ¶for some ***mysterious reason*** ある不可思議な理由で. ¶There is ***no reason*** to be afraid of him. 彼を恐れる理由は少しもない. ‖ for ***no*** other ***reason*** than that ... ...というだけで. ¶for ***obvious reasons*** 明白な理由で. ¶for some ***occult reason***, unknown to us われわれに分からないなにか不思議な理由で. ¶the ***only*** (=***sole***) ***reason*** is that ... ただ一つの理由は...である. ¶the ***ostensible reason*** 表面の理由. ¶for ***personal reasons*** 一身上の都合で. ¶for this ***plain reason*** この明りょうな理由で. ¶a ***plausible reason*** もっともらしい理由. ¶There is no ***pure reason*** in it to speak of. それには別に取り立てていうほどの理由がない. ¶for the ***quaint reason*** that ... ...というおかしな理由で. ¶***rational reasons*** もっともな理由. ¶the ***real reason*** for the failure is to be sought in ... その失敗の真の理由は...に求めるべきである. ¶a ***reasonable reason*** 当然の理由. ¶men rejected for ***physical*** or ***mental reasons*** 肉体的あるいは精神的理由で不合格となった人々. ¶for ***religious reasons*** 宗教上の理由で. ¶for ***selfish reasons*** 身勝手な理由で. ¶for ***sentimental reasons*** 感傷的な理由で. ¶for the ***silliest reason*** きわめてばかばかしい理由で. ¶for a ***similar*** (=***like***) ***reason*** 同様な理由で. ¶for this ***single reason*** この簡単な理由で. ¶a ***slender reason*** 貧弱な理由. ¶sever the sacred tie for the ***slightest reasons*** きわめてささいな理由で神聖なきずなを断つ(離婚する). ¶his ***sole reason*** for a tour to Sweden 彼がスエーデンへ旅行するただ一つの理由. ¶for ***some reason***, not explained なんだかはっきりしない理由で ‖ for ***some reason*** or other なんかの都合で. ¶a ***sound reason*** 確固たる理由. ¶he has some ***strong reason*** for ... 彼は...に対していく分有力な理由がある ‖ there are ***strong reasons*** for believing that ... ...と信ずべき有力な理由がある. ¶for some ***strange reason*** ある妙な理由で. ¶there is no ***sufficient reason*** for ... ...に対し十分な理由がない. 【類】that hardly furnishes a ***sufficient reason*** for ... ¶for ***trivial reasons*** つまらない理由で. ¶the ***true reason*** why ... なぜ...であるかの真の理由. ¶for the ***twin reasons*** of ... ...の二つの理由で. ¶My ***reasons*** for ... have been ***twofold***. ...に対する私の理由は二つある. ¶for some ***unaccountable reason*** なにか訳の分からない理由で. ¶for ***uncertain reasons*** どういうものだか. ¶there is ***undoubted reason*** to believe that ... ...ということを信じる確かな理由がある. ¶The ***reasons*** for this decision are ***unexplained***. この決定をなすに至った理由はまだ分かっていない. ¶for some ***unknown reason*** なにかしら訳があって. ¶***urgent reasons*** 緊急な理由. ¶there appears to be no ***valid reason*** for ... ...に対して有力な理由があるようには思われない. ¶for ***various reasons*** 色々な理由で. ¶a ***weighty reason*** 一つの容易ならない理由. ¶For ***what reason***? なぜですか.

Q² for ***economy reasons***=for reasons of economy 経済上の理由で. ¶for ***family reasons*** 家事の都合により. ¶the ***root reason*** is that ... 根本的理由は...である. ¶for ***security reasons*** 安全という理由で.

P ***above reason*** 理屈を超越して. ¶***according to reason*** 理性に従って. ¶It is ***against*** all ***reason***. それは全く理屈に反している. ¶The cost of labor and materials has advanced ***beyond*** all ***reason***. 賃金と資材が途方もなく騰貴した. ¶open to attacks and criticisms ***by reason*** of its novelty それが斬新なために攻撃非難を受ける ‖ be refuted ***by reason*** 理詰めにされる. 【類】***by reason*** of war / ***by reason*** of the fact that ... / The arrangement was cancelled ***by reason*** of his illness. / Today the great nations exist mainly ***by reason*** of their trade and commerce / ***By reason*** of its numbers, intelligence, and discipline the German Socialist Democracy takes the foremost place among the labor organizations of the world. ‖ ***by reason*** of its subject その問題が問題なので. ¶***for*** that (this) ***reason*** それゆえに, そういう訳で ‖ ***for reasons*** of health (unavoidable circumstances) 健康上(など)の理由で ‖ ***for*** a ***reason*** suggested earlier in this article 本文の前段で述べた理由で ‖ ***for*** one ***reason*** or another とにかく, いずれにせよ ‖ chiefly ***for*** (=***through***) ***reasons*** of convenience (=expediency) 主として便宜上 ‖ ***for reasons*** best known to himself [他の人には分からない]なにか彼の都合で ‖ ***for reasons*** which concern no one but myself 私自身以外のだれにも関係のない理由で ‖ ***for reasons*** not known somehow どういうものか. ¶***from*** the ***reasons*** I have cited elsewhere in detail 別の所で詳細に述べた理由で ‖ largely ***from*** sentimental ***reasons*** 主として感情から. ¶one bereft ***of reason*** 気の狂った人. ¶It is ***out of*** all ***reason***. それは全く狂気のさただ. ¶try to bring him ***to reason*** 彼を理性に立戻らせようと努める ‖ it stands ***to reason*** that ... ...ということは理の当然である ‖ contrary ***to reason*** 理に反して. ¶He complains ***with reason***. 彼が不平を言うのも無理はない. ☞現代語では He complains, and ***with reasons***. が通例. ‖ in accordance ***with reason*** 道理に従って ‖ he says ***with*** better ***reason*** that ... 彼は...と言っているがその方が理屈にかなっている ‖ Nothing can ***with reason*** be urged in justification of revenge. どんなに論じてもあだ討を正当化することは無理だ. 【類】justify (support) ... ***with reason***. ¶it is quite ***within reason*** to suggest that ... ...ということを提議するには全く十分の理由がある. ¶it is not altogether ***without reason*** to believe that ... ...と信じるのは理由のないことではない.

P² There is a ***reason behind*** the popularity of ... ...の人気は裏面に理由がある. ¶There is no ***reason for*** it. それにはなんの訳もない. 【類】the ***reason for*** this is probably to be found partly in ... / The ***reasons for*** the delay were threefold. / one of the ***reasons for*** the success of this system is that ... / The ***reason for*** this is not far to seek. ‖ ***reasons for*** and ***against*** doing a thing あることをするについての賛否の理由. ¶The ***reason of*** this is obvious. この訳は明白である. ¶unless there are strong ***reasons to*** the contrary それと反対の有力な理由があるのでなければ.

O there is ***reason*** to believe that ... ...と信ずべき理由がある. ¶The ***reasons*** why ... are not far to seek. なぜ...であるかの理由は分かり難くはない. ¶it stands to ***reason*** that ... ...は理の当然である.

reason, *v.* 論断する, 推論する.

M ***reason badly*** 誤った推論をやる. ¶***reason out*** a conclusion 結論を出す ‖ ***reason out*** the answer to the question その問題の解決を考え出す. 【類】***reason out*** the case. ¶***properly reason*** a proposition 適正に提案を論証する. ¶***reason soundly*** しっかりした推論をやる. ¶***well reason*** a statement 陳述を十分理論づける.

M² ***reason*** a person ***down*** 人を説き伏せる.

P ***reason about*** ... ...について推論する. ¶***reason against*** ... ...に反対な推論をやる. ¶***reason by*** syllogisms 三段論法で論じる. ¶***reason for*** ... ...を弁明する. ¶***reason from*** false premises 間違った前提から推論する. 【類】***reason from*** partiality (justice) / ***reason from*** experience. ¶***reason from*** the cause ***to*** the effect 原因から結果へと論究する. 【類】***reason from*** general laws ***to*** particular cases. ¶***reason in*** a circle 悪循環的に論じる. ¶He was ***reasoned into*** compliance. 彼は説き伏せられて承諾した. ¶***reason on*** a subject ある問題について論じる ‖ To ***reason on*** such a subject is of little use. こうした問題を論じるのは余り益がない. ¶***reason*** a person ***out of*** his anxiety (doing something) 道理を説いて懸念(など)を放棄させる. ¶***reason with*** a person ***on*** ... ...の問題で人と論じ合う. 【類】I tried to ***reason with*** him / You might as well ***reason with*** a horse [as ***with*** him].

reasonable, *a.* 理屈に合った.

M You aren't ***very reasonable*** if you expect children to stop romping about. 子供をふざけないようにしようたってそれは無理だ.

P ***reasonable in*** price 手ごろな値の.

reasoner, *n.* 推論家, 論究者.

Q an ***acute reasoner*** 明敏な推論家. ¶a ***close reasoner*** 綿密な論究者. ¶a ***cool reasoner*** 冷静な推論家.

reasoning, *n.* 推理, 推論, 理論.

V The ***reasonings*** you ***advance*** are those of an ignorant and stupid child! 君の述べる理論はまるで無知暗愚な子供の理論だ. ¶***detect*** the faulty ***reasoning*** 誤った推論を見破る. ¶***following*** this ***reasoning*** to a logical conclusion would be to state that ... この推考に従って論理的結論に到達しようとすると...と述べることになるだろう. ¶Its logical ***reasoning*** cannot be ***gainsaid***. その論理的推論は反ばくし得ない.

V² the same ***reasoning applies*** to ... 同じ論法が...にも当てはまる.

Q *bad reasoning* へたな推論. ¶ ***clear reasoning*** 明りょうな論法. ¶ ***deductive reasoning*** 演えき的論法. ¶The *reasoning* is ***fallacious.*** その推論は間違っている. ¶an instance of ***false reasoning*** 誤った推論の例. ¶***faulty reasoning*** 間違った論法. ¶***inductive reasoning*** 帰納的論法. ¶This is ***plausible*** *reasoning.* これは誠しやかな論法である. ¶by ***proper*** *reasoning* 正しい推論によって. ¶The *reasoning* seems ***rational.*** その論法は合理的であるようだ. ¶***sound*** *reasoning* しっかりした論法. ¶***sufficient*** and ***conclusive*** *reasoning* 充実して決定的な推論. ¶***wrong*** or ***faulty*** *reasoning* 間違ったまたは欠点のある論法.

P ***by*** the same *reasoning* これと同じ筆法で. ¶in a chain ***of*** *reasoning* 順次の推論で. ‖ the faculties ***of*** *reasoning* 推理力.

P^2 *reasoning* ***from*** analogy 類推による論法. ¶She knew that all the false *reasoning* ***in*** the world could never make wrong right. 彼女は間違った論法を幾ら重ねても邪を正になし得ないことを知っていた.

reassure, *v.* 気を取直させる, 安心させる.

M I was ***quickly*** *reassured* by his saying so. 彼がそう言ったので私は途端にほっとした.

rebate, *n.* 割戻し(リベート); 割引.

V ***allow*** a *rebate* of ... upon ... ...に...の払戻しをする. ¶***give*** *rebates* 割引をする.

Q^2 ***pro rata*** *rebate* あん分比例割戻し. ¶***tax*** *rebates* 税金の払戻し. ¶a ***10%*** *rebate* for immediate payment 即時払いに対し一割の割戻し.

rebel, *n.* 謀反人, 反逆人.

V ***chastise*** a *rebel* 反乱者を懲らす. ¶***defeat*** the *rebels* 反乱軍を打破る. ¶***suppress*** a *rebel* 反逆者を鎮圧する.

V^2 The *rebels* ***sprang up*** (=***arose***). 謀反が起った.

P^2 a *rebel* ***in*** the home 不幸者.

rebel, *v.* 謀反する, 反逆する.

P *rebel* ***against*** the government (ruler) 政府(など)にそむく. ¶*rebel* ***from*** ... ...にたて突く.

rebellion, *n.* 謀反, 反逆.

V ***crush out*** a *rebellion* 謀反を鎮圧する. ¶***excite*** a *rebellion* among the people 人民の間に反逆を教唆する. ¶the *rebellion* ***headed*** by ... ...を首領とする反逆. ¶***incite*** *rebellion* 謀反を扇動する. ¶speedily ***put down*** (=***suppress***) a *rebellion* すみやかに謀反を鎮定する. 【類】After much bloodshed the *rebellion* was ***put down.*** ¶***quash*** (=***quell***) a *rebellion* 謀反を鎮める. ¶***raise*** a *rebellion* 謀反を起す. ¶The *rebellion* was successfully ***repressed.*** 謀反をうまく鎮めた. ¶***stamp out*** a *rebellion* 謀反を撲滅する. ¶a *rebellion* ***broke out*** under ... ...を首領とする謀反がぼっ発した.

Q the ***Christian*** *rebellion* in the domain of Arima 有馬藩のキリシタン反乱. ¶The crew was ready for ***open*** *rebellion.* 乗組員は公然反乱の準備ができていた. ¶a ***simmering*** *rebellion* 徐々に盛り上った反乱.

P the army was then ***in*** *rebellion* against ... その軍隊は当時...に対し反乱を起していた ‖ rise ***in*** *rebellion* 謀反を起す.

P^2 a *rebellion* ***against*** rightful authority (nature) 正当な権威(など)に対する謀反 ‖ *Rebellion* ***to*** tyrant is obedience to God. 暴君に対する反逆は神に対する従順だ.

rebellious, *a.* 逆心のある, 反逆的な.

P *rebellious* ***to*** (=***against***) lawful authority 合法の権威に従わない.

rebirth, *n.* 再生, 復活.

V ***prevent*** the *rebirth* of Japanese militarism 日本の軍国主義の復活を予防する.

Q a ***moral*** *rebirth* 道徳的再生.

rebound, *n.* はね反り, 反動.

Q a ***spontaneous*** *rebound* of sympathy in all the joys and sorrows あらゆる喜びや悲しみに対する同情の自然的発露.

P^2 a *rebound* ***from*** a depression 失望からの反動. ¶hit (catch) a ball ***on*** the *rebound* バウンドした球を打つ(捕える).

rebound, *v.* はねかえる(バウンドする), はねかえる.

P *rebound* ***from*** the ground 地面からはねかえる. 【類】The ball *rebounded* ***from*** his racket ***into*** the net. ¶it *rebounds* ***to*** the honor of Japan that she ... 日本が...ということは日本の名誉になる ‖ *rebound* ***to*** the credit of ... ...の信用を増す. ¶One's evil doings will *rebound* ***upon*** oneself. 悪行はわが身に戻って来る.

rebuff, *n.* 打返し; 拒絶.

Q a ***polite*** but ***decided*** *rebuff* 丁重ながら断固たる拒絶.

P meet ***with*** a *rebuff* はねつけられる.

rebuild, *v.* 再建する, 改築する.

P *rebuild* a town ***from*** ruin 町を再建する.

O *rebuid* a wall (gate, house) 壁(など)を改築する.

rebuke, *n.* 非難, けん責, しっ責.

V ***utter*** a gentle *rebuke* やさしくしっ責する.

Q a ***quiet*** *rebuke* 穏かなしっ責. ¶a ***rough*** *rebuke* 激しいしっ責. ¶a ***scathing*** *rebuke* 名誉き損の非難. ¶a ***smart*** (=***strong***) *rebuke* 鋭い非難.

P ***without*** *rebuke* 非難されずに.

rebuke, *v.* しかる, とがめる.

M *rebuke* ***sharply*** 痛烈に非難する. ¶***Sternly*** and ***imperiously*** *rebuke* a person きびしくかさにかかって人を非難する.

P *rebuke* a person ***for*** what he has done 人のやったことを非難する.

rebuttal, *n.* 反ばく.

Q^2 ***labor*** *rebuttal* 労働者の反ばく. ¶a ***seven-point*** *rebuttal* 七点の論ばく.

recall, *n.* 呼返し, 召還; 〖政治〗リコール.

P It is gone ***beyond*** *recall.* それは去ってしまって呼返すことができない(機会など). ¶a drive ***for*** the *recall* of their Mayor 市長のリコール運動.

P^2 a *recall* ***to*** real life 夢うつつからの覚せい.

recall, *v.* 呼び戻す, 想起する, 回想する; 〖政治〗リコールする.

M *recall* ***distinctly*** はっきりと思い起す. ¶*recall* a scene ***vividly*** to one's mind はっきりその光景を記憶に呼び戻す.

P associations *recalled* ***by*** a word 語によって想起される連想 ‖ The Mayor was *recalled* ***by*** voting. 市長は票決でリコールされた. ¶we would *recall* ***to*** your remembrance the fact that ... ...という事実を想起していただきたい. 【類】*recalled* ***to*** life / it *recalls* us ***to*** the great truth that ... / *recall* it ***to*** our memory / the word ... *recalls* ***to*** the mind the picture of ... / *recall* a person ***to*** a sense of duties (義務の観念) ‖ He was *recalled* ***to*** Japan by cable. 彼は電報で日本に召還された.

recantation, *n.* 言い直し, 取消し; 変説.

V ***compel*** *recantation* 取消を迫る. ¶***feign*** a *recantation* of one's faith 自己の信条の改変を装う.

recapture, *v.* 取返す, 取戻す.

P *recaptured* ***from*** the enemy 敵から奪還した.

recast, *v.* 改鋳する; 書き直す.

P *recast* bells ***into*** guns 鐘を大砲に改鋳する.

O *recast* a sentence or two 文を一二カ所書き直す.

recede, *v.* 退く, 引込む.

P *recede* ***from*** one's position 職を退く ‖ *recede* ***from*** a contract 契約から手を引く. ¶The incident *receded* ***into*** the background. その事件は世人から忘れられた.

receipt, *n.* 領収, 受領; 受取書; 製法, 料理法.

V Kindly ***acknowledge*** [your] *receipt.* 御入手のむねを御通知下さい. 【類】***acknowledge*** the *receipt* of ... ¶***count up*** the cash *receipts* for the day 当日の現金受取を計算する. ¶***deposit*** a *receipt* with the library when lending out books 本を貸出すときその図書館に受取書を保存する. ¶***forward*** a *receipt* to ... ...に受取証を送る. ¶***get*** one's *receipt* for ... ...に対する領収書をもらう. ¶Will you kindly ***give*** me a *receipt* for it? どうぞその領収書を下さいませんか. ¶A *receipt* must be ***issued*** for the amount collected. 集金高に対して受取を出さねばならない. ¶***make*** one ***out*** a *receipt* 人に受取を出す. ¶***sign*** a *receipt* for ... ...の受取に署名する. ¶***take*** his *receipt* 先方から受取をもらう. ¶I ***want*** a *receipt* for ... 私は...の受取が欲しい.

Q a ***capital*** *receipt* for cooking oysters かきの素敵な料理法. ¶***gross*** *receipts* 総収入高. ¶***illegal*** *receipt* of rationing 配給の不正受配.

Q^2 an ***advance*** *receipt* 前受金. ¶***box-office*** *receipts* [映画館など] 切符売上高. ¶***gate*** *receipts* [野球などの] 入場料. ¶***net*** *receipts* 正味手取高. ¶a ***suspense*** *receipt* 仮受金. ¶***theatre*** *receipts* 劇場の入場料. ¶***traffic*** *receipts* [鉄道の] 運賃収入.

P We are ***in*** *receipt* of your favor dated the 9th inst. 本月九日付の貴書簡正に受取りました. ‖ he is ***in*** *receipt* of a wage of ... 彼は...の賃金を受取った. ¶I will pay the postman $1 ***on*** *receipt.* 品物引換えに郵便配達人に一ドル払います. ‖ samples sent ***on*** *receipt* of return postage—8 yen 郵券八円を受取って送った見本. 【類】pay money ***on*** *receipt* of an article / immediately ***on*** *receipt* of ... / ***on*** the *receipt* of a postcard (remittance, postage) / I will pay the money ***on*** *receipt* of the goods. / ***on*** *receipt* of the price above stated. ¶***since*** the *receipt* of this news この通知を受取ってから. ¶Ledger accounts will be opened ***upon*** *receipt* of satisfactory reference. 掛勘定取引は当方において適当と認める御指名を受取り次第開始します.

P² a *receipt* ***for*** money (payment) 金(など)の受取書. ¶*receipts* ***from*** sale of ... ...の売上金. ¶I am in almost daily *receipt* ***of*** letters commenting on ... 私は...批評の手紙を毎日のように受取っている.

receive, *v.* 受取る, もらう, 受ける; 迎える.

M A couple of days later I *received* it ***back***. それから二日ばかり経てそれが私の所に返送された. 【類】It will be *received* ***back*** if found unsatisfactory. / *receive* ***back*** the powers belonging to them under the constitution. ¶be *received* ***coldly*** (***warmly***) 冷たく(暖かく)迎えられる. ¶He was most ***cordially*** *received*. 彼はいとも丁寧に迎えられた. ¶*receive* a story ***credulously***＝swallow a story 話を直ちに真に受ける. ¶The book was ***favorably*** *received*. その本は評判がよかった. ¶it is a ***generally*** *received* opinion that ... ...は一般に認められた意見である. ¶*receive* a person ***graciously*** 人をいんぎんに迎える. ¶He was ***hospitably*** *received*. 彼は丁重に迎えられた. ¶The book was ***kindly*** *received* by the Press and by the public. その本は新聞にも一般社会にも受けがよかった. ¶Any suggestion will be ***thankfully*** *received*. 御注意は有難く承ります. ¶Even when I call, he *receives* ***unwillingly***. 私が訪問する時ですら彼はいやいやながら迎える. ¶His recent work was very ***warmly*** *received*. 彼の最近出した作品は非常に歓迎された. ¶The matter might ***well*** *receive* the serious attention of the authorities. その件は当然当局のまじめな注意を受けてよいことだ.

P He *received* it ***as*** a present. 彼はそれを進物としてもらった. ‖*receive* it ***as*** security それをかたに取る. 【類】*receive* ***as*** a gift from a lord. ¶injuries *received* ***at*** the hands of ... ...から受けた危害 ‖Applications must be *received* ***at*** the office not later than 1 p.m. on December 31, 1938. 申込書は一九三八年十二月三十一日午後一時までに事務所に届くようにせねばならない. ¶announcement *received* ***by*** telegraph 電報で受けた通知 ‖The magazine is *received* ***by*** members free. その雑誌は会員には無料で配布する. ¶*receive* a letter ***from*** one's father 父から手紙を受取る. ¶I trust that this answer will be *received* ***in*** the spirit in which it was written (＝given). この返事は筆者と同じ心持で受けられることと私は信じます. ‖He was *received* ***in*** audience by the Emperor. 彼は天皇陛下に拝謁を賜わった. ‖the amount *received* ***in*** taxes 受取った税額. 【類】*receive* persons ***in*** one's house for the pupose of education. ¶money *received* ***into*** the Exchequer 国庫に収納した金 ‖*receive* a person ***into*** one's house for the purpose of education 教育の目的で人を家にあずかる. 【類】*receive* a stranger for shelter / *receive* one ***into*** a hospital. ¶Information has not yet been *received* ***of*** the exact date. 正確な日取の通知がまだ来ていない. ‖*Received* ***of*** Mr. Smith the sum of 5,000 yen for house rent from the first of January to the first of April. スミス氏から一月一日から四月一日までの家賃五千円正に受取りました. ¶*receive* a letter ***through*** one ある人の手を経て手紙を受取る. ¶He was *received* ***with*** cheers on rising to reply. 答辞を述べようとして立ったとき彼はかっさいをもって迎えられた. 【類】The speech was *received* ***with*** loud cheering. / The book was *received* ***with*** favor (好評). / His book was *received* ***with*** universal praise. / The statement was *received* ***with*** great enthusiasm. / his remarks were *received* ***with*** murmurs of dissent (不満のささやき) from ... ‖He was *received* ***with*** respectful silence by the crowd. 彼は群集から厳しゅくに迎えられた. ‖The two brothers were *received* ***with*** honour by the Mongolian Prince. 二人の兄弟はモーコ王国賓の礼遇を受けた.

receiver, *n.* 受話器.

V ***apply*** (＝***put***) the *receiver* to one's ear 受話器を耳にあてる. ¶***hang up*** the *receiver* 受話器をフックに掛ける. ¶***hold on*** one's *receiver* 受話器をあて続ける. ¶***lift*** the *receiver* 受話器を取上げる. ¶She ***picked up*** the *receiver* and answered instantly. 彼女は受話器をはずしてすぐに答えた. ¶***remove*** the *receiver* from the hook 受話器を台からはずす. ¶***take up*** (***down***) the *receiver* 受話器を取る.

Q an ***official*** *receiver* 破産管財人.

Q² a ***radio*** *receiver*＝a radio receiving set ラジオ受信器.

P² the *receiver* ***of*** an action 行動の受身になった人.

recent, *a.* 最近の.

M be of ***comparatively*** *recent* date 比較的最近である. 【類】within ***comparatively*** *recent* times.

recently, *ad.* 近ごろ, このごろ.

M ***quite*** *recently* ほんの近ごろ.

M² ***as*** *recently* as a quarter of a century ago 二十五年前という近いころに.

P It was so hot ***until*** *recently*. ついこのごろまで実に暑かった.

receptacle, *n.* 入れ物, 容器.

Q² a ***garbage*** *receptacle* ごみ入れ.

P² a *receptacle* ***for*** ... ...の容器.

reception, *n.* 受取; 取立て; 歓迎, 接待; [歓迎]会(リセプション); 接見.

V an enthusiastic *reception* was ***accorded*** ... ...が熱心に迎えられた. ¶His *reception* is ***arranged*** for Monday. 氏の歓迎は月曜にきめられた. ¶The book should ***find*** a ready *reception* and a keen appreciation. その本はたちまち熱心な歓迎を受くべきである. ¶***get*** a cold *reception* 冷遇される. ¶***give*** a *reception* リセプションを開く. 【類】A *reception* was ***given*** in honor of the new Ambassador. ¶He ***had*** a most hearty *reception* from the crowd. 彼は群集から心からの歓迎を受けた. ‖I am afraid you have ***had*** but a poor *reception*. 君はほんの型だけの接待を受けたのじゃなかろうか. ¶***hold*** a *reception* at the Mansion House [ロンドン]市長邸宅でリセプションを開く.

Q a ***chill***[***ing***] (＝***frosty***) *reception* 冷淡な接待. ¶be given a ***cold*** (***warm***) *reception* すこぶる冷(厚)遇される. ¶a ***cordial*** *reception* 心からの歓迎. ¶a ***cyclonic popular*** *reception* 民衆の旋風的歓迎. ¶He was given a ***dry*** *reception*. 彼は冷かな接待を受けた. ¶receive ... an ***enthusiastic*** *reception* ...を熱烈に歓迎する. ¶a ***farewell*** *reception* to ... ...に対する送別の宴. ¶give a ***favorable*** *reception* to the publication その出版物を歓迎する. 【類】the ***favorable*** *reception* with which this book was honored by the public. ¶a ***flattering*** *reception* こびへつらう接待. ¶a ***frank*** *reception* of information 知識の率直な受入れ. ¶he met with a most ***friendly*** *reception* from ... 彼は...から友情のこもった歓迎を受けた. ¶the ***general*** *reception* of his theory 彼の学説の一般の気受け. ¶meet a ***generous*** *reception* which was accorded to its larger predecessor [辞書など] 一層大部な前著に与えられたと同じく大歓迎を受ける. ¶a ***heart-warming*** *reception* 心の暖まる(手厚い)歓迎. ¶The book met an ***indulgent*** and ***sympathetic*** *reception*. その本は寛大と同情とをもって迎えられた. ¶a ***noisy, demonstrative*** *reception* 騒々しいこれ見よがしの歓迎. ¶The American troops had a ***rousing*** *reception* in the streets of London. 米国の軍隊はロンドンの市街で熱狂的な歓迎を受けた. ¶a ***Royal*** (an ***Imperial***) *reception* 王(帝)室のリセプション. ¶a very ***satisfactory*** *reception* いかにも行き届いた接待ぶり. ¶The hard stones gave him a very ***severe*** *reception*. 堅い石に当ってひどい目に会った(まどから街に投げられた犬など). ¶a ***terrific*** *reception* was accorded ... [兵士慰問などで]圧倒的な接待を受けた. ¶He gave me such a ***warm*** *reception*. 盛んにお愛想をしてくれた.

Q² an ***afternoon*** *reception* with dancing ダンスのある午後の接待. ¶on the occasion of the ***New Year*** *reception* 新年宴会に際し. ¶***radio*** transmission and *reception* ラジオの発信及び受信. ¶a ***wedding*** *reception* 結婚披露会. ¶a ***welcome*** (＝welcoming) *reception* 歓迎会.

P ***at*** a *reception* held in honor of ... ...のために催された接待会で ‖remit ***at*** the *reception* of the goods 品物を受取ると同時に送金する. ¶meet ***with*** a cordial *reception* 丁重な接待を受ける.

P² the *reception* of the ladies of the Diplomatic Body ***by*** the Empress Dowager 皇太后陛下の外交団婦人御招宴. ¶a *reception* ***for*** new students 新入生の歓迎会. ¶He has met with the favorable *reception* ***from*** both the press and the public. 彼は新聞及び一般から好遇を受けた. ¶a *reception* ***to*** invited guests 招待客への接待.

receptive, *a.* 容れる, 受ける, 受容力ある.

P a mind *receptive of* new ideas 新思想を受け入れられる心. ¶The magazine is *receptive* ***to*** new writers. その雑誌は新作家を歓迎する.

recess, *n.* 休み, 中休み; 奥, 奥深い所.

V ***declare*** a *recess* 休憩を宣する. ¶A *recess* of ten minutes is ***given*** for recreation. 十分の休息を与える. ¶***take*** a *recess* 休憩する. 【類】a *recess* of half an hour was then ***taken***, after which ...

Q a ***curtained*** *recess* カーテンを下げた休憩所. ¶a ***fifteen minutes'*** *recess* 十五分の休憩. ¶in the ***innermost*** *recess* of their nature they have a belief that ... 彼らはその心の奥底に...という信念を持っている.

Q^2 before Parliament reconvene after the ***Christmas*** *recess* クリスマス休会後の議会再会前. ¶the ***Christmas holiday*** *recess* クリスマス休暇. ¶a ***mountain*** *recess* 山奥. ¶during the ***summer*** *recess* of Congress 米議会の夏季休会中. 【類】Parliament reconvened after the ***summer*** *recess.* ¶the ***Yuletide*** (***New Year's***) *recess* クリスマス(新年)の休暇.

P The children run out and play on the playground ***at*** *recess.* 児童らは休み時間に運動場にかけ出して遊ぶ. ¶hidden away ***in*** the green *recesses* of Regent's Park リーゼント公園の緑深い所に隠れて. 【類】deep ***in*** the *recess* of a forest.

P^2 a *recess* ***for*** holding ... ...を入れておく引込んだ所. ¶a *recess* ***in*** a room へやの引込んだ所. ¶in the inmost *recesses* ***of*** the Alps アルプス山の一番奥の所に. ¶a *recess* ***on*** the shore 海岸の入り込んだ所.

cess, *v.* 休憩する.

The session will *recess* ***at*** 5 p.m. 会議は午後五時休憩となる.

cession, *n.* 一時的な不況.

Q^2 [a] ***business recession*** 一時的事業不振.

recipe, *n.* 処方書, 薬方; (料理の)作り方.

P sauce prepared ***from*** the *recipe* of a nobleman in the country 地方の貴族の仕方書から調製したソース.

P^2 a number of *recipes* ***for*** cooking ... ...を料理する方法一括 ‖ a *recipe* ***for*** a powder 火薬の処方書 ‖ a *recipe* ***for*** success in life 成功の秘けつ.

recipient, *n.* 受領者.

Q^2 a ***degree*** *recipient* 学位受領者. ¶an ***honorary degree*** *recipient* 名誉学位受領者.

reciprocate, *v.* 交換する; 報いる.

P In return I will *reciprocate* ***to*** the best of my ability. その返礼に私のできるだけのことを致しましょう.

O *reciprocate* one's kindness (affection) 親切(など)に報いる.

reciprocity, *n.* 相互, 相互主義.

P ***by*** *reciprocity* we are going to ... 相互主義によってわれわれは...しようとしている.

recital, *n.* 暗誦, 吟誦, 朗誦; 独奏(唱)会(リサイタル); 説話, 詳述.

V ***give*** song *recitals* 歌の独唱会をやる. ¶***have*** a phonographic *recital* レコード・コンサートをやる.

Q mere ***frigid*** *recitals* of facts, dreary and uninspiring 退屈な面白くない事実の単に固苦しい詳説. ¶a ***Shakespearian*** *recital* シェークスピアの作品朗誦.

Q^2 a ***Chopin*** *recital* ショパン・リサイタル. ¶a ***music*** *recital* リサイタル. ¶an ***organ*** *recital* オルガンの演奏(会). ¶give a ***poem*** *recital* 詩を朗読する. ¶a ***song*** (***piano, violin***) *recital* 歌(など)独唱(奏)会.

P^2 a *recital* ***of*** one's own sufferings 自分のかん難物語.

recitation, *n.* 暗誦, 吟誦.

V ***give*** English *recitations* 英語の暗誦をやる.

Q^2 ***classroom*** *recitation* クラスの授業.

P^2 *recitations* ***in*** English 英語の暗誦. 【類】a *recitation* ***of*** poetry.

recite, *v.* 暗誦する, 朗誦する, 吟誦する.

P *recite* a poem ***from*** memory 詩をそらで朗吟する.

reciter, *n.* 語り手.

Q^2 a ***joruri*** *reciter* 義太夫語り.

reckless, *a.* 不注意な, 向う見ずな.

P *reckless* ***of*** the consequences 結果におかまいなく.

recklessness, *n.* 不注意, 無とん着, 怠慢.

Q spend money with ***absolute*** *recklessness* 全く無鉄砲に金を使う.

reckon, *v.* 数える, 計算する; 見なす.

M *reckoned* ***loosely*** at a hundred thousand ざっと十万にのぼる. ¶I *reckoned* ***short.*** 私の予想は控え目だった(それほどとは思わなかった). ¶*reckon* ***up*** the gains as well as the losses 損失及び利益を計上する. ¶It is *reckoned* very ***valuable.*** それははなはだ貴重だと考えられている.

P The basil is *reckoned* ***among*** sweet herbs. めぼうきは甘い草の部に入れられている. ‖ They are *reckoned* ***among*** civilized people. 彼らは文明人の仲間だと考えられている. 【類】You may *reckon* me ***among*** your patrons. ¶The railway has ... miles of track, *reckoned* ***as*** single track. その鉄道は単線に換算して...マイルの延長がある. ¶*reckoning* an ox ***at*** £10 雄牛一頭十ポンドと見て. ¶Charges are *reckoned* ***by*** distance. 料金は距離で計算する. ¶*reckoned* ***from*** the present 現在から計算して. ¶The civilized world *reckons* its time ***from*** that first Christmas Day. 文明世界は時日をあの最初のクリスマスの日から計算する. ¶That is a legacy which cannot be *reckoned* ***in*** pounds, shillings, and pence. それはポンド・シリング・ペンスをもって勘定し得ない遺産である. ¶I *reckon* ***on*** your being there in time. あなたが時間に間に合うようにそこに行くことを当てにしています. ¶In Belgium, Italy, Spain, and Portugal, time is *reckoned* ***to*** 24 o'clock. ベルギー・イタリア・スペイン及びポルトガルでは時間を(午前・午後各十二時に数えないで)二十四時に数える. ¶We *reckon* ***upon*** it. われわれはそれを当てにする. ¶The Chinese and Russian traders *reckon* so rapidly and correctly ***with*** ball-frames. 中国やロシアの商人はそろばんでじん速かつ正確に計算する. ‖ Socialism is a force to be *reckoned* ***with.*** 社会主義は慎重に考慮すべき力である. ‖ a power to be *reckoned* ***with*** 頼りになる力(機関紙など). ¶*reckon* ***without*** one's host 誤算する, 早合点する.

reckoning, *n.* 計算, 勘定; 計算書, つけ.

V ***lose*** one's *reckoning* of time 時間の立つのが分からなくなる. ¶***pay off*** old *reckoning* 古い勘定を支払う. ¶***settle*** one's *reckoning* (=account) 勘定を済ませる.

Q ***inclusive*** and ***exclusive*** *reckoning* 四捨五入的計算. ¶the tenth century of ***Western*** *reckoning* 西洋の計算による第十世紀.

P He is eighteen ***according to*** Japanese *reckoning.* 彼は日本流に数え(数え年)十八歳になる. ¶***in*** their *reckoning* 彼らの計算では. ¶He was ***out of*** his *reckoning.* 彼の計算が外れた.

reclaim, *n.* 矯正, 改心.

P He is ***past*** *reclaim.* 彼はもはや矯正ができない.

reclaim, *v.* 取戻す, 改心させる; 埋立てる.

P the land *reclaimed* ***from*** the lake (sea) 湖水(など)埋立地 ‖ woman *reclaimed* ***from*** a life of sin 罪悪の生活から改心した女. ¶*reclaimed* ***to*** civilization 文明に引戻された.

reclamation, *n.* 埋立.

P^2 *reclamation* ***of*** the foreshore (=water front) 海岸の埋立.

recline, *v.* 横たわはる, よりかかる.

M *recline* ***comfortably*** on a sofa reading a newspaper 新聞を読みながら気持よくソファによりかかる.

P *recline* [oneself] ***against*** the wall 壁によりかかる. ¶He *reclined* ***on*** a rug (the grass). 彼は敷物(など)の上に横になった. 【類】*recline* one's head ***on*** ...

recognition, *n.* 認知, 認識; 鑑賞.

V ***achieve*** *recognition* 認められる. ¶***claim*** a *recognition* 承認を要求する. ¶***command*** the *recognition* of the public 一般から認められるようになる. ¶***compel*** *recognition* of ... ...に認めさせる. ¶***deserve*** grateful *recognition* 感謝される価値がある. 【類】***deserve*** *recognition* for ... ¶He passed them rather hurriedly with his head down, as if anxious to ***escape*** *recognition.* 彼らは見られるのを避けたいかのごとくに頭をたれてかなり急いで彼らのそばを通り過ぎた. ¶The slang expression has not yet ***found*** *recognition* in the dictionary. その俗語はまだ辞書に採録されていない. ¶***gain*** the *recognition* of ... ...から認められる. 【類】***gain*** international *recognition* / He is rapidly ***gaining*** *recognition* as one of the most sympathetic interpreters of the genius of the race. ¶this ***gave*** him world-wide *recognition* as ... このために彼は広く世界的に...として認められるに至った. ¶***make*** some *recognition* of the services rendered by ... なにかの方法で...の功労を表彰する. ¶***obtain*** universal *recognition* 世界的に認められるようになる. ¶***pay*** due *recognition* to ... ...を十分認める. ¶He has not ***received*** *recognition* that is his due. 彼は当然受くべき認識を受けていない. 【類】***receive*** the *recognition* naturally to be expected from ... ¶***secure*** the *recognition* of Irish degrees by London hospitals ロンドンの病院でアイルラ

ンドの学位を認めてもらう. ¶*win recognition* from the public 世間から認められる.【類】At Cambridge modern studies are beginning to *win recognition.*

V² Slowly but surely there *dawned* the *recognition* of its need. 徐々にしかし確実にその必要が認められるようになった.

Q He is worthy of more ***appreciative recognition*** than he has as yet received. 彼はこれまで受けたよりも一層感謝を受ける価値がある. ¶a ***clear recognition*** of conditions as they exist あるがままの状態に対するはっきりした認識. ¶insist on ***complete recognition*** of our rights われわれの権利を完全に認めるよう主張する. ¶receive ***enthusiastic*** *recognition* 熱心な鑑賞を受ける. ¶He obtained a most ***flattering*** *recognition* of his efforts. 彼はその努力をばか丁寧にほめられた. ¶a ***frank*** *recognition* 率直な認識. ¶give it ***governmental*** *recognition* それを公認する. ¶in ***grateful*** *recognition* of your kindness 御親切を有難く思って. ¶have ***greater*** *recognition* 一層十分に認識される. ¶there is a ***growing*** *recognition* that … …ということが段段認識されつつある. ¶in ***honorable*** *recognition* of their brave defense 彼らの勇敢なる防衛を表彰して. ¶an ***informal official*** *recognition* of … …の非公式承認. ¶***literary*** *recognition* [文筆を執る政治家などの]文士としての認識. ¶be given an ***official*** *recognition* 公式に承認される. ¶***popular*** *recognition* 民衆の認識. ¶***post-facto*** *recognition* 事後承諾. ¶secure ***public*** *recognition* of … …を一般に認めてもらう ‖ escape ***public*** *recognition* 人目につかない.【類】***public*** *recognitin* of his services to science. ¶***social*** *recognition* 社会の認識. ¶not received ***sufficient*** *recognition* 十分に認められなかった. ¶***tacit*** *recognition* 黙認. ¶do dot receive ***universal*** *recognition* 一般に認められていない.【類】it has achieved the ***universal*** *recognition* that … ¶achieve ***wide*** *recognition* 広く認められる. ¶win ***world(nation)-wide*** *recognition* 世界(全国)的認識を得る.

Q² achieve ***dictionary*** *recognition* [新語など]辞書に採り上げられる. ¶***State*** *recognition* 公認; 国としての認識. ¶***union*** *recognition* 労組の承認.

P a building burned ***beyond*** *recognition* 見分けがつかないほどに焼けた建物. ¶bow ***in*** *recognition* 頭を下げてあいさつする ‖ ***in*** *recognition* of his services to the shipwrecked crew of the … 難破船…の船員に対する彼の奉仕を認めて. ¶He certainly deserved such a mark ***of*** *recognition.* 確かに彼はそうした報酬のしるしを受ける資格があった. ¶change ***past*** (=beyond) *recognition* 認識ができないまでに変る.

P² a *recognition* ***by*** the State of honorable service rendered to the nation 国家に尽したりっぱな功績を国家に認められること. ¶the *recognition* ***of*** the Soviet government 労農政府の承認. ¶He won *recognition* ***through*** his investigation in physiology. 彼は生理学研究で世に認められた. ¶in tardy *recognition* ***to*** his distinguished services to science 彼の科学に対する功績をおそまきながら認めて.

recognizable, *a.* 認めうる.

M be ***barely*** *recognizable* ほとんど人の目にとまらない.

recognizance, *n.* 承認.

Q enter ***into*** a *recognizance* 誓約する. ¶***upon*** his own *recognizance* he will … 彼は自分から認めて…するだろう.

recognize, *v.* 認める, 承認する.

M refuse to *recognize* it ***any longer*** もはやそれを認めようとしない. ¶***frankly*** *recognize* 率直に認める. ¶***fully*** *recognize* 十分に認める. ¶***gratefully*** *recognize* the kindness of … …の親切を心から感謝する. ¶can ***hardly*** *recognize* a person 人をみそれる. ¶He is *recognized* ***internationally*** as an authority in this field. 彼はこの方面における権威として国際的に認められている. ¶***officially*** *recognized* as … …と公認されて. ¶be ***sufficiently*** (***insufficiently***) *recognized* 十分認められている(られない). ¶***universally*** *recognized* as … 広く…と認められて. ¶be only ***unofficially*** *recognized* 非公式にしか認められていない.

P Landscape architecture is today *recognized* ***as*** one of the fine arts. 景園建築は今日では美術の一つと認められている.【類】it is now *recognized* ***as*** the work of … / *recognize* a woman ***as*** his legal wife. ¶*recognize* ***in*** those doings a crowning mercy それらの行為の中には大きな慈悲心がくみとれる.

O be *recognized* as important 重要と認められている. ¶One can *recognize* but not describe it. それはそれと感じられるが口には言えない.

recoil, *v.* 後戻りする, ひるむ.

M *recoil* ***back*** from the danger 危険を見て(感じて)ひるむ.

P *recoil* ***at*** seeing a snake in the path 道でへびを見てすくむ. ¶*recoil* ***before*** sufferings 苦難に際して意気しょう沈する. ¶*recoil* ***in*** horror ***from*** the spectacle その光景を見て後じさりする. ¶Revenge often *recoils* ***on*** (=***upon***) the avenger. かたきを取るとまた取られるものだ.

recollect, *v.* 思い出す, 想起する, 思い浮べる.

M if we *recollect* ***correctly*** われわれの記憶に誤りがなければ.

O as far as I *recollect* 私の記憶する限りでは.

recollect, *v.* 再び集める; [心を]落着ける.

P *recollect* oneself ***after*** a burst of anger かっと怒った後気を静める.

recollection, *n.* 想起, 追憶; 記憶.

V ***awaken*** *recollections* 追想を喚起する. ¶We shall ***carry away*** a pleasant and lasting *recollection* of Japan. われわれは愉快にして永続的な追憶をお土産に日本を辞し去るであろう. ¶write in order to ***fix*** *recollections* 記憶をはっきりさせるために書いておく. ¶***have*** the *recollections* of … …を回想する. ¶***lose*** all *recollection* of … …を全く忘れてしまう. ¶I still ***preserve*** a vivid *recollection* of … 私は今でも…をはっきりと覚えている.

Q I have a ***clear*** *recollection* of having seen … 私は…を見たことを明かに覚えている. ¶a ***confused*** and ***faulty*** *recollection* of what has passed あったことの混乱して間違っている記憶. ¶have a ***dim*** *recollection* ぼんやりと覚えている. ¶He replied that he had a ***distinct*** *recollection* of so doing. 彼はそうやったことをはっきり覚えていますと答えた. ¶a ***fond*** *recollection* なつかしい思い出. ¶I may have said so, but I have ***no*** *recollection* of it. そういったかも知れないが覚えがない. ¶a ***painful*** *recollection* 痛ましい記憶. ¶have a ***perfect*** *recollection* of … …を完全に覚えている. ¶have a ***personal*** *recollection* of … …を親しく覚えている. ¶scenes which arise in ***quiet*** *recollection* of the past 過去の静かな追憶の中に浮び上る場面. ¶some ***shadowy*** *recollections* ぼんやりした追憶. ¶have a ***vivid*** *recollection* of … …をはっきり覚えている.

P events ***beyond*** my *recollection* 私の思い出せないできごと. ¶sing an old song ***from*** *recollection* 古い歌を記憶から思い起して歌う. ¶it is ***in*** my *recollection* that … ということは私の記憶にある ‖ it may be ***in*** the *recollection* of many readers that … …ということは多くの読者諸君の記憶に存するであろう. ¶***to*** my *recollection* 私の記憶している所では.【類】***to*** the best of my *recollection* (せいぜい). ¶The Battle of Waterloo was well ***within*** his *recollection.* ウォーターローの戦いを彼はよく記憶していた(長寿者など).【類】it is well ***within*** the *recollection* of many that …

P² *recollections* ***to*** a classmate 級友の思い出.

O my *recollection* is that … 私は…ということを覚えている.

recommend, *v.* 勧める, 推挙する.

M I can very ***confidently*** *recommend* the book. 私は確信してその本を推挙することができる. ¶*recommend* it most ***cordially*** to … 心からそれをお勧めする. ¶He ***earnestly*** *recommended* to adopt this plan. 彼はこの計画を採用するよう熱心に勧めた. ¶I can ***conscientiously*** *recommend* the book most heartily. 私は良心的にその本を熱心に推挙することができる. ¶***emphatically*** *recommend* 力強く勧める. ¶I ***heartily*** *recommend* this … to … 私は衷心からこの…を…に勧める. ¶a book ***highly*** *recommended* 大いに推奨された本. ¶it may ***safely*** be *recommended* to … それを…に推薦して差支えない. ¶I have no one to ***specially*** *recommend.* 別にこれという推薦申上げる人もない. ¶***stoutly*** *recommend* 熱心に勧める. ¶it is to be ***strongly*** *recommended* to those who … それは…なる人々に熱心に勧めらるべきだ ‖ it can be ***strongly*** *recommended* to the attention of … それはぜひ…に考えていただきたいことである. ¶***unhesitatingly*** *recommend* ちゅうちょせず勧める. ¶can be ***unreservedly*** *recommended* 率直にお勧めできる. ¶***warmly*** *recommend* the scheme 熱心にその計画を勧める ‖ it cannot be *recommended* too ***warmly*** to … それは…に対して幾ら熱心に勧めても勧め過ぎることはない.

P We can warmly *recommend* this book ***as*** a useful book of reference. われわれはこの本を有益な参考書として熱心に推挙することができる.【類】it is *recommended* *as* a substitute (代用品) for ... / *recommend* a woman *as* a good cook. ¶I *recommended* him *as* a good agent for the sale (purchase) of ...の販売(買付け)代理人として彼を推薦した. ¶*recommend* one *for* the position 人をその位地に推薦する ‖ *recommend* a person *for* membership 人を会員に推挙する ‖ It is highly *recommended for* diseases of the liver, stomach, intestines, kidneys, etc. それは肝臓・胃・腸・じん臓などの病気に特効があるとされている. ¶I *recommend* you *to* ... 君を...に推薦する. ‖ We *recommend* these considerations *to* the attention of our readers. われわれは読者諸君がこれらのことをよく考えられんことをお勧めする. 【類】I can thoroughly *recommend* it *to* you. / Honesty will *recommend* any one *to* his employer. 正直だとだれでも主人の気に入られる. ¶I can *recommend* it *without* any reserve. 私はそれを心から推奨することができる.

recommendation, *n.* 推薦, 推挙, 勧告.

V *give* one's hearty *recommendation* to ... ...を熱心に推薦する. ¶*Have* you any further *recommendation?* その他何か御注意下さることはないでしょうか. ¶*implement recommendations* by ... ...して推薦を徹底させる. ¶*need* no *recommendation* 推薦を要しない.

Q a *good recommendation* りっぱな推薦. ¶a *poor recommendation* 貧弱な取柄. ¶deserve *strong recommendation* 熱心に推薦する値打がある. ¶*weighty recommendations* 有力な推薦.

Q² *Shoup recommendations* シャウプ勧告.

P *at* (=on) our *recommendation* われわれの推薦で. ¶*by* (= *through*) *recommendation* of ... ...の推薦により. ¶speak *in recommendation* of ... ...をほめる. ¶a letter *of recommendation* 推薦状. ¶He was appointed *on* the *recommendation* of the Secretary of War. 彼は陸軍長官の推薦で任命された.

recompense, *n.* 報酬, つぐない, 返報.

V *constitute* an ample *recompense* 十分の報酬になる. ¶*get* no *recompense* 報酬を全くもらわない. ¶*guarantee* a *recompense* 報酬を保証する. ¶I am afraid you will never *have* any *recompense* for your work. 私は君はその労力に対して決して報いられないだろうと心配する.

Q obtain a *handsome recompense* 結構な報酬を得る. ¶a *just recompense* for ... ...に対する当然の報酬. ¶*reasonable recompense* for ... ...に対する適当な報酬. ¶a *slender recompense* for all his pains 彼のあれほどの苦心に対しての薄謝.

P *in recompense* of one's trouble その労力に対する報酬として. ¶work *without recompense* 無報酬で働く.

P² a *recompense for* service 奉仕に対する報酬 ‖ a *recompense for* condolence 弔慰金. ¶I cannot cancel the contract *without* some *recompense.* いくらか弁償をしなければその契約を取消すことはできない.

recompense, *v.* 報いる, 報酬する, 償う.

M He will be *amply recompensed* some day. 彼は他日十分報いられるだろう.

P I feel more than *recompensed for* my task. 私は自分の仕事に対して十二分に報いられたと思う. ¶*recompense* good *with* evil 善に報いるに悪をもってする.

reconcile, *v.* 仲直りさせる; あきらめさせる.

P become *reconciled to* death 死ぬのが恐ろしくなくなる ‖ *reconcile* oneself *to* one's fate (lot, situation) 自分の運命(など)とあきらめる. 【類】*reconcile* oneself *to* the new mode of living ‖ *reconciled to* each other 互いに和解して ‖ I cannot *reconcile* it *to* my conscience. それでは私の良心がとがめる. ¶*reconcile* oneself *with* ... ...と仲直りする 【類】He *reconciled* himself *with* his friends. / *reconcile* one's statements *with* one's conduct 言行を一致させる.

reconciliation, *n.* 和解, 調停.

V *effect* a *reconciliation* with ... ...と和解する.

P² a *reconciliation between* ... and ... ...と...との間の和解. ¶a *reconciliation of* two conflicting interests 二つの相反する権益の調和. 【類】a *reconciliation of* religion and science. ¶a *reconciliation with* a person (country) 人(など)との和解.

reconnaissance, *n.* 偵察.

Q *aerial reconnaissance* 空中偵察.

reconsideration, *n.* 再考, 再審.

V *advise* a *reconsideration* 再考を勧める. ¶You should *give* it careful *reconsideration.* 君はそれを慎重に再考すべきだ.

P *after reconsideration* 再考の後. ¶*before reconsideration* 再考する前に. ¶take the matter *into reconsideration* その事柄を再審議する. ¶*on* (=*upon*) *reconsideration* 再考の上.

reconstruction, *n.* 再建, 改造, 復旧.

V *postwar reconstruction* 戦後の復興. ¶*undergo reconstruction* 再建を経る.

Q² *housing reconstruction* 再建築.

P It is *under* reconstruction. それは改築中である. ¶enter *upon* the *reconstruction* of ... ...の再建に着手する.

recopy, *v.* 写し直す, 書き直す.

P *recopy* another's composition *into* one's own autograph 他人の作文を自分の手で手写する.

record, *n.* (**1**) 記録; 経歴; 成績.

V *check up* one's *record* [警察など]身もとを洗う. ¶*collect* and *digest* scattered *records* bearing on the subject その問題に関する散逸した記録を収集抄録する. ¶The episode *deserves* [a] *record.* そのそう話は記録する価値がある. ¶*escape record* 記録から漏れる. ¶*find record* in the newspapers 新聞に出される. ¶*get* a photographic *record* of ... ...を写真に取る. ¶*have* a *record* to one's discredit その不名誉になるような経歴をもっている ‖ It *has* a *record* of 40 years behind its reputation. その名声の裏面には四十年の記録がある. ‖ The motorboat *has* a fine *record.* その発動機はりっぱな成績を示している. ‖ during the fifty-eight years of which we *have record* 記録に載っている五十年間. ¶*keep* a *record* of ... ...を控えておく. 【類】*keep records* according to a specified form / *keep* a careful *record* of ... / *keep* the *records straight* 正確に記する. ¶He has *left* a clean *record* while in our service. 同氏は当方に在任中何ら不都合な所為がなかった. ‖ The artist has practically *left* no *record* beyond his work. その画家は作品のみで何ら記録を残さなかった. ¶*make* a *record* of ... ...の記録を取る ‖ the *record* is yet to be *made* of ... ...の例は今までにない. ¶*merit record* 記録する価値がある. ¶we *possess* authentic *record* of ... ...について確かな記録がある. ¶history has not *preserved* any *record* of ... ...のことは歴史に記してない. ¶the ability to *read* the old Japanese *records* in the original 日本の古文書を原文で読む力. ¶He has *rescued* the obscure *records* of their lives and deeds from the dust of oblivion. 彼は彼らの生活や行動の乏しい記録が消滅して世人に忘れられるに至るのを救った. ¶*retain records* of ... ...を記録に留めておく. ¶*take* a picture *record* 映画に取る(記録映画など).

V² The earliest trustworthy historical *records* of Japan do not *antedate* the fifth century. 日本の信頼するに足る最も古い歴史上の記録は第五世紀以後のものである. ¶no *records exist* of ... ...の記録は現存していない. ¶*records fail* to show ... ...のことは記録が示していない. ¶The *record* in question *runs* from 1876 to 1903. その記録は一八七六年から一九〇三年にわたる. ¶Unquestionable *records show* that he is 131 years old. 彼が百三十一歳であることは確かな記録がある.

Q make a good *academic record* りっぱな学業成績をあげる. 【類】He had an indifferent (平凡な) *academic record.* ¶keep an *accurate record* of ... ...を正確に記録しておく. ¶*authentic records* 確かな記録. ¶He has a *brilliant record* as an alumnus of the university. 彼は同大学をりっぱな成績で卒業した. ¶a bald *chronological record* of events from 722 to 481 B.C.「春秋」. ¶be based on fragmentary and *broken records* 断片的な連続しない記録によっている. ¶men with a *clean record* 品行方正の人. 【類】His *record* is *clean,* no stain on it. ¶make a *complete record* of a language 一国語の完全な記録を作る. ¶keep a *correct record* 正確な控えを取っておく. ¶Films are of value as *documentary record.* 映画は文献として貴重である. ¶a *dry record* of facts 事実の無味乾燥な記録. ¶make an *excellent record* 好成績を示す. ¶a *faithful record* of facts 実録. ¶have a *fine record* in (=at) school 学業は優良である. ¶He has made a *good record* in Economics. 彼は(学校で)経済学の点がよかった. ¶a *grim record* 恐ろしい記録. ¶an *incomplete* and *fragmentary record* 不完全で断片的な記録. ¶There is *no record* of a wild cat ever having been tamed. 山ねこが飼ならされたためしがない. ¶an *official record* 公的記録. ¶keep ... in the note-books for *permanent record* ...を永久の記録としてその帳面に留めておく. ¶the *personal record* of every employee 各雇人の履歴. ¶a *random record* of travel 旅

行漫録. ¶be filed and retained as a ***semi-permanent record*** 半永久的保存記録としてとじ込み保管される. ¶a ***sorrow-laden record*** 悲惨な記録. ¶***statistical records*** show that ... 統計上の記録によると…だということが分かる. ¶a ***stenographic record*** 速記録. ¶a ***successful record*** behind him 彼の背後にあるりっぱな経歴. ¶a ***tabulated record*** 表にした記録. ¶a ***true pictorial record*** of jungle life 密林生活の生々した記録. ¶be taken from the earliest ***trustworthy records*** 最古の信ずべき記録から取られた. ¶a ***truthful record*** いつわりのない記録. ¶***unprinted records*** 印刷されていない記録. ¶the almost complete absence of reliable ***written records*** 信用のできる記録のほとんど絶無であること.

Q² an ***achievement record*** 実績記録. ¶an ***alumni record*** 卒業生の記録. ¶keep a ***class record*** クラスの成績を控えておく. ¶his brilliant ***college record*** 彼の大学におけるりっぱな成績. ¶dig in ***company records*** 会社の文書を調査する. ¶men who have no previous ***court record*** whatever 前科の全くない人々. ¶a ***crime record*** 前科 ‖ The United States has an unenviable ***crime record*** アメリカには残念ながら犯罪が多い. ¶an ***execution record*** 執行記録. ¶an ***expenditures record*** 支出額の記録. ¶make a ***facsimile record*** 複写を作る. ¶a ***family record*** [Bible などに記入した]家庭の記録. ¶***health record*** 健康の記録. ¶an ***identification record*** 身分証明記録. ¶make a ***film record*** of a trip (scientific value) 旅行(など)の活動写真を取る. ¶an ***interest record*** [学生などの]興味に関する記録. ¶a ***job application record*** [card] 求職者記録(カード). ¶a ***personal-history record*** 履歴. ¶a ***pictorial weekly record*** of current events 週刊時事画報. ¶have no previous ***police record*** 警察のやっかいになったことがない. ¶one's ***prison record*** その前科 ‖ The convicts were "short-timers" with good ***prison record***. その囚人たちは模範囚として勤務時間が短縮されていた. ¶have an excellent ***safety record*** りっぱな安全記録をもつ ‖ improve the ***safety record*** [空中]安全旅行の成績をあげる. ¶make a good ***scholarship record*** in college 大学で優秀の成績を示す. ¶have a good ***school record*** 学業成績がよい. ¶men with long ***service record*** 多年勤続の人々. 【類】His ***service record*** reached to 40 years. / have a total ***service record*** of less than four years. ¶a ***State record*** 公文書. ¶a ***travel record*** 旅行記録. ¶an officer with a fine ***war record*** 戦功のある将校. 【類】an outstanding ***war record*** / in recognition of his ***war record***.

P ***according to*** an ancient *record* 古い記録によると. ¶***as*** a pictorial *record* 絵画の記録として. ¶The data have been taken ***from*** official *records* covering 62 years. その参考資料は六十二年にわたる官庁の記録から得た. ¶***off*** the *record* 記録にのせない, 非公開の, 非公式の. ¶there is ***on*** *record* an anecdote of a great lady who ... …という偉大な婦人について逸話が記録されている ‖ cases are ***on*** *record* in which ... …という例が記録にある. 【類】There are only two cases ***on*** *record* of Frenchmen having made large fortunes in London. / of this several instances are ***on*** *record* in national history / Such a case certainly deserves to be placed (=put) ***on*** *record*. ‖ one of the longest droughts ***on*** *record* 今まで記録にある一番長い干ばつの一つ. 【類】one of the most extraordinary cases ***on*** *record*. ¶it is ***upon*** *record* that ... …ということが記録にある.

P² a *record* ***at*** examinations 試験の成績. ¶a *record* ***of*** work done 成績の記録 ‖ a *record* ***of*** a procedure 訴訟記録. ¶a *record* ***of*** a suit 訴訟記録. ¶First editions of this book are very rare and there is only one *record* ***of*** a sale of that edition at auction. この本の初版は非常にまれでありその初版が競売に出された実例はただ一度しかない.

(2) [蓄音機の]レコード.

V ***make*** *records* for the Victor Company ヴィクター会社で(歌手などが)レコードを作る. ¶***play*** (=***put***) a *record* on a phonograph (Victor instrument) 蓄音機(など)にレコードを掛ける.

Q ***double-faced*** (***single-faced***) ***records*** 両面(片面)レコード. ¶Let me play your ***favorite record***. 君の好きなレコードを掛けよう.

Q² a ***disc*** (=***disk***) ***record*** 円盤レコード(音盤). ¶a ***film record*** フィルム・レコード. ¶a ***phonograph record*** 音盤.

(3) 〖競技〗最優秀記録(レコード).

V ***approach*** his *record* 彼の塁を摩する. ¶easily ***beat*** all *records* in ... …で優にあらゆる記録を破る. 【類】***beat*** the *record* of 1896. ¶***better*** one's own *record* 自己の記録を更新する. 【類】She ***bettered*** the recognized world's *record* for amateur swimmers for 60 yards. ¶***break*** (=***smash***) a previous *record* 以前の記録を破る. ¶***complete*** a *record* レコードを作る. ¶The figures for the year ended March 31st last ***constitute*** a *record*. 去る三月三十一日に終了した一昨年度の数字は最高記録をなしている. ¶***create*** (=establish) a new speed *record* 速度の新記録を作る ‖ This ***created*** a new *record* in the annals of cricket. これでクリケットの歴史上新記録ができた. ¶***eclipse*** all *records* あらゆる記録を破る. ¶***equal*** the *record* そのレコードに匹敵する. ¶***establish*** a new *record* 新記録を作る. ¶He ***holds*** the *record* for the high jump. = He is a high-jump record holder. 彼は高飛びの記録保持者だ. 【類】He ***holds*** the *record* for life saving at his age. / The factory boasts of ***holding*** the world *record* in ... production with an output of ... a month. / London ***holds*** the *record* as the most dangerous city in the world. ¶***make*** a *record* of two hundred fifty-nine eggs in twelve months 十二カ月に二百五十九個産卵の記録を作る. ¶But on the present occasion we were hardly disturbed by a ripple, and ***made*** almost a *record* for smooth passage. しかし今度は波一つ立たずほとんど平穏な航海として一つの記録を作った. ¶The output ***reached*** a *record* in 1904. 生産高は一九〇四年に最高記録に達した. ¶***set*** [***up***] a new *record* at billiards 玉突の新記録を作る ‖ ***set*** a *record* of flying hours 滞空記録を作る. ¶February ***shattered*** all previous production *records* of the company. 二月になってその会社は以前の生産記録を断然突破した. ¶***show*** the greatest *record* of efficiency 能力の最大記録を示す. ¶***smash*** *records* in the matter of ... …の点で記録を破る. ¶***surpass*** all previous *records* in scope 規模の点であらゆる前の記録を上回る. ¶***touch*** (=***tie***) the world *record* 世界記録に達する. ¶The player ***won*** a world's *record*. その選手は世界記録を得た.

Q the ***best record*** 最善(高)のレコード. ¶He penetrated farther north than ***Dr. Nansen's record***. 彼はナンゼン博士の記録よりもさらに北方へ進入した. ¶newly ***established records*** 新に作られた記録. ¶beat the ***former record*** made in 1907 一九〇七年に作られた以前の記録を破る. ¶He set a ***new record*** in ski-jumping with a leap of 58 meters. 彼はスキーのジャンプで五八メートルを出し新記録を作った. ¶a ***postwar record*** 終戦後の記録. ¶eclipse all ***previous records*** 前代未聞のことである ‖ beat the ***previous*** "***record***" of ... by ... …によって以前の…の記録を破る. ¶The railway has a ***proud record*** of infrequency of accidents. その鉄道は事故が少ないのを誇りとしている. ¶break the ***world's record*** for speed 速力の世界記録を破る.

Q² set an ***attendance record*** of ... …という参会者の数における新記録を作る. ¶set a ***box-office record*** 切符売上の新記録を作る. ¶the longest ***Broadway run record*** in show history ショーの歴史で最も長い(ニューヨークの)ブロードウェー興行記録. ¶make a wonderful ***egg record*** 驚くべき産卵の記録を作る. ¶beat the ***height*** "***record***" 高さのレコードを破る. ¶excel his ***longevity record*** 彼の長命の記録をしのぐ. ¶set a new ***non-stop flight distance record*** 無着陸長距離飛行の新記録を打ち立てる. ¶set a new ***production record*** 生産の新記録をつくる ‖ mines with excellent ***production records*** すぐれた生産成績のある諸鉱山. ¶set a new ***speed record*** in crime 犯罪における早さの新記録を作る. ¶set a ***world record*** for ... …の世界記録を立てる. ¶the ***world's altitude record*** 高度新記録 ‖ establish a ***world record*** of ... seconds …秒の世界新記録を作る ‖ the ***world air speed record*** 世界最高航空速度記録. 【類】hold the ***world endurance swim record*** (世界長時間水泳記録) of 100 hours and 15 seconds.

P² the world *record* ***for*** the pole vault 棒高飛びの世界記録. 【類】The Crocker Building, San Francisco, holds the *record* ***for*** costly construction among the commercial buildings of the country—63 cents a cubic foot (一立方フート). ¶the world's *record* ***in*** quick shipbuilding じん速な造船の世界記録. 【類】an English *record* ***in*** railway speed.

record, *v*. 記録する, 登録する.

P *record in* a register 帳簿に記録する ‖ it is *recorded in* the history of ... それは...の歴史に記録されている.【類】be *recorded in* my notes (ノートブック) ¶ a song *recorded into* wax レコードに吹込んだ歌. ¶ it is *recorded of* him that ... ...ということが彼について記録されている. ¶ His action deserved to be *recorded on* a coin. 彼の行動は硬貨に刻まれるだけの値打があった.

recorder, *n*. 録音器.

Q a *magnetic recorder* 磁力録音器.

Q² a *disc recorder* 音盤録音器(レコードの). ¶ a *tape recorder* テープレコーダー. ¶ a *wax recorder* ろう録音器.

record-holder, *n*. 記録保持者.

P² the *record-holder*, so far, *for* ... 今日までの所...の記録保持者.

recording, *n*. 録音.

V *broadcast recordings* of his utterances 彼の言葉の放送用録音.

Q² *film recording* 映画録音.

P² the *recording of* minutes 議事録の作製.

recourse, *n*. 頼み, 依頼.

V *have recourse* to force (=violence, arms) 暴力(など)に訴える ‖ It seemed a pity that he should have been driven to *have recourse* to such expedients. 彼がそんな方法を採るにいたったとは遺憾なことに思われた. ‖ *have recourse* to lies うそをつく ‖ He was compelled to *have recourse* to self-tuition. 彼は独学によるの余儀なきにいたった.【類】he has *had* no other *recourse* but to ... ‖ *Recourse* was *had* to university professors of the highest repute. 名声の最も高い大学教授たちに教えを請うた.【類】instantly *have recourse* to the criminal law (刑法) / *Recourse* was *had* to a loan. / At present no one in England can spell correctly without *having recourse* to a dictionary. ¶ *make recourse* to ... ...の手段による.

Q Is there *any recourse?* なにか依る所があるか. ¶ *constant recourse* has had to be made to ... ...を絶えず頼りにせねばならなかった. ¶ have *frequent recourse* to a dictionary しきりに辞書を引く. ¶ a *last recourse* 最後の頼み. ¶ the *only recourse* ただ一つの頼み. ¶ I had no *other recourse*. 私は他に頼みがなかった.

P *by recourse* to excessive violence 法外な暴力に訴えて. ¶ *without recourse* to a dictionary 字引を引かないで.

P² *recourse to* law 上訴.【類】Our *recourse* (頼みの綱) when ill is a doctor.

recover, *v*. 回復する, 取戻す; [病気などが]直る.

M He has *almost recovered* [his health] already. 彼はもうほとんど回復した. ¶ *recover completely* 全快する. ¶ *fully recover* すっかり直る.【類】not yet *fully recovered*. ¶ He is now *happily recovering*. 彼は昨今回復しつつあるが結構なことだ. ¶ be *partially recovered* [鉄道など]一部回復している. ¶ How is your wife? Has she *quite recovered?* 奥さんはいかがですか, すっかりお直りになりましたか. ¶ *recover slowly* 徐々に回復する. ¶ I hope you will *soon recover*. あなたは間もなく回復するだろうと思います.

P *recover from* one's astonishment (burns, illness, the blow, discouragement) 驚き(など)から回復する.【類】My spirits could not yet *recover from* the violent shocks they had received. / I had not yet *recovered from* my terror. ‖ bodies *recovered from* the sea 海から取り上げた死体. ¶ become somewhat *recovered into* a calmer composure 少し気が落着くようになる ‖ He *recovered of* this. 彼はこれから回復した.

O He *recovered* himself. 彼は正気に返った. ¶ *recover* lost time 時間の損失をとり戻す.【類】*recover* one's health.

recovery, *n*. 回復, 取戻し; 克復.

V *crush* Japan's *recovery* 日本の復興をたたきつぶす. ¶ The patient *made* a perfect *recovery*. 患者は全快した. ¶ *retard* rather than *expedite recovery* 回復を早めないでかえって遅らす. ¶ *set back* her *recovery* その国の復興を遅らす.

Q a *brisk recovery* of prices めきめき物価が盛り返すこと. ¶ a *complete recovery* 全快. ¶ *French recovery* フランスの復興. ¶ *industrial recovery* 生産の復活. ¶ an astonishing *postwar recovery* 著しい戦後の復興. ¶ I wish your mother a *quick recovery*. お母さんが早く御全快なさいますように. ¶ make a *remarkable recovery* [戦果をこうむった都市が]めきめき復興する. ¶ a *valid recovery* of Japanese nationality. 日本国民の健実な復興.

Q² a sure index of *business recovery* 商業復興の確かな指標. ¶ *world recovery* would be better promoted by ... 世界の復興は...のために一層促進されるだろう. ¶ Without multilateral trade a *world recovery* is impossible. 多角貿易によらなければ世界の復興は不可能だ.

P He is quite *beyond recovery*. 彼は全く回復の見込がない. ¶ He has a good chance *for recovery*. 彼は回復の見込が十分ある. ¶ There is, however, little chance *of* his *recovery*. しかし彼は回復の見込がほとんどない. ¶ *on recovery* from the disease その病気が回復すると. ¶ The patient is well on *towards* (=the road to) *recovery*. 患者は十分回復に向っている.

P² since his *recovery from* the illness 彼の病気回復以来. ¶ a speedy *recovery to* health すみやかな健康回復.

recreation, *n*. 休養, 娯楽, 気晴らし(レクリエーション).

V Young people universally *crave recreation*. 青年は世界いたる所娯楽を熱求する. ¶ *find* one's *recreation* in these pastimes これらの娯楽によって気晴らしをする. ¶ You must *take* some *recreation*. 君は少し保養せねばならない.

Q *commercial recreations* 興行物. ¶ his *favorite recreation* 彼の好きな娯楽. ¶ Gardening is a *good recreation*. 庭いじりはいいレクリエーションになる. ¶ *healthy recreation* of mind and body 心身の健全な保養. ¶ an *outdoor recreation* 戸外の休養. ¶ a *popular recreation* 人気のあるレクリエーション.

Q² *open-air recreation* 野外のレクリエーション. ¶ Opportunities for *summer seashore* and *mountain recreation* are within easy reach by cheap transportation. 割引賃金で夏期海岸や山への行楽がらくにできる.

P dancing *as* a *recreation* 娯楽としての舞踏. ¶ facilities *for recreation* 娯楽機関 ‖ go to the seaside *for recreation* 海岸へレクリエーションに出かける.

P² a harmless *recreation for* the idle rich 有閑な金持にとっての無害な娯楽.

recrudescence, *n*. 復活.

P *with* the *recrudescence* of imperial sentiment 尊皇思想の復活に伴って.

recruit, *n*. 補充兵; 新加入者; 補充; 補給.

V *draft recruits* 補充兵を取る. ¶ *draw* most of their *recruits* from ... 彼らの補充者を大てい...から選り抜く. ¶ *drill recruits* 補充兵を訓練する. ¶ *enroll recruits* 新兵を編入する. ¶ *gain recruits* for the club クラブに新しい会員を入れる.

Q the enthusiasm of *new recruits* to the heresy 異教への新入門者の熱心さ. ¶ a *raw* (=*fresh*) *recruit* 新兵.

P² a new *recruit to* the ranks of the nation 新帰化国民.

recruit, *v*. 補う, 補充する, 強化する.

P Boards of Education and trustees should be *recruited* more largely *from* the ranks of physicians and scientific men. 学務局や学務委員はもっと医者や科学者を加えるべきである.【類】These witnesses are *recruited from* among the country or urban proletariat (無産階級). ¶ *recruit* (=reinforce) a team *with* new players 新人を入れてチームを強化する.

recruiting-ground, *n*. 補充地, 補給所.

Q India has always been a *favorite recruiting-ground* for British police officials. 古来インドは英国の警察官補給地である.

recruitment, *n*. 補充.

Q *direct recruitment* by employers 経営者による直接募集.

Q² *staff recruitment* 幹部の補充.

rectification, *n*. 改訂.

Q² *border rectification* 国境改訂.

recuperate, *v*. 健康に復する; 本復する, 元気になる.

P to *recuperate after* a severe attack of enteric fever 猛烈な腸チフスにかかって病後保養に. ¶ He is *recuperating at* Hayama. 彼は葉山で病後の保養をしている. ¶ There his wife is *recuperating from* an illness. そこで彼の妻は病後の保養をしている.

recur, *v*. 再発する; 再び胸に浮ぶ.

M The question *often recurs*. この問題は繰返し起る.

P The idea *recurs to* my mind. その考えが再び私の胸に浮ぶ. ‖ *recur to* some means《まれ》ある方法に頼る.

O Leap year *recurs* every four years. うるう年は四年毎にくる.

recurrence, *n*. 再現, 再発.

V prevent it and *hinder* its *recurrence* それを防ぎかつその再発を防ぐ. ¶ *prevent* a *recurrence* of disastrous floods

大洪水の再発を防ぐ.

Q the theory of ***eternal recurrence*** 永久循環の理. ¶***frequent*** *recurrence* of pregnancy ひんぱんな妊娠. ¶of ***incessant recurrence*** 絶間なく起ってくる.

red, *n.* 赤色; 《米》赤字; [しばしば R-] 赤(共産党).

Q² The leaves on the trees have just been touched with early ***autumn red***. 今や木の葉は初秋の紅色にちょっと染められたところだ.

Q ***bright red*** あざやかな赤色. ¶***Chinese Reds*** 中共軍. 【類】***Chinese*** and ***North Korean Reds***. ¶with cheeks glowing with a ***florid red*** 紅顔の. ¶a strong bloc of rabid ***Korean Reds*** who have sworn allegiance to the North Korean Regime 北鮮の政府に忠誠を誓った狂暴な北鮮軍の強固な団体.

P Business is ***in*** [the] *red*. 商売は赤字だ. ‖ Tell me how you like me ***in red***. 赤い服を着た私どう? ¶go ***into*** [the] *red* 赤字になる. ¶The business is getting ***out of*** the *red* at long last. ようやく商売は赤字を脱するところだ.

red, *a.* 赤い, 赤色の.

M ***fairly red*** 随分赤い. ¶A watermelon is ***red inside*** and green outside. すいかは中は赤くて外は緑色だ.

P ***red in*** the face ***with*** anger (=rage) 怒って顔を真赤にして ‖ ***red with*** rage かんかんに怒って.

redeem, *v.* あがなう; 身請けする.

P *redeem* a person ***from*** captivity 償金を出して人を捕虜から救出する ‖ Her eyes *redeem* the face ***from*** ugliness. 彼女は目がきれいなので顔の醜さがそれほど目立たない. ¶He had no way to *redeem* his furniture ***out of*** pawn. 彼は質に入れた家具を請出す手段がなかった.

O One good feature will *redeem* the other bad ones. 一つとり柄があればあとは悪くとも埋め合わせがつく.

redeemable, *a.* 請戻される, 償い得る.

P *redeemable* ***for*** merchandise 商品で償い得る. ¶*redeemable* ***in*** gold 金で償い得る.

redemption, *n.* 請戻し, 償ない.

P ***beyond*** (=***past***) *redemption* 償われない. ¶be due ***for*** *redemption* 償還の期限に達する(質受けなど). ¶***without*** *redemption* 済度しがたい.

P² *redemption* ***of*** borrowings 借入金返済 ‖ *redemption* ***of*** national bonds 国債償還. 【類】*redemption* ***of*** debts.

red-hot, *a.* 真赤な, 赤熱の.

P turn *red-hot* ***with*** warmth (rage) あつくて(など)真赤になる.

redistribution, *n.* 再分配.

Q² a ***land*** *redistribution* 土地再分配.

redolent, *a.* 芳ばしい, ふくいくたる.

P ceremonials *redolent* ***of*** national tradition 国民伝統の香り高い儀式 ‖ a house *redolent* ***of*** fresh paint 塗りたてのペンキがぷんぷんにおう家 ‖ a tale *redolent* ***of*** mystery 神秘な感じがあふれている物語. ¶The air is *redolent* ***with*** perfume. 空気は芳香で一杯だ. ‖ *redolent* ***with*** the scent of the incense 線香の香の高い.

redound, *v.* 結局…になる.

P *redound* ***to*** one's own good (=credit) 結局自分のためになる.

redress, *n.* 償い, 矯正, 救済.

V ***afford*** *redress* 救済する. ¶***have*** *redress* 弁償をしてもらう. ¶***obtain*** *redress* by … …によって償いを得る. ¶***seek*** *redress* in civil action 民事訴訟で賠償を求める.

Q There is no ***legal*** *redress* to be obtained. 法律の力で賠償を求めることはできない.

P² obtain *redress* ***for*** damage 損害の賠償を得る.

redress, *v.* 救う; 改める.

O know how to *redress* the afflicted 悩める者を救うこつを心得ている. 【類】*redress* those unfairly oppressed ‖ *redress* wrongs (distress, damages) 悪行(など)を改める.

red-tape, *n.* 繁文じょく礼, お役所風.

V ***abolish*** the *red-tape* of … …の繁文じょく礼を避ける.

Q There will be no ***annoying*** *red-tape* to go through. 面倒な手続きはいらないだろう.

P unhampered ***by*** *red-tape* 繁文じょく礼にわずらわされずに. ¶a stickler ***for*** *red-tape* 繁文じょく礼にとらわれた人.

red-tapism, *n.* お役所風, 形式主義.

Q People are fed up with ***bureaucratic*** *red-tapism*. 人民はお役所風の形式主義にはうんざりしている. ¶***inefficient*** *red-tapism* 非能率的なお役所風.

reduce, *v.* 下げる; 縮める; 減じる.

M She is ***easily*** *reduced* (=moved) to tears. 彼女は涙もろい. ¶It was ***materially*** *reduced* in number. それは著しく数が減じた.

P I can't *reduce* a cent ***beyond*** that. それ以上一セントも引けません. ¶*reduce* ***by*** half the number of … …の数を半減する ‖ *reduce* the amount ***by*** one-half その額を半減する ‖ *reduce* the price ***by*** 10 per cent. 一割だけ値段を引く ‖ *reduce* a fort ***by*** a sudden attack 奇襲攻撃でとりでを落す. ¶*reduce* a fact ***from***… …からある事実をつかむ. ¶The empire was *reduced* ***in*** extent and importance. その帝国は版図においてまた重要性において縮小した. ‖ books *reduced* ***in*** price 減価本. ¶*reduced* ***into*** splinters 粉砕された ‖ *reduce* it ***into*** possession それを手に入れる. ¶this craze for *reducing* everything ***to*** formulas, charts, graphs, curves, diagrams and statistical tables このなにもかも公式や図や図表や曲線や図式や統計表にして了うという流行熱 ‖ It can be *reduced* ***to*** rules fairly easily. それはかなり容易に法則化することができる. ‖ The usage is difficult to *reduce* ***to*** rule. その慣用法はこれを規則で示すことはむずかしい. ‖ *reduce* clods ***to*** powder 土塊を砕いて粉にする ‖ *reduced* ***to*** a system 切り詰めて系統立てた ‖ This *reduced* him ***to*** silence. これで彼は沈黙した. ‖ *reduce* a rule ***to*** practice 規則を実行する ‖ *reduce* an argument ***to*** its simplest form 議論をできるだけ簡素化する ‖ His prodigality *reduced* his parents ***to*** despair. 放とうで両親も彼を見放した. 【類】*reduce* one's views and words ***to*** actions ‖ *reduce* a person ***to*** reason 聞分けさせる ‖ *reduce* … ***to*** subjection …を征服する ‖ The district was *reduced* ***to*** a charred and smoldering waste. その地域は灰じんに帰した. 【類】*reduced* ***to*** ashes / The facts may be *reduced* ***to*** three heads. / The possibility of … is *reduced* ***to*** zero. / *reduce* ***to*** a minimum ‖ He was *reduced* ***to*** despair. 彼は絶望に陥った. 【類】He is almost *reduced* ***to*** beggary. / *reduce* him ***to*** starvation ‖ railway coaches *reduced* ***to*** kindling in collision 衝突してたきつけ同然に粉砕されてしまった車両 ‖ a factory dismantled and *reduced* ***to*** a skeleton 装置をはぎとられて骨組ばかりになった工場 ‖ war-prisoners *reduced* to mere skeletons 骨と皮ばかりになった捕虜たち ‖ *reduce* pounds ***to*** shillings ポンドをシリングに換算する ‖ The railway *reduces* the journey ***to*** A ***by*** one and a half days. 鉄道は…への旅行を一日半だけ短縮する. ‖ be *reduced* ***to*** its components その成分に分解する ‖ be *reduced* ***to*** writing 書面に認められる ‖ *reduce* it ***to*** two-thirds by boiling それを三分の二に煮つめる ‖ When a man is *reduced* ***to*** want, the beggar comes out. 〘諺〙貧すれば欲心が出て来る. ‖ In the Funk & Wagnalls New Standard Dictionary the compounding of words has been *reduced* ***to*** a scientific system. ファンク・ワグナルズのスタンダード新辞典では複合語は科学的方法で整理されている.

reduction, *n.* 減少, 割引, 軽減.

V ***accord*** substantial *reductions* of … …を思い切り割引する. ¶***afford*** a very considerable *reduction* (=discount) in price 値段を思い切り割引する. ¶***allow*** a *reduction* of … …の割引をする. ¶if we can ***get*** a *reduction* in the freight 運賃の割引が得られるなら. ¶Do you ***give*** a *reduction* for a month's stay? 一カ月とう留すると割引しますか. ¶***grant*** 10% *reduction* 一割引にする. 【類】A certain *reduction* is ***granted*** on the fare. ¶You will ***have*** a *reduction* for cash. 現金だと割引します. ¶***make*** a *reduction* 割引する ‖ No *reduction* will be ***made for*** meals taken elsewhere. よそで食事をしても(宿泊)料金から引かない. 【類】a *reduction* is ***made*** on orders of 10 copies and upwards (及びそれ以上の注文には) / What *reduction* can you ***make?*** ¶***receive*** a *reduction* of 50% on their fees 彼らの会費に対し五割の割引を受ける.

Q at a ***big*** *reduction* 大割引で. ¶make ***considerable*** *reductions* 余ほど割引する. ¶They are for sale at ***liberal*** *reductions*. 大割引で売っている. ¶***No*** *reduction* allowed. 〘掲示〙割引は一切おことわり. ¶effect a ***radical*** *reduction* in the cost of manufacture 工費を徹底的に引下げる. ¶a ***slight*** *reduction* in prices きん少な値段割引. ¶a ***small*** *reduction* 少額の割引. ¶offered at ***substantial*** *reductions* to ensure complete and rapid clearance 在荷全部をすみやかに処分するために大割引で提供した. 【類】***Substantial*** *reductions* have been made throughout the entire rate schedule (全賃金表にわたって). / A ***substantial*** *reduction* is made on large orders. / It has proved no ***substantial*** *reduction.* ¶at a *sweeping reduction* 大割引で. ¶*world-wide reduction* of armaments by international agreement 国際協定による世界的軍備縮少.

Q[2] *accident reduction* 事故低減. ¶*arms reduction* 軍備縮少. ¶a *personnel reduction* 減員. ¶a *price reduction* 値段の割引. ¶exceptional *railway reductions* 格外の鉄道賃金割引. ¶put through *tax reductions* 税金の引下げを決行する. ¶*world arms reduction* 世界軍備縮少. ¶at 10 *per cent reduction* 一割の割引で.

P They will not accept unless *at* a *reduction* of 10 per cent. 先方では一割引でないと引受けない. ‖ *at* a *reduction* in the *rate* 率を下げて. 【類】 sell *at* a *reduction* of 10 per cent off invoice (仕切状) / *at* a *reduction* of nearly 20 per cent off the ordinary prices.

P[2] Do you make any *reduction for* quantity (cash)? 沢山(現金で)買ったら割引しますか. ¶a very material *reduction from* the publisher's price 出版定価に対する大割引. ¶a *reduction in* working hours (armaments, prices) 労働時間(など)の縮小 ‖ *reduction in* advance 天引き. 【類】 a *reduction in* wages. ¶*reduction of* output 産出高の低下. 【類】 a *reduction of* rates / A *reduction of* charges will be made. ¶a *reduction on* quantities 大量の注文に対する割引. 【類】 a *reduction on* the regular rates ‖ *reductions* (=cut) *on* electric power supply 電力削減(切下げ). ¶*reduction to* clergymen 宗教家に対する割引. ¶sell at a considerable *reduction upon* the published price 定価を大割引して売る.

redundance, *n.* 冗語.

V You ought to *avoid* such *redundance* as "we two both had a pear each."「われわれ二人ともそれぞれ...」といった冗語は避けるべきだ.

reed, *n.* あし.

Q a *broken reed* 〖比ゆ〗あてにならない人.

P lean *on* a *reed* 当てにならない人(物)を頼みにする.

O as flexible as a *reed* あしのようにたわみやすい.

reef, *n.* 暗礁.

V *strike* an unknown *reef* 暗礁に乗り上げる.

Q[2] a *coral reef* さんご礁.

P The steamer went *on* the *reef*. その汽船は座礁した.

reek, *v.* 湯気を立てる, 悪臭を放つ.

P fish trawls *reeking of* their cargo 積荷のにおいがぷんぷんするトロール漁船 ‖ *reek of* tobacco (whisky) タバコ(など)のにおいがぷんぷんする. 【類】 The room *reeked of* tobacco smoke. ¶Russian journals *reek with* ... ロシアの新聞は...の色彩が濃厚だ. ‖ The book *reeks with* scraps of French and Latin. 同書にはフランス語やラテン語の語句がやたら出て来る. ‖ *reek with* sweat 汗でべとべとになる. 【類】 The room was *reeked with* an abominable odor.

reel, *n.* 糸車; 〖機〗リール; [フイルムの]巻.

Q[2] *news reels*=newsreels ニュース映画.

P unwind *from* a *reel* 糸車からほどく. ¶a picture *in* ten *reels*=a 10-reel picture 十巻もの. ¶*off* the *reel* [解けるように]すらすらと. 【類】 Words came *off* the *reel*. ¶wind ... *on* a *reel* ...を糸巻(リール)に巻く. ¶a *reel* of film.

P[2] a *reel of* cotton 一巻きの木綿糸(ミシン糸). 【類】 a *reel* of film.

reel, *v.* 旋回する, よろめく; 糸巻(リール)に巻く.

M *reel* a sail *rapidly* 急いで帆を巻きあげる. ¶*reel to and fro* あちこちよろめく.

M[2] *reel in* the wire ワイヤをリールに巻く ‖ *reel in* a fish [つり糸で]魚をさお車を巻いて引寄せる. ¶*reel off* a yarn (=story) 話をすらすらとしゃべる(書く)(糸を繰り出す意から) ‖ *reel off* the line つり糸をくり出してやる ‖ *reel off* the names of the American Presidents in order アメリカ大統領名を順次言って見る. ¶*reel up* a big fish 大きな魚をつり車で巻きあげる.

P He used to drink so much that he *reeled along* the streets. 彼はよく大酒を飲んで町をよろよろ歩いたものだ. ¶The street *reeled before* his eyes. [酔って]街がぐるぐるまわるように見えた. ¶go *reeling down* the street 町をよろよろ歩く. ¶reams of dry statistical studies *reeled off* governmental mimeograph machines 政府の謄写印刷となった大量の無味乾燥な統計学的書類. ¶*reel under* a heavy blow すごいパンチを一発食ってよろめく.

re-enlist, *v.* 再編入する.

P a soldier *re-enlisted in* the Army 陸軍に再帰の兵士.

re-entry, *n.* 再加入.

P[2] Japan's *re-entry into* the family of friendly and free nations 友好的な自由主義国家群に日本の再度の仲間入り.

re-establishment, *n.* 再興.

P[2] *re-establishment of* the shinto faith 神道信仰の再興.

refection, *n.* 食事.

Q take out one's *modest refection* from a newspaper package 新聞紙の包みから貧弱な弁当を取出す.

refer, *v.* 帰する; 委託する, 付託する; 参照する; 関して言う, 言及する.

M be *affectionately referred* to as "..." by his colleagues 同僚から...と愛称されている. ¶The matter was *referred back* to the committee. その件は委員再付託になった. ¶only *refer briefly* to ... ほんの簡単に...に言及する. ¶The subject has been *referred* to *cursorily* in the preface. その問題は序文でちょっと触れてある. ¶be *generally referred* to as ... 一般に...といわれる. ¶*jestingly refer* to ... 冗談交りに...に言及する. ¶*just referred* to たった今述べた. ¶Iva Torguri D'Aquino *often referred* to as "Tokyo Rose" 東京ローズの名で知られている I. T. ダキノ. 【類】 *Refer* to your dictionary as *often* as you can.

P be *referred for* decision *to* ... ...の裁判に付する ‖ I can not bear to *refer to* the subject. 私はその問題を口にするに忍びない. ‖ *refer to* a list 名簿を調べる ‖ *refer* it *to* another's judgment それを他の人の判断に譲る ‖ *referred to* in our letter of ... [いつ幾日]私どもの手紙で申上げた ‖ as *referred to* earlier 前に述べた通り ‖ on *referring to* my dictionary I find that ... 私の辞書を参照して...ということが分かる. 【類】 please *refer to* my letter of ... / *referring to* my remark in the letter of ... / *refer to* other books for study ‖ The enclosure *referred to* in your letter has been omitted. 御指示の同封書類は封入してありません. ‖ We *referred* him *to* the boss *for* further instructions. 彼を社長のもとにやってさらに指令を求めさした. ‖ Can you *refer* me *to* a good dentist in the city? 町のよい歯医者を御存じありませんか. ‖ *to* which we shall presently *refer* そのことについてはじきに述べるとしよう ‖ Manchuria was often *referred to* as the "life-line" of Japan. 満州はよく日本の生命線だと言われていた. ‖ A locomotive is always *referred to* as "she"; some say because it takes a man to handle it. 機関車はいつも「彼女」と女性で用いられる, それは男が操縦するからだという者がある. ☞ a locomotive (=an engine) を he で受けた例もある: The silver-shining engine gathered *his* speed as *he* moved on. ‖ *refer* a bill *to* a committee 議案を委員会付託とする. 【類】 *refer* the dispute *to* the committee ‖ the court of arbitration *to* which the case is referred 紛争事件を付託すべき仲裁々判所 ‖ *refer* it *to* them for consideration それを彼らの審議に付する ‖ *refer* the matter *to* the Privy Council for deliberation その件を枢密院会議の諮問に付する.

referable, *a.* 帰せられる.

P The typhoid was *referable* (=ascribable *or* assignable) *to* milk. そのチフスは牛乳が原因であった.

reference, *n.* 付託; 論及; 照会; 関係; 身元証明書.

V *bear reference* to ... ...に関係がある. ¶The book *contains* a *reference* to the event. その本にその事件に関する記事が載っている. ¶The table *facilitates reference* to Japanese historical dates. その表は日本歴史の年号の参照を容易にさせる. ‖ to *facilitate* quick *reference* 容易に検索ができるように. ¶I *find* no *reference* whatever to the subject in text-books. 教科書はその問題に全然触れていない. ¶frequent *references* to ... are *found* in ... ...の中に...に言及した記事が大分ある. ¶I can *furnish* A1 *reference*. 私は最も優秀な照会先を指名することができます. ¶*give references* to ... ...に関して述べる. 【類】 I *give* no *reference* to ... as his descriptions are utterly inaccurate. ¶*have reference* to this point この点に言及する ‖ She *has* a good *reference* from her last place. 彼女は前の雇主からりっぱな身元証明書をもらっている. ¶There are writers who "*lug in*" *references* merely to make themselves appear learned. ただただ学問をひけらかすために引用句を取入れる作家がある. ¶writing in the paper on the subject of ... he *makes reference* to ... ...の問題について同紙の中で彼は...について述べている. 【類】 *reference* may here be *made* to ... / *Reference* was *made* to it in the Times of March 2. / to which *reference* has already been *made* / to whom *reference* has been repeatedly *made* in the earlier portion of this narrative / A *reference* should be *made* in the margin (余白) to its source (出所). ¶You will ***pardon*** the personal *reference*. 一身上のことにわたったがそれはお許し願いたい.

Q The book has been compiled with ***constant reference*** to practical requiremets. 本書の編集においては実際上の要求を絶えず考慮した. ‖ the drudgery of ***constant reference*** to a dictionary 絶えず辞書を参考することのわずらわしさ. ¶***cross references*** 前後参照. ¶avoiding ***direct reference*** to it それとなしに. ¶for ***easy*** *reference* 容易に参照できるように. ¶The magazine made ***editorial*** *reference* to it in its issue for March. その雑誌はそのことを三月号の社説で論じている. ¶in ***further*** *reference* to your valued enquiry of the 28th ult. and our reply to the same of the 4th inst., we now have pleasure in handing you herein prices for ... なお先月二十八日付の貴問及びそれに対する今月四日付当方よりの回答に関しここに...の定価表をお送り申上げます. ¶It constitutes a convenient book of ***general*** *reference* それは一般参考用の便利な本である. ¶a ***highest*** *reference* [身もとなど]最高の照会先. ¶an ***indispensable*** [book of] *reference* to all who write すべての文筆家には欠くことのできない参考書. ¶there is ***no*** *reference* to it in ... そのことは一切...に書いてない. ¶with ***particular*** *reference* to ... 特に...に関して. ¶make a ***passing*** *reference* to ... ついでに...のことを述べる. ¶for ***quick*** *reference* すみやかに参照できるように. ¶designed especially for ***rapid*** *reference* 特にじん速な参照のためを計って. ¶be convenient for ***ready*** *reference* 急に調べるため参考するのに便利である ‖ Monthly credit accounts are opened subject to a ***satisfactory*** *reference*. 確実な照会先があれば月々の信用取引を始めてもよい. ¶***satistactory*** *references* 満足な照会先. ¶make a ***slight*** *reference* to the question ちょっとその問題に触れる. ¶an ***uncomplimentary*** *reference* [照会された人物に対して]悪しざまに言うこと.

Q² a ***bank*** *reference* 銀行である照会先. ¶a ***Bible*** *reference* 聖書に関する引用. ¶a ***business*** *reference* 商業上取調先. ¶a competent ***character*** *reference* 有力な人物照会先. ¶quote the ***file*** *reference* とじ込みの番号を記載する. ¶file this for ***future*** *reference* これを将来参考のためにつづっておく. ¶***letter*** *reference* 手紙の参照番号(など).

P The route is best seen ***by*** *reference* ***to*** the map. その経路は地図を見ると一番よく分かる ‖ ***by*** *reference* to ..., you will note that ... ...を参照なされば...ということに気がつくでしょう. ¶books ***for*** (=***of***) *reference*=reference books 参考書類. ¶keep it ***for*** *reference* それを参考用に取っておく ‖ very conveniently arranged ***for*** *reference* 参照にきわめて都合のよいように配列してある. ¶observation or complaints ***in*** *reference* to the service of ... should be addressed to ... ...の勤務振りについてお気付の点または御不満の点は...あてにお申出をお願い致します. ¶I found it ***on*** *reference* to ... 私は...を参照してそのことが分かった. ¶a question ***outside*** the *reference* [委員]付託(権限)外の問題. ¶I have nothing to say ***with*** *reference* (=regard *or* respect) to this question. この問題に関しては私は何も言うことはない. ‖ ***with*** some *reference* to ... 幾分...に関して ‖ a person ***with*** good (excellent) *references* [身もとや技術の]りっぱな証明書をもっている人. ¶***without*** *reference* to ... ...に関係なく.

P² good *references* ***from*** past employers 以前の雇主からのりっぱな勤務振証明書. ¶*references* ***to*** other sources [語などの]出所を示すこと. ¶*Reference* ***to*** footnotes is made by numbers. 脚注への参照は数字で示してある. ‖ *references* ***to*** sources and authorities 出所並に原本への参照 ‖ *reference* ***to*** self 自分のことへの言及 ‖ There is a *reference* ***to*** it in the book. その本にそのことを書いた所が一個所ある. ‖ There is no *reference* ***to*** cocks and hens in the Old Testament. 旧約聖書にはおん鳥とめん鳥について何も書いてない.

refine, *v.* みがく, 上品にする.

P *refine* ***on*** one's language 語学にみがきをかける. 【類】 *refine* [*on*] a theory (one's thought) / *refine* ***on*** one's intention.

refined, *a.* 上品な.

P *refined* ***in*** manner (speech, one's taste) 礼儀(など)が上品な.

refinement, *n.* 上品, 優雅, 洗練.

Q with the ***gradual*** *refinement* of the public taste 一般公衆の趣味が漸次向上するにつれて.

refinery, *n.* 精製所.

Q² ***copper*** (***lead, tin***) *refinery* 銅(など)精錬所. ¶an ***oil*** *refinery* 製油所. ¶a ***petroleum*** *refinery* 精油所. ¶a ***sugar*** *refinery* 精糖工場.

refining, *n.* 精製.

P² *refining* ***of*** metals 金属の精錬 ‖ *refining* of crude oil 精油.

reflect, *v.* 反映する; 思案する, 回顧する.

M the shapely figure of a mountain ***clearly*** *reflected* on the surface of a lake 湖面にはっきり映る山の美しい姿. ¶*reflect* ***deeply*** 三思する. ¶***faithfully*** *reflect* 如実に...を反映する. ¶*reflect* ***seriously*** on the future of ... ...の将来を真剣に考える. ¶*reflect* ***sorrowfully*** 悲しく思い起す.

P It is *reflected* ***in*** the literature of the time. それは当時の文学に反映している. 【類】 wisterias (藤) *reflecting* their purple blossoms ***in*** the water / The inverted cone of Fuji (逆さ富士) was *reflected* ***in*** the blue waters (glassy depths) of the lake. / She saw me *reflected* ***in*** the mirror. ¶His conduct *reflects* ***on*** his parents. 彼の行為は両親の面目に関する. ‖ *reflect* ***on*** one's honor その名誉にかかわる ‖ *reflect* no honor (=credit) ***on*** ... 一向...の名誉にはならない. ¶when we *reflect* ***upon*** the fact that ... われわれが...なる事実をつくづく考えて見ると ‖ *reflect* ***upon*** the future 思いを将来に致す.

reflection, *n.* 反射, 反影; 姿; 回顧; 非難.

V ***awaken*** *reflection* 反省を促す. ¶Mt. Fuji ***casting*** its sharply defined *reflection* into the waters くっきりその姿を水に投影する富士 ‖ ***cast*** a *reflection* on ... ...を(暗に)非難する. ¶***discover*** in ... a *reflection* of national character ...の中に国民的性格の反映を見る. ¶***intersperse*** *reflections* with descriptions 感想に説明を交ぜて書く. ¶a matter that ***merits*** our sober *reflection* われわれがまじめに考えて見る価値のある事柄. ¶***mirror*** the *reflection* of ... ...の影をうつす. ¶It ***requires*** (=***calls for***) grave *reflection*. それはまじめに考えて見る必要がある.

V² *Reflection* ***increases*** wisdom. 反省は知恵を増す. ¶This is a natural *reflection* which ***occurs***. これは自然に起る思慮である. ¶a moment's (=a little) *reflection* is likely to ***show*** that ... ちょっと考えて見れば...ということが分かるだろう.

Q ***dispassionate*** and ***uncolored*** *reflection* of contemporary thought 現代の思潮を冷静にかつ飾らないで反映したもの. ¶a ***faithful*** *reflection* of what he saw and heard 彼が見聞したものの忠実な反映. ¶on ***further*** *reflection*, he conceived the idea of ... さらに考えて見て彼は...という考えを起した. ¶the ***genuine*** *reflection* of the feelings of the nation 同国民の感情の純真な反映. ¶I do not wish to be understood as casting the ***least*** *reflection* upon the high character and standing of ... 私は...のりっぱな人格や身分を少しでも非難しているとは思われたくない. ¶the results of ***mature*** *reflection* 熟考の結果. ¶***melancholy*** *reflection* 悲しい思出. ¶***quiet*** *reflection* 沈思. ¶a source of ***sad*** *reflection* to his closest friends 彼の親友に取って悲しい思い出の種. ¶***serious*** *reflection*. 猛省. ¶***shrewd*** but ***sound*** *reflections* on the European situation ヨーロッパの情勢に関する鋭いが健全な考察. ¶too absurd for ***sober*** *reflection* まじめに考えるにはあまりにばかげている. 【類】 a matter that merits our ***sober*** *reflection*.

P ***after*** due *reflection* 相当考えた後. ¶I wish to have time ***for*** *reflection*. 私は考えて見る時日がほしい. ‖ call ***for*** one's *reflection* その人が考えて見る必要がある. ¶***on*** *reflection* 考えてみると. 【類】 Yet it is obvious enough ***on*** *reflection*. / ***on*** *reflection*, it will be found to ... / ***on*** *reflection*, we realize that ... ¶as will be seen ***upon*** a moment's *reflection* ちょっと考えて見ると分かるであろうが ‖ he will surely, ***upon*** *reflection*, perceive that ... 考え直して見れば彼は...ということがたしかに分かるだろう. ¶***With*** *reflection*, common sense rallied to my aid. 熟考したら常識がわいて来て解決がついた. ¶make one's choice ***without*** due *reflection* 十分考えずに選択する.

P² their *reflections* ***in*** a mirror 鏡に映った彼らの姿. ¶the *reflection* ***of*** light (heat, sound) 光(熱・音)の反射 ‖ the *reflection* ***of*** Mt. Fuji in Lake Ashi 芦の湖に映じた富士山の姿 ‖ *reflection* ***of*** Russian novels ***in*** English literature ロシア小説の英文学へ及ぼした影響. ¶*reflection* ***on*** a lake 湖面への反映 ‖ a *reflection* ***on*** one's honor (=fair name) 名折れ ‖ *reflections* ***on*** the world war 世界戦争に関する考察. ¶a *reflection* ***upon*** the intelligence of those who designed it それを計画した人々の頭脳への疑問(ばかさ加減).

reflex, *n.* 反映, 反射.

Q *conditioned reflex* 条件反射.

P² a *reflex from* the glory of ... ...の栄光の反映. ¶a *reflex of* public opinion 世論の反映. 【類】a *reflex of* the will of the people.

reform, *n.* 改革, 革新, 刷新.

V ***accomplish*** radical *reforms* in the government 政治機構の根本的改革を行う. ¶***advocate*** *reforms* 革新を唱える. ¶***bring about*** *reforms* 革新を招来する. ¶***carry*** a *reform* into effect 改革を実行する. ¶***carry out*** *reforms* 色々改革を行う. ¶***effect*** large *reforms* 大改新を行う. 【類】Unless a radical *reform* be ***effected*** one can foresee only one result from a state of things like this. ¶***found*** a *reform* 改革の基を開く. ¶***inaugurate*** great *reforms* in ... ...の大改革を始める. ¶***initiate*** a *reform* 改革に着手する. 【類】The city is a political theatre where plots are hatched and *reforms* ***initiated.*** ¶***institute*** *reforms* 改革を行う. ¶***introduce*** *reforms* into ... ...に改革を施す. ¶***make*** sweeping *reforms* 大改革をやる. 【類】the policy of ***making*** a few *reforms* at a time. ¶It is here that immediate *reform* is ***needed.*** 直ちに改革を要するのはこの点である. ¶***propose*** a *reform* 改革を提議する. ¶***start*** prison *reform* at ... ...において刑務所の改革を始める. ¶***urge*** *reform* 改革を説く.

Q ***administrative*** *reforms* 行政改革. ¶an ***agrarian*** *reform* 農地改革. ¶an ***constructive*** *reform* 建設的革新. ¶a ***drastic*** *reform* 思い切った改革. ¶carry through ***genuine*** *reforms* 真の改革を断行する. ¶***important*** *reforms* 重要な改革. ¶***legitimate*** *reforms* 合法的改革. ¶put through many ***needed*** *reforms* 必要な諸改革を実行する. ¶***political*** *reforms* 政治上の改革. 【類】conduct a ***political*** and ***religious*** *reform* of the country. ¶unless a ***radical*** *reform* be effected 根本的改革をしない限り. ¶a ***risky*** *reform* 危険な改革. ¶***social*** *reforms* 社会改造. ¶a ***tardy*** *reform* 遅々たる改革. ¶initiate ***vigorous*** *reforms* 改革を断行する. ¶a ***wholesale*** *reform* 大改革.

Q² the ***farmland*** *reform* 農地改革. ¶the ***farm system*** *reform* 農業組織改革. ¶***labor*** *reforms* 労働改革. ¶a ***land*** *reform* 土地改革 ‖ the agrariam ***land*** *reform* 農地改革. ¶***spelling*** *reform* つづり字法改正. ¶England, the birthplace of ***temperance*** *reform* 禁酒改革の本家英国.

P a step ***toward*** *reform* 改革への一歩. ¶*reform* ***from*** bottom ***to*** top 徹底的な改革. 【類】*reform* ***from*** root ***to*** basement.

P² *reform* ***in*** politics 政治上の革新.

reform, *v.* 改革する; 更正させる.

P *reform* juvenile criminals ***instead*** of punishing them 少年犯罪者を罰しないで更正させる. ¶The act should be *reformed* ***on*** the lines of ... その法令は...といった風に修正さるべきである.

reformation, *n.* 改正, 改革, 革新.

Q a ***drastic*** *reformation* of the present examination system 現在の試験制度の大改革. ¶***religious*** *reformation* 宗教改革.

Q² a ***deathbed*** *reformation* 臨終の改しゅん.

reformer, *n.* 改革者, 改良者.

Q an ***out-and-out*** *reformer* 徹底的な改革者. ¶a ***sanguine*** *reformer* 熱烈な改革者. ¶a ***social*** *reformer* 社会改良家. ¶***utopian*** "*reformers*" 空想的な社会改革者. ¶a ***vigorous, uncompromising*** *reformer* 精力的, 非妥協的な改革家.

refract, *v.* 屈折させる.

O Light is *refracted* when passing through water or glass. 光は水やガラスを通ると屈折する.

refrain, *n.* [歌詩の]くり返し.

Q² ***nonsense*** *refrain* [俗謡などの]意味のない合の手.

refrain, *v.* 差控える, 慎しむ, 遠慮する.

M ***kindly*** *refrain* from ... ing どうぞ...を御遠慮下さい. ¶***purposely*** *refrain* from ... 考えがあって...を慎しむ.

P *refrain* ***from*** flesh meat 肉食を避ける ‖ *refrain* ***from*** further words それ以上に言うことを避ける ‖ *refrain* ***from*** women 女を遠ざける. 【類】*refrain* ***from*** doing evil / You should *refrain* ***from*** judging others harshly. ‖ I could not *refrain* ***from*** laughing. 私は笑わずにはいられなかった. ‖ a subject so hackneyed that we *refrain* ***from*** quoting 敢えて引用の必要もないごく言いふるされた問題 ‖ I *refrain* ***from*** giving the name. 名前はあずかるが.

refresh, *v.* さわやかにする, 元気づける; 記憶を新たにする.

P *refreshed* ***by*** sleep 睡眠によって元気を回復して ‖ *refresh* one's memory ***by*** a glance at ... ...を一べつして思い出す. ¶*refreshed* ***from*** fatigue 疲労が取れて. ¶*refreshed* ***in*** mind and body 心身ともにそう快になって. ¶a mind *refreshed* ***with*** a nap 仮睡をやって清々した頭 ‖ *refresh* oneself ***with*** a cup of coffee コーヒー一杯で元気をつける.

refreshing, *a.* そう快な.

P *refreshing* ***to*** the eyes 見る目にそう快な.

refreshment, *n.* 元気回復; *pl.* 飲食物.

V He ***craved*** the *refreshment* of the bath after his tedious and dusty journey. 退屈でじんあいにまみれた旅行の後彼は湯に入ってさっぱりした気持になりたくてたまらなかった. ¶***enjoy*** *refreshments* at one's expense ごちそうになる. ¶***have*** *refreshments* 茶菓を食べる. ¶***order*** *refreshments* 茶菓を注文する. ¶***provide*** *refreshment* for ... ...に茶菓の用意をする. ¶***serve*** light *refreshments* 茶菓を出す. 【類】***serve*** *refreshments* at a party. ¶*Refreshments* were ***set*** before them. 彼らの前に茶菓が出された. ¶***take*** some *refreshment* 何か食べる. 【類】We ***took*** *refreshments* with us (携帯して) for a trip.

Q ***appetising*** *refreshments* 食指の動くごちそう. ¶***liquid*** *refreshments* 飲み物. ¶*refreshments*, either ***solid*** or ***liquid*** 飲食物.

Q² ***between-meals*** *refreshment* お茶受け. ¶***buffet*** *refreshments* 売店の飲食物(園遊会などの).

P partake ***of*** *refreshments* in the tea-room 喫茶室で茶菓をとる. ¶entertained ***with*** *refreshments* 茶菓のちそうになって.

P² a *refreshment* ***to*** the eyes 目の保養.

refrigerator, *n.* 冷蔵庫.

Q an ***electric*** *refrigerator* 電気冷蔵庫. ¶keep meat, fruit, etc. ***in*** a *refrigerator* 冷蔵庫に肉・くだものなどを貯蔵する.

refuge *n.* 隠れ場所, 避難所.

V ***find*** *refuge* in a hut 山小屋に避難する ‖ to ***find*** *refuge* and peace in ... ...に隠家と安心を見出すために. ¶***give*** *refuge* to ... ...に避難所を与える. ¶***seek*** *refuge* at a place ある場所に避難を求める ‖ ***seek*** *refuge* from an enemy 敵から逃れる ‖ ***seek*** some *refuge* from the stern demands of reality 現実のきびしい要求からなんとかして逃避しようとする ‖ ***seek*** *refuge* with a neighbor 隣人の家に隠れる. 【類】He ***sought*** *refuge* in the harbor of literature (文学という避難所). / ***seek*** *refuge* on board the ... ¶***take*** *refuge* and make a stand against ... in a castle 城に逃げ込んで...に抵抗する ‖ ***take*** *refuge* behind a door 戸のかげに隠れる ‖ ***take*** *refuge* in a citadel (foreign country) 城さい(など)に逃込む. 【類】***take*** *refuge* in the mountain of Yoshino ‖ ***take*** *refuge* with ... ...に身を寄せる ‖ ***take*** *refuge* in saying that ... ...と言い抜ける.

P fled to ... ***for*** *refuge* ...に逃げ込んで避難した.

P² a grateful *refuge* ***from*** the din and bustle of modern life 現代生活のけんそうと騒じょうからの有難い逃避. ¶*refuge* ***from*** oppression 圧迫からの逃避.

refugee, *n.* 避難者, 亡命客.

Q a ***political*** *refugee* 亡命者.

Q² rehabilitate ***war*** *refugees* 戦争疎開者を復帰させる.

P² a *refugee* ***from*** Petrograd ペトログラードからの亡命者 ‖ *refugees* ***from*** law (=justice) 法律からの逃避者(お尋ねもの).

refund, *n.* 払い戻し, 返還, 償却.

V ***allow*** (=***make***) no *refund* 返金をしない. ¶***claim*** a full *refund* of the amount paid 払った金の全額償却を請求する. ¶***obtain*** a *refund* of this amount on his behalf 彼に代ってこの金額を償還してもらう.

Q² ***tax*** *refunds* 税金の払い戻し.

refund, *v.* 返金する.

M If these shoes do not wear well, your money will be ***readily*** *refunded.* このくつがお足に合わなかったらお代はすぐ返金します.

refusal, *n.* 拒絶, 辞退, 不認可; 先取権.

V They ***announced*** their *refusal* to attend the conference. 彼らは同会議へ彼らが出席しないむねを公表した. ¶***brook*** no *refusal* 拒絶を許さない. ¶***get*** (=***meet with***) a *refusal* 拒絶される. ¶If you refer it to me, I will ***give*** you a flat *refusal.* 私の方へそれを持って来られるなら私はきっぱりお断りします. ¶Will you let me ***have*** the *refusal* of it till tomorrow? それを売らずにあしたまで取っておいてもらえませんか. ¶***receive*** a *refusal* 拒絶される. ¶He would ***take*** no *refusal.* いやとは言わせない.

Q a *curt refusal* そっけない拒絶. ¶a *firm refusal* to meet the demand その要求に対する断固たる拒絶. ¶It is tantamount to a *flat* (=*square*) *refusal*. それは断然拒絶したことになる. ¶an *obdurate refusal* 峻拒(しゅんきょ). ¶meet with a *square refusal* きっぱり拒絶される. ¶a *stubborn refusal* がん強な拒絶. ¶*ungracious refusals* にべもない拒絶. ¶an *unqualified refusal* 無条件の拒絶.

P persist *in* one's *refusal* to ... あくまで...することを拒絶する. ¶meet *with* a flat *refusal* きっぱり断わられる.

refuse, *n.* 廃物, 廃棄物.

V *carry off* the *refuse* 廃品を運び去る.

Q² *animal refuse* 動物性のごみ. ¶*garden refuse* 庭のごみ. ¶*household refuse* 家庭の廃品. ¶*kitchen refuse*=《米》garbage 台所のごみ.

P² a *refuse from* ... ...の廃物.

refuse, *v.* 拒む, 拒絶する, 辞退する.

M *refuse categorically* 無条件に拒む. ¶*bluntly refuse* すげもなく断る. ¶The request was *curtly refused* その頼みごとはすげなく断わられた. ¶*refuse gracefully* 遠曲に断わる. ¶*refuse flatly* きっぱり断わる. ¶We were *modestly refused*. われわれは体よく断わられた. ¶*obstinately refuse* がん強に拒む ¶*peremptorily refuse* 厳として拒む. ¶*refuse point-blank* すげなく断る. ¶*refuse* very *positively* 断固断る. ¶*resolutely refuse* to answer 断固返事を拒む ‖ *resolutely refuse* admittance (one's request) きっぱり入場(など)を断る. ¶*steadily refuse* to ... いつも...することを断わる. ¶*stubbornly refuse* がん固に拒む. ¶He *stupidly refuse* to be taught by these mistakes. 彼は愚かにもこれらの誤びゅうによって学ぼうとしない.

P *refuse* to budge *from* his original stand 彼の元来の立場を少しも変えようとしない.

O *refuse* to give her consent 彼女の承諾を与えることを拒む. ¶Three times the trap *refused* to work. 三度も落し穴がうまくきかなかった.

refutation, *n.* 論ばく, 反ばく.

V Such an argument scarcely *needs refutation*. そんな議論は反ばくを要しない. ¶The error is too obvious to *require* a particular *refutation*. その誤りはあまりにも明らかで特に反ばくを要しない.

regain, *v.* 回復する.

O *regain* one's health 健康を回復する. 【類】*regain* one's consciousness (footing).

regale, *v.* ごちそうする, 供応する.

P We were *regaled with* tea and cakes. われわれに茶菓の供応をした. 【類】*regale* oneself *with* feast (beer).

regard, *n.* 留意; 尊重; 注目; 関係; 敬意.

P Please *convey* my kind *regards* to your father. どうぞお父さんによろしくお伝え下さい. ¶*earn* a public *regard* 世人から尊敬を受ける. ¶we *entertain* the highest *regard* for ... われわれは...をこの上なく大事に思う. ¶*extend* my cordial and grateful *regards* to ... ...に対して敬意と感謝を払う. ¶*Give* my *regards* to your friends. 君の友人たちによろしく ‖ *give* no *regard* to ... ...を考えに入れない. 【類】Please *give* him my *regards*. ¶*have* a high *regard* for ... ...を大いに尊敬する. 【類】*regard* should be *had* of ... ‖ *having regard* to (=considering, *or* in view of) the fact that ... ...という事実にかんがみ ‖ In using cipher messages *regard* must be *had* to the Regulations relating to "Foreign telegrams" as published in the official "Post-office Guide." 暗号電報を用いる場合は「郵便案内」に公表してある外国電報規則に従わねばならない. ¶*level* their stern *regards* at ... ...をすごい目付で注視する. ¶*pay regard* to public opinion 世論を尊重する. 【類】*pay* no *regard* to ... ¶Our friend Mr. ... *sends* his *regards* to you. 友人...君から君によろしくとのことです. ¶*take regard* also of the question as to ... ...に関する問題をも考慮する. ¶*testify* one's affectionate *regards* 敬意を表明する. ¶He has *won* my *regards*. 私は彼に敬意を表している.

Q give my *affectionate regards* to ... ...によろしく. ¶I pay *deep regard* to all he says. 私は彼の言うことは何でも大いに尊重する. ¶give *due regard* to ... ...に相当の敬意を払う ‖ have *due regard* to ... ...に関して相当しん酌する. 【類】with *due regards*. ¶have a *great regard* for ... ...を大いに尊敬する. ¶I have come to have a *high regard* for ... 私は...を尊重するに至った. ¶give one's *kind regards* to ... ...によろしくと言う ‖ with *kind regards* to all 皆様によろしく. ¶*lingering regard* 今なお消えぬ敬意. ¶pay *little regard* to ... ...を重んじない. ¶bind together rich and poor in ties of sympathy and *mutual regard* 同情と相互的敬意のきずなで貧富の間をつなぐ. ¶He has *no regard* for the feelings of others. 彼は他人の感情を考慮しない. 【類】He has *no regard* for himself. ¶*patriotic regard* for our flag われわれの国旗に対する愛国的敬意. ¶with *sincere personal regards* from ... ...からくれぐれもよろしく. ¶He is held in *slight regard*. 彼はあまり重んじられていない. ¶with *strict regard* for ... ...の点を十分考慮して.

P We should not always act merely *from* a *regard* to ourselves. われわれは常に単に自己本位で行動してはならない. ¶What have you to say *in regard* to that subject? その問題に関して何か御意見がおありですか. ‖ *in* this *regard* この点で. ¶a man *of regard* 注意深い人. ¶*out of regard* for (=considering) their welfare 彼らの幸福を顧慮して. 【類】I kept silent *out of regard* for his feelings. ¶*with regard* to ... ...に関して ‖ *with* every *regard* to ... ...を十分考慮して. ¶promote its own interests *without regard* for the whole 全体を顧慮せずそれだけの利益を増進する ‖ *without regard* to time (age, sex, race, creed, cost, color) 時間(など)にお構いなく. 【類】*without regard* to his family conditions.

P² I have a great *regard for* him. 彼を大いに尊敬している.

regard, *v.* 思う; 注視する; 顧慮する, 尊重する.

M I do not *regard* the prospects of the company *favorably*. 私は会社の前途を楽観しない. ¶he is *generally regarded* as ... 彼は一般に...と認められている. ¶*highly regard* ... ...を重んじる. ¶*icily regard* each other お互いに冷やかに見合う. ¶In most Christian nations Friday is *popularly regarded* with superstition. 大抵のキリスト教国では金曜日を一般に迷信の目をもって見ている. ¶*properly* (=*rightly*) *regarded* 本当の見方では. ¶He *regarded* me *sternly*. 私をすごい顔でにらみつけた.

P The dove is poetically *regarded as* the symbol of purity, gentleness, and peace. はとは詩の方では純潔・温順・平和の象徴と見なされている. 【類】*regard* it *as* a scandal / *regard* them *as* an anachronism / Americans are said to *regard* the amount of money a man makes *as* a criterion of his ability.

O The idol is *regarded as* miraculous in power reputed to have supernatural powers. その神様(偶像)は御利益があるという評判である. ‖ *regard* him *as* among my friends 彼を私の友人中に入れて考える. 【類】In measures of practical socialism New Zealand may well be *regarded as* foremost among the nations of the world. / *regard* it *as* impossible (difficult, easy) / In England the classics are still *regarded as* essential to the making of an educated or cultured man. ¶*regarded from* one standpoint it may appear ... ある見地から見るとそれは...のように見えるかも知れない. ¶*regard* it *in* deep distress それについて非常に心配する. ¶The study of a language may be *regarded under* two aspects. 語学の研究は二つの方面から見ることができる. ¶*regard* it *with* abhorrence (fear, respect) それをけんお(など)の目で見る ‖ *regard* ... *with* wonder and admiration ...に舌を巻く ‖ *regard* ... *with* disfavor ...を排斥する. 【類】*regard with* sympathy the shortcomings of fellow workers in the same field.

regardless, *a.* 留意しない, 無とん着な.

P They were secured *regardless of* cost. それらを値段に構わず手に入れた. 【類】almost *regardless of* cost (出費) ‖ *regardless of* expense (consequences, sex, age) 費用(など)を構わず. 【類】use every means *regardless of* expense to ... / *regardless of* their ability to pay / *regardless of* courtly etiquette / seek to win by pure mass power, *regardless of* manpower losses.

regatta, *n.* ボートレース, ヨットレース.

V, V² *hold* a *regatta* ボートレガッタを催す. ¶the annual *regatta* of ... *took place* at ... 例年の...ボートレース会は...で催された.

Q the *annual regatta* of the yacht club ヨットクラブ例年のヨットレース.

P row *in* a *regatta* ボートレースで漕ぐ ‖ take part *in* a *regatta* ボートレースに参加する.

regeneration, *n.* 再生, 新生, 改新.

Q *constant regeneration* of hair 毛髪の不断の更生.

¶dawning of ***spiritual*** *regeneration* 精神改造の端緒(きざし).

P² the *regeneration* ***of*** Russia ロシアの改新. 【類】 *regeneration* ***of*** woolen cloth (毛ものの再生).

regent, *n.* 摂政.

Q² a ***prince*** *regent* 摂政の宮; 摂政親王. ¶a ***queen*** *regent* (=*regnant*) 摂政女王.

regime, régime, *n.* 制度, 政体, 管理.

V ***establish*** a new *regime* on a sound, permanent basis 健全にして恒久的な基礎の上に新しい政体を建設する. ¶***institute*** a new *regime* 新政体を立てる. ¶***upset*** (=***overthrow***) a *regime* 政権を倒す.

Q place ... under an ***international*** *regime* ...を国際管理の下におく. ¶recognize ***Mao Tse-tung's*** *regime* in China 中国における毛沢東政府を承認する. ¶go back to the ***old*** *regime* 昔の制度に復帰する. 【類】 under the ***old*** *regime*. ¶the exile ***Polish*** *regime* 亡命ポーランド政権. ¶overturn the ***Shogunate*** *regime* 幕府を打倒する.

Q² the abolition of the ***capitalist*** *regime* 資本主義制度の廃止. ¶the main supply route for the ***Chiang Kai-shek*** *regime* 蒋介石政権に対する主要供給路. ¶the establishment of the new ***Communist*** *regime* in China 中国における新共産政権の設立. ¶the elimination of the ***Fascist*** *regime* in Spain スペインにおけるファシズム政権の廃除. ¶disclaim the ***Franco*** *regime* フランコ政権を否認する. ¶the then ***Nationalist*** *regime* in China 中国における当時の国民党政権. ¶the ***one-party Kuomintang*** *regime* of Generalissimo Chiang Kai-shek 蒋介石総統の国民党単独政権. ¶the ***Peiping*** *regime* 北平政府. ¶set up a ***puppet*** *regime* かいらい政府を打立てる. ¶a ***rebel*** *regime* 反乱軍政権.

P ***during*** the Salisbury *regime* (=ministry) ソールズベリ内閣の間 ‖ ***during*** the Tokugawa *regime* 徳川幕府の執政中. ¶***under*** the present *regime* 現在の制度の下に.

P² the Bolshevist *regime* ***in*** Russia ロシアの過激(多数)派政権.

regimen, *n.* 正規食, 栄養食, 養生法.

V He was ***prescribed*** a severe *regimen*. 彼は厳重な正規食(摂養食)を取るように命ぜられた.

regiment, *n.* 連隊.

V ***review*** a *regiment* 連隊を検閲する.

Q an ***air-borne*** *regiment* 空輸部隊. ¶a ***whole*** *regiment* of starlings むくどりの一群.

P desert ***from*** one's *regiment* 脱営する. ¶He served ***with*** the *regiment*. 彼はその連隊付きであった.

P² a *regiment* ***of*** cavalry (foot) 騎兵(歩兵)連隊.

regimentation, *n.* 統制.

Q² ***war-time*** *regimentation* of industry, labor, food, clothing, etc. 戦時の産業·労力·食料·衣料などの統制.

P² *regimentation* ***of*** industries ***for*** war purposes 戦争目的の産業統制.

region, *n.* 地方, 地域; 部; 域, 界.

Q ***abdominal*** *regions* 下腹部. ¶***adjacent regions*** 隣接地区. ¶***Alpine*** *regions* アルプス地方. ¶the ***anal*** *region* しりの辺. ¶in more ***barbaric*** *regions* さらに野蛮な地方で. ¶***colonial*** or ***outlying*** *regions* 外地. ¶those ***exclusive*** *regions* which no mortal had ever penetrated before 先人未踏の地. ¶a ***faraway*** *region* 遠方の地域. ¶a ***fertile*** *region* 肥よくな地方. ¶a ***great coal-producing*** *region* 大石炭生産地方. ¶a ***humid*** *region* 湿潤な地方. ¶***mountainous*** *regions* 山岳地方. ¶the ***polar*** *region* 極地. ¶in these ***remote*** *regions* これらの辺ぴな地方では. ¶The paper is largely circulated in the ***rural*** *regions*. その新聞は地方に多数の読者を持っている. ¶***southern*** *regions* 南方の諸地域. ¶a ***troubled*** *region* 紛争地域. ¶the data collected from ***various*** *regions* of the world 世界の各方面から収集した資料. ¶***wooded*** or ***unwooded*** *regions* 森林または非森林地帯.

Q² a ***border*** *region* 境界地方. ¶***boundary*** *regions* 境界地域. ¶in ***country*** *regions* いなかの地方で. ¶make ***desert*** *regions* fertile 不毛地方を肥やす. ¶a ***forest*** *region* 森林地帯. ¶a ***half-desert*** *region* 半さばく地方. ¶the ***Lake Superior*** *region* シューペリオル湖地方. ¶a newly-opened ***lumber*** *region* 新たに開拓された木材地域. ¶the ***money*** *region*, the land of stocks and shares 株の本場金融街. ¶an ***oil*** *region* 油の産地, 油田地域.

P ***in*** the *region* of the ear 耳の辺に.

register, *n.* 記録, 登録; 帳簿, 登録簿.

V ***establish*** a *register* of trained nurses 訓練を経た看護婦の登録簿を作成する. ¶Each class ***has*** a *register* of 70 to 100 students. 各組七十名ないし百名の学生がある. ¶***keep*** a *register* of their sales (names and addresses) その売上(など)を帳簿に記入する.

Q² an ***army*** *register* 陸軍将校名鑑. ¶The Columbia ***Alumni*** *Register*, 1754–1931 一七五四年から一九三一年までのコロンビア大学校友名簿. ¶a ***hotel*** *register* 宿帳. ¶a ***shipping*** *register* 船舶登記簿. ¶be left off the ***voting*** *register* 選挙人名簿から除かれる.

P write one's address ***in*** a *register* 住所を名簿に記入する ‖ enter names ***in*** the *register* of the school 学校の名簿に記名する. ¶The school has 1,444 students ***on*** the *register*. その学校は在籍学生千四百四十四名を有する. 【類】 any person ***on*** the *register* of the school / He is not ***on*** the *register*.

P² a *register* ***of*** births and deaths 出生死亡の登録簿.

register, *v.* 記録する, 記入する, 登録する.

M *register* it ***dearly*** in one's memory それをはっきりその記憶に刻みつける.

P *register* ***as*** a student at a university 大学の学生として登録する. 【類】 He *registered* himself ***as*** a doctor. ¶guests *registered* ***at*** the Imperial Hotel 帝国ホテル投宿者 ‖ The ship is *registered* ***at*** the port. その船は同港登録になっている. ‖ *Registered* and entered ***at*** Stationers' Hall 版権登録所で登録した. ¶*register* ***for*** a course 学校のある科に入学の手続をする. ¶It was *registered* ***in*** U.S. Patent Office, 1876. それは一八七六年合衆国の特許局に登録した. ‖ *register* one's name ***in*** the book at a hotel ホテルで名を帳簿に記入する ‖ be *registered* ***in*** the name of ... ...という名前で登録(記帳)されている. ¶The trade-mark is *registered* ***on*** the book of the Patent Office. その商標は特許局の帳簿に登録してある. ¶luggage *registered* ***to*** destination 到着先受取として預けた手荷物. ¶*register* ***with*** an office 事務所に登録する ‖ Before leaving passengers are requested to *register* ***with*** us the address to which their letters are to be sent. お客様の出立前にお手紙回送のため御住所をお書留め願います. 【類】 his name must be *registered* ***with*** the clerk of ...

registration, *n.* 記入, 登記, 登録.

V ***close*** their *registrations* [生徒などの]募集を締切る. ¶The university ***has*** a large *registration* (=enrollment) of Chinese students. その大学には中国の学生が多数在籍している.

V² New *registrations* ***take place*** almost every night. [学校に]ほとんど毎晩新入生がある.

Q In October, 1912, the ***total*** *registration* of students in New York University was 4,428. 一九一二年十月ニューヨーク大学の名簿に登録した学生の数は四千四百二十八名であった.

Q² New York has a ***motor*** *registration* of nearly 800,000. ニューヨークにはほとんど 80 万台の自動車が登録されている. ¶***vehicle*** *registration* 車両登録.

P² *Registration* ***for*** 19..., ... students. 19...年度募集, 学生...名.

regret, *n.* 後悔, 悔み; 哀悼; 遺憾, 残念; [通例 *pl.*] 断わり

V He well ***deserved*** the *regrets* with which he was followed to the grave. 彼の永眠が伝わると世人は深い哀惜の情を寄せたがまことにゆえあることであった. ¶widespread *regret* has been ***excited*** here by the sudden death of Mr. ... ...氏の急死で当地は一般に哀惜の意を表した. ¶We have to ***express*** our *regret* at the inadvertence. その不注意に対して私どもは遺憾の意を表せねばなりません. 【類】 ***express*** one's deep *regret* at the untimely death (若死) of ... / ***express*** *regret* over the death of ... ¶***feel*** great *regret* at parting from ... ...と別れることを深く残念に思う. ¶His death has ***occasioned*** widespread *regret*. 彼の死去は広く一般の哀惜を喚起した. ¶***proffer*** *regrets* at ... ...に対して遺憾の意を表する. ¶***profess*** *regret* 遺憾の意を表する. ¶***send*** one's *regrets* on a post-card 葉書で断わる. 【類】 He did not come but ***sent*** *regrets*. ¶***suffer*** in silence sharp *regrets* which arise from ... ...に起因する痛切な遺憾の念を黙々と忍ぶ.

Q to my ***bitter*** *regret* 私が残念にたえないことは. ¶express ***deep*** *regret* at ... ...に対して深い遺憾の意を表する. 【類】 it is with ***deep*** *regret* that we announce the death of ... ¶with ***deep-felt*** *regret* 深い遺憾の意を表して. ¶***general*** *regret* 一般の人々の哀惜. ¶to his ***infinite*** *regret* 彼が非常に遺憾に思うことは. ¶a ***keen*** *regret* 深い遺憾. ¶***morbid*** *regret* over the passing of the old order 昔の制度のなくなったことに対する病的な残念がりよう. ¶a ***sharp*** *regret* 痛恨. ¶we cannot but express our ***sincere*** *regret* at ... われわれは...に対して心から遺憾の意を表さざるを得ない. ¶with ***unfeigned*** *regret* いつわらざる遺憾の念をもって. ¶***Universal*** *regret* is expressed in Japan at his death. 彼の死に対して日本では広く哀悼の意を表している. ¶waste time in ***useless*** *regrets* [くやんでも]つまらぬことに時を徒費する.

P it is a matter ***for*** *regret* that ... ...ということは遺憾の次第である.【類】It is a matter ***for*** deep *regret.* ¶lose heart ***in*** *regret* 哀悼のあまり意気消沈する. ¶***To*** my deep *regret* I cannot accept your invitation. はなはだ遺憾ながら御招待に応じ兼ねます. ¶it was ***with*** keen *regret* that ... ...ということは遺憾千万のことであった ‖ refuse it ***with*** much *regret* はなはだ遺憾ながらそれを断わる.

P² receive a letter of *regret* ***at*** the occurrence そのできごとに対して悔みの手紙を受取る. ¶the greatest *regret* ***of*** my life 私の一生の最大恨事.

O What is done is done and *regret* is of no avail. やってしまったことは過ぎたことで後悔しても役に立たない.

regret, *v.* 後悔する, 悔む, 哀惜する.

M as a patriotic Japanese, I ***deeply*** *regret* that ... 国を愛する日本人として私は...を深く遺憾に思う. ¶make us ***greatly*** *regret* that ... ...はわれわれを非常に残念がらせる. ¶***keenly*** *regret* 深く遺憾に思う. ¶it is to be ***much*** *regretted* that ... ...はまことに残念だ(惜しい). ¶It is a matter ***sincerely*** to be *regretted.* 本当に残念なことである.

O it is to be *regretted* that ... ...ということは遺憾である. ¶I *regret* to say that ... 私は...ということを遺憾とする.

regretful, *a.* 残念な.

M One can imagine ***how*** *regretful* he was. どんなに残念がったことだろう.

P be *regretful* ***for*** what one has done 自分の行為を後悔している.

regular, *n.* 正規兵.

Q² ***Chinese Army*** *regulars* 中国陸軍の正規兵.

P The army is made up ***of*** *regulars* and volunteers. その軍は正規兵と不正規兵とから成っている.

regular, *a.* 規則正しい, 秩序整然たる.

P *regular* ***in*** one's habits (payment) 日常の慣習(など)が規則正しい.

regularity, *n.* 正確, きちょう面.

V *Regularity* ought to be ***observed,*** as regularity is very conducive to health. 規則正しくなければいけない, 規則正しくすることは非常に健康によいから.

Q act with ***mechanical*** *regularity* 機械のように規則正しく行動する. ¶with ***monotonous*** *regularity* 単調に規則正しく. ¶observe these rules with ***religious*** *regularity* この規則を厳粛に守る. ⌊のように規則正しく.

Q² with ***clockwork*** (=clocklike) *regularity* ぜんまい仕掛け

P He paid all his accounts ***with*** *regularity.* 彼はすべての勘定をきちんと払った.

P² *regularity* ***in*** one's life 生活上のきちょう面.

regulate, *v.* 整える, 取締る, 調整する.

M This device will ***automatically*** *regulate* the temperature of the room. この装置で室内の温度は自動的に調整される. ¶*regulate* ***strictly*** 厳重に取締る.

P taxi fares *regulated* ***by*** distance (time, weight) 距離(など)によって規定したタクシー料金. ¶*regulate* finances ***into*** normalcy 財政を平常の状態に調節する.

regulation, *n.* 調整, 調節; 規則.

V ***abolish*** the *regulation* providing ... ...に関する規定を廃止する. ¶***adopt*** stringent *regulations* against ... ...禁止の厳重な規定を採用する. ¶***break*** a *regulation* 規則を破る. ¶***carry out*** *regulations* 規程を実施する. ¶These are things that ***defy*** all *regulation.* これらは規則ではどうにもすることができないものだ. ¶***enforce*** a *regulation* 規則を励行する. ¶***establish*** a *regulation* 規則を設ける. ¶***frame*** *regulations* to control ... ...管理の規則を作る. ¶***infringe*** the *regulations* 規則に違反する. ¶***issue*** *regulations* 規則を出す. ¶through drastic *regulations* ***laid down*** and rigidly ***enforced*** by the authorities 当局者が設けかつ厳重に強制した徹底的な規則によって. ¶***make*** a *regulation* compelling ... to ... ...をして強制的に...させる規則を設ける. ¶***urge*** strict *regulations* 厳重な規則を強制する. ¶***violate*** (=***infringe***) these *regulations* これらの規則を破る.

V² *regulations* ***affecting*** trade marks 商標に関する規則.

Q any Member deemed guilty of an infringement of the ***above*** *Regulations* 上記の規則に違犯したと思われる会員はだれでも. ¶by ***departmental*** *regulations* 省令で. ¶***detailed*** *regulations* (=by-law) 細則. ¶... shall remain subject to the ***existing*** *regulations* ...は引続き現行規則の適用を受ける. ¶according to the ***following*** *regulations* 次の規則によって. ¶***minor*** *regulations* 細則. ¶under the ***new*** *regulations* 新しい規則の下に. ¶***sanitary*** *regulations* 衛生に関する規則.

Q² enforce the ***customs*** *regulations* 関税規則を励行する. ¶issue an ***emergency powers*** *regulation* 非常時権力の規則を発布する. ¶***enforcement*** *regulations* 施行規則. ¶a speech infringing the ***government*** *regulations* 政令に違反する演説 ‖ ***Government*** *regulation* of economic life 経済生活に関する政令. ¶by ***police*** *regulations* 警察取締規則によって. ¶violations of the ***price-control*** *regulations* 物価統制違反. ¶Under the ***school*** *regulations,* every student must ... 校則により学生はすべて...しなければならない. ¶***traffic*** *regulations* 交通規則.

P ***According to*** *regulations,* school closes to-day. 規定に従って学校は本日休校する. ¶it is ***against*** the *regulations* of ... それは...の規則違反である. ¶rule ... ***by*** *regulations* ...を規則で取締る. ¶a stickler ***for*** *regulations* 規則に拘泥する者. ¶***under*** *regulations* made in 1885 一八八五年に制定した規則の下に. 【類】***Under*** the *regulations* of the University, doctor's thesis (博士論文) must be printed.

P² break the street-car *regulation* ***against*** carrying living animals in the cars 生きた動物を乗せてはならないという電車規定に抵触する. ¶*regulations* ***for*** the transaction of business 商取引の規則. ¶*regulations* ***governing*** examinations 試験に関する規定. ¶the *regulations* ***of*** a university (club) 大学(など)の規則. ¶*regulations* ***respecting*** (=***regarding, relating to*** or ***pertaining to***) ... ...に関する規則. ¶*regulations* ***with regard to*** ... ...に関する規則.

regulator, *n.* 調節器.

Q² a ***thermostat*** *regulator* 整温器調節装置.

rehabilitate, *v.* 更生させる.

M *rehabilitate* former criminals ***completely*** 前科者を更正させる.

rehabilitation, *n.* 復旧.

Q² ***forest*** *rehabilitation* 森林復旧. ¶***school*** *rehabilitation* 学校復興. ¶Japan's ***postwar*** *rehabilitation* 日本の戦後の復興.【類】a sound program of ***postwar*** *rehabilitation.* ¶***world*** *rehabilitation* 世界復興.

rehash, *v.* やり直す, まき直す.

M The program was *rehashed* ***again and again.*** その計画は何べんも作り変えられた.

O *rehash* an old story 古い話を焼き直す.

rehearsal, *n.* 演習, 復誦, 温習会(リハーサル); 繰り返し, 物語.

V ***attend*** a *rehearsal* 下げいこに出る.

Q a ***public*** *rehearsal* 公開のリハーサル(独奏·独唱など).

Q² stage a ***dress*** *rehearsal* [コスチュームをつけて]本げいこをやる.

P² a *rehearsal* ***of*** her troubles 彼女の苦労のかずかず. ‖ a *rehearsal* ***of*** his recent experience 最近の経験談. 【類】a *rehearsal* ***of*** grievances.

rehearse, *v.* 演習する, 下げいこをする.

P *rehearse* ***for*** a new play 新劇の下げいこをやる. ¶*rehearse* a symphony ***for*** the occasion [演奏会などの]演奏の練習する.

Reich, *n.* ドイツ国.

Q² the collapse of the ***Hitler*** *Reich* ヒットラー政権の崩壊. ¶the ***Nazi*** *Reich* ナチ政権. ☞ ヒットラー時代には the Third Reich [第三帝国]と呼称された.

reign, *n.* 治世; 支配, 主権; 全盛, 流行.

Q the ***despotic*** *reign* of ... ...の専制政治. ¶a ***long*** and ***splendid*** *reign* 永続した光輝ある時代.

P ***during*** his *reign* 彼の治世中 ‖ ***during*** the five successive *reigns* 五代にわたって. ¶***in*** the *reign* of ... ...の御代に. ¶***under*** the *reign* of ... ...の治世の下に.

P² the *reign* ***of*** literature (the gramophone) 文学(など)の流行 ‖ the *reign* ***of*** the Emperor Meiji 明治天皇の御治世 ‖ the *Reign* ***of*** Terror [フランス革命の]恐怖時代. ¶in her *reign* ***over*** subject people 女王の治政時代に.

reign, *v.* 支配する, 全盛をきわめる.

M Silence *reigned* ***all over.*** あたりはしんとなった. ¶***Long*** *reign* the Emperor! 皇帝万歳. ¶Baseball *reigns* ***supreme*** in the summer months. 夏季は野球が全盛をきわめる.

P reign over people (subjects) 臣下を統治する. 【類】 reign over a vast domain.

reimburse, v. 払い戻す, 弁償する.

P reimburse a person for loss (damages, time, expenses) 人の損失(など)を償う.

rein, n. 手綱; 制御, 統御.

V adjust reins 手綱をさばく. ¶draw one's rein=draw in the reins 手綱を引く, 馬を止める. ¶gather [up] one's reins 手綱を引締める. ¶give the rein to fancy 想像をたくましくうする. 【類】 give rein to one's passions (情欲) / give rein to the licentious desires (いん欲). ¶hand over the reins of office=resign 辞職する. ¶hold the reins [手綱を取る意から]政権を握る. ¶hold the reins of government 政権を握る. ¶loosen (=let go) one's rein 手綱をゆるめる. ¶pull up the reins 手綱を引締める. ¶The Shogun resigned the reins of government into the hands of his son. 将軍はその世子に政権を譲った. ¶take the reins in (=into) one's hands 支配権を握る. 【類】 take the reins of power out of the hands of ... / take the reins of government (政権). ¶take over the reins of housekeeping 家政の任に当る.

Q hold the domestic reins 家政に当る. ¶give a (=the) free rein to conjecture (one's imagination) 推測(など)をたくましくする ‖ give a free rein to one's desires (wishes) その欲望(など)のおもむくままにする. ¶give loose rein to one's passions 放縦に身を持ちくずす. 【類】 those to whom from early childhood sensibility and impulsiveness have been given a loose rein.

P check with reins 手綱で制御する.

P² hold the reins of State 国家の主権を握る.

rein, v. 手綱を引く.

M rein back a horse 馬を(手綱を引いて)留める.

M² rein up (=halt) a horse 馬を留める.

reinforce, v. 強化する.

M The supply will be greatly reinforced. 補給は大いに強化されるだろう. 「ど).

Q with nylon-reinforced soles ナイロン強化底の(くつ下な

P socks reinforced at the points and the heels つま先とかかとを特別に丈夫にしたくつ下. 「を強化する.

O reinforce a bank (fortress, wall, provision) 土手(など)

reinforcement, n. 援兵, 援軍, 加勢.

V bring up reinforcements 援軍をくり出す. ¶dispatch reinforcements to ... …に援軍を急派する. ¶receive reinforcements 加勢を受ける. ¶send naval reinforcements 艦

Q² steel reinforcement 鉄鋼の支柱(など). 」隊を増派する.

reinstate, v. 元通りにする, 原状に復させる.

P She was reinstated as a wife. 彼女は妻としてもとのさやに収まった. ¶reinstate him in his post (=former office)

reissue, v. 再発行する. 」彼を復職させる.

M reissue a book partly revised 一部改訂した本を再出版す

reiteration, n. 繰返し, 反復. 」る.

P occur with painful reiteration うるさく反復して起る.

reject, v. 棄てる, 棄却する; 拒む, 否む.

M reject categorically 無条件に拒絶する. ¶decidedly reject a proposal 提案を断然はねつける. ¶reject an offer (appeal, a request, a demand) flatly 申し入れ(など)を断固ことわる. ¶reject positively 断固としてはねつける. ¶scornfully reject the proposal その申出をぶべつしてはねつける. ¶reject summarily あっさりはねつける.

P rejected as erroneous (wrong, irreligious) 間違(など)としてはねつけられて. ¶All Quiet on the Western Front was rejected by several publishers. 「西部戦線異状なし」は数人の出版者にはねつけられた. ¶He was rejected for physical defects. 彼は体に欠陥があって不合格になった. ¶rejected from a factory 工場からはねつけられて. ¶reject ... with contempt (=scorn) ばかにしてはねつける.

rejection, n. 拒絶.

V take a rejection of manuscript cheerfully and philosophically 没書を楽観的にあきらめる.

Q a point-blank rejection ぶっきらぼうの拒絶.

rejoice, v. 喜ぶ, 悦に入る, うれしく思う.

M heartily rejoice in ... …を心から喜ぶ. ¶The Poles openly rejoiced over the news of the Japanese victory. ポーランド人は日本が勝利を得たという報道に接して大っぴらに喜んだ. ¶Let us rejoice together on your success. 御成功をみんなでお喜び申上げます.

P the child rejoiced at the sight (news) of ... その子は…を見て(聞いて)喜んだ ‖ rejoice at seeing ... …を見て喜ぶ ‖ rejoice at the idea of ... …を思って喜ぶ ‖ He is rejoiced at their success. 彼は彼らの成功を喜んでいる. ¶rejoice in ... …に恵まれている, …をもっている ‖ Croydon rejoices in ([joc.]=has) quite a colony of Frenchmen. クロイドンには随分フランス人がいる. ‖ an odd character, rejoicing in the nickname of ... …というあだ名のある変った人物 ‖ while seemingly rejoicing in life's pleasures 見かけは人生を享楽しているようだが ‖ rejoice in one's youth (=is young) 年が若い. 【類】 rejoice in good health / rejoice in the birth of a son / rejoice in another's joy as one's own. ¶rejoice over the good news 吉報を得て喜ぶ. ¶I rejoice with him over his joys and success. 私は彼の喜びと成功をともに祝う.

O rejoice to hear of a person's success 人の成功を聞いて喜ぶ. 【類】 rejoice to see a person.

rejoicing, n. 喜び, 喜悦, 歓喜, 祝い.

V the news caused great rejoicing among ... そのニュースが…間に大なる喜びを呼び起した. ¶great rejoicing took place there upon the receipt of the news of ... …の報を受けるとそこでは大喜びであった.

Q an exuberant rejoicing 盛んな喜び. ¶popular rejoicing 民衆の喜び. ¶There is universal rejoicing. だれもかれもが喜んでいる.

Q² a quiet family rejoicing ひそかな一家の喜び.

P² great rejoicings at the festival (wedding) お祭(など)の大祝い. ¶rejoicings in Tokyo over a victory 勝利に対す

rejoin, v. 復帰させる. 」る東京人の喜び.

P be rejoined to (=with) the former regiment 前の連隊

rejoinder, n. 返答; 言い返し. 」に復帰させられる.

V make a sharp rejoinder しっぺ返しする.

Q a crisp rejoinder はきはきした答弁. ¶a "cutting" rejoinder 辛らつな答弁. ¶a slightly sarcastic rejoinder 少し皮肉な返答. ¶a witty rejoinder 機知に富んだ返答.

rejuvenation, n. 若返り, 回春.

V undergo a complete rejuvenation すっかり若返る.

P undergo an operation for rejuvenation 若返りの手術を

rekindle, v. 再燃する. 」受ける.

P Our hopes rekindled for a brief period. ちょっとの間ま

relapse, n. 後戻り; ぶり返し, 再発. 」た希望がわいた.

V have a relapse [of a disease] ぶり返す. ¶suffer a relapse 再発する. ¶Relapses occur. 再発する.

relapse, v. 後戻りする, 再発する.

M The country soon relapsed into a divided state. 同国は間もなくもとの分割国家に戻った.

P relapse into a brown study once more 再び思案にくれる ‖ relapse into silence (idleness, poverty, vice) また沈黙(など)にかえる ‖ relapse into a state of barbarism 野蛮状態に逆行する. 「せる.

relate, v. 委細を語る, 述べる, 話す; 関係させる, 縁者にさ

M relate briefly 簡単に述べる. ¶closely related 密接な関係をもって ‖ closely related in thought 思想的に密接な関係がある. ¶distantly related to ... …と遠縁の. 【類】 The cat is distantly related to the tiger. ¶How are you related to her? 彼女とはどういう御関係ですか. ¶be intimately related with ... …と密接に関係している ‖ once so intimately related as to have a child born to them 子までなした仲. ¶be very loosely related to ... …とは関係が薄い. ¶mutually related 相互的に関係して. ¶nearly related 近縁の. ¶be related only slightly ほんのわずかの関係がある. ¶relate one's adventures vividly (=graphically) 冒険談を真に迫ったように話す.

P related by blood (marriage) 血族(など)関係のある. ¶it is related of Mr. F that ... F氏について…という話が伝えられている. ¶related on the father's side 父方の縁者で. ¶Are you related to Count T? あなたはT伯とご縁筋ですか. ¶It is difficult to relate it with (=to) any known cause. その原因をつきとめることはむずかしい.

O Curious to relate, the giraffe has no voice. おかしな話だが, ジラフには声がない.

relation, n. [しばしば pl.] 関係; 縁故, 親類; 物語.

V affect friendly relations 親密な関係をそこなう. ¶He assimilated the relation between the Emperor and his people to that between father and son. 彼は天皇と人民の関係を父子の関係と同一と考えた. ¶A bears the same *relation* to B that C bears to D. C が D に対すると同様の関係を A は B に対して持っている. ‖ ***bear*** no *relation* to ... ...に対して関係がない. ¶ He ***broke*** [*off*] all *relations* with her. 彼は彼女とぷっつり縁を切った. 【類】 ***break off*** the *relation* of teacher and pupil. / the diplomatic *relations* have been ***broken off*** between ... ¶ ***bring about*** better *relations* by the removal of the sources of misunderstanding and prejudices 誤解や偏見の根源を除去して一層の親善関係をもたらす. 【類】 He is working actively to ***bring about*** closer *relations* between Italy and the United States. ¶ ***build up*** a commercial *relation* 商業上の関係を打立てる. ¶ ***carry on*** a Platonic *relation* with ... ...と純潔な関係を持続する. ¶ He has done so much to ***cement*** the *relations* between England and Japan. 彼は日英両国の関係を強固にするために大いに尽力した. 【類】 It would do much to further ***cement*** the cordial *relations* existing between the two countries. ¶ ***continue*** the strained *relations* 緊張した関係を続ける. ¶ ***credit*** a *relation* 話を信じる. ¶ ***cultivate*** closer *relations* with ... ...と一層の親善関係を結ぶ. 【類】 ***cultivate*** friendly *relations* between the two nations. ¶ ***develop*** friendly *relations* between ... ...間の親交関係を増進する. 【類】 ***develop*** better *relations* among the nations. ¶ ***discontinue*** all *relations* with ... ...と一切関係を絶つ. ¶ ***dissolve*** one's business *relation* with ... ...と商取引を絶つ. ¶ ***disturb*** the amicable *relations* 親善関係を乱す. ¶ ***encourage*** more friendly *relations* between the two neighbourly peoples この二隣邦間に一層の親善関係を結ぶように努める. ¶ ***endanger*** the friendly *relations* now existing between ... ...間に現存する親交関係を危機に落し入れる. ¶ He ***enjoys*** friendly *relations* with his workmen. 彼はその職工たちと親密な間柄である. ¶ ***establish*** the best *relations* with ... ...とできるだけの親善関係を打立てる. 【類】 ***establish*** trade (=commercial *or* business) *relations* / ***establish*** and maintain friendly *relations*. ¶ in order to ***facilitate*** their trading *relations* with the Far East 彼らの極東との商取引を容易にさせるために. ¶ ***form*** a *relation* by marriage 結婚によって縁者となる. ¶ ***further*** the trade *relations* between ... and ... ...間の商取引を拡張する. ¶ ***have*** no *relation* to ... ...と無関係である. 【類】 a woman who ***has*** *relations* with a man. ¶ I can in no way better ***illustrate*** the *relation* of A to B than by saying ... A の B に対する関係を説明するに...というのが一番よい方法と思う. ¶ ***impair*** (=affect *or* hurt) the *relations* between ... ...間の関係をそこなう. ¶ ***improve*** the friendly *relations* between ... and ... ...間の親交関係を増進する. 【類】 ***improve*** international *relations* between Japan and America. ¶ ***intensify*** the happy *relations* which prevail between the two nations 二国間に現存する友交関係を深める. ¶ ***maintain*** a *relation* of vassalage to ... ...に対する従属関係を維持する. ¶ ***open*** commercial *relations* with ... ...と商取引を開く. ¶ ***perceive*** the *relations* of thought to thought 思想対思想の関係を知る. ¶ seriously ***prejudice*** the friendly *relations* between ... ...間の親交関係を大いにそこなう. ¶ ***promote*** cordial *relations* between Japan and America 日米間の親密な関係を増進する. ¶ ***promote*** and ***consolidate*** business *relations* between ... ...間の商取引を助成し強固にさせる. ¶ ***re-establish*** former *relations* 以前の関係を復活する. ¶ ***re-open*** commercial *relations* with Japan 再び日本と商取引を開始する. ¶ ***resume*** trade *relations* with Germany ドイツと再び商取引を始める. ¶ ***secure*** closer *relations* with ... ...と一層近接な関係をつける. ¶ I go home every summer to ***see*** my family *relations*. 私は毎夏父母兄弟と会いに帰省する. ‖ ***sever*** (=break) diplomatic *relations* with ... ...との国交関係を絶つ. ¶ ***strain*** the *relations* between the two countries 二国間の関係を緊張させる. 【類】 ***strain*** the *relations* of the two Powers. / The *relations* between nations now are ***strained*** in many ways. ¶ ***strengthen*** the cordial *relations* which have [*for*] so long subsisted between ... ...間に非常に永い間存在して来た親密な関係を強固にさせる. ¶ ***unsettle*** the diplomatic *relations* of ... ...の外交関係を危くする.

v² Their *relations* with ... were gradually ***becoming*** more and more ***estranged***, until their differences culminated in open rupture. ...との彼らの関係は疎遠そ隔になり遂に公然の断絶となった. 【類】 *relations* ***became*** so ***strained*** that ... ¶ cement friendly *relations* which have ***exsisted*** between ... ...間に存在してきた親善関係を強固にする. ¶ An intimate ***relation grew up***. 親密な関係が生じた. ¶ the re-establishment of those friendly *relations* which once ***subsisted*** between ... ...間に存在したあの親交関係の再建.

Q maintain ***amicable*** *relations* with foreign nations 外国と親善関係を維持する. ¶ His ***amorous relations*** with her is suspected. 彼はその女と怪しいと思われている. ¶ the improvement of ***Anglo-French commercial*** *relations* 英仏商業関係の進展. ¶ improve ***brotherly*** *relations* between ... ...間の友交関係を増進する. ¶ It stands in a ***causal*** *relation* to the event. それはその事件の原因をなしている. ¶ The somewhat ***chilly*** *relations* between Japan and the United States are beginning to thaw out. 日米間の少しく気まずい関係が今や融和しかかっている. ¶ a ***chronological*** *relation* 年代上の関係. ¶ bring about ***closer*** *relations* between East and West 東西両洋の関係を更に親密にさせる. ¶ have ***commercial*** *relations* with ... ...と商取引をしている. ¶ restoration of their ***conjugal*** *relations* 彼らの夫婦関係の復活. ¶ Self-control is the very basis of ***co-operative*** and ***constructive*** *relations* with one's fellows. 自制は友だちとの協力一致的関係を持続するそもそもの土台である. ¶ ***cordial*** *relations* 親しい間柄. ¶ promote ***cultural*** *relations* between ... ...の間に文化の交流を助成する. 【類】 the ***cultural*** *relations* of the West and the East. ¶ ***diagonal*** *relation* of position はすっかい. ¶ a rupture of ***diplomatsc*** *relations* 国交の断絶 ‖ resumption of full ***diplomatic*** *relations* 全面的外交関係の再開. 【類】 This made cordial ***diplomatic*** *relations* somewhat difficult to maintain. ¶ He was placed in ***direct personal*** *relation* with his instructor. 彼はその先生のけいがいに接するようになった. ¶ ***distant*** *relations* (=relatives) 遠縁の者. ¶ the ***early*** *relations* of the East with Greece 古代における東洋とギリシアとの交渉. ¶ my ***female*** *relations* 私の女の親せきたち. ¶ establish ***friendly*** *relations* with ... ...と親交を結ぶ. ¶ I would have no ***further*** *relations* with him. 私は彼とこれ以上の関係を持つことを欲しない. ¶ ***grammatical*** *relations* 文法的関係. ¶ ***happy domestic*** *relations* 幸福な家庭. ¶ ***harmonious*** *relations* むつまじい間柄. ¶ ***human*** *relations* 人倫. ¶ ***industrial*** *relations* 産業関係. ¶ bring about ***international friendly*** *relations* 国際的友交をもたらす. ¶ stand in ***intimate*** *relations* to ... ...と親密な間柄にある. ¶ in the interest of good ***Japanese-American*** *relations* 日米親善のために. ¶ ***legal*** *relation* 法律関係. ¶ ***logical*** *relation* 論理的関係. ¶ have ***marital*** *relations* with ... ...と夫婦関係を結んでいる. ¶ ***near*** *relations* of ours われわれの近親. ¶ cultivate the best ***neighborly*** *relations* with ... ...と最好の善隣関係を結ぶ. ¶ re-establish ***normal*** *relations* 正常な関係を再び結ぶ. ¶ The girl lives with her parents in very ***painful*** *relations*. その娘は両親と始終いがみあって暮している. ¶ break ***peaceful*** *relations* with ... ...との平和な関係を破る. ¶ have ***personal*** *relations* with ... ...親しく関係している ‖ be expert at ***personal*** *relations* 人事関係を手がけている. ¶ His ***poor*** *relations* are a great drag on him. 貧しい親類は彼にとってはやっかいだ. ¶ lay bare his ***private*** *relations* to ... ...との彼の私的関係を暴露する. ¶ in their ***proper*** *relations* 彼らの正当な関係で. ¶ build better ***public*** *relations* 一層親密な渉外関係を結ぶ. ¶ seem to have no ***recognizable*** *relation* to ... ...と認められるような関係はないらしい. ¶ a ***remote*** (=distant) *relation* 遠縁. ¶ set them in ***right*** *relation* to each other 彼らに正当な相互関係を結ばせる. ¶ it bears the ***same*** *relations* to ... それは...に対して同じ関係がある. ¶ have ***sexual*** *relations* with ... ...と性的に関係する ‖ abstain from ***sexual*** *relations* 性的関係を控える. ¶ bear ***some*** *relation* to ... ...に幾分の関係がある. ¶ ***spatial*** and ***temporal*** *relation* 空間的時間的関係. ¶ ***strained*** *relations* 断絶しかかっている不和な間柄. ¶ the ***syntactical*** *relations* of a word, as a unit of speech, with its environment 言葉の一単位としての一つの語とその前後の部分との構文的関係. ¶ ***social*** *relations* 社会的関係. ¶ put things in their ***true*** *relations* 物事の相互関係を明かにする.

Q² becloud ***Big Three*** *relations* 三大強国の関係に陰影を投じる. ¶ ***blood*** *relations* 血のつながり. ¶ have ***business*** *relations* with ... ...と取引関係がある. 【類】 those with whom he has ***business relations*** / I want to express the hope that our pleasant ***business relations*** will continue. ¶***employer-employe*** *relations* 雇主雇人の関係. ¶***labor*** *relations* 労働関係 ‖ an expert in ***labor*** *relations* 労働関係の専門家. 【類】a well integrated mechanism to adjust ***labor*** *relations* in the interests of continued production. ¶***labor-industry*** *relations* 労働者と産業の関係. ¶improve ***labor-management*** *relations* 労使関係を改善する. ¶***land-owner-tenant*** *relations* 地主と借地人の関係. ¶He was a member of the 1931 conference of the Institute of the *Pacific Relations*. 彼は太平洋関係研究所の 1931 年度会議に出席した. ¶better ***race*** *relations* 人種関係を改善する. 【類】seek to improve ***race*** *relations* in the South. ¶***student-faculty*** (=faculty and student) *relations* 学生と教授の関係. ¶the ***student-instructor*** *relations* 師弟の関係. ¶***tenant-landlord*** *relations* 家主と借家人の関係. ¶***thought*** *relations* [文章の]思想の関係. ¶develop ***trade*** *relations* with ... ...との貿易関係を増進する. ¶the earliest ***trade*** *relations* with ... ...との初期の貿易関係 ‖ We are in intimate ***trade*** *relations* with that country. わが国とその国とは親密な通商関係がある. 【類】establish new ***trade*** *relations* between / Japanese participation in world ***trade*** *relations* ... / worldwide ***trade*** *relations* / Japan's resumption of normal ***trade*** *relations* with the outside world / resume normal ***trade*** *relations* with the rest of the world. ¶***wage-price*** *relations* 賃金と価格の関係.

P sex ***in*** *relation* to society 社会的に見た性 ‖ seeing parts ***in*** *relation* to a whole 部分を全体に関連して観察すること. 【類】the cinema ***in*** its *relations* to intellectual life ‖ a great danger ***in*** our *relations* with ... ...との関係における一大危険. ¶come ***into*** intimate *relations* with ... ...と親交を結ぶにいたる. ¶the country is ***on*** hostile *relations* with ... その国は...と敵対関係にある. ¶***with*** *relation* to that affair その件に関して.

P² the *relations* ***between*** secondary schools and colleges 中等学校と大学専門学校との関係 ‖ the promotion of better *relations* ***between*** Japan and America 日米間の親善促進 ‖ the principle of the invariability of the *relation* ***between*** cause and effect 原因結果の不変原理. ¶*relation* ***by*** marriage (blood) 結婚(血統)による縁続き ‖ a *relation* ***by*** mother's side 母方の親類. ¶a *relation* ***in*** the fourth degree 第四等親. ¶he is a *relation* ***of*** Mr. ... あの人は...氏の親類である. ¶the *relations* ***of*** the sexes 男女関係 ‖ the *relations* ***of*** geography and history 地理と歴史の関係. 【類】the *relations* ***of*** art ***to*** morality / the *relation* ***of*** Confucianism (儒教) ***to*** Buddhism. ¶My *relations* ***with*** him are now quite friendly. 私の彼に対する関係は今はきわめて良好である. ‖ the cultivation of good *relations* ***with*** China 中国との親善関係の開拓.

relationship, *n.* 関係, 親類, 親族関係.

V ***bear*** no *relationship* to ... ...と何等関係がない. ¶***bring about*** a closer *relationship* between ... ...間を一層親密にする. ¶further ***cement*** the *relationship* and friendship which exist between ... ...間に現存する親密な関係と交わりとを更に強固にする. ¶***change*** one's love *relationships* frequently しばしば恋愛関係の相手を替える. ¶***create*** an intimate *relationship* with ... ...と親密な関係を作る. ¶***cultivate*** confidential *relationship* of ... ...の信頼を得ようと努める. ¶***determine*** the *relationship* of ... ...との関係を決定する. ¶***establish*** a closer *relationship* with the peoples of the world in order to secure the course of international peace and justice 国際平和と正義を確立するために世界各国民と一層親密な関係を結ぶ. ¶***form*** an intimate *relationship* with ... ...と親密な関係を作る. ¶it ***has*** a *relationship*, both direct and indirect, to ... それは...に対して直接間接関係がある ‖ ***have*** a *relationship* to ... ...に関係がある. 【類】***have*** no *relationship* with ... ¶Shelley did not ***legalize*** his *relationship* to Mary Godwin until after the suicide of Harriet, his first wife, in 1816. シェリーは 1816 年彼の最初の妻ハリエットの自殺後までメリー・ゴドウィンを正式の妻とは認めなかった. ¶***recognize*** the *relationship* その関係を認める. ¶***steady*** the *relationships* between ... ...間の関係を確固たるものにする. ¶***trace*** the *relationship* between ... ...間の関係を研究する.

Q if we consider them in their ***broadest*** *relationships* 最も広い意味で彼らを考えるならば. ¶by a curious ***causal*** *relationship* 不思議な縁で. ¶there is a ***close*** *relationship* between ... and ... ...と...との間には密接な関係がある. ¶have a ***direct*** *relationship* to ... ...と直接関係がある. ¶***happier social*** *relationships* 一層幸福な社会関係. ¶***near*** or ***remote*** *relationships* 近いまたは遠い親類. ¶a wife's carelessness about personal attractiveness and ***physical*** *relationships* of marriage 個人的魅力と結婚の肉体的関係について妻の無関心. ¶She formed a ***secret*** *relationship* with a lover. 彼女は愛人と秘密関係を作った. ¶***sexual*** *relationship* 性的関係. ¶bring about a ***strained*** *relationship* 緊張した関係を招来する.

Q² persons connected by ***blood*** *relationship* 血のつながっている人々. ¶degrees of ***family*** *relationship* 親族関係の等級. ¶form a ***love*** *relationship* with ... ...との恋愛関係を結ぶ. 【類】He has had four ***love*** *relationships* in the past three years. ¶the ***price-wage*** *relationship* 物価と賃金の関係. ¶***teacher-pupil*** *relationships* 教師と生徒の関係. ¶the '***oyabun-kobun***' (***boss-henchman***) *relationship* 親分子分の関係.「係にある.

P stand ***in*** the same *relationship* to ... ...に対して同じ関

P² There is some deep *relationship* ***between*** them. 彼らの間には何か深い関係がある. 【類】the *relationship* ***between*** God and Man. ¶*relationship* ***by*** blood 血族関係. ¶a *relationship* ***of*** unquestioning political loyalty, given and returned, between "the boss" and his subordinates 親分と子分の間に取交わされる絶対性の政治的忠誠 Lの関係.

relative, *n.* 親類, 縁者, 血族.

V I ***have*** no *relatives* or in-laws in this town. 私はこの町に親類も縁者もない.

Q a ***distant*** *relative* 遠い親類. ¶***humble*** *relatives* 身分の卑しい親類. ¶***near*** *relatives* 近い親類. 【類】a ***near*** *relative* of mine. ¶***rascally*** *relatives* with empty pockets すかんぴんで無頼な親類たち. ¶the word "tour" and its ***younger*** *relatives* "tourism" and "tourist." "tour" という語とその後にできた血族語 "tourism" と "tour- List."

P associate ***as*** *relatives* 親類としてつき合う.

P² *relatives* ***by*** affinity 姻族.

relative, *a.* 関する, 対立的の.

P Supply is *relative* ***to*** demand. 供給は需要と相関関係がある. 【類】They are *relative* ***to*** each other. / *relative* (=relating) ***to*** a question (matter) / casualties *relative* ***to*** traffic accidents.

relax, *v.* ゆるめる; ゆるむ, 緩やかになる.

P Discipline seems *relaxed* among the soldiers. 兵士間の規律がゆるんだようだ. ¶Do not *relax* ***in*** your exertions. 努力をゆるめるな. ¶His features *relaxed* ***into*** a smile. 彼はにっこり和らいだ顔を見せた. 【類】faces *relax* ***into*** amused (愉快そうな) smiles. 「で休養したまえ.

O Take a day or two off and *relax* [yourself]. 一二日休ん

relaxation, *n.* ゆるみ; くつろぎ, 気晴らし.

V He ***requires*** a little *relaxation*. 彼は少し気晴らしをする必要がある. ¶***seek*** *relaxation* after a hard day's work 一日うんと働いた後休養を求める. ¶***undergo*** *relaxation* 気がゆるむ.

P² Gardening is a *relaxation* ***after*** business (fatigues). 園芸は仕事(など)の後では気晴らしになる. ¶A hobby gives you *relaxation* ***from*** your labors. 道楽は骨休みにな Lる.

relay, *n.* 代り人; 継馬, 駅伝(リレー); 〖放送〗中継.

V ***require*** a *relay* of horses at every eight miles 八マイルごとに馬を乗り継ぐ必要がある. ¶***send*** *relays* of runners to long distances with verbal messages 伝言を帯びて遠距離へ中継飛脚を出す.

Q a ***fresh*** *relay* of workers (missionaries) 新しい労働者(など)の交替. ¶***New*** *relays* of men were dispatched to the battle front. 戦線へ増援部隊を急派した.

Q² ***broadcast*** *relays* 放送中継. ¶a ***vacuum tube*** *relay* 真空管継電器.

P work ***by*** (=***in***) *relays* 交替で働く ‖ The coffin was borne ***in*** *relays* of men, 18 in number. 棺は十八人の男が交替でかついだ.

relay, *v.* 駅伝で送る, 交替させる; 〖ラジオ〗中継放送する.

P *relay* a message (news) ***to*** a place ある場所へ伝言を中継する.

O *relay* broadcast music 音楽を中継放送する. L継する.

release, *n.* 放免, 解放, 解除; 慰安.

V ***obtain*** *release* from an obligation 責務を解除される.

Q It was a really ***happy*** *release* from great suffering. そ

れが苦しみを免かれる救いの神だった. ¶since his *last release* from prison 彼の最後の出所以来.

Q² a *casualty release* 死傷者の発表. ¶a *food release* 食糧の放出. ¶a *press* (=*news*) *release* 記事解禁.

P² the *release of* 600,000 tons of American foodstuffs 米国食糧六十万トンの放出.

release, *v.* 解放する, 釈放する, 免除する;〖映〗封切る.

M a *very recently released* French film ごく最近封切られたフランス映画.

P *release* a bomb *from* a warplane 軍用機から爆弾を落す ‖ *release* him *from* his debt 彼の借金を免除してやる ‖ He was *released from* the gaol (=prison). 彼はろう獄から釈放された. ‖ be *released from* duty 解職される ‖ workers *released from* toil for the day 一日の労働を終えた労働者たち. 【類】a British prisoner (捕虜) *released from* Germany / The agonies he suffered until death *released* him *from* his torments. / *release* a person *from* the responsibility for ... / war prisoners *released from* a German camp /be *released from* the purge list (追放のリスト) / *release* a person *from* custody (拘留) / be *released from* employment without prejudice (権利を侵害せずに) as of 31 August 1951. ¶an American film *released in* Japan 日本で封切の米国映画. ¶General Grodekoff has been *released of* his command of the Russian military forces in the Far East. グロデコフ将軍は極東におけるロシア陸軍の司令官を解任された. ¶He was *released on* parole. 彼は宣誓の上釈放された. ¶the seized goods will be *released upon* payment of a fine of ... 没収品は...の罰金を払うと同時に引渡す.

relegate, *v.* 追放する, しりぞける, 排斥する.

P be *relegated to* appendices 付録の方に回す ‖ She was *relegated to* the second place amidst the Great Powers of the world. その国は世界の列強中第二位にけ落された. ‖ I think that should be *relegated to* the past. それは過去のものとして葬り去るべきだと思う. ‖ It is *relegated* entirely *to* the background. それは全く後方へ押しのけられた. ‖ *relegate* magazines *to* the waste-paper basket 雑誌をくずかごに投入する.

relent, *v.* 不びんに思う.

P *relent toward* ... ...に対してあわれみを感じる.

relevance, *n.* 関連, 適当, 適切.

V *have relevance* to ... ...に関連している.

relevant, *a.* 関連する, 関係する.

P matters not strictly *relevant to* the subject 厳密にはその問題に関係のない事柄 ‖ data *relevant to* (=bearing upon) eugenic research 優生学の研究に関係のある資料.

reliable, *a.* 信頼できる.

M The news is *most reliable.* そのニュースは大いに信頼できる.

reliance, *n.* 頼み, 依頼, 信頼; よりどころ.

V *place* every *reliance* upon ... ...に全面的に信頼する. ¶*place* no *reliance* on ... ...を信用しない. 【類】In the absence of actual data no *reliance* can be *placed* (=*put*) on such figures.

Q I place *great reliance* on his judgment. 私は彼の判断を大いに信頼している. ¶place *implicit reliance* on the thorough correctness of ... ...の全く正しいことを暗黙のうちに信用する. ¶*much reliance* cannot be placed on ... ...はあまり信用ができない.

P *reliance on* one's promise (judgment) その約束(など)を信用すること. ¶*reliance upon* God神 を信頼すること.

relic, *n.* 遺物, 遺品, 記念物, かたみ.

Q *Dickens's relics* ディケンズの遺品. ¶a *genuine relic* of ancient days 昔の日本の遺物. ¶a *hoary relic* 大昔の遺物. ¶a *sacred relic* 神聖な遺物. ¶*venerable relics* of the past 貴重な古物.

P² a *relic of* early civilization 古代文明の遺物 ‖ *relics of* superstition 迷信の名残り. ¶*relics pertaining to* Carlyle カーライルに関する遺品.

relief, *n.* (**1**) 救済, 救助, 援助; 軽減, 慰藉(じゃ), 気晴らし; 交代.

V This *affords* great *relief* to the pain. これはその苦痛には大変よくきく. ¶A thunderstorm in hot weather *brings relief.* 暑い時のにわか雨は助かる. ¶*distribute relief* あまねく慰藉を与える. ¶*feel* intense *relief* 大助かりだと思う. ¶The drunkard pretends that he drinks to *find relief* from his domestic troubles, while in fact his intemperance has caused them. 酔漢は家庭のいざこざから免れるために飲むのだと言っているが実は自分の不節制が家庭争議の原因なのだ. ‖ *find relief* from taking a medicine 薬を飲んで楽になる. ¶The momentary *relief* was *followed* by worse suffering. その一時的慰藉の後には一層の苦痛が続いて来た. ¶*give relief* 慰藉を与える, 楽にする. 【類】The medicine will *give* immediate *relief.* ¶*have relief* from pain 苦痛を免れる. ¶*obtain relief* 楽になる. ¶*seek relief* from suffering 苦悩から免れようとする. 【類】*seek relief* from a tiresome journey.

Q Speak English. I know it well.—Thank you, that is a *great relief.* 僕は英語をよく知っているから英語でやりたまえ—有難う, そりゃ大いに助かります. ¶*indoor* (*outdoor*) *relief* [救貧院の]院内(外)救助. ¶An injection of morphine always affords *instantaneous relief.* モヒ注射は何時も即効がある. ¶there was an *intense relief* to find that ... ...してまあよかったと思う. ¶It came as a *merciful relief.* それは大助かりであった. ¶obtain *permanent relief* 全治する. ¶*poor relief* 貧民救済. ¶I find it a *pleasant relief* now and again to ... 折々...することが愉快な慰安となる. ¶give *quick relief* 即効がある. ¶bring *sudden relief* 突然効験を示す. ¶It brought such *sweet relief* to me. それで私は非常に慰安を得た. ¶give only *temporary relief* ほんの一時しのぎになるだけである.

Q² *emergency relief* 非常救済. ¶*farm relief* 農村救済. ¶*stop-gap relief* 一時しのぎの救済. ¶a *welcome relief* from ... ...からのありがたい救い.

P He has now been ordered complete rest *as* a *relief* from the nervous exhaustion from which he is suffering. 彼は神経衰弱をなおすために完全な休養を命じられた. ¶*by way of relief* 救助として. ¶*for* the (=in) *relief* of the sufferers by the typhoid outbreak at ... ...における腸チフス発生の救助に. ¶He is in need *of relief.* 彼は救助の必要がある. ¶troops came *to* the *relief* of ... 軍隊が...の救援にやって来た ‖ *to* one's *relief* ほっとしたことには. 【類】it was a *relief to* me that ... / *To* my great *relief* the pain is gone. ¶travel across wide stretches of Siberia *without relief* 無味単調なシベリアの大平原を横断する.

P² die to find *relief from* remorse 死んで悔恨(の苦痛)をのがれる.

(**2**) 浮き彫り; くっきり.

Q Mt. Fuji stands out in *bold relief* against the blue sky. 富士山が青空にくっきりそびえている. ¶in *full relief* くっきりと. ¶bring into *harsh relief* 半浮彫にする. ¶curve in *high* (*low*)*relief* 厚(薄)肉彫をする. ¶stand out in *marked relief* くっきり目立っている. ¶His action stood out in *strong relief.* 彼の行動は目に立った.

P a figure sculptured *in relief* 浮彫にした像 ‖ a pattern woven *in relief* on a white ground 白地に浮彫にした模様 ‖ work *in relief* 浮出し細工. ¶bring ... *into* bold *relief* ... をくっきり出す.

P² stand out in strong *relief against* the blue sky [山など]こんぺきの空にくっきりと見える.

relieve, *v.* 救済する, 安心させる, 軽減する, 交代させる; 解任する; 目立たす.

M I was *greatly relieved* at the news. そのニュースで大安心した.

P *relieved against* the background 背景からくっきり浮出して. ¶Sentinels are *relieved at* intervals. ほしょう兵は時々交代する. ‖ be *relieved at* noon 正午交代になる ‖ I was *relieved at* the news. 私はその報道を聞いて安心した. ¶He was *relieved by* another person. 彼は別の人と交代した. ¶*relieve* a person *from* pain (suffering, temptation) 人を苦(など)から救う ‖ *relieve* a person *from* the charge of ... その人の非難がぬぐわれる ‖ He cannot be *relieved from* fulfilling the agreement. 彼はその協定の実施を回避することはできない. 【類】be *relieved from* the necessity of ... / be *relieved from* the fulfilment of the agreement. ¶*relieve* a person *of* the burden of ... 人から...の重荷を除いてやる ‖ The general was *relieved of* his office as a supreme commander. 同将軍は最高司令官の職を解かれた. ¶There are in her home three maids who *relieve* her *of* all house work. ‖ Let me *relieve* you *of* your jewels. その宝石をよこせ(強盗が婦人に). ¶*relieved with* a pattern 模様が浮出して.

religion, *n.* 宗教, 宗旨.

V *abjure* one's *religion* 自分の宗旨を棄てる. ¶*ban* a *religion* 宗教を禁止する. ¶*cherish* in secret their old *reli-*

gion 彼らの昔からの宗旨をこっそり信じている. ¶*embrace* a *religion* 宗教に帰依する. ¶*establish* a world *religion* which will unite all creeds 全宗旨を統一する世界的宗教を創設する. ¶*experience religion* (俗) 発心する. ¶*exterminate* a *religion* 宗教を根絶する. ¶*found* a *religion* 宗教の始祖となる. ¶*identify religion* with religious rites 宗教と宗教的儀式を同一視する. ¶*persecute* a *religion* 宗教を迫害する. ¶*preach* (=*teach*) *religion* 宗教を説く. ¶*profess* a *religion* 宗教を信奉する. 【類】What *religion* do you *profess*? ¶*proscribe* a *religion* 宗教を禁じる. ¶*remodel* an old *religion* 古い宗教を改造する. ¶*renounce* the Christian *religion* キリスト教を捨てる.

Q an *alien religion* 外来宗教. ¶*ancestral religions* 祖先の宗教. ¶Buddhism is one of *Asia's greatest religions*. 仏教は東洋の大宗教の一つである. ¶a *banned religion* 禁止されている宗教. ¶the *Christian religion* キリスト教. ¶a *diabolical religion* 邪教. ¶the *dominant religion* of Japan 日本で最も広く行われている宗教. ¶the *established religion* 国教. ¶*extra-Christian religions* キリスト教以外の宗教. ¶tolerate a *foreign religion* 外国の宗教を許容する. ¶the *humanistic religion* of service for the common weal, a social honor which puts the health and happiness of all first and the wealth of self second 万人の健康幸福を第一として自己の富を第二とするような一般の幸福, 社会の名誉のために奉仕する人道的宗教. ¶Shintoism is the *national religion* of Japan. 神道は日本の国教である. ¶There is uncertainty concerning the *oldest religion* of the Chinese. 中国の最古の宗教については不明の点がある. ¶*pre-Christian religions* キリスト教以前の諸宗教. ¶the *three imported religions* 外来の三宗教.

Q² *Buddhist religion*=Buddhism 仏教. ¶*lip religion* 口先ばかりの宗教. ¶a *living religion* 生きた宗教. ¶make Roman Catholicism the official *state religion* ローマカトリック教を公式の国教とする. 【類】abolish Shinto as a *state religion*. ¶a *world religion* 世界的宗教.

P sneer *at religion* 宗教を軽視する. ¶elevated *by religion* 宗教によって向上して. ¶believe *in religion* 宗教を信じる. ¶lead the life *of religion* 宗教生活を送る ‖ Shintoism and Buddhism are the chief forms *of religion* in Japan. 神道と仏教が日本の主たる宗教である.

religious, *a.* 宗教の, 宗教を信奉する, 信心の.

M with *almost religious* care 厳格ともいうべきほど気をつけて. ¶*passionately religious* 狂信的な. ¶*profoundly religious* 深く宗教を信奉して.

relinquish, *v.* 棄てる, 辞する.

P *relinquish* the task *from* the difficulty of deciding where to begin どこから手をつけてよいかを決定することの困難なためにその仕事を廃棄する.

O *relinquish* all hope of going abroad 洋行の希望を捨てる.

relish, *n.* 味, 美味, 風味; 趣, 趣味.

V *add* a *relish* to food 食物に風味を添える. ¶try to *find* a new *relish* for his jaded appetite 彼の減退した食欲に対して新しい嗜好物を見出そうと努める. ¶*give relish* to ... =flavor ... ...に味をつける. ¶I *have* no *relish* for that sort of novels. 僕はそんな小説は好かない. 【類】I *have* no *relish* for my food. ¶*lose* its *relish* その風味を失う. 【類】Such a game will *lose* its *relish* (おもしろ味) when you grow old.

Q turn with *renewed relish* to the work その仕事に新しい興味を感じて再びかかる.

P It is eaten *as* a *relish*. それは味付として食べる. ¶eat *with* keen *relish* 非常においしく食べる.

relish, *v.* おいしく味わう.

P He didn't *relish* anything academic *after* his school life. 学校を出てからは学問的なものは一さいいやになった. ¶The meat *relishes of* pork. その肉は豚の味がする.

reluctance, *n.* きらい, いや味.

V He *feels* no *reluctance* in acknowledging errors. 彼は誤りを認めるにやぶさかでない. ¶*show reluctance* to ... ...に対していやな顔をする.

Q he felt it his duty, though with *extreme reluctance*, to ... 彼はきわめていやいやながら...することを彼の義務と感じた. ¶the *modest* and *coy reluctance* characteristic of the maiden 処女に特有のけんそんにして内気なけんお. ¶with *some reluctance* いく分不本意ながら.

P sacrifice ..., *without reluctance* おし気なく...を犠牲にする.

reluctant, *a.* いやがる, 気が進まない.

M He was *very reluctant* to give his money away. 彼は自分の金を人にやるのはとてもいやだった.

P a soil *reluctant to* the plow 耕作に向かない土地.

O be *reluctant* to accept the invitation その招待に応じるのを好まない.

rely, *v.* 頼む, 当てにする, 信頼する.

M You may *always rely* upon my assistance. いつでもきっとあなたの力になります. ¶*rely mainly* on ... 主に...を頼りにする. ¶Aren't you *relying too much* on appearances? 君はあまり外形に重きをおき過ぎはしないか. ¶you may *safely rely* on ... 君は...を当てにしても大丈夫だ.

P I *rely on* your honor to keep it secret. 君は名誉にかけてそれを秘密にしてくれると思う. ‖ He cannot be *relied on*. あの男は当てにならない. ‖ *rely on* ... for counsel (support, assistance) ...の助言(など)に待つ ‖ *rely on* one's promise (word) 人の約束(など)を当てにする ‖ *rely on* rule of thumb 目の子算でやる. 【類】*rely on* memory / *rely on* re-enforcement (応援) / *rely on* ... for part of one's living / *rely on* instinct rather than on judgment / *rely on* guesses or *on* memory rather than *on* actual records / *rely on* (=*upon*) others for success. ¶*Rely upon* my discretion. 悪いようにはしないから私にお任せなさい. 【類】I *rely upon* your honor to respect my wishes. / You may *rely upon* my remittance (送金).

remain, *v.* 残る, 余る; 残留する, 滞在する; 依存する.

M She *remained alone* on the platform. 彼女はホームにたった一人残った. ¶The visit will *always remain* in my memory. その訪問は永久に私の思い出となるでしょう. ¶He will not *remain any longer* in Japan. もうこの上は日本に滞在しないだろう. ¶*remain* (=stay) *away* from school 学校を欠席する ‖ *remain away* from the polls 投票に行かない. ¶It *remains* terribly *backward* in transit facilities. そこは交通の便がひどく遅れている. ¶*remain composed* じっと落着いている. ¶*remain concealed* for a long time 長い間隠れている. ¶The good will not *long remain lonely*. 徳必ず隣りあらん. ¶*Not much remains* to be done. もうやることはいくらもない. ¶The strikers *remain obdurate*. 罷業者側は依然がん強である. ¶the exhibition will *remain open* till ... その展覧会は...までであるだろう. ¶*remain satisfied* with ... 相変らず...に満足している. ¶In some civilized nations, population *remains stationary* owing to the decrease in the birth-rate. ある文明国では出産率減少のため人口が停止状態になっている. ¶*remain still* じっとしている ‖ A few apples *still remain* on the tree. その木にはまだりんごが少し残っている. ¶The town *remains the same* year after year. その町は年々歳々変らない. ¶The building *remained unburned*. その建物は焼けずに残った. ¶*remain uncovered* in the presence of a superior 目上の面前で帽子をかぶらずにいる. ¶He *remained unmarried* (=*single*). 彼は結婚せずにいた. ¶One incident *remains* very *vivid* in my mind. 一つのできごとが私の記憶に明りょうに残っている.

M² Ill-effect *remains* (=hangs) *over*. 副作用はあとをひく.

P He *remained at* his post. 彼は辞職せずにいた. 【類】*remain at* the seashore till ... ¶there only *remains for* consideration ... 最後に考慮したいことは...である. ¶he will *remain in* London until ... ...彼は...までロンドンにとう留する ‖ your membership of the Club will *remain in* effect until ... そのクラブのあなたの会員資格は...まで有効になっています. 【類】so long as this contract *remains in* force. / Canada *remains in* the Imperial connexion. ‖ as long as his party *remains in* power 彼の党が政権を握ってる限りは ‖ *remain in* charge of ... なお...を担当している. ¶*remain on* the memory 記憶に残る ‖ long *remain in* service 長年勤めている. 【類】He *remained in* office for fifteen years. ¶His reign will *remain on* record as the most dissolute and immoral reign which modern history has known. 彼の治世は近代史上最も放縦にしてかつ非倫な治世として記録に残るであろう. ‖ *remain on* the job その職場に留まる. ¶*remain out of* office 野に在る. ¶He *remained* a bachelor *through* (=*during*) his life. 彼は一生独身で通した. ¶They *remained* steadfast *to* their faith. 彼らはその信仰を固守した. ‖ *remain to* luncheon (dinner) 残って昼食(など)を食べる. ¶*remain under* water for a few minutes 二三分水の中にもぐっている. ¶She *remained* a widow *until* death.

一生未亡人で通した. ¶*remain with* a person throughout one's life 一生ある人を棄てないでいる. ¶Come what may, the final victory will *remain with* the Japanese. なにごとが起ろうとも最後の勝利は日本の手に帰するであろう. ‖ The captain *remained with* the wreck. 船長は難破船と運命をともにした.

O It *remains* to be seen if it will last. それが続くかどうかは今後にならないと分からない. ¶That *remains* to be proved. それは今後の証明にまつのみ. ¶There *remains* no more to be said. これ以上言うことはない.

remainder, *n.* 残り, 残余, 残部.

V He ***passed*** the *remainder* of his life in writing. 彼は文筆で余生を送った. ¶***spend*** in retirement the *remainder* of one's life 隠居して余生を送る.

P ***for*** the *remainder* of the night その夜はそれからずっと朝まで. ¶The figure can be divided ***without*** a *remainder*. その数は割り切れる.

P² *remainder* ***after*** selection よりっかす. ¶the *remainder* ***of*** the money その残金.

O Take 2 from 5, and the *remainder* is 3. 五引く二は三だ.

remains, *n. pl.* 遺跡, 遺がい.

V the train ***bearing*** his mortal *remains* 彼の遺がいを乗せている汽車. ¶The museum ***contains*** the *remains* of Japanese antiquity. その博物館には日本古代の遺物がある. ¶I wonder whether the *remains* will be ***cremated***? その遺がいは火葬にするのかしら. ¶His *remains* were ***interred*** in the cemetery. 彼の遺がいはその墓地に葬られた. ¶his *remains* were ***laid*** in the churchyard at ... 彼の遺がいは…の墓地に葬られた. ¶His *remains* ***lie*** (=***repose***) in the cemetery. 彼の遺がいはその墓地に葬られている. ¶there ***rest*** the mortal *remains* of ... そこに…の遺がいが葬られてある.

Q ***archaeological*** *remains* 考古学的遺物. ¶***fossil*** *remains* 化石の遺物. ¶***historic*** *remains* of a bygone age 往昔の歴史的遺物. ¶***literary*** *remains* 文学上の遺稿. ¶his ***mortal*** *remains* 彼の遺がい. ¶***osseous*** *remains* of animals 動物の遺骨.

P² *remains* ***of*** a wreck 難破船の残がい. ¶*remains* ***of*** youth 若き日のおもかげ. 【類】*remains* ***of*** ancient Rome (古ローマ).

remand, *n.* 召還, 再拘留.

P he was charged ***on remand*** with conspiring with ... 彼は召還され…と共謀のかどで起訴された. ¶he is ***under remand*** on suspicion of being ... 彼は…のけん疑で召還されている.

remand, *v.* 召還する, 再拘留する.

P soldiers *remanded* ***to*** the post 帰営を命ぜられた兵士たち ‖ be *remanded* ***to*** prison 入所を命ぜられる.

remark, *n.* 短評; 評, 言説; 注目.

V ***address*** some impolite *remark* to ... …に対して不そんな言説を述べる. ¶***brighten*** one's *remarks* with many humorous touches こっけい味を多分に交ぜて話に精彩を添える. ¶A few *remarks* on ... are perhaps ***called for***. …について二三の評言を必要とするだろう. ¶***call up*** the *remark* of ... …の言を想起させる. ¶I didn't quite ***catch*** your *remark*. あなたのお言葉はよく分かりませんでした. ¶***close*** one's *remarks* with ... …と言って結ぶ. ¶With these words he ***drew*** his *remarks* to a close. こう言って彼は演説を結んだ. ¶***exchange*** a few *remarks* in a low voice 低い声で二三の言葉を交わす. ¶***excite*** *remark* なんとか言われる, 物議をかもす. ¶***let fall*** some offending *remarks* なにか気にさわることを言う. 【類】***let fall*** (=***drop***) the *remark* that ... ¶I should be pleased to ***have*** your *remarks*. 貴下のお言葉をお伺いしたい. 【類】on this point I ***have*** many *remarks* to make, but ... / ***have*** you any *remark* to make on ...? ¶I ***hazarded*** some *remark* to break the monotony of the journey. 私は旅の退屈しのぎに話し出して見た. ¶heartily ***indorse*** the *remarks* of ... …の言葉に衷心から賛成する. ¶I listened, hardly ***interposing*** a *remark*. 私はほとんど一言も言わずに傾聴した. ¶***Keep back*** some pretty mean *remarks*. 口ぎたない評言を避けよ. ¶I ***make*** a *remark* about the weather 天気について一言述べる. 【類】***make*** a *remark* upon ... / he was overheard to ***make*** this *remark* to ... / ***make*** the *remark* that ... / a *remark* [which] he ***made*** at the recent dinner of ... / He ***made*** some *remarks* I could not catch. / I have been led into ***making*** these *remarks* by the wish to explain why ... / in ***making*** this *remark*. ¶***offer*** a few *remarks* about ... …について数言述べる. ¶I frequently ***overheard*** *remarks* from ... such as ... …からしばしば…というような話をもれ聞いた. ¶***pass*** *remarks* なんとか話合う. 【類】***pass*** a few *remarks* on ... / ***pass*** a *remark* or two. ¶***premise*** a *remark* 前提をおく. ¶***reserve*** one's *remark* 言葉を控える. ¶***retract*** a *remark* 言ったことを取消す. ¶***shout*** derisive *remarks* 大声にあざける. ¶let ***slip*** some offhand *remark* うっかり言う. ¶***soften*** a *remark* 言葉を和らげる. ¶***substantiate*** the above *remarks* 上の説を確かめる. ¶***suggest*** a few passing *remarks* 二三思いついたことを注意する. ¶step in and ***thrust*** their *remarks* upon the discussion 横合からその議論に口を出す. ¶***utter*** a witty *remark* 気のきいたことを言う. ¶***venture*** a *remark* あえて説をなす.

V² similar *remarks* ***apply*** to ... 同じような説が…にも適用される. ¶in an article on ... the following sensible *remarks* ***occur*** ... …に関する記事の中に次のような気のきいた説がある.

Q make some ***abusive*** *remarks* 二三の悪評を下す. ¶***adulatory*** *remarks* へつらいの言. ¶an ***astonishing*** *remark* 驚くべき言説. ¶make ***audible*** *remarks* to one's disparagement その人をひぼうする聞えよがしの言を吐く. ¶The matter calls for more than ***casual*** *remark*. その件はあっさり片付ける訳にはいかない. ¶It is a ***common*** *remark*. それは世人常とうの語である. ¶the most ***commonplace*** *remark* 最も平凡な説. ¶make ***complimentary*** *remarks* お愛想を言う. ¶***concluding*** *remarks* 結語. ¶***conversational*** *remarks* 談話. ¶a ***cruel*** *remark* 酷評. ¶make ***cutting*** and ***cold*** *remarks* 辛らつな冷評をする. ¶his usual ***cut*** and ***dried*** *remarks* 例のあじもそっけもない言葉. ¶a ***cynical*** *remark* 皮肉な評. ¶a ***facetious*** *remark* こっけいな言. ¶a ***feeling*** *remark* 同情味のある評言. ¶make a ***few*** *remarks* 二三の評言を下す. 【類】add a ***few*** *remarks* on ... ¶Discussing ... he has the ***following*** *remarks*. …を論じて彼は次の説を述べる. ¶***funny*** *remarks* 面白い説. ¶premise one or two ***general*** *remarks* 一二の一般的のことを前提にする. ¶***germane*** *remarks* 適切な説. ¶***humorous*** *remarks* こっけい味のある言葉. ¶***illuminating*** *remarks* 啓もう的な説. ¶***immodest*** *remarks* たしなみのない言葉. ¶***impetuous*** *remarks* 急激な言葉. ¶utter some ***incoherent*** *remarks* つじつまの合わないことを言う. ¶an ***inconsequent*** *remark* 不得要領な言葉. ¶***inconsiderate*** *remarks* 心ない言葉. ¶In his book there are some ***interesting*** *remarks* on this point. 彼の本にこの点に関して二三面白い説がある. ¶***invidious*** *remarks* しゃくにさわるような言説. ¶an ***ironical*** *remark* 皮肉な言葉. ¶make ***irresponsible*** *remarks* 与太を飛ばす. ¶a ***judicial*** *remark* 公平な説. ¶a ***just*** *remark* 正しい説. ¶a ***laughing*** *remark* 笑いながらの言葉. ¶***malapropos*** *remarks* 見当違いの評言. ¶***miscellaneous*** *remarks* 漫言. ¶a ***mollifying*** *remark* なだめの言葉. ¶a ***naive*** *remark* 飾り気のない言葉. ¶I took him up on account of his ***naughty*** *remark*. けしからんことをいうからしかりつけてやった. ¶make an ***obscene*** *remark* いやらしいことを言う. ¶***opinionated*** *remarks* 独断的な説. ¶one ***other*** *remark* has to be made with reference to ... …に関して今一言述べねばならない. ¶We have no need on this occasion to make more than a ***passing*** *remark*. われわれはこの場合ほんの一通りのことを述べれば足りる. ¶make some ***penetrating*** *remarks* うがったことをいう. ¶Don't make ***personal*** *remarks* (=abuse). 人身攻撃はよし給え. ¶a ***pointed*** *remark* 寸鉄的な評言. ¶***pointless*** *remarks* 不得要領な説. ¶***pregnant*** *remarks* 意味深長の説. ¶make a ***preliminary*** *remark* 冒頭する. ¶pass a ***rude*** *remark*=say something rude 失礼な言葉をはく. ¶a ***sapient*** *remark* 賢明な説. ¶a ***sarcastic*** *remark* 皮肉な言. ¶make a few ***scathing*** *remarks* on the folly of ... …の愚をひどくこき下ろす. ¶make ***short*** *remarks* 短評を下す. ¶a ***side*** *remark* ちょっと中にはさんだ言葉(ところで…など). ¶after an exchange of ***snappy, controversial*** *remarks* 威勢のよい議論を戦かわしてから. ¶a ***sour*** *remark* 気むずかしい言葉. ¶a ***sphinxlike*** *remark* なぞの言葉. ¶a ***staccato*** *remark* 短い力のこもった言葉; 『音』断音符. ¶a ***stock*** *remark* of politicians 政治家の口癖. ¶***suggestive*** and ***timely*** *remarks* on the subject その問題に関する暗示に富みかつ時宜を得た説. ¶a ***trivial*** *remark* つまらない説. ¶***uncalled-for*** *remarks* 差し出口. ¶some very ***uncomplimentary*** *remarks* were made about ... …に関してはなはだ無礼なことが言われた. ¶make ***undisguised*** *remarks*

思い切ったことを言う. ¶an *untimely remark* 時宜を得ない言葉. ¶a *usual remark* 例の説. ¶a *wise remark* 賢明な説. ¶*witty remarks* 機知に富む言葉.

Q² *closing remarks* 結びの言葉. ¶in his *opening remarks* 彼の開会のあいさつで ‖ the *opening remark* in conversation 会話の口切り. ¶*weather remarks* 天気のうわさ.

P *after* a few *remarks* 二三述べた後. ¶He took the remark *as* a personal *remark*. 彼はその言を人身攻撃と見なした. ¶*from* your *remarks* あなたの説からすると. ¶*in* a few passing *remarks* 手短かに, 無造作に. ¶*without* a remark 一言も言わずに. 【類】Let it pass *without remark*.

P² *remarks for* reference 備考. ¶A few *remarks from* you on that subject would be welcome. その問題についてあなたから一言述べていただきたいものです. ¶a stock *remark of* politicians 政論家のおきまり文句 ‖ I have nothing worthy *of remark*. 申上げるほどのこともない. ¶None of those present ventured to make any *remark on* this assertion. この所説については列座のうちだれ一人として意見を述べようとする者がなかった.

remark, *v*. 一言する, 説く; 気付く.

M as *remarked above*=remarked as above 上説の通り. ¶*calmly remark* 静かに述べる. ¶*casually remark* 偶然言う. ¶*cynically remark* 皮肉に評する. ¶*remark gravely* 真顔に言う. ¶it may here be *remarked incidentally* that ... 序でにここで...と言ってよかろう. ¶*remark jokingly* 冗談に言う. ¶as he *justly remarks* 彼がそう言うのも至当なことであるが. ¶*remark laconically* (=with loconic brevity) 春秋の筆法をもって説く. ¶*laughingly remark* to ... ...に対して笑いながら説く. ¶*naively remark* 天真らん漫に言う. ¶*oppositely remark* 反対に述べる. ¶*pertinently remark* on ... ...に関して適切なことを言う. ¶as the author of this work *rightly remarks* この本の作者がそう言うのも至当なことである. ¶*remark* rather *sharply* かなり痛烈に言う. ¶*truthfully remark* 正直に言う.

P This point has often been *remarked upon*. この点はしばしば言及されている.

remarkable, *a*. 著しい, 非凡な, 目立つ.

M be *more remarkable* for promise than for performance 約束だけはりっぱだがその履行が伴わない. ¶it is *not a little remarkable* to note that ... ...という点は大いに注意すべきだ. ¶This is *really remarkable*. これは本当に大したことだ.

P The family was *remarkable for* longevity. その家族は長寿で有名だった. ‖ This has been a year *remarkable for* disasters. 今年は災害の多い年だった. ‖ not being *remarkable for* the clearness of head 余り頭のいい方ではないので ‖ Journalism is seldom *remarkable for* its patience in any country. 新聞記者はどこの国でも気が早い.

remedy, *n*. 医薬, 療法; 救済策.

V *apply* a *remedy* 医薬を用いる ‖ *apply* several *remedies* to ... ...に数種の医薬を使う ‖ seek to *apply* to existing ills an inadequate *remedy* 現在の害悪に対して手ぬるい手段を講じようとする. ¶*discover* an infallible *remedy* for *mal de mer* 船酔いにてき面にきく薬を発見する. ¶*find* the *remedy* in ... その療法は...であることを発見する ‖ Some *remedy* must be *found*. 何か療法を見つけねばならない. ¶I *have* no legal *remedy*. 私には合法的な救済策がない. ¶I *know* a good *remedy* for a cold. 私はかぜのよい治療法を知っている. ¶*need* strong *remedies* 手荒い治療が必要である. ¶*prescribe* a single *remedy* for all diseases あらゆる病気に対してただ一つの薬を処方する ‖ Before *prescibing* a *remedy*, it is necessary to diagnose the disease. 薬の処方を書く前に病人の診察をする必要がある. ¶Some heroic *remedy* must be *resorted to*. 何か断固たる治療法を施さねばならない. ¶*suggest* a *remedy* 治療法を注意する. ¶*think out* a *remedy* for the evil その弊害救治策を考案する. ¶*try* various *remedies* 種々救治策を試みる. ¶*work out* (=*devise*) some *remedy* 何か救済策を考え出す.

Q Is there *any remedy* for fever? 何か解熱剤がありますか. ¶What is the *best remedy* against the air sickness. 飛行機病の療法はどうするのが一番よいか. ¶*chemical remedies* [草根木皮を用いる漢法薬に対して]西洋式の治療薬. ¶a *domestic remedy* in diarrhea 下痢の家庭薬. ¶a *drastic remedy* 荒療治. ¶an *effectual remedy* 有効な治療. ¶a *good remedy* for a cold よいかぜ薬. ¶a *heroic remedy* 荒療治. ¶Rebellion is the *last remedy* against tyranny. 謀反は専横に対する最後の療法である. ¶The *remedy* is *obvious* and near at hand. その救済策は明らかでかつ手近にある. ¶a believer in *old-fashioned remedies* 昔風の治療法を信じる人. ¶That is the *only remedy* for the situation. それが時局に対する唯一の救済策である. ¶a *popular remedy* against colds かぜの民間療法. ¶apply the *proper remedy* 適切な治療法を用いる. ¶the *quickest, safest,* and *best remedy* for ... ...に対する最もじん速で安全でかつ最善の方法. ¶a *simple remedy* for ... ...の簡単な治療法 ‖ a *simple* and effective *remedy* 簡単で有効な療法. ¶a *sovereign* (an *infallible*) *remedy* for colds かぜの妙薬. ¶a *stringent remedy* 緊急な救済策. ¶the *surest remedy* 最も確実な療法. ¶Water is a *universal remedy*. 水は万人にきく薬である.

Q² *cough* and *cold remedies* せきとかぜの薬. ¶a favorite *household remedy* 愛用される家庭薬. ¶*quack remedies* インチキ療法. ¶resist the *stock remedies* ありふれた療法はきかない. ¶apply all types of *stop-gap remedies* あらゆる一時おさえの薬を使う.

P it is used *as* a *remedy* for ... それは...の治療薬として用いられる. ¶He is *past* (=*beyond*) *remedy*. 彼はもう手おくれだ.

P² a sovereign *remedy against* all diseases 万病の妙薬 ‖ a *remedy against* poison (seasickness) 解毒(など)剤. ¶a *remedy for* consumption (toothache, indigestion) 肺病(など)の薬 ‖ *remedies for* crime 犯罪救治諸策. ¶it is of sovereign *remedy in* curing ... それは...の治療に特効がある.

remember, *v*. 記憶する, 覚えている, 想起する, 心に留める, 忘れない; 伝言する.

M I *always remember* that ... 私は...ということをいつも思出す. ¶*remember clearly* はっきり覚えている. ¶if I *remember correctly* 私の記憶が正しければ, たしか. ¶*distinctly remember* はっきり想起する. ¶deserve to be *gratefully remembered* よい記念となります. ¶*remember imperfectly* ばく然と記憶する. ¶She could *just remember* hearing, as a very little girl, of the Battle of Trafalgar. まだほんの少女のころ彼女はトラファルガーの戦のうわさを聞いたことをやっと思出すことができた. ¶Will you *kindly remember* me to her in the best of terms? どうぞ彼女にくれぐれもよろしくお伝え下さい. ¶*Now* I *remember* ...? そうだったっけ; そんなこともあったっけ. ¶if I *remember right[ly]* たしか. ¶I can't *simply remember* its name. どうしてもその名が思い出せない. ¶*still* I *remember* 忘れもしない. ¶I *suddenly remembered* that ... 私は...ということをふと思出した. ¶The lesson should be *thoroughly remembered*. その教訓ははっきり肝に銘じるべきである. ¶*remember vaguely* ばく然と覚えている.

P It is historically *remembered as* the Shimabara Revolt. これを世に島原の乱という. ¶Grandfather *remembered* us all *in* his will. おじいさんはわれわれみんなの名を遺言状に書いておいてくれた(遺産を分けてくれた). ¶It makes one *remember of* a fact (person). それである事実(など)を想起する. ¶*Remember* Mrs. Watson and myself kindly *to* your wife, and with every good wish to yourself. どうぞ私及妻からも奥様によろしく, 同時にあなたの御健康を祈ります. 【類】Please *remember* me kindly *to* Mr. ... the next time you meet him. / I wish to be *remembered to* ... / Mrs. ... wishes me to be kindly *remembered to* you.

O it is to be *remembered* that ... 記憶すべきことは... ¶I don't *remember* having ever seen you. [前に]あなたにお会いした記憶はありません. ‖ Please *remember* the porter. 赤帽にチップをやって下さい.

remembrance, *n*. 記憶, 思出, 回想.

V *call up* dim *remembrances* of the scene その光景をかすかに記憶に呼び起す. ¶*deserve* permanent *remembrance* 永久に記憶するだけの価値がある. ¶*escape* one's *remembrance* その記憶から逸し去る. ¶*Give* my kind *remembrances* to him. 彼によろしくお伝え下さい. ¶I *have* no distinct *remembrance* of it now. 私は今それをはっきり覚えていません. ¶I *retain* only the haziest *remembrance* of what took place. 当時のできごとをほんのぼんやり覚えているにすぎない. ¶*shaking off* all the *remembrance* of his late disgrace 彼が過般受けた不面目の思出をすっかりかなぐり棄てて.

V² The *remembrance* of your kindness will never *fade* from my memory. 御親切はいつまでも私の記憶から消え

ません.

Q My sister joins me in ***affectionate*** *remembrance* to you. 妹からもよろしくと申しました. ¶His name deserves to be kept in ***evergreen*** *remembrance.* 彼の名はいつも変らない思出として心に秘めておく価値がある. ¶His name will ever be held in ***grateful*** *remembrance* here in their country. 彼の名はこの国でいつまでも感謝の念をもって記憶されるであろう. ¶Let us send you a ***small*** *remembrance.* ささやかな贈りものですがお受取り下さい. ¶***vague*** *remembrance* うろ覚え. ¶a ***vivid*** *remembrance* 鮮明な記憶.

P preserve it carefully ***as*** a *remembrance* of her affections それを彼女の愛情のかたみとして大事にとっておく ‖ ***as*** a *remembrance* of the day 当時の思出として. ¶***at*** the *remembrance* of ... ...を思出して. ¶***for*** *remembrance* 思出のため. ¶***in*** *remembrance* of years of friendship 多年の友情の記念として ‖ Keep it ***in*** *remembrance* of me. 私の思出にそれを納めておいて下さい. 【類】He still lives ***in*** my *remembrance.* ¶to the best ***of*** my *remembrance* 私の記憶している所では. ¶call ***to*** *remembrance* 記憶に呼び起す. ¶***within*** my *remembrance* 私の覚えている範囲内に.

P² in kind *remembrance* ***of*** me 親切にも私の記念に ‖ *Remembrance* ***of*** Things Past" 『小説の題名』「過去の思出」.

remind, *v.* 思出させる, 気付かせる.

M I am ***constantly*** *reminded* of ... 私はいつも...を心にかけている. ¶*remind* me ***forcibly*** (=***vividly***) of ... 私に...をはっきり思起させる. ¶be ***gently*** *reminded* that ......のことを静かに注意される.

P You *remind* me ***of*** my brother. 君を見ると僕の兄(または弟)を思出す. 【類】It *reminds* me ***of*** home (the past). ‖ I must *remind* you ***of*** your promise. 君の約束を忘れないようにしてもらいたい. 【類】Those who do not know this little classic are to be *reminded* ***of*** the pleasure which awaits them. / It *reminded* me ***of*** Shakespeare's saying, " Sweet is the uses of adversity (逆境の効用は甘美なり)."

reminder, *n.* 思出さす人(もの); 名残り.

V He seems to have forgotton his promise. I must ***send*** him a *reminder.* 彼は約束を忘れたらしい. 思出すように手紙を出そう.

Q a ***consoling*** *reminder* 思出すと心を慰める人または物. ¶a ***gentle*** *reminder* ほのめかし. ¶a ***sad*** *reminder* 悲しい思い出. ¶a ***significant*** *reminder* that ... ...という大切な注意(書); 思い出. ¶a ***timely*** *reminder* 折よく思出さすもの. ¶a ***vivid*** *reminder* of the truth that ... ...という事理を克明に思出さすもの.

P² a *reminder* ***of*** the Spanish occupation of the Philippines スペインのフィリッピン占領の名残り.

reminiscence, *n.* 回想, 思い出, 回顧談(録).

V The journey will ***afford*** a most pleasing *reminiscence* in later years. その旅行は後にはなはだ愉快な思出となるであろう. ¶***call forth*** one's *reminiscences* 人の追憶を呼び起す. ¶names that ***conjure up*** *reminscences* of those days 当時の追憶を呼び起す名前. ¶***exchange*** *reminiscences* 互に旧を談じる. ¶***give*** one an interesting *reminiscences* of ... ...についてのおもしろい思出話を人にしてやる. ¶He knows how to ***put*** his *reminiscences* into a form that cannot fail to be interesting. 彼はその追憶をどう表現したら間違いなく興味を与えるかを知っている.

Q ***autobiographical*** *reminiscences* 自叙伝的回顧録. ¶carry away with one ***grateful*** and ***happy*** *reminiscences* of ... ...の有難いかつ愉快な思出をもって帰る. ¶***literary*** *reminiscences* of Mr. Gladstone グラッドストーン氏に関する文学的回顧. ¶***personal*** *reminiscences* about historical events 歴史的事件に関する個人的追想. ¶It is associated with many ***pleasant*** *reminiscences.* それは幾多の愉快な思出と関連している. ¶***rambling*** *reminiscences* 漫然たる回想.

Q² my ***boyhood*** *reminiscences* 私の少年時代の思出.

P He sighed ***in*** *reminiscence.* 彼は昔を回想してため息をついた. ¶a book ***of*** *reminiscences* 回想録.

P² *reminiscences* ***of*** the past 過去の追憶. 【類】*reminiscences* ***of*** the war.

reminiscent, *a.* 懐旧の, 昔をしのぶ, 想起させる.

P a manner *reminiscent* (=suggestive) ***of*** her mother. 彼女の母をしのばせる態度 ‖ mountain-meadows *reminiscent* ***of*** the pictures of a fairy-tale おとぎ話の絵画をしのばせる山間の牧場. 【類】the scene was *reminiscent* ***of*** ... / It made me *reminiscent* ***of*** old times (昔). / be *reminiscent* ***of*** one's young days / a fine landscape *reminiscent* ***of*** the pictures of a fairy tale.

remiss, *a.* 怠る, 怠慢な, 緩慢な.

M I have been ***sadly*** *remiss* about calling upon you. 御無さたしてすみません. ¶He is ***very*** *remiss* in handling business. 彼は仕事がとてものろい.

P I have been very *remiss* ***in*** writing to you. 大変御無さた致しておりました. ‖ *remiss* ***in*** one's duties (conduct, payment) 職務(など)に怠慢な.

remission, *n.* 免除.

V ***allow*** the *remission* of the entrance fee 入学金を免除する.

P² *remission* ***of*** sins (debts) 免罪(など).

remissness, *n.* 怠慢, 油断, 不行届.

P ***through*** the *remissness* of ... ...が怠慢のため.

remit, *v.* 回送する, 為替で送る, 送金する.

M ***Kindly*** *remit* by return of mail (=《英》return post) 折返し御送金願います.

P *remit* ***by*** bank draft (money-order, mail) 銀行為替(など)で送金する. ¶*remit* money ***to*** a person (place) 人(など)へ金を送る ‖ The case was *remitted* ***to*** the higher court. その訴訟は上級裁判に回付された.

remittance, *n.* 送金; 回送; 送金為替.

V *remittances*, if mailed, should be ***addressed*** to ... 郵便為替の送金は...あてのこと. ¶A prompt *remittance* would be ***appreciated.*** すみやかに送金下されば有難い. ¶***delay*** *remittance* until ... ...まで送金を遅らす. ¶***discount*** one's *remittance* その送金を為替割引する. ¶***enclose*** a *remittance* of 21 shillings 二十一シリングの送金為替を封入する. 【類】a letter ***enclosing*** a *remittance.* ¶***expect*** a *remittance* at latest tomorrow 遅くもあす金を送って来る当てがある. ¶***forward*** a prompt *remittance* 迅速に送金する. ¶have a *remittance* from ... ...から送金を受ける. ¶***make*** all *remittances* to ... 送金はすべて...にあてに ‖ *Remittance* was ***made*** through a bank. 銀行を通じて送金した. ‖ a convenient mode of ***making*** *remittance* 送金の便法. ¶he ***promised*** a *remittance* not later than ... 彼は遅くも...までに送金することを約した. ¶I have ***received*** your *remittance.* 私は御送金を入手しました. ‖ after ***receiving*** *remittance* of ... ...の送金を受取った後. ¶A *remittance* of ... is ***required.*** ...の送金が必要である. ¶When can you ***send*** *remittance?* いつ御送金できますか. 【類】What *remittance* do you intend ***sending***? / *Remittance* will be ***sent*** by air mail.

Q An ***additional*** *remittance* of ... is required. その上...の送金が必要である. ¶make a ***direct*** *remittance* to ... ...に直接送金する. ¶an ***enclosed*** *remittance* 封入した送金為替. ¶make ***immediate*** *remittance* 直ちに送金する. 【類】press for an ***immediate*** *remmittance.* ¶a ***large*** *remittance* 多額の送金. ¶***telegraphic*** *remittance* 電報為替送金.

Q² a ***cable*** *remittance* 電信送金. ¶***emigrants*** *remittances* 移民の送金.

P Orders from abroad should be accompanied ***by*** *remittance* to their value. 外国への御注文はその金高を同時に御送金願います. ¶charge ***for*** *remittance* 送金の手数料を取る. ¶form ***of*** *remittance* 送金の形式.

P² *Remittances* ***by*** bankers' draft on London can be converted at any bank in America. ロンドンへの銀行為替による送金はアメリカのどの銀行でも引換えることができる. 【類】a *remittance* ***by*** check. ¶*remittance* ***to*** a person or place 人または場所への送金.

O all *remittances* to be made through a bank すべて送金は銀行の手を経てすること.

remnant, *n.* 残り, 残余, 残部; 面影.

Q The Ainu settlers in Hokkaido are the ***last*** *remnant* of a great prehistoric race. 北海道のアイヌ移住民は有史以前に住んでいた大民族の最後の面影である. ¶destruction of ***political*** and ***economic*** *remnants* of nazism ナチズムの政治的経済的残さいの撲滅.

Q² a ***museum*** *remnant* 博物館に保存すべき遺物.

P² The castle is a *remnant* (=relic) ***of*** feudal times. その城は封建時代の遺物である. ‖ *remnants* ***of*** former glory 昔の栄華の名残り.

remodel, *v.* 作りかえる, 模様がえする.

P *remodelled* ***after*** the style of ... ...の様式にならって作りかえた. ¶The building has been *remodelled* ***into*** a department store. その建物はデパートに改造された. 【類】

remodel a barn *into* a living house. ¶*remodelled on* … …に基づいて作りかえた. ¶*remodel* everyone else *to* his own pattern 他人をうまく自分の型に合わせて作りかえる.

remonstrance, *n.* 抗議, 抗弁, 忠告. 「を持出される.
V *draw* a formal *remonstrance* from … …から正式の抗弁
V^2 *remonstrances* ***have*** no sort of effect upon … 忠告も…には一向ききめがない.
Q ***strong*** *remonstrances* of friends 友だちの強意見.
P ***in spite of*** all the *remonstrances* of … …のあらゆる抗議にもかかわらず. 「為に対する忠告.
P^2 *remonstrances* ***with*** one ***against*** one's conduct その行

remonstrate, *v.* 抗論する, 忠告する.
P *remonstrate* ***against*** cruelty to war-prisoners 捕虜虐待に抗議する. ¶*remonstrate* ***with*** one's master 主人に忠告する. ¶*remonstrate* ***with*** one ***against*** one's conduct (proceedings) その行為(など)を(改めるように)いさめる. ¶*remonstrate* ***with*** him ***on*** his course 彼のやり口について忠告する. 【類】I *remonstrated* ***with*** him ***on*** the danger of ill-effect (悪影響) of reading in bed.

remorse, *n.* 後悔, 悔恨, 悔み.
V A great *remorse* ***came*** upon him. 悔恨の情が彼の胸にこみあげてきた. ¶***feel*** *remorse* for what he has done 自分の行為に対し悔恨を感じる.
Q a ***bitter*** *remorse* はげしい悔恨.
P ***in*** deep *remorse* 深く後悔して. ¶seized (=touched) ***with*** *remorse* for … …のために悔恨の念に駆られて. ¶***without*** *remorse* 容赦なく.
P^2 *remorse* ***for*** the past (a crime) 過去(など)に対する悔恨. ¶*remorse* ***of*** conscience 良心のかしゃく.

remote, *a.* はるかな, 遠い, 遠隔の.
P *remote* ***from*** life 人里遠く離れた. 【類】live *remote* ***from*** cities (the sea) ‖ principles *remote* ***from*** actions 行動と一致しない主義 ‖ *remote* ***from*** common practice 変っ

removal, *n.* 移転, 立退; 撤去; 解任. 」たやり方の.
V The store has ***announced*** its *removal* to larger quarters. 同店はもっと手広い場所への移転を通知した. ¶***order*** *removal* to hospital 入院させる.
Q the ***operative*** *removal* of the ovary 手術による卵巣の除去. ¶***surgical*** *removal* (外科の)切除.
Q^2 ***garbage*** *removal* 台所のごみ(臓物など)の排棄. ¶a ***short-distance*** *removal* 小距離移転. ¶***snow*** *removal* 雪かき.
P^2 *removal* ***of*** grievances 怨恨の除去 ‖ *removal* ***of*** a piece of the skin 擦過傷. ¶*removal* ***of*** cases 事件の移送. ¶*removal* ***to*** more commodious quarters もっと便利な場所へ

remove, *n.* 移転, 移動; 進級. 」の移転.
V ***get*** a *remove* at school 学校で進級する. ¶The last *remove* was ***made*** in 1927 to 32 Old Bond Street. 最後の移転をやったのは一九二七年オールド・ボンド街三十二番へであった.
P^2 It is but one *remove* ***from*** slang. それは俗語とえらぶ所がない. 【類】He is only one *remove* ***from*** a fool.

remove, *v.* 除く; 移転する.
M be ***far*** *removed* from … …からほど遠い. ¶a cousin ***once*** (***twice***) *removed* またいとこ(またまたいとこ).
P He was *removed* ***by*** death. 彼は死んでしまった. ‖ *remove* hair ***by*** a razor かみそりで毛をそり落す ‖ *remove* a person ***by*** poison 人を毒殺する. 【類】The wreckage was *removed* ***by*** dynamite. ¶He was *removed* ***from*** office. 彼は職を解かれた. ‖ The people are little *removed* ***from*** barbarism. その民族は野蛮の域をほとんど脱していない. ‖ *remove* grease (spots, stains) ***from*** one's coat (clothes, hands) 着物(など)から脂のしみ(など)を除く ‖ *remove* ***from*** the city to escape wartime damage [戦時都市から]疎開する. 【類】be *removed* ***from*** active service. ¶*remove* ***into*** new offices at 26, African House, 6, Water Street, Liverpool リバァープールのウォーター街六番地アフリカ館二十六号の新事務所に引越す. ¶Let me know where you are *removing* ***to***. どこへお引越か知らせてください. 【類】*remove* ***to*** a new house.

removed, *a.* 隔った; [血族の]…等親の.
M a [first] cousin ***once*** *removed*=a second cousin またいとこ ‖ a [first] cousin ***twice*** *removed*=a third cousin また

remover, *n.* 動かす人, 除くもの(人). 」またいとこ.
Q^2 a ***furniture*** *remover* 引越し運送屋. ¶a miracle ***spot*** *remover* 卓効あるしみ取り.

remunerate, *v.* 報酬する.
M He claims that their toil was ***insufficiently*** *remunerated*. 彼は彼らの労力が十分に報いられなかったことを主張している.
P They are *remunerated* ***by*** a bonus or a commission. 賞与金かまたは手数料で報いられる. ¶I must *remunerate* him ***for*** his trouble. 私は彼の労に報いなければならない. 【類】*remunerate* a person ***for*** his time and labor.

remuneration, *n.* 報酬.
V we ***accept*** no *remuneration* whatever for our service. 手前では奉仕に対して何ら報酬を受けません. ¶***give*** inadequate *remuneration* to … …に不十分な報酬を与える. ¶***make*** generous *remuneration* for … …に対して寛大な報酬をする. ¶No member ***receives*** *remuneration*. 会員はだれも報酬を受けません.
Q ***adequate*** *remuneration* 相当な報酬. ¶the principle that men and women should receive ***equal*** *remuneration* for work of equal value 同一価値の労働に対しては男女同額の報酬を受くべき原則. ¶He earns the not too ***generous*** *remuneration* of £121 per annum. 彼は年々121ポンドという大した金高でもない報酬を受ける. ¶***great*** *remuneration* 大きな報酬. ¶***proper*** *remuneration* 適当な報酬.
P He is paid for his work ***at*** high *remuneration*. 彼はその労に対して高い報酬を受けている. 「る適当な報酬.
P^2 a suitable *remuneration* ***for*** one's trouble 苦労に対す

renaissance, *n.* 復活; [R-] 文芸復興.
Q a ***remarkable*** *renaissance* of poetry 著しい詩の復興.
P The wonderful re-birth of Europe ***at*** the *Renaissance* was at least in part due to the revival of human hope after the crushing calamity of the Black Death. 文芸復興時におけるヨーロッパの驚くべき再生はペストの恐ろしい災やくの後に人間の希望が復活したことに少なくともその一部が基因していた.
P^2 *renaissance* ***in*** literature 文学復興. ¶a *renaissance* ***of*** the interest in … …における興味の復活.

rend, *v.* 裂く, 寸断する, 分裂させる. 「ずたに裂いた.
M^2 She *rent* ***up*** all her clothes. 彼女は自分の着物をずた
P His mind was *rent* ***by*** (=***with***) fears and doubts. 彼の心は恐れと疑いで千々に乱れた. 【類】Her heart was *rent* ***with*** grief. ¶*rent* ***from*** the empire 帝国から割取した. ¶*rend* ***in*** two 二つに分裂させる. ¶*rend* ***to*** pieces ずたずたに裂く. ¶*rend* the air ***with*** cries 空も割れよと叫ぶ.

render, *v.* なす, …させる; 訳する.
M All our efforts were *rendered* ***futile***. われわれの努力もみな水のあわとなった. ¶It cannot be ***literally*** *rendered*. それは文字通りには訳されない. ¶Age has *rendered* him ***peevish***. 年のせいで彼は気むずかしくなった. ¶The piano solo was ***well*** *rendered*. ピアノ独奏は上出来だった. 【類】the part (配役) was ***well*** *rendered* by …
P *render* good ***for*** evil 悪に報いるには善をもってする. 【類】*render* blow ***for*** blow. ¶poems *rendered* ***from*** the French ***by*** … …によって仏文から翻訳した詩. ¶The book is important enough to be *rendered* ***into*** a foreign tongue. その本は外国語に訳すだけの価値がある. ¶*render* oneself ***up to*** … …に身をゆだねる; に降参する.

rendering, *n.* 翻訳, 訳文; 描出.
Q classical and other quotations with ***English*** *renderings* 英訳付の古典及びその他の引用文. ¶a somewhat ***free*** *rendering* of … …のやや自由な訳. ¶a ***literal*** *rendering* (=translation) 逐字訳.
Q^2 a ***prose*** *rendering* of the Odyssey オディッセーの散文訳. ¶a ***word-for-word*** *rendering* into English 逐字英訳.
P^2 an English *rendering* ***of*** a *haiku* 俳句の英語訳.

rendezvous, *n. F.* 指定集合地; ランデブー.
V arrange and ***carry out*** a *rendezvous* 打合わせをしておいて会合する; あいびきをする.
Q an ***educational*** *rendezvous* 教育上の会合をする場所. ¶a ***favorite*** *rendezvous* of … …のおきまり集合所. ¶a place assigned for ***political*** *rendezvous* 政治家連の会合所. ¶a ***secret*** *rendezvous* 密会.
P It became notorious ***as*** a *rendezvous* for gamblers. それはばくち打ちの集合所として有名になった.
O make it their *rendezvous* それを彼らの集合所にする.

rendezvous, *v.* 会合する.
P The U.N. expeditionary forces *rendezvoused* ***at*** Cai-

ro. 国連遠征軍はカイロで会合した.

rendition, *n.* 演出, 演奏.

Q² the reproduction on gramophone disks of ***radio rendition*** of songs, lectures, and other forms of art 歌曲, 講演, その他の芸能の放送演奏の音盤(レコード)での再現.

renew, *v.* 更新する.

P *renew* one's effort ***for*** ... …に対し努力を新たにする ‖ *renew* a lease ***for*** a further period of ... 借地権の期間を延長して…に更新する. ¶a coat *renewed* ***in*** places ところどころつぎの当った上衣 ‖ *renew* water ***in*** a tank 水そうの水をとりかえる.

renewal, *n.* 更新, 一新, 改新, 仕直し.

V ***urge*** the *renewal* of a subscription to a periodical 雑誌の購読継続を勧誘する.

P ***on*** a *renewal* of our lease 借家再契約の際.

P² *renewal* ***of*** procedure 再審. ¶in recent years there has been *renewal* ***of*** interest in ... 近年…に対する興味の復活があった.

renounce, *v.* 放棄する.

P *renounce* luxury ***for*** honor 名誉のためにぜいたくをやめる. ¶*renounce* all pleasures ***in*** life 浮世の楽しみを捨てる.

O *renounce* the idea of going to Europe 欧州行きを断念する. 【類】*renounce* one's claim (right, authority, principle, etc.).

renouncing, *n.* 放棄.

P² *renouncing* ***of*** war 戦争の放棄.

renovation, *n.* 改善.

Q a ***costly*** *renovation* 金のかかる改善.

renown, *n.* 名声, 高名, 令名.

V He ***attained*** some *renown* as an artist. 彼は芸術家として幾分有名になった. ¶***give*** imperishable *renown* to ... …に不朽の名声を与える. ¶***have*** great *renown* for ... …で非常に有名だ. ¶***obtain*** *renown* by deeds of prowess 勇名をとどろかす. ¶***win*** one's *renown* 名声を得る.

Q give an ***undying*** *renown* to ... の名声を不朽にする.

P a man ***of*** *renown* 令名ある人. ¶***of*** great *renown* 非常に有名な.

P² he gained most of his *renown* ***as*** ... 彼はその名声を主に…として獲得したのだ. ¶his *renown* ***in*** arms 彼の武勲.

renowned, *a.* 名声のある, 有名な.

P *renowned* ***for*** one's bravery (beauty, skill) 勇敢(など)で名高い.

rent, *n.* 裂目, 破れ目.

V ***mend*** a *rent* in her skirt 彼女のスカートの破れをつくろう. ¶***sew up*** *rents* in clothing 着物の破れ目を縫う.

P² a *rent* ***in*** the rock 岩の裂目.

rent, *n.* 地代, 家賃, 貸借料.

V ***demand*** exorbitant *rent* 法外な家賃を請求する. ¶***levy*** ground *rent* upon it それに地代を課する. ¶***lower*** the *rent* 料金を下げる. ¶Why do you ***pay*** *rent* instead of owning your home? なぜ君は自分で家を持たないで借家住いをするのか. ¶***put up*** (=***raise***) the *rent* 家賃を上げる.

Q let good houses at a ***low*** *rent* 良い家を安い家賃で貸す. ¶at ***moderate*** *rents* 適当な家賃で. ¶at a ***suitable*** *rent* 格好な家賃で.

Q² ***box*** *rents* 観覧料. ¶***farm*** *rents* 小作料. ¶***land*** (=***ground***) *rent* 地代.

P pay ***as*** *rent* 家賃として払う. ¶***at*** a *rent* of ... per annum 一年…の家賃で. ¶bungalows ***for*** *rent* バンガロー風の貸家 ‖ Apartments ***for*** *Rent* 貸室あり(アパートの掲示). ☞ 英語用法は to let である a houre *for rent*=《英》a house *to let*. ¶He is far back ***on*** his *rent*. 彼は家賃が大分たまっている.

P² It is for *rent* ***for*** a song. それはただのような家賃で貸す. ¶*rent* ***in*** money 金で支払う小作料 ‖ *rent* ***in*** kind 現物小作料. ¶the *rent* ***of*** films フィルムの使用料. 【類】The lease (租借権) was renewed for a further period of eighty years, at a ground *rent* ***of*** £2,000 per annum.

rent, *v.* 貸す, 借りる, 貸出される.

M He *rents* a house ***low***. 彼は家賃を安くする.

P The house *rents* (=lets) ***at*** $100 a month. その家賃は月百ドルだ. ¶It was the sort of house that *rents* ***for*** about ¥5,000 a month. それは月五千円程度で貸すような家であった. ‖ The house *rents* ***for*** 5,000 yen a month. その家は一カ月五千円の家賃だ. 【類】The cottages *rent* ***for*** from [$]6 to $10 a month. ¶*rent* a house ***from*** Mr. ... …氏から家を借りる. ¶*rent* a house (room) ***to*** a person 人に家(など)を貸す.

rental, *n.* 地代, 損料.

V The estate ***yields*** a *rental* of 25,000 yen. その地所から二万五千円の地代があがる.

Q at the ***monthly*** *rental* of ¥27,000 月二万七千円の地代で. ¶at a ***small*** (=***moderate***) *rental* わずかの地代で. 【類】lodgings at a very ***small*** *rental*.

Q² ***film*** *rental* 映画の損料. ¶increase in ***land*** *rentals* 地代の値上げ. ¶high ***office*** *rentals* 高い事務所の家賃. ¶***tenant*** *rental* 小作料.

P ***at*** a *rental* of £400 per annum 年四百ポンドの地代で. ¶The educational picture is available ***for*** *rental* at $4.50 a showing. その教育映画は一回 4.50 ドルの使用料で借りられる.

renunciation, *n.* 放棄.

Q² ***citizenship*** *renunciations* 市民権放棄.

P² *renunciation* ***of*** citizenship=citizenship renunciation ‖ *renunciation* ***of*** nationality 国籍の離脱.

reopen, *v.* 再開する.

P a port *reopened* ***after*** the war 戦後再開された港. ¶*reopen* negotiations ***between*** ... and ... …と…間の交渉を再開する.

reopening, *n.* 再開.

P² *reopening* ***of*** oral proceedings 口頭弁論の再開.

reorganization, *n.* 再編成.

Q² ***curriculum*** *reorganization* 学科目再編成.

repair, *n.* 修理, 修繕, 修復.

V ***carry out*** large *repairs* 大修理を行う. ¶***commence*** the *repairs* 修繕を始める. ¶after ***completing*** *repairs* 修理完了後. ¶***do*** some *repairs* 少し修繕を施す. ¶***finish*** the *repairs* 修繕を終る. ¶***effect*** *repairs* 修繕を行う. ¶***make*** *repairs* upon ... …に修理を施す. ¶to ***undergo*** *repairs* to her propeller 推進器修繕のため.

V² The *repairs* are expected to ***take*** a fortnight. その修繕は二週間を要する予定である.

Q require ***expensive*** *repairs* 金のかかる修繕を要する. ¶The house is in ***good*** (***bad***) *repairs*. その家は修理が行届いている(いない). ¶put her into a dry dock to effect the ***necessary*** *repairs* 必要な修理を行うために船を乾ドックに入れる. ¶make ***petty*** *repairs*=tinker, patch up こそくな修理をする. ¶***small*** *repairs* 小修理. ¶***thorough*** *repairs* 徹底的修理. ¶after ***temporary*** *repairs* 仮修繕の後. ¶for the execution of ***urgent*** *repairs* to disabled ship 破損した船に緊急修理を施すため.

Q² ***lightning*** *repairs* 突貫修理. ¶facilities for ***motor-car*** *repairs* 自動車修理施設.

P ruin the brain ***beyond*** *repair* 回復の見込ないまでに頭脳を使い果す ‖ smashed ***beyond*** *repair* 修理がきかないほど破れて. 【類】The ship is damaged ***beyond*** *repair*. ¶***during*** the *repair* of ... …の修理中. ¶The steamer is to be docked ***for*** *repairs*. その汽船は修理のためドック入りするはず. ¶The house is not ***in*** proper *repair*. その家は適当に修理ができていない. ¶The machine is ***out of*** *repair*. その機械は修理ができてない(使用不能だ). ¶***past*** (=beyond) *repair* 修理の見込がない. ¶***under*** *repairs*. 『掲示』修理中. 【類】The houses ***under*** *repairs*. / whilst ***under*** *repair*. 「修理工事.

P² *repair* ***of*** injury 損傷修理. ¶*repairs* ***on*** the building

repair, *v.* 修繕する.

M it is ***amply*** *repaired* by ... それは…によって十分修繕されている. ¶a wall ***partly*** *repaired* 一部補修した壁. ¶be ***provisionally*** (=***temporarily***) *repaired* 一時的に修理する.

repair, *v.* 赴く, 行く.

P *repair* ***for*** safety ***to*** a place ... …に避難する.

repairing, *n.* 修理.

V ***require*** *repairing* 修繕を要する.

reparation, *n.* 修繕; [通例 *pl.*] 賠償.

V ***demand*** *reparation* for the injury 損害賠償を請求する. ¶***make*** *reparation* for damages 損害賠償をする. ¶***pay*** *reparations* to the countries which suffered from its aggression その侵略によって損害をこうむった国々に賠償を払う. 「争賠償.

Q² ***war*** *reparations* to Indonesia インドネシアに対する戦

P ***in*** *reparation* of ... …の賠償として.

P² *reparation* ***for*** the destruction of ... …の破損修繕. 【類】German *reparations* ***for*** the War.

repast, *n.* 食物; 休養.

Q a ***dainty*** *repast* うまい食物. ¶a ***light*** *repast* 軽い食事.

P² a *repast* ***at*** noon 昼休み.

repatriate, *v.* 本国に送還する.

P war prisoners *repatriated* ***in*** a steam boat 汽船で本国に返された捕虜たち.

repatriation, *n.* 本国送還.

Q *enforced repatriation* 強制送還.

P^2 the *repatriation* ***of*** prisoners of war 捕虜の送還.

repay, *v.* 払い戻す, 報いる, 返報する.

M It will *repay* a ***hundred-fold***. 百倍も報いるだろう. ¶The pleasure will ***richly*** *repay* him for his long journey. その喜びで彼の長い旅は十分に報いられるだろう. ¶It ***well*** *repays* a visit. 行って見る価値が十分ある.

P will be *repaid* ***by*** a perusal of this book 本書を熟読して得る所があろう. 【類】His effort was *repaid* ***by*** the success. = The success repaid him for his effort. ¶*repay* scorn ***for*** scorn 軽べつをもって軽べつに報いる ‖ The magnificent prospect from its summit will *repay* us ***for*** our fatigue in the ascent. その頂上からの壮麗なながめは登山の疲労に報いるだろう. ¶*repay* him exactly ***in*** the same coin 先方のした通りにして報復する. ¶*repay* it ***with*** ... ...をもってそれに報いる.

repayment, *n.* 弁償, 償還.

V ***urge*** *repayment* 弁償を迫る.

P^2 receipt and *repayment* ***of*** money 金の受払い.

repeal, *n.* 廃止, 取消, 廃棄.

Q a ***total*** (=***complete***) *repeal* 全廃.

repeat, *v.* 繰返す, 反復する.

M words ***awkwardly*** *repeated* 無格好に繰返した言葉. ¶a statement has ***often*** been *repeated* that ... ...という言葉はこれまでしばしば繰返された. ¶He *repeated* the word ***several times***. 彼はその言葉を五六度繰返した. ¶The statement has been ***uncritically*** *repeated* by other writers. その陳述が他の文筆家によって無批判に繰返された.

P *repeat* it ***by*** heart それを暗しょうする. ¶*repeat* a word ***for*** emphasis 強調のため語を繰返す. ¶Now *repeat* it ***from*** memory. さあそれを暗しょうしてご覧なさい. ¶*repeat* oneself ***in*** one's speech その演説に同じことを繰返して言う.

O History (Fashion) *repeats* itself. 歴史(流行)は繰返す.

repeater, *n.* 繰返し手.

Q ***parrot-like*** *repeaters* of ... ...をおうむのように繰返す人.

repeating, *n.* 繰返し言うこと.

V There is a story of ..., told by ..., which will ***bear*** *repeating*. ...の言った...という話があるがそれは繰返して言う価値がある.

repel, *v.* 不快を感じさせる.

P She was *repelled* ***by*** his rustic manners. 彼女は彼のいなかくさい態度にいや気がさした.

O Water *repels* oil. 水と油は混合しない.

repellent, *n.* [うみなど]散らし薬.

Q^2 a ***mosquito*** *repellent* 蚊の駆除剤.

repent, *v.* 悔む, 後悔する.

M *repent* ***inwardly*** 内心悔む.

P *repent* [***of***] one's sin 罪を悔む ‖ He *repents* ***of*** it as well he may. さすがに彼はそれを悔いている. 【類】He *repented* ***of*** having been idle. / *repent* ***of*** one's late conduct.

repentance, *n.* 後悔, 改悟, 悔恨.

V ***show*** *repentance* 悔悟の色を示す.

Q a ***late*** *repentance* 後悔. ¶***sincere*** *repentance* 真心からの悔悟. ¶***true*** *repentance* 本当の悔悟.

Q^2 a ***death-bed*** *repentance* 死際の悔悟.

P Confession is one mark ***of*** *repentance*. 自白は悔悟のしるしである. ¶*pray* God ***with*** *repentance* 改悟して神に祈る.

P^2 *repentance* ***before*** (=***toward***) God 神に対しての改悟. ¶*repentance* ***for*** one's sins (folly) 己が罪(など)の悔悟.

repentant, *a.* 悔いる, 後悔する.

P *repentant* ***for*** one's sin 己が罪を悔いる.

repercussion, *n.* 反響.

P^2 The *repercussions* ***of*** the last War are still felt in many walks of life. 前大戦の影響はいまだに各方面に響いている. 【類】the *repercussion* ***of*** the waves from the rocks.

repertoire, *n.* 曲目, レパートリー.

Q^2 his ***juke box*** *repertoire* 彼の自動電蓄のレコード愛用曲目.

repertory, *n.* 貯蔵.

P^2 a *repertory* ***of*** useful information 有益な知識の泉(百科全書など).

repetition, *n.* 繰返し, 反復, 重復.

V ***avoid*** an awkward *repetition* 不体裁な反復を避ける. ¶It is too well known to ***bear*** (=***need***) *repetition* here. それはあまりにもよく知られているのでここに繰返す必要はない. 【類】It ***needs*** no *repetition* here. ¶To ***save*** the burdensome *repetition* of nouns, we have the pronouns as brief and much-used substitutes. 名詞反復のわずらわしさを避けるために簡単な代名詞なるものを繁用する.

Q by ***continued*** *repetition* 絶えず反復するため. ¶***disagreeable*** *repetition* of ... 不愉快な...の反復. ¶through ***frequent*** *repetition* しばしば反復するために. ¶Breakfast was a ***mere*** *repetition* of supper. 朝飯は夕飯と全く同じ献立であった. ¶at the risk of ***tedious*** (=***tiresome***) *repetition* くどいようだが.

P ***by*** *repetitions* of effort ぐいぐい引張って. ¶***for*** a *repetition* of the offense 重犯の場合は.

repine, *v.* 愚痴を言う; 心を悩ます.

P *repine* ***at*** one's misfortunes (=hard lot) 自分の不幸をかこつ. ¶He *repined* ***for*** the pleasures which had gone. 彼は過ぎ去った愉快を思って愚痴をこぼした.

replace, *v.* おき換える, 交代する.

P *replace* autocratic ***by*** constitutional government 立憲政治をもって独裁政治に替える ‖ be *replaced* ***by*** a newcomer 新陳代謝する. ¶*replaced* ***with*** another 他のものと取り代えて.

replacement, *n.* 取替, 交代.

P ***in*** *replacement* of ... と引替に.

replenish, *v.* 補充する.

P a pipe *replenished* ***with*** tobacco タバコをつめかえたパイプ.

replete, *a.* 充満した, 豊富な.

P The guide-book is *replete* ***with*** useful information. その案内書は有益な記事が豊富だ. 【類】*replete* ***with*** historical interest. 【類】The house is *replete* ***with*** every modern requirement (新式の設備).

replica, *n.* 模写, 複製物.

Q the ***exact*** *replica* of the Daibutsu of Kamakura 鎌倉の大仏の現物写し.

Q^2 a ***half-size*** *replica* 二分の一の複製品. ¶a ***miniature*** *replica* 小形の複製品.

P^2 a *replica* ***in*** silver (bronze) 銀(など)で作った模造品.

reply, *n.* 返事, 回答.

V ***await*** (=***wait for***) your *reply* お返事を待つ. ¶***delay*** *reply* 返事を遅らす. ¶***desire*** a prompt *reply* ぜひ即答を願う. ¶I ***expect*** a *reply* of some sort in a few days. 二三日中に何とか返事があるはずです. ¶***finish*** one's *reply* to an examination paper 試験問題の答案を書き終える. ¶***furnish*** an ample *reply* 十分な返事を与える. ¶Don't forget to ***get*** a *reply* to this letter. この手紙の返事をもらうことを忘れるな. ¶***give*** no definite *reply* 確答しない. ¶I ***have*** no *reply* yet. まだ返事をもらっていない. 【類】We will let you ***have*** a *reply* as early as possible. ¶***make*** a suitable *reply* 適当な回答をする. ¶a letter ***needing*** immediate *reply* 即答を要する手紙. ¶To this I ***offered*** no *reply*. これに対して私は何とも返事をしなかった. ¶***receive*** a courteous *reply* 丁重な返事を受取る. 【類】The editor ***received*** hundreds of *replies* to each question. ¶*replies* ***submitted*** to a ***questionnaire*** アンケートに対する回答. ¶***wire*** (=***cable***) a reply to ... ...に返電を打つ.

Q an ***absent-minded*** *reply* 上の空の返事. ¶an ***affirmative*** *reply* 受諾の返事. ¶an ***apt*** *reply* 適切な返事. ¶Such was his ***astounding*** *reply*. これが彼の驚くべき返事であった. ¶a ***brief monosyllabic*** *reply* 簡単な一綴語の返事 ('yes,' 'no,' 'well' など). ¶a ***conciliatory*** *reply* 折れて出た返事. ¶To this his *reply* was as ***conclusive*** as it was brief. これに対する彼の返事は簡単であると同時に決定的であった. ¶a ***courteous*** and ***polite*** *reply* 非常に丁重な返事. ¶I must have a ***definite*** *reply* by ... ...までに確答してもらわねばならない. ¶trusting we shall receive your ***favorable*** *reply* 御賛成の御返事をいただくことを信じて. ¶a ***flippant*** *reply* 軽率な返事. ¶a ***gruff*** *reply* 無愛想な返事. ¶have an ***immediate*** *reply* 早速返事をもらう. ¶an ***impolite*** and ***sarcastic*** *reply* 無礼で皮肉な返事. ¶an ***indignant*** (=***angry***) *reply* 怒った返事. ¶a ***laconic*** *reply* 簡潔な返事. ¶This was the ***laughing*** *reply*. これが笑いながらの返事であった. ¶an ***oral*** *reply* 口頭での答. ¶a ***pat*** *reply* 適切な返事. ¶a ***peremptory*** *reply* 厳然たる返事. ¶His *reply* was ***prompt*** and ***emphatic***. 彼の返事は迅速で力強かった. 【類】looking forward to a ***prompt*** *reply*. ¶***returned*** *replies* to a *questionnaire* on ... which was sent by ... to ... ...から...へ送られた...に関するアンケートの回答. ¶make a ***rude*** *reply* 無作法な返事をする. ¶a ***telegraphic*** *reply* 返電. ¶a ***temporizing*** *reply* その場のがれの答弁. ¶There is a ***twofold*** *reply*. ¶In the first instance, ..., secondly, ... これ

には二通りの答がある. 第一は…第二は… ¶a *vague reply* ばく然たる返事.

Q[2] a *non-committal reply* 当らずさわらずの返事.

P nod *in reply* これに答えてうなずく ‖ *in reply* to a remark from … …からの評に答えて. 【類】*in reply* to your letter of Dec. 5 / *in reply* to queries addressed to them. ¶the letter now *under reply* 今返事をしている手紙. ¶trusting to be favored *with* a *reply* by return 折返し御返事をいただけることと信じて.

P[2] I have never received a clear *reply to* this question. 私はこの質問に対していまだかって明確な解答を得たことがない.

reply, *v.* 答える, 返答する.

M *reply angrily* 怒って答える. ¶*reply approvingly* その通りと答える. ¶*reply brusquely* 無愛想に答える. ¶*reply* very *decisively* きわめてはっきり答える. ¶*diplomatically reply* 外交的に答える. ¶*immediately reply* 即答する. ¶*indignantly reply* 憤然と答える. ¶*reply promptly* 即答する. ¶*reply rudely* 荒々しく答える. ¶*reply tersely* 言葉短かに答える. ¶*reply unhesitatingly* in the affirmative ちゅうちょなく然りと答える

P Please *reply at* your earliest convenience. どうぞなるべく早く御返事下さい. ¶*reply by* letter 手紙で返事する. ¶I cannot *reply for* a few days. ここ二三日は御返事は出来ない. ‖ *reply for* the members on hand 出席会員に代って答弁する. ¶*reply in* the negative (positive) 否(然り)と答える ‖ *reply in* the rush あわただしく答える. ¶*reply to* a question 質問に対して答える. 【類】*reply to* a toast (乾杯) / *reply to* (=answer) roll-call (点呼) / *reply to* a query from … ‖ *reply to* the enemy's attack 応戦する. ¶*reply with* spirit 元気よく答える.

report, *n.* 報告(書), [大学の]リポート; 評判, 風説; 銃声, 砲声, 爆音.

V *accept* the *report* of a committee 委員会の報告を承認する. ¶*circulate* a false and malicious *report* 虚偽にして悪意ある報道を流布する. ¶*collate* a *report* 報告を照校する. ¶The *report* is necessarily *colored* by the political bias of the particular newspaper. その報道には勢い関係新聞の政治的偏見が加味されている. ¶*compile* a *report* 報告を編集する. ¶*confirm* a *report* 報道を確証する. 【類】The *report* is *confirmed*. ¶*contradict* the *reports* started by a newspaper ある新聞のたてた風説を全然打消す. ¶*deny* the *report* that … …という風説を否定する. ¶*discredit* a *report* 報道を信用しない. ¶The authorities *doctored* (=*cooked*) the *reports* before publishing them. 当局はその報道を公表する前に手を入れた. ¶*draw up* a provisionary *report* 仮の報告を作る. ¶The *report* has been *contradicted*. その報道は否認された. ¶give a brief *report* of … …の簡単な報告をする. ¶*have* bad *reports* 悪いうわさがある. ¶*hear* the *report* of a revolver けん銃の音を聞きつける. ¶a map to *illustrate* the war *reports* 戦況報告説明の地図. ¶*lay* a *report* before … …に報告を提出する. ¶*make* a *report* to … …に報告をする ‖ *make* a full *report* on … …に関して詳細な報告をする. ¶*make* and *publish* a *report* 報告書を作成しこれを公表する. ¶*pass* a *report* from one to another うわさをそれからそれへと伝える. ¶*prepare* a *report* in chemistry 化学上の報告を作製する. ¶a *report presented* by … at the request of … …の要請で…の提出した報告 ‖ two *reports* have been *presented* by … for … …のために…によって二つの報告が提出された. ¶a *report printed* in The Journal of the American Medical Association 米国医学雑誌に掲載された報告. ¶*produce* a *report* 報告を提出する. ¶*publish* (=*issue*) a *report* on … …に関して報告を発表する. ¶for the purpose of *receiving* the Committee's *report* 委員会の報告を受けるために. 【類】Though the *report* was favorably *received*, it was only partially put into operation. ¶*receive* and *examine reports* 報告を受理しかつ審理する. ¶The *report* we very much *regret* is too true. はなはだ残念ながらその報道は全く事実だ. ¶*retract* a *report* 報道を撤回する. ¶*send in* a brief *report* concerning … …に関して簡単な報告を提出する. ¶to *silence* mischievous *reports* 悪宣伝を沈黙させるために. ¶*spread* the harmful *report* that … …という悪宣伝をする ‖ this *report* being *spread* abroad この報道は世間に広まっているので. ¶a *report* is *started* here today that … …というらわさがきょう当地に立っている. ¶*submit* a *report* to a meeting 報告を会に提出する. 【類】*submit* a *report* covering the activities of the Committee on … ¶The *report* has been *substantiated*. その報道は確実となった. ¶*take* a *report* as read at a meeting 報告を会で読んだ通り受入れる. ¶*test* the *report* その報告通りやってみる. ¶*turn in* a *report* リポートを出す.

V[2] the *report goes* that … …というらわさがある. ¶*report has* it that … …という. ¶The *report runs* as follows. その報道は次の通りである. ¶the *report sprang* from … そのうわさは…から出た. ¶The *report* of this affair soon *spread* all over Edo. その事件の報道は間もなく江戸中に広まった.

Q I wonder who it was that started such an *absurd report*. そんなばかげたうわさを始めたのはだれかしら. ¶an *alarming report* 驚くべき報道. ¶The sixth *annual report* of the Library records a successful year. その図書館の第六年報は同館がその一年間好成績をあげたことを記録している. ¶*authentic reports* 確実な報道. ¶give a *biased report* of … …について片手落の報道をする. ¶a *calumnious report* 非難的報道. ¶a *circumstantial report* of an accident 事故の詳報. ¶a *condensed report* 要約した報告. ¶*conflicting reports* 前後が合わない報道. ¶a *correct report* 正しい報道. ¶a *report* was *current* that … …という風説が立っていた. ¶This gave occasion to *disagreeable reports*. このためにおもしろくない評判が立った. ¶a *disparaging* (=*damaging*) *report* was going about … …についてその声価を落すような報道が伝えられていた. ¶The *report* is very *doubltful* and should be taken with all reserve. その報道ははなはだ疑わしいので十分控目に受入れねばならない. ¶Francis Xavier's letters from Japan were the *earliest first-hand reports* of that country to come to Europe. フランシス・ザヴィエルの日本からの手紙はヨーロッパに伝えられた日本の最も早い直接の報道であった. ¶make an *effective report* 効果な報告をする. ¶an *elaborate report* 念の入った報告. ¶give rise to *evil reports* 悪評を立たせる. ¶The meeting was held for the purpose of receiving the *Executive Committee's Report* and Accounts for the year 1918. 一九一八年に対する実行委員の報告と記録を受ける目的でその会が開かれた. ¶The *false report* of his death alarmed us. 彼が死んだという虚報はわれわれを驚かした. ¶make a *favorable report* on … …に関する有利な報告をする. ¶registration and *financial reports* of labor union 労働組合の登記及び財政報告. ¶make a *formal report* 正式の報告をする. ¶a *fragmentary report* of an event 一事件の断片的報告. ¶a *full report* 詳細の報告. ¶His *reports* are generally *good*. 彼の成績は概して良い[学生など]. ¶a *heart-rending report* 悲痛な報道. ¶*incorrect reports* 誤った報道. ¶an *interim report* 中間報告. ¶a *lengthy report* 長たらしい報道. ¶There was a *loud report*, and the harpoon shot through the air. ごう然一発もりが空を切って飛んだ. ¶*majority* and *minority Reports* of the Divorce Commission 離婚委員会の多数者及び少数者代表報告. ¶a *mischievous report* 罪作りなうわさ. ¶make an *oral report* on … …に関して口頭で報告する. ¶as indicated in *prior reports* 前に数回の報道で指摘した通り. ¶*public report* 世評. ¶*scandalous report* 人の名誉に関するうわさ. ¶a *scrappy report* 断片的の報告. ¶a *semi-official report* 半公式の報道. ¶a number of *sensational reports* 幾多の人騒がせな報道. ¶make a *summarized report* of … …の概略の報告をする. ¶an official *top-secret report* 厳秘公報. ¶a *true report* 真実の報道. ¶an utterly *unfounded report* 全然無根の報道. ¶*unofficial reports* from … …からの非公式の報道. ¶an *unwarrantable report* 保証し難い報道. ¶*reports* are so *various* about … …については風評はなはだまちまちである. ¶a *verbal report* 口頭報告. ¶a *verbatim report* of a speech 演説の逐語的報道. ¶a *well-grounded report* 十分根拠のある報道. ¶a *written report* 文書による報告.

Q[2] an *April 1 report* 一杯食わされた報道. ¶a *committee report* 委員会の報告. ¶a *delinquency report* on traffic violations 交通違反に関する報告. ¶an *expert report* 専門家の報告. ¶a *field report* said that 現場の報道によると. ¶get a *first-hand report* on … …に関する直接の報告を入手する. ¶a *fitness report* 人事考課表. ¶*Follow-up reports* must be made each year. 毎年相次いで報告をしなければならない. ¶a *hearsay report* 風説の報道. ¶an *in-*

spection report 視察報告. ¶an ***investigation*** *report* 調査報告. ¶a ***mid-July*** *report* 七月中旬付の報告. ¶***news*** *reports* on ... ...に関する新聞報道. ¶according to ***newspaper*** *reports*, it would appear that ... 新聞報道によると...ということになるらしい. ¶***organization*** *reports* and proceedings 協会の報告及び議事録. ¶a ***Paris*** *report* パリからの報道. ¶a ***police*** *report* 警察の報告. ¶current ***press*** *reports* 時事に関する新聞報道 ‖ according to ***press*** *reports* 新聞の報道によると. 【類】 ***press*** *reports* said that ... ¶a ***research*** *report* 研究報告. ¶The ***school*** *report* was not very favorable. 学業成績の通知は余り香ばしくなかった. ¶a ***short-hand*** *report* 速記録. ¶a conflicting ***war*** *report* つじつまの合わない戦報. ¶a ***weather*** *report* 天気報道.

P ***according to*** later *reports* その後の報道によると. ¶***in*** a *report* on ... ...に関する報告中に ‖ Is there any truth ***in*** the *report?* その報道には本当の所があるか. ¶No confirmation ***of*** the *report* has yet been received. その報道の真偽がまだ分かっていない.

P² No *report* ***about*** it can be relied on. それについての報道は一切信を置けない. ¶the *report* ***for*** the half-year ended December 31 十二月三十一日に終る下半期の報告. ¶according to *reports* ***from*** official sources in ... ...における官庁筋からの報道によると ‖ a *report* ***from*** the committee on ... ...に関する委員会の報告. ¶the *report* ***of*** the Committee of Seven on ... 七人委員会の...に関する報告 ‖ a *report* ***of*** absence 欠席届 ‖ the *report* ***of*** the committee on telephones 電話に関する委員会の報告. 【類】 a *report* ***of*** an investigation ‖ a *report* ***of*** one's score on a test 試験成績報告. 【類】 a false *report* (虚報) ***of*** the death of ... ¶an exhaustive *report* ***on*** this subject この問題に関する至れり尽せりの報告. ¶*reports* ***to*** headquarters 本部への報告.

O there is a *report* that ... ...という風評がある.

report, *v.* 報道する, うわさする; 出頭する.

M *report* ***back*** to Parliament after the Christmas recess クリスマス休暇後再開の議会に報告する. ¶***badly*** *report* of ... ...のことを悪評する. ¶His Excellency stated that his utterances had not been ***correctly*** *reported* by the Vienna newspaper. 閣下はその発言がウインナの新聞によって誤り伝えられたと述べた. ¶The Committee has *reported* ***favorably*** on the Bill. 同委員会は同案に有利な報告をした. ¶it is ***further*** *reported* that さらに...と報ぜられている. ¶***immediately*** *report* 直ちに報告する. ¶*report* ***personally*** to ... ...に本人出頭する. ¶as ***previously*** *reported* 既報の通り. 【類】 The market continues in the same depressed state as ***previously*** *reported.* ¶it is ***telegraphically*** *reported* that ... ...という入電があった. ¶*report* ***verbatim*** 逐語的に報告する. ¶He is ***well*** (***badly***) *reported* of among diplomatic circles 彼は外交界で評判がよい(悪い).

P *report* ***against*** ... ...に反対(不利)な報告をする. ¶he is *reported* ***as*** saying that ... 彼が...と言ったと伝えられている. ¶The teacher did not *report* ***at*** his class. 教師が教場に出なかった. ‖ He was told to *report* [himself] ***at*** the office on Monday morning. 彼は月曜の朝社に出頭するように命ぜられた. 【類】 You are respectfully requested to *report* ***at*** the office at No. 55 ... Street. ¶*report* ***for*** the Times タイムズ紙のために種取りをやる ‖ fail to *report* ***for*** duty on the date indicated 指定の日に出勤しない ‖ *report* ***for*** work at six a.m. 午前六時に出勤する. ¶it is *reported* ***from*** Shanghai that ... 上海から...という報道がある. ¶*report* ***on*** one's trip to Europe and America 欧米への旅行の報告をする. ¶*report* a person ***to*** the police 人を警察へ告発する ‖ *report* a fact ***to*** the police (committee) 事実を警察(など)に報告する ‖ be *reported* ***to*** the floor 委員会から本会議に報告する ‖ the warship *reported* in ***to*** the West coast to take a new assignment 新任務につくため西海岸に向っているという軍艦. ¶a commission appointed to *report* ***upon*** the condition of ... ...の情況報告を任命された委員会.

Q He is *reported* to be in Paris. 彼はパリ在住とのことだ.

reporter, *n.* 報告者, 申告者; 探訪記者.

Q² a ***cub*** *reporter* on the paper その新聞のかけだし記者. ¶***never-say-die*** *reporters* 不とう不屈の報道記者. ¶besieged by ***newspaper*** *reporters* on arrival there, to tell ... そこへ到着するや...を語れと探訪記者に取巻かれて.

P² a *reporter* ***for*** a newspaper 新聞の探訪記者.

repose, *n.* 休み, 休息, 安静; 落着.

V ***disturb*** complete *repose* 完全な休息を妨げる. ¶***enjoy*** *repose* 休息を楽しむ. ¶***snatch*** a brief *repose* 暫時の休息を楽しむ.

Q ***magnetic*** *repose* 磁針の静止. ¶***sublime*** *repose* of manner りばな落着いた態度. ¶***well-earned*** *repose* 十分働いたあげくの休息.

P ***for*** the *repose* of the soul of the dead 死者の霊が安らかに眠れるように.

repose, *v.* 休む, 安住する; [死者が]眠っている.

P Every thing around us seemed to *repose* ***in*** beauty and happiness. われらの周囲の物がすべて美と幸福のうちに眠っているように思われた. ‖ *repose* there ***in*** peace そこに安らかに眠っている. ¶the copy has been *reposing* ***on*** a shelf in the library since ... その本は...以来図書館のたなに上げてあった ‖ *repose* ***on*** a bed ベッドに横になる.

repository, *n.* 容器, 倉庫.

Q The warehouse is a ***mere*** *repository* for empty cans and boxes. その倉庫は空かんや空箱の置場に過ぎない. ¶a ***valuable*** *repository* of encyclopaedic information 貴重な百般の知識の宝庫.

Q² a ***fireproof*** *repository* 耐火倉庫.

P² a *repository* ***of*** useful information 知識の宝庫(百科全書など).

reprehension, *n.* しっ責.

V ***earn*** the *reprehension* of ... ...ということでしっ責される.

represent, *v.* 代表する, 表わす, 描出する, 演じる.

M Japan is ***ably*** *represented* in the conference. 日本はその会議に有力な代表を送っている. ¶The distribution is *represented* ***graphically*** in Figure 6. この配分は第六図にグラフで示してある. ¶The idea is ***inadequately*** *represented.* その思想が十分に表わされていない. ¶America was ***largely*** *represented* at the conference. その会議には米国から多数の代数者が出席した. ¶Germany was not ***officially*** *represented* at the conference. その会議にはドイツの正式代表者が出席していなかった. ¶the moneyed interest, ***powerfully*** *represented* in Parliament 国会に力強く代表されている財閥(ばつ). ¶Russia will be ***strongly*** *represented* in the Olympic Games. ロシアはオリムピック競技に多数の選手を送るだろう.

P She *represented* herself ***as*** his wife. 彼女は彼の妻だと言触らした. 【類】 Balzac, in his novel Madame Jules, *represents* (...ということにする) the husband of the dead Lady ***as*** ... / *represent* a club ***as*** its chief executive ¶These countries will be *represented* ***at*** the conference. これらの国々はその会議に代表者を送るであろう. ¶The King was *represented* ***by*** ... at the funeral. 皇帝はその葬儀に...を御名代につかわされた. ‖ His knowledge of ... is *represented* ***by*** zero. ...に関する彼の知識はゼロである. ¶The State was *represented* ***by*** three Republicans. その州の共和党代議士は三名だ. ¶James Russel Lowell *represented* the United States ***in*** Spain from 1877 to 1880. ゼームス・ラッセル・ロウエルは一八七七年から一八八〇年までスペイン駐在北米合衆国の代表であった. ‖ What types of magazines are *represented* ***in*** your school library? 君の学校の図書館ではどんな種類の雑誌を購入しているか. ‖ More than twelve languages are *represented* ***in*** his library. 彼の蔵書には十二カ国以上の外国語がはいっている. ‖ firms *represented* ***in*** the foreign trade of Great Britain 大英国の外国貿易を代表している商会. 【類】 They are elected to *represent* us ***in*** the government. / *represent* one's government ***in*** the conference. ¶be not *represented* ***on*** the Council 理事会に代表せられていない ‖ Each child *represented* an animal ***on*** the stage. 子供たちはそれぞれ動物を演じた. ¶Ogui, the Hindoo god of fire and lightning, is *represented* ***with*** two faces, seven arms, and three legs. 火と稲妻の印度の神たるオグイは二面七手三脚の神となっている. ‖ Fukurokuju is *represented* ***with*** a very high cranium. 福祿寿は非常に頭の長い人として表わされている.

representation, *n.* 表示, 表現, 表象; 申立, 開陳; 説明, 説述; 代表.

V an allegorical *representation* of ... ***carried out*** by a figure of ... ...の形像を借りて風刺的に示したもの. ¶a frame ***containing*** the *representation* of a pagoda constructed of copper cash 銅銭で造た塔の額. ¶***find*** *representation* in the catalogue そのカタログにのせてある. ¶He ***had*** *representations* of them ***carved*** and ***painted*** upon the walls of his house. 彼はそれらを自分の家の壁に彫刻にしたり絵に描いたりさせた. ¶after ***hearing*** their *representations*

彼らの陳述を聞終ってから. ¶*make* a *representation* to the Government 政府に建議する. ¶The popular *representation* was *recognized.* 民衆の陳情は認められた. ¶We *want* good *representation.* [代理店などの]よい代表が入用だ.

Q ***adequate*** *representation* of the parties interested 多数関係者の参加. ¶***diagrammatic*** *representation* of the idea that … …という思想の図解. ¶make a ***false*** *representation* of a person 人をざんぼうする. ¶he made ***frequent*** *representations* upon matters vitally affecting … 彼は…に重大な影響を与える事件についてしばしば陳情した. ¶The child learning to read in the vernacular has a fund of language knowledge acquired before he sees his ***graphic*** *representation.* 母国語で読方を学ぶ児童は文字を見ない内に言葉の知識を豊富に獲得している. ¶The country has a ***large*** *representation* in the exhibition. その博覧会にその国の出品が沢山ある. ¶right of ***legal*** *representation* 法定代理権. ¶One can almost say that ***mental*** *representation* is already an act begun. 心に思ったことはすでに行動に移ったものとも言えそうだ. ¶form the most ***perfect*** *representation* of … …を最も完全に代表する. ¶a ***phonetic*** *representation* 発音の表示. ¶a ***symbolic*** *representation* 象徴. ¶***territorial*** *representation* 土地の代表. ¶a ***theatrical*** *representation* 演芸. ¶a ***true*** *representation* of the circumstances その境遇の実情. ¶a ***vivid*** *representation* of Russian life and character ロシア人の生活と性格の鮮明な描写.

Q² the principle of ***class*** *representation* 社会各層代表の原則. ¶It has a diverse ***nationality*** *representation* on the staff. その部は種々の国籍のものから成っている.

P ***for*** *representation* on the Council 国会に代表させるため. ¶***on*** a false *representation* that … …というその陳述に基づいて. ¶***through*** his favorable *representations* 彼が好意をもって取なしてくれたため. ¶ornamented ***with*** a *representation* of the oshidori おしどりの彫刻または絵画で飾った.

P² make a strong *representation* ***against*** such a proceeding こうした処置に反対して強硬な陳情をやる. ¶Japanese *representation* ***at*** the Exhibition その博覧会における日本の参加. ¶*representations* ***in*** marble or bronze 大理石または青銅の画像.

representative, *n.* 代表者, 代表物, 代議士; 特派員.

V ***delegate*** a *representative* 代表者を派遣する. ¶Christianity ***has*** no fit *representatives* there. そこにはキリスト教をりっぱに代表しているものは一人もない.

Q an English humorous magazine and an ***American*** *representative* of the type 英国のユーモア雑誌と同種の米国雑誌. ¶one of the most ***authoritative*** *representatives* of the school その学校の最も有力な派の一つ. ¶an ***authorized*** *representative* 責任代表者. ¶a ***buying*** (***selling***) *representative* 購買(販売)代行者. ¶***chosen*** *representatives* 選抜代表者. ¶A consul is a ***commercial*** *representative* of a foreign government. 領事は外国政府の商業上の代表者である. ¶a ***consular*** *representative* 領事. ¶a ***diplomatic*** *representative* 外交官. ¶***distinguished*** *representatives* of the various departments of science and art 文理各部門の著名な代表者. ¶Sir Rutherford Alcock, the ***first British*** *Representative* to Japan 日本への最初の英国代表たるラザーフォード・アルコック卿. ¶He was welcomed on his arrival at the terminus by the ***leading*** *representatives* of the belles-lettres in the capital. 彼が停車場へ到着するや首都の代表的文士によって歓迎された. ¶a ***learned*** *representative* of the young generation of Oxford scholars オクスフォード大学少壮学者の学識ある代表者. ¶a ***legal*** *representative* 法定代理人. ¶the ***nation's*** *representatives* 国民の選良. ¶a ***prominent*** *representative* 知名の代表者. ¶a special *representative* 特別代理人. ¶a ***travel[l]ing*** *representative* 注文取り. ¶a ***typical*** *representative* of … …の典型的代表者. ¶***various*** *representatives* of hard-working poverty 各方面の貧困労働者.

Q² the British ***Commonwealth*** *representatives* on the Allied Council for Japan 対日連合国理事会における英連邦の代表者. ¶a ***company*** *representative* 会社の代表者. ¶the Japanese ***Diet*** *representatives* 日本国会議員. ¶an ***ex-Socialist*** *Representative* 前社会党代議士. ¶an ***overseas*** *representative* 在外代表. ¶as ***Japan*** *representative* of … …の日本代表として. ¶***press*** *representatives* 新聞代表. ¶***Socialist*** *Representative* from Tottori. 鳥取県選出社会党代議士. ¶the ***trade*** *representative* of the Government of Thailand タイ国政府の貿易代表. ¶Every important party has ***women*** *representatives.* 各大政党には婦人代議士がある.

P act ***as*** the *representative* of … …の代理を勤める. ¶the House ***of*** *Representatives* 衆議院. ¶Governments have formally accepted invitations to participate, ***through*** *representatives,* in the congress. 諸国政府はそれぞれ代表を派遣してその会議に参加することを正式に承諾した.

P² *representatives* ***at*** the convention 大会への代表. ¶K. Kiyokawa, *Representative* ***for*** the Clifford-Wilkinson Tansan Mineral Water Co., Ltd. クリフォード・ウィルキンソン炭酸鉱水株式会社の代表者たる清川氏. ‖ *representative* ***for*** Japan 日本の代表者. ¶*Representative* ***from*** Pennsylvania ペンシルヴァニア選出代議士. ¶when one's father was the *representative* ***of*** the family その親の代(だい)に. ¶Japan's *representatives* (=delegates) ***to*** the United Nations 日本の国連代表.

representative, *a.* 代表的の, 模範的な.

M a government that will be ***directly*** *representative* of the popular will 民意を直接代表する政府. ¶an organ ***fully*** *representative* of popular will 民意を代表する機関. ¶be ***fully*** *representative* of modern Oxford scholarship (著作が)現代オクスフォードの学殖を十分代表している. ¶a government ***truly*** *representative* of the people 真に人民を代表する政府.

P *representative* ***of*** Oriental civilization 東洋文明を表わす / The audience was *representative* ***of*** all creeds (宗派) and political parties.

repress, *v.* 圧する, 抑制する, 制止する.

M Christianity was then ***sternly*** *repressed.* 当時キリスト教は禁厳されていた.

repression, *n.* 抑圧.

P² the *repression* ***of*** one's emotions その感情の抑制.

reprimand, *n.* しっ責, けん責, 非難.

V ***incur*** a gentle *reprimand* やさしくたしなめられる. ¶***receive*** an official *reprimand* for … …に対して官庁のおしかりを受ける.

Q a ***severe*** *reprimand* きびしいしっ責. ¶a ***sharp*** *reprimand* 鋭いしっ責.

P He was let off ***with*** a *reprimand.* 彼はけん責の上放免された.

reprimand, *v.* しかる, しっ責する, けん責する.

M ***severely*** *reprimand* きびしくしっ責する. ¶***sternly*** *reprimand* 厳重にけん責する.

P be *reprimanded* ***by*** a policeman 警官にしっ責される. ¶He was sharply *reprimanded* ***for*** indulgence in this habit. 彼はこの習慣にふけったというのでひどくしっ責された.

reprint, *n.* 再版, 翻刻.

Q an ***abridged*** *reprint* of the 1817 edition 1817年版の簡約復製本. ¶***cheap*** *reprints* 安価な翻刻. ¶present typographically ***perfect*** *reprints* of the best existing text 現行の最善のテキストによった完全な復刻版を示す.

P² a *reprint* ***from*** an article in the magazine 同誌の論文の別刷. ¶a *reprint* ***of*** a volume 本の再版.

reprint, *v.* 翻刻する.

P volumes *reprinted* ***from*** the original 原本から翻刻した本.

reprisal, *n.* 返報, 仕返し, 復しゅう.

V ***make*** a *reprisal* on … …に仕返しする.

Q² Leftist excesses and ***Rightist*** *reprisals* 極左の行き過ぎと極右の報復.

P ***in*** *reprisal* for … …への報復として.

P² They made *reprisals* ***for*** what they suffered. 彼らはそのこうむった損害に対して仕返しをした.

reproach, *n.* しっ責, 非難の言葉.

V He must ***bear*** the *reproach.* 彼がその非難を受けなければならない. ¶***bring*** *reproach* upon … …(の名誉)をきそんする. ¶***cast*** *reproach* on … …を非難する. ¶***hurl*** *reproaches* 盛んに非難する. ¶They have foolishly ***incurred*** that *reproach.* 彼らは愚かにもその非難を招いた. ¶***level*** a *reproach* against … …を非難攻撃する. ¶***merit*** *reproach* 非難されるだけのことはある. ¶The soft *reproach* I had ***prepared*** for him expired before it reached my lips. 彼に加えようと思っていた穏かなしっ責は私のくちびるを出ないうちに消えてしまった. ¶***wipe away*** a *reproach* 恥をそそぐ.

Q a *cutting reproach* しんらつなしっ責. ¶a *disguised reproach* あてこすり. ¶turn a look of ***keen reproach*** on … …に鋭い非難の目を向ける. ¶I saw a ***mute reproach*** in his eyes. 私は彼の目に無言のしっ責を認めた. ¶a ***stinging reproach*** 身を刺すような鋭い非難. ¶a ***soft reproach*** 穏かな非難. ¶This *reproach* is ***unjust***. この非難は不当らない.

P His morals are ***above reproach***. 彼の行状には非難すべき点がない. 【類】Their characters were not ***above reproach***. ¶His character is ***beyond reproach***. 彼は非難の余地がない人物だ. ¶***without*** *reproach* 非の打ち所がなく. 【類】a life ***without*** *reproach*.

P² The state of roads in that country is a *reproach* ***to*** civilization. その国の悪道路は文明の名折れである.

reproach, *v.* しっ責する, とがめる, 非難する.

M *reproach* ***openly*** for … …に対して公然しっ責する.

P *reproach* a person ***for*** his carelessness (forgetfulness, ingratitude) 人の不注意(など)をとがめる. ¶a term ***of*** *reproach* 非難の言葉. ¶Do not *reproach* him ***with*** laziness; he has done his utmost. 彼の怠惰をせめるな, 彼は精一杯やったのだから. 【類】*reproach* a person ***with*** his want of firmness (しっかりしたところ).

O *reproach* oneself 自責する.

reproachable, *a.* 非難すべき.

M ***very*** *reproachable* ふとどき至極な.

reproachful, *a.* 非難がましい.

P be *reproachful* ***of*** the lack of sincerity on the part of … …側の不誠意を非難している.

reprobation, *n.* 否認.

P ***in*** *reprobation* 否認して.

reproduce, *v.* 再現する, 複製する.

M *reproduced* ***direct*** from the objects themselves 本物から直接に複製した.

P illustrations *reproduced* ***from*** rare prints or comparatively inacessible originals まれな版画や比較的得がたい原版から複製したさし絵. 【類】*reproduce* an article ***from*** a magazine (newspaper). ¶*reproduced* ***in*** photogravure and collotype グラビア写真やコロタイプ版で複写した. ¶*reproduce* the scene they represent ***to*** the life 彼らが描く光景を如実に現わす.

reproduction, *n.* 再現; 翻刻; 転載; 演出.

V *Reproduction* ***prohibited***. 不許複製.

Q ***exact*** *reproductions* of famous statues 有名な彫像の正確な複製. ¶a ***facsimile*** *reproduction* 複写. ¶***faithful*** *reproductions* of the beautiful art objects of the past 昔の美術品の忠実な複写. ¶the ***photographic*** *reproduction* depicts … その複製写真版は…を示している ‖ illustrated by ***photographic*** *reproductions* 写真入りの ‖ a ***photographic*** *reproduction* in reduced size 縮写複製写真版.

Q² ***amateur*** *reproduction* of Hamlet しろうとのハムレット演出. ¶***art*** *reproductions* of famous pictures 名画の芸術的複製. ¶a ***facsimile*** *reproduction* of a rare book 珍本の複製. ¶a ***gravure*** *reproduction* グラビア版複製. ¶***plant*** *reproduction* 植物の生殖. ¶a Japanese ***woodblock print*** *reproduction* 日本の複製木版画.

P² *reproductions* ***from*** Chinese paintings 支那の絵画の複写. 【類】*reproductions* ***from*** an old print (古い版画) illustrating … / *reproductions* ***from*** photographs. ¶a *reproduction* ***in*** little of … …の縮小版. ¶his scholarly *reproduction* ***of*** The Midsummer Night's Dream at the Globe グローブ座における「真夏の夜の夢」の彼の学者的な演出.

reproof, *n.* 非難, しっ責, 説諭.

V I ***drew*** from him a *reproof*. 私は彼からお小言をちょうだいした. ¶***give*** sharp *reproof* こっぴどくしかる. ¶He was summoned to ***receive*** a *reproof*. 彼は呼ばれてしっ責を受けた. ¶***take*** one's *reproof* in good part そのしっ責を好意に解する. ¶***utter*** *reproof* against … …に小言を言う.

Q a ***mild*** *reproof* 穏かなしっ責. ¶I gave him this ***serious*** *reproof*. 私はこう言ってきびしく彼をしっ責した. ¶in ***silent*** *reproof* 心中では非難しながらも口に出さないで.

reprove, *v.* しかる, 非難する, とがめる.

M ***sharply*** *reprove* 激しくしかる.

P His master *reproved* him ***for*** his behavior. 彼の主人は彼の行状をしっ責した. 【類】*reprove* a person ***for*** his carelessness.

republic, *n.* 共和政体, 共和国; 社会.

Q an ***autonomous*** *republic* 自治共和国. ¶a ***crowned*** *republic* 君主共和国.

Q² the Constitution of the ***pre-Hitler Weimar*** *Republic* ヒットラー前のワイマール共和国憲法.

P the establishment ***of*** the Czecho-Slovak *Republic* チェッコスロヴァキア共和国の設立.

P² the *republic* ***of*** letters 文学界.

republication, *n.* 再版, 翻刻.

V The book will ***bear*** European *republication*. その本はヨーロッパで複製する価値があろう.

repudiation, *n.* 放棄.

P² *repudiation* ***of*** loans as an economic measure 徳政.

repugnance, *n.* いやな思い, けん忌.

V ***engender*** an early *repugnance* to study in the mind of the pupil 生徒の心に早くも勉強に対するいやな思いをいだかせる. ¶***feel*** a *repugnance* for … …に対していや気がさす. ¶***have*** a great *repugnance* to … …を大いにきらう.

P² *repugnance* ***to*** figures (publicity) 数字(宣伝)に対するけんしん悪.

repugnant, *a.* いとわしい, いやな, 相いれない.

P *repugnant* ***to*** the intellect and moral sense of all thinking men あらゆる心ある者の知性及び道徳的観念と相いれない. 【類】a mind *repugnant* ***to*** knowledge.

repulse, *n.* 撃退, 拒絶, 拒否.

V ***encounter*** a *repulse* はねつけられる. ¶***suffer*** a disastrous *repulse* 惨敗する.

P meet ***with*** a *repulse* はねつけられる.

repulse, *v.* 撃退する, 拒絶する.

M The attempts were ***brusquely*** *repulsed*. その試みはそっけなく拒絶された.

P I was not *repulsed* ***by*** these difficulties. 私はこれらの困難にひるまなかった. ¶The enemy was *repulsed* ***with*** a great slaughter. 大殺りくを加えて敵を撃退した.

repulsion, *n.* けんえん.

V ***feel*** *repulsion* toward a person 人に対していやな思いをいだく.

repulsive, *a.* いとわしい, いやな.

P *repulsive* ***to*** … …にとっていとわしい.

reputation, *n.* 名声, 令名; 体面, 外聞.

V He ***achieved*** a *reputation* as an artist in *shippo*. 彼は七宝焼の工芸家たる名声を博した. ¶***acquire*** a *reputation* as a bibliographer (a Latin scholar) 書史学者(など)として名を成す. 【類】He was gradually ***acquiring*** a European *reputation* by his novels and stories. ¶***affect*** the country's *reputation* その国の声誉を傷つける. ¶***attain*** international *reputations* 海外の評判を得る. 【類】He ***attained*** a world-wide *reputation* by his pioneer researches in chemistry and physics. ¶the *reputation* they ***bear*** 彼らのになう声価. 【類】he has long and deservedly ***borne*** the *reputation* of being … ¶He ***bears out*** this *reputation*. 彼はどこまでも名声を落さない. ¶***blacken*** (=***tarnish***) the *reputation* of the author 作者の名声を傷つける. ¶***build up*** a *reputation* in literary circles 文名を確立する. 【類】The year-book has ***built up*** a *reputation* for completeness and accuracy. / ***build up*** and ***maintain*** a high *reputation* as … ¶***cheapen*** the *reputation* of … …の名声を落す. ¶***clear*** one's *reputation* 身のあかしを立てる. ¶***compromise*** one's *reputation* 外聞が悪い. ¶greatly ***damage*** their *reputation* 大いに彼らの評判を傷つける. ¶It ***deserves*** the *reputation* it has won. その評判だけのことはある ‖ he richly ***deserves*** the *reputation* of being … 彼が…だという評判は誠に故あることである. ¶***destroy*** one's *reputation* 人の評判を害する. ¶The priest ***earned*** a high *reputation* for learning and sanctity. ¶to ***enhance*** (=increase) his own *reputation* 彼自身の評判を高めるために. ¶***enjoy*** the *reputation* of a model principal 名校長の名をほしいままにしている. 【類】He ***enjoys*** a high *reputation* as a friend of international justice and right (国際正義の味方). ¶The work ***established*** his *reputation* as a philosopher. その著作が哲学者としての彼の名声を築きあげた. 【類】The guide-book has ***established*** a *reputation* for accuracy (正確). ¶***forfeit*** (=ruin) one's *reputation* その名声を落す. ¶***gain*** a great *reputation* as … …として非常に評判になる. 【類】***gain*** a *reputation* of being an exceedingly able (働きのある) engineer. / ***gain*** a wide *reputation* for integrity (正直) in all transactions (取引). ¶***get*** an unfavorable *reputation* 面白くない評判をとる. ¶***give*** … a wide *reputation* …にひろく評判を得させる. ¶He ***has*** *reputation* well established. 彼は評判をりっぱに築きあげた. 【類】He ***has*** a *reputation* of never letting a student go to sleep in his class room. / The peach-tree ***has*** the *reputation* of being short-lived, the growers in some countries being compelled to renew their orchards every few years. / You ***have*** not the *reputation* of being a diligent student. / ***have*** a *reputation* for idleness (being a miser) / ***have*** deservedly the *reputation* of being ... / It ***has*** a *reputation* of many years' standing for good quality. / respectable shops whose (=where the) proprietors ***have*** a *reputation* to lose (信用を大事にする) / great writers ***having*** a *reputation* to support. ¶he ***holds*** a high *reputation* for ... 彼は…という高評を有する. 【類】 The "Great Paul" at St. Paul's Cathedral ***holds*** the *reputation* of the largest bell in England. / ***hold*** a *reputation* for supreme bravery. ¶***hurt*** (=***impair*** *or* ***mar***) one's *reputation* 人の評判を傷つける. 【類】 ***impair*** her *reputation* among the native population. ¶its already evil *reputation* has been ***increased*** of late years by the fact that ... そのすでにこうむっていた悪評が…と言う事実のために近年一層ひどくなった. ¶he ***injured*** his *reputation* for genius by ... 彼は…によってその天才家たる名声を傷つけた. ¶***justify*** one's *reputation* その評判を実証する. ¶***keep up*** *reputation* 名声を維持する. ¶***lose*** one's *reputation* その面目を失う. ¶***lower*** one's *reputation* as a ... …としての声価をおとす. 【類】 ***lower*** or ***injure*** one's *reputation.* ¶***maintain*** its old *reputation* その古くからの名声を維持する. 【類】 Throughout a long public life he ***maintained*** a *reputation* for unassailable integrity. / ***maintain*** the *reputation* which has attached the name of ... for nearly 200 years. ¶***maintain*** and ***enhance*** the high *reputation* of ... …の評判を維持しかつ高める. ¶he ***made*** an international *reputation* for success in ... 彼は…に成功して世界的名声を博した ‖ ***make*** (=win) a *reputation* as a classical scholar 古典学者としての評判を得る. 【類】 He ***made*** his *reputation* with the book as one of the first of European critics. ¶The old, sinister *reputation* of ... has been entirely ***obliterated.*** …と言う昔からの悪評は全く一掃された. ¶***obtain*** a *reputation* for ... …で評判を得る. ¶***raise*** the *reputation* of the country in regard to its military force その国の兵力について評判を高める. ¶***redeem*** the *reputation* for ... …の評判を取り返す. ¶***retain*** a *reputation* 名声を維持する. ¶***revive*** one's *reputation* その名誉を回復する. ¶***ruin*** her *reputation* 彼女の評判を失墜する. ¶the wish to ***save*** her *reputation* その評判を失わないようにしようとの念願 ‖ ***save*** two *reputations* 二人の顔を立てる. ¶***seek*** the bubble *reputation* 一時的な評判を求める. ¶***slur*** our *reputation* われわれの評判を汚す. ¶***soil*** one's *reputation* 人の評判を害する. ¶***stake*** one's *reputation* その名声をとする. ¶***sully*** the *reputation* which our ancestors have bequeathed to us われわれの祖先の名を汚す. ¶It will not add to, but ***sustain,*** his *reputation* as a painstaking historian. それは丹念な歴史家としての評判を増さないまでも維持するであろう. 【類】 They are admirably ***sustaining*** the ancient and glorious *reputation* of the University. / fully ***sustain*** the *reputation* won by "Lost Horizon." ¶***unmake*** *reputations* 評判を落す. ¶***uphold*** the *reputation* and honor of one's college その大学の名声を維持する. ¶***win*** a *reputation* for ... …で評判を取る. ¶***work up*** (=raise) a *reputation* 評判をあげる. ¶***wound*** one's *reputation* その評判を傷つける.

v² The high *reputation* of the lecturer has ***attracted*** a very large audience. 講演者の評判が高いので非常に大勢の聴衆を引きつけた. ¶His *reputation* is ***declining.*** 彼の評判は下り坂だ. ¶His *reputation* has not yet ***died out.*** 彼の名声はいまだ地に落ちていない. ¶His *reputation* is steadily ***growing.*** 彼の評判は着々高まりつつある. 【類】 His *reputation* as an authority on American affairs has steadily ***grown.*** ¶His *reputation* ***spread*** to the Continent. 彼の名は大陸まで鳴響いた. 【類】 Its *reputation* as ... is ***spreading.*** ¶His *reputation* ***suffered*** a great deal. 彼の名声は大分落ちた.

Q This gave him not only an ***academic*** but also a ***popular*** *reputation* throughout France. このために彼はフランス国内においてただに一学者としてばかりでなくまた一般的にも名声を博した. ¶a man with a ***bad*** *reputation* in my neighborhood 私の近所で評判の悪い人. ¶earn a ***better*** *reputation* for one's product その作品で一層評判を高める. ¶his ***brilliant*** *reputation* 彼の輝かしい名声. ¶a woman of ***chaste*** *reputation* 操の聞え高い婦人. ¶he has acquired ***considerable*** *reputation* by his lecture on ... 彼はその…に関する講演で大評判を取った. 【類】 He had a ***considerable*** *reputation* as an antiquarian. ¶a ***cosmopolitan*** *reputation* 世界的名声. ¶a ***cracked*** *reputation* 傷ついた声価. ¶men of ***eminent*** *reputation* 評判の高い人々. ¶have an ***enormous*** *reputation* with ... …の間に評判が高い. ¶He acquired an ***enviable*** *reputation* for integrity, scholarship, and artistic ability. 彼は公正で学識に富み芸術的才能がすぐれているというらやましい評判を得た. ¶a woman of ***equivocal*** *reputation* あやしい評判の女. ¶firms enjoying (= having) an ***established*** *reputation* and world-wide connections 動かすべからざる評判と世界中に広い取引関係のある商会. 【類】 He has an ***established*** *reputation,* being favorably known by ... over the country. / authors of ***established*** *reputation.* ¶having an ***evil*** (=***bad***) *reputation* 評判の悪い. ¶The London B.A. has an ***excellent*** *reputation.* ロンドン大学の B.A.(文学士)は評判がよい. ¶gain an ***extraordinary*** *reputation* as an orator 雄弁家として非常な評判を得る. ¶acquire a ***favorable*** *reputation* 好評を得る. ¶gain a ***fine*** *reputation* りっぱな評判を得る. ¶in a hurry to achieve a ***fleeting*** *reputation* 一時的の評判を得ようと急いで. ¶The physician has a ***good*** *reputation.* その医者は評判がよい. ¶He acquired a ***great*** *reputation* as a physician. 彼は医者として大いに評判がよかった. ¶His lectures won for him a ***high*** *reputation.* 彼はその講演で評判を取った. 【類】 achieve a ***high*** *reputation* as a poet. / It justifies the ***high*** *reputation* he has won. / He enjoyed a ***high*** *reputation* in his day (盛んなころ). ¶an ***ever-increasing*** *reputation* どこまでも増して行く評判. ¶have a most ***honorable*** *reputation* はなはだ尊敬に値する名声を博している. ¶of ***international*** *reputation* 国の内外に名声のある. 【類】 he made an ***international*** *reputation* as ... ¶build up an ***irreproachable*** *reputation* for ... …に対し申分のない名声を築き上げる. ¶he gained a ***literary*** *reputation* by the publication of ... 彼は…の出版によって作家としての声価を得た. 【類】 establish a lasting ***literary*** *reputation.* ¶a ***malodorous*** *reputation* 悪い評判. ¶He enjoys a ***merited*** *reputation.* 彼は評判だけのことはある. ¶a specialist of ***national*** and ***international*** *reputation* 国の内外に令名高い専門家. ¶an actress of ***nation-wide*** *reputation* 国中に名の響いた女優. ¶win a ***popular*** *reputation* as a magician 魔術家として広く評判を得る. ¶I don't care a bit about ***public*** *reputation.* 世間体など一向かまわん. ¶visit cafes and even places of ***questionable*** (=***doubtful***) *reputation* カフェーやいかがわしい場所にも出入する. ¶his *reputation* is already ***secure*** among ... 彼はもう…の間に押しも押されもしないものとなった. ¶a ***spotless*** (=an ***immaculate***) *reputation* 一点曇りなき評判. ¶a ***smirched*** *reputation* 悪い評判. ¶the Times with its ***thundering*** *reputation* 名声天下にとどろくタイムズ紙. ¶have a ***time-honored*** *reputation* 昔からよいとされている. ¶Japan has earned a most ***unenviable*** *reputation* for ... 日本は…ではなはだ香ばしからぬ評判を取った. ¶have an ***unpleasant*** *reputation* for ... …でおもしろくない評判を取っている. ¶The firm has an ***unrivaled*** *reputation* of nearly thirty years' standing. その店は約三十年も無比の声価を持続してきた. ¶The store has the ***unsavory*** *reputation* of making a practice of overcharging. その店は高売をするというおもしろくない評判がある. ¶have a ***well-deserved*** *reputation* for ... …で好評を受けるだけの価値がある. ¶This gained for him a ***well-merited*** *reputation.* これがために彼はりっぱな評判をとった. ¶As a jewel mart, Colombo has a ***wide*** *reputation.* コロンボは宝石市場として世界に知れ渡っている. ¶The firm enjoys a ***widespread*** *reputation.* その商会は広く知られている. ¶bent on ***winning*** *reputation* 評判をとろうと熱心になって. ¶achieve a ***wonderful*** *reputation* for ... …で大評判を取る. ¶men of ***world-wide*** *reputation* 世界的名声のある人々. 【類】 It gained for him a ***world-wide*** *reputation.*

Q² ***A 1*** *reputation* 最高の名声. ¶seek the ***bubble*** *reputation* 虚名を求める. ¶That will add greatly to his ***business*** *reputation.* それで彼の商売上の名声があがるだろう.

¶The Company upholds a ***115-year reputation*** for quality and service. 弊社は品質と奉仕により百十五年にわたり名声を維持しております.

P I know him well ***by reputation***. 私は評判で彼をよく知っている. 【類】I know the book ***by reputation***. ¶decline ***in reputation*** 評判が衰える. ¶a journalist (hotel) ***of*** high *reputation* 評判の高い新聞記者(など) ‖ acquire the worst ***of*** all *reputations*, that of a bore うるさいやつという一番悪い評判を取る. ¶a stain ***on*** one's *reputation* 面目上の汚点. ¶His position was obtained ***on account of*** his earned *reputation*. 彼はりっぱな評判を得たのでその地位を与えられた. ¶His recent work has not added much ***to*** his *reputation*. 最近作では大して名声があがらなかった. ¶live (act) ***up to*** one's *reputation* その名声に恥じない生活(行動)をする. ¶obscure writers ***with*** no *reputation* to lose 取るに足らない無名の作家 ‖ No moralist ***with*** a *reputation* to lose would like to back his remark. 名声を重んじる道徳家なら彼の説を支持しようとは思うまい. ‖ men ***with*** *reputations* already established すでに定評のある人々. 【類】He filled the chair ***with*** high *reputation* for a few years. / a batch of hotels ***with*** great German *reputations* (ドイツ人に大好評の) / authors ***with*** "great names" and established *reputations*. ¶Sandow, then a youth ***without*** *reputations* 当時年若くまだ無名のサンドウ.

P² authors who have a high *reputation* ***among*** publishers 出版者の間に評判が高い著述家たち. ¶found one's *reputation* ***as*** a great traveller 大の旅行家たる評判を取る. 【類】he has an international *reputation* ***as*** an expert on ... / He gained a high *reputation* ***as*** a skilful surgeon (外科医). ¶acquire a European *reputation* ***by*** his novels and stories 彼の小説や物語によってヨーロッパに名声を博する. ¶men of world-wide *reputation* ***for*** business sagacity 実務の才をもって世界的に有名な人々 ‖ the Frenchman's *reputation* ***for*** volubility フランス人が口達者であるという評判. 【類】a *reputation* ***for*** impartiality (公平無私) / have a *reputation* ***for*** interfering too much in the affairs of others (他人のこと). ¶a *reputation* ***of*** being a great scholar 大学者だという評判. ¶save one's *reputation* ***with*** the neighbors 隣人から悪く言われないようにする.

O His *reputation* is on the wane. 彼の評判は下り坂だ.

repute, *n.* 評判, 名声, 令名, 美名.

V She ***attained*** a high *repute* as a poetess. 彼女は閨秀歌人として有名になった. ¶***bear*** the *repute* of being a brave soldier 勇敢な軍人たる名声を担う. ¶He ***earned*** (=***won***) great *repute* as an author. 彼は著作家として大の評判を得た. ¶he ***gained*** considerable *repute* on account of his talent for ... 彼は...の才能があるので非常な評判を得た. ¶The name ***has*** a bad *repute*. その人は評判が悪い. ¶Assuan has ***obtained*** a world-wide *repute* as a valuable health resort. アスアン(エジプト)はすぐれた保養地として世界的名声を博した.

Q He (The firm) is of ***bad*** *repute*. その人(など)は評判が悪い. ¶He is placed by ***common*** *repute* at the head of them. 彼は皆から長と仰がれている. ¶fall into ***evil*** *repute* 評判が悪くなる. ¶Japanese firm of ***good*** *repute* 日本の確実な商社. ¶of ***high*** *repute* 高評のある. 【類】makers of the ***highest*** *repute*. ¶a remedy of ***imperial*** *repute* 非常に評判のよい薬. ¶authorities of ***international*** *repute* 国際的名声のある権威者. ¶be held in ***low*** *repute* by much of the public 多勢の者から軽べつされる. ¶of ***no small*** *repute* かなりの評判の. ¶a man of ***solid*** *repute* 評判のよい人. ¶an artist of ***some*** *repute* 多少名の知れた画家. ¶a well-known school of ***unimpeachable*** *repute* 評判の高い有名な学校. ¶It is of ***well-established*** *repute*. それは定評がある. ¶a diplomat of ***world-wide*** *repute* 世界的名声のある外交官.

P books hitherto known only ***by*** *repute* これまで名前だけで知られていた本. ¶The wine of Shiraz is ***in*** high *repute*. シラーズのぶどう酒は評判がよい. ¶authors (concerns) ***of*** *repute* 名高い作家(商店).

P² It is in high medicinal *repute* ***as*** a stimulant. それは興奮剤として医薬上有名だ.

repute, *v.* 思う, 見なす; 評判する.

M ***much*** *reputed* among ... ...の間で大評判の.

P be *reputed* ***as*** a physicist 物理学者として名がある. ¶He is *reputed* ***for*** his originality. 彼はその独創力で有名だ.

O He is *reputed* to be a great linguist. 彼は語学者として名が高い.

request, *n.* 依頼, 請願, 頼みごと.

V upon receipt of a *request* ***addressed*** to ... ...あての申出を受取り次第. ¶***advance*** a *request* 要求を提出する. ¶Your *request* will be ***allowed***. あなたの願はかなうだろう. ¶***concede*** a *request* 願を聞き届ける. ¶***decline*** a *request* 依頼を断わる. ¶***deny*** a *request* 要求を拒む. ¶***fulfil*** a *request* 願い事をかなえてやる. ¶I should with pleasure ***grant*** your *request*. 喜んで御依頼に応じます. 【類】Heaven has ***granted*** my *request!* ¶The dying man ***groaned out*** a *request*. ひん死の男が願いごとをうめき声で言った. ¶I ***have*** a *request* to make of you. あなたにお願いがあります. ¶I would like to ***make*** a *request*. 一つお願いをしたい. ‖ on *request* ***made*** to him for that purpose その目的で彼に願い出ると. ¶upon my ***pressing*** the *request* 私がそのことをせがんだ時に. ¶***proffer*** one's *request* その願を持出す. ¶***refuse*** a *request* 要求を拒む. ¶A *request* to omit name will be ***respected***. 匿名の要求は尊重します[新聞・雑誌など]. ¶***send*** a post-card *request* for ... ...請求の葉書を送る. ¶***whisper*** a *request* 頼みごとをささやく. ¶***write*** a *request* to him for permission of ... ...の許可を彼に手紙で願い出る.

Q if ***advanced*** *request* is made=if requested in advance 前もって願い出れば. ¶a ***ceremonial*** *request* 正式の願い. ¶a ***cool*** (=***calm***) *request* 虫の好い頼み. ¶an ***easy*** *request* おやすい御用. ¶at my ***express*** *request* 特に私の希望で. ¶It continues in ***good*** *request*. それは相変らず需要がある. ¶He is in ***great*** *request*. [芸人など]非常に持てはやされている. ¶The goods are in ***moderate*** *request*. その品は相当売行がよい. ‖ Money is in very ***moderate*** *request*. 金融が至極緩慢である. ¶a ***reasonable*** (an ***unreasonable***) *request* 当然(不当)な要求. ¶I approached him with a ***respectful*** *request* that ... 私は辞を低くして彼に...ということを頼み込んだ. ¶***several*** *requests* have come to us for information about ... ...に対する照会が数件あった. ¶except by ***special*** *request* 特別の請求がなければ. ¶at one's ***urgent*** *request* of たっての願いで. ¶there has been a ***wide-spread*** *request* that ... ...という広く一般の要求があった. ¶a ***written*** *request* 書面での申出. 【類】Additional information regarding ... will gladly be furnished by ... upon ***written*** *request*. / if a ***written*** *request* to that effect is made by ...

Q² at ***Government*** *request* 政府の請求で. ¶forward a ***two-point*** *request* to ... 二点の要求を...に提出する.

P ***at*** the *request* of ... ...の請求があれば. 【類】A copy of our catalogue will be promptly sent ***at*** your *request*. / He retired ***at*** his own *request*. ¶No flowers ***by*** *request*. 〖掲示〗遺志により贈花は御辞退申上げます. 【類】***by*** his own *requests* / ***by*** *request* from ... ¶***concerning*** your *request* あなたの願について. ¶It is much ***in*** *request*. それは大いに需要がある. ¶***in answer*** (=reply) ***to*** his *request* for help 助けてくれという彼の願に応じて. ¶***in response to*** an earnest *request* from ... ...からの熱心な希望を入れて. ¶A catalogue will be mailed free ***on*** *request*(=application). 目録は御請求次第無料で郵送します. 【類】***on*** the *request* of ... ‖ except ***on*** a *request* made by ... ...の請求ある場合を除くの外. ¶accede ***to*** a *request* 要求に応じる. ¶application blanks will be furnished ***upon*** *request* addressed to ... 申込用紙は...あてに請求されれば送付します. 【類】mailed ***upon*** *request*, addressed or telephoned to ... ¶comply ***with*** one's *request* その要求に応じる.

P² He is in great *request* ***as*** a popular lecturer. 彼は通俗講演者として大いにもてはやされている. ¶a *request* ***for*** an autograph 自筆をもとめること. 【類】There is a great *request* ***for*** teaching of English. / a *request* ***for*** information (問合わせ).

request, *v.* 願う, 頼む, 請う.

M ***earnestly*** *request* 折り入って頼む. ¶I ***hereby*** *request* you to ... ここに...することをお願いする. ¶***politely*** *request* it いんぎんにそれを頼む. ¶you are ***respectfully*** *requested* to ... どうか...していただきたいものです.

P Photographs are *requested* ***with*** articles. [寄稿などの]文にはさし絵用写真を添えていただきたい.

requiem, *n.* 安息, 平安; 鎮魂歌.

V ***chant*** one's *requiem* その鎮魂歌を歌う. ¶***say*** a *requiem* 引導を渡す. ¶a chorus of praise ***sounding*** the *requiem* of a great man 偉人の鎮魂祭に響きわたる賛美歌の合唱.

require, *v.* 要求する, 請う, 頼む, 願う.

M Zeal is ***greatly required***. 大いに熱意が要る. ¶***how long*** will it be *required* to…? …するにはどの位かかりますか. ¶***urgently required*** 切に希望されて.

P *required* ***by*** its regulations 規則で定めてある. 【類】be *required* ***by*** law to … ¶*required* ***for*** the purpose その目的に必要な ‖ There were only 50 present against the 69 *required* ***for*** a quorum. 定員数六十九人に対して五十人しか出席していなかった. ‖ the number of high school units *required* ***for*** admission 入学に必要な高校の単位数. ¶an explanation must be *required* ***from*** Mr.… …氏から説明を求めねばならない. ¶Too much work is *required* ***of*** students. 過度の勉強が学生に要求されている. 【類】I will do all that is *required* ***of*** me. ¶time *required* ***on*** ships (trains, cabs) 船(など)に要する時間.

O If you *require* me, send for me. 私に御用があったらお呼び下さい.

requirement, *n.* 要求, 需要; 入用物; 要件.

V ***fill*** one's *requirements* その必要を満たす. ¶It will ***fulfil*** your *requirements*. それはあなたの需要を満たすでしょう. ¶fail to ***grasp*** the *requirements* of … …の要求を解し兼ねる. ¶satisfactorily ***meet*** the *requirements* prescribed 規格にぴったりする ‖ ***meet*** every *requirement* あらゆる要求に応じる. 【類】***meet*** all these *requirements* / best ***meet*** these *requirements* / will probably ***meet*** *requirements* of the times / promptly ***meet*** the *requirements* of the new order / ***meet*** the *requirements* of the public (times). ¶***outline*** one's *requirements* …の要求を略説する. ¶Students are accepted on ***passing*** the entrance *requirements*. 学生は入学の要件に応じ得た場合に入学を許される. ¶***satisfy*** the entrance *requirements* for a regular coruse 正科の入学試験に合格する. ¶***set out*** (=***put forth***) *requirements* 条件を出す. ¶***suit*** the *requirements* of the case その場合の要求に適する. ¶***supply*** your present *requirements* あなたの現在の要求を満たす.

Q ***essential*** *requirements* 必須の要件. 【類】fulfil three ***essential*** *requirements*. ¶His *requirements* are most ***exacting***. 彼の要求は非常にやかましい. ¶the ***first*** *requirement* is to … 第一に…することが必要なのである. ¶cope with ***increasing*** *requirements* 増加して行く需要に応じる. ¶suit ***individual*** *requirements* それぞれの要求に適する. ¶meet the ***necessary legal*** *requirements* 必要な法律上の要求に合する. ¶The ***physical*** *requirements* for enlistment in the army are moderate. 入営についての身体上の要件はやかましくない. ‖ in order to meet their ***physiological*** *requirements* 彼らの生理的要求に対処するために. ¶meet ***public*** *requirements* 一般の要求に合する. ¶*Requirements* for home study are too ***severe***. 宿題の要求がきびし過ぎる.

Q^2 ***admission*** *requirements* [大学などの]入学資格. ¶supply one's ***coal*** *requirements* その必要とする石炭を供給する. ¶***college entrance*** *requirements* in English 英語の大学入学試験科目. ¶***contract*** *requirements* 契約の要件. ¶Books in the college library are made quickly available for ***course*** *requirements*. 大学図書館の書物は課程の需要に応じすみやかに閲覧ができるようになっている. ¶***Documentation*** *requirements*, such as passports, visé, health certificate, etc., will gladly be supplied. 旅行免状・査証・健康証明書などの証明書は手軽に発行します. ¶The school will make ***entrance*** *requirements* more difficult. その学校は入学試験を一層むずかしくするだろう. ‖ rigorous ***entrance*** *requirements* 苛酷な入学試験 ‖ present language study merely as an ***entrance*** *requirement* 単に入学の一つの要件としての語学の勉強. ¶rigid ***entrance*** *requirements* 厳密な入学試験. ¶***Food*** *requirements* of Orientals are at least 20 per cent less than for Occidentals. 東洋人の食糧の需要は西洋人のそれより少くも 20 パーセント少ない. ¶***graduation*** *requirements* 卒業資格. ¶failure to meet ***height*** and ***weight*** *requirements* 必要とする高さと重量の不足. ¶discriminatory ***hiring*** *requirements* 差別的雇用条件. ¶***import*** and ***export licensing*** *requirements* 輸出入許可条件. ¶fill the army's ***manpower*** *requirements* of 1,070,000 百七万の陸軍兵員の需要を満たす. ¶***registration*** *requirement* 登録に必要な条件; 入学の資格. ¶minimum ***residence*** *requirements* 最小限度に必要な住宅. ¶meet ***standard*** *requirements* 規格に合う. ¶***travel*** *requirements* 旅行必需品.

P accommodations far ***behind*** modern *requirements* 現代の要求からはるかに遅れている設備. ¶The supply of tonnage is greatly ***below*** (***in excess of***) *requirements*. トン数(船舶)の供給が需要よりはるか下(上)回っている. ¶Present supplies are ***beyond*** (***not equal to***) *requirements* 現代の供給は需要以上(下)である. ¶It is insufficient ***for*** my *requirement*. それは私の要求に対して不十分である. ¶conform ***to*** its *requirements* その要求にそう.

P^2 *requirements* ***for*** admission = admission requirements 入学上の資格. 【類】the entrance *requirements* ***for*** the course.

requisite, *n.* 必要物, 必須物; 要件, 要素.

Q To be a good animal is the ***first*** *requisite* to success in life, and to be a nation of good animals is the first condition of national prosperity.—Herbert Spencer. りっぱな動物たることは成功の第一要件であり, りっぱな動物から成る国民たることは国家繁栄の第一条件である. ¶***indispensable*** *requisites* 必須要件. ¶an ***occupational*** *requisite*=a capital in trade 商売道具. ¶a ***primary*** *requisite* 根本要件. ¶the ***prime*** *requisite* 第一要件. ¶a ***standard*** *requisite* 標準必要物.

Q^2 ***household*** *requisites* 世帯道具類. ¶***kitchen*** *requisites* 台所諸道具. ¶***toilet*** *requisites* 化粧用品. ¶a basket of ***traveling*** *requisites* 旅行用品を入れたかご.

P Neatness and cleanliness are among the first *requisites* ***of*** decent society. 清潔整とんは上品な社会の第一要件に属する.

P^2 *requisites* ***to*** good health 健康保持の諸条件.

requisite, *a.* 必須の, 必要の.

P *requisite* ***for*** the purpose その目的に入用の. ¶*requisite* ***to*** happiness (health, success) 幸福(など)にとって必要な.

requisition, *n.* 要求, 請求.

V ***make*** *requisition* for a week's leave of absence 一週間の賜暇を願い出る.

P It is ***in*** particular *requisition*. 特にそれが要求されている. ¶***on*** the *requisition* of … …の要求で. ¶A Special General Meeting shall be called by the General Committee ***upon*** the written *requisition* of ten members. 会員十名の文書による請求により特別総会が委員総会によって召集される.

P^2 *requisition* ***for*** provisions 糧食の需要.

requisition, *v.* 徴発する.

P be *requisitioned* ***for*** war material 戦争物資として徴発される ‖ *requisition* a house ***for*** a soldiers' billet 兵士の宿舎に家屋を接収する. 【類】*requisition* horses ***for*** war purposes.

requital, *n.* 報償, 返礼, 返報.

Q too ***poor*** *requital* for one's service その労力にしては貧弱すぎる報酬.

P ***in*** *requital* of the outrage of … …の暴行に対する報復として.

requite, *v.* 報いる, 返報する, 償う.

P *requite* like ***for*** like 類をもって類に報いる. ¶*requite* a person ***for*** a benefit 恩義に対して報いる. ¶*requite* good ***with*** evil 善に報いるに悪をもってする ‖ His servility was *requited* ***with*** cold contempt. 彼の屈従は冷たいぶべつで報いられた.

rescript, *n.* 勅書, 詔書.

V ***issue*** a Royal *Rescript* 詔書をかん発する.

Q the ***Imperial*** *Rescript* on Education 教育勅語.

rescue, *n.* 救い, 救助, 救援.

V ***effect*** the *rescue* of … …の救助を全うする.

Q a ***heroic*** *rescue* 勇敢な救助.

Q^2 a ***last minute*** *rescue* 際どい救助.

P rush to the scene ***for*** the *rescue* of … …の救助に現場に急行する. ¶go (come) ***to*** one's *rescue* それを助けにおもむく(来る).

P^2 a plucky *rescue* ***at*** a fire 火災時の勇敢な救助.

rescue, *v.* 救う, 救助する, 救援する.

P That boy has just been *rescued* ***from*** drowning. あの子は危くでき死するところを助けられた. 【類】She was *rescued* ***from*** a burning building. / *rescue* a tomb ***from*** oblivion.

research, *n.* 調査, 精査, 研究, 探究.

V ***carry on*** a *research* 調査を続ける. ¶***conduct*** *researches* into (=in the field of) … …の研究を行う. ¶His *researches* are ***contained*** in a book recently published. 彼の研究は最近発行された書物に収めてある. ¶***continue*** one's *research* in anthropology 人類学の研究を続ける. ¶a work ***displaying*** wide *research* and keen discernment 広範な研究と鋭敏な眼識を示している著作. ¶***do*** *research* 調査をやる. ¶***extend*** one's *researches* farther afield 研究の手をさらに広範囲にわたって広げる. ¶***institute*** exact *researches* into … …の正確な研究を始める. ¶***prosecute*** *research* on a subject ある問題の調査を行う. ¶***pursue*** his linguistic *researches* 彼の言語学上の研究を進める. ¶***stimulate*** and *promote* research 研究を刺激し助長する.

V² scientific *researches* have *shown* that ... 科学的な研究で...ということが分かった.

Q purely *academic researches* 純然たる学問上の研究. ¶after years of failure and seemingly *barren research* 多年の失敗と一見無だな研究の末に. ¶*comprehensive research* 広範な研究. ¶do *considerable research* for ... ...の相当重要な研究をする. ¶the result of twenty years of *continuous research* 二十年にわたる絶間ない研究の結果. ¶*experimental research* 実験的研究. ¶*fruitful researches* 成果のあがる研究. ¶*futile research* 無だな研究. ¶*genealogical research* 系図の研究. ¶*historical* and *antiquarian research* 歴史及び考古学的研究. ¶*indefatigable research* 不屈不とうの研究. ¶*independent research* 独立の研究. ¶*inexhaustible research* 無尽蔵の研究. ¶*intensive research* 熱心な研究. ¶very *interesting research* has already been done on ... ...に関して非常に興味ある研究がすでにとげられた. ¶the *Judicial Research* and Training Institute of the Attorney-General's Office 法務府研究所. ¶make *laborious research*=delve 骨の折れる研究をやる. 【類】the results of *laborious research*. ¶according to the light of the *latest researches* of medical science 最近医学研究の見解によれば. ¶the fruits of his *life-long research* 氏の一生がいにわたる研究の成果. ¶This essay treats of the progress of *medical research*. この論文は医学研究の進歩を取扱っている. ¶*modern researches* 近代の研究. ¶*Oriental research* in America アメリカにおける東洋研究. ¶after extended *original research* 長期の独創的研究を重ねた後. 【類】The occupant of a university chair (大学教授) is expected to spend much of his time in *original research*. ¶*painstaking researches* 丹念な研究. ¶years of *patient research* 多年にわたる根気のよい研究. ¶persons engaged in *scholarly research* 学究的研究に従事する人々. ¶make *scientific researches* on the subject of sex 性の問題について科学的研究をする.

Q² *atomic bomb research* 原爆研究. ¶According to *BBC Listener Research*, the most popular radio program is "Have a Go." イギリスの BBC 聴取者調査によれば最も人気のある放送番組は「やって見ろ」だ. ¶*institute research* 研究所における研究. ¶*market research* 市況調査. ¶*playtime research* 道楽の研究. ¶the German institute for statistical *public opinion research* ドイツ統計的世論調査所. ¶a director of *student research* 学生研究指導者. ¶*undergraduate research* 大学生の研究. ¶*university researches* on archeology 大学の考古学研究. ¶*word study research* 語の研究.

P *after* a careful *research* 注意深い研究の後. ¶he found *by research* that ... 彼は研究して...ということを知り得た. ¶Every facility is given *for* original *research*. 独創的研究にあらゆる利便が与えられている. ¶He is engaged *in research*. 彼は研究に従事している. ¶*through* analytical *researches* 分析調査の結果.

P² a *research after* facts 事実の調査. ¶*research among* fusty records of long forgotten facts 久しい以前に忘れられた事実を記したかび臭い記録の渉猟. ¶new *researches concerning* ... ...に関する新研究. ¶*research in* Eastern languages and literatures 東洋語と東洋文学の研究. ¶*researches into* the history of ... ...の歴史の研究 ‖ *researches into* the origin of ... ...の起源の研究. ¶his *researches on* Mars (explosives) 火星(など)に関する彼の研究. ¶He prosecuted his beneficent *researches on behalf of* humanity. 彼は人類のために慈善的な研究を行った.

researcher, *n.* 研究者.

Q² *market researcher* 市場調査員.

P² busy *researchers at* the British Museum 英国博物館における多忙な研究者.

resemblance, *n.* 類似, 似寄り; 類似物.

V *accentuate* (=*heighten*) the *resemblance* [...のため]いよいよ似て来る. ¶His face *bears* some *resemblance* to the first Napoleon. 彼の顔はどこかナポレオン一世に似ている. ¶to *complete* the *resemblance* いよいよ似るように. ¶*have* great *resemblance* to ... ...によく似ている. ¶*offer* a curious *resemblance* to ... ...に不思議によく似ている. ¶*present* a personal *resemblance* to ... ...に容ぼうが似ている. ¶*show* striking *resemblances* among one another お互い同志驚くほどよく似ている. ¶*strengthen* the *resemblance* between the two 二者間の類似を強化する.

Q an *accidental resemblance* 空似. ¶the *resemblance* is so *close* that ... 非常によく似ているので... 【類】There is a *close resemblance* btween the two (うり二つ). ¶stones bearing *curious resemblance* to animal forms 動物の形体に不思議に似ている珍らしい岩石. ¶present a *deceptive resemblance* to ... ...と間違うほど似ている. ¶These apes bear some *distant resemblance* to men. これらのさるは人間にほんの少し似ている. ¶an *exact resemblance* 酷似. ¶recall in him a *facial resemblance* to ... 彼を見ると容ぼうが...に似ていることを思い出す. ¶bear but a *faint resemblance* to ... ほんのちょっと...に似ているに過ぎない. ¶bear a *fancied resemblance* to ... ...と似ているような気がする. ¶there is *little resemblance* between ... ...間には類似点がほとんどない. ¶of *real* or *supposed resemblance* 実際に似ているあるいは似ていると思われる. ¶a *remarkable resemblance* 著しい類似. ¶bear a *remote resemblance* only to ... ただ...にだけほんの少し似ている. ¶a *singular resemblance* 著しい類似. ¶a *slight resemblance* ちょっとした類似. ¶bear many *startling resemblances* to ... ...と多くの著しい類似点がある. ¶a *striking resemblance* 目に立つ類似. ¶a *strong resemblance* 著しい類似. ¶bear *superficial resemblances* 表面だけ似ている. ¶*supposed resemblance* to ... ...に似た感じ. 【類】Many of the rocks and cliffs along the rapids have been given fanciful names by the boatmen and the passengers because of some *supposed resemblance* to various objects.

P *from* its *resemblance* to ... それが...に似ているので. ¶the name is founded *on* the fancied *resemblance* to ... その名は...に似ているという想像に基づいている. ¶*with* no *resemblance* to ... ...に似ないで. ¶it is not *without resemblance* to ... それは...に似ていないこともない.

P² *resemblances among* ... ...間の類似. ¶The *resemblance between* you and your sister is very striking. 君と君の妹さんとはよく似ている.

resemble, *v.* 似る, 類似する.

M *closely resemble* よく似る. ¶*remotely* (=*faintly*) *resemble* わずかに似る. ¶*strongly resemble* 非常によく似る.

P *resemble in* appearance (shape) 外ぼう(など)が似る.

resent, *v.* 憤る.

M *deeply resent* a person's remark (action) 人の言葉を憤る.

resentful, *a.* 憤る.

P *resentful of* ... ...を憤って, ...にぷんとして. 【類】*resentful of* what she said / *resentful of* the way of her speaking.

resentment, *n.* 憤慨, 遺恨.

V *allay resentment* 憤怒を静める. ¶*arouse* (*awake*) the *resentment* of ... ...を憤慨させる. ¶*bear* no *resentment* against ... ...には何のうらみももっていない. ¶*cherish resentment* 意趣を含む. ¶the whole *resentment* of ... was *directed* against (=toward) ... ...の憤怒がことごとく...に向けられた. ¶*feel* no *resentment* なんら憤怒を感じない. ¶*harbor resentment* against ... ...に対して恨みをいだく. ¶*rouse* the deep-seated *resentment* of all classes あらゆる階級の深く根ざした憤怒を喚起する. ¶*show* one's *resentment* by electing Democrats 民主党を選挙してうつ憤を晴らす. ¶*stir up resentment* 怒らす. 「恨みをいだく.

Q harbor *quiet resentment* against ... ...に対してひそかに

P² *resentment against* a person (government) 人(など)に対する憤り.

reservation, *n.* 留保, 制限, 遠慮; [しばしば *pl.*] 予約; 「《米》指定保留地.

V Early *reservations advised*. 早くお申込おきをお勧め致します(旅館など). ¶*reservations* can be *arranged* for through ... 予約は...を通じてすることができます. ¶*cancel reservations* 予約を取消す. ¶The *reservation* for the luncheon is *limited* to 500 plates. 昼食の申込は五百人前までに制限されている. ¶*Make reservation*[s] for me on the Empire. エンパイア号に予約して下さい. 【類】*Reservations* can be *made* by letter, cable or wireless. ¶*obtain* sleeper *reservations* 寝台の予約を取る. ¶*secure* their *reservations* well in advance 彼らの予約をずっと前に取っておく. 【類】I had difficulty in *securing* a steamship *reservation*. ¶The *reservation* has not been *taken up*. 予約をしていなかった(汽船・汽車など).

Q make *advance reservations* 前もって申込んでおく. ¶with *certain reservation* in the interests of truth, it may be said that ... 事実尊重の意味でいく分加減する必要はあるが先ず...と言って差支えない. ¶a ***Federal reservation*** 連邦留保地域. ¶an ***Indian reservation*** インディアン専有地(アメリカ政府の指定した).

Q^2 a ***bathing reservation*** 海水浴場. ¶***big game*** and ***bird*** *reservations* 大狩猟獣鳥類の保存. ¶***Hotel*** *reservations* may be made in distant cities and watering places. ホテルの予約は遠く離れた都市や海水浴場でできる. ¶***passage*** *reservations* 通行制限. ¶a ***sleeper reservation*** 寝台車予約. ¶secure ***sleeping-car*** *reservations* 寝台車の予約をする. ¶a ***steamer reservation*** 汽船の予約.

P This fact must be taken ***with*** some *reservation.* この事実は少し控え目に考えねばならない. ¶from my own observations of ..., I would say ***without reservation*** that ... 私の...に対する観察から私は遠慮なく...と申上げたい. 【類】accept the offer ***without reservation.***

P^2 *reservations* ***for*** accommodation at hotels 旅館の宿泊申込.

reserve, *n.* 差控え, 腹蔵; 予備; 予備軍.

V Good wine soon ***banished*** all *reserve.* 間もなく上等のぶどう酒ですっかりくつろいでしまった. ¶***break down*** all *reserve* 全く打解ける. ¶The *reserve* is ***called out*** (=called to arms) when war is impending. 戦争が差し迫って来ると予備軍が召集される. ¶***call up*** the *reserves* 予備軍を召集する. ¶***exhibit*** *reserve* on political matters 政治上のことに口をつつしむ. ¶We ***felt*** some cold *reserves* between ourselves. われわれの間に少し冷たい遠慮を感じた. ¶He ***has*** a great *reserve* of energy. 彼は大いに精力を貯えている. ¶the bank ***holds*** a gold *reserve* of ... その銀行には...の金貨準備がある. ¶***keep*** a *reserve* of money 予備金を取っておく. ¶He ***laid up*** no *reserves* out of his annuity. 彼は年金の内から貯蓄をしなかった. ¶***maintain*** *reserve* 沈黙を守る. ¶***mobilize*** the *reserve* 予備軍を動員する. ¶We must ***observe*** the greatest *reserve* in forming (=formulating) our conclusions. 結論を下す場合はできるだけ控え目にしなければならない. ¶A *reserve* is ***set up*** for that special purpose. その特別の目的のために予備金が積立ててある. ¶***throw off*** one's *reserve* 遠慮を捨てる.

V^2 his *reserve* ***melted away*** as he replied, "..." 彼が「...」と答えたときに遠慮がなくなっていた.

Q ***haughty*** *reserve* ごう岸なへだて心. ¶a ***legal reserve*** [銀行などの]法定準備金. ¶his ***provoking*** *reserve* 彼の腹立たしい遠慮. ¶a colonel in the ***second*** *reserve* 後備役大佐.

Q^2 a ***forest reserve*** 保安林. ¶a ***rainy day*** *reserve* 万一の場合の予備金. ¶the security of a ***specie*** *reserve* 正貨準備積立金.

P be put up to (=at) auction ***for*** the surplus *reserve* 剰余資金用として競売に付せられる. ¶a Minister Plenipotentiary ***in reserve*** 待命中の特命全権公使 ‖ a soldier ***in*** the *reserve* 予備軍人 ‖ He had enough strength ***in reserve*** to overcome the obstacles. 彼はその障害に打勝つだけの力を貯えていた. ¶go ***into reserve*** 予備に回る. ¶He is registered ***on*** the *reserve.* 彼は予備役に編入されている. ¶The report is very doubtful and should be taken ***with*** all *reserve.* その報告ははなはだ怪しいから大いに割引して受入れるべきだ. ¶converse ***without reserve*** 遠慮なしに話を交わす ‖ sell ***without reserve*** 値段に制限を設けずに売る. 【類】Tell me your idea on the subject ***without*** any *reserve.*

P^2 a *reserve* ***against*** loss 損失に備える準備金. ¶***in reserve for*** a rainy day 困るときの用意に. ¶a *reserve* ***of*** force 底力 ‖ a *reserve* ***of*** provisions 予備食糧.

reserve, *v.* 保存する; 予約する; 差控える.

P Seats may be *reserved* ***against*** a small fee. わずかの料金で席を取っておくことができる. ¶They entered the carriage *reserved* ***for*** them. 彼らは用意してあった(貸切の)車両に乗った. ‖ They are *reserved* ***for*** another job それらは別口の取引に使うことになっている. ‖ The fate that was *reserved* ***for*** me was too clear. 自分の運命はあまりにもはっきりしていた(死より他になかった). ‖ *Reserve* (=Share) your energy ***for*** other work. 【類】You'd better *reserve* your strength ***for*** tomorrow's climb. ¶cargo space *reserved* ***with*** the local shipping firms 土地の海運会社専用の荷揚おろし場.

O All the seats were *reserved.* 席は全部売り切れだった.

reserved, *a.* 遠慮した.

P He is *reserved* ***by*** nature. 彼は生れつき遠慮勝ちである.

reservoir, *n.* 貯水池, 貯蔵器.

Q^2 an ***air*** *reservoir* 〚機〛空気だめ. ¶***receiving*** *reservoir* 集水池.

P a *reservoir* ***for*** holding ... ...を入れるための貯蔵器. ¶His mind was a *reservoir* ***of*** facts. 彼は生字引だった. ‖ a *reservoir* ***of*** oil 石油貯蔵所.

reset, *v.* [骨折を]つぐ.

M He's got his arm broken and has to be *reset* ***immediately.*** 彼は腕を折ったのですぐ骨つぎをせねばならない.

reshuffle, *n.* 改造, 入れかえ.

Q^2 a partial ***Cabinet*** *reshuffle* 内閣の一部改組. ¶a *reshuffle* ***of*** the Cabinet 閣僚の入れかえ.

reside, *v.* 住む, 居住する, 居留する.

M *reside* ***abroad*** 海外に居住する. ¶*reside* ***permanently*** in Paris パリに永住する.

P *reside* ***at*** a house abutting on the seashore 海岸に臨む家に住む. ¶*reside* ***in*** England 英国に居住する ‖ the value *resides* solely ***in*** ... その価値は全然...の点にある ‖ All power *resides* ***in*** the people. 権力はすべて人民にある. ¶He purchased the land several years ago and now *resides* ***upon*** it. 彼は数年前に土地を買って今そこに住んでいる. ¶*reside* ***with*** a person 人の家に住む(同居する).

residence, *n.* 居住, 住所, 居所; 邸宅.

V ***change*** one's *residence* 移転する. 【類】***change*** the *residence* during the rebuilding (改築中) from ... to ... ¶he ***fixed*** his *residence* at ... 彼は...に居を定めた. 【類】***fix*** one's *residence* in the country (いなか). ¶He ***has*** no settled *residence.* 彼には一定の住所がない. ¶***make*** one's *residence* here 当地に住む. ¶***move*** one's *residence* from ... to ... その住所を...から...へ移す. ¶***relinquish*** a *residence* 住宅を手放す. ¶***shift*** one's *residence* 移転する. ¶He married an English woman and ***took up*** his *residence* in London. あの人は英人を妻にしてロンドンに家を持った. 【類】The King ***took up*** his *residence* at St. James's Palace. / ***take up*** one's *residence* with a person (in a boardinghouse) / Yedo was denominated (命名された) Tokyo when the Emperor Meiji ***took up*** his *residence* there. ¶***transfer*** one's *residence* to ... ...にその居を移す.

Q a ***bijou*** *residence* 小じんまりした優雅な邸宅. ¶be released from a ***compulsory*** *residence* at Yedo [大名が]江戸に強制居住を免除される. ¶a ***desirable*** *residence* 望ましい住宅. ¶***fixed residence*** 一定の住所. ¶two years' ***foreign*** *residence* 二年間の外国在住. ¶a ***handsome*** *residence* りっぱな邸宅. ¶his ***late*** *residence* 彼のこの前の住宅. ¶make a ***lengthy*** *residence* in China 中国に長く住む. ¶a ***magnificent*** *residence* 堂々たる邸宅. ¶***official*** *residences* 公邸. ¶***palatial*** *residences* 宮殿のような邸宅. ¶their place of ***permanent*** *residence* 彼ら永住の地. 【類】make the hotel their ***permanent*** *residence* / take up his ***permanent*** *residence* in California. ¶one's ***private*** *residence* 私宅. ¶a ***protracted*** *residence* 永年の居住. ¶a ***provisional*** *residence* 仮住所. ¶a ***suburban*** *residence* with all its conveniences, elegancies, and snuggeries 便利で優雅で住心地のよい郊外住宅.

Q^2 For more than eight hundred years Windsor Castle has been the ***country*** *residence* of the British monarchs. 八百年以上ウィンザー城は英国君主の市外邸宅であった. ¶a ***family*** *residence* 家族向住宅. ¶Buckingham Palace is the King's London *residence.* バッキンガム宮はロンドンにおける国王の邸宅だ. ¶a delightful ***seaside*** *residence* 快適な海岸住宅. ¶a ***summer*** *residence* (=house) 避暑別荘. ¶one's ***town*** *residence* [別荘に対し]都市の居住. ¶***villa*** *residence* 別荘暮し. ¶a ***week-end*** *residence* 週末保養住宅.

P ***after*** a long *residence* 永年居住の後. ¶I met him ***at*** the *residence* of Mr. ... 私は...氏の邸宅であの人に会った. ¶***during*** my *residence* in ... 私が...に居住した間. ¶boys and girls ***in residence*** in the orphanage その孤児院に収容されている少年少女. 【類】There are fifty-four students at present ***at residence.*** / He was for some time ***in residence at*** the University of Oxford.

resident, *n.* 居住者, 居留者.

Q an ***American*** *resident* 居留米人. ¶***foreign*** *residents* 居留外人.

Q^2 a ***hotel*** *resident* ホテル宿泊者. ¶a ***journalist*** *resident* in Tokyo 東京居住の新聞記者. ¶a former ***Kobe*** *resident* 以前神戸にいた人. ¶a ***long-time*** *resident* of Japan 日本永住の人. ¶Japanese ***alien*** and ***Nisei*** *residents* of the West Coast. アメリカ西岸地方の日本人及び二世居住者. ¶***summer*** *residents* at Karuizwa 軽井沢における夏季居住者.

P^2 a *resident of* Paris パリの居住者.

resident, *a.* 居住する, 駐在する.

M on behalf of the parties *resident* ***abroad*** 海外在留民に代って.

P the number of foreigners *resident* ***in*** Japan 日本に在住する外人の数 ‖ Certain force *resident* ***in*** us seems to impel the mind in this direction. われわれの内に宿る一種の力が心をこの方向に駆るようである.

residue, *n.* 残り, 残余, 残物.

V ***bequeath*** the *residue* of his estate to ... 彼の財産の残余を…に残す.

resign, *v.* 辞する, 退く; あきらめる.

M He was ***cheerfully*** *resigned* 彼は朗かな気持であきらめた. ¶ She *resigned* herself ***entirely*** to his will. 彼女は彼に身を委せた. ¶ ***suddenly*** *resign* 突然辞する.

P *resign* ***as*** ... …の職を辞する. ¶ *resign* ***from*** public life 公職から退く. 【類】*resign* ***from*** the service (職) of ... / *resign* ***from*** a place (位置) / The professor *resigned* (引退する) ***from*** his university. ¶ *resign* office ***in favor of*** the younger 後輩のために道を開く. ¶ He has *resigned* ***on*** the ground of ill-health. 彼は健康がすぐれないという理由で退職した. ¶ *resign* oneself ***to*** fate (Heaven's will, the inevitable) 運命(など)とあきらめる ‖ *resign* them ***to*** their fate 彼らを運命に任せる. 【類】be *resigned* ***to*** the situation ‖ The poor boy *resigned* himself ***to*** passing the night under the stars. かわいそうにその少年はその晩は野宿と決めた. ‖ *resign* ***to*** it ***as*** predestination 前世の約束とあきらめる.

resignation, *n.* 辞職, 退職, 辞表; あきらめ.

V ***accept*** one's *resignation* その辞表を受理する. ¶ They ***handed*** their *resignations* to ... for transmission to the Emperor. 彼らは…へ辞表を提出して陛下に執奏をこうた. ¶ ***hand in*** one's *resignation* 辞表を出す. ¶ ***reject*** one's *resignation* 辞表を突き返す. ¶ ***rescind*** one's *resignation* その辞職を取消す. ¶ ***send in*** one's *resignation* 辞表を出す. ¶ ***show*** great *resignation* きっぱりあきらめる. ¶ He has ***tendered*** his *resignation* effective at the close of the academical year. 彼は同学年度の終了をもって職を辞するむねを申出た. 【類】they ***tendered*** their *resignations* to ... ¶ ***withdraw*** one's *resignation* 辞表を撤回する.

Q a ***collective*** *resignation* 総辞職. ¶ commit ourselves to ***fatalistic*** *resignation* 運命とあきらめる. ¶ the ***general*** *resignation* of the Socialist Cabinet 社会党内閣の総辞職. ¶ ***sullen*** *resignation* 渋々のあきらめ. ¶ a ***wholesale*** *resignation* = a resignation in a body (= en bloc) 総辞職.

P ***with*** *resignation* あきらめて.

P^2 his *resignation* ***from*** the army 軍隊からの彼の退職. ¶ The resignation ***of*** failure 失敗のあきらめ. ¶ a proud *resignation* ***to*** the decrees of Fate and Fortune, of Destiny and Predestination 宿命や運命, 天命や定命に対するあきらめ. ¶ *resignation* ***under*** instruction 諭旨退職.

resilience, *n.* 弾性.

V Rubber tires ***provide*** luxurious *resilience.* ゴムのタイヤには誠に乗心地のよい弾力性がある.

resin, *n.* 樹脂.

Q ***synthetic*** *resin* 合成樹脂.

resist, *v.* 抵抗する, 阻止する, 反抗する.

M *resist* ***feebly*** 弱々しく抵抗する. ¶ ***never*** can *resist* her charm 彼女の魅力にふらふらとする. ¶ ***strenuously*** *resist* がん強に抵抗する. ¶ *resist* ***vigorously*** 激しく抵抗する.

P *resist* the enemy (violence) ***to*** the utmost あくまで敵(など)に抵抗する.

O be unable to *resist* laughing 笑いが止まらひない.

resistance, *n.* 抵抗, 対抗, 反抗; 抵抗力.

V ***break down*** the resistance of the enemy 敵の抵抗を打破する. ¶ ***conquer*** *resistance* 反抗に打ち勝つ. ¶ The pavement ***gives*** little *resistance* to the tires. 舗道がタイヤにほとんど抵抗を与えない. ¶ Alcohol ***lessens*** *resistance* to diseases. アルコールは病気に対する抵抗力を減殺する. ¶ ***lower*** the vital *resistance* of the body 身体の抵抗力を低下させる. ¶ Surrounded as I was on all sides, I could ***make*** no *resistance.* あんなに四方から取囲まれて私は抵抗ができなかった. ‖ without ***making*** any *resistance* ひとたまりもなく. ¶ She ***offered*** no *resistance.* 彼女は(相手の)自由にまかせた. ‖ ***offer*** *resistance* to the law 法律に反抗する. ¶ ***stiffen*** *resistance* 反抗を強める. ¶ ***weaken*** the *resistance* of the Socialists 社会党の抵抗を軟化する.

Q ***armed*** *resistance* 武力抵抗. ¶ his ***bitter*** *resistance* against the tide of militarism 軍国主義の風潮に対する彼の手きびしい反抗. ¶ their ***bold*** and ***uncompromising*** *resistance* to the powers that be 現在の権力者に対する彼らの大胆にしてがん固な抵抗. ¶ offer ***considerable*** *resistance* 相当抵抗を試みる. ¶ make a ***determined*** *resistance* がん強な抵抗をやる. ¶ ***feeble*** *resistance* やせ我慢の抵抗. ¶ ***firm*** *resistance* 強硬な抵抗. ¶ People generally choose the line of ***least*** *resistance.* 世人は通常最も抵抗の少い所を選ぶ(事を行う場合など). ¶ ***lingering*** *resistance* ねちねちした抵抗. ¶ ***low*** *resistance* to infection 伝染に対する弱い抵抗. ¶ ***passive*** *resistance* 消極的抵抗. ¶ feel ***pleasing*** *resistance* to the touch さわって見て気持のよい弾力性がある. ¶ without offering the ***slightest*** *resistance* to ... …に少しも手向いをしないで. ¶ a ***stout*** (= ***stubborn***) *resistance* がん固な抵抗. ¶ There are signs of ***strong*** *resistance.* 手ごわい抵抗の徴候がある. ¶ offer a ***stubborn*** *resistence* がん強に抵抗する. ¶ ***tenacious*** *resistance* がん強な抵抗. ¶ ***tough*** *resistance* 強硬な抵抗. ¶ a ***vigorous*** *resistance* 力強い抵抗. ¶ ***violent*** *resistance* 猛烈な抵抗.

P He made no effort ***at*** *resistance.* 彼は抵抗しようとしなかった. ¶ conquer ***beyond*** *resistance* 抵抗できないほどに征服する. ¶ He met ***with*** but little *resistance.* 彼はほとんど抵抗を受けなかった. ¶ yield ***without*** *resistance* 手もなく言うことをきく. 【類】***without*** the least *resistance.*

P^2 *resistance* ***to*** corrosion 腐食に対する抵抗. 【類】*resistance* ***to*** disease / *resistance* ***to*** laws.

resistant, *a.* 抵抗する, 反対する.

M a fence wire ***more*** ***resistant*** to atmospheric corrosion 酸化に耐え得るさく用鉄条.

P Gutta-percha is ***resistant*** ***to*** the action of salt water. ペルチャゴムは塩水に抵抗する力がある.

resister, *n.* 抵抗するもの.

Q^2 a ***poison*** *resister* 抗毒剤.

resolution, *n.* 決心, 決議, 決議案; 分解; 解決.

V the meeting rose as one man and unanimously ***adopted*** a *resolution* to the effect that ... その会は満場一致で…という意味の決議案を可決した. 【類】A *resolution* advocating ... was ***adopted.*** ¶ ***break*** one's New Year's *resolutions* 元旦(たん)の決心を破る. ¶ ***carry*** a *resolution* unanimously 満場一致決議案を可決する. 【類】The *resolution* was ***carried*** amid applause (wild cheering from thousands of people present). ¶ ***draft*** a *resolution* on ... …の草案を作る. ¶ ***form*** the *resolution* to ... …しようと決心する. ¶ ***introduce*** the *resolution* calling for ... …を要求する決議案を提出する. ¶ She resolved not to do it again, and she ***kept*** her *resolution.* 彼女は再びそれをすまいと決心しそうしてその決心を守った. ¶ ***kill*** a *resolution* 決議案を否決する. ¶ ***maintain*** a *resolution* 決心を持続する. ¶ He ***made*** a *resolution* to give up the drink. ¶ a *resolution* was ***moved*** on behalf of ... urging the Government to ... 政府を激励して…せしめる決議案が…のために動議された. ¶ ***offer*** a *resolution* 決議案を提出する. ¶ ***pass*** a *resolution* of thanks 感謝の決議案を可決する. 【類】***pass*** a *resolution* declaring (宣言する) that ... / ***pass*** a *resolution* in favor of (against) ... ¶ ***present*** a *resolution* to the House of Commons 下院に決議案を提出する. ¶ ***propose*** a *resolution* 決議案を提議する. ¶ before the *resolution* was ***put*** 決を取る前に. ¶ ***reconsider*** one's *resolution* その決心を再考する. ¶ ***revoke*** the *resolution* to ... …の決議を撤回する. ¶ ***second*** a *resolution* 決議に賛成する. ¶ ***shake*** one's *resolution* その決心をゆるがす. ¶ ***show*** great *resolution* 大決心を示す. ¶ ***stiffen*** one's *resolution* その決心を固めさせる. ¶ ***take*** a firm *resolution* 堅く決心する. ¶ ***throw out*** a *resolution* 決心を捨てる. ¶ ***vote down*** a *resolution* 決議案を否決する.

V^2 His *resolution* began to ***stagger.*** 彼の決心はゆるみかけた.

Q ***determined*** *resolution* 断固たる決心. ¶ a ***dogged*** *resolution* がん強な決心. ¶ a ***firm*** *resolution* 固い決心. ¶ a ***good*** *resolution* 正しい決心. ¶ form the ***heroic*** *resolution* to ... …する悲壮な決心をする. ¶ ***Indomitable*** *resolution* and dogged pertinacity marked his career at Oxford. 彼はオクスフォードに在学中不屈の決心と不抜の志と強情がその特徴であった. ¶ an ***inflexible*** *resolution* 不屈の決心. ¶ a man of ***no*** *resolution* of character ちっともしっかりした所のない男. ¶ a ***sluggish*** *resolution* 鈍い決心. ¶ a look of ***stoic*** *resolution* came over the pale face of ... き然たる決意が…の青白い顔に現われた. ¶ The conference passed a ***strong*** *resolution* condemning (in favour of) the measure. 会議はその方策を難詰する(方策に賛成の)強硬な決議案を通過した. ¶***unflinching*** *resolution* ひるまない決心. ¶***unshakable*** *resolution* ゆるがぬ決心. ¶make ***vain*** *resolutions* never to repeat the act 再び決してそんなことはしまいという実行不可能な決心をいく度かする.

Q² a ***draft*** *resolution* 決議の草案. ¶a ***non-confidence*** *resolution* 不信任決議. ¶a ***seventy-seven-word*** *resolution* 七十七語の決議案.

P a man ***of*** great *resolution* 果断家. ¶go back ***on*** one's *resolution* その決心にむそく. ¶talk one ***out of*** one's *resolution* よく話してその決心を翻えさせる. ¶adhere ***to*** one's *resolution* あくまで決心を貫く ‖ come ***to*** (=reach) a *resolution* 決心する.

P² *resolutions* ***against*** war 戦争に反対の決議. ¶the *resolutions* ***for*** the annexation of … …併合の決議. ¶A *resolution* ***of*** … in the Government was passed unanimously. 政府の…の決議案は満場一致で通過した. ¶a *resolution* ***on*** a matter あることに関する決議. ¶a *resolution* ***to*** the effect that … …という意味の決議.

resolve, *n.* 決心, 決意, 覚悟.

V ***abandon*** one's first *resolve* 初志を捨てる. ¶***form*** a *resolve* 決心する. ¶*Resolve* must be ***had*** to an operation. 手術をする必要がある. ¶***keep*** one's *resolve* 決心を持続する. ¶***make*** new *resolves* 新たに決心をする. ¶This *resolve* he immediately ***put*** into execution. この決心を彼は直ちに実行した. ¶***register*** one's *resolve* to … …しようとして心に誓う. ¶***renew*** *resolves* for the future 将来に対して決心を新たにする. ¶This did not ***shake*** his calm *resolve*. 彼の熟考の上の決心はこのために動かされなかった. ¶***strengthen*** one's *resolve* 決意を固める. ¶His *resolve* was ***taken***. 彼は決意した. ¶***upset*** his *rosolve* 彼の決心をくつがえす.

V² a *resolve* slowly ***grew up*** within me that … 私は…という一つの決心が徐々にできてきた.

Q a ***brave*** *resolve* 勇敢な決心. ¶a ***firm*** *resolve* to do or die やり終えるか死ぬかの断固たる決心. ¶***heroic*** *resolve* 悲壮な決意. ¶a ***high*** *resolve* 気高い決心. ¶an ***indomitable*** *resolve* 不退転の決意. ¶a ***mad*** *resolve* 気違いじみた決意.

P ***by*** noble *resolve* りっぱな決心によって. ¶firm ***in*** *resolve* never again to … 断然二度と…しないという決心を固めて. ¶***with*** a full *resolve* to … …しようとの十分の決意をもって.

resolve, *v.* 解く; 溶解する; 帰着する; 決心する; [はれものが]散る.

M be firmly *resolved* to … 固く…する決心をする. ¶the question *resolve* itself largely into … その問題は主として…に帰着する. ¶it ***really*** *resolves* itself into this, that … 結局…ということになる. ¶The tumor will ***soon*** be resolved. はれものはすぐ散る.

M² the question *resolves* itself ***down*** to a matter of … その問題は…ということに帰着する.

P *resolve* it ***into*** its component elements それをその構成要素に分解する. 【類】Water may be *resolved* ***into*** oxygen and hydrogen. ‖ The assembly *resolved* itself ***into*** a committee 議会は委員会(付託)となった. ¶The Government *resolved* ***on*** a bold policy. 政府は大胆な政策を行うことに決心した. ‖ a prostitute *resolving* ***on*** (=***upon***) amendment 更生を決心する売春婦. 【類】*resolve* ***upon*** amendment (vengeance) / He *resolved* ***upon*** his future course in life. / I have *resolved* ***upon*** going out.

O I cannot *resolve* to … 私には…する決心ができない.

resort, *n.* (1) 人出場所, 遊び場, 保養地, 「になっている.

V It ***forms*** a popular picnic *resort*. それは一般の行楽地

Q a ***bracing ozone-impregnated*** seaside *resort* そう快なオゾーンに富んだ海岸の行楽地. ¶a ***delightful*** *resort* 愉快な遊び場. ¶frequent a place of ***evil*** (=***immoral***) *resort* 悪所通いをする. ¶a ***favorable*** *resort* for foreign residents in Japan 日本在留外人に受ける行楽地. ¶The Row in Hyde Park is a ***fashionable*** *resort* for riding and driving. ハイドパークのロー馬場は上流社会が乗馬や自動車乗りに行く場所である. ¶a ***gastronomical*** *resort* 美食家の集まる場所. ¶no more ***ideal*** *resort* for duck shooting かも射ちにはもって来いの場所. ¶a ***popular*** *resort* 盛り場. ¶a ***quiet*** *resort* 静かな行楽地. ¶a ***sacred*** *resort* 霊場. ¶a ***scenic*** *resort* 景勝の地.

Q² an ***all-year*** *resort* 年中人の行く保養地. ¶a ***bathing*** *resort* of the good old kind 昔風の温泉場. ¶one of the ***beach*** *resorts* on the Pacific coast 太平洋岸の海水浴場の一つ. ¶a fashionable ***coast*** *resort* 多くの人の行く海水浴場. ¶a great ***fishing*** *resort* 魚つりに屈強な場所. ¶a most delightful ***health*** *resort* 非常に快適な保養地 ‖ two months' "sweet-do-nothing," passed in one of the many pleasant ***health*** *resorts* 数多い愉快な保養地の一つで過した二カ月の楽しい生活. ¶a ***holiday*** *resort* 休日遊山場. ¶a ***honeymoon*** *resort* 新婚旅行者がよく行く地. ¶an ideal ***holiday*** *resort* 理想的な保養地. ¶***mineral bath*** *resorts* 鉱泉地. ¶a ***hot-spring*** *resort* 温泉場. ¶Kusatsu is a ***mountain*** *resort* with celebrated hot springs. 草津は有名な温泉のある山の保養地である. 【類】***mountain, lake*** and ***shore*** *resorts*. ¶an ***outing*** resort 遠足地. ¶***picnic*** *resorts* 行楽地. ¶Nagano is one of the most popular ***pilgrim*** *resorts*. 長野は最も人気のある巡礼地の一つである. ¶a ***pleasure*** *resort* 遊山場. 【類】an advertisement at a Japanese railway station describing the attractions of a neighboring ***pleasure*** *resort*. ¶a ***seaside health*** *resort* 海岸の保養地. 【類】a residential ***seaside*** *resort*. ¶a great ***shopping*** *resort* 一大商店街. ¶fashionable ***summer*** *resorts* 上流人士の避暑地. 【類】a new international ***summer*** *resort*. ¶towns and places of ***tourist*** *resort* 旅行者の集まる町や場所. 【類】Hawaii is an all-the-year-round ***tourist*** *resort* / Mt. Buffalo National Park is the premier ***tourist*** *resort* of Victoria. ¶a ***vacation*** *resort* 休暇旅行に好適の地. ¶a ***week-end*** *resorst* 週末旅行者の集まる地.

P ***at*** an amusement *resort* 娯楽地で.

P² a notorious *resort* ***for*** pleasure and dissipation 有名な花柳街. ¶it is a great *resort* ***in*** summer for picnic parties from … それは夏季…から遊山団体が繰り込む有名な場所である. ¶a favorite *resort* ***of*** holidaymakers 休日の休養に人気のある行楽地 ‖ a *resort* ***of*** beggars こじきの集まり場所. ¶a very popular *resort* ***with*** (=***among***) … …間に非常に人気のある行楽地.

(2) 手段.

V ***have*** [a] *resort* to various devices for raising money 募金のため種々手段を講じる.

Q as a means of ***last*** *resort* 最後の手段として ‖ was his ***last*** *resort* 彼の最後の手段であった ‖ the court of ***last*** *resort* 終審裁判所. ¶The carriage and pair was the ***only*** *resort* then available to the tourist. 当時は二頭立ての馬車が唯一の乗りものだった.

P ***as*** a last (=final) *resort* せっぱ詰って. ¶The delight is, ***in*** the last *resort*, quite untranslatable into so many words. その愉快は結局言語に尽し難い. ¶***without*** *resort* to compulsion (force) 強制手段(腕力)によらずに. ¶a *resort* ***to*** arms 武力に訴えること.

resort, *v.* 頼る; 往く, 寄り集まる.

M Artificial respiration was ***immediately*** *resorted* to. 直ちに人工呼吸を施した.

P *resort* ***to*** violence (force, arms, harsh words, a strike, the sword, an extreme measure) 暴力(など)に訴える. 【類】*resort* ***to*** various (all sorts of) expedients / *resort* ***to*** bribery (わいろ) / *resort* ***to*** the old practice / *resort* ***to*** the law=procedure of the law=legal proceedings / *resort* ***to*** war / The Government had to *resort* ***to*** a policy of coercion. / *resort* ***to*** outrage against … ‖ *resort* ***to*** writing to make one's desires known 自分の希望を書面で述べる ‖ habitual *resorting* ***to*** bars 酒場に行く習慣. 【類】Many people *resort* ***to*** the beaches in hot weather.

resound, *v.* 反響する.

M The echo *resounded* ***back*** to us. こだまが返って来た.

P The hall *resounded* ***with*** a storm of applause. 会場は拍手のあらしで響き渡った.

resource, *n.* (1) [通例 *pl.*] 資源, 資力.

V ***develop*** (=***tap***) the *resources* of a country 国の資源を開発する. ¶She ***drained*** her *resources* by war. その国は戦争のためにその財源を枯渇させた. ¶***exhaust*** the *resources* of diplomacy 外交のあらゆる手段を尽す. ¶Italy has succeeded in ***expanding*** the hydro-electric *resources* of her Alpine frontiers. イタリアはアルプス国境における水力資源の開発に成功した. ¶***exploit*** all its *resources* その資源をことごとく開発する. ¶The country ***has*** ample *resources* at command. その国は豊富な資源が自由に入手で

きる. ¶English, like German, possesses the ability of ***increasing*** its *resources* by forming compounds. 英語はドイツ語のように複合語を作ることによってその語数を増すことができる. ¶***sap*** *resources* 資源を枯渇させる.

Q a ***cultural*** *resource* 文化財. ¶the ***dormant*** *resources* of China 中国の未開発の資源. ¶***economic*** *resources* 経済上の資源. ¶***financial*** *resources* 財力. ¶develop its ***illimitable*** *resources* その限りない資源を開発する. ¶***human*** *resources* 人的資源. ¶the ***intellectual*** and ***literary*** *resources* of the country その国の知的及び文学的資源. ¶its ***material*** *resources* その物資. ¶with quite ***modest*** *resources* 財政の豊かでない. ¶***natural*** *resources* 天然資源. ¶explore and develop all the ***potential*** *resources* of a country 国のあらゆる潜在資源を探究し開発する. ¶Labor is Japan's most ***plentiful*** *resource.* 労力は日本が有する最も豊富な資源だ. ¶***scenic*** *resources* 風景の美.

Q² New York's ***bank*** *resources* of over $15,000,000. ニューヨークの一千五百万ドル以上の銀行資力. ¶protect the ***forest*** *resources* of the country against exhaustion 国の森林資源を荒廃から守る. ¶***manpower*** *resources* 人的資源. 【類】The ***manpower*** *resources* were weakened. ¶the exploitation of ***water-power*** *resources* 水力資源の開発.

P rich ***in*** *resources* 資源に富む.

(**2**) 手段, 方法; 機知; 頼み.

V ***employ*** all the *resources* at their disposal 彼らの力に及ぶ限りの手段を講じる. ¶***find*** a *resource* of pleasure in ... ...を慰楽の手段と考える. ¶They ***had*** no other *resource* but to weep. 彼らは泣くより他手がなかった.

Q appeal to arms as the ***last*** *resource* 最後の手段として武力に訴える. ¶Fight was his ***only*** *resource.* けんかが彼のただ一つの手段であった. ¶Smiling was her ***usual*** *resource.* 彼女はいつも微笑でごまかした. ¶She finds an ***unfailing*** *resource* in music. いつも音楽が彼女のなぐさみとなる.

P finally ***as*** my despairing *resource* 終に私は仕方なく. ¶a man ***of*** great *resources* 賢者 ‖ at the end ***of*** one's *resources* 百計尽きて ‖ be full ***of*** *resources* at a crisis 危機に際して臨機応変である. ¶His death left her ***on*** her own *resources.* 彼が死んで彼女は自分でやって行かねばならなかった.

resourcefulness, *n.* 策略に富むこと.

V severely ***tax*** the *resourcefulness* of ... 大いに...の知恵を絞らせる.

respect, *n.* (**1**) 尊敬, 敬意, 尊重.

V ***challenge*** *respect* 尊敬を要求する. ¶The one way to command successfully is to ***command*** *respect.* りっぱに支配するただ一つの方法は尊敬されることである. ¶***conquer*** *respect* 尊敬をかち得る. ¶***deepen*** one's *respect* for ... ...に対する敬意を深める. ¶He rightly ***deserves*** *respect* for his scholarship. 彼はその学識に対して十分尊敬される価値がある. ¶He ***desires*** his *respects* to you. 彼から君によろしくとのことです. ¶***earn*** the *respect* of the world 世人の尊敬を得る. ¶***entertain*** a profound *respect* for ... ...に対して敬意をいだく. ¶***feel*** great *respect* for his knowledge of ... 彼の...の知識を大いに尊敬する. ¶***forfeit*** *respect* 尊敬されなくなる. ¶***Give*** him my *respects.* 彼によろしく言って下さい. ¶He ***has*** great *respect* for age. 彼は老人を大いに尊敬する. ¶***inculcate*** *respect* for elders 年長者を尊敬することを教え込む. ¶***inspire*** *respect* in all men すべての人に尊敬心を起させる. ¶tend to ***lessen*** the *respect* for ......に対する敬意を減殺させることになる. ¶***lose*** all *respect* for ... ...に対する敬意を全く失う. ¶***pay*** one's *respects* at the shrine 神社を参拝する ‖ ***pay*** *respect* to one's wishes 人の希望をしんしゃくする. 【類】***pay*** our *respects* (敬意) at the American Embassy / ***pay*** one's *respects* before a shrine (the Imperial Palace) ‖ ***pay*** one's *respect* to a person 人に敬意を払う. 【類】***pay*** one's *respects* to the dead (死者) / ***pay*** *respect* to one's national language / On the 1st, 15th, and 28th days of each month all Daimyos went to Court to ***pay*** their *respects* to the Shogun. ¶***present*** one's *respects* in person 自身敬意を表する. ¶***receive*** more *respects* 一層の敬意を受ける. ¶***secure*** one the *respect* of ... ...に...の敬意を得さす. ¶***send*** one's *respects* to ... ...にごきげん伺いの手紙を送る. ¶Every nation ***shows*** *respect* to its flag. どの国民もその国旗を尊重する. 【類】***show*** *respect* for public property (公有財産). ¶***subvert*** the *respect* for decency and morality 礼譲と道徳に対する敬意をくつがえす. ¶***win*** the *respect* of all classes of society 社会のあらゆる階級の尊敬を得る.

Q stand in ***bareheaded*** *respect* 起立脱帽して敬意を示す. ¶have a ***boundless*** *respect* for ... ...を無限に尊敬する. ¶express ***deep*** *respect* 深甚な敬意を表する. 【類】with ***deep*** *respect* / show their ***deepest*** *respect* and sincere affection. ¶entertain a ***deep-seated*** *respect* for authority 権威に対して深い敬意をいだく. ¶treat the gods with ***due*** *respect* 神々を相当の敬意をもって扱う. ¶have ***every*** *respect* for ... ...をどこまでも尊敬する. ¶have the ***highest*** *respect* for ... ...に対して最高の敬意を持つ. ¶He added to my already ***large*** *respect* for him. 彼に対する私の深い尊敬が一段と増した. ¶pay their ***last*** *respects* [死者に]最後の敬意を払う. ¶a sound, wholesome relationship based upon ***mutual*** *respect* 相互の尊敬に基づく健全な間柄. ¶They seem to have ***no*** *respect* for the old. 彼らは老人を尊敬していないらしい. ¶with ***profound*** *respect* and humility 深甚なる敬意と謙そんとをもって. ¶regard ... with ***reverent*** *respect* 敬けんの念をもて...を見る. ¶pay ***scant*** (=***little***) *respect* to ... ...にあまり敬意を払わない. ¶have a ***scrupulous*** *respect* for all treaty obligations 厳に一切の条約の義務を尊重する. ¶treat ... with the ***utmost*** *respect* and reverence 最上の敬意と敬けんとをもって...を扱う.

Q² win back ***world*** *respect* 世界の尊敬を取戻す.

P bend the knee ***in*** *respect* 敬意を表してひざを屈する. ¶Many Jewish houses in London close on Saturday ***out of*** *respect* for the Hebrew Sabbath. ロンドンのユダヤ人の商店はユダヤ教の聖日に対する敬意の念から土曜日に休業するものが多い. ¶receive ... ***with*** *respect* 敬意をもって...を迎える ‖ ***with*** *respect* due to one's worth 礼を厚くして ‖ treat one ***with*** great *respect* 大いに敬意を払って...を遇する.

P² a *respect* ***for*** international law 国際法に対する敬意. ¶*respect* ***to*** ancestors 祖先崇拝. ¶They are not wanting in their *respect* ***for*** mammon. 彼らは金銭崇拝の念に欠けてはいない.

(**2**) 関係; 点.

Q in an ***essential*** *respect* 必須の点において. ¶in ***every*** *respect* すべての点で. ¶in ***many*** *respects* 多くの点で. ¶in ***that*** and in ***other*** *respects* それとその他の点において. ¶in ***what*** *respect* どういう点で.

P ***as*** *respects* (=regards) ...=in (=with) respect to, respecting ... ...に関して. ¶***in*** *respect* that ... ...という点を考えれば ‖ ***in*** all *respects* あらゆる点において, 万事万端 ‖ ***in*** some *respects* ある点では ‖ People are often very thoughtless ***in*** this *respect.* 世人はこの点においてしばしばはなはだ無とん着である. 【類】He is senior to me ***in*** *respect* of service. / ***in*** *respect* of style his writings recall ... ¶***with*** *respect* to the matter (question) その件(など)について. ¶***without*** *respect* to (=of) ... ...を無視して. 【類】The Japanese name for all foreigners, ***without*** *respect* to nationality, was "tojin."

P² *respect* ***for*** elders (women) 長者(など)に対する尊敬 ‖ *respect* ***for*** truth (authority, law and order) 真実(など)の尊重.

respect, *v.* 尊重する, 尊敬する.

M *respect* him ***a great deal*** as ... ...として彼を大いに尊敬する.

P² I *respect* him ***as*** my superior (=senior). 私は彼を先輩として敬意を表する. ¶All *respect* him ***for*** his integrity. 彼が正直なので皆のものが彼を尊敬する.

respectable, *a.* 敬うべき; 《口語》かなりの, まともな, 見苦しくない.

M Externally, the house looked *respectable* ***enough.*** その家の外観は結構りっぱなものだった. ¶be considered ***highly*** *respectable* 大いに尊敬に値すると考えられている ‖ The firm is ***highly*** *respectable.* その商会は大いに信用がある. ¶***perfectly*** *respectable* and well-conducted 全く尊むべくりっぱな行いの.

O His record is *respectable*, though not brilliant. 彼の成績はすばらしいというほどじゃないがまずまずだ. 【類】They are all poor, but *respectable* people (正直な, まともな人々). / *respectable* clothes (behavior).

respectful, *a.* 丁寧な, 尊重する.

P *respectful* ***of*** tradition 伝統を重んじて. ¶*respectful* ***to*** one's superiors 長上に対していんぎんな. ¶You should be *respectful* ***towards*** your parents. 君は両親を尊重すべきだ.

respiration, *n.* 呼吸, 呼吸作用.

V almost ***intercept*** one's *respiration* ほとんど呼吸を止める. ¶***practice*** (***try***) artificial *respiration* 人工呼吸法を施す(など).

Q ***abdominal*** *respiration* 腹式呼吸. ¶***artificial*** ***respiration*** 人工呼吸. ¶***deep*** and ***slow*** *respiration* 緩慢な深呼吸. ¶The *respiration* is ***normal.*** 呼吸は普通だ. ¶***shallow*** and ***rapid*** *respiration* 浅く迅速な呼吸.

respire, *v.* 一息つく.

M *respire* ***briefly*** (=***just awhile***) ちょっと一息する.

P *respire* ***after*** hard work 骨折りのあとで一服する.

respite, *n.* 延期; 猶予; 休憩, 休養.

V The G.P.O. (=General Post Office) ***has*** no *respite* while London sleeps. ロンドン人が眠っている時でも中央郵便局は休まない. ¶***take*** a brief *respite* from ... ...を暫時休む.

Q^2 a ***32-hour*** *respite* 三十二時間猶予.

P^2 *respite* ***for*** the murderer 殺害者に対する執行猶予 ‖ *respite* ***for*** the condemned 被宣告者に対する執行猶予. ¶*respite* ***from*** work (suffering, march) 仕事(など)の中休み.

respond, *v.* 答える, 返事する, 応じる.

M ***briefly*** *respond* 簡単に答える. ¶*respond* ***excellently*** to an increasing demand 増大する要求にりっぱに応じる. ¶very ***gladly*** *respond* to his invitation to ... ...の招請に大喜びで応じる. ¶*respond* very ***heartily*** はなはだ熱心に唱和する. ¶The public has *responded* ***magnificently*** to our efforts. 公衆はわれわれの努力に対してりっぱに報いた. ¶***occasionally*** *respond* to the call of the mountains 折々山の招きに応じる(登山をする). ¶She *responded* ***passionately*** to his kisses. 彼女は彼のキスに対して熱情的に応じた. ¶*respond* ***promptly*** to the requirements of ... すみやかに...の要求に応じる. ¶*respond* ***quickly*** and ***splendidly*** to the appeal for subscriptions 寄付の求めにすみやかにかつ気前よく応じる. ¶*respond* ***willingly*** 喜んで答える. ¶***wittily*** *respond* 気のきいた答をする.

P *respond* ***to*** consultation 相談に乗る ‖ *respond* ***to*** every bow of recognition すべての会釈に答礼する ‖ *respond* ***to*** the call of duty 義務の命じる所に従う ‖ *respond* ***to*** a call for a speech 演説の求めに応じる ‖ *respond* ***to*** the call of nature 大(小)便をたす. 【類】*respond* ***to*** a request (要請に応じる) / an enduring memorial (永久の記念物) to those brave men who *responded* ***to*** the call of patriotism / He was not slow to *respond* ***to*** the humor of the situation. ‖ Performance continued to *respond* ***to*** public encouragement 好評につき続映. ‖ The celebration was *responded* ***to*** by a large attendance. その祝賀会には多数の人が出席した. ‖ He was too far gone to *respond* ***to*** the efforts to resuscitate him. 彼を生き返らせようと努力したがもう手遅れになっていた[水死人など]. ¶*respond* ***with*** a smile and a wave にっこりして手を振りあいさつに答える.

response, *n.* 応答, 唱和, 感応.

V ***awaken*** a *response* in ... ...を動かして感応させる. ¶The pathetic appeal ***called forth*** no *response* in his breast. その哀訴も彼の胸にこたえなかった. ¶It has ***found*** a *response* in the heart of every man. それはすべての人の心に反響があった. ¶He was unable to ***get*** any *response* to his tapping. 彼は戸をたたいたが何の応答もなかった. ¶***have*** no *response* 反響がない. ¶***make*** a sharp *response* 激しい口答をする. ¶***receive*** a most emphatic *response* 非常に力強い返事を受ける. ¶***return*** an encouraging *response* 色よい返事をする.

Q make an ***agreeable*** *response* あいづちを打つ. ¶with an air of ***amiable*** *response* 愛きょうのある返事振りで. ¶make an ***effective*** *response* to a situation 情勢に即応する. ¶The *response* was not ***encouraging.*** その反応はあまり思わしくなかった(募集など). ¶A ***generous*** *response* should be made to the appeals for funds. 資金募集に対し寛大な寄付をなすべきである. ¶meet with a ***gratifying*** *response* 満足な応答を得る. ¶The movement has met with a ***hearty*** *response.* その運動には熱心な反応があった. ¶the ***inevitable*** *response* to instincts of self-preservation 自己保存の本能に対する必然の感応. ¶an ***inner*** *response* to an outward impulse 外界の刺激に対する内的感応. ¶"Yes", was the ***laconic*** *response.* 「はい」と簡単な返事であった. ¶meet with such a ***lukewarm*** *response* このような気乗りのしない返答を与えられる. ¶a ***nervous, stammering*** *response* 神経的などもった返事. ¶A curt "no" was the ***only*** *response* made. 簡単に「だめ」と答えただけであった. ¶a ***quick*** *response* 即答. ¶find ***ready*** *response* 即答を受ける. ¶a ***splendid*** *response* to an appeal by the public 公衆の哀願に対する寛大な寄付. ¶make a ***stereotyped*** *response* ありふれたあいさつをする. ¶The appeal met with ***sufficient*** *response.* その哀願は十分な反応を見た. ¶a note that roused in me the most ***thrilling*** *response* 私にとってきわめて会心の点. ¶an ***unfavorable*** *response* 都合の悪い返事.

P be ready ***in*** *response* 即座に答える ‖ He murmured something ***in*** *response.* 彼はそれに答えて何やらつぶやいた. ‖ ***in*** *response* to an invitation 招待状に対して. 【類】***in*** *response* to your enquiry / The lectures have been published in book form ***in*** *response* to numerous (=many) requests. / bow ***in*** *response* to the plaudits of the audience / grow up ***in*** *response* to ... / ***in*** *response* to the prayers of ... / ***in*** *response* to a resolution passed by various public bodies (各種公共団体) / ***in*** *response* to a written request / ***in*** *response* to the desire expressed by ...

P^2 the *response* ***of*** the individual to the expectation of society 個人が社会の期待に添うこと. ¶*Responses* ***to*** the appeal have not been numerous. その哀願に応じた者は多くなかった.

O This is my *response.* 左様御承知を願います.

responsibility, *n.* 責任, 負担.

V completely ***abrogate*** *responsibility* 全然責任を解除する. ¶I cannot ***accept*** (=***undertake***) the *responsibility* for ... 私は...の責任を引受けることができない. ¶***administer*** effectively executive *responsibilities* 効果的に管理上の責任を果す. ¶do not ***admit*** any *responsibility* 責任を認めない. ¶***appreciate*** one's *responsibility* [大いに]その責任を認める. ¶***assume*** the *responsibility* of ... ...の責任を負う. 【類】***assume*** no *responsibility* for ... ¶No one can ***avoid*** the *responsibility* of example. 何人も他人の手本となる責任を回避し得ない. ¶***bear*** the *responsibility* of (=a responsibility for) ... ...の責任を持つ. 【類】can ***bear*** no *responsibility* whatever for ... ¶***claim*** (***disclaim***) all *responsibility* for the absolute accuracy of the following list 次表の絶対的正確に対しては一切責任を負う(負わない). ¶***decline*** all *responsibility* about your complaint あなたの苦情について一切責任をとらない. ¶***discharge*** *responsibility* 責任を果す. ¶***dissolve*** the *responsibility* その責任を解消する. ¶***divert*** the *responsibility* for the war from the Kaiser 戦争の責任をドイツ皇帝から他に転嫁する. ¶***divide*** *responsibilities* 責任を分かつ. ¶***dodge*** *responsibility* 責任をのがれる. ¶***escape*** *responsibility* 責任をのがれる. ¶seek to ***evade*** all *responsibility* for ... ...への責任を一切避けようとする. ¶***feel*** a great deal of *responsibility* 大いに責任を感じる. ¶***fix*** the *responsibility* of ... upon ... ...の責任を...に帰する. ¶***incur*** a heavy *responsibility* 重責を負わされる. ¶his duties do not ***involve*** *responsibilities* for ... 彼の職務には...に対する責任は含まれていない. ¶***locate*** the *responsibility* 責任の所在を明かにする. ¶***perform*** one's *responsibility* その責任を果す. ¶***place*** (=***put or thrust***) the *responsibility* for ... on ... ...の責任を...に帰する. ¶***realize*** the *responsibility* of using Australia as well as holding it 豪州を領有すると同時にこれを活用することの責任を感じる. ¶***relinquish*** the *responsibility* 責任を放棄する. ¶***repudiate*** all *responsibility* in the proceeding その行為における責任をことごとく放棄する. ¶***shake off*** any further *responsibility* それ以上の責任を負わない. ¶***share*** the *responsibility* of ... with ... ...と...の責任をわかつ. ¶***shift*** the *responsibility* on to someone else 責任を他に転嫁する. ¶***shirk*** *responsibility* 責任を回避する. ¶bravely ***shoulder*** *responsibility* for one's own acts 勇敢に自分の行為に対して責任を持つ. 【類】***shoulder*** all the *responsibilities* of ... ¶***shuffle*** every *responsibility* on to the shoulders of ... すべての責任を...に転嫁する. ¶***take*** the *responsibility* to (=on) oneself その責任を自分に引受ける. ¶***throw*** (=***cast***) our *responsibility* upon (=on to) the shoulders of ... われわれの責任を...に負わせる. 【類】It is not right to ***throw*** the *responsibility* on him. ¶***throw off*** one's own *responsibility* and put it upon ... 自分の責任を回避して...に負わせる. ¶***undertake*** the *responsibility* of ... ...の責任を引受ける.

V^2 the *responsibility* of ... ***ceases*** as soon as ... ...の責任は...するやいなや消滅する. ¶on him ***devolves*** the *responsibility* of ... ...の責任は彼の肩にかかってる. 【類】My *responsibility* ***ceases*** upon shipment (発送). ¶my *responsibility* ***ends*** with ... 私の責任は...とともに解除される. 【類】

There my *responsibility* *ends*. ¶the *responsibility falls* on ... …にその責任がかかる. ¶over his head *hangs* the great *responsibility* of ... 彼の頭上に…の大責任がかかっている. ¶the *responsibility lies* with (=in the hands of)... その責任は…にある. ¶The *responsibility rests* upon (=with) you. その責任は君にある.

Q its *accompanying responsibilities* それに付随する責任. ¶he had the *chief responsibility* for the success of ... 彼は…の成功に対して最もあずかって力があった. ¶*collective responsibility* [内閣などの]連帯責任. ¶accept *complete responsibility* 全責任を負う. ¶assume *entire* (=*full*) *responsibility* for ... …の全責任を負う. ¶*ethical* (=*moral*) *responsibility* 道徳上の責任. ¶assume *executive responsibilities* 運営上の責任を引受ける. ¶a very *grave responsibility* きわめて重大な責任. ¶assume the *heavy responsibility* of ... …の重責を引受ける. ¶*high responsibility* 重い責任. ¶*immense responsibilities* 大責任. ¶*legal responsibilities* 法律上の責任. ¶as a *major responsibility* 主な責任として. ¶*primary responsibility* 主要な責任. ¶persons of *public responsibility* 公職についている人々. ¶a *serious responsibility* 重大責任. ¶*social responsibility* 社会的責任. ¶This imposes upon us a *special responsibility*. これがわれわれに特別な責任を課する. ¶take upon my shoulders the *whole responsibility* 全責任を私の肩に担う.

Q² He has *family responsibilities*. 一家扶養の責任がある. ¶*trade* (=*labor*) *union responsibility* 労働組合としての責任. ¶deny one's *war responsibility* 戦争責任を否認する ‖ those with special "*war responsibility*" 特別戦争責任者. ¶*war crimes responsibility* 戦争犯罪の責任.

P absolved (=relieved) *from responsibility* 責任を解除されて. ¶with a sense *of responsibility* 責任を感じて. ¶The thing was done *on* (=*upon*) his own *responsibility*. そのことは彼の一存でやったのだ.

P² *responsibility for* blame (the fulfilment of obligations) 過失(など)に対する責任. ¶duties and *resonsibilities of* office 職務内容. ¶the *responsibility for* ... is chiefly *with* ... …に対する責任は主として…にある.

responsible, *a*. 責を負うべき, 責任ある.

M The Cabinet, in the exercise of executive power, shall be *collectively responsible* to the Diet. 〘憲法〙内閣は, 行政権の行使については, 国会に対し連帯して責任を負う. ¶*directly responsible* for ... 直接…に責任のある. 【類】 All the Cabinet members are *responsible directly* to the President. ¶*largely responsible* for ... 大いに…に責任がある. ¶It is hard to say how far he was *personally responsible* for this. この点についてどの程度彼に個人的責任があるかちょっと分からない. ¶He is not *primarily responsible* for it. 彼はそれに対する主な責任者ではない. ¶he is *solely responsible* for ... 彼は…に対して専ら責任がある.

P he is held *responsible* for ... …に対し彼に責任がある ‖ Age (Weather) is *responsible* for it. 年(陽気)のせいだ. ¶The gale was *responsible for* her being 36 hours late. その船が三十六時間遅れたのは暴風のためであった. ‖ He must be made *responsible for* it. 彼がその責任を負うべきである. ‖ Diseased teeth are *responsible for* an almost inconceivable amount of ill health and misery. 歯の病気がもとで計り知れないほどの病気や不幸な目に会う. ‖ He was *responsible for* the introduction of the American college system into Japan. アメリカの大学教育制度を日本に紹介したのは彼だ. 【類】 The weather is *responsible for* the delay. / It was Miss Murata who was *responsible for* the best piece of acting in the play, her Ophelia being something quite charming and sincere. / The central position of Kobe is *responsible for* its rapid growth. / The Chicago News is *responsible for* a story which might prove libellous were names mentioned. / hold oneself *responsible for* ... / The frequent practice of contraception (妊娠中絶) is *responsible for* sterility (不妊症). ¶*responsible in* morals and *in* law 道徳及び法律上責任がある.

responsive, *a*. 応答する, 感応しやすい.

M be *quickly responsive* to external influences 外的影響を受けやすい. ¶I did not find him *very responsive* when I talked about it. 話してみたが彼は気乗り薄だった.

P The Turks were little *responsive to* civilizing influences from without. トルコ人は外部からの文化的影響に対してほとんど感応しなかった. ‖ I found in him nothing very *responsive to* my earnest advice. 熱心に忠告したがぬかにくぎだった. 【類】 *responsive to* the wishes of ... / *responsive to* kindness.

rest, *n*. 休息, 休憩 ; 永眠.

V We *appreciate* a *rest* after hard work. 労働の後の休息は身にしみてありがたい. ¶*enjoy* a well-earned *rest* 十分働いた後の休息を楽しむ. ¶I hope you are *having* (=*getting*) a good and well-deserved *rest*. 君は本当によく働いて得た休息を楽しんでいられることと思います. ¶*give* the enemy no *rest* from anxiety 敵に安心をさせない. ¶Let's *have* a *rest*. 一休みしよう. ¶The police station *knows* no *rest* throughout the year. 警察署は一年中気の安まる時がない. ¶*make* a *rest* from ... …を休む. ¶*need rest* 休息が必要である. ¶*obtain* a short *rest* ちょっと休む. ¶*snatch* an hour's *rest* 忙しい中を一時間休憩する. ¶Let us sit down and *take* a *rest*. すわって休みましょう. 【類】 retire to *take rest* / *Take rest* after toil (=labor). / I visited the spa to *take* a *rest* after the fatigue of my journey.

Q *absolute rest* 絶対安静. ¶He is ordered a *complete rest* for the present. 当分絶対安静を命じられている. ¶take a *good rest* 十分休息する. ¶enjoy a *good night's rest* 一晩ぐっすり休む. ¶*healthful rest* 体によい休息. ¶take a *little rest* ちょっと休憩する. ¶take a *momentary rest* from ... …をちょっと休む. ¶We had *several rests* on our way up the mountain. 登山の途中数回休息した. ¶a *short rest* ちょっとの休息. ¶enjoy a *well-earned rest* [働いた後の]骨休めを楽しむ.

Q² an *elbow rest* 脇息.

P *after* a good *rest* 十分に休息した後. ¶an object *at rest* 静物 ‖ lie *at rest* 横になって休む ‖ Doubts were set *at rest*. 疑いが晴れた. ‖ have one's mind quite *at rest* 安心しきっている. 【類】 set one's mind *at rest*. ¶go away *for* a *rest* あっちへ行って休む. ¶go *to rest* 休む, 床につく ‖ He ritired *to rest*. 彼は寝所に入った. ‖ be laid *to rest* [in peace] [安らかに]葬られてある. ¶*without* any Sunday *rest* 日曜も休みなしに.

P² a *rest about* noon 正午前後の休憩. ¶isolation and *rest in* bed [病気などで]面会を避け床についての静養.

rest, *v*. 休む, 休憩する.

M *rest completely* すっかり気がゆるむ. ¶*rest content* with this state of things この状態をもって満足している. ¶cannot *rest easy* until ... …までは安心ができない. ¶Good deeds *rest easily* on one's conscience. よいことをするといい気持ちになる. ¶the blame *rests entirely* with ... その責は全く…に在る. ¶It *rests heavily* on my spirit. それは私の心の重荷になる. 【類】 the responsibility *rests* as *heavily* upon ... as upon ... ¶the responsibilities *rest largely* in the hands of ... 責任は主として…にある. ¶His fame *mainly rests* on this book. 彼が名声を得たのは主としてその本を著わしたためだ. ¶*Rest* is *necessary* after hard work. 骨を折った後に休息は必要だ. ¶He cannot *rest quietly* in his grave. 彼は死んでも浮ばれない. ¶*rest satisfied* 満足している. ¶*rest well* at night 夜安眠する.

M² be kept in warehouses to "*rest up*" from its voyage その航海中の動揺から落付くように入庫しておく(酒など).

P *rest against* the wall 壁にもたれて休息する. ¶*rest for* a new endeavor さらに努力するために休む. ¶*rest from* one's labors (duty, lesson, studies) 仕事(など)の中休をする ‖ *rest from* the heat 避暑する. ¶May his soul *rest in* peace! 彼の霊に平和あれ(なむあみだぶつ). ‖ We *rest in* (=*on*) your promise. 君の約束をあてにしている. ‖ We *rest* our hopes *in* you. われわれは君に期待を寄せている. 【類】 *rest in* eternal peace / *rest in* the grave ‖ now *resting in* the British Museum それは大英博物館所蔵になっている ‖ ‖ *rest on* a couch 長いすで休息する ‖ *rest on* (=*upon*) one's oars こぐ手を止める ; 〘比ゆ〙休憩する ‖ The legal systems of France and England *rest on* different foundations. 仏・英の法制は成立の根本が違っている. 【類】 Modern civilization *rests on* a foundation of science and education. / the basis *on* which these conclusions *rest* / Spenser's glory *rests on* a surer basis than that of popularity. / The argument *rests on* an illusion. ¶I made up the *rest out of* my own pocket. 残額は自腹を切って始末した. ¶A strange quiet *rests over* the entire city. 異様な静けさが全市を支配している. ¶with his chin *resting*

upon his hand あごを片手で支えて ‖ the philosophy (theory) of ... *rests* ***upon*** ... …の原理は…である ‖ Something like an expression of doubt, of uncertainty, was seen to *rest* ***upon*** his features. 疑惑や不安の表情が彼の顔に見えた. ‖ His eyes *rested* ***upon*** a terrible thing. 恐ろしいものが彼の目に留まった. 【類】He is not the sort of man to *rest* ***upon*** his laurels. ¶The time required for acquiring an art will *rest* almost entirely ***with*** the student himself. ある芸能を覚え込むに要する時間は十中八九これを学ぶ者によってきまるのである. ‖ the priority of the invention *rests* ***with*** ... その発明に先べんをつけたのは…である. ‖ It *rests* ***with*** you to decide. それを決定するのは君だ. 【類】The next move (次の手) *rests* ***with*** you. / The choice *rests* ***with*** you. / the primary responsibility *rests* ***with*** ... (第一の責) / the entire responsibility will *rest* ***with*** ... / the ultimate responsibility *rests* ***with*** him.

O We stopped at a wayside inn to *rest* ourselves. われわれは休憩のため路傍の旅宿に泊った. ¶Let's *rest* the matter there. その件はそれでほって置こう.

rest, *n.* 残り, 残余, 残部.

V ***devote*** the *rest* of the day to ... その日の残りの時間は…に使用する. ¶Nature will ***do*** the *rest*. それから先は自然にできてしまう. ¶I'll ***handle*** the *rest*. あとは(それから先は)おれが引受けた. ¶***Keep*** the *rest* for yourself. おつりはお前にやる. ¶You ***know*** the *rest*. それから先は君の承知の通り(ちょうちょうする必要がない). ¶***leave*** the *rest* to the survival of the fittest その他のことは適者生存の作用に任せる. ¶If you give 10,000 yen, they will ***make up*** the *rest*. 君が一万円出すとあとはみんながやってくれる. ¶***outdo*** the *rest* in ... …において他の者をはるかにしのぐ.

V² The *rest* ***needs*** no telling. それから先のことは語る必要がない. ¶All you have to do is just [to] plug in, and the *rest* will ***take care*** of itseslf. 〖広告〗スイッチを入れさえすれば自然にでき上ります(電気冷蔵庫など).

P ***among*** the *rest* その中に加わって ‖ Mr. ... himself was ***among*** the *rest*. …氏自身その仲間の一人であった. ¶***as*** for the *rest* その他の点については. ¶He lived in the country ***for*** the *rest* of his life. 彼はその余生をいなかで送った.

restaurant, *n.* 料理店, かっぽう店.

V ***run*** (=***operate***) a *restaurant* 料理店を経営する.

Q a ***Bohemian*** *restaurant* 手軽な料理屋. ¶a ***Chinese*** *restaurant* 中華料理店. ¶***fashionable*** *restaurants* 高級料理店. ¶their ***favorite*** *restaurant* 彼ら行きつけの料理店. ¶a ***first-class*** *restaurant* 一流の料理店. ¶a much ***frequented*** *restaurant* 客の多い料理店. ¶a widely ***patronized*** *restaurant* はやる料理屋. ¶In 1932 the average tip in a ***popular*** *restaurant* was ten cents. 一九三二年における人衆料理店で普通のチップは十セントであった. ¶a ***respectable*** *restaurant* 上品な料理店.

Q² a ***bona fide*** *restaurant* [食事専門の]料理屋. ¶a ***cafe*** *restaurant* 喫茶料理店. ¶a swell ***Chicago*** *restaurant* シカゴの高級料理店. ¶a ***foreign-style*** *restaurant* 西洋料理店. ¶a ***self-service*** *restaurant*=a cafeteria 自分給仕の飲食店, キャフェテリア.

P ***at*** a *restaurant* 料理店で.

resting-place, *n.* 休憩所; 墓.

V specimens which have ***found*** *resting-places* on the shelves of museums and in collectors' cabinets 博物館のたなや収集家のたんすにしまってある標本. ¶No grave mound ***marks*** their *resting-place*. 彼らが永眠の地を示すような塚一つない. ‖ without even a stone to ***mark*** his *resting-place* 彼が永眠の地を示す墓石さえなく.

Q He wished some other spot for his ***final*** *resting-place*. 彼は永眠の地として他の場所が欲しかった. ¶the ***last*** *resting-place* of his body 彼の(遺がい)永眠の地. 【類】More than twenty-five thousand people follow him to his ***last*** *resting-places*.

restitution, *n.* 回復.

V ***make*** *restitution* 弁償する, 返還する.

P² a *restitution* ***of*** energy after fatigue 疲労後勢力の回復.

restless, *a.* 落ちつかない.

M She seemed *restless* ***all the time***. 彼女はずっともじもじしていたようだった.

restoration, *n.* 回復, 復旧, 修復.

V ***apply*** *restorations* with success りっぱに復旧する. ¶The *restoration* of his health is practically ***assured***. 彼の健康回復はまず確実である.

Q There are hopes for your ***complete*** *restoration* to health. 貴方は全快する見込がある. ¶the ***Imperial*** ***Restoration*** 王政復古. ¶The castle is a ***mere*** *restoration*. その城は(昔のままのではなく)再建したものである.

P ***at*** the *Restoration* of Meiji 明治維新の際. ¶***with*** the *restoration* of the Emperor to absolute power 王政全く旧に復するとともに.

P² the *restoration* ***of*** the Imperial regime (=Mikado to temporal power) 王政復古 ‖ *restoration* ***of*** rights (peace) 復権(など).

restorative, *n.* 気付薬, 強壮剤.

P Massage is a capital *restorative* ***from*** fatigue after hard exercise. マッサージはうんと働いた後の疲労回復には一番だ.

restore, *v.* 回復する, 復興する.

P He is now completely *restored* ***in*** health. 彼は今は健康がすっかり回復している. ¶*restore* the sovereign power ***into*** the hands of the sovereign 主権を帝王の手に復帰させる. ¶The country has *restored* order ***out of*** chaos. その国は混乱から秩序を取戻した. ¶The city was *restored* ***to*** tranquillity. 同市は平穏に復した. ‖ He was *restored* ***to*** his sight. 彼は目が見えるようになった. ‖ *restore* one ***to*** life (full health, normal conditions) 人を復活(など)させる ‖ be *restored* ***to*** the community of peaceful nations 平和国家群の仲間に復帰する. 【類】be *restored* ***to*** the pre-war condition / be *restored* ***to*** former friendship / be *restored* ***to*** power / The stolen goods were all *restored* ***to*** their owner[s].

restorer, *n.* 再生剤.

Q² ***hair*** *restorer* 毛はえ薬.

restrain, *v.* 抑制する, 抑圧する, 束縛する.

P The English puritans, *restrained* ***at*** home, fled for freedom. 英国の清教徒は本国で束縛されたので自由を求めて本国をのがれた. ¶*restrain* oneself ***from*** making further discussion それ以上の議論は差控える. ¶be *restrained* ***in*** drinking 節酒している. ¶You must not *restrain* them ***of*** their liberty. 君は彼らの自由を妨げてはいけない. 【類】*restrain* a child ***from*** doing mischief. ¶*restrain* tears ***with*** difficulty やっと涙をおさえる.

O *restrain* one's curiourity (passion, ambition) 興味(など)を抑える.

restraint, *n.* 制止, 拘束, 束縛; 遠慮.

V ***apply*** *restraint* 制止する. ¶***break*** all *restraint* 十分打とけさせる(遠慮を抜きにする). ¶***exercise*** its *restraints* upon ... その抑制を…に加える. ¶Flushed with alcohol they are likely to ***forget*** the *restraints* of money. 酒で元気づくと彼らは財布に制限のあることを忘れがちだ. ¶***impose*** no *restraint* on ... …に制限を加えない. ¶***lay*** *restraints* on ... …に抑制を加える. ¶***lose*** all *restraint* and yield to the force of emotion 全く自制力を失い感情に走る. ¶***show*** *restraint* in ... …について控え目にするようにする. ¶***throw*** (=***shake or cast***) ***off*** all *restraint* 全く遠慮を捨てる ¶***use*** *restraint* 控え目にする.

Q ***moral*** *restraint* 道徳的束縛. ¶***social*** *restraints* 社会的制裁. ¶impose ***unreasonable*** *restraints* on ... …に不合理な抑制を加える.

P His anger was ***beyond*** *restraint*. 彼は腹が立って抑え切れなかった. ¶free ***from*** *restraint* 束縛がない. ¶get rid ***of*** *restraints* 束縛を脱する ‖ be impatient ***of*** *restraint* 抑制に我慢ができない. ¶submit ***to*** *restraint* 拘束を受ける. ¶place ... ***under*** *restraint* …に束縛を加える, 監禁する ‖ I feel ***under*** some *restraint* in ... …について束縛を受けている気持がする. ¶speak ***without*** *restraint* 遠慮なしにいう.

P² *restraint* ***of*** trade 〖経済〗[価格維持のため取引きの]自由競争の制限. 【類】the *restraints* ***of*** poverty.

restrict, *v.* 制限する, 拘束する.

M His action was ***severely*** *restricted*. 彼の行動は厳重に限定された.

P I am *restricted* ***by*** time. 私には時の制限がある. ¶They were *restricted* ***in*** their movements. 彼らはその行動を制限されていた. ¶*restricted* ***to*** a certain number (place, light diet) 一定数(など)に制限されて. ¶*restrict* his activity ***within*** narrow limits 彼の活動を狭い範囲に局限する.

restriction, *n.* 制限, 束縛, 拘束.

V ***have*** *restrictions* 制ちゅうを受ける. ¶***heed*** certain *restrictions* placed upon their conduct 彼らの行状に加えられたある制限に注意する. ¶employment which would ***impose*** *restrictions* on their liberty 彼らの自由に制限を加える仕事. ¶***lay down*** a *restriction* on ... …に制限を加える. ¶***lift*** all *restrictions* on commerce 商業に対するあらゆる制限を解除する. ¶***lighten*** *restrictions* on ... …に対する制限を軽くする. ¶***place*** (=***put***) *restrictions* on foreign trade

貿易に制限を加える. ¶ ***relax** restrictions* for ... …の制限をゆるめる. ¶ ***remove*** the *restriction*=raise the ban 制限を撤回する. ¶ ***withdraw** restrictions* regarding ... …に関する制限を除く.

Q ***absurd*** *restriction* 理に反した束縛. ¶ ***final*** *restriction* upon ... …の拘束権. ¶ under ***galling*** *restrictions* 苦しい束縛の下に. ¶ be admitted only under ***great*** *restrictions* いかめしい制限つきで始めて許される. ¶ ***immigration*** *restriction* 移民制限. ¶ ***naval*** *restriction* 軍備縮小. ¶ a very ***wise*** *restriction* はなはだ賢明な制限.

Q² ***government*** *restrictions* of industry 政府の産業制限. ¶ ***migration*** *restrictions* 移住制限. ¶ be subject to ***quota*** *restrictions* 割当て制限を受ける.

P ***under*** certain *restrictions* ある制限を設けて ‖ They are ***under*** many *restrictions*. 彼らはいく多の束縛を受けている. ¶ ***with*** no *restriction* 無制限に. ¶ ***without*** *restriction* 無制限に.

P² there will be no *restrictions* ***as to*** ... …については制限がないだろう. ¶ *restriction* ***of*** production 生産制限. ¶ *restriction* ***on*** strike activity スト活動制限. 【類】 *restriction* ***on*** water supply / *restrictions* ***on*** the sale of liquor.

result, *n.* 結果, 成績, 成行き.

V ***accomplish*** *results* satisfactory to ... …に満足な結果を収める. ¶ ***achieve*** good *results* よい結果をあげる. ¶ In my judgment certain factors ***affecting*** the *result* have been overlooked. 私の考えでは結果に影響する要素が看過されていると思う. ¶ ***announce*** the *result* その結果を発表する. ¶ in order to ***avoid*** disastrous *results* 悲惨な結果を避けるために. ¶ ***bear*** a *result* 結果を生じる. ¶ It will ***bring*** *results* to our mutual benefit. それはお互のためになる結果をもたらすだろう. ¶ It is not the knowing, but the doing of these rules, that ***brings** results*. ¶ ***bring about*** better *results* 一層好い結果をもたらす. ¶ in order to ***bring out*** this desired *result* この念願とする結果を得るため. ¶ ***communicate*** the *result* to ... 結果を…に知らせる. ¶ The book ***contains*** the *result* of some ten years' labor (=his researches of some ten years). その本にはおよそ十年にわたる彼の努力の結果が収められている. ¶ ***declare*** the *result* of ballot 投票の結果を発表する. ¶ if the best *results* are to be ***effected*** 最善の結果を得んとするならば. ¶ ***embody*** the *results* of investigations in a volume 彼の研究の結果を一冊の本にまとめる. 【類】 The book ***embodies*** the *results* of his own original research. ¶ ***ensure*** a successful *result* 好結果を確実にする. ¶ ***expect*** a good *result* 好結果を予期する. ¶ need not ***fear*** the *result* その結果を恐れるに及ばない. ¶ ***give*** (=***afford** or **furnish***) the *results* of their researches to the world 彼らの研究の結果を世の中に発表する. ¶ ***give*** better *results* …した方が成績が良い. ¶ ***have*** three most beneficial *results* 三つの最も有益な結果を示す ‖ ***have*** the *result* of bidding people out of being that way 人の戒めとなる. ¶ the best *results* may be ***hoped*** for by ... …によって最善の結果を期することができる. ¶ ***improve*** *results* さらに好成績をあげる. ¶ ***increase*** *results* さらに成績をあげる. ¶ in order to ***insure*** the most satisfactory *results* 必ず最も満足な結果を得られるために. ¶ ***leave** results* for Divine law 運を天に任せる. ¶ He hasn't ***left*** much *result* behind him. 大した成果を残さずに死んだ. ¶ ***measure*** the *results* of teaching 教育の効果を測定する. ¶ ***obtain*** (=***get, attain, gain, win** or **secure***) excellent *results* with the roughest means 最も粗末な道具で優秀な成績をあげる ‖ if the best *results* are to be ***obtained*** for ..., it seems to me imperative that ... …に対する善最の結果を得ようとするならばどうしても…が必要であると思う. ¶ ***produce** results* 成果を生じる. ¶ ***promise*** excellent *results* きわめて好い結果を産む見込がある. ¶ ***publish*** the *result* of his study in a magazine 研究の結果を雑誌に発表する. ¶ eager to ***reach** results* 成績をあげるのに熱心 ‖ ***reach*** substantially the same *results* as ... 大体…と同一結果に達する. ¶ ***realize*** satisfactory *results* 満足な結果をあげる. ¶ ***regard*** the *results* with satisfaction 結果を満足に思う. ¶ It ***represents*** the *result* of ten years' labor. それは十年にわたる努力の結果を示す. ¶ ***secure*** the best *result* 最上の結果をあげる. ¶ ***seeing*** no ill *results* 別にどうもないので(健康を害しそうなことをしたとき). ¶ ***show*** remarkable *results* 顕著な結果を示す. ¶ ***summarize*** the *results* of one's investigations その研究の結果を要約する. ¶ We may ***tabulate*** the *result* as follows. その結果を次のように表示することができる. ¶ We ***want** results*, not talk. 成果が問題なんで, 話じゅない. ¶ ***watch*** the *result* of ... …の結果を見まもる. ¶ design to ***yield*** the best *result* at a minimum of cost and trouble 最小限度の費用と労力で最善の結果をあげようと企画する ‖ It will ***yield*** no *result* that is worth while. それはひまをつぶすだけのことにしかならないであろう.

V² the best possible *results* have invariably ***followed*** from ... 従来最善の結果が間違いなく…からでてきた.

Q ***adequate*** *results* 十分の成果. ¶ achieve ***admirable*** *results* 賞賛に値する結果を収める. ¶ an ***annoying*** *result* 困った結果. ¶ without having attained ***any*** *result* 別にこれぞという成績を見ずに. ¶ produce no ***appreciable*** *result* 目立つほどの結果を生じない. ¶ It might have ***awkward*** *results*. そうすると面白くないことになるかも知れない. ¶ produce the most ***beneficial*** *results* on ... …に最も有利な結果を生じる. ¶ with the ***consequent*** *result* that ... それによって…と言う結果を生じて. ¶ achieve ***decisive*** *results* 決定的な成果を収める. ¶ The attempt was without ***definite*** *result*. その試みは徒労に終った. ¶ produce ***desirable*** *results* 願わしい結果を生じる. ¶ in order to accomplish ***desired*** *result* 目的とする結果を得るために. 【類】 The measure failed to bring about the ***desired** result*. ¶ ***Dire*** *results* may follow. 由々しいことになるかも知れない. ¶ as a ***direct** result* of ... …の直接の結果として. ¶ The *result* is fairly ***disappointing***. その結果はあまり思わしくない. ¶ The *result* is most ***disastrous***. その結果ははなはだ悲惨だ. ¶ ***discouraging** results* 悲観的な結果. ¶ ***distinguished*** *results* 抜群の成果. ¶ great ***educative** results* 大なる教育的効果. ¶ give the most ***effective** results* 最も効果的な成績を示す. ¶ meet with ***encouraging** results* はげみになる結果を見る. ¶ the ***eventual** result* of ... …の終局の結果. ¶ ***examination** results* 試験の結果. ¶ with ***excellent** results* すこぶる好結果をおさめて. ¶ obtain ***exceptional** results* 例外的な成績をあげる. ¶ get an ***expected** result* 期待した結果をあげる. ¶ with ***fatal** results* その結果命をとられて. ¶ It is in use in Scotland, with, I hear, ***favorable** results*. それはスコットランドで用いられているが聞くところによると好成績を示しているとのことだ. ¶ ***final*** (=***ultimate***) *results* 最後の成績 ‖ as the ***final** result* あげくのはてに. ¶ obtain better ***financial*** *results* 一層よい財政上の成績をあげる. 【類】 The ***financial** results* of the company for the last (=latter) half year were very satisfactory. ¶ have ***fruitful** result* 好結果を得る. ¶ with fruitless or worse than ***fruitless*** *results* 成績をあげ得ないかまたは成績をあげ得ないより更に悪い成績(赤字)を見て. ¶ I will let you know the ***general** result* by telegraph. 大体の成績を電報でお知らせします. ¶ It leads to ***good** results*. それは良い結果をあげることになる. 【類】 give ***good*** *results* in ... ‖ if the ***best** results* are to be obtained 最高の成績をあげようとすれば. ¶ The movement yielded the most ***gratifying*** *results*. その運動は最も満足な結果を産んだ. ¶ bring very ***grave*** *results* はなはだ重大な結果をもたらす. ¶ give the ***happiest** result* 最も喜ばしい結果を生じる. ¶ ***harmful*** *results* 有害な結果. ¶ achieve the ***highest** result* from ... …から最高の結果をあげる. ¶ the ***immediate** result* 直接の結果. ¶ the ***inevitable*** *result* of ... …の避けることのできない結果. ¶ produce ***lasting** results* 永続する結果を生じる. ¶ the ***latest** results* of European scholarship and criticism ヨーロッパの学識及び批評の最近の結果. ¶ the ***latest*** and ***anthoritative** results* of scholarly research in ... …に関する学術的研究の最近のかつ権威ある結果. ¶ the ***literary** result* of his visit to Japan 彼の日本来遊の文学的結果[著作となって現われなどした]. ¶ with ***little** result* 成績がはかばかしくなく. ¶ carry it to its ***logical** results* それを(理論的に)徹底させる. ¶ the ***mature** results* of many years' work 多年研究の結果 ¶ obtain ***maximum** results* with a minimum expenditure 最小の経費で最大の結果をあげる. ¶ ***meager** results* 貧弱な結果. ¶ the ***mean** results* of these observations これらの観察のつまらない結果. ¶ as a ***natural*** *result* 自然の結果として. ¶ As the ***necessary*** *result* of a life of devotion to some particular field of labor, he comes less proficient than others in practical affairs. 特殊な仕事に身をささげた必然の結果として彼は実際的の事務にかけては他の人々ほどなれていない. ¶ The experiments gave absolutely ***negative results***. その実験は全く反対の結果を生じた. ¶the ***net result*** of ... ...の正味の結果. ¶It has arrived at ***no result***. それは何らの成果も結ばなかった. ¶Though only a year old this organization has already achieved some ***notable results***. ほんの一年にしかならないがこの団体はすでに二三注目に値する成績をあげた. ¶achieve some ***noteworthy result*** ある注目に値する成果をおさめる. ¶There is also an ***objectionable result***. 弊害もある. ¶an ***opposite result*** 反対の結果. ¶be productive of ***poor results*** 貧弱な結果を生じる. ¶No ***practical results*** have as yet been arrived at. 何ら実際的成果を得ていない.【類】The negotiations came to no ***practical result***. ¶***principal*** (=***salient***) ***results*** 主なる結果. ¶yield ***profitable results*** 有益な結果をうむ. ¶***prompt result*** てき面. ¶a ***regretable result*** 遺憾な結果. ¶a very ***satisfactory result*** はなはだ満足な結果.【類】If ..., the ***results*** are bound to be ***satisfactory***. / with the most ***satisfactory results***. ¶produce ***sensational results*** 非常な成績をあげる. ¶a very ***signal result*** はなはだ顕著な結果. ¶gain a ***solid result*** 充実した結果を得る. ¶give ***splendid results*** すばらしい成績をあげる. ¶***statistical results*** 統計で示した成績. ¶***striking results*** 顕著な結果. ¶achieve ***substantial results*** 充実した成果をおさめる. ¶arrive at a ***successful result*** りっぱな結果に到達する. ¶without accomplishing any ***tangible results*** in the way of ... ...の点では何ら見るべき結果をうまずに. ¶both the ***tangible*** and ***intangible results*** of its work その事業の有形及び無形の結果. ¶often produce ***tragic results*** 往々悲惨な結果を生じる. ¶the ***ultimate result*** was that ... あげくのはては...であった. ¶The ***result*** is very ***uncertain***. 結果ははなはだ不確実である. ¶an ***unexpected result*** 思いがけない結果. ¶The ***result*** is very ***unfavorable***. 結果ははなはだ思わしくない. ¶it has sometimes an ***unfortunate result*** on ... それは時時...に不幸な結果をきたす. ¶one of the ***unhappy results*** of ... ...の不幸な結果の一つ. ¶yield the most ***valuable results*** 最も貴重な結果を生む.

Q² begin to yield ***box-office results*** [興業など]採算が取れ始める. ¶tabulation of the ***election results*** disclosed that ... 選挙の結果の表は...ということを明かにした. ¶***examination results*** 試験の成績. ¶Have you seen the ***football results***? しゅう球はどうなったか御覧でしたか. ¶***sales results*** 販売成績. ¶***test results*** 試験成績. ¶be considerably implementing ***war results*** 大いに戦果をあげつつある.

P He was injured ***as*** the ***result*** of a boiler explosion. 彼は汽かん爆発で負傷した.【類】Several people were killed ***as*** a ***result*** of the storm. / ***as*** a ***result*** of negotiations between ... / ***as*** the ***result*** of an agreement ‖ ***as*** a ***result*** largely of ... 主として...の結果として. ¶***in*** the last ***result*** 最終の成績で. ¶a table ***of results*** [競走などの]成績表. ¶***with*** the ***result*** that ... ...と言う結果になって.【類】***with*** the ***results*** known to our readers / disappointed ***with*** the ***result*** / ***with*** little ***result***. ¶at first ***without result*** 最初は成果を見ずに.【類】He tried all kinds of reliefs ***without results***. / All efforts to ... have, up to the present, been ***without result***. ‖ a race ***without results***=a dead heat 勝負なしの競走 ‖ The meeting ended ***without result***. その会合は結局むだであった.

P² the ***result of*** one's work at the last term-examination 最終学期試験における学業の成績.【類】The fire is said to be the ***result of*** incendiarism (放火). ‖ the ***result of*** the inquiry 調査の結果.【類】the ***results of*** work of investigators / The book is the ***result of*** many years' research among folklore (土俗) of all nations. / The ***result of*** the fall was a broken leg.

O The ***result*** is not up to expectation. その結果は期待に「そわない.

result, *v*. 成行く, 結果になる.

M ***result badly*** 悪い結果になる. ¶***necessarily result*** in ... きっと...に終る. ¶I believe that great good will ***result therefrom***. 私はそれから大なる善果が生じるだろうと信じる.

P the damage which ***resulted from*** the fire at ... ...の火事で生じた損害.【類】advantages ***resulting from*** ... / death ***resulted from*** ... ¶a triumph ***resulting from*** research 研究の努力の勝利 ‖ imagine the confusion ***resulting from*** the fact that ... ...ということから生じた混乱は大変なものであった.【類】a crack ***resulting from*** drying up (乾燥) / obligations (義務) ***resulting from*** ... ¶Their efforts ***resulted in*** sterility (=failure). 彼らの努力は徒労に帰した. ‖ failure to observe this would ***result in*** ... これを順守しないと...に終るだろう. ‖ ***result in*** stunted growth そのため生長が止まる ‖ It has ***resulted in*** nothing. 結局むだに終った. ‖ examination ***resulted in*** the discovery of ... 調べて見たら...がわかった ‖ He received a chill, which ***resulted in*** pleuritic inflammation. 彼は風を引いてそれがもとでろく膜炎になった.【類】it ***resulted in*** the death of ... / the match ***resulted in*** a victory for ... / The game ***resulted in*** a draw (=tie). / The investigations ***resulted in*** a fade out (うやむや). / ***result in*** the greatest good to society / ***resulted in*** very serious delays / ***result in*** increased income / such a course as will ***result in*** the settlement of ... / ***result in*** something undesirable / Inventions and new machines ***result in*** more jobs and higher wages.

resultant, *a*. 結果として.

P ***resultant from*** a mistaken policy 方針の誤りから生じ「た.

resume, *v*. 再び始める.

M Traffic is expected to be ***resumed shortly***. 交通はすぐ「回復するだろう.

résumé, *n*. *F*. 摘要, 要約.

V ***make*** (=***draw up***) a very hasty ***résumé*** of a conference 会議の概要を記する.

Q a ***brief résumé*** 大要. ¶a ***clever résumé*** of conclusion 結論の手際よい要約. ¶a ***statistical résumé*** 統計的概覧. ¶a ***trustworthy résumé*** of facts 事実の信頼しうる概要.

P² a ***résumé of*** the contents of ... ...の内容の概要.

resumption, *n*. 回復.

Q ***partial resumption*** of railway traffic [一時不通となった]「鉄道の一部開通.

P ***with*** the ***resumption*** of peace 平和克復とともに.

P² the ***resumption of*** government by the Mikado 王政復古.【類】***resumption of*** duties after absence.

resurgence, *n*. 復活.

P² ***resurgence of*** Japanese militarism 日本軍国主義の復「活.

resurrection *n*. 復活, そ生, 再起.

Q In hopes of a ***glorious resurrection***. 光栄ある復活を望「んで[墓銘].

P² the ***resurrection of*** hope 希望の復活.

resuscitate, *v*. そ生させる; そ生する.

M ***successfully resuscitate*** those who have been nearly drowned おぼれかかっていた連中をうまく生き返らせる.

P ***resuscitate from*** apparent death 仮死からそ生する.

resuscitation, *n*. そ生, 復活.

P² a ***resuscitation of*** a controversy (an argument) 論争の「むし返し.

retail, *n*. 小売, 受売.

P sell ***at*** (=***by***) ***retail*** 小売をする ‖ price for purchasers ***at retail*** 小売の値段. ☞「小(卸)売する」意には《主に米》sell ***at*** retail (wholesale) と《英》sell ***by*** retail (wholesale) がある. retail (wholesale) を副詞に使って sell (buy) ***retail*** (***wholesale***) という用法もある.

retail, *v*. 小売する, 受売する.

P ***retail ... at*** ...yen ...を...円で小売する.

retailer, *n*. 小売商人, 受売人.

Q² ***hand-to-mouth retailers*** その日暮しの小売商人.

retain, *v*. 保つ.

M China vessels ***retain*** heat ***longer*** than metal ones. せとものの方が金ものより保温がよい.

retainer, *n*. 家臣.

Q ***civil retainers*** of the Crown 文官. ¶a ***senior retainer*** 「of a *daimyo* 家老.

Q² a ***key retainer*** 重臣. ¶an old ***family retainer*** 老僕.

retaliate, *v*. 報いる, 復しゅうする, 返報する.

P ***retaliate on*** (=***upon***) the offender (one's foe) 犯人(な「ど)に復しゅうする.

retaliation, *n*. 報復.

P, P² ***in retaliation*** for Germany's submarine campaign ドイツの潜水艦攻撃の仕返しに.

retard, *v*. 遅らせる.

M His death was ***retarded several days*** by the skill of his doctor. 彼の死は医師の医療によって数日遅れた.

O ***retard*** the progress of ... ...の進歩を遅らせる.

retentive, *a*. 保持力ある.

P ***retentive of*** moisture 湿気を保持する.

reticence, *n*. 沈黙, 無言, 無口.

V Extreme ***reticence*** is ***observed*** in official circles in (=on) the affair. その事件については官辺ではかたく口をふさいでいる.

V² His ***reticence*** is more ***revealing*** than his speech. だまっていると口に出すよりかえってはっきりして来る.

Q *undue reticence* 不当の沈黙.

retricent, *a.* 無言の, 沈黙の, 口数の少ない.

M *remarkably reticent* concerning ... …については容易に口を開かない. ¶ *wisely reticent* on the subject 賢明にもその問題に触れないで.

P Records are very *reticent about* (=*as to*) sexual matters. 性のことについての記録ははなはだ乏しい.

retinue, *n.* 従者, 供奉員.

V The King *had* a large *retinue* of servants. 王には召使が多数あった.

Q a *numerous retinue* 多数の随行員. ¶ with a *small retinue* 微行で(少数の従者をつれて).

P accompanied *by* a large *retinue* 従者を多数従えて. ¶ He was *in* the *retinue* of the Prince. 彼はその皇子の一供奉員であった.

retire, *v.* 退く, 退去する; 寝床に入る; 隠退する.

M *retire altogether* from business 仕事からまったく隠退する. ¶ *retire early* to rest 早く床につく. ¶ He *retired hurt.* [ゲームなどで]負傷して退いた. ¶ *retire late* 夜ふかしをする. ¶ *retire permanently* from the political world 政界から永久に隠退する. ¶ *stealthily retire* to ... こっそり…に引きさがる.

P before *retiring at* night 夜寝る前に. ¶ *retire before* midnight 真夜中前に寝る. ¶ *retire for* the night 寝所に引っ込む. ¶ *retire from* public (active) life 公(活動)生活を退く ‖ *retire from* active participation (=work, service *or* business) 実務から退く ‖ *retire from* the presidency 総(会)長の職を退く ‖ *retire from* pictures 銀幕から引退する. 【類】*retire from* the editorship (主筆の職) of ... / *retire from* the management of his grocery business / He *retired from* practice (office) some time ago on account of failing health. / *retire from* a firm (an official post) / *retire from* the firm of ... / sea-dogs (老水夫) who have *retired from* the service / *retire from* politics (政界). ¶ *retire in* defeat 負けて退却する ‖ more (=rather) *retiring in* disposition than otherwise どっちかと言えば引込み思案な. ¶ *retire into* private life 隠退する ‖ *retire into* the country いなかへ引っ込む ‖ *retire into* private life 官界を去る, 野に下る. ¶ *retire on* a pension 恩給を取って引っ込む ‖ There are not enough savings to *retire on.* 隠退して食えるだけの貯蓄がない. ¶ *retire to* private life 隠退する ‖ *retire to rest* (=bed) 寝床に入る. 【類】*retire to* the country / Papa has *retired to* his den (居間) with the evening papers. / *retire to* bed for the purpose of poetic composition. ¶ *retire upon* a handsome competence かなりの財産をもらって隠退する. ¶ *retire with* a pension 年金を受けて引込む.

retirement, *n.* 隠退, 隠居, 退職.

Q spend the rest of one's days in *dignified retirement* りっぱな隠退生活に余生を送る. ¶ a *graceful retirement* 円満退職. ¶ He died in *quiet retirement* at the advanced age of 82 years. 彼は八十二歳の高齢で静かな余生を終った.

Q^2 get *disability retirement* 無能のため退職させられる.

P the allowance *for retirement*=a retiring allowance 退職金. ¶ live *in retirement* from the world 世間から隠退して暮す.

P^2 a prudent *retirement*, for a short time, *from* political life しばらくの間政界からの賢明な隠退. 【類】one's *retirement from* city (public) life.

retiring, *n.* 退くこと.

P *upon retiring* 寝しなに.

retort, *n.* 反論, 口答, 逆襲的返答.

V *give* a sharp *retort* 鋭く口答えする. ¶ *provoke* a humorous *retort* かいぎゃく的な反論を買う.

Q a *derisive retort* ちょう笑的な逆襲. ¶ an *effective retort* 有効な反ばく. ¶ a *neat retort* 抜かりのない返答(当意即妙). ¶ a *witty retort* 機知に富んだ逆襲的返答.

P *in retort* しっぺい返しに.

P^2 a sharp *retort on* the criticism of ... …の批評に対する鋭い反ばく.

retort, *v.* 返報する, 言い返しをする.

P *retort* blow *for* blow なぐり返す. ¶ he *retorted upon* me saying ... 彼は…と言って私にくってかかった.

O He *retorted* an insult (affront, a sarcasm). 彼は侮辱(など)の仕返しをした.

retort, *n.* [化学実験用]レトルト(蒸溜器).

Q a *tubulated retort* 管状レトルト.

retract, *v.* 引込む; 撤回する.

P Muscles *retract after* amputation. 切断後筋肉は収縮する. ¶ *retract from* an engagement 約束を撤回する.

retraction, *n.* 取消し, 撤回.

V *make* a formal *retraction* of what one said against ... …に反対した言を正式に取消す.

P^2 *retraction of* a bill 法案の撤回.

retreat, *n.* 退却; 避難; 避難所.

V Karuizawa *affords* a cool *retreat* during the heated season. 軽井沢は夏の間涼しい避暑地になる. ¶ he *beat* a safe *retreat* by saying: 彼は…と言ってうまくその場を逃げた. ¶ *cover* the *retreat* of ... …の退却を援護する. ¶ *cut off* (=*intercept*) the enemy's *retreat* 敵の退路を断つ. ¶ *have* its *retreat cut off* その退路を断たれる. ¶ *make* a *retreat* 退却する ‖ *make* a pre-arranged *retreat* 予定の退却をやる. ¶ *make good* one's *retreat* 首尾よく退却する. ¶ *order* a *retreat* 退却を命じる. ¶ *sound* a (=the) *retreat* 退却のらっぱを吹奏する.

Q a *delightful rural retreat* いなかの隠居所. ¶ *in full retreat* 総退却をして. ¶ a *graceful retreat* 上品な隠宅. ¶ beat a *hurried* (=*hasty*) *retreat* 急いで退却する. ¶ a *safe retreat* to end his days 彼の生がいを終るに安全な隠退所. ¶ a *sequestered retreat* 幽居. ¶ an *unseemly retreat* 見かけの悪い隠宅.

Q^2 a *summer retreat* 避暑地. ¶ a snug *winter retreat* 住み心地のよい避寒地.

P It is *beyond retreat* now. それは最早のっぴきならない. ¶ a signal *for retreat* 退却の合図. ¶ an army *in retreat* 退却軍.

P^2 a *retreat to* the west 西方への退却.

retreat, *v.* 退却する, 引込む, 退居する.

M *retreat further* into the distance さらに遠く退却する.

P *retreat before* German foes ドイツ軍に追われて退却する. 【類】*retreat before* the advance of the enemy. ¶ *retreat from* the oppressive heat of the capital 首都の炎暑を避ける. ¶ His lustreless eyes *retreated* way back *into* dark-ringed sockets. 彼のどろっとした目はまわりの黒ずんだ眼窩(がん)に落込んでしまった. ¶ *retreat on* a place 引きあげる.

retrenchment, *n.* 節約, 緊縮.

V *make* a *retrenchment* of 1,000 workers owing to shortage of orders 注文減少のため従業員を千人減らす. ¶ *push retrenchment* to an extreme 極端に節減する.

Q^2 *personnel retrenchment* 人員節減.

P^2 *retrenchment in* expenditure=economic retrenchment 経費節減.

retribution, *n.* 返報, 報い, 応報.

V certainly *bring* its natural *retribution* 確かにその自然の応報を招く. ¶ Nature has *devised* a *retribution* for illicit intercourse in the form of venereal disease.—Dr. Wingfield Scott Hall. 自然は不正の性交に対する応報として性病なるものを工夫した. ¶ Nature often *exacts* a severe *retribution.* 自然は往々にして峻(しゅん)烈な報復を断行する. ¶ Nature always *metes out* a *retribution* for any transgression of her law. 自然はいつもその法則を破るものに対して天罰を加える. ¶ *prophesy* the swift *retribution* that will overtake their persecutors 彼らの迫害者に加わるであろうすみやかな天罰を予言する.

V^2 The *retribution* at last *overtook* him. とうとう彼に天罰が加えられた.

Q *divine retribution* 天罰. ¶ It brings with it *inevitable retribution.* そうすると必ず応報がある. ¶ *tardy retribution* 遅まきの仕返し.

P^2 a *retribution for* one's sin 罪の報い.

retrieve, *n.* 救出.

V be *given* a *retrieve* [建物の取りくずしなど]猶予される.

P *beyond* (=*past*) *retrieve* 回復の見込みなく.

retrieve, *v.* 救出する.

P *retrieve* a person *from* ruin (misfortune) 人を破滅(不幸)から救い出す.

retroact, *v.* さかのぼる.

P The wage increase *retroacts to* January 1. 値上賃金は一月一日にさかのぼる.

retroactive, *a.* さかのぼって.

P be effective *retroactive to* ... [法令の施行など]…にさかのぼって有効である.

retrocession, *n.* 還付, 返却.

P^2 the *retrocession of* Alsace-Lorraine *to* France フランスへアルサス・ローレンの還付.

retrograde, *v.* 退歩する.

P *retrograde in* civilization 文明が退歩する.

retrogression, *n.* 後退, 逆行, 退歩.
P a tendency *towards retrogression* 退歩への傾向.
P² the *retrogression of* civilization 文明の逆行. ¶regard free love as a *retrogression towards* the rude sexual habits of savage peoples 自由恋愛を野蛮民族の盲目的な性生活への逆転と見なす.

retrospect, *n.* 回顧, 回想, 追懐.
V *carry on retrospect* some distance back さらに以前にさかのぼって追想する.
Q a *brief historical retrospect* 簡単な史的回顧.
P review 1956 *in retrospect* 一九五六年を回顧する. 【類】glance *in retrospect* over the past twelve months.

retrospection, *n.* 回顧.
Q indulge in *dreamy retrospections* 夢のような追想にふける.

retrospective, さかのぼって.
M The law is *not retrospective.* 法律は既往にさかのぼらない.

return, *n.* 帰還; 返答; [しばしば *pl.*] 報告; 利得.
V *ask* the *return* of ... ...の返却をこう. ¶*bring* them a fair *return* 彼らに公平な報酬をもたらす. ¶The goods *bring in* small *returns.* その商品はもうけが薄い. ¶*commemorate* the triumphal *return* of ... ...のがい旋を記念する. ¶*compile returns* 報告を編集する. ¶*earn* a fair *return* on the capital invested 投資に対し正当な報酬を得る. ¶*expect* a good *return* on one's capital 投下資本で相当の利益を見込む. ¶*file* an income-tax *return* 所得税の報告を提出する. ¶*get* a good *return* よい報酬を得る. ¶*give* a *return* もうけがある. ¶I hope you will not *have* any *return* of your illness. 御病気の再発のないように致したいものです. ‖ In the event of your *having* a *return* of the pain, take this medicine. また痛むようでしたらこの薬を服用なさい. ¶*increase* box-office *returns* 切符売場の収入を増す. ¶*make return* of a portion of the money 金の一部を返還する ‖ *make* a *return* for something done or given=reciprocate やってもらったことまたはもらった物に対して返礼する ‖ *Return* may be *made* to ... by rail or steamer. ...へは汽車または汽船で帰れる.【類】The *return* may be *made* the same day (on the same steamship). ¶a sure method of *obtaining* a *return* on spare capital 遊金を運転させる確実な方法. ¶a *return prepared* in August shows that ... 八月に作成した報告によると...ということが分かる. ¶*realize* large *returns* from ... ...から大なる利益を得る. ¶*seek* a higher *return* on one's capital その資本でもっと多くの利得を求める. ¶at prices which *show* reasonable *returns* upon the investment in them それらに対する投資に対して相当な利益を示すような値段で. ¶*speed* one's *return* to health 健康回復を早める. ¶the *return* may be *varied* by ... 帰りは...によって目先を変えることができる. ¶*welcome* the *return* of ... ...の帰還を歓迎する. ¶*yield* [one] a fair (an adequate) *return* on capital (one's investment) 資本(その投資)に対して十分(相当)の利得を産む.
Q It brings us an *adequate return.* それでわれわれに相当な利得がある. ¶get *fair returns* over expenses 出費に対し相当の利益を得る.【類】pay *fair returns* on one's investment. ¶bring in a *fat return* たくさんの利益をもたらす. ¶the *financial returns* of authorship 著者の収入. ¶yield *good returns* to ... ...に対してよいもうけを産み出す. 【類】get *good returns* from ... / a *good return* on an investment. ¶Many *happy returns* of the day! お目出度う(誕生日などの祝詞). ¶with *infinitesimal returns* きわめて少ない利得で. ¶obtain the *maximum return* 最大の利得を得る. ¶the latest year for which *official returns* are available 官庁の統計で調べられる最近の年. ¶Probably men of science will always have to be content with relatively *poor financial returns* for their work. 科学者は恐らくいつも彼らの努力に対して比較的貧弱な報酬をもって甘んじねばならないであろう. ¶yield *profitable returns* 利益を産み出す. ¶These articles make a *quick return.* これらの品は足が早い. ‖ small profits and *quick returns* 薄利多売. ¶*reasonable return* upon the money invested 投資金に対する相当な報酬. ¶the *said return* その申告書. ¶make *some return* for this kindness in the form of ... この親切に対し...をもって報いる. ¶ask for a *speedy return* of proof-sheets 校正刷を早く返すように求める. ¶a *triumphant return* がい旋. ¶a *weekly return* of lost ships 沈没船の週報.
Q² *census returns* 国勢調査申告. ¶*election returns* 選挙結果報告. ¶*mortality returns* 死亡率報告. ¶*property returns* from ... ...の資産報告表. ¶a report on *questionnaire returns* 質問状の回答に関する報告. ¶a Board of *Trade return* [英国]貿易庁の統計表. ¶*traffic returns* on railways 鉄道交通報告書.
P *according to* the most recent *returns* 最近の報告によれば. ¶*after* one's *return* from abroad 海外から帰国後. ¶We ordered a lunch to be ready *against* our *return.* われわれの帰ってから食べる昼食を用意しておくように命じた. ¶answer (=reply) *by return* of post 折返し返事する. ¶buy *in return* about ... of American goods 帰りに米国の品物を約...買う ‖ a natural impulse to love and to be loved *in return* 愛し愛されたいという自然の衝動 ‖ hand money *in return* for a receipt 受取証と引換に金を渡す ‖ *in return* for this courtesy (=favor) この好意に対する返礼に. 【類】He asked me for a loan *in return* for recommending me for the post. ‖ he is entitled to a holiday *in return* for his many years of work at ... 彼が...における多年の労に対し休暇を与えられる資格がある ‖ Please state how I can be of some service to you *in return.* どうしたらあなたの労に報いることができるか教えて下さい. ¶*on* my *return* home from college (abroad) 大学(外国)から私が帰ったとき ‖ Good-bye, old chap, I'll see you *on* my *return.* じゃ失敬, 帰りに会おう. ‖ Have you received any present from your uncle *on* his *return*? 君の叔父さんが帰ったとき何かおもらいでしたか. 【類】*on* the *return* of spring. ¶*upon* his *return* to society 出所後に. ¶*with* the *return* of peace (the New Year) 平和克服(など)とともに. ¶*without return* もうけなしに.
P² a *return for* a present received 贈答品のおかえし. 【類】I hope you will accept this small present as some *return for* your kindness on Thursday last. ¶*returns from* his books 彼の著作の収入 ‖ on my *return* (=way home) *from* Europe 私が欧州から帰るとき ‖ yield the largest *returns from* one's investment その投資から最大の利益を生む. ¶the *return of* the foreign trade of Japan for March shows that ... 日本の外国貿易三月分の報告によると...ということが分かる ‖ the *return of* the seasons to the earth 季節の変遷. ¶a *return on* an investment 投資に対する利得. 【類】The *return on* the loan (公債) is £3.4s.3d. ¶He will visit this country again on his *return to* India. 彼はインドへ帰る途中再びこの国を訪れるだろう. 【類】leave London on his *return to* America / a *return to* health / a *return to* nature.

return, *v.* 帰る; 返す, 報いる; 《英》 選出する.
M *Return* it *back* to me. それを私に返してくれ. ¶He *returned hence.* ここから帰った. ¶*return homeward* 帰路につく. ¶*return* home *safe and sound* 無事で家に帰る. ¶I've *just returned.* 今帰ったばかりのところ. ¶*return swiftly* すみやかに帰る.
P *return* the book *promptly* すぐ本を返す. ¶*return after* many years from a foreign clime 多年の外国滞在から帰朝する. ¶He was *returned by* ... votes. 彼は...票で選出された. ¶He will *return* home *by way of* the Pacific Islands and the United States. 彼は太平洋諸島と合衆国を経て帰国するであろう. ¶he has been *returned for* ... 彼は...から選出された ‖ *return* good *for* evil 恨みに報いるに徳をもってする. ¶*return from* an absence 留守をしていて帰る. 【類】he *returned from* a holiday at ... / *return from* a trip in Europe (an American tour) / He will *return from* his vacation next week. / a visitor *returning from* Europe / business men *returning from* their occupation / Her husband *returned from* work. ‖ But to *return from* this digression. それはそうと, 閑話休題. ¶The poem *returns to* my memory. その詩が記憶に浮ぶ. ‖ But to *return to* our subject. それはさておき(本文へもどって). ‖ *return to* their countries of origin 彼らの本国へ帰る ‖ *return to* consciousness=regain consciousness 正気になる ‖ *return to* work [ストの後で]職場に復帰する. 【類】*return to* one's duty / Strikers have been notified that unless they *return to* duty today they must consider themselves dismissed. ‖ The dying man *returned to* life. そのひん死の人が回生した. ‖ *return to* Mother Earth =die 永眠する ‖ ... appear to be *returning to* fashion ... がまた流行しだしたらしい ‖ *return* again *to* the world 還

俗する ‖ ***return to*** one's old form again もとの姿に返る; 正体を現わす ‖ ***return to*** nature 本然の姿に返る.【類】***return to*** normalcy ‖ ***return to*** its place in the family of nations 国際社会に復帰する ‖ ***return to*** power 再び政権を握る ‖ till he ***returns to*** his senses しょう(性)がつくまで ‖ he was ***returned to*** the House of Representatives for ... 彼は…から代議士に選出された. ¶ ***return upon*** a handsome competence 相当の金を手にして隠退する. ¶ The robins ***return with*** the spring. こま鳥は春になると帰って来る.

O *returning*, the steamer will leave there at ... その船は帰りはそこを…時に出るだろう.

return-card, *n.* 往復はがき.

P notify one ***by return-card*** 往復はがきで人に通知する.

returning, *n.* 帰路.

P ***in returning*** もどりには.

reunion, *n.* 再会, 懇親会.

V ***enjoy*** their *reunion* 彼らの再会を喜こぶ. ¶ The three brothers ***held*** their first *reunion* in seventeen years. その三人の兄弟は十七年目で一堂に会した.

Q the ***annual*** *reunion* of the alumni 年一度の卒業生の懇親会.

Q² an ***alumni reunion*** and banquet 卒業生の懇親会及び宴会. ¶ We have a ***family reunion*** every Thanksgiving Day. われわれは毎年感謝祭に親せきの懇親会をする.

revamp, *v.* 改訂する.

M *revamp* an old edition ***up to date*** 旧版を改訂する.

revamping, *n.* 修理.

Q² a ***large-scale*** *revamping* 大規模の修理.

reveal, *v.* 現わす.

M ***clearly*** *reveal* あらわに…を物語っている.

P *reveal* an aptitude ***for*** science 科学者に向く.

revel, *n.* 酒宴, どんちゃん騒ぎ.

Q an ***unrestrained*** *revel* 無礼講.

revel, *v.* 大いに楽しむ, たんできする.

P ***revel in*** the scenery of ... …の景に見とれる ‖ ***revel in*** luxury (vice, mischief, music) ぜいたく(など)にふける.【類】The children ***revel in*** country life.

revelation, *n.* 啓示; [意外な]新事実.

Q a ***divine*** *revelation* 神の啓示. ¶ some ***fresh*** *revelation* of the laboratory 同研究所のある新しい発見. ¶ a ***startling*** *revelation* 驚異すべき発見.

P² a ***revelation of*** the modern map-makers' skill 今日の地図製作者の技術を示す驚くべき一例 ‖ The ***revelation of*** the thief's hiding place ***by*** ... …による盗賊の隠れ場所の判明. ¶ It was a ***revelation to*** me. それは私にとって全く意外であった.

revenge, *n.* 復しゅう, かたき討.

V The best way to ***get*** *revenge* is to avoid being like the one who has injured you.—Marcus Aurelius. 復しゅうの最良の方法は君に損害を加えた者の様にならぬことである.【類】***get*** (=have) one's *revenge*. ¶ ***give*** a card-player the *revenge* カルタのあだをとる. ¶ You will ***have*** your *revenge?*—Enough for today. 君はかたきを取る気か—きょうはもうたくさんだ(競技など). ¶ ***inflict*** a terrible *revenge* upon ... …に恐ろしい復しゅうを加える. ¶ ***mediate*** *revenge* 復しゅうを仲裁する. ¶ ***seek*** *revenge* 復しゅうの機会をねらう. ¶ ***take*** *revenge* (=vengeance) for one's father's death 父のあだを討つ.【類】***take*** one's *revenge* on (=upon) a person. ¶ ***threaten*** *revenge* 復しゅうするとおどす. ¶ ***vow*** *revenge* 復しゅうを誓う. ¶ ***wreak*** a *revenge* on ... …に復しゅうする.

Q take a ***bitter*** *revenge* for ... 心行くまで…のあだを報いる. ¶ the ***bloodiest*** *revenge* 残忍きわまる復しゅう. ¶ a ***slashing*** *revenge* for ... …に対する大々的復しゅう.

Q² ***blood*** (=***bloodshed***) *revenge* 流血の復しゅう.

P fly to arms ***in revenge*** for wrong 非行に報いようとして武器を取る.【類】kill ... ***in revenge*** for a murder / done ***in revenge*** for the slights (ぶべつ) put upon ... ¶ ***out of revenge*** he contrived the murder of ... 復しゅうのため彼は…の殺害を企てた.【類】burn properly ***out of revenge.***

revenge, *v.* 報いる, 復しゅうする.

P resolve to be ***revenged for*** ... …のあだを取ろうと決心する. ¶ *revenge* oneself ***on*** (=***upon***) ... …にあだを報いる.【類】*revenge* ***on*** an insult / He wished to *revenge* ***on*** his tormentors. ¶ *revenge* ***upon*** a person ***for*** the loss その損害を受けた人に補償する. ¶ *revenge* wrong ***with*** wrong 悪には悪を(目には目を).

revenue, *n.* 収入, 所得, 歳入.

V ***defraud*** the *revenue* 脱税する. ¶ ***drain*** national *revenues* 国家の収入を枯渇させる. ¶ a samurai ***enjoying*** a *revenue* of 10,000 ducats 一万両の収入ある武士. ¶ ***obtain*** a *revenue* from ... …から収入を得る. ¶ ***raise*** *revenue* for national purposes 国家のために収税する.

Q enjoy an ***immense*** *revenue* 巨額の収入がある. ¶ bring in a ***large*** *revenue* 多額の歳入をもたらす. ¶ ***national*** *revenue* 国家歳入. ¶ the ***rich*** *revenue* of the B.B.C. from the listeners[-in] 英国放送局の聴取料から得る多大の収入.

Q² ***customs*** *revenues* 関税諸収入. ¶ China's ***salt tax*** *revenue* and ***maritime customs*** *revenue* 中国の塩税収入及び関税収入. ¶ Italy's "***invisible export***" *revenue* イタリアの「無形輸出」の収益(観光客の落した金など). ¶ ***tax*** *revenues* 税諸収入.

P heavy losses ***in*** *revenue* 歳入上の大損失.

P² *revenue* ***from*** that source その方面からの所得.

reverberate, *v.* 反響する, とどろく.

P The report of the gun *reverberated* loudly ***through*** the hills. 銃砲の音が山々に高く反響した.【類】The sound *reverberated* ***through*** the quiet room. ¶ The air *reverberated* ***with*** the booming of guns. 大砲の音が響きわたった.

reverberation, *n.* 反響.

V It ***had*** its *reverberation* in the English labor world. それは英国の労働界に反響があった.

reverence, *n.* 尊敬, 敬神.

V He ***deserves*** all our *reverence.* 彼はわれわれすべての尊敬に値する. ¶ ***do*** him *reverence*=do reverence to him 彼を尊敬する. ¶ ***feel*** (=***have***) *reverence* for ... …に対して尊敬の念を感じる. ¶ ***make*** a *reverence* to ... …に敬礼する. ¶ ***pay*** *reverence* at a tomb of ... …の墓に参拝する ‖ The *reverence* continues to be ***paid*** to her memory at the present day. 今日なお彼女の霊に敬意が払われている. ¶ Aged parents ***receive*** filial *reverence.* 老齢の両親は子供の尊敬を受ける. ¶ ***show*** one's *reverence* by certain forms of obeisance あるお辞儀の形式によって敬意を示す.

Q in the ***deepest*** *reverence* 最も深く敬って. ¶ bow in ***humble*** *reverence* うやうやしく頭を下げる. ¶ ***sentimental*** *reverence* for ... …に対する感傷的な敬意.

P hold one ***in*** *reverence* 人を尊敬する. ¶ I retired ***with*** three profound *reverences* (=bows). 私は三度最敬礼して退いた.

P² *reverence* ***for*** parents (scholarship and research) 両親(学問及び研究)に対する尊敬.【類】a great *reverence* ***for*** virtue. / my *reverence* ***for*** Christianity. ¶ *Reverence* ***of*** Heaven and love of man 敬天愛人. ¶ *reverence* ***toward*** God 敬神.

reverie, *n.* 夢想, 幻想.

P wake ***from*** one's *reverie* 幻想からさめる(われに返る). ¶ indulge ***in*** *reverie* 空想にふける ‖ He was ***in*** a deep *reverie.* 彼は深い幻想にふけっていた.

reversal, *n.* 転倒, 反転; 破棄.

V The news ***brought about*** a *reversal* of feeling in the wheat market. そのニュースで小麦市場は大変動をきたした. ¶ ***obtain*** a *reversal* of the censor's ruling 検閲者の判定を撤回させる.

Q² ***last-minute*** *reversals* in policy 最後の瞬間における施政方針の逆転.

P An appeal resulted ***in*** a *reversal* of the decision. 上告の結果判決が逆転した.

P² a *reversal* ***of*** the order of host and guest 主客転倒.【類】the *reversal* ***of*** the seasons in north and south.

reverse, *n.* 反対, 逆, 転変; 不幸, わざわい.

V a gentleman who has ***had*** *reverses* of fortune 幾多の辛酸をなめてきた紳士. ¶ ***prove*** the *reverse* 反証を与える. ¶ The army ***sustained*** a *reverse.* その軍隊は(形勢逆転して)敗亡するに至った.

Q The ***exact*** *reverse* was the case. 事実はその正反対であった. ¶ ***financial*** *reverses* 財政の逆転. ¶ I heard of the ***sudden*** *reverse* of fortune that had happened to him. 私は彼が突然不幸に見舞われたことを聞いた. ¶ under the stroke of ***unexpected*** *reverses* 思いがけない不幸に出会って. ¶ the ***very*** *reverse* of what has really happened 実際起ったことのちょうど反対.

Q² ***business*** *reverse* 商売の下向.

P ***on*** the *reverse* of the cover 表紙の見返しに.【類】***on*** the *reverse* of this page you find ... ‖ A copy of the current issue will be sent free of charge if you will fill up the form *on* the *reverse* and post this card. この裏にあるカードに記入して御郵送下されば本月号は無料で送ります. ¶smart *under* a *reverse* 失敗のうき目に会う.

P² a *reverse in* my affairs 突然私の身に降りかった不幸. ¶It is the *reverse of* (=far from being) friendly. それは親密どころかその反対だ.

O abundant or the *reverse* 豊富であるかあるいはその反対.

reverse, *v.* 反する.

M This *exactly reverses* what we might expect. 正に期待に反する. ¶Their positions are *now reversed*. 彼らの地位は今や逆になった.

P *reverse* a resolution *against* a Government policy 政府の政策に対する反対決議を逆転させる.

reversion, *n.* 復帰.

P² *reversion of* course 逆転. ¶a *reversion to* a more primitive civilization 一層原始的文明への復帰.

revert, *v.* 復帰する; 元へ戻って説く.

M one's attention *naturally reverts* to ... 自然注目は...に戻る.

P The manufactory was taken up by the State and carried on till ..., when it again *reverted into* private hands. その工場は政府に買収され...まで経営されたがその後また個人の手に戻った. ¶*reverting* (=to revert) *to* the question of ... ...の問題に戻って ‖ *revert to* its old state 復旧する ‖ *revert to* a status of full sovereignty 完全独立国に復帰する ‖ the property that *reverted to* the State 国家に没収された資産. 【類】*reverting to* the original topic / *reverting to* the original statement, I think ...

review, *n.* 評論; 検閲; 閲兵, 観艦式(など).

V *hold* a naval *review* 観艦式を催す.

Q a brief *review* of principal features of the ...'s work during last year is presented below: 昨年中の...事業の主たる点を簡単に回顧して見ると次のようになる. ¶a *favorable* (an *unfavorable*) *review* 好(不)評 ‖ skill in advertising and procuring *favorable reviews* 広告と好評獲得の手腕. ¶a *grand triumphal review* がい旋大観兵式. ¶make *hasty* (*rapid*) *review* of ... ...をざっと検閲する(批評する). ¶a *historical review* 回顧. ¶a *weekly review* 週刊評論.

Q² an *air review* 空中分列式. ¶a *book review* 書評.

P pass *in review* before ... ...の前を分列行進する. ¶the work *under review* 批評中の著作 ‖ the period *under review* 調査の期間. 【類】the works that came *under review* / The number of postal packages (郵便物) delivered in the United Kingdom during the year *under review* was 5,483,000,000.

P² a grand *review of* troops for inspection by the President 大統領検閲の大観兵式.

review, *v.* 評論する.

P one who *reviews* books *by* profession=a book reviewer 書評家. ¶*review* one's lessons *for* tomorrow. あすの予習をする. ¶The book was kindly and favorably *reviewed in* the principal papers. その本は主な新聞の好評を博した.

reviewer, *n.* 評論家.

Q² a *book reviewer* 書評を書く人.

revise, *v.* 校訂する.

M *carefully revise* ... 注意して...を校訂する. ¶*revise thoroughly* 大改訂を加える. ¶a book *revised to date* 最新版の本.

P *revised* and brought up to date *by* Mr. ... ...氏により現状に合致するように修正された. ¶*revised to* June, 1908 一九〇八年六月現在の訂正を加えて ‖ *revised to* prices in 1958 一九五八年の定価に改正されて.

reviser, *n.* 校訂者, 修正者.

Q the *literary reviser* of the Japan Times ジャパン・タイムズ紙の文章校閲者.

revision, *n.* 校訂, 校閲; 修正.

V *carry out revision* 修正を実施する. ¶*effect* a downward *revision* in the existing import duties on ... ...の現行輸入税率を引下げる. ¶*make* a thorough *revision* of ... ...に大修正を加える. ¶*procure* a *revision* of the treaties 条約改正を承諾させる. ¶*undergo* considerable *revision* 著しく修正される. 【類】The standards are *undergoing revision*.

Q submit a book to a *careful revision* 本を念入りに訂正する. ¶a greatly *augmented revision* 大増訂. ¶a *drastic revision* 大改正. ¶a *general* overhauling *revision* of treaties 諸条約の全般にわたる大修正. ¶a *radical revision* of ... ...の根本的改正. ¶institute *thorough-going revisions* 徹底的修正を行う.

Q² a *boundary revision* 境界の訂正. ¶a *frontier revision* 国境の修正. ¶a *wage revision* 賃銀修正.

P The catalogue is *under revision*. その目録は目下改訂中である.

revival, *n.* 復活, 復興, 再興.

Q *economic revival* 経済的復活. ¶an *enthusiastic* and *overwhelming revival* of ... ...の熱心で圧倒的な復興. ¶a *wide revival* of interest in ... ...に対する興味の広範にわたる復活.

Q² a *miracle revival* 奇跡的な復活. ¶*trade revival* 貿易の復興.

P² the *revival of* learning (letters) 学問(など)の復興.

revive, *v.* よみがえる.

P *revive from* a swoon 失神状態からよみがえる. ¶an old play *revived on* the stage 再演された古い劇.

revocation, *n.* 取消し.

P² the *revocation of* a license 免許の取消.

revolt, *n.* 謀反, 反乱, 一き.

V *quell* (=*suppress, put down or get under*) a *revolt* 反乱を静める.

V² A *revolt broke out*. 反乱がぼっ発した. ¶The *revolt* has *come* to a height. 反乱は高まった.

Q an *agrarian revolt* 小作争議. ¶*moral revolt* 義憤. ¶an *open revolt* against the Pope 教皇に対する公然たる謀反.

Q² a *peasant revolt* 百姓の暴動, 一き.

P rise *in revolt* against the government 政府に反抗する.

P² a *revolt against* capitalism 資本主義への反逆. 【類】*revolt against* a person (the government, the rule). ¶the *revolt of* the weak against the strong 強者に対する弱者の反逆.

revolt, *v.* 反抗する; いやな気持がする, 胸が悪くなる.

P He *revolted against* the fixed ideas of his age. 彼は当時の固定した思想に反抗した. ‖ when the Spanish colonies were *revolting against* the mother country スペイン植民地がその母国に反旗をひるがえした時. ¶My mind *revolts at* the idea (sight). 私はその考え(など)に対し反抗する. ‖ My stomach *revolts at* such food. 私はそれを食べると吐く. 【類】*revolt at* a bad smell. ¶his blunted sense does not *revolt from* ... 彼はその感覚がにぶっているので...をいとわない.

revolting, *a.* 胸の悪くなるような.

P It is very *revolting to* an Englishman's idea of fair play and true sport. それは英国人の公正と真実な競技の精神から言って大いに唾棄(だき)すべきことである. 【類】*revolting to* the sensitive conscience (敏感な良心) of ... / *revolting to* a person.

revolution, *n.* 回転; 大改革, 革命.

V *accomplish* a great *revolution* in poetry 詩に大改革を行う. ¶*bring about* (=*cause*) a *revolution* in the art of war 戦術に一大革新をもたらす. ¶*effect* a rapid *revolution* in the life of the people その国民生活の上に一大急変を生ぜしめる. ¶The medical world has *had* its *revolution*. 医学界に大改革が起った. ¶a remarkable *revolution* in thought was *initiated* by ... 思想上の一大改革が...によって主唱された. ¶The earth *makes* one *revolution* round the sun in about 365 days. 地球は約三百六十五日で太陽の周囲を一回転する. ‖ The warship *makes* a *revolution* in naval construction. その軍艦は建艦史上画期的のものである. ¶*precipitate* a *revolution* 改革を激成する. ¶*start* (=*raise*) a *revolution* 改革を始める. ¶*work* a *revolution* in human thinking (navigation, industry) 人間の思考上(など)に一大改革をきたす. ‖ Between that day and this a great *revolution* has been *wrought*. その当時と今日との間には一大改変が行われた.

V² a *revolution broke out* in ... ...に革命が起った.

Q a *bloodless revolution* 無血革命. ¶the *Bolshevik Revolution* 過激派革命. ¶a *complete revolution* in the world of taste 世人趣味の一大変革. ¶bring about a 2nd *industrial revolution* 第二の産業革命をもたらす. ¶a *mental revolution* 心機一転. ¶a *peaceful revolution* 平和革命.

Q² *Communist world revolution* 共産主義世界革命. ¶a *Fascist revolution* ファッショ革命. ¶the *talkie revolution* 発声映画のもたらした革命. ¶a program of *world revolution* 世界革命計画 ‖ the Communist doctrine of *world revolution* 共産党の世界革命綱領.

P Mexico *in revolution* 革命のメキシコ.

P² a *revolution against* the government (the king) 政府(など)に対する反乱. ¶the earth's *revolution around* (=

round or about) the sun 太陽を一周する地球の回転. ¶a *revolution in* opinion (our accepted habits of thought) 意見(など)の激変. ¶a *revolution of* ideas 思想の革命.‖a *revolution of* government 政変. 【類】a *revolution of* taste.

revolutionary, *a.* 革命的な.

M too *violently revolutionary* あまりにも急激に革命的な.

revolve, *v.* 回転する, 運行する.

M *ceaselessly revolve* 絶間なく回転する(水車など).

P The library *around* which student life *revolves* is one of the most important problems to be solved. 学生生活の中心となっている図書館は解決を要すべき最も重要な問題の一つである. ‖Planets *revolve around* (=*round*) the sun. 遊星は太陽の周囲を公転する. ¶I have long *revolved in* my mind whether I should not try to ... 私は...すべきでないか否かを長い間思い回らした. ¶*revolve on* its axis その軸を中心に回転する(自転する).

revolver, *n.* 《米》けん銃(ピストル).

V *carry* a *revolver* at one's side 腰にけん銃をさげる. 【類】The police are *carrying revolvers* for their own protection. ¶suddenly *draw out* (=*pull out, take out or produce*) a *revolver* from one's pocket 突然ポケットからピストルを取出す. ¶*fire* a *revolver* at ... ...をねらってピストルを打つ. ¶*level* (=*point*) a *revolver* at ... ...にピストルを向ける. ¶*whip* [*out*] (=take) a *revolver* from one's overcoat pocket その外とうのポケットからけん銃をぱっと取出す.

Q a fully *loaded revolver* 全部装てんしたけん銃. ¶a *six-chamber*[*ed*] *revolver* 六連発ピストル.

P *with* a *revolver* cocked ピストルの打金を上げて.

revue, *n.* レビュー.

Q a *spectacular revue* on the ice 壮観な氷上レビュー.

revulsion, *n.* 激変, 急変.

V This *brought about* a *revulsion* in the attitude of the Government towards foreigners. このために政府の外国人に対する態度に激変をきたした. ¶The feeling of the age *underwent* a *revulsion*. その時代の人心に急変を生じた.

Q an *immense revulsion* of feeling 感情の一大急変. ¶by a *natural revulsion* of feeling 自然に起った感情の反動で. ¶a *strong revulsion* of feeling 感情の激変.

reward, *n.* 報酬, 賞与, ほうび.

V I *ask* no *reward* besides ... ...以外にはほう美を欲しない. ¶the *reward* has never been *claimed* [懸賞の]賞を請求するものがなかった. ¶*confer* a *reward* for ... ...に対してほう美を与える. ¶*deserve* a *reward* 報酬を受ける価値がある. ¶You have well *earned* your *reward*. 君がほうびをもらったのは全く当然なことだ. ¶The officers of mercenary troops *expected* substantial *rewards* for their championship of Boer interests. 雇兵の士官たちはブーア軍のために戦ったので手厚い報酬が得られるものと期待した. ¶Follow this rule religiously and you will *find* your *reward*. まじめに守るとそれだけのことはありますよ. ¶*give* a *reward* for ... ...に対して謝礼をする. ¶*have* no *reward* for ... ...に対する報酬をもらわない. 【類】Whoever finds it and returns it to me shall *have* a liberal *reward* (多額の謝礼). ¶*hold out* a *reward* to ... ...に報酬を呈する. ¶He *offered* a *reward* of £100 for information which will lead to the recovery of the property. 彼はその物品を取りもどす手づるとなるような情報に対し百ポンドの礼をすると声明した. 【類】A *reward* of ... has been *offered* for information leading to the arrest of the thief. / publicly *offer* a *reward* to any one who ... / *offer* a $1,000 *reward* for ... ¶*pay* a *reward* to ... ...に報酬を払う. ¶he *proposed* the very large *reward* of £10,000 for the invention of ... 彼は...の発明に対し大枚一万ポンドの報酬を提供しようと申出た. ¶He *reaped* the *reward* to which he was undoubtedly entitled. 彼はその報酬を得たがたしかにその資格があった. 【類】*reap* the *reward* of virtue (善行). ¶*receive* the *reward* of one's labors 努力の報酬を受ける. ¶*yield* a rich *reward* to patient and careful study 根気のある注意深い研究をする人には十分な報酬が授かる.

Q find an *adequate reward* in the knowledge that ... ...を知ることが十分の報酬たることが分かる. ¶Her approbation was my *chief reward*. 彼女にほめてもらうことが私にとって第一のほうびであった. ¶such *fanciful reward* as a lady's smile 婦人の微笑というようなしゃれた報酬. ¶The work brought a great *financial reward*. その著作から著者は多大の収入を得た.‖reap the *financial reward* of his success as a breeder 飼育者としての成功に対し収入を得る. ¶a *fitting reward* for ... ...に対する適当な報酬. ¶receive *large* and *tangible reward* 大きな有形の報いを受ける. ¶He cares little about *monetary* (=*money*) *reward*. 彼は金銭上の報酬などは余り望んでいない.‖The labor of preparing the work has been its *own reward*. 労力そのものが報酬であった.‖bring a substantial *pecuniary reward* [それによって]多大の金銭上の報酬を得る. ¶*precarious rewards* of literature 文学のあてにならない報酬(小説などを書いて). ¶bring *rich rewards* 多大の報酬をもたらす. ¶*sundry rewards* 諸謝礼金. ¶a *well-earned reward* 当然受くべくして得た報酬. ¶a *well-won reward* 堂々と獲得した報酬.

Q² offer a *cash* (=*money*) *reward* for ... ...に対して現金報酬を提供する. ¶give *£100 reward* 百ポンドの賞を与える.

P *as* a *reward* for this courtesy この好意に対する返礼として. ¶*in reward* for one's services その勤労に対する報酬として.

P² *reward for* labor 作業賞与金‖*reward for* operation 作業賞与金. ¶the greatest *reward of* my labors 私の努力の最大の報酬.

reward, *v.* 報いる, 謝礼する.

M *reward abundantly* (=*amply*) 十分に報いる. ¶*reward bountifully* たっぷり報いる. ¶*reward generously* (=*nobly*) 気前よく報いる. ¶*reward* very *handsomely* たんまりと報酬をやる. ¶*richly reward* 豊かに報いる.

P he was *rewarded by* a gift from ... 彼は...からの贈物を頂だいした. 【類】For this discovery he has been *rewarded by* the Nobel prize. ¶His labors were *rewarded with* good fruit. 彼の努力はりっぱな成果をもって報いられた. 【類】We had a strenuous (骨の折れる) climb, but we were *rewarded with* a splendid view.

rewarding, *n.* 報い.

P² the *rewarding of* virtue and the punishment of evil 勧善懲悪.

rewriting, *n.* 書き替え.

V this *necessitated* the entire *rewriting* of the history of ... このために...の歴史をすっかり書き直す必要が生じた.

rhapsody, *n.* 狂詩曲(ラプソディー).

Q Liszt's *Hungarian Rhapsodies* リストのハンガリア狂詩曲.

P² a *rhapsody in* blue 《米》憂愁狂想曲. ¶a *rhapsody over* the charm of ... ...の美に対する狂詩曲.

rhetoric, *n.* 修辞学, 美辞.

V *attempt* no flowery *rhetoric* nor ambitious flights of eloquence けんらん花のごとき修辞も試みずまたとうとう懸河の弁をも試みない. ¶I *exhausted* all my *rhetoric* to persuade him to ... 私は口をすっぱくして彼に...することを勧めた.

Q a writing full of *stirring rhetoric* and biting satire 胸をおどらすような美辞と痛烈な皮肉に富んだ文. ¶*visionary rhetoric* 空論.

rheumatism, *n.* リューマチ.

V He *developed rheumatism* in his shoulder. 彼の肩がリューマチになった. ¶*ward off rheumatism* リューマチにかからないようにする.

Q *acute* (*chronic*) *rheumatism* 急(慢)性リューマチ.

P suffer *from rheumatism* リューマチに悩む. ¶He has a touch *of rheumatism*. 彼はリューマチの気味だ. ¶stiff *with rheumatism* リューマチで硬直して.

rhyme, *n.* 〖詩〗押韻, 韻語.

V The proper pronunciation of "hearth" *makes* a *rhyme* (=rhymes) with "garth" but not with "earth" hearth の正しい発音は garth とは韻が合うが earth とは合わない.

Q "Soldier, sailor, tinker, tailor, rich man, poor man, beggar, thief", as the *old rhyme* has it, they all dance. 兵隊も水兵も鋳掛屋も仕立屋も金持ち貧乏人もこじきも泥棒も, 古い言い草だがねこもしゃくしも皆ダンスをやる.

Q² sing a *nonsense rhyme* わけのわからない歌を歌う. ¶a *nursery rhyme* 子守歌.

P written *in rhyme* 韻文で書いた. ¶*without rhyme* or reason 分別のない, わけのわからない.

P² *Cat* is a *rhyme for mat*. Cat は mat と韻をふんでいる.

rhythm, *n.* 韻律, 律動.

Q the *faulty rhythm* of a sentence 文の誤ったリズム. ¶a *pleasing rhythm* 気持ちのよい韻律. ¶play in *quick*

rhythm 早い律動で奏する.
Q² *color rhythm* (=harmony) 配色の美. ¶the ***heart rhythm*** 心臓の鼓動.

rib, *n.* あばら骨.
P poke (=dig) a person ***in*** the ***ribs*** [意味ありげに]そっと人の横っぱらをこずく.

ribbon, *n.* ひも, リボン.
V ***hold*** the world's blue ***ribbon*** for ... ...では世界第一である. ¶I would like to have some hat to ***match*** this ***ribbon***. このリボンとあう帽子が欲しい. ¶***tie*** a ***ribbon*** in a hard knot リボンを固く結ぶ. ¶***wear*** a ***ribbon*** リボンを着ける.
Q a ***tawdry ribbon*** けばけばしくって安っぽいリボン.
Q² a ***baby ribbon*** 幅のせまいリボン. ¶a ***class ribbon*** 学級のリボン章. ¶pin a ***fourth-prize ribbon*** on the contestant 競技参加者に四等賞のリボンをピンでつける. ¶a ***typewriter ribbon*** タイプライターのリボン.
P clothes hanging ***in ribbons*** おんぼろ着物(ひじきの行列). ¶a piece (=length *or* trip) ***of ribbon*** 一本のリボン. ¶torn ***to ribbons*** ずたずたに裂けて.

rice, *n.* 米, 稲.
V ***cultivate*** (=***raise or grow***) ***rice*** 米を作る. ¶***harvest rice*** 米の収穫をする. ¶***hull rice*** もみ殻を除く. ¶***husk rice*** (=pound the rice from its husk) 米をつく. ¶***pound*** the steamed ***rice*** for mochi もちをつく. ¶***reap rice*** with a sickle かまで稲を刈る. ¶***thresh rice*** 稲を脱穀する.
Q ***boiled rice*** 飯. ¶***cleaned rice*** 白米. ¶***early*** (***late, middle-season***) ***rice*** 早(晩・中)稲. ¶***half-boiled rice*** しんのある飯. ¶***hulled rice*** 玄米. ¶***sprouted rice*** はい芽米. ¶***steamed rice*** むしご飯(赤飯など). ¶***unhusked rice*** もみ. ¶***white-polished rice*** 白米, 銀めし.
Q² ***black-mart rice*** やみ米. ¶***paddy rice*** 水稲. ¶farm deliveries of ***quota rice*** 割当て米の農家渡し(供米). ¶***upland rice*** 陸稲(おかぼ).
P a fine crop ***of rice*** 豊作. ¶feed ***on rice*** 米を常食とする.
P² ***rice in*** the husk もみ.

rich, *a.* 富んだ, 金持ちの; 高価の.
M ***enormously rich*** 非常に富裕な. ¶***exceptionally rich*** in ... ことに...に富んだ. ¶***intellectually rich*** 知性に富んだ. ¶His collection is ***particularly rich*** in works of this class. 彼の収集にはこの種の作が特に多い. ¶The soup is ***too rich*** (=thick). このスープはこ過ぎる. ‖ The color is ***too rich*** for real gold. 本ものの金にしては色がこ過ぎる.
P The soil of Russia is ***rich in*** ores of all kinds. ロシアの土壌は各種の鉱石に富んでいる. ‖ Japan is ***rich in*** contrasts. 日本は(新旧・東西など)対象の豊富な国である. 【類】 words ***rich in*** variety of senses and applications / ***rich in*** suggestions (experience, forms and colors) / an old man whose life has been ***rich in*** experiences / grow ***richer in*** experience (vocabulary) / Each session of the conference was ***rich in*** accomplishment (成果). / The museum is ***rich in*** fine specimens (標本). / The library is ***rich in*** historical and antiquarian works. ¶The annals of Yedo Castle are ***rich with*** (=in) incidents of interest. 江戸城の歴史は興味あるできごとに富んでいる.
Q² the ***new yen rich*** 新円成金.
O The ***rich*** are not always happy. 富める者必ずしも幸福とは限らない. ¶the idle ***rich*** 遊んでいる金持ち連. ¶The newly ***rich*** have not yet learned to give. 成金はいまだ与えることを知っていない. ¶get ***rich*** honestly 正直に金を作る. 【類】 get ***rich*** quick (成金).

riches, *n.* 富.
V ***amass*** tremendous ***riches*** 巨大な富を作る. ¶One cannot ***carry*** one's ***riches away*** with one. めい途まで金を持って行くわけにはいかない. ¶***despise riches*** 富をさげすむ. ¶***make riches*** 金持ちになる. ¶***pile up riches*** 富を築き上げる.
V² ***Riches*** do not always ***bring*** wealth. 富必ずしも幸ならず. ¶***Riches have*** wings. 〘諺〙 おかねは羽根が生えている.
Q ***great riches*** 巨万の富.
P greedy ***after riches*** 無性に富を欲しがって. ¶I would not do such a thing ***for*** all the ***riches*** of the world. 世界中の富をもらっても私はそんなことはしない.

richness, *n.* 豊富.
Q a mine of ***inexhaustible richness*** 無尽蔵の鉱山. ¶The ***verbal richness*** of the English language is marvellous. 英語の語いの豊富なことは実に驚く.

ricksha, *n.* 人力車.
V ***pull*** a ***ricksha*** 人力車を引く.
Q ***jumpy-bumpy rickshas*** ぴょこぴょこはね上りながら進んで行く人力車.
P photographed ***in*** a ***ricksha*** 人力車に乗って写した.

rid, *v.* 脱せしめる, 除去する, 追払う.
P ***rid*** the patient's mind ***of*** all ideas of ... 患者の心から...の考えをすべて除去する ‖ It is not easy to ***rid*** oneself ***of*** a bad habit. 悪い癖はなかなか抜けないものだ. 【類】 ***rid*** the house ***of*** the rats / ***rid*** the patient's mind ***of*** all ideas of organic affection (精神的でない肉体的の病気). ¶get ***rid of*** a troublesome burden やっかい払いをする ‖ visit Japan in order to ***get rid*** of the effects of a divorce 離婚のほとぼりをさますために日本に来る ‖ Holders appear anxious to get ***rid of*** stock. 保有者は在庫品を手離したがっているらしい. ‖ You can get ***rid of*** anything on him. 何でもあの人におっつければいいのさ. ‖ He is ***rid*** of fever. 彼は熱がとれた. ‖ The world is well ***rid of*** him. あんなやつが死んでいいやっかい払いをした.

riddance, *n.* 除去.
Q make ***clear riddance*** of street roughs (rats) まちのよたもの(など)を一掃する. ¶***Good riddance!*** やっかい払いをしてせいせいした. ‖ I had a ***good riddance***. やく払いをした. 【類】 It was a ***good riddance***.

riddle, *n.* なぞ, 判じ物.
V ***ask*** a ***riddle*** なぞをかける. ¶Shakespeare does not ***explain*** the dark ***riddle*** of life. シェイクスピアは人生の暗黒ななぞに触れていない. ¶***guess*** (=***find out***) a ***riddle*** なぞを当てる. ¶***propose*** (=***propound***) a ***riddle*** to ... ...になぞをかける. ¶attempts at ***solving*** the great ***riddle*** of existence 人生の大なるなぞを解こうとする種々の試み.
Q the ***eternal riddles*** of life 人生永遠のなぞ. ¶That is one of the great ***unsolved riddles***. それはまだ解けない大きななぞの一つである.
P You speak ***in riddles***. 君はなぞのようなことを言う.
P² It is still a ***riddle to*** us. それはいまだにとけないなぞだ.

riddle, *v.* なぞをとく.
O *Riddle* me a *riddle*, what's this?=*Riddle* me, *riddle* me what it is. なぞなぞなあに. 【類】 *Riddle* me this, can't you?

riddle, *v.* 数個所射たれる.
P The bird was ***riddled with*** shots. その鳥は数カ所散弾を食っていた.

ride, *n.* 乗馬, 騎行, 馬路.
V tourists ***enjoying*** a ***riksha ride*** 人力車に乗って行く観光客. ¶***get rides*** into a city (多数の人が bus などで) 市に乗込む. ¶I will ***give*** you a ***ride***. 君を乗せてあげましょう. ‖ ***give*** a child a ***ride*** on one's shoulders 子供を肩車に乗せる. 【類】 ***give*** him a ***ride*** in a boat. ¶***have*** a ***ride*** on a horse (bicycle, scooter, in a car) 馬(など)に乗る. 【類】 Let me ***have*** a ***ride*** in your car. ¶***offer*** one a ***ride*** 自動車に乗せて上げようという. ¶A train-jumper is one who ***steals*** a ***ride*** on a train. トレイン・ジャンパーとは汽車にただ乗りする人である. ¶get on a horse and ***take*** a ***ride*** 馬に乗って出かける. 【類】 ***take*** a ***ride*** in a boat (bus, buggy).
Q From ... to ... is a ***dusty ride*** of four or five hours. ...から...まではほこりだらけの道を馬に乗って四五時間かかる. ¶take one's ***first ride*** in the air 始めて飛行機に乗る. ¶a ***free ride*** on trains 列車の無賃乗車. 【類】 get a ***free ride*** in ... ¶a ***short*** (=***long***) ***ride*** on the electric cars 電車の短(長)時間乗車.
Q² enjoy an ***auto ride*** ドライブする. ¶a ***bicycle ride*** 自転車のひと乗り. ¶take a ***boat ride*** on the ocean ボートで海に出る. ¶a ***bus ride*** through the endless miles of streets はてしない街路のバスでの乗車. 【類】 go ***bus-ride*** / It's a 15-minute ***bus-ride***. ¶The hotel is within a ten minutes ***car ride*** of (=from) the station. ホテルは駅から十分位乗れば着く. ¶have an ***elephant ride*** 象に乗る. ¶a ***horseback ride*** 馬上で行くこと. ¶a ***joy ride*** ドライブ. ¶a ***nickel ride*** over short zones 五セントで短距離区間乗車. ¶a ***railroad ride*** of 110 miles through a wonderland of delight 楽しい驚異の国を通る百十マイルの汽車旅行. 【類】 a ***railway ride*** across Siberia. ¶a comfortable ***train ride*** 快適な汽車旅行. 【類】 a long, monotonous ***train ride***.
P go ***for*** a ***ride*** in a car (on a bicycle) 車(など)で出かける. ¶it is ***within*** two hours' train ***ride*** from ... それは...から汽車で二時間以内で行ける. 【類】 it is ***within*** an overnight's (一晩の) ***ride*** of ... / ***within*** [a] short streetcar ***ride*** of ...
P² a ***ride at*** a gallop かけ足乗馬. ¶it is only a short ***ride***

by rail from ... to ... ...から...までは汽車でほんのちょっとで行かれる. ¶a *ride in* an automobile 自動車での乗行.

ride, *v.* 乗る, 乗行する.

M cyclists ***riding alongside*** 自転車に並んで乗行する人々. ¶*ride* ***astride*** [馬に]またがって乗る. ¶*ride* ***away*** 馬に乗って去る; 自動車で去る. 【類】They *rode* ***away***, waving good-bye to us. ¶*ride* ***back*** in a car 車で帰る. ‖ *ride* a horse ***back*** to ... 馬に乗って...に帰る. ¶*ride* ***back*** and ***forth*** to one's work in a city 都市の職場に電車(バスなど)で通う. ¶*ride* ***barebacked*** はだか馬に乗る. ¶*ride* ***double*** (***single***) on an autocycle オートバイに相乗りする(一人で乗る). ¶*ride* ***full speed*** 全速力で駆ける(乗り回す). ¶The moon was *riding* ***high*** in mid-heaven. 月は高く天に昇っていた. ¶The country road *rides* ***hard***. そのいなか道は乗り心地が悪い. ¶*ride* ***horseback***=ride a horse 馬に乗る. ¶Teach me ***how*** to *ride* a bicycle. 自転車の乗り方を教えてくれ. ¶The boat *rode* ***out*** the storm in safety. 同船はしけを乗り切った. ¶*ride* ***roughshod*** over a person [比喩的]...にいばり散らす. ¶*ride* ***second-class*** 二等に乗る. ¶This car *rides* ***smoothly*** (***comfortably***). この車は揺れない(乗り心地がよい). ¶That horse *rides* ***well*** under the saddle. その馬は乗り心地がよい.

M^2 *ride* a bicycle ***down*** a country road 自転車でいなか道を行く ‖ He *rode* ***down*** three horses on his express mission. 彼は至急の用事で馬を三頭乗りつぶした. ¶*ride* ***in*** through a gateway 馬を門から乗り入れる. ¶*ride* ***up*** and ***down*** in an elevator エレベーターで昇降する.

P *ride* ***about*** London streets ロンドンの市街を乗り回す. ¶The moon is *riding* ***above*** the clouds. 月が雲の上にかかっている. ¶*ride* ***across*** a bridge 橋を馬上で渡る. ¶*ride* ***after*** ... ...の後を乗物で追う. ¶*ride* ***along*** the road one's bicycle=*ride* a bicycle ***along*** the road 自転車(など)で道を走る. ¶*ride* ***at*** full gallop 早かけで馬を飛ばす ‖ The fleets of eight nations *ride* ***at*** anchor in the harbour. 八国の艦隊が港に停泊している. ¶the horse was *ridden* ***by*** ... その馬には...が乗った. ¶*ride* ***down*** a hill on sledges そりに乗って小山を下る. ¶come back ***from*** a *ride* 乗馬(など)から帰って来る. ¶*ride* ***in*** an automobile (a streetcar) 自動車(など)に乗る. 【類】a man *riding* ***in*** a crowded car / *ride* ***in*** the train in the same compartment (室) / *ride* ***in*** a boat across (=over) a river (川を船で渡る) / He will take the baby for a *ride* ***in*** his wagon. ¶*ride* ***into*** a crowd 群衆の中に乗り入れる. ¶*ride* (=mount) ***on*** a horse 馬に乗る ‖ *ride* ***on*** a bus (train, bicycle, scooter) バス(など)に乗る. ☞ ride *on* a train (bus, plane) は米語用法. 【類】*ride* ***on*** horseback / let a child *ride* ***on*** one's back (shoulders) / The child *rode* ***on*** his father's back. / Many people can *ride* ***on*** this boat (船). / *ride* ***on*** a camel ‖ I was *riding* ***on*** a Nankai car last week reading a newspaper. 私は先週新聞を読みながら南海電車に乗っていた. ‖ *ride* a person ***on*** a rail《米》[リンチとして]人を横木に乗せる(黒人などを) ‖ *ride* ***on*** the beam (=on the wave of popularity) 人気の波に乗る. ¶*ride* ***over*** land 馬(車)で行く ‖ The moon was *riding* ***over*** the clouds. 月は雲を乗越えていた. ‖ *ride* one's horse ***over*** a fence 自分の馬にさくを乗り越えさせる. ¶He *rode* ***past*** our house. 彼は馬に乗ってわれわれの家の前を通った. ¶He *rode* ***through*** the train of the state procession of the prince of Satsuma. 彼は薩摩公の堂々たる行列を馬上で横切った. 【類】*ride* ***through*** the streets. ¶I *ride* ***to*** work in the cars. 私は電車で出勤する. ¶*ride* ***up*** the hill in a jeep ジープで丘を登る. ¶Ministers have been known upon occasion to *ride* ***up to*** a Cabinet Council upon their cycles. 大臣はときに自転車に乗って内閣々議に列することもあった. ¶*riding* ***upon*** an ox 雄牛に乗って. ¶*ride* ***with*** a great deal of dash 盛んに馬を走らせる.

rider, *n.* 騎手, 乗り手.

Q a ***good*** *rider* 巧みな騎手. ¶a ***bold*** and ***graceful*** *rider* 大胆で優美な乗馬者. ¶a ***splendid*** *rider* うまい騎手. ¶a daring ***trick*** *rider* 決死的曲乗芸人.

Q^2 a dare-devil ***auto*** *rider* 向う見ずな自動車運転手. ¶a ***bus*** *rider* バスに乗る人. ¶a ***circus*** *rider* 曲馬団の騎手. ¶a ***hobby*** *rider* (collector, etc.) 収集家(など). ¶A train slow-down plagued ***subway*** *riders* for two weeks. 鉄道員怠業のため二週間地下鉄の乗客が迷惑した.

P a horse ***without*** a *rider* 乗手のない馬.

P^2 a *rider* ***in*** a motor-car 自動車に乗る人 ‖ a *rider* ***in*** a bill 付属法案. ¶a *rider* ***on*** horseback 馬に乗る人, 騎馬の人.

ridge, *n.* うね, 峰.

Q The ***blue*** *ridges* of the Appalachian Mountains アパラチア山脈の青い群峰.

P^2 the *ridge* ***of*** an animal's back 動物の背の隆起部. ¶the *ridges* ***on*** corduroy cloth コール天地のうね.

ridicule, *n.* ちょうろう, 冷笑, ひやかし.

V without ***arousing*** *ridicule* ちょう笑を買うことなく. ¶***bring*** *ridicule* upon the heads of ... ...の頭上にちょう笑を招く. ¶***cast*** (=***throw***) *ridicule* upon (=on) ... ...をちょう笑する. ¶an object of ***deserved*** *ridicule* for foreigners 外国人から当然冷笑されるもの. ¶***direct*** *ridicule* against ... ...にちょう笑を向ける. ¶***draw*** *ridicule* upon oneself ちょう笑を招く. ¶say something that will ***excite*** *ridicule* ちょう笑を招くようなことを言う. ¶***heap*** further *ridicule* on ... ...に一層の笑いを買う. ¶***ignore*** *ridicule* ちょう笑を無視する. ¶without ***incurring*** *ridicule* ちょう笑を受けずに. ¶***launch forth*** keen *ridicule* against ... ...に痛烈なちょう笑を浴びせる. ¶***make*** one the *ridicule* of people ある人を世人の笑い物にさせる. ¶***pour*** (=***shower***) *ridicule* on ... ...にちょう笑をあびせる.

Q If ***good-natured*** *ridicule* is directed against you, meet it with good nature. 好意のひやかしはこれを好意で受けよ.

P a term applied ***in*** *ridicule* to ... ...をちょう弄する言葉 ‖ ***in*** *ridicule* of ... ...をちょう弄して. ¶turn everything ***into*** *ridicule* なにもかも笑いものにする. ¶hold up a person ***to*** *ridicule* 人をひやかす. ¶expose a person ***to*** *ridicule* 人をちょう笑の的にする. ¶overwhelmed ***with*** *ridicule* [あまりひどい]ちょう笑に面くらって.

P^2 In this we are the *ridicule* ***of*** other nations. この点においてわれわれは他国民の笑いものである.

ridiculous, *a.* ばかばかしい, あほらしい.

M ***extremely*** *ridiculous* 実にばかばかしい. ¶***utterly*** *ridiculous* 実にばか気た.

P *ridiculous* ***in*** dress (shape) 服装(など)がおかしい.

O It is *ridiculous* (=absurd) that ... ...とはばか気たことだ.

riding, *n.* 乗馬, 乗車.

Q^2 ***horseback*** *riding* 乗馬. ¶***autocycle*** (=***motor-bike*** or ***motorcycle***) *riding* オートバイ乗車.

rife, *a.* 盛んな, はやる.

P The English language is *rife* ***with*** maxims. 英語には格言が多い.

rifle, *n.* ライフル銃.

V carefully ***aim*** a shooting *rifle* 注意して猟銃をねらう. ¶***cock*** a *rifle* 小銃の引金を起す. ¶***fire off*** a *rifle* 小銃を発射する. ¶***handle*** a *rifle* 小銃を扱う. ¶***level*** a *rifle* at his head 小銃で彼の頭をねらう. ¶***shoot*** a *rifle* 発砲する. ¶***shoulder*** a *rifle* 銃を担う. ¶***slant*** a *rifle* across the chest 銃を胸に斜めに持つ. ¶***snap*** a shooting *rifle* 猟銃の引金を引く.

V^2 His *rifle* does not ***carry*** (=***reach***) ***far***. 彼の銃は遠くへ届かない.

Q a ***double-chambered*** *rifle* 二連発銃.

Q^2 a ***five-chamber*** *rifle* 五連発銃. ¶a ***toy*** *rifle* おもちゃの小銃. ¶a ***.22 caliber*** *rifle* .22 口径小銃.

P armed ***with*** a *rifle* 銃を持って.

rifleman, *n.* 射手.

Q an ***unerring*** *rifleman* 正確な射手.

rifle-range, *n.* 射程.

P ***out of*** (=***beyond***) *rifle-range* 小銃の射程外に. ¶***within*** *rifle-range* 小銃の射程内に.

rift, *n.* 裂け目, われ目.

V ***cause*** a *rift* in international friendship 国際関係に破たんを生ぜしめる.

P^2 There is a *rift* ***in*** the clouds. 雲に裂け目がある.

rig, *n.* 支度.

Q^2 ***working*** *rig* 作業服.

rig, *v.* 装備する, 艤(ぎ)装する, 着飾る.

M *rigged* ***out*** in full dress 美々しく着飾って ‖ *rig* one ***out*** completely 人に完全に服装をさせる. 【類】He is *rigged* ***out*** as a sailor (for a walk).

M^2 *rig* ***up*** a tent テントを急設する. 【類】*rig* ***up*** a shanty (山小屋) for a night's rest.

right, *n.* (**1**) 権, 権利.

V ***abridge*** a man's *rights* 人の権利を縮小する. ¶***abuse*** the *rights* 権利を乱用する. ¶***acquire*** the *right* in virtue of a treaty 条約によってその権利を獲得する. ¶***assert*** (=***insist on***) one's *right* to ... ...するその権利を主張する. ¶***buy*** the *right* of ... …の権利を買収する. ¶***claim*** one's *rights* その権利を要求する. 【類】***claim*** the *right* to ... ¶***concede*** fishing *rights* to ... …に漁業権を譲与する. ¶***defend*** the inalienable *rights* of life 生命という他に譲渡し得ない権利を防衛する. ¶No person shall be ***denied*** the *right* of access to the court. 〘憲法〙何人も裁判所において裁判を受ける権利を奪われない. ¶***devolve rights*** upon a person 人に権利を譲る. ¶He has not yet ***earned*** a *right* to a respectful hearing. 彼にはまだ敬意を払って聞いてもらうだけの貫ろくができていない. ¶***enjoy*** the same civil *rights* as other citizens 他の人同様の公民権を持つ. ¶***establish*** their *right* to live 彼らの生存権を確立する. ¶***exercise*** one's *rights* その権利を行使する‖***exercise*** the *right* of self-defense 自衛権を行使する. ¶***forfeit*** (=***lose***) one's *right* to ... …する権利を喪失する. ¶***give right*** to ... …に権利を与える‖***give*** a person the *right* to ... 人に…する権利を与える. ¶***give up*** (=***abandon***) the *right* of ... …の権利を放棄する. ¶***grant*** certain *rights* ある権利を付与する. ¶***guarantee rights*** 権利を保障する.【類】The freedoms and *rights* are ***guaranteed*** by this Constitution. ¶***have*** a *right* to the first place in the history of ... …の歴史において特筆大書さるべき権利を有する.【類】he ***has*** a full *right* to ... / In Mexico women do not ***have*** the *right* to vote. / ***have*** the *right* of voting / ***have*** the *right* of debating, but cannot vote. / A creditor ***has*** the *right* to demand payment. / What *right* ***have*** you to complain? ¶***hold*** prior *rights* 先取権を有する. ¶***ignore*** Japan's *right* to a voice in international politics 国際政治における日本の発言権を無視する. ¶***infringe*** the *right* 権利を侵害する. ¶***lose*** one's *right* to compete 競争する権利を失う. ¶***maintain*** one's *rights* その権利を保持する. ¶***obtain*** the *right* to place ... letters after one's name upon (=on) examination 試験によって自分の名前の後に…なる文字(学位)を付ける権利を得る. ¶Laws are made to ***protect*** our *rights* and not to take away our liberty. 法律はわれわれの権利を保護するためでわれわれの自由を奪うために作られたのではない. ¶No one ***questions*** the *right* of humanistic or scientific studies to university recognition. なに人も人文的または科学的科目が当然大学の課程たるべきことに異議はない. ¶***relinquish*** a *right* 権利を放棄する. ¶***renounce*** a *right* 権利を投げすてる. ¶***reserve*** the *right* to refuse the acceptance of ... …の引受拒絶の権利を保留する‖All *rights* ***reserved.*** 不許複製. ¶***respect*** the *rights* of others 他人の権利を尊重する. ¶***safeguard*** the *rights* of citizens 公民の権利を保護する. ¶***sell*** the *right* to ... …に権利を譲与する. ¶rigidly ***suppress*** the *right* of free speech 言論の自由を弾圧する. ¶***uphold*** their *rights* in the courts of law 法廷において彼らの権利を主張する. ¶properly ***use*** the *right* of franchise 普選の権利を正しく行使する. ¶***usurp*** the *rights* of ... …の権利を強奪する. ¶***waive*** one's *rights* 権利をすてる.

V^{2} One's *right* ***lapses.*** 権利を喪失する.

Q *right* ***alleged*** or ***recognized*** 主張されまたは認定された権利. ¶the protector of the people's ***civil rights*** 国民の人権の擁護者. ¶the ***divine right*** of creative instinct 創造的本能という神聖な権利. 【類】the ***divine rights*** of kings. ¶what ***earthly right*** has he to ...? 一体彼は…する権利があるか. ¶***equal right*** of men and women 男女同権. ¶have the ***exclusive*** *right* to ... …する独占権がある. 【類】a grant of the ***exclusive*** *right* of ... ¶Foreigners there enjoyed ***extra-territorial*** *rights.* そこの外人は治外法権を持っていた. ¶***friendly right*** 友誼的権利. ¶have the ***full right*** to that title その尊称を受ける十分な権利がある. ¶have a ***hereditary*** *right* to ... …する世襲権がある. ¶***human rights*** 人権‖the fundamental ***human rights*** 基本的人権. ¶an ***indefeasible*** *right* of man 人間の無効にしがたい権利. ¶***judicial right*** 司法権. ¶have a ***legal right*** to ... …する法律上の権利がある. ¶These belong to them by ***natural*** *right.* これらは生得の権利によって彼らのものである. ¶have a ***perfect right*** to ... …する完全な権利を有する. ¶a Parliament with wider ***popular*** *rights* さらに広い範囲にわたる民衆の権利を有する議会. ¶***preferential*** *right* 先取特権. ¶have the ***prior*** *right* to ... …に対して先取権を有する. ¶capacity for enjoying ***private*** *right* 権利能力. ¶trespass on some one's ***proprietary*** *rights* 人の所有権を侵害する. ¶***religious*** and ***civil*** *rights* 宗教上の権利及び民権. ¶have the ***sole right*** of ... …の独占権を有する‖the ***sole right*** of use 専用権. ¶be restored to the full exercise of his ***sovereign*** *rights* その主権の完全なる行使を回復する. ¶the ***unquestioned*** *right* of ... …の明白な権利. ¶a ***vested right*** 既得権利.

Q^{2} the ***acting*** *rights* in a play 脚本の上演権. ¶***book*** *rights* 版権. ¶***collective bargaining*** *rights* 〘労〙団体契約を行う権利. ¶***irrigation*** *rights* 用水権. ¶***labor*** *rights* 労働権. ¶first ***magazine*** (=serial) *rights* [小説などの]雑誌禁載権(複製権に対し). ¶***moving picture*** *rights* 映画版権. ¶infringe the ***patent*** *rights* of a rival firm 競争会社の特許権を侵害する. 【類】protected under United States ***patent*** *rights* of August 29, 1954. ¶***personal*** and ***property*** *rights* 人権及び財産権. ¶have ***priority*** *rights* over ... …に対して優先権を有する. ¶the infringement (=violation) of ***property*** *rights* 財産権侵害. ¶an ex-service man with ***reemployment*** *rights* 復職権を有する退役軍人. ¶***security*** *right* 担保権. ¶The ***surface*** *rights* here fetch about 4,000 yen per tsubo. 当地では地上権が坪約四千円で売れる. ¶***surface*** and ***subsurface*** *rights* 地上及び地下権. ¶***tenant*** *right* 小作権. ¶***treaty*** *rights* 条約上の権利. ¶***voting*** *rights* 選挙権. ¶***water*** *rights* 水利権.

P demand ***as*** a *right,* not to solicit as a favor お願いとして頼むのでなく権利として要求する. ¶***by*** *right* of conquest 征服の権利によって. ¶grant licenses ***for*** the *rights* to the invention その発明の権利に対して特許を与える‖stand up ***for*** one's *rights* その権利を擁護する. ¶***in*** one's own *right* [財産・爵位など]自分にその権利を所有している. 【類】The Baroness Beaumont, a peeress ***in*** her own *right,* was born in 1894 and succeeded to the title in 1896.‖From Shaw to Pellisier is not a great jump, for both are humorists ***in*** their own *right.* ショウからペリジアまでは大した隔りがない, どちらもそれぞれれっきとしたかいぎゃく家であるから. ¶It was, of course, wholly ***within*** my *right* to do so. もちろんそうすることは全く私の権限内にあった.‖it is ***within*** her technical *rights* to ... …することはその国が国際法で認められている権利である.

P^{2} *rights* ***for*** living=natural rights 生存権. ¶a *right* ***in*** ... …に関する権利‖*rights* ***of*** creditors against partners and partnerships 組合員及び組合に対する債権者の権利‖the *right* ***of*** preference (=priority) 優先権‖the *right* ***of*** veto 否定権. 【類】the *rights* ***of*** sovereignty of the state (主権)‖the *right* ***of*** way 通行権; 《米》鉄道[線路]用地‖Nor has he, as a right, *right* ***of*** way over the land of his neighbor. また彼は正当にその隣人の土地の通行権を持っているわけでもない. 【類】close to the *right* ***of*** way. ☞ 英語用法では the permanent way という.‖consideration of the *rights* ***of*** others 他人の権利の考慮. ¶a *right* ***to*** property (the use of land) 財産(土地使用)に対する権利‖*right* ***to*** a patent 特許権.

(**2**) 正義, 公道, 公義.

V ***dare*** the *right* 正義を無視する. ¶God ***defends*** the *right.* 神は正義を守る. 【類】It is man's duty to ***defend*** the *right.* ¶he has ***done*** right in ... 彼が…したのはもっともなことである. ¶I admit that they might ***have*** some *right* on their side. 私は彼らの方にもいくらか正しい所があるかも知れないということを認める. ¶***know*** *right* from wrong 正邪の区別を知る. ¶***scorn*** the *right* and choose the wrong 正義を軽んじ邪道を取る. 「しいか調べる.

V^{2} find out on which side the *right* ***lies*** どちらの方が正

P fight ***for*** *right* against wrong 正義のために邪道と戦う. ¶You are entirely ***in*** the *right.* 君は全く正しい.‖He contends that he is ***in*** the *right.* 彼は自分が正しいと主張する. 【類】I will not apologize because I am ***in*** the *right.* ¶set (=put) people ***to*** *rights* 人々の非を正す.

P^{2} the *right* ***of*** might 力の正義.

(**3**) 右, 右方.

O In the negative, *right* and left, and black and white are reversed. 陰画では右と左, 黒と白が逆になっている.

P sit ***at*** the *right* of ... …の右にすわる‖the picture ***at*** *right* shows ... 右は…の絵である(さし絵などの説明)‖I stood ***at*** her *right.* 私は彼女の右に立った.‖Three loud knocks are heard on the door ***at*** the *right.* 右手の戸を三度高くたたく音が聞える.‖To vote for a person mark a cross (×) ***at*** the *right* of the name. [選挙で]人を選挙するには名前の右側に × 印を付すること. 【類】***at*** the *right* of the main entrance. / the lofty mountains visible ***at*** the *right* are ... ¶turn to the neighbor ***on*** one's *right* その右側にいる人の方に向く.【類】If you go straight on, you will find a police-station ***on*** your *right*. / ***on*** the *right* of the entrance / sit ***on*** the *right* of one's hostess (女主人). ¶***to*** the reader's *right* 読者の右方に当って ‖ six miles ***to*** the *right* of ... ...の右六マイル ‖ We find ***to*** the *right* of the road a temple. 道路の右側にお寺がある. ‖ Keep ***to*** the *right* of the road. 右側通行.

right, *a.* 真すぐな, 正しい, 正確な.

M It is ***all*** *right*. それでよろしい. ‖ admitting it to be ***all*** *right* それはそれでいいとして.【類】Is it ***all*** *right* for me to come this evening? ‖ if things are ***all*** *right* with you 御都合よければ. ¶it is ***only*** *right* to ... ...して一向差支えない. ¶be only ***partially*** *right* ほんの少ししか正しくはない. ¶You are ***quite*** *right*. そうともそうとも.

P It is not *right* ***for*** children to sit up late. 子供が夜ふかしするのはよろしくない. ¶*right* ***in*** one's assumption (estimate) その説(など)が正しい.【類】am I *right* ***in*** assuming that ...? ¶it was quite *right* ***of*** you to ... 君が...したのは全く正しかった. ¶It is all *right* ***with*** him. 彼は大丈夫だ.

O set them *right* 彼らを正しくする. ¶*Right* you are.＝You're *right*. その通り.

right, *ad.* 正確に, ちょうど, 全く.

M Go *right* ***ahead***! 真すぐ行け; しっかりやれ. ¶*right* ***away*** 《米口》＝immediately 直ちに. ¶You'll find it *right* ***back*** of the building. その建物の背後にある. ¶I turned to find him *right* ***behind***. 振り返って見たら彼はすぐ後にいた. ¶*right* ***now*** 今すぐに. ¶He did his duty *right* ***nobly***. 彼は自分の本分を全くりっぱに果した. ¶The chorus rang out *right* ***heartily***. 唱歌隊が突如として熱心に歌い出した. ¶when the work is done *right* ***out*** 仕事が片づいたら.

M² *right* ***along*** 休まずに, ずんずん ‖ Come *right* ***along***, Tommy! トム公, 一緒にこいよ. ¶pay it *right* ***down*** 即金で支払う. ¶Come *right* ***in***! おはいり.

P It was *right* ***above*** my head. それは私の頭の真上にあった. ¶lean *right* ***against*** the wall 壁を背にしてもたれる. ¶fresh and sound tomatoes *right* ***from*** the vine 木から取りたての新鮮でいたみのないトマト. ¶Don't stand *right* ***in*** the middle of the road. 道路の真中に立つな. ¶read *right* ***through*** the book その本をずっと通読する. ¶*right* ***under*** your nose ちょうど君の鼻先に.

right, *v.* 正す.

P *right* her husband ***from*** the charge of murder 彼女の夫に対する殺害のけん疑を晴らす.

O *right* a wrong (an error, injustice) 不正(など)を正す.

right-about-face, *n.* 回れ右.

Q make a ***sharp*** *right-about-face* 回れ右をする, 百八十度の転換をする.

rigid, *a.* かたい.

P *rigid* ***in*** self-denial 自制心のごく強い ‖ *rigid* ***in*** one's views 考えがかたい.

rigo[u]r, *n.* 厳重, 厳格.

V ***escape*** (＝***avoid***) the *rigor* of winter きびしい冬を避ける.

Q prosecute ... with the ***utmost*** *rigor* of the law ...を法律の許す限り手きびしく処分する.

P enforce a law ***with*** *rigor* 法をきびしく施行する.

rikisha, *n.* 人力車.

Q a ***double*** *rikisha*＝a rikisha for two persons 二人乗の人力車. ¶one's ***own*** *rikisha* 抱え車.

P a *rikisha* ***with*** two men 二人びきの人力車.

rim, *n.* へり, ふち.

V ***protect*** the *rim* of a wheel 車輪のふちを保護する.

Q a straw hat with a ***broad*** *rim* つばの広い麦わら帽子. ¶a ***golden*** *rim* 王冠.

P² the *rim* ***of*** an eyeglass 鼻めがねのふち.【類】the *rim* ***of*** a teacup.

rind, *n.* 果皮, 外皮, 樹皮.

V ***strip*** the *rind* from (＝peel the rind off) cheese (a tree, a melon, an orange) チーズ(など)の外皮をはぐ.

ring, *n.* (1) 輪; 指輪.

V ***blow*** smoke *rings* タバコの輪を吹く. ¶All joined hands and ***formed*** a *ring*. 皆が手をつないで輪になった. ¶***have*** a *ring* on one's finger 指に指輪をはめている.【類】The moon ***has*** a *ring* about it.＝There is a *ring* around the ***moon***. ¶***make*** some *rings* of smoke 二三度タバコの輪を吹く. ¶***pass*** a *ring* over a finger 指輪をはめる. ¶***puff*** *rings* of smoke ぱっぱっとたばこの輪を吹く. ¶***put*** a *ring* on one's finger 指輪をはめる. ¶a *ring* ***set*** with a jewel 宝石をちりばめた指輪. ¶***wear*** a *ring* on one's finger 指輪をはめる.

Q² a ***diamond*** (***gold, silver***) *ring* ダイヤ(など)の指輪. ¶The moon has a ***gold*** *ring*. 月に金色のかさがかかっている. ¶a ***life*** *ring* 救命ゴム輪. ¶an ***engagement*** *ring* 婚約の指輪. ¶a ***marriage*** (＝***wedding***) *ring* 結婚指輪. ¶a ***napkin*** *ring* ナプキンはさみ輪. ¶a ***seal*** *ring* 印形付きの指輪. ¶a ***signet*** *ring* 印形付きの指輪.

P sit ***in*** a *ring* 車座にすわる ‖ dance ***in*** a *ring* 輪になって踊る ‖ a diamond ***in*** a *ring* 指輪のダイヤ. ¶keys ***on*** a *ring* 輪に入れてあるかぎ. ¶He looked very badly, ***with*** *rings* under his eyes. 彼は目の下に(黒い)輪ができてはなはだすぐれない顔をしていた.

P² *rings* ***of*** smoke from cigarettes 紙巻タバコの煙の輪 ‖ the *rings* ***of*** a tree 木の年輪. ¶a *ring* ***on*** (＝***upon***) one of one's fingers 一本の指にはめてる指輪.

(2) 仲間, 一団; 競技場(リング).

V ***keep*** the *ring* clear for the combatants [けん]闘士のためにリングを片づけておく.

Q In many American cities the government is controlled by a ***political*** *ring*. 多くのアメリカの都市では政府が一群の政治家に牛耳られている.

Q² a ***blackmarket*** *ring* やみ屋の一団. ¶a cigarette ***bootlegging*** *ring* 巻タバコ密売団. ¶a ***jeep theft*** *ring* ジープ窃盗団. ¶a ***narcotics*** *ring* 麻薬密売団. ¶a ***prize*** *ring* けん闘場. ¶a ***smuggling*** *ring* 密輸入の一団. ¶a ***spy*** *ring* スパイ団. ¶the ***Tammany*** *ring* タマニー派(ニューヨークのタマニーホールを根拠とする民主党の一派).

P meet ***in*** the *ring* リングで顔が合う.

(3) 鈴の音, 響き, 調子; 《口語》電話.

V ***answer*** the *rings* of the telephone bell 電話のベルの音に応じる. ¶***give*** a poetic *ring* 詩らしい響きを与える ‖ ***Give*** me a *ring*＝Give me a call. お電話を下さい. ¶His words ***have*** a *ring* of insincerity. 彼の言葉にはそらぞらしい調子がある.

V² A *ring* ***came*** to my door. 私の家の玄関のベルの音がした.

Q Names that have a ***familiar*** *ring* were played at as men behind the project. 知名の士をその計画の後援者ということにした. ¶a sort of forced laugh, with a ***hollow*** *ring* in it うつろな響きのある一種の作り笑い. ¶in words that have a very ***modern*** *ring* きわめて近代調の言葉で. ¶The expression has the ***old-fashioned*** *ring* about it. その言葉は古臭い. ¶There is a ***pleasant*** *ring* about it. それは聞いて気持ちがいい. ¶There is the ***true*** *ring* of romance in it. それには小説的な真の調子が出ている. ¶have a somewhat ***unfamiliar*** *ring* 耳遠い響きがする.

P ***at*** the third *ring* of the bell 三度目のベルの音で.

P² a *ring* ***at*** the bell ベルの鳴る音.【類】There was a *ring* ***at*** the door. ¶There is no *ring* ***of*** sincerity in the remark. その言にはまじめな響きがない.

ring, *v.* 鳴る, 《英》電話をかける.

M The bells *rang* ***clear***. ベルがはっきりした音で鳴った. ¶The warning bell began to *ring* ***furiously***. 警戒のベルがけたたましく鳴り出した. ¶His preachings *ring* ***hollow***. あの人の説教は上ついている. ¶The wedding bells are *ringing* ***merrily***. 結婚式のベルが愉快な音で鳴っている. ¶A bell *rings* ***out***. ベルが鳴り出す. ‖ *ring* ***out*** a temple bell 寺の鐘を鳴らす ‖ Two shots were *rung* ***out*** from the ship. 同船から二つ弾丸がずどんと発射された. ‖ *ring* ***out*** the Old Year and *ring* ***in*** the New 旧年を送り新年を迎える. ¶This coin *rings* ***true***. この貨幣は本物の音がする. ‖ The call *rings* ***true*** to one's heart. その呼びかけはぐっとこたえる.

M² *ring* ***off*** sharply がちゃんと電話を切る ‖ *rang* ***off*** in disgust at his importunities 押しつけがましいのでいやになって電話を切った. ¶His name is *ringing* the country ***over***. 彼の名声は全国に鳴り響いている. ¶*ring* ***up*** several times 《英》数回電話をかける ‖ *ring* ***up*** the Exchange＝《米》call the Central 電話局を呼び出す.【類】*ring* ***up*** a doctor / *ring* ***up*** late at night.

P Who is *ringing* ***at*** the door? 玄関のベルを鳴らしているのはだれだ. ‖ *ring* ***at*** the bell ベルを鳴らす. ¶*ring* ***for*** a servant ベルを鳴らして召使を呼ぶ.【類】*ring* ***for*** a porter (page) / *ring* ***for*** dinner (breakfast, etc.) / The bells are *ringing* ***for*** church (礼拝を告げる). ¶The bells are

still *ringing in* our ears. 鐘の音がまだわれわれの耳に残っている. 【類】The words are still *ringing in* my ears. ‖ *ring in* history 歴史に残る. ¶*ring* (=sound) *like* common sense 常識らしく響く. ¶His brilliant deeds in war *rang through* the country. 彼のはなばなしい戦功は国中に鳴り渡った. ¶The cashier *rang* the silver coins *upon* the counter. 出納係はその銀貨をカウンターの上で鳴らして見た. ¶The whole town *rings with* his fame. 町中に彼の名声が響き渡っている. ‖ The hall *rang with* cheers (laughter). 講堂はかっさいで鳴り響いた(笑いでどよめいた).
O I will *ring* if I want anything. 何か欲しい時はベルを鳴らします.

ringleader, *n*. 首謀者.
Q a *little ringleader* がき大将.

ringlet, *n*. [毛髪の]巻毛.
P [*with*] a *ringlet* or two over her forehead 巻毛が一本二本たれ下って.

rink, *n*. スケート場.
Q^2 an *ice-skating rink* スケート場. ¶a *roller-skating rink* ローラースケート場.

rinse, *v*. すすぐ, 洗い清める.
M Please *rinse out* this bottle. このびんをすすいで下さい. 【類】*rinse out* clothes in water / *rinse out* one's mouth.
M^2 *rinse* it *down* with a glass of beer 一杯のビールとともに飲み込む.

riot, *n*. 騒動, 乱暴; 放縦.
V *cause* a *riot* 騒動を起す. ¶He *got up* a *riot* in defiance of the law. 彼は法律を無視して暴動を起した. ¶*instigate* a *riot* 暴動を教唆する. ¶*make* a *riot* 乱暴する. ¶*put down* a *riot* 暴動を鎮定する. ¶send troops to *quell* a *riot* 暴動を鎮定すべく軍隊を派遣する. ¶*raise* (=*start*) a *riot* 暴動を起す. ¶*stage* a *riot* 暴動を起す. ¶*suppress* a *riot* 暴動を鎮圧する.
V^2 a serious *riot broke out* at ... ...で一大騒動がぼっ発した.
P a *riot of* color (sound) もろもろの色(音)の乱舞. 【類】The mountain slope is a *riot of* autumn coloring, the brilliant scarlet blending with the browns and toned with greens of every shade (色合い).
Q^2 an *election riot* 選挙騒ぎ. ¶*Food riots* are rife. 食糧暴動が盛んだ. ¶a *mass riot* 集団暴行. ¶a *May Day riot* メーデー騒動. ¶look as if a *miniature riot* is going on ひと騒動始まったように見える. ¶a *race riot* [アメリカの黒白人のような]人種問題の暴動. ¶a *student riot* 学校騒動.

rioter, *n*. 暴徒.
V *lead rioters* 暴徒を指揮する.
Q^2 the noise of *street rioters* 路上の酔漢のけんそう.

riotous, *a*. 騒々しい.
P be *riotous with* color 千紫万紅である.

rip, *v*. 切り開く, ひっ裂く.
M *rip away* the secrecy from ... ...から無理に秘密を聞き出す. ¶*rip open* an envelope (a letter) 封筒(手紙)を引き裂いてあける. 【類】*rip open* a bag. ¶*rip out* an oath のろいの言葉をはく(ば声をあげる). 【類】*rip out* a curse (悪口) when excited.
M^2 *rip off* the lining 裏をはぎとる. 【類】*rip off* a coupon. ¶*rip up* the belly 割腹する.
P *rip* buttons *off* the coat 上衣のボタンをむしりとる.

ripe, *a*. 熟している; 円熟した.
M *Soon ripe*, soon rotten. 〖諺〗早熟早老, 大器晩成.
P a girl (=maiden) *ripe for* marriage 結婚適齢の少女 ‖ The time is not yet *ripe for* it. まだその時期でない. ‖ confidential information or facts not yet *ripe for* publication まだ発表し得ない秘密な報道や事実. 【類】*ripe for* action (mischief). ¶*ripe in* judgment 分別盛りの. ¶*ripe with* experience 経験に富んだ.

ripen, *v*. 熟させる; 熟する, 成熟する.
M *ripen* just *good* for eating [果実が]ちょうど食べごろだ. ¶Time will *soon ripen*. まもなく機が熟する.
P *ripen* fruit *by* artificial heat 人工熱で果実を熟させる. ¶With some people acquaintanceship never *ripens into* friendship. 人によって顔見知りというだけで決して友人という所まで進展しないことがある. ‖ *ripen into* maturity 成熟する. 【類】Thinking *ripens into* resolve and *into* action.

ripeness, *n*. 成熟.
Q in the *full ripeness* of one's powers その力量が円熟しているので.

ripple, *n*. さざ波, 波紋.
P The moon (light) danced *on* the *ripples* of the lake. 月光が湖水のさざ波にちらちらした.
P^2 a *ripple of* talk and laughter ざわめく談笑.

rise, *n*. 上昇; 立身; 興起.
V *achieve* a wonderful *rise* 異常の立身をする. ¶*anticipate* a rise in the market 市況の上げを予想する. ¶*get* a *rise* of salary 俸給を上げてもらう. ¶The Japanese cherry flowers *give rise* to little fruits like cherries. 日本の桜は桜桃の小さな実を結ぶ. ‖ The news has *given rise* to a variety of conjectures and accounts. そのニュースが各種の推量憶測を生んだ. ‖ It may *give rise* to serious trouble. それが由々しいことになるやも知れない. 【類】*give rise* to doubts / I told him all the particulars that had *given rise* to the difficulty. / be likely to *give rise* to mistakes / *give rise* to much controversy / His going away at this time will *give rise* to evil reports. ¶Anglo-German hostility *had* its *rise* in trade competition. 英独戦争はその源を商業上の競争に発した. ¶*make* a spectacular *rise* 著しく出世する. ¶the elements of modern civilization which *owe* their *rise* to the Middle Ages 中世紀にその源を発した現代文明の要素. ¶expect to *see* an early *rise* in the price of ... ...の値段が遠からずあがるものと見る. ¶*sustain* a climactic *rise* of interest 興味が終局まで次第に増進するようにする. ¶The Hayakawa *takes* its *rise* in Lake Ashi. 早川は源を芦の湖に発する. ‖ *take* (=*get*) a *rise* out of ... ...をへこます; に一杯食わす ‖ The expression *took* its *rise* in America. その言回しはアメリカ製だ.
Q a *gentle rise* to ... ...までのなだらかな隆起. ¶its *gradual rise* in importance その重要性の漸進的増加. ¶a *great rise* in prices and wages 値段や賃銀の高騰. ¶a *sensational rise* in the price of building materials 建築材料費の突飛な高騰. ¶a *sharp rise* 急な上り坂 ‖ a *sharp rise* in quotations 相場の急騰. ¶a *sudden rise* in temperature 気温の急激な上昇. 【類】a *sudden rise* in price.
Q^2 a 12 per cent *pay rise* (=raise) 十二パーセントの昇給. ¶a *price rise* 物価騰貴. ¶be granted a *salary rise* 昇給される. ¶I had a *twenty-pounds rise* in pay. 私は給料が二十ポンド上った. ¶a 15 per cent *wage rise* 十五パーセント賃上げ.
P *at* the *rise* of the moon 月の出に. ¶hold it *for* a *rise* in price 物価騰貴を待ってそれを売らずにおく ‖ cry *for* a *rise* (=《米》 raise) in pay 昇給の必要を訴える ‖ ask *for* a *rise* in salary 昇給の請求をする. ¶speculate *on* a *rise* 騰貴を思わくする. ¶the town declined *with* the *rise* of ... その市は繁栄を...に奪われた.
P^2 a *rise in* blood-pressure 血圧高進 ‖ the *rise in* the cost of living 生活費の増加 ‖ a demand for a *rise in* salary (pay) 増給の要求. 【類】*rise in* rents and land values (地代と地価). ¶the *rise* and fall *of* Rome ローマの興亡 ‖ a *rise of* 1 in 30 三十分の一の上りこう配. ¶Japan's *rise to* supremacy in the Orient 東洋における日本の優越.

rise, *v*. 上がる, のぼる; 起きる; 高くなる.
M mountains *rise abruptly* from ... 山が...から急にそびえる. ¶*rise appreciably* 目立って上昇する. ¶The thought *rose dimly* in my mind. その考えがぼんやり私の心に浮んだ. ¶*rise early* [in the morning] 早起をする. ¶Coal prices had consequently *risen fabulously*. その結果石炭の値段がばかに騰貴した. ¶The river is *rising fast*. 川の水が急速に増している. ¶*gradually rise* to supremacy 漸次には権を握る. ¶Salmon *greedily rise* to the fly. さけが盛んに擬似えにつく. ¶as the sun *rises higher* 太陽が段々のぼるにつれて. ¶He *rose immensely* in our estimation. 彼はわれわれの間で大いに男をあげた. ¶Towering snow-capped peaks *rise majestically* from the very waterside. 天空にそびえる雪をいただく群峰がほんの水際から雄大にきつ立している. ‖ *rise majestically* above the neighboring peaks 隣れる群峰の上に厳然とそびえる. ¶Fish *rose merrily* to my fly. 魚が愉快そうに私の擬似えに食いついた. ¶Waves do not *rise more* than twelve feet above the level of calm water. 波浪はないだときの水面から十二フィート以上はあがらない. ¶*rise naturally* to the lips 自然口に出る. ¶A quarrel *often rises* from mere trifles. けんかはよくつまらないことがもとになる. ¶The cost *rose outrageously*. 生産費が法外に騰貴した. ¶hills *rising precipitously* from the water's edge 突こつとして水際からそそり立つ山々. ¶*rise quickly* from one's seat (=chair) 急いで席から立上る. ¶He *rose rapidly* into notice. 彼はとんとん拍子で有名になった. ¶with the mountains *rising sheer* from the shore 山々がじかに岸からそびえ立って. ¶Prices are *rising stead-*

ily. 値段がどんどんあがる. ¶*rise **steeply*** from the deep water 深い水際から急坂をなして立っている. ¶***suddenly** rise* in importance 急に重要なものになる. 【類】the price has ***suddenly** risen* very lately. ¶*rise **superior*** to ... ...をしのぐ.

M² *rise **up*** in revolt against ... ...にそむく ‖ *rise **up*** in protest むっとして立ち上る ‖ The castle *rose **up*** sheer from the lake. 城は湖畔真近に立っていた. ‖ *rise **up*** from kneeling ひざまずいた状態から起き上る.

P The sun *rises **above*** the horizon. 太陽は地平線からのぼる. ‖ Democracy cannot *rise **above*** the level of the human material of which its voters are made. デモクラシーはその投票者の人格以上に向上することはできない. 【類】*rise **above*** the level of common people / *rise **above*** mediocrity (=the ordinary level). ¶*rise **after*** a hundred falls 百たび倒れても起つ. ¶The people *rose **against*** the government (tyrant). 人民は政府(など)に反抗した. ‖ *rise **against*** a resolution (bill) 決議(など)に反対する. ¶The river *rises **among*** the hills. その川は山間に源を発している. ¶*rise **at*** a fixed early hour 一定の早い時間に起きる ‖ Salmon parr will *rise **at*** anything. 幼いさけは何を見ても飛びつく. ‖ *rise **at*** the summons 応召して立つ ‖ The House *rose **at*** 7 in the evening. 議会は午後七時散会した. ¶The idea *rose **before*** my mind. その考えが私に浮んだ. ¶Mists *rise **from*** the ground. 地上からもやが立ち上る. ‖ Tokyo *rose **from*** the ashes. 東京は灰じんの中から復興した. ‖ if it were possible for him to *rise **from*** the grave (=dead), he would ... もし彼が墓場から生き返ることができたら... ‖ They were just *rising **from*** dinner (the table). 彼らはちょうど晩さんの席(食卓)から立つところであった. 【類】*rise **from*** one's bed (seat) / *rose **from*** a low position (低い地位) / He *rose **from*** his seat to welcome us. / He *rose **from*** obscurity to fame (=renown). / *rise **from*** comparative penury (貧乏) to the possession of millions / *rise **from*** the ranks (下っぱ) / Trouble *rises **from*** misunderstanding. ‖ we *rise **from*** the book with a feeling of ... その本を読んで巻をおおう時われわれは...と感じる. ¶*rise **in*** life (=the world) 出世する ‖ *rise **in*** the scale of usefulness 有用な人となる ‖ The river *rises **in*** a mountain. その川は源を山地に発している. ‖ The land about Genoa *rises **in*** hills, which are backed by the Apennines. ゼノアの周囲は小山になっておりその後方はアペニン山脈に続いている. ‖ *rise **in*** power 権力が強まる. 【類】a singer *rising **in*** popularity / *rise **in*** price (pay, salary, wages). ‖ on *rising **in*** the morning 朝起きると ‖ The sun *rises **in*** the east and sets in the west. 太陽は東にのぼり西に没する. ‖ *rise **in*** a riot 暴動を起す. 【類】*rise **in*** revolution (revolt) against ... ‖ *rise **in*** arms 武器を取って立つ. ¶*rise **into*** importance (power, a dangerous ascendency) 重要な地位(など)にのぼる ‖ *rise **into*** an eloquence だんだん言葉に熱が出て来る ‖ Adams rapidly *rose **into*** favor with Ieyasu. アダムスはたちまち家康の気に入った. ‖ The Eiffel Tower *rises* 1000 feet ***into*** the air. エッフェル塔は高さ一千フィートに達する. ¶The Kurobe-gawa *rises **on*** Washigadake, on the boundaries of Etchu, Hida, and Shinano. 黒部川は越中・飛弾・信濃の国境たる鷲ケ岳に源を発する. ‖ *rise **on*** horseback 馬上に立つ ‖ feel one's hair *rise **on*** end 髪の毛がさかだつような気がする ‖ The color *rose **on*** her cheeks. 彼女のほおがぽっと赤くなった. ¶*rise **out of*** the crowd 群を抜く. ¶The sun *rose **over*** the wood and day was beginning. 朝日が森にさして夜が明けかけていた. ¶The hill *rises **to*** a thousand feet. その山は高さ一千フィートある. 【類】The mountain *rises **to*** a height (=an altitude) of ... above sea level. / The mountain *rises **to*** the westward (西方). / *rise **to*** a higher level (水準) ‖ He was not able to *rise **to*** the high level of the sacrifice demanded for kingship. 彼は王者たるに必要な犠牲を払うだけの義勇がなかった. ¶He went to work for the bank as office boy at 16 and *rose **to*** a $900 clerkship. 彼は十六歳のとき銀行の小僧を振出しに九百ドルの事務家にまで出世した. ‖ He has held most of the important offices of state, finally *rising **to*** premiership. 彼は国家の大抵の要職につき最後に首相になった. 【類】*rise **to*** the rank of a first-class military power (陸軍一等国) / *rise **to*** fame / *rise **to*** the Deputy-Governorship of New South Wales / *rise **to*** a position of importance and esteem in his community / *rise **to*** the highest station / This was the beginning of a career (経歴) in which he *rose **to*** the top of his profession. / *rise **to*** a height of prosperity / *rise **to*** high note (名声) / *rise **to*** high distinction / He has *risen **to*** national fame. / he *rose **to*** extraordinary eminence (抜群の高位) in the service of ... / He *rose **to*** eminence at Paris as a journalist and author. / The town soon *rose **to*** importance. / *rise **to*** great power and influence ‖ It does not *rise **to*** the dignity of a science. それはりっぱな一科学をなすまでになっていない. 【類】His language does not *rise **to*** the dignity of poetry. / provincialisms (方言) which have *risen **to*** literary rank ‖ The tears *rose **to*** his eyes. 彼の目に涙が浮んだ. ‖ *rise **to*** one's feet 起立する ‖ struggle [to *rise*] ***to*** one's feet 立ち上がろうと骨を折る ‖ *rise **to*** the occasion それにあたれるだけの力量を出す. ¶*rise **with*** the dawn (lark) 夜明け(など)とともに起きる.

riser, *n.* 起き手, 起きる人.

Q He is an ***early*** (a ***late***) *riser*. 彼は早起き(朝寝坊)である.

rising, *n.* 上り, 上昇; 起床; ほう起; 反乱.

V ***hail*** the *rising* of the sun 日の出を迎える.

Q ***early** rising* 早起き. ¶a ***popular** rising* 民衆のほう起.

Q² a ***peasants** rising* 百姓一き.

P ***at*** the *rising* of the moon 月の出に.

risk, *n.* 危険, 冒険.

V I cannot ***accept*** the *risk*. 私はその危険な仕事を引受けられない. ¶***assume*** the *risk* voluntarily 進んで危険な仕事を引受ける. ¶***cover*** all *risks* 全損害を負担する. ¶in order to ***decrease*** the pecuniary *risk* attending so large and costly a venture かく大きな費用のかかる事業に伴う金銭上の危険を軽減するために. ¶***diminish*** this *risk* この危険を少なくする. ¶totally ***eliminate*** the *risk* of ... ...の危険を全然のぞく. ¶***enhance*** the *risk* of ... ...の危険を増す. ¶***face*** the *risk* of ... ...の危険を冒す. ¶***incur*** the *risk* of certain penalties 必らず罰を受ける恐れがある. ¶***involve** risk* 危険を伴う. 【類】***involve*** a *risk* of life. ¶***lessen*** the *risk* of ... ...の危険を少なくする. ¶***minimize*** the *risk* of fire 火災の危険を最小限度にする. ¶***multiply*** our *risks* a hundred per cent. われわれの危険を百パーセント増す. ¶***reduce*** to a minimum the *risk* of ... ...の危険を最少限度に少なくする. ¶Some *risk* must be ***run***. 多少の冒険はやらねばならない. 【類】***run*** the *risk* of losing one's popularity / ***run*** the *risk* of carrying coals to Newcastle (だそくを添える). ¶***take*** a *risk* (=chance) 一か八かやってみる. ¶have the nerve (=courage) to ***take*** great *risks* to life and limb 生命と負傷の危険をおかすだけの勇気がある ‖ ***take** risk* with ... ...をやって見る. ¶***undertake*** the *risks* その危険を引き受ける.

Q at ***all** risks*=at any risk あらゆる危険をおかして, 是が非でも. ¶undertake a ***certain** risk* 幾分危険なことをやる. ¶He saved three men alive at ***considerable** risk* to himself. 彼は非常な危険をおかして三人を救助した. ¶There is a ***constant** risk* that a large-scaled organisation will become depersonalised to those who work in it. 大きな会社の使用人は会社が人であるという考えを持つことができなくなるおそれが絶えずある. ¶take ***foolish** risks*=be foolhardy 向う見ずなことをする. ¶run the ***formidable** risk* of ... ...という恐るべき危険をおかす. ¶at ***frightful** risk* to life and limb 生命及び手足への大きな危険をおかして. ¶run the ***grave** risk* of ... ...という非常な危険をおかす. 【類】take ***grave** risks* to save persons in peril. ¶at ***great** risk* to life 非常な生命の危険をおかして. 【類】There is a ***great** risk* of being icebound. / take ***great***, unusually ***foolish***, *risks*. ¶exposed to ***heavy** risks* of loss 非常な損失の危険にさらされて. ¶There is very ***little** risk*. 危険がきわめて少ない. ¶a step of ***much** risk* 大なる危険のともなう手段. ¶there is ***no** risk* of ... ...の危険がない. ¶at ***owner's** risk* 所有主負担で. ¶I am willing to take a ***reasonable** risk*. 私は相当危険があっても進んでやる積りだ. ¶run a ***serious** risk* of ... 大いに...のおそれがある. ¶take ***small** risks* あまり危険なことをやらない.

Q² ***fire** risk* 火災危険率. ¶***traffic** risk* 交通の危険. ¶***war** risk* 戦争の危険. 【類】***War** risk* to be covered by buyer (shipper).

P Some of the snaps (=photos) have been taken ***at*** [the] *risk* of life and limb. 写真の中には身命をかけてとったものもある. ‖ ***at*** the *risk* of repetition (=repeating) I must emphasize (=let me emphasize again) that ... くどいよ

うだが私は…と言うことを強調せねばならない ‖ ***at*** the *risk* of repeating facts with some of which you are doubtless already familiar 中には諸君がきっとすでに熟知していられるものもあってまたかと言われるかも知れないが ‖ ***at*** the *risk* of being considered obtrusive (=impolite) 差出口のようですが. 【類】 ***at*** the *risk* of being termed old-fashioned and conservative, we will repeat here advice that … / ***at*** the *risk* of being tedious (くどいようだが), I cite another illustration / ***at*** the *risk* of being tedious, I must repeat once more what I have said already—that … / ***at*** the *risk* of admitting a poor taste in literature, I may confess at once that … / ***at*** the *risk* of being accused of sensationalism (…とのお小言もあろうが) ‖ prohibit … to be employed ***at*** the *risk* of incurring a fine 違反は科料に処するということで…の使用を禁止する ‖ ship ***at*** the *risk* of … …の負担で出荷する. ¶free ***from*** *risk* 危険がない. ¶***on*** (=at) one's own *risk* 自分の負担で.

P^2 It was a *risk* ***of*** a thousand to one in my favor. それは九分九厘まで自分に有利な思わくであった.

risk, *v.* 冒険する.

P *risk* one's life ***for*** honor's sake 名誉のために生命をかける.

risky, *a.* 危険な, けんのんな.

P *risky* ***to*** life 生命に危険を及ぼす.

rite, *n.* 祭式, 儀式.

V the funeral *rite* was ***performed*** over the body of … …の遺がいに対して葬式が行われた.

Q ***burial*** (=***funeral***) *rites* 葬式. ¶***conjugal*** (=***nuptial***) *rites* 夫婦のちぎり. ¶hold ***funeral*** *rites* for … …の葬式を営む. ¶***liturgical*** *rites* 礼拝式. ¶a ***sacred*** *rite* 祭式. ¶celebrate its jubilee with ***various*** *rites* 種々な儀式でその祝典を催す.

Q^2 ***church*** *rites* 教会の諸儀式. ¶The funeral will be performed according to ***Shinto*** *rites*. 葬式は神式で挙行する.

P ***according to*** the consecrated *rites* 祭式によって. ¶The funeral service will be ***in*** Buddhistic *rites*. 葬式は仏式による. ¶The service was conducted ***with*** Buddhist *rites*. その儀式は仏式で行われた.

P^2 the last *rites* ***over*** the dead [告別式など]最後の儀式.

ritual, *n.* 儀式, 礼式, 式典.

Q ***ornate*** *rituals* はなやかな儀式.

P ***with*** a duly prescribed *ritual* 一定の式に従って.

P^2 a *ritual* ***for*** the worship of deities 敬神の儀式.

rival, *n.* 敵手, 競争者, 相手.

V ***crush*** one's *rival* その対手をまいらせる. ¶***defeat*** (=***beat***) one's *rival* 相手をやっつける. 【類】 He ***defeated*** his nearest *rival* … by 483 votes to 296. ¶successfully ***defy*** all *rivals* あらゆる敵手と戦って勝つ. ¶vastly ***excel*** one's *rivals* その敵手をはるかにしのいでいる. ¶We ***expect*** *rivals* in the field. われわれはその方面に競争者があるものと見ている. ¶They have ***had*** no *rival*. 彼らには競争者がなかった. ¶***humble*** a *rival* 競争者をへこます. ¶***outbid*** the *rivals* 競争者よりも高価をつける. ¶***outdo*** (=***surpass*** *or* ***overcome***) one's *rival* 自分の競争者を負かす. ¶***outplace*** these foreign *rivals* これら外国の競争者を排除する. ¶***run down*** one's *rivals* 対手を弱らせる. ¶***undersell*** one's *rivals* 相手より安く売る.

V^2 A formidable *rival* ***came*** to the front. 強敵が現われた.

Q an ***aggressive*** *rival* 攻勢に出る敵手. ¶a very ***close*** *rival* to … …にとって兄たり難く弟たりがたいもの. 【類】 his ***closest*** *rival*. ¶a ***defeated*** (=***beaten***) *rival* 負けた相手. ¶***doughty*** *rivals* 勇敢な敵手. ¶our ***enterprising*** *rival* われわれの進取的な競争者. ¶a ***formidable*** *rival* 強敵. ¶The town is a ***neighbouring railway-born*** *rival*. その町は鉄道のためにできた隣接の競争地である. ¶a ***powerful*** *rival* 有力な敵手. ¶a ***strong*** *rival* 強敵. ¶The book has no ***successful*** *rival* in its particular field. 同書はこの種のものとしては比較しうるものはない. ¶find a ***worthy*** *rival* in him 彼が手ごわい相手と分かる.

Q^2 ***business*** (=***trade***) *rivals* 商売がたき.

P a game ***with*** *rivals* 対手との一勝負. ¶It is ***without*** a *rival*. それと肩を並べるものがない. 【類】 remain ***without*** a *rival* among …

P^2 he has few *rivals* ***among*** … …の間に彼と肩を並べる者は少ない. ¶*rivals* ***for*** the trade 商売がたき ‖ his *rival* ***for*** the hand of Miss … …嬢に対する恋の競争者. ¶a *rival* ***in*** love 恋がたき. 【類】 They were good *rivals* ***in*** wealth. ¶a *rival* ***of*** equal skill 技巧の劣らない相手. ¶a serious *rival* ***to*** … …に取って由々しい競争相手.

rival, *v.* 競う; 匹敵する.

M No one could even ***remotely*** *rival* him. 何人も遠く彼に及ばなかった.

P *rival* ***for*** priority 先を争う. ¶Her cheeks *rival* the rose ***in*** hue. 彼女のほおはばらのように赤い. ‖ No other nation can *rival* England ***in*** this respect. この点ではどの国民も英国と比肩しえない. 【類】 It *rivals* ***in*** magnitude and splendor (壮大豪華) any of the cities of the whole world. / None in this part can *rival* him ***in*** wealth. / She will never *rival* … ***in*** popularity. ¶*rival* ***with*** … ***for*** a prize 賞を得ようと…の向うを張る.

rivalry, *n.* 競争, きっ抗.

V ***stimulate*** healthy *rivalry* 健全な競争を刺激する.

V^2 Keen *rivalry* ***sprang up***. 激烈な競争が起った.

Q ***acute*** *rivalry* 鋭い競争. ¶***Anglo-Japanese commercial*** *rivalry* in the Orient 東洋における日英両国の商戦. ¶there was ***bitter*** *rivalry* between … …間には激しい競争があった. ¶***friendly*** *rivalry* 友好的競争. ¶***professional*** *rivalry* 職業上の競争. ¶the spirit of ***strenuous***, but ***friendly*** *rivalry* 奮闘的でしかも友情的な競争精神. ¶***unfair*** *rivalry* 不公正な競争.

Q^2 ***Hindu-Moslem*** *rivalries* 回・印教徒の争い. ¶***trade*** (=***business***) *rivalry* 同業者同士の競争, 商売がたき.

P This puts us ***above*** *rivalry*. このためにわれわれは他の追随を許さないのである. ¶***in*** bitter *rivalry* 激しく競争して. ¶enter ***into*** *rivalry* with … …と競争を始める. ¶the keenness ***of*** their *rivalry* 彼らの競争の激烈さ.

P^2 *rivalry* ***against*** … …との競争. ¶the *rivalry* ***between*** the two powers 二国間の競争. ¶There is keen *rivalry* ***for*** these appointments. これらの就職には激烈な競争がある. ¶the *rivalry* ***in*** ostentation 見せびらかしの競争. ¶get (=enter) ***into*** *rivalry* with … …と競争を始める. ¶friendly *rivalry* ***with*** the trade of foreign nations 貿易上他国家との友情的競争.

river, *n.* 川.

V ***ascend*** (=***go up***) a *river* 川をさかのぼる. ¶rain ***caused*** the *river* to rise to a height of … 雨で川は…の高さまで増水した. ¶The *river* is ***crossed*** by a fine iron bridge. その川にはりっぱな鉄橋がかかっている. 【類】 The Yenisei *River* is ***crossed*** by the trans-Siberian railway at Krasnoyarsk. ¶***descend*** (=***go down***) a *river* 川を下る. ¶***deepen*** a *river* 川を深くする. ¶The frost ***enchained*** the *river*. 川が氷結した. ¶***ford*** a *river* 川を徒渉する. ¶All the *rivers* have been ***inundated*** since the recent heavy rainfall. 最近の豪雨以来すべての川がはんらんした. ¶the street ***lines*** the *river* from … to … …から…までは川沿いの片側町になっている. ¶***navigate*** a *river* 川を航行する. ¶A steel railway bridge ***spans*** the Yalu *River*. 鉄道の鉄橋が鴨緑江にかけてある. ¶***straighten*** a *river* 川筋を真すぐにする. ¶Floods ***turn*** *rivers* out of their course. 洪水は川の方向を変える. ¶***widen*** a *river* 川幅を広げる.

V^2 The *river* has ***dried up***. その河水がかれた. ¶The *river* ***falls*** (=***discharges, enters or empties***) into the Pacific. その川は太平洋に注ぐ. ¶The *river* ***flows*** through hills and fields. その川は山や野を流れている. ¶the *river* ***joins on*** to … その川は…と合流する. ¶The *river* is ***meandering*** through hills and fields. 川は山や野をまがりくねって流れている. ¶*rivers* ***meet*** each other at … 諸川が…で合流する. ¶The *river* ***rose*** (=***swelled***). その川は増水した. ‖ wait for the *river* to ***rise*** 水かさが増すまで待つ. ¶The *river* ***runs*** (=***rushes***) into a lake. その川は湖水に注ぐ. ¶The *river* ***sinks***. 河水が減る. ¶The *river* ***sweeps*** past some chalk cliffs curiously hollowed out by water. その川は水のために珍しいかっこうに削られた白亜質のがけに沿って流れて行く. ¶Here the *river* ***trends off*** to the west. ここでその川は西方へ転向する. ¶The *river* ***wanders eastward***. その河は東方へ流れて行く. ¶A *river* ***winds*** through a plain. 一条の川が原野をうねって流れる.

Q an ***affluent*** *river* とうとうたる河流. ¶The ***bloated*** *river* began to subside rapidly. ふくらんだ河水は急速に減り始めた. ¶a ***busy*** *river* 交通のさかんな川. ¶Irving has made the Hudson a ***classic*** *river*. アービングはハドソン川

を古典的なものにした. ¶*commercial rivers* 通商上重要な河. ¶a firmly *frozen river* かたく結氷している川. ¶The *river* is *higher* than usual at this season on account of recent heavy rains. 近ごろの大雨で川はこの季節の平常水準より高くなっている. ¶a very *large* and *commodious river* 非常に大きく便利な川. ¶a *long, winding river* 長い曲りくねった川. ¶a *magnificent river* 壮大な川. ¶a *meandering river* 曲りくねった川. ¶a large *navigable river* 大きな航行に便利な川. ¶a *narrow* (*wide*) *river* 狭い(広)い川. ¶a *swift limpid river* 急流で水の澄んだ川. ¶a *swollen river* 増水した川. 【類】The *river* is *swollen* by rain. ¶a *tidal river* 潮入りの川. ¶a *turbulent stony river* 水音はげしい岩石の多い川. 【類】*turbulent rivers* rushing merrily along over rocks and pebbles, making sweet music as they go to join the sea. ¶an *unfordable river* 徒渉できない川.

P throw a bridge *across* a *river* 川に橋をかける ‖ a cottage *across* the *river* 川向いのかやぶきの小屋. ¶the scenery *along* the *river* 川岸の風景. ¶Excellent trout-fishing can be obtained *at* the *river*. その川のますつりはすてきだ. ¶*beyond* the *river* 川向うに. ¶go (sail) *down* a *river* 川を(船で)下る. ¶catch fish *in* the *rivers* 川で魚を捕える. 【類】He was drowned *in* the Sumida *River*. / A ferry-boat capsized *in* the Tone *River*. / John baptized Christ *in* the *river* Jordan. ¶the boat race *on* the Thames テムズ川のボートレース ‖ a display of fireworks *on* a *river* 川の上での花火の打上げ ‖ the collapse of embankments *on* a *river* 川の中に築堤の崩壊 ‖ a sluice *on* a *river* 水門 ‖ rafts *on* the Yalu *River* 鴨緑江上のいかだ. ☞ the *River* (or *river*) Thames は英国式で, the Hudson *River* は米国式. 【類】maple leaves *on* the Tatsuta *River* / artificial propagation of salmon *on* the Columbia *River* / a cargo junk (荷船) *on* the Yangtze[-kiang] *river* (揚子江) / I had a few days' fishing *on* the *river*. / There is hardly any traffic *on* the *river*. ¶A new bridge *over* the *river* was publicly opened yesterday. その川の新橋はきのう開通した. ‖ cross *over* a *river* 川を渡る. ¶... miles *up* the *river* from ... ...から川を上って...マイル. ¶boat races *upon* the *river* その川のボート・レース.

P[2] a *river of* lava 溶岩の流れ.

river-side, *n.* 河岸. 「テル.

P a hotel *by* the *river-side*＝a river-side hotel 河岸のホ

rivet, *n.* びょう(リベット).

Q[2] a *boiler rivet* ボイラー用のリベット(びょう). ¶a *steel rivet* 鋼鉄のびょう.

rivet, *v.* くぎづけにする, 固定する.

M tin plates *riveted together* リベットで留めてあるブリキ

M[2] be *riveted up* びょうで留めてある. 「板.

P The incident is *riveted in* my mind. その事件は私の記憶にはっきりしている. ¶The speaker's eyes were *riveted on* his manuscript. 弁士は草稿と首引きで演説をやった. ‖ All the eyes were *riveted on* the speaker. みんなの目は演者に集中された. 【類】*rivet* one's attention *on* (＝*upon*) ... ¶*rivet* one's eyes *to* ... ...に目を据える.

road, *n.* 道路, 路, 行路; 方法, 手段; 《米》劇団の回る地方; 《米》鉄道.

V *bar* the *road* to betterment 改善の途をふさぐ. ¶*block* a *road* 道路をふさぐ. ¶trees *bordering* a *road* 道の境になっている立木. ¶*break* a *road* through new country 新開地に道路を作る. ¶*break up roads* 道路を掘り返す. ¶*build* [*up*] a *road* to ... ...へ道路を建設する. 【類】*build up roads* and bridges. ¶*clear* the *road* 道の障害物を除く. ¶*find* the right *road* 正しい路を見つける. ¶*follow* the *road* running along the banks of the river その川沿いの道路について行く. 【類】We *followed* the *road* with difficulty. ¶*lay out roads* 道路を敷設する. ¶*macadamize* a *road* 道路に砕石舗装をする. ¶*make* a *road* to ... ...へ道をつける. ¶*mend* the *road* 道路を修理する. ¶*mistake* the *road* 道を間違える. ¶*obstruct* the *road* 道路の妨害をする. ¶A new *road* was *opened* to traffic. 新道が開通した. ¶*return* the *road* followed 行った道を戻る. ¶*rut* a *road* 道路に(車輪の)わだちをつける. ¶*show* a person the *road* to ... ...への道を人に教える. ¶The *road* ahead is temporarily *stopped* for repairs. これから先きの道路は修繕のため一時通行止. ¶*strike* a *road* 道路を切り開く. ¶*take* the *road* 〔劇〕地方巡業に出かける ‖ *take* the first *road* to the left 最初の道を左に取る. 【類】*taking* this *road*, the traveler soon comes to ... ‖ cars ready to *take* the *road* 運転の用意のできた自動車. ¶*traverse* a rough and difficult *road* でこぼこしていて困難な道路を踏破する. ¶It is tiresome to *walk* the same *road* every day. 毎日同じ道を歩くのはあきあきする.

V[2] the *road ascends* rapidly to ... ...への道は急に上り坂になっている. ¶the *road branches* off at ... 道は...で二またになっている. ¶There the *road breaks* into three. ここでは道は三方に分かれる. ¶The *road crosses* the river by a bridge. 道は橋で川向うへ通じる. ¶The *road descends* steeply. 急に下り坂になる. ¶a point where the *road divides* 道路の交差点. 【類】We arrived at a place where the *road divided* into two. ¶this *road extends* from ... to ... この道路は...から...へ通じている. ¶the *road forks* for either ... or ... その道は...と...へ分かれる. ¶the *road goes* to ... その道は...へ通じる. ¶*roads intersect* at ... 道路は...で交差する. ¶Here two *roads join*. ここで二つの道が一しょになる. ¶two *roads lead* to ... from ... ...から...へは道が二つついている. 【類】Where does that *road lead*? ¶Your *road lies straight* before you. 君はこの道路を真すぐ行けばよい. ¶This *road operates* 20 trains a day. 《米》この鉄道は一日二十列車を運転する. ¶The *road runs southward*. その道路は南方へ通じる. 【類】a good *road runs* from ... to ... ¶here the *road turns* up the valley of ... この所で道は...の谷を上って行くことになる. ¶An automobile *road winds* along the precipices. 断がいにそって自動車道がうねっている.

Q a *broad road* 広い道路. ¶It was a *busy road* that day. その日は交通がひん繁だった. ¶*different roads* to the same end 同じ目的(地)へ達する色々な路(方法). ¶a long *dusty road* 長いほこりっぽい道路. ¶a *fine road*, running for some three miles straight as a die 真すぐに三マイルばかり走っているりっぱな道路. ¶a *forked road* 二また道, 追分け. ¶a much (＝well) *frequented road* 往来のはげしい道路. ¶There is no *golden road* to success. 成功に至る王道なし. ¶a *hard-surfaced road* 表面の固い道路(舗装した). ¶a *heavy road* full of stones and ruts 石やわだちだらけの悪路. ¶a *high road* to fortune 幸運への大道. ¶take the *left road* 左の道を取る. ¶a *level road* 平らな道路. ¶a *lonely road* さびしい道. ¶a *long dusty road* 長いほこりだらけの道路. ¶take the *main road* 本道を取る. ¶a *motor road* 自動車道. ¶a *muddy road* 泥んこの道路. ¶the *only road* to success lies in ... 成功へのただ一つの近道は...である. ¶a *precipitous road* 急坂路. ¶a *prefectural road* 県道. ¶a *rough road* laying bare small rocks all along 一面に小石がでているでこぼこした道路. 【類】A cart rattled down a *rough road*. ¶a *round-about* (＝*circuitous*) *road* 回り路. ¶There is no *royal road* to learning. 学問に王道なし. ¶a very *rugged road* ひどいでこぼこ道. ¶a *rural road* いなか道. ¶a deeply *rutted road* [車輪の]わだちの深いあとのある道路. ¶Our *road* is the *same*. あなたも私も行く道は同じである. ¶a *shorter* (*longer*) *road* 近(遠)道. ¶a *sloppy road* 水たまりだらけの道路. ¶The *roads* must be *slushy*. 雪融けで道が悪いに違いない. ¶a *smooth road* なめらかな道路. ¶a *snow-drifted road* 雪だまり道. ¶a *stony road* 石ころ道. ¶a *straight* and *easy road* 真すぐで楽な道. ¶the *surest road* to success 成功への最も確実な道. ¶a *tortuous road* 曲りくねった道路. ¶The car tipped on an *uneven road*. 道路のでこぼこで車が傾いた. ¶places where the *road* is "*up*" [修理などで]道路の「掘上げてある」場所. ¶a *wide road* 広い道路. ¶go (＝take) the *wrong road* 違った道を行く.

Q[2] an *accommodation road* 特設道路. ¶a *carriage road* 車道. ¶a *coast road* runs to ... 海岸添いの道が...に通じる. ¶a *concrete road* コンクリート道路. ¶two hours' ride over the *cog road* アプト式鉄路二時間の旅. ¶a *corduroy road*＝a road made of logs 木材舗道. ¶stand at the *cross-roads* of world's history 世界史の十字路に立つ. ¶a *dark country road* 暗いいなか道. ¶a *gravel road* 砂利道. ¶a *macadam road* 砕石舗道. ¶a *motoring road* 自動車道路(ドライブウエイ). ¶an inn on a *mountain road* 山道にある宿屋 ‖ The heavy cart bumped along the rough *mountain road*. でこぼこ山道を重い荷車がごとごと行った. ¶a *night road* 夜道. ¶an excellent *red-earth road* すばらしい赤土道路. ¶the *Silk Road* 〔中国〕絹街道. ¶a *town road* 町道. ¶an ***uphill*** *road* 上り坂道. ¶a ***village*** *road* 村道. ¶a ***wagon*** *road* 馬車(トラック)道路.

P A big tree lay ***across*** the *road*. 大木が道に横になっていた. ¶go ***along*** the *road* 道にそうて行く ‖ troops encamped ***along*** the *road* 道路にそうて露営した軍隊. ¶Bolshevism ***at*** the cross-*roads* (＝crossroads) 岐路に立つ過激主義. ¶A big tree lies ***athwart*** (＝across) the *road*. 大木が道に横になっている. ¶tramp or ride ***by*** *road* or rail てくるか汽車かで行く ‖ go to London from the North ***by*** *road* 北方陸路からロンドンへ行く. ¶walk ***down*** a *road* 道路にそうて歩く ‖ They took to their heels ***down*** the *road*. 彼らは道路を逃げて行った. ¶Change ***for*** the Delaware and Schuyler Valley *roads*. 《米》〖掲示〗デラウエア及びシューワイラーバレー線行の方はお乗り換え. ☞米語の road は英語の line に当る. 米国では鉄道の方が州(公)道などより先にできたためという. ¶They met ***in*** the *road*. 彼らは道路で出会った. ¶pave the surface ***of*** a *road* 道路の表面を舗装する. ¶companions ***on*** the *road* 道連れ ‖ accidents ***on*** the *road* 路上事故 ‖ milestones ***on*** the *road* of death 死出の旅路の一里づか ‖ a young woman only a little way gone ***on*** the *road* to vice ほんのちょっと悪に染まっただけの若い女. 【類】be ***on*** the *road* to success / He is well ***on*** the *road* to recovery. / The patient is ***on*** the *road* to improvement. ‖ The jinrikisha is ***on*** the *road* to extinction. 人力車はなくなりかかっている. ‖ play ***on*** the *road* [劇団の]地方巡業をやる ‖ troupe ***on*** the *road*＝an itinerant troupe. 旅役者の一座. ¶walk ***over*** a *road* 路上を歩く. ¶The course will be over the *road* ***from*** Nagoya ***to*** Kobe. 進路は名古屋から神戸への路上にある(競走など). ¶the *road* ***to*** ruin (wealth, success) 破滅(など)に至る路 ‖ on the *road* ***to*** Tokyo 東京への途上に ‖ take ***to*** the road 旅行に出かける.

roadhouse, *n.* 街道の宿屋(レストランなど).

P stop ***at*** a *roadhouse* for a meal ロードハウスに立寄って食事をとる.

roadside, *n.* 路傍.

P I saw some yellow flowers growing in the grass ***at*** the *roadside*. 路傍の草の中に黄色い草花が生えているのを見た. ¶a tea house ***by*** the *roadside* 路傍の茶屋. 【類】a guidepost (道標) ***by*** the *roadside* / a shrine standing ***by*** the *roadside* / a stone put up ***by*** the *roadside* to mark the distance. ¶trees ***on*** the *roadside* 路傍の木. 【類】an inn ***on*** the *roadside*＝a roadside inn, a roadhouse.

roam, *v.* うろうろする; 遊歴する.

P *roam* ***about*** the second-hand bookstores in Kanda looking for ... ...を探して神田の古本街をうろつき回る. 【類】*roam* ***about*** the world. ¶*roam* ***from*** place ***to*** place 所々を放浪する. ¶*roam* ***over*** the country 国中を放浪する.

roar, *n.* 怒号, うなり, とどろき.

V ***hear*** the *roar* of the waves 波の怒号を聞く. ¶The *roar* of the city is ***hushed***. 市のけん騒が静まる.

Q ***angry*** *roars* 怒号. ¶***cannon's*** *roar* 大砲のとどろき. ¶motors running with a ***great*** *roar* ごうごうと音をたてて回るモーター. ¶a ***loud*** *roar* of laughter 高い笑い声. ¶The rain came down in a ***steady*** *roar*. 雨は絶えず音を立てて降った.

P ***in*** the *roar* of the sea 怒とうの中に. ¶***with*** a terrible *roar* 恐ろしい音を立てて.

P² the *roars* ***of*** a lion しし く. ¶The *roar* ***of*** the fire was audible for an incredible distance. 火事場のどよめきが信じ得ないほど遠くまで聞えていた. 【類】the *roar* ***of*** a tempest (暴風) / There was a *roar* ***of*** buying and selling in the market.

roar, *v.* どなる, 怒号する.

M A train *roared* ***away*** overhead. 列車は頭上をごうごう通り過ぎた. ¶*roar* ***fearsomely*** [野獣などが]恐ろしくたける. ¶*roar* oneself ***hoarse*** どなって声をからす. ¶*roar* ***out*** どなり立てる. ¶The train *roared* ***past***. 列車がごう音を立てて通過した.

M² *roar* ***down*** 大声でしかりつける.

P *roar* ***at*** a person 人にどなりつける. ¶The train *roared* ***past*** the bridge. 列車はごうと音をたてて橋を通過した. ¶Storm *roared* ***through*** the forest. 暴風が森林をほえて通った. ¶*roar* ***with*** laughter 爆笑する.

roast, *v.* やく, あぶる.

M The burglar was *roasted* ***alive***. その夜盗は火あぶりの刑に処せられた.

P *roast* oneself ***at*** the fire 熱くなる位火にあたる. ¶The meat is *roasted* ***to*** a turn. 肉がころ合にやけている.

rob, *v.* 奪う, 略奪する, 強奪する.

M The house next to mine was *robbed* ***last week***. 先週隣家に泥棒がはいった.

P Gangsters *robbed* a bank ***of*** $10,000. ギャングが銀行から一万ドルを奪った. ‖ I got a glorious view, ***of*** which the bad weather of the year before last had *robbed* me. 私は一昨年天気が悪くて見ることができなかった美しい景色をながめた. 【類】Prejudice, more than anything else, *robs* life ***of*** its educational value. / *robbed* ***of*** the fruits of victory / *rob* an apple-tree ***of*** its fruit / *rob* it ***of*** its efficiency / The ocean voyage has been *robbed* ***of*** its perils. / The changes now beginning in Syria have *robbed* it ***of*** its ancient dresses and customs. / The word "..." *robs* this sentence ***of*** its dignity. / They were *robbed* ***of*** their means of existence. / A change in the personnel of the Department *robbed* him ***of*** his support in high quarters (有力な支持者). ‖ This *robbed* him ***of*** all liberty of thought. これで彼はなにがなんだか夢中になってしまった.

robber, *n.* 盗賊, 泥棒, 強盗.

V The *robber* was ***caught*** red-handed (＝in his act). 強盗は現行中を捕われた. ¶***intensify*** the *robber* as ... その泥棒は...であると判定する. ¶***outwit*** the *robber* 泥棒をだしぬく.

V² The *robber* ***fell*** upon him. 強盗は彼を襲撃した.

Q a gang of ***armed*** *robbers* 凶器携帯の強盗団. ¶a ***banded*** *robbers* 集団強盗.

Q² a ***highway*** *robber* 追いはぎ. ¶a gang of ***train*** *robbers* 集団列車強盗の一味. ¶a ***woman*** *robber* 女白浪.

P² a *robber* ***in*** a bank 銀行強盗.

robbery, *n.* 強奪, 強盗.

V ***commit*** *robbery* 強盗をやる. ¶The *robbery* was ***reported*** at the Central Police Station at eight o'clock the next morning. 翌朝八時にその強盗事件は中央警察署に報告された.

V² a *robbery* ***took place*** at ... ...に強盗事件があった.

Q ***armed*** *robbery* 凶器携帯強盗. ¶***audacious*** *robbery* 大胆不敵な強奪. ¶a ***bold*** and ***successful*** *robbery* 大胆にやり遂げた強奪. ¶***daring*** *robbery* 大胆な強奪. ¶***daylight*** *robberies* 白昼の強奪. ¶***highway*** *robbery* 追いはぎ(行為). ¶***extensive*** *robbery* 広はんにわたる強奪. ¶it would be ***sheer*** *robbery* to ... ...するならば全く強盗も同然であろう.

Q² organized ***bank*** *robbery* 集団銀行ギャング. ¶a ***daylight*** *robbery* 白昼の強盗行為. ¶a ***gang*** *robbery* 集団強盗. ¶a ***pearl*** *robbery* 真珠泥棒. ¶*robbery* ***with*** (＝***by***) violence 強盗(行為).

P live ***by*** *robbery* 強盗を商売にする.

robe, *n.* 外衣; [一般に *pl.*] 着物, 衣服.

V ***don*** the *robe* of ... ...の式服をまとう. ¶***wear*** the flowing *robe* ひらひら垂れる外衣を着る.

Q a ***black flowing*** *robe* ひらひら垂れる黒い外衣. ¶clad in ***ceremonial*** *robe* 式服を着た. ¶clad in very ***costly*** *robes* 高価なドレスを着て ‖ a very ***costly*** *robe* of silk 非常に高価な絹の着物. ¶newest London styles in ***dainty*** *robes* 最新ロンドン流行の美しいドレス. ¶priests in ***gorgeous*** *robes* 華美な法衣姿の僧りょ. ¶with her ***loose*** *robes* flying in the wind 彼女のゆるやかな着物を風にひらめかして. ¶wearing his ***official*** *robes* 官服を着て. ¶***royal*** *robes* 王服. ¶a lady in ***white*** *robe* 白服の婦人.

Q² a ***bath*** *robe* 浴衣 ‖ a quilted ***bath*** *robe* [羽毛入れ]さし子の浴衣. ¶Her majesty will be represented in her ***Coronation*** *robes*. 女王陛下は戴冠式礼装で表わされる(写真などで).

P a woman ***in*** her trailing *robes* 長いすその着物を着ている女.

P² in the *robes* ***of*** state 礼装をして ‖ in the *robes* ***of*** Chancellor of Oxford University オックスフォード大学名誉総長服を着て.

robe, *v.* 着る, 装う.

P *robed* ***in*** black (purple, white) 黒(など)の衣を着て.

robot, *n.* ロボット.

Q like a ***lifeless*** *robot* 生命のないロボットのように.

rock *n.* 岩, 岩石, 暗礁; 《米》小石.

V ***strike*** *rock* 座礁する ‖ The ship ***struck*** a *rock* at the entrance. その船はその入口で暗礁に乗り上げた. ¶Waves ***wear away*** *rocks*. 波は岩を磨滅する. ¶A *rock* is ***weathered*** by exposure. 岩は風雨にさらされて風化する.

Q a ***crumbling*** *rock* くずれる岩石. ¶a ***high steep*** *rock* 高くきり立った岩. ¶an ***igneous*** (***aqueous***) *rock* 火(水)成岩. ¶dig down to ***impenetrable*** *rock* [地下の]堅岩まで掘下げ

る. ¶*jagged* (=*ragged*) *rocks* ががたる岩. ¶a *lofty rock* 高い岩. ¶a *naked rock* はだか岩. ¶Slate, limestone and sandstone are *sedimentary rocks*. 粘板岩, 石灰岩, 砂岩は水成岩である. ¶He picked up a *small rock* and threw it at the gate. 《米》彼は小石を拾って門に投げつけた. ¶a *solid rock* がん丈な岩. ¶a *sunken rock* on the chart 海図にのっている暗礁. 【類】The ship struck on a *sunken rock* and sank. ¶*uncharted rocks* 海図にのっていない暗礁. ¶*water-worn rocks* 水に浸食された岩. ¶a *wave-beaten rock* 波に打たれる岩. 「嶙(りん)岩.

Q² the *mother* (*father*) *rock* 母(父)岩. ¶*phosphate rock*

P run *against* (=on) the *rocks* 岩に突き当る ‖ The steamer was dashed *against* a *rock*. その汽船は岩に衝突した. ¶The ship wrecked *on* a sunken *rock*. その船は暗礁に乗り上げて難破した. ‖ a lighthouse built *on* a *rock* 岩の上に

rock, *v.* 揺る, 震動する, 揺れる. 〔建てた灯台.

M The boat *rocked a great deal*. 小舟は激しく揺れた.

P The earth *rocked beneath* his feet. 大地は彼の足下で揺れた. ¶*rocked by* the waves 波に揺られて. ¶He sat *rocking* himself *in* his chair. 彼はいすに身を揺りながらすわっていた. ¶The ship was *rocking on* the waves. 船は波に揺れていた. ¶The baby was *rocked to* sleep in a cradle. 赤ん坊はゆりかごでゆられて眠った. ¶*rock with* merriment おかしさに体を揺る.

rocket, *n.* のろし.

V *send up* a *rocket* のろしを上げる.

rod, *n.* さお, むち; つりざお.

V *escape* the chastising *rod* こらしめのむちを免れる. ¶*Spare* the *rod* and spoil the child. 〚諺〛かわいい子には旅をさせよ. ¶*use* the *rod* むちを用いる.

Q a *hot rod* 《米俗》オートレース用の小型自動車. 【類】A *hot rod* steered in to the curb and she climbed into it.

Q² a *birch rod* かばの木むち(かばの小枝で作った不良生徒を罰する道具). ¶*computing rods* 算木, ぜいちく. ¶a *curtain rod* 窓かけ棒. ¶a *lightning rod* 避雷針. ¶a *piston rod* 〚機〛ピストンロッド. ¶a *two-way radio rod* [自動車などの]無線電話用アンテナ.

P His wife rules him "*with* a *rod* of iron." 彼の妻は彼を虐待している. ‖ He went out [*with*] a *rod* and line on shoulder. つりざお肩に出かけた.

roe, *n.* [集団的に]魚卵.

Q² *salmon roe* すじこ.

rogue, *n.* 悪者; いたずら者.

V *play* the *rogue* 詐欺を働く.

Q a *great rogue* 大悪党, 大ぺてん師. ¶You dear *little rogue!* このいたずらっ子(お母さんが). ¶Such a *wicked rogue* he is! 何て悪いやつだろう.

roguery, *n.* ぺてん.

V *play roguery* on (=upon) ... ...をぺてんにかける.

P romances *of roguery* 放浪奇談.

role, rôle, *n.* 役割, 役, 役目.

V *allot* (=*assign*) the *role* to... その役を...に割当てる. ¶*assume* the *role* of a princess 王女の役を演じる ‖ *assume* the same *role* 同じ役わりを演じる. ¶*avoid* the *role* of the mere iconoclast 単に偶像破壊者に過ぎないような役目を避ける. ¶*change* one's *role* 役目を変える. ¶*fill* (=*fulfil*) the *role* of ...=act as ... ...の役をつとめる ‖ *fill* two *roles* at one and the same time 二足のわらじをはく. ¶*have* a *role* to play 一役買っている ‖ *have* no *role* to play 出る幕じゃない. ¶*impersonate* the *role* of ... ...の役にふんする. ¶*play* the *role* of a prophet 予言者の役目をつとめる. 【類】*play* the *role* of a gentleman ‖ He *played* the *role* in society for which he was cast. 彼は社会にあって自分の振当てられた役をつとめた. 【類】He *played* a *role* of historical importance in Japanese affairs. ¶In the *kabuki* the female *roles* are *taken* by men. 歌舞伎では女役は男がやる. ¶*take on* (=assume) a *role* 役割を勤める.

Q men playing the *feminine roles* 女形. ¶play a still more *important role* in ... ...においてさらに重要な役を勤める. ¶take the *leading role* 主役を演じる ‖ with ... in the *leading role* ...が主役をつとめて. ¶The graphic arts, familiarly known as "printing," plays a *major role* in modern civilization. 一般に「印刷」といっている筆写芸術は現代文明に重要な役割を演じる. ¶Imitation plays a very *minor role* in the acquisition of manual habits. 手仕事を覚えるには模倣はあまり役に立たない. ¶the *new role* of woman in modern societies 現代社会の婦人の新しい役割. ¶Woman as mother and wife is an *obscure* but *important role*. 母たり妻たる女は表に現われないが重要な役目である. ¶assume the *principal role* 主役を引受ける. ¶play a *prominent role* おもだった役割を勤める. ¶*self-appointed role* of ... ...をもって自ら任じる役割. ¶her first *starring role* opposite ... 彼女が...の合役で始めてスターとして演じた役割. ¶A *static role* as an exhibit gallery and store-house is inadequate for the museum of today. 陳列場や倉庫という静的な役割だけでは今日の博物館は不十分である. ¶play a *subordinate role* 女房役(次官など)をつとめる. ¶one's *successful role* その当り芸.

Q² the *beau role* 色男役. ¶have the *title role* in ... ...では題名(ハムレットの劇のハムレットのような)役を持っている.

P reappearance on the scene *in* the *role* of a leader of ... ...の首領の役をつとめて再活躍.

P² the young lady who plays the little *role in* the novel その小説で端役を演じる若い婦人.

roll, *n.* 人名簿, 出席簿, 表; とどろき; ロールパン; 《米》弁護士録.

V *call* the *roll* 出席を取る ‖ *call* the *roll* on a question= take the ayes and noes ある問題に関して(賛否を問うため)指名点呼をする. ¶*have* a *roll* and a cup of coffee ロールパンにコーヒー一杯のむ. ¶*strike off* the *rolls* 弁護士名簿から名を除く.

V² The society's *roll* at present *shows* ... members. 現在その会の名簿には ... 名の会員が載っている. ¶the *roll* of members *totals* ... 会員名簿の総計は...名である.

Q *crushing rolls* of thunder 激しい雷鳴. ¶a *distant roll* of thunder 遠雷のとどろき. ¶Swift is one of the strangest personalities in the *entire roll* of English men of letters. スウィフトは英国文学史上最も変った人物の一人である. ¶a *long roll* of paper 長い巻紙 ‖ a *long roll* of illustrious names 多数の有名な人の名前をのせた表. ¶a *memorial roll* of the Association since 1872 一八七二年以来同協会の死亡会員人名表. ¶with a *strong roll* of the "r" r を強く響かして.

Q² I applied to him to place my son on his English *class roll*. 私は彼に英語のクラスにむすこを入れてくれと申込んだ. ¶swell the *death roll* of ... ...の死亡者数を高める. ¶an *employment roll* 職員名簿. ¶a *fire roll* 出火の際の呼出太鼓. ¶a *heavy death roll* in a disaster 災害による多数の死者. ¶the *honor roll*=the roll of honor. ¶a *merit roll* 士官候補生試験成績表. ¶the civil service *pay roll* 文官俸給表. 【類】*pay rolls* for employees ‖ keep an employee in illness on the *pay roll* 病欠の雇人に給料支給を続ける. ¶The *personnel roll* has increased to 621. 職員は総数六百二十一名に増加した.

P He was struck *off* the *rolls*. 彼は除名された. ¶His name is not mentioned *on* the *roll*. 彼の名は名簿にのっていない. ‖ The school has now ... students *on* the *roll*. その学校は目下...名の学生を有している. 【類】He stands first *on* the *roll*. / *On* the membership *roll* are three princes, several earls, baronets, judges, barristers, medical men, officers in the Army and Navy, and many well-known merchants. ‖ He is fifth in seniority *on* the *roll* of Cardinals. 彼は(ローマ法王庁の)枢機官の名簿での席次は五番目である. ‖ put (=place) ... *on* a *roll* ...を名簿にのせる. ¶His name has been *upon* the *roll* of the club for ... years. 彼の名は...年間クラブの名簿にのっていた.

P² *rolls for* breakfast 朝食のロールパン. ¶a *roll of* bread ロールパン一つ ‖ the *roll of* honor 戦死者, 入選者人名 ‖ the *roll of* voters 投票者名簿 ‖ a *roll of* cloth (paper, carpet) 布地(など)の一巻き ‖ a *roll of* silk for painting or writing on [書画用]絹地.

roll, *v.* 丸く巻く, 回転する; 移り行く; 横揺れする; ごろごろ鳴る.

M The carriage *rolled away*. その馬車はがらがらと音を立てて遠ざかって行った. ¶The organ *rolls forth* its music. オルガンからそのメロデーが流れる. ¶The ship *rolled heavily*. 船がはげしく横揺れした. ¶*roll out* in one's car 自家用の自動車で出かける ‖ *roll out* a drum 太鼓をどろどろ打鳴らす ‖ bravely *roll out* their hymns 勇敢に賛美歌を合唱し出す ‖ *roll out* by hand 手でのばす. ¶A wheel *rolls round*. 車輪が回転する. ¶*roll spirally* らせん状にめぐる. ¶This ink *rolls well*. この(印刷用の)インキはのびがよい.

M² *roll about* in intoxication 酔っぱらってころげ回る. ¶a ball *rolling along* ころがるボール. ¶as the months *roll around* 月日がたつにつれて ‖ until the next meeting *rolls around* 次の会が開かれるまで. ¶as the years *rolled by* 歳月のたつにつれて. 【類】two years more *rolled by* before ... ¶Waves *rolled in*. 波が打ちよせてきた. ¶Time *rolls on*. 時は移る. ‖ Centuries *rolled on*. 数世紀は過ぎ去った. 【類】Time *rolls on* in its ceaseless course. ¶*roll over* to (=on) the other side 向う側にころげて行く. 【類】*roll over* and *over* on the ground. ¶Smoke *rolls up*. 煙は輪になって上る. ‖ *roll up* a carpet (rug, map) 毛せん(敷もの)を巻く. 【類】*roll up* a scroll (巻もの) / *roll* them *up* in wrapping paper ‖ *roll* oneself *up* in a blanket 毛布にくるまる ‖ *roll up* one's eyes 目をくるくるさせる ‖ *roll up* one's umbrella かさをたたむ ‖ *roll up* one's shirt sleeves and start working ワイシャツのそでをたくしあげて仕事に着手する.

P A drunken fellow was *rolling about* (=in) the street. 酔漢が街上をよろよろしていた. ¶*roll along* (*by*, *past*) [車両など]ごろごろ通る. ¶Destructive floods *rolled down* valleys. 恐ろしい洪水が谷間を流れ下った. 【類】Rocks and stones *rolled down* the hillside. ¶The words *rolled from* his lips like a cataract of music. その言葉が音楽の滝のように彼のくちびるをついて出た. ¶*roll from* side *to* side 左右に揺ゆれる. ¶He *rolls in* wealth (=money) and riots in debauchery. 彼はぜいたく三まいに暮し放とうに身を持ち崩している. 【類】*roll in* luxury ‖ chopped meat *rolled in* cabbage leaves ロールキャベツ ‖ ... all *rolled in* one ... を打って一丸とした. ¶It is somewhat like Christmas and a Birthday Feast *rolled into* one. クリスマスと誕生日を一しょにしたようなものだ. ¶He *rolled* his eyes *on* us. 彼は目をぎょろぎょろさせてわれわれを見た. ‖ *rolled on* a stick 棒に巻いた. ¶*roll out of* bed ベッドから出る.

O Thunder *rolls* in the distance. 遠雷がとどろく.

roll-call, *n.* 点呼.

V *make* a *roll-call* 点呼を取る.

Q² a *surprise roll-call* 不時点呼.

P *at roll-call* 点呼のとき.

roller, *n.* 〖機〗ローラー; ローラ・カナリヤ.

Q *German rollers* ドイツのローラ・カナリヤ. ¶an *inky roller* 〖印刷〗インキローラー.

Q² a *road roller* [舗装用の]ロードローラー. ¶a *steam roller* スチーム・ローラー. ¶a *street roller* ロード・ローラー. ¶a *tandem rollor* くし形ローラー.

rolling, *n.* ごろという音.

V All the presses have *started rolling*. 印刷機が皆運転し始めた.

Q the *distant rolling* of a cascade 遠くの滝のどうという音(など). ¶a *solemn rolling* of a church organ 教会オルガンの荘重なひびき.

romance, *n.* 小説, 伝奇, 情話(ロマンス).

V *rub away* the *romance* of life 人生からロマンスを取去る(平凡化する). ¶You can't *spell romance* without a man (a woman). 男(女)なしではロマンスは生れないよ. ¶This *stirred romance*. こうしてお安くないことができ上った. ¶*taste* the *romance* of clerical life 牧師生活の情調を味う.

V² the *romance attaching* to ... ...に付随する情話. ¶A curious *romance happened* in his family. 彼の家庭におもしろい恋愛事件が起った. ¶The *romance started* in 1950. その恋愛関係が一九五〇年に始った.

Q Gil Blas is the *classic romance* of roguery. ジル・ブラースは悪漢小説として古典的のものである. ¶a *fascinating romance* 魅惑的な小説. ¶a *legendary romance* 伝説物語. It forms one of the *living romances* of life, beside which all the inventions of the novelist are tame and cold. それはおもしろい人生の実話の一つで, これに比べると小説家の創案はことごとく陳腐にして無味乾燥なものとなる. ¶a *military* (=*martial*) *romance* 武勇伝. ¶There is *no romance*. 曲がない. ¶a *powerful* and *impressive romance* 力強い印象的なロマン小説. ¶Our meeting was *quite* a *romance*. われわれの会合は全く偶然だった. ¶a *three-cornered romance* 三角関係物語 ‖ a principal in a *three-cornered romance* 三角関係の一人. ¶be full of *thrilling romance* 大いに刺激的な空想で満ちている.

Q² a *teen-age romance* 十台の恋愛関係.

P a girl full *of romance* 夢の多い少女.

P² Her story is a *romance in* real life. 彼女の経歴は小説的実話である. ¶a *romance of* real life, striking in its dramatic effect 劇的効果の著しい小説的実話.

Romanization, *n.* ローマ体活字印刷.

V *Romanization* in this map is *based* on the Chinese Post Office spelling. この地図のローマ体活字は中国郵便局のつづり字法による.

romantic, *a.* 小説的な, ロマンチックな.

M it is *quite romantic* to say that ... ...ということは全くロマンチックだ.

P There is something *romantic* felt *about* the old castle. その古城には何か伝奇的なものが感じられる.

romanticist, *n.* 空想家.

Q a *born romanticist* 生れながらのロマンチスト.

roof, *n.* 屋根; 住家, 居室.

V The wind *blew off* the *roof*. 風が屋根をめくった. ¶*get* one's *roof retiled* かわら屋根をふき直す. ¶He *left* the parental *roof* before he was out of his teens. 彼はまだ十代を越さない中に両親のひざ下を去った. ¶A bolt of lightning *struck* the *roof* of the house. 雷がその家の屋根に落ちた. ¶*thatch* (=*tile*) the *roof* [屋根を草かわら]ぶきにする.

V² The *roof* has *fallen in*. 屋根がくずれ落ちた. ¶The *roof leaked* and we caught water in a tub. 屋根が漏っておけで水を受けた. ¶The *roof* was *peeling off* in the wind. 屋根が風ではげかかっていた.

Q a *curved roof* 曲線の屋根. ¶Some houses have *flat roofs*. 平たい屋根の家もある. ¶I spent the night under his *hospitable roof*. 私はその家に一晩世話になった. ¶a *leaky roof* 漏る屋根. ¶leave the *parental roof* and enter college 両親のひざ下を辞して大学にはいる. ¶a *pitched roof* ピッチで塗り固めた屋根. ¶a *slanting roof* 傾斜屋根. ¶a *thatched roof* 草ぶき屋根.

Q² the ridge of the *chapel roof* 教会堂の屋根のむね. ¶a *rain-proof* (*weather-proof*) *roof* 雨もりのしない屋根. ¶a vivid *red-tile roof* あざやかな赤がわらの屋根. ¶It has a *shingle* or *slate roof*. その屋根はこけら板ぶきかスレート張りである. ¶a *tile roof* かわらの屋根.

P We have dwelt *beneath* the same *roof* for many years. われわれは長年同じ屋根の下に住んできた. ¶reform *from roof* to basement 家中を全部改築する. ¶live *under* one's parental *roof* 両親の下にいる ‖ The university welcomes *under* its *roof* students of all creeds and colors. その大学はあらゆる宗教あらゆる人種の学生をその校舎内に歓迎する. ¶houses *with* tiled *roofs* タイル屋根の家 ‖ The house is not yet covered *with* a *roof*. その家はまだ屋根ができていない. ¶sleep *without* any *roof* over one's head 青天井の下に眠る.

roof, *v.* 屋根を付ける, 屋内に囲う.

M The pond is *roofed in* by huge trees growing all around. その池は回りの巨木におおわれている. ¶huts *roofed over* with grass 草で屋根をふいた粗末な小屋. ¶a cottage *roofed with* tiles タイル(かわら)ぶきの小屋.

room, *n.* **(1)** 室, へや.

V *air* a *room* へやに風を通す. ¶The *room* is delightfully *appointed* へやは気持よく設備してある. ¶The hotel clerk *assigned* me a good *room*. ホテルの番頭が私に好いへやを当てがってくれた. ¶*board up* a *room* へやを板でふさぐ(はいれないように). ¶*book rooms* at a boarding-house 下宿屋でへやを予約する. ¶*brisk* one's *room* [来客などで]室をにぎやかにする. ¶*clean* a *room* 室を掃除する. ¶They were desired to *clear* the *room*. 彼らは座をはずすようにといわれた. ¶*clear up* a *room* へやを片付ける. ¶*consign* a *room* to one's use 一室を自分の専用にする. ¶*cross* the *room* to the window へやを通って窓に行く. ¶*crowd* (=*throng*) a *room* へやに一杯はいる. ¶*divide* a *room* between two families 一つのへやを二家族で分けて住む. ¶a maid *doing* the *room* へやを掃除する女中. ¶The *room* was *draped* with Italian flags. へやにはイタリアの旗が飾ってあった. ¶*dust* a *room* へやにはたきをかける. ¶*engage rooms* at a hotel ホテルにへやを取る. ¶*enter* a *room* 室に入る. ¶*fix up* a *room* in a hotel 旅館でへやを決める. ¶*flood* the *room* with light へやを(電灯で)こうこうと照す. ¶*floor* a *room* 部屋に床を張る. ¶*furnish* a *room* へやに家具を取付ける. ¶*give up* (=*devote*) a *room* to a collection of ... 一室を...の収集陳列に当てる. ¶*have* a *room reserved* へやを予約する. ¶*Hold room* for self and wife, ten days. 私と妻とで十日間へやが欲しい(旅館への電報). ¶He *kept* his *room* for six weeks. 彼は六週間引きこもった. ‖ *keep* the

room tidy (***untidy***) へやをきちんと(乱雑に)しておく. ¶***let*** the ***rooms out*** for a small amount わずかの料金でへやを貸す. ¶A lamp ***lighted up*** the ***room***. ランプが一つへやについていた. ¶***litter*** a ***room*** へやをちらかす. ¶***maintain*** extensive exhibition ***rooms*** at the corner of ... and ... streets ...及び...街の角に広範にわたる陳列室を設置している. ¶***occupy*** a ***room*** that faces south 南向のへやを占める. ¶***paper*** a ***room***＝hang a room with paper 室に壁紙を張る. ¶The maid ***quit*** the ***room***. 女中はそのへやから去った. ¶***relet*** a ***room*** engaged へやをまた貸しする. ¶***rent*** furnished ***rooms*** 家具付のへやを貸す. ¶***reserve*** a ***room*** for one's own use 自己用にへやを取っておく. ¶***secure*** a ***room*** in advance by telegram 電報でへやを予約する. 【類】 ***Rooms*** may be ***secured*** at $5 a day. ¶***set*** the ***room*** to rights へやをきちんと整理する ‖ He ***set*** the whole ***room*** in a roar. 彼は一座をわっと笑わせた. ¶A ***room*** is specially ***set apart*** for this purpose. このために特にへやが取ってある. ¶***share*** a ***room*** with another 他人と同室する. ¶I'll have her ***sweep*** the ***room clean***. 彼女にへやを掃除させよう. ¶***take*** (＝engage) a ***room*** in a hotel ホテルにへやを取る. 【類】 ***take*** the ***rooms*** by the month (月ぎめで). ¶***tidy*** [***up***] a ***room*** へやを片付ける. ¶***whitewash*** a ***room*** へやを白く塗る.

V² The ***room looks*** to the north. へやは北向だ. ¶The ***room opens*** into a beautiful Italian garden. そのへやは美しいイタリア風の庭園に面している.

Q an ***adjoining room*** 隣室. ¶an ***airy room*** 風通しのよい部屋. ¶***back rooms*** 奥の間. ¶a ***bare*** and ***miserable room***, destitute of furniture 家具のないがらんとしたみすぼらしい室. ¶a ***bright airy room*** 明るくて風通しのよいへや. ¶a ***commodious room*** 広い室. ¶***common rooms*** for students 学生の控室. ¶***complimentary rooms*** [ホテルの]特別室. ¶a ***dimly lighted room*** 薄暗いへや. ¶***dingy, cramped, narrow rooms*** きたなくて窮屈で狭い室. ¶a ***double room*** knocked into one 二へやぶちぬきのへや. ¶a ***double-windowed room*** 二重窓付の室. ¶a ***dusty, littered room*** ほこりだらけで乱雑なへや. ¶an ***empty room*** 空室. ¶***exhibit rooms*** 陳列室. ¶a ***forbidden room*** あけずの間. ¶a ***front room*** on the third floor 四(または三)階の正面のへや. ¶superbly ***furnished rooms*** りっぱな家具を備付けたへや. ¶a ***general room*** [レストランなど]一般お客用のへや. ¶a poorly ***illuminated room*** 照明の悪いへや. ¶***ill-ventilated*** and ***insanitary rooms*** 風通しの悪い非衛生的なへや. ¶an ***inner room*** 奥まったへや. ¶The ***room*** was ***large, lofty*** and ***well-lighted***. へやは大きくって天井が高くって明るかった. ¶a ***large-numbered*** (***small-numbered***) ***room*** 番号の高い(若い)へや. ¶a ***light room*** 明るいへや. ¶a workmen's ***meal room*** 職工の食事へや. ¶an ***outside room*** of a hotel ホテルの外側のへや. ¶***overcrowded*** and ***ill-ventilated rooms*** 人数の多過ぎる風通しの悪い室. ¶a ***padded room*** for violent lunatics 狂暴な狂人収容の周囲をしとね張りにした室. ¶a ***poky room*** 見すぼらしい室. ¶a ***private room*** 私室 ‖ a ***private room*** for parties [レストランなど]会合のへや. ¶a ***smoke-filled room***＝a room filled with smoke 煙のたちこめたへや(たばこなどで). ¶a ***snug little room*** こじんまりしたへや. ¶a ***south-ward room*** 南向のへや. ¶a ***spare room*** [来客用など]予備室. ¶On the ship there is a ***special room*** allocated for the storage of mail. その船には郵便物を収容するため特に設けた室がある. ¶a ***squalid room*** occupied by the two orphaned brothers 二人の孤児の兄弟が住っているこぎたない室. ¶***strong rooms*** [船などの]貴重品収蔵室. ¶The ***room*** is ***stuffy*** and ***oppressive*** in summer. そのへやは夏は蒸暑く息詰まるようだ. ¶a ***sunny room*** 日当りのよいへや. ¶a ***tidy room*** きちんとしたへや. ¶***unhealthy rooms*** 健康によくない部屋. ¶an ***upstair room*** 階上のへや. ¶Have you any ***vacant rooms?*** へやが空いていますか. ¶a ***warm*** and ***lighted room***, full of friendly faces 親しい友だちが一杯いる暖かくて明るい室.

Q² an ***audit room*** 教会の事務所. ¶an ***assembly room*** 会議室; 舞踏場; 〖機〗組立作業室. ¶a little ***attic room*** 狭い屋根裏のへや. ¶an ***audience room*** 接見室, 拝謁の間. ¶a ***bath room*** 浴室. ¶go up to one's ***bed room*** 自分の寝所に行く(寝る). ¶a ***blue-print room*** 青写真室.

P walk ***across*** a ***room*** へやを横切る. ¶use it ***as*** a store ***room*** それを貯蔵室に使う. ¶walk ***down*** a ***room*** へやの出口の方へ歩いて行く. ¶He is ***in*** the ***room*** above. 彼は上の室にいる. ¶***inside*** a ***room*** へやの内部に. ¶come ***into*** a ***room*** 室にはいる. ¶Show him ***into*** my ***room***. 僕のへやに案内してくれ. ¶partition off part ***of*** the ***room*** へやの一部を仕切る ‖ rent a suite ***of rooms*** 続きへやを借りる. 【類】 Wanted: a house or a suite ***of rooms*** partly or fully furnished (造作つき). ¶sneak (＝slip *or* steal) ***out of*** the ***room*** へやからこっそり抜けだす. ¶Take this up ***to*** my ***room***—Room 4. これを僕のへやに持って行ってくれ—四番だ. ¶walk ***up*** and ***down*** a ***room*** ‖ walk ***up*** a ***room*** へやを上手の方に歩く.

P² a ***room for*** refreshments 喫茶室 ‖ a ***room for*** rent 《米》貸間. ¶a ***room in*** a hotel ホテルのへや. ¶a ***room with*** a veranda えん側付きの室.

(2) 余地, 余裕, 場所.

V A street-car platform ***affords room*** for baggage. 電車の昇降台に荷物をおく場所がある. ¶Japan must ***find room*** for the expansion of her surplus population. 日本はその過剰人口のはけ場所を見いださねばならない. ¶***give room*** to ...＝make room for ... ...に(席などを)譲る. ¶The concourse ***has room*** for hundreds of people. その停車場の待合所は数百人を収容できる. ¶***leave*** no ***room*** for criticism 批評の余地がない. 【類】 ***leave*** no ***room for*** doubt / These facts ***leave*** little ***room*** to doubt the success of the scheme. ¶Would you kindly ***make room*** for my friend here? も少しお寄り下さって僕の友人をここへ入れてやって下さい. ¶This ***takes up*** no ***room***. これは場所を取らない. ¶The garage ***provides room*** for over 200 cars. そのガレージは二百台以上の自動車を収容することができる.

Q there is ***ample room*** for doubt as to ... ...について疑う余地が十分ある. ¶fight for ***elbow room*** 活動の余地を得ようと努める ‖ a home with rather less ***elbow room*** than a railway compartment 汽車の車室より狭い家. ¶***Freight room*** per steamer is scarce. 汽船の(荷物に対する)船腹が不足している. ¶have not ***head room*** [天井が低くって]頭がつかえる. ¶There is but little ***leg room***. 足が窮屈だ. ¶there is ***little room*** for doubt that ... ...ということを疑う余地はほとんどない. ¶There is ***much room*** for improvement. 改良の余地は十分ある. ‖ As to ... there is ***much room*** for argument. ...については大いに議論の余地がある. ¶There is ***no room*** to stand (＝step) in. 足を入れる余地がない. 【類】 There is ***no room*** for further improvement. / There is ***no room*** for argument on that point. / Thus far there is ***no room*** for difference of opinion. ¶Any ***sitting room?*** 座席がありますか(バスなどで). ¶***Standing room*** only. 〖映画〗立見席だけ(座席満員) ☞ SRO と略す: an *SRO* sign.

P² Have you ***room for*** me in your car? あなたの車に乗せていただく席がありましょうか. ‖ There is only ***room for*** standing. 立見席しかない. 【類】 There is ***room for*** argument. ‖ There is no ***room for*** sentimentality in the army. 軍隊では感傷的なことは許されない.

O There is scarcely ***room*** to turn. 身動きもならない.

room, *v*. 室を借りる, 同室する.

M The two students ***roomed together***. その二人の学生は同室した.

P ***room at*** the house of Mrs. ... ...夫人の家に同居する.

roomful, *n*. へや一杯.

P² a ***roomful of*** people へや一杯の人.

roommate, *n*. 同室人.

P He is one ***of*** my ***roommates***. 彼は私と同室の者だ.

roost, *n*. ねぐら.

V Mother ***rules*** the ***roost*** in his family. 彼の家ではお母さんが権力がある.

P Their chickens sit ***on*** the ***roost***. ひな鳥たちはやどり木に止まる. ¶go ***to roost*** ねぐらに帰る ‖ come home ***to roost*** もとへ帰る; 身から出たさびとなる. 【類】〖諺〗 Curses, like chickens, come home ***to roost***.

roost, *v*. ねぐらにつく, 宿る, 休む.

P Birds ***roost in*** (＝on) the trees. 鳥は木にとまって寝る. ¶***roost on*** poles さおの上にとまる.

rooster, *n*. 《米》おんどり.

V² A ***rooster crows***. おんどりはときをつくる.

Q a ***soft rooster*** 去勢されたおんどり.

root, *n*. 根; ふもと; 基礎, 根本; 〖言語〗語根.

V ***blight*** the ***root*** and fruit of our kind of civilization われわれのこの文明の根を枯らし実をしぼませる. ¶***brace roots*** of corn とうもろこしの根に(倒れないように)支柱をする. ¶***dig up roots*** 根を掘返す. ¶the story ***found root*** in ... その物語は...に基いた ‖ The tree has ***found root***. その木

は根がついた. ¶***gain*** firm *root* 確固たる根底を得る. ¶***give*** the *roots* the full benefit of the growing season 成長期に根を十分に成育させる. ¶***grow*** strong *roots* in … …に強固な基礎をすえる. ¶***grub up*** *roots* 根を掘りかえす. ¶it ***has*** its *roots* deep down in the soil of … それは…の地下にしっかり根をおろしている. ¶traditions which ***have*** their *roots* in fact 事実に根底を有する伝統.【類】All development ***has*** its *root* in a desire. / Almost all Japanese institutions ***have*** their *roots* in China. ¶Bursts of temper are exhausting to the system, and may ***lay*** the *roots* of mental disease. 激怒は心身を極度に疲労せしめるので精神病の源となることもある. ¶Buddhism ***planted*** its *roots* deeply in Japanese soil. 仏教はその根を深く日本の国土におろした. ¶***sap*** the *root* of enterprise 計画の根底を崩す. ¶***send out*** *roots* 根を出す. ¶***stick*** its *roots* firmly into the soil その根をしっかと地中に張る. ¶***strike*** its *roots* deep into the ground その根を深く地中におろす.【類】***strike*** its *roots* deep down into the heart of humanity (人類) / His popularity has ***struck*** *root*. ¶***take*** *roots* in … …に根がつく.【類】my aversion had ***taken*** already such deep *root* in me that … / Socialism has ***taken*** *root* (=gained a footing) in South Africa among … / ***took*** *root* and flourished / It is gradually ***taking*** deeper *root*.

Q the ***cubic*** (***square***) *root*〘数〙立(平)方根. ¶a good soil for love to strike ***deep roots*** in 愛情が深く根づくによい下地. ¶an ***even*** (***odd***) *root*〘数〙偶(奇)数根. ¶take ***firm*** *root* in Japanese soil 日本の国土にしかと根ざす. ¶The idea took ***strong*** *root*. その思想は確立した. ¶The cento did not take very ***vigorous*** *root* in British soil. その抜粋形式の詩文は英国の国土にあまりしっかと根付かなかった.

Q^2 a ***tulip*** *root* チューリップ根. ¶a ***verb*** *root*=the root of a verb〘文法〙動詞の原形.

P lie ***at*** the *root* of … …の基本を成している ‖ get [down] ***at*** (=***to***) the *root* (=bottom) of a matter 物事の真髄を突く ‖ It is ***at*** *root* (=radically) a question of biology. それは結局生物学の問題である. ‖ He said that ignorance was ***at*** the *root* of a great deal of infantile mortality. 幼児に死亡の多いのは世人の無知に基因する所が多いと彼は言った.【類】Self-interest is ***at*** the *root* of all his actions. ¶torn up ***by*** the *roots* 根こそぎにして. 【類】pull (= pluck) it out ***by*** the *root*.

P^2 the strong *root* ***at*** Scotland Yard スコットランド・ヤード(ロンドン警視庁の旧所在地)の強固な土台. ¶eliminate the *root* ***of*** evil 悪の根を除く.【類】remove the *root* ***of*** trouble / Uncleanliness is the *root* ***of*** various diseases. / the *root* ***of*** a word=a word root 語根.

root, *v.* 根付かす; 根絶する; 根付く, 根ざす.

M too ***deeply rooted*** to eradicate 非常に深く根付いているので根絶することのできない. ¶It is ***firmly rooted*** in experience. それはしかと経験に立脚している.【類】stories ***firmly rooted*** in the older traditions. / The idea that … is ***firmly rooted***. ¶***root out*** errors 誤りを根絶する.【類】***root out*** the causes of war / ***root out*** guerrillas / ***root out*** the system we dislike / ***root*** them ***out*** one by one.

M^2 ***root up*** weeds 雑草を根こそぎする.【類】***root up*** the garden / ***root up*** all evils / ***root up*** (=uproot) the cause of trouble.

P War is ***rooted in*** economic causes. 戦争は経済的原因から起る. ‖ It is ***rooted in*** the doctrine that "Might is right." それは「力は正義なり」という説に根ざしている.【類】Their evolutionary ideas of the sovereignty of the people and the rights of man are ***rooted in*** British soil. ‖ ***root*** a principle ***in*** the mind ある主義を心に植えつける. ¶Communism was ***rooted out of*** the country. 共産主義はその国からさん除された. ¶He was ***rooted to*** the ground by fear. 恐怖のあまり彼は根が生えたように棒立ちになった.【類】Fear ***rooted*** him ***to*** the ground.

root, *v.* 《米俗》応援する.

P The crowd ***rooted for*** the home team. 観衆は(遠征軍に対し)国内チームに応援した. 【類】Let's ***root for*** him. *Rah, rah, Dick!*

root-cause, *n.* 根原.

V ***eradicate*** the *root-cause* of a trouble 紛争の根原を絶滅する.

rooted, *a.* 根ざした.

M a ***deeply*** *rooted* prejudice 深く根ざした偏見.

rope, *n.* なわ, 綱; こつ, ひけつ.

V ***coil ropes*** neatly ロープをきちんと巻く. ¶***draw*** (=***pull***) a *rope* 綱を引く. ¶***draw up*** (=***in***) ***a rope*** 綱を引き入れる. ¶***haul up*** (=***in***) a *rope* 綱をたぐり込む. ¶Madge liked to ***jump*** the *rope*. マッジはなわ飛びが好きであった.【類】The girl ***jumped*** the *rope* again and again. ¶He ***knows*** the *ropes* 彼は心得たものだ. ‖ if you "***know*** the *ropes*" やり方によっては, うまく立回れば.【類】He does not ***know*** the *ropes*. ¶***let go*** [of] the *rope* ロープから手を離す. ¶slowly ***let out*** a *rope* 綱を徐々に繰りだす. ¶***lower*** the *rope* to let us pass 張り綱を下げてわれわれを通してくれる. ¶***pass*** a *rope* round a log 丸太にロープをかける. ¶***put*** the *rope* through a wrong hole 違った穴になわを通す. ¶Can you ***reach*** the *rope?* ロープに手が届くか. ¶***run*** a *rope* through … …に綱を通す. ¶***strand*** a *rope* 綱をなう. ¶***stretch*** *ropes* round … …の回りに綱をかける. ¶***twist*** a *rope* なわをよる. ¶***undo*** (=***untie***) the *rope* なわをほどく. ¶***use*** a *rope* to tie up a dog 犬をロープで縛る.

V^2 The *rope* ***gave way***. 綱が切れた.

Q know ***all*** the *ropes* あの手この手に通じている. ¶a ***flat*** *rope* 偏平な(編み)ロープ. ¶mend a ***frayed*** *rope* すり切れてぼろぼろの綱を修理する. ¶a net made of ***heavy*** *rope* 太綱の網(動物捕獲用の).

Q^2 ***cotton*** (***hemp***) *rope* 綿(麻)ロープ. ¶a strong ***Manila*** *rope* 丈夫なマニラロープ. ¶the ***straw*** *rope* suspended before Shinto shrines 神社のしめなわ. ¶a ***three-ply*** *rope* 三つこロープ. ¶The ***tow*** *rope* broke (slipped). [船の]ひき綱が切れた(スリップした).

P It was lowered ***by*** a *rope*. それは綱でおろした.【類】be lowered, ***by*** a *rope*, down the face of the cliff (がけぞいに). ¶The snake coiled itself ***like*** a *rope*. へびはロープのようにとぐろを巻いた. ¶lay (=catch *or* take) hold ***of*** the *rope* そのなわをつかまえる. ¶The bell is rung by means of a swinging wooden pole hung ***on*** a rope. 鐘は綱でつるしたしゅ木で鳴らす. ¶***on*** the *ropes*〘けん闘〙ロープにつかまって; 窮地に落入って. ¶bind ***with*** a *rope* なわでつかねる.

rope, *v.* なわでしきる, なわ張りする.

M ***roped off*** from pedestrians 徒歩通行人の通る所からなわ張りでしきった.【類】The police ***roped off*** the entrance to keep the crowd back (群集が入らないように). / ***rope off*** the arena (闘技場).

rose, *n.* ばら.

V ***cultivate*** *roses* ばらを栽培する. ¶***grow*** *roses* ばらを植える. ¶Her complexion ***outbloomed*** the lovely colored *rose*. 彼女の血色はばらの花も恥じるばかりであった.

V^2 Every *rose* ***has*** its thorn=No rose without a thorn. どんな幸福にも不幸は伴う(楽あれば苦あり). ¶The *rose* ***smells*** sweet. ばらはよいにおいがする.

Q a lovely ***flesh-colored*** *rose* nestling in maiden hair 少女の髪にさした美しい肉色のばら. ¶a ***perpetual*** *rose* 四季咲きのばら.

P the (=a) bed ***of*** *roses* 安楽な生活. 【類】repose on a bed ***of*** *roses*. ¶hear ***under*** the *rose* that … ひそかに…ということを聞く. ¶the *roses* ***in*** the garden 庭のばら.

P^2 She was the *rose* ***of*** the party. 彼女は一行の花だった.

O a *rose* about to blow 咲きかけたばらの花.

roster, *n.* 名簿.

Q a ***full*** *roster* of the faculty 全教授名簿.

rostrum, *n.* 演壇.

V A speaker ***mounted*** the *rostrum*. 一人の弁士が登壇した.

Q the ***auctioneer's*** *rostrum* 競売者の演台.

P Who is the speaker ***in*** the *rostrum?* 演壇の弁士はだれか.

rosy, *a.* ばら色の.

P She came in, *rosy* ***from*** a long bath. 彼女は長湯で顔が真赤になって入って来た.

rotate, *v.* 回転する, 自転する.

P The earth *rotates* ***from*** west ***to*** east. 地球は西から東へ自転する. ¶*rotate* men ***in*** office たらい回しに任命する. ¶*rotate* ***upon*** (=***on***) an axis 軸を中心に回転する.

rotation, *n.* 回転, 循環, 交代.

Q ***right-handed*** *rotation* 右回り回転.

P Magazines, like governments, are benefited ***by*** *rotation* in office. 雑誌は政府と同様当事者の交代によってよくなる. ¶Orders are executed ***in*** *rotation* as received. 注文は受けた順に取扱う.

rote, *n.* 暗誦.

P say the whole of the English Bible ***by*** *rote* 英語の聖書を全部そらで言う ‖ recite ***by*** *rote* 暗誦する. 【類】Do not learn anything ***by*** *rote* (=heart).

rotten, *a.* 腐った, 腐敗した.
P *rotten at* (=*to*) the core 心(しん)が(まで)腐った.
O The wheather is *rotten.* いやな天気だ.

rottenness, *n.* 腐敗, 腐朽.
V ***expose*** the *rottenness* of ... ...の腐敗をあばく.

rotundity, *n.* 円形, 球状. 「る.
V ***recognize*** the *rotundity* of the earth 地球の球形を認め
Q pigs of ***marvelous rotundity***=plump pigs 丸々と肥えた

rouge, *n.* べに(ルージュ). 」豚.
V ***put on*** *rouge* 口べにを着ける.
P cheeks touched ***with*** *rouge* ルージュをつけたほお.

rouge, *v.* べにをつける. 「けた口びる(ほお).
M ***slightly*** (=***lightly***) *rouged* lips (cheeks) 薄くべにをつ

rough, *n.* 粗造, 未加工品.
P a diamond ***in*** the ***rough*** 加工していないダイヤモンド ‖ write out the essay ***in*** the ***rough*** その論文の下書をする. 【類】The plan is yet ***in*** the ***rough***.

rough, *a.* あらい, 粗雑な, 乱暴な.
P ***rough in*** manner (speech, voice, dress) 行儀(など)が粗暴な. ¶***rough of*** speech 言葉が粗野な. ¶You are ***rough on*** him in saying so. そう言っては彼に対して酷だ.

rough, *v.* ざっとやる.
M ***rough out*** a statuette 小像をあら細工で造る ‖ ***rough out*** a city plan 都市計画の立案をする.

roughness, *n.* ぶしつけ.
Q ***honest roughness*** and manly straight-forwardness 飾り気のないぶしつけと男らしい率直. 「負.

round, *n.* 連続; 巡回, 一巡; [はしごの]段(だん); 一試合, 一勝
V ***arrange*** a *round* of festivities in honor of their guest 彼らの客のために連続的な祝いごとを計画する. ¶***attain*** the topmost *round* of the newspaper ladder 新聞界の最上位に達する. ¶One New Year's Day I was ***doing*** my *round* of calls. ある正月に私は年賀回りをしていた. ¶***draw*** *rounds* of applause 繰返し歓呼を受ける. ¶Five *rounds* were ***fought***. 五回勝負があった. ¶A good story about a certain peer is ***going*** the *round*. ある貴族についておもしろい話が今世間に伝わっている. 【類】War rumors are ***going*** the *round*. ‖ a postman ***going*** his *rounds* 配達をしている郵便夫 ‖ A censer ***goes*** the *round* of the party. 香炉を一座のものに回す(香道の会などで). 【類】It has been ***going*** the *round*[s] of the American (daily) press. / a paragraph ***going*** the *rounds* of various Tokyo papers (=journals). ¶***make*** (=***go***) one's *rounds* [その持場を]巡回する. 【類】The newly married couple ***made*** a *round* of calls. / ***make*** a *round* of visits (=calls) / doctors ***making*** their morning *round* / The teacher ***made*** his *round* among the benches. / ***make*** the *rounds* of the various advertising quacks. ¶***pay*** a *round* of New Year's calls 年始回りをする. 【類】***pay*** a *round* of one's patrons. ¶***raise*** a *round* of cheers 続けて万歳三唱する. ¶***repeat*** the tiring *round* 同じことをあきるほど繰返してやる. ¶***serve out*** a *round* of beer to all 皆に一杯ずつビールを出す. ¶a night watchman ***walking*** his *round* 巡回する夜番.
Q the ***common*** *round* of life ありふれた人生. ¶an almost ***continuous*** *round* of pleasure ほとんど続けざまの快楽. ¶the ***daily*** *round* of life 日常生活 ‖ take a person out of the ***daily dull*** *round* 日々の紋切型の仕事から解放してやる. ¶the ***first*** *round* of fighting will probably go to ... [けん闘の]第一ラウンドは多分...の勝ちだろう. ¶The road you came was a ***long*** *round*. あなたのきた道は遠回りでした. ¶a ***perpetual*** *round* of petty cares いつまで続くつまらない苦労. ¶a bout of ***ten*** *rounds* 〘けん闘〙十回戦. ¶in the ***whole double*** *round* of the clock 二十四時間に. ¶the ***yearly*** *round* of the earth=the earth's yearly round 地球の公転.
Q^2 The duration of the ***life*** *round* of a housefly is approximately ten days. 家ばいの一生は約十日だ.
P dance ***in*** a *round* (=circle) 輪になって踊る. ¶a policeman ***on*** his *rounds* 巡回中の警官 ‖ The ragman set out ***on*** his *rounds*. そのくず屋は仕事に出かけた. ‖ set out ***on*** a *round* of official calls 巡察に出掛ける.
P^2 a complete and perfect representation of a lumberman's ***round of*** duties きこりの務めを克明に描写したもの ‖ A good story is going the ***round of*** the clubs. おもしろい話が方々のクラブの部員の口に上っている. ‖ a ***round of*** beef 牛肉のももの肉.

round, *ad.* 回って, 遠回りして.
P the country ***round about*** ... ...近郷. ¶I shall be *round* ***at*** your office tomorrow about ... 私はあす...時ごろあなたの事務所に回りましょう. 「わたるほどあるか.
O Have we enough ***sake*** to go *round?* 酒はみんなに行き

round, *v.* 丸くする, 丸める.
M a form ***rounded out*** with health 丸々と肥えた健康体 ‖ Their talent is one-sided—incomplete. It needs ***rounding out***. 彼らの才能は一方に偏して不完全だ, かどをとらなくちゃ. ‖ ***round out*** a scheme properly 計画を手ぎわよくまとめる ‖ The bust was well ***rounded out***. 胸像に巧みに丸みをつけた. ‖ ***round out*** (=off) an essay 文章をうまく潤色する.
M^2 ***round off*** rough corners 角のざらざらをすり落す ‖ ***round off*** a cape toward ... みさきを回って...に向う ‖ He has corners yet to be ***rounded off***. 彼はまだ角がとれない(人間ができていない). 【類】The corners of his character are not ***rounded off***. ‖ ***round off*** the argument with a repetition, in varied terms, of the main idea 議論の主張を繰り返し表現を変えて丸味を持たせる ‖ ***round off*** one's career with the crown of success 成功で終生を飾る. 【類】***round off*** an evening party with a dance / ***round off*** an essay well. ¶***round up*** a scattered herd of cattle 散在する牛を狩り集める. 【類】***round up*** a gang of street roughs (町のよたもの). 「かった.
P He ***rounded on*** me in a rage. 彼は憤怒して私に食ってか

roundup, *n.* 狩集め. 「を総合するに...
Q the ***latest*** *roundup* of information is that ... 最近の情報
P^2 make a ***roundup of*** gamblers (criminals, street-girls, etc.) ばくち打(など)の手入れをする.

rouse, *v.* めざめさす, 起す; 起きる, 覚せいする. 「る.
M^2 ***rouse*** (brace) oneself ***up*** to action [緊こん一番]奮起す
P ***roused from*** dreamy thoughts by his footfall 彼の足音によって夢想からめざめて. ‖ *rouse* a person ***from*** his sleep その眠りをさます. ¶*rouse* a person ***to*** action 人を奮起させる ‖ *rouse* one's audience ***to*** enthusiasm 聴衆を熱狂させる. 【類】*rouse* them ***to*** a sense of their mission and

rouser, *n.* 騒ぎ立てる人. 」destiny.
Q^2 a ***rabble rouser*** わいわい騒ぎ回る人.

rout, *n.* 敗北, 敗走; 《古》群集.
Q an utterly ***disorganized*** *rout* 算を乱しての敗走. ¶a ***jovial*** *rout* of country folk いなかの人たちのにぎやかなざわめき. ¶an ***utter*** *rout* 大敗.
P put the enemy ***to*** *rout* 敵を敗北させる.

rout, *v.* 追出す, 引きずり出す.
M^2 ***rout up*** a person 人をたたき起す.
P *rout* a person ***out of*** home 人をその家から追出す ‖ *rout* a person ***out of*** his bed 人をたたき起す.

route, *n.* 路, 線路, 道程, 交通路, 航路.
V ***arrange*** the *route* so that the journey may prove a pleasant one その旅行を愉快なようにする経路を取る. ¶a return journey ***covers*** the same *route* as far as ... 帰路は...までは同じ経路を取る. ¶the *route* ***followed*** in the present journey この旅行で取った経路. ¶The newsboy ***has*** a *route* of sixty-three customers. その新聞配達は六十三軒の顧客先がある. ‖ the tourist ***has*** many *routes* to choose from ... and to ... ...への往復は経路が幾通りもある. ¶***lay out*** one's *route* in advance 旅程をあらかじめ作る. ¶Throngs ***line*** the *route*. 多数の人が道筋に行列を作る. 【類】The *route* was ***lined*** by 100,000 admirers (ファン). ¶***map out*** a *route* 経路をきめる. ¶Printed signs ***point*** the *route* to be followed by visitors. 印刷した掲示があって参観者の取るべき順路を示してある(博物館など). ¶the *route* from ... to ... is ***shortened*** by ... ...から...への道程は...だけ短縮される. ¶***take*** a *route* more to the north 路をさらに北方に取る. 【類】On his way back, he will ***take*** the Siberian *route*. ¶The three-mile *route* was ***thronged***. 三マイルにわたる道筋は群衆で一杯だった(歓迎・葬式など). ¶This *route* is not frequently ***used*** by travellers. この経路は旅行者があまり利用しません.
V^2 The *route* ***branches off*** here. その道はここで分かれる. ¶the point whence two *routes* ***diverge*** 追分. ¶the *route* ***lies*** through ... その線路は...を通過している(電車など). ¶*routes* ***reaching*** the point その地点に達する経路. ¶the *route* ***starts*** and ***finishes*** at ... その経路は...を発着点としている.

Q the ***cheapest route*** 最も安価な経路. ¶take a ***circuitous*** *route* 回り道をする. ¶a ***circular*** *route* 環状線路. ¶a ***commercial*** *route* 商路. ¶the most ***expeditious*** (=***quickest***) *route* to Europe ヨーロッパへ最も迅速に行ける経路. ¶a ***homeward*** *route* 帰りの経路. ¶an ***important tram*** *route* 重要な電車線. ¶This is no doubt an easier if a somewhat more ***lengthy*** *route*. この方はちと遠いがたしかに楽な経路です. ¶an ***overland*** *route* 陸路. ¶a ***pleasanter*** *route* 一層愉快な経路. ¶the most ***popular*** and most ***traveled*** *route* 最も人気のあるまた最も利用者の多い経路. ¶a ***quick*** *route* 近路. 【類】ship (発送する) by the ***quickest*** (***cheapest***) *route*. ¶on his ***return*** *route* 彼の帰路に. ¶go by a ***roundabout*** *route* 遠回りをする. ¶a ***scenic*** *route* 景色のよい経路. ¶a ***shorter*** *route* 距離の一層短い経路.【類】the ***shortest*** *route* available. ¶the diversion of ***trade*** *routes* 貿易路線の変更.

Q² an ***air*** *route* (=airway) by way of (=across) the Arctic 北極回りの空路. ¶an ***all-water*** *route* to India インドへの全部海路による行程. ¶the terminals of an ***air*** *route* 航空路の発着点. ¶the termini of ***bus*** *routes* バスの終点. ¶by a ***land*** (***water***, ***rail***) *route* 陸(など)路によって. ¶***ocean*** *routes* 外洋諸航路.【類】an ***ocean*** *route* to Japan. ¶a regular ***ration*** *route* 正規配給ルート. ¶the shortest ***sea*** *route* 最短航路. ¶a ***steamship*** *route* to a foreign port 外国港への航路. ¶follow the ***Suez*** *route* スエズ航路を通る. ¶world ***trade*** *routes* 数々の世界の貿易ルート. ¶a ***transportation*** *route* 輸送路.

P the party got an ovation ***along*** the *route* to ... 一行は...の途中大歓迎を受けた. ¶with the option of a return ***by*** *routes* different from the outgoing ones 行きと違った路を帰れる自由があって ‖ ship ***by*** some other *route* 他のルートから発送する. ¶The strait is ***in*** the *route* of ships. 同海峡は船の通路に当っている. ¶sights ***on*** the *route* to ... ...への経路にある風景 ‖ He is ***on*** my *route*. その人は自分の[牛乳などの]配達先になる. ‖ The Airlines fly five clippers ***on*** its Pacific *route*. 同航空会社はその太平洋空路に旅客機五機を運航している. ¶travelers ***over*** the trans-Siberian *route* シベリア経由で行く旅行者. ¶send ***via*** a different *route* 別な経路で送る.

P² A worse *route* ***for*** sightseers could hardly be imagined. 観光者にとってこれ以上悪い路線は想像できない. ¶push forward to India by the eastward *route* ***round*** the Cape of Good Hope 希望峰を回って東方経路によってインドへ進む. ¶a fast *route* ***to*** Japan 日本への早い路線.

O the *route* to be followed 順路.

route, *v.* 送る, 発送する.

P letters *routed* ***via*** ... ...経由にした手紙.

routine, *n.* [毎日の]きまり切った仕事.

V ***break*** the *routine* 変ったことをやる. ¶***follow*** a regular *routine* of business 正規の仕事をやる. ¶The business world ***resumes*** its *routine* on the fourth day after the New Year holiday. 実業界は正月休み後四日に仕事始めをやる. ¶***shake off*** *routine* for a time しばらく日課を休む. ¶He will be able to ***take up*** his normal (=habitual) *routine* shortly. 彼はじきに事務が執れるようになるだろう(病人など).

Q in your ***daily*** *routine* あなたの日課中に. 【類】***daily*** *routine* of his work. ¶emancipation from ***dull*** *routine* つまらない常務からの解放. ¶***clerical*** *routine* 牧師の日常の勤行. ¶***familiar*** *routine* 慣れている務め. ¶the ***humdrum*** *routine* of teaching 単調な教壇生活. ¶mere ***mechanical*** *routine* 全く機械的な仕事. ¶in the ***normal*** *routine* of events 当り前ならば. ¶***ordinary*** *routine* of office work きまり切った事務所の仕事.

Q² ***classroom*** *routine* クラスの日課. ¶***office*** *routine* 会社の事務. ¶***red-tape*** *routine*=redtapism [お役所の]わずらわしい手続き. ¶***school*** *routines* 学校の日課. 【類】the daily ***school-room*** *routine*.

rove, *n.* うろつき.

P ***on*** the *rove*=roving 漂泊して.

rove, *v.* うろつく.

M *rove* ***far*** into the forest 森林深く入り込む.

P *rove* ***in*** distant lands 遠い土地に漂泊する. ¶*rove* ***over*** sea and land 海やら陸やらを漂泊する.

row, *n.* 舟こぎ, 舟遊び.

V We want to ***have*** a *row* on the lake. 湖上で一こぎやりたいものだ.

Q² a ***practice*** *row* [ボートこぎの]練習.

P Let us go ***for*** a *row*. ボートこぎに行こう.

row, *v.* こぐ, こいで運ぶ.

M *row* a person ***ashore*** 舟をこいで人を岸に送り届ける. ¶*row* ***out*** こぎ出る. ¶He *rowed* ***stroke*** (***bow***) in the boat-race. 彼はそのボートレースで整調(など)を受持った. ¶*row* ***upstream*** 川をこぎ上る. ¶*row* ***wet*** (***dry***) 水をとばして(とばさないで)こぐ.

M² *row* ***off*** a boat ボートをこぎ出す.

P *row* ***across*** a stream 川をこいで横ぎる ‖ I'll *row* you ***across*** [the river]. 私が向う岸に渡してあげよう. ¶*row* ***against*** wind (current) 風(など)に向ってこぐ. 【類】The Cambridge University crew, which *rows* ***against*** (対抗の) Oxford every year, is selected from the best oarsmen in the university. ¶*row* ***in*** a regatta 短艇競そうで(ボートを)こぐ ‖ *row* ***in*** the same boat 同じボートでこぐ; [比ゆ的に] 同じ運命にある. ¶We are going to *row* ***on*** the Sumida this afternoon. われわれは今日午後隅田川にボートをこぎに行く. ¶The Oxford crew *rowed* ***over*** the Cambridge eleven. オックスフォード組はケンブリッジをボートレースで破った. ¶*row* ***towards*** the shore 岸の方へこぐ.

row, *n.* 列, 行, 並び.

V ***occupy*** the front *row* of a gallery さじきの前列を占める.

Q sit in ***alternative*** *rows* 交互の列にすわる. ¶be placed in a ***back*** *row* 後列におかれる. ¶a ***double*** *row* of trees 並木. ¶sit in the ***first*** (***second***, ***middle***) *row* 第一(など)列にすわる. ¶take a seat on a ***front*** *row* 前列に席をとる. ¶He thought it necessary to develop his voice loud enough to "reach the ***last*** *row*." 彼は自分の声が会場のすみずみにまで通らせるように大きくすることは必要だと思った. ¶in ***longitudinal*** *rows* 縦の列に.

P those sitting ***in*** the back *row* 後列にいる人々 ‖ arrange ... ***in*** four *rows* ... ...を四列に並べる. ¶the first one ***of*** the *row* その列の一番初めの者.

row, *n.* 騒ぎ, 騒動; けんか.

V ***have*** a *row* with a person 人とけんかをする. ¶***kick up*** a *row* やかましい音を立てる; けんかを始める. ¶***make*** a *row* 大騒ぎをする. ¶***start*** a *row* けんかを起させる.

V² when the *row* ***broke out*** けんかが起って.

Q They kicked up a ***jolly old*** *row*. いつものどたばた騒ぎをやった.

Q² an ***intra-party*** *row* 党内のごたごた. ¶a ***street*** *row* まちのけんか.

O What's the *row?* どうしたのだ.

royalty, *n.* 王権; 王; 印税.

V ***get in*** *royalty* on "..."「...」の著書で印税をもらう. ¶***offer*** a low *royalty* 安い印税を出す. ¶***pay*** a *royalty* to ten per cent upon the published price of the book その本の定価に対し一割の印税を払う. ¶***receive*** a *royalty* 印税をもらう.

Q a ***wealthy Continental*** *Royalty* 金持の大陸の王.

P money got ***in*** *royalties* 印税(特許権)として取った金. ¶in the presence ***of*** *royalty* 王の御前で.

P² the *royalties* ***of*** Europe ヨーロッパの諸国王. ¶*royalties* ***on*** a book 本の印税.

rub, *n.* 摩擦.

V ***have*** a brisk *rub* with a rough towel あらいタオルで敏速に摩擦する.

rub, *v.* さする, 摩擦する.

M *rub* ***down*** a horse 馬をくしけずる. ¶*rub* ***off*** color (paint) 色(など)をすり落す. ¶*rub* ***out*** (=***efface or wipe out***) chalk marks with an eraser 黒板ふきで白墨の跡を消す. ¶*rub* ***sore*** 痛いほどこする ‖ *rub* ***out*** pencil marks [ゴムで]鉛筆の字を消す.【類】*rub* ***out*** paint ‖ Let's *rub* him ***out***. 《俗》やつをばらそう. ¶*rub* one's hands ***together*** もみ手をする.

M² *rub* ***along*** (=***on***) 《俗》どうにか暮して行く. ¶*rub* ***down*** rough points かどをこすり落す. ¶*rub* ***off*** rust さびを落す ‖ *rub* ***off*** the rough edges かどをすり落す. ¶*rub* ***on*** from hand to month 辛うじて生活を立てる. ¶*rub* ***through*** with effort 努力してやり通す. ¶*rub* ***up*** (=refresh) one's memory 記憶を新たにする ‖ *rub* ***up*** furniture 家具をみがきこむ ‖ *rub* ***up*** against ...=come in contact with ... ...と接触する.

P *rub* ***against*** ... ...にこすりつける. ¶*rub* ointment (plaster) ***into*** the skin 皮膚に油(など)をこすり込む. ¶*rub* the sleep ***out of*** one's eyes 目をこすってねむけをさます. ¶*rub* ***through*** the world 細々と暮しを立てる. ¶*rub* ***to*** powder 粉になるほどこする. ¶*rub* ***with*** a stone (towel, hand) 石(など)でこする.

rubber, *n.* ゴム; *pl.* オーバシューズ.

V ***wear*** *rubbers* on one's shoes オーバシューズをつける.

Q impoverished rubber 弾力のなくなったゴム. ¶india rubber 消しゴム.

P insulate a live wire with rubber ゴムで電流を絶縁する.

rubbing, *n.* 拓本.

V make rubbings of monumental brasses 記念真ちゅう板の銘を拓本に取る.

rubbish, *n.* くず, ごみ, かけら.

V clear away rubbish ごみを掃除する. ¶dump rubbish ごみを捨てる. ¶gather up the rubbish ごみを集める. ¶sweep away rubbish ごみを掃除する. ¶talk rubbish つまらないことを話す. ¶write rubbish つまらないものを書く.

Q What rubbish=Nonsense! 何んだ詰らない.

P a pile of rubbish ごみの山; たわ言. ☞米国ではしばしば trash が使われる: throw trash on the street.

rudder, *n.* かじ, 方向かじ; 指導者.

V dismantle an old rudder of a ship 船の古いかじを取外す. ¶hold the rudder of the Stateship 国政のかじを取る.

rude, *a.* 粗野な, 粗暴な.

P rude in manner 態度が粗暴な. ¶It was very rude of me not to have replied sooner. 御返事が遅れて誠に失礼を致しました.【類】It is rude of me to have kept you waiting. ¶rude to a person 人に対して粗暴な.

rudeness, *n.* 無作法, 粗末, ぞんざい.

V Kindly excuse my rudeness in keeping you waiting. お待たせして失礼致しました. ¶forgive my rudeness 御無礼をお許し下さい. ¶Pray pardon my rudeness. 御無礼の段どうぞお許し下さい.

P I cannot put up with such rudeness. 私はこの無礼は容赦できない.

rudiment, *n.* 端緒, 初歩, 基礎.

V give the rudiments of education to China's 320,000,000 illiterates 中国の三億二千万という文盲の民に初歩の教育を施す. ¶learn the rudiments of arithmetic 算術の初歩を学ぶ.

P^2 the rudiments of chemistry (grammar) 化学(など)の基礎.

rueful, *a.* 悲しげな.

O an expression that sounds rueful=a rueful expression あわれっぽい表現.

ruffian, *n.* 悪徒, ろうぜき者, 曲者.

Q brutal ruffians 残忍な悪漢. ¶renowned ruffians 有名な悪党.

ruffle, *v.* [毛が]逆立つ.

M Nothing ever ruffled him. 彼が怒ったためしがない.

M^2 The crow ruffled up his black feathers. からすはその黒い羽根を逆立てた.【類】There was not a breath of air to ruffle up the glassy surface of the lake (鏡のような水面).

rug, *n.* 敷物(ラグ).

V weave a rug 敷物を織る.

Q^2 a hearth rug 炉辺の敷物. ¶a prayer rug (=mat) [回教徒の祈とうの際使う]ひざ敷き. ¶a little scatter rug 小さい敷物. ¶a three-ply rug 三枚合わせの敷物. ¶wrap up a woolen rug 毛のラグを巻く.

rugged, *a.* ごつごつした.

O climb rocks, rugged and steep ががとして切り立った岩をのぼる.

ruin, *n.* (**1**) 破滅, 没落, 零落.

V He accomplished her ruin. 彼は彼女を完全に破滅に落し入れた. ¶bring ruin upon oneself わが身の破滅を招く. ¶His folly brought about his ruin. 彼はばかをやって身の破滅を招いた. ¶face utter ruin 全くの破滅に面する. ¶It means his ruin. それは彼の破滅ということになる. ¶it would only serve to precipitate (=hasten) his ruin. そうするとただ彼の破滅を早めることになるだろう. ¶It spells ruin to him. それは彼の身の破滅ということになる. ‖ spell the ruin of the business 商売上ったりである. ¶work one's own ruin わが身の破滅をきたす.

V^2 Ruin now stares him in the face. 彼は今や破滅に直面している.

Q financial ruin 財政上の破滅. ¶national ruin 国家の滅亡. ¶social ruin 社会の破滅.

P fall into ruin 破滅に陥る. ¶go (=fall) to ruin 破滅となる.

P^2 This blackout business will be the ruin of me. この灯火管制で私の商売は上ったりだ.

(**2**) 廃虚, 旧跡.

V contemplate the ruins of Rome ローマの廃虚をしのぶ. ¶dig out ruins 廃虚を発掘する. ¶The castle is now forming an imposing ruin. その城は今や物々しい廃虚になっている.

V^2 whose ruins still stand in ... ...に今その廃虚が残っている.

Q an ivy-laden ruin つたのからまった廃虚. ¶Ruins are majestic. 廃虚は荘厳だ. ¶the moldering ruins of an old castle 累々たる古城の廃虚. ¶a mass of smoking ruins 煙がもうもう立上る廃虚. ¶The ruins of a fire are still smoldering. 火事の焼け跡がまだくすぶっている.

Q^2 a bomb ruin 爆撃による破壊の跡.

P his activity among the ruins of the past 旧跡の間における彼の活動[考古学者など]. ¶The whole superstructure would come down in ruins. 上層建築は全部くずれて廃虚に帰するであろう. ‖ The city is now in ruins. その市は廃虚となっている. ¶a heap of ruins うず高い廃虚. ¶under the ruins of the building 建物のくずれた下に.

P^2 the ruins of Rome ローマの廃虚.

ruin, *v.* 零落させる, 落ちぶれさせる.

M He was ruined financially. 彼は遂に零落した. ¶My dignity as a man is sadly ruined. 私の人間としての誇りはひどく傷つけられた.

P ruin oneself by ... ...によって身を滅ぼす. ¶ruined in health 健康を損じた.

O Marry her and ruin yourself! あの女と結婚してどうでもなれ.

ruinous, *a.* 破滅した.

P ruinous to his prestige 彼の威信にとって破滅的な.

rule, *n.* (**1**) 規則, 法則, 規定; 標準.

V abolish (=do away with) a rule 規則を廃する. ¶if the rules are administered by men of tact and experience 法規が世の経験に富んだ人士によって運用されると. ¶apply a rule unerringly 規則を的確に適用する. ¶break the rules of health 不養生をする ‖ these exceptions do not break the rule that ... これらの例外はあっても...という法則には変りはない ‖ guys who have broken the rules 法に触れた男たち(犯罪人). ¶carry out rules (instructions) 規定(など)を実行する. ¶disregard the rule 規則を軽視する. ¶The rule was rigorously (rigidly) enforced. 規則は厳重(など)に励行された. ‖ Rules were only occasionally and capriciously enforced. 規則は思い出したように気まぐれに励行された. ¶I have evolved the following rule as a guide. 私は次の規則を立ててこれによることにした. ¶follow the rules 規則に従う.【類】rules we may safely follow. ¶formulate rules 規則を作る. ¶frame rules of etiquette 礼式を定める ‖ rules framed by competent authorities for the use of ... ...の用に供するため有能な当局者によって定められた規定 ‖ It is impossible to frame rigid and at the same time safe rules. 厳重であって同時に安全な規定を作ることは不可能である. ¶a sentence illustrating this rule『文法』この規則を例示する文. ¶infringe rules 規則を破る. ¶The rule of the left is very strictly kept in London. ロンドンでは左側通行の規則がはなはだ厳格に守られる. ¶lay down rules of conduct 行為の準則を定める. ¶make a rule never to ... 決して...しないことにしている ‖ make a rule forbidding ... ...禁止の規則を作る. ¶obey rules 規則に従う. ¶observe all rules cheerfully 気持よくすべての規則を守る. ‖ rules to be observed in examination 受験規定.【類】observe the rules of priority (優先の規則). ¶prescribe rules 規則を定める. ¶promulgate rules against ... ...禁止の規則を公布する. ¶Such is only the exception that proves the rule. こんなのが通例になる唯一の例外である.【類】Exception proves the rule. ¶put rules into practice 規則を実施する. ¶remodel the rules 規則を改正する. ¶respect the rules 規則を尊重する. ¶see the rules go right 規則が正しく行われるように注意する. ¶set rules at defiance 規則を無視する. ¶set down rules 規則を定める. ¶show how the rule applies 規則の適用を示す. ¶The rule is sustained by the best modern usage. その規則は現代最善の慣習によって支持されている. ¶transgress the rules of debate 討議の規則にそむく. ¶violate a rule of syntax 文章法の規則を破る.【類】violate the rules of nature. ¶There is a rule against it, but on this occasion the rule is waived. それを禁止する規則があるがしかしこの場合その規則は無視する. ¶work out rules for their own use 自分たちだけに通用する内規を作る.

V^2 the rule bends for ... 規則は...に対していく分しんしゃくする. ¶the rules declare that ... 規則によれば... ¶rules governing the award of the ... medal ...賞はい授与に関する規定.【類】rules governing the competition for the prize / rules governing stopover privileges (途中下車). ¶This rule still holds good. この規定はいまだに有効である. ¶one of the rules of ... permits ... ...の規則に...を許す一条がある.

Q No absolute rules can be given. 絶対的な法則などあろ

うはずがない. ¶the ***big*** and ***little rules*** of the game of living 生活という競技の大小様々な法則. ¶***broad rules*** 広範な規定. ¶be reduced to a ***common rule*** 結局常道に落着く. ¶a violation of the ***established rules*** of decorum 守られている礼節の一つの違反.【類】disregard the ***established rules***. ¶it has no ***exact rule*** to guide the learners. それには学習者の参考になるたしかな法則がない. ¶Punctuality is the ***first rule*** in business. きちょう面は実業の骨子である. ¶there is no ***fixed rule*** as to ... ...については一定の規則がない. ¶a ***flexible rule*** 融通のきく規則. ¶***fundamental rules*** 根本の規則. ¶lay down a ***general rule*** 通則を定める.【類】With regard to ... there is no safe ***general rule***. / as a ***general rule*** / the ***general rule*** is ... / we might expect it a ***general rule*** that ... / a good ***general rule*** for ... is to ... ¶as a ***general*** though not ***invariable rule*** 一定不変ではなくとも一般の規則として. ¶live up to the ***Golden Rule*** 黄金律に従って生活する. ¶a ***good rule*** is to ... よい方法は...することだ. ¶So various are we as individuals that no ***hard-and-fast rule*** can be laid down. われわれは個人として非常に相違しているからしゃくし定規に規則を設けることはできない. ‖ It is not easy to lay down ***hard*** and ***fast rules*** for punctuation. 句読法に対して厳則を設けることは容易でない.【類】can lay down no ***hard*** and ***fast rule*** for ... ¶A most ***important hygienic rule*** is to maintain a strict regularity of the bowels. 一つのごく大切な衛生法は規則正しく通じをつけることである. ¶there are no ***infallible rules*** for ... ...にはあらゆる場合に通じるという法則はない. ¶There is an ***inflexible rule*** of the club which forbids any stranger to take a meal within its walls. そのクラブには外来者には絶対に食事をさせないという規定がある. ¶***invariable*** and ***inflexible rule*** 不変不動の規則. ¶an ***inviolable rule*** 破るべからざる規定. ¶break one of the ***minor rules*** of the university 大学のさほど重要でない規則の一つを破る. ¶There are some ***misleading rules*** in currency. 人を惑わすような規則が行われている. ¶***miscellaneous rules*** 雑則. ¶the ***normal rule*** of life 人生の常規. ¶observe the ***ordinary rules*** of decent society 上品な社会の普通の規律を守る. ¶make it a ***positive rule*** to ... ...することをはっきり習慣づける. ¶***practical rules*** 実際的な規則. ¶frame ***precise rules*** for ... ...に対する正確な規定を作る. ¶***printed rules*** regulating the work of a huge house-hold 印刷した大家の家憲. ¶***provisional rules*** 仮規定. ¶a ***rigid rule*** 厳重な規定. ¶***rough rules*** 大体の規定. ¶a ***rough-and-ready*** (=***thumbnail***) ***rule*** 大ざっぱなやり方. ¶the ***safe rule*** to follow is to ... 安全なやり方は...すること だ. ¶***sanitary rules*** 衛生上の規則. ¶There is no ***set rule*** for dressing on board [a] ship. 船の中では服装についてきまった規則はない. ¶a ***sound rule*** 堅実な規則. ¶I have never lived by any ***special rule*** of life. 私には別にこれという処生法もありません. ¶That is one of our ***strictest rules***. それが私たちの最も厳重な規定の一つです. ¶a ***stringent rule*** 厳重な規定. ¶***supplementary rules*** 補助規定. ¶The ***rule*** is by no means ***universal***. その規則は決して普遍的ではない. ¶***unsafe rules*** of conduct 不安な行為の軌範. ¶one of the ***unwritten rules*** of the club そのクラブの不文律の一つ. ¶***useful rules*** to follow やって役に立つ色色な方法(健康法など). ¶***vexatious rules*** and regulations わずらわしい諸規則や規定. ¶a ***wise rule*** 賢明な規則.

Q^2 under ***army rules*** 軍の法規によれば. ¶There is no ***cast-iron*** (=fixed *or* hard and fast) ***rule***. 別に鉄則といったものはない. ¶Our ***club rules*** provide that dues must be paid monthly. 当クラブでは会費は毎月収める規定になっている. ¶***everyday rule*** to go by 守るべき日常の規律. ¶***ground rules*** 運動場の諸規則. ¶***house rules*** 会館の内規. ¶***inn rules*** 宿屋の規則. ¶"Victory or death" was the ***iron rule*** governing the Imperial Forces.「勝利か死か」は皇軍を支配した鉄則であった. ¶the ***non-credit rule*** 現金主義. ¶***office rules*** 会社の内規. ¶the ***one hour rule*** [米国会議員の]一時間以上の演説禁止規程. ¶***playing rules*** 競技のルール. ¶***procedure rules*** in a debate 討論の方法に関する規程. ¶***road rules*** 道路法. ¶It is permitted by ***Rugby rules***. それはラクビーのルールで許されている. ¶***seniority rule*** 年功制度. ¶***side-bar rules*** 裁判所の内規. ¶***spelling rules*** つづり字法. ¶***standing rules*** 議事規則. ¶a ***textbook rule*** 教科書に載せてある法則(文法など). ¶break ***traffic rules*** 交通規則に触れる. ¶The ***three-halfpenny rule*** came into force. [書物など]一ペンス半の値が普通になった. ¶the ***two-meals-a-day rule*** 一日二食主義. ¶***working rules*** 作業の法則. ¶infringements of ***workshop rules*** 工場法の違反.

P ***according to*** the ***rule*** laid down 定められた規則に従って. ¶It is ***against*** the ***rule*** for an employee to whistle while on duty. 雇人が仕事中口笛を吹くのは規則違反である.【類】It is ***against*** the ***rules***. ¶***as*** a ***rule*** 原則として ‖ ***as*** a general ***rule*** 概して ‖ The artist is not a propagandist ***as*** a ***rule***. 芸術家は概して宣伝がまずい. ¶***by rule*** of the company 会社の規則で ‖ live ***by rule*** 規律を定めて生活する. ¶***in*** the ***rules*** of the association 同協会の規定中に. ¶a list (=set) ***of rules*** 一束の規定. ¶obedience ***to*** the ***rule*** 規則への服従 ‖ ***To*** this ***rule*** there are two exceptions. この規則には二つの例外がある. ¶A foreigner said, "It does not seem possible for the Japanese to work except ***under rules***."「日本人は規則によらないと仕事がやれないらしい」と一外人は言った. ‖ ***under*** this ***rule*** この(一カ条の)規則により.【類】work strictly ***under*** the ***rules*** of the association. ¶act ***upon*** (=***on***) a ***rule*** 規則に基いて行動する.

P^2 ***rules about*** ... ...に関する規定. ¶there is no ***rules against*** ... ...を禁止する規則がない. ¶***rules as to*** lectures 講義に関する規定. ¶Small classes are the ***rule at*** Denison, the majority having 20 or fewer students. デニソン校では小クラス主義で大概のクラスは二十名またはそれ以下の生徒である. ¶the ***rules for*** success 成功法 ‖ ***rules for*** practical (=the management of) life 処世法 ‖ ***rules for*** contestants コンテスト参加者の守るべき規定 ‖ ***rules for*** the management of life 処世法 ‖ ***rules for*** (=of) punctuation (spelling) 句読(など)法 ‖ ***rules for*** the pronunciation of words from Latin and Greek ラテン及びギリシア語から来た語の発音規則 ‖ lay down ***rules for*** our guidance われわれの参考のための規則を作る. ¶a ***rule of*** the common law 慣習法の一項目.【類】***rules of*** the library / ***rules of*** contest / ***rules of*** health ‖ the ***rules of*** decorum 礼法 ‖ the ***rule of*** right 右側通行の規則. ¶***rules on*** (=***for*** *or* ***regarding***) pronunciation 発音に関する規則. ¶It is a ***rule with*** me to go to bed early. 早寝が私の主義です.

O Cecil's mother made it a ***rule*** that if he came to the dinner table late he was not to speak a single word during the meal. セシルの母は彼が晩の食卓におそく来ると食事中黙っていなくてはならないという規則を作った. ¶you should make it a ***rule*** never to ... 君は決して...しないくせをつけるべきだ. ¶Failure is the ***rule***, success the exception.〘諺〙失敗が通例で成功は例外だ. ¶Only a hundred years ago, illiteracy was the ***rule***, not the exception. ほんの百年前までは文字を知らないことは例外ではなく通例であった.

(2) 支配, 統治.

V ***bear rule*** over the colonies 植民地を統治する. ¶***maintain rule*** 統治を続ける. ¶***consolidate*** their ***rule*** by creating new and more appropriate means of communication 新しい一層適当な通信方法を設けて彼らの支配を強固にする ‖ Iemitsu ably carried out the task of ***consolidating*** the Tokugawa ***rule***. 家光は徳川の統治を強化する事業をりっぱに成し遂げた. ¶He ***established*** the French ***rule*** in Canada. 彼がカナダにフランスの統治を建設した. ¶***spread*** his ***rule*** over ... 彼の支配を...に及ぼす.

Q the ***British rule*** in India インドにおける英国の統治. ¶be under ***foreign rule*** 外国の支配下にある. ¶Egypt under ***Roman rule*** ローマ統治下のエジプト.

Q^2 ***Bolshevik rule*** [ロシア]過激派の支配. ¶***boss rule*** ボス支配. ¶***closure*** or "***gag***" ***rule*** 言論抑圧支配. ¶the ***home rule***《英》内政自治. ¶***minority rule*** 少数者支配. ¶end its 21-year-old ***one-party rule*** of China 中国における二十一年にわたる一党支配を終える. ¶***trusteeship rule*** 信託統治. ¶***world rule*** 世界支配.

P revolt ***against*** the Chinese ***rule*** 中国の支配に反抗する. ¶***during*** the Tokugawa ***rule*** 徳川幕府の間. ¶There were some forty native peoples ***under*** the ***rule*** of Queen Wilhelmina. ウイルヘルミナ女王の治下には四十種族ほどの土着民がいた.【類】be brought ***under*** the same ***rule***.

P^2 ***rule by*** one person 一人による支配 ‖ ***rule by*** majorities 多数決政治. ¶the supremacy of British ***rule in*** South Africa 南アフリカにおける英国統治の優越性.

(3) ものさし, 定規.

Q a ***dotted rule*** 点線けい.

Q^2 a *foot rule* 一フィートもの差し. ¶a ***meter rule*** メートルざし. ¶a ***slide rule*** 計算尺. ¶the ***thumb rule***=the rule of thumb 目分量. ¶a ***wave rule*** 波線けい.

(**4**)〖数学〗比例.

P^2 the *rule* ***of*** three 比例 ‖ the double *rule* ***of*** three 複比例.

rule, *v.* 支配する; [相場など]保合う; 支配する; けいを引く.

M Exchange rate *rules* ***high*** (***low***). 為替相場が高い(安い). 【類】Prices of wheat and corn *ruled* ***high*** all the year. / Freight *rules* ***low*** owing to severe competition. ¶be *ruled* ***out*** 除外(名)される.

P *rule* ***by*** the sword 武力で治める. ¶*rule* lines ***on*** paper =rule paper with lines 紙上にけいを引く. ¶*rule* ***over*** a country 一国を支配する. 【類】The king *rules* ***over*** his people.

ruler, *n.* 統治者, 支配者; 元首.

V They prefer to ***obey*** a *ruler* rather than to rule themselves. 彼らは自治よりも統治者に服従する方を希望する.

Q an ***administrative*** *ruler* 執政官, 総督(将軍). ¶a ***brilliant*** *ruler* すばらしい統治者. ¶a ***deified*** *ruler* 神格化された支配者. ¶a ***despotic*** *ruler* 専制支配者, 暴君. ¶an ***efficient*** *ruler* 有能な支配者. ¶A dictator is an ***irresponsible*** *ruler*. 独裁者は無責任な支配者である. ¶a ***vicarious*** *ruler* 代理の支配者.

Q^2 a ***home*** *ruler* [アイルランドの]自治制主唱者.

ruling, *n.* 支配; 判決.

V ***accept*** a *ruling* 判決に服する.

Q^2 the ***Supreme Court*** *ruling* 最高裁判所の裁定.

P^2 according to a recent *ruling* ***of*** the Supreme Court 最高裁の先ごろの判決によれば ‖ a *ruling* ***of*** rectification 更正決定.

rumble, *n.* とどろき.

Q hear the ***far-off*** *rumble* of thunder 遠雷のとどろきを聞く. ¶the ***whispering*** *rumble* of the ocean 大洋の低いうなり声.

rumble, *v.* [雷や砲声が]ごろごろ鳴る.

M^2 The train is *rumbling* ***on.*** 汽車がごうっと通過する. ¶Day and night trains *rumble* ***past***, at the rate of 200 every 20 hours. 昼夜の差別なく二十時間ごとに二百の割で列車がごう音をたてて通る.

P All day a distant cannonading *rumbled* ***on*** the ear. 終日遠方からの砲声が耳にとどろいた.

ruminate, *v.* 反すうする; 思い回らす.

P *ruminate* ***on*** one's misfortunes 自分の不幸をかこつ.

rummage, *v.* 捜索する, くまなく捜す.

P *rummage* ***among*** one's effects 自分の所持品をくまなく捜す. ¶*rummage* ***in*** the desk drawer ***for*** ... 机の引出しの...を捜し回す.

rumo[u]r, *n.* うわさ, 風聞, 評判, 流言.

V It helped to ***beget*** various fantastic *rumors.* そのために色々な流言飛語を生むに至った. ¶*rumors* have been ***circulated*** of late to the effect that ... 近ごろ...といううわさが立った. ¶***deny*** *rumors* うわさを否定する. ¶Such *rumors* should be entirely ***disregarded.*** かかる風説は全然無視すべきものである. ¶***encourage*** a *rumor* うわさを立てる. ¶***hush up*** (=***burke or stifle***) a *rumor* うわさをもみ消す. ¶I have not ***heard*** the slightest *rumor* on the subject. その問題については私はちっとも風説を聞いていない. 【類】I ***heard*** a *rumor* that ... ¶The *rumor* was carefully ***nourished*** by interested persons. 関係者によってそのうわさが入念に立てられた. ¶***oppose*** the war *rumors* 開戦の風説を否定する. ¶a newspaper ***publishes*** a sensational *rumor* from Nagasaki to the effect that ... ある新聞に長崎からの...という意味の扇動的なうわさが出ている. ¶***put*** a *rumor* into currency 流言を放つ. ¶***revive*** the *rumor* of ... ...の風説を復活する. ¶***set at rest*** all *rumors* of ... ...のうわさを全部静める. ¶***spread*** a *rumor* うわさを流す. ¶***start*** a *rumor*=***put*** a *rumor* into circulation うわさを立てる.

V^2 the *rumor* is ***circulating*** that ... ...といううわさが立っている. ¶*rumors* ***came*** to Tokyo that ... ...といううわさが東京に伝わった. ¶there are *rumors* ***flying about*** that ... ...といううわさが立っている. ¶occasionally a *rumor* ***gets about*** that ... 折々...といううわさが立つ. ¶The *rumor* has ***got wind.*** そのうわさが立った. ¶a *rumor* ***goes forth*** that ... ...といううわさが立つ. ¶[a] *rumor* ***has*** it that ... ...といううわさが立つ. ¶The *rumor* ***passed*** from mouth to mouth. うわさが口々に伝わった. ¶*rumors* were ***prevailing*** in the city that ... ...といううわさが市内に広まっていた. ¶a *rumor* ***says*** that ... うわさによると... ¶the *rumor* ***spread*** that ... ...といううわさが立った.

Q an ***absurd*** *rumor* ばかげたうわさ. ¶for a long time *rumors* have been ***afloat*** of ... 長い間...のうわさが立っている. ¶***alarming*** *rumors* as to the imminence of war 戦争が切迫したという物騒なうわさ. ¶a *rumor* is ***apt*** to rise that ... ...といううわさが立ちやすい. ¶according to a ***current*** *rumor* 世間のうわさによると. ¶***dark*** *rumors* けしからぬうわさ. ¶***disquieting*** *rumors* 穏やかでない(人騒がせな)うわさ. ¶The *rumor* has turned out to be ***false.*** そのうわさは結局事実無根であった. 【類】spread ***false*** *rumors.* ¶***flying*** *rumors* 早く伝わる風評. ¶***frequent*** *rumors* ひん繁な風評. ¶a ***groundless*** *rumor* 根も葉もない風評. ¶circulate ***malicious*** *rumors* 悪宣伝をやる. ¶a ***persistent*** *rumor* 仲々消えないうわさ. ¶There is a ***queer*** *rumor* afloat. 妙なうわさが立っている. ¶a persistently ***recurrent*** *rumor* しつこく立てられる風説. ¶*rumors* were ***rife*** concerning ... ...に関してうわさがひどかった. ¶a ***silly*** and ***mischievous*** *rumors* ばかげている中傷的なうわさ. ¶a ***sinister*** *rumor* 悪宣伝. ¶The *rumor* is as yet ***unconfirmed.*** そのうわさはまだ確かめてない. ¶***unfounded*** *rumor* 根拠のない風評. ¶there was a ***vague*** *rumor* to the effect that ... ...という意味のぼんやりしたうわさがあった. ¶when ***warlike*** *rumors* were afloat 戦争のうわさが立ったときに. 【類】***Warlike*** *rumors* have caused quite a panic (恐慌) in the markets. ¶there are ***wide-spread*** *rumors* as to ... ...についてうわさが広く伝わっている.

Q^2 ***alarmist*** *rumors* 人騒がせなうわさ. ¶deny ***war*** *rumors* 戦争デマを打消す ‖ ***War*** *rumors* are in the air. 戦争のうわさが飛んでいる.

P the author ***of*** the *rumor* うわさの生みの親.

P^2 a *rumor* ***as to*** (=***about***) ... ...についてのうわさ. ¶the *rumor* ***on*** the subject その問題に関する風評.

O there is a *rumor* that ... ...といううわさがある. ¶*Rumor* is in the air (=rife). うわさが立っている.

rumo[u]r, *v.* うわさする, 風評する.

P it is *rumored* ***from*** London that ... ロンドンからのうわさでは...

rumple, *v.* しわにする, しわくちゃにする.

P *rumple* ***out of*** shape by pressure 押しつけてしわくちゃにする.

run, *n.* (**1**) 走り; 旅行, 遠足, 航行; 取付け.

V She can ***cover*** the New York-Hamburg *run* in eight days. その船はニューヨーク・ハンブルグ間の航程を八日で行ける. ‖ Tokyo-Shimonoseki special [express] ***covers*** its entire 700-mile *run* in 25 hours. 東京下関間の特急は七百マイルの全行程を二十五時間で走る. ¶***give*** a good *run* to a car 車を十分走らせる ‖ ***give*** it free *run* それを思う存分走らせる. ¶The steamer ***made*** the *run* in ... days and ... hours. その汽船はその航海を...日...時間で終えた. ‖ Depositors ***made*** a *run* on the bank. 預金者がその銀行に取付けをした.

V^2 if there ***comes*** a *run* on the bank その銀行に取付けでもあると. ¶if a *run* ***sets in*** 取付けが始まると.

Q the ship made a ***famous*** *run* of 14,511 knots from ... to ..., leaving ... on ... and reaching ... on ... その船は...から...まで一万四千五百十一海里の行程で...を...出発し...に...到着したというすばしい航海をやった. ¶make a ***hurried*** *run* to ... ...へ飛脚旅行をする. ¶the ***last*** *run* of the day その日の最終運転(列車の). ¶Joinville is a ***mere half-hour's*** *run* from Paris. ジョアンヴィルはパリーからわずか三十分という短時間で行ける.

Q^2 a ***century*** *run* 百マイルの(自転車)疾走. ¶Steamers placed on the ***China*** *run* 中国航路就航の諸汽船. ¶a ***nonstop*** *run* to ... ...への無停車運転. ¶an 8-hour ***railroad*** *run* from ... ...からの汽車旅行. ¶These steamers sail together on a ***shuttle*** *run* from Kagoshima to Shanghai and return. これらの船はいっしょに鹿児島上海間の航路に使われる. ¶set off on a ***skiing*** *run* スキーに出かける. ¶a ***takeoff*** *run* 〖飛〗離陸場. ¶a ***trial*** *run* 試運転. 【類】The U.S. submarine made a successful test dive on its ***trial*** *run* in the wintry Atlantic. ¶This is a ***two-hour*** motor *run.* 自動車で二時間で行ける.

P depart ***at*** a *run* towards ... ...の方へかけ足で行く. ¶go out ***for*** a *run* 一走りやりに出かける. ¶***in*** the long *run* 長い中には, 結局は. ‖ Cheap materials and cheap workmanship always prove the most expensive ***in*** the long *run.* 安い材料と安い細工ものはいつも結局一番高いものにつく. 【類】***In*** the long *run,* it is always the intellectual and spiritual forces that count most in the affairs of men. / An appeal to the reason (理性への訴え) of the people has never been known to fail ***in*** the long ***run***.—Lowell. ¶ vessels ***on*** the Australian ***run*** 豪州航路の船 ‖ one of the smaller vessels ***on*** this ***run*** この航路通いの小型の方の船の一つ. ¶ His pace lengthened almost ***to*** a ***run***. 大またになってまるでかけ足みたいになった. ¶ Prices (The barometer) came down ***with*** a ***run***. 相場(晴雨計)がどかっと下った.

P² vessels on the weekly ***run between*** … …間を毎週航行する船. ¶ From this place it is only a 20-minute ***run by*** rail to Osaka. ここから大阪へは汽車でわずか二十分で行ける. ¶ The ship was destroyed by fire on ***run from*** New York in 1840. その船は一八四〇年ニューヨークからの航海中火災にかかった.

(2) 〘劇・映〙連続興業; すう勢; 流行; 売行き; 囲い内; 使用; 〘野球〙得点; 《米》[たて糸の]ほつれ, 電線病; [銀行の]受付け.

V It ***created*** a great ***run*** upon popular literature relating to the subject. そのためにその問題に関する大衆文学の大流行をきたした. ¶ after he had ***finished*** his ***run*** in London 彼(俳優)のロンドン興行を終えてから. ¶ That piece of slang ***has*** a great ***run***. その俗語は非常に流行している. ‖ The play has ***had*** its ***run***. 芝居が千秋楽になる. ‖ ***have*** a ***run*** of ill luck 不幸が続く ‖ There one can ***have*** the ***run*** of every variety of bath. そこではあらゆる種類の水浴ができる. ‖ I ***had*** the ***run*** (=free use) of a well-stocked library. 私は蔵書の多い図書館を自由に使用することができた. 【類】He has ***had*** the ***run*** of the Apsly House archives. ¶ ***score*** a ***run*** in the 9th inning 〘野球〙九回目に一点入れる ‖ The play ***scored*** a phenomenal ***run***. その劇は奇跡的な長期興行をやった. ¶ ***taking*** the ordinary ***run*** of cases 普通の場合をとって考えるに.

Q They are not outstanding but they are rather better than the ***average run***. 抜群ではないがちょっと並以上だ. ¶ above the ***common run*** of mankind 人並以上の. ¶ an ***earned run*** 〘野球〙安打で入れた一点. ¶ be a fair ***run*** for one's money 代価相当のものである. ¶ I had the ***free run*** of the place. 私はその場所を自由に使用することができた. ¶ the ***general*** (=common) ***run*** of men 一般普通の人. ¶ The new novel has a ***good run*** among young readers. その新小説は若い読者間で好評だ. ¶ There is a ***great run*** on that style of dress. あの型の服が大流行だ. ¶ I have now a ***great many runs*** on my purse. 今は出費が多い. ¶ a ***long run*** of ill-luck 不運続き ‖ Peace has had a ***long run***. 平和が長く続いた. ‖ have a ***long run*** [映画・劇など] 長期興行をする ‖ The Conservatives have had a ***long run*** of power (=office). 保守党は長く政権についている. ‖ a bill at a ***long run*** 長期の手形. ¶ quite above (=out of) the ***ordinary run*** 全く類を異にした, けたはずれの. 【類】above the ***ordinary run*** of mankind. ¶ in the ***short run*** 差当りは. ¶ out of the ***usual run*** 並はずれた.

Q² swat a ***home run*** 〘野球〙ホームランをかっとばす. ¶ a ***nylon run*** (=ladder) ナイロンくつ下の電線病. ¶ a ***poultry*** (***sheep***) ***run*** 養鶏(飼羊)場. ¶ an 8-***hour run*** of work 八時間継続作業.

P ***after*** a ***run*** of bad luck 悪運続きの後. ¶ be so ***unlike*** the ***run*** of current French fiction in subject, method, and style 題目, 方法, 文体の点で今日の一般フランス小説とは非常に違っている.

P² There is a ***run in*** the stocking. 《米》くつ下に一本ほつれがある. ¶ the ***run of*** the market 市場気配 ‖ the ***run of*** events ことの成行(形勢). ¶ The play had a ***run of*** 222-day performances (ninety nights). その狂言は二百二十二日(など)打通し興行をやった. ¶ a ***run on*** a bank 銀行の取付け ‖ a great ***run on*** the war story 戦争ものの大好評(売行き). ¶ There will be nothing ***out of*** the usual ***run***. 普通以外のものは何もなかろう. 「転する; 経営する.

run, *v.* 走る, かける, 急ぐ; 経過する, 継続する; 走らす, 運

M The ship ***ran aground***. その船は座礁した. ¶ ***run*** (=go) ***ahead*** of … in … …ではより上だ ‖ ***run ahead*** of the (=one's) ticket 《米》他の味方候補者の平均得点よりも多数の投票を得る. ¶ ***run amuck*** at … …に向って猛進する, を滅多打にする. ¶ The ship ***ran ashore*** to avoid sinking. 同船は沈没を防ぐため浅瀬に乗上げた. ¶ A coward will ***run away*** rather than fight. おく病者は戦わないで逃げてしまう. ‖ ***run away*** from home 家出をする ‖ ***running away*** from life 人生からの逃避. 【類】***run away*** from her husband and children / ***run away*** from there back to home / He ***ran away*** from his first job as a book-binder (製本屋の職人), so that he might learn the violin. ‖ ***run away*** (=elope) with a girl 娘をかどわかす. 【類】***run away*** with one's master's money ‖ Her mind seemed ***running away*** with him. 彼女の心は彼のもとに行ってるように思えた. ‖ please don't ***run away*** with the idea that … …と早合点してくれるな. ¶ He ***ran back*** for an umbrella he had left. 彼はおき忘れたかさをとりにかけ戻った. ‖ ***run back*** to its source その出所を調べる. ¶ He ***runs*** me ***close*** in mathematics. 彼は数学ではほとんど私と同じ位だ(学力が). ¶ The Japanese national policy does by no means ***run counter*** to democratic principles. 日本の国策は決して民主々義に反しない. / ***run counter*** to the modern spirit in ethics / ***run counter*** to recognized usage (世人の慣習) / His conduct ***ran counter*** (=is opposed) to all rules of propriety (行儀作法). / His plan ***ran counter*** to mine. / Few persons have enough strength of mind to ***run counter*** to the general custom. ¶ Steamers ***run daily***. 汽船は毎日出る. ¶ The fish does not ***run deep***. その魚は(浮魚で)深い所にはいない. ¶ They may ***eventually run*** to a considerable number. 結局相当大きな数に上るかも知れない. ¶ ***run forward*** to meet (greet) … …に会おう(あいさつをしよう)と飛び出す. ¶ The cars ***ran foul*** of each other. 車が衝突した. ¶ ***run headlong*** into danger 危険の中に身を投じる ‖ The feeling of enmity against the Japanese was reportedly still ***running high*** among the Filippino people. 日本人に対する反感はいまだに比島人間に強かったそうだ. ‖ Feeling still ***runs high***. 感情が依然激興している. ‖ Hopes ***run high***. 希望がたかまる. ¶ ***How*** does the first verse ***run?*** [歌など] 最初の一節は何というの. ¶ ***run lengthwise*** [廊下など](たてに)長く走っている. ¶ ***run low*** on fuel [飛行機など]燃料が不足する. ¶ The stock of raw material is ***running low***. 持合わせの原料が段々乏しくなりかかっている. ¶ he ***ran mad*** on (=went wild about) … 彼は…に夢中になった. ¶ Waves were ***running mountain-high***. 波は山のように高くあがっていた. ¶ ***run naked*** from the bath はだかのまま風呂から走り出る. ¶ ***run out*** into the street 通りへ飛び出る ‖ prevent its ***running out*** by paying the pawnbroker's interest 利を入れて質が流れないようにする ‖ A little peninsula ***runs out*** to the middle of the lake. 小さな半島が湖水の真中に突き出ている. ‖ His enlistment has ***ran out***. 彼の在役期間は切れた. ‖ The coffee ***ran out*** a month before the relief ship put in. コーヒーは輸送船が入る一カ月前に品切れとなった. 【類】The fuel was rapidly ***running out***. / The food supplies have ***run out*** and the new harvest is not yet in. ‖ Time is ***running out***. 時間が迫っている. ‖ His luck ***ran out***. 彼の運が尽きた. 【類】The contract is nearly ***run out***. ¶ ***run parallel*** with (=to) … …と並行して走る. ¶ ***run plump*** into … …にばったりぶっつかる. ¶ ***run*** very ***rapidly*** 猛スピードで走る. ¶ The water ***ran red*** with the blood of dead and wounded men. 死傷者の血で水が赤くなった. ¶ This color will ***readily run*** when the dress is washed. 洗たくすればこの色はすぐ流れる. ¶ ***run riot*** in praise of … …をめちゃめちゃにほめそやす. ¶ He attends to the elevators to see that they ***run safely***. エレベーターが安全に動くかどうかを注意する. ¶ The paper is ***running serially*** the latest of his novels. その新聞は彼の最近の小説を連続小説として載せている. ¶ The supplies ***ran short***. 貯蔵品が尽きかけた. 【類】Stock is ***running short***. / The oil is ***running short***. ¶ The musical drama ***ran sixty nights***. その歌劇は六十夜続いた. ¶ ***run*** a car ***slowly*** (***fast***) 車をゆっくりやる(走らせる). ¶ The machine refused to ***run smoothly***. その機械はどうしても工合よく運転しなかった. ‖ The programme is ***running smoothly***. 番組が故障なく進行している. ‖ These verses ***run smoothly*** (=***regularly***). これらの詩は流ちょうである. 【類】The book ***runs*** more ***smoothly*** than translations commonly do. / His sentences ***run smoothly*** and ***easily***. ¶ The book ***speedily ran*** into a second edition. その本はたちまち再版になった. ¶ I think the blockade can be ***successfully run***. 封鎖線はうまく突破できると思う. ¶ ***run swiftly*** 早く走る. ¶ The words ***run thus***. その言葉はこうだ. ¶ ***run together*** when attacked from outside 外部からの攻撃を受けると急いで集合する. ¶ ***run wild*** 度を過す; 脱線する.

M² There is a joke that has been ***running around*** like wildfire this week. この一週間猛烈にはやった冗談がある.

¶A person was *run* ***down*** (=*over*) and killed by a train. 人が汽車にひかれて死んだ. ‖ *run* a man ***down*** 人をくさす ‖ My watch has *run* ***down***. 僕の時計は止まった. ‖ Our school has *run* ***down***. 学校は休みになった. ‖ I feel myself *running* ***down***. からだがだんだん衰弱するのがわかる. ‖ be *run* ***down*** by overwork 過労で健康を害する ‖ I generally *run* ***down*** once a fortnight. 私は大概二週間に一度いなかへ行く. ‖ *run* ***down*** to one's home 帰郷する ‖ *run* ***down*** criminals 犯人たちを追いつめる ‖ *run* ***down*** a gang of smugglers 密輸入団を抑える ‖ *run* ***down*** [a runner] between 3rd base and home plate 〘野球〙三本間できょう殺される ‖ a house, desolated, ready to *run* ***down*** 今にも倒れそうなあばら屋 ‖ *run* ***down*** (=sink) a vessel [突当って]船を沈める. 【類】The steamer was *run* ***down*** by a liner and sank. ¶*run* ***in*** with a person 人と意見が一致する ‖ *run* ***in*** at ... …のもとに立寄る. ¶*run* ***off*** with the idea that ... …だと早のみ込をする ‖ The reader must not *run* ***off*** with the idea that ... …読者は…と早合点してはいけない. ‖ *run* ***off*** (=away) with ... …とかけ落ちする ‖ *run* ***off*** to ... …へ走り去る. ¶*run* ***round*** for ... 急いで…を呼びに行く. ¶I *ran* him ***through***.=I thrust my sword through him. ‖ *run* ***through*** with=squander ... …を徒費する. ¶*run* ***up*** the flag 旗を揚げる. 【類】*run* ***up*** a signal ‖ *run* (=put) ***up*** a block of building 《英》ブロック家屋(アパート)を建てる ‖ *run* ***up*** the steps 階段をかけあがる. 【類】The cat *ran* ***up*** the tree. ¶sales *ran* ***up*** to ... 売上は…に上った ‖ *run* well ***up*** into the thousands ゆうに何千という数に上る ‖ Accounts are *running* ***up*** very fast. 勘定はどしどしふえる. ‖ *run* ***up*** bills at the grocer's 食料品屋の勘定がかさむ ‖ take care not to let one's inclinations *run* ***up*** into a habit この傾向が習性にならないように気をつける ‖ *run* ***up*** against ... …出会わす; …と衝突する.

P I accidentally *ran* ***across*** a little book entitled ... 私は偶然…という小冊子を見つけた. ‖ I *ran* ***across*** him.=I met him by chance. 私は偶然彼に会った. ‖ *run* ***across*** the plain 平原を横断する. ¶*run* ***after*** the fashion 流行を追う ‖ *run* ***after*** a thief 盗人を追かける ‖ Don't *run* ***after*** chickies. ひよっこを追いかけちゃいかん. 【類】The cat *ran* ***after*** the mouse. ‖ He is much *run* ***after***. 方々で引張りだこだ. ¶Fortune *ran* ***against*** him. あの人は運が悪かった. ‖ *run* ***against*** an acquaintance 知人にばったり会う ‖ *run* ***against*** the pier 波止場に突き当る. 【類】*run* ***against*** a rock ‖ be *run* ***against*** by a streetcar 電車にはねられる. ¶The horse *ran* ***along*** the street. 馬は街路に沿うて走った. ¶*run* one's eyes ***around*** the room へやをぐるっと見回す. ¶The novel is *running* ***as*** a serial in the Asahi. その小説は朝日に続き物として載っている. ¶The dog *ran* ***at*** the boy. その犬は子供に向って走った. ‖ *run* ***at*** full speed 全速力で走る ‖ the saying *runs* ***as*** follows: ことわざにいわく ‖ Races *run* ***at*** 10 a.m. 十時発走(競輪など). ‖ a troop of children *ran* ***at*** their heels 小供たちの一群は続いてばたばた走り出した ‖ *run* ***at*** the nose (=nostrils) 鼻汁が出ている ‖ with a pulse *running* ***at*** 100 or so 脈はくは百位で. ¶*run* ***before*** the enemy 敵に追われて逃げる ‖ *run* (=sail) ***before*** the wind 順風に帆をあげる. 【類】*run* ***before*** a gale. ¶We *ran* ***behind*** nearly $100. われわれの会計が約百ドル不足した. ‖ The concern has been *running* ***behind*** some from ¥200,000 to ¥300,000 yearly. その会社は年に二十万円から三十万円の赤字を出している. 【類】We *run* ***behind*** nearly 30,000 yen. ¶*run* ***by*** electric power 電力で運転させる ‖ These music halls are virtually *run* ***by*** one syndicate. これらの寄席は事実上一つの企業団体によって経営されている. ¶*run* ***down*** a hill 小山をかけ下る ‖ Sweat *ran* ***down*** my face. 汗が顔を流れた. 【類】The squirrel *ran* ***down*** the tree. ¶He *ran* ***for*** his life. 彼は命がけで走った. ‖ *run* ***for*** the rescue of ... …の救助にかけつける ‖ *run* ***for*** Congress 《米》代議士に立候補する ☞ 英語用法は *stand* for Parliament である. ‖ *run* ***for*** the election 選挙戦に打って出る ‖ *run* ***for*** President 大統領候補に立つ. 【類】candidates *running* ***for*** prefectural assemblymen (県会議員) / He has announced his intention to *run* ***for*** the Diet representing Tokyo. / They are *running* Mr. T ***for*** the House of Representatives (代議士に推薦している). ‖ The Geisha, a musical comedy, by Owen Hall, *ran* ***for*** 760 performances at Daly's Theatre, London. オーエン・ホール作喜歌劇「芸者」はロンドンのデーリー劇場で七百六十回の連続興行を打った. ‖ It is *run* ***for*** profit それは営利事業である. ¶The rates *run* ***from*** eight shillings a day up. 料金は一日八シリングからである[ホテルなど]. ‖ The offenders were sent to jail on sentences *running* ***from*** 7 to 14 days. 違反者は七日ないし十四日の拘留に処せられた. 【類】The term *runs* ***from*** April ***till*** July. ¶*run* an ad ***in*** a daily 日刊紙に広告を出す ‖ A taste for painting, and indeed for all the fine arts *runs* ***in*** our family. 絵画を始めあらゆる美術趣味は私たちの家族の共通点です. 【類】The disease seems to *run* ***in*** the family. / Genius *runs* ***in*** his family. / Longevity (長命) seems to *run* ***in*** families. ‖ The tune *ran* ***in*** his head. その歌が彼の頭にちょいちょい浮んだ. ¶The price *ran* ***into*** the millions. 値段は何百万円という額に上った. 【類】The annual sales (年間販売高) of the firm *run* ***into*** the hundreds of thousands of yen. / The expense will *run* ***into*** thousands of yen. / The money spent by Americans in Europe *runs* ***into*** many millions. / The London Gazette sometimes *runs* ***into*** hundreds of pages. / *run* ***into*** more than one paragraph / The numbers *run* ***into*** thousands. ‖ She was *run* ***into*** by an unknown vessel. 国籍不明船と衝突した. 【類】two things *running* ***into*** each other / An awkward driver carelessly *ran* ***into*** and damaged a family car on a highway. / He made a fortune *running* ***into*** six figures (なん十万) / The thermometer *runs* ***into*** the 90°F. ‖ *run* ***into*** trouble 事故を起す, 厄介なことになる ‖ *run* ***into*** a second edition [本が]重版する. 【類】*run* ***into*** editions of twenty, thirty, or fifty thousand ‖ Talking *ran* ***into*** all kinds of channels. 話は色々のことにわたった. ‖ *run* ***into*** heavy weather 悪天候に遭遇する ‖ The engine *ran* ***into*** a siding to water up. 機関車は給水のために側線にはいった. ‖ The river *runs* (=flows) ***into*** a lake. その川は湖に注ぐ. ‖ He caught a severe cold, which *ran* ***into*** pleurisy, and laid him up for about two months. 彼はひどいかぜを引いてそれがろく膜炎になり約二カ月床についた. ‖ *run* ***into*** debt 借金する. 【類】This cold of mine seems to be getting worse, and it may *run* ***into*** something serious. ‖ Ah Mr. ...! I'm happy in *running* ***into*** you. やあ…さん! お目に掛ってうれしいです. 【類】I was *run* ***into*** by a newspaper boy. ‖ *run* (=mould) lead ***into*** bullets 鉛をいて銃弾を作る. ¶*run* ***like*** a scared rabbit 脱とのごとく走る. ¶The train *ran* ***off*** [the line] (=jumped the metals) at ... 《英》その列車は…で脱線した. ☞ 米語用法は jump the track とか The train was ditched. という. ¶*run* ***on*** 〘印刷〙追込む ‖ *run* ***on*** a reef 暗礁に乗り上げる ‖ The factory is *run* ***on*** scientific lines. その工場は科学的に経営している. 【類】Trains are *run* ***on*** the following schedule, subject to usual summer changes. ‖ His mind *ran* ***on*** his own trouble. 彼は個人的な心配に悩まされた. ‖ The streetcar *runs* ***on*** rails (=track). 市電は線路上を走る. ‖ *run* ***on*** the rock 岩にぶっつかる. 【類】*run* ***on*** shore. ¶I am *run* ***out of*** tobacco=I have used all my tobacco. 私はたばこが切れた. 【類】*run* ***out of*** food / *run* ***out of*** stock / We are *running* ***out of*** food supplies (食料のたくわえ) / Our car is *running* ***out of*** gas (=gasolin). ‖ like the water *running* ***out of*** the basket 水がかごからもれるように ‖ *run* it ***out of*** business それと競争して廃業させる ‖ He *ran* ***out of*** the room. 彼はへやから走り出た. ¶The business it handles *runs* ***over*** two hundred millions a year. それが取扱う商売は一年二億以上になる. ‖ Short stories should not *run* ***over*** (=exceed) 3,000 words. 短編小説は三千字以内のこと. ‖ The book *runs* ***over*** 1,200 octavo pages. その本は八つ折判千二百ページ以上になる. ‖ The chauffeur *ran* ***over*** a pedestrian, who had not gone out of his way quickly. 一人の通行人がぐずぐずしてのかなかったものだから運転手がひいてしまった. ‖ *run* ***over*** a list 表を一覧する. 【類】*run* (=go) ***over*** papers ‖ Water *runs* ***over*** its banks. 川があふれている. ‖ The last drop makes the cup *run* ***over***. 〘諺〙最後の一滴で茶わんがあふれる(もう少しもう少しとやると行き過ぎる). ‖ They *run* trial cars ***over*** the section. その区間で試運転をする. ¶An automobile *ran* ***past*** me. 一台の自動車が私の傍を走って行った. ¶A fence *runs* ***round*** the house. その家の回りに垣がある. ¶The tunnel of a railroad *runs* ***through*** that mountain. 鉄道のトンネルが山を貫通している. ‖ *run* ***through*** Mss. ざっと原稿に目を通す ‖ *run* ***through*** one's money 金をどんどん使ってしまう ‖ It will first *run* *through* Scribner's Magazine beginning in the January number of 1900. それは先ず一九〇〇年一月号から始まってスクリブナー雑誌に連載される. 【類】The article is now *running through* the ... Magazine. / His last book has *run through* ten editions. ‖ *Through* all that he said there *runs* the evidence of a great heart as well as a great intellect. 彼がそこで述べた全部にわたって偉大なる知力と精神とが明瞭に現われている. ¶not let it *run to* waste それをむだにしない ‖ the constable *ran* the criminal *to* earth at ... 警官が犯人を…で捕縛した ‖ I should like to keep a horse, but I can't *run to* (=afford) it. 私は馬を飼いたいが費用にたえない. ‖ Apple-trees have *run to* seed. りんごの花時が過ぎて実になった. ‖ The book *runs to* nearly 120 pages. その本は約百二十ページになる. ‖ His tastes *run to* (=*toward*) law. 彼は法律が好きだ. ‖ when the machinery is *running to* capacity 機械が最大能力を発揮すると ‖ *run* (=ride) a horse *to* death 馬を乗りつぶして殺す ‖ *run to* ruin (=waste) 破滅する ‖ Nothing did he see but the sand *running to* a rim against the sky 目に見えるものは地平線まで大空に舞上る砂ほこりだけだった. ‖ *run to* seed じじむさくなる ‖ The figures *run* up *to* $50,000. 数字は五万ドルに上った. ¶*run up* a hill 小山をかけ上る.

O You had better cut and *run*. 君は默ってさっさと行ったがよい.

run-down, *a*. 健康を害した; 荒廃した.

P be *run-down from* overwork 過労で病気になっている.

O an old villa, *run-down*, dilapidated 古くなってこわれかかった別荘.

rung, *n*. はしごの桟.

Q men who are as yet on the *lower rungs* of the ladder まだ社会の下積になっている人々. 【類】start one's career at the *lowest rung*.

runner, *n*. 走者(ランナー); 細長い布地.

M assist a *runner out* 補殺する.

Q a *fast* (*slow*) *runner* 早(おそ)い走者.

Q² a *gun runner* 銃(ピストル)密輸入者. ¶a *hotel runner* 宿引き. ¶a *rickshaw runner* 人力車夫. ¶a *sled runner* そり乗り.

P² a *runner of* carpet (run) 細長いじゅうたん(など). 【類】a *runner of* lace on a bureau.

running, *n*. 走ること.

V The buses have *ceased running*. バスは運転をやめた. ¶trains *make* close *running* between ... 汽車は…間をひんぱんに運転される.

Q With *constant running* up and down stairs, her legs are now swollen. ひっきりなしに階段を上り下りするので彼女の足がはれている. ¶an *honest* and *efficient running* of the government 政府の正しく能率的な運営.

Q² *base running*〘野球〙走塁.

P be *in* (*out of*) the *running* 勝つチャンスがある(ない). ¶He is out of breath *with running*. 彼は走ったので息を切らしている.

rupture, *n*. 破裂, 破談; 不和.

V *avoid* a *rupture* by sitting "on the fence" between the conflicting parties=straddle 日より見主義で両者の決裂をさける.

Q *irremediable rupture* 調停不可能の不和.

Q² a *treaty rupture* 条約の決裂.

P The negotiations came *to* a *rupture*. 交渉は決裂した. ¶*upon* the *rupture* of negotiations with ... …との交渉が決裂して.

P² The *rupture of* friendliness between the two was never healed. 二者間の友情の破たんは終に結ばれなかった. ¶a *rupture of* athletic relations *with* Keio 慶応との競技関係の破たん ‖ the *rupture of* a blood vessel 血管の破裂.

ruse, *n*. 偽計, 計略.

V, V² *discover* a *ruse* 偽計に気ずく. ¶a *ruse intended* to ... …しようとする計略. ¶The *ruse failed*. その計略は失敗した.

Q a *diplomatic ruse* concocted by ... …のたくらんだ外交手段. ¶a *pious ruse* 方便のうそ.

P *by* some subtle *ruse* なにかずるい策略で.

rush, *n*. 突進, 押寄せ, 殺到; 流行.

V *attract* a *rush* of immigrants 移民の殺到をきたす ‖ *attract* the great *rush* of gold miners 金山鉱夫の殺到をきたす. ¶to *avoid* the *rush* 殺到を避けるために. ¶*have* a *rush* of blood to the head のぼせる. ¶*make* a *rush* for the door 入口に押寄せる. ¶a letter *marked* "*Rush*"《米》「速達」と印された手紙. ☞ 英語用法では "Urgent."

Q an *enormous rush* of mails at the General Post Office 中央郵便局における郵便物の恐ろしい殺到. ¶make the *final rush* on ... …に最後の突撃を加える. ¶There was a *great rush* of women folk to the windows. [何か見ようとして]女連が大勢窓口に押寄せた. ¶the *home-going rush* of city workers 都市勤労者の帰宅を急ぐあわただしさ. ¶The *red-hot rush* of the fire engine whirls down the narrow streets of the crowded city. 消防自動車が人だかりの狭い通りを火のつくように突進する. ¶A *sudden rush* of business kept us working hard. 仕事が急に忙しくなってわれわれは大わらわに働き続けた. ¶a *wild rush* to the house of ... …の家への盲目的突進.

Q² the *Christmas rush* クリスマスの書入時. ¶during the period of *morning* or *evening rush* 朝晩のラッシュアワーには. ¶the *gold rush* 黄金熱. ¶a *pell-mell rush* ごった返し, てんやわんや. ¶The *holiday rush* is over. 休日の雑踏も終る. ¶the *noon rush* at a restaurant 料理店の昼の混雑. ¶*traffic rush*=traffic jam 交通の混雑.

P carry it *at* the first *rush* 一挙にそれを攻略する. ¶be swept away *by* the *rush* of the river 激流に押し流される. ¶live *in* a *rush* 忙しく生活する ‖ *in* the *rush* of business 仕事が忙しいので ‖ reply *in* the *rush* あわてて返事をする. ¶He was *on* the *rush* (=in a rush). 彼は大多忙だった. ¶War books are coming out *with* a *rush*. 戦争物がどしどし現われて来る. 【類】fill an order *with* a *rush*.

P² The *rush for* cars is a typical night scene in the Strand after the play. あわてて自動車に乗る光景は芝居のはねた後のストランドでよく見る図である. ‖ a *rush for* straw hats 麦わら帽の流行 ‖ the *rush of* blood 流血. ¶the *rush of* city life 都会生活の騒々しさ. 【類】amid the *rush of* modern life. ¶Trains have been running late in consequence of the *rush of* holiday makers. 休日行楽者が多いので汽車が遅れている. ¶the *rush of* American youth *to* the colleges and universities for learning 米国青年が修学のため単科大学や総合大学に押寄せること. 【類】the *rush of* city life. ¶the *rush to* city life 都市生活への殺到.

rush, *n*. い草;《口語》つまらないもの.

V I don't *care* a *rush* (=bit). なんとも思わない.

Q It is not *worth* a *rush* (=fig). 三文の価値もない.

Q² *Dutch rushes* とくさ.

rush, *v*. 突進する; 急がせる.

M An electric train *rushed away* with great noise. 電車が音を立てて通り過ぎた. ¶*rush back* to ... 大急ぎで…に帰る. ¶*rush forward* 飛び出す. ¶*rush headlong* into a war (a general strike) まっしぐらに戦争(ゼネスト)に突入する. ¶Motor-cars, buses, and trucks *rushing incessantly* in the roadway make the crossing difficult and even perilous. 自動車・バス・トラックが絶えず車道を通るので道路横断が困難になりまた危険にさえなるのである. ¶*rush out* with a coat unbottoned and boots unfastened 上衣のボタンもかけずくつのひもも結ばないで飛び出す. 【類】*rush out* into the street.

M² The animal *rushed about* in great fury. その動物はたけり狂って走り回った. ¶*rush* in *for* seats 席を取ろうとなだれ込む. ¶*rush off* to ... …に急行する. ¶Let's *rush* it *through* to earn time for pleasure. 急いでそれをやってしまって遊ぼうじゃないか. ‖ *rush* a bill *through* 議案を急速に通す.

P *rush against* ... …に突進する. ¶The lion *rushed at* its prey. ししはその獲物に食ってかかった. ‖ *rush at* one's enemy 敵に向って突進する. ¶*rush down* (*up*) the stairs 階段を大急ぎで降りる(上る). ¶*rush for* a seat 席を取ろうと競う. ¶*rush into* each other's arms 急にだきつく ‖ *rush into* marriage 急いで結婚する ‖ *rush into* extremes 極端に走る ‖ *rush into* print with news that ... …のニュースの発表を急ぐ. ¶*rush on* one's coat あわてて上衣を着る. ¶water *rushing over* a rocky bed 岩床を流れる水. ¶*rush through* the crowd 群集の中を突進する ‖ A thousand conflicting thoughts *rushed through* his mind. 多く矛盾する考えが彼の心にわいた. ‖ *rush through* one's supper 急いで夕飯を取る. ¶*rush to* his assistance 急いで彼の救助に行く ‖ *rush to* the scene その場にかけつける ‖ *rush to* the other extreme 一方の極端に走る ‖ *rush to* a conclusion 結論を急ぐ. ¶The printers are terribly *rushed with* work. 印刷所は非常に仕事が忙しい.

O I have no work to *rush* right now. 《米》今急ぐ仕事はない.

Russia, *n.* ロシア.

Q He knows most of ***European Russia*** from the Black to the White Sea. 彼は欧州ロシアを端から端まで知っている. ¶ the state of affairs in ***Soviet Russia*** 労農ロシアにおける事態.

P the Slavic race ***of Russia*** ロシアのスラブ民族.

P^2 ***Russia in*** East London 東ロンドンのロシア街.

rust, *n.* さび.

V ***clean*** the *rust* さびをおとす. ¶ Iron ***gathers rust*** easily. 鉄はさびがつきやすい. ¶ ***prevent rust*** (=rusting) さびを止める. ¶ ***resist rust*** さびがつかない. ¶ ***rub off*** the *rust* さびをこすり落す. ¶ ***scour rust*** from a knife ナイフのさびをみがきおとす. ¶ The town ***wears*** the "*rust* of antiquity." その市は古色そう然たるものがある.

P a preventive ***against rust*** さび止め. ¶ eaten away ***by rust*** さびに腐食されて. ¶ corrode ***with rust*** さびで腐食する.

rust, *v.* さびを生じる, さびさせる.

M In spite of his exceptional abilities, he just *rusted* ***away.*** 非凡な才能があるのに彼は全く宝の持ちぐされだった. ¶ *rust* ***unused*** 使わずにさびさせる. ¶ Better wear out than *rust* ***out.*** 使わずにさびをつける位なら使って消耗させた方がよい.

P *rust* ***from*** disuse 使わないのでさびる.

rustic, *n.* いなか者.

Q an ***ingenuous rustic*** 純真ないなか者.

rustle, *n.* そよぐ音.

P^2 a *rustle* ***of*** branches in the breeze そよ風に吹かれて木の枝のそよぐ音.

rustle, *v.* [風の音に]ざわざわと鳴る, そよぐ; 《米俗》[仕事など]さっさとやる.

M^2 *rustle* ***along*** in silks きぬものを着てさらさらと音を立てて歩く.

P The low wind *rustles* ***in*** the reeds. そよ風であしがざわつく. ¶ At 4 a.m. we *rustled* ourselves ***into*** shape and made a start. 午前四時に大急ぎで支度して出掛けた.

rustling, *n.* かさかさ音.

Q ***mysterious rustlings*** at night 夜間の神秘なかさかさ音. ¶ a ***slight rustling*** in the trees 木のささやかなそよぎ.

P^2 the *rustling* ***of*** the corn in the light wind 微風にそよぐとうもろこし.

rusty, *a.* さびた.

P get *rusty* ***in*** memory 記憶力がにぶくなる.

O Your head (memory) is getting *rusty,* I fear. 君は頭(記憶)がにぶくなったんじゃないか.

rut, *n.* さかり時, 発情期.

P sheep ***in rut*** さかりのついた羊.

S

sabbath, *n.* 安息日.

V ***break*** the *sabbath* [仕事などをして]安息日を犯す. ¶ He has not ***missed*** a *sabbath* for many a year. 彼は多年の間安息日を一日も欠かさず守って来た. ¶ ***observe*** (=***keep***) the *sabbath* 安息日を守る.

sabotage, *n.* 〘労〙サボタージュ(ストの器具破損行為).

P acts ***of*** *sabotage* サボ行為.

saber, 《英》**sabre,** *n.* 洋刀, サーベル.

V They ***drew*** their *sabers* and injured several more or less seriously. 彼らはサーベルを抜いて数名に重軽傷を負わした. ¶ ***rattle*** the *saber* サーベルをがちゃがちゃ鳴らす.

P the rule ***of*** the *sabre* 武断政治.

saccharin, *n.* サッカリン.

Q ***soluble*** *saccharin* 溶性サッカリン.

sack, *n.* 袋.

V ***get*** (=***have***) the *sack* 《俗》解雇される. ¶ He has ***given*** his servant the *sack.* 彼は召使に暇を出した. ¶ ***put*** the *sack* on his back その袋を背負う.

Q a ***knitted*** *sack* for a baby 赤ん坊用のメリヤス製の着物(チャックで開閉する).

Q^2 a ***canvas*** (=***duck***) *sack* ズックの袋.

P^2 a *sack* ***of*** candy 《米》キャンデーの入った袋. 【類】a *sack* ***of*** flour (sugar).

sacrament, *n.* 聖礼; 聖晩さん.

V ***administer*** the last *sacrament* to the dying 臨終の人に最後の聖さん式を施す. ¶ ***receive*** (=***take***) the *sacrament* [誓いの印として]聖さんを受ける.

P^2 the *sacrament* ***of*** the Lord's supper 聖さん.

sacred, *a.* 神聖な; 神にささげた, 祭った.

P No place was *sacred* ***from*** outrage. 残るくまなく踏み荒された. ¶ It is *sacred* ***in*** popular belief. それは世俗の信仰では神聖視されている. ¶ a shrine *sacred* ***to*** a god ある神を祭ったやしろ ‖ For centuries Lombard Street has been *sacred* ***to*** the banking interest. 幾百年にわたってロンバード街は金融業者の天地となっている. 【類】Miyajima is *sacred* ***to*** Benten. ‖ The ivy is *sacred* ***to*** Bacchus and Osiris. / The month of December is *sacred* ***to*** the festival of Christmas. / This house is *sacred* ***to*** the memory (かたみ) of my parents. / Berlin was to have a theatre *sacred* ***to*** Shakespeare. / a monument *sacred* ***to*** the memory of unknown soldiers. ¶ In Africa the snake is still *sacred* ***with*** many tribes. アフリカの多くの土人の間ではへびは今なお神の御(み)物とあがめられている.

sacrifice, *n.* 犠牲, いけにえ; 見切り売り.

V A war ***demands*** of us enormous *sacrifices* of life and property. 戦争はわれわれに生命財産のばく大な犠牲を要求する. ‖ His health was the *sacrifice* ***demanded*** of him. 彼は健康を犠牲にしなければならなかった. ¶ A war ***involves*** the *sacrifice* of brave lives. 戦争があれば勇士の生命が必ず犠牲になる. ¶ ***make*** *sacrifice* of (=prey on) one's own flesh and blood 自分の子を食いものにする ‖ A mother will ***make*** *sacrifices* for her child. 母親は子供のために犠牲になる. 【類】We are prepared to ***make*** great *sacrifices.* / She ***made*** to him a *sacrifice* of her happiness. ¶ ***offer*** [***up***] a *sacrifice* 生けにえをささげる ‖ a *sacrifice* willingly ***offered*** 進んで払った犠牲. ¶ ***take*** *sacrifices* 犠牲を受ける.

Q Goods are cleared off at an "***alarming*** *sacrifice.*" 品物をいわゆる「出血値段」で処分する. ¶ at a ***conscious*** *sacrifice* 損を承知で. ¶ involve a very ***considerable*** *sacrifice* of … …という大きな犠牲を伴う. 【類】at ***considerable*** *sacrifices* to themselves. ¶ for quick sale at ***extraordinary*** *sacrifice* 大見切り大売出のため. ¶ ***fanatical*** *sacrifices* 熱狂的犠牲. ¶ surplus stock for sale at a ***great*** *sacrifice* 残品の大見切り売. ¶ ***gustatory*** *sacrifices* 飲食を断つこと(祈願のために). ¶ make a ***heroic*** *sacrifice* 悲壮な犠牲を払う. ¶ a toll of ***human*** *sacrifice* 人命の犠牲. ¶ a ***living*** *sacrifice* 生けにえ. ¶ a ***monetary*** *sacrifice* 金銭の犠牲. ¶ a ***needless*** *sacrifice* 無益な犠牲. ¶ make ***no small*** *sarcrifices* to … …に少なからぬ犠牲を払う. ¶ a ***painful*** *sacrifice* 痛ましい犠牲. ¶ a life of ***remarkable*** *sacrifices* 著しい犠牲の生がい. ¶ at a ***ruinous*** *sacrifice* to … …には大損で. ¶ make ***substantial*** *sacrifices* 実質的に犠牲になる. ¶ a ***terrible*** (=***horrible***) *sacrifice* of life 生命の恐ろしい犠牲. ¶ make an ***unnecessary*** *sacrifice* 不必要な犠牲を払う. ¶ a ***vicarious*** *sacrifice* 身代りの犠牲.

P sell ***at*** a *sacrifice* コストを割っても売る ‖ I will part with the goods ***at*** a *sacrifice* for ready cash. 即金なら大負にして手離します. ‖ It must be done ***at*** any *sacrifice* (=cost). どんな犠牲を払ってもやらなければならない. ¶ He gained nothing ***by*** the *sacrifice* of his principles. 彼は主義を犠牲にして何も得る所がなかった. ¶ offer animals ***in*** *sacrifice* 動物を生けにえにささげる. ¶ ***with*** a great *sacrifice* of time 非常に時間をつぶして. ¶ It must be done ***without*** *sacrifice.* 損をしないで取引しなければならない. ¶ go through it ***without*** a *sacrifice* of dignity 威厳を損せずにそれを遂行する.

P^2 a *sacrifice* ***of*** a hundred oxen 牛百頭の生けにえ ‖ with

little *sacrifice of* comfort and great saving of expenditure 格別の不自由もなくしかも費用は大節約ができて. ¶the *sacrifice of* interest *to* pleasure 快楽のための利益の犠牲. ¶fall a *sacrifice to* ... ...の犠牲となる.

sacrifice, *v.* 犠牲にする.

P Mothers often *sacrifice* themselves *for* their children. 母親は子供のため自分を犠牲にすることがよくある. 【類】*sacrifice* one's life *for* the country ‖ *sacrifice* business *for* pleasure 仕事を休んで楽しむ. ¶*sacrifice* one's personal interest *to* public good 公益のために一身の利益を犠牲にする ‖ *sacrifice* accuracy *to* vividness [ニュースなど]生々させるために正確を犠牲にする. 【類】*sacrifice* clearness *to* terseness (簡潔) / *sacrifice* beauty *to* accuracy / *sacrifice* one's comfort *to* the study of ... ‖ *sacrifice* the "dramatic" *to* the "theatrical" element 劇的要素を捨てて興行的要素をとる.

sad, *a.* 悲しい, 悲しんでいる.

M He is ***inexpressibly sad.*** 彼は言い知れず悲しんでいる.

P I am *sad for* (=*at or with*) his death. 私は彼の死を悲しむ. ¶I am *sad* and sorry *in* my heart. 私は心の中で悲しんでいる. ¶*sad of* appearance 悲しそうに見える. ¶He is *sad on account of* it. 彼はそのために悲しんでいる. ¶feel *sad over* the mishap その不幸を悲しく思う.

O it makes me *sad* to think that ... ...と考えると悲しくなる.

saddle, *n.* くら.

V ladies who "*affect* the *saddle*" いわゆる「くら好き」な女. ¶He could not *keep* the *saddle*. 彼は落馬した. ¶*put* a *saddle* on a horse 馬にくらをおく.

Q a ***ladies' (=side-)saddle*** 婦人くら. ¶The *saddle* is *secure*. そのくらは安全だ.

P horses *for* the *saddle* 乗馬. ¶perform a journey *in* the *saddle* 馬上で旅行する ‖ a man *in* the *saddle* 馬上の人; [比ゆ的に] 支配(指導)的立場にある人. 【類】outdoor girls *in* the *saddle*. ¶leap *into* the *saddle* 馬に飛び乗る. ¶*put* a *saddle on* くらをおく. ¶the leg-rest *on* a woman's *saddle* 婦人くらの足掛け. ¶He jumped *out of* the *saddle*. 彼は馬から飛び下りた. ¶horses *with* foreign *saddles* 洋くらを着けた馬.

saddle, *v.* 負わせる, 課する.

P *saddle* heavy taxes *upon* (=*on*) people 人民に重税を課する. ¶*saddle* oneself *with* responsibility 責任を負う ‖ *saddle* a gift *with* onerous (=troublesome) conditions [学校などへ]やっかいな条件を付けて寄付をする ‖ He is *saddled with* a large family to support. 彼は多数の扶養家族に苦しんでいる. 【類】He is *saddled with* a heavy debt (large family).

saddle-horse, *n.* あん馬, 乗馬.

V *hire* (=have the loan of) a *saddle-horse* 乗馬を借りる.

sadness, *n.* 悲しみ; 陰気.

Q these ***accumulated*** *sadnesses* これらの積り積った悲しみ. ¶record, with ***deeply felt*** *sadness*, the death of ... 心から悲しんで...の死を記す. ¶***plaintive*** *sadness* 哀愁. ¶***religious*** *sadness* 宗教上の悲哀. ¶be merged in a sentiment of ***unutterable*** *sadness* and compassion 言いしれない悲しみと同情の感じにふける.

Q[2] ***spring*** *sadness* 春愁.

P His heart is full *of sadness*. 彼の心は悲嘆に満ちている. ‖ He has an air *of sadness*. 彼は悲しそうな様子をしている. ¶He is grave *to sadness*. 彼は陰気なほどまじめだ. ¶He said *with* deep *sadness*. 彼は痛く悲しんで言った.

safe, *n.* 金庫.

V ***break*** a *safe* 金庫を破る. ¶***force*** [***upon***] a *safe*=force a safe open 金庫をこじあける. ¶***rob*** a *safe* of ... 金庫から...を盗み出す.

Q a ***fire-proof*** *safe* 耐火金庫.

Q[2] a ***meat*** *safe* 食肉貯蔵庫(冷蔵庫など). ¶a ***wall*** *safe* はめ込み金庫.

safe, *a.* 安全な.

M ***absolutely*** (***perfectly***) *safe* 絶対安全な. ¶be not ***quite*** *safe* あまり安全とはいえない.

P This is *safe against* all possibilities. これならどうころんでも大丈夫だ. ¶She was always pilfering; nothing was *safe from* her fingers. あの女は始終物をとる, 手癖が悪いってありゃしない. ‖ *safe from* danger (harm, criticism, enemies, interruption) 危険(など)の憂いはない. 【類】The house is not *safe from* theft. / The game is *safe from* pursuit (discovery). ¶You are *safe in* accepting the offer. その申入れは応じても危険はない.

sefeguard, *n.* 防護, 予防.

V ***constitute*** an excellent *safeguard* against ... ...のりっぱな予防になる.

Q the ***best*** *safeguard* against accidents and loss of time 事故や時間つぶしの何よりの予防. ¶a love of reading as a ***moral*** *safeguard* 道徳的な安全弁としての読書愛好. ¶It is ***no*** *safeguard* (=proof) against malarial fever. それはマラリア熱には効がない.

Q[2] ***atomic energy*** *safeguards* 原子力安全諸装置.

P *under safeguard* of ... ...の保護を受けて.

P[2] The Dutch people believe that the presence of a pair of turtle-doves is a *safeguard against* rheumatism. オランダ人は一つがいのきじばとがいればリュウマチスにかからないと信じている. ‖ Keeping clean is a *safeguard against* disease. 清潔は病気予防になる.

safeguard, *v.* 安全をまもる.

M ***jealously*** *safeguard* the honored name and great position it has won in the past 過去の栄誉や地位を固守するのにきゅうきゅうとする.

safeguarding, *n.* 擁護, 予防.

Q[2] ***fire*** *safeguarding* 火災予防.

P[2] *safeguarding of* living 生活擁護.

safe-keeping, *n.* 保管.

P *for* the *safe-keeping* of its property その財産保管のために. ¶My property is *in* his *safe-keeping*. 私の財産は彼が保管している.

safety, *n.* 安全; 安否; 警護.

V The *safety* of the party is ***apprehended***. 一行の安否が気使われている. ¶A state of ***complete*** *safety* is not quite re-established. 絶対安全はまだ十分確立されていない. ¶***compromise*** the *safety* of the country 国家を危くする. ¶***endanger*** the *safety* of ... ...の安全をおびやかす. ¶as an aid to ***ensure*** the *safety* of the documents 書類の安全を確保する一手段として. ¶The captain of a big liner ***has*** the *safety* of thousands of lives in his keeping. 大きな定期船の船長は数千人の生命をあずかっている. ¶take measures to ***insure*** one's *safety* その安全を守る手段を講じる. ¶***jeopardize*** the *safety* of navigation 航海の安全を危くする. ¶***menace*** another's *safety* 人の安全をおびやかす. ¶***provide*** *safety* against ... ...の警備をする. ¶***secure*** personal *safety* 一身の安全を得る. ¶***seek*** *safety* in flight 逃避して安全を求める. 【類】***seek*** *safety* in anonymity (変名で).

Q There is ***absolute*** *safety* for us in these woods. この森はわれわれに取って絶対に安全だ. ¶for its ***greater*** *safety* さらにその安全を計るため(宝物など). ¶***public*** *safety* 公衆の安全.

Q[2] ***air*** *safety* 空路の安全. ¶attain ***investment*** *safety* 投資の安全が確保される. ¶***road*** *safety* 道路の安全. ¶***traffic*** *safety* 交通安全.

P worry ***about*** one's *safety* その安否について心配する. ¶a gun *at safety* 安全装置を施した銃(砲). ¶much concern is felt *for* the *safety* of ... ...の安否が気使われる. 【類】deposit money in a bank *for safety* ‖ *for* extra *safety* 安全確保のため. ¶escape *in safety* 無事に逃れる ‖ My long errand has been completed *in safety*. 私の遠国への使はつつがなく済んだ. 【類】keep it *in safety*. ¶a place (zone) *of safety* 安全な場所(地帯). ¶*with safety* 無難に.

P[2] *safety for* life and property 生命財産の安全. ¶in *safety* (=safe) *from* fire 火災の心配なく. ¶*Safety in* aviation is improving. 航空の安全は改善せられつつある. 【類】the *safety of* human life.

safety-valve, *n.* 安全弁.

Q ***political*** *safety-valve* 政治上の安全弁. ¶a ***psychological*** *safety-valve* 心理上の安全弁.

sag, *n.* へこみ.

Q There is a ***deep*** *sag* in the seat of that chair. そのいすのシートは深々と沈む.

sag, *v.* 下がる.

P Her dress *sagged in* the back. 彼女のドレスは後がさがっていた.

O The market is *sagging*. 市況は下押しだ.

sagacity, *n.* そう明; [動物の]独特の知恵.

Q a man of ***commercial*** (***business***) *sagacity* 商才(実務の才)のある人.

P I am surprised *at* your *sagacity*. 君の利口なのには驚く. ¶a man *of sagacity* そう明な人.

P[2] The *sagacity of* a spider is wonderful. くもの知恵には驚くべきものがある.

sage, *n.* 賢人.

Q Mencius, China's *second sage*. 中国第二の聖人孟子.
P An owl sat there ***like*** a *sage*. ふくろうが聖人づらをしてすわっていた. ☞ ふくろうは聖人や哲学者の風ぼうがあると言われている.
P^2 the *sage* ***of*** old 先哲 ‖ *sages* ***of*** antiquity 古聖たち.

sail, *n.* 帆; 帆船; 隻; 帆走, 航海; 航程.
V ***carry*** a *sail* 帆を揚げる. ¶***crowd*** all *sails* 帆を残らず張る. ¶***discover*** a *sail* on the horizon 水平線上に白帆を見つける. ¶***furl*** *sails* 帆を巻き上げる. ¶***lift*** a *sail* 帆を揚げる. ¶We ***had*** an easy *sail*. われわれは楽に帆走した. ¶***hoist*** [***up***] a (all) *sail* 帆を(全部)揚げる. ¶***lower*** (=***douse***) a *sail* 帆を下ろす. ¶***make*** *sail* with the first favorable wind 順風になり次第出帆する. 【類】 boldly ***make*** *sail* for ... ¶***mend*** *sail* 帆を巻き直す. ¶***put up*** a *sail* 帆を揚げる. ¶***reef*** the *sails* 縮帆する. ¶***reverse*** *sails* 帆を逆にする ‖ ***set*** *sail* from ... for ... ...へ向け...を出帆する. 【類】 ***set*** *sail* in a ship / ***set*** *sail* homeward bound. ¶***shorten*** *sails* 帆を絞る. ¶***spread*** (=***unfurl***) *sails* 帆を揚げる. ¶***strike*** (=***lower down***) a *sail* 帆を下ろす. ¶Wind ***swells*** (=***fills***) the *sails*. 風が帆をはらます. ¶***take*** a *sail* with ... ...と同船する. ¶***take in*** *sails* 帆を下げる; [比ゆ的に] 野心が衰える, 動きがにぶくなる. ¶***trim*** the *sails* 帆のつり合を取る. ¶***unbend*** a *sail* 帆を取りはずす. ¶***unfurl*** a *sail* 帆をひろげる.
V^2 *Sails* ***flap***. 帆があおる.
Q ***bellying*** (***swelling***) *sails* 風をはらんだ帆. ¶under ***easy*** *sail* 追手に帆を揚げて. ¶***fore-and-aft*** *sail* たて帆(支索及び斜けたに掛ける帆). ¶[at] ***full*** *sail*[*s*]=in full sail [汽船など]全速力で. ¶a ***happy*** and ***delightful*** *sail* 楽しい船旅. ¶an ***hour's*** *sail* from ... ...から一時間の航程. ¶***main*** (***head***) *sail* 主(前)帆. ¶a fleet of ***twenty*** *sails* 二十隻からなる船隊.
P It is moved ***by*** *sail*. それは帆で動く. ¶go ***for*** a *sail* 帆走遊びに行く. 【類】 I took him out ***for*** a *sail*. ¶***in*** (=under) full *sail* 満帆を張って. ¶He has taken the wind ***out of*** my *sails*. 彼は私を不利な地位に陥れた. ¶The steamer was ***under*** *sail* with her engines broken down. 汽船は機関がこわれたので帆を掛けていた. ‖ get ***under*** *sail* 出帆する ‖ be ***under*** *sail* with machinery broken down 機関破損帆走中. 【類】 The ship has arrived ***under*** *sail* having lost the propeller. ¶The sea is covered ***with*** *sails*. 海は帆で一杯だ. ‖ a boat ***with*** a *sail* on it 帆かけ舟. ¶Bermuda is ***within*** two days' *sail* of New York. ベルムダ島はニューヨークから二日以内の航程である.

sail, *v.* 帆走する; 航行する; 出帆する; [大空を]飛ぶ; さっそうと歩く.
M *sail* ***away*** from home 故国を出帆する. ¶*sail* ***back*** from ... ...から帰帆する. ¶*sail* ***close*** to the wind 〚航〛[順風と逆風の中間を]船首を風に向けて航行する; 際どい行動をする. ¶Will she *sail* there ***direct***? 船はそこへ直航しますか. ¶*sail* ***homeward*** 帰航する. ¶*sail* ***leeward*** (***aloof***) [帆船が]風下(上)に進む. ¶The boat *sailed* ***out*** to sea. 同船は出帆した. ‖ She *sailed* ***out*** in her best. 彼女は晴着を着てさっそうと出かけた. ¶*sail* ***serenely on*** unruffled 人にとん着せず自分の信じる通りにやって行く. ¶The boat *sails* ***swiftly***. 舟が早く走る. ¶The steamer *sails* ***weekly***. その汽船は毎週出る. ¶*sail* ***west*** (***east***) 西(東)に向け航行する.
M^2 Wild ducks were *sailing* ***by*** in a large flock. かもが大群をなして飛び去って行った. ¶The boat *sailed* ***down*** the river. その舟は川を流れ下った. ¶*sail* ***in*** 入港する. ¶*sail* ***off*** in a few days 二三日で出帆する. ¶They *sailed* ***up*** to the head of the bay. 彼らは湾頭まで航行した.
P *sail* ***about*** a lake 湖水を船で乗りまわす. ¶*sail* ***across*** the Atlantic 大西洋を渡航する ‖ Clouds *sail* ***across*** the sky. 雲が大空を横切ってすーっと行く. ¶*sail* ***against*** the wind (tide) 風(など)に逆って航行する. ¶*sail* ***along*** the coast 沿岸を航行する. ¶*sail* ***before*** the wind 追手に帆走する. ¶*sail* ***down*** a river 川下に航行する. ¶*sail* ***for*** home 帰航する. 【類】 *sail* ***for*** America on the Asama Maru. ¶The ship *sailed* ***from*** Vladivostok ***for*** Nagasaki. 船はウラジオストックから長崎へ向け出帆した. 【類】 They *sailed* ***from*** London ***to*** Canton. ¶*sail* ***in*** a boat 舟で航行する. ¶Steamers from all parts of the world *sail* ***into*** the port of Yokohama. 世界の各地からの汽船が横浜に入港する. ‖ Mrs. G *sailed* ***into*** the room. G夫人は静々と入って来た. ¶Boats *sail* ***on*** the water. 舟は水面を走る. 【類】 They *sailed* ***on*** the Empress of Japan at four o'clock p.m. ¶We *sailed* ***out of*** the harbor ***toward*** the Pacific. われわれは港から太平洋へ乗り出した. ¶*sail* ***over*** the sea 海上を渡航する. ¶A glider (kite) was seen *sailing* ***over*** the sky. グライダー(など)がゆうゆう大空を舞っていた. ¶He *sailed* all ***round*** the world. 彼は世界を周航した. ¶*sail* ***through*** the channel 海峡を通って航行する. ¶*sail* ***under*** the American flag (British colors) 米国旗(など)を掲げて航行する ‖ *sail* ***under*** false colors 《俗》 世間体をごまかす. ¶*sail* ***up*** a river 川上に航行する. ¶*sail* ***with*** the wind 順風に帆走する ‖ *sail* ***with*** a cargo 荷を積んで航行する.

sailing, *n.* 航海; 速力; 出帆.
V the company ***has*** four *sailings* from ... to ... その会社の船は...から...へ四度航海する. ¶***postpone*** (=***delay***) her *sailing* [船が]その出帆を延期する. ¶The company ***provides*** two *sailings* a week. 同社の船が一週二回出る.
Q ***coastwise*** *sailings* 沿岸航海. ¶a vessel remarkable for her ***fast*** *sailing* 速力の早いので有名な船. ¶***fixed*** *sailings* 定期航海. ¶there is ***frequent*** steamship *sailing* from ... ...からはひんぱんに汽船が出る. ¶*Sailings* are quite ***irregular***. 出帆は至って不規則だ. ¶It's ***plain*** *sailing*. [比喩的] なんでもない, 平ちゃらだ. 【類】 it would not be all ***plain*** *sailing* for ... ¶***smooth*** *sailing* 静かな航海; [比ゆ] とんとんびょうしに行くこと. ¶***trans-Atlantic*** *sailing* 大西洋横断航海. ¶these liners provide ***weekly*** *sailings* to ... これらの定期船が毎週...に通っている.
Q^2 ***ocean*** *sailings* 外洋航海.
P ***during*** his *sailing* across the Atlantic 彼の大西洋航海中に. ¶the date ***for*** *sailing* 出帆期日 ‖ the signal ***for*** *sailing* 出帆信号. ¶I am fond ***of*** *sailing*. 私は舟遊びが好きだ.
P^2 *sailing* ***from*** New York at 12 noon Eastern standard time 東部標準時正午十二時にニューヨーク出帆 ‖ the list of *sailings* ***from*** London [船舶の]ロンドン出帆表. ¶the *sailing* ***of*** the boat その船の出帆.

sailor, *n.* 水夫, 船乗.
V He will ***make*** a good *sailor*. 彼はりっぱな水夫になるだろう. ¶***put up*** (=***lodge or house***) shipwrecked *sailors* in private houses 難船した水夫を民家に収容する.
V^2 The *sailor* ***went*** on shore (=ashore) and never came back. その水夫は上陸して帰って来なかった.
Q The sea was too stormy for me, as I am a ***bad*** *sailor*. 僕は船に弱いからその波では船には乗れなかった. ¶a ***capital*** *sailor* 非常に船に強い人. ¶I am a ***good*** *sailor*. 僕は船に強い. ¶***merry-faced*** *sailors* 陽気な顔付をした水夫. ¶***shipwrecked*** *sailors* 難破船の船員たち. ¶***weather-beaten*** *sailors* [いく多の風雨を経て]潮(しお)焼けした水夫.
Q^2 a ***turnpike*** *sailor* 水兵をよそおったこじき(泥棒仲間の言葉).
P He is rigged out ***as*** a *sailor*. 《俗》 彼は船員の格好をしている. ¶He looks ***like*** a *sailor* 彼は水夫らしい. ¶a *sailor* ***without*** a chart 海図なしの船乗(木から落ちたさる).
O become (=turn) a *sailor*=go to sea 水夫になる.

sailorman, *n.* 《俗》 水夫.
Q ***hard-as-nails*** *sailormen* 非常に強健な水夫.

saint, *n.* 聖徒, 聖人.
V It would ***provoke*** a *saint*. それでは聖人でも怒る.
Q the most ***famous*** *saint* of early Christian England 初期キリスト教英国の最も有名な聖僧. ¶an ***immaculate*** *saint* けがれのない聖人. ¶I am ***no*** *saint*. 僕は聖人じゃない(普通の人間だ). ¶a ***self-mortifying*** *saint* 難行苦行する聖徒. ¶the ***tutelary*** *saint* of the city その市の守護神.
Q^2 Bosatsu, a ***Buddhist*** *saint* 菩薩(ぼさつ). ¶the ***patron*** *saint* of the sailors 海員の守り本尊. 【類】 George, Andrew, Patrick and David are the ***Patron*** *Saints* of the different states of the United Kingdom. ¶***plaster*** *saints* 聖徒の石こう像.
P He has led the life ***of*** a *saint*. 彼は聖人のような一生を送った.
P^2 He is a *saint* ***of*** man. 彼は聖徒のような人だ.
O I no longer knew which *saint* to invoke. どうしてよいのかわからなくなってしまった.

sake, *n.* 利益, ため.
Q for ***appearance'***[***s***] *sake* 体裁上. ¶let us grant, for ***argument's*** *sake*, that ... 仮に...として. ¶art for ***art's*** *sake* 芸術のための芸術, 芸術至上主義. ¶for ***brevity's*** *sake* 簡略のために. ¶for ***caution's*** *sake* 用心に. ¶Do it all for ***charity's*** *sake*. 後生だからして下さい. ¶suffer all things for ***Christ's*** *sake* キリストのためにすべてを忍ぶ.

¶drink for ***company's sake*** おつき合に飲む. ¶for ***conscience' sake*** 良心の(満足を得る)ために. ¶for ***convenience' sake*** 便宜上. ¶for ***courtesy's sake*** 礼儀上. ¶No man is fit to be a professor who, for ***expediency's sake***, suppresses his own freedom. 便宜上自己の自由を抑圧するような人は大学教授たるに適しない. ¶for ***form's sake*** 形式上. ¶for ***freindship's sake*** 友だちのよしみに. ¶Save me for ***God's*** (=***goodness', Heaven's, mercy's or pity's***) *sake*. 後生だから助けて下さい. ¶for your ***health's sake*** 君の健康のために. ¶for ***humanity's sake*** 人道のために. ¶love literature for ***its own sake*** 文学その物のために文学を愛する. 【類】He was delighted with the war for his ***own sake***. ¶for ***my own sake*** as well as yours われわれ双方のために. ¶for one's ***name's sake*** その名誉のために. ¶for ***old acquaintance' sake*** 昔のよしみで. ¶for ***old remembrance' sake*** 昔なじみに. ¶send a present for ***old time's sake*** 昔を忘れないように贈物をする. ¶for ***opinion's sake*** 持論のために. ¶He opposes me for ***opposition's sake***. 彼は単に反対のために私に反対する. ¶for both ***our sakes*** われわれ両人のために. ¶for ***precaution's sake*** 用心に. ¶for ***remembrance' sake*** 忘れないように. ¶for our ***reputation's sake*** われわれの名誉のために. ¶for ***safety's sake*** 安全のために. ¶Deny thyself, for ***self's sake***. 自分のために自制せよ. ¶for ***shortness'*** *sake*=for short 略して. ¶I will for ***simplicity's sake*** call him ... 私は便宜上彼を...という簡単な名で呼ぶことにする. ¶for ***their sakes*** alone 彼らのためだけに. ¶the love of truth for ***truth's sake*** 真理のための真理の愛. ¶a return route may be made, for ***variety's sake***, by [way of] ... 帰りの道筋は趣向を変えて...にしてもよい. ¶the gospel of work for ***work's sake*** 働きのための働きという福音.

P admitting, ***for*** the *sake* of argument, that ... 仮に...とするも ‖ ***for*** the *sake* of appearances (=good form) 体裁上, 世間体もあるので ‖ ***for*** the *sake* of brevity 繁を避けて ‖ ***for*** the *sake* of comparison 比較上 ‖ ***for*** my *sake* 私に免じて ‖ ***for*** the *sake* of peace 問題を起さないように ‖ ***for*** the *sake* of convenient reference 参照の便宜のため ‖ quote only a few of them ***for*** the *sake* of example 例に二三だけを引く ‖ we may call it, ***for*** the *sake* of a name, ... 仮に(便宜上)...と呼ぶこととしよう. 【類】***for*** the *sake* of financial gain / study the past ***for*** the *sake* of the future / ***for*** the *sake* of future ages / ***for*** the *sake* of humanity (人道) ‖ even ***for*** the *sake* of justice (義理) / Society exists ***for*** the *sake* of the individual rather than the individual ***for*** the *sake* of society. / Many idle wars have been undertaken at one time or another ***for*** the *sake* of national prestige.—Froude. / ***for*** the *sake* of personal gain / ***for*** the *sake* of posterity / retreat to ... ***for*** the *sake* of rest / ***for*** the *sake* of scholarship in America / ***for*** the *sake* of simplicity I will assume that ... ‖ Keep this ***for*** his *sake*. 彼の形見にしまっておきなさい. 【類】Keep this ***for*** your own *sake*.

saké-cup, *n.* さかずき.

V ***exchange*** *saké-cups* with ... ...と杯をかわす. ¶***present*** a *saké-cup* to be filled 杯をさす.

salad, *n.* サラダ.

V ***dress*** *salad* サラダを作る.

Q² ***fruit*** *salad* フルーツサラダ. ¶***pineapple*** (lettuce) *salad* パイナップル(など)サラダ. ¶***vegetable*** (***fruit***) *salad* 野菜(など)サラダ.

P Cheese belongs ***with*** *salad* quite as much as it does with coffee. チーズはコーヒーと同様サラダに合う.

P² a dish of *salad* ***with*** meal and eggs 肉と卵の入ったサラダ.

salary, *n.* 俸給, 給料.

V I am willing to ***accept*** a *salary* of 35 yen, to begin with. 初任給は三十五円で結構です. ¶***augment*** the *salaries* of the teaching staff 教員の俸給を増す. ¶the *salaries* ***attached*** to the offices 職務給. 【類】A *salary* of £10,000 is ***attached*** to that position. ¶One must work twenty years to ***attain*** a *salary* of 150 yen. 百五十円の給料になるまでには二十年も勤めなくてはならない. ¶that kind of managerial ability that ***commands*** a five-figure yearly *salary* 五けた (10,000—99,999) の年俸に値するような管理の才. ¶They ***drew*** *salaries* in proportion to their supposed usefulness. 彼らの勤務の能率に比例して俸給をもらった. 【類】a man who ***draws*** a twenty-thousand-dollar-a-year *salary* at ... / ***draw*** [a *salary* of] $40.00 a week from the firm. ¶places in which they could ***earn*** *salaries* of from $3,000 to $5,000 a year 彼らが年三千ドルないし五千ドルの俸給を取り得た地位. ¶***eke out*** one's *salary* with odd jobs アルバイトで給料の不足を補なう. ¶I ***expect*** a moderate *salary*. 並の給料はいただきたい. ¶***fix*** the *salary* at ... 給料を...に定める. ¶***get*** a small *salary* 薄給を取る. ¶***give*** one a *salary* common in the world 人に世間並の俸給を与える. ¶He ***grudges*** them their *salaries*. 彼は彼らに出す俸給をけちけちしている. ¶he ***has*** a *salary* of ... 彼は...の給料を受けている. ¶***hypothecate*** one's *salary* 俸給を抵当に入れる. ¶***increase*** a *salary* 増俸する. ¶How can I do such things on the moderate *salary* I am ***making*** (=drawing). 私がもらっているような俸給でどうしてこんなことができましょう. ¶***measure*** one's *salary* by thousands 数千金の給料を取る. ¶***Name*** your own *salary*. お望みの給料をおっしゃって下さい. ¶***offer*** a high *salary* 高給を出そうという. ¶offices that ***pay*** large *salaries* 高給を払う社. ¶***raise*** one's *salary* 俸給を上げる. ¶***receive*** (=***take***) *salaries* from the Government 政府から俸給をもらう. ¶The employees saw their *salaries* ***slashed*** (=***cut***) from ten to fifty per cent. 使用人は給料を一割ないし五割方下げられた.

Q responsible positions and ***advanced*** *salaries* 責任ある地位と高い俸給. ¶at an ***annual*** *salary* of ... ...の年俸で. ¶***back*** *salary* 給料の滞り. ¶earn a small ***beginner's*** *salary* 新参者としての薄給をもらう. ¶at a ***big*** *salary* 高給で. ¶a ***comfortable*** *salary* かなりの俸給. ¶on a ***commencing*** *salary* of ... 初任給...で. ¶***fabulous*** *salaries* 滅法もない高給. ¶a ***fair*** *salary* かなりの俸給. ¶***fat*** *salaries* 多分の俸給. ¶a member of the staff with a ***fixed*** *salary* 固定給を受けている社員. ¶earn a ***good*** *salary* かなりの俸給を取る. ¶a ***handsome*** *salary* いい給料. ¶a ***high*** *salary* 高給. ¶utterly ***inadequate*** *salaries* 全く不十分な俸給. ¶He has a ***large*** *salary*. 彼は巨額の給料をもらっている. ¶***low*** *salaries* 薄給. ¶a ***meager*** *salary* わずかの給料. ¶work at a ***moderate*** *salary* 並程度の給料で働く. ¶receive one's ***monthly*** *salary* in two instalments 月給を二回に分割してもらう. ¶young men of ***modest*** *salary* or income 並の給料または収入の青年. ¶a ***paltry*** *salary* けちな給料. ¶a ***pitiful*** *salary* みじめな給料. ¶a humble village priest at a ***precarious*** *salary* of £2 per month 二ポンドという貧弱な月給を受けているいなかのつまらない牧師. ¶the (=a) ***princely*** *salary* of $15,000 a year 年一万五千ドルという豪勢な俸給. ¶draw one's ***regular*** *salary* 正規の給料をもらう. ¶a ***slender*** *salary* 貧弱な給料. ¶a young girl on a ***small*** *salary* 薄給の少女. 【類】He is willing to serve at a ***small*** *salary*. ¶***splendid*** *salary* すてきな俸給. ¶***starting*** *salary* 初任給. ¶pay ***substantial*** *salaries* たくさんの給料を払う. ¶I had a family of four children and it became increasingly hard to support them properly on a ***teacher's*** *salary*. 子供四人の家族を擁していた私は教師の俸給でりっぱにこれを支えて行くのが段々むずかしくなった. ¶a clerk at a ***trifling*** *salary* 薄給の書記.

Q² an ***entrance*** *salary* 初任給. ¶a ***life*** *salary* 一生の俸給. ¶earn ***living*** *salaries* 生活のできる程度の給料を取る. ¶the ***maximum*** *salary* provided in the Classification Act of 1949 一九四九年度の俸給令によって支給される最高給. 【類】guarantee a $60 a week ***minimum*** *salary*. ¶a ***starvation*** *salary* 飢餓給料.

P get a loan ***against*** my *salary* 月給の前借りをする. ¶He was engaged ***at*** a *salary* of $10,000 a year. 彼は年一万ドルの俸給で雇われた. ¶I would not accept such an office ***for*** any *salary* however high. どんな高給でもそんな役はご免だ. ‖ A competent man cannot be procured ***for*** such a small *salary*. そんな薄給で有能の士は得られない. ¶receive ... yen ***in*** *salary* 給料として...円もらう. ¶a rise (=an increase) ***of*** *salary* 増給. ☞ 米語用法は a ***raise*** in salary (pay) となる. ¶clerks ***on*** (=with) small *salaries* 薄給の事務員 ‖ He will not accept the appointment ***on*** that *salary*. 彼はその給料では就職すまい. ‖ a representation ***on*** *salary* and commission 有給歩合制の取次店 ‖ live ***on*** a small *salary* 少ない給料で生活する. 【類】He saved $5,000 in three years ***on*** a *salary* of $18 per week. / He was then ***on*** a *salary* of seventeen dollars a month. ¶He is ***under*** a big *salary* not to write for any other paper. 彼はばく大な俸給を受けていて他の新聞へは書かないことになっている. ¶an office ***with*** a *salary* 俸給ある役. 【類】He was offered a situation as ... ***with*** a *salary* of ... per annum. / hold an office ***with*** a good *salary*. ¶serve ***without*** *salary* (=pay) 無給で働く.

P² my *salary* ***for*** last month 私の先月分の給料. ¶a *salary* ***of*** 7,000 yen a month 七千円の月給. 【類】a *salary* ***of*** no less (more) than 50,000 yen.

sale, *n.* 販売, 売行; 競売.

V ***achieve*** sensational *sale* とっぴな売上成績を示す. ¶***advertise*** the *sale* of ... ...の競売を広告する. ¶The new book has ***attained*** a *sale* of three hundred thousand copies その新刊書は三十万部売れた. ¶***attend*** Christie's *sales* クリスティの競売場に出掛ける. ¶***ban*** the *sale* of ... ...の販売を禁止する. ¶to ***boost*** his *sales* of ... 彼の...の販売成績をあげるために. ¶***cancel*** a *sale* 販売を取消す. ¶This article will no doubt ***command*** a large *sale* in the Far East. この品は極東ではきっと売行がよかろう. ¶We have ***commenced*** the *sale* and it is proceeding very slowly. 販売を始めたがまだ売行きははかばかしくない. ¶***confirm*** the *sale* to the buyer 買手に売物を確約する. ¶There must be a price or consideration to ***constitute*** a *sale*, otherwise the transaction is a gift. 販売には価格もしくは手数料が含まるるべきだ, でなければ取引は贈りものになる. ¶The *sales* have been seriously ***diminished***. 売行が非常に減じた. ¶I want to ***effect*** a *sale*. 私は品を買ってもらいたい. ¶The book continues to ***enjoy*** a large *sale*. その本は相変らず売行がよい. ¶***find*** a large *sale* 大いに売れる. 【類】Stocks ***find*** no *sale*. / A small *sale* was ***found*** for it. ¶Its *sale* was immediately ***forbidden***. その販売は直ちに禁止された. ¶***force*** *sale* even at a loss (損をしても). ¶a patent medicine ***having*** a very large *sale* 大層よく売れる売薬. 【類】We have not ***had*** a *sale* for two months. ¶This will not ***hurt*** the *sale* of the book. このためにその本の売行を悪くするというようなことはなかろう. ¶***importune*** *sale* 押売りをする. ¶in order to ***increase*** *sales* 売高を増すために. ¶***interdict*** the *sale* of a book 書籍の販売を禁止する. ¶***lose*** a *sale* for [the] want of change つり銭がないので売りそこなう. ¶***make*** the *sale* of alcoholic drinks a state monopoly 酒精飲料を国家の専売にする ‖ ***make*** a *sale* 一回の販売をする. 【類】*sales* you have ***made***. ¶***meet*** a ready *sale* たちまち売れる. ¶This book ***obtained*** an immense *sale*. この本はすばらしく売れた. ¶***place*** the *sale* of one's produce to another's hands その製作品の販売をある人に託する. ¶***prohibit*** the *sale* of ... ...の販売を禁止する. ¶***promote*** the *sale* of home manufactures 国産品の販売を促進する. ¶***push*** the *sale* of ... ...を売広める. ¶The book has already ***reached*** a *sale* of over 10,000 copies. その本の売高はすでに一万以上に達した. ¶***secure*** larger *sales* 一層売広める. ¶***spread*** the *sale* of ... among ... ...を...の間に売広める. ¶***stimulate*** the *sale* 販売を奨励する.

V² the *sale* of ... almost ***ceased*** ...の売行はほとんど止った. ¶The *sales* ***fell off*** considerably. 売上げが大分減った. ¶Their *sales* are ***improving***. その売上げは増している.

Q the ***advance*** *sale* for tickets 切符の前売. ¶***annual*** (***biannual***) *sales* 年(半年の)売上高. ¶***average*** *sale* 平均売上高. ¶have the ***best*** *sales* 最高の売上げである. ¶***brisk*** *sale* 良好の売行. ¶the ***colossal*** *sales* that a popular novel attained before the World War 大戦前における大衆小説のすばらしい売行. ¶***compulsory*** *sale* by auction 強制競売. ¶have a ***considerable*** *sale* 大いに売れる. ¶***direct*** *sale* [売主から買主への]直接販売. ¶***dull*** *sale* はかばかしくない売行. ¶The *sales* were ***enormous***. 売高は非常なものだった. ¶there has been a very ***fair*** *sale* among ... これが...間にかなりよく売れる. ¶a ***forced*** *sale* by auction 強制競売. ¶The magazine is not on ***general*** *sale*. その雑誌は店売はしない(非売品になっている). ¶have a ***good*** *sale* よく売れる. ¶It had a ***great*** *sale* because of its cheapness. それは安いのでよく売れた. ¶***gross*** (***net***) *sales* 総(純)売上高. ¶the ***illicit*** *sale* of opium アヘンの不正販売. ¶***immediate*** *sale* 即売. ¶***indirect*** *sale* [注文書・電報などによる]間接販売. ¶enjoy ***large*** *sales* 売行は盛んだ. ¶intended to have a ***limited*** *sale* among ... ...間に限定はん布を目的とした. ¶I bought it at ***marked down*** *sales*. 私はそれを見切りで買った. ¶These articles had a ***moderate*** *sale*. この品は相当売れた. ¶***monthly*** *sale* 月売上高. ¶find ***no*** *sale*=have no demand 少しも売れない ‖ ***No*** *sale* after 4 o'clock 四時以後は販売お断り. ¶at ***one*** *sale* 一回の販売で. ¶It has had a ***phenomenal*** *sale*. それは非常に売れた. ¶***poor*** *sale* 売行不振. ¶dispose of it at a ***private*** *sale* それを個人取引で売る(公売などにかけないで). ¶at a ***public*** *sale* 競売で. ¶***quick*** *sales* and small profits 薄利多売. 【類】find the ***quickest*** *sale*. ¶The book met with a ***rapid*** *sale*. その本は売行が早かった. ¶command (=have) a ***ready*** *sale* 客足が早い, ばたばた売れる ‖ find a ***ready*** *sale* すぐ買手がつく. ¶a ***remnant*** *sale* 残品売出し. ¶at the ***same*** *sale* それと同じ売立で. ¶a ***short*** *sale* 〚株式〛空売り. ¶***slow*** *sale* 遅々たる売行. ¶a ***special*** *sale* 特売. ¶there is a ***steady*** *sale* of ... ...は着実に売れる. ¶have a ***wide*** *sale* 広く売れる. ¶It secured a ***world-wide*** *sale*. それは世界中に売れた.

Q² ***account*** *sales* 〚商〛売上勘定書. ¶land for ***allotment*** *sales* 分譲地. ¶***auction*** *sales* 競売. ¶hunt for ***bargain*** *sales* 特売ものをあさる. ¶a ***bulk*** *sale* 大量販売. ¶***cash*** *sale* 現金売買 ‖ petty ***cash*** *sales* わずかな現金売. ¶***Christmas*** *sale* クリスマスの売出し. ¶offer ***clearance*** *sales* たな卸し売出しをする. 【類】Saturday ***clearance*** *sales*. ¶***consignment*** *sale* 委託販売. ¶All the stores are having ***dollar*** *sales* on white goods today. どの店も白地もの一ドル均一売りをやっている. ¶special ***fall*** *sale* 秋の特別売出し. ¶***half-price*** *sale* 半値売. ¶***hour*** *sales* 時間売り. ¶***instalment*** *sales* of goods 品物の月賦販売. ¶a ***mark-down*** *sales* 値下げ販売. ¶a ***memorandum*** *sale* 送付売買. ¶a ***merchandise*** *sale* 商品売出し. ¶a great ***October*** *sale* 十月大売出し. ¶***opening*** *sales* 売出し. ¶A ***record*** *sale* may be predicted. 記録的売上げが予想される. ¶a ***reduction*** *sale* 割引販売(廉売). ¶look as if dug up from a ***rummage*** *sale* ぼろ市から掘出したように見える. ¶***season*** *sale* 季節売出し. ¶a ***seat*** *sale* 劇場の切符販売. ¶***Street*** *sale*, 10 cents. [新聞の]立ち売り十セント. ¶a ***tax*** *sale* 公売処分. ¶a ***tie-in*** *sale* 《米》リンク制販売. ¶a "***Today Only***" *sale*「本日限り」式販売. ¶***trade*** *sale* 仲間売買. ¶a ***X'mas*** *sale* クリスマスセール.

P It brought ... ***at*** the *sale*. それは売立てになった. 【類】***At*** their *sale* the sum of ... was realized (はいった). / Be careful when you buy things ***at*** a *sale* (廉売). / The book he secured ***at*** the *sale* of Thackeray's library in 1864. ¶dispose of ... ***by*** *sale* ...を売りさばく. ¶a house (factory, an automobile) ***for*** *sale* 売家(など) ‖ Postage Stamps ***for*** *sale* 〚掲示〛郵便切手売りさばき所. ‖ articles not ***for*** *sale* 非売品 ‖ cry ***for*** *sale* 呼び売りする ‖ expose ***for*** *sale* 売品として出して置く ‖ offer ***for*** *sale* 売り出す ‖ be up ***for*** *sale* 売物に出ている ‖ put up ***for*** (=***to***) *sale* 競売に付する. ¶dull ***of*** *sale* 売れ行きの緩漫な. ¶***on*** *sale* by ... [本など] ...発売の ‖ Every article on view (=at the exhibition) will be ***on*** *sale*. その展覧会の出品はどれでも売品です. ‖ send out books to booksellers ***on*** *sale* or return 委託で本屋に本を送る. 【類】I think Maruzen has it ***on*** *sale*. / Macmillan books are ***on*** *sale* at bookstores throughout the English speaking world. / it has been put ***on*** *sale* at ¥... / It has been offered ***on*** *sale* to the public. ¶set it ***to*** *sale* それを売りに出す.

P² have an enormous *sale* ***among*** the poor 貧民間にえらく売れる. ¶Duplicate specimens of the plants are for *sale* ***at*** the office of the Koishikawa Botanical Garden. 標本として出ている植物は小石川の植物園事務所で売っている. ¶*sale* ***by*** prescription 予約販売 ‖ *sale* ***by*** sealed tender 入札販売. ‖ *sale* ***by*** sample (brand, pattern) 見本(など)売り. ¶*sale* ***for*** cash (account) 現金(延べ)取引 ‖ There is no *sale* ***for*** old-fashioned goods. 古臭い品は売れない. ¶the great *sale* ***of*** a book 書物の非常な売行. ¶*sale* ***on*** consignment 委託販売 ‖ *sale* ***on*** credit=credit sale かけ売り ‖ *sale* ***on*** description 銘柄売買 ‖ *sale* ***on*** trial 試売. 【類】have a *sale* ***on*** suits (shoes, bags).

sal[e]able, *a.* 売るに適した.

P It is very *saleable* ***at*** present. それは目下のところ非常に売行きがよい.

salesclerk, *n.* 《米》店員.

V *saleclerks* ***assigned*** to second-floor counters 二階売場の店員.

salesgirl, *n.* 《米》女店員.

V ***hire*** a *salesgirl* 女店員を雇う.

V² a *salesgirl* ***attending*** at the counter (on a customer) 売場(接客)の女店員.

salesman, *n.* 外交販売員.

V ***dispatch*** a *salesman* 外交販売員を派遣する.

Q a ***sleek*** *salesman* 口のうまい外交員(セールスマン).

Q² a ***hot-air*** *salesman* 大業に効能を述べたてるセールスマ

ン. ¶a ***house-to-house*** *salesman* 戸別訪問販売者. ¶an ***insurance*** *salesman* 保険勧誘員. ¶***souvenir*** *salesmen* みやげ物販売外交員. ¶a ***traveling*** *salesman*=《英》a commercial traveller 地方回りの外交販売係.

saliva, *n.* だ液.

V ***eject*** *saliva* つばを吐く. ¶***run*** *saliva* つばを垂らす. ¶His mouth was half open, the *saliva* ***dribbling away*** uncontrolled. 彼の口は半分あいてよだれがだらだら垂れていた.

sally, *n.* 出撃; 出遊; 突発.

V ***make*** a *sally* into the country いなかに出遊する ‖ The garrison ***made*** a *sally*. 守備隊は突撃をやった.

Q a ***nocturnal*** *sally* in search of romance ロマンス探検の夜遊び.

P² a *sally* ***of*** wit (anger) とんち(など)のほとばしり.

sally, *v.* 出かける

M *sally* ***forth*** (=***out***) for an evening walk 夕方の散歩に出かける. 【類】*sally* ***forth*** in triumph (意気揚々と).

Sally, *n.* 女子の名.

Q² a ***Salvation*** *Sally* 救世軍婦人兵士.

salmon, *n.* さけ.

Q a ***kippered*** *salmon* さけのくん製. ¶***pink*** *salmon* 紅ます.

salon, *n.* 広間(サロン).

Q a ***literary*** *salon* 文学クラブ.

saloon, *n.* 広場; 《米》酒場.

V He ***entered*** the *saloon* and continued drinking there until two. 彼はバーに入って二時まで飲み続けた.

Q² a ***beauty*** *saloon* 美容室. ¶a ***billiards*** *saloon* どう球場. ¶a ***dining*** *saloon* [船内の]食堂. ¶a ***dancing*** *saloon* ダンス場. ¶a ***fencing*** *saloon* 剣道場. ¶a ***hairdressing*** *saloon* 美髪所(髪床). ¶a ***shooting*** (***pinball***) *saloon* 射的(パチンコ)場.

salt, *n.* 塩; とんち; しんしゃく; 《俗》水夫.

V Wit ***loses*** its *salt* on the written page. とんちは文に書くとうま味がなくなる. ¶***rub*** *salt* into the wounds of ... ...に対し死馬にむちうつような仕打をする. ¶***spill*** *salt* 塩をこぼす.

Q ***industrial*** *salt* 工業塩. ¶a ***typical old*** *salt* 模範的な老練水夫. ¶He is not ***worth*** his *salt*. 彼は給金だけの働きがない.

Q² ***cooking*** *salt* 料理用食塩. ¶***Epsom*** *salts* しゃり塩. ¶***table*** *salt* 食塩.

P ***above*** the *salt* [きょう宴の席で]上座に着いて. ¶***beneath*** (=***below***) the *salt* [きょう宴の席で]下座に着いて. ¶May I trouble you ***for*** the *salt?* [食卓で]その食塩をとっていただけませんか. ¶Let it remain ***in*** *salt* during twelve hours. 十二時間塩につけておきなさい. ¶a talk full ***of*** *salt* とんちに富んだ話 ‖ This report must of course be taken with a grain ***of*** *salt*. この報告は無論控え目に聞いて置かなければならない. ‖ a spoonful ***of*** *salt* 一さじの塩. ¶***under*** *salt* [漁夫用語]塩づけにして.

P² the *salt* ***of*** the earth「地の塩」(社会風教の維持者を意味する聖書中の句) ‖ Adventure is the *salt* ***of*** life to him. 冒険は彼にとって人生のスリルだ.

salt, *v.* 調味する.

M *salt* ***away*** (=down) 塩蔵する; 《俗》貯蓄する, 安全に投資する. ¶***lightly*** *salted* あま塩にした.

M² *salt* ***down*** 《米》塩づけにする; [比ゆ的に]金などを貯えておく. 【類】*salt* them ***down*** for winter food.

P His every phrase is *salted* ***with*** personality. 彼の一言一句みな個性の表われだ. 【類】*salt* one's language ***with*** jests (poems) ‖ a conversation *salted* ***with*** wit 機知に富んだ会話.

salty, *a.* 塩気のある.

M be not ***sufficiently*** *salty* 塩気が少ない.

salutary, *a.* 有益な.

P *salutary* ***to*** the state 国家に有益な.

salutation, *n.* あいさつ, 敬礼, 祝賀.

V omit to ***return*** his *salutation* 答礼を欠く.

Q the ***complimentary*** *salutation* at the beginning of a speech 演説の始めの呼びかけ (Ladies and gentlemen など). ¶A cold bow was her ***parting*** *salutation*. 無表情に頭を下げたのが彼女の別れのあいさつだった.

P nod ***in*** *salutation* あいさつにうなずく ‖ drink a glass of wine ***in*** *salutation* to ... ...を祝して一杯のぶどう酒を飲む.

P² a *salutation* ***at*** (=***on***) meeting in the morning 朝会った時のあいさつ. ¶a *salutation* ***to*** the Virgin Mary 聖母マリアへの礼拝.

salute, *n.* あいさつ, 敬礼, 祝賀; 祝砲, 礼砲.

V ***acknowledge*** the *salute* of ... ...のあいさつに答礼する. ¶***answer*** a *salute* 答礼する. ¶***boom*** a *salute* 祝砲を放つ. ¶***exchange*** *salutes* 礼砲を交換する. ¶***fire*** a *salute* at noon [軍艦など]正午に礼砲を放つ ‖ ***fire*** a *salute* in honor of the occasion 礼典を祝して祝砲を放つ. 【類】A *salute* was also ***fired*** by the shore batteries (海岸砲台). / While the statue was being unveiled, a *salute* was ***fired*** from the guns at the fort. / ***firing*** the *salute* over a soldier's grave (兵士の墓). ¶***give*** a *salute* of ... guns ...発の祝砲を放つ. ¶***make*** a *salute*=salute 敬礼する. ¶He ***received*** a tremendous *salute* from 52 warships of all nationalities. 彼は五十二隻の各国の軍艦から空もとどろく礼砲を受けた. ¶***return*** the *salute* 答礼する; 答砲を行う. ¶***roar*** a *salute* in one's honor [大砲など]それに敬意を表して礼砲をとどろかす. ¶***shout*** a *salute* in his honor 彼のために大声をあげてあいさつする. ¶***take*** the *salute* [高位の将校が]敬礼を受ける. 【類】***take*** the *salute* of a military review (閲兵式). ¶A *salute* of 21 guns was ***thundered forth*** from the fort. 二十一発の礼砲が要さいからとどろいた.

Q fire an ***Imperial*** (a ***Royal***) *salute* 皇礼(王礼)砲を放つ. ¶the ***military*** *salute* 軍隊式敬礼. 【類】In that school whenever and wherever a student encounters one of his teachers, he is required to halt, bring his feet together, draw himself erect, and give the ***military*** *salute*. ¶a ***naval*** *salute* 海軍礼砲. ¶receive a ***parting*** *salute* of 15 guns [軍隊訪問の顕官など]十五発の決別の礼砲を受ける. ¶***personal*** *salute* 個人に対する礼砲. ¶a ***return*** *salute* 答礼(砲). ¶a ***Royal*** *salute* was fired by ... 王礼砲が...によって放たれた.

Q² ***flag*** *salute* [旗手が]旗を下げて敬礼する. ¶the ***hand*** *salute* 挙手の敬礼. ¶give a ***Hitler-type*** *salute* [ヒットラー式の]片手をあげて礼をする. ¶give a ***V-letter*** *salute* [大戦中の]勝利を意味する礼をする(人さし指と中指で V 字を作って). ¶a ***19 gun*** *salute* was fired in honor of Gen. ... 将軍...に対し十九発の礼砲が発せられた. 【類】thunder (=fire) a ***21-gun*** *salute*.

P stand ***at*** the *salute* [兵士など]敬礼の姿勢を取る. ¶*salute* each other ***by*** raising their hats 帽子をとってあいさつをする. ¶***by way of*** *salute* 敬礼として. ¶raise one's hand ***in*** *salute* 挙手の礼を行う. ¶in reply ***to*** a *salute* 敬礼に答えて. ¶***under*** a *salute* of thirteen guns 十三発の祝砲を放って. ¶honor ***with*** a *salute* 敬礼する.

P² a *salute* ***at*** attention 停止敬礼. ¶a *salute* ***from*** deck 登げん礼.

salute, *v.* 敬礼する; 礼砲を放つ; 浴びせる.

P They were *saluted* ***by*** a salvo of seventeen guns. 彼らは十七砲門の一斉発射の敬礼を受けた. ¶*salute* him ***with*** cheers 彼にかっさいを浴びせる ‖ *salute* the enemy ***with*** a volley 敵に一せい射撃を食わす ‖ *salute* ***with*** a hand 挙手の礼を行う ‖ *salute* ***with*** a sword 捧刀礼をする ‖ My flag was *saluted* ***with*** 17 guns on arrival. 到着と同時にわが提督旗に対し十七発の礼砲を受けた.

salvage, *n.* [船体などの]引上げ.

P² the *salvage* ***of*** the ship and cargo 船体と積荷の引上げ.

salvation, *n.* 救済, 済度.

V ***attain*** (=***obtain***) *salvation* 済度される. ¶***find*** *salvation* 信仰によって救いを見出す. ¶Shinshu ***teaches*** *salvation* by faith in Buddha. 真宗はみ仏の信仰によって救われると説く. ¶***work*** the *salvation* of ... ...を救う. ¶***work out*** one's own *salvation* 自己を済度する.

P² the *salvation* ***of*** Christ キリストの救世 ‖ the *salvation* ***of*** a vessel そう難船救助.

same, *n.* 同じもの, 同一の事.

V ***look*** the *same* 同じように見える. ¶***mean*** precisely the *same* [thing] 全く同じ意味になる. ¶Please ***repeat*** the *same*. どうぞそれを繰返して下さい. ¶the *same* may be ***said*** of ... ...についても同様のことが言える.

V² the *same* ***holds*** good of ... 同様のことが...にも当てはまる.

Q ***all*** (=***just***) the *same* = nevertheless それでもやはり. ‖ There is much point in what you say; we adhere to our opinion ***all*** the *same*. お説はごもっともだが僕らはやっぱり僕らの説を固執する. 【類】***All*** the *same* he wouldn't go. ‖ You can pay me or later—it's ***all*** the *same* to me. 即金でもあと払いでもどちらでも結構です. ¶***substantially*** the *same* 大体同様. ¶The *same* is ***true*** in Japan. 日本でも同様である.

P² the *same* ***as*** before 従前通り, 相も変らず ‖ These are exactly the *same* ***as*** those. これはあれと全く同一だ. ¶It is the *same* ***in*** other countries. それは他国でも同様である.

¶He is always the *same to* me. 彼は私に対しては何時も同じ調子だ. ‖ This is the *same to* all intents and purposes. これは実際上同じだ. ‖ Merry X'mas!—The *same to* you. クリスマスおめでとう.—おめでとう. ¶His salary is the *same with* mine. 彼の俸給は私と同じだ. ‖ It is the *same with* men as *with* plants. その点は人も植物も同じだ.

sameness, *n.* 同様.

Q There is ***considerable samenses*** about the subways. 地下鉄はどれも大体同じだ. ¶reduce all boys and girls to a ***dead sameness*** すべての少年少女を同じ型に入れる.

sample, *n.* 見本.

V ***furnish sample*** 見本を供する. ¶***send*** some *samples* 見本を少し送る. ¶***Show*** me a *sample,* please. 見本を一つ見せてくれ. ¶***submit*** a *sample* 見本を渡す.

Q the ***average sample*** 平均見本. ¶a ***duplicate sample*** 控え見本. ¶give a ***fair sample*** of ... ...の現品通りの見本を見せる. ¶a ***fair average sample*** of ... ...の中等品見本. ¶a ***mild sample*** of ... ...の極端でない一例. ¶Send ***new samples*** immediately. 新しい見本を至急送れ. ¶send an assortment of ***standard samples*** 標準品見本を一そろい送る.

Q² a ***production run sample*** 生産見本. ¶a ***trade sample*** 商品見本.

P ***according to sample*** 見本通りに. ¶***as per sample*** 見本通り. ¶It is ***below sample.*** それは見本より劣っている. ¶sale ***by sample*** 見本売買. ¶test the quantity of fatty substance ***in*** the *sample* of milk 見本の牛乳中の脂肪の分量を試験する. ¶sell ***on samples*** 見本で売る. ¶equal ***to sample*** 見本に等しい. ¶come ***up to sample*** 見本通りだ. ¶correspond ***with sample*** 見本と合う.

sampling, *n.* 見本. 「of ... ...の一部見本.

Q ***composite sampling*** 混成見本取り. ¶a ***small sampling***

Q² ***Gallup samplings*** of public opinion show that ... ギャラップ世論調査によれば...

sanatorium, *n.* 療養所.

P² a *sanatorium* ***for*** consumptives 結核療養所.

sanction, *n.* 裁可; 是認; 制裁; 賞罰.

V ***apply sanctions*** against an aggressor 侵略国に対して制裁を加える. ¶***express*** implied *sanction* 黙認を表明する. ¶***get*** the *sanction* of ... to ... ...すべき...の許可を得る. ¶***give sanction*** to ... ...を裁可する. ¶***grant*** Parliamentary *sanction* 議会の承認を与える. ¶It ***has*** the *sanction* of good usage. それは慣例上りっぱに認められている. ¶***obtain*** the *sanction* of public opinion 世論の是認を得る. ¶***receive*** the *sanction* of good usage 慣例上りっぱに認められる. ¶***refuse*** one's *sanction* to ... ...すべき承認を拒む. ¶***secure*** the Imperial *sanction* to ... ...すべき勅許を得る.

Q the adoption of ***economic sanctions*** against ... ...に対する経済制裁の採用. ¶have the ***full sanction*** of ... ...の正式許可を得ている. ¶***legal sanction*** 法律上の制裁. ¶***moral sanction*** 道徳上の制裁. ¶***punitive*** (=***vindictive***) ***sanction*** 処罰. ¶***remunerative sanction*** ほう賞. ¶***social sanction*** 社会の制裁. ¶The usage has ***wide sanction*** in literature. その(語法の)慣用は文学上広く認められている.

P It was done ***without*** my *sanction.* それは私の承認なしでやったことだ.

P² receive the *sanction* ***of*** Parliament 議会の承認を得る. ¶one's *sanction* ***to*** marriage (plan, proposal) 結婚(など)

sanction, *v.* 是認する. 」に対するその承認.

P Slavery was *sanctioned* ***by*** Plato. どれい制度をプラトーは是認した. ‖ The wrong use of the word is *sanctioned* ***by*** usage. その語の誤用は慣用によって是認されている.【類】a marriage *sanctioned* ***by*** society.

sanctity, *n.* 神聖, 清浄.

V as ***befitted*** the *sanctity* of the Christian day of rest キリスト教の安息日の神聖にふさわしく. ¶***invade*** the *sanctity* of ... ...の神聖を犯す. ¶***uphold*** the *sanctity* of the marriage tie 結婚のきずなの神聖を維持する. ¶***violate*** the *sanctity* of (=desecrate) marriage 婚姻の神聖を汚す.

Q ***Christian sanctity*** キリスト教徒の清浄な生活. ¶men of ***eminent sanctity*** 清浄潔白の士. ¶a spot of ***great sanctity*** 神々しい場所.

P² *sanctities* ***of*** the home 家庭の神聖な義務 ‖ the *sanctity* ***of*** treaties 条約の神聖.

sanctuary, *n.* 聖堂; 避難所.

V ***break*** (=***violate***) ***sanctuary*** 教会の保護権を無視して罪人捕縛のためにちん入する. ¶The escaped convict ***found sanctuary*** in the temple. その脱獄囚は寺院をいい隠れ場所とした. ¶***take*** (=***seek***) ***sanctuary*** [罪人など]かくまってもらうために寺院へ逃げ込む.

Q an ***inviolable sanctuary*** 不可侵の聖堂.

Q² a ***bird sanctuary*** 鳥のいこいの場所, 禁猟地.

P² a *sanctuary* ***for*** study 研学の聖堂. ¶a *sanctuary* ***from*** care わずらいのない所. ¶Soho of London is the *sanctuary* ***of*** political refugees, conspirators, deserters, and defaulters of all nations. ロンドンのソホーは万国の亡命者・謀反人・逃亡者及び義務不履行者の逃避地である ‖ the *sanctuary* ***of*** sciences 科学の殿堂.

sanctum, *n.* 私室.

Q the ***editorial sanctum*** 編集室.

sand, *n.* 砂; *pl.* 砂原, 砂浜; 洲(す); 《米俗》元気.

V ***number*** (=***plow***) ***sands*** むだ骨を折る. ¶***sprinkle sand*** 砂を散布する.【類】***sprinkle*** dry *sand* over the muddy spot. ¶***strike*** the *sands* [船が]砂洲に乗り上げる. ¶it ***takes*** *sand* to go into a football scrimmage しゅう球のスクラムを組むことは勇気がいる.

Q ***fine sand*** 細かい砂. ¶***gravelly sand*** 小石混りの砂(砂利). ¶***loose sand*** 散砂. ¶***sun-baked sand*** 日に焼けた砂. ¶on the ***sunny sands*** 日当りのよい砂浜で.

Q² ***emery sand*** 金剛砂.

P obtain gold by washing it ***from sand*** and gravel 砂や砂利から洗い落して金を採る. ¶sink ***in*** the *sand* 砂中にめりこむ. ¶an ocean ***of*** *sand* 大砂原. ¶a house built ***on*** the *sand* 砂上に建てた家(基礎のしっかりしないもの) ‖ play ***on*** the *sand* 砂の上で遊ぶ. ¶a great figure well-nigh covered ***with*** the *sands* of (=buried in) oblivion [砂ほこりをかぶったように]世人から忘れられかかっている大人物.

P² numberless as the *sands* ***on*** the seashore 浜の真さご

sandal, *n.* わらぐつ, サンダル. 」のごとく無数な.

Q² ***beach sandals*** 海水浴場用のサンダル. ¶wear ***straw sandals*** わらぞうり(わらじ)をはく.

sandman, *n.* 砂袋のおじさん. 「だよ).

V² A *sandman* ***comes!*** そら目にはとが止った(ねんねするん

sandpaper, *n.* サンドペーパー.

P polish ... ***with sandpaper*** ...をサンドペーパーでみがく.

sandwich, *n.* サンドイッチ.

Q² ***eggs*** (***ham***) ***sandwich*** 卵(ハム)サンドイッチ. ¶***jelly*** (***lettuce***) ***sandwiches*** ジェリ(サラダ菜)サンドイッチ. ¶a ***three-decker sandwich*** 三重サンド.

P² a *sandwich* ***of*** good and bad 善と悪との背中合わせ.

sandwich, *v.* はさむ.

M be *sandwiched* ***in*** between the hunks of a camel らくだのこぶとこぶの間にはさまる ‖ His academic work is *sandwiched* ***in*** between his working-hours. 彼の研究は労務時間の合間にはさまれている.

P *sandwich* a picture ***between*** two pieces of pasteboard 絵を二枚の台紙の間にはさむ.【類】a bank *sandwiched* ***between*** warehouses. ¶Study should always be *sandwiched* ***with*** periods of rest. 勉強はいつも休息の時間をその間にはさんで行かなければいけない.

sang-froid, *n. F.* 冷静.

V He did not ***lose*** *sang-froid.* 彼は冷静を失わなかった.

Q Her *sang-froid* was ***astounding.*** 彼女の平気なのには驚

sanguine, *a.* のん気な, 楽観的な. 」き入った.

M Is it ***too sanguine*** to expect that ...? ...を当てにするのはのん気過ぎるか. 「みにしている.

P He is *sanguine* ***of*** success (victory). 彼は成功(など)を頼

O Not one of us was *sanguine* that it could be achieved by that time. われわれの中一人としてそのときまでにそれが実現されようと思うほど楽観するものはなかった.

sanity, *n.* 正気, 本気.

V I ***doubt*** his *sanity.* 正気のさたじゃない. ¶***lose*** one's *sanity* 気が違う. ¶***retain*** one's *sanity* 気はたしかである.

P² *sanity* ***of*** thought (judgment) 思想(判定)の穏健 ‖ *sanity* ***of*** outlook 観察の正しさ.

sap, *n.* 液汁; 血気.

Q² ***rubber sap*** ゴム樹液.

P² the *sap* ***of*** youth 青年の血気.

sap, *v.* 徐々にぶちこわす.

M The extreme heat ***gradually sapped*** our strength. 酷熱でわれわれのからだはだんだん弱って来た.

P His health has been ***sapped by*** the damp climate. 彼の健康は湿気の多い気候のために次第に衰えて行った. ‖ The walls had been *sapped* **by** the waves. 岩壁は波浪でこわれていた.【類】virtues *sapped* **by** luxury.

sarcasm, *n.* 風刺. 「風刺が過ぎた.
V *fear sarcasm* 皮肉を恐れる. ¶The *sarcasm* is **overdone.**
Q **biting** (=**cutting** or **keen**) *sarcasm* 痛烈な皮肉.【類】I wished to squelch him with **biting** *sarcasm.* ¶with **bitter** *sarcasm* 痛烈な風刺で.
P "How unselfish you are!" cried Ellen **in** *sarcasm.* 「まあ思いやりがあること」とエレンは皮肉たっぷりに言った. ¶**with** gentle *sarcasm* おとなしい風刺で.

sarcastic, *a.* 皮肉な.
P *sarcastic* **about** … …に皮肉な.

sash, *n.* 帯. 「る.
V She **has** a *sash* around her waist. 彼女は帯をしめてい

satchel, *n.* 手さげかばん.
V **carry** a *satchel* かばんを持つ. ¶**take** a *satchel* **along** かばんを持って行く.

sate, *v.* たん能させる.
P be *sated* **with** pleasure (food) 十分楽しむ(食べる).

satellite, *n.* 衛星国.
Q[2] shoot up an **earth** *satellite* 人工衛星をうちあげる. ¶the three **Soviet** *satellites* of Albania, Yugoslavia and Bulgaria ソ連の三衛星国であるアルバニア, ユーゴー, ブルガリア. ¶the minor **Axis** *satellites* 枢軸側小国.

satiate, *v.* あきさせる.
P Nothing would *satiate* his lust **for** power. いかなるものも彼の権勢欲を抑えることはできないだろう. ¶He is *satiated* **with** pleasures. 彼は快楽にあきあきしている.

satiety, *n.* 飽満.
V **experience** *satiety* あきあきする.
P feast **to** *satiety* あきるほど飲み食いする.

satire, *n.* 風刺.
V The book is a *satire* **directed** at the so-called "smart" society. この本はいわゆる「流行界」を皮肉ったものである.
Q a **bitter** (=**keen**) *satire* 痛烈な風刺. ¶a **good-natured** *satire* on … …に関する善意の風刺. ¶a **scathing** *satire* 手きびしい風刺.
Q[2] a **blackboard** *satire* 黒板の風刺(らく書).
P a *satire* **against** follies 愚行に対する風刺. ¶a *satire* **on** some person (society) ある人(社会)に加えた風刺.

satirist, *n.* 風刺家.
Q a **great social** *satirist* 偉大な社会風刺家. ¶a **political** *satirist* 政治風刺家.

satisfaction, *n.* 満足, 得心; 返済; 決闘.
V **afford** great *satisfaction* to … …に大なる満足を与える. ¶**attain** full and complete *satisfaction* 十分な満足を得る. ¶**demand** *satisfaction* 弁解を要求する, 責める; 決闘を申し込む ‖ The fleet set sail on the 20th of July to **demand** *satisfaction* from the Chinese. 中国人の不当を詰問するために同艦隊は七月二十日に出発した. ¶Mr. Folger was **denied** the *satisfaction* of witnessing the fulfilment of his life's dream. フォルジャー氏は自分の一生の夢想の実現を見ることができなかった. ¶**derive** great *satisfaction* from … …から大きな満足を得る. ¶**enjoy** plenary *satisfaction* 十分の満足を感じる. ¶I **expect** some *satisfaction* for that loss. その損害に対しては何らかの賠償があると思う. ¶**experience** intense *satisfaction* at … …に対して大満足に思う. ¶**express** *satisfaction* with … に満足を表する.【類】I **express** the *satisfaction* at the success which attended the meeting. ¶**feel** great *satisfaction* over … …を非常に喜ぶ. ¶**find** *satisfaction* in … …で満足する. ¶If you **give** me *satisfaction,* you shall in future have my custom. 気に入ればこれから得意になってあげる.【類】Endeavor all you can to **give** *satisfaction.* ¶*Satisfaction* **guaranteed.** [広告] 必らずご満足を得るように致します. ¶At least I **have** the *satisfaction* of knowing that I have done my best. 少なくとも私は自分でできるだけのことをやったということを知って満足する. ¶**make** *satisfaction* for a debt 借金を返済する ‖ once *satisfaction* is **made** 一たん要求を満たすと. ¶**obtain** *satisfaction* 満足を得る. ¶**reach** complete *satisfaction* 本懐を遂げる. ¶**receive** *satisfaction* 満足する. ¶**take** *satisfaction* for the injuries done to … …の損害賠償を取る. ¶seldom **yield** *satisfaction* めったに満足を与えない.
Q give **complete** *satisfaction* in every particular 細目にわたってすっかり満足させる. ¶a **deep** *satisfaction* from … …から生じる深い満足.【類】a matter for **deep** *satisfaction* / derive **deep** *satisfaction* from … ¶**entire** *satisfaction* 十分の満足. ¶**esthetic** *satisfaction* 美的満足. ¶**full** *satisfaction* 十分な満足. ¶**great** *satisfaction* 大満足. ¶with **huge** *satisfaction* 大満足で. ¶derive a very **imperfect** *satisfaction* from … …からきわめて不完全な満足を得る. ¶a **keen** *satisfaction* 大満足. ¶express **lively** *satisfaction* at … …に対して多大の満足を表する. ¶for the **physical** *satisfaction* of … …の肉体上の満足のために. ¶a **pleasurable** *satisfaction* 楽しい満足. ¶the public will hear with **profound** *satisfaction* of … 公衆は…を聞いて深い満足を覚えるだろう. ¶a **savage** *satisfaction* 残忍な満足感. ¶find a **secret** *satisfaction* in … …を心ひそかにうれしく思う. ¶a matter of **solid** *satisfaction* 真に喜ぶべきこと. ¶take a **special** *satisfaction* in … …を特に喜ぶ. ¶**unalloyed** *satisfaction* 心からの満足.
P **For** your *satisfaction* I will let you know the truth. 君の得心が行くように事実を申上げましょう. ¶He paid 100,000 yen **in** *satisfaction* of the claim. 彼はその弁償として十万円を払った. ¶a source **of** *satisfaction* 満足の原因の一つ. ¶The amount of compensation has been arranged **to** the *satisfaction* of all concerned. 賠償額は関係者全部の満足するように話をまとめた. ¶dress it **to** *satisfaction* それを着こなす.【類】He settled the matter **to** the satisfaction of all. / He did his duty entirely **to** my *satisfaction.* / **to** the *satisfaction* of all the parties to it / The paper was at last written **to** my *satisfaction.* / It has been proved **to** the *satisfaction* of statisticians that a continued spell (長続き) of wet weather results in an unusual crop of murders (いつもより多くの死者を出す). / It has not been demonstrated **to** my *satisfaction.* / This will prove it **to** your *satisfaction.* / **to** the *satisfaction* of all concerned (関係者一同). ¶**with** a great deal of *satisfaction* ほくほくして.【類】I can say **with** the greatest *satisfaction* that …
P[2] express *satisfaction* **at** the success which attends the meeting 盛会に対して満足を表する. ¶take great *satisfaction* **in** recommending … 喜んで…を推奨する. ¶the *satisfaction* **of** ambition 野心の満足. ¶it is a *satisfaction* **to** him that … …は彼に取って満足すべきことだ. ¶express one's *satisfaction* **with** the result of the conference 会議の結果に満足を表する.

satisfactory, *a.* 満足な, 申分のない.
M be **barely** *satisfactory* どうやらというところ. ¶These goods are **by no means** *satisfactory.* この品はどうも気に入らない. ¶The arrangement is **entirely** *satisfactory.* その取きめは全く申分がない. ¶The news is **highly** *satisfactory.* それは非常に結構なたよりだ. ¶The result is **most** *satisfactory.* 結果は申分がない. ¶The references given are **quite** *satisfactory.* 御指示の照会先は至極結構に存じます. ¶The result is not **very** *satisfactory.* 成績はあまりかんばしくない. ¶though not **wholly** *satisfactory* 十分とまでは行かないが. 「には満足できなかった.
P The answer was not *satisfactory* **to** him. その返事は彼

satisfy, *v.* 満足させる, 得心させる; 償う.
M I am **fully** *satisfied* of the truth of his statement. 私は彼の話の真実なことを十分認めている. ‖ *satisfy* one's appetite **fully** 食欲を十分満足させる. ¶be **heartily** *satisfied* with the result その結果に対し心から満足している. ¶I shall *satisfy* him very **perfectly** of that matter. この件については私が彼にすっかり得心させます.【類】He seemed **perfectly** *satisfied* with my offer. ¶He is **quite** *satisfied* with his lot. 彼は自分の運命に満足している. ¶**thoroughly** *satisfied* with … …にまったく満足して. ¶My customers are **very** much *satisfied.* お客さん方は大いに満足しています. ¶I am not very **well** *satisfied* with … 私は…には余り感心しない.
P He is *satisfied* **at** the success of his mission. 彼はその使命を果したのを喜んでいる. ¶*satisfy* a person **for** labor その労に酬いる ‖ *satisfy* one's desire **for** motoring (=auto-ing) 自動車を乗回してドライブ熱を満足させる. ¶I have *satisfied* myself **of** the truth of the report by inquiry. 私は調べて見てその報告に間違いないことを確かめた. ¶*satisfy* one's appetite **on** potato じゃが芋でその飢えをしのぐ. ¶I am *satisfied* **with** your explanation. 私は君の説明に満足だ. ‖ Are you *satisfied* **with** my answer? 私の返事で納得ができましたか. ‖ He will not be *satisfied* **with** such a

small salary. 彼はこんな薄給では満足すまい.【類】be *satisfied **with*** small success / The Government was *satisfied **with*** the results of the negotiations. / He was *satisfied **with*** a competence which (ほどの資力) enabled him to travel, to read, and to write.

saturate, *v.* しみ込ませる.

M The air was ***somewhat saturated*** with moisture. 空気はいく分湿気が多かった.

P *saturate* a sponge ***with*** water 海綿に水をしみ込ませる ‖ The fuel is ***saturated with*** kerosene. その燃料には石油を含ませてある.【類】English literature is thoroughly ***saturated with*** the poison of prejudice and hostility to the Catholic Church. / the moss ***saturated with*** water.

saturation, *n.* 飽満.

P Here is romance ***to saturation.*** これは粋(ｽｲ)百パーセントである.

Saturday, *n.* 土曜日.

V What a busy *Saturday* we have ***had***! 実に忙しい土曜日だった.

P He comes up ***of*** a *Saturday*. 彼は土曜日などにやって来る. ¶***upon*** (=on) some *Saturday* いつか土曜日にでも.

sauce, *n.* ソース;《米》くだものの砂糖煮.

V ***put*** sauce on ... ...にソースを掛ける.

Q put a ***sweet*** *sauce* over the pudding あまい(果汁)ソースをプデング(プリン)にかける.

Q^2 ***apple*** *sauce* 《米》アップルソース. ¶eat ***cranberry*** *sauce* with one's turkey 《米》七面鳥にクランベリソースをかけて食べる. ¶***soya*** *sauce* しょう油. ¶***tomato*** *sauce* トマトソース.

P serve a person ***with*** the same *sauce* 《俗》同じ手で仕返しをする. ¶It is tame ***without*** the *sauce* of danger. 危険味がないとおもしろ味が薄い.

saucer, *n.* 台ざら.

Q a ***flying*** *saucer* (=disk) 空飛ぶ円盤.

saucy, *a.* 生意気な.

P I'm very sorry I was *saucy* ***to*** you. 《米》あんたにつらく当ってご免なさいね.

V You are ***getting*** too *saucy*, but now I'll ***take*** the *sauce* out of you. 《米》お前はなんて生意気になったんだ, 今その生意気さを引っこ抜いてやるから.

saunter, *n.* 漫歩, 散歩.

V ***take*** an evening *saunter* 夕刻の散歩をする.

Q^2 take an ***evening saunter*** through one of the streets 通りを夕方散歩する.

saunter, *v.* ぶらぶら歩く.

M *saunter* ***away*** one's time of study 勉強の時間を空しく過ごす.【類】*saunter **away*** one's life.

M^2 ***saunter over*** to ... ...まで散歩する.

P *saunter* ***on*** its paths その道をぶらつく. ¶*saunter* ***through*** the Ginza 銀ぶらをする. ¶*saunter* leisurely ***toward*** ... ...の方へぶらぶら行く.

sausage, *n.* ソーセージ.

P slices of bread ***with*** *sausage* between ソーセージ入りのパン.

savage, *n.* 蛮民.

Q a ***ferocious*** *savage* どう猛な野蛮人. ¶***illiterate*** *savages* 無学文盲の蛮人. ¶a ***naked*** *savage* 裸体の蛮人.

P a horde ***of*** *savages* 蛮民の群.

savagery, *n.* どう猛.

Q ***unbridled*** *savagery* 勝手放題のどう猛.

savant, *n.* [著名の]学者.

Q ***celebrated*** *savants* 知名の大学者. ¶a ***great German*** *savant* ドイツの大学者.

save, *v.* 救う; 節約する, 貯蓄する.

M This will *save* you ***a lot***. これは大へんお徳用です. ¶This machine will ***certainly*** *save* you a lot of time and labor. この機械で時間と労力を大いに節約出来ます(洗たく器など).

M^2 *save* ***up*** money 金をためこむ ‖ *save* ***up*** for a rainy day 将来に備える.

P *Saving* ***at*** the spigot and wasting at the bung-hole. 一文惜みの百失い[格言]. ¶You *save* a mile ***by*** taking a short cut. 近道をすれば一マイル得する. ¶*save* money ***for*** tomorrow (a rainy day) 後々のために(不慮に備えて)金を積む ‖ *Save* your strength ***for*** further attempts. 今からそう張切るなよ. ¶*save* one ***from*** drowning 人のおぼれる所を救う.【類】*save* a house ***from*** burning / *save* a family ***from*** ruin / The building has been *saved **from*** destruction. ‖ He was *saved **from*** further harm. 彼はそれ以上の害は免かれた. ‖ *save* money ***from*** one's salary 俸給の中から貯金する. ¶This will *save* you fifty per cent ***on*** your gas bill. これでガス代が五割節約できる. ‖ *save* ***on*** one's wages 給金の中から貯金する. ¶*save* a thousand yen ***out of*** one's pay 給料の中から千円貯蓄する.

O I had my hat washed, and it *saved* my buying a new one. 私は帽子を洗たくさせたので新らしいのを買わずに済んだ. ‖ Soap *saves* rubbing. 石けんを使うともまないですむ.

saving, *n.* (**1**) 救助; 節約.

V ***afford*** an appreciable *saving* on ... ...がかなり節約される.【類】***afford*** a *saving* of 50% in time. ¶This ***allows*** a *saving* of 50 per cent in time. これで時間が五割節約される. ¶***effect*** (=***achieve***) a *saving* of 50 per cent in fuel 燃料において五割の節約になる ‖ ***effect*** a very great *saving* 大変な節約になる. ¶That ***means*** a *saving* of ten yen. それで十円浮く. ¶***practice*** close *saving* 十分出費をつめる.

Q a ***considerable*** *saving* of money 余ほどの金の節約. ¶It will be a ***great*** *saving* of expense in many ways. それは色々の点で費用の大節約となるだろう. ¶the ***pecuniary*** *saving* effected by ... is far outweighed by ... ...によって得られた金銭上の節約よりも...の方がはるかに重大だ. ¶a ***precious*** *saving* 大事にとってあるもの.

Q^2 ***daylight*** *saving* 日光の節約(夏時間など). ¶at a big ***money*** *saving* 大きな金の節約で. ¶***time*** (***labor***) *saving* 時間(労力)の節約.

P Machinery now does the business ***at*** a great *saving* of time and labor (=muscle). 今日は機械が仕事をするので時間と労働の大節約ができる.【類】We can produce ***at*** a *saving* of 20 per cent by the use of the machine.

P^2 a *saving* ***in*** time and trouble 時間と労力の節約. ¶a *saving* ***of*** $1.50 each week during the next two years would provide ample funds for ... 次の二カ年間毎週一ドル五十セントずつ節約すれば...のりっぱな資金ができるだろう ‖ a *saving* ***of*** work and time ***to*** ... ...に取っての労力と時間の節約. ¶a *saving* ***to*** the consumer 買手の徳.

(**2**) *pl.* 貯蓄, 貯金.

V ***deposit*** one's *savings* in a bank 銀行に預金する. ¶***draw*** one' *savings* from a bank 銀行からその預金を引き出す. ¶***encourage*** postal *savings* 郵便貯金を奨励する. ¶***exhaust*** one'e *savings* 貯金を使い果す. ¶***invest*** our *savings* われわれの貯金を投資する. ¶***keep*** one's hard-earned *savings* in a bank 辛苦してもうけた金を銀行に預けておく. ¶***withdraw*** one's *savings* from a bank 銀行から預金を引き出す.

Q ***postal*** *savings* 郵便貯金.

P ***pay out of*** *savings* from one's salary 俸給の内からした貯金で払う.

saving, *a.* つましい.

P He is very *saving* ***of*** his money. 彼は非常に金につましい.

savio[u]r, *n.* 救世主.

Q^2 a picture of the Wise Men adoring the ***infant*** *Savior* 救世の幼児(キリスト)を称える賢人の絵.

savo[u]r, *n.* 風味.

V Danger ***gives*** a *savor* to rock climbing. 危険だということが岩のぼりを面白くする.

Q food with ***pleasant*** *savor* 風味のよい食物. ¶the ***stinging*** *savor* of new slang 新しい俗語のぴりっとした味.

P the *savor **of*** a rose ばらの香 ‖ The soap has a *savor **of*** fish. この石けんはなま臭い.

savo[u]r, *v.* 風味がある; 臭味がある.

M He *savours **somewhat*** of the politician. 彼は少し政治家臭い. ¶His conduct *savors **strongly*** of hypocrisy. 彼の行いにはすこぶる偽善者臭い所がある.

P food that *savors **of*** onions ねぎの味のする食物 ‖ *savor **of*** Buddhism (Christianity) 仏教(など)臭い ‖ a request that *savors **of*** a command 命令みたいな依頼 ‖ This drink *savors **of*** the orange (lemon). この飲みものはオレンジ(レモン)の味がする.【類】His answers *savor **of*** impertinence. / This *savors* rather ***of*** a mercantile transaction. / *savor **of*** an old-school education (旧式教育) / His language (物の言い方) *savors **of*** pedantry (もの知りぶった). / College baseball men should not *savor **of*** professionalism. / declare with a tone *savoring **of*** pride and disdain (ごうまんと侮べつ).

saw, *n.* ことわざ, 格言.

Q a ***legal*** *saw* 法律の格言. ¶a ***silly old*** *saw* ばかげた古いことわざ. ¶a ***wise*** *saw* 賢明なことわざ.

saw, *n.* のこ, のこぎり.

V ***grease*** one's *saw* のこぎりに油を塗る. ¶***set*** a *saw* のこぎりの目立をする.

Q a ***cross-cut*** *saw* 横ひきのこぎり.

Q^2 a ***buzz*** *saw* 《米》丸のこ. ¶a ***hand*** *saw* 手のこ. ¶a ***pit*** *saw* 縦びき大のこ.

P the teeth ***of*** a *saw* のこぎりの歯. ¶cut ***with*** a *saw* のこぎりでひく.

saw, *v.* ひく.

M wood that *saws* ***easily*** (***badly***) [のこで]引きやすい(引きにくい)木.

M^2 *saw* ***off*** horns [のこで]角を切り取る. ¶*saw* ***up*** logs 製材する.

P *saw* timber ***into*** planks 材木を板にひく.

say, *n.* 言いたいこと.

V I ***condensed*** all my *say* into a letter. 私は言いたいことを一通の手紙に縮めた. ¶Let him ***have*** his say=Let's hear him say. 彼に言うだけのことを言わせろ. 【類】 I ***have*** my *say.* / have no (little) say. ‖ He rarely ***has*** a *say* in the matter. 彼は滅多にそのことには口を出さない. ¶***Say*** your *say.* 言うだけのことを言え. 【類】 When you have ***said*** your *say* you should finish up.

Q He has the ***last*** *say* in the matter. その件を決定する権利は彼にある. ¶I should like to say my ***little*** *say* on ... 私は...についていささか申述べたい.

say, *v.* 言う; 仮定する, まず...とする.

M Did he ***actually*** *say* so? 彼は本当にそう言ったか. ¶we *say* ... ***advisedly,*** for ... ...だからわれわれはあえて...と言う. ¶He did not dare to *say* anything ***aloud.*** 彼は声に出して言おうとはしなかった. ¶*say* ***apologetically*** 弁解的に言う. ¶I can only *say* ***approximately.*** 私はおおよそのことしか言えない. ¶I very much liked to *say* ***as much,*** but desisted. よっぽどそう言ってやろうかと思ったがやめた. ¶*say* ***autocratically*** to ... ...に独裁的に言う. ¶America, or, ***better said,*** the United States of America アメリカ正しくはアメリカ合衆国. ¶*say* ***brusquely*** 無愛想に言う. ¶Have something worth saying, and *say* it ***clearly,*** or ***impressively.*** ここで一言という場合ははっきりかまたは印象づけるようにか言い給え. ¶it is ***commonly said*** of him that ... 世間では彼のことを普通...と言っている. ¶we may ***confidently say,*** from the fact before us, that ... われわれは眼前の事実から安心して...と言える. ¶we cannot ***conscientiously say*** that ... ...とは断言し兼ねる. ¶he ***said,*** a little ***constrainedly,*** ... 彼は...とちょっと気がねしながら言った. ¶*say* ***coolly*** 平気で言う. ¶*say* ***cryptically*** 神秘的に言う. ¶*say* ***definitely*** きっぱりと言う. ¶I *said* it ***deliberately.*** 私は故意にそう言った. ¶I am a waitress, as you ***despisingly*** *say.* どうせあたしは女給ですよ. ¶She *said* it ***half*** to herself. 彼女はそれをつぶやくように言った. ¶*say* ***happily*** うまいことを言う. ¶he ***hardly*** *said* it than ... そういうが早いか. ¶*say,* ***half musingly*** 半分は自分に言って聞かせる. ¶*say* ***distinctly*** はっきりと言う. ¶It was ***easier*** *said* than done. それは言うはやすく行うは難しという訳だったのである. ¶it has been *said* ***elsewhere*** that ... 別の所で述べたように. ¶let it be ***emphatically*** *said* 特に断っておくが. ¶***enough*** has been *said* as to ... ...に関してはこれ以上言う必要はあるまい. ¶it is ***even*** *said* that ... ...とさえ言われている. ¶*say* ***exactly*** and ***felicitously*** what we mean 思うことを正確に巧みに表現する. ¶***flatly*** *say* 断固として言う. ¶***frankly*** *say* ... 率直に言う. ¶He knows how to *say* "No" ***gracefully.*** 彼は人の気を悪くしないで「いいえ」と言うこつをのみ込んでいる. ¶*say* ***hesitantly*** ためらって言う. ¶*say* ***hoarsely*** しゃがれ声で言う. ¶we can ***honestly*** *say* that ... われわれは正直に...と言える. ¶***How*** do you *say* this in English? これは英語でなんと言うか. ¶*say* ***humbly*** 謙そんして言う. ¶*say* ***indulgingly*** 甘えて言う. ¶*say* ***ironically*** 皮肉たっぷりに言う. ¶as has ***just*** been *said* 今言ったように. ¶***Magnificently*** *said!* よくも言ったり. ¶I cannot *say* ***much*** for his style. 彼の文体は余り感心できない. ‖ As to the style, I have ***much*** to *say.* 文体については私にも大いに文句がある. ‖ That is not *saying* very ***much.*** それだけでは言い尽していない. ¶*Say* ***no more,*** please! もう言わないでくれ, 頼む. ¶That's what people ***often*** *say.* 世間でよくいうことだ. ¶I *say* ***once*** for all that ... はっきり言っておくが... ¶I can ***only*** *say* that ... 私はただ...と言いうるのみだ. ¶None of us will dare to *say* it ***openly*** before him. 彼の目の前でそれをはっきり言える者はなかろう. ¶*say* ***over*** again what has been much better *said* before 前に人の言ったことをもっとずっと拙劣にまねをして言う. ¶*say* ***peevishly*** つけつけ言う. ¶*say* ***peremptorily*** けんもほろろに言う. ¶The proverb ***pithily*** *says.* ことわざは簡潔だ. ¶I cannot *say* ***positively*** 断言はできない. ¶as we have ***previously*** *said* 前に述べた通り. ¶*say* ***reproachfully*** つけつけ言う. ¶"Personal experience," it has been ***rightly said,*** "is the basis of all real literature." 「一個人の経験があらゆる真の文学の基礎である」という言葉は当を得ている. ¶we may ***safely*** *say* that ... ...といっても不当ではあるまい. ¶*say* ***sardonically*** 皮肉に言う. ¶*say* very ***sensibly*** that ... ...と賢明に言う. ¶I came very near to *saying* ***so.*** よっぽどそう言ってやろうかと思った. ‖ You don't *say* ***so!*** まさか! ‖ *Saying* ***so*** would serve no purpose. そんなこと言ったて始まらない. ‖ Why didn't you *say* ***so*** at the outset? なぜ最初にそう言わなかったんだ. ¶She ***sobbingly*** *said* to ... 彼女は泣きじゃくりながら...に言った. ¶No ***sooner*** *said* than done. 言うが早いか直ちに実行した. ¶*say* ***soothingly*** なだめるように言う. ¶*say* ***stoutly*** しっかり言う. ¶*say* ***succinctly*** 手短かに言う. ¶You cannot *say* so ***sweepingly.*** 一口にそうは言えない. ¶*say* ***too much*** 言い過ぎる. ¶it is ***traditionally said*** to be ... それは...であるという言伝えがある. ¶I can ***truly*** *say* with him, "..." 私は「...」といった彼に同感である. ¶we may ***truthfully*** *say* that ... ...といっても正当であろう. ¶*say* ***unthinkingly*** うっかり言う. ¶*say* ***wedgewise*** 横合から口を出す. ¶Have something to say and *say* it ***well.*** 言うことを持てそしてそれをうまく言え. ‖ it is ***well said*** that ... ...とはよく言ったものだ ‖ it might as ***well*** be *said* that ... ...とも言えないこともない. ¶he *says* ***wisely*** and ***well*** that ... ...というのは至言である.

P Do not for your life *say* anything ***about*** it. 命に掛けてもそのことはなにも言うな. ‖ Don't *say* unkind things ***about*** your playmates. 遊び仲間の悪口を言うな. ¶Do not believe what her detractors *say* ***against*** her. 彼女をけなす者の悪口を信じるな. ‖ Not one word was *said* ***against*** it. それをちょっとでも悪く言うものはなかった. ‖ *say* something ***against*** one 人の悪口を言う. 【類】 They had nothing to *say* ***against*** him. ‖ There is nothing to be *said* ***against*** it. それに対しては別に文句はない. ¶*say* so ***before*** people 人前でそう言う. ¶I can *say* it ***by*** heart (=rote). 私は空(そら)でそれを言える. ¶there is much to be *said* ***for*** looking upon it as ... それを...と見なすには大いに理屈がある ‖ *say* a good word ***for*** a person 人のことを良く言う ‖ *say* ***for*** [a] certainty 確言する. ¶*say* ***from*** one's heart 衷心から言う ‖ *say* ***from*** memory そらで言う. ¶He *says* nothing ***in*** his defense. 彼は一向自分のことを弁護しない. ‖ Much was *said* ***in*** his praise (=praise of him). 大分彼はほめられた. ‖ He *said* it ***in*** jest. 彼は冗談にそう言った. ¶What have you to *say* ***in regard to*** that subject? その問題についての君の意見はどうだ. ¶What do people *say* ***of*** me? 人は私のことをなんと言っていますか. ‖ it was maliciously *said* ***of*** him that ... 彼のことを...と悪口を言うものがあった. ¶I have nothing to *say* ***on*** that subject. その問題に関して私はなにも言うことはない. ‖ The last word has not yet been *said* ***on*** this subject. この研究はまだ行く所まで行っていない. ‖ There is a good deal much to be *said* ***on*** both sides. 双方に言い分がたくさんある. ‖ There is a good deal to be *said* ***on*** the other side. 一方にも大いに言うべき理屈がある. ¶They *say* such things ***out of*** (=***through***) envy. 彼らはねたんでそんなことを言うのだ. ‖ *say* ***out of*** the dark 暗がりから声を出す. ¶I *said* ***to*** the children, "Don't make such a noise." 私は「そんなに騒ぐな」と子供らに言った. ‖ Did he *say* anything ***to*** you about me? 彼は僕のことをなんとか言ったか. ‖ *say* ***to*** oneself 独言を言う ‖ *say* No ***to*** a question 質問に「違う」と言う. 【類】 *say* "Goodbye" ***to*** ... / *say* hello ***to*** Mrs. D / I must *say* good night ***to*** her before leaving. ‖ *say* ***to*** one's face 人に面と向って言う ‖ he *said* ***to*** what he thought was Mr. ... 彼は...氏だと思った人に言った ‖ What *say* you ***to*** 500 yen? 五百円ではどうです. ¶He *said* ***under*** the breath. 彼は小声で言った. ¶I *said* goodbye ***with*** a heavy heart. 私はいやいや別れを告げた. ‖ "*Say* it ***with*** (=***in***) flowers." あなたの心を花で表わしましょう(花屋のモットー). ¶I *say* this ***without*** vanity. 私はこれは自慢で言うのではない.

O *Say* which you prefer. どちらがよいか言って見給え. ‖ *Say* (=If) it were true, what then? それが本当とした所でそれがどうなのか. ‖ Any one, let us *say* yourself, might have done so. だれにしろよし君自身にしてもそうやったかも知れない. ‖ The number left behind was not great, *say* only ten. 残った数は大したものではなかった, まず十位だ. ¶a month ahead today, that's to *say*, October 10 来月の今日, すなわち十月十日.

saying, *n.* 言; ことわざ.

v His life ***illustrates*** the *saying* of Buffon, "Genius is infinite patience." 彼の生がいは「天才とは無限の忍耐なり」というビュッフォンの言を例証している. ¶It ***needs*** no *saying*. それは言うまでもない. ¶to ***paraphrase*** the *saying* of Kipling ... ...というキップリングの言葉の意味を換言する. ¶***prove*** the well-known *saying* that ... ...という人口に広く知られた言葉の真理性を証明する. ¶to ***quote*** a *saying* of ... ...の言葉を引用すれば.

v^2 as the *saying* ***goes*** (=***runs***) ことわざにある通り.

Q an ***antiquated*** *saying* 陳腐な言. ¶***bright*** *sayings* of children 子供の知言. ¶a ***classical*** *saying* 古言. ¶a ***clever*** *saying* うまい言葉. ¶a ***common*** *saying* 俚(り)言. ¶to use a ***common*** *saying* 俗に言う. 【類】Plutarch says, "It is a ***common saying*** that poetry is vocal painting, and painting, silent poetry." ¶offensively ***dirty*** or ***indecent*** *sayings* ひどく聞き苦しいまたはみだらな言葉. ¶the ***favorite*** *saying* of ... ...のよく言う言葉. ¶"An ounce of prevention is worth a pound of cure" is a ***fine old saying***, full of good, plain common sense「一オンスの予防は一ポンドの治療に値す」とははっきりした常識のこもったりっぱな古言である. ¶a ***golden*** *saying* 金言. ¶Hazlitt's Table Talk is a veritable mine of good *sayings* about life. ハズリットのテーブル・トークは真に人生訓の宝庫である. ¶a ***hard*** *saying* ひどい口げんか. ¶***homely*** *sayings* 俚(り)言. ¶He will not come, but there is ***no*** *saying*. 彼は来ないだろうが何とも言えない. ‖There is ***no*** *saying* what may happen if you neglect your studies. 君が学業を怠ればどうなるか分からない. ¶an ***old*** *saying* 古言. ¶a ***pithy*** *saying* 含蓄のある格言. ¶***popular*** *sayings* よく人の言うこと. ¶***proverbial*** *sayings*=proverbs ことわざ. ¶a ***self-coined*** *saying* 自分で造った言い回し. ¶a short ***sententious*** *saying* 寸鉄, 警句. ¶a ***significant*** *saying* 意味深い言葉. ¶a ***smart*** *saying* 痛切な言. ¶a ***sublime*** *saying* 崇高な言. ¶a ***time-worn*** *saying* 昔からよく言われる言. ¶It is a ***true*** *saying*. それは至言だ. ¶His talk is full of ***wise*** *sayings* 彼の話には名言が多くこもっている. ¶a ***witty*** *saying* 奇警の言.

P ***according to*** Nietzsche's *saying* ニーチェの言う所によると. ¶It goes ***without*** *saying* that the proposal will not be accepted. その提議が採用されないのは言うまでもない. ‖it goes ***without*** *saying*, of course, that ... もちろん...は言うまでもないことだ.

P^2 There is an old *saying* ***about*** the impossibility of making silken purses out of pigs' ears. 豚の耳では絹財布ができないという古いことわざがある.

O it is a *saying* that ... ...とは人のよく言うことだ.

scaffold, *n.* [建築の]足場; 絞首台.

V ***climb*** a *scaffold* 足場に登る. ¶***mount*** (=***go to***) the *scaffold* 死刑台にのぼる.

scald, *n.* やけど.

V ***produce*** a deep *scald* 深いやけどのあとを生じる.

scald, *v.* やけどさせる.

P He was *scalded* ***to*** death ***by*** the steam. 彼は蒸気で焼死した. ¶He was *scalded* ***with*** hot water. 彼は熱湯でやけどをした.

scale, *n.* (**1**) はかり, 天びん.

V ***hold*** the *scales* ***even*** 公正に判断する. ¶He stands six feet two inches and ***tips*** the *scales* at (=weighs) 225 pounds. 彼は身長六フィート二インチ, 重量は二百二十五ポンドある. ¶***turn*** the *scale* 〖比ゆ〗決定する, はっきりさせる ‖He ***turns*** the *scale* at 150 pounds. あの人は百五十ポンド(など)ある. 【類】If her size does not mislead us, she must ***turn*** the *scale* at fourteen stone. ‖***turn*** the *scale* toward profit (in one's favor) 利益になるよう(つごうのよいように)になる. 【類】That evidence ***turned*** the *scale* in the prisoner's favor.

Q an ***automatic*** *scale* 自動ばかり. ¶put it into the ***left*** *scale* of the balance それを天びんの左のさらに入れる.

P hang ***in*** the *scale* 懸案となっている. ¶a pair ***of*** *scales* 天びん.

P^2 turn the *scale* ***against*** ... ...とって(形勢が)不利となる.

(**2**) 目盛り, 尺度; 進法, 記法; 等級; 規模(スケール); 音階.

V ***enlarge*** the *scale* 規模を拡張する. ¶the comprehensive *scale* of their enterprise can be ***gauged*** by ... 彼らの計画の広大な規模は...で知れる. ¶***play scales*** [指の練習に]ピアノで音階をひく. ¶***practice*** the *scales* on the piano ピアノで音階の練習をする. ¶***sing*** *scales* [声の練習に]音階を歌う.

Q on a more ***active*** *scale* もっと活発に. ¶on an ***adequate*** *scale* 適度に. ¶on an ***ambitious*** *scale* 大がかりで. ¶on a more ***ample*** *scale* 一層大規模に. ¶on a much ***broader*** *scale* もっと広く ‖a ***calculating*** *scale* 計算尺. ¶thieving on a ***colossal*** *scale* 大仕掛の窃盗行為. ¶manufacture on a ***commercial*** *scale* 営利的に引合う規模での製造. 【類】poultry raising (養鶏) on a large ***commercial*** *scale*. ¶the ***decimal*** *scale* 十進法. ¶in a ***descending*** *scale* we have ... 上から下へと順に言うと... ¶on a gradually ***diminishing*** *scale* 漸次減少するように排列して. ¶a ***drafting*** *scale* 製図尺. ¶rise in the ***economic***, ***moral***, and ***intellectual*** *scale* 経済・道徳及び知力的に向上する. ¶practice on an ***enormous*** *scale* 大規模でやる. ¶on an ***exceptional*** *scale* 普通以上に. ¶consider a revision of the ***existing*** *scale* of wages. 現在の賃銀率の改正を考慮する. ¶an examination on an ***extended*** *scale* 広範囲の試験. ¶on an ***extensive*** *scale* 大規模で(手広く). ¶on an ***extraordinary*** *scale* 大々的規模で. ¶a ***folding*** *scale* 折尺. ¶a *scale* ***full*** (***half***) ***size*** 実(半)大図. ¶on a ***gigantic*** *scale* 大々的規模で. ¶on a ***great*** (***grand or extensive***) *scale* 大規模で. ¶rivalries on a ***half-inch*** *scale* 小さな争い. ¶pensions on a ***handsome*** *scale* 大分割のよい年金. ¶a ***higher*** *scale* of remuneration 一層高率の報酬. ¶on a ***huge*** (=***immense***) *scale* 大規模で. ¶one step lower in the ***juvenile*** *scale* 一段年が下って. ¶on a ***large*** *scale* 大規模で. 【類】on a still ***larger*** *scale*. ¶his ***lavish*** *scale* of living 彼のぜいたくな生活振り ‖The Northampton Institute is planned and equipped on the most ***lavish*** *scale*. ノーサムプトン協会は最もぜいたくな規模で経営されている. ¶The *scale* of payment is ***liberal***. 支払は割がよい. ¶operation on a ***limited*** *scale* 小規模での経営. ¶on a ***magnificent*** *scale* 堂々たる規模で. ¶Transactions are on a ***moderate*** *scale*. 取引は並である. ‖a ***moderate*** *scale* of living つつましい生活. ¶mass action on a ***national*** *scale* 全国的な大衆運動. 【類】on a ***national*** or even ***world-wide*** *scale*. ¶on a ***nation-wide*** *scale* 全国的に. ¶It is not plain that it is, in its ***present*** *scale*, a permanent, rather than a temporary, movement. その現今の規模では一時的と言うよりはむしろ永久的の運動と見るべきものであるかどうかが明りょうでない. ¶on a ***reduced*** *scale* 小規模で. ¶on a ***similar*** *scale* 同規模で. ¶on a much ***simpler*** *scale* もっと簡単に. ¶a building of ***small*** *scale* 小規模の建物. ¶descend in the ***social*** *scale* 落はくする ‖as we ascend the ***social*** *scale* 社会的地位が高まるにつれ ‖those higher (lower) in the ***social*** *scale* 上流(下層)の人. 【類】exalted in the ***social*** *scale* / as we pass upwards in the ***social*** *scale* / He is at the bottom of the ***social*** *scale*. / a desire to rise in the ***social*** *scale* / rise from bottom to top of the ***social*** *scale* / put the merchants lowest in the ***social*** *scale* / The trading class was placed lower in the ***social*** *scale* than that of the peasant. ¶a ***taxation*** *scale* of 2 per cent. 百分の二の比例税法. ¶on an ***unexampled*** *scale* 比類のない規模で. ¶on a ***vast*** *scale* 大仕掛に. ¶gather material on a ***wide*** *scale* 広大な規模で材料を集める. ¶as we rise in the ***zoological*** *scale* 動物が段段高等になるに従って.

Q^2 ***pay*** (***salary***, ***wage***) *scales* 俸給(賃金)率. ¶the nation's spiral ***price*** *scale* 全国的ら旋状物価率(スケール). ¶the ***sliding*** *scale* 〖労〗スライド制. ¶on a ***world*** *scale* 世界的規模で.

P can be reproduced ***at*** any *scale* desired 大小望み通りに複製ができる. ¶the position of man ***in*** the *scale* of existence 生活程度から見た人類の地位 ‖They are rated higher ***in*** the *scale* of civilization. 彼らは文化の程度が一層高いと見られている. 【類】rise higher ***in*** the *scale* of living / be weighed ***in*** the *scales* of a new social philosophy ‖the higher we go ***in*** the *scale* of animal life 高等動物になればなるほど. ¶***on*** a *scale* of great magnitude 広大な規模で ‖***on*** a *scale* of unusual grandeur 堂々たる規模で ‖a map ***on*** the *scale* of one inch to a (=the) mile (=a mile to one inch) 一マイル一インチの割の縮尺地図 ‖a map of the world ***on*** the *scale* of one-millionth (=one in a million=1/1,000,000) 百万分の一の地図 ‖mark examination papers ***on*** the *scale* of one hundred per cent. 百点満点で試験答案を採点する. 【類】grade (等別する)

compositions **on** the *scale* of 100 per cent. ¶a drawing made **to** *scale* 比例尺に合わせた図 ‖ a map drawn **to** a *scale* of one inch to the mile 一マイル一インチの縮尺地図.【類】maps **on** the *scale* of 1: 1,000,000 (百万分の一) / a world map drawn **to** the *scale* of one inch for each 100 miles / The drawings (製図) must be **to** the *scale* of ... feet in the inch. ¶The business is conducted **upon** a *scale* of unprecedented immensity. 事業は先例のない大規模で経営されている.

P² a *scale* **of** miles for a map 地図に用いるマイルの尺度 ‖ a *scale* **of** 1 inch to the mile 一マイルにつき一インチの縮尺 ‖ the *scale* **of** society 社会の等級 ‖ the *scale* **of** thermometer 寒暖計の目盛 ‖ the *scales* **of** justice [比ゆ的に]正義の尺度 ‖ The *scale* **of** wages in this factory ranges from three to twelve dollars a day. この工場の賃金率は三ドルから十二ドルまで段階がある.

scale, *n.* うろこ; りん片; 目の曇り.

V ***remove*** the *scales* from one's eyes 目の曇りをとり去る; 目を開かせる, 非を悟らせる.

P crystallize **in** small *scales* 小さいうろこ形に結晶する. ¶a bud covered **with** *scales* りん片でおおわれたつぼみ ‖ fishes **with** placoid *scales* 楯鱗(じゅんりん)を有する魚 ‖ a fish covered **with** *scales* うろこのついた魚.

P² *Scales* **of** skin peel off when heated. 皮膚のうろこは熱すると落ちる.

scale, *v.* 目方が…ある; [山などに]登る; 率に応じて増減する; はげる.

M ***How heavy*** does it *scale?* 目方はどの位か.

M² The prices were *scaled* **down** (**up**) 10 percent. 物価は十パーセントさが(あが)った. ¶*scale* **off** a boiler ボイラーの湯あかを取る ‖ The paint is half *scaling* **off**. ペンキが半分ほどはげている.

P *scale* a tree **by** ladders はしごで木に登る.

scamp, *v.* いいかげんにやる.

M The work has been ***shamefully*** *scamped.* 仕事はひどくぞんざいだ.

scamper, *v.* かける, 疾走する.

M He *scampered* ***away*** into the next room. 彼は隣室へかけ込んだ. ¶The mice tried to *scamper* ***away*** through a crack on the wall. ねずみは壁のすきまから逃げ出そうとした. ¶The boys *scampered* ***off*** in all directions. 子供らは八方へかけ出した. ‖ *scamper* ***off*** over a fence さくを越えて逃げて行く.

P *scamper* ***through*** a yard 庭をかけて通る ‖ *scamper* ***through*** a book 書物を急いで通読する.

scan, *v.* 〖詩〗韻律を調べる; じろじろ見る; ざっと見る; 〖テレビ〗走査する.

M The sailors ***anxiously*** *scanned* the horizon. 船員たちは心配そうに水平線をながめた. ¶*scan* it ***attentively*** 心を留めて調べる. ¶The verse *scans* ***badly*** (***smoothly***). その詩は音脚は整っていない(整っている).

P She *scanned* her son's face **for** some minutes. 彼女は息子の顔をしばらくじっと見つめた. ¶*scan* a picture (an image) **on** the TV screen テレビの画面に映像する.

O *scan* a verse [詩の]一節の韻律を調べる ‖ *scan* a morning paper 朝刊にざっと目を通す.

scandal, *n.* 汚名; 醜聞, 疑獄(スキャンダル); 反感.

V a great public *scandal* would be ***caused*** if (=were *or* should) ... もし…すると一大事が起るだろう. ¶***circulate*** wholly unfounded *scandals* about ... …について全然根拠のない醜聞を流布する. ¶***conceal*** a *scandal* 醜聞を秘す. ¶It will ***give*** *scandal.* それは反感を起させる. ‖ ***give*** *scandal* to ... …の評判を悪くする. ¶***hawk*** *scandal* all round the country 醜聞を国中にふれ回る. ¶***hush up*** a *scandal* 醜聞を内密にする. ¶***keep quiet*** (=***blanket***) a *scandal* 醜聞をもみ消す. ¶***make up*** a *scandal* 悪評を立てる. ¶The *scandal* was ***noised*** abroad. 醜聞が世間に広まった. ¶move into the country to ***outdistance*** the *scandal* 世間の口がうるさいのでいなかへ移転する. ¶***raise*** a *scandal* 世間の物議をかもす.【類】It will ***raise*** *scandal.* ¶***talk*** *scandal* 悪口を言う. ¶A grave *scandal* has ***occurred.*** 一大疑獄が起った.

Q a ***horrible*** *scandal* 恐ろしい疑獄. ¶a ***national*** *scandal* 国辱. ¶a ***naval*** *scandal* 海軍疑獄. ¶It is ***perfect*** *scandal.* それは全く業さらしだ. ¶***political*** *scandals* 政治汚職. ¶a ***public*** *scandal* [官公吏の]汚職, 醜聞. ¶give rise to ***serious*** *scandal* 体面上重大な事件を起す. ¶***What*** a *scandal!* 恥辱だ.

Q² He is involved in the ***iron-pipe*** *scandal.* 彼は鉄管不正事件に関係している. ¶a ***text-book*** *scandal* 教科書事件.

P give rise **to** *scandal* 世人に反感を起させる ‖ **to** the great *scandal* of his name 彼の恥ざらしに.

P² a *scandal* **about** a person ある人についての醜聞. ¶the *scandal* **of** the town その町の疑獄. ¶a *scandal* **to** our civilization わが文明の名折れ.【類】a big *scandal* **to** the nation (country, family).

scandalize, *v.* 反感を起させる, 憤慨させる.

P He was *scandalized* **at** my question. 彼は私の質問に反感を持った. ¶He was a great deal *scandalized* **by** the free-and-easy style of the modern student in dress. 彼は今の学生の服装がだらしないのに憤慨した. ‖ He was *scandalized* **by** his misconduct. 彼は不品行で愛想を尽かされた.

scant, *a.* 乏しい.

P He is *scant* **in** sense. 彼は分別に乏しい. ¶*scant* **of** breath 息を切らして.【類】We are *scant* **of** money (fuel, furniture).

scanty, *a.* 乏しい.

M The bed accommodation was ***somewhat*** *scanty.* 寝台数が幾分不十分だった.

P He is *scanty* **of** words. 彼は口数が少ない.

scar, *n.* 傷あと; こん跡.

V ***bear*** no *scars* 傷の跡がない ‖ ***bear*** the *scars* of honorable service 名誉の傷跡がある(戦傷など). ¶He ***has*** on his neck a *scar* from a saber wound received at the battle of Mukden. 彼はくびに奉天の戦で受けたサーベルの傷跡がある. ¶The cut will not ***leave*** any *scar.* その切傷は跡にならないだろう.

V² The *scar* ***died away.*** 傷あとがなくなってしまった. ¶The *scar* still ***remains.*** 傷跡がいまだにある.

Q a ***hideous*** *scar* みにくい傷跡. ¶A vaccination leaves a ***permanent*** *scar.* 種痘は一生あとが残る.

Q² a ***vaccination*** *scar* 種痘の跡. ¶Slowly the ***war*** *scars* faded. 戦傷の跡がだんだん消えていった. ¶a ***vaccine*** *scar* 種痘の跡.

P a hollow cheek **with** a *scar* across 切傷の跡が斜めについているこけた片ほお.

P² a *scar* **from** the bite of a dog 犬にかまれた跡. ¶the *scars* **of** life's battle in his face 彼の顔に現われた苦労の跡. ¶a *scar* **on** one's face 顔の傷跡.

scarce, *a.* 乏しい, 少ない.

M Produce is ***comparatively*** *scarce.* 製品は割方乏しい. ¶Silver is *scarce* ***now*** in England. 銀は今英国には少ない.

P We are *scarce* **of** provisions. われらは食糧に乏しい.

scarcity, *n.* 欠乏, 払底; ききん.

V ***cause*** a *scarcity* of ... …の不足を来たす. ¶***relieve*** the *scarcity* of ... …の欠乏(ききん)を救う.

V² should a *scarcity* ***arise*** 品不足の節は.

Q a ***general*** *scarcity* of money 貨幣の一般的払底. ¶there is ***great*** *scarcity* of ... …は非常に不足している. ¶***growing*** *scarcity* of timber ますます募る木材の払底. ¶books of ***wonderful*** *scarcity* 大の稀こう書(珍本).

Q² ***consumer*** *scarcities* 品不足(消費物資の). ¶***food*** *scarcities* 食料不足. ¶***labor*** *scarcity* 労力不足(人手不足). ¶***power*** *scarcity* 動力不足. ¶the ***world*** *scarcity* of the raw materials of reconstruction 再建資材の世界的欠乏.

P ***owing to*** the *scarcity* of stocks 在庫品払底のため.【類】Rates have advanced ***owing to*** the *scarcity* of tonnage (船腹不足). ¶***through*** *scarcity* of funds 資金欠乏のため.

P² a *scarcity* **of** foodstuffs 食料品の払底.

scare, *n.* おどし, 恐怖.

V ***get*** a *scare* ひどい目に会う. ¶***give*** a good *scare* 大いにおどす. ¶the greatest *scare* I ever ***had*** 私がこれまでに経験したことのない恐怖.

Q² a ***rabies*** *scare* 狂犬病の恐怖. ¶American "***Red*** *scares*" アメリカの「赤(共産主義)恐怖」. ¶a ***war*** *scare* 戦争の恐怖.

scare, *v.* おどかす.

M *scare* ***away*** birds 鳥をおどして追払う.

M² *scare* children ***off*** the scene. 子供たちをどなってその場から追い出す.

P he was *scared* **at** the sight of ... 彼は…を一見して驚いた. ‖ That should be enough to *scare* any man **into** grey hair. それを見てはどんな人でも恐ろしさに頭髪が白くなってしまうだろう. ¶be *scared* ***out of*** one's senses びっくりして度を失う.

O Wow! I'm *scared.* わあー. おどかすなよ.【類】Don't *scare* me, please.

scarecrow, *n.* かかし.

V *set up* a *scarecrow* かかしを立てる.

scarf, *n.* スカーフ.

Q have a ***woolen*** *scarf* around one's neck 毛のえりまきを「首に巻いている.

scatter, *v.* まき散らす; 四散させる.

M *scatter* seed (literature) ***broadcast*** 種子(文献)をばらまく.

P Leaves are *scattered* ***by*** the breeze. 葉が風に散っている. ¶ Many isles are *scattered* ***in*** the sea. 多くの島が海中に散在している. ¶ *scatter* gravel ***on*** the road 道路に砂利を散布する. ¶ The Jews are *scattered* ***over*** the world. ユダヤ人は世界中に散在している. ¶ Hitherto the information on this subject has been *scattered* ***through*** many volumes. 従来この問題に関する事項は数巻の書冊中に散在していた. ¶ Its population was *scattered* ***to*** the four winds. その人人は四散した. ‖ *scatter* money ***to*** the winds 金を浪費する. ¶ *scatter* the road ***with*** flowers 道路に花をまき散らす.

scavenger, *n.* 掃除夫.

Q a ***municipal*** *scavenger* 市の掃除夫.

scenario, *n.* シナリオ.

Q^2 a ***film*** *scenario* 映画の脚本.

scenarist, *n.* 脚本作家(シナリオ・ライター).

Q^2 a ***movie*** *scenarist* 映画の脚本作家.

scene, *n.*〘劇〙場,〘映〙場面(シーン); 道具立, 背景; 光景, 風景; 現場; 大騒ぎ.

V to ***avoid*** a *scene* 人目をはばかる; 物議をかもしそうなことを避ける. ¶ ***close*** the *scene* [劇の]一場を終える. ¶ Meeting him in another lady's company his wife ***created*** a *scene*. 夫が他の婦人と連立っているのを見て細君が乱痴気騒ぎを起した. ¶ ***dominate*** the *scene* 場を圧する(断然優勢を示す). ¶ *Scenes* like this have often been ***enacted***. こうした光景を度々演出した. ¶ ***enliven*** the whole *scene* 場面全体を引立てる. ¶ ***enter*** the *scene* 登場する. ¶ ***inspect*** the *scene* 現場を検査する. ¶ The *scene* is ***laid*** in Paris. [劇・小説など]場面はパリーである. 【類】More than one *scene* in Thackeray's novels is ***laid*** within the walls of White's. / Mr. Arthur Morrison stands foremost among the novelists who have ***laid*** their *scenes* in the East End (東部ロンドンの貧民区域). ¶ ***leave*** the *scene* to one's labors その活動の土地を去る; 世を去る. ¶ ***make*** a *scene* 大騒ぎする; 醜態を演じる. 【類】In her jealousy she ***made*** "*scenes*" on several occasions. / ***make*** a *scene* of trifles / Don't ***make*** a *scene* before them. ¶ the *scene* ***pictured*** above 上に描いた場面. ¶ ***present*** a *scene* of extraordinary beauty 非常に美しい光景を呈する. ¶ ... combine to ***produce*** a highly attractive *scene* ...が総合して非常に魅力ある光景を現出する. ¶ ***quit*** the *scene* 現場を去る; 死ぬ. ¶ ***reach*** one's new *scene* of labor 新任地に到着する. ¶ The novelist ***removed*** the *scene* from Rome to Venice. その小説家は(話の)場面をローマからヴェニスに移した. ¶ ***represent*** a night *scene* 夜景を写し出す. ¶ ***revisit*** the *scenes* of one's childhood 幼少時代見て暮した土地を再び訪れる. ¶ ***see*** the whole *scene* ***through*** 全場面を見終える. ¶ He ***sets*** his *scenes* in distant times 彼の小説場面は遠い昔である. ¶ ***shift*** the *scenes* 道具立を替える. 【類】***shift*** the *scenes* of their activities (活躍舞台). ¶ ***shoot*** *scenes* of present-day Japan 現代の日本を撮影する. ¶ ***survey*** the *scene* with keen enjoyment 多大の興味を持ってその光景をながめる. ¶ ***tragedize*** a *scene* 場面を悲劇的にする. ¶ ***transform*** the *scene* 面目を一新する. ¶ ***visit*** the *scene* of the disaster 惨事の現場を訪問する.

V^2 the *scene* ***changes*** now; ... 今度は場面が変って... 【類】The *scene* ***changes*** from London to New York. ¶ an amusing *scene* ***occurred*** at college when ... おもしろい活劇が大学に起ったその時に... ¶ The *scene* of the story now ***shifts*** to London. ここで話の場面がロンドンに移る. ¶ Riotous *scenes* ***took place*** in the Diet today. 乱暴な活劇がきょう議会に起った.

Q a strangely ***animated*** *scene* 妙に活気ある場面. ¶ take a shot of (=snap) a ***beautiful*** *scene* 美しい風景をスナップ(早取り)する. ¶ The picture presents the ***bleak, bare, greyish*** *scene* of a February morning. その絵は二月の朝の木枯し吹きすさぶ灰色の風景を表わしている. ¶ ... supply the ***chief*** *scenes* [小説など]...が主な場面となる. ¶ Japan is far from the ***chief*** *scene* of this grim conflict. 日本はこの恐ろしい戦闘の本舞台から離れている. ¶ a ***disgraceful*** *scene* 恥ずべき光景. ¶ a ***dismal*** *scene* 薄気味の悪い場面. ¶ ***distressing*** *scenes* 憂うべき情景. ¶ create a ***domestic*** *scene* 夫婦げんかを起させる. ¶ an ***episodic*** *scene* そう話的情景. ¶ an ***exciting*** *scene* 興奮的場面. ¶ a ***familiar*** *scene* よく見る場面. ¶ a ***favorite*** *scene* in the drama その劇の好きな場面. ¶ in the ***first*** *scene* of Act II 第二幕の第一場で. ¶ ***horrible*** *scenes* of domestic brawling 家庭紛争の恐ろしい情景. ¶ an ***impressive*** *scene* 印象の深い光景. ¶ the ***kaleidoscopic*** street *scenes* of the metropolis 首都の走馬灯のような街頭風景. ¶ a ***lovely*** *scene* 美しい風景. ¶ the ***main*** *scene* of the play 劇のやま場(クライマックス). ¶ There are some ***pretty*** *scenes* in the park. その公園にはよい風景の所がある. ¶ a ***repugnant*** *scene* いやらしい場面. ¶ a ***ridiculous*** *scene* こっけいな場面. ¶ a ***romantic*** *scene* ラブシーン. ¶ a ***rural*** *scene* 田園風景. ¶ a ***sad*** *scene* 悲しい情景. ¶ A ***shocking*** *scene* was observed. ぞっとするような光景を展開する. ¶ a ***somber*** (=***gloomy***) *scene* 陰気な光景. ¶ a ***striking*** *scene* 目ざましい光景. ¶ a ***sylvan*** *scene* 森林の光景. ¶ a ***thrilling*** *scene* はらはら(ぞっと)する場面. ¶ a ***tragic*** *scene* 悲惨な情景. ¶ a ***typical*** *scene* of ruin 荒城の代表的情景 ‖ a few of the ***typical*** *scenes* of the London termini ロンドンの始発駅でよく見かける光景二三. ¶ cover the ***whole*** *scene* of operation to the war その戦争の全戦闘場面を収めている.

Q^2 the ***balcony*** *scene* in "Romeo and Juliet"「ロメオとジューリエット」劇中の露台の場. ¶ a ***courtroom*** *scene* 法廷(白洲)の場. ¶ a ***crash*** *scene* [飛行機の]墜落現場. ¶ a ***deathbed*** *scene* 臨終の場. ¶ a New York ***departure*** *scene* [船など]ニューヨーク出帆の情景. ¶ a ***fight*** *scene* 殺陣. ¶ a ***kitchen*** *scene* at the Carlton カールトン(ホテル)の料理場光景. ¶ a ***life*** *scene* 人生の一こま. ¶ a ***love*** *scene* ラブシーン(ぬれ場). ¶ a ***mob*** *scene* 群集の場面. ¶ a ***night*** (=nocturnal) *scene* 夜景. ¶ a ***parting*** *scene* 別離の場. ¶ a ***rehearsal*** *scene* 舞台げいこのシーン. ¶ a ***snow*** *scene* in Hokkaido 北海道の雪げ色. ¶ a ***spring*** *scene* in Japan 日本の春げ色. ¶ the ***trial*** *scene* of the "Merchant of Venice"「ベニスの商人」の裁判の場. ¶ a typical ***street*** *scene* 代表的の街頭風景. ¶ a ***woodland*** *scene* 山林の一風景.

P The crowds gathered ***about*** the *scene* of the disaster. 群集は遭難現場の周囲に集った. ¶ ***amid*** a *scene* of indescribable excitement (great enthusiasm) 名状すべからざる興奮(など)の情景のうちに. ¶ find oneself ***among*** the *scenes* of youth again 青年時代を送った場所へ再び帰る. ¶ He was present ***at*** the *scene* of the performance in a little theatre. 彼は小さな劇場で芝居を見物していた. ¶ ***behind*** the *scene* 舞台裏で; 裏面で; 黒幕に; 内密に ‖ a story ***behind*** the *scenes* at the Peace Conference 平和会議の内幕 ‖ The book takes one ***behind*** the *scenes*. その本で内幕が分かる. 【類】There might be somebody ***behind*** the *scenes*. / glances ***behind*** the *scenes* / peep "***behind*** the *scenes*" / study the history from ***behind*** the *scenes*. ¶ The police were soon ***on*** the *scene*. 警官(たち)が直ちに現場にかけつけた. ‖ ***on*** the *scene* of the crime (murder) 犯罪(殺人)現場で. ¶ The policemen were dispatched ***to*** the *scene*. 警官が現場へ派遣された. 【類】rush ***to*** the *scene* for the rescue of ...

P^2 the *scene* ***after*** the earthquake 震災後の光景. ¶ a *scene* ***along*** the beach 海岸一帯の風景. ¶ riotous *scenes* ***among*** spectators 見物人間の立回り. ¶ *Scenes* ***at*** the Jubilee picnic. 五十年祭の野遊会における場面[さし絵の説明など]. ¶ as he looked upon the *scene* ***before*** him 彼が眼前の光景を見たときに. ¶ *scenes* ***from*** famous plays 有名な劇の場面 ‖ *scenes* ***from*** London slum land (country life, the war) ロンドン貧民くつ(など)の光景 ‖ *scenes* ***from*** Liaoyang 遼陽の風景. ¶ like a *scene* ***in*** the fairy land おとぎの国の情景のように ¶ the *scene* ***of*** the accident (a great battle) 事故(など)の現場 ‖ It was recently the *scene* ***of*** a serious disaster. 最近そこに大ちん事があった. ‖ the *scene* ***of*** the play is laid in ... その劇の場面は...においてある ‖ the *scene* ***of*** action 活動の舞台. 【類】The Municipal Exposition Halls (市設展覧館) have been the *scene* of many international gatherings during the last ten years. ‖ a *scene* ***of*** wonderful beauty 非常に美しい光景 ‖ a *scene* ***of*** devastation [火事場などの]荒涼たる場面. 【類】The world is a *scene* ***of*** strife. / a *scene* ***of*** wild excitement (much animation and bustle) ‖ a *scene* ***of*** carnage (bloodshed) 修

らのちまた.

O a *scene* which a painter might transfer to his canvas 画家が絵にしそうな情景.

scenery, *n.* 風景, 景色; 道具立.

V ***admire*** *scenery* 風景を賞する. ¶***enjoy*** natural *scenery* 天然の風景を楽しむ. ¶***explore*** the romantic *scenery* of ... ...の勝景を探る. ¶The *scenery* is strongly ***impressed*** on my memory. その風景は深く私の記憶に残っている. ¶The *scenery* about here is ***marred*** by ironworks. この辺の風景は鉄工所で滅茶苦茶にされている. ¶***overlook*** the surrounding *scenery* 周囲の風景を見下ろす. ¶***spoil*** beautiful *scenery* 美景を損じる.

Q a region of ***attractive*** *scenery* 風光明美な地域. ¶The road passes through most ***charming*** *scenery*. 路はきわめて明美な風景の間を通っている. ¶***dry*** and ***monotonous*** *scenery* 無味乾燥な光景. ¶***fine*** (=***beautiful***) *scenery* 明美な風光. ¶***grand*** *scenery* 雄大な風景. ¶***idyllic*** *scenery* 田園的風景. ¶***imposing*** *scenery* 雄大な風景. ¶The *scenery* of the Tenryugawa is ***impressive***. 天竜川の風景は印象が深い. ¶***lovely*** and ***picturesque*** *scenery* 美しい絵のような風景. ¶***majestic*** *scenery* 荘厳な風景. ¶***mediocre*** *scenery* 平凡な風景. ¶highly ***picturesque*** *scenery* きわめて明美な風景. 【類】The hotel is in the midst of very ***picturesque*** *scenery*. ¶***rustic*** *scenery* 野趣. ¶The *scenery* is just ***superb***. 風景が実によい. ¶***tame*** *scenery* 平凡な風景. ¶The *scenery* is ***unrivalled***. 景色が絶景だ. ¶***varied*** and ***inspiring*** *scenery* 変化に富みかつ霊感に打たれるような風景.

Q² ***landscape*** *scenery* 山水の景. ¶***coast*** *scenery* 海岸の風景. ¶explore the ***Maya*** *scenery* [中米]マヤの風景を探検する. ¶***mountain*** *scenery* 山景. ¶***rock*** *scenery* 岩石の景観(奇岩など). ¶***stage*** *scenery* 〖舞台〗道具立. ¶***woodland*** *scenery* 森林地帯の光景.

P ***amid*** nature's *scenery* 自然の風景の中で. ¶The region is remarkable ***for*** its *scenery*. その辺は非常に風景が良い. ¶gems ***of*** English *scenery* 英国風景美の秀逸. ¶travel ***through*** magnificent *scenery* 壮麗な風景美の中を旅行する.

P² the *scenery* ***about*** Nikko 日光辺の風景. ¶the *scenery* ***along*** the valley その流域の風景. ¶the *scenery* ***in*** the neighborhood of ... ...付近の風景. ☞ a scene は限られた一場面. scenery は集合的の意味で, 特に自然の風景を指すことが多い.

scent, *n.* 香気, 臭気; 嗅(ｷｭｳ)覚; 看破力.

V The dogs ***follow*** [***up***] the *scent* of a fox. 犬がきつねの臭跡をたどる. ¶***give forth*** a strong *scent* 強い臭気を発する. ¶He ***has*** a *scent* of it. 彼はうすうす感付いている. ‖ it ***has*** a strong *scent* resembling ... それには...に似た強い臭気がある. ¶***lose*** the *scent* 手掛りを失う. ¶adroitly ***throw out*** false *scents* 巧みに追跡をくらます. ¶***use*** strong *scents* 強い香料を用いる. ¶the *scent* of lilacs ***drifting*** across the road 道に漂ってくる沈丁花の香.

Q ***absorbed*** *scent* 移り香. ¶He has an ***acute*** (=a ***keen***) *scent* for roguery. 彼は詐欺を見抜く鋭い眼力を持っている. ¶a ***burning*** (=***hot***) *scent* [獣などの]強い臭気. ¶put one on a ***false*** (=wrong) *scent* 追手をまく. ¶It has a ***fine*** *scent*. それは良い香がする. ¶***liquid*** *scents* 香水. ¶a dog of ***nice*** *scent* 鼻の鋭い犬. ¶a ***powerful*** *scent* 強い香. ¶You are on the ***right*** (***wrong***) *scent*. 君は正しい(間違った)方向に追っている. ¶a ***sweet*** *scent* 芳香.

P pursue ***by*** *scent* 臭気をかいで追う. 【類】follow a criminal ***by*** *scent*. ¶put one ***off*** the *scent* 後をくらまして追手をまく. ¶The police are ***on*** the *scent* of a new plot. 警察では新規に陰謀を企てていることに感付いている. ‖ The umbrella he carried with him put the police ***on*** the *scent*. 彼が持っていたかさから足が付いた. ‖ put a person ***on*** the wrong *scent* 人をまく. ¶They have put me ***upon*** (=on) an entirely wrong *scent*. 彼らはすっかり僕をまいた.

P² the *scent* ***of*** fruits (flowers, hay) 果物(など)の香.

scent, *v.* におう; におわせる.

M *scent* [***out***] treachery 不信行為をかぎ付ける.

M² The dog *scented* ***about*** till he found the trail. 犬はくんくんかぎ回り(獲物の)跡を見つけた.

P *scent* ***of*** sulfur 硫黄のにおいがする. ¶The air was *scented* ***with*** perfume. 芳香がしていた. 【類】*scent* one's clothes ***with*** musk (じゃ香) ‖ You are given a Turkish towel sipped in ice-water and delicately *scented* ***with*** perfume to wipe your perspiring face. 汗の出た顔をふくために氷水に浸し芳ばしい香を付けたトルコタオルが出される.

scepter, 《英》 **sceptre,** *n.* しゃく; 王威.

V Paris is still supposed to ***hold*** the *scepter* as far as feminine dress is concerned. パリーは婦人服に関する限り依然王座を占めるものと考えられている. ¶***sway*** the *scepter* of Japan 日本に君臨する.

V² Perhaps the *scepter* has already ***passed*** from their hands. 恐らく支配権はすでに彼らの手を去った.

sceptical, *a.* 懐疑的な.

P be *sceptical* ***about*** its existence その存在については懐疑的である. ¶I am very *sceptical* indeed ***as to*** ... 私は実際...に関しては非常に疑をいだいている. ¶*sceptical* ***on*** ... ...に懐疑的な.

scepticism, *n.* 懐疑.

Q a ***wholesome*** *scepticism* 健全な懐疑.

schedule, *n.* 一覧表; 《米》 時間表; 《米》 予定, 日取り.

V Air transport lines converging on Chicago are ***increasing*** their *schedules* to accommodate travellers to the Expositions. シカゴを中心とする空輸線は博覧会への旅客の便を計ってその航行の回数を増そうとしている. ¶***lay out*** a *schedule* for the coming vacation 来るべき休暇の計画を立てる. ¶This *schedule* is not ***maintained***. この時間表通りにやってはいない[汽船の発着など]. ¶The *schedule* of games is not yet completely ***made out***. 競技の番組はまだ完全にでき上がっていない.

Q a ***daily*** *schedule* of hours 時間表. ¶under the ***original*** *schedule* 最初の予定では. ¶These steamers make runs on ***regular*** *schedules*. これらの汽船は定期航海をする.

Q² a ***consumer price*** *schedule* for rice 米の消費者価格表. ¶a ***job*** *schedule* 職務予定表. ¶speed up ***production*** *schedules* 生産計画を促進させる. 【類】It had its ***production*** *schedules* interrupted seriously by strikes. ¶a ***progress*** *schedule* 進捗予定表. ¶a ***railroad*** *schedule* = 《英》 a railway time-table [鉄道の]時間表. ¶a ***recitation*** *schedule* 《米》 授業時間表. ¶a ***sailing*** *schedule* 出帆予定表. ¶a ***shipping*** *schedule* 積出予定表. ¶a ***train*** *schedule* 列車時刻表. ¶a [railroad] ***transportation*** *schedule* [鉄道の]輸送計画. ¶map out a ***vacation*** *schedule* 休暇旅行の計画を立てる. ¶provide streetcar service on a ***24-hour*** *schedule* 二十四時間制で市電を運転する.

P a little ***ahead of*** *schedule* 《米》 少し予定より早く. ¶***as per*** (=***according to***) *schedule* = as scheduled 予定通り, 筋書通り. ¶***behind*** [the] *schedule* 《米》 予定より遅れて. 【類】The steamer was in two hours ***behind*** her *schedule*. / The train was in an hour ***behind*** *schedule*. ¶a *schedule* ***of*** prices 物価表. ¶Trains are sure to arrive ***on*** *schedule* (=time). 列車は時間通りに必ず到着する. 【類】The train was in ***on*** *schedule*. / The strike will begin ***on*** *schedule*. ‖ Plants and factories went ***on*** shorter *schedules*. 各種工場は操業短縮をやり出した.

P² *schedules* ***of*** games 競技の日取.

schedule, *v.* 表に作る; 予定する.

M as ***previously*** *scheduled* 予定通り.

P The arrival of the steamer is *scheduled* ***for*** the 16th inst. 汽船は本月十六日に着くことになっている. 【類】The game (試合) is *scheduled* ***for*** Saturday. / He is *scheduled* ***for*** a speech.

O He was *scheduled* to attend the luncheon, but was unable to be present. 彼は午さん会に出る予定であったが出席することができなかった. ‖ the liner is *scheduled* to sail from ... to ... 【類】The plane took off for Honolulu as *scheduled*.

scheme, *n.* 案, 設計; 悪計; 機構.

V Russia has ***abandoned*** her long-cherished *scheme* of an ice-free port on the Pacific. ロシアは太平洋上に不凍港構築の宿案を放棄した. ¶***adopt*** a *scheme* 考案を採用する. ¶The *scheme* is now well ***advanced***. その計画は今りっぱに進んでいる. ¶***bring*** the *scheme* to a successful issue その計画を首尾よく達成する. ¶***carry*** the *scheme* a step further 一歩その計画を進める. ¶***carry forward*** a *scheme* 計画を前進させる. ¶***carry out*** one's *scheme* その計画を実施する. ¶***complete*** a *scheme* 計画を完成する. ¶***conceive*** a ***grand*** *scheme* 一大計画を立てる. ¶***concoct*** a *scheme* 計画を立てる. ¶***contrive*** (=form) a *scheme* 立案する. ¶***countenance*** a *scheme* 計画を援助する. ¶***develop*** a *scheme* 計画を発展せしめる. ¶***devise*** a *scheme* 企画する. ¶***elaborate*** a *scheme* 念入りに企画する. ¶The *scheme* is now firmly ***estab-***

lished. その考案は確立した. ¶expedite the scheme of … …の計画をはかどらせる. ¶finance a scheme 計画の資金を出す. ¶float a scheme 計画の実施ができるまでにする. ¶follow out the scheme of work outlined below 下に略記した通りの計画を実行する. ¶formulate a scheme to raise money 金策案を立てる. ¶frame a scheme 案を立てる. ¶the scheme was frustrated by … その計画は…のためにとんざした. ¶They promised to do all that lay in their power to further the scheme. 彼らは該案の前進に全力を尽すことを約した. ¶get out a scheme 案を持ち出す. ¶he has under consideration a scheme for … 彼は…の計画を考慮中だ. ¶inaugurate a new scheme 新計画に着手する. ¶initiate a more ambitious scheme 一層大仕掛の計画を起す. ¶The scheme was practically killed by the war, but has been recently revived. その計画は事実上戦争のために停とんしていたが近ごろ復活した. ¶a scheme is being launched among … for … …間に…の計画を起している. ¶lay a scheme 計画を立てる. ¶lay (=work or map) out a vast scheme of work 一大計画を立てる. ¶the scheme was first mooted by … その計画は最初…が発起した. ¶The scheme has been nipped in the bud. その計画は物にならなかった. ¶outline a scheme 計画の概略を示す. ¶prepare a comprehensive scheme 大規模の計画を準備する. ¶project a scheme for … …の計画を立てる. ¶desire to cooperate in promoting the scheme 計画の促進に協力を望む. ¶a scheme has been proposed to … …という提案が出された. ¶put one's scheme into execution その計画を実施する ‖ put the scheme through 計画をやり通す ‖ put in hand a scheme 計画に着手する. ¶put forward a scheme 計画を起す. . ¶The Government will not sanction such a scheme. 政府はこういう計画は認可すまい. ¶The scheme has been set in motion. その計画を起した. ¶start an anti-profiteering scheme 暴利反対運動を起す. ¶support a scheme 計画を支持する. ¶welcome the scheme その計画を歓迎する. ¶work out their own schemes according to their own ideas and ambitions 彼ら自身の考案と抱負に従って自己の計画を遂行する.

V² The scheme has failed. その計画は失敗に終った. ¶The scheme fell (=[colloq.] slumped) througth. その計画はお流れになった. ¶The scheme has miscarried. 計画は失敗に終った. ¶A devilish scheme began to unfold itself in his ingenious but unscrupulous brain. 利口ではあるが良心の欠けている彼の頭に一つの非道な計画が展開され始めた. ¶The scheme worked. その計画はうまくいった.

Q an abortive scheme 無効の計画. ¶an ambitious scheme 大仕掛の計画. ¶a chimerical scheme 架空の案. ¶a decorative scheme 装飾意匠. ¶a deep-laid scheme 陰険な計画. ¶a diabolical scheme 悪どい計画. ¶a drastic scheme 果断的の計画. ¶a dubious scheme for making money あやし気な金もうけ策. ¶an expansionist scheme《米》[領土の]拡張案. ¶a far-seeing scheme 遠大な計画. ¶His financial scheme crashed disastrously. 彼の財政計画は無惨に砕かれた. ¶fraudulent schemes of every type あらゆるインチキ計画. ¶an impracticable scheme 実行不可能な計画. ¶an improvement scheme 改良案. ¶as part of an incentive scheme 報奨の一つとして. ¶a laudable scheme 賞賛に値する計画. ¶a mature scheme 十分に練った案. ¶a momentous scheme 重要計画. ¶a notorious "get-rich-quick" scheme 有名な一夜成金計画. ¶hit on a novel scheme 目新しい案を思付く. ¶a onesided scheme 片手落の案. ¶his pet (=favorite) scheme 彼の得意の考案. ¶a plausible scheme is being put forward to … …というもっともらしい計画が提出されている. ¶the postwar scheme of society 戦後の社会機構. ¶work out a practical scheme 実用的考案を作成する. 【類】A practical scheme has yet to be devised. ¶a preposterous scheme 没常識の計画. ¶promote a rival scheme 対抗策を講じる. ¶a silly scheme ばかげた計画. ¶schemes actually started or in contemplation すでに着手しまたは考案中の計画. ¶carry out a unique scheme 独特の計画を実施する. ¶a villainous scheme 悪計. ¶a visionary scheme 夢のような計画. ¶a well-devised (=well-thought-out) scheme 名案. ¶a wise scheme of reform 名改革案. ¶It is not a workable scheme. それは実行性のある案ではない. ¶support a carefully worked-out scheme 周到な計画を支持する.

Q² the exquisite color scheme of the parlor その客間のせん細な色彩設計 ‖ an effective color scheme of decoration 効果的な色彩装飾設計 ‖ a delightful color scheme 美しい色の配合. ¶a long-range scheme 遠大な計画. ¶implement some of their paper schemes 彼らの机上案の一部を実行する. ¶a water-power scheme 水力(電気)計画. ¶a wildcat scheme でたらめな計画.

P It has to play an important rôle in the great scheme of nature. それは自然の大機構において一大役を勤めることになっている. ‖ get entangled in a scheme ある悪計に巻込まれる ‖ take part in the scheme その計画に参加すはる. ¶enter into some scheme for … …のある計画に参加する. ¶the overthrow of a scheme 計画の崩壊 ‖ the prime mover of a scheme 計画の主動者. ¶a harbor construction on a five years' scheme 五カ年計画の築港. ¶under the proposed scheme 推案によると.

P² a scheme for the conquest of the world 世界征服の計画. 【類】There is a scheme for building a new road. ¶a scheme of distribution 配当表 ‖ a scheme of operations 作戦計画. 【類】the scheme of color=a color scheme.

O a scheme is on foot for … …の計画がある. ¶The scheme is very much to the front. 同案は大分表面化している.

scheme, *v.* 計画する; たくらむ.

M scheme out a new method of language teaching 新語学教授法を考案する.

O scheme the downfall of the present Government 現内「閣の打倒をたくらむ.

schism, *n.* 分離, 分裂.

V occasion a schism 分裂をきたす.

scholar, *n.* 学者; 学生, 生徒.

V discover promising scholars 有望な学者を見出す. ¶he would certainly make a scholar if … 彼は…ならきっと学者になるだろう. ¶spell down any scholar in the class 級中のどの生徒もつづり字で負かす. ¶turn well-rounded scholars [学校などが]円満な学者を造る.

Q an accomplished scholar 大学者. ¶an accurate scholar 正確な学徒. ¶an alert-minded scholar すばしっこい生徒. ¶an all-round scholar 万能の学者. ¶antiquated scholars 老朽学者. ¶an apt (=a bright) scholar よくできる生徒. ¶a backward scholar 低能な生徒. ¶a brilliant scholar 出色の学者. ¶a competent scholar in English 有能の英学者. ¶Napoleon was spoken of at school as the "dull scholar." ナポレオンは学校では低能児だといわれた. ¶an eminent German scohlar ドイツ一流の学者. ¶the most erudite scholar 最も博識な学者. ¶He was an excellent Japanese scholar, reading the characters with great proficiency. 彼は達者に文字の読めるりっぱな日本語学者であった. ¶the finest Chinese scholar 最も優秀な漢学者. ¶a finished scholar 円熟した学者. ¶He is a good (poor) scholar. 彼はできのよい(悪い)生徒だ. ¶a good French scholar りっぱなフランス語学者. ¶a great scholar 大学者. ¶an illustrious scholar 著名な学者. ¶independent scholars [大学教授などでない]民間の学者. ¶a most assiduously industrious scholar 非常に勤勉な生徒. ¶a King's scholar《英》官費生(国家から奨学金をもらう). ¶scholars both native and foreign 内外の学者. ¶disciples and followers of a notable scholar 著名学者の門弟と学徒. ¶a painstaking scholar 業に忠実な学者. ¶a productive scholar 多作の学者. ¶a profound scholar in Chinese 造詣の深い漢学者. ¶a raw peasant scholar なま半可の百姓学者. ¶a remarkable English scholar 著名な英語学者. ¶a ripe scholar 老熟の学者. ¶help the rival scholar 学問上の競争者を援助する. ¶a sound scholar 堅実な学者. ¶a tardy scholar よく遅刻をする学生. ¶a thorough Japanese scholar of English しっかりした日本の英語学者. ¶It has often been said that Humboldt was the last universal scholar. 万能学者はフンボルトが最後だとはよく言われることだ. ¶an unrecognized scholar 隠れた学者.

Q² a Chaucer scholar チョーサーの研究家. ¶an English scholar of no mean order 一かどの英学者. ¶an expert scholar 専門学者(会社の顧問). ¶a language scholar 言語学者. 【類】a competent language scholar. ¶a research scholar 研究家. ¶a university scholar 大学の先生.

P He ranks high as a scholar. 彼は学者として一流の位置を占めている. ¶He sets up for a scholar=He assumes the air of a scholar. 彼は学者ぶる. ‖ He is not much of a scholar. 彼は大した学者ではない. 【類】be something of a scholar.

P² a *scholar* ***by*** name 名ばかりの学者. ¶a *scholar* ***in*** English 英語学者. ¶*scholars* ***of*** high standing and attainments 名望学識ともにすぐれた学者.

scholarship, *n.* 学識; 給費; 奨学金.

V ***award*** a *scholarship* of £250 [優秀学生などに]二百五十ポンドの奨学金を与える.【類】The *scholarship* was ***awarded*** to the best scholar of the school. ¶***create*** a *scholarship* 奨学金を設定する. ¶***establish*** *scholarships* 奨学金を設定する. ¶The university has ***founded*** by bequest a *scholarship* of £60 a year for three years. その大学は遺贈によって三年間年六十ポンドの奨励金制度を設けた. ¶He has ***gained*** an open *scholarship* at the university of Cambridge. 彼はケンブリッヂ大学の公開奨学金を獲得した. ¶He ***has*** a *scholarship* at the middle school. 彼は中学校の特待生だ. ¶At Oxford he ***held*** the Sir Thomas White *scholarship* in modern history. オックスフォードで彼はサー・トマス・ホワイト近代史奨学金を受けていた. ¶***obtain*** a *scholarship* 奨学金を得る. ¶***offer*** a *scholarship* 奨学金を提供する. ¶***possess*** tolerable *scholarship* かなりの学識を有する. ¶***provide*** a *scholarship* for proficiency in anatomy to the value of $120 per annum 解剖学の優等生に年百二十ドルの奨学金を支給する. ¶He was educated at Magdalen College School and ***won*** a *scholarship* in English History to Oxford. 彼はモードリン学院に学びオックスフォード大学英国史科の奨学金を得た.

Q As a matter of fact, civilization needs something more than ***classical*** *scholarship*. 事実上文明には古典の学識以上のなにものかを必要とする. ¶***creative*** *scholarship* 独創的学才. ¶a man of ***profound*** *scholarship* in ... ...に造けいの深い人. ¶his ***ripe*** *scholarship* and great experience in teaching 彼の深い学識と大なる教授の経験 ‖ a readable book embodying the ***ripe*** *scholarship* of ... ...の円熟した学問を具体化した読みごたえのする本. ¶***sound*** *scholarship* 健全な学識. ¶At Oxford various Rhodes *scholarships* are ***tenable*** for three years. オックスフォードでは各種のローズ奨学金は三カ年間受けられる. ¶That's ***true*** *scholarship*. それが本当の学者というものだ. ¶***wide*** and ***thorough*** *scholarship* 広く深い学識.

Q² ***English*** *scholarship* 英語の力. 【類】for the steady advance of ***English*** *scholarship* in Japan. ¶based on ***present-day*** *scholarship* 現在成し遂げられた研究を基礎にした.

P They were supported ***by*** *scholarships*. 彼らは奨学金を支給されていた. ¶a man excelled ***in*** *scholarship* 学識優秀の士.【類】He is a rival ***in*** *scholarship*. ¶a student ***on*** *scholarship*=a scholar 奨学金給付学生. 【類】They were sent abroad ***on*** *scholarships* awarded by Government institutions.

P² *scholarship* ***in*** botany 植物学の学識.

school, *n.* **(1)** 学校; 練習所, 道場; 教室; 授業; 在校生徒.

V He ***attended*** school three years. 彼は三カ年通学した. ‖ he was ***attending*** a *school* kept by ... 彼は...経営の学校に通っていた. ¶The child was just ***beginning*** *school*. その子は学校へはいったばかりであった. ¶*School* has ***broken up***. [夏休などで]休校となった. 【類】***break up*** a meeting (party). ¶***close*** *school* 授業を終る. ¶The city ***contains*** *school* of law, medicine, and other institutions of learning. その市には法律・医学その他の学校がある. ¶***cut*** *school* 《米俗》授業をさぼる. ¶The principal ***dismissed*** *school* at noon. 校長は授業を正午仕舞にした. ¶Since the year 1884 the *school* has been ***domiciled*** in its imposing home at Kensington. 一八八四年以来同校はケンシントンの堂々たる校舎に落着いていた. ¶We ***enjoy*** *school*. 学校がおもしろい. ¶***enter*** (=***join***) a *school* 入学する. ¶***found*** a *school* 学校を創立する. ¶We ***have*** *school* till 4 in the afternoon today. きょうは午後四時まで授業がある. ‖ ***have*** a small *school* 生徒が少ない. ¶***hold*** a summer *school* 夏期学校を開く. ¶a little village *school* ***kept*** by the village priest 村の牧師が経営している村の小さな学校 ‖ ***leave*** *school* 退学する, 卒業する. 【類】He had to ***leave*** *school* (退学) at the early age of twelve. ‖ After ***leaving*** *school*, university graduates still want to be identified as "College Men." 卒業後も大学生は「大学出」のレッテルを欲している. ¶***maintain*** a *school* 学校を維持する. ¶***manage*** a *school* 学校を経営する. ¶***open*** *school* at 7 in the morning 朝七時に授業を始める. ¶He ***operates*** three *schools* all for mercenary purposes. 彼は事業として三つの学校を経営している. ¶***organize*** a *school* 学校をたてる. ¶***play*** *school* 学校ごっこをやる. ¶***reopen*** a *school* 学校を復興する. ¶***run*** (=***conduct***) a *school* 学校を経営する. ¶***set up*** a *school* 学校をたてる. ¶***start*** a rival *school* 競争学校を起す. ¶He ***taught*** *school* for twenty years. 彼は二十年間教べんを執った.

V² *School* has ***begun***. 授業が始まった. ¶The whole *school* ***knows*** it. 全校の生徒が皆そのことを知っている. ¶*school* ***lets*** out at ... 学校は...時に引ける. ¶I waited till *school* ***went in***. 私は授業が済むまで待った.

Q an ***endowed*** *school* 寄付でできた学校. ¶an ***exclusive*** *school* 《米》特殊学校(金持の子弟などの入学する). ¶***fully-staffed*** *school* 教師の充実している学校. ¶a ***girls'*** *school* 女学校. ¶a ***good-sized*** *school* かなり大きな学校. ¶learn in the ***hard*** *school* of experience 経験の猛訓練を受けて覚える. ¶trained in the ***hard*** *school* of adversity (war) 逆境(など)という激しい訓練を受けて. ¶a ***high*** *school* for girls =a girls' ***high*** *school* 女子高校 ‖ a junior ***high*** *school* 中学校. ☞米国の high school は四年制と, junior high school をふくめた六年制がある. 前者は九年級ー十二年級で, 後者は七年級ー十二年級 [8+4=12; 6+3+3=12]. ¶a ***higher normal*** *school* for girls女子高等師範学校. ¶an ***influential*** *school* 有力な学校. ¶a ***large*** (***small***) *school* 生徒の多い(少ない)学校. ¶in ***life's*** *school* 人生の学校で. ¶The London Hospital is the ***medical*** *school* of London University. ロンドン病院はロンドン大学の医学部である. 【類】The ***medical*** *school* has two hospitals attached. ¶a ***middle*** *school* 中学校. ¶a ***mission*** *school* 宗教学校. ¶There will be ***no*** *school* today. きょうは授業はない. ¶a ***non-provided*** *school* 私立学校(特に政府などからの助成金のない). ¶one's ***old*** *school* (alma mater) 母校. ¶when *school* is ***over*** (=***out***)=after school hours 放課後. ¶a ***parochial*** *school* 教区学校. ¶***preparatory*** *schools* and their consequential colleges 予備校(予科)とその連絡大学. ¶a ***primary*** *school* 小学校. ¶a day boy at a ***private*** *school* 私立学校の通学生. ¶a ***professional*** *school* 専門学校. ¶a ***proprietary*** *school* [月謝で経営する]営利学校. ¶a ***public*** *school* 公衆学校, 公立学校. ☞public school: 英国では主に上流子弟の大学進学のための予備教育を目的とする, 寄宿制の私立中等学校. 米国では公(州及び市)費で経営される初等及び中等学校を総称する. ¶a ***secondary*** *school* 中等学校. ¶a ***secretarial*** *school* 秘書養成学校. ¶He has grown up to a man in a ***severe*** *school*. 彼は厳格な訓練の下に人となった. 【類】be trained in the ***severest*** *school*. ¶colleges and ***specialized*** *schools* 専門学校. ¶***technical*** *schools* 工業学校. ¶a ***theological*** *school* 神学校. ¶an ***ungraded*** *school* 年級制でない小学校.

Q² an ***adult***[***-education***] *school* 成人[教育]学校. ¶a ***board*** (=***boarding***) *school* 寄宿学校. ¶a ***branch*** *school* 分校. ¶a ***business*** *school* 実業学校. ¶a ***charity*** *school* 貧民学校. ¶a medieval ***cloister*** *school* 寺子屋. ¶It is coupled with a ***companion*** *school* for girls. それには付属女子学校がある. ¶a ***continuation*** *school* 補習学校. 【類】The public should be made to see the library in a ***continuation*** *school*. ¶a ***day*** *school* 昼間学校(通学々校). ¶a ***district*** *school* 《米》地区小学校(地方の). ¶attend ***evening*** *school* 夜学に通う. ¶a fire ***fighting*** *school* 消防学校. ¶a ***finishing*** *school* 完成学校(花嫁学校の類) ‖ a boys' ***finishing*** *school* 男子技能完成学校 ‖ a girls' ***finishing*** *school* 花嫁学校. ¶a ***fitting*** *school* 《米》予備校. ¶a ***government***[***al***] *school* 国立学校(公立学校). ¶a ***grade***[***d***] *school* 《米》小学校. ¶a ***graduate*** *school* 《米》大学院(修・博士課程の). ¶a ***home*** *school* for young girls needing individual attention 個人教授を必要とする少女の私塾. ¶a ***law*** *school* 法律学校. ¶a ***moonlight*** *school* 月夜学校(米国で adult illiterates を教える夜学校). ¶a ***night*** *school* for day workers 労務者の夜学校. ¶a ***one-teacher*** *school* 教師一人の学校. ¶a ***non-government***[***al***] *school* 私立学校. ¶a ***police-***[***training***] *school* 警察学校. ¶an ***open-air*** *school* 青空学校. ¶an ***orphan*** *school* 孤児院. ¶a ***poor*** *school* 貧民学校. ¶a ***practice*** *school* 実務学校. ¶a "***prep***" *school* 《口語》予備校 (a preparatory school). ☞"prep school" は米国では大学予備学校, 予科の意だが, 英国では public school 進学準備の中間予備校. ¶a ***reform*** *school*=a reformatory 感化院. ¶a ***riding*** *school* 乗馬学校. ¶establish a ***rival*** *school* 競争学校を設立する. ¶a ***summer*** *school* 夏期学校. ¶a ***teacher training*** *school* 教員養成所. ¶a ***trade*** *school* 徒弟学校(職業学校). ¶The newspaper office is a good ***training*** *school*. 新聞社は良い訓練所だ. ‖ a manual ***training*** *school* 手工芸学校. ¶a ***truant*** *school* 不良児学校. ¶a [summer] ***vacation*** *school* 夏期学校. ¶the Washington ***University Medical*** *School* ワシントン大学医学部. ¶a ***watch*** *school* 時計学校.

P He was kept ***after*** *school*. 彼は放課後残された. ¶He is ***at*** *school* in England. 彼は英国の学校にいる. ‖ He is clever ***at*** *school*. 彼は学校でできがよい. 【類】He has never been ill ever since he was ***at*** *school*. ‖ a course ***at*** a business *school* 実業学校の課程 ‖ They teach well ***at*** that *school*. あの学校は教え方がうまい. 【類】I take my lunch ***at*** the *school*. ¶***before*** the whole *school* 全校生徒の前で. ¶I leave [home] ***for*** *school* at eight. 私は八時に学校へ行く. ¶come home ***from*** *school* 学校から帰る ‖ stay away ***from*** *school* 学校を欠席する ‖ play truant ***from*** *school* 学校をずるける ‖ He was expelled ***from*** *school*. 彼は放校された. ¶I am ***in*** *school* again. 私は復校した. ‖ We recite lessons ***in*** *school* every day. 私たちは学校で毎日学課を暗しょうする. ‖ when (=while) ***in*** *school* 在校中 ‖ He teaches ***in*** a *school*. 彼はある学校の教師をしている. ‖ ***in*** the *school* of adversity 苦難の訓練を受けて. ¶go ***into*** *school* with a purpose 目的をいだいて入学する. ¶a girl just ***out of*** *school* 学校を出たばかりの少女. ¶pass ***through*** a *school* 学校を卒業する ‖ work one's way ***through*** *school* アルバイトしながら卒業する. ¶I am going ***to*** *school*. 私は学校へ行く所だ. ‖ return ***to*** *school* 復校する.

P² a *school* ***for*** gymnastics 体操学校 ‖ The surroundings of imprisonment are a real *school* ***for*** crime. 刑務所の環境は真に犯罪の養成所の感がある. ¶a hard *school* ***with*** a rough master 手荒い教師のいるきびしい学校.

(2) 学派, 流派; 流儀.

V ***create*** a new *school* of fiction 小説の新派を起す. ¶He ***founded*** a *school* of his own. 彼は一派を立てた. 【類】***found*** a *school* of theology (神学). ¶He ***left*** no *school* behind him. 彼は流派を立てずに死んで行った.

V² A new *school* of fiction has ***grown up***. 小説の新流派が「起った.

Q a ***fleshly*** *school* of poetry 肉感的な詩の一派. ¶the study of ***foreign*** *schools* of thought 諸外国思想の研究. ¶psychoanalysis of the ***Freudian*** *school* フロイド派の精神分析. ¶a painter of ***Italian*** *school* イタリア派の画家. ¶the judiciary of the ***modern*** *school* of thought 新しい頭の裁判官たち ‖ a Quaker of the ***modern*** *school* 新派のクェーカー教徒. ¶the authorities who belong to the ***newer*** *school* 革新派の権威者. ¶a diplomat of the ***old*** *school* 旧式の外交家. 【類】He is a Wall Street man (株屋さん) of the ***old*** *school*. / an ***old*** *school* of oratory ‖ ladies (gentlemen) of the ***old*** *school* 昔風の女(男). ¶those who belong to an ***opposing*** *school* 反対派の人々. ¶a novelist of the ***psychological*** *school* 心理派の小説家. ¶the ***Scotch*** *school* of philosophy スコットランド派の哲学. ¶the ***Socratic*** *school* ソクラテスの学派. ¶a sportsman of the ***true*** *school* 正統派の野外運動家. ¶the futurist and others of ***ultramodern*** *school* 未来派その他超現代派の人人.

Q² paintings of the ***Kano*** *school* 狩野派の絵画. ¶a well-known landscape artist of the ***print*** *school* 有名な風景浮世絵画家. ¶the "get tough with ***Russia***" *school* of thought 「ロシアをよう懲せよ」型の思想.

P an artist ***of*** the Shijo *school* 四条派の画家.

P² found a *school* ***in*** music 音楽に一派を立てる. ¶Heretofore there have been two *schools* ***of*** thought on this question. この問題についてはこれまで二派の議論があった.

school, *v.* 教育する, しつける, 鍛錬する.

M a people ***abundantly*** *schooled* and newspapered 学校や新聞がたくさんある国民. ¶***well*** *schooled* 良くしつけられた.

P be *schooled* ***by*** adversity 困窮に鍛えられる. 【類】*schooled* ***by*** love and sorrows. ¶*school* oneself ***in*** adversity 苦難の中で自己を鍛練する. 【類】*school* oneself ***to*** the austerity of life (耐乏生活) ‖ inexplicable to a mind *schooled* ***in*** the ways of Western civilization 西洋風に教育された人には不可解の.

school, *n.* 群.

P a *school* ***of*** whales (dolphins, tunas, herring) 一群の「鯨(など).

school, *v.* 群来する.

M² *school* ***up*** (魚が)水面近く群がる.

schooling, *n.* 教育.

V He ***finished*** his public *schooling* in Brooklyn when he was fifteen. 彼は十五歳のときブルックリンで初等教育を終えた. ¶He has ***had*** little *schooling*. 彼は教育がない.

Q lack ***formal*** *schooling* 正式の教育を受けていない. ¶go through ***regular*** *schooling* 正規の学校を出る. 【類】had only one year's ***regular*** *schooling* / a man with no ***regular*** *schooling*. ¶He has not had ***much*** *schooling*. 彼は余り教育を受けなかった.

Q² ***grade*** *schooling* 《米》初学教育.

P send a boy ***for*** *schooling* 少年を学校に入れる.

schoolboy, *n.* [男の]児童, 生徒.

V² Every *schoolboy* ***knows*** it. 三尺の童子もなおよくこれを「知る.

school child, 小学児童.

P a film good ***for*** *school children* 小学生向きの映画.

school-hour, *n.* 授業時間.

P ***during*** *school-hours* 授業時間中.

schoolmaster, *n.* 小学校の教師.

Q² a ***village*** *schoolmaster* 村の学校の先生.

schoolmate, *n.* 同級生.

Q a ***contemporaneous*** *schoolmate* 同期生.

schoolwork, *n.* 学業.

V ***neglect*** one's *schoolwork* 勉強を怠ける.

P attend closely ***to*** one's *schoolwork* 学業に精を出す.

science, *n.* 科学; 科学の一分科.

V ***advance*** *science* 学術を進める. ¶***apply*** *science* for farming 農耕に科学をとり入れる. ¶the steps by which modern medical *science* has been gradually ***built up*** 現代医学が漸次に築き上げられた段階. ¶Physical *sciences* are now much ***cultivated*** in Japan. 自然科学は今日日本で大いに開拓されつつある. ¶***enrich*** *science* with many new and well-ascertained facts りっぱに確立した多くの新事実で科学の内容を豊富にする. ¶He ***professes*** a *science*. 彼はある科学の教師である. ¶***revive*** a *science* 科学を復興する. ¶***take up*** a *science* 一つの科学の研究に取掛る.

Q ***absolute*** *science* 絶対科学. ¶***abstract*** *science* 純理科学. ¶***applied*** *science* 応用科学. ¶***assistant*** (=***auxiliary***) *science* 補助科学. ¶***Biblical*** *science* 聖書科学. ¶***cultural*** *science* 人文科学. ¶Psychology is a rapidly ***developing*** *science*. 心理学は急速に発達している科学である. ¶***domestic*** *science* 家政学. ¶***economic*** (***electrical, historical, sanitary, statistical, technical***) *science* 経済(電気・史・衛生・統計・工)学. ¶the ***European*** *sciences* 欧州の科学. ¶***exact*** *science* 精密科学(特に数学). ¶Arithmetic is the one ***fundamental*** *science*, underlying all other physical sciences. 算術はすべての他の自然科学の土台となる一つの基礎科学である. ¶that ***ill-defined*** *science* called aesthetics 美学という輪郭の鮮明でない科学. ¶***industrial*** *science* 工業科学. ¶medicine and the ***kindred*** *sciences* 医学並びに関連科学. ¶the be-all and end-all of ***linguistic*** *science* 言語学の全部(一切合切). ¶modern developments of ***mechanical*** *science* 機械学の近代の発達. ¶the ***mental*** or ***cultural*** *sciences* 精神並に人文科学. ¶***military*** *science* 軍事科学. ¶the latest discoveries of ***modern*** *science* 現代科学の最近の発見 ‖ TV is one of the wonders of ***modern*** *science* テレビは現代科学の驚異の一つである. ¶the ***natural*** *sciences* 自然科学. ¶Astronomy is a ***noble*** *science*. 天文学は高尚な科学である. ¶***physical*** *sciences*, the foundation of Western civilization 西洋文明の基礎たる自然科学. ¶***political*** *science* 政治学. ¶***practical*** *science* 実際科学. ¶***pure*** (="***raw***") *science* 純正科学. 【類】in ***pure*** and ***applied*** *science*. ¶***scientific*** *science* scientifically taught 科学的に教えられた科学的科学. ¶***social*** *sciences* 社会科学. ¶be denied by ***western*** *science* 西欧科学が認めていない.

Q² when it was a ***baby*** *science* その科学が幼稚だったころ. ¶***fishery*** *science* 水産学. ¶***newspaper*** *science* 新聞学. ¶***Soviet*** *science* ソ連の科学.

P grind ***at*** one's *science* 専門の科学をこつこつ勉強する. ¶the latest discovery ***in*** *science* 最近の科学的発見. ¶advancement ***of*** *science* 科学の進歩 ‖ early cultivators ***of*** this *science* この科学の開拓者 ‖ a man ***of*** *science*=a scientist 科学者 ‖ popularizers ***of*** *science* 科学普及者.

P² the *science* ***of*** government 行政学.

scientist, *n.* 科学者.

V Whatever course this work takes, the problem of radiation will long be present to ***plague*** the *scientists*. その研究がどんなコースをとっても放射線問題は永久に残って科学者を苦しめることだろう. ¶***puzzle*** *scientists* 科学者を閉口させる.

Q ***abstract*** *scientists* 純理科学者. ¶the ***atomic*** *scientist* in his laboratory 彼の研究所に働く原子科学者. ¶***illustrious*** *scientists* 有名な科学者. ¶a ***top-flight*** (=***first-rate***) *scientist* 一流科学者.

Q² a ***cotton*** *scientist* 綿の研究家. ¶a ***GI*** *scientist* 兵士の科学者(科学兵器を扱うなどの). ¶an eminent ***plant*** *scientist* 著名な植物学者. ¶a ***research*** *scientist* 研究家, 研究所員. 【類】a noted atomic ***research*** *scientist*.

P a coterie ***of*** *scientists* 科学者の一団.

scion, *n.* 子弟.

Q a ***wealthy*** *scion* of nobility 富裕貴族の子弟.

scissors, *n. pl.* はさみ.

V ***sharpen*** *scissors* はさみをとぐ.

P a pair ***of*** *scissors* 一ちょうのはさみ. ¶trim one's hear ***with*** *scissors* 理髪する.

scoff, *v.* 冷笑する.

M *scoff* ***aloud*** 大声で笑いとばす.

P *scoff* ***at*** the idea of ... …の考えを鼻であしらう. 【類】*scoff* ***at*** such attempts / *scoff* ***at*** a person / *scoff* ***at*** religion.

scold, *v.* しかりつける.

M *scold* ***away*** しかり飛ばす. ¶Her tongue was ***incessantly*** *scolding*. 彼女の口からは小言の絶間がない.

P He was *scolded* ***about*** it. 彼はそのことでしかられた. ¶*scold* [***at***] a person 人をしかる. ¶I *scolded* him ***for*** having left the door open. ドアを明け放しにしたので彼をしかりつけた. 【類】*scold* children ***for*** tormenting animals.

scolding, *n.* 小言(ごと).

V ***catch*** a *scolding* お小言を食う. ¶***fear*** a paternal *scolding* 父のしっ責を恐れる. ¶***get*** [a] *scolding* しかられる. ¶***give*** a mild *scolding* やさしくしかる ‖ I ***gave*** him a sharp *scolding*. 私は彼をきびしくしかった. 【類】be ***given*** a good *scolding* / give a person a ***hearty*** *scolding*. ¶I ***had*** a good *scolding*. 私はうんとしかられた.

scoop, *n.* シャベル; 大さじ; 〚新聞〛特種.

V ***get*** a *scoop* on (=scoop) a rival paper 特種をとって他紙を出し抜く.

Q a ***clear*** *scoop* 独占の特種.

P dig up ***with*** a *scoop* シャベルで土を掘返す ‖ take out sugar ***with*** (=***in***) a *scoop* 大さじで砂糖を出す.

scoop, *v.* 穴を掘る.

P *scoop* a hole ***in*** the sand 砂地に穴を(スコップで)掘る.

scooter, *n.* スクーター.

V ***ride*** a *scooter* スクーターに乗る.

Q² a ***motor*** *scooter* スクーター. ☞ a scooter だけでも a motor scooter の意がある.

scope, *n.* 範囲, 活動範囲; 余地, 余裕.

V ***afford*** a *scope* for energies 才能を伸ばす余地がある. ¶***allow*** free *scope* for a further stage of development 一層の発展に対して自由活動の余地を与える. ¶***broaden*** the *scope* of the work of ... …の仕事の範囲を広げる. ¶The proceedings of the conference ***cover*** a wide *scope*. 会議事項は広範囲にわたる. ¶***enlarge*** the *scope* of the work 仕事の範囲を拡大する ‖ ***enlarge*** the *scope* of successful military operations いよいよ戦果を拡大する. ¶***extend*** the *scope* of operations 手を広げる. ¶He ***gives*** full *scope* to his imagination. 彼は想像をたくましくする. ‖ No *scope* is ***given*** for his originality. 彼の独創力を働かす余地が与えられていない. 【類】Football will ***give*** you *scope* for courage and quick moving. ¶He ***has*** full *scope*. 彼は十分活動の自由を有する. ‖ He ***has*** no *scope* for his ability. 彼は手腕を揮う余地がない. ¶***leave*** a certain *scope* for the exercise of feminine vanity 女子の虚栄心を発揮する幾分の余地を残す. ¶There is little ***scope left*** for further activities. これ以上活動の余地はまずない. ¶***limit*** its *scope* to ... その範囲を…に限る. ¶***narrow*** its *scope* その範囲をせばめる. ¶***seek*** *scope* for one's energies その活動の方面を求める.

V² the editorial *scope* ***embraces*** ... その雑誌は…関係の事項を掲載する.

Q His position affords him ***ample*** *scope*. 彼の地位は彼が十分活動ができるようになっている. ¶offer ***fine*** *scope* for his activities 彼が活動するりっぱな余地を与える. ¶The most effectual method that has been devised for diverting men from vice is to give ***free*** *scope* to a higher ambition.—Lecky. 悪から人を転向させる最も有効な方法はより高尚なる功名心を自由に活動させるにある. ¶give ***full*** *scope* to one's genius 天才を十分に発揮させる ‖ give ***full*** *scope* to one's imagination 想像をたくましくする. ¶a ***great*** *scope* of land 広い地面. ¶a person of ***limited*** (***wide***) *scope* 見解の狭(広)い人. ¶offer a ***splendid*** *scope* for ... to ... …に…すべきりっぱな余地を与える. ¶an investigation of ***wide*** *scope* 広範囲の調査.

Q² the expansion of the ***purge*** *scope* 追放範囲の拡大.

P ***beyond*** the *scope* of ... …の範囲外に. ¶include ... ***in*** the *scope* of its activities その活動範囲内に…を含む ‖ be limited ***in*** *scope* 範囲は狭く限られている. ¶it is ***outside*** my *scope* to deal in any detail with ... 細かに…を論議するは私の領分外だ. 【類】Their consideration (それらのことの考慮) is ***outside*** the *scope* of the present book. ¶It hardly falls ***within*** the *scope* of the present article. それはほとんどこの論文の範囲内にはいらない. 【類】***within*** the *scope* of this volume it is impossible even to mention briefly ... / do not fall ***within*** the *scope* of this book.

P² There is considerable *scope* ***for*** expansion in South America. 南米にはかなり発展の余地がある. ¶the *scope* ***of*** military (naval) operations [陸海]軍作戦の範囲. 【類】the *scope* ***of*** union activities (組合活動) / the *scope* ***of*** the law.

scorch, *v.* 焦げる, 焼ける.

P grass *scorched* ***by*** the sun 太陽の熱で焦げた芝生. ¶*scorch* a shirt ***in*** ironing アイロンでワイシャツに焼けこげをつける. ¶be *scorched* ***to*** death 焼死ぬ.

O The cake tastes *scorched*. ケーキはこげすぎてまずい.

score, *n.* 借金; 得点数; 理由; 二十; *pl.* 多数.

V ***achieve*** a perfect *score* 満点を取る. ¶***count*** the *score* 得点を数える. ¶***falsify*** *scores* 採点をごまかす, 勝負でずるをする. ¶***have*** many old *scores* to clear off 返済しなければならない旧債がうんとある. ¶***keep*** (=***mark***) the *score* 得点を記録する ‖ ***keep*** *score* accurately in tennis テニスのスコアを正確に取る. ¶***make*** *scores* 点を取る ‖ ***make*** a poorer *score* もっと悪い点を取る. ¶They ***number*** *scores*. 数は何十とある. ¶***pay*** one's *score* 借りを払う. ¶***pay off*** (=***settle***) old *scores* 旧債を片付ける; [比ゆ的に] 旧恨を晴らす. ¶***quit*** *scores* 債務を相殺する; 行掛りを一掃する. ¶***run up*** a *score* at grocery 食料品店に借がふえる. ¶The *score* ***stood*** at 5 to 1. 得点は五対一であった. ¶The *score* in each case, however, was ***tied*** in the ninth inning, and the game was not finished until the twelfth inning. しかし九回目で同点になり十二回で勝負がついた.

Q with ***deep*** *scores* of pain and sorrow on the forehead 深い苦悩のあとを額に刻んで. ¶an ***even*** *score* 五分五分の点(勝負). ¶beat the opposing team by a ***large*** *score* 大きな得点で相手のチームを破る. ¶be of the ***same*** *score* 同点, あいこである. ¶the ***three*** *score* and ten years of human life 人生七十年.

Q² a ***baseball*** *score* 野球の得点. ¶a ***cricket*** *score* クリケットの得点(勝負). ¶officers with the ***highest point*** *scores* 最高の軍務点数を持つ士官たち. ¶a ***piano*** *score* ピアノの楽譜.

P defeat ... ***by*** a (=the) *score* of five to three 五対三の得点で…を破る ‖ gather together ***by*** the *score* 数十人の人が集合する ‖ a paper which brought in appreciative letters ***by*** the *score* たくさんの謝状をもらった新聞 ‖ The disease killed men ***by*** *scores*. その病気で数十人の人が死んだ. ¶The soldiers went down ***in*** (=by) *scores*. 兵士が多数たおれた. ¶***on*** this (that) *score* こ(そ)の点では. 【類】You may make yourself perfectly easy ***on*** this *score*. ‖ It is advantageous ***on*** the *score* (=in respect) of economy. それは経済という点が有利だ. ‖ it leaves nothing to be desired ***on*** the *score* of ... それは…の点では申分がない. 【類】retire from service ***on*** the *score* of illness / deserve comment ***on*** another *score*. ¶Waseda won the game ***with*** the *score* of 7 to 3. 早稲田が七対三で勝った.

P² *scores* of men 多数の人 ‖ a *score* ***of*** reasons may be alleged for ... …には数多くの理屈がつけられよう. 【類】*Scores* [***of*** people] died in the epidemic. / *scores* ***of*** thousands of people. ☞ 数詞を伴う場合は a (two, three, four) *score* of eggs となる.

score, *v.* 得点する; 《米口》こきおろす.

P *score* (=win) four runs ***for*** the team 〚野球〛そのチーム

のため四点あげる. ¶He *scored* me ***like*** anything. 彼は私をくそみそにこきおろした.

scorn, *n.* 軽べつ; 軽べつの態度.

V ***feel*** (=***have***) *scorn* for ... ...に軽べつの念を持つ. ¶***pour*** bitter *scorn* on ... ...に向って毒づく.

Q with ***black*** and ***bitter*** *scorn* 恐ろしい軽べつの態度で. ¶eye a person with a ***terrible*** *scorn* ひどく見くだす. ¶in terms of ***withering*** *scorn* しょげさせるような軽べつの言葉で.

P say (laugh, shout) ***in*** *scorn* ばかにして言う(など) ‖ ***in*** *scorn* of their sneers みんなひやかしても平気で ‖ hold a person ***in*** *scorn* 人をさげすむ. 【類】 hold him ***in*** high *scorn* (ばかにしきる). ¶They laughed him ***to*** *scorn.* 彼らは彼をあざ笑った. ‖ He was raised to novel feeling ***to*** the *scorn* of death. 彼は死をも恐れぬ不思議な気持を始めて味わった. ¶He was treated ***with*** *scorn.* 彼は軽べつされた. ¶look in *scorn* ***at*** ... ...を軽視する.

scorn, *v.* 軽べつする.

M ***loftily*** *scorn* to ... 高く構えて...することを潔しとしない.

P *scorn* ***at*** a person (an idea, thing) 人(など)を軽べつする.

scorner, *n.* 軽べつ者.

V *scorn* the *scorner* 軽べつする者を軽べつする.

scoundrel, *n.* ならず者.

Q an ***artful*** *scoundrel* 老かいな無頼漢. ¶a ***cowardly*** *scoundrel* ひきょうな無頼漢. ¶a ***double-dyed*** *scoundrel* 一筋なわでは行かない無法者. ¶a ***thorough-faced*** *scoundrel* よくよくのならず者. ¶a ***worthless*** *scoundrel* やくざ.

Q² a ***penny novel*** *scoundrel* 三文小説に出てくる悪漢.

scour, *v.* かけ歩く; うろうろする; さがし回る.

P *scour* [***through***] the woods ***after*** game [犬が]獲物を求めて森の中を捜し回る. ¶*scour* the woods ***for*** game 獲物を捜して山林をかけ歩く ‖ *scour* a book ***for*** quotations 引用句を求めて書物を渉猟する ‖ *scour* the country over ***for*** a lost child 迷い子を見つけようと土地をくまなく捜し回る. ¶He *scours* the country ***in*** his motorcar. 彼は自分の自動車でいなかを走り回る.

scour, *v.* 掃とうする.

P *scour* the invaders ***from*** the land 侵略者を国土から掃とうする. ¶*scour* (=clear) the sea ***of*** pirates 海から海賊を一掃する.

O *scour* a ditch to carry off the water みぞを掃除して水を流す.

scourge, *n.* 罰, 天罰.

V ***stay*** the *scourge* [病気などの]災禍を防ぐ.

Q a ***dread*** *scourge* 恐ろしい災害(病気など). ¶the ***great*** *scourges* of humanity—cholera, bubonic plague, tuberculosis, enteric typhus, and yellow fever 人類のこうむる大罰—コレラ・腺ペスト・肺結核・腸チブス及び黄熱. ¶a ***terrible*** *scourge* 恐ろしい天罰. ¶the ***white*** ***scourge*** 肺病.

P Cancer is a *scourge* ***of*** mankind. がんは人類がうける天罰である. ‖ a *scourge* ***of*** Heaven (=God) 天罰 ‖ the *scourge* ***of*** war 戦争の惨禍.

scourging, *n.* 罰, たたり.

Q² ***fire*** and ***sword*** *scourging* 火難と剣難.

scout, *n.* 引きぬき係(スカウト).

Q a ***regular*** *scout* (=guy) 《俗》 いいやつ. ¶a ***good old*** *scout* 好漢.

Q² a ***talent*** *scout* [芸人 (talent) の] 引っこ抜き係.

P be ***on*** the *scout* for ... ...を偵察している.

scout, *v.* **(1)** さがし求める.

M² *scout* ***about*** for food 食物をあさる.

P *scout* ***for*** talents 芸人(新人など)を捜し出す.

(2) はねつける, 問題にしない.

M The Ruskinian social economy is ***still*** ***scouted*** as grotesque and fanciful. ラスキン流の社会経済は今尚怪奇で空想的と非難されている.

scowl, *v.* 顔をしかめる.

M *scowl* a person ***away*** 顔をしかめて人を追払う.

P *scowl* ***at*** (=***on***) a person 人ににがい顔を見せる ‖ *scowl* ***at*** ... ...するのを見て顔をしかめる. ¶*scowl* a person ***into*** silence 顔をしかめてだまらせる.

scramble, *v.* よじ上る; 争奪する.

M² *scramble on* (=***along***) in the world 刻苦して世を渡る.

P *scramble* ***after*** office 争って猟官する. ¶*scramble* ***for*** pennies thrown to them [子供やこじきなどが]投げてやった小銭の奪合をする ‖ *scramble* ***for*** seats 席を争奪する ‖ *scramble* ***for*** bare existence 辛うじてのりをすするに過ぎない. ¶*scramble* ***through*** difficulties やっと困難を切り抜ける. ¶*scramble* ***up*** a hill 山をよじ上る.

scrap, *n.* 切片, 断片; つぶし(スクラップ).

V ***collect*** *scraps* くずを集める. ¶***give*** some *scraps* to the dog 犬に肉を少しやる. ¶pick up some *scraps* ***of*** English knowledge ちょっと英語をかじる. ¶***write*** one a short *scrap* 人に短かい手紙を書き送る.

Q² ***codfish*** and ***pork*** *scraps* for supper 夕飯用のたらと豚肉のくず. ¶***beef*** (***fish***) *scrap* 牛肉(など)のくず. ¶***iron*** and ***steel*** *scrap* 鉄と鋼鉄のスクラップ(くず).

P dismantle a submarine and sell her ***as*** *scrap* 潜水艦を解体してつぶしで売る. ¶be ***like*** a *scrap* of paper ほご同様である.

P² *scraps* ***of*** paper (cloth) 紙(など)くず ‖ *scraps* ***of*** meat =meat scraps 肉のくず ‖ a *scrap* ***of*** poetry 一小詩 ‖ a *scrap* ***of*** evidence 一個の証拠 ‖ She read aloud *scraps* ***of*** the letter. 彼女はその手紙の所々を声をあげて読んだ. ‖ There is not a *scrap* ***of*** chow in the whole house. 家の内どこにも食べる物なんかなんにもない. ‖ *scraps* ***of*** conversation with ... ...との会話の断片.

scrape, *n.* 苦境, 窮地.

P He is always ***in*** some *scrape* or other. 彼はいつもなにかしら悩みがある. ¶He has got ***into*** a great *scrape.* 彼は一大窮地に陥った. ¶get a person ***out of*** a *scrape* 人を窮地から救い出す.

P² the *scrape* ***from*** the bow of a violin バイオリンのきーきーという音.

scrape, *v.* こする; 削り取る; かき集める.

M *scrape* ***together*** enough money for college education 大学教育の学資金をかき集める. 【類】 *scrape* ***together*** some money for one's old age / *scrape* ***together*** a good parcel (=quite a sum) of money ‖ He *scraped* ***together*** enough to wipe off the debt. 彼はどうにか算段をしてその負債を済ました.

M² They can just *scrape* ***along*** without asking for charity. 他人の恵みを請わないでどうにか細々と暮している. ¶*scrape* (=rub) ***off*** dirt 泥を擦り落とす ‖ *scrape* ***off*** the paint ぺんきをこすって落す. ¶He *scraped* ***through*** the examination. 彼はようやく試験に合格した. ¶*scrape* ***up*** enough money to ... ...する資金を集める.

P *scrape* the skin ***from*** one's sole 足裏から皮を削り取る. ¶*scrape* mud ***off*** one's shoes くつの泥をこすり落とす. ¶*scrape* one's shoes ***on*** the scraper くつの泥落しでくつの底をこする. ¶*scrape* a slate ***with*** a fingernail 指のつめで石盤をきーきーこする.

scraper, *n.* 泥落とし.

Q² a ***dirt*** *scraper* 泥落とし. ¶a ***shoe*** *scraper* くつの泥落とし.

scratch, *n.* かき傷; 悪筆.

V ***get*** an ugly *scratch* 醜いかき傷を受ける. ¶I ***received*** a mere *scratch.* 私はほんのかすり傷を受けただけだ. ¶He ***writes*** a miserable *scratch.* 《俗》 彼はなさけないほど悪筆だ.

Q a ***mere*** *scratch* ほんのかすり傷. ¶a very ***slight*** *scratch* ほんのかすり傷. ¶get an ***ugly*** *scratch* [ねこなどに]ひどくひっかかれる.

P He got off ***with*** a *scratch* or two. 彼は一二カ所微傷を受けただけで免れた. ¶escape ***without*** a *scratch* 微傷も受けずに免れる.

P² the *scratch* ***of*** a pen ペンのさらさらという音 ‖ just a *scratch* ***of*** the pen 一筆. ¶He received only some slight *scratches* ***on*** his face. 彼は顔にほんの少しのかすり傷を受けただけだった.

scratch, *v.* かく; なぐり書する; かき消す.

M This pen *scratches* a ***little.*** このペンは少しひっかかる. ¶The hens *scratched* the plants ***away.*** 鶏が草をかき除けた. ¶*scratch* ***out*** (=off) the paint (stains) ペンキ(など)をかき落す ‖ *scratch* ***out*** a word 一語削る. ¶*scratch* ***together*** a sizable sum [of money] 相当の金額をかき集める.

M² *scratch* ***about*** for ... ...を求めて引っかき回す. ¶*scratch* ***along*** 《俗》 どうにかやって行く. ¶*scratch* ***down*** a rough sketch 走り書で略図を作る. ¶*scratch* ***off*** a pimple にきびをかきつぶす ‖ *scratch* ***off*** a letter 急いで手紙を書く. ¶*scratch* ***up*** a little money 少額の金をかき集める.

P *scratch* one's head ***in*** trouble 困って頭をかく. ¶*scratch* a match ***on*** the wall 壁でろうマッチをする ‖ *scratch* a letter ***on*** the stone 石に文字を彫りつける. ¶*scratch* his name ***out of*** the list 名簿から彼の名を削除する. ¶I was *scratched* ***with*** thorns. 私はとげで引っかいた. 【類】 The cat *scratches* ***with*** her claws.

scrawl, *n.* 悪筆.

Q a ***hideous*** *scrawl* ひどい悪筆. ¶an ***unintelligible*** *scrawl* 読み取れない筆跡(ひじきの行列). ¶His penmanship is a *wretched scrawl*. 彼の筆跡はひじきの行列だ.

scrawl, *v*. 走り書きする.

P *scrawl* notes ***with*** a pencil 鉛筆でメモをとる.

scream, *n*. 金切声, 絶叫, 悲鳴.

V ***fetch*** a *scream* 絶叫する. ¶***give*** a *scream* 金切声を出す. ¶***hear*** a *scream* 叫声が聞える ‖ I ***heard*** his *scream* mingling with the wind. 風に混る彼の悲鳴を聞きつけた. ¶utter a *scream* 叫ぶ.

Q a ***discordant*** *scream* 耳ざわりな叫声. ¶give a ***great*** *scream* 大悲鳴をあげる. ¶a ***hysterical*** *scream* ヒステリックな金切声. ¶give a ***loud*** *scream* きゃっと叫ぶ. ¶a ***startling*** *scream* けたたましい悲鳴.

P ***with*** a stunning *scream* 耳をろうするばかりの叫声で.

P² A woman's *scream* ***of*** "murder" proceeded from the second floor.「人殺し」という女の叫び声が三階(《米》二階)から聞えて来た.

scream, *v*. 絶叫する, 悲鳴をあげる.

M *scream* oneself ***black*** in the face 顔が真っ赤になるまで叫ぶ. ¶*scream* oneself ***hoarse*** 叫んで声をからす. ¶*scream* ***out*** one's laughter きゃっきゃっと笑う.

P *scream* ***for*** help 助けてくれと叫ぶ. ¶The wind *screamed* ***into*** the house. 風がひゅーひゅー音を立てて屋内に吹込んで来た. ¶*scream* ***with*** laughter きゃっきゃっと笑う ‖ *scream* ***with*** pain 痛いので悲鳴をあげる. 【類】*scream* ***with*** fright (fear).

screen, *n*. びょうぶ, すだれ; しゃへい物; 映写幕, 映画.

V ***set up*** a *screen* びょうぶを立てる. ¶***put*** a *screen* in front of the fireplace 炉の前にびょうぶを建てる.

V² A *screen* of trees ***hides*** his cottage from the road. 並んだ木立で彼の小屋は道路から見えない.

Q an ***artistic four-fold tapestry*** *screen* 美術的なつづれ織の四枚折びょうぶ. ¶a ***bedside*** *screen* まくらびょうぶ. ¶a ***folding*** *screen* of six panels 六枚びょうぶ. ¶a ***sliding*** *screen* 障子.

Q² the ***radar*** *screen* レーダーしゃへい壁. ¶a gilded ***six-leaf*** *screen* 金の六枚びょうぶ. ¶lay down a ***smoke*** *screen* 煙幕を張る. ¶a ***storm*** *screen* 雨戸. ¶enjoy pro-wrestling on the ***television*** *screen* テレビでプロレスを見る. ¶a ***window*** *screen* 窓わく網(か・はえを防ぐための); 窓すだれ.

P ***behind*** the *screen* of trees 樹木のかげに隠れて. ¶a pair ***of*** *screens* 一双のびょうぶ. ¶***Off*** the *screen* she looks a little older than her eighteen years. 素顔だとあの映画女優は十八よりちょっと老けて見える. ¶the supremacy of American picture ***on*** the *screens* of the world 世界の映画界における米国もののは権.【類】He looks much younger and handsomer than ***on*** the *screen*. ¶***under*** *screen* of night 夜陰に乗じて.

P² a *screen* ***against*** mosquitoes か除けの幕. ¶a *screen* ***at*** the window (=a window screen) to keep out flies. ¶A *screen* ***of*** trees hides our house from the evening sun. 僕らの家は植込みで夕陽がよけられる.

screen, *v*. さえぎる; 映画に写る; 審査する.

M She *screens* ***well***. 彼女は映画に向く(よく写る).

M² *screen* ***off*** part of the room へやの一部を仕切る.

P *screen* a person ***from*** danger 人をかばって危険を避けさせる ‖ *screen* one's face ***from*** the fire 顔をかばって火をさえぎる. ¶an orchard *screened* ***from*** north winds ***by*** a hill 小山で北風を避ける果樹園. ¶it is *screened* ***from*** view ***with*** … それは…で見通しができないようになっている. ¶be *screened* ***under*** the provisions of Imperial Ordinance No. 109 of 1946 昭和二十一年勅令第九号により審査される.

screening, *n*. 審査.

Q ***initial*** *screening* 初審査.

screw, *n*. ねじ; [汽船の]スクリュー.

V ***adjust*** a loose *screw* ゆるんだねじを調節する. ¶He ***has*** a *screw* ***loose***. あいつは変っている(ねじが一本ゆるんでいる). ¶***loosen*** a *screw* one or two turns 一二回転ねじをゆるめる. ¶***put*** the *screw[s]* on …=apply the screw[s] to … …に圧迫を加える; [取締りなどを]厳重にする. ¶***tighten*** the *screw* on … …に圧迫を加える. ¶***tighten up*** the *screws* ねじをしめる. ¶***turn*** a *screw* to get it into a board ねじくぎを板にねじ込む.

Q One of the *screws* is ***loose***. ねじが一つゆるんでいる. ‖ There is a *screw* ***loose*** in your affairs. 君の事業にはどこか手抜かりがある. ¶He is an ***old*** *screw*. 彼は因業おやじだ. ¶a ***regular*** *screw* 因業もの. ¶a ***male*** (=an ***external***) *screw* おねじ.

Q² a ***female*** (=an ***internal***) *screw* めねじ. ¶an ***iron*** (a ***brass***) *screw* 鉄(など)ねじ. ¶a ***right(left)-hand*** *screw* お(め)ねじ.

P The steamer is propelled ***by*** *screw*. その汽船はスクリューで推進する.

screw, *v*. ねじで締める; 緊張させる.

M He *screwed* ***out*** half a crown for the contribution. 彼はしぶしぶ半クラウンを寄付した. ¶be ***regularly*** *screwed* 《俗》したたか酔っている. ¶*screw* a book ***tight*** 本をしっかり締め付ける.

M² I am *screwed* ***down*** to certain fixed rules. 私はある一定の規則に縛られている. ¶*screw* ***up*** one's courage 元気を出す ‖ *screw* oneself ***up*** to … …しようと大いに意気込む ‖ He wants (=needs) *screwing* ***up***. あれはねじがゆるんでいる.

P *screw* a bolt ***in*** (=***into***) a hole ボルトを穴にさし込む. ¶*screw* money ***out of*** a person 人から金をしぼり取る. ¶*screw* oneself ***under*** a bed 寝床にもぐり込む.

screwball, *n*. 《米俗》変り者.

Q an ***incorrigible*** *screwball* しまつにおえない変りもの.

scribble, *v*. 走り書き(楽書き)する.

M² *scribble* ***down*** 無造作に書下す.

P Those boys have *scribbled* ***on*** our fence. あの子供らがうちのへいに楽き書した. ¶*scribble* ***with*** one's pen on a sheet of paper ペンで紙に走り書きする.

script, *n*. 書体, 草書体; [映画・放送の]台本.

Q in the ***ordinary*** *script* 普通の草書体で. ¶write words in the ***phonetic*** *script* 音標文字で語を書く.

Q² a ***radio*** (=***broadcast***) *script* 放送台本. ¶a ***talkie*** *script* 映画(トーキー)台本.

scriptural, *a*. 聖書に基く.

P He holds the doctrine that it is perfectly *scriptural* ***for*** a man to beat his wife. 彼は男がその妻を打つのは完全に聖書の教えにかなっているという説を持っている.

scripture, *n*. 聖書.

V *Scripture* ***says*** that …聖書に…とある.

Q the ***Holy*** *Scriptures*=the Scriptures 聖書. ¶the ***Mohammedan*** *Scriptures* 回教経典.

Q² a ***New Testament*** *scripture* 新約聖書.

scroll, *n*. 巻物.

V ***roll up*** a *scroll* 巻物を巻く. ¶***unroll*** a *scroll* 巻物を解く(広げる).

Q² a ***calligraphy*** *scroll* 書の軸もの.

scrub, *n*. 洗い掃除.

V ***give*** a good *scrub* to … …をよくこする. ¶This floor (wall) ***needs*** a good *scrub*. この床(など)はよくみがかないといけない.

scrub, *v*. こする.

M *scrub* the floor ***clean*** 床をこすってきれいにする.

P *scrub* dirt ***off*** the wall 壁をこすってよごれをとる. ¶*scrub* a person's back ***with*** a sponge 人の背中をスポンジでながす.

scruple, *n*. ちゅうちょ, 遠慮.

V I ***feel*** certain *scruples* about … 私は…についていく分ちゅうちょする. ¶You need no longer ***have*** any *scruples* on my account. 君は最早私のために遠慮するに及ばない. ¶He ***makes*** little or no *scruple* of lying. 彼はほとんど平気でうそをつく. ¶***put away*** one's *scruples* ちゅうちょしない. ¶***silence*** one's *scruples* 良心のとがめを抑え付ける.

Q ***conscientious*** *scruples* 小心翼々たること. ¶a man of ***no*** *scruple* どんなことでも平気でやりかねない人.

P stand ***on*** *scruple* 遠慮している. ¶He is a fellow ***with*** few *scruples*. あいつは遠慮のない男だ. ¶He did it ***without*** *scruple*. 彼はちゅうちょせずそれをやった.

P² I have no *scruples* ***about*** the matter. 私はそのことにはためらいはしない.

scruple, *v*. ためらう.

P *scruple* ***at*** … …をためらう.

scrupulous, *a*. 用心深い, 慎重な.

M He is ***very*** *scrupulous*. 彼は非常に用心深い.

P He is very *scrupulous* ***about*** the choice of his word. 彼は言葉の選択にごく慎重だ. ¶He is *scrupulous* ***to*** a fault. 彼は用心し過ぎる.

scrutinize, *v*. 検査する, 吟味する.

M *scrutinize* ***keenly*** 鋭く吟味する. ¶*scrutinize* … ***narrowly*** …を綿密に検査する.

scrutiny, *n*. 吟味, 考査.

V It does not ***bear*** close *scrutiny*. それは厳重に吟味されてはたまらない. ¶construct a sentence which could not ***endure*** the strictest grammatical *scrutiny* やかましく文法的に吟味されるとあらの出る文を作る. ¶***escape*** their *scrutiny* その吟味を免れる ‖ ***escape*** the *scrutiny* of many eyes [誤植など]多数の鋭い目を抜ける. ¶ ***make*** *scrutiny* into ...＝scrutinize ... ...を吟味する.

Q after ***careful*** *scrutiny* 精査の上. ¶It was subjected to ***close*** *scrutiny*. それは綿密な考査を受けた. ¶It is subject to ***critical*** *scrutiny*. それは批評的に吟味されることを免かれない. ¶by a ***microscopic*** *scrutiny* 精査して. ¶a ***rigid*** *scrutiny* 厳重な吟味.

scud, *v.* 疾走する.

M *scud* ***pell-mell*** toward ... ...の方へ無茶苦茶に疾走する.

scull, *n.* ともがい.

P push a boat forward ***with*** a *scull* ともがいで舟を前進させる.

sculpture, *n.* 彫刻.

P He is skilled ***in*** *sculpture*. 彼は彫刻に巧みだ. ¶decorated ***with*** rich *sculpture* りっぱな彫刻で飾られた.

scum, *n.* 浮きかす; くず.

Q the ***unlettered*** *scum* 無学な人間のくず.

P The liquid is covered ***with*** *scum*. その液体には浮きかすができている.

P² the *scum* ***of*** society (＝the earth) 人間のくず ‖ the *scum* ***of*** the town 町の浮浪者(など).

scuttle, *v.* ちょこちょこ走る.

M *scuttle* ***away*** (＝***off***) ほうほうの体で逃げる. ¶*scuttle* ***out*** into the darkness たちまち暗やみに姿を消す.【類】*scuttle* ***out*** into the garden.

M² The dog *scuttled* ***off*** into the woods. 犬は森の中に逃込んだ. 「ちょこちょこ走った.

P The mice *scuttled* ***to*** their holes. はつかねずみが穴へ

sea, *n.* 海, 大うねり, 潮流; 海上生活; 海ほど沢山.

V ***command*** the *sea* 制海権を握る.【類】Whosoever ***commands*** the *sea* commands the trade; whosoever commands the trade of the world commands the riches of the world, and consequently the world itself.—Raleigh. ¶***cross*** the *sea* 海を渡る. ¶***defy*** the *sea* 海を物ともしない. ¶Here the river ***enters*** the *sea*. ここでその川は海にはいる. ¶mariners who ***explore*** strange *seas* 異国の海を探検する海員. ¶My villa ***faces*** the *sea*. 僕の別荘は海を見晴している. ¶***follow*** the *sea* 船乗りをやる. 【類】The mariner ***followed*** the *sea* for fifty years. ¶***head*** the *sea* 波に逆らって航行する. ¶The pirates then ***infested*** the *seas*. 当時海上には海賊が横行していた. ¶***inhabit*** the *sea* [魚など]海に住む. ¶The U-boat could ***keep*** the *sea* for three months. ドイツの潜水艦は海中作業を三カ月続けることができた. ¶***navigate*** the high *seas* 公海を航行する. ¶a cliff ***overhanging*** the *sea* 海を見おろすがけ. ¶a verandah that ***overlooks*** the *sea* 海を見おろすベランダ. ¶the luxurious giant liners, superbly ***riding*** the *seas* 堂々と海を航行する豪華巨大な定期船. ¶those who had ***sailed*** the *seas* 海外渡航した人々. ¶The boat ***shipped*** ***a*** *sea*. 舟が波をかぶった. ¶***sound*** the *sea* 海の深さを計る. ¶A furious gale ***stirred up*** the *seas*. 恐ろしい強風で海が荒れた. ¶***sweep*** the *sea* for mines 水雷を除くために掃海する. ¶a newly-built ship ***taking*** the *sea* 進水する新造船 ‖ ships capable of ***taking*** the *sea* 航海にたえる船. ¶***take up*** the *sea* as a career＝go to sea 海員になる.

V² *sea* ***breaking*** over the rocks 岩に砕ける波. ¶The *sea* ***gets up***. 波が立つ. ¶The *sea* ***goes down***. 波が静まる. ¶The *sea* ***roars***. 波が怒号する. ¶Heavy *seas* were ***running***. 高浪が立っていた.

Q an ***agitated*** *sea* 動乱の海. ¶An ***angry*** *sea* of faces greeted him as he emerged. 彼が姿を現わすと怒りを顔に出した人の海が彼を迎えた. ¶a ***boundless*** *sea* 果てしない海. ¶a ***broken*** *sea* 砕け波. ¶a ***calm*** (＝***placid***) *sea* 穏かな海. ¶a ***chopping*** (＝***cross***) *sea* 三角波(の海) ‖ raise a ***chopping*** *sea* 三角波を起す. ¶The *sea* was ***choppy***, as a rather stiff north-east wind was blowing. やや激しい北東風が吹いていたので海は荒れていた. ¶a ***closed*** *sea* 領海. ¶***Considerable*** *sea*. [信号用語]波かなり高し. ¶***deep*** *seas* 深海. ¶a ***freshening*** *sea* さわやかな海. ¶a ***glassy*** *sea* 鏡のような海面. ¶at ***full*** *sea* 満潮に. ¶***ground*** *sea* 余波. ¶***Heavy*** *sea* swept the vessel. 荒波が船の甲板を洗った.【類】There during ***heavy*** *seas* lightering is impossible. / There is a strong gale with ***heavy*** *sea*. ¶in a ***high*** *sea* and heavy fog 荒海と濃霧の中に ‖ piracy on the ***high*** *seas* 公海上の海賊行為 ‖ the ownerless ***high*** *seas* 公海 ‖ labor through the ***high*** *seas* of life 人生の荒海をこぎ抜ける. ¶an ***ice-free*** *sea* 不凍海. ¶an ***island-studded*** *sea* 大小の島が点在している海. ¶***long***[***-rolling***] *sea* 長波, 大うねり. ¶the ***main*** *sea* 外海, 大洋. ¶a ***mine-infected*** *sea* 水雷を敷設した海. ¶***mountainous*** *seas* 山のような波浪. ¶*seas* ***mountain-high*** 山なす高浪. ¶an ***open*** *sea* 外海. 【類】He is now on the ***open*** *sea*. ¶the same kind of feeling that brought Coleridge's old mariner to tears at the sight of his sweet English haven after voyaging in ***perilous*** and ***terrible*** *seas* コールリッジの老水夫が危険な恐ろしい航海の後に楽しい英国の港を見て泣いたのと同じような感じ. ¶in a ***rough*** *sea* 荒波に. ¶a ***ruffled*** (＝***troubled***) *sea* 波の荒い海. ¶finish a passage on a ***smooth*** *sea* 平穏に航海を終る. ¶the ***sparkling*** ***blue*** *sea* きらきら輝くこんぺきの海. ¶a ***storm-swept*** *sea* 暴風の吹きまくる海. ¶a ***stormy*** *sea* 荒れた海. ¶a ***troubled*** *sea* of life 浮世の荒波. ¶The *sea* became very ***turbulent***. 海がばかに荒れて来た. ¶embark on an ***uncharted*** *sea* full of sunken rocks 海図にのっていない暗礁の多い海に乗り出す. ¶a ***wide*** *sea* びょうぼうたる海.

Q² ***Fifteen-foot*** *seas* battered against her hull. 十五フイートの波が船体に当って砕けた. ¶a ***head*** *sea* 逆浪(さかなみ). ¶an ***inland*** *sea* 小海. ¶an ***ocean*** *sea* 大海, 大洋. ¶fly over the ***South*** *Seas* toward ... 南海を越えて...に向って飛ぶ. ¶a calm ***spring*** *sea* おだやかな春の海. ¶a rough ***winter*** *sea* 荒い冬の海.

P 19,900 feet ***above*** the *sea*[*-level*] 海抜一万九千九百フィート. ¶***across*** the *sea* 海外に, 外国に. ¶He is now ***at*** *sea*. 彼は今航海中だ. ‖ a voyage ***at*** *sea* 航海 ‖ an officer ***at*** *sea* 船上勤務の高級海員. 【類】when a ship is ***at*** *sea* / our first morning ***at*** *sea* ‖ burial ***at*** *sea* 水葬 ‖ heroism ***at*** *sea* [救人などの]海上の勇敢な行為. 【類】He spent some years ***at*** *sea*. / He was born (drowned) ***at*** *sea*. / I was ***at*** the *sea* for two months last summer. ‖ be ***at*** *sea* between ... and ...と...とどっちにしようかと迷う ‖ I am quite (＝completely) ***at*** *sea* in regard to ... ...に関しては五里霧中にだ. ¶a vast expansion of the Empire ***beyond*** *seas* 海外における帝国の大発展. ¶the Dragon Empire ***beneath*** the *sea* 海の底の竜宮. ¶the British dominions ***beyond*** the *seas* 海外の英国領土 ‖ the "Britains ***beyond*** the *seas*" いわゆる「海外の英国」. 【類】the Greater Britains ***beyond*** the *Seas*. / her development ***beyond*** the *seas*. / our cousins (同一または友邦民族) ***beyond*** the *seas* ‖ a country girdled ***by*** the *sea*＝a sea girt country ‖ I will take her down ***by*** the *sea*. 私は海辺へ彼女をつれて行きましょう.【類】a holiday ***by*** the *sea* (＝at the seaside) ‖ a villa ***by*** the *sea* 海辺の別荘.【類】a town (cottage) ***by*** the *sea* ‖ He proceeded to Osaka ***by*** *sea*. 彼は海路大阪に赴いた.【類】a traveller ***by*** *sea* / perils ***by*** *sea* / by land and [***by***] *sea*. ¶Such a boat is fit only ***for*** a calm *sea*. こんな舟は穏かな海にしか適しない. ¶a gale ***from*** the *sea* 海上からの強風. 【類】a cool breeze ***from*** the *sea*. ¶It was sent us ***from over*** the *seas*. それは海外から送り越された. ¶treasures ***in*** the *sea* 海中の財宝. ‖ burial ***in*** the *sea* 水葬 ‖ a current ***in*** the *sea* 海中の潮流 ‖ far away ***in*** the *sea* 沖合に ‖ the sea fight ***in*** the Yellow *Sea* 黄海の海戦 ‖ fish common ***in*** almost all *seas* ほとんどすべての海に住む魚. ¶flow ***into*** the *sea* 海に流れ入る ‖ He jumped ***into*** the *sea* from the deck of the steamer. 彼は汽船の甲板から海へ飛び込んだ. ‖ a point of land running out ***into*** the *sea* 海中に突出するみさき. ¶green ***like*** the *sea* 海のように緑の. ¶It is situated ***near*** the *sea*. それは海の近くにある. ¶the control (＝command) ***of*** the *sea* 制海権 ‖ a chart ***of*** the *sea* 海図 ‖ an expanse ***of*** *sea* びょうぼうたる海 ‖ freedom ***of*** the *seas* 航海の自由. ¶either ***on*** *sea* or on shore 海陸ともに ‖ Uwajima is a quiet old-fashioned town ***on*** the *sea*. 宇和島は閑静で古風な海辺の町である ‖ The house faces ***on*** the *sea*. その家は海に面している. 【類】Amano-Hashidate is situated ***on*** the *Sea* of Japan, in the province of Tango, to the north-west of Kyoto. ‖ May and October are charming months to sail ***on*** the Mediterranean *Sea* 地中海を帆走するには五月と十月が楽しい. 【類】***On*** the *sea*, sails remained the general motive power for more than five hundred years—from the latter part of the middle ages down to the middle of the nineteenth century. ‖ Her ships are ***on*** every *sea*. その国の船はどこの海にも航行している. ‖ the principal Treaty Ports ***on*** the China *Sea* シナ海の主要条約港. ¶sail ***over*** a *sea* 海上を帆走する ‖ Birds fly *over* the *sea*. 鳥が海の上を飛ぶ. ‖ His home is *over* the *sea*. 彼の故郷は海外だ. ¶go out ***to sea*** 海に乗出す ‖ go ***to*** *sea* 船員になる. 【類】 He went ***to*** *sea* at eighteen years of age. ‖ put ***to*** *sea*=set sail 出帆する. 【類】 The ship put out ***to*** *sea*. ‖ go ***to*** the *sea* during one's holidays 休暇中海辺に行く ‖ the land adjacent ***to*** the *sea* 臨海地. ¶look ***towards*** the *sea* [家など]海に面している. ¶sink deep ***under*** the *sea* 海中深く沈む. ¶a victory ***upon*** the *seas* 海上の勝利. ¶***within*** the four *seas* 海内に.

P^2 a *sea **of*** faces 見渡す限りの顔(人の海) ‖ There was a *sea **of*** heads. [会合などで]見渡す限りみな頭だった. 【類】 a *sea **of*** blood / a *sea **of*** wooden crosses (十字架): a cemetery near Bitterfeld containing 5,000 dead Germans. / a *sea **of*** troubles. ‖ a *sea **of*** impersonal faces 無表情な顔の集り ‖ the *sea **of*** cloud 雲海. ¶on the *sea **off*** (off the coast of) Misaki 三崎沖で.

sea-bathing, *n.* 海水浴.

P It is very much frequented ***for** sea-bathing*. そこは海水浴の人出が大分多い.

seaboard, *n.* 海岸.

Q the ***Atlantic*** *seaboard* 大西洋沿岸.

P the states ***on*** the *seaboard* 沿海各州.

seacoast, *n.* 海岸.

P build forts ***along*** the *seacoast* 海岸に沿うて要さいを築く.

sea-gull, *n.* 海ねこ.

V^2 *Sea-gulls* were ***mewing*** in a flock 海ねこの群がぎゃーぎゃー鳴いていた.

seal, *n.* 印章; 封印.

V ***affix*** (=***stamp** or* put) a *seal* to an instrument 証書に印を押す ‖ ***affix*** a *seal* at the joining of two papers 割印を押す ‖ ***affix*** a corporate *seal* 社印を押す. 【類】 ***affix*** one's *seal* to a contract (document) / make up a contract and ***affix*** their *seals* to it. ¶***break*** the *seal* 封を切る. ¶These facts ***gave*** the *seal* to his theory. これらの事実は彼の理論を証明した. ¶***have*** one's *seal* ***engraved*** 印形を彫らせる. ¶***impress*** one's *seal* on the wax その印を封ろうの上に押す. ¶***place*** a *seal* なつ印する ‖ ***place*** the *seal* of one's approval 賛成の印を押す. ¶***put*** the *seal* on (=upon) ... ...になつ印する. ¶I ***set*** my *seal* to it. 私はそれになつ印した(承認した). ‖ ***set*** one's *seal* to the truth of ...=endorse ... ...の事実に裏書する.

Q under ***flying*** *seal* 開封で. ¶the ***Great Seal***=the Seal of the State 国璽(じ). ¶the ***Imperial*** *seal* 御璽(ぎょ).

P a written contract ***under*** *seal* なつ印証書 ‖ ***under*** one's hand and *seal* 署名なつ印して ‖ He told me this ***under*** the *seal* of secrecy. 彼は口留をして私にこのことを話した. ¶a document stamped ***with*** his *seal* 彼のなつ印した書類.

seal, *v.* 印を押す; 封じる; 密閉する.

M be ***hermetically*** *sealed* 密閉されている. ¶be kept ***tightly*** *sealed* 厳重に封印してある.

M^2 *seal **off*** 封印をする. ¶*seal **up*** a letter (official documents) 手形(など)を封印する ‖ *seal **up*** a tin かんを封ろうする ‖ *seal **up*** the gas hermetically within the vessel その容器内にガスを密閉する ‖ We were *sealed **up*** in ice. われわれは氷の中に閉込められた. ‖ Please show it to me a minute before you *seal* it ***up***. それを封じないうちにちょっと私に見せて下さい. ‖ His fate is *sealed* [***up***]. 彼の運命はきまった. ¶*seal **up*** rooms for fumigation くん蒸消毒のためへやを密閉する.

P The treaty was signed and *sealed **by*** both governments. その条約は両国政府が署名なつ印した. ¶Her eyes were *sealed **to*** the holy book. 彼女は一心不乱に聖書を見詰めていた. ¶*seal* a letter ***with*** a wafer (gum) 封かん紙(など)で手紙を封印する ‖ *seal* it ***with*** one's blood それに血判する.

seal, *n.* あざらし.

Q the ***common*** (=harbor) *seal* 普通のあざらし.

Q^2 the ***fur*** *seal* あざらし. ☞「あしか」は sea lion.

sea-level, *n.* 海面.

P 12,000 feet ***above*** [the] *sea-level* 海抜一万二千フィート.

seam, *n.* 縫い目, 合わせ目.

V ***calk*** (=***caulk***) a *seam* 継目にまいはだを詰める. ¶***cut*** a *seam **open*** 縫い目を切り開く. ¶***make*** a *seam* in ... ...に縫い目を付ける. ¶***rip up*** the *seams* 縫い目をほころばす. ¶***saw*** and ***caulk*** a *seam* [くつ直しなど]合わせ目を縫って締め合わせる. ¶***undo*** a *seam* 縫い目を解く.

V^2 A *seam **gapes***. 縫い目に口があく. ¶The *seam **runs***. 縫い目がほころびる. ¶The *seam* has ***started***. 縫い目がほどけた.

Q a ***French*** *seam* 袋縫い.

P unite ***by*** a *seam* 縫合わせる. ¶underwear ***without*** *seam* 縫い目なしのはだ着.

P^2 a *seam **between*** pieces of cloth 布片と布片との縫い目. ¶the *seams **of*** a ship 船の継ぎ目 ‖ a *seam **of*** coal 石炭層.

seam, *v.* しわをよらせる.

P His face was *seamed **with*** wrinkles. 彼の顔はしわで一杯だ.

seaman, *n.* 水兵, 海員.

Q an ***able***[***-bodied***] *seaman* [英]二等水兵. ¶a ***bronzed*** *seaman* 真黒になった海員. ¶a ***leading seaman*** 《英》一等水兵. ¶an ***ordinary seaman*** 《英》三等水兵, 平水兵.

Q^2 an ***apprentice*** *seaman* 《米》練習兵. ¶a ***first-class*** *seaman* 一等水兵. ¶a ***merchant*** *seaman* 船員.

séance, *n. F.* 降霊会.

V The suggester ***gave*** (=***held***) *séances* in different towns of Germany and Switzerland. その暗示者はドイツとスイスの方々の町で降霊会を催した.

Q a ***hypnotic*** *séance* 催眠術実演の会. ¶a ***psychotherapeutic*** *séances* 精神療法実験の会.

seaport, *n.* 海港; 港市.

Q a ***thriving*** (***decaying***) *seaport* 栄える(衰える)港市.

Q^2 a warm ***water*** *seaport* 暖水港.

sear, *v.* 焼印を押す.

M^2 *sear **up*** 焼きふさぐ, 焼しゃくしてふさぐ.

P It is *seared **into*** my memory. それは私の記憶に焼付けられている.

search, *n.* 捜索; せん索, 研究.

V ***assist*** *search* 捜索の便をはかる. ¶the police at once ***began*** a *search* for ... 警察では直ちに...の捜索を始めた. ¶***cause*** a *search* to be made 捜索させる. ¶***encourage*** the *search* for truth 真理の探求を奨励する. ¶***facilitate*** the *search* for words 語の検索を便利にする. ¶A *search* was ***instituted***, but he could not be found anywhere. 捜索を始めたが彼のいどころは分からなかった. ¶***make*** *search* for ... ...を捜す ‖ after ***making*** a *search* 捜索をしてから. 【類】 The *search* was ***made*** in every direction. / *Search* was ***made*** without results. / A *search* was ***made*** at once of his room. ¶***prosecute*** a diligent *search* たん念に捜索する.

Q The police began to make an ***active*** *search* 警察では鋭意捜索を始めた. ¶an ***arduous*** *search* through many volumes of newspapers 数巻につづった新聞紙の丹念な検索. ¶a ***careful*** *search* 念入りな捜索. ¶a ***close*** *search* 厳密な捜索. ¶a ***domiciliary*** *search* 家宅捜索. ¶an ***eager*** *search* for truth 熱心な真理の追求. ¶***Every*** *search* was made for him. 百方手を尽して彼を捜した. ¶freedom of thought and the ***free*** *search* for knowledge 思想の自由と自由な研究. ¶a ***fruitless*** *search* for ... ...の無効な捜索. ¶the ***incessant*** *search* after new truth 絶えず新しい真理の追求. ¶a ***long*** and ***tedious*** *search* 長い間の退屈な捜索. ¶a ***nation-wide*** *search* for a criminal 犯人に対する全国的な捜索. ¶a ***patient*** *search* 根気のよい捜索. ¶a ***quiet, single-minded*** *search* 心静かに専心やる研究. ¶a ***rigorous*** *search* 厳重な捜索. ¶institute a ***thorough*** *search* 徹底的捜索を始める. 【類】 make a ***thorough*** *search* for ... ¶the ***unending*** *search* for truth 果てしない真理の追求. ¶in a ***vain*** *search* for ... いたずらに...を求めて. 【類】 after a ***vain*** *search*. ¶a ***weary*** *search* for employment らちの明かない就職運動.

Q^2 Teams began ***farm-to-farm*** *searches* for hoarded food. いくつかの組は農村から農村へと退蔵食料の追求を始めた. ¶a ***hole-and-corner*** *search* 秘密の捜索. ¶***house-to-house*** *searches* 戸別調査. ¶a ***surprise*** *search* for ... ...の突然の捜索.

P ***during*** my *search* for data regarding ... 私が...の資料調査中に. ¶I am at present ***in*** *search* of a house (good servant). 私は目下家(など)を捜している. ‖ They went out to Australia ***in*** *search* of gold. 彼らは金鉱を捜しに豪州へ出かけた. ‖ ***in*** *search* of a roof for their heads 貸家捜しに ‖ travel ***in*** *search* of the picturesque 勝景を尋ねて旅行する ‖ ***in*** *search* of poetic adventure 風雅を尋ねて. 【類】 wander about the continent of Europe ***in*** *search* of (=a search for) health. / ***in*** *search* of suspected pirates / drift (流れ込む) to the capital ***in*** *search* of employment (a job) / scientists ***in*** *search* of facts / adventures ***in*** *search* of gold / He went to America ***in*** *search* of fortune (運命開拓のため). / an expedition to Japan ***in*** *search* of literary material / go to London ***in*** *search* of literary work (文筆の仕事) / travel *in search* of warmth (change) / *in search* of an opportunity to rise / *in search* of relief from the current heatwave ‖ artists sincere *in* the *search* for new expression 新らしい表現法の研究に忠実な芸術家. 【類】 an artist traveling *in* the *search* for material and ideas for future work (将来の作品に対する資料と考案) ‖ breakers of the mold of the society from which they emerge *in* their *search* for ... 研究のため旧弊を脱する社会の型(かた)破り. 【類】 *in* the *search* after truth. ¶*in spite of* a wide *search* by relatives and friends 親せきや友人の広く行渡った捜索にもかかわらず. ¶*on* diligent *search* 苦心研究の上で.

P² The *search after* (=for) happiness is the great problem of life. 幸福の追求は人生の大問題だ. ¶make a most useful *search among* the old records and newspapers of ... ...の古い記録や新聞紙の中できわめて有益な研究をする. ¶a *search for* suitable gifts 適当な贈物のせん索. 【類】 the *search for* [the] truth. ¶a *search through* medical literature for some explanation as to ... ...について何か説明の記事があるかと医学の文献をあさること.

search, *v.* 捜索する, 検査する; 取調べる.

M *search carefully* for clues 念入りに手がかりを捜す. ¶*narrowly* search 厳密に捜す. ¶*search nation-wide* for uranium mines ウラン鉱を国中捜し回る. ¶*search out* facts (details) 事実(など)を捜し出す. ¶*search patiently* for new facts 辛抱強く新事実を捜す. ¶*search thoroughly* くまなく捜す. ¶*search vainly* for ... いたずらに...を捜す.

P *search* about *for* food 食物をあさる. 【類】 *search after* a lost child (迷い子) / One must keep on investigating and *searching after* truth, always maintaining a scientific skepticism and a philosophic doubt. ¶Luggage is *searched at* the custom-house. 荷物は税関で調べられる. ¶*search for* health 保養する ‖ *search for* the missing men 失そう者を尋ねる. 【類】 *search for* hidden treasure (things lost, things stolen) / *search for* a meaning in a dictionary ‖ tugs were sent out to *search for* ... ...捜索のため引船が出動した ‖ Special wants *searched for*. 御希望のもの(本など)はお捜しします. ‖ The swindlers are busy *searching for* victims. ぺてん師はのみ取りまなこでむく鳥を捜している. 【類】 the most effective method of *searching for* the truth / They were *searched for* concealed weapons. / *search* the dictionary *for* a word=look up a word in the dictionary. 【類】 *search* a book *for* a passage worth quoting ‖ He who would *search for* pearls must dive below. 虎口に入らずんば虎児を得ず. ‖ *search* in vain *for* ... ...いたずらに捜す. 【類】 They are *searching* in the ruins *for* bodies. ¶*search into* a matter (secret, the cause of a disaster) 事件(など)を調べる. ¶We have *searched* all *over* the city. 町中捜した. ¶*search through* many a dusty document たくさんのほこりだらけの書類を捜しぬく. ¶*search to* the root of it 根掘り葉掘り調べる.

searcher, *n.* 探索者; 研究家.

Q a *genealogical* and *biographical searcher* 系図及び伝記の研究家.

Q² a *record searcher* 記録を調べる人.

P² a *searcher after* truth (=a truth searcher) 真理の探索者.

searching, *n.* 検索.

Q *tireless searching* たゆまない検索.

Q² *library searching* 図書館での調べもの.

search-light, *n.* 探照灯.

V *turn* the *search-light* of common sense upon ... ...に常識の探照灯を向ける.

Q turn the *cold search-light* of science on the problem その問題に冷静な科学の光を向ける.

search-party, *n.* 捜索隊.

V *send out* a *search-party* for him 彼のために捜索隊を派遣する.

seashore, *n.* 海浜.

P Let's go for a walk *along* the *seashore*. 海浜を散歩しよう. ¶a reverie *at* the *seashore* 海浜でのめい想. ¶*off* the *seashore* of ... ...の沖合に. ¶a house abutting *on* the *seashore* 海辺の家. ¶go *to* the *seashore* for the summer 夏期(避暑に)海浜へ行く.

seaside, *n.* 海岸, 海辺.

P Didn't it rain a good deal while you were *at* the *seaside*? 海辺においでの間は雨が多かったじゃないですか. ‖ a cool summer evening *at* the *seaside* 海辺の涼しい夏の夕. ¶a summer cottage *by* the *seaside* 海の家. ¶go *to* the *seaside* (=beach) [保養・海水浴のため]海浜に行く.

season, *n.* 季節, 時期; 盛り時.

V The bathing resort *enjoys* an exceptionally prosperous *season*. その海水浴場はこの季節はことの外人出があった. ¶*expect* a big tourist *season* next year 来年の観光季節は好景気だと見越す. ¶It *has* its *season*. それには季節がある. ‖ The summer resort has *had* the busiest *season* in years. その避暑地はこの夏は近年になくにぎやかであった. ‖ Japan has *had* a good (bad) tourist *season*. 日本はこの季節は観光客が多(少な)かった. ¶The couple came to *spend* a *season* at Paris. その夫婦は一季節を送るためにパリーにきた.

V² The *season comes* (*draws*) *near*. 季節が来る(近づく). ¶the *season extends* from ... to ... その季節は...から...まで続く. ¶The *season opens* propitiously (unfavorably). 季節が景気良く(悪く)始まった. ‖ The herring *season* has just *opened*. 丁度にしんの季節になった.

Q The *season* is not sufficiently (too far) *advanced*. 季節はまだ早い(もうおそい). ¶form a popular resort at *all seasons* 四季ともに受けのよい行楽地になっている ‖ in *all* the *seasons* of the year 年中. ¶wishing you the compliments of the *approaching season* 間近い季節(クリスマスなど)のお祝を申上げて. ¶at the *appropriate season* 適当な時期に. ¶The *season* is *backward*. 季節が遅れている. 【類】 a *backward season*. ¶The *season* is much *behind*. 季節が大分遅れている. ¶Autumn is the *best season* for travel 旅行は秋に限る. ¶for a *brief season* 暫時. ¶the *burgling season* 夜盗の往行する季節. ¶a *busy season* 繁忙期 ‖ The *busy season* is over. 忙しい季節は済んだ. 【類】 the *busy season* in trade. ¶at *certain seasons* of the year 一年の一定の季節に. ¶this year's *climbing season* 今年の登山季節. ¶a *close season* for *ayu* fishing is prescribed from ... to ... あゆの禁漁期は...から...までと規定されている. ¶owing to the approach of the *cold season* 冬季が近づいたので. ¶stay over the *coldest season* 越冬する. ¶this *coming season* 今度のシーズン. ¶the *dead season* 霜がれ時. ¶at *different seasons* of the year 一年の中の別別の季節に. ¶the *dry season* 乾燥期. ¶in *due season* 時機が来れば. ¶a *dull season* [旅館などの]客の少ない季節. ¶at *each season* 季節ごとに. ¶The *season* is *early*. 季節が早い. ¶June is London's *fashionable season*. 六月はロンドンで上流人士が活動する季節だ. ¶Spring and summer are the *favorite seasons* for committing suicide. 春と夏は自殺のよくある季節だ. ¶at *festival seasons* 祭典の季節に. ¶a *festive season* 祝節. ¶the *four seasons* of the year 四季(春夏秋冬). ¶in *good season*=in good time 好時機に. ¶during the *high season* 出盛り中 ‖ The resort was then at its *highest season*. その遊び場はそのときが盛りであった. ¶in the *hot season* 夏場は. ¶There is no *off season* for France. フランスには季節はずれの時はない(いつ行ってもよい). ‖ in the *off season* シーズンオフには ‖ This year is *off season* for fruit. 今年は果物ははずれた. ¶the *oncoming* (=*forthcoming*) *season* 今度の季節. ¶the *open season* for trout ます解禁期. ¶do it at the *proper season* それを適当の時期にやる. ¶the *publishing season* 出版季節. ¶the *rainy* (=*wet*) *season* 雨季. ¶the *revolving seasons* めぐる四季. ¶like the animal in the *rutting season* 交尾期の動物のように. ¶in the *slack season* 不景気な季節に. ¶The *stormy season* is now upon us. 暴風雨の季節が迫っている. ¶the 1948-56 *theatrical season* 一九四八年-五六年の観劇シーズン. ¶this very *trying season* この非常に苦しい季節. ¶The *season* is yet *young*. その季期になってからまだ間がない.

Q² during the *blossom season* 花の季節には. ¶in the *breeding season* 繁殖期に. ¶at the *cherry season* さくらんぼのしゅんには; [桜の]花時には. ¶a gift bazaar for the *Christmas season* クリスマスの贈答品市. ¶the *Christmas shopping season* クリスマス売出しの季節. ¶The *climbing season* at Mt. Fuji opened yesterday. 富士の山開きは昨日だった. 【類】 the best *climbing season*. ¶the *football* (*baseball*) *season* しゅう球(など)シーズン. ¶the *game season* 狩猟期. ¶the *harvest season* 収穫(とり入り)の季節. ¶at *holiday* (=*vacation*) *seasons* 休暇旅行のシーズンには. ¶the *London season* ロンドンの社交季節. ¶the *nesting season* [鳥の]巣ごもり期. ¶This is the farewell *New York season* of the troupe. これはその一座のニューヨークお名残

り興行だ. ¶the ***pairing*** (=***coupling***) *season* 交尾期.【類】A bird loses its sexual plumage when the ***pairing*** *season* is over. ¶the ***peach*** *season* ももの季節. ¶the ***seaside*** *season* 海水浴の季節. ¶the ***shooting*** *season* opens today. 狩猟はきょう解禁となった. ¶at the ***spawning*** *season* 産卵期に. ¶a resort with a ***summer*** and a ***winter*** *season* 夏冬ともによい保養地. ¶the ***swim*** *season* 水泳シーズン. ¶a ***tourist*** *season* 旅行シーズン, 観光シーズン.【類】The 1950 ***tourist*** *season* was a success. ¶the opening of the ***trout fishing*** *season* ます解禁. ¶the ***whaling*** *season* 捕鯨期. ¶the ***working*** *season* 作業季節(季節労働者などの).

P It is ***about*** the *season* for cherries. そろそろ桜んぼの季節だ. ¶***according to*** the *season* 季節に従って. ¶***at*** any *season* of the year 一年中いつでも ‖ ***at*** this *season* of the year この季節に ‖ Japanese landscapes ***at*** all *seasons* of the year 四季の日本風景.【類】There is a festival ***at*** every *season*. / Have you ever been in this part ***at*** the cherry *season*? ¶The flowers have come out ***before*** their *season*. 花が季節よりも早く咲いた. ¶***behind*** the *season* 季節遅れに. ¶***during*** the "off" *season* 季節はずれの間. ¶***for*** a brief *season* 短期間. ¶be very warm (cold) ***for*** the *season* 季節にしては大変暖かい(寒い).【類】Isn't it warm ***for*** the *season* right now? / It is very dry ***for*** this *season* of the year. ¶a word ***in season*** 時宜を得た忠告 ‖ Strawberries are ***in season*** now. いちごは今が旬(しゅん)だ. ‖ The farmer is a busy man ***in season***. 農夫は季節になると忙しい. ‖ Fishes are ***in season*** for the table. 魚類は今や食いごろだ. ‖ ***in season*** from ... to ... ...から...までが季節 ‖ ***in*** all *seasons* 四季ともに. ¶***in*** and ***out of*** *season*=season in and season out 季節を論ぜず(いつでも). ¶***on*** a *season* ある時, いつか. ¶Fruits ***out of*** *season* require more skill and cultivation to force them. 季節外の果実はその促成のために一層の熟練と栽培を必要とする. ‖ The fish is ***out of*** *season*. その魚は旬(しゅん)はずれだ. ¶***through*** the four *seasons* 四季を通じて.

P² the *season* ***for*** a journey 旅行の好時節.【類】It is just the *season* ***for*** shooting now. / Mid-autumn, not late spring, is the proper *season* ***for*** transplanting (移植). / Is this the *season* ***for*** clams (oysters, salmon)? ¶the *season* ***of*** flowers 花の季節 ‖ Christmas, the *season* ***of*** good will 親善の季節クリスマス. ¶The open *season* ***on*** turkey is from Dec. 26 to Jan. 2. 七面鳥の季節は十二月二十六日から一月二日までである.

O The trout *season* is on (off). ますの季節だ(終った).

season, *v.* 味をつける; 慣らす.

M ***highly seasoned*** dishes 強く味をつけた料理.

P utter platitudes *seasoned* ***by*** epigram 陳腐な話にぴりっとわさびをきかせる. ¶He is *seasoned* ***for*** the passage. 彼は(身体が)航海に差支えなくなっている. ¶*season* oneself ***to*** cold (heat, hunger) 寒気(など)に身をならす.【類】They *seasoned* themselves ***to*** the rigorous climate. ¶*season* food ***with*** salt (pepper, vinegar) 塩(など)で食物に味をつける ‖ a statement *seasoned* ***with*** humor ユーモア混りの説明.【類】a conversation *seasoned* ***with*** wit.

seasoning, *n.* 味付け.

V ***add*** *seasoning* 味をつける.

seat, *n.* 座席, 地位; 議席; 場所; 邸宅.

V *Seats* are ***assigned*** according to priority of orders. [劇場などの]席は申込順できめる. ¶***book*** *seats* in a theatre 劇場の座席を取る.【類】***book*** one's *seat* at a cinema (the box-office). / *Seats* must be ***booked*** in advance (前もって). ¶***buy*** a country *seat* いなかの庭園付屋敷を買う. ¶***change*** *seats* with ... ...と座席を変える. ¶The hall ***contains*** *seats* for about 3,000 persons. その会館には約三千人の座席がある. ¶***contest*** a *seat* in the Diet 国会の議席を争う. ¶***engage*** a *seat* in the train 汽車の座席を取っておく. ¶***establish*** the *seat* of the league その同盟の本部を設置する. ¶I wonder if we can ***find*** good *seats*. 良い席があるだろうか. ¶***get*** a *seat* in a car 車内で座席が取れる. ¶He was ***given*** a *seat* of honor. 彼は上座にすえられた. ‖ ***give*** one's *seat* in a street car to a woman 市電で婦人に席をゆずる. ¶***give up*** one's *seat* in a crowded streetcar for an old woman. ¶He ***has*** a *seat* on the executive board. 彼は幹部のいすを占めている. ‖ ***Have*** your *seats*, gentlemen. 皆さん御着席願います.【類】He ***has*** a *seat* on the Commission. / ***have*** a *seat* in Parliament (the Cabinet) ‖ It ***has*** its *seat* in London. それはロンドンに本部がある. ‖ He ***has*** a *seat* in Norfolk. 彼はノーフォークに屋敷を持っている. ‖ The disease probably ***has*** its *seat* in the brain. その病気は多分脳が原因だろう. ¶He ***held*** the *seat* till the last general election. 彼はこの前の総選挙まで議席を有していた. ¶His directorships ***include*** a *seat* on the Hudson Bay Company. 彼はハドソン・ベイ会社の重役もやっている. ¶***Keep*** your *seat*. どうぞそのままに(席を離れず). ‖ He has ***kept*** his *seat* for fifteen years. 彼は十五年勤続した. ‖ ***keep*** *seats* for one's companions つれのために席を取っておく. ¶***leave*** (=***quit***) one's *seat* 座を立つ. ¶He has ***lost*** his *seat* in Parliament. 《英》国会の席を失った. ¶He has ***obtained*** a *seat* in his Majesty's Government. 彼は政府の役人になった. ‖ ***obtain*** a *seat* in Parliament 《英》国会議員になる. ¶the unpleasantness of the sensation felt on ***occupying*** a *seat* still warm from the body of another person 他の人の体熱の温みがまださめない席にすわるときの不愉快な感じ. ¶It is a man's duty to ***offer*** his *seat* in the train to a woman. 汽車内で婦人に席を譲るのは男子の義務だ. ¶***provide*** a *seat* 座を設ける. ¶***reserve*** *seats* [劇場などの]席を予約する. ¶***resign*** one's *seat* [国会議員など]辞職する. ¶***resume*** one's *seat* 復席する. ¶***retain*** a *seat* 座席を取っておく. ¶***secure*** a *seat* in the bus バス内に座席を取る. ¶*Seat* will be ***sold*** in all parts of the theatre for 200 yen. その劇場の席料は二百円均一. ¶***snap up*** the best *seats* for ... ...のために一番よい席を急いで取る. ¶***surrender*** one's *seat* 席を譲る. ¶Pray ***take*** a *seat*. どうぞお掛け下さい.【類】***take*** one's *seat* again on one's chair / ***take*** a *seat* by the hearth / All *seats* are ***taken*** (予約済み). ‖ Russia refused to ***take*** a *seat* in the commission. ロシアは委員会参加を拒んだ. ¶***vacate*** one's *seat* on a council 評議員の職を辞する. ¶He failed to ***win*** a *seat* in the Diet in the general election. 彼は総選挙で落選した. ‖ The opposition ***won*** 57 *seats*. 野党は(選挙で)五十七の議席を獲得した.

V² Does this *seat* ***belong*** to anybody? この席にはどなたかおいででしょうか. ¶A *seat* ***costs*** ¥6.30. 一人席料六円三十銭(劇場など). ¶The *seats* in the large enclosure immediately round the bandstand soon ***fill***. その音楽堂の広い囲い内の座席はじきに満員になる.

Q ***ancient*** *seats* of civilization 古代文明の所在地. ¶take a ***back*** *seat* 後の方の席につく; 引立たない. ¶***bad*** *seats* with a bad view of the screen 映画がよく見えない悪い席. ¶a ***berthable*** *seat* [旅客機などの]寝台兼用いす. ¶the ***chief*** *seat* of commerce 商業の中心地 ‖ the ***chief*** *seat* of the ... manufacture ...工業の本場. ¶a ***comfortable*** *seat* 気持のよい席. ¶a ***cushioned*** (=***padded***) *seat* しとね付の座席. ¶Here the beggar takes his ***daily*** *seat*. そのこじきはいつもここに陣取っている. ¶Belgium is an ***early*** *seat* of the iron manufacture. ベルギーは早くから製鉄事業の行われた土地だ.【類】Bizen was one of the ***earliest*** *seats* of the manufacture of pottery in Japan. / the ***early*** *seat* of this manufacture. ¶The performance was a failure, and there were ***empty*** *seats* galore. その興行は失敗で席はがらあきであった. ¶As a matter of course, reporters are given ***front*** *seats* at almost every kind of public occasion. 当然新聞記者はほとんどすべての公開の席で前列の座席を与えられる. ¶***inexpensive*** *seats* [劇場などの]安直な座席. ¶an ***inside*** *seat* in a coach 乗合馬車の中の方の席. ¶Canterbury is the ecclesiastical capital of England, being the ***oldest*** *seat* of Christianity in that country. カンタベリはその国で一番古くキリスト教の行われた所で英国における宗教上の首府である. ¶A district of North Staffordshire called The Potteries is the ***principal*** *seat* of the china and earthenware industry in England. ザ・ポッタリズと称せられるスタッフォードシャの北部地方は英国における陶磁器の本場だ. ¶***reserved*** *seats* 予約席. ¶Peking was the Imperial *seat* of Chinese Emperor. 北京は中国皇帝の王城であった. ¶***tiered*** *seats* in the bleachers 外野の階段席.【類】***tiered*** *seats* round an amphitheatre (円形劇場). ¶***unbookable*** *seats* 予約のできない座席. ¶an ***uneasy*** (=***uncomfortable***) *seat* すわり心地の悪い席. ¶an ***unreserved*** *seat* 普通席. ¶an ***upper*** *seat* [劇場の]二階さじき席. ¶***velvet-padded*** *seats* びろうどのしとねの付いた席.

Q² ***back-to-back*** *seats* 背中合わせの席. ¶a ***Cabinet*** *seat* 内閣のいす. ¶a ***councilor*** *seat* 顧問(参事官)のいす. ¶a *country seat* 別荘. ¶of 464 ***Diet seats*** the Socialists got only 90, the Communists 5. 四百六十四議席中社会党は九十，共産党は五をとったに過ぎない. ¶a ***front-row seat*** 前列の席. ¶buy two ***orchestra seats*** 《米》一階前列の二席を買う. ¶a ***ringside seat*** [けん闘などの]リングサイド. ¶a ***school seat*** 学校の所在地. ¶"***tipup" theater seats*** 劇場の上げ起しいす. ¶Some paid $300 and $400 for vantage ***window seats***. [戴冠式の行列などを見るため]窓わきの席に三百ドルから四百ドル払った人もあった.

P The Peace Conference designated Geneva ***as*** the *seat* of the League of Nations. 平和会議はジュネーブを国際連盟の本部に指定した. ¶sit down ***at*** a vacant *seat* 空席にすわる ‖ ***at*** the *seat* of war 戦地で. ¶fall ***from*** one's *seat* with astonishment 驚いていすから落ちる ‖ rise ***from*** one's *seat* 起立する. ¶place ... ***in*** a *seat* ...を座につかせる ‖ sit ***in*** one's *seat* 座席にすわる ‖ The boy squirmed ***in*** his *seat*. 男の子は席でもじもじ身を動かした. ¶a front row ***of*** *seats* 前列の座席. ¶He is just ***off*** his *seat*. 今ちょっと席をはずしています. ¶***on*** the front *seat* of a car 電車の正面の席に. ¶apply an ice-bag ***over*** the *seat* of pain 痛みの箇所に氷のうを当てる. ¶show a person ***to*** a *seat* 座席に人を案内する.

P² take one's *seat* ***at*** table 食卓につく. ¶*seats* ***for*** ladies 婦人席. ¶a *seat* ***in*** reserve 予約席 ‖ hold a *seat* ***in*** the Cabinet 内閣のいすを占める ‖ engage a *seat* ***in*** the train 汽車の席を取っておく ‖ a country-*seat* ***in*** Kent ケント州にある地方紳士の邸宅. ¶a *seat* ***next*** the window [汽車などの]窓際の席. ¶Already in remote antiquity Arabia was the *seat* ***of*** advanced culture. 遠い昔においてすでにアラビアは進歩した文化の国であった. ‖ Williamstown is the *seat* ***of*** Williams College. ウィリアムズタウンはウィリアムズ大学の所在地だ. ‖ the *seat* ***of*** fierce fighting in 1916 一九一六年に激戦のあった場所 ‖ a *seat* ***of*** learning 学問の中心地 ‖ the *seat* and heart ***of*** commerce 商業の中心地 ‖ the *seat* ***of*** gods 高天が原 ‖ a *seat* ***of*** honor 正座 ‖ the *seat* (=theater) ***of*** war 戦争地区(戦区) ‖ the *seat* ***of*** a chair いすの座 ‖ the *seat* ***of*** the pants ずぼんのおしり ‖ the *seat* (=part) ***of*** incessant pain 絶えず痛む箇所. 【類】The stomach is the *seat* ***of*** all ailments (病気). / The capital city of all Canada is Ottawa, *seat* ***of*** government for the Dominion's nine provinces and two territories. / the *seat* ***of*** a university. ¶the driver's *seat* ***on*** a carriage=a cabman's seat 馬車の御者台.

seat, *v.* すわらせる, 就任させる.

M We are ***all seated***. われわれは一同着席している. ¶The disease had become too ***deeply seated*** for recovery. 病はすでにこうもうに入っていたので回復は覚つかなかった. 【類】His influence is ***deeply seated*** in political circles.

P He *seated* himself ***at*** a table (desk). 彼は食卓(など)についた. ¶he was *seated* ***between*** ... 彼は...の間にすわっていた. ¶The hall is *seated* ***for*** three thousand. 会館には三千の座席がある. 【類】a carriage which is *seated* ***for*** five. ¶*seat* oneself ***in*** a chair いすにすわる ‖ be *seated* ***in*** a car 車中の人となる. 【類】A man *seated* ***in*** an office (執務中) is not expected to rise when a woman speaks to him. ¶He *seated* himself ***on*** the bench. 彼はベンチに腰をおろした. ‖ He is *seated* ***on*** a chair (cushion). 彼はいす(など)にすわっている. ‖ He is *seated* ***on*** the back of a bull. 彼は雄牛に乗っている. ‖ *seated* ***on*** their heels 彼らのすぐ後にすわって. ¶The white-headed old man was *seated*—like the Lord Chancellor—***upon*** a bale of wool. 白髪の老人が大法官のように羊毛袋の上にでんとすわっていた.

seaweed, *n.* 海草.

V² rocks with *seaweed* ***growing*** on 海草の生えている岩.

Q ***flavored*** *seaweed* 味付のり.

secede, *v.* 脱退する.

P *secede* ***from*** a political party (an organization, an association) 政党(など)から脱退する.

seceder, *n.* 脱退者.

P a *seceder* ***from*** the party 脱党者.

seclude, *v.* 引込む.

P *seclude* oneself ***from*** the world 世間から引込む(隠退する). 【類】live *secluded* ***from*** the world.

seclusion, *n.* 隠退.

V ***keep*** one's *seclusion* from the world 世間から隠退している. ¶***seek*** the *seclusion* of one's cabin 自分の船室に引込む. ¶Japan ***shook off*** her *seclusion* and voluntarily adopted the most vital parts of Western civilization. 日本はその鎖国主義を振り捨て進んで西洋文明の最も重要な部分を採り入れた.

Q spend the remainder of one's life in ***pious*** *seclusion* 信心三まいにその余生を送る. ¶be in a ***shy*** *seclusion* [人ぎらいで]引っこんでいる. ¶***thirty days' penitentiary*** *seclusion* 三十日間の謹慎(閉門). ¶the period of Japan's ***voluntary*** *seclusion* 日本の自発的鎖国時代.

P live ***in*** complete *seclusion* 全く世間と離れて生活する. 【類】live ***in*** *seclusion* apart from one's friends. ¶a place ***of*** *seclusion* 隠退所 ‖ a policy ***of*** *seclusion* 鎖国政策.

P² live in *seclusion* ***from*** the world 世を捨てる.

second, *n.* 第二位者, 第二流者;〘けん闘〙介添え(セコンド); 補佐.

V ***make*** a close *second* in a race 競技でわずかの差で第二位になる. ¶***take*** *seconds* 再入営する.

Q a ***bad*** *second* 第一位者よりはるかに劣る第二位者. ¶a ***close*** *second* to ... ほとんど...の塁を摩する第二流者 ‖ run a ***close*** *second* 接近した第二位になる. ¶a ***good*** *second* 第一位に余り劣らない第二位者. ¶an ***insignificant*** *second* 徴々たる第二流者. ¶He is ***no man's*** *second* in patriotism. 彼は愛国心においては人後に落ちない. ¶a ***poor*** *second* 第一位者と大差ある第二位者. ¶he proved a most ***useful*** *second* to ... 彼は...にとってふところ刀であることが分った.

P act ***as*** a *second* to a pugilist=second pugilist けん闘選手のセコンドをやる. ¶his *second* ***in*** command 彼の副官.

second, *a.* 第二位の.

P *second* ***in*** hardness only ***to*** the diamond 硬度は金剛石を除いて一番の ‖ *second* ***to*** none 一番の. 【類】*second* ***in*** importance only ***to*** ... / Germany is *second* ***to*** the United States ***in*** glass production. / a country *second* ***to*** none ***in*** resources (資源) / give it a place *second* ***to*** none / In those days of chivalry (武士制度) fencers were *second* ***to*** none ***in*** popular esteem (世人の尊重).

second, *v.* 補助する; 仮転勤する.

P It was *seconded* ***by*** government assistance. それは政府の補助があった. ¶be *seconded* ***for*** service on the staff 参謀本部付を命ぜられる. ¶*second* words ***with*** deeds 行いで言葉を補う.

second, *n.* 秒; 少時.

Q ***every*** *second* 刻々. ¶She lingered a few ***leisurely*** *seconds*. 彼女は二三秒(辞去するのを)ためらっていた. ¶in a ***split*** *second* たちまち, 突如.

P I can't do without it ***for*** a *second*. 私はすこしの間もそれなしでは済まされない. ¶Flames licked up a row of buildings ***in*** a *second*. 火炎は瞬間に一並びの建物をなめ尽した. ‖ ***in*** a few *seconds* 数秒間に.

secondary, *a.* 第二の; 副次的の.

P rather *secondary* ***in*** meaning (importance) むしろ第二義(など)的な. ¶a case of atrophy of the reproductive organs *secondary* ***to*** diabetes 糖尿病に付随する生殖器萎縮の一例.

second-hand, *n.* 古手物, 中古品.

V I ***want*** a *second-hand*. 私は古手がほしい.

P buy books ***at*** *second-hand* 古本を買う ‖ deal in eminent scholars' views ***at*** *second-hand* 著名学者の意見を受売する ‖ information obtained ***at*** *second-hand*=second-hand information 間接に得た情報.

second-hand, *a., ad.* 古手の(で).

O buy books *second-hand* 本を古で買う.

secrecy, *n.* 秘密.

V ***ensure*** absolute *secrecy* 絶対秘密を保証する. ¶***maintain*** *secrecy* about ... ...について秘密を守る. ¶Absolute *secrecy* is ***observed***. 絶対秘密が守られている. ¶A wonderful *secrecy* is ***preserved*** with regard to all that pertains to these meetings. これらの会合に関する一切の件は驚くほどに秘密が守られている. ¶***swear*** most perfect *secrecy* 絶対秘密を誓う.

Q the maintenance of ***complete*** *secrecy* concerning ... ...に関する秘密の厳守. ¶***Strict*** *secrecy* is observed in connection with depositors' accounts. 預金者の勘定に関しては秘密を厳守する(銀行などで).

P The proceedings were conducted ***in*** profound *secrecy*. 議事は極秘の内に行われた. ¶Conspirators were sworn ***to*** *secrecy*. 陰謀の仲間は秘密を守ることを誓わされた. ¶The conference was held ***with*** elaborate *secrecy*. 会議はつとめて秘密に行われた.

P^2 *secrecy* ***of*** letters 信書の秘密.

secret, *n.* 秘密, 密事; 秘けつ.

V ***break*** a *secret* 秘密を漏らす. ¶***confide*** one's *secret* to … …に秘密を打明ける. ¶The following few rules ***contain*** the *secret* of correct book-keeping. 次の数則に正確な簿記の秘けつが載せてある. ¶***disclose***(=***expose***) a *secret* 秘密をあばく. ¶he ***discovered*** the *secret* of the manufacture of… 彼は…製造の秘けつを発見した. 【類】***discover*** the *secret* of perpetual youth (不老). ¶***divulge*** (=let out) a *secret* to … …に秘密を漏す. ¶***explore*** *secrets* 秘密を探査する. ¶***ferret out*** *secrets* 秘密を探り出す. ¶The *secret* was ***found out***. 秘密が分かった. ¶***give away*** one's *secret* その秘密を漏らす. ¶jealously ***guard*** a *secret* 後生大事に秘密を守る. 【類】***guard*** the *secrets* of its production (製作の秘けつ) with the most jealous care. ¶***guess*** the *secret* その秘密を察しる. ¶They ***have*** no *secrets* from each other. 彼らはお互になんの隠し立てもしない. 【類】You are my second self (腹心の友), from whom I ***have*** no *secrets*. ‖ Oh, I ***have*** the *secret*! ああ(そのこつが)分かった. ☞I have it! ともいう. ¶rigidly ***keep*** a *secret* 秘密を厳守する ‖ ***keep*** one's *secret* deeply in one's breast 密事を胸の内に深く秘めておく. 【類】***keep*** a *secret* very closely to oneself ‖ I ***keep*** nothing a *secret* from you. 私は君にはなにも隠しだてはしない. ‖ He ***kept*** the *secret* to himself. 彼は秘密を胸にたたんでおいた. ¶I ***know*** his *secret*. 私は彼の秘密を知っている. ¶***lay bare*** (=***discover***) the *secrets* of nature 自然の神秘をうかがう. ¶He was on the point of ***letting out*** the *secret*, when he checked himself. 彼はすんでのことに秘密を漏らす所であったが気が付いて差控えた. ‖ Mind you; don't ***let*** the *secret* ***out***. いいかね, 秘密をもらしちゃいかん. ¶***lock*** a *secret* in one's breast 秘密を胸に秘めておく. ¶***make*** a *secret* of … …を秘する ‖ ***make*** no *secret* of one's ignorance 知らないことは知らないと言う. ¶You have ***mastered*** the *secret* and made it your own. 君はその秘けつをのみ込んでお手のものにした. ¶***offer*** French naval *secrets* to Germany ドイツにフランス海軍の秘密を提供する. ¶he ***passed*** the *secret* of his formula ***on*** to… 彼はその製法の秘密を…に伝えた. ¶***penetrate*** the *secret* of … …の秘密を見抜く. ¶***pluck*** Nature's *secrets* from her repository 自然の宝庫からその秘密物を奪い取る. ¶The Japanese alone ***possess*** this *secret*. 日本人だけがこの秘けつを知っている. ¶***preserve*** (=***retain***) another's *secret* 他人の秘密を守る. ¶***reveal*** the *secrets* of Nature 自然界の秘密をあばく ‖ ***reveal*** the *secret* of one's sex 女(男)装を見やぶる. ¶***smell out*** *secrets* 秘密をかぎ出す. ¶Never ***talk*** *secrets* ***before*** a child. 子供の前で秘密を話すな. ¶***tell*** *secrets* to … …に秘密を話す. ¶***trace*** the *secret* その秘密を探る. ¶***unlock*** the *secrets* of … …の秘けつを発見する. ¶***unroll*** the *secrets* of the human mind 人心の機微を啓(ひら)く. ¶***win*** from nature her inmost *secrets* 自然の神秘の奥底を見届ける. ¶Nature has contrived to ***withhold*** the *secret* from man's prying eyes for such a long time. 自然はこんなに長い間人類のせんさく好きな目にその秘密を見抜かれないように工夫した. ¶***worm out*** a *secret* こっそり秘密を探り出す. ¶He ***wrested*** the *secret* from me. 彼は無理やり私に秘密を漏らさせた. 【類】***wrest*** scientific *secrets* from nature. ¶***wring*** from Nature her jealously guarded *secrets* 自然がとらの子のように隠しておいた密事を無理やりにあかさせる. ¶***yield up*** *secrets* 秘密をあかす.

V^2 The *secret* ***leaked*** (=***oozed or slipped***) ***out***. その秘密が漏れた.

Q It is kept a ***close*** *secret*. それは極秘になっている. ¶***diplomatic*** *secrets* 外交上の秘密. ¶a ***disgraceful*** *secret* 不名誉な秘密. ¶a carefully ***guarded*** *secret* 厳秘. ¶an ***individual*** *secret* 一個人の秘密. ¶an ***inner*** *secret* 奥にひそんだ秘密. ¶***inside*** *secrets* 内部の秘密. ¶The process of manufacture is a ***jealously-guarded*** *secret*. その製法は絶対に他に漏らさない秘密である. ¶a ***military*** *secret* 軍機. ¶it is ***no*** *secret* that … …は世人周知のことだ. ¶It is now an ***open*** *secret* that these two ministers are to exchange posts at once. この二大臣が入替えになるということは今や公然の秘密だ. ¶***professional*** *secrets* 職務上の秘密. ¶keep it a ***profound*** *secret* それを厳秘に付する. ¶It has long been a ***public*** *secret* of the photo-play world that a good cameraman can make or break an actor. 腕のある撮影技師なら俳優を生かすも殺すも自由だということは長い間映画界公然の秘密になっている. ¶an ***ugly*** *secret* 醜悪な秘密. ¶***valuable*** *secrets* 貴重な秘けつ. ¶The ***whole*** *secret* of oratory is to feel passionately.—Mirabeau. 雄弁の秘けつは自ら熱情を持つことである.

Q^2 disclose ***atom*** *secrets* to Russia ロシアに原子の秘密を漏らす. ¶the retention of the ***atomic bomb*** *secret* 原子爆弾秘密の保有. ¶reveal ***atomic bomb production*** *secrets* 原子爆弾生産の機密を漏らす. ¶***atomic research*** *secrets* 原子研究の秘密. ¶***bosom*** *secrets* 胸に秘めた密事. ¶let out valuable ***business*** *secrets* 大事な商売上の秘密を漏らす. 【類】the disclosure of valuable ***business*** *secrets* / procure the ***business*** or ***trade*** *secrets* of competitors by espionage (スパイで). ¶an ***office*** *secret* 職務上の秘密. ¶pass ***state*** *secrets* to a foreign government 国家の機密を他国に漏らす. ¶an open, well-gossiped ***town*** *secret* 公然と相当話題になっている町の秘密.

P She wept ***in*** *secret*. 彼女はひそかに泣いた. ‖ people ***in*** the *secret* その秘密を知っている人々 ‖ keep one's picture ***in*** *secret* その写真を隠しておく. ¶pry ***into*** a *secret* 秘密をほじくる. ¶an iron box ***with*** a *secret* to its lock 錠前に仕掛のある鉄の箱.

P^2 Let this be a *secret* ***between*** you and me. これは君と僕と二人きりで承知していることにしておこう. ¶*secrets* ***for*** the cure of disease 療法の秘けつ. ¶the *secrets* ***of*** nature 自然の妙法 ‖ The *secret* of success is constancy to purpose. 成功の秘けつは目的を変えないことだ. 【類】the *secret* ***of*** his strength (longevity, youth, health) / Christanity is the *secret* ***of*** the highest civilization. / Equality between the sexes is the *secret* ***of*** married happiness.

O The *secret* is out. 秘密が漏れた.

secret, *a.* 秘密な; 不思議な.

M It is to be kept ***absolutely*** *secret*. それは絶対秘密だ. ¶make it ***strictly*** *secret* それを絶対に伏せておく.

P There is nothing *secret* ***about*** it. それにはなにも不思議なことはない.

secretary, *n.* 書記官, 幹事; 大臣.

Q a ***chief*** *secretary* 書記長, 幹事長. ¶a ***commercial*** *secretary* [大公使館の]商務書記官. ¶a ***corresponding*** *secretary* 通信係. ¶an ***executive*** *secretary* 主事. ¶a ***financial*** *secretary* 財務書記官. ¶a ***first*** (***second, third***) *secretary* of the embassy 大使館一(二・三)等書記官 ‖ Mr.—, ***First*** *Secretary* of the Communist Party 共産党第一書記…氏. ¶a ***general*** *secretary* 書記長. ¶an ***honorary*** *secretary* 名誉幹事. ¶an ***interim*** *secretary* 臨時書記官. ¶a ***parliamentary*** *secretary* 政務次官. ¶He is ***private*** *secretary* to the Minister. 彼はその大臣の秘書官だ. ¶a ***recording*** *secretary* 記録係. ¶a ***social*** *secretary* [従業員]厚生部主任. ¶an ***unpaid*** *Secretary* in the U.S. war Cabinet 米戦時内閣の無給(名誉職)長官.

Q^2 the Chief ***Cabinet*** *Secretary* 官房長官. ¶a ***class*** *secretary* クラス委員. ¶a ***court*** *secretary* 裁判所事務官. ¶a President's (White House) ***press*** *secretary* 大統領の新聞秘書. ¶a ***school*** *secretary* 学校の主事. ¶the ***State*** *Secretary* (=the Secretary of State) 《米》国務長官.

P^2 act ***as*** *secretary* to … …の秘書を勤める. ¶a *secretary* ***of*** the society その協会幹事 ‖ the *Secretary* ***of*** State 《米》国務長官; 《英》国務相 ‖ the *Secretary* ***of*** the Interior (the Treasury, Agriculture, Commerce, Labor, Defense, etc.) [米国]米国務(など)長官. ¶Mr. —, *secretary* ***to*** the Education Department 文部書記官—氏 ‖ a *secretary* ***to*** the Royal Geographical Society 王立地理学協会幹事.

secretary-general, *n.* 事務総長.

Q the ***first*** *Secretary-General* of the United Nations 第一次国連事務総長.

secretion, *n.* 分泌.

Q^2 ***hormone*** *secretion* ホルモンの分泌. ¶a suspension of the ***milk*** *secretion* 乳分泌の閉止.

sect, *n.* 宗派; 学派.

Q a ***depraved*** *sect* 邪宗. ¶***medical*** *sects* (allopathy, homeopathy, electrotherapy, osteopathy) [対症療法・同種療法・電気療法・整骨法のごとき]医療科目.

Q^2 the ***Jodo*** *sect* 浄土宗.

section, *n.* 部分, 部門; 項, 課(部); 派.

Q in ***all*** *sections* of our land わが国至るところ. ¶the business and ***industrial*** *sections* of the city その市の商工区域. ¶These books deserve a place in the ***active*** *section* of one's library shelves. これらの本は書架の常用部に備付

ける価値がある. ¶the *conservative section* 保守派. ¶a rail in *cross section* 軌条の断面図. ¶the most *crowded section* of a large city 大都市の最も繁華な街. ¶a *cyclic section* 週期(循環期). ¶the *Eastern* and *Midwestern sectinos* of the United States 米国の東部及び中西部. ¶the *enlightened section* of the people 人民のインテリ層. ¶a *large section* of the citizens 平民の大部分. ¶in the *farming sections* of Poland ポーランドの農業地域. ¶a *longitudinal* (=*lengthwise*) *section* 縦断面. ¶an *oblique section* 斜断面. ¶The European *residential section* of Yokohama is known as the "Bluff." 横浜の外人住宅区域を「山手」といっている. ¶a *Secretarial Section* 秘書課. ¶a *transverse section* 横断面. ¶a *vertical section* 縦横面. ¶in *warm sections* of the country [その国の]温暖地方では.

Q^2 an *accounts* (=accounting) *section* 《米》会計課. ¶an *administration section* 管理部. ¶an *amnesty section* 恩赦課. ¶a *business* or '*down-town*' *section* 商業地区即ち下町方面. ¶a *data section* 資料課. ¶an *information section* 情報部. ¶an *inspection section* 監察課. ¶a *liaison section* 渉外課. ¶a *personnel affairs section* 人事課. ¶the *photogravure picture section* of the New York Times ニューヨークタイムス紙のグラビヤ写真版. ¶the *Protection* and *Guidance Section* 補導課. ¶the *residence sections* of the city 都市の住宅地域. ¶the *statistics section* 統計課. ¶the *supplies section* 用度課. ¶the *terrorist* (militant) *section* of anarchism 無政府主義のテロ派. ¶the *Welfare* and *Health Section* 養護課.

P *in* all the *sections* of the public 公衆のすべての層に. ¶a bookcase built *in sections* 組立式の本箱.

sectionalism, *n.* なわ張り根性(セクショナリズム).

Q *bureaucratic sectionalism* 官界のセクショナリズム.

sector, *n.* 扇形地区.

Q^2 the four *Allied sectors* of Berlin ベルリンの四連合国分割占領地区. ¶an *amusement sector* さかり場, 歓楽街.

secure, *a.* 危険のない, 安全な.

P *secure against* the attacks of the enemy 敵の攻撃を受ける恐れのない. ¶*secure from* invasion (attack, harm, danger, interruption) 侵略などの憂いのない ‖ an excellent port *secure from* every wind どんな風にも安全な良港. 【類】be *secure from* any loss at sea. ¶*secure of* advantage 有利なこと疑いない ‖ *secure of* a welcome 歓迎されるに相違ない ‖ be *secure of* his livelihood 生活の安定を得ている. 【類】You may feel perfectly *secure of* one thing. / Nobody is here *secure of* life. / be *secure of* advantage over … …より優位を確保されている.

secure, *v.* 防護する; 担保におく.

M *Secure* your tickets *early.* 早目に切符を買っておきなさい.

P *secure us against* (=*from*) our enemies 敵が来てもわれわれを大丈夫にしておく ‖ He has been *secured against* loss by fire. 彼は(所有物に)火災保険を付けた. ‖ be *secured against* damage 損害は保証されている. ¶a city *secured by* fortifications 保塁で防備した都市 ‖ *secure* a debt *by* mortgage 抵当を入れて金を借りる. ¶Please *secure* a seat *for* me. どうぞ私に席を取っておいて下さい. ‖ *Secure* the locks *on* the windows. 窓のかぎを確めなさい. ¶The door is *secured with* bolts. 戸はかんぬきで開かないようになっている.

security, *n.* 安全; 安心; 確実; 担保; 証明.

V The *security* offered will be *accepted.* 提供の担保は承認されるだろう. ¶I must *decline* the *security* offered. 私は提供の担保を拒絶しなければならない. ¶*deposit security* with … …に担保を入れる. 【類】*deposit* ¥600 *security* with … ¶Such offenses as his profoundly *endanger* public security. 彼のこうした罪科は大いに公安を害する. 【類】*endanger* the *security* of the nations. ¶*furnish security* 担保を提供する. ¶*give security* for repayment 借金の担保を入れる ‖ *give security* against … …に対して保護する ‖ *give security* for 5,000 yen 保証金を五千円出す. ¶*go* one's *security* その保証に立つ ‖ *go* (=*stand*) *security* for … …の身元を引受ける. ¶I must *have* some approved *security*. なにか確実な担保を入れてもらいたい. ¶*hold* good *security* よい担保を持っている. ¶*increase* public *security* 治安を強化する. ¶*obtain* the best *security* possible できるだけ良い担保を手に入れる. ¶*offer* a *security* 担保を入れる. 【類】What *security* can you *offer* for it? ¶*threaten* its national *security* その国家を危くする.

Q lend money on *ample security* 十分な担保で金を貸す ‖ must have good *ample security* 十分確実な担保をとらねばならない. ¶The *security* is only *apparent* and *illusory*. 安全と思われるのは全く外見的で錯覚的である. ¶*approved securities* 受諾した担保. ¶You may safely accept orders from him without *collateral security*. 彼からの注文は見返り担保なしで引受けても大丈夫だ. ¶*convertible securities* 引換有価証券. ¶*double securities* 二重担保. ¶*dividend-paying securities* 配当のある証券. ¶*economic security* 経済保障. ¶*fatal security* 空頼み. ¶Do not deliver the bill of lading without *full security*. 十分の担保なしで船荷証券(荷為替)を引渡してはならない. ¶*gilt-edged securities* 一流証券. ¶He lends money on *good security*. 彼は確実な担保で金を貸す. ¶*good* and *sufficient security* 確実で満足な担保. ¶a position of *great security* きわめて安全な地位. 【類】A well-informed public is the world's *greatest security*. ¶deposit *heavy securities* for … …に対して十分の担保を入れる. ¶endanger *internal security* 国内治安を脅かす. ¶*material security* 物質的保証(担保). ¶a menace to our *national security* われわれの国家的保安に対する脅威. ¶give the *necessary security* 必要な担保を入れる. ¶a *negotiable security* 有価証券. ¶a *personal security* 対人担保, 対人信用. ¶The *security* is *poor*. その担保は貧弱だ. ¶give *satisfactory security* 満足な担保を入れる. ¶*social security* 社会保障. ¶a *substantial* and *undeniable security* 実価のあるりっぱな担保. ¶*tax-exempt* (=*non-taxable*) *securities* 免税証券. ¶a *valuable security* 有価証券.

Q^2 *employment* (=*job*) *security* 就職保証. ¶*government securities* 公債. ¶*railroad securities* 《米》鉄道の株券. ¶offer the real danger to *world security* 世界の安全保障にとって真に危険性をはらむ.

P deposit bonds with a creditor *as security* 担保として有価証券を債権者に預ける ‖ give (receive) … *as security* …を担保に入れる(取る). ¶live *in* peace and *security* 安泰に暮らす. ¶borrow (advance) money *on* (=*upon*) [the] *security* of … …の担保で金を借りる(貸す). ¶lull a person *to security* 人を安心させる. ¶borrow money *without security* 無担保で金を借りる.

P^2 Insurance is *security against* loss. 保険は損害に対する保証だ. ‖ No *security against* "line tapping" and "listening-in" is afforded by the telephone. 電話では盗聴や(他人の)聴取がないとは保証できない. ¶*security for* life and property 生命財産に対する保証 ‖ *security for* good conduct 〖労〗身元保証 ‖ become *security for* a friend 友人の保証人になる. 【類】*security for* the payment of a debt. ¶*security of* reward 報酬の確実性. ¶*Security to* life and property was obtained. 生命財産に対する保証が得られた.

sediment, *n.* おり, よどみ.

V The *sediment* of wine *settles*. 酒のおりはよどむ.

sedition, *n.* 反乱, 暴動.

V *foment* (=*stir up*) *sedition* 反乱を扇動する.

seduce, *v.* 誘う; たぶらかす; おびき出す.

M The pleasant air *seduced* me *abroad.* 気持の好い外気に誘われて表へ出た. ¶She was *seduced alright* by his honeyed words. 彼女は彼のうまい口にすっかりたらしこまれた.

P *seduce* a girl *by* fair speech 甘口で女をたらし込む. ¶*seduce* him *from* his home 彼を家から誘かいする. ¶His doctrines have *seduced* many *into* error. 彼の説は多くの人を誤らせた. ¶*seduce* him *out of* the right way 彼をたぶらかして邪道に踏入らせる. ¶They *seduced* him *to* (=into) the other party. 彼らは彼をくどいて他党へ引入れた.

see, *v.* 見る, [物が]見える; 察知する, 会う; 見送る.

M I *saw* him *aboard.* 彼を船まで見送った. ¶Well, so long. *See* you *again* tomorrow. あばよ, またあしたあおうぜ. ¶I couldn't *see* a foot *ahead.* 一尺先も見えなかった. ¶I wish to *see* you *alone.* あなただけにお目にかかりたい. ¶I have not *seen* you *a long while.* 久しくお目にかかりませんでした. ¶I *saw at a glance* that … 私は一見して…と見て取った. ¶I *saw* the boy *beaten.* 私は男の子が打たれたのを見た. ¶I never *saw* him *before*. 私は一度も彼に会ったことはない. ¶The owl *sees best* at night. ふくろは夜が一番よく見える. ¶I *clearly see* that … 私は…だとはっきり見ている. ¶Even the finest landscape, *seen daily,* becomes monotonous どんなに美しい風景でも毎日見ていると単調になる. ¶*see deeply* into things 物事を深く考察する. ¶I *see* life *dif-*

ferently now. 僕の人生観は前と違って来た. ¶be ***dimly seen*** ほの見える. ¶I can *see* it ***distinctly***. 私にそれがはっきり見える. ¶One may *see* ***double*** when drunk. 酔っぱらうと物が二つに見える. ¶Have you *seen* ***enough***? もう十分見たか. ¶no one ***ever*** *saw* ... だれも...を見たものはない. ¶*see* ***fair*** 中立の態度を取って黒白を判断する. ¶A hungry man *sees* ***far***. 腹がすいた人は遠目がきく. ‖ *see* ***far*** in the distance はるかかなたを見る.【類】*see* ***far ahead*** in life. ¶those who can *see* ***farther*** than others 先見の明ある人々. ¶I *saw* him ***for the first time***. 私は彼に始めて会った. ¶I *see* it ***fit*** to say something. 当然なにか一言すべきだと考える.【類】You may go if you *see* ***fit*** to do so. ¶I *saw* her safely ***home***. 私は彼女を無事宅まで送り届けた. ¶To the poet is accorded the high faculty of *seeing* the truth ***intuitively***. 詩人には真理を直覚的に悟るという高度の機能が与えられている. ¶***Kindly*** *see* that our wishes are regarded. われわれの念願が尊重されることを望みます. ¶When did you ***last*** *see* him? この前あの人に会ったのはいつですか.【類】It is a long time since I *saw* him ***last***. / the baggage was ***last*** *seen* at ... ¶I have not *seen* much of him ***lately***. 私はこのごろ彼に余り会わない. ¶*See* you ***later*** (***tomorrow***). あとで会おう(あすまた会おう). ¶I ***never*** *saw* anything of the sort before. そういう物はまだ見たことがない. ‖ I ***never*** *saw* a greater man. あんな偉い人は見たことがない. ‖ She was ***never*** *seen* angry. 彼女の怒った顔を見た人はなかった. ‖ He will ***never*** *see* 60 again. 彼はもう六十を越している. ¶He is *seen* ***no more***. 彼はもう見られない(死んだ). ¶I have ***often*** *seen* him of late. 私は近ごろ度々彼に会った. ¶I am happy to *see* you ***once more***. またお目にかかれてうれしゅうございます. ¶*see* a play ***out*** 芝居を終りまで見る ‖ *see* a person ***out*** (=***off***) at the door 人を玄関まで見送る ‖ *see* it ***out*** 結末まで見る. ¶*See* ***overleaf***. 裏面を見よ. ¶*see* ***plainly*** [それが]はっきり分かる. ¶*see* one ***professionally*** [医師など]職務上人に会う. ¶*see* her ***safely*** into a conveyance 彼女を無事に乗物まで見送る. ¶It is likely that I *saw* him ***somewhere before***. あの方どっかで見たことがあるようだ. ¶it will ***thus*** be *seen* that ... 従って...が明りょうとなるであろう. ¶I will never ***willingly*** *see* him again. 私は二度と彼に会う気にはなれない.

M² *see* her ***off*** into the train 列車に乗るまで見送る.【類】*see* him ***off*** at the station / Many thanks for your kindness in *seeing* me ***off*** at Yokohama. ¶*see* the job ***through*** 仕事をやり通す ‖ Look closer, and you will *see* it ***through***. よく見たらそのことが見抜ける.

P *see* a person ***aboard*** the railway car 人を汽車まで見送る. ¶I will *see* ***about*** it. まあ考えて見ましょう. ¶He hired a man to *see* ***after*** his flock. 彼は羊(やぎなど)の番人を雇った. ‖ Kindly *see* ***after*** my children while I'm away. 留守中は子供をお頼みします. ¶*see* a play ***at*** a theatre 劇場で芝居を見る ‖ It can conveniently be *seen* ***at*** a glance. それはらくに一目で分かるようになっている. ¶*see* ***below*** the surface ***into*** the inner truth 奥底の事実を見抜く. ¶statesmen who *see* ***beyond*** the moment 先見の明ある政治家. ¶It had never been seen ***by*** European eyes. それを欧州人が見たことはまだなかった. ¶I *see* ***from*** my diary that I am expected to see you on Saturday next, but ... 日記を見ると今度の土曜日にお目にかかるはずですが...【類】when first *seen* ***from*** shipboard (甲板から) ‖ ***from*** this it will be *seen* that ... これから...が察せられよう, 従って.【類】it can easily be *seen* ***from*** the fact that ... ‖ Tokyo *seen* ***from*** the air 航空機上から見た東京. ¶*see* one ***in*** one's true colors 人をありのままに見る ‖ I *saw* him ***in*** the street. 私は往来で彼に会った. ‖ *seen* ***in*** this light こう考えて見ると ‖ *see* a person ***in*** the face 人を正視する ‖ Can you *see* anything green ***in*** my eye? そんな甘ちゃんじゃないよ. ‖ one *sees* ***in*** it, telescoped, many of the problems concerning ... その中に...のごたごたの縮図が見られる. ¶I will *see* ***into*** this thing (matter). このことを調べて見ましょう. ‖ the wisdom and power of *seeing* ***into*** the future 将来を洞察するの明. ¶The airship was *seen* ***like*** a speck in the sky. 飛行船は大空に一つの点となって見えた. ¶I don't think we shall *see* anything more ***of*** him today. きょうはもうあの人に会えはしまいと思う. ‖ be anxious to see what there is to be *seen* ***of*** the county 是非その国で見られるものを見たいと思っている ‖ My opinion is that each youth or girl should personally *see* enough ***of*** the other sex at an early period. 少年少女は各幼少の折に異性を十分見ておくべきものだいうのが僕の持論だ. ¶Mind you *see* him ***off*** the premises. 忘れないでお客様のお帰りをお送りするのだよ. ‖ *see* ***off*** a book よそ見をする(本を見ているとき). ¶*see* ***through*** a crack on the wall 壁のすき間からのぞく ‖ Her arms are *seen* ***through*** her thin dress 彼女の腕は薄い衣服からすけて見える. ‖ *see* ***through*** (=finish up) one's literary work 著作を終える ‖ *see* ***through*** one's motives (game, trick) その動機(など)を見抜く.【類】*see* ***through*** what he has in mind ‖ *see* a person ***through*** his trouble (financial difficulties) 人を困難(など)から救い出す. ¶The mother kissed her children and *saw* them ***to*** bed. 母はその子供らにキスしてベッドにつれて行った. ‖ *see* a friend ***to*** the station 友人を停車場まで見送る.【類】*see* her ***to*** her mother's door ‖ I will *see* ***to*** that. そうなるように力を尽しましょう(私に任せない). ‖ he always *saw* ***to*** it that ... 彼はいつも...することに気をくばった.【類】it is his duty to *see* ***to*** it that it should not ... / The employer *sees* ***to*** it that the time he buys is not wasted. / Please *see* ***to*** this immediately. / *See* ***to*** the fire. ‖ *See* ***to*** it, at once! 直ちにやれ. ¶*see* ***with*** clearness 明りょうに見る ‖ *see* ***with*** our eyes われわれの目で見る ‖ *see* ***with*** half an eye ちらと見る.【類】I would not care to be *seen* ***with*** him. / can be *seen* ***with*** naked eyes (肉眼で).

O *See* the dog run. 犬が走るのをご覧なさい.【類】I *saw* them running out at the gate. ¶He was *seen* to walk. 彼が散歩するのを見た者があった. ¶in the picture he is *seen* talking to ... 彼が...に話している所がその写真にのっている. ¶You shall *see*. 今に分かる. ¶I am curious to *see* whether ...かどうだか見たいものだ.【類】it remains to be *seen* whether ... ¶as you *see* ご覧の通り; ご存じの通り. ¶Let me *see*. [考えるとき]こうっと. ‖ Just let ***me*** *see* it. それをちょっと見せてくれ. ¶I *see* it ***necessary*** to ... ...を必要と考える. ¶Please *see* that this seal is to be kept intact. この封が破れないように注意して下さい. ¶we have *seen* it stated that ... ...ということが書いてあるのをどこかで見た. ¶Thy charity is commendable, but *see* that it beginth at home. そなたの慈善は結構だが仁は家庭に始まることが肝要だ.【類】*See* that you do. / *See* that the letter is posted without fail. / I will *see* that everything is properly arranged. / *See* that all the lights and fires are safe before going to bed. / *See* that you return it immediately.

seed, *n*. 種子; 本(もと).

V ***contain*** the *seeds* of another war 戦禍をはらむ. ¶***devour*** the *seed* [鳥が]種をついばむ. ¶***engender seed*** [花など]種子を生じる. ¶Bees help to ***fertilize seed***. みつばちは結実の手伝をする. ¶***grow*** the *seed* from which the oil is extracted その油の取れる種を植える. ¶***plant*** 10 *seeds* in the sand 砂の中に種子を十個まく ‖ ***plant*** the *seeds* of disease 病の種をまく. ¶Farmers ***put*** *seed* in the ground. 農夫は地中に種子をまく. ¶***remove*** *seeds* from a water melon すいかの種をとる. ¶***scatter seeds*** 種をまき散らす. ¶***sow seeds*** in a field 畑に種子をまく.【類】We ***sow*** many *seeds* to obtain a few flowers. ‖ ***sow*** the *seed* of disease 病の種をまく ‖ ***sow*** the good *seed* よい種をまく; 福音を説く.【類】There the *seed* of so much evil is ***sown***. / ***sow*** the *seed* of lofty ideals / This oppression ***sowed*** the *seeds* of the French Revolution. / try to ***sow*** the *seeds* of dissension (不和) / ***sow*** the *seeds* of mutual hatred and distrust between two nations. / ***sow*** the *seeds* of mischief in the hereafter (将来) / ***sow*** the *seeds* of sympathy and understanding (strife and discord) / ***sow*** the *seeds* of world disaster / Youth is the time when *seeds* of character are ***sown***. ¶***spit out seeds*** 種子をはき出す. ¶Successful gardeners always ***test seeds*** before planting. 巧者な庭師はいつもまく前に種子を吟味する. ¶***throw*** the seeds on the ground 地上に種をまく.

V² The *seeds* are ***coming up***. 種子の芽が出て来た. ¶The *seed* ***fell*** on fertile soil, and ***germinated*** and ***developed*** into a healthy plant. その種子がよく土の上に落ち芽を出して見事な木になった. ¶*Seeds* ***grow*** in a fruit 種は果実の中にできる. ¶The *seed* that he sowed will ***ripen***. 彼がまいた種子が成熟するだろう. ¶a *seed* ***sending up*** a stem 茎をのばしつつある種子. ¶The *seed* ***sprouts***. 種が芽を出す.

Q² as large as an ***apricot*** *seed* あんずの種ほどの大きさの. ¶***grain*** *seeds* 穀物の種. ¶***potato*** *seeds* たねいも. ¶a ***hay-***

seed=hayseed《俗》おのぼりさん. ¶scatter ***herb seeds*** 牧草の種をまく.

P It cannot be grown ***from*** *seed.* それは種子からの栽培はできない. ¶it was found ***in*** the *seeds* of ... それは...の種の中にあった. ¶press oil ***out of*** the *seeds* of ... ...の種から油をしぼる. ¶go (=run) ***to*** *seed* 花の盛りが過ぎて実がなる; [比ゆ的に]盛りが過ぎる, 衰える. 【類】Flowers run ***to*** *seeds.* ¶a plant ***with*** aromatic *seeds* 芳しい種子のなる植物.

P^2 the *seed* ***of*** the oak かしわの種子 ‖ *seeds* ***of*** discord 不和の原因. 【類】*seeds* ***of*** trouble / She planted the *seeds* ***of*** virtue in her children.

seed, *v.* 種をまく; 〔競技〕[選手を]シードする.

M^2 *seed* ***down*** [草種など]まく.

P *seed* a player ***in*** a tournament トーナメントで選手をシードする. ¶*seed* a field ***with*** barley 畑に大麦の種をまく.

seeding, *n.* 種まき.

Q^2 ***cloud*** *seeding* 雨雲の種の植付け(人工降雨で).

P It is time ***for*** the *seeding* of rice (wheat, barley, etc). L稲(など)の植付の時期だ.

seedling, *n.* 苗木.

Q^2 ***mulberry*** *seedlings* 桑の苗木. ¶plant cedar and ***pine tree*** *seedlings* 米杉及び松の苗木を植える.

seek, *v.* さがす; 求める, こう.

M I have been *seeking* it ***all round*** あっちこっち捜し回った. ¶***assiduously*** *seek* ... 勤勉に...を求める. ¶***eagerly*** *seek* knowledge 熱心に知識を求める. ¶*seek* ***elsewhere*** ほかから手に入れる. ¶one has to *seek* ***far*** to find ... ...は容易に見つからない. ¶*seek* ***in vain*** いたずらに求める. ¶His friendship is ***keenly*** *sought* and treasured. 彼の友情は切実に求められ大切にされる. 【類】That will make you ***keenly*** *sought* (売れっ子にする). ¶This is just what I have ***long*** *sought* for. これは正しく私が久しく求めていたものだ. ¶*seek* ***out*** a gamblers' den ばく徒のどやをさぐり出す. 【類】*seek* ***out*** some retreat of more security / *seek* ***out*** methods for ... / I can *seek* you ***out*** wherever you may hide yourself. ¶*seek* ***vigilantly*** after ... ...をうの目たかの目でさがす.

P *seek* ***after*** the truth (God) 真理(など)を求める ‖ He is always *seeking* ***after*** wealth (happiness, fame). 彼は始終富(など)を求めている. ‖ The works of this novelist are much *sought* ***after.*** この小説家の作は大層持てはやされている. ‖ She is *sought* ***after*** as a guest and admired as a hostess. 彼女は客としては気受がよく女主人としては感心される. ‖ a prize much *sought* ***after*** by contestants 〔競技〕参加者の目標である賞. 【類】They are much *sought* ***after*** by specialists. ¶She is much *sought* ***for*** [in] marriage. 彼女は大層嫁に欲しがられている. ‖ *seek* ***for*** information (employment) 情報(など)を求める. 【類】*seek* ***for*** (=hunt) a house / *seek* ***for*** light on religious questions / *seek* ***for*** salvation / To *seek* ***for*** sleep is only to drive it away. / *seek* ***for*** the root of the evil in ... ¶*seek* assistance ***from*** ... ...の助力を請う. 【類】information which has to be *sought* ***from*** many and various sources / *seek* shelter ***from*** rain.

O Being sleepy, he *sought* his bed. 眠くなって寝床が恋しくなった.

seeker, *n.* 追求者.

Q the ***pure*** *seekers* after God 純真の心で神を求める人々.

Q^2 ***amusement*** *seekers* 娯楽を求める人々. ¶a ***bargain*** *seeker* (=hunter) 安売(特売)ものをあさる人. ¶a successful ***job*** *seeker* 職にありついた失業者. ¶an ***office*** *seeker* 役人志望者. ¶a ***pleasure*** *seeker* 快楽を求める人. ¶a ***treasure*** *seeker* 宝を捜す人.

P^2 *seekers* ***after*** new truth 新らしい真理の追求者 ‖ a *seeker* ***after*** novelty (pleasure) 新奇(など)をあさる人 ‖ *seekers* ***after*** knowledge 知識の探求者 ‖ *seekers* ***after*** health 保養する人々. ¶*seekers* ***of*** work in pictures 映画の仕事を求めている人々.

seeking, *n.* 追求.

Q^2 ***office*** *seeking* 役人志望. ¶***street*** *seeking* 街頭での客引き(やみの女などの). 「明の追求.

P^2 devout and unwearied *seeking* ***for*** light 熱誠不屈の光

seem, *v.* ...らしい, ようだ, 思われる.

M it certainly *seems* ***anomalous*** that ... ...はたしかに異例らしい. ¶It *seemed* ***as if*** he would recover. 彼は回復するかと思われた. ¶He *seems* [to be] ***aware*** of the fact. 彼はそのことを承知しているらしい. ¶Do as it *seems* ***best*** to you. 君が一番良いと思うようにやれ. ¶His whole frame *seemed* ***collapsed*** and ***shrinking.*** 彼は全くぺちゃんこになって縮む思いがした. ¶The statement *seems* ***correct.*** その話は本当らしい. ¶The premises *seem* very ***extensive.*** その建物は大層広そうだ. ¶At first sight it may *seem* ***fantastic.*** 一見異様に見えるかも知れない. ¶It would *seem* perhaps most ***fitting*** to say that ... ...と言うのがおそらくもっとも妥当であろう. ¶It *seems* unspeakably ***funny*** to me. それは私にとっては全くこっけいに思われる. ¶You may act as *seems* ***good*** to you. 君の良いようにやってよい. ¶He *seems* [to be] ***honest*** (***happy, clever***). 彼は正直(など)らしい. ¶He *seems* ***ill*** (***well***). 彼は病気(達者)らしい. ¶All his efforts *seem* ***in vain*** (=fruitless). 彼の努力も水の泡らしい. ¶To me it *seems* ***outrageous.*** 私にはそれは乱暴に思われる. ¶It *seems* ***incredible*** (=***preposterous***). 信じられないほどだ. ¶He *seemed* much ***pleased.*** 彼は大層気に入ったらしい. ¶He *seems* ***proud*** of his knowledge. 彼は学問が自慢らしい. ¶His curiosity *seemed* ***quenched.*** 彼の好奇心は満足したらしかった. ¶it may *seem* a little ***strange,*** but ... ...ちょっと変に思われるかも知れないが. ¶You *seem* (=look) ***tired.*** 君は疲れているようだ. ¶It *seems* ***undecided.*** それは未定らしい. ¶Such conduct *seems* to me ***unjustifiable.*** そのような行為は弁解の余地がないように思われる.

P it will *seem* ***as*** nothing when compared with ... それは...とは到底比べものにならない. ¶Time flies! it *seems* ***like*** yesterday, but eight years have gone by since ... 月日のたつのは早いものだ! つい昨今のように思われるが...から八年たっている. ¶It *seems* ***to*** me as if I saw you somewhere. どこかでお目にかかったような気がします.

O the truth *seems* to be that ... 事実は...らしい. ¶It *seems* that he is a soldier. 彼は軍人らしい. ‖ It *seems* that he likes study.=He *seems* to like study. 彼は勉強が好きらしい. ‖ It *seems* that ... is the case.=... is the case, it *seems.* ...が事実らしい. ¶[It] *seems* like it's going to rain. 雨になりそうだ.

seeming, *n.* 外見, 外観.

V ***put on*** a fair outside *seeming* りっぱに外観を装う.

P ***to*** all *seeming* 見た所どうしても. ¶***without*** *seeming* to exaggerate 誇張しないで(全く) ‖ perceive, ***without*** *seeming* to perceive it, that ... ...を知覚しないようでいて知覚する.

seethe, *v.* 沸き返る; 興奮する.

P enthusiasm *seething* ***in*** his brain 彼の頭に沸き返る熱心. ¶The country *seethed* ***over*** the question. 国中その問題で沸き返った. ¶Water was *seething* ***under*** the fall. たきつぼの水があわ立っていた. ¶The city is *seething* ***with*** discontent. 不満の声は市中に沸き返っていた. 【類】The scene was *seething* ***with*** men. ‖ His mind was *seething* ***with*** conflicting emotions. 彼の胸の中は千々にくだけるのであった.

segment, *n.* 区分; 〔数〕線分, [円の]弧.

Q The work of the Department of Justice cuts across ***every*** *segment* of American life. 司法省の仕事はアメリカの社会の各層に行きわたっている. ¶the ***shaded*** *segment* of the moon [月食の]月の暗くなった部分. 「袋(ひときれ).

Q^2 a ***tangerine*** (an ***orange***) *segment* みかん(オレンジ)の一

P An orange is easily pulled apart ***into*** its *segments.* オレンジの実は容易に一つ一つ引き離せる.

P^2 a *segment* ***of*** a circle (sphere, line) 円の弧(など).

segregate, *v.* 分ける.

P *segregate* (=separate) men ***from*** women 男と女を分ける ‖ a patient *segregated* ***from*** the others 隔離された患者. 【類】become *segregated* ***from*** the rest of mankind.

segregation, *n.* 分離. 「黒人種の分離.

Q^2 ***race*** (=racial) *segregation* 人種の分離; 《米》[特に]白・

P^2 *segregation* ***of*** the colored population 黒人の分離.

seize, *v.* つかまえる, 奪取する; 襲う.

M He was ***suddenly*** *seized* with an illness. 彼は突然病気にかかった. ¶The throne was ***unlawfully*** *seized.* 王位が不法に奪われた.

P *seize* one ***by*** the neck (hand, arm, ear) 人の首(など)をつかまえる ‖ *seize* him ***by*** force (authority) 腕力(など)で彼を捕える ‖ He was *seized* ***by*** apoplexy (a demon). 彼は卒中にかかった(悪魔にとりつかれた). ¶He *seized* the package ***from*** my hand. 彼は私の手から包みを奪い取った. ¶He was *seized* ***of*** some property. 彼は財産を幾らか差押えられた. ¶They *seized* ***on*** the ship, and imprisoned the crew. 彼らは船を押収して船員を監禁した. ‖ Madness *seized* ***on*** their mother. 彼らの母親は気が狂った. ¶*seize* ***upon*** a chance (pretext) 機会(など)をとらえる. 【類】The event was *seized* ***upon*** by the daily press reporters. / A great fear *seized* ***upon*** him. / *seize* ***upon*** an estate (財産). ¶ be *seized* ***with*** sexual passion 性欲のとりことなる. ‖ He was *seized* ***with*** death while reading Aristotle. 彼はアリストテレスを読んでいる時突然死んだ. ‖ I was *seized* ***with*** terror (misgivings, an inordinate desire). 私は恐ろしさ(など)を感じた. ‖ Upon taking at his work he was *seized* ***with*** a prompt relapse. 彼は仕事をやり出すとたちまち(病気が)ぶり返した. ‖ *seized* ***with*** a sudden freak [of mind] ふとした出来心で. 【類】She thought of her future, and was *seized* ***with*** a magnificent resolve. / He was *seized*, first ***with*** surprise, secondly ***with*** indignation, and lastly ***with*** alarm. / He was *seized* ***with*** cramp (an attack of epilepsy, a violent fever, a severe pain in his stomach, a sudden fit, cholera). / He is *seized* ***with*** violent insanity.

seizure, *n.* 差押え; 強奪; 突発, 発作.

V ***effect*** a *seizure* 差押える.

Q after a third ***apoplectic*** *seizure* 三回目の卒中が起ってから. ¶ ***forcible*** *seizure* 強奪. ¶ ***lawful*** *seizure* 差し押え. ¶ a ***permanent*** *seizure* 永久的掌握.

Q² a ***Communist*** *seizure* of power in Greece ギリシアにおける共産党の権力掌握. ¶ ***government*** *seizure* of properties 私有物没収. ¶ a ***heart*** *seizure* 心臓まひ

P² a *seizure* ***of*** disease 病の突発 ‖ a *seizure* ***of*** grief 突然の悲痛.

select, *v.* 選ぶ.

M be ***cunningly*** *selected* さがしこく選びとられてある. ¶ be ***first*** *selected* by ... ...が第一次に選定する. ¶ *selected* ***haphazard[ly]*** from ... ...から漫然と選んだ. ¶ be ***rigidly*** *selected* 厳選される. ¶ he has been ***providentially*** *selected* for ... 彼は天から...に選ばれた.

P *select* ***among*** various makes and patterns 色々の造りや型の中から選ぶ. ¶ it was *selected* ***as*** the site for ... それは...の敷地に選ばれた. 【類】The International Olympic Committee *selected* Japan ***as*** the place where the XIIth Olympic Games would be held. ¶ *select ...* ***by*** vote 投票で...を選ぶ. ¶ he was *selected* ***for*** promotion to the rank of ... 彼は...の位に抜てきされた. 【類】good books *selected* ***for*** reading. ¶ We have over 30 beautiful designs to *select* ***from***. われわれが選択すべき図案は三十以上ある. ¶ They were *selected* ***from among*** many applicants (= candidates). 彼らは多数応募者の中から選ばれた. ¶ He was *selected* ***out of*** a great number of candidates. 彼は多数の候補者中から選ばれた.

selection, *n.* 選択, とうた; 精選物.

V ***exercise*** no *selection* 選択をしない. ¶ There are two important factors that ***govern*** the *selection*. 取捨選択を左右する二つの重要な要因がある. ¶ ***make*** *selections* from ... ...中から選択する ‖ without ***making*** any *selection* of your food 食物を選ばないで. ¶ The music band ***played*** *selections*. その音楽隊が選曲を演奏した. ¶ ***read*** *selections* of classics 古典選集を読む. ¶ The band, under the direction of Mr.—, will ***render*** the following *selections*: その楽隊は...氏の指揮で次の選曲を演奏する.

Q ***artificial*** *selection* 人為とうた. ¶ a ***choice*** *selection* of American short stories アメリカ短編選集. ¶ an ***excellent*** *selection* 特選(品). ¶ a ***fine*** *selection* of summer goods 夏物の特上品. ¶ The new principal is a ***good*** *selection*. 今度の校長は適任者だ. ¶ ***human*** *selection* 人為とうた. ¶ ***indiscriminate*** *selection* めちゃめちゃな選択. ¶ ***intelligent*** *selection* そう明な選択. ¶ by ***judicial*** *selection* 公平な選択によって. 【類】make a ***judicious*** *selection* out of a variety of articles (色々な記事). ¶ a very ***large*** *selection* たくさんえらび集めたもの. ¶ a ***misguided*** *selection* of a hobby 道楽の無茶な選択. ¶ play some ***musical*** *selections* 選曲を若干演奏する. ¶ by ***natural*** *selection* 自然とうたによって. ¶ ***occupational*** (=***vocational***) *selection* 職業の選択. ¶ guide one to a ***proper*** *selection* 選択を誤らないように指導する. ¶ a ***representative*** *selection* 代表的選集. ¶ a ***varied*** and ***amusing*** *selection* 変化に富むおもしろい選集. ¶ The library has a ***wide*** *selection* of current newspapers and periodicals. その図書館には現代の新聞や雑誌が多数集めてある. ¶ a ***wise*** *selection* of material 材料選択のよろしきを得ていること.

P The geographical range of the country is such that except in the height of summer, almost any climate can be found ***by*** *selection* of locality. その国の地理的範囲は, 盛夏は別として場所を選べばほとんどどんな気候にでも出会えるようになっている.

P² a *selection* ***from*** the Works of Wordsworth ウァーズウァース選集. 【類】*selections* ***from*** great authors (poets).

self, *n.* 自己, 自我.

V ***control*** the *self* 自制する. ¶ She must be ready to ***sacrifice*** *self*. 彼女は自己を犠牲にする覚悟をもっているに相違ない.

Q She is ***beauty's*** *self*. 彼女は美そのものだ. ¶ one's ***better*** *self* (=half) その愛妻. ¶ so far from her ***bright, natural*** *self* 明朗な自然ないつもの彼女とは打って変って. ¶ one's ***former*** (***present***) *self* 以前(今)の自分 ‖ There is no vestige of his ***former*** *self*. 彼の以前の面影がない. ¶ our ***full*** *self* 自己の全ぼう. ¶ one's ***larger*** *self* 大我. ¶ my ***other*** *self* 第二の我. ¶ my ***single*** *self* 私一個人. ¶ my ***unworthy*** *self* 不肖. ¶ her ***old*** *self* [性格・風さいなどから見ての]昔の彼女. ¶ one's ***own*** *self* 自分自身. 【類】have no thought of one's ***own*** *self*. ¶ our ***two*** *selves* 私ども二人. ¶ reveal one's ***real*** *self* 本音を吐く. ¶ the ***second*** *self* 親友; 片腕. ¶ reveal its ***true*** *self* その本性を現わす. ¶ Be your ***natural*** *self*. 生来のままの自我たれ. ¶ You should be your ***own*** *self*. 自分がしっかりしなければいけない.

P Few men are great enough to be ***above*** *self*. 自我に勝つようなえらい人は少ない. ¶ ***beside*** one's *self* 気が変になって. ¶ ***by*** one's *self* 自分で, 自分独りで. ¶ He thinks ***of*** *self* only. 彼は自分のことだけしか考えない. ¶ He refers every thing ***to*** *self*. 彼は何もかも自己中心でやる.

-self, *suf.* [*pl.* *-selves*].

V ***abandon*** *oneself* to boundless grief 悲痛のどん底に落ち込む ‖ ***abandon*** *oneself* to day dreams 空想にふける ‖ ***abandon*** *oneself* to the saving hands of Amida あみだ如来の慈悲の手にすがる. 【類】***abandon*** *oneself* to the gratification of lust (いん欲) / Some alcoholics (酒のみ) ***abandon*** *themselves* to drink on account of financial ruin. ¶ ***abase*** *oneself* before a superior 目上のものの前でぺこぺこする. ¶ They ***absented*** themselves for that day. 彼らはその日は休んだ. ‖ ***absent*** *oneself* from the ceremony 式に欠席する. 【類】***absent*** *oneself* from school / ***absent*** *oneself* from home / ***absent*** *oneself* from duty / ***absent*** *oneself* from office under false pretenses (うまい口実で). ¶ ***absolve*** *oneself* of responsibility for ... ...の責任のがれをする. ¶ a plant which has ***acclimated*** *itself* to the new soil 新しい土壌に慣れた植物. ¶ ***accommodate*** *oneself* to the new order of things 新しい社会に慣れる ‖ ***accommodate*** *oneself* to other's wishes 人の希望に添うようにする. 【類】One must ***accommodate*** *oneself* to circumstances (環境). ¶ gradually ***accustom*** *oneself* to ... 次第に...に慣れる. 【類】***accustom*** *oneself* to European habits / ***accustom*** *oneself* to early rising. ¶ ***acknowledge*** *oneself* in the wrong 誤りを自認する. ¶ ***acquaint*** *oneself* of ... ...を知る ‖ ***acquaint*** *oneself*, as far as practicable, with ... できるだけ...を知るようにする. 【類】***acquaint*** *oneself* with one's duties (the country) / must first ***acquaint*** *themselves* with ... / ***acquaint*** *oneself* with the actual situation in Japan. ¶ ***acquit*** *oneself* (=perform one's part) well (ill) りっぱに(まずく)振舞う ‖ ***acquit*** *oneself* of social duties 自己の社会的義務を果す ‖ The crew ***acquitted*** *themselves* well in trying circumstances. 船員たちは苦境にあってよく働いた. 【類】***acquitted*** *himself* well in a task which might have daunted (へき易させる) the most daring / ***acquit*** *oneself* of the responsibility entrusted to one / ***acquit*** *oneself* well towards ... / ***acquit*** *myself* to your satisfaction / ***acquit*** *oneself* with distinction and discretion (りっぱにかつ慎重に) / ***acquit*** *oneself* ***with*** respectability / ***acquit*** *oneself* with credit (りっぱに). ¶ ***accuse*** *oneself* to be guilty of a crime 犯罪で自責する. ¶ be busy ***adapting*** *themselves* to the new position 新しい職務に慣れようと一生懸命である ‖ ***adapt*** *oneself* to altering (= changing) conditions 臨機応変する. 【類】He found a great deal of difficulty in ***adapting*** *himself* to his altered cirumstances. / ***adapt*** *itself* to the need of the present / ***adapt*** *oneself* to the new mode of living / ***adapt*** *oneself* to English manners and habits / a world wanderer who cannot ***adapt*** *himself* to a sybaritic life (ぜいたくな暮し) / My mind was slow to ***adapt*** *itself* to all I have seen and heard. / A man must be master of *himself* (沈着) in order to ***adapt*** *himself* to the requirements of the moment. / The common law ***adapts itself*** to the general in exclusion of the particular good. ¶***addict*** *oneself* to a scandalous kind of life 見苦しい生活にふける ‖ ***addict*** *oneself* to drinking (bad habits) 飲酒(悪癖)にふける.【類】***addict*** *oneself* to the use of alcoholic stimulants (酒). ¶I ***addressed*** *myself* in good earnest to my repose, but could obtain none. 本当に眠ろうという気になったが眠れなかった. ¶***address*** *oneself* to an assigned task 課せられた仕事にとりかかる ‖ ***address*** *itself* to the eyes それが目に訴える ‖ ***address*** *oneself* to the public (audience, chairman) 大衆(など)に呼びかける.【類】I am ***addressing*** *myself* to you in the hope that you may be able to aid me in the job. / ***address*** *oneself* to the oppressed / he ***addressed*** *himself* to them to the effect that ... / ***address*** *oneself* to a small circle ‖ ***address*** *oneself* to the task of ... ...の仕事にとりかかる ‖ the state should ***address*** *itself* with all its might to its prevention 国家はその防止のため全力を尽すべきである.【類】***address*** *oneself* energetically to its solution. ¶***adjust*** *oneself* to new situations 新状勢に順応する. ¶***adjust*** *ourselves* to world conditions.【類】***adjust*** *itself* to the changed economic environment / ***adjust*** *themselves* to life in a democracy / ***adjust*** *oneself* to new circumstances (= environments) / Chinese ***adjusted*** *themselves* very readily to Mongol rule seven hundred years ago and to Manchu rule three hundred years ago. ¶***admire*** *oneself* うぬぼれる. ¶***adorn*** *oneself* for the occasion その式に出るため盛装する. ¶go abroad to ***advance*** *himself* in his profession 修業のため洋行する ‖ ***advance*** *oneself* to a place of greater responsibility and a better salary 責任は重く給与もよい地位に昇進する. ¶***adventure*** *oneself* in poetry 作詩を試みる. ¶He is not fond of ***advertising*** *himself*. 彼は自己宣伝は好きじゃない.【類】Low's theatre ***advertised*** *itself* as "the nation's leading vaudeville theatre." ¶***affiliate*** *oneself* with (=to) a party (an association) 党(会)に加入する. ¶The king sought to ***aggrandize*** *himself* at the expense of his people. 王は国民を犠牲にして自己の権力の強化を計った. ¶Don't ***alarm*** *yourself*. 驚いちゃいけない. ¶openly ***align*** *themselves* with Moscow's policy and satellites 大っぴらにモスコーの政策及びその衛星国と歩調を合わせる. ¶The low-grade prostitute tends to ***align*** *herself* with crime. 下等な売春婦はとかく罪を犯しがちだ.【類】The armies were ***aligning*** *themselves* with the Communist forces in South China. ¶***allow*** *oneself* three dollars a day for one's personal expense 一日の小づかいとして三ドル使う ‖ One should not ***allow*** *oneself* to be impressed merely by externals. 人は外観だけで判断してはいけない. ‖ ***allow*** *oneself* in gambling (drinking) とばく(など)にふける. ¶Japan ***allied*** *himself* to (=with) Great Britain. 日本は英国と同盟した. ‖ ***ally*** *oneself* with a club (society) クラブ(会)に入会する ‖ ***ally*** *themselves* with ... against ... ...と協力して...に当る. ¶***amuse*** *oneself* by reading 読書で楽しむ ‖ ***amuse*** *oneself* in folly 道楽をやる ‖ ***amuse*** *oneself* in one's own way 勝手なことをして楽しむ.【類】***amuse*** *ourselves* by playing at cards / while I was ***amusing*** *myself* by looking out of the window / children ***amusing*** *themselves* in gardens / We ***amused*** *ourselves* in various ways—swimming, walking, and so on. / ***amuse*** *oneself* with a toy (puzzle) / ***amuse*** *oneself* with funnies (漫画) / ***amuse*** *oneself* with various devices (色々な考案) / ***amuse*** *oneself* with disk music (レコード音楽) / ***amuse*** *oneself* with photography ‖ How America ***Amuses*** *Herself*〘書名〙アメリカ人の娯楽. ¶***announce*** *oneself* publicly as a candidate for the Republican nomination 共和党の指名選挙に名乗りをあげる ‖ ***announce*** *oneself* in favor of the plan その計画に賛意を表する. ¶***apply*** *oneself* for a job 求職する ‖ ***apply*** *oneself* to the exercise of arms 専心武をみがく ‖ ***apply*** *itself* to the problems that confront it それに直面する諸問題の解決にとりかかる.【類】***apply*** *oneself* to work with a whole heart / ***applied*** *herself* assiduously to the tasks given her / ***apply*** *oneself* to the study of ... / ***apply*** *oneself* with great zeal to ... / ***apply*** *oneself* to the reading of philosophical works / ***apply*** *oneself* to the best of one's ability to the attainment of that objective. ¶***apprentice*** *oneself* to a cabinet-maker さしもの師の所へ弟子入りをする. ¶The assumption will not ***approve*** (=***commend***) *itself* to all philosophers. その仮定は哲学者の中には異論のあることであろう. ¶***arm*** *oneself* against danger 危険を警戒する ‖ ***arm*** *oneself* with a revolver (camera, lantern) ピストル(など)を携帯する ‖ ***arm*** *oneself* with a permit from the powers that be その筋からの許可証を携行する ‖ ***arm*** *oneself* with knowledge and convictions 知識と信念を身につける. ¶***arrange*** *themselves* in two fundamental categories おのずから二つの基礎部門に分かれる ¶The fighting forces of the two countries were ***arraying*** *themselves* against each other. 両国の戦闘部隊は相対じした. ‖ ***array*** *oneself* in one's best clothes 盛装する.【類】***array*** *oneself* in white (白衣). ¶Just ***ask*** *yourself*. まず身に聞いて見給え. ¶Meantime hunger began to ***assert*** *itself*. やがて空腹を感じ始めた. ‖ Justice will in time ***assert*** *itself*. 正道はやがて行われるようになる.【類】His genius ***asserted*** *itself* at an early age. ‖ Their common sense ***asserted*** *itself*. 彼らの常識が働き出した.【類】Now conscience has ***asserted*** *itself*. ‖ The equilibrium which had been arrested for a time again ***asserted*** *itself*. しばらくとまっていた力の均衡が再び出現してきた. ‖ Women are ***asserting*** *themselves* gradually in Japan. 日本では婦人が次第に自我に目覚めつつある. ‖ The noble generosity of his nature at once ***asserted*** *itself*. 彼の天性である寛大さがたちまち表面に出てきた.【類】His native (持って生れた) ability for leadership ***asserted*** *itself*. / ***assert*** *itself* as a virtue under the guise of friendship (友情という名の美徳). ¶I have fulfilled the object that I ***assigned*** *myself*. 私は自分でたてた目的を完遂した. ‖ He had to ***assign*** *himself* to a week's rest in bed on account of the wound. 彼は負傷のため一週間床につかねばならなかった. ‖ They ***assigned*** *themselves* to guard their fortress. 彼らはとりでの防衛に立上った. ¶***assimilate*** *oneself* to European ways 欧州風に自身を同化させる. ¶***associate*** *oneself* with a political movement 政治運動に参加する ‖ ***associate*** *oneself* with a proposal 提議に加わる(加盟する) ‖ labor ***associating*** *itself* into organized groups for the advancement of its legitimate interests その正当な利益増進のために組織化した労働者たち.【類】***associated*** *oneself* with the firm now known as ... ‖ the idea which ***associates*** *itself* with ... ...と関連している考え ‖ I wish to ***associate*** myself with your expression of sympathy with ... 私もあなたと同様...のおくやみを述べさしていただきたい. ‖ ***associate*** *oneself* with writing 文筆に従事する ‖ ***Associate*** *yourself* with men of good character. りっぱな人格者と交際しなさい. ¶I ***assured*** *myself* by careful search that there was really no ground in the rumor. 風説は事実無根であることをよく調べて安心した. ‖ ***assure*** *himself* from observation that ... 実地...を見て納得する ‖ ***assure*** *oneself* of one's success 自分の成功を確信する. ¶***attach*** *oneself* to a school [画家など]ある派に属する. ¶***attire*** *oneself* in clerical vestment ... 僧服を身にまとう ‖ ***attire*** *oneself* with ... ...で身仕度する.【類】***attire*** *oneself* for the season. ¶willingly ***avail*** *oneself* of another's kind offer 人の好意を喜こんで受ける ‖ ***avail*** *oneself* of the cooperation of ... ...の協力を利用する.【類】***avail*** *oneself* of the very latest publications bearing upon the subject / ***avail*** *oneself* of an early opportunity to ... / I desire to ***avail*** *myself* of this opportunity to ... / his ability to ***avail*** *himself* of other men's knowledge / ***availing*** *oneself* of the opportunity presented by ... / ***avail*** *oneself* of the advantages offered to the full / ***avail*** *themselves* of the resources of their wardrobe (着飾る). ¶***avenge*** [*oneself* of] one's father on ... ...に対して父のあだを打つ ‖ ***avenge*** *oneself* on a person 人に対しあだを打つ.【類】***avenge*** *oneself* on one's enemies. ¶She ***balanced*** *herself* well on a tight rope. 彼女はぴんと張ったロープの上でうまく身体のつり合をとった. ¶***band*** *themselves* against a person (the enemy) 結束して相手(敵)に当る ‖ ***band*** *themselves* into an association (club, sect) 集って会(など)を作る.【類】They have ***banded*** *themselves* into what they termed "the Farmers' Corps for the Service to the Country." ¶***baptize*** *oneself* with a Western thought 西洋思想の洗礼を受ける. ¶Scientific socialism ***bases*** *itself* on economic facts and realities. 科学的社会主義とは経済的事実と現実に基礎をおいたものである. ‖ ***basing*** *itself* upon these principles これらの原則に立脚して.【類】***base*** *themselves* upon historic data and facts. ¶ lie ***basking oneself*** abroad in the sun 外で身を横たえて日光浴する. ¶ ***bath oneself*** (bathe) in a stream 流れで水浴びをする. ¶ ***bear oneself*** with considerable bravado [裁判を受けている囚人など]大見えを切って見せる ‖ ***bear oneself*** in such a manner as to gain respect from the public 大衆から尊敬を受けるような行動をする. ¶ ***beautify oneself*** おめかしする. ¶ ***behave oneself*** well りっぱに振舞う. 【類】 ***behave oneself*** in a proper way / ***behave oneself*** as one should do (あるべきように) / ***behave oneself*** so as not to give offense to others (人の感情を害さないように) ‖ I'd teach him to ***behave himself***. あいつを懲らしめてやる. ‖ He doesn't seem to know how to ***behave himself***. 彼は行儀作法を知らないらしい. ‖ ***behave oneself*** with insolence to those below one 下の者に横柄に振舞う. ¶ ***bend oneself*** to another's will 人の意志に服従する. ¶ ***bestir oneself*** for this cause この目的のために活動する ‖ Soon others began to ***bestir themselves***. じき他の連中も起き出してきた. ‖ ***bestir oneself*** in a predicament 逆境で苦闘する. 【類】 The city began to show, in places, signs of ***bestirring itself***. ‖ The earliest workers now ***bestir themselves***. 一番早い労務者はもう就業している. 【類】 When gaslights twinkle like stars, and arc lamps shine out like moons, Dancing London ***bestirs itself***. ¶ ***betake oneself*** to … …へ行く; 仕方なしに…をやる. ¶ Having no other resource, he ***betook*** (***took***) ***himself*** to teaching. 他に仕事もないので彼は教職についた. 【類】 ***betake oneself*** to the study of … ‖ Tired of work on shore, he ***betook himself*** to the sea. 陸上の仕事にあきて彼は海員になった. ¶ the descendants of the British who ***betook themselves*** to fresh fields of enterprise 新天地開拓に乗り出した英国人の子孫. 【類】 Those who cannot afford the high-priced hotels ***betake themselves*** to boarding and lodging houses. / ***betake oneself*** with all speed to … / He ***betook himself*** back to his old quarters (古巣に). ‖ ***betake oneself*** with indefatigable ardor to the study of philosophy 哲学の勉強に熱中する ‖ ***betake oneself*** to one's heels (=legs) 逃げ出す ‖ ***betake oneself*** to flight 逃げ出す. ¶ He ***bethought himself*** of an excellent plan. すばらしい考えを思いついた. 【類】 ***bethink oneself*** of a new idea / At last he ***bethought himself*** of this contrivance. ¶ ***betray oneself*** 本性をあらわす, お里が知れる. ¶ a native of Berlin, who ***bills herself*** as Victorina ビクトリーナという芸名をもつベルリン子. ¶ ***bind oneself*** by a solemn agreement 厳粛な協定を結ぶ ‖ a large proportion of film actors ***bind themselves*** under contract for a period of years to one producer 映画俳優の大部分は契約によって何年間か一製作者に所属する ‖ ***bind myself*** to total abstinence 断然禁酒を誓う. ¶ He ***blamed himself*** for the accident. 彼はその事故の責任を感じた. 【類】 He ***blamed himself*** for neglecting it. ¶ ***bleed oneself*** to death 出血で死ぬ. ¶ ***bless oneself*** 十字を切る; 自分を祝福する ‖ ***bless oneself*** against evil powers 悪魔を払いおとす; 身を清める (みそぎ) ‖ He has not a penny to ***bless himself*** with. 彼はびた一文も持たない. ‖ He ***blessed himself***. 彼はまあよかったと言った. ☞ "Bless me!" などと言ったこと. ¶ ***blind ourselves*** to the dangers of … …の危険に目を覆う ‖ to write or talk of them as … is to ***blind oneself*** to the truth (真理に目をつむる). ¶ ***blindfold oneself*** 自分を目かくしする, 自分の目を覆う. ¶ ***blow oneself*** to bits (爆撃などで)木っ葉みじんになる. ¶ He ***boasted himself*** to be an Englishman. 彼は英国人たることを誇った. ¶ he ***booked himself*** for … 彼は…行の切符を買った. ¶ ***bore myself*** by his tedious talk 退屈な話でうんざりする ‖ I ***bored myself*** to death with a stupid novel. 私はつまらない小説を読んでうんざりした. 【類】 I am not going to ***bore myself*** with sight-seeing. ¶ ***bother oneself*** about … …のことで自分をわずらわす. ¶ ***bow oneself*** before a shrine 社の前で頭を下げる. ‖ I ***bowed myself*** from his office. 私はえしゃくして彼の事務所から出た. ‖ With this, he ***bowed himself off***. こう言いながら彼はえしゃくして立去った. 【類】 ***bowed himself*** out of court to pay his fine (罰金を支払うため) / ***bow oneself*** reverently before a Buddhist temple. ¶ ***brace oneself*** against a difficulty 困難を踏みこたえる ‖ ***brace oneself*** up to some determined aim 目的完遂のため気を引締める. 【類】 ***brace oneself*** up for a fight (task, undertaking). ¶ ***break oneself*** into the habit of work 働き癖をつける ‖ One does not readily ***break oneself*** of a bad habit. 悪い癖は仲々直るものじゃない. 【類】 ***break oneself*** of a habit of many years' standing / ***break oneself*** of a practice (やって来たこと). ¶ ***breast oneself*** to danger 敢然危険に立向う. ¶ ***bring oneself*** in touch with much of the best in modern thought 最高の近代思想を大いに吸収する ‖ ***bring oneself*** into favor with=ingratiate oneself with … …によく思われるようにする ‖ ***bring itself*** back into a place of respect in the world (会などを)再び世人から敬意を表されるようにする ‖ ***bring oneself*** immediately into contempt すぐ人から軽べつされるようになる ‖ ***bring oneself*** (=go) to great expense 大散財をする ‖ He has ***brought himself*** to poverty. 彼は貧乏暮しをするようになった. ‖ He could never ***bring himself*** to like his new surroundings. 彼は新しい環境がどうしても好きになれなかった. ‖ He could not ***bring himself*** to break the sad news. その悲報を告げる気にはなれなかった. ¶ ***bristle oneself*** up [猫など]毛を逆立てる; 大いに怒る. ¶ ***brutalize oneself*** 畜生道に落ちる, 堕落する. ¶ ***buckle oneself*** to a job 仕事にとっかかる. ¶ ***build themselves up*** as an industrial nation 工業国民に造り上げる ‖ The patient must ***build himself up*** with a nourishing diet. 患者は栄養食をとってからだを造らなければならない. 【類】 The world will ***build itself anew*** on fresh foundations. ¶ ***bulwark oneself*** behind authority 権威者の説を引いて自分を弁護する. ¶ ***bundle oneself up*** 暖かそうに(または重苦しく)くるまる. ¶ ***burden oneself*** with the responsibility for … …する責任を負う. ¶ ***burn oneself*** やけどする; 焼き切る ‖ maple leaf, "***burning itself*** away" in the autumn 秋に「真赤に燃える」紅葉 ‖ The lamp has ***burned itself*** out. ランプ(電球)が焼き切れた. ‖ like a candle slowly ***burning itself*** out ろうそくの火が次第に消えて行くように ‖ The fire has pretty nearly ***burnt itself*** out now. 火事はもう下火になった. 【類】 His zeal will soon ***burn itself*** out. ‖ ***burn itself*** deep in her heart [語などが]深く肝に銘じる ‖ He ***burned himself*** to death while (=whilst) tipsy. 彼は酔っぱらっていてやけど(火傷)で死んだ. ‖ ***burn itself*** more deeply into one's memory 記憶がはっきり焼きつく. ¶ ***bury oneself*** among books 書籍の中に身を埋める ‖ ***bury oneself*** in novels and romances 小説(など)に読みふける ‖ The knife ***buried itself*** in wood. ナイフが木にささった. ‖ ***bury oneself*** in solitude (one's work, the country) 埋木になる(没頭する, 幽居する). ¶ ***busy oneself*** about (=with) … …に奔走する ‖ ***busy oneself*** to exhaustion 多忙でへとへとになる, 奔命に疲れる ‖ begin to ***busy oneself*** with (=take to) stamp-collecting 盛んに切手収集をやるようになる. 【類】 ***busy oneself*** with the problem of … / ***busy oneself*** with one's work. ¶ It ***calls itself*** as the Amalgamated Society. その名は合同協会という. ‖ They ***call themselves*** by fancy names. 彼らは自分に芸名をつけている. ¶ ***Calm yourself***. まあ落付いてお聞きなさい. ¶ She ***carries herself*** rather insolently. 彼女は相当振(ﾌ)っている. ‖ ***carry oneself*** in manly fashion 男らしく振舞う. 【類】 For a lad of nineteen he ***carries himself*** remarkably well. / ***carry oneself*** creditably in a matter ‖ ***carry oneself*** with an air without assuming airs. 気どる風もなくおのずから一種の風格を備えている. ‖ the way he ***carries himself*** その様子っぷり ‖ A pound of coal has enough energy to ***carry itself*** around the world. 一ポンドの石炭はそれ自体に世界一週できるほどのエネルギーを持っている. 【類】 If I take any more, I fear I shall be unable to ***carry myself*** home. ¶ ***cast oneself*** into the water 水中に身を投げる ‖ ***cast herself*** on his neck. 女が男の首っ玉にかじりつく. ¶ ***catch oneself*** up ぽつんと言葉を切る. ¶ ***caution oneself*** against snares わなにかからないように注意する. ¶ A fox ***changed itself*** into a human form. きつねが人間に化けた. ‖ I ***change myself*** twice a day. 私は一日二回着物を着換える. ¶ He ***charged himself*** with all the sea risk of such vessels. 彼はこのような船舶の海上の危険の責任を引受けた. ¶ I cannot ***cheat myself*** into the belief that … [良心がとがめて] …とはどうしても信じ切れない. ¶ ***check oneself*** (=refrain) from … …から身を避ける. ¶ ***cheer oneself up*** 元気を出す. ¶ ***chin oneself*** 『体操』懸垂をする. ¶ ***clear oneself*** from (=of) the charge その明しを立てる ‖ ***clear oneself*** of doubts (suspicions) 疑いを晴らす. ¶ ***cloaking itself*** under a philanthropic garb 博愛に名を仮りて. ¶ ***clothe oneself*** very warmly ぬくぬくと

厚着をする ‖ ***clothe oneself*** in the skin of a sheep 羊の皮を着る(表面はやさしく見せかける). ¶***club themselves*** against ... 共同して...に当る. 【類】***club themselves*** for a cause. ¶***coddle oneself*** からだを大事にしすぎる. ¶A snake ***coils itself***. へびはとぐろを巻く. ¶I ***comfort myself*** by the fact that ... ...という事で安心する. ‖ ***comfort oneself*** with the thought that ... ...と考えて自ら慰める. 【類】***comfort oneself*** with this reflection (考え) that ... ¶This book does not ***commend itself*** to me. 私はこの本は感心しない. ‖ The book will ***commend itself*** to the admirers of Keats. その本はキーツ愛好者に喜ばれるだろう. 【類】that view is not likely to ***commend itself*** to the masses. ‖ ***commend itself*** to its own merits その価値が買われるだろう ‖ The action will hardly ***commend itself*** to the reflective. 思慮ある人々には恐らくこの行為は気に入らないであろう. 【類】Simplicity and directness are the qualities which ***commend themselves*** most to the young in both prose and poetry. ¶decline to ***commit oneself*** 言質を与えようとしない ‖ ***commit oneself*** on a problem ある問題について言質をとられる ‖ ***commit oneself*** for the information その報道に対し責任をとる ‖ ***commit oneself*** to the cause of freedom 自由のために働く ‖ ***commit oneself*** to an issue 責任をもって問題にとりかかる. 【類】***commit oneself*** to do the work of ... / The Secretary refused to ***commit himself*** to any promise. / We do not feel inclined to ***commit ourselves*** as regards this information. / the writers who have ***committed themselves*** to such utterances ‖ ***commit herself*** to his care 女が男の世話になる. 【類】***commit oneself*** to a doctor's care ‖ ***commit ourselves*** to fatalistic resignation 宿命とあきらめる ‖ ***commit oneself*** to the current of evil 悪の道をたどる ‖ ***commit oneself*** formally to the office 正式に就任する ‖ He is one of the last men likely to ***commit himself*** to an imprudent promise. 彼に限って無思慮に約束をするようなことはない. ‖ ***commit oneself*** for trial 進んで裁判を受ける ‖ The Japanese nation, through its new Constitution, has ***committed itself*** to a policy of perpetual disarmament. 日本国民は新憲法によって永久非武装の方針を定めた. ‖ ***commit oneself*** upon the unsafe subject of ... ...という危険な問題にとりかかる. ¶be found to ***communicate itself*** to practically all other segments of the economy 事実経済のすべての面に影響を及ぼしている. ¶***compensate oneself*** in ... ...で埋合わせをする. ¶***comport oneself*** with dignity [裁判官など]いかめしい態度を取る ‖ ***comport oneself*** in a more or less extraordinary manner 多少変ったふるまいをする. ¶it was some time before he could ***compose himself*** [笑いくずれなどした後で]気を落ちつけるのにしばらくかかった. ¶***conceal oneself*** behind a tree (under a desk, in a ditch) 木の陰(など)に身を潜める. ¶***conceit oneself*** [to be] ... ...とうぬぼれる. ¶so far as it ***concerns myself*** 私に関する限りは ‖ Do not ***concern yourself*** about my affairs 私のことは心配しないで下さい. ‖ ***concern oneself*** deeply in a matter ある事に深く関係する. 【類】You do not have to ***concern yourself*** about it. / You need ***concern yourself*** a little on this point. / too much occupied with it to ***concern themselves*** with the practical affairs of life ‖ The subjects with which the writer most ***concerned himself*** were ... 筆者が主として取扱った題目は ... ‖ the science ***concerns itself*** with ... その科学は...を説明する. 【類】***concern oneself*** with private affairs / ***concern oneself*** with Government / ***concern oneself*** with public work / Botany ***concerns itself*** with the study of plants ¶***conduct oneself*** badly = misconduct oneself 不行跡をする ‖ ***conduct oneself*** creditably りっぱに振舞う. 【類】I had all the necessary previous instructions how to act and ***conduct myself***. / ***conduct oneself*** well (= properly) / ***conduct oneself*** against one's own interest / ***conduct oneself*** like a mad man / ***conduct oneself*** in a proper manner = behave oneself / ***conduct oneself*** in a way that the world approves / the manner in which she ***conducted herself*** towards ... / ***conduct oneself*** with propriety (正しく) / ***conduct oneself*** with discretion (慎重に) / ***conduct oneself*** with Christian meekness. ¶***confide oneself*** 打ちあける. ¶***confine oneself*** to liquid food [食事は]流動食だけにする. 【類】***confine oneself*** wholly to the milk diet. ¶so far as one ***confines oneself*** to ... ...する分には ‖ ***confine oneself*** to one's sick bed 病気でふせっている. 【類】***confine oneself*** almost entirely to ... / the study ***confines itself*** to ... ¶***congratulate themselves*** for ... ...に対して互いに喜ぶ ‖ can ***congratulate themselves*** on the results of their efforts この成果に対して一同祝福できる. 【類】I ***congratulated myself*** on having got under shelter before the storm came on. ¶***consecrate oneself*** to the cause of humanity 人類の正義のために身をささげる ‖ ***consecrated herself*** to God by a vow of chastity 純潔を誓って彼女の一生を神にささげる. ¶***consider ourselves*** under a deep gratitude 深く感銘している. ¶***console oneself*** by thinking of (= with the thought that) ... ...と考えて自分を慰める. ¶What right have you to ***constitute yourself*** a judge of my conduct? 君は何の権利があって僕の行為の批判をするのか. ‖ He ***constituted himself*** our guide. 彼はガイドの役を買って出た ‖ ***constitute itself*** into a distinct class 別の種類に属する. ¶***consume oneself*** in inanity つまらないことで身をすり減らす. ¶Finally he could ***contain himself*** no longer and burst out. 我慢がしきれなくなって爆発した. 【類】I scarce knew how to ***contain*** (= refrain) ***myself***. ‖ He could not ***contain himself*** for joy. 喜びに我を忘れた. ¶we will ***content ourselves*** by ... われわれは...することで満足しよう. 【類】***content oneself*** by making a few short remarks / be forced to ***content ourselves*** with the hope that ... / the philosopher may ***content himself*** with the reflection (達観して) that ... / so let us ***content ourselves*** with the knowledge that ... / ***content oneself*** with one's lot (自分の運命) / I shall ***content myself*** with (= by) pointing out that ... ‖ ***contented himself*** with saying, "We shall see." 「今に見ろ」と言うだけで自己満足した. ¶***contradict oneself*** 自己矛盾をきたす. ¶He was unable to ***control himself***. 彼は自我を制することができなかった. ¶Conviction is worthless till it ***converts itself*** into conduct. 信念はそれが行動化されないと価値がない. ¶***convince*** (= ***persuade***) ***oneself*** of ... ...を堅く信じる. ¶***cool oneself*** 涼む, 気を静める. ¶But no I must ***correct myself***. いいや, そりゃ間違いだった(言い直さなければならない). ‖ These irregularities will ***correct themselves*** in time. これらの不規律はそのうち直るだろう. 【類】The situation will soon ***correct itself***. ¶He ***coughed himself*** into a fit. 彼は発作的にせきをした. ¶***count oneself*** among the number その数にはいる ‖ ***count oneself*** among the fortunate 自分を幸福者と思う ‖ irrevocably ***count oneself out*** 〘けん闘〙ノックアウトを宣告される. ¶***cover oneself*** with one's garments 衣服を身につける. ¶***cram oneself*** with food 腹一杯食べる ‖ ***cram oneself*** for an exam 一夜づけの猛勉をやる. ¶No one is bound to ***criminate himself***. 何人も自分に不利な証言をする必要はない. ¶***cross oneself*** 自分の胸に十字を切る. 【類】She ***crossed herself*** before the altar. ¶***cry oneself blind*** 目を泣きつぶす ‖ ***cry oneself*** to sleep [子供が]泣き寝入りする. ¶He ***cultivated himself*** by various reading and extensive travel. 彼は読書と多方面への旅行で自己修養を積んだ. ¶***cumber oneself*** about ... ...で心を悩ます. 【類】***cumber oneself*** with a lot of worries. ¶***cure oneself*** of a bad habit 悪癖を直す ‖ Christian scientists declare that by the exercise of the will power we may ***cure ourselves*** of any disease. キリスト教医学の信徒たちは意志の力で何の病気でも直ると言っている. 【類】Anarchy, by its very nature, ***cures itself***, sooner or later, by one means or another. ¶If I ***cut myself*** into four quarters, they would not be sufficient. 体が二つあっても足りない. ‖ ***cut oneself*** when one shaves ひげそりでけがをする. ¶***dash oneself*** against ... ...にぶっつかる; ...に体当りする. 【類】***dash themselves*** on their prey. ¶***debase oneself*** その権威をおとす. ¶***deceive oneself*** as to ... ...について自分をあざむく. ¶***deck herself*** in all her finery 晴着で着飾る, 盛装する. ¶***declare oneself*** 所信を公言する; その旗色を鮮明にする ‖ The malady first ***declared itself*** in 1897. その病気は一八九七年に始めて現われた. ‖ ***declare oneself*** after the following manner 次のように所信を述べる ‖ openly ***declared themselves*** against ... ...に対し反対の態度を表明する. 【類】***declare themselves*** strongly in favor of ... / ***declare oneself*** its author. ¶***dedicate oneself*** to the work of ... ...の仕事に専念する. ¶There is an accuracy that ***defeats itself*** by the overemphasis of details. 細目を強調

し過ぎて正確を欠くということがある. ¶give a chance to ***defend oneself*** 自己弁護の機会を与える ‖ ***defend oneself*** against number 大勢を相手にして防戦する. 【類】he ***defended himself*** so energetically that ... / ***defend oneself*** against a false accusation / ***defend oneself*** against a charge / He wanted to kiss her, but she ***defended herself***. / be in a position to ***defend themselves*** against aggression / ***defend oneself*** against an attack (enemy) / ***defended himself*** by stating that ... / The country is prepared to ***defend itself*** from attack from any quarter. / ***defend oneself*** from wrong / ***defend themselves*** with great bravery. ¶The term ***defines itself***. その語は定義なしに明りょうである. ¶***degrade oneself*** 身を持ちくずす ‖ ***degrade oneself*** to the level of the brute 畜生道に落ちる. ¶***delight oneself*** with gazing at the sleeping infant 眠る幼児をながめて喜びに浸る. ¶***deliver oneself*** of an opinion (a joke) 意見を述べる(冗談を言う). 【類】he ***delivered himself*** as follows ‖ ***deliver herself*** of a seven-pound baby 七ポンドの赤ん坊を産む ‖ ***deliver oneself*** of an address to ... ...に向って演説をする ‖ ***deliver himself*** of a stream of crackling language ものすごい言葉を連続的に吐き出す(怒ったタクシーの運転手など). ¶***delude oneself*** into a pretense that ... ...と断じる錯覚に陥る ‖ ***delude himself*** into the belief that he understands when he does not understand 自分で分からないことを分かったかのように思い込む. 【類】***delude oneself*** into thinking that ... / he ***deluded himself*** with the idea that ... ¶***demean oneself*** to a beggar こじきに身を落す. ¶***denationalize oneself*** 国籍を離れる. ¶***denounce oneself*** [to the authorities] 自首する. ¶***deny oneself*** 自己を捨てる ‖ ***deny oneself*** to callers (=visitors) 面会を謝絶する ‖ ***deny oneself*** the pleasure of smoking 禁煙する ‖ ***deny himself*** for the good of his family 家族の幸福のため犠牲になる. ¶***deport oneself*** like a gentleman 紳士らしく振舞う. ¶He ***deprived himself*** of many pleasures in order to give his children a good education. 子供たちを教育しようと色々な楽しみを捨てた. 【類】finally ***deprived themselves*** of the bare creature comforts of life (日常の安楽) in the interest of ... / He ***deprived himself*** of the necessaries of life (生活必需品), and gave all his income to the poor. ¶***describe itself*** 名でその性質が分かる(クラブなど) ‖ ***describe oneself*** as ... ...だと自称する. ¶***destroy oneself*** 自滅する. ¶***detach itself*** from the line 脱線する(列車が) ‖ ***detach oneself*** from some organization 脱会する. ¶***develop itself*** strongly 強力に発展する. 【類】a new tyranny ***developing itself*** under the external forms of ... / ***develop itself*** into full growth. ¶***devote oneself*** chiefly to ... ...に専念する. 【類】***devote oneself*** with great enthusiasm and success to ... / ***devoted themselves*** with great ardor (=zeal) to ... / ***devote oneself*** to the pursuit of pleasure / give up all other literary work (執筆) to ***devote oneself*** to ... / ***devote oneself*** to deep meditation denying all worldly affairs / ***devote oneself*** to the study of sociology / ***devote oneself*** to the investigation of ... / ***devote themselves*** exclusively to the company's service (会社の仕事) / ***devote oneself*** to the life of a scholar / ***devote themselves*** with great assiduity (うまずたゆまず) to ... / ***devote oneself*** tranquilly to study / leave all earthly attractions and ***devote oneself*** to a life of prayer and penance (祈りとざんげの生活) / ***devote oneself*** with unceasing energy (こつこつと) to obtaining mastery of English / ***devote oneself*** too much to athletics (politics) / ***devote oneself*** more to one's family / ***devote oneself*** to the fine art of writing (書道). ¶***diet oneself*** 一定の食料を取る. ¶Under the benign superintendence of the director the spirit of love ***diffused itself*** through all its members. 監督の慈愛深い指導の下に愛の精神は会員全部に浸み込んだ. ¶***dig oneself in***=prepare a defensive trench or pit 護身のためざんごうを掘る ‖ ***dig oneself out*** through a fence さくの下を堀って抜け出る. ¶those who know not how to ***direct*** (=***control***) ***themselves*** 自制心のない人々. ¶The river ***disburdens*** (=***discharges***) ***itself*** into the sea. 川は海にそそぐ. ‖ ***disburden oneself*** of grief (care) 悲しみ(心配)を人に打ちあける. ¶The rubbish carts ***disburden themselves*** into a metallic conveyor. 清掃車のごみは金属製のコンベイヤーにあけられる. ¶***discharge oneself*** of one's duty. その義務からのがれる. ¶***disembarrass oneself*** of an old girl 以前の女と手を切る. ¶***disembowel oneself*** 切腹する ‖ ***disembowel oneself*** rather than survive the disgrace 恥辱に生きるよりはむしろ切腹する. ¶***disengage oneself*** from slavery 自由の身となる ‖ She was unable to ***disengage*** herself from him. 彼との腐れ縁が続いた. ‖ softly ***disengage himself*** from her fond embrace 彼女の愛の抱擁からそっと身を離す ‖ ***disengage oneself*** from sensual passion 煩悩を払いのける. 【類】***disengage oneself*** of racial prejudices. ¶***disgrace oneself*** before ... ...の面前で恥をかく. ¶***disguise itself*** as a man 人間にばける ‖ He ***disguised himself*** the best as he could. 彼は苦心して変装した. ¶***dispatch oneself*** to ... at the invitation of ... ...の招待で...に出かける. ¶***disport oneself*** at will 勝手なことをする(振舞う) ‖ tortoises ***disporting themselves*** in water 水中で遊び回るかめ ‖ ***disport*** (=enjoy) ***oneself*** over wine 酒を飲んで浮かれる ‖ ***disport themselves*** to their heart's content 思う存分遊ぶ. 【類】***disport oneself*** according to one's taste / Crowds watched the boys ***disporting themselves***. / Practically all London is ***disporting itself*** away from home. / dragons and other fabulous monsters ***disporting themselves*** in clouds. ¶***disqualify oneself*** by ... ...のため失格する. ¶***disrobe oneself*** 着物をぬぐ. ¶***dissociate oneself*** from an organization (a club, party) 脱会する. ‖ The train service gradually ***dissociates itself*** from the time tables. 列車のダイヤルはだんだん狂って来る(降雪・出水などで). ¶Does oil ***dissolve itself*** in water? 油は水に溶けるか. 【類】Ice ***dissolves itself***. ¶***distinguish oneself*** 群を抜く ‖ he ***distinguished himself*** at the battle of ... ...の戦闘で手柄を立てた. 【類】He worked hard and ***distinguished himself*** at mathematics. / ***distinguish oneself*** in life / ***distinguish oneself*** by gifts of speech (雄弁の才) / ***distinguish oneself*** by scholarship (courage) / one who greatly ***distinguished oneself*** in the affairs of men / he ***distinguished himself*** in various actions, especially in the capture of ... / ***distinguish oneself*** in a battle / ***distinguish oneself*** in literature. ¶He ***distressed himself*** about the matter. 彼はその件で心を痛めた. ‖ Come, come, my dear, don't ***distress yourself***. 君, 君, そう心配するなよ. ¶The army ***distributed itself*** over the country. 軍隊は全国に駐留した. ¶***divert themselves*** with a free talk 雑談で気を晴らす. 【類】***divert oneself*** by reading books (listening to music). ¶***divest oneself*** of a habit 癖を直す ‖ ***divest oneself*** of one's robes 着物をぬぐ. 【類】***divest oneself*** of one's clothes (everything one has on) / ***divest oneself*** of every article of dress (all one's garment) / ***divest herself*** of all but the drawers ‖ ***divest oneself*** of a party (club, an association) 党(クラブ, 会)を脱退する ‖ ***divest oneself*** of one's ownership その所有権を放棄する. 【類】***divest itself*** of authority (権力) / Human nature is never able to ***divest itself*** completely of its inborn prejudices and prepossessions. / She ***divested herself*** of every trace of feminine daintiness (しおらしさ) / ***divest ourselves*** of the hostile attitude towards ... / ***divest oneself*** of the character of agent (代理店の資格) / ***divest oneself*** of responsibility for ... / ***divest oneself*** of ***oneself***—that second self (第二の我) one has unconsciously acquired. ¶At this point the story ***divides itself*** into halves ここでその話は二つに分かれる ‖ ***divide themselves*** roughly into two classes 大体二つの種類に分かれる ‖ ***divide itself*** into two periods of development 発展過程は二段階に分かれる. 【類】Carpets ***divide themselves*** into two classes: those which are made by hand, and those which are made by machine. / Roughly speaking the matter ***divides itself*** into three principal heads (主な項目). ¶***divorce oneself*** from the 20th century 二十世紀から離れる. ¶***dose oneself*** with medicine of unknown composition 調合のはっきりしない薬を服用する. ¶The American export trade with ... ***doubled itself*** within three years. ...とのアメリカの輸出貿易額は三年間に倍になった. 【類】The population has ***doubled itself*** in the past ten years. ¶***drag oneself along*** 足を引ずって歩く ‖ ***drag oneself*** to ... 無理に...に行く ‖ He ***dragged himself up*** to his feet. 彼はようやくからだを起して立ちあがった. ¶***draw oneself up*** in dignity 胸をはって威厳を示す. 【類】***draw oneself up*** with offended dignity (無礼に対して) ‖

he *drew himself up* angrily, and said ... 【類】*draw oneself up* to one's full height. ¶The little boy can *dress himself*. その幼ない子は自分で着物が着れる. ‖ quickly *dress oneself* 急いで着物を着る ‖ *dress oneself up* for a party パーティに行くため着飾る ‖ *dress oneself* in woman's clothing 女装する. 【類】*dress oneself* in one's best clothes / *dress oneself* in silk. ¶*drill oneself* for examination by re-reading one's books or notes 本やノートを読み直して試験準備をする ‖ *drill oneself* on the meanings of these words これらの語の意味をよく覚える. ¶*drink himself* into a limp condition ぐでんぐでんに酔っぱらう ‖ *drink oneself* into unconsciousness (illness) 自分が分からなく(病気に)なるほど飲む ‖ *drink oneself* out of a situation 悪酒で職を失う ‖ *drink oneself* to death 酒で死ぬ. ¶*drown oneself* in a well 井戸に投身する ‖ *drown oneself* voluntarily 投身自殺をする. 【類】try to *drown oneself* in a river. ¶*dry oneself* on a towel タオルで体をふく. ¶*ease oneself* 便通する; くつろぐ ‖ *ease oneself* by cursing one's enemy 敵をののしってうさを晴らす. ¶*eat oneself sick* (death) 食い過ぎて病気になる(死ぬ). ¶It was a chance of *edging himself* into the daily. それが彼のその新聞社にはいり込む機会だった. ¶*educate oneself* 独学する. ¶*efface oneself* 私を滅する. ¶Human thought *elaborates itself* with the progress of intelligence. 人間の思想は知能の進むにつれて複雑になる. ¶*emancipate themselves* from the thraldom of ... ...の束縛から脱する. ¶*employ oneself* by reading or by writing 読書または作文で日々を暮す ‖ How do you *employ* (What do you do with) *yourself* on Sunday? 日曜日には何をなさいますか. ‖ I think it best fit to *employ myself* in ... ...するのが私には一番適していると思う ‖ Let every one *employ himself* in what he knows. それぞれ自分のなれていることをやらせることだ ‖ *employ oneself* on education 教育に従事する. 【類】He thinks that the business is one which is fit to *employ himself*. / He *employed himself* with so much sweetness and warmth to soothe and comfort me in my misfortune. ¶The Ohio *empties itself* (=flows) into the Mississippi. オハイオ川はミシシッピー川に注ぐ. ¶*encumber oneself* with worldly cares 浮世の苦労で悩む. ¶*endear oneself* to womankind 女に可愛がられる ‖ *endear oneself* to everyone of one's neighborhood 近所のみんなから好かれる. 【類】Next to the dog and the cat, rabbits have *endeared themselves* to all children. / He *endeared himself* to the hearts of the people (人から慕われる) / He *endeared himself* to them by his kindness and courtesy. / John D. Rockefeller, Jr., has *endeared himself* to all humanity by his generous benefactions (多大の寄付) toward the welfare of mankind in general. ¶*engage oneself* in the study of ... ...の研究に従事する ‖ *engage oneself* in an affair ある事件に関係する ‖ *engage oneself* to perform one's duties 義務を果すと約束する ‖ *engage oneself* to a merchant 商人と契約する. 【類】I have *engaged myself* to nothing. / *engage himself* (婚約する) to a rich widow. ¶*engross oneself* in gambling (sport, autoing) ばくち(など)に夢中になる. ¶I *enjoyed myself* professionally in finding out all its workings. その機能を全部会得して技術上の喜びを味わった. ‖ *enjoy oneself* over one's wine 一杯やって御機げんになる ‖ *enjoy oneself* to the full (=to one's heart's content) 十分に歓を尽す ‖ *Enjoy yourself* with this magazine. この雑誌でも見てらっしゃい. 【類】*enjoy oneself* so well / Good-bye ... *Enjoy yourself* (=Have a good time). / *enjoy oneself* without going to excess. ¶*enlarge oneself* on a subject ある問題に対する自分の理解を深める. ¶I prefer to *enlist myself* among those who ... 私は...という人たちの仲間に入りたい. ‖ *enlist oneself* for the army 軍隊に入る. ¶*enmesh oneself* in difficulties 困難に陥る. 【類】*enmesh itself* in complications. ¶*enrich oneself* 金持になる. ¶*enroll oneself* 兵士になる ‖ *enroll oneself* as a member 会員となる. 【類】*enroll oneself* in the service (軍務) ‖ *enroll oneself* under the banner of Venus 色男になる. ¶*ensconce oneself* in a hotel ホテルに落着く ‖ The cat *ensconced itself* in the arm-chair. ねこがひじかけいすに気持ちよげに納まっていた. 【類】*ensconce oneself* in flush cushions (ビロードの座ぶとん). ¶*enshroud oneself* in mist もやに包まれる ‖ *enshroud oneself* in obscurity 世間から忘れられるようにする. ¶The situation *entangled itself* to the annoyance of all concerned. 事情がこんがらかって関係者一同が当惑した. ¶*enter oneself* as a clerk 事務員と記帳する ‖ go to ... to *enter oneself* in a school ある学校に入学するために...に行く. ¶The crowd *entertained itself* with speechless staring. 群集はあっけにとられてながめていた. ¶The landscape *envisaged itself* before me. 山水の景色が目前に現われた. ¶*equip oneself* for a battle 戦闘準備をする ‖ *equip oneself* with a camera カメラを携帯する. ¶*erect oneself* 直立する. ¶try to *establish oneself* as dictator 独裁者となろうとする ‖ He *established himself* at Malacca. 彼はマラッカに身を落付けた. 【類】*establish oneself* as an artist (a fiction writer) / She *established herself* as one of America's foremost actresses. / *establish oneself* as commission agent under the style of ... (...の屋号で). / We have *established ourselves* as commission merchants for American goods at the above address. / *establish oneself* in business / *establish oneself* in a new home / *establish oneself* in a chair / *establish oneself* in a comfortable room / *establish oneself* in a small provincial town / The guide book has *established itself* in public favor. / The book has quickly *established itself* as the true and trusted friend of many teachers and students. / The Dutch *established themselves* in Java during the early years of the seventeenth century. / A new doctor has *established himself* on this street. / The party *established itself* on a firm footing. ‖ *establish herself* in strength 強国になる ‖ She *established herself* with considerable courage. 彼女はしっかりしていた. ‖ *establish oneself* in practice 開業する(医者・弁護士が). ¶*estrange oneself* from city life = rusticate いなかへ引っ込む ‖ *estrange oneself* from practical life 実務から引退する, 隠居する. 【類】*estrange oneself* from politics (政界). ¶*Europeanize herself* upon Prussian lines プロシア流に欧化する. ¶*evaluate oneself* 自己評価をやる. ¶to *exalt oneself* in another's eyes 人によく思われようとして ‖ *exalt oneself* to the position of ... ...の地位に昇格する. ¶*examine oneself* on occasions as to what one has done 自分のやったことを時々内省する. ¶*exculpate oneself* 弁解する. ¶He says he wants to *excuse himself*. 彼はこれで失礼(辞去)したいと言ってます. 【類】Now I must excuse *myself*. ‖ I can't *excuse myself*. 申訳がない. ‖ I called on him to *excuse myself*. 断りに彼を訪問した. 【類】I really don't know how to *excuse myself*. / We sometimes *excuse ourselves* by saying, "I have a poor memory." / *excuse oneself* for absence / She *excused herself* for not returning your call. / *excuse myself* on the ground that ... / He sent me a letter *excusing himself* on the ground of illness. ‖ *excuse oneself* from seeing him 彼との面会を断る ‖ *excuse oneself* from the exercise of one's function その職務執行を回避する. ¶*exercise oneself* in music 音楽の練習をやる ‖ *exercise oneself* in a foreign language 外国語の練習をやる ‖ *exercise oneself* over the question その問題を考える. ¶*exert oneself* for ... ...のために努力する. 【類】*exert oneself* in study / *exert oneself* to the utmost / They are obliged to *exert themselves* to the fullest extent of their ability. ¶*exhale oneself* of enthusiasm (wrath) 熱心さ(怒気)を示す. ¶I have *exhausted myself* walking miles all day. 一日中何マイルも歩いてくたくたになった. ¶A slight smoke in the distance shows that the fire is *exhausting itself*. 遠方のちょっとした煙りで火事は消えかかっていると分かる. ¶One would not wish to *exhibit themselves* in a hopeless guise. 人は絶望の姿を見せたくないだろう. ‖ *exhibit oneself* to others 人前で裸体になる. ¶They *exiled themselves* for the sake of money-making. 彼らは海外に出かせぎした. ‖ *exile oneself* from Germany ドイツから亡命する. ¶*expiate oneself* (=do penance) in ... ...の苦行をして罪亡ぼしをする. ¶I cannot *explain myself*. どう説明してよいか分からない. ‖ Let me *explain myself*. わけをお話しましょう. ‖ Be good enough to *explain yourself* again. すみませんがもう一度説明して下さい. 【類】I pressed him to *explain himself*. / The enclosed letter *explained itself*. / The name easily *explains itself*. / The figures (数字) almost *explain themselves* (=speak for themselves). / I received the following communication, which *explained itself*. ¶He was very embarrassed in the attempt to

explain himself. 弁明しようとして非常に困った. ¶***expose oneself*** to the suspicion of being ... ...という疑いを受けるようにする ‖ you ***expose yourself*** needlessly (=unnecessarily) to ... それでは...に対してやぶへびになる. 【類】They ***exposed themselves*** to abundance of ridicule. / ***expose oneself*** to the danger (=hazard) of ... / ***expose oneself*** to public odium (きらわれ者) / ***expose oneself*** to the hatred of some and the contempt of others / ***expose oneself*** to the jibes (あざけり) of ... / I don't care a crap (ちっとも) to ***expose myself*** to criticism. / ***expose oneself*** to sunlight. ¶***exonerate myself*** in one or two particulars 一二の点で身のあかしを立てる. ¶***expatriate oneself***=renounce citizenship 市民権を返上する(捨てる) ‖ ***expatriate oneself*** 本国を去る, 国籍を捨てる. 【類】In 1916 a law was passed in Japan opening a way for Japanese in Hawaii to ***expatriate themselves***, that is, to rid *themselves* of their Japanese citizenship. ¶bluntly ***express oneself*** against ... ...に向って露骨に反対意見を吐く ‖ ***express itself*** in many ways 色々な形で表われる. 【類】***express oneself*** strongly (clearly) / those who can ***express themselves*** in good English / ***express oneself*** well in English / ***express oneself*** as follows: / He ***expresses himself*** thus: / ***expressed himself*** as greatly pleased with ... / ***express oneself*** as displeased with (には不賛成) ... / ***express themselves*** as being greatly concerned (大いに関心を持っている) about ... / ***express oneself*** entirely in favor of ... / ***express oneself*** in mathematical formulas (数学式に議論を述べる) / ***express oneself*** in strong language / ***express oneself*** in good form (りっぱに) / freely ***express oneself*** as to ... / He ***expressed himself*** only by gestures, pretending to be deaf and dumb. / ***express oneself*** in technical language / He ***expressed himself*** in the following language (次のように). / There are only a few Westerners in Japan who can ***express themselves*** intimately in Japanese. / ability to ***express oneself*** in public / ***express oneself*** in violent language (ひどい言葉) / ***express oneself*** in a manner interesting and agreeable to others / I could not resist ***expressing myself*** / He went too far in the manner in which he ***expressed himself***. / He ***expresses himself*** in speech and in writing most fluently in English. / ***express oneself*** in other language than his own / ***expresses himself*** to a similar effect / I can ***express myself*** with certainty. / He generally ***expresses himself*** with a frankness which is bordering on rudeness. / ***express themselves*** with clearness, directness, and force / ***express oneself*** with strong feeling ‖ ***express oneself*** in high terms of ... ...を称賛する ‖ the artistic spirit of the nation ***expresses itself*** in ... 同国民の芸術心は...に現われている. ¶***extricate oneself*** from difficulties 困難を克服する. 【類】***extricate oneself*** (脱出する) from a difficult position / ***extricate themselves*** from the wreckage (破船). ¶***fag oneself*** to death 働き過ぎて死ぬ. ¶***familiarize oneself*** with (=to) ... ...に慣れる. 【類】***familiarize oneself*** with the manners and customs of a country. ¶calmly ***fan oneself*** おちついて扇子を使う. 【類】***fan herself*** with her handkerchief. ¶This idea ***fastened itself*** upon me. その考えが私の心にしっかり根をおろした. ‖ The account of the terrific fight will ***fasten itself*** on the mind of the readers. ¶***feast oneself*** upon a picture 絵を見て楽しむ. 【類】***feast oneself*** with music / ***feast oneself*** with the pleasure of ... ¶***feed themselves*** and their families 自分たちとその家族を養う. 【類】enable the Japanese to help ***feed themselves*** (自給). ¶I don't ***feel myself*** tonight 今夜は気分が悪い. ‖ I ***feel*** quite ***myself*** today. きょうはすっかりもとの身体のような気がする(病気上りなど). ‖ ***feel oneself*** above the work offered 与えられた仕事を役不足だと思う. 【類】They ***felt themselves*** in a position (立場) to announce the plan of ... / I ***feel myself*** under particular obligations to ... ‖ He ***felt himself*** flattered by the invitation. 彼はその招待を受けて得意であった. ‖ ***feel oneself*** running down 《米》からだが弱るように思う. ¶***fence oneself*** against the enemy 敵の攻撃に備える. ¶The university has had great difficulty in ***financing itself***. 同大学は財政上非常な困難に陥っている. ¶***find oneself*** 自分の長所に気付く; 宿とまかないを自分で持つ ‖ He learned to ***find himself*** in his early days. 彼は年少にして自立の道を学んだ ‖ a world very different from that in which we find ourselves today 今日われわれの住む世界とは非常に違った世界. ‖ How do you ***find yourself*** today? きょうはいかがですか. 【類】How does the patient ***find himself?*** / He does not seem to know how to ***find himself*** with his present income. / He has ***found himself*** barely above want (生きるのがやっと). ‖ ***find oneself*** more at ease with ... ...だと気が楽だ. ‖ ***find oneself*** between two fires 板ばさみになる ‖ the economic plight in which Europe now ***finds itself*** 欧州の経済的現状 ‖ you will ***find yourself progressing*** easily through the world 順調に世渡りができよう ‖ Masters help their pupils to ***find themselves***. 教師たちは弟子たちが銘々の天分を伸ばすように面倒をみてやる. ‖ In a word, my mind has ***found itself***. 一言で言うと私は本心に帰ったわけだ(迷っていたことに目覚めて). ‖ How to help the young man "***find himself***" as early as possible is the thing desired. いかにして青年をしてできるだけ早く各自の使命を認識させるよう補導するかということが願わしいのである. ‖ ***find oneself*** at a momentary loss for words ちょっと言葉が出て来ない ‖ ***find oneself*** at the door of death=face to face with death 死に直面する ‖ ***find oneself*** before a movie camera 映写機に映されている ‖ ***find oneself*** in unison with ... in one's judgments 私の判断は...のと全く一致している ‖ ***find oneself*** at a disadvantage 不利な地位に立っていることに気ずく. 【類】One who knows only his dialect ***finds himself*** at a disadvantage in social life. / ***find oneself*** in difficulties / ***find oneself*** in a sorry plight (情けない状態) / He ***found himself*** in the midst of insurmountable difficulties. / ***find itself*** in a squeeze (=fix) / ***find oneself*** in a tight squeeze (のっぴきならない羽目) ‖ ***find oneself*** in a car (class) with ... / It was ten days or more before I ***found myself*** once again in that restaurant. / I followed him, and ***found myself*** in a small apartment. / before he ***found himself*** in Japan / ***find oneself*** in a precarious condition (不安定な状態) / ***find oneself*** in an embarrassing position / There French is now ***finding itself*** in competition with other languages. / ***find oneself*** in line with ... (...と一致して) / I ***find myself*** in complete agreement with his views. / I am glad to ***find myself*** on this point in agreement with ... ‖ ***find oneself*** up to the neck in an affair 事件に深入りする ‖ I don't know how to ***find myself out***. 出口が分からない. ‖ ***find oneself*** under an obligation to do ... ...する羽目になる. 【類】***find oneself*** under the necessity of doing ‖ ***find oneself*** face to face with trials 試練に直面する. ‖ I ***found myself*** with 10,000 yen to my credit at the end of the year. 私は一年の終りには一万円の貸しになっていた. ‖ He ***found himself*** within sight of his home. いつの間にか家が見えてきた. ‖ ***find themselves*** on graduation without any prospects of a job 卒業はしたが就職の当もない ‖ ***find oneself struck*** for want of funds 資金欠乏で行詰る. ¶***fit oneself*** for one's chosen work 自分で選んだ仕事につく準備をする ‖ ***fit ourselves*** to a new situation 新境界に順応する ‖ ***fit themselves*** for the responsibilities of the strenuous years which lie ahead 今後何年間か骨の折れる仕事の責任をとる用意をする ‖ ***fit oneself*** for school (college) 入学の準備をする ‖ ***fix myself*** in the memory 記憶に残る. ¶***fix herself up*** a bit [女が]ちょっとしたくする, 身じまいをする. ¶***flatter oneself*** with such hopes そのような希望で気をよくする. ¶it may sound I'm ***flattering myself***, but ... 口幅ったいことを言うようですが... ‖ I don't mean to ***flatter myself*** when I say that ... 自分の口から言うのも何ですが... 【類】I ***flatter myself*** with the hope that I have done my duty. / ***flatter oneself*** with having passed the examination with approval. ¶***fling oneself*** down on the ground 大地に身を投げる. 【類】The mother bird ***flung herself*** against the big animal. / ***fling oneself*** into a pond / She ***flung herself*** into her lover's arms. / ***fling oneself*** into an arm-chair / ***fling oneself*** into the life of journalism / He ***flung himself*** on a couch (長いす) / He ***flung himself*** on the ground and pretended to be dead. ‖ ***fling oneself out*** (=***about***). じだんだを踏む; 怒ってあばれ出す ‖ ***fling herself*** at a man's head 男に夢中になる; 男を自分に引きつけようとする. ¶***fold itself up*** [巻きものなど]ひとりでに巻ける. ¶The idea ***forced itself*** into his mind. いや応なしにその考えが頭に浮んできた. ‖ The tears ***forced themselves*** into his eyes. 彼は涙がこら

えられなかった. ‖ I had to ***force myself*** to ... いや応なしに...しなければならなくなった. ‖ I recoil from ***forcing myself*** upon his notice. 私には彼に自分を見せつけるようなことはできない. 【類】 It constantly ***forces itself*** on the notice of careful observers. / the truth ***forces itself*** upon the attention of ... / the question that ***forces itself*** upon us is ... ¶my eyes ***focused themselves*** on ... 私の目は...に止まった. ¶They ***fool themselves*** into thinking ... 彼らは愚にも...と思う. ¶***forgetting oneself*** われを忘れて ‖ I will never ***forget myself***. 私は決して本心を失わない. 【類】 an angry woman who ***forgets herself*** / ***forget oneself*** about love affairs / ***forget oneself*** and one's soul in giving joy to others / ***forget oneself*** on one's studies / ***forget oneself*** to such an extent as to ... ¶After the habit has ***formed itself*** it is very difficult to get rid of it. 癖はいったんついたら仲々抜けないものだ. ‖ ***form themselves*** in groups いくつかのグループを作る ‖ ***form themselves*** into a band (an association) 一隊(協会)を組織する ‖ I had not intended thus to encourage her, but the words fairly ***formed themselves*** upon my lips. 私はそういって彼女を元気づける積りはなかったが言葉が自然と口に出て来た. 【類】 The respective followers of Wesley and Whitefield ***formed themselves*** into separate organizations. / ***formed themselves*** into a committee to carry out the purposes in view. ¶***forswear oneself*** and desert his colors 誓いにそむいて彼の旗下から脱走する. ¶***fortify themselves*** in a trench ざんごうで身を護る ‖ ***fortify oneself*** against a cold (disease) かぜ(病気)にかからないように身体を丈夫にする. 【類】 after he had ***fortified himself*** by several glasses of absinthe / ***fortify oneself*** by citing many illustrations (自説をかためる) / ***fortify*** (=arm) ***oneself*** with necessary information. ¶***free oneself*** by force 無理に振り切る ‖ ***free oneself*** from anxiety 心配をなくす ‖ ***free oneself*** of obligations 義務(負債)がなくなる. 【類】 ***free oneself*** from embarrassment=get out / ***free oneself*** from debts / a nation trying to ***free itself*** from the curse of slavery. ¶Do not ***frighten yourself*** so about nothing. 影を見てそうおびえるな. ¶***fulfil oneself*** (=one's promise *or* one's prophecy) 約束(予言など)を守る(実行する). ¶He ***gambled himself*** out of all the money and property then in his possession. 彼はばくちで当時所有していた財産全部を失った. ¶***gather themselves*** together from the four points of the compass 四方から集まる ‖ The panther ***gathered herself*** [***up***] for a vigorous spring. ひょうは猛烈に飛び上ろうと身構えをした. ¶***get oneself*** into serious trouble 厄介なことになる. 【類】 Go through life without ***getting yourself*** into trouble. ‖ ***get oneself*** into a bad fix 窮地に陥る ‖ ***get*** [***oneself***] into a bad habit 悪い癖がつく ‖ ***get oneself*** out of the room (house) へや(家)から出て行く ‖ ***get oneself well up*** in the part その演じる役になりきる. ¶***gird oneself*** to get through the difficulty 困難をやり通す覚悟を定める ‖ ***gird oneself up*** for a fight (game) けんか(勝負)しようと緊こん一番する. ¶women who ***give themselves*** for money 金のために身を売る女たち ‖ ***give herself*** for love 愛情に身を任せる. 【類】 She ***gave herself*** to him. ‖ ***give oneself*** to despair 途方にくれる ‖ ***give oneself*** to teaching 教職につく ‖ ***give themselves*** to prostitution 売春婦になる ‖ The soldiers ***gave themselves*** to plunder. 兵士たちは略奪をほしいままにした. 【類】 He ***gave himself*** to innumerable forms of public and friendly service. / ***give oneself*** wholly up (信仰する) to Christianity. ¶***give oneself away*** 心中を披瀝する ‖ She ***gives herself*** to actions which in the next she will regret. 彼女は後で悔むようなことをやる. ¶The mountains ***glass themselves*** in the lake. 山々が湖水に影を映している. ¶***glorify oneself*** もったいをつける. ¶***glut oneself*** with ... ...をたらふく食べる. ¶***gorge oneself*** with ... ...を腹一杯食う ‖ ***gorge oneself*** with the victuals placed before one 出された食物をぱくつく. ¶In the United States the people ***govern themselves***. 米国では国民自身が政治をとる. ‖ He failed to ***govern himself*** at the news. その知らせを聞いて心が乱れた. 【類】 This is a just and reasonable rule for men to ***govern themselves*** by. / ***govern itself*** without outside aid. ¶***gratify oneself*** by accepting a sacrifice 犠牲を甘んじて引受ける. ¶***ground oneself*** in Russian ロシア語の初歩を独修する ‖ ***ground oneself*** on scientific ideas 科学思想の基礎を学ぶ. ¶naturally ***group themselves*** in two main classes 自然二大別になる ‖ ***group themselves*** in combinations それらは組合わせができる. ¶Let me ***guard myself*** against misunderstanding. 誤解のないようにこれだけ申上げておこう. ‖ ***guard oneself*** against disease (accidents) 病気(など)に備える. ¶***habituate oneself*** to vice 悪の道に染まる ‖ ***habituate oneself*** to hard work (hardships, a cold climate) 労働(など)になれる. ¶He ***hanged himself*** in the kitchen (on a tree). 彼は台所(立木)で首をくくった. ¶***harmonize itself*** in color with ... ...と色のうつりがよい. ¶I ***hate myself***. おのが身にあいそがつきる. ¶***haul*** (=***pull***) ***oneself up*** by a rope ロープをよじ上る. ¶She ***heaped herself*** with reproaches. 彼女は非難を浴びた ‖ The sand ***heaped itself*** up while sea-winds were sweeping. 海風が吹きまくる間に砂丘ができた. ¶***Help yourself***. 召上って下さい. ‖ You must help him to ***help himself***. 自分でやれるように教えてやらなけりゃいけない. ‖ No man can help others who wants ***help himself***. 人の助けを必要とする人は人を助けることはできない. 【類】 I'll just ***help myself***. / ***Help yourself***, please, to a fan. / ***help oneself*** to *saké* freely / The point is not simply to help the people, but to help the people to ***help themselves***. / help Europe to ***help itself*** toward a reconstruction / ***help oneself*** out of financial difficulties / Nature suffers nothing to remain in her kingdoms which cannot ***help themselves***. / liberally ***help oneself*** to the other fellow's savings / ***help themselves*** to a little portable property (ハンドバッグなど) / ***help oneself*** to apples from sidewalk stands / ***help oneself*** freely to another's property / ***help oneself*** to money from one's mother's bureau / He ***helped himself*** to 30,000 rubles and fled on foot. / They tied up the manager and ***helped themselves*** to $3,000 from his safe. / No power has a right to ***help itself*** to enemy properties. / Every nation ***helps itself*** to the idea of others. ¶***hide oneself*** among the rocks (behind a tree, in a cave) 岩の間(など)に身を隠す ‖ He ***hid himself*** in the hold of the ocean-steamer with a view to obtaining a free passage. 彼は密航しようとして外洋船の船倉に身を隠した. 【類】 ***hide oneself*** in deep mountain recesses, far from the ken of man / ***hide oneself*** under a heap of straw. ¶***hire oneself*** out as a servant to... 雇われて...の召使となる ‖ The labourer, being destitute of the instruments of labor, must ***hire himself*** to the possessor of capital. 労働者は機具がないので資本家の下で働かなければならない. ¶***hold oneself*** responsible for ... ...に対する責任を負う ‖ ***hold themselves*** out to the public as ... 世間に...と吹聴する ‖ We readily ***hold ourselves*** at your command. お指図をお待ちしています. ‖ ***hold oneself*** in readiness to ... ...する覚悟をしている ‖ ***hold themselves*** in armed readiness [軍が]待機している. 【類】 The regiment has been ordered to ***hold itself*** in readiness for active service. ‖ ***hold oneself*** to it by one's own effort 務めてそれを固守する. ¶***huddle themselves up*** in a corner すみっこにかたまる. 【類】 ***huddle oneself up*** in bed (in a blanket) / ***huddle themselves together*** for warmth. ¶***hug oneself*** over the scene その光景を見てうれしがる ‖ ***hug oneself*** on success (victory) 成功(勝利)で喜こぶ. 【類】 ***hug themselves together*** with joy. ¶***humble oneself*** before one's seniors 上役の前でぺこぺこする. 【類】 ***humble oneself*** before one's creditors. ¶That will serve only to ***humiliate yourself***. そんなことすれば恥をかくだけだ. ¶***hurl oneself*** at ... ...に体当りする ‖ ***hurl oneself*** from the third floor window of a building ビルの三階の窓から身を投げる ‖ ***hurl oneself*** over a cliff (=precipice) がけから身を投げる. ¶The boy ***hurt himself***. その少年はけがをした. 【類】 ***hurt oneself*** through fatigue. ¶***Identify yourself!*** 身分証明書をお出し. ‖ The guard asked him to ***identify himself***. 守衛は彼に身分証明書を示すように要請した. 【類】 carry a card with a person to ***identify himself*** / He ***identified himself*** as George Mason. / He was made to ***identify himself***. ‖ He early ***identified himself*** with the Restoration movement. 彼は早くから維新の大業に参加した. ‖ ***identify oneself*** with the heroes of novels 小説の主人公になりきる(その気持ちになる) ‖ The Democratic Party ***identifies itself*** with revised capitalism. 民主党は修正資本主義を標榜している. 【類】 There have always been men of British stock who have ***identified themselves***, heart and soul, with the service of alien races. ‖ ***identify oneself*** with many schemes of reform 色々な改革案に関係する.【類】***identify oneself*** actively with the project / ***identify oneself*** with the objects of the association / ***identify themselves*** with the national cause (大義) / entirely ***identify oneself*** with the eugenic movement (優生運動). ¶***imagine*** (=***fancy***) ***oneself*** in fairyland 自分がおとぎの国にいると想像する ‖ strive to ***imagine oneself*** in another's place 人の身になってみようと努力する. ¶***illuminate oneself*** by the Gospel 福音の教化に浴する. ¶the bullet passed through ... and ***imbedded itself*** in ... 弾丸は...に貫通し...で止まった. ¶people who have never ***immersed themselves*** in French life フランス人の生活にはいり込んだことがない人々. ¶Colonel Charles A. Lindbergh ***immortalized himself*** by making the first successful solo-flight across the Atlantic. リンドバーグ大佐は始めて大西洋横断単独飛行に成功しその名を子孫に残した. ¶***immunize themselves*** against ... ...に対して免疫となる. ¶the person with whom one has ***immured oneself*** for life 人が一生をともにした人. ¶***impoverish oneself*** 貧困の身となる. ¶a picture that ***impresses itself*** on the imagination. 想像力に訴える絵 ‖ These are a few of the main features that ***impress themselves*** on the memory. これらが記憶に残る二三の主な点である. ‖ This remark of the speaker ***impressed itself*** forcibly upon the mind of the audience. この弁士の言葉は聴衆の胸を強く打った.【類】Two scenes ***impress themselves*** upon my mind in particular. / ***impress itself*** upon the least observant. ¶people who want to ***improve themselves*** by reading 読書によって向上しようとする人々 ‖ show evidence of effort to ***improve oneself*** 改善への努力のあとが見られる.【類】***improve oneself*** by practice. ¶***indulge oneself*** with a glass of wine 楽しみの一杯を傾ける ‖ ***indulge oneself*** while one is still in the secondary school まだ中学校時代にすでに身を持ちくずす ‖ ***indulge oneself*** at home by a quiet hearth 家庭の静かな炉の側で身体を楽にする ‖ ***indulge themselves*** in some hobby 何かの道楽にふける ‖ ***indulge oneself*** in frequent excursions into other byways of politics, letters, art, and morals 傍ら政治, 文学, 芸術, 道徳など色々な方面にも進出する ‖ ***indulge oneself*** with a nap いい気持ちでうたた寝をする. ¶try to ***inform oneself*** as to ... ...について知ろうとする ‖ ***inform oneself*** about a rumor うわさを確かめる ‖ ***inform oneself*** of the current movements of the world 世界の動きに通じる.【類】***inform oneself*** of the laws affecting one's occupation / neglect to ***inform oneself*** on (=upon) such matters. ¶***ingratiate oneself*** with her mamma 彼女の母に取入る ‖ ***ingratiate oneself*** into the favor of ... ...のご気げんをとる ‖ ***ingratiate himself*** with rich or influential people 金持や勢力家にとり入る ‖ ***ingratiate oneself*** with the Almighty 全能の神の恩ちようにあずかろうとする. ¶The ivy ***insinuates itself*** into every crevice. つたはどこにでも入りこむ. ‖ ***insinuate oneself*** into the favor (=good opinion or good graces) of ... 手を尽して...に取入る ‖ ***insinuate oneself*** from a poor mean condition into a good estate 貧窮状態から相当の資産家にのしあがる. ¶***install oneself*** in one's seat 席に落つく ‖ The cat ***installed itself*** on a chair. ねこがいすにおさまった. / gladly ***installing myself*** as his personal servant 喜んでその召使代りになって. ¶***insure oneself*** for £3,000 三千ポンドの生命保険をつける ‖ ***insure oneself*** with a commercial company 保険会社で保険をつける. ¶***intensify itself*** in durability その耐久力が増す. ¶***interest oneself*** in trading business (manufacturing industry) 貿易業(など)に関係する ‖ ***interest oneself*** actively in ... ...に奔走する ‖ ***interest oneself*** in the cause of laborers 労働者の利益のために働く ‖ ***interest oneself*** in another's affairs 人のことに興味を持つ.【類】***interest oneself*** in the study of financial problems / He ***interested himself*** in my welfare. / ***interest oneself*** in the socialist ideas ‖ the bureau ***interests itself*** in matters relative to ... その局は...に関する問題を取扱う. ¶***interpose onesilf*** between ... ...の中に割り込む; に干渉する. ¶***intoxicate oneself*** 酒に酔う. ¶You don't know me, so I must ***introduce myself***. 私を御存じないでしょうから自己紹介をします. ‖ ***introduce oneself*** into an assembly of ... ...の会合に自分を紹介する ‖ ***introduce oneself*** as ... ...と名乗る.【類】At the concert two new singers ***introduced themselves*** for the first time (デビュー) to an English audience. ¶***intrude oneself*** upon a person 人の邪魔をする. ‖ ***intrude oneself*** into a house (an office) 家(役所)に押入る ‖ ***intrude oneself*** into another's affair 人のことに干渉する. ¶***inure oneself*** to cold (heat) 寒気(暑熱)に慣れる ‖ ***inure oneself*** to hardship (distress, drudgery) / Diogenes ***inured himself*** to severe privations, relying on alms for the supply of his simple wants. ¶***invigorate oneself*** 元気づく. ¶***involve oneself*** in expenses 出費をするようになる ‖ ***involve oneself*** in trouble 困難に巻込まれる.【類】***involve oneself*** in intrigues / he was charged with having ***involved himself*** in ... ¶***join oneself*** to the opposite party 反対党にはいる. ¶try to ***justify oneself*** 自己を弁護しようとする ‖ to ***justify himself*** he declared that ... 自分の正しいことを証明しようとして彼は...と言った.【類】***justify oneself*** by saying ... ¶I wonder how he manages to ***keep himself well*** with so much work to do. あんなに働いてよくからだが続くものだ. ‖ The house will not ***keep itself***. その家はもつまい. ‖ manage to ***keep oneself*** above water どうやら水面に首を出している; 何とか借金しないで暮す ‖ ***keep oneself*** from being seen 人目につかないようにする ‖ You ought to ***keep yourself*** in the background. 君の出る幕じゃない. ‖ ***keep oneself*** in touch with the outside world 外界と接触を保つ ‖ ***keep oneself*** in the public eye いつも人目につくようにする ‖ ***keep itself*** in running order 活動体制を保つ ‖ His battalion received orders to ***keep itself*** in readiness for active service in India. 彼の砲兵隊はインドでの戦闘に待機するよう命令を受けた. ‖ ***keep oneself*** out of danger 危険に近づかないようにしている ‖ ***keep himself*** to himself=adopt a restrained attitude in the company of strangers 人と打解けない ‖ ***keep oneself*** up to date about events at home and abroad 内外における最近の情勢を心得ているようにする ‖ ***keep oneself*** under a secure guard 自分に厳重な護衛をつけておく ‖ ***keep oneself*** informed of ... 絶えず...の情報を受ける. ¶***kill oneself*** by accident 事故で死ぬ.【類】He ***killed himself*** by poison. / ***killed himself*** for love / ***kill oneself*** by a plane crash (飛行機事故) / He ***killed himself*** with grief. ¶***laugh oneself*** into convulsions. 腹を抱えて笑う. ‖ ***laugh oneself*** into the fits of coughing あんまり笑ってせき込む ‖ ***laugh oneself*** to death 笑い過ぎて死ぬ. ¶***launch oneself*** on a new voyage into the unknown future 未知の将来に向って船出をする. ¶He ***laid himself*** on her. 彼は彼女の上に身をおいた. ‖ ***lay oneself down*** on the grass 草に横たわる ‖ ***lay oneself open*** to criticism (an attack) 非難(攻撃)を受ける.【類】***lay oneself open*** to the suspicion of ... ‖ ***lay oneself out***=take great pains 骨を折る. ¶***leave oneself*** to the current 流のまにまに漂う. ¶It easily (=readily) ***lends itself*** to investigation. それは研究しやすい. ‖ specially ***lend itself*** to ... 特に...に適する.【類】The London climate does not ***lend itself*** to outdoor life in such a marked degree as does the climate of Paris or Vienna. ‖ avoid subjects ***lending themselves*** to misunderstanding 誤解を招きやすい題目を避ける ‖ He never ***lends himself*** to meanness. 彼は決していやしいことはしない. ‖ ***lend himself*** to the cause of peace 平和のために尽す ‖ Sawdust ***lends itself*** to many uses. おがくずは色々用途がある. ‖ A Fork does not ***lend itself*** to a spoon. フォークはスプーンの代りにならない. ‖ ***lend itself*** to quotation そこは引用ができる.【類】***lend themselves*** to this treatment (治療に役立つ) / This arrangement ***lends itself*** to clear exposition (明解な説明). ¶***let oneself*** down the wall by a rope ロープで壁伝いに降りる ‖ ***let oneself*** in with a latch key ドアのラッチをあけて中に入る ‖ ***let oneself out*** of the back door 裏口から出る. ¶***lift oneself*** by one's boot strap=attempt what is impossible《比ゆ》不可能をえあてやる ‖ ***lift oneself*** out of obscurity 無名から有名になる ‖ ***lift oneself*** to a pinnacle of fame by ... ...によって名誉の絶頂に達する. ¶I am trying to ***limit oneself*** strictly to ... 私は(他事に触れないで)...のことだけを述べようとしている. ‖ ***limit oneself*** to the description of ... ...を述べるに止める.【類】I shall ***limit myself*** to the mention of ... / There I ***limit myself*** to one or two main points. / I shall have to ***limit myself*** to the citation of one case. / I shall ***limit myself*** to general considerations. / ***limit** oneself* to an endeavor to … …することに努力を集中する. ¶***link** itself* with … …と関連する. ¶***list** oneself* among … …に加勢する. ¶***load** oneself* 株を大いに買こむ. ¶***lock** oneself **up*** in a room へやに閉じこもる ‖ ***lock** myself* always from the rest of the world 家に閉じこもって人に会わない ‖ ***lock** oneself* into a hotel suite ホテルの客室に錠を下して閉じこもる. ¶***look** oneself **over*** very carefully 自分の身体を念入りにながめる ‖ She ***looked** herself* in the mirror and gave her hat a little pull. 鏡に映る自分の姿を見て帽子をちょっと下げた. ¶***lose** oneself* in gambling (reading) とばく(など)に夢中になる ‖ ***lose** oneself* in thought 物思いに沈む. 【類】***lose** oneself* in business (没頭する) / ***lose** oneself* in admiration of … ‖ ***lose** oneself* in a riot of exuberant hyperbole 自己陶酔に入る. 【類】***lose** herself* in a reverie (空想) ‖ ***lose** oneself* in love for … …にうつつを抜かす. ‖ The stream ***lost** itself* in a marsh. 流れは沼沢に姿を消した. ‖ I'll answer for it that she ***loses** herself*. 今に見ろきっと彼女は途方にくれるから. ‖ ***lose** oneself* and one's loneliness in motion pictures 熱心に映画を見てさびしさを忘れる ‖ The carbonic acid gas ***lost** itself* in the air. 炭酸ガスは空中に発散した. ‖ ***lose** oneself* in the forest 森の中で道に迷う. 【類】***lose** oneself* in back alleys (裏の路地) ‖ ***lose** oneself* to the world 世に見捨てられる. ¶An unselfish man rather loves others than he ***loves** himself*. 没我的な人は自分の身よりむしろ他人を愛する. ¶***lower** oneself* in public estimation 評判をおとす. ¶He ***lulled** himself* into a feeling of false security by an illusion of wealth. 金持ちになったような錯覚を起して誤った安全感に陥った. ¶The crowd, unable to gain admittance, ***madded** themselves* against the walls of the arena. 群集は入場できないで闘技場の壁に気狂いのようにぶつかった. ¶***magnify** oneself* 尊大に構える; ほらを吹く ‖ ***magnily** oneself* against …を見くびる, …に対して横柄な態度を採る. ¶***maintain** themselves* against repeated assaults 波状攻撃に対抗する ‖ Britain is struggling to ***maintain** herself* as a great power in the post-war world. 英国は戦後の大国としての地位を保とうと努力している. ‖ ***maintain** itself* in the face of … …直面して譲らない ‖ ***maintain** himself* and family as a bookseller 本屋をやって一家を支える. 【類】A wife must ***maintain** herself* as a companion (伴りょ) to her husband. / ***maintain** oneself* in perfect physiological equilibrium / ***maintain** oneself* in a state of purity. ¶I cannot ***make** myself* to … …する気になれない. ‖ ***make** oneself* at home くつろぐ ‖ ***make** oneself **up*** for the stage (screen) [俳優が]メーキャップする. 【類】He helped her to ***make** herself **up*** for the part. ‖ ***make*** a fool of *oneself* ばかを見る. ¶unable to ***manage** oneself* 自分の始末もできないで. ¶a symptom ***manifests** itself* ある徴候が現われる ‖ After four o'clock the desire for tea begins to ***manifest** itself*. 四時を過ぎるとお茶を一杯という気持が出て来る. ‖ ***manifest** itself* as … or in other ways …か何かになって現われる. 【類】Meanwhile the opposite trend is ***manifesting** itself*. / Strikes or discontent was openly ***manifesting** themselves* amongst the work-people of certain firms / it ***manifests** itself* in the form of … / Heroism ***manifests** itself* in its varied forms (=manifold ways). ¶his spirit ***materialized** itself* in … 彼の霊が…に乗移った. ¶***measure** oneself* against the enemy 敵と争う(戦う) ‖ ***measure** oneself* with one's rival (competitor) 競争相手と取組む(技を競う). ¶***metamorphose** itself* [昆虫など]変態する. ¶***misconduct** oneself* 不行跡をやる ‖ ***misconduct** oneself* with Mrs. X X 夫人と密通する. ¶***misbehave** oneself* 身持ちが悪い. 【類】Has he ***misbehaved** himself* in any way? ¶***misrepresent** oneself* as an American アメリカ人と詐称する. ¶***mix** oneself* among the common people 大衆の中にはいりこむ. 【類】***mix** oneself* with the crowd. ¶***model** oneself* on … …に範をとる. 【類】For a time modern Japan largely ***modelled** herself* upon Germany. / ***model** itself* in political, industrial, and social matters after the Western type. ¶***mold** itself* into new forms 新式に改める. ¶***multiply** themselves* その数がふえる ‖ The literary man cannot ***multiply** himself*. 文士は代りがきかない. ¶***nerve** oneself* to the point of … 元気をつけて…する ‖ ***Nerving** himself* for the fate, he tore the envelope open. どうともなれと思い切って手紙の封を切った. ‖ ***nerve** oneself* for an ordeal 試練にたえるよう元気を出す. ¶The children ***nestled** themselves* in their beds. 子供たちはベッドにはいり込んでいた. ¶***obligate** oneself* to another to do 人に対し…する責任を負う. ¶***obtrude** oneself* on the notice of others 人目につくようにする. 【類】the defect ***obtruded** itself* more and more upon the attention of … ¶***occupy** oneself* in doing something 何か仕事に屈託する ‖ the author has ***occupied** himself* with … 同著者は…で多忙だ. 【類】***occupy** themselves* with farming (野良仕事) / ***occupy** oneself* with literature and intellectual culture ‖ the meeting ***occupied** itself* in some detail with the question as to how … 会は…の方法について幾分掘下げて検討した. ¶***offer** oneself* as a candidate against … …の向こうを張って候補に立つ ‖ ***offered** themselves* as victims to be experimented upon 実験台に登ろうと申出る ‖ till a better chance ***offers** itself* もっといい機会が来るまで. 【類】A striking example has recently ***offered** itself*. ‖ ***offer** itself* as a suitable title 適切な題目となる ‖ ***offer** oneself* for admission 採用を志願する. 【類】I beg to ***offer** myself* for the vacant position. / ***offer** oneself* for the service / A charming prospect ***offered** itself* to our view from the top of the mountain. ‖ women who work in public places ***offering** themselves* for immoral purposes すすんで売春をやる酒場の女たち ‖ ***offer** oneself* in marriage 結婚を申込む. ¶***open*** (=*unbosom*) *oneself* 本心を打明ける. ¶It ***operates** itself*. それは自働式である. ¶***oppose** oneself* to it それに反対する. ¶***organize*** (=*form*) *themselves* into an association (a union, a body) 会(組合, 団体)を作る. 【類】***organized** themselves* into guerrilla units (ゲリラ部隊) / ***organize** itself* as a nation-wide movement. ¶***orient** oneself* 順応する ‖ ***orient** oneself* to changed conditions 新事態に順応する. 【類】Filled with worry, probably homesick, struggling to ***orient** himself* in a strange academic and social environment, the boy writes a despairing letter to his father. ¶***outdo** oneself* いままでになくよくやる. 【類】In their enthusiasm they ***outdid** themselves* in endeavors to … ¶***overeat** oneself* 食い過ぎる. ¶***overexert** oneself* 過労になる. ¶***overgrow** oneself* 成長し過ぎる, 大きくなりすぎる. ¶Tiles were laid to ***overlap** themselves*. かわらはお互い重なるように列べた. ¶***overleap** oneself* 飛び過ごす; 飛び過ぎる. ¶It has ***overplayed** itself*. [労働組合などが]やり過ぎた. ¶Too much cunning ***overreaches** itself*. こうかつも過ぎるとかえって失敗する(策士策に倒れる). ¶***overshoot** oneself* in … …でやり過ごす(度をはずす). ¶***oversleep** oneself* 寝過ごす. ¶***overtire** oneself* へとへとに疲れる. ¶He ***overworked** himself* and fell into ill health. 彼は過労で健康を害した. 【類】***overwork** oneself* in learning a foreign language. / Take care not to ***overwork** yourself*. ¶***overstrain** oneself* 緊張し過ぎる; 過労になる. ¶***own** oneself* in the wrong 自分の非を認める. ¶storm the train and ***pack** themselves* in their places どうっと汽車に乗り込みそれぞれ場所に収まる(修学旅行などで). ¶***pamper** oneself* わがままになる. ¶***pass** oneself **off*** as … …と見せかける; …で通る. 【類】She is ***passing** herself **off*** as a white. / ***pass** oneself* [***off***] for (=as) a peer. ¶***pattern** oneself* after … …をお手本にする(まねる). ¶***perfect** themselves* in their respective crafts それぞれの特技を完成する ‖ ***perfect** oneself* in warlike attainments 武術の修業をする ‖ to ***perfect** oneself* in (=make oneself conversant with) the English language 英語に熟達するために. 【類】***perfect** oneself* in the art of fencing (judo, wrestling). ¶***perfume** oneself* with musk じゃ香の香水をつける. ¶***perjure** oneself* 偽証する. 【類】The witness ***perjured*** (=forswore) *himself*. ¶***perk*** (=plume) *oneself* on … …を自慢する. ¶here I must ***permit** myself* some necessary remarks on the subject of … ここで私は…の問題について必要な発言をしなければならない ‖ we have ***permitted** ourselves* to be deceived with the notion that … われわれは…という考えに欺かれたのである. ¶I cannot ***persuade** myself* of his death. 彼の死は信ぜられない. ‖ ***persuade** oneself* of the justice of it それが正当だということを自分に納得させようとする. ¶***pick** oneself* up はね起きる, 起上る. ¶His vanity always ***pictured** himself* in the place of the hero, rescueing beautiful women. 彼はうぬぼれが強くいつも美女を救う英雄といった自分を想像した. ¶With the heroine dead, all the broken ends of the story *piece themselves.* 女主人公が死んですべての物語の切れ切れがまとまる. ¶The snow had ***piled itself*** against his shoulders and chest, and added a white crest to the burden he carried. 雪が彼の肩や胸まで積り背中の荷物の上まで白くなった. ¶***pinch oneself*** to make sure that one is awake 夢じゃないかと身をつねる. ¶***pique*** (=***plume***) *oneself* of (=on) one's personal appearance. 自分の容姿を誇る. ¶***place oneself*** at ease くつろぐ ‖ He ***placed himself*** at the head of the conspiracy 彼は陰謀の首領となった ‖ ***place oneself*** in command of a regiment 連隊長となる ‖ ***place oneself*** in intelligent contact with ... ...と賢明な接触をする ‖ ***place oneself*** in an attitude of defense 防御の身構えをする ‖ ***place oneself*** upon the throne 王位につく ‖ ***place oneself*** in another's stead 人の身になって見る ‖ ***place oneself*** in communication with ... ...に照会する ‖ ***place oneself*** on the side of ... ...に組する, ...の味方になる ‖ ***place oneself*** under the protection of ... ...の保護を受けるようにする. 【類】***place oneself*** under the tuition of ... / ***place oneself*** under obligations / ***place themselves*** in a row in front. ¶***plant oneself*** on a vacant chair 空席に腰をおろす. ¶***play oneself*** in as a chairman 座長になる ‖ The forces of inflation have not ***played themselves*** out. インフレの波がまだ衰えない. ¶As to that you may ***please yourself***. その点は御自由に. ‖ ***Please yourself***, good sir! よいようになさい. ‖ if it ***pleases yourself*** それでよければ ‖ You cannot in this matter ***please yourself***. この件では気ままにならない. ‖ just to ***please myself*** 自分で楽しむために. ¶***pledge oneself*** in the cause of liberty 自由のために戦うことを誓う ‖ ***pledge oneself*** to secrecy 秘密を守ることを誓う. 【類】***pledge oneself*** by one's Christian faith to the truth of the matter / ***pledge oneself*** to Parliamentary reform (議会改革) / ***pledge oneself*** to one's country / They ***pledged themselves*** to each other. / ***pledge themselves*** to an association / the publisher of this journal ***pledges himself*** to ... / the meeting ***pledged itself*** with enthusiasm to ... ¶***plume oneself*** on one's ability (skill, talent, powers) 能力(など)を自慢する ‖ people ***pluming themselves*** on being able to trace ancestry back to William the Conqueror 祖先を尋ねるとウイリヤム征服王である点で得意になる. ¶***plump oneself down*** in a chair どっかといすに腰を掛ける. ¶***poise oneself*** on one's toes 足のゆび先でつり合を保つ(トーダンスなど) ‖ The Chinese Communist troops ***poised themselves*** to encircle the city. 中国共産軍は同市包囲の気勢を示した. ¶He ***poisoned himself*** in despairing fanaticism. 彼は絶望的な狂信から服毒自殺をした. ¶***possess oneself*** in patience じっと辛棒する ‖ ***possess oneself*** under all trials あらゆる試練にじっとたえる ‖ ***possess oneself*** of an estate 土地家屋を所有する ‖ ***possess oneself*** of an accomplishment 一芸を身につけている. 【類】***possess oneself*** of all helpful knowledge / They ***possessed themselves*** completely of the island. / contrive by some means to ***possess oneself*** of ... / come to ***possess oneself*** of every kind of information. ¶***post oneself*** at the end of a street 街路のはずれでこじきをする. ¶Here the stream ***pours itself*** into the sea. ここで流れが海中に注ぐ. ¶***practice oneself*** in English (skating) 英語を独習する(スケートを自分で習う). ¶***precipitate oneself*** from a tall building 高いビルから投身する ‖ ***precipitate oneself*** into danger 自分を危機に落し入れる. 【類】***precipitate oneself*** over the precipice into the whirlpool / ***precipitate oneself*** upon the enemy. ¶Our regional pride naturally ***preens*** (=***trims***) ***itself*** at the prospect. われわれの郷土の誇りがその期待で自然高まってくる. ‖ ***preen oneself up*** 盛装する. ¶***prepare himself*** for admission to the bar 弁護士試験の準備をする. 【類】***prepare oneself*** for the task / ***prepare oneself*** for a commercial career (商人) / ***prepare oneself*** for one's examination / She ***prepared herself*** so well for the business of wifehood (花嫁修業). / ***prepare oneself*** fully for the fight. ¶when an opportunity (=occasion) ***presents itself*** あわよくば ‖ He ***presented himself*** as a candidate at the general election. 彼は総選挙に立候補した ‖ ***present oneself*** to offer congratulations (greetings of the season) 参賀する ‖ Grammar deals with the dress in which our thoughts ***present themselves***. 文法はわれわれが発表する思想を包む衣装を取扱うものだ ‖ the first question that ***presents itself*** is that ... 最初に起る問題は...である. ¶the probability ***presented itself*** of ... ...ができそうであった. 【類】if a favorable opportunity ***presents*** [*itself*] / if propitious circumstances (好機) ***present themselves*** / But here a difficulty ***presented itself*** / when difficulties ***present themselves*** / olfactory evidence ***presents itself*** of the immediate vicinity of ... / The problem has ***presented itself*** for solution / the idea of ... began to ***present itself*** / Two different problems ***present themselves***. / The first question that ***presents itself*** is "Has ...?" / ***present oneself*** at the door of a house ‖ ***present oneself*** at the above address 前記の宿所を訪問する. 【類】He failed to ***present himeself*** at the examination. / He ***presented himself*** before me. / ***present oneself*** before ... in the semblance of (姿で) ... / this difficulty surmounted, another ***presented itself*** in the shape of ... / several difficulties ***presented themselves*** on account of ... / A speculation of this kind ***presented itself*** to my mind. / ***present itself*** to the eyes of ... / ***present themselves*** under different guises (それぞれ変った姿で) / greatly astonished at the scene which ***presented itself***. ¶***preserve ourselves*** from being tainted and infected with their manners 彼らの無作法が伝染しないように気をつける. ¶***press oneself*** against another 人にからだを押しつける ‖ I beckoned to cabmen and several ***pressed themselves*** upon me. 車屋を呼んだら五六人わっと押寄せてきた. ¶to ***prevent myself*** from misunderstanding 自分の誤解を避けるために. ¶***pride oneself*** in "advanced" sex-views いわゆる進歩的な性道徳感を自慢する. 【類】He ***prides himself*** on his success (being a self-made man). / She ***prides herself*** on her good cooking (巧みな料理法). / Boston ***prides itself*** on its intellectual and historic superiority. / At the age of eighty-three, he still ***prided himself*** on doing a good day's work. / a master-potter who ***prided himself*** on his dexterity (腕前) / ***pride oneself*** on his vigorous mental powers (強力な頭脳の活動力) / those who ***pride themselves*** on being well-informed (博識を誇る) / He ***prides himself*** upon his almost wild disregard of the usages of society. ¶So he had ***primed himself*** before coming. 来る前に一杯きこしめしたというわけか. ¶***primp*** (=dress) ***oneself*** up めかす. 【類】***primp themselves*** for a public show (party). ¶The party ***proclaimed itself*** as socialist in its tendencies. 同党は社会主義的傾向にあることを宣言した. ‖ the neighborhood of the sea ***proclaimed itself*** by ... ...で海の近いことが分かった. ¶She ***professed hereself*** a nun. 修道女だと明言した. ¶***project oneself*** 人の身になって見る; 思いを将来にはせる; [交霊術で]自分の姿を遠方の人に見せる. ¶He ***promised himself*** not to be gone out long. 彼は帰りはあまりおそくならないと言った. ‖ ***promise oneself*** a pleasant party 楽しいパーティを楽しみにして待つ. 【類】a trip that I had been ***promising myself*** for years. ¶***propel itself*** with its own power 自力で推進する ‖ a super-rocket ***propels itself*** at a speed of 50 miles per minute. 超ロケットは一分間に五十マイルの速度で推進する. ¶I ***proposed myself*** to ... ...することにした.... ¶***prostitute herself*** on the street 夜の女としてかせぐ. 【類】young women forced to ***prostitute themselves*** for their living (生活のために売春) / a woman who ***prostitute herself*** for money ‖ ***prostitute oneself*** to the enemy 敵に通じる. ¶***prostrate oneself*** in the dust before ... 平身低頭する. 【類】***prostrate themselves*** before the altar (祭壇). ¶***protect ourselves*** from disease 病気の予防をする ‖ ***protect oneself*** by patent 特許をとって自分の利益を守る ‖ He had nothing to ***protect himself*** from rain (against danger) 雨(危険)を防ぐすべがなかった. ¶the firm has ***proved itself*** of immeasurable advantage to the public by enabling them to ... 同会社はその...するという事業によって公衆にとって計り知れない利益を与えた. ¶***provide oneself*** with a guide-book to one's trip 旅行案内書を携帯する. 【類】***provide oneself*** with a passport of one's country / ***provide oneself*** with money (arms, weapons) / The family could not ever ***provide themselves*** with daily food. ‖ ***provide oneself*** with a way of retreat 逃道を作っておく ‖ Some say that Japan is no place for those who ***provide themselves*** on "speaking their mind." 日本は自分の本心はあかされない国だという人がある. ¶***puff oneself up*** when praised ほめられるといい気になる ‖ we need not ***puff ourselves up*** by asserting that ... …といって鼻を高くすることもない. ¶***pull oneself together*** 元気づく; 落着く; 元気を回復する ‖ ***pull itself*** out of an economic crisis [会社などが]経済危機を免れる. 【類】***pull oneself*** out of one's present difficulties / The country will ***pull itself*** out of the slump (スランプを脱する) ‖ Poland has ***pulled herself*** out of the chaos left by the second World War to a position where she stands today. ポーランドは第二次世界大戦の混乱から立ち上り今日の地位にまで回復した. ‖ ***pull oneself together*** 元気を出す, しゃんとなる. ¶***purge oneself*** of suspicion 身のあかしを立てる. ¶***purify oneself*** 身を清める; 水ごりを取る. ¶***push oneself ahead*** 前進する ‖ ***push oneself*** among ... …の中に割込む. ¶***put oneself*** behind the scenes 陰に回る, 黒幕となる ‖ ***put oneself forward*** おく面もなく出しゃばる ‖ ***put oneself*** mentally in the speaker's place 演説をする人の身になって考える. 【類】***put oneself*** in imagination in the place of ... ‖ Just ***put yourself*** into my place. まあ私の身にもなって御覧. ‖ You ***put yourselves*** in the category of snakes when you hiss. そんなにやじるとへびの仲間にはいるぞ(弁士が騒ぐ聴衆に向って). ‖ ***put oneself down*** as a believer in an occult, unseen world 自分を神秘な未知の世界を信じる者とする ‖ ***put oneself out*** 心配する ‖ ***put oneself up*** into the skilled or trained ranks 熟練工の仲間に入る ‖ ***put oneself*** in correspondence with ... …と文通する ‖ ***put themselves*** in communication with ... to arrange ... 手はずを定めるため…と連絡する ‖ ***put oneself*** into a clean shirt よごれていないワイシャツを着る ‖ He has ***put himself*** into its pages. 彼はその著作に精神をこめた. ‖ ***Put yourself*** into your work. 仕事に精神を打込め. ‖ ***put oneself*** into competition with another 人と競争する ‖ ***put oneself*** on the progressive side 進歩の方向をたどる ‖ ***put oneself*** over one's audience 聴(観)衆に自分を印象づける ‖ ***put oneself*** out of the way [衝突しないように]よける ‖ Don't ***put yourself*** out of the way on my account. 私のためにわざわざそうなさらないで下さい. ‖ ***put oneself*** to death 自殺する ‖ ***put oneself*** to great personal inconvenience to do one a favor 人に頼まれたことをやって不自由な思いをする ‖ ***put oneself*** to pains that he may appear ... …らしく見せようと苦心する ‖ ***put*** (=set) ***oneself*** to work 仕事を始める ‖ ***put oneself*** to trouble 厄介なことになる. 【類】Pray do not ***put yourself*** to any trouble for me, I insist. ‖ ***put oneself*** to expenses [払いで]金がかかる ‖ ***put oneself*** under the direction of medical men 医者の指導に従う. 【類】Every country, however democratic, has to ***put itself*** under a temporary dictatorship in case of war. / ***put oneself*** under the guidance of the wise ‖ ***put oneself together***=compose oneself [乱れた]心を落付ける. ¶He has ***qualified himself*** for the job. 彼はその職業の資格をとった. ‖ "crammed" to ***qualify himself*** as ... …の資格をとろうと「猛勉」した ‖ ***qualify oneself*** for the bar 弁護士の資格をとる. ¶the troops ***quarter themselves*** in ... 軍隊が…に駐留する. ¶***question oneself*** about ... …に対して自問する. ¶***quit oneself*** in a manner worthy of his high position その高い位置にふさわしいりっぱな振舞をする ‖ ***quit oneself*** like a man 男らしく振舞う. ¶It has ***rained itself up***= The rain has ceased. 雨が降りやんだ. ¶***raise itself*** upon its hinder legs 後脚で立ち上る ‖ after many years of poverty and hard work he ***raised himself*** to the position of ... 長年の貧窮と勤勉の後に彼は…の地位にのし上った. 【類】to ***raise oneself*** (=rise) by one's own exertion (独力で) / ***raise oneself*** to a higher moral or intellectual plane (=level) / ***raise oneself*** in another's favor (取入る) / ***raise oneself*** into the managerial class (支配人級) / By sheer force of military genius, Napoleon ***raised himself*** to an Imperial throne. ¶***range oneself*** [結婚などで]身を固める, 定職を得る ‖ ***range oneself*** with ... …に味方する ‖ ***range itself*** alongside of the League in that judgment その判断では連盟と歩調をともにする ‖ The nation ***ranged itself*** into three parties. 国民は三派に分かれた. 【類】... readily ***range themselves*** into two classes, namely, those that ... and those that ... / ***range oneself*** on the side of ... / ***range oneself*** on the side of the advocate of radical reform / ***range themselves*** on opposite sides in an issue. ¶***rave oneself*** out 疲れ切るまで暴言を吐く. ¶***read oneself*** into a nap 読書しながらうとうと眠る. ¶I think things will ***readjust themselves***. 事態はもと通りになるだろう. ‖ veterans ***readjusting themselves*** to civilian life 民間生活に慣れつつある帰還勇士たち ‖ enable the physically disabled to ***readjust themselves*** into useful members of society 不具者を社会の有用な一員に更生させる. 【類】***readjust itself*** to peace / a capacity for ***readjusting oneself*** to new conditions. ¶The idea is rapidly ***realizing itself*** in actual life. その考えが急速に実社会で実現されて来つつある. ¶His ingrained bad habit ***reasserted itself***. 彼の深く根ざした悪癖が再び頭をもたげた. ¶The city began to ***rebuild itself*** among the ruins. 同市は荒廃から立ち直り始めた. ¶***reclaim oneself*** from a life of shame or crime 足を洗う. ¶In general it may be truly said that insanity is a disease which does not ***recognize itself***. 一般に精神異状はそれ自身の存在を認めないものだと言える. ¶***recollect oneself*** 気を落着ける. ¶it has much to ***recommend itself*** on account of ... それは…のために大いに世間に歓迎されよう ‖ The work should ***recommend itself*** to the student of English. 同書は英学生に役に立つ. 【類】I am sure the book will ***recommend itself*** to every thoughtful reader. ¶***recompose oneself*** by degrees だんだん落着く ‖ ***recompose oneself*** to sleep 心を静めて眠る. ¶***reconcile oneself*** to one's fate 運命に甘んじる ‖ When one cannot ***reconcile oneself*** to the language one cannot ***reconcile oneself*** to the people. 言葉が分からないとその国民を理解することができない ‖ ***reconcile oneself*** with ... …で我慢する(甘んじる). 【類】***reconcile oneself*** to the inevitability of the situation / ***reconcile oneself*** to being ill for a long time / ***reconcile oneself*** to a life of obscurity (不遇の身). ¶assist industry to ***reconvert*** and ***re-equip itself*** 産業の転換及び再装備を助ける. ¶The publishers might ***recoup themselves*** part of their generous outlay. 出版屋はこの大きな支出の一部は回収できるかも知れない. ¶***recover oneself***=come to [one's senses] 正気になる; 落着く; 手足が自由になる ‖ The bended tree ***recovered itself*** from the strong wind. 強風にあたって倒れかかった木が直った. ¶***reduce oneself*** to want and beggary 困窮状態に陥る. ¶***re-establish oneself*** 再出発する, 再起する. ¶The mountain ***reflects itself*** in the mirror of the lake 山は鏡のような湖面にその姿を映す. ¶***reform oneself*** 改心する ‖ the experience of a drunkard in his efforts to ***reform himself*** 更正しようと努力する大飲酒家の経験. ¶The Malthusian League dissolved and ***re-formed itself*** as the New Generation Leagues マルサス連盟は解散し新時代連盟として再組織した. ¶***refrain oneself*** from tears 涙を抑える. ¶***refresh oneself*** with a hearty meal of ... …を腹一杯食べて元気をつける. 【類】***refresh oneself*** with milk. ¶The charge ***refutes itself*** by its absurdity. その罪科そのものに無理があるので成立しない. ¶***regale oneself*** with treat (beer, feast) ごちそう(ビールなど)で大いに楽しむ. 【類】They ***regaled themselves*** with food and wine (tea and cakes). ¶***regard oneself*** as dead 自分が死んだものと思う. 【類】The Chinese regard ***themselves*** as aborigines (原住民). / ***regard oneself*** as a fool / playwrights who ***regard themselves*** as doctors of the world's evils / He ***regarded himself*** as a child of a good position just about to enter on a life of good luck. ¶His ambition soon ***registered itself***. 間もなく彼の野心が頭をもたげ出した. ‖ ***register oneself*** with the association その会の会員になる. ¶***regulate oneself*** in drinking (smoking) 飲酒(など)を節制する. ¶The huge and highly productive Manchurian industrial area is unable to ***rehabilitate itself*** without outside help. 満州の巨大な大生産地域は外部からの援助なしには再起不可能である. ¶sell the security to ***reimburse oneself*** 償還のため担保を売る ‖ ***reimburse oneself*** from the proceeds of ... …の売上から償還する. ¶***relax oneself*** くつろぐ. 【類】Take off your coat and ***relax yourself***. ¶***relieve oneself*** 便通する(大小便) ‖ ***relieve oneself*** from liability 負債を片付ける ‖ ***relieve ourselves*** of the burden we have assumed 責任の重荷をおろす. ¶Continually I ***reminded myself*** of this resolution. この自分の決意を絶えず思い出すようにした. ¶***reorient oneself*** for ... …のため新方針を定める. 【類】***reorient herself*** for the changing situation. ¶He can ***repay himself*** from my wages. 彼はそれを私の賃銀から差

引いてもらえる. ¶*repeat oneself* 再言する; 再び行う ‖ History *repeats itself*. 歴史は繰返す. 【類】*repeat oneself* in one's speech / he *repeats himself* in his books that.... ¶*report oneself* at the office of... ...の役所に出頭する. 【類】The players have to *report themselves*, as a rule, some time before the curtain rises ‖ *report oneself* to... ...に復命する. ¶calmly *repose oneself* 身を安静にする. ¶*repossess oneself* of... ...を取返す. ¶*represent oneself* as... ...と言触らす. ¶*reproach oneself* 自責する. ¶*reproduce oneself* 生殖する, 繁殖する. ¶*requite oneself* for some past injury 昔の恨みの仕返しをする. ¶*reserve oneself* for... ...のために精力を貯えておく. ¶*resign oneself* to the inevitable 運命とあきらめる ‖ *resign oneself* to captivity とらわれの身となる. 【類】we had to *resign ourselves* to fate / *resign oneself* to sleep (rest) / *resign oneself* without complaint to... / *resign themselves* to a lower (=reduced) standard of living / *resign oneself* to the hands of... ¶the whole problem of... *resolves itself* into... 全問題は...に帰着する ‖ the question, then, *resolves itself* into whether... 問題は故に...かどうかに帰着する. 【類】This question *resolves itself* into two distinct inquiries, as follows: Why...? Why...? / The obstacle *resolves itself* into a question of money. ¶*respect* others as well as *oneself* 自分同様他人も尊敬する. ¶*rest oneself* in the shade (under a tree) 日(木)陰で休む. 【類】We stopped at a road house to *rest ourselves*. ¶*rest* and *refresh oneself* 休息して元気を回復する. ¶*restrain oneself* 自制する, つつしむ. 【類】unable to *restrain oneself* at the sight of... / *restrain oneself* from anger / He could not *restrain himself* from laughing at the sight. ¶it is too wide a subject for this small volume, which must *restrict itself* to dealing with... この小著には問題が大きすぎるので...を扱うだけに限定せざるを得ない. ¶*reveal oneself* in the form of... ...の形で現われる ‖ much interest has of late *revealed itself* in... 最近...に大いに関心が示されている ‖ They would *reveal themselves* as heroes in the hour of national peril. 彼らは一たん国家の危機となると英雄の本領を発揮するだろう. ¶*revenge oneself* by... ...で腹いせをする ‖ *revenge oneself* on... for... ...に...の仕返しをする. ¶*rid oneself* of the responsibility 責任をのがれる ‖ *rid oneself* by degrees of the habit of... 次第に...の癖が直る ‖ *rid oneself* of an unpleasant visitor いやな来客を撃退する ‖ a happy way of *ridding oneself* of applicants for office 求職運動の連中から手際よく手を抜く方法 ‖ I cannot *rid myself* of the belief that... 私は...と信ぜざるを得ない. 【類】*rid oneself* of one's perplexity (苦境) / he could not *rid himself* of that urge to... / *rid oneself* of one's Japanese citizenship / *rid ourselves* of the notion that... / We frequently find it impossible to *rid ourselves* of painful memories which cling to us. ¶*right itself* by degrees 次第に起直る, だんだんによくなる ‖ But these faults are *righting themselves*. しかしこれらの誤りは自然に直りつつある. 【類】There is the general feeling that conditions will *right themselves* in some way. ¶*rip oneself up* 切腹する. ¶*roast oneself* before a fire よく燃えている炉火にあたる. ¶He sat *rocking himself* in his chair. いすにすわって身体をゆすっていた. ‖ *rock oneself* to sleep 身体をゆすって眠る. ¶She *rolled herself up* in the blankets. 彼女は毛布にくるまった. ‖ The practice *rooted itself* into a habit. そのやり方はしみ込んで癖になった. ¶parasitically *root itself* on... 寄生虫のように...に定着する. ‖ He finally *rooted himself* at Brookfield School. 彼はついにブルックフィールド・スクールに落着いた(色々職業を転じて). ¶*rouse oneself*=awake 目覚める. 【類】Nature *rouses itself* from its winter's sleep. ¶*rub oneself* against... ...にこすりつける. ¶Marry her and *ruin yourself!* あの女と一しょになってどうにでもなれ. ‖ *ruin oneself* by gambling とばくで身を持ちくずす. ¶Is the country ready to *rule herself?* その国は独立の用意ができているでしょうか. ‖ demonstrate that she can *rule herself* その国に自治の能力あることを実証する ‖ a man who can *rule himself* 自制心のある人. ¶*run oneself* into inconveniences by... ...で不便な思いをする ‖ He *ran himself* out of breath. 走って息を切らした. ¶*rush ourselves* into shape いそいで身仕度をする. ¶They *sacrificed themselves* nobly to a grand cause. 彼らは大義のため気高くも身を犠牲にした. ‖ *sacrifice oneself* on the altar of publicity 自己宣伝に浮身をやつす. 【類】The willingness to *sacrifice oneself* for the common good is one of the noblest concepts of the human mind. ¶*saddle oneself* with responsibility 責任を負う. ¶*safeguard oneself* from... ...から身を護る. ¶*satisfy oneself* by... ...でりゅう飲を下げる ‖ *satisfy oneself* of the truth of... ...の真偽を確かめる ‖ unless he can *satisfy himself* to the contrary その反対を確かめ得たのでなければ ‖ *satisfy oneself* as to the purity of the water [飲料の]水が清潔であるかどうか確かめる. ¶He leapt out of the window to *save himself* 助かろうとして窓から飛び出した. 【類】*save oneself* by swimming to the shore / *save oneself* from falling (drowning). ¶*school oneself* to patience 忍耐の訓練をする. ¶*screw oneself* up 緊こん一番する ‖ *screw oneself* under a bed ベッドの下に身体をよじってもぐり込む ‖ You will perhaps have to *screw yourself* up to it as an unpleasant and irksome task. 不愉快で退屈な仕事だから無理にがん張らねばなるまい. ¶The word is repeated again and again till it *sears itself* on the brain. その語を頭に焼きつくまで何べんも繰返す. ¶the company *seated itself* at... [旅役者の]一行は...に落着いた ‖ *seat themselves* around a table 食卓を囲んですわる. 【類】*seat oneself* in a quiet corner / *seat oneself* in (=on) a chair / *seat oneself* on the bench / The Manchu invaders *seated themselves* on the throne of Peking. ¶*seclude oneself* from the world 引こもる, 隠とんする. 【類】*seclude oneself* from society. ¶design to *secure oneself* 身の安全を計る ‖ *secure itself* against aggression 侵略から国を護る. 【類】*secure oneself* against loss. ¶*See yourself* as others see you. 客観的に自分を見よ. ‖ I don't *see myself* living in a native's house. 土人の家に住む気にはなれない. ‖ It is a pleasure to *see oneself* in print. 自分の書いたものが活字となったのを見るのは楽しいものだ. 【類】The monkey *saw himself* in the mirror. / *see oneself* in the water ‖ O that some power would give us the knack of *seeing ourselves* as others see us! 自分を他人の目で見ることができるようなこつを授けてくれるものがあると有難いんだがな. ¶Dandelions *seed themselves*. たんぽぽは自分で自分の種をまく. ¶women who *sell themselves* 売春婦 ‖ *sell oneself* for money 売色(春)する ‖ *sell oneself* for publicity《米》自己宣伝する. 【類】those who *sell themselves* to prostitution. ¶live *separating oneself* from... ...と別居する ‖ *separate itself* from the trunk [鉄道が]幹線から分岐する. ¶*sequester oneself* from the world 世を捨てる, いんとんする. ¶At a cafeteria patrons *serve themselves*. カフェテリヤでは客が自分でサービスする(食事を運ぶ). ‖ *serve* (=avail) *oneself* of an opportunity 機会を利用する. ¶I did not realize the magnitude of the work I had *set myself* to. 自分で手をつけた仕事の重大性がよく分からなかった. ‖ That was the problem which the nineteenth century *set itself* to solve. それが十九世紀が解決しようとした問題だった. ‖ *set oneself down* 腰をおろす ‖ *set oneself* against (=oppose) an idea (a movement) ある考え(運動)に反対する. 【類】*set oneself* against the spirit of his age ‖ *set oneself* to the task of solving the problem その問題解決に本気で乗り出す. ¶*settle oneself* by marriage 身を固める ‖ *settle oneself* in an armchair 安楽いすに腰をおろす. 【類】*settle oneself* on the seat ‖ the veterans who have *settled themselves* successfully as civilians [復員して]市民としてうまく腰を落着けた勇士たち. ¶*sever oneself* from a society (party) 脱会(党)する ‖ *sever oneself* from public affairs 公生活から引退する. 【類】*sever oneself* in mind and soul from the world ‖ *shake oneself* in laughter からだを揺がして笑う ‖ *shake oneself loose* from... ...から離れる ‖ *shake oneself free* off the fetters of... ...の因襲を脱する. ¶His idea began to *shape itself*. 彼の考えは具体化し出した. ¶I prefer to *shave myself*. 私はひげは自分でそる方が好きだ. ¶*shelter oneself* from the storm (a downpour) あらし(どしゃぶり)を避ける ‖ *shelter onself* in a cave (under a tree) どう穴に身を隠す(木陰に宿る). ¶*shield oneself* behind the fact that...という事実をたてに弁護する ‖ *shield oneself* under [the shelter of] a great tree 大木の陰に身を隠す. ¶*ship oneself* 乗船する. ¶*shiver oneself* into illness (to death) 恐れおののいて病気になる(死ぬ). ¶*shoot oneself* in the temple 自分で自分のこめかみを射つ. 【類】

shoot oneself in the mouth / He tried to commit suicide by *shooting himself* in the chest. / *shoot oneself* to death. ¶alarming symptoms *show themselves* 危険な徴候が現われる ‖ They would have killed each other if the police had not *shown themselves*. もし警官が来なかったらお互い殺し合ったであろう. 【類】Bats *show themselves* after dark. / He seldom *shows himself* here. / *show himself* in the likeness (=form) of a ... / *show oneself* in a state of nudity / Chorus girls *show themselves* in a semi-nude condition / The sun has *shown itself* above the horizon. / It *showed itself* in the shape of a great snake. / He did not *show himself* to his friends for a long time. / his skill *shows itself* in ... / *show itself* in its simplest shape in ... / make him *show himself* in his true colors (化の皮をはぐ) ‖ *show itself* to perfection in ... ...において完全に表われる ‖ his love for letters *showed itself* in ... 彼の文学好きは...で明らかにされた ‖ ingrained idleness, *showing itself* in a strong dislike of work 仕事は大きらいという根っからの怠惰ぐせ. 【類】The effect of smoking on women will *show itself* in future generations. ¶*shrive oneself* ざんげして免罪を求める. ¶*shut oneself* inside one's own four walls and work independent of the outer world 自分のへやに閉じこもり世間と没交渉で仕事をする. ¶*sink oneself* deep under water 水中深く沈む. ‖ *sink oneself* in the study of ... ...の研究に没頭する. ‖ *sink oneself* for the public good 公益のために自己を犠牲にする. ¶*smarten* (=preen) *oneself* めかす. ¶The cigarette *smokes itself* away. シガレットが燃え切る. ¶*smuggle oneself* into Japan 日本に密入国する. ¶unwilling to *snatch ourselves* away from the scene その場を立去りがたく. ¶*sob oneself* to sleep (=slumber) 泣寝入りする. ¶*solace oneself* by ... ...で自分を慰める. 【類】*solace oneself* with the thought that ... ¶If left alone, the problem will in time *solve itself*. 放っておけば問題はそのうち自然と片づく. ¶Ship life, like hotel life, soon *sorts itself out* into congenial cliques. 船の生活ではホテルの生活の場合同様じきに気の合った同志がそれぞれグループをつくる. ¶*spare oneself* 骨を惜しむ. ¶he has never *spared himself* in his honest endeavors to ... 彼は誠心誠意...しようとして骨身を惜まない. ¶*specialize oneself* in political economy 経済学を専攻する. ¶He *spells himself* with two "r's." 彼は自分の名前を書くときに r を二つつける. ¶The fire is *spending itself*. 火事が下火になりつつある. ‖ He *spends himself* for his friends. 彼は友人のために骨を折る. 【類】His violence soon *spent itself*. / Wait until his anger *spends itself*. ¶The worm has *spun itself* out. その虫は糸を皆な出してしまった(まゆを作ってしまった). ¶The party *split itself* into two minor ones. 党は仲間割れして二つの小党になった. ¶*spread oneself* 気炎をはく ‖ *spread oneself* in adjectives 盛んに形容詞を並べる ‖ *spread itself* like a fan over ... [木が]...の上に扇のように開いておおいかぶさる ‖ A modest, dignified, serene smile *spread itself* over her face. つつましく, 落着きはらった静かな微笑が彼女の顔に現われた. 【類】the contagion (伝染病) *spreads itself* over ... / The subject is of sufficient importance to justify a writer in *spreading himself* to the extent of more than 3,500 words. ¶fight a duel to *square oneself* 決闘をやって報復する ‖ *square oneself* with... ...で仕返しをする. ¶*squat oneself* by the fireside 炉辺でしゃがむ ‖ *squat oneself* on the mats which covered the floor 床上の敷物の上にあぐらをかく. ¶*squeeze oneself* through the crowd 群集の中を無理に通り抜ける. ¶*squirm oneself* in bed ベッドで身をもがく. ¶*stab oneself* with a sword 刀でわが身を突く. ¶All the sharp conditions of the new life *stamped themselves* on his consciousness. その新生活のあらゆるつらさが彼の意識にはっきり刻みこまれた. ¶*starve oneself* to death 餓死する. ¶*station* (=settle) *oneself* 腰をおろす, おみこしを据える ‖ I begged him to *station himself* among the more honored guests. 私はもっと上席に着くように彼に要請した. ¶*steel oneself* to greater patience さらに意志を強固にしてがん張る. ¶*steep oneself* in a book 本を読みふける ‖ *steep oneself* in science 科学に没頭する. ¶*step oneself* in a position of immediate danger 直接の危険に足を入れる. ¶*stick oneself* out of ... ...から身体を乗り出す ‖ *stick oneself up*=assert *oneself* 《俗》お高く止まる, 威張る. ¶*stint oneself* つましくする ‖ *stint oneself* of food to give to ... ...に与えようと食を節する. ¶Three women had *stowed themselves away* on board the steamer. 三人の婦人が同船で密行した. ¶*straighten oneself* solemnly 厳粛にそりみになる ‖ *straighten oneself up* そりみになる ‖ *straighten oneself* like a soldier at attention「気をつけ」の兵士のように直立不動の姿勢をとる. ¶*strain oneself* 身体を無理する, 過労になる. ¶He *stretched himself*, yawning deeply. 背のびをして大きなあくびをした. ‖ *stretch oneself* at full length on the lawn 芝生の上に大の字になる ‖ *stretch oneself out* on a sofa ソファーの上で身体を伸ばす. ¶*strip oneself* of all pleasures in life 人生のあらゆる快楽をとり去る ‖ *strip oneself* of incumbrances 厄介払いをする. 【類】*strip oneself* of one's station and wealth. ¶The student *supported himself* meanwhile by teaching. その学生はその間教師のアルバイトをやった. ¶*stultify oneself* ばかを見る. ¶That would *stultify yourself* hopelessly. そんなことをすれば君の面目丸つぶれだ. ¶*stupefy oneself* in wonder あっとたまげる. ¶*subject themselves* to the general good 公益にてい身する ‖ *subject ourselves* to the danger of ... ...の危険に進んで身をさらす ‖ *subject oneself* to all conditions as required by ... ...に必要なすべての条件に従う. 【類】*submit oneself* to the inexorable logic of facts / *submit oneself* to a trial ‖ be required to *submit oneself* to examination by ... / meekly *submit themselves* to the rule of ... / reverentially *submit themselves* to the absolute authority of ... / He *subjected himself* to the savage seriousness of the training. / In those days for a Chinese to teach the language to foreigners was to *subject himself* to the penalty of death. ¶*subordinate itself* to ... 劣る; ...の下位に立つ. ¶*subscribe oneself* for books 本の購入を予約する. ¶*substitute itself* for ... ...の代りになる. ¶She gave birth to several children, all of whom she *suckled herself*. 彼女は五六人の子供を産んだが, それらを全部母乳で育てた. ¶*suffer oneself* to be led by the nose あごで指図される; 鼻であしらわれる. ¶in the study of ... one question *suggests itself* at once ... の研究では一つの問題が直ちに念頭に浮ぶ ‖ those whose names will at once *suggest themselves* to everybody. その名前はだれにでも思い出される人々. ‖ Another question *suggests itself*. そこでもう一つの問題が起る. 【類】an explanation that has *suggested itself* to ... / The idea *suggested itself* to his mind. / This is a thought that has frequently *suggested itself* to us. / I was quite at a loss what to do when the idea of going to him for advice suddenly *suggested itself* (=occurred) to me. / Any corrections or additions which *suggest themselves* to the careful reader will be gratefully received. / Upon second thoughts, an alternative *suggests itself* to me. ¶Please, *suit yourself*. どうぞおよろしいように. ‖ *suit oneself* to one's company 相手と調子を合わせる, 合いづちを打つ. 【類】*suit oneself* to the times (situation). ¶*sun oneself* 日なたぼっこをする. ¶*supply oneself* with ... ...を買込む. ¶*support oneself* at good wages ... 相当よい賃金をもらって自活する ‖ *support oneself* on a poor income わずかの収入で自活する. 【類】She decided to *support herself* on her musical talents. / *support oneself* (元気をつける) with a glass of wine or two. ¶*surfeit oneself* with sweets 甘いものを食べ過ぎる. ¶*surpass oneself* いつにないでき栄えを示す. ¶*surrender oneself* at ... ...に自首して出る ‖ *surrender oneself* to one's fate 運命に身を任せる ‖ *surrendering oneself* to the mercy of Heaven 運を天に任せて ‖ *surrender oneself* to indolence 怠惰にふける. 【類】*surrender oneself* to sorrow (grief, indignation) / *surrender oneself* to the police authorities / He *surrendered himself* to a quiet despair. ¶*surround oneself* with competent assistants and employees 有能な助手や従業員を使う. ¶She was *surveying herself* in the pier glass on her wardrobe door. たんすのドアにはまっている鏡で自分の姿をつくづく見ていた. ¶He *swilled himself* with wine. 彼は酒をがぶがぶ飲んだ. ‖ He must *take himself* for better for worse as his portion. よかれ悪かれ自分の運命としてあきらめねばならない. ‖ *take oneself* out of political life 政界から引退する ‖ She *took herself off* from this world. 彼女は自殺した. ‖ He suddenly *took himself off*. 彼は突然その場を去った. ‖ *take oneself* to flight

逃げ出す. ¶*talk oneself* out of breath 疲れるほどしゃべり続ける ‖ All those present had an opportunity to *talk themselves out* on the subject. 出席者は全員その問題について十分に話す機会を持った. ¶"Oh," laughed back the other, *tapping himself* on the breast, "I am he."「うん」と今一人が笑顔を向け, 自分の胸をたたいて「僕がその人なんだ」. ¶*tax oneself* for … …しようと努力する. ¶I could not *tear myself away* from my friends. 友から別れるのが心残りだった. 【類】*tear oneself away* from the crowd and the hubbub (混雑) / I *tore myself* [*away*] from him with a bleeding heart (生木を割くように) / It was with regret that we *tore ourselves away* at dinner-time, resolving, however, that our first visit should not be the last. ¶You may *thank yourself* for that. それは有難いことだと思っているでしょう. ¶*think oneself* above working 自分は働く必要はない身分だと考える. 【類】Just *think yourself*. / He always *thinks himself* in luck, at the start, whatever may be his feeling at the finish. / I was on the point of forgetting your message, but I suddenly *thought myself* of (=recalled) it. ¶*throw oneself* against the sliding-door and burst it open 体当りし戸を無理に開ける ‖ She *threw herself* at the heads of the young men. 彼女は青年たちに水を向けた(誘惑した) ‖ *throw oneself* at full length 大の字になる ‖ He *threw himself* upon his knees at his father's feet. 彼は父の足下にひざまずいた. ‖ He *threw himself* from a window at his residence 彼は自宅の窓から身を投げた ‖ *throw oneself* in front of an express 急行列車に飛込む. 【類】*throw oneself* into the river (volcano) / *throw oneself* upon the bed ‖ *throw oneself* into the jaws of death 身を死地に投じる. ¶*throw oneself* into the vortex (渦中) of revolution / try to *throw herself* out of the window / *throw oneself* over a waterfall / She *threw herself*, in despair, into the sea. ‖ *throw oneself* into its affairs with the keenest zest 極度の熱意をもってそのことに没頭する ‖ *throw oneself* upon a task with zeal 鋭意仕事に取りかかる ‖ *throw oneself* into others' state of mind 人の気持になってみる ‖ *throw oneself* into the spirit of the East 東洋精神に溶け込む. 【類】*throw oneself* into the task of … / *throw oneself* into the struggle / *throw oneself* into one's speech / *throw oneself* into an argument (議論) / She has never *thrown herself* whole-heartedly into her film work. / *throw oneself* into the socialist movement / throw *oneself* with enthusiasm into the study of … / *throw oneself* with ardor into Asiatic studies (東洋研究) / *throw oneself* into one's career with perfect confidence / he *threw himself* with great warmth into an attack on … / the zeal with which the Romans *threw themselves* with the study of Greek resulted in … ‖ the Government *threw itself* on the side of … 政府は…に加勢した ‖ *throw herself* at his knees ひざまずく ‖ plead guilty and *throw oneself* on the mercy of the court 罪を認め恐れ入ったと言う ‖ *throw oneself* into the arms of sin あえて罪を犯す ‖ *throw oneself* into the arms of refuge (friendship) 保護(友情)の手にすがる ‖ Then you advise me to *throw myself* on the generosity of Mr. T? では君は僕に T 氏の寛容にすがれと言うんだね. 【類】May I *throw myself* upon your mercy?. / I now *threw myself* upon his protection. / I *throw myself* on the indulgence of the public. / With these few remarks the writer *throws himself* upon the kind indulgence of his readers. / *throw oneself* with all one's energy into (全力をあげて) the task of … ‖ *throw themselves* on the town [軍隊が]町を攻撃する ‖ *throw oneself* upon one's enemy 敵に打ってかかる ‖ *threw myself* upon my face うつ伏せに倒れた ‖ *throw himself* into a cataleptic trance 人事不省に陥る ‖ *throw oneself* from one side to the other 左右に身体を強く振る ‖ *throw oneself back* in one's seat もとの席にどっかり腰をおろす ‖ *throw oneself on* to railway track [鉄道で]飛込み自殺をやる. ¶*thrust oneself in* 自分を押込む(割込む) ‖ *thrust oneself* into danger 自ら危地に立つ ‖ How dare you *thrust yourself* into my private affair? 人の個人的な問題に立ち入るなんて不都合千万だ. ‖ *thrust themselves* on a person at every turn あらゆる機会に…を非難攻撃する ‖ a branch line *thrusting itself* toward the east from … …から東に分かれる支線. ¶*thrust oneself* でしゃばる. ¶*tidy oneself* [*up*] 服装をきちんとする, 身づくろいをする. ¶*tire oneself out* 疲れ切る. 【類】They *tired themselves* by walking. ¶*train oneself* for a new job 新しい仕事の準備をする ‖ specially *train oneself* in philosophy 特に哲学を勉強する. 【類】He *trained himself* with a view to winning the match. / *train oneself* for the game. ¶*transfer oneself* to another ship 別の船に乗換える. ¶*transform itself* into love 愛情に変る ‖ *transform oneself* into … …に化ける. 【類】*transform oneself* into shapes attractive to … ¶Thoughts and feelings *translate themselves* into action. 思想や感情は行動化する. ¶*transport oneself* with joy 有頂天になる ‖ *transport oneself* in imagination into a room where … 自分が…のへやに入るような想像をする ‖ *trasport oneself* to … at 5.30 a.m. 朝五時半に…へ行って見る. ¶*treat oneself* 自分で療治する ‖ *treat oneself* to … …を奮発する, …をはりこむ ‖ *treat oneself* to a visit to Atami 熱海行としゃれる ‖ *treat oneself* to the luxury of … …というぜいたくをやる. 【類】*treat oneself* to the pleasure of … ‖ *treat oneself* to some chocolates (tea, a strong drink) / *treat oneself* to a little shooting trip / I want to *treat myself* to a good long sleep. / *treat oneself* to a new pair of spectacles (新しい目がね). ¶try to *trick oneself* out in borrowed plumes 借り着でめかそうとする. ¶*trim oneself up* きちんと服装をととのえる. ¶Why *trouble yourself?* 《口語》くよくよすることはない. 【類】You won't have to *trouble yourself* any longer. / She does not *trouble herself* about household matters. / *trouble oneself* about one's daily bread (日々の食事) / Don't *trouble yourself* about that; I'll take it upon *myself*. ‖ He does not *trouble himself* with trifles. 彼は小事にこだわらない. 【類】Very few men *trouble themselves* with morality and justice. ¶*trust oneself* in the hands of … 自分を…の手に任せる ‖ *trust oneself* to "Shanks' mare" (=foot it) てくる ‖ I would not *trust myself* with you. 君を信用する積りはない. ¶*trumpet oneself forth* with what is known as a "one-man" show いわゆる「独演」と自己宣伝をする. ¶*turn itself* in our direction こっちに向かって来る(野獣など). ¶*twine itself* round … …に巻きつく. ¶*unbosom oneself* to one's friend 友人に打ちあける ‖ *unbosom herself* on these extremely delicate, and sometimes painful matters to … …に対しこれらのきわめて微妙な時として苦痛でもある問題について打ち明け話をする. ¶*unburden oneself* of … …の重荷をおろす(自供などして) ‖ *unburden* (=unbosom) *oneself* to a confidant 腹心に打ち明ける. ¶*undeceive oneself* of one's errors 自分の誤りに気がつく. ¶A clergyman will *underfeed himself* for years in order to send his son to a public school. 牧師が息子をパブリックスクールにあげるとなると何年間も食うや食わずの生活をするだろう. ¶cannot *undersell oneself* 自分の安売りはできない. ¶assist students better to *understand themselves* 学生たちに一層よく自己を理解するように導く. ¶proceed to *undress oneself* 着物を脱ぎかける. ¶*unfold itself* [しきものなど]ひとりでにとける ‖ a glorious panorama of … *unfolds itself* …のすばらしい遠望が展開する ‖ the sensational military and political drama *unfolding itself* in South-eastern Europe 東南欧州で展開している注目すべき軍事及び政治劇. ¶allow the dark curtain of discouragement to *unfurl itself* too far 失望の暗いカーテンをあまりにも広く拡がらせ過ぎる. ¶The bats *unhooked themselves* at our approach. われわれが近づくとこうもりが(かぎの手をはなし)飛び去った. ¶*unlade oneself* of … …の荷をおろす. ¶women who have *unsexed themselves* 女らしさを失った女性 (M が強くなる). ¶*unshoe oneself* くつを脱ぐ. ¶That will *unveil himself* sooner or later. 早晩化けの皮がはげるだろう. ‖ *unveil oneself* before the face of the world 全世界の面前で自分の正体を現わす. ¶The clock *unwound itself* (=ran down) and stopped. 時計のぜんまいがすっかりとけて止った. ¶*uproot oneself* and go away 腰をあげて去る. ¶*use oneself* in the service of mankind 人類のために奉仕する. ¶*value oneself* on (=is proud of) one's tact 腕前を誇る. 【類】*value* (=pride) *oneself* on one's conversational powers (会話の巧みさ). ¶*venture oneself* in an ill-chosen place 不適当な地位につく. ¶*view oneself* in the glass 鏡を見る. ¶*vindicate oneself* 自分の主張を弁護する. ¶*vote itself* out of existence 票決で解散する(団体など) ‖ The League of Nations *voted itself* out of existence in 1946. 国際連盟は一九四六年議決の結果解散した. ¶Many a pedestrian ***walks himself*** to death. 街路を横断歩道によらないで向うに渡ろうとして死んだ者がたくさんある. ¶***wallow*** [*oneself*] in ashes 灰の中をころがる. ¶***warm*** *oneself* at the fire 火で身体を暖める.【類】They often drink wine in cold weather to ***warm*** *themselves*. / Sit nearer to the fire and ***warm*** *yourself*. ¶***wash*** *oneself* 顔や手を洗う. ¶***wean*** *oneself* from bad habits 悪習慣を直す ‖ ***wean*** *oneself* from stimulants 酒をやめる. ¶The novelty soon ***wore*** *itself* ***out***. じき新味がなくなった. ‖ When the mood of rage ***wore*** *itself* ***out***, we made it up with tears. 怒りの気持ちが去ると涙が出て来た(悲しくなって来た).【類】One should not ***wear*** one's *self* ***out*** with work. / wait till the fever ***wears*** *itself* ***out*** (熱が抜けるまで) / While the dreamer frets and ***wears*** *himself* ***out*** over the unattainable, the happy, practical man is satisfied with what can be attained. ¶***weary*** *oneself* with thought 考え悩む ‖ ***weary*** *oneself* with labor 過労でつかれる. ¶***wedge*** *oneself* in between ... ...の中に割込む. ¶***weep*** *oneself* ***out*** 涙に暮れる ‖ Niobe ***wept*** *herself* into a stone. ニオベは嘆き悲しんで石に化した. ¶***withdraw*** *oneself* from the business その仕事から手を引く ‖ ***withdraw*** *oneself* into a cave どう穴に引っ込む. ¶***withhold*** *oneself* as much as possible できるだけ控える. ¶***will*** *oneself* into contentment しいて満足する. ¶***wind*** *oneself* about ... ...にからみつく.【類】The serpent ***wound*** *itself* round a victim. ¶He started life on the last rung of the ladder and ***worked*** *himself* ***up***. 彼は下っぱから身を起し努力して出世した.【類】Edwin Wendell Panley ***worked*** *himself* from an oil-field hand to one of California's wealthiest oil men. ‖ ***work*** *oneself* to death 過労で死ぬ ‖ The problem will in time ***work*** *itself* ***out***. その問題はそのうち自然に解決する. ‖ These tendencies have been ***working*** *themselves* ***out***. これらの傾向は自然にはっきりして来た. ‖ ***work*** and ***support*** *oneself* 自活する ‖ ***work*** *oneself* into a passion 感情に走る ‖ The promising lad ***worked*** *himself* to death with study. その前途有望な青年は勉強の度が過ぎて死んだ.【類】He ***worked*** *himself* to death in the interests of the nation. ¶***worm*** *oneself* through the bush 茂みからはい出る ‖ ***worm*** *oneself* into another's favor 人にとり入る.【類】***worm*** *oneself* into another's business. ¶***worry*** *oneself* about trifles つまらないことにくよくよする ‖ ***worry*** *oneself* almost into a nervous breakdown for fear that ... ...することを恐れ心配のあまりほとんど神経衰弱になる. ¶***wrap*** *oneself* up in a warm winter cloak 冬の外とうに身を包む ‖ ***wrap*** *oneself* in the mantle of impenetrable dignity おかし難い威厳の衣を身にまとう ‖ The mountains ***wrapped*** *themselves* up in deep slumber. 山々は深い眠りに落ちた. ‖ a flame began to ***wrap*** *itself* round ... ...の回りを炎が包み始めた. ¶A good story, once clearly conceived, almost ***writes*** *itself*. いったん構想がまとまればりっぱな小説がほとんどひとりでに書ける. ¶The author seems to have ***written*** *himself* ***out***. 作家は種切れになったらしい. ¶She ***yielded*** *herself* to his desire. 彼女は彼の欲情に身を任せた. ¶***yield*** *oneself* to a strong passion. 激情に身をゆだねる.

P Mr. B deplores the frequent publication of rumors ***about*** *himself* and his wife. B氏は自分と妻に関する風説がしばしば公表されるのを嘆く. ¶He is living ***above*** *himself*. 彼は身分不相応な暮しをしている. ¶I confess, ***against*** *myself*, that ... 実は...なのです ‖ Europe alone of all the continents is divided ***against*** *itself*. すべての大陸の中でヨーロッパだけは(それぞれ)割れている. ‖ A kingdom divided ***against*** *itself* is brought to desolation. 仲間割れをしている王国は荒廃する. ‖ very much ***against*** *oneself* 不本意千万であるが. ¶be at variance ***among*** *themselves* 仲間割れがしている ‖ quarrel ***among*** *themselves* 仲間同士でけんかする ‖ they agree ***among*** *themselves* that ... 仲間同士...で妥協する ‖ We called it "..." ***amongst*** *ourselves*. それを仲間で「...」とわれわれは呼んでいた. ¶a girl of about the same age ***as*** *herself* 彼女とおなじ年位の少女. ¶Have a look ***at*** *yourself* in that mirror. その鏡に姿を写して御覧なさい. ‖ look ***at*** *himself* as a component part of a group 彼を一集団の一構成員と見なす ‖ look ***at*** *oneself* in a mirror 鏡をみる. ¶He was almost ***beside*** *himself* with joy. 彼はうれしさでほとんど有頂天だった ‖ be ***beside*** *oneself* with rage 怒ってわれを忘れる ‖ be half ***beside*** *oneself* with glee (うれしさで) / ***beside*** *oneself* with terror (fear) / He was quite ***beside*** *himself* with passion (かんしゃく). / I felt quite ***beside*** *myself* for joy and gratitude. / be ***beside*** *oneself* with age (年のせいで) ‖ There were two other guests ***beside*** *myself*. 私の外に客が二人あった. ‖ The compiler ventures to hope that the information here, for the first time, summarized will be of service to many ***besides*** *himself*. 編者はここに始めて総括した知識が編者以外多数の方々のお役に立つことを祈る. ¶***between*** *ourselves* ここだけの話だが.【類】This is ***between*** *ourselves*. ¶He sat ***by*** *himself* (alone) under a tree. 彼は木の下にひとりすわっていた. ‖ I ventured out ***by*** *myself*. 私は思いきって一人で出掛けた. ‖ It is not ***by*** *itself* and ***in*** *itself* an obstacle. それだけではまたそれ自体邪魔物ではない.【類】I like to go there ***by*** *myself*. / The barn stood in the field all ***by*** *itself*. / Set them apart ***by*** *themselves*. / I made it all ***by*** *myself*. / leave ***by*** *oneself* for ... / How could I let her go ***by*** *herself*? / set off ***by*** *ourselves* / Can your child walk ***by*** *himself*? / I was never less alone than when ***by*** *myself* (ひとりの方がさびしくない). / I visited him ***by*** *myself*. / settle the matter ***by*** *themselves* / He did not like to leave his daughter ***by*** *herself*. / I do not fear communism ***by*** *itself* (共産主義そのもの). / when ***by*** *himself* (=alone) / I spent a good deal of time ***by*** *myself*. / It was done entirely ***by*** *myself*. / stand ***by*** *ourselves* as much as possible / It can do nothing ***by*** *itself*. / One of the first things that a man has to learn in business is how little he can do ***by*** *himself*. / A child, eighteen months old, ought to be able to toddle along ***by*** *itself*. / The teacher found him studying ***by*** *himself*. / learn English ***by*** *oneself* / practice ***by*** *oneself* / let them play ***by*** *themselves* ‖ stand ***by*** *itself* 孤立する; 比類がない.【類】Mt. Fuji stands ***by*** *itself*, rising with one majestic sweep from a plain almost surrounded by mountains. ‖ Power is the product obtained by multiplying a number ***by*** *itself* one or more times.〘数学〙べきは一つの数を一回から数回自乗して得た積である. ‖ For sheer destruction power the atomic bomb is in a class ***by*** *itself*. 破壊力では原子爆弾は他にその類を見ないものである. ‖ The work holds a place ***by*** *itself* in biographical literature. その著作は伝記文学に独自の位置を占める. ‖ This places him in a class ***by*** *himself*. このために彼は独特の位置を占めている.【類】be practically in a class ***by*** *himself* as ... / be placed in a category ***by*** *itself* / give it a separate place ***by*** *itself* / Filipino English is in a class ***by*** *itself*. / The book has the most distinctive feature which removes it from the ordinary category of such works and puts it in a class ***by*** *itself*. ‖ judge others ***by*** *oneself* 自分を土台にして他人を判断する ‖ The males and females dance ***by*** *themselves* without intermingling. 男女別々に踊る. ‖ In correspondence instruction each student is a class ***by*** *himself*. 通信教授では銘々の学生が一つのクラスになる. ‖ London forms a county ***by*** *itself*. ロンドンは単独で一州を構成している.【類】they form a caste (階級) ***by*** *themselves* / form a class ***by*** *themselves* ‖ perform duties ***by*** *oneself* or substitute 自分であるいは代理を頼んで仕事をする ‖ a business all ***by*** *itself* 全く専門の商売 ‖ I refrained from this ***by*** *myself*. 私は自分の考えで控えた ‖ feed it ***by*** *itself* (他のものと交ぜないで)それだけ食わせる ‖ quite enough ***by*** *itself* to give interest to ... それだけで十分...に興味を与えられる ‖ That would require a book ***by*** *itself*. それだけで一冊の本になる位だ(簡単には述べられない).【類】deal it in a chapter ***by*** *itself*. ¶I have no one to blame ***but*** *myself*. ただただ自分を責めるだけである. ‖ Who should do it ***but*** *himself*? あの男でなくてだれがそれをやるだろう. ¶That you must decide ***for*** *yourself*. それは君自身できめなければいけない. ‖ ***For*** *myself* I cannot accept these views. 私としてはこの意見は承認できない. ‖ act ***for*** *oneself* 自由行動をとる ‖ they have built a big name ***for*** *themselves* in ... 彼らは自力で...で大ものになった ‖ He did not buy the book ***for*** *himself* but for you. 彼はその本を自分のためでなく君のために買ったのだ. ‖ the gift which he claims uniquely ***for*** *himself* 彼独特のものと主張する天分 ‖ cook ***for*** *oneself* 自炊する.【類】Test and compare ***for*** *yourself*. / Count them ***for*** *your-*

self. / He will not take it for granted that twice two are four until he has counted ***for** himself*. / decide ***for** themselves* what steps are most likely to be successful in their own districts / discover new facts about things ***for** himself* / They discovered this fact ***for** themselves.* / leave him to decide ***for** himself* / go to London to see what he can do ***for** himself* there / He has done it all ***for** himself.* / He does everything ***for** himself.* / I must do it ***for** myself.* ‖ the innovation would earn ***for** itself* the everlasting thanks of ... その革新は永久に…から感謝されるだろう ‖ examine impartially ***for** himself* the true value of his own qualities 彼自身の性質の真価を自分で公平に検討する ‖ Acquire it out ***for** yourself.* 自分で計算して御覧 ‖ You must find the solution of this problem ***for** yourself.* 君はこの問題を自分で解かなければならない. ‖ find it out ***for** themselves* それを自分で捜し出す(解決する) ‖ gain ***for** oneself* an enduring reputation 永続的名声を自分でかちうる ‖ There is no way under the sun to get valuable employees except by giving them a chance to get ahead ***for** themselves.* 自力で頭角を現わす機会を与えてやる以外によい雇人を得る方法は全然ない. 【類】I am not going to tell you. Find out ***for** yourself.* / He went into business ***for** himself* in Yokohama. / It is a term he invented ***for** himself.* ‖ Pampered and spoiled, she lives only ***for** herself.* 勝手気ままにさしておいたので彼女は自分の事しか考えない. ‖ If each individual looks out ***for** himself*, society will take care of itself. めいめいが注意すれば社会はおのずから治まる. ‖ Judge ***for** yourself.* 自分で考えて御覧. 【類】he may judge ***for** himself* as to ... ‖ Keep it ***for** yourself.* 君それを取っておけ. ‖ keep knowledge ***for** himself* 知識を一人じめする ‖ know ***for** themselves* 彼ら自身の力で知る ‖ learn ***for** himself* 独力で学ぶ. 【類】learn it ***for** oneself* ‖ leave you to judge ***for** yourself* whether ... 果して…かどうか君の判断に任せる ‖ live ***for** oneself* 自活する. 【類】live not ***for** himself* alone, but for the social life at large / unable to make a better living ***for** himself* and his family ‖ make ***for** himself* a place in ... 自分で…に地位を得る ‖ He will probably make ***for** himself* many friends. 彼は多くの友人がつくれるだろう. 【類】Crusoe made ***for** himself* a cap of goatskin. ‖ make good ***for** itself* by ... …で[事業が]収支つぐなうようにする. 【類】make observations ***for** himself* ‖ Last year he opened a shoe-store ***for** himself.* 彼は去年自分でくつ屋を始めた. ‖ It pays ***for** itself.* それは引合う(赤字にならない). ‖ Hold room ***for** self* and wife, ten days. 自分と妻が十日間滞在する室を頼む(ホテルへの電報). ‖ The machines quickly pay ***for** themselves.* その機械はすぐに原価が浮く. 【類】When if ever, civil aviation is going to pay ***for** itself?* ‖ puzzle things out ***for** oneself* 物を自分で考え出す(問題などを解く) ‖ Her eyes have so failed that she can no longer read ***for** herself.* 彼女は視力が衰えてもう自分で読むことができない. ‖ incite children to read further ***for** themselves* もっと自分で読書するよう子供たちを激励する. 【類】Read these volumes ***for** yourself.* ‖ He had no more to say ***for** himself.* 彼はそれ以上の弁明をする必要がなかったた. ‖ say ***for** oneself* that ... …と弁護する ‖ set it ***for** oneself* それを自分に課す ‖ secure ***for** itself* a recognized place among ... …の中で認められている位置を確保する ‖ he will see ***for** himself* that ... 彼は…が自分で分かるだろう. 【類】If you will read the paper, you will see ***for** yourself.* ‖ see to it ***for** yourself* that ... …するように自分で気をつける / see [to it] ***for** themselves* that their country is up against. 【類】He set up a business ***for** himself* at the sign (看板) of the Sun and Crown. ‖ The curves speak so plainly ***for** themselves* that any comment are almost superfluous. そのグラフの曲線が明かに示しているので注釈はほとんど不必要だ. ‖ leave others to shift ***for** themselves* 他のものは自分で始末をするようにほおっておく. 【類】let him shift ***for** himself* as much as he can / The parents should cherish and provide for their child, till it is able to shift ***for** itself.* ‖ It speaks ***for** itself.* それを見ると分かる. 【類】These figures speak ***for** themselves.* / The list speaks ***for** itself.* / I cannot do better than allow him to speak ***for** himself.* / let one's actions speak ***for** themselves* / In this respect recent events speak ***for** themselves.* ‖ start (=set up) in business ***for** oneself* 自分で商売を始める. 【類】Some day I am going to start out ***for** myself.* ‖ think ***for** oneself* 自分で考える. 【類】I want to think it ***for** myself.* / He thinks only of others and has no regard ***for** himself.* / those who think ***for** themselves* / think ***for** oneself*, from unconventional standpoints (自由な立場から), on many subjects / This saved them the trouble of thinking ***for** themselves.* / The best teaching is that which stimulates and encourages the student to think ***for** himself.* ‖ In his youth he took ***for** himself* the motto, "Nothing is impossible." 彼は青年時代に「世に不可能のことなし」という標語を座右の銘とした. ‖ try the experiment ***for** myself* 自分で実験して見る ‖ pick out (=choose) things one wants ***for** oneself.* 自分に入用な物を選り抜く ‖ they won ***for** themselves* an honored place in ... 彼らは…における名誉ある地位を自分の力で築いた ‖ The university won laurels ***for** herself* from outside sources. その大学は外部との試合で幾度か勝利を獲得した. ‖ work out their own problems ***for** themselves* 彼ら自身の問題を自力で解決する ‖ Who is it for?—It's ***for** myself.* それはどなたのですか—私がはいるんです(貸間など). ‖ ***for** myself*, I have had opportunities to ... 自分は…する幾多の機会に遭遇した ‖ each person ***for** himself*, and the devil take the hindermost 銘々自分のため, 人はどうなろうとも ‖ I would rather be in business ***for** myself* than employed by others. 人に使われるよりは自分で商売をやりたい. ¶ be absorbed ***in** oneself* 考え込む ‖ a huge subject ***in** itself* これだけで一大問題 ‖ write a book ***in** itself* その問題だけ取扱った本を書く ‖ the pursuit of knowledge as an end ***in** itself* 目的そのものとしての知識の追求 ‖ to be with a man who ... was ***in** itself* an education …の人とともにあることがすでに教育だった ‖ Almost a meal ***in** itself.* それだけで一回の食事といってもよい物(バナナなど). ‖ I can hardly find any trace of my father ***in** myself*, except an inborn faculty for drawing. 私には生得の画才を除き父の遺伝がほとんどない. ‖ a miniature world ***in** itself* それ自体一小世界 ‖ a contradiction ***in** itself* それ自体矛盾していること ‖ Each volume is complete ***in** itself.* 各巻それぞれ読み切りになっている. ‖ Football journalism is a profession ***in** itself*, with all its own editors, specialists, and reporters. フットボールの報道はそれぞれ主任記者・専門家・報道員があって一つの専門職業である. 【類】Each volume, though a unit ***in** itself*, is still an organic part of the whole series. / a complete unit ***in** itself* ‖ *What* contains an antecedent ***in** itself.* What はその中に先行詞が含まれている. ‖ be much perplexed ***in** himself* what it means どういう意味か分からないでほとほと困る ‖ The study of our own language is an education ***in** itself*; it is two of the three R's. 自国語の勉強そのものは一つの教育だ, それは三 R (reading, writing, and arithmetic) の二つを占めている. ‖ however desirable ***in** itself* その物は結構だが. 【類】The book is really a small library ***in** itself.* / be a complete cyclopedia ***in** itself* / The Aquitania (アキタニア号) is a city ***in** herself.* / Each borough (自治区) is ***in** itself* a large town. / things ***in** themselves* insignificant / Macy's (メーシー百貨店) is an actual city ***in** itself.* / It is a whole world ***in** itself.* / London is a little world ***in** itself.* / this incident appears negligible ***in** itself*, but ... / Isolated words, ***in*** and ***by** themselves*, are not language. / These petty troubles, each one ***in** itself* nothing serious, but added together, make quite a problem. / this is ***in** itself* proof of the fact that ... / be a cosmos (宇宙) ***in** itself* / The building is a picture ***in** itself*—art could no further go. / This ***in** itself* should be sufficient to guarantee its success. / To answer questions well is an art ***in** itself.* / Money is but a measure of commodities, which are ***in** themselves* for a measure of labor. / Something that is not always interesting ***in** itself* but which is none the less important. / Jesus Christ was perfect ***in** himself.* / This act does not constitute ***in** itself* a misdemeanor or an immoral act (不行跡あるいは不倫な行為). / Conrad was a literary phenomenon ***in** itself* unmatched. / Antinomians hold that faith ***in** itself* is sufficient for salvation. ¶ laugh ***in spite*** of *oneself* 思わず笑う. 【類】He yawned again and again ***in spite of** himself.* ¶ go down ***into** oneself* われに返る; 自己反省する. ¶ The door shuts (opens) ***of itself*** 戸が自然と閉まる(開く). ‖ unfold ***of itself*** [つぼみなどが]自然に開く ‖ unroll ***of itself*** [巻いたものが]ひとりでに解ける ‖ Those kind words were ***of themselves*** to make them happy. そのような親切な言葉はそれだけでも彼らを喜ばせるものだった. ‖ The movement died [away] ***of itself***. その運動は自然消滅になった. 【類】All animals move ***of themselves***. / The world goes ***of itself***. / It could not disappear ***of itself***, could it? / The wall fell ***of itself***. / I think you must have done something to it: it cannot break ***of itself***. / The reason was that it was then midwinter, which ***of itself*** drew closer all household ties. / Let us take care of the elementary stage (初歩の段階), and the advanced stage will take care ***of itself***. / A well-known writer said, " Be pleasant until 10 o'clock in the morning and the rest of the day will take care ***of itself***." / If you can control the mind, the body will be able to take care ***of itself***. / The likelihood is that he will come home ***of himself*** tomorrow morning. / I did this ***of myself***. ‖ Life Insurance Speaks ***of Itself***. 生命保険案内(宣伝文). ‖ He spoke ***of himself*** as a florist. 彼は自分は花屋だと言った. ‖ Pity indeed is, ***of itself***, but poor comfort at any time. たしかにあわれみそのものはどんな時でも大した慰めにはならない. ‖ A monosyllable has, ***of itself***, no accent. 単てつ語にはそれ自体にアクセントはない. ‖ This ***of itself*** was unusual. このこと自体が既に異例であった. ‖ Change of work ***of itself*** is a relaxation. 仕事を変えることはそれ自体一つの気晴しだ. ‖ The act of killing does not ***of itself*** constitute the guilt. 殺人行為そのものは犯罪を構成しない. 【類】London seems like a world ***of itself;*** you might walk about for a year, and go into some new street every day. ‖ be master ***of oneself*** 自制する ‖ He was no longer master ***of himself***. 彼は夢中になっていた. ‖ " Tempered " glass is a glass which ***of itself*** possesses exceptional tensile strength and marked safety features. 付加物質を加えたガラスは異常な張力と著しい安全性を具えている. ‖ He began to take care ***of himself*** at 14. 彼は十四歳で独立した生活を始めた. ‖ the necessary wearing apparel and bedding ***of himself***, his wife, and children 彼と妻子の必要とする着物と寝具 ‖ Rembrandt's famous portrait ***of himself***. レンブラントの有名な自画像. ‖ make these good rules a part ***of oneself*** これらの金言を実行する ‖ I judged that Robert and you were happy enough ***of yourselves***. ロバートと君は二人だけで十分幸福だと私は判断した. ¶make a fool ***of oneself*** ばかを見る. 【類】make a laughing-stock ***of oneself*** ‖ when one is sure ***of himself***, why shouldn't he say so? 自分でたしかだと思っているのにどうしてそう言ってはいけないの. 【類】That made me feel ashamed ***of myself*** ‖ They make a point of giving me news ***of themselves*** with great regularity. 彼らはきちんときちんとその安否を私に知らせることにしてる. ‖ American youth gave a magnificent account ***of himself*** in the war. アメリカの青年は戦争ですばらしい功績を立てた. ¶wait ***on oneself***＝serve oneself 自分で給仕する ‖ I take the blame ***on myself***. 私が悪かった. ‖ impose ***on oneself*** the task of ... ...の仕事を引受ける ‖ take a burden ***on oneself*** 責任を取る. 【類】take ***on oneself*** the responsibility of ... ‖ double over ***on itself*** 一回折りたたむ ‖ fold ***on itself*** 二つに折る ‖ bend ***on itself*** 二つ折りになる. 【類】a thread folded ***on itself*** several times / a carpet rolled ***on itself*** ‖ carry out ***on oneself*** observations of this kind 自分を対象にこういう観察を行う ‖ French public opinion is lenient to abortion, especially to women who perform the operation ***on themselves***. フランスの世論は堕胎に対して寛大だ, 特に自分で自分の胎児を手術する女に対して. ¶I was transported, confused, and ***out of*** (＝beside) ***myself***. 私は有頂天で, まごまごして, われを忘れた. ‖ wait patiently till the epidemic dies [*out*] ***of itself*** 伝染病が自然に終わるまで辛抱する ‖ go ***out of oneself*** into the world of external human life and activity 自分の精神生活から外面的の人生並に活動の世界に進出する. ¶She chuckled ***to herself***. 彼女は独りでクスクス笑った. ‖ number ***to oneself*** 独り言をつぶやく ‖ hum over ***to himself*** the verses of ... ...の詩を独りで口ずさむ ‖ mutter ***to oneself*** ぶつぶつ独り言をいう ‖ repeat it ***to oneself*** 自分でそれを繰返す ‖ " Death or life now," said he ***to himself***. 「死か生か」と彼は独り言を言った. ‖ whisper ***to oneself*** the name of ... ...の名を独りでささやく ‖ he said, half ***to himself***, ... 彼は独り言のように...と言った ‖ sing away ***to oneself*** in a corner すみっこで歌を口ずさむ. 【類】Something like this is what he must have said ***to himself***. / When I open a noble volume, I say ***to myself***, " Now the only Croesus that I envy is he who is reading a better book than this." ‖ What are you talking ***to yourself?*** 何を独り言をいっているのだ. ‖ talking ***to oneself*** by means of interior speech 心の中で独り言をいって ‖ think ***to oneself*** 腹で思う. 【類】I could not help thinking ***to myself*** ... ‖ I vowed ***to myself*** that ... 私は...を自分の心に誓った ‖ wondering ***to myself*** if ... ...かどうかと怪しんで ‖ I admit ***to myself***, now, miserably that I was not equal to the situation. 遺憾ながら今私はその任に耐えられなかったことを自認する. ‖ ally ***to itself*** the strength of ... それに...の力を加える ‖ Be good ***to yourself!*** お体をお大事に(御気げんよろしゅう). ‖ bring one ***to oneself*** 正気づく, われに返る. 【類】when she came ***to herself*** again ‖ cry ***to oneself*** しのび泣をする ‖ It deserves a paragraph ***to itself***. それだけに一節を費す値打がある. ‖ A dictionary of proverbs deserves a volume ***to itself***. 諺語辞典はそれだけで一冊の本にする値打がある. ‖ The subject has a chapter ***to itself*** (＝is treated in a separate chapter). その題目だけで一章できている. ‖ a matter which should really have a book ***to itself*** 実際それ専門の本があって然るべき事柄 ‖ We had the car ***to ourselves***. われわれは一車を独占した. ‖ I have not a minute ***to myself***. 私は自分の自由になる時間は一分もない. ‖ Elephants have a building all ***to themselves***. 象には象だけの建物がある(動物園で). ‖ form a class ***to itself*** 独得のものである ‖ Each flower has a page ***to itself***. 一つの花に一ページが当ててある. ‖ She had a room in her father's house ***to herself***. 彼女は父の家の一室を占領していた. 【類】We had the whole compartment ***to ourselves***. / as soon as we were in the room together, left ***to ourselves***, ... ‖ To ... would require a volume ***to itself***. ...するとなるとそれだけで一冊の本になるだろう. ‖ In " Living London " it has a special article ***to itself***. 「現代のロンドン」にはそれだけで一編の文になっている. ‖ have attention drawn ***to oneself*** 自分に注意を向けさせる ‖ just imagine ***to yourself*** how ... ...か思っても御覧なさい ‖ just picture ***to yourselves*** the horror with which ... ...の恐怖をちょっと想像して見給え. 【類】figure (＝picture) it ***to oneself*** ‖ You may keep it ***to youself***. それをしまってお き給え(あげるよ). ‖ keep it all ***to oneself*** それを独占する ‖ It lightens one's troubles to tell them to others, rather than to keep them ***to oneself***. 自分の胸に秘めておくより他人にそれを打明けた方が苦しみが楽になる. 【類】keep one's feelings ***to oneself*** / He kept the secret ***to himself***. / He kept his indignation ***to himself***. / He laughed ***to himself*** grimly. / laugh ***to oneself*** at the credulity of ... ‖ live ***to oneself***＝live selfishly 自分勝手の生活をする ‖ No nation can now live ***to itself*** alone. 今では自国だけで立って行かれる国はない. ‖ He was mumbling some inarticulate words ***to himself***. 彼は発音の不明白な言葉を独りでつぶやいていた. ‖ You owe it ***to yourself*** and to others to ... 君が...するのは自分並に他人に対する義務である. 【類】Each person owes it ***to himself*** as well as to society to observe rules of hygiene (衛生規則). ‖ the object I propose ***to myself*** 私が心がけている目的 ‖ read ***to oneself*** 独りで読む ‖ reason ***to oneself*** 自分で判断する ‖ remain true ***to oneself*** 自分を欺かないでいる ‖ secure ***to oneself*** the advantage of ... ...の利益を確保する ‖ He will not uncover himself even ***to himself***. 自分独りのときでも彼は裸にはならない. ‖ commodities peculiar ***to itself*** 土地の特産品 ‖ entire sincerity ***to oneself*** 自己に対する完全の忠実 ‖ Look ***to yourself***, dear Sir—or Madam. 男の方も女の方も反省なさい. ¶Each case is a law ***unto itself***, and the physician must take into consideration the characteristics of the particular patient. 病気は人によって違う, で医者は特殊の患者の特徴をしんしゃくしなければならない. ‖ In these matters every man must be a law ***unto himself***. こういうことは人によって違う(銘々が自分だけの規律を作らなければならない). ‖ In ancient times every man was a law ***unto himself***. 古代人はすべて自分の勝手にふるまったものだ(人の作った規律など守らないで). ¶take ***upon oneself*** the responsibility of ... ...の責任を負う. 【類】take ***upon*** *itself* the task of ... / He took it ***upon himself*** to see that it was done. ‖ take ***upon himself*** the mission of ... ...をもって自ら任じる ‖ take ***upon ourselves*** unnecessary trouble 無用の手数を背負い込む. 【類】take ***upon oneself*** the office of president (会長) / take ***upon oneself*** the exercise of judicial functions (裁判官の職務) ‖ The jest came to be turned home ***upon himself***. そのしゃれはかえって自分をあざける結果となった. ‖ That depends ***upon yourself***. それは君次第だ. ‖ bring ***upon oneself*** a great inconvenience 非常に不便を感じさせる ‖ bring down ***upon oneself*** an immediate refusal from ... ...から即座に拒絶される ‖ observations ***upon oneself*** 自己を対象とした観察 ‖ draw a censure down ***upon oneself*** 非難を受ける ‖ draw ***upon himself*** in consequence a torrent of abuse [その結果として]猛烈な非難を浴びる. ¶He that falls in love ***with himself*** will find no rival.—Franklin. 自分で自分にほれた場合は恋敵はない. ‖ play ***with oneself***=masturbate 手いんする ‖ For several minutes I was debating ***with myself*** the question—"Shall I tip him?" 数分間私は「彼に心付をやろうか」ということを心に決しかねていた. ‖ It rests ***with yourselves*** whether it proves a curse or a benediction. 幸となるか不幸になるかは銘々の心掛け次第だ. ‖ commune ***with oneself*** 黙考する ‖ I don't know what to do ***with myself*** today. きょうはからだの置場に困る. ‖ If things are only right ***with himself***, he does not care about other people's trouble. 彼は自分さえ好ければ他人の悩みなどは一向構わない. ‖ mope away ***with oneself*** 自殺する ‖ The world does not begin and end ***with oneself***. 人は世の中で銘々相互的連関がある. ¶think ***within oneself*** that ... 心の内で…と思う ‖ swear ***within myself*** 心に誓う ‖ They contain ***within themselves*** the seeds of their own destruction. それらの中には自己破滅の因を蔵している. ‖ The New Yorker is a city ***within itself***. ニューヨーカー[ホテル]は市の中の市だ.

self-abnegation, *n.* 自己犠牲.

Q an act of ***noble*** *self-abnegation* 高尚な自己犠牲の行為. ¶with ***utter*** *self-abnegation* (=complete self-forgetfulness) 完全に自己を滅却して.

self-acting, *a.* 自動的な.

M The plant is ***entirely*** *self-acting* (automated). その工場は完全に機械化している(オートメーションだ).

self-assumption, *n.* うぬぼれ, てんぐ.

V ***gratify*** one's *self-assumption* うぬぼれを満足させる, い⌊い気になる.

self-centered, *a.* 自己中心の.

M ***egotistically*** *self-centered* 自我でかたまった.

self-confidence, *n.* 自信.

V ***acquire*** *self-confidence* 度胸がすわる. ¶***gain*** *self-confidence* 自信を得る. ¶The time has changed and national *self-confidence* is ***restored*** again. 時勢が変って国民的自信が復活して来た. ¶***undermine*** his *self-confidence* and render him vacillating in action 彼の自信をくつがえしてその行動をぐらつかせる.

Q with ***superhuman*** *self-confidence* 自信にみちみちた.

self-consciousness, *n.* 自己意識.

V ***cast aside*** *self-consciousness* 自己意識を捨てる. ¶***regain*** one's *self-consciousness* 自己意識をとり戻す.

Q The spectators put me in a state of ***sacred*** *self-consciousness*. 観覧者を前にすると私には神聖な自己意識がもり⌊上った.

self-containment, *n.* 自足.

V ***achieve*** economic *self-containment* 経済的自足の域に達⌊する.

self-control, *n.* 自制, 克己.

V ***exercise*** *self-control* 自制する. ¶***lack*** *self-control* 自制心を欠く. ¶***lose*** *self-control* 自制を失う(あわてる). ¶***preserve*** one's *self-control* in all circumstances あらゆる場合に自制を失わない.

Q with ***admirable*** *self-control* 驚嘆すべき自制力で. ¶***social*** *self-control* 社会的自制.

P He is lacking ***in*** *self-control*. 彼は自制心を欠いている. ¶a loss ***of*** *self*-control 自制心の喪失. 【類】the power ***of*** ⌊*self-control*.

self-defense, 《英》**-ce**, *n.* 自己防衛.

Q ***legitimate*** *self-defense* 正当防衛.

P use a revolver ***in*** *self-defense* 自己防衛のために連発けん銃を使用する. 【類】He killed a man ***in*** *self-defense*. ¶a measure ***of*** *self-defence* 自衛手段.

self-denial, *n.* 自制.

V ***exercise*** (=***practice***) *self-denial* 自制する.

P He is very rigid ***in*** *self-denial*. 彼は自己を制することが⌊きわめて厳である.

self-destruction, *n.* 自殺.

Q a ***double*** *self-destruction* 心中.

self-discipline, *n.* 自己訓練.

Q ***laborious*** *self-discipline* 骨の折れる自己修養.

self-examination, *n.* 自省, 反省.

Q after ***honest*** *self-examination* 正直に自省した後に.

self-expression, *n.* 自己表現.

V ***develop*** *self-expression* 自己表現を発展させる.

self-governing, *a.* 自治の.

M which are not ***fully*** *self-governing* 完全なる自治を有し「ない.

self-government, *n.* 自治.

P[2] *self-government* ***through*** elected representatives 代議⌊員による自治.

self-guidance, *n.* 独り案内.

Q ***vocational*** *self-guidance* 就職独り案内.

self-interest, *n.* 利己, 私利.

Q the ***enlightened*** *self-interest* of the employer 雇主の(使用人の利益を考慮する)進歩的利己主義.

selfish, *a.* わがままな, 自分勝手の.

M ***incurably*** *selfish* 矯正すべからざるほどにわがままな. ¶That's ***too*** *selfish* それじゃあんまり虫がよすぎる.

P it was *selfish* ***of*** me that ... ...のは私がわがままだった.

selfishness, *n.* わがまま.

Q ***brutal*** *selfishness* and low passions 獣的なわがままと劣情. ¶***self-centered*** *selfishness* 自己中心のわがまま.

self-perfecting, *n.* 自己完成.

Q ***spiritual*** *self-perfecting* 精神的自己完成.

self-possession, *n.* 沈着, 落着き.

V When one speaks to him he ***loses*** his *self-possession*. 人が彼に話しかけると彼はあわてる. 【類】***lose*** all *self-possession* / He did not ***lose*** his perfect *self-possession*. ¶***recover*** (=***regain***) one's *self-possession* 心を落着ける.

self-reliance, *n.* 自信.

V ***cultivate*** *self-reliance* 自信をつける.

self-respect, *n.* 自尊, 自重.

V The look which the young man bestowed upon me would have ***aroused*** the *self-respect* of a door-mat. 私を見たその青年の顔付はどんなお人よしだってこれを見ては虫がおさまらないものであった. ¶***destroy*** one's *self-respect* 自敬心を破棄する, 恥知らずになる. ¶***hurt*** (=***wound***) one's *self-respect* 自尊心を傷つける. ¶He was anxious to ***keep*** his *self-respect*. 彼は自尊心を傷つけまいと気をもんでいた. ¶***lose*** one's *self-respect* 自尊心を失う. ¶***lower*** one's *self-respect* 自尊心を傷つける. ¶***maintain*** the national *self-respect* 国民的自尊心を維持する. ¶in a way that will ***preserve*** one's *self-respect* and independence ... その自重心と独立心を失わせないような風に.

Q He is a man of ***great*** *self-respect*. 彼は自尊心の強い男だ.

P the spirit ***of*** *self-respect* 自尊心.

self-restraint, *n.* 自制.

V ***exercise*** increasing *self-restraint* ますます自制する.

P schooled ***in*** *self-restraint* 自制力できたえられて. ¶the power ***of*** *self-restraint* 自制力.

self-sacrifice, *n.* 自己犠牲.

Q ***heroic*** *self-sacrifice* 勇壮な自己犠牲. ¶The planes sank four cruisers through ***voluntary*** *self-sacrifice*. それらの飛行機はそのとう乗員の献身的犠牲によって巡洋艦四隻を爆⌊沈した.

P the spirit ***of*** *self-sacrifice* 犠牲的精神.

self-satisfaction, *n.* 自己満足.

Q ***breed*** *self-satisfaction* 自己満足に安んじさせる.

self-scrutiny, *n.* 反省.

Q ***national*** *self-scrutiny* 国民的反省.

self-seeker, *n.* 利己主義者.

Q an ***ambitious*** *self-seeker* 利己主義な野心家. ¶a ***mere*** *self-seeker* 全くの利己主義者.

self-sufficiency, *n.* 自給自足.

V ***achieve*** economic *self-sufficiency* 経済的自足の域に達す「る.

Q acquire those skills which will mean ***economic*** *self-sufficiency* 経済的自給自足に達しうるような技術を獲得する.

Q[2] ***foodstuff*** *self-sufficiency* 食料の自給自足.

P We have attained, or are attaining, *self-sufficiency* ***in*** chemicals. われわれは化学薬品において自給自足の域に達したかまたはまさに達しようとしている.

self-survey, *n.* 自己反省.

V ***make*** a thorough *self-survey* 自己を深く内省する.

self-sustaining, *a.* 自活の.

M become *economically self-sustaining* 経済的に自活できるようになる.

self-taught, *a.* 独学の.

M He was almost ***entirely*** *self-taught.* 彼はほとんど全く独学だった.

sell, *v.* 売る; 敵に売る, 裏切る; 売れる; 《米》[宣伝して]売り出す, 売込む.

M *Sold again!* やられた! ¶*sell* it ***away*** それを売飛ばす. ¶Corn is *selling* ***briskly.*** 穀物は活発に売れている. ¶That is *sold* very ***cheap.*** それは非常に安く売っている. ¶buy goods cheap and *sell* them ***dear*** 品物を安く買って高く売る【類】Butter *sells* very ***dear.*** ¶*sell* one's life ***dearly*** 高価に一命を売る(敵に多大の損害を与えて討死する). ¶*sell* ***direct*** to ... ...に直接売る. ¶It can very ***easily*** be *sold* for ¥2,000. 默っていても二千円には売れる. ¶It can *sell* ***high.*** 高く売れる. ¶*sell* ***immediately*** 即時に売れる. ¶*sell* ***individually*** 別々に売る. ¶Books are *selling* ***languidly.*** 本の売行は思わしくない. ¶continue to *sell* very ***largely*** 依然売行がすばらしい. ¶I am *selling* very ***low*** (=***poorly***) now. 私の所は目下売行が非常に悪い. ¶It will ***never*** *sell.* それはとても売れまい. ¶*sold* ***openly*** (secretly) 大っぴらに(こそこそ)売る. ¶*sell* ***out*** ... ...を売切る, 一切売払う ‖ Tobacco allotment for today *sold* ***out.*** タバコ本日分売切れ. ‖ Bears are *selling* ***out*** their purchases. 弱気筋では手持ちを投げに出している.【類】The New Year number was *sold* ***out*** in December. / *sell* ***out*** one's property / The large stock we had laid in was soon *sold* ***out.*** ¶*sell* hand-made dolls ***outright*** 手製人形を即売する.【類】*sell* one's manuscript (原稿) ***outright.*** ¶*sell* ***over*** 売渡す. ¶*sell* it ***piecemeal*** それを一個売にする. ¶*sell* ***poorly*** 売足がかんばしくない. ¶*sell* ***privately*** to ... ...に秘密に売る. ¶It will *sell* ***promptly.*** それはすぐに売れるだろう. ¶*sell* ***quickly*** 売足が早い. ¶*sell* ***short*** 空売する. ¶Books are *selling* ***smartly.*** 本の売行は上景気だ. ¶*sell* ***sparingly*** ちょびちょび売れる. ¶What can I *sell* you ***this morning***? 今朝は何かお買上の御用がありませんか. ¶Corn is *selling* remarkably ***well.*** 穀物は非常によく売れている. ¶The concert promotors tried to "*sell*" that type of music very ***widely.*** 楽団屋連はその型の音楽を大いに売り出そうとした. ¶*sell* ***wholesale*** (***retail***) おろし(小)売をする.

M² *sell* ***off*** all the property in possession 所持品を全部売払う. ¶*sell* ***up*** ... ...を公売に付す.

P This *sells* ***at*** $3 a yard. この織物は一ヤール三ドルで売る.【類】*sell* ***at*** one pound apiece (=each) ‖ *sell* ***at*** a bargain 安売する ‖ *sell* ***at*** current market-price 時価で売る ‖ *sell* ***at*** my limit 私の指値で売る ‖ *sell* ***at*** a loss (profit) 損をして(もうけて)売る ‖ *sell* ***at*** market 一般に売出す ‖ *sell* ***at*** the market price 市価で売る ‖ *sell* ***at*** a fancy price 法外の値で売る ‖ *sell* ***at*** a premium 割増金付で売る ‖ *sell* ***at*** the latest quotation 最近の相場で売る ‖ *sell* ***at*** auction 《米》競売する ‖ *sell* ***at*** retail (wholesale) 《米》小(卸し)売する.【類】*sell* ***at*** fixed prices / *sell* ***at*** a discount (=reduction) / *sell* ***at*** a fair (high) price / will be *sold* ***at*** a very much higher price than is asked now / Our goods are *sold* only ***at*** this one store. ‖ It was *sold* ***at*** Christie's ***for*** £1,700. それはクリスティズ(在ロンドン美術品競売場)で千七百ポンドに売れた.【類】The picture was *sold* ***at*** Sotheby's (在ロンドン書店) in 1874 ***for*** £495. ¶*sell* ***below*** cost コストを割って売る. ¶*sell* ***by*** auction 《英》競売する.【類】*sell* ***by*** retail (wholesale) / The goods shelved will be *sold* ***by*** public auction. ☞米語用法の *sell* ***at*** auction (retail, wholesale) は英語用法では "by" ‖ The books are *sold* ***by*** all booksellers. その本はどの書店でも売っている. ‖ *sell* ***by*** the cask 一たるいくらで売る ‖ It is *sold* ***by*** all chemists. それはどの薬種屋でも売っている. ‖ *sell* ***by*** subscription 予約で売る.【類】Eggs are *sold* ***by*** the dozen. / It is *sold* ***by*** measure or weight (はかりと目方で). / Tea is *sold* ***by*** the pound. / *sell* ***by*** private contract ‖ Cloth is *sold* ***by*** the yard. 布は一ヤールいくらで売る. ‖ *sell* ***by*** tender 入札で売る. ¶*sell* ***ex*** lighter (ship, pier, quay, rail) はしけ船(など)渡しで売る. ¶*sell* ***for*** future delivery 先物で売る ‖ It can be *sold* ***for*** a good price (large sum). それは良い値(など)で売れる.【類】It wouldn't pay to *sell* it ***for*** less than five dollars. / How much do you *sell* this ***for***? / I won't *sell* it ***for*** a cent less. / *sell* ***for*** a song (trifle, nothing) ‖ *sell* oneself ***for*** money 金で身を売る.【類】He was *sold* ***for*** a slave. / *sell* one's country ***for*** money ‖ *sell* ***for*** immediate delivery 直渡しで売る ‖ *sell* ***for*** next settlement 次期決算で売る ‖ *sell* ***for*** spot cash 即金で売る ‖ *sell* it ***for*** what it brings 売れる値で売る. ¶The book has *sold* exceedingly well ***in*** America. その本はアメリカでは非常によく売れた. ‖ *sell* ***in*** bottles (bundles, casks) びん詰(など)にして売る ‖ *sell* ***in*** bulk ばらで売る ‖ *sell* ***in*** gross こみで売る ‖ *sell* ***in*** the lump 込みで売る ‖ *sell* ***in*** small lots 小さく分けて売る.【類】*sell* goods ***in*** (=***by***) lots (数口に分けて). ¶He was *sold* ***into*** slavery. 彼はどれいに売られた.【類】*sell* the king ***into*** the hands of the enemy. ¶*sell* ***like*** wildfire (=hot cakes) どしどし売れる. ¶*sell* ***on*** commission 手数料を取って売る ‖ *sell* ***on*** credit (trust) 掛(信用)で売る ‖ *sell* ***on*** note 手形で売る.【類】*sell* ***on*** chit (伝票) / *sell* ***on*** sample / *sell* ***on*** spot (現物で). ¶*sell* it ***through*** ... ***to*** ... ...を通じてそれを...に売る ‖ *sell* ***through*** a commission merchant 仲買人の手を経て売る. ¶*sell* ***to*** the highest bidder 一番の高値をつけた人に売る ‖ *sell* an idea ***to*** ... 《米》...に新考案を売り込む.【類】*sell* one's name ***to*** the public ‖ Through tickets are *sold* ***to*** all points on the line. 通し切符はその線の各地点に対して発売する. ¶*sell* ***under*** prime cost 仕入原価以下で売る ‖ I cannot *sell* it ***under*** a hundred thousand yen. それは十万円以下では売れない. ‖ *sell* "***under*** the counter" 《英》やみ取引する. ¶We are *selling* almost ***without*** any profit. お取次同様です.

O ***You're sold!*** [競売などで]君に落ちた.

seller, *n.* 販売人; よく売れる商品.

Q ***best*** *sellers* 一番よく売れる物[本など]. ¶a ***poor*** *seller* よく売れない商品.

Q² a ***newspaper*** *seller* 新聞販売人. ¶a ***street*** *seller* 街頭の売屋(流し屋).

selling, *n.* 販売.

V ***delay*** *selling* as long as possible できるだけ売りを延ばす ‖ Producers are holding off *selling* ***in*** anticipation of a rise in price. 生産者は値上りを見越して売り惜しんでる.

Q ***competitive*** *selling* 競争販売. ¶It is not so ***good*** *selling* as it once was. 今は一ころのようには売れない. ¶***intensive*** *selling* 売りあおり. ¶We have very ***little*** *selling* now. 一向売れない. ¶***panicky*** *selling* of securities 有価証券の乱売. ¶have ***poor*** *selling* 売行きが悪い. ¶***public*** *selling* 公売.

P a flood ***of*** *selling* 売手の続出.

P² *selling* ***by*** tender 入札払.

semblance, *n.* 似より; 似顔; 見かけ.

V He ***bears*** the *semblance* of an angel and the heart of a devil. 彼は外面(げめん)如菩薩(にょぼさつ)内面如夜叉(にょやしゃ)だ. ‖ He ***bears*** a manly *semblance.* 彼は見かけは男らしい. ‖ The country ***bears*** the *semblance* of wealth. その国は裕福そうに見える. ¶***draw*** his *semblance* 彼の似顔を描く. ¶***give*** a *semblance* of truth to ... ...をまことらしく見せかける. ¶It ***had*** more the *semblance* of a rapid dream than of actual occurrence. それは実際のできごとというよりは急速度の夢のようだった. ‖ ***have*** no *semblance* of ... ...に似ていない. ¶The statement ***lacks*** even the *semblance* of truth. その声明は見え透いたでたらめだ. ¶***put on*** (=***assume***) a *semblance* of indignation 憤怒を装う. ¶I ***recognize*** in him a *semblance* to his father. あの人は父親に似よったところがある.

Q a ***mere*** *semblance* ただ似ているだけ. ¶in ***outer*** *semblance* 外部の類似点では. ¶without the ***slightest*** *semblance* of hostility 紛争らしいものすらなく(平穏無事に). ¶There is ***some*** *semblance* between the two stories. その二つの話には似よったところがある.

P ***under*** the *semblance* of ... ...の仮面をかぶって. ¶He greeted ***with*** sad *semsblance.* 彼は悲しそうな様子をしてあいさつした. ¶They put him to death ***without*** even the *semblance* of a trial. 彼らは型だけの審問さえもせずに彼を死刑に処した.

semi-circle, *n.* 半円.

V ***form*** a *semi-circle* round ... ...のまわりに半円形を造る.

seminar, *n.* 研究科(ゼミナール).

Q² a ***painting*** *seminar* conducted by ... ...指導の絵画研究科.

P² a graduate *seminar* ***in*** political science 大学院の政治学研究科. ¶a *seminar* ***of*** political economy 経済学のゼミ.

seminary, *n.* 専門学校.

P² a *seminary* ***for*** young ladies 女子専門学校 ‖ our *seminaries* ***for*** the study of the law わが法律専門学校. ¶a *seminary* ***of*** learning 学問所, [専門の]学校.

senate *n.* [S-] 上院.

Q² the ***state*** *senate* [米国]州の上院. ¶the ***United States*** *Senate* 米国上院.

senator, *n.* 上院議員.

Q He is a *strong* (=*powerful*) *Senator*. 彼は有力な上院議員だ.

Q^2 a *U.S. Senator* from Virginia バージニア選出上院議員.

P^2 He is *Senator from* Massachusetts. 彼はマサチューセッツ州選出の上院議員だ.

send, *v.* 派遣する; 送る; 発射する.

M *send abroad* 海外へ派遣する. ¶He has *sent away* his servant. 彼は召使を解雇した. 【類】Boats were *sent away* to the rescue (急援に). ‖ a clerk *sent away* for the order 注文とり. ¶*send back* a thing to some person ある人に物を送り返す ‖ His body will be *sent back* to Sendai. 彼の身柄は仙台へ送還されるだろう. 【類】*send* them *back* to work / All persons arriving without passports are *sent back*. ¶*send directly* 直送する. ¶The tree *sends forth* (=*out*) branches. 木が枝を出す. 【類】The flowers *send forth* (=*out*) fragrance. / trees *sending forth* twigs and branches ‖ *send* it *forward* with a letter 手紙をつけてそれを送ってやる ‖ *send* him *forward* 彼を派遣する. ¶*send gratis* and *post free* 代価郵便税共無料で送る. ¶As the chairman got sick, he was *sent instead*. 議長が病気のため彼が代理として派遣された. ‖ *send out* a warning to ... ...に警告を発する ‖ *send out* word that ... ...という布令を出す. 【類】*send out* a proclamation (布告) / *send out* a questionnaire (質問書) / *send out* circulars (回状) concerning... / *send out* invitations to the marriage of ... and ... / The prospectus (趣意書) has been *sent out* today. / The commandant of the district *sent out* a signal to cease fire. ‖ *send* a book *out* to the world 一書を公刊する ‖ *send out* a colony to ... 移民団を...に送り込む / *send out* an expedition (遠征隊) / *send out* students into the world (卒業) ‖ The rose *sends out* strong fragrance. バラはにおいが強い. ‖ I *sent* the children *out* that the house might be quiet. 私は家の中が静かになるように子供らを外へ出した. 【類】He was *sent out* in the country for the benefit of his health. / He was *sent out* on an errand (使いに) by his master. ¶*Send* me the newspaper *regularly* until further orders. 新聞を続けて送ってください.

M^2 The tradesman *sent in* his account. 商人が勘定書をよこした. ‖ *send in* one's card 名刺を通じる ‖ *send in* an application at ... ...に願書を提出する ‖ He *sent in* his resignation. 彼は辞表を提出した. ‖ The report has not yet been *sent* in. レポートはまだ出していない. 【類】*Send in* your papers (答案). / *send in* a complaint (苦情書) / *send in* an application (申込み書) at ... / be required to *send in* their applications not later than the 15th inst. / *send in* an alarm (警報) ‖ *send* in one's name to ... 名前を...に書き送る ‖ *send in* one's promised donation 約束の寄付金を出す ‖ *send in* a proposal to ... for an insurance upon one's premises その家屋保険の申込を...にする. ¶*send* it *off* instantly to ... ...にすぐそれを発送する. 【類】I should advise you to *send* the goods *off* early. ‖ *send* a person *off* 人を見送る. ¶It should be *sent on* before June 1. それは六月一日前に発送しなければならない. ‖ A letter was to be *sent on* to him. 彼の許へ手紙を出すことになっていた. ¶*send* him *over* to the police 彼を警察に突き出す. ¶*send* him *over* to England 彼を英国にやる ‖ *Send* them *over* to the laundry. それら(洗たくものなど)を洗たく屋に回しなさい. ¶I have *sent* him *round* to my customers. 彼に得意先を回らした. ¶*send* a *sake* bottle *round* [酒の]おちょうしを回す ‖ Shall I *send* them *round*, or will you call for them? お送りしましょうか, それとも取りにお出で下さいますか. ¶*send up* rockets ロケットを飛ばす ‖ *send up* a trial balloon in the form of ... ...という観測気球をあげる(瀬踏みをする). 【類】*send* clouds of smoke *up* into the air ‖ hoard goods to *send* prices *up*. 物価つりあげのため品物を退蔵する.

P I have *sent* my servant *about* his business. 私は召使をたたき出した. ¶an army *sent against* the Hitler regime ヒットラー政権打倒軍. ¶*send* a shell *among* the enemy 敵の中に砲弾を放つ. ¶He *sent* me a gold watch *as* a Christmas present. 彼はクリスマスの贈物に金時計を送ってよこした. ¶*send by* mail (post, rail) 郵便(など)で送る ‖ *send* goods *by* express 品を急行便で送る. 【類】The length is too great for *sending by* parcel post. ‖ *send by* water 船で送る ‖ He *sent* a message *by* me. 彼は僕に伝言をした. 【類】*send* a parcel *by* a messenger / *send* a package *by* air mail. ¶*send for* a doctor (policeman) 医者(など)を呼びにやる ‖ I *sent* a servant *for* the luggage (=baggage). 荷物を取りに召使をやった. ‖ I am the carpenter your master *sent for*. 私は御主人がお呼びになった大工です. ‖ He was *sent for* down. 彼は二階から降りて来いと言われた. ‖ *send for* show at the exhibition 博覧会の陳列のため送る. ¶*send* a person *into* the country 人をいなかにやる ‖ They *sent* him *into* exile (=banishment). 彼らは彼を追放した. 【類】He was *sent into* a hospital. ¶*send* a boy *on* errands 少年を使いにやる ‖ *send* a person *on* a mission 人をある用向で派遣する ‖ *send* the blessings *on* a person 人に祝福の言葉を送る. ¶I *sent* the children *out of* the house. 私は子供らを外へ出した. ‖ *send* the children *out of* the way 子供を追い出す. ¶*send* goods all *over* the world 貨物を世界各地に送る. ¶*send* a parcel *through* the medium of a goods-agent 運送店に頼んで小荷物を送る ‖ mails *sent through* (=*via*) Siberia シベリヤ経由の郵便物. ¶will be *sent to* your address 貴名あてにお送りします ‖ be *sent to* penal servitude 刑務所に送られる. 【類】be *sent to* jail / be *sent to* hospital (school). ¶*send* the children *to* bed 子供らを寝かす ‖ *send* a vessel *to* the bottom 船を沈める ‖ *send* it *to* the wash (=laundry) それを洗たくに出す ‖ *send* one's regards *to* ... ...によろしくと伝言してやる ‖ He *sent* [a letter] *to* me asking for a loan of money. 手紙で借金の申込みをして来た. ‖ He was *sent* (=returned) *to* the House of Commons. 彼は下院議員に選出された. ¶I will *send* it *to* your place *by* a servant this evening. 今夕召使に持たせてお宅にお届けします. ¶be *sent to* the care of ... ...気付で送る. ¶be *sent via* Suez Canal スエズ運河経由で送られる. ¶Please *send* us a boy *with* change. つり銭を持たせて小僧さんをよこして下さい.

O The gun *sends* a ball 2,000 yards. その大砲は二千ヤードの着弾距離がある.

sender, *n.* 差出人, 荷送人.

P^2 a *sender* (=addresser) *of* a letter 手紙の差出人. 【類】a *sender of* a package (parcel).

send-off, *n.* 送別; 《俗》門出を祝うこと.

V to *give* him a *send-off* 彼の門出をさかんにするために. ¶The new play *had* a poor *send-off*. 新狂言はさい先が悪かった. ¶The villagers *made* a showy *send-off* in honor of a newly-enlisted soldier. 村民は入営兵のために盛んな見送をした. ¶*receive* a hearty *send-off* 心からの見送りを受ける.

Q We will give him a *good send-off*. 大いに彼の門出をさかんにする考えです. ¶His Majesty was given a *rousing send-off* by the workers. 国王陛下は労働者から割れるような歓送を受けた. ¶a *royal send-off* 大々的の見送り.

P arrange a spectacular funeral to provide him with a brilliant *send-off to* the other world 彼の最後を飾るためにりっぱな葬式を行う.

senility, *n.* 老衰.

Q *premature senility* 早老.

senior, *n.* 年長者; 先輩; 《米》[大学・高校の]上級生.

Q I was slightly *his senior*. 私は彼よりもちょっと年上だ. ¶the *village seniors* 村の長老.

P^2 He is now a *senior at* Lincoln High School. 彼はもうリンカン高校の上級生だ. 【類】a *senior at* Harvard Law School (ハーバード大学法律学部). ☞米国の大学及び四年制高校では senior, junior, soph (sophomore), freshman の四学年級になっている. ¶He is my *senior by* three years. 彼は私よりも三つ年上だ. ¶one's *senior in* office その上役.

senior, *a,* 年上の; 上席の.

P *senior in* office 上役の. ¶He is two years *senior to* me. 彼は私よりは二つ年上だ.

seniority, *n.* 年長; 古参.

V the system of *determining seniority* by the number of marks gained upon exit. 学年末に得た点数で席次をきめる制度.

Q^2 *service seniority* 先任.

P arranged *according to seniority* (=by order of precedence) 年長(あるいは地位)の順に配列して. ¶He is entitled to the place *by seniority*. 彼は古参なのでその地位につく資格がある.

sensation, *n.* 感じ; 感動; 世上の評判(センセーション).

V *awake* a pleasant *sensation* 快感を喚起する. ¶Working with one's head *causes* a *sensation* of hunger quite as much as, if not more than, muscular work. 頭脳労働は

筋肉労働以上ではないにしても同程度には飢えを覚えさせる. 【類】His new theory has ***caused*** an enormous *sensation* throughout the civilized world. ¶***chill*** the *sensation* 感興をさます. ¶The new invention has ***created*** a great *sensation*. その新発明は大評判になった. ‖ His death ***created*** a great *sensation*. 彼の死は大いに世間を騒がした. ‖ to ***create*** a *sensation* and gather an audience [大道で]人気をあおって人を寄せるために. ¶***dull*** the *sensation* 感覚を鈍らす. ¶***excite*** the *sensation* of heat 熱いという感じを起させる. ¶He ***experienced*** a *sensation* of heaviness in his legs. 彼は脚が重くるしく感じた. ¶I ***feel*** a *sensation* of distress (pride, pleasure). 私は苦悩(など)を感じる. ¶I ***have*** a *sensation* of giddiness (heat, thirst, pain, deafness). 目まい(など)がする. ‖ I ***had*** the *sensation* of being borne aloft on the shoulders of men. 人の肩に乗って意気揚々と運ばれるような気がした. ¶***produce*** a great *sensation* 大評判になる. 【類】His speech ***produced*** a great *sensation* among the audience. ‖ Pressing the eyeball in the darkness will ***produce*** the *sensation* of light. 暗いところで眼球を圧すると光が出るような感じがする.

Q experience the ***bitter*** *sensation* of being "cut out" 大いに面目を失する思いをする(恥をかく). ¶a ***blank*** *sensation* あ然とした心状. ¶a ***burning*** *sensation* 焼けるような感じ. ¶I attempted to get out a few words of consolation but a ***choking*** *sensation* in my throat stopped my utterance. 少し慰めの言葉を述べようとしたが胸が一杯になって声が出なかった. ¶A ***cooling***, ***soothing*** *sensation* resulted. その結果涼しいすがすがしい感じがした. ¶It caused me a most ***delicious*** *sensation*. それが私に非常な快感を起させた. ¶feel a ***delightful*** and ***novel*** *sensation* 楽しい新鮮な感じがする. ¶cause a ***disagreeable*** *sensation* to the teeth 歯に不快な感じを与える. ¶***hazy*** *sensations* ぼんやりとした感じ. ¶The *sensation* produced by this work was ***immense***. この著作の起した人気は大したものであった. ¶have an ***irritating*** *sensation* いらいらする. ¶***keen*** *sensation* 鋭い感覚. ¶The new opera did not cause the ***least*** *sensation* in the capital. 新歌劇は首府で何らの評判も立たなかった. ¶a ***literary*** *sensation* 文学界の評判. ¶***optical*** and ***tactile*** *sensations* 視覚と触覚. ¶***pleasurable*** *sensasion* 快感. ¶have a ***pricking*** *sensation* ちくちくする. ¶a ***profound*** *sensation* 深い感動. ¶a ***queer*** *sensation* 妙な感じ. ¶His victory at ... was the ***reigning*** *sensation* of the Britsh parliamentary elections. 彼が…で首尾よく当選したのは英国議会選挙において最も人気をわかしたものであった. ¶I felt a ***slight*** *sensation* of pleasure. 私はいささか愉快になった. ¶***tactual*** *sensation* 触覚. ¶the latest ***theatrical*** *sensation* 劇界最近の問題. ¶a ***three-day's*** *sensation* きわもの. ¶a ***tickling*** *sensation* くすぐったい感じ. ¶an ***unpleasant*** *sensation* いやな感じ. ¶It created a ***veritable*** *sensation*. それはすばらしいセンセーションを引起した. ¶experience ***voluptuous*** *sensations* 肉感をそそられる. ¶create a ***wonderful*** *sensation* 一大センセーションを起す. ¶cause a ***world-wide*** *sensation* 全世界の評判になる.

Q² the season's ***comedy*** *sensation* そのシーズンの喜劇の大人気. ¶a new ***taste*** *sensation* 味覚の新風味.

P ***with*** a *sensation* of gimlets boring into his temples 手きりでこめかみをもまれるような感じがして.

P² a *sensation* ***of*** dizziness 目まい ‖ a *sensation* ***of*** fear 恐怖感.

sensational, *a.* 扇情的な, 人気取りの.

M those New York Sunday papers that are more or less ***notoriously*** *sensational* これらの多少人気取りで知られたニューヨークの日曜新聞.

sensationalism, *n.* センセーション.

Q² as a result of ***newspaper*** *sensationalism* 新聞が騒ぎ立てたので.

sense, *n.* (**1**) 感覚(五感など); 肉感; 意識; 思慮, 分別; *pl.* 正気, 本性.

V I beg you to ***accept*** my deep *sense* of gratitude for your courtesy on the occasion of ... …の際の御厚情に対し有難くお礼申上げます. ¶serve to ***accentuate*** the *sense* of ... そのため…の感を深くする. ¶***acknowledge*** one's deep *sense* of obligation to ... …に対しその深い感謝の意を表する. ¶His *sense* of gallantry was ***aroused***. 彼はきょう気を出した. 【類】***arouse*** the *sense* of the ludicrous (ばかばかしさ). ¶***awaken*** a *sense* of the beautiful in ... …に美感を呼び起す. 【類】***awaken*** in ... a deeper *sense* of obligation to mankind. ¶***blunt*** the moral *sense* 道徳心を鈍らせる. ¶I managed to ***collect*** my *senses* a bit. 私はどうにか少し心を落着けた. ¶***conserve*** our common *sense* われわれの常識を養う. ¶***cultivate*** a critical *sense* 批評眼を養成する. 【類】***cultivate*** one's *sense* of system and order (組織と秩序). ¶***deepen*** the *sense* of reverence to ... …に対する尊敬の念を深める. ¶***delight*** the artistic *sense* 芸術感を満足させる. ¶***develop*** a *sense* of individual responsibility 個々の責任感を養成する. 【類】***develop*** a *sense* of service (奉仕) to ... / before the sexual *sense* (性欲) is ***developed***. ¶***display*** (=***show***) a *sense* of humor ユーモアが分かる. ¶Drunkenness ***dulls*** the *sense* of the present evil. 飲酒は目前の悪事に対する感覚を鈍らせる. ¶Not everybody ***enjoys*** chromatic *sense* to the same extent. みんながみんな色感が同じ程度になってはいない. ¶***excite*** the *senses* 五感を刺激する. ¶we wish to ***express*** our *sense* of indebtedness (gratitude, deep obligation) to ... われわれは…に対し感謝(など)の意を表したい. ¶***feel*** a *sense* of cold 寒気を感じる ‖ he ***feels*** little *sense* of concern about ... 彼は…についてはほとんど無関心だ. ¶His speech ***gave*** us the *sense* of the vast scheme. 彼の演説でその大計画の内容が分かった. ¶***gratify*** one's *senses* 五感(肉感)を満足させる. ¶***Has*** a plant *sense?* 植物には感覚があるだろうか. ‖ ***have*** the *sense* of shame 恥を知る ‖ He ***has*** no *sense* of discretion (responsibility, the beautiful, right, music). 彼にはいささかの分別(など)もない. 【類】The rodents (ねずみ類) ***have*** a remarkable *sense* of smell. / one who ***has*** the *sense* of style (文体) ‖ ***have*** (=***possess***) both robust common *sense* and high ideals 健全な常識と高尚な理想を二つながら備えている ‖ ***haven't*** you the *sense* to see that ...? 君には…が分からないのか. ¶a person who ***has*** no *sense* of music 音痴. 【類】***have*** no *sense* of smell / ***have*** no *sense* of humor ‖ she ***had*** the *sense* [enough] to ... 彼女は…するだけの頭のよさを持っていた. ¶a historian who can ***impart*** a *sense* of reality into their reconstruction of such far-off times このような古い時代の再建に現実性を与えうる歴史家. ¶***instill*** a *sense* of social responsibility 社会的責任感を漸次に注入する. ¶***intoxicate*** one's *senses* 感覚を麻ひさせる. ¶***keep*** one's *senses* 気をたしかに持つ. ¶***lack*** all *sense* of proportion つり合いという観念が全然欠けている. 【類】***lack*** a *sense* of responsibility / ***lack*** a *sense* of time (distance, beauty). ¶The story ***leaves*** a *sense* of after-delight. その話は後味がよい. ¶***lose*** all *sense* of decency (shame) 恥かしいという感じが全然ない ‖ ***lose*** one's *senses* 気が狂う. ¶***lull*** to sleep the *sense* of this busy living world about us 忙しいこの実社会の感じをおだやかにする. ¶This small present ***marks*** in some degree my *sense* of your kindness. 御厚意に対する感謝の印までにこの粗品を差上げます. ‖ ***mark*** their *sense* of his importance 彼の重要性を彼らが感得していることを示す. ¶***mortify*** the *senses* 情欲を抑える. ¶The sight of an injustice ***offends*** the *sense* of justice. 義人は不義を見て憤る. ‖ ***offend*** a nice *sense* of logic 微妙な論理的観念に逆らう. ¶***outrage*** one's *sense* of proportion つり合の感じに逆らう. ¶I ***owe*** a deep *sense* of gratitude to him. 私は深く彼に感謝しなければならない. ¶***please*** one's own *sense* of beauty 自身の美感を喜ばす. ¶The use of Calox ***produces*** a *sense* of freshness and purity only possible as the result of a chemically-clean mouth. カロックスを使用すると化学的に清潔な口のみが与えるそう快と純潔の感じが味わえる. ¶***quicken*** the artistic *sense* 芸術感を鋭敏にする. 【類】***quicken*** one's *sense* of words. ¶***recall*** one's *sense* of shame しゅう恥心を起す. ¶***recover*** (=come to *or* come round) one's *senses*=regain one's consciousness 正気づく. ¶***reflect*** the artistic *sense* of the maker 作者の芸術感を示す. ¶at this instant of my ***regaining*** my *senses* このわれに返った瞬間. ¶***rouse*** the historical *sense* in children 子供に歴史的観念を起させる. ¶***ruin*** the *sense* of honor (morality) 名誉(道徳)感を打ちこわす. ¶fail to ***satisfy*** the esthetic *sense* 審美感を満足させ得ない. ¶***sharpen*** one's *sense* その感覚を鋭敏にする. 【類】His *sense* of values may be ***sharpened*** by coming into contact with the world through his job. ¶***stale*** our *senses* われを忘れさせる. ¶***stimulate*** a *sense* of honor 名誉心を刺激する. ¶The joy of seeing him again ***swallowed up*** every other *sense* or concern. 再び彼に会った喜びで一切他の感じや屈託を忘

れてしまった. ¶***talk*** (***write***) *sense* 物の分かったことを言う(書く). ¶***tickle*** the *sense* of humor くすっと笑わせる. ¶***train*** and ***foster*** the *sense* of beauty 美感を養成する. ¶***use*** a little *sense* 少し頭を使う.

V² *Sense* ***comes*** with age. かめの甲より年の劫. ¶When moral *sense* ***disappears*** from a nation the whole social structure commences to crumble away. 道徳感が国民から消失すると社会の全組織が崩壊し始める. ¶when his *senses* ***returned*** 彼が正気づいたとき.

Q Dogs have an ***acute*** *sense* of smell 犬は鋭いきゅう覚を持っている. 【類】an ***acute*** *sense* of the picturesque (雅致). ¶appeal to a jaded ***aesthetic*** *sense* 衰えた美感を刺激する. ¶I use the word in no ***censorious*** *sense*. 私は非難の意味でその言葉を使いはしない. ¶***chivalrous*** *sense* of fairness 公平という武士道的観念. ¶the ***comic*** *sense* こっけい感. ¶The House of Commons ought to be the house of ***common*** *sense*.—Chesterton. 下院は常識の府であるべきだ. ‖ the exercise of a little ***common*** *sense* will enable you to ... 常識をちょっと働かせば...することができるだろう. 【類】He has ***common*** *sense* in an uncommon degree. ‖ showing good ***common*** *sense* 良識的に ‖ show a sound ***common*** *sense* 健全な常識を示す ‖ the robust (=strong) ***common*** *sense* しっかりした常識 ‖ have sober ***common*** *sense* まじめな常識を持つ. ¶with a ***deep*** *sense* of ... ...を深く意識して ‖ with a ***deep*** *sense* of gratitude 深い感謝の念をもって. 【類】express one's ***deep*** *sense* of gratitude / I beg you to accept my ***deep*** *sense* of gratitude for ... on this occasion. ¶persons with ***defective chromatic*** *sense* 色盲の人. ¶have a ***delicate*** *sense* of natural beauty 自然美に対し鋭い感覚を持つ. ¶***diplomatic*** *sense* 外交感覚. ¶He has a highly ***developed*** *sense* of humor. 彼は非常に発達したかいぎゃく精神の持主だ. ¶have a ***dull*** *sense* of right or wrong 正邪の感じが鈍い. 【類】His *sense* of smell is exceedingly ***dull***. ¶a serious breach of ***economic good*** *sense* 経済観念のはなはだしい欠陥. ¶A ***faint*** *sense* of compunctions moved her. 軽い悔恨の情が彼女を動かした. ¶The cat possesses a ***fair*** *sense* of the ridiculous. ねこは結構ユーモアが分かる. ¶He has a ***fine*** *sense* of humor. 彼には微妙なかいぎゃく精神がある. ¶the ***five*** *senses* 五官 (sight, hearing, smell, taste and touch). ¶with a ***full*** *sense* of responsibility 十分責任感をもって ‖ history, in the ***full*** *sense* 真の意味の歴史. ¶He had the ***good*** *sense*, good manners, and tact to repress it. 彼にはそれを押えるだけの良識も礼儀も気転もあった. 【類】He had the ***good*** *sense* to make a wise choice. / deal with it with ***good*** *sense* and tact / have a ***good*** *sense* of humor. ¶people whose ***grammatical*** *sense* is weak 文法的感覚の弱い人々. ¶have a ***high*** *sense* of its obligations to the public 公衆に対する高尚な責任感を持つ. ¶a ***high*** *sense* of honor 高尚な名誉心. ¶display a lack of ***historical*** *sense* 歴史眼を欠いていることを示す. ¶the ***humiliating*** *sense* of defeat 敗北に対する屈辱感. ¶have a good ***hygienic*** *sense* 健全な衛生観念をもっている. ¶He has ***keen*** *senses*. 彼は感覚が鋭敏だ. 【類】He has a ***keen*** *sense* of beauty (smell). / He had a ***keen*** *sense* of the miseries of mankind. / Scott was endowed with a ***keen*** *sense* of the value of words. / The French have a ***keen*** *sense* for form. / with a ***keen*** *sense* of irony / have a ***keen*** *sense* of justice (正邪感) / the development among parents of a ***keener*** *sense* of responsibility for their children. ¶outrage (=destroy) their ***literary*** *sense* その文学的感覚をこわす. ¶have a ***lively*** *sense* of humor 敏活にユーモアを解する. ¶from a ***mere*** *sense* of obligation 全くの責任感から. ¶***Moral*** *sense* is more important than intelligence. 道徳心は知能より大事だ. ‖ devoid (=destitute) of ***moral*** *sense* 道徳心を欠いた. ¶He has ***more*** *sense* than to go where he is not wanted. 彼は用のない所へ首を突込むようなばかな男ではない. ¶He has not ***much*** *sense*. 彼は余り利口でない. 【類】I thought you had ***more*** *sense* than that. ¶***musical*** *sense* 音感. 【類】He has no ***musical*** *sense* (音痴). ¶A ***nice*** *sense* of proportion is worth a thousand etiquette books. つり合という微妙な観念は千の作法書に値する. ¶lack of ***poetical*** *sense* 無風流. ¶There is something wrong with their ***political*** *sense*. 彼らの政治感覚には欠けるものがある. ¶He has a good deal of ***practical*** *sense*. 彼は大いに常識がある. ¶a ***previous*** *sense* of one's misfortune 不幸の予感. ¶***professional*** *sense* 職業意識. ¶with a ***profound*** *sense* of ... ...を深く感じて. ¶offend the ***public*** *sense* of decency 公衆の風紀を害する. ¶the ***religious*** *sense* 宗教心. ¶He is regarded as not quite in his ***right*** *senses*. 彼はどうかしているんじゃないかと思われている. ¶He was blessed with a ***saving*** *sense* of humor. 彼は幸にしてユーモアの分かる男だった. ¶***scientific common*** *sense* 科学的常識. ¶the awakening of the ***sexual*** *sense* 性の目ざめ. ¶a ***sharp*** *sense* of smell 鋭いきゅう覚. ¶a ***sickening*** *sense* of vertigo 目がまわる感じ. ¶a sort of ***sixth*** *sense* 一種の第六感 ‖ a gift reminiscent of the ***sixth*** *sense* 第六感と思われる一つの能力. ¶in one's ***sober*** *senses* 冷静に. ¶***Some*** *sense* of humor! さぞおもしろかったろうね. ¶a ***sound*** *sense* of judgement 健全な判断力. ¶He has a ***strong*** *sense* of justice. 彼は正義感が強い. ‖ He has a ***strong*** *sense* of his own importance. 彼はもったい振る. ¶have ***sufficient*** *sense* to ... ...するだけの常識がある. ¶No one who lacks a ***tonal*** *sense* can be a writer of prose of the first order. 音感のない人は一流の文章家にはなれない. ¶an ***uncommon*** *sense* 非凡な感覚力. ¶readers with an ***undeveloped*** *sense* of art 芸術の鑑賞力の乏しい読者. ¶in a ***world-wide*** *sense* 世界的に見て.

Q² it is good ***business*** *sense* to ... ...するのはりっぱな事務的な考えだ. 【類】have a good ***business*** *sense*. ¶***color*** *sense* 色感. ¶***dress*** *sense* 服装の感覚. ¶cultivate one's ***horse*** *sense* 《米》基礎的な常識を身につける. ¶have a good (no) ***language*** *sense* 語感が鋭い(ない). ¶***news*** *sense* ニュースセンス(新聞記者の感). ¶have the ***newspaper*** *sense* ニュースの勘を持っている. ¶Sailors have "***weather*** *sense*." 船員は天候に敏感だ.

P detect ***by*** the *sense* of smell きゅう覚で探り出す ‖ dictated ***by*** common *sense* 常識で判断して. ¶***from*** a *sense* of duty 義務感から. ¶No man ***in*** his *senses* would have done so. 正気の人ならだれだってそうはしなかったろう. ¶***in*** his [sober] *senses* 正気のときは. ¶errors ***of*** *sense* 知覚の錯誤 ‖ the gratification ***of*** *sense* 肉感の満足. ¶be ***devoid of*** *sense* センスがない. ¶***out of*** (=***from***) a *sense* of duty 責任感から. ¶This does not seem what he has done ***in*** his *senses*. これは彼が正気でやったことじゃないらしい. ¶***through*** a *sense* of duty 義務観念から ‖ receive ***through*** the *senses* 五官を通して受ける. ¶bring one ***to*** his *senses* 正気に立返らせる ‖ come ***to*** one's *senses* 正気に返る. ¶***under*** a *sense* of duty (wrong) 義務(虐待されたという)観念の下に. ¶***with*** a *sense* of relief ほっとした気持で. 【類】***with*** the *sense* of security ‖ She was gripped ***with*** a *sense* of suffocation and panic. 彼女は今にも窒息しそうな恐怖感にとらわれた. ‖ a man ***with*** a *sense* of humor ユーモアを解する人 ‖ be ***without*** a *sense* of contrast 対照という感覚が欠けている. ¶accept the term ***without*** any *sense* of shame 厚顔にもその条件に同意する. 【類】a woman ***without*** a *sense* for color / It can be read ***without*** the slightest *sense* of boredom (たいくつ).

P² common *sense* ***about*** ... ...に関する常識. ¶appeal less to the European *sense* ***of*** beauty 欧州人はさほど美しいと思わない ‖ Their *sense* ***of*** citizenship is low. 彼らの市民たるの観念は低い. ‖ It gave me a *sense* ***of*** delight. それは私に快感を与えた. ‖ the *sense* ***of*** hearing (sight, smell, taste, touch) 聴(視・きゅう・味・触)覚 ‖ *sense* ***of*** national honor 国民的名誉心 ‖ The editor's *sense* ***of*** proportion seems to have failed him. その編集者はつり合という感覚が働らかなかったらしい. ‖ A *sense* ***of*** desolation and disillusionment overwhelmed me. 私は悲しい幻滅感に圧倒された. ‖ have no *sense* ***of*** humor ユーモアを解しない. 【類】appeal to one's *sense* ***of*** humor / a *sense* ***of*** public duty / a *sense* ***of*** shame (honor) / the *sense* ***of*** guilt / a sense ***of*** justice (right) / call a person to a *sense* ***of*** his responsibilities / a *sense* ***of*** uneasiness. ¶A film actress must develop a sixth *sense* ***with regard to*** the photographic effect of her drapery. 映画女優は自分の服装の写真効果について第六感を発達させねばならない.

(**2**) 意義.

V ***acquire*** a different *sense* [語句などが]違った意味を持つようになる. ¶The word can be omitted without ***affecting*** the *sense*. その語は削除しても意味は変らない. ¶***alter*** the *sense* of ... ...の意義を変える. ¶***attach*** a *sense* to a word 言葉にある意義を付与する. ¶***bring out*** the *sense* その意義を明かにする. ¶***complete*** the *sense* 意味を徹底さ

せる. ¶***confound*** the *sense* その意義を混同する. ¶***convey*** a *sense* of opprobrium 悪い意味を持つ. ¶***develop*** the *sense* of a passage 一部の意味を布えんする. 【類】***develop*** new *senses* of words. ¶***fix*** the *sense* of a word 語の意義を一定する. ¶The students cannot ***follow*** the *sense* of a speech made in English. その学生たちは英語演説の意味を聴取できない. ‖ In a free translation the *sense* is ***followed*** rather than diction. 自由訳では語調よりも意味をとって訳される. ¶The sentence does not ***give*** complete *sense*. その文は完全な意味を成さない. ¶***grasp*** fully the *sense* of his words 彼の言葉の意味を十分把握する. ¶***interpret*** the *sense* of a word 語の意味を解釈する. ¶***make*** *sense* 意味をなす, 理くつに合う. 【類】It does not ***make*** *sense*. / It ***makes*** no *sense* at all. ‖ ***make*** a *sense* out of a sentence 文の意義を解する ‖ Subordinate clauses do not ***make*** *sense* by themselves. 〖文法〗従属部だけでは意味をなさない. ‖ ***make sense*** out of nonsense たわ言の意味を判じる ‖ I cannot ***make out*** the *sense*. 私にはその意味が分らない. ¶***obscure*** the *sense*. 意義を不明ならしめる. ¶***retain*** its old *sense* その古い意義を保持する. ¶***sacrifice*** *sense* to sound 意義を犠牲にして句調をよくする. ¶***unfold*** the *sense* of spoken or written words 口語または文語の意義を解釈する.

Q in an ***absolute*** *sense* 絶対に. ¶in the generally ***accepted*** *sense* of the word その語の一般に認められた意味で. ¶They have never come of age in any ***adequate*** *sense*. 彼らはなんら正当な意味の成年には達しはしなかった. ¶in ***all*** *senses* どの点から見ても. ¶These words have ***acquired*** special ***American*** *senses*. これらの語は米国特有の意味を持つようになった. ¶It is not intended in ***any*** *sense* to be exhaustive. それは決して徹底的という考えでやったのではない. ¶in a ***bad*** *sense* 悪い意味で. ¶in this, the ***best*** *sense*. この最善の意味で ¶He may be regarded in the ***broad*** *sense* as the real founder of the institution. 彼は広義で言えばその協会の真の創立者と見なされる. ‖ in a ***broad*** *sense* of the word 広義では. 【類】in the ***broadest*** *sense* of the term. ¶in a ***certain*** *sense* 見ようによっては. 【類】Schools in a ***certain*** *sense* are like factories turning out a product, in this case, splendid young graduates. ¶in a ***commercial*** *sense* 商業上から言えば. ¶make ***complete*** *sense* 完全な意味を成す. 【類】The sentence does not give ***complete*** *sense*. ¶She used the word " kiss " in the more ***comprehensive*** *sense* in which the French sometimes employ it. 彼女は「キッス」という言葉をフランス人が折々面白く使っているようなきわめて広い意味で使った. ¶Handwriting can not be used in a ***concrete*** *sense*. 筆跡という語は具体的の意味には使えない. ¶in its ***Continental*** *sense* [欧州]大陸的な意味では(イギリス人から見て). ¶take in a ***contrary*** *sense* 反対の意味に取る. ¶It is not ... in the ***customary*** *sense*. それは普通の意味の...ではない. ¶in a ***depreciatory*** *sense* 軽べつの意味で. ¶apply a word in a ***derogatory*** (=***contemptuous***) *sense* 語を軽べつの意味に使う. ¶in a ***detrimental*** *sense* 侮辱の意味で. ¶spoil the ***delicate*** *sense* of the lines [詩の]微妙な意味を打ちこわす. ¶acquire a ***different*** *sense* 異なった意味を持つようになる. ¶used in a ***disparaging*** *sense* くさす意味に使用した. ¶a word used in a ***double*** *sense* as ... and as ... ...と...と二つの意味に使われた語. 【類】The Russian word ' soviet ' has the ***double*** *sense* of council and congress. ¶in its ***enlarged*** *sense* その広い意味では. ¶very far from being a circle in the ***Euclidean*** *sense* ユークリッド幾何学のいわゆる円とは大いに相違して. ¶a fine man in ***every*** *sense* of the word どの点から見てもりっぱな人. 【類】The marriage was in ***every*** *sense* happy. / He was, in ***every*** *sense* of the word, a born merchant. ¶in the ***fashionable*** *sense* of the word その語の当世風の意味で. ¶in a ***favorable*** *sense* 都合の好い意味で. ¶in its ***figurative*** *sense* 比ゆ的には. ¶in a ***fuller*** *sense* of the word その言葉のもっと広い意味で. 【類】use the foreign language in the ***fullest*** *sense* of the term. ‖ The work is creditable, in the ***fullest*** *sense*, to the industry, the accuracy, and the learning of the compiler. その著述は十二分に編者の勤勉・正確及び学識を裏書する. ¶I use the word in a ***general*** *sense*. 私はその言葉を普通の意味で使う. ¶The telegram does not make ***good*** *sense*. その電文は明りょうでない. ¶be used in an ***ill*** *sense* 悪い意味に使われる. ¶a word used in a very ***inclusive*** *sense* 非常に広義な意味に用いた語. ¶In a ***large*** *sense*, civilization is measured by how well people can get along with each other and work together. 広義にいえば文明の高低は人民が互に仲よく働く程度で計られる. 【類】He was a martyr (殉難者) in a ***large*** *sense* of the word. ¶in a ***legal*** *sense* of the term 法律用語としては. ¶in a ***limited*** *sense* 狭義で. ¶those who can no longer in a strictly ***literal*** *sense* be described as young 厳格に文字通りの意味でもう若いといわれない人たち. ¶in a ***literary*** *sense* of the term その語の文学的意味では. ¶in a ***loose*** *sense* ばく然とした意味で. ¶an encyclopedia in the ***modern*** *sense* 現代の意味の百科事典. ¶in ***more*** *senses* than one 色々の意味で. ¶literature in the ***narrow*** *sense* of the word 狭義の文学. ¶These words make ***no*** *sense*. これらの語は意味をなさない. ‖ I'm in ***no*** *sense* of the word an Anglomania. 私は決していわゆる英国心酔者ではない. ¶an ***obscure*** *sense* あいまいな意味. ¶I use the word " sentiment " in no ***offensive*** *sense*. 私はセンチメントという語を悪い意味に使っているのではない. ¶be used in a ***low*** *sense* 卑俗な意味に使われている. ¶the ***main*** *sense* of ... ... の主旨. ¶in a ***metaphorical*** rather than a ***material*** *sense* 具体的よりむしろ比ゆ的な意味で. ¶in the ***narrow*** *sense* 狭義における. ¶old words in a ***new*** *sense* 新しい意味に用いた古い語. ¶What he says makes ***no*** *sense* at all. 彼の言うことはちっとも分からない. ‖ there is ***no*** *sense* in taking measures beyond ... ...を越えた方策は意味がない(むだだ). ¶acquire an ***opprobrious*** *sense* 侮辱した意味になる. ¶in the ***ordinary*** *sense* 普通の意味で. ¶in its ***original*** and ***strict*** *sense* その原意による厳正な意味では. ¶be used in a ***peculiar*** *sense* 特殊の意味に使われている. ¶I speak in a ***Pickwickian*** *sense*. 私は冗談にそういっているのである. ¶in a ***popular*** *sense* 通俗には. ¶the ***primary*** *sense* of the word is ... その語の第一義は...である. ¶in the ***proper*** *sense* of the term その語の本来の意味で. ¶in a ***real*** *sense* 真の意味で, 本当は. 【類】in the ***real old English*** *sense*. ¶in a ***relative*** *sense* 比較的に. ¶in a more ***restricted*** *sense* 一層狭義に. ¶It is used in much the ***same*** *sense*. それはほとんど同じ意味に用いられる. ¶in a ***selective*** *sense* 正しい意味で. ¶in ***some*** *sense* ある意味で. ¶Mr Balfour cannot be called a man of letters in the ***strict*** *sense* of the term. バルフォア氏は厳正の意味の文人とは言われない. 【類】in the ***strictest*** *sense* of the word. ¶in the ***technical*** *sense* of the term その言葉の専門的な意味で. ¶in ***this*** *sense* it is not too much to say that ... その意味で...というのは過言ではない. ¶He was in a very ***true*** *sense* of the word cultured. 彼は本当に教養のある人であった. 【類】Science is in the ***true*** *sense* of the word international. / in the ***truest*** *sense* of the term / a ***true*** *sense* of art. ¶politics in the ***true*** and the ***nobler*** *sense* of the term (= word) 真の一段高尚な意味の政治. ¶a word used in an ***unfamiliar*** *sense* 変った意味に用いられた語. ¶in an ***unfavorable*** *sense* 悪い意味で. ¶Shintoism is hardly a religion in the ***usual*** *sense* of the term. 神道は普通の意味ではほとんど宗教とはいわれない. ¶in a ***vague*** *sense* ばく然たる意味で. ¶It has ***various*** *senses*. それには種々の意味がある. ¶in the most ***vulgar utilitarian*** *sense* きわめて俗な実利的な意味で. ¶use the word in a ***wide*** *sense* その語を広義に用いる. 【類】in a ***wider*** *sense* / using that term in the ***widest*** *sense*. ¶understand a word in a ***wrong*** *sense* 語を間違った意味に解する.

Q² use a word in its ***everyday*** *sense* 語を普通の意味に使う. ¶in a ***slang*** *sense* 俗語的には.

P arrive ***at*** the *sense* of a word 語の意義に到達する. ¶***in*** a *sense* ある意味で, ある程度 ‖ ***in*** no *sense* ... 断じて(...ではない). 【類】it might be said ***in*** a *sense* that ... / Whatever his position, he is ***in*** a *sense* a representative of his firm. / ***In*** what *sense* is the Bible the word of God? ‖ be complete ***in*** *sense* 意味はまとまっている. ‖ " people " ***in*** the *sense* of persons 人間としての意味の「人々」(国民でなく) ‖ use a word ***in*** two *senses* 語を二義に使う ‖ He was a superior man ***in*** the *sense* of Confucius. 彼は孔子のいわゆる君子であった. ‖ It is not ... ***in*** the *sense* of the German law. それは独法でいう...にはならない. ¶void ***of*** *sense* 意味のない.

P² the *sense* ***of*** indignity 不面目の意義 ‖ the *senses* and sub-senses ***of*** a word 語の本義と分義.

sense, *v.* 感知する；《米》感づく，悟る.

M He ***fully*** *sensed* of his danger. 自分の危険を十分感づいた. ¶***vaguely*** *sense* it おぼろげにそれを感知する.

O I *sensed* that she would go to kill herself. 彼女は自殺するような予感がした.

sensibility, *n.* 感覚；敏感；感受性.

V ***blunt*** *sensibility* 感覚を鈍らす. ¶***have*** the *sensibility* of a poet 詩人のような感性を持つ ‖ He ***has*** little artistic *sensibility*. 彼には芸術的感受性がほとんどない. ¶***injure*** (=***hurt or wound***) one's *sensibility* 感受性を傷つける，その感情を害する.【類】***injure*** the *sensibilities* of the French. ¶The skin has ***lost*** its *sensibility*. 皮膚に感覚がなくなった. ¶It may ***offend*** some people's *sensibilities* (=susceptibilities). それは差障りがあるかも知れない. ¶***possess*** a fine *sensibility* [芸術家など]鋭敏な感受性を持っている. ¶when his *sensibility* ***returned*** 正気に返ると. ¶***shock*** the *sensibilities* of ... …を驚倒させる. ¶***show*** a marked *sensibility* as regards odors 臭気に関しては著しい敏感を示す.

Q a college professor with more ***delicate literary*** *sensibilities* 一層微妙な文学意識を有する大学教授. ¶repugnant to our ***esthetic*** *sensibilities* われわれの審美眼にあわない.【類】millionaires with no ***esthetic*** *sensibilities*. ¶find one's ***gastronomic*** *sensibilities* greatly upset at the thoughts of partaking of such a dish こんな料理のお相伴をしなければならないのかと思うと美食に慣れた胃の働きが止まってしまう. ¶***olfactory*** *sensibility* (=acuity) きゅう覚の鋭敏. ¶***tactile*** *sensibility* 触角力. ¶have an ***unusual*** *sensibility* for colors 色彩感覚が非凡だ.

P² the *sensibility* ***of*** the magnetic needle 磁針の敏感性. ¶*sensibility* ***to*** ... …に対する敏感性.

sensible, *a.* 感じられる；分別のある.

M I am ***deeply*** *sensible* of my indebtedness to ... …に恩義をこうむっていることを私は深く感じる. ¶It is *sensible* ***enough.*** 至極もっともな話である. ¶***piercingly*** *sensible* 洞察力の鋭い.

P I am *sensible* ***of*** difference (smell, pain). 私に相違(など)が分かる.【類】He was *sensible* ***of*** your kindness. / be *sensible* ***of*** the responsibility ‖ He is *sensible* ***of*** the vicissitudes of life. 彼は人生の転変に対して敏感である. ‖ That is very *sensible* ***of*** him. それが彼の利口な所だ.

sensitive, *a.* 感じやすい，敏感な.

M ***extremely*** *sensitive* to cold 極端に寒さを感じる. ¶be ***highly*** *sensitive* to ... …に鋭敏である，…に神経を起しやすい. ¶***morbidly*** *sensitive* to ... 病的に…に敏感な.

P *sensitive* ***on*** the subject of ... …の問題に敏感な. ¶*sensitive* ***over*** one's inability to read or write 読み書きのできないのを気にやむ. ¶Butter is very *sensitive* ***to*** odors. バターは非常に香がうつりやすい. ‖ *sensitive* ***to*** abuse and calumny ののしりやかげ口を気にしやすい.【類】be *sensitive* ***to*** cold and heat / The eye is *sensitive* ***to*** light.

sensitiveness, *n.* 敏感，感受性.

V ***develop*** a *sensitiveness* to artistic beauty 芸術美に対する感受性を発達させる. ¶He ***has*** the *sensitiveness* of a young girl. 彼は少女のように敏感だ.

Q Ruskin had a ***rare*** *sensitiveness* to beauty in every form. ラスキンはあらゆる形態の美に対する珍らしい感受性を持っていた.

P² Hearn had a *sensitiveness* ***to*** beauty. ハーンは美に対する感受性を持っていた.【類】have *sensitiveness* ***to*** cold (heat).

sensuality, *n.* いん行，好色ぶり.

Q the most ***bestial*** *sensuality* 最も獣的ないん行.

sentence, *n.* (**1**)〘文法〙文；格言，警句.

V ***analyze*** *sentences* 〘文法〙文を分析する. ¶***anatomize*** a *sentence* 〘文法〙文を解剖する. ¶He ***begins*** almost every *sentence* with the pronoun "I". 彼はほとんどすべての文を代名詞 I で始める. ¶***build*** a *sentence* [文法的に]文を作る. ¶***choose*** a good closing *sentence* 結末の文として適当なものを選ぶ. ¶***coin*** an epigrammatic *sentence* 寸鉄的文章を創作する. ¶***complete*** elliptical *sentences* by inserting words omitted 略した語をそう入して省略文を完全な文にする. ¶the ability to ***compose*** a pregnant *sentence* 含蓄のある文を作る才.【類】***compose*** *sentences* correctly. ¶***correct*** a *sentence* 一文を訂正する. ¶***disentangle*** a complicated *sentence* 複雑な文を分解する. ¶It is a recognized rule not to ***end*** a *sentence* with a weak little word, especially in written composition. 弱い微々たる語で文章を結ばないというのが特に作文の場合認められた法則である. ¶***form*** a *sentence* 一文を作る. ¶***frame*** *sentences* with simple words 簡単な語で文をつづる. ¶***make up*** *sentences* correctly 正しく文を作り上げる. ¶***pen*** impressive and well-constructed *sentences* 印象の深い構文のりっぱな文を書く. ¶***polish*** a *sentence* 一文を洗練する. ¶***recast*** a *sentence* 一文を改作する. ¶***resolve*** a *sentence* into its subject and predicate 一文をその主部と叙述部に分解する. ¶***rewrite*** *sentences* in the emphatic order 強意の順に文を書換える. ¶***sing*** the opening *sentences* of the Burial Service 埋葬式辞の初めの句を読む. ¶***split*** a long *sentence* into shorter sentences 長文を短文に分割する. ¶***stop*** a *sentence* 一文にピリオドを付ける. ¶***throw*** the two *sentences* into one 二文を一つにまとめる ‖ ***throw*** (=***render***) an English *sentence* into Latin 一英文をラテン語に訳する. ¶The *sentence* is so ***worded*** as to be misleading. その文は正しく意味が取れないような書き方だ. ¶***write*** good *sentences* りっぱな文を書く.

Q a ***clear*** and ***coherent*** *sentence* 明析で条理の立った一文. ¶the ***closing*** *sentence* of an address 演説の結びの文. ¶a ***clumsy*** *sentence* 拙文. ¶give answers in ***complete*** *sentences* [省略でない]完全な文で返答をする. ¶***detached*** *sentences* 離れ離れの文. ¶clarify a ***difficult*** *sentence* 難解な文を明りょうに書き直す. ¶an ***elliptical*** *sentence* 省略文. ¶***high-flown*** *sentences* 誇大な文. ¶the evolution of the ***literary*** *sentence* in modern English prose 現代の英語散文における文学的文章の発達. ¶write on paper five ***negative*** *sentences* 紙上に五つの否定文を書く. ¶***ornate literary*** *sentences* 雅文. ¶a ***passive*** *sentence* 〘文法〙受身の文. ¶dilate in ***polished*** *sentences* upon ... …を洗練された文で解説する. ¶a very ***pregnant*** *sentence* 非常に含蓄ある一文. ¶***priceless*** *sentences* 一字千金の文. ¶***proverbial*** *sentences* ことわざ風の文章. ¶***Stilted*** *sentences* gleaned from the book are inadequate for everyday conversation. 本から集めた気取った文は日常の会話には不適当だ. ¶a ***straggling*** and ***weak*** *sentence* しまりがなくて弱々しい文. ¶a ***terse*** *sentence* 簡潔な一文. ¶a ***telling*** *sentence* ぴんと答える文. ¶a ***weighty*** *sentence* 一句千均.

P ***in*** one *sentence* 一文で ‖ It cannot well be expressed ***in*** a single *sentence*. 一文ではよく表わせない.

P² *sentences* ***of*** this type この型の文.

(**2**) 裁判判決，宣告；刑.

V ***carry out*** a *sentence* 宣告を執行する. ¶***commute*** a *sentence* 減刑を宣言する.【類】***commute*** his *sentence* to exile (追放に減刑). ¶He has ***completed*** his *sentence*. 彼の刑期は満了した. ‖ The thief was sent to Tokyo in charge of a police-sergeant to ***complete*** his *sentence* in Ichigaya Prison. 盗賊は市ケ谷刑務所で服役すべく巡査部長の監視で東京へ送られた. ¶***defer*** a *sentence* until next day 宣告を翌日まで延期する. ¶***impose*** an extremely heavy *sentence* upon a prisoner 被告に極端に重い判決を下す. ¶His *sentence* has been ***mitigated.*** 彼の判決は減刑になった. ¶***pass*** (=***pronounce***) *sentence* of death on (=upon) ... …に死刑の判決を下す. ¶***pronounce*** a *sentence* 判決を言渡す. ¶***recall*** (=***repeal***) a former *sentence* 前の判決を取消す. ¶He ***received*** a six months' *sentence*. 彼は六カ月服役の判決を受けた. ¶***reduce*** a *sentence* to ... …に減刑する. ¶***reverse*** a *sentence* 判決を撤回する. ¶***serve*** a *sentence* in jail 刑務所で服役する. ¶He will be made to ***undergo*** a *sentence* of 15 years' imprisonment for murder. 彼は殺人罪で禁固十五カ年の判決を受けるようになるだろう. ‖ a criminal ***undergoing*** the *sentence* 処罰中の犯人. ¶the *sentence* ***runs*** as follows: その判決は次のような文面になっている.

Q a ***capital*** *sentence* 死刑宣告. ¶an American criminal serving a ***life*** *sentence* at Folsom Prison, California カリフォルニア州のフォルサム監獄で終身刑に服している米国の犯罪人. ¶He is undergoing a ***long*** *sentence* for burglary. 彼は夜盗罪で長期の刑に服している. ¶cassation of the ***original*** *sentence* 原判決破棄. ¶those who served ***previous*** *sentences* 前科者. ¶serve a ***short*** *sentence* 短期の刑に服する.

Q² be under a ***death*** *sentence* for murder 殺人罪で死刑の宣告を受けている ‖ execution of a ***death*** *sentence* 死刑執行.【類】pass (申渡す) a ***death*** *sentence* on ... ¶a ***jail*** *sentence* 懲役の判決. ¶serve a ***larceny*** *sentence* 窃盗罪の刑に服する. ¶impose a ***life prison*** *sentence* on ... …を無

期刑に処す ‖ serve a ***10-year prison*** *sentence* 十年間の刑に服する.

P a convict ***under*** *sentence* of death 死刑の宣告を受けた囚徒 ‖ a prisoner ***under*** *sentence* 受刑者.

P² release prisoners serving *sentences* ***for*** political offenses 政治犯で服役中の囚徒を釈放する. ¶*sentence* ***of*** death has been passed on (=against) ... 死刑の宣告が...に下された.

sentence, *v.* 処刑を宣告する, 申渡す.

P He was *sentenced* ***to*** capital punishment (penal servitude, two years' imprisonment with hard labor). 彼は死刑(など)を申渡された. ‖ He was *sentenced* ***to*** five years at hard labor. 《米》彼は五カ年の重労働を宣告された. ☞ 英語用法では five years' hard labor. 【類】be *sentenced* ***to*** a fine (罰金刑) for trespass (私有地侵害) / be *sentenced* ***to*** death / be *sentenced* ***to*** prison (=jail).

sentiment, *n.* 感情, 情操; 意見; 感想.

V ***appreciate*** his *sentiments* 彼の意見に共鳴する. ¶***arouse*** *sentiment* for some form of cooperative work 何らかの形式で協力がなされるように世論を呼び起す. ¶***conceal*** a *sentiment* 感情を隠す. ¶***conciliate*** *sentiment* 感情をやわらげる. ¶***create*** public *sentiment* 与論を呼び起す ‖ ***create*** a *sentiment* in favor of ... ...に有利な世論を作る. ¶***echo*** his *sentiments* 彼の意見をそのまま繰返す. ¶I would not go so far as to ***endorse*** that *sentiment*, but it must be admitted that ... 私はその意見に裏書する所までは行かれないが...は認めねばならない. ¶***entertain*** charitable *sentiments* 慈愛の念をいだく. ¶he ***explained*** the *sentiments* of his government concerning ... 彼は...に関する政府の意向を説明した. ¶***expose*** one's *sentiments* to ... その感想を...に発表する. ¶***express*** one's *sentiment* on a subject 問題について意見を述べる. 【類】***express*** friendly *sentiments*. ¶***further*** the jingo *sentiment* 示威的外交政策の感情を助長する. ¶a very unusual opportunity of ***gauging*** the *sentiment* of Japan 日本の感情を測定する絶好の機会. ¶***give off*** grand lofty *sentiments* 雄大崇高の感情を発揮する. ¶He has ***illustrated*** this *sentiment* very thoroughly in a drama. 彼は一つの脚本にこの感情をきわめて徹底的に表現した. ¶***make*** one's *sentiments* ***known*** to ... 所感を...に開陳する. ¶***mask*** one's *sentinmets* by art 技巧によってその感情に仮面をかぶせる. ¶***placate*** *sentiment* 《米》反対党などの黙認を得るような手段を講じる. ¶***recipirocate*** most cordially the very courteous and friendly *sentiments* expressed by ... ...によって表明されたきわめて丁寧で友情ある言葉に最も懇篤に報いる. ¶***rouse*** public *sentiment* against ... ...に対する公衆の反感を起させる. ¶***share*** a similar *sentiment* with ... ...と感を同じくする. ¶***shock*** public *sentiment* 世人の感情を刺激する. ¶Those words of praise are acceptable as they ***show*** a real *sentiment*. その称賛の語は真情から出ているのであるから喜んで受入れる. ¶***talk*** mawkish *sentiment* 余りに感傷的なことを言う. ¶Thinking of dictionaries alone, one might today ***voice*** Solomon's *sentiment* about the making of many books. 辞書だけについて言ってもソロモンの著作についての感想は今日においても同様のことが言えるであろう. 【類】This utterance ***voiced*** the *sentiments* of the crowd.

Q ***adverse*** *sentiment* 反感. ¶***aesthetic*** (=***esthetic***) *sentiment* 美的情操. ¶the beauties of ***altruistic*** *sentiments* 利他的精神の美. ¶***Anti-British*** *sentiment* was in full blast. 反英感情が最高潮であった. ¶The ***anti-foreign*** *sentiment* was brewing among the reactionaries. 排外思想が反動主義者の中でくすぶっていた. ¶***beautiful*** *sentiments* 麗わしい感情. ¶***elevated*** *sentiments* 高尚な情操. ¶the ***enlightened*** *sentiments* of the age その時代の進んだ考え. ¶dedicated with ***every*** *sentiment* of duty and respect 義務と敬意の念を十分に示して献呈した[本など]. ¶The *sentiment* is ***good*** though the words are injudicious. 用語は感心しないが意見はよい. ¶there is a ***growing*** *sentiment* that ... ...という考えは段々増大して来る. ¶a ***healthy*** *sentiment* 健全な情操. ¶appeal to the ***highest*** and ***best*** *sentiments* of both patriotism and morality 最高最善の愛国心並びに道徳心に訴える. ¶an ***honorable*** *sentiment* りっぱな考え. ¶***hostile*** *sentiments* 反感. ¶a ***lofty*** *sentiment* 高い情操. ¶a ***low*** *sentiment* 卑しい情操. ¶***mawkish*** *sentiment* ぐちっぽい感情. ¶quite a ***modern*** *sentiment* 全く近代的な考え. ¶***moral*** *sentiments* 道徳の観念. ¶there arose a ***national*** *sentiment* ***in*** favor of (against) ... ...に賛意(反対)の国民感情が起った. ¶He had a heart which promptly responded to such ***noble*** *sentiments* as these. 彼はこうした高尚な情操に敏速に感応するような心情を持っていた. ¶***popular*** *sentiments* 一般の受けのよい意見. ¶a ***predominant*** *sentiment* 圧倒的な感情. ¶***pretty*** *sentiment* 美しい感情. ¶a ***prevailing*** *sentiment* 一般に行われる意見. ¶a champion of the ***pro-German*** *sentiment* 親独主義の闘士. ¶But ***public*** *sentiment* has since done an about-face. しかし世論はその後百八十度の転回をした. ‖ The movement is supported by strong ***public*** *sentiment*. その運動は堅固な世論によって支持されている. ¶men of deep ***religious*** *sentiments* 宗教的情操の深い人. ¶It was received with ***respectful*** and ***sincere*** *sentiments* of enthusiasm. それは恭敬かつ真剣な熱情をもって迎えられた. ¶express ***revolutionary*** *sentiments* 革命的意見を述べる. ¶***rose-water*** *sentiment* 温和な感情. ¶he voices the ***same*** *sentiment* when he affirms that ... 彼は...を肯定して同じ感想を述べている. ¶***shocking*** *sentiment* いやな感情. ¶***sound*** *sentiment* 堅実な情操. ¶***stirring***, ***patriotic***, and ***loyal*** *sentiments* 感動的で愛国的な忠誠心. ¶a *sentiment* ***stronger*** than reason 理性よりも強い感情.

Q² ***class-room*** *sentiment* 教室(学校生徒)の受け(人気). ¶***hand-across-the-sea*** *sentiments* 対岸の国と提携すべしという意見. ¶the ***majority*** *sentiment* of a party (in the country) 党(その国)の大多数の意向.

P We are often influenced ***by*** *sentiment*. われわれは往々感情に支配される. ¶tender ***in*** *sentiment* 気立の優しい. ¶unity ***of*** *sentiment* 感情の一致. ¶I will conclude my speech ***with*** a *sentiment*. 私は終りにのぞんで一言致します.

P² the fast-increasing dissemination of socialistic *sentiments* ***among*** the laboring and the uneducated classes 労働階級及び無識階級間に迅速に増加する社会主義思想の伝ぱ. ¶a *sentiment* ***of*** joy 喜悦の情 ‖ a *sentiment* ***of*** inexpressible loneliness 言い難いせきばくの情 ‖ the *sentiments* ***of*** the people 庶民の感想 ‖ the *sentiment* ***of*** patriotism 愛国の情.

O *Sentiment* is the life and soul of fine art. 情操は美術の生命及び精神である.

sentimental, *a.* 情のこもった.

M ***effusively*** *sentimental* (=maudlin) あふれるばかりに情のこもった.

sentimentality, *n.* 感傷性.

Q ***maudlin*** *sentimentality* 涙もろい感傷性.

sentinel, *n.* しょう兵, 歩しょう.

V ***post*** (=***station***) a *sentinel* しょう兵を配置する.

Q² a ***box*** *sentinel* しょう舎の側に立つしょう兵.

P get ***past*** a *sentinel* without detection 見つけられずに歩しょうの所を通り抜ける.

O The *sentinel* is on guard. しょう兵が番をしている.

sentry, *n.* しょう兵; 見張り.

V ***pass*** a *sentry* [歩しょう]警かいを通り抜ける. ¶***post*** (=***station***) a *sentry* しょう兵を配置する. ¶The *sentry* is ***relieved*** at intervals. 歩しょうは時々交代になる.

P to the hail ***of*** our *sentry* came the ready response of "..." われわれのしょう兵の掛声に対して「...」という即答が聞えた. ¶come ***off*** *sentry* 歩しょうの非番になる. ¶go (=stand) ***on*** *sentry* 歩しょうに立つ ‖ soldiers ***on*** *sentry* 勤務中のしょう兵.

O stand *sentry* 歩しょうに立つ.

separate, *a.* 分れた.

P live *separate* ***from*** others 他の人と別居する.

O The prisoners are kept *separate* one from the other. 囚人は各自独房に入れられている.

separate, *v.* 分ける; 別れる.

M They are *separated* ***for the present***. 彼らは当分別れている. ¶***violently*** *separate* them from the others 他としゅん別する.

P *separate* a word ***by*** a hyphen 語をハイフンで分ける ‖ *separate* cream ***by*** machinery 器械でクリームを分離する. 【類】*separated* ***by*** a wall ‖ be *separated* ***by*** a comma コンマで切る. ¶*separate* a person ***from*** his wife 某を妻と別居させる ‖ *separate* the worthy ***from*** the unworthy 価値あるものと無価値のものを分ける. 【類】live *separated* ***from*** one's wife / *separate* gold ***from*** sand / *separate* metal ***from*** ore (鉱石) / *separate* religion ***from*** politics ‖ *separate* flour ***from*** the bran by sieving ふるいにかけて粉からふすまを取去る ‖ He had his spirit *separated* ***from*** his soul and body. 彼の精神は彼の心身から離れた(天国に昇った). ‖ Being *separated* ***from*** my attendants, I lost my way. 私は従者と別れてから道に迷った. 【類】In some way he became *separated* ***from*** his companions. / Beasts are *separated* ***from*** man by a great gulf. / live *separate* (=apart) ***from*** ... / I *separated* ***from*** my companions there and returned home. ¶They are *separated* ***in*** time ***by*** one hundred years. 彼らは時代が百年違う. ¶*separate* ***into*** two parties to ... 二手に別れて…する ‖ *separate* ... ***into*** classes (parts) …を組(など)に別ける ‖ It is *separated* ***into*** couples ***by*** six-feet high partitions. 高さ6フィートの中じきりで二つずつに分けてある. ¶The rope *separated* ***under*** the strain. ロープは引っぱられて切れた.

separation, *n.* 分離, 分裂; 離婚.

V ***bring*** *separation* between us われわれの間に分裂を生じる. ¶***get*** a *separation* from her husband 夫と離婚する.

Q a ***judicial*** *separation* of married persons 結婚者の合法的別居. ¶after a ***long*** *separation* (silence) 長い離別(ごぶさた)の後に. ¶a ***rigid*** *separation* of the sexes 男女の厳格な分離. ¶a ***sad*** *separation* 悲しい別れ.

P ***after*** his *separation* from his wife 妻と別れてから.

P^2 the *separation* ***between*** (=***of***) Sweden and Norway スエーデン・ノルウェー間の分裂. ¶*separation* ***by*** consent 合意上の離別. ¶*separation* ***from*** a person (one's wife, party) 人(など)からの分離. 【類】after nearly 300 years of *separation* ***from*** the mother country. ¶a *separation* ***into*** two parts 二分.

separator, *n.* 分離器.

Q^2 a ***chaff*** *separator* もみがら分離器. ¶a ***wheat*** *separator* 小麦ごみ砂分離器(もみ分け器).

sepulcher, *n.* 墓.

Q a ***whited*** *sepulcher* 偽善者(聖書から).

sequel, *n.* 続き; 結果.

V ***form*** a *sequel* to ... …の続きになる. ¶***mark*** the *sequel* その結果を示す.

Q The story has an ***amusing*** *sequel.* その話は続きが面白い. ¶The *sequel* was ***tragic.*** その結果は悲惨であった.

P Typhoid fever is apt to leave epilepsy ***as*** a *sequel.* 腸チフスは結果としててんかんを起しやすい. ¶***in*** the *sequel* of much deliberation とくと協議の結果.

P^2 the book is a *sequel* ***to*** ... その本は…の続編である ‖ a supplement rather than a *sequel* ***to*** a romance 小説の結末というよりは寧ろその付録.

sequence, *n.* 連続; 順序.

V ***follow*** the *sequence* of events 事件を発生順に調べる. ¶The story ***lacks*** *sequence.* 話が前後している.

Q place them in ***chronological*** *sequence* それらを年代順に並べる. ¶short, clear sentences, arranged in ***logical*** *sequence* 筋を通して列べた簡潔な短文. ¶a ***long*** *sequence* of narrative 長い続きの物語. ¶the ***natural*** *sequence* to folly 愚行の報い(天罰). ¶Calamities fall in ***rapid*** *sequence.* 不幸は後から後からと連続的に来る. ¶Occurrences are reported in ***regular*** *sequence.* 事件は(発生の)順序に報告される.

P ***in*** *sequence* 次ぎ次ぎに ‖ ***in*** *sequence* of date 時日順に.

P^2 the *secuence* ***of*** events できごとの連続 ‖ *sequence* ***of*** tenses 時制連続法 ‖ the *sequence* ***of*** thought 思想の一致. ‖ a *sequence* ***to*** a story 後日物語.

serenade, *n.* 〘音楽〙セレナーデ, 小夜曲.

V ***sing*** (***play***) *serenade* for one's love under her windows 恋人のために窓下でセレナーデを歌う(奏する).

serenity, *n.* 平静.

V ***disturb*** his *serenity* 彼の平静を乱す. 【類】***disturb*** the *serenity* of her neighbor (隣国).

Q^2 ***summer*** *serenity* 夏の静寂.

P ***with*** the *serenity* of mind 澄み切た心境で.

P^2 the *serenity* ***of*** the weather おだやかな日より.

serge, *n.* サージ, セル.

Q There is nothing like ***blue*** *serge* for men's wear. 男には青のサージが一番似合う. ¶***fade-proof blue*** *serge* 色のあせないこんサージ.

Q^2 ***silk*** *serge* 絹セル.

sergeant, *n.* 〘陸軍〙軍曹(又は曹長).

Q^2 an ***Air Corps*** *sergeant* 空軍曹長. ¶a ***color*** *sergeant* 軍旗護衛軍曹. ¶a ***customs*** *sergeant* on sentry 臨検税関監視員. ¶a ***drill*** *sergeant* 訓練係軍曹. ¶a ***master*** *sergeant* 上級曹長. ¶a ***police*** *sergeant* 巡査部長. ¶a ***recruiting*** *sergeant* 募兵係軍曹. ¶a ***staff*** *sergeant* 中隊付曹長. ¶a ***tech-[nical]*** *sergeant* 技術曹長 ☞ 現在は sergeant first class と呼称している.

P^2 a *sergeant* ***at*** arms [議院・王宮などの]守衛官.

serial, *n.* 続き物.

V some *serials* now ***running*** in the magazines 目下雑誌に掲載中の続き物.

Q^2 a ***magazine*** (***newspaper***) *serial* 雑誌(新聞)連載もの. ¶a ***radio show*** *serial* 連続ラジオショー. ¶a ***soap opera*** (=sob story) *serial* 《米》〘ラジオ〙お涙頂だいもの(主婦向け連続恋劇もの).

series, *n.* 連続; 連続物, 双書.

V It ***awakens*** a *series* of associations of ideas. それにつれて色々な連想が起る. ¶Collectors sometimes pay big prices for pieces they want or need to ***complete*** a *series.* 収集家はその希望するまたはそろいを完成するために必要な品に折々ばく大な価を払うことがある. ¶***conclude*** a *series* 続き物を終了する. ¶***organize*** a *series* of lectures 連続講演会を編成する. ¶***raise*** a *series* of questions あとからあとから質問をする. ¶***suffer*** a *series* of misfortunes 打続く不幸に苦しむ.

Q make a ***careful*** *series* of scientific observations of ... …の慎重な科学的観察を続行する. ¶in a ***continued*** *series* 続いて. ¶a ***first*** *series* 第一集. ¶The pelvis enlarges as we rise in the ***human*** *series.* 骨盤は人種が高級になるに従って拡大される. ¶one ***long*** *series* of blunders 失錯の長い連続 ‖ a ***long*** *series* of lectures 長期連続講演 ‖ by a ***long*** *series* of gradations いくつも段階を通って. ¶in ***regular*** *series* 順次に. ¶an ***unbroken*** *series* of defeats on sea and on shore 海陸ともに重なる連敗.

Q^2 an intercollegeate ***championship*** *series* 大学対抗選手権大会. ¶one of the "***How to*** ..." *series*「…のやり方」双書の一巻. ¶the "***man-of-letters***" *series* 文人双書. ¶a ***World Series*** 〘野球〙ワールドシリーズ(世界選手権大会).

P ***after*** a *series* of wet days 雨天続きの後. ¶***for*** a *series* of years 引続き数年間. ¶***in*** *series* 連続的に ‖ ***in*** a *series* of 43 lessons 全四十三課の連続授業で. ¶put it ***through*** an extended *series* of tests to determine its point of weakness その弱点を検出するために長期連続試験を行う.

P^2 Thenceforth his life was a *series* ***of*** most brilliant discoveries. その後彼の生がいはいく多の大発見の連続であった ‖ a *series.* ***of*** battles (kings, dynasties, years, victories, pictures, entertainments, misfortunes) 戦(など)の連続. 【類】a *series* ***of*** rainy days.

seriousness, *n.* 重大性, 真剣.

V ***feel*** (***realize***) the *seriousness* of the situation 局面の重大性を感じ(認知す)る. ¶thought ***lacking*** *seriousness* 浮いた考え. ¶***take in*** the *seriousness* of the situation 事態容易ならずと見て取る.

P ***in*** all *seriousness* 全く真剣に.

sermon, *n.* 説教, 談義; 教訓.

V ***deliver*** a *sermon* 説教する. ¶***draw out*** a *sermon* 談義を引伸ばす. ¶***find*** *sermons* in stones 石を見ても教えられる. ¶***get*** a *sermon* on table manners 食事の作法について講釈を一席伺う. ¶***give*** a person a *sermon* on ... …について人にお説教をする. ¶***hear*** a fine *sermon* りっぱな説教を聴く. ¶***preach*** a *sermon* 説教をする. ¶***read off*** a *sermon* [教会で]説教を朗読する. ¶***stud*** one's *sermon* with gems of wit and wisdom とん知と学識の珠玉で説教を飾る.

Q ***academic*** *sermons* representing Oxford and Cambridge thought respectively オクスフォードやケンブリッジの思想をそれぞれ代表する学問的な説教. ¶The ***funeral*** *sermon* on Charles Dickens was preached by the Dean of Westminster, in Westminster Abbey. チャールズ・ディケンズの葬儀の説教はウェストミンスター寺院でウェストミンスター副監督が行った. ¶a ***living*** *sermon* 生きた教訓. ¶a *sermon* two hours ***long*** 二時間にわたる説教. ¶a ***long-winded*** *sermon* 長たらしい説教. ¶a ***matterless*** *sermon* 実のない説教. ¶***moral*** *sermons* 道話. ¶a ***sleepy*** *sermon* 眠気を催す説教. ¶He is noted for his ***tiresome*** *sermons.* 彼は退屈な説教で有名だ.

Q^2 a ***bosom*** *sermon* 暗誦説教. ¶a ***day*** *sermon* 昼の説教. ¶***election*** *sermons* 就任式説教(米国で州吏の就任式にする).

P He fell asleep ***during*** the *sermon.* 彼は説教を聴きながら眠ってしまった. ‖ fall into a doze ***during*** a *sermon* 説教中いねむりする. ¶He slept ***through*** the *sermon.* 彼は説教中眠っていた. ¶listen ***to*** a *sermon* on the air 説教を放送で聞く ‖ treat him ***to*** a *sermon* 彼に小言を言う ‖ little *sermons* ***to*** girls 少女たちへのちょっとした注意.

P^2 *Sermon* ***on*** the Mount 〘聖書〙山上の垂訓.

serpent, *n.* へび.

v² *Serpents hiss.* へびがしゅーしゅーと音を立てる.

Q in the form of a ***coiled serpent*** とぐろを巻いたへびの形に. ¶a ***loathsome serpent*** いやらしいへび.

serpentine, *n.* テープ.

V ***throw serpentines*** of all colors at departing friends 色様々のテープを出発する友人に投げつける.

serum, *n.* 血清.

Q a ***preventive serum*** 予防血清.

servant, *n.* 雇人, 召使, 奉公人.

V ***discharge*** (=***dismiss***) a *servant* 召使を解雇する. ¶He ***employs*** four *servants.* 彼は召使を四人使っている. ¶***engage*** a *servant* 召使を雇う. ¶***get rid of*** one's bad *servant* 悪い召使を追払う. ¶He ***has*** many *servants.* 彼は召使をたくさんおいている. ¶***hire*** a *servant* 召使をやとう. ¶***keep*** (=***maintain***) two female *servants* 女中を二人おく ‖ discuss the advisability of ***keeping*** a *servant* 召使をおくことの可否を論じる. ¶***make*** *servants* of one's passions 情欲を制する. ¶He knows how to ***manage*** his *servants.* 彼は召使の取扱方をわきまえている. ¶***pack off*** a *servant* 召使をたたき出す. ¶***procure*** respectable *servants* 卑しからぬ召使を雇入れる. ¶She ***raised*** the *servant* with her cries. 彼女のさけび声で召使が起きた. ¶***scold*** a *servant* for ... …に対し召使をしかる. ¶***send*** a *servant* for ... 召使を迎えにやる. ¶***send out*** one's *servant* to post it 郵便を出しに召使をやる. ¶He ***slanged*** his *servant* for his misconduct. 《俗》彼は召使の不都合をしかりとばした. ¶He does not ***spare*** his *servants.* 彼は召使をこき使う. ¶***starve*** one's *servants* 召使をひぼしにする. ¶***sweat*** one's *servants* 召使をこきつかう. ¶***turn away*** a *servant* 召使を解雇する. ¶***turn*** a *servant* ***off*** for misconduct 不都合のかどで召使を解雇する. ¶***use*** one's *servants* kindly 召使をいたわって使う. ¶***Wanted*** a good, honest *servant.* [広告] 善良正直の召使一名入用. ¶I am glad to say that my *servant* has ***reformed.*** 私の召使は善くなってよかった. ¶My *servant* does not ***stop*** with me. 私の所へは召使がいつかない.

Q an ***anonymous*** *servant* of humanity 人道のための無名奉仕者. ¶***civil*** *servants* in all departments of the United Kingdom 連合王国各省の文官. ¶***dishonest public*** *servants* 不正公吏. ¶a ***domestic*** *servant* 家僕, 女中. ¶a ***faithful*** *servant* to his paper その新聞に忠実な記者. ¶a ***female*** *servant* 女中. ¶I'll do my best to deserve it, and be a ***good*** *servant* to you. ご厚意に報いるように最善を尽しよい御奉仕ができるように努めます. ¶***good general*** *servants* 善良な小使. ¶a ***hired*** *servant* 使用人. ¶a ***humble*** *servant* 身分の卑い奉仕者. ¶***indoor*** *servants* [料理人・女中のような]屋内勤務の召使. ¶***liveried*** *servants* 定服着用の従僕. ¶The lot of the ***maid*** *servant* is a hard one. 女中奉公はつらい. ¶a ***male*** *servant* 下男. ¶***outdoor*** *servants* [園丁・馬丁のごとき]屋外勤務の召使. ¶***paid*** *servants* of the state 有給の官吏. ¶a ***parlor*** *servant* 仲働き. ¶a ***public*** *servant* 公僕. ¶one of the best ***public*** *servants* the country ever had その国の最も勲功のあった官吏の一人. ¶a ***shiftless*** *servant* よく働かない召使. ¶a ***trusty*** *servant* 信用のできる召使.

Q² a ***body*** *servant* 小間使. ¶a ***farm*** *servant* 農家の手伝. ¶a ***home*** *servant* 女中. ¶a ***post-office*** *servant* (=clerk) 郵便局員. ¶a ***railway*** *servant*=a railwayman, 《米》 a rail roader 鉄道職員.

P I will send it to your place ***by*** a *servant.* 召使に持たせてやりましょう. ¶Ring ***for*** the *servant* 鈴を鳴らして小使を呼んで下さい.

P² a *servant* ***at*** an inn 旅館の召使. ¶a *servant* ***of*** all work 小使 ‖ a *servant* ***of*** the people 国民の奉仕者 ‖ a *servant* ***of*** the State 公務員. ¶This woman was *servant* ***to*** your wife. この女は奥さんに使われていた者です.

serve, *v.* 仕える; 役に立つ; 配膳する.

M Thou wilt *serve* thyself ***best*** by serving others well. 最も良く自己に仕うるの道は他に良く仕うるにあり. ¶food well cooked and ***cleanly*** *served* 料理もうまくきれい盛った食物. ¶***faithfully*** *serve* one's master 忠実に主人に仕える. ¶Ladies must always be *served* ***first.*** 婦人方をいつでも先きにすべきものだ. ‖ Soup is ***first*** *served.* スープが一番先きに出る. ¶*serve* ***gratuitously*** 無料奉仕する. ¶***hardly*** *serve* the purpose of ... ほとんど…の目的には添わない. ¶*serve* coffee (tea) ***hot*** 熱いコーヒー(紅茶)を出す. ¶***loyally*** *serve* one's country 国家に忠誠を尽す. ¶With whom did you *serve* ***last***? 最後に奉公したのはだれの所か. ¶He ***once*** *served* as an artillery officer under his command かって彼の部下として砲兵将校であった. ¶*serve* ***out*** food 食物を盛る ‖ *serve* ***out*** shellmeat for supper 夕飯に貝料理を出す. ‖ *serve* [***out***] one's sentence 刑期を終える ‖ *serve* ***out*** medicine to the poor 貧民に薬品を配給する ‖ *serve* ***out*** the remainder of their terms 彼らの残余の刑を終了する. ¶*Serve* you ***right***!=It serves you right. ざまあ見ろ! ¶if my memory *serves* me ***right*** 私の覚えている所では ‖ It *serves* him perfectly ***right.*** 彼にはそれが当然のむくいだ. ¶He *served* ***some time*** as a waiter in a restaurant. 彼はある料理店に給仕をしていたことがある. ¶he *served* ***successively*** as manager of ... and editor of ... 彼は順次に…の支配人お及び…の編集人として勤めた. ¶The dinner was well *served* ***up.*** ごちそうはじょうずにつけて出された. ¶My servant *serves* ***well.*** うちの召使はよく勤める.

P He *served* ***as*** a private soldier in the war. 彼は一兵卒として従軍した. 【類】 He *served* ***as*** governor of a prefecture (県知事). ‖ This will *serve* ***as*** a model (an illustration). これは手本(例証)になるだろう. 【類】 Park seats *serve* ***as*** free dormitories for tramps and outcasts (ルンペンや無宿者の宿泊所). / *serve* ***as*** a pattern to human society / will *serve* ***as*** a specimen (標本) / It *served* ***as*** a lesson (hint) to him. ‖ *serve* ***as*** a background [知識など]背景として役立つ ‖ It *served* ***as*** a clue to a criminal's tracing. それで犯人の足が付いた. ‖ *serve* ***as*** a portal of entry to ... への入門になる ‖ *serve* the Russian Government ***as*** an engineer. ロシア政府に技術官として勤める. ‖ Relishes *serve* ***as*** a fillip to the appetite 風味品は食欲をそそる. 【類】 *serve* ***as*** witness (証人に) / *serve* ***as*** minister plenipotentiary to Spain (全権公使) ‖ *serve* ***as*** a foil to the principal clown 主役の道化師の引立役をする. ¶*serve* ***at*** a hospital 病院に勤める ‖ *serve* ***at*** the front 戦地で服務する ‖ No wines will be *served* ***at*** the dinner. その晩さんには酒類は一切出さない. ‖ be willing to *serve* ***at*** a small salary 安い給与で喜んで働く. ¶All floors (decks) are *served* ***by*** elevators. 各階(甲板)ともエレベーターで行かれる. ¶*serve* ***for*** both purposes 双方の役に立つ ‖ *serve* ***for*** an illustration 説明になる. 【類】 *serve* ***for*** an excuse ‖ *serve* ***for*** nothing (something) 何の役にも立たない(何かの役に立つ) ‖ This will *serve* [me] ***for*** some time. これで一時間に合う. ‖ ready to *serve* anybody ***for*** money 金になるならだれのためでも喜んで働く. ¶Tea is *served* ***from*** a teapot. 茶は土びんから注ぐ. ¶He *serves* ***in*** the army (Foreign Office). 彼は陸軍(など)に勤めている. ‖ He *served* ***in*** the war (twenty campaigns). 彼はその戦争(など)に従軍した. ‖ *serve* one's full term ***in*** office 任期を勤めあげる. 【類】 *serve* one's term ***in*** prison / He has *served* ***in*** the diplomatic service. / He *served* ***in*** many important public capacities. / get practical knowledge of English that will *serve* him ***in*** good stead in the affairs of life 世の中でりっぱに役に立つような英語の実用的知識を得る ‖ No excuse *serves* you ***in*** this case. この場合何と言いわけしてもだめだ. ¶He *served* ***on*** the U. S. North Dakota ***as*** ensign, United States Navy. 彼はノース・ダコタ艦上に合衆国海軍の少尉として勤めた. 【類】 He *served* ***on*** the Royal Commission. / He *served* ***on*** several campaigns in the army. / He *serves* ***on*** the staff. ¶He *served* ***under*** the Government of India ***as*** consulting architect. 彼は建築顧問としてインド政府に仕えた. ‖ He *served* ***under*** Admiral Togo. 彼は東郷大将の部下であった. ¶*serve* ***with*** the British army 英国陸軍に勤める. 【類】 During the war he *served* ***with*** the French Air Forces. / I was *served* ***with*** tea and cake. ‖ *serve* a town ***with*** water 水を市に給する ‖ he *served* ***with*** distinction as ... 彼は…として勤務成績をあげた. ¶*serve* ***without*** salaries 無給で勤める.

O This will *serve* the purpose for the moment. 当分これで間に合う.

service, *n.* (**1**) 勤務, 軍務; 奉仕(サービス); 尽力; 功労.

V ***abandon*** a *service* 辞任する. ¶I declined to ***accept*** his *service.* 私は彼の好意を断った. ¶efficiently ***administer*** *services* 能率的に仕事をする. ¶***appreciate*** the *service* その労を多とする. ¶to ***commemorate*** his *services* 彼の功績を記念するために. ¶He has ***completed*** his 20 years' *service* on the board. 彼は重役就任以来二十年になる. 【類】

They have ***completed*** *service* under indentures (年季奉公). ¶He ***continued*** his unbroken *service* in the Foreign Department up to the time of his death. 彼は死ぬまでずっと外務省に勤めていた. ¶these societies ***devote*** their *services* to ... これらの協会は...のためにその力を尽す. ¶Please ***do*** me a *service*. 一つ頼まれて下さい. 【類】***do*** a *service* for the public (to English philology, to the community). / he has ***done*** great *service* to the world in ... / ***do*** no small *service* to ... ¶***employ*** the *services* of ... ...を起用する. ¶***engage*** the *service[s]* of a guide 案内者を雇う. ¶***enjoy*** the exclusive *services* of ... ...を専用する. ¶***enlist*** the *service* of the work in ... その仕事を...に頼む. 【類】***enlist*** the *services* of the most experienced teachers. ¶***enter*** the *service* (=military *service*) 兵役に入る(入隊する) ‖ ***enter*** the *service* of a firm (school) 社(など)に奉職する. 【類】He ***entered*** the *service* of this journal as apprentice boy. ¶***escape*** (=***evade***) the military *service* 兵役を忌避する. 【類】The most heinous political offence which a Frenchman or a German can commit, is attempting to ***evade*** military *service*. ¶He ***exaggerates*** his own *services*. 彼は自分の功労を大げさに言う. ¶***extend*** its *service* to ... そのサービスを...に及ぼす. ¶***find*** *service* 職につく. ¶In order to ***get*** the best and most satisfactory *service* from this machine, it must be kept thoroughly cleaned and oiled. この機械の最善最大の能率をあげるには掃除と塗油に十分注意しなければならない. ‖ ***get*** one's *services* for nothing ただで使う. ¶They willingly ***give*** their *services* free. 彼らは喜んで無給で働く. ‖ That store ***gives*** good *service*. あの店は勉強する. ¶***have*** long (twenty years') *service* 永年(など)務める. ¶***join*** the *service* of a company 会社の社員になる. ¶***leave*** one's (the Government) *service* その職(官職)を去る ‖ ***leave*** (=***give up***) the *service* 軍籍を脱する ‖ ***leave*** his *service* for that of ... 彼の所から...へくらがえする. 【類】***leave*** the *service* of a company. ¶***lend*** one's *services* 手を貸す. ¶***lose*** one's *services* 失職する. ¶***man*** a *service* 部署に人員を補充する. ¶Your *services* are ***needed***. 君は(社などに)必要な人だ. ¶***obtain*** *service* under the Niger Protectorate ナイジャー保護領で就職する. ¶***obtrude*** one's *services* upon another 余計な世話を焼く. ¶***offer*** one's *services* as a peace-maker 調停者の役を買って出る. 【類】She ***offered*** her *services* to the Red Cross. / ***offer*** one's *service* as trouble-shooter (火消役). ¶***perform*** a *service* of inestimable value 非常に貴重な奉仕をする. 【類】***perform*** great *services* in the community. / ***perform*** a valuable *service* in behalf of the friendship between ... and ... ¶***place*** one's *services* at the disposal of ... ...のために働く. ¶***proffer*** one's *services* 労務を提供する. ¶***purchase*** the *services* of a licensed messenger 認可を得た用達業者を使う. ¶Rotary teaches us to ***put*** *service* before self. ロータリークラブは自分のことより人のことを先にせよと教える. ¶***quit*** one's *service* やって来た仕事をやめる. ¶I have ***received*** good *service* from this watch. この時計は良い時計だった. ‖ His *services* to learning are ***recognized*** throughout the world. 学問に対する彼の功績は世界から認められている. 【類】***recognize*** *services* to philology and scholarship / ***recognize*** the *services* he has rendered to the cause of education. ¶the *services* offered were ***refused*** by ... 申し出た協力を...に断られた. ¶***render*** *service* to our fellows (the country) 世(など)のために尽す. 【類】***render*** *services* to mankind. / He has ***rendered*** many *services* to the cause of education. ¶We do not ***require*** the *services* of an interpreter. われわれには通訳の必要はない. ¶Your *service* shall be well ***rewarded***. 君の労には十分報いる積りだ. ¶The school is very fortunate in being able to ***secure*** his *services*. 学校が彼を招用することができたのは非常に仕合わせだ. ¶He ***saw*** [active] *service* in the World War. 彼は世界戦争に参加した. ‖ a coat that has ***seen*** *service* 大分くたびれた上衣. 【類】He ***saw*** active *service* in Cuba as private (一兵卒). / He first ***saw*** active *service* during the Great War. / an officer who has ***seen*** much *service* ‖ one who has ***seen*** *service* (経験) on a newspaper / American missionaries, who have ***seen*** *service* in Japan and China. / ***saw*** military *service* during World War II. ¶***seek*** *service* under other masters 他の主人に仕えようとする. ¶***stint*** *service* 骨惜しみをする. ¶***take*** *service* in a regiment 連隊に勤務する ‖ ***take*** *service* under a second lord 次の君主に仕える ‖ He ***took*** *service* with the legation at Athens. 彼はアテネの公使館に勤めた. 【類】***take*** *service* (=serve) with a firm (the government). ¶***tender*** one's *services* as a teacher 教員の口に採用を申込む. ¶***utilize*** the *services* of homing pigeons 伝書ばとを利用する. ¶***value*** one's *services* highly その功労を大いに多とする. ¶Students have ***volunteered*** their *services* to escort them round the sights of the city. 学生たちは彼らの市中見物の案内をしようと申し出た. ¶***wind up*** one's *service* as ... ...の職務を終える. 【類】he ***wound up*** his war *service* as a lieutenant.

Q render an ***acceptable*** *service* to the book-collector 書籍収集家の喜ぶように尽力する. 【類】Both character and knowledge are required to render ***acceptable*** *service* in positions of public trust (要職). ¶the preacher who has grown too old to perform ***active*** *service* 年を取り過ぎて活動のできなくなった伝道師 ‖ while in ***active*** *service* at the front [兵隊として]戦地で活躍中. 【類】a soldier in ***active*** *service*. ¶There is no charge for this ***advisory*** *service*. この相談は無料で応じる. ¶the ***armed*** *services* 軍部(三軍). ¶***bad*** *service* 不行届. ¶do ***better*** *service* 一層よく尽す. ¶his ***brilliant*** *services* 彼のさえた手腕. ¶***civil*** *service* 文官[の勤務]. ¶***clerical*** *service* 聖職. ¶he gave his ***competent*** *services* in ... 彼は...にあずかって力があった. ¶He has rendered ***considerable*** *service* to the cause of commercial education. 彼は商業教育のために多大の貢献をした. 【類】do a ***considerable public*** *service* (公益). ¶the ***consular*** *service* 領事の事務. ¶The machinery has been in ***continuous*** *service* for a large number of years. その機械は多年間断なく使用してきた. ¶***courteous*** *service* 丁寧な客扱い. ¶thanks to the ***devoted*** *services* of the doctors 医師たちの熱心な骨折りのおかげで. ¶top officials in the ***diplomatic*** *service* 外交畑の最高幹部. 【類】enter the ***diplomatic*** *service*. ¶inaugurate a ***direct*** *service* of a steamer 汽船を始めて就役させる. ¶He has done a ***distinct*** *service* to Japanese commercial education. 彼は日本の商業教育に功労があった. ¶do the cause of English education a ***distinct*** and ***lasting*** *service* by ... ing ...することによって英国の教育のために特殊の永続的勲功をたてる. ¶his ***distinguished*** *service* in the last War この前の大戦における彼の功績. ¶You need ***doctor's*** *service*. 医者にかからなくてはいけない. ¶***domestic*** *service* 召使奉公. ¶It has done us a ***double*** *service*. それはわれわれにとって二重に役立った. ¶be in the ***educational*** *service* 教職にある. ¶render ***efficient*** *service* to the State 国のためにりっぱに御奉公をする. ¶in recognition of his ***eminent*** *service* to literature 彼の文学上の顕著な功労を認めて. ¶give years of ***enthusiastic*** *service* to ... ...のために多年熱心に尽力する. ¶The dictionary is of ***enormous*** *service* to students. その辞書は学徒の大いに参考になる. ¶do an ***essential*** *service* to ... ...に対し重要な仕事をする. ¶do ***excellent*** *service* in ... ...にりっぱに役立つ. ¶an *animierkneipe* with ***female*** *service* 女給のいる(ドイツの)酒店. ¶a soldier hired into ***foreign*** *service* 外国軍隊に雇われている兵士. 【類】Part of the battalion is now on ***foreign*** *service*. ¶render helpful ***free*** *service* to ... ...に無償で有益な助力をする. ¶He has done ***good*** *service* to the cause of truth and justice. 彼は真理と正義のためにりっぱに尽した. 【類】Those woollen shirts have done us ***good*** *service*. ¶enter the ***Government*** *service* 官界に入る. ¶His *services* are ***gratuitous***. 彼の仕事は無報酬だ. ¶his ***great*** *service* to learning 彼の学術上の大勲功. 【類】He rendered ***great*** *services* to medical science. / he has done a ***great*** *service* by ... ‖ A trip to the coast and sea-bathing, in such a case, is often of ***great*** *service*. こうした場合には海岸や海水浴に出掛けると非常にいいことが往々ある. 【類】The book will be of ***great*** *service* to all who wish to use good English. ¶He saw ***hard*** and ***honorable*** *service* under Lafayette. ラファイエット(将軍)の下で困難だが名誉ある戦功をたてた. ¶do ***heroic*** *service* at the front 戦場で勇ましい働きをする. ¶render ***high*** *service* りっぱな仕事をする. ¶render ***immeasurable*** *services* to the community at large 一般社会のために絶大の功績がある. ¶The American cinema has done ***immense*** *service* in patriotic propaganda. 米国の映画は愛国的宣伝に非常に役立っている. ¶He has rendered the country ***important*** *service*. 彼は国家に大功があった.【類】He has rendered a most ***important*** *service* to our knowledge of ... by his valuable work. ¶He has rendered ***inestimable*** *service* to the Japanese people. 彼は日本国民のために非常に尽した. ¶***inside*** and ***outside*** *service* 内勤外勤. ¶an opportunity for ***international*** *service* 国際的功労をたてる機会. ¶a ***lasting*** *service* to mankind 人類への永久の功績. ¶The machine will give ***long*** *service* with minimum attention and upkeep. その機械は手入れや維持はごくわずかで長持ちがする.【類】He has had ***long*** *service* at the Foreign Office. ¶get ***loyal, enthusiastic*** *service* from the entire force 全部員から忠実熱誠の助力を得る. ¶perform ***manual*** *service* 筋肉労働をする. ¶render ***material*** *service* to one in learning 人が学習するに当って大いに参考になる ‖ do a ***material*** *service* to ... ...のために実質的に役立つ. ¶perform ***menial*** *services* いやしい勤めをする. ¶a sailor in the ***merchant*** *service* 商船の水夫. ¶***meritorious*** *service* 勲功. ¶undergo a year of ***military*** *service* 一年間兵役に服する ‖ ***Military*** *service* is at once a duty and a right. 軍務は義務でもあり権利でもある.【類】rendered valuable ***military*** *service* to the American cause. ¶***multifarious*** *services* to ... ...への種々の援助. ¶the relationship of ***mutual*** *service* 互助的関係.【類】The spirit of ***mutual*** *service* lives and thrives amongst us. ¶***national*** *service* through occupation 職域奉公 ‖ in the ***nation's*** *service* 国民のために. ¶a hospital for men in the ***naval*** *service* 海軍病院. ¶do a ***noble*** *service* to one's father's memory 父の記念に(寄付などの)りっぱな仕事をする. ¶for his ***past*** *services* 彼の過去の功労に対して. ¶***personal*** *service* at a hotel ホテルの客扱い. ¶***poor*** *service* 不行届き ‖ To say that ... is to do him a ***poor*** *service*. ...と言っては彼にとって気の毒だ. ¶It is of ***practical*** *service*. それは実際上役に立つ. ¶give customers ***prompt*** and ***satisfactory*** *service* 顧客に敏速かつ満足に奉仕する. ¶I am sure you will get ***proper*** *service* in that inn. あの宿屋なら客扱いはたしかです. ¶the spirit of ***public*** *service* 奉公の精神 ‖ remarkable opportunities for ***public*** *service* 公に奉じる絶好の機会.【類】Newspapers do a great ***public*** *service* for a very small return. ‖ Such a magazine renders a ***public*** *service* of great value. こうした雑誌はりっぱな公益機関だ. ‖ whether in the ***public*** or in commercial life 官界においても実業界においても. ¶perform a ***real*** *service* for the public 社会のため真に奉仕する.【類】He has rendered me a ***real*** *service*. ¶do ***realistic*** *services* to the students 実際に学生の面倒をみてやる. ¶in ***regular*** *service* 常雇の. ¶***Reuter's*** *service* to the Japan Advertizer ジャパン・アドヴァタイザー社着のロイター電報. ¶the ***secret*** *service* 秘密情報部(特に軍関係の). ¶the ***secret military*** *service* 特務機関. ¶the ***signal*** *services* rendered to ... by ... ...の...に致した大奉仕. ¶I think he will not consent to do him even that ***small*** *service*. 彼はそんなささいな世話でも彼のために尽すことを承知しないと私は思う. ¶render the greatest ***social*** *service* 最大の社会奉仕をする. ¶I found him of ***some*** *service* to me. 彼がいくらか私のためになることが分かった. ¶offer ***some slight*** (=***little***) *service* 少しばかり骨を折る. ¶send off on ***special*** *service* 特別任務で派遣する. ¶***subsidiary*** *service* 副業. ¶He did a ***substantial*** *service* to anthropology. 彼は人類学のために実質的に尽した. ¶the ***three*** *services* of land, sea, and air=the armed services 陸海空三軍. ¶give ***unselfish*** *service* 利他的に尽力する. ¶perform a ***useful*** *service* 有益な社会奉仕をする.【類】render ***useful*** *service* to the community. ¶He rendered ***valuable*** *services* to the cause of education (good lighting, historical learning). 彼は教育(など)のために貴重な貢献をした.【類】rendered ***valuable*** *services* to literature as an editor of reprints (複刻). ¶enlist the ***voluntary*** *service* of ... ...の自発的奉仕を募集する.

Q² ***beauty*** *services* 美容院の仕事. ¶the three ***fighting*** *services* 三軍. ¶be in the ***full-time*** (***part-time***) *service* 専任(嘱託)である. ‖ secure the ***full-time*** *service* of ... ...を専任する. ¶map [up] ***future*** *services* for youth 青年たちのため将来の仕事を考えてやる. ¶enter (leave) ***Government*** *service* 公務員になる(をやめる) ‖ an expert in the ***Government*** *service* 政府専門事務官 ‖ screen employes considered disloyal from ***Government*** *service* 国家に不忠実と見なされる公務員を整理する ‖ reinstatement in ***Government*** service 官職への復帰.【類】during his years of ***Government*** *service*. ¶the reader's ***guide*** *service* in a library 図書館の閲覧案内係. ¶enter the ***hospital*** *service* 病院に奉職する. ¶pay ***lip*** *service* to ... ...に口先だけいいことを言う ‖ It is true that the great majority of people pay only ***lip*** *service* to the classics of their own literature. 多数の国民は口先で言うだけで自国の古典文学を読まないのは事実だ. ¶bad ***maid*** *service* 女中の悪い働き振り. ¶***out-patient*** *services* [病院の]外来患者診察. ¶a veteran of 52 months ***overseas*** *service* 五十二カ月の海外勤務の古参兵. ¶A ***photostatic reproduction*** *service* is maintained in the library. その図書館では必要に応じて書籍の複製写真を取ってくれる. ¶a warship unfit for further ***sea*** *service* これ以上使用にたえない老朽艦. ¶a ***shopping*** *service* 購買部. ¶the Army and its ***sister*** *service*, the Navy 陸軍及びその姉妹格の海軍. ¶complete one's ***six-year*** *service* as a trustee of the university 大学理事として六カ年の任期を完了する. ¶international ***travel*** *service* 国際旅行業務. ¶***visiting nurse*** *service* 派出看護婦業. ¶his ***war*** *service* marked him as a great American. 彼は戦功によってアメリカの偉人と目されるに至った. ‖ vessels that have seen long ***war*** *service* 多年実戦に参加した艦船. ¶***war-time*** *service* 戦時の功績.

P He retired ***after*** 46 years' *service* with the Mersey Mission to Seamen. 彼はマージー船員伝道会に四十六年勤務の後引退した. ¶***as*** a friendly *service* 好誼上. ¶it is ***at*** the *service* of ... それを...の使用に任せる ‖ My name is ..., ***at*** your *service*. 私は...と申す者で御用の仰せ付けを待っております. ‖ I am altogether (=entirely) ***at*** your *service*. 私は全く御意次第です.【類】You will find me ever ***at*** your *service*. ‖ There good hotels are ***at*** the *service* of the visitor. そこへ行く人はいいホテルに宿泊ができる. ¶***during*** his *service* with the railway authorities 彼の鉄道に勤務中. ¶a gift ***for*** *service* done 骨折りの謝礼 ‖ he was decorated ***for*** *services* with the French Red Cross at the time of ... ...の際仏国赤十字に勤務したので叙勲された. ‖ a soldier disabled ***for*** active *service* 現役に不適当になった兵士 ‖ ***for*** the *service* of the fatherland 祖国のために. ¶discharged ***from*** military *service* 除隊となった ‖ exemption ***from*** military *service* 兵役免除 ‖ dismiss ***from*** one's *service* 解職する.【類】He is released ***from*** active *service* (現役). ‖ She has been ***in*** my *service* only a few months. 彼女はほんの二三カ月私の所に奉公していた.【類】He was ***in*** the *service* successively of Francis I. and Henry II. of France (歴任した). / work ***in*** the *service* of humanity / be long ***in*** the *service* of ... ‖ He died ***in*** *service*. 彼は戦死した. ‖ wives or daughters of men ***in*** *service* 出征軍人の妻または娘 ‖ atomic energy ***in*** the *service* of man 人類に奉仕する原子力 ‖ We have ***in*** our *service* first class couriers. 手前どもは一流の案内人を使っております(旅行会社など). ‖ foreign troops ***in*** the *service* of a nation at war 交戦国に雇われている外人兵.【類】a meteorologist (気象学者) ***in*** the *service* of the United States Weather Bureau / the horse which has worn [out] its energies ***in*** the *service* of man (人間のために) / employ riches ***in*** the *service* of mankind. ¶I will parden him ***in consideration of*** his past *services*. 私は過去の功労に免じて彼を許してやろう. ¶***in recognition of*** his *services* to scholarship 彼の学界への功績により. ¶go ***into*** *service* 奉公に出る ‖ send one out ***into*** *service* 人を奉公に出す ‖ I begged to be taken ***into*** his *service*. 彼に雇ってくれるように頼んだ. ¶Will it be ***of*** *service* to you? それは君のためになるだろうか. ‖ Can I be ***of*** *service* to you?=Can I do anything for you? 私がなにかお役に立ちましょうか.【類】I shall be happy to be ***of*** *service* to you. / I'm just wondering if it could be ***of*** any *service* to you. / prove ***of*** no (little) *service* to ... ‖ a means ***of*** *service* to the public 奉公の一手段 ‖ He was ***of*** great *service* to me. 彼は私に大層役に立った. ¶while ***on*** *service* in Portugal and elsewhere ポルトガルその他に出征中.【類】a soldier ***on*** *service* (=duty). / owing to the absence of ... ***on*** *service* in South Africa. ‖ He was disabled when ***on*** active *service*. 彼は出征中に廃兵となった. ‖ die ***on*** active *service*=die in action.【類】They sent him ***on*** some important *service*. / firemen ***on*** *service* fighting the flames / while ***on*** active *service* in the field. ¶***on ac-***

count of his *services* to literature 彼の文学への貢献のために. ¶He has a right ***to*** my *service*. 彼は私に用を命じる権利がある. ¶Pray show him this letter, ***with*** my *service* to him. どうぞこの手紙を彼に見せてよろしく言って下さい.

P^2 he entered the *service* ***as*** ... 彼は...として軍籍に入った. ‖ give their *services* ***as*** instructors 講師として尽す. ¶The *service* ***at*** the hotel is good (bad). その旅館は世話が行届く(行届かない).【類】The *service* ***at*** large receptions is usually so poor. ¶their "war of *service* ***for*** humanity" 彼らのいわゆる「人道のための戦争」. ¶Of all the public *services* ***in*** London it may safely be said that none exceeds in importance the supply of water. ロンドンにおけるすべての公共事業の中で重要の点で給水に及ぶものはないといっても過言ではあるまい. ¶a Portuguese in the *service* ***of*** France フランスに雇われたポルトガル人. ¶a master worker in the difficult field of international *service* ***through*** journalism 新聞による国際奉仕という困難な分野での敏腕家. ¶in recognition of his *services* ***to*** scholarship 学問に対する彼の功労を認めて ‖ his greatest *service* ***to*** science was ... 彼の科学への最大貢献は...であった.【類】a *service* ***to*** civilization (society, a cause). ¶on *service* ***with*** the American ambulance. 米国野戦病院勤務の(軍医など). ¶during the thirty-two years of his *service* ***with*** Edison 彼が三十二年間エディソンに使われている間.【類】the second year of my *service* ***with*** that company.

(2) [一般]公共事務(業務); 施設; 勤行, 礼拝.

V attend divine *service* 礼拝に出る. ¶The fire last night completely ***blocked*** the tram *service* in the street. ゆうべの火事で市街電車の交通が完全にと絶した. ¶The tram car *service* was ***carried on*** without a hitch. 市街電車の交通は故障なく行われた. ¶In June of 1921 she had a memorial mass and *service* ***celebrated*** for him in the church at Warsaw. 一九二一年六月に彼女はワルソーの教会で彼のために記念の供養と礼拝を行ってもらった. ¶***call in*** the *services* of a decorator 装飾屋に用を命じる. ¶The *service* in that church is ***conducted*** in French. あの教会の礼拝はフランス語で行う.【類】The unveiling (除幕) was preceded by a short *service* ***conducted*** by the Bishop of Winchester and the Rev. A. Saunders. ¶The hospital ***contains*** a *service* of 750 beds. その病院には七百五十の寝台がある. ¶***correlate*** railway *services* with those of the buses and the airplanes バス及び飛行機の業務と鉄道業務を連絡させる. ¶The company will ***discontinue*** its Mediterranean *service*. その汽船会社は地中海の航路を廃止するだろう. ¶***establish*** a daily *service* of steam ferry-boats between ... ...間に毎日の連絡汽船往復を開始する. ¶The hosipital ***has*** a *service* of 500 beds. その病院は五百名の患者を収容する寝台の設備がある. ¶This church ***holds*** three *services* every Sunday. この教会では毎日曜日に三回の礼拝式を行う. ‖ *Services* are ***held*** in honor of those who fell in the Saga trouble of 1873. 一八七三年佐賀の乱に倒れた人々のために礼拝式が行われる. ¶***improve*** postal (=mail) *service* 郵便事務を改善する. ¶***inaugurate*** a *service* of passenger steamers 客船の往復を開始する.【類】***inaugurate*** regular air *services* between ... ¶***install*** telephone *service* 電話を架設する. ¶***institute*** a new steamer *service* between ... ...間に新航路を開始する. ¶The railway *service* on the Hokuriku Line is ***interrupted***. 北陸線の汽車が止まっている. ¶The company ***maintains*** a *service* from Alexandria via Naples to Marseilles. 会社はアレキサンドリアからナポリ経由マルセィユ行の航路を経営している.【類】A daily steamer *service* is ***maintained*** by the Government Railways between Shimonoseki and Fusan. ¶***open*** a *service* to Germany [汽船会社など]ドイツへの航路を開始する. ¶***operate*** regular *services* to ... [汽船会社など]...への定期航路を経営する. ¶The Marconi Company ***organized*** a *service* of long-distance transmission of news to ships in the Atlantic. マルコニー会社は大西洋上の船舶にニュースの長距離送信を始めた. ¶***popularize*** the *service* その公益機関を民衆化する. ¶***provide*** two *services* weekly to ... [汽船・航空など]...へ毎週二回往復する. ¶***read*** a *service* お経を読む. ¶13,760 *services* were ***rendered*** last year by the Japan Travel Bureau 日本旅行協会では昨年中一万三千七百六十人にサービスした. ¶Normal train *services* will be ***restored*** next week. 来週平常通り列車運転する. ¶***resume*** a normal train *service* [ストライキや事故の後など]正規の列車運転に復帰する. ¶railway companies ***run services*** to ... 鉄道会社が...へ列車運転を行う. ¶***speed up*** *service* [鉄道など]運転速度を増す. ¶***start*** a *service* of omnibuses between ... ...間に乗合自動車の運転を始める.【類】before the streetcar *service* was ***started***. ¶***supplant*** streetcar *service* with buses, supplemented with automobiles バスを用いて電車を廃しハイヤーで補う. ¶***suspend*** the *service* of steamboats 汽船の往復を中止する. ¶***undertake*** a direct steamship *service* 直行の汽船便を起す. ¶***use*** the rental *service* of a library 図書館の貸出を利用する.

V^2 When does *service* ***begin***? 礼拝はいつ始まりますか. ¶*Service* is ***going on*** in the church. 教会では今礼拝をやっている. ¶a *service* of motor-omnibuses is now ***working*** between ... 乗合自動車は今...間を運転している.

Q There was a ***brief*** *service* at the grave too. 墓地でも簡単な式があった. ¶A third of a century of ***continuous*** *service*. 創業三十余年. ¶attend ***divine*** *services* at ... church ...教会で礼拝に出る. ¶a transport put into ***European*** (***Pacific***) *service* 欧州(など)航路についている輸送船. ¶There is a ***good*** *service* of trains. りっぱな汽車の便がある. ¶***high*** *service* [水道の]水の出のよいこと. ¶an ***impressive*** *service* 荘厳な宗教の儀式. ¶in the ***industrial*** *service* of Japan 日本の産業部門で. ¶the shipping company maintains a ***joint*** *service* with ... その汽船会社は...と合同経営をやっている. ¶***linked*** *services* of Cunard White Star Limited and Imperial Airways キューナード汽船会社と帝国航空会社の連絡輸送. ¶ships performing a ***magnificent*** *service* between ... ...間を往復している設備優秀の船. ¶conduct a ***memorial*** *service* for the dead 故人のために法要を営む. ¶***postal*** *services* 郵便事業. ¶a department of the ***public*** *service* 公益事業部(政府の一部門) ‖ perform a ***public*** *service* 公共事業をやる. ¶there is a ***regular*** *service* of launches between ... ...間にランチの定期往復がある ‖ run a ***regular*** *service* of trains at forty-two miles an hour 一時間四十二マイルの速度で定期列車を運転する. ¶***religious*** *services* 礼拝式 ‖ hold a ***religious*** *service* for the repose of the deceased 故人の法要を営む. ¶***reverential*** *service* of mourning 敬けんな追悼式. ¶a ***seven-day*** *service* for the benefit of the souls of the departed 故人追善のための七日間の法事. ¶inaugurate ***through*** *service* between France and America, via Liverpool リヴァプール経由仏米直通航路を開始する. ¶maintain a ***weekly*** *service* between ... ...間を毎週往復する.

Q^2 ***aerial*** (=***air***) ***mail*** *service* 航空郵便.【類】a Tokyo-Sydney ***aerial mail*** *service*. ¶set up (=establish) a regular ***air*** *service* between ... and ... ...間の定期航空路を新設する.【類】***air*** *service* was started between ... ¶Pacific ***airline*** *service* 太平洋空路運航. ¶hold an ***all-night*** *service* 徹宵礼拝をする. ¶***Armed Forces Radio*** ***Service*** (AFRS) [進駐軍の]軍部の放送班. ¶***auto*** (=***motor***) *services* between ... ...間の自動車運転(ハイヤーなど). ¶the B.B.C. overseas ***broadcasting*** *service* [英国の] BBC 海外放送班. ¶***Buddhist*** *services* are performed. 法事が営まれる. ¶There is no ***bus*** *service* available in this part. この辺はバスの便がない. ‖ The growth of the ***bus*** *service* is almost phenomenal. バス輸送の進歩は実に驚くべきものがある. ¶***cab*** *service* 馬車業, タクシー業. ¶attend ***church*** *services* 教会の礼拝に出る. ¶the ***communion*** *service* 〖宗教〗聖さん式. ¶purchase goods through a ***consumer cooperative*** *service* 消費組合を通じて物資を購入する. ¶the ***custom*** *service* 関税事務. ¶hold a ***dedication*** *service* 献納式を開催する. ¶***delivery*** and ***collection*** *service* [荷物の運送などの]集配業務. ¶a moderately-priced ***dining-car*** *service* 低廉な食堂車の設備. ¶the ***distribution*** *service* of the Stores そのデパートの配達部. ¶There is an ***electric train*** *service* every thirty minutes. 三十分ごとに電車の便がある. ¶The present ***emergency*** *service* will be continued for some time. この臨時運転は当分継続する. ¶the United States ***Employment*** ***Service*** 米国職業紹介部. ¶operate an ***express*** *service* between ... ...間に急行列車を運転する ‖ ***express*** *service* 《米》小運送業. ¶The priest was intoning the ***evening*** *service*. 僧は晩の読経をしていた. ¶The Cunard ships provide the most luxurious ***ferry*** *service* in the world. キューナード社の汽船は世界で最も豪華な連絡の便を提供している.

¶temporary ***ferryboat service*** 臨時連絡船. ¶***fetch and carry services*** 集配小運送業. ¶women on ***fire service*** 婦人消防官. ¶the U.S. ***Forest Service*** 米国森林部. ¶conduct ***funeral*** (***burial***) ***service*** (埋)葬式を行う. ¶***Government security services*** 政府の安全保障事業. ¶the ***Government operated Star route service*** 政府経営のスター航空路線. ¶***Harmony Service*** 米国における一種の共産主義の宗教団体. ¶a school (student) ***health service*** 学校(学生)保険部 ‖ a modern public ***health service*** 近代的公衆健康相談所. ¶the U.S. ***Information Service*** 米国報道班(略 USIS). ¶a capable ***intelligence service*** 有能な情報班. ¶***low-cost service*** 費用低廉制. ¶***mail service*** 郵便業務 ‖ quick-delivery ***mail service*** 速達郵便制度. ¶a ***marriage service*** 結婚式. ¶a ***memorial service*** 記念祭. ¶***merchant service*** 商用船舶; 海商. ¶the ***money-order service*** both domestic and international 国内及び国際間の為替制度. ¶***morning service*** 朝の勤行. ¶***motor transportation service*** トラック業務. ¶a ***news service*** ニュース(報道)配給会社(通信社の). ¶a ***nonprofit service*** 非営利事業. ¶The churches held ***noontime services***. 教会で正午礼拝を行った. ¶***nurse service*** 看護(育児)の仕事. ¶The excellence of the ***N.Y.K. service*** was known throughout the world. 日本郵船の輸送業務のすばらしさは世界で有名だった. ¶during ***occupation service*** in Japan 在日占領軍行政期間中. ¶an ***omnibus service*** バス事業. ¶The steamship company runs an ***opposition service***. その汽船会社は競争航路を経営している. ¶***party-line service***〖電話〗共同加入線制. ¶establish a ***passenger steamboat service*** on the Thames 客船のテームズ川航行業務を開始する. ¶the ***pneumatic-tube service*** 気送管装置. ¶S connects with K by a ten-hour ***sea service***. S は K と十時間の航海で連絡する. ¶***probation service*** [裁判所の]保護観察部. ¶***quick freight service*** 貨物の急行便. ¶***radiocast*** (=***radio broadcast***) ***service*** ラジオ放送. ¶***railroad transportation service*** 鉄道輸送業務. ¶a curtailment of ***railway service*** 鉄道業務の縮小 ‖ Part of the ***railway service*** was crippled (=paralyzed). 鉄道は一部不通になった. 【類】The ***railway service*** grew steadily more irregular and less efficient. ¶operate a ***rapid-car service*** 急行電車を運転する. ¶***road*** and ***rail services*** 道路及び鉄道の便. ¶a ***round-the-world air service*** 世界一週航空業務. ¶The bus stop will be skipped during the ***rush-hour express service***. ラッシュアワーの急行運転期間はその停留所は止まらない. ¶***special-delivery service*** 特別配達制. ¶a ***state service*** 国営の事業. ¶excellent ***steamboat service*** is run direct to ... by ... ...を経由して...まですばらしい汽船の便が直通している. ¶paralyze the capital's ***street-car telephone, gas*** and ***electric light services*** [ストライキなどが]首都の市電, 電話, ガス及び電灯を麻ひさせる. ¶The ***street-cleaning service*** has become lax. 街路清掃の作業が不行届きになってきた. ¶***subway*** and ***elevated train service*** 地下鉄及び高架鉄道業務. ¶***sunrise services*** 日の出の礼拝. ¶***student personnel services*** 学生厚生業務. 【類】improve ***student personnel services*** on the campus (大学). ¶***taxi*** (=***taxi cab***) ***service*** タクシー業. 【類】There is a ***taxi service*** available from ... to ... ¶***telecast*** (=***television broadcast***) ***service*** テレビ放送. ¶***telegraph*** and ***telephone services*** 電信電話事業. ¶a poor ***telephone service*** 不完全な電話施設. ¶disrupt ***telephone, electric*** and ***transport services*** 電話, 電気及び輸送業務を阻害する. ¶electrified ***train service*** 列車の電化運転 ‖ ***Train service*** was disrupted by washouts. 列車の運行は沿線の土砂流出のため一時不通となった. ‖ fast through ***train service*** 準急直行列車運転. ¶the ***United States Fish*** and ***Wild-life Service*** 米国魚類・野生課. ¶***utility services*** 雑役務 ‖ public ***utility services*** 公益事業. ¶a "***watch-night***" ***service*** at church on New Year Eve 除夜の教会の徹宵礼拝. ¶***water*** (***gas, light***) ***service*** 配水(など). ¶operate a ***water taxi service*** across Boston Harbor to the airport ボストン港から空港まで有料水道給水をやる. ¶***weather*** [***observation***] ***service*** 天気測候事業. ¶***weekday*** (***weekend***) [operation] ***service*** [列車・バスなど]平日(週末)運転. ¶a ***wireless*** (=***radio***) ***service*** between ships at sea and ... 航海中の船と...との無線通信施設.

P The two places are connected ***by*** a good ***service*** of steamboats. その二つの場所はりっぱな汽船連絡がついている. ¶What ***service*** is the vessel ***for***? その船はどの航路についていますか. ¶steamers ***in service*** between ... ...間を往復している汽船. 【類】steamers will be placed ***in service*** between ... ¶Three 24 to 25 knot turbine steamers are now ***on*** the ***service***. 二十四ノットないし二十五ノットの三隻のタービン式汽船を目下その航路に使用している. ‖ one of the trio ***on*** the Japan-American ***service*** 日米間を航海する三姉妹船の一隻.

P² There are three ***services*** weekly ***between*** Marseilles and Port Said. マルセイユとポートサイドの間に一週三回汽船が往復している. ¶a Buddhist memorial ***service for*** animals 動物の供養 ‖ a religious ***service for*** the repose of the soul of ... ...の追善供養. ¶a ***service of*** public utility 公益機関. ¶attend the funeral ***services over*** ... ...の葬式に参列する. ¶its ***services to*** the cause of popular education [映画など]その民衆教育のための事業.

(**3**) 食器一そろい.

Q² a ***dinner service*** 食膳の調度(主として陶器). ¶a ***table service*** 食器一式. ¶a ***tea*** (***dinner, coffee***) ***service*** 茶道具(食器類)一組. 【類】a solid silver ***tea service***.

serviceable, *a.* 役に立つ.

M be ***serviceable enough*** for the purpose intended 最初の目的に十分適合する. ¶a book of this kind will ***no longer*** be ***serviceable*** for the study of ... この種の本は...の研究にはもはや役に立たないだろう. ¶though quite worn out, it is ***still serviceable*** 相当使い古したがまだ使える.

P It is quite ***serviceable*** enough ***for*** the purpose intended. その目的には十分役に立つ. ¶A practical knowledge of English is ***serviceable to*** one in functioning as an international worker. 英語の実用的知識は国際人として活動する者の役に立つ.

serviceman, *n.* 兵隊.

Q a ***demobilized serviceman*** 復員軍人. ¶a ***former serviceman***=an ex-serviceman 予(後)備兵. ¶a ***soon-to-be discharged serviceman*** 解除まじかの軍人.

servicing, *n.* 施設.

Q² ***radio servicing*** ラジオ放送.

P² the ***servicing*** and repair ***of*** machinery 工場の欠品補充.

servile, *a.* 追従する, 従順な.

P ***servile to*** public opinion 世論に追従する ‖ ***servile to*** one's superiors 先輩に一目おく.

servility, *n.* どれい根性.

V ***betray*** one's ***servility*** どれい根性を出す. ¶***show servility*** to ... ...にどれい根性で対する.

serving, *n.* [料理など]一人前. 「四人分です.

P A can is approximately ***for*** four ***servings***. 一かんは約

servitude, *n.* 懲役; どれいたること. 「服する.

V ***do*** two years' penal ***servitude*** for ... ...で二年の懲役に

Q ***involuntary servitude*** 強制労働. ¶***penal servitude*** 徴役 ‖ limited ***penal servitude*** 有期懲役. 【類】***penal servitude*** for an indeterminate period (無期) / discharged from ***penal servitude***.

P be driven ***into servitude*** of evil passions 邪欲のとりこになる. ¶deliver a country ***out of*** (=***from***) ***servitude*** 国家をどれいの状態から救い出す. ¶sentence him ***to*** three years' penal ***servitude*** 彼を三年の懲役に処する.

P² penal ***servitude for*** life 無期徒刑. ¶***servitude to*** vice 悪への盲従.

session, *n.* 会合; 会期; 開廷; 課業時間.

V ***adjourn*** its ***session*** until ... ...まで(議会などが)休会する. ¶A stormy ***session*** is ***anticipated***. 会議の雲行がすこぶる険悪だ. ¶***begin*** its ***sessions*** [国会など]開会する. ¶***call*** the ***session*** of the Diet 議会を召集する. ¶***convene*** (=***summon***) a special ***session*** of the Diet 臨時議会を召集する. ¶***have*** a long ***session*** 開会が長期にわたる. ¶The Council will ***hold*** a ***session*** on Monday. 会議は月曜日に開会する ‖ ***hold*** its ***sessions*** [法廷など]開廷する. ¶A stormy ***session occurred*** in the Chamber of Commerce and Industry. その商工会議所では会議があって議論百出であった.

Q the ***autumnal session*** of the conference その会議の秋の会議. ¶an ***extra session*** of Congress [米国の]臨時議会. ¶the ***first session*** of the Diet 第一議会. ¶in ***full session*** 総会で. ¶submit to a ***plenary session*** 本会議にかける. 【類】the final ***plenary session*** of a conference. ¶The committee held a ***short session*** today reporting progress. 委員が本日委員会を開き経過を報告しほどなく散会した.

¶hold ***two sessions***〖株式〗二回の立会を催す.

Q² Parliament had an ***all night session.*** 議会が徹宵審議した. ¶a ***council session*** 会議の集会. ¶a ***country session*** 州治案裁判廷(英国で四季に開廷). ¶a ***Diet session*** 議会の会議.【類】in the last ***Diet session.*** ¶a ***five-hour session*** of a council 会議の五時間にわたる会議. ¶a ***morning*** and an ***afternoon session*** [学校などの]午前の課業時間と午後の課業時間. ¶hold a ***night session*** 夜間会議を開く. ¶Most of these schools have ***night sessions.*** これらの学校には大抵夜学がある. ¶an ***opening*** (a closing) ***session*** 初(終)回の会合. ¶a ***round-table session*** 円卓会議. ¶the ***summer session*** of a university 大学の夏季授業. ¶***this year's session*** of Congress 今年の議会の会期. ¶meet for a ***three-day session*** 三日間の会期に参集する.【類】a ***three-day session*** of the Council.

P present bills ***at*** this ***session*** 今回の会議に議案を提出する. ¶***during*** the ***sessions*** of the convention 同会議開会中. ¶The Diet (court) is now ***in session.*** 議会(など)開会中である.【類】keep a conference ***in session*** until ... / ***in*** its 2nd ***session*** for the year.

P² a ***session of*** Parliament (a legislature) [英国]国会(など)の開会.

set, *n.* 一そろいの人または物(セット), 仲間 ; 形勢, 方向.

V ***break*** a ***set*** [そろった器具など]はんぱにする. ¶The three ***make*** a ***set.*** 三つで一組になる ‖ ***make*** a ***set*** at a person 断然人に打ってかかる.

Q a ***blackguardly set*** of people ごろつきの一団. ¶A ***complete set*** of Walter Scott in French is now difficult to obtain. スコットの仏訳を全部そろえるのは今ではむずかしい. ¶He made a ***dead set*** (=determined attack) at me. 彼はやっきとなって僕に食ってかかった.【類】make a ***dead set*** against this practice (やり方). ¶an ***entire set*** 完全な一そろい. ¶a ***fast set*** 道楽仲間. ¶a ***fine set*** of china cups りっぱな一組の磁器茶わん ‖ a ***fine set*** of men そうそうたる連中. ¶a ***literary set*** 文学の仲間. ¶We are in the ***same set.*** われわれは同じ仲間だ. ¶of ***short*** and ***thick set*** ずんぐり(むっくり)した. ¶the ***smart set***《米》〖集合的〗[社交界の]しゃれ者.

Q² a ***burn-injury set*** やけど手当用備品. ¶a ***chemistry set*** [試験管など]化学実験用品. ¶a ***clock set*** 飾り時計のセット. ¶a ***desk set*** 文房具一そろい. ¶***Dial sets*** can be operated without a girl at the switchboard. 幾組もの数字盤が交換嬢をわずらわさずに運転することができる. ¶an ***emergency lighting set*** 非常用照明具一そろい. ¶a ***French Sevres set*** フランス・セーヴルの陶器一そろい. ¶a ***radio set*** and parts (=components) ラジオ受信機及び部分品. ¶a five-tube ***radio set*** 五球ラジオ受信機.【類】switch on one's ***radio set.*** ¶a ***razor set*** 顔そり用具一そろい. ¶a ***shaving set*** ひげそり用具一式. ¶a ***tête-à-tête set*** 二人前の食器一式. ¶a ***two-volume set*** 二巻もの(本). ¶a ***TV*** (=television) ***set*** テレビ受像機. ¶be equipped with ***wireless receiving set*** 無電受信機を備えてある. ¶a ***dinner set*** 一組の正さん用品.

P ***in sets*** of five 五つあて組んで.

P² After a ***set at*** tennis, a dip in this refreshing pool is delightful. テニスを一勝負やった後でこの清涼なプールに浸るのは気持がよい. ¶a ***set of*** buttons 一組のボタン ‖ a ***set of*** chairs (parlor furniture) 一組のいす(など).【類】three thousand ***sets of*** cavalry uniform / a ***set of*** silver cups (forks, spoons) ‖ a ***set of*** observations 連続的の観測 ‖ a ***set of*** hills 一連の小山 ‖ a ***set*** (=gang) ***of*** thieves (swindlers) 一団の盗賊(など) ‖ the ***set of*** public opinion 世論の動向 ‖ the ***set of*** the wind (a current) 風(など)の方向.

set, *v.* おく ; 当てがう ; 植える ; [時間などを]合わせる ; きめる ; 植字する ; [日が]没する ; 向う ; 取りかかる.

M ***set abroad*** [うわさ・病などを]伝染する. ¶***set afire*** 火をつける. ¶***set*** the building ***alight*** その建物を焼く. ¶***set apart*** some money 金を別にしておく ‖ ***set*** it ***apart*** for ... ...のためにそれを別にしておく.【類】***set*** a day ***apart*** (= aside) for Thanksgiving / the day is officially ***set apart*** for ... / A room is ***set apart*** for the purpose. ¶***set ashore*** [風・潮などが]陸へ方向を取る. ¶***set*** it ***aside***=disregard *or* lay it out of the question それを無視する ‖ ***set aside*** (= abrogate) a verdict〖法〗判決を破棄する ‖ I will ***set*** this ***aside*** for future use. 私はこれを取っておいて後で使おう.【類】***set aside*** part of one's income for ... / ***set aside*** a little for a rainy day ‖ ***set aside*** a claim 要求をしりぞける ‖ ***setting aside*** his own dissipation 自分の放らつはたなに上げて ‖ ***setting aside*** anything else=above all 何はさておき ‖ ***setting aside*** the question of expense, ... 経費の問題は別にして. ¶This ***set*** it ***back*** almost where it had started. これでそれが振り出しへ逆戻りした. ‖ be ***set back*** fully half a century in her program of ... その国の...の計画が丸半世紀遅れるようになる ‖ I saw that the houses were all ***set*** well ***back*** from the sidewalk. 家はみんな人道からずっと引込んでいた. ¶The tide ***set definitely*** in the opposite direction. 潮が明かに反対の方向に変った. ¶***set forth*** (=move, march, begin to march *or* advance) ... ...を進める ‖ ***set forth*** a program of improvement 改善計画を提示する ‖ ***set forth*** its aims その目的を述べる ‖ succinctly ***set forth*** 要約して述べる ‖ the conditions and terms ***set forth*** in your letter お手紙に書いてある条件.【類】as ***set forth*** herein / ***set forth*** a clear statement of ... / be fully ***set forth*** in a statement / ***set forth*** essential facts regarding ... / clearly ***set forth*** one's theory / ***set forth*** the facts / ***set forth*** the merit of ... / ***set forth*** one's stand clearly / ***set forth*** his argument of ... ‖ ***set*** it ***forth*** in detail それをくわしく述べる ‖ explicitly ***set forth*** the bases for one's reason's conclusions ... ...の理性の断定に対する根拠を明示する ‖ clear up many points once enigmatic or wrongly ***set forth*** 前に不可解だったあるいは説明を誤った多くの点を明かにする.【類】A constitution ***sets forth*** the powers and duties of the citizens of a nation. ¶***set forward*** clocks one hour 時計を一時間進める ‖ ***set forward*** [計画などを]進行させる. ¶The prisoners were ***set free.*** 捕虜は釈放された. ‖ they were ***set free*** from the thraldom of ... 彼は...の束縛から解放された. ¶The rainy season ***generally sets*** in about the middle of June. 雨季は大抵六月中旬ごろ始まる. ¶***set*** one ***home*** 人をその宅に送り届ける. ¶***set*** a dog ***loose*** 犬を放してやる. ¶***set out*** for home 家路につく ‖ ***set out*** in business 仕事を始める ‖ ***set out*** in the world 世の中へ出る.【類】***set out*** in search of it ‖ emigrants ***setting out*** on new careers 運命開拓に向う移民たち ‖ ***set out*** on one's travels (pleasure excursion) 旅(など)に出る.【類】***set out*** on the expedition against ... / ***set out*** upon a voyage ‖ a Japanese ***setting out*** to learn Russian ロシア語の研究を始める日本人 ‖ The tide ***sets out*** at 4 p.m. 潮は午後四時に退く. ‖ ***set out*** northward 北地へ押かける ‖ ***set out*** to show that ... 進んで...のことを示す ‖ ***set out*** thirty men-of-war in case of emergency 非常の際には三十隻の軍艦を派遣する ‖ When a woman ***sets out*** to be cruel, she beats the record. 女が残酷なことをやり出すととんでもないことをやる. ‖ ***set out*** the flags of ... ...の旗を掲げる. ‖ The parlor is ***set out*** with pictures. 客間は絵画で飾ってある. ‖ ***set out*** one's complaint 苦情を並べ立てる ‖ ***set out*** plants 植物を植える ‖ the functions ***set out*** in this article 本条に定めた職能 ‖ ***set out*** requirements 必要条件を指示する. ¶Plaster of Paris ***sets quickly.*** 石こう粉はじきに固まる. ¶***set*** oneself ***resolutely*** to the task of ... 堅い決心で...の仕事にかかる. ¶I can soon ***set*** that ***right***! 私が直ちにいいようにしてやる. ¶***set*** things ***straight*** 物のきまりをつける. ¶This ***set*** me ***wide*** of the truth. このために私は飛んでもない見当違いをした.

M² ***set*** a burden ***down*** 荷物を降ろす ‖ ***Set*** me ***down*** at the station. 私をその駅で降ろしてくれ. ‖ ***set*** it ***down*** in one's diary precisely as it occurred 起った通り正確にそれを日記に記す ‖ There is something that I want to ***set down*** in words. 書きつけておきたいと思うことがある.【類】***set*** them ***down*** in a list (表に作る) / notes ***set down*** for remembrance (reference) / ***set down*** the generalization of ... ‖ ***set*** a person ***down*** as a liar (dunce) 人をうそつき(のろま)ときめつける ‖ I ***set*** it ***down*** as an impossibility. 私はそれを不可能と考える. ‖ ***set down*** one's success to luck その成功を幸運に帰する ‖ I was obliged to ***set*** him ***down.*** 私はやむを得ず彼をへこましてやった. ‖ ***set*** (=put) it ***down*** in cold black and white それを冷静な文字で表現する. ¶The rainy season is now ***set in.*** 雨季になった. ‖ The tide ***sets in*** (=moves towards the shore) 潮が差して来る.【類】A reaction has ***set in.*** / The hot (bad) weather has now ***set in.*** / Great heat now ***sets in*** here. / Drought appears to have ***set in.*** / Winter ***sets in*** about December in England. ‖ Ice is ***setting in*** fast. 氷がずんずん張っている.【類】before ice ***sets in*** ‖ A most decidedly peaceful tone has *set* ***in***. きわめてはっきりと平和的な雰囲気がかもし出された. ¶*set* ***off*** for home 家路につく ‖ He *set* ***off*** to Paris. 彼はパリへ立った. 【類】He *set* ***off*** on his travels. / *set* ***off*** for a trip / *set* ***off*** for a holiday at ... ‖ She does not need finery to *set* her ***off***. 彼女は(そのままで美しいから)美装をする必要がない. 【類】The frame (額) *sets* ***off*** (引き立てる) the picture. / *set* it ***off*** to advantage (有利に) / delightfully (美事に) *set* it ***off*** / *set* it ***off*** by contrast / Her dress *set* herself ***off*** to the best advantage / *set* him ***off*** from others ‖ If uncontrolled, the shortage would *set* ***off*** a new upsurge in meat prices. 統制を加えないと品不足のため肉価の暴騰を来すだろう. ‖ *set* a room ***off*** with colored tapes and flags 色テープや旗で室を飾り立てる ‖ be *set* ***off*** by a comma コンマで区切られる ‖ *set* it ***off*** against ... [記入済の項]と向い合わせに記入して相殺または差引する ‖ An atomic bomb was *set* ***off*** over Hiroshima. 原爆が広島の上空で爆発した. 【類】The ship exploded and *set* ***off*** a chain of explosions. / His landing *set* ***off*** a nation-wide demonstration. ‖ *set* ***off*** with a furious rush すごい勢いでかけ出す ‖ *set* ***off*** a clause by a comma カンマで区切る. ¶*set* another ***on*** to commit a crime 人に罪を犯させる ‖ *set* a dog ***on*** 犬をけしかける. ¶*set* ***over*** one's property to his creditors 債権者にその財産を引渡す. ¶*set* ***up*** a building (post, wall, school, factory) 建物(など)を造る ‖ *set* ***up*** (=erect) a bronze statue 銅像を立てる ‖ *set* ***up*** (=establish) a monarchy 君主国を建設する ‖ *set* ***up*** a standard 標準を立てる ‖ *set* ***up*** a steam-engine 蒸気機関を組立てる ‖ He has *set* ***up*** a new business. 彼は新らしい商売を始めた. ‖ *set* ***up*** a plant 植物を植える ‖ *set* ***up*** one's easel [画家が]画架を立てる. 【類】*set* ***up*** a tent ‖ *set* ***up*** machines in their places 機械をそれぞれの場所に据えつける. 【類】*set* ***up*** a monument to the memory of ... / *set* ***up*** a notice (signal) ‖ *set* ***up*** a program 番組を作製する ‖ *set* ***up*** a scarecrow かかしを立てる ‖ *set* ***up*** a stand on a street and call on passers-by to sign petitions 路上に台を据えて通行人に対し請願書に署名を求める ‖ *set* ***up*** a new theory 新説をたてる. 【類】*set* ***up*** rules / *set* ***up*** regulations to be followed by ... / *set* ***up*** a new economic order (経済新秩序) in East Asia ‖ *set* ***up*** a home 世帯を持つ. 【類】*set* ***up*** a simple home / *set* ***up*** a new home there ‖ *set* ***up*** a quota for ... ...に対する割当てをきめる ‖ *set* ***up*** a false claim 虚偽の要求を提起する ‖ *set* ***up*** a train of evils 悪いことを続けて起す ‖ A Latin inscription was *set* ***up*** on the tablet. ラテン語の銘がその記念板に彫りつけられた. ‖ *set* ***up*** machinery to carry out the program. その計画実行のために機構を設ける. 【類】*set* ***up*** the machinery to guard the world against the atomic bomb ‖ *set* ***up*** a small bookshop 小さい本屋の店を出す. 【類】*set* ***up*** a school / *set* ***up*** classes for ... / *set* ***up*** a National Science Foundation (国民科学財団) / The Security Council *set* ***up*** a shop at New York's Hunter College. ‖ *set* ***up*** a distinction between ... ...の間の区別をつける ‖ *set* ***up*** a government-sponsored corporation 政府後援の公団を創立する. 【類】*set* ***up*** a provisional government (仮政府) / *set* ***up*** a puppet government in Peiping / *set* ***up*** a democratic regime / *set* ***up*** a monarchy (君主国) / *set* ***up*** a strong government in New China / *set* ***up*** a new national state / *set* ***up*** a weak buffer state (緩衝国) / *set* ***up*** headquarters (military command) / *set* ***up*** an Institute of Industrial Administration (産業行政研究所) / *set* ***up*** a national control of electric power / *set* ***up*** an office in the Department of Agriculture / *set* ***up*** one's office in one of the rooms in the building / *set* ***up*** an international organization to maintain peace / *set* ***up*** a commission composed of ... / *set* ***up*** a special committee / *set* ***up*** an international tribunal (国際裁判所) to try Japanese war criminals / *set* ***up*** a policy board or group at high Government level / *set* ***up*** a fund / *set* ***up*** a standard of excellence / *set* ***up*** friendly relations with ... / a new telegraph line has been *set* ***up*** from ... to ... / *set* ***up*** (=start) a vicious circle of price and wage (物価と賃金の悪循環) ‖ *set* ***up*** a cry for home rule 自治を唱道する ‖ *set* ***up*** inflammation on the wound 傷の炎症を起す ‖ cannot be *set* ***up*** against ... ...に対抗することは出来ない ‖ once the habit is *set* ***up*** 一度その癖がつくと ‖ *set* ***up*** for oneself [卒業生など]独り立ちになる ‖ *set* oneself ***up*** on one's own legs 一本立になる. 【類】*set* oneself ***up*** as a judge (merchant, lawyer) / *set* oneself ***up*** in life / He wishes to *set* himself ***up*** in business all for himself. ‖ The university *set* itself ***up*** there after moving from Peking. その大学は北京から移転後その地で開校した. ‖ *set* ***up*** for a gentleman 紳士を気取る ‖ He *sets* ***up*** for a man of wits. あの人は機知のある人のような風をする. ‖ *set* ***up*** a shout (clamor) わめき立てる ‖ *set* ***up*** a terrific howl 恐ろしくどなり立てる. 【類】*set* ***up*** a loud cry / *set* ***up*** a laugh (roar) / *set* ***up*** a claim / *set* ***up*** an opposition to ... ‖ *Set* her (him, you) ***up***! えらいよ(見栄を張る人をなぶる言葉). ‖ This fine air quite *sets* me ***up***. ここの空気がすてきなので私は元気がつく. ‖ The wheels immediately *set* ***up*** a tremendous creaking. 車輪が直ちにすさまじくきーきー音を立てて回転を始めた. ‖ be *set* ***up*** for auction 競売にかけられる ‖ *set* ***up*** a page of copy 一ページの原稿を版に組む ‖ *set* it ***up*** in type それを活字に組む. 【類】The manuscripts are already *set* ***up***. ‖ Although he did not *set* ***up*** as a poet he was one. 彼は詩人振らなかったが詩人であったのだ. ‖ *set* him ***up*** for a new business 新商売の資金を融通してやる. ‖ *set* a person ***up*** in business 店(など)を出してやる.

P *set* ***about*** stamp-collecting 郵便切手の収集を始める ‖ *set* ***about*** one's work (an active canvass, writing) 仕事(など)を始める. 【類】He asked me how he should *set* ***about*** learning the German language. ‖ *set* ***about*** the study of mineralogy (鉱物学). ¶*set* one ***across*** the river 人を川向うへ渡す. ¶*set* it ***against*** the wall 壁にそれを立掛ける ‖ *set* a friend ***against*** another 一友人に他の友人を悪く思わせるように持ちかける ‖ be *set* over ***against*** ... ...と対抗させる ‖ He *set* his face ***against*** the scheme from the first. 彼は始めからその計画に反対した. 【類】He (=His mind) is *set* ***against*** all reforms. ‖ ***against*** these gains must be *set* the loss of ... これらの利益に対して一方...の損失を考慮しなければならない ‖ England can *set* no native-born dancer ***against*** ... 英国には...に匹敵する本国生れのダンサーがいない. ¶*set* it ***as*** one's goal ... ...をその目標とする ‖ a jewel worthy to be *set* ***as*** a solitaire [演芸家など]一本立の出来る者. ¶*set* ***at*** defiance the civilization and culture of the present day 今日の文明文化を無視する ‖ *set* one's mind ***at*** ease (=rest) 心を安んじる ‖ *set* a guard ***at*** the gate 門に番人を置く ‖ *set* a war prisoner ***at*** liberty 戦犯を釈放する ‖ *set* a person ***at*** defiance 人を眼中におかない ‖ *set him* ***at*** his ease 彼をくつろがせる ‖ *set* ... ***at*** nought ...を眼中に置かない ‖ *set* the alarm hand ***at*** the time one wants it to ring 目ざまし時計の針を所要の時間に掛ける ‖ *set* a person ***at*** odds with another 甲と乙を争わせる. 【類】He *set* them ***at*** variance. ‖ *set* the public opinion ***at*** defiance 世論を無視する ‖ *set* the death of ... ***at*** 1796 ...の死を一七九六年と断定する. ¶*set* food ***before*** a guest 客に食物を出す ‖ the object he has *set* ***before*** himself 彼が目指した目的 ‖ *set* ***before*** him as his task ... 彼の仕事として彼に...を当てがう. ¶The sun *sets* ***behind*** the western range of mountains. 日が西山に傾く. ¶can be *set* ***beside*** ... ...と並べおくことが出来る. ¶*set* one's watch ***by*** another clock (a railroad station clock) その懐中時計を別の時計(など)に合わせる. 【類】*set* one's watch ***by*** the radio time signal ‖ *set* other nations ***by*** the ears 他国民を不和にさせる ‖ *set* all Europe ***by*** the ears 全欧州の耳目をしょう動する ‖ the standard *set* ***by*** law 法令により定めた標準 ‖ be *set* ***by*** monotype 〖印刷〗モノタイプで組版される. ¶*set* a time ***for*** a meeting 会合の時間を極める ‖ The vote was *set* ***for*** today. きょう票決を行うことになった. ‖ His departure is *set* ***for*** May 2. 彼の出発は五月二日ときまった. ‖ on the date *set* ***for*** the examination 試験に当てた日に. ¶*set* them ***in*** line それを一列に並べる ‖ *set* a room ***in*** order 室を整とんする ‖ A pageant and a mass meeting *set* London ***in*** a ferment. 戸外劇や大会でロンドンが沸き返るようになっていた. ‖ a ruby *set* ***in*** a gold 金の指輪にはめたルビー ‖ *set* a machine ***in*** motion 器械を運転する. 【類】A very large part of the machinery of the Russian government had to be *set* ***in*** motion. ‖ *set* foot ***in*** a native city 本国人の町に足を踏み入れる ‖ *set* a person in the dock 人をその上に置く(批判する) ‖ be *set* ***in*** type 〖印刷〗活字に組まれる. ¶*set* it ***into*** motion again 再びそれを運転させる ‖ a stir as of a heavy body being *set* ***into*** motion 重い物体が動き出すような気配(大男が起きあがる時の形容) ‖ sparks that *set* ***into*** a flame the smouldering insensate fury which lurks in every human heart すべての人の心中に潜在する残忍な狂暴性を爆発させた火花. ¶Her question *set* him ***off*** thinking. 彼女に質問されたので彼は考えを中止した. ¶*set* one brick ***on*** another れんがを積み重ねる ‖ *set* one ***on*** one's guard 人に警戒させる ‖ *set* a dish ***on*** the table 食卓の上にさらを置く ‖ I never *set* eyes ***on*** his like. 私はあんな人間を見たことがない. ‖ *set* one's heart ***on*** going abroad 洋行することにはらをきめる ‖ *set* a house ***on*** a rock 岩石の上に家を建てる ‖ He has *set* ***on*** foot a new scheme. 彼は新計画に着手した. ‖ *set* a house ***on*** fire 家に火をつける ‖ *set* the river ***on*** fire 驚天動地の業を成しとげる. 【類】The vessel was *set* ***on*** fire before being left. / The building was *set* ***on*** fire. ‖ *set* a trunk ***on*** its end トランクを立てておく ‖ *set* him ***on*** his feet again 再び彼の地位を安定させる ‖ an inquiry being *set* ***on*** foot, it was discovered that ... 調査に着手したら…ということが分かった. 【類】A subscription was *set* ***on*** foot. ‖ The sun never *sets* ***on*** the British dominions. 太陽は決して英国の領土に没しない. 【類】Englishmen have a proud phrase that the sun never *sets* ***on*** their empire. / The sun never *sets* ***on*** the N.Y.K. flag. / The sun never *sets* ***on*** American soil. / The saying, "The sun never *sets* ***on*** the empire," was at first used not in reference to England, but to Spain. ¶*set* ***out of*** adjustment その調節を狂わす. ¶*set* a person ***over*** others ある人を他の人々の上位に置く, 長にする ‖ The sun *set* ***over*** the sea. 太陽が海上に没した. ‖ officers *set* ***over*** me 私の上官たち. ¶*set* seriously ***to*** work on one's studies 研究にまじめに取掛かる. 【類】*set* ***to*** work in earnest / *set* oneself ***to*** the task of ... / *set* a person ***to*** work. ‖ *set* a bugle ***to*** one's lips らっぱを口に当てる ‖ *set* the clock ***to*** the proper hour of day 時計を正しい時間に合わせる ‖ *set* a child ***to*** crying 子供を泣かせる ‖ There was a hint in his talk which *set* me ***to*** thinking. 彼の話には私を考えさせる一つの暗示があった. ‖ *set* a pen ***to*** paper ペンを紙に当てて書く ‖ *set* a fire ***to*** a house 家に放火する ‖ *set* spurs ***to*** a horse 馬に拍車を当てる ‖ be *set* to music 作曲される. 【類】It was *set* ***to*** music by an American composer. ‖ This hymn is *set* ***to*** the tune of "Kimigayo." その賛美歌は君が代に合わせてある. ‖ Two powerful hydrants were *set* ***to*** work. 強力な消火せんを二つ使った(火災の時など). ‖ The tide *sets* ***to*** the west. 潮が西に流れる. ‖ *set* ***to*** work in real earnest 真剣になって仕事に掛る ‖ *set* things ***to*** rights 物事を片づける(きちんとする). ¶*set* one's face ***toward*** the East 東方に顔を向ける. ¶eggs *set* ***under*** hens めんどりにだかせた卵. ¶*set* a boy ***upon*** the back of a camel 男の子をらくだの背に乗せる. ¶a room *set* ***with*** tables and chairs 食卓といすを備え付けたへや ‖ the land *set* ***with*** beans 豆を植える畑地 ‖ an 18 carat gold ring *set* ***with*** two fine diamonds 二個のりっぱなダイヤモンドをはめた十八金の指輪. 【類】a ring *set* ***with*** rubies / a valuable ornament *set* ***with*** precious stones.

set-aside, *n.* 貯蔵.

Q² ***government*** *set-asides* of food 政府保有食糧.

setback, *n.* つまずき.

V the movement ***received*** a serious *setback* when ... その運動は…で大打撃をこうむった. ¶***suffer*** a *setback* 障害を受ける, つまずく.

P a *setback* ***in*** trade 商売のつまずき.

set-off, *n.* 〚商〛差引き.

P ***as*** a *set-off* against ... …の差引勘定として.

setter, *n.* 調節器; 〚印刷〛植字工; セッター種の猟犬.

Q an ***Irish*** *setter* アイルランド・セッター(くり毛の犬).

Q² an ***anti-aircraft fuse*** *setter* 高射砲弾信管調節器. ¶a ***sword*** *setter* 刀剣とぎ師.

P² a *setter* ***of*** type＝a type setter 植字工.

setting, *n.* 背景(セット); 台, 台座; 四囲.

V ***choose*** appropriate *settings* in time and place [短編小説などで]時と場所の適当な背景を選ぶ. ¶Orchids or other rare and expensive flowers ***have*** a most appropriate *setting* in a silver receptacle. 蘭やその他高価で珍奇な花は銀の容器がきわめてふさわしい.

Q the ***geographic*** *setting* of Japan 日本の地理的環境. ¶the ***natural*** *setting* 自然の環境.

Q² a diamond encrusted ***platinum*** *setting* ダイヤモンドをちりばめた白金台. ¶***stage*** *setting* 舞台のセット.

P with the lake ***as*** its *setting* 湖水をその背景として. ¶a residence with the pretty garden ***for*** a *setting* 背景に美しい庭園のある邸宅. ¶a diamond ***in*** a gold *setting* 金台のダイヤモンド ‖ a vale ***in*** its *setting* of mountains 四方山に囲まれている谷.

P² the *setting* ***of*** a saw のこぎりの目立て ‖ the *setting* ***of*** a radio (TV) show 放送劇のセット.

settle, *v.* 据える; 植民する; 取決める; よどむ; 身を落着ける; 勘定をつける.

M The dispute was ***amicably*** *settled*. その係争は示談で済んだ. 【類】An apology on his part *settled* the quarrel ***amicably***. / I intervened between the two parties to *settle* the matter ***amicably***. ¶***comfortably*** *settled* 気持よく腰をおろして. ¶It has not yet ***definitely*** *settled*. それはまだ未確定だ. ¶the question is ***finally*** *settled* その問題はいよいよ解決された. ¶be ***irrevocably*** *settled* 最後的に解決を見る. ¶a question which has ***never*** been *settled* 未解決に終った問題. ¶*settle* a dispute ***peacefully*** 紛争を穏かに解決する. ¶*settle* ***positively*** the existence or nonexistence of ... …の実在いかんを確定する. ¶have the matter *settled* ***privately*** そのことを内済にしてもらう. ¶***satisfactorily*** *settle* a matter 事件を満足に解決する. ¶It will be *settled* ***somehow***. どうにか収まるだろう. ¶He had to *settle* his abode ***somewhere***. 彼はどこかに住所を定めなければならなかった. ¶***sparsely*** *settled* regions 人煙まれな地方. ¶The matter is ***unalterably*** *settled*. その事件はきっぱり解決した. ¶*settle* ***decisively***＝clinch きっぱり片をつける.

M² *settle* oneself ***down*** in an armchair ひじ掛けいすに腰をおろす ‖ Darkness *settled* ***down***. やみがあたりを包んだ. ‖ Night was *settling* ***down*** when we neared our journey's end. われわれが行先に近づいた時はあたりが暗くなりかかっていた. ‖ *settle* ***down*** to dinner 晩さんにつく ‖ *settle* ***down*** in a little cottage at ... …にある小さないなかの家に居を占める ‖ *settle* ***down*** to married life (a life of study) 結婚生活(など)に着く ‖ *settle* ***down*** to farming (literature) 農業(など)に身を固める ‖ *settle* ***down*** to a bachelor life 独身生活を送ることに決める. 【類】*settle* ***down*** to the job of ... / *settle* ***down*** very happily to life in Japan / *settle* ***down*** to a new career / Let's *settle* ***down*** to our studies. / *settle* ***down*** to their normal routine (いつもの仕事) / *settle* ***down*** to the enjoyment of a weekly paper / *settle* ***down*** to steady work at ... / opinion *settled* ***down*** to the conclusion that ... / when the market *settles* ***down*** / The panic is *settling* ***down***. ¶*settle* ***in*** for the night ゆっくり一晩おちつく. ¶*settle* (＝pay) ***off*** one's old score 古い勘定を済ませる; 復しゅうする. ¶*settle* ***up*** a dispute (quarrel) 係争(けんか)を解決する. 【類】We have to get it *settled* ***up***.

P They have *settled* the matter ***among*** themselves. 彼ら同士でその事件を解決した. ¶*settle* ***at*** the bottom 底によどむ ‖ *settle* ***at*** the town of ... …の町に定住する. ¶We have *settled* the matter ***between*** ourselves. われわれ両人で事件を解決した. ¶*settle* a controversy ***by*** mutual concession (＝compromise) 譲り合って争論を解決する ‖ *settle* a daughter ***by*** marriage 結婚で娘の身を固めさせる ‖ the first town *settled* ***by*** the English in North America 英国が北米に植民した最初の都市 ‖ be *settled* ***by*** lot くじできめられる. 【類】This is the sort of problem which might well be *settled* ***by*** plebiscites (人民投票). ¶*settle* oneself ***for*** a nap 腰を下ろして昼寝をする ‖ Will you *settle* ***for*** me? 私の勘定を払ってくれないか. ¶He *settled* ***in*** America. 彼はアメリカに定住した. ‖ *settle* oneself ***in*** an armchair ひじ掛けいすに腰をおろす ‖ *settle* ***in*** distant lands 遠隔の地に移転する. 【類】*settle* ***in*** a new house / *settle* a clergyman ***in*** a parish / *settle* a young man ***in*** a trade ‖ *settle* a thing ***in*** one's heart あることを心に銘記する ‖ *settle* one's feet ***in*** the stirrups あぶみに足を入れる. ¶*settled* her ***into*** a comfortable chair under the trees 木陰の居心地のいいいすに彼女を落着かせた ‖ The great city had ceased its busy murmuring and *settled* ***into*** sleep. 大都市はその気ぜわしいざわめきもやんで静まり返ってしまった. ‖ Things will soon *settle* ***into*** shape. 万事間もなく片がつくだろう. ‖ The wind *settled* ***into*** the northwest. 風が北東になった. ‖ The matter has been *settled* ***to*** the unspeakable relief of everybody. そのことが解決したのでみなのものがほっとした. ¶*settle* ***into*** silence 静まる. ¶*settle* oneself ***on*** a seat 座席にすわりこむ ‖ Do not *settle* ***on*** terms proposed as they are not suitable. 提出条件が適当でないから譲歩するな. ‖ What have you *settled* ***on***? 君はどういう条件できめたか. ‖ Silence *settled* ***on*** the lone wood. 静じゃくがうらさびしい森にただよっていた. ¶*settle* it ***out of*** court それを示談にする. ¶*settle* a child ***to*** his sleep 子供を眠らせる ‖ She *settled* herself ***to*** her work. 彼女は落着いて仕事をした. 【類】*settle* ***to*** work again after interruption ‖ *settle* ***to*** the bottom 底によどむ ‖ I could *settle* ***to*** nothing. 私は仕事に少しも手がつかなかった. ¶*settle* the matter ***upon*** a sound basis そのことを確固たる基礎の上に置く ‖ *settle* ***upon*** a plan 方法を決定する ‖ Gloom *settled* ***upon*** my heart. 私は暗い気持になった. 【類】Despair *settled* ***upon*** his heart. ¶*settle* ***with*** creditors 債権者と話をつける ‖ Upon the maturity of the debt he was unable to *settle* ***with*** the bank. 彼は債務の満期日について銀行と話合がつかなかった. 【類】Didn't I tell you this morning that I should *settle* ***with*** you for your bad behavior?

O *settle* who plays who 役割をきめる. ¶Britishers *settled* New England. 英人がニューイングランドに植民した.

settlement, *n.* 居留地; 解決; 決算.

V A *settlement* has been ***arrived at*** without friction. 円満に解決した. ¶***bring about*** a satisfactory *settlement* 満足な解決をもたらす. ¶***defer*** the *settlement* of ... ...の解決を遅らせる.

¶***effect*** a *settlement* out of court 示談にする. ¶***establish*** a *settlement* on a communistic basis 共産主義の原則に基いて植民地を建設する. ¶***obtain*** a *settlement* of a claim クレームの問題が解決する. ¶***plant*** a *settlement* 植民地を建設する. ¶Hitler expected to ***precipitate*** the *settlement* of Danzig issues. ヒットラーはダンチッヒ係争問題解決の促進を期待した. ¶A *settlement* was ***reached***. 解決がついた. ¶take proper steps to ***secure*** a satisfactory *settlement* of the affair その事件を満足に解決するために適当な手段を取る.

Q arrive at (=come to *or* reach) an ***amiable*** *settlement* 平和的解決に達する. ¶the ***foreign*** *settlement* 外人居留地(租界). ¶arrive at an ***honorable*** *settlement* of a question 問題のりっぱな解決に到達する. ¶work out a ***just*** *settlment* of the affair その事件の公正な解決をつける. ¶an ***international*** *settlement* 居留地. ¶In general, a ***minor's*** *settlement* is that of his parent. 一般から言えば未成年者の住所は親の所にある. ¶***pacific*** *settlement* of international disputes 国際紛争の平和的解決. ¶effect a ***peaceful*** *settlement* on ... ...の穏便な解決をつける. 【類】submit all international disputes to ***peaceful*** *settlement* ‖ For many years the Bonin Islands served as a Japanese ***penal*** *settlement*. 小笠原諸島は長い間日本の罪人流刑の地となっていた. ¶be compelled to insist on prompt ***monthly*** *settlements* in order to meet our own obligations 当方の債務を弁済するために月々敏速に支払を受ける方針を固持しなければならない. ¶***prompt*** *settlement* of bills 手形の敏速な決済. ¶It was brought to a ***satisfactory*** *settlement*. それは満足に落着した. ¶At the end of the sixteenth century England was not possessed of a ***single foreign*** *settlement*. 十六世紀の終には英国は海外植民地を一つも持っていなかった. ¶one of the most momentous ***political*** *settlements* of our times 現代の最も重要な政治的解決の一つ(インドの独立など). ¶a ***speedy*** *settlement* 早急解決.

Q^{2} ***boundary*** *settlement* 境界決定. ¶a ***compromise*** *settlement* 和解. ¶a ***convict*** *settlement* 囚徒植民地. ¶a ***dependent housing*** *settlement* [駐留軍]家族住宅区域. ¶***grievance*** *settlement* 紛争(苦情)解決. ¶***lend-lease*** *settlements* 《米》武器貸与取決め. ¶a ***peace*** *settlement* for Japan 対日平和解決. ¶a ***reparation*** *settlement* 賠償解決. 【類】the final ***reparations*** *settlement*. ¶Singapore, the capital of the ***Straits Settlements*** 海峡植民地の首府シンガポール. ¶a ***white*** *settlement* 白人居留地.

P land left ***for*** *settlement* 居住所として残された土地. ¶***In*** *settlement* of your account please pay a sum of 200 yen against the receipt presented by the bearer. 貴殿の勘定決済として持参人の提出する領収証に対して金二百円也を御支払下さい.

P^{2} the *settlement* ***after*** the war 戦後の整理. ¶penal *settlements* ***for*** convicts sentenced to hard labor 懲役人の流刑地. ¶a *settlement* ***in*** the woods 森林地の部落. ¶*settlement* ***of*** a dispute 紛争解決. 【類】the *settlement* ***of*** the matter / a peaceful *settlement* ***of*** a question ‖ the *settlement* ***of*** a new country 新開地の植民.

settler, *n.* 移民.

V The *settlers* were soon ***acclimated***. 移民はほどなく風土に慣れた. ¶***plant*** *settlers* on ... ...に住民を移植する.

P^{2} English *settlers* ***in*** America アメリカにおける英国の移民. 【類】the early *settlers* ***in*** New England.

setup, *n.* 《米》機構, 態勢.

V ***readjust*** today's financial *setup* 金融の現制度を再編する.

Q the ***economic*** *setup* of our national life 国民の経済状態. ¶a ***new*** *setup* regarding the housing problem 住宅問題に関する新機構. ¶Much the ***same*** *setup* exists in Arab areas. 大体これと同じ態勢がアラビア人居住地域にもある.

Q^{2} revamp Japan's ***school*** *setup* 日本の学校制度を改正する.

sever, *v.* 引離す; 切断する; 弁別する.

P *sever* one's head ***from*** his body 頭を胴体から切断する ‖ *sever* wife ***from*** husband 妻を夫から引離す. 【類】*sever* the good ***from*** the bad. ¶The church was *severed* ***into*** two great divisions. 教会は二大派に分かれた. 【類】a party *severed* ***into*** several factions (数派). ¶*sever* one's connection ***with*** it それと関係を絶つ.

several, *n.* 数人, 数個.

P^{2} I have heard it ***from*** *several*. 私はそれを二三の人から聞いた.

P^{2} *Several* ***of*** us know about it. 私たちの中でいく人もそれを知っている.

severance, *n.* 切断.

P^{2} the *severance* ***of*** relations 関係の断絶.

severe, *a.* きびしい; 厳粛な.

M No punishment is ***too*** *severe* for his crime. 彼の罪はいかなる厳罰をもってするも重過ぎるということはない.

P We must not be too *severe* ***against*** him. われわれは彼に対してきびし過ぎてはならない. ¶*severe* ***in*** countenance 顔付のいかめしい ‖ *severe* ***in*** criticism (judgment) 批評(など)のきびしい ‖ He is *severe* ***on*** (=***upon***) his enemies. 彼は敵にはきびしい. ¶He is *severe* ***with*** his children (students). 彼は子供(など)にはやかましい.

severity, *n.* 厳格, 厳重; 苛酷.

V ***mitigate*** its *severity* and hasten convalescence その(病気など)劇烈さを緩和して健康回復を促進する. ¶***taste*** the *severity* of the law 法の制裁を受ける.

Q^{2} The frost continues with ***increased*** *severity*. 寒気がますますきびしくなる. ¶With all the ***outward*** *severity* he is kind at heart. 彼はうわべはとても厳格だが内心はやさしい. ¶train pupils with ***relentless*** *severity* かしゃくせずきびしく生徒を訓練する. ¶with ***rigorous*** *severity* 厳格に, 苛酷に. ¶He spoke with ***utmost*** *severity*. 彼はきわめて激しい口調で言った.

P denounce a person ***with*** some *severity* 人を相当手痛く非難する.

P^{2} *severity* ***of*** an accident 災害強度率.

sew, *v.* 縫う; 縫いつける.

M *sew* ***well*** うまく縫う. ¶*sew* two pieces ***together*** 二枚の布を縫合わせる.

M^{2} *sew* ***in*** a band バンドを縫いつける. ¶*sew* ***on*** a button that has come off とれたボタンを縫いつける. ¶*sew* ***up*** a rip (wound) ほころび(など)を縫う. 【類】*sew* ***up*** a hole in one's coat.

P *sew* it ***by*** hand それを手で縫う. ¶*sew* money ***into*** one's belt 金を帯に縫い込む. ¶A plaited strip is *sewed* ***to*** the skirt of the dress. 編んだひもが着物のすそに縫いつけてある. ¶*sew* ***with*** a needle and thread 針と糸で縫う. 【類】*sew* it ***with*** a machine (ミシン).

sewer, *n.* 下水みぞ.

V ***sluice*** a *sewer* 下水みぞを放出する.

Q an ***egg-shaped*** *sewer* 卵形下水渠(きょ).

sewing, *n.* 縫物.

V ***do*** some *sewings* なにか縫物をする. ¶***gather up*** her *sewing* 縫物をよせ集める. ¶***learn*** (=take lessons in) *sewing* 縫物のけい古をする.

Q the ***final*** *sewing* 本縫.

sewing machine, ミシン.

V how to ***handle*** a *sewing machine* ミシンの扱い方.

V^{2} The *sewing machine* is ***buzzing*** (=***humming***). ミシンがかたかた動いている.

Q² a ***treadle** **sewing machine*** 足踏みミシン.
P stitch a curtain ***on*** the ***sewing machine*** ミシンでカーテンを縫いとりする.

sex, *n.* 性.
V ***attribute*** *sex* to stones of different form 形によって石に陰陽の性を配する. ¶***betray*** one's *sex* その性を見破られる(男装の女など). ¶***disregarding*** (=without regard to) age and *sex* 老若男女を論ぜず. ¶frankly ***discuss*** *sex* あけすけに性の問題を論じる. ¶She ***disguised*** her true *sex* under a man's garment. 彼女は男装をして女ということを隠していた.
Q persons of ***both*** *sexes* 男女とも. ¶persons of ***different*** *sex* 男女. ¶members of ***either*** *sex* 男女いずれかの会員. ¶the ***fair***[***er*** (=***gentle***[***r***], ***soft***[***er***], *or* ***weak***[***er***]) *sex* 女. ¶persons (children) of ***female*** *sex* 女(女児). ¶There are 2,000 members, of whom 500 are of the ***gentler*** *sex*. 会員二千名あるがその中五百名は婦人である. ¶the ***male*** (=***rougher***, ***stronger*** *or* ***sterner***) *sex* 男性. ¶an illicit intimacy between persons of ***opposite*** *sexes* 私通. ¶of the ***other*** *sex* 異性の. ¶a co-worker with the ***sterner*** *sex* 男子とともに働く女. ¶the ***trousered*** *sex* 男性.
P a school ***for*** both *sexes* 男女共学の学校. ¶without distinction ***of*** *sex* 男女の区別なく ‖ the equality ***of*** the *sexes* 男女の平等. ¶objects ***without*** *sex* 無性物.

shabby, *a.* 貧弱な, みすぼらしい.
O a boy who looks *shabby*=a shabby-looking boy みすぼらしい少年.

shack, *n.* 《米》小屋.
Q² a ***tin-plate*** *shack* トタン張りのバラック. ¶a ***mountain*** (***beach***) *shack* 山小屋(海の家).

shackle, *n.* かせ; 束縛, きずな.
V ***break down*** *shackles* きずなを断つ. ¶***throw off*** the *shackles* of that slavery その苦役の束縛を脱する.
P² *shackles* ***for*** the legs 足かせ ‖ the *shackles* ***of*** convention 因襲の束縛. 【類】the *shackles* ***of*** habit (debt).

shackle, *v.* かせをはめる.
M emancipate them from the bonds in which they have ***long*** been *shackled* 永い間のきずなから彼らを解放する.

shade, *n.* かげ; 《米》日除け; 色合; 幽魂.
V The shadows of trees ***afford*** welcome *shade*. 木かげで気持のよい日陰ができる. ¶It ***has*** several *shades* of meaning. それには少しずつ違った色々の意味がある. ¶The maple tree ***makes*** *shade*. そのかえでの木で日陰ができる. ¶The road ***offered*** little *shade*. 道路には余り日かげがなかった. ¶***pull up*** (***down***) the *shade* [店頭の]日よけを上げる(下げる). ¶***seek*** the *shade* of the park 公園の日陰に行く. ¶***throw*** a thin *shade* on ... …に薄い陰を投げる.
V² The *shades* ***dispersed away***. 夜が明けた. ¶The *shades* of night were ***falling*** fast. 夜陰はひしひしと迫って来た. ¶The *shade* does not ***match***. 色が合っていない[封筒と用紙など].
Q Our party consists of men of ***all*** *shades* of political belief. われわれの党派はそれぞれ政見の違った人から成っている. ¶under the ***cool*** *shade* of the trees 涼しい木陰で. ¶There are ***countless*** *shades* of color. 色合は無限にある. ¶a ***dark*** *shade* of blue 濃青色 ‖ the ***dark*** *shade* of brown こげ茶. ¶a ***deep*** *shade* 濃色. ¶***delicate*** *shades* of meaning 微妙な意味の相違. ¶the ***different*** *shades* of meaning 色々違った意味合い ‖ others of a ***different*** *shade* of political opinion 政見を異にする他の人々. ¶***dull*** *shades* くすんだ色合. ¶clothing fabrics of ***fancy*** *shades* 変った色合の服地. ¶His face has become a ***few*** *shades* darker. 彼の顔は心持黒くなった. ¶trees that give ***grateful*** *shade* 有難い陰をつくる木々. ¶with a ***green*** *shade* over my eyes 目に緑色のシェードをかけて. ¶in the ***leafy*** *shade* 葉の茂る木かげに. ¶***minute*** *shades* of meaning 細かい意味の相違. ¶discriminate the ***nicer*** *shades* of meaning 微妙な意味の相違を区別する. ¶The tree makes a ***pleasant*** *shade*. その木が気持のよい日陰をつくる. ¶It is difficult to convey a ***precise*** *shade* of meaning in a translation. 翻訳では言葉のあやを正確に伝えることは困難だ. ¶fry it to exactly the ***right*** *shade* of brown それをちゃんときつね色に揚げる. ¶***soft*** *shades* of blue and green 青と緑の柔かい色. ¶The trees offer ***welcome*** *shade*. その木で気持のよいかげができる.
Q² powder, rouge, and lipstick in all ***color harmony*** *shades* 全体で色合のよく調和したおしろい, ほお紅及び口紅. ¶a ***metal*** (***porcelain***, ***paper***) *shade* 金属(など)製のかさ. ¶a ***sun*** *shade*=sunshade 日よけ. ¶a ***window*** *shade* 《米》窓の日よけ. ☞英語用法では a window-blind.
P go to the tomb and prostrate oneself ***before*** that *shade* その墓に行ってその霊前に平伏する. ¶the mossy seat ***beneath*** the *shade* of a tree 木かげにあるこけの付いた腰掛. ¶lie (read, sit) ***in*** the *shade* of the palm trees しゅろの木の陰で横になる(など). 【類】The mercury (水銀柱) indicated 85 degrees ***in*** the *shade*. / walk ***in*** the *shade* of trees / It is cool in the *shade*. ‖ remain ***in*** the *shades* 隠退している. ‖ dry ***in*** *shade* 陰干(かげぼし)にする ‖ They differ ***in*** *shade*. それらは色合が異なる. 【類】clothing materials ***in*** numerous *shades* of blue ‖ he has been thrown ***into*** the *shade* by ... 彼は…のために顔色なしである. ‖ fall ***into*** *shade* 世間から忘れられる. ¶ministers of religion ***of*** all *shades* あらゆる宗派の僧侶たち. 【類】people ***of*** all *shades* of opinion. ¶take one's noon's rest ***under*** the *shade* of a great spreading oak-tree 大きな枝を張っているかしわの木陰に昼休みをする. 【類】***Under*** the *shade* of a tree the aisukuriimu-ya takes his stand (店を出している). ¶***without*** a *shade* of confidence 一向に信用しないで ‖ a desk lamp ***without*** a *shade*=a shadeless desk lamp かさのないスタンド.
P² *shades* ***for*** the eyes 目のおおい. ¶a *shade* ***of*** doubt わずかな疑い ‖ the *shades* ***of*** evening 暮色 ‖ *shades* ***of*** color 色合 ‖ all *shades* ***of*** purple あらゆる色合の紫 ‖ the *shades* of meaning of synonyms 類語の意味の微細な相違. 【類】There is a *shade* ***of*** difference in meaning between the two forms of the word. ‖ friends of all *shades* ***of*** political thought 皆少しずつ政治上の思想の違った友だち. ‖ the *shades* ***of*** departed heroes 死せる英雄たちの幽魂. 【類】memory of the *shade* ***of*** Hazlitt will pardon us, we may perhaps venture to criticize ...

shade, *v.* 日よけする; 暗くする; ぼかす.
M *shade* ***imperceptibly*** into each other 目につかないほどずつ段々色合がとけあう. ¶The garden is ***well*** *shaded*. その庭は木陰が十分造られている.
M² *shade* ***off*** gradually without definite border はっきりした境がなく次第にぼかしてある.
P *shade* it ***from*** the sun それに日よけをする. 【類】a blending of tints, as in a damaged photograph, which *shades* ***from*** clear white to the deepest black. ¶*shade* colors ***into*** one another 色が互にとけ合う ‖ a phase of extreme socialism *shading* ***into*** anarchism 漸次無政府主義に推移する極端な社会主義の一面. ¶*shade* one's eyes ***with*** one's hand 手を目にかざす. ‖ a face *shaded* ***with*** melancholy 憂うつに曇った顔.
O It was rather *shaded* than hid. それは隠れたというより薄くおおったというものであった.

shading, *n.* 意味合い.
V ***appreciate*** *shadings* of meaning 意味のわずかな相違を味う.

shadow, *n.* 影; 蔭(かげ); 前兆; 面影, 幽霊.
V ***cast*** its *shadow* over (=upon) ... …にその影を投げる. 【類】a person's *shadow* ***cast*** on a wall by lamplight ‖ Coming events ***cast*** their *shadows* before. 事件が起ろうとするとまず前兆がある(霜を踏んで堅氷至る). ¶***catch at*** *shadows* 影をとらえようとする. ¶We cannot ***jump off*** our *shadows*, and as little can we escape the influence of the society in which we live. われわれは自分の影から飛びのくことができないように自分の住んでいる社会の影響を免れる訳には行かない. ¶***project*** a *shadow* 影を投げる. ¶***seek*** the *shadow* and lose the substance 影を求めて実体を失う. ¶***throw*** a *shadow* over ... …に影を投げる.
V² Evening *shadows* ***fell***. 日が暮れた. ‖ those upon whom the *shadow* of death has already ***fallen*** 死にひんした人々. ¶The *shadows* of twilight were ***gathering*** over the village. 村は暮色に包まれていた. ¶the *shadow* of a tragedy ***hung*** over the lordly mansion of ... 悲劇の影が…の堂々たる邸宅の上にさしていた. ¶A *shadow* ***passed*** over the kindly face of the old woman. 老婦人のやさしい顔には憂いの影がちらっと見えた. ¶Black, indeed, is the *shadow* that ***rests*** upon the home of such a wife. こうした妻の家庭は実に悲惨なものである.
Q the ***dancing*** *shadow* of the trees 木の躍る影. ¶***inky*** *shadows* 黒い影. ¶He is a ***mere*** *shadow* of his former self. 彼はありし昔をわずかにしのばせるに過ぎない(ほどしょうすいしている). 【類】now ***mere*** *shadows* of former

greatness. ¶The street-trees cast ***inviting*** *shadows* during the hot days. 街路樹は暑い日中に人を引付ける(涼しい)陰を作る. ¶There is ***no*** *shadow* of truth in it. それには真実性の片影もない. ¶He is afraid of his ***own*** *shadow*. 彼は自分の影を恐ろしがっている(おく病だ).

Q[2] The ***evening*** *shadows* were creeping over the valley. 夕やみが谷に迫っていた. ¶in a ***twilight*** *shadow* of evening (morning) 夕やみせまる(朝が白む)ころ.

P catch ***at*** *shadows* 影を捕えようとする. ¶***beneath*** the *shadow* of cocoa-palms やしの木陰に. ¶It is ***beyond*** *shadow* of question. それはいささかの疑義をいれない. 【類】it has been shown ***beyond*** the *shadow* of doubt that ... ¶be darkened ***by*** *shadows* 影で暗くなる. ¶live ***in*** the *shadow* 退隠して余生を送る ‖ hidden ***in*** the woodland *shadows* 森林の奥に隠れて ‖ half buried ***in*** the *shadows* that swathe the square 方形の広場を包むかげの中に半ば埋もれて. ¶worn ***to*** a *shadow* by a constant diarrhoea 絶え間ない下痢のため見る影もなくやつれて. ¶***under*** the *shadow* of a tree 木陰で ‖ ***under*** the *shadow* of the Almighty 神のおかげをこうむって ‖ It lies ***under*** the *shadow* of the castle. それはその城のすぐ近くだ. ¶***within*** the *shadow* of the grove 森の影の内に. ¶***without*** a *shadow* of doubt 少しの疑もなく ‖ a man ***without*** a *shadow* 影なき男 (Chamisso 作の Peter Schlemihl の主人公).

P[2] The *shadow* ***of*** death was on his face. 死の影が彼の顔にさしていた. ‖ under the *shadow* ***of*** misfortune 不運に陥って ‖ There was not a *shadow* ***of*** hope. 一るの望みもなかった. ‖ the *shadow* ***of*** freedom 名ばかりの自由. 【類】There is not a *shadow* ***of*** doubt about it. ¶Sorrow is *shadow* ***to*** life. 悲哀は人生に付物だ.

shadow, *v.* かげにする; かすかに予示する; 尾行する.

M It is ***densely*** *shadowed* by a grove. それは樹林ですっかり陰になっている. ¶*shadow* ***forth*** (=***out***) future events 将来のできごとをかすかに予示する.

P He was *shadowed* ***by*** the police (spies). 彼は警官(など)に跡をつけられた. ¶His face was *shadowed* ***from*** the light. 彼の顔はあかりの影になっていた.

shady, *a.* うしろ暗い.

M be engaged in a ***rather*** *shady* occupation いささか怪しげな職についている.

shaft, *n.* 矢; 光ぼう, 鋒芒(ほう)); [馬車の]ながえ; たて坑.

V ***descend*** (=go down) a *shaft* たて坑を下る. ¶Two of my critics have ***directed*** the *shaft* of feeble ridicule. 二人の批評家が私に薄弱なちょう笑のほこを向けた. ¶*shafts* ***discharged*** by archers 射手の放った矢. ¶***sink*** a *shaft* たて坑を掘り下げる.

Q a ***venomed*** *shaft* 毒矢.

Q[2] an ***elevator*** *shaft* エレベーターのたて孔. ¶The first ***moonstone*** *shafts* of morning light were creeping over the Mediterranean. 朝日の最初の月長石色の光ぼうが地中海上に輝き初めた. ¶a ***propeller*** *shaft* プロペラの回転軸. ¶a ***ventilating*** *shaft* 換気孔.

P The cab is driven with one horse ***in*** the *shafts*. その馬は一頭立てだ. ¶It is fixed ***on*** a long *shaft*. それは長い柄に付けてある.

P[2] *shafts* ***of*** envy (malice, satire) しっと(など)のほさき ‖ *shafts* ***of*** light 光ぼう.

shafting, *n.* 〚機〛軸受装置.

Q ***square*** *shafting* 角形軸受装置.

Q[2] polished ***steel*** *shafting* みがいた鋼鉄の軸受装置.

shake, *n.* 振ること, 動揺; 〚複〛おこり.

V ***give*** a tree a *shake* 木をゆすぶる. ¶He ***gave*** me a *shake* of the hand. 彼は私と握手した. ¶***have*** a *shake* [家など]揺れる ‖ ***have*** the *shakes* おこりがする.

Q a ***cordial*** *shake* of the hand 心をこめた握手. ¶with an ***ominous*** *shake* of the head 縁起が悪いと言ったように頭を振って. ¶give a ***sharp*** *shake* 激しく振る.

Q[2] a hearty ***hand*** *shake* (=handshake) 心からの握手.

P ***in*** the *shake* of a lamb's tail 瞬間に.

shake, *v.* 振る, 揮う; 振り切る.

M *shake* the earth ***away*** from the roots 根の土を振り落す. ¶You should not *shake* yourself ***free*** from the feeling of responsibility. 責任感を捨ててはならない. ¶***heartily*** *shake* hands 熱誠の握手をする. ¶We drove on a rough road and were ***much*** *shaken*. 悪い道を乗り回わしたので大分揺られた. ¶His faith was ***severely*** *shaken*. 彼の信仰がひどく動揺した. ¶I ***shook*** him ***warmly*** by the hand. 彼とあつい握手を交した.

M[2] ***shake down*** 揺り落す; 環境などになれる; 《米俗》[金など]おどし取る, 収賄する ‖ Apples ***shook down*** with the last night's storm. りんごが昨夜のあらしで揺れ落ちた. 【類】***shake down*** fruit from a tree ‖ ***shake*** [oneself] ***down*** in a new environment 新しい環境に立ってこれに順応する. ‖ Things are ***shaking down*** rapidly. 秩序がずんずん回復されつつある. ‖ ***shake down*** for the night 一夜の宿を取る. ¶The dog flew at me, but I ***shook*** him ***off***. 犬が私に飛び掛ってきたが払いのけた. ‖ I can't ***shake off*** (=get rid of) my cold. どうもかぜが抜けない. 【類】***shake off*** the yoke (くびき) / ***shake off*** drowsiness (眠気) / I cannot ***shake off*** the feeling that ... / ***shake off*** all remembrance of one's late disgrace / ***shake off*** a bad habit / ***shake off*** the shackles (fetters) ‖ so as to ***shake off*** after-effects ほとぼり(酔い)をさますために. ¶***shake up*** fresh milk なまの牛乳をよくかきまわす ‖ ***shake*** (=stir) ***up*** a feather bed 羽根ぶとんを揺すぶって形を調える ‖ ***shake*** (=stir) ***up*** a dull market 不振市場に活を入れる ‖ ***Shake*** yourself ***up***. 元気を出せ. ¶The motor-car ***shakes*** me ***up*** too much. 私の自動車はばかに揺れる. ‖ He is lazy and must be ***shaken up***. 彼はなまけ者だから奮起させなければならない.

P He *shook* his fist ***at*** me. 彼はこぶしを振って私に手向いした. ¶I look forward with pleasure to the time when I shall once again *shaking* you ***by*** the hand. 君と再び握手する日を喜んで待つ. ‖ *shake* a person ***by*** the shoulder 人の肩をゆすぶる. 【類】It is *shaken* ***by*** the wind. ¶She was as angry as the sleeper who is *shaken* ***from*** some fair dream that he would fain hold fast. 彼女はいつまでも見ていたいと思うような楽しい夢から覚まされた人のように怒っていた. ¶*shake* hands ***in*** friendship むつまじく握手する. ¶I *shook* him ***off*** me. 私は彼を振り離した. ¶She has been *shaken* ***out of*** all reason. 彼女はあらゆる理性を失った. ¶*shake* the government (country) ***to*** its foundations 政府(など)をその根底までゆさぶる. ¶*shake* ***with*** laughter 腹を抱えて笑う. 【類】His body *shook* ***with*** emotion. / He *shook* ***with*** terror (fear, cold). ‖ He *shook* hands ***with*** me. 彼は私と握手した.

shakedown, *n.* 《米》かりの寝床.

V ***make*** a *shakedown* of straw and blankets on the floor 床上にわらと毛布を敷いて寝床を作る.

shakedown, *n.* 《米俗》頭はね(リベート), 収賄.

Q ***infamous*** *shakedowns* of party leaders 政党幹部の恥辱的な収賄.

shaker, *n.* 振り動かすもの.

Q[2] a ***cocktail*** *shaker* カクテル振り混ぜ器. ¶a ***floor*** *shaker* [ストーブの]灰落し. ¶a ***pepper*** *shaker* こしょう振り. ¶a ***salt*** *shaker* 塩振り.

shake-up, *n.* 《米》大異動.

Q a ***sweeping*** *shake-up* in officialdom 官界の大異動.

P[2] a *shake-up* ***of*** top Government personnel 政府高官連の大異動.

sham, *n.* 見せかけ, 虚偽.

V ***hate*** *shams* 虚偽を憎む.

Q a mere ***clumsy*** *sham* へたなにせもの. ¶a ***transparent*** *sham* 見えすいたうそ.

shame, *n.* しゅう恥; 恥辱.

V ***adding*** another *shame* to a shame 恥の上塗り. ¶***bear*** a *shame* 恥を忍ぶ. 【類】I ***bore*** *shame* to ask the question. ¶***bring*** *shame* on ... …に恥をかかせる. ¶***cause*** *shame* to ... …を辱かしめる. ¶***cry*** *shame* upon ... …に恥を知れと叫ぶ. ¶***dread*** *shame* 恥を知る. ¶***exhibit*** *shame* 恥かしがる. ¶***feel*** *shame* to ... …することを恥じる. ¶***lose*** all *shame* about ... …を少しも恥と思わない. ¶His family ***shares*** the *shame*. 彼の家族にその恥が及ぶ. ¶***show*** *shame* 恥じる. ¶***suffer*** the *shame* of ... …を恥かしく思う. ¶I ***take*** *shame* to myself. 私は恥かしく思う.

Q a ***burning*** *shame* 赤恥. ¶a ***crying*** *shame* はなはだしい恥辱. ¶***false*** *shame* よそおった恥かしさ. 【類】He had a good deal of ***false*** *shame* about it. ¶It is a ***great*** *shame* that you should be compelled to toil thus painfully. こんなに骨を折って働かされるのは非常な屈辱だ. ¶***indelible*** *shame* 忘るべからざる恥辱. ¶a ***jolly*** *shame* 《俗》えらい恥辱. ¶***open*** *shame* あかるみの恥.

P *Shame* ***at*** his conduct was felt by his friends. 彼の行為を恥じる気持が彼の友人たちに見られた. ¶***What*** a *shame!* まあひどい. ¶He said other things I cannot repeat ***for*** *shame*. 彼はこの外に恥かしくって今言うことがで

きないことも言った. ‖ cry *for shame* 恥じて泣く ‖ I cannot do it *for* very *shame*. 恥かしくて私にはそんなことはとてもできない. ‖ *For shame*, Mr. ...! ...君見っともない. ¶hide one's face *from shame* 恥じて顔を隠す. 【類】blush *from shame* or modesty. ¶He hung his head *in* (=for) *shame*. 彼は恥じて頭をたれた. ¶She is past all sense *of shame*. 彼女は全く恥を知らない. ‖ feel a touch *of shame* 少しく恥かしく思う ‖ a child *of shame* 私生児. ¶*out of* (=*through*) *shame* 恥かしいので. ¶That puts (brings) *to shame* even a professional singer. それでは本職の歌手もはだしだ. ‖ I was put *to shame*. 私は恥をかかされた, 赤面した. 【類】That puts me *to shame*. ‖ He is lost (=dead, *or* past) *to shame*. 彼は恥を知らない. ‖ *to* my *shame* be it confessed that ... 恥かしながら白状すると...である. 【類】*to* our *shame* it must be owned that ... ¶blush *with shame* 恥じて赤面する ‖ it must be owned *with shame* that ... 恥かしいことだが...なのだ. 【類】His face was hot *with shame*. / fill him *with shame*. ¶go about naked *without shame* 平気で裸体で歩き回る.

P² They think it a *shame for* a man to work. 彼らは働くことを人の恥と考えている. ¶You will be the *shame of* your own sex. [女子に向って]お前などは女の名折れだ. ¶*Shame on* you! 恥さらしめ! ¶He is a *shame to* his parents (family). 彼は両親(など)の面汚しだ. ‖ a *shame* and a disgrace *to* civilization 文明の名折れ. ¶Why, *shame upon* you, man! 君恥ずかしくないか.

shame, *v.* 恥じる.

P *shame at* (=*of or for*) one's fault 自分のあやまちを恥じる. ¶he *shamed* me *by* knowing more about ... 彼が...のことでは私よりもよく知っているので私は赤面した. ¶*shame* one *into* doing good 辱かしめて善に立返るようにする ‖ *shame* a person *into* behaving himself 恥じて身をつつしむようにさせる. ¶*shame* a person *out of* his course 恥じて転向させる ‖ That *shamed* me *out of* it. そのために私は恥じてそれをやめた. ¶*shame* a person *to* death 人をざん死させる. ¶those who *shame* not *with* their sin 自己の罪を恥じない人々.

shank, *n.* 柄; すね.

Q a *lean shank* 蚊の(細い)すね.

Q² a *camp shank* 天幕の柱. ¶a *spindle shank* 紡錘の柄.

shanty, *n.* 仮小屋.

Q² a *road construction shanty* 道路工事の仮小屋.

shape, *n.* 形; 実体; 型, 形式; 〖俗〗形勢.

V *assume* (=take) the *shape* of ... ...に化ける ‖ *assume* [the] human *shape* 人間に化ける ‖ *assume* her own *shape* その女性の正体を現わす ‖ The result is now *assuming* visible *shape*. 結果が今はっきり見えてきた. ¶slowly *gather shape* 徐々に形をなす. ¶*give shape* to a plan 計画を具体化する ‖ *give shape* to some rude lump 形を成さぬ塊片にかっこうをつける ‖ *give* a new *shape* to ... ...を造り変える. ¶*have* the *shape* of the letter "U" U字形を成している ‖ *have* a bad *shape* おもしろくない形勢になっている. ¶to *hold* its *shape* その形をくずさないように. ¶*keep* its *shape* [衣服など]型がくずれない. ¶Keep your shoes from *losing shape* by using shoe-trees. くつ型を使ってくつの形がくずれないようにせよ. ¶*retain* its *shape* [帽子など]形がくずれない. ¶*see shapes* in the fire 火の中に色々な形(幻影)が見える. ¶*take shape* きまった形になる, 具体化する. ¶These doubts *took shape*. 疑いが本ものになった. 【類】The intention *took shape* in action. ‖ His literary work is beginning to *take shape*. 彼の著作(の出版)は目鼻がつき出した. ‖ *take* the *shape* of a human being 人間に化ける. 【類】*take* more *shape* / The building is now *taking shape*. / The plan *took* practical *shape* in November, 1906. / the idea of ... seems to be *taking* practical *shape*. / The work *took shape* as the Concise Oxford Dictionary. / The dream is beginning to *take shape*. / The idea *took shape* in the minds of the promoters many years ago. / the festival *takes* the *shape* of ... / The principle *takes shape* in different ways. ¶The plan is *taking on* the *shape*. その計画は具体化しつつある.

Q of *abnormal shape* 奇形の. ¶*Angular shapes* are the most easily recognized in road signs. 角形が道路標として最も目につきやすい. ¶The patient (My lawn) is in *bad shape*. 〖俗〗病人(私のところの芝生)は調子が悪い(順調に行っていない). 【類】The business seems to go on in *bad shape*. ¶a *comical shape* こっけいな形. ¶The plan began to take *definite shape*. その案は具体化し始めた. ¶assume an *extraordinary shape* 変な形になる. ¶*fantastic shapes* 奇異な形. ¶The athletes tried to keep themselves in *good shape*. 競技者たちはコンディションをととのえるようにつとめた. ‖ The market is in *good shape*. 〖俗〗市場は好況だ. ¶Mt. Fuji has an exceptionally *graceful shape*. 富士山の形は実に優美だ. ¶My people are all in *great shape*=They are all in good health. 私の家族は一同すこぶる壮健です. ¶Two stone lions, of *grotesque shape*, guard the entrance. 異様な形をした二つの石のこま犬が入口を守っている(神社など). ¶gods in *human shape* 人間の形をした神々. 【類】a monster (devil) in *human shape*. ¶a stone of *irregular shape* 不規則な形の石. ¶It is of the *lozenge shape*. それはひし形だ. ¶resume their *normal shapes* [化けたものが]彼ら本然の姿に帰る. ¶of an *oval shape* 卵形(長円形)の. ¶re-issue ... in a more *permanent shape* ...を一層装ていをよくし再発行(単行本など). ¶Their colors are rich as their *shapes* are *quaint*. [菊など]形も変っているが色も豊かだ. ¶a *round shape* 円形. ¶receive an acknowledgement in a more *solid shape* than mere thanks 単に謝辞というだけでなくもっと実質的な謝礼を受ける. ¶A snail-shell has a *spiral shape*. かたつむりの殼は渦巻形だ. ¶take *tangible shape* 具体化する. ¶gymnastics under a *thousand shapes* 種々様々の形式の体操. ¶*vague shapes* looking ghostly in the darkness 暗黒の中で幽霊のように見えるぼんやりした形. ¶of *various shape* 様々の形の. ¶*What shape* shall I make the meeting seats? 会合の座席をどんな風に配列しましょうか.

Q² reproductions of photographs in *album shape* アルバムの形式にした写真の複製. ¶of a *corkscrew shape* せん抜き形の. ¶a Delft bottle of *double gourd shape* ひょうたん形をしたデルフト焼のびん.

P The ocarina is sometimes called sweet potato *from* its *shape*. オカリナは形が似ているので甘しょと呼ばれることがある. ¶Dogs differ from wolves *in shape*. 犬はおおかみと形が違う. ‖ It resembles a pear *in shape*. それは形が西洋なしのようだ. ‖ pottery queer *in shape* and quaint in design 形が変って意匠の奇抜な陶器 ‖ He would on no terms, no entreaties, no *shape* I could put it *in*, receive the money. 彼は私が何といってもその金を受取ろうとはしなかった. ‖ rectangular *in shape* く形の ‖ keep it *in shape* その形のくずれないようにする ‖ commission *in* any *shape* or form 何らかの形式における口銭 ‖ receive awards *in* the *shape* of ... 賞として...をもらう ‖ wear a badge *in* the *shape* of a silver-fish 銀魚形の記章をつける. 【類】exercise *in* the *shape* of callisthenics (美容体操) / a red mark *in* the *shape* of the letter S / a controversy of very long standing has been revived of late days *in* the *shape* of the question regarding ... ‖ the moon *in* the *shape* of a man 人に化けたお月様 ‖ distinguish by the difference *in* their *shapes* 形の違いで区別する. ¶beat *into shape* 打って形をつける ‖ develop *into* a definite *shape* 発達して一定の形になる(おたまじゃくしなど) ‖ get one's thoughts *into shape* 自分の考えをまとめる ‖ put one's ideas *into shape* その考えをまとめる ‖ put *into* written *shape* 書物にする. ¶a building *of* a square *shape* 四角形の建物. ¶The box was crushed *out of shape*. 箱はめちゃめちゃにつぶされた. 【類】The suit (衣服) was pulled *out of shape*. ¶*without shape* or form 形のない.

P² in the *shape of* a horseshoe てい鉄形の.

shape, *v.* 形造る.

M children *shaping satisfactorily* 申し分なく成育する子供たち.

M² see how things *shape up* どんなことになるか見ている ‖ plans began *shaping up* for ... ...のための計画の目鼻がついてきた ‖ Everything is *shaping up* well. 万事うまく行っている. 【類】The program will *shape up* as follows:

P It is *shaped into* a tub-like form. それはおけのような形にできている. ¶*shaped like* a pear なしのような形をした. ¶*shape* one's course *to* (=*toward*) ... ...の方へ進む. ¶*shape* a hat (shoes) *to* one's head (feet) 帽子(など)を頭(など)にあわせて作る.

share, *n.* 分前, 持分; 貢献; 〖主に英〗株, 株式.

V *allot* a *share* to ... ...に分前を与える. ¶*bear* (=have *or* take) one's *share* in ... ...にあずかる, ...を分担する. 【類】he has had to *bear* the lion's *share* (衝に当る) of attacks made on ... / He must *bear* his *share* of responsibility. /

bear our *share* in the great national work of reconstruction. ¶Marriage is a partnership to which each ***brings*** a *share* of the investment. 結婚は夫婦互に投資の分担額をもたらす合資会社のようなものだ. ¶***claim*** a *share* in the profits 利益の分前を要求する ‖ can ***claim*** its due *share* of attention 当然注意されてよい ‖ Oxford ***claims*** a large *share* in the making of England. オクスフォード大学は英国の建設にもちろん大いに貢献している. ¶***contribute*** one's *share* to the national prosperity 国民の繁栄に貢献する ‖ ***contribute*** one's *share* of work toward ... ...に助力する. ¶***cry*** *shares* 等分にすることを要求する. ¶***do*** one's *share* of work その仕事を分担する ‖ They have ***done*** their *share* in adding to the universal enjoyment. 彼らは一般娯楽の増進に貢献した. 【類】They wanted to ***do*** their man's *share* in a crisis of the world. ¶***enjoy*** a *share* in its advantage その利益にあずかる ‖ ***enjoy*** a fair *share* of public appreciation 相当に公衆に認識される. ¶***fulfil*** one's *share* in ... ...におけるその分担を果たす. ¶***get*** a large *share* of the world's trade 世界貿易の大きな部分を占める. 【類】He ***got*** no *share* of booty (分捕品). ¶***go*** *shares* with ... ...と山わけする. ¶***have*** a *share* in a bank (company) 銀行(など)の株を持っている ‖ He ***has*** a *share* in the profits. 彼は利益の分配を受けることになっている. ‖ He ***had*** a large *share* in bringing it about. 彼はそれをなし遂げるにあずかって大いに力があった. 【類】He ***has*** a *share* in the business. / ***have*** no *share* in ... ‖ a woman who has ***had*** her *share* of the world's troubles 苦労をしてきた女. ¶He ***holds*** 100 *shares* in the railway. 彼はその鉄道に株を百株持っている. ¶***issue*** *shares* 株を発行する. ¶We shall continue to ***merit*** even a larger *share* of patronage in the future. われわれは今後一層のご愛顧を受けるに足るものになるよう努力します. ¶***offer*** *shares* for sale 株を売出す ‖ I ***offered*** him my *share* of the bill. その勘定の中で自分の分前を出そうと言った. ‖ ***offer*** a *share* in the railroad as security その鉄道の株を担保として提供する. ¶***receive*** a *share* of the profits of the business その商売の利益の分前を受ける ‖ He should ***receive*** a generous *share* of praise. 彼は大いに賞賛を博すべきだ. ¶***secure*** the lion's *share* of ... ...の一番大きな分前を獲得する. ¶***sell*** one's *share* at a good price 株を良い値で売る. ¶they were compelled to ***take*** their *share* in ... 彼らは...に参加すべく余儀なくされた. 【類】A large *share* is ***taken*** by women in this branch of research. ‖ Will you ***take*** half *share?* 半口乗ってくれるか. 【類】***take*** half *share* on a venture. ¶***undertake*** a full *share* of the labor その労力を十分々担する. ¶*shares* ***boomed*** to over ... 株が...以上にはね上った. ¶*Shares* are ***falling.*** 株が下がり出した. ¶The *shares* ***yield*** (=***pay***) five per cent. その株の配当は五分だ.

Q have a ***conspicuous*** *share* 大いに貢献する. ¶a ***deferred*** *share* 利益後取り株. ¶a ***due*** *share* 当然の分担. ¶bear an ***equal*** *share* 同じ割合を分担する. 【類】I divided the money among the six men giving an ***equal*** *share* each. ¶That is your ***fair*** *share.* それは君の当然の分前だ. ¶entitle the holder to a ***full*** *share* of the profits of the company 株券の所有者に会社の利益の十分な配当を受ける権利を与える. ¶take ***half*** *share* in the venture その投機事業に半口乗る. ¶he has taken no ***insignificant*** *share* in ... 彼は...に有意義な助力をした. ¶contribute a ***large*** and ***brilliant*** *share* 多大のかくかくたる貢献をする. ¶assistants who have taken a ***leading*** *share* in the preparation of the dictionary are ... その辞書編集にあずかった主なる助手たちは...である. ¶the ***new*** (***old***) *shares* of the Tokyo Gas Company 東京ガス会社の新(旧)株. ¶He has had ***no small*** *share* in framing the destinies of our country. 彼はわが国の運命を築き上げるに当って少なからず貢献した. ¶an ***ordinary*** *share* 通常株. ¶take out just a ***slight*** *share* in the concerns of this world 現世のことはあまり苦にしない. ¶an ***unreasonable*** *share* 法外な割当. ¶contribute a ***valuable*** *share* to ... ...に貴重な貢献をする. ¶The linguist takes a ***worthy*** *share* in the international life of Japan. その語学者は日本の国際的生活に重要な貢献をしている.

Q² a ***gilt-edge*** (=gilt-edged) *share* 一流(花形)株. ¶a ***preference*** (=***preferred***) *share* 優先株. ¶"***slump***" *shares* 暴落株.

P come in ***for*** a *share* 分前にあずかる. ¶speculation ***in*** *shares* 株式投機. ¶Part of the profits falls ***to*** his *share.* 利益の幾分は彼の取分になる.

P² *shares* ***in*** companies=company shares 会社の株 ‖ one's *share* ***in*** the crime その犯罪への関与. ¶a *share* ***of*** the profits 利益配当.

share, *v.* 分与する; 共にする; 分前を受ける.

M All must *share* ***alike.*** 皆一様に分前を受けねばならない. ¶They ***generously*** *shared* it with us. 彼らは気前よくそれをわれわれにも分けてくれた.

P *share* one's fortune ***among*** one's children 子供たちに...その財産を分ける. ¶*share* the profits ***between*** them 利益を彼ら二人で分ける. ¶The worry is *shared* ***by*** her family. 彼女の家のものもそれを心配している. ¶I will *share* with you ***in*** the undertaking. 私はその事業を君と一緒にやりたい. ‖ *share* ***in*** profits 利益の分配にあずかる ‖ *share* ***in*** the privilege 恩典に浴する. 【類】*share* ***in*** the amusement / *share* with him ***in*** his distress / eagerly *share* ***in*** the joy of the occasion. ¶*share* ***with*** the world the sorrow of his death 世界の人々とともに彼の死を悲しむ ‖ If you have an umbrella, let me *share* it ***with*** you. かさがあるなら入れてくれ給え. ‖ It was a fire which he *shared* ***with*** others. その火事で彼の家も類焼した. ‖ *share* ***with*** him the battle of life 一生の苦楽を彼とともにする. 【類】*share* the room ***with*** a person / Gentile *shares* ***with*** Croce the leadership (覇(は)権) of Italian thought today. / *share* one's lunch (bed, room) ***with*** ... / *share* ***with*** a person a taste for ...

shareholder, *n.* 株主.

Q a ***heavy*** *shareholder* 大株主. ¶a ***principal*** *shareholder* 「主な株主.

P a general meeting ***of*** *shareholders* 株主総会. ¶dividends ***to*** *shareholders* 株主配当金.

P² *shareholders* ***in*** (=***of***) a company 会社の株主.

sharing, *n.* 分配.

Q² ***profit*** *sharing* 利潤分配.

shark, *n.* 《米》名手.

Q² a ***gospel*** *shark* in ... ...では名手だ.

shark, *v.* 詐取する.

M He *sharks* ***out*** for a living. 詐欺で食っている.

sharp, *n.* 《米》専門家, くろうと.

Q² a ***billiard*** *sharp* 玉突の名人. ¶a ***business*** *sharp* 腕きき「の商売人.

sharp, *a., ad.* 鋭い; きびしい; ちょうど.

P be *sharp* ***at*** reckoning (a bargain) 計算(など)がうまい ‖ be *sharp* ***at*** cornerwork 〚野〛コーナーワークがうまい. ¶I want you to have the Kuruma *sharp* ***to*** time. 時間きっちりに車にきてもらいたい. ¶I have to be *sharp* ***with*** him. 私は彼にきびしくしなければならない.

O Look *sharp!* 気をつけろ.

sharpen, *v.* 鋭くする, とぐ.

M be *sharpening* ***up*** せん鋭化している.

P² *sharpen* a razor ***on*** the strop かみそりを皮とでとぐ.

sharpener, *n.* とぐもの(人).

Q² a ***knife*** *sharpener* ナイフとぎ器. ¶a ***pencil*** *sharpener* 鉛筆削り. ¶a ***sword*** *sharpener* 刀とぎ師.

sharpness, *n.* 切味.

V *Sharpness* is ***dulled.*** 切味が鈍る. ¶You shall ***feel*** the *sharpness* of my sword. この刀の切味をお前に見せてやる. ¶***test*** the *sharpness* of a sword 刀の切味をためす.

shatter, *v.* 砕く; 砕ける.

M But such words ***simply*** *shatter* themselves on the hard fact. しかしかような言葉は冷厳な事実に会うと一たまりもなくくずれてしまう.

P *shatter* ***into*** splinters こっぱみじんになる.

shave, *n.* そること; すれすれ, 間一髪.

V ***get*** (=***have***) a *shave* ひげをそる. ¶Few women care to be seen with a man who ***needs*** a *shave.* 顔をきれいにそっていない男と同席して平気でいる女はほとんどない. ¶I ***want*** a *shave.* ひげをそってくれ.

Q appear in public without a ***clean*** *shave* 顔をきれいにそらずに公開の席に出る. ¶A sharp razor gives you a ***close*** *shave.* かみそりがきれるとよく顔がそれる. ‖ That was a ***close*** *shave!* 《米》危機一髪だったよ. 【類】have a ***close*** *shave* [from danger]. ¶miss it by a ***narrow*** *shave* 《俗》わずかのことではずす. ¶with ***near*** (=***close***) *shaves* of a collision 《俗》も少しで衝突しそうになって.

Q² a ***lather*** *shave* 石けんをつけてひげそり.

P pass ***by*** a *shave* 《俗》すれすれに通過する. 【類】escape death ***by*** a *shave.*

shave, *v.* [ひげを]そる.

M *cleanly shaven*=clean-shaven 顔をきれいにそって. ¶His beard was *freshly shaven*. 彼のひげはそり立てだった. ¶*neatly shaven* きれいにそって. ¶most *scrupulously shaved* きわめて念入りにそった[顔など]. ¶*smoothly shaven* [顔など]すべすべにそった.

M^2 *shave off* one's whiskers (beard, mustache) ほおひげ(など)をそり落す. ¶*shave up* さかぞりにそる.

shaver, *n.* かみそり.

Q an *electric shaver* 電気かみそり.

shaving, *n.* ひげそり; [しばしば *pl.*] 削りくず.

Q^2 *ice shaving* 氷のけずった片. ¶*pencil shavings* 鉛筆のけずりくず. ¶*shavings of* wood かんなくず.

shawl, *n.* 肩掛, ショール.

V *put on* one's *shawl* 肩掛を掛ける. ¶She *sported* her *shawl*. 肩掛をこれ見よがしに着てきた.

P wrap a baby *in* a *shawl* 赤ん坊をショールにくるむ.

sheaf, *n.* [穀物など]束.

Q a *little sheaf* of original essays 独創的論文小集.

P a pile of hay *in sheaves* 乾草のたばの積重ね.

P^2 a *sheaf of* letters 一束の手紙 ‖ He searched for and found a *sheaf of* papers in a filing cabinet.

shear, *v.* はさみで切る; はく奪する.

P *shear* [wool *from*] a sheep 羊の毛を刈る. ¶be *shorn of* glory 栄誉をはぎ取られる ‖ He was *shorn of* his privileges. 彼は特権をはく奪された.

shears, *n. pl.* はさみ.

P clip it *with shears* はさみでそれを刈る.

sheath, *n.* さや.

V *put up* a *sheath* to ... …をさやにおさめる.

Q a *contraceptive sheath* ルーデサック.

P a knife carried *in* a *sheath* さや入りのナイフ. ¶put it *into* a *sheath* それをさやに入れる. ¶cover it *with* a *sheath* それをさやに入れる.

sheathe, *v.* さやにおさめる; 覆う.

P a scroll *sheathed in* silk 絹に包んだ巻物. ¶a box *sheathed with* copper plates 銅板で覆うた箱.

shed, *n.* 小屋; 置場.

V *knock up* a *shed* 小屋を急いで造り上げる. ¶*put up* a *shed* 小屋を建てる. ¶*raise* a lowly *shed* 粗末な小屋を建てる.

Q^2 an *army shed* 兵舎. ¶an *assembly shed* 集会用差掛小屋. ¶a *car* (*wagon*) *shed* 車庫. ¶a *goods shed* 貨物庫. ¶a *locomotive shed* 機関車庫. ¶a *tool shed* 道具小屋.

shed, *v.* 落す; 流す; 放つ.

M *shed* tears *profusely* 涙の雨を降らせる.

P *shed in* small drops 小さいしずくになって落ちる. ¶Trees *shed* their leaves *in* autumn. 木は秋に葉が落ちる. ¶*shed* light *on* a subject 問題に光明を与える. ¶*shed* tears *over* what is past 過ぎ去ったことを思い出して涙を流す.

sheen, *n.* 光輝.

Q *ivory-like sheen* [陶器など]象げのような光沢.

sheep, *n.* 羊.

V shepherd *driving* his *sheep* to fold 羊を羊欄に追って行く羊飼い. ¶*herd sheep* 羊の世話をする. ¶*separate* the *sheep* from the goats 黒と白(悪玉と善玉)を分ける. ¶*shear* a *sheep* 羊毛を刈り込む.

V^2 *Sheep bleat*. 羊が鳴く. ¶The *sheep flocked out* (*in*). 羊がぞろぞろ出て行った(入ってきた). ¶Dogs *guard sheep*. 犬が羊の番をする. ¶*Sheep* are *grazing*. 羊が草を食っている.

Q He is a *black sheep* in my family. 彼は私の家族の厄介者だ. ¶a *lost sheep* 道に迷える人, 亡羊. ¶a *stray sheep* 迷える羊.

P a flock *of sheep* 一群の羊.

sheet, *n.* 敷布(シーツ); 新聞紙; 一枚; 一面, 一帯.

V *air sheets* 敷布を乾(ほ)す. ¶*fold* the *sheet* and thrust it into an envelope 紙をたたんで封筒に入れる. ¶*pull* [*off*] a *sheet* (用せんなどを)一枚はぎとる. ¶*put* clean *sheets* on the bed 寝床にきれいな敷布を敷く.

Q a *beautiful little sheet* of water 美しい小さな池・湖など. ¶put *clean sheets* and pillowcases on one's bed ...の寝台の上に清潔なシーツとまくらおおいをかける. ¶250 pages in a *duodecimo sheet* 四六版で二百五十ページ. ¶iron roof with *flat* (*corrugated*) *sheets* 平板(波形板)を張ったブリキ屋根. ¶*sheets hot* from the press 刷りたての新聞. ¶*mimeographed sheets* of teaching material 謄写版の教材. ¶a *scurrilous sheet* 悪口新聞(赤新聞). ¶a *silvery sheet* of water 銀白の滝. ¶be *three sheets* in the wind 《俗》ずぶ六に酔っている. ¶a *supplementary sheet* 補助紙. ¶a *venomous sheet* 有害な新聞紙. ¶a *white sheet* of blossom 一面に咲いた白い花.

Q^2 draw up a *balance sheet* of European resources and needs ヨーロッパの資源と欠乏の対照表を作製する. 【類】 be able to show a favorable yearly *balance sheet*. ¶a *bed sheet* 敷布(シート). ¶insert a *carbon sheet* below a tissue *sheet* 薄紙の下に炭酸紙をはさむ. ¶a *continuation sheet* to the item (2) 第2項の連続紙(継ぎたし). ¶a *fly sheet* ちらし. ¶an *iron sheet* 鉄板. ¶an *iron* corrugated *sheet* 波形鉄板. ¶an *order sheet* 注文伝票. ¶a *penny sheet* 一ペニーの新聞. ¶a *police charge sheet* 警察告発票. ¶read the *proof sheets* 校正刷を読む. ¶the *silver sheet* as an artistic medium 芸術的表現の一様式としての銀幕.

P get in *between sheets* 寝床に入る ‖ The rain fell *in sheets*. 雨がざーざー降った. ‖ zinc *in sheets* 亜鉛板. ¶throw magnified images *on* a *sheet* 拡大した画像を幕に映す. ¶a *sheet of* ice (water, flame) 一面の氷(など) ‖ a *sheet of* iron (glass) 一枚の鉄板(など) ‖ a *sheet of* paper (letter-paper, newspaper) 一枚の紙(など).

sheik, *n.* 《米俗》色男.

P^2 He is a *sheik among* young ladies, who can play football. しゅう球のできる男は女の子にもてる.

shelf, *n.* たな; 砂州(す).

V the volumes that *line* the *shelves* of our public libraries わが国の公立図書館のたなに並んでいる書物. ¶*put up* a *shelf* たなをつる.

V^2 Their achievements are recorded in volumes under which our *shelves* already *groan*. その功績を記した書物は非常な数に上る.

Q a *continetanl shelf* 大陸だな. ¶*shallow shelves* 浅瀬. ¶the heavily *stocked shelves* of leading druggists 一流薬種屋の商品のぎっしり詰ったたな. ¶the *top shelf* in the bookcase 本箱の一番上のたな.

Q^2 a *clock shelf* 時計をのせるたな. ¶a *display shelves* (賞杯などの)飾りだな. ¶a *five-foot shelf* of books=a 5-foot bookshelf 高さ5フィートの書だな. ¶a *store shelf* 商品だな.

P replace (=put back) books *on* the *shelves* たなへ本を戻しておく.

P^2 a *shelf over* a fireplace 炉架.

shell, *n.* 殻; 貝.

V *cast* the *shell* 殻を脱する ‖ These *shells* have been *cast up* by the sea. この貝は波で打上げられた. ¶A tortoise *has* a *shell* on his back. かめは背に甲らがある. ¶*send shells* among the enemy 敵中に弾丸を打ちこむ.

Q a *hollow shell* 抜けがら.

Q^2 an *abalone shell* あわび貝(南カリフォルニア語). ¶a *paper shell* 薄紙弾薬包; 花火. ¶hunt *sea shells* 海の貝を採集する.

shell, *v.* 《俗》手渡す.

M He *shells out* whatever money she needs for a living. 彼女の生活費はいくらでも出す.

shellfish, *n.* からのある海産物, 貝(類).

V Lobsters are sometimes *called shellfish*. えびも時には'shellfish'と呼ばれる.

shelter, *n.* 避難所; ひ護, えん護, 避難.

V *afford* temporary *shelter* [山間の岩屋など]仮りの宿になる. ¶The ship *found shelter* in a safe harbor. 船は安全な港に避難した. 【類】 *find* a *shelter* from a storm. ¶The trees *formed* a *shelter* over our heads. 木がわれわれの頭の上をおおっていた. ¶*give* (=*furnish*) *shelter* to=harbor ... …をかばう. ¶Will you *grant* a poor traveler the *shelter* of your roof (=in your home) tonight? あわれな旅行者に一夜の宿を貸して下さるまいか. ¶*make* a *shelter* from war fires 戦火の避難所になる. ¶The harbor *offers* good *shelter* for vessels from all winds. その港に停泊する船はどんな風も受けない. ¶*provide shelter* for ... …をかばう. ¶*reach shelter* 避難所に着く. ¶*seek shelter* from a shower (the sun) 雨宿りをする(日かげへはいる). 【類】 *seek shelter* in a deserted house / *seek shelter* under a tree during a sudden thunderstorm. ¶*take shelter* from the rain under a tree 木の下で雨宿りをする. 【類】 *take shelter* in a pure falsehood.

Q a *good shelter* for ... …のよい避難所. ¶have *perfect shelter* 完全にひ護されている. ¶a *poor shelter* 感心しない避難所.

Q^2 an *air raid shelter* 防空避難所. ¶a *bomb shelter* 空襲

避難所. ¶an ideal ***bomb-proof*** *shelter* 理想的な防空避難所.

P publish a book ***beneath*** the *shelter* of anonymity 匿名で著書を公にする. ¶ ***for*** *shelter* from rain 雨宿りに. ¶The town is ***under*** the *shelter* of a fortress. その町は城さいに守られている. ‖ ***under*** the *shelter* of the hospitality of ... ...の家に厄介になって. ¶for the night's *shelter* ***at*** an inn 旅館に一泊のため. ¶a *shelter* ***for*** the needy 貧民の(雨露をしのぐ)仮の宿. ¶a *shelter* ***from*** the wind 風よけ.

shelter, *v.* かくまう; 隠す; 避難する.

P *shelter* oneself ***behind*** one's superiors 上役の威光をかさに着る. ¶The harbor is *sheltered* ***by*** hills ***from*** (=***against***) the north wind. 港は小山で北風をよけている. ¶We are *sheltered* ***from*** the enemy's fire. われわれは敵の砲火からえん護されている. / The roof *sheltered* us comfortably ***from*** the shower. / *shelter* us ***from*** the weather (sun's rays) / *shelter* slaves ***from*** their pursuers. ¶The ship is *sheltered* ***in*** a haven. その船は港に避難している. ¶*shelter* ***under*** a roof ***from*** the storm 屋根の下にあらしを避ける ‖ *shelter* oneself ***under*** (=beneath *or* behind) one's father's influence 父親の威光をかさに着る. ¶*shelter* it ***with*** trees それを樹木でおおう. ¶*shelter* ***within*** the walls 壁の内に隠れる.

shield, *n.* たて.

P look only at one side ***of*** the *shield* たての一面(問題の一方面)のみを見る. 【類】the other (=opposite) side ***of*** the *shield*. ¶devices ***on*** *shields* たての模様(紋).

shield *v.* 防護する, かばう.

P *shield* oneself ***behind*** someone else 他の人の影になって自身を防護する. ¶*shield* ***from*** danger (suspicion) 危険(など)を防ぐ. 【類】*shield* a person ***from*** punishment (blame) / *shield* cattle ***from*** the wind (cold weather). ¶*shield* one's daughter ***with*** one's own body わが身をもって娘をかばう.

shift, *n.* 変更; 間に合わせ; 交代, 交代時間.

V I must ***make*** *shift* with what I have. 私はある物で間に合わしておかねばならない. ‖ ***make*** *shift* for the present お茶をにごす. 【類】***make*** *shift* with a small income / He ***makes*** *shift* to pick up a scanty livelihood. ‖ I just ***made*** a *shift* (=managed) to stammer out my business to him. 私はどもりながらやっと用事を彼に話した. ¶***relieve*** a *shift* 交替する. ¶***try*** many *shifts* 百方手を尽す.

Q in ***alternating*** *shift* 交替で. ¶practice ***artful*** *shifts* こすく立回る. ¶He was reduced to ***desperate*** *shifts*. 彼は捨ばちにでなければならないようになった. ¶work in a ***double*** *shift* 昼夜交替(二部制)で働く. ¶the ***last*** *shift* 最後の手段. ¶a ***mere*** *shift* ほんのごまかし. ¶a ***petty*** *shift* 小刀細工.

Q² the ***Communist*** *shift* of tactics 共産党の戦術変更. ¶workers on the ***night*** *shifts* 夜の交替を務める職工たち, 夜勤者. ¶work in ***six-hour*** *shifts* 六時間交替で働く.

P He was ***at*** his last *shift*[*s*]. 彼は絶体絶命に陥った. ¶***by*** the *shift* 一時の間にあわせに ‖ live ***by*** *shift*[*s*] やりくりして暮しを立てる. ¶***for*** a *shift* 一時の間に合わせに. ¶work ***in*** *shifts* day and night 昼夜交替で働く ‖ work ***in*** *shifts* of ten hours 十時間交替で働く. ¶The mill is operating ***on*** two 12-hour *shifts* その工場は二回の十二時間交替で操業している. ¶***with*** one *shift* of the eye ちょっと目を移しただけで.

P² a *shift* ***of*** clothes 着換え ‖ *shift* ***of*** crops 〘農〙輪作 ‖ a *shift* ***of*** scene 場面の転換 ‖ a *shift* ***of*** the wind 風向の変更.

shift, *v.* 変える; 移す; 取換える; やりくり算段をする.

M *shift* the lovers ***apart*** 二人の愛人を引離す. ¶*shift* ***back*** a day 一日繰上げる.

M² *shift* ***about*** 反対の方角へ向変る. ¶*shift* ***off*** the duties of religion 宗教上の務を後回しにする. 【類】*shift* ***off*** a responsibility. ¶*shift* the blame ***on*** to another 非難を人のせいにする. ¶*shift* ***over*** to ... ...に転換する, 取替える. ¶The wind *shifted* ***round*** to the east. 風がぐるりと東に変った.

P *shift* ***for*** a living 生活のためにやりくりをする ‖ He can *shift* ***for*** himself somehow. どうにかやって行くだろう. 【類】They were left to *shift* ***for*** themselves as best they could. ¶The wind *shifted* ***from*** north ***to*** west. 風が北から西へ変った. ¶*shift* the load ***to*** the other shoulder 荷物の肩がわりをする ‖ *shift* the blame ***to*** a person 罪を人に転嫁する. ¶*shift* responsibility ***upon*** a person (another's shoulders) 人に責任を転嫁する. ¶*shift* ***with*** little money なけなしの金でどうにかやって行く. ¶*shift* ***without*** money 金なしでどうにか切抜ける.

shiftiness, *n.* 応急手段.

P appeal ***to*** *shiftiness* 応急手段に訴える.

P² *shiftiness* ***in*** an emergency ことあるとき応急手段に窮しないこと(臨機応変).

shifting, *n.* 交替; 働き.

Q There is a ***subtle*** *shifting* in the political situation. 政局微妙に動く.

P² *shifting* ***of*** a burden ***from*** one shoulder to another 肩替り.

shimmer, *n.* ちらちらする光.

P² a *shimmer* ***of*** golden sun shaking through the trees 木の間をちらちらする金色の日光.

shin, *n.* 向こうずね.

P kick a person ***on*** the *shin* その向うずねをける.

shin, *v.* よじ登る.

M² *shin* ***up*** a pole (tree) 棒(など)にだき付いて登る.

shine, *n.* 光輝; つや; 晴天.

V ***Give*** your shoes a *shine*, sir?=Shine, sir? だんなくつみがきはいかが. ¶***put*** a good *shine* on one's boots くつをぴかぴかにみがく. ¶***take*** the *shine* out of (=off) ... 《俗》...を顔色なからしめる ‖ ***take*** a *shine* to ... ...が好きになる.

Q a ***refulgent*** *shine* さんらんたる光輝. ¶the ***warm*** *shine* of the sun 太陽の暖い光.

P ***in*** rain or *shine* 晴雨にかかわらず.

shine, *v.* 輝く; 映(は)える; 卓出する; [靴の]つやを出す.

M The moon *shone* ***beautifully*** last night. 昨夜はよい月だった. ¶The sun *shines* ***bright*** (=***brightly***). 太陽がこうこうと輝く. 【類】*shine* ***bright*** like so many stars. ¶The stars are *shining* ***brilliantly***. 星がきらきら輝いている. ¶It now *shines* forth with all its strength. それは今全盛である. ¶The sun *shines* ***gloriously***. 太陽がかくかくと輝く. ¶The stars are ***keenly*** *shining*. 星がきらきら輝く. ¶*shine* ***out*** so clear and bright こうこうと輝き渡る. ¶*shine* ***supreme*** as ... ...として断然光っている.

M² The sun *shines* ***in*** through the window. 日が窓からさし込む. ¶*shine* ***up*** to ... 《米俗》...の気げんをとる.

P *shine* ***as*** an executive 責任者として手腕を示す. ¶*shine* ***from*** reflected glory 他人のおかげで光る. ¶The stars *shine* ***in*** the sky. 星が大空に輝く. ‖ She *shines* ***in*** school. 彼女は学校では光っている. 【類】*shine* ***in*** society ‖ He does not *shine* ***in*** conversation. 彼は座談の方は映(は)えない. ¶The sun was *shining* full ***into*** her room. 日は彼女のへやに一杯に射(さ)していた. ¶*shine* ***like*** polished silver みがいた銀のようにぴかぴか光る. ¶The sun *shines* ***on*** (=***over***) the earth. 太陽は地球を照らす. ‖ The moon is *shining* ***on*** the water. 月が水面を照らしている. ‖ Pleasure *shone* ***on*** her face. 喜色が彼女の顔に輝いていた. ¶The moon *shines* ***over*** the marsh. 月が沼を照らしている. ¶The moon (lamplight) *shines* ***through*** the trees. 月(など)が木立の間からさしている. 【類】The sun did not *shine* ***through*** the leaves. ¶His face *shines* ***with*** health. 彼は健康で顔がつやつやしている. ‖ *shine* ***with*** its own light [星など]それ自身の光で輝く ‖ the future *shining* ***with*** hope 希望に輝く将来 ‖ his face *shining* ***with*** triumph 勝利に輝く彼の顔色.

O rain or *shine* 晴雨にかかわらず. ¶*Shine*, sir! 靴みがきいかがですか.

shingle, *n.* 屋根板; 《米俗》看板.

V The wind has ***blown*** some *shingles* off the barn. 風が屋根板を幾枚かはいだ. ¶***hang out*** one's *shingle* [医師・弁護士など]看板を掲げる, 開業する.

Q² a delicately curved roof of ***hinoki*** *shingles* ひのきぶきの美しくわん曲した屋根.

shining, *n.* つや出し.

Q² ***shoe*** *shining* くつみがき.

ship, *n.* 船, 艦.

V ***abandon*** a *ship* [船から]総員退去する. ¶***anchor*** a *ship* just off the coast 海岸をちょっと離れた所に船を停泊させる. ¶***board*** (=***go aboard or go on board***) a *ship* 乗船する. ¶***bring*** a *ship* to anchor 投びょうする ‖ ***bring*** a *ship* to 船を停止させる. ¶***calk*** a ship 船の底部のすき間をふさぐ. ¶Suddenly great billows rose and threatened to ***capsize*** the *ship*. 突然大波が起って今にも船を転覆させそうだった. ¶a failure to ***catch*** a *ship* 船の乗遅れ. ¶***clear*** a *ship* for action 戦闘準備で甲板を片づける ‖ ***clear*** a *ship* at the custom-house 税関で出港手続をする. ¶***commission*** a *ship*= put a ship in commission 軍艦を就役させる. ¶***decorate*** *ships* with bunting 旗で船を飾る. ¶***desert*** a *ship* 船を捨て

る. ¶*disarm* a *ship* 船の武装を解く. ¶The *ship* was ***dismasted*** and waterlogged. その船は帆柱を折られ水浸しだ. ¶***dress*** a *ship* rainbow fashion 満船飾を施す ‖ Ships are ***dressed*** full. 船は満艦飾を施してある. ¶***dress*** [*up*] a *ship* 満船飾をする. ¶The *ship* was ***driven*** into the harbour by stress of weather. 船は荒天のために港に追込まれた. ¶***electrify*** *ships* 船を電化する. ¶***equip*** a *ship* 船をぎ装する. ¶***fit out*** a *ship* 船をぎ装する. ¶***freight*** a *ship* 船に荷物を積込む. ¶*Ships* are ***guided*** through channels by pilots. 水先案内が船舶の海峡通過を案内する. ¶a pilot ***guiding*** a *ship* ***in*** 船舶の安全入港をさせる水先案内. ¶***hail*** a *ship* 船を呼ぶ. ¶***handle*** a *ship* 船を操縦する. ¶***hire*** a *ship* 船を雇う. ¶***launch*** a *ship* 船を進水させる. ¶***lay down*** a *ship* [風波が]船を傾ける. ¶***leave*** a *ship* 下船する. ¶***load*** and ***unload*** *ships* 船に荷を積込みまた積降ろす. 【類】***load*** a *ship* with coal. ¶***moor*** a *ship* to No. 3 buoy 船を第三号ブイにけい留する. 【類】Our *ship* was ***moored*** safely in Yokohama harbour. ¶***name*** (=***christen***) a *ship* 船に命名する. ¶On the bridge the officers of the watch are ***navigating*** their *ship*. ブリッジで当番士官が船を指揮している. ¶***pay off*** a *ship* 船を解役する(予備にする). ¶***pilot*** a *ship* to the Orient 東洋諸国へ船舶を案内する. ¶***place*** a *ship* in service 新造船を就役させる. ¶***pump*** a *ship* ポンプで船の排水をする. ¶***put*** a *ship* into the water=launch a ship ‖ ***put*** a *ship* out of commission (=in the reserve) 予備艦とする. ¶***raise*** a sunken *ship* 沈没船を引揚げる. ¶***re-deliver*** a *ship* to its owners 所有者に船を戻す. ¶The *ship* was ***requisitioned*** as a transport. その船は運送船として徴発された. ¶***run*** a *ship* on a sunken rock 船を暗礁に乗上げる. ¶***sail*** a *ship* 帆船を操縦する. ¶***scuttle*** a *ship* 穴をあけて船を沈める. ¶***send*** a *ship* to the bottom 船を沈める. ¶The *ship* was ***sunk*** by the violence of the gale (a wave, a cannonball, an explosion). 船は強風(など)のために沈められた. ¶***speak*** a *ship* [航海中]他船に通報する. ¶***strike*** a *ship* out of the active list 予備船にする. ¶***survey*** *ships* 船を検査する. ¶The *ship* was ***swallowed up*** by the waves. 船は波にのまれた. ¶***take*** *ship* (train) for ... 船(汽車)で…に行く. 【類】He ***took*** *ship* from ... and no one has heard of him since. / ***take*** *ship* at ... for ... ¶***tie*** a *ship* to a pier さん橋に船をつなぐ. ¶The *ship* was ***tossed about*** by the waves. 船は波でゆれた. ¶***wind*** a *ship* 船の向きを反対にする. ¶The *ship* was ***wrecked***. 難船した.

V^2 The *ship* ***became*** so ***battered*** by storm as to be no longer seaworthy. その船はもう航海にたえないまでに暴風に破壊された. ¶The *ship* ***careens*** to the port. 船が左げんへ傾く. ¶when one's *ship* ***comes home*** (=***in***) [比ゆ的に] 運が向いて来ると, 金が出来ると. ¶The *ship* ***draws*** deep (fifteen feet of water). その船は喫水が深い(十五フィートある). ¶The *ship* ***went down*** with all hands in a storm. 船は暴風で乗組員もろとも沈没した. ¶The *ship* has ***righted*** itself (=herself). 船は(航行中傾いた)船体を起した. ¶The *ship* ***pitches up*** and ***down***, and ***rolls*** heavily from side to side. 船は上下に縦揺れしまた激しく横揺れする. ¶The *ship* ***rolled*** and ***lurched*** very heavily in a storm. 船は暴風で横揺れしてひどく傾いた. ¶The *ship* ***ran ashore***. 船はかくざした. ¶The *ship* ***sailed*** down the river. 船は川下へ帆走した. ¶The *ship* was ***sinking*** rapidly. 船がずんずん沈んで行った. ¶The *ship* is ***steering*** due south. 船は真南に進行している. ¶The *ship* ***struck*** on a rock and ***sank***. 船は暗礁に乗上げて沈没した. ¶The *ship* ***tacks*** (=***beats***) against the wind. 船は風を間切って進む.

Q an irruption of ***armed*** *ships* from the western world 西世界からの武装船の侵入. ¶a ***capital*** *ship* 主力艦. ¶***foreign-going*** *ships* 外国行の船. ¶an ***ill-starred*** *ship* 不運な船. ¶***obsolete*** *ships* 廃船. ¶a ***ocean-going*** *ship* 外洋航海船. ¶an ***outgoing*** *ship* 出港船. ¶a ***sinking*** *ship* 没落しつつある船. ¶salvage a ***sunken*** *ship* 沈没船を引上げる. ¶***swift*** *ships* 快速船. ¶The *ship* is ***weather-beaten***. 船は大分老朽している.

Q^2 an ***amenities*** *ship* 慰問船. ¶a ***cable*** *ship* 海底電線敷設船. ¶a ***cargo*** *ship* (=boat) 貨物船. ¶a ***clipper*** *ship* 一種の快速帆船. ¶a ***deep sea*** *ship* 遠洋航行船. ¶an ***excursion*** *ship* 遊覧船. ¶a ***flag*** *ship* 旗艦. ¶a ***full-dress*** *ship* 満艦飾を施した船. ¶A modern ***giant*** *ship* is worth probably over £3,000,000. 近代の巨船は三百万ポンド以上かかるだろう. ¶a ***hospital*** *ship* 病院船. ¶a ***look-out*** *ship* 警戒艦, 見張船. ¶a ***luxury*** *ship* 豪華船. ¶a ***merchant*** *ship*=a merchantman 商船. ¶a ***mercy*** *ship* with supplies for internees 抑留者に渡す物品を運ぶ慰問船. ¶a ***monster*** *ship* 巨船. ¶an ***ocean*** *ship* 外洋航海船. ¶a ***passenger*** *ship* 客船. ¶a ***patrol*** *ship* 監視船. ¶a ***picket*** *ship* 監視船. ¶a ***prison*** *ship* 監獄船. ¶a ***register*** *ship* 積載量登録船(昔スペインの西インド諸島へ通商した船舶). ¶a ***refugee*** *ship* 避難民輸送船. ¶a ***repatriation*** *ship* 送還船. ¶a ***rescue*** *ship* 救助船. ¶a ***salvage*** *ship* 海難救助船. ¶a ***sister*** *ship* of (=to) ... …の姉妹船. ¶a ***slave*** *ship* どれい船. ¶The whalers hunt in ***small steam*** or ***oil-burning*** *ships* called whale-chasers. 捕鯨者はキャッチャー・ボートという小型の汽船あるいは油船で鯨をとる. ¶a ***supply*** *ship* 補給船. ¶a ***surveying*** *ship* 測量船. ¶a ***target*** *ship* 標的用の船. ¶a ***transport*** [*ship*] 運送船.

P be ***aboard*** (=on board) a *ship* 乗船している. ¶barges anchored ***alongside*** the *ship* 本船横付の荷揚船. ¶go (transport) ***by*** *ship* 船で行く(輸送する). ¶they sailed ***in*** the *ship* ... 彼らは…という船で出帆した. ¶run ***into*** a *ship* 船に衝突する. ¶a machine ***on*** a *ship* 船上備付の機械 ‖ sail ***on*** the same *ship* with ... …と同船で出帆する. 【類】travel ***on*** *ships*.

P^2 a merchant *ship* ***of*** 4,500 tons 四千五百トンの 商船.

O About *ship*! 右旋回!

ship, *v.* 船積する; 回送する; 《米》輸送する; 船に乗込む.

M pack them so that they can be safely *shipped* ***abroad*** 海外へ送っても大丈夫のように荷造りする. ¶*ship* a person (thing) ***back*** to ... …へ人(物)を送り返す. ¶Our goods are *shipped* ***extensively*** to all quarters of the globe. 弊店の商品は手広く世界至る所に輸出している. ¶*ship* ***out*** emigrants 移民を船で送り出す.

M^2 *ship* ***off*** 船で回送する.

P He *shipped* ***as*** a sailor in a French vessel plying between Europe and Japan. 彼は欧州・日本間を往復するフランス船に水夫として乗込んだ ‖ *ship* personal baggage ***as*** freight 手荷物を運送貨物として船積みする ‖ to be *shipped* ***at*** the seller's convenience 売主の都合のよいときに船積みされる. ¶*ship* goods ***at*** Liverpool ***for*** New York 貨物をニューヨークへ向けリヴァプールで船積みする. ¶*ship* goods ***by*** express or ***by*** freight 急行便または鉄道便で貨物を送る ☞ ship goods by express 《米》トラックなどで急送する意. ‖ *ship* ***by*** the first steamer to ... …行きの最初の汽船で送る. 【類】***By*** what ship have you *shipped*?. ¶goods *shipped* ***for*** England 英国に向け船積みした貨物. 【類】goods *shipped* ***from*** America ***for*** ... ¶goods *shipped* ***on*** the steamer for ... …行きの汽船に船積みした荷物 ‖ *ship* ***on*** consignment 委託品として送る. ¶The corn was *shipped* ***to*** Russia. 穀物は船でロシアに運送された. ‖ be *shipped* ***to*** order 注文通り発送される.

shipboard, *n.* 船上, 甲板; 船.

P go ***on*** *shipboard* 乗船する ‖ days ***on*** *shipboard* 船上の日日. ¶the Jesuits were sent ***by*** the *shipboards* to ... 幾隻かの船に乗せてヤソ会派の牧師が…に送られた.

shipment, *n.* 船積み, 積込み; 出荷貨物.

V ***effect*** *shipment* 船積みを終る. ¶The *shipments* are being ***expedited*** as much as possible. 船積みはできるだけ急いでいます. ¶*shipments* are ***made to*** ... …へ出荷する. ¶*Shipment* has been ***paralysed*** in consequence of strikes. ストライキのため船積みがと絶した. ¶***send*** a trial *shipment* 試みに送荷する. ¶refuse to ***take*** *shipments* for Chinese ports [回そう店など]中国諸港への積出しを拒絶する.

Q a ***combined*** *shipment* of horses and cattle 馬と牛の合併積込. ¶***partial*** *shipment* 一部積み. ¶***short*** *shipment* 積残り貨物. ¶the ***total*** *shipment* will be divided into three parts, each going by a separate vessel. 全部の積込は三部に分け, それぞれ別の船に積まれる.

Q^2 ***carload*** *shipment* [貨車の]貸切積み. ¶ban ***copper*** *shipments* to ... 銅の…向け積出しを禁止する. ¶American ***food*** *shipments* to Japan アメリカ食糧の日本向け積出. ¶a ***fresh-fruit*** *shipment* 果実積出. ¶***January*** (***summer***) *shipments* 一月(夏)の積出. ¶bear ***long-distance*** *shipments* 遠方送荷に耐える. ¶an ***overseas*** *shipment* 海外への発送.

P a port ***of*** *shipment* 船積港.

P^2 *shipment* ***by*** freight (parcel post) 船荷(小包)としての発送.

shipping, *n.* 船舶.

Q^2 ***merchant*** *shipping* 商船.

shipwreck, *n.* 難船；破滅.
V *suffer* (=*make*) *shipwreck* of one's hopes 希望がめちゃめちゃになる.
P vessels lost *by shipwreck* 難破のために失った船. ¶survivors *from* a *shipwreck* 難船の生存者. ¶They perished *in* a *shipwreck*. 彼らは難船で死んだ.

shirk, *v.* 怠ける.
M² *shirk off* (=*out*) こそこそ抜け出す.
P *shirk* [*from*] one's duty 義務を怠る.

shirt, *n.* シャツ, ワイシャツ.
V *Air* me a *shirt*. 私のシャツに風を当ててくれ. ¶He *has* not a *shirt* to his back. 彼は無一物だ. ¶*lay aside* one's *shirt* シャツを脱ぐ. ¶*slip* one's *shirt* over one's head シャツを頭からかぶる. ¶*strip* (=*take*) *off* one's *shirt* シャツを脱ぐ. ¶*wear* a dirty white *shirt* きたない白ワイシャツを着ている.
Q a *shirt fleeced inside* 裏毛のシャツ. ¶a *ready-made shirt* でき合いのワイシャツ. ¶a *stiff-collared shirt* えりの堅いワイシャツ.
Q² a *nylon shirt* ナイロンのシャツ. ¶a *knit shirt* メリヤスシャツ. ¶a *merino shirt* 純毛のメリヤスシャツ. ¶a *sport shirt* スポーツシャツ. ¶a good *Sunday shirt* よそ行きのワイシャツ. ¶a *sweat shirt* [晩春から初夏にかけて着る]薄手の婦人用セーター ‖ the fluffy blonde in pale lemon *sweat shirt* 薄いレモン色のセーターを着たうぶ毛のブロンドの女. ☞外国婦人は顔をそらない人が多い. ¶a *uniform shirt* 軍人用のシャツ. ¶a *utility shirt* 徳用シャツ(上衣をぬいで着るブラウス式のもの). ¶a 100% *wool shirt* 純毛シャツ. ¶a *work shirt* 労働用シャツ.
P work *in* one's *shirt* ワイシャツだけで(上衣をぬいで)働く. ¶stripped *to* the *shirt* ワイシャツ一枚になって. ¶put one's coat on *without* a *shirt* ワイシャツなしで上衣を着る.

shirt-sleeve, *n.* シャツのそで.
P a man sitting *in* his *shirt-sleeves* at a desk 上衣を脱いで(ワイシャツだけで)デスクに向っている人. 【類】work *in* one's *shirt-sleeves*.

shiver, *n.* 身震い.
V *cause* a *shiver* to permeate the reader 読者をりつ然たらしめる. ¶*feel* the *shiver* down one's spine 背筋がぞっとする. ¶It *gave* me the *shivers*. 私はぞっと身震いした.
V² A *shiver ran* through me and my teeth chattered. ぞっと身震いがして私の歯ががちがち鳴った. ‖ It made the cold *shivers run* over me. それで私はぞっとした.
Q It gives me the *cold shivers* when I think what might have become of me. 私の身がどうなっていたことだろうと思うとぞっとする. ¶A *sudden shiver* came upon him. 彼は突然身震いした.
P² something like a *shiver of* horror passed over me when ... ...の時恐ろしさに私は身震いのようなものを感じた.

shiver, *v.* 震える.
P *shiver with* cold (fright) 寒くて(など)震える.

shoal, *n.* 群.
P fish *in shoals* 群魚. 「の群.
P² a *shoal of* fish (porpoises, whales, herrings) 魚(など)の群.

shock, *n.* 衝突；震動, 地震；衝激(ショック), 打撃.
V a device for *absorbing* a *shock* 震動を除く工夫(スプリングなど). ¶*administer* a mild *shock* to ... ...に軽い衝激を与える. ¶*experience* a *shock* 衝激を受ける. ¶I *felt* a *shock*. 私はぎょっとした. ‖ We *felt* a smart *shock* of earthquake. 激震があった. ¶I *got* (=*experienced*) a great *shock* when I heard the news. その話を聞いたとき私は非常にびっくりした. ¶*give* a *shock* to ... ...をぎょっとさせる. ¶for the purpose of *producing* emotional *shock* 感情を刺激するために. ¶*receive* an electric *shock* 感電する. ¶Experience has shown that reenforced concrete buildings best *withstand* earthquake *shocks*. 補強コンクリートの建物が一番よく地震に耐えるということが経験で分かっている.
V² a *shock came* to them when ... ...したとき衝激を感じた. ¶A slight *shock* of earthquake *occurred*. 軽い地震があった. ¶An electric *shock ran* along the nerve. 電気が神経を伝わった.
Q A muscle contracts when irritated by an *electric shock*. 電気で刺激すると筋肉が収縮する. ¶be killed by an *electric shock* 感電して死ぬ. ¶The sight was a *great shock* to the wife. 妻はこれを見てびっくりした. ¶*horizontal shock* 〘地震〙水平動. ¶a *mental shock* 精神的打撃. ¶receive a *mild shock* ちょっと驚く. ¶we received a *profound shock* when it became known that ... ...が分かったときにわれわれは心から驚いた. ¶a great *psychical shock* 精神的大打撃. ¶give a person a *rude shock* ひどくどきんとさせる. ¶a *sad shock* to his mother [子息の死など]彼の母に取っては悲しい打撃. ¶receive a *serious shock* 重大な打撃を受ける. ¶*Several shocks* of earthquake were felt. 地震が数回あった. ¶There were two *severe shocks* of earthquake in Tokyo. 東京にひどい地震が二回あった. 【類】It gave a *severe shock* to his constitution (体). 【類】We have had a *severe shock* of earthquake. ¶feel a *slight shock* 軽微な震動を感じる. ¶give a *terrific shock* to ... ...に恐ろしいショックを与える. ¶collide with a *tremendous shock* 激しく衝突する. ¶*vertical shock* [地震の]上下動. 「経のショック.
Q² a sharp *earthquake shock* 強い地震. ¶*nerve shock* 神経のショック.
P He is suffering *from shock*. 彼は打撃を受けて悩んでいる. ¶He died *of shock*. 彼は悲痛の余り死んだ. ¶without coming *to* the *shock* 衝突するまでにならないで. ¶The news came upon me *with* a great *shock*. その話を聞いて私はどきんとした.
P² a *shock of* grief or joy 身にこたえるほどの悲しみまたは喜び. ¶a *shock to* the moral sense of a community 社会道徳の通念に対する一衝撃. 【類】The *shock to* public feeling was very great. / His announcement that he was going on the stage was a *shock to* the family.

shock, *v.* ぞっとさせる.
P I was *shocked at* (=*by*) his conduct. 彼のやり口に私は驚いた. 【類】He was *shocked at* her abandonments (しなだれかかって来たので). ¶I was almost *shocked with* the spectacle of ... 私は...の光景にほとんど衝激に近いものを感じた. 「びっくりしている.
O I am *shocked* to hear of his death. 彼の死を聞いて私はびっくりしている.

shocker, *n.* 《俗》扇情的な小説.
Q² a *shilling shocker* 一シリングの扇情小説.

shoe, *n.* くつ.
V *blacken shoes* くつに墨を塗る. ¶*shoes blacked* and *polished* till you can see your face in them 顔が映るまでにみがき上げたくつ. ¶*brush* [*up*] the *shoes* くつにブラシをかける. ¶*change* one's wet *shoes* for dry ones ぬれぐつを乾いたくつにはき換える. ¶*clean* one's *shoes* くつを奇麗にする. ¶*dust off* one's *shoes* with long-handled brushes ere entering はいる前に長柄のブラシでくつのちりを掃う. ¶I am not worthy to *fasten* (=*tie*) his *shoes*. 私は彼のくつのひもを結ぶだけの値打もない. ¶*get* one's *shoes polished* (=*shined*) くつをみがいてもらう. ¶*get* (=put) *on* one's *shoes* くつをはく. ¶*have* the right *shoe* in the wrong foot くつの右と左をはき違える. ¶*have* one's *shoes* partly *resoled* くつ底の半張りをしてもらう. 【類】*have* one's *shoes resoled* at the front (半張り). ¶You may *keep* your *shoes on*. くつをはいたままでよい. ¶*lace shoes* くつのひもを結ぶ. ¶*lay off* one's *shoes* くつをぬぐ. ¶*polish shoes* くつをみがく. ¶*pull off* (*on*) one's *shoes* and stockings くつとくつ下を脱ぐ(はく). ¶*put* one's *shoes* on the shoetrees くつ型にくつをはめる. ¶*put on shoes* くつをはく. ¶*resole* (*reheel*, *revamp*) *shoes* くつの底(かかと)を張替える. ¶*scrape* one's *shoes* on the scraper 泥ふきでくつをこする. ¶*shine shoes* 靴をぴかぴかにみがく. ¶*Shoes* are *slipped off* in the porch. くつは玄関で脱ぐ. ¶*take off* (=*remove*) one's *shoes* くつを脱ぐ. ¶*unbutton* her *shoes* for her 彼女のくつのボタンをはずしてやる. ¶*unlace* a *shoe* くつのひもを解く. ¶I am not worthy to stoop down and *unloose* his *shoes* (tie his shoe-lace). 私は身をかがめて彼のくつのひもを解く(結ぶ)にも足らない. ¶*wear* unsightly "health" *shoes* 不体裁な衛生ぐつをはく. ¶*wipe* one's *shoes* on the mat マットでくつをぬぐう.
V² My *shoes bite* [me]. くつが窮屈で痛い. ¶My *shoes creak*. 私のくつはきゅうきゅう鳴る. ¶The *shoes pinch* me. くつがきつい.
Q *comfortable shoes* はき心地のよいくつ. ¶pair of *creaky shoes* 一足のきゅーきゅー言うくつ. ¶The skin was off my feet owing to the *hard shoes*. くつが堅いので足の皮がむけた. ¶*high shoes* 長ぐつ. ¶*high-heeled shoes* かかとの高いくつ. ¶*low shoes* 短ぐつ. ¶*low-heeled shoes* かかとの低いくつ. ¶*pat shoes* 足にしっくり合うくつ. ¶*pointless* (*heelless*) *shoes* for women's wear 婦人用先なし(ヒールのない)のくつ. ¶*russet shoes* あずき革のくつ. ¶*sensible shoes* 飾りっ気のない女のくつ. ¶*soaked shoes* and dripping

umbrellas 水のしみ込んだくつと雨水のたらたら落ちるかさ. ¶***square-toed*** *shoes* つまさきの角張ったくつ. ¶***squeaky*** *shoes* きゅーきゅーいうくつ. ¶***tan*** *shoes* 濃茶革のくつ. ¶***thin-soled*** *shoes* 薄底のくつ. ¶***tight*** (loose) *shoes* きっちりした(ゆるい)くつ. ¶***ungainly*** *shoes* 不かっこうなくつ. ¶***wellworn*** *shoes* くたびれたくつ.

Q^2 ***at-home*** *shoes* 家庭用ぐつ. ¶***baby*** *shoes* 赤ん坊ぐつ. ¶***canvas*** *shoes* ズックぐつ. ¶***combat*** *shoes* 兵隊ぐつ. ¶***dress*** *shoes* 礼式用ぐつ. ¶***felt*** *shoes* フェルトぐつ. ¶***gymnasium*** *shoes* 運動ぐつ. ¶***lace*** *shoes* 編上げぐつ. ¶glossy patent ***leather*** *shoes* 紳士用のエナメルぐつ. ¶***low cut*** *shoes* 浅く作った婦人ぐつ. ¶***rain*** *shoes* 雨ぐつ. ¶***rubber*** *shoes* ゴムぐつ. ¶galoshes—***snow*** *shoes* 雪ぐつ(婦人用雨ぐつ式のもの) ‖ fur-lined ***snow*** *shoes* 毛裏の雪ぐつ. ¶***tennis*** *shoes*＝sneakers 庭球用ぐつ. ¶heavy ***walking*** *shoes* 重い歩行ぐつ. ¶***What size*** [*shoe*] do you wear?—I wear size 8, width E. どんな寸法のくつをおはきですか.—私は大きさ 8 幅 E のをはいています. ¶***white satin*** *shoes* 白じゅすのくつ. ¶***work*** *shoes* 作業ぐつ.

P One cannot ask a stately goddess, five feet ten ***in*** her *shoes*, to clean plates and dishes.—Kipling. だれしもくつをはいて五フィート十インチというりっぱな女神にさらばちを洗えとは言いかねる. ‖ stand ***in*** a person's *shoes* その代りをしている ‖ shake ***in*** one's *shoes* ふるえている. ¶step ***into*** a person's *shoes* その後がまにすわる. ¶three pair ***of*** *shoes* 三足のくつ. ¶brush mud ***off*** one's *shoes* くつの泥を落す. ¶[***with***] one *shoe* off and one shoe on 片足だけくつをはいて.

P^2 a *shoe* ***with*** a strap 革帯のついたくつ ‖ wooden *shoes* ***with*** loose heels かかとのゆるやかな木ぐつ.

shoe, *v.* くつをはく.

M ***heavily*** *shod* がん丈なくつをはいて. ¶a shoemaker is always ***ill*** *shod* くつ屋のやぶれくつ(こう屋の白ばかま).

shoe-lace, *n.* くつひも.

V one who is not worthy to ***tie*** her *shoe-lace* 彼女の足もとにも寄りつけないつまらない男.

shoestring, *n.* くつひも;《米口》小額の資本.

P start a business ***on*** a *shoestring*. わずかの資本で商売を始める.

shogunate, *n.* 将軍政治, 幕府.

P Japan ***under*** the *shogunate* 幕治下の日本.

shoot, *n.* 若枝, 新芽; 発射; 銃猟.

V ***have*** a *shoot* at ... ...を(銃で)撃つ. ¶workers ***transplanting*** the young *shoots* in a ricefield 田植の農夫たち.

Q a ***sudden*** *shoot* of light せん光. ¶the ***tender*** *shoots* in spring 春先に出る若芽.

Q^2 a ***bamboo*** *shoot* たけのこ. ¶out on a ***winter morning*** *shoot* 冬の朝の銃猟に出て.

P *shoots* ***from*** old stumps 古株の新芽.

shoot, *v.* 射撃する; 急に進める.

M *shoot* ***ahead*** 急に先頭へとび出す. ¶*shoot* a boat ***ahead*** ボートを矢のように進める. ¶We have *shot* ***away*** all our ammunition. われわれは弾薬をことごとく撃ち尽した. ¶He *shot* ***back*** to his home. 彼はわが家にはせ帰った. ¶He *shoots* ***better*** than he rides. 彼は乗馬よりも射撃の方が得意だ. ¶I *shot* it ***dead*** in two bullets. 私は二弾でそれを射殺した. ¶The leaves *shoot* ***forth***. 木の葉が発芽する. ‖ The shore *shoots* ***forth*** into the sea. 海岸は海に突出している. ¶*shoot* ***out*** the lips 口をとがらす ‖ *shoot* ***out*** one's tongue [ばかにして]舌を出す. ‖ A volcano *shoots* ***out*** flame and rocks. 火山は火炎や岩石を噴出する ‖ *shoot* ***out*** a sudden peal of laughter 急に声高に笑い出す ‖ Passengers were *shot* ***out*** of the bus. 乗客がどっとバスから出た. ‖ A plant *shoots* ***out*** buds. 植物が芽を出す. ‖ rice plants *shooting* ***out*** into ears 穂の出た稲. ¶He cannot *shoot* ***straight***. 彼は正確に撃てない. ¶*shoot* ***well*** 射撃がうまい.

M^2 The enemy's raider was *shot* ***down*** by an AA gun. 敵の爆撃機が高射砲で撃ち落された. 【類】A bobsleigh *shoots* ***down*** like an arrow. ¶*shoot* ***off*** firecrackers 爆竹を鳴らす ‖ *shoot* ***off*** one's (＝at the) mouth《俗》ぺらぺらしゃべる. ¶*shoot* ***off*** down a stream 川を(いかだなどで矢のように)はせ下る ‖ He had his arm *shot* ***off***. 彼は腕を射ち落された. ¶The boy is *shooting* ***up***. その男の子はずんずん育つ. ‖ The flames (A fountain) *shoot(s)* ***up***. 火の手(など)が上がる. 【類】Flames and smoke *shot* ***up*** from the burning house. ‖ See those rockets *shooting* ***up*** into the air! 空に上がるあののろしを見給え. ‖ A tree *shoots* ***up*** against the sky. 一本の木が大空にそびえている.

P *shoot* ***across*** one's mind 突然心に浮ぶ. ¶*shoot* ***at*** a mark (target) 目標(的)を目がけて撃つ. ‖ They are *shooting* ***at*** the wrong mark. 彼らは見当違いをしている. ¶*shoot* the ball ***between*** the posts [しゅう球で]ポストの間に球を送る. ¶He was *shot* ***by*** a robber. 彼は盗賊に撃たれた. ¶*shoot* ***down*** a slope [そりなど]坂道を矢のように下る ‖ Prices are *shooting* ***up***. 物価が上ってきた ‖ Unemployment *shot* ***up*** to a total of two million workers receiving State doles. 国家の失業救済手当を受ける失業労働者の総数は二百万人に達した. ‖ Tall trees *shoot* ***up*** to the clouds. 大木が高くそびえている. ‖ The corn is *shooting* ***up*** in warm weather. 気候が暖いので小麦が芽を出してきた. 【類】Soon a stalk has *shot* ***up***. / After the rain mushrooms *shoot* ***up*** as by magic. ¶He was *shot* ***for*** a spy. 彼は軍事探偵として銃殺された. ¶He *shot* ***from*** ambush. 彼は身を隠して射撃した. ¶He was *shot* ***in*** the arm. 彼は腕を撃たれた. ‖ *shoot* oneself ***in*** the mouth 口中を撃って自殺する. ‖ *shoot* nets ***in*** a river across the whole width 川幅全体に網を張る. ¶peaks that *shoot* ***into*** the blue (sky) 天空にそびえる峰々. ¶The express train *shot* ***into*** the crowded station. 急行列車は雑とうしている停車場へ矢のようにばく進して来た. 【類】*shoot* an arrow ***into*** the air. ¶*shoot* ***out of*** (＝through) a tunnel [汽車が]トンネルから走り出る. ‖ The flame *shot* ***out of*** the roof. 火炎は屋根から矢のように吹だした. ¶*shoot* oneself ***through*** the head 頭を打ち抜いて自殺する. 【類】He was *shot* ***through*** the head (heart). ¶He was *shot* ***to*** death (＝shot dead). 彼は銃殺された. ¶*shoot* ***with*** a rifle at a mark 施条銃で的を射撃する. 【類】He was *shot* ***with*** a pistol. ‖ silk *shot* ***with*** gold 金糸を織込んだ絹布. 【類】Her dress is *shot* ***with*** threads of gold and silver. ‖ His black hair was a little *shot* ***with*** gray. 彼の黒髪は少し白髪が混っていた. 【類】His hair was *shot* with gray not by age but by grief.

shooter, *n.* 射手.

Q^2 a ***snipe*** *shooter*《口語》もく拾い. ¶a ***trouble*** *shooter* けんかのまとめ役.

shooting, *n.* 射撃, 銃猟.

V *Shooting* and fishing may be ***pursued*** all the year round. 銃猟と漁猟は年中できる.

Q^2 ***clay-pegeon*** *shooting* 土ばと射撃(土製のはとを飛ばせて撃つ練習射撃). ¶***Duck*** *shooting* is easily the first of gun sports. かも猟は優に銃猟の首位を占める. ¶***fancy*** (＝***trick***) *shooting* 曲射撃. ¶*shooting*, ***feather*** or ***fur*** 鳥獣の猟. ¶***outdoor*** *shooting* 野外撮影. ¶***trap*** *shooting* 射出物射撃.

P The weather was rather unfavorable ***for*** *shooting* 天候が銃猟にはいささか不向だった.

shop, *n.* 商店; 工場.

V ***close*** one's *shop* 休業する. ¶The police ***closed down*** all the *shops* concerned. 警察がそれに関係ある店を全部閉鎖した. ¶***close up*** a *shop* 店をたたむ. ¶***hire*** untenanted *shops* at low rentals 安い店賃で空いている店を借りる. ¶***keep*** *shop* 店を持っている. 【類】He ***keeps*** a *shop* in the Ginza. ¶Owing to stress of work, I cannot ***leave*** my *shop*. 忙しいので店を明けられない. ¶***open*** [a] *shop* on one's own account 独力で開店する. ¶***open up*** *shop* 開店する. ¶***operate*** a shoe *shop* くつ店を経営する. ¶***restock*** a *shop* 店の仕入替をする. ¶***set up*** (＝***start***) a *shop* 店を出す. ¶The *shop* is ***shut***. 店がしまっている. ¶***shut up*** *shop* ＝give up business《口語》廃業する. ¶The *shop* is richly ***stocked***. その店は商品が豊富に仕入れてある. ¶***talk*** *shop*《俗》専ら商売(または職業上)の話をする.

Q a ***barber's*** [*shop*]＝《米》a barbershop 理髪店. ¶a ***bookseller's*** [*shop*]＝《米》a book store 本屋. ¶a ***broker's*** *shop* 仲買人事務所. ¶a ***closed*** *shop*〔労〕クローズドショップ. ¶He keeps a ***confectioner's*** *shop*. 彼は菓子屋をしている. ¶a ***dingy small*** *shop* with a sign "..." 「...」と看板の出ているきたない小さな店. ¶a ***double-fronted*** *shop* 店先が二つに分かれている商店. ¶an ***exclusive*** *shop* 高級店. ¶an ***extensive*** *shop* 手広く商売する店. ¶***fashionable*** *shops* 上流向きの店. ¶a ***mammoth*** *shop* 非常に大きな店. ¶a ***modest*** *shop* 小さな店. ¶His is an ***old-established*** *shop*. 彼の店は老舗(しにせ)だ. ¶an ***open*** *shop*〔労〕オープン・ショップ. ¶***reputable*** *shops* 評判のよいりっぱな店. ¶an ***unorganized*** *shop*〔労〕労組の未組織工場. ¶a ***tailor's*** [*shop*]＝《米》a tailor-shop. ☞ 商店の意では英は shop, 米は store とい

う．例えば菓子屋の意では a sweet *shop*《英》, a candy *store*《米》．なお《米》の shop は仕事場の意．例：a barber*shop*, a meat *shop*.

Q² an ***antique*** *shop* こっとう屋．¶a ***beauty*** *shop* (＝salon) 美容院．¶a ***beer*** *shop* ビヤホール．¶a ***bird*** *shop* 小鳥屋．¶a ***blacksmith*** *shop*＝《英》a blacksmith's [shop] かじ屋．¶a ***boiler*** *shop*＝《英》a boilersmith's 湯わかし製作所．¶a ***brass*** *shop* 真ちゅう製品商．¶a ***cake*** *shop* 菓子屋．¶a ***camera*** *shop* 写真機商．¶a ***chocolate*** and ***sweet*** *shop* 菓子屋．¶a ***chow-chow*** (＝general *or* ***variety***) *shop* 雑貨店；よろず屋．¶a small ***clothing*** *shop* 小さい呉服屋．¶a ***coffee*** *shop* コーヒー店．¶a ***collar*** and ***tie*** *shop* 洋品屋．¶a ***delicatessen*** [*shop*] 食品店；即席料理店．¶a ***dog*** *shop* 犬商．¶a ***dolly*** *shop* くず屋；無鑑札の質屋．¶a ***fancy goods*** *shop* 小間物店．¶a ***farthing*** *shop* in the East-End [ロンドンの] イーストエンドの一文菓子屋．¶a ***florist*** *shop* 花屋．¶a ***food*** *shop* 食料品店．¶a ***foundry*** *shop* 金物屋．¶a ***good-service*** *shop* 親切な店．¶a ***jerry*** *shop*《俗》下等なビール店．¶a ***liquor*** *shop* 酒屋．¶a ***meat*** *shop*＝《英》a butcher's [shop] 肉屋．¶a ***men's wear*** *shop* 洋服屋．¶a ***milk*** *shop* (＝bar) 牛乳屋．¶a ***multiple*** *shop* なんでも屋．¶a ***novelty*** *shop* 小間物屋(外人相手のみやげ物店など)．¶a ***pack*** *shop* キャラメルなど箱入の candy を自動的に売る飾台(映画館などに設けてある)．¶a ***painting*** *shop* 塗装工場．¶a ***pastry*** *shop* パン屋．¶a ***pet*** *shop* 愛がん動物商．¶a ***print*** *shop*《米》印刷所．¶a ***provision*** *shop* 食料品店．¶a ***repair*** *shop* 修理工場．¶a ***repairing*** *shop* for bicycles 自転車修繕工場．¶a ***retail*** *shop* 小売商．¶reopen a ***shoe*** *shop*《米》くつ屋を再び開業する．¶a ***shoe-repair*** *shop* くつ修理工場．¶a ***slap-bang*** *shop*《ロンドン語》《俗》下等な飲食店．¶a ***souvenir*** (＝***gift***) *shop* みやげ物屋．¶a ***sweat*** *shop*《米》酷使工場(安給料で長時間職工をこき使う)．¶a ***tea*** *shop* 喫茶店．¶a ***trade*** *shop* (school) 徒弟練習所．¶a ***union*** *shop* 組合工場．

P We buy provisions ***at*** a *shop* in the neighbourhood. うちでは食料品を近所の店で買っている．‖I deal ***at*** his *shop*. 私は彼の店が買付けだ．¶The books ***in*** that *shop* are mostly novels. あの店の本は大抵小説だ．‖a boy employed ***in*** our *shop* うちの小僧‖serve ***in*** a *shop* 店に勤める‖people who work ***in*** shops 工場に勤めている人々．¶He smells ***of*** the *shop*. 彼は商人臭い．

P² stores and *shops* ***along*** the street 表通りの商店．¶a *shop* ***for*** milk 牛乳屋．¶The *shops* ***in*** this town are very tempting. この町の商店は大いに人を引きつける．

shop-front, *n.* 店付, 店の構え．

V ***smash*** *shop-fronts* 店頭を破って物を盗む．

Q a ***flaming*** *shop-front* はでな店付．

shopman, *n.* 売子, 店員；《米》職工．

Q² The strike of ***railroad*** *shopmen* was called. 鉄道工場のストが中止になった．

P² a *shopman* ***at*** (＝***behind***) a counter 売場の店員．

shopper, *n.* 買いもの客．

Q a ***purposeless*** *shopper*＝a shop tramp ひやかしの客．

Q² a personal ***service*** *shopper* 自分でサービスする買物客(代金は出口でまとめて払う)．

shopping, *n.* 買物．

V ***do*** one's *shopping* and marketing 店や市場の買物をする‖the store where I usually ***do*** my *shopping* 私がいつも買物をする店．【類】***do*** some *shopping*＝make some purchases.

Q² ***Christmas*** *shopping* クリスマスの買物．¶for ***holiday*** *shopping* [クリスマスなどの]祝日の買物に．¶***window*** *shopping* 目正月(飾窓の陳列品をながめるだけで満足すること)．

P I did a lot ***of*** *shopping*. 私はたくさん買物をした．¶She's ***off*** (＝***out***) *shopping*. 彼女は買物に出かけている．

shore, *n.* 海岸, 海浜；陸．

V ***coast*** the *shores* of Central America 中央アメリカの海岸に沿うて航行する．¶Long rows of fantastic pine-trees ***flank*** the *shore*. おもしろい形の松の木の長い列が海浜に連なっている．¶The line ***follows*** the *shore* of Lake Baikal. その線(鉄道の)はバイカル湖畔を通っている．¶***leave*** our *shores* わが国を去る．¶Fishing hamlets ***line*** the *shore*. 漁村が海岸に沿うて並んでいる．¶***reach*** British *shores* イギリスの海岸に着く．¶***skirt*** the *shore* of a lake 湖水の周囲を巡っている．¶The tourist party will be the first to ***touch*** these *shores* this year. その観光団が今年になって始めての来朝者だろう．【類】A Western ship had never ***touched*** our *shores* before. ¶The sea ***washes*** the *shore*. 海水が岸を洗う．【類】the lands whose *shores* are ***washed*** by the same waters.

Q a ***flat sandy*** *shore* 平たんな砂浜．¶those visiting ***foreign*** *shores* 洋行する人々．¶the ***Greek-colonized*** *shores* of the Black Sea ギリシア人の植民した黒海沿岸．¶***heavenly*** *shores* 天がい．¶Japan is endeavouring to attract an increasing volume of American tourist traffic to its ***hospitable*** *shores*. 日本はその外客歓迎の自国へますます多数の米国旅行者を引付けようと努めている．¶an ***inhospitable*** *shore* 荒涼たる海岸．¶a ***low sloping*** *shore* 低く傾斜した海岸．¶on returning to his ***native*** *shores* 帰国後．¶the ***opposite*** *shore* of Tokyo Bay 東京湾の対岸．¶a ***palm-shaded*** *shore* しゅろの木の茂った海岸．

Q² a ***lee*** *shore* 船の風下に当る海岸．

P waves breaking ***against*** the *shore* 海岸にぶつかって砕ける波．¶walk ***along*** the *shore* of the lake その湖水の岸に沿うて歩く．¶They know little of the wide world ***beyond*** their hermetic *shores*. 彼らは鎖国した自国の外の広い世界についてはほとんどなにも知る所がなかった．¶play (sit) ***by*** the *shore* of a lake 湖辺に遊ぶ(など)．¶***from*** transoceanic *shores* 海洋のかなたの国から．¶He fell overboard and struck out ***for*** the *shore*. 彼は船から落ちそして岸の方へ泳ぎ出した．‖make ***for*** (＝proceed towards) the *shore* 岸の方へ行く．¶a transport ***in*** *shore* 近海にいる輸送船．¶***near*** the *shore* 海岸の近くに．¶***off*** the *shores* of ... ...の岸を離れて．¶1,000 miles ***off*** *shore* 海岸を離れる千マイル．【類】The ship stopped a little way ***off*** the *shore*. ¶The ship was driven ***on*** *shore*. 船は海岸に乗上げた．‖Passengers can speak to their friends ***on*** *shore* through wireless telephone. 乗客は無線電話で陸上の友と話ができる．‖get ***on*** *shore* 上陸する‖a visitor ***on*** our *shores* 来朝中の外客‖The ship was driven ***on*** *shore*. その船は海岸に打上げられた．【類】***on*** the *shores* of the Mediterranean / The marines (海兵) serve both at sea and ***on*** *shore*. / "I feel," said Newton, "like a small child ***on*** the *shore* of the ocean who has picked up a pebble (小石) or a pretty shell." ¶He was safely brought ***to*** *shore*. 彼は無事陸に引上げられた．

shore, *v.* [支柱で]支える．

M² *shore* ***up*** an economy weakened by the devastation of war 戦争の荒廃で衰えた経済を強化する．

shore-front, *n.* 岸頭．

Q² The Manhattan's ***East River*** *shore-front* マンハッタンのイースト河岸地域．

short, *n.* 簡約, 要領；*pl.* 不足物；〘映〙短編もの．

V to ***make*** *short* of the matter 手短かに言えば．

Q² a "***quota-quickie***" *short*〘映〙[配給の都合上]間に合わせの短編もの．

P It is called ***for*** *short* the Y.M.C.A. それは略してワイ・エム・シー・エイと呼ぶ．¶***in*** *short* 要するに．

short, *a.* 短い；足りない, 不十分な．

M The time required is ***amazingly*** *short*. 所要時間は驚くほど短い．¶be ***far*** *short* of the goal 目的にはまだほど遠い．【類】It is ***far*** *short* of one million. / be ***far*** *short* of meeting the requirements. ¶it would be ***little*** *short* of a miracle if ... もし...ならほとんど奇跡というべきだ．‖His escape was ***little*** *short* of miraculous (＝a miracle). 彼が助かったのはほとんど奇跡だ．【類】He is ***little*** *short* of genius. / The progress that has been made is ***little*** *short* of marvelous. / It will be ***little*** *short* of a national calamity (国難) if this occurs. ¶This year's crop will fall ***much*** *short* of that of last year. 今年の収穫は去年より余程減るだろう．¶be ***rather*** *short* than tall どっちかというと身長の低い方．¶The time allowed is ***too*** *short*. 与えられた期間が余りに短い．¶be ***very*** *short* of cash 現金が大いに欠乏している．

P be *short* ***for*** ... ...の略である．【類】"Despite" is *short* ***for*** "in spite of." / The UNO, *short* ***for*** the United Nations Organization, ... ¶*short* ***in*** needed material 入用の材料が足りない‖*short* ***in*** understanding 理解力の足りない．¶We are *short* ***of*** men (＝hands). 手が足りない．‖a hand which is *short* ***of*** three fingers 三本指のない手‖We are *short* ***of*** change. われわれは小銭が欠乏している．‖be *short* ***of*** breath 息を切らしている‖He is *short*

of (=straitened for) money. 彼は金に困っている. 【類】a lady whose age is *short **of*** thirty / It is still a few minutes *short **of*** the hour of seven. ‖ water just *short **of*** boiling 沸騰直前の湯 ‖ Exercise must be taken *short **of*** fatigue. 運動は疲労しない程度にしなければならない. ‖ *short **of*** stature 身長の低い. 【類】*short **of*** sleep / be *short **of*** weight / Present supplies of fruit are *short **of*** requirements (需要). / Tokyo ran *short **of*** water. ‖ fall *short **of*** one's expectations 期待に達しない. 【類】fall *short **of*** the mark (=goal) ‖ Nothing *short **of*** that will do. それまで行かないものではだめだ. 【類】Nothing *short **of*** war will avail. / Nothing *short **of*** a miracle could have saved him. ¶They are *short **on*** housing. 彼らは住宅が不足している.

O to be *short* 手短かに言えば. ¶to cut a long story *short* 簡略すると.

shortage, *n.* 不足.

V the *shortage* of world tonnage ***caused*** by ravages of the submarines and the mines 潜水艦や機械水雷からの被害によって生じた世界の船舶不足. ¶***make good*** (=***cover or fill up***) the *shortage* of ... ...の不足を補う. ¶to ***meet*** the *shortage* of ... ...の不足を補充するために.

Q ***basic*** *shortage* 絶対的不足. ¶***domestic*** *shortages* 家庭における物資の不足. ¶a ***great*** *shotage* of farm labor 農園労働者の大不足. ¶There is at present a ***serious*** *shortage* of horses in this country. 目下この国では馬が非常に不足している. 【類】a ***serious*** *shortage* in the supply of ... ¶There was s ***world-wide*** *shortage* of food. 世界的に食物が不足していた.

Q² ease the pressing ***bread*** *shortage* 差迫ったパンの不足を緩和する. ¶the acute ***clothing*** *shortage* ひどい衣料の不足. 【類】a solution to ***clothing*** *shortage*. ¶a ***coal*** (***fuel, oil***) *shortage* 石炭(など)不足. ¶alleviate the ***dollar*** *shortage* ドル不足を緩和する. ¶a ***dwelling*** *shortage* 住宅不足. ¶a serious ***electricity*** *shortage* 重大な電力不足. ¶***fabric*** *shortages* 繊維品不足. ¶in case of any emergency ***food*** *shortage* 非常時食糧不足に際しては. 【類】world ***food*** *shortages* / tide over the critical ***food*** *shortage*. ¶***feed*** *shortage* 飼料の不足. ¶world ***grain*** *shortages* 世界的穀物不足. ¶ease the ***housing*** *shortage* 住宅不足を緩和する. 【類】suffer an acute ***housing*** *shortage* / because of the continuing ***housing*** *shortage*. ¶in the face of drastic ***labor*** and ***material*** *shortages* 労働者及び物資のはなはだしい不足にもかかわらず. ¶when ***manpower*** and ***materials*** *shortages* ease 人員及び物資不足が緩和すると. ¶make up ***money*** *shortage* by ... ...で金の不足を補う. ¶A ***newsprint*** *shortage* made most papers look like leaflets. 新聞用紙不足のため大がいの新聞がちらしのような体裁になった. 【類】The war induced (=caused) ***newsprint*** *shortage*. ‖ skip 1945 because of the ***wartime paper*** *shortage* 戦時で用紙払底のため 1945 年度分を略して出版しない(年鑑など). ¶***power*** *shortage* 動力不足. ¶***summer*** *shortage* of electric power supply 電力の夏枯. ¶make the ***teacher*** *shortage* even more critical 教員不足が一層深刻になる. ¶an acute ***water*** *shortage* 深刻な水不足. ¶***world*** *shortages* of wheat 世界的小麦不足.

P² *Shortages* ***in*** his accounts were discovered. 帳簿の穴が見つかった. ¶the *shortage* ***of*** workers (man power) 労力の不足. 【類】*shortage* ***of*** shipping (fund).

shortcake, *n.* ショートケーキ.

Q² a ***strawberry*** *shortcake* いちご入りショートケーキ.

shortcoming, *n.* 欠点, 短所.

V ***atone for*** its numerous *shortcomings* その多数の短所を埋合わせる. ¶***fulfil*** one another's *shortcomings* in such a way that the one cannot exist without the other 甲がなければ乙は立ち行かないという風に互の欠点を埋合わせる. ¶We all ***have*** some *shortcomings*. だれにもなにか短所がある. ¶***overlook*** a *shortcoming* 欠点を見のがす. ¶***remedy*** *shortcomings* 欠点を矯正する.

Q ***sartorial*** *shortcomings* 裁縫の欠点.

P ***despite*** (=***with***) all his *shortcomings* 欠点はたくさんあるが ‖ ***in spite of*** the *shortcomings* we pointed out われわれが指摘した欠点にもかかわらず. ¶a man ***with*** many *shortcomings* 欠点の多い人.

shorten, *v.* 縮める; なくする.

M The days are ***rapidly*** *shortening*. 日あしは急に短かくなっている. ¶The full name of violoncello is ***usually*** *shortened* to the more convenient 'cello. バイオロンチェロという完全な名称は通例略して一層便利なチェロの名で呼ばれる.

M² *shorten* ***in*** a tree 木をかり込む,剪(き)り込む.

P *shortened* ***from*** a long article 長い文から要約した. ¶may be *shortened* ***into*** ... ...と省略される. ¶the name *shortened* ***of*** the "Mr." Mr. を略した名前. ¶The name Amida is sometimes *shortened* ***to*** Mida. あみだは往々縮めて「みだ」という.

shorthand, *n.* 速記術.

V by ***using*** *shorthand* 速記で.

P take the conversation down ***in*** *shorthand* 会話を速記する ‖ write ***in*** *shorthand* 速記する.

short-handed, *a.* 手不足の.

M They find themselves there ***extremely*** *short-handed* for cultivation. 彼らはそこの開墾にはきわめて手不足なことが分かった.

shortness, *n.* 簡単.

P ***for*** *shortness* (=for short, for brevity's sake) 略して.

shot, *n.* 弾; 射程; そ撃; 射手; 勘定; 《俗》[モルヒネなどの]注射; 《俗》スナップ写真.

V ***discharge*** *shots* 弾丸を発射する. ¶***draw*** *shots* 射撃される. ¶***exchange*** *shots* with the enemy fleet 敵艦隊と砲火を交える. ¶Several *shot*[*s*] were ***extracted*** from his arm. 彼の腕から数個の弾丸を抜き取った. ¶***fire*** four *shots* 弾丸を四発々射する ‖ *Shot* after shot was ***fired*** without effect. 何発も撃ったがだめだった. ‖ without ***firing*** a *shot* 一発も打たずに. ¶He sprang to his feet as if he ***got*** a *shot* in the arm. 彼は腕に(モヒの)注射でもしたかのように元気よく立ち上った. ¶***have*** (=***take or try***) a *shot* at a bird 鳥をねらって打つ. ¶I ***heard*** revolver *shots*. けん銃の音が私に聞えた. 【類】Several *shots* were ***heard***. ¶I ***made*** (=had) a good *shot* at a bird. 鳥をねらいうちした. ‖ ***make*** a *shot*, hit or miss 一か八かやってみる ‖ ***make*** hopelessly bad *shots* at guessing とんでもない推量をする. ¶***miss*** one's *shot* at a deer しかを打損じる. ¶***pay*** one's *shot* [宿屋などで]勘定を払う. ¶***resist*** a *shot* from musket 小銃の弾(たま)を通さない. ¶***send*** a *shot* from a field gun at ... ...目がけて野砲を放つ. ¶A *shot* ***passed*** through the wall. 弾丸が壁を打ち抜いた. ¶He says he will ***take*** a *shot* of us all. 《俗》彼はみんなの写真をとってやるといっている. ¶Every *shot* ***told*** (=was a hit). 百発百中だった.

Q He is a ***bad*** *shot*. 彼は射撃がへただ. ¶He is one of the ***best*** *shots* in country where good marksmen abound. 彼は射撃の名人の多い国での一流射手だ. ¶a ***big*** *shot* 《米俗》大もの, おえら方. ¶a ***competent*** *shot* 射撃の達人. ¶a ***dead*** *shot* 必中弾; 射撃の名手. ¶***Good*** *shot!* うまくあたった. ¶a ***lucky*** *shot* まぐれ当り. ¶a ***random*** *shot* 乱発. ¶a ***remarkable*** *shot* with a rifle 銃を持っては非凡な射手. ¶fire ***some*** *shots* 数発打つ. ¶He was a victim of ***stray*** *shots*. 彼は流弾に当って死んだ.

Q² a ***crack*** *shot* 射撃の名手. ¶an ***expert*** *shot* 射撃の名人. ¶a ***fashion*** *shot* [デザイナーの]流行の当り. ¶a ***gag*** *shot* 演技の間に場当りを言うこと. ¶a ***gun*** *shot* 砲弾射撃. ¶a ***pistol*** *shot* けん銃射撃. ¶exchange ***revolver*** *shots* けん銃で撃ち合う. ¶a ***speed*** *shot*=a snapshot [写真の]早取り. ¶a ***trick*** *shot* トリック映画. ¶a ***winning*** *shot* 〖野〗決め球.

P proof ***against*** *shot* 弾丸の通らない. ¶turn tail ***at*** the first *shot* 最初の一発で後ろを見せる(逃げる). ¶I did it ***like*** a *shot*. 私は電光石火の早業でやった. ¶***out of*** *shot* 射程外に, 弾丸の届かない所に. ¶strike ***with*** a *shot* 弾丸で撃つ ‖ load a gun ***with*** *shot* 銃に弾(たま)を込める. ¶***within*** *shot* 射程内に.

P² a *shot* ***at*** a bird on the wing 飛んでいる鳥に一発. ¶*shots* ***of*** the same ink 《俗》一つ穴のむじな. ¶a crack *shot* ***with*** rifle (revolver) ライフル銃(など)の名人.

shoulder, *n.* 肩; 肩状部分.

V ***bare*** one's *shoulder* はだを脱ぐ. ¶***dislocate*** (=***put out***) one's *shoulder* 肩の骨を違わす(脱きゅうする). ¶***draw up*** the *shoulders* 肩をいからせる. ¶Now, ***give*** me a *shoulder*. さあ一つ肩を貸してくれ給え. ‖ He ***gave*** me the cold *shoulder*. 彼は私を冷遇した. ¶***have*** broad (narrow) *shoulders* 肩幅が広い(狭い). ¶***put*** one's *shoulder* against a wagon 本腰を据えて仕事に掛かる ‖ ***put*** (=***set***) one's *shoulder* vigorously to the wheel 鋭意ことに当る. ¶***put back*** the dislocated *shoulder* into place 脱きゅうした肩を復位させる. ¶***raise*** the *shoulder* 肩をそびやかす. ¶***reduce*** a dislocated *shoulder* 脱きゅうした肩を復位させる. ¶***rub*** one's *shoulders* with many people 多くの人と交際する. ¶***shrug*** one's *shoulders* 肩をすくめる ☞ いやなやつ, 勝手にしろ, 仕方がないといったときの表情. ¶***swing*** one's *shoulders* 肩を振り動かす. ¶***tap*** one's *shoulder* familiarly なれなれしく人の肩をぽんとたたく. ¶***throw back*** one's *shoulders* そり身になる. ¶***turn*** (give *or* show) the cold *shoulder* to ... ...を冷遇する.

V² My *shoulder* ***aches.*** 肩が痛む.

Q give the ***cold*** *shoulder* to ... ...を冷遇する. ¶***drooping*** *shoulders* なで肩. ¶***padded*** *shoulders* 〘服飾〙パッドを入れた肩. ¶***round*** *shoulders* 丸肩. ¶***sagging*** *shoulders* 〘服飾〙ゆるく下った肩. ¶She carries a burden far too great for her ***slender*** *shoulders*. 彼女の細腕では余りに荷が勝ちすぎている. ¶a ***sloping*** *shoulder* なで肩. ¶a ***square*** *shoulder* 角張った肩. ¶rub ***sympathetic*** *shoulders* with the favorites of bygone days and the hopes of the years to come 先進後輩ともに談笑.

Q² graceful length of limbs and ***fall*** *shoulders* ほどのよい長さの手足となで肩.

P carrying a little satchel slung ***across*** his *shoulder* 小さな胴乱を肩に掛けて. 【類】They have race-glasses (双眼鏡) slung ***across*** their *shoulders*. / carry a coupled packages (振りわけ荷物) ***across*** the *shoulder*. ¶a company of soldiers walking down a village street with muskets ***at*** their *shoulders* 小銃を肩にして村の往来を練って行く一隊の兵士. ¶wounded ***in*** the *shoulder* 肩に負傷した. ¶The onus (=responsibility) of ... is ***off*** your *shoulder*. 君は...の責任を解除された. ¶He has a rifle ***on*** his *shoulder*. 彼は銃をかついでいる.【類】He went out, gun ***on*** *shoulder*. ‖The crowd carried the speaker ***on*** their *shoulders*. 群集は弁士を胴上げにした. ‖strike him ***on*** the *shoulder* 彼の肩を打つ. 【類】He patted me ***on*** the *shoulder*. ‖have a head ***on*** one's *shoulders* 抜目がない ‖The blame (=responsibility) rests ***on*** my *shoulders*. その責任は私にある. ¶preachments of morality ***over*** the left *shoulder* 間違った道徳の説教. ‖look ***over*** one's *shoulder* 肩越しに見る ‖say ***over*** one's *shoulder* 捨ぜりふを言う ‖carry a rod and line ***over*** one's *shoulder* つりざおをかつぐ. ¶with his gun ***upon*** his *shoulder* 鉄砲をかついで ‖put a burden ***upon*** one's *shoulders* 重荷を人に負わす ‖take it ***upon*** one's *shoulders* その責任を負う.

P² the *shoulder* ***of*** a mountain (type) 山(活字)の肩. ¶stand *shoulder* ***to*** shoulder 肩を並べて立つ; 共同一致する ‖shift the blame on ***to*** other *shoulders* 責めを人に転嫁する.

shoulder, *v.* 肩にかつぐ; 肩から下げる.

M *shoulder* fire arms ***all at once*** 銃を一せいにになう. ¶*shoulder* a task (responsibilities) ***like a man*** 男らしく仕事(など)を引受ける.

P *shoulder* one's way ***through*** a crowd 肩で人中を押分けて進む.

shout, *n.* 叫び声.

V ***give*** a great *shout* 大声を揚げる. ¶***raise*** a joyous *shout* 歓喜の叫びを揚げる. ¶***set up*** *shouts* of joy (alarm) 歓喜(など)の声を揚げる. ¶***shout*** a *shout* 叫ぶ. ¶A *shout* of admiration ***burst*** simultaneously from the crowd. 称賛のさけび声が一斉に群集から起った. ¶A *shout* ***went up*** from the army. さけび声が軍の中から起った.

Q amid ***deafening*** *shouts* 耳もろうせんばかりの叫び声の中に. ¶a ***loud ringing*** *shout* of joy 響き渡る歓呼の声. ¶a ***stentorian*** *shout* 大音声の叫び声. ¶amid the ***thunderous*** *shouts* of "Banzai" raised by their friends 彼らの友だちの揚げた雷鳴のごとき万歳の叫びの中に. ¶amid ***universal*** *shout* of applause 全国民のかっさいの中に.

P He rose to speak ***amid*** wild welcoming *shout*. 彼は熱狂せる歓呼のうちに立って演説を始めた. ¶The train moved off ***amidst*** deafening *shouts* of viva. 耳をろうせんばかりの万歳の叫びの中に列車は動き出した. ¶***with*** *shouts* どなって. 【類】He ran off ***with*** a *shout*.

P² *shouts* ***of*** assent and disapproval 賛否の叫び ‖*shouts* ***of*** encouragement 声援 ‖there was a *shout* ***of*** joy from ... ...から歓呼の声が起った ‖*shouts* ***of*** victory 勝どき.

shout, *v.* 叫ぶ.

M *shout* ***angrily*** 怒号する. ¶They *shouted* ***as with one voice.*** 彼らは異口同音に叫んだ. ¶*shout* ***back*** to ... ...に怒鳴り返す. ¶*shout* ***derisively*** at ... ばかにして...を怒鳴りつける. ¶I *shouted* myself ***hoarse.*** 私は叫んで声をからした. ¶*shout* ***out*** loudly 声高に叫び出す ‖He *shouted* ***out*** "Thief!" 彼は「泥棒」と叫んだ. ‖They *shouted* ***out*** to each other with a river between. 彼らは川をはさんで怒鳴り合った. 【類】*shout* ***out*** at the top of one's voice.

M² Boss *shouted* him ***down***. 親分がだまれ! と彼にいった.

P *shout* ***at*** a person in anger 人にどなりつける ‖*shout* ***at*** the top of one's voice 声を限りに叫ぶ. ¶*shout* ***for*** delight (joy, victory) 喜んで(など)叫ぶ. ¶I *shouted* ***to*** him to come. 私は大声で彼に来いと言った. ¶*shout* ***with*** the utmost strength 声を限りに叫ぶ.

shove, *v.* 強く押す.

M He *shoved* me ***back*** out of the room. 彼は私をへやから突き出した. 【類】*shove* a book ***back*** in the shelf.

M² *shove* ***down*** 押倒す. ¶*shove* ***off*** for a trip 《米俗》旅に出発する. ¶*shove* ***in*** (***out***) 押し込める(押し出す).

P *shove* a salt-shaker ***across*** a table to ... 食卓塩をテーブルの向側に押して...の方にやる. ¶*shove* one's shovel ***into*** the ground シャベルを地面にさし込む. ¶*shove* them ***off*** the sidewalk 彼らを人道から押し出す. ¶*shove* a person ***with*** the elbow ひじ鉄砲を食わす.

shovel, *n.* シャベル.

Q² a ***steam*** *shovel* 蒸気シャベル. ¶a ***trenching*** *shovel* ざんごう用シャベル.

shovel, *v.* シャベルですくう.

P *shovel* the food ***into*** one's mouth 食物を口に詰め込む. ¶*shovel* a path ***through*** the snow シャベルで雪道をつける.

shovel[l]er, *n.* [雪・泥など]すくうもの.

Q² a ***snow*** *shoveler* 雪かき.

show, *n.* 見世物; 陳列; 光景; 表示; 外観.

V ***boss*** a *show* 牛耳る, 親分となる. ¶He had to ***do*** at least seven *shows* a day. 彼は一日に少くとも七回の興行をしなければならなかった. ¶a room where a *show* is ***exhibited*** 展覧品陳列室. ¶The theatre ***gives*** two *shows* in one day. その劇場では一日二回興行がある. ‖They ***give*** a much better *show* at the theatre. その劇場の方がずっといい. ¶***have*** (=***bear*** *or* ***carry***) a *show* of respectability 重々しく見える ‖He ***has*** no *show* (=prospect) of winning 彼には勝味がない. ¶***hold*** a *show* 催し物をする. ¶***make*** a great *show* of zeal (politeness, friendship) 大層熱心(など)らしく見せかける ‖I do not like to ***make*** a *show* of myself before strangers. 私は見ず知らずの人の前でさらし者になりたくない. ‖***make*** a good *show* 好成績をあげる; 見ばえがする. ¶***stand*** no *show* 《口語》見込みがない. ¶***substitute*** dumb *show* for words 口をきかずに身振りをする. ¶***take*** a *show* of hands 挙手採決をする. ¶***take over*** the *show* その事業を引継ぐ.

Q ***automatic*** *shows* 自動のぞき絵. ¶a ***beautiful*** *show* of blossom 花の美観. ¶make a ***big*** *show* of oneself 自分を誇示する. ¶a ***burlesque*** *show* 道化芝居. ¶It does not have a ***fair*** *show*. それは有利の地位に立っていない. ¶make a ***false*** *show*=pretend みせかける, よそおう. ¶make a ***fine*** *show* [宝石など]見ばえがする. ¶make a ***good*** (***poor***) *show* in a class クラスで良(不良の)成績を示す. ¶make ***great*** *show* of grief 非常に悲しげに見せかける. 【類】the world's ***greatest*** *show* on ice. ¶***low-toned picture*** *shows* 低級の映画館. ¶This is a ***mere*** *show*. これはほんの見せ掛けだ. ¶a ***musical*** *show* 音楽入りの興行物. ¶***outward*** *show* 外観, 見てくれ. 【類】attach much importance to ***outward*** *show* 外見を重んじる. ¶a ***public*** *show* 公開の催し物. ¶make a ***sorry*** *show* みすぼらしい格好をする. ¶***yearly*** (=***annual***) *shows* 例年の催し物.

Q² put on an ***air*** *show* 空中演習をやる. ¶a ***big laugh*** *show* お笑い大会. ¶a ***black-cattle*** *show* 《俗》教会人の寄合. ¶a ***business*** *show* (=a trade display) 商店の飾り付け. ¶a ***catchpenny*** *show* 銭取り主義の見世物. ¶a ***cattle*** *show* 家畜品評会. ¶The ***circus*** *show* is on. 曲馬団が興行中. ¶his one-man song and ***dance*** *show* 彼一人の歌謡と舞踊のショー. ¶a ***floor*** *show* 客席のショー(キャバレーなどの). ¶a ***flower*** *show* 花の展覧会. ¶a ***giveaway*** *show* 〘ラジオ〙賞品つきの番組. ¶a ***hit*** *show* 好評の見世物. ¶a ***leg*** *show* 脚線美ショー(レビューなど). ¶a ***marionette*** *show* あやつり人形芝居. ¶a ***motion picture*** (=***cinema*** *or* ***picture***) *show* 映画. ¶a "***no-admission***" *show* 《米》無料興行. ¶a "***nudity***" *show* ヌード・ショー. ¶a "***one-man***" *show* 個展. ¶a ***peep*** *show* のぞきショー(ストリップショーなど). ¶a ***poultry*** *show* 家きん品評会. ¶a ***premiere*** *show* 〘映〙封切. ¶a ***radio*** (***TV***) *show* ラジオ(テレビ)の催し物. ¶a ***radio quiz*** *show* ラジオのクイズの番組. ¶a ***road*** *show* (映画の)一般に公開しない特別興行. ¶a ***side*** *show* 寸劇, 余興. ¶televise a *stage show* 舞台劇などテレビ放送する. ¶a *strip[-tease] show* ヌードショー. ¶American circuses are all *tent shows*. アメリカの曲馬はみなテント張りである. ¶a *traveling show* 旅回りの見世物. ¶a *variety show* よせ.

P win a medal *at* a cattle *show* 家畜展覧会で賞はいを授与される. ¶express *by* dumb *show* 身振りで示す ‖ decide it *by* a *show* of hand それを挙手できめる. ¶He wears glasses *for show*. 彼はだてに眼鏡を掛けている. ‖ wild beasts *for* a *show* 見世物にする野獣 ‖ linen shirts *for show* 見本用のリンネルのワイシャツ. ¶a friend only *in show* うわべだけの友 ‖ Many of its performances are *in* dumb *show*. その演芸は大体身振り狂言(だんまり)でやる[神楽など]. ‖ *in* open *show* 公然と. ¶She is very fond *of show*. 彼女は見えを張るのが好きだ. ¶Xmas novelties now *on show*. 目新しいクリスマス贈答品目下陳列中. 【類】new-look hats (新型帽子) *on show* ‖ *On* a *show* of hands the motion was negatived by a large majority. 挙手でその動議は大多数をもって否決された. ¶*with* some little *show* of alarm いくらか驚いたらしい様子で ‖ *with* a *show* of nervousness いらいらしたようすで ‖ He was dismissed *with* little *show* of courtesty. 彼はそこそこに暇を出された. ‖ *with* some *show* of reason 幾分もっともらしく. 【類】*with* a great *show* of indignation / *with* a *show* of determination / people who live *with* more *show* than is justified by their income. ¶some suggest, not *without* good *show* of reason, that ... ある人が...と言ったのも無理はない.

P² call for a *show of* hands from those who are in favor of ... ...に賛成の人々に挙手を求める.

show, *v.* 示す; 見える; 案内する.

M Just let me know in advance and we'll be mighty glad to *show* you *around*. 前もってちょっとお知らせ下さいますれば喜んで近所の御案内を致します. ¶Oil paintings *show best* at a distance. 油絵は離れて見るのが一番よい. ¶*show clearly* and *conclusively* 明りょうにかつ決定的に表示する. ¶scientific investigations *conclusively show* that ...科学の研究が...と決定的に示している. ¶it has been *definitely shown* by him that ... 彼によって...が明らかにされた. ¶The lights of the city *showed dimly* through the fog. 町の明りが霧を通してぼんやり見えた. ¶it can be *easily shown* that ... ...ということが容易にわかる. ¶*show forth* 発表する. ¶*show* more *fully* 一層十分に説明する. ¶It is *shown graphically* in diagram. 図表に明りょうに示されている. ¶*Show* him *in*. その方をお通し申しなさい. ¶*show minutely* and beyond the shadow of a doubt ... 詳細に一点の疑いのないように...を示す. ¶It *only shows* how little you know. それは君の知識が浅薄だということを示すだけだ. ¶*showed* them *out* at the gate 彼らを門まで送り出した. ¶The pattern *shows plainly*. 模様がはっきり見える. ¶I was *shown upstairs* into his den. 私は二階の彼の私室に案内された.

M² *show* itself in ... それが...となって現われる. ¶the amount of money *shown in* 出して見せた金の高. ¶*show off* 見えをはる, 見せびらかす. 【類】*show* [oneself] *off* / *show off* one's talent (=knowledge, skill) / The sea lion (あしか) seems to enjoy *showing off*. / *show off* their beauty to the best advantage / *show off* her figure to perfection. ¶He was *shown* the new building *over*. 彼は新しい建物をずっと見せてもらった. ¶*show* a person *round* 人を案内して(工場などを)見せる. ¶*show up* at ... ...に顔を出す ‖ failed to *show up* [会などへ]出席しなかった. 【類】Why doesn't daddy *show up*? ‖ *show up* the character of a man 人の性格を発揮させる ‖ ‖ *show up* important matters 重大な事項を指示する. 【類】*show up* one's faults / As the train continues westward, the mountain *shows up* conspicuously on the right.

P The sun has *shown* itself *above* the horizon. 太陽が地平線上に現われた. ‖ A tower *shows above* the wood. 森の上に塔が見える. ¶Bats *show* themselves *after* dark. こうもりは暗くなってから出て来る. ¶*show at* a glance 一見して分かる. ¶*show by* a diagram 図で示す. ¶as *shown in* the illustration (table) 図(など)の示す通り ‖ be *shown in* detail くわしく示されてある. ¶The servant *showed* them *into* the drawing room. 召使は応接間へ彼らを通した. ¶the amount *shown on* the meter メートルに表われた分量. ¶He *showed* me *out of* his study. 彼は私を書斎から送り出した. ¶He *showed* us *over* the ship (works, city). 彼はわれわれに船(工場)を見せてくれた. 【類】The servant *showed* the prospective lodger (下宿希望の人) *over* the house. ¶*show* one's country uncle *round* [the sights of] the city いなかのおじに町中を案内する. ¶I was *shown through* the rooms of the hotel. 私はそのホテルの各室を案内された. ‖ The blood *shows through* the skin. 血液は皮膚を通して透いて見える. ‖ *show through* the clothing 着物から透いて見える. ¶*show* a person *to* his seat 座席に人を案内する ‖ *Show* this gentleman *to* the door. この方を戸口へご案内申しなさい. ‖ Her beautiful figure will *show to* advantage in a silk dress. 彼女のあで姿は絹物を着るとよく引立つ. ‖ the odd variety of things *shown to* view 陳列された種々雑多の物.

showdown, *n.* 対決.

V This would *make* a *showdown* sooner or later *inevitable*. そういう訳で早晩対決しなければならないだろう.

Q² the *Berlin showdown* ベルリンの対決(米ソの).

shower, *n.* にわか雨, 夕立.

V We are going to *have* a *shower*. 夕立が来る. ¶Many drops *make* a *shower*. ちりも積れば山となる. ¶The waterproof [coat] *stands* a *shower*. そのレーン・コートは大雨にたえる.

V² There is a *shower coming* [down]. 夕立が来る. ¶A heavy *shower fell* today. きょうひどいにわか雨があった. ¶Heavy *showers* have *occurred* today over the large portion of the prefecture. その県の大部分にわたってきょう大雨があった.

Q a *delicious* (=*nice*) *shower* そう快な雨. ¶a *fertile shower* おしめり. ¶unless a *golden shower* comes in my way 私に運が向いて来なければ. ¶a *hail shower* あられの混った雨. ¶be caught in a *heavy shower* ひどい夕立に会う. ¶a *plenteous shower* 豪雨. ¶a *sudden shower* 夕立.

Q² like the *April showers* [本の出版など]雨後のたけのこのように. ¶a *hail* [*stone*] *shower* ひょうまじりの夕立. ¶a *snow shower* 降りしきる雪. ¶a *spring shower* 春の大雨. ¶a heavy *thunder shower* 大雷雨.

P I was overtaken *by* a *shower*. 私は夕立に会った. ¶Letters came *in showers*. 手紙が盛んに来た. ‖ I was caught *in* the *shower*. 私はその夕立に会った. ¶It looks *like* a *shower*. 夕立が来そうだ. ¶They greeted us *with* a *shower* of stones. 彼らはわれわれに雨あられと石を投げつけた.

P² a *shower of* bullets 雨と降る弾丸 ‖ a *shower of* rain 大雨. 【類】a *shower of* blows (arrows, dust) / a *shower of* sparks from an engine.

shower, *v.* 雨下する.

V *shower* blows *on* a person 人にげん骨を雨と浴びせ掛ける. ¶He was *showered with* congratulations. 彼は「お目出とう」を浴びせ掛けられた.

shower-bath, *n.* シャワー.

V *take* a *shower-bath* シャワーを浴びる.

P² a *shower-bath from* the rain 雨の水浴.

showing, *n.* 示すこと; 成績.

V *give* a fine *showing* りっぱな成績をあげる. ¶*make* a wonderful *showing* すばらしい成績をあげる.

Q make a *better showing* 一層成績をあげる. ¶a *brilliant showing* りっぱな成績. ¶give a *creditable showing* 好成績を収める. ¶make a *fair showing* 相当の好成績を示す. ¶The concern made a not altogether *favorable showing* at the end of last year. その会社の昨年末の成績は余り芳しくなかった. 【類】make a more *favorable showing*. ¶a firm with a poor (bad) *financial showing* 金ぐりのよくない会社. ¶make a *good* (*bad*) *showing* りっぱにやる(やらない), 成績をあげる(あげない). 【類】make a *good* (*poor*) *showing* in school ‖ That is certainly a *good showing* in a bad year. それは不景気の年としてはたしかに好成績だ. 【類】make a *better showing* / make one of the *best showings* in the past decade (十年). ¶a *grim showing* 悲惨な成績. ¶The store made a *wonderful showing* in the furniture department. その店の家具部は驚くべき成績をあげた.

P He seems guilty *on* the *showing* of the witnesses. 証人の言うのを見ると彼は有罪らしい.

P² the first showing (=release) *of* a film *before* the public 映画の封切.

show-room, *n.* 陳列室.

Q a *commercial show-room* 商品陳列室.

shred, *n.* 小片.

P a flag *in* (=*into*) *shreds* きれぎれになった旗. ¶It was torn *to shreds*. それはずたずたに裂けていた.

shrew, *n*. あばずれ女.

V *tame* the *shrew* あばずれ女の根性を直す, じゃじゃ馬をならす.

shrewd, *a*. 抜目のない.

M be *shrewd enough* to ... 抜目なく...

P *shrewd at* a bargain 取引きのうまい. ¶*shrewd in* business (trade) 商売に抜目がない.

shrewdness, *n*. 抜目ないこと.

P^2 have *shrewdness in* trade 商魂たくましい.

shriek, *n*. 叫び, 悲鳴.

V He *gave* a piercing *shriek* of joy. 彼は金切声を揚げて喜んだ. ¶*utter* a *shriek* 悲鳴を揚げる.

Q a *dreadful shriek* 恐ろしい悲鳴. ¶with one *wild shriek* 一声けたたましい叫びを揚げて.

P *with* a *shriek* of joy 喜びの叫びを揚げて.

shriek, *v*. 悲鳴を揚げる.

M *shriek out*＝say in shrill agonized tones 悲鳴を揚げる.

P *shriek with* laughter きゃっきゃっと笑う ‖ *shriek with* terror びっくりして悲鳴を揚げる.

shrieking, *n*. 悲鳴.

Q a *timorous shrieking* from danger 危険におびえた悲鳴.

shrill, *v*. かん高い声を出す.

P He *shrilled with* joy (fear, fright). 彼はかんばしった声を出して喜んだ(など).

shrine, *n*. 霊廟(びょう), 神社; 霊場.

V *desecrate* a *shrine* 神社を汚す. ¶*raise* a *shrine* to Kannon 観音堂を建立する.

Q an *ancestral shrine* 仏壇 ‖ the *Ancestral Shrine* in the Imperial Palace 賢所(かしこどころ). ¶The George Washington Home at Mount Vernon is America's most *hallowed shrine*. ヴァーノン山ろくにあるワシントンの家はアメリカ中で一番神聖な霊場である. ¶the *Grand Shrines* at Ise 伊勢神宮. ¶a *literary shrine* 文学上の霊場. ¶the *main shrine* of a Shinto temple 神社の本殿. ¶the *mortuary shrine* of Ieyasu at Nikko 日光にある家康の霊殿. ¶one of the most *sacred shrines* of India インドの最も神聖な霊場の一つ.

P worship *at* the *shrine* 神社に参拝する. ¶bow *before* the household *shrine* 氏神を拝する. ¶lay one's life *on* the *shrine* of patriotism 一命を君国に捧げる.

P^2 a suitable *shrine for* great works of art 芸術の大作品にふさわしい殿堂. 【類】a *shrine for* drama lovers (George Bernard Shaw's home など). ¶the *shrine of* affection for thousands of students 数千学生の敬愛の殿堂. ¶a small *shrine to* the Goddess Benten ささやかな弁天堂.

shrink, *v*. 畏(い)縮する, しりごみする, 収縮する.

M *shrink aside* 引込める. ¶*shrink away* 縮み上がる. ¶*shrink back* frightened びっくりしてしりごみする. 【類】To *shrink back* before obstacles is not to overcome them.

M^2 *shrink up* into oneself like a snail かたつむりのようにい縮する.

P *shrink at* the thought of obstacles 障害を考えてしりごみする. ¶*shrink before* the influence of ... ...の力の前にしりごみする. ¶He does not *shrink from* danger. 彼は危険を恐れない. ‖ England does not *shrink from* comparison with Continental Europe in matters dramatic. 英国は劇にかけては欧州大陸諸国に比較してそん色がない. 【類】He does not *shrink from* infinite research (際限ない研究). / They *shrink from* no task, however arduous or unpleasant. / *shrink from* making new acquaintances / He *shrank from* any direct participation in politics. / *shrink from* it as *from* a lizard ‖ Flannel *shrinks in* the wash. フランネルは洗うと縮む. ¶*shrink into* comparative insignificance 比較すると顔色なしということになる ‖ *shrink into* ridges しわになる. ¶Those halfcotton suits are likely to *shrink out of* shape if worn in the rain. その混織木綿の着物は雨降りに着て出ると縮んで形がくずれがちだ. ¶*shrink with* fear こわいので縮み上がる ‖ Wool sweaters often *shrink with* water. 純毛のセーターは水につけるとよく縮む.

shrinking, *n*. 短縮.

P^2 the *shrinking of* space 距離の短縮(交通機関の迅速化による).

shrivel, *v*. しなびる.

M^2 The leaves are *shrivelled up* by the frost. 葉が霜でしなびてしまった.

P *shrivel to* the size of ... 縮んで...の大きさになる.

shroud, *n*. とばり.

P wrapped (＝enveloped) *in* a *shroud* of mystery 神秘の幕にとざされて.

P^2 a *shroud of* darkness (mist) やみ(霧)のとばり.

shroud, *v*. 包む, おおう.

P The hills are *shrouded by* fog. 山は霧に包まれている. ¶a woman *shrouded from* head to foot in a black cloak 頭からつまさきまで黒外とうで包まれた女. ¶He is *shrouded in* a black coat. 彼は黒衣をまとっている. ‖ The crime is *shrouded in* mystery. その罪悪は秘密に包まれている.

shrub, *n*. かん木.

Q a *climbing shrub* からまるかん木. ¶*flowering shrub* 花の咲くかん木.

shrug, *n*. 肩すくめ.

Q with a *dramatic shrug* of the shoulders 芝居がかりに肩をすくめて.

P "Russian," said others, dismissing the matter *with* a *shrug* of their shoulders. 「それがロシア式さ」と他の連中は肩をちょっと上げて表情よろしくあっさり片づけた.

shrug, *v*. 肩をすくめる.

M He *just shrugged* his shoulders. 彼は(だまって)ちょっと肩をすくめた. 【類】He *just shrugged* and gave no answer.

shudder, *n*. 身震い, 戦りつ.

V *cause* a *shudder* 身震いさせる. ¶*send* a *shudder* through ... ...を戦りつさせる.

V^2 A *shudder passed* over me. 私は全身がぞっとした. ¶A *shudder ran* through my frame. 私は体がぞっとした.

P it is not *without* a *shudder* that I recall ... ...を思い出すとぞっとする.

shudder, *v*. 身震いする, ぞっとする.

P *shudder at* the bare thought (＝idea) of ... ...と考えるだけで身震いがする. 【類】All Europe *shuddered at* the name of Tartar (ダッタン人). / Who does not *shudder at* the fear of being called "unpatriotic"? ¶*shudder with* cold (fright, horror) 寒さ(など)で震える.

shuffle, *n*. 調査.

Q after a *hasty shuffle* through one's papers 書類を大急ぎで調べた後で.

shuffle, *v*. 足をひきずって歩く; [トランプを]切る.

M *shuffle* cards *carefully* 念を入れてトランプ札を混ぜる. ¶The old man *shuffled feebly* along. その老人は弱々しく足をひきずって歩いた.

M^2 *shuffle along* 足をひきずって歩く. ¶*shuffle off* a duty on some one else 他の人に義務を転嫁する ‖ *shuffle off* upon posterity the burden of ... ...の負担を子孫に押しつける. ¶The ambassador *shuffled up* a treaty which was not satisfactory to either nation. 大使は双方の国民に満足を与えない条約をでっち上げた.

P *shuffle off* one's responsibilities onto others 自分の責任を人に転嫁する. ¶He came *shuffling into* the room. 彼は足をひきずって室にはいってきた. ‖ *shuffle into* one's clothes 無造作に着物を着る.

shun, *v*. 避ける.

P try to *shun* danger (risk) *in* business 商売上の危険を避けようとする.

shunt, *v*. 入換する, 回避する.

M be *shunted aside* 転嫁される.

P a train *shunted to* a siding 側線に入っている列車.

shut, *v*. 閉じる; はさむ; 締まる.

M The door *shuts easily* (*hard*). 戸が楽に締まる(中々締まらない). ¶The door *shuts of itself*. 戸が独りでに締まる. ¶*shut out* the light 光をさえぎる ‖ *shut out* new comers. 新来者を拒絶する. 【類】The workers were *shut out* from work. ‖ The blinds *shut out* the garden. 窓の日よけで庭が見えない. 【類】a house *shut out* from the street by trees / *shut* one *out* from social amenities ‖ cargo *shut out* from a steamer 積込不能の船貨 ‖ *shut out* an opposing team 〖野球〗相手のチームを完封する ‖ *shut out* the rain 雨を防ぐ ‖ *shut out* the late comers 遅く来た者をしめ出しする. ¶All the doors and openings were *shut securely* against any possible intrusion. すべての戸口と窓をだれも乱入できないようにしっかり閉じた. ¶The door *shuts suddenly*. 戸が急に締まる.

M^2 shut (＝close) *down* a mine (factory, shop) 鉱山(工場, 商店)を閉鎖する ‖ *shut* (＝calm) *down* upon one's anger 怒りを静める. ¶night *shut in* (＝fell) 日が暮れた ‖ The house was *shut in* by trees. その家は木立ちにかこまれていた. ¶*shut off* the in-flow of a stream 水流をせきとめる. 【類】The water supply was *shut off* for two whole days. / *shut off* electric service to nearly 2,000,000 people in a 50-mile area ‖ above banks of clouds that *shut off* the earth below 下界をさえぎる雲層の上に ‖ *shut off* aid funds at any stage どんな段階においてでも援助資金を中断する ‖ be *shut off* from attending a conference 会議列席を禁止される. 【類】*shut* oneself *off* from his friends and neighbors / *shut* oneself *off* from the world. ¶*Shut up*!《俗》だまれ.【類】"*Shut up*!" cried he. ‖ *shut* them *up* in a drawer それを引出しにしまいこむ ‖ He *shut* himself *up* in his room. 彼は自分のへやに閉じこもっていた.【類】The Japanese in those days were kept *shut up* from the world. / *shut* oneself *up* in one's ivory tower (象牙の塔) / be *shut up* in a dungeon ‖ *shut up* a school 学校を閉鎖する.【類】The stores are usually *shut up* at nine at night. / *shut* oneself *up* in a monastery ‖ It *shut* them *up*. そのために彼らは沈黙した.

P He *shut* the door ***after*** him. 彼ははいって(出て)から戸を締めた. ¶*shut* doors ***against*** a person 人のはいれない(出られない)ように戸を締める. ¶The post-office will *shut* ***at*** 4 p.m. 郵便局は午後四時に締まる. ¶He *shut* the door ***behind*** him. 彼は戸を締めて出た(はいった). ¶*shut* the ports ***by*** a blockade 封鎖して港にはいれないようにする. ¶*shut* a cottage ***for*** the winter (summer) 冬(夏)の使用を打切って小屋を閉鎖する ‖ *shut* in ***from*** all the outside world 外界から切断されて. ¶*shut* a man ***in*** prison (a chamber) 獄舎(など)に人を閉じこめる ‖ She *shut* her dress ***in*** the door. 彼女は締める拍子に戸に着物をはさまれた. ¶*shut* the door ***on*** (=***upon***) a person 人のはいられない(出られない)ように戸を締める. ¶*shut* a person ***out of*** his room 人をへやから締め出す. ¶I cannot *shut* my eyes ***to*** the fact. 私はその事実を無視する訳には行かない. ¶The door *shut* ***with*** a bang. 戸がばたんと締まった. ¶*shut* a man ***within*** the walls 壁内に人を閉じ込める.

shut-down, *n.* 休業.

Q a ***complete*** *shut-down* of commerce 商店の総休業.

Q² a ***coal*** *shut-down* 炭坑の休業.

shutoff, *n.* せん. 「動しゃ熱装置.

Q the ***automatic*** *shutoff* on a heater〔電気〕ストーブの自

shut-out, *n.* しめ出し;〚競技〛ゼロ敗. 「する.

Q get a ***complete*** *shut-out* 完全に締め出しを食う; ゼロ敗

shutter, *n.* 雨戸, よろい戸;〚写真〛シャッター.

V ***click*** the *shutter* カチリとシャッターを切る. ¶***put up*** the *shutters*=close the shop 表戸をしめる; 閉店する.

shutting, *n.* 閉じること.

Q There is ***no*** *shutting* of the mouth of Mrs. Grundy. 人の口には戸が立てられない.

shy, *a.* 気の進まない, 恥かしい; 恐れる;《米》足りない.

P I am *shy* ***of*** doing it. 私はそれをするのは気が進まない. ‖ He is *shy* ***of*** telling the truth. 彼は事実を告げるのをはばかっている.【類】A chinese woman is as *shy* ***of*** showing her feet to a man as a European woman her breasts. ‖ be a bit *shy* (=short) ***of*** the amount《米》金額が少し不足している.【類】be *shy* ***of*** funds ‖ The boatmen were *shy* ***of*** the rapids. 船頭はその急流をこわがっていた. ‖ fight *shy* ***of*** a cop《口語》お巡りがきらいだ.

shy, *v.* 恥かしがる; てれる. 「かしがった.

M *shy* ***away*** 避ける. ¶He ***bashfully*** ***shyed***. 彼は大いに恥

P *shy* ***at*** their names 名を聞いて敬遠する ‖ The horse *shyed* ***at*** an automobile. 馬は自動車を見て驚いてはねた.

shyness, *n.* 恥かしがり, はにかみ.

V ***coax away*** one's *shyness* すかしてその恥かしい気分を取直させる. ¶***get over*** one's *shyness* 恥かしさを感じなくなる. ¶she ***had*** very great *shyness* about telling ... 彼女は…のことを話すのを大層恥かしがった. ¶***lose*** one's *shyness* すれる, ずうずうしくなる. ¶***throw aside*** all *shyness* in his anxiety to ... …しようとする熱心のあまり恥かしいと思わなくなる.

V² *Shyness* ***came*** over her. 彼女は恥かしくなって来た.

Q ***ingrained*** *shyness* 深く染み込んだ内気.

P She has no sense ***of*** *shyness* or discretion. 彼女は恥かしいとか慎しみとかいうものを知らない.

sick, *a.* 病気の; 胸の悪い; 恋しがる.

M be *sick* ***abed*** with flu 流感で床についている. ¶He is ***awfully*** *sick* at being beaten. 彼は負けたのをひどく苦にしている. ¶Say! I'm getting ***dead*** *sick* of this. おい僕はこのことがやけにいやになって来た. ¶I am ***heartily*** *sick* of it. 僕はそれがつくづくいやになった. ¶He is lying ***mortally*** *sick*. 彼は重病で寝ている. ¶He is ***somewhat*** *sick* with croup. 彼はクループの気味だ. ¶I am, to tell you the truth, ***thoroughly*** *sick* of the business. 実を言えば僕はつくづくあの仕事がいやになった.

P He is very *sick* ***about*** it. 彼はそのことを非常に苦にしている. ¶I am *sick* ***at*** heart. 私はつくづくいやだ. ¶It makes me *sick* ***at*** my stomach to look at him.《米》あいつを見ると胸がむかむかする. ¶He is *sick* ***for*** his home. 彼は故郷を恋しがっている.【類】*sick* ***for*** a sight of home. ¶be *sick* ***in*** bed with flu 流感で床についている. ¶lie *sick* ***of*** a fever 熱病で床につく ‖ I am *sick* ***of*** flattery (rain, waiting). お世辞(など)はご免だ.【類】I am *sick* ***of*** life. / I am *sick* ***of*** the subject. / I am about *sick* ***of*** it. / I'm getting *sick* ***of*** his lies. ¶be *sick* ***with*** a cold 風を引いている ‖ She is *sick* ***with*** envy. 彼女はしっとで悩んでいる.【類】*sick* ***with*** fear (jealousy). ☞ 米語用法では sick は ill より口語的である. 英語用法の sick は「気分が悪い」意・例: I feel *sick*.《米》からだの具合がわるい;《英》胸がむかむかする. cf.《米》be sick at the stomach=《英》feel sick.

sick, *n. pl.* 病人.

V ***heal*** the *sick* 病人をなおす. ¶***nurse*** the *sick* 病人を看護する. ¶***serve*** the *sick* in a hospital 病院で病人に付添う. ¶The *sick* were carefully ***tended***. 病人は手厚く看護された. ¶***watch over*** (=***look after***) the *sick* 病人を看護する.

sick-bed, *n.* 病床.

P sleepless attendance ***at*** *sick-beds* 病床に不眠の付添. ¶rise ***from*** a *sick-bed* [病人が]床上をする. ¶I left him ***on*** a *sick-bed*. 私は病床に彼を残した.

sicken, *v.* 病気になる; 胸が悪くなる. 「て.

M ***soon*** *sickening* of one's new wife じき新妻が鼻につい

P *sicken* ***at*** the very sight (sound) of the name of ... …の名を見(聞い)ただけで胸が悪くなる.【類】Good citizens *sicken* ***at*** municipal corruption (市の腐敗). ¶The child is *sickening* ***for*** the measles. 子供がはしかをしている. ¶*sickened* ***in*** the palace for the old, free romantic life. 宮殿にいて昔の自由な楽しい生活にあこがれて. ¶be *sickening* (=getting sick) ***of*** life 人生がいやになる.【類】*Sickening* ***of*** hotel life, I decided to live with Mrs. X.

sickness, *n.* 病気; はき気.

V ***feign*** *sickness* 病気を装う. ¶He went to ... to ***fight*** *sickness*. 彼は病気療養のため…に行った. ¶until *sickness* ***overtakes*** him 彼が病気になるまで.

Q ***mental*** *sickness* 精神病. ¶a ***severe*** *sickness* 重病. ¶a ***slight*** *sickness* 軽症.

Q² ***mountain*** *sickness* 山岳病. ¶***radiation*** *sickness* ふく射病. ¶***sea*** *sickness* 船酔. ¶***trolley*** *sickness*《米》電車病.

P ***after*** *sickness* 病後. ¶He is confined to bed ***by*** *sickness*. 彼は病気で寝ている. ¶***during*** one's *sickness* 病中. ¶recover ***from*** a *sickness* 病気が本復する ‖ death ***from*** *sickness* 病死. ¶either ***in*** *sickness* or in health 病気の時も健康の時も ‖ He is far gone ***in*** his *sickness*. 彼は病勢がよほど進んでいる. ¶an attack ***of*** *sickness* 発病 ‖ die ***of*** a *sickness* 病死する. ¶He is seized ***with*** a painful *sickness*. 彼は苦しい病にかかっている. ‖ The steamer arrived here ***with*** *sickness* on board. 船は発病者を乗せて当地に着いた.

P² *sickness* ***at*** the stomach はき気.

sickle, *n.* かま.

P² the *sickle* ***of*** the moon 三日月. ¶a hammer and *sickle* ***on*** a red flag ソ連国旗.

side, *n.* わき; 側(ｶﾞﾜ); 面(ﾒﾝ); 方面; 味方; 血筋.

V He ***championed*** enthusiastically the American *side* in the War of Independence. 彼は独立戦争の時熱心にアメリカ側を擁護した. ¶***change*** *sides* 脱党する, 党派を変える. ¶***choose*** *sides* [競技などで]組を決める. ¶He ***depicts*** the sordid, vulgar, and unclean *sides* of life exclusively. 彼はもっぱら人生のいやしさや不潔な方面を描く. ¶Cambridge ***has*** a strong *side*. ケンブリッジには強い組がいる. ‖ His character ***has*** many *sides*. 彼の性格には色々の方面がある. ¶I must ***hear*** both *sides* before I judge. 私は双方の申立を聴いてからでなくては判断は下せない.【類】He is fairminded enough to want to ***hear*** both *sides* of the questions at issue (問題). ¶***hold*** one's *sides* with laughter 腹をかかえて笑う. ¶He has ***joined*** the *side* of the Liberals. 彼は自由党の側にくみした. ¶***keep*** the right *side* ***up*** [荷物など]さかさに置かないようにする. ¶someone who ***knows*** both *sides* of the question 問題の両面を知っている人. ¶***Look on*** the reverse *side* of this wrapper (=jacket). この(本の)カバーの裏を見よ.【類】with an inclination to habitually ***look upon*** (=***on***) the gloomy *side* of life (人生の暗黒面). ¶If you try to ***please*** both *sides*, you will please neither. 双方の気に入るようにしようとすればどちらの気にも入るまい. ¶it ***provides*** the third *side* completing the triangle of ... それは…の三角形を作る第三辺となる. ¶***receive*** the practical *side* of their professional education その専門教育の実際方面を受ける. ¶carefully ***repress*** the animal *side* of one's nature 天性の動物的方面を念入りに抑制する. ¶***reveal*** a more general and charming *side* of Ruskin's personality ラスキンの個性の一層全体的で魅力的な方面を表わす. ¶***see*** the both *sides* of the shield たての両面(物事の表裏)を見る ‖ Be like the sun which never ***sees*** the dark *side* of anything. 何物に対しても決してその暗黒面を見ない太陽の如くあれ. ¶***shake*** one's ***sides*** 腹をかかえて笑う. ¶***show*** the seamy *side* of human nature 人性の裏面を示す. ¶***split*** one's ***sides*** with laughter 横腹をかかえて笑う. ¶***state*** one *side* of the case 事件の一方を陳述する. ¶***study*** all *sides* of a question 問題の各方面を研究する. ¶in that war he fervently ***took*** the *side* of ... その戦争で彼は熱心に…側に味方した. ‖ It ***takes*** both *sides* to tell the truth. 話というものは双方聞いてみないと分からないものだ. ‖ decline to ***take*** *sides* with him in the dispute. その争議で彼にくみすることを断る. 【類】Don't ***take*** *sides* in servants' quarrels. / avoid ***taking*** *sides* in a lovers' quarrel. ¶***uphold*** the other *side* of a question 問題の他の側を支持する. ¶***use*** one *side* of the page only 紙の片面だけを使う. 「ほど笑った.

v² He laughed till his *sides* ***ached***. 彼は横腹が痛くなる

Q on the ***advantageous*** *side* we may put the fact that ... われわれは有利な事項として…を述べることができる. ¶be on the ***affirmative side*** 賛成の側に立っている. ¶He is on the ***alcoholic*** *side*. あいつはのんべいだ. ¶from ***all*** *sides* 四方から ‖ a lake rounded by low hills on ***all*** *sides* 低い丘でとり巻かれている湖水 ‖ On ***all*** *sides* war is believed to be inevitable. 戦争は不可避だと信じられている. ¶on the ***back*** *side* of ... …の裏面に. ¶appeal to the ***better*** *side* of our nature われわれの性質の一層よい面に訴える. ¶the peoples on ***both*** *sides* of the Atlantic 大西洋の両岸にある国民 ‖ the parents on both *sides* [夫婦]双方の親たち ‖ There is a good deal to be said on ***both*** *sides* of the question. その問題の双方に沢山の言分がある. 【類】There is right and wrong on ***both*** *sides*. ‖ I will agree to arbitrate if ***both*** *sides* wish it. 双方の希望とあれば仲裁の労をとろう. ‖ the man who sees ***both*** *sides* of a question 問題の両面を見る人. ¶Look on the ***bright*** (***dark***) *side* of a thing. 物事の明るい(暗い)半面を見るべきだ. ‖ the ***brighter*** *side* of existence 生活の明るい(楽しい)半面. ¶a ***certain*** *side* of a great subject 大問題のある一つの面. ¶reveal a more general and ***charming*** *side* of his personality 彼の人物の一層全体的の美しい面を現わす. ¶the ***commercial*** *side* of literature 文学の商業的方面. ¶its ***dangerous*** *side* その危険な方面. ¶his wide experience of the ***darker*** *side* of London life ロンドン生活の暗黒な半面における彼の広い経験. ¶cubes of ***different*** *sides* 種々の側面を有する立方体. ¶the ***disreputable*** *sides* of life 人生の外聞の悪い方面. ¶on ***each*** *side* 双方の側に. ¶the ***economic*** *side* of the question その問題の経済的方面. ¶The fertile valley of Comondu has precipitous rocky cliffs at ***either*** *side*. コモンジュの肥よくなけい谷の両側にけわしい岩の断がいがある. 【類】Grass grows on ***either*** *side* of the road. ¶on the ***employers'*** *side* 雇主の側に. ¶the ***ethical*** *side* of art 芸術の倫理的方面. ¶hemmed in on ***every*** *side* by ... 四方…に囲まれて. ¶the ***expressional*** *side* of literary training 文学修業の表現的方面. ¶the ***farther*** *side* of the hill その岡の向う側. ¶my grandparents on my ***father's*** *side* 私の父方の祖父母. ¶the ***flat*** *side* of a sword 剣の峰. ¶the ***gloomy*** *side* of life 人生の暗黒面. ¶The idea has its ***good*** *sides*. その思いつきにはよい所がある. ¶the ***graver*** *side* of hospital life 病院生活の厳粛な半面. ¶the ***higher*** *side* of human nature 人性の高尚な半面. ¶wear a shirt ***hind*** *side* before シャツを後ろ前に着る. ¶He was very witty, and always saw the ***humorous*** *side* of things. 彼は非常に機知があっていつも物事のユーモラス的な半面を見た. ¶the most ***important***, certainly the most ***remunerative***, *side* of the firm's activities その商会の事業の中で最も重要でたしかに最も有利な方面. ¶the ***intellectual*** *side* of a feast きょう宴の知的方面[演説など]. ¶cast anchor on the ***lee*** *side* of the island 島の風下の側にいかりを降ろす. ¶A bow is always to be found on the ***left*** *side* of a man's hat. 男子の帽子はちょう形の結びがいつも左側に出るようにかぶるものだ. ¶the ***lighter*** *side* of German life ドイツ生活の明るい半面. ¶He is on the ***managerial*** *side*. 彼は幹部だ. ¶On his ***mother's*** *side* he is related to King. 母方では彼は国王の縁者になっている. ¶***mountain*** *sides* 山腹. ¶the ***near*** and ***off*** *sides* [馬の]左側及び右側. ¶stand on the ***negative*** *side* [討論会などの]反対の側に立つ. ¶You should take ***neither*** *side*. 君はどちらへも付いてはならない. ¶The club's emblem is a small silver badge, upon ***one*** *side* of which appears a miniature heart, pierced by a small dart, and on the ***obverse*** *side* the inscription "Nit." クラブの標章は一面に小さい矢の通った小形の心臓があり裏面には "Nit" と銘を打った小さい銀の記章である. ¶Write on only ***one*** *side* of each sheet of paper. 用紙は各葉一面だけに書け. ¶go to the ***opposing*** *side* 反対側へ行く. ¶on the ***opposite*** *side* of ... …の向側に ‖ ***opposite*** *sides* of a parallelogram 平行四辺形の対辺 ‖ play ... on ***opposite*** *sides* in the game その競技で二組に分かれて…をプレーする. ¶turn the ***other*** *side* out 裏返しにする ‖ on the ***other*** *side* of the Atlantic 大西洋の向う側に ‖ upon the ***other*** *side* of this box この箱のへりの相対する側に. ¶fight on ***our*** *side* われわれに味方して戦う ‖ on ***our*** *side* of the pond 米国では(英国へ渡った米人が自国を指す). ¶Artistic London has its ***pathetic*** *side*. ロンドンの画壇には悲そうな半面がある. ¶approach a problem rather from the literary than from the ***philological*** *side* 言語学方面からよりはむしろ文学的方面から問題を取扱う. ¶the ***physical*** *side* of love 恋愛の肉的半面. ¶the ***practical*** *side* of science 科学の実際的方面. ¶the ***psychic*** *side* of the human being 人間の心理的方面. ¶take the ***Republican*** *side* of the question その問題については共和党側に味方をする. ¶on the ***reverse*** *side* of this wrapper (folder) この包装紙(など)の裏面に ‖ There is a ***reverse*** *side* of this. これには裏がある. ‖ He is on the ***reverse*** *side* of life. 彼は下り坂(老人)だ. ¶the ***right*** *side* of cloth 布の表 ‖ We find the balance still on the ***right*** *side*. 帳じりはまだ赤字になっていない. ‖ Keep to your ***right*** *side* of the road. 路の右側を歩け. 【類】the store on the ***right***[***-hand***] *side*. ¶It is not without its ***romantic*** *side*. それにはロマンチックな面がないでもない. 【類】appeal to the ***romantic*** *side* of human nature. ¶There is a ***sad*** *side* to the story. その話には悲しい半面がある. ¶err on the ***safe*** *side* 万全をとり過ぎる. ¶stand on the ***safe*** *side*＝be prudent 大事を取る. ¶He and I were aligned on the ***same*** *side* in the contest. その競技で彼と私は味方同志となった. ¶the ***seamy*** *side* of life 人生の裏面 ‖ ***seamy*** *sides* of human nature 人間性の弱点. 【類】show (＝reveal) the ***seamy*** *side* of humanity. ¶Human nature is weak on the ***sexual*** *side*. 人間性は性の方面には弱いものだ. ¶He is on the ***shady*** *side* of forty (middle life). 彼は四十(など)を越している. ¶the ***social*** *side* of history 歴史の社会的方面. ¶He is rather on the ***solid*** (***soft***) *side*. 《口語》彼はどっちかというとまじめの(だらしない)方だ. ¶He is still on the ***sunny*** *side* of thirty. 彼はまだ三十前だ. ¶the ***successful*** (＝winning) *side* 勝った方. ¶We are on the ***sunny*** *side* of the car. われわれは自動車の日の当る側に乗っている. ‖ He is, say, on the ***sunny*** *side* of 50. 彼はまあ五十になっていない. ¶on its ***theoretical*** *side* その理論的方面に. ¶on ***this*** *side* of the Channel 海峡のこちら側(即ち英国)において. 【類】on ***this*** (***that***) *side* of the river ‖ on ***this*** *side* of ten o'clock 十時前に ‖ He is on ***this*** *side* of thirty. 彼は三十にはまだならない. ¶***three sides*** of a triangle 三角形の三辺. ¶There are ***two*** *sides* to the question. その問題は二つの面がある. ¶the ***upper*** and ***under*** *sides* of a plank 板の上と下の面(表と裏). 【類】the ***upper*** (***under***) *side* of a box. ¶on ***various*** *sides* 種々の方面で. ¶He made practical acquaintance with the ***warm*** *side* of the prison walls. 彼は刑務所生活を体験した(幽囚の身となったことがある). ¶the ***weak*** *side* of music 音楽の短所. ¶on its ***west*** *side* その西側に. 【類】Democracy has its ***weak*** *side*. ¶He knows on ***which*** *side* his bread is buttered. 彼はどうすれば自分の利益になるかを心得ている. ¶those belonging to the ***winning*** (***losing***) *side* 勝っ(負け)た方の人々. ¶Your socks are on ***wrong*** *side* out. 君のくつ下は裏返しだ. 【類】wear a ***kimono wrong*** *side* out ‖ The widow was on the ***wrong*** *side* of 40—probably 48. 未亡人は四十以上で多分四十八ぐらいだった.

Q² She entered the war on the ***Axis*** *side*. その国は枢軸側

について戦争に参加した. ¶the ***business side*** of a tool [柄などに対して]道具の働く方の先. ¶on the ***credit*** (***debit***) *side* 貸方(借方)の側に. ¶the ***creditor*** *side* of an account 帳簿の貸方. ¶the ***distaff*** *side* 女系. ¶on the ***lake*** (***river***) *side* 湖(河)畔に. ¶from the ***land*** *side* 陸地側から. ¶the ***money-making*** *side* of the matter その事件の金もうけの方面. ¶the ***night*** *side* of London 夜のロンドン. ¶on the ***port*** (***starboard***) *side* 左(右)げんに. ¶Her business was at the ***post-office*** *side*. [郵便局と薬局を兼ねている店などで]彼女は郵便局の部に勤務していた. ¶on the ***right*** (***left***) ***hand*** *side* of the page そのページの右(左)側に. ¶the ***silver*** *side* 牛肉のロースの類. ¶the ***spear*** *side* 父方.

P sit ***at*** her *side* 彼女のわきにすわる‖This character has what is called nim-ben ***at*** its *side*. この字にはいわゆる人偏がある. ‖I said to a friend ***at*** my *side*. 私は私のわきの友だちに言った. ‖with my love ***at*** my *side* 私のわきに恋人を控えて. 【類】have the dictionary ***at*** his *side* / ***at*** the *side* of a pool. ¶He appeared quite a pigmy ***by*** her *side*. 彼は彼女のわきへ来るとまるで小人(こびと)のように見えた. ‖fight ***by*** the *side* of … …に味方して戦う. ¶The ink ran ***down*** the *side* of the ink-well. インキがインキつぼの側面を流れ落ちた. ¶viewed ***from*** the *side* 側面から見て‖***from*** the land *side* 陸の方から‖The ship rolled ***from*** *side* to side. 船が横に揺れた. ¶a thorn ***in*** the *side* 身に付きまとうわずらい‖pain ***in*** the *side* 横腹の痛み‖Some birds build nests ***in*** the *sides* of hills. 鳥の中には山の側面に巣を作るものがある. ¶The room is ***on*** the north *side* of the house. そのへやは家の北側にある. ‖be ***on*** the *side* of the working people 労働者に味方している. 【類】We have America ***on*** our *side*. / Public sympathy is ***on*** the *side* of … ‖***On*** the *side* of the French 13,000 were slain. フランス側は一万三千人殺された. ‖We have right ***on*** our *side*, and we are bound to win. われわれの方に正義があるのだから勝つにきまっている. 【類】There is no reason ***on*** his *side*. ‖The winds and waves are always ***on*** the *side* of the ablest navigators. 〖諺〗波は常に有能な航海者に味方する. 【類】The mistake is ***on*** your *side*. / The fault must be ***on*** your *side*. / The obligation if anything was ***on*** your *side*. ‖Directions ***on*** other *side*. 用法は裏面に. ‖He is ***on*** this *side* of forty, I should think. 彼は四十を越してはいないと思う. ‖be well ***on*** this *side* of the century mark 百歳よりずっと下である‖***on*** the *side* 《米》内職に, 片手間に‖He wrote ***on*** the *side*, with little success. 彼はアルバイトに文筆をとったが成功しなかった. 【類】And he got me a teacher to tutor me ***on*** the *side*. / do literary work ***on*** the *side*‖Our photograph shows the vessel lying ***on*** its *side*. この写真には船が横倒しになっている所が取ってある. ‖The load is too much ***on*** one *side*. 荷が片方に寄りすぎている. ‖err ***on*** the *side* of liberality (charity, optimism) 寛大(など)に失する‖The wolf lay ***on*** (=upon) its *side* dead. そのおおかみは死んで横たわっていた. ‖slide the screen ***on*** one *side* [障子など]一方に引く. ¶draw back ***to*** one *side* [道路で]一方の側に後退する‖I'll go ***to*** his *side*. 彼の組に行こう. ¶A boy sat weeping ***upon*** the *side* of a well. 一人の男の子が井戸のかたわらに泣きながらすわっていた. ¶The incident was not ***without*** its amusing *side*. その出来事にはおかしな半面がないでもなかった.

P² walk *side* ***by*** side with … …と並んで歩く. ¶the German *side* ***of*** the case 該事件のドイツ側. ¶There is another *side* ***to*** the question. その問題には別の半面がある.

side, *v.* 与(くみ)する; 味方する.

P *side* ***against*** … …の反対側に与(くみ)する. ¶They *sided* ***with*** … in the war. 彼らは戦争で…に味方した. 【類】I would rather *side* ***with*** the intelligent few than ***with*** ignorant many. ‖they ***sided with*** … ***against*** … 彼らは…に反対して…に味方した.

side-glance, *n.* 横目.

V ***cast*** *side-glances* at … …に横目を使う.

side-light, *n.* 〘比ゆ〙側光.

V ***throw*** *side-light* upon … …を側面から説明する. 【類】***throw*** many *side-lights* on the discussion.

Q ***curious*** *side-lights* upon history 歴史上の興味ある側面観. ¶throw ***interesting*** *side-lights* on persons and events 人及び事件につき興味ある側面観を示す.

P² an interesting *side-light* is furnished ***by*** … ***about*** his personality 彼の個性に関する興味ある側面観を…が提供している. ¶*side-lights* ***to*** history 歴史の側面観.

sideline, *n.* 副業.

P ***as*** a *sideline* 副業として.

side-show, *n.* 寸劇.

Q² a ***circus*** *side-show* 曲馬団の余興.

side-step, *v.* [問題などの決定を]避ける.

M He has ***deftly*** *side-stepped* the issue. 彼はたくみにその論点を避けた.

side-street, *n.* 横町.

Q a ***sunless*** *side-street* 日の目を見ない横町.

side-track, *n.* [鉄道の]側線.

P² *side-track* ***on*** a question (issue, subject) 問題の枝葉.

sidewalk, *n.* 《米》歩道.

Q scatter ashes on the ***icy*** *sidewalk* 凍った歩道に灰をまく(滑らないように). ¶the ***roofed-over*** *sidewalk* of a new street 新しい街路のおおいのある歩道.

siding, *n.* 待避線.

Q² ***railway*** *siding* 鉄道の待避線.

sidle, *v.* にじり寄る.

M ***timidly*** *sidle* up 恐る恐る寄る.

siege, *n.* 囲み, 包囲, 攻撃.

V ***abandon*** a *siege* 包囲を断念する. ¶***conduct*** a *siege* 包囲軍を指揮する. ¶***endure*** a *siege* 包囲攻撃にたえる. ¶***lay*** *siege* to a fortress 城砦を包囲する‖***lay siege*** to a woman's heart 女をくどく. ¶***lift*** (=***raise***) a *siege* 囲みを解く. ¶***push*** the *siege* 猛烈に攻めたてる. ¶***raise*** a *siege* 包囲を解く. ¶***stand*** a long *siege* 長攻撃にたえる. 【類】¶No city in the world has ***stood*** so many *sieges* as Constantinople. ¶The *siege* was ***sustained*** for three years. その城は三年間守り通した.

Q ***regular*** *siege* 正攻法.

P he fell in battle ***at*** the *siege* of … 彼は…の包囲中戦死した. ¶***during*** the *siege* 攻囲中. ¶he served ***in*** the *siege* of … 彼は…の攻囲戦に参加した. ¶Port Arthur ***under*** the *siege* 包囲の下にある旅順港.

P² a *siege* ***of*** nearly a year 約一年にわたる攻囲.

siesta, *n.* うたたね.

V ***take*** a *siesta* 昼寝をする.

sieve, *n.* ふるい.

Q² a ***hair*** *sieve* 毛ぶるい.

P remove lumps ***through*** a *sieve* ふるって塊を除く.

sift, *v.* ふるう, ふるい分ける; ふるい落す; [雪・光など]入りこむ.

M The snow *sifted* ***softly*** down. 小雪が静かに降った. ¶*sift* ***out*** flour 麦粉をふるい分ける‖The judge had to *sift* ***out*** the truth from the conflicting testimony of the two parties. 判事は原被両告の矛盾する陳述から真相をは握しなければならなかった. ¶***painstakingly*** *sift* 骨を折ってふるい分ける.

M² The snow (rain) was falling *sifting* ***down***. 粉雪(ぬか雨)が降っていた.

P *sift* sand ***along*** the road 道路に沿って砂をふるい落す. ¶*sift* flour ***from*** bran 麦粉とぬかとをふるい分ける. 【類】*sift* the good ***from*** the bad / *sift* the fabulous ***from*** the trustworthy. ¶sand *sifted* ***into*** one's shoe くつに入った砂. ¶*sift* sand ***over*** the ground 地面に砂をふるい落す. ¶*sift* sand ***through*** the fingers 指の間から砂を通す. 【類】The sunshine *sifts* ***through*** the cloud (crevices). / Snow *sifted* ***through*** cracks in the wall. ¶The affair should be *sifted* ***to*** the bottom. その事件は徹底的に調査をすべきである. ¶*sift* sugar ***upon*** a cake 菓子に砂糖を振りかける.

sifting, *n.* ふるい分け, 精査.

V The alleged facts ***need*** further careful *sifting*. 申立ての事実は一層入念の精査を要する. ¶It ***requires*** a good deal *sifting* to get a few grains of truth from a large measure of chaff. 多量のくずからほんの少しの真実を拾い出すには十分ふるいにかける必要がある.

sigh, *n.* ため息, 嘆息, 嘆声.

V ***breathe*** (=***give or heave***) a *sigh* of relief 安心の吐息(といき)をつく. ¶***draw*** a long *sigh* of gratification 満足の長い吐息をする. ¶***heave*** a *sigh* of grief 嘆声を漏らす. ¶***sigh*** a deep *sigh* 吐息する. 【類】***sigh*** (=***utter***) a *sigh* of relief.

Q heave an ***amorous*** *sigh* 恋こがれてほっと吐息をつく‖with a ***deep*** *sigh* 吐息して. ¶a ***deep-drawn*** *sigh* 深いため息. ¶with a ***long*** *sigh* 長大息して.

P ***with*** a *sigh* of contentment (grief, admiration) 満足(など)の吐息をついて. 【類】He sat slowly on the seat ***with*** a *sigh*.

sigh, *v.* 嘆息する; あこがれ悲しむ.

M *sigh **away*** one's days 歳月を嘆息して過ごす. ¶*sigh **deeply*** 長大息する. ¶*sigh **heavily*** 重くるしくため息をつく. ¶One man *sighs **in vain*** for such works today. 今日こんな作品を望んでもむだかも知れない. ¶*sigh **lugubriously*** 悲しそうにため息をつく. ¶*sigh **out*** ため息をつく. 【類】*sigh **out*** one's grief (love). ¶*sigh **softly*** 静かに吐息をつく.

P *sigh **after*** (=for) ... ...を渇望する. ¶*sigh **at*** (=*over*) one's misfortune 不運を嘆息する. ¶But it is no use *sighing **for*** the unattainable. しかし得られないものを渇望するのはなんの役にも立たない. ‖ *sigh **for*** the old days of ... ...の昔を恋しがる. 【類】*sigh **for*** better days / *sigh **for*** home and one's parents / well may we *sigh **for*** the good old days when ... ¶The wind *sighed **in*** the treetops. 風がこずえを鳴らした. ¶*sigh **over*** one's unhappy fate 不運を嘆息する. ¶I *sighed **with*** relief on hearing that ... 私は...を聞いて安心の吐息をついた.

sight, *n.* 視力; 光景; 視界; 照準; 《俗》多数.

V ***abhor*** the *sight* of man 人目を恐れる. ¶***adjust*** the *sight* 照準を合わせる. ¶It ***affords*** a *sight* of unequalled beauty. それはまたとなく美しい. ¶unable to ***bear*** the *sight* any longer もう見ていられない. ¶You may ***catch*** *sight* of it from the railway. それは汽車から見える. ‖ ***catch*** *sight* of ... ...を見かける. ¶***destroy*** the *sight* of the right eye 右眼の視力を害する. ¶***do*** the *sights* of London ロンドン見物をする. ¶***dread*** the *sight* of ... ...を見るのを恐ろしがる. ¶a crowd ***enjoying*** a free *sight* 無料の立見をして喜んでいる群集. ¶***feast*** one's *sight* with ... ...で目の正月をする. ¶***fix*** one's *sight* upon a distant landmark 遠くの目標に注目する. ¶It ***forms*** a *sight* which once seen can never be forgotten. それは一度見たら決して忘れられない光景だ. ¶***get*** a *sight* of ... を見る, 認める. ¶***give*** a *sight* to a blind man by making the sign of the Cross over him 十字を切って盲人の目をあける. ¶I ***hate*** the *sight* of him. 私は彼を見るのもいやだ. ¶***keep*** *sight* of one その人を見失わないようにする. ¶***lay by*** a *sight* of money somewhere どこかにたくさんの金銭をしまっておく. ¶The ship ***lost*** *sight* of the coast. その船は海岸が見えない所に出た. ‖ We ***lost*** *sight* of him in the crowd. われわれは群集の中に彼を見失った. 【類】be ***lost*** *sight* of (ゆくえ不明) for some years / Never ***lose*** *sight* of the main purpose of your life / ***lose*** *sight* (=forget) the fact that ... / I have ***lost*** *sight* of my old friend. / In trials of skill the distinction between master and servant should be ***lost*** *sight* of. ‖ She ***lost*** her *sight* at the age of three. 彼女は三歳のときに失明した. 【類】He ***lost*** the *sight* of the right eye. ¶***make*** a *sight* of oneself 見っともない風をする. ¶one must not ***miss*** the *sight* of ... ...を見失ってはならない. ¶***present*** a colorful *sight* 色彩に富んだ光景を呈する. ¶***preserve*** the *sight* 視力を保存する. ¶***provide*** interesting *sights* for visitors 参けい人のために興味ある観覧物を用意する. ¶The blind ***received*** their *sights*. 盲人は目があいた. ¶***recover*** one's *sight* 視力を回復する. ¶***restore*** one's *sight* 視力を回復する. 【類】***restore*** *sight* to the blind. ¶***save*** a *sight* (=lot) of money しこたま金をためこむ. ¶***see*** the *sights* of ... ...を見物する. ¶***show*** one the *sights* 人に名所を見せる. ¶***strain*** one's *sight* 目をみはる. ¶***take*** *sight* 照準を定める, ねらう ‖ ***take*** a *sight* of ... ...を見る ‖ It must have ***taken*** a *sight* of work. それは大層手が掛ったに相違ない. ¶***view*** the *sights* of the city 町の名所を見物する. ¶I ***want*** a lot more *sight* of it. それをもっともっと見たい. ¶***witness*** a beautiful *sight* 美しい光景を見る. ¶His *sight* is ***failing***. 彼の視力が衰えてきた.

Q have an ***acute*** *sight* 鋭い眼力を持つ. ¶an ***artistic*** *sight* 芸術上の眼識. ¶***attractive*** *sights* 興味ある見もの. ¶I have ***bad*** (***good***) *sight*. 私は目が悪い(いい). ¶The sunset is a ***beautiful*** *sight*. 日没は美しいものだ. ¶That blue serge makes you a ***better*** *sight*. その青いサージは君を引立たせる. ¶a ***breath-catching*** (***-taking***) *sight* for the spectator 見ていて息づまるような光景. 【類】The Grand Canyon is one of the most ***breathtaking*** *sights* in the world. ¶***captivating*** *sights* 見とれるような風景. ¶take a ***careful*** *sight* 注意して照準する. ¶a ***cheerful*** *sight* おもしろい光景. ¶the ***chief*** *sights* in Tokyo 東京名所. ¶a half ***comic***, half ***pathetic*** *sight* おかしくもあり痛ましくもある光景. ¶a ***common*** *sight* ありふれた風景. ¶a ***commonplace*** *sight* 平凡な風景. ¶enjoy the ***cooling*** *sight* of a waterfall 滝の涼味を満喫する. ¶a ***dazzling*** *sight* 目がくらむような光景. ¶My *sight* is ***dim***. 私は目がかすむ. ¶a ***disgusting*** *sight* へどを催させる光景. ¶present a ***dreadful*** *sight* 恐ろしい光景を呈する. ¶a ***familiar*** *sight* in a bustling street 雑とうの往来には珍らしくない光景. ¶a ***fascinating*** *sight* 人をうっとりさせる光景. ¶be of ***feeble*** *sight* 視力が弱い. ¶What a ***fine*** *sight* it must be! さぞよい景色でしょう. ¶if paradoxical at ***first*** *sight* 一見矛盾しているようでも ‖ the ***first*** *sight* that struck me was ... 最初に目についたのは...であった ‖ He fell in love with her at ***first*** *sight*. 彼は彼女を一目で見初めた. 【類】nor is it apparent at ***first*** *sight* why ... ¶London ***free*** *sights* ロンドン市中の無料で見られるもの. ¶a ***frightening*** *sight* 恐ろしい光景. ¶***ghastly*** *sights* 恐ろしい光景. ¶He has ***good*** *sight*. 彼は目がよい. ¶The review was a ***grand*** *sight*. 観兵式は壮観だった. ¶a ***heart-rending*** *sight* 悲惨極まりない光景. ¶a ***horrible*** *sight* 恐ろしい光景. ¶a centenarian whose *sight* and hearing are somewhat ***impaired*** 目と耳が少し弱っている百歳の人. ¶an ***impressive*** *sight* 肝に徹する光景. ¶it is not an ***infrequent*** *sight* to see ... ...を見るのは珍らしいことでない. ¶an ***inspiring*** *sight* 感激的光景. ¶It is an ***interesting*** *sight* to see them work. 彼らの仕事をしているのを見るのは興味あることだ. ¶have ***keen*** *sight* and hearing 視力も聴力も鋭い. ¶have ***long*** *sight* 遠視眼だ ‖ This is worth a ***long*** *sight* ([colloq.]=good deal) more than that. この方がそれよりよっぽど値打がある. ¶a ***marvelous*** *sight* 驚くべき光景. ¶a ***memorable*** *sight* 記憶すべき(忘るべからざる)光景. ¶be a ***miserable*** *sight* 見るかげもない有様. ¶***near*** *sight* 近視眼. ¶***noted*** *sights* 名所. ¶stars visible to ***ordinary*** *sight* 肉眼で見える星. ¶He is a ***perfect*** *sight*. 彼のざまは実に見ものだ[反語]. ¶a ***picturesque*** *sight* 絵のような風景. ¶It was a ***piteous*** *sight* to see. それは見るも悲惨であった. ¶not a ***pleasant*** *sight* 見て心地よいものではない. ¶***popular*** *sights* of Japan 日本で評判の見もの. ¶A ***prettier*** *sight* than this could not well be imagined. これ以上美しいながめは想像できない. ¶the ***principal*** *sights* of Kyoto 京都の主な名所. ¶An open fire is a ***rare*** *sight*. 開いた炉はまれにしか見られない. ¶a ***repugnant*** *sight* いまわしい光景. ¶a ***revolting*** *sight* 見るもいやな物. ¶a ***rueful*** *sight* 暗たんたる光景. ¶show a very ***sad*** *sight* はなはだ痛ましい光景を呈する. ¶a ***scenic*** *sight* 勝景. ¶the ***second*** *sight* of a seer 予言者の千里眼 ‖ on ***second*** *sight* I noticed that ... 見直して私は...に気が付いた. ¶***short*** *sight* 近視眼; 短見. ¶a ***sickening*** *sight* いやな光景. ¶a ***spectacular*** *sight* 壮観. ¶Grand! ***Splendid*** *sight!* すばらしい, すてきだ! ¶a result of ***strained*** *sight* 目を疲らした結果. ¶He who has not seen Niagara in its winter robe has missed one of the ***striking beautiful*** *sights* of the world. 冬の装いをしたナイアガラを見ない人は世界絶景の一を見そこなったことになる. ¶a ***thrilling*** *sight* 胸躍る光景. ¶beyond the range of ***unassisted*** *sight* 肉眼では見えない所に. ¶it is not ***uncommon*** *sight* to see ... ...を見るのは珍らしくない. ¶at the ***unexpected*** *sight* of ... ...を不意に見て. ¶The ***very*** *sight* of him is quite disgusting. 彼を見るだけでも胸が悪くなる. ¶***weak*** *sight* 弱視.

Q[2] it is an ***every-day*** (=daily) *sight* to see ... ...を見るのは毎日のことだ.

P ***after*** *sight* 一覧の上, 一覧後[手形の支払など]. ¶translate ***at*** *sight* passages of Homer ちょっと見たばかりでホーマーの句を翻訳する ‖ He started ***at*** *sight* of something. 彼は何か見てびくっとした. ‖ like a thief ***at*** [the] *sight* of a detective 刑事を見た泥棒のように ‖ a cheque payable ***at*** *sight* 一覧払の小切手 ‖ draw a bill ***at*** *sight* 手形を一覧払で振出す ‖ parliamentary law ***at*** *sight* 議院法一覧 ‖ He can play and sing ***at*** *sight*. 彼は譜を見てすぐ楽器を奏したり歌ったりできる. 【類】***at*** the very *sight* of ... / she began to cry ***at*** the *sight* of ... / she was unable to restrain herself ***at*** the *sight* of ... / my blood rose ***at*** the *sight* of ... / She wept ***at*** the *sight* of his distress. ‖ spend the afternoon ***at*** the *sights* 見物して午後を暮す. ¶The prairie stretched ***beyond*** the *sight*. 大草原は際限なく広がっていた. ¶I know him only ***by*** *sight*. 私はあの人は顔だけ見知っている. ¶buried ***from*** *sight* 世に埋れた(りっぱな作品など) ‖ vanish ***from*** *sight* 見えなくなる. ¶We came ***in*** *sight* of land. われわれは陸の見える所へ来た. 【類】Land came ***in*** *sight*. /

The burglars were nowhere *in sight.* ‖ The end of the task is not yet *in sight*. その仕事の結末はまだ見当がつかない. 【類】The next election was already *in sight.* ‖ The accident happened *in* my *sight.* そのできごとは私の見ている所で起った. ‖ All human beings are equal *in* the *sight* of God. すべての人間は神から見れば平等だ. 【類】We are mere worms *in* his *sight.* ¶loss *of sight* 失明 ‖ There is nothing worthy *of* our *sight.* われわれが見るに足るものはない. ¶I can tell a reporter *on sight.* 私には新聞社の人は見て分かる. ¶*Out of sight*, out of mind. 去る者は日にうとし. ‖ The steamer is now *out of sight.* 汽船はもう見えない. ‖ Get *out of* my *sight!* 出て失せろ, 消えてなくなれ! 【類】sail *out of sight* of land. ¶unaccustomed *to* the *sight* of foreigners 外国人を見なれていない ‖ be lost *to sight*＝disappear 見えなくなる. 【類】The head was lost *to sight* among the rank growth of weeds (雑草のしげみ). ¶It is by no means a dream; it is, in fact, already *within sight.* それは決して夢ではない, すでに実現しかけている. ‖ He cannot be trusted *within sight* of a brandy bottle. 彼はブランディーのびんが見える所にあると飲まずにはいられない. ‖ We were every day in peril and *within sight* of death. われわれは毎日危険に取巻かれいつ死ぬか判らなかった.

P² a *sight for* sore eyes 見るもうれしい人また物; 珍客. ¶the *sights of* the town 町の名所 ‖ a *sight of* people たくさんの人.

O It was a *sight* to see (＝to be seen). それは見られたざまじゃなかった. ¶a *sight* which we should not have seen 見るべきではなかったもの ‖ a *sight* not to be forgotton 忘れられない光景. 【類】a *sight* one cannot soon forget.

sight, *v.* 見る; 照準する.

P *sight at* 5,000 meters 五千メートルに照準する. ¶A lighthouse was *sighted in* the distance. 灯台が遠方に見えた.

sight-seeing, *n.* 見物.

V *do sight-seeing* and shopping 見物と買物をする ‖ *do* much *sight-seeing* 色々見物をする.

sight-seer, *n.* 観光客.

V *attract* many *sight-seers* from ... ...からの多くの観光客を引きつける.

Q a group of *foreign sight-seers* 一団の外国観光客.

sign, *n.* (**1**) 記号; 徴候, 形勢; 証跡.

V The book *bears* all the *signs* of being the product of a ripe scholar. その本は円熟した学者の著作であるというこん跡が十分に見える. 【類】Her face *bore signs* of many years' sufferings. ‖ *bear* no *signs* of life 生きている様子はない. ¶*develop signs* of an oncoming cold 感冒当初の徴候を示す. ¶*discern* the *signs* of the times 時代の形勢を看取する. ¶I could not *discover* any *sign* of houses or inhabitants. 私は人家や住民のこん跡も発見し得なかった. ¶*display signs* of nervousness 神経質の徴候を示す. ¶He *gave* me a *sign* to withdraw. 彼は私に引込めと手まねをした. ‖ *give* the *sign* of battle 合戦の合図をする. 【類】I *gave* him a *sign* to come to me. ¶without *having* a *sign* of a burn やけどのこん跡を残さずに. ¶*interpret* aright those significant *signs* of the times 時代のそうした重要なすう勢を正しく解釈する. ¶*make* a *sign* by fire (with the eye) 火(など)で合図をする. 【類】a *sign* was *made* to me by ... to ... ‖ I could not write my name, so I *made* the *sign* of the cross. 私は自分の名が書けなかったので十文字を記した. 【類】*make* the *sign* of the cross on one's breast (十字を切る) on entering a church. ¶*read* the *signs* of the times aright (more wisely) 時勢の帰向を正解する(など). ¶a tiny gold charm *representing* the *sign* of the zodiac under which the child was born 子供の生れた宮(十二支に当る)をかたどった小さな金の護符. ¶*see signs* of decay 衰微の徴候を見る. 【類】*see* the *signs* of a coming change. ¶*show* (＝*exhibit*) *signs* of madness 狂気の徴候を示す ‖ *show signs* of spring 春めく ‖ begin to *show signs* of life よみがえり出す ‖ His face *showed signs* that he had been bewitched. きつねにつままれたような顔つきをしていた. ‖ Old age will not fail to *show* its *signs*. 年は争えない. 【類】*show signs* of hostility (敵意) to one's plan / The vogue is just now *showing signs* of abatement. / *show signs* of a relapse (再発) / Old formulae of belief are *showing signs* of dissolution. / *show signs* of future promise / *show signs* of annoyance (dilapidation, deep emotion, fatigue) / The weather *shows* no *signs* of improving. / *show* no *signs* of decline / The weather *shows signs* of change. / come to *show signs* of activity / It seems that animals sometimes *show signs* of reasoning. / The flood *shows* no *signs* of decreasing. / The flood of ... literature *shows* no *signs* of abating. / *show* a *sign* of anger. ¶Statesmen should *study* the *signs* of the times. 政治家は時勢の帰向をきわめなければならない. ¶*use signs* 手まねをする.

V² *signs* are daily *increasing* that ... ...の徴候が日々増大しつつある. ¶*signs indicate* that ... ...の徴候が見える. ¶today *signs* are *multiplying* that ... 今日...の徴候が増加しつつある. ¶These *signs point* to the general gravity of the condition. これらの徴候は一般に事態の重大性を示す.

Q an *absolute sign* 動かない証拠. ¶*algebraic signs* 代数の記号. ¶*arbitrary signs* 勝手にきめた符号. ¶*astronomical signs* 天文学上の記号. ¶an *auspicious sign* 吉兆. ¶The most *certain sign* of a Cockney is his pronunciation of the letter *i*, which he invariably sounds *oi*. ロンドン児の一番確かな証拠は*i*文字をきまってオィと発音することだ. ¶it is a *clear sign* that ... それは...の明らかな証拠だ. ¶a "*closed*" *sign* put up over the door of a bank 銀行の入口に出ている"休業"の掲示. ¶*deaf-and-dumb signs* ろうあ文字. ¶one of the most *encouraging signs* of the times is apparent in the fact that ... この時代の最も有望な動向の一つは...の事実に明かに示されている. ¶there is *every sign* to show that ... どこから見ても...らしい ‖ He suppressed *every sign* of surprise. 彼は少しも驚かないような振りをした. 【類】It bears *every sign* of composition by a Japanese. ¶listen with *every outward sign* of sympathy すっかり同情した様子で拝聴する. ¶a *favorable sign* 都合のよい徴候. ¶He fled away at the *first sign* of danger. 彼は危険と見るが早いか逃げてしまった. ‖ youths with *first sign* of hair on the lip 口ひげが出たばかりの若者. ¶*genuine signs* of a better understanding between the two peoples 両国民間により良い理解の成立した真の証拠. ¶a *happy* and *healthy sign* of the times 時代の喜ばしい健全な風潮. ¶a very *healthful sign* きわめて健全な兆候. ¶*hopeful signs* of the times 時代の有望な徴候. ¶a *hostile sign* 敵意ある証拠. ¶an *interesting sign* of the times is the fact that ...時代の興味あるすう勢は...の事実である. ¶*irrefutable signs* 争われない証拠. ¶*signs* are not *lacking* (＝there are not wanting in signs) that ... ...という証拠が見られる. ¶without showing the *least sign* of reluctance いやな顔一つせず. ¶bear *manifest signs* of ... ...の明白なこん跡がある ‖ *Signs* of pregnancy have become *manifest* in her. 妊娠の徴候が明白になった. ¶*mathematical signs* 数学上の記号. ¶There was *no sign* of him there. 彼はそこには影も形もなかった. ‖ There is *no sign* of immediate rain. 差当り雨は降りそうもない. ¶The ability to handle with some accuracy the mechanics of written English has long been regarded as the most *obvious sign* of the educated man. 英文という機械を多少正確に操縦する手腕は教育ある人の最も明りょうな証拠と見なされた. ¶an *ominous sign* 凶兆. ¶in spite of all the *outward signs* to the contrary 外面上は反対の証拠十分なのにもかかわらず. ¶give *outward* and *visible signs* of the warmth of their affection 彼らの愛情のこまやかさをはっきり表面に示す. ¶*Physical signs* of age are noticeable in him. 年をとったという印が彼の顔に現われている. ¶a *pleasing sign* of ... ...の喜ばしい徴候. ¶*promising signs* of peace 有望な平和の徴候. ¶the *radical sign* 根の記号(√). ¶one of the most *remarkable signs* of the times 注目すべき現時風潮の一つ. ¶write in *secret signs* 秘密の記号で書く. ¶a very *sinister signs* おもしろくない前兆. ¶do not show the *slightest signs* of ... ...はおくびにも出さない. ¶show *some signs* of improvement 多少改善のこん跡を示す. ¶one of the most *striking signs* of the times 時局の最も顕著なる形勢の一. ¶a *sure sign* of ... ...の確かな証拠. ¶There are *undeniable signs* of improvement. 好転のきざしがたしかに見えている. ¶An *unfavorable sign* is to be seen. 見たところ不利な形勢だ. ¶there are *unmistakable signs* of ... ...のまぎれもない徴候がある. 【類】Black clouds are an *unmistakable sign* of coming rain. / Age brings its *unmistakable signs* with it. ¶a *welcome sign* of the times 時局の喜ばしい形勢.

Q^{2} ***spring signs*** 春のきざし.

P It is looked upon ***as*** a *sign* of noble breeding. それはりっぱな育ちの証拠と見なされている. ‖ ***as*** a *sign* of caution 注意の合図として. ¶***At*** a *sign* from her eyes he glided out of the room on tiptoe. 彼女の目くばせで彼は抜足差足で室外へ忍び出た. ‖ denote ***by*** a *sign* 記号で示す ‖ if sounds were expressible ***by*** *signs* 音が記号で表わせるものなら ‖ speak ***by*** *signs* 手まねで話す.【類】The dumb man made himself understood ***by*** *signs.* ¶foretell ***from*** *signs* 徴候を見て予言する.【類】I can tell ***from*** every *sign.* ¶a thing given ***in*** *sign* of love＝a love token 愛の印の贈物 ‖ something offered ***in*** *sign* of peace 平和の印に捧げた物. ¶The dog barked at the man ***on*** (＝***at***) a *sign* from his master. 主人が合図をすると犬はその人にほえついた. ¶a corpse ***with*** evident *signs* of murder 明らかに他殺の証跡のある死がい ‖ mark ***with*** a plus *sign* ＋の記号をつける. ¶I found him ***without*** *sign* of life. 私が行ったら彼は気絶していた.

P^{2} Yawning is a *sign* ***of*** sleepiness. あくびをするのは眠い証拠だ. ‖ The ruin is a *sign* ***of*** past grandeur. その廃虚は当時の壮麗を物語る証跡である.【類】To sneeze is often a *sign* ***of*** catching cold. / a *sign* ***of*** old age.【類】There are *signs* ***of*** improvemet. / A nod is a *sign* ***of*** agreement. / Violence is a *sign* ***of*** weakness. ‖ There are no *signs* ***of*** life about the plants. その植物は枯れてしまったらしい. ‖ *signs* ***of*** the zodiac 黄道の十二宮.

(2) 看板; 掲示.

V the building ***bears*** a huge *sign* on which are the words ..., その建物に...という字の大きな看板が出してある. ¶The *sign* "Standing Room Only" was ***displayed*** at the theatre.「座席満員」という掲示がその劇場に出ていた. ¶***erect*** a "No Trespass" *sign*「無用の者入るべからず」の立札を立てる. ¶I can ***find*** a *sign* that reads ... ...と書いた看板がある. ¶by ***following*** these *signs* 道標を見て行けば. ¶Shopkeepers ***hang up*** a *sign* of their business in front of their shops. 店主はその店の前にその商売の看板を出す. ¶The car ***has*** the *sign* "No Smoking." その車には「禁煙」の掲示が出ている. ¶***post*** a "No Trespassing" *sign*「みだりに立入るべからず」の掲示を出す.【類】***post*** a *sign* declaring that (＝reading) ... ‖ a *sign* conspicuously ***posted*** in all places 各所に目立つように掲げた看板. ¶***put up*** *signs* telling people to ...するように掲示を出す.【類】*signs* were ***put up*** in hotel rooms notifying guests that ... ¶***set up*** one's *sign* as ... ...の看板を立てる.

V^{2} there is a *sign* ***announcing*** that ... ...という看板が出ている.

Q I noticed a ***large sign*** over the building which announced that ... その建物の上の...という大看板が私の目についた.

Q^{2} the ***call sign*** JOAK... 呼出符号 JOAK. ¶the "***closed for the summer***" *sign*「夏季休業」の掲示. ¶a ***desk sign*** 卓上標札. ¶a ***detour sign*** う回せよという掲示(通行止に付). ¶a ***dollar sign*** ドルの記号 ($). ¶put up a "***For Sale***" *sign* on one's truck ...の貨物自動車に「売り物」の札をはる ‖ In those days celebrities' mansions were often stuck up with "***for sale***" *signs.* そのころは名士の邸宅によく「売家」の札がはってあった. ¶a "***Don't Touch***" *sign*「手を触るべからず」の掲示. ¶a "***For rent***" *sign* 貸家札. ¶a ***neon sign*** ネオン・サイン. ¶an "***off limits***" *sign* on a hotel 旅館の「立入禁止」の掲示. ¶an ***on-again-off-again flashing*** *sign* 点滅する(ネオンの)看板. ¶bottles with the ***poison sign*** on them 毒薬のはり紙をしたびん. ¶a ***road sign*** 道路標. ¶***shadow signs*** on side-walks 歩道にある(光線で映す)影看板. ¶the "***Silence***" *sign* in the library 図書館の「静粛」の掲示.【類】a "***Silence***" or "***Please-do-not-handle***" *sign.* ¶put up an ***SRO sign*** 座席満員 (＝standing-room-only) の掲示をする. ¶a ***stop-go*** (＝***go-stop***) *sign* 止まれ進めの標示. ¶a ***street sign*** in both English and Japanese 和英両語で書いた街路掲示. ¶a ***tavern sign*** 居酒屋の看板. ¶the ***telltale signs*** suggest that ... そこに表われていることで...が察知される. ¶a luminous ***tube sign*** ネオン・サイン. ¶a ***wayside sign*** 路傍の掲示.

P It was specially shown ***by*** *signs.* 特に掲示を出してそのことが示されてあった.

P^{2} run to the *sign* ***of*** the three brass balls 一六銀行(質屋)にかけつける. ¶the *sign* ***on*** the door reads ... 入口の看板に...と書いてある.【類】the *sign* ***on*** a telephone pole. ¶the wording of a *sign* ***over*** a shop 店に掲げてある看板の文句.

sign, *v.* 署名する; 手まねなどで示す.

M ***sign away*** one's rights 証書に署名して権利を譲渡する.【類】***sign away*** their citizenship. ¶He ***blindly*** *signed* an instrument tendered to him. 彼は提出された証書に盲判を押した. ¶***sign clear*** of an agreement 契約解除承認の署名をする. ¶If you fail to ***sign out*** you will be considered AWOL. 署名しないと無届欠席とみなされるだろう. ¶***sign unread*** 盲判を押す.

M^{2} *sign* ***off*** drinking 署名して酒をやめる ‖ The radio *signed* ***off*** at midnight. 放送が真夜中に終了を告げた. ¶Those ex-marines came back to ***sign up.*** それらの前海兵隊員は再入隊署名のため戻ってきた. ‖ ***sign up*** with one's old outfit 再入営する ‖ ***sign up*** as a salesman with ... ...と外交販売員として契約する.【類】***sign up*** for a job / The actor *signed* ***up*** for a new film production.

P articles of agreement were *signed* ***between*** ... 協定条項は...間に調印された. ¶The letter is *signed* ***by*** him. その手紙には彼の署名がしてある. ¶*sign* ***for*** a telegram (a parcel) 電報(小包)を送るので署名する. ¶He *signed* ***for*** paper and pencil. 彼は手まねで紙と鉛筆を求めた. ‖ The patrolman *signed* ***for*** him to halt there. 巡回中の警官が止まれと彼に合図した. ¶be required to be *signed* ***in*** ink ***by*** ... ...がインクで署名することになっている. ¶The firm *signed* ***on*** another group of workers. 会社は他の一組の職工を署名させて雇入れることにした. ¶He *signed* ***to*** me to take a seat. 彼はすわれと私に手まねをした. ‖ *sign* a name ***to*** an instrument 証書に署名する. ¶The screen star has *signed* ***with*** Shochiku. その映画スターは松竹と契約を結んだ. ‖ pottery *signed* ***with*** his name 彼の銘のある陶器.

O initials *signed* 略式署名(頭字の).

signal, *n.* 合図, 信号.

V ***break*** a *signal* 信号を発する. ¶***catch*** the *signal* 合図を見てとる(悟る). ¶Urgent *signals* of distress (＝SOS) were ***flashed*** ashore. 緊急難船信号が陸に打電された. ¶A *signal* will be ***given*** from ... by the sounding of a bell. 鐘を鳴らして...から合図をする. ‖ on a *signal* being ***given*** 合図をすると. ¶***hoist*** the *signal* 信号を掲げる. ¶***ignore*** a *signal* (列車・運転手など)信号を無視する. ¶***make*** a *signal* by the motion of the head 首を動かして信号する.【類】***make*** *signals* to ... ¶***make out*** a *signal* 信号を判じる. ¶fail to ***observe*** a *signal* 信号を無視する. ¶***pull*** the alarm *signal* 警報器を引く. ¶***put up*** a *signal* of distress 難船信号を掲げる. ¶***raise*** (＝***display***) a *signal* 信号を掲げる. ¶***repeat*** a *signal* 信号を繰返す. ¶***set*** a wrong *signal* 信号を誤る. ¶***sound*** a *signal* 号音で報知する. ¶***strike*** a *signal* 信号を発する. ¶***transmit*** *signals* 信号を伝える. ¶***work*** the *signals* 信号を行う.

V^{2} The *signal* does not work. 信号がきかない.

Q an ***audible*** *signal* 音響信号. ¶make a ***mute*** *signal* to ... ...に無音信号をする. ¶on a ***prearranged*** *signal*＝on a signal as prearranged あらかじめ示し合わして.

Q^{2} an ***alarm*** *signal* 警報. ¶a ***black*** *signal*〖鉄道〗閉鎖信号. ¶a ***call*** *signal* 呼び出し信号. ¶a ***caution*** *signal* 警戒警報. ¶a ***clear*** *signal* [航路など]安全信号; [空襲時の]敵機なしの信号. ¶***color light*** *signals,* red, blue and orange 赤, 青, 及びだいだい色の色灯信号. ¶set up a ***danger*** *signal* to warn the general public 一般大衆に警告するため危険信号を発する. ¶send out a ***distress*** *signal* そう難信号を発する. ¶a flag (lamp) *signal* 手旗(など)信号. ¶a ***fog*** *signal* 濃霧信号. ¶a ***go-ahead*** *signal* 進めの信号. ¶exhibit a ***hand*** *signal* 手信号を送る.【類】use ***hand*** and ***horn*** *signals.* ¶a ***home*** (***starting***) *signal*〖鉄道〗場内(出発)信号. ¶an ***information*** *signal* 暴風雨の警報旗(米国気象庁などの). ¶The ***railroad*** *signal* was not working. 鉄道信号が止まっていた. ¶a ***slowdown*** *signal* 徐行信号. ¶observe a ***stop*** *signal* 停止信号に従う. ¶***storm*** *signals* are flying. 暴風雨警報が発令されている. ¶***time*** *signal,* Greenwich, at 4.45 四時四十五分のグリニチ天文台の時報. ¶a radio ***time*** *signal* ラジオの時報.【類】the six-o'clock ***time*** *signal.* ¶a ***traffic*** *signal* 交通信号. ¶send out an ***urgent distress*** *signal* (＝an SOS) 緊急難船信号を発する. ¶send out a ***warning*** *signal* to ... ...に対して警報を発する.

P raise one's hand ***as*** a *signal* to ... ...の合図に手をあげる ‖ ***as*** a *signal* for ... ...の合図に. ¶***at*** a *signal* from below

下から合図をすると ‖ *at* a given *signal* 合図があがると. ¶ask *by signal* 信号で尋ねる. ¶*on* (=*upon*) a *signal* being made 合図をすると ‖ *on* (=at) a *signal* from ... ...からの合図を見て ‖ as if *on* a *signal* 合図でもしたように.

P² a *signal* ***for*** starting 出発の信号 ‖ a *signal* ***for*** attention (order) 注意(命令)の合図. ¶a *signal* ***of*** danger 危険信号 ‖ a *signal* ***of*** recognition 承認の合図.

signal, *v.* 信号する.

P *signal* ***for*** a pilot 水先案内を呼ぶ信号を発する.

O The time-keeper *signals* him to move on. 作業係が彼に発車の合図をする[バスなど].

signalize, *v.* 著名にする; 目立たせる.

P He *signalized* himself ***by*** a speech. 彼は一回の演説で名をあげた. ‖ *signalize* his entrance into the State Legislature ***by*** promoting a Bill providing for ... ...案の通過に努めて彼の米国州議会入りを目立たせる.

signatory, *n.* 記名調印者(国).

Q² a San Francisco ***Peace Treaty*** *signatory* サンフランシスコ平和条約署名国.

P² the *signatories* ***to*** the London Treaty were ... ロンドン条約の署名国は...であった.

signatory, *a.* 記名調印している.

P one of the powers *signatory* ***to*** the Hague Convention ヘーグ平和会議に記名調印する列国の一つ.

signature, *n.* 署名.

V ***add*** one's *signature* to a document 証書に署名する. ¶***affix*** one's *signature* to a typewritten letter タイプした手紙に署名する. 【類】 ***affix*** one's *signature* and seal to an agreement. ¶***append*** one's *signature* ...の署名を付加する. ¶***attach*** a *signature* to ... ...に署名する. ¶present one with a testimonial ***bearing*** the *signature* of ... ...の署名ある推薦状を人に差出す. ¶***carry*** the *signature* of ... (書類など)...の署名がある. ¶***get*** (=***obtain***) one's *signature* to ... ...にその署名をしてもらう. ¶Old masters seldom ***put*** their *signatures* to a canvas. 昔の画伯はめったに絵画に署名しなかった. ¶***withhold*** one's *signature* from ... ...の署名を差控える. ¶***write*** one's *signature* 署名する. ¶***write down*** one's *signature* on it その上に自署する.

Q the ***chief*** *signatures* of the manifesto are ... そのげき文の主な署名者は...だ. ¶an ***indecipherable*** *signature* 難読の署名. ¶a ***shaky*** *signature* 字の震えた署名.

Q² a ***specimen*** *signature* 署名の見本.

P consent ***by*** *signature* 署名による承諾. ¶***under*** the *signature* of ... ...の署名の下に. ¶a statement ***with*** *signature* 署名してある声明書. ¶a ballot ***without*** *signature* 無記名投票.

P² *signatures* ***to*** the Treaty of Peace 平和条約への署名.

signboard, *n.* 看板.

V ***exhibit*** a *signboard* 看板を掲げる. ¶***repaint*** its *signboard* その看板を塗替える.

Q² ***metal*** (***gold, silver, copper***) *signboard* 金属製(など)の看板. 【類】 a ***gold*** *signboard* over the door.

signer, *n.* 署名者.

P² a *signer* ***to*** ... ...の署名者.

significance, *n.* 意味, 意義; 重要.

V ***acquire*** a deeper *significance* 一層意義が深くなる. ¶***attach*** a deep *significance* to ... ...に深い意義を与える. ¶***attain*** a broader *significance* 一層意義が広くなる. ¶***bring home*** to parents the *significance* of ... 父母たる人々に...の意義をしみじみ感じさせる. ¶***derive*** fresh *significance* from ... ...から新たな意義を見出す. ¶***divine*** the full *significance* of ... ...の意義を十分推知する. ¶***explain*** the *significance* of one's knowledge of English 英語知識の意義を説明する. ¶***give*** ... a deeper *significance* ...に更に深刻な意義を与える. ¶clearly ***grasp*** the *significance* of ... はっきり...の意義を解する. ¶The movement ***has*** a national *significance*. その運動には国家的意義がある. ¶***make*** its *significance* quite ***clear*** その意義を十分明らかにする. ¶***increase*** the *significance* of the day in many ways 多くの点でその日の重要性を増す. ¶***misinterpret*** its *significance* その意義を誤解する. ¶***point out*** the real *significance* of ... ...の真義を指摘する. ¶***read*** surely the *significance* of events or forecast their trend clearly でき事の意義を確実に解しあるいはそのすう勢を明りょうに予測する. ¶***realize*** the full *significance* of ... ...の意義を十分に会得する. ¶The child did not ***understand*** the full *significance* of death. その子には死というものが本当に分っていなかった.

Q Eugenics has a ***biological*** *significance*. 優生学には生物学上の意義がある. ¶the ***commercial*** *significance* of an invention 発明の商業的意義. ¶***considerable*** *significance* is attached to ... ...を重要視している. ¶the ***etymological*** *significance* of a word 語原による言葉の意義. ¶The 1904 Olympics had little ***international*** *significance*, as virtually all the competitors were Americans. 一九〇四年のオリムピック大会はほとんどすべての参加者が米国人であったからあまり国際的意義を有しなかった. ¶***literal*** *significance* 文字通りの意義. ¶an event of ***no little*** *significance* 相当に重要な事件. ¶in its ***original*** and ***fundamental*** *significance* その根本的意義において. ¶attach a ***peculiar*** *significance* to the word その言葉に一種特別な意義を付する. ¶have no ***political*** *significance* 政治的意義は全然ない. ¶an event of ***profound*** (=***deep***) ***political*** *significance* 政治的に重要な出来事. ¶the ***psychological*** *significance* of the kiss キスの心理学的意義. ¶grasp the ***real*** *significance* of ... の真義を会得する. ¶***religious*** *significance* 宗教的な意義. ¶***secular*** *significance* (非宗教的な)凡俗の意義. ¶of ***small*** *significance* あまり重要でない. ¶be of ***special*** *significance* 特殊の意義を有する. ¶There is a ***strategic*** *significance* in the construction of this railway. この鉄道の敷設には軍事上の意義がある. ¶"Adamant" has no ***technical*** *significance*. adamant という語は術語ではない. ¶It has no ***warlike*** *significance*. それにはなんら好戦的の意味はない. ¶It has a ***wider*** *significance*. それにはもっと広い意味がある. ¶a question of ***world-wide*** *significance* 世界的意義(重要性)を有する問題.

Q² have ***world*** *significance* 世界的重要性を有する.

P ***in*** its true *significance* その真の意義において. ¶a matter ***of*** *significance* 重大な事件. 【類】 ***of*** deep *significance* / What he thinks about it is ***of*** no *significance*. ¶***with*** some *significance* in his face 何か意味ありげな顔をして. 【類】 ***with*** no *significance*.

P² There was no *significance* ***in*** his eyes. 彼はぼんやりした目付をしていた.

significant, *a.* ...を表示する.

M July 4, 1776 is a date ***most*** *significant* for Americans. 一七七六年七月四日は米人にとってもっとも意義深い日である.

P a gesture *significant* ***of*** consent 承諾を示す身振り. 【類】 an act *significant* ***of*** one's intentions.

signification, *n.* 意義, 意味.

V ***affix*** new *significations* to old words 古語に新しい意義を付加する. ¶Sounds like right, rail, list, and many others ***have*** from three to five *significations*. ライト・レール・リストその他の多数の音には三つまたは五つの意義がある.

Q have a ***different*** *signification* from ... ...と異なる意義がある. ¶It has a ***double*** *signification*. それには二重の意味がある. ¶fix a ***new*** *signification* to a word 言葉に新意義を付する. ¶a newly ***received*** *signification* of a word ある語の新たに持った意義. ¶in their ***widest*** *signification* その最も広い意味で.

P ***in*** its proper *signification* その本当の意味において.

signify, *v.* 影響する, 重要である.

M It *signifies* ***little*** (***much***). それはさほど重要でない(大いに重要だ).

P *signify* one's consent ***with*** a nod うなずいて承諾の意を示す.

O It *signifies* nothing. それはなんの意味もない. ¶What does a little loss *signify?* 少しばかりの損が何であろう.

signing, *n.* 署名.

Q The ***formal*** *signing* of a treaty. 条約の正式調印.

silence, *n.* 沈黙; 静粛, 静寂; 黙過.

V He was the first to ***break*** that *silence*. 彼が先ず口を開いた. 【類】 The hoarse barking (しわがれたほえ声) of dogs occasionally ***broke*** the *silence* of the night. / The *silence* was only ***broken*** by the whirr and buzz (騒音) of the machinery operating the projector (映写機). ¶I ***construed*** his *silence* into a tacit rejection. 私は彼の沈黙を無言の拒否と解釈した. ¶***keep*** *silence* 沈黙を守る. ¶***maintain*** a strict *silence* 堅く沈黙を守る. ¶***observe*** a *silence* on the point その点に関して沈黙を守る. 【類】 Two minutes' *silence* is ***observed*** (黙とうする) for the remembrances of the sacrifice made by Canadian soldiers in the Great War. ¶***preserve*** *silence* 沈黙を守る. ¶*silence* ***purchased*** at a high price 高価を払って得た沈黙(口止め). ¶ ***secure*** the *silence* of ... ...の口止めをする. ¶ ***take*** *silence* for consent 無言を承諾したことと解する. ¶ I cannot ***understand*** your *silence*. 君がだまっているのは私には解(げ)せない.

V² A deep *silence* ***broods***. ひっそりかんとしている. ¶ A dead *silence* ***fell*** upon (=over) the court. 満廷寂として声がなかった. ¶ Then ***followed*** a stupefied *silence*. それから(麻酔剤でもかけられたように)静まりかえった. ¶ *Silence* ***prevailed*** on the assembly. 満場黙して語るものはなかった. ¶ *Silence* ***reigned*** for a while. しばし寂として物音がなかった. ¶ *Silence* ***settled down*** once more upon the room. へやはまた始めの沈黙に戻った.

Q in ***absolute*** *silence* 全く静粛に. ¶ look in ***admiring*** *silence* これはこれはとばかり無言にながめる. ¶ She plodded on in an ***angry*** *silence* 彼女は腹が立つので口もきかずこつこつ歩いて行った. ¶ There was an ***awkward*** *silence*. 言葉が途切れてばつが悪かった. ¶ his ***complete*** *silence* on the subject その問題に関する彼の絶対沈黙. 【類】There fell a ***complete*** *silence*. ¶ There was a ***dead*** *silence* when the orator rose to speak. 弁士が起って演説を始めると水を打ったように静まりかえった. 【類】There was an instant of ***dead*** *silence*. / in ***dead*** *silence*. ¶ ***death-like*** *silence* 死のような静寂. ¶ ***deep*** (=profound) *silence* 静寂. ¶ a ***dense*** *silence* 深い静寂. ¶ a ***dreadful*** *silence* before a storm 暴風雨の前の物すごい静けさ. ¶ They fell into a ***dreamy*** *silence*. 彼らは夢心地の沈黙に落ちた. ¶ ***eloquent*** *silence* 雄弁な沈黙. ¶ For a few moments there was a ***hushed, tense*** *silence*. ちょっとの間水を打ったような緊張した沈黙が続いた. ¶ maintain a ***judicious*** *silence* 賢明に沈黙を続ける. ¶ an excuse for ***long*** *silence* ぶさたのわび. 【類】Forgive me for my ***long*** *silence*. ¶ in ***moody*** *silence* むっつり黙って. ¶ in ***mournful*** *silence* 悲しげに黙して. ¶ an ***ominous*** *silence* 薄気味悪い沈黙. ¶ In the dead tranquility of night, the bell broke the ***oppressive*** *silence*. 穏かな夜に鐘声が重苦しい静寂を破った. 【類】the *silence* becoming ***oppressive***. ¶ Ten minutes of ***painful*** *silence* ensued. それから十分間の苦しい沈黙が続いた. ¶ maintain a ***perfect*** *silence* 堅く沈黙を守る. 【類】Around the house prevailed a ***perfect*** *silence*. ¶ observe (=keep) a ***profound*** *silence* あくまで静粛にしている. ¶ after a ***short*** *silence* しばし黙っていてから. ¶ maintain a ***sulky*** *silence* ふくれて黙っている. ¶ There was a ***tense*** *silence* for a minute. ちょっと張りつめた沈黙が続いた. ¶ the *silence* of the peace is almost ***unbroken*** except by ... 静寂を破るものは先ず...だけである. ¶ in the ***utmost*** *silence* 静まり返って. ¶ an ***utter*** *silence* 深い静寂.

P kill ***by*** *silence* 黙殺する. ¶ The chairman rapped ***for*** *silence*. 議長は静粛にとこつこつ卓をたたいた. ¶ pass it over ***in*** *silence* だまってそれを見逃がす. 【類】pray ***in*** *silence* / ***in*** the *silence* of night. ¶ pass ***into*** *silence* (=obscurity) (世の中から)忘れられる ‖ He relapsed ***into*** *silence*. 彼はまた黙って仕舞った. 【類】abashed ***into*** *silence* / be bullied (おどされて) ***into*** *silence* / be forced ***into*** *silence* / He cried them down ***into*** *silence*. ¶ a man ***of*** *silence* 無口な人. ¶ ***through*** the *silence*, they could hear ... 静寂の中に...が彼らの耳に聞えてきた. ¶ He was put ***to*** *silence*. 彼は黙らされた. ‖ reduce a person ***to*** *silence* 人を黙らしてしまう. 【類】The gossip was put ***to*** *silence*. / shout (scold) a person ***to*** *silence*. ¶ ***with*** unanimous *silence* だれ一人口をきく者もなく ‖ pass ***with*** *silence* 黙殺する.

P² There was *silence* ***between*** them. 彼らは二人とも黙っていた. ¶ the *silence* ***of*** midnight 夜半の静寂.

silent, *a.* 口をきかない, 無言の; 言及しない.

M be ***conspicuously*** *silent* 際立って静粛だ. ¶ be ***prudently*** *silent* on that matter そのことに関しては慎重に沈黙している. ¶ history has ***strangely*** been *silent* about ... ...のことは不思議に歴史には見えていない.

P We will be *silent* ***about*** your conduct. われわれは君の行については黙っていることにしよう. ¶ B is *silent* ***in*** "doubt". "doubt" の b は発音されない. ☞ 音声学の黙字はmute という. ¶ The record is *silent* ***of*** (=***as to***) the subject. 記録にはその問題がのっていない. ¶ History is *silent* ***on*** (=***upon***) the subject. 歴史はその問題に言及していない. ¶ He was *silent* ***with*** surprise. 彼はぼう然としていた.

O keep *silent* 黙っている.

silhouette, *n.* 輪郭; 影法師.

V ***give*** a fine *silhouette* against the sky 空に美しい影を映す.

P Spain ***in*** *silhouette* スペインの外ぼう ‖ figures shown ***in*** *silhouette* 影絵(など).

P² this year's *silhouette* ***of*** lady's fashion 今年の婦人流行概観.

silhouette, *v.* 影絵のように現わす.

P *silhouetted* (=outlined) ***against*** the evening sky 夕方の空に黒々と現われて. 【類】He saw a human figure dimly *silhouetted* ***against*** the darkness. / dark forms of men *silhouetted* ***against*** the yellow light of lamps / *silhouetted* black ***against*** the blue sky.

silk, *n.* 絹糸, 生糸; [しばしば *pl.*] 絹もの.

V ***condition*** *silk* 生糸を検査する. ¶ ***reel off*** raw *silk* from cocoons まゆから生糸を紡ぐ. ¶ ***take*** (=***obtain or receive***) [the] *silk* [比ゆ的に]王室弁護士になる. ¶ ***wear*** *silks* 絹のくつ下をはく. ¶ ***weave*** *silk* with exquisite skill 巧妙に絹布を織る.

Q ***artificial*** *silk*=rayon 人絹. ¶ The bride wore a ***lizard-green*** *silk*. 花嫁はとかげのような緑色の絹の衣しょうをつけていた. ¶ a ***rich*** *silk* りっぱな絹布. ¶ woven from ***spun*** *silk* 絹糸で織った. ¶ ***thrown*** *silk* より(絹)糸. ¶ ***waste*** *silk* くず糸. ¶ ***watered*** *silk* 波紋のある絹.

Q² ***imitation*** *silk* 人絹.

P She is dressed (=arrayed) ***in*** *silk*[*s*]. 彼女は絹の着物を着ている ‖ ***in*** *silks* and satins おかいこぐるみで. ¶ a thin kind ***of*** *silk* 薄手の絹布. ¶ The picture is painted ***on*** *silk*. その絵は絹地に描いてある.

silkworm, *n.* 蚕.

V ***breed*** (=***raise or rear***) *silkworms* 蚕を飼う.

sill, *n.* 敷居.

Q² on the ***window*** *sill* 窓敷居に.

silliness, *n.* 愚かさ.

P ***in*** the *silliness* of her tender years 若気の至りで.

silly, *a.* 知恵の足りない; たわいもない.

M She is a ***trifle*** *silly*. 彼女は少々(知恵が)足りない.

P I was very *silly* ***of*** me. われながら愚であった. ¶ He was *silly* ***over*** a pretty woman. 彼は美人にうつつを抜かしていた.

silver, *n.* 銀; 銀貨; 銀器.

V ***clean*** the silver 銀器をみがく. ¶ ***Have*** you any *silver* on you? 銀貨をお持ちですか. ¶ ***rub up*** *silver* 銀をみがいて光らせる.

Q It looks and feels like ***sterling*** *silver*. それは見た所も手触りも純銀そっくりである.

Q² ***table*** *silver* 食卓用銀器.

P 2,000 yen ***in*** *silver* 銀貨で二千円 ‖ a small sum ***in*** *silver* 銀貨で少額 ‖ a statue ***in*** *silver* 銀製立像 ‖ wrought ***in*** *silver* 銀細工の. ¶ change paper money ***into*** *silver* and copper 札を銀貨や銅貨に換える. ¶ white ***like*** (=as white as) *silver* 銀のように白い. ¶ inlaid ***with*** *silver* 銀で象眼した ‖ wash over ***with*** *silver* 銀をきせる.

similar, *a.* 同様の, 類似の, 似寄りの.

M ***exactly*** *similar* to ... すっかり...と同じな. ¶ ***slightly*** *similar* to ... やや...に似ている. ¶ ***somewhat*** *similar* to ... やや...に似た. ¶ This is ***very*** *similar* to that. ここはそれによく似ている.

P *similar* ***in*** every respect どこからどこまで同じような ‖ *similar* ***in*** appearance (essence, form, style) ***to*** ... 外見(など)の...に似寄った.

similarity, *n.* 相似, 類似; 類似点.

V ***bear*** a certain *similarity* in sound to ... ...と音が幾分似通っている. ¶ ***present*** an almost complete *similarity* to ... ...とほとんど同一と言ってよいほど似ている.

V² But here the *similarity* ***stops***. しかし似ている点はそれだけだ.

Q show ***striking*** *similarities* 著しい類似を示す. ¶ There was a ***wonderful*** *similarity* between the twins. その双生児は驚くほどよく似ていた.

P² an extraordinary *similarity* ***between*** ... ...間の酷似. ¶ the *similarity* ***in*** (=of) sound 音の類似. ¶ a *similarity* ***of*** tastes 趣味の類似. 【類】a *similarity* ***of*** feature (姿) ***between*** them. ¶ The *similarity* ***to*** his brother was noticeable. 彼の兄(弟)と似ている所が目立った.

simile, *n.* たとえ, 直喩(ゆ).

V send the school's output to market, if one may ***use*** the commercial *simile* 商業式にたとえて言えば学校の製品を市場に送る. 【類】to ***use*** a familiar *simile*.

Q ***novel*** *similes* ざん新な直喩. ¶ a ***strained*** *simile* 不調和な直喩. ¶ a ***threadbare*** *simile* 陳腐なたとえ.

simmer, *v.* [湯が]ちんちん言う, 沸く.

M² *simmer down* 熱がさめる.

P The kettle is *simmering on* the stove. やかんがストーブの上でちんちん言っている. ¶Though *simmered with* indignation, he didn't say a word. 怒りに燃えていたが彼は一言も言わなかった. ‖ The air is *simmering with* heat. 熱でかげろうが立っている.

simper, *n.* にやにや笑い.

P *with* a *simper* にやと笑って.

simple, *a.* 単純な; ばかな.

M *severely* (=*extremely or utterly*) *simple* きわめて単純な. ¶It is *very simple* of you to leave school. 退学するとは君も余ほどの大ばかだ.

P a table *simple in* shape 形の単純なテーブル.

simplicity, *n.* 単純; 質素.

V Cambridge *retains* more *simplicity of* habits than Oxford. ケンブリッジにはオクスフォードより質素な風が残っている.

V² Could *simplicity* further *go*? [式など]これ以上質素にはできまい.

Q with an almost *austere simplicity* ほとんど極端な単純さで. ¶*businesslike simplicity* 事務的な簡易さ. ¶possess minds of *childlike simplicity* 子供らしい単純な心をもっている. ¶*classic simplicity* 古典的単純. ¶a *democratic simplicity* 平民的な質朴. ¶The building has *dignified simplicity*. その建物は質素で気品がある. ¶*elegant simplicity* さび. ¶*noble simplicity* 気品のある簡素. ¶*rustic simplicity* 質朴さ. ¶a *severe simplicity* 全く飾り抜きの単純さ. ¶*soldierly simplicity* 軍人らしい質朴. ¶*stark simplicity* しゃちこ張った単純さ.

simplification, *n.* 簡易化.

V *undergo* a *simplification* 簡易化される.

Q a *wonderful simplification* 驚くべき簡易化.

P² *simplification of* living 生活の簡易化 ‖ the *simplification of* hospital rooms 病室の簡素化.

simplify, *v.* 単純化する.

M Can't you *simplify* the method *any bit*? もう少しやり方が簡単になりませんか.

simultaneous, *a.* 同時の.

P almost *simultaneous with* ... ほとんど...と同時の.

simultaneously, *ad.* 同時に.

P *Simultaneously with* the earthquake came the conflagration. 地震と同時にあの大火が起った.

sin, *n.* 罪, 罪悪; 違反.

V His *sins* are all *blotted out*. 彼の罪悪はことごとく消滅した. ¶*cloak* a *sin* 罪を隠す. ¶*commit* a *sin* 罪を犯す. ¶*expiate* one's *sin* 罪をあがなう. ¶*forgive* a *sin* 罪を赦す. ¶*nip* a *sin* in the bud 罪を当初にくじく. ¶*palliate* a *sin* 罪を言いつくろう; [ある事情が]罪悪の弁解となる. ¶*sin* a *sin* 罪を犯す.

V² His *sin* has *come* to roost. (比ゆ的) 彼は年貢の納めどきがきた.

Q an *actual sin* 現実の罪 (original sin すなわち原罪に対して). ¶the *besetting sin* 陥りやすい罪. ¶his *crowning sin* 彼の犯した最悪の罪. ¶a *deadly sin* 恐ろしい罪 ‖ Mankind has not yet discovered a fourth cardinal virtue or an *eighth deadly sin*. 人類はまだ第四の大徳や第八の大罪というものを発見していない. ¶To miss the Derby is considered a *grave social sin*. ダービーの競馬を見に行かないのは大きな社交上の失態とされている. ¶a *high sin* 深い罪. ¶a *mortal sin* 大罪. ¶an *open sin* 明らかな罪. ¶*original sin* 原罪. ¶the *social sin* of consuming without producing 生産せずに消費する社会の罪. ¶a *trifling* (=*little*) *sin* 小さな罪. ¶a *venial sin* 赦すべき罪. ¶an *unpardonable sin* 赦し得ない罪.

P He is debased *by sin*. 彼は罪で悪化している. ¶purify *from* all *sins* 一切の罪を清める.

P² a *sin against* elegance 不しつけ ‖ *sins against* unity 不統一 ‖ a *sin against* good manners 不作法. ¶a *sin of* good taste 無趣味 ‖ *sins of* commission and omission [原稿などの]過誤と脱落.

sin, *v.* 罪を犯して...する; 違反する.

M *sin away* one's health 不節制をして健康を損じる.

P *sin against* God 神にそむく ‖ At the risk of *sinning against* modesty, we will state another defect. 不そんをも顧みずわれわれはもう一つの欠点をあげよう.

since, *ad.* 以前に.

M He went out *a little while since*. 彼は少し前に出かけた. ¶*ever since* それ以来ずっと. ¶I haven't seen him *long since*. 彼とは随分会わない. ¶*many years since* 数年前. ¶*since then* それ以来.

sincere, *a.* 誠実な.

M be *utterly sincere* in ... ...にかけてわ全く誠実である.

P He is *sincere in* his promises (statement). 彼は約束(など)に誠実だ.

sincerity, *n.* 誠実.

V *doubt* his *sincerity* 彼の誠実を疑う. ¶*lack sincerity* 誠実を欠く.

Q *artistic sincerity* 芸術的良心(誠意). ¶*passionate sincerity* of emotion 情熱. ¶the *transparent sincerity* of his nature 彼の天性のれいろうたる誠実. ¶His *sincerity* is *undoubted*. 彼の誠実は疑うべくもない.

P do (reply) *in* all *sincerity* 十分誠実にやる(など). ¶None could hope to do it with anything short *of sincerity*. ちょっとでも誠意を欠いたらとてもできるものじゃない. ¶He told us, *with* very evident *sincerity*, how he was eager to learn. 彼は学問がしたいと誠意をこめてわれわれに話した.

P² *sincerity in* friendship 誠意ある友情.

sinew, *n.* 腱(けん); *pl* 精力; 資金.

V necessary to *maintain* the *sinews* of her national life その国家的生命の精力を維持するに必要な. ¶*raise* the *sinews* of war 軍資金を調達する. ¶*supply* the *sinews* of war 軍資金を供給する.

sing, *v.* 歌う; さえずる, 鳴く.

M It was shocking to hear him *singing away* at his ugly old sea-song. 彼がいやな船歌をどなり立てるのは実にいやだった. ¶She *sang beautifully*. 彼女は見事に歌った. ¶This song *sings* more *easily* than that. この歌はあの歌より楽に歌える. ¶*sing flat* 〖音楽〗半音さげて歌う; 低い調子で歌う. ¶a couple of jovial sailors, arm-in-arm, flourishing their pipes and *singing lustily* 腕を組みパイプを振回し威勢よく歌を歌う二人の陽気な水夫. ¶Birds were *singing merrily*. 鳥が楽しそうにさえずっていた. ¶*sing out*=shout 叫ぶ, 大声で呼ぶ. 【類】Men *sang out* their feelings long before they were able to speak their thoughts. / *sing out* the old year and *sing in* the new. ¶Birds were *singing rapturously* all round. 四面一帯に鳥が夢中になって歌っていた. ¶*sing sharp* 高い調子で歌う. ¶*sing small* 弱音(よわね)を吐く, しょげる. ¶*sing softly* やわらかい調子で歌う. ¶*sing sweetly* 麗しく歌う.

P He can *sing at* sight. 彼は(譜を)見てすらすらと歌える. ‖ I cannot *sing at* so high a pitch. そんな高い調子では歌えない. ¶*sing by* ear 譜を見ずに歌う ‖ It was *sung by* a geisha to the samisen. それを芸者が三味線に合わせて歌った. ¶*sing* a hymn *from* a hymn-book 賛美歌集で賛美歌を歌う. ¶*sing in* adoration 礼賛する ‖ *sing in* chorus 合唱する ‖ *sing in* deep low voice 太くて低い声で歌う ‖ *sing in* the nose 鼻に掛けて歌う ‖ *sing in* tune 調子に合わせて歌う ‖ *sing in* an undertone 低調に歌う. ¶*sing* "satsumabiwa" *into* the gramophone 蓄音機にさつまびわを吹込む ‖ *sing* one *into* good humor 歌を歌って人の機げんを直させる. ¶He *sings of* war. 彼は戦争をほめたたえた. ¶*sing out of* tune 調子はずれに歌う. ¶*sing over* one's work as cheerily as birds in an aviary 鳥小屋の小鳥のように朗らかに仕事をしながら歌う. ¶*sing through* one's nose=hum 鼻歌を歌う. ¶*sing to* the harp たて琴に合わせて歌う ‖ Come and *sing to* us. さあ一つ歌って聞かせて下さい. ‖ *sing* a child *to* sleep 歌を歌って子供を寝付かせる ‖ *sing to* the praise of God 神を賛美する. ¶*sing with* skill (spirit) うまく(活発に)歌う.

O My ears *sing*. 耳鳴りがする. ¶*sing* the same old tune 同じことをくどくどと言う.

singer, *n.* 歌手; 歌人.

V The *singer* was *cheered*. その歌手はかっさいされた. ¶The new *singer* is much *sought after*. 今度の歌手は大もてだ.

V² A good *singer draws*. 歌手がよいと入りがよい. ¶A great *singer performs* tonight. 有名な歌手が今晩歌う.

Q an *operatic singer* 歌劇の歌手. ¶*unlettered* and *peasant singers* 無学な百姓歌手.

Q² a *folk song singer* 俗曲歌手. ¶a new *hit singer* 最近大いに当った歌手.

P a *singer in* a chorus 合唱団の歌手.

singing, *n.* 唱歌.

V *have* a *singing* in the ears 耳鳴りがする. ¶*practice singing* 唱歌を練習する. ¶He *teaches* them *singing*. 彼は彼らに唱歌を教える.

Q *concerted singing* 合唱.

Q² *church singing* 教会の唱歌.

P praise ***with*** *singing* 賛美する ‖ He was cheered ***with*** *singing*. 彼を慰さめるために歌が歌われた.

singing-girl, *n.* 歌姫(芸者など).

V ***hire*** *singing-girls* 芸者をあげる.

single, *v.* 選抜する.

M He has *singled* you ***out*** from all the swarming millions. 彼は雲集する数百万人の中から君を選抜した. 【類】 It is not easy to *single* any ***out*** for attention (special mention).

P He was *singled* ***out of*** the many candidates. 彼は多くの候補者中から選抜された.

singles, *n.* 〘庭球〙 *pl.* 単試合(シングル).

V ***play*** *singles* 単試合をする.

singsong, *n.* 抑揚のない話しぶり.

P speak (chant) ***in*** *singsong* 抑揚のない調子で話す(など).

singular, *n.* 単数.

P The noun is ***in*** the *singular*. その名詞は単数だ.

singular, *a.* 風変りの.

P He is very *singular* ***in*** his behavior. 彼は挙動が一風変っている.

O *singular* to say 妙なことだが.

singularity, *n.* 奇妙さ, 風変り.

P² the *singularity* ***of*** his appearance attracted our attention. 風さいが変っているのでわれわれの目をひいた.

sink, *n.* 汚水こう, [調理場の]流し.

Q² a ***kitchen*** *sink* 台所の流し.

P² a *sink* ***of*** iniquity 罪悪の巣くつ.

sink, *v.* 沈む, 落込む; [資本など]投じる.

M *sink* ***back*** in one's chair 自分のいすにがっくりしりを落す ‖ *sink* ***back*** into apathy again 再びもとの冷淡に帰る. 【類】 The capital *sank* ***back*** into the position of a provincial town. ¶His kindness *sank* ***deep*** into my soul. 彼の親切が私の身にしみた. ‖ *sink* ***deep*** in the armchair 安楽いすに深々とすわる. ¶The hill *sinks* ***downward*** to an extensive plain. 小山は下り坂になって広野に続いている. ¶The patient is *sinking* ***fast***. 病人はどんどん衰弱して来る. ¶His eyes (cheeks) *sank* ***in***. 彼の目(ほお)がくぼんだ. ¶His heart *sank* ***low***. 彼は意気消沈した. ¶The Lusitania was ***practically*** *sunk*. ルシタニヤ号は事実上沈没してしまった. ¶He *sank* ***quietly*** and died on the 1st of May. 彼は徐々に衰弱して五月一日に死んだ. ¶*sink* ***rapidly*** [病人など]どんどん衰弱する. ¶*sink* evidence ***somewhere else*** 証拠をどこかへ隠す.

M² *sink* ***down*** to a lower level 下級に下がる ‖ The wind has *sunk* ***down***. 風がないだ.

P The sun is *sinking* ***below*** the horizon. 太陽は地平線下に没しようとしている. 【類】 The sun is gradually *sinking* ***below*** the horizon. ¶*sink* ***beneath*** the waves (a heavy load) 波(など)の下に沈む. ¶The sun *sank* ***beyond*** the mountain 太陽が山の端に入った. ¶*sink* ***by*** (=***from***) its weight [船など]その重量で沈む ‖ The ship was *sunk* ***by*** a storm (hurricane, explosion). 船はあらし(など)のために沈んだ. ¶*sink* a caisson ***for*** engineering work 土木工事のために潜函を水に沈める. ¶*sink* ***in*** a mire 泥中に没する ‖ *sink* ***in*** deep slumber=sleep soundly ぐっすり眠る. 【類】 *sink* ***in*** the deep sleep of drunkenness / *sink* ***in*** dreamy slumbers / He is *sunk* ***in*** the deeper thought. / *sink* ***in*** despair / He is now *sunk* ***in*** oblivion (世間から忘れられて). ‖ He *sank* ***in*** our opinion. 彼はわれわれの間に評判を落した. ‖ *sink* ***in*** price 価格が下がる ‖ *sink* ***in*** the social scale 身分が下がる ‖ *sink* ***in*** (=***into***) a chair いすにどかっと腰を下ろす ‖ The sun is *sinking* ***in*** the west. 日は西に没しようとしている. ‖ *sink* the head of a screw ***in*** a hole らせんくぎの頭を穴にさし込む ‖ *sink* money ***in*** an enterprise (business, investment) 事業(など)に金を注ぎ込む. 【類】 an enormous sum *sunk* ***in*** war. ¶*sink* ***into*** deep meditation 深いめい想に沈む ‖ The fangs of a dog *sank* ***into*** his flesh. 犬のきばが彼の肉に食い入った. ‖ *sink* ***into*** the grave 死ぬ ‖ *sink* ***into*** the ground 地にめり込む ‖ The oil *sank* ***into*** the wood. 油が木にしみ通った. ‖ The lesson *sank* ***into*** his mind. その教訓は彼の心にしみた. ‖ *sink* ***into*** Nirvana ねはんに入る ‖ *sink* ***into*** the background [問題など]世間から忘れられる ‖ He has *sunk* ***into*** the second place (=a secondary position). 彼は第二位に落ちた. ‖ *sink* ***into*** insignificance beside ... ...と比較するとつまらないものになってしまう ‖ gradually *sink* ***into*** oblivion 次第に世間から忘れられてしまう. 【類】 *sank* ***into*** obscurity and died almost unknown / *sink* ***into*** poverty / *sink* ***into*** the depths of misery ‖ Buddhism *sank* ***into*** degraded forms. 仏教が堕落した. ‖ *sink* ***into*** reverie 夢うつつになる. 【類】 *sink* ***into*** a deep thought / *sink* ***into*** a deep (refreshing) sleep / *sink* ***into*** silence / *sink* ***into*** vice / The war *sank* ***into*** peace. ‖ I felt inclined to *sink* ***into*** the ground with shame. 私ははずかしくて穴があったら入りたいような気持がした. ¶*sink* ***like*** lead 鉛のように沈む. ¶*sink* ***on*** one's knees ひざまずく ‖ Darkness (Night) *sank* ***on*** the sea. 海は(夜になって)真暗になった. ‖ *sink* one's head ***on*** one's breast うなだれる ‖ *sink* ***on*** (=***upon***) a couch (bed) 長いす(など)にどっかと腰を下ろす. ¶Her head *sank* ***onto*** her chest. 彼女は頭を胸の所にたれた. ¶He *sank* ***out of*** sight. 彼は姿を隠した. ¶The rain *sank* ***through*** the clothes. 雨が着物にしみ込んだ ‖ *sink* ***to*** the bottom 沈む ‖ She *sank* ***to*** the floor in a faint. 彼女は気が遠くなってどっと倒れた. ‖ The moon *sank* ***to*** the horizon. 月は地平線下に落ちた. ‖ *sink* ***to*** poverty and impotency [国民が]窮乏と無力に陥る. 【類】 *sink* ***to*** the lowest depths ‖ *sink* ***to*** a state of chaos 混とん状態に陥る ‖ *sink* one's voice ***to*** a whisper 声を低くしてささやく. ¶The sun was *sinking* ***towards*** the horizon. 日は地平線に傾いていた. ‖ The road *sinks* ***towards*** the river. 道は川の方へ下り坂になる. ¶*sink* ***under*** [the] water 水中に沈む ‖ *sink* ***under*** misfortune 不幸に落入る ‖ *sink* ***under*** the weight of year (disease, burden, cares) 寄る年波(など)で弱る. ¶He *sank* his head ***upon*** his breast. 彼は首をたれた. ¶*sink* ***with*** fatigue 疲れて力なげに倒れる. ¶The house *sank* ***within*** the ground. 家が地面にめり込んだ ‖ His heart *sank* [***within*** him]. 彼は意気そそうした.

sinking, *n.* 沈むこと.

V one ***feels*** a *sinking* of one's heart when one contemplates ... ...を考えると心細くなる. ¶***suffer*** horrid *sinking* of the heart and depression of spirits 恐ろしく憂うつになって気がめ入る.

sinner, *n.* 罪人(ざい), 悪漢.

V ***reclaim*** the *sinner* その罪人を改心させる.

Q a ***hardened old*** *sinner* 改心の望みない老悪漢. ¶a ***repentant*** *sinner* 悔悟した罪人.

sip, *n.* すすること.

V I'll just ***take*** a *sip*. 一口いただきましょう.

P drink ***by*** *sips* ちびりちびり飲む. ¶drink saké ***in*** small *sips*. ちびりちびり酒を飲む.

sip, *v.* すする.

P *sip* ***at*** the wine 酒をちびりちびり飲む. ¶*sip* a little more ***of*** the wine もう少しぶどう酒を飲む.

siphon, *v.* サイフォンで吸う.

M² High taxes *siphoned* ***off*** so much money that life was hard for the people. 重税が多額の金をしぼり取るので国民の生活が苦しかった.

P *siphon* water ***from*** the cellar 地下から水を吸い揚げる.

sir, *n.* 貴下, 足下.

Q ***Dear*** *Sir* 親愛なる足下; 拝啓. ¶***Reverend*** *Sir* 尊師(牧師に対する敬語).

siren, *n.* サイレン.

V² *Sirens* ***wailed out***. サイレンが鳴り響いた.

Q² a ***fire-engine*** *siren* 消防自動車のサイレン. ¶the ***noon*** *siren* 正午のサイレン.

sirup, *n.* シロップ.

Q² ***maple*** (***cane***) *sirup* 楓糖(蔗糖)のシロップ.

sis, *n.* 《米俗》=sister.

Q This is my ***littlest*** *sis*. 《米口》 これは一番下の妹です(紹介など).

sister, *n.* 姉妹.

V He ***gave away*** his *sister* in marriage. 彼はその妹を嫁がせた. ¶I ***have*** no brother or *sister*. 私には兄弟も姉妹もない.

Q one's ***big*** *sister* 姉. ¶Many of the Japanese women of today, like her ***European*** *sisters*, receive a university education. 今日の日本婦人の多数は欧州の姉妹のように大学教育を受ける. ¶***gifted*** *sisters* 天分豊かな姉妹. ¶***little*** *sisters* 少女たち. ¶punctuality, and its ***twin*** *sister*, regular attendance 時間の厳守とその双生の姉妹たる出席の励行. ¶an ***older*** *sister* 姉. ¶her ***small*** *sister* 彼女の妹. ¶the ***youngest*** *sister* in the circle of commercial nations 商業国民中の最後進国.

Q² her ***artist*** *sister* 彼女の画家の姉(妹). ¶She carried her ***baby*** *sister* to safety. 彼女は赤ん坊の妹を安全な所へ連れて

行った. ¶their ***Continent sisters*** 彼らの欧州大陸の姉妹たち(英国人から見て). ¶a "***sob sister***"《米俗》哀れっぽい話(sob story) を書く婦人作家.

P　a ***Sister of*** Charity〘カトリック〙尼僧(シスター).

P²　She is ***sister to*** my uncle. 彼女は私のおじの姉(妹)だ. ‖ Four ***sisters to*** the battleship are to be built. その戦闘艦の姉妹艦四隻が建造されるはずである. ‖ languages which are brothers and ***sisters to*** English, as it were いわば英語と兄弟姉妹の関係にある言語 ‖ be "a ***sister***" ***to*** the rest of the public 売春婦となる.

sit, *v.* すわる, 開会する; [衣服など]似合う; [食物が]もたれる.

M　***sit alone*** in one's study 書斎に独座する. ¶***sit astride*** 馬乗りになる. 【類】***sit astride*** [of] a horse. ¶***sit back*** in an arm chair ひじ掛けいすにふんぞり返る. ¶***sit back to back*** with ... ...と背中合わせにすわる. ¶***sit closer*** together もっと詰めてすわる. ¶***sit correctly*** at the table 食卓にちゃんとすわる. ¶***sit cross-legged*** あぐらをかく. ¶***sit erect*** 体をまっすぐにしてすわる. ¶***sit face to face*** with ... ...と差向いにすわる. ¶***sit fully*** on the chair, and not on its edge いすの端の方でなく深く腰を掛ける. ¶Food ***sits heavy*** on the stomach. 食物がひどく腹にもたれる. ¶My sorrows ***sit heavily*** on me. 悲しみがたえ難いほどひどく私の身にこたえる. ‖ Care ***sat heavy*** on his brow. 心配が彼の額にありあり現われていた. ¶***sit idle*** 安閑とすわっている. ¶The name of reformer ***sits ill*** on him. 彼を改革家と呼ぶのはふさわしくない. ¶***sit lazily*** in an armchair ひじ掛けいすにものうげにすわる. ¶Grief ***sits light*** on a youthful heart. 悲しみは若人の胸には軽く感じる. ¶His principles ***sit loose*** (=***loosely***) on him. 彼は自分の主義などにはあまり束縛されない. ¶***sit motionless*** じっとすわっている. ¶***sit mute*** 黙ってすわる. ¶***sit opposite*** 向うにすわる. ¶***sit*** all the other guests ***out*** 他の客が皆帰ってしまうまですわっている ‖ I ***sat out*** the lecture. 私はその講義が済むまで席を立たなかった. 【類】***sit out*** the whole play / ***sit out*** a meeting / ***sit out*** an entertainment. ¶***sit pensively*** at the window (by the fire) 窓の側(など)に物思わしげにすわる. ¶***sit praying*** for hours 何時間もすわってお祈りする. ¶***sit*** quite ***still*** in the middle of one's bed その寝台の真中に身動きもせずにすわっている. ¶The committee ***sit*** (=meet) ***regularly*** on Thursday. 委員会はきまって木曜日に開かれる. ¶***sit side by side*** 並んですわる. ¶***sit silent*** 黙ってすわっている. ¶***sit*** perfectly ***still*** 少しも身動きをしないですわっている. ¶***sit tailor-fashion*** (=tailorwise) あぐらをかく. ¶***sit tight*** 動かずにじっとしている. ¶The vessel ***sat upright***. その器はきちんとおいてあった. ¶Her dress ***sits well*** (***ill***) on her. 彼女の着物はよく似合う(似合わない). 【類】Her riding-habit (乗馬服) does not ***sit*** her ***well***. ‖ He ***sits well*** on horseback. 彼は巧みに馬に乗る. ‖ It doesn't ***sit well***. それはすわりが悪い. ‖ The food does not ***sit well*** on the stomach. その食物は腹にもたれる. ‖ it does not ***sit well*** with ... それは...の性に合わない. ¶He ***sat writing*** (***thinking***, ***weeping***). 彼はすわって書き物(など)をしていた.

M²　***sit around*** at a mahogany table マホガニーのテーブルを囲んでぐるっと席につく. ¶***sit*** [***down***] on a bench ベンチに掛ける ‖ ***sit down*** at [the] table 食卓につく. 【類】They ***sat down*** to their meal. / ***sit down*** to a table spread with all sorts of good things to eat. / They ***sat down*** to a merry game of cards. / ***sit down*** at a piano / ***sit down*** to a meal (banquet) / ***sit down*** to one's work / He ***sat*** himself ***down*** as gingerly (=warily) as possible. / ***sit down*** to write ¶***sit up*** far (=late) into the night and study 夜ふかしして勉強する ‖ The patient ***sat up*** in bed. 病人が床の上にすわった. ‖ ***sit up*** with an invalid 病人を看護する ‖ All the pupils ***sat up*** straight when the teacher came into the room. 先生が教室に入って来ると生徒は皆姿勢を正した. ‖ Can't you ***sit up*** right like a good boy? お行儀よくおすわりできないの. ‖ ***sit up*** all night with (=attending) one's sick child 病気のこどもの看護で徹夜する. 【類】***sit up*** to nurse her father / How late do you ***sit up*** at night? ‖ ***sit up*** half the night reading a novel 小説を読んで夜中まで起きている. 【類】cannot ***sit up*** / She ***sat up*** for her husband.

P　***sit above*** ... ...の上座にすわる. ¶***sit around*** the fire 火を囲んですわる. ¶***sit at*** a book at intervals 折々読書する ‖ ***sit at*** a desk (the table, the piano) 机(など)に向う ‖ ***sit at*** the board with ... ...と食卓をともにする ‖ ***sit at*** home 家にいる ‖ ***sit at*** their places 彼らの席に着く. 【類】***sit at*** meal / ***sit at*** tea / She was ***sitting at*** needle-work (針仕事) / ***sit at*** the fire / A sprucely dressed clerk in shirt sleeves ***sat at*** a typewriter. ¶***sit beside*** the brazier 火ばちのそばにすわる. ¶***sit by*** the fireside (window) 炉辺(など)にすわる. 【類】***sit by*** the fireless hearth (火の気のない炉) / ***sit by*** the roadside / He ***sat by*** himself. 彼は独りですわっていた. ¶become eligible to ***sit for*** an examination 受験の資格ができる. 【類】without ***sitting for*** examination at all / ***sit*** (=pose) ***for*** a photograph (portrait) / He has never ***sat for*** his picture. / A photographer once asked him to ***sit for*** him. ‖ He ***sits for*** Liverpool. 彼はリヴァプール選出議員である. ‖ Representatives ***sit for*** their respective constituencies. 代議士は各選挙区を代表する. ‖ ***sit*** up ***for*** a person 人が帰るまで起きている. ¶***sit in*** a chair [ひじ掛]いすに掛ける ‖ ***sit in*** a circle 車座になる ‖ They ***sat in*** conference. 彼らは会議を開いた ‖ ***sit in*** Parliament (Congress) 国会に議席を有する ‖ not qualified to ***sit in*** judgment 批評を加える資格がない ‖ ***sit in*** council together 会議をする ‖ ***sit in*** pews 教会の長いすにすわる ‖ ***sit in*** a tree [鳥など]木にとまる. ¶He ***sits in front of*** me at school. 彼は学校で僕の前にすわる. ¶***sit into*** (=***near***) the fire 火のそばにすわる ‖ ***sit into*** the early hours of the morning 真夜中過ぎまで起きている ‖ ***sit*** far ***into*** the night 夜ふかしをする. 【類】***sit into*** midnight. ¶He ***sat*** himself ***next*** me=He sat next to me. 彼は私の次にすわった. ¶***sit on*** a bench (stool) 腰掛に掛ける ‖ ***sit on*** the extreme edge of a chair いすの端に掛ける ‖ ***sit on*** a branch (bough) 枝にとまる ‖ ***sit on*** the floor 床の上にすわる ‖ ***sit on*** one's heels (=legs) かしこまる ‖ ***sit on*** one's knees ひざまずく ‖ The glass ***sits*** (=lies *or* stands) ***on*** the table. コップが卓上においてある. ‖ ***sit on*** the tribunal 裁判に列する ‖ He ***sits on*** the fence. 《米》彼はどっちつかずにいる(あいまいな立場をとる). ‖ The hen ***sits on*** her eggs. めん鶏が卵をだく. 【類】***sit on*** glass or china eggs ‖ ***sit on*** a committee 委員会に列する. ‖ An empress was then ***sitting on*** the throne. 皇后が当時皇位についていた. ¶***sit over*** one's piano for hours 何時間もピアノをひき続ける. ¶***sit round*** the open fire たき火のまわりにすわる. ¶***sit through*** a performance 演芸のはねるまでいる. ¶***sit to*** a painter ***for*** one's portrait 画家に肖像を描かせる(ために腰かける). ¶The book is the outcome of the notes of the students who ***sat under*** Hearn. その本はハーンの講義を聞いた学生の筆記の産物だ. ‖ ***sit under*** the shade of a tree 樹陰にすわる. ¶The responsibility ***sits upon*** your shoulder. 責任が君の肩にかかっている. ¶***sit with*** them at a council-table (roundtable) 彼らと一緒に会議に列する(円卓につく) ‖ I ***sat with*** him all night. 私は夜通し彼を看護した.

site, *n.* 位置, 場所; 敷地; 遺跡.

V　The ***site*** of the new school is not definitely ***fixed*** yet. その新設学校の敷地はまだはっきりきまっていない. ¶It has ***formed*** the ***site*** of a mighty city. そこには一大都市ができ上がった. ¶***give*** a free ***site*** for a purpose of the library building その図書館建築のために敷地を寄付する. ¶Kyoto is the ancient capital of Japan and ***has*** (=***contains***) many noted ***sites***. 京都は日本の古都でいく多の名高い遺跡がある. ¶Building ***sites*** are ***let*** on long-termed leases, ground rents varying according to position chosen. 宅地長期賃貸に応じます, 地代はお選びの場所で違います. ¶***mark*** historic ***sites*** 史跡を標識する. ¶His premises ***occupy*** the ***site***. 彼の店がその場所にある. ¶***purchase*** a ***site*** 敷地を買入れる. ¶***select*** a ***site*** 敷地を選定する.

Q　***archaeological sites*** in Honan 河南の古跡. ¶a ***ceremonial site*** 式場. ¶Inhabitants of beri-beri countries should build their houses on the ***highest*** and ***driest sites*** possible. 脚気国に住む人はできるだけ高燥の地に家を建てるべきである. ¶preservation of ***historic sites*** 史跡保存. ¶***residential*** and ***business sites*** 住宅地と商業区. ¶the most ***suitable site*** for ... ...に最好適の地.

Q²　an old ***battlefield site*** 古戦場. ¶a ***building site*** 建物の敷地. ¶a ***camp***[***ing***] ***site*** キャンプ場. ¶a ***garden site*** 庭の位置. ¶a ***holiday site*** 休日に行く場所. ¶a ***housing site*** 家の敷地. ¶a ***school site*** 学校の敷地. ¶a ***storage site*** 置場. ¶a ***town site***=a townsite 都市計画の敷地.

P　***at*** the ***site*** of the recent fire 最近火事のあった所に. ¶It was rebuilt ***on*** the *site* of the old building. それは古い建物のあった場所に建て直したものだ.【類】The barracks (兵営) stand ***on*** the *site* of the castle. ¶The estate costs, ***with*** *site*, 10,000 yen. その家は敷地付一万円である.

P² a *site* ***for*** a factory 工場敷地. ¶a *site* ***of*** many a battle 数次戦争のあった場所.【類】Tokyo was to be the *site* ***of*** the 14th Olympic Games. / the *site* ***of*** a recent fire.

sitter, *n.* すわり込む人.

Q² a ***baby*** *sitter* 《米》赤ん坊の守りをする人(女学生などのアルバイト). ¶a ***chimney*** (***flag-pole***) *sitter* 煙突(旗柱)男.

sitting, *n.* 着席; 開会, 会期.

V the commission ***began*** its *sittings* under the chairmanship of ... その委員会は…を議長として開会した. ¶***hold*** a *sitting* 会議を開く. ¶Can you ***give*** me four *sittings?* 四回御着席を願われましょうか[画家が肖像を描く時など]. ‖ portraits painted from *sittings* ***given*** by the originals 本人をモデルとして直接描いた肖像. ¶The hall ***has*** 800 *sittings*. その会館には八百の座席がある. ¶***hold*** its *sittings* in ...でその会議を開く ‖ after eighteen *sittings* ***held*** in the college その大学で十八回会合を重ねてから.

Q a ***humdrum*** *sitting* of Parliament 〖英国〗議会の平凡な一日. ¶an ***inaugural*** *sitting* 創立総会. ¶The question will be finally settled at a ***joint*** *sitting* of both Houses. 同問題は結局両院連合協議会で解決されるだろう. ¶The trial was not finished at a ***single*** *sitting*. その審問は一回の開廷では終了しなかった.

Q² The "***all-night*** *sitting*" is essentially a British institution. [議会など]終夜会議は特に英国の習慣である. ¶get 50 cents an hour for ***baby*** *sitting* 《米》時間ぎめ子守りをして一時間五十セントもらう.【類】do ***baby*** *sitting* for ...

P read from cover to cover ***at*** a *sitting* 一気に全巻を読了する.【類】read a book [straight] through (通読する) ***at*** a *sitting*. ¶bleachers ***with*** thirty-five hundred *sittings* 座席が三千五百ある露天観覧席.

P² *sitting* ***in*** banc 合議裁判. ¶*sitting* ***of*** the court 開廷. ¶I have had the privilege of *sitting* ***on*** the editorial board with him. 私は光栄にも彼と一しょに編集局に務めていた.

situated, *a.* ...にある, 位している.

M it is *situated* ***about hundred miles*** from ... それは…から約百マイルのところにある. ¶It is ***centrally*** *situated*. それは中央に位している. ¶It is ***charmingly*** *situated*. その位置は素敵だ. ¶be (in) ***conveniently*** *situated* for transit facilities 出場がいい(悪い). ¶The town is ***favorably*** *situated* for transportation. その町は交通の便利な所にある. ¶The house is ***nicely*** *situated*. その家は場所がよい. ¶The house is ***pleasantly*** *situated*. その家は快的な場所にある. ¶be ***similarly*** *situated* with ... …と似たような立場にある. ¶Wyoming is *situated* ***south*** of Montana. ワイオミング州はモンタナ州の南にある.

P It is prettily *situated* ***among*** hills. それは丘に包まれて風景のよいところだ. ¶The village is cosily *situated* ***at*** the foot of a hill. その村はちんまりと小山のすそにある. ‖ The company is *situated* ***at*** the corner of ... street. その会社は…町の角にある. ¶The house is *situated* ***in*** a ravine. その家は谷間にある. ¶It is *situated* ***near*** the sea. それは海辺にある. ¶London is *situated* ***on*** the Thames. ロンドンはテームズ川にまたがっている.【類】be *situated* ***on*** the east coast of ... ¶*situated* [***to*** the] east of ... …の東にある. ¶My house is *situated* ***within*** five minutes' walk of the station. 私の家は停車場から歩いて五分以内のところにある.【類】be *situated* ***within*** an hour's car-ride from ...

Q Life is not worth living *situated* as I am. 私の境遇では生きているかいがない.

situation, *n.* (**1**) 位置, 場所; 立場; 事態, 局面; (劇などの)場面.

V regretfully ***accept*** the *situation* 仕方がないとあきらめる. ¶***affect*** the *situation* 局面に影響する. ¶***aggravate*** the *situation* 情勢を悪化する. ¶***alter*** the *situation* 局面を変える. ¶The *situation* is being ***ameliorated***. 事態は改善されつつある. ¶***analyze*** a *situation* 局面を分析する. ¶There is right on both sides, but naturally each looks at the matter from its own point of view and sometimes fails to ***appreciate*** the other's *situation*. 両方に道理があるが自然どちらもそれ自身の見地から問題を考察し時として他方の側への認識を欠く. ¶***better*** the *situation* 局面を改善する. ¶***bring about*** a remarkable *situation* 由々しい事態を招来する. ¶***canvass*** the *situation* with a view to ... …を目あてに事態を調査する. ¶Tomorrow the *situation* may be ***changed***. あすにも形勢が変るかも知れない. ¶The *situation* is ***charged*** with danger. 時局は危険をはらんでいる. ¶***clarify*** the present *situation* 時局を釈明する. ¶***clear up*** the *situation* 事態を明りょうにする. ¶***command*** the *situation* 形勢を支配する. ¶the *situation* is further ***complicated*** by the fact that ... 事態は…の事実で一層複雑になっている. ¶He was not slow to ***comprehend*** the *situation*. 彼は早くもその情勢を見てとった. ¶***confide*** one's *situation* to ... 事情を…に打明ける. ¶Another meeting will be held today to ***consider*** the *situation*. 事態を議するためまたきょう集会を開く ‖ The *situation* is ***considered*** serious. 形勢は重大視されている. ¶***discuss*** the *situation* 時局を論じる. ¶***dominate*** a *situation* 情勢を支配する. ¶***ease*** the *situation* 事態を緩和する. ¶complicate the dispute by ***embittering*** the *situation* 事態を悪化して紛争を増大させる. ¶***encounter*** a *situation* やっかいな事態に出っくわす. ¶***examine*** the *situation* at first hand 現状を直接調査する. ¶The cruel state of anxiety I was in can be judged of only by those who have ***experienced*** a similar *situation*. 私と同じような経験をした人々でなければ私の陥っていた恐ろしい憂慮の状態はわからない. ¶It ***explains*** the *situation* which led to the Boer War. それがブーア戦争の導火線となった情勢を説明している. ¶All the revolutionary elements are doing their best to ***exploit*** the *situation*. すべての革命的分子がこの情勢を利用することに努力を傾けている. ¶This aptly ***expresses*** the *situation*. これが適切に情勢を示している. ¶It takes a great deal of courage to ***face*** the *situation* bravely (=squarely). 大胆にこの情勢に対抗するには多大の勇気を要する. ¶***find*** the *situation* galling この情勢はたえ難いものと思う. ¶***grasp*** (=***take in***) the *situation* 情勢を見て取る. ¶be well qualified to ***handle*** the difficult *situation* 難局を処理するだけのりっぱな資格がある. ¶Strawberries should ***have*** a sunny *situation* in the garden. オランダいちごは日当りのよい畑で栽培しなければならない. ‖ The government ***has*** the *situation* well in hand. 政府は情勢をよくつかんでいる. ¶***improve*** the present *situation* in English teaching 英語教授の現状を改善する. ¶***make*** their *situation* singularly ***painful*** 彼らの立場を非常に苦しくする. ¶***make clear*** the *situation* we are placed in by ... われわれの立場を…ではっきりさせる. ¶He is incapable of ***managing*** the *situation*. 彼は時局に善処することができない. ¶***manipulate*** a difficult *situation* 難局に処する. ¶***meet*** the *situation* by recourse to ... …の手段によって時局に当る.【類】Measures must be taken to ***meet*** the *situation*. / They are ***meeting*** the *situation* successfully. / the best method of ***meeting*** this difficult *situation*. ¶***observe*** the *situation* 情勢を注視する. ¶***occupy*** a fairly picturesque *situation* かなり景色のいい位置を占める. ¶***portend*** a grave *situation* 重大な事態の前兆を示す. ¶***precipitate*** a difficult *situation* 時局の悪化を昂進させる. ¶***produce*** a *situation* 事態を生む. ¶***realize*** the *situation* 事態を悟る.【類】***Realising*** the *situation* I was determined to fight to the last. ¶***review*** the *situation* 時局を批判する. ¶The nation cannot afford to ***regard*** the *situation* with indifference. 国民はこの形勢に対して無関心ではあり得ない. ¶***relieve*** the *situation* 事態を緩和する. ¶The *situation* has been completely ***reversed***. 事態が全く逆転した. ¶The *situation* was completely ***saved***. 形勢がまったく好転していた. ‖ I did what very little could be done to ***save*** the *situation*. 私はその場を取つくろうためにわずかながらできるだけの事をした. ¶***sense*** the *situation* 実情を悟る. ¶***settle*** a difficult *situation* 難局を収拾する. ¶It's time to ***size up*** the *situation*. 今や情勢を判断すべき時期だ. ¶***solve*** the *situation* 事態を解決する. ¶***straighten out*** a bad *situation* 難局の始末をつける. ¶a current epigram of the time ***summed up*** the *situation* thus:— 当時流行の警句は時局を次のように概括した. ¶***take in*** the *situation* 場合を考える. ¶***talk over*** the political *situation* of the day 現下の政局を談議する.【類】I will ***talk over*** the *situation* fully with you. ¶be ***unbefitting*** the *situation* その場合にそぐわない. ¶thoroughly ***understand*** the *situation* 完全に事態を解する. ¶***view*** the *situation* with alarm その事態を由々しいと見る. ¶***watch*** the *situation* with interest 興

味をもって事態を見守る.

v² The *situation* is ***becoming*** intense. 形勢は深刻化しつつある. 【類】The *situation* ***becomes*** more strained. ¶The *situation* ***deteriorated.*** 情勢が悪化した. ¶should the *situation* ***improve*** 情勢が好転すれば. ¶That is what the *situation* ***needs.*** それが時局の要求するところだ. ¶Let me know how the *situation* ***stands.*** 事態はどうなっているか知らせてください. ‖ as the *situation* now ***stands***=as things go 目下のところ.

Q with the ***above situation*** in view 前記の情勢を考慮して. ¶foreign trade conducted without any specific knowledge of the ***actual*** *situation* of the market concerned. 関係市場の実情について特殊の知識なしに行われた外国貿易. ¶the present ***acute*** *situation* in South Africa 南アにおける目下のせん鋭化した情勢. ¶I found myself in an ***awkward*** *situation.* 私は全くまずい立場にあった. ‖ to save one's ***awkward*** *situation* その場をとりつくろうために. ¶The *situation* was as ***bad*** as it could be. 事態はこのうえもなく悪化していた. ¶a ***compromising*** *situation* 疑われそうな立場. ¶I wish to buy a small quantity of land somewhere in a ***convenient*** *situation.* 私はどこか便利なところに土地を少し買いたい. ¶a ***conversational*** *situation* 一つの会話の場合(始めて会った時などの). ¶be in a ***difficult*** *situation* 難局に立つ. ¶a very ***delicate*** *situation* きわめて微妙な情勢. ¶The *situation* is ***desperate.*** 形勢は最早いかんともし難い. ¶the ***diplomatic*** *situation* 外交的情勢. ¶a ***dramatic*** *situation* [小説などの]やま. ¶a ***dreadful*** *situation* 恐るべき形勢. ¶This is my ***economic*** *situation.* これが私の経済状態だ. ¶He was confronted with an ***embarrassing*** *situation.* 彼は難局に直面した. ‖ ingenious dodge of ***embarrassing*** *situations* 巧妙な難局切抜け. ¶take in the ***extraordinary*** *situation* ただならぬ形勢を見てとる. ¶the ***general*** *situation* 大勢. ¶the ***geographical*** *situation* 地勢. ¶The market is in a ***gloomy*** *situation.* 市場は心細い情勢にある. ¶a ***good*** (***bad***) *situation* よい(悪い)状態. ¶The *situation* is still ***grave.*** 事態は依然重大である. ¶a ***hackneyed*** *situation* ありふれた一場面(脚本など). ¶The *situation* is none too ***happy*** at present, and we do not want to complicate it. 事態は目下決して好都合に行っていないからわれわれはそれを複雑化させたくない. ¶a ***healthy*** (=***wholesome***) *situation* 健全な事態. ¶The *situation* is ***hopeful.*** 形勢は有望だ. ¶a ***hopeless*** *situation* 見込のない情勢. ¶a ***humiliating*** *situation* 屈辱的立場. ¶a ***ludicrous*** *situation* ばかげた事態. ¶the ***national*** *situation* 国民の形勢. ¶a ***noisy*** *situation* 騒がしい場所. ¶He is noted for his cool-headedness when placed in a ***perilous*** *situation.* 彼は危地に臨んで冷静だというので有名である. ¶discuss the ***political*** *situation* with ... ...と政局を談じる. ¶the ***present*** *situation* of the world 世界の現状. ¶a ***tantalizing*** *situation* 歯がゆい局面. ¶a ***tense*** *situation* 緊張した情勢. ¶a ***threatening*** *situation* 険悪な形勢. ¶a ***thrilling*** *situation* [劇などの]身の毛のよだつような場面. ¶a ***ticklish*** *situation* 歯がゆい事態. ¶a ***touching*** *situation* 悲壮な場面. ¶a ***triangular*** *situation* 三角関係. ¶a lack of knowledge of the ***true*** *situation* 認識不足. ¶This is a very ***trying*** *situation.* これは非常に苦しい立場だ. ¶an ***unfavorable*** *situation* 逆境. ¶The *situation* of this city is ***unrivalled.*** この市の位置は無類だ.

Q² a ***crime*** *situation* 犯罪の実情. ¶in view of the ***emergency*** *situation* 非常時局にかんがみ. ¶meet the ***emergency*** *situation* 非常時局に対応する. 【類】except in an ***emergency*** *situation.* ¶real needs in ***everyday*** *situations* 日々の実情において真に必要なもの. ¶meet the ***famine*** *situation* ききんの事態に対処する ‖ as one means of alleviating the ***food*** *situation* 食糧事情を緩和する一手段として. 【類】a serious (=acute) ***food*** *situation* / the world ***food*** *situation* / until the crops came in to ease (=alleviate) the ***food*** *situation* / The ***food*** *situation* has become better. / remedy (=improve) the ***food*** *situation* / The ***food*** *situation* is aggravating. ¶the ***food rationing*** *situation* 食糧配給状況. ¶the acute ***food supply*** *situation* 切迫した食糧配給状態. ¶***home*** *situation* 家庭の事情. ¶ease the ***housing*** *situation* 住宅事情を緩和する. 【類】The ***housing*** *situation* is catastrophic. ¶an ***import*** *situation* 輸入状況. ¶one's ***life*** *situation* 社会におけるその人の立場. ¶the ***labor*** *situation* in California カリホルニアにおける労働状況. ¶the ***market*** *situation* 市況. ¶the ***money*** (=***monetary***) *situation* 金融界の情勢. ¶the ***nutrition*** *situation* of the Japanese people 日本人の栄養状態. ¶improvement in the ***power*** *situation* 動力情況の好転. ¶a "***tight-money***" *situation* in business circles 実業界の金融ひっ迫情勢. ¶the ***trade*** *situation* 貿易状況. 【類】the European ***travel*** *situation.* ¶live according to the ***wartime*** *situation* 戦時情勢に応じた生活をする. ¶bring about the Alice in ***Wonderland*** *situation* 不思議の国のアリス同様の事態を将来する ‖ the critical ***world*** *situation* 切迫した世界情勢. 【類】the tense ***world*** *situation* / in the present ***world*** *situation* / cause a radical change in the ***world*** *situation* / the ***world*** *situation* of the day (現勢) / the ***world*** *situation* in population / adapt ourselves to a changing ***world*** *situation.*

P The country is ***in*** a critical *situation.* その国は危急の状態にある. ¶take stock ***of*** the *situation* 事態を調査する. ¶***on*** (=***under***) the present *situation* 現状では. ¶deal ***with*** the *situation* [書物など]時局を取扱う.

P² the *situation* ***between*** Turkey and Greece トルコ・ギリシア間の事態. ¶the present *situation* ***in*** Egypt エジプトの現状.

(**2**) 勤め口, 地位.

V I am unable to ***find*** a *situation.* 就職口が見つからない. ¶***get*** a respectable *situation* 恥ずかしくない職を得る. ¶*Situations* are ***guaranteed*** to all students trained at the college. その大学で教育された学生全部に就職が保証されている. ¶He ***has*** a good *situation.* 彼はよい勤め口を持っている. ¶***hold*** a responsible *situation* 責任ある地位についている. ¶***lose*** one's *situation* 失職する. ¶cannot ***obtain*** a *situation* 職が得られない. ¶***offer*** *situations* with high wages 高給で人員を募集する. ¶help ***secure*** *situations* 就職の世話をする. ¶servants ***seeking*** *situations* 職を求めている召使. ¶The maid says that she is unwilling to ***take*** a *situation* in a house where there are young people. その女中は子供のいる家に勤めるのはいやだと言っている. ¶***throw up*** one's *situation* 勤め口をやめる.

Q hold a ***subordinate*** *situation* 部下の地位に就いている. ¶a ***well-paying*** *situation* 報酬の多い地位.

P apply ***for*** a *situation* 勤め口を志願する. 【類】apply to ... ***for*** the situation.

six, *n.* 六.

Q the ***secular*** *six*=weekdays 日曜日以外の週日.

P The men of the house were all ***at*** *sixes* and sevens. その家の人々は互いに折合が悪かった. ‖ Everything in the city was ***at*** *sixes* and sevens. この市は万事ごたついている. ¶It is *six* ***of*** one and half-a-dozen of the other. 似たり寄ったりだ.

six-shooter, *n.* 六連発けん銃.

V ***draw*** one's *six-shooter* 六連発けん銃をさやから抜く.

sixteen, *n.* 十六.

Q The date of Shakespeare's death, which is ***double*** *sixteen,* is easily remembered. シェークスピア死去の年代は十六を二つ重ねた一六一六年だから覚えやすい. ¶a girl of ***sweet*** *sixteen* 花もつぼみの十六娘.

size, *n.* 大きさ, 寸法(サイズ).

V ***attain*** the *size* of a pea えんどう豆の大きさになる ‖ The plant has ***attained*** a great *size.* その木は非常に大きくなった. ¶***compare*** the *sizes* of two things 物の大小を比較する. ¶This box is very light when we ***consider*** its *size.* この箱は大きさの割に非常に軽い. ¶***contrast*** relative *sizes* of ... and ... ...と...との相対的の大きさを対照する. ¶***double*** its *size* その大きさを倍にする. ¶***exceed*** the middle *size* 中位より大きい. ¶***give*** the *size* of a book in inches 本の大きさをインチで示す. ¶a minister trying to ***increase*** the *size* of his flock 信者の数をふやそうとしている牧師. ¶The massive *size* of the figure is ***indicated*** by the presence of a man standing on its right. その像の巨大なことは右側に立っている人を見て察せられる. ¶***multiply*** its *size* several times その大きさを数倍にする. ¶***preserve*** the handy *size* of the book その本の手ごろな大きさを失わないようにする. ¶***regulate*** the *size* of families 産児の数を調節する. ¶***take*** the *size* of ... ...の寸法を取る. ¶The average Americans ***worship*** *size.* 一般に米人は大きいものが好きだ. ¶What *size* do you ***want***?—I want a seven (=No. 7). 形は何番がお入用です—七番です.

V² *Size* ***matters*** less than quality. 大きさよりも質の方が大事だ.

Q It was reproduced here in its ***actual*** *size.* それを実物大にここで複製した. ¶of ***all*** *sizes* and shapes あらゆる大

きさと形の. ¶the ***average size*** 平均の大きさ. ¶***children's sizes*** of shoes 大小色々の子供ぐつ. ¶a tree of ***commanding size*** 付近を圧する大木. ¶It is of a ***convenient size*** for the pocket. それはポケットに入れるに便利な大きさだ. ¶of ***different*** (=***various***) ***sizes*** 大小様々の. ¶of ***diminished size*** [型の]小さい. ¶of ***diminutive size*** ちっぽけな. ¶a nail of the ***eight size*** 八番くぎ. ¶of ***enormous size*** 巨大な. ¶of a ***fixed size*** 一定の大きさの. ¶The scale is ***full size***. 縮尺は実物大. ¶woollen blankets in ***generous sizes*** 大きさがたっぷりした毛布. ¶of ***gigantic size*** すばらしい大きさの. ¶cooks' knives in ***graduated sizes*** 小型から順次大型になっている料理ナイフ. ¶of ***great size*** 非常に大きい. ¶books of ***handy size*** 手ごろの大きさの本. ¶an animal of ***huge size*** 非常に大きい動物. ¶This hat is one ***size*** too ***large*** (***small***) for me. この帽子はサイズが一つ大き(小さ)すぎる. ‖ a stone of ***large size*** 大きな石. ¶clothes ***many sizes*** too large 幾まわりも大きすぎる着物. ‖ of ***many sizes*** 大小色々の. ¶a house of ***medium size*** 中位の大きさの家. ¶a town of ***middling size*** 中位の大きさの町. ¶of ***moderate size*** 並の大きさの. ¶of ***natural size*** 実物大の. ¶of ***ordinary sizes*** 並の大きさの. ¶of ***phenomenal size*** ばかに大きな. ¶of conveniently ***portable size*** 携帯に便利な大きさの. ¶expand to its ***proper size*** その適当の大きさに膨張する. ¶larger than the ***real size*** 実際の型よりも大きな. ¶in ***reduced size*** 大きさをつめて. ¶boards of the ***required size*** 注文通りの大きさの板. ¶Each of these skyscrapers houses a population of a town of ***respectable size***. これらの摩天楼の一つ一つはそれぞれ相当大きな町と同じ人口がある. ¶It is of the ***right size***. それは本式の大きさだ. ¶We have it in ***several sizes***. それは大小色々持合わしております. ¶He wears a huge pair of brown leather riding-boots about ***six sizes*** too large for him. 彼は約六番(六まわり)も大きすぎる大きな赤皮の乗馬ぐつをはいている. ¶animals of ***small size*** 小動物. ¶of ***some size*** かなりの大きさの. ¶***special size*** of paper 紙の特別の大きさ. ¶a ***standard size*** 標準の大きさ. ¶volumes of ***uniform size*** 一様の大きさの本. ¶***various size*** of type 様々の大きさの活字. ¶***What size*** do you want your table made? どの位の大きさに食卓をお造りしましょうか. ‖ ***What size*** do you wear? サイズはどの位ですか(帽子・靴など).

Q^2 an ***inch-cube size*** of it その一インチ立方の大きさ. ¶in various ***can sizes*** 寸法の違ったかんに入れて. ¶The picture is larger than ***life size***. その絵は実物より大きい. ¶a book of ***magazine size*** 雑誌型の本. ¶a dictionary of ***pocket size***=a pocket-size[d] dictionary ポケット型辞典. ¶You are what tailors call a "***stock size***." あなたはでき合いがあうからだです. ¶a weekly of the ***tabloid size*** タブロイド判の週刊紙. ¶The linotype can handle all ***type sizes*** up to 36-points. ライノタイプ(植字鋳造機)は三十六ポイントまですべての寸法の活字を扱える.

P ***about*** the ***size*** of the little finger 小指ぐらいの大きさ ‖ That's ***about*** the ***size*** of it. それはほとんどその位の大きさだ. ¶***according to size*** 大きさによって. ¶***below*** the usual ***size*** 普通のよりも小さい. ¶***beyond*** the natural ***size*** 実物より大きい. ¶Its importance is not to be measured by ***size***. その重要性は大きさでは計られない. ¶judging ***from*** its ***size*** その大きさから判断すると. ¶handy ***in size*** 手ごろの大きさの ‖ be reduced ***in size*** 寸法が詰っている ‖ It is equal ***in size*** to a turkey. その大きさは七面鳥に等しい. 【類】 increase (grow) ***in size*** / Here is placed a huge pipe organ that is seventh ***in size*** in the world. ¶***of*** a ***size*** 同じ大きさの. 【類】 They are much ***of*** a ***size***. ‖ one of the most beautiful art galleries ***of*** its ***size*** in America アメリカにおけるその規模の美術館の中で最も美しいものの一つ ‖ ***Of*** what ***size*** is that man? あの人はどの位大きいか. ‖ a man of [large] ***size*** 大がらの人. 【類】 ***of*** all ***sizes*** / ***of*** no small ***size*** / ***of*** smaller ***size***. ¶grow ***to*** an enormous ***size*** 法外な大きさになる. ¶She is ***under size***. 彼女は並より小さい.

P^2 the ***size of*** a book (house, city) 本(など)の大きさ ‖ be about the ***size of*** a pegion's heart およそはとの心臓ほどの大きさだ. 【類】 a tiger about the ***size of*** a horse.

size, *v.* 大きさを測る.

M ***size up*** Japan 日本を評価する ‖ ***size up*** a situation 事態を看取する ‖ They ***sized*** me ***up*** for ..., instead of ... 彼らは私を…でなく…と見当をつけた. 【類】 after carefully ***sizing*** her ***up***, he said ... / ***size up*** a customer at a glance / ***size up*** one's political qualifications / ***size up*** the outlook for the year 1958.

skate, *n. pl.* スケートぐつ. 「一組.

Q^2 a pair of ***roller*** (***ice***) ***skates*** ローラー(アイス)スケート

P ***on skates*** スケートをはいて.

skate, *v.* スケートぐつで走る.

P ***skate over*** the ice 氷上を滑走する ‖ skate ***over*** (=***on***) thin ice 〖比ゆ〗危険な(難しい)状態になる. ¶The ice is seldom strong enough to ***skate upon***. スケートのできるぐらい氷が厚く張ることは滅多にない.

skating, *n.* 氷すべり.

P^2 ***skating on*** a pond 池での氷すべり ‖ ***skating on*** wheels ローラースケート滑走. 【類】 ***skating on*** the ice.

Q^2 ***figure skating*** 図形滑走. ¶***free skating*** 自由滑走.

skeleton, *n.* がい骨; 骨組.

V ***air*** one's family ***skeleton*** 内輪の恥を表に出す.

Q a ***bleached skeleton*** 野ざらしのがい骨. 【類】 a ***bleached human skeleton***. ¶a ***mere skeleton*** 骨と皮ばかりの人. ¶an ***unhappy skeleton*** of a horse あわれなやせ馬.

Q^2 a maze of ***building skeletons*** and walled-in basement holes 建物の残がいと壁でふさがれた地階の穴の迷路. ¶the ***family skeleton*** 一家内の秘密. 【類】 air (=tip off) one's ***family skeleton***. ¶a ***living skeleton*** 骨皮筋右衛門. ¶Many modern buildings are constructed upon ***steel skeletons***. 近代の建物は多くは鉄骨だ. ¶a ***walking skeleton*** weighing only seventy-five pounds わずかに七十五ポンドのやせ男.

P He was reduced (=worn) ***to*** a ***skeleton***. 彼はやせて骨と皮ばかりになった. ‖ Our regiment was reduced ***to*** a ***skeleton***. わが連隊は人員が非常にわずかになった. 【類】 The prisoner was worn ***to*** a ***skeleton***.

P^2 a ***skeleton in*** the closet (=***cupboard or house***)=the family skeleton. ¶the ***skeleton of*** a house 家屋の骨組 ‖ the ***skeletons of*** war plants 軍需工場の残がい ‖ He is the ***skeleton of*** his former self. 彼はやせ衰えてわずかに以前の面影を止めているに過ぎない.

skeptical, *a.* 懐疑的な.

P I am ***skeptical over*** the real efficacy of these means. 私はこうした手段が本当に効果的かどうか疑わしいと思う.

skepticism, *n.* 懐疑.

V ***maintain*** a scientific ***skepticism*** and a philosophic doubt 科学的懐疑と哲学的懐疑を持続する.

sketch, *n.* スケッチ; 略図; 小品; 概略.

V ***do*** a musical ***sketch*** at the piano ピアノで小曲を奏する. ¶***give*** a short ***sketch*** of ... …の概略を示す. ¶***make*** a ***sketch*** in oils of a view ある風景を油絵でスケッチする. ¶***take*** a ***sketch*** on the spot 現場でスケッチを取る.

Q a ***biographical sketch*** 略伝. ¶a ***brief sketch*** of one's career (=life) その略歴. ¶a ***clear*** and ***succinct historical sketch*** of ... …の簡単明りょうな歴史的概略. ¶***dramatic sketches*** made up of boiled-down plays 寸劇. ¶an ***elaborate sketch*** 精巧な見取図. ¶a concise ***historical sketch*** of the progress of the art その芸術の簡明な史的記述. ¶a ***modern sensational dramatic sketch*** 近代の扇情的な寸劇. ¶make a ***rough sketch*** 略図を作る. ¶I took ***several sketches*** on the way. 私は途中色々のスケッチを取った. ¶a very ***short sketch*** of one's life 略伝. ¶a ***vivacious sketch*** 生き生きした小品.

Q^2 a ***character sketch*** 人物評. ¶a ***freehand sketch*** [器具を使わずに]手で描いたスケッチ. ¶a ***lightning sketch*** in colors 絵具を使った素早い写生. ¶a ***pen-and-ink sketch*** ペン画, 小品. ¶a ***personality sketch*** 人物寸描. ¶a ***silhouette sketch*** 素描, 横顔. ¶a ***thumb-nail sketch*** of life 世相寸描. 【類】 make a ***thumb-nail sketch*** of British character. ¶a ***travel sketch*** 旅行記.

P a ***sketch in*** black and white 墨絵, コンテのスケッチ.

P^2 ***sketches from*** my life 自伝断片.

sketch, *v.* 図取りする, 写生する; 概説する.

M ***sketch briefly*** 簡単にスケッチする. ¶***sketched directly*** from Nature instead of from books 書物から写したのでなく直接自然から写生した. ¶***sketch rapidly*** the course of events that led to ... …の導火線となった事件の経過をざっと述べる. ¶the plan thus ***roughly sketched*** out 以上概説した計画.

P ***sketch from*** nature 写生する.

O go ***sketching*** 写生に出掛ける.

ski, *n.* スキー.

P traverse snow fields ***in*** *skis* スキーで雪原を横断する. ¶I have never been ***on*** *skis*. 私はスキーをやったことがない.

skid, *v*. すべる; 空転する.
P The car *skidded* ***on*** the slippery road. 自動車がすべる道で空転した.

skidding, *n*. 空転.
V chain tires to ***stop*** *skidding* 空転防止のためタイヤに鎖を巻く.
P Beware ***of*** *skidding*. 空転注意.

skilful, =skillful.

skill, *n*. 熟練, 巧妙; 手腕, 手並.
V ***acquire*** *skill* in writing 文章が上達する.【類】there is nothing like practice in ***acquiring*** *skill*. ¶***attain*** considerable *skill* (=become proficient) on the organ オルガンが大分うまくなる.【類】***attain*** *skill* through frequent practice. ¶The case ***baffles*** the *skill* of our most experienced medical men. その病人には最も老練な医者もさじを投げている. ¶***bring*** *skill* to bear upon a work 熟練にものをいわせてある仕事をやる. ¶***capitalize*** one's *skill* 熟練を元手にする. ¶***develop*** *skill* 腕をみがく. ¶***display*** one's *skill* at the game その競技に手腕を見せる. ¶a method of teaching which will ***ensure*** *skill* in the handling of the language その国語に必ず熟達させる教授法. ¶***exercise*** one's *skill* in ... …に手腕を揮う. ¶***exert*** one's utmost *skill* ありったけの腕を揮う. ¶***exhibit*** one's *skill* 熟練を示す. ¶He ***has*** great *skill* in handwork. 彼は手工が非常にうまい. ¶***improve*** one's *skill* 腕をみがく. ¶***measure*** one's *skill* with a rival 相手と腕比べをする. ¶It ***needs*** *skill* to tune a piano. ピアノの調律は熟練を要する. ¶***outwit*** the *skill* of ... …にまさる腕前を示す. ¶***possess*** some *skill* at sleight of hand 奇術がかなりうまい. ¶***require*** much *skill* 大いに熟練を要する. ¶***show*** great *skill* in condensation [表現の]要約に大いに腕前を見せる. ¶***show off*** one's *skill* 手腕を誇示する. ¶***tax*** the physician's *skill* 医師を悩ます. ¶***try*** one's *skill* at flying a kite たこ揚をやってみる.【類】We ***tried*** our *skill* in wrestling. ¶***use*** one's *skill* in ... …に手腕を揮う.
Q a task which calls for the highest ***administrative*** *skill* 経営上大いに熟練を要する仕事. ¶He has more than the ***amateur's*** *skill*. 彼はしろうと離れがしている. ¶He possesses ***astonishing*** *skill* in calligraphy. 彼はめざましく書道に達している. ¶do with ***consummate*** *skill* 十分巧みにやる. ¶***constructive*** *skill* 構成上の技術. ¶the delights of the products of American ***culinary*** *skill* 米国の料理人が腕によりをかけて作った珍味. ¶The condition baffled the ***diagnostic*** *skill* of many physicians. その病状診断には多くの医者がさじを投げた. ¶***diplomatic*** *skill* 外交的手腕. ¶a rival of ***equal*** *skill* 同じように熟練した相手. ¶with ***exceptional*** *skill* ことの外巧妙に. ¶show ***great*** *skill* 非常な腕前を見せる. ¶girls who possess some form of ***industrial*** *skill* 何か仕事の熟練を有する娘たち. ¶***inventive*** *skill* 発明の才. ¶show much ***literary*** *skill* 大いに文学上の技量を示す ‖ The essays are written with much ***literary*** *skill*. その論文は非常な才筆で書いてある. ¶Any one with a ***little*** *skill* in carpentry can make it. それは少し大工仕事の心得のある者ならだれにでも作れる. ¶***manual*** *skill* (=dexterity) 手先の熟練. ¶display ***marvelous*** *skill* at the game その競技にすばらしい腕前を示す. ¶with ***masterly*** *skill* 名人芸で. ¶He has ***much*** *skill* in intrigue. 彼は悪知恵にたけている. ¶The workmen of the present day are deficient in the ***patient*** *skill* of the artists of a bygone age. 現代の職工は昔の工芸人の丹念さを欠いている. ¶***pedagogic*** *skill* 教授上の手腕. ¶a great masterpiece of ***photographic*** *skill* 写真術の大傑作. ¶examples of ***primitive engineering*** *skill* 原始人の工事上の手腕を示す実例. ¶***professional*** *skill* 職業上の手腕. ¶an exercise of ***pure*** *skill* 真の腕前の発揮. ¶he showed ***remarkable*** *skill* in ... 彼は…に非凡の腕前を見せた. ¶acquire a reputation for ***special*** *skill* in one's calling …の職業上の特殊技能のために名声を博する. ¶lack of ***technical*** *skill* 専門的技術の欠如. ¶***traditional*** craft *skill* 伝統的の技巧. ¶with ***unerring*** *skill* 確かな腕前で. ¶with ***wonderful*** *skill* 実に巧みに.
Q² ***bargaining*** *skill* 掴出しじようず. ¶***Engineering*** *skill* of a high order was required in the construction. その工事には高度の工学上の手腕を必要とした. ¶***marketing*** *skill* 買物じようず. ¶lack of technical ***production*** *skill* 専門的生産技術の欠如. ¶***reading*** *skills* 読書術. ¶use their ***wartime*** *skills* in peacetime jobs 戦時の熟練を平和時の仕事に使う.
P He lacks (=is wanting) ***in*** *skill*. 彼は未熟だ. ¶gain ***in*** *skill* 腕が上がる. ¶a man ***of*** *skill* 名人 ‖ a trial ***of*** *skill* 腕比べ. ¶plume oneself ***on*** one's *skill* その腕前を鼻にかける. ¶***through*** the *skill* in war or diplomacy 戦争または外交の手腕によって. ¶This anyone ***with*** a little *skill* in carpentry can make in half an hour. 少しでも大工の腕のある人ならこんなことは半時間でできる. ‖ a picture painted ***with*** great *skill* 非常にうまく描いてある絵.
P² one's *skill* ***at*** embroidery 刺しゅうの腕前. ¶one's *skill* ***in*** the art of expression in English (modern languages) 英語(など)表現上の手腕. ¶one's *skill* ***on*** [the] organ (flute) オルガン(など)の演奏技術.

skilled, *a*. 熟練している; 巧者な.
P "old hands" *skilled* ***at*** their jobs 仕事には腕に覚えのベテラン. ¶be *skilled* ***in*** technique 技巧に熟練している.【類】one *skilled* ***in*** music (keeping accounts, the carpenters' trade).

skillful, *a*. 熟練な, 巧妙な.
M become ***amazingly*** *skillful* びっくりするほど巧みになる. ¶***tolerably*** *skillful* at ... …がかなりうまい.
P very *skillful* ***at*** dancing (billiards, treating eye diseases, painting birds) ダンス(など)が非常に巧みな. ¶*skillful* ***in*** teaching (negotiation, managing a school, the detection of crime) 授業(など)に熟練した.【類】become *skillful* ***in*** reading and writing. ¶*skillful* ***with*** their fingers 指先の器用な ‖ very *skillful* ***with*** his rod つりが非常にうまい.【類】He is *skillful* ***with*** a tool of any kind.

skim, *v*. ざっと目を通す; すれすれに通る(飛ぶ).
M² Swallows are *skimming* ***by*** all day. つばめは終日地面をかすめて飛んでいる.
P *skim* ***on*** the surface of the water 水面をかすめ飛ぶ. ¶A bird *skimmed* ***over*** the stream. 鳥が流れの上をかすめて飛んだ. ¶*skim* ***over*** a newspaper (book, volume) 新聞(など)にざっと目を通す. ¶*skim* ***through*** a book (magazine) 本(など)を早々に読過する.【類】The book is worth *skimming* ***through***.
O The gulls are *skimming* the waters. かもめが水上をかすめてとんでいる.【類】skaters *skimming* the ice. / Read carefully; don't *skim*.

skin, *n*. 皮膚, 皮.
V ***abrade*** the *skin* 皮をすりむく. ¶She ***bears*** a white *skin*. 彼女は皮膚が白い. ¶a preparation for ***beautifying*** the *skin* はだを美しくする調合剤. ¶***break*** the *skin* けがをする.【類】The *skin* (flesh) is ***broken*** (***bruised***). ¶***bronze*** the *skin* 日に焼ける. ¶Serpents ***cast*** their *skin* once a year. へびは一年に一回脱皮する. ¶***change*** one's *skin* 急変する. ¶***clear*** the *skin* はだをきれいにする. ¶The frost has ***cracked*** my *skin*. 寒さでひびが切れた. ¶***develop*** a *skin* that's "elephant-thick" 象のような皮膚になる. ¶She ***has*** a clear *skin*. 彼女ははだがきれいだ. ¶a new cosmetic to ***improve*** one's *skin* はだをよくするための新しい化粧品. ¶***irritate*** the *skin* 皮膚をただらせる. ¶***keep*** the *skin* ***warm*** 皮膚を暖かにしておく. ¶The cold ***makes*** the *skin* ***smart***. 寒気で皮膚がひりひりする. ¶***pale*** the *skin* 皮膚を青ざめさせる. ¶***pare off*** the *skin* of an apple りんごの皮をむく. ¶***polish*** the *skin* はだをみがく. ¶***puncture*** the *skin* 皮に穴をあける. ¶***roughen*** the *skin* 皮膚を粗くする. ¶***rub*** the *skin* till it glows 皮膚を真赤になるまでこする. ¶***save*** one's *skin* 皮膚を傷つけないようにする; [比ゆ的に]危難を脱する. ¶***slough*** the *skin* [へびなど]皮を脱する. ¶Talc powder ***soothes*** the *skin*. タルク粉は皮膚をやわらげる. ¶***strip*** the *skin* from a banana バナナの皮をむく. ¶***strip off*** the *skin* 皮をはぐ. ¶***take*** the *skin* ***off*** my hand 手の皮をむく. ¶***tan*** *skins* into leather 獣皮をなめす. ¶The *skin* ***tans*** (=***burns***). 日に焼ける. ¶***tear*** the *skin* ***off*** ... …から皮をはぐ. ¶***throw off*** its *skin* その皮を脱ぎ捨てる. ¶They ***wore*** *skins* of animals for clothing. 彼らは被服として獣皮を着けていた.
V² The *skin* ***freckles***. 皮膚に斑点ができる. ¶The *skin* ***peels*** when sunburnt. 日にやけると皮がむける. ¶His *skin* ***remained*** in a fold when pinched together. 彼の皮膚はつまんでもそのままになっていた.
Q ***black*** (***brown***, ***copper-colored***, ***dark***, ***fair***, ***yellow***) *skin* 黒い(とび色の・銅色の・浅黒い・白い・黄色い)皮膚. ¶the ***cast-off*** *skin* of a cicada せみの抜け殻. ¶***chafed*** *skin* すりむいた皮膚. ¶a ***coarse*** *skin* 荒はだ. ¶the ***delicate*** *skin*

of infants 幼児の弱い皮膚. ¶a *dry* (*parched*) *skin* かさかさした皮膚. ¶have a *fair* (*dark*) *skin* 色が白い(黒い). ¶her *finegrained skin* きめのこまかい皮膚. ¶a *greasy skin* あぶらはだ. ¶an ass in a *lion's skin* とらの威を借るきつね. ¶*oily skin* あぶらぎった皮膚. ¶a *pale milky skin* 青ざめた乳色の皮膚. ¶*raw* or *dressed skin* 生またはなめした獣皮. ¶have a *rough skin* 皮膚が荒れている. ¶*satiny skin* しゅすのような皮膚. ¶*slimy skin* ぬるぬるした皮. ¶a *soft fair skin* もちはだ.【類】a *soft* and *velvety skin*. ¶a *spotty skin* しみだらけの皮膚. ¶a badly *sunburnt skin* ひどく日に焼けた皮膚. ¶a [*sun-*]*tanned skin* 日焼けした皮膚. ¶A lion has a *tawny skin*. ライオンの皮は黄かっ色だ. ¶a *tender skin* 柔かい皮膚. ¶a *thick* (*thin*) *skin* 厚(薄)皮; [比ゆ的に]鈍(敏)感. ¶come off with a *whole skin* けがなしで済む.

Q² skid on a *banana skin* バナナの皮を踏んですべる. ¶tread on *fruit skins* くだものの皮を踏む. ¶a *potato skin* じゃがいもの皮. ¶*Rattle-snake skin* is used for fancy bags and purses. ガラガラへびの皮はしゃれたかばんやがま口に使われる.

P *by* the *skin* of one's teeth《俗》あやうく. ¶abrasions *in* our *skin* 皮膚のすりむき ‖ have an irritating sensation *in* the *skin* 皮膚がぴりぴりする. ¶spots (eruptions, swellings) *on* the *skin* 皮膚のはん点(など). ¶I was wet *to* the *skin*. 私はびしょぬれになった. ‖ The rain soaked *to* the *skin*. 雨がはだまで通った. ¶a wart *on* the *skin* 皮膚のいぼ. ¶wear a yukata next *to* the *skin* じかにゆかたを着る. ¶inject medicine *under* the *skin* 皮下注射をする. ¶peoples *with* tinted *skins* 有色民族 ‖ escape *with* a whole *skin* (無傷で)無事にのがれる.

P² the *skin of* a human being 人間の皮膚.

skin, *v.* 皮をむく.

P *skin* the cream *from* the milk 牛乳からクリームをすくい取る. ¶*skin* a person *of* every shilling《口語》金を全部巻きあげる. 【類】He was *skinned of* all the money he had then on. ¶*skin off* one's gloves 手袋をめくって脱ぐ.

skip, *n.* 軽跳び.

V *give* a *skip* of joy 小おどりして喜ぶ.

P *without* a *skip* ＝without a hitch 何事もなく.

skip, *v.* とびとびに読む; とばす;《米》急ぐ, 急行する.

M² *skip over* to America アメリカに急行する. 【類】*skip over* to Paris for the weekend. ‖ *skip over* to page 105 百五ページまで飛ばして読む.

P *skip in* reading とびとびに読む. ¶*skip* stones *on* the pond 池で石切りをする. ¶Here the historian *skips over* half a century. ここでその歴史家は半世紀とばして先へ行っている. ‖ *skip over* difficult passages むずかしい節をとばして読む. 【類】*skip over* a chapter (a few pages).

skipper, *n.* とぶ人(もの).

Q² a *water skipper* あめんぼ.

skipping, *n.* 飛ぶこと.

Q² *wage skipping* 一足飛びの昇給.

skipping-rope, *n.* なわ飛びのなわ.

V *turn* a *skipping-rope* なわ飛をする.

skirmish, *n.* 小ぜり合, 小衝突.

Q *domestic skirmishes*＝family jars 夫婦げんか. ¶*preliminary skirmishes* leading up to a big encounter 大会戦になるまでの前しょう的小せり合い. ¶*Some skirmishes* between Japan and Soviet Russia 日ソ間の小衝突. ¶*border skirmishes* 国境の小戦闘.

skirmish, *v.* 小ぜりあいをする.

P *skirmish with* the enemy 敵軍と小ぜりあいをする.

skirt, *n.* すそ; スカート; [通例 *pl.*] 都市の周辺.

V *draw* one's *skirts together* すそを引寄せる. ¶*gather up* one's *skirts* すそを引寄せる. ¶*hold up* the *skirt* つまを取る. ¶She *tucked up* her *skirts*. 彼女はすそをからげた. ¶*make* a *skirt* an inch *longer* (*shorter*) スカートを一インチ長(短か)くする. ¶It was immodest to *wear skirts* above the ankles. くるぶしを出してスカートを着けるのはぶしつけであった. 「パッと開いている.

V² The *skirt flares* at the bottom. そのスカートは下部で

Q *divided skirts* 二またのスカート. ¶a *flared skirt* フレヤスカート. ¶a *gathered skirt* ギャザスカート(つまみ縫いしたスカート). ¶children's *shirred skirts* 子供のギャザスカート. ¶a *trailing skirt* 後ろに引きずる(貴婦人などの)長すそ.

Q² a *blue-serge skirt* 紺サージのスカート. ¶a *grass skirt* 草のスカート. ¶a "*hula-hula*" *skirt* フラ・ダンスの腰みの. ¶a *tweed skirt* スコッチ織りのスカート.

P *at* the *skirts* of the wood 森の端(はし)で. ¶a man *in skirts* 女装した男子 ‖ *in* a trailing *skirt* すそを引きずって. ¶*on* the *skirts* (＝outskirts) of the city 市の周辺で, 郊外で. ¶pleats *on* a *skirt* スカートのひだ.

P² the *skirts of* a coat 上衣のすそ.

skirt, *v.* 囲む; めぐる.

O a road *skirting* a city 都市をめぐる道路. 【類】*skirt* a town to avoid heavy traffic.

skit, *n.* 落首(らくしゅ). 「な落首ができた.

V It *evoked* a droll *skit* " ... ". それで「...」というこっけい

Q a *musical skit* [映画の]音楽入りの軽い風刺.

skittles, *n. pl.* 九柱戯.

V *play skittles* 九柱戯をする.

skulk, *v.* こそこそ隠れる.

M *skulk away* from sight 姿を消す.

skull, *n.* 頭がい骨.

V *fracture* the *skull* 頭がい骨をくじく.

Q a *grinning skull* 歯をむきだしている頭がい骨.

skunk, *n.*《口語》卑劣なやつ.

Q You *dirty old skunk!* このげじげじ野郎.

sky, *n.* [the s-] 空; [しばしば *pl.*] 上空; 空模様.

V The *sky* is *blotted out* by clouds. 空は雲で一面おおわれている. ¶the domes that *cut* the *sky* 空にくっきり見える丸屋根. 【類】search-lights *cutting* the night *sky*. ¶The clouds *darkened* the *sky*. 雲が空を暗くした. ¶The setting sun was *illuminating* the western *sky*. 夕日が西の空を照らしていた. ¶The *sky* was *overspread* with clouds. 空は雲でおおわれていた. ¶The dawn begins to *redden* the *sky*. 暁が空を赤くし始める. ¶*rend* the *skies* with loud applause 歓呼で天をつんざく. ¶the wires that *score* the *sky* in a very cat's-cradle あや取りそのままに空に引いてある電線. ¶Not a cloud *specked* the deep blue *sky* above. 頭上のこんぺきの空をさえぎる一点の雲もなかった. ¶The peak *touches* the *sky*. 峰が天空を摩する. 【類】sky-scrapers that *touch* the *skies*.

V² The *sky* has *become* a good deal *brighter*. 空が大分明るくなった. ¶The *sky clears*. 空が晴れる. ¶The *sky* is *threatening* 雨模様だ.

Q the *azure sky* 青天. ¶*balmy skies* うららかな空. ¶the *blue sky* 青空. 【類】*blue skies*. ¶with a *bright sky* overhead 頭上にうららかな青空をいただいて. ¶*clear skies* 晴れた空. ¶in a *cloudless sky* 雲のない空に. ¶A *cloudy sky* is not always a sign of rain. 曇天必ずしも雨の降る徴候ではない. ¶the *dark blue sky* 黒ずんだ青空. ¶a *dull sky* どんよりした空. ¶an *emerald sky* 青空. ¶a *gray sky* in the morning 朝の灰色の空. ¶the *indigo-blue sky* 濃藍(らん)の空. ¶a *lambent sky* なごやかに輝く空. ¶a *leaden sky* どんよりした空. ¶A haze of light is reflected against the *murky sky*. 光のもやが小暗い空に映っている. ¶watch the British *literary skies* in hopes of some new stars of genius swimming into their ken 新しい天才の出現を待望してイギリスの文壇を注視する. ¶beneath our *northern skies* わが北国において. ¶the *opalescent sky* オパール色の空. ¶the *overarching sky* 弓形に広がる空. ¶The *sky* is *overcast*. 空は曇っている. 【類】look up nervously at an *overcast sky* which is threatening to rain. ¶A *red sky* at night is a sailor's delight. 赤い夜空は船乗の喜びだ. ¶a *rosy sky* at sunset 日没の淡紅色の空. ¶a motor tour under the *sapphire skies* of Italy イタリアの青玉色の空をいただいての自動車旅行. ¶the *scintillant sky* きらめく空. ¶a *serene sky* 晴朗な空. ¶under *smiling skies* うるわしい空の下に. ¶look up into the broad *starlit sky* 星明りの空を仰ぐ. ¶a *starry sky* 星空. ¶beneath a *stormy sky* 荒れた空の下で. ¶a *sullen sky* 曇って憂うつな空. ¶the land of *sunny skies* うららかな空の土地. 【類】the *sunny skies* of Honolulu. ¶the *sunrise* (*sunset*) *sky* 日の出(日没)の空. ¶invade Japanese *territorial skies* over and around Hokkaido 北海道及びその周囲の日本上空を侵犯する. ¶*threatening skies* 雨模様の空. ¶the *turquoise sky* トルコ玉のような青緑色の空. ¶a *water-clear sky* 水のように澄んだ空. ¶the *watery sky* 雨もよいの空. ¶in the *western sky* 西の空に.

Q² suddenly change the overcast *industrial relations skies* 暗たんたる産業関係を突然変化させる. ¶a *mackerel* sky さば雲の空. ¶Rifts appeared in the dull gray of a ***November*** sky. 十一月の空のくすんだ灰空の中に切れ目が見えた.

P its graceful silhouette ***against*** the *sky* 青空にはえるその優美な黒影 ‖ The castle stands out ***against*** the *sky*. 城は青空にきつ立している. ¶look ***at*** the *sky* 空を見上げる. ¶***beneath*** a *sky* of cloudless blue 一点の雲もない青空の下に ‖ gaudy chocolate boxes tied with every shade of ribbon ***beneath*** the *skies* 世にありとあらゆる色のリボンで結んだ花やかなチョコレートの箱. ¶a thunderbolt ***from*** a clear *sky* 青天のへきれき. 【類】The Divine Wind (神風号) gave the Prince and Princess a greeting ***from*** the *skies*. ¶A war-cloud appeared ***in*** the *sky*. 戦雲が空に現われた. ‖ Planes wrote " Welcome home " ***in*** the *sky* above him. 飛行機が彼の頭上の空に「歓迎」の煙文字を描いた. 【類】The weather was at its best, without a cloud ***in*** the *sky*. / Stars are ***in*** the *sky* at night. ¶from the look ***of*** the *sky* 空模様からみると. ¶***out of*** a clear *sky*= all of a sudden 突然, 不意に. 【類】It came to me suddenly ***out of*** a clear *sky*. ¶The moon and the stars move ***through*** the *sky* 月と星は空を運行する. ¶ascend ***to*** the *sky* (煙・風・船など)天に上る ‖ extol (=praise) a person ***to*** the *skies* ほめちぎる. ¶the top of some mountain reaching up ***towards*** the *sky* 天空にそびえるある山のいただき. ¶***under*** the black night *sky* やみ夜の空の下に. 【類】The very thing we most admire at home seems a grotesque absurdity to our neighbors living abroad ***under*** another *sky*. ¶They praised him ***up to*** the *skies*. 彼らは彼をほめそやした. ¶***with*** sapphire *skies* overhead 上には青玉色の空をいただいて.

P² It can be seen in the *sky* ***after*** sunset. それは日没後の空に見られる. ¶all-red *sky* ***at*** sunset. 日没の真赤な空. ¶a *sky* ***without*** clouds 雲のない空.

sky-line, *n.* 起伏する地平線, 界空線; 輪郭線.

V Smoke-stacks ***break*** the *sky-line*. 煙突が地平線を破って空高くそびえている. ¶The lofty range of ... ***cuts*** (=***stabs***) the *sky-line* ...の高い山脈が空高くそびえている. ¶Fully fifty huge skyscrapers ***dot*** the *sky-line* of Lower Manhattan. [ニューヨーク市]マンハッタン下区の空に点てつする摩天楼はたしかに五十はある. ¶The mountain range ***presents*** a jagged *sky-line*. その山脈がのこぎり形の輪郭線を成している. ¶We eagerly ***scanned*** the *sky-line* for the first glimpse of Mount Fuji. われわれ(船上の人々)は真先に富士を見ようと熱心に水平線に目をくばった. ¶vividly ***show*** the *sky-line* of the metropolis その都市の空をバックに建物の起伏する線をはっきり現わす.

Q The exterior of the edifice, owing chiefly to the ***irregular*** *sky-line*, is very picturesque and pleasing. 建物の外部は主に輪郭線が不規則なために非常に画趣があって気持がよい.

Q² Toronto's ***skyscraper*** *sky-line* トロント市の摩天楼の輪郭線.

skyscraper, *n.* 摩天楼.

V ***erect*** a *skyscraper* 摩天楼を建てる.

Q one of Tokyo's ***newest*** *skyscrapers* of steel and concrete 東京最新の鉄筋コンクリート摩天楼の一. ¶***towering*** *skyscrapers* 天にそびえる摩天楼. ¶the Empire State Building, ***world's highest*** *skyscraper* 世界最高の摩天楼エンパイアステートビル.

Q² a ***forty-five-storey*** *skyscraper* 四十五階の摩天楼. ¶a ***mammoth*** *skyscraper* 大摩天楼.

slab, *n.* 石板.

Q² a ***marble*** *slab* 大理石板.

slack, *v.* ゆるむ; ゆるめる.

M *slack* ***away*** (=***out***) ゆるめる; [仕事など]手をぬく.

M² *slack* ***off*** one's efforts (speed) 努力(速力)をゆるめる. ¶*slack* (=slow) ***up*** 速度をゆるめる ‖ *slack* ***up*** [船など]速力を減じる ‖ Can't you *slack* ***up*** a little? も少しゆっくり歩けませんか.

slack, *a.* ゆるんだ.

P Business is *slack* ***at*** this season. この季節は商売が不景気だ. ¶*slack* ***in*** stays 回転のおそい(帆船が).

slacks, *n.* 〖服飾〗替ずぼん.

Q ***tailored*** *slacks* for women 婦人用の仕立ずぼん.

Q² ***corduroy*** *slacks* コールジュロイのずぼん. ¶worsted ***gabardine*** *slacks* ウステッド・ギャバずぼん.

slacken, *v.* ゆるめる.

M His pace has ***gradually*** *slackened*. 彼の歩調は次第におそくなった.

M² The freights have *slackened* ***off***. 貨物の出が減った.

P *slacken* one's pace ***to*** a walk 歩調を並足にゆるめる.

slackness, *n.* 沈滞.

P² *slackness* ***of*** trade 不景気.

slam, *v.* [ドアなど]ばたんとしめる; 《米口》酷評する.

M *slam* a door ***shut*** ドアをばたんとしめる.

M² *slam* a book ***down*** on the table 本をテーブルにばたんと置く.

P He *slammed* the door ***in*** my face. 彼は私の鼻先でドアをばたんとしめた. ‖ *slam* a ball ***into*** outfield 〖野球〗ボールを外野へ飛ばす.

slander, *n.* 悪口; 非難, ひぼう.

V ***get up*** a *slander* ざん言を仕組む.

V² the copious *slanders* ***scattered*** broadcast against ... in books and papers 書物や新聞紙で...に対してばらまいたおびただしい非難.

Q an ***absurd*** *slander* which has been spread abroad concerning him 彼に関して言いふらしたばかばかしいひぼう. ¶a most ***cruel*** *slander* 非常に残酷なひぼう. ¶To say that ... is a ***gross*** *slander*. ...と言うのははなはだしいざん言だ. ¶***journalistic*** *slanders* were spread by ... ...が新聞式の悪宣伝をやった. ¶an ***unprincipled*** *slander* 不らちなざん言. ¶The report is a ***vile*** *slander*. その報道はろう劣な中傷だ.

P² a sort of *slander* ***on*** the real Japan 真実の日本に対する一種のひぼう.

slander, *v.* ひぼうする.

M He was ***basely*** *slandered* by his enemies. 彼は敵からひどくひぼうされた.

slang, *n.* 俗語(スラング); 通り言葉; 通語.

V ***talk*** *slang* 俗語を語る. ¶***use*** *slang* 俗語を使う.

Q a bit of ***American*** *slang* 一つのアメリカ俗語. ¶***downright*** *slang* よくよくの俗語. ¶in the ***expressive*** *slang* of the Stock Exchange 株式取引所の調法な通語で. ¶Crib means *cheat* in ***students'*** *slang*. 虎は学生語でカンニングのことだ. ¶***thieves'*** *slang* 盗賊仲間の隠語.

Q² ***college*** *slang* 学生の通り言葉. ¶***gangster*** *slang* ギャングの隠語. ¶drop back into ***school*** *slang* in writing 文章を書くとき思わず学生語を使う. ¶***service*** *slang* 軍隊用語. ¶***sports*** *slang* スポーツ用語. ¶***trade*** *slang* 商売上の通り言葉. ¶***underworld*** *slang* 暗黒街の隠語. ¶" Brass " is ***U.S.*** *slang* for top-ranking officers in the Army and Navy. 「金ピカ」は陸海軍の最高級軍人をさすアメリカ俗語だ.

P² " Dough " is *slang* ***for*** " money." 「ねり粉」は「かね」の俗語だ.

slant, *n.* 傾斜.

Q an ***inward*** *slant* of the eyes あがり眼(さがり目に対し). ¶The roof has a ***sharp*** *slant* その屋根はこう配が急だ.

P ***on*** the (=a) *slant* 斜めに, 傾斜して.

slant, *v.* 傾斜する, 傾く.

M² *slant* ***off*** from the road (path) 道路(小路)からはすっかいになる.

P That picture *slants* ***to*** the right. その絵は右の方へ傾く. ¶He *slants* ***towards*** drinking too much. 彼はとかく飲み過ぎる.

slap, *n.* 平手打, 平打.

V He ***gave*** me a nice *slap* in the face. 彼は僕の顔をしたたか平手打ちした. ¶The one who lets the shuttle-cock drop ***has*** a *slap* on the back with the battledores of all engaged in the game. 羽根を落したものは競技に加わっている者全部から羽子板で背中を打たれる. ¶He ***received*** (=***got***) a *slap* in the face. 彼は平手で顔を打たれた(ひじ鉄砲を食った).

Q He hit the man a ***violent*** *slap* with the palm of his hand on the cheek. 彼は平手で激しくその男のほおを打った.

P² a *slap* ***in*** the eye 目の平手打ち ‖ a *slap* ***in*** the face 顔の平手打. ¶a *slap* ***on*** the shoulder with ... ...で肩をぴしゃりと一打.

slap, *v.* ぴしゃりと打つ.

P *slap* a person ***in*** the face 人の顔をぴしゃりと打つ. ¶I *slapped* him vigorously ***on*** the back (shoulder, cheek). 私は彼の背中(など)を強くぴしゃりと打った.

slash, *n.* 削減.

Q² a ***10 percent*** *slash* in all retail prices 小売値段一割引.

slash, *v.* 切りつける; 削る.

P He fears his salary will be *slashed* ***at*** this time of depression. 彼は不景気になると減給になりはしないかと心配している. ¶be *slashed* ***over*** the head with a cutlass 短剣で頭を切りつけられる. ¶Occupation costs to the Japanese were *slashed* ***to*** the bone. 日本の駐留軍負担は最小限度に節約された.

slasher, *n.* 削減する人.

Q² a ***budget*** *slasher* 予算を削減する人(大蔵大臣など).

slat, *n.* 細長い板.
Q a ***wooden*** *slat* 木板.
slate, *n.* 石板(スレート)；石盤.
Q a man with a ***clean*** *slate* (=record) 汚点のない経歴の人. ¶***covering*** (=***roofing***) *slate* 屋根用スレート.
Q^2 a ***paper*** *slate* 紙石盤. ¶a ***pencil*** *slate* 石盤. ¶a ***ridge*** *slate* 棟スレート.
slate, *v.* 《米》候補者名簿に登録する；予定する；《米》酷評する.
P be *slated* ***for*** the office (chairmanship) その役(など)につくことになっている. ¶be *slated* ***in*** the daily 新聞でたたかれる.
O He is *slated* to leave Japan on Jan. 10. 彼は一月十日に離日の予定だ.
slaughter, *n.* 殺りく，虐殺.
Q The Chinese were routed with ***immense*** *slaughter*. 中国軍は恐ろしく多数の死者を出して敗走した. ¶The Persians were defeated with ***terrible*** *slaughter*. ペルシア人は多数の兵を失って敗北した. 【類】a ***terrible American*** *slaughter*.
Q^2 ***mass*** *slaughter* 集団虐殺.
P The enemy was driven back ***with*** great *slaughter*. 敵は多数の兵を失って撃退された.
P^2 a *slaughter* ***of*** the innocents 罪なき者の殺りく.
slave, *n.* どれい.
V ***emancipate*** *slaves* どれいを解放する.
Q ***absolute*** *slaves* to money lenders 金貸の完全などれい(借金で苦しめられている人々). ¶a ***crowned*** *slave* 王冠をつけたどれい(王の苦境をいう). ¶***eager*** *slaves* of duty 本分を熱心に守る人. ¶a ***faithful*** *slave* 忠実などれい. ¶a ***redeemed*** *slave* 買い戻されたどれい. ¶a ***white*** *slave* 売笑婦として売られる白人の女.
Q^2 a ***galley*** *slave* 船こぎどれい. ¶the boss and his ***wage*** *slaves* 親分と彼の子分の賃銀労務者.
P They were sold ***for*** *slaves*. 彼らはどれいに売られた. ¶trade (traffic) ***in*** *slaves* どれいを売買する. ¶work ***like*** a *slave* どれいのように働く.
P^2 I could not bear to be the *slave* ***of*** a habit. 習慣のどれいになるのは忍び得ない. ‖a *slave* ***of*** fashion (opium, drugs) 流行(など)のどれい. ¶a *slave* ***to*** (=of) drinking (money) 飲酒(など)のどれい‖a *slave* ***to*** cleanliness 大のきれい好き‖a *slave* ***to*** constipation 便秘に悩む人‖a *slave* ***to*** tradition (illusion) 伝統(錯覚)にとらわれている人.【類】He is a *slave* ***to*** his passions (情欲のとりこ).
slave, *v.* どれいのように働く.
P *slave* ***for*** one's master 主人のためにあくせく働く.
slavery, *n.* どれいたること，どれいの身分.
Q ***abject*** *slavery* 浅ましいどれいの身分. ¶be in ***gilded*** *slavery* 体裁のよいどれいの境がいにある. ¶***white*** *slavery* 白人女の売春.【類】She was driven by poverty to ***white*** *slavery*.
Q^2 ***chattel*** *slavery* どれいを財産視する制度.
P He was released ***from*** *slavery*. 彼はどれいの境遇から解放された. ¶***in*** gilded *slavery* 体のいいどれいの境遇にある.
P^2 *slavery* ***to*** cigars 喫煙のどれいとなること.
slaving, *n.* どれいのように働くこと.
Q ***white*** *slaving* 白人女の売春.
slay, *v.* 殺す.
M ***treacherously*** *slay* one at a feast ひきょうにも宴会の席で人を殺す.
P He was *slain* ***in*** battle. 彼は戦死した. ¶*slay* one ***with*** a look 人を一目で殺す.
slaying, *n.* 虐殺.
Q^2 ***mass*** *slayings* 大量虐殺.
sledge, *n.* そり.
V ***steer*** a *sledge* そりを操縦する.
Q a ***dog-drawn*** *sledge* 犬ぞり.
P through Siberia ***by*** *sledge* そりでシベリアを通って. ¶go ***in*** a *sledge* そりで行く‖drive ***in*** a *sledge* そりを駆る.
sleep, *n.* 睡眠；永眠，死；静寂.
V In the middle of the night his *sleep* was ***broken*** by a strange noise. 真夜中に彼の眠りは不思議な物音で破られた. ¶***cause*** *sleep* 眠らせる. ¶***curtail*** *sleep* 睡眠時間を短縮する. ¶by ***cutting down*** *sleep* 睡眠時間を減らして. ¶***disturb*** one's sweet *sleep* 安眠を妨害する. ¶***feign*** (=***sham***) a sound *sleep* 熟睡をよそおう. ¶***forget*** *sleep* and food 寝食を忘れる. ¶He could ***get*** no *sleep*. 彼は少しも眠れなかった.【類】I didn't ***get*** much *sleep*. ¶***get back*** one's *sleep* 眠られるようになる. ¶I ***had*** (=got) a good *sleep* last night. 昨夜はよく眠った. ¶***induce*** *sleep* 眠りを催うさせる. ¶The *sleep* was ***interrupted*** by nightmares. 睡眠は悪夢のために妨げられた. ¶***lose*** *sleep* trying to decide whether ... …かを決しようとして眠れなくなる.【類】She ***lost*** her *sleep* over it. ¶unable to ***obtain*** the *sleep* for which one longs 眠ろうとしても眠れないで. ¶***produce*** *sleep* 眠らせる. ¶***promote*** *sleep* 眠りを催させる. ¶***sleep*** the *sleep* of the just 心にやましい所のない者にして得られる安らかな眠りを得る‖***sleep*** the *sleep* of death 永眠する.【類】The traveller ***slept*** the *sleep* of the weary. / ***sleep*** the ***sleep*** of the man who has done his duty. ¶***take*** *sleep* 睡眠を取る. ¶My *sleep* was ***troubled*** by dreams. 私は夢に悩まされて眠れなかった.
V^2 *Sleep* does not ***come***. 寝つけない.【類】Deep *sleep* ***came*** to him. ¶***sleep fell*** upon me 眠りに落ちた. ¶*sleep* and appetites ***improved*** 睡眠と食欲が回復した. ¶My ***sleep returned***. 私は以前のように眠れるようになった.
Q a ***broken*** *sleep* とぎれとぎれの眠り. ¶***comatose*** *sleep* こん睡. ¶fall into a ***comfortable*** *sleep* 快い眠に入る. ¶My nerves were on edge from ***curtailed*** *sleep*. 私は睡眠不足で神経がとがっていた. ¶a ***dead*** *sleep* 熟睡. ¶a ***deep*** *sleep* of exhaustion 疲れて熟睡すること‖the ***deep*** *sleep* of the city 市の静寂. ¶enjoy a ***deep, sound*** *sleep* ぐっすり安眠する. ¶a ***dreamless*** *sleep* 夢を見ない睡眠(安眠). ¶sleep the ***final*** (***eternal***) *sleep* 死ぬ. ¶two hours of ***fitful*** *sleep* 二時間の落着かない睡眠. ¶a ***fitful, tossing*** *sleep* 絶えず目がさめる悩ましい眠り. ¶Have a ***good night's*** *sleep*. お休みなさい.【類】I wish you a ***good night's*** *sleep*. ¶I was wrapped in a ***heavy*** *sleep*. 私はぐっすり寝込んだ.【類】She slept at first the ***heavy*** *sleep* of exhaustion—blessed *sleep* that came to us and lightened our sorrows. ¶a ***hypnotic*** *sleep* 催眠術をかけられての睡眠. ¶have an ***interrupted*** and ***disturbed*** *sleep* [暴風などで]おちおち寝られない睡眠. ¶a ***lengthy*** *sleep* 長寝. ¶a ***light*** *sleep* (=dog-sleep) 浅い睡眠. ¶I got a ***little*** *sleep*. 私は少し眠った. ¶have a ***long*** *sleep* 長寝をする‖Here they sleep their ***long*** *sleep*. 彼らはここに永眠する. ¶fall into a ***miraculous*** *sleep* 不思議な眠りに落ちる. ¶a ***night's*** *sleep* 一夜の眠り. ¶plunge into a ***noisy*** *sleep* たちまち寝込んでいびきをかく. ¶I slept my first ***peaceful*** *sleep* in three weeks. 三週間ぶりで始めてよく眠った. ¶a ***profound*** *sleep* 熟睡. ¶a ***quiet*** *sleep* 安眠. ¶induce ***quiet*** and ***restorative*** *sleep* 安らかに元気を回復するように眠らせる. ¶***refreshing*** *sleep* 気分をさわやかにする睡眠. ¶a ***restful*** *sleep* 気の休まる睡眠. ¶a ***sham*** *sleep* たぬき寝入り. ¶a ***short*** *sleep* 微睡. ¶a ***soft*** *sleep* まどろみ. ¶I slept a ***sound*** *sleep*. 私は熟睡した. ¶the difficulty of securing ***sufficient*** *sleep* 十分眠ることの困難. ¶have one's ***sweet*** *sleep* disturbed 安眠を妨げられる. ¶***troubled*** *sleep* 落着かない眠り. ¶a ***troubled dreamy*** *sleep* 夢ばかり見て寝苦しい眠り. ¶***unquiet*** *sleep* 不安な眠り. ¶***winter*** *sleep* [動物などの]冬眠.
Q^2 She is a society belle and takes her ***beauty*** *sleep* long after the ordinary world is astir. 彼女は社交界の麗人で世間の人が起きた後長い間美ぼうを維持するための睡眠をとる. ¶have a restless ***morning*** *sleep* 落ちつかない朝寝をする. ¶the so-called "***twilight*** *sleep*" induced during parturition 分べん時に適用されるいわゆる「黄昏睡眠」(無痛分べん法). ¶***winter*** *sleep* 冬眠.
P rouse one ***from*** one's *sleep* 目をさまさせる‖awake ***from*** one's *sleep* 目をさます.【類】awakened ***from*** *sleep*. ¶I remained ***in*** *sleep*. 私は眠ったままでいた.‖I found him ***in*** *sleep*. 私が行って見たら彼は眠っていた.‖talk ***in*** one's *sleep* 寝言を言う‖He walks ***in*** his *sleep*=He is a sleep-walker. 彼は夢遊病にかかっている.【類】He frequently started ***in*** his *sleep*. / She was murdered ***in*** her *sleep* (=while she was asleep) / talk nonsense ***in*** one's *sleep* (うわ言)‖turn round ***in*** one's *sleep* 寝返りを打つ. ¶fall ***into*** a deep *sleep* 熟睡する. ¶on account of loss ***of*** *sleep* 眠れなかったので‖Twenty hours ***of*** *sleep* out of the twenty-four are not too many for the new-born baby. 二十四時間の中二十時間の睡眠は生れたての赤ん坊にとって長すぎない. ¶fall ***on*** *sleep* 寝付く. ¶I woke up ***out of*** a sound *sleep* one night to find that ... 一夜熟睡からさめると…であった. ¶He walks ***through*** (=in) his *sleep*. 彼は寝ぼけて歩く. ¶drop off ***to*** *sleep* 寝込む‖get ***to*** *sleep* 寝付く‖put a baby ***to*** *sleep* 赤ん坊を寝かし付ける‖I read him ***to*** *sleep*. 私は本を読んで聞かせて彼を寝付かせた.‖rock (=lull) a child ***to*** *sleep* 子供を揺すって寝かせつける.【類】put a child ***to*** *sleep* / sing a child ***to*** *sleep*. ¶***with-***

out sleep 眠らずに.

sleep, *v.* 眠る; 眠って過ごす.

M *sleep **abundantly*** 十分に眠る. ¶*sleep **apart*** from each other 別々に寝る. ¶*sleep **atrociously*** ばかによく眠る. ¶He *sleeps **audibly*** and ***convincingly***. 彼は恐ろしいいびきをかく. ¶*sleep **away*** one's life (time) 一生(など)をぼんやり過ごす. 【類】*sleep **away*** the whole morning. ¶I *slept* very ***badly*** last night. ゆうべ私はろくに眠れなかった. ¶*sleep **heavily*** ぐっすり眠る. ¶*sleep **late*** in the morning 朝寝をする. 【類】*sleep **late*** into the next morning / the habit of *sleeping **late***. ¶*sleep* a day ***out*** 一日寝て暮らす. ¶*sleep **peacefully*** 安眠する. ¶*sleep* very ***restfully*** よく眠る. ¶A child *sleeps **sounder*** and ***sweeter*** in a dark than in a light room. 子供は明るい室内よりも暗い室内の方がぐっすり気持よく眠る. ¶I can *sleep **soundly***, free from fears of ... 私は...の心配なく熟睡ができる. ¶having *slept **sufficiently*** 十分眠ったので. ¶*sleep **together*** 共寝する. ¶I do not *sleep **well*** at night. 私は夜分よく眠れない.

M[2] *sleep **off*** one's headache (vexation, fatigue, disappointment) 頭痛(など)を眠って直す ‖ *sleep **off*** the effect of one's drink 寝て酔いをさます. ¶*sleep **on*** for hours 何時間も眠り続ける. ¶*sleep* the clock ***round*** 十二時間ぶっ通しに眠る.

P The sentinel was accused of *sleeping **at*** his post. 番兵はとん所で眠ったので求刑された. ¶*sleep **beneath*** the willows やなぎの下に眠る. ¶*sleep **beyond*** one's usual time 平常より寝過ごす. ¶I cannot *sleep **for*** (***from***) thinking of ... ...のことを考えて私は眠れない. ¶*sleep **in*** peace 安らかに眠る. 【類】the habit of *sleeping **in*** pyjamas / *sleep **in*** the open air (=under the open sky) ‖ His bed had not been *slept **in***. 彼は床についた形跡がなかった. ¶*sleep **like*** a top (=log) 熟睡する. ¶*sleep **on*** a pillow まくらをして眠る ‖ *sleep **on*** one's side 横向きになって眠る ‖ *sleep **on*** the job その仕事に没頭する. ¶*sleep **over*** a question before deciding it 問題をきめずに翌朝までそのままにしておく. ¶He *slept **through*** a lecture (sermon). 彼は講義(など)の済むまで眠ってしまった. ¶*sleep **with*** one's eyes open 目をあけたまま眠る(疲れて).

sleeper, *n.* 睡眠者.

V The shouts ***raised*** the *sleepers* from their beds. その叫び声で眠っていた人々は寝床から起上がった.

Q a ***good*** (***bad***) *sleeper* 熟睡のできる(できない)人. ¶a very ***heavy*** *sleeper* 熟睡する人. ¶a ***light*** *sleeper* 目ざめ勝ちな人. ¶a ***restless*** *sleeper* 落着いて眠れない人. ¶a ***sound*** *sleeper* 熟睡する人. ¶an ***uneasy*** *sleeper* 安眠のできない人.

sleeper, *n.* 〘鉄道〙まくら木.

Q[2] a ***longitudinal*** *sleeper* 縦まくら木. ¶a ***steel*** *sleeper* 鋼鉄製まくら木. ¶a ***timber*** *sleeper* 木製まくら木. ¶a ***transverse*** *sleeper* 横まくら木. ¶a ***wood*** *sleeper* 木製まくら木.

sleeplessness, *n.* 不眠.

Q ***persistent*** *sleeplessness* がん固な不眠状態.

sleepy, *a.* ねむい, ねむっているような.

M feel ***very*** *sleepy* とてもねむい.

O It was a *sleepy* village as they say. そこはいわゆる眠っている村だった.

sleeve, *n.* そで.

V ***brace back*** the *sleeves* of a dress たすきをかける. ¶***pull up*** one's *sleeve* いざという時の用意をしておく. ¶Mrs. Yasuda ***rolled*** (=***turned***) ***up*** her *sleeves* and set to work. 安田の細君はそでをまくり上げて働き出した.

Q the ***empty*** *sleeve* of a war-veteran 片腕を失った出征者兵. ¶***long flowing*** *sleeves* 長くたれたそで.

P pull (pluck, seize) a person ***by*** the *sleeve* 人のそでを引く(など). ¶conceal ***in*** one's *sleeves* そでに隠している; 奥の手がある ‖ have it ***in*** (=***up***) one's *sleeves* それをそでに入れている; 覚悟ができている ‖ laugh ***in*** one's *sleeves* かげで笑う(腹の中でわらう). 【類】weep ***in*** one's *sleeve* ‖ He works ***in*** his shirt *sleeves*. 彼はシャツ一枚になって働く. ¶embroider ***on*** one's *sleeve* そのそで口を刺しゅうする. ¶cling ***to*** one's *sleeve* 人のそでにすがる. ¶wipe away one's tears ***with*** one's *sleeve* そでで涙をふく.

P[2] a *sleeve* ***for*** the forearm 前腕をおおうそで.

sleigh, *n.* そり.

P cross ***by*** *sleigh* そりで渡る. ¶convey it ***in*** a *sleigh* そりでそれを運ぶ.

sleigh-ride, *n.* そり乗り.

P go ***for*** a *sleigh-ride*=go sleigh-riding そり乗りに行く.

sleight, *n.* 手[わざ].

Q ***forty-eight*** *sleights* in the art of wrestling 相撲道の四十八手.

slender, *a.* きゃしゃな.

P *slender **in*** build=of slender build 体格のきゃしゃな.

sleuthing, *n.* 探偵.

Q ***undercover*** *sleuthing* 秘密探偵.

slice, *n.* 薄片.

Q a ***thick*** (***thin***) *slice* of cake ケーキの厚(薄)い一切れ.

P raw fish cut ***in*** *slices* (魚肉の)刺身. ¶cut it ***into*** thin *slices* それを薄片に切る.

P[2] a *slice **of*** bread (ham, beef, cake) パン(など)の薄片.

slice, *v.* 薄く切る.

M[2] *slice **off*** pieces of a loaf パンを薄く切る ‖ *slice **off*** an end 端を薄くそぐ ‖ *slice **off*** one piece after another of Chinese territory 中国の領土を次ぎ次ぎにさん食する. ¶*slice* [***up***] a loaf of bread 一本のパンを薄く切る.

slick, *a.* すべすべした, すべりやすい.

P The road was *slick **with*** wet mud (snow and ice). 道路は泥(など)ですべりやすかった.

slide, *n.* 滑走; すべり台.

V ***have*** a *slide* on ... ...に乗って滑走する. ¶***make*** *slides* on the ice 氷すべりをする.

Q[2] be projected from ***color*** *slides* 色彩スライドを映写する. ¶a ***land*** *slide* 山くずれ. ¶a ***lantern*** *slide* 幻灯のスライド. ¶a ***paper*** *slide* 障子. ¶a ***stereopticon*** *slide* 幻灯の画板.

P slip ***on*** a *slide* すべり台の上ですべる.

slide, *v.* すべる, 滑動する; すらすらと進む.

M The years *slide **away*** swiftly. 歳月はずんずんたって行く. ¶*slide **back*** into free enterprise 自由企業に復帰する. ¶The drawers ***easily*** *slide* in and out. その引出しは楽に出し入れができる. ¶The piston *slides **noiselessly*** up and down. ピストンは音を立てずに上下に滑動する.

M[2] *slide **down*** a slide スライドを差し込む. 【類】The snow is *sliding **down*** to the river. ¶The book *slid **off*** her knee. 本が彼女のひざからすべり落ちた. ¶The thief *slid **in*** by the window. 泥棒は窓からしのび入った.

P *slide **along*** a piece of timber 一本の木材に沿ってすべって行く. ¶*slide **down*** a slope (rope) 坂(など)をすべり下る ‖ *slide **down*** the banisters 欄干をすべり降る. 【類】*slide **down*** the hill (=downhill) on a sled / Snow *slides **down*** the mountain's sides. ¶Boys *slide **for*** a pastime in winter. 子供らは冬はすべって遊ぶ. ¶*slide **into*** the first base 一塁にすべり込む ‖ *slide **into*** sin (evil ways) 知らず識らず罪悪(など)に陥る. 【類】*slide **into*** a bad habit. ¶*slide **on*** the ice 氷上をすべる. ¶*slide **over*** the surface of the water 水面をすべるように進む. ¶A boat *slides **through*** the water. 舟が水を分けてするすると進む.

slight, *a.* きゃしゃな.

P She is *slight **of*** figure (=stature). 彼女は姿がきゃしゃだ.

slim, *a.* 細い.

O It's a *slim* excuse. そんな言いわけはだめだ. ‖ This will make you appear *slimmer* and more graceful. [広告] これを御使用になればほっそりして姿もよくなります.

slime, *v.* ぬるぬるする.

P *slime **out of*** the grip つかんだ手から抜け出る. ¶*slime **through*** fingers 指からすべり抜ける.

sling, *n.* 投石機; つり包帯.

P *sling* a stone ***at***... 石を...に投げる. ¶He had to carry his arm ***in*** a *sling*. 彼は腕につり包帯をかけねばならなかった. ‖ with his right arm ***in*** a *sling* 右腕につり包帯を掛けて. ¶throw stones ***with*** a *sling* ぱちんこで石を投げる.

sling, *v.* 投げる; [肩などに]かける.

P having race-glasses *slung **across*** one's shoulder 競馬用眼鏡を肩にかけて. ¶*sling **into*** one's coat 外とうをひっかける. ¶*sling* it ***over*** one's shoulder 肩越しにそれを投げる.

slink, *v.* こっそり行く.

P *slink **into*** a back seat こっそり後方の席にさがる.

slip, *n.* すべること; 過失; 細長い紙片; 一片; 〘服飾〙スリップ.

V He ***gave*** his creditors the *slip*. 彼は借金取りをはずした. ¶***hold together*** *slips* by an elastic band ゴムひもで紙片をくくる. ¶***Give*** me a *slip* of paper. 紙切れを一枚下さい. ¶He has ***made*** several *slips* in his translation. 彼は大分誤訳をした. 【類】***make*** a big *slip* in one's calculation as to ... / ***make*** a *slip* of the tongue (pen). ¶The film ***received*** the white *slip*, which means total rejection. その

映画は白書せんを受取った, これは全然不認可という検閲係からの通知である. ¶She ***wears*** a *slip* under her dress. 彼女は服の下にスリップを着ている.

Q by a ***curious*** *slip* of the editorial pen 編集者の妙な書誤りで. ¶a ***trifling grammatical*** *slip* 細かな文法上の誤りで. ¶a ***mere*** *slip* of a girl 娘っこ. ¶***trifling*** *slips* 小さな過失. ¶He was an ***undersized*** *slip*. 彼は小柄なきゃしゃな男だった.

Q² a ***complaint*** *slip* 修理請求票(借家人などの). ¶an ***identification*** *slip* attached to a dead body 死体に付けた身元鑑定票. ¶***pillow*** *slips* まくらおおい. ¶a ***rejection*** *slip* 不受理投稿返送用せん. ¶a ***voting*** *slip* 投票用紙.

P ***by*** a *slip* of the pen 書誤りで. ¶He wrote something ***on*** a *slip* of paper. 彼は紙きれに何か書いた.

P² a *slip* ***in*** pronunciation 発音の間違い ‖ A few *slips* ***in*** youth are inevitable. 若いときには少しの過失は免れない. ¶a *slip* ***of*** earth＝a land-slide 地すべり ‖ a *slip* ***of*** memory (the tongue) 記憶(など)の誤り. 【類】a *slip* ***of*** the pen ‖ a *slip* ***of*** paper 細長い紙片. ¶He had a *slip* ***on*** [the] ice. 彼は氷の上で一度すべった.

slip, *v.* すべらせる; すべる; そっと抜ける; 失錯する.

M *slip* ***away*** beyond recall [機会など]取返しのつかないようにすーっと去る ‖ The time is *slipping* ***away***. 時がずんずんたって行く. ‖ The guests began to *slip* ***away***, one by one, unnoticed. 客は一人一人そっと抜け出し始めた. ¶I must *slip* ***out*** to post a letter. 手紙を出しにちょっと出なければならない. 【類】He *slipped* ***out***, nobody knew when. ¶*slip* ***quietly*** underground 静粛に地下潜行に移る.

M² *slip* ***down*** from one's chair いすからすべり落ちる ‖ The spoon *slipped* ***down*** from the table. さじが食卓からすべり落ちた. ¶Errors are sure to *slip* ***in***. とかく間違は起りやすい. ¶*slip* ***off*** (***on***) one's coat (shoes) 上衣(など)を急いでぬぐ(着る) ‖ Her shawl *slipped* ***off*** with a gust of wind. 彼女のショールが一陣の風ですべり落ちた. 【類】My shoes *slipped* ***off*** when I started running.

P *slip* ***between*** the sheets [ベッドの]敷布の間へすべり込む ‖ *slip* a marker ***between*** the pages しおりをページの間にさす. ¶*slip* ***from*** memory 失念する ‖ *slip* ***from*** a buoy ブイを離れて出港する. ¶The motor-car *slipped* ***in*** the mud. 自動車が泥の中へすべり込んだ. ‖ He *slipped* ***in*** (＝into) the house. 彼はそっと家へはいった. ‖ He often *slips* ***in*** his grammar. 彼は時々文法で間違いをする. ¶*slip* a bill ***into*** another hand 札を握らせる. ¶She *slipped* the note ***into*** her pocket (hand). 彼女はその手紙をポケット(など)にそっと入れた. 【類】*slip* five shillings ***into*** the woman's hand / *slip* one's feet ***into*** one's slippers / a little book which can easily be *slipped* ***into*** quite a small pocket / *slip* poison ***into*** one's drink ‖ *slip* ***into*** obscurity 次第に世間から忘れられる ‖ *slip* a few things ***into*** a handbag ハンドバッグに二三の品を入れる. ¶The trolley *slipped* ***off*** the wire. トローリー・バスが架線からはずれた. ‖ *slip* ***off*** the chiff がけをすべり落ちる. ¶the laughter of a street urchin at the sight of a fat gentleman *slipping* ***on*** a banana peel バナナの皮ですべった肥満紳士を見た町のいたずら小僧の笑い声 ‖ *slip* ***on*** the ice (stairs) 氷(など)の上ですべる. ¶easily *slip* ***out of*** the memory すぐに忘れる ‖ My purse has *slipped* ***out of*** my pocket. 私は財布を落した. 【類】The lamp *slipped* right ***out of*** my hand. ‖ The word *slipped* ***out of*** my mouth before my thought. 私はひょっくり口がすべった. ‖ Its elaborate mechanism *slipped* ***out of*** order. その複雑な機構がちょっと狂った. ‖ She gave me a peek (＝peep) and *slipped* ***out of*** the room. 彼女は私をのぞいて室からそっと出て行った. ¶*slip* a letter (money) ***to*** a person 手紙(など)を人にそっと握らせる. ¶The opportunity *slipped* ***through*** his fingers. 彼はその機会を逸した. ¶*slip* ***under*** a mosquito net かやの中へもぐり込む.

slippers, *n.* 室内ぐつ.

Q² ***bed*** *slippers* 寝室用ばき.

P be ***in*** *slippers* 室内ぐつをはいている. ☞日本語のスリッパーに近いものは scuffs という. scuffs: loose-fitting house slippers without heels and counters (かかと皮).

slit, *n.* 細長い穴.

V ***open*** a narrow *slit* of window 窓を細目に明ける. ¶A *slit* is ***provided*** for the coin to drop through. 銭を投入するための細長い穴が明けてある.

P² a *slit* ***in*** a letter-box 郵便受けの口 ‖ a *slit* ***in*** a bag かばんの口.

slogan *n.* 標語.

Q a ***favorite*** *slogan* of the advocates of ... ...の擁護者たちの得意の標語. ¶a ***national*** *slogan* 国民の標語.

Q² a ***propaganda*** *slogan* 宣伝標語. ¶the "***See America First***" *slogan* [海外旅行の前に]「まずアメリカを見よ」という標語.

P the 2nd week was celebrated ***under*** the *slogan* "..." 第二週が...の標語の下に行われた. 【類】Fight cancer with knowledge—***under*** this *slogan* the women of America are uniting in the first national campaign to fight cancer and its allies, fear and ignorance.

slop, *n.* 汚水.

V ***empty*** the *slop* 汚水をあける.

Q² ***kitchen*** *slops* 台所の汚水.

slop, *v.* こぼれる.

M *slop* ***out*** (＝***over***) こぼれる.

slope, *n.* 斜面; 傾斜, こう配; 坂路, 坂.

V It ***has*** a general *slope* from west to east. それは一体に西から東へ傾斜している.

Q ***forest-clad*** *slopes* 樹木のある山腹. ¶a ***gentle*** *slope* ran up from the beach to the entrance of his villa. 海浜から彼の別荘の入口までなだらかな登り坂になっていた. ¶***grassy*** *slopes* of a mountain 草の茂った山の面. ¶an ***upward*** (***downward***) *slope* 上(下)り坂.

Q² a ***skiing*** *slope* スキーをする斜面. ¶on a ***steep*** *slope* 急斜面で. ¶***terraced mountain*** *slopes* ひな壇状になっている山の斜面.

P ***at*** (＝***in***) a *slope* 傾斜して, 斜に. ¶go ***down*** (***up***) a *slope* 坂を下って(上って)行く. ¶trees growing ***on*** the *slopes* of a mountain 山の斜面に生じる樹木. ¶***with*** a *slope* 斜めにして, 斜めになって.

P² The *slope* ***of*** the roof is low. 屋根のこう配が低い. ¶a *slope* ***with*** a gentle gradient だんだら坂.

slope, *v.* 傾斜する, 坂になる.

M The road *slopes* ***gradually*** to the village. その道路は村の方へ段々下り坂になっている. ¶*slope* ***rapidly*** 急に傾斜する.

M² The valley *slopes* ***down*** to the sea. その谷は海の方へ傾斜している. ¶*slope* ***upwards*** (***downwards***) 上(下)り坂になる.

P *slope* eastward ***into*** the Pacific Ocean 東に傾斜して太平洋に面している. ¶the turf which *slopes* ***to*** the river 川の方へ坂になっている芝地.

slot, *n.* 細い穴(硬貨入れの).

P put a coin ***in*** a *slot* 硬貨を細穴に入れる. ¶drop a nickel ***into*** a *slot* 穴に五セント白銅を一つ入れる.

slot, *v.* あとをつける.

M² be *slotted* ***in*** 穴まで追い込まれる(きつね狩りなどで獲物が).

sloth, *n.* 怠慢.

V ***induce*** *sloth* 怠慢を生じさせる.

slothful, *a.* 怠ける.

P *slothful* ***in*** business 仕事を怠ける.

slough, *n.* ぬかるみ.

P stuck up ***in*** a *slough* ぬかるみにはまって.

P² sink in a *slough* ***of*** despondence 絶望(のふち)に沈む.

slough, *n.* [へびなどの]抜けがら.

Q find a ***cold*** *slough* ***hot*** 空巣かと思ったら人がいた.

slough, *v.* 脱ぎ捨てる.

M² *slough* ***off*** old customs (prejudices, bad habits) 古い習慣(など)を捨てる.

slovenly, *a.* だらしのない.

P He is *slovenly* ***in*** his dress (habits, appearance). 彼は服装(など)がだらしない.

slow, *a.* のろい, 遅鈍な, 遅れて.

M ***Dead*** *slow*.〘掲示〙最徐行(道路標識). ¶***despairingly*** *slow* がっかりするほどのろい. ¶***desperately*** *slow* in results 気抜けがするほど成績が上らない. ¶The progress is ***discouragingly*** *slow*. 進行がのろいので張合がない. ¶You are ***painfully*** *slow* with your figures. 君は計算がいかにものろい. ¶My watch is ***three minutes*** *slow*. 私の時計は三分遅れている. ¶My watch is five minutes ***too*** *slow*. 私の時計は五分遅れている. ¶Oxford is ***traditionally*** *slow* to move. オクスフォードは伝統的に行動が緩慢だ.

P He is *slow* ***at*** arithmetic (＝accounts). 彼は計算がのろい ‖ Things are *slow* ***at*** the office. 事務所は万事スロモー

だ. ‖ He is *slow* ***at*** learning. 彼は物覚えが悪い. 【類】He is very *slow* ***at*** his work (business). ¶*slow* ***in*** coming 来るのがおそい ‖ *slow* ***in*** current 流れがのろい; [金融·気流·流行など]緩慢な. 【類】*slow* ***in*** progress (moving, payment) / I am very *slow* ***in*** understanding, but once in my head, I never forget it. ¶He is *slow* ***of*** understanding (=apprehension *or* wit). 彼は血のめぐりがにぶい. 【類】be *slow* ***of*** learning / He is *slow* ***of*** speech (foot). / one hour *slow* ***of*** the time.

O *slow* to recognize (mature) なかなか認識(成熟)しない. ¶He is *slow* to sympathize with the sufferings of others. 彼は仲々他人の難儀に同情しない. ‖ He is *slow* to take offense. 彼は容易に怒らない. ‖ He was not *slow* to take advantage of it. 彼はいち早くそれを利用した. ‖ He was not *slow* to say so. 彼は遠慮なくそうだといった.

slow, *v.* おそくなる.

M^2 The train *slowed* ***down*** (=up) and stopped. 汽車は速度がゆるくなって止まった. 【類】*slow* ***down*** efficiency / be *slowed* ***down*** to twenty miles an hour / The wheel *slowed* ***down*** / *slow* ***down*** the car=do not run the car so fast / *slow* ***down*** reconstruction / The increase in ... has now *slowed* ***down***. / A small quantity of alcohol *slows* ***down*** a man's reactions. / The economic machine is likely to *slow* ***down***. ¶*slow* ***up*** (=down) 速度が落ちる ‖ The car *slowed* ***up*** over the bridge. 自動車が橋の上で速力をゆるめた. ‖ *slow* ***up*** the nation's export business その国の輸出業を緩漫にする ‖ *Slow* ***up*** while you're driving through a city street. 街路を走る間は速力を落せ.

O the *slowing* down of enthusiasm 熱のさめて来ること.

slugger, *n.* 〘野球〙強打者.

Q^2 a ***hurricane*** *slugger* すごい強打者.

sluice, *v.* 流す.

M^2 *sluice* ***off*** 側へよける, 別にしておく; 除く.

P Water *sluiced* ***down*** the channel. 水が海峡をどんどん流れた.

slum, *n.* 貧民くつ.

Q^2 the poor in a ***West-end*** *slum* [ロンドンの]ウェストエンドの貧民くつの貧民たち.

P^2 the *slums* ***of*** a large city 大都市の貧民くつ.

slumber, *n.* 睡眠.

V ***break*** our *slumber* われらの睡眠を破る. ¶***disturb*** the *slumbers* of ... ...の安眠を妨害する.

Q a ***deep*** *slumber* 熟睡. ¶a ***profound*** *slumber* 深い眠り. ¶a most ***refreshing*** *slumber* 非常に気持のよい眠り. ¶a ***sweet*** *slumber* 快い眠り. ¶fall into a ***troubled, broken*** *slumber* 不安な眠りに入る.

Q^2 an ***open-air*** *slumber* 戸外の睡眠.

P He is lost ***in*** *slumber*. 彼はぐっすり寝込んでいる. ¶fall ***into*** a *slumber* 寝入る.

slumber, *v.* 眠る.

M *slumber* ***away*** one's life 人生を無為に過す. ¶*slumber* ***healthily*** すこやかに眠る. ¶*slumber* ***heavily*** 熟睡する.

P a volcano that has *slumbered* ***for*** centuries 何世紀も爆発しない火山(休火山).

slumming, *n.* 貧民くつ訪問.

Q^2 a ***curate*** *slumming* 牧師の貧民くつ視察.

slump, *n.* 暴落, がら落.

V ***bring about*** a heavy *slump* in prices 物価の非常な暴落をきたす.

Q as a result of the ***bad*** *slump* in business 商売がひどく不振に陥った結果. ¶There was a ***great*** *slump* in the price of railway shares in the market. 市場で鉄道株の大暴落があった. ¶The speculative sentiment is wiped out as a result of the ***recent unprecedented*** *slump*. 近ごろの空前の暴落で投機心は一掃された. ¶a ***severe*** *slump* in the price of ... ...の物価の非常な暴落. ¶the ***worst*** *slump* in ten years ここ十年間最悪の不景気.

Q^2 ***business*** *slump* in the theatre 劇場の事業不振. ¶***price*** *slumps* (jumps) 物価の急落(はね上り).

P^2 a *slump* ***in*** the trade その商売における物価の大暴落. 【類】a *slump* ***in*** prices ‖ a *slump* ***in*** flour メリケン粉の暴落. ¶the recent *slump* ***on*** the Japanese share markets 日本の株式市場の最近の暴落.

slump, *v.* 落ちる, 暴落する.

P *slump* ***in*** a chair いすにどかっとすわる. ¶It *slumped* ***to*** $50. それが五十ドルに暴落した.

slur, *n.* 汚点.

V ***cast*** a *slur* on one's character 人の評判に汚点をつける.

P a *slur* ***on*** one's reputation 名折れ ‖ There is no *slur* ***on*** his career. 彼の一生には全く汚点がない. 【類】This is a *slur* ***on*** his good name.

slur, *v.* 軽く取扱う.

M ***hurriedly*** *slur* over the subject その題目を(深入りしないで)あっさり片付ける.

P Never *slur* ***over*** your work. 自分の仕事を決していい加減にするな. 【類】be *slurred* ***over*** (made light of) as trivial.

slush, *n.* 雪どけ.

P The streets are slick (=slippery) ***with*** *slush*. 街路が雪どけですべりやすい.

sly, *a.* 内証の.

P She received letters, ***on*** the *sly*, from young men. 彼女はこっそり若い男から手紙を受取った. ‖ He often bought opium ***on*** the *sly*. 彼は度々内証でアヘンを買った.

smack, *n.* 香味; なまかじり.

V He ***has*** a *smack* of bravado. 彼にはいなせな所がある. ‖ ***have*** a *smack* of ginger しょうがの味がする. 【類】It ***has*** a *smack* of novelty about it.

P^2 a *smack* ***of*** learning なまかじりの学問.

smack, *v.* ...の味がする; ...臭い.

M *smack* ***strongly*** of ... 大いに...を思わせる.

P His talk *smacks* ***of*** Buddhism. 彼の話は仏教臭い. 【類】It *smacks* ***of*** the nineteenth century (古くさい). / have a *smack* ***of*** Buddhism / *smack* ***of*** the cask / His speech *smacks* ***of*** affectation (気取り). / His manner *smacks* ***of*** pride. / His talk *smacks* ***of*** the sea (船乗らしい). / His manner *smacks* ***of*** self-conceit (うぬぼれっ気).

smack, *n.* 舌打; 平打; 音の高いキッス.

V ***get*** a *smack* on the face 顔をぴしゃりと打たれる. ¶She ***gave*** him a *smack*. 彼女は音を立てて彼にキッスした. ¶He ***hit*** me a *smack* upon the shoulder. 彼は私の肩をぴしゃりと打った. ¶He ***planted*** a resounding *smack* on her glowing cheek. 彼は彼女の真赤なほおに音がするほど(強い)キッスをした.

Q a ***sounding*** *smack* ぴしゃりと音がするほどの平打ち.

P ***with*** a *smack* 舌打ちして. 【類】kiss her lips ***with*** a *smack*=smack her lips.

P^2 a *smack* ***on*** (=***of***) the lips キッス.

smack, *v.* 舌打ちする.

P *smack* one's lips ***over*** *saké* 酒を舌打して賞味する.

small, *a.* 小さい; 小量の.

M ***distressingly*** *small* 痛ましいほど小さな[数など]. ¶***infinitesimally*** *small* ごく小さい. ¶The price is ***ridiculously*** *small*. 代価がおかしいほど安い. ¶use a ***surprisingly*** *small* vocabulary 使う語いが恐ろしく少ない. ¶The house is ***too*** *small* for the family. その家では手ぜまだ.

P The boy is *small* ***for*** his age. その男の子は年の割に小さい. ¶*small* ***in*** number (quantity, stature, size, price) 数(など)の少ない(わずかな). ¶He is *small* ***of*** his age (=years). 彼は幼少だ.

smallness, *n.* 小さいこと.

Q written in letters of ***microscopic*** *smallness* 顕微鏡で見るほどの細字で書いた.

smallpox, *n.* 天然痘.

V ***have*** [the] *smallpox* 天然痘にかかる ‖ be immune ***from*** *smallpox* as the result of vaccination 種痘しているので天然痘にかからない.

P suffer ***from*** *smallpox* 天然痘にかかる. ¶He was taken ill ***of*** *smallpox*. 彼は天然痘にかかった ‖ should a case ***of*** *smallpox* occur in the neighborhood 天然痘が近所に発生したときは ‖ owing to the prevalence ***of*** *smallpox* 天然痘流行のため. ¶He was seized ***with*** *smallpox*. 彼は天然痘にかかった.

smart, *n.* 痛み.

V^2 The *smart* began to ***go off***. 痛みがとれだした.

P^2 the *smart* ***of*** a cut 切りきずの痛み.

smart, *a.* 気がきいている, スマートな; 抜目のない.

M He looks ***quite*** *smart* in his uniform. 彼の制服姿は全く気がきいている.

P He is *smart* ***about*** business. 彼は商売には抜目がない. ¶He is *smart* ***in*** all things. 彼は万事に抜目がない. ‖ *smart* ***in*** dress (appearance)=smartly dressed (=attired) スマートな服装をして.

smart, *v.* ずきずき痛む; 傷心する.

M The cut *smarts* ***terribly*** (=***violently***). 切り傷がひどく痛む.

P *smart* ***at*** remarks made by ... ...の言葉に憤慨する. ¶You shall *smart* ***for*** this. このことで君に痛い思いをさせてやる(いまに見ていろ). ¶still *smarting* ***from*** the memories of ... ...のにがい経験が今に忘れられないで. ¶*smart* under a sense of injustice 不正義を痛感する. ¶smart with pain 痛みを覚える. 【類】smart with a burn (cut) ‖ smart with neglect 怠慢を痛感する.

smarten, *v*. スマートにする.

M^2 smarten oneself up めかす.

smash, *n*. 粉砕.

P come (go) to smash ぺちゃんこになる.

smash, *v*. みじんに砕く; こなごなになる.

P smash (=rush) in for seats どっと座席奪いに押掛ける. ¶The glass fell and was smashed into a dozen pieces. コップが落ちて粉みじんになった. ¶smash a person on the nose 人の鼻を強打する. 【類】The dishes dropped and smashed on the floor. ¶smash onto the rocks 暗礁に乗りあげる. ¶smashed to atoms (pieces, splinters, bits) 粉みじん(など)になった.

smatterer, *n*. 半可通.

Q a mere smatterer 生(なま)物識り.

smattering, *n*. なまかじり, 聞きかじり.

V acquire a smattering of the Japanese language 日本語を少しかじる. ¶He has a smattering of Latin. 彼はラテン語を少しかじっている. 【類】have a smattering of knowledge in ... / have a smattering of English literature. ¶obtain a smattering of superficial knowledge on many subjects 色々のことを生かじりする. ¶possess a smattering of the technical terms in use in one's special profession 特別の職業で使う専門語を聞きかじっている.

P^2 a smattering of several languages 数カ国語の生かじり. 【類】a smattering of scientific subjects.

smear, *n*. よごれ.

P^2 there is a smear of blood on the cloth. その布地に血こんがついている. 【類】a smear of oil (grease, paint).

smear, *v*. 塗る; 塗ってよごす; よごれる.

M smear away (=out) 塗りつぶす. ¶It smears easily. それはすぐよごれる.

P smear with oil (mud) 油(など)を塗る ‖ be smeared with blood 血まみれになる ‖ smear the wall with finger-marks (Indian ink) 指跡(など)で壁をよごす.

smell, *n*. きゅう覚; 香, 臭気.

V I cannot bear (=stand) the smell of tobacco. 私はタバコのにおいが我慢できない. ¶destroy (=remove) bad smell 臭気を消す. ¶disguise a smell 臭気を紛らす. ¶exude a smell 香を発する. ¶give a nice smell 良い香を発する. ¶give off an offensive smell いやな臭気を放つ. ¶give out (=emit) a smell 香気を放つ. ¶have a smell 香がする. ¶mask (=drown) the unpleasant smell いやなにおいを消す. ¶notice a sulfurous smell 硫黄のにおいに気がつく. ¶overpower a smell においを消す. ¶perceive the smell その臭気に気がつく. ¶smell a smell of cooking 料理のにおいがして来る. ¶take a smell at ... ...を一度かぐ. ¶A breeze wafts the smell of roses. 風がばらの香を吹き送る.

V^2 A faint smell of ... hangs in the air. ...のかすかな香が空中にただよう. 【類】All over the house there hangs a smell of fresh (塗りたての) paint.

Q an agreeable (a disagreeable) smell よい(いやな)におい. ¶It has an agreeable aromatic smell. それは気持のよいこうばしい香がする. ¶its awful smell その恐ろしい臭気. ¶a bad smell 悪いにおい. ¶a burnt smell きな臭いにおい. ¶a close smell むっとするにおい. ¶a disgusting smell いやなにおい. ¶a faint smell かすかなにおい. ¶a fetid smell むれくさい臭気. ¶a fish-like smell なま臭いにおい. ¶a foul smell いやなにおい. ¶What a horrid smell! いやなにおいだなあ. ¶What a nasty smell of gasoline it leaves behind it! 後に残るガソリンの臭気といったら実に胸がむかむかする. ¶a not-unpleasant smell あまりいやでもないにおい. ¶an objectionable smell いやなにおい. ¶The streets are not very clean and in some the smells are offensive. 市街は清潔な方ではなく所によってはいやなにおいがする. ¶have no perceptible smell, either good or bad 良いにも悪いにも気のつくほどの香はない. ¶a pleasant smell 芳香. ¶there began to be a pleasing smell of ... ...のうまそうな香がし始めた. ¶It has a pungent and nauseous smell. つんとした胸の悪くなるようなにおいがする. ¶a putrid smell 腐っているにおい. ¶repugnant (=repulsive) smells いやなにおい. ¶a savory smell おいしそうな香. ¶give off a very strong smell はなはだ強いにおいを発する. ¶strong musky smell 強いじゃ香のような香. ¶a sweet smell 芳香. 【類】The sweet smell of the hay rose to my window. ¶an unforgettable smell of fresh paint 鼻についた新しいペンキのにおい. ¶have an unpleasant smell いやなにおいがする. ¶a villainous smell 毒々しいにおい.

P He has an acute sense of smell. 彼は鼻がよくきく. ‖ a fine sense of smell 鋭敏なきゅう覚 ‖ It is destitute of smell. それは臭気がない. ¶agreeable to the smell 香の良い. ¶a colorless liquid with a sweet smell 香の良い無色液. ¶a liquid without smell 無臭の液体.

P^2 There is a smell of gas. ガスのにおいがする. 【類】the smell of a rose / There is a smell of cooking.

smell, *v*. かぐ; 香がする, 臭い.

M smell awful 恐ろしく臭い. ¶This meat smells bad. この肉は生きの悪いにおいがする. ¶It smells delicious. うまそうな香がする. ¶I smell it faintly. 私にはその香がかすかにする. ¶The butter smells quite good. そのバタはいいにおいがする. ¶He smelled horribly of cigar and wine. 彼は恐ろしくタバコと酒のにおいがしていた. ¶It smells musty. かび臭い. ¶The dish smells nice. そのお料理はおいしそうなにおいがする. ¶smell offensive (agreeable) いやな(よい)香がする. ¶smell out another's secrets 他人の秘密をかぎ出す. 【類】smell out a thief ‖ smell it out into purity それを精錬する. ¶The milk smells sour. その牛乳は酸い. ‖ smell sour 酸いにおいがする. ¶A rose (violet, lily) smells sweet. ばら(すみれ, ゆり)は香がよい. ¶smell strongly ぷんぷんにおう. ¶smell violently ひどくぷんぷんする.

P smell at a bottle びんをかいで見る. 【類】smell at a flower. ¶smell like musk じゃ香のような香がする. ¶smell of burning きなくさい ‖ smell of drink 酒臭い ‖ smell of fish 生臭い ‖ The plan smells of something tricky. その計画はいんちきのような感じがする. 【類】The knife smells of onions. / His breath always smells of strong tobacco. / smell of sweat / Just smell of this flower. / smell of something burning (いぶり臭い). ¶We smell with our noses. われわれは鼻でかぐ.

smile, *n*. 笑顔, 微笑; 喜色.

V arouse a smile にこにこさせる. ¶I couldn't check a smile. 私は微笑を禁じ得なかった. ¶conceal the smile that played over his features 彼の顔にちらと現われた微笑を隠す. ¶crack a smile にっこり笑う. ¶draw (=evoke) a smile from the surly Mr.— 気むずかしい—さんをにこにこさせる. ¶exchange smiles with ... ...と微笑をかわす. 【類】exchange smiles and greetings. ¶excite a smile on the life of ... [運命の神が]...の生がいにほほえみかける. ¶force a smile 作り笑いをする. ¶grin a ghostly smile にたりとすごい笑いをもらす. ¶She had a kind smile on her face. 彼女はやさしくにこにこ笑った. ¶provoke smiles 微笑を催させる. ¶She put a smile into her voice. 彼女はほほほと笑い声を立てた. ¶put on one's best smile できるだけにこにこしてみせる. ¶raise a smile by force 無理に笑わせる. ¶receive a welcome smile from ... ...ににこにこ迎えられる. ¶I could not repress a smile at ... 私は...を見て(聞いて, など)微笑を禁じ得なかった. ¶I couldn't resist a smile for the life of me. 自分はどうしても微笑を禁じ得なかった. ¶He did badly at trying to suppress a smile. 彼は笑わずにいようとしたがうまく行かなかった. ¶She threw me a radiant smile. 彼女は私に晴々しい笑顔を向けた. ¶wear a smile on one's face にこにこしている. ¶to win a smile from ... ...の微笑を得ようとして.

V^2 A smile beamed over his countenance. 微笑が彼の顔に輝いた. ¶A smile came to the lips of the patient. その病人はにっこり笑った. ¶A faint smile crept across his face. 彼はかすかに笑った. ¶Smiles of derision faded from their faces. ちょう笑は彼らの顔から次第に消えて行った. ¶A little smile, half a grin, flickered on his face. にやりと薄笑いが彼の顔にちらっと浮んだ. ¶A smile passed over his face. 彼はにっこり笑った. ¶A pleasant smile spread over his face. 彼は満面に微笑をたたえた.

Q an accommodating smile 人をそらさない笑顔. ¶with an amused smile おもしろそうに笑顔をして. ¶an angelic smile 天使のような微笑. ¶an apologetic smile 申訳がないという微笑. ¶the saint's face wore a beatific smile. その聖者は天福に輝く笑顔をしていた. ¶a beautiful smile 美しい笑顔. ¶a benevolent smile 好意の微笑. ¶a benignant (=benign) smile やさしい笑顔. ¶She gave him a be-

witching** smile*. 彼女は彼にようえんな笑顔を見せた. ¶with a ***bland** smile* にこにこして. ¶a ***bright** smile* of welcome 明朗な歓迎のえみ. ¶with a ***broad** smile* on his face 満面に微笑をたたえて. ¶His ***charming** smile* is worn only for public. 彼の愛きょう笑いは人前に出た時だけだ. ¶a ***complacent** smile* 満足の微笑. ¶a ***contemptuous** (=**disdainful**) smile* 軽べつ的な笑い. ¶with a ***coquettish** smile* あだっぽい笑顔をして. ¶a ***cordial** smile* 心からのえみ. ¶a ***cryptic** smile* 薄気味の悪い笑い. ¶a ***cynical** smile* 皮肉なえみ. ¶derisive** smile* あざけりの笑い. ¶an ***engaging** smile* 愛きょうのある微笑. ¶She forced a ***faint quivering** smile*. 彼女は口びるをふるわせて無理に笑い顔をした. ¶A ***faint, wistful** smile* lightened her brooding face. 懐しそうなかすかな笑いが彼女の思案顔を明るくした. ¶a ***fatherly** (**motherly**) smile* 慈父(母)らしい微笑. ¶a ***forced** smile* 作り笑い. 【類】She hid her concern with a ***forced** smile*. ¶***fortune's** smile* 好運. ¶the ***frank** smile* and instant bow of recognition きさくな微笑と即座のお辞儀. ¶approach a customer with a ***friendly** smile* 愛想笑いをしながらお客に近づく. ¶a ***genial** smile* 晴れやかな微笑. ¶smile a ***grim** smile* うすきみ悪くにやっとする. ¶A ***happy** smile* spread across her face. うれしそうな微笑が彼女の顔をほころばせた. ¶a ***healthy** smile* すこやかな微笑. ¶an ***illuminating** smile* 晴晴した微笑. ¶an ***incredulous** smile* [信じられないといった]疑いの笑い. ¶an ***innocent** smile* 罪のない(天真らんまんな)微笑. ¶an ***ironical** smile* 皮肉な微笑. ¶hold a ***kind** smile* on her face 彼女の顔にやさしい微笑をたたえる. ¶a ***kindly** smile* やさしい笑顔. ¶a ***merry** smile* 上気げんの笑顔. ¶a ***mocking** smile* 冷笑. ¶a ***modest** smile* つつましやかな微笑. ¶a ***patronizing** smile* mingled with a little disdain 人をこばかにしたような恩人ぶった微笑. ¶a ***piquant** smile* 気にさわる微笑. ¶a ***pitying** smile* 哀れむような微笑. ¶with a ***pleasant** smile* にこにこして. ¶a ***pretty** (=**lovely**) smile* かわいらしい笑顔. ¶a ***provoking** smile* しゃくにさわる微笑. ¶a ***quizzical** smile* からかい半分の笑い. ¶a ***radiant** smile* 明るい微笑. ¶a ***refulgent** (=gloriously bright) smile* ほがらかな微笑. ¶He broke into a ***reminiscent** smile*. 彼は思いだし笑をした. ¶A ***sad** smile* passed over her tear-marked face. 彼女の涙にぬれた顔に悲しそうな微笑が浮んだ. ¶a ***sardonic** smile* 皮肉な笑い, 冷笑. 【類】with a ***sardonic** smile* upon his lips. ¶a kind of ***satanic** smile* 一種悪魔的な笑い. ¶a ***satirical** smile* 皮肉な微笑. ¶a ***self-satisfied** smile* 会心の微笑. ¶a ***saucy** smile* 図々しい微笑. ¶a ***senile** smile* 老人の微笑. ¶a *smile* almost ***seraphic*** in its beauty ほとんど天使の美しさを持つ微笑. ¶a ***serene** smile* 静かな微笑. ¶a ***set** smile* 作り笑い. ¶a ***sickly** smile* 病人のような弱々しい微笑. ¶I met with a ***skeptical*** and ***sneering** smile* at my innocence and lack of worldly understanding. 私が世間知らずなので相手は半信半疑のあざけるような微笑をした. ¶wear a ***slight** smile* かすかにほほえむ. ¶a ***sly** smile* しのび笑い. ¶a ***sparkling** smile* 輝やかしい微笑. ¶A ***sunny** smile* beautifies a countenance. 陽気な笑は顔を美化する. ¶view it with a ***supercilious** smile* ばかにして相手にしないといった微笑をもってそれを見る. ¶with a ***sweet** smile* 愛らしくにっこりして. ¶a ***sympathetic** smile* 同情的な微笑. ¶a ***taking** smile* ほれぼれする微笑. ¶a ***toothy** smile* 歯を見せた笑い. ¶a ***wan** smile* 陰気な微笑. ¶receive a ***welcome** smile* from ... ...から暖い微笑で迎えられる. ¶a ***winning** (=engaging) smile* 愛きょうのある微笑. ¶a ***winsome** smile* 愛くるしい微笑. ¶a ***wry** smile* 苦笑.

Q² smile a broad "***I-told-you-so***" *smile*「だから言わないことじゃない」というような遠慮のない笑顔をする. ¶a ***saccharine** smile* 甘ったるい微笑. ¶a ***suave, man-of-the-world** smile* 人をそらさない世なれた微笑.

P She smiled a tired sort ***of** smile*. 彼女は疲れたような微笑をもらした. ¶He replied ***with*** a *smile*. 彼は微笑しながら答えた. 【類】a face beaming ***with*** a *smile* ‖ ***with*** a *smile* of triumph 得意そうににこにこして ‖ ***with*** a *smile* that spoke volumes of gratitude 微笑の中に多大の感謝をこめて ‖ He passed me ***with*** a *smile* of recognition. 彼はにっこり会釈して私の前を通り過ぎた.

P² There was a forced *smile* ***on*** his countenance. 彼は不自然な笑顔を見せていた. ‖ with a *smile* ***on*** (=***upon***) his lips 口のあたりに微笑を浮べて. ¶go to martyrdom with a *smile* ***upon*** one's lips にっこりして教えの道に殉じる ‖ Fortune began to *smile* ***upon*** him. 彼に運が向いてきた.

smile, *v.* 微笑する; 冷笑する.

M *smiling* ***all over*** 満面微笑の. ¶*smile* ***alluringly*** 人目を引くようににっこりと笑う. ¶*smile* tears (grief, fear) ***away*** にっこりして涙(など)を隠す. ¶*smile* ***back*** at ... ...をにこにこ見返す. ¶*smile* ***benignly*** 優しく微笑する. ¶*smile* ***bitterly*** 苦笑する. ¶*smile* ***charmingly*** at ... ...に愛きょう笑いをする. ¶*smile* ***coyly*** はにかんで微笑する. ¶***faintly** smiling* 薄笑いして. ¶*smile* ***frankly*** あけっぱなしにこにこする. ¶*smile* ***broadly*** 相好をくずして微笑する. ¶*smile* ***contemptuously*** ちょう笑する. ¶*smile* ***disdainfully*** 軽べつ的に微笑する. ¶*smile* ***faintly*** かすかに微笑する. ¶*smile* ***fatuously*** 無意味にほほえむ. ¶*smile* ***genially*** ほがらかに微笑する. ¶*smile* ***grimly*** すごく笑う. ¶*smile* ***happily*** うれしげにほほえむ. ¶*smile* ***hideously*** きみ悪く笑う. ¶*smile* ***incredulously*** 疑っているようにせせら笑う. ¶*smile* ***knowingly*** 心得顔に微笑する. ¶*smile* ***mechanically*** わけもなくほほえむ. ¶***patronizingly** smile* 先輩顔でほほえむ. ¶*smile* ***radiantly*** 朗かに微笑する. ¶*smile* ***sadly*** 悲しげに微笑する. ¶*smile* ***sardonically*** せせら笑う. ¶*smile* ***seductively*** たらし込むように微笑する. ¶*smile* ***slyly*** こうかつに微笑する. ¶*smile* ***sweetly*** 愛らしくにっこり笑う. ¶*smile* ***sympathetically*** 共鳴してほほえむ.

M² His wife *smiled* ***down*** from the balcony. 彼の妻は露台からにっこりした顔を下に向けた. ¶*smile* tears ***up*** にっこりして涙をかくす.

P She *smiled* ***at*** him. 彼女は彼に微笑を投げた. ‖ I *smiled* ***at*** her credulity (ignorance). 彼女の軽信(など)には笑ってしまった. 【類】What are you *smiling* ***at***? ‖ *smile* ***at*** his menace (threats) 彼のおどかしを一笑に付す. 【類】He only *smiled* ***at*** the idea. / It is *smiled* ***at*** as most desirable in itself, but absolutely out of the question as a practical problem. ¶*smile* ***in*** his face 彼の顔をじっと見てにっこりする. ¶She *smiled* ***on*** him. 彼女はにこにこして彼をながめた. ‖ Fortune at length *smiled* ***on*** him. 終に彼に運が向いて来た. ¶He *smiled* all ***over*** his face. 彼は満面に微笑をたたえた. ¶*smile* ***through*** one's tears 涙を流しながら微笑する. ¶She *smiled* ***to*** me from her window. 彼女は窓から私に微笑を投げた. ¶craftily *smile* ***upon*** him 彼に向ってずるそうに笑う. 【類】Fortune began to *smile* ***upon*** him. ¶*smile* ***with*** admiration 感心してほほえむ.

smirch, *v.* けがす.

P He is *smirched* ***with*** dishonor. 彼は不名誉を身に負っている.

smite, *v.* 打つ; ひどい目にあわせる.

M *smite* a person ***dead*** 人をたたき殺す. ¶He is ***deeply*** (=***greatly***) *smitten* with her beauty. 彼はすっかり彼女の色香に迷っている. ¶He is ***quite*** *smitten* with the girl. 彼はぞっこんその娘にほれこんだ. ¶*smite* the hands ***together*** 両手を打つ. ¶He was ***violently*** *smitten* with her at first sight. 彼は一目で彼女にまいった.

M² *smite* ***off*** one's head 首を打ち落す.

P He was *smitten* ***by*** (=with) paralysis. 彼は中風にかかった. ¶A sound *smote* ***on*** my ear. 音が強く私の耳に響いた. ¶He is *smitten* ***with*** amazement (her charms). 彼は驚き(など)に打たれた. ‖ He has been *smitten* ***with*** the plague. 彼は疫病にかかった. ‖ a city *smitten* ***with*** pestilence 疫病にわざわいされた都市.

smith, *n.* かじ屋(人).

Q a ***sooty** smith* すすだらけのかじ屋.

Q² a ***village** smith* 村のかじ屋.

smithy, *n.* かじ屋.

Q² a ***village** smithy* 村のかじ屋.

smock, *n.* 〚服飾〛上っ張り(スモック).

Q an ***artist's** smock* 画家の仕事着.

P a salesgirl ***in*** her navy blue *smock* こん色のスモックを着た女店員.

smog, *n.* 《米》煙霧.

V² A heavy *smog* was ***hanging*** low over the city. 重い煙霧がその都市に低くたれこめていた.

smoke, *n.* 煙, ばい煙; 喫煙.

V Tall chimneys ***belch*** (=***vomit***) ***forth*** *smoke*. 高い煙突が煙を吐き出す. ¶***emit*** black *smoke* 黒煙を吐く. ¶***enjoy*** a *smoke* 一服やる. ¶***evolve*** *smoke* 煙を出す. ¶***force*** tobacco *smoke* on the public 公衆にタバコをしいる. ¶***give forth*** (=***off or out***) *smoke* 煙を出す. ¶***have*** (=***take***) a *smoke* 一服やる. ¶produce a cigar-case and ***offer*** a person a *smoke* 葉巻のケースを出して人に一服進める. ¶***pour***

forth *smoke* 煙を放出する. ¶***produce*** *smoke* 煙を発する. ¶***puff*** *smoke* 煙をぱっぱっと吐く. ¶***puff out*** (=***off***) *smoke* [機関車が]ぱっぱっと煙を出す. ¶***remove*** *smoke* ばい煙を除く. ¶I do ***smell*** *smoke;* where is it? くすぶるにおいがするがどこだろう.

V^{2} The *smoke* is ***ascending*** slowly from the chimney. 煙突から煙が昇っている. ¶The *smoke* is ***coiling up.*** 煙が渦を巻いて昇っている. ¶the *smoke* which ***issues*** from cigars and pipes and cigarettes 葉巻やパイプや紙巻たばこから出る煙. ¶With *smoke* ***pluming*** from her four great red funnels, the liner was steaming across the ocean. 四本の赤い大煙突から煙を吐きながらその定期船は大洋を航行していた. ☞ a plume of smoke (ふわふわ浮ぶ煙). ¶The *smoke* ***rises*** in the air. 煙が空にのぼる.

Q a column of ***black*** *smoke* 黒煙の柱. ¶a ***choking*** *smoke* むせっぽい煙. ¶a ***heavy*** *smoke* すさまじい煙. ¶There is ***no*** *smoke* without some fire. 火のない所に煙はない. ¶have a ***quiet*** *smoke* after ... …後に落ちついて一服やる. ¶a ***snatched*** *smoke* 暇をぬすんでの一服. ¶a scent of ***stale*** *smoke* from cheap cigars 安葉巻の古臭い煙の香.

Q^{2} blackened with ***powder*** *smoke* 火薬の煙で黒くなった.

P He was stifled (=choked) ***by*** *smoke.* 彼は煙にむせんだ. ¶dry [a fish] ***in*** *smoke* くん製にする ‖ a herring cured ***in*** *smoke* くん製にしん ‖ He was enveloped ***in*** *smoke.* 彼は煙に包まれた. ‖ The plan has ended ***in*** *smoke.* その計画は煙と消えた. ‖ vanish (=disappear) ***in*** *smoke* 煙と消える. ¶volumes ***of*** *smoke* もうもうたる煙. 【類】puff clouds ***of*** *smoke* ‖ a puff ***of*** *smoke* ぽっと出る煙. ¶fumigate rooms ***with*** *smoke* 煙で室をいぶす. ¶The room was filled ***with*** *smoke.* 室内に煙がもうもうとこもっていた. ‖ be stained ***with*** *smoke* (=smoke-stained) 煙でくすんでいる.

P^{2} the *smoke* ***from*** a volcano (fire, cannon) 火山(など)の煙.

smoke, *v.* いぶす; 喫煙する; 煙る.

M *smoke* ***away*** one's time 喫煙で時間をつぶす ‖ sit *smoking* ***away*** たばこをくゆらしてすわる. ¶*smoke* ***freely*** 自由に喫煙する. ¶*smoke* very ***heavily*** 盛に喫煙する. ¶*smoke* ***out*** mosquitoes (a fox) 蚊(きつね)をいぶし出す. ¶*smoke* ***placidly*** ゆう然とたばこをふかす. ¶*smoke* oneself ***sick*** たばこを吸って気分が悪くなる. ¶He *smokes* ***too much.*** 彼はたばこを吸い過ぎる.

P *smoke* ***to*** excess 過度に喫煙する.

smoker, *n.* 喫煙家.

Q a ***confirmed*** *smoker* やめようとしてもやめられない喫煙家. ¶a ***discerning*** *smoker* [品質に対し]批判力のある愛煙家. ¶an ***enthusiastic*** *smoker* 大の喫煙家. ¶a ***great*** *smoker* 大の喫煙家. ¶a ***habitual*** *smoker* 常習の喫煙家. ¶a ***hard*** *smoker* 大の喫煙家. ¶a ***hardened*** *smoker* 常習的の喫煙家. ¶A man who smokes more than six Havana cigars in the day is a ***heavy*** *smoker.* 一日にハバナ葉巻を六本以上吸う人は大の愛煙家だ. 【類】Asked if he had any vices, she replied that he was a ***heavy*** *smoker.* ¶an ***incorrigible*** *smoker* 矯正し難い喫煙家. ¶***inveterate*** *smokers* who cannot exist without tobacco タバコなくしては生きていられない手におえない喫煙家. ¶a ***light*** *smoker* 軽度の喫煙家. ¶a ***passionate*** *smoker* 激しい喫煙家. ¶a ***persistent cigarette*** *smoker* 執ような葉巻の喫煙家. ¶a ***tremendous*** *smoker* どえらい喫煙家.

Q^{2} a loyal ***Camel*** *smoker* キャメルの愛用者. ¶a ***chain*** *smoker* 連続的にくゆらす喫煙家. ¶a ***cigar*** *smoker* 葉巻の愛用者. ¶a ***pipe*** *smoker* パイプの喫煙家.

smokestack, *n.* 煙突.

Q a ***tall*** *smokestack* of a steel mill (steamer, locomotive) 鉄工場(など)の高い煙突.

smoking, *n.* 喫煙.

V No *smoking* ***allowed.*** 禁煙. ¶***give up*** *smoking* タバコをやめる. ¶***knock*** off *smoking* 喫煙をやめる. ¶Do you ***mind*** *smoking?* タバコを吸ってもいいですか. ¶*Smoking* is ***prohibited*** in the school buildings. 校舎内での喫煙は禁じられている. ‖ "*Smoking* ***prohibited.***" 禁煙[掲示]. ¶He never ***stops*** *smoking* for a moment. 彼は少しもタバコを離さない. ¶***suppress*** cigarette *smoking* among little boys 少年の喫煙を禁止する.

Q ***excessive*** *smoking* 過度の喫煙. ¶***incessant*** *smoking* 間断ない喫煙. ¶***juvenile*** *smoking* 少年の喫煙. ¶"***No*** *smoking.*" 禁煙[掲示].

Q^{2} ***cigarette*** and ***pipe*** *smoking* 巻タバコとパイプタバコの喫煙.

P I am fond ***of*** *smoking.* 私はタバコが好きだ. ¶I cannot bear to be ***without*** *smoking* for a moment. ちょっとの間もタバコを吸わずにいられない.

smo[u]lder, *v.* くすぶる.

M The faggots ***simply*** *smolder* and do not burn. その薪たばはいぶるだけで燃えない.

P *smolder* ***for*** hours after the blaze dies down 炎が消えてからなん時間もいぶっている.

O smell something *smoldering* きなくさい.

smooth, *a.* なめらかな.

M ***as*** *smooth* as satin しゅすのようになめらかな.

P Milk is delightfully *smooth* ***on*** the palate. 牛乳は舌ざわりがよい. ¶*smooth* ***to*** the touch すべすべした.

smooth, *v.* なめらかにする.

M *smooth* ***away*** difficulties (troubles) 困難(など)を克服する. ¶*smooth* ***out*** the unevenness でこぼこを直す ‖ *smooth* ***out*** difficulties 困難を打開する. 【類】*smooth* ***out*** wrinkles.

M^{2} *smooth* ***down*** hair 髪をなでつける ‖ *smooth* ***down*** a quarrel けんかをなだめる. 【類】*smooth* (=calm) ***down*** one's anger (passion, enthusiasm). ¶*smooth* ***over*** difficulties 困難を和げる.

P *smooth* the way ***for*** a contract (treaty) 契約(など)の進捗を進める.

smoothness *n.* なめらかさ.

V ***lack*** *smoothness* なめらかでない.

Q ***velvety*** *smoothness* ビロードのようななめらかさ.

smother, *v.* 窒息させる; 包む.

M The smoke has ***almost*** *smothered* me. 私は煙でほとんど息がつけなかった.

M^{2} The scandal was *smothered* ***up.*** 疑獄事件はもみ消された ‖ *smother* ***[up]*** a yawn あくびをかみ殺す. 【類】The recommendation of the committee was *smothered* ***up.***

P I was *smothered* ***by*** the crowd. 人込にもまれて私は息もつけなくなった. 【類】be *smothered* ***by*** smoke (dust). ¶The cottage was *smothered* ***in*** green foliage. 小屋はすっかり青葉に包まれていた. ¶He was *smothered* ***to*** death. 彼は窒息して死んだ. ¶*smother* a fire ***with*** ashes 灰をかけて火をいける ‖ She *smothered* me ***with*** a kiss. 彼女はキッスで私を息もつけなくした. 【類】He was *smothered* ***with*** smoke.

smudge, *n.* しみ, よごれ; 《米》いぶし火.

V ***make*** a *smudge* to drive away insects いぶし火をつくって虫を追い出す. ¶We ***saw*** a *smudge* of smoke far out on the horizon. はるか水平線上に一条のけむりを見た.

smudge, *v.* 《米》いぶす.

M *smudge* mosquitos ***out*** 蚊をいぶり出す.

P *smudge* it ***out of*** existence それをいぶし殺す.

smuggle, *v.* 密輸出(入)する.

M, M^{2} *smuggle* ***abroad*** 密輸出する. ¶try to *smuggle* ... ***in*** …をそっと中へ入れようとする.

P *smuggle* opium ***into*** the country アヘンをその国に密輸入する ‖ *smuggle* a letter ***into*** a person's hand 人の手に手紙をそっと渡す. 【類】*smuggle* a person ***into*** a meeting. ¶*smuggle* a bag ***out of*** the room へやからそっとカバンを持出す. ¶*smuggle* him ***through*** the window 窓から彼をそっと出す.

smuggler, *n.* 密輸入者.

P a ring ***of*** *smugglers*=a smuggling ring 密輸入団.

smuggling, *n.* 密輸入.

Q ***organized*** *smuggling* of aliens into this country 外人の組織的密輸入.

Q^{2} a hidden industry—***arms*** *smuggling* 秘密産業—武器密貿易.

smutch, *v.* 汚す.

P *smutch* (=smudge) ***with*** soot すすで汚す.

snack, *n.* 大急ぎの食事; おやつ.

V ***eat*** a *snack* between meals 間食をする. ¶I ***took*** a hasty *snack* of cold meat and bread. 冷肉とパンを大急ぎで食べた.

snag, *a.* 沈み木; 暗礁.

V ***strike*** a *snag* 沈み木(または暗礁)にぶっつかる.

P He ran ***against*** a *snag* in his enterprise. 彼は事業で暗礁に乗り上げた.

snail, *n.* かたつむり.

Q^{2} a ***father*** *snail* 父のかたつむり.

P move on slowly ***like*** a *snail* 牛の歩みを続ける.

snake, *n.* へび.

V You can ***pick up*** a *snake* by holding it behind its head and using the other hand to grab the body and the tail. 頭の後ろの所を持ち片方の手で胴と尾をつかまえるとへびをつまみ上げることができる.

V^2 A snake coils up. へびはとぐろを巻く. ¶A snake is crawling away in the grass. へびがのそのそ草の中へはいって行く. ¶Snakes hiss. へびはしゅーという. ¶The snake uncoiled itself and crawled slowly away. へびがとぐろを解いてのろのろとはって行った.

Q a poisonous snake 毒へび. ¶a venomous snake 毒へび.

snap, n. ぽきっと折れること; ぽきっ, ぱちり, ぴしゃっ[音]; 《米》[写真の]早取り; 酷寒.

V make a snap at ... …にかじり付く. ¶take a snap of ... [写真機で]…のスナップをとる. 【類】Hold on (=Stop) there! I'll take a snap of you.

Q The cold snap continued for several days. 寒い天気が数日続いた. ¶a severe snap ひどく寒い陽気.

P The stick broke with a snap. そのつえがぽきっと折れた. ‖ shut a book with a snap 本をぴしゃっと閉じる ‖ move with snap and energy てきぱきと動く.

P^2 the snap of glass ガラスがぴちんとわれる音 ‖ a snap of whip むちのぴしっという音.

snap, v. ぽきっと折れる; ぱっくりと食いつく; がなりつける; 《米》[写真]スナップをとる.

M snap the lever back to its original position てこをもとの位置にパチンと戻す ‖ He snapped back at me, saying, "..." 彼は私に「…」としっぺい返しをした. ¶His nerves snapped there. 彼の意力もそこでぽきんとくだけた.

M^2 snap off the handle of a cup 茶わんのとってをぽきっと折る. 【類】snap off the tail. ¶snap up a bone [犬など]骨に食い付く. 【類】The dog snapped up the meat. / They are snapped up by collectors at high prices. ‖ The merchant ship was snapped up by a cruiser of the enemy. その商船は敵の巡洋艦に不意にだ捕された. ‖ Don't snap him up so fiercely. そんなにひどく彼にがなりつけるな.

P snap at ... …にとびつく, 食いつく; …に小言をいう ‖ The dog snapped at the visitor. 犬は来客にかみ付いた. ‖ snap at the chance 機会をとらえる ‖ snap one's fingers at ... …を指弾する, べっ視する. 【類】"What's it for?" he snapped at me. / A big fish snapped at bait (えさ). ¶Snap into it. 《米口》ぐずぐずするな, てきぱきやれ. ¶Snap out of it. 《米口》よせ, やめろ. ¶snap off a twig 小枝をポキッと折る. ¶snap on a stopwatch ストップ・ウォッチを動かす. ¶snap up the meat 肉に飛びつく.

snapshot, n. 早取写真.

V develop and print snapshots 早取写真を現像して焼付ける. ¶get (=take or spread) a snapshot of ... …を早取写真に取る.

snare, n. わな.

V avoid the snare so craftily set 非常に巧みにかけたわなを避ける. ¶escape a snare わなから抜ける. ¶lay (=set or spread) a snare for ... …のわなをかける ‖ fall into the snare spread for ... by ... …が…を目的にかけたわなにかかる.

P a wild cat caught by a rabbit snare うさぎわなにかかった山ねこ. ¶catch ... in a snare わなで…を捕える. 【類】feel like a rabbit taken in a snare. ¶allure a lion into a snare わなにライオンをおびき込む.

snarl, v. うなる.

P snarl at a person [犬など]人にうなりかかる. 【類】The dog snarls at a stranger.

snatch, n. 引っつかみ; 断片; 少時.

V eat a snatch ひと口食う. ¶give a snatch at ... …をぱっとひったくる. ¶I heard snatches of their conversation. 私は彼らの談話をとぎれとぎれに聞いた. ¶make a snatch at a flying ball 飛球を捕ろうとする ‖ make snatches at the truth 色々と真相をつかまえようとする. ¶overhear snatches of conversation 談話をところどころ立聞きする. ¶take a snatch 食物を急いで食べる.

Q a short snatch of verse 詩の短い一節.

P work (read) by snatches ときどき思い出したように働く(読書する).

P^2 have a snatch of sleep ちょっと居眠りをする ‖ snatches of song 歌のきれぎれの文句.

snatch, v. ひっつかむ, ひっさらう.

M He was snatched away by premature death. 彼は若死にした. 【類】The death suddenly snatched away his mother. / snatch away a bag from a passer-by / All his hope was snatched away. ¶hastily snatch up one's camera 写真機を引っさらう.

M^2 The wind snatched my hat off. 風が私の帽子をひっさらって行った.

P He snatched at the book. 彼はその本をひったくろうとした. ‖ snatch at a straw わらにでもつかまろうとする ‖ snatch at an opportunity (offer) 機会(など)をつかまえようとする. 【類】snatch at the reflection / snatch at the chance to make money from ... ¶moments snatched from a busy life 忙中に得た零細な時間 ‖ He snatched the hand-bag from (=out of) her hand. 彼は彼女の手から手さげかばんをひったくった. 【類】snatch a victory out of ... / snatch a person out of danger.

sneak, v. そーっと去る.

M sneak away from company 人中からそーっと脱け出る.

M^2 sneak about for a chance to steal a dog 犬を盗む機会をうかがってこっそり歩き回る. ¶sneak in (out) そーっと入る(出る) ‖ sneak in on a person こっそり会いにやって来る. ¶sneak off into dark corners こっそり暗い片すみへ隠れ去る.

P sneak to a corner こっそりと片すみに隠れる.

sneakers, n. 《米》ゴム底の運動ぐつ.

P walk in sneakers ゴム底ぐつをはいて歩く.

sneer, n. 冷笑, あざけり.

Q a veiled sneer 包み隠したあざけり.

P respond with a sneer 冷笑して答える ‖ sting a person with sneers さげすんで人を刺す.

P^2 with a sneer of contempt 軽べつ的に冷笑して.

sneer, v. 冷笑的に言う; 冷笑する.

M sneer his fame away 彼の名声をちょう笑し去る. ¶sneer back an answer 冷笑的な返答をする. ¶sneer him down 彼をこき下ろす.

P sneer at religion (learning) 宗教(など)を冷笑する ‖ sneer at his speech 彼の演説を冷笑する. ¶sneer him into insignificance 彼をくそみそにこき下ろす. ¶sneer him out of countenance 彼を冷笑して面目を失わせる.

sneeze, n. くしゃみ.

V emit a formidable sneeze 恐ろしいくしゃみをする.

sneeze, v. くしゃみをする; 《口語》軽べつする.

M sneeze violently ひどくくしゃみをする.

P sneeze at another's opinion 他人の説を軽べつする. 【類】This is not to be sneezed at.

sneezing, n. くしゃみ.

V do one's sneezing くしゃみをする.

sniff, v. 鼻でにおいをかぐ.

M sniff something burning 何か焦げくさい. ¶sniff out the trace of ... …の足跡をかぎ出す. ¶The dog sniffed suspiciously at a stranger. 犬は見知らぬ人をうさん臭そうにくんくんかいだ.

P sniff at ... …をかいで見る, 鼻をくんくんいわせる; …を軽べつしてかかる.

snigger, n. くすくす笑い.

Q a subdued snigger 抑えつけたくすくす笑い.

snips, n. はさみ.

Q^2 tin snips ブリキばさみ.

snobbery, n. 俗物根性.

Q intellectual snobbery 学者ぶる俗物根性.

snoop, v. 《米口》のぞきまわる.

M^2 snoop around from door to door 家から家へとうろつき回る. 【類】a dog snooping around for food.

P snoop for information [刑事などが]聞込みをやる.

snooper, n. のぞく人.

Q an inquisitive snooper しつっこく聞きただす人. ¶a sly snooper 油断のならない空巣ねらい.

snooze, n. うたた寝.

V take a snooze (=nap) うたた寝する.

snooze, v. のらくらする.

M snooze away one's time のらくらと時を過す.

O snooze while on a train 列車でいねむりする.

snore, v. いびきをかく.

M snore oneself awake いびきで目をさます. ¶snore horribly 恐ろしくいびきをかく. ¶snore loudly 大きないびきをかく.

snorer, n. いびきをかく人.

Q a terrific snorer 恐ろしくいびきをかく人.

snow, n. 雪.

V bear snow [山頂など]雪をいただいている. ¶clear away (=off) the snow 雪を取片づける. ¶We had snow last night. ゆうべ雪が降った. ‖ We shall have snow. 雪が降るでしょう. ¶knock the snow from one's shoes くつの雪をたたき落す. ¶The snow was piled in great drifts. 雪が吹だまりになって積っていた. ¶shovel snow from the pavement 舗道の雪をかく. ¶thaw away snow 雪を融かす. ¶The sky threatens snow. 空は雪模様だ.

V^2 There the *snow* often ***drifts*** to a depth of fifteen or twenty feet. そこでは雪が往々十五フィートから二十フィートも吹きだまりになっている. ¶About once in ten years *snow* ***falls*** on Mexico City. メキシコ市では十年に一度位雪が降る. 【類】The *snow* was ***falling*** thickly (=thick and fast).. ‖ The *snow* ***fell*** in a whirl. 雪はまんじともえに降りしきった. ¶*Snow* ***flurries***. 雪がひらひら飛ぶ. ¶In October the first *snow* ***flies***. 十月には初雪が降る. ¶Does the *snow* ever ***lie*** in Tokyo? 東京では雪が積るか. ‖ The *snow* ***lay thick*** on the ground. 雪が厚く積っていた. ¶Five to six feet of *snow* ***remains*** on the ground for weeks on end. 五六フィートの雪が幾週間も消えずにいる. ¶The *snow* is ***thawing***. 雪が融けている.

Q ***deep*** *snow* 深雪 ‖ the *snow* two feet ***deep*** 深さ二フィートの積雪. ¶in ***driving*** (=***blinding***) *snow* ふぶきの中を. ¶***everlasting*** *snow* 千古の雪. ¶freshly ***fallen*** *snow* 新たに降った雪. ¶in the ***falling*** *snow* 雪の降る中で. ¶We had the ***first*** *snow* of the season yesterday. きのう初雪が降った. ¶a ***heavy*** *snow* 大雪. ¶***lingering*** *snows* 残雪. ¶a region of ***perpetual*** *snow* 年中雪のある国. ¶mountain-tops covered with ***unsoiled*** *snow* 清浄の雪でおおわれた山頂. ¶***virgin*** *snow* 処女雪.

Q^2 ***glacier*** *snow* (=***névé*** *or* ***firn***) 万年雪.

P It is buried ***in*** *snow*. それは雪に埋もれている. 【類】He perished ***in*** the *snow*. / be buried deep ***in*** the *snow*. ¶footprints ***in*** the *snow* 雪中の足跡. ¶It looks ***like*** *snow*. どうやら雪になりそうだ. ¶a fall ***of*** *snow* 雪の一降り ‖ a storm ***of*** *snow*=a snow-storm 暴風雪 ‖ The town is under many feet ***of*** *snow*. その市は幾尺も雪の下になっている. ¶***on*** the *snow* 雪の上で. ¶travel ***through*** the *snow* 雪の中を旅行する. ¶Tokyo ***under*** the *snow* 雪の東京 ‖ be buried deep ***under*** the *snow* 深く雪に埋もれる. 【類】Kyoto's famous cherrytrees ***under*** spring *snow*. ¶The road is covered ***with*** *snow*. 道は雪に埋まっている. ‖ Mount Asama was crowned ***with*** *snow* on May 8th. 五月八日浅間山に降雪があった.

snow, *v*. 雪で閉ざす; 雪が降る.

M It is *snowing* ***fast***. どんどん雪が降っている. ¶It *snows* ***hard***. 大雪だ. ¶It *snowed* ***heavily*** last night. ゆうべは大雪だった. ¶It ***seldom*** *snows* in Tokyo. 東京は滅多に雪が降らない.

M^2 We were *snowed* ***in***, in a railway train. われわれは汽車内に雪で閉じこめられた. 【類】be *snowed* ***in*** all winter. ¶The train was *snowed* ***under***. 汽車は雪で埋まった. ‖ His opponent was *snowed* ***under*** (=defeated by an overwhelming majority). 《俗》彼の敵は圧倒的多数で負けた. ‖ The desk was *snowed* ***under*** by letters and cards of complaint. 机の上は苦情の投書が山積していた. 【類】The Democrats were *snowed* ***under*** in that election. ¶The train was *snowed* ***up***. 汽車は雪で閉じこめられた.

P It is *snowing* ***in*** great flakes. 綿のような雪が降っている. ¶*snow* ***with*** a mingling of rain 雨まじりの雪が降る.

snowball, *n*. 雪だま, 雪つぶて.

V ***fling*** *snowballs* at ... ...に雪だまをぶつける. ¶***roll*** a *snowball* 雪球をころがして作る.

V^2 A *snowball* ***gathers*** as it goes on. 雪球はころがって行くうちに大きくなる.

P play ***at*** *snowballs* 雪合戦をやる.

snowfall, *n*. 降雪.

Q We have ***frequent*** *snowfalls* in this part. この辺はよく雪が降る. ¶a ***heavy*** (***light***) *snowfall* 大(小)雪. ¶a ***slight*** *snowfall* in srping 春の淡雪.

Q^2 ***paper*** *snowfall* [歓迎などの]紙ふぶき.

P^2 There was a *snowfall* ***of*** from 5 to 15 inches. 五インチから十五インチの降雪があった.

snowflake, *n*. 雪片.

V^2 *Snowflakes* are ***dancing*** in the air. 雪片がひらひら舞っている.

Q ***feathery*** *snowflakes* 羽毛に似た雪片.

snow-line, *n*. 雪線.

V The *snow-line* is ***found*** at about 10,700 feet. その雪線は約一万七百フィートのところにある.

snowman, *n*. 雪だるま.

V ***make*** (=***build***) a *snowman* 雪だるまを作る.

Q a ***half-thawed, disfigured*** *snowman* 融けかかって形のくずれた雪だるま.

snowshoe, *n*. 雪ぐつ.

P walk ***in*** *snowshoes* 雪ぐつをはいて歩く.

snow-storm, *n*. 吹雪.

Q in a ***blinding*** *snow-storm* 目のあけられないふぶき中に. ¶a ***protracted*** *snow-storm* 長引いたふぶき.

P^2 a *snow-storm* ***of*** cherry blossoms 花ふぶき.

snuff, *n*. かぎタバコ.

V Do you ***take*** *snuff*? かぎタバコをおやりですか.

P a pinch ***of*** *snuff* 一つまみのかぎタバコ.

snuff, *v*. [ろうそくなどの]心(しん)を切る; 香をかぐ.

M The lives of 161 men, women, and children have been *snuffed* ***out*** (=died). 百六十一人の男女小児が落命した.

M^2 *snuff* ***up*** one's nose 鼻をくんくんさせる.

P The dog *snuffed* ***at*** the track of the fox. 犬がきつねの通った道をかいだ.

snug, *a*. 安楽な, 居心地のいい.

M We are ***very*** *snug* here. われわれはここで非常に居心地よくしている.

P The baby lay *snug* ***in*** its cradle. 赤ん坊は気持よくゆりかごの中に寝ていた. 【類】He is very *snug* in his new quarters (今度の住い).

O a *snug* little cottage こじんまりした小屋.

snuggle, *v*. 寄り添う.

M^2 *snuggle* ***up*** to her lover 愛人のもとにすりよる.

P *snuggle* ***against*** a person 人に寄り添う.

so, *ad*. その通りに.

M ***just*** (=***precisely or exactly***) *so* その通り ‖ It is ***just*** *so* with me. 僕もその通り. ¶*So* ***long***! 失礼. ¶*So* ***much*** for today. [先生が]きょうはこれでおしまい. 【類】*So* ***with*** a man of humble birth like me. ¶***quite*** *so* 全くその通り.

O *so* to speak (=say) いわば.

soak, *v*. 浸す, つける; しみ込む.

M I was ***thoroughly*** *soaked*. 私はびしょぬれになった. ¶It is *soaking* ***wet***. それはびしょぬれだ.

M^2 A sponge *soaks* ***up*** water. 海綿は水を吸込む.

P *soak* dirty clothes ***in*** water ぬれた着物を水につける. 【類】*soak* bread ***in*** broth (肉汁) / bread *soaked* ***in*** milk / be *soaked* ***in*** the surf (波) ‖ *soak* oneself ***in*** ... ...に夢中になる. ¶The idea *soaked* ***into*** him. 彼にその思想がしみ込んだ. ¶*soak* ***through*** a carpet (cushion, cloth) [水やインクが]じゅうたん(など)にしみ込む. 【類】The water *soaks* its way ***through*** the soil (=earth). ¶I was *soaked* to the skin (=bone). 私はびしょぬれになった. ¶*soak* a sponge ***with*** water 水を海綿に含ます. 【類】*soak* a book ***with*** a scent. ‖ He was *soaked* ***with*** rain (water). 彼は雨(など)でびしょぬれになった.

soap, *n*. 石けん.

V^2 This *soap* ***lathers*** so nicely. この石けんはすばらしくあわ立ちがよい.

Q an ***evil***(=***ill***)***-smelling*** *soap* においの悪い石けん. ¶***hard*** (=***insoluble***) *soap* 硬質石けん. ¶a ***scented*** *soap* 香料入り石けん. ¶***soft*** *soap* 軟質石けん.

Q^2 ***bath*** *soap* 浴用石けん. ¶a piece of yellow ***laundry*** (=washing) *soap* 黄色洗たく石けん一個 ‖ a stick of ***laundry*** *soap* 洗たく用棒石けん一本. ¶***liquid*** *soap* 液体石けん. ¶***palm-oil*** *soap* やし油製石けん. ¶***toilet*** and ***shaving*** *soap* 洗顔用及びひげそり用の石けん. ¶***whale oil*** *soap* 鯨油製石けん.

P a cake ***of*** *soap* 石けん一個. ¶wash ***with*** *soap* [and water] 石けんで洗う.

P^2 a fine *soap* ***for*** laundry work 上等洗たく石けん

soar, *v*. 空中高く飛ぶ; 高くそびえる.

M *soar* ***high*** [建物・山など]高くそびえる.

M^2 The prices seemed *soaring* ***up*** without limit. 物価が無限に騰貴するように思われた.

P A skylark *soars* ***above*** the clouds. ひばりは雲の上をかける. ¶Her hope *soared* ***at*** the news. そのニュースで彼女の希望が高まった. ¶*soar* ***in*** price as a result of ... ...の結果として価格が暴騰する. ¶*soar* high ***into*** the air 空高く飛び上がる. ¶Their ambitions *soared* ***to*** the skies. 彼らは雄志天を突く概があった. ¶*soar* ***on*** the wing 翼で飛ぶ. ¶The aeroplane (eagle) *soared* ***through*** the air. 飛行機(など)が空中をかけた. ¶Its summit *soars* ***to*** an enormous height. その頂上は非常に高くそびえる. ‖ The mountain *soars* ***to*** heaven above all rivals. その山が群峰の上に高くそびえている. 【類】Miss Hutcheson, New York actress who *soared* ***to*** stage stardom (一流の舞台俳優の域) in "Alice in Wonderland." ¶The eagle and kite can *soar* ***without*** flapping their wings. わしととびは羽ばたきせずに飛べる.

sob, *n*. しゃくり泣き, むせび泣き.

Q in ***broken*** *sobs* とぎれるしゃくり泣きをして. ¶***deep, con-***

vulsive *sobs* burst forth from ... ...が激しいけいれん的なしゃくり泣きをし出した. ¶***spasmodic*** *sobs* しゃくりあげ泣き.

P She said ***between*** her *sobs*. 彼女はしゃくり泣きをしながら言った. ¶She burst ***into*** a convulsive *sob*. 彼女はしゃくり泣きを始めた. ¶ask ***with*** a *sob* 泣きじゃくりながら頼む. ¶Not ***without*** *sobs* could she conclude her story. 彼女は泣きじゃくらずには話を終ることができなかった.

sob, *v.* 泣きじゃくる.

M *sob* ***bitterly*** はげしくしゃくり上げる. ¶*sob* ***hysterically*** ヒステリックにしゃくり上げる. ¶*sob* ***unseen*** 人知れずしゃくり泣く.

P *sob* ***to*** oneself 独りでしゃくり泣く.

sober, *v.* まじめになる.

M He *sobered* ***down*** at the age of discretion. 彼は分別のつく年齢(英法では満十四歳)になってからまじめになった. ‖ The class *sobered* ***down*** as the teacher came into the room. 先生が教室に入って来ると生徒がおとなしくなった. ¶*sober* ***up*** (=*off*) 酔がさめる, 正気づく.

soberness, *n.* まじめ, しらふ.

P I can't talk about it ***in*** *soberness*. しらふではその話はできない.

sobriquet, *n.* あだ名.

V the Grand Old Man, a *sobriquet* ***applied*** to Gladstone グラッドストーンに付けたあだ名グランド・オールド・マン. ¶he ***earned*** (=***obtained***) the *sobriquet* of ... 彼は...というあだ名をつけられた.

sociability, *n.* 親ぼく.

V ***encourage*** *sociability* among the student body 学生たちの間の親ぼくを奨励する.

Q ***friendly*** *sociability* 親ぼく.

sociable, *n.* 《口語》懇親会.

V ***attend*** the *sociables* and public meetings of the Neighbourhood Association むつみ会の懇親会や例会に出席する.

Q[2] a ***church*** *sociable* 教会の懇談会.

socialism, *n.* 社会主義.

V ***advocate*** *socialism* 社会主義を唱道する. ¶***profess*** *socialism* 社会主義を標榜(ぼう)する. ¶***repudiate*** *socialism* 社会主義を否認する. ¶***stamp out*** *socialism* 社会主義を撲滅する.

Q ***Christian*** *socialism* キリスト教社会主義. ¶In measures of ***practical*** *socialism* New Zealand may well be regarded as foremost among the nations of the world. 実践的社会主義の政策においてはニュージーランドは世界諸国民中首位に立つものと見て差支えない. ¶***state*** *socialism* 国家社会主義.

socialist, *n.* 社会主義者; [S-] 社会党員.

Q a ***Christian*** *socialists* キリスト教社会主義者. ¶a ***revolutionary*** *socialist* 革命的社会主義者. ¶an ***unequivocal*** *socialist* 正真正銘(金ぱく付)の社会主義者. ¶a ***Utopian*** *socialist* 空想社会主義者.

Q[2] a ***library*** *socialist* [実際活動をしない]書斎社会主義者. ¶the trend toward ***Marxist*** *socialist* マルクス社会主義的傾向. ¶a ***rightist*** *Socialist* 右派社会党員. ¶the ***right*** (***left***)-***wing*** *Socialists* 社会党右(左)派.

P[2] a *Socialist* ***to*** the core (=backbone) すじ金入りの社会党員.

socialistic, *a.* 社会主義的.

M ***intensely*** *socialistic* in one's views その思想がきわめて社会主義的な.

society, *n.* (**1**) 社会; 社交界, 交際場裡(り); 交際.

V ***abjure*** man's *society* 世を捨てる. ¶***affect*** the *society* of ladies 婦人との交際を好む. ¶***avoid*** his *society* 彼との交際を避ける. 【類】***avoid*** the *society* of the vicious (邪悪な人). ¶***benefit*** *society* 社会を利する. ¶***build*** an efficient *society* on ... ...の上に有利な社会を建設する. ¶***contaminate*** *society* 社会に毒を流す. ¶tend to ***corrupt*** *society* 社会に害を及ぼす傾向がある. ¶His *society* was much ***courted*** by a circle of choice friends. 彼は少数有力な友人たちから盛んに持てはやされていた. ¶***cultivate*** the *society* of the opposite sex 異性との交際を求める. ¶***degrade*** *society* 社会を堕落させる. ¶***destroy*** *society* as constituted now 現状の(既成)社会を破壊する. ¶***disgrace*** *society* 社会をはずかしめる. ¶***dislike*** *society* 交際をきらう. ¶***enjoy*** the *society* of women (children) 婦人(など)との交際を好む. 【類】***enjoy*** the *society* of "our dumb friends" (動物) / ***enjoy*** each other's *society* after the day's separation which business in the city demands. ¶***feel*** *society* in (=enjoy the companionship of) books 読書して寂しさを忘れる. ¶***forsake*** human *society* 世の中を捨てる. ¶***frequent*** the *society* of foreign gentlemen 外人の社会に出入する. ¶***hate*** feminine *society* 婦人との交際をきらう. ¶***improve*** *society* 社会を改良する. ¶women who ***lead*** *society* 社交会の牛耳をとる婦人たち. ¶He ***likes*** the *society* of interesting people. 彼はおもしろい人たちと交際するのが好きだ. ¶He ***loves*** the *society* of children. 彼は子供らを相手にするのが好きだ. ¶the elements which go to ***make up*** a civilized *society* 文明社会を組成するに必要な諸要素. ¶***remodel*** *society* on a democratic basis 民主主義的基礎の上に社会を改造する. ¶***renovate*** *society* 社会を革新する. ¶***re-organize*** *society* 社会の組織を改める. ¶***seek*** the *society* of the opposite sex assiduously 異性との交際を熱心に求める. 【類】They ***sought*** my *society* with the interested motive of exercising their French. ¶***serve*** *society* 社会に奉仕する. ¶***serve*** *society* by children 産児報国をする ‖ ***shun*** the *society* of women 婦人仲間を避ける ‖ ***shun*** his *society* 彼に会わないようにする. ¶He ***stirred*** the *society* of Boston to its depth. 彼はボストンの社交界でで大持てであった. ¶***worsen*** *society* 社会を悪化する.

Q the ***best*** *society* of Tokyo 東京の上流社会. ¶in ***civilized*** *society* 文化社会において. 【類】a highly ***civilized*** *society*. ¶the ***congenial*** *society* of ... ...の意気投合した仲間. ¶the corrupt and frivorous section of ***contemporary*** *society* 現代の腐敗した浮薄な部分. ¶He was bred in the most ***cultivated*** *society*. 彼は最も上品な社会で育った. ¶a ***debating*** *society* 討論会. ¶a ***democratic*** *society* 民主的社会. ¶in ***European*** *societies* ヨーロッパの社会において. ¶She is the queen in the ***fashionable*** *society* of London. 彼女はロンドン社交界の女王だ. ¶be mixed in ***good*** *society* よい人たちの仲間にはいる ‖ pronunciations current in ***good*** *society* 上流社会で通用する発音. ¶***high-bred*** *society* 上流育ちの人たち. ¶evils incident to ***human*** *society* 人間社会に付随する弊害. ¶fond of ***intellectual*** *society* 学問のある人々と交際するのが好きな. ¶in ***modern*** *society* 近代社会においては. ¶***polite*** *society* 上流社会. ¶a member of a ***reactionary patriotic*** *society* 反動的愛国会の一員. ¶***refined*** *society* 上流社会. ¶***select*** *society* 上流社会. ¶a successfully ***socialized*** *society* 社会化の達成された社会. ¶a ***well-organized*** *society* りっぱに組織された社会.

Q[2] ***adult*** *society* 大人の世界. ¶astonish ***London*** *society* ロンドンの社交界をあっと言わせる. ¶the ***bourgeois*** *society* ブルジョア仲間. ¶a ***capitalist*** *society* 資本家仲間. ¶***law*** and ***order*** *societies* 法律あり秩序ある社会. ¶the ***poetry*** *society* of America アメリカの詩人仲間. ¶in ***present-day*** *society* 現代社会においては. ¶***upper-class*** *society* 上流社会.

P sigh ***for*** the *society* of his wife 彼の妻が一緒にいたらよいと思う. ¶He keeps aloof ***from*** *society* 彼は世間と交際しない ‖ retire ***from*** *society* 隠退する. ¶He is of a higher class ***in*** *society* 彼は身分が一段良い. ‖ get on ***in*** *society* 出世する ‖ Do you go out much ***in*** *society?* 君は人と交際するか ‖ He is embarrassed ***in*** *society*. 彼は人前に出るときまりわるがる. ‖ He shines ***in*** *society*. 彼は交際社会に異彩を放っている. 【類】Profound thinkers are often helpless ***in*** *society*, while shallow men have nimble and ready minds. / be influential ***in*** *society* ‖ ***in*** the *society* of ladies 婦人の前で ‖ ***in*** the *society* of books 書籍を友として. ¶go ***into*** *society* 社交会に入る ‖ We do not go much ***into*** *society*. われわれは余り世間へ顔を出さない. ‖ introduce a person ***into*** *society* 人を社交会に入れてやる. ¶men of the highest classes ***of*** *society* 上流の人々. 【類】the upper class ***of*** *society* ‖ the lower strata ***of*** *society* 下層社会 ‖ in any strata ***of*** *society* 社会のいかなる層においても ‖ the welfare ***of*** *society* 社会の幸福 ‖ give her less and less ***of*** his *society* [夫など]彼女(妻)に段々寄りつかなくなる. ¶We were displeased ***with*** their *society*. われわれは彼らとの交際を不快に思った. ‖ He is in (out of) touch ***with*** *society*. 彼は世間と接触している(いない).

P[2] His *society* ***at*** sea I greatly enjoyed. 海上でのその人との交際は非常に面白かった. ¶the *society* ***of*** the learned 学者の社会.

(**2**) 会, 協会, 団体.

V The *society* was ***brought*** to an end in 1896. その会は一八九六年に解散した. ¶***form*** a *society* 会を組織する. ¶***found*** (=***organize***) a *society* for ... ...のために会を創立する. ¶***join*** a *society* for the annual subscription of one guinea 一年一ギニーの会費で入会する. ¶***keep up*** a *society* 会を維持する. ¶***leave*** a *society* 脱会する. ¶***manage***

(=*direct*) a *society* 会の事務を管理する.

Q a *benevolent society* 共済組合. ¶a *choral society* 音楽会. ¶a *cooperative society* 消費組合. ¶the *Educational* (*Economical*) *Society* 教育(など)会. ¶a *friendly society* 友愛会. ¶the *Japanese-American Society* 日米協会. ¶*kindred societies* 同種の協会. ¶the *Ladies' Patriotic Society* 愛国婦人会. ¶a *literary society* 文学会. ¶a *mutual aid society* 相互救済会. ¶the *Philosophical Society* 哲学会. ¶a *secret society* 秘密結社.

Q² a *benefit society* 共済会. ¶At the instance of their teachers, the students have started an *English speaking society*. 先生たちに勧められて学生が英語会を創立した. ¶a "*fresh air*" *society* 小児保健組合(子供に holidays in the country または holidays at the seashore を与える). ¶a *hunting safety society* 狩猟事故防止協会. ¶a *loan society* 貸金会社. ¶a *mutual aid society* 互助会. ¶a *rescue society* 救済会. ¶a *socialist society* 社会主義者の団体. ¶*tract society* 布教図書出版会社. ¶a *trade protection society* 代行的に掛を取り立てる会.

P receive him *into* a *society* as a member 彼を会員として入会させる.

P² a *society for* the promotion of science 科学振興会 ‖ the *Society for* the Abolition of ... ...廃止期成会.

sock, *n.* 半くつ下(ソックス).

V *darn socks* くつ下を修繕する. ¶*knit socks* くつ下を編む. ¶*pull up* one's *socks* きんこん一番.

Q *nylon-reinforced socks* ナイロンで補強したくつ下 ¶You *old socks!* ばか野郎. ¶*baby socks* 赤ん坊のくつ下.

Q² *dress socks* 男子正装用くつ下. ¶*knee socks* ひざまでのくつ下. ¶spun *nylon dress socks*, guaranteed 6 months 平織ナイロン正装用くつ下, 六カ月保証. ¶*skating* (*skiing*) *socks* スケート(スキー)用くつ下.

P a pair (two pair) *of socks* くつ下一(二)足.

P² *Socks for* Gents [広告] 紳士用くつ下.

socket, *n.* 穴.

P His eyes started *from* their *sockets*, and he stared fixedly downward. 彼は目を思いきり開いてじっと下を見つめていた.

sod, *n.* 芝土.

V *turn* the first *sod* of a railway 鉄道の起工式を行う.

Q the *old sod* [俗] 故郷. ¶with the *springy sod* beneath me, and a carolling lark above 足は湿(しめ)った土をふみ耳には空にさえずるひばりの声を聞いて.

P He is *under* the *sod*. 彼は草葉のかげにいる. ¶cover *with sod* 芝土でおおう.

soda, *n.* ソーダ.

Q² *washing soda* 洗たくソーダ.

sodden, *a.* 浸した.

P He is *sodden in* evil habits. 彼は悪習に浸っている. ¶*sodden with* drink 酒浸りになって.

sofa, *n.* ソファー.

V *wheel* the *sofa* round 車付きの長いすの向きをかえる.

Q a *broad sofa* with a padded back and also padded arms on each side 後ろ両ひじパッド付幅広の長いす. ¶an *upholstered sofa* [シートなどを]張り変えたソファー.

P She sank *on* to a *sofa*. 彼女はソファーにどっかり腰をおろした.

soft, *a.* 柔らかな; 柔和な; 知恵の足りない.

M I think he is *a bit soft*. 彼は少し足りないようだ. ¶He is *rather soft*. 彼は人が好い方だ.

P Moss is *soft like* velvet. こけはビロードのように柔らかい. ¶He was *soft of* tongue. 彼は言葉つきがやさしかった. ¶Velvets are *soft to* the touch (=feel). ビロードは手ざわりが柔らかい.

soften, *v.* 柔らかにする; 柔らかになる; 和らぐ.

M *soften away* harshness 和らぐ.

P His heart *softened at* the pitiable sight. 彼の心はその不びんな光景を見て哀れを催した. ¶*soften* ... *by* heat (moisture) 熱(など)で...を柔らかにする. 【類】a light *softened by* a blue shade (青色のかさ) / the dictates of propriety (正義の命令) *softened by* humanity. ¶Wax *softens in* heat. ろうは熱すると柔らかになる. ¶*soften into* tears 感きわまって涙を催す. ¶My heart *softened towards* him. 彼に対する私の心は和らいだ. ¶Iron *softens with* heat. 鉄は熱で柔らかになる.

O *soften* one's attitude (voice) 態度(など)を和らげる.

softener, *n.* 軟化剤.

Q² a sanitary *beard softener* for shaving [そりよくするための]衛生ひげそりクリーム(など).

softling, *n.* 若様.

Q a *pap-nerved softling* 乳臭い若殿様.

softness, *n.* 柔らかいこと.

V *give* a velvety *softness* to the skin 皮膚をびろうどのように柔らかにする.

Q The breeze rustled tree leaves with almost *caressing softness*. 微風がなでるように優しく木の葉をサラサラ鳴らした. ¶*fluffy softness* にこ毛のような柔らかさ[粉などにいう]. ¶*physical softness* and deterioration 身体の虚弱と低下.

soil, *n.* 土壌, 地味; 土地, 国; 生地.

V *cultivate* the *soil* 地を耕作する. ¶*exhaust soil* 地味を疲弊させる. ¶*farm* poor *soil* やせた土地を耕作する. ¶*fertilize soil* 土に施肥する. ¶Naturally it is among the gullible rustic populations that these traditions and sentiments *find* their most complacent *soil*. こうした伝統や感情が欺きやすい農民の間に最も盛んになるのは当然である. ¶It will help to *furnish* a *soil* on which such an idea develop unimpeded. それはこうした思想が思うままに発育する土壌を作ることになるだろう. ¶*furrow soil* 畑土をすく. ¶Central and South America, and more especially Brazil, *have* a *soil* of extraordinary fertility. 中南米特にブラジルには非常に肥えた土地がある. ¶Weeds *impoverish* the *soil*. 雑草は地味を荒らす. ¶*prepare* the *soil* for seed 種子をまくように土地をこしらえる. ¶*provide soil* favorable to ... ...に有利な下地を作る. ¶The king demanded that the French troops should forthwith *quit* German *soil*. 国王は仏軍が直ちにドイツ国土を撤退すべきことを要求した. ¶*stir up* the sandy *soil* into a perfect dust-storm 砂地をかき乱して完全に砂じんをまき起す. ¶*till* the *soil* 地を耕す. ¶the first Europeans that ever *trod* Japanese *soil* (=the soil of Japan) 日本の地を踏んだ一番最初のヨーロッパ人. ¶*turn* [*up*] the *soil* 土を掘返す. ¶Japanese *soil* (=Japan) has not been *violated* by foreign hoof. 日本の土地は外敵に汚されたことがない.

V² The *soil settles*. 土が固まる.

Q *arable soil* 耕作適地. ¶no crops will grow in *arid soil* 乾燥した土壌には作物ができない. ¶the *burning soil* of Africa アフリカの熱地. ¶a residence on a *damp soil* 湿地にある住宅. ¶grow in *dry* (*wet*) *soil*. ¶raise life-sustaining crops from the *earth's soil* 土地に命をつなぐ作物を作る. ¶find *favorable soil* in ... ...をその温床になるものと見る. ¶a *fertile soil* よく土. ¶tread on *foreign soil* 外国の地を踏む. ¶a *fruitful soil* 肥よくな土地. ¶fall on *good soil* and bear fruit (種子など)肥よくの土地に落ちて実を結ぶ. ¶a *moist soil* 湿地. ¶one's *native soil* 生れ故郷. ¶*poor* (=*sterile, hungry*) *soil* やせ地. 【類】grass that are found on *poor soil*. ¶a *porous soil* 多孔質の土壌. ¶a *productive* (=*teeming*) *soil* よく実る地味. ¶The *soil* is *rich* here. ここは地味が肥えている. ¶till the *stubborn soil* 荒地を耕す. ¶*sunbaked soil* 日光で乾いた土地. ¶*virgin soil* 処女地. ¶*workable soil* 耕作可能の土壌.

Q² heavy *clay soils* 重い粘土質土壌. ¶a *forest soil* 森林の土壌. ¶the use of "*night soil*" as fertilizer 肥料として下肥の利用. ¶small shafts of ice which form under the *surface soil* 表土の下にできる霜柱.

P transplant ... *in* American *soil* ...をアメリカの土に移植する ‖ grow *on* chalky *soil* 白亜質の地に生じる ‖ A noble literature is not likely to flourish *on* such *soil*. こうした国土には高尚な文学は栄えそうもない. ‖ tread *on* Japanese *soil* 日本の地を踏む. ¶*under* the *soil* 地下に, 地中に. ¶the greatest genius ever produced *upon* American *soil* 米国の産んだ最大の天才.

soil, *v.* よごす.

P *soil with* mud 泥でよごす ‖ *soil* one's hands *with* ... ...で手をよごす; [比ゆ的に] 不正事件に関係する.

soiling, *n.* よごれ.

V It quickly *shows soiling*. それはよごれが目立つ.

sojourn, *n.* とう留, 滞在.

V *make* a *sojourn* in a mountain 山中に滞在する. 【類】*make* a lengthy *sojourn*.

Q a *short sojourn* 短いとう留. ¶a *year's sojourn* 一年間の滞在.

P *during* one's *sojourn* とう留中. ¶a place *of sojourn* 滞在地.

P² a *sojourn in* an asylum (sanitarium) 精神病院(など)での静養.

sojourn, *v.* とう留する, 滞在する.

P *sojourn among* (=*with*) one's relatives (friends) 親族(など)ととう留する. ¶*sojourn at* an inn 旅館に滞在する. ¶*sojourn in* some place ある所にとう留する.

sojourner, *n.* 滞在者, 居留者.

Q a *temporary* (=*transient*) *sojourner* 短期間のとう留客. ¶the *Western sojourners* in the East 東洋における西洋人の滞在者.

P There are about 21,000 French *sojourners* ***in*** England, and about 11,000 of them live in the metropolis. 英国には約二万一千のフランスの居留者がいるがその中約一万一千は首府に住んでいる.

solace, *n.* 慰み, 慰安.

V The unsuccessful fisherman ***finds*** *solace* in the scenery. 不漁の漁師は風景の美に慰安を得る. 【類】He ***finds*** *solace* in religion. ¶***seek*** *solace* from her trials by indulging in drink 飲酒にふけって辛苦に対する慰安を求める.

Q find in it a ***compensatory*** *solace* それで埋合わせの慰安を得る. ¶find the ***greatest*** *solace* in ... ...で最大の慰安を得る. ¶find ***no*** *solace* in his company 彼との交際では何らの慰安も得られない. ¶tobacco, the ***poor man's*** *solace* 貧者の慰安物たるタバコ. ¶his ***sole*** *solace* in his sick bed was the company of books. 病床における唯一の慰安は本だった.

P one *solace* ***amid*** ... ...の中の一つの慰め. ¶***as*** a *solace* to his own soul 彼自身の精神に対する慰安として. ¶turn to books ***for*** *solace* 慰みに書物を見る.

solace, *v.* 慰める.

P *solace* oneself ***with*** the conviction that ... ...と確信して自ら心を慰める.

solatium, *n.* 慰謝料.

V ***obtain*** ... yen *solatium* ...円の慰謝料をもらう.

soldier, *n.* 軍人, 兵士, 兵卒.

V *soldiers* ***armed*** with muskets 小銃を携える兵士. ¶***draw*** *soldiers* from the Tokyo garrison 東京守備隊から兵士を抜てきする. ¶The *soldiers* were ***lined up***. 兵士を整列させた. ¶He will ***make*** a good *soldier*. 彼はりっぱな軍人になるだろう. ¶***pick*** *soldiers* 兵士を選抜する. ¶***play*** *soldiers* 兵隊ごっこをして遊ぶ. ¶He ***proved*** a good *soldier*. 彼はりっぱな軍人になった. ¶***train*** *soldiers* 兵卒を教練する. ¶*Soldiers* were ***put up*** (=***lodged***) in private houses. 兵士は民家に宿泊した. ¶***unhorse*** a *soldier* 兵士を馬から落す. ¶*Soldiers* ***came*** to close quarters. 兵士は接戦した.

V² The *soldier* ***deserted*** from his regiment. その兵卒は連隊を脱走した. ¶a *soldier* who has ***gone*** to the front 出征した軍人. ¶Time-expired *soldiers* have ***returned*** from Formosa. 満期兵が台湾から帰って来た. ¶He has ***turned*** [a] *soldier*. 彼は軍人になった.

Q ***admirable*** *soldiers* りっぱな軍人. ¶a ***bluff old*** *soldier* ざっくばらんの老兵. ¶***common*** (=***private***) *soldiers* 兵卒. ¶the ***crippled*** *soldier* in industry 実業についた傷い軍人. ¶a ***gallant*** *soldier* りりしい軍人. ¶a ***great*** *soldier* あっぱれの武将. ¶a ***hired*** *soldier*, ready to fight in any cause 正邪を眼中におかずに戦う雇用兵. ¶***merry-faced*** *soldiers* 元気な顔をした兵士. ¶a ***mounted*** *soldier* 騎兵. ¶He is ***no*** *soldier*. 彼は軍人の器ではない. ¶an ***old*** *soldier* 老兵, 老将; 老練家. ¶a ***private*** *soldier* 一兵卒. ¶a ***professional*** *soldier* 職業軍人. ¶a ***recruited*** *soldier* 応召軍人. ¶a ***smart*** *soldier* ハイカラな軍人. ¶***time-expired*** *soldiers* who have completed their time with the colors 満期除隊兵. ¶***uniformed*** *soldiers* 制服姿の軍人 ¶the tomb of the ***Unknown*** *Soldier* 無名戦士の墓.

Q² a ***back-to-the-farm*** *soldier* 帰農兵士. ¶a ***career*** *soldier* はえ抜きの軍人. ¶a ***citizen*** *soldier* 非職業軍人. ¶an ***embryo*** *soldier* 兵隊の卵. ¶a ***feather bed*** *soldier* 《俗》よくよくの道楽者. ¶a ***foot*** *soldier* 歩兵. ¶a ***line*** *soldier* 戦線にある兵. ¶an ***occupation*** *soldier* 職業軍人. ¶a ***Royalist*** *soldier* 王党の兵. ¶***tin*** (=***toy***) *soldiers* おもちゃの兵隊さん. ¶the sex life of the ***U.S.*** *soldier* アメリカ兵の性生活.

P serve ***as*** a *soldier* 軍人になる. ¶go ***for*** a *soldier* 軍人になる ‖ He is cut out ***for*** a *soldier*. 彼は軍人に適している. ¶He looks ***like*** a *soldier*. 彼は軍人らしい. ¶a company ***of*** *soldiers* 一個中隊の兵.

P² He is a *soldier* ***by*** profession. 彼は軍人だ. ¶every *soldier* ***in*** the battalion 大隊の各兵士 ‖ a *soldier* ***in*** science 科学界の勇士. ¶a *soldier* ***of*** the artillery 砲兵隊の兵士 ‖ *soldiers* ***of*** fortune 風雲児 ‖ a *soldier* ***of*** industry 産業戦士 ‖ a *soldier* ***on*** sentry しょう兵.

soldier, *v.* 《米俗》なまける.

P *soldier* ***on*** one's job 《俗》仕事に身を入れない(油を売る).

sole, *n.* 足裏; くつ底.

V ***tap*** [leather] *soles* on one's shoes くつの半張りをする. ¶***tickle*** the *soles* of the feet 足の裏をくすぐる.

Q For hiking women wear shoes of stout leather with ***heavy*** *soles* and flat heels. 女はハイキングに底のがん丈なかかとの平たいしっかりした皮ぐつをはく. ¶a doubly ***reinforced*** *sole* 鬼底. ¶The *soles* are ***thick*** (***thin, double***). くつ底は厚い(など).

P He stood exactly six feet ***in*** his stocking *soles*. 彼は(くつをはかずに)くつ下の足で六フィートあった. ¶walk ***on*** the *sole* of the foot [くつをはかずに]素足で歩く. ¶He was a business man ***to*** the *soles* of his boots. 彼は徹頭徹尾実業家だった. ¶fasten a shoe ***with*** a wooden *sole* くつに木底を付ける.

solemnity, *n.* 厳粛.

V ***add*** an indescribable *solemnity* to the scene その光景にえも言われない厳粛な趣きを添える. ¶***inspire*** *solemnity* 厳粛な気分を起させる.

solicit, *v.* 懇願する.

M We ***respectfully*** *solicit* your continuous patronage. 相変らず御愛顧のほど幾重にもお願い致します.

P *solicit* ***for*** one's views (subscriptions, contributions) その所見(など)を求める ‖ I *solicited* him ***for*** his help. 私は彼の助力を懇願した. 【類】*solicit* ***for*** another's favor / We *solicit* you ***for*** your custom (favors). ¶*solicit* contributions ***from*** him 彼に寄稿を依頼する.

solicitation, *n.* 懇願.

Q ***at*** the *solicitation* of ... ...の懇願で. ¶***through*** his *solicitation* or influence 彼の懇願もしくは勢力によって. ¶This testimonial is written by me ***without*** *solicitation*. この証明書は私が(依頼されたのでなく)自分から進んで書いたものである.

solicitous, *a.* 心配する; 切望する.

P I am *solicitous* ***about*** (=***concerning***) the future. 私は将来が心配だ. ¶She is *solicitous* ***for*** her son's welfare. 彼女は息子の幸福を願っている. ¶I am *solicitous* ***of*** his help. 彼の助力を得たいものだ.

solicitude, *n.* 配慮.

V ***show*** *solicitude* for his comfort and convenience 彼の安楽と便宜に対する切望を示す.

Q with ***apprehensive*** *solicitude* about the future 将来について気づかって. ¶***divine*** *solicitude* 神の配慮.

P inquire ***with*** *solicitude* 心配して尋ねる. ¶*solicitude* ***for*** one's welfare 幸福に対する切望.

solid, *n.* 固形物.

V No *solids* to be ***given***. 固形物は一切与えてはいけない.

solid, *a.* 結束した.

Q the ***most*** *solid* of realities 少しも疑う余地のない現実.

P People were *solid* ***for*** (***against***) their government. 人民は政府を支持(に反対)した. ‖ be *solid* for (***in*** favor of) ... こぞって...に賛成する.

solidarity, *n.* 共同一致, 団結.

V ***strengthen*** its *solidarity* [国家など]その一致団結を強固にする.

Q ***human*** *solidarity* 人類の共同一致. ¶the sense of ***social*** *solidarity* 社会連帯の観念.

Q² ***Empire*** *solidarity* 帝国の一致団結.

solidify, *v.* 団結する.

P *solidify* people ***into*** a party 党派を組織して人々を団結させる.

solitaire, *n.* ひとりトランプ.

V ***play*** *solitaire* 一人トランプをする.

solitude, *n.* 孤独, 独居; 辺地.

V ***find*** *solitude* 孤独の境地を得る. ¶They seemed to ***make*** the *solitude* more sensibly ***felt***. その(よしきりの鳴く声など)ためにさびしさが一段と増すように思われた. ¶***love*** *solitude* 孤独を好む.

Q in the ***leafy*** *solitude* of the garden 庭の葉の茂った閑静な所で. ¶a ***snowy*** *solitude* 雪中の幽境.

P ***in*** the *solitude* of one's own room そのへやに独居して ‖ live ***in*** *solitude* 独りで住む. ¶I am fond ***of*** *solitude*. 私は孤独が好きだ. ‖ in the midst ***of*** a vast *solitude* 広ばくたる辺地の真中に.

solo, *n.* 独唱, 独奏; 単独飛行.

V ***dance*** a *solo* 一人だけで踊る. ¶***fly*** a *solo* 単独飛行をする. ☞ a solo flight (単独飛行). ¶***play*** a *solo* 独奏する.

Q a ***vocal*** *solo* 独唱.

Q² a ***concertina*** (***accordion***) *solo* 手風琴(アコーディオン)独奏. ¶a ***violin*** (***piano***) *solo* バイオリン(ピアノ)独奏.

solstice, *n.* 至.

Q² the ***summer*** *solstice* 夏至. ¶the ***winter*** *solstice* 冬至.

soluble, *a.* とけやすい.

M It is ***easily*** *soluble* in water. それは容易に水に溶ける.

P A dry powder is readily *soluble* ***in*** water. 乾いた粉は容易に水に溶ける.

solution, *n.* (**1**) 解決, 解答; 解法.

V problems ***awaiting*** *solution* 解決を待っている諸問題. ¶***bring about*** a satisfactory *solution* 満足な解決をもたらす. ¶***find*** a *solution* of (=for) a problem 問題の解決法を見出す. ¶It ***furnishes*** a *solution* of the problem. それはその問題の一つの解決法になる. ¶It is ***nearing*** a *solution.* それは解決に近づきつつある. ¶Two *solutions* are ***offered*** as a way out of the dilemma. その難局打破の二つの方法が提案されている.【類】I can ***offer*** no *solution* of the problem. ¶***reach*** (=***come to***) a wise *solusion* 賢明な解決に達する.【類】failure to ***reach*** a *solution.* ¶***seek*** a *solution* of the problem その問題の解答を求める. ¶***work out*** a *solution* for a problem 問題を解決する.

Q an ***amicable*** *solution* through friendly negotiations 友交的交渉による円満解決. ¶a ***correct*** *solution* to a puzzle なぞの正しい解答. ¶an ***easy*** *solution* 容易な解決. ¶a ***fair working*** *solution* of the problem その問題の実行性のあるりっぱな解決法. ¶a ***half-way*** *solution* 不徹底な解決. ¶the ***happiest*** *solution* of the problem would seem to be ... その問題の最も適切な解決法は...であると思われる. ¶a ***lame*** *solution* 片手落的な解決. ¶Is there ***no other*** *solution?* 他の解決法はないか. ¶a ***pacific*** *solution* 平和的解決. ¶a ***partial*** *solution* of the labor problem 労働問題の部分的解決. ¶find a ***peaceful*** and ***adequate*** *solution* for the vexed question その紛争に対する平和的で適切な解決法を見出す. ¶a ***perfect*** *solution* for ... ...の完全な解決. ¶reach a ***practical*** *solution* of a problem 問題の実際的な解決に達する. ¶a ***prompt*** and ***intelligent*** *solution* of a problem 問題の敏速そう明な解決. ¶the ***right*** *solution* of the problem その問題の正しい解決. ¶The problem does not come to a ***satisfactory*** *solution.* その問題はいまだに満足な解決がついていない. ¶There must be ***some*** *solution* to the problem. その問題は何とか解決ができるに相違ない. ¶my own ***tentative*** *solution* 私自身の暫定的解決. ¶a most ***unsatisfactory*** *solution* of the problem of ... 問題のきわめて不満足な解決. ¶a ***workable*** *solution* of the labor problem 労働問題の実行し得べき解決法.

Q^2 a ***long-run*** *solution* to the problem その問題の長期解決. ¶one of those ***two-bird-one-stone*** *solutions* 一石二鳥的解決の一つ.

P^2 a *solution* ***for*** (***of, to***) a problem 問題の解決法 ‖ a partial *solution* ***of*** the financial problem 財政問題の局部的解決. ¶a *solution* ***to*** problem No. 765. 第七百六十五問の解答 ‖ a *solution* ***to*** a grievance 苦情に対する解決.

(**2**) 溶解; 溶液.

V ***make*** a *solution* of ammonia アンモニア溶液を造る.

Q ***aqueous*** *solution* 水液. ¶thoroughly wash in a 1 in 40 ***carbolic*** *solution* 四十倍の石炭酸水でよく洗う. ¶***chemical*** (***mechanical***) *solution* 化学(機械)的溶解. ¶in a ***dilute*** *solution* of ... ...の希薄な溶液中に. ¶a ***saline*** *solution* 塩の溶液. ¶a 1/3000 ***silver-nitrate*** *solution* 三千倍の硝酸銀液. ¶a ***weak*** *solution* of carbolic acid 石炭酸の希薄な溶液.

Q^2 a boracic ***acid*** *solution* ほう酸水. ¶a ***75%*** *solution* of a drug 薬品の七十五パーセント溶液.

P The sea-water holds many salts ***in*** *solution.* 海水には多くの塩類が溶けて含まれている. ‖ His ideas are ***in*** *solution.* 彼の考えは(固まらずに)ぐらついている. ‖ Water always holds a quantity of air ***in*** *solution.* 水の中には必ず一定量の溶解した空気がある. ¶a 1 to 2,000 *solution* ***of*** perchloride of mercury. 二千倍の水銀塩化物.

solve, *v.* 解決する.

M The problem can ***easily*** be *solved.* その問題はじきに解決がつく.

solvency, *n.* 資力, 支払能力.

V it will seriously ***jeopardize*** the *solvency* of ... それは大いに...の財政的基礎を弱めるであろう.

Q institutions or individuals of ***recognized*** *solvency* 財政的基礎の確実な団体または個人.

solvent, *n.* 溶剤; 薄弱にするもの.

Q a ***liquid*** *solvent* 液体溶剤.

P It is used ***as*** a *solvent.* それは溶剤に用いる. ‖ science ***as*** a *solvent* of religious belief 宗教上の信仰を弱める科学.

somebody, *n.* だれか; ひとかどの人物.

V ***get*** *somebody* to sweep the room clean だれかに室の掃除をしてもらう.

P He is *somebody* ***in*** his circle. 彼はその仲間の中で一かどの人物だ.

P^2 There are lots of *somebodies* and nobodies on the list. その表にはたくさんの有名無名人が載っている.

somersault, *n.* とんぼ返り.

V ***perform*** a *somersault* 宙返りをする. ¶He ***turned*** a *somersault* in mid-air. 彼は宙返りをした.

Q turn ***forward*** and ***backward*** *somersaults* 前と後ろへとんぼ返りをする.

P ***in*** a *somersault* 宙返えりをして.

something, *n.* 何か; 幾分; 一かどの人物.

V ***achieve*** *something* great in the world 世の中で何かえらいことを仕遂げる. ¶***add*** *something* to the appearance of the city その市の外観を幾分よくする. ¶***bring*** *something* like order into the city その市にどうにか秩序らしいものをもたらす. ¶*something* must be ***done*** with respect to ... ...について何とかしなければならない.【類】*something* will have to be ***done*** by ... / *Something* is going to be ***done*** about it. / *Something* can yet be ***done.*** / spend time in ***doing*** *something.* ¶There is *something* to ***eat***, but nothing to drink. 食べる物はあるが飲む物がない. ¶She ***felt*** *something* oppressive in his presence. 彼の前に出ると彼女は何か重苦しい感じがした. ¶It is hard to ***get*** *something* for nothing. どんな物でもただでは得難い. ‖ We've ***got*** *something* nice for you. 君にあげるいい物がある. ¶***Give*** the beggar *something.* こじきに何か少しやれ. ¶I ***have*** *something* to say to you. 君にちょっと言うことがある. ‖ ***have*** *something* to do with it 幾分それに関係がある ‖ You ***have*** *something* in your eye=You are considering something. 君は何か考えている. ‖ Father ***has*** *something* for my birthday. 父は私の誕生日に何かくれることになっている. ‖ ***have*** *something* to be clarified ふに落ちない, 割切れないものが残る. ¶***hear*** *something* unpleasant from ... ...のお小言を頂だいする. ¶***inherit*** *something* of its father's constitution and temperament 父の体質と気質を幾分受ける. ¶It ***leaves*** *something* to be desired. 物足りない. ¶***make*** *something* out of leisure 暇を何かに利用する. ¶The old maid has the feeling of having ***missed*** *something* in life. その未婚の老女は何か世の中でなすべきことをしなかったような感じがしている. ¶They are planning to ***present*** *something* of novelty. 彼らは何か目新しいものを持出そうとしている. ¶The book ***reflects*** *something* of the character of the author. その本は著者の性格を幾分反映している. ¶***save*** *something* handsome for a rainy day 不慮の備えに相当な貯えをする. ¶***say*** *something* of ... ...について少し言う.【類】I have *something* to ***say*** to you. ¶***see*** *something* of Europe ヨーロッパを少し見物する ‖ I hope to ***see*** *something* of you. 時には顔を見せて下さいよ. ¶***spare*** *something* out of so much それだけの中から幾らか余す. ¶***take*** *something* 何か食べる. ¶I want to ***tell*** you *something.* 君にお話したいことがある.

V^2 *something* ***happened*** that obliged me to ... 私が...せざるを得ないような事件が起った. ¶*Something* ***told*** me you would come today. きょうお出下さることを虫が知らせた. ¶*Something* is ***wanting.*** 何だか物足りない. ¶There was *something* that ***weighed*** on her mind. 何かしらないが彼女の気掛りになっていることがあった.

Q You're the only girl I've ever seen that actually did look like *something* ***blooming.*** 私が今まで会った中で何か花が咲いているように感じる少女と言ったらあなただけである. ¶He has caught cold, but at first he thought it was *something* ***else*** (***different***). 彼はかぜを引いているのだが初めは何か別な(違った)病気だと思った. ¶There is *something* almost ***epic*** about the long voyage of the Baltic Fleet. バルチック艦隊の長途の航海についてはどこか雄壮といった所がある. ¶There is *something* ***fascinating*** about his manner of speech. 彼の話し方にはどこか魅惑的な所がある. ¶Almost every one has *something* ***finny*** to show for his outing. [魚が豊富だから]釣りにでかけるとほとんどだれでもなにか獲物がある. ¶He has that ***hard-to-define*** but easily recognizable *something* called talent. ちょっと説明するには困るがたやすく認識される手腕というものが彼にはある. ¶*something* ***hot*** (***cold***) to drink なにか熱い(冷い)飲物. ¶an ***indefinable*** *something* 説明しにくいある物. ¶an ***indescribable*** *something* 名状すべからざるある物. ¶The relic has an ***intangible*** *something* that years alone can print on it. その遺物には時代のみが付けうる微妙なある物(古色)が見られた. ¶an *indeterminate something* なんだかわけのわからないもの. ¶He is *something more* than an ordinary artist. 彼は普通の美術家よりもえらい所がある. ¶I have *something new* to tell you. 君に聞かせる珍らしいことがある. ¶*something noticeable* in his manner 彼の態度で目につく点. ¶*something peculiar* なにか変ったもの. ¶*something rare* なにか珍らしいもの. ¶chaffer at the fish-stall for *something toothsome* to take home for supper 夕飯の菜に買って行くなにかおいしいものを魚屋の店で値切る. ¶There was *something unusual* in his expression. 彼の言い振りにはどこか変った所があった. 【類】*something extraordinary* (=*unusual or uncommon*). ¶There is *something wholesome* in all disappointment. どんな失望にも人を益する所があるものだ. ¶He must have done *something wrong*. 彼はなにか悪いことをしたに相違ない.

P *with something* of impatience 多少じれ気味で.

P² He has *something besides* his salary. 彼は俸給以外にいくらか収入がある. ¶He is *something between* knave and fool. 彼は悪党と低能の合の子だ. ¶Here is *something for* you. これを君に上げます. ¶I want *something* to drink water *from*. なにか水を飲む物が欲しい. ¶There is *something in* him. 彼には多少取得がある. ‖ There is *something in* what you say. 君の言うことには一理ある. ‖ He is *something in* the Customs. 彼は税関では相当の所にいる. ¶for *something like* two years 約二カ年間. 【類】This book cost me *something like* twenty yen. ‖ it is *something like* sacrilege to say anything against ... ...に反することを言うのはなんとなく神聖を汚すような気がする ‖ This is *something like* a dinner. これは相当のごちそうだ. ¶It is *something of* anachronism. それは先ず時代錯誤だ. ‖ He is *something of* an athlete. 彼はちょっとした運動家だ. 【類】He is *something of* a carpenter (musician, hero, gentleman). / it is *something of* a shock to him to ... / *Something of* doubt remains. / *somethig of* the kind. ¶I want *something* to cover my hair *with*. 髪をおおう物がほしい. 【類】*something* to write *with* (ペンかなにか).

somewhere, *ad.* どこか; ころ.

P A young man appeared *from somewhere*. どこからか一人の青年が現われた. ¶He lives *somewhere about* Shinagawa. 彼はどこか品川辺に住んでいる. ‖ *somewhere about* 1588 一五八八年ごろ. ¶*somewhere in* this neighborhood どこかこの近所に. ¶*somewhere near* us どこかわれわれの近くに.

son, *n.* 息子.

V He *acknowledged* his *son*. 彼は自分のせがれであることを認めた. ¶At the end of another year Fusa *bore* another *son*. 翌年の末に房子はもう一人男の子を生んだ. ‖ Did his first wife *bear* a *son* to him? あの人の最初の奥さんに男の子がありましたか. ¶parents wishing to *enter* their *sons* at Eton school せがれをイートン校に入れたいと思う両親たち. ¶*Sons follow* fathers in the service. 子は親を継いで同じ勤務(商売)をする. ¶He *has* a *son* to succeed him. 彼には跡取りの息子がある. ¶A married man, he *left* two *sons* [*behind*]. 彼は結婚しており二人の子を残して死んだ. ¶They have *lost* their little *son* through scarlet fever. 彼らはしょう紅熱で小さい男の子をなくした. ¶He *outlived* his *son* by four years. 彼はその子供の死後四年生きながらえた. ¶*renounce* one's *son* せがれを勘当する.

Q one's *beloved son* いとしいせがれ. ¶my *dear son* いとしいせがれよ. ¶a *disinherited son* 勘当されたせがれ. ¶a *dissipated son* ほうとうむすこ. ¶his *eldest* and *youngest sons* 彼の長男と末のむすこ. ¶Britain's *famous fighting sons* 英国知名の勇士. ¶He is his *father's son*. 彼はお父さん似だ(容ぼう・性格などが). ¶a *favorite son* of the people 《米》国民の人気のある政治家. ¶a *half Japanese son* of a Scotchman スコットランド人と日本人の合の子. ¶a *horny-handed son* of toil 手の硬くなった労働者. ¶*idle sons* of pleasure 遊惰むすこ. ¶an *infant son* 未成年の息子. ¶People born in New York are *native sons* and daughters of New York. ニューヨーク生れの人はニューヨークのむすこであり娘である. ¶Goldwin Smith, the greatest of Canada's *literary sons* カナダ文士中の最大偉人たるゴールドウィン・スミス. ¶He was the *only son* of a father. 彼は一人っ子であった. ¶a *prodigal son* どらむすこ. ¶America's most *prominent* and *respected sons* 米国の最も傑出した名士たち. ¶a *spoiled son* 甘やかしたむすこ. ¶his *unworthy son* 彼の不似合なむすこ. ¶a *wayward son* わがままなむすこ. ¶their *wellbeloved only son* 彼らのいとしい独りむすこ. ¶a *wicked son* 不良むすこ.

Q² a Chinese *peasant son* 中国の百姓のせがれ. ¶a *soldier son* 軍人になったむすこ. ¶a *teen-age son* 十代のむすこ.

P handed down from father *to son* 親から子に伝えられる(宝物など). ¶*without* a *son* むすこのない.

P² Masatsura was *son of* Masashige. 正行は正成の子であった. ‖ a *son of* France フランス人 ‖ the *son of* the soil =the peasant 農夫, 百姓 ‖ *sons of* liberty 《米》自由の子(特に独立戦争当時の) ‖ a *son of* a gun 《米俗》ばか, とんま; [叫び声]あっ驚いた, さあ困った. ¶*son to* the king 王子 ‖ the *Son of* God (=Man) キリストの別称 ‖ the *sons of* Adam 人間.

sonata, *n.* 『音楽』ソナタ, 奏鳴曲.

Q² the *Moonlight Sonata* 月光の曲 (Beethoven 作曲の).

P in the form *of sonata*=in *sonata* form ソナタ形式で.

song, *n.* 歌, さえずり声; 詩歌; 《俗》さ少.

V *chant* a *song* 歌を歌う. ¶Let us *have* a *song*. だれか一つ歌いませんか. ¶*hum* a *song* 鼻歌を歌う. ¶The sun upon the lake is low; the wild birds *hush* their songs. 湖上に輝く日は沈もうとし野鳥は歌をやめる. ¶The bird *pours out* a ceaseless *song*. その鳥はひっきりなしにさえずる. ¶*roar* student *songs* 学生歌を大声で歌う. ¶*set* a *song* to music 歌詞に作曲する. ¶*sing* a *song* 歌を歌う ‖ *sing* in unison a *song* 斉唱する.

V² as the old *song goes* 古歌にある通り. ¶A popular *song rang out* loud and clear. 流行歌が音高くはっきりと聞えた.

Q a *charming song* 楽しい歌. ¶a *choral song* 合唱曲. ¶*comic songs* こっけい歌. ¶one's *favorite song* 愛唱歌. ¶The bird is in *full song*. 鳥が盛に歌う. ¶a *funeral song* ばん歌. ¶the *latest* music-hall *patriotic song* 最近よせでやる愛国の歌. ¶a *mellow song* 甘美な歌. ¶the *national song* 国歌. ¶not worth an *old song* ただでもいらない位の. ¶a *plaintive song* 哀れっぽい歌. ¶a *popular song* of the moment 目下の流行歌. ¶sing a *pretty song* 美しい歌を歌う. ¶*ribald songs* いんわいな歌. ¶a *rollicking song* さんざめく歌. ¶a *rustic song* 俗謡. ¶a *sacred song* 聖歌, 賛美歌. ¶a *smutty song* わいせつな歌. ¶a *spicy song* 下がかった歌. ¶a *sweet song* 調子のよい歌.

Q² singing their *drinking songs* 酒宴の歌を歌いながら. ¶a *folk song* 民謡. ¶a *hit song* 当り歌. ¶a *home song* ホーム・ソング. ¶a *humming song* 鼻歌. ¶sing Red "*Liberation*" *songs* 共産党の「解放」歌を歌う. ¶a *sea song* 海の歌. ¶a *swan song* 絶唱 ‖ the *swan song* of a poet 詩人の絶吟. ¶a *theme song* 主題歌 ‖ his *theme song* was ... 彼の主義は...であった. ¶a *three-man song* 三部合唱歌. ¶a *working class song* 労働歌.

P It was sold *for* a mere *song*. それは二束三文で売られた. ¶placcs renowned *in song* 歌(の文句)で名高い名所. ¶burst forth *into song* 歌いだす. ¶keep time *to* a *song* 歌に調子を合わせる.

P² *songs about* birds 鳥を歌った歌. ¶a *song for* one voice 一人で歌う歌. ¶the *song of* a lark ひばりの歌(さえずり声) ‖ a *song of* praise 賛美歌, 頌(しょう)歌 ‖ the *song of* the wind 風声.

songster, *n.* [男性]歌手.

Q a nation's most *favorite songster* 人気歌手.

Q² *TV songsters* and songstresses テレビ出演の歌手たち.

soon, *ad.* すぐに.

M I will come *as soon* as I can (=possible). できるだけ早く来ます. ‖ He got married *as soon* as he graduated. 彼は卒業すると直ちに結婚した. ‖ *as soon* as the signal was given 合図があると直ちに. ¶*How soon* can you come? いつごろ来られるか. ¶He had *no sooner* faltered it than he fell down. 彼はどもりながらそう言うや否や倒れてしまった. ¶*pretty soon* 間もなく. ¶Winter has come *rather soon* this year. ことしは冬がちょっと早かった. ¶What makes you come *so soon?* 君はなぜこんなに早く来たのか. ¶You spoke *too soon*. 君の言ったのは時日が早過ぎた. ¶*very soon* ほどなく.

P I cannot get there in two days *at* (the) *soonest*. いくら早くとも二日では行けない.

O *sooner* or later おそかれ早かれ ‖ I'd *soon* (=rather) stay here than go out and get a cold. 外出してかぜでも引くよりはここにじっとしていた方がよい.

soot, *n.* すす.

V *brush* the *soot off* the wall 壁にブラシをかけてすすをお

とす. ¶*sweep* (*wipe*) *off* the *soot* すすをはき(ふき)とる.

sooth, *n.* 真実, 事実.

P ***for** sooth* 本当に, 確かに. ¶***in*** (good) *sooth* 実に, 本当に.
O *sooth* to say 実を言えば, 実際の所.

soothe, *v.* きげんをとる.

P *soothe **with*** praise ほめてきげんをとる. 【類】*soothe* a crying child ***with*** sweets.

soothing, *a.* うれしい.

M The absence of advertisements there is ***very** soothing*. そこ(名所など)に広告が見えないのは非常にうれしい.

sop, *v.* ぬれる.

M² be *sopped* ***through*** and ***through*** びしょぬれになる. ¶*sop **up*** water with a cloth 水を布切れでふきとる.
P be *sopped* (=soaked) ***in*** the rain 雨でびしょぬれになる. 【類】Don't *sop* your bread ***in*** your gravy (スープ).

sophism, *n.* き弁.

V The *sophisms* by which these murders have been defended may be ***passed over*** in scorn. これらの殺害を弁護したき弁は一笑に付してもよかろう.

sophisticate, *v.* すれっからしにする.

M a girl, once naive, now ***greatly** sophisticated* かつては純真だったが今はとても悪ずれした女. ¶the ***politically** sophisticated* 政治の裏に通じている人々. ¶a person ***too much** sophisticated* すれっからし.

sophistry, *n.* き弁.

Q It is ***pure** sophistry* to justify those exasperated acts. そのような言語道断な行為を弁明するのは純然たるき弁である.

soprano, *n.* ソプラノ歌手.

Q a ***coloratura** soprano* コロラチューラ・ソプラノ歌手.

sorcery, *n.* 魔術.

P charm ***by** sorcery* 魔術でばかす.

sore, *n.* 傷; はれ物; 心痛.

V ***cure*** a *sore* 傷をなおす. ¶The burn ***made*** a *sore* on my hand. やけどで手にあざができた. ¶***reopen*** old *sores* 古傷をつつく; 忘れかかったけんかなどをまた始める.
Q an ***angry*** *sore* きん衝しているはれもの. ¶have a ***cold** sore* on one's lip からすに灸を据えられる. ¶an ***eating** sore* 内部に食い込むはれ物. ¶a ***festering** sore* 痛むはれ物. ¶a ***running** sore* うみの出るはれ物.
P discharge matter ***in*** a *sore* はれ物からうみを出す. ¶a *sore **on*** the foot 足の痛む個所.

sore, *a.* ただれた; 気に病む.

P He is very *sore **about*** it. 彼はそれを大層気に病んでいる. ¶He looked *sore **at*** the sight. 彼はそれを見て不きげんな顔をしていた. ¶My heart was *sore **for*** them. かわいそうで胸がしめつけられるようだった. ¶an arm *sore **from*** vaccination 種とうでただれた腕. ¶He is *sore **over*** his defeat. 彼は負けたのを気に病んでいる.

sorrow, *n.* 悲しみ, 悲哀; うき目, 不幸.

V ***assuage** sorrow* 悲痛を和らげる. ¶***banish** sorrow* 悲しみを一掃する. ¶This news of his death will ***bring** sorrow* to many hearts. 彼のこの悪い知らせは多くの人の心を痛めることであろう. ¶***cause*** a great deal of *sorrow* to ... ...を非常に悲しませる. ¶*sorrow* that cannot be ***comforted*** 慰めようのない悲しみ. ¶***disguise*** one's *sorrow* 悲しみを顔に出さない. ¶***drown*** one's *sorrows* in drink 酒にうさを晴らす. ¶***experience** sorrow* 悲しみに会う. ¶He ***expressed*** his *sorrow* for my sufferings. 彼は私の苦痛を気の毒だと言った. ¶***feel** sorrow* 悲しむ ‖ ***feel*** (=***have***) the *sorrow* of parting 別れを惜しむ. ¶***forget*** every care and *sorrow* 一切の心配や悲しみを忘れる. ¶Life ***has*** its *sorrows*, as every rose has its thorns. ばらにはばらのとげがあるように人生には人生の悲哀がある. 【類】He has ***had*** many *sorrows*. ¶***inspire** sorrow* 哀れを催させる. ¶In such circumstances an entertainment would seem to ***insult*** the public *sorrow*. こんな場合に娯楽の催しは公衆の悲哀を侮辱するように取られるだろう. ¶***lighten*** (=***mitigate***) our *sorrows* 悲痛を軽減する. ¶He still ***nurses*** his *sorrow* for his wife's death. 彼は今にその妻の死を悲しんでいる. ¶***respect*** a person's *sorrow* 人の悲痛を思いやる. ¶***sow** sorrow* 悲しみの種をまく. ¶***strike** sorrow* into every heart 万人の胸に悲痛を与える. ¶***suffer*** some great *sorrow* ある非常な悲哀を感じる.
V² His *sorrow* did not ***abate***. 彼の悲哀は薄らがなかった. ¶*sorrow* and pleasure ***alternate*** 悲喜こもごも至る.
Q cause ***acute** sorrow* ひどく悲しませる. ¶a ***great*** (=***heavy***) *sorrow* 大悲哀. ¶He had a ***hidden** sorrow*. 彼には人の知らない悲しみがあった. ¶a ***national** sorrow* 国患. ¶She found it difficult to get over the very ***natural** sorrow* at leaving home. 彼女にはさすがに家を離れるときの大きな悲しみを抑え兼ねた. ¶a ***personal** sorrow* 自分の身の悲しみ. ¶her ***secret, life-long** sorrow* 彼女の一生つきまとったひそかな悲しみ. ¶Parting is such ***sweet** sorrow*.—Shakespeare. 別れというものは懐かしい悲しみだ.
P ***After*** that great *sorrow* he never was the same. あの大不幸後彼は全く別人になった. ¶be prevented ***by** sorrow* 悲嘆の余りそれができない. ¶He is living ***in** sorrow*. 彼は悲しみつつ暮している. ¶She died ***of** sorrow* at her great bereavement. 彼女はその(夫などの)死別を大いに悲しんで死んだ. ¶She wept ***through** sorrow*. 彼女は悲しくて泣いた. ¶I learned ***to*** my *sorrow* that ... 私は...と分かって悲しんだ. 【類】learn ***to*** one's *sorrow* the impossibility of ... ¶He was overcome ***with** sorrow*. 彼は悲嘆に暮れた. ¶leave each other ***without*** much *sorrow* わりと平気で別れる.
P² *sorrow **for*** one's misfortunes その不幸に対する悲しみ. ¶the *sorrows **of*** future years 将来の悲哀 ‖ *sorrows **of*** travel 旅愁. ¶A foolish son is a *sorrow **to*** his mother. ばかむすこは母の苦労の種だ.

sorrow, *v.* 悲しむ.

M *sorrow **out*** with tears 悲しみを涙に流す.
P *sorrow **over*** my hard fate わが身の不運を嘆く ‖ an old woman who *sorrows **over*** the passing of sixty winters 六十の坂を越した老女.

sorry, *a.* 残念な, 気の毒な; みじめな, くだらない.

M I am ***heartily** sorry*. 実にお気の毒だ. ¶I'm ***so** sorry* to hear that. それはほんとにお気の毒です. 【類】I'm ***so** sorry* for your father's death. ¶I am ***terribly** sorry* for (=about) the accident. その事故ははなはだお気の毒なことです.
P I am *sorry **about*** it. それは残念だ. ¶I am *sorry **at*** hearing of your failure. 私は君の失敗を聞いて残念です. ¶I am (=feel) *sorry **for*** you. お気の毒です ‖ I am *sorry **for*** your sufferings. さぞお困りのことでしょう. 【類】I am *sorry **for*** giving you trouble. / I am *sorry **for*** putting you to such expense. / You will be *sorry **for*** what you have done some day.
O I shall not be *sorry* if ... 私は...してもかまわない. ‖ I'm *sorry* I startled you so. そんなに君をびっくりさせて済みません. ‖ I am *sorry* to trouble you, but ... すみませんが... ‖ a *sorry* sight みじめな有様. 【類】a *sorry* excuse / a *sorry* performance.

sort, *n.* 種類; 《俗》ある性質の人.

V ***exercise*** a *sort* of paternal control over ... ...に対し父としての一種の監督を行う. ¶After a spell of dull weather the country is ***experiencing*** a *sort* of second summer. うっとうしい天気が続いた後でその地方は二度目の夏といったような陽気である. ¶they actively ***propagated*** all *sorts* of calumnies against ... 彼らは...に対してありとあらゆる非難を盛んに流布した. ¶***take*** all *sorts* of pains with ... ...に対して色々骨を折る. ¶***try*** all *sorts* of devices あらゆる種類の手段を試みる.
Q machinery of ***all** sorts* 各種の機械 ‖ ***all** sorts* and conditions of men 種々様々な人 ‖ We talked of ***all** sorts* of subjects. われわれはあらゆる問題について語った. 【類】***all** sorts* of things / ***all** sorts* of nationalities and races. ¶the ***better** sort* 高級な人々. ¶sorcery of the ***blacker** sort* 恐ろしいよう術. ¶the ***common** sort* 平民 ‖ ***common** sorts* なみもの. ¶a ***crude** sort* of cloak-room for the employees 雇人用の粗末な携帯品預り所. ¶a ***curious** sort* of jacket 妙な型のジャケツ. ¶He surveyed me a moment in a ***dazed** sort* of fashion. 彼は面食ったような風でちょっと私を見守った. ¶a ***different** sort* of man 別のタイプの人. ¶a ***dull, stagnant** sort* of life with boredom as its keynote けん怠に満ちたつまらない沈滞した生活. ¶I will take three of ***each** sort*. それぞれの口を三個ずつ下さい. ¶peploe of ***every** sort* and kind あらゆる種類の人々. ¶people of ***evil** sort* たちの悪い人々. ¶What a ***funny** sort* of man! 実におもしろい人だ. ¶a ***gloomy** sort* of house 陰気な家. ¶a ***good** sort* of man 性質の良い人. ¶a clergyman of the ***good** old **sort*** 昔風の人のよい牧師. ¶a fairly ***humdrum** sort* of place 全く平々凡々の場所. ¶of ***inferior** sort* 低級

な. ¶With a ***joyful*** *sort* of stoicism she neglected her pains. 一種歓喜に満ちた冷静さで彼女はその苦難をものともしなかった. ¶His instructions were of the ***laconic*** *sort*. 彼の訓示は寸鉄的のものであった. ¶in the ***like*** *sort* 同じ様に. ¶among the ***lower*** *sort* of people 下層社会の人々に混って. ¶men of the ***meaner*** *sort* 地位の低い人々 ‖ the ***meaner*** *sort* 低級な人々. ¶with a ***mock*** *sort* of shyness わざとはずかしそうな振りをして. ¶a ***motherly*** *sort* of woman 母性型の女. ¶biscuits of ***one*** *sort* 一と色のビスケット. ¶a very ***poor*** *sort* of place はなはだつまらない場所. ¶What a ***pretty*** *sort* of judges you are! 君(たち)は実にりっぱな鑑識家だ. ¶a ***queer*** *sort* of guy へんなやつ. ¶He is a ***quiet*** *sort* of man. 彼は物静かな人だ. ¶a woman of the ***right*** *sort* 正道を歩む女 ‖ election of the ***right*** *sort* of officials 適任者の選挙 ‖ have not the ***right*** *sort* of heart to ... ...するという本当の気持がない. ¶***rougher*** and more ***brutal*** *sorts* of European outcasts 欧州浮浪者の中でも特に乱暴で野蛮な連中. ¶biscuits of ***several*** *sorts* 数種のビスケット. ¶He began business in the ***smallest*** *sort* of way. 彼はごく小規模に商売を始めた. ¶a meeting of ***some*** *sort* ある種の会合. 【類】I require ***some*** *sort* of portmanteau (トランク) for my journey. / There is sure to be ***some*** *sort* of dinner going. ¶seeds of well-known ***standard*** *sorts* 有名な品種の種子. ¶This is a ***strange*** *sort* of story. これは奇妙な話だ. ¶This kind of view is of the most ***superficial*** *sort*. こうした意見が一番皮相なものである. ¶a few coffee-shops of the ***superior*** *sort* 高級な二三のコーヒー店. ¶For some varieties of stock the male clerk still is the most ***suitable*** and ***successful*** *sort* of salesman. ある種の商品には相変らず男の店員が売子として最も適当でありまた最も好成績をあげている. ¶***that*** (***this***) *sort* of person. あの(この)様な人. ☞ these (those) などの次に sort と単数に用いるのは俗語体. ‖ ***That*** *sort* of thing is not much in my way. [カルタ会など]そういったことは私は余り好まない. 【類】He is not a man of ***that*** *sort*. ¶in a ***troubled*** *sort* of way 困ったという風に. ¶of ***various*** *sorts* 様々の. ¶***What*** *sort* of man is he? どんな人だ. ‖ ***What*** *sort* of clothes does he wear? 彼はどんな着物を着ているか. ¶crimes of ***whatever*** *sort* どういう種類の犯罪でも. ¶people of ***your*** *sort* 君のような人々.

P He is wise ***after*** a *sort*. 彼はどこか利口な所がある. ¶***as*** a *sort* of reward 一種の報酬として. ¶He is a good hand ***at*** all *sorts* of games. 彼はどんな競技でもうまい. ¶***by*** a *sort* of accident ちょっとしたことで. ¶***in*** (=after) a *sort* いく分, どうやら ‖ The crane is held ***in*** a *sort* of semi-veneration by all classes of the community. つるはその社会のあらゆる階級によって半ば神様扱いにされている. 【類】He is honest ***in*** a *sort*. ‖ They are classified ***in*** *sorts*. それは種類分けにしてある. ¶These goods are all ***of*** a *sort*. この品は皆一つ手だ ‖ He could speak English ***of*** a *sort*. 彼は英語といえばまあ英語のようなものを話すことができた. ‖ cranks ***of*** one *sort* or another 色々のクランク. ‖ I never saw anything ***of*** the *sort* before. 私はそんな物はこれまで見たことがない. 【類】I will make no attempt ***of*** the *sort*. / "Do you mean to insult me?" "Nothing ***of*** the *sort*." ¶I am a little ***out of*** *sorts* today. きょうは少し気分が悪い.

P² He is a *sort* ***of*** a hero. 彼は一種の英雄だ. 【類】a prison, a *sort* ***of*** social quarantine / ..., and all that *sort* ***of*** thing ... ‖ it serves as a *sort* ***of*** touchstone to test ... それは...を試験する一種の試金石となる ‖ a *sort* ***of*** companion and servant united 友だちと下男を兼ねたようなもの ‖ a *sort* ***of*** cross between ... and ... ...と...との合の子.

sort, *v.* 口分けする; えり分ける; 一致する.

M *sort* ***out*** the good from the evil 善悪を択り分ける.

P *sort* clothes ***by*** colors 織物を色別けにする. ¶His actions *sort* ill ***with*** his professions. 彼の行動はその言う所と一致しない.

sorta, *ad.* [=sort of] 《米俗》いく分, ...みたい.

O I *sorta* (=sort of) expected it. 《米俗》まあそう期待していたわけだ. ‖ *Sorta* interesting, ain't it? ちょっと面白いじゃないか. ☞ sorta (=sort of), kinda (=kind of) は副詞用法で somewhat, rather, almost 位の意. sorter, kinder ともつづる.

sortie, *n.* 出撃.

V ***make*** a *sortie* (=sally) from the fortress [城兵など]城さいから出撃する.

soul, *n.* 霊魂; 精神; 要義; 生気; 人間.

V ***absorb*** the *soul* 魂を奪う. ¶in order to ***benefit*** the *souls* of their ancestors その祖先の霊を成仏せさるために. ¶a woman who ***degraded*** her *soul* 心の堕落した婦人. ¶the doll babies which so ***delight*** the *souls* of our little sisters at home われわれの家の少女たちの心を非常に喜ばせるひな人形. ¶***deprave*** the *soul* 心を堕落させる. ¶***develop*** the *soul* 精神を啓発する. ¶***elevate*** the *soul* 精神を向上させる. ¶***find*** in him a kindred *soul* 彼と気が合う. ¶***freeze*** one's *soul* 肝を冷やす. ¶***gain*** numerous *souls* to Christ 数多の人をキリスト教に転向させる. ¶The lovers ***have*** but one *soul* between them. その相愛の二人は一心同体である. ‖ He ***has*** no *soul* for art. 芸術鑑賞眼がない. ¶***keep*** body and *soul* ***together*** 露命をつなぐ. ¶not ***knowing*** a *soul* だれ一人知っている人がいないで. ¶His pictures ***lack*** *soul*. 彼の絵には生気がない. ¶***nourish*** one's *soul* 精神を養う. ¶the destruction of false ideas and of the illusions which ***obsess*** the *soul* of man 人間の精神に付きまとうびゅう見もう想の打破. ¶***put*** *soul* into one's work 仕事に身を入れる. ¶***save*** a *soul* 魂を救済する. ¶***sear*** the *soul* 精神をまひさせる. ¶I did not ***see*** a *soul* in the street. 往来には人っ子ひとり見えなかった. 【類】Not a *soul* was to be ***seen*** all around. ¶She ***sold*** her *soul* for money (the luxury and magnificence). 彼女は金(など)のためにその魂を売った. ¶Melancholy ***steeps*** my *soul*. 憂うつが私の心にしみ込む. ¶***throw*** one's whole *soul* into ... ...に魂を打込む. ¶***train*** the *soul* 精神を修養する. ¶***win*** *souls* to Christ 人々をキリスト教に入れる. ¶***worry*** one's *soul* about ... ...に心を悩ます.

V² May his *soul* ***rest*** in peace! =God rest his soul! [邦語なら]なむあみだぶつ. ¶his *soul* ***yearned*** to ... 彼は心の中で...したいと願った.

Q an ***artistic*** *soul* 芸術的な人. ¶a ***booklovìng*** *soul* 愛書家. ¶a ***cheery*** *soul* 快活な人物. ¶a ***cheery old*** *soul* of 87 八十七歳の快活な老人. ¶be a pair of ***congenial*** *souls* 意気投合する仲である. ¶a ***dear good*** *soul* 好人物. ¶the ***deceased*** *soul* of a man 故人の霊. ¶***delicate*** *souls* 情のこまやかな人人. ¶***departed*** *souls* 故人の霊. ¶an ***eccentric*** *soul* 変人. ¶a ***genial*** *soul* 親切な人物. ¶a ***good*** *soul* 良い人 ‖ My ***good*** *soul*. お前. ¶a ***grand, simple, chivalrous*** *soul* 英まい単純で義気ある人物. ¶the ***greatest*** *souls* of antiquity 古代の最大人物. ¶a ***high-minded*** *soul* 気高い人. ¶He is a ***hopeful*** *soul*, and looks to the future with confidence. 彼は確信を持って将来に対する希望に満ちた人である. ¶a feast of ***hungry*** *souls* 施餓鬼. ¶an ***irascible*** *soul* かんしゃく持. ¶a ***kindly*** *soul* 情のある人. ¶a ***kindred*** *soul* 同志. ¶***like-minded*** *souls* 同志. ¶***little*** *souls* 小人. ¶a ***lost*** *soul* 済度しがたい人. ¶the ***national*** *soul* of India インドの国民精神. ¶He has ***no*** *soul*. 彼には熱がない. ¶newly ***parted*** *soul* 新仏. ¶people possessed of ***pioneering*** *souls* 新地開拓の志ある人々. ¶He is a ***poor*** *soul* to whom none of these things appeal. 彼はこうしたものを見ても何の感じも起らないかわいそうな人間だ. ‖ ***Poor*** *soul!* かわいそうに. ¶except a few ***prophetic*** *souls* 先見の明のある二三人の外は. ¶Some ***prudish*** *souls* are always ready to be shocked. 謹厳をよそおう人の中には(少し下品なことを言われると)じきに驚く者がある. ¶She was (=had) a ***religious*** *soul*. 彼女は宗教心があった. ¶some ***romantic*** *souls* may wish that ... 空想的な人間の中には...を望むものがあるかも知れない. ¶Not a ***single*** *soul* was to be seen. 人っ子ひとり見えなかった. ¶a ***sordid*** *soul* 卑劣な人. ¶a ***thirsty*** *soul* 飲み助. ¶***two*** *souls* in one breast=duality 二重人格. ¶an ***unconquerable*** *soul* 征服されない気魂. ¶a man with an ***upright*** *soul* 心の正しい人. ¶a ***worthy*** *soul* りっぱな人物.

P ***by*** (=***for***) my *soul*=on (=upon) my soul 真心から, 神かけて ‖ ***by*** the *soul* of me, you shall ... どうしても...したまえ. ¶He played as if ***from*** his *soul*. 彼は心をこめて演じた. ¶infuse a spirit ***into*** one's *soul* 人の精神に活気を吹込む. ¶***with*** one's whole *soul*=[with] heart and soul 誠心誠意 ‖ The ship sank ***with*** 300 *souls* on board. その船は三百人の乗客を乗せたまま沈没した.

P² The *soul* ***of*** commerce is upright dealing. 商業の要義は正直な取引にある. 【類】Simplicity is the *soul* ***of*** conversations. ‖ the *soul* ***of*** the enterprise その事業の主脳者 ‖ the *soul* ***of*** a movement 運動の中心人物 ‖ He is the *soul* ***of*** honor. 彼は高潔な人格者だ.

sound, *n.* 音響; 音調, 音声; 音響距離.

V These *sounds* can only be ***approximated*** by a Japanese equivalent. これらの音は日本語では十分に表わせない. ¶I can't ***bear*** the *sound.* 私はその音は聞いていられない. ¶***catch*** the *sound* of ... ...の音を聞取る. ¶hissing *sound* ***caused*** by plunging red-hot metal into water しゃく熱した金属を水中に突込んだときに立つしゅーという音. ¶***emit*** (=***give forth***) a *sound* 音を発する. ¶***enunciate*** correctly those *sounds* それらの音を正しく発音する. ¶In Spanish J ***has*** the *sound* of H. スペイン語では J を H のように発音する. ¶Presently he ***heard*** the *sound* of footsteps. ほどなく彼は足音を聞いた.【類】Not a *sound* was ***heard.*** ¶All *sound* of music was ***hushed*** throughout the land. 全国にわたって音曲は停止になった. ¶***infer*** *sound* from printed letters 印刷した文字から音を推測する. ¶***make*** a *sound* 音を立てる. ¶***produce*** a *sound* 音を出す. ¶***take*** the *sound* to be imaginary その音を気のせいだと思う.

V^2 *Sounds* ***carry*** well in this hall. この会堂は音がよく通る. ¶Not a *sound* ***escaped*** him. 彼は少しの音も聞き漏らさなかった. ¶The familiar *sound* of dance music ***floated*** out of the dining-room which was well filled. 舞踏曲の聞き慣れた音が満員の食堂から流れて来た. ¶The *sound* of his footsteps was ***gone.*** 彼の足音が聞えなくなった. ¶The *sound* ***swelled*** from a murmur to a roar. その音はつぶやきから段々高まって怒号になった.

Q The sentence has an ***abrupt, truncated*** *sound.* その文はぶっきらぼうで頭が取れているような感じだ. ¶***articulate*** *sounds* はっきりした音. ¶have an ***artificial*** and ***hollow*** *sound* 不自然なうつろに響く音だ. ¶a ***charming*** *sound* 美音. ¶emit a ***curious*** *sound* 妙な音を出す. ¶The earthquake began with a ***deep*** (***low***) ***rumbling*** *sound.* 地震は太い(低い)ごろごろいう音とともに始まった. ¶a ***deep hollow*** *sound* 底力のあるうつろに響く音. ¶give forth a ***deep*** and ***lingering*** *sound* 底力のある長く尾を引く音を発する. ¶a ***dulcet*** *sound* 美音. ¶a ***dull*** *sound* にぶい音. ¶an ***ear-deafening*** *sound* 耳をろうするばかりの大音響. ¶one of the cities' ***familiar*** *sounds* 都市の聞き慣れた音の一. ¶a ***hideous*** *sound* ぞっとするような音. ¶a ***hissing*** *sound* しゅーしゅーいう音. ¶make an ***inarticulate*** *sound* ろれつが回らない. ¶a ***joyful*** *sound* 歓声. ¶a ***mournful*** *sound* 悲しい泣声. ¶the ***muffled*** *sound* of the gong 低く沈んだどらの音. ¶He uttered with a ***nasal*** *sound.* 彼は鼻声で言った. ¶The sentence has an ***odd*** *sound.* [その文は]調子が変だ. ¶I heard an ***ominous*** *sound* near by. すぐそばに気味の悪い音がした. ¶a ***penetrating*** *sound* よく通る音. ¶The bell has a ***quaint*** old-world *sound* about it. そのつり鐘には昔をしのばせる異様な響きがある. ¶A ***queer*** *sound* escaped then. へんな音がそのとき漏れた. ‖ This may have a ***queer*** *sound.* =This may sound queer. こう言うと変に聞えるだろうが. ¶a ***rumbling*** *sound* [雷などの]ごろごろいう音. ¶The bullet grazed past with a ***sharp*** *sound.* 弾丸がすれすれにびゅーとんで行った. ¶***sharp metallic*** *sound* かちんという鋭い音. ¶a ***signal*** *sound* 号音. ¶a ***sonorous*** *sound* 朗々と響き渡る音. ¶a ***splashing*** *sound* of a waterfall 滝のとばしる音. ¶It has a ***strange*** *sound.* それは変に聞える. ¶emit ***subterranean*** *sounds* [火山など]地底から音響を発する. ¶a ***sweet*** *sound* うるわしい音声. ¶hear the ***tinkling*** *sound* of a bell 鈴のちりんちりん鳴るのを聞く. ¶a ***tinkling, metallic*** *sound* きんきんいう金属的な音.

Q^2 a ***buzzer*** *sound* of a slot-machine 自動販売器のザーという音. ¶a ***consonant*** *sound* 子音. ¶The "***ground***" *sounds* irritate the ear. 地音が耳ざわりだ(トーキーなど). ¶a ***speech*** *sound* 声音. ¶***traffic*** *sounds* 交通の騒音. ¶a ***vowel*** *sound* 母音. ¶a ***whistling*** *sound* ひゅーひゅーという音.

P ***at*** the *sound* of a bugle らっぱが鳴ると.【類】We got up ***at*** the *sound.* / startle even ***at*** the *sound* of footsteps. ¶***beyond*** the *sound* of human voice 人声も聞かれない所に. ¶I was awakened ***by*** a singular *sound.* 私は妙な音で眼がさめた. ¶The hall is bad ***for*** *sound.* その会館は音響効果が悪い. ¶About a fourth ***of*** the *sound* now used in talkies is faked. トーキーで今聞かれる音のおよそ四分の一は擬音である. ¶***out of*** [the] *sound* of ... ...の音の聞えないところに. ¶dance ***to*** the *sound* of music 音楽の音に連れて踊る.【類】The funeral procession moved slowly along ***to*** the *sound* of muffled drum. ¶The church clocks strike ***with*** a muffled *sound.* 教会の時計は低く沈んだ音で鳴る. ‖ ***with*** the *sound* of trumpets らっぱを吹奏して. ¶***within*** ***sound*** of the sea 波の音の聞える所で ‖ He was born ***within*** ***sound*** of Bow Bells. 彼はロンドンの Bow Church の鐘声の聞えるところで産声をあげた. ☞日本なら「神田川の水で産湯を使った」とでもいう所.

P^2 The *sound* ***of*** the footsteps died away. 足音が消えて行った.【類】the *sound* ***of*** thunder (human voice) / the *sound* ***of*** an automobile horn (自動車の警笛) / Through the half-opened door came the *sound* ***of*** many voices. ‖ the *sounds* ***of*** spring 春の調べ.

sound, *v.* 鳴らす; 鳴る; 響く, 聞える; 思われる.

M It *sounds* very ***alluring.*** 心をそそるように響く. ¶... *sounds* ***better*** from a man's mouth 男は...という方が一層適当である. ¶That *sounds* ***beautiful.*** そりゃ美しい話ですね. ¶*sound* ***childish*** 子供っぽく聞える. ¶His voice *sounds* ***clear.*** 彼の声ははっきりしている. ¶The bell *sounds* ***cracked.*** あの鐘はひびの入った音がする. ¶it may *sound* ***cynical*** that I say, ... 私が...というと皮肉に聞えるだろうが ... ¶The "l" in "cold" *sounds* ***darker*** than the "l" in "light". "cold" の "l" は "light" の "l" ほど明りょうに響かない. ¶*sound* ***elegant*** 優美に聞える. ¶The report *sounded* ***everywhere.*** その報道は至るところに伝わった. ¶The expression *sounds* ***familiar.*** その言回わしは平凡に聞える. ¶That excuse *sounds* ***false.*** その申訳はうそらしい. ¶His voice *sounds* ***feeble.*** 彼の声は力がない. ¶The music *sounded* ***frightful*** like a serpent's song. その音楽はへびの歌のように恐ろしい音色だった. ¶*sounds* ***funny*** こっけいに聞える.【類】It may *sound* ***funny*** if I say that ... ¶His voice *sounds* ***harsh.*** 彼の声はざらざらしている. ¶a voice that *sounds* ***hollow*** and ***deep*** うつろにひびく太い声. ¶***How did*** the story *sound* to you? その話は君にはどう聞えたか. ¶The story *sounds* ***incredible.*** その話はどうも信じ難い. ¶It *sounds* ***interesting.*** おもしろそうな話だ. ¶Those words *sound* very ***lofty*** and ***big.*** その言葉ははなはだ高尚かつ壮大に聞える. ¶The wind *sounds* ***melancholy.*** 風が物悲しく聞える. ¶This *sounds* more ***natural.*** こう言った方が不自然でない. ¶It would *sound* ***odd*** so to speak of ... ...のことをそう言うのは変に聞えるだろう. ¶*sound* ***paradoxical*** [言論など]逆説的に聞える. ¶It *sounds* ***plausible.*** もっともらしく聞える. ¶His speech *sounds* ***quaint.*** 彼の言葉は奇抜に聞える. ¶It *sounds* ***queer.*** それは変に聞える. ¶It may *sound* ***queerly*** in Japanese ears. それは日本人の耳には変に聞えるかも知れない. ¶It *sounds* very ***ridiculous.*** それを聞くとはなはだばからしく感じる. ¶That explanation *sounds* all ***right.*** その説明はもっともらしい. ¶The answer does not *sound* ***satisfactory.*** その回答は満足とは思われない. ¶His voice *sounds* ***shrill.*** 彼の声はかんばしっている. ¶The plan *sounds* very ***silly.*** その計画はばかばかしく思われる. ¶His voice *sounds* ***soft.*** 彼の声はやさしい. ¶***strange*** as it may *sound* そう言うと変に聞えるだろうが. ¶The bell *sounds* ***sweet.*** その鐘はいい音がする. ‖ Every word of hers *sounds* ***sweet.*** 彼女の一語一語が魅力だ. ¶That explanation *sounds* ***true.*** その説明は正しく思われる. ¶The silver coin does not *sound* ***well.*** その銀貨はよい音がしない(にせ物らしい). ‖ Your plan *sounds* ***well.*** 君の案はよさそうに思われる.

P It *sounds* ***like*** thunder. それは雷のように聞える. ‖ *Sounds* ***like*** fun. おもしろそうね.【類】The statement *sounds* ***like*** fiction. / it may *sound* ***like*** a paradox, but it is true that ... / It *sounds* ***like*** an animal howling. ¶*sound* an alarm ***on*** the bugle or drums ラッパまたは太鼓で警報する. ¶Suddenly the note of a whippoorwill *sounded* ***through*** the trees. 突然よたかの鳴声が木の間から聞えた.

sound, *v.* ...の意中を探る.

M *sound* a person ***as to*** ... ...について人の考えにさぐりを入れる. ¶He is looking at you, trying to *sound* you ***out.*** 彼は君の顔色を見て君の意向を探ろうとしている. ‖ *sound* ***out*** public opinion 世論を探り出す.【類】*sound* ***out*** sentiment on ... ‖ *sound* him ***out*** on the idea その計画に関する彼の意図を探る.

P *sound* a person ***on*** (=***about*** *or* ***as to***) a matter (question, subject) ある事柄(など)について人の意中を探る ‖ *sound* a person ***on*** his opinion 人の意見に探りを入れる. ¶*sound* one ***upon*** the point その点について探りを入れる.

sound, *a.* 確実な, 着実な, 健全な.

M ***financially sound*** [会社・銀行など]財政的に確実な. ¶be ***logically sound*** 筋道が立っている. ¶The view is ***morally sound***. その見解は道徳的に健全だ. ¶The method is ***pedagogically sound***. その教授法は学理に適っている. ¶***perfectly sound*** in mind and body 心身ともに全く健全な. ¶The view is ***philosophically sound***. その見解は哲学的に正確だ. 「trine 学説の正しい.

P ***sound in*** body and mind 身心の健全な ‖ ***sound in*** doc-

O a *sound* policy (mind) 健全政策(など) ‖ a *sound* whipping 容赦のないむち打.

sounding, *n.* 水深測量; 測鉛の到達点.

V ***strike soundings*** 水深を測量する. ¶***take soundings*** for ... ...の瀬踏みをする.

P come ***into soundings*** 水の浅い所に来る. ¶get ***off soundings*** 測鉛の届かない所へ行く; 自分の手に余ることに取掛る. ¶get ***on soundings*** 測鉛の届く所へ来る; [比ゆ的] 自分の得意のことに取掛る. ¶The ship was soon ***out of soundings***.

soundness, *n.* 健全. └船はすぐ深海に出た.

V He now ***enjoys*** perfect mental *soundness*. 彼は今は申分のない健全な精神状態である.

Q ***sanitary soundness*** 衛生の健全. ¶the ***theoretical soundness*** of the argument 立論の理論的確実性.

soup, *n.* 吸物, スープ.

V ***heat*** the *soup* on a fire 火にかけてスープを暖める. ¶***dispose of*** one's *soup* with speed and noise 急いで音を立ててスープを平げる. ¶***drink*** one's *soup* from a cup 茶わんから[直接]スープを飲む. ¶***eat soup*** from a plate [スプーンで]スープをさらから吸う. ¶I ***had*** some *soup* for lunch. 私は昼食にスープを吸った. ¶***stir soup*** スープをかき回す. ¶***take soup*** スープを吸う. ¶***soup thickened*** with peas and barely えんどう豆と大麦入の濃いスープ.

Q a ***clear*** (***thick***) *soup* 澄んだ(濃い)スープ. ¶a ***rich soup*** 味の濃厚なスープ. ¶a ***thick custardy egg soup*** 茶わん蒸し. ¶***watery soup*** 水っぽいスープ.

Q[2] hot ***noodle soup*** 熱いうどん入りスープ. ¶***rice-cake red-bean soup*** しるこ. ¶***tomato*** (***chicken, pea***) ***soup*** トマト(など)スープ. ¶***vegetable soup*** 野菜スープ.

P be ***in*** the *soup* 窮境にある.

sour, *a.* すい. 「と!

M ***How sour*** these grapes taste! このぶどうのすっぱいこ

P make one's face ***sour at*** ... ...を見(聞い)て顔をしかめる. ¶***sour to*** the taste すい味の.

O taste (smell) *sour* [牛乳など]すばい味(香)がする.

source, *n.* 水源(地); 源, 出所, もと.

V ***credit*** the *source* of an article 文の出所を明かにする. ¶***disclose*** one's *source* of information 情報の出所を明かす. ¶***discover*** the *source* of the Nile ナイル川の水源を発見する. ¶This *source* has not yet been ***enlisted*** for the study of the question. この方はまだその問題研究に利用されていない. ¶***exploit*** the *sources* of wealth 富源を開発する. ¶***form*** a *source* for future trouble 将来の禍根となる ‖ ***form*** a never-failing *source* of interest いつも興味の源泉となる. 【類】***form*** the *source* of his profit. ¶These streams ***have*** their *source* in the forests high up the mountain-side. これらの水流は山腹の上方部にある森に源を発する. ‖ It ***has*** its *source* in envy (jealousy). それはしっとに原因している. ¶***indicate*** the *source*, where possible できうる場合にはその出所を示す. ¶***locate*** the *source* of one's infection その伝染した場所を突きとめる. ¶***name*** the *source* of information 情報の出所を明記する. ¶***put away*** all *sources* of sorrow and pain from the world 憂愁と苦痛の源を世界から除く. ¶***remove*** the *sources* of misunderstanding 誤解の原因を除く. ¶The stream ***takes*** its *source* from the lake. その流れはその湖水から出ている. ¶***tap*** a new *source* of revenue 新しい財源を作る. ¶cannot ***trace*** the *source* of the report その報道の出所を突きとめることはできない ‖ ***trace*** its *source* to India その起源はインドにさかのぼる. ¶The *source* of this information is ***withheld***. この報道の出所は伏せてある.

Q an ***abundant*** *source* of pleasure and profit for any intelligent mind あらゆる識者に取って快楽と利益の豊富な源. ¶the ***Alpine*** *sources* of the Rhine アルプス山のライン川水源地. ¶statistics compiled from ***authentic sources*** 信頼すべき材料から作った統計. ¶***authoritative sources*** 権威ある出所. ¶I have it from the very ***best source*** that ... 私はきわめて確かな筋から...ということを聞いた. ¶one of Britain's ***biggest source*** of badly needed dollars イギリスが非常に必要とするドルの最大源泉の一つ. ¶Their ***chief sources*** of income are their fisheries. 彼らの収入の主なる財源は漁業である. 【類】his ***chief source*** of inspiration / America's ***chief source*** of rubber. ¶a ***constant source*** of anxiety 始終心配の種 ‖ The prevailing chaos in English with regard to hyphenation is a ***constant source*** of perplexity to the compiler of a dictionary. ハイフン使用に関しては英語はでたらめなので辞書編集者にとってはいつも悩みの種だ. ¶an ***endless*** (=an ***inexhaustible***) *source* of interest 尽きない興味の泉. ¶a ***favorite source*** of pleasure 人に好まれる娯楽のたね. ¶The bestowal of wet umbrellas in omnibuses and tramcars is a ***fertile source*** of trouble. バスや電車の中ではぬれた洋がさの始末にこまる. ¶***fruitful sources*** of disease よく病気の本となるもの. 【類】The next-door neighbors are a ***fruitful source*** of a wife's little worries (ちょっとした苦労). / one of the ***fruitful sources*** of waste in economic life. ¶a very ***handsome source*** of income 非常に結構な財源. ¶from an ***impeachable source*** いかがわしい筋から. ¶an ***inexhaustible source*** of wealth (energy, strength) 無尽蔵な富源(など). ¶He possesses great ***intellectual sources*** and intuitive judgment. 彼には豊富な知力と直覚的な判断力がある. ¶a perfectly ***legitimate source*** of income 全く合法的な収入の道. ¶information supplied from some ***mischief-making source*** だれかのいたずらから出た報道. ¶a ***never-failing source*** of interest (regret, pleasure) 必ず興味(など)をもたらす源泉. ¶be collected from ***numerous sources*** 多くの出典の中から集められている. ¶information (data) from an ***official source*** その筋からの報道(材料). ¶an ***organic*** (***inorganic***) ***source*** 有(無)機源. ¶***original sources*** of information 報道の出所. 【類】study history from the ***original sources*** (根本資料). ¶a most ***pernicious source*** of evil きわめて有害な罪悪の源. ¶***primary*** (=***original***) ***sources*** 最初の出所. ¶his ***principal source*** of income 彼の主な収入源. ¶a ***prolific source*** of litigation 訴訟の多くの原因. ¶***recondite*** manuscript *sources* 世間に余り知れていない筆写の種本. ¶figures gathered from ***reliable sources*** 確かな筋から採った統計. ¶a ***rich source*** of information 豊富な知識の泉(百科全書など). ¶a ***secondary source*** of historical knowledge 第二次的史料. ¶crimes of violence having a ***sexual source*** 性に原因する暴行犯. ¶the ***standard sources*** of information 報道の本筋. ¶from figures obtained from a ***trustworthy source*** it appears that ... 信頼すべき筋から得た数字では...らしい. 【類】This item of news came from a ***trustworthy source***. ¶the ***ultimate source*** 根本の源. ¶an ***unfailing source*** of solace and encouragement 間違いなく慰さめと激励を与えるもの[伝記など]. ¶information from ***unimpeachable sources*** 確実な筋からの報道. ¶a book edited from ***various sources*** 諸々の出所から採って編集した書物. ¶***well-informed sources*** say that ... 消息通の語る所によれば... 【類】learn from a ***well-informed source*** that ...

Q[2] the International Bank and other ***credit sources*** 国際銀行及び他の融資源. ¶direct one to ***information sources*** 報道の出所を...に教える. ¶a ***government source*** said that ... 政府筋の語る所では ‖ statistical data obtained from ***government sources*** 政府筋から得た統計資料. ¶official ***news sources*** 官辺筋の報道. ¶have been descended from one ***parent source*** 同祖の子孫だ. ¶unless our ***reference sources*** have failed us われわれの見た参考書に誤りがなければ... ¶the political barriers to ***supply sources*** of materials 物資供給源に対する政治的障害. ¶the ***water supply sources*** of a country 一国の水の供給源. ¶a compilation of evidence from ***world sources*** 世界中から集めた証拠の編集.

P the fowl ***as*** a *source* of food supply 食糧供給源としての鶏. ¶build a hydraulic power plant ***at*** the *source* of a river 川の水源地に水力発電所を設ける ‖ imposition of taxes ***at source*** 源泉課税 ‖ cut off the evil ***at*** its *source* 禍根を断つ.

P[2] go to the best *sources* ***for*** one's information 参考に一番良い本を見る. ¶gradually spread ***from*** a single *source* 一つの根元から次第に広がる ‖ The materials are drawn ***from*** all *sources*. 材料は各方面から集めた. 【類】gather data *from* many *sources*. ¶The river has its *source* ***in*** the ... mountains. その川は...山脈に源を発する. ¶Intemperance is the *source* ***of*** many evils. 大酒は多くの害悪の源である. 【類】Pride is a *source* ***of*** ill manners (無作法). / a *source* ***of*** untold (無数の) evils. ‖ the earth and the sun—two great *sources* ***of*** life 生の二大源泉たる地球と太陽 ‖ a *source* ***of*** sorrowful memory 悲しい思い出の種. 【類】It is a *source* ***of*** great pleasure to me. / a *source* ***of*** profit / a *source* ***of*** national weakness / a *source* ***of*** trouble (=worry *or* unxiety) / a *source* ***of*** funds / a *source* ***of*** income / a *source* ***of*** wonder / This *source* ***of*** inspiration has dried up. ‖ Guano is a *source* ***of*** fertilizer. グアノ(海鳥のふん)は肥料になる. ‖ a *source* ***of*** money out 出費の一項目.

souse, *v.* 突込む.

P *souse* the dog ***in*** a pond 池に犬を突込む. ¶*souse* ***with*** water 水に浸す.

south, *n.* 南, 南方; 南部; [the S-] (《米》) 南部.

V The house ***faces*** [the] *south.* 家は南向きだ. ¶***travel*** *south* 南方へ旅行する.

Q about two miles ***due*** *south* to ... ...の真南約二マイル ‖ streets running due north and ***due*** *south* 真北と真南に通っている街. ¶at the ***extreme*** *south* of South America 南米の南端に. ¶the ***slave-owning*** *south* どれいを所有している南部.

P Ceylon is an island ***at*** the *south* of India. セイロンはインドの南にある島である. 【類】***At*** the *south* of the long, straggling street, which follows the sweep (曲り道) of the lower end of the lake, and which is known as Moto Hakone, you will find an avenue leading to some stone steps, suggesting a shrine beyond. / a noted whirpool ***at*** the *south* of the Lofoten Is. off Norway. ¶A hot breeze blew ***from*** the *south.* 熱風が南方から吹いて来た. ‖ a wind ***from*** the *south*=a southerly wind 南風. ¶***in*** the *south* of Japan 日本の南部に ‖ down ***in*** the *South* (《米》) 南部に(で). ☞ up in the North に対する句. 【類】a famous street ***in*** the *south* of London / the glow ***in*** the *south* of the sky ‖ It (=The wind) is ***in*** the *south.* 南風だ. ¶inhabitants ***of*** the *south* 南方の住人. ¶It is bounded ***on*** the *south* by France. 南はフランスに接している. ¶Mexico and other countries ***to*** the *south* メキシコ及び(米国から見て)南方の諸国 ‖ The garden lies ***to*** the *south* of the house. 庭は家の南にある. 【類】Sakai is a seaport town, about 6 miles from Osaka ***to*** the *south,* on the Yamato-gawa. / Mount Fuji rises ***to*** the *south* of the town. / It is situated ***to*** the *south* of the bay. ‖ The wind has changed ***to*** the *south.* 風は南に変った. ¶The house faces ***towards*** the *south.* その家は南向きだ.

south, *a.* 南の.

P *south* ***by*** east 南微東. ¶The swallows go *south* ***in*** winter. つばめは冬南に行く. ¶Nikko lies thirty miles *south* ***of*** Tokyo Station 日光は東京駅から南へ三十マイルの所にある. ‖ Is Manchester north or *south* ***of*** London? マンチェスターはロンドンの北か南か.

O go (travel, sail) *south* 南方に行く(など).

souvenir, *n.* 記念物, みやげ.

V ***collect*** a few *souvenirs* of ... ...の記念物を少し集める. ¶***form*** an attractive *souvenir* of ... ...の目ぼしい記念物になる. ¶***make*** a pleasant *souvenir* for home friends わが家の人たちには楽しいみやげになる.

Q an ***artistic*** *souvenir* of Westminster Abbey ウェストミンスター寺院の雅致ある記念物. ¶to form a ***permanent*** *souvenir* of ... ...の永久の記念に. ¶form ***pretty*** *souvenirs* りっぱな記念物になる. ¶a ***unique*** *souveir* of W.E. Gladstone グラッドストンの無比の記念物.

Q² a ***London*** *souvenir*=a souvenir from London ロンドンみやげ.

P give it ***as*** a *souvenir* of the occasion その折の記念としてそれを与える. 【類】Presented by ... to ... ***as*** *souvenir* of February, 1895. / keep it ***as*** a *souvenir* of ... ¶***for*** a *souvenir* 記念物に. 【類】give them to the children ***for*** little *souvenirs.*

P² a *souvenir* ***for*** travelers 旅行者への記念品. ¶a little *souvenir* ***of*** Thackeray サッカレイのちょっとした記念物.

sovereign, *n.* 君主.

V ***depose*** a *sovereign* 君主を廃する. ¶***re-establish*** a *sovereign* on the throne 君主を玉座に復する. ¶Since then five *sovereigns* have ***reigned.*** それ以来五人の君主が君臨した.

Q an ***actual*** *sovereign* [名目だけでなく]実際の君主. ¶our ***Gracious*** *Sovereign,* King Edward VII. わが情深い君主エドワード七世王. ¶Tsung-ching, the ***last*** *sovereign* of the Ming dynasty 明(みん)朝の最後の君主崇禎. ¶our ***present*** *Sovereign* わが国の現君主. ¶a ***reigning*** *sovereign* 現君主, 今上陛下. ¶the ***ruling*** *sovereign* 現君主. ¶Well is it that they, so worthy a people, have so ***worthy*** a *sovereign.* そうしたりっぱな国民がそうしたりっぱな君主をいただくことは結構なことである.

sovereignty, *n.* 主権, 統治権.

V ***acknowledge*** the *sovereignty* of ... over ... ...に対する...の主権を承認する. ¶The *sovereignty* of the country was ***divided*** between two rulers. 国家の主権は二人の統治者に分有された. ¶***extend*** Germany's *sovereignty* over Austria ドイツの主権をオーストリアの上に伸ばす. ¶***found*** a dual *sovereignty* [朝廷と幕府のような]二元的主権の基礎を据える. ¶***regain*** *sovereignty* 主権を回復する. ¶***respect*** China's *sovereignty* 中国の主権を尊重する. ¶***restore*** full *sovereignty* to the Japanese people 日本国民に対する完全な主権を回復する. ¶***violate*** the *sovereignty* of ... ...の主権を侵す. ¶***yield*** the *sovereignty* without a struggle 一戦もせずに統治権を放棄する.

V² the people with whom ***resides*** *sovereignty* 主権を有する国民.

Q after ***full*** *sovereignty* is secured 完全な主権を得た後. ¶the territory of ***Japanese*** *sovereignty* 日本の統治権内の土地. ¶Japanese recovery of ***national*** *sovereignty* 日本の国家主権の回復. ¶government by ***popular*** *sovereignty* 民主主義の政治. ¶establish an ***independent*** *sovereignty* 独立国家を建設する. 【類】a State with a ***separate*** and ***independent*** *sovereignty.*

Q² The shaved head and pigtail were the signs of Tatar *sovereignty* in China. てい髪と弁髪はだったん人の中国統治の証跡だった.

P oppose the erection of American *sovereignty* ***in*** their country 彼らの国における米国の主権建設に反対する. ¶be ***within*** the *sovereignty* of a country 一国の統治権の範囲内にある.

P² *sovereignty* ***of*** the people 国民の主権 ‖ the *sovereignty* ***of*** the sea 海上の統治権 ‖ *sovereignty* ***of*** the will 意志の統制力. ¶*sovereignty* ***over*** a country 一国に対する統治権 ‖ China's *sovereignty* ***over*** Formosa 中国の台湾統治権.

Soviet, *n.* [ソ連]会議.

P the Union Congress ***of*** *Soviets*=the Supreme Soviet ソ連最高会議. ☞ 最高会議の下に village soviets, town soviets など地方議会がある.

sovietism, *n.* 労農政治.

V overthrow their Government and ***establish*** *Sovietism* in its stead 彼らの政府を倒してその代りに労農政治を建設する.

sow, *v.* まく, 種をまく.

M The grain was *sown* ***broadcast.*** 穀物をばらまきにした. 【類】They *sowed* sedition (騒動の種) ***broadcast*** over the country.

P *sow* ***in*** autumn 秋種子をまく ‖ *sow* seed ***in*** the soil 地に種子をまく. ¶... acres are *sown* ***to*** rice ...エーカーは稲が作ってある. ¶*sow* one's field ***with*** flax 畑に亜麻の種子をまく. 【類】*sow* the soil ***with*** seed. ‖ a sky *sown* ***with*** stars 星をばらまいた空 ‖ A letter heavily *sown* ***with*** "I" is, in the true sense of the word, "egotistic." 「私」という字を繁用した手紙は文字通り全く「自我的」なものである.

O As a man *sows,* so shall he reap. 〖諺〗まいた種は刈らねばならぬ(身から出たさび).

sowing, *n.* 種まき.

Q a ***broadcast*** *sowing* of seed 種子のばらまき. ¶***spring*** *sowing* 春の種まき.

soy, *n.* しょう油.

P boil (cook) it ***in*** *soy* それをしょう油で煮る(料理する).

spa, *n.* 鉱泉; 温泉場.

V² *Spa* ***comes*** from the name of a Belgian resort city. スパーというのはベルギーの温泉町の名から出ている.

Q a ***hydropathic*** *spa* 水療温泉場. ¶a ***sulfurous*** *spa* 硫黄泉.

space, *n.* 空間; 場所; 空所; 時間; しばらくの間.

V The room ***affords*** an ample *space* for 200 people. そのへやはらくに二百人は収容できる. ¶I cannot, in the limited *space* ***allotted*** to me, discuss ... 私に割当てられた限りある時間(たま紙面)では...を論じることはできない. ¶if you would ***allow*** me a little *space* in your paper, I should be able to ... 貴紙面を少しく割愛して下されば私は...することができる. ¶*annihilate space* [電話など]空間をなくする. ¶*block up* the entire *space* 全体の空所を閉鎖する. ¶*buy* newspaper *space* 新聞に広告を出す. ¶*clear* a *space* 場所の邪魔物を取除く. ¶*cover* a *space* of 70 ft. by 40 ft. [建物など]縦七十フィートに横四十フィートの面積を占めている. ¶*devote* a good deal of *space* to a description of ... ...の記事に多くの紙面を費す. ¶*Space* for the advertisement was *donated* by the magazine. その広告はその雑誌の厚意で無料にしてくれた. ¶with a view to *economizing space* 紙面節約のために. ¶*enclose* a *space* of 100 acres with fences 百エーカーの場所にかきねをめぐらす. ¶*fill* a *space* as directed 指示の通り空所に入れる ‖ *Fill* [*in*] the blank *spaces* with right words. 空所に適当の語をそう入せよ. 【類】*fill in* the *spaces* as directed. ¶we should be obliged if you would *find space* for ... ...を掲載していただければありがたい. 【類】trusting that *space* may be *found* for the publication of this acknowledgement / Harper's Magazine *finds space* (掲載する) for poetry. ¶*give* large *space* to ... ...にたっぷり紙面を与える. ¶*have* no more *space* to fill an ad in / we *have* only *space* here to note ... / I *haven't space* enough for its full description. / we *have* no *space* to criticize the book in detail. ¶I wish I *had space* in this connection to quote ... これに関して...を引用すべき余白があるといいんだが. 【類】There are more ... than we *have space* to mention. ¶*lack space* to continue the subject further これ以上問題を継続すべき余白を有しない. ¶*leave* a *space* for ... ...のために間を明ける ‖ *leave* no *space* between lines 行間を詰める. ¶as *space* is *limited* 紙面が限られているので. ¶It will not *occupy* much *space*. それは余り場所を取らない; かさ張らない. ‖ It will *occupy* (=*require*) more *space* than is here available. それは大き過ぎてここへははいるまい. 【類】*occupy* less *space*. ¶the editor courteously *offered* me *space* in his pages to ... 編集者が...するためその編集する雑誌(新聞)のページを好意的に私に提供してくれた. ¶*provide* sufficient *space* for ... ...に十分の場所を当てがう. ¶*save space* 場所を節用する. ¶To illustrate ... would *take* much more *space* than at our command. ...を説明するにはわれわれの使える紙面では足りないだろう. ‖ *take* advertising *space* in a magazine 雑誌に広告を出す. ¶*take up* little (comparatively small) *space* 余り(など)場所を取らない. 【類】It would *take up* too much *space* (紙面) to go into detail. ¶*Watch* this *space*. [新聞などの広告]この所に御注意.

V² Did *space allow* (=*permit*), I should like to quote it. 紙面が許せばそれを引用したいのだが.

Q The room affords an *ample space* for 200 people. そのへやは優に二百人収容することができる. ¶The *blank spaces* are words which could not be deciphered. 空白になっていた所は判読のできなかった言葉のあった所だ. ¶*boxed-off spaces* 別々に仕切った場所. ¶"*breathing spaces*" for the masses 大衆の息つき場所. ¶in an incredibly *brief space* of time ほんのちょっとの間に. ¶We will appreciate if you would give him *complimentary space* at your hotel. 貴ホテルにおいて同氏を(無料で)御優待下さいますればあり難く存じます. ¶after a *considerable space* of time ほどへて. ¶can *economize space* 場所をとらない. ¶an *empty space* 空所. ¶My *space* is *exhausted*. 私に割当てられた紙数が尽きた. ¶Paragraphs are indented one inch, or, if the manuscript is type-written, *five spaces*, from the right to the left-hand margin. 各項の書出しは(行の)右端から左側の余白まで一インチ下げることになっているが原稿をタイプライターで打つ場合は五字下げる. ¶an *inclosed space* 囲いをした場所. ¶The *space* is *in sufficient*. 場所が足りない. ¶the *intervening space* その間にはさまった場所. ¶*leave* a wider *space* between the lines 行間をもっとあけておく. ¶devote *liberal space* to ... [新聞紙など]...にたっぷり紙面をあてる. ¶The good quality and the cheapness of the food more than atone for *limited space*. 食物が上等で安いのが場所の狭いのを償って余りがある. ¶be forced into a *narrow space* 狭い所に追込まれている. ¶an *open space* in a city 都市の広場(空地). ¶launch (=fire *or* shoot) a super-missile through the *outer space* 大気圏を突破して超ミサイルを発射する. ¶in the *short space* of this little booklet この小冊子のわずかな紙面に ‖ in the *short space* of ten minutes (a couple of hours) 十分(など)の短時間内に. 【類】in a comparatively (an incredibly) *short space* of time. ¶state in a much *smaller space* もっと手短かに述べる. ¶a *stellar space* 星の輝く大空. ¶gaze into *vacant space* 何もない所を見詰める. ¶in conclusion (not to occupy too much of your *valuable space*) 終りに臨んで(余り多く貴重な紙面を取らないように). ¶a *walled-in space* 壁で囲んだ場所.

Q² with an *air space* between them その間に空気が介在して. ¶give the nation a *breathing space* 国民に一息つかせる. ¶*ear space* 〖出版〗耳(新聞図書などの端の白い部分). ¶a building with 650,000 square feet of *floor space* 建坪650,000平方フィートの建物. 【類】a 15×10 ft. *floor space*. ¶occupy a *ground space* of 180 by 120 ft. 縦百八十フィートに横百二十フィートの面積を占める. ¶The news takes *major press space*. ニュースが一番紙面を取る. ¶buy *newspaper* and *magazine space* 新聞雑誌に広告を出す. ¶*parking space* for 500 cars 自動車五百台を収容する駐車場. ¶There is *seating space* for only 300 spectators. わずか三百人の観客を入れる座席しかない. ¶*shipping space* 船の積載余地. ¶cover a *water space* of ... acres ...エーカーの水面を占める.

P *after* a *space* 暫時の後. ¶It is quite *beyond* the *space* of this article (book). それはこの論文(書物など)の紙面ではとても書き切れない. ¶separated by nothing *but space* 間に空地があるだけで. ¶*for* a brief *space* [of time] 少しの間 ‖ *for* the *space* of three days 三日間. 【類】*for* the long *space* of fifty years. ¶*in* the *space* of a moment (two hours) 一瞬間(など). 【類】*In* the short *space* of fifty years Japan has passed from the age of chivalry to the age of machinery. ‖ The hall is very limited *in space*. そのホールは手ぜまだ. ¶It has disappeared *into space*. それは空に消えてしまった. ‖ force it *into* a narrow *space* それを狭い場所へ無理に押込む. ¶the immensity *of space* 空間の広大無辺 ‖ owing to the lack *of space* for further details 詳説する余白がないので. 【類】for want *of space* 余白がないので. ¶They converged *on* the central open *space*. 彼らは中央の空地に寄り集まった. ¶They scattered *over* a wide *space*. 彼らは広い空所に散らばった. ¶roll along *through space* [天体など]空間を転回して行く.

P² two houses *with* the *space* of ten feet between them 十フィートの間隔を置いて隣り合っている二軒の家. ¶I regret that the *space at* my disposal is so limited as to preclude my citing cases illustrative of ... 使える紙面が限られているので...を説明する例をあげ得ないのを遺憾に思う. ¶leave a *space between* the lines for the necessary corrections 必要な修正のために行間に余白を残す. ¶the *space of* a mile 一マイルの間隔.

space, *v*. 間隔をおく.

M two hyphens not *spaced away* from the neighboring words 隣接語から間隔をおいてない二つのハイフン(これが普通の dash である). ¶*space out* スペース(余白)をあける (letters や words の間隔を).

spacing, *n*. 間隔を置くこと.

Q type with *double spacing* 二行おきにタイプを打つ. ¶print with *thin spacings* to show syllabication [字書など]音節を示すために少し間隔をおいて印刷する.

spade, *n*. すき; [トランプの]スペード.

V Rich treasures *await* their *spades*. 貴重な宝物がまだ発掘されないでいる. ¶*call* a *spade* a spade 遠慮なく(率直に)物を言う. ¶*drive* a *spade* into the earth すきを土に打込む. ¶*Say* a *spade* a spade. あけすけに物を言え. ¶In these excavations the *spade acts* as the humble handmaid of history. これらの発掘においてすきは史学のために犬馬の労を取っているのである.

P the queen (king, jack) *of spades* スペードの女王(など). ¶cultivate *with* a *spade* すきで耕す.

spadework, *n*. 最初の仕事.

V *do spadework* for ... ...の最初の仕事をする.

span, *n*. 親指と小指とを張った長さ; 短時間.

V *complete* the natural *span* of man's life 天寿を全うする. ¶at an age which had considerably *exceded* the *span* fixed by the Psalmist 詩編の作者が定めた寿命(七十歳)を大分越した年齢で. ¶*have* a *span* of two feet 長さ二フィートある. ¶*lengthen* (*shortern*) the *span* of life 寿命を延ばす(縮める). ¶He has *reached* the allotted *span* of life. 彼は定命(ていめい)に達した. ¶widen the span of knowledge 知識の範囲を広める.

Q in a brief span of year (=time) 短時日に ‖ our brief span of life この短い人生. ¶the ordinary span of life 普通の寿命. ¶a bridge of four spans 四径間(けいかん)の橋. ¶the whole span of Roman history ローマ史の全幅.

Q^2 a suspension bridge of about 180 feet span 長さ約百八十フィートのつり橋. ¶extend the life span 寿命を延ばす. ¶The plane has a wing span of 230 feet. その飛行機は翼の差渡しが 230 フィートある.

P measure by spans 指尺で計る. ¶in a span of twenty years 二十年の間に.

P^2 the span of a bridge 橋の長さ ‖ the span of memory 記憶の範囲.

span, *v.* (橋を)かける.

P span a river with a bridge 川に橋をかける. 【類】The river is spanned with arches (めがね橋) of solid masonry.

spangle, *n.* [舞台衣裳などにつける]ぴかぴかした飾り.

P a costume covered with spangles スパンゴールの一杯ついたコスチューム.

spangle, *v.* 光る.

P grass spangled with dewdrops 露の玉で光る草.

spanking, *n.* しりをなぐること.

V You are both going to get a spanking! お前たち二人のおしりをぶってやるぞ.

Q give a boy a good spanking 少年のおしりをうんとひっぱたく.

spare, *a.* つましい, 粗末な; 慎重な.

P The study is simple and very spare of furniture. 書斎は質素で家具はきわめて粗末だ. ‖ He is spare of speech. 彼は容易に口をきかない.

O live on a spare diet 粗食で生活する.

spare, *v.* さいてやる; 倹約する; とっておく.

M I can't spare time away from my work. 私は仕事の時間をさくことはできない. ¶sell what one can badly spare 手離せないものを売却する. ¶I cannot spare it just now. 今ちょっとそれを手離すことはできない.

P spare against the evil day 不慮に備える. ¶I can spare you for tomorrow. あすは君はいなくてもよい. ‖ spare land for a garden 庭を作る地所を取っておく ‖ Spare your energy for some other work. その努力を他のことに使え. ‖ I cannot spare time for it. 私にはそれをする暇がない. 【類】Can you spare this book for a little while? ¶spare time from business 用事の時間をさく ‖ He spent nearly all the time he could spare from his duties in study. 彼はその職務の暇をほとんど全部勉学に使った.

O Can't you spare me one of those books? その本の中一冊譲っていただけませんか. ‖ Can't you spare me a few minutes? ちょっとお話がありますが… ¶spare oneself 骨を惜しむ. 【類】not to spare oneself.

spareness, *n.* やせること.

P^2 spareness of flesh やせぎす.

sparing, *a.* 惜しむ.

P be sparing of one's praise 控え目にほめる ‖ be sparing of oneself 骨身を惜しむ. 【類】be sparing of one's labor.

spark, *n.* 火花, 火粉; せん光; こん跡.

V emit sparks 火花を散らす. ¶He has no spark of generosity (gratitude, anger). 彼には寛容さ(など)はみじんもない. 【類】have not a spark of interest in it. ¶keep the spark of life burning until morning 朝まで命を持たせる. ¶His eyes shot sparks of fire. 彼の目はきらめいた. ¶strike sparks from flint and steel 火打石と鋼鉄で火を切る ‖ strike sparks out of a person 人から知恵などを引き出す. ¶strike out sparks [火打石などで]火花を出す. ¶The burning wood threw up sparks. 燃える木から火花が上った. ¶We witnessed the first spark of the fearful conflagration. われわれはその恐ろしい大火の最初の火の粉を目にした.

V^2 The sparks flew up the chimney. 火花が煙突の中を立ち昇った. ‖ as the sparks fly upward [火花が上へ飛ぶように]確かに. ¶Not a sprak of life remained. もう少しの息もなかった. ¶The sparks shot up like thousands of shooting stars into the still night air. 火の粉が幾千の流星のように静かな夜の空に吹き上がった.

Q an electric spark 電気の火花. ¶Ten times hourly does a mortal spark return to its Maker in this mighty metropolis, leaving its earthly tabernacle to descend to the dust from which it sprang. この巨大な首都(ロンドン)では毎時間十人の人がその肉体をもとの土くれに返し造物主の許に帰る. ¶The appeal failed to strike a responsive spark in him. その哀訴も彼の同情を引くことはできなかった. ¶There was a wild spark in his eyes. 彼の目はすごく光った.

P^2 Sparks from the chimney ignited the shingles. 煙突から出た火の粉が屋根板を焼いた. ‖ sparks from red-hot iron しゃく熱の鉄から発する火花. ¶sparks of wit (a gem) 才気(など)のせん光. 【類】have a spark of interest in ...

sparkle, *n.* きらめき.

Q the crisp sparkle of the sea 海の生き生きしたきらめき.

P^2 the sparkle of one's eyes 目の光り.

sparkle, *v.* ひらめく, きらきらする.

P Diamonds sparkle in the dark. ダイヤはくらやみで光る. ¶sparkle with delight [目など]喜びで輝く. 【類】her eyes sparpled with hope.

sparrow, *n.* すずめ.

V^2 Sparrows chirp (=twitter). すずめがちゅーちゅー鳴く.

P a flock of sparrows 一群のすずめ.

spasm, *n.* けいれん.

V have a spasm (=paroxysm) of coughing ひどくせき込む.

V^2 The spasm passed off. そのけいれんが収まった.

P^2 a spasm of pain (fear, excitement, temper) 痛み(など)の発作.

spat, *n.* こぜり合い.

Q Though very fond of his wife, he has an occasional spat (=tiff) with her. 彼は妻が大好きなのだがときどき妻とこぜりあいをする.

spats, *n.* 短いゲートル.

Q^2 cloth spats 布ゲートル.

spatter, *n.* [水の]しぶき.

P^2 a spatter of rain (bullets) 雨の飛まつ(など).

spatter, *v.* はねかける, はねかす.

P spatter water on a pavement 舗道に水をまく ‖ spatter ink on one's dress 着物にインキをはねかす. 【類】The rain spattered [down] on my umbrella. ¶He was spattered with mud (water) by a passing cart. 彼は往来の車に泥(など)をはねかけられた.

spatula, *n.* へら.

V In the pond the lotus was spreading its broad spatulas. 池にははすが広いへら形の花弁を拡げていた.

speak, *v.* 言う; 語る; 演説する.

M speak accurately 正確に話す. ¶speak English admirably 英語を見事に話す. ¶speak admiringly of one's own wife 妻ののろけをいう. ¶speak agreeably 気持よく話す. ¶speak aloud 高声に話す. ¶speak amorously of one's sweetheart 恋人ののろけをいう. ¶speak approvingly of ... …をほめる. ¶approximately speaking 概言すれば. ¶speak aside [台詞を]独語する. ¶He is badly spoken of. 彼は評判が悪い. ¶speak English badly but understandably 英語をまずいが分かるように話す. ¶speak English beautifully りっぱに英語を話す. ¶speak bitterly of ... …をずけずけ言う. ¶speak out bluntly ぶっきら棒に言う. ¶speak boastingly of ... …を自慢する. ¶speak out boldly しゃあしゃあと言う. ¶speak briefly 簡単に話す. ¶speaking broadly 概して, 大体. ¶speak brokenly とぎれとぎれに言う. ¶speak candidly 打明けて言う. ¶speak chaffingly about the matter そのことをからかう. ¶speak civilly 丁寧に言う. ¶comparatively speaking 比較的に言えば. ¶speak complimentarily on ... …に世辞を言う. ¶speak concretely 具体的に言う. ¶speak contemptuously 侮辱して言う. ¶speak correctly 正しく話す. ¶I know enough of music to speak decidedly on that point. 私はその点について断言できる位の音楽の知識はある. ¶It is impossible to speak decisively on this point. この点は断言はできない. ¶It does not become a young man to speak so dictatorially before his elders. 先輩の前であんなに横柄な口をきくのは若い人にふさわしくない. ¶speak disarmingly [突っ込めないように]無邪気に言う. ¶speak very disparagingly of ... …をぼろくそにいう. ¶speak disrespectfully 失敬な物の言い方をする. ¶speak distinctly はっきりと物を言う. ¶speak dramatically 芝居がかりに物を言う. ¶speak English effectively 効果的に英語を話す. ¶We have spoken elsewhere of this. このことはすでに述べた. ¶speak evil of his wife 細君を悪しざまに言う. ¶speak falsely 誤った言い方をする. ¶He stammers when he tries to speak fast. 彼は早く話そうとするとどもる. ¶speak fast and incoherently 口早にとんちんかんな言い方

をする. ¶*speak* ***feelingly*** しみじみと言う. ¶*speak* ***firmly*** 確言する. ¶a word ***fitly*** ***spoken*** 適切な語. ¶*speak* ***fluently*** in English 英語で流ちょうに話す. ¶*speak* ***foolishly*** ばかなことを言う. ¶*speak* ***frankly*** 卒直に言う. ¶*speak* ***freely*** 遠慮なく話す. ¶He *speaks* ***friendly*** to everybody. 彼はだれにも親しげに話しかける. ¶*Speaking* ***generally,*** this is the case. 一言に言えばこうだ. 【類】***Generally*** *speaking*, you may be right; but as far as I am concerned (私には), it is really not the case. ¶*speak* ***glibly*** ぺらぺら話す. ¶*speak* ***guardedly*** (=***cautiously***) on that point その点に関し用心深く話す. ¶*speak* ***harshly*** つけつけ言う. ¶*speak* ***highly*** of his talents 彼の才能をほめる ‖ We cannot *speak* too ***highly*** of its value. その値打はいくらほめてもよい. ¶***How*** do people *speak* of me? 僕のことを人は何と言っているか. ¶*speak* ***idiomatically*** 語法にかなった話し方をする. ¶One should not *speak* ***ill*** of others. 他人を悪しざまに言うのはよくない. ¶***inadvertently*** *speak* うっかり言う. ¶*speak* ***intelligibly*** 分かるように(明りょうに)言う. ¶*speak* ***interestingly*** and ***learnedly*** おもしろくかつ学者らしく話す. ¶*speak* ***ironically*** 当てこすって言う. ¶*speak* ***irresponsibly*** でたらめを言う. ¶*speak* ***jeeringly*** ばかにした言い方をする. ¶*speak* ***jestingly*** 冗談に言う. ¶*speak* ***kindly*** of ... ...について親切に話す. ¶***legally*** *speaking* 法律的に言えば. ¶*speak* ***lightly*** of ... ...を軽く見て言う. ¶*speak* ***loud*** 大声で話す. ¶*speak* ***low*** 低い声で話す. ¶*speak* ***long-windedly*** 長談義をする. ¶***mentally*** *speaking* 精神について言えば. ¶I ***merely*** *spoke* as a friend. 私は友人として話しただけなのさ. ¶***metaphorically*** *speaking* 比ゆ的に言えば. ¶It is now ***much*** *spoken* of. それは目下大評判だ. ¶*speak* English ***naturally*** 英語を無理がなく話す. ¶*speak* ***nervously*** 神経的に話す. ¶***objectively*** *speaking* 客観的に見て. ¶*speak* ***off-hand*** (=extempore) 即席に演説する. ¶*speak* ***openly*** of ... ...を大っぴらに話す. ¶*speak* ***oratorically*** in public=declaim 公開で雄弁を揮う. ¶Please *speak* ***out***. どうぞ思った通り(遠慮なく)言って下さい. ‖ *speak* ***out*** one's thought 自分の考えを打明ける. ¶***paradoxically*** *speaking* 逆説的に言えば. ¶*speak* ***passionately*** about ... ...について熱烈に語る. ¶I *speak* to you ***peaceably***, yet you will not listen. 私は穏かに言っているのにお前は私の言うことを聞かない. ¶***philosophically*** *speaking* 哲学的に言えば. ¶To *speak* ***plainly***, you have no right to spend the money. ざっくばらんに言えば君にはその金を使う権利はない. ¶We *speak* ***poetically*** of such a costly picture as "silver film." こうした高価な映画を詩的にシルヴァ・フィルムという. ¶***practically*** *speaking* 実際的に言えば. ¶Of this I shall *speak* ***presently***. このことをじきに後段でお話ししましょう. ¶***properly*** *speaking* 正しく言えば. ¶You *speak* too ***quickly*** (=***rapidly***). 君は余り早口だ. ¶*speak* ***respectfully*** 丁寧に話す. ¶***relatively*** *speaking* どっちかといえば. ¶***roughly*** *speaking* ざっと言えば ‖ *speak* to a person ***roughly*** ぞんざいに人に話し掛ける. ¶He *spoke* ***scornfully*** as if addressing a dog. 彼は犬にでも言っているようにさげすんで話した. ¶words that are ***seldom*** *spoken* めったに話されない言葉. ¶*speak* ***seriously*** 真剣に話す. ¶be ***severely*** *spoken* of ひどく非難されている. ¶*speak* ***sharply*** 甲高(ｶﾝﾀﾞｶ)に物を言う. ¶*speak* ***slightingly*** of his writings 彼の文章をけなす. ¶*speak* ***slower*** もっとゆっくり話す. ¶***so*** to *speak* 言わば ‖ when ***so*** *spoken* そう言われた時は. ¶*speak* ***softly*** やわらかい声で言う ‖ His way was to *speak* ***softly*** but carry a big stick. 圧力をちらつかせながら口先だけはやさしくというのが彼のやり口であった. ¶***statistically*** *speaking* 統計的に言えば. ¶***strictly*** *speaking* 厳密に言えば. ¶*speak* ***strongly*** against ... 盛んに...の悪口を言う. ¶***technically*** *speaking* 専門的に言えば. ¶*speak* ***thoughtlessly*** 不用意に物を言う. ¶*Speaking* ***thus*** he hurried away. こう言いながら彼は急いで去った. ¶*speak* ***truthfully*** 正直に話す. ¶He never *speaks* ***unadvisedly*** about anything. 彼はどんな事についても不用意なことは言わない. ¶*speak* ***unfavorably*** 悪く言う. ¶*speak* ***unkindly*** of ... ...の悪口をいう. ¶to *speak* ***vulgarly*** 下品な言葉で言えば. ¶*speak* ***warmly*** of the use of note-books ノートの使用を熱心に勧める. ¶He *speaks* English ***well***. 彼は英語を巧みに話す. ‖ Your health *speaks* ***well*** for your mode of life. 君の健康なのは君の生活法が正しい証拠だ. ‖ Deserve to be ***well*** *spoken* of. よく言われるだけのことをしろ. ¶That child does not learn to *speak* ***yet***. その子はまだ物が言えない.

M² ***speak up*** (=***out***) 大声で話す; はっきり言い切る ‖ I'll *speak* ***up*** for you about it. それについて君の弁護をしよう. ‖ *speak* ***up*** through the mike マイクを通して語る ‖ Come, now, *speak* ***up*** at once. さあ早くなんとか言いなさい.

P Just as we were *speaking* ***about*** him, he came. 彼の話をしていたとき丁度彼がやって来た. ‖ He *spoke* ***about*** his travels. 彼は旅行談をやった. ¶*speak* ***above*** one's breath 聞える位に話す. ¶He *spoke* ***against*** me behind my back. 彼はかげで私の悪口を言った. ¶*speak* ***at*** a large gathering (=audience) 多数の群集に対して演説する. 【類】*speaking* ***at*** a meeting of ..., he said that ... ‖ He *spoke* ***at*** a great length on the matter. 彼はそのことをくわしく話した. ‖ He *spoke* ***at*** random. 彼はでまかせに話した. ¶*speak* ***before*** a company (the public, an annual convention) 一同(など)の前で演説する. ¶*speak* ***by*** the card はっきりと話す ‖ *speak* ***by*** signs (gestures) 手まね(身ぶり)で話をする ‖ *speak* ***by*** telephone 電話で話す. ¶He could not *speak* ***for*** fear (joy). 彼は恐ろしくて(うれしくて)口がきけなかった. ‖ *speak* ***for*** countless others who ... ...の無数の人の代弁をする. 【類】Please speak ***for*** me to the director. ‖ It *speaks* ***for*** itself. それは自然に分かる. ‖ This action *speaks* volumes ***for*** his probity. この行動をみると彼の正直さがよく分かる. ‖ *Speak* ***for*** the candy, Fido. [犬に]さあチョコレートをあげるからわんと言え. ¶*speak* ***from*** the platform 演壇から演説する ‖ *speak* ***from*** experience 経験から話す. 【類】I am *speaking* ***from*** a constant experience of 30 years. / Of course I am *speaking* only ***from*** memory. / *speak* ***from*** a written manuscript / I do not *speak* ***from*** hearsay(うわさ), but ***from*** actual observation. ¶*speak* ***in*** defense 弁護する ‖ I *speak* ***in*** (=on) your behalf. 私は君のために言う. ‖ *speak* ***in*** sober earnest まじめに言う ‖ *speak* ***in*** English 英語で話す ‖ *speak* ***in*** fun 冗談にいう ‖ *speak* ***in*** public 公開演説をやる ‖ *speak* ***in*** earnest 本気でいう ‖ words *spoken* ***in*** lead humor 重々しい気持で言った言葉 ‖ *speak* ***in*** the highest terms (terms of high praises) with regard to ... ...を口をきわめて(など)ほめる. 【類】*speak* ***in*** the most flattering terms / *speak* ***in*** a loose sort of way (締りのない言い方) / They *spoke* ***in*** whispers. ¶*speak* ***into*** a telephone 電話口に向って話す. ¶I have heard him *speak* ***of*** it. 私は彼がそのことを話しているのを聞いたことがある. ‖ *speak* ***of*** the old days on the campus 学窓の昔を語る ‖ I have no luggage to *speak* ***of***. 私にはこれというほどの荷物もない. ‖ He is *spoken* ***of*** as a good teacher. 彼は良教師という評判だ. ‖ The wealth and honor of a man are usually *spoken* ***of*** as his "credit." 人間の富と名誉は通例その人の信用と言われている. ‖ I can not afford to buy a silver watch, not to *speak* ***of*** a gold one. 私は銀時計が買えないのだから金時計などはなおさらのことだ. 【類】No progress worth *speaking* ***of*** is ever made in any study where the learner himself is not interested in the subject. ¶Tonight he *speaks* ***on*** temperance. 今夕彼は禁酒のことについて演説する. ‖ I am not empowered to *speak* ***on*** the topic. 私はその問題について語る自由を有しない(権限はない). ‖ *speak* ***on*** (=in) behalf of others 人のために言う ‖ *speak* ***on*** a national network broadcast 全国放送で演説する ‖ he *spoke* at length ***on*** ... 彼は...について長々と話した. ¶*speak* ***out of*** (=from) a full heart 胸がつまって言う. ¶*speak* ***through*** an interpreter 通訳を通して言う ‖ He declared that God *spoke* ***through*** him. 彼は神が彼を通して語るのだと言放った. ‖ those who *speak* ***through*** pen or type ペンまたは活字を通して語る人々(文士など). 【類】*speak* ***through*** the telephone ‖ He *speaks* ***through*** the nose. 彼は声が鼻にかかる. ¶*speak* ***to*** a large audience 多数の聴衆に向って演説する ‖ I'd like to *speak* ***to*** Mr. K. [電話などで] K さんをお願いします. ‖ He was *spoken* ***to*** by the general. 彼は将軍に話しかけられた. ‖ He *speaks* ***to*** nobody. 彼はだれにも口をきかない. ‖ *speak* ***to*** oneself 独りごとを言う. 【類】I want to *speak* ***to*** you a moment. ‖ Clergymen who occupy the position of canon of a cathedral are *spoken* of as "Canon So-and-so," but ***to*** as "Mr." 本山役付の僧は第三者としては「カノンなに某」と言うが面と向っては「ミスター」と言う. ‖ He *spoke* ***to*** the same effect. 彼もやはりそういう意味のことを言った. ‖ He *speaks* ***to*** the point. 彼

の言うことは要領を得ている. ‖ *speak* ***to*** the purpose 効果的に言う. ¶*speak* ***under*** one's breath ささやく. ¶*speak* ***upon*** the telephone 電話で話す ‖ *speak* feelingly ***upon*** a subject ある問題についてしみじみ話す. ¶I *spoke* ***with*** him in private. 私は彼と内々で話した. ‖ *speak* English ***with*** … …と英語を話す ‖ We *speak* ***with*** our mouths (lips). われわれは口で物を言う. ‖ *speak* ***with*** the warmest praise 激賞する. 【類】*speak* ***with*** certainty (emphasis, freedom, hesitation, insolence, spirit, great composure, great effect) / On this subject he *speaks* ***with*** an authority commanding respect (傾聴させずにはおかない権威をもって). ‖ He *spoke* ***with*** tears in his eyes. 彼は涙ながらに話した. ¶*speak* ***without*** being asked くちばしを入れる ‖ *speak* ***without*** reserve 腹蔵なく(また遠慮なく)話す.

O so to *speak* いわば. 【類】He is, so to *speak*, a grown-up baby.

speaker, *n.* 話し手; 演説者, 弁士; 議長.

V ***applaud*** a *speaker* 弁士を拍手かっさいしてほめる. 【類】The *speaker* was warmly ***applauded***. ¶***cheer*** a *speaker* to the echo 弁士を盛んに応援する. ¶***groan down*** a public *speaker* 演説者をやじり倒す. ¶The audience ***hissed*** the *speaker* off the stage. 聴衆はしっーしっーとやじって弁士を引込ませた. ¶The crowd ***howled down*** the *speaker*. 群衆は弁士をどなって沈黙させた. ¶***interrupt*** a *speaker* 話の腰を折る. ¶The stenographer is able to ***take*** the fastest *speaker*. その速記者はどんな早口の弁士の演説でも書き取れる.

V² The *speaker* ***draws*** large audiences. その弁士はたくさんの聴衆を引付ける. ¶The *speaker* ***warmed up*** as he went on. 弁士は演説しているうちに油が乗ってきた.

Q an ***able*** and ***accurate*** *speaker* of English 力があって正確な英語を話す人. ¶a ***bad*** (=***poor***) *speaker* 話しべたな人. ¶a ***careful*** *speaker* 言葉に気を付けて話す人. ¶a ***careless*** *speaker* 不注意に物を言う人. ¶a ***convincing*** *speaker* 聴衆を信服させる弁士. ¶a ***crisp*** *speaker* きびきびした弁士. ¶a ***cultivated*** *speaker* 洗練された弁士. ¶a ***dramatic*** *speaker* 芝居がかりの弁士. ¶***educated*** *speakers* of English 教育のある英語の話し手. ¶a ***fast*** *speaker* 早口の人. ¶a ***fluent*** and ***earnest*** *speaker* 能弁で熱心な演説家. ¶a ***forceful, convincing*** *speaker* 聴衆を信服させる力強い弁士. ¶a ***forcible*** *speaker* 力強い弁士. ¶***foreign*** *speakers* of Japanese 日本語を話す外国人. ¶a ***good*** *speaker* 話しじょうずな人. ¶a ***laconic*** *speaker* 含蓄のある言い方をする弁士. ¶a ***lucid*** *speaker* 論旨明せきな弁士. ¶a ***polished*** *speaker* of Standard English 標準英語を上品に話す人. ¶a ***political*** *speaker* 政談演説の弁士. ¶a ***public*** *speaker* 公開演説家. ¶a ***refined*** *speaker* 上品な口をきく人. ¶speeches by ***rival*** *speakers* 立会演説. ¶a ***slovenly*** *speaker* だらしない口のきき方をする人. ¶He is a ***slow*** *speaker*. 彼は口がおもい. ¶a ***social*** *speaker* 社交的座談家. ¶a ***vehement*** *speaker* 熱心な弁士. ¶a ***veteran*** *speaker* of wide experience 老練な弁士.

Q² an ***after-dinner*** *speaker* 晩さん後の演説者. ¶a ***deputy*** *speaker* [下院の]副議長. ¶a ***guest*** *speaker* 来賓演説者. ¶the ***keynote*** *speaker* at the convention その会議における方針演説者. ¶a powerful ***platform*** *speaker* 力強い弁士. ¶a ***street radio*** *speaker* 街頭のラジオ広告放送者. ¶a ***stump*** *speaker* 《米》選挙演説家.

P² a *speaker* ***of*** extraordinary brilliancy 非常にはなやかな弁士. ¶the *Speaker* ***of*** the House of Representatives 下院議長.

speaking, *n.* 話すこと; 演説.

V if you will ***excuse*** [my] plain *speaking* 直言をお許し下さるなら.

Q ***formal*** *speaking* 四角ばった話し方. ¶***Japanese*** *speaking* by foreigners 外国人の日本語を話すこと. ¶***plain*** *speaking* 直言. ¶***public*** *speaking* 公開演説.

Q² ***microphone*** *speaking* マイクで話すこと. ¶***stump*** *speaking* 《米》選挙演説(遊説).

P Your bounty is ***beyond*** my *speaking*. 御恩は口には尽せません. ¶one's proficiency ***in*** *speaking* 演説の熟達. ¶owing to his quick way ***of*** *speaking* 彼が早口なために. ¶There is no *speaking* ***with*** obstinate people. がん固な人間には話してもむだだ.

spear, *n.* やり.

V ***thrust*** a *spear* やりを突込む. 【類】***thrust*** a *spear* into an enemy's heart.

P catch a fish ***with*** a *spear* やりで魚を捕える.

spearhead, *n.* 〘軍〙最前線.

P² the *spearhead* ***of*** an advance 軍の最前線.

special, *n.* 特別のもの, 特別仕立.

Q ***Olympic Special*** 〘航空〙オリンピック選手用特別仕立.

Q² "***Bargain Special***" [売場の掲示]特売. ¶a London *special* ***to*** the Mainichi says that … 毎日新聞あてロンドン特電によれば. ¶***racing*** *specials* 競馬特別列車. ¶***Sunday*** *Special* 《米》日曜特別料理. ¶a one-million-dollar "***Super*** *Special*" 〘映画〙百万ドル超特作.

specialist, *n.* 専門家, 専門医.

V ***consult*** a *specialist* in nervous diseases 神経病の専門家に診てもらう.

Q a ***ceramic*** *specialist* 陶磁器の専門家. ¶the ***chief*** *specialist* on English municipal institutions 英国都市制度の主な専門家. ¶an ***eminent*** *specialist* 専門大家. ¶a ***genito-urinary*** *specialist* 性病泌尿科の専門家. ¶a ***mental*** *specialist* 精神病専門医. ¶a ***scientific*** *specialist* 科学の専門家. ¶a ***trained*** *specialist* 熟練した専門家. ¶a ***well-known*** *specialist* in laryngology (children's diseases) こう頭科(など)の著名な専門家.

Q² consult an ***eye*** *specialist* 眼科専門医に診てもらう. ¶a ***fishing tackle*** *specialist* つり具専門店. ¶a ***food*** *specialist* 食料品専門店. ¶a ***hair*** *specialist* 毛髪専門家. ¶a ***modern language*** *specialist* 近代語の専門家. ¶a ***plant disease*** *specialist* 植物病害専門家. ¶a ***stomach*** *specialist* 胃病専門医. ¶the frank analyses of ***visitor*** *specialists* 往診医のはっきりした病状診断. ¶a ***V.D.*** *specialist* 性病専門医.

P² *specialists* ***in*** modern languages (geography, skin and surgery) 近代語(など)の専門家. 【類】*specialists* ***in*** the field (この方面の) / We are *specialists* ***in*** this line of business (この方面の商売). / a *specialist* (=expert) ***in*** the subject / Teachers are all *specialists* ***in*** their respective departments. ‖ a *specialist* ***in*** heart (lung) diseases 心臓(肺)病専門医. 【類】a *specialist* ***in*** diseases of the nose and throat. ¶one of our greatest *specialists* ***on*** hygiene says that … 衛生学専門大家の一人が…と言っている ‖ he does not claim to be a *specialist* ***on*** … 彼は…の専門家だとは言っていない.

speciality, *n.* 専門; 特色.

V ***choose*** one's *speciality* after a fair degree of general learning 普通学を相当に修めてから専門を選ぶ. ¶***make*** a *speciality* of this business (poultry) この商売(養鶏)を専門にやる ‖ We ***make*** a *speciality* of the manufacture. 手前どもはその製造が専門です. ‖ ***make*** a *speciality* of entering empty dwellings and breaking open slot-machines あきすねらいや自動販売機のこじ明けを専門にする. 【類】There are but few London dealers who ***make*** a *speciality* of puzzles (考え物). / the late T.R. McClatchie, the one European who ***made*** a *speciality* of the Japanese stage.

Q a ***local*** *speciality* 名物.

P² A *speciality* ***of*** Victoria Park is the "sand pit." ビクトリア公園の一つの特色はいわゆる「砂穴」である. ¶It is a *speciality* ***with*** him. それは彼の専門だ.

O Philology is my *speciality*. 言語学が私の専門だ.

specialization, *n.* 専門化.

Q a ***premature*** *specialization* in education 普通学を終えぬうちに専門の学問に入ること.

P² *specialization* ***in*** research 研究の専門化.

specialize, *v.* 専門化する.

M The business is now ***highly*** *specialized*. その商売は非常に専門化している.

P we *specialize* ***in*** the manufacture of … われわれは…製造を専門にしている ‖ Pittsburg *specializes* ***in*** glass-making. ピッツバーグはガラス製造が専門だ. ‖ *specialize* ***in*** the study of … …研究を専門にする. 【類】*specialize* ***in*** child portraiture / a medical man who has *specialized* ***in*** the subject / The cinema *specializes* ***in*** Italian films. ¶collectors who *specialize* ***on*** this line この方面を専門にする収集家.

specialty, *n.* 《主に米》専門.

V ***make*** a *specialty* of political economy (natural science, philology) 経済学(など)を専攻する ‖ The store ***makes*** a *specialty* of children's clothes. そこは子供用服の専門店だ.

O Phonetics is Prof. B's *specialty*. 音声学はB教授の専攻だ.

specie, *n.* 正金, 正貨.

V *specie* ***held abroad*** 在外正貨.

P one thousand dollars ***in*** *specie* 正金で千ドル ‖ payable

***in** specie* 正貨で支払いうる. ¶the outflow (inflow) ***of** specie* 正貨の流出(流入) ‖ shortness ***of** specie* 正貨の欠乏.

species, *n.* [単・複同形] 種(しゅ), 種類.

Q ***cognate** species* 同一系統の種類. ¶This is a ***curious** species* of rose. これは珍らしい種類のばらだ. ¶an ***extinct** species* of fish 今絶種となった魚. ¶the ***human** species* 人類. ¶a ***large** species* of ... ...の大きな種類. ¶The *species* are very ***numerous***. その種類は非常にたくさんある. ¶***our** species* 人類.

P the Origin ***of** Species* 種の起源(C. Darwin の著書). ¶a *species **of*** fern (fish) しだ(など)の一種 ‖ a *species **of*** shame 一種の恥辱. 【類】a *species **of*** crime.

P² butterflies ***of*** many *species* 各種のちょう.

specific, *n.* 特効薬, 妙薬.

Q There is no ***sovereign** specific* for the malady. その病には妙薬がない.

P Rattle-snake oil is highly esteemed ***as*** a *specific* for rheumatism. がらがらへびの油はリュウマチの特効薬として非常に珍重される.

P² a *specific **against*** headache 頭痛の特効薬. ¶an alleged *specific **for*** the white plague 肺結核の特効薬と称せられるもの ‖ ***For*** a jaded and overtaxed brain, recreation is the *specific*. 使い過ぎて疲れた頭には保養が一番よくきく.

specification, *n.* 明細書.

Q² ***building** specification* [建物の]設計明細書. ¶a ***job** specification* 仕事の明細書. ¶a ***shipping** specification* 積荷の明細書.

P ***as per** specification* attached 添付仕訳書通り.

specify, *v.* 明示する.

P be *specified **by*** name 氏名を明示される. ¶*specify* date (time) ***for*** ... ...の日どり(など)を明示する.

specimen, *n.* 見本, 標本; 参考品.

V exactly ***follow*** this *specimen* 精密にこの標本にならう. ¶Can you ***show*** me some *specimens* of your work? 君の細工の見本を少し見せていただけますか.

Q an ***average** specimen* of ... ...の普通の標本. ¶***botanical** specimens* 植物標本. ¶a ***capital** specimen* of the Chinese 中国人の絶好の標本. ¶a ***choice** specimen* えり抜きの標本. very ***creditable** specimens* of Japanese gentlemen 日本紳士のりっぱな標本. ¶***degraded** specimens* of humanity (the softer sex) 堕落した人間(女)の標本. ¶the ***extant** specimens* 今なお残存している参考品. ¶He is a ***fair** specimen* of manhood. 彼は人としてりっぱな手本となるべき人だ. ¶The ship is the ***fine** specimen* of the builder's craft. その船は造船技師の手腕の好見本だ. ¶This is indeed the ***finest** specimen* of bronze work I have ever seen. これは真に銅細工として私がこれまで見たことのないほどすぐれたものだ. 【類】The Koraku-en is the ***finest** specimen* of the Japanese landscape gardener's art to be seen in the capital. ¶***genuine old** specimens* from the collection of ... ...収集中の真正の古物. ¶In a ***good** specimen* the narrower end of the hen's egg is about one half as thick as the wider end. よい鶏卵ではとがった方の端の大きさは丸い方の端の約半分だ. ¶He is a remarkably ***handsome** specimen* of his race. 彼はその人種のりっぱな標本である. ¶a very ***inferior** specimen* of the art of the Japanese gardener 日本園芸のきわめて劣等なひな形. ¶***poor** specimens* of pottery 陶器の下等品. ¶This stamp is a ***rare** specimen*. この郵便切手は珍品だ. ¶***stuffed** specimens* はく製の標本. ¶a ***tough** specimen* 強情っぱり. ¶a ***typical** specimen* 代表的標本. ¶a ***unique** specimen* of the Nara period 奈良時代の無類の参考品. ¶a particularly ***unpleasant** specimen* of Japanese commercial methods 日本の商業習慣の特に不愉快な例. ¶***worthy** specimens* of the race その民族のりっぱな代表者. ¶***zoological** specimens* 動物標本.

Q² a ***museum** specimen* 博物館陳列の標本.

P serve ***as*** a *specimen* of ... ...の見本となる. ¶***by way of** specimen* 見本に.

P² *specimens **for*** reference 参考品. ¶*specimens **of*** copper ore 銅の鉱石の標本 ‖ *specimens **of*** Oriental craftsmanship 東洋工芸の標本 ‖ a *specimen **of*** one's handwriting 筆跡の見本. 【類】a *specimen **of*** his skill / a *specimen **of*** one's work.

speck, *n.* はん点; 小片, 微片.

V I've ***got*** a *speck* of dust in my eye. 目にごみが入った. ¶He ***has*** not a *speck* of generosity. 彼には寛大という所は少しもない.

Q² a ***fly** speck* はえのつけた汚点.

P² without a *speck **of*** cloud 一点の雲もなく. 【類】Not a *speck **of*** cloud was to be seen. ¶a *speck **on*** paper 紙についている一つのはん点.

speckle, *v.* しみをつける.

P The pond is *speckled **with*** foam. 池はあわだらけになっている. ‖ A page *speckled **with*** dashes is unsightly. ダッシュの多く用いてあるページは見苦しい.

spectacle, *n.* (**1**) 見もの, 光景.

V ***enjoy*** the *spectacle* with inhuman mirth 浅ましい歓喜をもってその光景に見入る. ¶***make*** a *spectacle* of oneself 自分のはじをさらす. ¶***present*** (=***offer***) an amusing *spectacles* 滑けいな光景(いい格好)を呈する. ¶***provide*** a very attractive *spectacle* きわめて興味ある光景を呈する. ¶Such a *spectacle* has seldom been ***seen*** of late years. こんな光景は近年まれに見るところだ. ¶A curious *spectacle* was ***witnessed***. 妙な光景を見た.

Q a ***beautiful*** but ***melancholy** spectacle* 美しいがさびしい風景. ¶a ***brilliant** spectacle* すばらしい光景. ¶one of the ***capital's gratis** spectacles* 首府の無料観覧物の一. ¶a ***charming** spectacle* 美観. ¶a ***dazzling** spectacle* さんらんたる光景. ¶a ***delightful** spectacle* 楽しい見もの. ¶a ***deplorable** spectacle* 惨たんたる光景. ¶a ***distressing** spectacle* 悲惨な光景. ¶a ***dramatic** spectacle* 劇的場面. ¶an ***entertaining** spectacle* おもしろい見もの. ¶The sunrise as is seen from the top of Mt. Fuji is a ***famous** spectacle*. 富士山頂の日の出(御来迎)は有名な光景だ. ¶a ***fine** spectacle* 壮観. ¶a conflagration—the grandest of London's ***free** spectacles* 大火事—ロンドンの無料観覧物中最大の偉観. ¶a ***frightful** spectacle* 恐ろしい光景. ¶a ***gay** spectacle* きらびやかな光景. ¶an ***imposing*** and even ***showy** spectacle* いかめしくしかも花やかでさえある光景. ¶a very ***lively** spectacle* 非常に活気のある光景. ¶it was a ***ludicrous** spectacle* to behold ... ...を見るのはばかばかしかった. ¶a ***magnificent** spectacle* 壮観. ¶a ***military** spectacle* 軍隊の行列. ¶a ***pathetic** spectacle* 悲そうな光景. ¶a ***piteous** spectacle* 哀れな光景. ¶a ***pitiable** spectacle* なさけない光景. ¶a ***pitiful** spectacle* 痛ましい光景. ¶a ***public** spectacle* 公開のショー(競技など). ¶He was a ***sorry** spectacle* 彼は見るも気の毒であった. ¶a ***splendid** spectacle* りっぱな光景. ¶a ***striking** spectacle* すばらしい光景. ¶a ***terrible** spectacle* 恐ろしい光景. ¶a ***theatrical** spectacle* 劇の一場面. ¶a ***thrilling** spectacle* 痛快な(ぞっとする)光景. ¶a ***wonderful*** and ***never-to-be-forgotten** spectacle* すばらしい忘れられない光景.

P² The *spectacle* was that ***of*** sheep going to the slaughter. それは屠(と)所に引かれて行く羊の光景であった. ‖ it is a *spectacle **of*** no small interest to see ... ...を見るのは中々おもしろい.

O a *spectacle* to see 見ておくべき景色, 見もの.

(**2**) *pl.* めがね.

V ***put on*** one's *spectacles* めがねをかける. ¶***take off*** one's *spectacles* めがねをはずす. ¶He ***wears spectacles***. 彼はめがねをかけている. ¶***wipe*** one's *spectacles* めがねをふく.

Q ***frameless** spectacles* 縁なしめがね. ¶***gold-rimmed*** (***horn-rimmed***) *spectacles* 金縁(ロイド)めがね.

Q² a gentleman in the ***tortoise-shell** spectacles* べっ甲縁めがねをかけた紳士. ¶***water** spectacles* 潜水めがね.

P glaring at me ***behind*** his *spectacles* めがね越しに私をねめつけながら. ¶a gentleman ***in*** (=wearing) *spectacles* めがねをかけた紳士. ¶a pair ***of*** *spectacles* めがね. ¶He looked at me ***over*** [the edge of] his *spectacles*. 彼はめがね越しに私を見た. ¶the English stage ***through*** foreign *spectacles* 外人の目で見た英国の演劇 ‖ see everything ***through*** rose-colored *spectacles* 何ごとにも楽観する. ¶He is reading ***with*** his *spectacles* on. 彼はめがねをかけて物を読んでいる. ‖ ***with*** his *spectacles* upon his forehead ひたいにめがねを上げて. 「鏡.

P² *spectacles **for*** short-sighted persons 近視めがね, 近眼

spectator, *n.* 見物人; 傍観者.

V ***draw*** over 10,000 *spectators* 一万以上の観客を呼ぶ(入りがある). ¶The *spectators* were ***moved*** to tears. 見物人は感動して涙を流した.

Q ***gaping** spectators* あっけにとられている観客. ¶***horrified** spectators* びっくり仰天した傍観人. ¶an ***interested** spec-*

tator おもしろがっている見物人. ¶a ***mere*** *spectator* 全くの傍観者. ¶watch ... as a ***silent*** and ***helpless*** *spectator* 施すすべもなく黙って...をながめる. ¶an ***unconcerned*** *spectator* 高見の見物人. ¶an ***uninitiated*** *spectator* might imagine that ... 見なれない人は...と想像するかも知れない.

Q² a ***court*** *spectator* 裁判傍聴人.

P sit ***as*** *spectators* to the scene その現場を傍観する. ¶a large gathering ***of*** *spectators* たくさんの見物人.

P² *spectators* ***in*** the pit of a theatre 土間の見物人.

specter, 《英》**-re,** *n.* 幽霊.

V ***exorcise*** forever the *specter* of ... 永久に悪魔を払う(迷夢を解く). ¶They ***raised*** a *specter* they could not lay. 彼らは退散させることのできない幽霊を出現させた.

Q a ***hollow-cheeked*** *specter* of his former husky self 以前がん丈であった人のやつれた姿.

P believe ***in*** *specter* 幽霊のあることを信じる.

spectrum, *n.* 〖光学〗スペクトル.

Q² ***absorption*** *spectrum* 吸収スペクトル. ¶***diffraction*** (***line***) *spectrum* 回折(輝線)スペクトル. ¶***radio*** *spectrum* 〖ラジオ〗波長のスペクトル分布.

speculate, *v.* 思索する; 投機をする.

M *speculate* ***moonily*** about ... ...に遠く思いをはせる.

P It is useless to *speculate* ***about*** it. それについて思案するのは無益だ. ¶*speculate* ***as to*** (=***concerning***) the cause of ... ...の理由を考察する. ¶*speculate* ***for*** a rise (fall) 値が出る(下がる)と思って投機する. ¶*speculate* ***in*** stocks (=shares) 株をやる ‖ *speculate* ***in*** sugar 砂糖でやまをやる(株を買う). ¶*speculate* ***on*** the origin of the universe 宇宙の起源について思索する ‖ *speculate* ***on*** the issue of the war 戦争の結果を反省する ‖ *speculate* ***on*** a rise (fall) 値が出る(下がる)と思ってやまを張る. 【類】He *speculated* heavily ***on*** the favorite horse (好きな馬).

speculation, *n.* 思索, 思案; 理論; 投機.

V I am sorry to ***disturb*** your *speculation.* 考えごとの邪魔をしてすみません. ¶Many *speculations* were from time to time ***hazarded*** as to its results. その成行に関して時折色々の推測をやって見た人がある. ¶***make*** rash *speculations* 無鉄砲なやまをかける. ¶The *speculation* has ***failed.*** やまがはずれた.

Q ***abstract*** *speculations* 難解の理論. ¶not a ***bad*** *speculation* 悪いやまではない. ¶a ***commercial*** *speculation* 商業上のやま. ¶***intellectual*** *speculation* 知的思索. ¶In the corridors and lounges of the Assembly hall there was ***intense*** *speculation.* 会議場の廊下や休憩室で盛んに思わくが飛んだ. ¶***metaphysical*** *speculation* 形而上学的思索. ¶***political*** *speculation* 政治上のおもわく. ¶He lost money by ***rash*** *speculation.* 彼は無鉄砲な投機で金をなくした. ¶*speculation* is ***rife*** about ... ...についてうわさとりどりである. ¶***sublime*** *speculations* 高尚な思索. ¶***vain*** *speculations* 空想.

Q² a ***wild-cat*** *speculation* 無鉄砲なやま.

P He bought it ***as*** a *speculation.* 彼は思わくでそれを買った. ¶failure brought about ***by*** *speculation* in ... ...の投機で招いた失敗. 【類】He has ruined himself ***by*** *speculation.* ¶go in ***for*** *speculation* 投機に手を出す. ¶refrain ***from*** *speculation* 投機を控える. ¶dabble ***in*** *speculation* 投機に手を出す ‖ fail (succeed) ***in*** a *speculation* 投機で失敗(成功)する ‖ He threw away all his property ***in*** *speculation.* 彼は投機で全財産をすった. ‖ He invested money ***in*** that *speculation.* 彼はその投機に金をつぎ込んだ. ¶I bought it ***on*** [a] *speculation.* 私はやまでそれを買った. ¶He is much given ***to*** *speculation.* 彼は考えごとばかりしている.

P² The *speculation* ***concerning*** the Japanese swimming success at Los Angeles was rife. ロスアンゼルスにおける日本水泳の勝敗に関するかけが盛んに行われた. ¶a *speculation* ***in*** stocks 株式の投機. ¶*speculation* ***on*** the stock market 株式市場での投機.

speculative, *a.* 投機的な.

M The buying is ***purely*** *speculative* その買入れは全くの投機だ.

P There is nothing whatever *speculative* ***about*** it. それには何ら投機的なところがない.

speculator, *n.* 投機業者, 相場師.

Q² a ***real estate*** *speculator* 土地家屋の投機業者.

P² *speculators* ***for*** a fall 値下りを予想しての投機者. ¶a *speculator* ***in*** rice 米相場師.

speech, *n.* (**1**) 談話; 言葉; 弁舌; 話しぶり.

V any one desiring to ***acquire*** refined *speech* 上品な言葉使いをしたいと思う人. ¶***carry on*** *speech* with ... ...と話をする. ¶***clip*** *speech* なるべく手短かに話す. ¶***get*** (=have) *speech* 談話の機会を得る. ¶***give*** *speech* to one's feelings 感情を口に出す. ¶I ***had*** *speech* with him. 私は彼と話をした. ¶***improve*** one's *speech* 言葉使い(話し方, 演説の仕方)を改善する. ¶***lose*** one's *speech* 口がきけなくなる. ¶I ***made*** this *speech* to my patient. 私は患者にこう言って聞かせた. ¶***recovering*** *speech* with difficulty ようようのことで口を開いて. ¶***utter*** such a *speech* こんなことを言う.

Q an ***abusive*** *speech* ばとう的な談話. ¶people of ***affected*** *speech* 気取った言葉使いの人々. ¶the colloquial style of ***American*** *speech* 米語の口語体 ‖ in ***colloquial*** *speech* 口語で. ¶in ***common*** *speech* (=parlance) it is called ... 俗にそれを...という. ¶locutions which are not permissible in ***correct*** *speech* 正しい言葉使いと見なされない言い方. ¶a ***crisp*** *speech* 歯切れのいい談話. ¶***cryptic*** *speech* 密談. ¶***current*** *speech* 現代語. ¶a ***cutting*** *speech* 辛らつな談話. ¶a ***cynical*** *speech* 皮肉な談話. ¶Even ***dull*** *speeches* are better than dull silence. おもしろくない話でもおもしろくなく黙っているよりはまだよい. ¶an ***educated*** *speech* 教養ある談話. ¶take a person in by ***fair*** *speech* 人を口車に乗せる. ¶be permissible in ***familiar*** *speech* 打ちとけた談話では使って差支えない. ¶quick ***flashing*** *speech* of challenge and reply 電光のような会話のやりとり. ¶by ***flattering*** *speech* お世辞を言って. ¶In Greece, during the epoch of the Tyrants, when ***free*** *speech* was dangerous, the fable was largely used for political purposes. 自由の言論が危険であった専制君主時代のギリシアでは政治上の目的にぐう話が広く用いられた. ¶in ***general*** *speech* 一般に通用する言葉で. ¶***glib*** *speech* 能弁. ¶the ***guttural*** *speech* of Germans のど発音の多いドイツ人の言葉. ¶***hasty*** and ***thoughtless*** *speech* 口から出まかせの言葉. ¶***homely downright*** *speech*=the vernacular くだけた言葉. ¶the diversity of ***human*** *speech* 人類言語の多様性. 【類】Parrots imitate ***human*** *speech.* ¶***indigenous*** *speech* [その国]特有の言い方. ¶His *speech* is as ***laconic*** as of a military commander in the midst of an engagement. 彼の言葉は戦場に立つ司令官のように簡潔である. ¶a ***long-winded*** *speech* 回りくどい話. ¶a ***mawkish*** and ***affected*** *speech* 胸が悪くなる気取った言葉使い. ¶the Bible in ***modern*** *speech* 現代語聖書. ¶a striking example of ***national*** *speech,* as well as of national thought and philosophy 国民の思想哲学並に国語の著しい実例. ¶in an ***oblique*** *speech* 遠回しに. ¶out of place in ***ordinary*** *speech* 日常の談話には不適当な. ¶Vulgarism signifies English that is not used in ***polite*** *speech.* 卑語とは上品な言葉には用いられない英語のことである. ¶proverbs long current in ***popular*** *speech* 久しく言い古された格言. ¶the southern ***provincial*** *speech* 南部諸州の言葉. ¶in ***rapid*** *speech* 早口で. ¶I was charmed with his ***ready*** *speech.* 私は彼のよどみない弁舌に魅せられた. ¶***rustic*** *speech* in England 英国のいなか言葉. ¶the ***second*** *speech* of all men 人類の第二国語. ¶***simple*** and ***direct*** *speech* 簡潔直接的な言葉. ¶***sloppy*** *speech* だらしのない話しぶり. ¶***slovenly*** *speech* だらしのない話しぶり. ¶***slow, measured*** *speech* ゆっくりしたリズミカルな話し方. ¶a ***smart*** *speech* for a five year old 五歳にしてはきびきびした物の言いぶり. ¶***soft*** *speech* 物やさしい言いぶり. ¶***standard educated*** *speech* 標準的教養人の話し方. ¶***standardized*** *speech* 標準化された言葉. ¶a people of ***strange*** *speech* 言語の異った人民. ¶a ***sulfurous*** *speech* 火のような熱弁. ¶***terse*** *speech* 簡潔な言葉. ¶***Ungrammatical*** *speech* is the chief sign of illiteracy. 文法はずれの言葉は無学の主な証拠である. ¶an ***unspoken*** *speech* 口に出さない言葉. ¶***visible*** *speech* 視話法.

Q² in ***everyday*** *speech* 日常語では. ¶***infant*** *speech* 幼児の言葉. ¶in ***London*** *speech* ロンドン言葉で. ¶He said it in ***Malay*** *speech.* 彼はそれをマレー語でいった. ¶the ***peasant*** *speech* of Ireland アイルランドの農民の言葉. ¶formal ***platform*** *speech* 堅苦しい演説の言葉.

P be startled ***beyond*** *speech* 何とも言えないほどびっくりする. ¶I was offended ***by*** his blunt *speech.* 彼の無遠慮な言方が私のしゃくにさわった. ¶conciseness ***in*** *speech* 言葉の簡潔さ ‖ poverty ***in*** *speech* 言葉の貧弱 ‖ hesitation ***in*** *speech* 言葉のつまること ‖ He has an impediment ***in*** his *speech.* 彼はどもる. ‖ He used nasty words ***in*** *speech.* 彼はきたな

い言葉を使った. 【類】 graceful ***in speech*** / He is rough ***in speech.*** ‖ He is thick ***in*** (=***of***) ***speech.*** 彼はろれつが回らない. ¶ the faculty ***of speech*** 言語の能力 ‖ a figure ***of speech*** 言葉のあや ‖ part ***of speech*** 〖文法〗品詞. 【類】 the parts ***of speech*** ‖ freedom ***of speech*** 言論の自由 ‖ a man ***of*** low ***speech*** 言葉のいやしい人 ‖ He is slow (rapid) ***of speech.*** 彼はとつ弁(早口)である. ¶ All were ***without speech.*** 一同は黙っていた.

P² Music is a common ***speech for*** humanity. 音楽は人類共通の言語である.

(**2**) 演説.

V ***address*** stirring ***speeches*** of encouragement 血をわかすような激励演説をやる. ¶ ***compose*** a ***speech*** 演説の草稿を作る. ¶ ***construct*** a ***speech*** 演説の文章をつづる. ¶ ***deliver*** a ***speech*** extemporaneously 即席演説をする. ¶ a ***speech given*** before the New York Chamber of Commerce ニューヨーク商業会議所でやった演説. ¶ ***hear*** a ***speech out*** 演説を終りまで聞く. ¶ ***improvise*** a ***speech*** 即席演説をやる. ¶ ***indite*** a ***speech*** 演説を草案する. ¶ ***make*** a ***speech*** from one's notes ノートを見ながら演説する ‖ ***make speeches*** of more or less coherence 多少筋の立った演説をする. 【類】 I was called upon to ***make*** a ***speech*** on the occasion. ¶ ***plan*** a ***speech*** 演説を立案する. ¶ ***prepare*** a ***speech*** which he intends to deliver やらうとする演説の準備をする. ¶ The ***speech*** was ***punctuated*** with cheers. その演説はかっさいでしばしばとぎれた. ¶ ***read*** one's ***speech*** 朗読演説をやる. ¶ His ***speech*** was fully ***reported*** in The Times of Oct. 4th. 彼の演説は十月四日のタイムズ紙に全部載った. ¶ ***shout*** one's ***speech*** 演説で声を張りあげる. ¶ His ***speech smacks*** of affectation. 彼の演説は気どった所がある. ¶ this ***speech*** was ***spoken*** on the occasion of ... この演説は…の折にやったものだ. ¶ ***write*** one's ***speech out*** beforehand あらかじめ演説の草稿を作る.

Q an ***admirable speech*** あっぱれな演説. ¶ an ***animated speech*** 活気ある演説. ¶ an ***arid, tiresome speech*** 無味乾燥で退屈な演説. ¶ a ***brief*** and very ***happy speech*** 簡潔なしかも非常に適切な演説. ¶ a ***clean, uplifting speech*** 上品な修養になる演説. ¶ a ***congratulatory speech*** 祝辞. ¶ a ***cut and dry*** (=***dried***) ***speech*** きまりきった(月並な)演説. ¶ The President addressed the people in an ***eloquent speech.*** 大統領が民衆に向って雄弁を振った. ¶ an ***eloquent*** and ***appealing speech*** 雄弁で同情を引く演説. ¶ an ***empty speech*** 内容のない演説. ¶ an ***excellent speech*** りっぱな演説. ¶ an ***extemporaneous speech*** 即席演説. ¶ a ***farewell speech*** 告別演説. ¶ a ***fiery speech*** 火のような演説. ¶ a ***flat speech*** 活気のない演説. ¶ a ***formal*** and ***majestic speech*** 正式の荘厳な演説. ¶ a ***graceful speech*** 上品な演説. ¶ an ***impassioned speech*** 熱のこもった演説. ¶ an ***impromptu speech*** 即席演説. ¶ an ***incendiary speech*** 扇動的演説. ¶ an ***incoherent speech*** 筋の立たない演説. ¶ an ***introductory speech*** 紹介演説. ¶ a carefully ***learned speech*** [前から作って]よく覚えた演説. ¶ a ***long*** and ***boring*** (=tiresome) ***speech*** 長い退屈な演説. ¶ a ***long rambling speech*** 長いまとまりのつかない演説. ¶ His ***speech*** is ***longwinded.*** 彼の演説は冗長だ. ¶ a ***maiden speech*** 処女演説. ¶ a ***masterly speech*** 巧妙な演説. ¶ an ***off-hand*** (=***extempore***) ***speech*** 即席演説. ¶ an ***open speech*** 公開演説. ¶ make a ***passionate speech*** 熱烈な演説をする. ¶ a ***patriotic speech*** 憂国的な演説. ¶ a ***pointless speech*** 要領を得ない演説. ¶ He was rudely interrupted in the course of the ***political speech.*** 彼は政談演説中乱暴な妨害を受けた. ¶ a ***poor speech*** へたな演説. ¶ a ***post-prandial speech*** 正さん後の演説. ¶ a ***pretentious speech*** 仰々しい演説. ¶ a ***prolix speech*** 長たらしい演説. ¶ a ***public speech*** 公開演説. ¶ a ***rambling speech*** まとまりのない演説. ¶ a ***read speech*** 朗読演説. ¶ a ***ready-made speech*** 予め用意された演説. ¶ make a ***reply speech*** 応戦演説をする. ¶ a ***sententious speech*** 警句に富んだ演説. ¶ a ***set speech*** 用意した演説. ¶ a ***splendid speech*** りっぱな演説. ¶ a ***strong speech*** against ... …に反対する熱烈な演説. ¶ The ***speech*** is very ***suggestive.*** その演説は非常に示唆に富んでいる. ¶ a ***tame speech*** 平々凡々の演説. ¶ His ***speech*** was ***tedious.*** 彼の演説はくどくどしかった. ¶ deliver a ***telling speech*** on the subject その問題について効果的な演説をする. ¶ ***temperate speech*** 穏当な言葉. ¶ a ***touching speech*** 人を動かす演説. ¶ a ***violent speech*** 劇烈な演説. ¶ His ***speech*** was ***washy.*** 彼の演説は活気がなかった. ¶ a ***wordy speech*** 冗長な演説.

Q² an ***after-dinner speech*** 食後の演説. ¶ a ***campaign speech*** 選挙[応援]演説. ¶ a ***curtain speech*** 就寝後細君のお説教. ¶ an ***election-rally speech*** 選挙応援演説. ¶ a ***farewell speech*** お名残り演説. ¶ a ***five-minute speech*** 五分間演説. ¶ a ***holiday speech*** お世辞演説. ¶ the ***opening speech*** of Mr. ... …氏の開会の辞. ¶ a ***Presidential nomination acceptance speech*** 大統領候補指名受諾演説. ¶ make a coast-to-coast ***radio speech*** 全米放送網演説をする. ¶ a ***stump speech*** 《米》 選挙演説. ¶ a ***throne speech*** 開(閉)院式勅語. ¶ a ***40-minute speech*** 四十分にわたる演説.

P I believe I'm down ***for*** a ***speech***—or something. 演説かなにかやるはずになっている. ¶ He wandered (stopped short) ***in*** his ***speech.*** 彼は演説中話が横道にはいった(突然やめた). ¶ the keynote (subject) ***of*** a ***speech*** 演説の要点(題目).

P² Most ***Speeches from*** the Throne are proverbially dull, conventional, and colorless. [英国議会]開院式勅語は大抵きまって無趣味で紋切形で色彩のないものだ. ¶ make an eloquent ***speech in*** English 流ちょうな英語演説をやる. ¶ make a ***speech of*** welcome 歓迎演説をやる. ¶ a ***speech on*** (=***upon***) the war 戦争に関する演説 ‖ his ***speech on*** that occasion was ... その際の彼の演説は…であった. 【類】 ***speeches on*** fruit culture.

speed, *n.* 速力, 速度; 急速.

V ***accelerate*** the ***speed*** 速力を早める. ¶ ***achieve*** (=***develop***) a ***speed*** of ... [自動車など]…の速力を出す. ¶ she ***attained*** on her official trials a ***speed*** of ... [船など]正式試運転で…の速力を出した. ¶ ***gain speed*** 速度を増す, はかが行く. ¶ ***gathering speed*** as it goes down 下るに従って次第に速力を増して. 【類】 It goes more slowly at first, but ***gathers speed*** the farther it advances, until, at last, its course is irresistible (破竹の勢で). ¶ ***get*** a ***speed*** of 40 miles an hour 時速四十マイルの速力を出す. ¶ ***get up speed*** 速力を出す. ¶ She ***has*** an extreme ***speed*** of thirty knots. その船は最高速力三十ノットを有する. ¶ ***increase*** its ***speed*** その速力を増す. ¶ ***maintain*** full ***speed*** 全速力を続ける. ¶ ***make*** a ***speed*** of thirty-three knots an hour 一時間三十三ノットの速力を出す. 【類】 large steamers ***making*** a ***speed*** of eighteen knots. ¶ ***put on*** a tremendous ***speed*** 恐ろしい速力を出す. ¶ ***reduce*** the ***speed*** 速力を減じる. ¶ ***slacken*** the ***speed*** of one's horse 馬の足を緩める. ¶ ***slow up*** (=***down***) ***speed*** 速度を緩める. ¶ ***try*** the ***speed*** of a steamer 汽船の速力をためす. ¶ I ***wish*** you good ***speed*** (=luck) on your journey. 道中御無事で.

Q with ***accelerating speed*** 加速度で. ¶ make an ***average speed*** of 25 knots an hour 一時間平均二十五ノットの速力を出す. ¶ the ***breath-catching speed*** of 309 miles per hour 一時間三百九マイルというかたずをのませる速度. ¶ with ***breathless speed*** 息もつけない速度で. ¶ with all ***convenient speed*** なるべく早く. ¶ ***easy speed*** 楽な速度. ¶ drive at ***excess speed*** 過度の速力で駆る. ¶ at ***devil-defying speed*** ものすごいスピードで. ¶ at an ***exhilarating speed*** 快速度で. ¶ Everything goes on at ***express speed.*** 万事が特急で進行する. 【類】 travel (visit) at ***express speed.*** ¶ go (run, sail) [at] ***full speed*** 全速力で進む(など). 【類】 The horse galloped at ***full speed.*** ¶ rush along at a ***furious speed*** 猛烈な速力で突進する. ¶ at a ***giddy speed*** 目の回るような速度で. ¶ at a ***good speed*** かなりの速度で ‖ bid him ***good speed*** forward the goal 目的地に向って十分な速力を彼に命じる. ¶ They were running at their ***greatest speed.*** 彼らは最大速力で走っていた. ¶ at a ***headlong speed*** 大速力で. ¶ travel at a ***high speed*** [汽車など]高速度で走る. ¶ More haste, ***less speed.*** 急がば回れ. ¶ at ***lower speed*** 速度をゆるめて. ¶ with a ***maximum speed*** 最高速度で. 【類】 travel at ***maximum speed.*** ¶ with a ***mean speed*** of 100 miles an hour 一時間平均百マイルの速力で. ¶ at ***minimum speed*** 最低速度で. ¶ at ***moderate speed*** 適度の速度で. ¶ ***normal speed*** 正常速力. ¶ I shall work at it with all ***possible speed.*** なるたけ早くやりましょう. ¶ at ***quick speed*** 高速度で. ¶ at a ***reckless speed*** 突飛な速度で. ¶ The torpedo-boat destroyer attained the ***record speed*** of a little over 39 miles an hour. その駆逐艦は一時間三十九マイルちょっとという記録的な速度に達した. ¶ at ***reduced speed*** 速度をゆるめて. ¶ ***slow speed*** 緩速度. ¶ with ***surprising speed*** 驚くべき速力で. ¶ at a ***terrific speed*** 恐ろしい速力で. ¶ work at ***top speed*** 最高速度

で働く.【類】with a ***top*** *speed* of 660 miles an hour. ¶at ***tremendous*** *speed* 恐ろしい速度で. ¶go at ***utmost*** *speed* 最高速度で進む. ¶with ***vertiginous*** *speed* 目が回るような速度で. ¶At ***what*** *speed* does the steamer run? その汽船の速力はどの位ですか.

Q[2] a car traveling at ***breakneck*** *speed* はらはらするような速度で走る自動車.【類】Events in France were moving at ***breakneck*** *speed*. ¶The helicopter has a ***cruising*** *speed* of 100 miles an hour. そのヘリコプターの航空速力は毎時百マイルである. ¶with ***lightning*** *speed* 目ばたくまに, たちまち. ¶the ***surface*** (***under-water***) *speed* of a submarine 潜水艦の水上(水中)速力. ¶***trial*** *speed* 試験速力.

P ***at*** a *speed* of ... ...の速力で.【類】We are being whirled around the sun ***at*** a (=the) *speed* of nineteen miles a second. ¶fast (slow) ***in*** *speed* 速力の早い(おそい) ‖ lose heavily ***in*** *speed* [船など]非常に速力が落ちる. ¶go at a high rate ***of*** *speed* 高速度で進む. ¶***on*** high *speed* 高速度で. ¶put ***to*** *speed* 速力を出す. ¶a ship ***under*** full *speed* 全速力で航行する船.【類】***under*** an average hourly *speed* of 23.58 knots an hour. ¶***with*** the *speed* of a whirlwind 破竹の勢で ‖ ***with*** all *speed* 全速力で.【類】He brought down his sword ***with*** the *speed* of a sunbeam (電光石火のごとく) on the neck of the victim.

P[2] *speed* ***at*** reading 読方の速度.

speed, *v.* 急ぐ.

M *speed* ***away*** 急いで走る. ¶*speed* ***back*** to town 急いで町へ戻る. ¶*speed* ***homeward*** from abroad 外国から急いで帰朝の途につく.

M[2] sweating, *speeding* ***on*** あくせくやること. ¶*speed* ***up*** 速度をあげる ‖ *speed* ***up*** one's sales 売り急ぐ.【類】*speed* ***up*** the tempo / *speed* ***up*** housework / *speed* ***up*** the rehabilitation of the war-devastated areas / work is being *sped* ***up*** on the projects / *speed* ***up*** the production of aircraft / *speed* ***up*** the work to completion / *speed* ***up*** growth process (生長過程).

P They *sped* ***down*** the street. 彼らは街を急いで通って行った. ‖ *speed* ***down*** the hill 坂を急いで下る. ¶He *sped* ***on*** his way with breathless speed. 彼は息を切らして進んで行った. ¶The news *sped* swiftly ***over*** the country. そのニュースが国中にぱっと広がった. ¶*speed* ***through*** a task 仕事を急いでやってしまう.

speeding, *n.* 急速度を出すこと.

Q ***reckless*** *speeding* 無謀な急速運転.

P be arrested ***for*** *speeding* 規定外速度を出したために逮捕される.

speeding-up *n.* 速度上昇.

P[2] the *speeding-up* ***of*** the services [電車など]運転の高速度化.【類】the *speeding-up* ***of*** industrial production.

speedway, *n.* 《米》高速道路(自動車専用の).

P He hurried his car across the white glare ***of*** the *speedway*. 白くぴかぴか光る高速道路を彼は車を走らした.

spell, *n.* 仕事の交代; 休息時間; 一しきり.

V Each man ***does*** a six hours' *spell* of duty, followed by twelve hours' freedom ere his turn arrives again. 銘々が六時間続けて仕事をするとその後で次の順番が来るまで十二時間自由な時間がもらえる. ¶a rain ***following*** a dry *spell* 天気続きの後に来る雨天. ¶***give*** the horses a *spell* and have a pot of tea 馬を休ませて茶を一杯飲む. ¶We ***had*** a long *spell* of dry weather. 長いことよい天気が続いた. ‖ Sentimental girls often ***have*** a crying *spell*. 感情的な少女は一しきり泣き続けることがよくある.

Q ***dry*** (***wet, cold, hot***)*spell* for over one month 一カ月以上の天気(雨天・寒さ・暑さ)続き. ¶after a ***grievous*** *spell* of eighteen months on board the galley そのガリー船で十八カ月の辛い月日を送った後で. ¶a summertime ***hot*** *spell* 夏の暑さ続き. ¶a ***long*** *spell* of depression 長い間の不景気続き.【類】a ***long*** *spell* of north-east winds / a ***long*** *spell* of dry weather / They are used to ***long*** *spells* of work (長時間作業). ¶the ***prolonged*** *spell* of hot weather 暑気の長続き. ¶a ***severe*** *spell* of cold weather 一時のひどく寒い陽気. ¶in a ***single*** *spell*=at a stretch 一気に.

Q[2] a ***breathing*** *spell* ちょっとの息抜き ‖ ***breathing*** *spells* of peace 短期間の平和.【類】provide a temporary ***breathing*** *spell*. ¶have a ***fainting*** *spell* 一時気を失う.

P ***after*** a *spell* of about seven weeks of almost unbroken fine weather 約七週間もずーっと晴天が続いた後. ¶***during*** the late cold *spell* このごろの寒さ続きの間. ¶***for*** a brief *spell* ちょっとの間.

P[2] His *spell* ***of*** duty is then at an end for the nonce. それで彼は一時(当分)明番(非番)になる. ‖ a *spell* ***of*** ill-luck (bad weather) 不運(悪い天気)続き.【類】a *spell* ***of*** severe frost ‖ a *spell* ***of*** coughing 一しきりのせき.

spell, *n.* まじない; 魔力.

V ***break*** the *spell* 魔力を破る; 迷夢をさます; 正気に返らせる ‖ The *spell* of ... was ***broken*** ...のまじないがきかなくなった. ¶***cast*** a *spell* over ... ...を魅する ‖ ***cast*** a *spell* on the reader 読者を魅する.【類】Her beauty ***cast*** a *spell* over him. ¶They ***laid*** their powerful *spell* on the present generation. 彼らは現代の人々の上に彼らの力強い魔力を投げた. ¶***remove*** the *spell* from which one suffers かけられたのろいを払う. ¶The *spell* was ***snapped***. その通力がきかなくなった. ¶She said that some one had ***thrown*** a *spell* over her. 彼女は私はだれかにのろわれたのだと言った.

Q a ***magic*** *spell* 魔力.

P bind a person ***by*** a *spell* 人をまじないにかける. ¶***under*** the *spell* of bashfulness 気恥かしさを感じて.【類】***under*** the *spell* of beauty (eloquence).

spell, *v.* [語を]つづる, つづり字する.

M *spell* ***abominably*** つづり字の誤りがひどい. ¶*spell* ***backward*** 逆に字をつづる. ¶Here the answer must be *spelled* ***chiefly*** by the name of the teacher. 要するにこれは教師によりけりである. ¶*spell* the word ***correctly*** その語を正確につづる. ¶***grotesquely*** *spelt* words へんてこにつづった語. ¶***How*** do you *spell* 'cough?'「コーフ」という語はどうつづるか. ¶*spell* numbers ***out***, without using figures 数を数字でなく語で示す ‖ *spell* ***out*** (=over) =read with difficulty 苦労して読む.【類】*spell* ***out*** the meaning of ... ¶Take care to *spell* every word ***right***. どの語も正確につづるように注意せよ. ¶You have *spelt* this word ***wrong***. 君はこの語のつづりを間違えた. ¶***wrongly*** *spelled* (=spelt) words 間違ってつづった語.

P The word is *spelt* ***as*** "slaughter." その語は slaughter とつづる. ¶*spell* ***by*** guesswork いい加減につづる. ¶*spell* one's name ***in*** full 名前を略さずに書く ‖ *spell* ***in*** £ s.d. ポンド・シリング・ペンス(すなわち金高)で示す.

spelling, *n.* つづり字; 語のつづり方.

V ***phoneticize*** *spelling* つづりを発音通りにする. ¶***take*** the *spelling* as a guide to the sound つづり字を発音の目当てにする.

Q ***another*** *spelling* of the same word 同一語の別なつづり方. ¶incorrigibly ***bad*** *spelling* 途方もなく間違ったつづり方. ¶the complicated ***English*** *spelling* 複雑な英語のつづり. ¶***etymological*** *spelling* 語原的なつづり. ¶***good*** *spelling* 正しいつづり方. ¶***incorrect*** *spelling* 正しくないつづり方. ¶Some inflected words have ***irregular*** *spellings*. 屈折語の中には不規則なつづりのものもある. ¶in ***normal*** *spelling* 標準的つづり方で. ¶***official*** *spelling* 正式なつづり方. ¶in ***phonetic*** *spelling* 音標文字のつづり方で. ¶The *spelling* of English words is often ***puzzling***. 英語のつづり方ははっきりしない場合が多い. ¶In French, as in English, there are often ***several*** *spellings* for one sound and several sounds for one spelling. フランス語には英語同様同じ音を色々のつづりで示し同じつづりに色々の音があることが往々ある. ¶*Eon* is a ***simpler*** *spelling* of *aeon*. eon は aeon の略だ. ¶***variant*** *spellings* of the same word 同一語の多様のつづり. ¶His *spelling* is ***weak***. 彼のつづり方は怪しい. ¶The *spelling* of this word is ***wrong***. この語のつづりは間違っている.

Q[2] the ***Hepburn*** *spelling* in Romanization ローマ字のヘボン式つづり方.

P make a mistake ***in*** one's *spelling* つづりを間違える.【類】an error ***in*** one's *spelling*.

spend, *v.* 使う; 費す, 過ごす; 消費する.

M *spend* the winter ***abroad*** 外国で冬を過ごす.【類】He *spent* more than half his life ***abroad***. ¶Our ammunition was ***all*** *spent*. われわれの弾薬は皆尽きた. ¶*spend* money ***cautiously*** 慎重に金を使う. ¶*spend* one's money more ***efficiently*** 一層有効に金を使う. ¶Part of the time may be ***enjoyably*** *spent* in fishing. 時間の一部をさいてつりをするとおもしろく遊べる. ¶The month of June is ***far*** *spent*. 六月の月も大部過ぎた. ¶*spend* money ***freely*** on ... ...に金銭を惜気なく使う. ¶a life ***honestly*** *spent* in the faithful service of the common weal 公益のために忠

実に尽した生がい. ¶spend the hour idly 時間を徒消する. ¶It cannot be called ill spent. それは損にはならない. ¶spend money lavishly and foolishly on a mere hobby ほんの道楽に金銭を惜気なく無茶苦茶に使う. ¶A week may be pleasantly spent in seeing the interesting sights of the city. 一週間位は市内の見物でおもしろく過ごせる. ¶He spends money profusely. 彼は金を浪費する. ¶spend money rashly 無鉄砲に金を使う. ¶spend money right and left 金銭を濫費する. ¶His anger will soon spend itself. 彼の怒りもすぐ収まるだろう. ‖ Ill-gotten money is soon spent. 〖諺〗悪銭身につかず. ¶a long life well spent 有効に送った長い一生.

P spend a day at the beach 海辺(海水浴場)で一日過す. ¶spend ... for public purposes 公共の目的に…を使う ‖ spent a lot of money for clothes 金をたくさん衣服に使った ‖ spend for nought くだらなく使う. ¶We spent many hours in a pleasant conversation. われわれは幾時間も愉快に話をした. 【類】He has spent a long life in the study. / spend money in drinking (gambling) / He spends his time in reading. / The United Sates spent more than $300,000,000,000 in the war. ‖ He spent the remainder of his years in Japan. 彼は余生を日本で送った. ¶He spends most (a good deal) of his money on books. 彼は金を大概(大分)本に使う. 【類】spend (=lay out) a great deal of money on curios (骨とう品) / In 1934 American tourists are reckoned to have spent £38,000,000 on foreign travel. / We spent nearly twenty years on the project. / spend a lifetime of study on ... / He spent very little money on himself (自分のことに). ¶reduce the time we spend over newspapers 新聞を読んで費す時間を短縮する. ¶He contributed a lot of money to be spent towards the improvement of public libraries. 彼は図書館改善費に大金を寄付した. ¶I shall come to spend an evening (afternoon) with you. いつか一晩(午後に)遊びに行こう. 【類】Come and spend the day with us. / He spent the holiday with his friends.

spending, n. 支出, 消費.

V make one's spending and one's earning meet 収支を償わせる. ¶plan the spending of one's money ahead of time 前もって金を使う計画をたてる.

Q big spending 多額の消費. ¶wanton spending だらしのない消費. ¶wrong spending 間違った消費. ¶get some money for one's own personal spending 小使かせぎをする. ¶Wise spending is planned spending. 賢明な消費は計画的な消費だ.

Q² consumer spending 消費者の仕払い. ¶economy in government spending 政府支出の節約.

spendthrift, a. 金使いのあらい.

P be spendthrift of courage 勇気を惜まず出す.

sphere, n. 球; 本分, 地位; 勢力範囲, 圏.

V enlarge one's sphere of influence 勢力範囲(なわ張り)を広げる. 【類】the study of foreign languages as a means of enlarging one's sphere of interest and widening one's outlook. ¶establish and consolidate spheres of influence 勢力範囲を確立しかつ強固にする. ¶extend its sphere of usefulness それを一層役に立たせる. ¶have a wider sphere of usefulness 用途が一層広い. ¶increase its sphere of influence [国家など]その勢力範囲を増大する. ¶Women everywhere are invading the spheres of men. 女子は各方面に男子の領分を侵しつつある. ¶widen one's sphere of knowledge 知識の範囲を広める. 【類】widen (=enlarge) its sphere of influence.

Q He moves in quite another's sphere. 彼は全く違った畑で活動している. ¶He moves in a different sphere from us. われわれとは違った社会で活動している. ¶confinement of women to the domestic sphere 家庭内への婦人の拘束. ¶the French sphere of influence in Africa アフリカにおけるフランスの勢力範囲. ¶a heavenly sphere 天体. ¶He moves in a higher (lower) sphere. 彼が活動している社会はもっと高い(低い). ¶men and women of importance in all the manifold spheres of human activity 人類の多様な活動舞台における重要な男女. ¶on this mundane sphere 現世において. ¶Statesman, legislator, administrator, orator, scientist and philosopher, the late Duke of Argyll was a bright ornament of the noble sphere in which he was born. 政治家・立法者・行政官・雄弁家・科学者兼哲学者であった故アーガイル公爵は彼の生れた貴族社会の大立物であった. ¶woman's proper sphere 女子の本領. ¶if he could revisit this sublunary sphere 彼がこの世に再来したら. ¶the supernal sphere 天界. ¶He has a wide sphere of action (=activity). 彼は活動の舞台が広い. ¶The home is a woman's shere. 家庭が女の本拠だ.

P in the spheres of action and thought 活動及び思想の舞台に ‖ life in cultured sphere 教養ある社会の生活. ¶the enlargement of the sphere of woman 女子活動範囲の拡張 ¶a map of the world drawn on a sphere 球に描いた世界地図(地球儀). ¶out of the sphere of ... …の範囲外に. ¶outside the sphere of a woman 女子の領域外に. ¶within the sphere of ... …の範囲内に ‖ remain within one's proper sphere 自己の本分を守っている.

P² The position is not the proper sphere for your talents. その地位は君の技両を発揮する適当な舞台ではない. ¶the sphere of fortress=the fortified zone 要さい地帯 ‖ a sphere of interest 利益圏 ‖ one's sphere of influence 勢力範囲, なわばり.

spice, n. 香料; 加味物; 気味.

V Spices give relish to a dish. 香料は食品に風味を添える. ¶interlard our daily discourse with foreign quotations that lend spice to our speech 言葉に生彩を添えるために日常の話題に外国語の引用句をそう入する.

P It is used as a spice. それは香料に使う.

P² a spice of humor 滑けい味 ‖ There was a spice of irony in his speech. 彼の演説にはちょっと皮肉なところがあった. ‖ Variety is the spice of life. 変化というものは人生の薬味になる. ‖ There is a spice of madness in his character. 彼の性格には気狂いじみた所がある.

spice, v. 調味する.

P It is spiced with ginger. それはしょうがで調味してある.

spider, n. くも.

V² Spiders crawl. くもははって歩く.

spill, n. こより.

P twist paper into a spill 紙をこよりにする.

spill, n. [乗物から]落ちること.

V have a spill [乗物から]落ちる ‖ He had a nice spill. 彼はひどくほうり出された.

spill, v. こぼす; [乗物から]落ちる.

P spill milk from a cup 茶わんから牛乳をこぼす ‖ Water spilled from the pail. バケツから水がこぼれた. ¶You have spilled some gravy on the table-cloth. お前はテーブル掛の上に肉汁をこぼした. ¶be spilled out of a cab 車から投げ出される. ¶She has spilt boiling water over herself. 彼女は煮え湯を浴びた. ¶water spilt upon a table 食卓の上にこぼれた水.

spin, n. 旋回; 疾走; [自転車などの]一走り.

V give a coin a spin 銭(銅貨など)をぐるぐる回す. ¶have a pleasant spin 自転車で一走りを試みる. ¶take a spin on the lake 湖水にボートを一こぎやる.

Q set forth on a long spin into the country 自転車でいなかへ遠乗りをする. ¶It is the last hour of this two and a half spin that is the most delightful. [バスなど]最も愉快なのはこの二時間半の快走の最後の一時間だ.

P He went for a spin (=biking). 彼は自転車で遊びに出かけた.

P² the spin of a top こまの旋回. ¶a spin on a bicycle 自転車での一走り.

spin, v. つむぐ; 物語りをする; 繰り延べる; 回す.

M spin out long discourses 長談義をする ‖ spin out the time by discussion 議論で時間を長引かせる ‖ The story is too much spun out. その話はくど過ぎる ‖ He endeavored, however, to gain further time by spinning out the negotiation. しかし彼は交渉を引延ばして時をかせごうとした.

M² The room seems to spin round. へやがぐるぐる回るようだ. 【類】The wheels spin round.

P spun at home (home-spun) 手織りの. ¶spin by hand 手でつむぐ. ¶spin a yarn about adventures at sea 海の冒険談をする. ¶Cotton is spun into thread. 綿が糸になる. ¶spin a coin on a table テーブルの上で銭を回す. ¶Thread is spun out of cotton. 糸が綿からつむがれる. ¶Without saying a word, he span upon his heel and went out. 彼は一言も言わずくるっと向きを変えて出て行った.

spiral, n. らせん, 渦巻状.

Q an inflationary (deflationary) spiral インフレ(デフレ)の進行.

Q² stop the price spiral 物価高騰の悪循環を阻止する. ¶launch (halt) the wage-price-profit spiral 賃銀・物価・利

潤の悪循環が始まる(阻止する).

spiral, *v.* らせん状に進む.

M² *spiral down* [飛行機など]らせん状に降下する. ¶a few wisps of smoke *spiraled up* from ... 数条の煙が...から渦巻き昇った.

spirit, *n.* (**1**) 精神; *pl.* 元気, 気分; [精神から]人.

V I at least ***admire*** their *spirit*. とにかく彼らの精神を私は高く買う. ¶***assimilate*** the *spirit* その精神を同化する. ¶***awaken*** a *spirit* of inquiry 研究心をそそる. ¶the *spirit* of the age was strongly ***bent*** on ... 時代精神は強く...に傾いていた. ¶Heavy domestic grief ***bowed down*** his *spirit*. 家庭に非常な不幸があって彼は力を落した. ¶***brace up*** the *spirits* of the down-hearted 落胆した人たちの気分を引立たせる. ¶***break*** one's *spirits* その元気をくじく. ¶To whatever he did he ***carried*** the same *spirit* of unfailing correctness. 何をやっても彼はあくまで正確を期するという精神を捨てなかった. ¶***catch*** the *spirit* of the day 時代の精神をつかむ ‖ I ***caught*** the *spirit* of the occasion. その場合の空気が飲込めた. 【類】 The most faithful translation can never ***catch*** quite the *spirit* of the original (原作). / Hearn accurately ***caught*** the Japanese *spirit*. ¶***cheer*** the drooping *spirits* of ... ...の消沈した気分を引立たせる. ¶***chill*** the *spirits* 元気をくじく. ¶***complete*** the gay *spirit* of festivity and mirth with ... ...があってはじめて陽気なお祭り気分を出せる. ¶His writings ***contain*** the *spirit*, the aroma, of the age in which he lived. 彼の著作には彼の生活した時代の精神と香りが出ている. ¶***cow*** the *spirit* 心をおじけさす. ¶***create*** a public *spirit* 公共心を起させる. ¶All the *spirit* of manhood seems to have been ***crushed*** of him. 彼は全く壮者の意気がそそうしてしまったらしい. ¶***cultivate*** the *spirit* of fair play (boldness and fearlessness) 公正(など)の精神を養う. 【類】 ***cultivate*** a *spirit* of self-help (mutual help). ¶***damp*** high *spirits* 元気をそそうさせる ‖ ***damp*** the rising *spirit* of a conversation 話の腰を折る. ¶***depress*** one's *spirits* その気をふさがせる. ¶***develop*** the *spirit* of loyalty 忠義心を啓発する. ¶***display*** *spirits* in the presence of danger 危険に臨んで勇気を示す. 【類】 The audience ***displayed*** a properly appreciative *spirit*. ¶Lottery ***encourages*** a *spirit* of gambling and speculation. 富くじはとばく及び投機心を助長する. ¶***enlarge*** the narrow *spirit* of ... ...の偏狭な精神を広くする. ¶***enliven*** one's *spirits* 元気を出させる. ¶***entertain*** no *spirit* of revenge 復しゅう心をいだいていない. ¶***exhibit*** a *spirit* of liberality and sweet reasonableness 寛容と穏当の気持を示す. ¶***foment*** the *spirit* of dissension 不和の気分を醸成する. ¶Lottery ***fosters*** the *spirit* of gambling. 富くじはとばくを助長する. ¶The translator has succeeded in ***grasping*** the *spirit* of the original. その翻訳者は原作の精神をつかんでいる. ¶He ***had*** not the *spirit* to complete the task. 彼には仕事をやり遂げようとする元気がなかった. 【類】 he ***had*** *spirit* enough to ... ¶***heighten*** one's *spirits* 気を引立てる. ¶***imbibe*** the *spirit* その精神をのみ込む. ¶***impart*** a more or less humane *spirit* to one's decisions 処分(判決)に多少人情を加味する. ¶***inflame*** the war *spirit* of the nation 国民の戦争熱をあおる. ¶He ***infused*** his *spirit* into his men. 彼は部下に自分の意気を吹込んだ. ¶***inspire*** the *spirit* of outrage 狂暴な精神を鼓吹する. ¶***instil*** the *spirit* of military discipline 軍人精神を吹き込む. 【類】 The schools ***instil*** a *spirit* of learning which continues through life. ¶***Keep up*** your *spirits!* しっかりしろ. ¶***lose*** one's *spirits* 気を落す. ¶***nourish*** the *spirits* 元気をかん養する. ¶They failed to ***penetrate*** thoroughly the *spirit* of the Russian people. 彼らはロシア人の精神を十分理解し得なかった. ¶***promote*** the *spirit* of nationalism 国家主義の精神を振興する. 【類】 ***promote*** a *spirit* of friendship and of honorable (堂々たる) peace. ¶***protect*** and ***foster*** the *spirit* of manly independence 男らしい独立の精神を保護しかつ養成する. ¶***put*** much *spirit* into ... ...に多大の力を入れる. ¶***quicken*** (=stir up) martial *spirit* 士気を鼓舞する. ¶***raise*** our *spirits* from the lowest depths われわれの消沈しきった意気を引立たせる. 【類】 ***raise*** the *spirits* of his men. ¶***re-animate*** the *spirit* 気を取り直す. ¶***recover*** one's *spirits* 元気を回復する. ¶***re-energize*** the drooping *spirits* 消沈した意気をよみがえらせる. ¶***reflect*** the *spirit* of the times (=age) 時代の精神を反映する. 【類】 faithfully ***reflect*** the *spirit* of his day. ¶***repress*** the *spirit* of militarism 軍国主義の意気を押える. ¶***revive*** the drooping *spirits* of the army 軍のそそうした士気を振い起す. ¶***sense*** the *spirit* and learn the essential requirements of reporting 報道の精神を感得しその基本的諸要件を悟る. ¶***show*** a little *spirit* 少し元気を出す ‖ ***show*** a *spirit* of compromise 妥協の気持を示す. ¶***stir*** [***up***] one's *spirit* 精神を鼓舞する. ¶It does not ***suit*** the *spirit* of the age. それは時代精神にそわない. ¶His absence ***took off*** the *spirit* of the evening. 彼の不参でその晩の会はさびしかった. ¶he who would ***understand*** the *spirit* of Japan must ... 日本精神を理解しようとするものは...しなければならない. ¶***voice*** the *spirit* of his times aright その時代精神を正しく表現する. ¶***weaken*** the *spirit* of self-reliance 自立の精神を弱める. ¶***weigh down*** one's *spirits* 意気をくじく.

V² The *spirits* of the troops ***flagged***. 軍隊の士気がそそうした. ¶In his nature there still ***lingered*** the *spirit* of romance. 彼にはなおローマンスを愛する心が多少残っていた. ¶While this splendid *spirit* ***lives*** in the hearts of her youth, Japan should have little to fear for the future. この輝かしい精神が青年の胸に脈打っている限り日本はその将来について少しも心配はいらない. ¶Whether the *spirit* ***moves*** him or not he must take up his pen. 気が向いても向かないでも彼は執筆しなければならない. ¶His *spirits* ***rose***. 彼は元気づいた. ¶A *spirit* of adventure ***seized*** us. われわれは冒険心が燃えた.

Q ***abject*** *spirit* 見さげはてた精神. ¶He is gifted with an ***active*** and ***inquiring*** *spirit*. 彼はおう盛でせんさく好きな精神をさずけられている. ¶It appealed to some ***adventurous*** *spirits* eager to escape the humdrum of life at home. それは国内の単調な生活を脱したいと熱望していた冒険的な人々の心を動かした. 【類】 one of the most ***adventurous*** *spirits* the world has ever bred. ¶of an ***ambitious*** *spirit* 向上心の強い. ¶the ***American*** *spirit* of hurry 米人のせっかちな気質. ¶an ***animating*** *spirit* of the rebellion 燃え上る反乱熱. ¶an ***ardent*** *spirit* 烈士. ¶a manifestation of the ***artistic*** *spirit* of a race 一民族の芸術心の表われ. ¶His letter was not written in a ***bad*** *spirit*. 彼の手紙は腹を立てて書いたものではなかった. ¶in ***best*** *spirits* 大元気で. ¶the ***Bohemian*** *spirit* 野人かたぎ. ¶a ***bold*** *spirit* 大胆な人. ¶those who have a ***brave*** *spirit* 勇敢な人人. ¶a ***brutal*** *spirit* 獣的な人. ¶He is in ***buoyant*** *spirits*. 彼は浮き浮きしている. ¶a ***bureaucratic*** *spirit* 官僚的精神. ¶in a ***business-like*** *spirit* 実務的精神で, てきぱきと. ¶His objections were made in a ***captious*** *spirit*. 彼はあげ足を取る気で反対を唱えだした. ¶a ***catholic*** *spirit* 広量. ¶He was in ***cheerful*** *spirits*. 彼はきんきん然としていた. ¶the ***chivalrous*** *spirit* 武士気質. ¶his ***civic*** *spirit* 彼の市を愛する心. ¶a ***clubbable*** *spirit* 社交心. ¶It was in ***commercial*** *spirit* that he embarked on the enterprise. 彼がその事業に関係したのは商売気からであった. ¶show a ***compromising*** *spirit* 折れて出る. ¶in a ***conciliatory*** *spirit* 妥協的態度で, 折れて. ¶the affinity between ***congenial*** *spirits* 気の合った同志の和合性. ¶the ***controlling*** *spirit* 主動者. ¶The ***cooperative*** *spirit* has become a cornerstone of our economic structure. 協同精神が経済機構の基礎となった. ¶***corporate*** *spirit*＝team work 団体精神. ¶the ***cosmopolitan*** *spirit* 世界的精神. ¶a ***creative*** *spirit* 創造的精神. ¶The intensely ***critical*** *spirit* is often the narrow-minded, ignorant one. はなはだしく批評的な根性は往々偏狭無知なものだ. ¶the ***critical, questioning*** *spirit* 批判的なせんさく好きの性分. ¶the ***deadly*** *spirit* of dilettantism 有害な好事家気分. ¶his ***democratic*** *spirit* 彼の民主的精神. ¶a ***devoted*** *spirit* 熱心. ¶animated by a ***devout*** *spirit* 敬けんな精神に燃えて. ¶in a wholly ***different*** *spirit* 全く違った精神で. ¶The ***discontented*** *spirits* were all arrested. 不平分子は皆拘引された. ¶These plain facts are not presented here in any ***disparaging*** *spirit*. これらの事実をここに述べたのは決して悪口を言おうという気持でしたのではない. ¶the ***drooping*** *spirits* of the people were revived as they heard of ... 人民の消沈した意気は...の報道が伝わって元気を持直した. ¶the growth of the ***English national*** *spirit* 英国国民精神の発達. ¶an ***enterprising*** *spirit* 進取の気象. ¶in ***excellent*** *spirits* 上きげんで. ¶with an ***exemplary*** *spirit* of philanthropy 模範とすべき博愛の精神をもって. ¶in a ***fair, open,*** and ***liberal*** *spirit* 公平で

腹蔵なく寛仁の気持で. ¶the ***festal*** *spirit* お祭気分. ¶He was in ***fine*** *spirits*. 彼は大元気だった. ¶in a ***friendly*** *spirit* 親切に. ¶with a ***gallant*** *spirit* かいがいしく. ¶show one's ***generous*** *spirit* 気前を見せる. ¶He is in ***good*** *spirits*. 彼は元気だ. ‖ He is in the ***best*** *spirits*. 彼は上きげんだ. ¶He shows ***great*** *spirit*. 彼は元気おう盛だ. ‖ one of the ***greatest*** *spirits* of the day 現代の代表的人物の一人. ¶not in a ***grudging*** *spirit* いやいやでなく. ¶the ***guiding*** *spirit* 主動者. ¶a ***healthful*** *spirit* of emulation 健全な競争心. ¶in ***high*** *spirits* 上きげんで. ¶in a ***hostile*** and ***destructive*** *spirit* 敵対の破壊的気分で. ¶a ***humane*** *spirit* 人情のある人. ¶in an ***impartial*** *spirit* 公平な態度で. ¶He is of an ***independent*** *spirit*. 彼には独立の精神がある. ¶***indomitable*** and ***tireless*** *spirit* 不とう不屈の精神. ¶be full of ***initiative*** and ***offensive*** *spirit* as an automobile salesman or a book agent 自動車の販売員や本屋の外務員のように心臓が強い. ¶***irrepressive high*** *spirits* わきあがる意気. ¶the ***Japanese national*** *spirit* 日本の国民精神. ¶in ***kindly*** *spirit* 親切な気持で. 【類】His letter shows a ***kindly*** *spirit*. ¶with a ***kindly*** and ***good-humored*** *spirit* ¶I found in him a ***kindred*** *spirit*. 私は彼とよく気が合った. ‖ a ***kindred*** *spirit* with ... …の同志. ¶one of the ***leading*** *spirits* in the founding of the University 大学創立者の一人. 【類】the ***leading*** *spirits* of the movement (運動). ¶respond in a ***liberal*** *spirit* to ... 寛大な気分で…に応じる. ¶with that ***love-like*** *spirit* common to every collector of ceramics 陶器収集家に共通の恋愛めいた精神. ¶in ***low*** *spirits*＝depressed＝dejected 意気消沈して. ¶the ***martial*** *spirit* 士気. ¶a ***mean*** *spirit* 卑しい心. ¶the ***mercenary*** (＝***mercantile***) *spirit* 商人根性, もうけ主義. ¶the ***militant*** *spirit* 士気. ¶lack of ***military*** *spirit* 軍人精神の欠乏. 【類】fierce ***military*** *spirit* / foster ***military*** *spirit*. ¶the ***modern inquisitive*** *spirit* 現代的探究精神. ¶the ***moving*** *spirit* of the club クラブの主動者. ¶***narrow sectarian*** *spirit* 偏狭な教派心. ¶***neighborly*** *spirit* 親和の精神. ¶the birth of a ***new*** *spirit* and a new philosophic attitude in our university life わが大学生活における新精神と新哲学的態度の発生. ¶approach the subject in an ***objective*** *spirit* 客観的精神でその問題に対する. ¶animated by a ***patriotic*** *spirit* 愛国心に鼓舞されて. ¶It was not written in a ***pessimistic*** *spirit*. それは悲観的な気分で書かれてはいなかった. ¶in a ***philosophical*** *spirit* 哲学的精神で. ¶the ***pioneering*** *spirit* 開拓精神. ¶in the ***pious*** spirit of the period その時代の敬けんな精神で. ¶in ***poor*** *spirits* 意気消沈して. ¶He is of a ***proud*** *spirit*. 彼はごう慢だ. ¶a man with plenty of ***public*** *spirits* 公共心に富んだ人. 【類】actuated entirely by a ***public*** *spirit*. ¶one of the ***rarest*** and ***brightest*** *spirits* in the world 世にもまれな明朗な人. ¶a ***rebellious*** *spirit* 謀反心. ¶***rectified*** *spirits* 矯正された精神, 入れ替わった魂. ¶awaken the ***reflective*** *spirit* 反省心を起させる. ¶with a ***relieved*** *spirit* ほっとして. ¶undertake married life in a ***responsible*** *spirit* 責任感を持って結婚生活にはいる. ¶a ***revengeful*** *spirit* 復しゅう心. ¶***revolutionary*** *spirits* 革命気分の人々. ¶That's the ***right*** *spirit*. それはよい心掛だ. 【類】approach the subject in the ***right*** *spirit*. ¶the ***ruling*** *spirit* of ... …の主動者(首脳). ¶The ***sanitary*** *spirit* is as yet quite undeveloped. 衛生思想がまだ発達していない. ¶in a strictly ***scientific*** *spirit* 厳密の科学的精神で. ¶investigate the question in a ***scientific*** and ***impartial*** *spirit* 科学的な不偏の精神でその問題を検討する. ¶a ***self-helping*** *spirit* 自助の精神. ¶a ***selfish*** *spirit* 利己的精神. ¶develop a ***self-reliant national*** *spirit* 独立独行の国民精神を啓発する. ¶the ***tolerant*** *spirit* 寛大な精神. ¶He had the ***true*** *spirit* of an Edoite. 彼は生粋の江戸っ子であった. ¶conduct an investigation in the ***true scientific*** *spirit* 真の科学的精神で研究を行う. ¶investigate the life of Jesus in a ***truth-loving historical*** *spirits* 事実尊重の歴史的精神でキリストの生がいを研究する. ¶He is of an ***unbending*** *spirit*. 彼は剛直だ. ¶with an ***unvarying*** *spirit* of liberality 不変の寛大な気持で. ¶a ***warlike*** *spirit* 好戦的気質. ¶a man of ***young*** *spirit* 気の若い人. ¶Though old, he has a ***youthful*** *spirit*. 彼は(年はとっているが)気は若い.

Q² an exhibition of one's ***animal*** *spirits* 血気の表われ. 【類】high ***animal*** *spirits*. ¶catch the ***association*** *spirit* at last とうとう協会精神にかぶれる. ¶have the ***Christmas*** *spirit* クリスマス気分になっている. ¶***class*** *spirit* 学校の同級精神. ¶the true ***club*** *spirit* characteristic of Britain 英国特有の真正のクラブ精神. ¶***college*** *spirit* is something more than the noisy ebullition of boyishness set free from restraint. 大学気分というのは解放された少年らしさのあふれでた以上のものである. ¶***compromise*** *spirit* 妥協的精神. ¶***comrades-in-arms*** *spirit* 戦友精神. ¶with the ***do-or-die*** *spirit* 死して後やむの意気で. ¶instill a ***fighting*** *spirit* 闘志を鼓吹する ‖ the ***fighting*** *spirit* in an army 軍の闘志. 【類】stir up their ***fighting*** *spirit*. ¶a ***forgiving*** *spirit* 寛恕(じょ)の精神. ¶the ***frontier*** *spirit* [米国]辺境開拓精神. ¶the ***holiday*** *spirit* 休暇気分. ¶a ***master*** *spirit* (＝mind) 豪傑, 偉人. ¶the ***mob*** *spirit* 野次気分. ¶***party*** *spirit* 党派心. ¶the ***research*** *spirit* 研究精神. ¶the ***sporting*** *spirit* スポーツ精神. ¶the ***team*** *spirit* チーム精神. ¶stimulate ***war*** *spirit* 戦時精神を振作する. ¶creation of the "***warrior*** *spirit*" 武士的精神のかん養 ‖ the four ***warrior*** *spirits* or archangels 四天王. ¶the most adventurous type of ***Yankee*** *spirit* もっとも冒険型のヤンキー精神. ¶dampen the ***Yuletide*** *spirit* キリスト降誕祭気分をぶちこわす.

P still strong and mighty ***in*** *spirit* [老人だが]まだがん丈ですこぶる元気な ‖ ***in*** *spirit* participate in gathering [出席はしないが]精神ではその集会に参加する. 【類】I am very sorry that my engagements prevent my attending your charity concert but I shall be with you ***in*** *spirit*. ‖ travel ***in*** *spirit* over the vast East 広大な東洋を想像で旅をする ‖ depressed ***in*** *spirits* 気のふさいだ ‖ ***in*** a *spirit* of broad-minded fairness (gravity) かっ達公平(など)の精神で ‖ be young ***in*** *spirit* 気は若い ‖ ***in*** a *spirit* ***of*** rhetorical imagination [白髪三千丈のような]修辞的架空の気分で ‖ ***in*** a *spirit* of mischief でき心で ‖ ***in*** a *spirit* of jest ふざけ気分で. 【類】criticize it not ***in*** a *spirit* of fault-finding (あらさがしの積りでなく) / ***in*** a *spirit* of gratitude for ... / ***in*** a *spirit* of compromise / ***in*** the *spirit* of revolt (むほん気) / I trust that you will understand the above ***in*** the *spirit* in which it is written. / more true ***in*** the *spirit* than in the letter ‖ ***In*** (＝With) what *spirit* did you say so? 君はどんなつもりでそう言ったのか. ¶elation ***of*** *spirits* 意気高揚 ‖ dullness ***of*** *spirits* 気分の沈滞 ‖ He is a man ***of*** *spirits*. 彼は元気だ. ‖ at the top ***of*** his *spirits* and health 最高のコンディションで. ¶You are quite ***out of*** *spirits*. 君はまるで元気がない. ¶it is contrary ***to*** the *spirit* of ... それは…の精神に反する. ¶***under*** his guiding *spirit* 彼の指導精神の下に. ¶cast a damp ***upon*** one's *spirits* の元気をくじく. ¶answer ***with*** *spirit* 元気よく答える. 【類】He speaks ***with*** *spirit* and animation. / ***with*** a *spirit* of world-wide citizenship.

P² He was one of the moving *spirits* ***in*** the formation of the organization. 彼はその団体組織における主動者の一人であった. ¶the *spirit* ***of*** self-sacrifice 自己犠牲の精神 ‖ the *spirit* ***of*** the age 時代精神 ‖ the *spirit* ***of*** inquiry＝the inquiring mind 研究心 ‖ the *spirit* ***of*** revolt 反骨 ‖ a *spirit* ***of*** learning abroad (海外)留学熱 ‖ a remarkable indication of the *spirit* ***of*** the times 時代精神の著しい徴候 ‖ the *spirit* ***of*** inquiry 探究心. 【類】the *spirit* ***of*** a law (法の精神) is more important than its words.

(**2**) 霊魂, 亡霊; 精, 魔.

V ***appease*** the evil *spirits* 悪魔をしずめる. ¶***behold*** his *spirit* 彼の幽霊を見る. ¶***call up*** *spirits*, good or evil 善又は悪の精霊を呼び出す. ¶***chase away*** evil *spirits* 悪まを払う. ¶***conjure*** *spirits* to appear before ... 魔法を使って霊魂を目前に現わす. ¶***drive away*** (＝***banish or dispel***) evil *spirits* 悪魔払いをやる. ¶The evil *spirit* is ***exorcised*** that it may come out of the victim. [取りつかれた者から]悪魔を払う. ¶until my *spirit* shall be finally ***gathered*** to my fathers 私がやがて死んでしまうまで. ¶***give up*** the *spirit* 死ぬ. ¶***invoke*** *spirits* 魔術で招魂する. ¶***keep off*** evil *spirits*＝***keep*** evil *spirits* ***away*** 魔除けをする. ¶***release*** evil *spirits* 悪魔を払う. ¶***reverence*** the *spirits* of those who ... …した人々の霊に敬意を表する. ¶***scour away*** *spirits* 亡霊を退散させる. ¶***see*** a *spirit* 幽霊を見る. ¶***summon*** the *spirits* of the absent by burning incense 香をたいて招魂する. ¶***turn away*** evil *spirits* 魔除けをする. ¶The *spirit* had already ***departed***. [そのとき]既にこと切れていた.

Q ***ancestral*** *spirits* 祖先の霊. ¶a ***departed*** *spirit* 亡霊.

¶She has abundant faith in the appearance of ***disembodied*** *spirits*, and in their occasional intervention in human affairs. 彼女は亡霊が出て折々人事に立入ることを深く信じていた. ¶***good*** *spirits* 善霊. ¶the ***Holy Spirit***=the Spirit 聖霊. ¶grasp the hempen rope that hangs in front, sway it against the gong across which it is suspended to summon the ***presiding*** *spirit* 前に下っている麻の綱を掴みそれを揺すぶってつり下げてあるわに口に当てて祭神に呼びかける. ¶The disturbances were believed to have been caused by the ***troubled*** *spirit* of a man who was murdered in the house. その騒動はその家で殺された人の浮ばれない亡霊が起したものと信じられた.

Q^2 the ***forest*** *spirit* 森の精. ¶a ***water*** *spirit* 水のよう精.

P He is possessed ***by*** (=***with***) an evil *spirit*. 彼は悪霊につかれている. ¶associate ***in*** *spirit* with great historical characters 歴史上の大人物と霊交する. ¶the world ***of*** *spirit* 霊界 ‖ lead the life ***of*** the *spirit* 霊の生活を送る.

P^2 *spirits* ***of*** wine 酒精.

(3) [しばしば *pl.*] 酒(特に強い酒).

V He ***drinks*** *spirits*. 彼は強い酒を飲む.

Q ***raw*** *spirits* 生一本の酒; 水をわらないアルコール.

Q^2 Whisky is a ***grain*** *spirit*. ウイスキーは穀物から造った酒だ. ¶***rice*** (***potato***) *spirit* 酒(いもしょうちゅう).

P freaks preserved ***in*** *spirits* アルコールづけの奇形物.

O He drinks beer but no *spirits*. ビールは飲むがほかの酒は飲まない.

spirit, *v.* 励ます, 元気づける; 神隠しにする.

M *spirit* ***away*** (=***off***) a boy 子供を神隠しにする. ¶*spirit* one ***on*** for the attempt 元気づけてその企てをやらせる.

P *spirit* the people ***up to*** (=***into***) rebellion 人民を教唆して反乱を起させる. ¶*spirit* a person ***with*** whisky 人をウイスキーで元気づける.

spit, *v.* 吐く; つばを吐く, つばする.

M *spit* ***out*** blood 血を吐く ‖ *Spit* it ***out***! 泥をはけ(白状しろ).

M^2 Don't *spit* ***up*** into the air: it may fall back on you. 上を向いてつばを吐くな, 結局はわが身にふりかかるから.

P *spit* ***at*** him 彼につばをする ‖ *spit* ***at*** the idea その考えをばかにする. ¶*spit* ***in*** (=***into***) his face 彼の顔につばをかける ‖ Please do not *spit* ***in*** the car. 車中でつばを吐かないように願います. ¶*spit* ***on*** (=***upon***) the pavement (floor) 道路(など)につばを吐く ‖ *spit* ***on*** (=***upon***) one's hand 手につばをする.

spite, *n.* うらみ; 悪意.

V I ***have*** a *spite* against him. 私は彼に恨みがある. ¶He ***owes*** (=***bears***) me a *spite*. 彼は私に恨みがある. ¶***vent*** one's *spite* on ... ...にうっ憤を漏らす.

Q a ***petty*** *spite* ちょっとした恨み.

P He did it ***from*** pure (=just for) *spite*. 彼はほんの意地でそうしたのだ. 【類】This was all done ***from*** *spite*. ¶***in*** *spite* 腹いせに ‖ He persevered ***in*** *spite* of difficulties. 彼は困難をも顧みず辛抱した. ‖ ***in*** *spite* of protests 抗議をも顧みず ‖ ***in*** *spite* of his eighty-six years 彼の八十六歳(の高齢)にもかかわらず ‖ This made him a hero ***in*** *spite* of himself. このために彼は否応なしに人気者にされてしまった. ‖ ***in*** *spite* of him 彼には気の毒だが ‖ ***in*** *spite* of that それだのに ‖ The judge laughed ***in*** *spite* of himself. 裁判官は思わず吹き出した. ‖ My spirits became, ***in*** *spite* of me, more and more somber. 私は陰うつになってどうにもならなかった. ‖ those who succeeded ***in*** *spite* of the hardship 苦難に打勝って成功した人たち. 【類】***In*** *spite* of all his riches, he is never contented. / He is poor ***in*** *spite* of all his labors (かせぎ). ¶gratification ***of*** one's own *spite* 遺恨を晴らすこと. ¶He did it ***out of*** *spite*. 彼はつらあてにそれをやった. 【類】drink heavily ***out of*** *spite* / ruin the flowers ***out of*** *spite*.

spite, *v.* いじめる.

M *spite* a person ***cruelly*** つらくあたる.

spiteful, *a.* 恨みを含む, 執念深い.

P *spiteful* ***against*** a person 人に恨みを含んで.

splash, *n.* ばしゃり, ざんぶり; 《俗》見え.

V boys and girls ***enjoying*** a *splash* 水のかけっくらをして遊んでいる少年少女. ¶He ***made*** a great *splash* in the water. 彼は水の中でばしゃと大きな音をさせた. ‖ ***make*** (=***cut***) a *splash* 《俗》はでにやる, 大評判を取る ‖ ***making*** a *splash* of red where the throng is drabbest [群集の]万緑草中紅一点をいろどって.

Q a dog with ***brown*** *splashes* 茶色のぶちのある犬. ¶Ornamentally dressed ladies made ***strong*** *splashes* of color among the dark-coated men. その美装した婦人たちは黒ずんだ服装の男子の間に強い色彩を点出していた.

P Waves *splash* ***against*** the rock. 波が岩に打寄せる. ¶He jumped into the water ***with*** a *splash*. 彼はざんぶと水に飛込んだ.

P^2 a *splash* ***of*** water 水のはね返り ‖ a *splash* ***of*** muddy water 泥水のはね ‖ have *splashes* ***of*** grease on one's dress その衣しょうは油の汚点(しみ)がある.

splash, *v.* はね返す; はねかける; はねる.

P *splash* ***across*** a stream (creek) 小川をざぶざぶ渡る. ¶The rain *splashes* ***on*** the window-panes. 雨が窓ガラスにはねる. ‖ *splash* dirty water ***on*** one 人に泥水をはねかける ‖ The waves *splashed* ***on*** the beach. 波が浜に打寄せた. ¶The mud was *splashed* ***over*** the garment. 泥が着物にはねた. ‖ The water *splashed* ***over*** the deck. 波が甲板を洗った. ‖ *splash* mud ***over*** a person 泥を人にはねかす. ¶*splash* ***through*** the water 水中をばしゃばしゃさせて行く. ¶*splash* a person ***with*** mud 泥を人にはねかす. 【類】We had our car all *splashed* ***with*** mud.

spleen, *n.* ひ臓; 悪感情, 腹立ち; 憂うつ.

V ***bear*** a *spleen* against ... ...に対して悪感情をいだく. ¶This room ***gives*** me the *spleen*. 私はこのへやへはいると気がふさぐ. ¶Even a fly ***has*** its *spleen*. 一寸の虫にも五分の魂. ¶***vent*** one's *spleen* on everybody around やつあたりする.

P He is suffering ***from*** (=in the) *spleen*. むしゃくしゃしている. ¶in a fit ***of*** *spleen* 腹立ちまぎれに. ¶He acted so ***out of*** *spleen*. 彼は腹を立ててそうした. ¶He came in ***with*** [a fit of] *spleen*. 彼は憂うつな顔をして入って来た.

splendid, *a.* すばらしい.

P Oh, how *splendid* ***of*** you! まあ御親切に.

splendo[u]r, *n.* 輝き; 華美, 華麗.

V the town ***attained*** great *splendor* under ... その町は...の統治の下に隆盛の域に達した. ¶***boast*** a scenic *splendor* 風景の美を誇る.

Q ***extravagant*** *splendor* 法外な華美. ¶vice in its ***fulsome*** *splendor* and virtue in its radiant purity 威丈高の悪徳と清らかに輝く美徳. ¶***gilded*** *splendor* [劇場・寺院など]金ぴか. ¶live in ***great*** *splendor* 豪しゃな生活をする. ¶***massive*** *splendor* どっしりした壮麗. ¶***Oriental*** *splendor* 東洋風の業々しさ. ¶the ***retreating*** *splendor* of autumn 去り行く秋の花やかさ. ¶folk from the country slightly overawed by the ***surrounding*** *splendor* あたりがりっぱなのでちょと顔負けのしたいなか出の人々.

Q^2 the ***noonday*** *splendor* of the sun 日光の真昼の輝き.

P He vied with the king ***in*** *splendor*. 彼は国王と華美を競った. ¶rise ***into*** *splendor* りっぱになる.

P^2 the *splendor* ***of*** his art as a playwright 劇作者としての彼の腕のさえ. ¶a *splendor* ***of*** diamonds and low-necked dresses half hidden under loose cloaks ゆるやかな外とうに半ば隠れたダイヤや胸をずっとあらわした晴着の壮麗さ.

splicer, *n.* 接合者(物).

Q^2 a ***cable*** *splicer* 海底電線を接合する人(あるいは物).

splint, *n.* 副木.

V ***apply*** *splint* 副木を当てる.

P patients ***in*** *splints* 副木を当てた患者.

splinter, *n.* 破片.

V ***run*** a *splinter* into one's hand 手に破片を突き刺す.

P ***in*** *splinter* 切れ切れに, ばらばらに ‖ The plane crashed down ***into*** *splinters*. その飛行機は墜落してばらばらに分解した.

split, *n.* 裂れ目; 分離, 分裂.

Q It may ultimately lead to a ***serious*** *split* in the party. 結局それはゆゆしい党派割れとなるかも知れない.

P a *split* ***in*** a board 板の割れ目 ‖ a *split* ***in*** the cabinet 内閣の分裂.

P^2 the *split* ***into*** sects 数派への分裂. ¶the *split* ***of*** Buddhism ***into*** sects 仏教の数派への分裂.

split, *v.* 割る; 裂ける; 《俗》密告する.

M *split* ***asunder*** きれぎれに裂ける. ¶The kingdom *split* ***away*** from the empire. その王国が帝国から分離した. ¶Good mushrooms ***easily*** *split* from end to end. 良いきのこは簡単にたてに裂ける. ¶The road *splits* ***off*** from the main street. 路が大通りから分かれている. ¶*split* ***open*** 張り裂ける, はじける.

M^2 A minority which disagreed *split* ***off***. 少数の反対者が分離した. ¶The wood must be *split* ***up*** for fuel. 木を

割ってまきをこしらえなければならない. ‖ The party *split* **up** into two groups (=camps) その政党は二派に分裂した.

P *split* the cost **between** ... 費用を折半して…分担する. ¶*split* **from** ... over the question その問題で…と分裂する. ¶*split* it **in** two それを二つに割る ‖ *split* **in** half 半分に裂ける. ¶The State was *split* **into** large counties. その州は大きな郡に区画された. 【類】*split* **into** two factions (groups) ‖ Water *splits* **into** hydrogen and oxygen. 水は水素と酸素とに分解する. ‖ The old farm was *split* up **into** house lots. 昔からの畑が住宅地として分譲された. ¶The House *split* **on** the vote. 議院はその票決で満場一致を見なかった. 【類】The Liberals *split* **on** the Home Rule question. ‖ *split* **on** a rock 暗礁に乗上げて砕ける ‖ I *split* **on** him. 《俗》私は彼のことを密告した. ¶*split* **with** laughter 笑って腹をよる ‖ *split* **with** one's partners 仲間と割れる ‖ *split* one's sides **with** laughter 抱腹絶倒する.

O My head is *splitting*. 頭が痛くて割れそうだ. ¶*split* hairs こまかく区別し過ぎる.

split-second, *n*. 瞬時.

P **in** a *split-second* 瞬時に.

spoil, *n*. 戦利品, 分捕品; 獲物.

V **carry home** their ill-gotten *spoils* 不義の分捕品を持って帰る. ¶**divide** a *spoil* 分捕品を分配する.

P be taken **as** *spoils* of war 戦利品としてとられる.

P^2 the *spoils* **of** office 役得 ‖ the *spoils* **of** the chase 狩猟の獲物.

spoil, *v*. だめにする, …の物をかすめる.

P The plan was quite *spoiled* **by** the rain. その企ては雨で全くだめになった. ¶be *spoiled* by **favors** ひいきされて甘い人間になる. ¶They *spoiled* him **of** a gold watch. 彼らは彼の金時計を奪った. ¶*spoil* a child **with** praise ほめて子供を甘やかしてしまう.

O Spare the rod and *spoil* the child. 〖諺〗かわいい子には旅.

spoke, *n*. [車輪の]輻(や).

V He **put** a *spoke* in my wheel. 彼は僕の仕事の邪魔をした.

spokesman, *n*. 代弁者(スポークスマン).

Q^2 a **French Government** *spokesman* said that ... フランス政府のスポークスマンは…と言った. ¶a **Foreign Office** *spokesman* 外務省のスポークスマン.

P act **as** *spokesman* for the family 家族を代表して述べる.

P^2 a *spokesman* **of** the working men 労働者の代弁者.

sponge, *n*. 海綿.

V **pass** a *sponge* over his past and wipe out ... 彼の過去のことは水に流し…をぬぐい去る. ¶**throw up** (=**in**) the *sponge* 〖拳闘〗[スポンジを投げて]負けを認める; 参ったと言う.

Q a **regular** *sponge* 大の酒好き.

Q^2 **vegetable** *sponge* 繊維だけにしたへちま. ¶a **velvet** *sponge* 柔らかい海綿.

P wipe **with** a *sponge* 海綿でふく.

sponge, *v*. [スポンジで]ふく, 寄食する, 居候をする.

M *sponge* **away** (=**off**) sweat and dust 汗とほこりを洗い流す.

P *sponge* oneself **in** the bath ふろでからだを流す. ☞外人はふろおけの中でからだを洗う. ¶*sponge* **on** (**upon**) one's father 親のすねをかじる ‖ an idler who *sponges* **upon** his friends 友だちのところを居候をして歩く怠け者. 【類】*sponge* **on** a person for a living.

sponsor, *n*. 保証人; 名親; 〖放送〗スポンサー(広告主).

V **stand** one's *sponsor* その(身もとなどの)保証人となる. 【類】**stand** *sponsor* for ...

Q^2 a **parade** *sponsor* 行列の主催者. ¶a **radio program** *sponsor* ラジオ番組のスポンサー. ¶a **TV** *sponsor* テレビのスポンサー.

P^2 a *sponsor* **for** a warship 軍艦の名親. ¶a *sponsor* **in** baptism 洗礼のときの名親. ¶the *sponsor* **of** the proposal その提案者 ‖ the *sponsor* **of** a system 制度の支持者. ¶stand *sponsor* **to** ... [船の]名親になる.

sponsor, *v*. 支持する; 主催する.

P the exposition will be *sponsored* **by** ... その博覧会は…の主催で開かれる. 【類】The Journal of Educational Sociology, *sponsored* **by** the Department of Educational Sociology of New York University, is the only one of its kind in the field of educational sociology. / TV (radio) programs *sponsored* **by** ...

sponsorship, *n*. 後援, あっせん, 保証.

P **Through** the *sponsorship* of ..., a league of ... has been formed. …の後援で…連盟ができた. ‖ **through** his *sponsorship* 彼のあっせんで. ¶The meeting was held **under** the *sponsorship* of the Municipality. その会合は都の後援の下に催された. 【類】It was published **under** the *sponsorship* of the ... Association.

spook, *n*. 《米》幽霊, 化けもの.

V^2 *Spooks* **haunt** that old villa. あの古別荘には幽霊が出る.

spool, *n*. 糸巻.

Q^2 a **wire** *spool* 針金を巻くわく.

P wind thread **on** a *spool* 糸を糸巻に巻く.

P^2 a *spool* **of** thread = a reel of thread 一巻きの糸 ‖ a *spool* **of** film 一巻のフィルム.

spoon, *n*. さじ.

V a pair of lovers **having** a quiet *spoon* しんみりと楽しむ一組の愛人. ¶It's not proper to **leave** your *spoon* in your cup of coffee. コーヒー茶わんの中にさじを入れっぱなしにするのは無作法だ. ¶Baby **put** the *spoon* in her mouth. 赤ん坊がさじを口に入れた.

Q^2 a **dessert** *spoon* デザート用のさじ. ¶a **medicine** *spoon* 薬剤用のさじ. ¶a **soup** *spoon* スープさじ. ¶a **table** *spoon* [大形の]食卓さじ. ¶a **drilling** *spoon* 穴掘り用シャベル.

P a set **of** *spoons* 一組のさじ. ¶eat **with** a *spoon* さじで食べる.

spoonful, *n*. さじ一杯.

Q a **heaped** *spoonful* of (salt, sugar, tea) さじに山盛りの塩.

P^2 a *spoonful* **of** sugar (salt) 一さじの砂糖(など)

spoony, *a*. 《俗》[女に]まいって.

P be *spoony* **on** a girl 女の子にまいっている.

sport, *n*. 娯楽; 競技, 競技会; *pl*. 遊猟; 戯れ; がんろう物.

V The carp is a powerful fish **affording** great *sport* to the angler. こいは強魚で, 釣るには非常におもしろい. ¶His hat blew off and **became** the *sport* of the wind. 帽子が飛んで風にほんろうされた. ¶Three cheers for the ladies and donors of prizes **closed** the good afternoon *sport*. 婦人連と賞品寄贈者とに三度かっさいを送って楽しい午後の競技を終えた. ¶**conduct** athletic *sports* in a gentlemanly manner 紳士的態度で競技を行う. ¶We **had** good *sport*. たくさん猟があった. ‖ He **had** fine *sport* with his new skates. 彼は新らしいスケートで愉快に遊んだ. ¶**hold** annual athletic *sports* 例年の運動会を催す. ¶They **made** a *sport* of him. 彼らは彼をなぶりものにした. ‖ **make** *sport* of one's stammering 人のどもるのをからかう. 【類】**make** *sport* of a woman. ¶The *sports* were **postponed**. 運動会は延期された. ¶It **provided** capital *sport* for those taking part. それに参加した者は非常におもしろかった. ¶Here the angler can successfully **pursue** his favorite *sport*. ここでおもしろい釣りができる. ¶It **yields** excellent *sport*. それは実におもしろい.

Q **aquatic** *sports*, such as fishing, sailing, bathing, motor-boating, canoeing つり・帆走・海水浴・モーターボート・カヌーなどの水上遊戯. ¶They were off for a **day's** *sport*. 彼らは一日の遊びに出かけていた. ¶new records made in **different** *sports* 種々の競技で造られた新記録. ¶**equestrian** *sports* 乗馬スポーツ. ¶The game is a **favorite** *sport* with every class in Japan. その競技は日本では各層の人が好む. ¶It is **fine** *sport* to sail in a boat. ボートで帆走するのはおもしろい. ‖ Making money is the **finest** *sport* in the world. 金もうけは世界で一番おもしろい道楽だ. ¶a **good** *sport* = a good fellow 好漢 ‖ Be a **good** *sport*! 堂々とやれ(競技で). ¶he thought it **great** *sport* to ... …することを非常におもしろいと思った. ¶**healthy** *sport* 健康的なスポーツ. ¶**inter-university** *sports* 大学対校競技. ¶for the sake of a **little** *sport* ちょっと慰みに. ¶**major** and **minor** *sports* 大小の競技. ¶**manly** *sports* 男らしい遊戯. ¶in a **merry** *sport* 冗談に. ¶Skiing is the **national** *sport* of Norway. スキーはノールウェーの国技だ. ¶one of **nature's** *sports* (=freaks) 造化のいたずらの一つ. ¶suppose one to beat one's **old** *sport* その人の例のことだと思う. ¶Archery is an **old-time** *sport*. 弓術は昔からの遊戯だ. ¶**outdoor** (**indoor**) *sports* 戸外(室内)遊戯. ¶**What** *sport*! 愉快々々!

Q^2 **house** *sports* 会社などでやる運動会. ¶**school** *sport* 学校の運動会. ¶lovers of **snow** *sports* 雪上遊戯の愛好者たち. ¶**track and field** *sports* トラック及びフィールドの競技. ¶**water** *sports* 水上遊戯. ¶Bobsleighing is a popular **winter** *sport* in America. ボブスレー(そり競走)はアメリカで流行の冬のスポーツだ.

P whales **at** *sport* 遊泳中の鯨 ‖ **at** the *sport* of the wind 風のまにまに. ¶catching birds **for** *sport* or for gain 慰みまたは金もうけの小鳥捕り ‖ He has a passion **for** *sport*.

彼はスポーツが大好きだ. ¶Dogs fight ***in** sport.* 犬はふざけてかみ合う. ‖ He did it merely ***in** sport.* 彼はほんの戯れにしたのだ. ¶I am very partial ***to** sport.* 私はスポーツが大好きだ. ‖ turn it ***to** sport* それをひやかす.

P^2 be the *sport **of*** one's fortune (circumstances) 運命の神(など)にもてあそばれる. 【類】The ship was the *sport **of*** the winds. ¶It may be *sport **to*** you, but it is death to us. それは君らにはおもしろかろうがわれわれに取っては生死の問題だ. ¶*Sport **with*** this fish can be obtained in the lake. この魚つりはその湖水でできる.

Q He is quite a *sport.* あいつはいい男だ.

sport, *v.* もてあそぶ; 自由自在に出す.

M *sport **off*** epigrams 警句を連発する. ¶***proudly** sport* the badge 誇らしげにその記章を着用する.

P He is *sporting **with*** us. 彼はわれわれをもてあそんでいる. 【類】A high west wind was *sporting* gaily ***with*** the flags. / *sport **with*** a woman.

sportive, *a.* ふざけ気分の.

M^2 The old man seemed ***as** sportive* as a young boy. その老人は子供のようにはしゃいでいたようだ.

sportsdom, *n.* スポーツ界.

Q the re-entrance of Japan in ***international** sportsdom* 国際競技への日本の復帰.

sportsman, *n.* 遊猟家.

Q He was a ***keen** sportsman* and an excellent shot. 彼は熱心な遊猟家でありまた射撃の名人でもあった.

Q^2 an ***air-gun** sportsman* 空気銃遊猟家. ¶A well-known ***millionaire** sportsman* ある有名な富豪の運動家.

spot, *n.* 場所; はん点; 汚点.

V How did I ***get*** this *spot?* このしみはどうしてついたんだろう. ‖ I cannot ***get out*** these *spots.* このはん点は取れない. ¶He ***has*** a black *spot* on his forehead. 彼は額にほくろがある. ¶You ***hit*** the *spot!* 《口語》全くその通り(そのものずばり). ¶***mark*** the *spot* where ... once stood かつて…のあった地点を示す ‖ a monument to ***mark*** a sacred *spot* その神聖な場所を示す記念碑. ¶dare to ***profane*** a *spot* sacred to ... …を祭った神聖な場所をあえてけがそうとする. ¶***remove*** grease *spots* from clothing 着物の油の汚点を抜きとる. ¶***show*** *spots* easily 汚れが目立つ. ¶***take out*** *spots* of oil 油のしみを抜く.

V^2 These *spots* won't ***come out.*** このはん点は取れない.

Q an ***attractive** spot* 人目を引く場所. ¶pick out for display the ***black** spots* in the record of ... …の記録にあるその失行をやり玉にあげる. ¶a ***bright** spot* on the Japanese production horizon is ... 日本生産界の有望な点は…だ. ¶There is no ***busier** spot* in the universe than a tobacco factory. どこが忙しいといったってタバコ工場位忙しい所はない. ¶a ***clear** spot* among clouds 雲の切間. ¶quite a ***delightful** spot* in which to spend an hour or two on a summer's day 夏の日一二時間遊ぶのに快適な場所. ¶the ***exact** spot* where it happened そのことの起った現場. ¶a ***fair** spot* 美景. ¶The most ***famous** spot* for cherry-blossom in all Japan is Yoshino amid the mountains of Yamato. 日本一の桜の名所は大和の山中にある吉野だ. ¶a ***fine** spot* 景勝地. ¶a ***high** spot* 《俗》盛り場 ‖ a ***high** spot* in one's life 一生の中で得意の場面. ¶housed in a bright, sunny room situated in some ***high, dry** spot* ある高い乾燥した場所にある明るい日当りのよいへやに宿泊した. ¶a ***historic** spot* 史跡. ¶an ***isolated** spot* in the world 世とかけ離れた場所. ¶a ***likely** spot* for fishing 好い釣場. ¶a ***lovely** spot* to spend a vacation 休暇を過ごすに適したよい場所. ¶a ***peaceful** spot* in the heart of London ロンドンの真中の静かな場所. ¶a ***romantic** spot* 名所. ¶a ***sequestered** spot* 閑静な場所. ¶a ***shady** spot* 木陰のある場所. ¶one of the ***sickliest** spots* on the Continent [欧州]大陸における不健康地の一つ. ¶a ***sluggish, restful, old-world** spot* 活気のない, 静かな, 古臭い場所. ¶a ***soft** spot* 《俗》弱点. ¶a ***sore** spot* 痛む個所. ¶a ***sunny** spot* 日当りのよい場所. 【類】one of the ***sunniest** spots* (もっとも輝かしい場面) in his whole life. ¶a ***vital** spot* 急所. ¶a ***vulnerable** spot* 弱点. ¶the ***weak** spot* of English civilization 英国文明の弱点. ¶The vulgar of Europe call the ***white** spots* on the nails "gifts," because they portend presents. 教育のないヨーロッパ人はつめの白はんを「贈物」といっている, それは物をもらう前兆だというのだ.

Q^2 a ***beauty** spot* [婦人のほおにつける]美人ほくろ; 《口語》景勝の地 ‖ develop some of the lesser known ***beauty** spots* of Japan 日本の余り知られていない美景の地を発展させる. 【類】one of the famed ***beauty** spots* of that region. ¶a ***breathing** spot* いこいの場所. ¶a potential ***danger** spot* 危険のおそれある場所. ¶a suitable ***embarkation** spot* for warships 軍艦とう乗に好適の地点. ¶a ***gambling** spot* とばく場. ¶an ***ink** spot* インキのしみ. ¶The café is a popular ***night** spot.* カフェーは人気のある夜の遊び場だ. ¶a ***sun** spot* 太陽の黒点. ¶an old ***trouble** spot*—Roumania 昔からの係争地ルーマニア. 【類】Greece and other ***trouble** spots* of the Mediterranean. ¶his favorite ***vacation** spot* 彼が休暇に好んで行く場所.

P We met ***at*** the stated *spot.* われわれは所定の場所で会合した. ¶Children are fond of rotating ***in*** one *spot* until dizzy. 子供らは目まいするまで一つの場所で回っているのが好きだ. ‖ ***in*** the *spot* where he was shot 彼が撃たれたその場に ‖ a sack coat threadbare ***in*** *spots* 所々すり切れている上下の背広服. ¶***on*** the *spot* 現場で; 即座に, 直ちに ‖ sell ... ***on*** the *spot* …を即売する ‖ a policeman ***on*** the *spot* 現場におった警官 ‖ drawings made ***on*** the *spot* 現場で作った絵図. 【類】He was run over and killed ***on*** the *spot.* / study ***on*** the *spot* the facts of ... / investigate ***on*** the *spot* the subject of the Canadian book trade. ¶I stood rooted ***to*** the *spot.* 私はそこに根がついたように(動かずに)立っていた. ‖ He ran ***to*** the *spot* immediately. 彼はすぐ現場へかけつけた. ¶marked ***with*** black *spots* 黒いはん点のある(獣皮など). ¶***without*** a *spot* はん点のない.

P^2 a favorite *spot **for*** pleasure-parties (picnic parties, holiday-makers, pleasure-seekers) 遊覧団体(など)のよく行く所. ¶a *spot **on*** the face (skin) 顔面(など)のはん点 ‖ a *spot **on*** one's name (fame) その名声(など)の汚点.

spot, *v.* はん点をつける; 目星をつける; [名声などに]傷をつける.

P *spot* a friend ***among*** people (***in*** a crowd) 人中(など)で友人を見つける. ¶I *spotted* him at once ***as*** an American. 私は彼を直ちに米人と目星をつけた. ¶*spot* one's reputation ***by*** lying repeadtely うそ八百で名声を落す. ¶*spotted **with*** various colors 種々の色のはん点のある.

spouse, *n.* 配偶.

Q She is going abroad to rejoin her ***beloved** spouse.* 彼女はその夫の後を追って洋行する.

spout, *v.* ふく; ふき出る.

P Water *spouted **from*** the break of a pipe. 管の割れ目から水がふき出した. ‖ Blood *spouts **from*** an artery. 血が動脈からふき出る. ¶*spout* water ***into*** the air 水を空中にふき上げる.

sprain, *v.* [手・足など]くじく.

P have one's ankle (wrist) *sprained **by*** ... …して足くび(など)をくじく.

sprawl, *v.* 寝そべる.

P *sprawl **on*** the beach 海辺に腹ばう.

spray, *n.* 飛まつ, しぶき.

V The fountain ***throws*** its silvery *spray* into the air. その噴水は空中に銀色のしぶきを放射する. ¶The waves ***toss up*** much *spray* on the beach. 波がしぶきを立てて浜に打上げる.

Q the ***blinding** spray* 目のあけられないしぶき.

Q^2 ***dust** spray* 塵(ちり)煙. ¶get wet with ***sea** spray* 波のしぶきでぬれる.

P^2 the *spray **of*** a waterfall 滝のしぶき. 【類】a *spray **of*** bullets.

spray, *v.* 散布する.

P *spray* plants ***with*** an insecticide = spray an insecticide over (= on) plants 植物に駆虫剤をふりかける.

spraying, *n.* 散布.

Q^2 ***fruit** spraying* 果実の薬剤散布.

spread, *n.* 拡張; 幅, 広さ; 普及, まん延.

V ***alleviate*** the *spread* of disease まん延を減じさせる. ¶***check*** the *spread* of a disease 病気のまん延を食止める. ¶***give*** a royal *spread* to ... …にぜいたくなごちそうを出す. ¶The bird's wing ***has*** a large *spread.* その鳥の翼は幅が大きい. ‖ Gionzakura ***has*** a *spread* of more than thirty yards. ぎおん桜の(枝の)広がりは三十ヤード以上ある. ¶***prevent*** the *spread* of a disease = prevent a disease from spreading 病気のまん延を防ぐ. ¶***promote*** the *spread* of civilization 文化の普及を助成する. ¶***stay*** the *spread* of the habit その風習のまん延を防ぐ.

Q the ***westward** spread* of the United States 米国の西部への発展. ¶a ***wide** spread* of prairie 広い草原.

Q^2 a ***bed** spread* 寝台かけ; [寝台用]かけぶとん. ¶The

craft has a *wing spread* of 230 feet. その飛行機は全翼長が230フィートある.

P ***through*** the *spread* of education amongst the natives 土民間に教育が普及したために.

P[2] the *spread **of*** learning 学問の普及 ‖ the *spread **of*** infection 伝染病のまん延. 【類】 when the *spread **of*** education is more marked.

spread, *v.* 広げる; 広がる; まん延する.

M *spread* its branches ***abroad*** [樹など]枝を広く張る. ¶The news is ***already*** *spread* all over the town. その話はすでに町中に広まっている. ¶The story of the poor boy was *spread **broadcast*** in the newspapers. そのあわれな少年の話は新聞で広く伝えられた. ¶Its branches *spread* [themselves] ***far*** and ***wide***. その枝が広く張った. ¶*spread **out*** a rug on the grass 草の上にラグ(敷物)を布く ‖ The view *spread **out*** before us. その風景はわれわれの前に展開した. ‖ *spread **out*** one's payment for ... over a long period of months ...に対する仕払を長期月払いにする ‖ *spread* [*out*] one's arms 腕を広げる. 【類】 *spread* [*out*] a map. ¶The news ***quickly*** *spread.* その話が急速に広まった. ¶Aided by a fresh wind the fire *spread **rapidly***. 強い風が手伝って火はずんずん広がった. 【類】 The report is *spreading **rapidly***.

P *spread* one's hands ***before*** the fire [暖まろうと]火に手をかざす. ¶The table was *spread **for*** supper. 夕飯のおぜん立をした. ¶*spread **from*** mouth ***to*** mouth [うわさなど]口から口へ伝わる. ¶The news (reports) *spread **like*** wild-fire. その話(など)がりょう原の火のように早く広がった. ¶*spread* butter ***on*** bread=spread bread with butter バターをパンに塗る. 【類】 *spread* paint ***on*** fences / *spread* a table-cloth ***on*** the table. ¶From India Buddhism *spread **over*** the countries of the East. 仏教はインドから東洋諸国に広まった. 【類】 *spread **over*** Europe like epidemic ‖ The clouds *spread* [themselves] ***over*** the sky. 雲が空に広がった. ‖ *spread* payments ***over*** a term of years 支払いを数年間で済しくずすようにする. 【類】 The instalments were *spread **over*** twelve months. ¶the revolt *spread **through*** the whole of ... 反乱は...の全部に広がった. 【類】 An epidemic of cholera *spread **throughout*** the land. ¶It spread ***to*** dreadful extent. それ(病気など)が恐ろしくまん延した. 【類】 The flames *spread **to*** the other buildings. ‖ His fame has *spread **to*** the remotest villages. 彼の名声は片いなかにまでも広まった. 【類】 Interest in the movement (その運動に対する興味) is also *spreading **to*** France. ¶a table *spread **with*** dainties ごちそうを並べた食卓 ‖ *spread* the floor ***with*** mats 床にござを敷く ‖ the meadow *spread **with*** daisies ひなぎくの咲き乱れた草原. 【類】 a field *spread **with*** wild flowers / A large table was *spread **with*** an abundant supply.

spreading, *n.* 広がること.

P[2] *spreading **of*** disease 病気のまん延.

spree, *n.* 歓楽; 遊戯.

V ***have*** a *spree* 浮かれ騒ぐ.

P He was ***on*** a *spree.* 彼は酔って浮かれていた. 【類】 He is out ***on*** the *spree* somewhere.

spring, *n.* (1) 春.

V The nightingale is already with us to ***herald*** the coming *spring.* 来る春の先触れにナイチンゲールがもうやって来た. ¶Birds strained their little throats to ***proclaim*** *spring.* 鳥は春を告げようとその小さい声を張上げた.

V[2] *Spring **awakens***. 春が目ざめる. ¶When the swallow returns, *spring **begins***. つばめが帰って来ると春になる. ¶*Spring* has ***come***. 春が来た. ¶as *spring **comes round*** 春が来ると. ¶*Spring **enters*** Europe through Southern Italy. ヨーロッパの春は南イタリアから. ¶*Spring **flew*** swiftly ***by***, and summer followed. 春は早くも過ぎ去って夏が来た.

Q in the ***early*** *spring* 初春に. ¶***last*** *spring* 過ぎし春. ¶*Spring* is ***over***. 春が過ぎた.

P ***during*** the *spring* 春の間. ¶She is planning an exhibition of her work ***for*** the early *spring.* 彼女は来春早々その作品展示会を開く計画をしている. ¶The trees put forth buds and leaves ***in*** *spring.* 木は春に芽や葉を出す. ‖ late ***in*** the *spring* 春の末に. 【類】 ***in*** the *spring* of 1899. ¶the mild days ***of*** *spring* 春ののどかな日.

P[2] the *spring **of*** life 人生の春.

(2) 泉, 水源; 根源, 起原; 原動力.

V ***analyse*** its *springs* [どうして起るか]その原因を調べる, 分析する. ¶***dig*** a *spring* 水源を掘りあける. ¶The custom ***has*** its *spring* in another country. その習慣は他国から伝来したものだ. ¶***tap*** the *springs* of merriment 歓楽のちまたをあさる.

V[2] The Wakulla *Spring* in Florida ***flows*** at the rate of 120,000 gallons a minute. フロリダのワクラ泉は毎分十二万ガロンの噴出量がある. ¶The *spring* has ***revived***. その泉が再びでるようになった. ¶The *spring* has ***run dry***. その泉がかれた.

Q a ***boiling*** *spring* 熱泉. ¶a ***bubbling*** *spring* ぶくぶくわき出す泉. ¶a ***cool*** *spring* 冷泉. ¶a ***fresh*** *spring* in the wilderness 荒野にわき出る清水. ¶the most ***health-giving hot*** *springs* in Japan 日本で一番効験のある温泉. ¶***medicinal*** *springs* 薬泉. ¶bathers at ***mineral*** *springs* 鉱泉地の浴客. ¶the most ***ordinary*** *spring* of action 行為の最も普通の原動力. ¶***thermal*** (=***hot*** *or* ***warm***) *springs* 温泉.

P[2] a little *spring **by*** the hillside 山腹の小さな泉. ¶a great *spring **of*** human happiness 人類の幸福の一大源泉 ‖ the *springs **of*** social progress 社会進歩の原動力 ‖ a *spring **of*** water 泉.

(3) 飛ぶこと; ぜんまい, ばね.

V The rabbit ***gave*** a *spring.* うさぎがぴょんと飛んだ. ¶The old man's legs have ***lost*** their *spring.* 老人の脚はねばりがなくなった. ¶***make*** a *spring* at a person 人に飛びつく. 【類】 The dog ***made*** a *spring* at the horse's head. ¶***take*** a *spring* 一躍する.

Q I know that the game is ***worth*** the *springs.* 私はその仕事は本気になってやるかいがあると思っている.

Q[2] coils of ***copper wire*** *springs* 銅線発条のコイル. ¶Torsion ***rubber*** *springs* developed during the war. 戦争中に発達したねじりゴムばね. ¶a ***steel leaf*** *spring* 鋼鉄板製ばね.

P worked ***by*** a *spring* ぜんまい仕掛の(おもちゃなど).

spring, *v.* 飛ぶ; 発生する; 出て来る.

M *spring **aside*** 飛びのく. ¶*spring **away*** 飛び去る. ¶*spring **back*** はね返る. ¶*spring **forth*** 飛び出る; [植物が土中から]発生する. 【類】 *spring **forth*** (=out) like a rabbit / A young plant *springs **forth*** from the soil. ¶The lid *sprang **open***. [時計など]ふたがぱっと開いた. ¶It *sprang **suddenly*** into world-wide fame. それは急に世界中に名高くなった.

M[2] The grass *springs **up***. 草がもえ出る. ‖ The breeze has *sprung **up***. 風が出た. ‖ A custom has *sprung **up***. 一つの習慣が起った. ‖ He *sprang **up*** from his seat. 彼は席から飛び立った. 【類】 The town has *sprung **up*** from a poor fishing village. / So many ideas *spring **up*** within me as I think of it. / New factories are *springing **up*** in rapid succession. / A new power *sprang **up***. ‖ A coolness *sprang **up*** between them. 二人の間が冷くなった.

P *spring **at*** each other's throat お互ののどを目掛けて飛びつく. 【類】 Fish *spring **at*** flies (羽虫). ¶He is *sprung **from*** an ancient family (a noble ancestry). 彼は古い家柄(など)の人だ. 【類】 He had a good luck to *spring **from*** an old family. ‖ He *sprang **from*** a humble origin (the common people). 彼は低い身分(など)から起った. 【類】 *spring **from*** obscurity (無名の人) to eminence (=renown). / His actions *spring **from*** a false conviction. / the ***popularity*** *springs* from ... / The water *springs **from*** the ground. ‖ charges *springing **from*** revenge or envy 復しゅうかまたはせん望から来る中傷 ‖ ***from*** this union *sprang* ... この結婚から...が生れた. ¶The great muscles on his bare arms *sprung* up ***into*** knots at every rapid stroke. 矢継ぎ早に打ち込むたんびにむきだした彼の腕に大きな力こぶがでた. ‖ I *sprang **into*** the sea resolved to attempt to reach the shore by swimming. 私は岸に泳ぎつこうと決心して海中に飛び込んだ. ‖ The tears of joy *sprang **into*** his eyes. うれし涙が彼の目に浮んだ. ‖ *spring **into*** existence in immense numbers ばく大の数が出現する ‖ *spring **into*** life 生れる ‖ His name *sprang **into*** fame. 彼はたちまち有名になった. 【類】 The book has *sprung **into*** immediate popularity. / *spring* suddenly ***into*** view from apparently nowhere. ¶***Of*** what family is he *sprung?* 彼はどういう家柄の人か. ¶*spring **on*** (=upon) a person 人に飛びかかる. ‖ *spring **on*** one's feet ぱっと立ち上る. ¶*spring **over*** a fence かき根を飛び越す. ¶Involuntarily the tears *sprang **to*** her eyes. 彼女の目には独りでに涙が出た. ‖ Blood *sprang to* her face. 血が彼女の顔にのぼった, ぱっと赤くなった. ‖ *spring to* one's feet 飛びあがる, けっ起する. ¶He *sprang upon* his enemy. 彼は敵に飛びかかった.

springboard, *n.* 飛込み板. 「する.
Q^2 use it as a ***propaganda springboard*** それを宣伝に利用
P with these ***as*** its *springboard* これを足場として.

springtime, *n.* 春.
Q in the light rains of ***early springtime*** 早春の細雨の中に.

springy, *a.* 弾力のある.
P flesh *springy* ***to*** the touch 弾力のある肉付.

sprinkle, *n.* 小雨.
O It's just a *sprinkle*. ほんのぱらぱら(小雨)だ.

sprinkle, *v.* 振りかける, まく.
M The sky was ***heavily sprinkled*** with stars. 空一面に星がまき散らされていた. ¶leaves ***thickly sprinkled*** with dews (=bedewed) 露しげき葉.
P *sprinkle* water ***on*** the flowers 花に水をそそぐ. 【類】*sprinkle* salt ***on*** meat. ¶churches *sprinkled* ***over*** the city 市のあちこちに散見する教会堂. ¶*sprinkle* the street ***with*** water 往来に水をまく ‖ *sprinkle* a fish ***with*** salt 魚に塩を振る ‖ His composition is *sprinkled* ***with*** mistakes. 彼の作文にはちょいちょい間違いがある.

sprinkler, *n.* 水まき器.
Q^2 a ***garden sprinkler*** 庭園水まき器. ¶a ***holy-water sprinkler*** (=sprinkle) 聖水まき器; 大くぎを一面に植えた一種のほこ; 〖狩〗きつねの尾. ¶a ***self sprinkler*** 自動消火器.

sprinkling, *n.* ふりまき; [雨などの]ぱらつき; 小数, ちら
V ***have*** a *sprinkling* of rain 雨がぽつぽつ降る. Lほら.
Q There was a ***considerable sprinkling*** of Japanese students among the audience. 聴衆中には日本の学生がかなり多く交っていた. ¶There was a ***tiny sprinkling*** of foreigners in the meeting. その会には少数の外人が出席していた.
P^2 a good *sprinkling* ***of*** colored people 黒人のちらほら見えること ‖ a *sprinkling* ***of*** knowledge 少しばかりの知識.

sprout, *n.* 新芽.
V ***thin out*** the *sprouts* 新芽をすぐる.
P early *sprouts* ***of*** rice 早苗.

sprout, *v.* 発芽する, 発芽させる.
M Potatoes *sprout* ***twice*** a year. じゃがいもは一年に二回発芽する. ¶expect rain to *sprout* seed ***well*** 雨で種がよくでてくれればいいがと思う.

spruce, *v.* 小ぎれいにする.
M^2 *spruce* ***up*** the surrounding neighborhood 付近をきれいにする ‖ *spruce* oneself ***up for*** ... 《口語》に出ようとめか

spruce, *a.* こぎれいな. Lす.
P She looks *spruce* ***in*** that suit. 彼女はあのスーツを着る

spunk, *n.* 元気. Lとスマートに見える.
V^2 ***get*** one's *spunk* ***up*** 《米口》元気を出す.

spur, *n.* 拍車; 刺激物.
V ***apply*** the *spur* to ... ...に拍車を当てる, 刺激する. ¶He ***needs*** the *spur*. 彼はのろまだ. ¶***set*** (=***put***) *spurs* to one's horse 馬に拍車をかける. ¶He ***touched*** *spurs* to his horse. 彼は馬に拍車を当てた. ¶***win*** one's *spurs* (=reputation) 名声を得る.
P act ***as*** a *spur* to one's ambition 野心の刺激物となる. ¶***on*** the *spur* of the moment その場のはずみで. 【類】He acts ***on*** the *spur* of the moment.
P^2 the *spur* ***of*** ambition 野心の刺激. ¶the *spur* ***to*** exertion 努力への刺激 ‖ the *spur* ***to*** higher attainment 上達への刺激 ‖ He knew no failure, save as a *spur* ***to*** renewed efforts. 彼は失敗するとこれを刺激として必ず努力を新たにした. 【類】To him difficulties were simply *spurs* ***to*** endeavor. / a *spur* ***to*** the sluggard (怠け者).

spur, *v.* 拍車を当てる.
M *spur* one ***on*** to effort 人を刺激して努力させる ‖ He was *spurred* ***on*** by poverty to commit a crime. 彼は貧にかられて罪を犯した. ‖ *spurred* ***on*** by incentives in the form of ... ...という刺激にかられて ‖ *spurred* ***on*** by chagrin くやしまぎれに. ¶*spur* a person ***up*** to duty 人を刺激して本分を果させる.
P *spurred* ***by*** mother-love 母性愛に刺激されて ‖ *spurred* ***by*** anger 腹立ちまぎれに. ¶He was *spurred* ***to*** activity (action, industry). 彼は刺激されて活動(など)しだした.

spurn, *v.* はね付ける.
P *spurn* ***at*** a person (an offer) 人(など)をはねつける.

spurt, *n.* 大奮闘(努力).
V ***put on*** a *spurt* がん張る.
Q put forth one's ***last spurt*** 最後の努力をふりしぼる.
P^2 a *spurt* ***in*** prices 物価暴騰. ¶a *spurt* ***of*** flame 火炎の

spurt, *v.* ほとばしる. L噴出.
P Blood *spurted* ***from*** the wound. 血が傷口からほとばしった. ¶The runners *spurted* ***into*** the goal. 走者がゴールに飛込んだ.

sputter, *v.* せき込んで早口に言う; ぱちぱちとはねる.
P The cook *sputtered* ***at*** the housemaid. コックは女中にせき込んで言った. ¶fat *sputtering* ***in*** the flying pan フラ

spy, *n.* 間者, 探偵(スパイ). Lイパンではねる脂肉.
V ***employ*** a *spy* 間者を入れる. ¶We ***have*** a *spy* among us. われわれの中にスパイがいる. ¶***set*** a *spy* on ... ...の
Q a ***military spy*** 軍事探偵. L跡をつけさせる.
Q^2 a ***government spy*** 政府のスパイ. ¶an ***office spy*** 職場のスパイ. ¶a ***police spy*** 刑事. ¶a ***Tsarist spy*** 露探. ¶***women*** (=***lady***) *spies* 女スパイたち.
P The communist is shadowed ***by*** *spies*. その共産主義者は探偵につけられている.
P^2 He refused to be a *spy* ***on*** her conduct. 彼は彼女の操行を探偵することを拒んだ.

spy, *v.* 探り出す; 探偵する.
M *spy* ***out*** a secret 秘密をかぎ出す. 【類】*spy* ***out*** one's faults ‖ *spy* ***out*** "White Continent" 白大陸(南極)を踏査する.
P *spy* ***into*** a secret 秘密を探る. ¶*spy* ***on*** (=upon) a person 人をつける. 【類】*spy* ***on*** (=***upon***) one's movements (行動). ¶*spy* ***upon*** the enemy 敵の行動を偵察する. 【類】He has no intention of *spying* ***upon*** the secrets.

squabble, *n.* 口論.
Q^2 a ***labor squabble*** 労働争議.
P^2 *squabble* ***between*** (***among***) children 子供たちのけん

squabble, *v.* 口論する. Lか.
P *squabble* ***with*** a person ***about*** ... ...について人と口論す

squad, *n.* 小隊, 班. Lる.
Q^2 be executed by a ***firing squad*** 射撃班の手で銃殺される. 【類】The war criminal died before a ***firing squad***. ¶a member of the ***fire-fighting squad*** 消防班の一員. ¶a ***flying squad*** 〖警察〗特務班(白バイなどの). ¶a ***rescue squad*** 救護班. ¶a ***tear-gas squad*** 催涙ガス班.

squadron, *n.* 艦隊. 「る.
V ***station*** a *squadron* on the Pacific 太平洋に艦隊を配備す
Q the ***First Squadron*** 第一艦隊. ¶a ***standing squadron*** 常備艦隊.
Q^2 an ***air squadron*** 航空中隊[十・十二または十八機からな

squalid, *a.* 見すぼらしい. Lる].
P *squalid* ***in*** attire 服装の見すぼらしい.

squall, *n.* スコール.
Q a ***heavy squall*** 激しいスコール. ¶Before I had gone far, a ***regular squall*** struck me. それから先に余り行かない中に本格的なスコールに会った. ¶encounter a ***tremendous squall*** すさまじいスコールに会う.
P^2 a *squall* ***of*** sleet (snow, rain) みぞれ(雪, 雨)混じりの狂

squander, *v.* 浪費する, とう尽する. L風.
M ***recklessly squander*** [金銭を]向う見ずに浪費する.
P He *squandered* his wealth ***by*** the most riotous living. 彼はきわめて放らつな生活でその富を浪費した. ¶*squander* one's money ***in*** drink 飲酒に金銭を浪費する. 【類】*squander* time and money ***in*** gambling. ¶*squander* one's fortune ***on*** women 女に財産をとう尽する.

square, *n.* 正方形; 方陣; 広場; 定規.
V ***break*** a *square* 方陣を解く. ¶***form*** a *square* 方陣を布く.
Q The battalion was formed in a ***hollow square*** 大隊が方陣を作った. ¶a ***nice cozy square*** occupying half the block その地区の半ばを占める小じんまりしたよい広場. ¶a ***public square*** 公共広場. ¶a ***set square*** 三角定規. ¶a ***ten-by-ten square*** for dancing 十フィート四方のダンス用の床.
Q^2 ***Times Square*** [ニューヨーク市の]タイムス広場 (Broadway と 42 St. の交差点にある). ¶***Trafalgar Square*** [ロンドンの]トラファルガー広場.
P do anything ***by*** the *square* 何ごとでも正確にやる. ¶They are playing ***on*** the *square*. 彼らは広場で遊んでいる. ‖ He does everything ***on*** (=***upon***) the *square*. 彼は何でもきちょうめんにやる. ¶It is ***out of*** *square*. それは乱脈

square, *a.* 貸借のない. Lになっている.
M Everything is ***now*** *square*. 万事がちゃんとしている. ‖

Accounts between us are *now square*. 君と僕とはもう帳消しになった.

P I am *square with* all the world. 私はだれにもひけ目を感じない.

O Let't do business *square* (=square business). 商売は五分五分と行こう.

square, *v.* 律する；勘定をつける.

M *square away* 帆けたを直角にする(船を風前に進ませるために).

M^2 *square up* one's accounts すっかり勘定をつける ‖ *square up* to one's antagonist けん闘の身構えをして相手に詰めよる. ¶I will *square up* (=get even) with you tomorrow. あした君にお礼をするぞ(あだ打をする).

P I *squared* myself *by* his views. 彼の意見に従って私自身をただした. 【類】*square* one's action *by* the opinions of others. ¶*square* one's opinions *to* the prevailing tendencies 自己の所見を時代の傾向に適合させる. ¶*square* accounts *with* a creditor 債権者と勘定をつける ‖ His statement fails to *square with* the facts. 彼の陳述は事実と合致しない ‖ His actions do not *square with* his words. 彼は言行が一致しない. 【類】He does not *square* his practice *with* his principles. / His acts do not *square with* his promise. / His practice doesn't *square with* his principle. / Idiomatic expressions do not always *square with* the accepted rules of grammar.

squash, *n.* かぼちゃ.

Q^2 a *summer squash* 夏かぼちゃ.

squat, *v.* しゃがむ；すわる.

M *squat a la japonaise* 日本流にすわる. ¶He *squatted down* cross-legged. 彼はあぐらをかいた. ‖ *squat* [himself] *down* on the floor (mat) 床(など)の上にすわる.

P *squat about* (=*by*) the fire 火のそばにしゃがむ. ¶*squat on* one's haunches 腰を据える.

squeak, *v.* きゅーと鳴る.

M Mice were rampant, *squeaking everywhere.* ねずみがちゅーちゅー言ってあちこちで騒いでいた. ¶A Hare, being seized by an Eagle, *squeaked out* in a most woeful manner. [寓話]わしに捕えられたうさぎが悲痛な叫び声をあげた.

P The floor *squeaked at* every step. 一足ごとに床がきーきー鳴った.

squeamish, *a.* 気むずかしい.

P He is very *squeamish about* it. 彼はそのことについてばかに気むずかしい.

squeeze, *n.* 力のはいった握手；混雑.

V All the middlemen *get* a "*squeeze.*" 仲買人は皆搾取する. ¶She *gave* him a *squeeze* [of the hand]. 彼女はぎゅーっと彼の手を握った.

Q Our hands, locked in each other, repeated the most *passionate squeezes.* われわれの手はしっかと結ばれ繰返し繰返し力強く握りしめあった. ¶Hey there, Smithy, this is *some squeeze.* [電車などで]おいスミジー, ひどい込みようじゃないか.

Q^2 *dollar squeeze* ドルの金詰まり.

squeeze, *v.* しぼる, [手を]強く握る；押し込む；圧迫する.

M She *squeezed* my hand *again.* 彼女はまた私の手をぎゅっと握った. ¶*squeeze dry* 水気のないようにしぼる. ¶Sponge *squeezes easily.* 海綿はすぐしぼれる. ¶*squeeze* things *forcibly* into a trunk 品物を無理にトランクに詰め込む. ¶The boss has *squeezed* his men *mercilessly.* 親方はみんなをひどくこき使った. ¶*squeeze out* water 水を絞り出す ‖ *squeeze out* the water from the cloth 布から水を絞り出す.

P I was *squeezed in* between two stout men. 私は二人のがん丈な男の間にはさまれた. ¶*squeeze into* a crowded room 人の一杯いる室へむりやりにはいる. ¶*squeeze through* a crowded hallway 込み合っている廊下を押し通る.

P *squeeze* money *from* a person 人から金を絞り取る ‖ *squeeeze* juice *from* apples りんごから液汁を絞り出す. ¶*squeeze* the juice of the grape *into* a cup ぶどう汁をコップの中へ絞り込む ‖ *squeeze* one's hand *into* a glove 手を手袋にぎゅーっと押し込む ‖ *squeeze* passengers *into* the coach 乗客を馬車に無理やりに押込む. ¶*squeeze out of* shape めちゃめちゃに押しつぶす. ¶*squeeze* one's way *through* a crowd 群集の中を押し通る. ¶He was *squeezed to* death in the crowd. 彼は人込みで押しつぶされて死んだ.

squelch, *v.* 鎮定する.

M *squelch* [*out*] a riot 反乱を鎮定する.

squint, *n.* 斜視.

Q One of her eyes had a *slight squint.* 彼女の片方の目は少し斜視であった.

squint, *v.* 横目で見る.

P *squint at* ... ...を横目で見る；目を細めて見る(近眼など). ¶Glasses lost, he *squinted into* the dark. 目がねが見えなかったので彼は目を細めてやみをすかして見た.

squirm, *v.* もじもじする.

P The boy *squirmed in* the seat. その子供は席でもじもじした.

squirrel, *n.* りす.

V^2 a *squirrel shooting up* a tree 飛ぶように木にのぼるりす.

Q a *perky squirrel* 気どったりす.

stab, *n.* 刺し, 突き；試み.

V *give* a person a *stab* in the back 人を中傷する. ¶*have* a sharp *stab* of pain in ... ...が鋭く刺すように痛む. ¶*make* a *stab* at ... ...をやってみる.

P fall *by* the *stab* of an assassin 刺客の手にたおれる. ¶a sudden *stab with* a pointed instrument とがった道具で突然の一突き.

stab, *v.* 刺す, 突込む.

P *stab at* a person 人に突きかかる. ¶She was *stabbed by* him *with* a sword. 彼女は彼に刀で刺された. ¶He was *stabbed* violently *in* the heart. 彼は心臓を激しく刺された. ‖ *stab* a person *in* the back [比喩的に]人をかげで非難する(中傷する). ¶*stab* a dagger *into* a person=stab a person with a dagger 人に短刀を突き刺す. ¶*stab* a person *to* death 人を刺し殺す ‖ be *stabbed to* the heart 心臓を刺される. ¶*stab* a person *with* a knife 人をナイフで刺す. ¶*stab* oneself *with* a sword 自刃する.

stability, *n.* 安定, 強固.

V *secure* the *stability* of peace 平和の安定を得る.

Q *domestic stability* 家庭の安定. ¶conducive to *economic stability* 経済的安定を助ける. ¶*financial stability* 金融の安定.

Q^2 *trade stability* 通商の安定. ¶a formula for *world stability* 世界の安定方式.

P a man *of stability* しっかり者.

stabilization, *n.* 安定.

V *effect* economic and industrial *stabilization* 経済並に産業の安定を実現する.

Q^2 *currency stabilization* 貨幣の安定工作. ¶*wage* and *price stabilization* 賃金物価の安定工作.

P^2 the *stabilization of* the mark マルク(独貨)相場の安定.

stabilize, *v.* 安定する.

M *politically stabilize* Russia ロシアを政治的に安定させる.

O *stabilize* prices 物価を安定させる.

stable, *n.* 馬小屋.

P prices *stabilized after* inflationary fluctuations インフレの変動の後安定した物価.

Q^2 a *livery stable* 貸馬車屋；馬預り所. ¶the *riding stable* [集合的に]乗用馬.

P^2 the *stables for* racers 競馬調練場.

stack, *n.* たい積物；[汽車・汽船の]煙突；《俗》多額, 多数.

V I *have stacks* of work to get through. やってしまわなければならない用が山ほどある.

Q^2 a *chimney stack* 組み煙突. ¶a *corn stack* とうもろこしの束の山. ¶a *book stack*=a bookstack [図書館の]書架. ¶a *factory stack* 工場の大煙突.

P^2 a *stack of* hay 一積みの干草.

stadium, *n.* 運動競技場, スタジアム.

Q the *Olympic stadium* at Melbourne メルボルンのオリンピック大会場.

Q^2 a *baseball stadium* 野球場. ¶a *swimming stadium* 水泳競技場. 【類】a *swimming stadium* with accommodation for 18,000 spectators. ¶a *41,000-seat stadium* 四万一千人の座席のある競技場.

staff, *n.* (**1**) つえ, さお.

V *join* the *staff* of the newspaper その新聞に入社する. ¶*put down* one's *staff* in the ground つえを地面に立てる.

V^2 A *staff cracks.* 棒(つえ)がぴしっと折れる.

P a banner *on* a *staff* さおにつけた旗 ‖ lean *on* a *staff* つえにもたれる. ¶walk *with* a *staff* つえを突いて歩く.

P^2 Bread is the *staff of* life. パンは生命のつえだ. ‖ You are the *staff of* his old age. お前は彼の老後のつえだ.

(**2**) [団] 参謀, 幕僚本部；職員, 部員.

V *augment* the *staff* by the appointment of ... ...の任命によって増員を行う. ¶*cut down* the *staff* 人員をとうたする. ¶*employ* a very large *staff* 非常に多数の部員を使用する. ¶The general *has* a *staff* of officers to assist him. 将軍にはそれを補佐する幕僚がいる. ¶He *joined* the *staff* of the Tokyo Asahi. 彼は東京朝日の社員になった. 【類】he

joined the *staff* at the invitation of ... (...の招待で). ¶The library ***maintains*** (=***supports***) a *staff* of experts (=experienced consultants). その図書館は経験のある相談係を常置している.【類】***maintain*** a *staff* of several hundreds. ¶How large a *staff* will you ***need***? どの位部員が必要ですか. ¶***re-arrange*** a *staff* 職員の更迭を行う. ¶***reduce*** a *staff* to a minimum 社員を最少限に縮減する. ¶***reorganize*** its *staff* その部員を改組する.

Q the competence of the faculty and ***adminisrative*** *staff* 教授及び事務員側の能力. ¶He served on the ***consular*** *staff* in Osaka, Kobe, etc. 彼は大阪・神戸などの領事館員を勤めた. ¶the ***editorial*** *staff* of a newspaper 新聞の編集部.【類】He is on the ***editorial*** *staff*. ¶The ***entire*** *staff* are Germans. 社員は全部ドイツ人だ. ¶a ***faithful*** and ***industrious*** *staff* 忠実で勤勉な職員陣. ¶the ***General*** *Staff* 参謀本部. ¶The merchant has a ***large*** *staff* of clerks. その店にはたくさんの店員がいる. ¶join the ***managerial*** *staff* 幹部に加わる. ¶attended to by a ***numerous*** *staff* 多数の部下を持って. ¶the ***nursing*** *staff* [その部に属する]看護婦たち. ¶a ***permanent*** *staff* 常置部員. ¶the ***regimental*** *staff* 連隊本部. ¶He is on the ***regular*** *staff*. 彼は本官(または正社員)だ. ¶the ***reporting*** *staff* 探訪部員. ¶his ***skilled*** *staff* of assistants 彼の熟練した助手団. ¶The school has a ***small*** *staff* of teachers. その学校には少数の教師がいる. ¶a ***subordinate*** *staff* 属僚.

Q² an ***encyclopaedia*** *staff* 百科辞典編集陣. ¶an ***engineering*** *staff* 技術陣. ¶the college has a ***faculty*** *staff* of ... その大学は...名の教授団を有する. ¶a ***food inspection*** *staff* 食料検査団. ¶a ***government*** *staff* 政府の職員. ¶a ***hospital*** *staff* 医局(員). ¶an ***instruction*** *staff* 教職団. ¶be on a ***library*** *staff* 図書館員である. ¶the ***teaching*** *staff* and student body of a college 大学の教授団と学生団.【類】a splendid ***teaching*** *staff*. ¶"***uniform*** *staff*" and plain-clothes officers「正服」警官と和服(刑事).

P ***Among*** his *staff* and co-workers he was really beloved. 彼は部員及び同僚間に真に愛されていた. ¶assisted ***by*** a *staff* of trained specialists 教育を受けた専門家の部員に助けられて. ¶to fill the vacancies ***in*** the *staff* 欠員補充のために. ¶the members ***of*** his *staff* 彼の属僚. ¶while I was [serving] ***on*** the *staff* of the Japan Times 私がジャパンタイムス社に勤務中 ‖ men ***on*** the *staff* of a daily 日刊新聞社員 ‖ have the right men ***on*** the *staff* 部員には適任者がいる.【類】He is ***on*** the *staff* of the Boston Evening Transcript.

P² maintain a special *staff* ***for*** taking charge of the business 特別の業務担任部員を常置する. ¶a *staff* ***of*** professors=a [university] faculty 教授団.

staff, *v*. 職員をおく.

M an office ***sufficiently*** (***insufficiently***) *staffed* 人員のそろっている(足りない)事務所.

P be *staffed* ***with*** sufficient numbers of trained personnel to cope successfully with ... ...に対応するに差支えないように訓練を積んだ人員を十分配置してある.

stage, *n*. 舞台; 劇; 期, 段階; 駅; 駅馬車.

V He has ***advanced*** another *stage* in his career. 彼はその経歴にさらに一歩を進めた. ‖ It has not yet ***attained*** the scientific *stage*. それはまだ科学という程度には達していない. ¶***enter*** the *stage* 俳優になる. ¶***follow*** three *stages* 三つの段階を上る. ¶***leave*** (=***quit***) the *stage* [役者など]舞台から引退する. ¶She ***made*** the *stage* her profession. 彼女は俳優を職業とした. ¶***mark*** a *stage* in the field of ... ...の方面で(進歩の)一段階を示す ‖ it ***marked*** a new *stage* in the history of ... それは...の歴史に新紀元を画した.【類】One important *stage* in history is ***marked*** by religion taking to itself legal control (法律上の支配) over the conduct of a nation. ¶the desire to ***occupy*** the *stage* 一人舞台になりたいという欲望. ¶It has ***passed*** the experimental *stage*. それは試験期を経過した. ¶The youth is ***passing through*** the most critical *stage* of his life. その青年は人生の最大危機を今経過している. ¶He ***quit***[***ted***] the *stage* of politics. 彼は政界から引退した. ¶It has not yet ***reached*** the *stage* of ratification. それはまだ批准の運びに至らない. ‖ if the disease has ***reached*** this *stage* その病気がここまで進んだら. ¶***represent*** a *stage* in the social evolution of all races (=peoples) あらゆる民族の社会的発達における一段階を示す. ¶They ***ran*** four *stages* (=stage coaches) 一日に四回乗合馬車が出ていた. ¶The *stage* is ***set***. [比ゆ的に] 道具立ができた. ‖ ***set*** the *stage* for ... ...の下地を造る.

V² the *stage* ***leaves*** in three minutes 乗合馬車は三分おきに出る.

Q It has passed beyond the purely ***academic*** *stage*. それは研究から実行の段階にはいった. ¶in the ***acute*** *stages* of the disease その病気の最悪期に ‖ Its financial trouble reached an ***acute*** *stage*. その財政難は苦境に落入った. ¶Arrangements are now in an ***advanced*** *stage*. その準備が今進んでいる. ‖ an emaciated man in the ***advanced*** *stages* of consumption 肺病の進んだ時期にあるやせた人.【類】in the more ***advanced*** *stage* of linguistic study / a disease in its ***advanced*** *stage*. ¶fish in ***all*** *stages* of growth 生長の過程にある大小いろいろの魚 ‖ mark ***another*** *stage* in the progress of mechanic industry 機械工業における一進境を画する. ¶in the ***closing*** *stages* of his life 晩年に. ¶In 1912 Edison developed a talking motion picture, but did not bring it to the ***commercial*** *stage*. 一九一二年にエディソンは発声映画を創案したがこれを市場にのぼすまでには至らなかった. ¶a patient in the ***convalescent*** *stage* 回復期の患者. ¶a ***critical*** *stage* 危機. ¶in the ***dessert*** *stage* (course) デザートコースにはいって. ¶It marks a ***distinct*** *stage* of his growth. それは彼の発達の判然たる時期を画する. ¶check a plague during its ***early*** *stages* 疫病を初期に押える.【類】The science is still in an ***early*** *stage*. / in a very ***early*** *stage* of its progress / in the ***early*** *stages* of language teaching / in the ***earlier*** *stages* of her career / at a much ***earlier*** *stage* / a study of ***earlier*** *stages* of social evolution / In the ***earliest*** *stages* of human development nakedness was the rule. / the recognition of disease in its ***earliest*** stages. ¶detect disease in its ***early*** and ***curable*** *stages* その初期の回復のできる時期に病気を発見する. ¶It is still in an ***embryonic*** *stage*. それはまだ胎生期にある. ¶one of the ornaments of the ***English*** *stage* 英国劇壇を飾る名優の一人. ¶the ***experimental*** *stage* of a scheme 計画の試験期.【類】It is as yet in an ***experimental*** *stage*. ¶the ***first*** *stage* of a disease 病気の初期.【類】recognize the disease in its ***first*** *stages* / on the ***first*** *stage* of one's journey. ¶in the ***further*** *stage* of speaking the language その国語の会話力がもっと進むと. ¶reach a ***higher*** *stage* of perfection 一層完全の域に到達する. ¶She is now in the ***hoyden*** *stage*. 彼女は今おてんば盛りだ. ¶It is still in an ***inchoate*** *stage*. それはまだ揺らん期にある. ¶discover diseases in their ***incipient*** and ***curable*** *stages* 初期で手当のできる時期に病気を発見する. ¶a handful or two of dust—man in his most ***inglorious*** *stage* 一握か二握の土一人間の最もみじめな状態. ¶in the ***initial*** *stages* 初期に. ¶at the ***initiatory*** *stage* 初期に. ¶the ***junior*** (***middle***, ***senior***) *stage* of language training 語学教育の初(中・高)等段階. ¶A ***larger*** *stage* opened to him. 一層大きな活動舞台が彼に開けた. ¶the ***larval*** *stage* of insects こん虫の幼虫期. ¶a small crowd of men in the ***last*** *stage* of seediness 風体のきわめてよくない連中 ‖ trousers in the ***last*** *stage* of shockingness 見る影もないズボン. ¶pass through a ***long*** *stage* of inactivity 長い潜伏期を経過する. ¶How far is it to the ***next*** *stage*? 次の宿場までどの位あるか. ¶at the ***opening*** *stage* of a battle 序戦に. ¶her success on the ***Parisian*** *stage* パリ劇壇における彼女の成功. ¶He is a conspicuous figure on the ***political*** *stage*. 彼は政界の大立者だ. ¶***preliminary*** *stages* 予備的段階. ¶at the ***present*** *stage* of our knowledge われわれの現在の知識程度で. ¶the ***primary*** *stage* 初期. ¶the ***probationary*** *stage* 見習期間. ¶the ***progressive*** *stage* 進歩的時代. ¶the ***pupal*** *stage* さなぎ期. ¶a ***revolving*** (=***movable*** *or* ***rotative***) *stage* 回り舞台. ¶the ***second*** *stage* of the Siberian journey シベリア旅行の第二段階. ¶the ***secondary*** *stage* 第二期. ¶trace back through ***successive*** *stages* of development 順次発展の跡をたどる ‖ by ***successive*** *stages* 漸次に. ¶the ***tearful*** *stage* of drunkenness めいていの流涕(ﾃｲ)段階. ¶a ***transition***[***ary***] *stage* in the development of ... ...の発達における過渡期. ¶at ***this*** *stage* この段階において. ¶in an ***undeveloped*** *stage* 未発達期に. ¶the ***various*** *stages* of production from the raw material to the finished article 原料から仕上げ品に至るまで種々の製作の工程.【類】at ***various*** *stages* of evolution. ¶as we rise in the ***zoological*** *stage* 高等動物になればなるほど.

Q^2 be beyond the ***blue-print*** *stage* [建築など]施行期に入っている. ¶The Japanese when they migrated from the mainland were passing out of the ***Bronze Age stage*** of culture and entering the Iron Age. 日本人が大陸から移民したころは青銅時代の文化を過ぎて鉄器時代に入っていた. ¶the ***cocoon*** *stage* [かいこの]まゆの段階. ¶The bill has not even reached the ***committee*** *stage*. 議案はまだ委員会提出まで進んでいない. ¶It has not yet passed the ***discussion*** *stage*. まだ論議の段階を経ていない. ¶The project is out of the ***drawing board*** *stage*. 計画は青写真の段階を脱している. ¶The river, though rising, is not expected to reach ***flood*** *stage*. 川は水かさが増したが洪水にはならないという観測である. ¶students at the ***freshman*** *stage* [大学の]一年級の学生. ¶The experiments are still in the "***grammar school***" *stage*. その実験はまだ「小学校」の段階だ. ¶insects that do not have a ***grub*** *stage* 幼虫期のないこん虫. ¶be still in the ***laboratory*** *stage* まだ実験の段階である. ¶a ***landing*** *stage* for cattle [波止場の]家畜揚げ場. ¶put up a ***make-shift theatre*** *stage* 仮舞台を作る. ¶be still in the ***pioneer*** *stage* まだ草分け状態である. ¶be now in (out of) the ***planning*** *stage* 目下計画中(計画の段階を脱している). ¶when the corn reaches the ***pollination*** *stage* とうもろこしは受粉する程度まで成長すると. ¶those whose school education finishes at the ***post-primary*** or ***secondary school education*** *stage* 高等小学校もしくは中等学校を終えた人々. ¶the ***pupa*** *stage* さなぎの段階. ¶get beyond the ***slang*** *stage* 俗語の域を越える(口語になる). ¶the ***speaking*** *stage* as distinguished from the film *stage* 映画劇に対する舞台劇. ¶The plan is still in the ***talk*** *stage*. 計画はまだ話し合いの段階にある. ¶The boy has yet to reach the ***talking*** *stage*. その子はまだ口をきくまでになっていない. ¶in this critical ***transition*** *stage* この重大な過渡期に当って. ¶The idea is still in the ***trial*** *stage*. その案はまだ試験の段階だ. ¶go beyond the "***war-of-nerves***" *stage*「神経戦」の域を越える. ¶The scheme has now reached a ***working*** *stage*. その計画は今や実行の段階に達した.

P an actor strutting ***across*** the *stage* 舞台をもったいぶって歩く役者. ¶all sorts and conditions of men ***at*** all *stages* in their passage from the cradle to the grave 揺らんより墓穴に至るまでのあらゆる段階にあるあらゆる種類と境遇の人々 ‖ unsafe to predict ***at*** this *stage* that ... この時期に…を予言するのは心もとない. 【類】***at*** this *stage* in his career of development / make a slip ***at*** some *stage* of the process ‖ women ***at*** different *stage* of demoralization 種種のだらく段階にある女 ‖ It was discovered ***at*** a *stage* in which it could be successfully treated. それは治療が施せる段階で発見された(手遅れでなかった). ¶The scheme will never get ***beyond*** the talking *stage*. その計画は意見の交換程度で終るだろう. ‖ The question has now been carried ***beyond*** the *stage* of arguing for or against. その問題は賛否を論じるまでもない段階に到達した. ¶train one's will-power ***by*** easy *stages* 意志の力を徐々に養成する ‖ travel ***by*** long (easy *or* short) *stages* 急いで(ゆっくり)旅行する. ¶give up the pen ***for*** the *stage* 文士をやめて俳優になる. ¶The actress came ***from*** the legitimate *stage*. その女優は劇壇の出身だ. ¶The book is still ***in*** the *stage* of rough drafts. その本はまだ未定稿のままだ. ‖ a learner ***in*** the first *stage* 初学者. 【類】language teaching ***in*** the early *stages*. ¶go ***off*** the *stage* 劇壇を去る. 【類】***Off*** the *stage* she is an ordinary woman: Miss Burke is Mrs. Florenz Ziegfeld. ¶He is ***on*** the *stage*. 彼は役者だ. ‖ go ***on*** the *stage* 俳優になる ‖ perform (=play) ***on*** the *stage* 舞台で演じる. 【類】played both ***on*** *stage* and screen (映画) / The story has been represented ***on*** the *stage* (上演された). ¶if things come ***to*** this *stage* こうしたことになれば ‖ take to the *stage* 役者になる.

P^2 a *stage* ***for*** the performance of a "noh" dance 能楽の舞台. ¶at a comparatively early *stage* ***in*** his career 彼の生がいの比較的初期に. 【類】a *stage* ***in*** the history of this doctrine / a *stage* ***in*** an illness. ¶*stages* ***of*** culture 文化の段階 ‖ *stages* ***of*** growth in an animal or a plant 動物または植物の生長段階 ‖ the *stage* ***of*** his operations 彼の活動舞台.

stage, *v.* 上場する.

P This play was *staged* ***in*** London. この劇はロンドンで上場された.

stagecoach, *n.* 駅馬車.

V^2 The *stagecoach* ***rattled away*** through the village. 駅馬車ががらがらと村を通って行った.

stage-manager, *n.* 舞台監督.

V She ***chose*** a *stage-manager* for her husband. 彼女は舞台監督と結婚した.

stager, *n.* 熟練家.

Q an ***old*** *stager* at the game その競技の老練家.

stagger, *v.* よろめく, 仰天する.

M *stagger* ***back*** in surprise びっくり仰天する.

M^2 *stagger* ***around*** うろつき回る.

P He *staggered* ***at*** the price. その値(の高いの)にぎょっとした. ¶He was *staggered* ***by*** the news. 彼はその知らせでびっくりした. ‖ He was *staggered* ***by*** the blow. 彼は打たれてよろめいた. ¶The news *staggered* me ***for*** the moment. その報道に接して私は一時はっとした. ¶*stagger* ***in*** walking よろめいて歩く. ¶He *staggered* ***into*** the dining-room, where he fell dead. 彼は食堂へひょろひょろと歩いて行きそこで倒れて死んだ. ¶He *staggered* ***to*** his feet. 彼はよろよろしながら立上がった. ¶*stagger* ***under*** heavy burdens 荷が重くてよろめく.

staggering, *a.* ぎょっとするほどの.

M The price boom is ***really staggering***. 物価の高騰には全くあきれる.

stagnant, *a.* 沈滞した.

M The market is ***extremely stagnant***. 市場は極度に沈滞している.

stagnation, *n.* 沈滞, 不振.

Q^2 ***business*** *stagnation* 不況.

P fall ***into*** *stagnation* 不振に陥る.

P^2 *stagnation* ***in*** the market 市場の不振. ¶*stagnation* ***of*** commerce (=trade) 不景気 ‖ *stagnation* ***of*** price 良い値の出ないこと.

stain, *n.* しみ; 汚点, きず.

V ***bring*** a *stain* on the character of ... …の名声を傷つける. ¶***get out*** the *stain* しみを抜く. ¶Your collar ***has*** a *stain* on it. 君のカラにはしみがついている. ¶This ***leaves*** no *stain* on his character. これは別に彼の名声を傷つけはしない. ¶***remove*** *stains* from one's coat 上衣のしみを抜く. ¶***take*** the *stain* ***out*** しみを抜く. ¶***wash*** *stain* from one's inward self 内心の汚れを洗う. ¶***wash off*** *stains* しみを洗い落す. ¶***wipe out*** (=***off***) the *stain* of a former defeat 以前の失敗を雪辱する.

V^2 This *stain* on my coat will not ***come out***. 僕のこの上衣のしみは抜けない. ¶*Stains* often ***die away***. 不名誉はよく消えてしまうものだ.

Q It will remain an ***indelible*** *stain* on his memory. それは消し難い汚点として彼の記憶に残るだろう. ¶a ***slight*** *stain* ちょっとしたしみ. ¶a ***telltale*** *stain* 隠しきれない欠点.

Q^2 Finding ***blood*** *stains*, the police scented a crime. 血こんを見つけて警官は犯罪をかぎつけた. ¶***ink*** *stain* インキのしみ. ¶***rust*** *stain* さびのしみ.

P^2 a *stain* ***on*** one's clothes 着物のしみ ‖ a great *stain* ***on*** her reputation 彼女の名誉の大きな名折れ.

stain, *v.* よごす; 汚す, 染める.

M She *stained* her teeth ***black***. 彼女はお歯黒を付けた.

P *stain* ***in*** patterns 模様を付ける. ¶It is *stained* ***with*** blood. それは血でよごれている. ‖ All the near hills were *stained* ***with*** the tawny of autumn oaks. 近くの山々は皆秋のかしわの黄葉で色づいていた. 【類】His hands were *stained* ***with*** many crimes. / He was *stained* ***with*** every vice. / a mind *stained* ***with*** guilt (罪) / *stained* ***with*** ink (grease) / *stain* one's record ***with*** a scandal / try to *stain* another's name ***with*** slander.

stair, *n.* [はしごの]段; 階段; *pl.* はしご段.

V ***ascend*** a long stone *stair* 長い石段を上る. ¶***climb*** the *stair* of a prison 刑務所の階段を上る(絞首台に上る). ¶***mount*** many *stairs* たくさんの階段を上る. ¶***run up*** the *stairs* はしご段をかけ上る. ¶***slip on*** the *stairs* はしご段ですべる.

Q enter into a house by the ***back*** *stairs* 裏階段から家にはいる. ¶the ***top*** *stair* but one はしご段の上から二番目の段. ¶There were ***two*** *stairs* in the house. その家には二つの階段があった. ¶a ***winding*** *stair* 回り階段.

Q^2 an ***escape*** *stair* 避難(非常)階段. ¶a ***spiral*** (=***screw***) *stair* ら旋階段. ¶***steep*** *stairs* 急な階段.

P The matter has been noticed and discussed ***below*** *stairs*. そのことは奉公人べやの話題となった. ‖ life ***below*** *stairs* 下層生活. ¶go ***down*** (***up***) *stairs* はしご段を降りる

(上る). ‖ fall *down stairs* はしご段から落ちる. ¶at the foot *of* the *stairs* はしご段の下で ‖ a flight *of stairs* 一条の階段. 【類】go up two flights *of stairs*. ¶fall *off* the *stairs* はしご段から落ちる. ¶I passed him *on* the *stairs*. 私は階段で彼とすれ違った.

P² *stairs to* the ground floor 一階に行くはしご段.

staircase, *n.* 階段.

V *ascend* a *staircase* 階段を上る. ¶*fall off* the *staircase* 階段から落ちる. ¶He *ran up* the wooden *staircase*. 彼は木の階段をかけ上がった. 「を登って上に行く.

V² A *staircase* of 100 steps *leads* to the top. 百段の階段

Q a *back staircase* 裏の階段. ¶a *grand staircase* 大階段. ¶a *steep staircase* 急な階段. ¶a *winding staircase* 回り階

Q² a *corkscrew* (=spiral) *staircase* ら旋階段. 段.

P² a *staircase of* 12 steps 十二段の階段.

stair-climbing, *n.* 階段のぼり.

Q *tedious stair-climbing* あきあきする階段のぼり.

stake, *n.* (**1**) くい, 棒くい; 火刑柱, 火刑.

V *drive* a *stake* くいを打込む. ¶*plant* a *stake* くいを立てる. ¶*pull up stakes* くいを抜く; 《米口語》立ち去る. ¶A plant *winds up* a *stake*. 植物が棒ぐいにからみつく.

P The martyr died *at* the *stake*. その殉教者は火刑に処せられた. 【類】He was burned *at* the *stake*. / He suffered *at* the *stake*. ¶Horses are tethered *to* a *stake*. 馬はくいにつないである. ‖ He was condemned *to* the *stake*. 彼は火刑の宣告を受けた.

(**2**) かけ, かけ金; 利害関係; 危険.

V He *has* a *stake* in the enterprise. 彼はその事業に利害関係を持っている. 【類】*have* the deepest *stake* in the issue (問題).

Q play for *big stakes* 大きなかけをする. ¶I object to *high stakes*. 私は高いかけには反対だ. ‖ have *high stakes* 大ばくちをする. ¶for *low stakes* 低いかけ金で. ¶play at cards for *small stakes* 小さなかけでカルタ遊びをやる.

P His life is *at stake* (=in danger). 彼は生命が危い. ‖ His honor is *at stake*. 彼の不名誉を招く恐れがある. 【類】The very life of the nation was *at stake*. / My honor is *at stake*, so I cannot let the matter rest. ¶card-playing *for stakes* かけのカルタ遊び.

stake, *v.* かける; くいで仕切る.

M *stake* very *high* たくさん金をかける. ¶*stake off* (=*out*) [地所などを]くいで仕切る ‖ *stake out* a day for the meeting 一日を会合にとっておく.

P *stake* money *on* a race 競馬に金をかける ‖ *stake* one's life and fortune *on* the event of a war 戦争の勝敗に生命と財産とをかける. 【類】I am prepared to *stake* my fortune *on* that. / *stake* one's honor *on* ... ¶*stake* his all money *upon* a single throw 一勝負に有金全部をかける.

stalemate, *n.* 行き詰まり.

V *break* the *stalemate* 行き詰りを打破する. 「なる.

Q produce a *virtual stalemate* in ... ...が全く行き詰りに

P be *at* a *stalemate* 手(行き)詰りだ. ¶subject *to* a *stalemate* 手詰りになって.

stalk, *n.* [植物の] 茎.

Q a *woody* or *stringy stalk* 木のようなまたは筋張っている

Q² an *asparagus stalk* アスパラガスの茎. 茎.

P leaves growing *on* a stalk 茎に生じる葉.

stalk, *v.* ごう然かっ歩する; [疫病などが]広がる.

M *stalk abroad* 外をごう然かっ歩する. ¶A big negro cook *stalked out* from the kitchen. 大きな黒人の料理人がのっそり出て来た.

P *stalk along* the highway 大道を威張って通る. ¶Famine *stalked* the land *over*. 飢きんが国中に広がった.

stall, *n.* 畜舎の一仕切, 馬小屋; 露店.

V The stable *contains* eight *stalls*. この馬小屋には八つ仕切がある. ¶*set up* a little *stall* 小さな露店を建てる. ¶*Stalls* are beginning to *disappear*. 露店をしまいかけている.

Q² a *black-market stall* やみ市の屋台店. ¶a *book stall* 本屋. ¶an *open-air stall* 露店. ¶a *street stall* 街頭の屋台店. ¶a *vegetable stall* 八百屋(屋台店).

P sell ... *at* a *stall* 露店で...を売る.

stamina, *n.* 元気.

Q *moral stamina* 気骨.

stammer, *v.* どもって言う; どもる.

M He *stammers badly*. 彼はひどくどもる. ¶*stammer out* an excuse どもりどもり断りを言う.

P *stammering over* the words その言葉をどもりながら.

stammerer, *n.* どもり.

Q an *inveterate stammerer* ひどいどもり.

stamp, *n.* (**1**) 印章; 郵便切手; 足踏.

V *affix stamps* to the duplicate copy of this document この証書の写しに印紙をはる. ¶*bear* the *stamp* of the manufacturer 製造元の印がある. ¶*cancel* a *stamp* 切手に消印をする. ¶This indenture must *carry* a 2s. 6d. *stamp*. この証書には二シリング六ペンスの印紙をはらねばならない. ¶*collect stamps* 切手を収集する. ¶*enclose* a *stamp* 切手を封入する. ¶*give* a *stamp* with one's foot 足でどんと踏む. ¶New postage *stamps* are *issued*. 郵便切手が新たに発行された. ¶*place* a *stamp* over the stopper of a bottle びんのせんに商標をつける. 【類】*place* its *stamp* of approval (承認の印) on ... ¶*put* a *stamp* on an envelope 封筒に切手をはる. 【類】*put* an 8-yen *stamp* on each of those letters. ¶"*Stamps sold* here" [看板]印紙販売所. ¶*stick* a *stamp* in the corner (on a letter) すみ(など)に切手をはる. 【類】*stick stamps* in one's stamp-album.

Q a *bogus stamp* 偽の切手. ¶*memorial stamps* 記念切手. ¶a *used stamp* 消印のある切手.

Q² an *India-rubber stamp* ゴム印. ¶stick a *postage stamp* on a letter 書状に郵便切手をはる. ¶a *receipt stamp* 受取判. ¶a *rubber stamp* ゴム印; 《米俗》盲判を押す人(役人), 人の意見を無条件に受入れる人. ¶*revenue stamps* 収入印紙.

P send 20c *in stamps* 郵券で二十セント送る. 【類】enclose 4-yen *in stamps* (=a 4-yen stamp) for postage. ¶those *under* this *stamp* may be regarded as not valid. この印を押したものは無効である. ¶*with* a *stamp* of the foot 強く足踏みして. ¶None are genuine *without* our *stamp*. 弊店の商標のないものはすべて偽物です.

P² a *stamp for* impressing coins 貨幣の極印. ¶the *stamp on* a coin 貨幣面に打ちだした極印. ¶a receipt with a *stamp on* (=*upon*) it なつ印のある領収証.

(**2**) 特徴; 性質; きず跡.

V *bear* the *stamp* of the age その時代の特徴を持っている ‖ His face *bears* the *stamp* of suffering. 彼の顔には苦労のあとが見えている. 【類】His features *bear* the North Japanese *stamp*. / This book *bears* the *stamp* (=mark) of scholarship. / The "Webster" of 1828 was written throughout by one man, and it *bears* on every page the *stamp* of his personality. / His face *bears* the unmistakable *stamp* of goodness, consideration, and self-control. / *bear* the *stamp* of originality (独創性) ‖ The story *bears* the *stamp* of truth. その話は本当らしい. ¶they *left* the *stamp* of their own individuality on ... 彼らは...の上に彼ら自身の個性の証跡を残した. ¶they *wear* a *stamp* of inferiority in the eyes of ... 彼らは...から劣等のものと見られている.

Q a journalist of *literary stamp* 文士型の新聞記者. ¶These idioms give the language a *native stamp*. これらの慣用句はその国語に独自性を与える. ¶It was looked upon as the *necessary stamp* of refinement to a gentleman. それは紳士には必要な身だしなみとされていた. ¶bear its own *peculiar stamp* それ自身の特徴を持つ. ¶men of the *same stamp* (=type) 同じ型の人々.

P men *of* that *stamp* あのような性質の人々 ‖ *of* the same *stamp* 同型(種)の. 【類】I dislike a man *of* his *stamp*. ‖ socialists *of* the *stamp* of Henry George ヘンリージョージ派の社会学者.

P² the *stamp of* dishonesty 不正直の証明.

stamp, *v.* 印を押す; 切手を張る; 強く踏む; [比ゆ的]極印を押す.

M It is *clearly* (*indelibly*) *stamped* on everybody's memory. それは各人の記憶にはっきり(深く)銘記されている. ¶*stamp* a hat *flat* 帽子を踏んでぺちゃんこにする. ¶The letter is *insufficiently stamped*, and 12 cents is due from you. この手紙は切手不足ですから十二セントいただきます. ¶*stamp out* with vigor 力をこめて踏みにじる. ¶*stamp out* an epidemic (the plague, the typhus) 流行病などを根絶する. 【類】*stamp out* undesirable elements / *stamp out* social evils (社会悪) / *stamp out* an insurrection / *stamp out* poisonous doctrines (有害な理論) / *stamp out* the flames (fire) / *stamp out* individual liberties. ¶His individuality is ***strongly stamped*** on all his work. 彼の個性が全作品に強くしみ出ている. ‖ *stamp* ***out*** a coin 型で硬貨を打抜く.

P *stamp* a picture ***as*** a fake 絵をいかさま物と極印を押す. 【類】 *stamp* a story ***as*** false. ‖ His conduct *stamps* him ***as*** a villain. 彼の行は彼に悪人という極印を押す. ¶ *stamp* ***by*** hand 手で押す ‖ a clinical thermometer *stamped* "normal" ***by*** the sand blast 噴砂で「正」と印を押した体温器. ¶ *stamped* ***in*** Chinese characters with the name of ... 漢字で...の名を押した(製作品など). ¶ It has been pretty well *stamped* ***into*** the minds and memories of several generations of Londoners. それは数代のロンドン人の心と記憶にかなりよく印せられている. ‖ with drink *stamped* ***on*** every feature まごうことなく酒に酔って ‖ *stamp* ***on*** the ring 土俵で四こを踏む ‖ *stamp* one's name ***on*** a book 書物に自己の名を判で押す ‖ The deed is *stamped* ***on*** his memory. その行為は彼の記憶にはっきりと残っている. ‖ *stamp* a mark ***on*** the plate 板金に刻印を打つ. 【類】 Happiness, contentment, and good temper are *stamped* ***on*** every countenance (=feature). ‖ Her image was *stamped* ***on*** his heart. 彼女の姿が彼の胸に刻み込まれた. ¶ *stamp* it ***out of*** existence それを根絶する. ¶ *stamp* ***with*** the foot 足で踏む ‖ a coin *stamped* ***with*** a crown 王冠の極印のある貨幣 ‖ It is *stamped* ***with*** his seal. それには彼の印が押してある. ‖ The letter was *stamped* ***with*** this post-mark. その手紙はこの消印があった. ‖ a face *stamped* ***with*** sadness 悲哀の跡のありありと見える顔付. 【類】 *stamp* ***with*** rage / The entire work is *stamped* ***with*** industry and learning. 全部の仕事に勤勉と学才の跡がありありと見える. ‖ Time has *stamped* the cant ***with*** authority. 時がたってその俗語もりっぱな語になった.

stampede, *n.* 《米》殺到; 総逃げ, 総くずれ.

P² There was a *stampede* ***of*** panic-stricken crowd from the burning apartment. その焼けているアパートから狂気のように飛び出した人の波が見られた. ¶ a *stampede* ***to*** a newly-discovered gold field 新発見の金鉱への殺到.

stampede, *v.* 《米》どっと押しよせる; どっと逃げる.

P A panic-stricken crowd *stampeded* ***from*** the burning building. 恐怖にかられた群集が燃える建物からどっと出て来た.

「そろい.

stand, *n.* 立ちどまること; 抵抗; 位置; 台; 〖法〗証人台, 一

V ***adopt*** a *stand* 態度を取る. ¶ ***attain*** so high a *stand* 非常に高い地位に上る. ¶ ***define*** the Japanese *stand* on the situation 時局における日本の立場を確立する. ¶ About 350 firms have ***erected*** their *stands* on an area of 165,000 square feet in the fair grounds. 三百五十の商会が博覧会場内なる十六万五千平方フィートの広場にそれぞれの売店を設けた. ¶ ***illustrate*** one's *stand* on the Japanese question 日本問題に対するその立場を説明する. ¶ ***keep*** a *stand* 立場を守る. ¶ ***make*** a *stand* against the enemy 敵を防御する ‖ ***make*** a *stand* for the principle (good of the country) 主義(など)を擁護する. ¶ He will ***occupy*** the conductor's *stand*. 彼が(管弦楽などの)指揮者台に立つであろう. ¶ He ***took*** his *stand* near the door. 彼は戸口に近く立った. ‖ ***Take*** your *stand*. [裁判長が証人などに]お立ちなさい. 【類】 ***take*** one's *stand* at the counter (売場) / ***take*** one's *stand* by ... (...に味方して) / He ***took*** his *stand* on a broken bridge of London Bridge to sketch the ruins of St. Paul's. / ***take*** his *stand* to pay his devotions (拝する) to the rising sun ‖ ***take*** a *stand* against oppression 圧制に抗する. 【類】 ***take*** a *stand* for independence ‖ ***take*** a *stand* on firmer ground 一層強固な基礎に立脚する. 【類】 I ***take*** my *stand* on the precise wording of the act (法令) ‖ ***take*** the *stand* 《米》証人席につく. ☞ 英語用法は enter the witness box. 【類】 the witness ***took*** the *stand* and said: ‖ He can now ***take*** his *stand* with the great travelers of the world. 彼は今では世界の大旅行家と肩を並べられるようになった. ¶ We ***take up*** our *stand* on the eternal principles of right and justice. われわれは正義という永遠の原則に立脚している.

V² The *stand* ***gave way***. 観覧席が(こわれて)落ちた.

Q take a ***decisive*** *stand* 断固たる態度に出る. ¶ make a ***determined*** *stand* 踏み止って断固たる抵抗を試みる. ¶ make a ***final*** *stand* 踏止って最後の抵抗をする. ¶ make a ***firm*** *stand* 決然たる抵抗を試みる. ¶ He made his ***heroic*** *stand*. 彼は勇ましく抵抗した. ¶ take an ***intelligent*** *stand* against ... 理解ある態度で...に対立する. ¶ He made his ***last*** *stand* at the castle. 彼はこの城で最後の抵抗を試みた. 【類】 make the ***last*** *stand* against the enemy. ¶ He takes a ***premier*** *stand* in the theatrical world. 彼は劇界での第一人者である. ¶ make a ***resolute*** *stand* 思いきって踏み止まる. ¶ take a ***similar*** *stand* 同様の立場を取る. ¶ ***smokers'*** *stands* [灰などを落す高足の]喫煙台.

Q² an ***advertisement*** *stand* 広告塔. ¶ saw stage performance over the ***band*** *stand* 楽士席をへだてて舞台を見た. ¶ a ***book*** *stand* 本立て. ¶ the Police Gazette—a pink periodical with an enormous circulation among barber shops and ***boot-black*** *stands* 警察新報—床屋やくつみがき屋で大好評の桃色の雑誌. ¶ a ***desk-set*** *stand*=a desk lamp 卓上灯(スタンド). ¶ a ***fruit*** *stand* 果物店の屋台. ¶ a ***fruit drink*** *stand* 果物のジュースを飲ませるスタンド. ¶ a ***hot-dog*** *stand* ホットドック屋台. ¶ a ***news*** *stand* 新聞売店. ¶ an ***open-air soft-drink-and-frankfurter*** *stand* 飲物とソーセジを出す街頭の屋台店. ¶ a ***periodical*** *stand* 雑誌売店. ¶ a ***refreshment*** *stand* 喫茶洋菓子の売店. ¶ pass the ***reviewing*** *stand* [閲兵など]検閲台を通過する. ¶ a ***sidewalk*** *stand* 歩道の露店. ¶ a ***taxi*** *stand* タキシー駐車場. ¶ an ***umbrella*** *stand* かさ立て. ¶ on the [***witness***] *stand* 証人台に. ☞ 英語用法は in the [witness] box. 【類】 take the ***witness*** *stand* / be called to the ***witness*** *stand*.

P Business is ***at*** a *stand*. 商売は停止状態だ. ‖ We do business ***at*** the old *stand*. 手前ではもとの場所で営業しています. ‖ newspapers sold ***at*** *stands* 呼売の新聞 ‖ I was very much ***at*** the *stand*. 私は大いに当惑した. ¶ firm ***in*** one's *stand* 根拠の強固な. ¶ Business has been brought ***to*** a *stand*. 商売は停止状態になった.

P² a good *stand* ***for*** a hotel ホテルには好適の位置. ¶ a *stand* ***of*** arms 武器一式. ¶ His *stand* ***toward*** the matter has not changed. その事件に対する彼の立場は変らない.

stand, *v.* 立つ; 耐える; 振舞う, おごる.

M He *stood* ***accused*** of a crime. 彼は罪人とされていた. ¶ *stand* ***agape*** at the sight 口あんぐりでその光景を見ていた. ¶ He *stood* ***aghast*** at the sight. 彼はその光景にびっくりしていた. ¶ The door is *standing* ***ajar***. ドアが少しあいている. ¶ I was kept *standing* ***all the time***. 私は始終立ち続けだった. ¶ Can a nation *stand* ***alone***? 国は孤立していられるだろうか. ‖ *stand* almost ***alone*** in ... ...の点ではほとんど天下独歩 ‖ jelly stiff enough to *stand* ***alone*** おいてくずれない程度のジェリ. ¶ *stand* ***aloof*** from politics (the rush of life) 政界(など)から超然とする. 【類】 *stand* ***aloof*** from the madding crowd (狂騒). ¶ I can't *stand* this heat (cold) ***any longer***. もうこの暑(寒)さには堪えられない. ¶ a policy of *standing* ***apart*** from other nations 他国不干渉国策. ¶ The policeman motioned us to *stand* ***aside***. 警官は離れているようにわれわれに手で合図をした. ‖ *stand* a bit ***aside*** ちょっと離れている. ¶ I *stand* ***assured*** of his protection. 私は彼が保護してくれるものと確信している. ¶ *stand* ***avowedly*** for reform 公然改革に味方する. ¶ *Stand* ***back***! 後ろへさがれ. 【類】 *stand* ***back*** to let him pass. / *stand* ***back*** ten or fifteen feet. ¶ I *stood* ***bewildered*** for a moment. 私は暫時途方に暮れて立っていた. ¶ *stand* almost ***cheek by jowl*** [店など]目と鼻の所にある. ¶ *stand* ***clear*** of ... ...を避ける. ¶ *stand* ***close*** to it それに接して立つ. ¶ His name *stands* ***conspicuously*** on the list. 彼の名は名簿中で目立っている. ¶ She *stands* ***eighth*** in line of countries. その国は各国中第八位に立つ. ¶ *stand* ***erect*** 直立する. ¶ *stand* ***fast*** to one's resolution 堅く決心を守る. ¶ He *stood* ***firm***. 彼は泰然としていた. ‖ *stand* ***firm*** on the ground がっちり大地に足を踏みしめる. 【類】 *stand* ***firm*** in one's views ¶ *stand* ***firmly*** for loyalty 断固忠誠を守る. 【類】 *stand* ***fimly*** against... ¶ He *stands* ***first*** in his class. 彼はクラス中の首席だ. 【類】 His name *stands* ***first*** on the list. ‖ *stand* easily ***first*** 優に首席を占める. ¶ The fact clearly *stands* ***forth*** that ... ...という事実がはっきり現われる. ¶ I *stood* ***gazing*** at the scene. 私はその光景をながめながら立っていた. ¶ He *stood* a ***giant*** among them. 彼は彼らの中の大男(傑物)だった. ¶ *stand* ***godfather (sponsor, surety)*** to ... ...の名親(など)となる. ¶ The contract *stands* ***good*** for another year. 契約はもう一年有効だ. ¶ The cathedral *stands* ***grandly*** overlooking the town at the top of the hill. 本山は小山の頂上に町を見下ろして堂々と立っている. ¶ a tree which *stood* ***hard by*** 近くに生えていた一本の木.

¶He *stands* ***high*** in his class. 彼はクラス中で成績がよい. 【類】names which *stand* ***high*** in the list of savants (学者) / His credit *stands* ***high***. / *stand* ***higher*** in scientific achievement than … / He *stands* very ***high*** in his profession. / He *stands* ***high*** in the public estimation. / The credit of our firm *stands* ***high*** with him. / These films *stand* ***high*** in public favor. / He was appointed as the person *standing* ***highest*** in the competitive examination. ¶***how*** does America *stand* with regard to …? …に関して米国はどういう位置になるか. ¶He was *standing* ***idle***. 彼はぼんやり立っていた. ‖ The factory is *standing* ***idle***. 工場は休んでいる. ¶*stand* ***idly by*** 何もしないで立っている. ¶I *stand* ***indebted*** to this gentleman. 私はこの方には恩がある. ¶*stand* ***innocent*** of all evils あらゆる悪に染まらない. ¶*stand* ***loyally*** by their agreements and conventions 彼らの協約を忠実に守る. ¶Egypt *stood* ***midway*** between Christianity and classical Paganism エジプトはキリスト教と古典的異教(回教)の中間に立った. ¶She was tall and handsome, *standing* (=measuring) ***nearly*** 5 feet 11 inches. 彼女は身長約五フィート十一インチもあってたけが高くりっぱだった. ¶*stand* ***nervously*** on the kerb waiting to cross the road 道路を向側に渡ろうとして人道の辺石(ﾍﾘｲｼ)にいらいらしながら立つ. ¶*stand* ***neuter*** 中立でいる. ¶*stand* ***next*** to … …の次に位する. ¶an inevitable result of the system as it ***now*** *stands* 現今の組織の必然の結果. ¶There ***once*** *stood*, close by, the celebrated Ravelagh Gardens. そこに以前有名なラヴェラの庭園があった. ¶The door *stands* ***open***. 戸は明いている. 【類】The vault (地下金庫) *stood* ***open***. ¶*stand* ***opposed*** 抵抗する. ¶a flag *standing* ***out*** in the breeze above me 頭上を吹く微風になびく旗. ‖ The castle (tree, mountain) *stands* ***out*** against the sky. 城(など)が空にきつ立している. ‖ what do *stand* ***out*** in my memory are … 私の記憶に鮮かなのは…である ‖ It *stands* ***out*** clearly (very vividly) from other objects. 他の物より(一際)目立つ. ‖ *stand* ***out*** vividly against … …と対照して目立つ. 【類】The graceful figure of Mt. Fuji *stood* ***out*** clear and distinct against the blue sky. / Stone and marble effigies (像) *stand* ***out*** weirdly (薄気味悪く) against the night. / *stand* ***out*** prominently from … / there are two names, among …, which *stand* ***out*** above all others ‖ *stand* ***out*** from the crowd (among the crowd of mediocrities) 群(凡庸の群)を抜く. 【類】*stand* ***out*** above all the rest / Of the parks … Park *stands* ***out*** / *stand* ***out*** in history as the type of … / *stand* ***out*** [distinctly] in my memory. / It *stands* ***out*** with great effect. ‖ They *stood* ***out*** against all his persuasions and arguments. 彼らは彼のあらゆる説得や議論にも心を動かさなかった. ¶He left me *standing* ***outside***. 彼は僕を外に待たせておいた. ¶*stand* ***preeminent*** today among … 今日…間に断然頭角を現わしている. ¶We *stood* ***prepared*** to repel any attack. われわれはいかなる攻撃でも撃退の覚悟をしていた. ¶*stand* ***ready*** for … …は何時でも用意ができている. 【類】Thanking you for the kindness you have shown in the past, and always *standing* ***ready*** to reciprocate (御恩返しをする). ¶see the position as it ***really*** *stands* 真相(実態)を見きわめる. ¶He graduated from Yale, 1878, *standing* ***second*** in a class of 121. 彼は百二十一名のクラスの次席を占めてエイルを卒業した. ‖ *stand* ***second*** to none as … …としては一と言って二と下がらない. ¶he stood ***sentinel*** against … …に対し警戒の目を光らした. ¶let us *stand* ***shoulder to shoulder*** (=***side by side***) for (against) … 協力して…のためにやろう(反対しよう). ¶He *stood* ***silent***. 彼は無言で立っていた. ¶He *stands* ***six feet*** in his shoes. 彼はくつをはいて六フィートある. ¶*stand* ***squarely*** きちんと立つ. ¶I will *stand* ***squarely*** back of you in your attempt. 君の企画はしっかり応援する. ¶*standing* ***statuesquely*** in the sentry-box 見張所に彫像のように立って. ¶simply *stand* ***still*** and mark time 単に立止まったまま足踏みをする. ¶There she *stood* ***straight*** like a lily on its stem. そこで彼女はゆりの花のように真すぐに立った. ‖ The hair on his head *stood* up ***straight***. 彼の頭の毛が直立した. ¶*stand* ***surety*** for … …の保証に立つ. ¶*stand* ***suspiciously*** aloof 危しとして近よらない. ¶Costermongers' barrows *stand* ***thickly*** by the kerb. 大道商人の車が人道の側に所せましと並んでいる. ¶The matter *stands* ***thus***. それはこういうことになっている. ¶*stand* ***twenty-ninth*** in the list 名簿で二十九番目になっている. ¶It will *stand* ***20 feet*** from the ground. それは地面から高さ二十フォートある. ¶He *stood* ***uncovered***. 彼は無帽で立っていた. ¶*stand* absolutely ***unrivalled*** 絶対に比類がない. ¶*stand* ***upright*** 真すぐに立つ ‖ He *stood* ***upright***. 彼は直立していた. ¶He always *stand* ***well*** in his classes. 彼はいつもクラスで成績がよい. ‖ He *stands* ***well*** in the list of German poets. 彼はドイツ詩人中そうそうたるものだ. ‖ The name *stands* ***well***. それ(商店など)は評判がよい. ‖ he *stands* ***well*** with … 彼は…と仲がよい. ¶*stand* ***well back*** ずっと離れている. ¶It *stands* ***written***. そう書いてある.

M[2] *stand* ***off*** a creditor 債権者を避ける ‖ *stand* ***off*** from one's friends 友人を避ける. 【類】*stand* ***off*** assaults. ¶Let the matter *stand* ***over***. そのことはそのままにしておきなさい. ‖ Let the debt *stand* ***over*** for another month, and we'll square things up at Christmas. 返金はもう一カ月延ばして下さい, クリスマスには片を付けます. ¶*stand* ***up*** boldly for free trade 大胆に自由貿易を擁護する ‖ *stand* ***up*** stoutly for … 敢然として…を弁護する ‖ *stand* ***up*** from one's seat 席から立上る. 【類】I am ready to *stand* ***up*** for you. / *stand* ***up*** for one's favorite actor or actress on all occasions ‖ *stand* ***up*** for a great cause 大義のために立上る. 【類】*stand* ***up*** for peace (liberty) ‖ *stand* ***up*** against …=resist … …に抵抗する. 【類】*stand* ***up*** against any wind of fate / *stand* ***up*** together against the common enemy ‖ *stand* ***up*** to speak 発言しようと立上る ‖ *stand* [***up***] the heat (cold) 暑さ(寒)さにたえる ‖ None of these explanations can *stand* ***up*** under close examination. これらの説明は厳密な考査にたえるものは一つもない. ‖ How the American woman *stands* ***up*** in comparison with the European woman? 米国婦人は欧州婦人に比べるとどんなことになりますか. ‖ *stand* ***up*** to one's antagonist 敵手に敢然立ち向う. 【類】He *stood* ***up*** to us like a madman. ‖ Only first-rate merchandise can *stand* ***up*** to intensive publicity. 一級品だけが猛烈な宣伝に値する. ‖ the artificial protection of vegetables for a period longer than they normally "*stand* ***up***" on the market 普通野菜の市場での保存期間より長い期間の人工的保存 ‖ with the only clothes he *stood* ***up*** in 着のみ着のままで.

P *stand* ***against*** a person 人に抵抗する ‖ He has *stood* many years ***against*** storm and earthquake. 多年風雨や地震と戦ってきた. ‖ She *stood* ***against*** the grocery counter. 彼女は食料店のカウンターによりかかっていた. ‖ *stand* it ***against*** the wall それを壁に立てかける ‖ who can *stand* ***againt*** destiny だれだって運命にはかなわない. ¶a monument *standing* ***amid*** palms and beautiful shrubbery しゅろや美しいかん木の中に立っている記念碑. ¶It *stands* ***among*** the foremost universities of the world. それは世界一流大学の一つである. ¶They *stood* ***around*** him, while he spoke. 彼が話をしている間彼らは彼の周囲に立っていた. ¶*stand* ***as*** a candidate for the Presidency 大統領の候補に立つ. 【類】He *stood* ***as*** Labour candidate (労働党候補) at the 1923 election in the Epsom division of Surrey. / *stand* ***as*** a sentinel ***upon*** … / Here is a joke that might *stand* ***as*** a type of British humour. / In their general plan and their working arrangements they are so much alike that a description of one will *stand* ***as*** a description of all. / men whose discoveries *stand* ***as*** mileposts in the growth and development of scientific knowledge. ¶*stand* ***at*** attention 気を付けの姿勢を取っている ‖ *stand* ***at*** the door 戸口に立つ ‖ The stag *stood* ***at*** bay on the edge of the cliff. 雄じかはがけの突端まで追いつめられた. ‖ *Stand* ***at*** ease! [号令]休め ‖ *stand* ***at*** bay 追詰められる, 絶体絶命になる ‖ sentries *standing* ***at*** the salute 敬礼の姿勢を取っている番兵 ‖ *stand* ***at*** the head of one's class クラスの首席を占めている. 【類】The umbrella *stands* ***at*** the head of the articles that Londoners have a habit of losing. ‖ The thermometer *stands* ***at*** 90° in the shade. 寒暖計は日陰で九十度になっている. 【類】with the mercury (寒暖計) *standing* ***at*** over 75° / the score (得点) *stood* ***at*** … / The index figure (指数) *stood* ***at*** 119. / In 1902 the number *stood* ***at*** 15,231. / The reserve fund (準備金) *stands* ***at*** £150,011. ‖ Japan *stands* ***at*** a disadvantage in that respect. その点では日本は不利な地位に立っている. ‖ He will not *stand* (=hesitate) ***at*** murder. 彼は人を殺す位のことは何とも思わない. ¶I *stood* ***before*** him. 私は彼の前に立った.

¶He *stood* ***behind*** me. 彼は私の後ろに立った. ¶He *stood* ***below*** me in class. 彼はクラスでは私より下だった. ¶She *stood* ***beside*** her mother. 彼女は母のそばに立っていた. ‖ be worthy to *stand* ***beside*** ... …と比肩する. ¶*stand* ***between*** us われわれの中間に立つ. ¶*stand* ***by*** the fence かきねのそばに立つ ‖ I *stand* ***by*** it as true and unexaggerated. 私はそれを真実で誇張なきものとして支持する. 【類】I will *stand* ***by*** you in this matter. / He *stood* ***by*** him till the last hour. / We *stand* ***by*** him to the last (命のあらん限り). / I took it for granted that he would *stand* ***by*** me. ‖ *stand* ***by*** pocket-handed (=hand in pocket) / *stand* ***by*** him through thick and thin (順境逆境とも). ¶The castle has *stood* ***for*** centuries. その城は数世紀前のものだ. ‖ candidates who *stand* ***for*** election 選挙の候補者. 【類】He declined to *stand* ***for*** re-election. / he *stood* ***for*** the presidency (総裁など) against ... ‖ He always *stood* ***for*** straight dealing (the right). 彼はいつも公正な処置(など)に味方した. 【類】*stand* ***for*** idealism (唯心論) in philosophy. / He always *stood* ***for*** us and with us. ‖ *stand* ***for*** no fooling about ... …については何らのあなどりをも容認しない ‖ What do the letters N.B. *stand* ***for***? N.B. という字は何の略語か. ‖ Words *stand* ***for*** ideas. 語は意味を持つ. ‖ the principles ***for*** which the UN *stands* 国連の綱領. 【類】The crown *stands* ***for*** royal dignity (王位). ‖ Statues are made to look like people or the objects they *stand* ***for***. / the ideas ***for*** which a party *stands*. ‖ In his eyes a laugh *stands* ***for*** an argument. 彼は笑えばそれが議論(意見の発表)になると思っている. ‖ For a hundred and forty years the Nelsons have *stood* ***for*** all that is best in publishing. 過去百四十年間ネルソン社は出版界で重きをなしてきた. 【類】Oxford, and what it *stands* ***for***, is not easily appreciated in the outside world. ‖ He wouldn't "*stand* ***for*** a touch." 彼はからいくじがない. ¶The house *stands* fifteen yards ***from*** the road. その家は道路から十五フィートのところに立っている. ¶A stranger *stood* ***in*** the doorway. 戸口に見知らぬ人が立っていた. ‖ The house *stands* ***in*** a garden. 家は庭の中にある. ‖ *stand* ***in*** a circle 輪になって立つ. ‖ *stand* ***in*** a queue (=line) waiting for their turn 一列になって順番を待つ ‖ *stand* ***in*** a row ずらり並ぶ ‖ The teacher *stood* the boy ***in*** a corner. 教師は生徒をすみに立たせた. 【類】He's too old to have to *stand* in the corner for punishment. / *stand* the umbrella ***in*** a corner. ‖ *stand* ***in*** the way of one's promotion 人の出世の邪魔をする ‖ *stand* ***in*** the same circumstances 同じ事情にある ‖ *stand* ***in*** one's own light 自分に不利になるようなことをする ‖ *stand* ***in*** awe (fear) of ... …を畏敬(など)している ‖ *stand* ***in*** contrast to ... …と対照になる ‖ *stand* ***in*** need of money (clothes, food) 金(など)に窮している. 【類】He *stands* ***in*** an awkward position. / *stand* fast ***in*** the faith / The law still *stands* ***in*** force. ‖ be willing to *stand* ***in*** half profit and loss 喜んで損益は半々にする. ‖ That overcoat *stood* me ***in*** twenty dollars. その外とうには二十ドルかかった. ‖ The warm coat *stood* him ***in*** good stead when the sun set. 日が沈んでからはその暖い上衣が大いに役にたった. 【類】Mildness and forbearance are virtues which will *stand* the traveller ***in*** good stead. ‖ References must be from people of *standing* ***in*** the community from which the student comes. 照会先は学生出身地の著名人であること. ¶He *stood* ***next*** me. 彼は私の次に立っていた. ‖ Germany *stands* ***next*** the Great Britain among the mining countries of Europe. ドイツは欧州の鉱業国中英国の次に位する. ¶*stand* ***on*** one's head (and hands) さか立ちをする ‖ *stand* firmly ***on*** one's own feet (=legs) 敢然として独立独歩する ‖ *stand* ***on*** tiptoe つま先きで立つ ‖ *stand* ***on*** end 直立する, さか立つ ‖ *stand* a book ***on*** edge 本を立てる ‖ Her hair *stood* ***on*** edge (=end) with fright. びっくりして彼女の髪の毛はよだった. ‖ *stand* ***on*** high ground 高地による ‖ *stand* a man ***on*** his feet 人を立たせる ‖ Paris *stands* (=lies) ***on*** the Seine. パリーはセーヌ河畔にある. ‖ *stand* ***on*** one's basis 独立する ‖ *stand* ***on*** its own bottom 独立する ‖ A news story is a triangle *standing* ***on*** its apex. 新聞記事はさか立ちする三角である(紙面の都合で文尾を切るから). ‖ *stand* ***on*** one's rights どこまでも権利を主張する ‖ *stand* ***on*** a basis of equality 平等の立場に立つ ‖ One must not *stand* ***on*** trifles. 人は細かなことに拘泥してはいけない. ‖ Don't *stand* ***on*** ceremony with us. われわれに遠慮するな. ‖ *stand* ***on*** compliment 遠慮する ‖ *stand* ***on*** the defensive 守勢を取る ‖ like to *stand* on the safe side=be prudent 大事を取る ‖ *stand* ***on*** the threshold of a peace settlement 平和実現の一歩手前にある. ¶*stand* ***to*** one's assertion 所説を固執する ‖ *stand* ***to*** one's duty 本分を守る. 【類】You should *stand* ***to*** your promise (=what you said). ‖ it *stands* ***to*** a credit of his that ... …は彼の名誉となる ‖ it *stands* ***to*** reason that ...は理の当然である ‖ *stand* ***to*** one's oath 誓いを守る ‖ A long list of books *stands* ***to*** his credit, but none compare with those we have named. 彼にはたくさんの著述があるがいずれもわれわれがあげたものとは比較にならない. ‖ The enemy could not *stand* ***to*** their guns. 敵は彼らの砲火に抵抗できなかった. ‖ singly and unitedly *stand* ***to*** their post 単独にまた団結して彼らの持場を守る ‖ it *stands* ***to*** reason that ... …は理にかなっている ‖ The son *stands* ***to*** his father in sacred relation. 子は父に対して神聖な関係にある. ‖ He *stood* icecream (wine) ***to*** the company. 彼は仲間にアイスクリーム(など)をおごった. ¶The cottage *stands* ***under*** the tree. 小屋は木の下に立っている. ¶I have not a leg to *stand* ***upon***. 私は全く申訳がない. 【類】The Western civilization *stands* ***upon*** the foundation reared by the Greeks and the Romans. ‖ *stand* ***upon*** one's rights (claims) 権利(など)を主張する. ¶How does it *stand* ***with*** him? それは彼とどういう関係になっているか. ‖ *stand* ***with*** a person on terms of friendship 人と親密な間柄になっている ‖ *stand* ***with*** one's reputation その名声に符合する(そむかない).

o Let's *stand* her a drink. 彼女に一杯おごってやろう.

standard, *n.* 本位; 標準, 模範; 旗.

v ***abandon*** the gold *standard* 金本位制を廃する. ¶***adopt*** a *standard* of inclusion [語い選定の場合など]どの程度まで採用するかという標準を設ける. ¶***apply*** the *standard* of common sense 常識で断判する. ¶New *standards* of living have been ***created*** and many of the luxuries of 10 and 20 years ago are now considered necessities. 生活の新らしい標準が設けられて十年前や二十年前のぜいたく品の多くは今では必要品と考えられている. ¶***cultivate*** a high *standard* of public morality 高い標準の公徳心を養成する. ¶***debase*** its *standard* その標準をさげる. ¶***demand*** higher *standards* of comfort 一層高級の慰安物を要求する. ¶***elevate*** (=***better***) the *standard* of living 生活を豊かにする. ¶***encourage*** high ethical *standards* in the conduct of business 商業経営に高尚な道徳的標準の樹立を奨励する. ¶***establish*** a gold *standard* 金本位制を確立する ‖ ***establsh*** a new *standard* 新たに標準を設ける ‖ ***establish*** higher ethical *standards* in business 商業の一層高尚な道徳的標準を確立する. 【類】***establish*** higher *standards* for human conduct. ¶***fix*** the *standard* 標準を確定する ‖ How is the *standard* of correctness ***fixed***? [作文の]可否の標準はどうきめてあるのか. ¶***have*** a *standard* ***lower*** than ... …より程度が低い ‖ ***have*** a low *standard* of life (=living) 生活程度が低い. ¶***improve*** the intellectual *standard* of the masses 民衆の知的水準を高める. ¶***lower*** the *standard* of living 生活の標準を低くする. ¶***maintain*** the *standard* of ... …の水準を保つ. 【類】***maintain*** a fair American *standard* of living. ¶***promote*** a high personal *standard* of honor 高い名誉の基準をあげる. ¶***raise*** the *standard* of public appreciation of films 公衆の映画鑑賞の標準を高める. 【類】***raise*** the *standard* of living (home life) / ***raise*** materially the average social *standard* of the community / ***raise*** the artistic *standard* of translation / ***raise*** the *standard* of revolt (反旗). ¶***reach*** a *standard* 標準に達する. ¶***secure*** a *standard* of excellence 優秀の域に到達する. ¶***set*** a new *standard* in guidebook-making 案内書作製に新らしい標準を示す. 【類】***set*** a new *standard* for completeness and accuracy in dictionary compiling. ¶***set up*** a false *standard* of excellence 誤った優秀標準を設定する ‖ ***set up*** high *standards* of character 高い品性の標準を設ける. ¶***settle*** the *standard* 標準を定める. ¶***show*** a high *standard* of performance in English 英語の学習において好成績を示す. ¶***suspend*** the gold *standard* 金本位制を停止する. ¶***unfurl*** the *standard* to the air 旗を空中にひるがえす.

v² where the gold *standard* ***prevails*** 金本位制の行われて「いる所に.

Q A perfect oval face is the ***accepted*** *standard* of beauty in Hollywood. 完全な卵形の顔がハリウッドでは美人の標準

と認められている. ¶be measured by a ***certain*** *standard* 一定の規準で計ることになっている. ¶the ***current*** *standard* of ... ...の目下の標準. ¶The half of mankind that lives in Asia has never had a ***decent*** *standard* of living. アジアに住む人類の半数はいまだかつて相当の生活というものをしたことがない. ¶set up a ***different moral*** *standard* for men and women 男女のために別々の道徳標準を設定する. ¶a ***double*** (***single***) *standard* 複(単)本位制. ¶the more ***elaborate*** and ***expensive*** *standard* of life 一層こって費用のかかる生活標準. ¶high ***ethical*** *standards* in business and professions 実務並に知的職業における高級な道徳的標準. ¶a ***fixed*** *standard* 一定の標準. ¶raise the ***general*** *standard* of efficiency among workers 労働者間の能率の一般的標準を上げる. ¶The currency to the country was put on the ***gold*** *standard* in 1897. この国の通貨は一八九七年に金本位に定められた. ¶a ***high*** *standard* of journalism (commercial honor) 新聞事業(商業道徳)の高い標準. 【類】 maintain the ***high*** *standard* of quality / raise factories to the ***highest possible*** *standard* of comfort / be of the ***high*** *standard* of accuracy / acquire a ***higher*** *standard* of living. ¶an ***improved*** *standard* of living for the people 人民の一層向上した生活程度. ¶the ***intellectual*** *standard* of the pupils 生徒の知力程度. ¶the lowering of the ***literary*** *standard* of magazines 雑誌の文学的標準の低下. ¶a ***lofty*** *standard* of morality 道徳の高尚な標準. ¶The work was a ***low*** *standard.* その作品は中以下であった. ‖ set too ***low*** a *standard* 余りに低い標準を立てる. 【類】 The *standard* of behaviour and morality in those days was very ***low.*** / one of the countries of the ***lowest*** *standards* of living in the world. ¶set up certain ***minimum*** *standards* 一定の最低基準を設ける. ¶According to ***modern*** *standards* of wealth India is still extremely poor. 現代の富の標準ではインドはまだ非常に貧乏だ. ¶set up a ***new*** *standard* 新らしい標準を設ける. ¶make seven hours the ***normal*** *standard* of a day's labor 七時間を一日の労働正規標準とする. ¶It is modeled closely upon ***occidental*** *standards.* それは全然西洋の模倣である. ¶not to be measured by the ***ordinary*** *standard* 常規をもってしては律し得ない. ¶There is no ***permanent*** *standard* of taste. 趣味には永久の規準といったものはない. ¶***quantitative*** (***qualitative***) *standards* 量(質)の基準. ¶the ***recognized*** *standard* in these matters こういった方面で認められた規準. ¶***settled*** *standards* of life and conduct 処生の確固たる標準. ¶the ***single moral*** *standard* for men and women 男女に対する単一の道徳標準. ¶***variable*** *standards* 色々な規格. ¶the ***world-accepted*** *standard* 広く世間に認められた規準.

Q² ***collegiate-level*** *standards* 大学と同程度. ¶raise ***food*** and ***nutrition*** *standards* 食料と営養の程度をあげる. ¶establish a ***gold*** (***silver***) *standard* [貨幣の]金(銀)本位制を確立する. ¶The ***living*** *standard* of the people is low. 人民の生活水準は低い. 【類】 assure Germany a minimum ***living*** *standard* / high (low) ***living*** *standards* / bring about (= realize) higher ***living*** *standards* / have a decent ***living*** *standard.* ¶the fall (rise) in ***living*** *standards* 生活水準の低下(上昇) ‖ one of the lowest ***living*** *standards* of world nations 世界国家中最低生活水準の一つ. ¶rebel against ***Old World*** *standards* 古い世界(欧州)の伝統的基準にあきたらずこれに反抗する. ¶raising of ***pay*** *standard* 給与基準の引上げ. ¶at prices approximating ***peace-time*** *standards* 平和時標準に近い価格で. ¶conform to our ***present-day*** *standard* of beauty 現代における美の標準に合う. ¶***quality*** *standards* 品質規格. ¶students receiving instruction of ***university*** *standard* 大学程度の講義を受ける学生. ¶set the new ¥6,920 basic ***wage*** *standard* for workers in public service 六千九百二十円の公務員賃金ベースを新設する. 【類】 countries of lower ***wage*** *standards* / a ¥5,200-a-month ***wage*** *standard.* ¶***wartime*** *standards* 戦時規格.

P Prices are far ***above*** the prewar *standard.* 物価は戦前よりずっと上がっている. ¶honest ***according to*** the *standard* of his time 彼の時代の標準から見れば正直な. ¶set him up ***as*** a *standard* for others 他の模範とする ‖ It is accepted ***as*** a *standard.* それは標準として認められている. ¶pupils ***below*** the *standard* of average intelligence 平均以下の知能を有する生徒 ‖ Eggs ***below*** the *standard* are reserved for household use in the home family. 規格はずれの鶏卵は自家食用としてとっておく. ¶It is measured ***by*** the same *standard.* それは同一標準で計る. ¶***from*** the European *standard* 欧州の標準から. ¶fall short ***of*** the *standard* 標準に達しない. ¶pass an examination ***on*** a high *standard* 優等で及第する. ¶come up ***to*** the *standard* 標準に達する. ¶goods ***up to*** the *standards* 規格品. 【類】 The goods are not ***up to*** the *standard.* ¶***Upon*** what *standards* is she judged? 彼女はどういう標準で批判されるのか.

P² the legal *standard* ***for*** whole milk 全乳の法定規準 ‖ *standards* ***for*** judging acting 演技を判定する規準. ¶the moral *standard* ***in*** the home 家庭における道徳標準 ‖ The *standard* ***in*** the syllabus is high, but the standard of examination is low. 教材は高級だが試験の水準は低い. ¶Japan's *standards* ***of*** feminine beauty 女性美の日本での標準 ‖ a *standard* ***of*** comparison 比較の標準. 【類】 the *standard* ***of*** living ‖ The elephant is the *standard* (= symbol) ***of*** Thailand. 象はタイ国の象徴である. ¶*standards* ***on*** electrical insulating materials 電気絶縁材料の規格.

standardization, *n.* 規格化.

V ***size*** *standardization* of containers 容器の大きさの規格を定める.

P² *standardization* ***of*** machine parts 部品の規格化.

standing, *n.* 存続; 地位, 階級, 名望.

V ***attain*** the same scholastic *standing* as ... ...と同程度の学者的地位に達する. ¶***establish*** the *standing* of ... as the supreme authority 最高権威として...の地位を確立する. ¶The possession of the knowledge will ***give*** a good *standing* in business. その知識があると実業界で幅がきく. ¶He ***has*** no official *standing.* 彼は官等を持っていない. ¶***improve*** one's *standing* in one's studies 学力を進める. ¶***lose*** one's social *standing* 社会的地位を失う.

Q stand highest in ***academic*** *standing* among graduating students 卒業する学生中で学問的資格では最高に位する. 【類】 be high in ***academic*** *standing.* ¶a union in ***bad*** *standing* 資格不備の労組. ¶It has lost much of its ***early*** *standing.* それは初めの声価が大分落ちた. ¶of ***established*** *standing* 押しも押されもしない. ¶***financial*** *standing* of a firm 商社の経済状態. ¶The house has a ***fine commercial*** *standing.* その店にはりっぱな商業上の格式がある. ¶I owe him a debt of ***five years'*** *standing.* 彼に五年越しの借金がある. ¶a member of ***full*** *standing* 資格十分の会員. ¶be given a ***good*** *standing* in the literary world 文士として相当高い地位を与えられる. 【類】 The mere fact that a word is found in the dictionary should not lead one to assume that this word is in ***good*** *standing.* ‖ a man of ***good*** *standing* 身分のある人. ¶a firm of quite ***high*** *standing* 一流商店 ‖ he has long enjoyed a ***high*** *standing* in the sanitary world as the author of ... 彼は...の著者として長い間衛生の方面で高い地位を占めている. 【類】 an eminent antiquary (好古家) of ***high*** *standing* / attain the ***highest*** *standing* on competitive examination. ¶He had the ***highest general average*** *standing* in all studies. 彼はあらゆる学課目で最高の平均点を取った. ¶a man of ***high financial*** *standing* 財政的に名望ある人. ¶students of ***high scholastic*** *standing* 学殖の高い学者. ¶a family of the ***highest social*** *standing* 最も社会的地位の高い家族. ¶gain an ***honest*** *standing* in the working world 労働者仲間では正直者で通るようになる. ¶Baseball, before 1852, had ***little*** *standing* in American colleges. 一八五二年以前は野球は米国大学で余り認められていなかった. ¶an officer of ***long*** *standing* 長く勤めている官吏 ‖ a feud of ***long*** *standing* 長い間の確執. 【類】 a custom of ***long*** *standing* / a consumptive of ***long*** *standing* / a debt of ***long*** *standing* (こげつき) / There was a quarrel of ***long*** *standing* between the two families. ¶friends of ***many years'*** *standing* 多年の友人. 【類】 a problem (quarrel) of ***many years'*** *standing.* ¶degraded ***moral*** *standing* 堕落した道徳標準. ¶an educator of ***national*** *standing* 国家的名望のある教育家. ¶He is of ***no*** *standing* in society. 彼は身分が低い. ¶two friends of ***old*** *standing* 二人の昔からの友人. 【類】 an illness of ***old*** *standing.* ¶a concern of very ***old*** and ***wealthy*** *standing* 財政の豊かな老舗. ¶a friend of ***over ten years'*** *standing* 十年以上の友. ¶persons (speakers) of ***recognized*** *standing* 定評ある人々(弁士). 【類】 The firm is of ***recognized*** *standing,* qualified to render reliable and satisfactory service. ¶the ***relative*** *standing* of the five その五つの格付け ‖ change the ***relative*** *standings* 順序が変って来る(選挙の結果など). ¶attain ***reputable*** *standing* りっぱな地位を得る(俗語などが). 【類】be destined (運命になっている) to attain ***reputable standing*** in the future. ¶attain the same ***scholastic*** *standing* as ... ...と同等の学力を獲得する. ¶differ in ***social*** *standing* 社会的地位が違う. ¶an antiquary of ***some*** *standing* 相当の考古学者. ¶some institution of ***unquestioned*** *standing* あるたしかな協会.

Q² his ***average grade*** *standing* 彼の平均学業成績. ¶an institution of ***college*** *standing* 大学程度の学校. ¶lower one's ***criedt*** *standing* 信用を落す ‖ the ***credit*** *standing* of a corporation 会社の信用程度. ¶a technical school of ***junior college*** *standing* 短大程度の工業学校. ¶students of ***university*** *standing* 大学程度の学生.

P finish a work ***at*** one *standing* 一挙に仕事をしてしまう. ¶a man ***of*** *standing* 身分のある人 ‖ a Washington paper ***of*** *standing* ワシントンの一流新聞 ‖ a writer ***of*** *standing* 名のある執筆家.

P² an actor of high *standing* ***in*** his profession れっきとした俳優.

standpoint, *n.* 立脚地, 見地.

V ***explain*** one's *standpoint* publicly 天下に向って自分の立場を明かにする.

Q from an ***artistic*** (***aesthetic***, a ***biological***, ***economic***, a ***financial***, a ***geological***, ***industrial***, a ***literary***, a ***moral***, a ***practical***) *standpoint* 芸術的(美学的・生物学的・経済的・財政的・地質学的・産業的・文学的・道徳的・実際的)見地から. ¶From a ***commercial*** *standpoint* it was a failure. 商業的見地から見ればそれは失敗であった. ¶view the matter from a ***different*** *standpoint* (=angle *or* point of view) 異なった見地からそのことを見る. ¶an ***emotional*** and ***spiritual*** *standpoint* 感情的及び精神的見地. ¶The conduct is immoral from a high ***ethical*** *standpoint*. その行為は高い倫理的見地から言えば不道徳である. ¶an ***incorrect*** *standpoint* 誤っている観察点. ¶even from the mere ***monetary*** *standpoint* 単なる財政の見地から言っても. 【類】from a strictly ***moral*** *standpoint*. ¶judge the matter from an ***unbiased*** *standpoint* 不偏の見地からその件を判断する.

Q² from a ***box-office*** *standpoint* 〖映画〗営業の方(入場者数)からいうと. ¶from a ***common-sense*** *standpoint* 常識的にいって. ¶from a ***utility*** *standpoint* 実用の点から言うと.

P ***from*** the *standpoint* of an amateur in physiography 地文学におけるしろうとの見地から. 【類】***from*** the *standpoint* of a third party (第三者) / The book is a work of art, ***from*** the *standpoint* of typography (印刷), writing, and artistic photography.

standstill, *n.* 立止まり, 停止.

Q The work is at a ***complete*** *standstill*. その作業は全く停止している.

P The business is ***at*** a *standstill* for want of funds. 商売は資金欠乏のために行悩んでいる. ¶The war brought all foreign trade ***to*** a *standstill*. 戦争で外国貿易がぱったりやんだ. ‖ The train came ***to*** a *standstill*. その列車が立往生をした.

stanza, *n.* [詩の]節.

P a poem ***in*** six *stanzas* 六節から成る詩.

P² a *stanza* ***of*** six lines 六行から成る一節.

staple, *n.* 重要産物; 主成分.

V current words ***forming*** the *staple* of the language 国語の主成分を成す現代用語 ‖ The newspaper ***forms*** for many people the *staple* of daily reading. 新聞は多くの人人にとって日常読書の主体をなしている. 【類】Overwhelming ridicule and contempt are the elements which ***form*** the *staple* of their criticism.

Q the ***main*** *staple* of commerce 貿易の重要産物.

Q² the main ***food*** *staple* 主要食料品.

P² the *staple* ***of*** conversation 主要話題.

staple, *v.* 止め金でつづる.

M sheets *stapled* ***together*** with wire 止め金でつづられたなん枚かの紙.

star, *n.* 星; 運勢, 運; 花形(スター).

V ***add*** new *stars* to the celestial sphere of knowledge 知識の宇宙に新たな星を加える(学界に新知識を貢献するなど) ¶You may ***bless*** (=***thank***) your *stars* that you were not there. 君がそこにいなかったのは運がよかったのだ. ¶***catalogue*** *stars* 星の目録を作る. ¶***curse*** one's *stars* 自分の運勢をのろう. ¶***enter*** a lucky *star* うけに入る. ¶***have*** one's *star* in the ascendency うけに入る. ¶Everyone who goes to the movies ***has*** a favorite *star*. 映画見物にでかける人には皆ひいきのスターがある. ¶Last night the sky was so clear that it seemed to be ***raining*** *stars*. ゆうべは空が晴れて星が降るようであった. ¶The *stars* are ***seen*** only at night. 星は夜しか見えない. ‖ ***see*** *stars* [比ゆ的] 目から火が出る. 【類】He hit me so hard that it made me "***see*** *stars*." ¶***Thank*** my *stars!* ありがたい. ¶***trust*** one's *star* 自己の運勢を頼りにする. ¶***watch*** the *stars* in the sky at night 夜間大空の星をながめる.

V² The *star* of Spain was evidently ***setting*** in that part of the world. スペインの運勢は明かに衰えかけていた. ¶A *star* ***shot***. 星が飛んだ(流星). ¶The *stars* ***twinkle***. 星がきらきらする.

Q His *star* is ***ascendant*** (***descendant***). 彼の運勢は上り(下り)坂だ. ¶the ***bad*** *star* under which one was born 哀れな生れ合せ. ¶the Dog Star, or Sirius, is the most ***brilliant*** *star* in the heavens. おおかみ星(シリウス)は天界でもっとも明るい星である. ¶a ***first-rate*** *star* 最上の運勢. ¶delicately ***emerging*** *stars* かすかに光る星. ¶a ***flying*** *star* 夜ばい星(流星). ¶one of the most ***glamorous*** *stars* in filmdom (=cinemadom) 銀幕スター中最も光輝ある者の一人. ¶a ***guiding*** *star* 導きの星. ¶an ***international*** film *star* 国際的映画スター. ¶***literary*** *stars* of the first magnitude 文芸界の巨匠. ¶a ***lucid*** *star* 輝く星. ¶we have to thank our ***lucky*** *stars* that ... われわれは...の好運を天に謝さねばならない. 【類】He was born under a ***lucky*** *star* (好運の星). / if some ***lucky*** *star* enables one to ... ¶He is a ***new*** *star* in our team. 彼はわれわれのチームの花形新人だ. ¶an ***operatic*** *star* 歌劇界の花形. ¶The *stars* are ***out***. 星が見える. ¶the ***shining*** *star* of the truope その劇団のぴかー. ¶Oh, there goes a ***shooting*** *star!* おや, 流れ星だ! ¶a ***social*** *star* 社交界の花形. ¶the understudy of a ***theatrical*** *star* 有名な舞台俳優の代役. ¶the ***twin*** *stars* of the popular fiction firmament 大衆小説の両横綱.

Q² a ***battle*** *star* 戦闘の勇士. ¶a ***box-office*** *star* 座元のドル箱になっているスター. ¶a famous ***child*** *star* 有名な子役. ¶the ***evening*** (***morning***) *star* よい(明け)の明星. ¶a ***film*** (=***screen or movie***) *star* 映画スター. ¶a ***five-point*** *star* 星形. ¶She is the most sincerely flattered of ***Hollywood's*** *stars*. 彼女はハリウッドのスターの中で最もほめそやされている. ¶a ***horse opera*** (=western film) *star* 《米》西部もののスター(活劇王). ¶a ***motion picture*** *star* 映画スター. ¶an animal ***movie*** *star* 動物映画スター(出演動物). ¶a ***music-hall*** *star* バラエティ・ショーのスター. ¶a ***pro-ball*** *star* 《米》職業野球花形選手. ¶a ***screen cowboy*** *star* カウボーイ役の映画俳優. ¶a ***swimming*** *star* 花形水泳選手. ¶***tennis*** *stars* from all nations 各国代表のテニス選手. ¶a ***track*** *star* 陸上競技の(トラック)選手.

P ***below*** (=***beneath***) the *stars* 星の下に. ¶foretell future events ***by*** the *stars* 星で未来を予言する ‖ sleep ***under*** the *stars* 星空の下に眠る ‖ return home ***under*** the *stars* 星を載いて帰る.

P² the *stars* ***in*** the sky 空の星. ¶the *stars* ***of*** the English stage 英国劇壇の花形 ‖ She is a *star* ***of*** the first magnitude. 彼女は大立物だ.

star, *v.* 星形を付ける; 〖劇〗主役をつとめる.

P Next season she would *star* ***in*** a new play. 次季に彼女は新らしい劇のスターとなって登場するだろう. ‖ a new comedy ***in*** which Jeff and tiny tiger are *starred*. ジェフと子とらが主役を演じる新らしい喜劇 ‖ *star* it ***in*** the provinces [役者など]地方巡業をする. ¶The pages are *starred* ***with*** tears (blood, gore). その記録には涙(など)のあとが点点と付いている.

O an American film *starring* ... ...を主役にしたアメリカ映画.

starch, *n.* でん粉; のり.

V I would ***like*** more *starch* in my handkerchiefs. ハンカチにもっとのりをつけてもらいたい. ¶***put*** some *starch* in one's dress when it is washed 衣服を洗たくしてからのりをつける. ¶***take*** the *starch* out of ... ...ののりを抜く.

Q² ***corn*** (***potato, rice***) *starch* コーン(など)スターチ.

P It is formed ***from*** *starch*. それはでん粉で作る. ¶stiffen ***with*** *starch* のりで堅くする.

starch, *v.* のりをつける.

M My clothes are not *starched* ***enough***. 私の着物は十分のりがついていない. ¶It is very ***stiffly*** *starched*. それは非常に堅くのりがついている.

stardom, *n.* 花形格.

V young movie players likely to ***achieve stardom*** スターになりそうな若い映画俳優. ¶a talent that fully ***justifies*** the *stardom* she enjoys さすがは花形だけの値打がある演技力.

Q^{2} a leading figure of ***Hollywood*** *stardom* ハリウッド映画界の一流俳優.

stare, *n.* 凝視, 目をみはること.

V ***have*** a vacant *stare* ぼんやり目をみはる.

Q fix a person with an ***angry*** *stare* 人をにらみつける. ¶He gave her a ***baffled*** *stare.* 彼は力なげに彼女の顔をじっと見詰めた. ¶He looked at me with ***cold*** (***stony, glassy***) *stare.* 彼は私を冷淡に(仏頂面で, どんよりした目付で)見た. ¶all this while not a word on either side: a ***stupid*** *stare* was all the face I could put on this strange visit. すべてこの間双方とも一語もなく私はこの際ただぼんやりと目をみはるのみであった.

P ***in*** a *stare* of dumb surprise ぼう然と目をみはって. ¶***with*** a vacant *stare* ぼんやり目をみはって.

stare, *v.* 見つめる, じろじろ見る.

M *stare* ***directly*** in one's face 人の顔を真ともにじっと見る. ¶I *stared* him ***dumb.*** 彼をにらみつけてだまらした. ¶*stare* ***fixedly*** at ... ...を凝視する. ¶*stare* ***fully*** at ... ...をじっと見る. ¶*stare* ***hard*** at him 彼をじっと見つめる. ¶*stare* one's eyes ***out*** 目をむく. ¶*stare* ***vacantly*** あっけにとられる. ¶Crouching in the low chair, the young woman *stared* ***thoughtfully*** into the fire. 低いいすにうずくまってその若い婦人は考えに沈んでじっと火を見つめた. ¶*stare* ***wildly*** 恐ろしい見幕で見つめる.

M^{2} *stare* ***down*** from ... ...からじっと見おろす. ¶*stare* a person ***up*** and ***down*** 人を頭のさきから足のつまさきまでじろじろ見る.

P He continued to *stare* ***about*** her. 彼は彼女を見回わしていた. ¶He *stared* ***at*** me hard for a moment. 彼はしばし私をじっと見つめた. 【類】*stare* ***at*** a person in astonishment. ¶*stare* a person ***in*** the face 人の顔をじっと見る ‖ *stare* ***in*** bewilderment at ... あっけに取られて...を見つめる ‖ Death (Poverty, Ruin, Starvation) *stared* him ***in*** the face. 死(など)が彼の眼前に迫っていた. ‖ The fact *stares* us ***in*** the face. 厳然たる事実がわれわれに直面している. ¶*stare* ***in*** a mirror 鏡をじっと見る. ¶*stare* ***into*** the blackness (distance) 暗黒の中をのぞき込む(遠く思いをはせる) ‖ *stare* ***into*** their faces 彼らの顔をじっと見入る ‖ *stare* a person ***into*** silence 人をにらみつけて沈黙させる. ¶He *stared* ***like*** a fool. 彼はばかみたいに目をみはった. ¶He *stared* ***on*** the people around in wonder. 彼は驚いてあたりの人を見つめていた. ¶*stare* a person ***out of*** countenance 人を見つめて顔負けさせる. ¶*stare* ***with*** astonishment あ然として目をみはる ‖ *stare* ***with*** open mouth 口をぽかんとあけて見つめる ‖ I *stared* ***with*** all the eyes I had. 私は一心に見つめた.

starlet, *n.* 小役.

Q^{2} a ***film*** *starlet* 映画の子役(ベビースター).

starlight, *n.* 星明り.

P walk home ***by*** *starlight* 星明りで帰宅する. ¶***in*** the *starlight,* he saw that ... 星明りで彼は...を見た. ¶a ramble ***under*** the *starlight* 星月夜にぶらぶら歩く.

start, *n.* はっとすること; 開始, 出発; 機先.

V ***cheer*** their *start* 彼らの出発を激励する. ¶The *start* is ***fixed*** for 3 p.m. [競馬などの]始まりは午後三時ということになっている. ¶***gain*** a *start* スタートを切る. ¶He ***got*** his *start* in life in a dry goods store. 彼は呉服屋に奉公して人生のスタートを切った. ‖ You have ***got*** the *start* of me. 君は僕の機先を制した. ¶***give*** a sled (kite) a start そり(たこ)を走ら(飛ば)せる ‖ What a *start* you ***gave*** me! 君はひどく僕をおどかした(あっ, びっくりした). ¶I ***had*** the *start* of three minutes. 私は三分間先に出発した. ‖ ***have*** a *start* of ten yards in a race 競走の初めに十ヤード前に出ている. 【類】Ricci ***had*** the *start* of (より早く手を着けた) the first Protestant missionary in China by just two hundred and twenty-five years. / In elementary education Germany ***had*** a *start* of more than a century as compared with England. ¶***make*** a *start* in the morning 朝出発する ‖ ***make*** a *start* in the study of ... ...の研究を始める ‖ A *start* was ***made*** with fifty dollars for books. [図書館や本屋など]書籍費五十ドルで始めた. 【類】A *start* should be ***made*** at once. / It has not yet ***made*** a *start.* ¶the library ***owes*** its *start* to ... その図書館は...のおかげで設立された. ¶The dawn ***signaled*** the *start* of another day. 夜は明けてまた新らしい一日が始まった. ¶***take*** (=make) a fresh *start* 新規まき直しをする ‖ ***take*** one's *start* in life 世に出る.

Q The new President is to be congratulated on his ***auspicious*** *start.* 新大統領の幸先のよい出発は慶賀すべきだ. ¶He made a ***bad*** *start.* 彼は手始めがまずかった. ¶make a ***big*** *start* in this line この方面に巨歩を踏出す. ¶make an ***early*** *start* for ... ...へ早朝出発する. ¶make a ***fair*** *start* in ... 滞りなく...に着手する ‖ give A and B a ***fair*** *start* A と B を同様に不公平のないようにスタートさせる. ¶make ***false*** *starts* [競走者・力士など]スタートを誤る. ¶give ex-convicts a ***fresh*** *start* in life 前科者を更生させる. 【類】make a ***fresh*** *start* on one's problem. ¶get a ***good*** *start* in life 幸先よく世に出る ‖ A ***good*** *start* is half the battle. 〖諺〗出がよいと半ば成功したようなものだ. ¶in spite of a ***late*** *start* おそまきながら. ¶He had a ***long*** *start* of 60 yards. 彼はスタートで六十ヤードも前に出ていた. ¶try a ***new*** *start* 新らしくやり直す. ¶have a very ***promising*** *start* すこぶる有望なスタートを切る. ¶give them the ***right*** *start* in life 彼らを世の中に正しく出発させる ‖ give them a ***right*** *start* in their learning of English 彼らに英語学習の正しい道を踏出させる ‖ The ***right*** *start* in the making of the beautiful house is the proper decoration of the walls. 美しい家を造る本当の手始めは壁を巧みに装飾することだ. ¶give a ***sudden*** *start* to ... ...を急に動かす. ¶It has been a success from the ***very*** *start.* それはそもそもの始めから成功であった. ¶give it a ***violent*** *start* それを猛烈に動かす. ¶get a ***wrong*** *start* 間違った出方をする.

Q^{2} She got her ***movie*** *start* when she won a beauty contest. 彼女は美人コンクールで優勝してから映画界に入った. ¶I will give you ***60 yards*** (***fifteen seconds***) *start.* 君を六十ヤード(十五秒)前に出してやろう.

P soon ***after*** the *start* of the war 戦争ぼっ発の直後に. ¶***as*** a *start* 手始めに, まず第一に. ¶It is difficult work ***at*** the *start.* それは始めは困難な仕事だ. 【類】Three fundamental questions confront us ***at*** the *start.* / The salary ***at*** the *start* (初給) is from $900 to $1,000 a year. / ***at*** the very *start* 最初に / The idea was wrong ***at*** the *start.* ¶work ***by*** fits and *starts* 発作的に(思い出したように)働く. ¶It was doing fairly well ***for*** a *start.* それは始めにしてはかなりよく運んでいた. ‖ Lot 77. What shall I say ***for*** a *start,* gentlemen? 七十七番の口, さあ皆さん初口いくら(競売人の言葉). ¶a newsman ***from*** the *start* はえ抜きの新聞人. 【類】a success ***from*** the *start* / The game was thrilling ***from*** *start* to finish, and abounded with beautiful plays, both in the field and at bat. ‖ over again ***from*** the *start* 新規まき直しに. ¶***through*** its early *start* それが率先してやったため. ¶awake ***with*** a *start* 驚いて目を覚ます. 【類】spring (=jump) up ***with*** a *start.*

start, *v.* 出発させる; びっくりする; 飛び立つ; 始める; 出発する.

M We are ***about*** to *start.* われわれは立つ所だ. ¶*start* ***aside*** びっくりして飛びのく. ¶*start* ***away*** 飛びのく. ¶*start* ***back*** suddenly はっとして後にしりぞく. ¶*start* ***home*** 家路につく. ¶*start* ***out*** 旅行に出かける. 【類】*start* ***out*** on a speaking tour / *start* ***out*** at a full speed / They *started* ***out*** together. ‖ *start* ***out*** to reform the community in which he lives 自分の住む土地の社会改善に乗出す ‖ His eyes almost *started* ***out*** from his head. 彼は目のくり玉がとび出しそうだった. ‖ The spectacle *started* ***out*** to our view. その風景が目の前に現出した. ¶The A team *started* ***strong*** in the first inning. A チームは一回では優勢を示した.

M^{2} Will prices *start* ***down***? 物価は下るだろうか. ¶I stood squarely on my two feet and *started* ***in***! 私はしっかり足を踏みしめて演説を始めた. ¶*start* ***off*** for a ramble (journey) 散歩(など)に出掛ける ‖ *start* ***off*** at one's work 自分の仕事にとりかかる. 【類】*start* ***off*** on a holiday / *start* ***off*** upon one's expedition. / The phonebook (電話帳) *starts* ***off*** with the letter A. ¶He *started* ***up*** at the sound. 彼はその物音ではっとした. 【類】*start* ***up*** in horror ‖ Many difficulties have *started* ***up.*** 多くの困難が起った.

P I *started* ***after*** him in hot haste. 私は大急ぎで彼を追った. ¶*start* ***against*** ... ...に反対してけっ起する. ¶He *started* his career ***as*** a newspaperman. 彼は新聞記者を振出しにして世に立った. ¶We *start* ***at*** six. われわれは六時に

出発する. 【類】the train which *starts* ***at*** eight. ‖ He *started* ***at*** the sound of my voice. 彼は私の声を聞いてびっくりした. ‖ *starting* ***at*** the sight of him 彼を見てびっくりして ‖ *start* ***at*** the bottom instead of the top 上からでなく下から振出す(低い身分から立上がる) ‖ *start* ***at*** $250 a month 初任給二百五十ドルだ. ¶*start* ***down*** the street むこうの方へ歩き始める. ¶He will soon *start* ***for*** home. 彼はすぐ帰国する. 【類】I am going to *start* ***for*** London. / *start* ***for*** a visit to ... / *start* ***for*** a tour round the world / *start* ***for*** a sail / *start* ***for*** the seat (=theatre) of war (戦地) ‖ *start* ***for*** post 赴任の途に上る. ¶The tears *started* ***from*** her eyes. 涙が彼女の目から出た. ‖ He *started* ***from*** his seat. 彼はびっくりしていすから立った. ‖ The great railway lines of England all *start* ***from*** London. 英国の大鉄道線路は皆ロンドンから出ている. ‖ enable the next generation to *start* ***from*** a higher vantage ground than its predecessor 次の時代の人々がその先代の人々よりも一層有利な地点から出発できるようにさせる ‖ a fire *starting* ***from*** one's own house 自火 ‖ He *started* ***from*** his sleep. 彼はびっくりして目をさました. ¶*start* ***in*** business in Kobe 神戸で商売を始める ‖ *start* ***in*** life with these equipments こうした準備をして世の中へ出る, 世渡りを始める. 【類】a young man *starting* ***in*** life / He *started* ***in*** life very heavily handicapped (はなはだしく不利な立場で). ‖ The fire *started* ***in*** a cottage. 火は小屋から出た. ‖ The society was *started* ***in*** 1890. その協会は一八九〇年に出来た. ‖ *start* ***in*** pursuit of ... ...を追って行く ‖ *start* one's son ***in*** business 自分の子どもに商売を始めさせる ‖ *start* men ***in*** a race 競走でランナーにスタートを切らせる. ¶The statue is traditioned to have *started* ***into*** life. その立像は動き出したという伝説がある. ‖ *start* ***into*** song 急に歌い始める ‖ *start* ***into*** view たちまち現われる. ¶*start* ***on*** a tour in China 中国漫遊に出かける. 【類】*start* ***on*** one's tour of (= travel round) the world / holidaymakers *starting* ***on*** their trips. / a theatrical company (劇団) *starting* ***on*** a tour / *start* on one's journey ‖ Perspiration *started* ***on*** her brow. 汗が彼女の額に出た. ‖ *start* a party ***on*** an expedition 一行を遠足に出発させる ‖ *start* him ***on*** one of his favorite topics 彼に得意の問題の一つを話し出させる ‖ It is difficult to realize that in London a baby *starts* ***on*** its life march every five minutes. ロンドンでは五分ごとに赤ちゃんが生れるというがちょっと想像に浮ばないことだ. ‖ *start* ***on*** the trail of ... ...のあとをつける(追跡する) ‖ get *started* ***on*** one's literary work [文士が]作品にとりかかる. ¶*start* ***out of*** bed 寝床から飛び出す ‖ ... when his eyes were *starting* ***out of*** his head その時彼の目はとび出していた(びっくりして). ¶Tears *started* ***to*** their eyes. 涙が彼らの目に浮かんだ. ‖ *start* ***to*** one's feet びっくりして立上がる. ¶*start* ***up*** a mountain 山を登り始める. ¶He was *starting* ***upon*** the right way. 彼は正しい道を踏むようになった. ¶*start* ***with*** fright 驚いて飛び上る, はっとする ‖ *Starting* ***with*** little, he accomplished an outstanding achievement. 始めは微々たるものだったが彼は目ざましい成功をなし遂げた. ‖ to *start* (=bigin) ***with***=in the first place まず第一に. 【類】You have no right to be here, to *start* ***with***. ‖ He had no capital to *start* ***with***. 彼は第一資本がなかった. 【類】We had six members to *start* ***with***. / He has a respectable knowledge of Roman history to *start* ***with***. / I will pay you twelve dollars a week to *start* ***with***. ‖ This book *starts* ***with*** a tale of country. この本はいなかの物語から始まる. 【類】The dictionary *starts* [*off*] ***with*** the letter A.

O It is *starting* to rain. 雨が降り出して来た. ¶I *started* to turn away. 私はその場を去ろうとした.

starter, *n.* 始める人(もの).

P ***as*** (=***for***) a *starter* 手始めに, いの一番に. ¶***Of*** the 10 *starters*, only six finished. スタートした時は十人だったがゴールに入ったのは六人だけだった.

starting, *n.* 出発, 開始.

Q it is a ***good*** *starting* for those who wish to scale the peaks of ... それは...の諸峰を踏破しようとする人々にはよい足場である.

P I have not taken a round-trip ticket ***at*** *starting*. 私は出発するときに回遊乗車券を買わなかった.

starting-off, *n.* 出発.

P² the *starting-off* ***of*** a Sunday School treat 日曜学校生徒の遠足出発.

starting-point, *n.* 出発点.

V ***form*** the most appropriate *starting-point* 最も適当な出発場となる. ¶It was ***made*** the *starting-point*. そこから出発した. ¶This ***provides*** a new *starting-point*. これが新らしい出発点になる.

P² this is the best *starting-point* ***for*** the ascent of ... ... 登山にはこれが一番良い出発点である. ¶a *starting-point* ***of*** ships for Alaska アラスカ行船舶の出発点.

startle, *v.* びっくりさせる.

P I was *startled* ***at*** (=***by***) the news. その便りを聞いて(見て)びっくりした. ‖ He was *startled* ***at*** the sight. 彼はその有様を見てびっくりした. ¶*startle* a person ***from*** sleep 人をびっくりさせて目をさます. ¶be *startled* ***to*** swoon 目を回す.

starvation, *n.* 飢餓, 餓死.

V ***face*** *starvation* 飢餓に直面する. ¶***ward off*** *starvation* 飢餓を防ぐ.

Q² prevent ***mass*** *starvation* due to the great scarcity of rice 極度の米不足による大量飢餓を阻止する. ¶die from ***vitamin*** *starvation* ビタミンの欠乏で死ぬ.

P reduce a castle ***by*** *starvation* 城を兵糧攻めにする. ¶They had a miraculous escape ***from*** *starvation*. 彼らは奇跡的に餓死をまぬかれた. ¶They were reduced to the verge ***of*** *starvation*. 彼らは飢餓にひんするに至った. ¶We were brought face to face ***with*** *starvation*. われわれは飢餓に直面した.

starve, *v.* 餓死させる; 餓死する.

M I am ***almost*** *starved*. 非常に空腹だ. ¶The garrison was *starved* ***out***. 守備隊は兵糧攻めにされた.

P a child *starving* ***for*** affection 愛情に飢えている子供. 【類】*starve* ***for*** knowledge (information, news, friendship). ¶*starve* the garrison ***into*** surrender 守備隊を兵糧攻めにして降服させる ‖ *starve* ***into*** submission 食わせずにおいて言うことをきかせる. ¶be *starved* ***of*** food (drink, sleep) 食料(など)欠乏している. ¶He *starves* ***on*** a salary of 5,000 yen a month. 彼は月給五千円でひもじい思いをしている. ¶*starve* a person ***to*** death 人を餓死させる. 【類】He was *starved* ***to*** death. ¶*starve* ***with*** hunger (cold) 飢(など)で死ぬ.

O I'm simply *starving*. 腹ぺこだ.

state, *n.* (**1**) 状態, 形勢, 有様.

V It completely ***altered*** the *state* in Russia. それがロシアの国情を一変した. ¶***bring about*** a better *state* of affairs よりよい事態を生じさせる. ¶Motion pictures can ***create*** the *state* of mind that ultimately means peace or war. 映画は結局平和か戦争に持って行く精神状態を造り出すことができる. ¶***end*** the *state* of war between the two countries 両国間の戦争状態を終結する. ¶It only ***made*** the patient's *state* worse. そのためにかえって病人の容体が悪くなった. ¶***reach*** an advanced *state* of civilization 高度の文化に達する. ¶A *state* of complete safety is not quite ***re-established***. 完全な安全状態にはまだなっていない. ¶until the stomach ***resumes*** its normal *state* 胃が常態に復するまで. ¶***reveal*** the *state* of mind of ... ...の心理状態を明らかにする.

Q The ***actual*** *state* of the country is cheering. その国の実情は有望だ. ¶consumptive patients in an ***advanced*** *state* (=stage) 病勢の進んだ肺病患者 ‖ The corpse was in an ***advanced*** *state* of decomposition. 死体は相当腐敗していた. ¶In its ***amended*** *state* it will come into force. それは修正の上実施になるだろう. ¶an ***amorphous*** *state* of substance 物質の無定形態. ¶this ***appalling*** *state* of things この驚くべき形勢. ¶remain in a ***backward*** *state* of civilization 文化が遅れている. ¶I am in a ***bad*** *state* of health. 体の具合が悪い. ‖ My house is in a ***bad*** *state*. 私の家は荒れ果てている. ¶a ***better*** *state* of things よりよい情勢. ¶the attainment of a ***bilingual*** *state* 両国語併用状態の達成. ¶pass into a ***chronic*** *state* [病気が]慢性になる. ¶be in a ***chronic inflammatory*** *state* 慢性炎症を起している. ¶He has fallen into a ***comatose*** *state*. 彼はこん睡状態に陥った. ¶The street is in a ***congested*** *state*. 往来は雑踏している. 【類】the ***congested*** *state* of our schools and colleges / the ***congested*** *state* of traffic. ¶China was in a ***continual*** *state* of disturbance. 中国は始終乱れていた. ¶He is in a ***critical*** *state*. 彼は危篤の容態にある. ¶the ***crucial*** *state* of the world food problem 深刻な世界の食糧事情. 【類】The talks reached a ***crucial*** *state*. ¶be in a very ***dangerous*** *state* 危険状態にある. ¶the ***dark*** *state* of the weather 曇天. ¶a ***defective mental*** *state* 欠陥のある

精神状態. ¶a city in ***defenseless state*** 無防備状態にある都市. ¶one who is in a ***delicate state*** of health 健康のすぐれない人. ¶a very ***deplorable state*** of affairs きわめてなげかわしい形勢. ¶He is in a very ***depressed state.*** 彼は非常にふさいでいる. ‖ in the present ***depressed state*** of business この不況の場合に. 【類】the ***depressed state*** of trade. ¶in a ***desponding state*** of mind 力を落して. ¶in a ***dirty state*** よごれて. ¶this ***discouraging state*** of things この悲観的事態. ¶the ***disturbed state*** of the country 同国の混乱状態. 【類】owing to the ***disturbed state*** of the market. ¶in a ***dying state*** 死にひんして. ¶The finances of the company were in an ***embarrassed state.*** その会社は財政困難に陥っていた. ¶in an ***excellent state*** of preservation 見事に保存されて. ¶in an ***excited state*** of mind 興奮状態で ‖ the ***excited state*** of market 高騰市況. ¶the remedy for the ***existing unsatisfactory state*** of affairs 不満足な現状に対する救済策. ¶in a remarkably ***fine state*** of preservation 非常に見事に保存されて. ¶water in its ***frozen state*** 氷になった水. ¶the ***future state*** 来世(後生). ¶The patient is in a ***good state*** of nutrition. 病人の栄養は良好である. 【類】The book is in a ***good state*** of preservation. ¶a ***grave state*** of affairs 容易ならぬ形勢. ¶in a ***half finished state*** 半成の状態に. ¶What would be the ***happy state*** of mind of the people if ...? もし...なら人々の心はどんなに幸福だろう. ¶in a (=the) ***healthy state*** 健全な状態で. ¶in a ***high state*** of indignation 非常に憤慨して ‖ bring high schools to a ***high state*** of efficiency 高等学校の能率を上げる. 【類】a ***high state*** of civilization. ¶a ***lamentable state*** of things 嘆かわしい事態. ¶the ***larval state*** of an insect こん虫の幼虫態. ¶a ***liquid state*** 液状. ¶in the ***low state*** of the tides 退潮時には. ¶the analysis of ***mental states*** 精神状態の分析. 【類】the patient's ***mental state.*** ¶He sank into a ***misanthropic state*** of mind. 彼はえん世的な精神状態に陥った. ¶a ***miserable state*** 哀れな有様. ¶the existing ***national state*** 現今の国状. ¶The question is still in a ***nebulous state.*** その問題はまだ目鼻がつかない. ¶All is back to its ***normal state.*** すべてが平常に復した. 【類】The river is in its ***normal state.*** ¶in a partially ***nude state*** 一部裸体状態で. ¶a ***poetic state*** of mind 詩情. ¶The men injured are in a very ***precarious state.*** けが人は危篤だ. ¶the ***present state*** of things 現今の形勢. 【類】in the ***present state*** of our good health (great excitement, nudity, semi-nudity) / in the ***present state*** of public opinion / be unable in the ***present state*** of the copyright law (著作権法) to ... / Probably a complete explanation, in the ***present state*** of our knowledge, is not possible. / It is a question which cannot be answered in our ***present state*** of knowledge. / in the ***present state*** of our knowledge, we are not in a position to be precise as to ... / cannot be ascertained in the ***present state*** of our knowledge. ¶They believed that something connected with a ***previous state*** of existence determined what takes place in this life. 彼らは前世と現世との因果関係のあることを信じていた. ¶the ***psychic state*** in pregnancy 妊婦の精神状態. ¶emergence from the ***pupal state*** さなぎ状態からの脱出. ¶in a ***pure state*** 無垢(?)で. ¶The meat was in a ***putrid state.*** 肉は腐敗していた. ¶in a ***rudimentary state*** 発育不全で. ¶What a ***sad state*** of affairs! いかにも悲しいことだ. ¶I found him in the ***same state.*** 彼は相変らずであった. 【類】much the ***same state*** of things exist in ... ¶men in a ***savage state*** 野蛮人. ¶the ***scandalous state*** of ecclesiastical morals in the Middle Ages 中世における僧徒のなさけない堕落ぶり. ¶in a ***semi-nude state*** 半裸体で. ¶The markets are in a very ***sensitive state.*** 市況はすこぶる敏感になっている. ¶a ***serious state*** of affairs has risen at ... 由々しい事態が...に起った. ¶The ship was towed ashore in a ***sinking state*** 船は沈没状態で岸辺に引寄せられた. 【類】The ship was abandoned in a ***sinking state.*** ¶owing to the ***swollen state*** of the river by heavy rain 豪雨による川の増水のため. ¶a ***tranquil, untroubled state*** of mind 平静で苦労のない精神状態. ¶The country is in a ***troubled state.*** その国は乱れている. ¶a ***true state*** of its financial position その財政の実状. ¶an ***unsatisfactory state*** of affairs 不満足な事態. ¶The country is in an ***unsettled state.*** その国は不安状態にある. ¶Things were in an ***untidy state.*** なにやかや取散らかっていた. ¶in the ***waking (sleeping) state*** 目をさまして(眠って)いるとき. ¶***What*** a ***state*** you are in! なんというざまだ! ¶return to the ***wild state*** [家畜など]野生状態に還る.

Q² be in a ***transition state*** (=stage) 過渡期にある. ¶under the current ***world state*** of affairs 世界の現状では.

P ***in*** (=under) this ***state*** of things この状態で ‖ be ***in*** a ***state*** of flux あげ潮状態(上り坂)にある ‖ ***in*** a ***state*** of insensibility 人事不省となって ‖ The room was ***in*** a ***state*** of chaos after the burglar had left. へやは夜盗の去った後はてんやわんやだった. ‖ Owing to the Napoleonic wars, Germany was then ***in*** a ***state*** of extreme disorder. ナポレオン戦争の影響でドイツは目も当てられぬ状態だった. ‖ ***in*** a ***state*** of unstable equilibrium 不安定な均勢状態にある ‖ when the mind is still ***in*** a ***state*** of plasticity 心がまだ素直になっているときに ‖ The country was then ***in*** a ***state*** of nature. その国は当時未開の状態にあった. 【類】people living ***in*** a ***state*** of nature / he is ***in*** such a ***state*** of nervousness that ... / ***in*** a ***state*** of confusion (rest, transition, cultivation, depression, emergency) / ***in*** a ***state*** of ecstasy (=rapture ***or*** self absorption) / whilst ***in*** a ***state*** of intoxication (酔っぱらって). ¶We are ***in*** a ***state*** of peace with all nations. われわれは万邦と平和状態にある ‖ The industry was then ***in*** a ***state*** of doldrums. 当時産業は不振状態だった. ‖ ***in*** a ***state*** of primeval buff《俗》真裸で. ¶put an end ***to*** this ***state*** of matters (=affairs ***or*** things) この事態を打破する. ¶***under*** a civilized ***state*** of society 文明の社会状態の下に.

P² a ***state of*** mind so common among laborers 労働者間にきわめて普通の精神状態 ‖ with the desire of obviating this unsatisfactory ***state of*** things この不満足な形勢を一新しようとして ‖ the ***state of*** weather at Nikko 日光の天気模様. ¶a ***state of*** dejection 失意状態 ‖ a ***state of*** extremity 行き過ぎの状態. 【類】the ***state*** of his health / There was a ***state of*** war between the two countries / a ***state of*** peace has not yet been restored between ... / the ***state of*** the weather ‖ the ***state of*** things is such ⌊that ...

(**2**) [しばしば S-] 国家; 国務; 《米》[S-] 州.

V ***govern*** a ***state*** 国を治める. ¶***organize*** a ***state*** 国家を組織する. ¶***subvert*** a ***state*** 国家を滅ぼす. ¶Here is where ***State*** should ***interfere.*** こんな場合には国家が干渉すべきだ.

Q ***all*** the ***States*** in the Union《米》米全州. ¶highly ***armed states*** 軍備の充実した国家. ¶Maine, a ***cold bleak maritime State*** 寒くて殺風景な海浜の(米国)メイン州. ¶a ***constitutional state*** 立憲国. ¶***contending states*** 交戦国. ¶***dependent states*** 属国. ¶***friendly states*** 友好諸国家. ¶It has disappeared as an ***independent state.*** その国は滅びてしまった. ¶a ***maritime state*** 海洋国家. ¶all of the ***principal states*** of the world 全世界の主要国家. ¶a fully ***self-governing State*** 完全な自治を有する国. ¶the ***sovereign states*** of the western hemisphere 西半球の独立諸国家. ¶the ***sovereign Princely States*** of India インドの諸侯国. ¶a ***totalitarian state*** 全体主義国家. ¶a ***tributary state*** 進貢国(属国). ¶a ***vassal state*** 属国. ¶a ***well-ordered state*** 秩序のよく保たれている国家.

Q² the ***Arab States*** アラブ諸国. ¶the ***Atlantic seaboard States*** 大西洋岸諸国. ¶the ***banner State*** for ... ...では第一位の国. ¶the ***Badger State*** (Wisconsin 州の異称). ¶a ***buffer state*** 緩衝国 ‖ The British kept Afghanistan under control as a ***buffer state.*** 英国はアフガニスタンを緩衝国として支配下においていた. ¶a ***capitalist*** (socialist) ***State*** 資本(社会)主義諸国. ¶the ***city states*** of ancient Greece 古ギリシアの都市国家. ¶an ***enemy State*** 敵国. ¶an ***ex-enemy State*** 旧敵国. ¶a ***fascist state*** ファッショ国家. ¶his ***home State*** 彼の故国(の州). ¶Texas is still an ***infant State*** テキサスはいまだに幼児状態の州である. ¶***member States*** of the treaty 同条約の署名諸国. ¶a ***monarchist state*** 君主国. ¶a ***one-party State*** 一党国. ¶the ***Pacific coast States***《米》太平洋沿岸諸州. ¶a ***paper State*** 名目だけの国家. ¶a now defunct ***puppet State*** 消失したかいらい国. 【類】Manchukuo, one-time ***puppet State*** of Japan / the old Nazi ***puppet state*** of Slovakia. ¶former Germen ***satellite States*** in Europe 欧州の旧ドイツ衛星諸国. ¶European ***Soviet bloc States*** 欧州ソ連圏諸国. ¶a ***vassal State*** れい属国家. ¶a ***welfare State*** 福祉国家.

P offenses ***against*** the *state* 国家に対する罪. ¶the nobles ***in*** a *state* 一国の貴族. ¶Ministers ***of*** *State* 国務大臣 ‖ Secretary ***of*** *State* 《米》国務長官；《英》国務相 ‖ devote oneself to the service ***of*** the *state* 国務に一身をゆだねる. ‖ affairs ***of*** the *State*＝State affairs 国事.

(**3**) 身分；威儀, 儀礼.

V a style of dress ***befitting*** one's *state* 身分相応の服装様式. ¶***keep*** one's *state* 自己の威儀を保つ.

Q The ambassador travelled in ***great*** *state*. その大使は物物しい大名旅行をした. ¶The King went with ***royal*** *state* to the House of Lords. 国王は威儀堂々と上院に御出席になった.

P The King traveled ***in*** *state*. 国王は威儀堂々と旅行した. ‖ over there ***in*** the *States* アメリカでは(外国からみて). ¶a coach ***of*** *state* 儀式の馬車 ‖ on occasions ***of*** *state* 儀式の折に.

state, *v.* 述べる, 言う.

M to *state* it ***briefly*** それをかいつまんで言うと ‖ such, ***briefly*** *stated*, is the argument, pro and con, as to ... ...に関する賛否の意見は単的に言ってこのようなものである. ¶*state* ***categorically*** 一概に言う. ¶*state* ***clearly*** and ***impartially*** the cause of ... 明りょうかつ公平に...の理由を述べる. ¶*state* ***concisely*** 簡潔に述べる. ¶*state* ***definitely*** きっぱりと述べる. ¶to *state* it ***differently*** 言葉を換えて言えば. ¶***distinctly*** *state* はっきりと言う. ¶***emphatically*** *state* 力を入れて言う. ¶be ***erroneously*** *stated* 誤記してある. ¶*state* very ***explicitly*** きわめて明白に述べる. ¶***facetiously*** *state* たわむれに言う. ¶it must be ***frankly*** *stated* that ... ...は率直に述べねばならない. ¶as has been sometimes ***jocosely*** *stated* 時折冗談に言ったように. ¶Men of great learning are frequently unable to *state* ***lucidly*** what they know fully. 大学者は往々自分のよく知っていることを明りょうに述べられないことがある. ¶His definition of statistics is *stating* ***mathematically*** what the compiler does not know. 彼の統計学の定義は「編集者が知らないことを数学的に記述すること」である. ¶He *stated* the case ***mildly***. 彼はその事件を穏かに述べた. ¶*state* ***openly*** 腹蔵なく述べる. ‖ *state* it ***openly*** それを公然と言う. ¶it may be *stated* ***parenthetically***. 割り注的に述べると(ちなみに記す). ¶*state* ***plainly*** and ***unmistakably*** 率直にしかも誤りなく述べる. ¶*state* it ***practically*** by illustrations それを実例で示す. ¶as ***previously*** *stated* 前述のように. ¶*stated* ***reversely*** 裏を返せば. ¶it is ***semi-officially*** *stated* that ... ...と半官的に報じてある. ¶***unhesitatingly*** *state* that ... ためらいなく...と述べる. ¶*state* ***unreservedly*** 腹蔵なく述べる.

M² as *stated* ***above*** (***below***) 上(下)記の通り.

P the reason, *stated* ***in*** a word, is that ... 一言で言えばその理由は...だ ‖ *state* it ***in*** detail それを詳細に述べる. 【類】as *stated* ***in*** the preceding chapter. ¶*state* it ***on*** oath それを宣誓して述べる.

Q He *stated* such and such to be the case. 彼は事実はかくかくだと述べた.

statecraft, *n.* 政治的手腕.

P It gave him credit ***for*** his *statecraft*. それで彼の政治的手腕が確められた.

statehood, *n.* 《米》州制.

P realize their hope ***of*** *statehood* 州制への希望を達成する.

P² *Statehood* ***for*** Hawaii ハワイの州制(現在の準州に対して).

statement, *n.* 陳述；声明(ステートメント)；〔商〕明細書, 一覧表.

V His *statements* should not be ***accepted*** without verification. 彼の陳述は確証なしには真に受けてはいけない. ¶***affirm*** the *statement* to be true その陳述を確認する. ¶***back up*** general *statements* with specific illustrations 一般的な陳述を特殊の例証で補う. ¶This *statement* is not ***borne out*** by my experience. この陳述は私の経験によって実証されてはいない. ¶He ***called*** my *statement* in question. 彼は私の陳述に不審を言立てた. ¶I ***confirmed*** his *statement* by testimony. 私は証拠をあげて彼の陳述に偽りないことを証明した. ¶authoritatively ***contradict*** a *statement* 権威的に陳述に反対する. 【類】***contradict*** a *statement* point-blank (率直に). ¶strongly ***corroborate*** (＝bear out) one's *statement* その陳述を力強く確証する. ¶We can hardly ***credit*** his *statement*. 彼の言うことはほとんど信じられない. ¶***deny*** the *statement* made in ... ...で出した声明を否認する. ¶***disprove*** the *statement* that ... ...という陳述の反証をあげる. ¶***endorse*** most emphatically a *statement* made by ... ...の陳述をきわめて力強く是認する. ¶***give*** a complete and unprejudiced *statement* of ... ...を完全かつ公平に陳述する. ¶The educational authorities ***gave out*** the following *statement*. 文部省当局は次のステートメントを発表した. ¶occasionally one ***hears*** now the *statement* that ... われわれは昨今...ということをしばしば耳にする. ¶The authorities ***issued*** the following *statement*. 当局は次の声明を発した. 【類】***issue*** a *statement* saying that ... ¶We ***maintain*** our previous *statement*. われわれの考えは前述した所と変らない. ¶***make*** a *statement* 声明する. ¶***prepare*** a tabulated *statement* of ... ...の陳述事項を表に作る. ¶***present*** an impartial *statement* of the situation 事態の公平な陳述をする. ¶***prove*** one's *statement* その陳述を証拠立てる. 【類】The *statement* can be ***proved***. ¶***rectify*** a *statement* 声明を訂正する. ¶the *statement* ***referred to*** occurs in ... 前述の話は...に出ている. ¶a *statement* has often been ***repeated*** that ... ...という話はしばしば繰返された. ¶It ***requires*** clearer *statement*. それは一層明白な陳述を要する. ¶***retract*** one's former *statements* with the utmost frankness きわめていさぎよく前言を取消す. ¶***set forth*** a clear *statement* of ... ...を明りょうに陳述する. ¶I ***take*** your *statement* on trust. 私は君の言うがままに信じる. ‖ ***take*** a *statement* too generally 陳述を正直に取り過る. ¶***withdraw*** one's *statement* 陳述を取消す.

V² The *statement* ***reads*** well. その記事は分かりやすく書いてある. ¶His *statement* does not ***square*** with yours. 彼の言う所は君のと一致しない.

Q To assert that ... is to make too ***absolute*** a *statement*. ...と断言したのでは余りに言過ぎる. ¶The *statement* is too transparently ***absurd*** to need refutation. その論は余りばかさ加減が見えすいているので論ばくする必要を見ない. ¶He made this ***amazing*** *statement*. 彼がこの驚くべき話をした. ¶a ***bold*** *statement* 大胆な陳述. ¶the ***clear*** *statement* of a principle (facts) 原理(など)の明せきな所説. ¶***compact*** *statements* 簡潔な陳述. ¶***conflicting*** *statements* 矛盾する陳述. ¶This is the most ***conservative*** *statement* I have ever seen in print. これは印刷されたものでは始めて見る最も内輪の意見である. ¶a ***contradictory*** *statement* つじつまの合わない話. ¶The above is a ***correct*** *statement*. 右の通りです. ‖ a ***correct*** *statement* of financial condition 経済状態の正確な明細書. 【類】A ***correct*** *statement* is now under way. ¶a ***definite*** *statement* 明確な陳述. ¶a ***demi*** (＝***semi***)-***official*** *statement* 半公式の声明. ¶give a ***detailed*** *statement* of the finances of the Empire 帝国の財政を詳述する ‖ a ***detailed*** *statement* of profit and loss 損益明細計算書. ¶a ***dispassionate, authoritative*** *statement* of the Chinese position 中国の情勢の公平にして権威ある叙述. ¶various ***erroneous*** *statements* have been circulated concerning ... ...に関する色々な誤った意見が流布された. ¶a ***fair*** and ***unbiased*** *statement* of the facts 公平無私の事実の陳述. ¶a ***fake*** *statement* of one's academic career 学歴詐称. ¶***financial*** *statements* 財務諸表. ¶the ***first authentic*** *statement* about ... is made in A.D. ... ...について確実な最初の記事が見えているのは紀元...年である. ¶a ***foggy*** *statement* ばく然たる叙述. ¶the ***foregoing*** *statement* 以上の陳述. ¶a ***frank*** *statement* 赤裸々の陳述. ¶send a ***full*** *statement* 明細書を送る. ¶a ***general*** *statement* 概説. ¶an ***impartial*** *statement* of facts 事実の公平な陳述. ¶make the very ***inexact*** *statement* that ... というすこぶる不正確な陳述をする. ¶an ***itemized*** *statement* 内訳. ¶a ***lucid*** *statement* 明せきな陳述. ¶a ***mere*** *statement* of facts 単なる事実の陳述. ¶a very ***mild*** *statement* of the case 事件の内輪な言い方. ¶grossly ***misleading*** *statements* 大いに人を誤らせる陳述. ¶a grossly ***misrepresented*** *statement* 事実とはなはだしく相違した陳述. ¶To say that at the most it makes a mountain out of a molehill would be a very ***moderate*** *statement*. 高々それは針ほどのことを棒ほどに言うだけのことだと批評するのは至極穏当な所であろう. ¶give an ***objective*** *statement* of the background of an important event 重要事件の背景を客観的に記述する. ¶No ***official*** *statement* has been made. なんら公式の声明はない. ¶It was the ***only*** *statement* they made then. それが当時彼らのなしたただ一つの声明であった. ¶the ***opening*** *statement* [公判の]冒頭陳述. ¶an ***oral*** *statement* 口頭の陳述. ¶It is a ***plain*** *statement* of fact, without any coloring. それは少しも文飾を加えないありのままの事実の陳述だ ‖ a ***plain*** and ***truthful*** *statement* 簡潔で真実の陳述. 【類】

make a *plainer statement*. ¶a *pleasing statement* うれしい言葉. ¶a *poetical statement* 詩的な叙述. ¶a *prophetic statement* 予言的陳述. ¶make a *public statement* of its findings その査定の結果を公表する. ¶a *rambling statement* 冗漫な陳述. ¶make a *remarkable statement* 注目すべき陳述をする. ¶a *rough statement* 概説. ¶make a *startling statement* はっとするような陳述をする. ¶The *statement* has never been authoritatively *substantiated*. その声明に対してなんら力ある証明がなされなかった. ¶a *summarizing statement* 概説. ¶a *surprising statement*=a bolt from the blue 意外な陳述. ¶a *sweeping statement* 十ぱ一からげの話. ¶declare in a *sworn statement* that ... 誓って…と言明する ‖ a *sworn* (an *unsworn*) *statement* before a local notary 地方公証人を前にしての(無)宣誓陳述. ¶a *tabular statement* 図表的一覧. ¶a *temperate statement* 穏かな話. ¶a *tentative statement* might be made as follows: 次のような暫定的陳述がなされよう. ¶a *trite statement* 陳腐な話. ¶a *true* (an *untrue*) *statement* 本当(うそ)の話. ¶an *unfounded* (=a *groundless*) *statement* でたらめな陳述. ¶an *unsupported statement* 賛成されない意見. ¶a *vague statement* ばく然たる陳述. ¶a *verbal statement* 口述. ¶a *wild statement* 突飛な陳述(話). ¶a *written statement* 陳述書.

Q² an *alarmist statement* 戦争恐怖者の言葉. ¶a *liquidation statement* 〖商〗破産精算書. ¶*contract statements* made by ... …間の契約書. ¶a *fact statement* 事実の陳述. ¶a *first-person* (*second-person, third-person*) *statement* 当事者(相手方, 第三者)の陳述. ¶a *government statement* said that ... 政府の声明によれば…であった. ¶a *hearsay statement* 伝聞の陳述. ¶a *job statement* 職務の説明. ¶a *key statement* 主要陳述. ¶a *matter-of-fact statement* 無味乾燥な陳述. ¶a *policy statement* 政策綱領. ¶a *registration statement* 届書.

P *according to* the *statement* made by ... …の話では. ¶There is something *behind* his *statement*. 彼の話の裏面にはなにかある. ¶I have the best, the highest authority *for* my *statement*. 私の言うことには最善最高の典拠がある. ¶The truth cannot be known *from* (=on) his *statement* alone. 彼の陳述だけでは本当のことは分からない. ¶throw doubt *on* one's *statement* その言うことを疑う. ¶She is eighteen *upon* her own *statement*. 彼女は自分では十八歳だと言っている.

P² is being pressed on all sides to give a satisfactory *statement concerning* ... …に関して満足な陳述を与えるよう四方八方から迫られている. ¶the *statement of* a case 一事件の申立 ‖ simply a new *statement of* old truth 古い真理を新らしく言い直しただけ ‖ a *statement of* accounts 勘定書 ‖ a *statement of* reason 理由書. ¶make a *statement on* a question (subject) 問題(など)に関して陳述する. ¶make a *statement respecting* ... …に関して陳述する.

stateside, *a., ad.* [海外の米人からみて]米本国の(に).

P I haven't been *stateside for* three years. [米人が]三年本国に帰らない.

O *stateside* news (fashion) 米国だより(など).

statesman, *n.* 政治家.

V The *statesman* is much *occupied* with affairs of state. その政治家は国事に追われている. ¶A great *statesman* has *sprung up*. 一大政治家が出現した. 「だ.

V He is young as *statesmen go*. 政治家としては彼は若い方

Q *broad-minded* and *far-seeing statesmen* 心の広い考えの遠大な政治家. ¶a *clear-headed statesman* 頭脳明せきな政治家. ¶a *constructive statesman* 建設的政治家. ¶the *Elder Statesmen* [日本の]元老. ¶a *first-rank statesman* 一流政治家. ¶a *practical statesman* 実際的政治家.

Q² a *clear-vision statesman* 賢明な政治家. ¶a *warrior statesman* 軍人政治家.

P This monument is in memory *of* a great *statesman*. これはある大政治家の記念碑だ.

statesmanship, *n.* 政治的手腕; 経綸(りん).

Q *acquisitive statesmanship* 射利的政治手腕. ¶*blundering statesmanship* 失策の多い政治のやり方. ¶It was due to *British statesmanship* that war had been avoided. 戦争が避けられたのは英国政治家の手腕によったのであった. ¶*far-seeing statesmanship* 卓識の経綸(りん). ¶*high statesmanship* りっぱな政治家的手腕. ¶a *robust* and *vigorous statesmanship* 腰が強くて強力な政治的手腕.

station, *n.* (1) 部署; 地位; 場所.

V *fill* properly one's *station* in life 人生における自己の地位を適当に占める. ¶*install* a wireless *station* 無線放送所を設ける. ¶*keep* one's *station* [軍艦など]列位を保つ. ¶*know* one's *station* 自己の分をわきまえている. ¶amateur enthusiasts who *operate* their private wireless *stations* 自分の無線室を持っているしろうとの熱心家. ¶the *station* was further *re-enforced* by the arrival of ... その陣地は…の到着によって一層補強された. ¶*take* one's *station* before the outer gate 門前に陣取る. ¶He *took up* his *station* near the front. 彼は正面に近く陣取った. 【類】Just before her having the berth the officers *took up* their various *stations* (各部署についた) on the ship.

Q in *all stations* of life あらゆる社会層において. ¶I took up a *convenient station*. 私は便利な位置を占めた. ¶live in luxury due to his *exalted station* 彼の高い身分にふさわしいぜいたくをして暮す. ¶young men of undoubtedly *good station* 確かにりっぱな身分の青年. ¶Singapore is the *half-way station* of the world. シンガポールは世界の中間寄港地だ. ¶a man of *high station* 身分の高い人. ¶persons of *humble station* (=in a humble *station*) 卑しい身分の人. 【類】be in the *humblest station* in society (社会の下積). ¶a *local station* 〖ラジオ〗地方放送局 (key station に対し). ¶a *meteorological station* 測候所. ¶a *military station* 屯(とん)営地. ¶a *naval station* 海軍鎮守府. ¶a *penal station* 刑務所. ¶a *recruiting station* 募集事務所; 補充兵召集地. ¶They returned to their *several stations*. 彼らはそれぞれの詰所に帰った. ¶*social station* 社会的地位. ¶in *whatever station* of life one may be どういう身分であろうが.

Q² an *agricultural experiment station* 農事試験場. ¶a naval *air station* 海軍航空基地. ¶an *aviation station* 航空基地. ¶a *bathing station* 海水浴場. ¶*broadcasting station* 放送局. ¶establish a *coaling station* 給炭所を設ける. ¶a *coast-guard station* 沿岸警備隊詰所. ¶a *comfort station* 《米俗》共同便所. ¶a *consultation station* 相談所. ¶a *distributing station* 配電所. ¶erect an *electric power station* 電力発電所を建設する. ¶an *experiment* (=*experimental*) *station* 実験所. ¶a *field station* 野戦部(本部に対して). ¶a *filling station* 《米》ガソリンスタンド(給油所). ¶a *fire station* 消防署. ¶a *first-aid station* 救急所. ¶a *fueling station* for vessels 船舶給油所. ¶a *gas*[*-filling*] *station* 《米》ガソリンスタンド. ¶a [*gasoline*] *service station* ガソリンスタンド. ¶a *gendarmerie station* 憲兵とん所. ¶a *generating station* 発電所 ‖ an electrical *generating station* 発電所. ¶a [*hydroelectric*] power *station* 水力発電所. ¶an *immigrant station* 移民部(集合所). ¶a *key* (=central) *station* 〖ラジオ〗中央放送局. ¶a *leprosy investigation station* らい研究所. ¶a *life-saving station* 水難救済所. ¶a site of a *naval ordnance testing station*. 海軍兵器試験所の所在地. ¶a *packet station* 定期船発着所. ¶a *pay station* 自動電話. ¶a *petrol*[*-filling*] *station* ガソリンスタンド. ¶a *police station* 警察署. ¶a *polling station* 投票所. ¶a *protection and surveillance station* 保護観察所. ¶a *quarantine station* [船舶の]検疫所. ¶a *radar station* レーダー操作所. ¶a *radio station* 無線局; 放送局 ‖ a medium-wave *radio station* 中波通信(放送)局. ¶a [*radio-*]*broadcasting station* 放送局. ¶the *radio intercepting station* at Owada 大和田の無電(放送)傍受局. ¶a *radiotelephone station* 無線電話局. ¶a [*radio*] *short wave station* 短波通信(放送)局. ¶a *refuelling station* [ガソリン]給油所. ¶a *research station* 研究所. ¶a *spawning station* [魚類の]ふ化場. ¶a *stock station* [豪州語]牧畜地, 牧養地方. ¶a [*telephone*] *pay station* [有料]公衆電話(所). ¶a *weather station* 気象測候所. ¶a *wireless receiving station* 無線受信所. ¶a *wireless sending* (=*broadcasting*) *station* 無線送信局, 放送局.

P to be useful to his country, *according to* one's *station* その分に応じてその国のために尽すために. ¶He married a woman altogether *below* his *station*. 彼は自分よりずっと身分の低い女と結婚した. ¶those above one *in station* 自分より身分の高い人たち ‖ lower *in station* 身分のさらに低い ‖ be *in* (*out of*) *station* [軍艦など]列位を保つ(離れる). ¶be ahead *of station* [軍艦など]列位より進む ‖ be astern *of station* [軍艦など]列位より遅れる.

P² one in a *station below* him 彼より身分の低い人. ¶according to one's *station in* life その身分に応じて. 【類】

whatever our *station* ***in*** life may be. ¶the 8th *station* ***on*** Fuji 富士の八合目.
(2) 停車場, 駅.

Q the ***central*** *station* 中央停車場. ¶break one's journey at an ***intermediate*** *station* 途中の駅で下車する. ¶a ***roadside*** *station* 中間停車場. ¶a ***stop-over*** *station* 途中下車駅. ¶a ***terminal*** [*station*] =《米》a terminus 終着駅.

Q^2 a ***bus*** *station* (=stop) バス停留所. ¶the ***commencing*** *station* 出発駅. ¶a ***departing*** (an ***arrival***) *station* 発(着)駅. ¶an ***electric-car*** *station* 電車停留所. ¶a ***flag*** *station* 〖鉄道〗信号場. ¶a ***freight*** *station* 貨物駅. ¶a ***goods*** *station* =《米》a freight depot 貨物駅. ¶a ***junction*** *station* 連絡駅. ¶a ***passenger*** *station* 旅客駅. ¶a ***railway*** (=***railroad***) *station* 鉄道の駅. ¶a ***shunting*** *station* 待避駅. ¶a ***signal*** *station*=a flag station. ¶a ***transfer*** *station* 乗換駅. ¶a ***union*** *station* 《米》合同連絡駅(各鉄道会社の). ☞英国の joint station に当る. ¶a ***way*** *station* 《米》中間駅.

P ***at*** *station* 〖商〗停車場渡し ‖ We must get out ***at*** the next *station*. われわれは次の駅で降りねばならない. ‖ Driver, get me down (=drop me) ***at*** the *station*. 運転手さん停車場で降ろして下さい. ‖ I left my trunk ***at*** the *station*. 私は停車場へトランクをおいて来た. ‖ The train dropped me ***at*** the *station*. 私はその駅で下車した. ¶I went ***to*** the *station* to see my friend off. 私は友人の見送りに停車場へ行った.

station, *v.* 配置する, 置く.

P the consul is *stationed* ***at*** ... 領事は…に配置してある ‖ an officer who is *stationed* ***at*** the University of ... …大学配属将校. ¶The sentinel was *stationed* ***on*** a hill. 番兵は山の上に配置してあった. ¶The police were *stationed* ***outside*** the hall in large numbers. 警官が多数館外に配置された.

stationer, *n.* 文房具商.

P go ***to*** the *stationer's* 文房具屋へ行く.

stationery, *n.* 〔団〕文房具.

V ***get*** some *stationery* 文房具を少し買う.

Q^2 ***business*** *stationery* 業務用文房具.

P bear ... as our symbol ***on*** our *stationery* …をわれわれの(学校などの)記章として用せん及び封筒などについている.

statistics, *n. pl.* 統計.

V ***collate*** *statistics* 統計を比較研究する. ¶***collect*** *statistics* (=figures) 統計を集める.【類】*statistics* ***collected*** by me show that ... ¶***give*** actual *statistics* 実際の統計を示す. ¶*statistics* ***compiled*** from ... …から編集した統計. ¶We ***have*** *statistics* for the last annual festival. この前の年祭のときの統計ができている. ¶*statistics* ***issued*** by the Government 政府発行の統計. ¶*statistics* ***prepared*** by ... …の作製した統計. ¶*statistics* ***indicate*** that ... 統計では…となっている. ¶the *statistics* of 1908 for American streets and elevated railways ***show*** that ... 米国の市街高架両鉄道の一九〇八年の統計では…となっている.

Q ***basic*** *statistics* in social work 社会事業における基礎的統計. ¶***Exact*** *statistics* on the subject are not yet forthcoming. その問題に関する正確な統計はまだ発表されていない. ¶***horrible*** *statistics* [死亡率などの]ぞっとする統計. ¶***international literary*** *statistics* 世界の文学上の統計. ¶the ***latest*** *statistics* from all countries 各国最近の統計. ¶according to ***published*** *statistics* 公表された統計によれば. ¶***reliable*** (***unreliable***) *statistics* 信ずべき(信じるに足りない)統計. ¶***startling*** *statistics* 驚くべき統計. ¶***vital*** *statistics* 動態人口統計.

Q^2 ***Government*** *statistics* indicate that ... 政府の統計では…となっている. ¶a comprehensive ***table*** *statistics* 広範にわたる統計表. ¶***trade*** *statistics* 貿易統計.

P ***according to*** official *statistics* その筋の統計によれば. ¶a table ***of*** *statistics* 統計表.

P^2 *statistics* ***of*** life insurance 生命保険の統計 ‖ *statistics* ***of*** daytime population in a large city 大都市の昼間人口統計. ¶*statistics* ***on*** population (birth, death) 人口(など)の統計. ¶the *statistics* ***up to*** June of this year 今年六月までの統計.

statue, *n.* 彫像.

V ***carve*** (=***sculpture***) a *statue* 像を彫る. ¶***cast*** a bronze *statue* 銅像を鋳る. ¶***erect*** a bronze *statue* to his memory 彼を記念する銅像を建てる. ¶***inscribe*** a *statue* to ... …の像に銘を刻む.【類】this *statue* is ***inscribed*** to ... ¶***make*** a *statue* of a portrait 肖像画から立像を作製する. ¶A *statue* to Gladstone has recently been ***placed*** in Westminster Abbey on the spot marked for it years ago by Dean Stanley. グラッドストーンの彫像はウェストミンスター寺院内のスタンレー院長が数年前に指定した場所に最近据えられた. ¶The *statue* is ***railed in***. その彫像はさくで囲ってある. ¶***set up*** a *statue* 彫像を据える. ¶They ***tore*** his *statue* from its pedestal. 彼らは彼の彫像を台座から引離した. ¶***touch up*** a *statue* 彫像の仕上げをする. ¶the ceremony of ***unveiling*** the *statue* of ... …の彫像除幕式.【類】a *statue* of Cecil Rhodes was ***unveiled*** recently at ...

Q a most ***impressive*** *statue* 非常に印象の深い彫像.

Q^2 a ***bronze equestrian*** *statue* of ... …の青銅騎馬像. ¶a ***gold*** (***silver, marble***) *statue* 黄金(など)像.

P a *statue* ***by*** ... …作の彫像.

P^2 a *statue* ***in*** marble (bronze) 大理石(などの)像. ¶a *statue* ***of*** the Virgin 聖母マリアの彫像. ¶a *statue* ***to*** Captain Cook クック船長の彫像.

stature, *n.* 身長, 丈.

Q a man of ***gigantic*** *stature* おそろしく大きな人(巨人). ¶He is of ***great*** *stature*. 彼は背が高い. ¶a gentleman of ***imposing*** *stature* 堂々たるかっぷくの紳士. ¶of ***large*** (small) *stature* 大柄(小造り)の. ¶a ***low*** (=***small***) *stature* 小柄. ¶a man of ***mean*** (=***middle***) *stature* 中ぜいの人. ¶a ***middling*** *stature* 中ぜい. ¶a man of ***ordinary*** *stature* 身長の並の人. ¶a man of ***short, squab*** *stature* せいの低いずんぐりした人. ¶a lady of ***small*** *stature* and delicate frame 小柄でなよなよとした婦人. ¶be of ***unimposing*** *stature* あまり背の高くない.

P small (=short) ***in*** *stature* 背の低い.【類】He is five feet five inches ***in*** *stature* (=***tall***). ‖ grow (=increase) ***in*** *stature* 背が延びる. ¶short ***of*** *stature* 背の低い. ¶***on account of*** his small *stature* 小柄なので.

status, *n.* 地位; 形勢.

V Women have been regarded as inferior creatures and have contentedly ***accepted*** the *status* assigned to them. 女は劣等のものと見なされまたその与えられた地位に甘んじていた. ¶***assess*** the scholarly *status* of American universities 米国諸大学の学問上の地位を評価する. ¶***elevate*** the social *status* of women 婦人の社会的地位を高める. ¶***ennoble*** the *status* of working men 労働者の地位を高める. ¶***improve*** the *status* of the nursing profession 看護婦の職業的地位を向上させる. ¶***maintain*** one's social *status* 自己の社会的地位を維持する. ¶Your deeds would ***make*** the *status* of your ancestors blush upon their tombs. 君の行為は先祖をはずかしめることになろう.【類】***raise*** the *status* of the profession of letters. ¶None will ***question*** his *status* as a scholar. 彼が学者であることは疑問の余地はない. ¶***raise*** the *status* of women in society 婦人の社会的地位を高める. ¶***restore*** the *status* prior to ... …に先立って地位を回復する.

Q give the new science an ***assured*** *status* その新科学を確立させる. ¶Their *status* is wholly ***different***. 彼らの地位は全然違っている. ¶a man of ***doubtful*** *status* 身もとの怪しい人. ¶individuals of ***equal*** *status* 同じ位の地位の人々. ¶an ***extra*** *status* 別格. ¶one's ***financial*** *status* 財政上の地位(信用度). ¶faculty and students on ***full-time*** *status* 専任教授団と本科(全科修業の)学生. ¶citizens of ***high intellectual*** *status* 知能の高い国民. ¶be put on the ***inactive*** *status* 休止状態におかれる. ¶have ***legal*** *status* 合法性をもつ. ¶the ***low social*** *status* of women 女の低い社会的地位. ¶***marital*** *status* 配偶関係. ¶give an ***official*** *status* to ... …を本格にする. ¶***preferred*** *status* for a special group 特殊の人々に対する優先的地位. ¶the ***present*** *status* of affairs 現在の形勢. ¶Bibliography has no ***recognised*** *status* in England. 書史学は英国では認められていない. ¶the ***slighted*** *status* of the teacher 教師という軽視された地位. ¶the ***social*** *status* of the teacher 教師の社会的地位.【類】a person of lower ***social*** *status*. ¶Japan's resumption of full ***sovereign*** *status* 日本の国権完全回復.

Q^2 have a permanent ***civil-service*** *status* 本官となっている. ¶grant the ***dominion*** *status* to ... 《英》…に自治領の地位を与える. ¶a classified ***civil service*** *status* 職階制. ¶re-establish one's ***duty*** *status* (of men hospitalized or in confinement)〖軍〗(病気・監禁などの軍人を)復職させる. ¶clarify the ***immigration*** *status* of certain aliens 特定外人の移民資格を明白にする. ¶a ***self-government*** *status* 自治体の地位. ¶allow a "most favored nation" ***trading*** *status* 最恵通商国の待遇を与える. ¶the ***union*** *status* 労組の地位.

P a rise ***in*** *status* 地位の向上.

P^2 his status among novelists 小説家間の彼の地位. ¶her status as a housewife 主婦の座. ¶the status of women in Government service 公務員としての婦人の地位.

status quo, 《ラテン》現状.

V change the status quo overnight 一夜の中に現状を変える. ¶maintain the status quo in ... ...における現状を維持する. ¶restore the status quo 現状を回復する.

P remain in status quo 現状に止まる.

statute, *n.* 律令, 法令; 規程.

V pass a statute 法令を可決する.

Q statutes at large 一般法規. ¶general statute 一般法. ¶private statute 私法. ¶public statute 一般法.

Q^2 a city statute 市条例. ¶civil rights statutes 公民権法.

P It was declared by statute in 1920. それは一九二〇年法令で布告された.

P^2 a statute of 1919 providing ... ...を規定する一九一九年の法令. ¶the statutes of a school (university) 学則. ¶statutes on ... ...に関する法令.

stave, *v.* ...の側板をはずす; ...の来るのを防ぐ.

M^2 stave in 穴をあける; こわす. 【類】stave in the top of a box. ¶stave off a danger (an illness, trouble) 危険(など)を防ぐ ‖ stave off exposure あらわれないようにする ‖ stave off old age 若さを保つ. 【類】stave off the disastrous effects (悲惨な結果) of ... / stave off starvation / stave off a strike / stave off an evil day (凶日) / stave off the fatal day (運命の日) / stave off bankruptcy / stave off a creditor (借金取り) / stave off political chaos (政治的大混乱) / stave off a threatening famine (迫り来る飢きん). ¶stave to splinters [おけなど]ばらばらになる.

stay, *n.* 滞在, とう留; 〘法〙停止.

V How did you enjoy your stay in Japan? 日本の御滞在はいかがでした. ¶extend one's stay 滞在期間を延ばす. ¶I hope you will have an enjoyable stay in our country. この国で楽しく御滞在のほどを祈ります. ¶make some stay at ... ...にしばらく滞在する. 【類】make a stay of three weeks. ¶prolong one's stay 滞在を延期する. ¶put a stay upon one's activity その活動を妨害する.

Q I made a brief (=short) stay in ... 私は...にちょっとの間滞在した. ¶during a continuous stay in ... ...に長く滞在している間. ¶make an extended stay 長とう留をする. ¶Hotels reduce charges for lengthened stays or for parties. ホテルでは長とう留または団体には料金の割引をする. ¶make a long stay 長く滞在する. 【類】have a long stay in ... ¶a month's stay at ... ...に一カ月の滞在. ¶a prolonged stay in China 中国における長い滞在. ¶a restful stay 安らかな滞在. ¶Your stay has been very short. 御滞在は本当に短かかった. ¶with a two years' stay of execution 二年間の執行猶予で.

Q^2 an overnight stay 一泊. ¶enjoy a two-week stay in the country いなかで二週間遊ぶ.

P after the stay of a few days 二三日滞在後. ¶during my stay in England 私が英国滞在中.【類】Douglas Fairbanks, during his English stay, said he would like to live in England at least part of his time.

P^2 during my stay among you 貴地滞在中. ¶his long stay at Kobe 神戸における彼の長とう留. 【類】my stay at his home over Sunday (月曜まで). ¶make a stay of nine days 九日間滞在する ‖ stay of execution 刑の執行猶予. 【類】a request of a stay of execution ‖ stay of procedure 訴訟手続の中止.

P^2 There is a stay on heavy industry production. 重工業生産が止まっている.

stay, *n.* 支え; *pl.* 《英》コルセット.

V wear no stays underneath コルセットをつけない.

Q^2 port stays [船の]ワイヤロープ.

P^2 Her breasts stood erect in scorn of any stays. 彼女の乳房はコルセットなんか不要でぴんと立っていた.

stay, *v.* 止まる, 滞在する; 立止まる.

M stay all night 徹夜する. ¶She is never allowed to stay away from home overnight. 彼女は一晩家をあけることはどうあっても許されない. 【類】stay away from church / "Tourists" may be defined as persons who stay away from home for any period not exceeding one year. / stay away from the polls (投票) / stay away from school ‖ stay away after the liberty time is up [兵士など]許された時間が切れても帰って来ない. ¶stay back in the class [進級せずに]原級に止まる. ¶Don't stay fat—you can lose pounds easily and safely. 〘広告〙やせましょう—体重は簡単・安全に減らせます. ¶if the weather stays fine 天気が引続き晴れなら. 【類】The weather is going to stay fine. ¶Stay here till I return. 私の帰るまでここにいて下さい. ¶stay home alone 一人で留守番をする. ¶stay indoors うちに引こもっている. ¶The visitor stayed late. 客がおそくまでいた. ¶How long will you stay here? いつまで御滞在ですか. ‖ Could you stay longer? I'll fix you supper. ごゆっくり. 夕食を用意しますから. ¶stay one night (=overnight) 一泊する. ¶stay out 外泊する; 外出している ‖ He will stay out [till] late tonight. 彼は今晩帰りがおそくなる. ¶He stays out, I'm sorry. [電話で]ちょっと出かけています. ¶stay open till 8 at night 八時まで夜間営業する. ¶He stays overnight at his office every other day. 彼は隔日に役所に宿直します. ‖ stay overnight with a friend 一友人の所に泊る. ¶《米》stay put=remain where (=as) placed おいた所にある; [名声などが]残る ‖ stay put in the history of contemporary literature 現代文学史上に残る. 【類】His literary fame will soon stay put. ¶stay supper 夕飯までいる. ¶I stayed there ten years. 私はそこに十年いた. ¶stay young いつまでも若々しい.

M^2 Stay (=Stick) around. I'll soon be back with you. 《米口》この辺にいてくれ. すぐ戻って来るから. ¶stay in for a few days 二三日在宅する. ¶I want a place to stay in for the weekends. 週末を過す家(場所)が欲しい. ¶stay on for days 何日も居続ける ‖ The needles of a pine rtee stay on all winter. 松の針葉は冬中落ちない. ¶stay up [till] late at night 夜ふかしする ‖ stay up all night 徹夜する.

P stay after school 学校に居残る. ¶stay at home うちにいる ‖ There is no staying at home in such fine weather. こんないい天気に引込んではいられない. ‖ stay at a boarding-house (hotel) 下宿屋(など)に泊る. 【類】stay at a friend's. ¶I stayed very much beyond my time. 私は大分長居した. ¶stay for a day 一日滞在する. ¶stay in London ロンドンに滞在する.【類】stay in town all summer ‖ stay in business 営業を続ける. ¶You want to stay out of this affair. 君はこの問題には手を触れたくないんだね. 【類】stay out of the black market ‖ I wonder how he has stayed out of jail. どうしてあの男は刑務所に行かずに済んだのだろう. ¶stay over [the] night (=overnight) 泊る ‖ stay over Sunday 月曜日までいる. 【類】stay over the weekend. ¶He stayed there through the holidays. 彼は休暇中そこにいた. ¶He insisted on my staying to a meal. 彼は食事をして行けとしいた. ¶stay with his friend ... 彼の友だち...の所に滞在する. 【類】He left town to stay with his friends. / My cousin is staying with us on a visit.

O come to stay 長続きする. ¶Stay right where you are. 「そこ動くな.

stay-at-home, *n.* 出ぶしょう者.

Q He is a regular stay-at-home. 彼は全く出ぎらいだ.

stead, *n.* 代り; 用, 役.

Q What he learned there stood him in good (rich) stead later. そこで彼が習ったことは後に(大変)役に立った. ‖ It stands me in good stead. それは役に立つ.

P This stick has served me in stead. このつえは役に立った. ‖ Serfdom came in [the] stead of slavery. どれい制度に代って農ど制が行われた. 【類】David died, and Solomon reigned in his stead. / He could not come, so I have come in his stead (代りに). / in their stead.

steadfast, *a.* 忠実な.

P steadfast to one's principle (idea) その主義(など)に忠実な.

steady, *n.* 《米》愛人.

V My cook has a steady (=young man). 《米》うちのコック(女)にはいい人がいる.

steady, *a.* しっかりした; 実直な.

P steady in one's allegiance (purpose) 忠実な(志の堅い). ¶He is not steady on his legs. 彼は足がたしかでない(ひょろつく).

O Hold the ladder steady. はしごをちゃんと抑えていろ.

steak, *n.* ステーキ.

V cook a steak ステーキを料理する.

Q^2 beef steak=beefsteak. ¶I'll have Hamburg steak. 私はハンバーグステーキをもらおう. ¶the ossified mackerel steak of Japan かつお節.

steal, *v.* 盗む; そっとはいる.

M *steal* ***away*** to the seaside 海岸へひそかに去る ‖ *steal* ***away*** one's heart 巧みにその人に取入る ‖ *steal* ***away*** across the lawn こっそり芝生を抜けて行く. ¶*steal* ***cautiously*** around to the back door あたりに気を配りながら裏口に回る. ¶*steal* ***out*** unnoticed そっと抜け出す.【類】*steal* ***out*** into the yard. ¶*steal* ***softly*** out of a room こっそり部屋から抜け出す. ¶*steal* ***softly*** upstairs そっと二階へあがる. ¶*steal* ***up*** on unsuspecting people うっかりしている人々にそっと寄り付く.

M^2 The years *steal* ***by***. 知らない間に月日がたつ. ‖ The night is *stealing* ***in***. 夕やみがしのびよる.

P *steal* a glance ***at*** ... …をそっと見る. ¶The watch has been *stolen* ***from*** my person. その時計を私はすられた. ‖ *steal* a kiss ***from*** ... …からキッスを盗む. ¶*steal* ***into*** a house (room, hole) 家(など)へ忍び込む.【類】*steal* ***into*** its hole / A sunbeam *stole* ***into*** the gloomy room. ‖ *steal* ***into*** favor いつとはなしに人に取入る ‖ Fear *stole* ***into*** his heart. 彼は何となくこわくなってきた. ¶He *stole* ***out of*** the house. 彼はそっと家を出た. ‖ *steal* ***out of*** sight こっそり隠れる. ¶Mist *stole* ***over*** the valley. いつとなしに谷に霧がかかった. ‖ A strange drowsiness *stole* ***over*** him. 彼は妙に眠くなってきた. ‖ A smile *stole* ***over*** his face. 彼は顔に微笑を浮べた.【類】A lonely feeling *stole* ***over*** me. / A vague feeling of uneasiness began to *steal* ***over*** me. / A feeling of repulsion (discouragement) has *stolen* ***over*** her. / He felt a gentle warmth *steal* ***over*** his feet on putting his chilled feet on the ornamental brass rest. ¶*steal* ***toward*** ... …の方にしのび寄る. ¶*steal* softly ***to*** the door 戸口へそっと行く. ¶Disease is *stealing* ***upon*** him. 彼はじわじわ病魔におそわれている. ¶Terror *stole* ***upon*** his heart. 彼は知らぬ間に恐怖のとりこになっていた.

stealing, *n.* 窃盗.

P He is imprisoned ***for*** *stealing*. 彼は窃盗で禁固されている. ¶He is accused ***of*** *stealing*. 彼は窃盗したと言われている. ¶stoop ***to*** petty *stealing* こそどろに身を落す.

stealth, *n.* 秘密.

P do good ***by*** *stealth* 人知れず善を行う ‖ enter ***by*** *stealth* 「こっそりはいる.

steam, *n.* 蒸気, スチーム;《俗》勢力, 気力.

V ***blow off*** *steam* 蒸気を吹き出す; [比ゆ的に] うっ憤を漏らす, 苦情を言う. ¶*Steam* is ***employed*** as the motive power. 蒸気が動力に利用されている. ¶***generate*** *steam* in a boiler 汽かんに蒸気を発生させる. ¶The steamer ***gets up*** *steam*. 汽船が蒸気を立てる. ¶***keep up*** full *steam* in the boiler 汽かんに蒸気を十分におこさしておく ‖ manage to ***keep up*** a little *steam* in local industry 何とか地方産業が細々立って行けるようにする. ¶***let off*** *steam* ＝blow off steam ‖ ***let*** the *steam* ***off*** and then come to an agreement 気をとり直して妥協する.【類】***let off*** the *steam* (はしゃぐ) by dancing, shouting, and clapping hands all together / ways of ***letting off*** youthful *steam*. ¶***put*** new *steam* into it 新に力を出す. ¶***put on*** more *steam*, with the object of getting out to sea [船を]海上へ乗出す目的で一層蒸気を立てる. ¶***raise*** *steam* 蒸気を発生させる.【類】From twelve to twenty-four hours before the sailing of a ship *steam* has to be ***raised*** and the machinery warmed up. ¶***shut off*** *steam* 蒸気を(弁などで)しゃ断する. ¶***turn off*** (***on***) *steam* 蒸気を止める(出す). ¶***work off*** *steam* 蒸気を止める; 努力をやめる.

Q a steamer under ***easy*** *steam* 緩慢な速力で航行する汽船. ¶put on ***full*** *steam* 全速力を出す.

P ***at*** (＝***with***) full *steam* 全力をあげて. ¶travel ***by*** *steam* 汽船で旅行する ‖ It goes (＝is driven) ***by*** *steam*. それは蒸気で動く. ¶the generation ***of*** *steam* 蒸気の発生. ¶a ship ***under*** *steam* 航行中の船.

O The *steam* is ***on***. [暖房など]スチームが通っている.

steam, *v.* 蒸発する; 汽力で行く; 奮進する.

M *steam* ***ahead*** 前進する. ¶*steam* ***along*** [船など]汽走する. ¶*steam* ***away*** 迅速に汽走する. ¶*steam* ***on*** to ... [汽船が]…へ走り進む. ¶*steam* ***out*** to sea [船が]出港する. ¶The boiler *steams* ***well***. この汽かんはよく蒸気を発生する.

M^2 The vessel *steamed* ***off***. 汽船は出港した. ¶Vapors *steam* ***upward*** from the earth. 水蒸気は地上から気体となって上昇する. ¶The train *steamed* ***up*** to the platform. 汽車がプラットフォームへ進んで来た. ‖ *steam* ***up*** peace industries 平和産業に景気をつける.

P The horse *steamed* ***after*** a hard gallop. 馬は猛烈なかけ足の湯気を出していた. ¶*steam* ***against*** the wind 風に向って汽走する. ¶*steam* ***down*** (***up***) the river 汽船で川を下(上)る. ¶*steam* ***in*** the wind's eye 風上に向って汽走する. ¶The vessel *steamed* ***into*** (***out of***) the harbor. 船が港へ入った(を出た).【類】At half-past two we *steamed* ***into*** the station of Norfolk.

steamboat, *n.* 汽船.

V^2 the *steamboat* ***plies*** between ... 汽船が…間を往復している.

P a journey ***by*** *steamboat* 汽船旅行.

steamer, *n.* 汽船.

V The harbour ***accommodates*** the largest *steamers* afloat. その港には世界最大の汽船も停泊ができる. ¶the wharves where ocean *steamers* are ***berthed*** on arrival at Yokohama 横浜到着の際外洋航行船の停泊する波止場. ¶***board*** (***go aboard or go on board***) a *steamer* 乗船する. ¶***charter*** a *steamer* [契約して]船を雇う. ¶***coal*** a *steamer* 汽船に石炭を積込む. ¶***fit out*** a *steamer* 汽船をぎ装する. ¶***leave*** a *steamer* 下船する. ¶***load*** a *steamer* 汽船に荷物を積込む. ¶All *steamers* ***met***. [ホテルなどの掲示]すべての汽船にお出迎えをします. ¶***run*** *steamers* regularly to Europe [汽船会社など]欧州に定期船を出す.【類】the steamship company ***runs*** *steamers* between ... and ... ¶the *steamer* is ***scheduled*** to sail on ... その汽船は…に出帆する日取りになっている. ¶***secure*** a *steamer* on time charter 時間ぎめで汽船を借りる. ¶***take*** a *steamer* 汽船に乗る ‖ ***take*** the *steamer* for ... …行きの汽船に乗る. ¶***tow*** a *steamer* to ... 汽船を…へ引綱(または引船)で引く. ¶***use*** a river *steamer* 川蒸気船を利用する.

V^2 The *steamer* ***goes*** every other day. 汽船は隔日に出る. ¶The *steamer* ***pitches*** and ***rolls*** in a rough sea. 汽船が荒海で縦揺れ横揺れする. ¶the *steamer* ***plies*** between ... 汽船が…間を往復する. ¶The *steamer* ***puts in*** at several ports, and then ***puts out*** to sea again. 汽船が方々の港へ寄ってまた出掛ける. ¶The *steamer* ***runs*** daily. 汽船が毎日出る. ¶there are over half a dozen lines of *steamers* ***sailing*** from ... …から出帆する船は六航路以上ある. ¶The *steamer* ***starts*** at 8 o'clock. 汽船は八時に出港する.

Q a ***fast*** *steamer* 快速力の汽船. ¶a ***fine*** *steamer* りっぱな汽船. ¶ship per ***first*** *steamer* 最初の船便で送荷する. ¶***incoming*** and ***outgoing*** *steamers* 出入港の汽船. ¶***intermediate*** *steamers* 中間出帆汽船. ¶***local*** *steamers* 沿海航路汽船. ¶the ***mammoth*** *steamers* "Adriatic" and "Cedric" 巨船アドリアティック号とセドリック号. ¶***popular*** *steamers* 評判のよい汽船. ¶a ***slow*** *steamer* 速力ののろい汽船.

Q^2 ***coasting*** *steamers* 沿岸航路船. ¶a ***ferry*** *steamer* 連絡船. ¶a ***mail*** *steamer* 郵船. ¶an ***ocean***[***-going***] *steamer*＝an ocean-goer (liner) 外国航路船. ¶an ***oil*** *steamer* (＝tanker) on fire 火災中の油送船. ¶***paddle*** [***-wheel***] *steamers* 外輪汽船. ¶a ***passenger*** *steamer* 客船. ¶a ***pleasure*** *steamer* 遊覧船. ¶a ***river*** *steamer* 河船. ¶a ***screw cargo*** *steamer* スクリュー貨物船. ¶a ***shallow-draught*** *steamer* 喫水の浅い汽船. ¶a ***tank*** *steamer*＝a tanker 油送船. ¶sail a ***tramp*** *steamer* 不定期(貨物)船を運航する.

P return ***by*** *steamer* 汽船で帰る ‖ send it ***by*** *steamer* それを汽船で送る ‖ travel ***by*** *steamer* 汽船で旅行をする. ¶engage a cabin ***in*** a *steamer* 汽船の客室を申込んでおく ‖ embark ***in*** the *steamer* for ... …行の汽船に乗込む.【類】He crossed over the river ***in*** a *steamer*. ¶fire ***on*** a *steamer* 汽船の火事 ‖ go back to Kobe ***on*** the same *steamer* 同じ汽船で神戸へ帰る. ¶The train corresponds ***with*** the *steamer*. その汽車は汽船に連絡する.

P^2 the *steamer* ***between*** Aomori and Hakodate 青函連絡船. ¶the *steamers* ***for*** Kobe 神戸行の汽船.

steam-hammer, *n.* 蒸気ハンマー.

V ***employ*** a *steam-hammer* to crack a nut [比ゆ的に]鶏を裂くに牛刀を用いる.

steaming, *n.* 汽船旅行.

P ***within*** a couple of days' *steaming* from ... …から汽船で二日以内の(距離に).

steam-pipe, *n.* 蒸気管.

V^2 The *steam-pipe* ***burst***. 蒸気を送る管が破裂した.

steamship, *n.* 汽船.

V^2 the *steamship* Europe, ***bearing*** the remains of the late ... 故…の遺がいを載せた汽船コーロッパ号. ¶*steamships*

ply the channel. 汽船がその水道(海峡)を往来する.

P time required ***on steamships*** 汽船に要する時間(旅程) ‖ sail for Belgium ***on*** the *steamship* Lapland 汽船ラプランド号でベルギーに向け出帆する.

steed, *n.* 馬, 軍馬.

V ***rein in*** (=*up*) one's *steed* 馬を止める.

Q ride in on a ***bare-backed*** *steed* はだか馬で乗付ける. ¶a ***fiery*** *steed* かんの強い馬.

steel, *n.* 鋼鉄; 刀, 剣.

V ***decontrol*** *steel* 鋼鉄の統制を解く.

Q ***carbonic*** *steel* 炭化鋼. ¶***cold*** *steel* 白刃, 秋水. ¶***mild*** *steel* 軟鋼. ¶***stainless*** *steel* ステンレス鋼. ¶***Swedish*** *steel* スエーデン鋼.

Q² ***Bessemer*** *steel* ベッセマー鋼. ¶***conversion*** *steel* 変質鋼. ¶***ingot*** *steel* 〖冶金〗溶製鋼. ¶***nickel*** *steel* ニッケル鋼. ¶***scrap*** *steel* スクラップ鋼. ¶***tungsten*** *steel* タングステン鋼.

P worthy ***of*** one's *steel* 刀にかけるほどの価値ある, 敵として不足のない ‖ have nerves ***of*** *steel* 鋼鉄の心臓(勇気)を持っ └ている.

steel, *v.* 堅くする, 無感覚にする.

P *steel* one's heart (=oneself) ***against*** compassion 心を鬼にする. ¶*steel* oneself ***to*** some action 心を鬼にしてあ └る行動をとる.

steep, *v.* ぬらす; 没入させる; つかる.

M The herb *steeps* ***slowly***. その菜はつかりにくい.

P ***steeped in*** salt water 塩水に浸して. ¶***steeped in*** liquor 酒びたりになって ‖ be ***steeped in*** prejudice 偏見がしみ込んでいる ‖ ***steeped in*** Greek and Latin ギリシアやラテンの文学に没頭して ‖ *steep* oneself ***in*** the classics 古典に没頭する ‖ swords ***steeped in*** blood 血に染った刀剣 ‖ He is ***steeped in*** sleep. 彼は熟睡している. 【類】He is ***steeped in*** vice (misery).

steer, *n.* 《米俗》考え; 助言.

Q give a person a ***friendly*** *steer* 助言を与える. ¶a ***good*** └*steer* 名案.

steer, *v.* 操舵(だ)する; [進路を]取る, 向う.

M ***steer clear*** of rocks (difficulties, worry) 暗礁(など)を避ける ‖ *steer* ***clear*** of the movies 映画館に足を向けない ‖ ***steer clear*** of anything risky and dangerous 危い橋は一切渡らないようにする. ¶This ship *steers* ***easily***. この船はかじがよくきく. ¶The ship *steers* ***southward***. 船は南方に向って行く. ¶The ship *steers* ***straight***. 船は真すぐに進む.

P ***steer between*** extremes 両極端の間を取って行く. ¶We *steered* a course ***by*** compass. われわれはら針盤によって進んだ. ¶We *steered* ***for*** the railway station. われわれは駅を目指して行った. ‖ Where are you *steering* ***for***? どこへ行くのか. ¶*steer* ***through*** the high waves 怒とうの中を操縦する. ¶*steer* one's course ***to*** (=***toward***) the station 駅 └に向って進む.

steerage, *n.* 三等船室.

P I sailed ***in*** the *steerage* on a French liner. 私はフランス定期船の三等で航海した.

stem, *n.* 船首.

P ***from stem*** to stern 船首から船尾まで; 端から端まで.

stem, *n.* 茎; 家系; 〖言語〗語幹.

Q a ***collateral*** *stem* 傍系. ¶a ***noble*** *stem* 貴族の家系. ¶descend ***from*** an old (=ancient) *stem* 旧家の出である.

P a plant that flowers ***on*** long *stems* 長い茎に花の咲く植物.

P² "Run" is the *stem* ***of*** runner, running, etc. run は runner, running などの語幹だ.

stem, *v.* 分かれる.

M² ***stem off*** a disaster 災害を回避する.

P The theory ***stems from*** (=originates in) an ancient tradition. その説は古い伝統から派生している. 【類】languages *stemmed* ***from*** the Indo-European family (インド └ヨーロッパ語族).

stem, *v.* 止める, 抑える.

M² ***stem back*** communism 共産主義を食い止める.

P *stem* the current ***by***… 流れを…で止める.

stenographer, *n.* 速記者.

Q a ***fast accurate*** *stenographer* 正確で早い速記者. ¶***public*** *stenographers* 専属でない速記者.

step, *n.* 歩み; 階段; 昇級; 進歩; 手順, 手段; 歩調, 足取り; 足音; 足跡.

V ***aid*** her tottering *steps* よろめき歩く彼女に手を貸す. ¶***ascend*** 150 *steps* to … 階段を百五十上って…へ行く. ¶***bend*** one's *steps* homewards 帰路につく. ¶***break*** *steps* 歩調を乱す. ¶a good rule to ***conduct*** (=***guide***) one's *steps* 処世の良いしおり. ¶***descend*** the *steps* 階段を降りる. ¶I ***directed*** my *steps* homeward. 私は家路についた. ¶***dog*** one's *steps* 人の跡をつける. ¶***earn*** a *step* in the peerage 爵位が一級進む. ¶He will not ***endorse*** such *steps*. 彼はこんな処置には賛同しないだろう. ¶***get*** one's *step* 昇級する. ¶***give*** a person a *step* 昇級させる. ¶But we must ***hasten*** our *steps*. それはさて置き, 閑話休題. ¶He ***has*** a quick *step*. 彼は足がはやい. ¶I ***heard*** a light (heavy) *step* on the stairs. 階段に軽(重)い足音が聞えた. ¶***keep*** *step* with … …と歩調をそろえる. ¶***lose*** *step* with … …と疎遠になる. ¶a forward *step* was ***made*** to … …のため一歩を進めた. 【類】***make*** a big *step* ***forward*** in negotiations. ¶***mark*** a *step* toward peace for mankind 人類の平和への一進歩を画する. 【類】***mark*** a *step* in human progress. ¶***mind*** the *step* 足もとに気をつける. ¶***miss*** one's *step* 足を踏みはずす. ¶***move*** a *step* nearer to … …に一歩近づく. 【類】Don't ***move*** a *step*. ¶***perfect*** the legal *steps* necessary for … …に必要な法律上の手続を完了する. ¶***pick*** one's *steps* 足下に気をつけて歩く. ¶***prove*** a great *step* toward establishing … …建設への一大進歩を示す. ¶***quicken*** *steps* 足をはやめる ‖ His *steps* were ***quickend*** and ***lengthened*** as he neared his destination. 目的地に近づくに従って足は早く大またになった. ¶***repent*** the *step* その処置を遺憾に思う. ¶***retrace*** my *steps* towards … …の方へ来た道を戻る. 【類】too late to ***retrace*** his *steps* / hastily ***retrace*** one's *steps*. ¶***save*** many *steps* 大分手数を省く. ¶I ***saw*** his *steps* in the snow. 雪中に彼の足跡があった. ¶***take*** a *step* in the right direction by … …することによって正しい方向に一歩を進める ‖ ***take*** a *step* ***back*** 一歩退く. 【類】It resulted in his ***taking*** two or three *steps* ***upward*** in popularity. / ***take*** a new *step* ***forward*** / ***take*** some *steps* / urge British Government to ***take*** *steps* / We must ***take*** *steps* to protect our interests. / ***take*** *steps* toward adopting a similar scheme / ***take*** three *steps* ***forward*** toward the platform / ***Take*** such *steps* as you think best. / *Steps* must be ***taken*** immediately. / What *steps* are you going to ***take*** about that affair? / I have ***taken*** *steps* on your advice. / ***take*** a *step*. ¶avoid ***tangling*** one's *steps* in … …の巻きぞえを食わないようにする. ¶***turn*** our *steps* in the direction of (=toward) … …の方へわれわれの足を向ける. 【類】***turn*** their *steps* toward the waiting carriages / ***turn*** one's *steps* ***homeward***. ¶unable to ***walk*** a *step* [***ahead***] 一歩も前進出来ないで. ¶He will not ***warrant*** such a *step*. 彼はかかる処置を是認しないだろう. ¶***Watch*** your *step!* 足もとご用心.

V hear *steps* ***approaching*** … …に近ずく足音を聞く.

Q ***active*** *steps* are being taken to … …すべき手段が活発に講ぜられている. ¶take ***all possible*** *steps* to … …するためあらゆる手段を取る. ¶go ***another*** *step* in … …に更に一歩進む ‖ He was so fatigued that he was unable to take ***another*** *step*. 彼は疲れてもう一足も歩けなかった. ¶take ***another long*** *step* in advance. その(事業は)さらに一大進展に乗り出す. ¶take an ***appropriate*** *step* 適宜の措置をとる. ¶take the ***authorized*** *steps* for … …の正規の手続を踏む. ¶a *step* ***backward[s]*** 一歩退却. ¶take a ***bold*** *step* 大胆な手段をとる. ¶***Broad*** *steps* lead down into a garden. 広い階段を降りると庭に出る. ¶take ***certain*** *steps* 一定の手段を取る. ¶the ***chief*** *steps* in the argument 議論の要点. ¶take ***concrete*** *steps* 具体的な方法をとる. ¶take a ***courageous*** *step* 勇猛な手段を取る. ¶a ***decided*** *step* in advance 明かな一進歩. ¶take ***decisive*** *steps* 断然たる処置を取る. ¶take ***definite*** and ***determined*** *steps* 断固明確な手段をとる. ¶take ***diplomatic*** *steps* 外交的手段を取る. ¶a ***distinct*** *step* forward in English education 英語教育における明かな進歩. ¶***double-time*** (=***double-quick***) [*step*] 〖軍〗かけ足(行進). ¶take ***drastic*** *steps* 思い切った手段を取る. ¶***Easy*** *Steps* in Chinese Studies 中国語入門[書名]. ‖ trace with ***easy*** *steps* the natural development of … …の自然的発展を骨を折らずに調べる. ¶***effective*** *steps* 有効な手段. ¶no ***efficient*** *steps* have been taken to … …すべきなんら有効な手段が講ぜられてない. ¶at ***every*** *step* 一歩一歩(慎重に); 至る処に ‖ take advantage of ***every*** *step* forward in the progress of science 科学の進歩を遺漏なく利用する. ¶take an ***extreme*** *step* 極端な手段を取る. ¶make a ***false*** *step* 足を踏はずす. ¶one of the most ***fatal*** *steps* in the beginning of a boy's downfall 少年の堕落の初期における最も恐るべき段階の一つ. ¶walk with ***firm*** and ***steady*** *steps*

しっかりした足取りで歩く. ¶The one-act play is ideal as a ***first step*** in the appreciation of drama. 演劇鑑賞の第一歩として一幕物が理想的だ. 【類】This was for those imitators the ***first step*** to independence. / it marks the ***first step*** in the development of ... / the ***first step*** to golfing / In this the girl took her ***first step*** downward (堕落の第一歩). / Taking the ***first step*** (開拓は) proverbially costs the most. / The ***first step*** to a good name depends on the first steps he makes in the world. ¶a ***first necessary step*** 第一に必要な手順の一つ. ¶certainly a ***forward step*** たしかに一進歩 ‖ take each ***forward step*** 一歩一歩前進する. 【類】It marks a ***forward step*** in human progress. ¶A ***further step*** was subsequently taken. 次いで次の手段がとられた. 【類】no ***further steps*** will be taken until ... ¶move onward with ***giant steps*** 大またで前進する. ¶The field is a ***good*** (=long) ***step*** from a village. その畑は村からかなり隔っている. ¶by ***gradual steps*** 段々に. ¶***great steps*** forward were taken with regard to ... ...は大いに進歩した ‖ it marks a ***great step*** in advance toward ... それは...への一大進歩を画する. ¶a ***heroic step*** 勇ましい手段. ¶take a ***historic step*** forward 歴史的な一歩を踏み出す. ¶an ***ill-advised step*** 無分別なやり口. ¶take ***immediate steps*** for the introduction of ... 早速...を採用するようにする. ¶an ***important step*** toward ... ...に向って進む重要な一点. ¶an ***inevitable step*** in the evolution of society 社会発達に避くべからざる段取り. 【類】the next ***inevitable step*** is .... ¶as an ***initiative step*** in this activity この活動方面の第一歩として. ¶The ***irrevocable step*** is taken. 取返しのつかないことをした. ¶a ***justifiable step*** 正当な手段. ¶with ***light*** and ***cautious steps*** 軽快なしかも注意深い足どりで. ¶***light*** and ***elastic steps*** 軽く弾力のある足どり. ¶walk with ***long steps*** 大またに歩く ‖ That is a ***long step*** toward the prevention of war. それは戦争防止に大いに役立つ. ¶***mincing steps*** ちょこちょこ歩き. ¶walk with ***lively steps*** 元気よく歩く. ¶***muffled*** (=stealthy) ***steps*** 忍び足. ¶take the ***necessary steps*** 必要な手段を取る ‖ omit ***necessary steps*** in process of ... ...の手を抜く. ¶the ***next-to-final step*** (あと一回という)ぎりぎりの手. ¶with ***noiseless steps*** 足音をたてずに. ¶This is a ***notable step*** forward. これは目ざましい進歩だ. ¶go ***one step*** further さらに一歩を進める ‖ take ***one step*** at a time 一歩一歩進む. ¶take ***positive steps*** toward that end その目的達成のため積極的な手段をとる. ¶It is hoped that in the near future ***practical steps*** will be taken in this direction. 近い将来にその計画実行に着手されるよう希望する. ¶take the ***preliminary step*** of ... ...の予備工作をする. 【類】as a ***preliminary step***. ¶a ***preparatory step*** 準備工作. ¶make a ***prodigious step*** forward 一大進歩を遂げる. ¶take ***proper steps*** to meet the situation 事態に適合する適当な手段を取る. ¶hurry with ***quick steps*** toward ... ...の方へ早足で急ぐ. 【類】He has a ***quick step*** (足がはやい). ¶a ***radical*** and ***precarious step*** 急激な危なっかしい行動. ¶with a ***rapid step*** 早足で. ¶a ***rash step*** むやみな処置. ¶a ***reckless step*** 向う見ずの処置. ¶a ***retrograde step*** 逆行. ¶a ***second step*** to take toward ... ...のためとるべき次の措置. ¶with ***short steps*** 小またに ‖ it was but a ***short step*** to ... ...まではほんの一足だった. 【類】From ... to ... is a ***short step***. ¶take ***some wild step*** ある乱暴な処置を取る. ¶with ***steady steps*** 着々と. ¶a ***stealthy step*** of a beast 獣のしのび足取り ‖ approach ... with ***stealthy steps*** 抜足さし足で...に近づく. ¶take a few ***stumbling steps*** 二三歩つまづきつつ進む. ¶take ***tentative steps*** 試験的にやって見る. ¶the ***top step*** of the ladder はしごの一番上の段. ¶aid her ***tottering steps*** 彼女のよろめく足を支える. ¶with ***unsteady steps*** よろよろして. ¶take a ***wrong step*** [正道を]踏みはずす.

Q[2] mark one of the great ***advance steps*** in ... ...における大躍進を示す. ¶***area steps*** 地下室への階段. ¶sit on a ***stoop step*** [玄関先の]踏み段の一つに腰をおろす.

P I regard it ***as*** the first ***step*** toward an English teaching reform. 私はそれを英語教授改良への第一歩と見なす. ‖ ***as*** one ***step*** in its democratization その民主化の一歩として. ¶From the clerk of a stock broker he became a millionaire ***at*** a ***step***. 彼は株屋の番頭から一足飛びに百万長者になった. ‖ go ***at*** quick ***step*** 早足で行く. ¶The altar is approached ***by steps***. 祭壇へは段を登って行く. ‖ I missed seeing him just ***by*** a ***step***, so to speak. いわばひと足ちがいで彼に会いそこねた. ¶run ***down*** the ***steps*** 段々を走り降りる. ¶march ***in step*** with ... ...と歩調をそろえて行進する. 【類】not ***in step*** with the tempo (進歩) of modern business ‖ follow ***in*** one's ***steps*** 人にならう. ¶fall ***into step*** 足並がそろう. ¶a flight ***of steps*** 一本の階段. 【類】a flight ***of*** 50 ***steps***. ¶a cat lying ***on*** the ***steps*** half way up 階段の中ほどに横たわるねこ. ¶walk ***out of step*** 足並を乱して歩く ‖ be ***out of step*** with the times 時代にそぐわない ‖ Politics and economics are ***out of step*** today. 現今では政治と経済との歩調が合わない. ¶a series of pictures representing the art of sericulture ***through*** its consecutive ***steps*** 養蚕の手順を示す続き絵. ¶I hear the patter of feet coming ***up*** the verandah ***steps***. 縁側の階段を上って来るばたばたという足音が聞える. ¶walk forward ***with*** a firm ***step*** しっかりした足取で進む ‖ walk ***with*** quick (slow) ***steps*** 足早に(のろのろ)歩く.

P[2] retrace our ***steps across*** ... ...を横切ってもと来た道を帰る. ¶take stringent ***steps against*** ... ...に対して厳重な手段を取る. ¶There is but one ***step between*** the ludicrous and the sublime. こっけいと荘厳との差はただ一歩だ. ¶walk ***step by*** step 一歩一歩進む. 【類】***Step by*** step we gain knowledge. ¶It's only a ***step from*** here. ここからほんの一足です. ¶***steps in*** the development of American democracy 米国民主主義の発達の段取り. 【類】the ***steps in*** bookmaking ‖ It is one of those ***steps in*** the right direction. それは行くべき方向への第一歩である. ¶They were one ***step nearer*** defeat (victory). さらに一歩敗北(勝利)に近づいていた. ¶***steps of*** procedure 手順. ¶It is but a ***step to*** the station. 駅まではほんの一足だ. ‖ ***steps to*** success 成功への道 ‖ the first ***step to*** the saloon and the brothel 銘酒屋や売春宿へ流れ込む第一歩. ¶Realization of ignorance is a ***step toward*** knowledge. 無知の自覚は知識への第一歩だ. 【類】To know our ideal is one ***step towards*** attaining it. / a ***step toward*** their hope of statehood (州制昇格の希望). ¶first ***steps with*** British and American writers 英米作家研究の手始め.

step, *v.* 歩む; [精神的に]歩を進める.

M ***step aside***, to give way to ... わきへ寄って...に道を譲る ‖ "***Step aside***!" barked the chauffeur. 「どけ」と運転手がどなった. ¶We ***stepped back*** to let the carriage pass. われわれは後へ下がって馬車を通した. ‖ ***step back*** from meeting a person 人に会うのを避けようとして後へ引下がる ‖ ***step back*** into remote antiquity 太古にさかのぼって考える. ¶He ***stepped backward*** a pace or two. 彼は一二歩退いた. ¶***step briskly*** 活発に歩む. ¶***step forth*** 進みでる. ¶***step forward*** 前に踏み出す ‖ ***Step forward***, please. どうぞ前へ願います. ¶***step high*** 足を高くあげて歩を運ぶ. ¶Hey, Jack! ***Step inside***. Let's have a drink. おい, ジャック, 中へ入れよ, 一杯やろう. ¶***step lively*** さっそうと歩く. ¶I must ***step out*** for a moment to post a letter. 私は郵便をだしにちょっと出なければならない. ‖ We shall be late for the train if we don't ***step out***. 急がないと汽車に遅れる. 【類】***step out*** briskly for a mile and a half walk. / tell pupils to ***step out*** from their seats to the gangway (通路) / ***step out*** from a train / ***step out*** on the veranda ‖ It seemed China had ***stepped out*** on the road to unity. 当時中国は統一に向って前進したようだった. ‖ ***step out*** into the street 通りに出る. 【類】So saying he ***stepped out*** the door into the street. ¶***step over*** to a fruit shop 果実店へでかける. ¶***step short*** (***long***) 歩調を短く(長く)する. ¶***Step soft*** lest he should awake. 彼が目をさまさないようにそっと歩け. ¶Please ***step this way***. どうぞこちらへ. ¶***Step upstairs***! 二階へお上がりなさい.

M[2] ***step down*** from one's car 車から降りる ‖ ***step down*** from an office 辞職する. ¶***step in*** at one's uncle's (on one's friend) 伯父の家に立寄る(友人を訪れる) ‖ ***step in*** between the two parties 二つの党派の間に割り込む. ¶***step off*** a distance ある距離を歩幅で計る. ¶***step on*** to ... ...に進む. ¶***step up*** the tempo テンポを早める ‖ ***step up*** to the front of the room へやの前まで進んで行く ‖ vastly ***step up*** production 猛烈に生産をあげる. 【類】***step up*** manufacture of locomotives / ***step up*** industrial production / increase the incentives to miners to ***step up*** the coal output / The productivity has been ***stepped up*** (=increased) 50 per cent / help ***step up*** food production ‖ be ***stepped up*** from ... to ... ...から...の増産(額)になる.

P *step* ***across*** the street 街路の向側に行く. ¶*step* ***into*** a car (cab, train, room) 汽車(など)に乗込む ‖ *step* ***into*** journalism 新聞記者になる ‖ *step* ***into*** a fortune (an estate) 大身代(財産)を一挙にして獲得する(譲受ける) ‖ He *stepped* ***into*** his father's shoes and stretched them. 彼は父の事業を継いでますます盛大にした. ¶*step* ***off*** a ship (train) 下船(など)する. ¶*step* ***on*** the platform (a mat) 壇(など)に上る ‖ *step* ***on*** to a station 駅に入って行く. 【類】*step* ***on*** another's foot ‖ *Step* ***on*** it! 《口語》[車など]早くやれ; 急げ. ¶*step* ***out of*** a cab (car) 馬車(など)から降りる ‖ *step* ***out of*** college 大学を出る ‖ *step* ***out of*** character 柄にないことをする. ¶*step* ***over*** the cliff ***into*** the sea がけを踏みはずして海中に落ちる. ¶*step* ***to*** one side 一方へ寄る ‖ *step* ***to*** the next house 隣家に行く. ¶*step* ***upon*** the platform 登壇する.

stepping-stone, *n.* 飛石, 踏石; 階梯(ﾃｲ).

V *make* a *stepping-stone* of ... ...を踏台にする.

Q Law was the ***recognized*** *stepping-stone* to politics. 法律は政治への階梯(ﾃｲ)と認められていた.

P with it ***as*** a *stepping-stone* to ... ...を...への階梯として.

P^2 Gibraltar is the *stepping-stone* ***to*** Africa. ジブラルタルはアフリカへの飛石だ. ‖ Every failure is a *stepping-stone* ***to*** success. 失敗は皆成功への飛石だ. 【類】Newspaper work was his *stepping-stone* ***to*** films.

stereotype, *n.* 鉛版.

P a Negro portrayed ***as*** a *stereotype* きまりきった手法で描かれた黒人. ¶print ***with*** ***stereotypes*** 鉛版で印刷する.

stereotype, *v.* 鉛版にする.

P *stereotyped* ***into*** traditional systems 伝統的体系に固められて.

sterility, *n.* 不妊.

V The hot springs have a reputation for ***removing*** *sterility.* その温泉は不妊症に効能があるといわれる.

Q ***artificial*** *sterility* 避妊. ¶the ***literary*** *sterility* of America アメリカの文学不振. ¶***wilful*** *sterility* 計画的避妊.

sterilization, *n.* 断種.

Q the ***artificial*** *sterilization* of marriage 避妊.

sterilize, *v.* 殺菌する, 消毒する.

M *sterilize* ***chemically*** 化学的消毒をする.

P *sterilize*...***by*** steam ...を蒸気消毒をする. 【類】water (milk) *sterilized* ***by*** boiling.

stern, *n.* 船尾.

P sit ***at*** the *stern* of the State 国政を担当する. ¶It is placed ***in*** the *stern* of a boat. それは船尾におかれる.

stern, *a.* きびしい.

P be very *stern* ***in*** one's discipline 訓育がすこぶるきびしい. ¶*stern* ***to*** one's pupils 生徒にきびしい.

sternness, *n.* きびしさ.

Q with ***unrelenting*** *sternness* 情け容赦もなく.

stew, *n.* 《俗》はんもん, 憤慨.

P He was ***in*** a *stew.* 彼ははんもん(焦慮)している. ‖ *stew* ***in*** one's own juice [自分の行為を]後悔する.

stew, *v.* とろ火で煮る; 《口語》はんもんする.

P fruit *stewed* ***with*** sugar 砂糖を入れて煮たくだもの.

steward, *n.* 別当, 執事; 給仕.

Q a ***chief*** *steward* 職場委員長. ¶a ***ship's*** *steward* 船の給仕.

Q^2 a ***cabin*** (***table***) *steward* 船室(食卓)の給仕. ¶a ***shop*** *steward* 店の番頭.

P Lord *Steward* ***of*** the Household [英国の]宮内大臣. ¶Lord *Steward* ***to*** the Empress 皇后太夫.

stewardess, *n.* 女給仕; 〚航空〛スチュアデス.

Q a ***cute-looking*** *stewardess* in sky-blue uniform そら色の制服を着たきれいなスチュアデス.

Q^2 a ***JAL*** *stewerdess* 日航機のスチュアデス. ¶a ***train*** *stewardess* 列車の女ボーイ.

stick, *n.* 棒; つえ; 《口語》のろま.

V ***burn*** incense *sticks* 線香をたく. ¶***carry*** a *stick* つえを持つ. ¶***eat*** a person's *stick* つえでぶたれる, 痛棒を食う. ¶***flourish*** one's *stick* つえを振り回す. ¶I ***left*** my hat and *stick* in the hall. 帽子とつえを玄関において来た. ¶The *sticks* are ***tied*** together. 棒が束ねてある. ¶He ***wants*** the *stick.* 彼はなぐってやるがいい. ¶The *stick* ***snapped.*** つえがぽきっと折れた.

Q the ***Big*** *Stick* (=fellow) あの大男. ¶an ***odd*** *stick* 唐変木, 変り者. ¶a ***stout*** *stick* がん丈なつえ. ¶a ***queer old*** *stick* 変り者. ¶He is a ***regular*** *stick.* あいつはほんとの木偶だ.

Q^2 a ***composing*** *stick* 植字かまち, ステッキ. ¶a ***golf*** *stick* ゴルフ棒. ¶a Japanese ***fencing*** *stick* 竹刀(ｼﾅｲ). ¶put up an ***incense*** *stick* 線香を立てる. ¶a ***knitting*** *stick* 編棒. ¶a ***walking*** *stick*=《米》a cane ステッキ. ¶a ***yard*** *stick* ヤール尺.

P be supported ***by*** *sticks* 棒で支えてある. ¶without the help ***of*** a *stick* つえの助けをかりずに. ¶lean ***on*** one's *stick* つえに寄りかかる. ¶strike ***with*** a *stick* 棒で打つ ‖ walk ***with*** a *stick* つえをついて歩く.

P^2 a *stick* ***of*** candy (gum, soap, wax) [棒形の]キャンデー(など)一個 ‖ the *stick* ***of*** celery (asparagus) セロリ(アスパラガス)のくき ‖ a *stick* ***of*** timber 一本の材木.

stick, *v.* 突込む; さす; 張る; 《俗》動けなくする; 動かない; 立つ; 突出る; 固守する.

M The envelope *sticks* ***fast.*** 封筒がよく付く. ‖ *stick* ***fast*** in the mind (=memory) 心に深く銘記される ‖ The parley *stuck* ***fast*** (=bogged down). 談判(交渉)は行詰った. ‖ *stick* ***fast*** like a bar がっちり食いついて離れない. ¶He *stuck* his tongue ***out*** at me! 彼は私に向って舌を突き出した(嘲けって). 【類】"*Stick* ***out*** your tongue," said the doctor. ‖ *stick* one's head ***out*** [窓などから]頭を出す. ‖ *stick* ***out*** one's neck=rubberneck 首をのばす. 【類】His belly *stuck* ***out*** when he breathed in deeply. ¶*stick* so ***pertinaciously*** (=***tenaciously***) to this theory あくまでこの説を固執する. ¶*Stick* ***right*** where you are! そこ動くな. ¶*stick* things ***together*** 一緒にくっつける ‖ *stick* paper ***together*** with gum ゴムのりで紙を張り合わせる.

M^2 *Stick* ***around,*** can't you? I'll soon be back with you. 《米口》この辺で待っててくれ. すぐ戻るから. ¶Are you going to *stick* ***in*** all day? 君は一日中家にいるのか. ‖ If you *stick* ***in,*** there is quite a fair chance of your succeeding. 辛抱すれば君の成功のチャンスは大いにある ‖ *Stick* them ***up!*** [ギャングが]手をあげろ. ‖ I'll *stick* ***up*** for the woman speaker. あの婦人弁士の説に賛成する. 【類】I'll *stick* ***up*** for you on that (その点では). ‖ She is pretty much *stuck* ***up.*** 《米》彼女は相当お高くとまっている.

P *stick* ***at*** (=***to***) one's work 自分の仕事にかじりつく ‖ *stick* ***at*** it 《俗》辛抱する ‖ He *sticks* (=stops) ***at*** nothing. 彼は何ごとにもちゅうちょしない(向う見ずだ). ¶They *stick* ***at*** home. 彼らは外へ出ない. ¶*stick* a pen ***behind*** one's ear 耳にペンをはさむ. ¶We must *stick* ***by*** him. われわれは彼を裏切ってはいけない. ‖ The words seemed to *stick* ***in*** his throat when he tried to utter them. 彼がそれを言おうとした時に言葉がのどにつっかかったらしい. ‖ the mass of people *sticking* ***in*** the ruts of life 人生の旧態を墨守している民衆 ‖ *stick* a flower ***in*** one's button-hole ボタン穴に花を差す. 【類】*stick* a feather ***in*** the cap / *stick* one's hand ***in*** one's pocket ‖ *stick* ***in*** the mud 泥にはまり込む, 動きがとれない ‖ The boat (car) is *stuck* ***in*** the mud. 舟(など)が泥にはまって動けなくなっている. ¶*stick* a needle ***into*** cloth 布に針を刺す ‖ *stick* a skewer ***into*** meat 肉にくしを刺す ‖ A needle *stuck* ***into*** my finger. 針が私の指に刺さった. ¶*stick* a stamp ***on*** ... ...に切手をはる ‖ *stick* a potato ***on*** a fork フォークにじゃがいもを刺す ‖ He is *stuck* ***on*** the girl. 《口語》彼はその娘に参っている. ¶He *stuck* his head ***out of*** a window. 彼は窓から頭を突き出した. ‖ What is that *sticking* ***out of*** your pocket? 君のポケットから顔を出しているのは何か. ¶*stick* a bayonet ***through*** one's breast その胸に銃剣を突通す. ¶*stick* ***to*** one's agreement 約束(協約)を守る ‖ *stick* ***to*** one's business 熱心に仕事をする. 【類】*stick* ***to*** a job (position, work, post) ‖ *stick* ***to*** one's colors その主義を守る. 【類】*stick* ***to*** the principle through thick and thin (盛衰を一貫して) ‖ He always *sticks* ***to*** his country. 彼は常に国家に忠実だ. ‖ *stick* ***to*** it doggedly 剛情を張る ‖ *stick* ***to*** one's decision (resolution) 決心を変えない ‖ He *sticks* ***to*** nothing. 彼は何にもあきる. ‖ Birds-lime *sticks* ***to*** feathers. とりもちが羽につく. ‖ Glue *sticks* ***to*** the finger. にかわが指にくっつく. 【類】Habits *stick* ***to*** one. ‖ My tongue *stuck* ***to*** my throat. びっくり仰天した(はっとして舌がのどもとにひっついた). ¶*stick* ***with*** a needle 針で留める.

O The door *sticks* and doesn't move a bit. ドアーが堅くして開かない.

sticker, *n.* 《米》レッテル; とげ.

V ***plaster*** *stickers* on ... ...にレッテルをはりつける.

Q The thistle has ***sharp*** *stickers* on the stem. あざみは茎に鋭いとげがある.

Q^2 a ***price*** *sticker* 値段票(のり付の).

stickler, *n.* へりくつ屋.
P great *stickler* ***for*** ceremony (discipline, accuracy, forms) 儀式(など)のことを非常にやかましく言う人 ‖ I am no *stickler* ***for*** authority. 私はあえて出所のいかんなどをやかましく言うものではない.

sticky, *a.* べとべとした.
M I feel ***rather sticky*** here. ここにいると汗でべとべとする.
O It's warm and *sticky* inside. 中はむっとして汗ばむ.

stiff, *a.* こわばった；がん固な.
P feel *stiff* ***around*** (=about) the neck 首すじがこっている. ¶lie *stiff* ***in*** death 死んで体がこわばっている ‖ stand *stiff* ***in*** a foolish argument ばかげた議論をがんこに言い張る ‖ be *stiff* ***in*** one's negotiations 交渉がてごわい. ¶I am quite *stiff* ***with*** cold. 私は寒さで体がかたくなっている. 【類】He is *stiff* ***with*** rheumatism. / My fingers are *stiff* ***with*** cold (かじかんで).
O He was found dead lying *stiff* and cold. 彼を見つけた時は死体はもう冷たく堅くなっていた. ¶*stiff* prices 高値.

stiffen, *v.* こわばらせる；堅くなる.
P *stiffen* one's attitude ***at*** ... ...を聞いて(見て)態度を硬化させる. ¶*stiffen* ***in*** purpose 意志が堅くなる. ¶*stiffen* linen ***with*** starch のりをつけて麻布をこわばらせる ‖ He stood gazing on (=at) me, *stiffened* ***with*** astonishment. 彼は驚いて棒立ちになって私を見つめていた. ‖ *stiffened* ***with*** cold 寒さで体がこわばって.

stiffness, *n.* 固苦しさ.
Q The party was free from the ***detestable*** *stiffness* of ceremonies. その会は固苦しい儀式抜きで気持がよかった.

stifle, *v.* むせばせる, 窒息させる.
P *stifled* ***by*** the closeness of the room 密閉したへやの中で息苦しくなって ‖ He was *stifled* ***by*** gas. 彼はガスで窒息した. ¶*stifle* a person ***with*** smoke 煙にむせばせる.
O *stifle* one's sobs (laughter) すすり泣き(など)を抑える.

stigma, *n.* 汚名.
V ***fix*** an indelible *stigma* upon ... ...にそそぎ難い汚名をきせる. ¶***leave*** a *stigma* upon one's family その家名を汚す. ¶***place*** a severe social *stigma* on ... ...に一大汚名をきせる ¶***remove*** the *stigma* from the family 家族の汚名を除く.
V² the *stigma* ***attaching*** to domestic service 下女の仕事につきまとう肩身の狭さ.
Q place a ***heavy social*** *stigma* on ... 社会的一大汚名を...にきせる. ¶***no*** *stigma* rests on ... ...には汚点はない.

stigmatize, *v.* 汚名をきせる, 非難する.
P he is ***properly*** *stigmatized* as ... 彼が...と指弾されるのは当然だ.
P *stigmatize* a person ***as*** a coward 人をおく病者呼ばわりをする ‖ It is justly *stigmatized* ***as*** parrot work. それは人まねに過ぎないといわれているのはもっともなことだ.

stile, *n.* [かき根などを越すために設けた]踏段.
V ***cross*** a *stile* かきねの踏段を越す.

still, *n.* 静寂；〖映画〗スチール.
Q² ***midnight*** *still* 夜半の静寂. ¶collect ***movie-star*** *stills* 映画スターのスチールを集める.
P He passed away ***in*** the *still* of midnight. 彼は静寂な真夜中にこの世を去った.

still, *a.* 静まった.
M Everything was ***deadly*** *still*. 万物寂として声がなかった. ¶It was ***so*** *still* that you could have heard a pin drop. しんとして留針一つ落しても聞えるほどであった.

stillness, *n.* 静粛, 静けさ.
V But the sounds seemed only to ***accentuate*** the *stillness*. しかしその音はむしろ静粛を強めるように思われた. ¶***break*** the noontide *stillness* 正午の静けさを破る(鐘の音など). 【類】***break*** the *stillness* of the night. ¶A wild cry suddenly ***cleft*** the noontide *stillness*. 激しい叫び声が突然日中の静けさを破った. ¶***intensify*** the *stillness* of night 夜の静けさを強める.
V² A terrified *stillness* ***reigned***. 恐ろしく静まり返った.
Q There was a ***death-like*** *stillness* in the air. あたりは死のような静寂であった. ¶the ***deep*** *stillness* of the night 夜の深い静寂. ¶the ***sacred*** *stillness* of "God's Acre" 墓地の神々しい静けさ. ¶***solemn*** *stillness* おごそかな静寂.
P ***in*** the *stillness* of night 夜の静寂に.
P² The *stillness* ***of*** the room was broken by the ticking of the old clock in the corner. へやの静けさはすみの古時計のかちかちで破られた.

stilt, *n.* 竹馬, たかあし.
Q² ***bamboo*** *stilts* 竹馬.
P walk ***on*** *stilts* 竹馬で歩く.

stimulant, *n.* 刺激物, 興奮剤；酒.
V ***administer*** *stimulants* 興奮剤を服用させる. ¶***take*** *stimulants* 酒を飲む. ¶***use*** *stimulants* very sparingly 強精剤をごく少し用いる.
Q ***alcoholic*** *stimulants* 酒類. ¶a ***literary*** *stimulant*, such as tobacco, tea,etc. タバコ・茶などの文学活動の刺激物. ¶***psychic*** *stimulants* 精神の刺激物. ¶a ***sexual*** *stimulant* 性的興奮剤.
Q² a ***heart*** *stimulant* 強心剤.
P It is used ***as*** a *stimulant*. それは興奮剤に用いる. ¶He indulges too much ***in*** *stimulants*. 彼は酒などの刺激物を用い過ぎる.

stimulate, *v.* 刺激する.
M It *stimulates* ***mentally***. それは精神的に刺激する. ¶***sexually*** *stimulate* 性的に刺激する(薬剤など).
P *stimulated* ***by*** the criticism of ... ...の批評に刺激されて. 【類】*Stimulated* ***by*** a desire to tend his invalid mother, he studied medicine. ¶Success will *stimulate* a man ***to*** further efforts. 成功すると人は一層努力するものだ.

stimulation, *n.* 刺激, 興奮.
V ***receive*** powerful *stimulations* from ... ...から力強い刺激を受ける.
Q ***improper*** *stimulation* 不当の興奮.

stimulus, *n.* 刺激.
V ***give*** healthy *stimulus* to ... ...に健全な刺激を与える. ¶This will ***provide*** a good *stimulus* to young scholars of science. これは科学に志す青年学徒にとってよい刺激となろう. ¶***receive*** a powerful *stimulus* 力強い刺激を受ける.
Q ***environmental*** *stimulus* 環境の刺激. ¶susceptible to the influence of ***external*** *stimulus* 外界の刺激に動かされやすい. ¶***great*** *stimulus* to progress 進歩への大きな刺激. ¶***intellectual*** *stimulus* 知的刺激. ¶***literary*** *stimulus* 文学上の刺激. ¶***mental*** *stimulus* 精神的刺激. ¶a ***wholesome*** *stimulus* 健全な刺激.
P act ***as*** a powerful *stimulus* 強い刺激になる. ¶***under*** the *stimulus* of this hope この希望に刺激されて ‖ work ***under*** the *stimulus* of hunger 飢に迫って働く. ¶***with*** the *stimulus* of poverty and ambition 貧と野心に励まされて.
P² a *stimulus* ***to*** the ambitious 野望に燃える人々に対する刺激 ‖ Rivalry is often a *stimulus* ***to*** trade. 競争は往々商業の刺激になる. ‖ Hope is a *stimulus* ***to*** labor. 希望は労働の刺激になる.

sting, *n.* [こん虫の]はり, 針；刺傷；刺痛；[良心の]かしゃく.
V His words ***carry*** a *sting*. 彼の言葉には針がある. ¶***feel*** a *sting* of defeat 負けたことを残念がる. 【類】***feel*** a *sting* of remorse (後悔). ¶The wind ***has*** a *sting* in it. 風が痛い(身にしみる). ¶***take away*** the *sting* of one's sorrows 人の悲哀の痛みを除く.
Q Flattery is a ***honeyed*** *sting*. おべっかはみつのついた針だ. ¶a ***sharp*** *sting* 鋭い刺痛.
Q² an ***insect*** *sting* こん虫の一さし.
P He was hurt ***by*** a *sting*. 彼は針で刺された. ¶a jest ***with*** a *sting* in it 針のあるしゃれ.
P² the *stings* ***of*** conscience (shame) 良心(など)のかしゃく ‖ the *sting* ***of*** a wound 創傷の痛み. ¶a *sting* ***on*** the cheek ほおのさし傷.

sting, *v.* 刺す；刺激する.
M Conscience *stung* him ***sharply***. ひどく良心のかしゃくに苦しんだ.
P He was *stung* ***by*** a wasp. 彼はやまばちに刺された. ‖ It hurts to be *stung* ***by*** a bee. みつばちに刺されると痛い. ‖ *stung* ***by*** reproaches (remorse, insult) 非難(など)を苦にして. 【類】The boy was *stung* ***by*** the mockings of the other children. ¶He has been *stung* ***in*** the finger. 彼は指を刺された. ¶*sting* a person ***into*** action 人を刺激して活動させる. ¶The wasp *stung* me ***on*** the arm. そのやまばちは私の腕を刺した. ¶That *stung* me ***to*** the quick. その言葉がぐっと応えた. 【類】This will *sting* the sensitive Jap ***to*** the quick. ‖ He was *stung* ***to*** death. 彼は刺殺された. ‖ He was *stung* ***to*** fury. 彼は大いに憤慨した. ¶He was *stung* ***with*** desire. 彼に欲望がむらむらと起った.

stingy, *a.* けちな.
P He is good-natured, but *stingy* ***of*** tips. 彼は人は好いが祝儀を出し惜しむ ‖ *stingy* ***of*** effort 骨惜しみする.

stink, *v.* ...臭い, におう.
M *stink* ***out*** 悪臭で追い出す. 【類】*stink* ***out*** mosquitoes (rats, etc.).
M² *stinks* ***up*** violently すごく臭い.

P It *stinks of* onion (fish, ink) それはねぎ(など)臭い. ‖ He *stinks of* money. あいつはくさるほど金を持っている. 【類】*stink of* something smoky.

stint, *n.* 規定の仕事; 制限.

V *do* one's daily *stint* 日々課せられた仕事をする.

P *After* his *stint* as Lieutenant Colonel, he edited a weekly magazine. 中佐としての退役後彼は週刊誌を編集した. ¶ labor *without stint* 骨を惜しまず働く ‖ spend money *without stint* 惜気なく金を使う. 【類】Walking is the finest exercise that can be taken, and must be taken, and that *without stint* (十分に). / The work proceeded steadily, *without stint* or difficulty.

stint, *v.* 制限する.

P *stint* oneself *in* food 自分の食物を切詰める. ¶ He *stints* himself *of* the necessaries of life. 彼は日用品をけちけちする.

stipend, *n.* 給費.

P The *stipend attached* to such fellowships is $1,500. こうした大学特待生に対する給費は千五百ドルである. ¶ a graduate *holding* a *stipend* on condition of research = a fellow 特殊研究生.

P *with* a *stipend* of ... ...の俸給で.

stipulate, *v.* 約定する.

P *stipulate for* certain terms 一定の条件を設定する. ¶ it is *stipulated in* the contract that ... 契約に...と規定してある. 【類】as *stipulated in* the agreement.

stipulation, *n.* 契約条項.

V a contract *containing* so many *stipulations* 非常に多く条項を含む契約. ¶ *violate* the *stipulations* of a treaty 条約の条項にふれる.

Q² carry out *contract stipulations* 契約条項を実行する.

stir, *n.* かき回すこと; 動揺, 騒動; 刺激.

V It *caused* much *stir* in scientific and religious circles. それは科学界及び宗教界に多大の動揺を起した. ¶ The proclamation *created* a *stir* in the country. その布令で国内に騒動が起った. 【類】It *created* considerable *stir* in the medical world. / This didn't *create* much of a *stir*. ¶ It *excited* no small *stir* in the diplomatic world. それは外交界に少からざる動揺を与えた. ¶ He *gave* it a *stir* with his foot. 彼は足でそれを揺り動かした. ‖ *give* the fire a *stir* 火をかき回す. ¶ The event *made* a great *stir*. その事変で世間が大騒ぎをした. ‖ The arrival of the king *made* a great *stir*. 国王の到着で一層人気が立った. 【類】It *made* a great *stir* in the world. ¶ *produce* a great *stir* 大動揺を生じる. ¶ Public opinion *received* a great *stir*. 世論は大いに動揺した.

Q There was a *great stir* in the place. そこには大騒動があった. ¶ create an *immense stir* 大評判を取る. ¶ There is *no stir* felt in the open air. 戸外には風がちっともない.

P² The book created quite a *stir in* the medical world. その本は医学界に波紋を起した.

stir, *v.* かき回す; 動かす, 刺激する; 活動する; 《俗》起きる.

M He seldom *stirs abroad* (=out of the house). 彼は滅多に外出しない. ¶ He is *continually stirring*. 彼は常に活動している. ¶ *stir* a person *deeply* 人を深く感動させる. 【類】The audience was *deeply stirred* by his speech. ¶ *stir early* 朝早く起きる. ¶ Here I am not able to *stir outside*. [降りこめられなどして]私は外出ができない. ¶ *stir uneasily* もじもじする. ¶ He is not *stirring yet*. 彼はまだ寝ている.

M² *stir about* a good deal 大いに活躍する. ¶ *stirred on* by incentives in the form of ... ...という刺激によって元気づいて. ¶ A furious gale rose and it *stirred up* the seas. 猛烈な強風が起って海はしけになった. ¶ *stir up* one's mind 人の心を鼓舞する ‖ *stir up* curiosity 好奇心を刺激する. 【類】*stir up* wrath against ... / *stir up* much interest in ... / *stir up* a quarrel / *stir up* controversy / *stir up* civil war / *stir up* public opinion / *stir up* a nation to rebellion / *stir up* food strikes / *stir up* a reign of terror (恐怖政治) / *stir up* strife between nations / *stir up* violent discussions for and against (賛否の)... / *stir up* a reposing community (眠っている社会) / *stirred* them *up* to rebellion / The book *stirred up* a furor of excitement. ‖ *stir up* a nest of hornets 〘比喩〙てんやわんやの大騒動を引き起す ‖ *stir up* the passivity which tends to leave all decisions to others すべての決断を人に任せる傾向のある消極性にむち打って積極的にさせる ‖ be *stirred up* to mischief おだてられていたずらをする.

P The city was already *stirring about* the business of the day. 街はもうその日の仕事に従事していた. ¶ We could not *stir* him *from* his resolve. われわれは彼の決心を翻えさせることはできなかった. ¶ Odd sensations *stirred in* him. 変な気が彼の心に起った. ‖ No one was *stirring in* the house. 家の中では人の動くけはいがなかった. ¶ He is *stirred into* passionate anger. 彼は刺激されるとすぐにかっとなって怒りだす. ¶ He never *stirred out of* the house. 彼は家からでたことがない. ¶ The news *stirred* them *to* revolt. その報道は彼らを刺激して暴動を起させた. 【類】*stir* a person *to* action ‖ the archives of ... are *stirred to* the bottoms ...の文庫をねこそぎせんさくする. ¶ The failure seemed but to *stir* him *towards* renewed efforts. その失敗はかえって彼を駆って一層奮闘努力させたように思われた. ¶ *stir* the fire *with* a poker 火かきで火をかき回す. 【類】*stir* one's coffee *with* a spoon / His heart *stirred with* shame and anger. / The town was *stirring with* new life (活気). ¶ the thrill that was *stirred within* us われわれの心にわいたスリル(感激).

stirring, *n.* 動揺.

V *feel* a strange *stirring* of the heart 不思議な心の動揺を感じる.

Q a *deep stirring* of national feeling 国民的感情の深い動揺 ‖ the *deep stirring* of the soil 深耕.

P pour hot water *with stirring* かき回しながら湯を注ぐ.

stirrup, *n.* あぶみ.

P with a foot *in* the *stirrup* あぶみに片足を掛けて.

stitch, *n.* 一針(ひと); 縫い方.

V *drop* (=*let down*) a *stitch* 一目落す. ¶ I *have* a *stitch* in my side. 横腹がつる. ¶ I am *learning* a new *stitch*. 私は今新らしい縫い方をけいこしています. ¶ *put in* a *stitch* 一針縫う ‖ Fourteen *stitches* were *taken*. [傷などを]十四針縫った. ¶ *take up* a *stitch* 一目針をかける.

Q He has not a *dry stitch* on him. 彼はびしょぬれだ. ¶ an *ornamental stitch* 飾り縫い. ¶ take *several stitches* in the cloth 布に数針入れる.

Q² a *buttonhole stitch* ボタン穴のかがり.

P sew *with* large *stitches* 荒く縫う.

stitch, *v.* 縫う, かがる; 針仕事をする.

M *stitch assiduously* 精出して針仕事をする.

M² *stitch up* 縫い合わす, つくろう. 【類】*stitch up* a wound (rent) / *stitch up* a tent (net).

stock *n.* **(1)** 《米》株, 株式; 債券.

V *buy stock* 国庫債券を買う. ¶ *hold stock* 国庫債券を持っている ‖ *hold stocks* for a rise 株を売らずに上るのを待つ ‖ one who *hold* (=*owns*) *stocks* = a stockholder 株主. ¶ *issue* new *stock* 新株を発行する. ¶ *scalp stocks* and bonds 《口語》[資金回収のため]薄利で株を売る.

V² *Stock is going up* (*down*). 株は上って(下って)いる.

Q *active* (*inactive*) *stock* 人気(不人気)株. ¶ *capital stock* 資本株金. ¶ *common stock* 通常株. ¶ *founders' stock* 発起人株. ¶ *fresh stock* 新株. ¶ *fullpaid stock* 全額払込株. ¶ *part-paid stock* 一部払込株. ¶ *potential stock* 権利株. ¶ *preferred* (=*preference*) *stock* 優先株. ¶ *watered stock* 水まし株(帳面上の金額だけ増した).

Q² The *debenture stock* is redeemable between 19 ... and 19 ... at 102 yen. その債券は一九...と一九...の間に百二円で回収ができる. ¶ *premium stock* 割増金付株. ¶ a *railroad stock* 鉄道株.

P He has money *in stocks*. 彼は金を公債にして持っている. ‖ a fall *in stocks* 株の下落 ‖ speculate *in stocks* 株をやる ‖ £50,000 *in* the *stocks* 公債五万ポンド.

(2) 仕入品; 貯蔵物; 〘鉄道〙[集合]貨・客車両; 台木; *pl.* 造船台.

V *acquire* a good *stock* of common words 普通語をかなり豊富に覚える. ¶ We *carry* a very large *stock* of English, American, and French novels. 弊店は英米仏の小説の在庫品をたくさん持っています. ¶ *check* a *stock* 在庫品をつき合せる. ¶ Please order at once as our *stock* will soon be *cleared*. 手持品がじきに売切れますからどうぞすぐ御注文わ下さい. ¶ *corner* the *stock* of wheat on the market 小麦を買占める. ¶ *dispose of* a *stock* 在荷を処分する. ¶ The *stock* is nearly *exhausted*. 在庫品は切れかかっている. ‖ *exhaust* one's *stock* of patience 勘忍袋の緒が切れる. ¶ *find* a large *stock* to choose from その中から選択ができるたくさんの在庫品がある. ¶ *get in* a *stock* of ... ...を仕入

れる. ¶***have*** a great *stock* of hardware 金物の在庫品をたくさんに持っている ‖ ***have*** a rich *stock* of information 情報を豊富に持っている. 【類】***have*** a good *stock* of knowledge / ***have*** no *stock* of ... ¶***increase*** one's *stock* of words 語いの数を増大する. ¶***keep*** (=have *or* carry) a *stock* 在庫品を持っている. ¶***lay in*** a *stock* of coals 石炭を仕入れる ‖ ***lay in*** a good *stock* of ... ...を十分仕入れる. ¶***make*** *stock* of ... ...でもうける. ¶***reduce*** their *stocks* by attractive prices 値をこなして在庫品を売減らす. ¶***renew*** one's *stocks* 仕入れ替をする. ¶***replenish*** one's *stock* 仕入品を補充する. ¶rotate *stocks* 在庫品を古いのから順に出す. ¶***secure*** an enormous *stock* of ... ...をたくさん仕入れる. ¶try to ***sell off*** their surplus *stock* by auction 過剰在庫品を競売で売却しようとする. ¶***take stock*** たな卸しをする, [品物を]照合する ‖ ***take stocks*** of linen, crockery, and glassware 麻布・陶器・ガラス器などを仕入れる ‖ ***take stock*** of the progress made 進歩の跡を精査する ‖ He came intothe room, and, having ***taken stock*** of the position, went out. 彼はへやに入り様子を見てそれから出て行った. ‖ don't ***take*** much ***stock*** in the talk about ... ...の話に余り信をおくな.

V^2 Our *stock* is ***going off***. ストックが切れかかっている. ¶My *stock* of patience ***ran out***. 私の勘忍袋の緒が切れた.

Q lay in ***ample*** *stocks* of ... ...をたくさんに仕入れる. ¶***cleared*** *stock* 整理品. ¶a ***dead*** *stock* 売れ残り品. ¶***excessive*** *stocks* 余分の仕入品. ¶the two great nations of ***kindred*** *stock* 同種族の二大国民. ¶a ***large*** *stock* of ideas and experience 思想及び経験の大きな貯え. ¶He has a ***limited*** *stock* of words. 彼の語いは乏しい. ¶insects injurious to ***live*** *stock* 畜産に被害を与えるこん虫. ¶*Stocks* are ***low***. 在庫品が手薄だ. ¶a ***new*** (an ***old***) *stock* 新着(古)荷. ¶have a ***richer*** *stock* of ideas さらに思想が豊富だ. ¶have a ***small*** (***large***) *stock* on hand 手持ちが少ない(豊富だ).

Q^2 The ***coal*** *stock* has further dwindled. 石炭の貯蔵はさらに減少している. ¶an ***emergency*** *stock* 非常用の貯蔵. ¶***paper*** *stock* 製紙原料(ぼろ・パルプなど). ¶the ***parent*** *stock* 根原. ¶a ***reserve*** *stock* 予備品. ¶a ***rifle*** *stock* 小銃の台じり. ¶the ***rolling*** *stock* 〘鉄道〙[一鉄道会社所有の]機関車・客・貨車の全部. ¶the ***passenger*** (***goods***) ***rolling*** *stock* 〘集合〙客(貨)車. ¶replenishment of ***war*** *stocks* 戦争資材の補給.

P goods ***in*** *stock* 手持ちの品. 【類】I have them ***in*** *stock*. / Goods are kept ***in*** *stock*, and can be supplied without delay. / The book you write for (御注文の本) is not ***in*** *stock*. ¶ships ***on*** the *stocks* (=under construction) 建造中の船. ¶be ***out of*** *stock* 品切れになっている.

P^2 *stocks* ***in*** (=***on***) hand 手もと在荷 ‖ *stock* ***in*** trade 手持ち品; [大工などの]商売道具. ¶a *stock* ***of*** goods 仕入れてある品 ‖ One's *stock* ***of*** patience has run out 勘忍袋の緒が切れた.

(3) 血統, 家柄(ぎ); 種族; 家畜.

Q He belongs to a ***good old*** *stock*. 彼は旧家の出だ. ¶***growing*** *stock* 家禽家畜. ¶***live*** *stock* 家畜. ¶of the ***same ethnic*** *stock* 同種類の(民族など). ¶a ***tainted*** *stock* 悪い遺伝のある血統.

Q^2 ***farming*** *stock* 家畜家禽.

P He comes ***of*** a good *stock*. 彼は家柄がよい.

stock, *v.* 仕入れる; 貯蔵する.

M Wine is *stocked* ***all the year round***. ぶどう酒は年中貯蔵している. ¶The market is now ***fully*** *stocked*. 今市場には十分在荷がある. ¶*stock* ***heavily*** before holidays 休暇前にうんと仕入れをする. ¶a pond ***plentifully*** *stocked* with carp こいをたくさん囲っている池. ¶The shop is ***well*** *stocked*. あの店は品がたくさん仕入れてある. ‖ a large park ***well*** *stocked* with deer しかをたくさん飼ってある大公園. ¶The mountain streams in this vicinity are ***well*** *stocked* with rainbow trout. この近くの溪流には紅ますがたくさんいる.

M^2 *stock* ***up*** for the holiday trade 休日(クリスマスなど)売りの仕入れをする. 【類】goods *stocked* ***up*** in anticipation of higher prices.

P a garden *stocked* ***with*** rare trees and attractive rockeries 珍木やおもしろい岩を集めた庭園. 【類】districts well *stocked* ***with*** game (猟の目的物) ‖ *stock* land ***with*** clover クローバの種を地にまきつけておく ‖ *stock* one's mind ***with*** knowledge 頭に知識をたくわえる ‖ The library is well *stocked* ***with*** rare books. その図書館は珍書が多い.

stockade, *n.* さく; 収容所.

V ***make*** (=***erect***) a *stockade* さくを作る.

Q^2 a ***prisoner of war*** *stockade* 捕虜収容所.

stockings, *n. pl.* 長くつ下.

V ***darn*** (=***mend***) *stockings* くつ下をかがる. ¶***foot*** *stockings* くつ下の足部を付ける. ¶***hang up*** *stockings* [クリスマスなどに]くつ下をつるす. ¶***knit*** *stockings* くつ下を編む. ¶***pull off*** her *stockings* そのくつ下を脱ぐ. ¶***pull on*** her *stockings* そのくつ下をはく. ¶***stitch up*** one's *stockings* そのくつ下をつくろう. ¶***wear*** *stockings* くつ下をはく.

Q ***clocked*** *stockings* くるぶしに縫取飾りのあるくつ下. ¶***long, thick, ribbed*** *stockings* 長くて厚いうねのある毛糸くつ下.

Q^2 darn the ***family*** *stockings* 家族のくつ下をかがる. ¶***imitation, silk*** *stockings* 人絹くつ下. ¶***nylon*** *stockings* ナイロンくつ下. ¶***open-work*** *stockings* すかし細工のくつ下. ¶***woolly-nylon*** *stockings* ウーリーナイロンくつ下. ¶***yarn*** *stockings* 毛糸のくつ下.

P He stands six feet ***in*** his *stockings*. 彼は(くつをはかずに)くつ下で六フィートある. ¶a pair ***of*** *stockings* 一足のくつ下.

stock-in-trade, *n.* 商売品, 商売道具.

Q ***dead*** *stock-in-trade* 不さばき品. ¶a ***politician's*** *stock-in-trade* 政治家の商売道具(身上).

stockpile, *n.* 物資蓄積.

Q the nation's ***strategic*** *stockpile* その国家の戦略物資の蓄積.

Q^2 destroy all the ***atomic-bomb*** *stockpiles* 原子爆弾の貯蔵を全部破壊する.

P^2 a *stockpile* ***of*** war material 戦争資材のストックのたい積.

stocky, *a.* 肥えた.

P be *stocky* ***in*** build 太っちょである.

stoicism, *n.* ストア哲学; 冷静.

V ***manifest*** a calm *stoicism* 自若としている.

stoke, *v.* 《俗》食物をかっ込む.

M^2 "*stoke* ***up***" at coffee-house hard by the Docks ドックのすぐそばのコーヒー店で腹をこしらえる.

stomach, *n.* 胃; 腹; 食欲; 欲望; 気分.

V ***disarrange*** the *stomach* 胃をこわす. ¶***disorder*** the *stomach* 胃をそこねる. ¶***empty*** the *stomach* 胃をからにする. ¶***fill*** the *stomach* 腹ごしらえをする. ¶***have*** a *stomach* for fighting 闘志がある ‖ He ***has*** a disordered *stomach*. 彼は胃の調子が狂っている. ‖ ***have*** a good *stomach* for one's meals 食欲が進む ‖ ***have*** no *stomach* for continuing the opposition 反対を続けるだけの勇気がない. ¶***injure*** one's *stomach* by eating too much 食い過ぎでお腹をこわす. ¶***load*** one's *stomach* with sweets, fruit, and pastry 菓子・果物・ねり粉菓子を胃に詰め込む. ¶***overload*** the *stomach* late at night 夜おそくなって食べ過ごす. ¶***put*** the *stomach* out of order 胃をこわす. ¶***rip up*** one's own *stomach* 切腹する. ¶***satisfy*** the *stomachs* of the people 人民の欲望を満足させる. ¶***stay*** the *stomach* 一時空腹を抑える. ¶***strengthen*** a weak *stomach* 弱い胃を丈夫にする. ¶It is enough to ***turn*** one's *stomach* (=make one sick). 全く胸が悪くなる. 【類】literally (文字通りに) ***turn*** one's *stomach*. ¶Cocktails ***upset*** my *stomach*. 私はカクテル(混酒)で胃をこわした. ¶***wash out*** the *stomach* 胃を洗浄する.

V^2 My *stomach* ***aches***. 私は胃が痛む.

Q his ***bulging*** *stomach* 彼のほてい腹. ¶a ***dyspeptic*** *stomach* 消化不良の胃. ¶One cannot work on an ***empty*** *stomach*. 空腹では仕事はできない. ‖ go through a forenoon "on an ***empty*** *stomach*" 朝食を抜きにする. 【類】with an ***empty*** *stomach*. ¶A ***good*** *stomach* is the best sauce. 胃の善い人にまずい物なし. ¶a ***loaded*** *stomach* 食物のたまっている(満腹した)胃. ¶the ***protruding*** *stomach* 出腹. ¶a ***protuberant*** *stomach* 太鼓腹. ¶a ***queasy*** *stomach* むかつく(吐気のする)胃. ¶a ***sour*** *stomach* 胸やけ(胃酸過多). ¶poor sailors who have ***weak*** *stomachs* 胃が弱くってじきに船酔のする人たち. ¶spitchcock are too heavy for a person with a ***weak*** *stomach*. かば焼きは胃腸の弱い人にはもたれる.

P It makes me sick ***at*** my *stomach* to look at him. 彼を見ると胸が悪くなる. ¶food digestible ***by*** a weak *stomach* 弱い胃でも消化される食物. ¶It is bad ***for*** the *stomach*. それは胃に悪い. ¶I feel (=have) a pain ***in*** my *stomach*. 私は胃が痛む. ‖ I feel quite sick ***in*** the *stomach*. 私はどうも腹具合が悪い. ‖ I kicked him ***in*** the *stomach*. 私は彼の下腹をけった. ¶take it ***into*** the *stomach* それを胃に入れる. ¶a cancer ***of*** the *stomach* 胃がん. ¶lie ***on*** one's *stomach* in bed 寝床で腹ばいになる ‖ wind ***on*** the *stomach* 胃のガ

ス. ¶The way to a man's heart is ***through*** his *stomach.* 人にうんと言わせるにはごちそうするに限る. ¶go to bed ***with*** an empty *stomach* 空腹のまま寝る.

stone, *n.* 石; 結石; [果実の]さね, たね.

V ***break*** *stone* 石を割る. ¶***buzz*** a *stone* 《俗》石を力一杯に投げる. ¶The hard seeds in cherries, peaches, and other fruits are ***called*** pits or *stones.* さくらんぼ, 桃その他果実の固いたねをピットとかストーンとか呼んでいる. ¶***cast*** (=throw) a *stone* at ... ...に石をぶっつける; ...をひぼうする. ¶He has ***contributed*** many *stones* to the edifice. 彼は大いにその事業に貢献する所があった. ¶***cut*** *stone* 石を切る. ¶***dress*** *stone* 石をみがく. ¶***erect*** a *stone* on a grave bearing a suitable inscription 適当な碑銘を刻んだ石碑を墓の上に建てる. ¶***fling*** a *stone* into the pond 池に石を投げる. ¶***hurl*** a *stone* at a dog 犬に石を投げつける. ¶Plums ***have*** *stones* inside. 梅にはたねがある. ‖ ***have*** a *stone* in place of a heart 石のように無情である. ¶***leave*** no *stone* unturned to ... ...しようと百方手を尽す. 【類】I will not ***leave*** a *stone* unturned to bring it to a successful conclusion. ¶***lift*** a *stone* with a cry of heave=heave a stone どっこいしょと石を持ち上げる. ¶***quarry*** *stone* 石を切り出す. ¶***raise*** a *stone* with an effort うんと力を入れて石を持ち上あげる. ¶***remove*** the *stones* from peaches 桃の実からたねを取去る. ¶***rive*** a *stone* 石を割る. ¶***roll*** a big *stone* 大石をころがす. 【類】prevent the practice of ***rolling*** *stones* down the mountain slopes. ¶***skip*** a *stone* on the surface of the water 水面に石を飛ばす. ¶***throw*** *stones* over the fence へい越しに石を投げる.

Q ***crushed*** *stone* 砕石. ¶the ***oldest dated*** *stones* known to archaeology 年号入の石としては最古のもの. ¶a ***precious*** *stone* set in ... ...にちりばめた宝石. ¶a ***rolling*** *stone* 職業を始終取替える人; 放浪者. 【類】A ***rolling*** *stone* gathers no moss. ¶a ***rough*** *stone* 粗石(あらいし). ¶a ***water-rounded*** *stone* [川の]丸石. ¶***small round*** *stones* [海辺などの]角のとれた小石.

Q² ***building*** *stones* 建築用石材. ¶lay a ***corner*** *stone* すみ石を据える. ¶lay the ***foundation*** *stone* of ... ...の土台石を据える ‖ overturn the ***foundation*** *stones* of British freedom 英国の自由の土台をくつがえす. ¶a ***grape*** (***cherry, peach, plum***) *stone* ぶどう(など)のたね. ¶a ***graveyard*** *stone* 墓石. ¶a ***memorial*** *stone* 記念碑. ¶a ***mile*** *stone* on the road to ... ...に至る道中のマイル標. ¶a ***mill*** *stone* 石うす. ¶a ***sharpening*** *stone* と石.

P trip ***against*** (=***over***) a *stone* 石につまずく. ¶He is buried ***beneath*** this *stone.* 彼はこの石の下に葬られている. ¶print ***from*** *stone* 石版で印刷する. ¶a builder ***in*** *stone* 石造建築家. ¶It is built ***of*** *stone.* それは石造だ. ‖ He has a heart ***of*** *stone.* 彼は無情だ. ‖ a house ***of*** *stone* 石造の家. ‖ a piece (=bit) ***of*** *stone* 一片の石. ¶carve ***on*** *stone* 石に彫る ‖ stumble ***on*** a *stone* 石につまずく. ¶turn ***to*** *stone* 石につまずく. ¶turn ***to*** *stone* 石になる. ¶kill two birds ***with*** one *stone* 一石で二鳥を殺す.

P² a *stone* ***in*** the bladder ぼうこう内の結石.

stone, *v.* 石をぶっつける.

P *stone* a person ***to*** death 石を投げて人を殺す.

stooge, *n.* 《俗》のろま.

Q You ***big*** *stooge!* この大ばか野郎.

stool, *n.* [一人用の]こしかけ; 便器; 便通.

V My *stools* have ***become regular.*** 私は通じが規則正しくなった.

Q ***baby's*** *stools* 乳児の便. ¶***frequent*** *stools* ひん繁な便通.

Q² a ***camp*** *stool* [帆布製の]折たたみ式の腰かけ. ¶***cholera*** *stools* コレラ患者の便.

P ***after*** *stool* 便通後に. ¶strain ***at*** *stool* 便通にいきむ. ¶fall ***between*** two *stools* あぶはち取らずになる. ¶go ***to*** *stool* 大便に行く. 【類】He has not been ***to*** *stool* (=the closet) for two days.

stoop, *n.* かがむこと; 卑屈.

V ***have*** the carpenter's *stoop* 職人根性を持つ.

Q have a ***shocking*** *stoop* ひどい猫背だ.

P walk ***with*** a *stoop* 上半身をかがめて歩く.

stoop, *v.* かがむ; 身を落す, 屈従する.

M² *stoop* ***down*** to pick a flower 体をかがめて花を摘む.

P *stoop* ***from*** age 年とって腰が曲る. ¶*stoop* ***in*** walking かがんで歩く. ¶*stoop* ***over*** a desk 机にうつ伏せになる. ¶*stoop* ***to*** beggary こじきに身を落す ‖ *stoop* ***to*** flattery へいへいして機げんをとる ‖ *stoop* ***to*** humiliation 屈従する ‖ He *stooped* ***to*** such meanness. 彼はそんな卑しいことまでした. 【類】*stoop* ***to*** meanness and duplicity (かげひなた).

stop, *n.* 停止, 停車; 停留所, 駅; 滞留; 句読点.

V Every letter should ***have*** its proper *stops.* 手紙はどれも句読点をきちんとつけなければいけない. ‖ You ***have*** five more *stops* before you get to ... ...まであと五回停車する. ¶The train ***made*** a twenty-minute *stop* for refreshments. 汽車は食事のため二十分停車した. ‖ ***make*** three *stops* [汽車など]三度停車する. ¶***put*** a *stop* to the practice (this evil) その習慣(など)をやめる ‖ ***put*** a *stop* upon a vessel 船に停船を命じる. ¶***remove*** the *stop* 禁止を解く.

Q put a ***complete*** *stop* to ... ...を完全にやめる. ¶put an ***effective*** *stop* to ... ...をりっぱにやめる. ¶the ***first important*** *stop* in the railway journey その汽車旅行での最初の重要停車駅. ¶The horse came to a ***full*** *stop.* 馬がぴったり止まった. ¶the ***last*** *stop* (=terminus) [電車などの]終点. ¶come to a ***sudden*** *stop* 突然とまる, 急停車する. ¶The train makes a ***short*** (***long***) *stop* at this station. その列車はこの停車場でちょっと(長く)停車する.

Q² a ***bus*** (***car***) *stop* バス(など)停留所. ¶an ***emergency*** *stop* 『鉄道』非常停車. ¶with a ***one-day*** *stop* in Tokyo 東京で一日滞在して. ¶make an ***overnight*** (a ***two-night***) *stop* at ... ...に一泊(二泊)する. ¶a ***service*** *stop* 『鉄道』通常停車. ¶a ***whistle*** *stop* 《米口語》急行列車の停車しない小駅.

P The train is ***at*** a *stop.* 汽車は止まっている. ¶bring it ***to*** a *stop* それを停止させる. ¶run ***without*** a *stop* [急行列車など]止まらずに走る.

P² a *stop* ***for*** a time 暫時の停止. ¶be ***under*** a *stop* put by Board of Trade surveyor 《英》商務省検査官の命による(貿易)停止状態にある. ¶Paris is one of the *stops* ***in*** his itinerary. パリーは彼の巡歴における停留所の一つだ.

stop, *v.* 止める; 休む; 宿泊する.

M *Stop* ***a moment.*** ちょっと待って. ¶*stop* ***away*** 外泊する. ¶The horse *stopped* ***dead.*** 馬がぴったり止まった. ¶*stop* ***deprecatingly*** いけないと言ってしきりに止める. ¶business (work) is ***entirely*** *stopped* owing to (=in consequence of) ... ...のため商売(仕事)は全然休止状態である. ¶be ***loosely*** *stopped* せんをゆるくしてある. ¶He ***never*** *stops* to think. 彼は落着いて考えるということをしない. ¶*stop* ***out*** 外泊する. ¶See that your sentences are ***properly*** *stopped.* 文章の句読点を正しくせよ. ¶*stop* the window ***rattling*** 窓のがたがたする音をとめる. ¶The use ***seldom*** *stops* to notice the fact. 大半の(語句などの)使用者はこの事実に気がつくことはまれである. ¶*stop* ***short*** (=dead) ぴったりとまる. 【類】He *stopped* ***short*** in the middle of his speech. ‖ *stop* ***short*** of one's desire 希望が達せられない.

M² Please *stop* ***by*** (=***in***) when you come this way. こちらへお出での節はお立寄り下さい. ¶*stop* (=stay) ***in*** all day 一日中引きこもる(外出しない) ‖ He *stopped* ***in*** on us this morning. 彼は今朝われわれのところを訪問した. ¶*stop* ***off*** (=break one's journey) at ... ...で途中下車をする. ¶you may *stop* ***over*** at ... ...に途中下車してもよい. ¶*stop* ***up*** a hole 穴をふさぐ ‖ *stop* (=sit) ***up*** all night 一晩中起きている.

P *stop* ***at*** home [外出せずに]家にいる ‖ *stop* ***at*** an inn 宿屋に泊る ‖ *stop* ***at*** a tea-house 茶屋に休む. 【類】How long does this train *stop* ***at*** Kyoto? ‖ *stop* ***at*** difficulty 困難に出会ってがっかりする ‖ *stop* ***at*** no expense 入費を意としない ‖ *stop* (=stick) ***at*** nothing to obtain it それを手にするまではやめない ‖ *stop* ***at*** an inn for the night その晩そこに一泊する. ¶All work *stops* ***at*** six o'clock ***in*** this factory. この工場では仕事はすべて六時にやめる. ¶Work is *stopped* ***by*** bad weather. 天気が悪いので仕事は中止になっている. 【類】All traffic is *stopped* ***by*** snow. ¶They *stopped* work ***for*** a week. 二週間休業した. ‖ fail to *stop* ***for*** a red light 赤信号であるのに停止せずにいる. ¶*stop* a person ***from*** folly そのばかなことをやめさせる ‖ The ointment *stops* the hair ***from*** falling out. その塗薬をつけると抜け毛がとまる. 【類】*stop* him ***from*** drinking / It's a lot easier to *stop* something ***from*** happening than to fix it after it happens. ‖ *Stop* there ***from*** running. ほつれを止めてくれ(くつ下など). ¶I *stopped* ***to*** the end so as to see the whole of it. それを全部見ようと思って最後まで残った. ¶I am *stopping* ***with*** my nephew. 私はおいの家に泊っている. ‖ *stop* a bottle ***with*** a cork コルクでびんのふたをする.

O *stop* to think 考えて見る. ¶But we must not *stop* to

sentimentalize. しかしわれわれはいたずらに感傷的に流れてはならない.

stopgap, *n.* 埋草.
Q It is a ***mere stopgap*** for the space. それはほんの埋草だ.
P serve ***as*** a ***stopgap*** [一時の]間にあわせになる.

stopover, *n.* 《米》途中下車.
V ***allow stopover*** at all principal points [乗車券など]すべての主要地点で途中下車を許す. 【類】***allow stopovers*** anywhere. / on these tickets *stopovers* will be ***allowed*** at ... / *Stopover* at ... will be ***allowed*** on all through tickets (通し切符). / This ticket ***allows*** you two *stopovers* on your way. ¶All steamers ***grant*** thirty-day *stopover* at Honolulu. 汽船は皆ホノルルで三十日の途中下船を許す. ¶***make*** a *stopover* at ... 《米》...に途中下車する. ¶***permit*** *stopovers* at ... [乗車券など]...で途中下車を許す.
Q offer a ***pleasant*** *stopover* to ... ...は途中下車をして楽しめる.
Q^2 ***one day*** *stopover* at Honolulu ホノルルで一日の途中下船.
P^2 a *stopover* ***of*** eleven days ***at*** ... ...で十一日間の途中下船. ¶a *stopover* ***on*** first-class tickets 一等切符での途中下車.

stoppage, *n.* 休止.
Q^2 a ***production*** *stoppage* 生産休止. ¶strikes and ***work*** *stoppages* 争議と作業休止. 【類】without ***work*** *stoppage*.

stopper, *n.* [穴などを]ふさぐ(埋める)人(物), せん.
V That ***put*** the *stopper* on the business. これでその話はさたやみになった.

stopper, *v.* せんをする.
M ***loosely stoppered*** ゆるくせんをして.

storage, *n.* 貯蔵; 貯蔵所.
V ***hire*** *storage* 倉庫を賃借する.
Q in ***cold*** *storage* 冷蔵して.
P Three hundred bags of rice are ***in*** *storage*. 三百俵の米がたくわえられてある. 【類】The reservoirs still have ***in*** *storage* about 30 million cubic meters.

store, *n.* 貯蔵品, 用品; 《米》商店; *pl.* 《英》百貨店.
V ***close*** one's *store* 閉店する. ¶***close up*** the *store* 店を仕舞う(商売をやめる). ¶The press ***exhausted*** its *store* of vile epithets in opposition. 新聞紙は口をきわめてば倒した. ¶He ***has*** a *store* of learning. 彼は相当学問がある. ¶***husband*** the *store* [石炭などの]貯蔵品を節約する. ¶***keep*** *store* 店を持つ. ¶***lay up*** a reserve *store* of energy 余分の精力をたくわえる. ¶***open*** a *store* 店を開く. ¶***own*** a *store* 店主である. ¶***patronize*** a *store* 店をひいきにする. ¶***run*** a grocery *store* 雑貨店を経営する. ¶***set*** (no) *store* by ... ...を重(軽)んじる. 【類】***set*** most *store* by ... / ***set*** great *store* by ... / ***set*** little *store* by science ‖ Imagining it was only a copy, he ***set*** no *store* upon it. 写本だと思って彼はそれを大切にしなかった. ¶***set up*** one's *store* 店を出す. ¶That *store* seems to be well ***stocked***. あの店は豊富に仕入れがしてあるらしい.
Q ***co-operative*** *stores* 消費組合店. ¶the author is remarkable for his ***copious*** *store* of words and phrases その著者の使用語句の豊富さが目立つ. ¶a ***fashionable*** *store* 高級店. ¶your ***favorite*** *store* あなたの買いつけの店. 【類】her most ***favorite*** *store*. ¶a post-office and a ***general*** *store* 郵便局と雑貨店を兼ねた店. ¶a ***grocery*** [*store*] 《米》=a grocer's 《英》食料品店. 英国の grocer's は食料品の他に家庭用品も販売する. ¶***marine*** *stores* 古船具類. ¶***military*** and ***naval*** *stores* 陸海軍用品. ¶a ***respectable*** *store* 良心的な店. ¶a ***second-hand*** *store* 古物店. ¶***ship's*** *stores* 船舶用品. ¶look for a ***vacant*** *store* あき店を捜す. ¶a ***wholesale*** *store* 卸し売店.
Q^2 an ***all-night*** *store* 徹夜営業店. ¶a ***book*** *store* (*or* book-store)=《英》a bookseller's 本屋. ¶a ***chain*** *store* 連鎖店. ¶a ***cigar*** *store* 《米》=a tobacconist's 《英》タバコ屋. ¶a ***clothing*** *store* 衣服店. ☞ store clothes は「既製の服」. ¶a ***cooking*** *store* かっぽう店. ¶a ***corner*** *store* かど店. ¶an ill-stocked ***country*** *store* 仕入の不十分ないなか店. ¶a ***delicatessen*** *store* 食料品店(かん詰·あげもの, その他調製料理を売る). ¶a ***department*** *store* デパート. ¶a ***drug*** *store* 《米》薬店(飲物や化粧品·雑誌なども売る). ¶a ***dry goods*** *store* 《米》=a draper 《英》生地屋. ¶a small ***general merchandise*** *store* 小規模の雑貨店, よろず屋. ¶open a ***grocery*** *store* 《米》食料品店を開く. ¶a ***hardware*** *store* 金物店. ¶a ladys' (men's) ***hat*** *store* 《米》婦人(男子)帽子店. ¶$24,000 worth of jewelery stolen from a ***jewelery*** *store* in a hold-up ギャングが入って宝石店から盗んだ二万四千ドル相当の宝石. ¶the ***Macy*** *stores*=Macy's [米国]メーシイ百貨店. ¶a ***member*** *store* 加盟店. ¶an ***office equipment*** *store* 事務用品店. ¶a ***picture-frame*** *store* 額ぶち店. ¶a ***pioneer*** *store* 元祖店. ¶a ***ready-to-wear*** *store* 既製洋服店. ¶a ***school supply*** *store* 学校用品店. ¶a ***seed*** *store* 種屋. ¶a ***shoe*** *store* くつ屋. ☞ a shoe shop は製作·修理をやる. ¶a ***specialities*** *store* 専門品店. ¶a ***sports*** *store* 運動用具店. ¶a ***stationery*** *store*=《英》a stationer's 文房具店. ¶a ***ten cent*** *store* 十セント·ストア. ¶He owns a ***toy*** *store*. 彼はがん具店をやっている. ¶a ***used clothing*** *store*=a second-hand clothes store 古着屋. ¶a ***variety*** *store* 雑貨店.
P buy things ***at*** *stores* 品物を店で買う. 【類】It is now sold ***at*** drug *stores* for ten cents. ¶The wares ***in*** that *store* are dear. あの店の品は高い. ‖ have it ***in*** *store* それを持合わせる. 【類】What the future has ***in*** *store* for him no one can foretell. / I little thought of the calamity (災害) which was ***in*** *store* for us. / Many people must wonder what science has ***in*** *store* for us in 1940. ‖ What future is there ***in*** *store* for them, I wonder? 彼らにはどんな将来が待っているのであろうか. ‖ I have a surprise [***in*** *store*] for you. すばらしいニュースがあるぜ. ‖ You won't get that ***in*** every *store*. そうざらにはありません(売子の言葉). ¶***with*** a *store* of learning 相当学問があって.
P^2 *stores* ***for*** the troops 軍隊用品. ¶one's *stores* ***of*** observation その豊富な見聞 ‖ the *stores* ***of*** a family 家庭の必要物. 【類】The volume is a *store* ***of*** good things.

store, *v.* たくわえる, 貯蔵する; 仕込む.
M *store* a plant ***away*** from frost 木の霜よけをする ‖ *store* ***away*** goods for future sale 先売り用に商品を在庫しておく. ¶The museum is ***richly stored*** with such objects. 博物館はこの種の物品を豊富に収蔵している. 【類】His head is ***richly stored*** with knowledge.
M^2 Ants *store* ***up*** food against (=for) winter. ありは冬の用意に食物を貯蔵する. ‖ *store* ***up*** knowledge (wealth, strength) 知識(など)をたくわえる. 【類】*store* ***up*** grain against famine / the vast supply of knowledge that has been *stored* ***up*** in books / energy *stored* ***in*** atomic nuclei (原子核).
P *store* vegetables ***for*** winter 冬季用として野菜を貯蔵する. ¶*store* goods ***in*** a warehouse. 倉庫に商品を貯蔵する. ¶*store* a warehouse ***with*** goods 品物を倉庫にたくわえる. ‖ *store* one's memory ***with*** facts (knowledge, information) 事実(など)を覚え込む.

storehouse, *n.* 倉庫.
Q an ***inexhaustible*** *storehouse* of information 無尽蔵の知識の倉庫. ¶a ***perfect*** *storehouse* of literary treasure 真の文学の宝庫. ¶a ***vast*** *storehouse* of facts 事実(知識)の大宝庫.
P^2 a *storehouse* ***of*** knowledge 知識の蔵.

stork, *n.* こうのとり.
V^2 *Storks* ***clatter***. こうのとりが鳴く. ¶Who's brought the baby here?—A ***stork has***. だれが赤ちゃんを連れてきたの—こうのとりよ.

storm, *n.* 暴風雨, あらし; 動乱; 強襲.
V ***abide*** (=face) the *storm* 暴風雨に向って行く. ¶***brave*** a *storm* あらしを冒す. ¶***dare*** a *storm* 暴風雨を冒す. ¶the flashes of lightning ***heralding*** the *storm* あらしを予報する稲妻. ¶***lull*** (=***quiet***) a *storm* あらしを静める. ¶The dark low clouds ***presage*** the *storm*. 暗雲低迷はあらしの前兆である. ¶***raise*** a terrible *storm* 恐ろしいあらしを巻起す ‖ A *storm* was ***raised*** by the first edition of Malthus' book. マルサスの本(人口論)が出たとき一大センセーションを巻き起した. ‖ ***raise*** a *storm* in a tea-cup 内輪もめを起す. ¶I never ***saw*** such a *storm* in my life. 私はまだこんなあらしを見たことがない. ¶***still*** a *storm* 騒動を静める. ¶The ship has ***survived*** (=***weathered***) the *storm*. 船はしけをしのいだ. ¶***threaten*** a *storm* 風雲をはらむ. ¶***weather*** [***out***] (=come safely through) a *storm* あらしをしのぐ; 難局を切抜ける. 【類】The ship ***weathered*** the *storm*. ¶The tree has ***withstood*** the *storms* of 400 years. その木は四百年の風雨をしのいで来た.
V^2 when the *storm* ***abates*** あらしがなぐと. ¶A *storm* is ***approaching***. 暴風が押し寄せて来る. ¶A terrible *storm* of wind and rain ***arose***. 恐ろしい暴風雨が起った. ¶wait until the *storm* ***blows over*** あらしがやむまで待つ. ¶The *storm* ***breaks***. あらしが起る. ‖ The *storm* has ***broken out***. あらしが起った. ¶A *storm* is ***brewing*** (=***gathering***). あらしをはらんでいる. ¶The *storm* ***came on*** of a sudden. あ

らしが不意にやって来た. ¶A *storm* is ***coming up***. あらしがやって来る. ¶A sudden *storm* ***descended***. 突然あらしが襲来した. ¶The *storm* has ***passed off*** (=***over***). あらしが通り過ぎた. ¶A great *storm* was ***raging*** at the time. その時は大あらしだった. ¶A *storm* ***roars***. 暴風がうなる. ¶The *storm* of applause has ***subsided***. 拍手のあらしがやんだ.

Q mutter of ***departing*** *storm* 過ぎ去るあらしのうなり. ¶The ***economic*** *storm* hit the publishers. 経済のあらしが出版業に波及した. ¶a ***fearful*** *storm* 恐ろしいあらし. ¶There was a ***furious*** *storm* blowing. 猛烈な暴風が吹きまくっていた. ¶the ***gathering*** *storm* 次第に募る暴風. ¶A ***heavy*** *storm* is now raging here. ここではひどいあらしが今吹きまくっている. 【類】a ***heavy*** *storm* of lightning (wind and rain). ¶an unusually ***severe*** *storm* 珍らしいひどいあらし. ¶a ***severe electric*** *storm* 大雷雨. ¶a ***sudden*** *storm* arose and ... 突然暴風が起って… ¶a ***thunder-raged*** *storm* 大雷雨. ¶a ***violent*** *storm* 激しいあらし.

Q² raise an ***ash*** *storm* 灰かぐらをあげる. ¶a heavy ***dust*** *storm* ひどい砂あらし. ¶an ***ice*** *storm* 氷雪のあらし(吹雪). ¶The bill is now the center of an ***intra-party*** *storm*. その議案は今や党内紛争の中心である. ¶a ***rain*** *storm* 暴風雨. ¶a ***sleet*** *storm* みぞれ降るあらし. ¶a ***snow*** *storm* 大吹雪 ‖ a blinding ***snow*** *storm* 目もあけられない大吹雪. ¶a severe ***snow*** and ***wind*** *storm* すごい吹雪. ¶a ***thunder*** *storm* 雷雨. ¶a ***wind*** *storm* 暴風. ¶an icy cold ***winter*** *storm* 凍りつく冬のあらし.

P I was overtaken ***by*** a *storm*. 私はあらしに会った. ‖ The castle was taken ***by*** *storm*. その城は強襲で攻落された. ¶***during*** *storms* at sea しけの最中に. ¶The ship has been wrecked ***in*** a terrible *storm*. その船は恐ろしいあらしで難破した. ‖ I was caught ***in*** a *storm*. 私はあらしに会った. ¶the eye ***of*** a *storm* 暴風の目. ¶in the height ***of*** the *storm* 暴風雨の最中に. ¶***until*** the recent *storm* 先だってのあらしまでは.

P² a *storm* ***of*** wind and rain 暴風雨 ‖ a *storm* ***of*** applause あらしのようなかっさい ‖ a *storm* ***of*** bullets 雨あられと飛び来る弾丸 ‖ a *storm* ***of*** passion 情熱のあらし. 【類】a *storm* ***of*** indignation / a *storm* ***of*** wastepaper / a *storm* ***of*** angry words.

O The *storm* is over (=gone). あらしがやんだ.

storm, *v.* 荒れる; 怒鳴る.

M It *stormed* ***all day***. 終日荒れた.

M² *storm* ***in*** for a fight なぐり込みをかける.

P *storm* ***at*** a person 人をどなりつける ‖ He *storms* ***at*** nought. 彼はくだらないことにどなり散らす. ¶*storm* ***into*** one's office その事務所にあばれ込む. ¶*storm* ***out of*** the room へやからどかどかと出る. ¶*storm* a person ***with*** questions 質問の矢をそそぐ.

storm-center, *n.* 暴風雨の中心.

P² become a *storm-center* ***of*** controversy 論争の中心となる.

story, *n.* 物語; 経歴; 脚色; 《俗》うそ.

V I will ***abridge*** my *story*. かいつまんでお話しましょう. ¶this *story* is not now ***accepted*** because ... この(昔)話は今では信じるものはないというのは… ¶***accredit*** a *story* 話を信用する. ¶The *story* was ***bandied about***. この話が口から口に伝わった. ¶I dare say you ***believe*** the *story*. 君はその話を信じるでしょうね. ¶to ***bring*** my *story* to a close この話の終りに臨んで. 【類】The volume before us ***brings*** the *story* to 1940 and further volumes will continue it to 1955. ¶scandalous *stories* were ***circulated*** concerning ... …に関して悪評が立った. ¶The coming forth of the winged adult ***completes*** the *story* of the moth. 羽のある成虫がでて来るとそれで蛾(が)の一代記のまとまりがつく. ¶It does not ***constitute*** the whole *story*. それは全ぼうを尽していない. ¶***construct*** an admirable *story* 結構興味ある話になる. ¶T ***cooked*** him ***up*** a *story* so plausible of me. Tは私についてのいいかげんな作りごとをまことしやかに彼に話した. ¶well, to ***cut*** a long *story* short まあ手短かに言えば. ¶the manner of ***developing*** the *story* 物語の展開させ方. ¶The *story* is ***discredited*** by some. その話を信じない人もある. ¶***dramatize*** a *story* 小説を脚色する. ¶My sympathy ***elicited*** a pitiful *story* from the woman. 私が同情したのでその婦人は私に哀れな身の上話をした. ¶***end*** one's *story* 話を終る. ¶***enjoy*** printed *stories* 小説類を楽しむ. 【類】The reader cannot fail to ***enjoy*** a *story* so well written. ¶the whole *story* is ***fabricated*** to furnish a pretext for ... 全体が…の口実にするような工合にねつ造してある. ¶***filmize*** a *story* 小説を映画化する. ¶The *story* has been several times ***handled*** in both prose and verse. その物語はしばしば散文にもいん文にも取扱われた. ¶he ***had*** *stories* and even plays written around ... 彼は…を題材にして小説やら脚本やらを作らせた. ¶***have*** no *story* to tell 別に珍らしい話もない. ¶He ***invented*** a wicked *story* about her. 彼は彼女について悪い風説を立てた. ¶***keep*** the *story* to oneself その話を(人に聞かせないで)自分の腹に収めておく. ¶***knock out*** one's *story* on the typewriter [新聞記者などが]その記事をタイプで打つ. ¶***launch*** false *stories* about ... …について虚説を立てる. ¶It is impossible to ***lay down*** the *story* without finishing it. その話は話し出すと中途では止められない. ¶well, to ***make*** a long *story* short で, 手っ取り早く言えば ‖ ***make*** a good *story* out of it それを種におもしろい話を作る ‖ the *story* has been ***made*** into a film by ... その話は…が映画に作った ‖ ***make*** a *story* laid in Mars 金星を舞台に取った小説を書く ‖ ***make*** a *story* ***look*** as big as possible なるたけ話に山をかける. ¶***make up*** a *story* 話を作り上げる. ¶***outline*** a *story* in 500 words 五百語で物語の概略を説く. ¶The *story* is ***put*** into the mouth of the millionaire's nephew. その話はその百万長者のおいの口から出たことになっている. ¶***radiocast*** a children's *story* 少年物語を放送する. ¶Are you ***reading*** the *story* in that newspaper? その新聞の小説を読んでいますか. ‖ I ***read*** the whole *story* in her face. 私は彼女の顔付で全体の様子を察した. 【類】I ***read*** the whole *story* at the sight of ... (…を見て). / ***Read*** the *story* on page 10. ¶it ***recalled*** a certain famous *story* about ... それで…のある有名な話を思い出した. ¶***relate*** one's *story* その経歴を語る. ¶***repeat*** like parrots the *stories* of ... …の話を十分確めないで雷同する. ¶a *story* that will not be ***retold*** 二度とはない話(例). ¶***scribble*** *stories* 話のなぐり書をする. ¶***serialize*** a *story* 一つの小説を続き物にする. ¶***sift*** a *story* 話の真相を探る. ¶slightly ***sketch*** the *story* of one's life その生がいの経歴を略記する. ¶The reporter ***slapped*** a *story* ***together*** anyhow. 記者はどうにかその記事をまとめた. ¶***spin out*** a *story* 長々と話す. ¶***spread*** *stories* abroad うわさを世間に広める. ¶I really cannot ***swallow*** such a curious *story*. そんな妙な話は私には全く信じられない. ¶***take*** the *story* ***up*** on August 21, 1605 その歴史を一六〇五年の八月二十一日のことから書き始める. ¶***telecast*** a *story* 物語をテレビ放送する. ¶***tell*** a person a *story* 人に話をする ‖ ***tell*** the *story* of one's life 身の上話をする ‖ ***Tell*** the *story* as it is. ありのままにその話をしろ. 【類】Many curious (珍しい) *stories* are ***told*** about elephants. / the *story* is graphically (目に見るように) ***told*** in ... / The *story* is ***told*** with delightful gaiety, humor, and crispness (快活にこっけいにそしてきびきびと). / the *story* of ... has been ***told*** by many pens, but by none better than that of ... ‖ The advertisement is too brief to ***tell*** its *story*. 広告では十分その内容を示されない. ¶***throw*** a *story* into the form of correspondence. 小説を書翰体にする. ¶the *story* of ... is ***tinged*** with not a little of romance …の話は少なからず小説的色彩で色取られている. ¶***turn up*** a *story* 話をねつ造する.

V² a romantic *story* ***attaches*** to ... 小説的な話が…につきまとっている. ¶the *story* ***goes*** (=***runs***) that ... 話はかくかくだ, …という話だ ‖ as the *story* ***goes*** その話によると ‖ So the *story* ***goes***. 話にはそうある. ¶That *story* won't ***go down***. その話は信じられない. ¶the *story* ***opens*** with ... その物語は…から始まる. ¶The *story* ***sounds*** a little "steep." その話はいささか途方もないように聞える. ¶The *story* ***traveled*** far and wide. そのうわさは広く伝わった.

Q an ***adventurous*** *story* 冒険談. ¶an ***alarming*** *story* about ... …についての恐ろしい話. ¶an ***amazing*** *story* たまげた話. ¶But that is ***another*** *story*. だがそれは話が違う. ¶an ***authentic*** *story* 確実な話. ¶a ***baseless*** *story* 跡形もない話. ¶This is a ***beautiful*** *story*, isn't it? そりゃ美談ですね. ¶a ***black*** *story* 悲しい話. ¶a ***blue*** *story* びろうな話. ¶a ***breezy*** *story* 明朗な話. ¶a ***breathless*** *story* of love 息づまるような恋愛小説. ¶a ***charming*** *story* おもしろい話. ¶make a ***coherent*** *story* out of a medley of materials 雑多の材料から筋の通った話をつづる. ¶there are many ***conflicting*** *stories* as to ... …については矛盾する色々の説がある. ¶tell a ***connected*** *story* 関連のある話をする. ¶His *story* was not *convincing*. 彼の言うことは承服できなかった. ¶a ***cooked-up*** *story* でっち上げた話. ¶a ***credible story*** 確かな話. ¶a *story* is ***current*** that ... ...という風説がある. ¶print a ***detailed*** *story* 詳細記事を掲載する. ¶a ***detective*** *story* 探偵もの. ¶a ***dull*** *story* 無味乾燥な話. ¶an ***edifying*** *story* ためになる話. ¶a most ***entertaining*** *story* 非常におもしろい話. ¶The "Treasure Island" is an ***enthralling*** *story* of adventure.「宝島」は非常に面白い冒険小説だ. ¶***episodical short*** *stories* そう話的な短編. ¶His is an ***eventful*** *story*. 彼の経歴は波らんが多い. ¶There is an ***evil*** *story* abroad. 感心しない話が世間に伝えられている. ¶an ***exhilarating*** *story* 陽気な話. ¶a ***feeling*** (=***touching***) *story* 人を動かす話. ¶a ***filmized*** (***televised***) *story* 映画(テレビ)化した小説(脚本). ¶a ***fishy*** *story* 当にならない(信じ難い)話. ¶when the ***full*** *story* is known 全ぼうが明かになると. ¶a ***funny*** *story* おかしな話. ¶a ***good*** *story* well told おもしろく話したおもしろい話. ¶a ***gripping*** *story* 感銘深い話. ¶a ***grim*** *story* 気味の悪い話. ¶***hair-raising*** *stories* of narrow escapes from death 九死に一生を得たぞっとする話.¶Tongue cannot adequately tell, nor pen indite, the ***heart-moving*** *story* of London's missionary zeal. ロンドンの熱誠に人を動かす布教の話は口にも筆にも説き尽せない. ¶a ***heart-rending*** *story* 胸の張り裂けるような話. ¶*stories* both ***historical*** and ***legendary*** 歴史的並びに伝説的な物語. ¶a ***historical*** *story* 歴史小説. ¶Oh! what a ***horrid*** *story*, Jane! まあ, ジェーン, こわいわ. ¶a ***humorous*** *story* ユーモア小説. ¶***incredible*** *stories* 信じられない話. ¶an ***ingenious*** and ***exciting*** *story* 巧みではらはらさせる話. ¶the ***inside*** *story* of the Peace Conference 平和会議の内幕話. ¶the real ***inside*** *story* of ... ...の真相を明かにした内幕話. ¶I have an ***interesting*** *story* to tell. 僕におもしろい話がある. ¶***jolly, laughable*** *stories* おもしろおかしい話. ¶a ***legendary*** *story* 伝説, 伝奇物語. ¶A ***likely*** *story!* ありそうな話だ. ¶bore a person with a ***long*** *story* 長話で人をうんざりさせる ‖ to make a ***long*** *story* short かいつまんで言うと. ¶a ***ludicrous*** *story* ばかげた話. ¶there are ***many*** *stories* of ... ...について話が色々ある. ¶***milk-and-water*** *stories* 味もそっけもない話. ¶***moving*** *stories* 人を動かす話. ¶This *story* is probably more ***mythical*** than ***historical***. この物語は恐らく歴史的というよりはむしろ神話的である. ¶It is not a ***new*** *story*. それは珍らしい例ではない(世間によくあることだ). ¶a ***newsy*** and ***sensational*** *story* 珍らしい扇情的な話. ¶The Chinese are very fond of telling such ***nonsensical*** *stories*. 中国人は好んでこういうる無意味な話をする. ¶an ***off-color*** (=***risqué***) *story* 《米》いかがわしい話, 上品でない話. ¶an ***oft-told*** *story* 度々耳にする話. ¶There is an ***old*** *story* which tells how ... ...という古い話がある. ¶It's an ***old*** *story* now. もう古い話だが. ‖ To him fame is an ***old*** *story*. 彼は昨今有名になったのではない. 【類】 Yesterday is an ***old*** *story* in the annals of the "movies." ¶the ***old sweet*** *story* writ large (=written clearly) upon their happy faces 彼ら(恋人同士など)の幸福な顔にはっきりと書いてある昔からの楽しい物語. ¶the ***parent*** *story* 話のもと(原体). ¶a ***pathetic*** *story* 世にも哀れな話. ¶a ***plausible*** *story* もっともらしい話. ¶there is a ***pretty*** *story* about ... ...についてゆかしい話がある. ¶a ***queer*** *story* 変な話. ¶a ***readable*** *story* [読んで]おもしろい物語. ¶a ***realistic*** but ***fictive*** *story* 実話的な作り話. ¶learn to write a "***running*** *story*" as one listens to a speech 演説を聴いていながらまとまった記事を書きつづるようになる(議会担当の新聞記者など). ¶His is a ***sad*** *story*. 彼の来歴は悲惨だ. ¶the ***same*** *story* has to be told about ... ...も同様である. ¶a ***sensational*** *story* 扇情的(世間騒がせ)な話. ¶a ***serial*** [*story*] 続き物. ¶***sexual*** *stories* わい談. ¶a ***short*** *story* 短編小説. ¶a ***sordid*** *story* きたない話(わい談). ¶***splendid*** *stories* すばらしい話. ¶a ***stirring*** *story* of adventure 血わく冒険談. ¶a ***strange, wild*** *story* 変った空想的な話. ¶a ***thrilling*** *story*=《米》a thriller スリラー物. ¶a ***traveller's*** *story* 旅の話; ほら. ¶a ***true*** *story* 実話. ¶We are heartily glad that the whole *story* of the massacre was ***unfounded***. 虐殺の報道が全部無根であったことは心からうれしい. ¶a ***weird*** *story* 薄気味の悪い話. ¶a ***well-told*** *story* そつのない話. ¶a ***well-worn*** *story* 陳腐な話. ¶***Western*** *stories* 米国西部の話. ¶Oh, ***what*** a *story!* うそ, うそ! ¶He related the ***whole*** *story*. 彼は一部始終を語った. 【類】 Tell me the ***whole*** *story*. ‖ But that doesn't tell the ***whole*** *story*. それだけ話したのではまだ不十分だ.

Q² an ***adventure*** *story* 冒険談. ¶an ***animal*** *story* 動物の物語. ¶It sounds like an ***Arabian Nights*** *story* それは丁度アラビヤンナイト(千一夜物語)を聞く感じだ. ¶a ***bedtime*** *story*=a fairy tale おとぎ話. ¶a ***behind-the-scenes*** *story* 内幕(楽屋)話. ¶a ***Bible*** *story* 聖書物語. ¶a ***Christmas*** *story* クリスマス物語. ¶a ***cock-and-bull*** *story* だぼら, 大ぶろしき. ¶a ***copyright*** *story* 著作権のある小説. ¶a ***crime*** *story* 犯罪小説. ¶a ***day-to-day*** (=serial) *story* [新聞などの]連載小説. ¶a ***detective*** *story* 探偵もの. ¶a ***life*** *story* 伝記. ¶be interwoven with a ***touching love*** *story* 悲しいロマンスを織りまぜてある. ¶a ***dog*** *story* 犬の話. ¶a ***fairy*** *story* おとぎ話. ¶a ***film*** *story* of Gandhi's life ガンジー伝の映画物語. ¶a ***fish*** *story* ほら, でっかい話. ¶The paper carries ***front-page*** *stories* and editorials on ... その新聞には...に関する一面ニュースと社説が載っている. ¶a ***ghost*** *story* 幽霊の話. ¶a "***good-night***" *story* おとぎ話. ¶a ***hero*** *story* 英雄物語. ¶a ***high-tale*** *story* ほら話. ¶a ***horror*** *story* 恐ろしい物語. ¶a ***human interest*** *story* 新聞の社会(三面)記事. ¶a ***love*** *story* 恋愛もの. ¶a ***murder*** *story* 犯人物語(サスペンスもの) ☞《米俗》 whodunit (=who done it?) ともいう. ¶a master of ***mystery*** *stories* 推理小説の大家. ¶a ***news*** *story* 新聞記事. ¶not fit for a ***parlor*** *story* 人前では言えぬが(びろうな話だが). ¶a silly ***season*** *story* つまらないきわもの小説. ¶a ***smoking-room*** *story* 軽い物語. ¶a ***sob*** *story* (=stuff) 《米口》お涙もの. ¶a ***spook*** (=spooky) *story* 《米》怪談もの(怪奇小説). ¶The ***success*** *story* is the typical American story. 成功談は典型的なアメリカ小説である. ¶a ***war*** *story* 戦争物語. ¶a ***Western*** [*story*] 西部もの.

P ***according to*** his *story* 彼の言う所によれば. ¶I read only ***for*** the *story*. 私はただ筋を追って読んだだけだ. ¶a character famous ***in*** *story* and song 物語や詩歌に名高い人物. ¶entertain ***with*** (=***by***) a *story* ごちそうに話を聞かせる ‖ to go on ***with*** my *story* それから先をお話すれば ‖ a woman ***with*** a *story* いわくつきの女.

P² Various strange *stories* are told ***about*** him. 彼について色々妙なうわさがある. ¶*stories* ***from*** the ancient Japanese classics 古い日本の古典から取った物語. ¶a *story* ***in*** three chapters 三章から成る物語 ‖ a *story* ***in*** dialogue 対話体物語. 【類】 a *story* ***of*** warfare. ¶the *story* ***of*** one's life その経歴談 ‖ *stories* ***of*** detection, mystery and horror 探偵・怪談及び恐怖の物語. ¶a *story* ***on*** the subject その問題についてのうわさ. ¶It was an old *story* ***to*** him. それは彼には珍らしくないことであった. ¶placing of *stories* ***with*** magazines 小説を雑誌社に売込むこと.

story, 《英》 **storey,** *n.* 階, 階層.

Q the ***basement*** *storey* 地階. ¶the ***first*** (***second, third***) *storey* 《米》第一(二・三)階 ☞ 米国の the first story は英国の the ground floor に当り, 米国の the second (third) story 英国の(三)四階に当る. ¶a house of ***five*** *storeys* 五階建の家. ¶the ***ground*** *storey* 一階. ¶a building of ***thirty*** *storeys* in height 高さ三十階の建物. ¶the ***upper*** *storey* 上階 ‖ He is a little wrong in the ***upper*** *storey*. 彼は頭が少し狂っている.

Q² a ***mezzanine*** *story*=an entresol 中二階.

P His room is ***on*** the second *story*. 彼のへやは三階にある.

O The Empire State [Building] is 102 *stories* high. エンパイアステート・ビルは百二階だ. 【類】 new buildings are all five *stories* high.

story-cartoon, *n.* 物語漫画.

Q² a ***Walt Disney*** *story-cartoon* ウォルト・ディズニーの物語漫画.

story-teller, *n.* 話手; 短編小説作家.

Q a ***born*** *story-teller* 天才的な話じょうず. ¶a ***good*** *story-teller* 話じょうず; 《口語》じょうずなうそつき. ¶a ***humorous*** (***vivacious***) *story-teller* 話をおもしろく(生々と)聞かせる話手. ¶Stevenson was the ***master*** *story-teller* of all time. スティーヴンソンは他にまね手のない物語の大家であった.

stout, *a.* たくましい; 肥満した.

P He was *stout* ***of*** build. 彼はたくましい体格をしていた. ‖ He is *stout* ***of*** heart. 彼は豪胆だ.

O The old lady is *stout*.=She is a stout old lady. その老婦人はとっても肥えている.

stove, *n.* ストーブ.

V ***heat*** a *stove* ストーブをたく.

V² The *stove* was well ***burning***. ストーブはよく燃えていた. ☞「ストーブをもやす」意では burn a stove といわ

ず, burn coal[s] (wood) in a stove が普通.

Q a red ***glowing*** *stove* 真赤に燃えているストーブ. ¶The *stove* is well ***heated***. ストーブはよく燃えている.

Q^2 a ***coal*** *stove* 石炭ストーブ. ¶light a ***cooking*** *stove* 調理ストーブに火をつける. ¶cook on a ***gas*** *stove* ガスストーブで調理する. ¶a ***heating*** *stove* だん炉. ¶a ***kitchen*** *stove* 調理用ストーブ. ¶an ***oil*** *stove* 石油ストーブ. ¶a ***slow-combustion*** *stove* 燃えのおそいストーブ.

P make a fire ***in*** the *stove* ストーブに火をたく.

stow, *v.* 詰め込む.

M *stow* it ***away*** in a drawer 引出ししにそれをしまい込む. ¶*stow* ***away*** on a transport 輸送船で密航する. 【類】They *stowed* ***away*** on a ship and reached Japan.

M^2 The circus animals *stowed* ***down*** for shipping. 船に積込まれたサーカスの動物. ¶The cargo was *stowed* ***in*** the hold. 積荷は船倉に収めた. ‖ plates *stowed* ***in*** on the starboard side 右げんの作りつけ食器だなに収めてあるさら類.

P *stow* a little cabin ***with*** supplies for mountaineering 登山用品を小屋に入れる.

stowaway, *n.* 密航者.

P^2 a *stowaway* ***in*** a hold 船倉の密航者.

strafe, *v.* [空中から]掃射する.

O *strafe* an enemy position 敵陣地を掃射する.

straggle, *v.* 散在する; まん延する.

M *straggle* ***away*** ちりじりばらばらになって行ってしまう. ¶branches that *straggle* ***out*** too far 余り長くのびている枝. ‖ The village *straggles* ***out*** a mile long. 村が一マイルもだらだらと続いている.

M^2 The cows *straggled* ***along***. 雌牛がばらばらに歩いて行った. ¶She *straggled* ***behind*** when a car swished close by. 彼女は車がそばをしゅうと走り過ぎた時よろよろとあとずさりをした. ¶aid a fallen horse to *straggle* ***up*** 倒れた馬をよろよろ立ち上らせる.

P The hamlets *straggle* ***along*** the side of a creek. 村落がクリークに沿って散在している. ¶the roses *straggling* ***over*** the fence かきねの上にのさばっているばら. 【類】Weeds *straggle* ***over*** the garden. / Vines *straggling* ***over*** the wall.

straight, *a.* 真すぐな, 正直な; 《米》純粋な, 生(ᵏ)の.

V ***drink*** whisky (gin) *straight* ウイスキー(など)わらないで飲む.

M *straight* ***away*** (=***off***) 直ちに, すぐ.

P go *straignt* ***ahead*** 真すぐ進む. ¶live *straight* ***among*** the crooked 曲った連中の中で正しく暮す. ¶He is *straight* ***in*** all his dealings. 彼は万事に正直だ.

straighten, *v.* 真すぐになる(させる).

M *straighten* ***out*** a very complicated subject すこぶる複雑な問題を解明する. 【類】*straighten* ***out*** a sorry tangle. ‖ *straighten* ***out*** conflicts 意見の衝突を和解させる ‖ *straighten* ***out*** accounts 精算する ‖ be anxious to see world affairs *straightened* ***out*** 世界の現状が正常になるように切望している.

M^2 *straighten* ***up*** きちんと整理する; 《俗》地道に世を渡る. 【類】*straighten* ***up*** one's room.

straightforward, *a.* 正直な, 率直な.

P *straightforward* ***with*** a person 人に対して率直な.

straightforwardness, *n.* 率直.

Q ***manly*** *straightforwardness* 男らしい率直.

strain, *n.* 緊張; 筋違え; 過労.

V ***apply*** a *strain* to the stomach 腹にぐっと力を入れる. ¶The rope will ***bear*** the *strain*. そのなわは張りに耐えるだろう. ‖ The relations will not ***bear*** much further *strain*. その関係はこれ以上多くの緊張に耐えそうにもない. 【類】I left the scene unable to ***bear*** the *strain*. ¶***ease*** the *strain* =relax 緊張をやわらげる, 気を楽にする. ¶***impose*** heavy *strain* on the physical and nervous system 身体及び神経系統に重い負担を課する. ¶***lay*** a heavy *strain* upon the vital forces of students 学生の活力に重い負担を課する. ¶***relieve*** the *strain* 過労を緩和する. ¶***stand*** the *strain* of sleepless nights 数晩不眠の苦を忍ぶ. 【類】***stand*** the *strain* very well (no longer). ¶***sustain*** a *strain* 過労にたえる. ¶***withstand*** a *strain* of over half a ton 半トン以上の重量にたえる. ¶The *strain* of the last few days has ***told*** severely on his health. 最近二三日の過労が彼の健康にひどくこたえた.

Q the ***bursting*** *strain* of a balloon 気球の張り切れんばかりの緊張. ¶withstand ***enormous physical*** and ***mental*** *strain* 激しい心身の過労にたえる. ¶The danger can be realized without a ***great*** *strain* on the imagination. その危険は想像するに難くはない. ¶***hard physical*** *strain* 激しい身体の過労. ¶impose a great ***intellectual*** *strain* on ... …に大なる知能上の労苦を課する. ¶an almost ***intolerable*** *strain* ほとんどたえ難い過労. ¶at the expense of a smaller ***physical*** *strain* than of old 以前ほど身体にこたえないで. ¶a ***real*** *strain* on their purse and their time 彼らの財力と時間とに対して真に無理な要求. ¶impose ***severe*** *strain* on ... …にひどい負担をかける. ¶The *strain* is often very ***trying***. その過労は往々たえられないものがある. ¶impose an ***unnecessary*** *strain* on ... …に不必要な負担を課す.

Q^2 ease the ***housing*** *strain* 住宅不足を緩和する. ¶in these days of abnormal ***nerve*** *strain* この異常に神経を使う時代に.

P suffer ***from*** a *strain* ストレス病に悩む. ¶feel a certain sense ***of*** *strain* [聴衆を前にした弁士が]かたくなる. ¶All his senses are ***on*** the *strain*. 彼は気は張り切っている. ¶break down ***under*** the *strain* of heavy duties 重税の負担にたえない. ¶***without*** the smallest *strain* いささかの無理もなく, 順調に.

P^2 the *strain* ***of*** modern life 現代の生活難 ‖ be such a *strain* ***upon*** ... …にとって非常な重荷である. ¶the *strain* ***on*** the rope なわの張りつめ ‖ It was a great *strain* ***on*** my resources. それは私の資力から言って非常な無理であった. 【類】The expense is a *strain* ***on*** the model income (=pocketbook) of a professor. / This hard work is a great *strain* ***on*** the muscles (nerves) (気骨が折れる). / a *strain* ***on*** the memory of ... ‖ a *strain* ***on*** one's good nature お人よしにつけ込んでの圧迫.

strain, *n.* 調子; *pl.* 歌; 血統, 家柄.

V He suddenly ***changed*** his scolding *strain*. 彼は小言を言っていたが急にその調子を変えた. ¶He ***has*** a heroic *strain* in his character. 彼の性格には英雄的な所がある. ‖ ***have*** a *strain* of melancholy 憂うつな所がある. ¶The *strains* of the National Anthem ***filtered out*** from within. 国歌の音律が内から漏れて来た. ¶***sing*** the *strains* 歌をうたう.

Q in ***another*** *strain* 調子をかえて. ¶***discordant*** *strains* 耳ざわりな調子. ¶speak in a ***dismal*** *strain* ゆううつそうに話す. ¶The ***Irish*** *strain* in him makes him like jokes. アイルランド系の血は争われないもので彼は冗談が好きだ. ¶in a ***lofty*** *strain* 高調子で. ¶***martial*** *strains* 軍楽. ¶***melancholy*** *strains* 悲調の音楽. ¶His ambition was of a ***noble*** and ***generous*** *strain*. 彼の野心は高潔なたちのものであった. ¶He has an ***Oriental*** *strain* in his blood. 彼には東洋人の血が混っている. ¶***pathetic*** *strains* 悲そうな曲調. ¶Vigorous, independent, and accustomed to danger, Slavs added a ***powerful*** and ***virile*** *strain* to American blood. 元気よく独立心がありそして危険に慣れているのでスラブ人は米国人の血に力強い男性的な一素質を付加した. ¶***stirring*** *strains* 壮快な音楽.

P All the provincial papers speak more or less ***in*** the same *strain*. 地方新聞は皆多少同じ調子で論じている. ¶He comes ***of*** a good (noble) *strain*. 彼は家柄がよい(貴族の出だ).

P^2 There is a *strain* ***of*** insanity (=madness) in that family. あの家は気狂の血統だ. ‖ the *strain* ***of*** a nation 国民性 ‖ *strains* ***of*** music (a song) 音楽(など)の調子.

strain, *v.* 引締める; こす; [意味を]曲解する.

M *strain* ***out*** coffee grounds コーヒーのかすをこしてとる. ¶a plant *straining* ***upwards*** to the light 光線を求めて延び上がる植物.

P *strain* ***after*** originality 独創的になろうとして骨を折る. 【類】*strain* ***after*** (=for) effect. ¶*strain* ***at*** stool 大便でいきむ ‖ The rowers *strain* ***at*** the oar. こぎ手が精一杯にかいをこぐ. ‖ The dog is *straining* ***at*** the leash. 犬がしきりに自分の皮ひもを引っ張っている. ¶*strain* a horse ***by*** overloading 荷を負わせ過ぎて馬を痛める. ¶*strain* ***for*** a better view もっとよく見ようとする. ¶*strain* the provisions ***in*** favor of (against) ... …に都合いいように(わるいように)条文をこじつける. 【類】*strain* the meaning ***in*** one's favor. ¶*strain* it ***through*** a sieve それをふるいにかける. ¶Why do you *strain* ***to*** so poor an end? なぜそんなつまらない目的に骨を折るのか. ‖ *strain* a rope ***to*** the breaking-point なわを切れるほど引締める ‖ *strain* the probabilities ***to*** a breaking-point その可能性を尽す. ¶He is

straining under his load. 彼は一所懸命に荷物を担いでいる. 【類】*strain under* pressure. ¶*strain* one's face ***with*** anxiety 心配して顔を引締める.

O *strain* one's eyes to see it better それをよく見ようとして目を皿にする(見張る). 【類】*strain* one's ears (耳をすます) to hear …

strained, *a.* 緊張した.

M this ***seriously*** *strained* relations between … …間のこの非常に緊張した関係.

straining, *n.* 緊張.

Q the ***continual*** *straining* after perfection which marks the thorough workman りっぱな職人の特徴たる技術の完成をねらっての絶えざる努力.

strait, *n.* 海峡; 窮迫, 困難.

Q in the ***direst*** *straits* 進退きわまって. ¶students in ***financial*** *straits* 財政困難の学生. ¶He is in ***great*** *straits.* 彼は大層困難している. ¶only in the ***last*** *straits* せっぱつまって始めて. ¶a ***narrow*** (***wide***) *strait* せまい(広い)海峡. ¶if brought to ***similar*** *straits* 同様の窮状に陥れば.

Q² the ***Tsushima Straits*** 対馬海峡. ☞ 複数形で往々単数の意味に用いる.

P He is ***in*** *straits* for money. 彼は金に困っている. ¶go ***through*** a *strait* [船など]海峡を通過する. ¶They were reduced ***to*** the greatest *straits* by the failure of the rice crop. 彼らは稲の不作のために非常な困難に陥った.

P² He is in *straits* ***for*** money. 彼は金に困っている. ¶the *Straits* ***of*** Dover ドーバー海峡.

straiten, *v.* 窮迫させる.

P be *straitened* ***for*** money (time, room) 金(など)がなくて困っている. ¶He is *straitened* ***in*** money matters. 彼は金銭のことで困っている. ‖ a man *straitened* ***in*** his circumstances (=in straitened circumstances) 貧乏している人.

strand, *n.* 股(こ).

P a rope ***of*** three *strands* 三本よりの索.

strand, *v.* 座礁させる; かく座する.

P The ship has *stranded* ***on*** the Japanese shore. その船は日本の海岸で座礁した. ‖ She was *stranded* ***on*** a reef. その船は暗礁に乗上げた. ‖ The ship remained *stranded* ***on*** the mud till the tide rose. その船は上げ潮まで座洲(す)したままになっていた.

strange, *a.* 未知の, 不思議な, 変な; 不なれな.

M ***How*** *strange* that you should not have heard it! 君がそれを聞かなかったとは変だ. ¶I am ***quite*** *strange* here. 私はこの辺は全く不案内だ. ¶His manner is ***very*** *strange.* 彼の挙動はいかにも変だ.

P He felt *strange* ***in*** the palace. 彼は宮殿でどぎまぎした. ¶The idiom is *strange* ***to*** an English ear. その用語法は英人には妙に聞える. ‖ I am *strange* ***to*** these parts. 私はこの辺は知らない. ‖ being *strange* (=unaccustomed) ***to*** the work その仕事に不慣れのため.

O *strange* to say 変な話だが. ¶This may sound *strange* [to you]. こう言うと妙に聞えるだろうが.

strangeness, *n.* 異様.

V² The *strangeness* of her surroundings gradually ***wore off.*** 彼女はあたりの変っているのに段々なれて来た.

stranger, *n.* 面識のない人, 他人; 他国人.

V Do they ***admit*** *strangers* to the tennis court? そのテニスコートは一般の人もはいれますか. ¶A baby ***distinguishes*** *strangers.* 赤ん坊は人見知りをする. ¶***make*** a *stranger* of … …をよそよそしくする. 【類】He ***makes*** no *stranger* of me.

V² A little *stranger* ***comes.*** 赤ん坊が生れた.

Q a ***comparative*** *stranger* あまりよく知らない人. ¶I am a ***complete*** (=***total*** *or* an ***utter***) *stranger* to the place. 私はここは丸で不案内だ. 【類】He was born in a city and was a ***complete*** *stranger* to country life. ¶those to whose hands sword and pen are ***equal*** *strangers* 文も武もない人人. ¶a ***mere*** *stranger* 赤の他人. ¶I am ***no*** *stranger* to poverty. 私は貧乏の味は知っている. ¶He is a ***perfect*** (=***entire***) *stranger* to me. 彼は私とは一面識もない. ¶***Some*** *strangers* were at table. 客人が二三食卓についていた. ¶an ***unamiable*** *stranger* 感心しない(いやな)見知らぬ人. ¶an ***utter*** *stranger* to shame 全くの恥知らず.

P die ***among*** the *strangers* 他境の土となる. ¶live ***amongst*** *strangers* 他国人の中で暮らす. ¶The dog barks ***at*** a *stranger.* その犬は知らない人にほえる. ¶I was accosted (=hailed) ***by*** a *stranger.* 知らない人が私にあいさつをした.

P² I am a *stranger* ***in*** this neighborhood. 私はこの辺は不案内だ. ‖ a *stranger* ***in*** a strange land 他国における他国人. ¶I am a *stranger* ***to*** love (dissipation, music, art). 私は恋(など)というものは知らない. ‖ I'm no *stranger* ***to*** it. それはもう経験がある. 【類】I'm a *stranger* ***to*** this type of work. / He ceased to be a *stranger* ***to*** English readers. / a *stranger* ***to*** hard work / Most of them were *strangers* ***to*** me.

O You are quite a *stranger!* 《口語》まあお珍らしい(久し振りの会合で).

strangle, *v.* 絞殺す.

P He *strangled* her ***to*** death by a cord put around her neck. 彼は彼女を綱で絞め殺した. ¶*strangle* a man ***with*** a string ひもで人を絞め殺す.

O *strangle* a yawning (sob, sigh) あくび(など)をかみころす.

strap, *v.* ひもでくくりつける; ばんそうこうを張る.

M *strap* ***up*** one's wound 傷にこう薬を張る.

P with small babies *strapped* ***to*** their backs 赤ん坊をひもでおんぶして.

stratagem, *n.* 戦略; 謀計, 計略.

V ***adopt*** a *stratagem* 計略を用いる. ¶***contrive*** (=***devise***) *stratagems* 謀を巡らす. ¶the same *stratagem* was ***resorted to*** in the attack on … …の攻撃にも同じ戦法を用いた.

Q a ***subtle*** *stratagem* 抜目のない計略.

P It must be effected ***by*** *stratagem.* 計略でやり遂げねばならない. 【類】capture a castle ***by*** *stratagem* / escape ***by*** *stratagem.* ¶He failed in fighting, but succeeded ***in*** *stratagem.* 彼は戦では負けたが戦略では成功した.

strategist, *n.* 作戦家.

Q² the ***Kremlin*** *strategists* クレムリン(共産党)作戦家たち. ¶a ***party*** *strategist* 政党の作戦家.

strategy, *n.* 戦略.

Q an ***enlightened*** *strategy* 文化的戦略.

Q² ***long-range*** *strategy* 将来を見越しての戦略. ¶Japan is the key in American ***Pacific defense*** *strategy.* 日本はアメリカにとって太平洋防衛の中心基地である.

P overcome a maiden's coy reluctance ***by means of*** a tender *strategy.* やさしい手くだで内気で気の進まない娘をくどき落す.

straphanger, *n.* 《口語》[電車・バスの]つり革にぶら下っている人.

P² *straphangers* ***in*** a crowded bus (streetcar) 込んだバスのつり革客.

stratification, *n.* 『気象』成層.

Q² ***class*** *stratification* of society 社会の階級層.

stratum, *n.* 層.

V ***strike*** a *stratum* of sand then several stratums (=strata) of rock 砂の層につき当りそれから数段の岩層につき当る.

Q The modern Burmese, though a Buddhist, carries on much of the old worship of the spirits of the house and the forest, which belongs to a far ***earlier religious*** *stratum* than Buddhism. ビルマ人は仏教徒だが仏教よりもずっと以前の宗教層に属する家屋や森林の精霊礼拝を多く行っている. ¶in a ***higher*** *stratum* of life 上層社会に. ¶cater for the ***humblest*** *strata* of the middle class 下層中産階級を顧客とする. ¶the ***lower*** (***lowest***) *strata* of society (=social life) (最)下層社会 ‖ the ***lower*** *strata* of the vocabulary 語いの下層(俗語など). ¶in all ***social*** *strata* 社会の各層を通じて. ¶the ***well-to-do*** *strata* of society 社会の裕福階級.

P² the Iranian *stratum* ***in*** the structure of Chinese civilization 中国文明の構成中に占めるイラン[文化]層. ¶in all *strata* ***of*** society 社会のあらゆる階級に.

straw, *n.* 麦わら, わら.

V Not one of them has ***added*** one *straw* to the happiness of the human race. その人たちの内一人だって人類の幸福に少しも貢献していない. ¶***braid*** *straw* 麦わらを編む. ¶He doesn't ***care*** a *straw* about his personal appearance. 彼は少しも身なりにはとん着しない. ¶***cut*** *straw* into chaff わらをこまかに切る. ¶***draw*** *straws* わらくじを引く. ¶I would not ***give*** this *straw* for your life. 君の命は実に危ないもんだ. ¶any *straw* is eagerly ***seized*** on to … …するためにはどんなつまらないものでも利用しようとする. ¶***spread*** *straw* わらを敷く. ¶***throw*** *straws* against the wind とうろうのおのを揮う.

Q the ***last*** *straw* かすかな望み ‖ The ***last*** *straw* breaks the camel's back. 最後のちょっとしたことが破滅のもととなる. ‖

the *last straw* on the poor man's back 貧者の重荷最後の小づけ(それで倒れる). ¶It is not ***worth*** a *straw*. それは少しの価値もない.

P A drowning man will catch ***at*** a *straw*. 〖諺〗おぼれる者はわらをもつかむ. ¶a man ***in*** a white *straw* 白い麦わら帽をかぶった人. ¶a man ***of*** *straw* わら人形; 無資産の人. ¶suck (=imbibe) soda water ***through*** a *straw* [tube] ストローでソーダ水を吸う. ¶a house thatched ***with*** *straw* わらぶきの家.

O I don't care a *straw*. ちっともかまわない.

strawberry, *n.* いちご.

V *grow strawberries* in one's garden 畑にいちごを作る.

Q the ***first*** *strawberries* 走りのいちご.

stray, *v.* それる, はぐれる, 踏み迷う.

M² *stray* ***off*** into a wood 森林に迷い込む. 【類】The dog *strayed* ***off*** somewhere else.

P *stray* ***from*** one's companions つれにはぐれる ‖ *stray* ***from*** the question (main point) 問題(など)から脱線する ‖ *stray* ***from*** the right path (path of duty) 正道(など)を踏はずす.

streak, *n.* 線条, 筋; 気味.

V He ***has*** a *streak* of superstition in him. 彼には迷信的な所がある. ‖ He ***has*** a *streak* of humor. 彼にはちょっとこっけい味がある.

P ***like*** a *streak* 《口語》迅速に.

P² a *streak* ***in*** wood 木の線条(木目). ¶a *streak* ***of*** luck 好運続き. 【類】We've had a *streak* ***of*** bad luck. / a *streak* ***of*** lightning.

streak, *v.* 線条をつける.

P *streaked* ***with*** snow even in the height of summer 真夏でも雪の線条のついた(山腹など) ‖ be *streaked* ***with*** color 色のすじがついている ‖ hair *streaked* ***with*** gray しらが混りの毛.

stream, *n.* 水流, 川; 流れ; 風潮, 時勢.

V The accident ***delayed*** a long *stream* of buses, cabs, and trucks. その事故のためにバスや自動車やトラックがずっと並んで止まった. ¶***ford*** a *stream* 水流を歩いて渡る. ¶***foul*** the pure *stream* of charity 慈善という清い流れを汚す. ¶cliffs ***overhanging*** the *stream* 水流の上にかかった絶壁. ¶***pour*** a steady *stream* of intelligent, qualified women into the rank of the teaching profession (教員養成所など)教育界にそう明で, 有資格の婦人を着々送り出す. ¶Here the *stream* is ***spanned*** by a foot bridge. 川にはここに丸木橋がかけてある. ¶The child ***started*** the *stream*. その子は小便をし始めた. 【類】have some difficulty in ***starting*** the *stream* in urination (利尿のとき). ¶***swim up*** (***down***) the *stream* 流れを上る(下る). ¶***tap*** a *stream* by tunnel to irrigate a waterless region トンネルで水を送り無水地方をかんがいする. ¶***turn*** the *stream* of words into another channel (=topic) 話題を転換させる. ¶***whip*** a *stream* for trout [糸車付の竿を用いて]ます釣する.

V² The *stream* ***glides*** through the meadow. 川が草地をさらさらと流れている.

Q a ***brawling*** *stream* ごうごうという川. ¶a ***clear*** *stream* 清流. ¶a ***constant*** *stream* of health and pleasure seekers 健康及び快楽を求めて陸続としてやって来る人々. ¶***dancing*** *streams* 躍動する河流. ¶flow in and out of it in apparently ***endless*** *streams* ひきもきらずそれから出入する. ¶a ***fine fishing*** *stream* きれいな漁猟場. ¶a ***garrulous*** (***babbling***) *stream* 鳴りさざめく河流. ¶a ***laughing*** *stream* さざめく流れ(こぽこぽ音を立てて流れる川). ¶a ***lucid*** *stream* すき通る流れ. ¶a ***meandering*** *stream* 曲りくねる流れ. ¶a ***mighty*** *stream* of the Nile ナイルの巨流. ¶the ***moving*** *stream* of humanity 人の流れ. ¶There is little more than room for ***one*** *stream* of vehicles each way. ほとんど片側だけしか車両が通れない. ¶a ***placid*** *stream* 静かな流れ. ¶a ***quiet, sluggish*** *stream* 静かで緩漫な流. ¶a ***rapid*** *stream* 急流. ¶a ***running*** *stream* 水流. ¶ford a ***rushing*** *stream* 激流を渡る. ¶a ***silvery*** *stream* 銀のような流れ. ¶***snow-fed*** *streams* 雪どけ水の流れ. ¶***sparkling*** *streams* きらきら光る河流. ¶People come and go in a ***steady*** *stream*. 人の流れが引きも切らず去来する. ¶The flood of miscellaneous letters flows on in one ***steady, uninterrupted*** *stream*. 色々の手紙の洪水が引きも切らず押寄せて来る. ¶There is a ***strong*** *stream* in the river. その川は流れが強い. ¶***swollen*** *streams* 水かさの増した川. ¶a ***tiny*** *stream* meandering through the meadow 牧場を曲りくねる細流. ¶a ***tumultuous*** *stream* 奔流. ¶a ***turbulent*** *stream* 騒々しい流れ.

Q² a ***feeder*** *stream* 支流(本流に入る). ¶the ***Gulf*** *Stream* メキシコ湾流. ¶The ***Japan*** *Stream* 黒潮. ¶Little ***mountain*** *streams* are dashing down to the plain. 山のせせらぎが平原に突き下る. ¶***sun*** *streams* 太陽の光線.

P swim ***across*** (=***over***) a *stream*. 川を泳いで渡る. ¶swim ***against*** a *stream* 流れを泳ぎ上る ‖ row ***against*** the *stream* 水流に逆って舟をこぐ ‖ go ***against*** the *stream* 流れにさかのぼる; 時勢に逆う. ¶sail ***down*** [the] *stream* 流れをくだって帆走する. ¶Blood flows ***in*** *streams*. 血がひどく流れる. ¶a bridge ***over*** a foaming *stream* あわ立つ急流にかかる橋. ¶go ***up*** [the] *stream*=go upstream 流れをのぼる ‖ row ***up*** [the] *stream* 川上にこぐ ‖ It is ***up*** (***down***) *stream*. それは上流(下流)にある. ¶float ***with*** the *stream* 世と共に推移する ‖ It is easy to swim ***with*** the *stream*. 時勢に順応するはやすい.

P² The *stream* ***of*** cabs and omnibuses is growing thinner. 馬車や乗合馬車の流れが段々に減って来る. ‖ a *stream* ***of*** *tears* 流れ落ちる涙 ‖ the *stream* ***of*** thought 思潮 ‖ the *stream* ***of*** times 時勢 ‖ a *stream* ***of*** lava よう岩の流れ ‖ a *stream* ***of*** light 一条の光線 ‖ a *stream* ***of*** loose talk 勝手なおしゃべり, ぺらぺら. 【類】a *stream* ***of*** blood [tears] / *streams* ***of*** motor-vehicles.

stream, *v.* 流れる.

M Students dispersed by vacation are now *streaming* ***back*** to their schools. 休暇で散った学生が再び母校に帰りつつある. ¶the lights that *streamed* ***out*** from its windows 窓から流れ出る灯火.

M² Blood *streamed* ***down***. 血が流れ落ちた. ‖ watch the cars *stream* ***down*** into the business section of the city 車が市の商業区域に流れ込むのをながめる. ¶People *streamed* ***in***. 人が流れ込んだ. ¶The moonlight *streamed* ***in*** through the window. 月光が窓から差し込んだ. ¶*stream* ***off*** their jobs in protest 不服で続々職場を去る.

P Tears *streamed* ***down*** her cheeks. 涙が彼女のほおを流れ落ちた. ¶Tears *streamed* ***from*** his eyes. 涙が彼の目から流れ落ちた. ¶The flag is *streaming* ***in*** the wind. 旗が風にひるがえっている. ¶The sun *streams* ***into*** the room. 日光がへやに差し込む. ¶the workpeople who *streamed* ***out of*** the printing works その印刷工場から流れでた職工連. 【類】School children *streamed* ***out of*** their classrooms when the bell rang. ¶*stream* ***to*** her studio 流れをなしてスタジオに行く. ¶eyes that *stream* ***with*** tears 涙のこぼれる目 ‖ *streaming* ***with*** *sweat* 大汗をかいて.

streamer, *n.* 吹き流し.

P² *streamers* ***of*** ribbon hanging from her hat 帽子からたれさがっている飾りリボン. ¶carp *streamers* ***on*** a May pole 五月のこいの吹き流し.

street, *n.* 街, 往来; 市街.

V The *street* is ***barricaded*** (=***closed or barred***) to the public. その街は往来止めになっている. ¶***beautify*** city *streets* 都市の街路を美化する. ¶The *street* is ***blocked*** with snow. 往来は雪で不通になっている. 【類】The procession (行列) ***blocked*** the *street*. ¶Gay dresses ***brighten up*** the *streets*. 晴れの衣しょうが街を明るくする. ¶***clean*** *streets* 街を掃除する. ¶***close*** the *street* to traffic for an hour その街路の通行を一時間閉鎖する. ¶London ***contains*** 8,000 *streets*. ロンドンには八千の街がある. ¶***disfigure*** *streets* 街の美観をそこなう. ¶***cross*** a *street* by the crosswalk 横断歩道で向うに渡る. 【類】Pasted bills ***disfigure*** the *streets*. ¶The house ***faces*** (=***fronts***) the *street*. その家は往来に面している. ¶***gravel*** [***down***] a *street* 往来に砂利を敷き詰める. ¶Beggars ***infest*** the *streets*. こじきが往来に群をなしている. ¶***keep*** the *streets* ***clear*** of this nuisance 街頭にこの(こじきなどの)不体裁がないようにする. ¶***lay down*** a new *street* 新しい街路を作る. ¶*streets* ***laid out*** in straight parallel lines 並行直線に設計した街. ¶***lengthen*** a *street* 街を延ばす. ¶people ***lined*** the *streets* to see … 人々は…を見ようと往来に整列した. 【類】The *streets* were ***lined*** by troops, school children and the general public. ¶The parlor ***overlooks*** the *street*. その居間から街を見下せる. ¶The procession ***paraded*** the *streets*. その行列は街々を練り歩いた. 【類】Prostitutes ***parade*** the *streets* to seek patrons. ¶Sandwichmen ***perambulate*** *streets*. [胸と背に広告を下げた]広告屋が街をうろうろする. ¶***stride*** [down] a *street* 通りを大またに歩く. ¶***sweep*** *streets* ***clean*** 街を清掃する. ¶Enormous crowds ***thronged*** the *streets*. 非常な群集が街へ押し寄せた. ¶***stroll*** the *streets* at night 夜街路を

散歩する. ¶whitecollars ***tramping*** the *streets* during their off-duty hours 休み時間に町を散歩するサラリーマンたち. ¶***tread*** *streets* at midnight 夜半街上を歩く. ¶***walk*** the *streets* of London [売春の目的で]ロンドン市中をうろつき歩く. 【類】the clandestine prostitute (私娼) ***walking*** the *street*. ¶***water*** the *street* 街路に水をまく. ¶***widen*** a *street* 往来を広げる.

V² the *streets* of London ***boiled*** with passionate men shouting ... ロンドンの市街は…を叫ぶ熱烈な人士で沸騰していた. ¶Here three *streets* ***converge***. ここで三筋の街路が一つになる. ¶a point where *streets* ***intersect*** 街路が交差する地点. ¶*streets* that ***lead*** to railway stations 停車場まで延びている街路.

Q a ***back*** *street* 裏通り. ¶a ***broad*** *street* 大通り. ¶a ***bustling*** *street* 雑とうする街. ¶a ***busy*** *street* にぎやかな通り. ¶***congested*** *streets* 雑とうの街. ¶a ***cross*** *street* 横通り. ¶a ***crowded*** *street* 雑とうしている往来. ¶We groped our way through the ***dark*** *street*. 暗い通りを手さぐりで進んだ. ¶a ***deserted*** *street* 人通りのとだえた通り. 【類】The *streets* were well-nigh ***deserted***. ¶the ***dirty*** *streets* ぬかるみの往来. ¶a ***fashionable*** *street* 上流人の行く街. ¶a ***filthy*** *street* 不潔な街. ¶***frequented*** *streets* 人通りの多い街. ¶a ***hideous*** *street* 醜悪な街. ¶a ***high*** *street* 本通り, 大通り. ¶***hilly*** *streets* 坂の多い街. ¶fall on an ***icy*** *street* 凍りついた街路ですべってころぶ. ¶***lively*** *streets* 活気ある街. ¶a ***lonely*** *street* さびしい街. ¶He has a shop on the ***main*** *street* of the village. 彼は村の本通りに店を持っている. ¶a ***muddy*** *street* ぬかるんだ往来. ¶***narrow*** and ***mean*** *streets* 狭い下等な街. ¶a ***narrow, crooked*** *street* 狭い曲った通り. ¶a ***noisy*** *street* 騒々しい通り. ¶in ***open*** *streets* 街頭で. ¶the ***prosaic*** *streets* of an English country town 英国いなか町の殺風景な往来. ¶in the ***public*** *streets* 往来で. ¶a ***quaint*** *street* 風変りな街. ¶a ***residential*** *street* 住宅街. ¶a ***shabby little*** *street* むさくるしい小さな街. ¶a ***slippery*** *street* すべる通り. ¶a ***slushy*** *street* どろどろしている往来. ¶***snowy*** or ***slush-filled*** *streets* 雪の積もった, または雪どけの往来. ¶a ***solitary*** *street* しんとした街. ¶a ***stone-flagged*** *street* 石舗装街. ¶***straight*** *streets* まっすぐな街. ¶a ***sunless*** side *street* 日当りの悪い横町. ¶***tortuous*** *streets* 曲りくねった街. ¶***traffic-chocked*** *streets* 人通りのはげしい往来. ¶***traffic-laden*** *streets* of London 往来のはげしいロンドンの街. ¶***tree-lined*** *streets* 街路樹のある街. ¶an ***ugly*** *street* 醜い街. ¶***underground*** *streets* 地下街. ¶when the *streets* are "***up***" 街路が(修理で)「通行止」になっているとき. ¶***well laid-out*** *streets* and avenues 設計のよい通路や街路. ¶***well-paved*** *streets* りっぱに舗装した街. ¶The *streets* are ***wet***. 往来はぬれてぬかっている. ¶The ***whole*** *street* cheered as he rode past. 彼が通過すると全町をあげてかっさいした. ¶a ***wide, paved,*** properly ***curbed*** *street* with broad sidewalks 幅広の人道のある広い舗装してちゃんと車道との間にかさ石のある街.

Q² an ***artery*** *street* north and south 南北に延びている主要大通り. ¶an ***asphalt*** *street* アスファルト街. ¶a ***business*** *street* of the city 市の商店街. ¶a ***city*** *street* 都市の通路. 【類】beautify ***city*** *streets*. ¶a ***concrete*** *street* コンクリート道路. ¶a ***downtown*** *street* 下町通り. ¶a ***market*** *street* 市場通り. ¶***one-way*** *streets* [自動車など]一方通行街路. ¶a ***prospect*** *street* 見晴しのよい街. ¶Cornhill is a ***shop*** *street*. コーンヒルは商店街だ. ¶the Benten Dori, the principal ***shopping*** *street* of Yokohama 横浜主要な商店街の弁天通り. 【類】on the Ginza, Tokyo's chief ***shopping*** *street*. ¶a ***side*** *street* 横道, わき通り. ¶a ***theatre*** *street* 劇場通り. ¶a ***water-front*** *street* 海岸通り.

P hawk them ***about*** the *streets* of London ロンドンの市中でその品を呼売する. 【類】wander (うろうろする) ***about*** the *street*. ¶The house is just ***across*** the *street*. その家は通りの真向いだ. ¶The houses ***along*** the *streets* are decorated. 往来に沿っている家は装飾を施してある. 【類】The horse dashed (突進した) ***along*** the *street*. / totter (よろつく) ***along*** the *street*. ¶a tram accident ***at*** Main Street 本町での電車事故. ¶come ***down*** the *street* 街をやって来る. 【類】walk ***down*** a *street* / The wagon rattled ***down*** a *street*. ¶The house stands somewhat back ***from*** the *street*. その家は往来から少し引込んでいる. ¶He cut me ***in*** the *street*. 彼は往来で私に知らん顔をして通った. ‖ There it is dangerous to be ***in*** the *streets* after dark. そこでは日が暮れてから外出するのは危険だ. 【類】A stranger accosted me ***in*** the *street*. / stop a person ***in*** the *street* ‖ live ***in*** the *street* 始終家を外に出歩いている ‖ I met him ***in*** (=***on***) the *street*. 往来で彼に会った. ☞ on は米語用法. ‖ the man ***in*** the *street* [専門家に対して]門外漢; 一般人. 【類】meet ***in*** the *street* (街路で) / lie drunk ***in*** the *street* / He stopped me ***in*** the *street*. / There is little traffic (交通) ***in*** the *street*. / pick up a purse ***in*** the *street*. / There is a crowd ***in*** the *street*. ‖ a boy ***in*** the *street*=a street Arab. 浮浪少年 ‖ cut a person ***in*** the *street* 人と道で会って知らん顔をする. ¶go out ***into*** the *street* [家の中から]街へ出る ‖ rush out ***into*** the *street* 表に飛びだす. ¶at the bottom (top) ***of*** a *street* 街の下(上)手で ‖ at the end ***of*** a *street* 街はずれで ‖ in the middle ***of*** a *street* 街の真中で. ¶His home is ***on*** (=in) Fifteenth *Street*. 彼の家は十五番街にある. ‖ play catch ***on*** the *street* 通路でキャッチボールをやる ‖ go ***on*** the *streets* 売春をする ‖ live ***on*** Fifth *Street* 五番街に住む(通路に面して) ‖ make a living ***on*** the *streets* 売春を商売にをする ‖ One window looks out ***on*** the *street*. 一つの窓は往来に向いている. 【類】The door opens ***on*** the *street*. / Do not eat ***on*** the *street*. / Don't throw waste paper ***on*** the *streets*. / I met a lady ***on*** the *streets*. / He was found loitering ***on*** the *streets* at night. ¶march ***through*** the *streets* 市中を行進する. ¶My room looks ***to*** the *street*. 私のへやは通りに向いている. ¶The house is ***up*** the *street*. その家は通りの上手にある. ¶walk ***up*** and ***down*** the *street* 通りを行ったり来たりする.

P² The *streets* ***at*** night are unsafe. 夜分の街は物騒だ. ¶the most important *street* ***for*** wholesale business 卸売業には最も重要な通り. ¶Lombard Street is a *street* ***of*** banks. ロンバード通りは銀行街である.

streetcar, *n.* 《米》市内電車.

V ***drive*** *streetcars* 電車を運転する. ¶***operate*** *streetcars* 電車を運転する. ¶***take*** (=get in) a *streetcar* 電車に乗る.

Q an ***illuminated*** *streetcar* 花電車.

P a book to read ***on*** the *streetcars* 電車内で物を読む本.

street-door, *n.* 通りに面した戸口.

V ***secure*** the *street-door* 表通りの戸口に締りをする.

strength, *n.* 力, 勢力; 兵力, 兵数.

V It will ***add*** *strength* to his argument. それは彼の議論を一層力あるものにするであろう. 【類】***add*** *strength* to the tie of friendship between the two nations. ¶***borrow*** *strength* from ... …から力を借りる. ¶***bring*** *strength* to the weak 弱いものに力をつける ‖ ***bring*** all one's *strength* into play to ... 全力を揮って…する. ¶***build up*** *strength* 力を養う. ¶***collect*** *strength* 勇を鼓す, 元気を出す. ¶It ***composes*** the *strength* of a nation. それは国力を成している. ¶***concentrate*** one's *strength* (=energy) upon ... …にその力を集中する. ¶How have you managed to ***conserve*** *strength* and vigor? [老人に向って]どうして体力と気力とを保つことができましたか. ¶The middle classes ***constitute*** the real *strength* and backbone of the country. 中産階級はその国の真の力であり背骨である. ¶***cultivate*** national *strength* 国力を養う. ¶his argument ***draws*** *strength* from the fact that ... 彼の議論は…という事実と照し合わして有力となる. ¶***exceed*** one's *strength* その力に及ばない. ¶Talk ***fritters away*** one's mental *strength*. 談話は頭脳を消耗する. ¶"What's the matter?" I ***found*** *strength* to ask. 「どうしたんです」と私はやっとのことで尋ねた. ¶***gain*** (=***acquire***) *strength* 力を得る. ¶it ***gathers*** *strength* from the fact that ... その強味は…の点にある ‖ The sick man is ***gathering*** *strength*. あの病人は段々力がついて来た. ‖ ***gather*** *strength* for the renewed attack on ... 巻土重来…攻撃の力を養う. ¶I espoused the cause with *strength* my Creator has ***given*** me. 私は神が私に与えた力をもってその主義を擁護した. ‖ ***give*** it *strength* and color [文体など]それに力と色つやをつける. ¶My staff was so ill-fed that it ***had*** not the *strength* to be disloyal. 私の部員は栄養不良で不忠実になるだけの元気すらなかった. ‖ ***have*** the *strength* of a horse 馬ほどの大力である. 【類】He ***had*** the *strength* of a boy brought up on a farm. / ***have*** no *strength* to swim so far / ***have*** ten times the *strength* of an ordinary man (十人力). ¶***increase*** the *strength* of the army 軍隊を増員する ‖ ***increase*** the *strength* of a solution 溶解液の濃度を増す. ¶***keep up*** one's *strength* 元気を維持する. ¶***lose*** *strength* 力を失う.

¶***measure*** one's *strength* with ... ...と力比べをする. ¶***muster*** [***up***] (=***summon***) *strength* 力を振い起す. ¶***overtax*** (=***overtask***) one's *strength* 力以上の仕事をさせる. ¶***put forth*** (=***out***) *strength* 力を出す. ¶in order to ***recruit*** its *strength* その力を補うために. ¶***recuperate*** its used-up *strength* その消耗した気力を回復する. ¶***regain*** the *strength* he had lost through overwork 過労のために失った力を回復する. ¶***renew*** *strength* 力を回復する. ¶***sap*** one's *strength* 気力を消耗する. ¶***spend*** one's *strength* in ... ...に精力を使う. ¶***store up*** *strength* for ... ...のために精力を養う. ¶***summoning*** [***up***] all his *strength* 全力をあげて. ¶***task*** (=***tax***) one's *strength* 力を出させる. ¶***throw*** *strength* into ... ...に力を入れる. ¶***try*** one's *strength* with (=against) ... ...と腕だめしをする. ¶***undervalue*** (=***belittle***) the *strength* of ... ...の力を軽視する. ¶They ***united*** their *strength*. 彼らは協力した.

V² At last his *strength* ***gave out***. ついに彼の力が尽きた. ¶while our *strength* ***lasts*** われらの力の続く限り. ¶its *strength* ***lies*** in ... その強味は...にある. 【類】Herein ***lies*** their *strength*. ¶Man's physical *strength* ***wanes*** with age. 人の体力は年とともに衰えて行く.

Q ***additional*** *strength* 鬼に金棒. ¶***aggressive*** *strength* 攻撃力. ¶***alcoholic*** *strength* [ビールなどの]アルコール分. ¶the ***armed*** *strength* of a country 一国の軍事力. ¶***basic*** *strength* 底力. ¶***brute*** *strength* [熟練・知識などを伴わない]腕力. ¶We find in it his ***chief*** *strength* and his greatest weakness. われわれはその中に彼の主な強味と最大の弱点とを見出す. ¶***denominational*** *strength* 各宗派の勢力. ¶***exuberant*** *strength* あふれるばかりの力. ¶***financial*** *strength* 財力. ¶in ***full*** *strength* or diluted [酒など]生一本か割るかして ‖ a battalion at ***full*** *strength* 最強の状態の軍 ‖ with one's ***full*** *strength* 精一杯に, 力まかせに ‖ under ***full*** *strength* of work 用務繁多の際にも. ¶with a ***giant*** *strength* 怪力で. ¶***Herculean*** *strength* 怪力. ¶***impregnable*** *strength* 強固な力. ¶He felt his ***intellectual*** *strength* failing. 彼は自分の知力が衰えだしたのに気づいた. ¶an ***inner*** *strength* 精神の力. ¶the party has ***little*** *strength* in ... 党は...ではあまり勢力がない. ¶***lusty*** *strength* 元気. ¶***main*** *strength* 主力. ¶***military*** *strength* 兵力. ¶***mobilized*** *strength* 戦時定員. ¶***moral*** *strength* 精神力. ¶***national*** *strength* 国力. ¶the Japanese ***naval*** *strength* 日本の海軍力. ¶with the ***nominal*** *strength* of one hundred thousand 十万と称する兵力をもって. ¶***numerical*** *strength* [海軍など]数字上の戦闘力. ¶God is our ***only*** *strength*. 神がわれらのただ一つの頼みだ. ¶She has reached a vigor that will enable her to walk firmly in her ***own*** *strength*. 彼女は力が付いたから人手を借りないでちゃんと歩けるでしょう. ¶a man of great ***physical*** *strength* 非常な体力の人. ¶Benkei was a man renowned for his ***prodigious*** *strength* 弁慶はその怪力で有名な人であった. ¶the ***relative*** *strength* [党員など]数の比較割合. ¶***rugged*** *strength* 蛮勇. ¶a question of ***sheer*** *strength* 全く力づくの問題. ¶troops in ***sufficient*** *strength* 数の十分な兵. ¶by virture of their ***united*** *strength* 一致協力のおかげで.

Q² scale down the ***Army*** *strength* from ... to ... 陸軍力を...から...に縮少する. ¶the fleet's ***combat*** *strength* 艦隊の戦闘力. ¶***fighting*** *strength* 戦闘力. ¶***party*** *strength* in the Diet shown in the elections 選挙の結果による国会の党勢力. ¶a ***peace*** *strength* of roundly 600,000 men and a ***war*** *strength* of 8,000,000 or more 六十万の平時兵力と八百万の戦時兵力. ¶The U.S. Army reached its interim ***peace-time*** *strength* of 1,070, 000 only July 1, 1947. 米陸軍は一九四七年七月一日現在で百七万の中間平時兵力に達した. ¶***war*** *strength* 戦力.

P Attempt nothing ***beyond*** your *strength*. 力に及ばないことをしようとするな. 【類】It is ***beyond*** human *strength*. ¶***by*** sheer *strength*=***by*** *strength* alone 力だけで. ¶It is too much ***for*** my *strength*. それは私の力に余る. ¶They equalled us ***in*** *strength*. 彼らの力はわれわれに匹敵した. ‖ gain (diminish) ***in*** *strength* 力が増す(減る) ‖ The students of the school were present ***in*** great *strength*. その学校の生徒が大勢そろって出席していた. 【類】She can cope with England ***in*** naval *strength*. ¶feats ***of*** *strength* 力業 ‖ a test ***of*** *strength* 力だめし. ¶I dit it ***on*** the *strength* of your promise. 私は君の約束を当にしてそうやった. 【類】***on*** the *strength* of agreements concluded with ... / I did it ***on*** the *strength* of his statements. / ***on*** the *strength* of this assumption, the assertion is sometimes made that ... / ***on*** the *strength* of his own investigations, he is in opposition to ... / ***on*** the *strength* of relationship ‖ He presumes too much ***on*** his *strength*. 彼は力を鼻に掛け過ぎる. ¶***with*** all one's *strength* 力一杯に ‖ ***with*** full *strength* 全力で. 【類】a man ***with*** the *strength* of a Sandow ‖ come back ***with*** *strength* renewed / He is endowed ***with*** a giant's *strength*.

P² gather sufficient *strength* ***for*** active opposition 対抗できるような力を出す ‖ the *strength* ***of*** an army 兵力 ‖ *strength* ***of*** body 体力 ‖ *strength* ***of*** will (character, mind) 意志(など)の力 ‖ *strength* ***of*** grasp 握力 ‖ The *strength* ***of*** the solution is 1/3000. その溶液は三千倍になっている.

O My *strength* was nearly gone. 私は力がほとんど尽きた. ¶What is its *strength* is also its weakness. その長所が同時にその弱点だ.

stress, *n*. 重味; 努力, 緊張; 圧迫; 〖音声〗語勢(アクセント).

V ***cast*** an undue *stress* upon the brain 頭を過度に働かせる. ¶***feel*** the *stress* of hunger 空腹に苦しむ. ¶***impose*** a severe *stress* on ... ...に激しい圧迫を加える. ¶***lay*** (=***put, place***) *stress* on ... ...に重きをおく; ...に力を入れて言うまたは発音する. 【類】*stress* is ***laid*** on the point (fact) that ... / ***lay*** great *stress* upon ... ¶***put*** undue *stress* on one's faculty 能力の無理をする ‖ ***put*** *stress* on (=give stress to) the second syllable 第二音節にアクセントをおく. ¶***shift*** the *stress* on to the second syllable アクセントを第二音節に移す.

Q lay ***equal*** *stress* upon ... ...に同様重きをおく. ¶lay ***greater*** *stress* on ... than on ... ...よりは...に一層重きをおく. ¶The ***main*** *stress* is laid upon excellence in mathematics. 主として数学の力に重きをおく. ¶lay too ***much*** *stress* on ... 大いに...に重きをおき過ぎる. ¶lay ***particular*** *stress* on the fact that ... 特に...の事実に重きをおく. ¶the ***primary*** (***secondary***) *stress* 第一(二)アクセント. ¶a very ***severe*** *stress* is imposed on ... ...に非常に強い圧力を加える. ¶***special*** *stress* is laid on the fact that ... ...の事実に特に重きをおく. ¶the ***strong*** (***light***) *stress* 強(弱)アクセント. ¶cast an ***undue*** *stress* upon the brain 頭脳に不当な負担をかける. ¶subject a faculty to the ***utmost*** *stress* 才能の限り能力を働かす.

P driven ***by*** [*stress* of] poverty 貧に駆られて ‖ ***by*** *stress* of weather 天候険悪のため. ¶times ***of*** *stress* 非常時. ¶***Owing to*** *stress* of work I cannot leave my study. 私は忙しいので書斎を出られない. ¶The match was postponed ***through*** *stress* of ground conditions. グラウンドの状態が良くないのでその試合は延期になった. 【類】***through*** *stress* of weather. ¶do a thing ***under*** *stress* 迫られて(余儀なく)やる ‖ ***under*** the *stress* of circumstances 事情に迫られて ‖ acts performed ***under*** the *stress* of unavoidable necessity やむを得ない必要に迫られて出た行為. ¶syllables ***without*** *stress* アクセントのない音節.

P² But here was the *stress* ***of*** the joke. しかしここがこのしゃれのねらいどころであった. ‖ The *stress* ***of*** the negotiation has obliged him to reject the demand. 彼は談判の行掛り上その要請を拒絶した. ¶In most English words there is a strong *stress* ***on*** one syllable. 英語は大概どれか一つの音節にアクセントがある.

stress, *v*. 力を入れて発音する.

P *stressed* ***on*** the first syllable 最初のシラブルにアクセントのある.

stretch, *n*. 緊張; 延長, 範囲; 一気; 旅程.

Q a truly ***diabolical*** *stretch* of weather 悪天候の継続. ¶a ***great*** *stretch* of moorland 広い沼沢地. ¶a ***long*** *stretch* of hills 一帯の山 ‖ a ***long*** *stretch* of bad weather 長い間の悪い天気続き. 【類】a ***long*** *stretch* of white beach. ¶It is not difficult for one to foresee the result with the ***smallest possible*** *stretch* of fancy. ちょっと想像して見ればその結果どうなるかがたやすく分かる. ¶the ***utmost*** *stretch* of one's power 極度の努力. ¶The ***whole*** *stretch* of them will ultimately become a public park. その全部が結局公園になるだろう. ¶***wide*** *stretches* of moorland ぼうばくたる荒野.

Q² the ***home*** *stretch* 最後の曲路と決勝点との間(競走場の).

P sometimes from twenty-four to thirty-six hours ***at*** a *stretch* 時としては一気に二十四時間から三十六時間まで. 【類】sit four or five hours ***at*** a *stretch* / row for six hours *at* a *stretch.* ¶ ***beyond*** the *stretch* of reason 道理をはずれて. ¶ ***by*** a *stretch* of language こじつけて ‖ ***by*** any *stretch* of imagination どう想像をたくましくしても.【類】He could not ***by*** any possible *stretch* be considered [as] a gentleman. ¶work ten hours ***on*** a *stretch* 一気に十時間働く ‖ His duties keep his mind continually ***on*** the *stretch.* 彼は職務のために始終気を張り詰めている.

P² a *stretch* ***of*** five miles 五マイルの旅程 ‖ a *stretch* ***of*** authority 越権 ‖ There was a *stretch* ***of*** sand hills along the shore. 海岸沿いに砂丘がずっと伸びていた.

stretch, *v.* 引張る; 渡す; 差伸べる; 延びる.

M Rubber *stretches* ***easily.*** ゴムは引っ張ると容易に伸びる. ¶*stretch* ***out*** 手足を伸ばす.【類】*stretch* ***out*** one's legs / I lay still on the couch, quietly *stretched* ***out.*** ‖ *stretch* ***out***! 強くこげ! (ボート漕手への号令) ‖ *stretch* ***out*** (=***forth***) one's arms 腕を差し伸べる. ¶*stretch* a rope ***tight*** ロープをぴんと張りつめる. ¶cords *stretched* ***tightly*** on a wooden frame 木のわくに堅く張り巡らしたひも.

M² The ownership of the soil *stretches* ***down*** into the depths of the earth. 土地所有権は地球の深部まで伸びている.

P *stretch* a wire ***across*** a river 川に針金を渡す.【類】A bridge is *stretched* (架(か)して) ***across*** the river. / *stretching* ***across*** (=extending for) three-quarters of a century. ¶The town *stretches* ***along*** the bay. 町は湾に沿うて延び拡がっている. ¶garments *stretched* ***at*** the elbows ひじのところが延びた着物. ¶The Meiji era *stretched* ***from*** 1868 ***to*** 1912. 明治時代は西暦一八六八年から一九一二年にわたった. ‖ The Alps *stretch* ***from*** east ***to*** west. アルプス山脈は東から西へ延びている. ¶*stretch* the law ***in*** one's favor. 法を自分に都合いいように解釈する. ¶The war dragged on the months *stretched* ***into*** years. 何カ月が何カ年と延びて戦争は長引いた. ‖ *stretch* it ***into*** service 無理やりそれを流用する. ¶It *stretches* ***like*** elastic. それはゴムのひものように伸びる. ¶*stretch* oneself ***on*** the bed 寝床に身を横たえる. ¶*stretch* a curtain ***over*** an opening あいている所へ幕を張る ‖ the experiments *stretched* (=extended) ***over*** a period of ... その実験は…の期間にわたった. ¶The Turkish dominions *stretched* ***to*** the furthest point of Arabia. トルコの領土はアラビアの一番奥の地点まで延びた. ‖ *stretch* ***to*** the oar 一所懸命にかいをこぐ.

stretcher, *n.* つり台, 担架.

P carry a wounded man ***on*** a *stretcher* 担架にのせて負傷者を運ぶ.

strew, *v.* 振りまく.

P *strew* flowers ***on*** the path 道に花をまく. ¶*strew* flowers ***over*** the grave 墓に花をまく.【類】The parts of the crashed planes were *strewn* ***over*** an area of more than 5 acres. ¶The paths of virtue are *strewed* ***with*** roses eternally unfading. 徳の道には永遠にあせないばらがまいてある.【類】The table is *strewn* ***with*** books. ‖ Every field of victory is *strewn* ***with*** corpses. 勝戦の野には死体がばらまかれている(一将功成りて万骨枯る).

stricken, *pa.* → strike.

strict, *a.* きびしい; 厳正な.

M The teacher is ***very*** *strict* but not unfair. 先生はとてもきびしいがえこひいきはしない.

P He is not very *strict* ***about*** it. 彼はそのことにはあまり厳格でない. ¶*strict* ***in*** discipline 訓練のきびしい ‖ *strict* ***in*** morals 品行の厳正な ‖ He is *strict* ***in*** observing the Sabbath. 彼は安息日を厳守する.【類】She is *strict* ***with*** her pupils in the class.【類】You seem too *strict* ***with*** your young ones.

strictness, *n.* 厳格.

P it may not ***in*** *strictness* be considered as ... それは厳格に言えば…と考えられないかも知れない. ¶***with*** *strictness* きびしく.

stricture, *n.* [通常 *pl.*] 非難, 非議.

V ***lay*** (=***pass***) *strictures* on a person or a thing 人また物を攻撃する.

P² he is severe in his *strictures* ***on*** ... 彼の…に対する非難はきびしい.

stride, *n.* 大またの歩み; 足どり.

V ***hit*** (=***strike***) one's *stride* 自分の仕事の調子が出る. ¶***make*** great *strides* forward 長足の進歩をする ‖ Probably no science has ***made*** greater *strides* than psychology within the past few years. 恐らく過去数年間に心理学ぐらい長足の進歩をした科学はないだろう.【類】the great *stride* that education has ***made*** during recent times among civilized nations. ¶It has ***taken*** great *strides* in its progress. それは長足の進歩をした. ¶***take in*** one's *stride* 自己のペースでやる; [仕事など]軽くやってのける.

Q It has made such ***astonishing*** *strides.* それは驚くべき長足の進歩をした. ¶walk with ***big*** *strides* 大またに歩く. ¶It has made ***considerable*** *strides.* それは著しく進歩した. ¶The teaching art has made ***enormous*** *strides* since then. その後教授法は非常に進歩した. ¶the ***giant*** *strides* Japan has made since ... in ... 日本が…以来…において遂げた長足の大進歩. ¶make ***gigantic*** *strides* 長足の大進歩をする. ¶a ***great*** *stride* of progress 長足の進歩. ¶make the pace with ***heavy*** *strides* のっしのっしと大またに歩く. ¶take ***huge*** (=***large***) *strides* 長足の進歩をする. ¶Surgery has taken ***immense*** *strides.* 外科は非常に進歩した.【類】the country is making such ***immense*** *strides* forward in ... ¶make a ***long*** *stride* in mechanical civilization 機械文明に長足の進歩をとげる ‖ The movement has made ***long*** *strides* since the war. その運動は戦後長足の進歩をした. ¶a ***masculine*** *stride* 男らしいかっ歩. ¶Since then what ***mighty*** *strides* we have made! その時からえらい進歩をしたものだ. ¶After his return to Japan his illness made ***rapid*** *strides.* 帰朝後彼の病気はずんずん進んだ.【類】make surprisingly ***rapid*** *strides.* ¶step at a ***single*** *stride* from the "doss house" 一足飛びに木賃宿から(りっぱな住宅にはいるようになるなど). ¶march with ***stately*** *stride* through ... …の中を堂々と大またに進む. ¶make ***tremendous*** *strides* in one's studies 勉強にすばらしい進歩をする.【類】take ***tremendous*** *strides* toward ... ¶***Vast*** *strides* have been made in this comparatively short interval. この比較的短かい間にえらく進歩した. ¶walk with ***vigorous*** *strides* 大またで活発に歩く.

P ***at*** a *stride* 一足飛びに. ¶advance ***by*** rapid *strides* 急速に進む. ¶***in*** one *stride* 一またぎに. ¶move ***with*** gigantic *strides* 大またに歩く ‖ Her population is growing ***with*** great *strides.* その国の人口は非常な勢いで増加しつつある. ‖ Civilization has advanced ***with*** rapid *strides* in Japan. 日本の文化は急激な進歩をした.

P² It has made such vast *strides* ***in*** civilization. その文明は実際非常に進んだ.

stride, *v.* 大またに歩く(またぐ).

M *stride* ***across*** ... …をまたぐ. ¶*stride* ***ahead*** 大またに先に出る. ¶He *strode* ***along*** at a great pace. 彼は大またに歩いて行った. ¶*stride* ***boldly*** 大胆にかっ歩する.

P *stride* ***across*** a puddle 水たまりを大またにまたぐ. ¶*stride* ***along*** the corridor 廊下を大またに歩いて行く. ¶He *strode* fiercely ***out of*** the room. 彼はへやから恐ろしい勢いで飛び出した. ¶*stride* ***over*** a brook 小川をまたいで越える. ¶He *strode* ***to*** the window. 彼は大またに窓の方へ歩いた. ¶*stride* ***with*** dignified gait 威厳をつけて大またに歩く.

strife, *n.* 闘争.

V ***beget*** *strife* 闘争を起させる.

V² *strife* ***arose*** among ... …間に紛争が起った.

Q A ***civil*** *strife* is universally condemned as a crime. 内乱は世界を通じて犯罪と認められている. ¶carry on a ***friendly*** *strife* with Nature 自然と親しい闘争を続ける. ¶***sectarian*** *strife* 宗派争い. ¶***smoldering*** *strife* 暗闘.

Q² antisocial ***labor*** *strife* 反社会的労働争議.【類】head off a ***labor*** *strife* scheduled for June 15 / once the scene of bitter ***labor*** *strife.* ¶a major cause of ***labor-management*** *strife* 労使衝突の主因の一つ.

strike, *n.* (**1**) 同盟罷業, スト[ライキ].

V ***avert*** *strikes* 罷業を防止する. ¶The Union will ***bring about*** a *strike* of tramway men in that city. 組合はあの市の電車従業員のストを実行するだろう. ¶they determined to ***call*** a *strike* in order to ... 彼らは…のためにストを決行することに決定した. ¶The *strike* has been ***called off.*** そのストは中止された. ¶***carry on*** a *strike* of some months' duration 数カ月にわたるストを続行する ‖ At the meeting it was determined to ***continue*** the *strike.* その会合でスト継続に決定した. ¶***declare*** a *strike* ストを宣言する. ¶***organize*** a *strike* ストを計画する. ¶***proclaim*** a general *strike* 総罷業を宣言する. ¶***put down*** (=suppress) a *strike* ストを静める. ¶At a meeting of the masters it was determined to ***resist*** the *strike.* 雇傭主会議で争議に反抗することに決定した. ¶He made several attempts to ***settle*** the miners' *strike.* 彼は坑夫のストを解決すべく色々やって見た. ¶The *strike* was ***terminated*** and normal conditions were restored. そのストは終局をつげて常態に復した.

V² A *strike* has ***broken out.*** ストがぼっ発した. ¶The *strike* ***came off***. そのストが終った. ¶as the *strike* ***entered*** its third month スト開始後三カ月目に. ¶A *strike* ***went into effect*** yesterday. ストがきのう実行された.

Q call a ***general*** *strike* ゼネストを決行する. 【類】a 24-hour ***general*** *strike.* ¶an ***illegal*** *strike* 不法スト. ¶a "***light out***" *strike* 消灯を手段とするスト. ¶a ***long-protracted*** *strike* 長引いたスト. ¶The *strike* is ***on.*** スト中である. ¶a ***sporadic*** *strike* 散発的スト. ¶a ***sympathetic*** *strike* 同情スト. ¶an ***unofficial*** *strike* 非公式のスト.

Q² smash a ***coal*** *strike* 炭坑ストをたたきつぶす. ¶a "***go-slow***" *strike* サボスト(市電の「安全運転」など). ¶a ***guerrilla*** *strike* ゲリラスト. ¶a "***leave of absence***" ***holiday*** *strike* 欠勤休暇スト, 賜暇スト. ¶a ***hunger*** *strike* ハンスト. ¶stage a voluntary ***hunger*** *strike* 自由意志によるハンストをやる. ¶stage ***labor*** *strikes* in succession ストの波状攻撃を加える. ¶a ***nuisance*** *strike* いやがらせスト. ¶The workers left their jobs in a ***one-day general*** *strike* 労働者は一日ゼネストで職場を放棄した. ¶prevent nationwide "***paralysis***" *strikes* 全国的規模の麻ひストを防止する. ¶a "***piston***" *strike* ピストン・スト. ¶a nationwide ***protest*** *strike* against "anti-labor" legislation 「反労働」立法に反対する全国的抗議スト. ¶a ***sitdown*** *strike* in front of the premier's residence 首相官邸前のすわり込みスト. ¶a "***stay-in***" *strike* 職場すわり込み(ろう城)スト. ¶a 26-day-old ***steel*** *strike* 二十六日経過の鉄鋼スト. ¶walk out in "***sympathy***" *strikes* 同情ストで職場放棄をする. ¶a ***tramway*** *strike* 都(市)電スト. ¶a ***transport*** (=***transportation***) *strike* 輸送スト. ¶go on a ***wildcat*** *strike* 山ねこストを決行する.

P join ***in*** a *strike* ストに加わる. ¶The workers are ***on*** *strike.* 従業員がスト中である. 【類】Our men are ***on*** a *strike* for higher wages. / The students are out ***on*** *strike.* ¶*go on* [a] *strike*=《米》walk out ストを決行する. 【類】go [out] ***on*** *strike* / remain ***on*** *strike*=still idle (=out) / railroaders (=railway workers) ***on*** *strike.*

P² a *strike* ***of*** laborers=a labor strike 労働争議.

(**2**) 打つこと, 当てること.

V ***make*** a lucky *strike* in politics 政治で当りを取る. ¶*score* a *strike* 〖野球〗ストライクになる.

Q² carry out an ***air*** *strike* against ... …に空襲を加える. ¶a ***Navy carrier*** *strike* 航空母艦出撃.

P ten *strikes* ***from*** the old church tower 古い教会堂の塔から聞える十時の鐘.

O The count was two *strikes* and no ball. カウントはストライク二つにボールなしだ.

strike, *v.* (**1**) 打つ(など).

M *strike* ***aground*** 浅瀬に乗上げる, 座礁する. ¶The road *strikes* ***away*** to the left. 道は左にそれる. ¶*strike* ***back*** at ... …に打返す ‖ *strike* ***back*** from the first goal [レースで] 最初のゴールから打返す. ¶They *struck* him ***dead.*** 彼らは彼を打殺した. ‖ He was *struck* ***dead*** by lightning. 彼は雷に打たれて死んだ. ¶The tree *strikes* its roots ***deep.*** その木は深く根ざしている. 【類】The matter really *strikes* very much ***deeper*** than the police were at first inclined to think. ¶His eloquence *struck* them ***dumb.*** 彼の雄弁は彼らをあ然たらしめた. ‖ He was *struck* ***dumb*** with astonishment (by the news). 彼は(その報に接して)驚いてあ然とした. ¶I am *struck* ***favorably*** with the plan. 私はその案に感心した. ¶We were a good way from the top of the pass when we ***first*** *struck* snow. 峠の頂上からかなりの距離の所で初めて雪に出会わした. ¶It *struck* us most ***forcibly.*** それが非常に強くわれわれを感動させた. ¶be *struck* ***hard*** against ... …に猛烈にぶっつかる. ¶*strike* ***harshly*** upon the ear 耳ざわりが悪い. ¶it *struck* ***home*** それは…の急所に当った. ¶*strike* ***out*** (=delete) a name from a list 名簿から名前を削除する. ¶*strike* an item ***out*** 項目を削除する ‖ *strike* ***out*** the article 冠詞を除く ‖ He has *struck* ***out*** a new plan. 彼は新しい方法を案出した. ‖ The batter was *struck* ***out.*** 打者は三振した. ‖ *strike* ***out*** for the shore [水泳などで]岸の方に泳ぎだす ‖ boldly *strike* ***out*** into uncharted seas without a compass 大胆にもら針盤も持たずに海図にも出てない海洋に乗り出す ‖ *strike* ***out*** into the world [学窓から] 世間に進出する ‖ sparks *struck* ***out*** from a flint 火打石から飛ぶ火花. ¶what *strikes* us so ***remakably*** is that ... ひときわわれわれを感動させるものは…だ. ¶*strike* it ***rich***=strike oil《米口》大成金になる. ¶*strike* ***savagely*** at ... …を猛烈に攻撃する.

P What *strikes* me ***about*** him is his great patience. 私が彼について感心することはその忍耐力の強いことだ. ¶*strike* one ***across*** the face 顔を(真正面から)なぐりつける ‖ *strike* ***across*** the fields 田野を横断して行く.

P² *strike* (=knock) ***down*** one's foe (an adversary) かたき(敵手)を打倒する ‖ be *struck* ***down*** with flu 流感で倒れる. 【類】Thousands were *struck* ***down*** by the epidemic. ¶here another gentleman, who sat next to me, *struck* ***in*** with ... ここで私の隣りにすわっていた別の人が…と口をはさんだ. 【類】He *struck* ***in*** while we were talking. ¶*strike* a name ***off*** (会員名簿などから)除名する ‖ *strike* ***off*** anything superfluous (harmful) 不要(有害)のものを省く ‖ He *struck* ***off*** a hundred copies. 彼は百部刷った. ‖ His head was *struck* ***off.*** 彼は首をはねられた. ‖ *strike* ***off*** in a heat of enthusiasm 一気可成にやってのける. ¶*strike* ***up*** (=begin) a conversation 会話を始める. ¶I have *struck* ***up*** an acquaintance with him. 私は彼と懇意になった. 【類】*strike* ***up*** (=establish) friendship between nations. ‖ The band *struck* ***up*** a tune. 楽隊が曲を奏し始めた. 【類】The band *struck* ***up*** when the Queen entered. ¶The liner has *struck* ***against*** a rock and greatly damaged her keel. 船は暗礁に乗上げて大いに竜骨を損じた. ‖ *strike* one's foot ***against*** a stone 足を石に打ち当てる ‖ The light *strikes* ***against*** (=upon) the wall. 光線が壁に当る. ‖ *strike* ***against*** the proposed alteration 提出された改正案に反対する. ¶It *struck* me ***as*** strange. 私はそれを変に思った. 【類】*strike* one ***as*** peculiar / *strike* me ***as*** particularly curious / They *strike* us ***as*** being the production of an abler man. ¶*strike* ***at*** a person with a club 棒で人に打ってかかる ‖ *strike* ***at*** the ball 球を打とうとする ‖ *strike* ***at*** the air 空振りする ‖ *strike* ***at*** the root of the evil (mischief, government, power) 悪弊(など)を根底からくつがえす. 【類】go deeper and *strike* ***at*** the roots of the trouble. ‖ A pang of pity *struck* ***at*** my heart. 不びんだという感じが私の胸を痛めた. ‖ New coins are being *struck* ***at*** the mint. 新貨幣は造幣局で鋳造されている. ¶He was *struck* ***below*** the knee. 彼はひざの下を打たれた. ¶He was *struck* ***by*** a stone. 彼は石にあたった. 【類】I was *struck* ***by*** (出会った) a hurricane (つむじ風). / He was *struck* (打たれた) ***by*** lightning. ‖ be *struck* ***by*** a torpedo and sank 水雷にやられて沈没する. ¶*strike* ***for*** freedom (one's country) 自由(など)のために戦う. ¶*strike* a coin ***from*** a die (metal) 型(などで)貨幣を鋳造する. ¶*strike* ***in*** the dark やみ討をする ‖ They *struck* him ***in*** the face. 彼らは彼の顔を打った. 【類】he was *struck* ***in*** the eye with ... / *strike* an enemy ***in*** the rear (背後) ‖ with swords jauntily *struck* ***in*** their belts 得意然と大小を手ばさんで ‖ a man well *struck* (=advanced) ***in*** years かなり高齢の人. ¶*strike* (=enter suddenly) ***into*** conversation 急に話しだす ‖ *strike* ***into*** a song 歌いだす ‖ *strike* ***into*** a gallop かけだす ‖ *strike* ***into*** the harbor 入港する ‖ Cold *strikes* ***into*** one's marrow 寒気が骨身にしみる. ‖ Its roots are *striking* deep ***into*** earth. その根は深く地中に張っている ‖ *strike* a letter ***into*** an envelope 封筒に手紙を入れる. ¶*strike* (=erase) one's name ***off*** (=from) the list 除名する. 【類】His name was *struck* ***off*** the rolls (名簿). ¶The ship *struck* ***on*** the reef (rock, bar, sandy beach of ...) 船が暗礁(など)に乗り上げた. 【類】The ship *struck* ***on*** a sunken rock not laid down on any chart (海図). ‖ He *struck* three times ***on*** the door. 彼は戸を三度たたいた. 【類】He was *struck* ***on*** the head with a stone. / A bullet *struck* him ***on*** the back of the neck. / *strike* one's hand ***on*** the table ‖ *strike* ***on*** a novel means of ... …の新らしい方法を思いつく. ¶*strike* sparks (fire, light) ***out of*** a flint 火打石で火をきり出す ‖ *strike* a ball ***out of*** the court 球を球場外に打ちあげる. ¶The arrow *struck* ***through*** his armor. 矢が彼のよろいを貫いた. ‖ Cold *strikes* ***through*** one's clothes. 寒気が衣服を通す. ¶*strike* a person ***to*** the heart with a dagger 短刀で心臓まで刺す ‖ *strike* terror ***to*** one's heart 恐怖心をいだかせる. ¶*strike* ***upon*** an unknown path 知らない道に出る ‖ *strike* ***upon*** a happy thought うまい考えが出る. 【類】*strike* ***upon*** an idea ‖ His professors' lectures *strike **upon*** dull ears. 彼は教授連の講義には感心しなかった. ‖ The accident was caused by the vessel *striking **upon*** a sunken rock. その事件は船が暗礁にぶつかったので起った. ¶*strike* a horse ***with*** a whip むちで馬を打つ ‖ *strike* a person ***with*** fright (terror, wonder, remorse) 人に恐怖(など)の念を起させる. 【類】 be *struck **with*** her beauty / be *struck **with*** cerebral hemorrhage (脳出血) ‖ *strike **with*** the open hand 平手で打つ ‖ a man *stricken **with*** age 年を取った人 ‖ He was *stricken **with*** influenza (paralysis). 彼はインフルエンザ(など)にかかった. ‖ London is *stricken **with*** the craze for ... ロンドンでは...が大流行だ. ‖ he was *struck **with*** the idea that ... 彼は...を思いついた ‖ He was *struck **with*** shame. 彼は恥入った.

O Don't *strike* you that ...? = Does it not (= Doesn't it) *strike* you that ...? 君は...とは思わないか. 【類】 It *struck* me (気がついた) that he was telling a lie.

(**2**) ストをやる.

P *strike **against*** long hours (the proposed alteration) 就業時間短縮要求(など)のストをやる. 【類】 *strike **against*** an employer. ¶*strike **for*** higher wages 賃銀値上げを要求してストする. 【類】 Workmen have *struck **for*** less hours.

string, *n.* 糸, ひも; 〘楽器〙 弦; 一列; 一連.

V ***adjust*** the *strings* of a violin バイオリンの調子をととのえる. ¶***have*** two *strings* to one's bow 両天びんをかける. 【類】 The "koto" ***has*** 13 *strings*, which are plucked with plectra of ivory (象げのつめ) fixed to the fingers. ¶***hold*** the purse *strings* 財布のひもを握っている. ¶***pluck*** the *strings* (三味線などの) 弦をはじいて鳴らす. ¶***pull*** *strings* [かげから]糸を引く, 黒幕となる. ¶***tie** a string* to ... ...にひもを結ぶ ‖ He ***tied*** no *strings* to his gift. 彼はその寄付になんら条件を付けなかった. ¶***tighten*** the *strings* of ... ...のひもを締める ‖ ***tighten*** (***loosen***) one's purse *string* 〘比ゆ〙 財布のひもをしめる(ゆるめる) ‖ We must not neglect to ***tighten*** the helmet *strings* after victory. 勝ってかぶとの緒を締めよ, である. ¶***touch*** the *strings* [弦楽器を]奏する. 【類】 ***touch*** the lute *strings* (琴線) of his heart. ¶***twang*** *strings* 弦をはじく. ¶***untie*** a *string* ひもを解く. ¶She ***wants*** leading *strings*. 彼女には後見が要(い)る.

Q touch the ***emotional*** *strings* 情緒に触れる. ¶have a ***long*** *string* of degrees 学位をたくさんもっている. ¶a ***strong*** *string* 丈夫なひも.

Q^2 too old to be at his mother's ***apron*** *string* 母親にすがりついてる年じゃない(もう幼児じゃない). ¶***boot*** *strings* = shoestrings, shoelaces くつひも. ¶wear a ***G*** *string* with spangles or tassels [ストリッパーが]スパンゴールやふさのついた細ひもをつける. ¶touch the ***lute*** *strings* of her heart 彼女の心の琴線に触れる.

P They filed past ***in*** a long *string*. 彼らは長い縦列になって通った. ‖ knots tied ***in*** a *string* ひもについている結び目. ¶It is ***on*** a *string*. それは糸につないである. ‖ He is always harping ***on*** the same *string*. 彼はいつも一つことをくどくどと述べたてる. ‖ have a person ***on*** a *string* 人を自由にあやつる. ¶a musical instrument ***with*** ten *strings* 十弦の楽器 ‖ tie it ***with*** a *string* それを糸で結ぶ ‖ subsidies ***with*** no *strings* attached ひも付で(付帯条件の)ない補助金. 【類】 an offer ***with*** a *string* attached to it.

P^2 a *string **of*** carriages (apartments, islands) 一列の客車(など) ‖ He has a *string **of*** admirers. 彼には一団のファンがある. ‖ a *string **of*** porters 一列の人夫 ‖ a *string **of*** pearls (beads) 一連の真珠(など).

string, *v.* 緊張する; 興奮する; 引伸ばす.

M be ***highly*** *strung* for a fight 戦いを控えて大いに張切っている ‖ He is sensitive and ***highly*** *strung*. 彼は感じやすく興奮しやすい. ¶*string **out*** a lecture 講義を引きのばす ‖ *string **out*** scouts along the road 道路ぞいに見張りを配置する.

M^2 *string **up*** one's nerves 気を引しめる ‖ He was *strung **up*** to do the deed. 彼はやっきとなってその行為に出た. 【類】 He is *strung **up*** (緊張して) before the game.

P men *strung **in*** cradles [船体の塗装などの時の]つり板につるされた人々.

stringency, *n.* ひつ迫.

Q in view of general ***financial*** *stringency* caused by the European war 欧州戦争のために起った一般の財政ひつ迫にかんがみて.

Q^2 ***food*** *stringency* 食料事情の急迫. ¶***money*** *stringency* 金融ひつ迫.

strip, *n.* 一片, 断片.

聞などの]続き漫画.

Q a title on ***back*** *strip* [本の]背の標題. ¶a ***comic*** *strip* [新

Q^2 an ***air*** (= airplane) *strip* [飛行場の]滑走路. ¶the ***landing*** *strip* 着陸場(滑走路).

P cut ... ***into** strips* ...を小片に切る ‖ tear it ***into*** *strips* それをずたずたに裂く. ¶***without*** a *strip* of a gauze wrapper on 身に一枚の布(一糸)もまとわず.

P^2 a *strip **of*** land (garden) 一片の土地(など) ‖ a *strip **of*** paper (board) 一枚の紙(など).

strip, *v.* 裸かにする; はぎ取る; 切り離す.

M *strip **away*** all disguises 化けの皮をはぐ. ¶land that has been ***completely*** *stripped* of its timber 立木を全部切りとられた土地. ¶*stripped* stark (= perfectly) ***naked*** 全裸になって.

M^2 *strip **off*** one's coat (clothes, shirt) 上衣(など)を脱ぐ ‖ *strip **off*** a piece of salt fish 塩魚の一片を切り離す.

P *strip* a bamboo shoot ***by*** peeling off the skin 竹の子の皮をむく. ¶*strip* ***for*** a bath もく浴のために脱衣する. ¶*strip* the bark ***from*** a tree 木の皮をはぐ. 【類】 *strip* skin ***from*** a beast ‖ Practically every power was *stripped* ***from*** him. 事実上彼は一切の権力をはく奪された. ¶*strip* a cloth ***in*** pieces 布をきれぎれに引裂く. ¶*stripped* [***in***] ***to*** one's shirt シャツ一枚になって. ¶*strip* a person ***of*** his clothes 人の着物をはぎ取る ‖ *strip* him ***of*** estate or employment 彼の財産または職業を奪う. 【類】 All men are equal if *stripped **of*** their garments. ‖ a plant *stripped **of*** all its equipment 施設全部を取り去った工場. ¶*strip* paper ***off*** the wall 壁から紙をはぎとる. ¶They *stripped* him ***to*** the skin. 彼を裸にした. ‖ *strip* oneself ***to*** the waist はだを脱ぐ. 【類】 *stripped **to*** his shirt-sleeves.

stripe, *n.* しま.

Q A zebra has ***dark*** *stripes*. しま馬には黒ずんだしまがある. ¶a ***sergeant's*** *stripes* 軍そうの山形のすじ. ¶***service*** *stripes* 勤務年数を示すすじ.

P woolen cloth woven ***in*** (= ***with***) *stripes* しま織のラシャ地. 【類】 slacks marked ***with*** *stripes*. ¶a diplomat ***of*** that *stripe* 《米》 その型の外交官. 【類】 blue serge ***with*** pink *stripes*.

P^2 *stripes **on*** a soldier's trousers 兵隊ずぼんのすじ.

stripe, *v.* しまを立てる.

P *striped **in*** blue in a white ground 白地に青いしまを立てた(毛布など).

stripling, *n.* 若者.

Q then a ***mere*** *stripling* 当時ほんの若僧. ¶a ***raw*** *stripling* 未熟の若者.

P^2 He was but a *stripling **of*** sixteen. 彼はたった十六の若僧だった.

strive, *v.* 努力する; 争う.

M *strive **hard*** to ... ...しようと努力する. ¶*strive **mightily*** to check it それを防止しようとして大骨を折る. 【類】 *strive **mightily*** for victory. ¶***persistently*** and ***energetically*** *strive* to carry out one's aims たゆまず折れず自己の目的を貫徹しようと努力する. ¶*strive **strenuously*** to capture the market 市場獲得に骨を折る. ¶*strive **together*** for ... ...を求めて互いに競う. ¶*strive **upward*** 向上を目的に奮闘する. ¶*strive **vainly*** むだ骨を折る.

P *strive **after*** ideals impossible of realization 実現不可能の理想を目的に努力する. 【類】 *strive **after*** a mighty world supremacy (世界支配の大業). ¶*strive **against*** a person 人と争う ‖ *strive **against*** the stream 流れにさからう; 時代に逆行する ‖ *strive **against*** fate 逆運と戦う. 【類】 *strive **against*** great difficulties. ¶compelled to *strive* ***for*** their daily bread 彼らの日常の糧を得るために努力を余儀なくされて ‖ Mistakes are inevitable, but *strive **for*** accuracy. 間違いはやむを得ないが正確を期せよ. ‖ *strive* ***for*** mastery (victory, supremacy) 精通しよう(勝利を得よう)と努力する. 【類】 *strive **for*** the imperial crown ‖ *strive **for*** a place in his recognition 彼に認められようとあせる. ¶*strive **in*** vain to control oneself いたずらに自制しようと努める. ¶*strive **through*** waves 波浪を切って進む. ¶*strive **with*** difficulties 困難と戦う ‖ He *strove **with*** his fellow students ***for*** the prize. 彼は学友と賞与を争った.

O I have *striven* (= tried hard) to ... 私は...しようと努力した.

striving, *n.* 努力.

Q ***incessant*** *striving* 絶えざる努力.

P^2 self-examination (自省) and *striving **after*** the highest life. ¶a *striving **for*** (= ***after***) effect 効果をねらう努力.

stroke, *n.* 打撃; 発作; 脈はく; [ボートの]一こぎ.

V He *caught* the *stroke* on his stick. 彼は打込をステッキで受け留めた. ¶*do* a *stroke* of business at ... ...で大もうけする ‖ He has not *done* a *stroke* of work. 彼は仕事といって何もしていない. ¶*give* a finishing *stroke* 止めを刺す. ¶The bell *hammered out* 101 *strokes*. 鐘が百一度鳴った. ¶*have* a paralytic *stroke* (=a stroke of paralysis) 中風を病む. ¶*have* a *stroke* of good business うまいもうけをする. ¶*invent* a new *stroke* in cricket クリケットで新らしい打ち方を発明する. ¶When rowing with others you must *keep stroke*. 人とこぐときはかいをそろえねばならない. ¶*make* a *stroke* with a pen 一筆揮う. ¶*pull stroke* in a race ボートレースで整調をする. ¶He *received* twenty *strokes* of the lash (whip). 彼はかばむち(など)で二十打たれた. ¶*row* a fast *stroke* 早こぎする. ¶*set* the *stroke* こぎ方を整調する. ¶He cannot *swim* a *stroke*. 彼は一かきも泳げない. 【類】*swim* a few *strokes*. ¶*vary* a *stroke* こぎ方を変える.

Q suffer an *apoplectic stroke* 中風にかかる. ¶a *back-handed stroke*=a backhand 〖テニス〗バックハンド. ¶by a *brilliant stroke* of diplomacy 花々しい外交手腕で. ¶be written with uncertain *childish strokes* 稚拙な筆づかいで書いてある. ¶a *clever stroke* 上出来. ¶his *crowning stroke* 彼の最大の手柄. ¶resolve on a *decisive stroke* 断固たる攻撃に出ることに決心する ‖ portrayed with *few rapid strokes* わずかの筆数で早描きに描いた(絵画など). ¶a *fine stroke* of business 見事な手腕の取引. ¶a *good stroke* of business 一もうけ ‖ by a *good stroke* of bad luck 不幸が幸になって. 【類】A *good stroke* of fortune came to him. ¶a *great stroke* of diplomacy 外交の一大成功. ¶a *light stroke* 軽い一こぎ. ¶pull a *long stroke* 長こぎする. ¶swim with a *long* and *slow stroke* 長くおそいかきぶりで泳ぐ. ¶a *poor stroke* まずい細工. ¶The boatman pulls a *short stroke* with his oar. こぎ手は短いこぎ方をする. ¶swim with a *short* and *quick stroke* 短い急ピッチで泳ぐ. ¶a *smart stroke* of work 鮮やかな細工. ¶He rowed with a *strong stroke* of the oars. 彼は力強くオールをこいだ. ¶a *thick* (*thin*) *stroke* 肉太(細肉)の書体. ¶an *unexpected stroke* of policy 予期しなかった策動. ¶It is painted with *vigorous strokes*. その絵は雄健な筆で描いてある.

Q^2 a *master stroke* in the rubber industry ゴム工業における一大傑作.

P make a fortune *at* a *stroke* 一かく千金を得る ‖ *At* one *stroke* he severed the head from the body. 彼は一撃で首をはねてしまった. ‖ *At* the *stroke* of the clock 時計が鳴ると ‖ just *at* the *stroke* of eleven ちょうど十一時を打つときに ‖ It is *at* the *stroke* of six. ちょうど六時を打つ所だ. ¶*by* a *stroke* of good luck (=fortune) 運よく. 【類】*by* a bad *stroke* of fortune ‖ *by* a bold *stroke* 一大英断をもって ‖ be hit *by* a *stroke* of lightning=be struck by lightning 落雷に打たれる. ¶*on* the *stroke* of four [o'clock] 四時を打つと. 【類】exactly *on* the *stroke* of the hour / It was *on* the *stroke* of six when I arrived. ¶it must have been almost *upon* the *stroke* of twelve when ... ...したのは十二時を打とうとしていた時であったに相違ない. ¶He was punished *with* the forty *strokes* of the bamboo. 彼は罰として竹で四十打たれた. ‖ *with* one *stroke* 一筆で ‖ dash off a picture *with* a few *strokes* 二三の筆使いで絵を(早々に)描き上げる ‖ *with* one *stroke* of the oar オールを一こぎして. ¶He won a kingdom *without* a *stroke*. 彼は一撃をも加えずに王国を得た.

P^2 *stroke by* stroke 一こぎ一こぎに. ¶a *stroke of* death 死の一撃(卒中など) ‖ a *stroke of* misfortune 不幸 ‖ the *stroke of* the pulse 脈はく ‖ a *stroke of* wit 奇警の文句 ‖ a *stroke of* a sword 一太刀. 【類】a *stroke of* a whip.

stroke, *v.* なでる.

M^2 *stroke down* one's hair 髪をなでつける. ¶*stroke* one's hair *up* (=the wrong way) [比ゆ的] 人を怒らす.

stroll, *n.* 散歩, さまよい.

V *take* a *stroll* to (along) ... ...へ(づたいに)散歩する.

Q take a *long breezy stroll* 風に吹かれながらゆっくり散歩する. ¶I am rather fond of taking a *solitary stroll* in the country. 僕はむしろ一人でいなか道をぶらつく方が好きだ.

Q^2 an *evening stroll* through a Canton street 広東街の夕方の散歩.

P^2 a *stroll over* the ruins 廃墟のさまよい. ¶a *stroll through* a street 街のぶらつき.

stroll, *v.* ぶらぶら歩く, 散歩する.

M *stroll about* through a town 町中をぶらつく. ¶*stroll aimlessly* through the streets あてどもなく街をぶらつく. ¶*stroll homeward* 家の方へぶらぶら歩く.

P *stroll about* the town (street, park) 街(など)をぶらつく. ¶*stroll along* the beach 浜づたいに散歩する. ¶*stroll around* the city (park) 市中(など)をぶらつく. ¶*stroll in* a wood in the cool of evening 夕涼みに森の中をぶらつく. ¶*stroll into* a park ぶらりと公園にはいり込む. ¶*stroll over* the place その辺をぶらつく. ¶*stroll through* the streets 街中をぶらつく ‖ *stroll through* Asia アジアを漫遊する. 【類】*stroll* [*through*] the countryside ‖ I *strolled to* the opposite side of the street. 街の向側へぶらぶら歩いた.

stroller, *n.* ぶらつく人; うば車.

V *push along* a *stroller* うば車を押して行く.

Q *surging strollers* 波を打って行く人の群.

Q^2 *afternoon* (*evening*) *strollers* 午後(夕べ)の散歩をする人々.

P an endless train (=line) *of strollers* どこまでも続く人の列.

strong, *a.* 強い; ...の人数を有する.

M I am not yet *strong enough* to go to school. 体が本当でないのでまだ学校へは行かれない. 【類】He is now *strong enough* to get about (動き回れる). ¶*financially stronger* men 財政的に一層豊かな人々. ¶*How many strong* are you? 君の方の人数はどのくらいか. ¶a little school, not yet *a hundred strong* counting both students and faculty 生徒と教師でまだ百人に満たない小さな学校. 【類】The party is *nine hundred strong*. ¶*numerically strong* 数的に優勢な. ¶be not very *strong physically* からだはあまり丈夫じゃない. ¶Are you *quite strong* again? もと通りすっかり丈夫になりましたか. ¶This coffee (tea) is *too strong* for me. このコーヒー(など)は僕にはこすぎる.

P He is *strong against* compromise. 彼は譲歩しないとりきんでいる. ‖ The evidence is *strong against* him. その証拠は彼にとってすこぶる不利だ. ‖ be *strong at* heart しんが強い. ¶She was always *strong for* peace and happiness in the house. 彼女は家内の平和と幸福とのためにはいつも熱心であった. ¶The wind was *strong from* the north-east. 北東の風が強かった. ¶*strong in* body (constitution, health) 身体(など)の強健な. 【類】those sound in character and *strong in* body (志操堅実体格優良). ‖ He is *strong in* arithmetic. 彼は算術が達者だ. ‖ they are *strong in* their feeling that ... 彼らは...の感じが強い ‖ *strong in* judgment 判断のしっかりした ‖ *strong in* number 数において優勢な ‖ the idea that the *stronger* are always *in* the right 強者は常に正しいという考え. ¶He is *strong of* will. 彼は意志が強い. ¶He is not *strong on* literature. 彼は文学は不得手だ. ‖ The odour of alcohol was *strong on* him. 彼は酒のにおいがぷんぷんした.

O That is where he is at his *strongest*. そこが彼の強みだ. ¶The battle is to the *strong*. 戦いは強い方が勝つ. ¶a task force 600 *strong* 六百の遊撃隊.

stronghold, *n.* 堅城.

Q^2 a *Communist stronghold* 共産党の牙城.

P^2 those districts in Holland which were *stronghold of* Roman Catholicism オランダの旧教の根拠地であった地方. 【類】That city was a *stronghold of* Protestantism (新教).

structure, *n.* 建築物; 構造, 組織.

V *build* a *structure* 建物を造る. ¶*erect* a temporary *structure* 仮の建物を作る. ¶*exhibit* a highly complex *structure* 非常に複雑な構造を示す. ¶*shake* the economic *structure* of the State その国の経済組織をぐらつかせる. 【類】*shake* a *structure* to its foundation (土台まで). ¶*simplify* sentence *structure* 文の構造を簡単にする. ¶*study* the *structure* of the human body 人体の構造を研究する.

Q simplify the *administrative structure* 行政機構を簡素化する. ¶*arched brick structures* アーチ造りのれんが建物. ¶his *brawny structure*, strong-made limbs, and rough shaggy breast 彼のがっちりした体, がん丈な手足, そうして荒々しい毛むくじゃらな胸. ¶*corporate structure* 事業形態. ¶a *durable structure* 持ちのよい(堅固な)建物. ¶an *economic structure* of society 社会の経済的組織. ¶of *elegant structure* しゃれた造りの. ¶the *existing structure* of society 現存の社会組織. ¶Viscount Shibusawa erected Japan's *financial structure*. 渋沢子爵が日本の財政機構を建てた. ‖ sound *financial structure* and operation 健全な財

政機構とその運営. ¶a *fine fire-proof structure* built of brick れんが造りのりっぱな耐火建築物. ¶a *Gargantuan structure*=a skyscraper 巨大な建物(高層ビル). ¶an *inflammable structure* 燃えやすい建物. ¶*modern structures* 現代式の建築物. ¶threaten the stability of the *national structure* 国家組織の安定をおびやかす. ¶a *palatial structure* 堂々たる建物. ¶a *structure peculiar* to England 英国特有の建築物. ¶a *slight structure* 貧弱な建物. ¶defects in the *social structure* 社会組織における欠陥. ¶*unsightly structures* 醜い建物.

Q² a *business structure* 営業上の建物. ¶work on *business* and *residential structures* 会社や住宅建造の工事をする. ¶*customs structure* 税関機構. ¶an *engineering structure* 工学上の建造物. ¶a fine *marble structure* りっぱな大理石の建築物. ¶the new *price structure* to be fixed in the near future 近い将来決定さるべき新物価機構.【類】the streamlining of the present *price structure*. ¶a *single-story structure* 平屋建て. ¶a *six-story ferroconcrete structure* with a total floor space of 2,500 *tsubo* 総建坪二千五百の鉄筋コンクリートの建物. ¶*surface structures* [鉱山の]地上建物. ¶Back from the main road was a *two-story colonial structure*. 本道から引込んだところに二階建の植民地式建物があった. ¶a stucco-covered, *two-story frame structure* しっくい塗りした二階木造建て. ¶*union structure* 組合機構. ¶*wage-price structure* 賃金•価格機構.

P The buildings are Japanese *in structure*. 建物の構造は日本式だ. ‖ All human bodies are uniform *in* their *structure*. 人体は皆構造が一様だ.

P² a brick *structure in* foreign (western) style 洋風のれんが建築. ¶a *structure of* red brick 赤れんがの建物.

struggle, *n.* 苦闘, 戦争, 戦闘.

V *continue* the *struggle* to the bitter end あくまで争い続ける. ¶He *experienced* a severe *struggle* for livelihood. 彼は激しい苦闘の生活を経験した. ¶*face* a *struggle* 戦闘に当る. ¶He *had* a hard *struggle* with poverty during his youth. 彼は青年時代に猛烈に貧苦と戦った. ‖ He *had* a hard *struggle* for existence through most of his life. 彼は一生の大部分にわたり激しい生存競争をやった. ‖ She has *had* a bitter enough *struggle* for recognition. 彼女は(自己を)認識させるために相当の苦闘をやってきた.

Q in the *after-war* (=*postwar*) *struggle* for commercial advantage 戦後の商業戦において. ¶a respite in the *bitter struggle* with cruel fortune 惨酷な運命との悪戦苦闘中の一休み. ¶avoid a *bloody* and *exhausting struggle* 流血消耗の戦闘を避ける. ¶He is free from the *bread and butter struggle*. 彼には生活の心配がない. ¶man's *centuries-old struggle* for freedom 人類の何世紀にわたる自由獲得闘争. ¶a *climacteric struggle* for world freedom and peace 世界の自由と平和のための画期的奮闘. ¶The election was a *close struggle*. その選挙は接戦であった. ¶have a *conclusive struggle* with ... ...と最後の決戦をする. ¶To me, her *courageous struggle* will always be an inspiration. 彼女の勇敢な奮闘振は私にとっていつも感激となるだろう. ¶engage in a *desperate struggle* with ... ...と決闘をする. ¶The ages between thirty-five and fifty years are the period of life in which the *struggle* for existence is *fiercest*. 三十五歳から五十歳までが生存競争の最も激しい時代である. ¶a *frantic struggle* 気違いじみた奮戦. ¶a *fruitless struggle* against the complaint 不平に対する効果なき抗争. ¶a *gigantic struggle* 大戦争. ¶a *grim* (=severe) *struggle* 激闘. ¶a *hard struggle* with circumstances 環境との激しい争い. ¶after some moments of *internal struggle* ちょっとはんもんした後. ¶*international struggle* 国際的戦闘. ¶*internecine struggle* 死にもの狂いの闘争. ¶His life was a *long struggle* with disease. 彼の一生は長い闘病の生活だった. 【類】The whole town was upset with joy over the ending of the *long struggle*. ¶after terrific *mental struggles* ひどい苦悩の後. ¶a *painful struggle* 苦闘. ¶a *perpetual struggle* 永久の奮闘. ¶after a *protracted struggle* 長期戦の後. ¶a *savage struggle* 野蛮な闘争. ¶the *spiritual struggle* of a recluse 隠者の霊のはんもん. ¶a *titanic struggle* 大戦闘. ¶fight a *tough struggle* 苦闘する. ¶a *victorious struggle* with ... ...に勝った戦争. ¶the *world-wide struggle* for the triumph of right and liberty 正義と自由の勝利のために全世界にわたる奮闘.

Q² *class struggle* 階級闘争. ¶in a *death struggle* for existence 生きんがための苦闘で. ¶*dying struggle* 断末魔の苦しみ. ¶*electioneering struggle* 選挙運動. ¶a fierce *hand-to-hand struggle* 壮烈な白兵戦. ¶terrible *life* and *death struggle* for liberty and freedom 自由獲得の生死の苦闘. ¶a *love struggle* 恋愛の争い. ¶a *step-by-step struggle* 堅実な努力.

P They gave in *after* a short *struggle*. 彼らは少し戦ってから降参した. ¶They were injured *in* the *struggle*. 彼らはその戦闘で負傷した. ¶a glory that has been attained *through struggles* 苦闘の後に獲得された栄光. ¶They gave way (=submitted) to his power *without* a *struggle*. 彼らは戦わずして彼に降参した.【類】The enemy is not likely to surrender *without* a *struggle*.

P² unite in the *struggle against* an enemy 連合して敵軍に当る. ¶the *struggle at* Waterloo ワーテルローの戦. ¶a *struggle* between labor and *management* 労使間の闘争. ¶The *struggle for* life grows fiercer. 生存競争が一層猛烈になる. ‖ a *struggle for* ascendancy 争覇(は) ‖ the stress of the *struggle for* existence 生存競争の圧迫. 【類】the *struggle for* bare subsistence (ただ生きんがための) / In spite of the bitter *struggle for* existence, a sentiment of altruism (利他主義) pervades humanity. ‖ a *struggle for* supremacy 争覇(は). 【類】*struggles for* international supremacy in commerce / this great *struggle for* right against wrong. ¶the *struggle of* death 断末魔の苦しみ. ¶the *struggle of* Christianity against Paganism キリスト教の異教との抗争. ¶a *struggle to* the death 死にもの狂い. ¶a *struggle toward* better things 向上への努力. ¶He went through a bitter *struggle with* poverty. 彼は貧窮と苦闘した. 【類】serious difficulties in their *struggle with* a strange tongue (外国語). / *struggles with* death.

struggle, *v.* 苦闘する, 努力する.

M *struggle bravely* against adverse fate 勇敢に逆境と抗争する. ¶*struggle desperately* 死闘する. ¶*struggle hard* for ... ...しようと苦闘する. 【類】*struggle hard* at an experiment. ¶He *struggled manfully* against these overwhelming misfortunes. 彼は男らしくこれらの圧倒的不幸と抗争した. ¶*struggle out* through ... ...からやっとのことで出る. ¶*struggle successfully* against difficulties 困難に打ち勝つ. ¶*struggle together* もみ合う. ¶*struggle wildly* 激しく争う.

M² *struggle in* やっとのことではいる. ¶*struggle on* in life 生存競争を続ける ‖ have the pluck to *struggle on* 勇敢にも奮闘を続ける.

P He *struggled across* the field against a high wind. 彼は強風を突いてかろうじて広野を横断した. ¶*struggle after* ... を得ようと骨折る. ¶*struggle against* the forces of nature 自然力と抗争する ‖ *struggle against* odds (oppression) 優勢(など)に対して苦闘する. 【類】*struggle against* the tide (stream). ¶*struggle for* their daily bread 日々のパンのために努力する. 【類】*struggle for* existence / *struggle for* independence (liberty) / *struggle for* supremacy (mastery). ¶*struggle through* the snow 雪を冒して行く.【類】*struggle through* the muddy pool on to the shore. ¶*struggle to* one's feet 立ちあがろうともがく. ¶*struggle with* adversity 逆境と戦う ‖ strangers *struggling with* the tongue 言葉を覚えようと努力している外国人. 【類】It is only a gracious method of helping a young writer, *struggling with* adverse circumstance, without wounding his pride. / *struggle with* a mathematical problem / *struggle with* the temptation / *struggle with* the waves.

O *struggle* to get free 自由になろうともだえる ‖ *struggle* to express oneself 自己を表現しようと苦心する. 【類】*struggle* to control one's feelings / She *struggled* to disengage from him.

strum, *v.* やたらにひく.

P *strum on* a piano (guitar) ピアノ(など)をめちゃめちゃにひく.

strut, *n.* 気取り歩き.

P walk *with* a *strut* 気取って歩く.

strut, *v.* 気取って歩く.

M² *strut along* (*about*) 気どって歩く(歩き回る).

P The turkey *strutted about* the yard. 七面鳥は飼養場を気どって歩き回った. ¶*strut in* borrowed plumes 借着で気取って歩く ‖ The actor *struts in* royal appendages. その俳優が王衣を着けて気取って歩く. ¶He *struts into* the room. 彼は気取って室内にはいる.

stub, *n.* 短くなった物;《米》控え(小切手・為替などの).
Q *perforated stubs* 切取線のついた控紙.
Q² *pencil stubs* 短くなった鉛筆. ¶a *cigar stub* 葉巻の吸いさし. ¶*ticket stubs* from ... to ... …から…までの切符のもぎとり券.
P² The pussy wagged the *stub of* her tail. 小ねこは短い尾を振動かした. ‖ the *stub* (=counterfoil) *of* a check (bill) 小切手(など)の控え. 【類】the *stub of* a tree (tooth).

stubble, *n.* ぶしょうひげ.
V He *had* three days' *stubble* on his unshaven face. 彼は三日も顔をそらずぶしょうひげを生やしていた.

stubborn, *a.* 執ような.
P *stubborn in* [the] *wrong* 悪に執ような.

stubbornness, *n.* がん固.
Q his *proverbial stubbornness* 彼の評判のがん固.
P² the *stubbornness of* the aged 老いの一徹.

stucco, *n.* しっくい.
P work *in stucco* しっくいで細工する ‖ plasterer *in stucco* 上塗りの左官.

stud, *n.* 飾りボタン.
Q a set *of studs* 一組の飾りボタン.

stud, *n.* 馬; 馬の飼育場.
Q² a *racing stud* (=racer) 競馬馬.
P horses and dogs *at stud* 飼養場の馬や犬.

stud, *v.* 飾りボタンで飾る; 散在する.
P a gold pin *studded with* jewels 宝石で飾った金製のピン. ‖ a door *studded with* nails 点々とくぎを打った戸 ‖ Japanese daimyo gates *studded with* big bronze bolt-heads 大きな青銅のねじくぎ頭で飾った日本の大名門. 【類】Its darkness was *studded with* the glow-worm lights of the shipping. / The sea is *studded* (=scattered) *with* islands. / a composition *studded with* errors.

student, *n.* 学生; 学者, 研究家.
V *accept students* by transfer from junior colleges 短大からの転学生の入学を許す. ¶*condition* a *student*《米》不合格学科のある生徒を仮進級にする. ¶*cram* the *student* with facts 学生に知識を詰込む. ¶There are in the United States several hundred colleges of recognized standing *enrolling* more than 100,000 *students* every year. 米国には世間から相当認められている大学が数百あって毎年十万以上の学生を登籍する. 【類】That college *enrolled* 1,668 *students* last year. / *enrol students* in a school. ¶*familiarize* the *student* with ... 学生に…と親しませる. ¶*equip* a *student* for life 学生に世の中へ出る準備をさせる. ¶That school *has* ... *students*. あの学校には…名の生徒がある. ¶The *students* were *headed* by their teacher. 生徒は教師に引率された. ¶*matriculate students* [大学など]学生の入学を許す. ¶It *numbers* its *students* by the thousand. 学生の数は何千というほどであ. ¶The *student* was *plucked* (=*spun*) in his examination. 《俗》その学生は落第した. ¶*prepare students* for examinations 生徒に試験の準備をさせる. ¶*send* its *students out* into life 学生を社会に送り出す.
V² Those *students belong* to Tokyo University. 彼らは東大の学生だ. ¶The *student* is always *poring* over his books. その学生はいつも書物と首引をしている.
Q *academic students* [大学などの]学生(自修者でない). ¶*advanced students* in research or in conference courses 研究科または実習科に籍をおいている高学年の学生. ¶*architectural students* 建築学専攻の学生. ¶*beginning students* 初学者. ¶Young Huntington was not a particularly *bright student* in his school days. ハンチントンは学校時代には特別そう明な少年ではなかった. ¶The *brilliant student* should not be compelled to linger with the majority of his classmates. 優秀な学生を大多数の同級生と一緒にぐずぐずさせておくべきでない. ¶a *Chaldean student* カルデア語の学者. ¶a *close student* 勉強家. 【類】a *close student* of national questions. ¶classes of *commercial students* 商科の学級. ¶a *competent student* of contemporary politics 現代政治の有能な研究家. ¶a *deep student* 篤学な学者. ¶a *deserving student* in need of a lift 財政的援助を必要とする優秀学生. ¶a *devout student* of literature 熱心な文学者. ¶Japan has been applauded as a *diligent student* of all the West has had to teach. 日本は西洋が教え得たすべてに渡って勤勉な学生として称賛された. ¶*dull plodding students* にぶいこつこつ型の学生. ¶an *earnest student* of the English tongue 熱心な英語学生. ¶*energetic students* 精力おう盛な学生. ¶an *enthusiastic student* of Browning 熱心なブラウニング研究家. ¶*female students* 女学生. ¶a *former student* of mine 私の旧弟子. ¶a *frolicsome student* 茶目な学生. ¶*full(half)-fledged students* 正規(聴講)生 ‖ be enrolled as a *full-fledged student* 正規の学生として入学を許される. ¶a *full-time* (*part-time*) *student* 正規(聴講)学生; 昼(夜)間学生. ¶a *good student* りっぱな学生. ¶*graduated students* 卒業生. ¶He is a *great students*. 彼は大の研究家だ. ¶Young Carlyle was a *hard student*. 青年時代のカーライルは非常に勤勉な学生であった. ¶a *high* (*low*)*-ranking student* 成績の良(悪)い学生. ¶Vienna has many charms both for *historic students* and the observers of social and racial contrasts. ウィーンは歴史研究家にも社会・民族の比較観察者にも色々な魅力がある. ¶a *hopeful student* of European methods 将来有望なヨーロッパ風の研究家. ¶*impartial*, *dispassionate*, and truly *scientific students* of political economy 公平無私で真に科学的な経済学者. ¶an *isolated student* [俗世間から]隔絶した学者. ¶a *keen student* of the game その遊戯の熱心な研究家. ¶a *laborious student* 勉強家の学生. ¶*lazy students* なまけものの学生. ¶a *literary student* 文学者. ¶*Marxian-minded students* マルクス主義的の学生. ¶*medical students* 医学生. ¶a *needy student* 苦学生. ¶*nonmatriculated students* まだ入学を許可されていない学生. ¶He was a *noted student* of jujitsu. 彼は有名な柔術家であった. ¶a party of the *old students* 同窓生の会. 【類】The *old students* of the Royal School of Mines resident in South Africa recently held their annual dinner in Johannesburg. ¶a *patient student* 根気強い学者. ¶a *plodding student* こつこつと勉強する学生(学者). ¶a *poor student* 貧書生. ¶*private students* 自修者. ¶*professed* (=*pretended*) *linguistic student* 自称語学者. ¶a *promising* and *energetic student* 有望で精力的な学生. ¶*prospective students* 入学希望者. ¶*returned students* 新帰朝留学生. ¶*self-boarding students* 自炊する学生. ¶*self-supporting student* 自立自給の(苦)学生. ¶*self-taught students* 独学でやる(やった)学生. ¶an entirely *self-trained student* 全然独学の学生. ¶a *senior* (*junior*) [*student*] 上(下)級生;《米》[大学及び四年制の高校で]四(三)年生. ¶a *serious student* of history まじめな歴史の研究家. ¶a *shrewd student* of the matter その問題のけい眼な研究家. ¶*slow students* 頭ののろい学生. ¶the *sober*, *thoughtful student* of economic condition 経済問題の謹直な思慮深い研究家. ¶a *struggling* art *student* 苦学する美術学生. ¶a very *subtle student* of human nature きわめてちみつな人間研究家. ¶a *technical student* 工芸の学生. ¶a students who have entered junior colleges as *terminal students* 最終学年生として短大に入学した学生. ¶An *unstudious student* is a contradiction in terms. 学問ぎらいの学生などという言葉は矛盾である. ¶*vocational students* 職業教育を受けている学生. ¶*zealous students* 熱心な研究家.
Q² an *adult student* 成人[学校]学生. ¶an *art student* 美校学生. ¶a *beginning student*=a beginner,《米》a freshman 一年生. ¶a *better class student* 恵まれた階級の学生. ¶a group of *Bible students* 聖書研修生の一団. ¶a *bird student* 鳥類研究者. ¶a *book student* 読書家. ¶a *charity student* 給費生. ¶a *college student* 大学生. ¶a *Cornell student* コーネル大学生. ¶a *day student* 通学生(寮生に対して). ¶an *English student* 英国の学生; 英語学徒. ¶a *foreign-language student* 外国語学生. ¶an *evening student* 夜間学生. ¶an *exchange student* 交換学生. ¶a *graduate student* 大学院学生. ¶a *high-school student* 高校生. ¶a great help to the *home student* 自宅学習者にとっての福音. ¶a *language student* 語学学生. ¶a *law student* 法律学生. ¶his *one-time student* 彼の昔の学生. ¶a *night-school student* 夜学生. ¶prepare texts for *non-class students* 独学生に適したテキストを編集する. ¶a *physics* (*chemistry*) *student* 物理(化学)専攻の学生. ¶a *pro-Communist* (*non-Communist*) *student* シンパ(反共)学生. ¶a *psychology student* 心理学専攻の学生. ¶a *research student* 研究生. ¶a *senior* (*junior*) *class student* 上(下)級生. ¶a *sociology student* 社会学専攻の学生. ¶a *State University of California student* 州立カリフォルニア大学学生. ¶a *tutor student* 下級生の個人指導をする学生. ¶an *undergraduate* [*student*] 大学生(学位をとっていない). ¶*war veteran students* at Columbia コロンビア大学の退役軍人学生たち.

P² a *student at* Harvard＝a Harvard *student* ハーバード大学生 ‖ a *student at* the head of his class 首席の学生. ¶a *student in* a college 大学生 ‖ a *student in* sociology 社会学研究生. ¶a *student of* antiquity 古代学者 ‖ a *student of* life (mankind) 人生(人間)の研究者. 【類】a *student of* philosophy at the University of Washington / a *student of* Buddhism (Japanese life) / He is a great *student of* stars—movie stars. / a *student of* the histories of words (philology, pedagogics). ¶a *student under* Dr. ... ...博士の門下生.

studio, *n.* 仕事べや, アトリエ, スタジオ.

V *fit up* a *studio* アトリエを設ける.

Q² a *CBS studio* 〘ラジオ〙[米国]コロンビヤ放送会社のスタジオ. ¶a *color print studio* 色彩版画制作所. ¶a *health studio* 衛生試験所. ¶a *movie studio* 映画のスタジオ. ¶a *photo[graph] studio* 写真屋. ¶a *recording studio* 録音室.

studious, *a.* 学問にこる; 勤勉な.

P *studious of* one's business 業務に勤勉な. ¶*studious* almost *to* excess ほとんど行過ぎと言っていいほどに勤勉な.

study, *n.* 勉学; 研究, 研究科目; 研究室, 書斎.

V *advocate* the *study* of English 英語研究の必要を唱道する. ¶It *affords* a pleasing *study*. それはおもしろい研究になる. ¶*begin* one's *studies* with ... ...について勉強を始める ‖ *begin* the *study* of stenography 速記術の勉強を始める. ¶*carry on* one's *studies* 研究を続行する. 【類】*carry on* various *studies*. ¶*commence* one's *studies* with ... ...について研究を始める. ¶having *completed* his *studies* at the universities of Bonn and Berlin ボン・ベルリン両大学で研究を済ませてから ‖ *complete* one's *studies* by foreign travel 外国旅行で研究の仕上をする. 【類】He did not *complete* his college *studies*. ¶this book *comprises* a *study* of ... 本書は...の研究の記録である. ¶He is *conducting* a *study* of the problem. 彼はその問題の研究をやっている. ¶He *continued* his musical *studies* while at Harvard. 彼はハーバード大学在学中音楽の研究を続けた. 【類】he *continued* his vocal *studies* for three years with (＝under) ... ¶*deserve* serious and enthusiastic *study* まじめで熱心な研究に値する. ¶He *detests study*. 彼は勉強ぎらいだ. ¶*devote* deep *study* to ... ...を深く研究する. ¶*direct study* 研究を指導する. ¶worthy and promising students compelled to *discontinue* their *studies* for lack of funds 学費欠乏のためやむなく中退する有望でりっぱな学生. ¶*dump* some useless *study* and take up ... ある無益な研究をなげうって...に着手する. ¶Perhaps, after all, it would be more sensible for you to remain here and *finish* your *studies*. 結局ここに留まって研究を済ます方が君としては得策だろう. 【類】after he *finished* his *studies* at Princeton. ¶*follow up* one's linguistic *studies* 語学の研究を続ける. ¶It *forms* an interesting *study*. それは興味ある研究材料となる. ¶a subject to which he has *given* special *study* 彼の専攻科目 ‖ For years he has *given* careful *study* to this subject. 多年彼はこの問題を慎重に研究した. ‖ Much *study* is being *given* that problem in many quarters. その問題は諸方面で大いに研究している. ¶*give up* the *study* その研究をやめる. ¶*help forward* the *study* of ... ...の研究を助成する. ¶*hinder* its *study* その研究を妨げる. ¶*involve* a life-long *study* 終生の研究を要する. ¶*leave off* one's scholastic *studies* 学業を廃する. ¶*make* a *study* of ... ...を熱心に研究する. ¶*merit* our *study* われわれの研究に値する. ¶He would *neglect* his *studies* when he was at school. 彼は在校中はいつもなまけていたものだ. ¶It can hardly fail to *present* an interesting and instructive *study*. それはほとんど確実におもしろくってためになる研究材料となる. ¶*promote* the *study* of Esperanto (the West) エスペラント語(など)の研究を進める. ¶*prosecute* further *studies* in this field さらにこの方面の研究に従事する ‖ *prosecute* the *study* of English literature 英文学の研究をやる. ¶*pursue* one's *studies* diligently at a university 大学の勉強をせっせとやる. ¶*pursue* the *study* of the law (classics, subject) / *pursue* their *studies* of anarchism (無政府主義) / *pursue* one's *studies* with less ardor / *pursue* one's *studies* with brilliance (好成績をあげて). ¶*put medical studies aside* 医学の研究を放棄する. ¶*quit study* for ever 勉強をすっかりやめる. ¶The problem is *receiving* careful *study*. その問題は慎重に研究されている. ¶His hobby has *relaxed* his *studies*. 彼は道楽のために勉強を怠るようになった. ¶*repay* a careful and minute *study* 慎重綿密な研究に報いる. ¶*require* patient *study* 根気強い研究を必要とする. ¶He *resumed* his interrupted *studies* at the university. 彼は中絶した研究を大学でまたやりだした. ¶Students *shun* real *study* by using cribs. 学生はとらの巻を使って真の勉強を避ける. ¶It *stimulated* the author's *study* of the problem. それがその問題に対する著者の研究を促した. 【類】*stimulate* the *study* of English. ¶*supplement* one's *study* 研究を補う. ¶*take* so many *studies* 色々な科目をとる. ¶*take up* the *study* of ... as a pastime 慰みに...の研究を始める.

V² Even a cursory *study* of ... *points* to this conclusion. ...をざっと研究してみてもこの結論になって来る.

Q a most *absorbing study* きわめて興味ある研究. ¶*accurate study* 精密な研究. ¶*active* reading and *study* 自発的な読書と研究. ¶pursue *advanced studies* 進んだ研究に従事する. ¶history and *allied studies* 歴史並に関係諸学科. ¶make an *anthropological study* of the subject その問題を人類学的に研究する. ¶*biographical studies* 伝記の研究. ¶a *booklined study* 書籍を四壁に並べた書斎. ¶be in a *brown study* 物思いに沈んでいる. ¶a *calm* and *unbiased study* of the history of ... tells us that ... ...史をおもむろにかつ公平に研究すれば...が分かる. ¶well worth a *careful study* 慎重研究に値する. 【類】make a most *careful study* of Whitman literature (ホイットマン文学) / repay *careful study* by those who can afford the time. ¶I made the subject the *chief study* of my life. 私はその問題を終生の主要研究科目とした. ¶make a *close study* of life in the Jewish quarters ユダヤ人街の生活状態を綿密に研究する. ¶two years of *close, concentrated study* 三カ年にわたる一心不乱の研究. ¶*collateral study* 付帯的研究. ¶make *comparative studies* before deciding where to place their orders 注文先をきめる前に比較研究をする. 【類】make a *comparative study* of Oriental languages. ¶make a *complete study* of ... ...を完全に研究する. ¶relaxation after *concentrated study* 根をつめて勉強した後の骨休め. ¶make a *conscientious study* of ... ...を良心的に研究する. ¶the fruit of his *constant study* of it 彼のそのことに関するたゆまぬ研究の結晶. 【類】it requires a *constant study* on the part of ... ¶*critical study* 批評的研究. ¶*cultural studies* 教養上の諸学科 ‖ the *cultural study* of foreign literatures 教養のための外国文学の研究. ¶a *deep study* 深い研究. ¶make a more *detailed study* of ... ...を一層細かに考察する. ¶a *diligent study* of his pages 彼の著書の精読. ¶a *dull study* with a dull teacher 遅鈍な教師について無味乾燥な勉強. ¶give *earnest study* to ... ...を熱心に勉強する. ¶an *elaborate study* of life in Russia ロシアにおける生活の熱心な研究. ¶make it one's *exclusive study* それを専攻する. ¶make an *exhaustive study* of a question ある問題を徹底的に研究する. 【類】an *exhaustive study* of their inter-relations (相互関係). ¶pursue the *fascinating study* among the larger text-books もっと詳しい教科書でこの興味ある研究を進める. 【類】It presents a *fascinating study*. ¶a *fascinating* as well as an extremely *profitable study* to ... ...に取って非常に有利であると同時にまた魅力ある研究. ¶make a *first-hand study* of the subject その問題を直接に研究する. ¶a *focused study* of needs in Japanese universities 日本の諸大学が必要とする事項の集中的研究. ¶Foreign artists make this part of Japan a *frequent study* in oils. 外国の画家は日本のこの地方をよく油絵に描く. ¶For several years *fundamental studies* have been in progress in this field. 数年間この方面の根本的研究が続けられた. ¶make a *further study* of ... ...を一層突込んで研究する. 【類】prosecute *further studies* in this field. ¶a method of *grammatical study* 文法的研究の一方法. ¶after several hours of *hard study* 幾時間も大いに勉強してから. ¶*historical study* of a language 言語の歴史的研究. ¶*humane studies* 人文学. ¶*humanistic studies* 古典文学の研究. ¶an *impartial study* of ... ...の公平な研究. ¶*informational studies* 事実に関する研究. ¶*intelligent study* of the dictionary 賢明な辞書の研究. 【類】I believe that an *intelligent study* of English is the shortest and safest way to attain (＝come up) to an intelligent and successful study of Latin and Greek. ¶an *intensive* and *extensive study* of the literature of the subject そのことに関する文献上の深いかつ広い研究. ¶Geography is an *interesting study*. 地理は興味ある学問

である. ¶an ***introductory*** *study* of pedagogics 教育学序説. ¶as a result of years of ***laborious*** and ***tiresome study*** 多年骨の折れるいやな研究を続けた結果. ¶he made a ***life-long study*** of ... 彼は...を終生の研究科目とした. ¶get good result with ***limited study*** ちょっとの研究で成績をあげる. ¶***linguistic studies*** 語学研究. ¶***literary studies*** 文学研究. ¶exchange letters with ... for ***mutual study*** 相互の研究のために書面を取交わす. ¶the ***nation-wide study*** of a foreign language 一外国語の全国的学習. ¶a ***new*** *study* of Shakespeare シェイクスピアの新研究. ¶History is a ***noble*** *study*. 歴史は高尚な学問だ. ¶The average man does not care for ***out-of-the-way historic*** *studies*. 普通の人は縁遠い歴史の研究なんか好きはしない. ¶make it a ***particular*** (=special) *study* 特にそれを研究する. ¶***part-time*** *study* after business hours 勤務終了後の(夜学生など). ¶exact research and the ***patient*** *study* of facts 正確な研究と事実の根気強い研究. 【類】 the outcome of many years of ***patient*** *study*. ¶***philological*** *studies* 言語学的研究. ¶George Gissing's "The Unclassed" is a ***powerful*** *study* of the life of a London prostitute. ジョージ・ギッシングの「階級なき人々」はロンドンの売春婦の生活を力強く描写したものである. ¶make a ***preliminary*** *study* of ... ...の予備的研究をする. ¶***preparatory*** *study* 予備的研究, 下調べ. ¶have no leisure for ***private*** *study* 自習の時間がない. ¶a ***profound*** and ***conscientious*** *study* of the subject その問題の徹底的良心的な研究. ¶after a ***prolonged*** *study* of the evidence collected by ... ...の集めた証拠を時をかけて研究してから. ¶The ***proper*** *study* of mankind is man. 人間の研究すべき問題は人間である. ¶a ***rapid*** *study* 概説. ¶***realistic*** *studies* of everyday life 日常生活の現実的な研究. ¶a ***scholarly*** (***practical***) *study* of a language 国語の学者的(実用的)研究. ¶a ***scientific*** *study* of the dramatic art 演劇の科学的研究 ‖ the pioneer step in the ***scientific*** *study* of ... ...の科学的研究の先駆. 【類】 his patient and brilliant ***scientific*** *studies*. ¶Much that is finest in man is cultivated by action rather than by ***sedentary*** *study*. 人間において最も尊ぶべきものの多くは独座(机上)の研究よりはむしろ行動(実行)の中に練磨されるのである. ¶deserve ***serious*** and ***enthusiastic*** *study* まじめで熱心な研究に値する. ¶He is a ***slow*** (***quick***) *study*. [せりふなど]覚えがおそい(早い)人だ. ¶***solitary*** *studies* 独学. ¶make ***some*** *study* of ... ...を多少研究する. ¶make a ***special*** *study* (=speciality) of ... ...を専攻する. 【類】 This was made the subject of ***special*** *study*. ¶the ***statistical*** *study* of human life 統計学から見た人間生活の研究. ¶give ***sufficient*** *study* to ... ...を十分研究する. ¶a ***systematic*** *study* 組織的研究. ¶take up the ***thorough*** *study* of ... ...をしっかり勉強する. ¶***unfinished*** *studies* 未完成研究. ¶make an ***unprejudiced*** *study* of ... ...を片寄らずに研究する. ¶a ***useful*** *study* 有益な学科. ¶***utilitarian*** *studies* 実用的な学科. ¶a ***valuable*** *study* 貴重な学問. ¶the progress of ***Virgilian*** *studies* [ローマの詩人]バージル研究の進歩. ¶***wider*** and ***deeper*** *study* 一層広く深い研究. ¶his ***worst*** (=***weakest***) *studies* 彼の一番不得意な学科.

Q² "***bread-and-butter***" *studies* すぐ役に立つ研究. ¶a ***case*** *study* 判例研究. ¶***classroom*** *study*=classwork 教室内の学習. ¶the advance in ***English*** *studies* 英語研究の進歩. ¶questions that demand the most serious ***expert*** *study* 専門家の最もまじめな研究を要する問題. ¶***field*** *studies* 現場(実地)研究. ¶make a ***first-hand*** *study* of ... ...を自分で直接研究する. ¶the advantages of ***foreign language*** *study* 外国語学習の利益. ¶***foundation*** *studies* in literature 文学の基礎的研究. ¶***graduate*** (***undergraduate***) *studies* 修(学)士課程 ‖ several years of intensive ***graduate*** *study* 数年間の熱心な修士課程専攻. ¶home *study* 家庭学習. ¶***language*** *study* 語学研究. ¶He has made it his ***life*** *study*. 彼はそれを一生の研究題目とした. ‖ He has made this book a ***life*** *study*. 彼はこの本を一生をかけて勉強した. ‖ Fabre has made a ***life*** *study* of the lives of insects. ファーブルはこん虫生活を終生の研究科目とした. ¶***midnight*** *studies* 夜半の学習. ¶***modern-language*** *studies* 近代語学の研究. ¶***research*** *study* 研修. ¶***school*** *studies* 学科(目). ¶***science*** *study* 科学研究. ¶***social*** *studies* 社会科. ¶This is a good subject for ***spare-time*** *study*. これは余暇の勉強にはもってこいだ. ¶job analysis, ***time*** *study* and ***motion*** *study* 職業の分析, 時間の研究及び動作(製作過程)の研究. ¶***thumb-nail*** *studies* in pets 愛がん動物の小点(絵または文). ¶the Carnegie committee on ***vocabulary*** *study* カーネギー語彙(ゐ)研究委員会. ¶a ***word*** *study* 語の研究.

P ***after*** an exhaustive *study* of the situation 時局を徹底的に研究してから. 【類】 ***after*** his ten years' *study* in America. ¶***as*** a *study* in English literature 英文学における...研究事項として. ¶He is ***at*** his *studies*. 彼は勉強している. ¶knowledge got ***by*** *study* 勉強で得た知識 ‖ ***by*** hard *study* 刻苦して ‖ ***by*** the *study* of the West 西洋研究によって. ¶go in ***for*** the *study* of English 英語の勉強に没頭する. ¶He is absorbed (=buried) ***in*** *study*. 彼は勉強に夢中だ. ‖ progress ***in*** one's *studies* その学力の進歩. 【類】 He had made great strides in his *studies*. / Be diligent ***in*** your *studies*. ‖ I found him ***in*** his *study*. 彼は書斎にいた. ‖ created ***in*** the *study* 書斎で造られた. ¶hours ***of*** *study* 勉強時間 ‖ the value ***of*** the *study* of geography 地理学研究の価値 ‖ branches ***of*** *study* 学問の部門 ‖ a four-year course ***of*** *study* 四年の修業課程. ¶He gives his hours (=time) ***to*** *study*. 彼は幾時間も勉強する. ‖ take ***to*** *study* 学問を好む; 学問に従事する ‖ He devoted all his life ***to*** the *study* of astronomy. 彼は一生を天文学の研究に捧げた. ‖ a magazine devoted ***to*** the *study* of human psychology 心理学専門の雑誌. 【類】 He applied himself ***to*** his *studies*. ¶works ***under*** *study* 研究中の書物. ¶go on ***with*** one's *study* 研究を続ける ‖ His absorption in sport interferes ***with*** his *studies*. スポーツ熱が彼の勉学の邪魔になる. ‖ get ahead (=on) ***with*** one's *studies* 学業が進歩する.

P² *studies* ***among*** the tenements of New York City ニューヨーク市の細民生活の現地研究. ¶complete one's *study* ***at*** Oxford オクスフォード(大学)で学業を仕上げる. ¶a *study* ***for*** an artist 美術家の研究問題. ¶The biography is a *study* ***from*** original documents. その伝記は根本史料によって編成したのだ. ‖ *studies* ***from*** nature 自然物のスケッチ. ¶a *study* ***in*** the evolution of man (political thought) 人間進化(など)の研究 ‖ The scene was a *study* ***in*** all degrees and positions of drowsiness. その光景は睡眠のあらゆる度合並びに姿勢を示したものであった(夜汽車などで). ‖ *studies* ***in*** humanism (the thought world) 人文主義(など)の研究 ‖ *Studies* ***in*** Honor of Professor ... [題名]...教授記念研究. ¶a *study* ***of*** Kant (American politics) カント(など)の一考察 ‖ *study* ***of*** methods 方法研究. 【類】 *studies* ***of*** chess (fish life, religious history, Buddhism in Japan, the Greek poets) ‖ *studies* ***of*** men 人物評論. ¶short *studies* ***on*** great subjects 大問題に関する小研究.

study, *v.* 研究する; 学習する.

M *study* ***abroad*** 外国で勉強する. ¶*study* a reader ***aloud*** 音読してリーダーを勉強する. ¶***assiduously*** *study* 精出して勉強する. ¶should be ***carefully*** *studied* 念を入れて勉強すべきだ. ¶*study* a subject ***closely*** 問題をとくと研究する. 【類】 *study* it more ***closely***. ¶*study* ***deeply*** into ... ...を突っこんで研究する. ¶***diligently*** and ***devoutly*** *study* the Bible 勤勉かつ敬けんに聖書を研究する. ¶*study* one's lesson ***faithfully*** 自分の課業をまじめに勉強する. ¶he *studied* ***first*** with ... and ***later*** with ... 彼は初め...後...について学問した. ¶*study* it ***gloatingly*** それを夢中に勉強する. ¶*study* ***hard*** 熱心に勉強する. ¶*study* and travel ***indefatigably*** 根気よく勉強しかつ旅行する. ¶*study* ***laboriously*** (=《米口》grind) こつこつ勉強する. ¶*study* ***late*** at night 夜ふかし勉強をする. ¶*study* ***omnivorously*** 手当り次第に勉強する. ¶*study* ***out*** the best way 最善の方法を案出する ‖ *study* ***out*** the mystery of ... ...の秘けつをきわめる ‖ *study* ***out*** a puzzle 骨を折ってなぞを解く. ¶*study* German ***privately*** ドイツ語を独学する. ¶can ***profitably*** *study* the report その報告書を研究すると得るところがある. ¶*study* too ***severely*** 勉強し過ぎる. ¶*study* ***silently*** 静粛に勉強する. ¶*study* ***strenuously*** 根気強く研究する. ¶*study* ***thoroughly*** 徹底的に研究する. ¶the foreign language that he so ***toilfully*** *studied* at school 彼が学校であんなに骨を折って勉強した外国語. ¶Biology is now ***widely*** *studied*, both in colleges and high schools. 生物学は今日では大学でも高等学校でも一般に研究されている.

P He *studied* ***at*** Westminster School. 彼はウェストミンスター校で学んだ. ¶*study* ***by*** oneself 独学する. ¶*study* ***for*** marks rather than for knowledge 知識修得のためよ

りはむしろ点のために勉強する ‖ study **for** a painter 画家を目的に勉強する ‖ study **for** the arm (bar, church, stage) 軍人(など)になろうと勉強する. 【類】study **for** pleasure such subjects as architecture and mineralogy. ¶study **from** every (this) angle あらゆる(この)角度から研究する. ¶We study **in** school. われわれは学校で勉強する. ¶He has not studied **into** the subject enough to really understand it. 彼は真に理解ができるほどにその問題をきわめなかった. ‖ study **into** the early morning hours 夜から早朝まで勉強する. 【類】study late **into** the night. ¶study **under** the advice of Dr. … …博士指導の下に勉強する ‖ I studied **under** him at Edinburgh University. 私はエジンバラ大学で彼について学んだ. ¶study **with** … …について学ぶ. 【類】study English **with** (=**from** or **under**) a foreign teacher ‖ study **with** text-books 教科書で勉強する. ¶learners studying **without** a teacher 独学者.

stuff, *n.* 材料; 物, 物質.

V **classify** stuff 材料を分類する. ¶I don't **eat** such an odious stuff. こんないやな物は食べない. ¶**have** too much stuff on hand [編集員の]手元に材料(原稿など)があり過ぎる ‖ **have** the stuff = **have** stuff on the ball 〘野球〙好投する. ¶I'm tired of people trying to **sell** me stuff I don't need. 欲しくもない品物を押売りされるにはうんざりだ. ¶can **write** printable stuff 出版のできるような物が書ける.

Q **bad** stuff 劣作, 粗悪品. ¶**clear** stuff きずのない品物(材木など). ¶Lava is **curious** stuff. 溶岩は(研究心をそそる)不思議なものだ. ¶**green** (=garden) stuff 青もの; 緑樹緑草など. ¶This is **good** stuff! こりゃ上ものだ(酒など). ¶I wish to have a pair of trousers of **gray** stuff. ねずみ色のズボンを一着こしらえたい. ¶**inferior** stuff 悪い品. ¶He rubbed some **medical** stuff on the burn. 彼はやけどに何か薬を塗りつけた. ¶This medicine is **nasty** stuff. これはいやな薬だ(とても飲みにくい). ¶That is tosh, and **old** stuff besides. その文句はナンセンスだ, しかも古い. ¶This wine (book) is **poor** stuff. このぶどう酒(など)はろくでもないものだ. ¶Men of the stuff are needed, enthusiastic, yet sane and patient; **practical** yet disinterested. ほんとに良い人物が必要だ, 熱があってそれでまじめで我慢強く, 実際的でそれで利己的でないといった風の. ¶This is **prewar** stuff. これは戦前の品物だ. ¶write **sad** stuff《米口》まずいものを書く. ¶**silk** stuff 絹布. ¶That's **sissy** stuff.《米口》めそめそするな(男じゃないか). ¶**sweet** stuff 甘いもの(菓子類). ¶**that** stuff そんなこと. ¶**woolen** stuff 毛織物.

Q² **feeding** stuffs 飼料(かいば). ¶Get out my **fishing** stuff and kit bag. つり道具とかばんを出してくれ. ¶Meat and vegetable are **food** stuffs (=foodstuffs). 肉や野菜は食料である. ¶**household** stuff = furniture 家具; 器具. ¶**sob** stuff《米口》お涙頂だいもの(放送劇など).

P My coat is made **of** good, strong stuff. 私の上衣の地は物が良くって丈夫だ.

stuff, *v.* 詰め込む; つめ物を入れる.

M stuff **out** one's purse with banknotes 財布に紙幣を詰め込む.

M² stuff **up** one's head with knowledge 頭に知識を詰め込む ‖ My nose is uncomfortably stuffed **up**. 私は鼻が詰って気持が悪い.

P stuff it **in** one's mouth 口にそれを詰め込む. ¶stuff a newspaper **into** one's pocket ポケットに新聞紙を押し込む. 【類】stuff food **into** one's mouth / He rolled up the newspaper and stuffed it **into** one of his coat pockets. ¶stuff the ears **with** cotton 耳に綿をつめる ‖ stuff a person **with** lies うそ八百を言って聞かせる ‖ a cushion stuffed **with** straw (cotton, down, feathers) わら(など)を詰めた座布団. 【類】a chimney stuffed **with** soot / a head stuffed **with** fancies.

stuffy, *a.* むっとする.

O I feel stuffy in this room. このへやはむんむんする.

stumble, *v.* つまずく; どもる.

M stumble **forward** つまずいて前の方にのめる. ¶stumble **out** よろけ出る.

M² stumble **along** つまずきながら行く. ¶stumble **down** よろけてころぶ. ¶stumble **off** into the water つまずいて水の中へのめる.

P stumble **across** … …にめぐり会う. ¶I stumbled **after** him. 彼の後をつまずきつまずき行った. ¶stumble **against** a person (chair) ふと人(など)に出っくわす. ¶stumble **at** a straw つまらないことにまごつく. ¶stumble **in** one's speech 演説でつかえる. ¶stumble **into** a chair つまずいていすにのめる ‖ stumble **into** a den of thieves 偶然盗賊の巣くつにはいり込む ‖ somehow or other he stumbled **into** greatness なんとかして彼は名を揚げるようになった. ¶He stumbled **on** the stairs and fell forward to the bottom. 彼は階段でつまずいて下へころげ落ちた. ¶stumble **over** (= against) a stone 石につまずく. 【類】stumble **over** pronunciation / stumble **over** words ‖ stumble **over** to … …へとぼとぼ出かけて行く. ¶stumble **through** a recitation (speech) ひっかかりながら朗読(など)する. ¶stumble **toward**[**s**] … …の方へよろける. ¶stumble **upon** a rare book 偶然珍本を見つける.

stumbling, *n.* つまずき, 失敗.

P go through **without** stumbling 間違わずにやり通す.

stumbling-block, *n.* 障害物.

Q a **great** stumbling-block with beginners 初学者にとっての大きな障害.

P² a stumbling-block **to** progress 進歩の障害物.

stump, *n.* 株, 根っこ; 短くなったもの;《米》遊説.

V use the stump of one cigarette to light the next のみさしでシガレットの新しいのに火をつける. ¶**take** the stump 遊説に出かける.

Q² a **pencil** stump (=stub) 短かくなった鉛筆.

P go **on** the stump 遊説に出掛ける. ¶be **up** a stump《米口》どぎまぎする(返事など), 閉口する.

stump, *v.* 閉口させる;《米》遊説する.

M² The candidates are stumping the country **over**. 候補者たちは全国遊説中だ.

P Quick-witted as he was, he was stumped **by** this. 彼は機敏だがこれには閉口した.

stun, *v.* 気絶させる; 肝をつぶさせる.

M He was **temporarily** stunned. 彼は一時気絶した.

P be stunned **by** a sudden blow 突然なぐられてのびる ‖ I was stunned **by** the news. 私はそれを聞いてぼうっとした. 【類】For a whole day he sat alone, stunned **by** despair. ¶stun an animal **with** a club 動物をこん棒で打って気絶させる.

stunt, *n.* 曲芸; 高等飛行.

V Her favorite actress is Pearl White, dressed like a man, **doing** stunts on horseback. 彼女の好きな女優は男装して馬上の曲芸をやるパール・ホワイトだ. ‖ **do** athletic stunts on bamboo ladders [消防夫など]はしご乗をやる. ¶**perform** a stunt 高等飛行を行う ‖ Circus riders **perform** stunts on horseback. サーカスの騎手は馬術の妙技を見せる.

Q² an **autocycle** stunt オートバイ曲乗り. ¶a **flying** stunt 高等(曲乗)飛行. ¶a **promotion** stunt to give a free hamburger to each of the first five customers 先着五名にハンバーグステーキを一個ずつ無料進呈という景気付け. ¶a **publicity** stunt 宣伝の変り種. ¶a **riding** stunt 馬術の妙技. ¶a **tight rope** stunt 綱渡りの曲芸.

stunt, *v.* いじけさせる.

P stunted **in** growth 生長を妨げられて.

stupefy, *v.* 知覚を失わせる.

P He was stupefied **by** a blow on the head. 彼は頭を打たれて気が遠くなった. ¶He is stupefied **with** drink (narcotics). 彼は酒(など)で正体なくなっている. ‖ I am quite stupefied **with** this noise. 私はこの騒ぎで全く気が遠くなった.

stupid, *a.* ぼんやりしている; 正気を失った.

M You're **a little** stupid. 君は少しぼんやりしている. ¶**How** stupid of you to overlook such an obvious mistake! こんな明りょうな間違いを見過ごすなんて君はなんというぼんやりだ. ¶be **incredibly** stupid ばかばかしいくらいまぬけである.

P I am afraid I am rather stupid **about** cricket. 私はどちらかというとクリケットに趣味がない方だ. ¶stupid **from** narcotics 麻酔剤で正気を失って. ¶It was very stupid **of** me to say yes. 承知するなんて僕もよほどぼんやりしていた. 【類】It's most stupid **of** me to have forgotten it. ¶stupid **with** drink 酔って正体なくなって.

stupid, *n.* のろま.

Q a **bottomless** stupid 底抜けのばか.

stupidity, *n.* 愚鈍; 愚行.

V Poverty **brings** stupidity. 貧すれば鈍する. ¶**commit** some stupidity なにかへまをやる.

Q **post-adolescent** stupidity or insanity [神童など]少年時代後の愚鈍または狂気.

Q² **blockhead** stupidity 愚行, まぬけ.

sturdy, *a.* がん丈な.

P be sturdy **in** argument 主張が強硬である.

stuttering, *n.* どもり; 渋滞.

Q *urinary stuttering* 利尿の渋滞.

style, *n.* **(1)** 流儀, 様式; 型; 品格, 気品; 商号.

V ***alter*** the *style* of one's hair 髪様式の型を変える. ¶***change*** one's *style* of living 生活法を変える. ¶***follow*** the native *style* of architecture 自国の建築風にならう. ¶***give*** one one's full *style* [人に言掛けるかまたは人の名を記す場合]その肩書を全部付ける. ¶She ***has*** a *style* of her own in everything. 彼女は何をするにも独特の型がある. ¶His painting ***lacks style***. 彼の絵には気品がない.

Q a house of ***antique style*** 古風な家. ¶an ***awkward style*** of walking ぎごちない歩きつき. ¶***bad style*** 不体裁, 不作法. ¶She has a ***beautiful style***. 彼女は容姿がよい. ¶in ***becoming style*** 体裁よく. ¶a gate in the ***Chinese style*** 唐門. ¶cafes in the ***continental style*** 大陸風のカフェー. ¶***different styles*** of rowing 色々のこぎ方. ¶a wooden building in ***European style*** 欧風の木造建物. ¶He lives in an ***expensive style***. 彼はぜいたくな暮しをしている. ¶an ***extravagant style*** of living ぜいたくな生活振り. ¶her ***fair, queenly style*** of beauty 彼女のくっきりした女王のような美しさ. ¶This *style* is very ***fashionable*** now. この様式は目下大流行だ. ¶in ***fine style*** 手際よく. ¶***finicking style*** いやに気取った風. ¶a room furnished in ***foreign style*** 洋式に造作を付けたへや. 【類】edifices (建物) in ***foreign style***. / We partook of an excellent meal in ***foreign style***. / His house is built in ***foreign style***. ¶it is ***good (bad) style*** to ... ...するのは上(下)品だ ‖ dressed in ***good style*** スマートな服装で. ¶the ***Gothic style*** of architecture 建築のゴシック式. ¶live in ***grand style*** 豪しゃな生活をする ‖ march in ***grand style*** 堂々と行進する. ¶live in ***great style*** りっぱな生活をする. ¶in the ***Gregorian style*** 太陽暦の. ¶the ***Italian style*** of painting イタリア風の画法. ¶a house in the ***Japanese style*** 日本風の家屋. ¶the ***latest (=newest) style*** 最新流行. 【類】They sell the ***latest styles*** in hats. / the ***latest styles*** in garments for beach wear. ¶in a ***masterful style*** [巨匠のように]巧妙に, 名人芸で. ¶of ***military style*** 武張った. ¶in thoroughly ***modern style*** 全然現代式に. ¶a ***national style*** in garden design 国民特有の庭園設計法. ¶a ***nervous style*** of writing 神経質な書き方. ¶June, 16 ***new (old) style*** 新(旧)暦六月十六日. ☞ 普通 N.S. または O.S. という略字形を用いる. ¶There is ***no style*** about her. 彼女には気品がない. ¶a ***novel style*** 変ったスタイル. ¶a gentleman (bicycle) of the ***old style*** 旧式の紳士(など). ¶look very queer in their ***old fashioned style*** of dress [肖像など]古風の着物でおかしく見える. ¶in a ***plain, common sense style*** ひらたく常識的に. ¶in ***pure Japanese style*** 純日本風に. ¶in a ***quaint style*** 妙な具合に. ¶in a ***racy style*** きびきびとして. ¶in ***rococo style*** ロココ式(建築)に. ¶He called me a stupid and more in the ***same style***. 彼は僕をばかだのなんだのとののしった. ¶Their home is built in ***semi-foreign style*** 彼らの家は半洋風に建ててある. ¶of ***similar style*** [衣服・帽子など]同じ型の. ¶dressed in a ***sporty style*** スポーティな服装をして. ¶in the ***stockingless style*** くつ下なしで. ¶She dresses her hair in a ***strange style***. 彼女は妙な風に髪を結っている. ¶an inn built in a ***typical national style*** 典型的なお国ぶりに建てた旅館. ¶in ***western style*** 西洋風に. ¶***What style*** of man is he? 彼はどんな人物か. ¶in ***womanly style*** 女のように.

Q² in ***rococo style*** 〘建築〙ロココ式に. ¶wear a fashionable ***hair style*** 流行型に髪を結う ‖ the Hepburn ***hair style*** ヘップバーン刈り. ¶a ***hair-cut style*** prevailing in Broadway ブロードウェイで流行している髪型. ¶The building is in the ***Italian Renaissance style***. その建築はイタリア復興式だ. ¶It was designed by ..., the architecture being of ***late Renaissance style*** それは...の設計に成ったもので建築は晩期の復興式だ. ¶in the Louis-Quatorze or ***Louis-Quinze style*** 〘建築・装飾〙ルイ十四世時代風もしくはルイ十五世時代風. ¶in a ***matter-of-fact style*** 実際的に. ¶***office style*** 官庁風. ¶the ***pre-Raphael style*** ラファエル前派の画風.

P something ***after*** the *style* of ... ...といったような物 ‖ ***after*** the *style* of the Pantheon [建物など]ローマの万神廟(びょう)にならった ‖ a room ***after*** Japanese *style* 日本風のへや. ¶ancient ***in*** *style* 古風の. 【類】similar ***in*** *style* of ... ‖ a blue serge suit—always ***in*** *style* and always in good taste いつでも気がきいていていつでも品のあるこんサージの合服 ‖ He lives ***in*** *style*. 彼ははでに暮している. 【類】live ***in*** the *style* of a nobleman / a man ***in*** the *style* of a servant / It is painted ***in*** the *style* of that master and perhaps by his hand. / designed ***in*** the *style* of Louis XIV. ‖ Rai Sanyo was an excellent poet ***in*** the Chinese *style*. 頼山陽は漢詩の大家だった. ‖ He called me a stupid and more ***in*** the same *style*. 彼は私をのろまだとか何とかののしった. ‖ She dressess ***in*** *style*. 彼女の着つけはいきだ.

P² her *style* ***of*** dressing 彼女の着こなし. ¶The frock is now ***out of*** *style*. フロックは旧式だ. ¶trade carried on ***under*** the *style* of Echigoya 越後屋という名儀での商売. 【類】This business was established in 1856 ***under*** the *style* of Rich & Sons. / he purchased the business and continued it ***under*** the *style* of ...

P² He lives in a *style* ***beyond (within)*** his means. 彼は収入以上(以内)の暮しをしている. ¶*style* then ***in*** vogue 当時流行の様式. ¶His clothes are of good material and well cut in the *style* ***of*** the day. 彼の服は品がよくて仕立も現代式だ.

(2) 文体.

V ***acquire*** an efficient *style* of composition 効果的な文体を習得する. ¶Don't ***copy*** anybody's *style*: ***develop*** your own. 他人の型を追うな, 自流をのばせ. ¶He ***has*** a *style* with many merits. 彼の文体にはいく多の長所がある. ¶***make*** a *style* of one's own 自己の流儀を作り出す. ¶***model*** one's *style* on accepted masterpieces 定評ある傑作にならって自分の様式を作る. ¶***polish up*** the *style* 文体を修飾する. ¶He ***possesses*** an easy, racy *style*. 彼の文体は平易でいてきびきびしている. ¶***use (=write in)*** a rough *style* 乱暴な文体を用いる.

Q possess an ***admirable style*** 見事な文体を持っている. ¶an ***affected style*** 気どった文体. ¶an ***antiquated style*** 古い文体. ¶an ***argumentative style*** 議論体. ¶an ***attractive style*** 人を引きつける文体. ¶written in a singularly ***beautiful style*** 特に流麗な文体で書いた. ¶***blunt, uncouth***, and scarcely even ***grammatical style*** ぶっきら棒で不体裁で文法的にもなっていない文体. ¶be written in a ***breezy style*** 軽妙に書かれている. ¶written in a ***bright*** and ***chatty style*** 明朗なくだけた文体で書いてある. 【類】in a ***bright*** and ***witty style*** / written in a ***bright*** and ***pleasing style***. ¶his ***charming*** "***colloqui-literary***" *style* 彼の魅力ある雅俗折衷の文体. ¶an excellent poem in the ***Chinese style*** 美事な漢詩. ¶a ***clear, attractive style*** 明せきな魅力ある文体. ¶a ***clear, forcible*** and ***convincing style*** 明せき雄健で人を信服させる筆致. ¶a ***clear*** and ***neat style*** 明快な文体. ¶a ***clear*** and ***pithy style*** 簡潔な文体. ¶***clear*** and ***precise style*** 明白で正確な文章. ¶a ***colloquial style*** 口語体. ¶a ***concise style*** 簡潔な文体. ¶a ***conversational style*** 会話体. ¶a ***crisp style*** きびきびした文体. ¶a ***crystal-clear style*** 玲瓏(ろう)玉のごとき文体. ¶a ***cursive style*** [字の]草書体. ¶a ***direct*** and ***unaffected style*** 率直でいや味のない文体. ¶in an ***easy conversational style*** すらすらと会話口調で. ¶written in an ***easy, flowing style*** 流ちょうな文体で書いた. 【類】***easy*** and ***fluent style*** ‖ written in an ***easy*** and ***gossiping style*** くだけた雑談調で書いた. ¶an ***elegant style*** 優雅な文体. ¶an ***elevated style*** 上品な文体. ¶written in an ***entertaining*** and ***humorous style*** おもしろい諧謔(ぎゃく)的な文体で書いてある. ¶the ***epic style*** 叙事詩体. ¶an ***epigrammatic style*** 風刺詩体. ¶an ***epistolary style*** 候文体. ¶be written in ***excellent style*** 名文である. ¶a master of a most ***exquisite style*** きわめて文章の巧みな人. ¶a ***familiar style*** 通俗体 ‖ He has a ***familiar, unpretentious style***. 彼の文は親しみがあってさっぱりしている. ¶in such a ***fascinating style*** 非常に愛きょうのある語調で ‖ the master of a most ***fascinating style*** 名文家. ¶talk in a ***flattering style*** おべっか口調で話す. ¶a ***florid style*** 流麗な文体. ¶a ***flowery style*** けんらんたる文体. ¶a ***forcible style*** 力のある文体. ¶This author has a ***good style***. この作者の文体はりっぱなものだ. ‖ acquire a ***good English style*** りっぱな英文が書けるようになる. ¶a ***grave style*** 重々しい文体. ¶archaic words used in ***higher style*** 調子の高い文に用いられる古語. ¶***inflated style*** 上ずった調子の文. ¶deal in ***interesting style*** with ... 興味深く...を説く. ¶written in ***journalistic style*** 新聞体に書いた. ¶a ***light style*** 軽い文体. ¶the perfection of ***literary style*** 文語体の極致. 【類】the charm of his ***literary style*** / a stiff ***literary style***. ¶write in a ***lively style***

生々した文体で書く. ¶a ***lively, conversational*** *style* 発らつとした会話体. ¶in the ***lofty*** *style* of writing 調子の高い文体で. ¶a ***loose*** *style* 締りのない文体. ¶a ***luscious*** *style* 余り色彩のあり過ぎる文体. ¶the ***magnificent*** *style* of Victor Hugo ビクトルユーゴーの堂々たる文体. ¶a ***meretricious*** *style* けばけばしい文体. ¶an ***obscure*** *style* 読みにくい文体. ¶written in a richly ***ornate*** *style*, with a wealth of figures and allusions 詩藻(ﾌ)・引喩(ﾕ)ともに豊かに非常に花やかに書いた. ¶***pedantic*** *style* げん学的な文体. ¶a ***pedestrian*** *style* of writing 粗雑な(無味乾燥な)文体. ¶Twain's ***pellucid*** *style* is easy to understand, トゥエーンの明白な文章は分りやすい. ¶a ***pellucid, passionate, trenchant*** *style* 明白で, 情熱的で, しんらつな文体. ¶a ***picturesque*** *style* 絵を見るような文体. ¶the ***plain, homely*** *style* of Tolstoy トルストイの平易で四角張らない文体. ¶written in a ***pleasant, chatty*** *style* おもしろく軽快に書いた. ¶a ***poetical*** *style* いん文体. ¶a ***polished*** *style* 洗練された文体. ¶written in ***popular*** *style* 通俗体に書いた. ¶a ***prolix*** *style* 冗漫な文体. ¶a ***pseudo-antique*** *style* 擬古体. ¶a writer of the ***purest English*** *style* きわめて純粋な英語で書く文士. ¶a ***racy*** *style* きびきびした文体. ¶a ***recondite*** *style* 難解の文体. ¶write a ***rollicking Irish*** *style* ふざけたアイルランド調で書く. ¶written in a ***simple*** and ***graphic***, sometimes ***ungrammatical*** *style* 時折文法の誤りはあるが簡単明りょうな文体で書いた. ¶The *style* is somewhat ***slangy*** and ***slipshod***. その文体はやや俗気を帯びてしまりがない. ¶His *style* is ***slovenly***. 彼の文はしまりがない. ¶a ***sonorous*** *style* of writing 句調のいい文体. ¶a ***stiff*** *style* 固い文体. ¶a ***tumid*** *style* 誇張的文体. ¶a *style* ***unobtrusive*** yet ***elegant*** 控目ではあるが優雅な様式. ¶a ***vicious*** *style* 悪文. ¶a ***vigorous*** *style* 強健な文体. ¶written in rather ***vulgar*** *style* 相当卑俗な調子で書かれた. ¶the ***winning*** *style* of Stevenson スティーヴンソンのほれぼれする文体.

Q² a private letter written in a ***business*** *style* 商用文の文体で書いた私信. ¶a ***diary*** *style* 日記体. ¶some tendencies of ***prose*** *style* 散文におけるある傾向.

P we constantly receive letters ***after*** the *style* of the following extract:—われわれは絶えず次の抜書のような書面に接する. ¶***in*** a *style* of his own 彼一流の文体で. 【類】Milton and Sir Thomas Browne wrote ***in*** a *style* crammed full of Latinisms. / written ***in*** the *style* of Byron ‖ There is much improvement ***in*** your *style*. 君は文章が大層よくなった. ‖ His writings are bright ***in*** *style*. 彼の書いたものにはその才筆がひらめいている.

style, *v*. 称する, 呼ぶ.

M Tasmania, ***appropriately*** *styled* "the Garden of Australia," is celebrated for its orchards, mountains, and ferns. 適切にもオーストラリアの庭園の称あるタスマニアはその果園・山岳及びしだで有名だ. ¶may be ***fairly*** *styled* ... ...と称してもよかろう. ¶***loosely*** *styled* ... 漫然...と称された. ¶be ***justly*** *styled* classic 古典風と言って不適当でない. ¶this department is ***officially*** *styled*... この部の正式の名称は...である. ¶it is ***popularly*** *styled* ... それは一般に...と呼んでいる. ¶One may ***so*** *style* it. そう呼んでも差支えない.

stylish, *a*. いきな, 上品な.

P He looks *stylish* ***in*** his uniform. 彼は制服を着るといきに見える. 【類】*stylish* ***in*** manner (dress, behavior).

stylist, *n*. 文章家; デザイナー.

Q a ***polished*** *stylist* 洗練された大文章家. ¶***second-rate*** *stylists* 二流の文章家.

Q² a ***table*** *stylist* 食卓飾りの専門家.

suasion, *n*. 説得, 説諭.

V ***apply*** gently coercive *suasion* やんわりとしかし威圧的な説得をする.

subdivide, *v*. 細分する.

P It is *subdivided* ***into*** two classes. それは二つに小分されている. ¶It may be conveniently *subdivided* ***under*** five captions. それは便宜上五つの見出しに細分される.

sub-editor, *n*. 〘新聞〙編集次長.

Q the ***chief*** *sub-editor* of a daily [paper] 日刊紙の編集次長.

subject, *n*. (**1**) 問題, 題; [実験]材料; 学科; 〘文法〙主語.

V ***approach*** the *subject* from a different (another) standpoint 異った見地からその問題に接する. 【類】***approach*** the *subject* with an open mind (虚心坦(ﾀﾝ)懐) / His experience allows him to ***approach*** the *subject* from a practical standpoint. ¶***attack*** a delicate *subject* 取扱いにくい問題に着手する. ¶***break up*** the *subject* into sections その問題を分割する. ¶***bring up*** the *subject* of ... in the course of conversation 会談中に...の問題を持出す. ¶***broach*** the *subject* with ... ...にそのことを言出す. ¶Let's ***change*** the *subject*. 話題を変えよう. ¶***choose*** a *subject* for an article 文題を選ぶ. ¶***close*** the *subject* その問題を打切る. ¶carefully ***consider*** a *subject* 慎重に問題を考察する. ¶A single word ***covers*** the whole *subject*. 一言で全問題を約言される. ¶***cram up*** a *subject* [学生が]学科を詰め込む. ¶***discuss*** a *subject* from a variety of points of view 種々の見地から問題を論議する. 【類】***discuss*** the *subject* in all its aspects (各方面から) / The *subject* is more fully ***discussed*** in Chapter III. ¶before ***dismissing*** this *subject* この問題を片付ける前に. ¶***divert*** the *subject* into another channel 話を転じる(そらす). ¶The artist ***drew*** many of his *subjects* from ... その美術家は...から多くの題材を得た. 【類】Let's ***drop*** the *subject* here. ¶***elucidate*** the *subject* その問題を釈明する. ¶***exhaust*** a *subject* 問題を十分に検討する. ¶***expound*** a *subject* ある問題を解説する. ¶This painter ***found*** most of his *subjects* in rural life and scenes. その画家は題材の大部分を田園生活及び風景の中から採った. ¶the episode ***forms*** the *subject* of ... ...はそのそう話題材としている ‖ It ***forms*** *subjects* of daily debate and newspaper articles. それが日常の話題や新聞記事の問題となる. 【類】The question whether ... ***forms*** the *subject* of the next chapter. / It ***forms*** the *subject* of his lecture (one of his poems). ¶***give*** the *subject* serious study (=careful thought) その問題をまじめに研究する. ¶***grapple*** a *subject* 問題を真剣に研究する. ¶***grip*** one's *subject* その取扱う問題をしっかりと把握する. ¶***handle*** the *subject* in all its aspects その問題をあらゆる面から取扱う. 【類】He ***handled*** Japanese *subjects* with great appreciation (感激して). / He is probably one of the best equipped (資格のある) men in the country to ***handle*** the *subject* clearly. / The *subject* is admirably ***handled*** by the author. / ***handle*** his *subject* in a masterly way (あざやかに). ¶***have*** the *subject* under serious consideration その問題をまじめに考慮する ‖ ***have*** *subjects* of common interest to talk about 話が合う. ¶We would like to ***have*** (=see) these *subjects* ***treated*** at greater length in your magazine. この問題を貴誌でもっと詳細に論じていただきたい. ¶his researches have ***illuminated*** the *subject* of ... 彼の研究が...の題目の説明に貢献した. ¶***illustrate*** a *subject* in hand with an appropriate quotation 適切な引用句を使って文を解説する. ¶***introduce*** a painful *subject* 痛ましい話題を持出す. ¶thoroughly ***investigate*** the *subject* 徹底的にその問題を研究する. ¶The writer evidently ***knows*** his *subject*. その筆者はたしかにその取扱った問題を理解している. 【類】show how thoroughly the author ***knows*** his *subject*. ¶***learn*** the *subject* その学科を学ぶ. ¶We ***leave*** the *subject* here. この問題はここで筆をおく. 【類】before ***leaving*** the *subject* of ..., mention must be made of ... / before ***leaving*** the *subject* it may be worth while to point out that ... ¶***make*** it a *subject* of experiment それを実験材料にする. ¶Patent medicine is often ***made*** the *subject* of extravagant advertising. 売薬は往々法外な広告をする. 【類】It was ***made*** a *subject* of interpellation (質問) in the Diet. / those whose characters were ***made*** the *subject* of unjust aspersions (非難). ¶***Mark*** the *subjects* in which you are interested 貴方が興味を感じた問題に印を付けて下さい. ¶***master*** a *subject* with facility ある問題を容易にきわめる. ¶***mention*** the *subject* to ... その題目を...に話す. ¶***narrow down*** one's *subject* to ... その取扱う問題の範囲を...に局限する. ¶He ***opened*** the *subject* of socialism. 彼は社会主義の問題を持出した. ¶***ponder*** a *subject* in philosophy 哲学の問題を考える. ¶*subjects* ***portrayed*** in Japanese color prints 日本のにしき絵の画題. ¶The *subject* was ***postponed*** for future consideration. その問題は繰り延べて他日考慮することにした. ¶***present*** a *subject* in its true perspective 問題の真面目を発揮する. ¶***propose*** a *subject* for the debate 討論題を提出する. ¶the student who wishes to ***pursue*** the *subject* further さらにその問題の研究を続行しようとする学徒. 【類】He ***pursued*** the *subject* no further. / ***pursue*** the *subject* in greater detail (all its ramifications). ¶before ***quitting*** the *subject* of ..., it is essential for me to add ... ...の問題を切上げる前に筆者

は是非…を付加しておかなければならない. ¶***see*** our *subject* in its proper perspective われわれの問題の正当な見方をする. ¶***select*** their *subjects* from … …から題材を取る. ¶***start*** a *subject* 問題を持出す. ¶***study*** the *subject* thoroughly 問題を徹底的に研究する. 【類】The *subject* has but imperfectly been ***studied*** in Japan. ¶***submit*** the *subject* to the judgment of several eminent scholars その問題を数名の著名学者の判断にゆだねる. ¶***survey*** the *subject* その問題を考査する. ¶***taboo*** (=***avoid***) the *subject* その問題を避ける. ¶***tackle*** a *subject* 問題に取掛かる. ¶***take*** the *subject* seriously その問題をまじめに考える. ¶***take up*** a *subject* 問題をとりあげる. ¶***treat*** the *subject* exhaustively その問題を徹底的に論述する. 【類】***treat*** a *subject* technically (専門的に) / a *subject* frequently ***treated*** by Japanese artists / The *subject* is there ***treated*** very fully and clearly. ¶Why do you ***turn*** the *subject* into ridicule? なぜ君はこの問題を一笑に付するのか. ¶I ***turned*** the *subject* ***over*** in my mind. 私はそのことを色々と考えて見た. ¶***view*** the *subject* from different angles 違った角度からその問題を見る. ¶to anyone disposed to ***weigh*** the *subject* dispassionately 冷静にその問題を比較考量せんとする人には. ¶The *subject* has been ***worked*** since the remotest ages. その問題は大昔から論じられてきた.

V² every time the *subject* ***comes up*** in Congress 議会でその問題が持ち上がるごとに. ¶the *subject* ***drifts away*** into …話題が知らず知らず…にはいって行く.

Q an ***abstruse*** *subject* 玄妙な問題. ¶***academic*** *subjects* 学科. ¶***animate*** or ***inanimate*** *subjects* 生物または静物の画題. ¶form ***attractive*** *subjects* of conversation 興味ある話題となる. ¶***basic*** *subjects*—literature, science, philosophy, mathematics, and history 文学・科学・哲学・数学及び歴史などの基礎学科. ¶My ***best*** (***weak***) *subject* is Latin. 私の一番得意(不得手)な学科はラテン語だ. ¶these and other ***cognate*** (=***kindred or allied***) *subjects* これら並びにその他の関連した諸題目. ¶expound a ***complex*** *subject* 複雑な問題を解説する. ¶A *subject* so ***complicated*** as the history and people of India cannot be satisfactorily treated in a few pages. インドの歴史及び国民のような複雑な問題は数ページで満足に論述することはできない. ¶a ***compulsory*** (=***obligatory***) *subject* 必修科目. ¶all ***conceivable*** *subjects* of interests to students 学生に興味あるあらゆる問題. 【類】on every ***conceivable*** *subject*. ¶a ***controversial*** *subject* 論議の多い問題. ¶The *subject* is too ***delicate*** to be treated here. その問題はさしさわりが多いのでここでは論ぜられない. ¶a ***difficult*** *subject* to tackle 取扱いにくい問題. ¶a ***disagreeable*** *subject* 不愉快な話題. ¶teachers of ***domestic*** *subjects* 家事科の教師. ¶a ***dull*** *subject* 無趣味な問題. ¶writers on ***economic*** *subjects* 経済方面の論文家. ¶***elective*** *subjects* 選択科目. ¶an ***enticing*** *subject* 魅力ある問題. ¶form an ***examination*** *subject* 試験科目になっている. ¶form a ***favorite*** *subject* of Japanese art 日本美術の得意の画題になっている. ¶It is ***fertile*** *subject*, where careful study would lead to constructive suggestion. それは内容豊富な題目で入念に研究すると建設的な示唆が得られるであろう. ¶form the ***excellent*** *subject* of … …の絶好の題目となっている. ¶a ***fascinating*** *subject* 魅力ある問題. ¶one's ***favorite*** *subject* その好きな題目(文などの) ‖ read a book on some ***favorite*** *subject* 何か得意の問題に関する本を読む. ¶form a ***fitting*** *subject* for a photograph 撮影の好題材である. ¶the ***fruitful*** *subject* of Gothic art in England 英国におけるゴシック芸術という有益な問題. ¶mathematics, physics, and other ***fundamental*** *subjects* 数学・物理学その他の基礎学科. ¶a ***genre*** *subject* of painting 風俗画題. ¶What a ***ghastly*** *subject!* なんといういやな問題だろう. ¶a ***good*** *subject* for discussion 討論の好題目. ¶a ***graduate*** *subjects* of study 卒業後大学院などでの研究科目. ¶the ***hackneyed*** *subjects* of politics 陳腐な政治問題. ¶that ***inexhaustible*** *subject*, Literary London 文学のロンドンというあの無尽蔵の問題. ¶an ***informative*** *subject* [実習などに対する]知識学科. ¶a very ***interesting*** *subject* of inquiry きわめて興味ある研究問題. ¶***kindred*** *subjects* of study 同種の研究問題. ¶an illuminating exposition of a ***learned*** *subject* 専門的な事項のわかりやすい解説. ¶a ***literary*** *subject* 文学上の問題. ¶the ***main*** *subject* 主要問題. ¶***major*** *subjects* 主要(必修)科目. ¶a ***much-discussed*** *subject* 盛んに論議された問題. ¶a ***never-ending*** *subject* 書いても書いても書ききれない問題. ¶I now come to consider the ***next*** *subject*. ここで次の問題に移ります. ¶an ***occult*** *subject* 神秘な問題. ¶an ***optional*** *subject* 随意科目. ¶articles on ***out-of-the-ordinary*** *subjects* 変り種の文. ¶the ***polemical*** *subject* of vivisection 生体解剖というやかましい問題. ¶***professional*** *subjects* 専門の学科. ¶a ***ready*** *subject* of conversation 直ちに使える話題. ¶***related*** *subjects* それに関連した諸問題. ¶All experts in their ***respective*** *subjects*. 皆それぞれの問題における専門家である. ¶***required*** *subjects* 必修科目. ¶a ***ridiculous*** *subject* to talk to … …に話すにはばかばかしい問題. ¶pictures of ***sacred*** *subjects* [キリストの昇天・はりつけなどを取扱った]聖画. ¶***scriptural*** *subjects* 聖書に基づく(詩歌・絵画などの)題. ¶Logics is not taught even in high schools as a ***separate*** *subject*. 論理学は独立した科目としては高校でも教えていない. ¶be a ***sore*** *subject* with … …にとってはおもしろくない題目である. ¶their ***staple*** *subject* of conversation 彼らの会話の主題目. ¶write essays on some ***stock*** *subjects* ありふれた問題で文をつづる. ¶a ***suggestive*** *subject* 示唆に富む問題. ¶a ***technical*** *subject* 技術的な問題. ¶a ***tender*** *subject* 扱いにくい問題. ¶Education remains a ***thorny*** *subject* for the Government. 教育は政府に取っては依然困難な問題になっている. 【類】a ***thorny*** *subject* to handle. ¶a ***threadbare*** *subject* 陳腐な問題. ¶attack a ***thorny*** *subject* 難問と取組む. ¶a ***timely*** *subject* 時機に投じた題目. ¶a ***topical*** *subject* 時事問題. ¶an ***undergraduate*** *subject* of study [大学]卒業前の研究問題. ¶an ***unpleasant*** *subject* 不愉快な問題. ¶a *subject* hitherto ***untouched*** in fiction これまで小説家の触れていなかった問題. ¶a ***vital*** *subject* 死活問題. ¶a ***weighty*** *subject* 重要題目.

Q² a ***curriculum*** *subject* 教科目. ¶***elementary-school*** *subjects* 小学校諸教科目. ¶an ***essay*** *subject* 小品の題, 作文の題. ¶an ***examination*** *subject* 試験科目. ¶the ***key*** *subject* 主要題目. ¶the academic ***liberal arts*** *subjecsts* [大学の]教養科目. ¶***off-the-record*** *subjects* オフレコの(速記録にのせない)問題. 【類】send out confidential notes on ***off-the-record*** *subjects*. ¶Most of the ***school*** *subjects* are informational. 大半の学科目は知識を与えるものである. ¶***secondary school*** *subjects* 中学諸学科目. ¶a ***skill*** *subject* 技能の科目(速記術など). ¶a ***thesis*** *subject* 論文題目. ¶about any ***travel*** *subject* on which information is desired 知りたいと思われるあらゆる旅行の問題について.

P arranged ***according to*** *subject* 問題別に分類した. ¶he chose ***as*** the *subject* of his lecture "…" 彼は演題に「…」を選んだ. ¶There is no restriction ***as to*** *subject*. 題目にはなんら制限がない. ¶It is ***beside*** the *subject* (=question). それは問題外だ. ¶It is a little aside ***from*** our *subject*. それはいささか問題をはずれている. ‖ Conversation strayed ***from*** *subject*. 話がそれていった. ¶go deep ***into*** a *subject* 問題に深入りする. ¶this phase ***of*** the *subject* その問題のこの観察面. ¶He is ***off*** the *subject*. 彼は脱線している. ¶***on*** the *subject* no one is better worthy of hearing than … その問題に関しては…の意見を徴すのが一番だ. ‖ A good deal is to be said ***on*** the *subject*. その問題については言うべきことが多々ある. ‖ dwell ***on*** the *subject* その問題を大いに論じる ‖ a work ***on*** this *subject* この問題に関する著作. 【類】a *subject* ***on*** which volumes (数巻の書) might be written / What you say has no bearing ***on*** the *subject*. / This is practically the only text-book ***on*** the *subject*. / Give me more accurate information ***on*** the *subject*. / the statistics available (手に入れられる) ***on*** this *subject* / whilst ***on*** the *subject* (この問題を論じるついでに), though it has nothing to do directly with it, it may be mentioned that … ¶ponder ***over*** (=***on***) a *subject* 問題をとくと考える. ¶It is foreign ***to*** our *subject*. それは問題外だ. ‖ Let us return ***to*** our *subject*. [それはさておき]本問題に帰ろう. ¶touch ***upon*** a *subject* 問題に触れる. 【類】touch briefly ***upon*** a *subject*.

P² *subjects* ***for*** examination 試験問題 ‖ a *subject* ***for*** inquiry 研究問題 ‖ a *subject* ***for*** laughter 笑い草 ‖ a *subject* ***for*** a painter 画題. ¶the *subject* ***in*** hand 当面の問題. ¶a *subject* ***of*** common conversation 平常の話題 ‖ a *subject* ***of*** discourse 話題 ‖ a *subject* ***of*** inquiry 調査の目標. 【類】a *subject* ***of*** discussion and controversy / this question has been the *subject* ***of*** investigation by … / a *subject* ***of*** endless dispute among … ¶A fisherman mending his net is the *subject of* this picture. これは網つくろいをしている漁夫を描いたのだ. ‖ *subjects of* public interest 公共問題.【類】a *subject of* praise / render it a *subject of* regret ‖ become a *subject of* remark 評判の種となる ‖ a *subject of* interesting study おもしろい研究題目.【類】make it a *subject of* a scientific study ‖ the *subject of* tax 租税の目的物 ‖ the *subject of* the sentence〘文法〙その文の主格 ‖ He became a *subject of* press comment. 彼は新聞に書き立てられた. ‖ the *subject of* this sketch この小伝の主人公. ¶a *subject to* a verb〘文法〙動詞の主語 ‖ the *subject* and object *of* thought 思想の主体と客体. ¶the *subject under* consideration 考慮中の問題. ¶a favorite *subject with* Japanese artists 日本美術家の得意の画題.【類】Christ at Emmaus breaking bread—a favorite *subject with* Rembrandt.

(**2**) 臣民; 患者.

Q T.S. Eliot became a ***British*** *subject* in 1927. エリオットは一九二七年に英国臣民となった. ☞アメリカは an American ***citizen***: This former British *subject* is now an American ***citizen***.

Q² our ***fellow*** *subjects* in Canada カナダの(英国人)同胞. ¶a ***good*** (***bad***) *subject* 本復の望みのある(望みのない)病人. ¶***hypnotizable*** (***refractory***) *subjects* 催眠術のかけられる(かけられない)人々. ¶a ***loyal*** *subject* 忠良な臣民. ¶***natural born*** *subiects* of Great Britain 大ブリテンの生来の臣民. ¶He became a ***naturalized*** *subject* of the Czar. 彼は露国に帰化した. ¶Mr. Conrad, the famous Anglo-Polish novelist, was a ***naturalized British*** *subject*. ¶turn them into ***peaceable*** *subjects* それを鎮撫(*)して平和的臣民とする. ¶***rebellious*** *subjects* 反逆的な臣民. ¶a ***rheumatic*** *subject* リュウマチス患者.

P The king is ***above*** the *subjects*. 国王は臣民の上に立っている. ¶A king rules ***over*** his *subjects*. 国王は臣民を統治する.

subject, *a.* 従属する; 受けやすい, かかりやすい.

M Japan is ***exceedingly*** *subject* to earthquakes. 日本には地震が非常に多い. ¶No condition of life is ***more*** *subject* to revolution than that of a woman of pleasure. 売春婦の境界ほど身の上に大変化の起り勝ちなものはない. ¶Vessels arriving from there are ***no longer*** *subject* to quarantine. そこから着港の船舶はもはや検疫は受けない. ¶The herbivora are ***scarcely*** ever *subject* to constipation. 草食類にはほとんど便秘というものがない.

P *subject **to*** the proviso that ... ...のただし書をつけて ‖ Issued *subject **to*** conditions printed on back hereof. [切符など]この裏面に記した条件によって発行. ‖ All men are *subject **to*** death. 人は皆死すべきものだ. ‖ Prices are *subject **to*** change (=revision) without notice. 値段の改正は一々予告しません.【類】*subject **to*** the following conditions. / The State of Pennsylvania now takes—*subiect **to*** some exceptions (幾分例外はあるが)—one-tenth of the property left by its citizens. / He is *subject **to*** fever (constipation, headaches, giddiness). / I used to be *subject **to*** very severe colds. / Excitement is liable to bring on fits (発作) in a person *subject **to*** them. / Fares are *subject **to*** alternation and should be confirmed by reference to... / *subject **to*** the buyer's approval / The contract is *subject **to*** your approval. / The treaty is *subject **to*** ratification (批准). ‖ The work is *subject **to*** a penalty for delay. 作業は遅延すれば罰を受けることになっている. ‖ Have you any article *subject **to*** duty? 課税される物がおありですか.【類】it will be *subject **to*** a duty of ... ‖ He is *subject **to*** anger. 彼は怒りっぽい.【類】be *subject **to*** a tax of ... ‖ He has done things that are *subject **to*** criticism. 彼は批判を招きやすいことをした.【類】be *subject **to*** approval on examination / be *subject **to*** a discount of 10% / be *subject **to*** the fluctuations of the market (相場の変動) / *subject **to*** confirmation in writing (文書による確認) ‖ a country *subject **to*** extreme heat or cold 寒暑の極端な国 ‖ The tomato is *subject **to*** a number of plant diseases. トマトには色々な病気がつく ‖ a state *subject **to*** foreign rule 外国の支配を受けている国 ‖ *Subject **to*** your consent, I propose to try again. 君が賛成ならまたやって見よう. ‖ *subject **to*** a reply in seven weeks 返信は七週間と限定して ‖ He will soon be *subject **to*** the conscription, and, to avoid the service, he is going to America. 彼はすぐ徴兵に応じなければならなくなるので渡米しようとしている.【類】We are all *subject **to*** the laws of nature. ‖ ...shall be *subject **to*** scrutiny by A ...はAが審査する / Jamaica is *subject **to*** Great Britain. / That district is more *subject **to*** fire than any other. / All men are *subject **to*** difficulties. / *subject **to*** heavy fines (重い科料) ‖ be *subject **to*** shrinkage in value 価値の減少を免れない ‖ The offer is *subject **to*** the goods being unsold on receipt of your reply 貴下から返信あるまで該商品が売れずにあればお売り致します ‖ districts *subject **to*** the jurisdiction of ...〘法〙その管轄区域 ‖ an economy already *subject **to*** inflationary pressures 既にインフレの重圧を受けている経済 ‖ *subject **to*** the provisions of this treaty 本条約の規定により.

subject, *v.* 受けさせる; 服従させる.

P *subject* one ***to*** bad treatment 人をひどい目に会わせる ‖ *subject* another ***to*** one's will 人を自分の思い通りにさせる ‖ Your conduct *subject* you ***to*** public ridicule. 君のようなことをすると世間から笑われる. ‖ Such conduct would *subject* the offender ***to*** a heavy penalty. こうした行為の違犯者は重刑に処せられるだろう.【類】*subject* it ***to*** thorough revision / *subject* it ***to*** a searching examination (=strict inquiry) / be *subjected **to*** indignity / if *subjected **to*** this test / *subject* it ***to*** an exhaustive scientific treatment (周到な科学的処理) / *subject* the teaching of Malthus (マルサスの人口論) ***to*** a critical examination. / *subject* their conduct ***to*** a very close scrutiny (考査) ‖ *subject* metal ***to*** a white heat 金属を白熱する ‖ *subject* their clothes ***to*** a disinfecting process 彼らの衣服を消毒する. ‖ Greeks were *subjected **to*** the Romans. ギリシア人はローマ人に服従した. ‖ *subject* them ***to*** his yoke 彼らを彼の支配下におく ‖ Our exports are *subjected **to*** a duty of one per cent in Canada. わが国の輸出品はカナダで一割の関税を課せられる. ‖ *subject* one's plan ***to*** the consideration ***to*** a committee その計画を委員会の審議にかける.【類】He was *subjected **to*** severe criticism. / he was *subjected **to*** the sharp criticism of ... / He was *subjected **to*** the treatment (operation). / The student was *subjected **to*** an examination. / the cruelty and mismanagement ***to*** which she was *subjected*.

subjection, *n.* 征服; 屈従, 服従.

P hold ***in*** *subjection* 服従させる. ¶The natives live in a state ***of*** *subjection*. 土民は服従している. ¶bring ***to*** *subjection* 服従させる.

P² *subjection **of*** the rebels 反乱者鎮定. ¶*subjection **of*** the individual ***to*** the State 個人の国家への服従. ¶*subjection **to*** the laws 法律への服従.

subject matter, 主題.

P The science of economics has ***for*** its *subject matter* the goods and the services of economic life. 経済学は経済的生活の物資並びに労務をその主題とする.

subjoin, *v.* 添加する.

P *subjoin* a postscript ***to*** a letter 手紙に追書を添える.

subjugate, *v.* 征服する.

P She has never been *subjugated **by*** the foreigner. その国はいまだかつて外国人に征服されたことはない.

subjugation, *n.* 征服, 克服.

Q ***financial*** *subjugation* 財政上の征服.

P the *subjugation **of*** passion ***by*** reason 理性による情欲克服.

sublet, *v.* 又貸しする.

P *sublet* one's house ***for*** the summer 夏期間中住宅を又貸しする. ¶*sublet* a house ***from*** the actual tenant 実際の借主から家屋の又借をする.

sublime, *a.* 壮厳な.

M No scene could be ***more*** *sublime*. あれほど荘厳な光景はあるまい.

sublimity, *n.* 荘厳.

P² the *sublimities **of*** nature 自然の荘厳さ.

submarine, *n.* 潜水艦.

Q the Nautilus, the world's first ***atom-powered*** *submarine* 世界最初の原子力潜水艦ノーチラス号.

Q² ***long distance*** *submarines* 長距離潜水艦. ¶a ***midget*** *submarine* 小型潜航艇. ¶an ***ultra-high-speed*** *submarine* capable of 25 knots 25ノットの速力の出せる超高速潜水艦.

P the look-out tower ***on*** a *submarine* 潜水艦の展望台.

submerge, *v.* 水に沈める.

P rocks *submerged **at*** high tide 高潮時には没する岩. ¶It was *submerged **beneath*** the sea. それは海底に沈んだ. ¶The factory is *submerged **with*** orders. その工場は注文はんらんの状態だ.

submersion, *n.* 沈没.

P The bell has been recovered *after* a *submersion* of three centuries. そのつり鐘は三百年間水中にあったが引揚げられた.
P² *submersion under* water 沈没, 冠水.

submission, *n.* 服従, 帰服; 付託.
V I *demand* the *submission* of the signature to an expert. 私は署名の真偽を鑑定人に見てもらいたい. ¶*effect submission* 付託する. ¶*exhibit* entire *submission* どこまでも従順にする. ¶The clans of the north and east *gave in* their *submission*. 北部及び東部の閥族は帰順を申し出た. ¶*offer* their *submission* 彼らの帰服を申出る. ¶*tender* one's *submission* to ... …に帰順を申し出る.
Q follow him with *blind* and *servile submission* 盲目的かつどれい的に彼に服従する. ¶I shall be satisfied with nothing short of *complete submission*. 私は全然の服従でなければ満足しない. ¶The *gentle submission* of woman to man is the basis of every solid social system. 女子の男子への従順があらゆる堅固な社会組織の基礎である. ¶*slavish submission* to power 事大根性. ¶*unquestioning submission* to the will of God 神の意志への絶対服従.
P frighten a person *into submission* 人をおどかして服従させる. ¶*with submission* へいへいして.
P² Patriotic altruism is the *submission of* the selfish interests and narrower lives to the wider life and prosperity of the State. 愛国的利他主義とは私利や偏狭な生がいを国家という一層広い生活と繁栄とに服従させることである. ¶the *submission* of a dispute *to* arbitration 争議の仲裁付託.

submissive, *a.* 従順な.
P *submissive to* superiors and kindly to inferiors 目上には従順に目下には親切に.

submit, *v.* 提出する, 付託する; 服従する.
M The manuscripts were *submitted anonymously*. [懸賞などで]原稿は匿名で提出した. ¶*submit grumblingly* 不平だらだら服従する. ¶*submit meekly* すなおに服従する. ¶*submit* to them too *passively* 彼らに従順すぎる. ¶*respectfully submitted* うやうやしくさし出した. ¶No one would *submit silently* to such an insult. こんなにはずかしめられてはだれだって黙ってはいまい. ¶He is the last man to *submit tamely* to another's opinion. 彼は人の意見におとなしく従うといった男じゃない.
P *submit* papers *for* inspection 検閲のため書類を提出する. 【類】*submit* it *for* approval (adoption). 【類】It was *submitted for* the approval (御裁可) of His Majesty the Emperor. ¶The question was *submitted to* the commission for its consideration. その問題はその委員会の審議に付せられた. ¶I will *submit to* arbitration. 私は調停に服します. ‖ *submit to* the public 世論に聞く ‖ *submit to* examination without objection [持物などの]検査を異議なく受ける. 【類】*submit to* defeat (indignity, necessity, God's will) / I will not *submit to* such treatment. / You must *submit to* my judgment (判断) in the matter. / *submit to* one's fate / *submit* oneself *to* another's direction (指図) / Do not *submit* yourself *to* insult. ‖ The minds of the people do not *submit to* him. 人心は彼に帰服しない. ‖ *submit to* authority (law) 権力(法)に服する. ‖ It was *submitted to* expert after expert. それはそれからそれと鑑定家に回された. ‖ *submit* the beliefs *to* the criticism of reason その信仰を理性によって批判する ‖ he *submitted to* the Throne a full report of ... 彼は…を委細陛下に上奏した. 【類】They, of their own will, *submitted to* the authority of ... / induce a person to *submit to* certain rules / He made Persia *submit to* the Mongol arms. / The Bill was *submitted to* the Diet. / *submit* a question *to* the court / *submit* a measure *to* a council of ministers (閣議). ¶*submit under* a protest 異議申立ての上で服する.

submittal, *n.* 付託.
P *for submittal* to ... …に出す(付託する)ため.

subordinate, *n.* 部下.
V *manage* one's *subordinates* 部下をあやつる.
P leave everything *to* one's *subordinates* 万事部下任せにする.

subordinate, *a.* 下級の.
P officials *subordinate to* ... …より下級の役員.

subordinate, *v.* 次位におく, 後にする; 服従させる.
P *subordinate* passions *to* reason 理性のために情をまげる ‖ *subordinate* the public good *to* one's own interest 公益を無視して私利を計る ‖ *subordinate* temporal *to* spiritual things 俗界のことを後にして霊界のことを先にする. 【類】*subordinate* the welfare of the country *to* their own advancement or convenience.

subordination, *n.* 従属.
V *force subordination upon* ... …を無理に従わせる.
Q one's *voluntary subordination* of self to the good of the world 世界の幸福のために進んでやる滅私.
P² *subordination of* individuals *to* the superior interests of state 個人のことを後にして国家の公益を先にすること.

subscribe, *v.* 応募する, 寄付する; 同意の上署名する.; [新聞・雑誌を]予約する.
M The large sum of £1,000 was *subscribed at once*. 千ポンドの大金もたちまち応募された. ¶*heartily subscribe* to the words of ... …の言に心から同意する. ¶The bank *subscribed heavily* to the Government loan. その銀行は政府の公債に多額の応募をした. ¶He *subscribed liberally* for the building fund. 彼は建築費に惜気もなく寄付した. ¶will *not subscribe* to anything unfair 不公平なことは一切認めない. ¶The sum needed was *subscribed several times over*. 所要の金額に対する応募は数倍に達した. ¶materials *voluntarily subscribed* 篤志家寄付の物資 ‖ *subscribe* oneself *voluntarily* to ... 進んで…に応じる.
P *subscribe for* a charitable object 慈善の目的に寄付する ‖ *subscribe for* (=take in) a newspaper 新聞紙の購読を申込む ‖ Please *subscribe* here *for* The Times. ロンドンタイムズ予約の方はここへお申込を願います. 【類】The library *subscribes for* 30 periodicals. ‖ *subscribe for* railway stock 鉄道株に応募する ‖ *subscribe for* the telephone communication 電話加入を申込む. ¶*subscribe* one's name *to* a document 文書に署名する. 【類】*subscribe to* a presentation (建議書) ‖ countries *subscribing to* the Berne Convention ベルン会議出席に同意する国々 ‖ *subscribe* £100 *to* a charity 慈善事業に百ポンド寄付する. 【類】*subscribe to* the relief-fund (救済費) ‖ *subscribe to* (=for) a newspaper 新聞紙の購読を申込む ‖ *subscribe to* an opinion ある意見に賛成する ‖ I cannot *subscribe to* (=endorse) this view (what he says, the opinions of ...). 私はこの意見(など)には賛成しかねる. 【類】Do you *subscribe to* that belief (所信)? / *subscribe to* some "ism" (主義) / *subscribe to* nearly every work of it. / He does not *subscribe to* anything unfair. ¶*subscribe toward* the City's wedding gift for ... 市から贈る…の結婚祝賀贈品基金に応じる.

subscriber, *n.* 署名者; 加入者, 申込人.
V *beat up subscribers* to our scheme われわれの計画に対する賛助者を募る. ¶Telephone operators *connect subscribers* to (=with) their desired numbers. 電話交換手は希望する番号に加入者をつないでくれる. ¶*secure subscribers* for ... …の予約者(寄付者)を獲得する.
Q *existing subscribers* 現在の加入者. ¶*monthly subscribers* 月ぎめ読者. ¶*present subscribers* 現在の加入者. ¶become a *regular subscriber* for ... …正規の購読者となる.
Q² special *discount subscribers* 特別割引の加入者. ¶a *telephone subscriber* 電話加入者.
P put down one's name *as* a *subscriber* for the newspaper その新聞紙の購読者として記名する. ¶become a *subscriber for* a magazine 雑誌の購読者となる. ¶a *subscriber to* the telephone [service] 電話加入者. 【類】I wish to become a *subscriber to* your magazine.

subscription, *n.* 予約, 購読申込; 会費.
V *accept subscription* 申込に応じる. ¶*advance subscriptions* to publications 出版物申込金を前払する. ¶*book subscriptions* to the magazine with ... …に雑誌の予約を申込む. ¶*cancel* a *subscription* 申込を取消す. ¶*collect subscriptions* for the building of a new temple 殿堂新築のきょ金をする. ¶The enclosed remittance of $... is to *cover* a *subscription* for ... for ... months in the name and at the address given below. 封入の金…ドルは下記あて名に対する…誌…月分の購読料です. ¶*discontinue* one's *subscription* to a paper 新聞の購読をやめる. ¶I herewith *enclose subscription* amounting to ... yen. …円の購読料を同封致します. ¶Please *enter* my *subscription* for one year to the Modern World. モダン・ワールド一カ年分の購読料お収め下さい. 【類】*enter* my *subscription* for The Oriental Outlook for I year and send me a bill for $100 to ... ¶*get up* a *subscription* for ... …のためにきょ金する. ¶*file* one's *subscription* 予約申込みをする. ¶*invite subscriptions* for a loan to the amount of ... 総計…の公債を

募集する. ¶*make* a private *subscription* 内輪の寄付を募集する. ¶*obtain subscriptions* from its members 会員から会費を取る. ¶*subscription* has been *opened* for … …に対する予約を受けつけている. 【類】He proposed to *open* a *subscription* in order to offer a testimonial of sympathy to the bereaved family of the late Mr. … / *open* a *subscription* for the relief of … ¶*pay* one's *subscription* 寄付金を払う. 【類】each member of the club *pays* a *subscription* of … ¶*raise* a *subscription* for the erection of a monument 建碑の寄付金を募る. 【類】*subscriptions* are being *raised* to … ¶*receive subscriptions* for "The Times Weekly Edition" 週刊タイムズの購読申込を受ける. 【類】*Subscriptions* are *received* for any newspaper or magazine published in the world. ‖ *receive subscriptions* towards the fund. ¶*renew* one's *subscription* to a magazine for another year 更に一カ年間雑誌の購読を継続する. ¶*secure subscriptions* from … …から寄付申込を受ける. 【類】We *secure* 89 *subscriptions*. / allot the summer vacation to *securing subscriptions* for a magazine. ¶*send* a *subscription* to a newspaper 新聞紙の購読を申込む. 【類】*send* one's *subscription* in advance (前金で), ¶*send in* one's *subscription* 払込金を(受取人に)引渡す. ¶A *subscription* was *set* on foot. きょ金に取り掛った. ¶*solicit subscriptions* for (=to) magazines 雑誌の購読を勧誘する. ¶*start* a private *subscription* 内輪のきょ金をする. ¶*take subscriptions* for (=to) magazines 雑誌購読の勧誘をする.

V² The *subscription* to date *amounts* to … from … persons. 今日までの申込は…名の人員からで金額は…に達する. ¶The *subscription came* [*up*] to above 500 yen. 申込は五百円以上に達した. ¶your *subscription expires* on … あなたの購読払込金は…で切れます.

Q an *annual subscription* of … …の一カ年分購読料. ¶The remainder of the price is payable by *monthly subscriptions* of 5s. 代価の残額は五シリングの月賦払ができる. ¶raise money by *popular subscription* 一般からの寄付によって資金を調達する. ¶The memorial was created by *public subscription*. その記念碑は一般からの寄付で建てた. 【類】erect a school building by *public subscription*. / The Union Jack Club was erected by *public subscription* chiefly as a national memorial to those who had fallen in the South Africa War. / money raised by *public subscription*. ¶All *uncovered subscriptions* will be duly refunded. [購読料]残額はすべて清算の上御返金申上げます(廃刊雑誌などの). ¶*voluntary subscriptions* toward the expenses その費用への篤志家からの寄付. 【類】supported by a *voluntary subscription* among …

Q² pay *arrear subscriptions* 滞納の料金を支払う. ¶a gift made by *class subscription* クラスの寄金による贈り物. ¶*season subscriptions* of a theatre 劇場のシーズン中の予約申込み数. ¶*trial subscription* to a magazine 雑誌の試験的購読.

P a series of books sold only *by subscription* 予約発売の双書. 【類】acquire one's magazine *by subscription*. / be published *by subscription*. ¶solicit persons *for subscription* 人に寄付を勧誘する ‖ Please put my name down *for* a *subscription*. 寄付者として私の名を御記入願います.

P² raise a *subscription among* themselves 彼ら自身の間できょ金する. ¶collection of *subscriptions for* relief 救済義えん金募集. ¶by *subscriptions from* alumni 校友からの寄付金で. ¶the suspension of one's *subscription to* a newspaper 新聞購読の中止 ‖ *subscriptions to* the fund (war loan) 基金(などの)応募.

sub-secretary, *n*. 副長官.

P three *co-equal sub-secretaries* 三人の同格副長官(米国防省の海・陸・空の副長官).

subsequent, *a*. 後の, …に続く.

P during the period *subsequent to* the war 戦争直後には ‖ on the day *subsequent to* your call お出で下さった日の翌日に. 【類】the course of affairs (事態の進行) *subsequent to* the 25th of February.

subsequently, *ad*. 後に.

P *subsequently to* the election 選挙後に.

subserve, *v*. 役立つ.

M Chewing food *well subserves* digestion. 食物をかむことは大いに消化作用を助ける.

subservient, *a*. 助けとなる.

P *subservient to* our enterprise われわれの計画の助けとなる. 【類】make it *subservient to* the purpose.

subside, *v*. 静まる; 納まり込む; 低下する.

M Cholera appears to have *entirely subsided*. コレラはもうすっかり静まったようだ. ¶Cholera is *subsiding rapidly*. コレラは急速に衰えている.

P He *subsided into* his armchair. 彼はひじかけいすに納まり込んだ. ¶The storm did not *subsided till* dawn. あらしは夜明けまで続いた. ¶The wind *subsided to* a calm. 凪がないだ. ¶The hills *subside toward* the shore. 山は海岸の方へ向って段々低くなる.

subsidence, *n*. 鎮静.

P *on* the *subsidence* of the affair 事件が静まると.

subsidiary, *n*. 補助物.

Q The bus line is a *mere subsidiary* to the railroad. バスは鉄道の補助機関に過ぎない.

P² a *subsidiary of* a company … …の傍系会社. 【類】*subsidiaries of* the Mitsui Head Office.

subsidiary, *a*. 補助の.

P *subsidiary to* the main business 本業の補助の(副業として).

O *subsidiary* coins 補助貨幣.

subsidize, *v*. 補助金を与える.

M *heavily subsidize* the press 新聞に多大の補助金を与える.

P The French theatres are *subsidized by* government. フランスの劇場は政府から補助金をもらっている. 【類】*subsidized by* the national exchequer (国庫) / The steamship line is *subsidized by* the Government at $150,000 per annum to carry mail between … and … on fortnightly service.

subsidy, *n*. 保護金, 補助金.

V It has neither *asked* nor *received* any *subsidy* from national, state or city government. それは連邦・州・または市の当局に助成金を出願したこともなくまたこうした助成金を受けてもいない. ¶*give* a *subsidy* of … yen to … …に…円の保護金を下付する. ¶*grant* heavy shipping *subsidies* 多額の海運補助金を下付する.

Q² a *cash subsidy* 補助金. ¶Air services are not yet sound enough economically to operate without *government subsidies*. 航空事業は政府の補助なしに経営ができるまでにまだ経済的に十分基礎が固まっていない. 【類】the development of a growing merchant marine (海運界), aided by heavy *government subsidies* / *Government subsidies* with several strings attacled [to them] (ひも付きの). ¶a *state subsidy* 国家の助成金.

P *as subsidy* for … …の補助金として.

P² a *subsidy for* the Association その会への補助 ‖ a *subsidy for* expenses for … …費の補助金. ¶as *subsidy to* a steamship company 汽船会社への補助金として.

subsist, *v*. 生活する.

P *subsist by* the pen ペンで生活する. 【類】*subsist by* begging. ¶*subsist on* rice (grass, vegetables, bread) 米(など)を常食とする ‖ The monks *subsist on* the charity of the people. 僧職者は人々の施しで生活する. 【類】*subsist on* a mere pittance (薄給). ¶*subsist upon* (=*on*) scanty food 乏しい食物で生活する. 【類】*subsist upon* charity.

subsistence, *n*. 生活, 生計; 生計の資.

V They have *drawn* so large a part of their *subsistence* from the river. 彼らはその生計の資を大部分川から得ていた. ¶He *earned* a *subsistence* in Paris by acting as tutor. 彼は家庭教師をやってパリにおける生計の資とした. ¶*eke out* one's *subsistence* by … …して細々と暮しを立てる. ¶*gain* their *subsistence* by … …して暮しを立てる. 【類】He *gain subsistence* (=a living) by "the sweat of his pencil", as he quaintly expressed it. ¶Competition among the men is so keen that they find it difficult to *get* a bare *subsistence*. その人たちの間には競争が激しいので細々暮して行くのさえも困難であると分かった. ¶*give* a bare *subsistence* ようよう暮しを立てさせる. ¶*obtain subsistence* 生計の資を得る. ¶work and *win subsistence* for oneself 自活する.

Q His work brings him something more than a *bare subsistence*. 彼の仕事から得る収入はやっと暮す以上多少の余裕がある. ¶get a *scanty subsistence* 口を糊(のり)する.

Q² *Army subsistence* 陸軍の存在.

P the minimum necessity *for* [a] bare *subsistence* 最小限度の生活必需品. 【類】What does he do *for* a *subsistence* (=livelihood)? / labor *for subsistence*. ¶His means *of subsistence* are limited. 彼の暮しは豊かでない.【類】Selling papers is the only means ***of*** his *subsistence*.

P² *subsistence* ***on*** rice 米食での生活.

substance, *n.* 物質, 実質; 要点.

V ***drop*** the *substance* for the shadow 虚を取って実を廃する. ¶***have*** the *substance* 実質を持つ. ¶***sacrifice*** the *substance* for the shadow 虚を実の犠牲にする. ¶I can ***tell*** you the *substance*, but not the exact words of the speech. その演説の要点は話せるが言葉は一々覚えていない. ¶***waste*** one's *substance* in riotous living 酒色にふけって財産を浪費する.

Q an ***antiseptic*** *substance* 防腐剤. ¶***chemical*** *substances* 化学的物質. ¶a highly ***deliquescent*** *substance* 潮解性の強い物質(湿気を吸いやすい). ¶an ***explosive*** *substance* 爆発物. ¶a ***fragrant*** *substance* 芳香物質. ¶iodoform or other ***germicide*** *substances* ヨードホルムその他の殺菌剤. ¶The *substance* is ***good,*** but the style repellent. 内容は良いが文章はひどい. ‖ a man of ***good*** *substance* 資産家. ¶The pond is covered up with ***green*** *substances*. その池は緑の植物でおおわれている. ¶engrave on ***hard*** *substances* 堅い物に彫る. ¶the soul as an ***immortal*** *substance* 不滅である魂. ¶The *substance* is more ***important*** than the form. 実質は形体よりも大切だ. ¶a man of ***large*** *substance* 財産家. ¶a ***lustrous, satiny*** *substance* ぴかぴか光沢のある物質(真珠など). ¶a fabric of ***little*** *substance* 質の良くない織物 ‖ an argument of ***little*** *substance* 実のない議論. ¶a ***medical*** *substance* 薬物. ¶***mineral*** *substances* 鉱物. ¶There is ***no*** *substance* in him. あの男には中味がない.【類】there is ***no*** *substance* in the reports now current in ... about ... ¶a ***solid*** *substance* 固体. ¶***strong-smelling*** *substances* like musk じゃ香のようなにおいの高いもの. ¶a ***translucent*** *substance* 半透明の品. ¶an ***yielding*** *substance* 押せばへこむ物.

Q² the ***food*** *substances* natural to milk 乳製品.

P It is [the] same (unlike) ***in*** *substance*. 質が同じだ(違う).【類】I agree with you ***in*** *substance* (大体). / Her account was ***in*** *substance* correct. / This, ***in*** *substance*, represents the opinion of two experts (専門家). / I'm one with you ***in*** *substance*.

P² a *substance* ***like*** wool 羊毛に似た物. ¶a man ***of*** *substance* 資産家.

substantial, *a.* 本質的な, 実質的な, しっかりした.

M The building is *substantial* ***enough*** to last a hundred more years. その建物はしっかりしているから百年は優に保つ.

substantiate, *v.* 証明する.

P *substantiate* one's theory ***by*** experiments その理論を実験によって実証する.

substantiation, *n.* 証明.

V I cannot ***discover*** any *substantiation* of the oft-repeated assertion that ... 私は…というしばしば繰返された所説の実証を得られない. ¶***lack*** *substantiation* 具体性を欠く.

substitute, *n.* 代用物.

V ***concoct*** a very good *substitute* for butter バタの非常に良い代用品を製する. ¶***make*** a very awkward *substitute* by ... …ですこぶるまずい代用品を造る. ¶Can you ***secure*** a *substitute?* 代用品が手にはいりますか.

Q an ***anemic*** *substitute* for the real thing 本物に代る貧弱な代用物. ¶***effective*** *substitutes* りっぱな代用物. ¶the ***next best*** *substitute* for foreign travel 外国旅行に代る次善の代用物(映画など). ¶***no perfect*** *substitute* for ... …の不完全な代用物. ¶a ***poor*** *substitute* for ... …の貧弱な代用物. ¶a ***satisfactory*** *substitute* for ... …の満足すべき代用品(代人・補欠など). ¶a ***spurious*** *substitute* [試験などの]替玉. ¶a ***time-saving*** *substitute* for ... 時間の節約ができる…の代用物. ¶a ***tolerable*** *substitute* 我慢のできる代用物. ¶Notoriety is an ***unstable*** *substitute* for Fame. 悪評とは安定性のない名声の代名詞である.

Q² a ***meat*** *substitute* 食肉の代替用品. ¶a ***rice*** *substitute* 米の代用食品.

P it is used ***as*** a *substitute* for ... それは…に代用されている. ¶an easy *substitute* ***for*** study 勉強の楽な代用物 ‖ There is no real *substitute* ***for*** mother's milk. 本当に母乳に代るべきものはない.【類】There can be no *substitute* ***for*** experience.

substitute, *v.* 代らせる; 代える.

P *substitute* a person ***by*** (=with) another 甲の人を乙の人に代える. ¶*substitute* oneself ***for*** ... …の身代りに立つ ‖ *substitute* experiment and observation ***for*** speculative theories 実験と観察をもって空理空論に代える.【類】*substitute* electric ***for*** horse traction on a tramway line. ☞自動詞の substitute は米語用法; Can I ask you to *substitute* for me till I return?

substitution, *n.* 代り; 代用.

Q² ***land*** *substitution* 換地.

P ***in*** *substitution* for ... …の代りに.

P² a *substitution* ***of*** equal ***for*** unequal treaties 対等条約の差別条約への代換(差別条約を廃止して対等条約を作ること).【類】*substitution* ***of*** machinery ***for*** labor (=handwork). / the *substitution* ***of*** mechanical ***for*** manual processes (power).

subterfuge, *n.* 言いのがれ.

V ***employ*** *subterfuges* 言いぬけを用いる.

sub-title, *n.* 小見出し.

P² the *sub-title* ***of*** an essay 論文の小見出し.

subtlety, *n.* 綿密.

Q ***hair-splitting*** *subtlety* 毛を裂くような細かさ. ¶***scholastic*** *subtlety* 学者的綿密.

P² *subtleties* ***in*** the pronunciation of foreign languages 外国語発音の微妙な諸点.

subtract, *v.* 減じる.

P *subtract* 5 ***from*** 10 十から五を減らす ‖ That will *subtract* nothing ***from*** his merit. それによって彼の価値が低下することはない.

suburb, *n.* 市外地; [the -s] 広く郊外.

Q a ***fashionable*** *suburb* 上流人士の住む郊外. ¶Chofu is increasing popularity as a ***residential*** *suburb*. 調布は郊外住宅地として評判が段々好くなって来ている.

P ***from*** various *suburbs* 方々の近郊から. ¶***in*** a London *suburb* ロンドン市外に.【類】***in*** the *suburbs* of Tokyo.

O the town of Thornton, Illinois, a *suburb* south of Chicago シカゴの南部イリノイ州ソーントン市.

subvention, *n.* 補助金.

P² *subventions* ***for*** study abroad 海外留学の補助金.

subversive, *a.* 壊乱する.

P *subversive* ***of*** discipline (good order, happiness) 規律(など)をかき乱す ‖ changes *subversive* ***of*** the entire social and political life of the Japanese 日本の社会及び政治の全機構をくつがえすほどの大変革.

subway, *n.* 地下道; 《米》地下鉄.

V the new *subway* is now being ***laid*** under ... の地下道が目下新たに…の下に敷設中だ. ¶The *subway* was ***tied up*** for two hours. 地下鉄は二時間運転休止となった. ¶***tunnel*** a new *subway* 新規に地下道を掘る.

Q² a ***monorail*** *subway* 単軌道地下鉄. ¶a ***single-track*** *subway* 単線地下鉄.

P There was a tie-up of twenty minutes ***on*** the *subway*. 地下鉄に二十分間の運転休止(停電)があった.

succeed, *v.* **(1)** 成功する.

M He *succeeded* ***admirably*** in his business. 彼は見事商売に成功した. ¶*succeed* ***badly*** うまく行かない. ¶He *succeeded* ***brilliantly*** in his attempt. 彼の企ては見事成功した. ¶***eventually*** *succeed* 結局成功する. ¶***fully*** *succeed* in one's plans 十分その計画に成功する. ¶*succeed* ***magnificently*** すばらしく成功する. ¶***measurably*** *succeed* 相当に成功する. ¶*succeed* ***partially*** in realizing it その実現に多少成功した. ¶whatever else be said of it, it has ***really*** *succeeded* in ... ing 何といっても…の点でそれはたしかに成功した. ¶***signally*** *succeed* 大いに成功する. ¶The business has *succeeded* wonderfully ***well*** with him. 彼は素晴らしく商売に成功した.

P He ought to *succeed* ***after*** his labors. 彼は働いたのだから成功するはずだ. ¶*succeed* ***at*** one's profession 職業に成功する ‖ He *succeeded* ***at*** matriculating at the college. 彼は首尾よくその大学に入学した. ¶He *succeeded* ***by*** (=through) your help (=assistance). 彼は君のおかげで成功した. ¶He *succeeded* ***by dint*** (=***means***) ***of*** perseverance. 彼は辛抱一つで成功した. ¶*succeed* ***in*** life 出世する ‖ *succeed* ***in*** everything 何事にも成功する.【類】*succeed* ***in*** foreign language study / He *succeeded* ***in*** solving the problem. / *succeed* ***in*** limiting his expenditure to ... / He is fortunate in not belonging to those who, in seeking to be everything, *succeed* ***in*** being nothing. / *succeed* ***in*** entering the House of Commons (下院議員) / *succeed* ***in*** getting a job / I have *succeeded* ***in*** persuading him. ‖ I have not yet *succeeded* ***in*** selling. まだいい買手が見つからない. ¶Nothing *succeeds* ***like*** success. 人気が人気を呼ぶ.

¶He *succeeded* ***to*** admiration. 彼は見事に成功した. ¶The business has *succeeded* ***with*** him alone. 彼だけがその商売に成功した. ‖ Did that affair *succeed* ***with*** him? 彼はその件に成功したか. ‖ *succeed* ***with*** a scheme (=plan) 計画を首尾よく実行する.

(**2**) 継ぐ, 相続する.

P The Marquis *succeeded* Mr. Gladstone ***as*** Prime Minister. 侯爵が首相としてグラッドストーン氏の跡を継いだ. ‖ In 1850 Tennyson *succeeded* Wordsworth ***as*** poet laureate. 一八五〇年にテニスンは桂冠詩人としてワーズワースのあとを継いだ. ¶Night is *succeeded* ***by*** day. 夜があける. 【類】Sooner or later the ebb is bound to be *succeeded* ***by*** the flood. ¶Land was *succeeded* ***by*** James Christie the second. ジェームス・クリスティー二世が土地を相続した. ¶He *succeeded* his father, Sir Richard, ***in*** the title. 彼はその父リチャード卿の爵位を継いだ. ‖ *succeed* ***in*** the chair of Mr. … …氏の後がまにすわる(委員長になる). ¶He was *succeeded* ***in*** the business ***by*** his son John. 息子のジョンが彼の商売を相続した. ¶*succeed* a person ***to*** his position その後継者となる ‖ He has *succeeded* ***to*** his father's estate (all his wealth). 彼が父の相続をした(財産全部を相続した). ‖ *succeed* ***to*** the crown (=throne) 王位を継ぐ ‖ The young lord *succeeded* ***to*** the title. 若主人が襲爵した. 【類】*succeed* ***to*** a large property (多大の財産) / *succeed* one's father ***to*** his fortune / *succeed* ***to*** the fortune bequeathed to him by his father (遺産) / *succeed* ***to*** the family business / *succeed* ***to*** the baronetcy (准男爵の位) / *succeed* ***to*** the peerage (貴族の位) / He *succeeded* ***to*** the mayoralty (市長). / *succeed* ***to*** the speakership (議長の職) left vacant by the death of … / Iyemitsu *succeeded* ***to*** the shogunate in 1653.

success, *n.* 成功, 上首尾; 成功者.

V folk[s] (=people) who have ***achieved*** *success* in some walk of life 人生のある方面で成功した人々. ¶***approach*** *success* 成功に近づく. ¶***attain*** *success* 成功する. ¶***attribute*** one's *success* in life entirely to … 人生におけるその成功をすべて…に帰する. ¶I do not ***believe*** his *success*. 彼が成功するものと信じない. ¶He ***bought*** his *success* dearly. 彼は高価な犠牲を払って成功を手に入れた. ¶His strenuous work will ***carry*** *success* in its train. 彼は奮闘の成果として成功するであろう. ¶***celebrate*** a *success* 成功を祝する. ¶***command*** *success* 成功を博す. ¶You richly ***deserve*** *success*. 君は成功の資格十分だ. ¶***drink*** *success* to the enterprise その事業の成功を祈って乾杯する. ¶***earn*** *success* as a pitcher 投手として成功する. ¶He has ***enjoyed*** great *success* in America. 彼は米国でえらく成功した. ¶confidently ***expect*** *success* 確信して成功を期待する. ¶***extenuate*** one's *success* 人の成功をけなす. ¶***following up*** his *success* その成功に乗じて. ¶***gain*** *success* 成功する. ¶***get*** *success* 成功する. ¶The use of … may ***give*** *success* …を使用するとうまく行くかも知れない. ¶I do not ***grudge*** his *success*. 私は彼の成功をねたまない. ¶***guarantee*** its *success* その成功を保証する. ¶The usual treatment ***had*** no *success*. あり触れた療法では成功しなかった. ¶It may ***imperil*** the *success* of the enterprise. その事業はそのために成功を危くするかも知れない. ¶***insure*** (=***ensure***) *success* 成功を確実にする. ¶***jeopardize*** *success* 成功を危くする. ¶***make*** [a] *success* in life (=the world) 出世する. 【類】He has come to Hollywood with the fond dream to ***make*** a *success* in filmdom (映画界). ¶That ***means*** *success*. そうなりゃもうしめたもんだ. ¶***measure*** one's *success* by the size of one's safe 金をつくった高によって成功の程度を計る. 【類】if one ***measures*** *success* by the number rather than the quality of readers (読者の質). ¶be ***nearing*** *success* もう山が見えた. ¶***obtain*** *success* 成功する ‖ Thanks to his ability, he has ***obtained*** great *success*. 腕があったので彼は大成功をした. ¶it ***owed*** its *success* largely to … その成功は大いに…に負う所があった. ¶assist in ***promoting*** the *success* of … …の成功を助成する. ¶***reach*** considerable (one's highest) *success* 多大(など)の成功を収める. ¶***register*** *success* 成果を収める. ¶***score*** a great *success* 大成功を遂げる. ¶***secure*** *success* 成功を確保する. ¶all who are ***seeking*** *success* 成功を望む者はすべて. ¶Details often ***spell*** *success*. 細目が成功の因を成すことが往々ある. ¶***trace*** *success* to … 成功の原因を…までさかのぼる. ¶***win*** (=gain) *success* 成功を得る. 【類】***win*** the greatest possible *success* in life. ¶I heartily ***wish*** you (more) *success*. (ますます)御成功を祈る. 【類】I ***wish*** *success* to the enterprise. / I ***wish*** the College even greater *success* in the future than it has achieved in the past. / ***wishing*** you every *success* in your sphere (方面) of labor. ¶***wrest*** *success* out of failure 努力して失敗を転じて成功たらしめる.

V² *Success* ***attend*** you! 御成功を祈る. ‖ Complete *success* ***attended*** his efforts. 彼の努力はりっぱに報いられた. ¶now that *success* has ***come*** to him 彼はいよいよ成功したから. 【類】In commercial relations, *success* has always ***come*** to him who masters the language of the customer. ¶*Success* has ***crowned*** his efforts. 成功が彼の努力に報いた. ¶He believed that *success* would ***follow***. 彼はやがて成功すべきことを信じた. ¶Big *success* does not usually ***occur*** early. 大器晩成.

Q He met with ***amazing*** *success*. 彼は驚くべき成功をした. ¶a ***bad*** *success* 不結果. ¶No ***better*** *success* could be attained. これ以上の成功は得られないだろう. ¶[a] ***big*** (***small***) *success* 大(小)成功. ¶a ***brilliant*** *success* かくかくたる成功. ¶*Success* is now ***certain***. 今や成功疑いなし. ¶The invention has been a ***commercial*** *success*. その発明は商業上の成功であった. ‖ achieve ***complete*** *success* 申分ない成果を収める. ¶The play scored a ***considerable*** *success*. その劇は相当あたった. 【類】with ***considerable*** *success*. ¶As a politician he was not a ***conspicuous*** *success*. 政治家としては彼は抜群の成功者ではなかった. ¶With best wishes for your ***continued*** *success*, I am yours sincerely. 今後さらに躍進を続けられんことを祈ります敬具. ¶a ***decided*** *success* 確かな成功. ¶a ***difficult*** *success* むずかしい成功. ¶with somewhat ***diminishing*** *success* 後になるほど幾分成績が不良になって. ¶achieve a ***distinct*** *success* 明かに成功する. ¶a ***doubtful*** *success* おぼつかない成功. ¶an ***enduring*** *success* 長期にわたる成功. ¶His book proved an ***enormous*** *success*. 彼の著書は大々的成功であった. ¶I most heartily wish you ***every*** *success*. 万事上首尾に行くよう心から祈っています. ¶an ***exceptional*** *success* 異数の成功. ¶He achieved an ***extraordinary*** *success*. 彼は非常な成功をした. ¶a ***fair*** *success* 相当の成功. ¶The enterprise was never a ***financial*** *success*. その事業は財政的には成功ではなかった. ¶achieve ***full*** *success* 十分の成果を収める ‖ an enemy to one's ***fullest*** *success* その十二分の成功に対する障害. ¶a ***glittering*** *success* かくかくたる成功. ¶a ***good*** *success* 好結果. ¶prove a ***great*** *success* 大成功となる. 【類】The meeting was (=had) a ***great*** *success*. / the industry was carried on with ***great*** *success*. ¶a ***howling*** *success* 《俗》どえらい成功. ¶his ***ill*** *success* in … 彼の…における不成功. ¶an ***immense*** *success* 大成功. ¶but with ***indifferent*** *success* 然し(結果は)可もなく不可もなかった. ¶This is a story of ***initial*** *success* followed by almost absolute failure. これは竜頭だ尾の一例である. ¶The novel was an ***instant*** *success*. その小説はたちまち好評を博した. ¶He met with ***invariable*** *success*. 彼はいつも成功した. ¶one of the greatest ***literary*** *successes* in the world's history 世界史中文学上最大成功の一. ¶meet with ***little*** *success* 満足な成功が得られない. ¶a ***magnificent*** *success* すばらしい成功. ¶He scored ***many*** *successes* in popular songs. 彼は流行歌手として数多く成功した. ¶a ***marked*** *success* 著しい成功. ¶From that time their *success* has been ***meteoric*** (=***dazzling***). それからというものは彼の成功は目ざましいものであった. ¶***military*** *successes* 武功. ¶The new opera was produced on April 2 with ***much*** *success*. 新歌劇は四月二日上演されて大当りを取った. ¶his ***outstanding*** *success* in writing for the press 新聞寄稿家としての彼の顕著な成功. ¶an ***overwhelming*** *success* 圧倒的な大成功. ¶a ***parliamentary*** *success* [政治家など]議会における成功. ¶have ***partial*** (=***fractional***) *success* 幾分成功する. 【類】with only ***partial*** *success* / have but ***partial*** *success*. ¶***pecuniary*** *success* 金銭上の成功. ¶a ***permanent*** *success* 永久的の成功. ¶a ***petty*** *success* 徼々たる成功. ¶a ***political*** *success* 政治上の成功. ¶a ***poor*** *success* 思わしくない結果. ¶win so ***prodigious*** a *success* とてつもない成功を収める. ¶a ***pronounced*** *success* 著しい成功. ¶The experiment proved only a ***qualified*** *success*. その実験は幾分の成功を見たに過ぎなかった. ¶The book achieved a ***remarkable*** *success*. その本は著しく成功した. ¶a ***roaring financial*** *success* すばらしい財政上の成功. ¶I trust it will meet with the ***same*** *success*. きっとそれもまた成功します. ¶a ***signal*** *suc-*

cess 大成功. 【類】mark a ***signal*** *success* in an undertaking. ¶a ***similar*** *success* attended to ... ...は同様に成功した. ¶All attempts at ... have met with ***small*** *success*. ...の試みはどれもこれも大した成功は見られなかった. ‖ it was by no means a ***small*** *success* for ... それは...にとっては決して小さな成果ではなかった. ¶a ***social*** *success* 社交界での成功. ¶He achieved ***some*** *success*. 彼は幾らか成功した. ¶a ***stunning*** *success* 驚くべき一大成功. ¶a ***thorough*** *success* 十分の成功. ¶a ***thrilling*** *success* 痛快な成功. ¶It proved a ***tremendous*** *success*. それは大々的成果を収めることとなった. ¶a ***triumphant*** *success* 圧倒的成功. ¶depend for its ***ultimate*** *success* upon ... その結局の成功は...による. ¶an ***unexpected*** *success* 思いがけない成功. ¶an ***unparalleled*** *success* 比類ない成功. ¶an ***unprecedented*** *success* 無類の成功. ¶meet with an ***unqualified*** *success* 十二分に成功する. ¶a record of ***unquestioning*** *success* 絶対的成功の記録. ¶The enterprise was attended with ***varying*** *success*. その事業には幾多消長があった. ¶a ***vulgar*** *success* 俗悪な成功. ¶a ***well-earned*** *success* りっぱにかち得た成功. ¶a ***well-merited*** *success* 当然の成功. ¶***What*** *success* did you have in finding a new cook? コックはうまく見つかりましたか. ¶reach the very pinnacle of ***worldly*** *success* 現世的成功の絶頂に達する.

Q² last season's ***Broadway*** *successes* 前期のブロードウェイ好評の出しもの. ¶a ***box-office*** *success*〘映画〙興業的成功; 大入りの出しもの. ¶***business*** *success* 営業上の成功. ¶a ***chance*** popular *success* 場当り. ¶the Chinese ***Communist*** *success* in China 中国における中国共産党の成功. ¶***life*** *success* 人生の成功. ¶talk of one's ***love*** *successes* のろけをいう. ¶***school*** *success* 学業優秀. ¶a great ***stage*** (***screen***) *success* [俳優の]舞台(映画)での大成功. 【類】make a ***stage*** *success* in "...".

P I am rejoiced ***at*** your *success*. 御成功を祝します. ¶He has been spoiled ***by*** *success*. 彼は成功してかえって悪くなった. ‖ encouraged ***by*** *success* 成功に気をよくして. ¶He hopes ***for*** *success*. 彼は成功を望んでいる. ‖ I'm greatly indebted to you ***for*** my *success*. 私の成功は全くあなたのおかげです. ¶It will result ***in*** *success*. それは結局成功するだろう. ¶This does not look ***like*** *success*. これは成功しそうもない. ¶the secret ***of*** *success* 成功の秘けつ ‖ achieve (=obtain) a measure ***of*** *success* 一通りの成功をおさめる. 【類】with a high degree ***of*** *success* / The attempts made in this direction have been attended with a very scant measure ***of*** *success* (芳しくなかった). ‖ I am desirous ***of*** *success*. 私は成功を望んでいる. 【類】be hopeful ***of*** *success*. ¶pride oneself ***on*** one's *success* おのれの成功を誇る ‖ Please accept my congratulations ***on*** your *success*. 御成功を祝します. ¶a guide ***to*** *success* in life 処世術のしおり ‖ the key (way) ***to*** *success* 成功の秘けつ(など) / Hard and honest work is the surest way ***to*** *success*. ¶***with*** *success* (=successful) 首尾よく. 【類】He will meet ***with*** most *success*. / His efforts were crowned (飾られた) ***with*** *success*. / He is puffed up (慢心している) ***with*** *success*. / He tried several lines (色々の商売) of business ***with*** no great *success*. ¶I tried to persuade him, but ***without*** *success* (=in vain). 彼を説きつけようとしたがだめだった. 【類】I attempted, ***without*** *success*, to ...

P² a remarkable *success* ***against*** malaria. マラリア熱予防の注目すべき成功. ¶He is a *success* ***as*** a teacher. 彼は教師として成功者である. ¶It turned out to be a *success* ***in*** every way. 万事首尾よく行った. ‖ his *success* ***in*** business 彼の事業上の成功. ¶the *success* ***of*** the photoplay ***with*** the public その映画の受けのよさ. ¶I wish *success* ***to*** the gathering. その会の成功を祈る.

successful, *a.* 好結果の, 上首尾の.

M The play was ***astonishingly*** *successful*. その芝居は大当りだった. ¶***completely*** *successful* 全く上首尾の. ¶be ***conspicuously*** *successful* in ... ...で顕著な成功を収める. ¶The experiment was ***eminently*** *successful*. その実験は非常に好結果であった. ¶The meeting was ***highly*** *successful*. その会は非常に盛会だった. ¶he has been ***remarkably*** *successful* in ... 彼は...に著しく成功した. ¶***socially*** *successful* people 社交的に成功した人々. ¶The trip was ***very*** *successful*. その旅行は誠に好成績だった. ¶The trial trip was ***wonderfully*** *successful*. その(汽船などの)試運転は大成功だった.

P He was *successful* ***from*** his very first attempt. 彼は初めっから上首尾だった. ¶He was very *successful* ***in*** business. 彼は商売をうまく当てた. ‖ He was *successful* ***in*** gaining the object. 彼は首尾よく目的を達した. 【類】men and women who have been *successful* ***in*** their work. ¶He was notoriously *successful* ***with*** women. 彼は女をうまく扱うことでは有名だった. 「(など).

O a *successful* attempt [enterprise, mission, war). 上首尾

succession, *n.* 連続; 相続, 継承権.

V ***claim*** the *succession* 継承権を要求する. ¶***gain*** a *succession* of victories (defeats) 連戦連勝(連敗する). ¶attempt to ***secure*** the *succession* to the office その職に就任運動をする.

Q in ***close*** *succession* 続々と. ¶follow each other in almost ***endless*** *succession* ほとんどのべつに続く. ¶in ***frequent*** *succession* ひんぴんと. ¶a ***life-long*** *succession* of honey-moons 終生続く密月. ¶Entertainments followed one another in ***quick*** *succession*. 余興が続々上演された. 【類】Three horse-shows succeeded one another in ***quick*** *succession*. ‖ Misfortunes came in ***quick*** (=***rapid***) *succession*. 不幸が続いた. ¶in ***regular*** *succession* 順次に.

Q² in ***white-hot*** *succession* 矢つぎ早に.

P ***by*** *succession* 継承権で. ¶Many soldiers ***in*** *succession* fell in the attempt. その攻略戦で多数の兵士が続々倒れた. 【類】He has had etchings (食刻版画) accepted, two years ***in*** *succession* (引続いて), for the Royal Academy. / three great victories ***in*** *succession*. / He served the five emperors ***in*** *succession*. / for two or three days ***in*** *succession* / for a number of years ***in*** *succession* ‖ He was appointed ... ***in*** *succession* to ..., resigned. 彼は...退職の後を受けて...に任じられた. 【類】he has been elected ... ***in*** *succession* to ... ¶order ***of*** *succession* 相続順.

P² a *succession* ***of*** (=a series of) surprises in the way of ... ...という意外な事件の続発. 【類】a *succession* ***of*** misunderstandings. ¶*succession* ***to*** a person's property 財産相続 ‖ *succession* ***to*** rights or obligations 権利義務の継承 ‖ *succession* ***to*** the throne 王位継承.

successor, *n.* 相続者, 継承者.

V A temporary *successor* has been ***appointed***. 代理の任命があった. ¶His *successor* has already been ***chosen***. 彼の後継者はすでに定っている. ¶We have ***found*** a good *successor* in Mr. T. Tさんというよい後継者を見つけた. ¶He ***left*** no *successors*. 彼は相続人を残さずに死んだ. ¶***secure*** a *successor* to ... ...の継承者を得る.

Q ***legitimate*** *successors* 法的な後継者. ¶Mr. A is a ***likely*** *successor*. その後継者として A 氏の呼声が高い. ¶a ***lineal*** *successor* 直系相続人. ¶a ruined bridge and its ***modern*** *successor* こわれた橋とそのあとに新しく架けた橋. ¶a ***probable*** *successor* 継承者となりそうな人. ¶had a not ***unworthy*** *successor* in ... ...というはずかしからぬ後継者が得られた ‖ a ***worthy*** *successor* to ... ...に相応な相続人.

P² He is his father's *successor* ***in*** his estate (business). 彼は父の財産(など)の後継者だ. ¶the *successor* ***to*** the throne 王位継承者 ‖ a *successor* ***to*** an action 訴訟継承人 ‖ *successor* ***to*** the mantles of ..., ..., and ... ...及び...の後を継ぐ者. 【類】The American Journal of Eugenics (優生学), *successor* ***to*** Lucifer the Light-bearer (雑誌名).

succo[u]r, *n.* 援兵; 援助.

V ***lend*** a person some *succor* (=help) 人に手を貸してやる. ¶***seek*** *succor* 救いを求める. ¶*Succor* was ***sent*** (=***dispatched***). 援兵を派遣した.

succumb, *v.* 屈する, 負ける.

M ***readily*** *succumb* to temptation すぐ誘惑にかかる.

P *succumb* ***before*** (=to) temptation 誘惑に陥る. ¶*succumb* ***to*** her charms (=fascinations) 彼女の色香に迷う ‖ *succumb* ***to*** grief 憂いに沈む ‖ *succumb* ***to*** disease (nervous prostration) 病(など)で倒れる. 【類】A few days later he *succumbed* ***to*** his injuries (負傷のため落命した). ‖ *succumb* ***to*** one's enemies 敵に降服する. 【類】*succumb* ***to*** irresistible force (不可抗力) / *succumb* ***to*** an attack of typhoid fever / He has trained himself to *succumb* ***to*** no obstacles (障害物) whatever / *succumb* ***to*** the attraction of ... ¶*succumb* ***under*** calamities 不幸に屈する.

such, *n.* かかる人または物.

Q So perish ***all such***! こういうやつは皆死んでしまえ!

P I am a gentleman, and will be treated ***as such***. 僕は紳

士だから紳士として取扱ってもらいたい. 【類】The leader, ***as such***, is entitled to respect.

O *such* being the case そういう訳であるから. ¶*Such* is the case with me. 私はそういう訳なのだ. ¶modern contrivances, *such* as the cinema, the radio and the television 映画・ラジオ・テレビといった近代施設. ¶*Such* as (＝Those who) have plenty of money will not want for friends. 富める者に友人の不自由はない.

suck, *n*. 乳を飲むこと; 吸うこと.

V ***give suck*** to ... ...に乳を飲ませる. ¶***have*** a ***suck*** of liquor 酒を一口やる. ¶***take*** a ***suck*** at ... ...を一吸い吸う.

suck, *v*. 吸う; 吸込む.

M *suck* an orange ***dry*** みかんを水気のなくなるまで吸う. ¶***suck out*** blood 血を吸い取る.

M² *suck* ***down*** a boat [渦巻など]舟を巻込む. ¶The whirlpool *sucked* ***down*** the boat 渦巻はそのボートをのみ込んだ. ¶Sponge *sucks* ***in*** water. 海綿は水を吸込む. ‖ *suck* ***in*** a boat 舟を吸込む. ¶Sponges *suck* ***up*** water 海綿は水を吸う. ‖ *suck* ***up*** all the juice from the poor 貧乏人の血を絞り尽す.

P *suck* ***at*** a cigar 葉巻を吸う. ¶Plants *suck* moisture ***from*** the ground. 植物は地から水を吸う. ¶Plants *suck* ***from*** the soil. 植物は土から養分を取る. ¶*suck* it ***into*** its maelstrom その大渦巻の中へそれを吸込む. 【類】The boats are being rapidly *sucked* ***into*** the same vortex (渦巻). ¶He *sucked* icecream-soda ***through*** a straw. 彼はストローでアイスクリームソーダを吸った.

sucker, *n*. 吸血鬼; 《俗》かも.

Q Here's a ***good*** *sucker* coming. Let's try it on him. いいかもがきた, やつに一つ試して見よう.

Q² a ***blood*** *sucker* 吸血動物(ひるなど); [比ゆ的]吸血鬼.

suckle, *v*. ほ乳する.

P *suckled* ***by*** a woman (cow) 女(など)にほ乳されて.

suction, *n*. 吸入.

P draw grape juice through a straw ***by*** *suction* グレープ・ジュースをストローで飲む.

sudden, *n*. 不意, 突然.

P [all] ***of*** a *sudden* 不意に, 突然. ¶***on*** a (＝the) *sudden* 突然. 【類】The fire broke out ***on*** a *sudden*.

sudden, *a*. 突然の, 急の.

M His death was ***awfully*** *sudden*. 彼の死は恐ろしく急だった. ¶But it was all ***so*** *sudden*. でもそれはあまりにも出し抜けだった.

suddenness, *n*. 不意, 突然.

Q it occurred with such ***alarming*** *suddenness* that ... それはいかにも急に起ったので... ¶with ***surprising*** *suddenness* いかにも突然. ¶Death came with ***tragic*** *suddenness*. 恐ろしく急な死に方をした.

P ***with*** great *suddenness* 突如.

sue, *v*. こう; [人を]訴える.

M *sue out* a pardon for an offender 犯行者をもらい下げる.

P *sue* ***at*** a court 訴訟を起す. ¶*sue* ***for*** peace (mercy) 和(など)を請う ‖ *sue* him ***for*** damages 彼を相手取って損害賠償の訴を起す. 【類】*Sue* ***for*** the damage if it cannot be obtained without (そうしないで). / I *sued* him ***for*** a debt. / *sue* a person ***for*** a divorce on grounds of (の理由で)...

suffer, *v*. 悩む; 損害を受ける.

M The country was *suffering* ***acutely*** from the reactions of the war. その国は大いに戦後の反動(影響)に悩んでいた. ¶I am still *suffering* ***a great deal***. 私はまだ大いに悩んでいる. ‖ The boy *suffered* ***much*** from rough *schoolmates*. その少年はクラスのいじめっ児にひどい目に会わされた. ☞ 口語の肯定文では much の代りに a lot, a great deal, greatly などを使う傾向がある. ¶Japan is *suffering* ***greatly*** from over-population. 日本は人口過剰で大いに悩んでいる. ¶The pioneers have not *suffered* ***in vain***. 開拓者が苦しんだかいがあった. ¶He knew how to *suffer* ***joyfully***. 彼は苦痛に甘んじることができる. ¶He *suffered* ***much*** for his faith. 彼はその信仰のために非常な受難をした. ¶*suffer* ***nothing*** by comparison それと比較して少しも見おとりがない. ¶*suffer* ***poignantly*** from the thought that ... ...と考えてひどく頭を悩ます. ¶*suffer* ***profoundly*** 大いに悩む. ¶The engine *suffered* ***severely***. その機関がひどく損害を受けた.

P it will not *suffer* ***by*** comparison with ... それは...と比較して見おとりがないだろう ‖ those who *sufferd* ***by*** wartime disasters 戦時り災者 ‖ do not *suffer* ***by*** comparison 見劣りがしない. 【類】The magazine has not *sufferd* ***by*** a change of editorship. ¶He *suffered* ***for*** his wisdom. 彼はその才があだとなった. ‖ *suffer* ***for*** one's country 邦家のために受難する ‖ He *suffered* death ***for*** his crime. 彼はその犯罪によって死刑に処せられた. ‖ The inhabitants are *suffering* ***for*** provisions. 住民は食糧がないので悩んでいる. ¶*suffer* ***from*** an incurable disease (a serious complaint, a nervous breakdown, ill health) 不治の病(など)にかかる. 【類】*suffer* ***from*** complications of the stomach (胃病) / He is *suffering* ***from*** some long trouble (持病). ‖ persons *suffering* ***from*** accident or sudden illness in the streets or public places 街路または公開の席で事故を起しまたは突然発病した人々. 【類】those who *suffer* ***from*** physical defects / *suffer* ***from*** two weaknesses / *suffer* ***from*** lack of water / *suffer* ***from*** poverty (貧) / people who do not *suffer* ***from*** stage fright (舞台度胸のないこと) / *suffer* ***from*** the fickleness of fame (名声の変りやすいこと) / *suffer* ***from*** a severe crisis / *suffer* ***from*** "emotional disturbance" / He *suffers* greatly ***from*** the heat. / *suffer* ***from*** cold, hunger, and insufficient clothing / *suffer* ***from*** the delusion (迷い) that ... / *suffer* ***from*** inconvenience / *suffer* ***from*** a lack of oxygen / *suffer* ***from*** the shortage of housing / *suffer* ***from*** lack of nourishment / Your reputation will *suffer* ***from*** such conduct. / The health *suffers* ***from*** overwork. / Trade is *suffering* ***from*** the war. / Schoolboys' eyes have *suffered* much ***from*** the bad type and paper of those books. ¶He *suffered* ***in*** his reputation＝His reputation suffered. 彼は名誉を傷つけた. 【類】*suffer* ***in*** a storm. ¶I have *suffered* much loss ***through*** him. 私は彼のために大損害を受けた. ¶the company *suffered* ***to*** the extent of $... その会社は...ドルほど損をした. ¶He *suffered* ***under*** the dentist. 彼は歯科医の治療を受けた. ‖ *suffer* ***under*** disadvantags 不利に立つ. ¶a person *suffering* ***with*** consumption＝comsumptive 肺病患者. 【類】children *suffering* ***with*** a desease (the measles, skin eruptions, aching tooth, chilbrains) ‖ *suffer* ***with*** anxiety (agony) 心配する(苦悩する).

O *suffer* (＝undergo) losses (death, defeats, reverses, etc) 損害(など)をこうむる ‖ He couldn't *suffer* (＝bear) criticism. 批判にはがまんができなかった.

sufferance, *n*. 黙許, 黙諾.

P be ***beyond*** *sufferance* 我慢ができない. ¶admitted ***on*** *sufferance* 大目に見られて ‖ He is here only ***on*** *sufferance*. 彼はお情けでここにいるのだ. 【類】They are employed (在職している) only ***on*** *sufferance*. ¶***through*** *sufferance* 黙許されて.

sufferer, *n*. り災者, 遭難者.

V heal a *sufferer* ***of*** his infirmity 患者の病気を直す. ¶***relieve*** the *sufferers* り災者を救う.

Q ***chronic*** *sufferers* えらい迷惑をこうむった人. ¶the ***chief*** *sufferer* from a crime 犯罪の主な被害者. ¶***chronic*** *sufferers* from ... ...が持病の人々. ¶the ***heaviest*** *sufferers* 一番ひどいり災者.

Q² ***air-raid*** *sufferers* 空襲災害者たち. ¶in that he was a ***fellow*** *sufferer* with ... その点では彼も...と同様被害者の一人だった. ¶***hunger*** *sufferers* 飢餓に苦しむ人々. ¶a ***syphilis*** *sufferer* 梅毒患者. ¶***war[-damage]*** *sufferers* 戦争被害者たち.

P render assistance ***to*** the *sufferers* り災者を救う.

P² express sympathy with the *sufferers* ***by*** the Chicago fire シカゴ大火のり災者に同情を表する. 【類】in aid of the *sufferers* ***by*** the floods / I hope you are not a *sufferer* ***by*** the dreadful floods. ¶*sufferers* ***from*** the earthquake その地震のり災者 ‖ The *sufferer* ***from*** a weak stomach (mental troubles). 胃弱(など)に悩む人. 【類】a *sufferers* ***from*** mental weakness (頭の悪い人). ¶*suffererers* ***in*** the war 戦争の被害者. ¶for the relief of the *sufferers* ***through*** the great fire at Chicago シカゴの大火り災者救済のために. ¶a chronic *sufferer* ***with*** nervous breakdown 神経衰弱の慢性患者.

suffering, *n*. 苦痛, 損害を受けること.

V ***alleviate*** human *sufferings* 人類の苦痛を軽減する. 【類】***alleviate*** the *sufferings* of ... ¶He has ***borne*** intense *suffering* for many years. 彼は多年激しい困苦にたえた. ¶***ease*** *suffering* 苦痛を和らげる. ¶***palliate*** (＝ease) the agonizing *sufferings* 苦悩を軽減する. ¶***prolong*** *suffering*

苦痛を長引かせる. ¶***recite*** his own *sufferings* at full length 彼自身の苦しみを長々と物語る. ¶***relieve*** the terrible *sufferings* of ... ...の痛ましい苦悩を救う. ¶***undergo*** much *sufferings* 多大の苦しみを受ける.

Q a ***life-long*** *suffering* 終生の苦悩. ¶***mental*** *sufferings* 精神的苦悩. ¶The greatest of all sufferings is ***moral*** *suffering*. 苦悩の最大なるものは道徳上の苦悩である. ¶***physical*** *sufferings* 肉体的苦痛. ¶***postwar*** *suffering* 戦後の苦難. ¶***resigned*** *suffering* 苦悩に対するあきらめ. ¶a ***vicarious*** *suffering* 身代りの受難.

P ***amidst*** *sufferings* 苦しみ最中に. ¶He is patient ***under*** his *sufferings*. 彼は苦悩を辛抱している. ¶***without*** *suffering* 苦しまずに.

P² after intense *sufferings* ***from*** thirst ひどく渇に苦しんだ後で. ¶the *sufferings* ***of*** the poor 貧民の苦しみ.

suffice, *v.* 足る, 間に合う.

P The rules will *suffice* ***for*** all ordinary needs. その規則で普通の場合はことごとく間に合う. ‖ The ship's provisions will *suffice* ***for*** the crew. 船の糧食は乗組員には十分だ. 【類】The stock in hand (持合わせ品) will only *suffice* ***for*** fifty or sixty days.

Q a little attention will *suffice* to show that ... 少し注意すれば...が分かる. ¶*suffice* it to say that ... ...と言えば足りる. 【類】*Suffice* it to say that he left his family in poverty.

sufficient, *a.* 十分な, 足る.

M ***amply*** *sufficient* to ... ...するに十分な. ¶***Not*** *Sufficient* 〖銀行〗支払不可(小切手など).

P The pension is not *sufficient* ***for*** living expenses. その年金は生活費に足りない. ‖ *sufficient* ***for*** one's needs (requirements, purpose) その入用(など)に十分な. ¶be *sufficient* ***unto*** the need of the hour 目下の必要を満たすに足りる.

O this is *sufficient* to show that ... これは...を示すに十分だ.

suffix, *v.* 語尾に添加する.

P *suffix* a syllable ***to*** a word 語尾に一音節を添える.

suffocate, *v.* 窒息させる.

P He was *suffocated* ***by*** (=***with***) grief (heavy smoke). 彼は悲嘆(など)にむせんだ. 【類】*suffocated* ***by*** the poisonous fumes (毒気). ¶He was *suffocated* ***in*** water. 彼はでき死した.

suffocation, *n.* 窒息, 息詰まり.

Q² an ***infant*** *suffocation* 幼児圧死.

P die ***by*** (=***from***) *suffocation* 窒息死する ‖ murder a person ***by*** *suffocation* 窒息させて人を殺す. ¶The place was crowded ***to*** *suffocation*. そこは息詰まるほどの人込みであった.

suffrage, *n.* 投票; 賛成; 選挙権.

V ***beg*** his *suffrage* 彼の賛成をこう. ¶***gain*** his *suffrage* 彼の賛成を得る. ¶***give*** one's *suffrage* to ... ...に投票する. 【類】The electors ***gave*** their *suffrages* for free trade (自由貿易賛成の). ¶My plan ***had*** his *suffrage*. 彼は私の案に賛成した. ‖ Women ***have*** the *suffrage*. 婦人は選挙権を有する.

Q ***political*** *suffrage* 参政権. ¶***popular*** *suffrage* 普通選挙権. ¶a government founded on ***universal*** *suffrage* 普通選挙に基礎をおいた政府.

Q² universal equal ***adult*** *suffrage* 成年男女普通選挙権. ¶***household*** *suffrage* 戸主選挙権. ¶***manhood*** *suffrage* 成年男子選挙権. 【類】***universal manhood*** *suffrage*. ¶We believe in ***woman*** (=female) *suffrage* われわれは婦人参政権をよいことと思う.

P He has been elected ***by*** general *suffrage*. 彼は総選挙で当選した.

suffuse, *v.* みなぎらす, 一面に漂わす.

P The scenery is *suffused* ***with*** moonlight. 風景は一面に月光を浴びている. ‖ a face *suffused* ***with*** blushes (a deep flush) さっと赤くなった顔(など). 【類】Her cheeks were *suffused* ***with*** blushes (もみじ). / The sky is *suffused* ***with*** purple. / The sky was *suffused* ***with*** afterglow color (夕焼). / Her eyes were *suffused* ***with*** tears (涙で一杯).

sugar, *n.* 砂糖.

V ***extract*** *sugar* from canes 砂糖きびから糖分を抽出する. ¶***put*** *sugar* into the tea 茶に砂糖を入れる. ¶***refine*** *sugar* 砂糖を精製する. ¶Will you ***take*** any *sugar* with your coffee? コーヒーに砂糖を入れてお上がりになりますか.

Q ***granulated*** *sugar* ざらめ糖. ¶***raw*** *sugar* 粗糖. ¶***refined*** *sugar* 精糖.

Q² ***beet*** *sugar* ビート糖. ¶Dextrose helps to overcome fatigue when ***body*** *sugar* is low. ぶどう糖は糖分が欠乏したとき疲労回復に役立つ. ¶***cane*** *sugar* 蔗(しょ)糖. ¶***castor*** *sugar* 粉砂糖. ¶***crystal*** *sugar* 氷砂糖. ¶***cube*** (=***cut***) *sugar* 角砂糖. ¶***grape*** *sugar* ぶどう糖. ¶***icing*** *sugar* 《英》粉砂糖(製菓用の). ¶***loaf*** *sugar* 棒砂糖. ☞一個は a loaf of sugar. ¶***maple*** *sugar* かえで糖. ¶***lump*** *sugar* 角砂糖. ☞一個は a lump of sugar. ¶***milk*** *sugar* 乳糖.

P fruits ***in*** *sugar* 砂糖づけの果物 ‖ preserved ***in*** (=***with***) *sugar* 砂糖づけにした. ¶coat ***with*** *sugar* 砂糖を掛ける ‖ sweeten ***with*** *sugar* 砂糖で甘くする ‖ have tea ***with*** or ***without*** *sugar* 砂糖を入れてまたは入れないで紅茶を飲む.

suggest, *v.* 暗示する; 言い出す.

M This is a thought that has ***frequently*** *suggested* itself to us. これはしばしばわれわれの胸に浮んだ考えだ. ¶it has been ***ingeniously*** *suggested* that ... ...という妙案が出された. ¶***insidiously*** *suggest* ひそかに暗示する. ¶The question ***naturally*** *suggested* itself. その問題が自然胸に浮んだ. ¶The idea was ***probably*** *suggested* by ... それはおそらく...からの着想だったろう. ¶The thing ***readily*** *suggests* itself. そのことはすぐ胸に浮ぶ. 【類】Those instances will ***readily*** *suggest* that ... ¶it has been ***tentatively*** *suggested* that ... 仮に...という説が立てられた. ¶it has been rather ***unkindly*** *suggested* that ... ...というような ちょっと同情のない説を立てるものもあった. ¶***vaguely*** *suggest* それとなくいう.

P The following points are *suggested* ***for*** consideration. 次の諸点を参考に供する. ¶I *suggested* a way ***out of*** the difficulty. 私は困難を脱すべき方法を持出した. ¶I *suggested* ***to*** him that he should adopt a different policy. 私は彼に別な方法を採ったらよかろうと言った. ‖ The idea *suggested* itself ***to*** his mind. その考えがおのずと彼の胸に浮んだ. 【類】The incident *suggested* these thoughts ***to*** the writer. / it was *suggested* ***to*** me that I might ...

O I *suggested* that we [might] go home. = I said, "Let us go home." 私はみんな帰ろうじゃないかと言った. ¶His pale face *suggests* [that he is in] bad health. 彼の青白い顔を見ると身体が悪いことが分かる.

suggestion, *n.* 暗示, 示唆; 思付, 提案.

V ***accept*** a *suggestion* put forward by ... ...の提議に同意する. ¶The *suggestion* was ***acted*** upon. その注意の通り実行した. ¶***adopt*** the *suggestion* made by ... ...の提議を採用する. ¶***advance*** the *suggestion* that ... ...という考案を提出する ‖ *suggestions* ***advanced*** as to the origin of ... ...の起源に関して立てられた説. ¶***carry*** a *suggestion* of ... ...を想起させる. ¶***convey*** a slight *suggestion* of vulgarity 少しく野卑な感じを与える. ¶***derive*** valuable *suggestions* from ... ...から貴重な暗示を得る. ¶***follow*** his *suggestions* 彼の注意に従う. ¶***follow out*** *suggestions* 注意通りにやる. ¶***gather*** *suggestions* 暗示を得る. ¶The expression ***has*** the *suggestions* of the streets and the kitchen. その言葉には下町や台所のにおいがある. ‖ I ***have*** some *suggestions* to submit. 二三御参考に申上げたい. ¶a *suggestion* is ***hazarded*** which ... ...という案が提出された. ¶***lend*** an unexpected *suggestion* of poetry to a prosaic scene 平凡な光景に思い掛けない詩趣を添える. ¶***make*** some pertinent *suggestions* regarding (=as to) ... ...に関してある適切な提議をする. ¶he ***offered*** us many *suggestions* as to ... 彼は...に関して色々参考になることを提議した. ¶I have ***put*** my *suggestions* in pencil so that they may be rubbed out if you do not approve of them. 君が不賛成なら消せるように私の思付きを鉛筆で記した. ¶The management will be pleased to ***receive*** any *suggestions* from customers which are likely to add to the comfort of the house. 当館経営につき改善の点御気付きの方はお申出を願います. ‖ helpful *suggestions* ***received*** from many quarters 諸方面から受けた有益な示唆. ¶***take*** the *suggestion* into consideration その提案を考慮する. ¶***throw away*** (=***turn down*** or ***toss off***) a *suggestion* 提案をしりぞける ¶***treat*** a *suggestion* with mere disdain 提案をてんで問題にしない. ¶if I may ***venture*** the *suggestion* 失礼ながら一言申上げますが. ¶***volunteer*** *suggestions* on a subject presented to one's consideration 提出された問題に関して進んで一言する.

V² The *suggestion* ***fell*** upon deaf ears. この注意は顧みられなかった(馬の耳にねんぶつ).

Q the ***bare*** *suggestion* that ... ...と言っただけで. ¶***copious*** and ***valuable*** *suggestions* 色々貴重な思いつき. ¶a ***dubious*** *suggestions* 余り感心できない意見 ¶a ***feeble*** sugges-

tion 力のない発議. ¶offer a *few suggestions* 二三気の付いたことを言う. ¶***foolish*** and ***puerile*** *suggestions* ばかげたたわいもない提議. ¶a ***happy*** *suggestion* よい思いつき. ¶***helpful*** and constructive *suggestions* 役に立つ建設的な案. ¶an ***idiotic*** *suggestion* ばかげた案. ¶***ingenious*** *suggestion* 巧妙な考え. ¶***invaluable*** *suggestions* 非常に貴重な思いつき. ¶his ***judicious*** *suggestions* 彼の賢明な注意事項. ¶The title gives ***little*** *suggestion* of the interest and value of the contents. 表題では内容の興味や価値がよく分からない. ¶This is a ***mere*** *suggestion* これは一つの案に過ぎい. ¶one's ***own*** *suggestion* 自分の案. ¶His *suggestion* is ***out of place.*** 彼の提議は現実に即しない. ¶a ***pertinent*** *suggestions* 適切な思いつき. ¶a ***powerful*** *suggestion* 有力な提案. ¶a ***ridiculous*** *suggestion* ばからしい思いつき. ¶***vague*** *suggestions* ばく然とした注意. ¶receive ***valuable*** *suggestions* 貴重な参考意見を聞かせてもらう.【類】derive ***valuable*** *suggestions* from ... ¶***valuable*** and ***workable*** *suggestions* 貴重でしかも役に立つ暗示. ¶***wise*** *suggestions* 賢明な助言.

Q² ***shopping*** *suggestions* お買物心得.

P He did it ***at*** my *suggestion*. 彼は私に言われてそれをやった. ¶***By*** his *suggestion* the contribution was raised. 彼の発議で寄付が募集された. ¶only ***by way of*** *suggestion* 単に参考までに. ¶quick ***in*** *suggestion* 着想の早い. ¶The article is full ***of*** *suggestions*. その論文は示唆に富んでいる. ¶act ***on*** one's *suggestion* その発議に基いてやる ‖ ***on*** the *suggestion* of ... …の発議で. ¶unripe persimmons ***with*** a *suggestion* of pucker 渋そうなまだ熟していないかき ‖ blue ***with*** a *suggestion* of yellow ちょっと黄味がかった青 ‖ It was buried in the earth to stain it ***with*** the *suggestion* of antiquity. それは古物に見せようとして土中に埋めてあった.

P² I was going to make a *suggestion* ***about*** it. 私はそれについて一言申上げる積りでした. ¶*suggestion* ***as to*** ... …の案. ¶*suggestions* ***for*** ... …に対する注意. ¶there is a *suggestion* ***of*** ... …に似通った所がある. ¶*suggestion* ***on*** how to ... …の方法に関する指針. ¶Crooking the elbow and raising the forearm is a potent *suggestion* ***to*** an initiated individual to have a drink. ひじを曲げて前腕をあげるのはその道の人には一杯やろうというりっぱな合図だ.

suggestive, *a.* 思い出させる; 暗示に富む.

M The book is *suggestive* ***rather*** than exhaustive. その本は余蘊(ようん)なしというよりむしろ暗示に富んだ方だ. ¶The poem is ***very*** *suggestive*. その詩は暗示に富んでいる.

P His face is *suggestive* ***of*** a monkey. 彼の顔はさるを思い出させる. ‖ be *suggestive* ***of*** refined taste 奥ゆかしい ‖ a picture *suggestive* ***of*** something lewd わいせつがかった絵.【類】The scene is more *suggestive* ***of*** Dante's "Inferno" than of Milton's "Paradise."

suggestiveness, *n.* 暗示性.

Q ***verbal*** *suggestiveness* 言葉づかいの暗示性.

suicide, *n.* 自殺; 自殺者.

V He ***attempted*** *suicide* in despair. 彼は自暴自棄になり自殺しようとした. ¶He ***committed*** *suicide* in the approved Japanese fashion by disembowelling himself. 彼は日本流にりっぱに切腹した. ‖ ***commit*** *suicide* following the death of ... …のあとを追って自殺する.【類】He failed in his attempt to ***commit*** *suicide*. / ***commit*** *suicide* by gas (hanging oneself) ‖ ***commit*** *suicide* by disembowelling (drowning) 切腹(など)する ‖ ***commit*** *suicide* to escape the perplexities to which we are all subjected 浮世のわずらわしさをのがれるために自殺する. ¶***contemplate*** *suicide* 自殺をはかる. ¶Jealousy ***courts*** *suicides*. しっとが自殺の因になる. ¶***pull*** a would-be *suicide* out of a river 自殺しようとする人を川から引上げる.

Q an ***attempted*** *suicide* 自殺未遂. ¶an ***attempted*** (***forced***) ***double*** *suicide* 心中未遂(無理心中). ¶a ***camouflaged*** *suicide* 自殺と見せかけた他殺. ¶prove ***economic*** *suicide* 経済的自殺となる. ¶commit ***financial*** *suicide*＝become bankrupt 破産する. ¶a ***hideous*** *suicide* 悲惨な自殺. ¶***intellectual*** *suicide* 自家撞(どう)着. ¶***joint*** *suicide* with a woman 心中. ¶a ***moral*** *suicide* 道義的自殺. ¶a ***patriotic*** *suicide* 憂国的自殺. ¶a ***political*** *suicide* 政治的自殺. ¶a ***spiritual*** *suicide* 精神的自殺.

Q² attempt a ***family*** *suicide* 一家心中を企てる. ¶the phrase '***race*** *suicide*' was coined by Dr. Ross, the famous professor of sociology in America. 民族の自殺という句はアメリカの社会学者ロス博士が初めて用いたものである.

P No cause ***for*** a *suicide* could be imagined. 自殺をする原因がどうも分からない. ¶a *suicide* ***for*** love 心中. ¶Despair drove him ***to*** *suicide*. 失望のあまり彼は自殺した. ¶a marked decrease in *suicides* ***from*** poison 毒薬自殺の著しい減少.

suit, *n.* (**1**) [洋服]一そろい, 一着; [カルタの]組札.

V ***follow*** *suit* after ... …にならう.【類】The Denver Public Library opened a circulating library for children, and by 1896 ten others had ***followed*** *suit*. ¶***make*** a *suit* of clothes to order 注文で服を一着仕立てる. ¶***put on*** a clean *suit* 汚れていない服と着替える. ¶***wear*** dress *suits* 夜会服を着る.

Q a ***civil*** *suit* 背広. ¶a man dressed in a ***dark*** *suit* of clothes 黒ずんだ服装をした人. ¶varieties of ***men's*** *suits* 紳士服各種. ¶a ***sporty*** *suit* スポーティな服.

Q² a ***bathing*** *suit* 海水着. ¶wear a ***business*** *suit* 背広を着る.【類】clad in an ordinary ***business*** *suit*. ¶wear ***cowboy*** *suits* カウボーイ姿をする. ¶a ***dining-room*** *suit* 晩さん用の礼服. ¶a ***dinner*** *suit* 正さん服(普通タキシードのことをいう). ¶a ***ditto*** *suit*＝a suit of dittoes 合服. ¶hire a ***dress*** *suit* 式服を賃借りする. ¶an ***every-day*** *suit* ふだん着. ¶a ***fall*** *suit* 秋向きのスーツ. ¶in a ***flying*** *suit* 飛行服で. ¶the usual ***gymnasium*** *suit* 普通の体操服. ¶a ***jacket*** *suit* of tweed dittoes《英》スコッチの上下そろいのジャケツ. ¶a ***lounge*** *suit* 背広. ¶girls in white ***middy*** *suits* with pink ties 白のセーラー服にピンクのネクタイ姿の少女. ¶a ***new-look*** *suit* for the season 季節向きの新型スーツ. ¶a pre-school boy in a ***play*** *suit* いたずら着を着た学齢前の男の子. ¶***ready-to-wear*** *suits* でき合いの服. ¶a gray ***sack*** *suit* ねずみの背広. ¶in a ***sailor*** *suit* セーラー服で. ¶a double-breasted ***sharkskin*** *suit* シャークスキン地のダブルの背広. ¶a ***sports*** *suit* 運動服. ¶a ***summer*** *suit* 夏服. ¶a ***sunday*** *suit* 晴衣. ¶a one-strap ***swim*** *suit* 肩掛けが一つの海水着. ¶a ***two-pants*** *suit* ずぼんのスペヤのついた服一着. ¶a ***two*** (***three***)***-piece*** *suit* 上下(三つぞろい).【類】a ***two-piece tweed*** *suit*. ¶a ***union*** *suit*《米》シャツのコンビネーション(シャツとずぼんが続いているもの). ¶a ***work*** *suit* 作業服.

P ***in*** a business *suit* 事務服で. ¶*suits* ***for*** misses and juniors お嬢様向きスーツ.

P² a *suit* ***of*** clothes 一着の服.【類】a *suit* ***of*** gray clothes ‖ a *suit* ***of*** armor 一領のよろい. ¶a *suit* ***with*** extra (＝spare) pants スペヤのずぼん付きの服 ‖ a *suit* ***of*** spades (hearts clubs, diamonds) [トランプ]スペード(など)の一組.

O a *suit* ready to wear 出来合服 ‖ a *suit* made of order 注文服.

(**2**) 嘆願, 懇願; 求婚; 訴訟.

V He ***began*** a *suit* in a local court. 彼は地方裁判所に提訴した. ¶***bring*** (＝***institute***) a *suit* against a firm 会社を相手取って訴訟を起す. ¶***commence*** (＝***start***) a *suit* to collect damages for ... …に対する損害賠償の訴訟を提起する. ¶***conduct*** a *suit* (＝case) 訴訟を起す. ¶***contest*** a *suit* 応訴する. ¶***defend*** a *suit* 訴訟の弁護をする. ¶***enter*** *suit* in a court 裁判を起す. ¶***file*** a *suit* against ... …を相手取って訴訟を起す.【類】***file*** *suit* in a court against ... / the *suit* was ***filed*** with the court (裁判所) by ... / ***file*** *suit* for divorce. ¶I ***have*** a *suit* to the director. 私はその理事に願いの筋がある. ¶***lose*** a damage *suit* 損害賠償の訴訟に敗訴する. ¶***make*** *suit* 嘆願する. ¶***press*** (＝***push***) one's *suit* 強引に求婚する. ¶***start*** a *suit* in a law-court＝go to law 訴訟を起す. ¶***win*** (＝***gain***) one's *suit* 勝訴する.【類】he ***won*** his *suit* against ... in an action to recover (取戻し訴訟).

Q a ***civil*** (＝***criminal***) *suit* 民事(刑事)訴訟.

Q² a ***back pay*** *suit*《米》給与遅配請求訴訟. ¶a ***charter revocation*** *suit* 用船契約破棄の訴訟. ¶a ***damage*** *suit* 損害賠償の訴訟.【類】file a 3,000,000 ***damage*** *suit* against ... ¶maintain a ***law*** *suit* 訴訟を続ける ‖ entail endless ***law*** *suits* 際限のない訴訟事件を必要とする. ¶bring a ***libel*** *suit* against ... …をひぼう罪で訴える.【類】file a $2,000,000 ***libel*** *suit* against ... ¶a ***test*** *suit* 試験的(それが先例となる)訴訟. ¶a ***winning*** (***losing***) *suit* 勝(敗)訴.

P ***After*** two years' *suit* we were married. 求婚後二年でわれわれは結婚した. ¶***with*** lowly *suit* 平に嘆願して.

P² He began a libel *suit* ***against*** a newspaper. 彼は一新聞社を相手取ってひぼう罪の訴訟を起した. ¶a *suit* ***for*** damages 損害賠償訴訟. ¶She has filed *suit* ***for*** divorce from her present husband. 彼女は現在の夫と離婚の訴訟を提起した. ¶a *suit* ***in*** law 訴訟.

suit, *v.* 適する; 適合させる; 似合う; 求婚する.

M This hat *suits* you ***admirably***. この帽子は君によく似合う ‖ The part *suits* him ***admirably***. その役は彼によくあてはまる. ¶Which date will *suit* you ***best***? 何日が一番御都合よろしいですか. ☞ what day ...? というと普通週日の意.【類】Which will *suit* you ***best***—the morning or afternoon? ¶my training was ***ill suited*** for ... 私の受けた教育は...には不向であった. ¶The young man is ***quite suited for*** the position. その青年はその任地にうってつけだ. ¶***well suited*** to the needs of the times 時代の要求にぴったりした.【類】The title of this book is ***well suited*** to its contents. ¶Either would *suit* me equally ***well***. 私はどちらでも好い.

P You can *suit* yourself ***about*** going or remaining. 行くなり止まるなり君の勝手にしてよい. ¶*suit* ***for*** a woman's hand in marriage 求婚する ‖ He is not *suited* ***for*** (=***to be***) an engineer. 彼は技師には適しない.【類】Democracy is not *suited* ***for*** (=***to***) barbarians. / He is not *suited* ***for*** such work. / be *suited* ***for*** teaching. ¶fail ***in*** one's *suit* 求婚に失敗する. ¶*suit* the action ***to*** the word 言いながらそうする ‖ *Suit* your style ***to*** your audience. 聴衆に合うような話し方をせよ.【類】be *suited* ***to*** a warm climate / The soil is *suited* ***to*** the cultivation of oranges. / music best *suited* ***to*** the occasion ‖ *suit* ... ***to*** a degree (=marvel) 大いに...に合う ‖ It will *suit* me ***to*** a T. それは私にきっちり合う. ¶*suit* ***with*** each other つり合う ‖ Red does not *suit* ***with*** her complexion. 赤は彼女の顔色とつり合わない. ‖ He is well *suited* ***with*** (=for) his place. 彼は適材適所だ.

suitability, *n.* 適合性.

Q² the ***adult*** (***family***) ***suitabitity*** of motion pictures 映画の成人(家族)に対する適性(適不適).

suitable, *a.* 適当な, 適合せる.

M ***barely*** *suitable* for ... ...にはあまり適しない. ¶***peculiarly*** *suitable* for women 特に婦人向の.

P It is *suitable* ***for*** the purpose intended. それはあつらえ向きだ. ‖ *suitable* ***for*** gifts or souvenirs 贈答またはみやげ向きの ‖ *suitable* ***for*** both sexes 男にも女にも適した.【類】a house to let *suitable* ***for*** residence (住宅向きの) / topics *suitable* ***for*** written composition / Some words are *suitable* ***for*** use in verse and others are unsuitable. / It is not *suitable* ***for*** the purpose intended / books *suitable* ***for*** Christmas presents. ¶*suitable* ***to*** the occasion 時宜に適した ‖ *suitable* ***to*** one's rank 身分相応の ‖ most *suitable* ***to*** one's particular requirements その特殊の要求に一番よく適合した.

suitcase, *n.* スーツケース.

V ***tag*** *a suitcase* トランクに荷札をつける.

P² a *suitcase* full ***of*** jewels トランク一杯の宝石.

suite, *n.* 随員, 供奉員, 一行; [室の]一続き; [家具の]セット.

V Two rooms and a bath ***form*** *a suite*. 二室と浴室で一組になっている.

V² the *suite* ***includes*** ... その一行には...が加わっている.

Q a ***snug*** *suite* of two rooms with a bath built in バス付き二間続きの感じのいいへや.

Q² an ***apartment suite*** アパートの居室 ☞ 普通二間か三間に kitchen がついている. ¶a ***dining-room suite*** セットになっている食堂用テーブルといす. ¶a ***drawing-room*** (***living-room***) ***suite*** 応接間(居間)のセット. ¶a luxurious ***four-room suite*** [船の]豪華な四間続きのへや. ¶book (=reserve) a ***hotel suite*** ホテルのへやを予約する. ¶an ***office suite*** 事務所用品一式.

P The captain accompanied ***by*** a small *suite* of officers, landed at the place indicated. 艦長は少数の士官を同伴して指定の場所に上陸した. ¶He went to Nikko ***in*** His Highness' *suite*. 彼は殿下に供奉して日光へ行った. ‖ ***in*** the *suite* of ... ...に随行して.

P² the *suite* ***of*** an ambassador 大使の一行 ‖ a *suite* ***of*** attendants 供奉員 ‖ a *suite* (=set) ***of*** furniture 一組の家具 ‖ a *suite* ***of*** rooms 二間(以上)続きのへや.

suitor, *n.* 懇願者; 求婚者.

P² a *suitor* ***for*** a favor 嘆願者 ‖ a *suitor* ***for*** a woman's hand 女への求婚者. ¶a *suitor* ***to*** one's daughter's hand 娘の求婚者.

sulfa-drug, *n.* ズルフォン剤.

V ***dispense*** a *sulfa-drug* ズルフォン剤を調剤する. ¶***import*** *sulfa-drugs* ズルフォン剤を輸入する.

sulfate, *n.* 硫酸塩.

Q² an ***ammonium*** *sulfate* アンモニア硫酸基.

sulk, *n.* 不きげん.

P He is ***in*** the *sulks* today. 彼はきょうは機げんが悪い.

sulk, *v.* すねる.

P He *sulked* himself ***to*** sleep. 彼はすねて寝てしまった.

sulky, *a.* 不きげんな.

P *sulky* ***at*** finding ... ...を見て機げんが悪く.

sullen, *a.* 不愛想な.

P *sullen* ***by*** nature 生得不愛想な.

sullenness, *n.* 渋い面持, 不愛想.

P ***in*** *sullenness* 渋い顔をして.

sum, *n.* 総計, 総額; 額; 《俗》*pl.* 算術, 計算.

V ***advance*** large *sums* 大金を前払いする. ¶***augment*** the *sum* of sorrow and suffering for mankind at large 一般人類の悲哀と苦難を増す. ¶***bequeath*** a *sum* of money to the institution その協会に若干の金額を遺贈する. ¶The modest *sum* of one shilling is ***charged*** for it. それは一シリングというわずかな料金だ. ¶***cheapen*** the *sum* of the indemnity 賠償額を少くする. ¶***complete*** the *sum* of misery 不幸の極に達する. ¶It ***costs*** an enormous *sum*. それには大変な金がかかる. ¶***do sums*** 算数をやる. ☞ 一つの問題をやる場合は do a sum.【類】A calculating machine is one that ***does sums*** automatically. ¶***donate*** to the university the *sum* of ... その大学に...の金額を寄贈する. ¶***expend*** vast *sums* 巨額を費す. ¶***figure out*** a *sum* 合計を出す. ¶King George of England ***gave*** the huge *sum* of £1,450 for a single stamp. 英国のジョージ王は一枚の切手に一千四百五十ポンドの巨額を投じた. ¶Next Monday I ***have*** a large *sum* due to me. 今度の月曜日に多額の金が手にはいる. ¶***increase*** the *sum* of human knowledge 人類の持つ知識を増す. ¶***lend*** a large *sum* to ... ...に大金を貸す. ¶***lay out*** a large *sum* in ... ...に大金を支出する. ¶There is a comfortable little ***sum left over*** after paying the debt. その借金を払ったあとかなり小金が後に残っている. ¶***name*** a large *sum* 高いことを言う. ¶***net*** a large *sum* 大金を手取りする. ¶***paying*** a small *sum* 少額を払って. ¶***place*** an immense *sum* in the hands of the manifestation as a symbol of devotion. 誠意を示すためその示威運動に多大の金を寄付する. ¶He was able to ***present*** a considerable *sum* to the Red Cross. 彼は赤十字へかなりの金額を贈ることができた. ¶***raise*** the *sum* needed 所要の金額を集める.【類】***raise*** a *sum* by mortgage on the property (財産を抵当にして). ¶The price of ... ***reaches*** a high *sum* of ... ...の価は...の巨額に達する. ¶***realize*** the *sum* of ... ...の金額を手に入れる. ¶***receive*** a certain *sum* for ... ...に対して一定の金額を受ける. ¶The total outlay ***represents*** a considerable *sum*. 総経費は巨額にのぼる. ¶This will ***save*** vast *sums* in production expense for picture producers. このために映画会社は製作費においてばく大の節約ができるだろう. ¶enormous *sums* are ***spent*** on ... ...に巨額の金が費される. ¶***stake*** huge *sums* on the result of a race (gambling) 競走(など)に巨額の金をかける. ¶***subscribe*** a substantial *sum* to ... ...に多額の金員を寄付する. ¶The expenditure ***totals*** the staggering *sum* of nearly $1,000,000,000. その支出はかれこれ十億ドルという突拍子もない総計に達する. ¶a handsome *sum* will be ***turned over*** to ... [慈善音楽会などの収入で]沢山の金が...の手に渡るだろう. ¶***work sums*** 運算する.

Q come to a very ***alarming*** *sum* 驚くべき額に達する. ¶a ***beggarly*** *sum* of $200 二百ドルのはした金. ¶a ***colossal*** *sum* of money 巨大の金額. ¶The total outlay represents a ***considerable*** *sum*. 全支出は相当の金高になる. ¶The *sum* is ***correct***. その計算は合っている. ¶a ***dazzling*** *sum* ばく大な金. ¶cost a ***fabulous*** *sum* 突飛な金がかかる. ¶a ***good*** *sum* 相当の金. ¶sell for a ***good round*** *sum* 相当よい値で売る. ¶a ***goodly*** *sum* かなりの金額. ¶***great*** *sums* of money 大金. ¶The taxes came up to a ***huge*** *sum*. その金が巨額にのぼった. ¶spend ***immense*** *sums* in ... ...に巨額を費す. ¶no ***inconsiderable*** *sum* for that period その当時としてはよほどの金額. ¶a ***large round*** *sum* 相当まとまった金. ¶pay in a ***lump*** *sum* instead of by monthly instalments 月賦でなく一まとめに払う. ¶for the ***modest*** *sum* of 6d. 六ペンスというわずかな金額で. ¶save a ***neat*** *little sum* 小金をためる. ¶the ***noble sum*** of half a crown 大枚半クラウンの金. ¶for the ***nominal sum*** of $500 五百ドルの名目だけという値で. ¶a preposterously ***paltry sum*** ほんのはした金. ¶do a ***rapid sum*** in one's head 素早く暗算する. ¶sell for ***ridiculous sums*** ばかばかしい値で売れる. ¶a ***round sum*** of money [端数のない]まとまった金. ¶sell the site for a ***small sum*** わずかの金でその敷地を売る. ¶a ***sizable sum*** [of money] 相当まとまった金. ¶a ***staggering sum*** of 150 million pounds 一億五千万ポンドというとっぴょうしもない巨額. ¶a ***stupendous sum*** 巨額. ¶save a ***tidy sum*** 小金をためる. ¶the *sum* ***total*** 総計. ¶purchase it for a relatively ***trifling sum*** それを比較的わずかな金で買う. ¶a ***trivial*** *sum* ささいな金. ¶***vast sums*** 巨額.

P He worked at carrying bricks ***at*** a small *sum* a week. 彼は一週わずかの金でれんが運びをやった. ‖ He is good ***at*** *sums*. 彼は算術(運算)がうまい. ¶He sold his house ***for*** a small *sum*. 彼はわずかな金で家を売った. ¶The court amerced the accused ***in*** the *sum* of 100 yen. 裁判所は被告人を百円の科料に処した. ‖ pay any balance due ***in*** one *sum* 残額は一口にまとめて支払う.

P² do a *sum* ***in*** addition 加え算の問題をやる.

sum, *v.* 摘要する; 総計する; のぼる.

M It *sums up* to $1,000. それは締めて千ドルになる. ‖ *sum* ***up*** bills at the grocery store その食料品店での買物の勘定を締める ‖ to *sum* ***up*** 要するに. 【類】 to *sum* ***up*** it may be said that ... / *summed* ***up***, it was ... / roughly *sum* ***up*** / The foregoing considerations may be *summed* ***up*** in a few words. / *sum* ***up*** very pithily / It may be briefly *summed* ***up*** as follows. / to *sum* it ***up*** in a few words / it may be *summed* ***up*** by saying that ... / *sum* ***up*** the contents (内容) in a few sentences / *sum* ***up*** the thought in two words / *sum* ***up*** the arguments which have been given / *sum* ***up*** the essence (本質) of the post-war problem / It *sums* ***up*** the situation pretty well. / *sum* ***up*** the main features (=points) of ... / *sum* ***up*** the feeling of the majority of the people / It may be *summed* ***up*** something like this ... / *sum* ***up*** the state of affairs (情勢) in the Council ‖ Probably this *sums* the matter ***up*** conclusively. おそらくこれがその問題の結論になるだろう. ‖ *sum* ***up*** one's character in a term 人物を寸評する.

summarize, *v.* 摘要する, 概説する.

M The situation is perhaps ***best*** *summarized* in two brief sentences as follows:—時局は簡単な二つの文で次のように要約するのが恐らく一番当を得ていよう. ¶It may be ***briefly*** *summarized* in the following outline. それは次の概要のように簡単に要約される. ¶***compactly*** (=concisely) *summarize* 要約する.

summary, *n.* 要略, 大略.

V ***give*** a *summary* of ... の大体を示す.

Q such are, in a ***brief*** *summary*, the leading principles of ... 要するにこれが...の主なる原則である ‖ a ***brief*** *summary* of the leading facts おもな事実の概略. ¶a ***brief critical*** *summary* 簡単な評論 ‖ a ***brief historical*** *summary* of... ...の歴史的概説. ¶a ***chronological*** *summary* 統計的概表. ¶give a ***clear*** *summary* of ... ...を簡潔に記述する. ¶a ***concise*** *summary* 要略. ¶a ***condensed*** *summary* 摘要. ¶a ***convenient*** *summary* 便利な要約. ¶a ***short*** *summary* 概略. ¶a ***statistic*** *summary* 統計的概表.

P present it ***in*** a *summary* その摘要を示す.

P² a *summary* ***of*** reports 報告の大要. 【類】 the following is a *summary* ***of*** the results.

summer, *n.* 夏; 年, 年齢.

V ***devote*** one's *summer* to playing golf 一夏ゴルフで過す. ¶go up-country to ***escape*** the *summer*. 内地へ避暑する. ¶I expect to ***finish*** the *summer* at Nikko. 私は日光で夏を過ごそうと思う. ¶One swallow does not ***make*** a *summer*. 〖諺〗一燕(ｴﾝ)夏を作(ﾅ)さず(つんぼの早合点). ¶***pass*** the *summer* 夏を過ごす ‖ How would you like to ***pass*** a *summer* in the country?—I shouldn't mind. いなかで夏を過ごしたらどうです—そうしてもいいです. ¶***spend*** a *summer* at ... ...で夏を過ごす.

V² as the *summer* ***advances*** 夏が進むにつれて. ¶*Summer* has ***come***. 夏が来た. ¶*Summer* is ***gone***. 夏が過ぎた. ¶as *summer* ***grows on*** だんだん夏の盛りになると. ¶when a third *summer* ***rolled around*** 三度目の夏が来たときに.

Q He stayed ***all*** the *summer*. 彼は夏中滞在した. ¶in ***early*** *summer*=early in summer 初夏に. ¶***full*** *summer* 盛夏. ¶***high*** *summer* 真夏. ¶the ***Indian*** *summer* 《米》小春. ☞英国では St. Luke's summer. ¶***last*** *summer* 昨夏. ¶a ***scorching*** (=***broiling***) *summer* 酷暑の候(三伏). ¶***second*** *summer* 残暑. ¶a girl of ***seventeen*** *summers* 十七歳の少女. ¶a ***sultry*** *summer* 酷暑の夏. ¶a ***torrid*** *summer* 炎熱の夏期. ¶I intend to go to Nikko ***this*** *summer*. この夏私は日光へ行く積りだ. ¶***two*** or ***three*** *summers* ago 二三年前に. ¶the ***whole*** *summer* 夏中.

P ***during*** the *summer* 夏中. ¶live out of town ***for*** the *summer* 夏の間都市を離れて暮す. ¶***In*** *summer* the days are long. 夏は日が長い. ¶in the height ***of*** *summer* 真夏に ‖ a boy ***of*** ten *summers* 十歳の男の子. ¶He worked hard ***through*** (=***throughout***) the *summer*. 彼は夏中一所懸命に働いた.

P² the *summer* ***of*** my day 私の壮年の時分 ‖ the *summer* ***of*** life 人生の盛り.

summer, *v.* 夏を過ごす.

P *summer* ***at*** Karuizawa 軽井沢で避暑する. ¶*summer* ***in*** Japan 日本で夏を過ごす.

summersault, *n.* とんぼ返り.

V ***throw*** (=turn) a *summersault* とんぼ返りを打つ.

summit, *n.* 絶頂, 頂上; 頂点.

V ***conquer*** the very *summit* of Mt. Everest エベレスト山頂を征服する. ¶***reach*** the *summit* of its glory その栄華の絶頂に達する. 【類】 In this masterpiece the gifted author has ***reached*** the *summit* of his art. ¶***surmount*** the *summit* of a peak 山頂を踏破する. ¶***tread*** the *summit* 山頂をきわめる.

Q the ***bold*** and ***ragged*** *summit* of ... ...の線の太い山骨稜稜とした絶頂. ¶***cloud-capped*** *summits* 雲にそびえる絶頂. ¶the ***icy*** *summits* of the Alps アルプス山脈の氷雪の山頂. ¶***snow-clad*** *summits* 雪をいただく絶頂.

P A cottage stands ***at*** the *summit* of the hill その丘の上に小屋が一つ建っている. ‖ when chivalry was ***at*** the *summit* of its honor 騎士道花やかなりしころ. ¶the crater ***on*** the *summit* of Mt. Asama 浅間山頂の噴火口. ¶***On*** the *summit* of this pillar stood the colossal statue of Apollo. この柱の頂上にアポロ神の巨像が立っていた.

P² The *summit* ***of*** the mountain can be reached in a day. 一日で山頂へ行ける. ‖ the *summit* ***of*** power (human fame, ambition) 権力(など)の頂点. 【類】 the *summit* ***of*** a crisis.

summon, *v.* 呼出す, 召喚する; 召集する.

M The ambassador has been *summoned* ***home***. 大使は本国に召喚された.

M² *summon up* courage (=spirit) 勇気を出す. 【類】 *summon* ***up*** all one's strength (=energy) ‖ *summon* ***up*** the blood 勇気を振い起す.

P He was *summoned* ***before*** a judge. 彼は裁判官の前に呼出された. 【類】 be *summoned* ***before*** a court / be *summoned* ***before*** a police magistrate. ¶The Emperor *summoned* the elder statesmen ***for*** a conference. 天皇陛下には会議に元老をお召しになった. ¶He was *summoned* ***from*** ... by telegraph. 彼は電報で...から召喚された. ¶be *summoned* ***into*** the presence of the king 王の御前に呼び出される. ¶be *summoned* ***on*** a jury 陪審官として招集される. ¶*summon* men ***to*** the defense of their country 人々を国防に召集する ‖ order them to be *summoned* ***to*** one's presence 彼らをその面前へ呼び寄せる ‖ The relatives were *summoned* ***to*** his bedside. 親族は彼のまくらもとに呼び寄せられた. 【類】 He was *summoned* ***to*** the Imperial presence. ‖ The call-boy *summoned* him ***to*** duty. [演芸場などで]呼び出しが彼を呼びに来た.

O He was *summoned* to appear in court. 彼は裁判所から召喚された. 【類】 *summon* men to defend their country.

summons, *n.* 呼出し, 召喚状.

V ***answer*** a *summons* at the telephone 電話の呼出しに応じる. ¶***ignore*** a *summons* from ... ...からの召喚を無視する. ¶***issue*** a *summons* against ... ...に召喚状を発する ‖ *Summons* after summons has been ***issued***, but without effect. 召喚状を後から後へと出したが効果がなかった. ¶***obey*** the *summons* of a court 裁判所の召喚に応じる. ¶***receive*** a *summons* to attend 呼出しを受ける. ¶***serve*** a *summons* on a person 人に召喚状を送達する. ¶The *summons* was ***withdrawn***. その召喚を取消した.

Q² serve ***court*** *summonses* 裁判所から召喚状を送達する.

【類】 issue a *court summons* for an offense.

P *at* one's *summons* その呼出しで. ¶He was served *with* the *summons* 彼は召喚を受けた.

P² a *summons from* the police (court) 警察(など)からの召喚. ¶a *summons on* a criminal charge 犯罪けん疑の召喚.

sun, *n.* 太陽; 日光, 日向(ひなた).

V *apostrophize* the *sun* thus ... 太陽にこう呼びかける. ¶to *avoid* the afternoon *sun* 西日をよけるために. ¶I will *call* the *sun*, the moon, and stars to witness that ... 日月星辰(しん)も御照覧あれ... ¶*exclude* the *sun* 日光をしゃ断する. ¶*fend off* the summer's *sun* 夏の日をよける. ¶*forsake* the setting *sun* and turn to the rising 景気のよい方へ寝返りを打つ. ¶The room never *gets* any *sun* at all. そのへやは日が当らぬ. ¶*hail* the rising *sun* 時めく権門にへつらう. ¶*keep off* the *sun* 日を避ける. ¶open the windows to *let* in the *sun* 窓をあけて日光を入れる. ¶*see* the *sun* 生きている(詩語). ¶*take* the *sun* 陽に当たる. ¶*worship* a (the) rising *sun* 日の出を礼拝する.

V² The *sun* *beats* on our garden. 日が庭に照りつける. ¶The *sun* was *beating down* on the uncovered head of this poor little fellow. 日はこの哀れな少年の無帽の頭を照りつけていた. ¶The *sun* was *bending* in the west. 日が西に傾きつつあった. ¶The *sun* is particularly *blazing* this morning, although it is only nine o'clock. やっと九時だがけさは日の照り方が格段に強い. ¶at last the *sun* *broke* through the clouds. ついに日は雲間を出た. ¶The *sun* is *coming up*. 日が上る所だ. ¶The *sun declines*. 日が傾く. ¶The *sun dipped* behind the hills. 太陽は丘のかげに没した. ¶The *sun* now *gleamed* on the crest of the mountains. 今や山頂に日がさした. ¶The *sun* was *glowing* in all its splendor. 太陽はさんさんと輝いていた. ¶The *sun peeped in* at her window. 彼女の窓から日が差込んだ. ¶The *sun rides* high in heaven. 太陽が大空にかかる. ¶The *sun sparkles* on keen axes and burnished helmets. 鋭いおのや光ったヘルメットに日が当ってきらきらした. ¶The *sun rises* in the east. 日は東に上る. 【類】 The *sun* was *rising* in all its splendid beauty. ¶The *sun sets* (=*goes down or downs*). 日が入る. ‖ His *sun* is *set*. 彼の盛りは過ぎた. ¶The *sun shines* in the sky. 太陽が大空に輝く. ‖ The *sun shines in* at the window. 日が窓に差込む. ¶The *sun sinks* below the horizon. 日が地平線下に没する. ‖ The *sun* was *sunk*. 日が沈んだ. ¶The *sun streams* into the room. 日が室内に差込む.

Q under the *blazing sun* 炎天に. ¶a *broiling sun* 焼けつくように熱い日. 【類】 walk five miles in a *broiling sun*. ¶under the *burning sun* of midsummer 真夏の燃えるような(熱い)日を浴びて. ¶a *dazzling sun* まばゆい日. ¶the *declining sun* 西日. ¶in August, when the *sun* is *hot* o'erhead. 日が頭の上で照りつく八月に. ¶the *irradiant black sun* in eclipse 日食で光線を放射した黒い太陽. ¶A *late November sun* was breaking through the clouds. 十一月末の日が雲から漏れていた. ¶The *sun* was *low* in the west. 日は西に傾いていた. ¶the *merciless sun* [夏の] 残酷な太陽. ¶a restorer of the *royal sun* to the darkened land やみの国に再びさんさんたる太陽を出現させた人. ¶a *scorching sun* 焼き付く太陽. ¶the *setting sun* 落陽. ¶a *smiling sun* ほほ笑む太陽. ¶The *sun* was so *strong* yesterday that we could not go out. きのうは日が強くて外出ができなかった. ¶like the setting of a *tropical sun* 熱帯地方の日没のように. ¶the *westering sun* 西へ回りかけた太陽.

Q² protect us from the heat of a *four-o'clock sun* 四時ごろの(強い)太陽の熱を避ける役に立つ. ¶the *midnight sun* 中夜の太陽(北極地方における). ¶the *morning* (*evening*) *sun* 朝(夕)日. ¶under the *noonday sun* 日盛りに. ¶under the warm *October sun* 暖い十月の日を受けて. ¶the *summer sun* 夏の(熱い)太陽 ‖ the excessive heat of the *summer sun* 夏の太陽の酷熱.

P the earth's revolution *about* (=*around or round*) the *sun* 地球の公転. ¶*below* (=*beneath*) the *sun* 太陽の下で. ¶the great continents *beyond* the setting *sun*= the great west かなた西の大陸(南北アメリカ). ¶a face burned *by* the *sun* 日に焼けた顔 ‖ boards warped *by* the *sun* 日にあたってそった板. ¶protect it *from* the *sun* それを太陽に当らないようにする. ¶*from sun to* sun 日の出から日没まで. ¶placed *in* the *sun* 日なたに出して; [比ゆ的に] 順調な ‖ The cat likes to sit *in* the *sun*. ねこは日なたが好きだ. ‖ bask (=bathe) *in* the *sun* 日なたぼっこをする ‖ His character is as fickle as the icicle *in* the *sun*. 彼の性格は日を受けた氷柱のように変化する. 【類】 leave it to dry *in* the *sun* / The clothes are drying *in* the *sun*. / keep a pot-plant out *in* the *sun* / How brown you are, Miss Bosling, you've been *in* the *sun* lately, have't you? / glitter (glisten) *in* the *sun* / The streams sparkle and dance *in* the *sun*. ¶We have two hours *of sun* yet. 日の入りまでにはまだ二時間ある ‖ the rising (setting) *of* the *sun* 日の出(入). ¶spots *on* the *sun* 太陽のはん点. ¶a place *out of* the *sun* 日の当らない場所. ¶expose it *to* the *sun* それを日に当てる ‖ dry by exposure *to* the *sun* 日ぼしにする. ¶The sunflower turns *towards* the *sun*. ひまわりは日の方へ向く. ¶from every country *under* the *sun* 世界中の各国から. 【類】 everything of interest *under* the *sun* / There is nothing new *under* the *sun*. ‖ on every topic *under* the *sun*=on every conceivable subject 世界中のありとあらゆる問題に関して ‖ What *under* the *sun* (=in the world *or* on earth) do you mean? 一体君は何を言っているのか. 【類】 Where *under* the *sun* did you go? ¶rise *with* the *sun* 日とともに起きる.

sun, *v.* 日に当てる.

O *sun* and air clothings (beddings) 衣服(など)を日光と空気にあてる(虫干しする).

sunbeam, *n.* 日光.

V *sunbeams filter* through the foliage of ... 日光が...の葉から漏れる.

sunburn, *n.* 日焼け.

V *get* a *sunburn* 日に焼ける. ¶*ward off sunburn* 日焼けを防ぐ.

sunburn, *v.* 日焼けする.

P be *sunburned from* a day on the beach 海岸の一日で日焼けする.

Sunday, *n.* 日曜日.

V not *counting Sundays* 日曜を除いて. ¶*keep* (=*observe*) *Sundays* 日曜(安息)日を守る.

Q on *alternate Sundays* 一つおきの日曜に. ¶one of these *bright sunshining Sundays* 近ごろの上天気続きの日曜日. ¶the *first Sunday* of each month 毎月第一の日曜日. ¶The meeting will be held *next Sunday* (=on *Sunday next*). 会はこの次の日曜に開く. ¶*this Sunday* この日曜に. ¶on *Sunday last*=last Sunday この前の日曜に.

Q² *hospital Sunday* 病院義えん金募集日曜日. ¶*Passion Sunday* 復活祭の前々日曜日; 大斉第五主日. ¶*Renewal Sunday* 復活祭後第二主日(俗称). ¶one *summer Sunday* ある夏の日曜日.

P *after* next *Sunday* この次の日曜後に. ¶Call again *before Sunday*. 日曜前にまた来たまえ. ¶Do you usually go to church *on Sunday?* あなたは日曜にはいつも教会へ行きますか. ‖ The festival was *on Sunday*. その祭日は日曜にあった. ‖ The national holiday falls *on* a *Sunday*. その祭日は日曜にぶつかる. ‖ Such a revelry is not seemly *on* a *Sunday*. そんな底抜騒ぎは日曜にはふさわしくない. ¶I have been here *since Sunday*. 私は日曜からここへ来ている.

sundown, *n.* 《米》 日没.

P just *after sundown* 丁度日没後に. ¶the glow of the sky *at sundown* (=sunset) 夕焼け. ¶just *before sundown* ちょうど日没前に. ¶He will be home *by sundown*. 日暮れまでには家に帰れるだろう. ¶get home a little ahead *of sundown* 日没の少し前に帰宅する.

sunlight, *n.* 日光.

V open a window and *let in sunlight* まどを開けて日光を入れる.

Q The eyes are affected by the *glaring sunlight*. ぎらぎらする日光は目に悪い. ¶the fresh air and the *golden sunlight* 新鮮な空気と金色の日光.

P expose it *to sunlight* それを日光に当てる.

sunrise, *n.* 日の出.

V *see* the *sunrise* 日の出を見る.

Q on the *next sunrise* 翌朝の日の出に.

P The star is visible *about sunrise*. その星は日の出ごろに見える. ¶an hour *after sunrise* 日の出後一時間. ¶The daisy opens *at sunrise* and closes *at sunset*. ひなぎくは日の出に開き日没にしぼむ. 【類】 depart *at sunrise*. ¶go to one's work *before sunrise* 日の出前に働きに出掛ける. ¶I always get up *by sunrise*. 私はいつも日の出までには起きる. ¶*since sunrise* 日が出てからずっと.

sunset, *n.* 日没.

Q the beauty of a *flaming sunset* 燃えるような日没の美しさ. ¶a *golden sunset* 金色の日没. ¶a *gorgeous sunset* 美

しい夕焼. ¶a ***Hawaiian*** *sunset* ハワイの日没. ¶a ***summer*** *sunset* 夏の日没.

P It is seen in the sky ***after*** *sunset.* それは日没後空に見える. ¶***at*** *sunset* 日没に ‖ ***at*** about *sunset* 日没ごろに. ¶He will not be here ***before*** *sunset* today. 彼はきょうは日没前には来ないだろう. ¶He got through all his work ***by*** *sunset.* 彼は日没までに仕事を残らずやってしまった. ¶It was still half an hour ***from*** *sunset.* 日没にはまだ半時間あった. ¶He is now ***in*** the *sunset* of his days. 彼はもう老衰期に入った. ‖ ***in*** the *sunset* of his years (=life) 晩年に. ¶the hour ***past*** *sunset* 日没後の時間. ¶It is drawing ***toward*** *sunset.* 日没に近づいて来た. 【類】The wind went down ***toward*** *sunset.*

sunshade, *n.* 日おおい.

V ***pull down*** a *sunshade* 日おおいを降ろす.

sunshine, *n.* 日光; 日なた; 晴天.

V ***admit*** (=***let in***) the *sunshine* 日光を入れる. ¶to ***enjoy*** the *sunshine* for a day outside the surroundings of the city 一日郊外の日光を楽しむために. 【類】Rows of pigeons were ***enjoying*** the *sunshine* of the roof. ¶***flash back*** the *sunshine* 日光を反射する. ¶a room ***having*** much *sunshine* 日当りのいいへや.

Q There was ***bright*** *sunshine.* よい天気だった. ¶***Brilliant*** *sunshine* returned. 輝く晴天が来復した. ¶a light scarce inferior to that of ***broad*** *sunshine* 白昼にも劣らないほどの(強い)光. ¶***genial*** *sunshine* 気持ちよい日ざし. ¶a glimpse of ***golden*** *sunshine* 金色の日光の閃めき. ¶golf in the ***sparkling*** *sunshine* きらきらする日向でゴルフをやる. ¶a week of ***uninterrupted*** *sunshine* 晴天続きの一週間. ¶enjoy the ***warm*** *sunshine* in mid-fall 秋半ばの暖かい陽光を浴びる. 【類】in the ***warm spring*** *sunshine.*

P All the difficulties he apprehended dissolved like morning mist ***in*** *sunshine.* 彼があやぶんだ障害は朝霧が日光に溶けるように残らず消え失せた. ‖ ***in*** *sunshine* or rain = rain or shine 晴雨にかかわらず ‖ bathe (=bask) ***in*** [the] *sunshine* 日光浴をする.

sunstroke, *n.* 日射病.

V ***have*** (=suffer) *sunstroke* 日射病にかかる.

sunup, *n.* 《米》日の出.

P ***before*** (***after***) *sunup* 日の出前(後).

sup, *v.* 夕食を食べる.

P *sup* ***in*** town 外で夕食をする. ¶*sup* ***on*** some food ある食物を夕食に食べる.

superbomb, *n.* 超強力爆弾.

Q² a ***hydrogen*** *superbomb* 超水爆.

superimpose, *v.* 〘映画〙スーパーを入れる.

P *superimpose* propaganda ***upon*** the plot 〘映〙ストーリーの中に宣伝用のスーパーを入れる.

superintendence, *n.* 監督.

Q under the ***energetic*** *superintendence* of ... ...の力ある監督の下に. ¶under ***foreign*** *superintendence* 外人の監督の下に. ¶under the ***general*** *superintendence* of ... ...の総監督の下に.

P a dictionary prepared ***under*** the *superintendence* of Dr. ... ...博士監修の辞典. 【類】he was placed ***under*** the *superintendence* of ...

superintendent, *n.* 監督.

Q² a ***mine*** *superintendent* 鉱山監督.

superior, *n.* 優者, 長者, 上長官.

V Lippert tells us that the inferior ***copied*** the *superior* in ancient society. 古代社会においては下級者が上級者を見習ったとリペルトは説いている. ¶As a lecturer he ***had*** few *superiors.* 講演者として彼の右に出る者は多くなかった. 【類】***have*** no *superior* in courage / He ***has*** no *superior* as a prose writer. ¶Young people should ***reverence*** their *superiors.* 青年は長者を敬うべきだ. ¶***salute*** one's *superior* 上官に敬礼をする. ¶***treat*** *superiors* as equals 目上を同輩のように取扱う.

Q In the knowledge of the subject the author probably has ***few*** *superiors* in this country. その方面の知識にかけてはこの国に著者の右に出るものは恐らくないであろう. ¶the ***naval*** *superior* of Great Britain 英国海軍の長官. ¶he has ***no*** *superior* in ... ...では彼の右に出るものがない. ¶***social*** *superiors* 社会的に地位の高い人々(先輩).

Q² on the shore of ***Lake*** *Superior* スーペリオル湖畔で. ¶a ***mother*** *superior* 女の院長 (Catholic などの経営になる慈善団体など).

P show respect ***for*** one's *superiors* 長者を敬う. ¶assume the air ***of*** a *superior* 先輩づらをする. ¶impudent ***to*** *superiors* 上長に対して心臓の強い. ¶be submissive ***to*** *superiors* and kindly to inferiors 上にも下にもよい.

P² a *superior* ***in*** age (dignity, scholarship) 年齢(など)の上の人 ‖ You are my *superior* ***in*** ability and I am yours in application. 技術は君の方が上だが勤勉では僕が上だ. ¶the *superior* ***of*** monastery 僧院長, 修道院長 ‖ be the *superior* ***of*** others in ... ...では群を抜いている.

superior, *a.* すぐれた, まさった.

M ***decidedly*** *superior* to ... 断然...にすぐれた. ¶***incomparably*** *superior* to ... はるかに...にすぐれた. ¶text-books ***intellectually*** *superior* to the simple content of the earlier lessons 昔の簡単な内容のものよりは知的にすぐれた教本. ¶***numerically*** *superior* to ... 数では...よりすぐれた.

P *superior* ***in*** ability (quality) to ... 技術(など)では...よりすぐれた. ¶The Allies are *superior* in numbers ***to*** their enemies. 連合軍は数では敵にまさっている. ‖ *superior* in speed ***to*** any other machine 速力ではあらゆる他の機械にすぐれた ‖ He is *superior* ***to*** (=above) bribery. 彼は賄ろを取るような人間じゃない. ‖ rise *superior* ***to*** every obstacle どんな障害にも平気でいる. 【類】He is *superior* ***to*** envy (temptation). / He is *superior* ***to*** me in learning. ‖ A species is *superior* ***to*** a variety. 〘生物〙種は変種より高級である.

superiority, *n.* 優越, 優勝, 優位.

V ***claim*** *superiority* 優位を主張する. ¶***establish*** the incontestible *superiority* of ... over ... 争うまでもなく...以上に...の優秀性を実証する. ¶***give*** it *superiority* over ... それを...以上の優位におく. ¶He ***has*** a *superiority* over the others. 彼は他にすぐれている. ‖ He ***has*** the *superiority* of me. 彼は私より上だ(すぐれている). ¶***possess*** a decided intellectual *superiority* over ... 知識が断然...よりもすぐれている. ¶He ***showed*** decided *superiority.* 彼は断然傑出していた.

Q the former ***naval*** *superiority* of Great Britain 以前の大英国海軍の優勢. ¶***numerical*** *superiority* over ... ...に対する数的優勢. ¶a test of ***racial*** *superiority* 人種の優秀性の一証左. ¶attain ***social*** *superiority* 社会的優位に立つようになる. ¶His *superiority* is ***undisputed.*** 彼のすぐれていることは争われない. ¶the ***vast*** *superiority* of ... ...の偉大な優秀性.

Q² ***Air*** *superiority* is the prerequisite to war victory. 戦争に勝つには空の優位が前提条件である. ¶***class*** *superiority* 階級の優位.

P He assumes an air ***of*** *superiority.* 彼はえらそうな風をする.

P² the *superiority* ***of*** ... ***over*** ... ...の...に対する優勢. ¶It constitutes his *superiority* ***to*** other people. それが他の人より彼のえらい所だ.

superman, *n.* 《米》超人.

P² He is a *superman* ***in*** physical strength (mental faculties). 彼は体力(など)では超人的だ.

super-power, *n.* 超大国.

Q the ***two*** *super-powers,* the United States and the Soviet Union 超二大国米ソ.

supersede, *v.* 入替える.

P *supersede* A ***by*** B 甲を乙と入替える.

supersensitive, *a.* 感覚鋭敏な.

P *supersensitive* ***to*** ... ...に過度に敏感な.

superstition, *n.* 迷信.

V there are very many *superstitions* ***connected*** with ... ...に関連して非常に多くの迷信がある. ¶***explode*** (=***kill***) a *superstition* 迷信を打破する. ¶The dangers of a sea life ***foster*** *superstition* 海上生活は危険だからとかく迷信が行われる. ¶***generate*** and ***foster*** *superstitions* 迷信を産みかつ助長する. ¶A limited number of people appear to ***have*** pet *superstitions* of their own. 銘々独特の迷信を持つ人も多少はあるらしい. ¶***overcome*** one's *superstition* 迷信に打勝つ.

Q ***animistic*** *superstition* 万物有霊の迷信. ¶The luck of a black cat is a ***common*** enough *superstition.* 黒ねこは縁起がよいというのはきわめて一般的に行われている迷信である. ¶a ***favorite*** *superstition* お定まりの迷信. ¶It is a ***theatrical*** *superstition* that a bad dress rehearsal means a good first night. 演劇界では試演が悪いと初日がよいという迷信がある. ¶a ***vain*** *superstition* くだらない迷信. ¶a ***wide-spread*** *superstition* 広く広まっている迷信.

P certain *superstitions* ***about*** ... ...についてのある迷信. ¶There have been many idle *superstitions* ***as to*** the influence of the moon upon the earth and its inhabitants. 月が地球とその住民に及ぼす影響については色々ばかげた迷信があった.

supervene, *v.* 併発する.

P The cause of his death was pneumonia *supervening* ***on*** influenza. 彼の死因は流感に肺炎の併発であった.

supervision, *n.* 管理, 監視, 監督.

V ***exercise*** a close (the closest) *supervision* over ... ...を(最も)厳重に監督する. ¶***have*** *supervision* over ... ...を監督する ‖ the work has ***had*** the *supervision* of ... その著作は...の校閲を受けた. ¶***relax*** *supervision* over ... ...の監視を寛大にする.

Q exercise ***careful*** *supervision* 細心に監視する. ¶colleges and universities under the ***direct*** *supervision* of the Government 国立諸大学. ¶exercise ***editorial*** *supervision* over the publication 出版物の編集を主宰する.【類】under the ***editorial*** *supervision* of ... ¶exercise ***efficient*** *supervision* in the matter of ... ...に関して効果的な監督をする. ¶exercise a ***general*** *supervision* 総監督をする.【類】prepared under the ***general*** *supervision* of ... ¶a ***humane*** *supervision* 人情味のある監督. ¶under the ***immediate*** *supervision* (=direct control) of government 政府直轄の. ¶a ***lax*** *supervision* 手ぬるい監督. ¶exercise ***necessary*** *supervision* 必要な監督を行う. ¶his will was executed under the ***personal*** *supervision* of ... 彼の遺言は...自身の管理の下に執行された. ¶exercise ***strict*** *supervision* over ... ...を厳重に監督する.【類】under the ***strict*** *supervision* of ... ¶the ***vigilant*** *supervision* of examinations by teachers 教師の周到な試験監督. ¶The business has the ***watchful*** *supervision* of the proprietor. その仕事は事業主が綿密に管理している.

Q² ***expert*** *supervision* 専門家の検閲. ¶under strict (=stringent) ***Government*** *supervision* 政府の厳重な監督の下に. ¶under strict ***police*** *supervision* 警察の厳重な監督下に. ¶***state*** *supervision* of economic life 経済生活の国家管理.

P He was blamed for lack ***of*** *supervision*. 彼は監督不行届のかどでけん責された. ¶first-class cuisine ***under*** the *supervision* of an experienced chief 熟練なコック長の監督する一流料理場.

P² *supervision* ***of*** an appeal 〘法〙上訴の管理 ‖ *supervision* ***of*** guardianship 〘法〙後見に対する監督人.

supervisor, *n.* 監督.

Q² a ***floor*** *supervisor* 売場監督. ¶a ***mess*** *supervisor* 食堂監督.

supper, *n.* 夕食.

V ***eat*** a hearty *supper* 腹一杯夕食を食う ‖ ***eat*** one's *supper* of bread and cheese パンとチーズで夕食をする. ¶Stay a little longer. I'll ***fix*** you *supper*. もう少しごゆっくり. 夕飯をさしあげますから. ¶We ***had*** a *supper* from a neighboring restaurant. われわれは近所の料理屋から夕飯を取った. ¶A cold *supper* was ***laid*** upon the table. 冷えた夕食が食卓に出された. ¶***prepare*** *supper* 夕飯の仕度をする. ¶*Supper* was ***served in***. 晩飯が出された. ¶***share*** a *supper* with ... ...と夕食をともにする. ¶***take*** *supper* 夕食を食べる. ¶I ***want*** a slight *supper*. 私は軽い夕食が欲しい.

Q have an ***early*** *supper* 早い夕食をする. ¶have a ***hearty*** *supper* 夕食を腹一杯食べる. ¶a ***light*** *supper* 軽い夕食. ¶a ***scanty*** *supper* 貧弱な夕食. ¶a ***substantial*** *supper* 食べごたえのある夕食.

Q² an ***after-theater*** *supper* 観劇後の夕食. ¶have a ***picnic*** *supper* in the grove 森の中でピクニックの夕飯をとる. ¶a ***seven o'clock*** *supper* 七時の夕飯.

P ***after*** *supper* 夕食後に. ¶He is ***at*** *supper*. 彼は夕食中だ.【類】take too much champagne ***at*** *supper*. ¶sit down ***to*** *supper* 夕食の卓につく.

supplant, *v.* 取って代る.

P Democracy has been *supplanted* ***by*** a plutocratic despotism. 財閥専制政治が民主主義に取って代った.

supplement, *n.* 補遺, 付録.

V The magazine ***has*** a Christmas *supplement* of complete stories. その雑誌には読切小説のクリスマス付録がついている. ¶***pay*** a *supplement* 不足を払う(切符など).

Q a ***literary*** *supplement* to an encyclopedia その百科事典の文学付録.

P² a *supplement* ***to*** The Times タイムス紙の付録.

supplement, *v.* 補う.

P *supplement* one's salary ***by*** outside work 他の仕事で俸給を補う. ¶The text is *supplemented* ***by*** an adequate glossary. 本文には適切な用語解を付してある.

supplementary, *a.* 補足の.

P The reading is *supplementary* ***to*** other studies. その読み物は他の学科の補いだ.

supplicate, *v.* 懇願する, 祈願する.

P *supplicate* one's master ***for*** pardon 主人の許しを願う. ¶*supplicate* ***to*** God ***for*** mercy 神の慈悲にすがる.

supplication, *n.* 祈願.

Q He is absorbed in his ***devout*** *supplication*. 彼は敬けんな祈願に余念がない. ¶Her eyes were raised in ***tearful*** *supplication* to Heaven to watch over and guard her little ones. 彼女は涙にうるむ目で天を仰ぎ子供たちを見守り給えと祈った.

supplier, *n.* 供給者.

Q² a ***war material*** *supplier* 戦争資材納入者.

supply, *n.* 供給; *pl.* 用度品, 糧食.

V ***abridge*** *supply* 供給を節約する. ¶The rivers ***afford*** an inexhaustible *supply* of fish. その川は魚を無尽蔵に供給する. ¶***balance*** *supply* with demand 供給と需要の均衡を取る. ¶The Japanese employers are able to ***command*** a large *supply* of cheap and efficient labor. 日本の雇主には低廉有効な労力の多大の供給が得られる. ¶***cut off*** the *supplies* 補給(食料など)を止める. ¶Japan ***derives*** its *supply* of oil from abroad. 日本は海外からその石油の供給を得る.【類】The city ***derives*** its *supply* of water from the river. ¶***draw*** one's *supplies* from ... ...からその物資の供給を仰ぐ. ¶***economize*** household *supplies* 家庭用品を節倹する. ¶***even up*** the *supply* to meet the demand 供給と需要の均衡をとる. ¶The demand for these goods ***exceeds*** the *supply*. この商品は供給より需用の方が多い. ¶The *supply* is ***exhausted***. 貯蔵が切れている. ¶***expect*** a fresh *supply* by next mail 今度の郵船で新規の供給を得られるものと見込む. ¶***forward*** another *supply* as previously 前と同じ品を重ねて送る. ¶***furnish*** *supplies* to ... ...に物資を供給する. ¶***get*** fresh *supplies* from Europe and America 欧米から新たに買入れる. ¶***have*** a plentiful *supply* of ... ...をたくさん持合わせている. ¶Producers are ***holding back*** *supplies*. 生産者は供給を控えている. ¶***lay in*** a *supply* of food 食糧を仕込む. ¶***make*** their own *supply* 自給する. ¶***obstruct*** food *supplies* 糧食の供給を妨げる. ¶The United Kingdom is the country whence Sweden ***obtains*** its chief *supply* of coal. 英本国はスエーデンがその石炭の供給を主として仰いでいる国である. ¶***order*** *supplies* to family dealers 御用聞きに注文をする. ¶***procure*** a constant *supply* of ... 絶えず...の供給を得る. ¶***produce*** a plentiful and cheap *supply* of ... ...を豊富かつ廉価に供給する. ¶***renew*** the *supply* of ... ...を新たに買入れる. ¶***replenish*** the *supply* 供給を補充する. ¶Bad weather will ***retard*** *supplies*. 悪天候のため品の出回りが悪くなる. ¶***shut off*** the *supply* of ... ...の供給をしゃ断する. ¶Those rates do not ***tempt*** *supplies* to come out. この相場では品物は出回りはよくなるまい.

V² The water *supply* to the room ***failed***. そのへやの給水が止まった. ¶Our *supplies* have ***fallen short***. われわれの糧食が少なくなってきた.

Q ***abundant*** *supply* of labor and its cheapness 労力の豊富なる供給とその低廉. ¶the ***ample*** *supply* of waterpower 水力の十分な供給.【類】The room is maintained by a number of iron pillars, round which is an ***ample*** *supply* of clothes hooks (着物を掛けるかぎがたくさん). ¶a ***cheap*** and ***beautiful*** *supply* of power by the white coal 水力による安価で豊富な電力の供給. ¶need a ***constant*** *supply* of ... ...が品切れにならないようにして欲しい.【類】obtain a ***constant*** *supply* of raw materials. ¶the ***earliest*** *supplies* [商品の]走り. ¶a ***free*** *supply* of food 無料の食料配給. ¶handle poultry to provide ***fresh*** *supplies* of eggs for the family table 各家庭の食卓に新鮮な卵をのぼすために養鶏をやる ‖ take in a ***fresh*** *supply* of fuel 新たに燃料を買入れる.【類】get ***fresh*** *supplies* from America. ¶a ***full*** *supply* of modern machinery 近代機械類の十分な供給. ¶We have a ***good*** *supply* on hand. 十分手持品がある. ¶a ***goodly*** *supply* of newspapers 新聞の相当多量な供給. ¶highly ***important basic*** *supplies*, such as iron and coal 鉄・石炭のような非常に重要な根本的物資. ¶there is an ***inadequate*** *supply* of police at ... ...では警察官が手不足

だ. ¶an ***inexhaustible*** *supply* of coal 無尽蔵の石炭. ¶a ***large supply*** of superior (inferior) sorts 上(なみ)品の大量出回り ‖ owing to the ***large supply*** of tonnage 船腹豊富のため ‖ the ***largest supplies*** are drawn from ... ¶a ***liberal*** (=***plentiful***) *supply* of ... ...の豊富な出回り. ¶***limited*** *supplies* 限りある糧食. ¶***military supplies*** 軍需品. ¶***moderate supplies*** of grain 穀類のまずまずの出回り. ¶***outside supplies*** for prisoners 差入物. ¶have a ***plentiful supply*** of ... ...が豊富に出回る. 【類】 produce a ***plentiful*** and ***cheap supply*** of ... ¶have a ***reserve supply*** of ... ...のストックがある. ¶The *supply* of money continues ***scarce***. 金融が依然切迫している. ¶The *supply* is ***short***. 供給が不足している. 【類】 *Supplies* (供給品) are very ***short***. / Around Paris as well as elsewhere fruits and vegetables are in very ***short supply*** (品不足). ¶a ***sufficient supply*** of necessities 十分な必要品の供給. ¶find in it an ***unfailing supply*** of firewood それでまきは必ず手に入る. ¶***visible*** (***invisible***) *supplies* 〖経〗顕(潜)在貨. ¶the ***world's supply*** of coal 世界の石炭供給.

Q² ***auto*** [***mobile***] *supplies* 自動車の供給. ¶***clothing supplies*** 衣料の供給. ¶increase ***coal supplies*** 石炭の出回りをよくする. 【類】 an inadequate ***coal supply***. ¶marshal Japan's available ***commodity supplies*** toward more equal distribution 日本の生産品の配給をさらに平等化するように操作する. ¶the ***drinking water supply*** 飲料水の供給. ¶***electric power supplies*** 電力供給. ¶an ***emergency food supply*** 非常食料の配給. 【類】 pour ***emergency food supplies*** into that country. ¶the purchase and distribution of departmental and ***field supplies*** 省の本部並びに支部の用品買入及び分配. ¶holders of huge ***food supplies*** 大量の食料手持ちのある人々 ‖ reserve ***food supplies*** held for emergencies 応急用食料を貯蔵する. 【類】 secure an ample ***food supply*** for Japan. ¶draw out ***ice supplies*** from ... ...から氷をとる. ¶***labor supply*** 労力の供給. ¶***landscaping supplies*** [日本式]庭園工事資材. ¶a source of ***material supplies*** 物資の供給源. ¶***maintenance supplies*** 営繕資材. ¶***manufacturing supplies*** 生産資材. ¶***nursery supplies*** 子供べや用品. ¶***office supplies*** 事務用品. ¶***post exchange*** (=PX) *supplies* PX の品物. ¶***power supply*** 動力配給(電力など). 【類】 There is a greater demand for ***power supply***. ¶the United States ***relief supplies*** to Russia 米国からロシアへの救済物資. ¶a good (poor) ***reserve supply*** of water 豊かな(乏しい)貯水. ¶***table supplies*** 食卓の用度品. ¶***timber supplies*** 木材. ¶***war supplies*** 軍需品. ¶the ***water supply*** of a town 町の水道(給水).

P a contract ***for*** the *supply* of coal 石炭供給の契約. ¶liberal ***in supply*** 供給の大まかな. ¶through scarcity ***of supply*** 在荷払底のため.

P² The *supply* ***of*** money is rather scanty (continues scarce, has increased, is more abundant). 金融がかなり緩慢だ(依然切迫している, よくなった, さらに豊富だ). ¶There is a *supply* ***on*** hand. 手持ちがある.

supply, *v.* 供給する, 支給する, 配給する.

M valuable information ***courteously*** *supplied* 好意をもって支給された貴重な報告. ¶The market is ***poorly*** (***well***) *supplied*. 市場は品不足(品が豊富)だ. ¶Goods will be *supplied* ***promptly*** to order. 品は御注文に応じて敏速に配達します. ¶but (=only) ***sparsely*** *supplied* with hair 毛の薄い. ¶The city is ***well*** *supplied* with churches of all the leading denominations. その市には主な宗派の教会が多数ある. 【類】 I am ***well*** *supplied* with clothing. / In iron ores, Japan is not ***well*** *supplied*.

P Rivers are *supplied* ***by*** smaller streams. 川の水は小さな流れから来る. ¶*supply* milk ***for*** them 牛乳を彼らに供給する. ¶I can *supply* ***from*** stock. 手持品を回せます. ¶*supply* goods ***to*** the army 品を陸軍に納める. ¶The cow *supplies* us ***with*** milk. 雌牛はわれわれに牛乳を供給する. ‖ rooms *supplied* (=fitted) ***with*** electric light 電灯の設備があるへや. 【類】 *supply* the poor ***with*** clothing (provisions) / *supply* a furnace ***with*** coal / pipes *supplied* ***with*** hot steams.

support, *n.* 支持; 支持物, 支持者.

V ***add*** *support* to the rumor that ... ...といううわさをさらに裏づける. ¶***administer*** moral *support* 精神的援助を与える. ¶***afford*** a *support* against pressure 圧迫の支えとなる. ¶***derive*** one's *support* in whole (in part) from ... 生活費は全部(一部)...から得る. ¶The school ***draws*** its *support* from public subscription. その学校は維持費を一般の寄付に仰いでいる. ¶***eke out*** one's scanty *support* by extra toil 乏しい生活の資をアルバイトで補う. ¶***enlist*** their *support* 彼らの援助を借りる ‖ ***enlist*** the financial *support* of ... in the work その事業に...の財政的援助を得るようにする. ¶***extend*** one's hearty *support* to ... その心からの援助を...に与える. ¶***find support*** in all quarters 各方面に賛成を得る. 【類】 *supoprt* for this supposition (想像) might be ***found*** in the fact that ... ¶***form*** a *support* to a person standing 立っている人の寄掛りになる. ¶***gain*** the *support* of ... ...の後援を得る. ¶***get support*** from ... ...から支持される. ¶***give support*** to a roof 屋根を支える ‖ ***give support*** to the poor 貧民を扶助する. 【類】 we ***give*** our hearty *support* to ... ¶The shelf must ***have*** *support*. そのたなには支柱が要る. ‖ The movement has ***had*** encouraging *support* from the technical professions. その運動には専門家の激励的援助があった. ¶***lack*** popular *support* 人気がない. 【類】 ***lack*** adequate *support*. ¶***lend support*** to this argument (opinion) この議論(など)に賛成する. 【類】 ***lend*** financial *support* to an enterprise (a scheme) / ***lend*** him the *support* of her prestige (名声). ¶***lose*** the *support* of the people 民心を失う. ¶We ***need*** his *support*. われわれは彼の支持を必要とする. ¶arouse the interest and ***obtain*** the *support* of American citizen 米国市民の感興を目ざめさしてその援助を得る. 【類】 ***obtain*** financial *support* for ... from ... ¶He ***pledged*** his *support* to the plan. 彼はその計画を援助することを約した. 【類】 ***pledge*** our hearty *support* and co-operation. ¶We failed to ***procure*** *support*. われわれは援助が得られなかった. ¶They ***promised*** their continued *support*. 彼らは引続いて援助することを約した. ¶They have already ***received*** *support* far exceeding their expectations. 彼らはすでにはるか予想以上の援助を受けた. 【類】 ***receive*** the heartiest *support* from all sections of the Chinese community. ¶***refuse support*** to ... ...への援助を断わる. ¶***render*** good *support* to the main rôles [二流所の俳優などが舞台で]大立物をよく引立たせる. ¶***require support*** 支持を要する. ¶We have never yet failed to ***secure*** a warm and hearty *support*. われわれはこれまでいつも熱心な援助を得ている. ‖ if it fails to ***secure*** the *support* of two-thirds of the votes cast by ... ...のやった票決の三分の二の同意を得ないときでも. ¶***solicit*** public *support* 公衆の援助をこう. ¶***throw*** its *support* to ... その支持を...に移す. ¶***win*** public *support* 公衆の援助を得る.

Q give ***active support*** to ... ...に活発な支援を与える. 【類】 I received his ***active personal support***. / maintain (続行する) their ***active support*** of ... ¶He is the ***chief support*** of his poor old mother. 彼は気の毒な老母のつえ柱だ. 【類】 the ***chief support*** of a family. ¶give one's ***cordial support*** to the movement その運動に心からの援助を与える. ¶give one's ***enthusiastic support*** to ... ...に熱心な援助を与える. ¶the ***financial support*** of the Government 政府の財政的援助. ¶a ***frail support*** 貧弱な支持. ¶receive the ***full support*** of ... ...から十分な援助を受ける. ¶give [a] ***generous support*** to ... ...に惜気ない援助を与える. ¶give ***generous financial support*** to the undertaking その事業に豊富多大な財政的援助を与える. ¶give only ***half-hearted support*** to ... ...に微温的な支持を与える. ¶a ***hearty*** and ***consistent support*** 心からの首尾一貫した援助. ¶deserve ***hearty*** and ***unstinted support*** 心からの惜気ない援助に値する. ¶The proposal has received ***influential support***. その提案は有力な援助を受けた. ¶***liberal support*** 大まかな援助. ¶the ***main support*** 主柱. ¶***mental support*** 精神的援助. ¶give ***moral support*** 声援する. 【類】 the ***moral support*** and encouragement to the nation. ¶get ***no support*** 支持を得ない. 【類】 give ***no support*** to ... ¶He is the ***only support*** of his mother. 彼は母の唯一のたよりだ. ¶give a ***passive support*** to ... ...に消極的援助を与える. ¶an institution seeking ***popular support*** 一般からの寄付を求めている会. ¶an only son who is the ***sole support*** of the widowed mother 未亡人である母の唯一のたよりになる一人むすこ. 【類】 become the ***sole support*** of the family. ¶give ***sympathetic support*** to the movement その運動に同情的援助を与える. ¶The idea has his ***warm support***. その考案は彼の厚い支持を得ている. ¶a ***whole-hearted support*** 全面支持.

Q² *artillery support* coming from ... ...から増援の砲兵隊. ¶secure *class support* クラスの支持を得る. ¶contribute to the *family support* 家族の生活を助ける. ¶have *Government support* 政府の後援を得ている. ¶*mass support* 大衆の支持. ¶*State support* of education 州(国家)の教育助成 ‖ remove *state support* from Shinto 神道への国家補助を止める.

P It is used *as* a *support* to the rail of a staircase. それは階段の欄干の支柱にする. ¶depend on alms *for* one's *support* 施しを受けて生活する ‖ the sum paid *for support* to him 彼の生活費として支給した額. ¶His life is an argument *in support* of this theory. 彼の一生はこの学説を証明する実証のようなものだ. 【類】*in support* of this theory it has been pointed out (指摘された) that ... / *in support* of our view we may quote the words of ... / the evidence *in support* of ... / He cited certain facts *in support* of this statement. / use the foreign colonies as milch-cows (金ぐら) *in support* of her own national life at home / hold a meeting *in support* of the movement / a meeting held *in support* (=aid) of the fund. ¶His means *of support* are limited. 彼は生活が豊かでない. ¶place it *on* a *support* それを柱で支える ‖ It is erected 4 feet above the ground *on* wooden *suppports*. それは木の支柱で地上四フィートの所に建ててある. ¶Will you kindly give something *towards* the *support* of the school? 学校の維持費へ幾分御寄付を願われませんか. ¶an academy founded *with* the *support* of the Carnegie Endowment for International Peace カーネギー国際平和基金の援助で立った学会. ¶The assumption is quite *without support*. その仮定には全然根拠がない.

P² a *support for* a musket 銃を載せる台 ‖ He gave his keen *support for* the scheme. 彼はその計画に熱心な援助を与えた. ¶receive *support from* the observations of ... ...の観測から支持を得る. ¶the *support of* a bridge 橋の台 ‖ the *support of* the family 家族の扶養 ‖ the *support of* life 生命の維持 ‖ He is a *support of* the state. 彼は国家の柱石だ.

support, *v.* 支持する; 証明する.

M This use of the word is *authoritatively supported*. その語をかく使用するについては確固たる根拠がある. ¶*support* oneself *economically* 経済的に独立する. ¶*support* it *financially* 財政的にそれを援助する. ¶I was *supported home*. 私は人に助けられて家に帰った. ¶*support* it *loyally* 忠実にそれを支持する. ¶*mutually support* one another 相互に支持する. ¶The theory (suggestion) is *poorly supported* by facts. その理論(説)は事実の証明が不十分だ. ¶I was *supported* by him both *materially* and *spiritually*. 私は彼から物心両面の支援を受けた. ¶*steadfastly support* the cause of ... 堅実に...の主張を支援する. ¶He is the most *strongly supported* candidate (successor). 彼が最も呼声が高い.

P *support* a person *against* ... ...に反対して人を助ける. ¶*support* a pier *by* chains 鎖で桟橋を止める ‖ universities *supported by* the Government 国立諸大学 ‖ The church is *supported by* subscription. その教会は寄付金で維持している. ‖ a theory *supported by* no facts whatever 何ら事実が証明していない学説. 【類】He is *supported by* charity (慈善) / He is *supported by* parents or other relatives. / a theory *supported by* observed (実現した) facts. / The usage (語法) is not *supported by* good authority (しっかりした権威). / it is *supported by* evidence from ... ¶He is *supported from* the society's funds. 彼はその会の基金から支給されている. 【類】students *supported from* Government grants (支給金). ¶The roof is *supported on* iron pillars. その屋根は鉄柱に支えられている. ‖ He is *supported on* (=*upon*) a pittance. 彼は薄給で暮している. ‖ She decided to *support* herself *on* her musical talents. 彼女は音楽で自活しようと決心した. ¶*support* it *with* a post それを柱で支える.

O He has a large family to *support*. 彼は扶養家族が多い.

supporter, *n.* 支持者, 後援者, 味方.

V I *found* a steady *supporter* in him. 彼こそ着実な後援者であった. 【類】we *found* in France an enthusiastic *supporter* in ... ¶He *has* many strong *supporters*. 彼には有力な援助者がたくさんある.

Q an *ardent supporter* of the movement その運動の熱烈なる支持者. ¶a *convinced* and *life-long supporter* of the work その事業に対する十分理解のある終生の支援者. ¶*enthusiastic supporters* of the scheme その計画の熱心な支持者. ¶the lack of *influential supporters* 有力な援助者を持たないこと. ¶one of the *keenest supporters* of the narrow gauge [鉄道の]狭軌の最も熱心な賛成者の一人. ¶The New York World, a *leading supporter* of the Administration その政府の主なる支持者たるニューヨークワールド紙. ¶a *loyal supporter* of a policy 政策などの忠実な支持者. ¶*stalwart supporters* 強力な支持者. ¶*staunch supporters* of the existing order 現在の事態の忠実なる維持者. ¶a *strong supporter* of the bill その法律案の有力な支持者. ¶an *unflinching supporter* 勇猛な支持者. ¶a *warm supporter* of the cause その主義の熱心な支持者.

Q² *Administration supporters* 政府支持層, 与党側. ¶*millionaire supporters* 富豪の後援者たち.

P² He is a *supporter of* the Cabinet. 彼は内閣の支持者だ.

suppose, *v.* 思ふ, 想像する.

M The question is more complicated than [is] *commonly supposed*. その問題は存外複雑である. ‖ the effect of it upon ... is not so great as is *commonly supposed* ...に与えるその影響は一般に考えるほど大きくはない. ¶you may *easily suppose* that ... ...とは容易に想像ができよう. ¶*even supposing* you to be in the wrong 君が間違っているとしても. ¶as is *generally supposed* 一般に想像されているように. ¶you *naturally suppose* that ... 君は当然...と思うだろう. ¶we may *reasonably suppose* that ... ...と思うのも無理がない. ¶"Will he come?" "I *suppose so*."「彼は来るか」「来るだろう」.

O *suppose* you make ... your starting point 君が...を出発点とすると仮定する. 【類】*Suppose* we (=Let's) go for a walk. ¶What are they *supposed* to be doing? この人たちは何をしているのか(絵の説明を求めるときなど). ¶*Supposing* [that] it rains, what shall we do? 雨が降ったらどうしよう.

supposition, *n.* 想像, 仮定.

V I cannot even *entertain* the *supposition* that ... 私には...という想像すらいだくことはできない. ¶This *favors* the *supposition* and even makes it almost matter of certainty. それはその想像には有利でほとんど確実とさえ思わせる. ¶*put on supposition* 想像を働かせる. ¶this *supposition* is *strengthened* by the fact that ... この想像に対して...の事実が力添えになる.

Q it is on the *safe supposition* that ... それは...という安全な仮定に立脚している.

P *on* the *suppositson* that ... ...と想像して ‖ a newspaper article based *on supposition* 仮定に基づく新聞記事. 【類】*on* this *supposition* / *on* the *supposition* of ...

suppository, *n.* 座薬.

V *insert* a *suppository* into ... ...に座薬を差込む.

suppress, *v.* 禁止する; 抑圧する.

M *firmly suppress* all propaganda against ... ...反対の宣伝を一切厳禁する. ¶*unlawfully suppress* the press (the Communists) 新聞(など)を不当に弾圧する. ¶*vigorously suppress* 弾圧する.

P Meetings were *suppressed by* the police. 会合は警官のために禁止された.

suppression, *n.* 禁止.

P² *suppression of* evidence 採証禁止.

suppuration, *n.* 化のう.

V *set up suppuration* in the wound その傷をうませる.

supremacy, *n.* 主権, 勝利.

V decline to *acknowledge* his *supremacy* [属国などが]彼の主権を否認する. ¶*assert* its *supremacy* その主権を主張する. ¶*challenge* the *supremacy* of ... ...という権力に挑戦する. ¶In the seventeenth century the Dutch became great sailors and *disputed* with England the *supremacy* of the ocean. 十七世紀においてオランダ人はりっぱな海員となって英国と海洋の支配権を争った. ¶Its *supremacy* was *established* stronger than ever. その覇(は)業の基礎がいよいよ強固となっていた. 【類】they *established* their *supremacy* over the whole of ... ¶*give* her the *supremacy* in the world market 世界市場における覇権をその国に与える. ¶*hold supremacy* in the Far East 極東において覇権を握る. ¶*maintain* our *supremacy* われわれの覇権を維持する. 【類】*maintain* the *supremacy* (優位) of Parliament. ¶Even as late as 1685 Bristol *retained* its *supremacy* as the first seaport in England. 降って一六八五年ごろまでもブリストルは英国における第一の海港としてその覇権を失わ

なかった. ¶*secure supremacy* in ... ...に最上権を獲得する. ¶*wrest* that *supremacy* from ... ...からその主権を奪い取る. 「と移った.
V² the *supremacy passed* from ... to ... 覇権は...から...へ
Q *Anglo-Saxon supremacy* アングロサクソン民族の制覇. ¶struggle for *commercial supremacy* in the markets of the world 世界の市場において商業の覇権を争う. ¶America's *economic supremacy* アメリカの経済上の覇権. ¶hold the *financial supremacy* 財政上の覇権を握る. ¶*maritime supremacy* 制海権. ¶British *mercantile supremacy* 英国の商業上の優位. ¶New York's *undisputed supremacy* as the wonder city of the world 世界驚異の都市としてニューヨークの押しも押されもしない優越性.
Q² America's *air supremacy* 米国空軍の優位. ¶hold *world supremacy* 世界的優位に立っている.
P struggle *for* athletic *supremacy* 競技上の覇権を争う.
P² They held *supremacy in* their respective fields. 彼らはそれぞれの活動範囲で覇権を握っていた. ¶the *supremacy of* the king *over* a country 国家に君臨する国王の主権.

surcharge, *v.* こめ過ぎる.
P *surcharged with* ozone オゾンをこめ過ぎた ‖ Her heart was *surcharged with* grief. 彼女は胸をかきむしられる思い
sure, *n.* 確実. ∟だった.
P I do not know it *for sure* (=certain). 私には確かなこと
sure, *a.* 確かな, 疑いない. ∟は分からない.
M an *absolutely sure* remedy 絶対確実な医療. ¶It is possible that he did so, but I am *almost sure* that he did not. 彼はそうしないとも限らないが私はまずしなかったものと信じる. ¶I'm *dead sure.* 大丈夫(まちがいなし). ¶*sure enough* 案の定, もち論. ¶I am *pretty sure* that ... 大抵...と私は思っている. ¶Are you *quite sure* of (=about) it? 君それはたしかか. ‖ Be *quite sure* before you do anything. 何ごとでも実行にかかる前に確かめることだ. ¶I am not *so sure* of that. 私にはあまり確信はない. 「だ.
M² It is *as sure* as you're living. それは大丈夫間違いなし
P I am not *sure about* it. それはしかとは言えない(疑わしい). ¶His name is ..., I'm *sure of* that. 彼の名はたしかに...と言った. ‖ I am *sure of* his living to 70. 僕は彼が七十までは確かに生きると信じている. ‖ You may be *sure of* his honesty. 君は彼の正直なことを信じてよい. ‖ make *sure of* the fact previously reported 前の報告の真偽を確かめる. 【類】make *sure of* the amount (quality, quantity) of ... / to make *sure of* one's success.
O Be *sure* to come. きっと来たまえ. ¶Be *sure* that you get one. 必ず一つお買いなさい. 【類】Be *sure* to close the door after you. ¶He is *sure* to succeed. 彼はきっと成功する. ¶Are you *going* to attend the party?—*Sure,* I am. 会に出るのか.—出るよ. ☞ *Sure,* I am. は Yes の感じだが, 否定は *Sure,* I ain't (=am not). となって No の感じ. 英
surety, *n.* 保証人; 保証. ∟語用法は Surely.
V *find sureties* 保証人になる人を求める. ¶*get* a *surety* 保証人を立てる. ¶*go* (=*stand*) *surety* 保証人になる.
P stand a *surety for* (*against*) ... ...の保証(反対証)人に立つ. ¶I will be *surety for* him. 私が彼の保証人になります. ¶be *surety on* a contract 契約の保証に立つ.
surf, *n.* 寄せ波, 砕け波.
V² *Surf booms* upon a desolate shore. 寄せ波が荒涼たる浜辺にごうごうと当る.
Q a *heavy surf* 激浪. ¶the *rhythmic surf* on the shore 岸に押寄せる韻律的な寄せ波. ¶The white *seething surf* fell exhausted along the shore. あわ立つ白波が力なく海岸に
surface, *n.* 表面, 面; うわべ, 皮相. ∟砕けた.
V Russia *covers* one-seventh of the land *surface* of the globe. ロシアは地球陸地面の七分一を占めている. ¶*fret* the *surface* of water [風など]水面を波立たせる. ¶A cube *has* six *surfaces.* 立方体には六面がある. ¶As yet, we have done no more than *scratch* the *surface* of the subject. 今までの所われわれはその問題研究の端緒を得たに過ぎない.
Q a *broad surface* 広い面. ¶This piece of wood has a *curved surface.* この木片の面はそっている. ¶This road has an *even surface.* この道路は平らだ. ¶a *flat surface* 平たい面. ¶on the *frozen surface* of a pond 池の凍った表面. ¶a *level surface* 水平面. ¶the *outer* (*inner*) *surface* of a bottle びんの外(内)側. ¶a *rough surface* ざらざらした面. ¶a *smooth surface* すべっこい面 ¶the *under surface* of cloth 布の裏. ¶*veneered* or *varnished surface* 着せ板をしたまたはワニスを塗った面. 「面.
Q² a *plane surface* 板の面. ¶the *land surface* 地域, 陸地
P It appears *above* the *surface.* それは表面に現われている. ¶*at* the earth's *surface* 地球の表面に ‖ look only *at* the *surface* of things 事物の皮相のみを見る. 【類】Straws swim *at* the *surface.* / *at* or *near* the *surface* of the water. ¶a rock four feet *below* (=*beneath*) the *surface* of the water 水面の四フィート下の所にある岩 ‖ if we look *below* the *surface* of controversy 議論の内面に立入って見れば ‖ He is kind *below* the *surface.* 彼は心は親切だ. ¶a depression *in* the *surface* 表面のくぼみ. ¶this region *of* the earth's *surface* 地球の表面のこの地域. ¶*on* the *surface* 表面は, ちょっと見には. 【類】not visible *on* the *surface.* ¶It does not appear *on* the *surface.* それは表面には現われない ‖ float *on* the *surface* 表面に浮ぶ ‖ His faults are *on* the *surface.* 彼の過失は明白だ. ‖ His politeness was all *on* the *surface.* 彼の丁寧はうわべだけだった. ¶rise *to* the *surface* [魚など]浮き上がる ‖ Wickedness is sure to come *to* the *surface* in time. 悪いことは早晩知れる. ¶two feet *under* the *surface* 表面下二フィートの所に. ¶It has made great progress at least *upon* the *surface.* それは少なくともうわべだけは著しく進歩した. ¶a board *with* a rough *surface* 表面のざらざらした板.
surfeit, *v.* 満腹させる.
P He *surfeits* us *with* compliments. 彼はわれわれにいやになるほどお世辞を言う. ‖ People are easily *surfeited with* that sort of entertainment. その種のもてなしはすぐいやになる. ‖ *surfeit* oneself *with* sweets 甘い物を食い過ぎる.
surf-riding, *n.* 波乗り.
V *enjoy surf-riding* 波乗りをやる.
O *Surf-riding* is a thrilling sport. 波乗りはスリルのある
surge, *n.* 大波. ∟スポーツだ.
V² where the *surges roll* 大波のうねる所に.
P a coast beaten *by* the *surge* 大波の打寄せる海岸.
P² a *surge of* flame 火炎の渦巻 ‖ A *surge of* anger rushed over him. 怒りの表情がさっと顔に現われた.
surge, *v.* 波打つ, 波動する; [群集が]押し寄せる.
M Indignation *surges up* within one. 憤慨の情が胸にわきたって来る. 【類】the longing that *surged up* from his very heart ‖ Prices *surge up.* 物価が高騰する.
P Smoke *surged from* the burning building. 煙が焼けている建物から渦巻いて出た. ¶When the door was opened, the crowd *surged into* the hall. 入口が開くと群集は潮のように館内へ流れ込んだ. ¶A big crowd *surged out of* the ball park. 大観衆が野球場からどっと流れ出た. ¶The crowd *surged through* the streets. 人波が街路を押し回った. ¶Blood *surges to* the face. 血が顔にさっと押寄せる ‖ *surge to* the fore again 『比ゆ』再び浮び上る.
surgeon, *n.* 外科医, 軍医.
Q a *naval surgeon* 海軍々医. ¶an *operating surgeon* 手術をする外科医. ¶an *orthopedic surgeon* 整形外科医. ¶a *veterinary surgeon* 獣医. 「科医.
Q² an *army surgeon* 陸軍々医. ¶a *plastic surgeon* 整形外
P He practises *as* a *surgeon.* 彼は外科医を開業している.
P² a *surgeon in* the British Army 英国陸軍勤務の軍医. ¶a *surgeon to* the hospital その病院付の外科医.
surgery, *n.* 外科手術.
Q *clinical surgery* 臨床外科手術. ¶*dental* and *oral surgery* 歯科及び口腔外科手術. ¶*major surgery* 大手術. ¶*operative surgery* 手術. ¶*orthopedic* (=plastic) *surgery*
Q² *brain surgery* 脳外科. ∟整形外科.
surmise, *n.* おく測.
V People *elicited* many *surmises* from the press. 新聞の記事を見て人々は種々のおく測をたくましくした.
surmise, *v.* 推測する.
P At least she *surmised* as much *from* his looks. 少なくとも彼女は彼の顔色でそう察した.
surmount, *v.* 頂上をおおう, 冠する.
P a gateway *surmounted by* the Royal Arms 王室御紋章を冠する門口. ¶a polygonal dome *surmounted by* a cupola 小丸屋根のついた正多角形のドーム(冠形屋根). ¶*surmount* a tower *with* a spire 塔の上にせん塔を付ける. 【類】peaks *surmounted with* snow.
O *surmount* difficulties 困難を切抜ける.
surname, *n.* 姓; あだ名.
V *drop* her own *surname* and take that of her husband

自分の姓をやめて夫の姓を名乗る. ¶William I *had* the *surname* " the Conqueror." ウイリヤム一世は「征服者」と称された. ¶*put* the *surname* あだ名を付ける.

P call one *by* one's *surname* 人を姓で呼ぶ.

surname, *v.* あだ名を付ける.

P He was *surnamed* the Owl, *from* his habit of burning the midnight oil. 彼は夜ふかしして勉強するので「ふくろう」とあだ名を付けられた.

surpass, *v.* …にまさる, …をしのぐ.

P he was *surpassed* as an orator only *by* … 演説で彼をおししのぐものは…だけであった. 【類】The silk industry in Lyons is *surpassed* ***by*** none in foreign countries. ¶*surpass* … ***in*** rank (strength) 位(など)が…にまさる.

surplus, *n.* 剰余, 余分.

V ***have*** a *surplus* 余剰がある. ¶***provide*** an ample *surplus* たくさんの剰余金を準備する. ¶***represent*** a *surplus* of … …の剰余を示す.

Q² ***food*** *surpluses* of the United States, Canada, Australia and Argentina 米, 加, 豪及びアルゼンチンの過剰食料. ¶***import*** *surplus* 輸入する余剰物資. ¶leave a ***treasury*** *surplus* 国庫に余剰金を残す. ¶***war*** *surpluses* located in foreign nations 諸外国に凍結してある戦争余剰資材.

P There is a *surplus* ***in*** the State's treasury ***of*** over $… 国庫には…ドル以上の剰余金がある. ¶a *surplus* ***of*** births ***over*** deaths 死亡数に対する出生数の超過.

surprise, *n.* びっくり, 奇襲.

V ***afford*** a welcome *surprise* うれしい驚きを与える. ¶***attempt*** a *surprise* 奇襲を試みる. ¶***cause*** one no *surprise* 人に案外と思わせない. ¶***excite*** the *surprise* of … …をびっくりさせる. 【類】it may, perhaps, ***excite*** *surprise* when I add that … ¶he ***exhibited*** no *surprise* at … 彼は…には少しも驚いた様子を見せなかった. ¶He ***expressed*** his *surprise* at seeing her look so ill. 彼は彼女がとても顔色が悪いのでびっくりした. 【類】***express*** much *surprise* on learning that … ¶***feel*** *surprise* at … …にびっくりする. ¶***give*** one *surprise* 人を驚かす. ¶I ***have*** a *surprise* for you. 君が驚くことがある. 【類】I ***have*** a great *surprise* in store for you. ¶one can ***imagine*** my *surprise* when it was announced … …が発表されたときの私の驚きは想像できよう. ¶no little *surprise* was ***occasioned*** by the outcome of … …の結果に少なからず驚かされた. 【類】it may therefore ***occasion*** no small *surprise* to find that … ¶***provide*** an unpleasant *surprise* for … …におもしろからぬ驚きを与える. ¶***show*** no *surprise* 少しも驚きの色を見せない.

Q an ***agreeable*** *surprise* うれしい驚き. 【類】one finds with ***agreeable*** *surprise* that … ¶get a ***big*** *surprise* あっという ‖ Here's a ***big*** *surprise* for you. 珍しい(すばらしい)ことがあるよ. ¶with an expression of ***blank*** *surprise* あっけに取られて. ¶a ***delightful*** *surprise* うれしい驚き. ¶a ***disconcerting*** *surprise* どぎまぎさせる不意打. ¶in ***dumb*** *surprise* あっけに取られて. ¶to my ***extreme*** *surprise* I found that … 私は…と知って非常に驚いた. ¶recover from the ***first*** *surprise* 最初の驚きから心が落着く. ¶a ***fresh*** *surprise* 新たな驚き. ¶a ***glad*** *surprise* 喜ばしい驚き. ¶It is a ***great*** *suprise* to me. それには私はひどくびっくりした. ‖ note, with ***great*** *surprise*, that … 非常に驚いて…であることに気がつく. ¶go away in ***grieved*** *surprise* 悲しみかつ驚いてその場を去る. ¶a ***happy*** *surprise* うれしい驚き. ¶a ***joyous*** *surprise* 喜ばしい驚き. ¶She looked at him in ***mute*** *surprise*. 彼女はローつきかず彼を見入った. ¶to their ***mutual*** *surprise* 彼ら双方驚いたことには. ¶It is ***no small*** *surprise* to … それは … に取っては少なからぬ驚きだ. ¶a ***painful*** *surprise* 痛ましい驚き. ¶His visit gave me a ***pleasant*** *surprise*. 彼の訪問を受けてうれしくもあり驚きもした. ¶a ***pleasing*** *surprise* 愉快な驚き. ¶it was a ***real*** *surprise* to find … …には本当に驚いた. ¶a ***stunning*** *surprise* 気絶するほどの驚き. ¶***What*** a *surprise!* これは驚いた(あきれた, お珍らしいなど). ¶to our ***utter*** *surprise* われわれが全く驚いたことには.

P The castle was taken ***by*** *surprise*. 城は奇襲で落された. ‖ You have taken me ***by*** *surprise*. 君は僕に不意打を食わした. 【類】The news took us rather ***by*** *surprise*. ¶This was done ***for*** a *surprise*. それはちょっとびっくりさせるためやった. ¶start up (=jump) ***in*** *surprise* 驚いて飛び上がる. 【類】" Why," she exclaimed ***in*** *surprise*. / " Why?" he asked ***in*** some *surprise*. ¶A thrill ***of*** *surprise* came over me. 私はぞっとするほどの驚きに襲われた. ¶***to*** my *surprise* 私の驚いたことには. 【類】Much ***to*** his *surprise* he found his dog dead. ¶he asked ***with*** *surprise* whether … 彼は驚いて…かを尋ねた. 【類】He turned pale (青くなった) ***with*** *surprise*.

P² express the liveliest *surprise* ***at*** the sight of … …を見てひどくびっくりする. ¶it is no *surprise* ***to*** us to find that … …ということが分かったところで別に驚きはすまい. 【類】it is a *surprise* ***to*** us to learn that …

surprise, *v.* びっくりさせる, 奇襲する.

M I was ***agreeably*** *surprised* to find that … …と分かって私は驚いたがうれしかった. ¶I be ***disagreeably*** *surprised* あきれる. ¶be ***greatly*** *surprised* at the scene その光景を見て大いに驚く. ¶***indignantly*** *surprised* 驚きかつ怒って. ¶I was ***much*** *surprised* at it. それには私は非常に驚きました. 【類】I was ***much*** *surprised* to hear about it (それを聞いて). ¶I was ***unpleasantly*** *surpirsed*. 私は驚きもし不愉快にもなった.

P I am *surprised* ***at*** you. 君には驚いた. 【類】I am not *surprised* ***at*** that. / He was greatly *surprised* ***at*** the news. / I am *surprised* ***at*** seeing that … / Were you *surprised* ***at*** finding me here? ¶I was *surprised* ***by*** the man's appearance. 私はその人の風さいに驚いた. 【類】*surprise* her ***by*** saying that … ¶A detective *surprised* him ***in*** the act. 探偵が現行犯で彼に不意打を食わせた. ¶*surprise* a person ***into*** confession 思いがけない所を突込んで白状させる ‖ He was *surprised* ***into*** consent. 彼は不意を打たれてつい承諾した.

O I am *surprised* to hear you say so. 君がそういうことを言うとは意外だ.

surprising, *a.* 意外な, 不思議な.

M what seems to me ***most*** *surprising* is … 私に一番意外に思われるのは…だ. ¶It is ***really*** *surprising*. 実に不思議だ.

P it is *surprising* ***for*** (=***to***) me to hear that …とは意外だ.

surrender, *n.* 降服; 交付.

V ***announce*** its unconditional *surrender* その無条件降服を通告する. ¶The *surrender* of the fort ***took place*** a few days after. その城塁はその後数日で陥落した.

Q an ***unconditional*** *surrender* 無条件降服.

P ***since*** the *surrender* 降服(敗戦)以来. ¶He was set free ***upon*** *surrender* of key. 彼がかぎを渡したので解放された.

P² by a complete *surrender* ***of*** self ***to*** art 芸術に没頭して.

surrender, *v.* 引渡す, 降服する.

M *surrender* ***unconditionally*** to … …に無条件で降服する. ¶*surrender* ***unresistingly*** to … …に抵抗せず降服する. ¶He *surrendered* ***voluntarily*** to the police. 彼は警察へ自首した.

P *surrender* it ***to*** the owner upon presentation of the receipt 領収証呈示次第それを所有主に引渡す. 【類】He *surrendered* his property ***to*** his creditors. ‖ women who refuse to *surrender* ***to*** the years なかなか年にめげない婦人 ‖ *surrender* oneself ***to*** indolence (a bad habit) 遊惰(など)に身を持くずす ‖ *surrender* oneself ***to*** a quiet despair 不運とあきらめる ‖ *surrender* oneself ***to*** justice 自首する. 【類】*surrender* oneself ***to*** grief.

surround, *v.* 取巻く, 囲む.

M The great hall of the temple is *surrounded* ***entirely*** by a wide gallery. 寺院の大本堂には広い回廊がついている.

P He stood *surrounded* ***by*** an eager crowd of listeners. 彼は熱心な多数の聴衆に取巻かれて立っていた. ‖ *surrounded* always ***by*** medicine-bottles いつも薬びんに取巻かれて(薬じに親しんで). 【類】He is *surrounded* ***by*** danger. / It is *surrounded* ***by*** hills. / *surrounded* ***by*** seas (=the sea) on all sides. ¶The house is *surrounded* ***with*** (=***by***) a moat (walls, trees). その家はほり(など)で囲まれている. ‖ It was *surrounded* ***with*** heaps of combustible materials consisting of fagots and straw. それはそだやわらの可燃物の山で囲まれていた. 【類】He found himself *surrounded* ***with*** an atmosphere of calm kindness.

surroundings, *n. pl.* 環境, 周囲の人々.

V ***recognize*** one's *surroundings* その周囲を認識する.

Q ***artistic*** *surroundings* 芸術的な環境. ¶present entertainment in ***clean*** and ***comfortable*** *surroundings* 清潔で心地よい環境で娯楽を与える. ¶***cultured*** *surroundings* 教養ある環境. ¶***dignified*** *surroundings* 気品のある周囲の人々. ¶in ***fancy*** *surroundings* しゃれた環境で. ¶***healthy*** *sur-*

roundings 衛生的な四囲の状態. ¶live in ***hostile surroundings*** 周囲から敵視されて生活する. ¶***picturesque surroundings*** 絵のように美しい四囲の情景. ¶We can work best in ***sympathetic surroundings***. あたりが親切だと一番よく働ける. ¶A genius seldom comes out of ***ugly surroundings***. 天才は環境が悪いと滅多に現われない. ¶amidst ***uncongenial*** (=disagreeable) *surroundings* 不愉快な環境の中で. ¶toil under ***unfavorable hygienic surroundings*** 不衛生な環境で作業する. ¶Good work cannot be done in ***unpleasant*** or ***uncomfortable surroundings***. よい仕事は不愉快なもしくは落着の悪い環境ではできない.

Q² *home surroundings* 家庭の環境.

P The opera-house stands on an open site ***amid*** beautiful *surroundings*. そのオペラ館は周囲の美しい空地に立っている. ¶A child learns ***from*** its *surroundings*. 子供はその四囲の事物から物を覚える. ¶a place ***with*** evil *surroundings* 環境の良くない場所.

surtax, *n.* 付加税.

P a *surtax* ***to*** ... ...の付加税.

surveillance, *n.* 監視.

V ***evade*** the *surveillance* of the police 警官の監視をくぐる. ¶***remove surveillance*** on ... ...の監視を解く.

Q under the ***close*** *surveillance* of ... ...の厳密な検査を経て. ¶He was placed under ***strict*** *surveillance*. 彼に厳重な監視が付けられた.

Q² bring it under ***government*** *surveillance* それを政府の監督下におく. ¶He is still under ***police*** *surveillance*. 彼は今でも警官の監視をつけられている.

P ***under*** the *surveillance* of the police 警官監視の下に.

survey, *n.* 測量; 検分, 概観; 調査.

V ***attempt*** a rapid *survey* of ... ...の概論を試みる. ¶***conduct*** *surveys* 検分を行う. ¶***give*** a comprehensive *survey* of the activities of the society from 1863 to 1913 一八六三年から一九一三年に至る同協会の事業の概括的調査報告をする. ¶Being interested, I cannot ***hold*** *survey*. 利害関係があるので私には検査はできない. ¶***institute*** a *survey* 調査を開始する. ¶***make*** a *survey* of the prospective town site 将来の都市指定地を検分する. 【類】***make*** a *survey* of education in Japan / ***make*** a *survey* of research in this field. ¶***obtain*** a careful *survey* of the goldfield その金山を細かに視察する. ¶***take*** a *survey* of the whole 全体を見渡す.

Q an ***adequate*** and ***up-to-date*** *survey* of the libraries in London ロンドンにおける図書館の詳細で現状に即した調査. ¶take a ***broad*** *survey* 広く観察する. ¶make a ***careful*** *survey* of ... ...について細心の調査をする. ¶a ***compact, accurate*** *survey* of the facts of ... ...という事実の簡潔で正確な調査. ¶get a ***complete*** *survey* of the news in the home country 自分の本国のニュースを徹底的に調べあげる. ¶make a ***factual*** *survey* 事実上の調査をする. ¶a ***general*** *survey* of the subject その問題の概観. ¶a ***hurried*** (=***cursory***) *survey* of ... ざっとやる...の調査. ¶an ***impartial*** *survey* 公平な観察. ¶a ***monthly*** *survey* of the French literary world フランス文学界月評. ¶s ***pictorial*** *survey* of recent events 近事画報. ¶take a ***rapid*** *survey* of the subject その問題を急速に調査する. ¶indulge in a certain ***retrospective*** *survey* of the history of ... ...の歴史の回顧的な調査を道楽にやる. ¶fail to pass ***satisfactory*** *survey* 満足な調査が出来ない. ¶a ***sectional*** *survey* 部分的観察. ¶***social*** *surveys* 社会調査. ¶a ***synthetic*** *survey* 総合的観測. ¶a ***topographical*** *survey* 地形測量. ¶a ***valuable*** *survey* of the results of previous researches 先人の研究に関する貴重な一般考査. ¶a ***vigilant*** *survey* of markets and of prices 市場及び物価の綿密な調査. ¶when we take a ***wide*** *survey*, we realize that ... 高所から概観すると...が分かる.

Q² an ***air*** *survey* 空中観測. ¶a ***magazine*** *survey* ある雑誌の調査. ¶***market*** *survey* 市場調査(大衆の購買力を科学的に調査すること). ¶a ***public opinion*** *survey* 世論調査.

P ***after*** a careful *survey* of the effect その結果をよく観測してから. ¶***on*** careful *survey* よく調べて見ると ‖ ***on*** a broad *survey* 大局から見れば.

P² a *survey* ***by*** travelling through ... ...の踏査. ¶a brief *survey* ***of*** his career 彼の閲歴の要略.

survey, *v.* 測量する; じろじろ見る; 概説する.

P The Prime Minister *surveyed* the current world situation ***in*** his speech. 首相はその演説で現在の世界の時局を概説した. ¶I *surveyed* him ***from*** head ***to*** foot. 私は彼の頭からつま先までじろじろ見た. 【類】*survey* a stranger ***from*** top ***to*** bottom.

O *survey* house lots 区割りした敷地を検分する.

surveyor, *n.* 測量技師.

Q get properly ***qualified*** *surveyors* 測量技師として適格者を得る.

survival, *n.* 生存, 残存; 残存物.

Q a ***curious*** *survival* of old-time usage 古い習慣のおもしろい遺物. ¶the three ***existing*** *survivals* 現存する三つの遺品. ¶the obscure laws of ***literary*** *survival* 文学作品の永続性に関する不明の法律. ¶only the ***pale*** *survival* of ... わずかに余命を保つ...の遺物. ¶an ***ultimate*** *survival* of the fittest 最適者の最終的生存.

P ***by*** a *survival* of the unfittest 最不適者の生存によって.

P² a *survival* ***from*** ancient (primitive, Roman) times 往古(など)からの残存物. 【類】a *survival* ***from*** a former period (往時). ¶*survivals* ***into*** our day of the barbarous practices of the middle ages 中世紀の蛮風の現代における名残り. ¶a *survival* ***of*** barbarism 野蛮な遺風 ‖ the *survival* ***of*** the fittest 適者生存.

survive, *v.* ...より長く生き延びる.

M His wife *survived* him ***a few years***. 彼の妻は彼の死後数年生きていた. ¶He did not ***long*** *survive* his humiliation. 彼はその恥辱を受けて間もなく死んで行った.

P *survive* ***beyond*** the period of its usefulness 時代が変って役に立たなくなる. ¶He is *survived* ***by*** his wife and their daughter, Mrs. ... 彼は妻と娘の...夫人を後に残して死んだ. 【類】He passed away being *survived* ***by*** his wife and two sons. ‖ She *survived* him ***by*** ... years. 彼女は彼の死後数年生きていた. ¶Few *survived* ***to*** our time (=the present day). 今日まで生き残っている人はほとんどない. ¶Mrs. ... *survives* him ***with*** a son and two daughters. ...夫人は一人の男の子と二人の娘とともに彼の亡き後に残っている.

survivor, *n.* 生存者.

Q One boat with a ***few*** *survivors* was picked up. 二三人の生残者を乗せた一そうのボートが発見された. ¶the ***only*** *survivors* of the accident その惨事の唯一の生存者. ¶the ***sole*** *survivor* from the shipwreck その難船のたった一人の生存者 ‖ the ***sole*** *survivor* of his class, which graduated fifty-nine members 五十九人卒業した彼のクラス中の唯一の生存者. 【類】***two*** *survivors* ***from*** the wreck.

P² one of the *survivors* ***of*** the famous class of 1837 at Yale College エール大学一八三七年度卒業の(偉人の輩出した)有名なクラスで今生残っている者の一人.

susceptibility, *n.* 感受性; 感情力, 感情.

V ***hurt*** the *susceptibilities* of ... ...の感情を害する. ¶***injure*** French *susceptibilities* フランス人の感情を害する. ¶***offend*** the *susceptibilities* of ... ...の感情を害する. ¶***shock*** the moral *susceptibilities* of ... ...の道徳的感受性に激動を起す. ¶***wound*** the *susceptibilities* of ... ...の感情を害する.

Q a man of ***keen*** *susceptibilities* 感受性の強い人 ‖ ***keen*** *susceptibility* of injustice 正邪(是非)に対する鋭い感受性. ¶His ***wounded*** *susceptibility* was healed with the lapse of time. 彼の傷つけられた感情は時がたつにつれていやされた.

P² *susceptibilities* ***of*** being moved 動かされやすいこと. ¶*susceptibility* ***to*** shame (criticism) 恥辱(など)に対する敏感 ‖ *susceptibility* ***to*** a disease 病身.

susceptible, *a.* ...のできる; ...に感じやすい.

M ***highly*** *susceptible* of cold 寒さにひどく感じやすい. ¶Children are ***more*** *susceptible* than adults. 小児は大人よりも感じやすいものだ.

P *susceptible* ***of*** change (improvement) 変更(改良)のできる ‖ a passage *susceptible* ***of*** several interpretations 色々に解釈のできる文句. 【類】The passage is *susceptible* (=admits) ***of*** another interpretation. / The fact is not *susceptible* (=does not admit) ***of*** proof (証明). / The word is not *susceptible* ***of*** exact definition. ¶*susceptible* ***to*** cajolery 甘言に動かされやすい. 【類】so *susceptible* ***to*** influences from the outside / He is very *susceptible* ***to*** female charms (女好き) / *susceptible* ***to*** the influence of fashion (流行) / *susceptible* ***to*** (=of) cold / *susceptible* ***to*** kindness / *susceptible* ***to*** pain.

suspect, *n.* 容疑者, 注意人物.

V ***arrest*** *suspects* 容疑者を捕縛する. ¶"***shadow***" a *sus-*

pect 怪しい人物の跡をつける.

Q photographs of ***criminal suspects*** 被疑者の写真. ¶a ***key suspect*** 有力な容疑者. ¶a ***political suspect*** 政治上の注意人物.

Q^2 a ***spy suspect*** スパイ容疑者. ¶a ***war crime*** (=criminal) *suspect* 戦争犯罪容疑者.【類】"Class A" ***war crime*** *suspects.*

P He is ***above suspect.*** 彼はけん疑など受くべき人物ではない. ¶An inspector sprang a surprise ***on*** a *suspect.* 警部がだし抜けに容疑者を取調べた.

P^2 a *suspect* ***in*** a murder 殺人容疑者.

suspect, *v.* 疑う, あるらしく思う.

M ***little*** *suspecting* a plot 企(たくら)みがあろうなどとはほとんど思いも寄らず. ¶I could not ***possibly*** *suspect* as much. よもやそうだとは気がつかなかった. ¶be ***strongly*** *suspected* けん疑が濃厚である. ¶be ***unjustly*** *suspected* of ... ...について不当なけん疑を受ける.

P He is *suspected* ***as*** an accomplice. 彼は共犯者として疑いをかけられている. ¶*suspect* one ***of*** murder (lying) 人に殺人(など)のけん疑をかける ‖ He is *suspected* ***of*** having a hand in the late affair. 彼は先だっての事件に関係があるとけん疑を掛けられている.【類】He is *suspected* ***of*** crime. / all persons *suspected* ***of*** infectious diseases (伝染病). ¶*suspect* ***without*** reason 邪推する.

Q I *suspected* him to be (=that he was) a swindler. 私は彼が山師だろうと思った.【類】I *suspect* the bill to be a counterfeit (偽造手形).

suspend, *v.* つるす; 停止する, 停止処分に付する.

P *suspend* a lamp ***above*** (=over) the table 食卓の上にランプをつるす. ¶*suspend* a ball ***by*** a thread まりを糸でつるす. ¶The public business was *suspended* ***for*** five days. 官庁は五日間休みになった.【類】Negotiations are *suspended* ***for*** the present. / Payment was *suspended* ***for*** a certain period. ¶*suspend* a lamp ***from*** the ceiling ランプを天井からつるす ‖ be *suspended* ***from*** a school for an indefinite period (無期停学).【類】He was *suspended* ***from*** his office. / He was *suspended* ***from*** church membership (教会から除名). / be *suspended* ***from*** a financial aid ‖ Her flower basket was *suspended* ***from*** her neck ***by*** a strap. 彼女は花かごを皮ひもでくびにつるしていた. ¶a balloon *suspended* ***in*** mid-air 中空にかかる気球 ‖ a particle *suspended* ***in*** a liquid 液体中に浮ぶ微粒子.【類】dust (withered leaves) *suspended* ***in*** the air. ¶a bridge *suspended* ***on*** chains くさりでつるした橋.

suspense, *n.* つり下がり; 不安, 気掛り.

Q look on in ***agonized*** *suspense* 不安にもだえながら傍観する. ¶wait in ***anxious*** *suspense* for his arrival 彼の到着を今か今かと気をもんで待つ. ¶keep one in [a] ***awful*** *suspense* 人に恐ろしく気をもませる. ¶Everyone in the room sat in the silence of ***deep*** *suspense.* へや中の人が深い不安におそわれ黙然としてすわっていた. ¶wait in ***great*** *suspense* for a doctor's opinion 医者の診断を心配しながら待つ.

P The matter now hangs ***in*** *suspense.* その事件は未解決のままになっている. ¶a story that keeps you ***in*** *suspense* until the last chapter=a thriller サスペンスもの(犯罪心理小説など).

suspension, *n.* つり下がり; 浮遊; 停止.

V ***force*** *suspension* of US Army Information Service offices 命令で米陸軍情報部を閉鎖する. ¶***release*** the *suspension* of a newspaper 新聞紙の発行停止を解除する.

P The issue was placed ***under*** (=subjected to) *suspension.* [新聞紙など]発行停止を食った.

P^2 *suspension* ***from*** a nail くぎからのたれ下り. ¶*suspension* ***in*** liquid 液体中の浮遊. ¶*suspension* ***of*** hostilities 休戦 ‖ the *suspension* ***of*** an official 官吏の停職 ‖ the *suspension* ***of*** a student 学生の停学 ‖ *suspension* ***of*** publication 発行停止.【類】*suspension* ***of*** the rules / *suspension* ***of*** execution / a *suspension* ***of*** the rain / *suspension* ***of*** payment (judgment).

suspicion, *n.* けん疑, 疑念;《俗》気味.

V ***allay*** *suspicion* 疑念を解く. ¶This ***aroused*** my *suspicion* at first sight. 私は一目見て怪しいと思った.【類】A *suspicion* was ***aroused.*** / without ***arousing*** *suspicion.* ¶***attach*** *suspicion* to ... ...にけん疑をかける. ¶I cannot ***avoid*** a haunting *suspicion* that ... 私にはどうしても...と思われてならない. ¶It ***awakened*** his *suspicions.* それが彼の疑念を呼び起した. ¶***breed*** the *suspicion* that ... ...という疑いを起す. ¶***cast*** (=***throw***) *suspicion* on ... ...にけん疑をかける. ¶What ***caused*** the *suspicion?* なんでけん疑がかかったのか. ¶***clear*** *suspicion* (=clear oneself) 身のあかしを立てる. ¶***confirm*** one's *suspicions* その疑念を強める. ¶***create*** *suspicion* 疑いを起させる. ¶***disarm*** *suspicion* 疑いを解く. ¶The *suspicion* was ***discovered*** to be utterly groundless (=unfounded) その容疑には全く根拠がないことが分かった. ¶***dispel*** *suspicion* and create confidence けん疑を晴らして信用させる.【類】*Suspicions* are ***dispelled.*** ¶***divest*** *suspicion* from ... ...からけん疑いを解く. ¶***encourage*** the *suspicion* that ... ...の疑いを強める. ¶***entertain*** a strong *suspicion* that という強い疑いをいだいている. ¶It is likely to ***excite*** *suspicion.* それは疑いを招きやすい.【類】There is nothing to ***excite*** *suspicion.* / no *suspicion* was ***excited*** on the part of ... (...の方には). ¶***favor*** the *suspicion* [色々の事情が]そのけん疑を確実と思わせる. ¶***fix*** one's *suspicions* upon ... ...にそのけん疑をかける. ¶***foster*** *suspicion* 疑いを増す. ¶I ***have*** a *suspicion* that ... 私は...の疑念をいだいている.【類】nobody ***had*** any *suspicion* that ... / he ***had*** some *suspicion* of ... ¶It merely served to ***increase*** my *suspicions.* それは私の疑いを増すばかりだった. ¶***incur*** *suspicion* 疑いを受ける. ¶The secrecy surrounding the whole affair ***inflamed*** *suspicion.* 事件全部が秘密にされていることがかえって疑いを高めた. ¶***lull*** the *suspicion* 疑念を静める. ¶Iago ***played off*** Othello's *suspicions* against Desdemona's simplicity. イヤゴーはオセロにデズデモーナの無邪気さを疑わせて漁夫の利を占めた. ¶***raise*** *suspicions* in their mind's 彼らの心に疑念をいだかせる.【類】His behavior ***raised*** *suspicions* ***in*** my mind. ¶***rouse*** *suspicion* 疑いを起す. ¶***start*** *suspicions* in one 人に疑念をいだかせる. ¶***strengthen*** one's *suspicion* 疑念を強める. ¶***wake*** *suspicion* 疑いを起させる.

V^2 Does no *suspicion* ***attach*** to him? 彼にけん疑が掛かっていないか.【類】no *suspicion* whatever ***attached*** to ... ¶*suspicions* ***fell*** on ... ...にけん疑が掛かった. ¶this *suspicion* still ***lingers*** in the minds of ... この疑念はまだ...の心から消えない. ¶to this day there ***lurks*** a *suspicion* that ... 今に至るまで...という疑惑が奥底にある. ¶*suspicion* ***points*** to ... ...が怪しいと思われる. ¶There ***prevailed*** a profound *suspicion.* けん疑が深まっていた. ¶*Suspicion* ***rested*** upon him, perhaps not unnaturally. けん疑が彼にかかったのは恐らく無理ではなかったろう.

Q the ***entire*** *suspicion* fell upon ... けん疑は全部...に掛かった. ¶***groundless*** (=***unfounded***) *suspicion* ぬれぎぬ. ¶a ***lurking*** *suspicion* 潜在する疑念. ¶He was detained for ten days upon a ***mere*** *suspicion.* 彼はけん疑だけで十日間拘留された. ¶have a ***secret*** *suspicion* that ... ...の疑念をひそかにいだいている. ¶there are ***strong*** *suspicions* that ... ...のけん疑が濃厚だ. ¶***unjust*** *suspicions* 不当のけん疑. ¶have ***well-grounded*** *suspicions* 疑いには十分根拠がある.

P His character is ***above*** *suspicion.* 彼はけん疑を受けるような人物でない.【類】Their business methods are ***above*** *suspicion.* ¶His absolute reliability is ***beyond*** *suspicion.* 彼に絶対信頼のおけることは疑いを入れない. ¶There is no cause ***for*** *suspicion.* けん疑をかける理由がない.【類】There is no room (余地) ***for*** *suspicion.* / the only cause ***for*** *suspicon* is ... ¶He was arrested ***on*** *suspicion.* 彼はけん疑で捕縛された.【類】He has been arrested ***on*** [the] *suspicion* of theft (complicity). / He is held ***on*** *suspicion* of being a spy. / ***on*** *suspicion* of being concerned in a robbery / ***on*** [a] *suspicion* of having been concerned in an outrage on ... ¶he was so given ***to*** *suspicion* that ... 彼は...ほど邪推深かった ‖ He is open ***to*** *suspicion.* 彼は疑いを受けても仕方がない. ¶He was arrested ***under*** *suspicion.* 彼はけん疑で捕縛された. ‖ fall ***under*** *suspicion* けん疑を受ける ‖ come ***under*** *suspicion* of having committed the murder その殺人事件の犯人だというけん疑を受ける. ¶come ***under*** *suspicion* for other crimes.【類】He is ***under*** *suspicion* as one of the murderers. / place a person ***under*** *suspicion* of theft. ¶view ***with*** *suspicion* 疑って見る ‖ He was regarded ***with*** *suspicion.* 彼は疑いの目で見られた. ¶Quite ***without*** *suspicion* I accepted his invitation.【類】He died not ***without*** *suspicion* of the poisoned cup. / ***without*** a slight *suspicion* of ...

P² There is a strong *suspicion against* him. 深いけん疑が彼にかかっている. 【類】There are several grounds of *suspicion against* him.

P² without a *suspicion of* humor 少しのユーモア味もなく ‖ a *suspicion of* brandy 少量のブランデー.

suspicious, *a.* 疑い深い.

P He was *suspicious of* all his neighbors. 彼は近所の人を残らず疑っていた. ‖ I am *suspicious of* his intentions (motives, promise). 私は彼の考え(など)を疑っている.

sustain, *v.* 支える; 受ける, こうむる.

P He has *sustained* a great loss *by* the death of his father. 彼は父が死んだのでえらい打撃を受けた. ¶He was *sustained during* his illness *by* hope (religion). 彼は病中希望(など)で持ちこたえた.

sustenance, *n.* 生計; 糧食.

V How shall we *get sustenance*? われわれはどうして生計を立てようか.

P He lived a week *without sustenance* of any kind. 彼は何も食わずに一週間暮した.

sutra, *n.* 経典.

V He *caused* the *sutras* to be recited for the little souls. 彼は亡き子供らのために経を読んでもらった. ¶priests *reciting* the *sutras* 経を読む僧りょたち.

Q² the *Buddhist sutras* 仏教徒の経典.

P some scrolls *of* the *sutras* 数巻の経文.

P² the *Sutra of* Nirvana ねはん経.

suzerainty, *n.* 宗主権, 保護権.

P *under* nominal *suzerainty* 有名無実の主権の下に.

P² *suzerainty on* a country (people) 一国(など)に対する宗主権.

swaddling-clothes, *n.* むつ着.

P The movies in that country are scarcely *out of swaddling-clothes*. その国で製作する映画はまだほとんど幼稚の域を脱していない.

swagger, *v.* 威張ってなびかせる; 豪語する.

P *swagger about* ... …を豪語する. ¶*swagger* a person *into* dread おどしつけて恐れさせる. ¶*swagger* a person *out of* opposition おどしつけて反抗の手を引かせる.

swain, *n.* 愛人(男).

Q her *faithless swain* 彼女の薄情な愛人.

swallow, *n.* つばめ.

V² *Swallows skimmed* about the eaves of the barns. つばめは納屋の軒をかすめて飛んだ. ¶The *swallow twitters*. つばめがさえずる.

V² The *swallows* are [*getting*] *about*. つばめが出始めた.

P a flight *of swallows* 一群のつばめ.

swallow, *n.* 嚥(えん)下; 一飲み込み.

V I *took* deep *swallow* of milk 牛乳をぐいと飲んだ.

Q drink milk slowly in *little swallows* そろそろと少しずつ牛乳を飲む.

P² a *swallow of* water 一口の水.

swallow, *v.* のみ込む.

M *swallow* one's food too *quickly* 食物を早くのみ込み過ぎる. ¶*swallow* it *whole* それをうのみにする. ¶His figure was *swallowed up* in the dark. 彼の姿はやみに吸込まれた. ‖ be fabled to suck in and *swallow up* vessels 船舶を吸いつけのみ込むと伝えられている. 【類】The ship was *swallowed up* by the waves. / be *swallowed up* in the mist ‖ The expenses *swallow up* the earnings. 費用が利得を食ってしまう(掛かり負けがする). 【類】In this situation I sat nearly half an hour, *swallowed up* in grief and despair.

P *swallow at* one gulp がぶっとのみ込む ‖ *swallow in* lumps うのみにする ‖ *swallow in* large draughts ぐいぐい飲む.

O *swallow* one's resentment (anger) 怒りを抑える. ¶*swallow* one's words 前言をとり消す.

swamp, *n.* 沼, 沢, 沼沢地.

V *drain* a *swamp* 沼を干す.

Q amid the *deadly swamps* and forests of the Niger country [アフリカの]ニゲル国の魔の沼沢と森林のまっただ中で. ¶an *impassable swamp* 人の通れない沼沢地. ¶a *marshy swamp* 卑湿の沼沢地. ¶a *mosquito-infested swamp* やぶ蚊のうなる沼沢地. ¶a *miry swamp* 泥深い沼沢地.

swamp, *v.* 水につかる; 殺到する.

P Japanese manufacturers are *swamped by* rush of foreign orders. 日本の生産業者たちは外国から続々注文が殺到して悲鳴をあげている. ‖ a boat *swamped by* waves 水舟. ¶The horse was *swamped in* the stream. 馬が川に流された.

swap, *v.* 交換する.

P *swap* a watch *for* money 時計を金に代える(質入れなどして).

swarm, *n.* 群.

P they came to the town *in swarms* from ... 彼らは…から群を成してその町へやって来た.

P² a *swarm of* bees (mosquitoes, insects, ants, people). 一群のはち(など).

swarm, *v.* 群集する; 群がり行く.

P Ants are *swarming about* the spilt sugar. ありはこぼれた砂糖の回りに群がっている. ¶The insects *swarmed by* thousands. 虫が幾千となく群がった. ¶They were *swarming out of* the inn. 彼らは旅館から群がって出て行った. ¶the streets and squares of Washington *swarmed with* statues ワシントンのつじつじは彫像で一杯だ. 【類】Every place *swarmed with* soldiers. / The beach is *swarming with* bathers. / His compositions *swarm with* blunders (間違いだらけ) / *swarm with* fish.

swat, *v.* ぴしゃっと打つ.

P *swat* a mosquito *with* a hand 手で蚊をぴしゃっと打つ.

O *swat* a fair ball 〘野球〙 好球を打つ.

swath, *n.* 一刈りの幅.

Q cut a *wide swath* 見せびらかす ‖ cut a *wide swath* of destruction [台風などが]わがもの顔の猛威を振う.

swathe, *v.* 巻く, くるむ.

P with limbs *swathed in* bandages 手足をほう帯で巻いて. 【類】with their heads *swathed in* a shawl / its steep rock *swathed in* trees / an old woman *swathed in* furs [毛皮のオーバー].

swatter, *n.* はいたたき.

Q² a *fly swatter* はいたたき.

sway, *n.* 勢力, 権勢; 支配.

V *bear* (=*hold*) *sway* 権勢を握る. ¶*exercise* no small *sway* over one's mind その心に少なからず威力を感じさせる. ¶*extend* its *sway* over ... …に威を揮う. ¶the men who *have* the *sway* of the world today 今日世界を支配する人々. 【類】*have* a great *sway*. ¶The belief *held sway* for centuries. その信仰は数世紀間勢力を揮った. 【類】In those provinces feudal lords *held sway*.

Q hold *dominating sway* among ... …間に圧倒的勢力を揮う. ¶under his *energetic sway* 彼のたくましい支配下で. ¶languish under the *oppressive sway* 暴政のために衰える. ¶The first of the Manchurian conquerors of China held *peaceful sway* over the Flowery Kingdom in the years between 1661 and 1722. 満州出身の中国征服者の初代は一六六一年から一七二二年まで中国に泰平の治世を布いた. ¶hold *regal sway* 王権を握る. ¶Fashion has held *tyrannical sway*. 流行が猛威をたくましくした. ¶It held *undisputed sway* for 2,500 years over ... それは二千五百年間…に対して押しも押されもしない勢力を持っていた.

P He united the whole empire of China *under* his *sway*. 彼は中国の全帝国を統一し支配した. 【類】one of those far-off lands which are *under* the British *sway*. ¶hold *sway in* ... …を支配する. ¶He held *sway over* the British stage. 彼は英国劇壇を風びした.

sway, *v.* 揺り動かす; 支配する; 揺れる.

M We are *too much swayed* by the needs of the moment. われわれは余りに目前の必要に支配される.

P We are *swayed by* sentiment. われわれは感情に支配される. ‖ trees *swayed by* the wind. 風に揺り動かされる樹木. 【類】judgement *swayed by* passion. ¶*sway* the mind *from* rectitude 正しい心をゆがめる ‖ *sway from* side *to* side=roll [船が]左右に揺れる. ¶The wind *swayed* a tree *to* the ground. その風で木が一本倒れた. ¶*sway with* the human tide *in* a jammed car 満員電車の人波で揺れ動く.

swear, *v.* 誓う, 宣誓する; 証言する.

M The witness was *duly sworn*. 証人は正式に宣誓させられた. ¶protest and *swear mightily* 反抗しかつ盛んに毒づく. ¶*swear roundly* 露骨に毒づく.

M² *swear* in 宣誓して(正式に)就任させる. 【類】He was elected on April 22, 1924, but has not been *sworn in*. / *swear in* as Secretary of the Treasury (a constable). ¶*swear off* smoking (drinking). タバコ(など)を誓って断つ.

P *swear against* (*in favor of*) the accused 被告に不利(有利)な証言をする. ¶*swear at* a person 人をののしる. ¶I *swear before* god I didn't mean it. 私はそんな積りではなかったことを神かけて誓う. ¶*swear by* Heaven (the name of God) 天に(神の名によって)誓う. ¶He will shortly be *sworn into* office. 彼は近日宣誓式をあげて任命されるだろう. ¶*swear like* a pirate 口ぎたなくののしる. ¶*swear on* one's sword 刀にかけて誓う. 【類】he *swore on* (=*upon*) the Bible never to ... ¶I *swear to* God 神かけて誓う. ‖ I could *swear to* the fact. そのことは私が受合う. ‖ *swear to* one's statement その陳述の虚偽でないことを誓言する ‖ The affidavit should be *sworn to* before a notary public. 供述人は公証人に対し宣誓して証言しなければいけない. ‖ The conspirators were *sworn to* secrecy. 謀反人は秘密を守ることを誓わせられた. ¶*swear within* oneself 心に誓う.

sweat, *n.* 汗; 発汗; 労苦.

V *exude* cold *sweat* 冷汗をかく. ¶I cannot *stand* the *sweat* of it. その労苦に私はたえきれない. ¶He *took* a *sweat* in the bath. 彼はふろにはいって汗を取った. ‖ He will not *take* the *sweat*. 彼はその労をとらないだろう. ¶*wipe* the *sweat* from one's face 顔の汗をぬぐう.

V² A *sweat* will *do* you *good*. 君汗を出すとよくなるだろう. ¶Cold *sweat* was *rolling* from his brow. 冷汗が彼の額から流れていた. ¶The *sweat stood* in beads upon his forehead. 彼の額には汗が玉になっていた. ¶The *sweat oozes out*. 汗がしみ出る.

Q put a person in a *cold sweat* 冷汗をかかせる. 【類】bring the *cold sweat* upon his brow / be in a *cold sweat* from fear (fright). ¶gain a pittance by *daily sweat* 日々汗水たらしてわずかな給料を得る. ¶It is a *horrid sweat*. それは恐ろしく骨の折れる仕事だ. 【類】It's a *horrible* (=an *awful*) *sweat*. ¶*nightly sweats* 寝汗.

P work *by* the *sweat* of one's brow 額に汗を出して働く. 【類】live (生活する) *by* the *sweat* of the brow. ¶Thou shalt eat thy bread *in* the *sweat* of thy brow. なんじは額に汗してなんじのパンを食うべし. 【類】earn our livelihood *in* the *sweat* of our brow ‖ You're all *in* a *sweat!* 君は汗びっしょりだ. ¶He trembled and broke *into* a *sweat*. 彼は身震いをしてだらだら汗を流した. ‖ throw one *into* a *sweat* 発汗させる. ¶He is covered *with sweat*. 彼は汗だらけだ. ‖ wet *with sweat* 汗びっしょりになって.

sweat, *v.* 発汗する; [労働者を]こき使う, 搾取する.

M be *sweated all over* 汗びっしょりになる. ¶*sweat easily* じきに汗をかく. ¶*sweat freely* 盛んに汗が出る. ¶The boss *sweated* his men *mercilessly*. 親方は若い者を冷酷にこき使った. ¶The disbanded soldiers were *sweating* [it] *out* for a boat to carry them home. 《米》除隊兵たちは帰国のため輸送船の到着を待ちわびていた. ‖ *sweat out* one's cold 汗を出してかぜを直す. ¶*sweat profusely* ひどく汗をかく. ¶The horse *sweated violently*. 馬がひどく汗をかいた.

P He shall *sweat for* it. あいつ今にひどい目に会わしてやる. 【類】I will make you *sweat for* it. ¶A pitcher of ice water sweats on a hot day. 氷水の入ってる水さしは暑い日には汗をかく.

sweater, *n.* セーター.

Q a *classic sweater* for misses お嬢さん向きの高級セーター. ¶a *tight* (*loose*) *sweater* ぴったりした(ゆるい)セーター.

Q² a *highneck sweater* ハイネックのセーター. ¶a *turtleneck sweater* (=a pullover) とっくり首のセーター. ☞ 英国の sweater は運動選手の着る厚手のもの. 薄手の身体にぴったりしたセーターは jersey という.

sweating, *n.* 発汗.

V *promote sweating* 発汗を促す.

sweep, *n.* 掃除; 掃討の眼界, 掃討の範囲.

V *command* an extensive *sweep* of ... ...を一帯に見晴らす. ¶*give* it a thorough *sweep* それを一掃する. ¶The fire has *made* a clean *sweep* of the village. 火事が村中を焼払って仕舞った. ‖ He *made* a *sweep* of the State. 彼は国内を風びした.

Q make a *clean sweep* of old furniture 古家具を一掃する. ¶row with an *easy sweep* ゆるやかにかいを揮ってこぐ. ¶the *eastward sweep* of Russia ロシアの東方発展. ¶The election was followed by a *general sweep* of officials. 選挙に次いで官界の大異動が行われた.

Q² a *chimney sweep* 煙突掃除人.

P *beyond* the *sweep* (=range) of a telescope 望遠鏡の視野外に. ¶*with* a *sweep* of the eye 一望の下に ‖ *with* a *sweep* of one's scythe かまで一なぎして. ¶*within sweep* of the eye (=sight) 眼界内に.

P² the *sweep of* human intelligence 人知の及ぶ範囲 ‖ the *sweep of* influence 勢力範囲 ‖ the *sweep of* a storm 暴風区域.

sweep, *v.* 掃く, 一掃する; 風びする; かすめる; 延び広がる.

M He *swept* his audience *along* with him. 彼は(雄弁で)聴衆をわかした. ¶*sweep away* the snow 雪をかく ‖ The bridge was *swept away* by the flood. 橋が出水でさらわれた. ‖ These doubts have now been *swept away*. これらの疑惑は今は一掃された. 【類】*sweep away* all the difficulties in one's path ‖ *sweep away* the tainted textbooks 悪教科書を追放する ‖ The land *swept away* to the east. 土地はずーっと東方に延び広がっている. ¶I'll have (=make) her *sweep* the room *clean*. 彼女にへやをきれいに掃除させよう. ¶*sweep* the dust *out* into the street 往来にちりを掃き出す ‖ The tide *swept* the boat *out* to sea. 潮流でボートが海に漂流した. ¶A flock of birds *swept by*. 一群の鳥が空をかすめて過ぎた. ¶A strong gale *swept down* on the Atlantic coast. 強風が大西洋岸を吹きまくった. ‖ The cavalry *swept down* on the enemy. 騎兵は猛烈に敵軍に殺到した. ¶Chill winds *sweep in* from the north. 寒い風(木枯)は北から吹く. 【類】The wind blew and the rain *swept in* under the umbrella. ¶The plague *swept off* multitudes. 疫病が多数の人を殺した. ‖ The valley *sweeps off* to the right. 谷は右方に延長している. ¶*sweep up* dust (rubbish, litter) ちり(など)を掃除する ‖ *sweep up* the room 室内をすっかり掃く.

P *sweep across* a continent 大陸を吹きまくる. ¶the area *swept by* the flames 焼失地域. ¶*sweep* the sea *for* mines 掃海する. ¶*sweep* all obstacles *from* one's path 邪魔物を一掃する ‖ *sweep* the pirate *from* the seas 海賊を一掃する. ¶He *swept* everything *into* his net. 彼は何もかもその網にさらい込んだ. ¶*sweep* the dirt *off* the floor 床のちりを掃く ‖ *sweep* a person *off* his feet 人の足をさらう. ¶*sweep* the dirt *out of* a room へやからちりを掃き出す. 【類】At last our army *swept* the Chinese *out of* Manchuria. / The rivers *swept out of* their confines, washing away valuable top-soil crop land. ¶Floods *swept over* the country on each side of the river. こう水は川の両岸からあふれあたり一面水びたしにした. ¶*sweep with* a broom ほうきで掃く ‖ *sweep with* fire 掃射する ‖ *sweep* the sea *with* a searchlight 探海灯で海上を掃照する. 【類】*sweep* (展望する) the heavens *with* a telescope.

sweeper, *n.* 掃除人, 掃除器.

Q² a *street sweeper* 道路掃除人(器).

sweeping, *n.* 掃除.

Q² a climbing-boy for *chimney sweeping* 煙突掃除にはい登る少年. ¶*street* (*floor*) *sweepings* 道路(床)をはいて集めたごみ.

sweep-up, *n.* 掃除.

Q give a *hasty* "*sweep-up*" そこそこにお掃除をする.

sweet, *n.* 菓子; 芳香; *pl.* 愉快, 快楽.

V *adulterate* the *sweets* 菓子の不正な造り方をする. ¶I *bought* him *sweets* at the village shop. 私は村の店で彼に菓子を買ってやった. ¶flowers *diffusing* their *sweets* on the air 空中に芳香を発散する花. ¶Little girls are *enjoying* the first *sweets* of motherhood in their tender attentions to the new doll. 少女たちは新らしい人形をやさしくいたわっている間は母としての最初の快楽を享受しているのだ. ¶*Sweets* were *served* as a dessert. 甘いものが食後に出た. ¶*taste* the *sweets* and bitters of life 人生の苦楽を知る.

Q *toothsome sweets* おいしい菓子.

P² the *sweets of* home 家庭の快楽. 【類】the *sweets of* success.

sweet, *a.* ふくいくたる, 芳ばしい; 温和な, やさしい.

M *How sweet* of you to come and see us. まあわざわざいらして下さいまして御親切ありがとうございます(女性の言葉). ¶They were *terribly sweet* to me. あの人たちは私に非常にやさしくしてくれた.

P She used to be *sweet on* (=*upon*) me before she got married. 《俗》彼女が他に片付く前までは僕にやさしかったものだ. ¶She is perfectly *sweet to* us. 彼女はわれわれに本当にやさしい. ¶meadows *sweet with* the incense of clover blossoms クロバーの花の香がぷんぷんする牧場.

sweeten, *v.* 甘くする.

P *sweeten* ... *with* sugar 砂糖で甘くする.

sweetheart, *n.* 愛人, 情人.

V a soldier *bidding* his *sweetheart* the last farewell 愛人に最後の告別をする(出征の)兵士. ¶*desert* (=*abandon*) one's *sweetheart* 恋人を捨てる.

Q an ***honest*** *sweetheart* 誠実な恋人. ¶an ***old*** *sweetheart* 古くからの愛人.

sweetie, *n.* 《米口》恋人.

O She is my *sweetie*. 彼女は私の恋人だ.

sweetmeat[s], *n.* [通例 *pl.*] 《英》菓子.

V *sweetmeats* ***made*** of fruit 果実製の菓子.

Q ***hard*** *sweetmeats* 堅い菓子. ☞「菓子」は英語では sweets とか sweetmeats, 米語の candy に当る; 《英》a *sweet* shop = 《米》a *candy* store.

sweetness, *n.* 愛きょう; 温和.

V She ***has*** the *sweetness* of an angel. 彼女は天使のようにやさしい.

Q lips that breathed more than ***Arabian*** *sweetness* アラビアの芳香にも増した息を漏らすくちびる. ¶the ***natural*** *sweetness* of his temper 彼の生れついた気立のやさしさ. ¶with ***perfect*** *sweetness* 実に優美に. ¶the ***sugared*** *sweetness* of her language 彼女の優しく甘い言葉使い. ¶with a ***winning*** *sweetness* of manner 愛きょうたっぷりで.

swell, *n.* 膨張. 波のうねり.

P² a *swell* ***in*** population 人口の増大. ¶a *swell* ***of*** the sea

swell, *n.* 《俗》ハイカラ, 見え坊; 大立物.

Q He is a ***great*** *swell*. 彼は大立物だ. ¶***What*** a *swell* you are! ばかにハイカラだね.

P He is a *swell* ***in*** politics. 彼は政界の大立物だ.

swell, *a.* 《米俗》すばらしい.

M It's ***darn*** *swell*. そいつはとってもすばらしい.

O He is a *swell* guy (=an excellent fellow). あれはすばらしいやつだ. ¶a *swell* room いいへや.

swell, *v.* ふくれる, 増水する; こうじる.

M The ankle was ***badly*** *swollen*. くるぶしがひどくはれ上っていた. ¶The balloon *swells* ***out*** with gas. 気球はガスでふくれる.

P expenditure *swollen* ***by*** extravagance ぜいたくのために膨張した支出. ¶The ground *swells* ***into*** an eminence. 地が高まって丘をなしている. ‖ A murmur *swelled* ***into*** a roar. つぶやきが段々怒鳴り声になった. 【類】The wind *swelled* ***into*** a tempest. ¶*swell* ***to*** the form of a stout man upon a camel [遠方の一点が]大きくなってらくだに乗ったがん丈な男の姿になる. ¶The river has *swelled* ***with*** the rain. 川は雨で増水した. ‖ *swell* ***with*** anger (indignation) 怒り(など)で胸いっぱいになる ‖ one's breast *swells* ***with*** pride 得意になる ‖ pouters *swelling* ***with*** the sense of their dignity くちびるをとがらしてえらそうに構えている人々 ‖ sails *swollen* ***with*** the wind 風をはらむ帆.

swelling, *n.* 膨張; 増大; はれ物.

V The *swelling* has ***gone down***. はれが退いた. ¶Bees stang him on the forehead and on the cheeks, and ***made*** big *swellings*. 彼は額とほおをはちに刺されて大きくはれができた.

V² *Swelling* ***subsides***. こぶ(はれ)が引く.

P² a *swelling* ***in*** the throat のどのはれ物. ¶the *swelling* ***of*** anger (emotion) 怒気(など)の高まり ‖ the *swelling* ***of*** a river 川の増水.. ¶a *swelling* ***on*** the body (skin) 体(など)のはれ物.

swerve, *v.* 正路を逸する, それる.

P The motor-car *swerved* ***at*** a corner and upset. 自動車がかどでそれて転覆した. ¶The bullet *swerved* ***from*** the mark. 弾丸が的からそれた. ‖ *swerve* ***from*** the path of right 正道を逸する. 【類】He never *swerves* ***from*** his duty. ¶The road here *swerves* ***to*** the right. 道はここで右にそれている.

swift, *a.* 速力の早い, 迅速な.

P a pandemic that is *swift* ***in*** its spread and high in its percentage of mortality まん延が迅速で死亡率の高い流行病 ‖ *swift* ***in*** motion 運動の迅速な. ¶*swift* ***of*** foot like a hare うさぎのように足の早い ‖ birds *swift* ***of*** wing 羽の早い鳥.. ¶*swift* ***to*** anger 怒りやすい. ¶He is *swift* ***with*** his judgments. 彼は判断が早い.

swiftness, *n.* じん速.

Q the ***rocket-like*** *swiftness* of ascent のろしのような上昇(出世)の早さ. ¶with ***surprising*** *swiftness* あっという間に.

swill, *v.* 鯨飲する.

P He *swilled* himself ***with*** wine. 彼はたらふく酒を飲んだ.

swim, *n.* 水泳.

V whilst ***having*** a *swim* 遊泳中に. ¶***take*** a *swim* 一泳ぎする.

Q² an ***ocean*** *swim* 外洋での水泳.

P ***after*** a *swim* 一泳ぎ泳いでから. ¶go down to the beach ***for*** a *swim* 浜へ泳ぎに行く. ¶He was coming out ***from*** his *swim*. 彼は泳ぎを終えてから出て来る所であった. ¶The interpreter was evidently "***in*** the *swim*." その通訳はたしかにぐるになっていた.

P² a short *swim* ***in*** the shallows 浅瀬での一泳ぎ.

swim, *v.* 泳ぐ; 浮く.

M *swim* ***ashore*** (=to the shore) 岸に泳ぎつく. ¶I cannot *swim* a ***stroke***. 私はちっとも泳げない. ¶*swim* ***back*** to the shore 岸辺に泳ぎ戻る. ¶*swim* ***hand over hand*** 抜手を切る. ¶The brig was so full of water that she could *swim* ***no longer***. その帆船はもう一時も浮いていられないほど一杯に浸水していた. ¶*swim* ***out*** to a wrecked ship (an island) 難破船まで泳ぎ出す.

M² *swim* ***about*** 泳ぎ回る. ¶*swim* ***up*** (***down***) 泳ぎのぼ(下)る.

P *swim* ***across*** (=***over***) a river 川を泳ぎ越す. ¶*swim* ***against*** a strong stream 激流を泳ぎのぼる ‖ *swim* ***against*** the current 大勢に逆行する. ¶Everything *swam* ***before*** his eyes. 彼は目が回った. ¶*swim* ***in*** the water 水中を泳ぐ ‖ Rafters *swim* ***in*** water. いかだは水に浮ぶ. 【類】Balloons *swim* ***in*** [the] air. ‖ Her eyes *swam* ***in*** happy tears. 彼女はうれし涙があふれた. ‖ the floor *swimming* ***in*** blood 血まみれの床. ¶He *swims* ***like*** a cork (stone). 彼は泳ぎが達者だ(てんでできない). ¶*swim* ***on*** one's back (chest, side) 背泳ぎ(平泳ぎ, 横泳ぎ)をする. 【類】Straws *swim* ***on*** the surface. ¶The swans *swim* ***over*** the lake. 白鳥が湖上に遊泳する. ‖ The light white cloud *swam* ***over*** us. 軽い白い雲が頭上に浮いていた. ¶*swim* ***to*** the shore 海岸に泳ぎつく ‖ The ship *swims* ***to*** the harbor. 船が静かに入港する. ¶*swim* ***under*** the water もぐって泳ぐ. ¶*swim* ***with*** the tide (stream or current) 大勢と共に進む ‖ The deck *swam* ***with*** water. 甲板は水をかぶった. ‖ Her eyes were *swimming* ***with*** tears of sadness. 彼女は悲しさで目に涙を一杯ためていた.

O The heat made my head *swim*. 暑さで頭がぐらぐらした.

swimmer, *n.* 泳ぎ手.

Q a ***good*** *swimmer* 巧みな泳ぎ手. ¶a ***poor*** *swimmer* へたな泳ぎ手. ¶a ***weak*** *swimmer* 水泳の余りできない人.

Q² He is an ***expert*** *swimmer*. 彼は水泳が達者だ. ¶a "***ten-miles-before-dinner***" *swimmer* 朝飯前に一泳ぎする人. ¶a ***woman*** *swimmer* = a mermaid 女流水泳選手.

swimming, *n.* 水泳.

Q ***supervised*** (=***escorted***) *swimming* 監督付の水泳.

P come up ***from*** *swimming* 水から上って来る. ¶the art ***of*** *swimming* 水泳法.

swindle, *n.* 詐欺.

Q an ***abominable*** *swindle* とんでもない詐欺. ¶***extensive*** *swindles* 大仕掛の詐欺. ¶a ***gigantic*** *swindle* 大々的の詐欺. ¶It is a ***perfect*** *swindle*. それは全くの詐欺だ.

swindle, *v.* かたる, 詐取する.

P *swindle* a person ***into*** buying an inferior imitation article 人をだましてくだらない模造品を買わせる. ¶*swindle* money ***out of*** (=***from***) a person 人から金をかたり取る ‖ *swindle* a person (firm) ***out of*** money 人(など)をだまして金を取る. 【類】He was *swindled* ***out of*** his $280.

swindler, *n.* 詐欺師.

Q an ***arrant*** *swindler* 金ぱく付きの詐欺師. ¶an ***impudent*** and ***unblushing*** *swindler* 厚顔無恥の詐欺師. ¶an ***international*** *swindler* 世界をまたにかけた詐欺師. ¶He is an ***out-and-out*** *swindler*. 彼はよくよくの詐欺師だ. ¶a ***regular*** *swindler* 札付きのぺてん師. ¶a ***thorough*** (=***perfect***) *swindler* 大ぺてん師. ¶an ***unscrupulous*** *swindler* 悪らつな詐欺師.

Q² a ***cheque*** *swindler* 小切手詐欺師.

P The police set a trap ***for*** the *swindler*. 警察はその詐欺師逮捕の網を張った. ¶a gang (=set) ***of*** *swindlers* 一団の詐欺師.

swing, *n.* 振動; ぶらんこ; 振幅.

V ***Give*** him full *swing*. 彼を自由にさせておけ. ¶***have*** a *swing* ぶらんこに乗る ‖ Let it ***have*** its *swing*. それに干渉せずに放っておけ. ‖ ***have*** one's *swing* of indulgence 存分にわがままをする ‖ His genius ***has*** full *swing*. 彼は天才を十分に発揮している.

Q an obstacle to the ***full*** *swing* of his genius 彼の天才を十分発揮させる障害物 ‖ The Christmas festivities are now in ***full*** *swing*. 今はクリスマス気分がみなぎっている. ‖ get into the ***full*** *swing* of the day's work 一日の仕事の盛りどきにはいる. 【類】This program will reach ***full*** *swing* in September. ‖ give one's wrath ***full*** *swing* かんかんに怒る.

P sit ***in*** a *swing* ぶらんこに乗る ‖ Business is ***in*** full *swing*. 商売は活躍している. ‖ The holiday season is now *in* full *swing*. 今は祭日季節の最中だ. 【類】The negotiations are *in* full *swing*. ¶a door *on* the *swing*＝a swing door スイング・ドアー. ¶He walks *with* a *swing* of the body. 彼は肩で風を切って歩く. ‖ The horse drove off flies *with* the *swing* of his tail. 馬はしっぽではえを追い払った.

P² The *swing of* the pendulum. 振子の振幅; 振子の振動; [比ゆ的に]政党の交代執権. ‖ I like the *swing of* the poem. その詩の句調が私の気に入った.

swing, *n*. 『音楽』スイング.

P hop (＝dance) *to* the *swing* 《米》スイングの曲に合わせて踊る.

P² The fad *of swing* swept the country over. スイング熱が全国に流行した.

swing, *v*. 振り動かす; 揺れる; 《俗》絞首される.

M *swing back* to ... 揺れて...に戻る. ¶The hammock *swings gently*. ハンモックが静かに揺れる. ¶the door *swings inward* (outward) ドアーは内(外)側に開く. ¶The door *swung open*. 戸がぎーっと開いた. ¶The door *swings to and fro*. 戸が前後に揺れる.

M² The soldiers went *swinging down* the street. 兵士が元気よく(手を振って)街路を進んで行った. ¶The ship *swings round* with the tide. 船が潮流につれてぐるりと回る.

P He shall *swing for* it. その罪で彼を絞罪にする. ¶*swing from* the saddle 馬からひらりと飛び降りる. ¶*swing in* the swing ブランコに乗ってこぐ ‖ The pendulum is already beginning to *swing in* the other direction. 『比ゆ』行き過ぎから正常に戻りつつある. ¶*swinging into* the saddle he started for ... ひらりと馬に打乗って彼は...に向った ‖ With the advent of June the summer season at White Spring is *swinging into* full bloom. 七月の声を聞くとホワイト・スプリングの夏の季節はぐんとはずみ出す. ¶be *swung on* a pivot ちょうつがいで旋回する. ¶a motor-car being *swung on board* ship 船に積込中の自動車. ¶The door *swung to*. ドアーがぎゅうと閉じた. ¶*swing* a club *with* the hand 手でこん棒を振る.

swirl, *v*. [風で]渦巻く.

P dust *swirling in* the air 空中に舞い上るほこり.

swish, *v*. しゅうと風を切る.

M² The racers *swished by*. [競馬で]馬が一瞬にして通り過ぎた. ¶*swish off* to catch a bus 飛んで行ってバスに乗る.

P The whip *swished through* the air. むちが空中でびゅうンと鳴った.

switch, *n*. 《米》むち; 『電』開閉器; 『鉄道』転てつ器(ポイント).

V *close* a *switch* 開閉器を閉じる. ¶The *switch* was often *used* to punish children. 子供を罰するにむちがよく使われた.

Q² a *ceiling switch* 天井スイッチ. ¶a *circuit-changing switch* 転換スイッチ. ¶a *door switch* 戸付けスイッチ. ¶a *knife switch* 刃型開閉器. ¶a *magnet switch* マグネット(磁気感応)スイッチ. ¶an "*on-off*" *switch* [電流などの]点滅スイッチ. ¶A *railroad switch* shifts a train from one track to another. 転てつ器によって列車を甲線から乙線に移す.

switch, *v*. スイッチをひねる; 転換する; 《米》むちで打つ.

M *switch* cars *back* and *forth* 車両をポイントを使って入れ換える.

M² *switch off* [列車・車両を]転てつする; [電話の接続を]切る; [電灯を]消す ‖ *switch off* the use of the telephone from another 電話を切る ‖ *switch off* from one subject into another 甲の問題から乙の問題に転じる. 【類】He began in English and then *swicthed off* into Japanese. / the conversation was forthwith *switched off* to the weather. ¶*switch on* [車両を]転てつする; [電話を]つなぐ; [スイッチを回して灯を]つける ‖ *switch on* the use of the telephone to another 電話をつなぐ ‖ *switch on* the light 電灯をつける. 【類】*switch on* the radio to hear the news bulletin and weather forecast. ¶be *switched over* to peace industry 平和(軽)産業に切り換える.

P *switch* conversation *from* a painful subject 会話を痛ましい問題から他に転じる. ¶*switch* carriages *from* one track (line) *to* another 車両を転てつする. ¶He *switched* it *out of* my hand. 彼はそれを私の手から引ったくった. ¶*switch to* ... ...にくら替えをする. ¶*switch* a boy [*with* a cane] 少年をむちで打つ.

switchboard, *n*. 交換台.

P plug in *on* the *switchboard* [交換手が]電話を交換台に接続する.

switching, *n*. むち打ち.

Q You deserve a *good switching* (＝caning or whipping). うんとひっぱたいてやるから.

swoon, *n*. 気絶, 卒倒.

Q Her fright and concern sunk her down in a *deep swoon*. 恐怖と心配とで彼女は深いこん睡状態に陥った.

P fall down *in* a *swoon* 卒倒する. 【類】He is *in* a *swoon*. ¶fall *into* a *swoon* 気絶する.

swoon, *v*. 気絶する.

P She *swooned at* the sight (news). 彼女はそれを見(聞い)て気絶した.

swoop, *n*. 搏(う)撃; 引っさらい.

V *make* a *swoop* at ... ...を突撃する.

P Bolsheviks try to do the impossible *at* one *swoop*. 共産主義者は一挙に不可能事をなし遂げようとする. ‖ carry off ... *at* one *swoop* ...を一さらいに持去る.

P² a *swoop of* the hawk たかの襲撃.

swoop, *v*. ひっさらう; 一挙しておそう.

M The eagle *swoops down* upon its prey. わしがえじきに飛びかかる. 【類】Pirates *swooped down* on the transport. / The bombers swooped *down* (急降下爆撃) upon the enemy positions. ¶*swoop up* (＝snatch) a handbag ハンドバッグをひったくる.

P The Arabs *swooped upon* the caravan. アラビア人が隊商を襲撃した.

swop, *v*. ＝swap.

sword, *n*. 刀, 剣.

V They have *beaten* their *swords* into plowshare. 彼らは剣をすきに打ち変えた. ¶*carry* a *sword* [*along*] 刀剣をはい用する. ¶*cross swords* with ... ...と一戦を交える. ¶*draw* one's *sword* from the scabbard (＝sheath) さやを払う ‖ *draw* her *sword* in co-operation with England 英国と共同して開戦する. 【類】The medieval knight was ever ready to *draw* his *sword* for his faith and his lady-love and in the cause of the feeble and the oppressed. ¶*drive* a *sword home* 刀を突き通す. ¶*gird on* a *sword* 帯刀する. ¶*hold* a *sword* by the hilt 刀の柄を取る. ¶*lift up* a *sword* against ... ...に刃向う. ¶*measure swords* with ... ...と真剣勝負をする. ¶It is like *putting* a *sword* into the hands of a child. それは子供に刃物を持たせるようなものだ. ¶Hold! *Put up* your *sword!* 待った, 刀を納めよ. ¶*recover sword* [刺した]刀を抜取る. ¶*run* a *sword* through the body 体に刀を突通す. ¶*sheathe* the *sword* 刀をさやに納める. ¶*sway* (＝*wield*) a *sword* 剣を揮う. ¶*swing* a *sword* 剣を振り回す. ¶*take up* a *sword* 刀を取上げる. ¶*temper* a *sword* to make its edge sharper 刀の刃に焼きを入れて切味をよくする. ¶*thrust* one's *sword* through ... ...に刀をさし通す. ¶*try* a *sword* on a person 試しぎりをする. ¶*unsheathe* (＝draw) a *sword* 剣を抜く. ¶*wear* a *sword* 刀を差す. 【類】privileged to *wear* two *swords* (帯刀御免の).

V² His *sword flashed* from the scabbard. 彼の剣がさやからひらめいた. ¶The *sword snapped*. 刀がぽきっと折れた.

Q a *celebrated sword* 名刀. ¶with a *drawn sword* 抜身で. ¶a *naked sword* 抜身, 白刃. ¶a *trenchant sword* よく切れる刀. ¶a *trusty sword* 頼みの一刀. ¶a *two-edged sword* もろ刃の刀.

P He who lives *by* the *sword* shall die *by* the *sword*. 剣によって生くるものは剣によって死す. ‖ die *by* the *sword* 剣難に会う. 【類】gain it *by* the *sword* (武力) / an empire won *by* the *sword* and held by the sword. ¶at the point *of* the *sword* 武力で(おどかして) ‖ a pair *of swords* 大小. ¶appeal *to* the *sword* 武力に訴える ‖ They were put *to* the *sword*. 彼らは刀のさびとなった. ¶I live *under* a *sword* suspended by a hair. 私は一本の毛でつった剣の下にいるようなものだ. ¶die *upon* one's own *sword* 自刃する. ¶attack *with* a *sword* 剣で打って掛かる. 【類】defend oneself *with* a *sword* / fight hand and hand *with swords* (白兵戦) / The criminal was executed *with* the *sword*. / He was killed *with* a *sword*.

P² *sword in* hand 剣を手にして.

swordsman, *n*. 剣客.

Q a *good swordsman* りっぱな剣客.

syllabary, *n*. 字音表.

Q the *Japanese syllabary* 五十音図.

syllable, *n*. 音節(シラブル).

V *abbreviate* a *syllable* 音節を略する. ¶*accentuate* the first, not second, *syllable* in the word "social" social という語の第二音節でなく第一音節にアクセントを付ける.

¶ ***articulate*** their *syllables* その音節をはっきり発音する. ¶ Please do not ***breathe*** a *syllable* of what I tell you. この話はおくびにも出すな. ¶ Till this instant I have not ***heard*** a *syllable* about him. 今が今まで私は彼のことは何も聞いていない. ¶ ***mumble*** one's *syllables* その音節を口ごもる. ¶ Don't ***say*** a *syllable*. 一言も言うな. ¶ ***stress*** the first *syllable* (of a word) (語の)第一音節を強く発音する. ¶ In speaking English do not ***swallow*** a single *syllable*, however short it may be. 英語を話すときはどんな短い音節でもうやむやにしてはならない. ¶ He never ***told*** me a *syllable* of the matter. 彼はそのことについては一言も僕に話さなかった. ¶ never ***utter*** a *syllable* of complaint 決して一言も不平を言わない.

P a word ***of*** two *syllables* 二音節の語. ¶ accent the word ***on*** the second *syllable* 第二音節にアクセントを付ける.

syllabus, *n.* 要項.

Q The program furnishes an ***attractive*** *syllabus* of literary and social enjoyment. その番組で文学的社会的な興味深い要領が修得される.

P² a *syllabus* ***of*** a course of lectures 講義要項.

syllogism, *n.* 推測式; 三段論法.

V It ***completes*** the *syllogism*. それで三段論法がまとまる.

Q a ***false*** *syllogism* えせ三段論法.

P reason ***by*** *syllogism* 推測式で推理する.

symbol, *n.* 象徴; 符号, 記号.

Q a ***chemical*** *symbol* 化学符号. ¶ a ***direct*** *symbol* of thought 思想の直接の符号. ¶ a ***divine*** *symbol* 神の信条. ¶ a ***graphic*** *symbol* 図解(グラフ)符号. ¶ a ***mathematical*** *symbol* 数学記号. ¶ ***phonetic*** *symbols* 発音符号.

Q² a ***letter*** *symbol* 文字符号.

P express ***by*** *symbols* 符号で示す. ¶ write ***in*** *symbols* 符号で書く.

P² C is the *symbol* ***of*** carbon. C は炭素の符号だ. 【類】 The Cross is the *symbol* ***of*** Christianity. / Among Chinese, the bat is a *symbol* ***of*** happiness. / a *symbol* ***of*** peace / The oak is a *symbol* ***of*** strength, the lion ***of*** courage, the cross ***of*** Christianity, white ***of*** purity. ‖ The Emperor shall be the *symbol* ***of*** the State and of the unity of the people. 〚憲法〛天皇は日本国の象徴であり, 日本国民統合の象徴である.

symbolic, symbolical, *a.* 象徴の.

P The eye is *symbolic* ***of*** sight and knowledge. 目は視力と知識の象徴である. ‖ It is *symbolic* ***of*** the fighting spirit of modern womanhood. それは現代女性の奮闘心を象徴する.

symbolism, *n.* 象徴.

V ***interpret*** the *symbolism* その象徴を解釈する.

symbolize, *v.* 象徴する.

P the five elements *symbolized* ***by*** a sphere, crescent, pyramid, circle, and square 球体・新月・角すい・円及び正方形によって象徴された五元素. ¶ the principle *symbolized* ***in*** the badge その記章が象徴する主義.

symbology, *n.* 象徴論.

Q² ***Buddhist*** *symbology* 仏教徒の象徴論.

symmetry, *n.* つり合, 均斉.

V The story ***lacks*** *symmetry*. その物語は均斉を欠いている. ¶ Only one incident of a slightly discordant nature occurred to ***mar*** the *symmetry* of the occasion. その席の気分をちょっと乱すような事件がたった一つあった.

Q ***stately*** *symmetry* of her figure 彼女の姿のりっぱなつり合.

P ***with*** (***without***) *symmetry* 均斉が取れて(ないで).

sympathetic, *a.* 同情的な, 共鳴する.

P be *sympathetic* ***to*** (=***toward***) the opinion (project) その意見(など)に共鳴的な. ¶ *sympathetic* ***with*** sufferers 遭難者に同情して.

sympathize, *v.* 同情する, 共鳴する.

M *sympathize* ***deeply*** with the cause of ... ...の主義に深く共鳴する. ¶ I *sympathize* ***heartily*** with you. 私は心からあなたに同情します. ¶ *sympathize* ***keenly*** 深く同情する. ¶ ***profoundly*** *sympathize* with に深く同情する. ¶ ***sincerely*** *sympathize* 心から同情する. ¶ ***thoroughly*** *sympathize* すっかり同情する.

P *sympathize* ***with*** one's anger 人の立腹に同情する ‖ *sympathize* ***with*** the object その目的に共鳴する. ¶ I *sympathize* ***with*** you ***from*** the bottom of my heart. 私は心からあなたに同情する. ¶ *sympathize* ***with*** a person ***in*** his sorrow (joy, feelings) 人の悲しみ(など)に同情する. 【類】 *sympathize* ***with*** a helpless orphan. ¶ *sympathize* ***with*** a friend ***upon*** his bereavement 友の(愛児などを失った)不幸に同情する.

sympathizer, *n.* 同情者; シンパ.

V ***discourage*** *sympathizers* 同情者を失望させる.

Q a ***great*** *sympathizer* with the Japanese cause in the Manchurian dispute 満州事変における日本への非常な同情者. ¶ a ***hearty*** *sympathizer* with ... ...の心からの同情者.

Q² a ***Communist*** (***Fascist***) *sympathizer* 共産党(など)のシンパ.

P a *sympathizer* ***with*** Bolshevism 過激主義の同調者.

sympathy, *n.* 同情, 哀れみ; 賛成.

V Please ***accept*** my sincere *sympathy* with you in your sorrow. 御愁傷の段心からご同情申上げます. ¶ ***alienate*** the *sympathy* and respect of ... ...の同情と尊敬とを失う. 【類】 ***alienate*** Russian *sympathy* / ***alienate*** the *sympathy* of the general public / ***alienate*** the reader's *sympathy*. ¶ ***arouse*** *sympathy* for ... ...に対する同情を喚起する. 【類】 ***arouse*** *sympathy* from the benevolent (慈善家たち). ¶ ***avow*** one's *sympathy* with ... ...に同調すると公言する. ¶ ***awake*** *sympathy* in ... ...の同情を喚起する. ¶ ***bring*** the *sympathy* on her side by ... ...によって彼女の方に同情を呼ぶ. ¶ He ***captured*** the *sympathies* of the world at once by his speech. 彼はその演説によって直ちに世界の同情を得た. ¶ ***command*** our *sympathy* われわれの同情を得る. ¶ ***cultivate*** *sympathy* 同情を得ようと努める. ¶ ***engage*** our *sympathy* in ... われわれの同情は...に注がれる. ¶ ***enjoy*** the warm *sympathy* of ... ...の暖かい同情を得ている. ¶ ***enlist*** his *sympathy* in the cause その主義に対して彼の賛成を得る. 【類】 The scheme ***enlisted*** the *sympathies* of the great majority. / ***enlist*** the active *sympathies* of many well-known ladies. ¶ ***evoke*** *sympathy* 同情を喚起する. ¶ ***excite*** one's *sympathy* その同情を喚起する. ¶ ***express*** *sympathy* with the movement その運動に同情を寄せる. 【類】 They have ***expressed*** their *sympathy* with the idea. / ***express*** one's great *sympathy* with him on the death of ... / ***express*** his *sympathy* with her in her sorrow. ¶ We lament his death and ***extend*** our *sympathy* to his bereaved family. われわれは彼の死をいたみその遺族に対し哀悼の意を表する. ¶ ***feel*** *sympathy* toward ... = sympathize with ... ...に同情を寄せる. 【類】 ***feel*** *sympathy* for his sad failure / much *sympathy* is ***felt*** with ... ¶ ***find*** active *sympathy* 盛んに同情される. ¶ ***forfeit*** *sympathy* by ... 同情を失う. ¶ ***gain*** (***lose***) our *sympathy* 同情を得る(失う). ¶ Certainly my own *sympathy* is unreservedly ***given*** to him. たしかに私自身は満腔(ɕ)の同情を彼に寄せている. ¶ You ***have*** (=***deserve***) our *sympathy*. われわれは君に同情する. ‖ ***have*** (=***possess***) the *sympathy* of ... ...の同情を得ている ‖ ***have*** *sympathy* for a person (country) 人(など)に同情を持つ ‖ ***have*** a *sympathy* with ... ...に同情する ‖ They ***have*** many *sympathies* in common. 彼らは共鳴する点が多い. 【類】 I ***have*** no *sympathy* for female suffrage. / He ***has*** great *sympathy* with the cause of reform. / we ***have*** no *sympathy* with the substitution of ... for ... ¶ ***lavish*** *sympathy* on ... ...に惜気なく同情を寄せる. ¶ ***offer*** *sympathy* 同情を示す. ¶ ***rouse*** our *sympathy* for ... ...に対する同情を呼び起す. ¶ I am not here to ***seek*** *sympathy* for ... 私は...に同情していただこうとしてお伺いしたのではありません. ¶ I have ***sent*** him my deep *sympathy*. 私は深い同情を表すると彼にいってやった. ‖ ***show*** *sympathy* toward ... = be kind to ... ...をいたわる ‖ He ***showed*** his practical *sympathy* with the hospital by becoming an annual subscriber. 彼は毎年寄付者となってその病院に対する同情の意を具体的に示した. ¶ ***speak*** one's *sympathy* for ... ...に対する同情を述べる. ¶ ***strengthen*** *sympathy* 同情を強める. ¶ ***telegraph*** one's *sympathy* to ... ...に慰問の電報を送る. ¶ I ***tender*** my heartfelt *sympathy* to you in your great loss. あなたの御不幸に対して心から御同情申上げる. ¶ ***win*** the *sympathies* of ... ...の同情をかち得る.

V² *Sympathy* ***flew back*** to them. たちまち同情が再び彼らの上に寄せられた. ¶ our *sympathy* ***goes*** to ... ...に同情を寄せる. ¶ our *sympathies* ***went*** out toward ... われわれの同情は...の方へ引かれた. ¶ *Sympathy* ***wells up*** in our hearts. 同情がわれわれの心にわいて出る.

Q persons suspected of ***communistic*** *sympathies* 共産主義のけん疑者. ¶ have ***cosmopolitan*** *sympathies* 世界的な同情を持っている. ¶ he expressed his ***deep*** *sympathy* with

... 彼は...に深い同情を寄せた. ¶a reporter of ***democratic*** *sympathies* 民主々義に同情のある記者. ¶I am in ***full*** *sympathy* with ... 私は...に十分同情している. 【類】 show him ***full*** *sympathy*. ¶***Heart-felt*** *sympathy* is extended to ... in their bereavement. ...の不幸に対し心から同情の言葉を述べる. ¶have the ***hearty*** *sympathy* of ... ...の心からの同情を得ている. ¶I read the history of that time with a great deal of ***historical*** *sympathy*. 私は多大の史的興味をもってその時代の歴史を読んだ. ¶a ***keen*** *sympathy* 熱烈な同情 ‖ in ***keen*** *sympathy* with ... ...に強い同情を持って. ¶the ***lukewarm*** *sympathy* of his supporters 彼の後援者の微温的同情. ¶I feel ***much*** *sympathy* for you. 大いに御同情致します. ¶Social intercourse is impossible where ***mutual*** *sympathy* is lacking. 相互の共鳴が欠けている所には社交というものは不可能だ. ¶show ***Platonic*** *sympathy* 精神的な愛を示す. ¶show ***practical*** *sympathy* with the society by becoming an annual subscriber. 毎年寄付を出してその協会に具体的な同情を示す. ¶express one's ***profound*** *sympathy* with ... ...に深い同情を表する. ¶***Public*** *sympathy* was active in his behalf. 彼に対する世間の同情は盛んであった. ¶have a ***strong*** *sympathy* with ... ...に強い同情を寄せている. ¶I heartily appreciate your ***thoughtful*** *sympathy*. 私は心からあなたの思慮ある御同情を感謝します. ¶I've heard of your loss with ***unfeigned*** *sympathy* あなたの損失を心からの同情の念をもって聞きました. ¶***universal*** *sympathy* 一般の同情. ¶***verbal*** *sympathy* 声援. ¶show a ***warm*** *sympathy* 暖かい同情を寄せる. 【類】 enlist the ***warmest*** *sympathy* of ... ¶He has ***wide*** *sympathies*. 彼は心(包容力)が大きい. 【類】 a man of ***wide*** *sympathies*.

Q² hide one's ***Communist party*** *sympathies* in order to obtain one's job その職を得ようと共産党のシンパであることを隠す. ¶***pro-labor*** *sympathies* 労働者層への同情.

P I am quite ***in*** *sympathy* with your opinions. 私は君の意見には大賛成だ. ‖ I was ***in*** complete *sympathy* with him on this point. 私はこの点については彼と意見が全く一致していた. 【類】 They are ***in*** *sympathy* with each other. ¶as a mark ***of*** *sympathy* with ... ...に対する同情の印に. ¶the staff resigned ***out of*** *sympathy* with ... 部員一同は...に反対して辞職した ‖ people ***out of*** *sympathy* with the policy その方策に不賛成な人々. ¶appeal ***to*** one's *sympathy* その同情に訴える. ¶overflow ***with sympathy*** 同情にあふれる. 【類】 a man, philanthropic, large-minded and large-hearted, ***with*** *sympathy* for all good men and good movements.

P² the *sympathy* ***between*** ... ...間の同情. ¶have no *sympathy* ***for*** (=***with***) beggars こじきには同情がない. ¶have the *sympathy* ***of*** the working classes 労働者層の同情を得ている. ¶They are in hearty *sympathy* ***with*** the project. 彼らはその計画に大賛成だ. 【類】 his *sympathy* ***with*** the down-trodden (しいたげられた者たち).

O My *sympathy* is with you. 私は君に同情している.

symphony, *n*. 交響曲, 調和.

P a *symphony* ***in*** color 色の調和.

symposium, *n*. 座談会, 討論会.

V The magazine ***carries*** (=***contains***) a *symposium* on sports. その雑誌にスポーツに関する座談会記事が載っている. ¶a periodical ***worked up*** a *symposium* on the value of ... ある雑誌が...の価値という題目で誌上座談会を計画した.

Q² a ***heart-to-heart*** *symposium* 打解けた座談会.

P² a *symposium* ***on*** biological problems of the day 今日の生物学問題に関する座談会. 【類】 a *symposium* ***on*** friendship (atomic energy, space travel, etc.).

symptom, *n*. 兆候; (病の)徴候.

V ***aggravate*** the acute *symptoms* 急性の症候をつのらせる. ¶***alleviate*** the *symptoms* of a disorder 症候を緩和する. ¶***develop*** the *symptom* of ... ...の徴候を悪化させる. ¶***discover*** in him *symptoms* of uncommon genius 彼の素質中に非凡の英才の特徴を発見する. ¶I ***have*** *symptoms* of appendicitis. 私には盲腸炎の症候がある. ¶properly ***interpret*** the *symptoms* 徴候を正しく診察する. ¶***observe*** the *symptoms* of arteriosclerosis 動脈硬化の症候を認める. ¶The patients ***present*** *symptoms* of widely different varieties. その患者はきわめて多様の病状を呈する. ¶The worst *symptoms* have ***subsided***. 症状も峠を越した. 【類】 after the acute *symptoms* have ***subsided***.

Q have ***all*** the *symptoms* of influenza 流行性感冒の徴候歴然である. ¶***disquieting*** *symptoms* 不穏の兆候. ¶a ***healthy*** *symptom* 健全な兆候. ¶***manifest*** *symptoms* 明白な徴候. ¶***premonitory*** *symptoms* of an earthquake 地震の前兆. ¶a ***reassuring*** *symptom* 心強い徴候. ¶I had ***slight*** *symptoms* of this illness for about a year back. 私には一年ほど前からこの病気の徴候が少しあった. ¶***unhealthy*** *symptoms* 不健全な徴候.

P distinguish a disease ***by*** its *symptoms* その徴候によって病気を見分ける. ¶ascertain ***from*** *symptoms* 徴候によって確定する.

P² a *symptom* ***of*** neurosis 神経症(ノイローゼ)の徴候 ‖ The owl is the *symptom* ***of*** wisdom. ふくろうは知恵の象徴である.

symptomatic, *a*. 徴候のある.

P *symptomatic* ***of*** ... ...の徴候のある.

synchronize, *v*. 同時に起る, 一致させる.

P *synchronize* all the clocks ***in*** the theater 劇場の時計の時間を全部合わせる. ¶One event *synchronizes* ***with*** another. 甲の事件が乙の事件と同時に起る. ‖ The film does not *synchronize* ***with*** sound. その映画は録音が不ぞろいだ. 【類】 Electric sparks *synchronize* ***with*** the movements of the switch.

synchronous, *a*. 同期の.

P at a period *synchronous* ***with*** ... ...と同期に.

synchronously, *ad*. 同時に.

P Talkies produce sound *synchronously* ***with*** action. 発声映画は動作と同時に音声を発する.

syndicate, *n*. 企業組合.

V ***form*** a *syndicate* 企業組合を組織する. ¶***join*** the *syndicate* その企業組合に加入する.

Q a ***cartoonists'*** *syndicate* 漫画家組合.

Q² a ***banking*** *syndicate* 銀行組合.

P join ***in*** a *syndicate* 企業組合に加入する. ¶It is ***under*** the same *syndicate*. それは同じ企業組合の経営である.

synonym, *n*. 同義語, 類語.

Q ***close*** *synonyms* ほとんど同義の語. ¶a ***perfect*** *synonym* 全く同義の言葉. ¶a ***popular*** *synonym* of a plant 植物の通俗名.

P² The English language is rich in *synonyms* ***for*** "say." 英語には「言う」という語の類語が多い. ‖ His name has become a (=the) *synonym* (=another name) ***for*** probity and magnificence. 彼の名は正直と偉大さの代名詞となった. 【類】 The word "ferrum" was employed in Latin as a *synonym* ***for*** a sword. ¶"Diligent" is a *synonym* ***of*** "industrious." diligent は industrious と同意語である.

synonymous, *a*. 同義の.

M ***almost*** *synonymous* with ... ...とほとんど同義の. ¶***closely*** and ***strictly*** *synonymous* すっかり同義の. ¶these words are ***so far*** *synonymous* in that they ... これらの語は...という点では同意語である.

P *synonymous* ***in*** signification 意義の同じな. ¶"Till" is *synonymous* ***with*** "until." till は until と同義だ. ‖ Leisure is often erroneously considered *synonymous* ***with*** idleness. 閑暇は往々誤って安逸と同一視される. 【類】 The term "management" is often used as *synonymous* ***with*** "administration." ‖ Ninteenth-century civilization is *synonymous* ***with*** Christianity. 十九世紀の文明はキリスト教と同義である. 【類】 The name of Keats has come to be *synonymous* ***with*** beauty.

synopsis, *n*. 要略, 概略.

V ***give*** a *synopsis* of the historical evolution of ... ...の歴史的発達の概略を示す.

P² a brief *synopsis* ***of*** the world's news 世界ニュース一覧.

syntax, *n*. 措辞法, 統語法.

Q ***bad*** (=***false***) *syntax* 誤った措辞法.

syphilis, *n*. 梅毒.

V ***contract*** *syphilis* 梅毒にかかる.

V² *Syphilis* ***developed*** a few days after the wedding. 結婚後二三日たって梅毒が出た.

Q ***florid*** (***latent***) *syphilis* 陽(陰)性梅毒. ¶***primary*** (***secondary, tertiary***) *syphilis* 初(二・三)期の梅毒.

syrup, *n*. シロップ.

Q² ***corn*** *syrup* コーン・シロップ. ¶***maple*** *syrup* on pancakes パンケーキにかけたメープル糖の糖みつ.

system, *n*. 組織, 制度; 系統; 規律; 身体.

V The feudal *system* was ***abolished***. 封建制度が廃された. ¶***adopt*** a uniform *system* of enumeration 一定の計算法を採用する. ¶***apply*** the *system* to ... ...にその方法を適用する. ¶***build up*** a *system* of etiquette 礼式を制定する. ¶It is better for students of all countries to ***complete*** their national *system* of education before going abroad to study. どの国の学生でも海外留学に先立って自国の教育系統を修了する方がよい. ¶***construct*** a modern water *system* 現代式の水道を敷設する. ¶***develop*** a *system* of one's own 自己独特のやり方をする. ¶***devise*** a *system* 一つの系統立った方法を案出する. ¶***erect*** a *system* of philosophy 哲学体系を建設する. ¶***establish*** a *system* of posts 郵便制度を確立する. ¶***evolve*** a *system* 系統を立てる. ¶***follow out*** the *system* of ... ...のやり方を襲用する. ¶***formulate*** a *system* 体系を編成する. ¶***found*** a *system* of political economy 経済学の一派を立てる. ¶***frame*** a *system* 一派を立てる. ¶I've ***got*** a *system* to ... ...させるやり方がある. ¶He ***has*** *system* in his business. 彼のすることには秩序がある. ‖ The city ***has*** an efficient tramway *system*. その市にはりっぱな電車系統ができている. ¶***improve*** our transportation *system* わが運輸系統を改善する. ¶***initiate*** a *system* of language teaching 語学教授の新案を立てる. ¶Telephone *system* has been ***installed*** in all rooms throughout the inn. その旅館は各室に電話を据え付けた. ‖ ***install*** a hot-water *system* 熱湯供給の装置をする. ¶***institute*** a splendid *system* of primary education りっぱな初等教育の制度を設ける. 【類】***institute*** a new *system*. ¶He has ***introduced*** a *system*. 彼は一派を立てた. 【類】the year in which the *system* was ***introduced***. ¶***keep*** the great drainage *system* in perfect working order 大規模の下水組織を完全に働かせる. ¶***keep up*** a good postal *system* りっぱな郵便制度を維持する. ¶He ***lacks*** (=has no) *system* in his study. 彼の研究は系統立っていない. ¶***maintain*** a *system* of omnibuses plying between the hotels and the station ホテルと停車場の間に旅客送迎車を往復させる. ¶In the United States the government ***operates*** the postal *system*. 米国では政府が郵便制度を経営する. ¶The town ***possesses*** an admirable telephone *system*. その市にはりっぱな電話の設備がある. ¶***renovate*** and ***transform*** the *system* of education now in existence 現行教育制度を刷新する. ¶He has ***struck out*** a new *system*. 彼は新方法を案出した. ¶***tone up*** one's *system* 体の調子を整える. 【類】It ***toned up*** my entire *system*. ¶***work out*** a *system* of shorthand 新速記術を考案する.

v² The *system* is not ***working well***. その方法はうまく行っていない.

Q the ***aerial*** *system* of external wiring. 架空式屋外線. ¶the ***ambulacral*** *system* 〘動〙管足系. ¶***Anglo-American*** *system* of oil mill machinery 英米式の石油採掘法. ¶The ***coddling*** *system* and the ***hardening*** *system* are both to be deprecated in education. 教育では軟式も硬式もいずれもこれを排しなければならない. ¶a ***complex*** *system* 複雑なやり方. ¶a ***crude*** *system* 粗雑な方法. ¶In the ***decimal*** *system*, each figure, or digit, has a place value ten times that of the next figure to the right. 十進法では各数字は右側の数字の十倍の価値を有する. ¶Japanese script contains a strange mixture of characters used both ideographically and phonetically, together with two ***different*** *systems* of native phonetic writing. 日本の文字には妙な訓及び音読による漢字が混っていてそれに本国創製の音標字が二通りある. ¶the ***dual*** *system* 二重制度. ¶under the present ***economic*** *system* 現在の経済組織下に. ¶a very ***elaborate*** *system* of rules 非常に複雑な規則. ¶the development of ***electric*** *systems* of railroads 鉄道電化施設の拡充. ¶*bushido* the ***ethical*** *system* of the military class 武士道. ¶the ***existing*** *system* of English spelling 現行英語つづり字法. ¶suppress the ***feudal*** *system* 封建制度を抑圧する. ¶The ***French*** *system* of numeration is followed in the United States. フランス式読数法は米国で採用されている. ¶the ***human*** *system* 人体. ¶the largest ***hydro-electric*** *system* in the world 世界最大の水力発電設備. ¶the inefficiency of Japan's ***industrial*** *system* 日本産業組織の無効力. ¶a ***maladjusted industrial*** *system* 調整不完全の産業組織. ¶the ***metric*** *system* メートル法. ¶a ***monetary*** *system* 貨幣制度. ¶the dissemination of doctrines which are fundamentally opposed to our ***national*** *system* わが国体と根本的に相反する主義の流布. ¶the ***nervous*** *system* 神経系統. ¶He is being instructed in English on the ***new*** *system*. 彼は新らしい教授法で英語を習っている. ‖ under the ***new*** *system* 新制度の下に. ¶under the ***old*** *system* 旧制度の下に. ¶His ***pilifereous*** (=***hairy***) *system* is well developed. 彼は毛深い. ‖ He has a poor ***piliferous*** *system*. 彼は毛が薄い. ¶the ***premium*** *system* of payment 割増金付支払方法. ¶under the ***present*** *system* 現在の制度では. ¶the ***ramified*** *system* of railways 鉄道の網状連絡系統(本線から分岐した). ¶Buddhism as a ***religious*** or ***philosophical*** *system* 宗教または哲学体系としての仏教. ¶a ***rigid*** and ***inelastic*** *system* 厳格で融通のきかない制度. ¶the ***single transferable*** *system* 一回乗換のできる制度. ¶the planets in our ***solar*** *system* われわれの太陽系内の遊星. ¶a ***suicidal competitive*** *system* 自殺的な競争制度. ¶our ***time-honored*** *system* 古くからのわれわれの間に行われている制度.

Q² the ***absentee landowner*** *system* 不在地主制度. ¶the ***allocation*** *system* 割当(配給)制度. ¶a ***banking*** *system* 銀行制度. ¶on the ***barter*** *system* 〘商〙交換貿易制により. ¶the Palestine ***broadcasting*** *system* said that ... パレスタイン放送によれば... ¶adopt a ***budget*** *system* 予算制度を採択する. ¶the present ***capitalist*** social *system* 現行の資本社会主義制度. ¶the catalogue arranged on the ***card*** *system* カード式の目録. ¶the ***case*** *system* 《米》判例主義. ¶the ***communications*** *system* 通信制度. ¶establish a ***Communist world*** *system* 共産党世界制度を打ち建てる. ¶the ***contents certification*** and ***delivery certification*** *systems* of the mail service 郵便事務の内容証明及び配達証明制度. ¶the ***conveyor*** (=assembly-line) *system* 流れ作業. ¶the ***credit*** *system* 〘教育〙単位[履修]制度. ¶the ***crossover*** *system* 〘映〙共映制(かけ持ち制). ¶improve the ***delivery*** *system* 荷渡しの方法を改善する. ¶The telephones there have been changed to the ***dial*** *system*. そこの電話はダイヤル式に変った. ¶the ***easy-payment*** (***down-payment***) *system* 月賦(即時払込)制度. ¶advocates of the ***eight-hour*** *system* of work 八時間労働制の主唱者たち. 【類】operate a factory on the ***eight-hour*** *system*. ¶the power house of an ***electric-lighting*** *system* 電灯配線専門の発電所. ¶the abolishment (reestablishment) of the ***emperor*** *system* 天皇制の廃止(復活). ¶the ***employment security*** *system* 職業安定制度. ¶the Soviet ***espionage*** *system* ソ連のスパイ網. ¶have a widespread ***espionage*** *system* 広く張り回らしたスパイ網. ¶the ***export incentive*** *system* 輸出報奨制. ¶the ***extra-ration*** *system* 特別配給制. ¶the ***factor analysis*** *system* 要素分析法. ¶the ***factor comparison*** *system* 要件比較法. ¶a ***fire-prevention*** *system* 防火組織. ¶a ***follow-up*** *system* 追いかけ式通信販売法(広告技術). ¶a ***fool-proof inspection*** and ***control*** *system* 絶対安全な点検操縦装置. ¶ under a ***free enterprise*** *system* 自由企業制の下では. ¶the ***free lecture*** *system* 無料講座制. ¶the ***good time*** *system* 善時制(成績のよい受刑者は服役時間を軽減される制度). ¶a ***grading*** *system* by means of such marks as ... ...といったような符号を用いた等級表示法. ¶on the ***gradual*** (=easy) ***payment*** *system* なしくずし制度で. ¶the ***great wind*** *systems* of the earth 地球上の大風力系統. ¶the ***Gregg*** *system* of shorthand グレグ式速記法. ¶instal a ***heating*** (***cooling***) *system* 暖房(冷却)設備をする ‖ the central ***heating*** *system* ボイラー式暖房設備. ¶the ***Hepburn*** *system* of romanization ヘボン式ローマ字. ¶have furniture on the ***hire*** *system* 損料で家具を借りている. ¶the ***hire-purchase*** *system* 賦払制度. ¶the Princeton ***honor*** *system* プリンストン大学の学生責任制度. ¶an ***incentive*** *system* 報奨制. ¶the ***informer*** *system* 第三者通報制. ¶the ***inheritance*** *system* 相続制度. ¶an ***inter-office telephone*** *system* 社(など)内電話. ¶the ***job classification*** *system* 職務分類法. ¶the ***labor boss*** *system* 労働ボス搾取制. ¶the ***land tenure*** *system* 土地賃貸法. ¶the ***living-in*** *system* in English shops 英国の商店住込み制度. ¶the ***long-term calculated*** *system* 長期計算方式. ¶a ***marking*** *system* 採点法. ¶the ***Nazi*** *system* of education ナチスの教育制度. ¶the ***one horse*** *system* 一馬式. ¶the ***one-pipe*** *system* 単管式. ¶an ***old-age-pension*** *system* 年金制度. ¶the multiple ***party*** *system* 多数党制. ¶the ***patrol*** *system* 〘海軍〙しょう戒制; 〘警察〙パトロール制. ¶on the "***pay-at-the-counter-please***" *system* カウンター払い(現金)制度(スーパーマーケットなどの). ¶the ***point*** *system* 点数制. ¶a ***police*** *system* 警察制度. ¶be put under a ***pool accounting*** *system* 〘経済〙共同計算制の下におく. ¶the ***premium*** *system* of payment 賃金支払の賞与制度. ¶the official ***price*** *system* 公定価(丸公)制. ¶a ***priority*** *system* 優先(重点)制度. ¶the

profit(-sharing) system 利益分配制度. ¶the ***purchase*** *system* 売官制度(古く英国陸軍部内に行われた). ¶the ***quota*** *system* 割当制. ¶the ***radio, telegraph, telephone,*** and ***cable*** *systems* of communications 無線, 電報, 電話及び海底電線による通信機関. ¶the ***ranking*** *system* 等級法. ¶an ***up-to-date rapid transit*** *system* 現代的な急行便制. ¶on the ***ready money*** *system* 現金払制度で. ¶a ***report*** *system* 報告制;〘教育〙リポート制度. ¶the ***river*** (***mountain***) *system* 河(山)系. ¶a ***road*** *system* 道路系統. ¶a ***rotation*** *system*〘農〙輪作制. ¶under the present ***royalty*** *system* 現行著作権制度では.【類】an agreement has been made on the ***royalty*** *system.* ¶an automatic (proficiency) ***salary raise period*** *system* 自動的(能率的)給与引上げ期間制. ¶a flexible ***school*** *system* 融通性のある学校制度. ¶reorientation of Japan's ***school*** *system* 日本の学制の新方針. ¶the ***secret-ballot*** *system* 秘密投票制. ¶In these industries the ***shift*** *system* of work prevails. これらの産業では労働交替制が行われている. ¶the ***shop steward*** *system*《労》職場委員制度. ¶the ***single*** (***double***)***-track*** *system*〘鉄道〙単(複)線系統. ¶the nation's ***sky*** *systems* その国の航空路. ¶the ***spoils*** *system*《米》猟官制(与党勝利の報酬として). ¶the ***spy*** *system* スパイ網. ¶the ***star*** *system* 太陽系. ¶the ***state police*** *system* 国家警察制度. ¶abolish the ***surface-car*** *system* 路面電車制を廃止する. ¶the ***sweating*** *system* [労働者に対する]搾取制度. ¶the ***tally*** *system* 短期掛売. ¶The town possesses an admirable ***telephone*** *system.* その町はすばらしい電話施設を持っている. ¶the ***tenant-farmer*** *system* 小作人制度. ¶democracy under the ***Tenno*** *system* 天皇制下の民主々義. ¶the ***touch*** *system* of typewriting タイプの軽いキーの打ち方. ¶on the ***ticket*** *system* of payment チケット制で. ¶electrify a ***tramway*** *system* 馬車鉄道を電化する. ¶cripple the ***transportation*** *systems* 運転系統を阻害する. ¶an electric tramway on the overhead ***trolley*** *system* 架線(トロリー)式市電. ¶a ***twentieth-century*** *system* of government 二十世紀式の統治体制. ¶work on the ***two-shift*** *system* 二部制で働く‖classes operated on the ***two-shift*** *system* 二部教授. ¶the incentive ***wage*** *system* 報奨賃金制度. ¶New York's ***water*** *system* is the largest and most extensive in the world. ニューヨークの水道は世界最大でもっとも広範囲にわたるものである. ¶a ***water-supply*** *system* 水道. ¶connected by a ***wireless telegraph*** *system* 無線電信施設で連絡した.

P fingerprints taken ***after*** the Bertillon *system* [仏国の]ベルチヨン式で取った指紋. ¶Judo is used ***as*** a *system* of physical training. 柔道は身体訓練の一つの方法とされている. ¶places ***beyond*** the tramway *system* 市街電車で行かれない場所. ¶***by*** a *system* of easy payments なしくずしで. ¶a change ***in*** the *system* of taxation 課税法の変更. ¶The poison has passed ***into*** the *system.* 毒が体に回った. ¶people in depressed conditions ***of*** the *system* 体が衰弱している人々. ¶work ***on*** *system* 規律的に仕事をする‖Language is taught here ***on*** *system.* ここでは国語を系統的に教えている.‖a railway ***on*** the Abt *system* アプト式鉄道.【類】The Italian and German clocks are both arranged ***on*** the 24-hours *system* (二十四時間制), the hours from midnight to midnight being numbered consecutively from 0 to 24. / rear chickens (養鶏する) ***on*** the most scientific *system*‖offer furniture ***on*** a *system* of weekly payments 週払い制で家具を売る. ¶They had six months' training ***under*** the new *system.* 彼らはその新式で六カ月習った.‖He kept the nation ***under*** a rigid *system* of officialism. 彼は厳格な官僚主義で政治を行った.‖***under*** (=***on***) the old *system* 旧式では.

P² The *system* now ***in*** existence 現行制度. ¶a *system* ***of*** classification 一つの分類法‖the *system* ***of*** inspection 監督制度‖a *system* ***of*** espionage=an espionage system‖a *system* ***of*** government 一つの政体‖The Hebrew and Roman are two great *systems* ***of*** law. ヘブライ法及びローマ法は法律の二大系統である‖a *system* ***of*** memory training 一つの記憶法.

systematize, *v.* 組織化する; 分類する.

P *systematize* an organization ***for*** ... 団体を…の目的で組織化する. ¶*systematize* (=classify) one's collection ***under*** several heads コレクションをいくつかの項目に分類する.

T

T, *n.*

P It will suit me ***to*** a *T.* それなら実に私は好都合だ.【類】The hat fits me ***to*** a *T* (ぴったり).

tab, *n.* 数.

V ***keep tab*** (=*tabs*) on ... …の勘定をする. ¶【類】***keep*** close *tabs* on daily sales (日々の売上げ).

tab, *v.* 張札をする.

P be *tabbed* ***as*** "..." …という折紙がつく, とみなされる.

table, *n.* (**1**) 食卓; 台; *pl.* 形勢.

V ***bedeck*** the *table* with flowers 食卓を花で飾る. ¶***clear*** the *table* 食卓を片付ける. ¶His *table,* if it does not actually "groan," is well ***covered*** with good things. 彼の食卓には山海の珍味を満載したとまでは行かなくともりっぱなごちそうがたくさん載っている. ¶***dust*** a *table* テーブルのちりを払う. ¶***jog*** a *table* テーブルをゆすぶる. ¶***keep*** a good *table* 口がおごっている. ¶He is a witty talker and ***keeps*** the *table* ***amused.*** 彼は話しが面白いから食卓に同座する人々は皆興がる. ¶***lay*** (=***set***) the *table* for three 三人前のぜん立てをする‖There was a *table* ***laid*** with three covers. 食卓には三人前のぜん立てがしてあった. ¶***leave*** the *table* 食卓を離れる. ¶books that ***litter*** the *tables* テーブルの上に散らかっている本. ¶***prepare*** a *table* 食事の用意をする. ¶The *table* is all ***set.*** 食卓の用意がすっかりできた.【類】***set*** the *table* for dinner‖***set*** a *table* on its feet テーブルを据える‖***set*** a good *table* ごちそうを出す. ¶***spread*** a *table* ぜん立てをする. ¶I ***turned*** the *tables* on him completely (=fairly). 私は彼にすっかりさかねじを食わしてやった.【類】I ***turned*** the *tables* upon him neatly by applying the same argument. / I confess you have fairly ***turned*** the *tables* upon me. / The *tables* were ***turned*** on the attacker (攻撃者). ¶***wait*** *table*=wait on a table 食事の給仕をする. ¶***wipe*** the *table* clean テーブルをきれいにふく.

V² The *tables* ***turned*** in our favor. 形勢がわれわれに有利「になった.

Q It is given in the ***accompanying*** *table.* それは次の表に掲げてある. ¶a ***bare*** *table* 貧弱な食卓. ¶Food is served at a ***common*** *table.* 食事は共同の食卓でする. ¶The matter was laid without hesitation or concealment upon the ***diplomatic*** *table* of the world. その事件はちゅうちょもせず取隠しもせず世界外交界の俎(*)上にのぼった. ¶a dinner party in which each contributes to the ***general*** *table* 持寄り宴会. ¶a ***humble*** *table* 粗末な食事. ¶a ***luxurious*** *table* ぜいたくな食事. ¶the ***main*** *table* 主卓. ¶a ***rickety*** *table* ぐらぐらする卓. ¶sit at a small ***round*** *table* 小円卓を囲む‖they sat around a "***round*** *table*" at the hotel to discuss problems of ... 一同はホテルで…の問題を討議するためにいわゆる円卓会議を開いた. ¶a ***sloppy*** *table* [水などで]ぬれている食卓. ¶a ***square*** *table* 四角の食卓. ¶a ***substantial*** *table* 実のある食卓. ¶a ***well-appointed*** *table* 食品の十分整った食事.

Q² a ***banquet*** *table* 宴会の食卓. ¶a ***billiard*** *table* 玉突き台. ¶at the ***breakfast*** *table* 朝食の食卓で. ¶a ***card*** *table* トランプ台. ¶a ***center*** *table* 中央テーブル(室の中央に据えるもの); 客室用テーブル. ¶a circular ***conference*** *table* 会議用円卓‖be placed on the ***conference*** *tables* of the United Nations 国際連合の会議にかけられる.【類】solve their differences around the ***conference*** *table.* ¶a ***dining*** *table* 食卓. ¶an ***extension*** *table* 伸縮自在食卓. ¶the food for the ***family table*** 家族用食卓に供する食物. ¶a ***horseshoe conference table*** 馬てい形の会議用テーブル. ¶She is at her ***make-up table.*** 鏡台に向っている(お化粧をしている). ¶a ***marble-top table*** 大理石張りのテーブル. ¶be given a light luncheon at ***open-air tables*** 戸外の軽食が出る. ¶an ***operating table*** 手術台. ¶We have a ***ping-pong table.*** Pardon me, we did have one. 宅にはピンポン台がある, 失敬, 以前はあった. ¶a ***work table***=a worktable 作業台, 裁縫台.

P Both sat facing each other ***across*** a *table.* 二人は卓でさし向いになった. ¶seated ***around*** the *table* 食卓を囲んで. ¶wait ***at*** (=***on***) *table* 食事の給仕をする ‖ be ***at*** *table* 食事中だ. 【類】They were ***at*** *table* when I went in. / Two gentlemen and two ladies are ***at*** a *table* playing cards. / sit ***at*** the *table* of ... ¶It is highly esteemed ***for*** the *table.* それは珍味とされている. ¶Dishes are served ***on*** the *table.* 料理が食卓に出してある. 【類】The supper is ***on*** the *table.* / We never have any but imported melons ***on*** our *table.* ‖ The bill was laid ***on*** the *table.* その議案はたな上げされた. ¶settle a dispute ***round*** a *table* instead of on a battlefield 紛争を戦場でなく会議(外交折衝)で解決する. ¶sit down ***to*** *table* 食卓につく ‖ dishes brought ***to*** *table* 食卓に運ばれた料理. ¶be ***under*** the *table* 《俗》酔いつぶれる. ¶The facts are ***upon*** the *table.* それらの事実は明りょうである.

(**2**) 表, 目録.

V ***compile*** (=***draw up, frame or make up***) a *table* 表を作成する. ¶***fix*** (=***make***) a *table* 表を作る. ¶this *table* ***shows*** at a glance ... この表で...が一目で分かる.

Q an ***attached*** *table* 付属表. ¶a ***classified*** *table* 分類表. ¶a ***comparative*** *table* of Japanese and Western dates 日本と西洋の日付の対照表. ¶a ***conversion*** *table* 換算表. ¶an ***exhaustive*** *table* of irregular verbs 不規則動詞の全表. ¶in the ***foregoing*** *table* 前掲の表に. ¶a ***genealogical*** *table* 系図. ¶a ***graphic*** *table* 図表. ¶a ***statistical*** *table* 統計表.

Q² a ***census*** *table* framed in 19— 千九百...年に作成された国勢調査表. ¶the Combined ***Experience*** *Table* 総合経験死亡率表. ¶a ***genealogy*** *table* 系図. ¶a ***multiplication*** *table* 九九表. ¶a ***personnel allotment*** *table* 人員配置表. ¶Dining halls and luncheon counters are marked thus † on ***time*** *table* (=timetable). 食堂や立食所は時間表に † の符号が付けてある.

P The imports of cotton during the last five years are seen ***from*** the following *table.* 過去五カ年間の綿の輸入高は次表に示してある. ¶as shown ***in*** the *table* 表に示したように. ¶make ... ***into*** a *table*=tabulate ... ...を表にする. ¶pleasures ***of*** the *table* 飲食の楽しみ.

P² a *table* ***of*** contents [書籍などの]内容目録. ¶a *table* ***with*** this inscription: "..." 「...」という銘を刻んだ平板.

table, *v.* 《米》[議案など]握りつぶす.

O The motion was *tabled* after all. その動議は結局握りつぶされた.

tablecloth, *n.* 卓布.

V ***fold up*** a *tablecloth* 食卓布を畳む. ¶***spread*** a *tablecloth* 食卓布を掛ける.

Q spread a very ***clean white*** *tablecloth* 純白の食卓布を掛ける.

tablespoonful, *n.* 大さじに一杯.

Q a ***scanty*** (***full, heaping or rounded***) *tablespoonful* 大さじに軽く(たっぷり, 山盛りに)一杯. 【類】an enema of a ***rounding*** *tablespoonful* of salt to two quarts of warm water.

tablet, *n.* 平板; はぎ取り紙; 錠剤.

V a ***commemorable*** *tablet* 記念牌(はい). ¶***dedicate*** a *tablet* to ... ...に記念板を奉献する. ¶***erect*** a *tablet* to the memory of ... ...を記念するために牌を建てる. ¶***unveil*** a *tablet* 記念牌の除幕式を行う.

Q an ***ancestral*** *tablet* 位牌. ¶Some medicine is round pills and some ***flat*** *tablets.* 薬には丸薬も錠剤もある. ¶a ***memorial*** *tablet* has been placed near the spot, recording that ... その近くに...と記した記念牌が取付けられた. ¶a Buddhist ***mortuary*** *tablet* 位牌. ¶a ***sugar-coated*** *tablet* 糖衣錠.

Q² a ***bronze*** (***marble***) *tablet* 青銅(など)の牌. ¶***cold*** *tablets* for quick remedy はやく治るかぜの錠剤. ¶a ***school*** *tablet* 学校で(ノートを取る)備忘録. ¶***water purification*** *tablets* 浄水用錠剤.

P the names inscribed ***on*** the *tablets* 記念牌に銘刻された姓名.

tableware, *n.* 食器.

Q² ***stainless steel*** *tableware* さびない鋼鉄の食器.

taboo, *n.* 禁忌.

V ***place*** (=***put***) a *taboo* ***on*** ... =taboo (*vt.*) ... ...を禁止する.

taboo, *a.* 禁忌の.

M the word is ***now*** *taboo* among ... その語は...の間で今では忌み言葉になっている.

tabulate, *v.* 表示する.

P the results of ... are *tabulated* ***as*** follows: その結果は次の表に示される.

tabulation, *n.* 表.

P² the *tabulation* ***of*** statistics 統計表 ‖ a *tabulation* ***of*** these opinions これらの意見を表に作ったもの.

tack, *n.* びょう; 方針.

V ***try*** another *tack* 別の方針を試みる.

Q² a ***thumb*** *tack* 画びょう.

P It is ***on*** the right (wrong) *tack.* それは方針が誤っている.

tack, *v.* 添える; 〖航〗針路を転じる.

M *tack* ***together*** 結合する; 結婚させる.

M² *tack* the picture ***up*** on the wall その絵をびょうで壁に留める.

P The ship *tacks* ***against*** the wind. 船が船首を風上に向けて上手回しにする. ¶*tack* one thing [on] ***to*** another 甲を乙に付加する.

tackle, *v.* 真剣にとり組む.

M ***squarely*** *tackle* [with] a problem 問題と真剣にとりくむ.

P *tackle* one's job ***with*** mastery skill 仕事をりっぱにやる.

O *tackle* the job (the art of gardening) 仕事(など)ととり組む.

tact, *n.* 手練; 気転.

V ***exercise*** *tact* 気転をきかせる. ¶he ***has*** *tact* in dealing with ... 彼は...をあしらう調子がうまい. ¶It ***requires*** *tact* to do so. そうするには手練を要する. ¶he ***showed*** great *tact* in ... 彼は...することが非常に巧みであった. ¶***use*** *tact* 気転をきかす. ¶***want*** *tact* 気がきかない ‖ It ***wants*** a certain *tact* to manage them. 彼らをあしらうにはちょっとこつがいる.

Q it requires ***considerable*** *tact* to ... ...するには大分手練を要する. ¶***consummate*** *tact* りっぱな手並. ¶***diplomatic*** *tact* 外交上の手腕. ¶***graceful*** *tact* 上品な如才なさ. ¶***inexhaustible*** *tact* 円転滑脱の才.

P gifted ***with*** extraordinary *tact* 生得非凡な機才のある.

tactful, *a.* 機知に富んだ.

M be ***so*** *tactful* as to ... 如才なく...する.

tactician, *n.* 戦術家.

Q an ***adroit*** and ***consummate*** *tactician* 機敏で万事に抜目のない策略家. ¶a ***clever*** *tactician* 賢明な戦術家. ¶a clever ***political*** *tactician* 賢明な政略家.

Q² a ***party*** *tactician* 党の策士.

tactics, *n. sing., pl.* 戦術, 策略.

V ***adopt*** the usual *tactics* いつもの手を用いる. ¶***change*** its *tactics* その戦術を変える. ¶***employ*** the same *tactics* 同じ策略を用いる.

Q ***defensive*** *tactics* 防御戦法. ¶***delaying*** *tactics* 引延ばし戦術. ¶***elementary*** *tactics* 基本戦術. ¶***false*** *tactics* 誤った策略. ¶***favorite*** *tactics* 例の手. ¶The ***same old*** *tactics!* また例のでんか. ¶***sharp*** *tactics* 巧妙な戦略.

Q² ***partisan*** *tactics* パルチザンの戦術. ¶"***blitzkrieg***" *tactics* 電撃戦術. ¶***campaign*** *tactics* [政治など]運動の戦術. ¶cease bargaining and begin ***dispute*** *tactics* 協定をやめて争議戦術を始める. ¶***gangster*** *tactics* 暴力団戦術. ¶Communist party ***infiltration*** *tactics* in non-Soviet areas. 非ソ連地域における共産党の漸侵戦術. ¶***money*** *tactics* 買収戦術. ¶***obstructionist*** *tactics* used to delay or kill legislation 法律制定を引延ばしあるいは葬り去るために用いた議事進行妨害者の戦術. ¶***on-again, off-again*** *tactics* さみだれ戦術. ¶***sabotage*** *tactics* 破壊戦術. ¶***steam-roller*** *tactics* [圧倒的勢力による]暴圧戦術. ¶***strong-arm*** *tactics* 実力戦術. ¶lawful ***struggle*** *tactics* 合法的闘争戦術. ¶use ***terrorist*** *tactics* 暴力戦法を用いる.

P lack ***in*** *tactics* 軍略が欠けている. ¶by a brilliant piece ***of*** *tactics* すばらしい策略を用いて.

taffy, 《英》**toffee,** *n.* 糖菓子.

Q² ***molasses*** *taffy* 糖みつ菓子.

tag, *n.* 札.

V ***attach*** (=***fix***) a *tag* to ... ...に札を付ける.

Q a ***released*** or ***condemned*** *tag* 取替品または廃品の票.

Q² a metal ***identification*** (=***identity***) *tag* 金属製身分証明票. ¶the ***metal*** *tag* of a shoestring くつひもの端金. ¶A ***price*** *tag* of 400 marks was attached. 四百マルクの正札が付いていた.

tag, *n.* 鬼ごっこ.

V ***play*** *tag* 鬼ごっこをして遊ぶ.

tag, *v.* 後について行く.

M² *tag along* with ... on a tour ...の遊覧旅行に随行する.
P The boy who is "it" *tagged after* his sister. 鬼になった少年が自分の妹を追いかけた. 【類】*tag after* mother. ¶*tag at* one's heels あとについて行く.

tag, *v.* 付ける.
M *tag* ... *together* ...を付け合わせる.
P *tag* one thing *on to* another 甲を乙に付ける.

tail, *n.* 尾.
V *dock* the *tail* of the horse 馬のしっぽを切る. ¶The earthworm *grew* a *tail*. そのみみずに尾が生えた. ¶*jerk* its *tail* from side to side その尾を左右に振る. ¶*lash* its *tail* strongly from side to side そのしっぽを強く左右に振る. ¶The dog *turned tail* and fled (=ran off). 犬が尾を巻いて逃げた. 【類】*turn tail* and quake (ふるえる). ¶a dog *wagging* (=*swinging*) its *tail* 尾を振っている犬.
Q a *bushy tail* 房々した尾. ¶a *docked tail* 短かく切った馬の尾. ¶a *short, crooked tail* 短くて曲った尾.
Q² an *ox tail* 牛の尾肉. ¶a *shirt tail*=the tail of a shirt ワイシャツのしり.
P His place is *at* the *tail* of the procession. 彼の位置は行列のしんがりだ. ¶followed *by* a *tail* of attendants 一列のお供を引連れて. ¶Boys go *into tails* at sixteen. 男は十六歳になるとえん尾服を着る. ¶sit *on* the *tail* of a van [ほろ付き]荷馬車の後部に乗る. ¶*with* a long *tail* 長いしっぽのある ‖ A dog speaks *with* his *tail* wagging. 犬は尾を振ってその気持を表わす. ‖ with his *tail* between his legs しりごみして小さくなって.

tail, *v.* 後をつける.
M *tail* (=trace) a suspicious person *all along* 疑わしい人の跡をつける. ¶*tail closely* behind ... ぴったり...について行く.
M² *tail off* (=stop *or* quit) drinking 禁酒する.
P *tail* a few coaches *on* a train at ... ...で列車の後部に客車を数両増結する.

tailor, *n.* 仕立屋.
V I've *changed tailors* and go to Smith's now. 私は仕立屋をかえて今ではスミスの店へ行く.
Q a *fashionable tailor* 上流相手の仕立屋. ¶a *first-class tailor* 第一流の仕立屋. ¶a *military tailor* 陸軍省御用達の仕立屋.
Q² an *army* (*navy*) *tailor* 陸(海)軍御用の洋服屋. ¶a *custom tailor* 注文で作る洋服屋. ¶a *merchant tailor* 服の生地を店に持っている仕立屋.
P He established himself *as* a *tailor*. 彼は仕立屋を開業した. ¶go *to* the *tailor's* 仕立屋へ行く. ☞「注文洋服店」は《英》a tailor's [shop], 《米》a tailor shop.

tailor, *v.* 仕立てる.
M *perfectly tailored* 仕立の申分のない. ¶He was a dandy and thought he could only be *properly tailored* in Bond Street. 彼はおしゃれで仕立はボンド街に限ると思っていた.
P a Hollywood movie script *tailored for* John Wayne ジョン・ウェインのために書下ろされたハリウッド映画シナリオ ¶His stories are well *tailored to* popular tastes. 彼の小説は大衆の趣味にぴったりだ.

tailoring, *n.* 仕立.
Q *high-quality tailoring* 高級仕立. ¶This suit bears *reversed tailoring*. その洋服は裏返しがきく.
P They are good *at tailoring*. あそこは仕立がうまい.

taint, *n.* 汚点.
V The sentence *has* the *taint* of tautology. その文は同じ事の繰り返しに近い. ¶Drinking *revived* in him some dormant *taint* of heritage. 彼は酒を飲み出したので潜伏していたある遺伝的素質が出てきた.
Q in case where a *congenital taint* exists 先天的な病根がある場合は. ¶those who suffer from the results of *inherited* (=*hereditary*) *taint* 悪い病気の遺伝がある人々. ¶The *moral taint* spread among all classes. その道徳上の害毒が各階級に広まった.
P athletes free *from* the *taint* of professionalism 職業選手的な臭味のない運動家. ¶*without taint* of commercialism 商人根生は全然なく.
P² There seems to be a *taint of* insanity in his family. 彼の家には精神病の遺伝があるらしい. ¶a *taint on* one's escutcheon 名折れ.

taint, *v.* 汚す, 腐らす.
M *hereditarily tainted* with insanity 精神病の遺伝のある. ¶Meat will *taint readily* in hot weather. 陽気が暑いと肉は悪くなりやすい.
P *tainted with* the touch of time 古色を帯びた ‖ The transaction is *tainted with* fraud. その取引には詐欺の疑いがある. ‖ The family is *tainted with* mental disease. その家は精神病の筋だ. ‖ *tainted with* prejudices 偏見のある.
O Bad books will *taint* the young mind. 悪い本は青少年を毒する.

take, *n.* 収穫.
V We *made* a large *take*. われわれは(穫物・刈納めなどが)たくさんあった.
Q a *great take* of fish 大漁.

take, *v.* 取る(など).
M be *taken aback* [不意をうたれて]あっけに取られる. 【類】I confess I was somewhat *taken aback*. ¶whilst the cargo was being *taken aboard* 貨物を船に積込中に. ¶*Taken all in all*, New York is one of the best governed cities in all the world. 全体から見てニューヨークは全世界で最も市政の整備した市の一つである. ¶I came back to *take* my wife *along* with me. 私は妻を連れに戻ってきた. ¶The imperial throne was to be occupied by mikados *taken alternately* from the rival houses. 競争している家族から交互に天皇が出て位につくことになっていた. ¶*taken altogether* これを総合して考えて見て. ¶*take amiss* 誤解する; 腹を立てる ‖ Don't *take* it *amiss* (=ill *or* in ill part). 悪く取るな. 【類】My good intentions were *taken amiss*. ¶*take* a machine *apart* and put it together again 機械を分解してまた組立てる. ¶he *took* me *aside* and whispered "..." 彼は僕を別席へ連れて行って「...」とささやいた. ¶*Take* it *away* with you それを持ってってくれ. ‖ In his tenth year his father *took* him *away* from school. 彼が十歳のときにその父が学校を退学させた. ‖ He contracted the illness which *took* him *away*. 彼はその病気にかかり遂に倒れた. ‖ *take away* one's breath あっけにとられる ‖ *take away* wrinkles しわをなくす ‖ *take* the spotlight *away* from ... ...からスポットライトを外(そ)らす ‖ *take away* one's custom from a shop ある店の顧客を奪う ‖ *take away* one's breath in surprise びっくりして息がとまる ‖ *take* one's life *away* 人の命をとる. ¶*take* a person (=thing) *back* to a place 人(物)をもとの所へ戻す ‖ *take* a thing *back* with a person 物を持って帰る ‖ *take back* one's pledge 質物を出す ‖ *take back* what I said about ... ...について私の言ったことを取消す ‖ *take back* a right 権利を取戻す ‖ We won't *take* that hat *back*. [売った]その帽子は引きとりません. ¶He might have been *taken bodily* from one of old Van Dyck's pictures. 彼はヴァン・ダイクの(肖像)画から抜出たとも思えた. ¶*boldly take* it in one's hand 大胆にそのことに当る. ¶*cheerfully take* upon himself the task of ... ...の仕事を喜んで引受ける. ¶*taken collectively* 全体として考えて見て. ¶*take* the number *conservatively* その数を内輪に見積る. ¶*take* it *easy* のんきに構える, あせらない ‖ "*Take* it *easy*, old man," said he as the last greeting. 「気をつけて」と彼は別れの際言った. ¶he *took* himself *firmly* in hand and practiced ... 意を決して断然...を実行した(自分の悪癖を直そうとする場合など). ¶I *gladly take* this opportunity to ... 私は喜んでこの機会を利用して...する. ¶*take* it *good-humoredly* それに対して気持を悪くしない. ¶*take* it very *grievously* to heart that ... ...をひどく気に病む. ¶The mind can *hardly take* in the fact that ... 人々には...の事実はほとんど信じられない. ¶*take* it *home* as mementoes of the city その市のみやげとしてそれを家に持ち帰る ‖ buy it to *take home* 家へ持って帰るためにそれを買う ‖ May I *take* you *home*? お宅までお送りしていいでしょうか. ¶*take* it *ill* (*good*) それを悪(良)く取る. ¶*How long* does a letter *take* to reach England from here. 手紙がここから英国に届くのにどの位かかるでしょう. ¶*take* a medicine *internally* 薬を内服する. ¶*take keenly* to the study of ... 鋭意...の研究に当る. ¶I should *take* it *kindly* if you would ... あなたが...して下されば私は有難い. ‖ The masses did not *take kindly* to the innovation. 大衆はその改革を喜ばなかった. 【類】The English public do not *take kindly* to the German novel. / He *takes* more *kindly* to Western diet (洋食). ¶It is a hyperbole and not to be *taken literally*. それは誇張で文字通りに解釈してはならない. ¶It does not *take long* to say. それは簡単に言える. ‖ It did not *take* them *long* to fall asleep. ほどなく彼らは寝ついてしまった. 【類】It *takes long* to wear it out. ¶I *merely took* you at your word. 僕はただ君の言うことを真に受けたまでだ. ¶They *take mightily* to each other. あの人たちはばかに気が合う. ¶*take naturally* to one's studies. 生来学問を好む ‖ *Take* me *out* to the ball game 野球に連れて行ってくれたまえ.

【類】*take* a person *out* for a walk (drive, trip, hike) ‖ *take out* a license 鑑札を受ける. 【類】a patent was *taken out* for ... ‖ *take out* a life insurance policy of ... on oneself 自分が(金高)の生命保険に加入する ‖ *take out* naturalization papers 帰化関係書類をもらう. ¶ *restfully taking* in the ever changing view 静かに絶えず変り行く眼前の風景をながめつつ. ¶ *take* it *seriously* to heart それを苦にする ‖ *take* a person *seriously* 人の言うことを真に受ける. 【類】The college student does not *take* the movies *seriously.* / I've learned not to *take* it *seriously.* ¶ He was *taken sick* with fever. 彼は熱病にかかっていた. ¶ all these *taken together* これらを総合すると. ¶ But its consideration would *take* me *too far* from our subject. しかしそのことを論じるのは当面の問題から大分それることになる. 【類】It would *take* us *too far* to attempt to treat these in detail. ¶ Seems like he *took* my words *wrong.* 僕の言葉を誤解したらしい.

M² You'd better *take* a lunch *along.* 弁当持参の方がよい. 【類】He *took* his gun *along.* ¶ *take down* (*up*) the receiver 受話器を下ろす(とり上げる) ‖ *take down* the tents テントをたたむ ‖ He was *taken down* with influenza (=flu). 彼は流行性感冒にかかった. ‖ The speech was *taken down* in shorthand. その演説は速記された. 【類】The stenographers who *took down* transcripts on the proceedings. / *take down* from one's dictation ‖ *take down* (=swallow) a draught (dose) 薬を一服のむ. ¶ *take in* money 収納する ‖ The ship *took in* supplies at ... その船は...で用品を積込んだ. ‖ Most ships stop at Suez to *take in* coal. 船は大抵石炭積込のためにスエズに寄港する. ‖ *take in* boarders 下宿人をおく. 【類】We reached a house which we had been told *took in* travelers. ‖ *take in* a pleasing glimpse of ... ...の美景をべっ見する ‖ *take in* the whole situation at a glance 一べつして情勢を見て取る ‖ *take in* the lines at a glance 一目で文の意味をとる ‖ *take in* arms against the government 政府に対して干戈(*)をとる ‖ Are you the lady that *takes in* washing? [婦人に向って]あなたがうちで洗たくをして下さるんですか. ‖ *take in* with ... ...に款を通じる ‖ *take in* fancy-work 売春婦となる ‖ be "*taken in*" by profiteers 暴利をむさぼる商人にだまされる. 【類】He told the story so well that I was *taken in.* ¶ *take off* one's coat (garment) その上衣を脱ぐ ‖ *take off* the hook かぎをはずす. 【類】*take off* (=remove) shoes ‖ breathing exercise for *taking off* fat 脂肪を除く(やせる)ための呼吸法 ‖ *take* one's hat *off* to ... ...にはかなわない(参る) ‖ He decided to *take* himself *off* that very day. その当日辞去しようと決心した. ‖ *take off* by plane (=in a plane) for ...に向って飛行機で立つ. 【類】The plane *took off* at 7 p.m. / *take off* from Haneda for ... / He *took off* with his writer friend for Algeria. ‖ The embargo is *taken off.* 出(入)港禁止が解除になった. ‖ *take* the chill *off* a liquid《俗》液体を暖める, かんをする ‖ *take off* the gloves〖比ゆ〗[争闘・議論に]はだ脱ぎになってかかる ‖ His arrival *took* a weight *off* my mind. 彼が到着したので安心した ‖ it *takes off* something from the reputation of a great soul who ... ...すると...の大人物の名声が幾分落ちる ‖ *take* a day *off* from work 一日勤めを休む. 【類】I want to *take* two days *off* next week. 来週二日休みを取りたい ‖ be *taken off* by an apoplexy 卒中で死ぬ ‖ *take off* the force of an argument 議論の鼻をくじく. ¶ *take on* a new life 新生活に入る ‖ *take on* an abnormal development 異常な発達をする ‖ A boat *takes on* a cargo (supplies) 船が荷(など)を積込む. ‖ *take on* its natural color そのものの自然の色彩を帯びてくる. 【類】*take on* a different character / *take on* a new importance of late as a result of ... / *take on* a new office ‖ an old term that has *taken on* a new meaning 新しい意味で使われるようになった古い語 ‖ So worded, the sentence *takes on* rhetorical flavor. そういう言葉にすると文が修辞的になる. ‖ *take on* a new lease of life 命が延びる ‖ In Los Angeles "barnyard golf" was *taking on* some of the popularity of bowling. ロスアンゼルスでは「裏庭ゴルフ」が球投げ場の人気を幾分奪った. ¶ *take over* the defense of the coast 海岸防備に当る ‖ The woman is *taking over* as head of the house. 段々婦人が家長の位置を占めるようになってきた. ‖ *take over* the leadership of ... ...の指揮に当る. 【類】*take over* the Presidency in a national crisis / *take over* the chairmanship of the board / *take over* command from ... ‖ *take over* the management 管理に当る. 【類】*take over* the management of all industry / *take over* ownership and management of ... ‖ *took over* from ... as Secretary of State 国務長官として...から事務を引継ぐ ‖ *take over* one's duties その任務を引継ぐ ‖ *take over* the occupation duties from ... 占領任務を...から引継ぐ ‖ *take over* the reins of government 政権をとる ‖ *take over* the business of a firm 会社の事務を譲り受ける. 【類】*take over* buildings occupied by ... / *take over* the assets of a firm (会社の資産) / *take over* the property as a German asset / An international atomic authority, if established, will *take over* the duties of the U.S. Atomic Energy Commission (原子力委員会) / He *took over* the office with an ease which gave the people a comfortable feeling. / a building *taken over* by the Occupation Army. ¶ *Take* this trunk *up* to my room. [ホテルで]このかばんを私のへやまで持って行ってくれ. ‖ *take* a person *up* into the air ...を空中に運ぶ ‖ *take up* one's pen ペンをとる, 執筆する ‖ *take up* the sword (gun) 剣(銃)を取る ‖ *take* [*up*] arms against ... ...に対して武器をとる(戦う). 【類】*take up* arms in defense of the country ‖ *take up* the profession of law 法律家になる ‖ *take up* one's old position as ... ...としてもとの地位に返り咲く ‖ *take up* the role of conciliator 調停者の役目を引受ける. 【類】*take up* one's duties as manager / *take up* one's duties in Congress (国会議員) / the causes which induced the prostitutes to *take up* their avocation / *take up* piracy (海賊行為) as a trade / *take up* employment overseas ‖ *take up* a berth [船が]停泊地につく ‖ *take up* begging こじきになる ‖ *take up* a quarrel about trifles 詰らないことでけんかをする ‖ *take up* a challenge 挑戦に応じる ‖ be ready to *take up* a fight against overwhelming odds 圧倒的多数を相手に戦う覚悟である ‖ *take up* the cudgel against ... ...を非難する ‖ *take up* the cudgel in the present war 現在の戦争に参加する ‖ *take up* the study of law 法律の研究を始める. 【類】He *took* up the study of English at the age of 14. / *take up* original investigation of ... / we shall *take up* in the next chapter the history of ... ‖ The author *takes up* the story where he broke off in his previous volume. 著者は前巻で筆をおいた所からその物語を始める. ‖ *take up* permanent residence there そこを本籍地と定める. 【類】Bonaparte *took up* his residence in the Tuileries in 1800. / *take up* one's quarters at ... / *take up* one's abode in a deserted hut ‖ *take up* moorings at ... ...浮標の所にけい留する ‖ This will *take up* too much room. これは余り場所を取り過ぎるだろう. ‖ I am sorry to *take up* your space by ... ...で貴紙をわずらわすのは恐縮です(投稿者の言葉). ‖ I'm afraid I've *taken up* too much of your time. 大変お邪魔をしてすみません. 【類】It may *take up* much of your time, I'm afraid. ‖ This *took up* the rest of the day. これでその日の残りはつぶれた. 【類】My time is entirely *taken up* with my office work. ‖ The authorities will *take up* the matter vigorously. 当局者はその問題を断然取上げるだろう. ‖ *take up* the issue (=question). その問題を取上げる. 【類】*take up* seriously the question of ... / *take up* the subject of ... / *take up* a new topic for discussion ‖ *take up* a suggestion 助言に従う. 【類】*take up* the idea / *take up* a proposal enthusiastically ‖ A streetcar conductor *takes up* (=collects) the tickets. 電車の車掌が切符を集める. 【類】*take up* contributions (寄付) / *take up* a collection to buy a present for a departing employee ‖ *take up* a heavy burden 重荷をになう ‖ *take up* one's mission ...の使命をになう ‖ *take up* a thief for examination 賊を逮捕して尋問する. 【類】He was *taken up* for disgracing the dignity of the Army to which he belongs. ‖ Sponges *take up* (=absorb) water 海綿は水を吸う. ‖ *take up* an insurance policy 保険に加入する ‖ He *took* me *up* for a great scholar. 彼は私を大学者と思った. ‖ All shares of the company have been *taken up.* 会社の株が全部引受済みになった. ‖ There was a short silence here, until he *took up* the thread of the narrative. ここでちょっと話が途切れ, やがて彼は話を続けた. ‖ their heads are *taken up* with ... 彼らは...に没頭している ‖ He thinks he can *take up* with his new neighbors alright. 彼は新しい隣人と仲よくつきあえると思っている. ‖ We had to *take* (=put) *up* with the berth in the steerage. われわれは船は三等で我慢しなければならなかった.

P He takes *after* his father. 彼は父に似ている. ¶*take* it *as* the center-point (basis) それを中心点(土台)と見なす ‖ *take* it *as* security それをかた(抵当)に取る ‖ You may not *take* me *as* such, but ... こう見えても ‖ The date of its invention may be *taken as* 1797. その発明の時代は一七九七年と思われる. ‖ *take* him (her) *as* a husband (wife) その人を夫(妻)にする ‖ *take* it *as* a whole それを全体的に見る ‖ I wouldn't *take* it *as* a gift. 私はそれをくれると言ってももらいたくない. ‖ A man's speech and manners are usually *taken as* a criterion of his social position. 人の言語と作法は通例その人の社会的地位を示すものと考えられている.【類】*take* them *as* models for imitation ... / may be *taken as* a proof that ... / *take* it *as* an authoritative standard. ¶*taking* the price *at* ... その値を...として ‖ *taking* the total population of the globe *at* ... 地球上の総人口を...として ‖ a hundred yen being *taken at* 2s. $^1/_2$d. 百円を二シリング半ペンスに換算して ‖ *take* one *at* a disadvantage その油断に乗じる ‖ All things considered, he connot be *taken at* his own valuation. どう見たって彼は自分の思っているほど偉い人物じゃない. ‖ *take* one *at* one's words その言葉を本気にする(真に受ける) ‖ Stories like these must be taken *at* what they are worth. このような物語はそれ相当に評価しなければならない(つまらないものもあるから). ¶proceedings *taken behind* one's back 本人のあずかり知らぬ議事. ¶*taking* me *by* the hand 私の手を取って ‖ The news *took* London (all England) quite *by* storm. そのニュースはロンドン人(など)をあっと言わせた. ‖ *taken by* surprise 不意打を食って. ¶I will *take* fifty yen *for* it. その代に五十円いただきましょう. ‖ They *took* me *for* him, for certain. 彼らはきっと私を彼と間違えたのだ. ‖ *take* Scott *for* one's model スコットを手本にする ‖ *take* it *for* the model それを模範とする ‖ *take* everything *for* Gospel 何でも真に受ける ‖ He *took* it *for* his cue of disappearing. 彼は気をきかしてその場を外した. ‖ Mother *took* baby *for* a ride in the gocart. 母が赤子を乳母車に乗せて出掛けた.【類】*take* a person out *for* a drive ‖ The speaker *took for* his subject "...". 弁士は「...」を演題とした. ‖ *take* the Chinese *for* instance 中国人を例に取る ‖ he has *taken for* his task ... 彼は...をそのなすべき事業に選んだ ‖ it may be *taken for* granted that ... ...と見て可なりである ‖ Either ... or ... may be *taken for* the starting point. [登山など]...かまたは...を出発点としてよろしい.【類】I *took* it *for* granted that he would stand by me. / it may be *taken for* granted that ... ‖ He *took* me *for* better than I am. 彼は私を買いかぶった.【類】*take* it *for* what it is worth ‖ *take* a person *for* all in all 人を無上の人物と見なす. ¶*take* it *from* a drawer (pocket) 引出し(など)からそれを取出す ‖ That flaw *takes from* the value. そのきずがあるために値打が下がる. ‖ be *taken* verbatim *from* the original 原文から逐語的に訳されている. ¶Do you *take* sugar *in* your tea? お茶に砂糖を入れますか. ‖ He officiously *took* me *in* a car. 彼はどうぞと言って私を車に同乗させた. ‖ *take* the laugh *in* good part 笑われても気にしない ‖ Remember the words of the Leader concerning the woman *taken in* adultery. 姦淫(かん)の現行犯を見付けられた女についてキリストの言った言葉を記憶せよ. ‖ The work is to be *taken in* hand shortly. その仕事は近々着手するはず. ‖ *take* it *in* earnest それを本気に考える ‖ *take* it *in* pieces. それを分解する. ¶all the circumstances being *taken into* consideration あらゆる事情を考慮して ‖ in estimating it we must never fail to *take into* consideration ... それを評価するには必ず...を考慮に入れる必要がある.【類】*take* it *into* serious consideration / *taking* all these facts *into* consideration, I am induced to believe that ... ‖ *take* it *into* account (=consideration) それを酌量する.【類】It must be *taken into* full account. / these are factors that must be *taken into* account ‖ I will *take* you *into* my confidence. 君に私の秘密を明かそう. ‖ *take* him *into* partnership (one's service) 彼を組合員(その使用人)にする ‖ *take into* partnership his son, ... 彼の息子...を組合員にする ‖ He *took* a friend *into* the secret. 彼はある友人にその秘密を明かした. ‖ *take* ... *into* custody ... ...を拘留する ‖ The bank will *take* it *into* its custody. その銀行がそれを保管してくれるだろう. ‖ he *took* it *into* his head to ... 彼は...を思い立った ‖ Don't hesitate to *take* our ads *into* your confidence. 本誌の広告は御懸念なく御信用下さい. ‖ I *took* him *into* my service. 私は彼を雇入れた. ¶*take* ten years off his age 十年若返る ‖ *take* the dead leaves and branches *off* a plant 植物の枯れた枝や葉を取る ‖ I will *take* it *off* your hands at 1,000 yen. 千円で引取りましょう. ‖ thus *taken off* his guard 不意打を食って. ¶I *take* it *on* myself to say that ... 私はあえて...と言う. ‖ *take* notes *on* (=of) a lecture 講議のノートを取る. ¶*take* a handkerchief *out of* one's pocket ポケットからハンケチを取り出す ‖ *take* a child *out of* school 子供を退学させる ‖ The shock *took* the breath *out of* him. その衝撃で息が止まった. ¶He was *taken round* (=*around*) the city by a competent guide. 彼はりっぱな案内者に導かれてその市を一周した. ¶save enough money to *take* a person *through* [the] college 卒業ができるだけの貯金をする. ¶The usher *took* me *to* my seat. 案内係は私を席に案内した. ‖ He was at once *taken to* a hospital. 彼はさっそく病院に入院させられた. ‖ *take* a friend *to* lunch (dinner) 友人を昼食(など)に連れて行く ‖ *take to* the branches of a tree 木に登る ‖ The cows *took to* the wood. 雌牛の群は林に入って行った. ‖ *take* it home *to* children それを子供へのみやげにする ‖ *take* the advice *to* heart その忠告を心に銘じる ‖ *take* her *to* wife 彼女を妻にする ‖ I *took* him *to* task about it (for what he had done). 私はそのこと(など)について彼を責めた. ‖ He *took to* drink again. 彼はまた酒を飲むようになった. ‖ *take to* (=begin) stealing pressed by want 貧に迫られて窃盗を始める ‖ *take to* (=enter) politics 政界にはいる ‖ *take to* stamp-collecting 切手の収集を始める ‖ He *took to* photography as a business. 彼は写真屋を始めた.【類】Can you tell me how you began to *take to* this work? / He *took to* the practice of smoking. / *take to* telegraphy / *take to* letters (文学) as a diversion ‖ *take to* the airwaves (放送による運動) ‖ The ship is ready to *take to* sea again. その船は再航海の用意ができている. ‖ He was forced to *take to* his bed for ten days. 彼は病気で十日間床につかねばならなかった. ‖ He has *taken to* his heels. 彼は逃げ出した. ‖ He has *taken to* the ice. 彼はスケートをやり出した. ‖ *take to* flight 逃げ出す ‖ Children *take to* me (=feel at home with me). 子供たちはよく私になつく.【類】The baby has *taken to* a new nurse-maid. ‖ *take* a clock *to* pieces 時計を分解する. ¶*take* a person *under* one's wing 人を保護する.【類】*take* a person *under* protection. ¶*take upon* oneself the office of president 会長としての就任を受諾する ‖ he *took upon* himself to ... 彼はあえて...した ‖ *take* a task *upon* oneself 仕事を引受ける. ¶He was *taken with* (=has taken) cold (smallpox, headaches and insomnia). 彼はかぜ(など)にかかった. ‖ a remark to be *taken with* a grain of salt まゆつばもの ‖ The report must be *taken with* discount. その報道は割引して聞かなければならない. ‖ He was *taken with* a serious illness. 彼は重病にかかった. ‖ He *took* £300 *with* him. 彼は三百ポンド持って行った. ‖ While swimming he was *taken with* the cramp and drowned. 彼は水泳中けいれんを起してでき死した. ‖ It would not *take with* the general reader. それは一般読者には向くまい. ‖ be *taken with* a shy fit はにかむ ‖ The Moors *took* this art *with* them *into* Spain. ムーア人はこの技術をスペインに伝えた.

O Years ago it used to *take* five yards to make a woman's dress. 数年前には婦人服を作るには五ヤールの切地を要したものだ. ¶Police officers—as we *took* them to be—came along. 警察官らしい人々がやって来た.

take-off *n.*〖航空〗離陸.

Q make a *good* (*bad*) *take-off* [飛行機が]うまく(まずく)離陸した.

Q² a *mass take-off* of planes 飛行機の集団離陸.

taking, *n.* とること.

Q *mutual taking* of life 命のやりとり.

Q² *leave taking* 告別. ¶*X-ray picture taking* レントゲン写真撮影.

P *taking of* evidence 証拠調べ.

takings, *n. pl.* 収入.

V The conductor is *checking* his last journey's *takings.* 車掌は今乗車勤務を終ってその間の収入を勘定している.

Q The previous day's *takings* were *small.* 前日の収入(売上高など)は少なかった.

P² the *takings* in *at* the box office 入場料の収入. ¶*tak-*

ings from one's pen (books, work, labor) 文筆(など)からの収入.

tale, *n.* 話., 物語

V ***contradict*** the *tale* その話を打消す. ¶***cook up*** (=***concoct***) a *tale* 話をでっち上げる. ¶I ***found*** a very different *tale*. 私は話が大分違っていることを知った. ¶***sob out*** a pitiful *tale* すすり泣きをしながら哀れな話をする. ¶Only three men escaped to ***tell*** the *tale*. たった三人命拾いをしてその口からその話が伝わった. ‖ Only ... are left to ***tell*** the *tale*. ...がわずかにその名ごりを留めている. ‖ Dead men ***tell*** no *tales*. 死人に口なし. ‖ ***tell*** the *tale*=count the number 数える ‖ These withered crops ***tell*** their own *tale* (=show the case clearly). この作物がしおれているので(かんばつのことが)推して知れる. ¶***unfold*** a *tale* お話をする.

V² His tale is ***getting high***. やつの話は大きくなってきた. ¶there ***hangs*** a wondrous *tale* to ... ...について不思議な話がある.

Q an ***absorbing*** *tale* of adventure 身のはいる冒険談. ¶an ***awesome*** *tale* 恐ろしい話. ¶a ***breathless*** *tale* of adventure 聞いていて息もつけないような冒険談. ¶a very ***cheery***, readable *tale* 愉快なおもしろい物語. ¶tell a ***false*** *tale* about him 彼についてありもしないことを言う. ¶a ***fascinating*** *tale* from beginning to end 徹頭徹尾魅力のある物語. ¶an ***exciting*** *tale* 興奮させる物語. ¶I had heard ***glowing*** *tales* about ... ...に関するすてきなうわさを前から聞いていた. ¶a ***hair-raising*** *tale* 身の毛もよだつ話. ¶a ***harrowing*** *tale* 痛ましい話. ¶tell the ***oft-told*** *tale* again 毎度の話を繰返す. ¶a ***plain*** *tale* ありふれた話. ¶a ***romantic*** *tale* ロマンティックな物語. ¶there is a ***sad*** *tale* of heroism told of ... ...にまつわる悲惨な義勇談がある. ¶There is yet room in the world of fiction for ***simple*** *tales* told simply. 小説界には飾り気なしに書いた単純な話をいれる余地がまだある. ¶a ***singular*** *tale* 珍奇な話. ¶a ***stale*** *tale* 古臭い話. ¶relate a ***strange*** *tale* of the wilderness 荒野の不思議な話をする. ¶a ***tall*** *tale* 大ぼら. ¶a ***thrilling*** *tale* 血沸き肉躍る話. ¶a ***tragic*** *tale* of her brother's death at the hands of her husband 彼女の兄(弟)がその夫に殺害されたという悲痛な話. ¶a mere ***traveller's*** *tale* 単なる外遊者のほら. ¶***true*** *tales* of mountain adventure 登山冒険の実話. ¶All this forms a ***twice-told*** *tale*. これは全然ありふれた話だ. ¶hear a ***weird*** *tale* 怪奇談を聞く. ¶a ***wonderful fairy*** *tale* すばらしいおとぎ話.

Q² a ***Canterbury*** *tale* カンタベリ巡礼物語, 架空の物語. ¶a ***folk*** *tale* 民間に伝わる話.

P² a gory *tale* ***concerning*** a mortal combat between a cock and a cat, with the dire result to the cat 雄鶏とねこが命がけで闘いねこが悲惨にも敗北するという血なまぐさい物語. ¶*tales* ***from*** mythology 神話から出た物語 ‖ Lamb's "*Tales* ***from*** Shakespeare" ラムの「シェークスピア物語」.【類】sound like a *tale* ***from*** fairyland. ¶the *Tale* ***of*** Troy トロイ物語 ‖ listen to the *tale* ***of*** woe (wrath, terror) 悲哀(など)の物語に耳を傾ける ‖ the same *tale* ***of*** woe was echoed in ... [不景気などの]同じ心細い話が...でも聞かれた.【類】a *tale* ***of*** misery. ¶this is a common *tale* ***with*** ... これは...には珍らしくない(有りふれたことだ.

talent, *n.* 手腕; 人材; [団] 芸能人.

V highly ***appreciate*** his *talent* 彼の手腕を高く買う. ¶***cultivate*** one's *talents* 技術をみがく. ¶***develop*** one's *talent* その才を延ばす ‖ ***develop*** one's special *talent* 特殊の才能を発達させる. ¶always eager to ***discover*** new *talent* 技能ある新人を見出そうと始終やっきとなっている. ¶He ***displays*** decided *talent*. 彼はりっぱに才幹を発揮している. ¶***draw out*** his native *talents* 彼の持って生れた才能を啓発する. ¶***engage*** cheaper *talents* 技能の低級な者を雇入れる. ¶***exercise*** one's *talents* on ... ...の才能を働かせる. ¶He ***found*** in himself a hidden *talent*. 彼は自己に隠れた才能があることを知った. ¶an artist who ***has*** more *talent* than recognition 世間に認識されている以上の才幹を有する芸術家 ‖ ***have*** *talent* for drawing 図画の才を有する.【類】***have*** a *talent* for organization (組織の才) / He ***has*** no *talent* for music. ¶***inherit*** the *talent* for acquiring foreign languages 外国語学習の才能を遺伝する. ¶his literary *talent* was first ***manifested*** in his virgin work "..." 彼の文才は処女作「...」に見られた. ¶his gift for ***picking out*** young *talent* 若い才人(新人)を掘り出す彼の腕. ¶***possess*** a *talent* for ... ...の才がある. ¶***prostitute*** one's *talent* to win poularity 人気を取るためにその才能を悪用する. ¶***release*** the *talent* 才を発揮させる. ¶***require*** special *talent* 特殊の才能を要する. ¶He early ***showed*** *talent* for drawing. 彼は幼時から図画の才が現われていた.【類】At a very early age she ***showed*** a *talent* for music. ¶***show off*** one's *talents* その才能を見せびらかす. ¶***suppress*** the *talents* of artists 芸術家の才を殺す. ¶To describe this perhaps ***transcends*** the *talent* of mortals. これはとうてい筆紙の尽す所でない. ¶He ***turned*** his *talents* to account. 彼はその腕前を役に立たした. ¶know how to ***use*** other people's *talents* 他人の技能の利用法を知る. ¶***utilize*** one's *talents* その才能を利用する.

Q his ***administrative*** *talents* 彼の行政的手腕. ¶***amateur histrionic*** *talent* and playwright 有能なしろうと俳優兼脚本作者. ¶His work shows no ***artistic*** *talent* 彼の作品には何ら芸術的才能が認められない. ¶***average*** *talents* 並の才能. ¶***brilliant*** *talents* すばらしい才. ¶a ***charming*** *talent* 人を魅する才知. ¶a young man of ***considerable*** *talent* 相当の才能を有する青年.【類】show considerable *talent* for characterization (人物描写). ¶***diplomatic*** *talent* 外交的手腕. ¶develop one's ***dramatic*** *talents* 劇作の才能を発達させる. ¶an ***exceptional*** *talent* for mimicry まれに見る模倣の才. ¶have a ***facile*** *talent* for pen-and-ink sketches ペンで見取図を書くことに妙を得ている. ¶He early displayed a ***great*** *talent* for music. 彼は幼い内から偉大な音楽の才を示した. ¶an ***inborn*** *talent* for ... ...の天才. ¶an ***innate*** *talent* for drawing 天賦の画才. ¶a decline in ***literary*** *talent* 文才の衰え.【類】His ***literary*** *talents* are inherited by two of his sons. ¶***local*** *talent* 地方の芸能人たち.【類】look out for ***local*** *talent*. ¶men of ***mediocre*** *talents* 凡才. ¶a commander of great ***military*** *talent* 非常に軍事上の才に長じた司令官. ¶He was born with a ***natural*** *talent* for reckoning. 彼は生来計算が達者であった. ¶show off (=air) one's ***oratorical*** *talent* 雄弁術の才を誇らしく示す. ¶the man of ***ordinary*** *talent* 十人並の才能を持った人. ¶He had a ***peculiar*** *talent* for making most of the labor of other people. 彼には他人の力を最大限度まで利用するという特殊の才があった. ¶show a ***remarkable*** *talent* for ... ...の非凡な才を示す. ¶a ***rugged, unpolished*** *talent* 生れついたままのみがきをかけてない才能. ¶win success by ***sheer*** *talent* 腕一本で成功する. ¶The House of Lords is representative of the ***sounder legal*** *talent* in the country. 上院にはその国のしっかりした法律家がそろっている. ¶He has no ***special*** *talent* for language study. 彼は別に語学の才があるというのではない. ¶display ***unusual*** *talent* 非常な才能を発揮する. ¶encourage ***young*** *talent* [芸能など]新人を激励する.

Q² ***amateur*** *talent* 余技. ¶Companies are recruiting college *talent*. 諸会社で大学出の人材を採用している. ¶***stage*** *talent* 俳優としての才能.

P scout ***for*** new *talent* [映画・芸能など]新人をスカウトする. ¶a young man ***of*** *talent* 才能ある青年. ¶endowed ***with*** *talents* 天賦の才能のある.

P² a *talent* ***for*** writing (music, painting) 文章(など)の才.

talisman, *n.* 護符, お守り.

P² a *talisman* ***against*** evil (misfortune) 禍(など)よけの護符. ¶a *talisman* ***for*** traffic safety 交通安全のお守り(タクシーなどの).

talk, *n.* 話.

V ***carry out*** *talks* (=conversation) 談話をする. ¶suddenly ***changing*** this *talk* 急にこの話題を転じて. ¶***contradict*** the idle *talk* この浮いたうわさを否定する. ¶***enliven*** one's *talk* with slang 俗語を交えて話をおもしろくする. ¶***get*** all the *talk* to himself [他人に言わせないで]自分独りでしゃべる. ¶***give*** a *talk* to young men 青年に向って一場の演説をする ‖ ***give*** a *talk* on ... ...に関する話をする. ¶I'd like to see you again and ***have*** a *talk* of old times. 君に会って昔話をしたい. ‖ ***have*** a long *talk* with ... over business ...と長時の用談をする. ¶one ***hears*** so much *talk* about ... ...のうわさは随分聞く. ¶***call off*** the *talks* as early as possible なるべく早く会談を打切る. ¶***make*** one's *talk* ***colorful*** 話につやをつける. ¶circles where the intelligentsia ***make*** *talk* together 知識階級が語り合う仲間. ¶try to ***overhear*** a private *talk* 内証話を立聞しようとする. ¶***preface*** one's *talk* by references to ... and ... まず...と...のことを述べておいてから話し始める. ¶***talk*** small *talk* 雑談をする.

V² the *talk chanced* to turn upon … たまたま話が…に移った. ¶our *talk drifted* to … われわれが話している中に…の話が出た. ¶the *talk* often *runs* on the affairs of … しばしば話が…のことに及ぶ.

Q an *animated talk* 気炎. ¶No *back talk!* 口返答はよせ. ¶*big talk* 大言壮語. ¶*breezy* and *bright talk* 明朗な話. ¶*candid talks* 打明け話. ¶in *careless talk* 不用意に話すときは. ¶it is *common talk* that … …とは人がよく言うことだ ‖ words used in *common talk* 普通用語. ¶*confidential talk* 打明け話. ¶have a *desultory talk* with … …と雑談をする. ¶a *foolish talk* ばかげた話. ¶*free talk* Y談. ¶amuse us with *gay talk* and entertaining jest 陽気な話をしおもしろい冗談を飛ばして私たちを喜ばせる. ¶His voice was heard above the *general talk*. 彼の声が皆の話声の中にはっきり聞えた. ¶fooled by the *glib, smooth talk* 口車に乗せられて. ¶an *honest talk* about … …についての正直な話. ¶an *illuminating talk* よく条理を尽した話. ¶an *impure* (=*indecent*) *talk* わい談. ¶enjoy the flavor of his *keen, incisive talk* 彼の鋭い痛切な談話を興味深く聞く. ¶have a *long talk* with … …と長時間話をする. 【類】We had a *long* and *serious talk*. ¶loose people and their *loose talk* いんわいな人のみだらな話. ¶Only *low talk* permitted here. 高声に談話すべからず(図書館などの掲示). ¶a *luscious talk* 味のある話. ¶there is *open talk* of the wish of … to … …が…しようという念願を持っているというわさが世間に立っている. ¶The word is not used in *ordinary talk*. その語は普通の話には用いない. ¶have one's *personal talk* with God in the bush やぶの中で神と親しく霊話をする. ¶a *pointless talk* 要領を得ない話. ¶*preliminary talks* on disarmament (peace) 軍縮(平和)に関する予備会談. ¶overhear a *private talk* 密談を立ち聞きする. ¶a *public talk* about … …の世間話. ¶a *rambling talk* むだ話. ¶there is *some talk* of … …というちょっとした風説がある. ¶a *silly talk* ばか話. ¶a *straight talk* to … …への直言. ¶"*straight from the shoulder*" *talks* 痛言. ¶indulge in some *tall talk* with regard to … …について気炎を吐く. ¶a *war talk* 戦争談. ¶a *washy talk* 実のない話. ¶there is a *wide talk* about … …についてうわさが広まっている. ¶indulge in *wild talk* とほうもないことを言う. ¶a *windy* (=empty) *talk* 内容のない話.

Q² an *after-dinner talk* 晩さん後の談話. ¶Stop your *baby talk*. 赤坊のような口をきくのはよせ. ¶a series of *broadcast talks* on … …に関する談話の連続放送. ¶a *business talk* 商売の話. ¶*deadlock talks* 行詰りの会談. ¶*evening talks* with … …を相手の夜話. ¶a *heart-to-heart talk* うちとけた話. ¶a free *public gallery talk* or lecture 無料の画廊講演. ¶a *radio talk* on … …に関する放送談話. ¶a *round-table talk* 座談会. ¶a *sales talk* 販売談. ¶a *sea talk* 海洋談. ¶a *shop talk* 商談 ‖ swap *shop talk* with … …と商談をかわす. ¶a *table talk* 食卓談話. ¶a symposium of *ten-minute talks* will be held in which the following will participate: 十分間の討論会が催され, 左記の人々が参加する. ¶*three Power money talks* 三大国財政談. ¶a *travel talk* 旅行談. ¶a *war talk* 戦争談.

P *in talk* we say … 話では…という. ¶in the heat *of* their *talk* 話につられて ‖ bits *of talk* overheard on the subway 地下鉄で拾った話. ¶amused *with* his *talk* 彼の話に興味を感じて.

P² *talks about* art 芸談. ¶She is the *talk of* the town. 彼女は町で評判だ. 【類】His store was beginning to be the *talk of* the town. ‖ the *talk of* the whole country 国をあげての話題. 【類】There is a *talk of* a new road being made. / the café that's the *talk of* the town. ¶a *talk on* literature (politics) 文学(など)の話 ‖ seven *talks on* England 英国に関する七回講演.

talk, *v.* 語る.

M *talk aside* with … 人と離れて(ひそかに)…と話す. ¶He has the ability of *talking at length* and talking nothing. 彼はなんでもないことを長々と話す才を持っている. ¶*talk at random* 出放題を言う. ¶*talk* one's fears *away* 人に説き聞かせて安心させる ‖ *talk* a night *away* 一夜を語り明かす. ¶*talk back* to a person 《米》人に口答えをする. ¶*talk big* 大口をたたく. ¶*talk briskly* 元気よく話す. ¶*talking broadly*, one may say that … 概して…といえる. ¶*talk* too *copiously* 余りしゃべり過ぎる. ¶*talk earnestly* しきりに話す. ¶*talk freely* of … …を遠慮なく話す. ¶*talk friendly* 友情をもって話す. ¶*talk glibly* 喋(ちょう)々と述べる ‖ *talk gruffly* あらっぽく話す. ¶*talk heart-to-heart* with … …と腹をわって話し合う. ¶*talk* oneself *hoarse* しゃべり過ぎて声をからす. ¶*How* she *talked!* [女が]しゃべるわ, しゃべるわ. ¶Don't *talk* so *impudently*. そんな生意気なことを言うな. ¶*talk incessantly* of … 絶えず…の話をする. ¶*talk knowingly* of … 知ったかぶりに…を語る. ¶*talk languidly* 身のはいらない話し方をする. ¶*talk long* and *confidentially* 長々と内証話をする. ¶*talk loudly* and *gleefully* 声高にうれしそうに話す. ¶it has become a subject *much talked* about. それはよく話題にのぼるようになった. ‖ What makes you *talk* so *much*? どうしてそんなにおしゃべりするのか. ¶*talk openly* of … …を大っぴらに話す. ¶*talk* it *out* 話をつける ‖ *talk out* loud 声高に話す. ¶*talk plain* 飾らずに話す. ¶*talk quick* (=*rapidly*) 早口に話す. ¶*talk seriously* to a person 人に向ってまじめに話す. ¶*talk shyly* おずおず話す. ¶*talk together* 相談する. ¶*talk unkindly* of one's neighbors 近所の人の悪口を言う. ¶*talk unrestrainedly* 腹蔵なく話す. ¶*talk viciously* 毒づく. ¶*talk volubly* of one's wares べらべらと商品の能書を並べる. ¶We *talked well on* to midnight. われわれは真夜中まで話し続けた. ¶The subject is *widely talked* about. その問題は評判になっている. ¶extremists who *talk wildly* 無軌道なことを言う極端論者.

M² It remains to be seen whether he can *talk* them *around*. 先方を説き付けることができるかどうかそれが見ものだ. ¶*talk* him *down* 彼をやり込める ‖ *talk down* to what one supposes to be the level of one's hearers 聴衆に適当と思われる程度に調子を下げて話す. ¶She *talks* our arms *off*. おしゃべりでうんざりさせられちゃうわ. ¶let a person *talk on* しゃべらせておく. 【類】*talk on* and *on*. ¶*talk* a person *over* to one's side 人をだき込む. 【類】"I know—I know," he said "I'll *talk* them *over*." ‖ *talk* it *over* with … …とそれを話し合う.

P a district more *talked about* than visited 話にはよく出るがあまり人の行かない地方 ‖ *talk* only *about* one's own concerns 自分に関係のことだけ話す. 【類】*talk about* other people's affairs. ¶*talk against* a person 人の不利なことを言う. ¶*talk at* a person 人に話しかける ‖ *talk at* table 食卓で話す. 【類】*talk at* each other across the table. ¶*talk before* one's audience 聴衆の前で話す. ¶I heard you *talking in* your sleep last night. ゆうべ寝言を言っていましたね. ‖ *talk in* a lofty strain (low tone, whispers) 高調子(など)で話す. ¶We *talked* far *into* the night. 私たちは夜ふけまで話した. ‖ political speeches *talked into* a phonograph 蓄音機へ吹き込んだ政談演説 ‖ He was *talked into* doing … 彼は…するように説得された. ¶*talk like* a book 文語調で話す. ¶He *talks of* going abroad. 彼は洋行する積りだと言う. ‖ people *talk* very lightly *of* elementary school teachers, but … 小学校の教師というと人はひどく軽べつするがしかし… ‖ *Talking of* being grateful, isn't there …? 有難いと言えば…じゃないですか. ¶*talk on* politics 政治を談じる. ¶He *talked* me *out of* my belief. 彼の話で私はもうそのことを信じなくなった. ¶He invited me to his home to *talk over* old times. 彼は昔話をしようと私を家に招待した. ‖ *talk over* business affairs 仕事の相談をする. 【類】*talk over* the happenings of the day / I've got something to *talk over* with you. ‖ foregather and *talk over* their ideas on art 集ってお互に芸術上のことを話し合う ‖ Don't *talk over* his head. 彼の頭にはいらないようなことを言うな. ‖ *talk over* the telephone to … 電話で…に話す. ¶*talk round* the subject その問題を中心にして話す. ¶*talk through* an interpreter 通訳付きで話す ‖ *talk through* the nose 鼻声で話す. ¶*talk to* oneself ひとり言を言う ‖ I want to *talk to* you of a very serious matter. 非常に大切な件についてあなたにお話したい. ‖ *talk to* the public 公衆に呼びかける ‖ But I was *talking to* the winds. 言っても聞かばこそ. ¶*talk with* a person on … …について人と話す ‖ *talk with* animation 元気よく話す.

O *talk* nonsense むだ話をいう. 【類】*talk* business (baby).

talker, *n.* 話し手.

Q an *able, influential talker* うまい力のある話し手. ¶a *brilliant talker* すばらしい能弁家. ¶a *charming talker* 魅力のある話をする人. ¶a *glib talker* 能弁家. ¶a *good talker* not in volume but in quality 言葉数は少いがしっかりした話をする人. ¶a ***long-winded talker*** 長たらしくしゃべる人. ¶a very ***original talker*** 非常に奇抜な話し手. ¶an ***overgifted*** and ***aggressive talker*** 能弁すぎて押しつけがましい話し手. ¶a ***stiff talker*** 固苦しい話し手.

talkie, *n.* トーキー映画.

V when *talkies* ***came*** トーキーができた時. ¶A fine *talkies* was ***released.*** よい映画が封切になった.

Q^2 ***pre-release talkies*** 封切前のトーキー.

talking, *n.* 談話.

V ***do*** very little *talking* ほとんど口をきかない. ¶***keep*** [***on***] *talking* during ... の間話し続ける.

Q ***loose talking*** and thinking on the subject その問題に関する散漫な言説並に思索. ¶in ***ordinary*** (***formal***) *talking* or writing 普通の(儀式張った)話または文において.

P He is very fond ***of*** *talking.* 彼は非常に話好きだ.

tall, *a.* たけが高い.

M^2 She is ***as tall*** as her mother. お母さん位のせいだ.

P *taller* ***by*** a head ...より頭だけ高い. ¶He is *tall* ***for*** his age. 彼は年にしてはせいが高い. ¶*tall* ***of*** stature せいが高い.

tally, *n.* 計算, 勘定; 《米》レッテル.

V ***pay*** the *tally* 勘定を払う.

Q keep a ***correct tally*** 正しく数を取る. ¶a ***running tally*** 累計の数.

P^2 the *tally* ***on*** a box (trunk) 箱(など)の荷札.

tally, *v.* 符合する, 一致する.

P The articles do not *tally* ***with*** the invoice. 品物が送り状と合わない. 【類】 your account *tallies* ***with*** mine.

talon, *n.* [猛鳥などの]つめ.

Q the young Thackeray ***sharpening*** his *talons* for future and large battles 将来一層大きい戦いに備えてつめをといでいる青年サッカレー.

tame, *v.* ならす.

O *tame* a wild tiger 野生のとらをならす.

tame, *a.* なれた; 無味単調な.

O a *tame* bear (squirrel) 人なれたくま(など). ¶a *tame* story (performance) つまらない話(など).

tamer, *n.* ならす人.

Q a ***dexterous tamer*** of horses 巧みに馬をならす人.

tamper, *v.* 手を触れる, いじる.

P Don't *tamper* ***with*** a lock (what does not belong to you). 錠前(など)に手をつけるな. ‖ *tamper* ***with*** the seal of an envelope [あて名の人でない者が]手紙の封を切る.

tan, *n.* 日焼け.

Q^2 get a ***sun tan*** 日に焼ける.

tan, *v.* 日焼けさせる.

M He was ***well tanned.*** 彼は大分日に焼けた.

P slightly *tanned* ***by*** (=***with***) the sun ちょっと日に焼けた ‖ complexion *tanned* ***by*** the sun 日に焼けた顔.

tang, *n.* 香味.

Q the ***clean, salty tang*** of the open sea 外海の清らかな塩辛いにおい.

P^2 the *tang* ***of*** salt from the sea 海から来る潮の香り.

tangible, *a.* 触知し得る, 具体的な, 明かな.

M Though the good will of a business is not ***so tangible*** as its buildings, ... 商売ののれん(信用)は建物ほどはっきりしていないが, ...

tangle, *n.* 紛議.

V ***straighten out*** the Mexican *tangle* メキシコの紛争を解決する. ¶***unravel*** the *tangles* 幾多の乱麻をほぐす.

P The financial condition of the company is ***in*** a hopeless *tangle.* その会社の財政は整理の見込が立たないほど乱れている. ¶get ***into tangles*** 混乱状態に陥る.

tangle *v.* もつれさせる.

M The trees and bushes in a jungle are all ***tangled together.*** 森林の中の樹木やかん木はみなからみ合っている.

P hedges ***tangled with*** wild rose bushes 野ばらのからみついたかき根.

tango, *n.* 〘音楽〙タンゴ.

V ***dance*** the *tango* タンゴを踊る.

tank, *n.* 水そう(タンク).

Q^2 a wooden ***bath tank*** 浴そう. ¶a ***gasoline tank*** ガソリンタンク. ¶an ***iron*** (***brickwork***) ***tank*** 鉄製(れんが積み)貯水そう. ¶a ***swimming tank*** 水泳用水槽.

tanker, *n.* 油送船.

Q a ***privately owned tanker*** 私有の油送船.

tantamount, *a.* 等しい.

P a step considered *tantamount* ***to*** recognizing 承認と同様に見なすべき行為.

tap, *n.* のみ口.

V ***put in*** the *tap* のみ口を入れる. ¶***turn on*** (***off***) a *tap*= ***turn*** a *tap* ***on*** (***off***) せんを開け(締め)る. 【類】 I ***turned on*** the *tap*, but no water flowed.

Q an ***excellent tap*** 良い酒.

P ***in*** the *tap* 酒場で. ¶coffee ***on tap*** のみ口で出すコーヒー ‖ beer ***on tap*** (=from the wood) 生ビール ‖ keep saké ***on tap*** 酒をのみ口で出せるようにしておく. ¶draw ***through*** a *tap* のみ口から出す. 【類】 Beer run ***through*** a *tap.*

tap, *v.* [知識などを]さぐる, ひき出す.

P *tap* a person ***for*** information [質問して]人から知識を引き出す ‖ *tap* news sources ***for*** the press (publication) [新聞などの]ニュース・ソースをさぐる.

tap, *n.* 軽打.

V ***give*** a *tap* at ... ...を軽くたたく. ¶I ***heard*** a *tap* at the door. 私は戸口をたたく音を聞いた.

P go to sleep ***at taps*** 《米》消灯らっぱが鳴ると就床する.

P^2 a *tap* ***at*** the gong どらのひと打ち. ¶Then there was a *tap* ***on*** (=at) the door. それから戸をたたく音がした.

tap, *v.* たたく.

M men ***tapping out*** news stories on their typewriters 新聞記事をタイプライターで打っている人々.

P *tap* one's stick ***against*** the window (pavement) つえで窓(など)をこつこつたたく. ¶*tap* ***at*** the door 戸をたたく ¶*tap* the ash ***from*** one's cigar 葉巻の灰をはたく. ¶*tap* the ashes ***out of*** (=***off***) a pipe パイプから灰をはたく. ¶*tap* a person ***upon*** (=***on***) the shoulder (back) 人の肩(など)をたたく. ¶*tap* the door ***with*** one's knuckles げんこで戸をとんとんたたく.

tape, *n.* 細ひも(テープ).

V ***break down*** (=***cut***) the red *tape* 繁文褥(じょく)礼を廃する. ¶***breast*** the *tape* [決勝点で]テープを切る; 勝つ. ¶***eliminate*** the red *tape* 繁文褥礼を廃する.

Q put one's words on the ***phonographic tape*** (disk) 人の言葉を録音する. ¶one example of ***red tape*** (redtapism) お役所仕事の一例 ‖ get through the ***red tape*** of admission 複雑な手続をする ‖ ***red tape*** and inflexibility 融通のきかないこと.

Q^2 ***fancy tape*** 変ったテープ.

tape, *v.* テープを張る.

M^2 ***tape up*** a wound 傷を包帯する.

taper, *v.* 段々細くなる.

M^2 ***taper down*** to a point 先細になる. ¶British aids ***taper off.*** 英国の援助が段々減じる. 【類】 A church spire ***tapers off*** to a point.

P ***taper*** ... ***into*** a sharp point ...を段々細くして端を鋭くとがらせる. ¶***taper*** [off] ***to*** a point 段々細くなって先がとがる.

tapis, *n.* 議席.

P come ***on*** the *tapis* 議題となる ‖ the question ***on*** the *tapis* 審議中の問題.

tar, *v.* タールを塗る.

P be ***tarred with*** the same brush (stick) 他人と同じ欠点がある(同類だ).

O *tar* and feather a black slave 《米》黒人どれいを私刑にする(タールを浴びせ, その上に鳥の羽を植えたりして).

tardy, *v.* 遅れた; ぐずぐずした

P be ***tardy at*** school 学校に遅れる. ¶be *tardy* ***for*** supper 夕飯に遅れる. ¶***tardy in*** one's response (payment) 返答(など)が渋る.

target, *n.* 標的.

V ***hit*** the *target* 的に当てる ‖ ***hit*** the *target* in the white 肯綮(こうけい)に当る. ¶***miss*** (=fail to hit) the *target* 的に当てそこねる; 見当がはずれる.

Q an ***admirable target*** for ... ...の垂涎(すいぜん)の的. ¶a ***movable target*** 移動標的.

Q^2 a ***fan target*** 扇の的. ¶Great Britain missed her 1947 coal ***production target.*** 英国は1947年度石炭生産目標に達しなかった. ¶a ***test target*** 試験目標.

P fire (=shoot) ***at*** the *target* 射的する.

P^2 the *target* ***for*** severe criticism 厳密な批評の的. ¶He was made the ***target of*** all manner of abuse. 彼は様々なののしりの的となった. ‖ It was the *target* ***of*** bitter criticism. それはひどくやり玉に上げられた.

tariff, *n.* 税率

V Hotels in most countries have ***lowered*** their *tariffs* [by] 36%. 大抵の国ではホテルが料金を三割六分下げた. ¶***raise*** the customs *tariff* 関税率を上げる. ¶***revise*** the *tariff* 税率を改正する.

Q according to a ***fixed tariff*** of prices 定価表によって. ¶countries which have ***high*** (***moderate***) ***tariffs*** 高(低)税率の諸国 ‖ a high-class hotel with ***moderate tariff*** 低廉で高級なホテル. ¶Hotel *tariffs* are ***reasonable.*** 旅館の宿泊料金は高くない. ¶establish a ***regular tariff*** 正常の税率を制定する.

Q² a ***customs tariff*** 関税率. ¶a ***railway tariff*** 鉄道運賃率. ¶***trade tariff*** 貿易の税率.

P hire ***at*** a fixed *tariff* 一定料金で借りる. ¶charges fixed ***by*** *tariff* 表で定められた料金. ¶the reduction ***of*** the *tariff* 料金の割引. ¶***under*** the existing *tariff* 現在の税率で.

P² *tariff* ***for*** carriage 運賃率. ¶*tariff* ***of*** charges (meals and apartments) [ホテルなどの]料金率(食事とへや代). ¶the *tariff* ***on*** lumber 材木の関税率.

tarry, *v.* とう留する; ぐずぐずする.

P *tarry* ***at*** a place ある場所にとう留する. ¶*tarry* ***for*** … ぐずぐず…を待つ. ¶*tarry* ***on*** the way 道草を食う.

task, *n.* 課せられた仕事.

V ***abandon*** one's *task* at the outset 最初から仕事を放棄する. ¶Now that I have ***accepted*** the *task*, I will do it without fail. その仕事を引受けた以上きっとやります. ¶***accomplish*** a *task* 仕事を成し遂げる. ¶***assign*** the *task* of … to … …の仕事を…に振り当てる. ¶***attempt*** a similar *task* 同様な仕事を企てる. ¶The author has ***attempted*** and ***accomplished*** an enormous *task*. その著作家は非常な大作を企てこれを完成した. ¶***begin*** (=***enter upon***) one's *task* その仕事を始める. ¶How can they possibly ***carry out*** this *task*? どうしてあいつらにこの仕事ができよう. 【類】 admirably ***carry out*** a task. ¶***commit*** the *task* to … その仕事を…に任せる. ¶My *task* is now ***completed***. 私の仕事はもうでき上った. ¶***complicate*** the teacher's *task* 教師の仕事を複雑にする. ¶***conclude*** one's *task* 仕事を完成する. ¶***do*** a *task* assigned to a person あてがわれた仕事をする. ¶***essay*** a hopeless *task* 完成の見込がない事業を企てる. ¶***execute*** a *task* well 首尾よく仕事を完成する. ¶In spite of all these deterrents, he boldly ***faced*** the *task*. 彼はかかる妨害を物ともせず敢然と事業に当った. ¶The *task* they had to ***fulfil*** was twofold. 彼らのなすべき仕事は二通りであった. ¶I ***have*** a heavy *task* before me. 私は困難な仕事を前に控えている. ¶***impose*** a *task* on … …に仕事を言いつける. ¶***lighten*** one's *task* その仕事を軽減する. ¶***neglect*** one's *task* 仕事を怠る ‖ the ability with which he has ***performed*** the *task* 仕事を仕遂げた彼の才能 ‖ ***perform*** one's *task* admirably (efficiently, mechanically, faithfully) りっぱに(成績をあげて, 機械的)に仕事をなし遂げる. ¶***quit*** one's *task* 仕事を投げる. ¶***set*** a *task* before oneself 自ら仕事に当る ‖ This is the *task* I ***set*** before myself when I commenced to write this volume. これが私がこの本の著作に着手したときの目標である. ¶He has ***set about*** his *task* very thoroughly. 彼は抜かりなく仕事に取り掛かった. ¶***shirk*** the *task* その仕事を回避する. ¶***shoulder*** the *task* その仕事を負担する. ¶Interest ***sweetens*** a *task*. 興味をもってすれば仕事がおもしろくなる. ¶***tackle*** one's *task* with no mean skill 仲々器用に仕事をさばく. ¶***take up*** the *task* under the direction of … …の指導のもとに仕事を始める. ¶***undertake*** a hopeless *task* 見込のない事業を始める. 【類】 be quite capable of ***undertaking*** the *task*. / ***undertake*** a *task* and carry it through.

V² on (=upon) Mr. … has ***devolved*** (=***fallen***) the *task* of … …氏がその仕事をやることになった ‖ the *task* of … ***fell*** on … …の仕事が…に回った. ¶The *task* ***seems*** one of deadly dullness. それは実におもしろくない仕事らしい.

Q perform thoroughly one's ***allotted*** *tasks* in the world's work この世で自分に割り当てられた仕事を徹底的にやる. ¶the divinely (=heaven-) ***appointed*** *tasks* 天職. ¶an ***arduous*** *task* 骨の折れる仕事. ¶an ***assigned*** *task* 割り当てられた仕事. ¶a ***back-breaking*** *task* 骨の折れる仕事. ¶a pretty ***big*** *task* かなりの大仕事. ¶perform one's ***biographical*** *task* 伝記を書く. ¶too ***burdensome*** a *task* 非常にやっかいな仕事. ¶a ***colossal*** *task* 大事業. ¶perform a ***complicated*** *task* 込み入った仕事をやりあげる. ¶He did not find it a ***congenial*** *task*. 彼はその仕事をやって見て自分の性に合わないことを知った. ¶a ***considerable*** *task*=quite a job 一仕事. ¶a ***daily*** *task* 日課. ¶a ***difficult*** *task* 困難な仕事. ¶a ***disagreeable*** *task* いやな仕事. ¶***a distasteful*** *task* おもしろくない仕事. ¶a ***divine*** *task* 神聖な仕事. ¶the ***double*** *task* of earning one's way while one is educating oneself 自活と独学という二重の仕事. ¶a ***dry*** *task* 無味乾燥な仕事. ¶It is not so ***easy*** a *task* as might be supposed. それは思ったほどやさしい仕事ではない. 【類】 an ***easy*** *task* / be no ***easy*** *task* to … ¶He has executed his ***elaborate*** *task* with conspicuous success. 彼はその骨が折れる仕事をりっぱにやりとげた. ¶an ***enormous*** *task* 非常な大仕事. ¶an ***exacting*** *task* 骨の折れる仕事. ¶a ***fascinating*** *task* 魅力のある仕事. ¶a ***formidable*** *task* 手ごわい仕事. ¶a ***fruitless*** *task* むだ骨. ¶the inception and the completion of a ***gigantic*** *task* 大事業の着手及び完成. ¶a ***grim*** *task* むごい仕事. ¶a ***hard*** *task* 困難な仕事. 【類】 Fretting and frowning (焦燥と渋面) make ***hard*** *tasks* all the harder. ¶a ***heavy*** *task* 大仕事. ¶a ***Herculean*** *task* 非常に骨の折れる仕事. 【類】 He has a ***herculean*** *task* in prospect (前途に). ¶It scarcely seems a ***hopeful*** *task*. それはどうも有望な仕事とも思えない. ¶An ***immense*** and ***glorious*** *task* indeed, the like of which was never offered to man before. 天が人間にこれまで課したことのない実に光栄ある大事業. ¶The ***immutable*** *task*, the sacred destiny, of women is to become the mother of new generations. 女子の不易の使命, その神聖な運命は新時代を生む母となることである. ¶an ***impossible*** *task* 到底できない仕事. ¶an ***insurmountable*** *task* 遂行のできない仕事. ¶an ***interminable*** *task* 際限のない仕事. ¶the ***invidious*** *task* of dwelling on… …を力説するという人からよく思われない仕事. ¶an exceedingly ***laborious*** *task* きわめて骨の折れる仕事. ¶a very ***large*** *task* 大仕事. ¶a ***light*** *task* 容易な業. 【類】 a ***lighter*** *task*. ¶a ***nerve-wrecking*** *task* 気骨の折れる仕事. ¶when it is done, the ***next*** *task* is to … それが終ったら次の仕事は…だ. ¶It is ***no light*** *task*. それは容易な業ではない. ¶an ***onerous*** *task* 骨の折れる仕事. ¶an ***overwhelming*** *task* 手の着けようもない仕事. ¶undertake a ***perilous*** *task* 危険な仕事を引受ける. ¶a ***ponderous*** *task* 大仕事. ¶a highly ***praiseworthy*** *task* 大いに称賛すべき仕事. ¶a ***prodigious*** *task* どえらい仕事. ¶a ***profitless*** *task* 利益のない仕事. ¶be ***quite*** a *task* (=job) 一骨だ. ¶discharge a ***responsible*** *task* 責任の重い仕事を果す. ¶a ***self-appointed*** *task* 自分の勝手でやる仕事. ¶a ***self-imposed*** *task* 自分から進んでやる仕事. ¶a most ***senseless*** *task* まるでばかげた仕事. ¶a ***slight*** *task* ちょっとした仕事. ¶This may seem a (no) ***small*** *task*. それはささたる(骨の折れる)仕事だと思うかも知れない. ¶a ***stupendous*** *task* どえらい仕事. 【類】 Shakespeare's ***stupendous*** *task* in writing King Lear. ¶the ***tedious*** *task* of collating texts 原文校合のわずらわしい仕事. ¶a ***thankless*** *task* 人から認められない仕事(縁の下の力持). ¶the ***threefold*** *task* of the high school principal as administrator, supervisor, and director of extra-curricular activities 中学校の校長の経営者・監督者・及び課外作業の指導者としての三重の仕事. ¶a ***toilsome*** *task* 骨の折れる仕事. ¶an ***uncongenial*** *task* 性に合わない仕事. ¶I shall not undertake the ***ungracious*** *task* of pointing out trifling errors, but … つまらない誤りを指摘するようないやなことはしないがしかし… ¶undertake an ***uninviting*** *task* 気乗りのしない仕事にかかる. ¶an ***uphill*** (=a hard) *task* [坂に車を押すような]困難な仕事. ¶an ***urgent*** *task* for … …にとって緊急のこと. ¶a ***useless*** *task* むだな仕事. ¶a ***weary*** *task* つくづくいやになる仕事. ¶A ***worthy*** *task*! 実にりっぱな(あっぱれな)仕事だ.

Q² a ***holiday*** *task* 休暇中の宿題 ‖ find it no ***holiday*** *task* それが仲々骨が折れると知る ‖ He thinks of writing, as a ***holiday*** *task*, during his tour. 彼は漫遊中道楽に執筆を考えている. ¶a ***home*** *task* 《英》 宿題. ☞米は one's home work ‖ make it his ***life['s]*** *task* それを彼の一生の仕事とする ‖ Chinese classics are so difficult that they make facility in reading almost a ***life*** *task*. 中国の古典は難解でそれを楽に読みこなすことはほとんど一生の仕事になる. ¶the end of the ***occupation*** *task* 占領関係の仕事の終了.

P busy ***at*** one's *task* 仕事がいそがしい. ¶He is not equal ***to*** the *task*. 彼はその仕事にたえない. ¶take (=***call or bring***) a person ***to*** *task* for … …に対し責任を問う(非難する) ‖ I took him ***to*** *task* for his carelessness. 私は彼の不注意をしかってやった. ¶to cope ***with*** the *task* of … …の仕事を達成しようと ‖ go on ***with*** one's *task* その仕事を進めて行く.

P² the main *task* ***before*** us is to … われわれが差当りなすべき主な仕事は…することだ. ¶a *task* ***of*** no small difficulty (magnitude) かなり困難(大き)な仕事. 【類】 He felt that it was the *task* ***of*** life (=a lifetime) to find a cure

for such a state of things. ‖ it is the *task of* the lexicographer to ... ...することが辞書編集者の仕事だ.
O It is not the *task* to be lightly undertaken. それは軽々に着手すべき仕事ではない.

task-work, *n.* 課せられた仕事.
V *do task-work* at a small salary 薄給で一定の仕事をする.

tassel, *n.* 房.
P sugar-cane ***in*** *tassel.* 穂の出たさとうきび. ¶a cap ***with*** a *tassel* on it ふさのついた帽子.

taste, *n.* 味; 好み; 趣味.
V ***acquire*** (=***attain***) a *taste* for history 歴史の趣味を持つようになる. ¶***admire*** one's *taste* 人の趣味を嘆賞する. ¶***broaden*** one's *taste* その趣味を広める. ¶gases and other matters which ***cause*** *tastes* or odors on water ガスその他水に味やにおいをつけるもの. ¶studiously ***consult*** the *tastes* of their customers 顧客の好みに投じるように苦心する. ¶***correct*** the *taste* of the masses 大衆の趣味を高める ¶***create*** a *taste* for literature 文学に趣味を持つ. ¶***cultivate*** (=foster, nourish) a *taste* for art 美術思想を養う ‖ ***cultivate*** an appreciative literary *taste* 文学の鑑賞力を養う. ¶The collector began to ***develop*** a *taste* for etchings. その収集家は蝕(ﾀﾞ)刻版画に趣味を持ち始めた. 【類】 ***develop*** a *taste* for good literature (English books). ¶***disseminate*** a *taste* for the subject その問題に対する趣味を普及する. ¶***educate*** the public *taste* 一般人の趣味を向上させる. ¶***elevate*** and ***refine*** public *taste* 一般人の趣味を高めかつ洗練する. ¶***exercise*** her *taste* in the color of her gloves 手袋の色でその趣味を示す. ¶but even then his *taste* for travel had not been ***exhausted*** しかしその時でも彼の旅行趣味はなくなってはいなかった. ¶***exhibit*** bad *taste* 趣味の悪さを示す ‖ His writings ***exhibit*** but little good *taste.* 彼の作品は余り趣味がよくない. ¶***flatter*** his *taste* 彼の好みにかなう. ¶This ***fostered*** and ***fed*** his *taste* for the pen. このために彼は文章に親しむようになった. ¶***get*** a first *taste* of ... ...に指を染める. ¶***give*** a *taste* for ... ...に趣味を持たせる. ¶He ***has*** a *taste* for researches of this kind. 彼はこの種の研究に趣味を持っている. ‖ ***have*** a *taste* for reading (going abroad) 読書(など)を好む ‖ ***have*** *taste* in dress 衣服の趣味がある. 【類】 ***have*** no *taste* for ... ¶fail to ***hit*** the public *taste* 一般人の好みに投じ得ない. ¶***improve*** one's *taste* for music 音楽趣味を向上させる. ¶***indulge*** one's *taste* (=habit) その好きな道楽をする ‖ ***indulge*** one's *taste* with ... ...で自己の趣味を満足させる. ¶The play has ***left*** a bad *taste* in the mouth of the audience. その劇は見物人にいやな後味を与えた. ¶***lose*** one's *taste* for pictures and music 絵画や音楽がいやになる. ¶***meet*** all *tastes* どんな好みにも適する(万人向き). 【類】 Booksellers naturally only stock to ***meet*** local *taste.* ¶Such a scene is fit to ***nauseate*** a good *taste.* こうした光景に対しては心ある人は嘔(ｵｳ)吐をもよおす. ¶Such illustrations will ***offend*** English *taste.* こうしたさし絵を英国人はきらう. ¶***please*** every *taste* だれの趣味(口)にも合う. 【類】 ***please*** the *taste* of the reading public. ¶***possess*** an attractive *taste* 魅力のある味を持っている. ¶***refine*** the *taste* 趣味を上品にする. ¶***reflect*** the varied *tastes* of ... ...の好みがさまざまであることを示す. ¶***reform*** and ***elevate*** the public *taste* 一般人の好みを矯正し向上させる. ¶The average Japanese does not ***relish*** the *taste* of cheese. 普通の日本人はチーズをきらう. ¶***satisfy*** Western *taste* 西洋人の好みを満たす. ¶***scorn*** American *tastes* 米人の趣味を軽べつする. ¶The pictures ***show*** good *taste* rather than original genius. その絵は独創力は見られないが良好の趣味は現われている. ‖ ***show*** bad *taste* in choice 選択に悪趣味を示す. ¶***spoil*** the *taste* of ... ...味を悪くする. ¶This ***suits*** my *taste* ***best.*** これが一番私の気に入った. 【類】 There are inns to ***suit*** all *tastes* and pockets (貧富). ¶***take*** a *taste* for retirement 隠退生活が好きになる. ¶It soon ***tires*** one's *taste.* それはじきにあきが来る. ¶***train*** one's *taste* for ... ...の趣味を養う. ¶He has ***used*** his *taste* in choosing the books. 従来彼は自分の趣味によって書物を選んだ. ¶***violate*** good *taste* 趣味の俗悪を示す.
V² *Tastes* has ***changed.*** 趣味が変った. ¶*Tastes* ***differ.*** 人の好みはさまざま.
Q It is an ***acquired*** *taste.* それはだんだんに好きになったのだ. ¶one's ***aesthetic*** *taste* その美の趣味. ¶***after*** *taste* あとあじ. ¶readers of ***all*** *tastes* さまざまな好みを持った読者. ¶He has an ***artistic*** and ***antiquarian*** *tastes.* 彼は芸術並に考古趣味を持っている. ¶The food has an ***attractive*** *taste.* その食物は味がよい. ¶It is his ***bad*** *taste* to act as such. そうするのは彼の悪い癖だ. ‖ ***bad*** *taste* in the mouth 口に入れたときのいやな味 ‖ a joke in ***bad*** *taste* だじゃれ ‖ That is the acme of ***bad*** *taste.* それは野暮の骨頂だ. 【類】 showiness (派手好き) is ***bad*** *taste.* ¶be more judicious and in ***better*** *taste* to ... ...するのは賢明でまたよい趣味である ‖ have a ***bitter*** *taste* にがい味がする ‖ the ***bitter*** *taste* of life. 人生のにがい経験. ¶have a ***burnt*** *taste* 焦げた味がする. ¶He has a ***catholic*** *taste* in reading. 読書の趣味が広い. ¶She was glad that they had ***certain*** *tastes* in common. 彼女は二人が同じ趣味をもってる点を喜んだ. ¶They are drawn together by some ***common*** *taste* in politics, or sport, or art. 彼らは政治とか運動とか芸術とかに対して多少趣味が同じなので互に引きつけられている. ¶a woman of the world of ***comprehensive*** *tastes* 趣味の広い世なれた婦人. ¶Your *taste* is ***correct.*** 君の趣味は正しい. ¶***cosmopolitan*** *taste* 何でもござれの趣味. ¶a "***cowy***" *taste* in milk 牛乳のなま臭い味. ¶That appeals to the most ***critical*** *taste.* それはどんなやかましい人でも喜ぶ. 【類】 The book should satisfy the most ***critical*** *taste* in criminal mysteries and sensation. ¶***crude*** *tastes* 粗野な趣味. ¶people of ***cultivated*** *tastes* 趣味の洗練された人々. ¶a man of ***cultured*** *tastes* 趣味の上品な人. ¶I have a ***decided*** *taste* for fiction, poetry and music. 私は小説・詩歌・音楽が断然好きだ. ¶***degraded literary*** *taste* 堕落した文学趣味. ¶It has a ***delicious, heavenly*** *taste.* それは何とも言えないよい味がする. ¶pander to ***depraved*** *tastes* 下劣な趣味に落ちる. ¶people of ***discriminating*** *tastes* 上品な趣味を持つ人々. ¶strike one as in ***doubtful*** *taste* その趣味には感心できない. ¶***eclectic*** *tastes* 多方面の趣味. ¶***elegant*** *taste* 優雅な趣味. ¶a more ***educated*** *taste* さらに高尚な趣味. ¶develop a more ***elevated*** and ***refined*** *taste* もっと高尚な洗練した趣味を養う. ¶The room is furnished in ***excellent*** *taste.* そのへやの調度品はすばらしく高尚だ. ¶with ***exceptional*** *taste* 際立った趣味の. ¶gratification of ***expensive*** *tastes* ぜいたくな好みの満足. ¶a woman of ***exquisite*** *taste* 繊細な趣味を持つ婦人. ¶satisfy the most ***fastidious*** and ***exacting*** *taste* 最も気むずかしくやかましい趣味を満足させる. ¶a ***fine*** *taste* in art 芸術上の上品な趣味. ¶give a ***fishy*** *taste* to ... ...をなまぐさくする. ¶a change in ***floral*** *taste* 花に対する好みの変化. ¶medicine with a ***foul*** *taste* いやな味の薬. ¶It is not in ***good*** *taste.* それは(趣味から言って)よくない. ‖ the formation of ***good*** *taste* よい趣味の養成 ‖ She had the ***good*** *taste* not to mention it. 彼女は気をきかしてそのことを言わずにいた. ‖ ***good*** *taste* shown in the selection (= choice) その選択に示されたよい趣味. 【類】 write in ***good*** *taste.* ¶display a ***great*** *taste* for painting 絵に対して非常な趣味を示す. ¶show a ***growing*** *taste* for ... ...に対する趣味が段々増して来る. ¶***impeccable*** *taste* 申し分のない趣味. ¶a matter of ***inborn*** *taste* 持って生れた趣味. ¶It is a matter to be settled by ***individual*** *taste.* それは銘々の好みによって決定さるべきことだ. ‖ ***Individual*** *tastes* differ so much in this matter. このことは各人の好みが非常に異なっている. ¶The cultivation of ***intellectual*** *taste* 知的趣味のかん養. ¶to the ***king's*** (***queen's***) *taste* 申し分なく, 十二分に. ¶Having some ***literary*** *taste,* he decided to become a bookseller. 彼は文学に趣味を持っていたので本屋になろうと決心した. ‖ men of similar ***literary*** *tastes* 似寄った文学趣味を持つ人たち. ¶His *tastes* are very ***luxurious.*** 彼にはきわめてぜいたくな趣味がある. ¶The two lads had ***many*** *tastes* in common, especially their love of poetry. この二人の若者は趣味において幾多共通の点を持っていたが特に詩を愛好した. ¶a woman with ***masculine*** *tastes* 男性的な趣味を持つ婦人. ¶***Modern*** *taste* in such matters does not allow it. それはこの方面の現代人の趣味に合わない. ¶improve the ***musical*** *tastes* of the people 民衆の音楽趣味を向上させる. ¶a change in the ***national*** *tastes* 国民の趣味における変化 ‖ meals cooked in accordance with their ***national*** *tastes* それぞれ異なった国人の口に合うように料理した食事. ¶the Yankee's ***native*** *taste* for trading アメリカ人の持って生れた商売気. ¶indulge his ***natural*** *taste* for political speculation 政治上の空論をろうする生来の道楽をほしいままにする. ¶It is highly entertaining to the not ***overrefined*** *taste* of the

audiences of this day. それは余り趣味の高尚でない今日の聴衆にとっては非常に興味がある. ¶It is a matter of ***personal taste***. それは銘々の趣味によることだ. ‖ my ***personal taste*** lies in the direction of ... 私一個の趣味としては…の方だ. ¶***perverted taste*** 邪道にはいった趣味. ¶show ***poor taste*** in one's dress その衣服に下品さを示す. ¶***poetical taste*** 詩歌の趣味. ¶elevate the ***popular taste*** 一般人の趣味を向上させる. ¶cater to a depraved ***public taste*** 下劣な一般人の趣好にこびる ‖ deprave and brutalize the ***public taste*** 大衆の趣味を堕落させ野獣化する. ¶It is ***questionable taste*** to say such things. そんなことを言うのは下品だ. ¶customers of ***refined taste*** 趣味の上品な顧客. ¶He has ***scientific tastes***. 彼には科学の趣味がある. ¶have a ***sharp taste*** 強烈な味がする. ¶a friend of ***similar tastes*** 同好の友. ¶***simple tastes*** あっさりした趣味. ¶a ***sound taste*** in reading 読書における健全な趣味(悪書を読まないという). ¶He has a ***strong pictorial taste***. 彼は非常に絵画が好きだ. ¶It gives a ***sweet taste***. それは甘い. ¶a ***sweetish taste*** 甘ったるい味. ¶the ***sybaritic tastes*** of the British officer 英国官吏の放縦なぜいたく趣味. ¶It leaves rather an ***unpleasant taste*** in the mouth. ちょっと後味が悪い. ¶low ***urban taste*** 野卑な都会趣味. ¶***versatile tastes*** 多方面の趣味. ¶***vitiated taste*** 堕落した趣味. ¶***vulgar tastes*** 俗悪な趣味.

Q[2] ***consumer tastes*** 消費者の好み. ¶The ***mass taste*** in public entertainment is not so depraved as some pessimists suppose. 公衆演芸に対する大衆の趣味は一部の悲観論者が想像するほど堕落していない. ¶***reading taste*** 読書の趣味.

P be not ***according to*** one's ***taste*** お歯に合わない. ¶it is ***against*** good ***taste*** to ... …するのは(趣味から言って)よろしくない. ¶simple ***in*** one's ***taste*** その趣味が単純な ‖ dress ***in*** good ***taste*** 上品な服装をする ‖ His remark was not ***in taste***. 彼の言い方はまずかった. ¶a man ***of*** Bohemian ***tastes*** らいらくな人 ‖ the catholicity ***of*** his ***tastes*** 彼の趣味の広さ. 【類】It is a matter ***of taste***. ‖ a man ***of taste*** 趣味のある人. ¶It is ***out of taste***. それは雅致がない. ¶sour (sweet, bitter) ***to*** the ***taste*** 味の酸い(など) ‖ Life in the metropolis was not ***to*** his ***taste***. 彼は首都の生活を好まなかった. ‖ He found her perfectly ***to*** his ***taste***. 彼は彼女と趣味がぴったり合った. ‖ add sugar ***to taste*** 砂糖をころ合に入れる. ¶She dresses her hair ***with taste***. 彼女は気のきいた結髪をする. ‖ flavored ***with*** the ***taste*** of ... …の風味を加えた ‖ a room decorated ***with*** much ***taste*** 中々上品に飾り立ててある室.

P[2] develop correct ***taste among*** the craftsmen 製作者の趣味を向上させる. ¶a ***taste for*** music (thrills) 音楽(など)の趣味 ‖ it shows the existence among them of a ***taste for*** ... それは彼らが…に趣味を持っていることを示す ‖ The stage-manager has a ***taste for*** light-light. その舞台監督は趣味として余り強い照明を用いない. ‖ The ***taste for*** food began to pall. 食物がまずくなり出した. ¶The half century just past has seen many changes of ***taste in*** art and literature. 最近半世紀間に文芸趣味に種々の変化が起った. 【類】good ***taste in*** dress. ¶The ***taste of*** the time has changed. 時好が変った.

taste, *v.* 味がする.

M ***taste acid*** 酸い味がする. ¶***taste burnt*** こげた味がする. ¶***taste puckery*** 渋い味がする. ¶***taste sweet*** (＝***sour, bitter or bad***) 甘い(など)味がする. ¶***taste good*** (＝***nice***) うまい.

P ***taste of*** lemon (orange, onions) レモン(など)の味がする ‖ He ***tastes of*** poverty. 彼は貧乏たらしい. 【類】This coffee ***tastes of*** pepper.

O ***taste*** the sweets and bitters of life 人生の苦楽を経験する.

taster, *n.* 鑑定家, 味きき.

Q ***expert tea*** (***sake***) ***taster*** 茶(など)の鑑定家.

tasting, *n.* 味見.

V ***make*** a trial ***tasting*** 塩かげんを見る.

tatar *n.* タタール人.

Q ***Manchoo*** (Mongol) ***Tatars*** 満州(モーコ)タタール人.

tatter, *n. pl.* ぼろ.

P a beggar ***in tatters*** (＝rags) ぼろぼろの着物を着たこじき ‖ Their clothes were ***in tatters***. 彼らの着物はぼろぼろに裂けていた. ¶worn ***to tatters*** ぼろぼろに切れて.

tattoo, *n.* こつこつたたく音.

V ***beat*** the ***tattoo*** on the stomach 腹づつみを打つ.

tattoo, *v.* いれずみする.

P ***tattoo*** a name (＝figure) ***on*** one's shoulder (arms). 肩(など)に名前(など)のいれずみをする ‖ ***tattoo*** one's arm ***with*** a name 腕に名前のいれずみをする.

taunt, *n.* ばとう, ちょうろう.

V ***endure*** the ***taunts*** of ... …のばとうを忍ぶ. ¶the ***taunt*** was ***flung*** in our teeth by ... …は悪態をわれわれに浴びせかけた. ¶***throw*** bitter ***taunt*** at ... …に毒々しいばとうを浴びせる.

P[2] He became a ***taunt to*** his neighbors. 彼は近所の人の笑いものになった.

taunt, *v.* ののしる.

P ***taunt*** a person ***with*** being ... …だといって人をののしる ‖ ***taunt*** a person ***with*** his conduct 人の振舞をあざける.

tautology, *n.* 《語》同義異語反覆, 冗言法.

Q an ***evident tautology*** 明りょうな同義異語の反覆.

tavern, *n.* 居酒屋.

Q[2] a ***beer tavern*** ビールを飲ませる店, ビヤホール.

tax, *n.* 税; 重荷.

V ***alter tax*** 税率を変更する. ¶***assess tax*** upon property 財産に課税する ‖ ***assess*** the land ***tax*** 地租を定める. ¶***clear up*** unpaid ***taxes*** 未納税金を払ってしまう. ¶***collect taxes*** 収税する. ¶***dodge*** (＝***evade***) a ***tax*** 脱税する. ¶***impose*** (＝***lay***) a ***tax*** of ... on ... …に…の税金を課する. ¶***levy*** a ***tax*** on persons 人に税を賦課する. 【類】***levy taxes*** on one's incomes / ***taxes levied*** on real estate and personal property (不動産及び動産) ‖ Certain resorts ***levy*** a residence (＝resident) ***tax***. ある客の入込む土地では住居税を徴収する. ¶***pay taxes*** to the city 都市に税を納める. ¶***place*** a ***tax*** on bachelors 独身の男子に課税する. ¶***put*** a large ***tax*** on ... …に巨額の税金を課する. ¶***raise*** a ***tax*** 税率を上げる. ¶***reduce*** (＝***lower***) ***taxes*** 減税する. ¶***remit*** the ***taxes*** of the people 国民の税金を免除する. ¶***repeal*** a ***tax*** 税を廃する. ¶***yield tax*** 税が取れる.

Q an ***additional tax*** on ... …の付加税. ¶a ***confiscatory tax*** 没収的(高率)課税. ¶a ***direct tax*** 直接国税. ¶***heavy taxes*** 重税. ¶a ***municipal*** (＝city) ***tax*** 市税. ¶***national*** (***state, local***) ***taxes*** 国(州, 地方)税. ¶an ***oppressive tax*** 重税. ¶a ***progressive tax*** 累進税. ¶***public taxes*** 公租. ¶only ***slight taxes*** ほんのわずかの課税. ¶It was a ***sore tax*** upon her family. それは彼女の家族に取って重い負担であった.

Q[2] ***business tax*** 営業税. ¶***commodity tax*** 物品税. ¶***consumption tax*** on salt 塩の消費税. ¶***corporation taxes*** 法人税. ¶the ***entertainment tax*** 遊興飲食税. ¶an ***excise tax*** 国内消費税. ¶***gift tax*** 《米》贈与税. ¶***Government tax*** 国税. ¶a ***graduated income tax*** 累進所得税. ¶***horse race tax*** 馬券税. ¶***income tax*** 所得税. ☞ income tax は corporate income tax (法人所得税)と individual income tax (個人所得税)に分かれる ‖ a 20 percent slash in ***income taxes*** 所得税の二割控除. ¶pay a ***land tax*** of ... …の地租を納める. ¶***legacy tax*** 遺産税(相続税). ¶***per capita tax*** 頭割り組合費. ¶***property levy tax*** 財産税. ¶a ***reservation tax*** 付加税. ¶***road traffic taxes*** 交通税. ¶a ***sales tax*** on ... …の販売税. ¶a ***succession tax*** 相続税. ¶***tonnage tax*** トン税. ¶***transit tax*** on the ticket 乗車券の通行税. ¶***war-profit tax*** 戦時利得税. ¶the ***wartime excess-profits tax*** 戦時超過利得税.

P ***plus tax*** 税込みで. ¶groan ***under taxes*** 税金に苦しむ.

P[2] a ***tax on*** land (house) 地租(など) ‖ the ***taxes on*** imports 輸入税 ‖ ***taxes on*** knowledge 知識(出版物などに対する)税 ‖ The ***tax on*** the eyes is enormous. 目の疲労は大変なものだ. ¶Climbing stairs is a ***tax to*** a weak heart. 階段の上り降りは心臓に悪い. ¶a ***tax upon*** the brain 頭脳の負担.

tax, *v.* 課税する; 重荷を負わせる.

M Reading in a poor light will ***certainly tax*** your eye. 薄暗いところで読書するときっと目を悪くするよ. ¶***heavily taxed*** 重税を課せられて. ¶***lightly taxed*** 税が軽い. ¶***taxed severely*** 過重な税金を課せられて.

P ***tax*** people ***to*** the bone 人民に血税を課す ‖ the factory is ***taxed to*** capacity to supply the orders from ... その工場は…から注文があって生産力一杯の仕事をしている. ¶He was ***taxed with*** ingratitude (fault). 彼はその不義理(など)を責められた.

taxation, *n.* 課税.

V ***bear taxation*** 課税にたえる. ¶***impose taxation*** upon people 人民に課税する.

Q ***graduated taxation*** 累進税. ¶suffer from ***heavy taxa-***

tion 重税で苦しむ. ¶complain bitterly of ***oppressive*** *taxation* 重税に対してひどく不平を鳴らす.

P groan under the heavy burden ***of*** *taxation* 重税に苦しむ.

taxi, *n.* タクシー.

V ***take*** a *taxi* one can but ill afford 大奮発をしてタクシーに乗る.

Q ***cruising*** *taxis* 流し円タク. ¶an ***oncoming*** *taxi* やってくるタクシー.

Q^2 a "***night-hawk***" *taxi* 深夜タクシー.

P go ***by*** *taxi* タクシーで行く.

taxpayer, *n.* 納税者.

Q^2 ***low-income*** *taxpayers* 低収入納税者たち.

tea, *n.* 茶(紅茶); 簡単な食事.

V ***brew*** *tea* from the petals of a wild flower for a patient 薬用に野花の弁から茶をせんじる. ¶***draw*** *tea* 茶をせんじる. ¶***drink*** *tea* from a cup 茶わんから茶を飲む. ¶***fire*** (=roast) *tea* 茶をせんじる. ¶***gather*** *tea* 茶をつむ. ¶Please stay till I ***fix*** you *tea* 茶を入れるから帰らないでいて下さい. ¶***have*** *tea* with milk 茶に牛乳を入れて飲む. 【類】***Have*** some more *tea*? ¶***make*** (=***brew***) *tea* 茶を入れる. ¶***offer*** *tea* to a visitor 訪問客にお茶を出す. ¶***pick*** *tea* 茶をつむ. ¶***pour*** (***out***) *tea* 茶を注ぐ. ¶Do you ***prefer*** (=like) *tea* or wine? お茶とお酒とどちらが宜しゅう御座いますか. ¶***Prepare*** some *tea* and bring it. お茶を入れて持ってきてくれ. ¶***serve*** *tea* and simple cakes お茶とちょっとした菓子を出す. ¶***sip*** the *tea* and nibble the delicious candy cakes お茶をすすりながらおいしい砂糖菓子をかじる. 【類】***sip*** one's *tea*. ¶***stir*** the *tea* with a spoon スプーンでお茶をかき回す. ¶***take*** (=***drink***) *tea* 茶を飲む. ¶***whip*** *tea* 茶を立てる.

V^2 This *tea* ***draws*** well. この茶は(せんじると)よく出る.

Q ***black*** *tea* 紅茶. ¶***brick*** *tea* 磚茶(たん). ¶***ceremonial*** *tea* 茶の湯. ¶make ***fresh*** *tea* 茶を入れ換える. ¶***green*** *tea* 緑茶. ¶***high*** *tea* 肉ざら付のお茶(簡単な食事). ¶***roasted*** *tea* ほうじ茶. ¶***strong*** (***weak***) *tea* 濃い(薄い)茶. ¶a ***sumptuous*** *tea* ごち走のあるお茶(簡単な食事). ¶a ***washy*** (=***watery***) *tea* (coffee) 水っぽい茶(など). ¶Without ***well-brewed*** *tea* I am never myself. よく出た茶がないと私は生きている気がしない.

Q^2 take ***afternoon*** *tea* with ... ...と一緒に午後のお茶を飲む. ¶***dry*** *tea* 味の抜けた茶. ¶***five-***(***three-***)***o'clock*** *tea* 五(三)時のお茶. ¶***gunpowder*** *tea* [中国産の]一種小粒の上等緑茶.

P The party is ***at*** *tea*. 会の人たちは簡単な食事を取っている. ¶He usually takes whisky ***in*** his *tea*. 彼は大抵お茶にウイスキーを入れて飲む. ¶buy a packet ***of*** *tea* 茶を一袋買う. ¶I am ***out of*** *tea*. もう茶が切れた. ¶talk much ***over*** *tea* お茶を飲みながら大いに話す ‖ hob-nob ***over*** one's *tea* 茶を飲み打解けて話す.

teach, *v.* 教える.

M For the young, history is ***best*** *taught* by means of biographies. 青少年に歴史を教えるには伝記によるのが一番よい. ¶*teach* ***competently*** りっぱに教える. ¶History is *taught* very ***poorly*** in the schools 学校の歴史教授は実に不完全だ. ¶be ***strictly*** *taught* not to use the word その語を使うことを厳禁されている.

P *taught* ***by*** the best masters in the best way 最良の教師に最良の教授法で教えられて ‖ *teach* ... ***by*** precept and examples 教訓を聞かせ手本を示して...を教える. ¶*teach* ***for*** a living 生活のため教える. ¶learn English ***from*** a *teacher* 師について英語を学ぶ ‖ *teach* the names of the states ***from*** a wall map 掛図で州の名を教える. ¶He *teaches* ***in*** a school. 彼はある学校で教べんを取っている. ‖ He was *taught* ***in*** the bitterest of all schools, that of experience. 彼は経験という一番つらい学校で訓練された. ¶grammar *taught* ***through*** composition 作文によって教える文法. ¶*teach* English ***to*** one's pupils 生徒に英語を教える. ¶learn French ***under*** a foreign *teacher* 外人教師についてフランス語を学ぶ. ¶*teach* composition ***with*** much success 大層巧みに作文を教授する.

O I'll *teach* you to refuse to give me what I want. おれの欲しいものをくれないとひどい目に合わしてやるぞ.

teacher, *n.* 教師.

V His parents could not ***afford*** a private *teacher*. 彼の両親の収入では家庭教師などは頼めなかった. ¶The salaries are inadequate to ***attract*** good *teachers*. その月給では良い教師は得られない. ¶the pupils now ***rival*** their *teachers* in the excellence of ... 今では...の点で弟子は先生に劣らない.

Q He was a good scholar but a ***bad*** *teacher*. 彼は学者としてはりっぱなものであったが教えるのはへただった. ¶***bilingual*** *teachers* 二国語のできる教師. ¶a ***capable*** *teacher* 有能な教師. ¶***certificated*** *teachers* 免許状のある教師. ¶a ***competent*** *teacher* 手腕のある教員. ¶a ***devoted*** *teacher* 熱心な教師. ¶my ***first*** *teacher* in English 私が最初に英語を習った先生. ¶Ruskin was a ***great ethical*** *teacher*. ラスキンは偉大なる倫理の指導者であった. ¶an ***inexorable*** *teacher* がん固な教師. ¶an ***ingenious*** and ***resourceful*** *teacher* 器用で知恵のある教師. ¶one of the most ***inspired*** and ***eloquent*** *teachers* of the new truth その新らしい真理をきわめて切実に体得しかつこれをきわめて雄弁に説くものの一人. ¶a ***kind old*** *teacher* 親切な老師. ¶an ***overworked*** and ***underpaid*** *teacher* 薄給で時間の多すぎる教師. ¶a ***peremptory*** *teacher* 横柄な教師. ¶a ***practical*** *teacher* 実地経験のある教師. ¶the ***public's*** *teachers* 公衆の指導者. ¶a ***rigorous*** *teacher* 厳格な教師. ¶a ***stimulating*** *teacher* 生徒の激励になる教師. ¶a ***torpid*** *teacher* 不活発な教師. ¶a ***vivacious*** *teacher* 活発な教師.

Q^2 a ***beginning*** *teacher* 初級の教師. ¶a ***business*** *teacher* 商業の教師. ¶a ***class*** *teacher* クラスの主任教師. ¶a ***grade*** *teacher* 《米》小学校の教師. ¶a ***lady*** (=***woman***) *teacher* 女教員. ¶a ***man*** *teacher* 男の教師. ¶a ***physical-training*** *teacher* 体操教師. ¶a ***science*** (***language***) *teacher* 理科(語学)の教師. ¶a ***secondary***(***primary***)***-school*** *teacher* 中等(小学校)教員. ¶***married***(***unmarried***)***-women*** *teachers* 既(未)婚女教師たち.

P the function of the newspaper ***as*** a great *teacher* of the people 民衆の偉大な指導者としての新聞の職能. ¶learn English ***under*** a skilful *teacher* 老練な教師について英語を学ぶ. ¶learn English ***with*** (=***upon***) a foreign *teacher* 英語を外人教師について学ぶ.

P^2 *teachers* ***in*** natural science or mathematics 自然科学または数学の教師. ¶great *teachers* ***like*** Confucius and Gautama 孔子や釈迦のような偉大な指導者. ¶a *teacher* ***of*** physiology ***at*** Lincoln High リンカン高校の生理学の教師 ‖ prospective *teachers* ***of*** English ***in*** secondary schools 将来中学校の英語教師たるべき人々.

teaching, *n.* 教え; 授業.

V ***accept*** the new *teaching* with an eager heart 新らしい教えを熱心に受入れる. ¶***adopt*** *teaching* as a profession 教師を職とする. ¶The principal ***did*** no *teaching*. 校長は何も授業を受持っていなかった. ¶***gain*** *teaching* from ... ...に教えを受ける. ¶***give up*** *teaching* 教員をやめる. ¶I ***have*** *teaching* at the time you mention. 御指定のときは私は授業があります. ¶***methodize*** the *teaching* of the mother tongue 母国語の教授を秩序立てる. ¶***take up*** *teaching* as a makeshift 一時の腰掛けに教師になる. ¶***twist*** its *teachings* purposely to suit one's own ends 自分の目的に適するよう故意にその教義をまげる.

Q ***individual*** *teaching* 個人教授. ¶***ethical*** *teaching* 倫理学の授業. ¶***first-rate*** *teaching* 第一流の授業. ¶supplement ***oral*** *teaching* by text-books 教科書で口頭授業を補足する. ¶The advocate of ***oral*** *teaching* of English deprecates translating 英語の口頭授業論者は翻訳を排斥する. ¶***popular moral*** *teaching* 通俗道徳教育(心学など). ¶the patriotic *teaching* at school 愛国的な学校教育. ¶one of the chief elements in ***successful*** *teaching* 巧みな教授法の一主要素.

Q^2 ***class***[***room***] *teaching* 教室授業. ¶modern methods of ***language*** *teaching* 近代的諸語学教授法.

P be experienced ***in*** *teaching* 教授に経験を積んでいる.

P^2 *teaching* ***by*** pouring in=cramming 注入教授. ¶*teaching* ***from*** books 書物による授業. ¶It is *teaching* ***of*** history. それは歴史の教える所である.

teacup, *n.* 茶わん.

P gossip ***over*** the *teacups* お茶を飲みながら雑談する ‖ ***Over*** the *teacups* they sat together in amity. 一同は集って茶を飲みうちくつろいだ.

team, *n.* [運動家の]チーム, 組.

V ***cheer*** a *team* to victory 応援して勝たせる. ¶***support*** the *team* with college yells 大学の応援歌を歌ってチームの応援をする.

Q ***contesting*** *teams* 交戦チーム. ¶***rival*** *teams* 対抗チーム. ¶a ***strong*** *team* on defense 守備の強いチーム. ¶the ***visiting*** *team* from the University of Chicago シカゴ大学か

らの来訪チーム. ¶a ***youthful team*** of dancers 若い一組の踊り手.

Q² Lefty O'Doul, one of baseball's former "greats", began taking ***ball teams*** to the Orient in 1931. 野球の前の「重鎮」の一人であるレフティ・オドールは 1931 年にチームの東洋遠征を始めた. ¶He was wanted on the varsity ***baseball team***. 彼は大学の野球チームに必要であった. ¶the captain of a ***basketball team*** バスケットチームの主将. ¶the ***home team*** 〘野球〙地元チーム. ¶appoint an ***investigation team*** to look into ... ...を調査するために調査団を任命する. ¶a ***landscaping team*** 庭園係. ¶***Outdoor teams*** will also be stationed at ... 野外部隊がまた...で部署につくだろう. ¶a ***pro-ball team*** 職業野球団.

P sledges drawn ***by teams*** of dogs 犬の群に引かれたそり. ¶Eery one ***on*** our ***team*** is a good fellow. われわれのチームは好人物ぞろいだ. 【類】Are you ***on*** the ***team?*** / She was swimming ***on*** the ***team*** of the Los Angeles Athletic Club in 1939.

P² a Japanese ***team on*** commercial mission 日本商業使節団.

teamster, *n.* 指導者.

Q² an ***AFL teamster*** アメリカ労働総同盟 (American Federation of Labor) の指導者.

teamwork, *n.* 協力.

Q ***fine teamwork*** りっぱに連絡のとれた仕事. ¶***harmonious*** and ***efficient teamwork*** 一致していて能率の高い協同作業.

tear, *n.* 涙(の一しずく).

V ***bring tears*** to one's eyes 目に涙を催させる ‖ a sight that ***brought tears*** to one's eyes 見て涙が出た光景. ¶***brush*** the ***tear*** away 涙を払う. ¶***call tears*** 涙を誘う. ¶***call forth*** the ***tears*** of his audience 聴衆の涙を誘う. ¶***choke down tears*** 涙をのみこむ. ¶though it ***cost*** him many ***tears*** 涙ながらに. ¶As every nurse knows, wee babies do not ***cry tears***. 子供の守はだれでも知っていることだがちっちゃな赤ん坊は泣いても涙を出さない. ¶Her account ***drew tears*** from me (=my eyes). 彼女の話を聞いて私は涙が出た. ¶***draw forth tears*** 涙を流させる. ¶The poor old Sam! ***Drop*** a ***tear*** for him, gentle reader. かわいそうに老サム! 親愛なる読者よ彼のために一滴の涙をささげたまえ. 【類】***dropping*** a ***tear*** on the letter. ¶***dry*** one's ***tears*** on a handkerchief ハンカチで涙をふく. 【類】I helped ***dry*** her ***tears***. ¶Only to think of it ***forces*** the ***tears*** from my eyes. ただそう思っただけで私は涙を催さずにはいられない. ¶I ***heard tears*** in her voice. 私は彼女が涙声になっているのに気が付いた. ¶***keep back*** one's ***tears*** 涙を押える. ¶***kiss away*** her ***tears*** 彼女の涙をキッスでふきとってやる. ¶***laugh away*** one's ***tears*** 涙を笑いにまぎらす. ¶***quicken tears*** 涙をそそる. ¶He could not ***restrain*** his ***tears***. 彼は涙を押えられなかった. ¶***shed tears*** abundantly おびただしく涙を流す ‖ without ***shedding*** a ***tear*** 涙一つ出さずに. 【類】***shed*** a ***tear*** in secret (ひそかに) / ***shed tears*** of gratitude (感涙) / ***shed*** bitter ***tears*** (くやし涙). ¶***waste tears*** on ... ...のためにむだな涙を流す. ¶***weep tears*** 泣いて涙をこぼす ‖ She ***wept*** a few bitter ***tears***. 彼女はぽろぽろくやし涙をこぼした. 【類】***weep tears*** of joy (pain). ¶***wipe away*** furtive ***tears*** 人知れずそでをぬらす. ¶***wring tears*** from the hardest heart どんな無情な人にも涙を出させる.

V² Every now and then ***tears came*** into the eyes. 時々涙が出た. ¶***Tears coursed*** down her face. 涙が彼女の顔を伝わった. ¶***Tears fell*** fast. 後から後へと涙が落ちた. ¶***Tears flowed*** plentifully (easily). 涙がしきりに(など)流れ出た. ¶***Tears gathered*** in her eyes. 涙が彼女の目にたまった. ¶***Tears glistened*** in her eyes. 彼女の目には涙が光った. ¶The big ***tears*** of grateful happiness ***gushed*** from his eyes. 感謝とうれしさで大粒の涙が彼の目からわき出た. 【類】***Tears*** of pleasure ***gushed*** from my eyes. ¶***Tears ran*** down her face (cheeks). 涙が彼女の顔(など)を伝わった. ¶The ***tears rolled*** down his cheeks. 涙が彼のほおを伝わって落ちた. ¶The ***tears stood*** in his eyes as he spoke. 語る彼の目には涙が宿っていた. ¶***Tears started*** from her eyes. 涙が彼の目から出た. 【類】***Tears started*** to his eyes ***unbidden*** (独りでに). ¶***Tears stole*** down her face. 涙が静かに彼女の顔を伝わって落ちた. ¶***Tears streamed*** down her cheeks. 涙がほおを伝わって流れた. 【類】***Tears streamed*** (=***trickled***) from her eyes. ¶***Tears swelled up*** in his eyes. 涙が彼の目にわき出た.

Q She sat in ***bitter tears***. 彼女は涙にくれていた. ¶***blinding tears*** 目を泣きつぶす涙. ¶shed ***copious tears*** さめざめと涙を流す. ¶shed a ***few tears*** ほろりと涙をこぼす. ¶weep ***glad tears*** over her dear lad 愛する若者に会ってうれし涙を流す. ¶with ***happy tears*** in my eyes 私はうれしさに涙が出て. ¶shed one's ***heart's tears*** 心からの涙を流す. ¶***hot tears*** 熱涙. 【類】***Hot tears*** trickled down in drops. ¶weep ***real tears*** 真実の涙を流す. ¶***regretful tears*** くやし涙. ¶The ***unbidden tears*** glistened in her eyes. おのずと浮んだ涙が彼女の目に光った. ¶She looked at him, her eyes brilliant with ***unwept tears***. 彼を見た彼女の目はせき止めた涙でまたたいていた.

Q² ***crocodile tears*** そら涙. ¶with an ***imitation tear*** in one's voice わざと涙声を出して. ¶***salt tears*** 血の涙. ¶a beauty's ***virgin tears*** 美人の初の涙.

P tell (say) ***between*** her ***tears*** 泣く泣く語る(など). ¶Nobody wept—it was ***beyond tears***. だれ一人泣くものはなかった—泣くどころではなかったのだ. ¶bathed ***in tears*** 涙にぬれて ‖ He was ***in tears***. 彼は泣いていた. 【類】answer ***in tears*** / confide her miseries (不幸を打明ける) while ***in tears***. ¶melt ***into tears*** 心がやわらいで泣き出す. ¶I burst ***into tears*** of mortification and anger. 私はくやし泣きにわっとばかり泣出した. ¶evidence given ***through tears*** 涙ながらに陳述された証言 ‖ ***through*** her ***tears*** she begged to ... 彼女は涙ながらに...と請願した. 【類】She smiled ***through*** her ***tears***. ¶She is easily moved ***to tears***. 彼女は涙もろい. ¶Her eyes were wet ***with tears***. 彼女の目は涙にぬれていた. ‖ ***with tears*** of penitential sorrow or grateful joy 後悔の涙かまたは感謝の涙を流して ‖ ***with tears*** in one's eyes 目に涙をためて. 【類】***with tears*** of tenderness in his eyes / cry out ***with tears*** in her voice. ¶One cannot read it ***wihout tears***. それを涙なしに読むことはできない. ‖ a German ***without tears*** 血も涙もないドイツ人.

P² ***tears of*** ecstatic happiness 有頂天のうれし涙 ‖ the ***tears of*** a brave man 丈夫の涙 ‖ ***tears of*** laughter あまり笑いすぎて出る涙.

tear, *v.* 引裂く, むしりとる; 裂ける, ほころびる; 《口語》かける, 走り回る.

M ***tear*** it ***apart*** それを裂き離す. ¶***tear*** it ***asunder***=pull apart それを引裂く. ¶I could not ***tear*** myself ***away*** from my friends. 私は心残りがして友だちと別れることができなかった. ¶The book is ***badly torn***. その本はひどく破れている. ¶Lace ***tears easily***. レースはほころびやすい. ¶***tear open*** a letter 手紙の封を裂いて開く. ¶***tear out*** the entrails 腸をつかみ出す ‖ ***tear out*** (=***off***) several pages 数ページむしり取る. 【類】***tear out*** the eyes of a fish.

M² ***tear down*** a poster ポスターを破り取る ‖ the old building is being ***torn down*** to make way for new premises. 古い建物が新築のために取こわされている. ¶***tear off*** a button (sleeve) ボタン(など)をもぎとる ‖ ***tear off*** a coupon クーポンをもぎる ‖ He couldn't ***tear*** himself ***off*** from the plot. 彼はその陰謀から身を引くことができなかった. ¶***tear*** it ***up*** それを引裂く ‖ ***tear up*** a tree by the root 木を根こぎにする. 【類】The Communists ***tore up*** much of the railway.

P ***tear about*** a house 家の回りを狂い回る. ¶***tear along*** a street 通りをひた走りに走る. ¶***tear at*** one's hair (clothes) 頭髪(など)をかきむしる. ¶The country is ***torn by*** factions. 国中は党派で分裂している. ¶The death of his only son ***tore from*** him his only joy on earth. 彼はたった一人の子を失ってこの世の唯一の楽みを奪われてしまった. ‖ He was rudely ***torn from*** his slumber. 彼はたたき起された. ‖ ***tear*** clothes ***from*** body 着物を体から引っぱがす. 【類】***tear*** arms ***from*** one's body. ¶***tear*** a ticket ***in*** two 切符を二つに裂く ‖ His clothes were ***torn in*** ribbons (=tiny bits). 彼の着物はずたずたに裂かれた. ¶***tear*** a sheet of paper ***into*** strips 紙一枚を細長く裂く ‖ He was ***torn into*** four quarters by infuriated bulls. 彼はたけり狂う牛に八裂きにされた. 【類】He ***tore*** the document (書付) ***into*** pieces. / a fabric ***torn into*** shreds. / ***tear*** a letter ***into*** tiny pieces. ¶***tear*** a page ***out of*** one's book 書物のページを一枚引き裂く. ¶***tear*** a button ***off*** a coat 上着のボタンを一つむしり取る. ¶He ***tore*** it ***to*** threads and flung it into the fireplace. 彼はそれをずたずたに裂いて炉の中に投げこんだ. ‖ ***tear*** one's argument ***to*** pieces その議論を粉砕する. ¶***tear*** it ***with*** rage 怒ってそれを引き裂く. 【類】***tear*** it ***with*** the teeth.

tease, *n.* いじめること.

Q² a *strip tease*=a strip show ストリップ・ショー.

tease, *v.* いじめる; ねだる.

M *tease* a child ***unmercifully*** じゃけんに子供をいじめる.

P *tease* a boy ***about*** his curly hair 少年のちぢれ毛をからかう. ¶*tease* mummy ***for*** money 母親に金をねだる. ¶*tease* a person ***with*** jest 冗談を言って人をからかう.

teaspoonful, *n.* 茶さじに一杯.

Q a conically ***heaped teaspoonful*** 茶さじに山盛一杯. ¶a ***rounded teaspoonful*** 茶さじに丸く一杯.

P² a *teaspoonful* of sugar (salt) 茶さじ山盛一杯の砂糖(など).

technical, *a.* 専門的な.

M ***severely*** (=***strictly***) *technical* きわめて専門的な.

technicality, *n.* 専門的なこと.

Q ***abstruse technicalities*** 難解な専門的のこと. ¶To describe the whole marvellous mechanism would mean to involve you, perhaps, in a maze of ***bewildering*** and ***boring*** *technicalities.* その巧妙な機構全体にわたって説明を加えることは恐らく専門事項を列べ立てていたずらに頭を混乱させるだけであろう. ¶***confusing technicalities*** ごたごたした専門的な事項. ¶the ***horrid*** *technicalities* of the author その著者の恐ろしい専門的なこと. ¶in language devoid of ***unnecessary*** *technicalities* 不必要な専門的の理屈を抜きにした通俗の言葉で.

P ***on*** *technicality* 技術上は.

technician, *n.* 専門家.

Q an eye (a limb) ***prosthetic*** *technician* 義眼(肢)製作者. ¶***linguistic*** (=language) *technicians* 語学者.

Q² a ***movie*** *technician* 映画技術者. ¶an ***X-ray*** *technician* X線技術者.

technicolor, *n.* 〘映〙[商標 T-] 色彩(映画).

Q ***all*** *Technicolor* 総天然色映画.

P an American film ***in*** *Technicolor* テクニカラーによるアメリカ映画.

technique, *n.* 技法, 手法.

V ***acquire*** the *technique* of one's art その技法を体得する. ¶***display*** a surprisingly advanced *technique* 驚くべき技術的進歩を示す. ¶***master*** *technique* 手法をのみ込む.

Q A very significant achievement in ***cinematic*** *technique* 映画の技法におけるきわめて著しい業績. ¶a ***newly-developed*** *technique* 新たに発達した技法. ¶the ***old*** (***new***) *technique* 従来の(新式の)やり方. ¶The mining *technique* is ***shaky.*** その採鉱の技術はなっていない. ¶a ***statistic*** *technique* 統計的技法.

Q² an ***arrest*** *technique* 逮捕術. ¶a ***motion picture*** *technique* 映画技法. ¶specialists without ***platform*** *technique* 講演のへたな専門家たち. ¶A basic ***propaganda*** *technique* of the Fifth Columnist is to create suspicion, doubt and hatred. 第五列の基本的宣伝法は邪推, 疑惑, 憎悪を生ぜしめるにある. ¶acquire the ***story-telling*** *technique* 話術を習得する. ¶the ***stump speaking*** *technique* 街頭政治演説のこつ. ¶a ***working*** *technique* 作業技法.

P² the *technique* ***of*** the art その芸術の手法. 【類】the *technique* ***of*** playwriting (劇作).

technology, *n.* 工業学.

Q² ***glass*** *technology* ガラス工業.

P study the science of art at a school ***of*** *technology* 工芸学校で工芸技術を勉強する.

P² the *technology* ***of*** sugar 製糖法.

tedious, *a.* 退屈した.

M It made me feel ***awfully*** *tedious.* それで私はとても退屈になった.

P *tedious* ***to*** a person 人をあきあきさせる.

tedium, *n.* 退屈.

V ***abolish*** train *tedium* 汽車中の退屈をしのぐ. ¶obviate the *tedium* of ... ...のわずらわしさを避ける. ¶***beguile*** the *tedium* of waiting by ... ...で待つ間の退屈をまぎらす. 【類】to ***beguile*** the *tedium* of a train journey. ¶While at work the girls ***keep away*** *tedium* with continuous songs. 作業中少女たちは絶えず歌を歌って退屈をしのぐ. ¶***relieve*** the *tedium* of the journey (wait) by reading 読書で旅(など)の憂さを晴らす. ¶***while away*** the *tedium* of a dreary day わびしい日の憂さを晴らす.

teem, *v.* 満ちる, 富む.

P His mind *teems* ***with*** ideas. 彼の頭はさまざまの考えで一杯だ. ‖ The pond *teems* ***with*** fish.=Fish *teem* ***in*** the pond. その池には魚がたくさんいる. ‖ The book *teems* ***with*** blunders. その本は誤りが多い. 【類】The canal traffic was *teeming* ***with*** boats of all shapes and sizes. / *teeming* ***with*** platitudes and empty phrases (陳腐な説と空疎な文句).

teen, *n.* [十三から十九までの]十代.

V ***enter*** (=grow into) one's *teens* 十三歳になる. ¶***pass*** one's *teens* 十代から二十代になる.

Q yet in her ***early*** *teens* まだ十三四で. ¶a girl in her ***late*** *teens* 十八九の少女.

P maidens ***in*** their *teens* 十代の娘たち ‖ He is still ***in*** his *teens.* 彼はまだ十代だ. ‖ ***in*** the *teens* of the cinematic art 映画芸術の初期において. 【類】a girl in her *teens* / Enthusiasm ***in*** the *teens* is not a trustworthy guide to an abiding taste or interest. ¶She is hardly ***out of*** her *teens.* 彼女は二十歳になったかならぬかという年ごろだ. ¶before they are ***through*** their *teens* 二十にならい内に.

teetotalism, *n.* 禁酒.

V He is ***preaching*** *teetotalism* to others. 彼は他人に(は)禁酒を勧める.

telegram, *n.* 電報.

V ***address*** a *telegram* of condolence to ... ...に弔電を送る. ¶Just then a *telegram* was ***brought*** in. ちょうどその時電報がきた. ¶We ***confirm*** the *telegrams* which have passed between us this day. 本日貴店と交換した電文を念のためここに書面をもって申し上げます. ¶***dispatch*** several *telegrams* 数通の電報を送る. ¶***forward*** a *telegram* 電報を打つ. ¶I ***had*** a *telegram* from ... 私は...からの電報を受取った. ¶a *telegram* has been ***received*** from ... intimating that ... ...から...の通知の電報が来た. 【類】I ***received*** a *telegram* announcing (=informing) that ... ¶***send*** a *telegram* expressing regret at inability to be present 残念ながら出席不可能のむねを電報で言ってやる. ¶***transmit*** *telegrams* 電報を伝達する. ¶I ***withdraw*** my *telegram* of ... and substitute the following. ...の電報を取消して次の...に代える.

V² How much did the *telegram* ***cost?*** 電報料はいくらでしたか. 【類】This *telegram* will ***cost*** you forty-five yen. ¶*telegrams* ***poured in*** on him from the anxious Mr. X, demanding to know ... X 氏が心配して...を知らせるようにと彼のもとへしきりに電報を打ってよこした. ¶a *telegram* from ... ***says*** that ... ...からの電報によれば...とのこと.

Q by means of a ***bogus*** *telegram* うその電報を打って. ¶a ***collated*** *telegram* 校合電報. ¶***congratulatory*** *telegrams* 祝電. ¶a ***deferred*** *telegram* 間送電報. ¶a ***mutilated*** and ***undecipherable*** *telegram* 文面が脱文があって判読し難い電報. ¶an ***official*** *telegram* 公電. ¶a ***startling*** *telegram* びっくりさせる電報. ¶an ***urgent*** *telegram* 至急電報. ¶a ***wireless*** *telegram*=《米》a radio message 無線電報.

Q² a ***business*** *telegram* 商用電報. ¶a ***greetings*** *telegram* あいさつ電報. ¶***Letter*** *telegrams* were formerly called ***night letter*** *telegrams* 間送電報は以前は夜間々送電報といった.

P ***according to*** a *telegram* from London ロンドン発電報によれば. ¶he was called away ***by*** *telegram* to ... 彼は電報で...へ呼ばれた ‖ remittance ***by*** *telegram* 電報為替. 【類】learn ***by*** *telegram* / a request ***by*** *telegram* / forward a message ***by*** *telegram.* ¶here it says ***in*** this *telegram* that ... この電報に...と書いてある.

P² a *telegram* ***by*** submarine telegraph=a cablegram 海底電報. ¶*telegrams* ***for*** foreign countries 外国行電報. ¶a *telegram* ***from*** London ***to*** the Tokyo Asahi ロンドン発東京朝日あて電報. ¶*telegrams* ***in*** plain language [暗号電報に対し]普通文電報. ¶a *telegram* ***of*** sympathy (congratulation, thanks, Xmas greetings) 見舞(など)の電報. ¶here is a *telegram* ***to*** the effect that ... ...という内容の電報が来た. ¶a *telegram* ***under*** date of ... ...日付の電報.

telegraph, *n.* 電信.

V The *telegraph* has been ***cut*** between Peking and Shanghai. 北京上海間は電信不通になった. ¶a *telegraph* was ***erected*** from ... to ... ...と...間に電信が開通された. ¶***extend*** *telegraphs* all over the country 国内一般に電信網を拡張する. ¶***fit*** a *telegraph* from ... to ... ...から...まで電信の装置をする. ¶***work*** a *telegraph* 電信機を使用する.

Q² a ***signal*** *telegraph* 信号電信機. ¶***submarine*** *telegraph* 海底電信.

P chess games played ***by*** *telegraph* 電信による将棋の手合わせ. 【類】answer ***by*** *telegraph* / announcement received ***by*** *telegraph* / inform ... ***by*** *telegraph.*

telegraph, *v.* 打電する.

M I ought to have *telegraphed* ***immediately.*** 直ちに打電すべきであった.

M² *telegraph* it ***on*** to ... それを...に電報で言ってやる.

P *telegraph* ***by*** wireless 無線電信を打つ ‖ *telegraph* ***by*** glances 目で知らせる. ¶I suppose the son will be *telegraphed* ***for***. 電報でせがれを呼寄せるでしょう. 【類】*telegraph* ***for*** a nurse. ¶Russia's sorrow is Germany's sorrow—Kaiser *telegraphed* ***to*** the Czar after the Petropavlosk disaster. ロシアの悲痛はこれすなわちドイツの悲痛―とドイツ皇帝はペトロパウロスクの災害後ロシアの皇帝に打電した. 【類】he *telegraphed* ***to*** his father [saying] that ... / *telegraph* a message to ...

telegraphy, *n.* 電信術.

Q establish ***wireless*** (***wired***) *telegraphy* 無(有)線電信を開設する.

Q^2 ***radio*** (=wireless) *telegraphy* 無電.

P reported ***by*** *telegraphy* 電報によって. ¶a code used ***in*** *telegraphy* 電信に使用する暗号. ¶steamers fitted ***with*** wireless *telegraphy* 無線電信の設備のある汽船.

telephone, *n.* 電話.

V ***answer*** the *telephone* 電話に出る. ¶***disconnect*** the *telephone* 電話を切る. ¶He ***has*** a *telephone* in his house. 彼の家には電話がある. ‖ He has recently ***had*** the *telephone* ***attached*** to his house. 彼は最近家に電話を引いた. ‖ ***have*** the *telephone* ***fixed*** by the bedside 寝台の側に電話を取付けてある ‖ We ***have*** a *telephone* ***put in***. 私の家には電話がある. ¶A *telephone* has been ***installed*** in the house. その家に電話が引かれた. 【類】Three *telephones* are ***installed*** in the house. / About 300 *telephones* will be ***installed*** this year. ¶***lift*** one's *telephone* 電話の受話機を取る. ¶***pick up*** a *telephone* 電話を受ける. ¶Those *telephones* are ***set up*** by the Government. それらの電話は政府で設置したものだ. ¶***ring on*** (***off***) the *telephone* 《英》電話をかける(切る). ¶***use*** the *telephone* for frivorous purposes つまらない用で電話を掛ける.

V^2 His *telephone* ***rings***. 彼の卓上の電話が鳴る. 【類】the *telephone* ***rang*** and he received a message to the effect that ...

Q A ***public*** *telephone* may be found there. そこに公衆電話があるかも知れない.

Q^2 a ***dial*** *telephone* ダイアル式電話機. ¶a ***long-distance*** *telephone* 長距離電話. ¶a ***radio*** (=wireless) *telephone* 無線電話. ¶***ship-to-shore*** *telephone* 海陸連絡の電話.

P look ***after*** the *telephone* 電話掛りをする. ¶There is somebody ***at*** the *telephone*. だれか電話を掛けている. ¶continue one's conversation ***at*** the *telephone*. 電話で話を続ける. ¶hold conversations with ... ***by*** *telephone* 電話で…と話をする ‖ Orders ***by*** *telephone* will receive prompt attention. 電話での御注文は早速お扱い致します. ‖ You're wanted ***by*** (=on the) *telephone*. 君に電話が掛ってきた. 【類】inform ***by*** *telephone* / speak ***by*** (=through the) *telephone*. ¶call him up ***on*** the *telephone* 彼に電話を掛ける. 【類】speak to ... ***on*** (=over) the *telephone* / ring up a person ***on*** the *telephone* ‖ the number ***on*** the *telephone*=the telephone number 電話の番号 ‖ Miss White ***on*** the *telephone*. ホワイト嬢からお電話です. ‖ get a person ***on*** the *telephone* 人を電話口に出す. ¶The matter was arranged ***over*** the *telephone*. その件は電話で取りきめた. ‖ talk (=speak) ***over*** the *telephone* 電話で話をする. 【類】have (=hold) a conversation ***over*** the *telephone*. ¶instruct his stockbroker ***through*** a *telephone* 電話で株式仲買人に命じる. 【類】I told him ***through*** the *telephone*. ¶call him ***to*** the *telephone* 彼を電話口に呼ぶ.

P^2 a *telephone* ***between*** ... …間の電話. ¶Here's [*tele-*] *phone* ***for*** you=This is for you. お電話です.

telephone, *v.* 電話する.

P *telephone* a person ***by*** long distance 人に長距離電話を掛ける. ¶The doctor was *telephoned* ***for***. 電話でその医者を呼んだ. ¶[*tele*]*phone* ***to*** ... …へ電話を掛ける.

O he *telephoned* (wrote, telegraphed, wired) to say that ... 彼は電話(など)で…と言ってきた.

telephoto, *n.* 電送写真.

P it was sent ***by*** *telephoto* from ... それは…から電送写真で送られた.

telescope, *n.* 望遠鏡.

V ***direct*** (=***point***) a *telescope* at ... …に望遠鏡を向ける.

Q an ***astronomical*** *telescope* 天体望遠鏡. ¶a ***binocular*** *telescope* 双眼鏡.

P He is ***at*** his *telescope*. 彼は望遠鏡でながめている. ¶If the moon be looked at ***through*** a *telescope* lofty mountains and deep valleys may be seen. 望遠鏡で月をのぞいてみると高山幽谷が見える. ¶upon examination ***with*** a powerful *telescope* 強度の望遠鏡で検査の上.

teletype, *n.* テレタイプ.

P send messages ***by*** *teletype*=teletype messages テレタイプで送信する.

television, *n.* テレビ.

Q^2 ordinary ***black-and-white*** *television* 普通の黒白テレビ. ¶***color*** *television* 色彩テレビ.

P enjoy wrestling ***on*** *television*. テレビで相撲を見る.

tell, *n.* 話.

V I have a *tell* (=talk) about it. それについて話がある.

tell, *v.* 話す; 数える; 分かる; こたえる.

M Her crew was reduced to four-and-twenty ***all*** *told*. その船の乗組員は全部で二十四人になってしまった. ¶These ***amply*** *tell* his past career as a diplomat. これらで彼がかつて外交官であったことが十分わかる. ¶It is difficult to *tell* the girls ***apart***. その(双子の)女の子は別にするとどっちがどっちだか分からない. ¶a story ***badly*** *told* へたな話. ¶he was very ***civilly*** *told* that ... 彼は非常に丁寧に…と教えられた. ¶***charmingly*** *told* 聞きほれるように話された. ¶The story was very ***cleverly*** *told*. その話は実に巧みに話された. ¶The matter is ***coherently*** *told*. 話がまとまっている. ¶he *told* me ***confidentially*** that ... 彼は私に…のことを内密に話した. ¶The story is ***cunningly*** *told*. その話がおもしろく話される. ¶The story is ***entertainingly*** *told* in his recent novel. その話は彼の近作小説におもしろく書いてある. ¶I cannot *tell* ***exactly*** when he will come back. いつ彼が戻るかはっきりしたことは言えない. ¶*tell* it ***fearlessly*** それを大胆に言う. ¶*tell* ***flatly*** 率直に話す. ¶***glibly*** *tell* 能弁に語る. ¶The story is only ***half*** *told*. その話はまだ先がある. ¶The recent rise in prices *tells* ***heavily*** on low-salaried employees. 最近の物価騰貴は大いに下級俸給生活者にこたえる. ¶***indiscreetly*** *tell* 後先の考えもなく話す. ¶can *tell* ***infallibly*** the genuine from the counterfeit 正確に真偽を見分けることができる. ¶***kindly*** *tell* the way to ... …に親切に道を教える. ¶be ***marvellously*** *told* 驚くほどに話される. ¶You ***never*** can *tell*. 世の中は何が幸福になるか分かったものじゃない, 人間万事塞翁(おう)が馬. ¶*tell* ***off-hand*** 即席に語る. ¶I *tell* you ***once for all*** that ... 私はきっぱり言っとくが… ¶He *told* ***out*** twenty sovereigns on the table. 彼は二十個の金貨を数え上げてテーブルの上においた. ¶***peremptorily*** *tell* ぶっきら棒に言う. ¶he *told* me ***regretfully*** that ... 彼は…と残念がって私に話した. ¶I *told* him ***roundly*** that ... 私はむき出しに…と彼に言った. ¶without your *telling* ***so*** 君の言うまでもなく, どうせ ‖ I *told* you ***so***! それ御覧言わないこっちゃない. ¶It'll ***soon*** be *told*. その話は簡単だ. ¶*tell* him ***straight*** 有りのままを彼に言って聞かせる. ¶*tell* ***succinctly*** 手短かに話す. ¶*tell* ***unasked*** 問われもしないのに言う. ¶a story ***well*** *told* うまい話.

M^2 Why has nobody *told* me this ***before***? なぜ今までこのことをだれも話してくれなかったんだろう. ¶*Tell* ***off***!=Number! [軍隊など]番号! ¶The workers were *told* ***off*** to their several tasks. 職工がそれぞれの仕事に配置された.

P You never can *tell* ***about*** a woman. 女というものはどうも分からないものだ. ‖ in this chapter you are *told* ***about*** ... この章には…のことが述べてある. 【類】many strange stories are *told* ***about*** / *Tell* me ***about*** yourself. ¶Your bad writing will *tell* ***against*** you in the examination. 君は字がまずいから試験で損をするだろう. ¶can *tell* ***at*** a glance 一見して分かる. ¶I can *tell* a woman's age ***by*** looking at her. 私にはその容ぼうを見て女の年齢が分かる. ¶We cannot *tell* ***for*** certain how many there are without counting them, can we? 数えて見なくってはいくつあるのか正確には分かりません. ¶*tell* the real ***from*** the false 真偽を識別する. 【類】Some people are color-blind (色盲): they cannot *tell* one color ***from*** another. / who cannot *tell* the imitation (模造品) ***from*** the original (原物) ‖ Can you *tell* ***from*** looking at a woman's hands whether she does her own work? 君は女の手を見て自分のことを自分でしているかどうか分かるか. ¶It can hardly be *told* ***in*** words. それは言葉ではほとんど言い表わせない. ‖ *tell* evidence ***in*** favor of the prisoner [刑事]被告に有利な陳述をする. ¶People don't like to be *told* [***of***] their faults. 人は短所をいわれるといやがるものだ. ‖ You mustn't *tell* tales ***of*** your little sister. お前は妹の言い付

けロをするものじゃない.【類】An interesting story is *told of* a country schoolboy. / Victor Hugo, in "Les Miserables" *tells of* an old man who never went out without a book, and who seldom came back without two. / He *told* us *of* the men and things that had interested him. ‖ Can you *tell* me *of* a good dentist? いい歯医者を知りませんか.【類】Can you *tell* me *of* a way to prevent milk, in hot weather, from turning sour? ‖ The castle has yet more to *tell of*. お城にはまだまだ色々な話がある. ¶It is beginning to *tell on* him. それが彼の身にこたえだした. ‖ A woman stops telling her age as soon as age begins *telling on* her. 女は年が争われなくなると年を言わなくなる. 【類】The strain *tells on* one's nerves. / The heat [work] *told on* him. ¶*tell* a story *to* a person 人に話をして聞かせる ‖ *Tell* that *to* the Jews. そんな話あてになるもんか. ¶The constant poring over fine print naturally *told upon* his eyesight. 始終細かい印刷物をじっと見ているので自然彼の目に障った. ‖ The great exertion *tells upon* his strength. あの大骨折が彼の体に障る. ‖ His unflinching industry has *told upon* his fortune. 彼のたゆまない勤勉がその運命を左右した. ¶it was *told with* a tenderness and pathos that remind one of ... それは人に...を思い出させるようにやさしく哀れっぽく語られた.

O I *tell* you it is a fine plan. そりゃ実に名案だ. ‖ I hate to see him, I *tell* you. 《口語》実を言うとあいつに会いたくないんだ. ‖ You're *telling* it! 正にその通りだ. ‖ Every blow *told*. 一発一発手ごたえがあった(効果があった).

teller, *n.* 話し手.

Q² a *master teller* of tales 話の名人. ¶a *paying teller* [銀行の]支払掛.

telling, *n.* 言うこと.

Q The story remains fresh in spite of *many tellings*. その話は幾度語っても新鮮味を失わない. ¶there is *no telling* what may be the outcome of ... ...がどんな結果になるか分からない. 【類】If you do so there is *no telling* what will happen.

Q² *fortune telling* 身の上判断.

temper, *n.* 気質; 立腹.

V *allay* an irritated *temper* 焦燥を静める. ¶His fiery *temper* was *aroused*. 彼はかっとなった. ¶*develop* a volcanic *temper* 非常に怒りっぽい人間になる. ¶In ordinary steel the *temper* is *drawn* when it gets very hot. 普通の鋼鉄は高熱になると焼が戻る. ¶*give* one's *temper* しゃくに障って応答する. ¶*have* a hot *temper* 怒りっぽい. ¶*keep* (=*control*) one's *temper* じっと我慢する. ¶I *know* her *temper*. 彼女の気心をのみ込んでいる. ¶Nothing is to be gained by *losing* your *temper*. 短気は損気 ‖ He *loses* his *temper* for nothing. 彼はつまらないことに怒る. 【類】I quite *lost* my *temper* with him at last. ¶*master* (=*control*) one's *temper* 怒りを抑える. ¶*recover* one's *temper* 平静に返る. ¶She ought to *restrain* her *temper*. 彼女は我慢すべきだ. ¶Don't let such a thing *ruffle* your *temper*. こんなことで腹を立てるな. 【類】Such trifles occasionally *ruffle tempers*. ¶*show temper*=behave petulantly かんしゃくを起す. ¶*sour* the *temper* of ... ...をひねくれさせる. ¶*spoil* one's *temper* by fretting 気を腐らす. ¶It would *sweeten* one's *temper* at any time to read it. どんな時でもその本を読めば気分がやわらぐでしょう. ¶My *temper* is often *tried* by noisy children. 子供たちが騒がしいので私はよくごうを煮やす. ¶*wreak* one's bad *temper* on ... [怒っている人が]...にあたる.

Q He has a *bad temper*, and, when angry, says things he doesn't mean. 彼は短気で怒ると心にないことを言う. ¶*cheerful* and *sociable temper* 快活で社交的な気質. ¶a *conciliatory temper* 折れ合う(妥協的な)気質. ¶a *cool temper* 冷静な気質. ¶*critical temper* 批評的気質. ¶Being of a *curious* and *inquiring* temper, I determined to seek some knowledge on the subject. 好奇心があって研究的な私はそのことを少し調べて見ようと思い込んだ. ¶a *diabolical temper* 極悪の性癖. ¶an *even* (=a *calm*) *temper* おだやかな気性. ¶He is possessed of a *fiery temper*. 彼は短気だ. ¶a *frigid temper* 冷淡な気質. ¶*genial temper* 温和な気質. ¶He has a *good temper*. 彼は気が練れている. ‖ be in a *good* (*bad*) *temper*. 機げんがよい(悪い). ¶a *harsh temper* 残酷な性質. ¶a life which is conceived in a purely *historical temper* [ためにする所がなく]全く歴史的精神で書いた伝記. ¶He said that out of *ill temper*. 彼はきげんが悪かったからあんなことを言ったのだ. ¶of *impetuous temper* 激しい気質の. ¶a man of but ordinary capacity, with an *irritable*, *peevish temper* 短気で気難かし屋のごく平凡な人間. ¶*meek temper* 素直な性質. ¶a man of *merciless temper* 無慈悲な男. ¶*moody temper* 気の変りやすいたち. ¶he lost *much temper* because ... 彼は...で非常に腹を立てた. ¶of *patient temper* 気の練れた. ¶It is written in a duly *patriotic temper* それは確かに愛国的感情から執筆してある. ¶a *placid temper* なごやかな気質. ¶have a *quick* (=*short*) *temper* 気が短い. ¶the *scientific temper* of the Germans ドイツ人の科学的性向. ¶a *stubborn temper* 強情なたち. ¶in none too *sweet* a *temper* 余り朗かな気分でなく. ¶a *tolerant temper* 寛容な気質. ¶appeal to the *urgent temper* of youth 青年の性急な気質に訴える. ¶*venerable temper* 敬老の念を起させる性質. ¶a *yielding temper* 従順な性質.

Q² raise *troop tempers* to a boil 兵士の感情を沸騰させる.

P He is *in* a *temper*. 彼は立腹している. 【類】*In* her *temper*, she broke the vase. ¶in a fit *of temper* かんしゃくを起して ‖ an outburst *of temper* かんしゃく玉の破裂. ¶*out of temper* 腹を立てて. 【類】He is a very good tempered fellow; I never saw him *out of temper* with any one.

temper, *v.* 鍛える; 融和する.

P *temper by* heat 熱で鍛える. ¶*temper* justice *to* the weak 弱者に対して情理をつくす. ¶*temper* justice *with* mercy 仁をもって義を緩和する(情理を尽す) ‖ *tempered with* taste 趣味を加味した.

temperament, *n.* 素質, 気質.

V He *has* no poetical *temperament*. 彼には詩的素質は全然ない. ¶*inherit* a warm *temperament* 情熱の気質を親から受ける.

Q of an *active*, *excitable temperament* 活発な感激しやすい性質の. ¶*cheerful temperament* 快活なたち. ¶*choleric temperament* 胆汁質. ¶the "femme de tête," the woman of *cold* and *intellectual temperament* 冷静で知的ないわゆる「頭の女」. ¶We are of *contrary temperaments*. われわれは性が合わない. ¶*English temperament* and English character 英国気質と英国々民性. ¶a people of an *imaginative* and *poetic temperament* 想像的詩的素質を持つ国民. ¶a *joyous* and *happy temperament* 陽気で愉快な気質. ¶a *melancholic temperament* 憂うつな気質. ¶persons of a *nervous temperament* 神経質な人々. ¶*neurotic temperament* 神経質. ¶*phlegmatic temperament* 粘液質(冷静な気質). ¶persons of a *pronounced erotic temperament* 著しく好色な人々. ¶of a *religious temperament* 宗教心のある. ¶of a *romantic temperament* ロマンチックな性質の. ¶of a *sanguine* and *ardent temperament* 快活で熱情的な性質の. ¶the *self-reliant temperament* of the British race イギリス民族の自立性.

P a young widow *of* ardent *temperament* 物事に熱中する性質の若い未亡人. ¶a person *with* the artistic *temperament* 芸術家はだの人.

temperance, *n.* 節制.

V *practice temperance* in ... ...を節制する.

P² *temperance in* drinking (diet, conduct, speech) 飲酒(など)の節制.

temperate, *a.* 節度のある.

P *temperate in* eating and drinking 飲食に節度のある ‖ *temperate in* tone 調子のおだやかな.

temperateness, *n.* 中庸.

Q a *mellow temperateness* of judgment 円熟した判断.

temperature, *n.* 温度; 体温.

V *acquire* a *temperature* of white heat 白熱化する. ¶*elevate temperature* 温度を上げる. ¶The hot springs *have* a *temperature* of 130 F. その温泉は華氏百三十度の温度がある. 【類】You *have* no *temperature*. / a place *having* a *temperature* of 75 to 80 degrees. ¶*raise* the *temperature* 温度を上げる. ¶*reach* a high *temperature* 高温になる. ¶The thermometer *recorded* a *temperature* of 107. 寒暖計は百七度を示した. ¶Now, I will *take* your *temperature*. さあ あなたの体温を取りましょう. ‖ It *takes* the *temperature* of the room. それにへやの温度がうつる(伝わる).

V² The *temperature declines*. 温度が下がる. ¶the *temperature dropped* to ... 温度が...に降った. ¶The *temparature fell* to (=*reached* the) normalcy. 体温が平熱に下がった. ‖ The *temperature* sometimes *falls* to 50° F[ahr]. below zero. 時には気温が華氏零下五十度に下る. ¶The *temperature reads* (=*registers or stands at*) 25° C. in the shade. 寒暖計は室内で摂氏 25 度だ. ¶The *temperature* ***remains*** at about 85° Fahrenheit. 気温は依然華氏八十五度内外に居据わる. ¶the *temperature* ***rises*** as high as ... 温度は...までも上る.

Q ***atmospheric*** *temperature* 気温. ¶Atlanta has an ***average*** *temperature* of 60°. アトランタの平均温度は六十度である. ¶hot water of the ***desired*** *temperature* 適度と思う温度の温湯. ¶He has a ***high*** *temperature.* 彼は熱が高い. 【類】 sterilization (殺菌) by cooking at a ***high*** *temperature.* ¶***icy*** *temperatures* 氷のような温度. ¶at ***lower*** *temperatures* 低温で. 【類】 the ***lowest*** *temperature* ever recorded. ¶the ***maximum*** *temperature* 最高温度. ¶You have ***no*** *temperature,* and your pulse is normal あなたは熱もなく脈はくも平脈です. ¶The ***normal*** *temperature* of the human body is 98.6 degrees. 人体の平熱は 98.6 度だ. ¶at an ***ordinary*** *temperature* 普通の温度で. ¶***outdoor*** *temperature* 屋外の温度. ¶at a ***suitable*** *temperature* 適度の気温で.

Q^2 ***air*** *temperature* 気温. ¶***sub-freezing*** *temperatures* ranging from 14 to 22 degrees 14 度から 22 度にわたる氷点下温度. ¶***sub-zero*** *temperatures* 氷点下温度. ¶***summer*** *temperature* 夏の気温. ¶correct ***water*** *temperature* 湯加減をする. ¶withstand a ***1,200-degree*** *temperature* 1,200 度の温度に耐える.

P Water begins to boil ***at*** *temperature* of 212°F. 水は華氏二百十二度の温度で沸騰し始める. 【類】 ***at*** these *temperatures.* ¶***in*** a *temperature* of 93° 九十三度の温度で.

P^2 a room maintained at a *temperature* ***between*** 60 and 70 degrees 温度を六十度から七十度に保ったへや.

tempest, *n.* あらし.

V ***stir up*** a *tempest* あらしを起す.

V^2 A *tempest* was ***raging.*** あらしが吹きまくっていた.

Q a ***frightful*** *tempest* 恐ろしいあらし.

P It is like the hush ***before*** a *tempest.* あらしの前の静けさのようだ. ¶Bullets came ***in*** a *tempest.* 弾丸が雨あられと降った. ¶the roar ***of*** a *tempest* あらしの怒号. ¶***through*** a *tempest* of shot and shell 実弾りゅう弾のあらしの中を突いて. ¶The wind grew ***to*** a *tempest.* 風は次第につのりあらしになった.

temple, *n.* 寺院.

V A small *temple* was ***dedicated*** to the service of Buddha. 小寺院が仏にささげられた. ¶***erect*** a *temple* to ... ...の神殿を築く. ¶***make*** a *temple* to his memory 彼の記念堂を建てる. ¶***use*** a *temple* as a dwelling-house 寺を住家にする. ¶***visit*** a *temple* お寺参りをする.

Q a ***Buddha*** (=***Buddhist***) *temple* [仏教の]寺院. ¶the ***Hase*** *Temple* 長谷寺. ¶***propitiatory*** *temples* [己に罪なくして苦しめられた人または不幸の人のための]慰霊の社. ¶a ***rock-hewn*** *temple* 岩くつ寺.

P ***at*** the *temple* of Ekoin in Tokyo 東京の回向院で. ¶go ***to*** a *temple* for worship 寺まいりに行く.

P^2 *temples* ***of*** luxury and beauty 金殿玉楼. ¶a *temple* ***to*** Confucius 孔子廟(びょう).

temple, *n.* こめかみ.

V The bullet ***pierced*** his left *temple.* 銃弾が彼の左のこめかみを貫いた.

P The veins stood out ***at*** the *temples.* 青筋がこめかみに立った. ¶a terrible pain ***in*** one's left *temple* 左のこめかみの劇痛.

tempo, *n.* テンポ.

Q the ***fast*** *tempo* of modern life 近代生活の早いテンポ. ¶move in ***quick*** (***slow***) *tempo* 早い(おそい)テンポで動く. 【類】 service paced to today's ***quick*** *tempo.* ¶***slow, stately*** *tempo* 徐々たる荘厳な拍子. ¶keep pace with the ***swift*** *tempo* of the day 時勢の急速な進歩に遅れないようにする.

tempt, *v.* 誘う.

M I was *tempted* ***out*** by pleasant weather yesterday. きのうは天気が好いのに浮かされて僕は遊びに出かけた. ¶be too ***strongly*** *tempted* to desist やむにやまれぬ.

P *tempted* ***by*** poverty to commit a crime 貧故につい罪悪を犯す ‖ be *tempted* ***by*** an evil spirit 魔がさす. 【類】 *tempted* ***by*** bribes. ¶*tempt* a person ***from*** his duty 誘惑して義務を怠らせる. ¶His ambition *tempted* him ***into*** politics. 彼は大望をいだいて政治に志した. ¶He was never to be *tempted* ***off*** the straight path. 彼は決して正道を踏外さなかった. ¶*tempt* a person ***to*** wrong (vice) 人を悪(邪道)に誘う.

O One is *tempted* to think so. ちょっとそう考えたくなる. ‖ we may be *tempted* to smile now at ... われわれは今では...に対して微笑を漏す気分になるかも知れない.

temptation, *n.* 誘惑.

V ***accept*** *temptation* 誘惑に屈する. ¶***face*** *temptation* 誘惑に直面する. ¶***feel*** *temptations* 誘惑を感知する. ¶***overcome*** *temptation* to evil 悪い誘惑に打勝つ. ¶***put*** new *temptation* into the hearts of young men 青年の心を新たに誘惑する. ¶***remove*** *temptation* 誘惑を除く. ¶***resist*** *temptation* 誘惑に耐える. ¶if the *temptation* is ***thrown*** in one's way もし誘惑にかかると. ¶***withstand*** the *temptation* to ... ...への誘惑にたえる.

V^2 Here *temptation* ***enters.*** 誘惑が生じるのはここだ.

Q resist ***all*** *temptations* (=***every*** *temptation*) あらゆる誘惑に耐える. ¶The *temptation* to move in the other direction were most ***alluring.*** もう一つの方面に向おうとする誘惑がきわめて強かった. ¶a ***mischievous*** *temptation* 危険な誘惑. ¶a ***sore*** *temptation* 激しい誘惑. ¶The *temptation* was too ***strong*** to be resisted. その誘惑が大きくてこれに打勝てなかった. 【類】 The sight of the purse on the table was a ***strong*** *temptation* to the thief.

P He is proof ***against*** *temptation.* 彼は誘惑に負けない. ¶***amidst*** *temptations* 誘惑を受けながら. ¶fall ***before*** *temption* 誘惑に屈服する. ¶lead a person ***into*** *temptation* 人を誘惑する. ¶victory ***over*** *temptation* 誘惑の克服. ¶yield (=succumb) ***to*** *temptation* 誘惑に負ける. ¶***under*** the Devil's *temptation* 魔がさして. ¶struggle ***with*** *temptation* 誘惑と戦う.

P^2 a *temptation* ***of*** drink 飲酒の誘惑.

tempter, *n.* 誘惑者.

Q Love is a ***great*** *tempter.* 恋は大の曲者.

tempting, *a.* 誘惑的な.

M Your proposal is not ***sufficiently*** *tempting.* 御提案には余り乗気になれない. ¶The offer was ***very*** *tempting.* その申し出は頗る魅惑的だった.

P a field *tempting* ***to*** historians 歴史家の研究心をそそる方面.

ten, *n.* 十.

P a boy ***of*** *ten* 十歳の男の子. ¶nine ***out of*** *ten*=most likely 恐らくは.

P^2 *tens* ***of*** thousands of ... 何千何万という... ¶*Ten* ***to*** one he will fail. 九分通り彼は失敗だろう.

tenable, *a.* 耐えうる.

P scholarships *tenable* ***at*** technical schools 工業学校に有効な奨学金. ¶the scholarship *tenable* ***for*** three years 三年間有効の奨学金.

tenacious, *a.* 強い.

P *tenacious* ***of*** memory 記憶力が強い ‖ *tenacious* ***of*** one's purpose (opinion, rights) あくまで志(など)を固守する.

tenacity, *n.* 執着, ねばり強さ.

V ***lack*** *tenacity* ねばりが足りない.

Q adhere to it with a ***dog-like*** *tenacity* あくまで根強くそれを固守する. ¶a ***praiseworthy*** *tenacity* in the right direction 殊勝にもあくまで正しい方面に向って進むこと. ¶with ***unremitting*** *tenacity* of purpose 不とう不屈の志をいだいて.

Q^2 with a ***bulldog*** *tenacity* がん強にねばって.

P^2 *tenacity* ***for*** life 生の執着. ¶*tenacity* ***of*** memory 記憶力の強さ.

tenancy, *n.* 借用期限.

P^2 His *tenancy* ***of*** the house has not very long to run. その家の彼の借用期限は近々満了する.

tenant, *n.* 借家(地)人.

Q landlords and their ***defiant*** *tenants* 地主とその反抗的な借地人. ¶***outgoing*** and ***incoming*** *tenants* 出る借家人と新たにはいる借家人.

P^2 the *tenant* ***of*** a house 借家人. ¶a *tenant* ***under*** an ordinary lease 普通の借地契約による借地人.

tend, *v.* ...する傾向がある.

M It *tends* ***rather*** to confusion than to clearness. それは明りょうにするよりむしろ混乱させる傾向がある.

P It *tends* ***to*** the increase of contentment among all classes of the community. それらは社会のあらゆる階級の幸福を増進するのに役立つ. ¶*tend* ***towards*** centralization 中央集権に傾く. 【類】 *tend* ***toward*** selfishness.

O Excessive drinking *tends* to produce disease of the liver. 過度の飲酒は肝臓病を起す.

tend, *v.* 世話をする.

P He *tends* a shop ***for*** his father. 彼は父に代って店を経営している.

O *tend* a flock of sheep (the sick and wounded).

tendency, *n.* 傾向, すう勢.

V efforts to ***correct*** this *tendency* by administrative devices この傾向を行政的手段で矯正しようとする努力. ¶***de-***

velop an anti-Japanese *tendency* 排日的すう勢を助長する. ¶***display*** fresh *tendencies* 新らしい傾向を示す. ¶***exhibit*** a *tendency* to (=toward)… …の傾向を示す. ¶***fight*** the *tendency* toward… …の動向と戦う. ¶Everything of real merit ***has*** a *tendency* to survive. 何でも真価のある物はすべて後まで残る傾向がある.【類】Wood ***has*** a *tendency* to swell when it gets wet. ¶***note*** an opposite *tendency* 反対の傾向があることを認める. ¶***outgrow*** these boyish *tendencies* 生長してこうした子供じみた癖が直る. ¶***repress*** *tendencies* toward… …への傾向を抑える. ¶***show*** a *tendency* to increase 増加の傾向を示す.【類】***show*** a *tendency* to stuttering (どもり). ¶***strengthen*** the *tendency*, already powerful, to… すでに有力な…の傾向を強める.

V^2 this *tendency* ***becomes*** more ***pronounced*** as… この傾向は…するに従って一層顕著になる. ¶the *tendency* now is ***turning*** toward… 現時の風潮は…に変りつつある.

Q The market shows an ***advancing*** *tendency*. 市況は上向きだ. ¶suspected of ***anarchistic*** *tendencies* 無政府主義の傾向があると見られて. ¶the ***cityward*** *tendency* of the population 人口の都市集中傾向. ¶***constiutional*** *tendency* to disease 病弱な体質. ¶resist all ***corrupting*** *tendencies* in a language 一国語の堕落する傾向をすべて抑制する. ¶correct their ***criminal*** *tendencies* 彼らの犯罪的傾向を矯正する. ¶***Current*** *tendency* is in just the reverse direction. 現時の傾向はその正反対である. ¶a ***decided*** *tendency* 明らかな傾向. ¶have a ***declining*** *tendency* 衰える傾向がある. ¶a ***deep-seated*** *tendency* 根強い傾向. ¶show ***delinquent*** *tendencies* 不良性を示す. ¶a ***democratic*** *tendency* 民主主義の風潮. ¶a ***deplorable*** *tendency* なげかわしい傾向. ¶take a ***downward*** *tendency* 下向きになる. ¶***evolutional*** *tendency* 進化的傾向. ¶In America there is a ***general*** *tendency* toward jumboism. アメリカには一般に巨大主義の傾向がある. ¶there is a ***growing*** *tendency* that… 次第に…という傾向が高まりつつある.【類】today there is ***growing*** *tendency* in political and juristic thought (法律的思想) to… ¶a ***healthy*** *tendency* of the time 時代の一つの健全な傾向. ¶***hereditary*** *tendency* to madness 遺伝的発狂の傾向. ¶the market has an ***improving*** *tendency* 市場は上向である. ¶there is an ***increasing*** *tendency* to… …への傾向がますます著しい. ¶the ***inevitable democratic*** *tendency* of civilization 文化の不可避的な民主々義への傾向. ¶the ***leveling*** *tendencies* of this present day 今日の平等主義の風潮. ¶a review of present ***literary*** *tendencies* 現代文学の傾向の評論. ¶show ***little*** *tendency* to… ほとんど…の傾向を見せない. ¶It shows a ***marked*** *tendency* to improvement. それは著しく改善されつつある. ¶a play with "***modern***" *tendencies* いわゆる近代的傾向を帯びた劇.【類】***modern*** *tendencies* toward circumlocutory phraseology (回りくどい言い方). ¶a ***natural*** *tendency* 自然的傾向. ¶there is an ***observable*** *tendency* to… …の傾向が認められる. ¶the well-known ***piratical*** *tendencies* of Parisian taxi-drivers パリーのタクシー運転手の有名な雲助的傾向. ¶a ***powerful*** *tendency* 有力な傾向. ¶***present-day*** *tendencies* in education 現代教育のすう勢. ¶The *tendency* is ***pronounced*** (=marked). その傾向は著しい. ‖ It is developing a ***pronounced*** *tendency* towards pessimism. そのために悲観的傾向を著しく促進せしめている. ¶a ***reactionary*** *tendency* 逆コースの風潮. ¶Prices show a ***receding*** *tendency*. 物価は後退的傾向を示している. ¶show a steady ***rising*** (***falling***) *tendency* じり高(弱気)の傾向を示す. ¶The love of early youth has a ***romantic, idealizing*** *tendency*. 若き青春期の恋には小説的で理想化の傾向がある. ¶there is a ***slight*** *tendency* to… 幾分か…の傾きがある. ¶show a ***strong*** *tendency* はなはだしい傾向を示す. ¶Every one has more or less of ***such*** a *tendency*. だれだって多少そういう気味がある. ¶there is an ***undisguised*** *tendency* in all European countries to… 欧州各国には明かに…の傾向がある. ¶an ***unhealthy*** *tendency* 悪風潮. ¶the ***universal*** *tendency* of human nature to exaggeration 人間が一般に持つ誇張癖. ¶Freights are well maintained with an ***upward*** *tendency*. 船賃は手堅く上向になっている. ¶***vicious*** *tendencies* 悪い風潮. ¶The market shows a ***weak*** *tendency*. 市場は弱腰だ.【類】In consequence of accommodation stocks (融通株), quotations show a ***weaker*** *tendency*. ¶a ***wholesome*** *tendency* 健全な風潮.

Q^2 Their alleged "***radical***" and "***Communist***" *tendencies* 彼らのいわゆる「急進的」かつ「共産主義的」傾向. ¶an acute ***inflation*** (=inflationary) *tendency* 急激なインフレ傾向. ¶***neo-Fascist*** *tendencies* 新ファシスト風潮. ¶writers with ***socialist*** *tendencies* 社会主義的傾向のある作家連.

P patients ***with*** suicidal *tendencies* 自殺でもしそうな病人.

P^2 there are *tendencies* ***at*** work which will bring about… …を招来しそうな傾向が動いている. ¶the newer *tendencies* ***in*** education 最近の教育すう勢. ¶the *tendency* ***of*** society 社会の風潮. ¶a *tendency* ***to*** melancholia 憂うつ症の傾向.【類】a *tendency* ***to*** "red tape" (繁文縟(じょく)礼) / a *tendency* ***to*** tears / a *tendency* ***to*** rebellion (反乱). ¶there is some *tendency* ***toward***… 幾分…の傾向がある.

P^2 this *tendency* ***of*** the day この今日のすう勢.

tender, *n.* 入札; 提供物, 法貨.

V His *tender* for the supply of coal has been ***accepted.*** 石炭供給の入札は彼に落ちた. ¶*Tenders* are being ***advertised*** for the supply of 2,000 tons of coal. 石炭二千トン供給の入札広告が出ている. ¶***invite*** *tenders* for repairing the vessel (the erection of a building) 船舶修理(など)の入札を募集する.【類】*tenders* are ***invited*** and will be ***received*** up to… by… for the supply of… ¶***make*** a *tender* for the supply of… …供給の入札をする.【類】All *tenders* must be ***made*** on forms which may be obtained on application to the Secretary. ¶***open*** the *tenders* for the purchase of… …購入の入札を開始する. ¶***place*** *tenders* 入札する. ¶advertise that they are prepared (=open) to ***receive*** *tenders* for the supply of… …供給の入札受付を開始するむねの広告をする ‖ *tenders* will not be ***received*** until… 入札の受付は…日から. ¶His *tender* was ***rejected.*** 彼の入札ははずれた. ¶***send in*** *tenders* for the supply of… …供給の入札をする. ¶***submit*** a *tender* for the construction of a bridge 橋りょう架設の入札をする. ¶*tenders* are ***wanted*** for iron work for… …に対する鉄工事の入札を募る.

Q invite ***fresh*** *tenders* 新規に入札を募る. ¶***legal*** *tender* 法貨. ¶the ***lowest*** *tender* 最低入札. ¶It is to be sold by ***public*** *tender*. その売却は一般入札に付するはず. ¶The ***successful*** *tenders* were a British firm. 落札者はある英国の商会だった. ‖ His *tender* was ***successful.*** 彼に落札した.

Q^2 his job as ***baby*** *tender* 子守としての彼の仕事. ¶a ***submarine*** *tender* 潜水艦補給船.

P sell ***by*** *tender* 入札で売却する. ¶call ***for*** *tenders* 入札を募る.

P^2 calling of *tenders* ***for***… …の入札募集 ‖ *Tenders* ***for*** the supply of… are invited. …供給の入札を募集する. ¶*tender* ***of*** evidence 証拠の申出.

tender, *v.* 入札する.

P You may *tender* ***for*** the contract on the following terms. その契約(請負)に対し入札をするものは次の条件によること.

tender, *a.* やさしい; いたみやすい.

M I feel the wound ***still*** *tender*. きずはまだふれると痛い.

P children *tender* ***in*** years 年はも行かぬ子供たち. ¶*tender* ***of*** heart 心のやさしい. ¶*tender* ***to*** a person 人にやさしい ‖ *tender* ***to*** weakness やさし過ぎる. ¶*tender* ***toward*** the bashful はずかしがるものを手柔かに取扱う.

tenderness, *n.* やさしさ, 親切, 愛情.

V ***retain*** a great *tenderness* for one's place of nativity 相変らず強い郷土愛を持っている.

Q ***excessive*** *tenderness* turned to hundred-fold hatred 可愛さ余って憎さが百倍. ¶Robert Burns had a ***great*** *tenderness* for all created things. ロバート・バーンズはすべての生物に深い愛情を持っていた.

P ***with*** the *tenderness* of a mother 母の慈愛をもって.

tenement, *n.* 住家.

Q In those unhappy children of genius an ***earthly*** *tenement* is unequal to the strain of the clamoring spirit. それらの不びんな天才たちは体が虚弱で発揚しようとする英才を十分に伸ばすことができない.

tenet, *n.* 教義.

V ***embrace*** the *tenets* of a sect 宗門に入る. ¶***preach*** the *tenets* of the "Religion of the Future" with the fervour of Apostles いわゆる「将来の宗教」の教理をキリストの使徒の熱誠をもって説く.

Q the ***fundamental*** *tenets* of Christianity キリスト教の根本的教義. ¶***social*** *tenets* 社会に関する諸説.

P² There are no absolute *tenets* ***for*** selection. 選択するについてぜひよらねばならない主義といっては別にない.

tennis, *n.* 庭球.

V ***play*** *tennis* 庭球をやる.

Q a ***swell*** *tennis* (=net) player すばらしいテニスの選手.

Q² ***shore*** *tennis* 陸上テニス (tennis on board に対して). ¶play ***table*** *tennis* 卓球をやる.

P beat the opponent ***at*** *tennis* 庭球で相手を負かす ‖ They are ***at*** *tennis*. 彼らは庭球をやっている. ‖ a wrong serve ***at*** *tennis* 庭球のサーブの出し損じ. ¶He is very keen ***on*** *tennis* 彼は庭球が大好きだ.

tenor, *n.* 内容; [人生の]行路.

Q the ***even*** *tenor* of one's life 平穏な人生行路 ‖ He kept on the ***even*** *tenor* of his way for sixty years. 彼(芸人など)は同じことを六十年もやっていた. 【類】Business and social life goes along on the ***even*** *tenor* of its ways. ¶complaints of ***similar*** *tenor* 同じような意味の苦情.

P² the *tenor* ***of*** a letter (document, speech) 手紙(など)の内容. 「一歌手.

tenor, *n.* 〘音楽〙テノール(バリトンとアルトの間の音); テナ

V ***sing*** *tenor* テノールで歌う.

Q an ***excellent*** *tenor* すばらしいテナー歌手.

tense, *n.* 〘文法〙時相, 時. 「時制.

Q a ***compound*** *tense* 複合時制. ¶a ***progressive*** *tense* 進行

Q² My travels there are all in the ***future*** *tense*. 私はまだ一度もそこへ旅行したことがない.

P a verb ***in*** the present *tense* 現在形の動詞.

tension, *n.* 緊張.

V ***ease*** the *tension* [局面などの]緊張を緩和する. ¶***lessen*** the international *tension* 国際的緊張を緩和する. ¶***reduce*** the *tensions* which now grip the world 目下世界を支配している緊張を和らげる. ¶***relax*** the *tension* 緊張を緩和する. ¶to ***relieve*** the *tension* ばつを合わせるために, てれ隠しに. 【類】***relieve*** the *tension* of the market.

V² the same *tension* ***runs*** throughout ... …を通じて同様な緊張がみなぎっている ‖ *Tension* ***runs*** high. 危機一髪.

Q ***International*** *tension* has become less acute. 国際関係が幾分緩和された. ¶relieve one's ***nervous*** *tension* 心の緊張を緩和する. ¶***social*** *tension* 社会的緊張.

Q² reassumption of a status of equality with other nations in the present state of ***world*** *tension* 現在の世界緊張のときに当り他国と平等の状態を回復すること.

P Overstrained nerves, ***on*** a *tension* all day, pass on their fatigue on the rest of the body. 終日の緊張に神経が興奮しその疲労が身体にこたえる.

tent, *n.* 天幕(テント).

V ***peg down*** a *tent* テントをくいで地面に止める. ¶***pitch*** a *tent* 天幕を張る. 【類】***pitch*** *tents* and lodge in them. ¶***pull down*** a *tent* テントを取りはずす. ¶***strike*** (=***lower***) a *tent* 天幕を取はずす. 「会場など).

Q a ***lost*** children's *tent* 迷子を収容しておくテント(博覧会

Q² an ***ambulance*** *tent* 野戦傷病兵収容テント. ¶an ***army squad*** *tent* 軍用分隊テント. ¶a ***bell*** *tent* 円すい形天幕. ¶a ***hospital*** *tent* 病院天幕, 仮設病院.

P spend the night ***in*** a *tent* 天幕で夜を明かす.

tentacle, *n.* 〘動物〙触手.

P² *tentacles* ***of*** the law 法網.

tentative, *a.* 試験的, 暫定的.

M ***purely*** *tentative* 全く試験的な.

tenth, *n.* 十分の一.

Q the ***submerged*** *tenth* 下積みとなっている人々.

P get rarities ***at*** a *tenth* of their real value 珍品を本値の十分の一で手に入れる.

tenure, *n.* 在任期間; 不動産の保有.

V He is ***promised*** a long *tenure* of office. 彼は長期在任が約束されている.

Q ***feudal*** *tenure* 封建制度の土地保有. ¶***precarious*** *tenure* いつ解職されるか分からない地位.

Q² collective ***land*** *tenure* 共同土地保有権. ¶These nations have finished their ***two-year*** *tenure* on the Council これらの国はその会議の二年間の在任期間を終った. 【類】a professorship (講座) of ***three years*** *tenure*.

P ***during*** his *tenure* of the office of ... 彼の…在職中. 【類】***during*** his *tenure* of the Headmastership of Wellington. ¶the security ***of*** *tenure* [農夫などの]土地保有権の確保. ¶***On*** what *tenure* does the tenant hold the land? どんな保有条件で借地人はその土地を借りているのか.

term, *n.* (1) *pl.* [契約・支払・料金などの]条件.

V ultimately ***accept*** (=comply with) the *terms* 結局その条件を承認する. ¶***carry out*** the *terms* of an agreement with ... …との契約諸条件を履行する. ¶***command*** one's own *terms* 自分の方で勝手な条件を定める. ¶***derive*** *terms* favorable to women and girls. 女子に有利な条件を獲得する. ¶***dictate*** the *terms* of peace 講和条件を強請する. ¶The *terms* were ***embodied*** in a contract. その条件が一つの契約の中に含められた. ¶land our army and ***enforce*** our own *terms* わが軍隊を上陸させてこっちの主張を押し通す. ¶***extort*** *terms* favorable to ... …に有利な条件を強請する. ¶***get*** better *terms* 条件をもっとよくしてもらう. ¶***give*** the *terms* asked 要求した条件を与える. ¶***make*** *terms* with ... …と妥協する. 【類】***make*** better *terms*. ¶desire him to ***name*** his own *terms* その希望条件を述べるようにと言い出す. ¶The same *terms* are ***offered*** by other sellers. 他の販売者も同じ条件を提供している. 【類】The opponents are ***offering*** better *terms*. ¶Better *terms* are ***opened*** by other buyers. もっと好い条件を他の買手が申し出ている. ¶***quote*** special *terms* 特別の条件を与える. ¶***reject*** *terms* 条件を拒否する. ¶***serve*** their *terms* in prison 彼らの刑期に服する.

V² if the *terms* do not ***suit*** その条件が気に入らなければ.

Q trade on ***advantageous*** *terms* with the natives 有利な条件で土人と取引する. ¶very ***attractive*** *terms* 飛びつくような好条件. ¶sell (buy) on ***better*** *terms* もっと好い値で売る. 【類】secure ***better*** *terms* / buy on ***best*** *terms* possible. ¶***Easy*** *terms* are available. 買手に有利な条件が得られる. ‖ sell on ***easy*** *terms* 買手に楽な条件で販売する. ¶negotiate on ***equal*** *terms* 同じ資格で交渉する. ¶offer to join him at ***exceptional*** *terms* 特別の条件で彼と合同しようと申出る. ¶on ***fair*** *terms* 公正な条件で. ¶on the most ***favorable*** *terms* 最も有利な条件で ‖ quote the most ***favorable*** *terms* 最も好都合な条件を提供する(取引で). ¶Both parties have agreed to the settlement of the dispute upon the ***following*** *terms*—viz., ... 次の条件の下に双方の和解が成立した, すなわち… ¶The article was sold on ***high*** (***low***) *terms*. その品は高く(安く)売れた. ¶***liberal*** *terms* of payment 寛大な支払条件. ¶***moderate*** *terms* 穏当な条件; 割安の料金 ‖ undertake estate management at ***moderate*** *terms* 低廉の手数料で不動産監理の世話をする. ¶He will not sell me his property on my ***own*** *terms*. 彼はこちらの言い値ではその財産を売るまい. ¶Your *terms* are ***obtainable***. あなたの希望条件は得られる. ¶The *terms* are too ***onerous*** for me to accept. そんなわずらわしい条件は承諾できない. ¶He was asked to submit to the most ***preposterous*** *terms*. 彼はきわめて無茶な条件に服従せよと言われた. ¶***reasonable*** *terms* もっともな条件. ¶mutually ***satisfactory*** *terms* 双方に満足な条件. ¶The railway will make ***special*** *terms* for parties. その鉄道は団体には特別割引をします. ¶***unfavorable*** *terms* 不利な条件. ¶***usual*** *terms* 普通の条件.

Q² "***cease-fire***" *terms* 休戦条件. ¶easy ***credit*** *terms* 楽な信用貸条件. ¶draw up ***peace*** *terms* for ... …の平和条件を起草する. ¶under the ***Potsdam*** *terms* ポツダム宣言の条件のもとに. ¶implement the ***surrender*** *terms* 降服条件を履行する. 【類】violate ***surrender*** *terms*. ¶reduced ***winter*** *terms* of hotels ホテルの冬季割引料金.

P ***according to*** *terms* 条件通りに. ¶write articles ***at*** *terms* [working out] somewhere near fourpence a line 原稿を一行四ペンス見当で書く. 【類】the *terms* ***at*** which he lends money. ¶capitulate ***on*** *terms* 条件を定めて降服する ‖ We cannot buy ***on*** *terms* mentioned. その値段では当方は買えない. ‖ trade ***on*** his *terms* 先方の言い値で. ¶bring the enemy ***to*** *terms* 敵を降服させる ‖ unless we come ***to*** *terms* at once 早速妥協ができなければ. 【類】come ***to*** *terms* with ... ¶***under*** the *terms* of the Portsmouth treaty ポーツマス条約の規定する所によって. 【類】***under*** the *terms* of this statute (法令) / ***under*** the *terms* of his will (遺言). ¶***upon*** especially favorable *terms* 特に有利な条件で.

P² *terms* ***for*** foreign orders 外国からの注文に対する条件 ‖ *Terms* ***for*** quantities. 大口取引の条件. ¶*terms* ***of*** payment (subscription) 支払(など)条件 ‖ the *terms* ***of*** the present treaty 本条約の条項.

O *Terms*, two guineas a week 料金は週二ギニー.

(**2**) *pl.* 関係, 間柄.

Q live on very ***bad terms*** with one's friends 友だちとひどく仲を悪くしている ‖ get on ***bad terms*** with ... …と仲が悪くなる. ¶be on ***cordial terms*** with ... …と懇意な間柄である. ¶be on very ***easy terms*** with ... …と非常に気楽な間柄である. ¶associate on ***equal terms*** 対等の交際をする. ¶He is on very ***familiar terms*** with idiomatic English. 彼は慣用英語によく通じている. ¶keep on ***friendly terms*** with ... …と懇意にしている. ¶a man who is hard to be on ***good terms*** with＝《米》a bad mixer つき合いにくい人 ‖ keep on ***good terms*** with ... …と友好関係を持続する. ¶be on ***good*** and ***neighborly terms*** 懇意にしている. ¶on ***intimate terms*** with ... …と親しくして. ¶live on more ***sociable terms*** with one's neighbors もっと近所付合いをよくする. ¶live on the most ***unpleasant terms*** with one's wife 妻との折合がきわめて悪い.

Q² on ***calling*** (＝***visiting***) ***terms*** with ... …とは互に往来する仲. ¶be on ***first-name terms*** with ... …と親しくしている(姓で呼ばず名で呼んでいる). ¶He has been on ***Sam and John terms*** with me for eighteen years. 彼と私は十八年間親友関係を続けてきた. ¶I am on ***speaking terms*** with him. 私と彼とは会えば互に言葉を交わす間柄だ. ¶be on ***thee-and-thou terms*** 君僕の間柄である. ¶on ***visiting*** (***writing***) ***terms*** with ... …とは訪問(など)し合う仲.

P her claims to be admitted ***on terms*** of equality into the comity of nations 対等の関係で国際友好を結ぼうというその国の主張. 【類】live ***on terms*** of equality / live ***on terms*** of brotherly love with ... / He was ***on terms*** of friendship with me. / They are ***on terms*** of friendly intimacy (親密). ‖ not ***on terms*** of harmony with ... …とは折合がよくない ‖ associate with people ***on terms*** of intimacy 人々と親しく交際する.

(**3**) 語; [専門]用語.

V There is a tendency throughout United States to ***adopt*** the ***term*** Memorial Day instead of Decoration Day. 米国ではデコレーションデーと言わずメモリアルデーという語を採用しようという意向が一般にある. ¶it is a misnomer to ***apply*** the ***term*** ... to ... …に…という言葉を用いるのは間違いである. ¶***define*** more accurately the ***terms*** employed in talking and writing about ... …について言ったり書いたりする言葉を一層正確にする. ¶***employ*** occasionally vulgar ***terms*** 時折下等な言葉を使う. ¶***let drop*** (＝***out***) the ***term*** うっかりその言葉を使う. ¶He claims the honor of ***originating*** the ***term***. 彼はその語の生みの親であると言っている. ¶There were no mechanics in those days, as we now ***understand*** the ***term*** (＝in the present sense). 今日われわれが使用している意味の機械工なるものはその当時はなかった. ‖ as we ***understand*** that ***term*** in the West われわれ西欧人が言う意味の.

Q ***abstract terms*** 抽象語. ¶the ***abusive terms*** popularly applied to ... …を悪しざまに言うとき普通用いる言葉. ¶Yamato is an ***ancient poetic term*** for Japan. 大和は詩的に言う日本の古称である. ¶in ***another term*** for ... …の代名詞(別名). ¶speak of ... in ***appreciative terms*** …を賞賛する. ¶Of "fable" and "apologue" the latter is the most ***bookish term***.「fable (ぐう話)」と「apologue (道話)」の両語中後者は多く書物に用いられる. ¶a glossary of ***botanical terms*** 植物学用語集. ¶reduced to the ***briefest terms*** these may be called "..." 約言すれば「…」となる. ¶Social welfare is a ***broad term***. 厚生とは意義の広い言葉だ. ¶expose in ***clear*** and ***concise terms*** 簡潔に陳述する. 【類】state in the ***clearest terms*** that ... ¶a ***colloquial term*** 通俗語. ¶speak of him in ***complimentary terms*** 彼のことをほめて言う. ¶in very ***decisive terms*** きわめて決定的な言葉で. ¶the ***term*** "***duly qualified***"「正式の資格がある」という言葉. ¶speak in ***disparaging terms*** of ... …を悪しざまに言う. ¶commend the results of their labors in ***eloquent*** and ***graceful terms*** 彼らの努力の結晶を流ちょうかつ優美な言葉で賞賛する. ¶***equivalent terms*** 同義語. ¶in ***express terms*** [法規などの]明文で. ¶I know of no more ***expressive term***. 私はこれ以上に表現力のある言葉を知らない. ¶speak of ... in ***favorable terms*** …をよくいう. ¶***figurative*** and ***metaphorical terms*** 比ゆ的語句. ¶The ***term*** "..." is not quite the ***fitting*** one.「…」という語は余り適当でない. ‖ be couched in ***fitting terms*** 適切な言葉で表現してある. ¶in very ***flattering terms*** 大いに称賛して. ¶His views were expressed in the ***following terms***. 次のように彼はその所見を述べた. 【類】It is described by him in the ***following terms***. ¶The ***term*** is not a ***fortunate*** one. 名が適切でない. ¶in ***general term*** 概括的な言葉で ‖ "Cat" is a ***general term*** for cats, lions and tigers. "Cat" はねこ, ライオン, とらの総称だ. ¶he spoke in ***glowing terms*** of ... 彼は…について大いに賛辞を呈した. ¶a ***generic term*** 総称. ¶scold a man in ***good, round terms*** みっちりしかる. ¶using ***grammatical terms***, we may say that ... 文法用語を使うと…といえる. ¶speak in ***high terms*** of ... …をしきりにほめそやす. 【類】speak in the ***highest terms*** (激賞する) with regard to ... ¶an ***honorary term*** 敬称. ¶***impathetic*** but ***dignified terms*** 無表情ではあるがしかし威厳のある言葉で. ¶in ***intelligible terms*** 分かりやすい言葉で. ¶in ***kindly terms*** やさしい言葉で. ¶speak in ***laudatory terms*** of ... …を嘆美する. ¶a ***legal term*** for ... …の法律語. ¶"Wasuregusa" is a Japanese ***literary term*** for tobacoo.「忘れ草」は日本語でタバコの雅語である. ¶a ***local term*** 地方的用語, 方言. ¶Pianoforte is a ***longer term*** for *piano*. Pianoforte は piano の長い語形だ. ¶speak of the King in the most ***loyal*** and ***loving terms*** 最も忠節な親愛な言葉で国王のことをいう. ¶describe it in ***lucid terms*** 明りょうな言葉でそれを記述する. ¶They abused each other in no ***measured terms***. 彼らは勝手に悪口を言い合った. ‖ He expressed his disapproval in no ***measured terms***. 彼は断固として不承知を唱えた. 【類】express one's likes and dislikes in no ***measured terms***. ¶a ***medicolegal term*** 法医学の術語. ¶to speak in the ***mildest term*** ごく穏か(内輪)に言っても. 【類】It is surely, to use the ***mildest term*** we can think of, pedantic. ¶a much ***misunderstood term*** 大分意味を取違えられた語. ¶think in ***new terms*** 新しい考え方をする. ¶a ***newly-coined term*** 新造語. ¶a ***pivotal term*** 要語, 字眼. ¶in ***plain terms*** 平易な言葉で言えば. ¶be fixed on ***private terms*** 示談できまる. ¶the most widely ***received*** technical ***term*** きわめて広く通用している術語. ¶a ***reproachful term*** 非難がましい言葉. ¶in ***rough terms***, we may say that ... 大まかに言えば…と言えるだろう. ¶in ***round terms*** 大ざっぱに言って. ¶in ***set terms*** きまり文句で. ¶reduced to their ***simplest terms*** 約言すれば. ¶his task, in ***simple terms***, is to ... 一口に言えば彼の仕事は…することだ. 【類】Simple facts are to be told in ***simple terms***. ¶***simple, straightforward terms*** 簡明直さいな言葉. ¶in ***such terms*** as you may think fit [だれが見ても]適当な言葉で. ¶Blindness and pauperism are no longer ***synonymous terms***. もはや今日では盲目は貧困の代名詞ではない. ¶state in ***unmistakable terms*** はっきりと述べる. ¶a ***vague term*** applied to ... …に用いる意味のばく然とした語. ¶denounce in the most ***violent terms*** 猛烈に非難する. ¶speak in ***warm terms*** of ... …を称賛する. 【類】speak in the ***warmest terms*** of ...

Q² ***art terms*** 芸術諸用語. ¶"Right" is the ***correlation term*** of "obligation." 権利は義務の相関語だ. ¶explain it in ***everyday terms*** それを日常の言葉で説明する. ¶the use of ***highbrow terms*** in place of honest English words 平易な英語の代りにやかましい言葉の使用. ¶an expressive ***slang term*** 意味深長な俗語. ¶definition of ***trade terms*** 商売用語の定義. ¶develop the ability to think in ***world terms*** 物を世界的視野で見る能力(国際的見識)を養成する. ¶***26,000 vocabulary terms*** 26,000 語の語い.

P call ***by*** a specific ***term*** 特殊の語を用いて言う. ¶see all life ***in terms*** of dollars and cents すべて人生を金銭の方面から見る. ¶let each child read ***in terms*** of his own tastes and choices 子供にそれぞれ自分の趣味と好みで本を読ませる. 【類】think ***in terms*** of the working man / let them have freedom to develop ***in terms*** of his own nature (その才能に応じ) / ***in terms*** of his ability and his interests ‖ speak of one ***in terms*** of respect 敬意を表して人のことを語る. 【類】we can speak ***in terms*** of the highest praise of ... ‖ Figures are stated ***in terms*** of the metric system. [統計などの]数字にはメートル制を用いてある. ‖ ***in terms*** of dollar value ドルで評価すると. 【類】appreciate the significance of knowledge ***in terms*** of profit / The industry is the largest of all in this country ***in terms*** of the numbers in employment (使用人の数からいうと) / set forth ***in terms*** that can be understood by ordinary intelligent readers (やさしい言葉で) / Expressed merely ***in terms*** of currency (通貨), the annual gain to Egypt from its winter visitor has been estimated at over a million sterling (英貨百万ポンド).—D.G. Hogarth. / In picture things are expressed ***in terms*** of light and shade (陰影) and form. / A word is primarily an idea expressed ***in terms*** of sound, the vocal representation of a mental image (心像). / express it ***in terms*** of philosophy (哲学的に) / express ***in terms*** of action (行動で) / Such kind of information can be expressed with greater clearness ***in terms*** of lines and numerals (グラフなど) / The letter was couched (書かれて) ***in*** very friendly ***terms***. / His success is but modest, reckoned ***in terms*** of money. / mention him ***in terms*** of thinly-veiled contempt or scorn / stated ***in terms*** of algebraic equation (代数方程式で) / restated (言直せば) ***in*** the *terms* of ... / We are prone to interpret the actions of the child ***in terms*** of our own experience. / It is impossible to define the essay ***in terms*** of either subject or length, for essays exist on all manner of subjects and vary in length from a page or so to several volumes.—J.B. Priestley. / explain life ***in terms*** of chemistry / explain mysteries ***in terms*** of chemical or physical law / The fact is explainable ***in terms*** of chemistry. / A Chicago antiquary (考古学者) has ascertained that the famous first voyage of Columbus cost only $7.000 ***in terms*** of our present currency (=the money of today). / ***in terms*** of cold, scientific analysis / ***In terms*** of [the numbers in] employment the hotel industry was the second largest Swiss industry in 1929. / ***In terms*** of Christianity it is called " the grace of God " (神の恩愛).

P² a *term* ***in*** astronomy 天文学の術語. ¶translate into *terms* ***of*** tone the feeling of ... ...の感情を音楽に移す ‖ *terms* ***of*** science 科学用語 ‖ a *term* ***of*** contempt (endearment) 侮辱(愛ぶ)の言葉 ‖ a *term* ***of*** courtesy (respect) 敬称.

(**4**) 学期; 期限, 期間; 満期, 産期; 項.

V ***extend*** the *term* of payment 支払期限を延期する. ¶***fix*** a *term* 期限をきめる. ¶He ***had*** a short *term* of imprisonment. 彼はしばらく禁固された. ¶***keep*** two *terms* 二学期間出席する. ¶***serve*** one's *term* of imprisonment 刑期を勤める ‖ How many *terms* has he ***served*** at the prison? 彼はその刑務所へ何度入れられたか. 【類】 ***serve*** a *term* of one month in a house of correction (penitentiary) / ***serve*** two *terms* in succession (二期続けて). ¶***wind up*** one's *term* of office 任期を終了する.

V² ***set*** a *term* to ... ...を制限する, 止める. ¶reprint established classics whose copyright *term* has ***expired*** 版権の喪失した定評のある名著を復刻する ‖ His *term* of appointment (=office) ***expires*** in August. 彼の任期は八月で満了する. ¶The *term* ***runs*** from September till Easter. 期間は九月から復活祭までである.

Q The Evening School will open again on March 3 for ***another*** *term*. 夜学は三月三日から新学期が始まる. ¶examinations for the ***final*** *term* 学期末試験. ¶a ***fresh*** *term* 新学期. ¶At (***full***) *term* she gave birth to a healthy girl. 月満ちて彼女は丈夫な女の子を産み落した. ¶since his ***last*** *term* in prison 彼の前の刑期以来. ¶for the ***like*** *term* 同様期間に対し. ¶a ***peremptory*** *term* 不変期間. ¶Men and women move across the face of the earth on ***long*** *term*, meaning to stay, or on ***short*** *term*, meaning to return. 人々があるいは一所に定住する考えであるいは一時滞在の考えで世界をあちらこちらと移動する. ¶for a ***short*** *term* 短期間.

Q² the ***fall*** *term* 秋の学期. ¶be appointed for a ***five-year*** *term* 五年の期間で任命される. 【類】 after completion of one's ***five-year*** *term* of office / a ***forty-hour*** *term* of instruction / The members were elected for ***six-year*** *term*. ¶suffer fines and ***jail*** *terms* 罰金と体刑に処せられる. ¶serve a ***life prison*** *term* 終身刑期を勤める ‖ be sentenced to ***two-year prison*** *terms* 二年の禁固刑を宣告される. 【類】 wind up (=complete) one's ***prison*** *term*. ¶a ***quarter*** *term* 四半期.

P a birth which takes place ***at*** *term* or prematurely. 月満ちての, または月足らずでの出産 ‖ She has delivered of a child ***at*** *term*. 月満ちて彼女は女の子を産み落した. ‖ The fetus was nearly ***at*** *term*. 胎児はほとんど産期になっていた. ¶***during*** his *term* of office 彼の任期中. ¶***for*** a *term* of five years 五年の期間にわたって ‖ an imprisonment either for life or ***for*** a *term* of years 終身かまたは数年の禁固. ¶***on*** long *terms* ***of*** payment 長期返済の方法で. ¶go ***through*** one's *term* of office=serve one's time 任期を勤め上げる.

P² during his second *term* ***as*** President 彼が大統領として二回目の任期中. ¶He previously served a *term* ***in*** a house of correction. 彼は以前感化院へ入れられたことがある. ¶the *term* ***of*** a loan [貸金]据置期限 ‖ *term* ***of*** validity =validity term 有効期間 ‖ at the expiration of his *term* ***of*** service (=office) 任期満了して.

term, *v*. 称する, 名づける.

M it may be ***conveniently*** *termed* ... それは便宜上...と呼んでよかろう. ¶though it is more ***correctly*** *termed* ... ...という方が正しいのであるが. ¶it may be not ***inaptly*** *termed* the "..." それは「...」と称して不適当ではない. ¶be ***justly*** *termed* "..." 「...」と呼ぶのは正しい. ¶as he is often ***lovingly*** *termed* 彼がしばしばこう愛称されているが. ¶be ***officially*** *termed* 公式には...と呼ばれる. ¶***picturesquely*** (=***fancifully***) *termed* ... ...というしゃれた名のついた. ¶***popularly*** *termed* ... 俗に...という. ¶it is ***slangily*** and ***vulgarly*** *termed* ... それは卑俗の言葉では...と言っている. ¶***variously*** *termed* 色々異名のある.

terminal, *n*. 《米》 終点.

Q² a huge ***bus*** *terminal* 大型バス終点. ¶a ***railroad*** *terminal*=《英》 a railway terminus 終着駅.

terminate, *v*. 終る.

M The case *terminated* ***fatally***. その病人は助からなかった. ¶The appeal has *terminated* ***favorably***. 上告が有利に終った.

P the tram-line *terminates* ***at*** ... その電車線は...が終点だ. ¶It was an unfortunate married life which *terminated* ***in*** divorce. それは不幸な結婚生活で結局離婚ということになった. ¶the proceedings *terminated* ***with*** ... その会の次第は...をもって終了した.

termination, *n*. 結末.

V The disaster ***hastened*** the fatal *termination*. その災禍がその没落を早めた.

Q the meeting came to an ***abrupt*** *termination* on account of ... その会は...のため突然散会となった. ¶in the case of a ***fatal*** *termination* [病人など]死んだ場合. ¶come to a ***happy*** *termination* 目出度く終了する. ¶the ***successful*** *termination* of the affair その事件の首尾よい落着.

Q² serve a five-day notice of ***contract*** *termination* 契約終了を五日前に通知する.

P ***at*** the *termination* of a spire せん塔の頂点に. ¶***on*** the *termination* of the present war この戦争が終った時. ¶***since*** the *termination* of the war 戦争が終ってから. ¶bring it ***to*** a *termination* それを終える. 【類】 The dispute was brought ***to*** a satisfactory *termination*. ¶***upon*** *termination* of employment in ... ...を退職するとき.

terminology, *n*. 用語, 術語.

V ***standardize*** the *terminology* of English grammar 英文典の用語を統一する. ¶to ***use*** logical *terminology* 論理学の術語で言えば.

Q The word is destined to disappear from ***medical*** *terminology*. その語は医学の術語としては将来用いられなくなるものと見られる. ¶***technical*** *terminology* 専門語.

terrace, *n*. 台地; ひな段式.

P formed ***in*** *terrace* ひな段式になっている.

P² There are on the hillside many ricefields, *terrace* ***above*** terrace. その小山の側面には段々になって田がたくさんにある. ¶a *terrace* ***in*** a hillside 山側の台地.

terrify, *v*. 脅かす.

P He was *terrified* ***at*** the occurrence. 彼はそのできごとに脅かされた. ¶*terrified* ***by*** ... ...に脅かされて. ¶He was *terrified* ***into*** compliance. 彼はこわくなって承知してしまった.

territory, *n*. 領土, 領域; 《米》 [T-] 准州.

V ***annex*** *territory* 領地を併合する. ¶***acquire*** *territory* 領土を獲得する. ¶***cede*** a *territory* in perpetuity 永久に領土を割譲する. ¶***extend*** her *territory* by conquest 領土を征服によって拡張する. ¶***restitute*** a *territory* to a country 領土を国へ償還する. ¶***seize*** a *territory* 領土を占領する.

Q The eastern bank of the Niagara River is ***American*** *territory*; the western bank Canadian. ナイアガラ川の東岸は米領で西岸はカナダ領である. ¶Gibraltar is ***British*** *territory*. ジブラルタルは英領だ. ¶***contiguous*** *territory* northward 北方隣接の地. ¶the *ex-Japanese territory* 日本の旧領土. ¶a *mandated territory* 委任統治の土地. ¶richly *mineralized territories* 鉱物を豊富に埋蔵する地域. ¶the mere acquisition of *new territory* 単なる新領土の獲得. ¶*outlying territories* 在外の領土.

Q² a *buffer territory* 緩衝地域. ¶the fertile *Saar territory* bordering France, Luxembourg and Germany フランス, ルクサンブルグ及びドイツに界する肥よくなザール領域. ¶the Soviet Union and its *satellite territory* ソ連及その衛星国. ¶a *trust territory* 委任領域.

P *in* the *Territory* (=sphere, field *or* domain) of psychiatry 精神病学の領域において. ¶the presence of foreign troops *on* her *territory* その国土における外国軍隊の駐在 ‖ At the St. James's the diplomatists of every nationality may meet *on territory* that is at once pleasant and neutral. セント・ジェームス宮では各国の外交官が愉快でしかも中立的な気持で会合ができる. ¶*within* Japanese *territory* 日本領土内に.

P² the *Territory of* Alaska (Hawaii) アラスカ(ハワイ)准州. ¶*territories under* their control その監理に属する地域.

terror, *n.* 恐怖.

V *cause terror* 恐怖の念を起させる. ¶*excite terror* 恐怖の念を呼び起す. ¶*heighten terror* to frenzy 恐怖の余り気を狂わす. ¶*inspire terror* 恐怖の念を吹込む. ¶*instil terror* into the audience 聴衆を戦りつさせる. ¶Death *lost* all *terrors* for them. 彼らは死を何とも思わないようになった. ¶*strike terror* into (=to) their cowardly hearts 彼らおく病者の心胆を寒からしめる. 【類】The aeroplanes *struck terror* among the savages.

Q *overpowering terror* たえ難い恐怖. ¶*superstitious terrors* 迷信から恐ろしく思う物.

Q² the *right-wing terror* 右翼のテロ.

P flee *in terror* from ... 恐ろしいので...から逃げる ‖ recoil *in terror* 恐れてたじろぐ. 【類】keep awake *in terror*. ¶I found *to* my *terror* that he was a "Red." 彼が「赤」であることを知って恐ろしく思った. ¶stupefied *with terror* 恐怖の余りぼう然として. 【類】look up *with terror* at ... ¶He became a *terror to* all who knew him. 彼は彼を知る者からこわがられるようになった.

terrorism, *n.* テロ.

Q² *Communist terrorism* 共産党のテロ. ¶The district was suffering from *mob terrorism*. その地方は暴民のテロに悩んでいた.

test, *n.* 試験.

V He cannot *abide* the *test*. 彼はその試験にたえ得ない. ¶Let us *apply* the practical *test*. 実験して見よう. ¶It cannot *bear* the *test* of scientific criticism. 科学の立場から批判するとそういうことはあり得ないということになる. ‖ *bear* the *test* of reason and experiment 理論及び実地の試験にたえる. 【類】valuable maxims which have *borne* the *test* and use for centuries. ¶*give* oral *tests* 口頭試問をする. ¶*make* some preliminary *tests* 少し予備試験をする. ¶The candidate has *passed* all the *tests*. その志願者は試験全部が通った. 【類】It is doubtful whether the present concrete buildings will successfully *pass* the *test* of time. ¶*resist* every known *test* ありとあらゆる試験にたえる. ¶It has *stood* the *test* of actual practice. 実地に使用して見ていよいよそれがよいということが分かった. 【類】*stand* the *test* of time and experience. ¶refuse to *take* the *test* きらってその考査を受けない. 【類】*take* one's *test* for an auto driver's license.

Q *accurate tests* 厳密な試験. ¶*chemical tests* 化学実験. ¶a *crucial test* 決定的試験. ¶an *experimental test* 実験. ¶an *infallible test* きわめてたしかな試験法. ¶face its first *major test* 始めての大試練に直面する. ¶successfully stand *many tests* 種々の試験に首尾よく合格する. ¶a *mental test* 知能テスト. ¶apply *objective tests* 客観的試験法を行う. ¶put the matter to a *practical test* それを実地に試験して見る. ¶a *rough test* for coffee コーヒー(品質)のざっとした(精密の反対)試験. ¶These textbooks have passed the *searching test* of the classroom. その教科書は教室(実地教授)の厳密な試験を経て良いとされたものである. ¶It was subjected to very *severe tests*. それは非常にきびしい試験に掛けられた. ¶a *simple test* is to ... ...のが一番簡単だ. ¶stand the *specified test* 指定された試験に合格する. ¶The ability to write is a *supreme test* of linguistic competence. 作文力は語学力をためす最高考査の一つである. ¶The *ultimate test* of "correctness" is usage. [文などの用法が]正しいかどうかを判定するのは結局慣用の有無だ.

Q² an *ability test* 性能検査. ¶an *achievement test* 業績考査. ¶an academic *aptitude test* 学力の適性考査. ¶an *acid test* [金の酸試験から]厳密な試験. ¶an *alpha test* 本国人の知能考査. ¶apply a *blood test* to ... ...の血液検査をする. ¶have a *color[vision] test* [目の]色神検査を受ける. ¶an *efficiency test* 性能検査. ¶an *endurance test* 耐久試験. ¶an *eye[sight] test* 視力試験. ¶the *H-bomb explosion test* 水素爆弾爆発試験. ¶*intelligence test* 知能考査. ¶a *literacy test* 読み書き試験. ¶a *loyalty test* 忠誠の試金石. ¶a *matriculation test* 入学考査. ¶a *mental hygiene test* 精神衛生試験. ¶a *matching test* 意味合わせの試験(語と意味とを連結する). ¶a *memory test* 記憶試験. ¶a *microphone voice test* マイクロフォンの音声試験. ¶a *true-false test* 当不当試験. ¶a *vocabulary test* 語い試験.

P put it *through* a preliminary *test* それに予備試験を施す. ¶put it *to* the *test* それをためす. 【類】Put it *to* the *test* and see how it will go. ¶I congratulate them on the proof they have given of their efficiency *under* severe *test*. きびしい試験を経てその人たちがその実力を証明し得たことに対し私は御喜びを申上げる.

P² *test for* coffee コーヒーの試験. ¶make *tests in* electricity 電気の実験をする. ¶Only the best manufactures will stand the *test of* advertising. 最優良品でなくては広告をしても結局だめだろう.

test, *v.* 試験する.

P *test* ... *at* law ...に法律の試験を行う. ¶*tested by* the touchstone of ... ...の標準で試験された ‖ be *tested by* time 時が試験する(時がたてば分かる). ¶The students were *tested for* tuberculosis. 学生は結核検査を受けた. 【類】*test* ore *for* gold (金の有無).

tester, *n.* 鑑別器, [電流の]テスター.

Q² a *chick tester* [鶏の]ひな鑑別器.

testify, *v.* 証明する.

M *testify falsely* against ... ...に不利益な偽証をする. ¶*sufficiently testify* to his capability for work 彼に力量があることを十分に証明する. ¶The endorsement of such a scholar *well testifies* to the truth of this. こうした学者が裏書するからにはこれが真理であることを十分証言されたものと見られる.

P *testify about* a matter ある件について保証する. ¶*testify against* an accused person 被告に不利な証言をする. ¶*testify before* courts 法廷で証言する. ¶it is *testified by* the fact that ... それは...という事実によって証明されている. ¶*testify on* oath as witness 証人として宣誓の上証言する. ¶*testify to* its excellence その卓越していることを証明する. 【類】*testify to* the fact that ... / *testify to* his fitness (適性) / *testify to* the progress which has been made by ... / I am pleased to *testify to* the splendid utility of your Fire Escape (火災避難用具) for high buildings. ¶he *testified under* oath that ... 彼は...と誓約した.

testimonial, *n.* [人格・技能などの]証明書.

V *give* a *testimonial* to an antique 古物にきめをつける. ¶He *has testimonials* from his teacher and former employer. 彼は先生や前雇主の人物証明書を持っている. ¶*make up* (=*prepare*) a *testimonial* 証明書を作成する.

Q the *highest testimonial* 最良の証明書. ¶*paid testimonials* 報酬を出して書いてもらった証明書. ¶*unsolicited testimonials* 自発的の証明書(頼まないで). ¶Applicants for this post must send copies of two *recent testimonials*. この職の志願者は最近の証明書の写しを二通送付しなければならない. ¶I now present for your acceptance this *slight testimonial*. この粗末なお印をどうか御受納下さい. ¶a *telling testimonial* 有効の証明書.

P² a *testimonial as to* character 人物証明書. ¶*testimonials from* customers 顧客の証明(店の信用など). ¶a *testimonial of* one's distinguished services 功労表彰状. ¶a *testimonial to* one's industry 精勤証.

testimony, *n.* 証明.

V *afford testimony* of this fact この事実の証拠になる. ¶I can *bear testimony* to his good character. 彼がりっぱな人物であることは私が証明できる. ¶*bring forward* the *testimony* of ... ...の証拠をあげる. ¶*give testimony* as to ... ...について証明する. ¶No stronger *testimony* could be *given*. これほど確かな証拠はない. ¶We *have* his *testi-*

mony for that. そのことについては彼が証明している. ‖ As regards ... we *have* the confirmatory *testimony* of Japanese writers. ...に関しては日本人が書いたものに確実な証拠がある. ¶*produce testimony* of ... ...の証拠をあげる. ¶*seal* one's *testimony* with one's blood 血判を押して証明する. ¶No one can *withstand* the silent *testimony* of hard facts. 何人も動かし難い事実が与える無言の証明に反抗することはできない.

V² the lithic *testimony* of ancient India *proves* that ... 古代インドの石文が...を証明している.

Q To this ... bears *abundunt testimony*. ...がこのことを十分に証拠立てている. ¶bear *ample testimony* to ... ...を十分に証拠立てる. ¶*eloquent testimony* 能弁な(十分の)証明. 【類】one can with difficulty conceive a more *eloquent testimony* to the immense importance of ... ¶maliciously give *false testimonies* against ... 悪意から...に不利な偽証を与える. ¶a *high testimony* of its usefulness それが有益であるというりっぱな証拠. ¶bear *little testimony* to ... ...についてほとんど何も証明していない. ¶bear *mute testimony* to ... ...に対して無言の(言葉では言わぬが自然)証明を与える. 【類】These stone lanterns are *mute testimony* of the devotion of past ages. ¶very *remarkable testimony* has come to ... from ... ...のきわめて顕著な証拠が...からあがった. ¶a bit of *side testimony* on this point may be gleaned from ... この点に関する一傍証が...から得られるだろう. ¶There is *strong negative testimony* against it. それに対する有力な反証がある. ¶bear *warm testimony* to ... 力強く...を証明する.

Q² a *deposition testimony* 口供書の証明.

P *by* the *testimony* of the witness 証人の証言により. ¶call one *in testimony* 人を証人として召喚する ‖ *in testimony* of our respect and affection われわれの尊敬と愛情のしるしとして(贈り物など). ¶rely *on* the *testimony* of ... ...の証明に頼る.

P² *testimony against* one's character その不品行の証明. ¶*testimony as to* ... ...に関する証明. ¶*testimony to* one's character その人物証明.

testing, *n.* 試験.

Q after *rigid testing* きびしく試験して後.

tête-à-tête, *n.* 内証話.

Q have a nice *little tête-à-tête* むつまじい話をする(恋人同士が). ¶have *several tête-à-têtes* with the statesmen 政治家と数回対談する.

tête-à-tête, *a.* 二人きりの.

P They sat *tête-à-tête at* table. 二人きりで食卓についた.

tether, *n.* 範囲.

P This is *beyond* my *tether*. これは僕の力には及ばない. ¶come to the end *of* one's *tether* 行き詰る.

tether, *v.* つなぐ.

P a horse *tethered to* a post くいにつなぎなわでつないだ馬.

text, *n.* 本文.

V *collate texts* 原文を校合する. ¶*illumine* his *text* with brilliant and instructive notes りっぱで有益な注釈を付して本文の意味を明かにする. ¶Eight colored maps and thirty nine other cuts *illustrate* the *text*. 八枚の彩色地図と他に三十九枚の木版画を本文に添えてある. ¶*interpret* the *text* 本文を解釈する. ¶In invitations the *text* is usually *worded* in this manner. 招待状の文句は大抵こんな風になっている.

Q an *authoritative text* 権威ある本文. ¶a *descriptive text* 解説(絵などに対する). ¶read it in an *English text* それを英文で書いたもので読む ‖ Of the present Treaty *French* and *English texts* are both authentic 本条約はフランス語及びイギリス語の本文をもってともに正文とする. ¶a *full text* 全文. ¶the *full text* of an address 演説の全文. 【類】the *full text* of the Regulations. ¶*nasty texts* of Scripture 聖書中文句のいかがわしい個所. ¶a *new* and *purer* (=purified) *text* of Shakespeare シェークスピアの校訂新版. ¶the *official text* of an agreement 協定書の正文. ¶a *written text* 本文 (maps, pictures, diagrams, and tables などに対して). ¶the *explanatory text* for the film 映画の説明文句.

Q² *Advance texts* of his speech were distributed in the city. 彼の演説の本文が前もってその都市に配布された. ¶an extensive *reading text* 補習用教科書.

P *from* the *text* 原文から. ¶a long sermon *on* the *text* that ... という題の長い説教.

textbook, *n.* 教科書.

Q a *beautifully-illustrated textbook* 美しいさし絵のある教科書.

Q² a *geography textbook* 地理の教科書.

P² a *textbook for* business administration 商業経営の教科書. ¶*textbooks in* English composition 英作文教科書. ¶*textbooks on* grammar 文法教科書 ‖ a *textbook on* knitting あみもの教本.

textile, *n.* 織物; 布地.

Q² *cotton* and *linen textiles* 木綿とリンネルの織物. ¶*rayon filament textiles* 人絹繊維織物. ¶*wool textiles* 毛織物.

P² *textiles for* export 輸出向け布地.

texture, *n.* 織物; [布]地.

V *feel* the *texture* of one's garments その着物の地にさわってみる.

Q *coarse* (=*rough*) *texture* あらい地. ¶Her skin is a *dark velvety texture*. 彼女の皮膚は黒くてきめがなめらかだ. ¶*delicate texture* はだのきめがこまかい. ¶be of *fine texture* 目がつんでいる. ¶his *flimsy consumptive texture* 彼のひ弱なせん病質体格. ¶garments of a *lighter texture* 薄物の衣類. ¶cloth of *loose* (*close*) *texture* 目のあらい(つんだ)布地.

P fine *in texture* 織目の細かな.

thank, *v.* 感謝する.

M I do not know how I can *adequately thank* for ... ...は何ともお礼の申しようもございません. ¶*Thanks a lot*= Thank you very much. ☞ 米国では男性が Thanks a lot, 女性が Thank you [ever] (=Thanks) so much. という. ¶*thank* very *cordially* 厚く礼を述べる. ¶*thank earnestly* 真心から感謝する. ¶*thank gratefully* 有難く感謝する. ¶*heartily thank* 衷心から感謝する. ¶*thank* most *kindly* 誠にねんごろに感謝する. ¶*thank lightly* あっさり礼を言う. ¶*thank profusely*. 大いに礼を言う ¶I cannot *sufficiently thank* him for his interest and help. 親切に助力して下さったあの方に何とお礼を申上げたらいいでしょう. ¶*thank* you *very much* indeed for ... ...はほんとうに有難う. ¶He *thanked* me *volubly*. 彼は口をきわめて私に礼を言った. ¶*warmly thank* 深謝する.

P I *thanked* him *for* the gift. 私は彼に贈物の礼を言った. 【類】I *thank* you *for* the information. / Please *thank* him *for* the trouble taken. ‖ He *thanked* those present *for* coming. 彼は出席者に来会の礼を述べた. ‖ *Thank* you *for* the salt. 塩を取って下さい(食卓などで). ‖ *Thank* her *for* me. 僕に代って彼女に礼を言ってくれ. ‖ *Thank* you *for* nothing. 有難いが実は迷惑. ‖ I *thank* you *for* including me in this party. 私も御招待下さって有難う存じます.

thankful, *a.* 感謝して.

M *deeply thankful* for ... ...を深く感謝して. ¶*devoutly thankful* 衷心より感謝して.

P *thankful for* kindness (assistance) 好意(など)を感謝して ‖ be *thankful for* one's appreciation 知遇に感じる. ¶be *thankful to* a person *for* ... ...に対して人に感謝する. 【類】I am *thankful to* you *for* your favors.

O I shall be *thankful* if you will ... ...して下さるとありがたいんですが.

thankfulness, *n.* 感謝.

P *in thankfulness* for ... ...を感謝して.

thank-offering, *n.* お礼の印.

P as a *thank-offering for* ... ...のお礼の印として.

thanks, *n. pl.* 感謝.

V Please *accept* our *thanks* in advance for the favor of a reply. 御回答の御厚意に対してここにまずお礼を申上げておきます. ‖ pray *accept* my *thanks* for ... ...に対する私の感謝をお受け下さい. ¶We wish to publicly *acknowledge* our sincere *thanks* for the good work done. われわれはその功績に厚い感謝の意を表したい(警察などに対して). ¶*bow* one's *thanks* 頭を下げて謝意を表する ‖ The lady *bowed* him most profuse *thanks*. その貴婦人は彼にいかにも丁重に謝意を表した. ¶She *cabled* joyous *thanks* to the flower sender. 彼女は花を贈ってくれた人に深い感謝の電報を打った. ¶I wish to *convey* my special *thanks* to ... 私は...に特に謝意を表したい. ¶*deserve* the *thanks* of the whole nation 全国民から感謝されるに足りる. 【類】He *deserves* our *thanks* for ... ¶He *earned* the *thanks* of the country. 彼は国民から当然感謝された. ¶*express* one's *thanks* to a person for ... ...に対し人に謝意を表わす. 【類】I don't know how to *express* my *thanks*. ¶To one and all of you I *extend* my *thanks* for your loyalty, fidelity and co-operation. 忠義・忠節を尽し一致協力して働いてくれた諸君に対し私は漏れなく感謝の意を表する. 【類】I desire to ***extend*** our best *thanks* for ... ¶You will never ***get*** any *thanks* for trying to do such a thing. そんなことをしようとしたってだれが感謝なんかするものか. ¶***give*** *thanks* to God 神に感謝する. ¶***let*** *thanks* be given to ... ...に感謝しましょう. ¶***make*** one's *thanks* to ... ...に謝する. ¶***murmur*** *thanks* to God that ... 小声で...と神に感謝の言葉をささげる. ¶***offer*** one's *thanks* at a shrine 神社で感謝の祈とうを上げる. ¶I ***owe*** you *thanks*. 私は君にお礼を言わねばならない. ‖ we ***owe*** the sincerest *thanks* to you for having ... われわれは君が...したことを心から感謝せねばならない. ¶***present*** you my most cordial *thanks* 厚くお礼申上げる. ¶***receive*** *thanks* 感謝を受ける. ¶I should also like to ***record*** my sincere *thanks* to ... for the very hearty and hospitable reception accorded me. なお真に誠意ある御歓待に対し私が衷心から...に感謝しておりますことをここに記しておきたいと存じます. ¶***render*** *thanks* to ... ...に謝意を述べる. ¶***return*** one's *thanks* to ... for ... ...に対し...に礼を言う. 【類】***return*** *thanks* to God ‖ as a token of ***returning*** *thanks* for favors received 報恩の一端として. ¶***say*** *thanks* 礼をいう. ¶She ***smiled*** her *thanks*. 彼女は微笑をもって感謝の意を表した. ¶To my many helpers I ***tender*** my sincerest *thanks*. 私のために助力せられた多数の方々に私は心から感謝の意を表する. 【類】The Commander-in-Chief ***tendered*** his and his fleet's *thanks* for the friendly reception given them. / The Editor ***tenders*** his best *thanks* to those who have co-operated (協力した) with him in the laborious undertaking. ¶***wave*** one's *thanks* with a handkerchief ハンカチを振って感謝の意を表する. ¶He ***wept*** the *thanks* he could not speak. 彼は口で言い表わせない感謝の意を涙で示した.

V² my *thanks* ***go*** to ... 私は...に感謝する.

Q I had nothing to give him in return but ***barren*** *thanks*. 私がお礼として彼にささげうるものはただ感謝の言葉あるのみである. ¶our ***best*** *thanks* are due to ... for ... 私たちは...に...を手厚くお礼を申述べなければならない. ¶deserve more than ***common*** *thanks* for ... 一方ならない感謝を受けるに足りる. ¶for ... our ***cordial*** *thanks* are due to ... ...に対しわれわれの心からの感謝を表します. ¶return my ***cordial*** and ***sincere*** *thanks* ... ...に厚く衷心からお礼を述べる. ¶Let me give you my ***earnest*** *thanks*. 衷心より感謝致します. ¶***graceful*** and ***unending*** *thanks* 限りない深謝. ¶I owe him ***grateful*** *thanks*. 私はあの人に大いに感謝しなければならない. 【類】to all of whom we extend our ***grateful*** *thanks*. ¶tender one's ***heartfelt*** *thanks* to the Almighty for all the love and kindness すべての愛と好意に対し神に心からの感謝をささげる. ¶extend my ***hearty*** *thanks* to ... ...に心から感謝する. ¶return ***many*** *thanks* for ... ...を多謝する. ¶owe ***much*** *thanks* to one for ... 人に対し...に多大の感謝をしなければならない. ¶acknowledge with ***profound*** *thanks* 深じんなる感謝の意をもってあいさつする. ¶my ***sincere*** *thanks* are due to him for ... 私は...に対し彼に衷心より感謝せねばならない. ¶A ***thousand*** *thanks* for your kindness. あなたの御親切に対し深謝致します. ¶offer you my very ***warm*** and ***cordial*** *thanks* for ... ...に対し心から深謝する. ¶one's ***warmest*** *thanks* その最も深い感謝. ¶***willing*** and ***hearty*** *thanks* 進んで衷心から述べる謝意.

P ***in*** *thanks* for ... ...のお礼に. ¶receive ***with*** *thanks* 有難く頂だいする ‖ decline ***with*** *thanks* 深謝して辞退する.

P² *thanks* ***to*** the eloquence which is their birthright 生来能弁であるため ‖ *thanks* largely ***to*** Irish influence 主としてアイルランドの影響で ‖ *thanks* ***to*** your patronage おかげ様で(商人が得意に対して). 【類】*thanks* ***to*** the assistance of the Benevolent Society (慈善協会).

thanksgiving, *n.* 感謝; 《米》[T-] 感謝祭.

P a votive offering ***in*** *thanksgiving* for ... ...のお礼のための奉納物. ¶***on*** *Thanksgiving* [Day] 感謝祭に.

that, *pron.* それ.

V ***Get*** *that?* 分かりましたか. ☞ Get it (=the idea)? ともいう.

V² *That* will ***do***. それでよろしい.

P He was a story-teller and a clever one ***at*** *that*. 彼はよく話をして聞かせたがしかもそれがじょうずだった. 【類】He is very young ***at*** *that*. / The tea was too high-priced and not a very good tea ***at*** *that*. ¶I'm not cut out ***for*** *that*. 僕はそんな風にできていない. ‖ This news is strange, but it is true ***for*** all *that*. このニュースは変だ, だが事実だ. ¶A differs from B ***in*** *that* the former is ..., while the latter is ... AはBと異っている, というのは前者は...であるが後者は...だ. 【類】He speaks poor Japanese ***in*** *that* he is foreign-born. ¶***instead of*** *that* それどころか. ¶I'm with you ***on*** *that*. その点君に賛成だ. ¶***with*** *that* そこで.

thatched, *a.* 《口語》頭髪が...な.

M the ***thinly*** *thatched* 頭髪の薄い人々.

thaw, *n.* 雪解けの陽気.

V We shall ***have*** a *thaw*. [陽気がゆるんで]雪解けがするだろう. ¶A *thaw* has ***set in***. 春暖になって雪解けして来た.

Q ***silver*** *thaw* 樹氷.

Q² ***spring*** *thaw* 春の雪解け.

theater, theatre, *n.* 劇場; 舞台.

V It ***constitutes*** the *theater* of his activities (=basis of his operations). それが彼の作戦根拠地である. ¶***enter*** a *theater* 劇場にはいる. ¶when the *theaters* are ***emptying*** 劇場がはねて観客が出場するとき. ¶***operate*** two movie *theaters* 二つの映画館を経営する. ¶***run*** a *theater* 芝居を打つ. ¶the main *theater* of activity has now been ***shifted*** from ... to ... 活動の本舞台は今や...から...に移動した.

Q ***cheap*** *theaters* 入場料の安い劇場. ¶***commercial*** *theaters* (amateur theater に対して)一般の劇場. ¶The *theater* is ***dark*** on Monday night. その劇場は月曜は休みだ. ¶imposingly ***designed*** and ornately ***appointed*** *theaters* 建築が堂々としていて設備の豪華な劇場. ¶a "***legitimate***" *theater* [映画劇場に対して]普通の劇場. ¶a ***little*** *theater* 小劇場. ¶on the ***main*** *theater* of war 主戦場で. ¶a ***marionette*** *theater* 人形劇場. ¶an ***operating*** *theater* 手術室. ¶the ***Pacific*** (***European***) *theater* of war 太平洋(欧州)戦場. ¶***palatial*** *theaters* 豪壮な劇場. ¶***popular-priced*** *theaters* 入場料の大衆向の劇場. ¶a ***public*** *theater* 公衆劇場. ¶the so-called "***regular***" *theater* [映画劇場に対して]いわゆる正劇場.

Q² American servicemen who have served in the ***China*** *theater* 中国の戦場に出征した米国軍人. ¶a popular variety and ***cinematograph*** *theater* 一般向きの諸芸と映画併演の劇場. ¶***combat*** *theaters* 戦争の舞台. ¶a ***drive-in*** *theater* 乗込み映画館(自動車に乗ったまま見られる戸外映画館). ¶be back from the ***fighting*** *theaters* 戦場から帰還している. ¶a ***first-run*** *theater* 封切館. ¶the ***future*** *theater* of world's commerce 世界通商の将来の舞台. ¶a ***lecture*** *theater* 階段講堂. ¶a ***movie*** (=***picture***) *theater* 映画劇場. ¶a ***news reel*** *theater* ニュース劇場. ¶an ***open-air*** *theater* 戸外劇場. ¶an "***ozone*** *theater*"=a drive-in *theater* 《米俗》戸外映画館(車に乗ったままで見るもの). ¶a ***patent*** *theater* 《英》勅許劇場. ¶a ***repertory*** *theater* [座付の劇団をもち狂言をさしかえて上演する]レパトリ劇場. ¶a ***strip***[***-tease***] ***show*** *theater* ストリップ・ショウ劇場. ¶a ***variety show*** *theater* 寄席(よせ). ¶a ***vaudeville*** *theater* 寄席. ¶withdraw troops from ... to reinforce other ***war*** *theaters* 他の戦場に増援するため...から軍隊を撤退する. ¶a ***West-End*** *theater* ロンドンの西部地区の劇場.

P It was acted ***at*** the Kabuki *Theater*. それは歌舞伎座で上演された. ‖ the ticket office ***at*** a *theater* 劇場の切符売場 ‖ an audience ***at*** a *theater* 劇場の観衆. ¶seek amusement ***in*** the *theater* 楽しみを芝居に求める. ¶I have never been ***inside*** a *theater*. 私はまだ劇場へはいったことがない. ¶go ***to*** the *theater* 劇場に行く.

P² his *theater* ***of*** command その司令下の地域 ‖ a *theater* ***of*** war 戦場 ‖ the *theater* ***of*** controversy and struggle 論争場裡(り).

theatrical, *n. pl.* しろうと芝居.

V ***give*** *theatricals* しろうと芝居をやる.

Q ***amateur*** (=private) *theatricals* 素人芝居.

theft, *n.* 窃盗.

V ***commit*** a *theft* 窃盗を働く. ¶to ***conceal*** one's *theft* ...の窃盗行為を隠匿するために.

Q a ***daring*** *theft* of a lady's purse-bag 婦人の財布を奪う大胆な窃盗. ¶***heinous*** *theft* 凶悪な窃盗. ¶***light*** *theft* ちょっとした窃盗. ¶a petty ***tiny*** *theft* こそこそ泥棒.

Q² an ***auto*** *theft* 自動車泥棒. ¶a ***bicycle*** *theft* 自転車泥棒. ¶a ***large-scale*** *theft* 大規模の窃盗. ¶a ***mail*** *theft* 郵便物泥棒.

P on a charge ***of*** *theft* 窃盗罪で. ¶charged ***with*** *theft* 窃盗罪を負わせられて.

P² the *thefts* ***from*** the Beaux-Arts Library in Paris パリーの美術図書館から盗み出した品 ‖ *theft* ***from*** an actress 女優の盗難.

theme, *n.* 題目；主題(テーマ)；《米》作文.

V My *theme* might be ***expanded*** to a volume. 私の論題は詳述すると一巻の書物にもなる. ¶It ***furnishes*** a good *theme* for a moving picture. それは映画の良い題材になる. ¶I admire the skill with which he has ***handled*** a delicate *theme*. 私は取扱いにくい題目を器用にこなした彼の手腕に感服する. ¶*Themes* two minutes late are not to be ***received*** whatever the accompanying excuse. いかなる理由ありとも二分後には作文は受取らない. ¶***select*** life *theme* 終生の研究題目を選ぶ. ¶*Themes* are to be ***sent in*** at eleven-thirty or earlier. 作文は十一時までに提出のこと. ¶the *themes* ***set*** on students in the examination just past 今度の試験で学生に出した問題.

Q an ***all-absorbing*** *theme* 一切を包括する題目. ¶an ***attractive*** *theme* おもしろい題目. ¶a ***comic*** *theme* こっけいな題目. ¶the ***constant*** *theme* of painters and sculptors 画家や彫刻家の常用題材. ¶a ***delectable*** *theme* おもしろい題目. ¶the ***dominant*** *theme* of the book その書物の主題. ¶The power of human kindness has ever been a ***favorite*** *theme* with the moralist. 人間の親切の力は古来道徳家が好んで論題とする所のものである. ¶***hackneyed*** *themes* 陳腐な題目. ¶these ***high*** *themes* これらの高級な題目. ¶be welcomed as ***inspiring*** *themes* fit for the artist's brush 画家が描くにふさわしい感激的な題目として喜ばれている. ¶***interesting*** *themes* 興味ある題目. ¶the ***main*** *theme* of discussion 議論の主題. ¶an ***oft-repeated*** *theme* 度々取扱われた題目. ¶Patriotism is the ***speaker's*** *theme*. その演説のテーマは愛国心である. ¶a ***threadbare*** *theme* 陳腐な論題 ¶a ***timely*** *theme* 時宜に適した題目. ¶a ***trifling*** *theme* つまらない題. ¶an ***uplifting*** *theme* 高尚な題目.

Q² a ***college*** *theme* 大学の課題作文. ¶an ***examination*** *theme* 試験の題目. ¶select a ***life*** *theme* 一生研究の題目を選ぶ. ¶a popular essayist on ***nature*** *themes* 自然を題目にした人気のある随筆家. ¶a ***student*** *theme* 学生の作文. ¶films with ***war*** *themes* 戦争をテーマにした諸映画.

P I had to write an essay ***on*** the *theme* of ... 私は…という題で論文を書かなければならなかった. ¶a profit *theme* ***upon*** which to converse にぎやかに座談のできる話題.

P² a fruitful *theme* ***for*** discussion 議論の容易に尽きない論題 ‖ a *theme* ***for*** the New Year's Poetry Party at Court 新年お歌会の勅題. ¶a favorite *theme* ***in*** poetry and art 詩や芸術でよく扱われるテーマ. ¶it has been the *theme* ***of*** more than one poem それは幾つかの詩のテーマとなった. 【類】The "expulsion of the outside barbarians" 攘夷(じょうい) was the favorite *theme* ***of*** ambitious patriots. ¶The Christmas bells have been a favorite *theme* ***with*** poets, great and small. クリスマスの鐘声は大小詩人が従来好んで扱った題材である.

then, *n.* 当時.

P I shall not start ***before then***. 私はその時までは出発しない. ¶if it is not finished ***by then*** それまでに終了しなければ. ¶***from then*** on=thence onward それ以来. ¶***since then*** それ以来. ¶[***up***] ***till then*** それまで. ¶Then, but not ***till then*** should you come. そのときになってから来なさい.

then, *ad.* その時；それから.

M ***even then*** それにしても. ¶***just then*** そこへ. ¶and *then* ***only*** ... そうしてこそはじめて.

theology, *n.* 神学.

Q ***scientific*** *theology* 科学的神学.

theorist, *n.* 理論家.

Q a ***hair-splitting*** *theorist* 徴細の区別を立てる理論家. ¶an ***impractical*** (=***unpractical***) *theorist*=a doctrinaire

Q² an ***arm-chair*** *theorist* 机上の理論家. ⌊空論家.

theorize, *v.* 理論づける.

P *theorize* ***on*** the matter of ... …の問題について説を立て ⌊る.

theory, *n.* 学理；説.

V those who ***accept*** this *theory* この学説を信じる人々. ¶he was long vacillated, irresolute what *theory* to ***adopt*** for ... …に対してどういう説を採用すべきかについて彼は長い間迷って決定し兼ねていた. ¶***advance*** a new *theory* concerning ... …について新しい説を立てる. ¶It is contrary to the true scientific spirit to ***advocate*** *theories* about matters of which we are profoundly ignorant. われわれが皆目知らないことについて説を立てるということは真の科学の精神に反する. ¶***apply*** an abstruse *theory* to the most ordinary uses 深遠な学理をきわめて普通の場合に応用する. ¶***bear out*** (=***confirm***) a *theory* 説を確証する. ¶***build up*** (=***erect***) a *theory* that ... …という説を立てる ‖ comfort each other, ***building up*** *theories* of hope 希望をつなぎうるような理屈を考えてお互に慰め合う. ¶***construct*** general *theories* 一般的な説を立てる. ¶***construe*** a *theory* that ... …という説を立てる. ¶***develop*** the (=a) *thoery* that ... …という説を立てる. ¶***discredit*** the *theory* その学理に信をおかぬ. ¶this *theory* is ***disproved*** by ... この説は…によって打破されている. ¶***enunciate*** a *theory* 説を立てる. ¶***establish*** a *theory* beyond doubt 一説を確立させる. ¶***evolve*** another *theory* 異説を出す. ¶***exclude*** accepted *theories* 一般に受入られた説を斥ける. ¶***explode*** a *theory* 理論を打破する. 【類】the *theory*, now happily ***exploded***, of ... ¶Regarding the formation of petroleum, many speculative *theories* have been ***expounded***. 石油の発生については こうもあろうかという色々なおく説が立てられた. ¶***form*** (=***formulate***) a *theory* 学説を立てる. ¶***found*** a *theory* on the ideas その思想を基礎にして説を立てる. ¶he ***has*** his own *theory* regarding ... 彼は…に関して独自の説を持っている ‖ In this connection psycho-analysis ***has*** four *theories* to advance. このことに関して精神分析家は四つの説を立てている. ¶those who ***hold*** this *theory* この説を支持する人々. ¶***hold up*** the *theory* of ... to ridicule この説を冷笑する. ¶***make*** the *theory* more ***plausible*** その説を一層もっともらしくする. ¶he has been ***nursing*** the *theory* that ... 彼は…という説をいだいてきた. ¶Wallace ***opposed*** Darwin's *theory* of natural selection. ウォレスはダーウィンの自然とうた説に反対した. ¶Sensible fathers allow their sons to ***outgrow*** their youthful *theories* in the school of life. 賢明な父たちはそのむすこたちが人生の道場に出てから青年として立てた説が幼稚なものだと考え直すようにさせる. ¶***overthrow*** a *theory* 説をくつがえす. ¶***place*** (=***put***) a *theory* on a solid historical foundation 学説を確固たる歴史的根拠の上に立たせる. ¶Several *theories* have been ***postulated*** in regard to the origin of speech. 言語の起源に関するおく説は数種ある. ¶***promulgate*** the *theory* that ... …なる学説を発表する. ¶He was careful to ***propound*** his *theory* as a hypothesis. 彼は慎重な態度を取りその説を仮定説として世に問うた. ‖ seriously ***propound*** the *theory* that ... 真剣に…という説を立てる. ¶***publish*** (=***ventilate***) *theories* 学説を発表する. ¶***put*** one's *theories* into practice 理論を実行する. ¶***put forward*** an interesting *theory* 興味ある説を唱える. ¶***reconcile*** *theory* and practicalities 理論と実際とを一致させる. ¶***reduce*** one's *theory* to practice 理論を実行する. ¶***refute*** the *theory* that ... …という説を論破する. ¶He ***set up*** a new *theory* of consumption. 彼は肺病について新説を立てた. ¶***strengthen*** the *theory* that ... …という説を有力にさせる. ¶***submit*** one's *theory* to the consideration of the scientific world その学説を発表して科学界に問う. ¶tentatively ***suggest*** a *theory* こころみに一説を唱える. ¶***support*** the *theory* that ... …という説を支持する ‖ The *theory* is ***supported*** by negative evidence only. その説は消極的な証拠だけで支持されている. ¶***upset*** one's *theory* about ... …に関するその説をくつがえす. ¶***use*** *theories* as a guide to experiments 実験の参考として学説を利用する. ¶***verify*** the *theories* 説を確証する.

V² It is doubtful if the *theory* will ***hold***. その説が維持されるかどうか疑わしい.

Q ***abstract*** *theory* 抽象的な理論. ¶the ***accepted*** *theory* as to the cause of the murder is that ... その殺人の原因について一般の説は…である. ¶an ***atavistic*** *theory* 隔世遺伝説. ¶a ***belated*** and ***exploded*** *theory* 陳腐で支持者のない説. ¶a ***crude*** *theory* 浅薄な理論. ¶use the novel as a vehicle for ***didactic*** *theories* on social, moral, and aesthetic subjects 社会・道徳及び美の問題を説明する理論を説く道具としてその小説を利用する. ¶Egotism is the ***ethical*** *theory* that self-interest is the basis of morality. 自己中心主義は私利が道徳の根底だという倫理学説だ. ¶***hidebound*** *theories* 偏狭な説. ¶a ***high-flown*** *theory* 誇大な説. ¶advance a very ***ingenious*** *theory* 非常に賢明な説を出す. ¶the ***Malthusian*** *theory* マルサス人口説. ¶a ***Marxian*** *theory* マルクス流の理論. ¶a ***measly, little, impossible*** *theory* つまらない取るに足らぬばか気た説. ¶set up a ***new*** *theory* of disease 病気に関して新説を出す ‖ a ***new-fangled*** *theory* せん端的学説. ¶The researches of these scholars have shown that the *old theory* is untenable. これらの学者の研究によれば旧学説の支持は不可能である. ¶*one theory* is that ... 一説では...である. ¶an *orthodox theory* 正統派の学理. ¶enlightened *penal theories* 進歩した諸刑法理論. ¶one's *pet theory* その得意の学理. ¶a *plausible theory* もっともらしい説. ¶insufficiently *pondered theories* 浅慮の説. ¶a *pure theory* 全くの仮説. ¶one's *social theories* その社会理論. ¶advance a *strange theory* 奇説を吐く. ¶a *tenable theory* 支持しうる学説. ¶an *undecided theory* 未決定の理論. ¶The *theory* is *untenable* その理論は立たない. 【類】The *theory* is not absolutely *untenable*, but the evidence advanced in its favor is very far from convincing. ¶This *theory* is wholly *unworkable*. この理論は全然実用的でない. ¶a *well-knit theory* しっかりした説. ¶a *whimsical theory* 気まぐれな説. ¶*wild theories* of visionaries 空想家の突飛な説.

Q² the *bow-wow theory* 声音模倣説(言語の発生に関する). ¶the *ding-dong theory* 言語自然発生説. ¶the *germ theory* of diseases 病気の細菌病原説. ¶the *Hitler theory* of German race superiority ヒットラーのドイツ民族優越説. ¶applying the *ill-wind-blowing-as-good theory* 甲の損は乙の得の理論を応用して. ¶the "*people's sovereignty*" (the "*Emperor's Sovereignty*") *theory* 人民主権(天皇主権)説. ¶according to the *socialist theory* 社会主義理論に従えば. ¶the *wave theory* of light 光の波動説.

P He is a Jumbo *at theory*, but weak in practice. 彼は説く所はすばらしいが実行力が欠けている. ¶*from theory* through method to practice 理論から方法をたどって実行へ. ¶It is not so easy in practice as *in theory*. それは実行してみると理論で考えたほど容易でない. ‖ It sounds right *in theory* 理論としては正しいようだ. 【類】It is very well *in theory*, but will it work? ¶*on* a new *theory* 新説によって ‖ *on* the *theory* that "what cannot be cured must be endured"「なおらないものは我慢しなければならない」というような訳で. ¶*upon* the *theory* that ... ...という説に基いて.

P² there are other *theories as to* ... ...については他の学説がある. ¶the Mendelian *theory of* heredity メンデルの遺伝説 ‖ his *theory of* life 彼の人生観. 【類】the *theory of* evolution (gravitation).

thermometer, *n.* 寒暖計, 温度計.

V² The *thermometer* rarely *drops* below 5° F. 寒暖計が華氏五度以下に下ることは滅多にない. ¶The *thermometer falls* to 5° or 6° below zero. 寒暖計が零下五度から六度に下がる. ¶*Thermometers* often *go* below zero. しばしば寒暖計が零度以下になる. ¶The *thermometer* often *marks* 120° Fahr. in the shade. しばしば寒暖計は日かげで華氏百二十度に上る. ¶the *thermometer ranges* between ... and ... 寒暖計は...度から...度の間を上下する. ¶The *thermometer registers* (=*reads, indicates or stands at*) 75 deg. in the shade. 寒暖計は日かげで七十五度を示す. ¶The *thermometer* rarely *rises* above 90°F. 寒暖計は滅多に華氏九十度以上には上らない. ¶The *thermometer runs* into the 90's. 寒暖計が九十度台に上る. ¶The *thermometer sank* very rapidly. 寒暖計がどんどん下がった.

Q a *clinial thermometer* 体温計 ¶a *maximum thermometer* 最高温度計.

Q² an *axilla thermometer* 検温器. ¶an *air thermometer* 用気寒暖計. ¶a *centigrade thermometer* 摂氏寒暖計.

P ... degrees *by* the Fahrenheit *thermometer* 華氏の...度. ¶The mercury *in* Singapore *thermometers* moves between 80 degrees and 84 degrees during the year. シンガポールでは寒暖計は年中八十度から八十四度である. ¶the lowest reading *of* the *thermometer* 寒暖計の最低示度.

thesis, *n.* 論文.

V *submit* a *thesis* 論文を提出する.

Q a *doctoral* (=*doctor's*) *thesis* 学位論文. 【類】write one's *doctor's thesis* on the subject of ... ¶But to return to our *fundamental thesis*. しかしわれわれの本論題に戻ることにする(岐路にはいったが). ¶a *Haxleyan thesis* ハックスレー一派の説.

Q² a *graduation thesis* 卒業論文.

P² a *thesis for* the doctorate (degree of Doctor of Philosophy) 博士(など)の学位論文. ¶a *thesis on* a subject ある問題に関する論文.

thick, *n.* 最も盛んなときまたは所.

P *in* the *thick* of a fight (=struggle) 戦闘(など)の最も激しい時に ‖ He is now *in* the *thick* of organizing a new scheme. 彼は昨今新計画立案に没頭している. ‖ *in* the *thick* of the forest 林の最も茂った所に. ¶He stuck to me *through thick* and thin. 彼は私が順境に立ったときも逆境に立ったときも私に忠実であった.

thick, *a.* 厚い.

M a *foot thick* 厚さ一フート ‖ *How thick* is it? その太(厚)さはどの位ですか. ¶They are *very thick*. 《俗》彼らは大の仲好しだ.

P *thick as* a cried fair 市のようににぎやか. ¶*thick of* hearing 耳が遠い. ¶*thick with* flowers (foliage, weeds) 花が一杯に着いた(など) ‖ The path was *thick with* dangers. その道は危険が多かった. ‖ The weather is *thick with* rain 雨が降って天気がはっきりしない.

O It is snowing *thick* and fast. 雪がどんどん降っている.

thicken, *v.* 濃くする.

M The weather is *quickly thickening*. 空が急に曇ってきた.

P *thicken by* boiling 煮詰めて濃くする.

thickness, *n.* 厚さ.

V *attain* a *thickness* of ... ...の厚さになる.

Q of *different thickness* 厚さの違った. ¶of *moderate thickness* 適当な厚さの. ¶a coal seam of *small thickness* 薄い炭層.

P ... inches *in thickness* (=thick) 厚さ...インチ. ¶coal seams *of* less *thickness* than four or five feet 四五フィート以下の薄い炭層. ¶*to* a *thickness* of two feet 二フィートの厚さに.

thief, *n.* 盗賊.

V *arrest* a *thief* 盗賊を逮捕する. ¶*catch* a *thief* 盗人を捕える. ¶a policeman *chasing* a *thief* 盗賊を追う巡査. ¶Opportunity *makes* the *thief*. 機会が与えられるので盗賊ができる. ¶The policeman has succeeded in *securing* the *thief*. 警察は首尾よくその賊を捕縛した. ¶*Stop thief!* 泥棒泥棒! ¶*take up* a *thief* 盗人を捕える. ¶*trace* a *thief* 盗賊の行方を探る. ¶The *thief* is *wanted* by the police. その賊は警察が手を回している.

V² The *thief got* (=*broke*) into the house. 賊はその家へ押入った. ¶The *thief gave* himself *up* to the police. 賊は警察に自首した.

Q a *born* (=*natural*) *thief* 生れついての泥棒. ¶a *downright thief* 正銘の泥棒. ¶a *petty thief* こそ泥.

Q² an *apple thief* りんご泥棒. ¶a *cow* (*horse*) *thief* 牛(馬)泥棒. ¶an *all-out home thief* 空巣ねらい. ¶a *sneak thief* こそ泥.

P Someone informed *against* the *thief*. だれかがその賊を密告した. ¶Beware *of thieves*=Be on your guard *against thieves!* 泥棒に御用心! ¶fall *among thieves* 泥棒仲間の手に掛かる.

P² a *thief on* the highroad=a highwayman 追はぎ.

thievery, *n.* 盗み.

Q *horse thievery* 馬盗み.

thigh, *n.* 太もも.

V *dislocate* a *thigh* 腰の骨を違える. ¶*pierce* one's *thigh* with an awl. きりでももを刺す.

P trickle *down thighs* in thick drops ぽとぽとと太ももをしたたり落ちる.

thimble, *n.* 指ぬき.

V *put* a *thimble* on one's finger 指ぬきをはめる. ¶*wear* a *thimble* when to use a needle 針仕事には指ぬきをはめる.

thin, *a.* 薄い; やせた.

M She used to be *very thin*. 彼女はもとは非常にやせていた.

O as *thin* as a lath 非常にやせて.

thin, *v.* まばらにする.

M I wish these lilies *thinned out*. このゆりをおろ抜(間引)きたいもんだが. ‖ *thin out* the coal dust to below the explosive point 破裂点以下まで石炭粉を希薄にする.

thing, *n.* 物, 事; 生きもの; 人.

V if we *analyze things* a little more deeply もう少し突込んで物を考えて見れば. ¶How does that *arrange things?* そうしたらどういうことになるだろう. ¶*attempt* new *things* in journalism 新聞事業において新しい試みをする. ¶*buy* American *things* 米国品を買う. ¶He scorns to *call things* by other than their real names. 彼は是を是とし非を非とする流儀だ. ¶The samurai of those days *carried things* with a high hand, acting on the principle that might is right. その時代の武士は力すなわち権利主義で何でも高飛車に出たものである. ¶*Carry up* my *things*. 私の

荷物を上へ持ってきてくれ(召使などに). ¶***clear*** breakfast ***things*** from the table 朝飯が済んだ食卓の後片付をする ‖ all *things* ***considered*** 大体から言って. ¶***cut things*** a little too fine [抜き差しのできないように]余りことを決め過ぎる. ¶the way they ***do things*** in Germany ドイツ流 ‖ He has ***done*** great *things* for his country. 彼は国家のために偉功があった. ‖ ***do things backward*** 物事を逆にやる ‖ I can't ***do*** a *thing* with ... ...は私の手におえない. ‖ He can ***do things a little better*** than most men. 彼はちょっと並以上に物ができる. 【類】 The Germans are noted for ***doing things*** methodically. ‖ I won't ***do*** a *thing* to you. 今に覚えていろ(しかえしをしてやるから). ¶I have hardly had time to ***embark*** my *things* yet. 自分の物を積込む時間がほとんどなかった. ¶***enjoy*** the good *things* of earth 現世の幸福を享有する. ¶Doesn't that ***even things up***? それでとんとんになるじゃないか. ¶How did you ***find things*** in America? アメリカはどうでした. ¶I think that will ***fix things***. それできまりが付くと私は思う. ¶manage to ***get things straight*** どうにか始末をつける. ¶***give*** the *thing* ***up*** in disgust いやになってそれをやめてしまう. ¶A farmer ***grows*** *things* to eat 百姓は食う物を作る. ¶he ***has*** many evil *things* to say against ... 彼は...のことを色々悪口をいう ‖ occasionally ***have things*** too much their own way 時々余り勝手にやり過ぎる. ¶I can't ***hear*** a *thing*. 私にはちっとも聞えない. ¶***help things forward*** considerably 著しく事態推進に役立つ. ¶***hush*** the *thing* ***up*** それを不問に付す(もみ消す). ¶I have still a little money left to ***keep things going*** till next payday. 次の給料日までやって行けるだけのわずかの金が私の手もとに残っている. ‖ A woman can't ***keep*** a *thing* to herself. 女は物事を自分の胸に仕舞っておくことができない. ‖ ***keep*** three *things* in view 三つのことを念頭におく. ¶You don't ***know*** a *thing* about riding. 君は乗馬のことは一向知っていない. ‖ I ***know*** a *thing* or two about ... 私は...のことはいくらか知っている. ¶He has been abroad and has ***learned*** a *thing* or two. あれは洋行していくらか物を覚えてきた. ¶***leave things alone*** (=***undone***) 放っておく ‖ ***leave*** a *thing* ***behind*** 忘れものをする. ¶***let things drift*** and ***wait*** for something to turn up 放っておいて成行を待つ. ¶***license*** a *thing* to be done 事を行う許可を与える. ¶***lock things up*** for safety 物をかぎのかかる所に入れておく. ¶***love*** the *things* of this world 現世の事物を愛する. ¶***make*** a good *thing* out of it それでうまい汁を吸う. 【類】 He ***made*** a good *thing* of the transaction. ‖ He fancied that he would ***make*** a good *thing* by the purchase. 彼はもうかる積りで買入れた. ¶That doesn't ***mean*** a *thing* to me. そんなことは何も私には関係がない. ¶That is the one *thing* ***needed***. それが何より必要なことだ. ¶the Divine Hand which " calmly and wisely ***orders*** all *things* " 万事心静かに賢明に取なし給う神の御手. ¶***palm*** a *thing* [***off***] on a person 物を人に押し付ける. ¶***poetize*** common *things* 平凡なことを詩化する. ¶do not ***possess*** such a *thing* as a dress coat えん尾服のようなものは持っていない. ¶***put things*** where they belong 物をおくべき場所におく. ¶***put*** the *thing* ***across*** その能率をあげる. ‖ He will have no difficulty in ***putting*** the *thing* ***through***. 彼はそれを遂行する上に少しの困難も感じはすまい. ¶***reason things out*** 物の理屈を考える. ¶***redeem*** the *things* pawned 質物を受出す. ¶***relate*** good *things* おもしろい話をする. ¶***revolutionize*** *things* 事物を根本的に変革する. ¶He ***says*** such sharp *things* about people. あの人は大の悪口屋だ. ‖ ***say*** one *thing* and mean another 口と心と違う ‖ ***say things*** that sound big えらそうなことを言う. ¶He ***sees things*** through the temperament of an artist. 彼は芸術家の立場から物を見る. 【類】 Foreign peoples ***see things*** differently from ourselves. ‖ ***see things*** as they are 物事を有りのままに看取する. 【類】 When one is young, it is always difficult to ***see things*** in their true proportions. / But he could not ***see things*** in this light. ¶The department store ***sells*** every conceivable (=[colloq.] mortal) *thing*. 百貨店は何から何まで売っている. ¶***set things*** to rights (=in order) いいように片を付ける. ¶*things* will be ***simplified*** if ... ...すればことが簡単になる. ¶I will ***smooth things*** for you. 私がいいようにお取計らいします. ¶I wouldn't ***speak*** to a *thing* like that! あんなやつに口をきくもんか. ¶***square things*** with China 中国の不正義を改めさせる. ¶***straighten things out*** 矯正する. ¶***take things*** as they are 物事をありのままに受入れる ‖ ***taking*** one *thing* with another 概して ‖ ***take*** a *thing* to the pawnbroker's to pledge it 物を質に入れに持って行く ‖ ***take things*** as they come 成行にまかせる. ¶***take away things*** 食事の後片付をする. ¶***take things easy*** 物事をのんきに考える. ¶***talk things*** over with ... ...と話し合う. ¶***think things out*** 物を考え抜く. ¶***treat*** serious *things* lightly まじめなことを軽々しく取扱う. ¶***waste things*** 物を粗末にする. ¶They had to ***work things out*** for themselves. 彼らは人の力を借りずにやらなければならなかった. ¶***undertake*** great *things* 大事を企てる. ¶***utter*** ungrateful *things* about ... ...の悪口を言う. ¶***wear*** the latest *thing* in shoes 最新流行型のくつをはく.

v² A sad *thing* ***befell*** [to] him. 悲惨な事件が彼に起った. ¶*Things* were ***beginning*** to look very serious. 形勢が不穏になりだしていた. ¶*Things* are ***getting hard*** on (=with) us. 世の中がだんだん住みにくくなる. ¶as *things* ***go*** 現状では ‖ when *things* ***go*** wrong 形勢が悪化すると. ¶How are *thing* ***going***? 景気はどうだい. 【類】 I hope *things* are ***going well*** with you. / *Things* did not always ***go*** according to his wish. / go there to see how *things* are ***going*** / *Things* did not ***go*** to his thorough liking. ¶regularly report to him how *things* are ***going on*** 経過をきちんきちん彼に報告する ‖ *Things* cannot ***go on*** in this way. もうこうしてはおけない. ¶*Things* ***look black***. 前途は暗たんたるものである. ¶No matter how ***hopeless*** *things* ***look***, there is always a way out, if you look for it hard enough.—De Forest. いかに絶望状態でも 求めてやまなければ必ず打開策は見つかるものだ. ¶*Things* ***look promising***. 形勢は有望である. ¶Well, I hope *things* will ***look up*** with you pretty soon. まあ, 君もじきに回り合わせがよくなるだろう. ¶perceiving that *things* would not ***mend*** (=improve) by his staying 長居は無用と. ¶*Things* ***moved*** slowly in those days. その時分は何事ものんびりしていた. ‖ *Things* ***moved*** quickly. ことが早く運んだ. ¶as *things* now ***stand*** 現状では ‖ state just how *things* ***stand*** 実情そのものを述べる. ¶It is difficult to say how *things* will ***turn out***. 見通しがつかない.

Q hold it to be an ***abhorrent*** *thing* それをきらうべきこととする. ¶an ***accursed*** *thing* 憎むべきこと. ¶One feels as if one is (=were) looking at ***actual*** *things* themselves. だれでも実物を眼前に見ているような感じがする. ¶There is moderation in ***all*** *things*. 物にはほどがある ‖ ***All*** *things* considered どう見ても, 全く. ¶He has ***amusing*** *things* to say. 彼はおもしろいことを言う. ¶The ***annoying*** *thing* is that ... うるさいことは... ¶New York City is always the center of *things* ***artistic***. 美術品ではニューヨーク市はいつも中心になっている. ¶do ***bad*** *things* 悪いことをする. 【類】 it is no ***bad*** *thing* to know something about ... ¶Young girls are ***bashful*** *things*. 若い娘ははずかしがり屋だ. ¶a ***basic*** *thing* in human nature 人間性の一つの根本. ¶the most ***beautiful*** *thing* about ... ...の一番良いところは. ¶That's the ***best*** *thing* to do. そうするに越したことはない. 【類】 The ***best*** *thing* of the kind that we have ever seen. ¶the ***biggest*** *thing* in the world 世界最大のもの. ¶The ***best*** and ***freshest*** *thing* of the kind yet published. 今まで発表された中で最もよく最も清新なもの. ¶It is a ***bitter hard*** *thing* to part thus. こんな風に別れるのはつらい. ¶***bright young things*** from the univesities 大学出のうら若い女たち. ¶***cheap*** and ***showy*** *things* 安くて見ばえのする品々. ¶It's likely to be a ***close*** *thing*. きわどいことになりそうだ. ¶it is not a ***common*** *thing* for him to ... ...は彼として珍しいことだ ‖ do ***common*** *things* uncommonly well 平凡な道を非凡に歩め. ¶a ***commonplace*** *thing* 平凡なこと. ¶It is not the ***correct*** *thing* for a student to do. 学生がそういうことをやってはいけない. ¶The houses along the coast were ***crazy old*** *things*. 海岸沿いの家は今にも倒れそうな古い家だった. ¶all ***created*** *things* この世のあらゆる物. ¶do a ***crooked*** *thing* 曲ったことをする. ¶That is a ***cruel*** *thing* to say. そんなことを言うのはひどい. ¶say ***cutting*** *things* ひどいことを言う. ¶He decided that it was a ***dangerous*** *thing* to do. 彼はそうするのは危険だと思った. ¶Well, who started the ***darned*** *thing*, anyway? 一体だれがそんなけったいなことをやり出したのだ. ¶a ***dear*** (=***cute***) ***little*** *thing* かわいい娘. ¶his insight into human character and ***deeper*** *things* of life 品性並びに人生の根底をなすものに対する彼のどう察力. ¶Death is a ***disagreeable*** *thing*. 死ぬのはいやなものだ. ¶a ***divine thing*** 神聖な事柄. ¶history and geography, and ***dry things*** of that sort 歴史とか地理とかそういった無味乾燥なもの. ¶it is by no means an ***easy thing*** to ... ...するのはどうして楽なことではない. ¶say an ***enigmatic thing*** なぞのようなことを言う. ¶an ***esoteric thing*** apart from life 人事とは別個の玄妙のこと. ¶an ***essential thing*** to learn is ... 大事なことは...を習うことである. 【類】The ***essential thing*** in religion is belief in the existence of spiritual beings. ¶It is an ***even thing***. それは五分五分だ. ¶Time is ***every thing***. 時は力なり. ¶an ***everyday prosaic thing*** 日常の平凡な事物. ¶do ***evil things*** 悪事をする. ¶an ***excellent thing*** すばらしいこと. ¶The most ***extraordinary thing*** about the judge's wig is that it is not considered extraordinary.—Chesterton. 裁判官のかつらについて最も不思議なことは人があのかつらを不思議と思わないことだ. ¶We take ***familiar things*** for granted. われわれはありふれたことを頭から信じる. ¶now it is a ***fashionable thing*** to ... 昨今は...するのが流行(ﾘｭｳｺｳ)である. ¶of course patriotism is a ***fine thing***, but ... 愛国もさることながら.... 【類】He thought it would be a ***fine thing*** to travel all over the world. ‖ talk ***fine things*** 調子のいいことを言う ‖ ***Fine thing*** that you call yourself a man and the head of a family! あんたそれでも男なの, それでも一家の主人なの. ¶Addition is the ***first thing*** of arithmetic. 加法は算術の根本だ. 【類】The ***first thing*** in language learning is to ... ‖ The ***first thing*** of its kind can never be what the last thing of its kind will be. 初めからうまく行くものではない. ‖ ***first things*** 事始め ‖ I did it [the] ***first thing*** in the morning. 朝起きがけにそれをやった. ¶the ***fleeting things*** of this world この世のはかないことども. ¶do ***foolish things*** ばかなことをする. ¶do ***funny things*** おかしなことをする. ¶as a ***general thing*** 概して. ¶It was a ***good thing*** he didn't have to have his arm amputated. あの人は腕を切らずにすんでよかった. ‖ It is a ***good thing*** for boys to know how to use tools. 男の子は道具の使い方を覚えるとよい. 【類】It's a ***good thing*** I came! / it would be a ***good thing*** if ... / He did many ***good things*** for his country. ‖ The ***good thing*** about inflation is that I lost 15 pounds worrying about it. インフレにも良い所がある, (肥満で困っていた)僕はそれを苦にして体重が十五ポンド減った. ‖ That's one ***good thing*** about Tom. ‖ have a share in the ***good things*** of life この世の福を受ける. ¶A nice voice, well trained and silvery, is a ***great thing*** in a lady. 十分訓練された銀のような美声を持つことは女としてはすてきなことだ. 【類】It is a ***great thing*** to be a queen. / T.V. (=Television) is a ***great thing***. ¶all ***growing things*** on the earth あらゆる地上の生物. ¶The encyclopedia is a ***handy thing***. その百科辞書は手ごろだ. ¶a ***hard thing*** to do 困難なこと. ¶say ***harsh things*** about ... ...についてひどいことを言う. ¶the ***honorable thing*** for you to do is ... 君の紳士としてなすべきことは...である. ¶In all ***human things*** there is a rise and a fall. 人事はすべて栄枯盛衰を免れない. ¶***imaginary things*** 色々な架空のこと. ¶The ***important thing***, however, is that ... だが, 重要な点は...だ. ¶The only ***inconvenient thing*** about the word is that it is heavy and lacks euphony. その語の欠点は重っ苦しくて語ろが悪いことだ. ¶an ***insignificant*** and ***negligible thing*** 無視し得べき細事. ¶say ***irresponsible things*** 出放題を言う. ¶He has a knowledge of ***things Japanese*** possessed by few foreigners. 彼は外国人にはほとんど皆無という位に日本の事情に通じている. ¶be ***just*** the ***thing*** for ... ...に持って来いだ. 【類】That's ***just*** the ***thing*** we want. ¶it would indeed be a ***lamentable thing*** if ... were ... ...だとすると実に嘆かわしいことだ. ¶The article was the ***last thing*** he did before dying. その記事は彼の絶筆であった. ‖ it is [the] ***last thing*** to suppose that ... まさかそんなことはあるまい ‖ Criticism is the ***last thing*** one looks for in a literary Year-Book. 文学年鑑で批評を求めても無理だ. ¶a ***lifeless*** (***living***) ***thing*** (無)生物. ¶a ***likely*** or ***possible thing*** ありそうなまたはあり得べきこと. ¶*Things* were pretty ***lively*** at the dinner party. その晩さん会は相当盛んであった. ¶never to let one's thought dwell on ***lustful things*** 断じて卑わいの考えを起させないように. ¶That, you may think, is a ***magical thing***. それは不思議だとお思いになるかも知れない. ¶the ***main thing*** 主眼. ¶say ***mean things*** 下品なことを言う. ¶It is a ***mortifying thing*** for a young lady that a man should court her for the sake of her fortune. 男が財産のために彼女に結婚を求めているということは若い女には我慢のならないことである. ¶the reality of ***mundane things*** 現在身にまつわる俗事. ¶the ***nearest thing*** to ... ...に一番よく似たもの. ¶It is no ***new thing*** in France. それはフランスでは新しいものではない. ‖ a ***new thing*** in drama 目新しい芝居. ¶the ***next thing*** to ... ...の一歩手前. ¶It is the ***next best thing*** to a real visit to America. 本当のアメリカ行きには及ばないがそれに一番近い(映画など). ¶Look here, my son, they don't say very ***nice things*** about your work. これせがれ, お前の仕事は人が余りよく言わないぞ. ‖ He has a ***nice thing*** to say. あの人はお世辞がうまい. ¶quite the ***normal thing*** for ... ...にとってごく普通のこと. ¶a highly ***objectionable thing*** to do もっての外のこと. ¶I am afraid that is the ***only thing*** to do. それ以外に方法がないのではあるまいか. ¶a very ***painful thing*** for me to do 私には本当にやりずらいこと. ¶***things personal*** 私有物. ¶***petty things*** ちっぽけなこと. ¶do all the proper ***Pickwickian things*** 本当にとぼけたことばかりやる. ¶say ***playful things*** ふざけたことを言う. ¶It's not a ***pleasant thing*** to hear that. それはおもしろくない話だ. ¶***Poor thing***, I am sorry to hear it. それはおかわいそうなことです(赤ん坊の病気など). ¶a ***poor make-believe thing*** 見え透いたごまかし. ¶for ***one thing*** 一つの例をあげれば. ¶talk ***pretty things*** 口先がうまい ‖ A ***pretty thing***, indeed, to be a waitress! なるほど女給になるのも結構だろうよ. ¶He does the ***proper things*** at the proper times. 彼は適当な時機に適当なことをする. ¶None of them seems ***quite*** the ***thing***. どれもぱっとしない. ¶*Things* ***read*** are much less affecting than things seen. 読んだことは見たことほどに身にしみない. ¶a ***real thing*** 本もの, 極上物 ‖ ***things real***=real property 不動産 ‖ the ***real thing*** 実物(模擬に対して). ¶What a ***ridiculous thing*** I've done! 何てばかなまねをしたんだ. ¶That's not the ***right thing*** to say here. ここでそんなこと言っちゃいかん. 【類】the ability of saying the ***right thing*** at the right moment / With good taste and a sense of discrimination, she does the ***right thing*** instinctively. ¶the ***saddest thing*** about ... is ... ...について最も悲惨なことは...だ. ¶She is very fond of ***salt things***. 彼女は塩辛い物が大好きだ. ¶mouth the ***same thing*** 同じことを言う ‖ Beauty and goodness are not two kindred things, but one and the ***same thing***. 美と善は二つの類似したものではなく同一のものだ. ¶say ***scandalous things*** 人聞きの悪いことをいう. ¶***secondary things*** 第二次的なこと. ¶say ***selfish things*** わがままを言う. ¶say a ***sensible thing*** 気のきいたことを言う. ¶a very ***serious thing*** 非常な重大事件. ¶a ***settled thing*** 決定したこと. ¶say some ***sharp things*** about ... ...の憎まれ口をたたく. ¶give better attention to "***small things*** that matter" 「大切な小事」に一層注意を払う. ¶a ***solemn thing*** おごそかなこと. ¶What a ***strange thing*** is man! 人間て何て変なものだろう! ‖ ***Stranger things*** have happened. もっと変ったこともあったのだ(だからそれが実現されないとも言えない). ¶a ***stupid thing*** 愚かなこと. ¶There is no ***such thing*** as an irregular verb in Esperanto. エスペラントには不規則動詞といったものはない. 【類】Then there was no ***such thing*** as applied psychology (応用心理学). ‖ How dare you say ***such*** a ***thing***! よくもこんなことが言えたものだ. ¶His death was a very ***sudden thing***. 彼の死は実に急だった. ¶a ***sweet young thing*** 美しくて若い娘. ¶***Sure thing!*** もちろん(大丈夫だ). ¶say ***tender things*** to ... ...にやさしい口をきく. ¶***three-dimensional things*** 三次の物[立体]. ¶But the most ***trying thing*** of all is yet to be mentioned. しかし中でも最も困難なことはこれから申し上げます. ¶say an ***uncalled-for thing*** 余計なことを言う. ¶It is not an ***uncommon thing*** to see. それはよく見かけることだ. 【類】it is no ***uncommon thing*** for them to ... ¶a quite ***unexpected thing*** 降ってわいたような話. ¶an ***unheard-of thing*** 前代未聞のこと. ¶do ***unkind things*** in a kind way 親切ごかしに不親切をする. ¶say ***unpleasant things*** on purpose いやがらせをいう. ¶An ***unusual thing*** happened. 珍らしいことが起った. ¶an ***unthinkable thing*** 考えの及ばないこと. ¶It is a ***useful thing*** to have. それは重宝なものだ. ¶There was a time when it was the ***usual thing*** for them to ... 彼らが...するのは当

り前だという時代があった. ¶This is the ***very thing*** I want. これは私にうってつけだ. ¶the ***vital thing*** in ... ...において肝要なこと. ¶an utterly ***wasteful thing*** 全然むだなこと. ¶do the ***whole thing*** over again 新規まき直しをやる. ¶say ***wild things*** 取止めのないことを言う. ¶it is a very ***wise*** (***foolish***) ***thing*** to ... ...するのは利口(ばか)なことだ. ¶the ***worst thing*** about it is ... その一番悪い点は...だ. ¶do a ***wrong thing*** 間違ったことをする.

Q[2] ***everyday things*** 日常の事物. ¶Don't make a ***play thing*** of what others say. 人の言うことを茶化しちゃいかん. ¶This ***Suez thing*** (=business *or* affair) was getting serious. このスエズ(運河)事件は大変なことになり出していた. ¶remove the ***tea things*** 茶の道具を(卓上から)片付ける.

P The medical art is, ***above*** all ***things***, an art of removing and abolishing pain. 医術とは第一に苦痛をのぞく術である. 【類】William Morris was, ***above*** all ***things***, an enthusiast. ¶***after*** all ***things*** considered あらゆる点を考えた末. ¶***among*** other ***things***, he said: 色々の言葉の中で彼は次のようなことも言った. 【類】***amongst*** other ***things***. ¶***as*** a general ***thing*** 概して. ¶an average boy ***at*** most ***things*** 何をやっても十人並の少年. ¶He is ***before*** all ***things*** a poet. 彼は第一に詩人だ. ¶***for*** one ***thing*** ちょっと言ってみれば ‖ It is useful ***for*** one ***thing*** or another. それは何につけかにつけ重宝だ. ‖ ***For*** one ***thing***, he drinks; for another, he likes gambling. 第一彼は酒好きだ, おまけにばくちまで好きだ. ¶careful ***in*** all ***things*** 万事に注意深い.

P[2] some ***things about*** frogs かえるのことども. ¶of all ***things in*** the world こともあろうに. ¶Influence is not a ***thing of*** numbers but of quality. 勢力とは数ではなく質だ. ‖ It is already (=That has become) a ***thing of*** the past. それは現在もう見られない物(事)だ. 【類】become a ***thing of*** the past / a ***thing of*** growth / a ***thing of*** taste ‖ To the book publisher the public is always a ***thing of*** moods and fancies. 書籍出版業者にとっては大衆はいつもむら気なものである. ¶Platonic love is a ***thing without*** existence, a self-deception, a false description of sexual sensations. 精神的恋愛などは存在するものでなくそれは自己欺まんであり性的感情の誤説である.

O He called me a "*thing!*" Impertinence! 人のことをやつだって! 失敬な. ¶***things*** to come 未来のできごと. ¶as ***things*** are now 現状では.

think, *v*. 考える.

M No two minds ***think alike***. 二人寄ればその考えは違う. ¶***think aloud*** 考えながらひとり言を言う. ¶He does not ***think*** it ***any trouble*** at all. 彼はそれを一向苦にしない. ¶I ***thought as much***. そんなことだろうと思った. ¶***think away*** a toothache 考えごとをして歯痛を忘れる. ¶Do as you ***think best***. 最善と考えたことをなさい. 【類】Do whatever you ***think best***. ‖ You must ***think better*** of it. そのことはもっとよくお考えにならなくてはいけない. ¶***think calmly*** 冷静に考える. ¶***carefully think*** it ***out*** 慎重にそれを案出する. ¶***think clearly, accurately, constructively*** and ***fearlessly*** 明りょうに正確に建設的に大胆に考える. ¶He was ***thought dead***. 彼は死んだものと思われた. ¶***think deeply*** 深く考える. 【類】things to ***think deeply*** about. ¶***think differently*** 異った考え方をする. ¶I cannot ***even think*** of it. 思いも寄らないことだ. ¶***first think*** of ... まず...のことを考える. ¶if he ***thinks fit*** (=good) to ... 彼が...するのがよいと思えば. ¶***fondly think*** 愚かにも考える, なつかしく思う. ¶***think geographically*** 地理的に考える. ¶***think harder*** and go down deeper さらに強く思索し深く掘下げる. ¶I can ***hardly think*** so. 私にはちょっとそうとは思われない. ¶***think*** very ***harshly*** of a person 人について酷な考え方をする. ¶It depends ***how*** you ***think*** of it. 気の持ちようだ. ¶***however hard*** I may ***think*** of it どう考えて見ても. ¶She ***thought hard*** of his teacher who had punished his son for it. 彼女はそれで自分のむすこを罰した先生のことをじっと考えてみた. ¶***think highly*** of ... ...に敬服する ‖ ***think*** too ***highly*** of oneself うぬぼれ過ぎる. ¶Do not ***think ill*** of me. 私を悪く思わないで下さい. ¶***think independently*** [人の説に雷同せず]自分で考える. ¶ability to "***think Indian***" アメリカの土人のような心持で考える能力. ¶***Just think!*** 考えても御覧なさい. ¶***think justly*** (=fairly) of ... ...を公平に考慮する. ¶***think leniently*** of ... ...を大目に見る. ¶***think light***[***ly***] of ... ...を軽視する. ¶***think little*** of fashion 流行を軽視する ‖ he ***little thinks*** that ... 彼は...とはほとんど考えていない. ¶If you were to ***think*** a ***little less***, and act a little more, it would be better for all parties. もし君がもう少し少なく考えもう少し多く実行したら関係の人たちのためになるだろう. ¶***think logically*** 論理的に考える. ¶***think*** too ***meanly*** of oneself 謙そんし過ぎる. ¶***think more*** and ***more*** もっともっと考える ‖ A girl ***thinks more*** of "looking nice" than a boy does. 女の子は男の子よりおしゃれだ. ¶***think*** too ***much*** of ... ...を思い過ごす. ¶I ***never thought*** that he himself would come. よもやあの人が来ようとは思わなかった. ¶***think no more*** of ... もう...のことは考えない. ¶***think nothing*** (***everything***) of it それを軽(重)視する. ¶***Only think*** of that! どうでしょう(案外のこと). ¶***think*** this matter ***out*** このことを考え抜く ‖ ***think out*** a plan ある計画を案出する. 【類】***think out*** (=solve) a chess problem / His theory is so complicated that nobody can hardly ***think*** it ***out***. ¶What we ***think persistently***, we do or become. 始終心がけているとそういうことができもするしまたそういう人になることもできる. ¶I will not ***think*** so ***poorly*** of the Turkish race. 僕はトルコ民族をそう見くびらない. ¶if you ***think*** it ***proper*** 君がそれでよいと思えば. ¶***think seriously*** about life 人生についてまじめに考える. ¶***think*** oneself ***silly***. 考えすぎて頭がどうかなる. ¶***think slightingly*** of ... ...を見くびる. ¶***so thinking*** そう思って ‖ I do not ***think so***. 私はそうは思わない. ¶You will not be disappointed if you ***think that way***. そう思っていれば間違いはない. ¶Even one of the most powerful of swimmers would ***think twice*** before tackling the current. この急流を乗切るということはいかに泳ぎが達者でも二の足を踏むであろう. 【類】I must ***think twice*** before I can promise. / But no one who could ***think twice*** about the matter could well make this mistake. ¶***think well*** of ... ...を好く思う ‖ Now ***think*** it ***well*** over again. まあもう一度よく考えて御覧.

M[2] ***think up*** a new gag《米》新しい手を考える ‖ ***think up*** ways to ... ...する方法を考え出す. 【類】***think up*** a new excuse / ***think up*** arguments of one's own / ***think up*** a plan.

P I am ***thinking about*** the friends I have lost. 私は失なった友だちのことを考えている. ¶***think*** it ***beneath*** one to ... そんなことをすると自分のこけんにかかわると思う. ¶***think from*** the first that ... 最初から...だと思う ‖ I ***thought from*** his accent he was a Tohoku man. そのなまりから察して彼は東北人だと私は思った. ¶***thinking in*** this way こう考えて. ¶I often ***think of*** you. 僕は時々君のことを思い出す. ‖ To ***think of*** it! それを考えると[たまらない]. 【類】We shudder to ***think of*** the accident. / What do you ***think of*** the idea? / ***think of*** other people first / Young persons who are ***thinking of*** the literary life. ‖ ***Think of*** the nerve of that fellow. そいつの心臓の強いといったら. ‖ It was ***thought of*** as impossible. それは不可能と考えられた. ‖ The piece is so high that I can not ***think of*** buying it. その品は値段が高過ぎるので買う気になれない. ‖ ***Think of*** it only 50 yen! どうですただの五十円(とは安い). ‖ I am ***thinking of*** purchasing a piano. 私はピアノを一台買おうかと思っている. ‖ It is ***thought of*** as impossible. それは不可能と思われている. ¶He has ***thought*** deeply ***on*** life, love, and death. 彼は人生・愛そして死のことを深く考えた. ‖ there is one fact which every beginner ought to ***think on*** if he wishes to ... 初学者が...したければだれでも考えるべき一つのことがある. ¶Just ***think*** it ***over***. ちょっと考えて御覧. ‖ I will give you three days to ***think*** it ***over***. 三日間の猶予を与えるからとくと考えて見たまえ. 【類】***Think over*** what I have said. / I am ***thinking over*** your proposal (提案). ¶he ***thought to*** himself that ... 彼は内心...だと思った. ¶I will ***think*** more seriously ***upon*** the matter. 私はその件についてもっと真剣に考えてみよう.

O He is ***thought*** to be a scholar. 彼は学者だと思われている. 【類】I didn't ***think*** (=expect) to find you here. / He ***thought*** (=intended) to deceive us.

thinkable, *a*. ありそうな.

M It's ***quite*** (***hardly***) ***thinkable***. 大いにあり得ることだ(ちょっと考えられない).

thinker, *n*. 思想家.

Q an ***acute thinker*** 頭が良い人. ¶These views fail to come up to the standard of the ***advanced thinkers*** of the present day. これらの見解は今日の進歩した思想家の標準には達していない. ¶an ***adventurous thinker*** 冒険的な思索家. ¶a ***clear thinker*** 頭のよい思想家. ¶a ***deep thinker*** 深い思索家. ¶a ***feeble thinker*** 思考力の弱い人々. ¶***great thinkers*** of antiquity 昔の大思想家. ¶an ***independent*** and ***original thinker*** 独自的で独創的な思想家. ¶a ***loose thinker*** 散漫な思索家. ¶a ***rapid thinker*** 考えの早い人. ¶a ***shallow thinker*** 浅薄な思索家. ¶a ***sharp thinker*** 鋭敏な思想家. ¶a ***subtle thinker*** 繊細な思想家. ¶the only ***theological thinker*** of Christendom キリスト教国唯一の神学思想家. ¶a ***veteran thinker*** 老練な思索家.

P^{2} the best *thinkers* ***on*** the subject その問題関係の最高権威者.

thinking, *n.* 思考.

V data on which to ***base*** one's *thinking* 思考の根底となる資料. ¶***clear*** muddled *thinking* on the subject その問題に関する混濁した考えを一掃する. ¶This has ***colored*** all their *thinking* with the yellow tinge of the dollar. このために彼らはドルの黄色い眼鏡越しに万事を見る. ¶***do*** one's own *thinking* 自分で考える. 【類】***do*** a little *thinking* for oneself. ¶***organize*** one's *thinking* その考えをまとめる. ¶It ***requires*** little *thinking* to see this. ちょっと考えればこんなことは分かる. ¶***stimulate*** independent *thinking* 自分で物事を考えるように刺激する.

Q ***correct*** (=***right***) *thinking* 正しい考え方. ¶***creative*** *thinking* 独創的考察. ¶be lost in ***deep*** *thinking* 深い考えに沈む. ¶***democratic*** *thinking* 民主的な考え. ¶changes in ***economic*** *thinking* 経済思想の変遷. ¶***free*** *thinking* and plain speaking 思想言論の自由. ¶the outcome of ***hard*** *thinking* 熟考の結果. ¶plain living and ***high*** *thinking* 生活は質素に考えは高尚に. ¶***honest*** *thinking* 正直な考え方. ¶avoid ***incorrect*** *thinking* 誤った考え方を避ける. ¶***independent*** *thinking* 独立的思索. ¶***logical*** *thinking* 論理的な考え. ¶fall into ***mistaken*** *thinking* that ... ...という誤った考えに陥る. ¶I have done ***much*** *thinking* along this line. 私はこの点について大いに考えた. ¶***quick*** *thinking* 敏速な思考. ¶***scientific*** *thinking* 科学的な考え. ¶it takes but ***short*** *thinking* to reach the conclusion that ... ...という結論に到達するには少し考えて見ればよい. ¶***straight*** *thinking* 率直な考え方. ¶***superficial*** *thinking* 浅はかな考え. ¶confound ***wishful*** *thinking* with reality 希望的観測と現実を混同する. 【類】***Wishful*** *thinking* is typical of the Oriental mind.

Q^{2} ***lightning*** *thinking* 電光石火の思考.

P one's way ***of*** *thinking* その考え方. ¶It is an outlandish kind of name, ***to*** my *thinking*. 僕にはそれは外国人の名のように思われる. ¶act ***without*** *thinking* 無思慮な振舞いをする.

P^{2} American *thinking* ***about*** Japan 米国人の日本観.

third, *n.* 第三.

V Soon another coming in ***made*** a *third*. やがて一人やってきて座が三人になった.

Q an ***awkward*** *third* 手持ぶさたな三人仲間の一人. ¶a ***close*** *third* [第二に]すぐ続いた第三. ¶the ***decisive*** *third* 三度目の勝負. ¶with ... a close second and ... a ***distant*** *third* ...が一番に接近して二番そして...がずっと離れて三番. ¶the ***first*** (***middle, last***) *third* of the century その世紀の始めの(中の, 終の)三分の一. ¶He is in the ***upper*** *third* of his class scholastically. 彼の成績はクラスの三分の一以内である.

P^{2} He was the *third* ***of*** a large family. 彼は大勢の兄弟の三番目であった. 【類】the *third* ***of*** three children.

thirst, *n.* のどのかわき.

V ***allay*** (=***assuage, quench or slake***) one's *thirst* at the fountain 泉でその渇をいやす. ¶***awaken*** a *thirst* for further and deeper study さらに深く研究しようという切なる念願を起させる. ¶***create*** *thirst* のどがかわく. ¶***feel*** intolerable *thirst* たえがたい渇を覚える. ¶I have a *thirst* [for drinking]. 一杯やりたい. ¶***quench*** *thirst* 渇をいやす. ¶***relieve*** one's *thirst* 渇をいやす. ¶***retain*** a *thirst* for knowledge 依然知識欲を持っている. ¶This ***roused*** their *thirst* for blood. この事件が彼ら(蛮人)を殺気立たせた. ¶***satisfy*** the *thirst* of gain 利欲を満たす. 【類】***satisfy*** one's *thirst* at a stream. ¶Such dry facts and figures do not ***slake*** one's intellectual *thirst*. こうした乾燥無味な事実や数字では知的渇望の満足は望まれない.

Q the ***ardent*** *thirst* for ... ...に対する切実な渇望 ¶a ***burning*** *thirst* for ... ...に対する熱烈な渇望. ¶parched with (=consumed by) a ***deadly*** *thirst* ひどくのどがかわいて. ¶feel a ***great*** *thirst* from one's exertions 努力したために非常に渇を覚える. ¶an ***insatiable*** *thirst* for ... ...に対する根強い渇望.

P the *thirst* ***for*** knowledge (honor, fame, publicity, novelty) 知識(など)の渇望. 【類】the *thirst* ***for*** Western learning / We live in an age that surpasses all others in the eagerness of its *thirst* ***for*** knowledge. / gratify a child's *thirst* ***for*** knowledge / a *thirst* ***for*** a fight. ¶the *thirst* ***of*** gold 富の渇望.

thirst, *v.* のどがかわく, 渇望する.

P *thirst* ***after*** knowledge (fame, honor) 彼は知識(など)を渇望する. ¶Our politicians are merely ambitious persons *thirsting* ***for*** power and wealth. わが国の政治家は権力と富を渇望する野心家に過ぎない.

O The sword *thirsts* to drink the blood of an enemy. その剣は敵の血に飢えている.

thirsty, *a.* かわいた.

M Politicians are ***more or less*** *thirsty* for publicity. 政治屋連は多かれ少かれ売名的だ.

P *thirsty* ***after*** (=***for*** or ***of***) knowledge (glory) 知識(など)を渇望している ‖ be *thirsty* ***for*** blood 殺気立っている ‖ He is *thirsty* ***for*** fame (more money). 彼は名声(など)を渇望している. ¶*thirsty* ***with*** running 走ったのでのどがかわいて.

thirteen, *n.* 十三.

Q^{2} the superstition of the ***number*** *thirteen*=the thirteen superstition 十三という数字の(不吉とする)迷信.

thirty, *n.* 三十.

Q men in their ***early*** *thirties* and their later twenties 三十前後の人々. ¶women in their ***late*** *thirties* 四十近い婦人連.

P a man ***in*** his *thirties* 三十台の人.

this, *pron.* これ.

V when *this* ***comes*** to pass このことが起ると.

Q when ***all*** *this* has been said, however とはいうものの.

P ***At*** *this*, he grew angry. すると彼は怒った. ¶Fold it ***like*** *this*. それをこうたため. ¶***On*** (=***Upon***) *this*, we separated. それからわれわれは別れた. ¶***With*** *this*, he left the room. こう言って彼はへやを出て行った.

thorn, *n.* とげ.

V ***run*** a *thorn* into one's finger 指にとげを立てる.

P It is unbearable to be always ***on*** *thorns*. 絶えず不安の気持でいるのはたまらない. ¶a twig covered ***with*** *thorns* とげだらけの小枝. ¶No rose ***without*** a *thorn*. 〘諺〙ばらにはとげがある(楽あれば苦あり).

P^{2} a *thorn* ***in*** one's side (=the flesh) 〘比ゆ〙なやみの種. ¶*thorns* ***on*** a plant 植物に生えているとげ.

thoroughfare, *n.* 道路; 往来.

V The *thoroughfare* is ***closed***. 通行止になっている. ¶People ***thronged*** the *thoroughfares*. 往来に人出があった. ¶***widen*** *thoroughfares* 道路を広める.

Q from its ***broadest*** *thoroughfare* to its narrowest byway その一番広い道路から一番狭い横道に至るまで. ¶flagstones of a ***busy*** *thoroughfare* にぎやかな往来の舗石. ¶These ***commonplace*** *thoroughfares* were strangely transfigured by a passing procession. 行列が通るのでこれらの平凡の通りも一種異様な趣を呈した. ¶a ***crowded*** *thoroughfare* 雑とうした往来. ¶less ***frequented*** *thoroughfares* 人通りの少い道路. ¶a ***leading*** *thoroughfare* 主要道路. ¶the ***main*** *thoroughfare* 本通り. ¶The Thames is London's ***natural*** *thoroughfare*. テムズ川はロンドンの自然の交通路である. ¶***No*** *thoroughfare* for vehicles. 〘掲示〙諸車通行止め. ¶in the ***public*** *thoroughfares* 大道において. ¶a ***scintillating*** *thoroughfare* blazing with countless electric lights and neon signs 電灯やネオンサインが数限りなくきらめくさんらんたる大通り.

Q^{2} a perfect network of ***underground*** *thoroughfares* 縦横無尽の地下道路網.

thoroughness, *n.* 徹底.

Q It has been carried out with ***exceptional*** *thoroughness*. それはまれに見る徹底さで実行された. ¶study it with ***some*** *thoroughness* 幾分徹底的にそれを研究する.

P be treated ***with*** the *thoroughness* of an encyclopedia 百科辞典のように徹底的に記述されている.

thought, *n.* 考え; 思想.

V It appears that in 1850, at the age of 30, Miss Nightingale had definitely ***abandoned*** all *thoughts* of marriage. 一八五〇年，ナイチンゲール嬢が三十歳のとき結婚するという考えを全然捨ててしまっていたものらしい. ‖ ***abandon*** any *thought* of a political career 政界を断念する. ¶The question is now ***absorbing*** the *thoughts* of the British people. その問題に対して目下英国民は大いに関心を持っている. ¶"Yes," he said, ***answering*** our *thoughts*. 「そうです」とこっちの心をくんで彼は言った. ¶***appreciate*** the kindly *thought* その親切な心づかいを有難く思う. ¶It ***arouses*** in us *thought* as well as laughter. それはわれわれを笑わせると同時にまた考えさせる. ¶***assimilate*** a *thought* 思想を同化する. ¶***avert*** (=***turn away***) one's *thought* from ... 考えを...から転じる. ¶***awake*** solemn *thought* 荘厳な考えを起させる. ¶he could not ***bear*** (=***endure***) the *thought* of living any longer; so ... 彼はこれ以上生きているに忍びなかった，そこで. ¶***bestow*** less *thought* on ... ...のことをそれほどに考えない. 【類】whoever has but once ***bestowed*** a *thought* on the subject will surely acknowledge that ... ‖ I have never ***bestowed*** any serious *thought* upon the matter. 私はそのことについてはまだとくと考えたことがない. ¶***build up*** the *thought* of the times 時代の思想を建設する. ¶***call up*** the *thoughts* of ... ...を思い起させる. ¶***carry*** one's *thought* ***back*** (***ahead***) 回顧する(将来を考える). ¶***carry out*** one's *thought* その考えを実行する. ¶A writer may ***cast*** his *thoughts* into various molds. 文士はその考えを色々の型で表現する. ‖ ***cast*** a *thought* to ... ...を一考する. ¶***clothe*** one's *thoughts* in appropriate words その思想を適当な言葉で表現する. 【類】We make the conscious intellectual effort to ***clothe*** our *thoughts* in new, unfamiliar garb when learning a foreign language. / words are all too inadequate to ***clothe*** the *thought* and feelings of those ... / ***clothe*** one's *thought* in a fitting way (適切に). ¶***collect*** one's *thoughts* 気を落着ける ‖ Give me time to ***collect*** my *thoughts*. ちょっと待って下さい，落ちついて考えてみるから. ‖ He endeavoured to ***collect*** his wandering *thoughts*. 彼は乱れる気持を落着けようとした. ¶***commit*** one's *thoughts* to paper 思想を紙に書付ける. ¶a means of ***communicating*** *thoughts* 思想伝達の一手段. ¶***conceive*** a *thought* 一つの考えを思いつく. ¶I cannot ***concentrate*** my *thoughts*. 私は精神の統一ができない. ¶his habit of ***condensing*** much *thought* into few words 多くの思想を数語でまとめる彼のくせ. ¶the book ***contains*** much pregnant *thought* on ... その本は...に関する含蓄ある思想に富んでいる. ¶***control*** public *thought* 公衆の思想を統制する. ¶Language was made to ***convey*** *thought*. 言語は思想を伝達するために作られた. ¶***cultivate*** healthy and happy *thoughts* 健全明朗な思想を養う. ¶***devote*** more earnest *thought* to ... 一層誠意をもって...を考慮する. ¶***direct*** one's *thoughts* toward ... ...に考えを向ける. 【類】It ***directs*** one's *thought* to the uncertainty of life (人生のはかなさ). ¶***dismiss*** from their minds the *thought* of ... ...の思想を彼らの頭の中から追い出す. ¶***distract*** *thoughts* from books and lessons 授業中気を散らす. ¶***divert*** one's *thoughts* from cares of business 気を紛らして仕事の苦労を忘れる ‖ ***divert*** her *thoughts* into intellectual channels 彼女の考えを知的方面に向ける. ¶*thought* ***divorced*** from life 人生と没交渉の思想. ¶At his height Hegel ***dominated*** German philosophic *thought*. その勢力が絶頂に達した時ヘーゲルはドイツの哲学界を風びした. ¶***dramatize*** one's *thoughts* その思想を戯曲に仕組む. ¶***echo*** the *thought* of ... ...の思想を伝える. ¶write a short article ***elaborating*** the *thought* that ... ...という思想を土台にして短文を書く. ¶***employ*** one's *thoughts* upon ... ...に心をくだく. ¶***encourage*** original, reflective *thought* on vital current problems 重要な時事問題に関して創意に富む深い思索を奨励する. ¶The problem of speech rhythm is now ***engaging*** much *thought*. 言語の韻律という問題は当今大分研究されている. ¶***ennoble*** the *thoughts* 思想を高尚にする. ¶His *thought* is clumsily ***expressed***. 彼は思想の表現がまずい. 【類】***express*** one's *thoughts* with propriety (適切な言葉で). ¶try to ***fathom*** the *thoughts* of ... ...の腹を探る. ¶These are English idiomatic expressions different from our way of ***framing*** the *thought*. これらはわれわれの思想表現法と異なる英語の特有の言回しである. ¶***gather*** my *thoughts* again 私の取乱した心を落着ける ‖ ***gather*** the world's *thought* on the subject その問題に関する世界の人々の考えを集める. ¶***get*** a *thought* (=an idea) from the printed page 読書によって一つの考えを得る ‖ train oneself to read English so as to ***get*** the *thought* quickly 内容が早くつかめるように英語を読む練習をする. ¶***give*** *thought* to one's clothes その着物のことを考える ‖ without ***giving*** a *thought* to ... ...のことはちっとも考えずに ‖ These few lines are just to prove that I have ***given*** you a *thought* away here on my trip. この手紙は遠くこちらに来ていてあなたのことを思い出したからです. 【類】few of us ever ***gave*** a *thought* to ... / This ought to be clear to any one who ***gives*** the matter any *thought*. / ***give*** little *thought* to the morrow / he does not ***give*** enough *thought* to the matter to realize that ... / without ***giving*** much *thought*. ¶***give*** one's own interests first *thought* 自己の利害をまず念頭におく. 【類】***give*** no *thought* to ... ¶***give up*** all *thoughts* of matrimony 結婚ということは全然考えないようになる. ¶***grasp*** the *thought* as a whole 思想の大体をつかむ. ¶You have ***guessed*** my *thoughts*. 私の心はあなたの察した通りです. ¶The matter ***haunted*** his *thoughts* even amid the stern duties of the field. 戦場のきびしい軍務の中にあってもなおそのことが彼の心につきまとっていた. ¶I ***have*** some *thought* of ... 私には幾分か...という考えもあった. ‖ I ***had*** no *thought* of offending him. 私には彼を怒らせようという気はなかった. ‖ He ***has*** always a kindly *thought* for you. 彼はいつも君に同情を持っている. ¶Schopenhauer's philosophy has profoundly ***influenced*** the *thought* of our time. ショーペンハウエルの哲学は現代思想に深く影響を及ぼしている. ¶***Inhibit*** such *thought* at once. こうした考えは即座に捨ててしまえ. ¶***inject*** the *thoughts* (=ideas) into the minds of ... その思想を...の心に注入する. ¶***interest*** speculative *thoughts* 思索を誘う. ¶He ***kept*** the *thoughts* to himself. 彼はその考えをだれにも言わずにいた. ¶***lay aside*** all *thoughts* of ... ...しようという考えを一切捨てる. ¶***lead*** one's *thoughts* ***off*** その考えを他に転向させる. ¶***lift*** the *thoughts* of men 人々の考えを向上させる. ¶***marshal*** one's *thoughts* その思想を整然と述べる. ¶***merit*** some *thought* 幾分考慮に値する. ¶***mold*** the *thoughts* and the actions of the next generation 次代の思想並びに行動を一定の型に入れる. ¶***nourish*** low or impure *thoughts* いやしいまたは不純な考えをいだく. ¶The matter has ***occupied*** my *thoughts* for years. その考えは多年私の頭にあった. ¶***organize*** *thought* 思想をまとめる. ¶***phrase*** the *thought* of a paragraph in one sentence 一節の思想を一文で言い表わす. ¶faithfully ***portray*** our *thoughts* and sentiments 忠実にわれわれの思想感情を述べる. ¶***pour out*** one's *thoughts* to a friend その思う所を友人に披歴する. ¶***present*** one's *thoughts* clearly 自己の思想を明りょうに表わす. ¶***put*** one's *thought* into words (English) その考えを言葉(英語)につづる ‖ ***put*** all *thoughts* of ... ***away*** ...を一切断念する ‖ ***put*** [***down***] one's *thoughts* on paper その考えを書く. ¶It ***puts*** good *thoughts* into my mind. それで名案が私の頭に浮んだ. ¶***read*** his *thoughts* 彼の心を読む. 【類】The *thoughts* can be ***read*** in their faces. ‖ ***read*** *thoughts* set forth in print or writing 印刷したまたは書いた文章の内容を理解する. ¶the inadequacy of speech to ***represent*** *thought* 思想表現における言語の不徹底さ ‖ precious books ***representing*** the world's best *thought* and experience 世界最良の思想と経験を盛った貴重な著作. ¶***require*** much *thought* 大いに考える必要がある. ¶***reveal*** the innermost *thoughts* of the Japanese nation 奥深い日本の国民精神をせん明する. ¶clearly ***set forth*** one's *thought* その考えをはっきり述べる. ¶***shape*** the *thought* of the future 将来における物の考え方を定める. 【類】his powers to ***shape*** his own *thoughts* in English (英語表現力). ¶we ***share*** this oldtime *thought* that ... われわれもまた...という古い考えを持っている. ¶***show*** some *thought* for others 人にいく分同情を示す. ¶***soothe*** one's troubled *thoughts* 心の悩みを慰める. ¶***speak*** one's *thought* その考えを語る. ¶I should ***speak out*** my *thoughts* were I in your place. 僕が君だったら遠慮なく考えを述べるのだが. ¶***steal*** *thoughts* 思想を盗み取る. ¶***stimulate*** *thought* 思考を刺激する. ¶***submit*** one's *thought* to paper その思想を文につづる. ¶He ***summed up*** the *thought* in these words. 彼はその思想をこの数語に

要約した. 【類】 ***sum up*** a *thought* in two words. ¶***systematize*** one's own *thoughts* 自己の思想を系統立てる. ¶***take*** no *thought* for the morrow あすのことを心配しない ‖ ***take*** *thought* about ... …に思いを致す ‖ ***take*** *thought* for a better way もっとよい方法を考える ‖ ***take*** no (little) *thought* of ... …はちっとも(など)考えない ‖ this ***takes*** my *thoughts* ***back*** to the time when ... これで私は…の昔を回想する. ¶***tell*** one's *thoughts* to others 自分の考えを他人に告げる. ¶***think*** one's *thoughts* 思案する ‖ ***think*** noble *thoughts* りっぱなことを考える. ¶***throw*** one's *thoughts* ***back*** to the scenes of childhood 幼年時代のことどもを追憶する. ¶***tinge*** one's *thoughts* その思想に幾分影響を与える. ¶***transplant*** foreign *thought* 外国思想を移植する. ¶let us ***turn*** our *thoughts* to ... …のことを考えて見よう. ¶***turn*** the patient's *thought* ***away*** from the symptom 病人に症状のことを気に掛けさせないようにする. ¶if we ***turn*** our *thoughts* ***back*** to the earliest days of ... …の初期を回顧してみるならば. ¶***turn*** one's *thoughts* ***inward*** 内省する. ¶***unfold*** one's *thought* to ... 自分の考えを…に打明ける. ¶For us English is the key to ***unlock*** world *thought*, past and present. われわれに取って英語は古今の世界思想の庫をあけるかぎである. ‖ find a difficulty in ***venting*** one's *thoughts* in one's mother tongue. その母国語で思想を表現することを困難に感じる. ¶Don't ***waste*** your *thoughts* on the matter: it can't be helped. そのことを考えるのはむだです, もう仕方がないのだから. ¶Into every seam is ***woven*** loving *thoughts* of the coming happiness. 一針一針に来るべき喜びに対する愛の心尽しが織込まれるのである(妊婦がお産の用意をする場合など). ¶***write down*** one's *thoughts* 考えを書き留める.

v² A happy *thought* ***came*** into his head. 名案が彼の頭に浮んだ. ‖ when a *thought* ***comes*** to one's mind 考えが浮ぶと. ¶Wild *thoughts* ***clash*** in my brain. 無軌道な考えが私の頭で相反撥する. ¶as the *thought* ***flashed*** upon him (=into his mind) その考えが彼の胸に浮んだ時. ¶at length the happy *thought* ***occurred*** to some one to ... やがて…という名案がだれかの胸に浮んだ. 【類】 This is just a *thought* that ***occurs*** to me. ¶***Perish*** the *thought*! ばかな! ¶The *thoughts* were ***precipitated*** (=***materialized***) in action. その思想は行動に現われた. ¶The *thoughts* of ... ***pressed*** upon her. …のことが彼女の気に掛かっていた. ¶*Thought* has ***progressed*** since then. その後思想は進歩した. ¶*thoughts* ***run*** on ... 考えが…に及ぶ. ¶A new *thought* ***sprang*** into his mind. 新しい考えが突然彼の胸に浮んだ. ¶Then a new *thought* ***struck*** me. その時に新しい考えが私に浮んだ. ¶*Thoughts* ***turned*** toward home. 思いが家庭のことに及んだ. ¶My *thoughts* ***wandered back*** to a melancholy past. 私の思いは憂うつな過去にさまよって行った.

Q give ***adequate*** *thought* to ... …を十分考慮する. ¶***Altruistic*** *thoughts* predominate. 利他的思想が主調をなす. ¶in the ***ancient*** and ***modern*** *thought* 古代及び近世の思想では. ¶penetrate the very core of the ***author's*** *thoughts* 作者の思想の心髄に徹する. ¶a ***beautiful*** *thought* 麗わしい思想. ¶the ***best*** *thoughts* of the best writers 最良の著者の最良の思想 ‖ It is a task worth a man's ***best*** *thought*. それは人間が頭脳を最もよく働かせる価値のある仕事だ. ¶a ***bitter*** *thought* 苦々しい感想. ¶a ***borrowed*** *thought* 他から借りた思想. ¶***bright, cheery, merry*** *thoughts* 明朗な快活な楽しい思想. ¶one of the ***central*** *thoughts* その中心思想(主眼)の一つ. 【類】 a quick grasp (速解) of the ***central*** *thought* / the ***central*** *thought* of a paragraph (節). ¶a ***cheering*** *thought* 心を引立てる思想. ¶put the ***choicest*** *thoughts* into the choicest language 最良の思想を最良の言葉で表現する. ¶a ***cloudy*** *thought* 不明りょうな思想. ¶put ***communistic*** *thought* into practice 共産主義の思想を実行する. ¶express a ***completed*** *thought* 完成された思想を表現する. ¶a ***complex*** *thought* 複雑な思想. ¶give ***considerable*** *thought* to ... …のことを大いに考える. ¶it is a ***consoling*** *thought* that ... …であると思えば気も休まる. ¶the suppression of "***dangerous*** *thoughts*" いわゆる危険思想の圧迫. ¶The world's *thought* was prevailingly ***deductive*** till the days of Francis Bacon. フランシス・ベイコンの時代までは世界人の考え方は主として演えき的であった. ¶It furnishes material for ***deep*** *thought*. それは深く思いを致す材料になる. 【類】 be in ***deep*** *thought*. ¶a ***depressing*** *thought* 悲観させる考え. ¶***disquieting*** *thoughts* おだやかならぬ(危険)思想. ¶one ***disturbing*** *thought* is that I may not be able to ... 一つ気になることは私が…することができないのではないかしらということだ. ¶the ***dominant*** *thought* in his mind 彼の思想の主流. ¶a very ***elusive*** and ***delicate*** *thought* はなはだ捕促しがたい微妙な思想. ¶the current ***English*** *thought* 現代イギリス思想. 【類】 ***English*** *thought* in the nineteenth century. ¶the ***essential*** *thought* 要旨. ¶be very useful as a means of ***expressing*** *thought* 思想を表現する手段としてきわめて有用である. ¶I have ***few*** *thoughts* that are new and worthy to express on the subject. 私はその問題に対し新らしいかつ表現する価値のある思想をほとんど持合わしていない. ¶a book containing so much ***fine*** and ***lofty*** *thought* 美しい高遠な思想をおびただしく盛っている本. ¶this should be the ***first*** *thought* and duty of ... これが…のまず第一に考えまたなさねばならないことである ‖ the ***first*** *thought* is, "What is ...?" まず考えることは「…とは何か?」である. 【類】 strange as it may appear at ***first*** *thought*. ¶***fragmentary*** *thoughts* 切れ切れな考え. ¶***fundamental*** *thoughts* in economics 経済学の根本思想. ¶The world of ***German*** *thought* was at that time dominated by the philosophy of Hegel. 当時のドイツ思想界はヘーゲル哲学で支配されていた. ¶He surrendered himself to ***gloomy*** *thought*. 彼はふさいでしまった. ¶***grand*** *thoughts* in beautiful language 美しい言葉で書かれた雄こんな思想. ¶He mused a little while in ***grave*** *thought*. 彼はしばらくの間深く考え込んだ. ¶some authorities who have given ***great*** *thought* to the subject claim that ... その問題を深く考慮した権威者で…だと主張している人もある. ¶***green*** *thought* which should have been laid by in the apple-chamber to mature 温室で熟させるべきであった生な思想. ¶At last a ***happy*** *thought* came to him. やがていい考えが彼の頭に浮んだ. ¶a ***hideous*** *thought* 恐ろしい考え. ¶the peculiarities of ***Hindu*** *thought* インド思想の特徴. ¶***Horrible*** *thought*! 恐ろしい考えだ. ¶***Human*** *thought* is in a state of flux. 人間の考えが混乱状態に陥っている. ¶virgins of the most ***immaculate*** *thoughts* 清浄むくの処女. ¶***independent*** *thought* 独立不きの思想. ¶***indigenous Japanese*** *thought* 日本固有の思想. ¶***inspiring*** *thoughts* 鼓吹的思想. ¶the main currents of ***Japanese*** *thought* 日本思想の主流. ¶a ***kindly*** *thought* 好意. ¶It was the ***last*** *thought* I had of him that he would do such a thing. あの人があんなことをしようとは夢にも考えていなかった. ¶***licentious*** *thoughts* みだらな考え. ¶A word is the skin of a ***living*** *thought*. 言葉は生きている思想の外皮である. ¶Emerson's ***lofty*** *thought* was merely the philosophy of Brahman filtered through a marvelous Western mind. エマーソンの高遠な思想もただバラモン哲学を西洋人の奇才を通して純化したものに過ぎない. ¶The book is an admirable example of ***luminous French*** *thought*. その本はさん然たるフランス思想の光った一例だ. ¶the ***main*** *thought* of a paragraph [文の]一節の主眼. ¶the result of more ***matured*** *thought* 一層深く考えた上の成果. ¶leaders of ***medical*** *thought* 医学思想の指導者. ¶***melancholy*** and ***depressing*** *thoughts* 気の滅入る陰気な考え. ¶***modern*** *thought* 近代思想. ¶on a ***moment's*** *thought* ちょっと考えると. 【類】 I do not think it worth a ***moment's*** *thought*. ¶I have given it ***much*** *thought*. 私はそのことを篤と考えて見た. ¶students of our ***national*** *thought* わが国民思想の研究家. 【類】 The trend (動向) of ***national*** *thought* is turning in the direction of commerce and industry with an enthusiasm never known in the history of Japan. ¶a ***noble*** *thought* 高い思想. ¶I have only ***one*** *thought*. 私はたった一つのことしか考えていない. ¶Such was my ***only*** *thought*. そうとばかり思っていた. 【類】 My ***only*** thought was to escape from prison. ¶highly ***organized*** *thought* りっぱに系統立った思想. ¶a man of wide study and ***original*** *thought* 博学で独創的思想の持主 ‖ ***original analytical*** *thought* 独創的な分析的思想 ‖ *thought* neither ***original*** nor ***profound*** 新しくもまた深みもない思想. ¶give a ***passing*** *thought* to ... …をざっと考える. ¶***pernicious*** *thought* 有害な思想. ¶it is a ***pleasant*** *thought* that ... …とは考えるも愉快なことだ. ¶enter into one's most ***private*** *thoughts* その内心に深く立入って考える. ¶centers of ***progressive*** *thought* 進歩的思想の中心地,

¶ ***random thoughts*** 随想. ¶ give ***real thought*** and study to educational questions 教育上の問題を真剣に思索研究する. ¶ ***roving thoughts*** 散漫な思想. ¶ ***Russian*** Communist *thought* ロシア共産思想. ¶ to express the ***same*** *thought* in a different way その思想を言葉を変えて言えば. ¶ I never gave it a ***second*** *thought*. 私はそれっきり考えて見たこともない. ¶ ***secular*** *thoughts* 俗念. ¶ dismiss any ***serious*** *thought* that ... ...ということは真剣には考えられない. ¶ ***sober*** *thought* 穏健な思想. ¶ various schools of ***social*** *thought* 社会思想の諸学派. ¶ the history of ***socialist*** *thought* 社会主義思想史. ¶ give it ***some*** *thought* そのことを多少考慮する. ¶ ***spiritual*** *thoughts* 霊的思索. ¶ a ***stately*** *thought* 堂々たる思想. ¶ ***stray*** *thoughts* 断想. ¶ His writings abound in ***striking*** *thoughts*. 彼の書いたものには奇抜な考えが多い. ¶ ***suggestive*** *thoughts* 示唆に富んだ思想. 【類】There is much ***suggestive*** *thought* in the classification of eras by St. Simon, who divided history into two alternating periods of analysis and synthesis, or criticism and belief. ¶ a ***superficial*** *thought* 皮相な考え. ¶ a ***tender*** *thought* やさしい思いやり. ¶ I have a ***troubled*** *thought*. 私は心配ごとがある. ¶ ***underlying*** *thought* 根底をなす思想. ¶ ***uninspired*** and ***ordinary*** *thoughts* 平々凡々の思想. ¶ ***vagrant*** *thoughts* 随想. ¶ the ***very*** *thought* of ... ...という考えそのもの. ¶ ***waking*** *thoughts* 頭がはっきりしている時の考え. ¶ The *thoughts* are ***wayward*** and hard to control. 思想はわがままでこれを統制することはむずかしい. ¶ ***Western*** *thought* 西洋思想. ¶ indulge in ***wicked*** *thoughts* 邪念にふける. ¶ a ***wild*** *thought* 暴論.

Q² ***autumn*** *thoughts* 秋の思い. ¶ be condemned as dangerous and branded "***Communist*** *thought*" 危険と非難され「共産思想」のらく印を押される. ¶ ***dream*** *thoughts* 夢想. ¶ ***Pacifist*** *thought* 平和(主義)思想. ¶ schools of ***socialist*** *thought* 社会主義思想の諸学派. ¶ gather the ***world*** *thought* on the problem of ... ...の問題に関する世界の思想を集める.

P ***after*** serious *thought* 篤と考えてから. ¶ ***At*** this *thought*, his legs stiffened under him and he could not run a step further. こう思うと足がこわ張って一歩もかけ出すことができなかった. ¶ I felt uneasy ***at*** the *thought* of ... 私は...のことを考えて不安に思った. ¶ He is poor ***in*** *thought*. 彼は思想が貧弱だ. ‖ go back ***in*** *thought* (=imagination) to one's birthplace 故郷に思いをはせる. 【類】I am at this moment in Japan—***in*** *thought*. ‖ be immersed (=lost) ***in*** *thought* 思いに沈んでいる ‖ I feel happy ***in*** the *thought* that ... 私は...のことを考えてうれしく思う. ‖ I at once guessed what had been passing ***in*** his *thoughts*. 私は直ちに彼の意中を察した. ¶ a language as an instrument ***of*** *thought* 思想表現の手段としての国語 ‖ an exponent ***of*** Japanese *thought* 日本思想の解説者 ‖ express every shade ***of*** *thought* from mild conjecture to positive assertion 穏健な推測から断固たる言明に至るまで色々な思想を表現する. ¶ ***on*** a moment's *thought* ちょっと考えて ‖ recognize it ***on*** second *thoughts* 考え直してそれを認識する ‖ ***on*** second *thought* I realised that ... 考え直してみたら...であることが私に分かった. ¶ ***To*** my *thought*, the answer is simple. 私の考えではその答は簡単だ. ¶ ***upon*** second *thought* 思い直して. ¶ a retiring scholar ***with*** no *thought* of a career 何かやろうという考えの一切ない引退学者 ¶ ***with*** no *thought* of the nature of the occasion 場所柄も考えずに. ¶ ***With*** these sweet *thoughts* I went home. こうした楽しい思いにふけりつつ私はうちへ帰った. ¶ To get the widest possible distribution for the book, we have priced it ***with*** no *thought* of profit. その本をできるだけ広く普及させたいという考えで採算を無視した値段を付けた. 【類】***with*** no *thought* of the consequences. ¶ ***without*** *thought* to expense 費用におかまいなしで ‖ act ***without*** *thought* 考えずに行動する. 【類】give in to a desire (希望をいれる) ***without*** a *thought* that ... / ***without*** any *thought* of ... / You can realize ***without*** much *thought* that ...

P² *thoughts* ***about*** (=on) Germany ドイツに関する考察. ¶ take *thought* ***for*** the morrow 明日(将来)のことを心配する. ¶ *thoughts* ***from*** Tolstoi トルストイの思想. ¶ fragments of his *thought* ***on*** philosophy 彼の哲学思想の断片. ¶ *thoughts* ***on*** hunting 猟に関する感想. ¶ *thoughts* ***upon*** the present and future of China 現在及び将来の中国に関する考察.

thoughtful, *a.* 考え深い.

M it's ***mighty*** *thoughtful* of you to ... ...するなんてほんとに気がきいている. ¶ He is ***very*** *thoughtful*. 彼は非常に考え深い.

P *thoughtful* ***about*** the business 業務に注意する. ¶ *thoughtful* ***for*** one's friend 友人に対する思いやりがある. ¶ *thoughtful* ***of*** the comfort of others 他人の幸福に対する思いやりがある. 【類】*thoughtful* ***of*** the future (one's safety).

thoughtfulness, *n.* 深い思慮.

P *thoughtfulness* ***for*** others 他人に対する思いやり.

thoughtless, *a.* 不注意な.

P Maybe it was *thoughtless* ***of*** me. 恐らく僕が不注意だったのだ. ‖ *thoughtless* ***of*** the future 将来を考えないで.

thoughtlessness, *n.* 不注意.

Q from ***mere*** *thoughtlessness* 全くの不注意から. ¶ ***utter*** *thoughtlessness* はなはだしい不注意.

thousand, *n.* 千.

V The plague ***carried off*** *thousands* of people. その疫病が何千という人命を奪った.

Q ***countless*** *thousands* of ... [何千とも知れない]無数の... ¶ a ***hundred*** *thousand* 十万. ¶ crowds ***some*** *thousands* strong 数千の群集. ¶ ***unnumbered*** (=***uncounted***) *thousands* 幾千か数えきれないほどの多数.

P The white ants came streaming out ***by*** *thousands*. 白ありが何千となく流れをなして出て来た. ‖ be sold ***by*** the *thousand* 千を単位で販売される. 【類】The birds flock together ***by*** [the] *thousands*. / "Rugger" has its followers (ラグビーをやるものが) ***by*** *thousands* in London. ¶ one man ***in*** a *thousand* 千人に一人という人. 【類】She is a devoted housemaid—plainly a girl ***in*** a *thousand*. / Its membership is counted ***in*** *thousands*. ‖ ***in*** *thousands* [統計など]千位で示した. 【類】people flock ***in*** their *thousands* to see ... / The townsfolk (市民) resorted ***in*** *thousands* to the florists' gardens of Dangozaka to see chrysanthemum shows (菊花展覧会) in November. ‖ The circulation is far up ***in*** the *thousands*. 発行部数は優に数千に上っている.

P² *thousands* ***of*** people 何万という人々. 【類】The great moving-picture companies purvey to *thousands* ***of*** theaters. / hundreds and *thousands* ***of*** people. ¶ It is a risk of a *thousand* ***to*** one in my favor. 九分九厘私はそれに成功する見込がある. ¶ ***in*** *thousands* ***upon*** *thousands* of ... ...が数万にもなって.

thrash, *v.* むちうつ, 打ちたたく ; [案などを]ねる.

M *thrash* ***soundly*** はげしくむち打つ. ¶ The subject is ***well*** *thrashed* ***out***. その題目は十分論じ尽した.

M² The patient *thrashed* ***about*** with pain. 患者は苦しんでのたうち回った.

P *thrash* ***with*** a stick 棒で打つ.

thrashing, *n.* 打ちたたくこと, むち打ち.

V The boy ***deserves*** a sound *thrashing*. その少年は激しくむち打ってやるべきだ. ¶ I ***got*** a *thrashing* for my pains. 私は骨を折ってぶたれた.

thread, *n.* 糸; 続き, 筋道.

V I was unable to ***follow*** the *thread* of the plot. 私にはその物語の筋をたどって行けなかった. ¶ ***free*** silk *threads* from cocoons まゆから糸を繰る. ¶ After the general discussion of the subject, the chairman skilfully ***gathered*** the *threads* together. その問題を一般に討議した後で議長は手際よく衆議をまとめた. ¶ The needle-eye is too small to ***hold*** the *thread*. 針のめどが小さいから糸が通らない. ‖ continue to ***hold*** the *threads* of the movement その運動と縁を切らないでいる. ¶ ***lose*** the *thread* of one's argument その議論の連絡が切れる ‖ if the speaker happens to ***lose*** the *thread* of his discourse もし弁士の演説中戸惑いをする(どう続けていいか分からなくなる)ようなことがあったら. ¶ ***pick up*** the *thread* of our conversation again 再び話の筋道をたどる(先を続ける). 【類】***pick up*** the *threads* of education and training, in many cases, broken by years of military service. ¶ ***push*** a *thread* through a needle 針の目に糸を通す. ¶ ***tangle*** the *threads* 糸をもつらかす. ¶ ***trace*** the *threads* that have gone to make up ... ...するに到った諸原因を探究する. 【類】***trace*** the *thread* of subversive activity (破壊的活動).

Q ***coarse*** (***fine***) *thread* 太(細)糸. ¶ Yarn is like a ***heavy*** *thread*. より糸は太糸に似ている.

Q² a reel of ***cotton thread*** カタン糸一つ. ¶***gold*** (***silver***) *threads* 金(銀)糸. ¶a ***silk thread*** 絹糸.

P We hold our lives ***by*** (=***on***) a *thread!* われわれは一すじの糸で命をつないでいるのだ. 【類】His life hangs ***by*** a *thread.* ¶drawn ***into*** a *thread* 引いて糸にした. ¶string beads ***on*** a *thread* 糸でガラス玉をつなぐ. ¶worn ***to*** a *thread* [衣服が]よれよれになって. 【類】a dress worn ***to*** the last thread.

P² the *thread* ***of*** a story 話の筋道.

thread, *v.* 縫うようにして通る, 押分けて通る.

P The ship *threaded* her way ***between*** the hidden rocks. 船は暗礁の間を縫って進んだ. ¶The district is *threaded* ***by*** a railroad. その地方には一路の鉄道が通じている. ¶*thread* eels ***on*** a stewer うなぎをくしに通す. ¶*thread* one's way ***through*** a crowd 群集の間を縫って行く.

threat, *n.* 威かく, 脅迫.

V The *threat* was ***carried out*** (into effect). そのおどかしは実行された. ¶***laugh*** one's *threat* to scorn その脅迫を一笑に付する. ¶***make*** *threats* against ... ...をおどす. ¶***present*** a greater *threat* to her than ... ...その国に取って...よりも恐ろしい. ¶Mad with rage, I commenced to ***put*** my *threat* into execution. 腹立まぎれに私はおどしだけでなくそれを実行し出した. ¶***try*** *threat* of violence 暴力に訴えるとおどしてみる. ¶***utter*** *threats* against ... ...におどし文句を言う. ¶***vent*** a *threat* おどすし文句を言う.

Q a ***dire*** *threat* to the freedom of the press 言論の自由に対する恐るべき威かく. ¶"I will write to the Times" is a ***favorite*** *threat* of Britons.「タイムズに投書するぞ」というのが英国人のおきまりのおどし文句である. ¶an ***implicit*** *threat* 暗默の脅迫. ¶a ***veiled*** *threat* それとなしのおどかし.

Q² a ***security*** *threat* 保安をおびやかすもの. ¶a ***storm*** *threat* 暴風雨の脅威. ¶a ***strike*** *threat* ストライキの脅威.

P ***by*** *threat* of force 腕力に訴えるとおどかして. ¶***on*** the *threat* of ... ...がおどかしたので. ¶yield ***to*** *threats* 威かくに屈服する.

P² *threats* ***against*** the life of ... ...の命を取ろうというおどかし. ¶a *threat* ***to*** the safety of ... ...の安全を脅かすもの ‖ *threats* ***to*** the maintenance of world peace 世界平和の維持に対する脅威 ‖ the *threat* ***to*** strike ストをやるぞという威かく.

threaten, *v.* おどす; 危くする; きざしがある.

M It will ***seriously*** *threaten* the prosperity of the town. それは大いに町の繁栄に影響するだろう.

P *threatened* ***by*** a person 人におどされて. ¶The company is *threatened* ***with*** bankruptcy. その会社は破産の恐れがある. ‖ *threatened* ***with*** danger 危険にひんして ‖ *threaten* a person ***with*** injury 人に危害を加えると言っておどす. 【類】*threaten* ***with*** an action (実力行使) ‖ He was *threatened* ***with*** pneumonia due to exposure. 彼は外気にさらされたので肺炎になりかかった. ‖ be *threatened* ***with*** death many times 死線をただよう.

O The practice *threatens* to become general. その慣習は一般化しようとしている. ¶The house *threatened* to topple over on them. その家が彼らの上に転覆しかけていた. ¶It *threatens* to rain. 今にも雨が降りそうだ.

three, *n.* 三, 三個.

Q the ***Big Three*** of living English literature 現代英文学の三大家.

P come into flower ***in*** twos and *threes* ぽつぽつ花が開く.

three-dimensional, *a.* 立体の.

P be *three-dimensional* ***in*** effect [ジオラマなど]立体的に見える.

three-year-old, *n.* 三つの子.

Q a ***toddling*** *three-year-old* よちよち歩きの三つになる子.

thresh, *v.* 検討する.

M *thresh* ***out*** the whole business 全事業を再検討する.

threshing, *n.* ばたばた打つこと.

P² Outside there was only the *threshing* ***of*** the rain. 外では雨がぱらぱら降っているだけだった.

threshold, *n.* しきい; 入口.

V ***cross*** (=***pass***) the *threshold* しきいをまたぐ ‖ ***cross*** the *threshold* of practical life 実生活にとびこむ.

P ***at*** the *threshold* of the Taisho reign 大正の当初に ‖ those ***at*** the *threshold* of a career [卒業生など]活世界に船出する人々 ‖ situated ***at*** the very *threshold* of ... ...のとっ鼻に位置して. ¶welcomed ***on*** the *threshold* 戸口で迎えられて ‖ stand ***on*** the *threshold* of a brilliant future かくかくたる未来へ乗り出そうとしている ‖ children ***on*** the *threshold* of thirteen 十三になりかけている子供たち ‖ ***on*** the *threshold* of manhood 大人になりかけている ‖ young men ***on*** (=***upon***) the *threshold* of life 人生の門出の青年. 【類】a young man who died ***on*** the *threshold* of a life full of promise.

thrift, *n.* 節約, 勤倹.

V ***practice*** *thrift* 節約を実行する.

thrill, *n.* 身震い, 感動.

V ***cause*** a *thrill* ぞっとさせる. ¶we ***experienced*** a pleasant *thrill* of excitement over the news that ... われわれは...という報道に接してその痛快さに胸を躍らせた. 【類】***experience*** a *thrill* of surprised pleasure. ¶***feel*** a pleasant *thrill* ***go*** through one うれしさにぞくぞくとする. ¶I ***got*** a big *thrill* out of it. ひどく感動した; [ゲームなど]非常に面白かった. ¶as long as love, sympathy and heroism ***rouse*** an answering *thrill* in the human heart 人の心が愛と同情と勇気に打たれる限りは. ¶***send*** a *thrill* through every individual すべての人の心をぞっとさせる ‖ The news ***sent*** a *thrill* of joy to my heart. 私はその知らせを聞いてうれしさが胸にこみ上げて来た. ¶the *thrill* that was ***stirred*** within us by ... ...がわれわれの心に与えた感動.

V² A *thrill* ***ran*** through the assembly touching the heart of each one. 会衆はだれも心を打たれ身にしみ渡る思いをした.

Q² a ***picture*** *thrill* 絵の感激. ¶a ***sex*** *thrill* 性的感激.

P play football ***for*** the *thrill* of it; not merely to win 単に勝つためでなくスリルのためにしゅう球をやる. ¶***in*** the *thrill* of the assignation 指定された場所に行くうれしさにぞくぞくして.

P² the *thrill* ***of*** seeing oneself in print 自分の書いたものが印刷されたときの感激.

thrill, *v.* ぞっとさせる, 感動させる.

M be ***so*** *thrilled* at going off 出かけるのを非常に喜んでいる.

P Fear *thrilled* ***through*** my veins. 恐ろしさが私の身にしみ渡った. ‖ The voice *thrilled* ***through*** the hall. 声は会堂にひびき渡った. ¶*thrill* one ***to*** the marrow 人を骨髄まで感動させる ‖ The sight *thrilled* ***to*** the very soul of me. その光景に対して私は心の奥底から感激した. ¶*thrill* ***with*** horror 恐ろしさに身震いする ‖ be *thrilled* ***with*** joy (=delight) うれしくてぞくぞくする.

thriller, *n.*《口語》スリラーもの.

Q This is one of the best of ***American*** *thrillers.* これは米国のスリラーものでは傑作の一つだ.

Q² a ***mystery*** *thriller* スリラーもの.

thrilling, *a.* スリルのある.

M "***How*** *thrilling!*" cried she.「まあすてき」と彼女は叫んだ.

thrive, *v.* 繁盛する, 栄える.

P Sheep do not *thrive* ***in*** Japan. 羊は日本ではよく育たない. ¶Japanese *thrive* ***on*** rice. 日本人は米食でりっぱにやっている. ‖ These vegetables do not *thrive* ***on*** this type of soil. これらの野菜はこういった土ではよくできない. 【類】*thrive* ***on*** sunshine and fresh air. ¶Flowers will not *thrive* ***without*** sunshine. 花は太陽に当らないとよく咲かない.

throat, *n.* のど.

V ***clear*** one's *throat* and say ... せき払いをして...と言う. 【類】He coughed a little and ***cleared*** his *throat.* ‖ The power of voluntarily ***clearing*** the *throat* of mucus, "hawking," is peculiar to man. 自発的にのどから粘液を除く力すなわちせき払いは人類特有のものだ. ¶***cut*** a man's *throat* 人ののどを切る. ¶***gargle*** the *throat* うがいをする. ¶with a costly silver fox ***glorifying*** her *throat* 首には高価な銀ぎつねを巻いて. ¶***grip*** one's *throat* そののどを締める. ¶***slit*** one's *throat* with a knife ナイフでのどを切る. ¶When the spring put in I felt charmed with the music of birds, which ***strained*** their little *throats* to proclaim it. 春がやって来ると小さなのどをしぼって立春を告げる小鳥の音楽に私は魅せられた. ¶***swab*** the *throat* with permanganate of potash 過マンガンサンカリをのどに塗布する. ¶***wash*** the *throat* のどを洗う. ¶***wrap up*** one's *throat* のどを布で巻く.

V² My *throat* ***pains*** when I swallow. 私は物をのみ込むときのどが痛む.

Q The ***brazen*** *throat* of war had ceased to roar. 当時戦争の砲火はすでにやんでいた. ¶a ***dry, husky, tickling*** *throat* harassed by coughing せきでいためつけられているかわいた, しわがれ声の, くすぐったいのど. ¶"Mad dog! Mad dog!" is the cry that comes from a hundred *throats.*「狂犬だ! 狂犬だ!」と大勢の人が叫ぶ. ¶They

yelled from those ***lusty young** throats*. その若者たちは威勢よく叫んだ. ¶have a ***sore** throat* のどが痛い.
P force it ***down*** one's *throat* それを無理に飲み下す. 【類】Food does not go ***down*** his *throat*. ¶The words stuck ***in*** my *throat*. その言葉が容易に私の口から出なかった. ‖ I felt a lump ***in*** my *throat*. 私はのどのつまる思いがした. 【類】a tiny bone stuck ***in*** my *throat*. ¶put it ***round*** one's *throat* それをのどに巻く.

throb, *n*. 鼓動. 「ろうふるえ.
Q a ***treacherous** throb* of her voice 彼女の声の上べをつくろうふるえ.
Q^2 tremulous with ***heart** throbs* 胸のとどろきでふるえて.
P^2 a *throb **of*** pain (joy) 苦痛(など)のためのふるえ ‖ the *throb **of*** a pulse 脈はく. 【類】the *throb **of*** distant gun-fire.

throb, *v*. 鼓動する, どよめく.
M My heart *throbbed **violently***. 心臓がはげしく鼓動した.
P The newsroom is a place *throbbing **with*** activity. 新聞社の編集室は大車輪に立働く場所である. ‖ cities *throbbing **with*** the pulse of modern industry 近代産業の鼓動する都市 ‖ news which will make London *throb **with*** pride ロンドンが誇りの胸を躍らせるニュース ‖ my wound *throbs **with*** pain きずがうずく.

throe, *n*. 激痛; [通例 *pl.*] 悩み.
Q^2 a ***birth** throe*=the throe of birth 出産の苦痛, 陣痛.
P The country was then ***in*** the *throes* of actual revolution. その国は当時革命騒ぎのさ中にあった. ‖ a nation ***in*** the *throes* of political and mental rebirth 政治的並びに精神的再生の悩みにある国民.
P^2 the *throes **of*** death 死の苦しみ.

throne, *n*. 玉座; 王位, 帝位.
V ***abdicate*** the *throne* 位を譲る. ¶***ascend*** (=***accede to** or **come to***) the *throne* 王位につく. ¶***claim*** the *throne* 王権を主張する. ¶***compass*** the *throne* of ... ...の王権を握る. ¶He ***desired*** the *throne* for himself. 彼は自ら王権を握ろうとした. ¶he continued to ***fill*** the *throne* of ... 彼は引続き...の王位についていた. ¶***lose*** one's *throne* 王位を失う. ¶***memorialize*** the *throne* 王(帝)に上訴する. ¶***mount*** the *throne* 王位につく. ¶***occupy*** a *throne* 王位を占める. ¶***renounce*** the *throne* 王権を放棄する. ¶***reverence*** the *Throne* 王を尊敬する. ¶***seize*** (=***usurp***) the *throne* 王位を奪う. ¶cause the emperor to ***vacate*** the *throne* 皇帝に王位を放棄させる.
Q a figure of Buddha on a ***lotus** throne* 蓮座の仏像. ¶with Innocent III upon the ***papal** throne* インノセント三世がローマ法王の位についていて.
Q^2 the ***peacock** throne* くじゃくの玉座(インド Delhi の王家に伝わり後ペルシア王の所有に帰した有名な玉座).
P a conference ***before*** the *throne* 御前会議. ¶He is still the great man (=power) ***behind*** the *throne*. 彼はいまだに帝王の偉大な後だてである. ¶a speech ***from*** the *Throne* 勅語. ¶he is ***on*** the *throne* of ... 彼は...の王位についている ‖ with George the Third ***upon*** the *Throne* ジョージ三世を王にいただいて. 【類】he was placed ***on*** the *throne* of ... ¶succeed ***to*** the *throne* of ... ...の王位を継ぐ ‖ succession ***to*** the *throne* 王位継承.

throng, *n*. 群集, 大勢.
V gay old gentlewomen ***quizzing*** the *throng* through their glasses 群集を眼鏡越しに物色する陽気な老淑女ら.
Q a ***bedraggled** and **dingy-looking** throng* 着物をずるずる引きずって汚い格好した群集. ¶a wildly ***cheering** throng* 夢中になって歓呼する群集. ¶***dense** and **frowzy** throngs* ごたごたしてむれ臭い群集. ¶a ***gay** throng* of strollers, shoppers, and businessmen 漫歩者や買物する人や商人のにぎやかな群. ¶a ***huge** throng* of 5,000 students 学生五千の大群. ¶a ***medley** throng* 雑然たる群集. ¶quell ***milling** throng* なぐり合う群集を静める. ¶standing aloof from the ***motley** throng* of the city その都市のう合の衆から超然として. ¶a ***vulgar** throng* 低俗な群集.
P^2 a *throng **of*** people 人の群.

throng, *v*. 群がる, 込み合う.
M ***thickly** thronged* 雑とうした.
P *throng **around*** a person ごたごたと人を取巻く. ¶The resort is *thronged* during the season ***by*** bathers. その温泉場は季節中は浴客が多い. ¶*throng **into*** a room へやの中にどやどや入る. ¶These thoughts *throng **on*** my mind. こういう考えが私の心にむらむらと浮んで来る. ¶*throng **to*** a place ある場所へどやどや押しかける. ¶Ginza is always *thronged **with*** promenaders strolling along the pavements. 銀座はいつも歩道をぶらつく人で一杯になっている.
O Multitudes *thronged* the church to hear the sermon. 大群集がその説教を聞こうと教会に押しかけた.

throttle, *v*. のどをしめる; 抑圧する.
P High tariffs *throttle* trade ***between*** nations. 高い関税は国家間の貿易を阻害する.

through, *ad*. 通して, 終りまで, 残らず.
P We had engaged an automobile *through **to*** Nikko. 日光まで通しの自動車をあらかじめ雇ってあった. ¶Are you *through **with*** this knife? このナイフはお済みですか. ‖ I'm *through **with*** her for good. もう彼女とは縁切りだ.
O The hotel is open the year *through*. そのホテルは年中やっている. ¶Give it back as soon as you're *through*. 終ったらすぐ返してくれ.

throw, *n*. 投げて届く距離; 機会.
Q It is your ***last** throw*. これが君の最後のチャンスだ. ¶a ***well-aimed** throw* at cricket クリケットでよくねらいをつけた投てき.
P ***at*** a stone's *throw* 石を投げて届く所に. ¶***within*** a stone's *throw* of (=from) the sea 海から石を投げて届くような所に(近くに).

throw, *v*. 投げる, 投射する.
M *throw **aside*** as useless 不用として捨てる ‖ *throw **aside*** all caution すっかり油断する ‖ *throw **aside*** all decorum 無遠慮に振舞う. ¶*throw **away*** one's life in one's country's cause 国家のために生命を投げうつ ‖ *throw* them ***away*** into the wastebasket それをくずかごに放り込む ‖ Kindness was never *thrown **away*** upon the lad. その若者に尽くした親切はむだではなかった. ‖ *throw **away*** (=reject) a good offer よい申し出を断る. 【類】It's folly to *throw* chances ***away***. / All his efforts were *thrown **away***. ¶*throw **back*** an assault 攻撃を撃退する ‖ He is *thrown **back*** a generation by shaving. 彼はひげをそったのでめっきり若くなった. ¶She *threw* herself ***blindly*** into his hands. 彼女は一図に彼に頼った. ¶*throw* oneself ***carelessly*** down on the floor かまわず床にころぶ. ¶a horse *thrown **completely*** out of the race 競馬ですっかり置いてけぼりを食った馬. ¶*throw* ourselves ***eagerly*** into the task of ... ...の仕事に打込む. ¶*throw* oneself ***headlong*** into the water 真逆様に水に飛び込む. ¶*throw* oneself ***heart** and **soul*** into a political contest やっきとなって政争の渦中に身を投じる. ¶*throw* oneself ***heartily*** into the movement その運動に専心する. ¶*thrown **open*** to foreign trade (the intercourse of the civilized world) 外国貿易(など)に開放された ‖ *throw **open*** a wide view 突然...の広い景色が眼前に開ける. 【類】The door was *thrown **open***. / The garden was *thrown **open*** to the public. ¶The motion has been *thrown **out***. その動議は否決された. ‖ *throw* it ***out*** at the window それを窓から投げる ‖ *throw **out*** roots 根を生じる ‖ The House of Lords has no power to *throw **out*** a Bill relating to money. 英国の上院は金銭に関する法案を否決する権限がない. ‖ *throw **out*** feelers=fly (=send out) a *ballon d'essai* 探りを入れる ‖ *throw **out*** the Labor Government 労働党政府を倒す ‖ *throw **out*** a suggestion that ... ...という暗示を与える. 【類】*throw **out*** a few hints ‖ *throw **out*** sparks 火花を散らす. 【類】The lamp *threw **out*** a dim light. ‖ *throw **out*** jest upon ... ...を冷やかす. ¶*throw **overboard*** about ... tons of cargo 約...トンの積荷を船から投げ出す ‖ *throw* oneself ***overboard*** 船から(海へ)飛び込む. ¶*throw* oneself ***quickly*** to the ground and feign to be dead さっと地上に身を伏せて死んだふりをする. ¶*Katakana* words are ***thickly** thrown* through the pages of our general literature. 片仮名語はわが国の一般読物によく出て来る. ¶Two rooms were *thrown **together*** to form a large gathering hall. 二つのへやをぶっ通して一つの大きな集会場にした. ¶*throw* oneself ***uneasily*** from side to side of the bed [寝苦しそうに]寝台の端から端へ寝返りする.
M^2 *throw* oneself ***about*** in a frightful manner 恐ろしいようにころげ回る. ¶*thrown **by*** ... as useless ...は無用として捨てられる ‖ Maybe she'll be *thrown **by*** like a scrap of paper. 彼女は多分紙きれのように捨てられるだろう. ¶*throw* oneself ***down*** on the grass いきなり草の上にからだを横にする ‖ *throw* oneself ***down*** into a couch 長いすにどっかと腰をおろす. ¶*throw **in*** (***out***) a circuit 回路を閉じる(開く)

‖ If you take 10 copies, I'll *throw* ***in*** another. 十部お買いになれば一部おまけします ‖ with ... *thrown* ***in*** おまけに...を添えて ‖ *throw* ***in*** one's lot with ... ...とその運命をともにする. ¶ briskly *throw* ***off*** one's clothes 手早く着物を脱ぐ ‖ *throw* ***off*** restraint 束縛を脱する. 【類】*throw* ***off*** one's yoke / The rebellion ended in *throwing* ***off*** the Chinese yoke. / *throw* ***off*** the shackles (束縛) ‖ *throw* ***off*** all disguise 一切の仮面を脱ぐ. 【類】*throw* ***off*** one's mask ‖ *throw* ***off*** one's acquaintance (friends, dependents) 知人(友人, 居候)を見捨てる ‖ *throw* ***off*** hesitation ためらいを捨てる. 【類】*throw* ***off*** impurities / *throw* ***off*** the cares of business / *throw* ***off*** one's own ***responsibility*** / *throw* ***off*** all feeling of restraint (窮屈な感じ) ‖ Our system is constantly *throwing* ***off*** waste matter. われわれの体は絶えず廃物を排せつしている. ‖ *throw* ***off*** the switch スイッチを切る ‖ *throw* ***off*** a poem 即興詩を作る ‖ In slopes water is more easily *thrown* ***off***. 傾斜地では水がよくはける. ¶ *throw* ***on*** one's garment (coat, etc.) 外とう(上着など)を引掛ける. ¶ *throw* ***up*** one's hands in despair 絶望して両手をさっとあげる ‖ *throw* ***up*** a ball in the air 空中にボールを投げ上げる ‖ *throw* ***up*** a position 断然その職を辞する ‖ *throw* ***up*** one's contract with ... ...との契約を破棄する. 【類】*throw* (=give) ***up*** painting in despair ‖ *throw* (=chuck *or* toss) ***up*** (=***in***) the sponge 負けたと自認する ‖ He *threw* ***up*** Annie for another girl. アニーを捨てて別の娘にくらがえした. ‖ *throw* ***up*** a battery 砲台を急造する.

P he had these words *thrown* ***at*** him: 彼は...としかりつけられた. ¶ *throw* a stone ***across*** a fence 石をさく越しに投げる. ¶ *Throwing* good money ***after*** bad. 〖諺〗泥棒に追銭. ¶ *throw* oneself ***againt*** ... 体を...に突当てる. ¶ *throw* a cordon ***around*** ... ...の回りに非常線を張る. ¶ *throw* a stone ***at*** a dog 犬に石を投げつける ‖ He *threw* himself ***at*** her feet. 彼は彼女の足下にひれ伏した. ¶ Angry words of disapproval were *thrown* ***from*** the audience. 聴衆から不賛成の怒語が投げつけられた. ‖ He *threw* himself ***from*** the tower. 彼は塔から投身した. ¶ *throw* it ***in*** the waste basket それをくずかごに投入れる. ¶ *throw* one's cap ***into*** the air 帽子を空中に投げ上げる ‖ It *threw* him ***into*** a high fever. それで彼は大熱が出た. ‖ She *threw* extreme tenderness ***into*** her voice and eyes. 彼女は急にその声やまなざしをいかにもやさしくした. ‖ *throw* it ***into*** the dust heap of useless rubbish それをがらくたの中に投げ込む ‖ *throw* oneself ***into*** a chair 体をどっかといすに投げる. ¶ The newspapers *threw* themselves ***into*** the arena. 諸新聞がその問題を論じ立てた. ‖ *throw* a manuscript book ***into*** a form suitable for publication 本の原稿を出版のできるように整理する ‖ *throw* a person ***into*** prison 人を投獄する ‖ He was *thrown* ***into*** a fit. 彼は気絶した. ‖ The whole assembly was *thrown* ***into*** fits of laughter. 会衆一同はどっと笑った. ‖ *throw* it ***into*** bolder relief それをさらにくっきりと目立たせる ‖ The whole country will be *thrown* ***into*** a state of anarchy. 国内が無政府状態に陥るだろう. ‖ the city was *thrown* ***into*** a panic through a report that ...同市は...という報道のために恐慌状態に陥った. 【類】The country was *thrown* ***into*** an upheaval (てんやわんや). / the conference was *thrown* ***into*** an uproar. 【類】*thrown* ***into*** confusion (discord, consternation and amazement, utter despair) by ... ‖ the ideas advanced in this article have been *thrown* ***into*** shape after a series of visits to ... 本論文に開陳した思想は...を数回訪問した後に草したものである ‖ *throw* a person ***into*** ecstasy 人をこうこつとさせる ‖ be *thrown* ***into*** a dilemma 窮境に陥る ‖ be *thrown* ***into*** the shade by ... ...のために顔色がなくなる. ¶ be *thrown* ***off*** the straight course [船などが]進路をくるわさせられる ‖ I have often noticed that a thick fog will *throw* the Londoner ***off*** his balance altogether. 濃霧のためにロンドン人の調子が狂っているのを私はしばしば見た. ‖ *throw* the keepers ***off*** their guard 看守を油断させる. ¶ be *thrown* ***on*** the streets 路頭に迷う ‖ That incident and its consequences *threw* her ***on*** the public. その事件とその後の成行のために彼女は江湖放浪の身となった. ‖ It appeared as if it had been suddenly *thrown* ***on*** a screen. それがあたかも突然幕の上に映写されたかのように現われた. ‖ be *thrown* ***on*** her own resources 彼女自身の力に頼らなければならないことになる ‖ be *thrown* ***on*** her beam ends 船が横っ倒しになる; 〖比ゆ〗困り切る ‖ new light has been *thrown* ***on*** the text of ... ...の本文に新たな光明が投げられた ‖ *throw* oneself face-down ***on*** a table 急に卓の上に身を伏せる. ¶ *throw* a person ***out of*** balance 人をろうばいさせる ‖ *throw* a person ***out of*** the house 人を戸外にほうり出す ‖ *throw* the workers ***out of*** employment 従業員を失業させる. 【類】be *thrown* ***out of*** work / *throw* it ***out of*** the market ‖ be *thrown* ***out of*** gear [工事の]順序を乱す; 調子がみだれる. ¶ *throw* a man ***over*** board 人を船から投げ出す ‖ *throw* a bridge ***over*** ... ...に橋をかける. ¶ He *threw* his arm ***round*** my neck. 彼は私の首に抱きついた. ¶ They *threw* ***to*** the wind all respect for things or persons. 彼らは物や人に対する尊敬の念を全く捨てた. ‖ *throw* one's eyes ***to*** the ground 視線を地上に投げる ‖ *throw* physic ***to*** the dogs 犬に薬をやる ‖ He hasn't a word to *throw* ***to*** a dog. あの男はひどく無口だ. ¶ *throw* oneself ***under*** an approaching train 近づく汽車の下に身を投げる. ¶ May I *throw* myself ***upon*** your kindness? あなたのお親切にすがってよろしいでしょうか. 【類】The author *throws* himself ***upon*** the kind indulgence of his readers. ¶ *throw* a stone ***with*** a sling 投石器で石を投げる ‖ *throw* himself ***with*** great warmth into an attack on ... やっきとなって...の攻撃に取掛る.

thrower, *n.* 投げる人(もの).

Q² a ***curve*** *thrower* 〖野〗曲球投手. ¶ a ***flame*** *thrower* 火炎放射機.

thrum, *v.* つまびきする; こつこつ打つ.

P *thrum* ***on*** the desk 机をこつこつたたく. ¶ *thrum* a guitar ***out of*** tune 調子っぱずれにギターをかき鳴らす. ¶ *thrum* ***over*** 一本調子で語り続ける.

thrush, *n.* 〖鳥〗つぐみの一種.

Q A ***solitary*** *thrush* was singing his spring song. 一羽のつぐみが春の歌を歌っていた.

thrust, *n.* 押し, 突き, 突撃.

V ***make*** a veiled *thrust* 暗に一矢酬いる. ¶ ***parry*** a *thrust* 突込みを受流す.

Q a ***sudden*** *thrust* in fencing 剣道のお突き.

Q² a ***bayonet*** *thrust* 突貫. ¶ This was a ***home*** *thrust*. これで止めを刺された. ¶ assassination by ***knife*** *thrusts* ナイフで刺した暗殺. ¶ sword 剣での一突き.

P² a big *thrust* ***from*** the air 大空襲. ¶ a *thrust* ***with*** a

thrust, *v.* 突く, 推す, 突込む.

M *thrust* a person ***aside*** 人を押しのける. ¶ *thrust* ***away*** 押しのける, はねのける. ¶ *thrust* ***out*** one's way 押しのけて進む. ¶ Viewless and unexpected events *thrust* themselves ***continually*** athwart our path. 目に見えず予期しない事件がわれわれの進路に絶えず現われる. ¶ She *thrust* herself ***forth*** into the storm. 彼女は暴風雨の中を飛び出した. ¶ *thrust* (=stick) ***out*** one's tongue at ... ...に向って舌を出す ‖ *thrust* ***out*** the problem from many angles 色々の角度からその問題を検討する. ¶ *thrust* ... ***pell-mell*** in a group ...をしゃにむに一まとめにする. ¶ *thrust* ***together*** 圧し固める.

M² *thrust* ***in*** 突入れる, 打込む. ¶ The trees have *thrust* ***off*** their leaves. 木の葉が落ちてしまった. ¶ *thrust* a person ***on*** to his duty ...を促して勤務させる. ¶ the white cone of Fuji *thrusting* ***up*** above the clouds 雲の上にそそり立つ白い円すい形の富士山.

P *thrust* one's resignation ***at*** one's superior 上役に辞表を突付ける. ¶ *thrust* ***at*** a person ***with*** a sword 剣で人を突こうとする. ¶ *thrust* it ***into*** the limbo of forgotten things それを過ぎ去ったものとして葬ってしまう ‖ *thrust* a guinea ***into*** his hands 彼に一ギニーを握らせる ‖ It was *thrust* (=thrown) ***into*** the background. それはもう世間から忘れられてしまった. ‖ *thrust* it ***into*** one's pocket それをポケットに突っ込む. 【類】be *thrust* ***into*** the car. ¶ *thrust* a person ***out of*** the house (room, office) 人を戸外(など)に押出す. ¶ *thrust* one's sword ***through*** another's bosom 他人の胸に剣を突刺す. 【類】He was *thrust* ***through*** with a lance by a common soldier. ¶ *thrust* a person ***to*** death with a sword 刀で人を突き殺す. ¶ Greatness was *thrust* ***upon*** him. 彼は(それほどの人物でもないのに)世間から偉い人に祭り上げられた. ‖ Honors were *thrust* ***upon*** him. 名誉が彼に押しつけられた. 【類】He showed great reluctance to accept the high position *thrust* ***upon*** him. 【類】*thrust* a person ***with*** a spear (sword, dagger) やり(など)で人を突き刺す. 【類】was *thrust* ***with*** a sharp weapon from behind.

thud, *n.* どさっという音.

Q with a *heavy thud* どさっと(音を立てて).

P The tree fell to the ground *with* a *thud*. その木はどさっと地上に倒れた.

thumb, *n.* 親指.

V He has *pinched* his *thumb* in the door. 彼は親指を戸にはさんだ. ¶*Put* your *thumbs up*!=Thumbs up! 悲観するな, しっかり; 賛成! 【類】*Put* your *thumbs up* (=Thumbs up) to show your approval (賛成の方は). ¶*rotate* one's *thumbs* 二つの親指を回転する. ¶A baby *sucks* its *thumb*. 赤ん坊は親指を吸う. ¶*thrust* the *thumb* between two fingers [指で]豆をこしらえる.

Q His fingers are *all thumbs*. 彼は不器用な男だ. ¶He knew fully well that *thumbs* were *down*. 彼はへまをやったとは百も承知していた.

P pinch it to dust *between thumb* and forefinger それを親指と人差指でひねりつぶす. ¶by rule *of thumb* めのこ算で, 目分量で. ¶She gets him *under* her *thumb*. 彼女はすっかり彼の頭を押えている(恐妻など). 【類】He is completely *under* her *thumb*. / remain *under* the *thumb* of ... ¶seal *with* the *thumb* ぼ印を押す.

thumb, *v.* 親指でよごす; ページをめくる.

M The book is *badly thumbed*. その本は(ふちが)ひどくすれている. ¶a *well-thumbed* family dictionary 手あかのついている家庭用辞書.

M² He took it down and busily *thumbed* it *through*. 彼はそれをおろしていそがしくページをくった. 【類】*thumb* [*through*] pages (leaves).

thumbtack, *n.* 《米》画びょう.

V *pull out* a *thumbtack* 画びょうを抜く. ¶*push in* a *thumbtack* 画びょうを刺す.

thump, *n.* ごつんという音.

P *thump against* a lamppost 外灯柱にごつんとぶつかる. ¶beat *with* a *thump* ごつんと打つ.

thump, *v.* どしんと打つ.

P *thump at* the door ドアにどしんとぶっつかる. ¶*thump* a table *with* a fist こぶしで卓をたたく.

thumping, *n.* ごつんという打撃.

P He reinforced his oratory by *thumping on* the table. 彼はテーブルをどんとたたいて彼の弁舌に力を添えた.

Q the *heavy thumping* of the heart 心臓の激しいどうき.

thunder, *n.* 雷, 雷鳴.

V We shall *have thunder* today. きょうは雷があるだろう. ‖ I calculate we're going to *have thunder*. 《米》雷がありそうだ.

V² The *thunder crashes* and *rumbles*. 雷ががらがらごろごろと鳴る. ¶A *thunder broke* suddenly. 雷が突然鳴り出した. ‖ The *thunder* had *ceased* outside. [そのとき]戸外では雷がすでに鳴りやんでいた. ¶The *thunder growls*. 雷がごろごろ鳴る. ¶The *thunder roared* and the lightning flashed. 雷がはためき電光がひらめいた. ¶The *thunder rolls*. 雷鳴がとどろく.

Q like *distant thunder* 遠雷のように. ¶a *roaring thunder* ごろごろと鳴る雷鳴.

P a charm *against thunder* 雷よけの護符. ¶a welcome *in thunder* 礼砲をもっての歓迎 ‖ Why, *in thunder*, didn't you let me know? 一体どうして君は僕に知らせなかったのか. ¶a peal (=clap) *of thunder* 一しきりの雷鳴.

P² *thunders of* applause われるようなかっさい.

thunder, *v.* 雷鳴する, とどろく.

M It *thunders hard*. 激しく雷が鳴る. ¶Trains are *thundering in* and *out* all the time at a subway station. 地下鉄は駅で絶えずごう音を立てて出入りしている. ¶*thunder out* one's indignation 怒って大かつ一声する.

P *thunder against* a person 人に向ってどなり立てる. 【類】Waves *thunder against* the rocks. ¶*thunder at* a person 人をどなりつける ‖ *thunder at* the castle gate 城門を砲撃する. ¶It *thunders in* the distance. 遠雷が鳴る.

O It's *thundering* and lightening. ごろごろぴかぴかやっている.

thunderbolt, *n.* 雷電; 脅迫.

V *scatter* editorial *thunderbolts* 社説で硬論を吐く. ¶The *thunderbolt falls*. 落雷する. ¶A *thunderbolt struck* a building. 建物に落雷した.

thundering, *n.* とどろき, 咆哮(ほう).

Q *subterranean thundering* 地下の鳴動.

P² *thunderings against* the corruption and abuses of the age 時代の腐敗悪弊に対する猛烈な叫び.

thunder-shower, *n.* 雷雨, 夕立.

Q² a *summer thunder-shower* 夏の夕立.

thunderstorm, *n.* 雷雨.

V We shall *have* a *thunderstorm*. 雷雨があるだろう.

V² A violent *thunderstorm broke over* ... last night. 昨夜...に激しい雷雨があった. ¶A very heavy *thunderstorm passed* over the city. 非常にはげしい雷雨が同市を通過した. ¶A *thunderstorm* was *raging*. 雷雨が激しかった.

Q a *sharp thunderstorm* 激しい雷雨. ¶a *sudden thunderstorm* 突然の雷雨.

Q² a *summer thunderstorm* 夏の夕立.

P go out *in* a *thunderstorm* 雷雨の中を出て行く.

O The *thunderstorm* is over. 夕立があがった.

thunderstruck, *a.* 落雷して; ぎょっとして.

P They seemed *thunderstruck at* the news. そのニュースできもをつぶしたらしかった.

Thursday, *n.* 木曜日.

Q on *alternate Thursdays* 隔週の木曜日に.

thwart, *v.* 横ぎる, 反対する; 邪魔する.

P *thwarted by* casualties 不慮のできごとに妨げられて. ¶*thwarted in* one's plans (wishes, purposes) その計画(など)が失敗に帰して.

tick, *n.* 《主に英》信用, 掛け.

P buy things *on tick* (=credit *or* charge) 掛けで物を買う.

tick, *v.* 合印のしるしをつける; かちかち音をたてる.

M A telegraph *ticks out* messages. 電信機がかちかちと通信文を打出す.

M² *tick off* 時を刻む; [引合わせの]しるしをつける ‖ *tick off* (=check up) the items one by one 一つずつ項目を照合する.

ticker, *n.* 受信機; 《俗》懐中(腕)時計.

V² What does your *ticker say*? 君の時計では何時だ.

Q² *news tickers* ニュース受信機.

ticket, *n.* 乗車券, 切符; 入場券.

V *book tickets* in advance from ... ...から切符を前買する ‖ *book* 2nd class *tickets* by the 10.30 express train from Tokyo 東京発十時半の急行二等切符を買う. ¶*buy* a return *ticket* for the Sunny South 南方暖地行きの往復切符を買う. ¶*collect tickets* 切符を取集める. ¶*deliver tickets* at the turnstile when entering a museum 博物館にはいるとき回り木戸の所で切符を渡す. ¶*engage tickets* 切符を予約する. ¶*examine tickets* 切符を調べる. ¶You can break the journey at Nagoya without *forfeiting* your *ticket*. 切符をむだにしないで名古屋で途中下車ができる. ¶*furnish* through *tickets* to destination 目的地への通し切符を売る. ¶*get* a *ticket* 切符を求める. ¶*give* a person a *ticket* 券を人に渡す(交通違反のカードを警官が渡すなど). ¶*give up* (=*surrender*) one's *ticket* to the ticket-collector 集札係へ切符を渡す. ¶*hold tickets* ready via ... ...経由の切符をすぐ見せられるように用意している. ¶*Tickets* sold for return from Vancouver will be *honored* for return from San Francisco and vice versa. ヴァンクーヴァー引返しの切符はサンフランシスコ引返しの場合にも有効として取扱う, その反対の場合もまた同じである. ¶*issue* a *ticket* to ... ...への切符を発行する ‖ Cheap *tickets* will be *issued* to Boulogne. ブーローニュ行きの割引切符が発行される. ¶*make out* a *ticket* 切符を作る. ¶*obtain* a *ticket* at a terminal 切符を終着駅で求める. ¶*offer* a free *ticket* to the performance その演技に対し無料入場券を提供する. ¶*place tickets* on public sale 切符を一般に売る. ¶*present* one's *ticket* その切符を示す. ¶*procure tickets* at ticket offices 切符売場で切符を求める. 【類】*procure* a *ticket* for one's heavier luggage (重量超過荷物). ¶*produce* a *ticket* 切符を出して見せる. ¶*provide* a free rail *ticket* 無賃乗車券を提供する. ¶The conductor *punches tickets*. 車掌が切符にはさみを入れる. ¶No *tickets redeemed* within 3 days before game. 競技三日以内の切符は料金払戻しできません. ¶*scalp* a ball *ticket* 野球の入場券をやみ値で売る. ¶*secure tickets* at gate 入口で入場券を買う. ¶You will be required to *show* your *ticket* at the door. 入口で切符を示すことを求められるでしょう. ‖ *show* one's *ticket* to ... ...にその切符を示す. ¶*snip* (=*clip*) *tickets* 切符を切る. ¶*take tickets* at games and concerts 競技や音楽会で切符を求める. ¶The conductor *took up tickets*. 車しょうは切符を手に取上げた. ¶This *ticket* must be *worn* visibly. この切符は見えるように持っていなくてはならない. ¶*tickets reading* between Chicago, M., and Columbus, O. シカゴ・コロンバス間と記してある切符 ‖ *tickets reading* via ... ...経由指定の切符.

Q ***admission** tickets* 入場券. ¶***charity** tickets* 慈善興業の入場券. ¶***circular tour** tickets* 回遊切符. ¶a ***complimentary** tickets* 招待券. ¶a ***consolidated** ticket* (=joint booking) office 共同切符売場. ¶travel on a ***half** ticket* 半額切符で旅行する. ¶the ***Democratic** ticket* 民主党の党是. 【類】He is too big for ***half** ticket*. ¶vote a ***straight** ticket* 《米》看板に偽りない政党の候補者に投票する. ¶passengers holding ***through** tickets* to ... ...への通し切符所持の乗客. ¶The *ticket* is ***valid*** for ... days. その切符は...日間有効である. ¶a ***whole** ticket* 大人の切符.

Q² an ***admission-order** ticket* 入場整理券. ¶a ***circular tour** ticket* 回遊切符. ¶a ***clothing** ticket* 衣料切符. ¶***combined rail*** and ***sea** tickets* 鉄道汽船連絡切符. ¶appeal to the electorate to shun the ***Communist** ticket* 共産党の党是をけんおするよう選挙民に訴える. ¶***commutation** tickets* 割引切符, 回数券. ¶a ***convertible admission** ticket* 入場引替. ¶a book of ***coupon** tickets* クーポン券のとじ込み. ¶***courtesy** ticket* 優待券. ¶a ***credit deposit** ticket*=a merchandise bond 商品券. ¶an ***excursion** ticket* 回遊乗車券. ¶a ***forecabin** ticket* 前部船室の切符. ¶***full fare** tickets* 割引でない切符. ¶a ***half** ticket* 半札. ¶***long-limit, low-rate, round-trip** tickets* 長距離・割引・回遊乗車券. ¶a ***lottery** ticket* 福引券. ¶a ***meal** ticket* 食券. ¶a ***mileage** ticket* マイル数切符. ¶***monthly commutation*** and ***school** tickets* 月ぎめ回数及び学生割引切符. ¶a ***movie** ticket* 映画館の入場券. ¶a ***newspaper** ticket* 新聞社への招待券. ¶a ***number** ticket* (=plate) 番号券(札). ¶a ***one-way** ticket* 片道切符. ¶an ***order** ticket* 整理票. ¶an ***outside meal** ticket* 外食券. ¶a ***pawn** ticket* 質札. ¶***party** tickets* 団体切符 ‖ new men running on their respective ***party** tickets* それぞれの政党の公認候補として立候補した新人たち. ¶a ***passage** ticket* 乗船券. ¶***periodical** tickets* 定期乗車券. ¶***platform** tickets* [駅の]入場券. ¶***privilege** tickets* allowing the holders to travel by rail at a reduced courtesy rate その所持者に割引で鉄道旅行を許す特別待遇の乗車券. ¶a ***reserved seat** ticket* 予約座席券. ¶a ***relief rice** ticket* 救援飯米券. ¶a ***return** ticket* 往復切符. ¶a ***round-trip** ticket* 《米》往復切符. 【類】the return half (帰り半分) of a ***round-trip** ticket*. ¶***Season** tickets* good for ... days are sold over the railroad. ...日間有効の定期券はその鉄道で売っている. ¶vote a ***split** ticket* 《米》[政治] 分割投票をする. ¶a ***steamer*** (=***steamship***) *ticket* 乗船切符. ¶a ***steerage** ticket* 三等乗船切符. ¶the advance sale of ***theater** tickets* 劇場切符の前売. ¶punch ***trolley** tickets* 《米》都(市)電の切符にはさみを入れる.

P Admission will be ***by** ticket* only. 入場は切符所持者に限る. ¶The prisoner came out ***on** ticket* of leave. その囚人は仮出所をした. ‖ run ***on*** the Democratic *ticket* 《米》民主党公認として立候補する. 【類】a convict ***on** ticket* of leave=a ticket-of-leave man. ¶***without*** a *ticket* 切符なしで.

P² a *ticket* ***for*** a concert (performance, entertainment) 音楽会(など)の入場券. ¶*Tickets* ***of*** admission may be obtained from the Secretary. 入場券は幹事に申込めば手に入る. ¶*tickets* ***on*** foreign railroads 外国鉄道の乗車券. ¶*tickets* ***to*** and ***from*** all parts of the world 世界の各地へ及び各地からの切符.

ticking, *n.* かちかちという音.

P² The *ticking* ***of*** the wall clock broke the silence. 掛時計の秒をきざむ音が静けさを破った.

tickle, *v.* くすぐる, うれしがらせる.

P I was hugely *tickled* ***at*** the idea of ... ...と考えると私はとてもうれしかった. ¶*tickle* his vanity ***by*** passing his work 彼の作品を入選させていい気にさせる. ¶*tickled* ***to*** death 苦しいほどくすぐられて. ¶*tickle* a person ***under*** his arm わきの下をくすぐる. ¶*Tickle* him ***with*** a feather 羽で彼をくすぐる. ‖ *tickled* ***with*** one's praise そのほめ言葉に甘やかされて.

ticklish, *a.* くすぐったい.

P *ticklish* ***at*** an idea (plan, proposal) あること(など)を考えてくすぐったく感じる. ¶The news is quite *ticklish* ***to*** the ear. それは耳よりの話だ.

tide, *n.* 潮,風潮; 時機, 機会.

V ***arrest*** that *tide* その風潮を阻止する. ¶the ship ***awaited*** a favorable *tide* to sail for ... その船は...に出帆するために好都合な潮を待った. ¶***reverse*** the *tide* その傾向が逆行する. ¶***stem*** the *tide* of the sea [船などが]潮流に対立または抗進する ‖ More heroic methods were necessary to ***stem*** the *tide*. 大勢ばん回のためにはもっと強硬なやり方が必要であった. 【類】attempt to ***stem*** the *tide* of change (すう勢の変化). ¶***turn*** the *tide* of ... ...の潮流を転じさせる ‖ he succeeded in ***turning*** the *tide* of public opinion against the barbarity of ... 彼は世論のすう勢を転じて...の野蛮性を認識させることに成功した.

V² The *tide* is ***coming in***. 潮が上げている. ¶The *tide* of exclusive nationalism which set in with the accession of Alexander III. was ***ebbing*** fast. アレキサンダー三世の即位とともに始まった極端な国家主義の風潮はどんどん衰退しつつあった. ¶The *tide* ***falls***. 潮が落ちる. ¶The *tide* begins to ***flow*** at four today. きょうは四時上げ潮になる. ¶The *tide* ***rises***. 上げ潮になる. ¶The *tide* is beginning to ***run down***. 下げ潮になりだした. ¶when the *tide* of life ***sets homewards*** [勤め人などが]皆な家に帰るとき. ¶The *tide* ***sets out*** (***flows out** or **ebbs***) at 2 p.m. 二時に下げ潮になる. ¶The *tides* ***sweep in*** and ***out***. 潮はさしひきする. ¶The *tide* ***turns*** at noon. 潮は正午に変る. ‖ The *tide* ***turned*** his way. 彼に運が向いてきた. ‖ The *tide* of affairs ***turned*** in his favor. 彼は順境に立つようになった. 【類】the *tide* (=tables) began to ***turn*** in favor of ...

Q The boat was borne seawards by an ***adverse** tide*. ボートは下げ潮で海の方へ持って行かれた. ¶the ***ebbing*** (=***falling***) *tide* ひき潮. ¶at ***full** tide* 満潮に. ¶happy as a clam at ***high** tide* 上げ潮時のはまぐりのように愉快で. 【類】It is midday, and London's business is at ***high** tide* (盛り). ¶the ***incoming** tide* さし潮. ¶stem the ***oncoming** tide* 大勢に対抗する. ¶wait until ***next** tide* 次の潮時まで待つ. ¶The *tide* is ***overwhelming***. 大勢いかんともすべからずである. ¶***rain-swollen** tides* 雨で水かさを増した潮. ¶***receding** tide* 引き潮. ¶The ***returning** tide* of pleasure seekers begins to move. 出遊者のむれがぞろぞろと帰りかけている. ¶the ***rising** tide* さし潮 ‖ a ***rising** tide* in interest on the part of the public in ... 公衆が...に対して持つ興味の高まり. 【類】for some years there has been a ***rising** tide* of protest (反対の声) against ... ¶a ***strong eastward** tide* of tourist travel 観光者がどしどし東洋に押しかける傾向. ¶***swelling** tide* ふくれる潮.

Q² repeated attempts to stem the ***black-market** tide* やみ市の風潮を抑止しようとする再三の試み. ¶at ***ebb** tide* 引潮に ‖ the ***ebb** tide* of English literature 英文学の衰退. 【類】His fortune is now at ***ebb** tide*. ¶the ***flood** tide* 満潮. ¶the ***spring*** (***neap***) *tide* 大(小)潮 ‖ the depth of high water at ***spring** tides* 大潮における満潮時の水深. ¶a rise in ***travel** tide* 旅行熱の高まり. ¶***weather*** (***weather-going***) *tide* 逆風潮(風下に流れる潮).

P ***against*** the *tide* 世の風潮に逆って. ¶***at*** flood *tide* 満潮に ‖ gather shell-fish ***at*** low *tide* 潮干狩をやる. ¶***between*** the *tides* 干満両潮の間に. ¶the range ***of*** *tide* 潮の干満する範囲 ‖ Boats are able to get alongside to the landing stage at any state ***of*** the *tides*. どんな潮のときでも船がさん橋に横づけにできる. ¶***on*** the next high *tide* 次の満潮時に. ¶go ***with*** the *tide* 世の風潮に従う.

P² There is a *tide* ***in*** the affairs of men. 人事には潮時がある. ¶The *tide* ***of*** events turns. 世の中の情勢は変って行く.

O The *tide* is on the ebb (flow). 潮が引い(さし)ている. ¶The *tide* is on the turn. 潮が(上げまたは下げに)変りつつある. ¶when the *tide* is in (out) 潮が満ち(引い)て来ると.

tide, *v.* 乗り越す, 切り抜ける.

P provide funds to *tide* its members ***over*** bad times その会員に不況を切抜けるだけの資金を供給する ‖ The money will be enough to *tide* him ***over*** his illness. その金で彼の病気を治るまで十分足りるだろう. ‖ *tide* oneself ***over*** until ... ...まで一時しのぎをする. 【類】*tide* one ***over*** the difficulties / *tide* ***over*** the crisis / *tide* ***over*** the present political crisis / *tide* ***over*** losses / *tide* ***over*** the period of hardship / *tide* ***over*** a period of difficulty. ¶*tide* ***into*** (***out of***) a harbor 港へ潮がさし込む(港から潮が落ちる).

tidings, *n.* [*sing., pl.* 同型] 報知, 消息, 音信.

V ***bear*** the *tidings* to ... ...に報知をもたらす. ¶***break*** the sad *tidings* to ... ...にその悲報を漏らす. ¶***bring** tidings* 消息をもたらす. ¶***get*** evil *tidings* 凶報に接する.

V² *Tidings* seldom ***comes*** (=***come***). 便りはめったに来な

い. ☞ tidings は元来 *pl.* だが, 今は news 同様 *sing.* にも用いられる.

Q the ***best*** *tidings* for the future 将来のために最も喜ぶべき報道. ¶***glad*** *tidings* うれしい音信, 快報. ¶***ill*** (=***evil***) *tidings* 凶報. ¶the ***mournful*** *tidings* of the death of ... ...が死去したという悲報. ¶***sad*** *tidings* 悲報.【類】when the ***sad*** *tidings* of his death were received. ¶***welcome*** (***unwelcome***) *tidings* 吉(凶)報.

P^2 It is greeted throughout the country as *tidings* ***of*** great joy. それは全国にわたって非常に喜ばしい報知として迎えられている. ¶good *tidings* ***to*** mothers 世の母親たちへの吉報.

tidy, *v.* きちんとする.

M *tidy* oneself ***up*** 服装を正す ‖ *tidy* her ***up*** a bit 彼女の服装を少しきちんとする.【類】*tidy* ***up*** one's room.

tidy, *a.* きちんとした.

O keep one's clothes (room) neat and *tidy* 衣服(など)を小ぎれいにきちんとしておく.

tie, *n.* 結束; *pl.* きずな, 縁; 〘服飾〙ネクタイ; 無勝負; 《米》〘鉄道〙まくら木.

V ***break*** the marriage *tie* 離縁する. ¶an excellent means of ***cementing*** and ***strengthening*** the *ties* that already bind us to the United States すでにわれわれとアメリカとをつないでいる友情をさらに強固にする絶好な手段. ¶***complete*** the *tie* 結束を完全にする. ¶***draw close*** the *ties* between the two countries 両国間の国交を親密にする. ¶***establish*** (=***forge***) new *ties* of friendship 新たに友好関係を結ぶ. ¶Too many boys go away and ***forget*** the home *ties*. 両親のひざ下を去って家のことを忘れて仕舞う少年の数が多過ぎる. ¶family *ties* ***knitted*** by bonds of mutual love 相互愛のひもで結びつけられた家庭の縁. ¶***loosen*** all *ties* from the mind 俗じんを洗う. ¶***rupture*** the *tie* そのきずなを断つ. ¶***strengthen*** the *ties* of friendshiip and of brotherhood which unite England and the U.S. 英米両国を結ぶ友愛親善の関係を強固にする.【類】***strengthen*** the *ties* of friendship and amity that bind the two peoples / still further ***strengthen*** those *ties* of friendship which so happily unite the two Empires. ¶***tie*** a *tie* ひもを結ぶ. ¶***weaken*** the *ties* of sympathy and fraternity between ... ...間の同情親和の関係を弱める. ¶***wear*** a red *tie* 赤いネクタイを着ける.

Q a ***bright*** *tie* 明るい色のネクタイ. ¶the ***conjugal*** *tie* 夫婦関係. ¶My office work is ***great*** *ties*. 私の事務所の仕事は非常に面倒だ. ¶a ***hand-made*** *tie* 手縫いのネクタイ. ¶for the strengthening of the ***international*** *ties* 国際的友誼(*)を強固にするために. ¶bound by ***legal*** or ***moral*** *tie* 法律上または道徳上の制限を受けて. ¶look upon ***marriage*** *ties* as made only to be loosened or even cut at pleasure 結婚の縁を勝手にゆるめたり切ったりすることのできるものと見なす. ¶***matrimonial*** *ties* 夫婦の縁. ¶***political*** *ties* 政治的な結合. ¶It tends to a better mutual understanding and to ***stronger*** *ties* of friendship between ... ...間に一層の相互的了解とさらに強固な親善関係とをもたらすことに役立つ. ¶the ***weakened*** *ties* of morality 薄弱になった道徳の制裁. ¶a ***woolen*** *tie* 毛織のネクタイ.

Q^2 a ***bow*** *tie* ちょう結びのネクタイ. ¶be suspected of ***Communist*** *ties* 共産党との関係を疑われる. ¶weaken ***Dominion*** *ties* 英国自治領間の結束を弱める. ¶abolish the ***family*** *ties* 家族関係を撤廃する ‖ lead to the rupture of ***family*** *ties* 家族の仲たがえとなる. ¶Many women have ***home*** *ties*. 多くの婦人は家庭に縛られている. ¶cut the ***language*** *tie* with Britain 英国と言語上の関係を絶つ. ¶the breaking of the ***marriage*** *tie* 離婚. ¶a ***railroad*** *tie* 《米》まくら木. ☞ 英国は a [railway] sleeper.

P united ***by*** some *tie* 何らかの縁で結ばれて. ¶a man ***in*** the white *tie* 白いネクタイをした男 ‖ The game (match) ended ***in*** a *tie*. その競技(など)は同点に終った. ¶***without*** a single human *tie* 身寄りとては一人もなく.

P^2 a *tie* ***for*** the neck えり飾り. ¶the *ties* ***of*** blood (friendship) 血縁(など).

tie, *v.* 結ぶ, 縛る, 束縛する; 《米》[交通を]不通にする.

M *tied* ***fast*** (=***hard***) しっかり結んだ. ¶be ***loosely*** *tied* だらしなく結んである. ¶***securedly*** *tied* しっかり結んだ. ¶*tied* ***together*** 結び合わせた.

M^2 He didn't want to be *tied* ***down*** to a steady job. 彼はきまった仕事にしばられたくなかった. ‖ *tied* ***down*** by the traditions of the past 過去の因襲にしばられて ‖ I'm *tied* ***down*** here all day. 終日ここに(仕事に)しばられている. ¶*tie* ***up*** a bundle 包を結ぶ.【類】*tie* ***up*** things in a handkerchief / The dog is *tied* ***up***. ‖ be inextricably *tied* ***up*** with ... ...と切っても切れない縁を結んでいる ‖ try to *tie* ***up*** with one's former rivals 旧敵と連けいしようとする ‖ The strike *tied* ***up*** the newspaper. ストライキでその新聞は休刊であった. ‖ *tie* ***up*** passengers 乗客の足を奪う ‖ *tie* ***up*** the nation's rail system その国の鉄道網を休止状態におく.【類】A strike *tied* ***up*** streetcar and bus lines. / The accident *tied* ***up*** traffic the entire day. / Business is *tied* ***up*** by bad transportation. / All the traffic was *tied* ***up*** by the snow-storm. ☞ tie up は「縛る, 制限する」以外は米語用法 ‖ He is a financier and does not believe in *tying* ***up*** unnecessary capital. 彼は財政家で不必要な資本を固定するようなことはしない. ‖ He has his money *tied* ***up*** in real estate. 彼は不動産に投資している.

P horses *tied* ***at*** hitching posts けい留柱につながれた馬. ¶her hands *tied* ***behind*** her back 後ろ手に縛られて. ¶much *tied* ***by*** ... ...のために大いに拘束されて. ¶I am *tied* ***for*** time. 私は暇がない. ¶*tie* a knot ***in*** a handkerchief to remind me of something あることを思い出すようにハンカチで結び目を作る ‖ *tied* ***in*** wedlock 夫婦の縁を結んだ. ¶*tie* ***into*** an ornamental knot 飾り結びに結ぶ ‖ *tie* ***into*** bundles 束に結ぶ. ¶*tie* a handkerchief ***round*** one's neck 首の回りにハンカチを結ぶ. ¶*tie* a fish-line ***to*** a fishing-rod 釣りざおに釣り糸を結びつける.【類】There's a message *tied* ***to*** his leg. ‖ *tie* a horse ***to*** the manger 馬にかいばおけを当てがう ‖ *tied* ***to*** it is the question of ... それと関連して...の問題がある ‖ be *tied* ***to*** the apron-strings of one's wife 妻のしりに敷かれる. ¶*tie* a dog ***to*** a tree ***with*** a cord 綱で犬を木に結びつける. ¶a box *tied* ***with*** colored ribbons 色リボンで結んだ箱.【類】a gift *tied* ***with*** a red tape.

tier, *n.* 並び, 列; 階段.

P seats arranged ***in*** *tier* 階段席.【類】with seats rising ***in*** many *tiers* from the center.

P^2 *tier* ***above*** (=***upon***) tier 階段になって. ¶*tiers* of seats at a baseball game=bleachers 野球場階段席.

tie-up, *n.* 《米》協力; 途絶.

Q a ***close*** *tie-up* between ... ...間の堅い提携.

Q^2 a ***transportation*** *tie-up* 《米》輸送の途絶(スト・事故のため).

P^2 a *tie-up* (=deadlock) ***in*** negotiations 交渉の行きづまり.

tiffin, *n.* 中食, 昼食.

V ***eat*** one's *tiffin* 中食を食べる.

tiger, *n.* とら; どう猛な人.

V ***face*** a *tiger* とらと向きあう. ¶***train*** a wild *tiger* for the show みせものにするために野生のとらをならす.

V^2 *Tigers* ***growl***. とらはほえる.

Q^2 a ***baby*** *tiger* とらの子.

P^2 The soldier was a *tiger* ***in*** fight. その兵士は戦うときは猛虎のごとくであった.

tight, *a.* 緊張した, 緊密な; 窮屈な.

M The stopper is ***so*** *tight* that it can't be withdrawn. せんがあまり固くて抜けない.

P He is very *tight* ***about*** money. 彼は金には締り屋だ. ¶I feel *tight* ***on*** the chest. 私は胸の辺が窮屈に感じる.

O Money is *tight*. 金づまりだ.

tighten, *v.* 引しめる.

M^2 *tighten* ***up*** loose fastenings ゆるい結び目を固くする ‖ *tighten* ***up*** on their credit [銀行が]信用貸を引締める.

P *tighten* one's belt ***for*** ... ...のためきんこん一番する.

tights, *n. pl.* [ぴったり身につく]肉じゅばん.

P ***in*** fighting *tights* きちんと戦いの身支度をして ‖ a woman ***in*** *tights* [サーカスの女など]ぴったりしたはだ着になった女.

tile, *n.* かわら(タイル).

Q a ***ceramic*** *tile* 陶製タイル. ¶a ***French*** *tile* フランス風タイル.

Q^2 an ***art*** *tile* 意匠をこらしたタイル. ¶a ***pan*** *tile* 波形かわら. ¶a ***paving*** *tile* 舗装用タイル. ¶a ***roof[ing]*** *tile* 屋根がわら.

P^2 *tiles* ***on*** a roof 屋根のかわら.

tillage, *n.* 耕作, 農耕.

P area ***under*** *tillage* 耕作地域.

tilt, *n.* 覆布, 車ほろ.

P^2 The clothes of the bed were raised by a "cradle", like the *tilt* ***of*** a wagon. 夜着が馬車のほろのように支架で高く上げてあった.

tilt, *v.* 傾く; 傾ける.

M *tilt* one's head ***forward*** 頭を前に傾ける. ¶*tilt* a hat

sideways (*backward, forward*) 帽子を横(後, 前)さがりにかぶる.

M^2 The table is apt to *tilt over*. その卓はよくかしぐ.

P *tilt at* an opponent 相手を目がけて(やり)で突き掛る. ¶*tilt* the case *to* one side 箱を一方へかしげる.

tilting, *n.* 傾向.

Q *literary tilting* 文学的傾向.

timber, *n.* 材木, 用材;《米》立木, 森;《米》人物.

V *cut timber* 材木を切る. ¶*dry timber* 木材を乾燥する. ¶The forests *yield* valuable *timber*. その森林は貴重な木材を産出する.

V^2 Seasoned *timber* does not *warp*. 枯らした木材はそらない.

Q *creosoted timber* クレオソートを塗った木材. ¶*dead timber* 枯れた木材. ¶cut *excess timber* from land 山から過剰の木材を伐採する. ¶*hard timber* 堅い木材. ¶*hewn timber* 切った木材. ¶a statesman of the *highest timber* 最も高潔な政治家. ¶*massive timber* 巨材. ¶gain *new timber* through growth 成長すると木材がとれる. ¶*soft timber* 軟い木材. ¶acquire a large area of *standing timber* 広い面積の立木を手に入れる ¶*unseasoned timber* なまがわきの木材. ¶*well-seasoned timber* よく枯らした木材. ¶be of *wooden timbers* [家など]木造である.

Q^2 *forest timber* 森の立木. ¶*a mine timber* [鉱山用]坑木.

P a dealer *in timber*=a timber dealer 材木商.

timber, *v.* 植える.

M an area *beautifully timbered* with grand old trees 堂堂たる古木の美しく生えた地域.

P a hill finely *timbered with* cryptomerias りっぱな杉の生えた小山.

time, *n.* (**1**) 時; 時間の余裕; 時勢; 現代.

V *abide* the better *time* さらに適当なときを待つ. ¶We could not *afford time* to visit all. 残らず見て回るだけの余裕がなかった. ¶matters that greatly *agitate* the *times* 大いに世間を騒がせている問題. ¶Ample *time* is *allowed* for meats, etc. 食事などの時間はたっぷり取ってある ‖ *allow* oneself a little breathing *time* 息抜をする ‖ *allow* sufficient *time* to ... ...するに十分な時間を与える ‖ *Time allowed*, $1^1/_2$ hours. 時間の制限一時間半(試験など). ¶*annihilate* space and *time* 空間と時間とを滅却する. ¶*anticipate time* 時の来るのを待たずにやる, さきがける. ¶Can you *appoint* a *time*? 何時にしたらよろしゅうございますか(時間の指定) ‖ *appoint* another *time* 別の時を指定する. ¶*arrange* one's *time* so as to ... ...するように時間を取りきめる. ¶*ascertain* definite *time* しかと時間を確める. ¶The *time assigned* to English is scanty. 英語の配当時間が少ない. ¶*await* a future *time* at which he should ... 彼が...すべき将来の時を待つ. ¶to *beguile* [the] *time* 暇つぶしに. 【類】*beguile* the *time* with dominoes. ¶*bide* one's *time* 機の熟するのを待つ. ¶*change* the *times* of the running of the trains 列車運転の時間を変更する ‖ *Times* are *changed*. 時世が変っている. ¶It is impossible for us to *choose* our *time* for coming home. 自分たちは帰宅の時間を勝手に決めるわけにはいかない. ‖ *choose* one's own *time* 自分で勝手に時間をきめる. ¶The *time* for ... is *closed*. ...の時代は過ぎ去った. ¶The Ainu have no mode of *computing time*, and do not know their own ages. アイヌ人は時の計算の仕方を知らないので自分の年も分からない. ¶*consume* a good *time* of ... ...の時を大分費す. ¶The author *contributes* his *time*, his work, his skill, or his learning on his book. 著者は彼の時間, 彼の努力, 彼の手腕, あるいは彼の学識を彼の著書にささげる. ¶*convert* one's spare *time* into money 余暇を使って金をもうける. ¶*cut down* by over half the *time* required 所要時間の半ば以上を短縮する. ¶*dedicate* the *time* to arms and religion その時を武術と宗教に用いる. ¶*deem* the *time* inexpedient いまだ機至らずとなす. ¶*depict* his *times* 彼の時代を描く. ¶more *time* is *deserved*, but make at least one day's visit to ... もっと時日をかけてもよいのだがせめて一日でも...を見物するようになさい. ¶He *devotes* all his spare *time* to his studies. 彼はその余暇を残らず研究に当てている. ¶*distinguish times* 時代の特徴を識別する. ¶She *divided* her *time* between office work and her little domestic cares. 彼女は勤めのかたわら家庭の雑事に気を配っていた. 【類】*divide* one's *time* between prayer and study. / *divide* one's *time* (掛持をする) between the Chicago and New York offices. / *divide* one's *time* in the study of ..., ..., and ... / *divide* one's time between criticism and production. ¶The city will *employ* the *time* of the visitor profitably and agreeably for days. 旅の人はその市で数日を有益におもしろく過せるだろう. 【類】*employ* one's *time* in writing / *employ* all one's *time* and wits in ... ¶*engross* all one's *time* 時間を全部とる. ¶*enjoy* a jolly good *time* 歓を尽す. ¶*enlarge* (=*extend*) the *time* for ... ...の日限を延ばす. ¶I *envisage* the *time* when ... ...する時代を頭に浮べる. ¶*extend* the *time* for executing an order 注文納品の期限を延ばす. 【類】*extend* the *time* to July 31. ¶I *felt* the *time* hanging on my hands. 私はひまで困っていた. ¶to *fill up time* 時間つぶしに. ¶I can never *find time* to do it. 私にはそれをする暇がない. ‖ He managed to *find time* to attend the funeral. 彼はどうにか時間の都合をして葬式に参列した. ‖ *find time* only at irregular intervals for ... ...する時間が不規則にしか得られない. 【類】He *found time* amid his absorbing duties (多忙の中から) to attend this festival. ¶*fix* a *time* for a call 訪問の時を決める. ¶*fleet* the *time* carelessly 時を利用しない. ¶*fool away* one's *time* 時間を徒費する. ¶*fritter away time* on ... ...で時間を徒費する. 【類】*fritter* all one's *time away* over flowers and tennis. ¶I wish to *gain time* (=have more time to decide). もう少し考えさしてもらいたい. ‖ The clock *gains time* (=runs fast). 時計が進む. ‖ Let's get it through to *gain time* for pleasure. 仕事を片ずけてあとで遊ぼう. ¶Go to the office and *get* your *time*. 事務所へ行って君の勤務の時間を見て来い. ¶Off he went, without *giving* me *time* to thank him. 私がお礼を述べようとしているうちにさっさと彼は立去った. ‖ *give* (=*grant*) *time* [支払など]猶予を与える ‖ professors *giving* their entire *time* to college and university work 専門学校や大学に全部の時間をささげている教授たち ‖ *give* one's full *time* to ... ...に掛りきりにする ‖ *Give* me *time*, and I will tell you the whole story. そのうちゆっくりお話しましょう. ¶We haven't *got time* for that. そんな時の余裕はない. ¶*grudge* the *time* and patience 時間と骨を惜しむ. ¶*guarantee* the *time* of delivery (arrival) 引渡し(到着)の期限を約束する. ¶*hasten* the *time* when ... ...の時機をはやめる. ¶It is twelwe o'clock now; I *have* just *time* to catch the train. 今十二時だ, やっと汽車に間に合う. ‖ I *have* scarcely *time* to breathe. 忙しくて私は息つくひまもない. 【類】I *have* but *time* to read a few books. / whenever he *has time* / I *haven't time* to argue the matter. / *have* no *time* to spare for reading ‖ arrest the culprit before he *has time* for flight 罪人を逃げない内に逮捕する ‖ *Have* you [got] the *time*, please? [時計は]今何時ですか. ‖ It has *had* its *time* (=day). もうそれは時代おくれだ. ‖ *have* no *time* to call their own during sunlight 昼間は自分のひまというものがない ‖ The easy-going, happy-go-lucky masses go out to *have* a good *time*. のんきで楽天的な連中が行楽する. ¶*idle away* ones *time* 怠けて時を過ごす. ¶*improve* one's *time* 時間を利用する ‖ *improve time* well 時間を十分利用する. ¶*invest* our *time* to the best advantage できるだけ時間を利用する. ¶My watch *keeps time* very well (=accurately). 私の時計はよく合う. ‖ The watch *keeps* good (=correct) *time*. 時計がよく合う. ‖ My watch *keeps* perfect *time*. 私の時計は時間がきわめて正確だ. ¶How do you manage to *kill* your *time* on Sundays? 日曜には退屈しのぎに何をなさいますか. ‖ take up painting to *kill time* 暇つぶしに絵をやり出す. 【類】to *kill time* on a rainy day / by way of *killing time*. ¶He *knows* the *time* without looking at a watch. 彼は時計を見ないで時間が分かる. ¶It will *last* a life *time*. それは一生もつだろう. 【類】It will *last* our *time*. ¶I shall probably *lay out* my *time* to most advantage if I ... もし私が...すれば最も有益に時間が使えよう. ¶I *loitered away* the *time* in looking through the shop windows. 私は店の飾窓を見て歩いてひまつぶしをした. ¶My watch *lost time*. 僕の時計は遅れた. ‖ I hope you don't *lose* your *time* in building castles on (=in) the air. 空想にふけったりして時間をむだにしないようにし給え. ‖ without *losing time* 時を移さず. 【類】He was not a man who *lost* much *time* in vain repinings (くよくよして). / I will *lose* no *time* in reading. / I shall *lose* no *time* in using every endeavor (全力を尽す) to ... / You should *lose* no *time* in communicating (文通をする) with ... ¶*lounge away time* むだに時を費す. ¶Could you *make time* to copy it for me? 時間

の都合してそれを写して下さいませんか. ‖ The subway is supposed to *make* better *time*. 地下鉄の方が早いということになっている. ‖ We are *making* very poor *time* this morning. 今朝はばかにのろい(電車など). 【類】 He *made* the best *time* in the auto race. ¶ *mark time* by the burning of a stick of incense 線香をたいて時の経過を示す(芸者のお座敷など). ¶ To one man, at all events, London never *metes out* hard *times*—and that is the chimney-sweep. ロンドンには少くとも一人の不景気知らずがいる, それは煙突掃除屋である. ¶ *misemploy* one's *time* 時間を濫用する. ¶ I don't wish to *monopolize* your *time*. 私はお邪魔をしたくない. ¶ *murder time* 時間をつぶす. ¶ I have *occupied* your *time*. お邪魔を致しました. ‖ best *occupy* one's *time* できるだけ時を利用する. ¶ The visitor *overstayed* his *time*. 訪問者は長座をした. ¶ *overstep* one's *time* 時間以上に居過ごす. ¶ *pass* the *time* playing billiards (reading) たまつき(など)をやって退屈をしのぐ ‖ *pass* the *time* of day [お早うなど]あいさつをする ‖ *pass* one's *time* idly 何もしないで時を過ごす ‖ just to *pass* [the] *time* ひまつぶしに. 【類】 *pass* one's leisure *time* in reading. ¶ *pass time away* pleasantly おもしろく時を過ごす. ¶ *Time* devoted to such training will be well *paid*. こうした訓練に使った時間は十分に報いられるだろう. ¶ *play away* one's *time* 時を遊んで過ごす. ¶ *reckon* in the *time* その時を計算に入れる. ¶ The railway has appreciably *reduced* the *time* of journeying to the place. その鉄道が同地へ旅行する時間を著しく短縮した. ¶ *repay* the *time* and labor spent upon ... ...に費した時間と労力とに報いる. ¶ *require* more *time* それ以上の時間がかかる. ¶ *rule* our *time* [ある思想などが]われわれの時代を支配する. ¶ *save* much *time* 多大の時間を節約する ‖ *save* both *time* and labor 時間と労力を節約する. ¶ *sell* one's *time* to ... ...に自己の時を売る. ¶ *serve time* for murder 殺人で受刑する. ¶ I was there before the *time set*. 私は定刻前にそこへ着いていた. ¶ All railway-clocks in England *show* Greenwich *time*. 英国の鉄道の時計はすべてグリニジの時間を示す. ¶ *smoke* one's *time away* タバコを吸って時を過ごす. ¶ I *snatch time* to read and study in the midst of great affairs. 重大事件の最中にあって読書かつ研究する時間を忙中につくる. ¶ I am so very busy every day that I cannot *spare* the *time* to go. 私は毎日とても忙しいので行く暇がありません. ‖ *sparing* no *time* (money) 暇(金)にあかして. ¶ *specify time* 時間を明示する. ¶ He *spends* his *time* wholly in writing and lecturing. 彼は著述と講演で日を送っている. 【類】 If my fortune allowed it I would *spend* all my *time* quietly in study. / *spend* one's *time* foolishly / He is well versed in English, having *spent* some *time* in the United States. ¶ I *spent* the *time up* to 2 in the afternoon seeing the sights of the city. 私は午後二時まで市内の見物に時を過ごした. ¶ *spin out* the *time* [わざと]時間を引きのばす. ¶ There is no *time* to *split* for it. いそがしくてそんなことにさく時間がない. ¶ *squander time* 時を浪費する. ¶ with *time stolen* from sleep 寝るめも寝ないで. ¶ be content to *take* one's *time* over ... ...しながら甘んじて時間をつぶす ‖ He *took* his *time* and made a careful inquiry. 彼は十分時間をかけて入念な調査を遂げた. ‖ After I am up, I *take* my *time* in looking through the paper. 私は起床後ゆっくり新聞を見る. ‖ *take time* to work it out 十分時間をかけてそれをやる. 【類】 *Take* your *time* and think it over. / *take time* to consider it calmly / *Take time* to eat your meals. / Since ..., I must *take time* to say a little more on this subject. ‖ it *takes* less *time* to change cars at ... ...で乗換える方が早く行ける ‖ *taking* [the] *time* by the forelock (=scruff) 機会をしかととらえて ‖ *take* the *time* from the booming notes of "Big Ben" broadcast from the London Houses of Parliament ロンドンの議事堂から打ち出す大時計のいんいんたる音で時間を知る. ¶ cheerfully *take away* the *time* 快談に時を移す. ¶ The clerks and the girls who do the typewriting *take time off* at noon for their lunch. タイプをやる男女の事務員は正午に休憩して昼食を取る. ‖ *take time off* from college to ... ...するために学校を休む ‖ Stick around till I can leave with you.—*Take* your *time*, please. 出かける用意ができるまで待っていてください.—どうぞごゆっくり. ¶ hardly *taking time out* for lunch ほとんど弁当を食べる暇も惜しんで. ¶ My *time* is fully *taken up*. 私の時間は一杯で暇がない. 【類】 His *time* is wholly *taken up* by school work. ¶ *telegraph* the *time* one leaves その出発時を電報で知らせる. ¶ Kindly *tell* me the *time*. 何時でしょうか. 【類】 A clock is used to *tell* the *time* of day. / Can you *tell* the *time?* ¶ *throw away* one's *time* 時間を浪費する. ¶ the lack of enough capital to *tide over* bad *times* 不況を切抜けるだけの資本の欠乏. ¶ *trifle away* one's *time* 時を徒費する. ¶ *value time* 時を重んじる. ¶ *wait* one's *time* 時機をまつ ‖ I cannot *wait* an indefinite *time*. 私は無期限に待つ訳には行かない. ¶ More *time* is *wanted*. もっと時日を要する. ¶ *waste time* on such light trash こんなつまらない読物に時を空費する. 【類】 Please don't *waste* any more *time* over it. / *waste time* in splitting straws (こまかいこと) / *waste* (=lose) no *time* in ... / *waste* much *time* in finding what they want. ¶ *weather* the *times* of receding trade 商売の不況にたえる. ¶ I *whiled away* the *time* by smoking my pipe and tobacco. 私はパイプをくゆらして時を過ごした. ‖ read a book to *while* the *time away* 書物を読んで時を過ごす. ¶ The building *withstood time* and earthquakes. その建物は長い歳月と数回の地震に耐えた.

v² as *time advanced* 時の経過につれて. ¶ those whose *time allows* it そうする時間の都合がつく人々. ¶ The *time* has *arrived*. その時が来た. ¶ But *times* have *changed*. しかし時代は変った. ‖ *Times* were *changing* rapidly. 時代がどんどん変って行った. ¶ the *time* has fully *come* for ... ...の時正に到れりだ ‖ when lunch *time came* ひる時になって ‖ The *time* will soon *come* when ... ...という時期が間もなく到来するだろう. ¶ *Time creeps on*. 知らない内に時がたつ. ¶ The *time draws near*. その時が近づく. ¶ when the *time expires* 期日満了の時. ¶ How [quickly] *time flies*! 時のたつのは早いものだ. ¶ How *goes* the *time?* [時間は]何時ですか. ¶ It will increase as *time goes by*. それは時がたつにつれて増加するだろう. ¶ as *time goes* (= *moves, runs or wears*) *on* 時のうつるにつれて ‖ as *time* has *gone on* [これまで]時がたつにつれて. ¶ those whose *time hangs* heavily on their hands 退屈で困る人々. 【類】 *Time hangs* a little monotonously on his hands. ¶ *Time marches on*. 時がたつ. ¶ as the *time* was rapidly *passing* 時がずんずんたつので ‖ as *time passed* 時がたつにつれ ‖ As *time passed on*, the practice of doing so became more and more common. 時がたつにつれてその習慣が段段一般化した. ¶ *Time* will not *permit* me to touch upon it more than very briefly. 時間がないので私はほんの簡単にしかそれに触れられない. ‖ should *time* and circumstances *permit* 時と場合によっては. ¶ when *time presses* 急ぐ時には. ¶ Dull *time prevails*. 不景気である. ¶ as *time progresses* 時の進むにつれて. ¶ The *time slipped by*. 時がいつの間にか過ぎてしまった. ¶ How far he will succeed in his ambitious work *time* alone will *solve* (can *tell*). 彼がその大事業にどの程度まで成功するかは時がたって見なければ分からない.

Q ...in these *advanced times* この進んだ世の中に. ¶ The steamer left port forty-eight hours after her *advertised time*. 汽船は掲示した時刻より四十八時間後に出港した. ¶ in *after times* 後世に至って. ¶ He has spent a most *agreeable time* there. 彼はその地で非常に愉快だった. ¶ The scenery of Japan is beautiful at *all times* of year. 日本の風景は一年中いつでも美しい. 【類】 Shimonoseki enjoys an excellent climate at *all times* of the year, owing to its southern frontage with hills behind, admitting the summer breezes and protecting it from northerly winter blasts. / Visitors are welcome at *all times*. / at *all times* of day and night / at *all times* there is something to study for the student of human nature (人間性) ‖ The people of this modern age are the busiest workers of *all time*. 現代の人々は古今を通じて最も多忙な労役者である. 【類】 one of the greatest astronomers of *all time* / Napoleon's Grand Army of *all time*. ‖ I find him working at desk *all* the *time*. 彼はいつ見ても机に向って働いている. ‖ What have you been fooling around *all* this *time?* 今までどこをうろついていたんだ. ¶ The *allotted time* quickly ran out. それに定めた時刻がたちまちたってしまった. ¶ there is *ample time* to ... ...する時間が十分ある ‖ He has *ample time* at his disposal. 彼は時間が十分にある. ¶ in *ancient times* 昔. 【類】 from *ancient times* down to the present day a wide spread belief has prevailed that ... ¶a hero the like of which has not been heard of (=known) in ***ancient*** or ***modern times*** (=days) 古今無双の勇士. ¶***any time*** tomorrow 明日いつでも ‖ ***Any time*** will suit me. [時は]いつでも結構です. ¶I shall not be able to answer by the ***appointed time.*** 私には約束の時間までに答えられそうもない. ‖ at the ***appointed time*** 指定の時間に. ¶***appropriate time*** for a visit to the place そこを訪れるに適当な時. ¶***approximate time*** occupied in ... ...に要する大体の時間. ¶It came at an ***auspicious time.*** それはちょうどよい折に来た. ¶***bad times*** 不景気 ‖ I had a ***bad time*** with the dentist. あの歯医者にかかってひどい目にあった. ‖ I had a jolly ***bad time*** of it. いやはやひどい目にあった. ‖ It was ***bed time.*** 床につく時刻だった. ¶at this ***belated time*** 今となっては. ¶Now is the ***best time*** for buying. 今が買い時だ. ¶The convict was living on ***borrowed time*** for a year since the current failed in an electric chair. その囚人は電気いすに電流が通じなかったので借りものの一年間を過していた. ¶in my ***boyhood's time*** 私の少年時代に. ¶in these ***bustling times*** この忙しい時代に. ¶the traders have a ***busy time*** その業者は景気が好い ‖ during ***busy times*** 繁忙期中. 【類】I have had a ***busy time.*** / The ***busiest time*** of the day are from 12 to 1 o'clock and from 3 to 5 o'clock. / Their ***busiest time*** is Saturday night. / at the ***busiest time*** of the day (say, nine in the morning or six in the evening). ¶a picture of ***by-gone times*** 往時のおもかげ. ¶at ***certain times*** of the day (year) 一日(年)の中で一定の時に. ¶a ***charming time*** 楽しい時. ¶in ***Christian*** or ***pre-Christian time*** 紀元後または紀元前において. ¶in early ***Christian times*** 西暦紀元の初めごろ. ¶in ***classical times*** ギリシア・ローマ時代に. 【類】men and women from ***classical times*** to the present. ¶poach salmon in ***close time*** 禁猟期にさけの密漁をする. ¶in ***colonial times*** [米国などの]植民時代に. ¶the most ***congested time*** of day 一日中最も混雑する時間. ¶be likely to remain some ***considerable time*** かなり長い間そのままに続きそうだ. ¶at some ***convenient time*** いつか都合のよい時に. ¶at a ***critical time*** of life 人生の危機に ‖ in these ***critical times*** これらの非常時において. ¶at a ***crucial time*** in world history 世界史上の危期において. ¶if one doesn't pay up within a ***decent time*** その支払いが少し滞り過ぎると. ¶We had a most ***delightful time.*** 非常に愉快だった. ¶at ***different times*** 色々な場合に. ¶the ***time*** is not far ***distant***, if not already here, when ... ...の日はまだ到来しないが遠い先きではない. ¶at ***diverse times*** 色々の場合に. ¶at ***due time*** 適当の時に ‖ in ***due time*** やがて. ¶***dull time*** 不景気. ¶***each time*** その都度, 毎回. ¶from (=since) very ***early times*** 大昔から ‖ The use of peas as a food dates back to very ***early times.*** えんどう豆を食用に供するようになったのはよほど昔のことである. 【類】Osaka has been prominent in the history of Japan from the very ***earliest times*** / in the ***earliest times.*** ¶at ***election time*** 選挙の際に. ¶in ***Elizabethan times*** エリザベス時代に. ¶the ***enormous time*** now spent over learning ... 今日...を学ぶのに費す多大の時間. ¶given ***enough time,*** he will ... 時を与えれば彼は...するだろう. 【類】We haven't ***enough time*** for it. ¶***every time*** I come 私が来る度に. ¶What is the ***exact time***? 正確なとこ今何時ですか. ‖ The clock keeps ***exact*** time. その時計はよく合う. ¶in the ***exceptional times*** through which we are now passing 今日の非常時に. ¶We had an ***exciting time.*** 壮快であった. ¶in these ***fast-moving times*** このテンポの早い世の中に. ¶a ***favorite time*** to buy them up is ... 買占めの好時期は...である. ¶in the ***feudal times*** 封建時代に. 【類】handed down (伝承した) from ***feudal times.*** ¶I have seen her a ***few times.*** 私は二三回彼女に会った. ¶in a ***few days' time*** 二三日中に. 【類】in a ***few hours' time.*** ¶have a ***fine time*** おもしろく時を過ごす. ¶You pronounce the words very well for a ***first time.*** 君は初めてにしてはその言葉の発音が仲々うまい. ‖ for the ***first time*** in years 数年ぶりに. ¶the ***first few times*** 最初の二三回. ¶so this seems a particularly ***fitting time*** to ... それで今が...するに特に適当の時期らしい. ¶in ***five years' time*** 五カ年に. ¶for a certain ***fixed time*** ある一定の期間. ¶***fleeting time*** 疾過する光陰. ¶in ***former times*** 以前は. ¶The movement comes at a ***fortunate time.*** その運動は時宜を得ている. ¶Every mill in the State is running ***full time.*** その州の工場は全力操業をやっている. ‖ When her ***full time*** had come, she gave birth to a son. 彼女は月満ちて男の子を産んだ. 【類】The Diet was dissolved before the expiration of the ***full time.*** ¶far back in ***geological time*** ずっとさかのぼって地質時代に. 【類】somewhere in the comparatively recent stretches (期間) of ***geological time.*** ¶determine what the weather shall be at any place at a ***given time*** 一定の時刻におけるある場合の天候を測定する. ¶Children have a ***glad time*** when the snow falls. 子供は雪が降ると喜ぶ. ¶We had some ***glorious good times*** being very young. われわれは大いに若かったので愉快なことが時々あった. ¶You have come at a ***good time.*** 君は丁度よい時に来た. 【類】reinforcements in ***good time*** / if ordered in ***good time*** ‖ have a reasonable number of ***good times*** and vacations 相当数の楽しい時と休暇がある. 【類】We had a ***good time,*** but missed you. ‖ when ***times*** are ***good*** (***bad***) 景気の好(悪)い時 ‖ There is a ***good time*** coming. だんだん景気がよくなってくる. ‖ for a ***good long time*** 大分長い間 ‖ a ***good many times*** 何度も ‖ think of ***good old times*** なつかしい昔をしのぶ ‖ Give me the ***good old times.*** 昔がなつかしい. ¶Boys and girls had a ***grand*** (=***mighty***) ***good time.*** 少年少女たちはすばらしく愉快に遊んだ. ¶We had a ***great time*** at the party. その会は実に愉快だった. ¶in about ***half an hour's time*** 半時間位で. ¶a ***happy time*** 楽しい時. ¶owing to the present ***hard times*** 昨今不景気のため ‖ have a ***hard time*** of it ひどい目に会う ‖ have a ***hard time*** believing it 容易に信じられない. ¶Is it not ***high time*** that this question should be gone into? この問題を研究すべき時が来ているのではなかろうか. 【類】The science of language-study does not exist, but it is ***high time*** that it should exist.—H.E. Palmer. ‖ Surely it is ***high time*** to put a period to this letter. この手紙もこのへんで筆をおかなければなるまい. 【類】He now thought it ***high time*** to interfere. ¶in ***historical times*** 有史以後に. ¶I tell you for the hundredth ***time*** that ... もう一ぺん言うが... ¶Springtime is an ***ideal time*** to go abroad. 春は洋行にはもってこいの時だ. ¶from ***time immemorial*** down to our own day 太古から現時に至るまで. 【類】From ***time immemorial*** the Swedes have been a sport-loving people. / The average woman has found delight in dress from ***time immemorial.*** ¶at ***inconvenient times*** 都合の悪い時に. ¶for an ***indefinite time*** いつまでも. ¶an ***interminable time*** 永久に. ¶the ***intervening time*** 中間の時期. ¶We wish him a ***jolly time*** with the old folk at home. われわれは彼(休暇を取って帰った水兵など)が家庭の老人たちとおもしろく暮すことを願っている. ¶have a ***joyous*** and ***carefree time*** 愉快にのん気に暮す. ¶in ***later times*** 後日になって. ¶***legendary times*** (=period) of Chinese history 中国史の伝説時代. ¶those who have ***less time*** to spare あまり暇のない人たち ‖ in ***less time*** than it takes to tell it 口で言うよりも早く. ¶What is the most ***likely time*** to find him at home? あの人はいつごろだと在宅しておられるでしょうか. ¶travellers with ***limited time*** 時間に余裕のない旅行家 ‖ should ***limited time*** be a consideration 時が十分にない場合は. ¶have ***little time*** to study 勉強の時間が乏しい ‖ this will leave us but ***little time*** for ... ...する時間は少ししか残らないだろう. ¶I had such a ***lonely time.*** 私はほんとにさびしかった. ¶after a ***long time*** 久しぶりで ‖ It will be a ***long time*** in coming. それはまだじきに来やしないだろう. ‖ it won't be a ***long time*** before ... ...の時はそう長くはないだろう ‖ I've been kept waiting a confounded (=***damned***) ***long time.*** べらぼうに長く待たされた. ‖ It's a ***long time*** ago now. 今は昔. ‖ for a ***long time*** to come. ¶***Lost time*** is never found again. 一度去った時は二度と来ない. ¶have a perfectly ***lovely time*** together 一緒にほんとに楽しく暮す. ¶***many*** a ***time*** and oft 幾度か. ¶at ***meal time[s]*** 食事時に. ¶in the ***mean time*** (=while) とかくする内に. ¶within ***measurable time*** 適度の時間内に. ¶***medieval times*** 中世に. 【類】The metal for the noted Damascus blades of ***medieval times*** was not made at Damascus, but at Kona Samundrum near Nirma in Haidarabad. ¶our ***modern time*** われわれの今の時代. 【類】in these ***modern times.*** ¶in a ***moment's time*** 瞬時に. ¶in this ***momentous time*** この重大な時期に. ¶devote ***much time*** to study in various subjects 種々な題目の研究に多くの時をささげる ‖ How ***much time*** do you have at noon? 正午にはどの位休みがありますか.【類】spend ***much time*** in travel. ¶His ***time*** is ***near.*** 彼の死期が近寄っている. ¶He saw clearly that ***new times*** were coming. 彼は時代が替るのをはっきり見てとった. ¶We have had a ***nice time*** of it (=terrible experience). [反語的に]われわれはえらい目に会った. ¶***nine times*** out of ten 十中の九回まで. ¶in ***no time*** 直ちに ‖ in less than ***no time*** またたく間に ‖ ***No time*** must be lost in making arrangement. さっそく手はずをしなければならない. ‖ I have ***no time*** to go. 私は行くひまがない. ¶as in ***normal times*** 平常と変りなく ‖ at (=in) ***normal times*** 平常は. ¶at ***odd times*** あいまあいまに. ¶Four p.m. is the ***official time*** for closing. 午後四時が規定の締切時間です. ¶We passed many pleasant hours in talking our ***old times***. われわれは昔話をして愉快な数時間を過ごした.【類】in the ***old times***=in ***olden times*** / as in ***old times.*** ¶***one time*** あるとき ‖ He was at ***one time*** a professor in that university. 彼は以前その大学の教授だった. ‖ at ***one time*** it seemed likely that ... 一時は…のように思われた.【類】At ***one time*** all systems of knowledge (知識の全体系) were embraced under the term Philosophy. / At ***one time*** the patient threatened to be fatal and another ... ¶***one*** or ***more times*** 一回または数回. ¶at an ***opportune time*** 適当の折に. ¶at ***ordinary time*** 平常は.【類】The Japanese community in London at an ***ordinary time*** numbers about 200 persons, chiefly clerks and students. ¶brief biographies of men and women of ***our time*** 現代男女の小伝 ‖ the extension of educational opportunity characteristic of ***our time*** 現代の特徴たる教育を受ける機会の拡張.【類】the sexual life (性的生活) of ***our time.*** ¶write in one's own home, in one's ***own time*** 自分の家で勝手の時に書く.【類】a history of our ***own time*** ‖ fix its ***own time*** of meeting その会議の期日をその団体自身が定める. ¶at a ***particular time*** 特定の時に. ¶the ***time*** is ***past*** when ... …の時代は過ぎた. ¶My watch keeps ***perfect time.*** 私の時計は少しも狂わない. ¶in [the] ***piping times*** of peace 太平の御代に. ¶I had a very ***pleasant time*** with my brother and friends. 私は兄(弟)や友人たちと非常におもしろく遊んだ. ¶at the earliest ***practicable time*** 都合のつく限り早く. ¶in ***pre-Columbian times*** コロンブスのアメリカ発見前に. ¶in ***prehistoric times*** 歴史以前に.【類】a survival (遺物) of ***prehistoric times.*** ¶the conditions of society at the ***present time*** are such that ... 現代の社会状態は…のようなものである ‖ even at the ***present time*** of writing この文を書いている今も.【類】up to the ***present time.*** ¶***pre-scientific times*** 科学前の時代. ¶at some ***previous time*** 以前に. ¶in ***prewar times*** 戦前に. ¶in the ***primitive times*** 原始時代に. ¶delivered to ***promised time*** 約束の期日通りに交付された. ¶at ***proper time*** ころを見計って ‖ These truths must be earned at the ***proper time*** and in the proper way これらの事実は適当な時に適当な方法で学ばねばならない. ¶in their most ***prosperous times*** 彼らの最も栄えた時代に. ¶come in ***quick time*** 急いで来る. ¶in much ***quicker time*** than ... …よりずっと早く. ¶have a ***rattling time*** すばらしく楽しい時を過す. ¶within a ***reasonable time*** 相当な期間内に. ¶in ***recent times*** 近代において ‖ coming to more ***recent times*** 下ってもっと近代になって.【類】until comparatively ***recent times*** / in more ***recent times*** / of ***recent times*** there has been a tendency to ... / within comparatively ***recent times.*** ¶from the earliest ***recorded times*** 記録にある最も早い時代から. ¶from ***remote times*** 昔から.【類】in ***remote times*** and places. ¶just at the ***right time*** 丁度適当な時に. ¶the ***time*** is ***ripe*** for ... …の機が熟している. ¶We had a ***ripping good time.*** すてきに面白かった. ¶from ***Roman times*** to the present ローマ時代から現在まで. ¶go in for a ***rough time*** えらいことになる ‖ give one a ***rough time*** [それで]頭を悩ます. ¶Ruskin, scientifically considered, is guilty of gross errors, and at the ***same time*** he reveals scientific insight of a high order.—Richard T. Ely. ラスキンは科学的に考察すると大きな誤りを犯しているがしかし同時に彼は非常にすぐれた科学的どう察を示している. ¶in ***savage times*** 野蛮時代に. ¶have but ***scant leisure time*** ひまがほとんどない. ¶Trains run to ***scheduled time.*** 汽車が予定の時間通りに運転される.【類】the ***scheduled time*** of departure. ¶go to bed at a fixed ***time***, and rise at a ***set time*** 一定の時に床につき一定の時に起きる. ¶in ***seven years' time*** 七年を経て. ¶It has happened three ***several times.*** それは三度(継続しないで)別々の時に起った. ‖ once or ***several times*** 一回または数回. ¶The firemen had a very ***severe time*** in trying to overcome the flames. 消防夫は火を消しとめようとして大分骨を折った. ¶in a ***short time*** 短時日に.【類】take an amazingly ***short time*** to ... ‖ work ***short time*** 操短をする / Some misprints and other inaccuracies may possibly be found in the following pages, in consequence of the ***short time*** which has been allowed us for correcting them. / There is so much to be done in a ***short time.*** / wait a ***short time*** for ... / have only a ***short time*** to run (老人など) ‖ The trains make ***short time*** between A and B. AB 間には汽車があるので短時間で行かれる.【類】in the ***shortest possible time.*** ¶***skittish times*** 戦々兢々の時代. ¶Now it is early in the afternoon—a ***slack time*** for busmen. 今は午後もまだ早いのでバスの運転手にはひまな時です. ¶at ***some time*** of the day 一日の内いつか ‖ go to the boss for ***some time*** off 少し休ましてもらうように主人の所へ話しに行く. ¶***some little time*** ago ちょっと前に ‖ ***some little time*** must elapse before ... …するまでに少し時間をおかねばならない. ¶***some other time*** いずれ. ¶The work has been carried on in ***spare time*** for five months. その仕事は五カ月にわたって暇々になされたものである. ¶put one's ***spare time*** to account その余暇を利用する. ¶devote ***special time*** to him 彼のために特に時間を割く. ¶at a ***specified time*** 指定の時間に. ¶have a ***splended time*** 非常に愉快に時を過す. ¶the ***standard time*** 標準時. ☞ 米国には four standard times がある. 即ち Eastern (E.S.T.), Central (C.S.T.), Mountain (M.S.T.) 及び Pacific (P.S.T.) の四つで, Eastern time, Pacific time などともいう. ¶make payments at ***stated time*** 一定の時に支払をする. ¶pictures depicting the ***stirring times*** of the period その時代の動乱期を描いた絵. ¶in those ***stormy times*** 当時の旋風時代に. ¶have a very ***strenuous time*** 極力奮闘する. ¶at a ***subsequent time*** その後に. ¶at ***such time*** こうしたときに. ¶at a ***suitable time*** and place 随時随所に. ¶We had the ***swellest time*** last week-end down at Balm springs. 《俗》この前の週末にはバーム温泉でとても愉快に過ごした. ¶a ***tedious*** and ***trying time*** 退屈に苦しむ時. ¶I may be excused in about ***ten minutes' time.*** 私は失礼ですが十分ばかりたってから退席します. ¶Burglars seem to be very prevalent ***these times.*** このごろは夜盗がよくあるようだ. ‖ In ***these times*** of international competition. この国際競争の時代において.【類】even in ***these times*** of depression / in ***these times*** of progress and civilization. ¶We had a very ***thin time*** of it. 一向つまらなかった. ¶at ***this time*** of day (night, year, season) この時刻(など)に ‖ another correspondent, ***this time*** a man, tells me that ... 別の手紙をよこした人(今度は男だ)が…と私の所へ言ってきた. ¶at ***those times*** of the year like Christmas and Easter クリスマスや復活祭のような季節に ‖ in ***those times*** of business depression 当時の不況時代に. ¶in ***those early times*** 当時のような初期に. ¶in ***those remote times*** その昔. ¶No! a ***thousand times***, no! 否, 断じて否. ¶***three times*** the number of ... …の三倍の数 ‖ is ***three times*** as large in population as ... 人口は…の三倍ある. ¶have a ***tough time*** [of it] 《米》ひどい目に会う. ¶the ***troublous times*** of the Revolutionary War 国歩多難な独立戦争の時代. ¶in the ***troubled time*** of 1715 一七一五年の動乱時代に. ¶have a ***trying time*** 苦しい目に会う. ¶in these ***turbulent times*** この騒々しい時代に. ¶He is a cinema fan. He visits a picture-house on an average ***two*** or ***more times*** a week. 彼は映画ファンだ, 平均一週に二度またはそれ以上映画館へ行く. ¶***two*** or ***three times*** 二三度 ‖ ***two*** or ***three times*** twenty thousand 二万の二倍から三倍. ¶***two weeks' time*** 二週間. ¶a man's ***unbought time***—his leisure 買手のない時間—すなわち閑暇. ¶in those ***undegenerate time*** 当時の健全な時代に. ¶for an ***unlimited time*** 期間を限定せず. ¶in those ***unsettled times*** 当時の乱世に. ¶There can be little doubt that the present is an ***unusual time*** in human history. 当今はたしかに人間歴史における異常時である. ¶at ***various times*** 色々な時に. ¶At ***what time?*** 何時に. ‖ ***What time*** of the day does the steamer arrive at Kure?

何時ごろ汽船が呉に着きますか. ¶give one's *whole time* to ... ...に没頭する ‖ the *whole time* it was besieged 包囲中ずーっと. ¶It is now the *worst time* of the year. 今が一年で一番悪い時だ. ¶You are here at the *wrong time* of the year. あなたは悪い時にここへいらしった.

Q² preliminary *activity time* consumed by a worker 労働者が活動準備に費す時間. ¶in *apple time* りんご成熟の時. ¶one's *arriving time* 到着する時間. ¶40 minutes ahead of its estimated *arrival time* 予定されたその到着時間より四十分早く. ¶at *Bank-holiday time* 例年の法定休業日に. ¶at *bathing time* 入浴時に. ¶just before *blooming time* 花時のちょっと前. ¶at *blossom time* 花期に. ¶at (=in) *boom time* 景気の好い時に. ¶at *breakfast time* 朝食時に. ¶as the *broadcast time* neared 放送時間が近づいたので. ¶Washington, D.C. in *cherry time* 桜のころのワシントン市. ¶at *Christmas time* クリスマス(の季節)に. ¶in *chrysanthemum time* 菊の季節に. ¶*clam-digging time* はまぐり取りの季節. ¶*clean-up time* 清掃時間. ¶*Clock time* is moved back one hour. 時計を一時間遅らす. ¶a *closing time* 締切時 ‖ at *closing time* [店などを]締める時に. ¶a college campus at *Commencement time* 卒業式の時の校庭. ¶within the *contract time* 契約の期限以内に. ¶the *curtain time* 幕あき. ¶It is eleven o'clock, *daylight-saving time* 夏時間の十一時だ. ¶*departure time* 出発時刻. ¶at *dusk time* 夕暮に. ¶during *election times* 選挙の期間. ¶in *examination times* 試験期には. ¶at *feed time* えさをやる時間に. ¶at *flowering time* 花時に. ¶at *harvest time* 収穫時に. ¶Fall *house-cleaning time* is here. 秋の大掃除が始まった. ¶Some *future time* will do. いつか今度の時でいい. 【類】[at] some *future time* / in *future times*. ¶the *glory time* of year (October, etc.) 一年中の一番よい季節. ¶at the *Han time* 漢時代に. ¶in *harvest time* 収獲時に. ¶at *holiday time[s]* 休暇の時に ‖ in *holiday time* 休暇の時に. 【類】The New Year is a great *holiday time* for the Japanese. ¶till the *home-going time* arrives 帰宅する時まで. ¶at *husking time* とうもろこしの皮をはぐ時期に. ¶in *leisure time* 余暇に ‖ devote their *leisure time* to ... 余暇を...に当てる. 【類】the *leisure time* between labor and rest. ¶give up one's *leisure time* for the study of ... 余暇を利用して...の研究をする. ¶spend *liberty time* in rational amusements [仕事から解放された]自由な時間を合理的な娯楽に費す. ¶the *life time* of a man 人間の一生. ¶*lighting-up time* for cyclists 自転車乗用者が点灯する時刻. ¶It is about *lunch* (=*luncheon*) *time* now. 今は大体昼食時だ. 【類】see another at *lunch time*. ¶at *meal time[s]* 食事時に. ¶at *night time* 夜中に ‖ It is dark (light) in the *night* (*day*) *time*. 夜(昼)は暗い(明るい). ¶It was *noon time* of a very warm day in August. 八月のある暑い日の真昼時のことであった. ¶at *pairing time* 交尾期に. ¶in *peace time[s]*= in times of peace 平時に. ¶at *picking time* 摘取時期に(茶・果実など). ¶give 15% of the possible *radio time* to education 放送しうる時間の十五パーセントを教育に向ける. ¶the *railway time* 鉄道時(鉄道運営のために定めた). ¶win in *record time* 新記録で勝つ. 【類】a criminal arrested in *record time* / in the *record time* of ... min. ... sec. ¶We were nearly twice the *regulation time* in getting there. そこへ行くのに規定時間のほとんど二倍かかった. ¶We had a *rollicking time*. [会などが]すてきに面白かった. ¶The *running time* of trains on the road has been cut from ... to ... 同線の運転時間は...から...に短縮された. 【類】The train maintains a *running time* of eight minutes. ‖ the *running time* for a film 映画の映写時間 ‖ *sale* (=*selling*) *time* [店で]売出しのある時. ¶land within one minute of its *schedule time* その予定の時間の一分以内に着陸する. 【類】The train was in (到着した) right on [*schedule*] *time*. / The vessel (train) reached its destination on *schedule time*. / an hour behind its *schedule time* / The train failed to keep her *schedule time*. ¶It's *school time* now. もう授業時間だ. ¶*cut* one's *shaving time* in half ひげそりに要する時間を半減する. ¶mariners spend *shore time* in ... ...海員は上陸時間を...して送る. ¶at *slump time* 不況時に. ¶a reduction of wasted *student time* and energy 浪費される学生の時間と体力の軽減. ¶*study time* 勉強時間. ¶*Summer time*=《米》 [the] daylight saving time 夏時間. ¶*take-off time* 飛行出発時.

¶The *train time* between Naples and Rome is five hours. ナポリ・ローマ間の列車時間は五時間である. ¶cut *travel time* 旅行に要する時間を短縮する. 【類】four days including *travel time*. ¶in *Tudor* and *Stuart times* チュードル及びスチュアート時代に. ¶in about *twenty years time* 約二十年間に. ¶This is *vacation time*. 今は休暇だ. ¶*waiting time* 手持時間. ¶in *war time[s]*=in *times* of war 戦時に. ¶in [the] *winter time* 冬季に. ¶the *witching time* of night 草木も眠るうしみつ時.

P It is *about time* that the thing should be done. もうそれをなすべきころ合だ. ¶*after a time* しばらくして ‖ Don't be uneasy; we are never *after time*. 心配し給うな, 間に合わないことは決してない. ‖ just *after* the *time* when ... ...の直後に ‖ time *after time* 幾度か. ¶write rapidly, *against time*, an article for a magazine わずかな時しかなくて大急ぎで雑誌へ送る原稿を書く ‖ provide *against* the *time* of need 窮乏の時に備える. ¶it occurs *at times* that ... 時々...ということが起る ‖ *at times* to be fixed between November 30th and December 5th 十一月三十日と十二月五日との期間において決定さるべき時日に ‖ two *at* a (=the same) *time* 一度に二つ ‖ He spoke two hours *at a time* (=stretch). 彼は二時間ぶっ通しの演説をやった. 【類】for months *at a time* (引続いて) / It is possible for a model to be unemployed for weeks *at a time*. ‖ *at a time* convenient to ... ...に都合のよい時に ‖ *at a time* when international agreements come hard 国際協定がうまく行かない時に ‖ *at* the *time* of which I write 私が今論じている時代に ‖ *at* the *time* it is due そうす(なる)べき時に ‖ *at* the *time* of receipt of ... ...を受取った時に. 【類】*at* the *time* of the collapse of feudalism / *at* the *time* of [present] writing / *at* the *time* of the writing of this notice (注意書) / *At* the *time* of this writing the Pacific coast states are much concerned over the problem of the Japanese in their midst (米国在住の). / *at* the *time* of their bitterest poverty (一番貧苦に悩んでいた) / The bride was but fifteen years old *at* the *time* of her marriage. / The goods were carefully weighed *at* [the] *time* of shipment. / *at* the *time* appointed / *at* a *time* of life when ... ‖ *at* that *time* その時 ‖ *at* my *time* of life 私ぐらいの年になると. 【類】*at* this *time* of his life / *at* this *time* of jubilation (歓喜) / *at* this *time* tomorrow ‖ *at* any *time* of its history その歴史中いずれの時にも. 【類】*at* any *time* between ... and ... in the afternoon / [*at*] each *time* / *at* such *times* / *at* other *times* ‖ It is difficult *at times* to determine which is the principal or important term in a phrase. 一つの句の中でどれが主要なあるいは重要な語であるか決定に苦しむことが時々ある. ‖ *at* the *time* of his wife's first confinement 彼の妻が初産の時. ¶become bald-headed *before* one's *time* まだ若いのに頭がはげる ‖ become old *before* one's *time* 早く年を取る ‖ Children often die *before* their *time*. 子供はよく早死をする. ‖ He came *before* his *time*. 彼は時刻より早く来た. ‖ Such a great man as Dante or Carlyle was born *before* his *time*. ダンテやカーライルのような偉人は時代に先だって生れた予言者だった. 【類】The mail steamer has arrived two days *before* her *time*. ‖ whether *before* the *time* of memory or not 有史以前か以後かいずれにしても. ¶fall hopelessly *behind* the *times* 取返しのつかないほど時勢に遅れる ‖ enormously *behind* the *times* 恐ろしく時世に遅れて. 【類】His way of thinking is a century *behind* the *times*. ‖ You are always *behind time* with your work. 君はいつも仕事が遅れる. 【類】He was *behind time* for his appointment. / In England we are for the most part lamentably *behind* the *times* in our advertising ideas. ¶take three full meals a day with milk *between times* 一日三食を十分に取り合間合間に牛乳を飲む. ¶I have stayed very much *beyond* my *time*. 僕は予定よりもずっと長く滞在した. ¶fares *by times* 時間制の賃銀 ‖ healed *by time* 時がたったので(その気持が)なおって ‖ wear out *by time* [物が]古くなっていたむ ‖ You ought to know *by* this *time* that such things should not be done in an office. 事務所でそんなことをしてはいけないくらいのことは君にもう分かっておるべきはずだ. ‖ He must have got there *by* this *time*. 彼は今ごろは先方に着いたはずだ. ¶*disregarding* the *time* and place 時と場所にお構いなく. ¶*during* the disturbed *times* from 1868 to 1871 一八六八年から一八七一年に至る

動乱中に ‖ You can study at home ***during*** spare *time.* 君は家で暇な時に勉強ができる. ¶ that work will remain ***for*** all *time* to come as a monument to ... その作は将来いつまでも...の記念として残るだろう. 【類】 ***for*** some *time* ahead (＝to come) / for ***some time*** past ‖ ***for*** a few *times* 二三度 ‖ ***for*** the *time* being 当分の内; さし当り ‖ He was ***for*** a *time* a professor at Cambridge. 彼は一時ケンブリッジ大学の教授であった. ‖ be pressed ***for*** *time* and money 時間と金がなくて困る. ¶ Look in ***from*** *time* to time and see me. 時々いらっしゃい. 【類】 Education is an admirable thing, but it is well to remember ***from*** *time* to time that nothing that is worth knowing can be taught.—Oscar Wilde. ‖ two weeks, lacking one hour, ***from*** the *time* of starting 出発の時から計算して (一時間だけ不足だが)二週間 ‖ ***from*** that (this) *time* on (＝onward) その(今)後は. 【類】 ***from*** that *time* to the present / ***from*** Greek *times* down to our own day ‖ ***from*** *times* of old (high antiquity) (大)昔から ‖ ***from*** Ben Jonson's to Addison's *time* ベン・ジョンスンからアディスンに至るまでの時代に. ¶ I wish you would come ***in*** *time.* 間に合うようにいらして下さい. 【類】 I finished my work ***in*** *time.* / He was warned (警告された) just ***in*** *time.* / Cancer can be cured if discovered ***in*** *time.* / Why did you not let me know ***in*** *time?* / They left the restaurant ***in*** *time* for the one-o'clock lecture. ‖ just ***in*** *time* not to be left おいてけぼりにされないように丁度間に合って. 【類】 I started ***in*** *time* to arrive at her house by seven o'clock. ‖ My article shall be finished ***in*** *time* for your March number. 貴誌三月号に間に合うように原稿を書き上げます. ‖ I will do it ***in*** [the course of] *time.* その内やりましょう. 【類】 The candle-light will ***in*** *time* go out of itself (独りでに消える). ‖ ***in*** *time* of war 戦時に ‖ ***in*** *times* of scarcity 物資不足の時代に. 【類】 ***in*** *time* of need (sickness, emergency) / ***in*** a *time* of transition (過渡期に), at the end of the age and the beginning of another / training for war ***in*** a *time* of peace ‖ a kitchen ***in*** the *time* of Edward III. エドワード三世時代の台所. 【類】 ***in*** the *time* of Nobunaga / agriculture ***in*** the *time* of Edward III / Genoa, ***in*** the *time* of Columbus, was a very great city. / ***in*** the *time* of one generation (一世代) / It existed ***in*** the *time* of ... ‖ ***in*** this *time* of change この変り行く時代に ‖ It had a large sale and use ***in*** its *time.* それはもとはよく売れて使われたものだ. ‖ ***In*** her *time* it enjoyed considerable vogue. それは彼女の若いころは非常に流行したものだ. ‖ It won't come ***in*** my *time.* 僕の生きている内にはそうはなるまい. 【類】 The college was small ***in*** my *time* (私の若い時分). / Some of them have been sailors ***in*** their *time.* ‖ not being ready ***in*** the *time* stipulated 契約の時期に用意ができていないので ‖ ***in*** between *times* 合間合間に ‖ ***in*** *times* of antiquity 古代に ‖ ***in*** *times* of stress 一朝ことある時に当って. 【類】 ***in*** *times* of industrial distress (産業受難) / ***in*** *times* of peace (war) / ***in*** *times* of drought (かんばつ) / ***in*** *times* of heavy storms (大あらし) / ***in*** *times* of prolonged frost (霜が長く続いた) / The antique trade is always the first to suffer and the last to recover ***in*** [the] *times* of economic crisis. ‖ ***in*** Alexander's *time* アレキサンダー時代に. 【類】 ***in*** Stuart *times* / ***in*** the *time* of the Incas (インカ王国) / ***in*** the *time* of Shakespeare ‖ ***in*** *times* long past. よほど以前には ‖ ***in*** *times* (＝days) gone by＝in bygone days 往時は ‖ ***in*** *time* to the music 音楽に拍子を合わせて. ¶ She is ***near*** her *time.* 彼女の分べん時が近づいた. ¶ for lack ***of*** *time* 時間がないので ‖ in an incredibly brief space ***of*** *time* 信じ得ないほどの短い時間に ‖ in the required space ***of*** *time* 要求された時間内に ‖ What a short span ***of*** *time* is a period of ten years! 十年といっても短いものだ ‖ disposition ***of*** *time* 時の配置 ‖ He takes no account ***of*** *time.* 彼は時間を考慮に入れない. ‖ from the infancy ***of*** *time* 太古から ‖ have lots ***of*** *time* たくさん時間がある ‖ What a pity he chose today ***of*** all *times!* 日もあろうに今日を選ぶとは! 【類】 in a moment ***of*** *time* ‖ the noted people ***of*** the *time* 当代の名士 ‖ like all men ***of*** his *time* 彼も当時のあらゆる人々と同様 ‖ the men ***of*** the *time* 現代の人々. 【類】 the strongest man ***of*** his *time* ‖ in [the] course ***of*** *time* 日を追うて, やがて. 【類】 in due course ***of*** *time* ‖ in process ***of*** *time* 時の立つ内に. ¶ Trains are ***off*** *time.* 汽車の発着が時間通りでない. ¶ ***on*** *time* (＝schedule) 《米》 時刻通り(正確に). ☞ 英用法は to time. ‖ Be here tomorrow ***on*** *time.* あす遅れずにここへ来なさい. ‖ exactly ***on*** *time* [汽車・汽船など]きっちり時間通りに. 【類】 The train was in right ***on*** *time.* ‖ buy ... ***on*** *time* 好期に...を買う ‖ once ***on*** (＝upon) a *time* 昔[ある時] ¶ The baby was born ***out of*** *time.* その赤ん坊は月足らずで生れた. ¶ I have waited a fortnight ***over*** the *time.* 私は約束の日から二週間も待った. ¶ ***since*** the oldest *time* 太古から ‖ ***since*** early *times* 昔から ‖ ***since*** (＝***from***) *time* immemorial 大昔から ‖ ***since*** ancient *times* 古代から. ¶ ***through*** *times* of stress and of peace 戦時平時を通じて ‖ He will learn ***through*** (＝***in***) *time.* 《スコット》 彼は早晩分るだろう. ¶ As a collector of fine specimens of Japanese art, Mr. Fenollosa's name will live ***to*** all *time.* 日本の優秀美術品収集家としてのフェノローサ氏の名はいつまでも記憶されるであろう. ‖ The train is running ***to*** (＝on) *time.* 《英》 その列車は時間通り運転している. 【類】 It was found impossible to get the mail-ship away ***to*** *time* owing to the fact that the firemen were drunk and refused to get steam up. ‖ The letter was posted ***to*** *time.* その手紙は時間に間に合うように投かんされた. ¶ rest ***until*** train *time* 汽車の時間まで休む. ¶ once ***upon*** a *time* 昔昔, ある時. 【類】 Once ***upon*** a *time* the editorial writer and the editorial column were more powerful and certainly more vigorous than they are now. ¶ ***up to*** the present *time* 現在まで. ¶ He will succeed ***with*** (＝in) *time.* 彼は今に成功するでしょう. ‖ increase in price ***with*** *time* 段々値段が上がる ‖ contend ***with*** *times* of stress 難関に当る ‖ keep up (＝keep pace) ***with*** the *times* 時代と歩調を合わせる. ¶ ***within*** the *time* mentioned 前述の期限内に ‖ ***within*** the *time* specified 所定の期間内に ‖ ***within*** historical *times* 有史以来.

P² The *time* ***between*** two and four is convenient. 二時から四時までは都合がよろしい. 【類】 This is a *time* ***for*** nervous excitement for all concerned. / The usual (customary, proper, fashionable) *time* ***for*** call (訪問時間) is between 4 and 6 p.m. ‖ He decided it was *time* ***for*** him to be his own boss (＝master). 彼は今や一本立になるべきだと決心した. ‖ Hey, Jack! It's *time* ***for*** bed now. ジャックや, もう寝る時間だよ. ‖ There is a *time* ***for*** everything. 何事にも時機がある. ¶ a *time* ***of*** rejoicing 歓喜の時 ‖ when a *time* ***of*** trouble comes 財政困難の時機に際して ‖ The setting is the Virginia of the *time* ***of*** James. [劇・小説などの]背景はゼームス時代のヴァージニアである. ¶ travelers with *time* ***on*** hand 急がない旅客 ‖ *Time* ***on*** his hands, maybe. (＝He is free, perhaps.) 多分ひまだろう. ¶ *time* ***out of*** mind 大昔.

O *time* and again しばしば. ¶ *time* and *time* again＝very often 折々. ¶ If you intend to fulfil your promise to Jack, it is *time* [that] you went. ジャックとの約束を守る積りなら君もう出かける時だ. ¶ there was a *time* (＝there were times) when ... ...という時もあった. ¶ And it's *time* the truth be told. そして今や真相を語るべき時だ. ¶ night is the *time* to see ... 夜が...を見るによい時だ. ¶ It's *time* you were going. もう出かける時間だよ. 【類】 It is *time* to get up. ¶ *time* was when ... ...という時代であった. ¶ But *times* are not what they were. しかし昔とは時勢がちがう.

(2) 兵役期; [奉公の]年季; 《口語》 刑期.

V He is ***doing*** *time* at Ichigaya. 彼は市ケ谷で服役している. ¶ In Italy every man must ***serve*** his *time* in the army. イタリアでは皆兵役に服さねばならない. ‖ He has ***served*** *time* at Sugamo for larceny. 彼は窃盗犯で巣鴨刑務所に服役した. ‖ ***serve*** one's full *time* 満期服役する. ¶ ***serve out*** (＝***wind up***) one's *time* [年季など]つとめあげる.

(3) 拍子.

V The conductor ***beats*** *time.* [楽団の]指揮者は拍子を取る. ¶ ***keep*** *time* with the drum 太鼓に拍子を合わせる ‖ ***keeping*** *time* to music 音楽に拍子を合わせて. ¶ The soldiers ***mark*** *time.* 兵士が足踏みをする. ‖ The business is ***marking*** *time* only. 商況が動かない. ‖ The priest beat his "mokugyo" in order to ***mark*** *time* to his monotonous chant. 僧はその単調な読経に拍子を合わせるため木魚をたたいた.

Q ***triple*** (＝***ternary***) *time* 三拍子.

P ***out of*** *time* 拍子がはずれて.

time, *v.* 時に合わす; 拍子を合わせる.

M It was time that they knew it and *timed* ***accordingly.***

もう彼らはそれを知ってそれに調節して行くべき時だった.

P The start of the race is *timed for* 11 o'clock. 競走の出発は十一時となっている. ¶*time* one's steps *to* music [ダンスなど]音楽にステップを合わせる. 【類】The boatmen's stroke was *timed to* their song.

O The afternoon service is *timed* to leave at 3.30 p.m. 午後の汽車(船)は三時三十分に出発することになっている. ¶He *timed* his visit to find her in. 彼女の在宅の時間を計って訪問した.

timekeeper, *n.* 時計, タイムレコーダー.

Q a *good* (*bad*) *timekeeper* 時間の合う(合わない)時計.

Q^2 the *factory timekeeper* 工場のタイムレコーダー.

timer, *n.* 時間記録係.

Q an *old timer* 古参者, 会社などの主(ぬし).

time-signal, *n.* 時報.

Q^2 I set my watch by the *wireless time-signal* at lunch time today. きょう昼食時間に僕はラジオの時報に時計を合わせた.

timetable, *n.* 時刻表.

V *change* one's *timetable* その(旅行滞在などの)日取を変更する.

Q^2 a *railway timetable* 鉄道時刻表.

P *on timetable* (=schedule) [汽車の発着など]時間表通りに.

timid, *a.* おく病な, 小胆な, 気の弱い.

P *timid by* nature 天性おく病な. ¶*timid of* earthquakes 地震を恐れて ‖ *timid of* disposition おく病な性質の.

timidity, *n.* おく病, 小胆.

V *cast off* one's *timidity* おく病をふり捨てる. ¶*conquer* one's *timidity* そのおく病を征服する. ¶gradually *losing* her *timidity* 段々彼女は気が大きくなって. ¶*show* an almost childlike *timidity* in ... ...においてほとんど子供のようなおく病さを見せる.

Q *nervous timidity* 神経的なおく病. ¶*shy timidity* 内気のおじけ.

P a person *of* great *timidity* 非常に小心な人. ¶*without timidity* 恐れないで.

tin, *n.* すず; 《英》[ブリキ]かん.

V *Keep tin* tightly *closed.* かんをしっかり締めておいて下さい(レッテルの注意書).

Q *air-tight tins* 気密かん. ¶biscuits in *sealed tins* 密封したかん入りのビスケット.

P sausages *in tins*=tinned sausages かん詰ソーセージ ‖ work *in tin* ブリキ細工をする ‖ a reel of film carefully packed *in* its own *tin* 大事に専用のかんに入れてある一巻の映画.

P^2 eat [up] a whole *tin of* salmon (biscuits) さけ(など)一かん食ってしまう.

O *tinned* (=canned) food かん詰め.

tincture, *n.* 色合, 気味; 〖薬〗チンキ.

V *have a tincture* of Western learning 西洋の学問をちょっとかじっている.

Q have a *faint tincture* of tobacco (vanilla) タバコ(など)のかすかなにおい. ¶all who have the *least tincture* of learning 学問を少しでもかじっているすべての人.

P^2 *tincture of* quinine 規那塩チンキ ‖ *tincture of* iodine ヨードチンキ.

tincture, *v.* 色を着ける, 味をつける.

P *tincture* it *with* red それに赤味をつける.

tinge, *n.* 色合, 気味.

V *carry* with a *tinge* of ... ...の気味を帯びている. ¶*give* his genius a certain *tinge* of pessimism 彼の天才に一種の悲観的色彩を添える. ¶*have* a strong *tinge* of Chinese or Korean blood in them 彼らは多分に中国人または朝鮮人の血を受けている.

Q a word of a *literary tinge* 文学がかった言葉. ¶The words have a *poetic tinge.* その語には詩的な色彩がある. ¶assume a *religious tinge* 宗教的色彩を帯びる. ¶There is a *slight tinge* of humor in it. それにはちょっとユーモアがある.

P a political party *with* a *tinge* of communism 共産主義の色彩を帯びた政党.

P^2 a *tinge of* pedantry 学識をひけらかし気味. 【類】a *tinge of* affection / He has not a *tinge of* humor.

tinge, *v.* 色合をつける, かすかに色づく.

P Their religions are *tinged by* superstition. 彼らの宗教は迷信臭い. ¶white flowers *tinged with* red 赤味を帯びた白い花 ‖ words *tinged with* cynicism 皮肉めいた言葉.

【類】She was *tinged with* envy.

tingle, *v.* 鳴る, 響く.

P His words still *tingle in* my ears. 彼の言葉が今なお耳に響く. ¶The words *tingled* her *to* her very fingers' end. その言葉で彼女は指先までぞくぞくした. ¶I was *tingling with* excitement. 私は気が立ってうずうずしていた.

【類】Her memory was *tingled with* sorrow.

tinker, *v.* 鋳掛する; へたにつくろう.

M *tinker up* 鋳掛する.

P Do not *tinker at* a doubtful sentence; reconstruct it thoroughly. できの悪い文は小細工をやらないですっかり造り直しなさい. ¶*tinker with* ... ...をいじくり回す, こね回す.

tinkle, *v.* ちりんとひびく.

P a tea-house *thinkling with shamisen* 三味線でさんざめく茶屋.

tinkling, *n.* ちりんちりん.

P^2 the *tinkling of* sleigh bells ちりんちりんというそりの鈴の音.

tint, *n.* 色彩.

V The clouds *acquire* new *tints* at sunset. 雲は日没に新しい色彩を帯びる. ¶The forest *displays* glorious *tints* of red and gold. 林は赤と黄金の輝かしい色彩を示す. ¶Maples *put on* their crimson *tints.* 紅葉が深紅の色を帯びる.

Q the *gorgeous tints* of color seen in the soap-bubble シャボン玉に見られる華美な色彩. ¶*neutral tints* 中間色. ¶foliage in *rich autumn[al] tints* 豊かな秋の色に染む木の葉.

Q^2 *autumn tints* of yellow and gold 秋色.

P a painting *in* one *tint* only [墨絵のように]単色の絵画.

【類】painted *in* several *tints* of color (blue, green).

tint, *v.* 色づける.

P *tinted with* rouge べに色をした; ルージュを(ほおなどへ)塗った.

tip, *n.* 先き, 端.

Q a Communist to his *finger tips* 徹底した共産主義者. 【類】Edison was a utilitarian (実利主義者) to his *finger tips.*

P She has half a dozen languages *at* the *tip* of her tongue. 彼女は五六カ国の言葉を自由に操る. ¶The albatross measures seventeen feet *from tip* to tip of his wings. あほうどりは翼の端から端まで十七フィートある. ¶A question was *on* the *tip* of my tongue. 私は一つ質問が口の先へ出た. 【類】The word is just *on* the *tip* of my tongue. ‖ walk *on* the *tips* of one's toes つま先で歩く. ¶a sailor *to* the *tips* of one's fingers ベテランの水夫. ¶curved *toward* the *tip* せん端の方へと屈曲して.

tip, *v.* せん頭をつける.

P a church-spire *tipped with* a weather-cock 先頭に風見のついている教会のせん塔.

tip, *v.* 傾かす, 傾く.

P He *tips* the beam (=scales) *at* ... pounds. 彼は体重...ポンドある.

M *tip out* 飲み干す; 傾けてあける; 覆えす.

M^2 *tip off* 傾け尽す. ¶*tip over* ひっくり返す. ¶*tip up* 傾ける; ひっくり返す. The boat *tipped over* (=capsized). そのボートが転覆した.

tip, *n.* 心付, 祝儀(チップ).

V *Tips* are most emphatically not *accepted.* 心付は決してお受けしません. ¶*distribute* large *tips* 多額の心付をばらまく. ¶*expect* a *tip* 心付をもらう気でいる. ¶*fix* a porter a sizable *tip* 赤帽に沢山のチップをやる. ¶*give* a *tip* 祝儀をやる ‖ *give tips* all round 総花をやる. ¶*offer* a *tip* 祝儀を出す. ¶*receive* a *tip* 祝儀をもらう.

Q The *fat tips* of war days are over. 世間一般の戦時の気ばった心付はもう見られない. ¶a *good tip* 多分の心付. ¶a *small tip* わずかな心付. ¶*weighty tips* 多分の祝儀.

P including a *tip for* the waiter 給仕への祝儀を含めて.

tip, *v.* 心付(チップ)をやる, 祝儀を出す.

M *generously* (=*handsomely*) *tip* a waiter 給仕にふんばつしたチップをやる.

M^2 My father often *tips* me *up.* 時々父が小使いをくれる.

P *tip* the servant *into* telling the whole story 召使に心付をやってそのことを全部話させる.

tip, *n.* 工夫, 秘けつ; 内報.

V It *supplies* many a good *tip*. それから良いヒントがたくさん得られる.

Q an *anonymous* "*tip*" 密告.

P a *tip for* extracting grease-spots 油のしみを抜き取る法.

tip, *v.* 《口語》[秘密を]漏らす.

M^2 *tip off* one's secret 秘密を漏らす ‖ Thanks for *tipping* me *off*. [金もうけなど]いいことを教えてくれて有難う.

tipping, *n.* チップを出すこと.

Q *No tipping* accepted. 〖掲示〗御祝儀はいただきません.

tipsy, *a.* 酒に酔って, 酒気を帯びて.

M *slightly tipsy* 少しく酒気を帯びて.

tiptoe, *n.* つま先き, 抜足差足.

V *steal* a *tiptoe* to the door 戸口の方へ抜足差足で行く.
P Everybody was ***on tiptoe*** with excitement. だれもかも今か今かと待ち構えていた. ‖ step ***on tiptoe*** つま立てて歩く. 【類】stand (raise oneself, walk) ***on tiptoe*** ‖ they were ***on*** the *tiptoe* of expectation for ... 彼らは...を首を長くして待っていた.

tiptoe, *a.* つまさきの.
P stand *tiptoe* ***for*** ... ...を待ちかまえる.

tire, tyre, *n.* ごむ輪(タイヤ).
V *inflate* the *tires* タイヤに空気を入れる. ¶The cyclist (motorist) ***punctured*** his *tire*. 自転車(など)がパンクした.
Q a *spare tire* 予備タイヤ, スペヤー.
Q² an ***aircraft*** *tire* 航空機のゴム輪. ¶a busted ***autocycle*** *tire* パンクしたオートバイのタイヤ. ¶a skidless ***Dunlop*** *tire* 空転しないダンロップタイヤ. ¶a ***truck tire*** トラックのタイヤ.

tire, *v.* 疲労させる; あきさせる, あきる.
M get ***awfully tired*** of ... ...にあきあきする. ¶I am ***dead*** (***a little***) *tired*. 私はばかに(ちょっと)疲れた. ¶I am ***tired out***. 私はくたくたに疲れた. ‖ ***tire out*** one's patience 辛抱し切れない. ¶get ***quite tired*** 全く疲れる. ¶***very tired*** with ... ...で大いに疲れて.
P ***tired after*** one's journey 旅の後で疲れて. ¶***tired from*** traveling (work, ride, waiting) 旅行(など)で疲れて. ¶He *tires* ***of*** everything. 彼は何にでもあきる. ‖ *tired* ***of*** the monotony of wealth 富貴の単調にあきて. 【類】*tired* ***of*** hearing it / *tired* ***of*** waiting / a saying, which he was never *tired* ***of*** quoting. ¶I am very *tired* ***with*** that long walk. 私はあの長い散歩で非常に疲れた. ‖ ***tired with*** one's resistance 根負けがして ‖ ***tired with*** teaching all day 終日の授業に疲労して. 【類】be *tired* ***with*** exertions.

tireless, *a.* 疲れない, あきない.
P *tireless* ***in*** one's activity 根気よく活動して.

tirelessness, *n.* 根気よさ.
P a *tirelessness* ***in*** research 研究に対する精力.

tiro, *n.* =tyro.

tissue, *n.* 薄紙.
Q² ***toilet*** *tissue* 落し紙.
P² a *tissue* ***of*** lies (falsehoods) うそのかたまり.

tit, *n.* 軽打.
V ***give*** a person *tit* for tat しっぺい返しをする.
P² *tit* ***for*** tat しっぺい返し.

titillation, *n.* くすぐり, くすぐったさ.
V ***feel*** *titillation* くすぐったく感じる.

title, *n.* 題目, 称号; [本などの]書名, 表題; 爵(しゃく)位; 権利; 〘拳闘・レスリング〙選手権.
V He ***abdicated*** his *titles* to a young brother. 彼は栄誉(爵位など)を弟に譲った. ¶***acquire*** *title* to property (land) 財産(など)の所有権を得る. ¶The Association ***adopted*** its present *title* in 1908. その協会は一九〇八年に今の称号を採用した. ¶He had his *title* ***advanced*** from "Mr." to "Marquis" and "Prince" 彼はその称号を「様」(平民)から「侯」へそれから「公」へと進められた. ¶***append*** a *title* 称号を付記する. ¶***assume*** the *title* of king 王と称する. ¶The book ***bears*** the *title* "..." その本は「...」という表題である. ‖ women ***bearing*** *titles* 有爵の婦人たち ‖ a magazine ***bearing*** the *title* of *Literature* 文学という題名の雑誌. ¶***bestow*** a *title* to ... ...に称号を与える. ¶The *title* of the country was ***changed*** to Chosen. その国の名称は朝鮮に変った. ¶***confer*** the honorific *title* of ... on ... ...に...の名誉称号を授ける ‖ The Emperor ***confers*** *titles* of nobility, rank, orders and other marks of honor. 〘旧憲法〙天皇は爵位・勲章及びその他の栄典を授与する. ¶a catalouge ***containing*** over 3,000 *titles* 三千以上の書名を含む目録. ¶***defend*** the *title* 〘拳闘〙選手権を防衛する. ¶***deserve*** the *title* of ... ...の称号に値する. ¶he will ***drop*** the *title* and be known as ... 彼はその称号を捨てて...ということになるだろう. ¶he has just ***earned*** its *title*, "..." 彼は丁度その称号「...」を得たところだ. 【類】He fully ***earned*** the *title* of "Father" of New Japan. ¶Its iridescent appearance has ***earned*** for it the *title* of the Pearl. その外観が真珠光りがしているので真珠館と呼ばれるに至った. ¶To ... is to ***forfeit*** the *title* of world's champion. ...すると世界選手の資格を失うことになる. ¶This ***gained*** for him the *title* of leading poet of his age. このために彼は当代屈指の詩人と称せられるようになった. ¶***give*** a fantastic *title* to a book 書物に珍妙な名をつける ‖ the poem which ***gives*** the *tilte* to the book その本の表題になっている詩. ¶He ***has*** many *titles* to distinction. 彼は高名となるべき幾多の資格を有している. ¶one who ***holds*** a *title*=a title-holder 選手権保持者. ¶***inherit*** the *title* of the father 父の名称を受継ぐ ‖ ***inherit*** his father's estates and *titles* 彼の父の財産と爵位を受継ぐ. ¶The contents ***justify*** the *title* of the book. 表題がその本の内容をよく現わしている. ¶He has ***lost*** the *title*. 選手権を喪失した. ¶***prefix*** *title*, Mr., Mrs., Master or Miss to name, as the case may be その場合場合で様・夫人・君・嬢の称号を姓名の前に付ける. ¶***put*** a *title* to a book 書物に題名を付ける. ¶a picture that ***requires*** no *title* [見ればそれとすぐ分かるので]題名を付ける必要のない絵. ¶***select*** a *title* for a short story 短編小説の題目を選ぶ. ¶***take*** the *title* Pius XI. ピオ十一世の名称を用いる. ¶***transfer*** *title* to ... ...に対する権利を譲渡する. ¶***wear*** a *title* 爵位を持っている. ¶***want*** *title* to ... ...に対する権利を取りたい ‖ He ***won*** for him among his friends the *title* of the "Boy Burbank of the Danube." 彼は友人間に「ダニューブの少年バーバンク」の名で知られるに至った. 【類】He has ***won*** for him the proud *title* of "..." / Colonel Higginson ***won*** his *title* by service in the Civil War at the head of a regiment of negroes. ¶***write*** a *title* to a picture 絵の題名を書く.
Q an ***academic*** *title* 学位. ¶an ***apposite*** *title* 適切な題名. ¶published under an ***attractive*** *title* 興味ある表題の下に刊行された本. ¶a ***bogus*** *title* いんちきな肩書. ¶a book with a ***captivating*** *title* 魅力ある表題の本. ¶a doubtfully ***complimentary*** *title* [ちょっとまゆつばもの程度に称賛した]実は有難くない称号. ¶an ***elegant*** *title* 上品な名称. ¶Ruskin loved ***fanciful*** *titles* for his books. ラスキンは著書に変った表題をつけるのが好きだった. ¶The Royal Society, the ***full*** *title* of which is The Royal Society of London for the Promotion of Natural Knowledge, has its anniversary meeting and dieting on St. Andrew's Day. 自然科学研究ロンドン王立学会(略称王立学会)は毎年の記念会と晩さん会を聖アンデレ祭の当日に催す. ¶a ***functional*** *title* [官名に対する]職名. ¶a ***graceful*** and ***suggestive*** *title* [本の]優美にして暗示に富んだ表題. ¶***high-sounding*** *titles* 仰々しい肩書. ¶he is known under the ***honorable*** *title* of ... 彼は...という敬称で知られている. ¶the ***legitimate*** *title* to a throne 王位を継承する正当な権利. ¶a ***lengthy*** *title* of a book 長たらしい本の表題. ¶dyspepsia, or, to call it by a more ***modern*** *title*, indigestion 胃弱すなわちもっと近代的な名称でいうと消化不良. ¶a dictionary of ***occupational*** *titles* 職業名称辞典. ¶an ***official*** *title* 正式の呼称. ¶an ***ornamental*** *title* 装飾的肩書. ¶a premier with ***ponderous*** *titles* いかめしい肩書のある首相. ¶a ***posthumous*** *title* 死後の位階. ¶a ***professional*** *title* 職業上の肩書. ¶***seductive*** *titles* 引つけられる見出し. ¶a ***spurious*** *title* 偽の肩書. ¶a very ***unpromising*** *title* はなはだ人ずきのしない題名. ¶not a ***well-chosen*** *title* 選択よろしきを得ない題名.
Q² a ***chapter*** *title* 章の表題. ¶a ***courtesy*** *title* [Viscount の長男を Baron と呼ぶなど]礼儀上の敬称. ¶a ***cover*** *title* =title on outside cover 表紙に出ている書名. ¶a ***job*** *title* 職名. ¶a ***newspaper*** *title* 新聞紙の名. ¶an ***occupation*** *title* 職種. ¶the ***photo-play*** *title* of a novel 映画化した小説の題名.
P having ***for*** its *title* ... ...その題目は...で ‖ marry ***for*** a *title* 爵位を目当に結婚する. ¶a book ***under*** the *title*, "..." 「...」という題名の本. 【類】published ***under*** the *title* of ... / be published ***under*** the *title* "..." ‖ a corporation was created ***under*** the *title* of ... ...という名の会社が組織された. 【類】the formation, ***under*** the *title* of the ..., of an association for ... ‖ After his death, he was deified ***under*** the *title* of Myogi Dai-Gongen. 死後彼は妙義大権現として神に祭られた. ¶He was created a peer ***with*** the *title* of Baron. 氏は男爵に叙せられた. ¶a man ***without*** *title* 爵位のない人 ‖ call one's name ***without*** *title* 人を呼捨にする ‖ a picture ***without*** a *title* 無題の絵.
P² the *title* ***of*** Colonel 大佐の肩書. 【類】... will be the *title* ***of*** his work (著作の題名). ¶His *title* ***to*** fame rests on his literary accomplishments. 彼が有名なのは文芸上の業績のためだ. ‖ The *title* ***to*** it he claimed to be in himself. それに対する権利は自分にあると彼は主張した.

tittle, *n.* 少量, 微量.
P ***to*** a *tittle*=〘米〙to a dot 正確に ‖ Her face is her

mother's *to* a *tittle*. 彼女の顔は母親そっくりだ.

toast, *n*. 乾杯; 祝詞.

V To his memory let us ***drink*** a *toast* of honor. 彼の霊につつしんで乾杯しましょう. ‖ ***drink*** a *toast* to … …のために祝杯をあげる. ¶***exchange*** *toasts* 祝杯を酌み交わす. ¶***give*** a *toast* to the flag その旗に対して乾杯する. ¶The *toast* was enthusiastically ***honored,*** being greeted with shouts of "Banzai." 乾杯は万歳歓呼のうちに熱心にあげられた.【類】The *toast* of the King having been ***honored,*** he proposed "Liberal Women and the Liberal Course." ¶***propose*** the *toast* of the club クラブを代表する乾杯を発議する.【類】in ***proposing*** the *toast* of "Miss Nation," he said that …

Q after the ***royal toasts*** had been duly honored 王室のため祝杯を正式にあげてから.【類】The ***royal*** *toast* was heartily drunk, the band playing "God save the King." ¶a "***standing***" *toast* 起立乾杯.

P replying ***to*** the *toast* of his health, he said that … その健康を祝された彼は…と答えた.

P^{2} Here is a *toast* ***to*** …, may he live long and prosper well. [乾杯の詞]…の御健康と御繁栄を祝します.

toast, *v*. 健康を祝して杯をあげる.

P *toast* back ***to*** the host 主人に祝杯を返す.

toast, *n*. 焼パン(トースト).

V ***make*** *toast* in a toaster トースターでトーストを作る.

P a slice ***of*** *toast* 一片の焼パン.

toast, *v*. トーストを作る.

P *toast* slices of bread ***for*** lunch 昼飯用のトーストを作る.

tobacco, *n*. タバコ.

V ***cultivate*** (=***raise***) *tobacco* タバコを栽培する. ¶***gvie up*** *tobacco*=quite smoking タバコをやめる. ¶***smoke*** *tobacco* in one's pipe パイプでタバコを吸う.

Q ***cut*** *tobacco* 刻みタバコ. ¶***mild*** *tobacco* 軽いタバコ.

Q^{2} ***leaf*** *tobacco* 葉タバコ. ¶***pipe*** *tobacco* パイプ(に詰める)タバコ. ¶***plug*** *tobacco* 板タバコ.

P a fill ***of*** *tobacco* 一服のタバコ.

toboggan, *v*. [競争用そりの意から]急落する.

O Prices have been *tobogganing* in the past year. ここ一年物価が急落している.

today, *n*. 今日; 現今.

V We ***have*** *today* for a holiday. 今日は一日休みだ. ¶It's only three days ***from*** *today*. もう三つ寝るとね. ¶No business ***for*** *today*.〚掲示〛本日休業.【類】I have finished my work ***for*** *today*.

Q ***all*** *today* きょう一日.

P a week ***from*** *today* 今日から一週間. ¶Oxford ***of*** *today* 現今のオクスフォード.【類】young men ***of*** *today* ‖ in the course ***of*** *today* きょう中に. ¶***on*** and ***after*** *today* 今日以後. ¶***up to*** *today* 今日まで.

O It was two years ago *today* that he left Japan. 彼が日本を去ったのは丁度二年前のきょうだった.

toddle, *v*. よちよち歩く.

M *toddle* ***along*** [幼児など]よっちよっち歩く.

to-do, *n*.〘口語〙大騒ぎ.

Q The chickens made a ***great*** *to-do* when the cat came near. ねこがそばへ来たのでひよこが大騒ぎをした.

toe, *n*. 足指, 足の先.

V ***curl*** *toes* 足の指を曲げる. ¶***incline*** the *toes* inside (outside) when walking 内(外)足で歩く. ¶These boots are too tight, and they ***pinch*** my *toes*. くつが窮過ぎて指に当る. ¶***stub*** (=***dash***) one's *toes* against a stone 石にけつまずく. ¶***toast*** one's *toes* 足の指を火で暖める.

Q one's ***naked*** *toes* はだしの足先. ¶shoes with ***pointed*** *toes* 先のとがったくつ.

P My shoes are tight ***at*** the *toes*. 私のくつは指の所が窮屈だ. ¶step (=tread) ***on*** one's *toes* 人の足を踏む; [比ゆ的に]腹を立たせる.【類】walk ***on*** the *toes* ‖ tread ***on*** the *toes* of men in power 長上の御機げんを損じる ‖ be ***on*** one's *toes* for … …する準備が出来ている, 油断がない.

P^{2} wet from top ***to*** *toe* 頭の先からつま先までぬれて. ¶walk ***with*** the *toes* turned in (out) つま先を内(外)に向けて歩く.

toe, *v*. つま先を動かす.

M *toe* ***in*** (***out***) 内(外)輪に歩く.

together, *ad*. 一緒に.

P *together* ***with*** … …と一緒に.

togs, *n. pl*. 衣服.

Q^{2} don ***bathing*** *togs* 海水着を着る. ¶in ***business*** *togs* 平常服で.

toil, *n*. 骨折, 辛苦; 網.

V ***beguile*** *toil* 仕事の苦労を紛らす. ¶***endure*** the *toil* 辛苦を忍ぶ. ¶***lighten*** *toil* 骨折を軽くする. ¶Mountain-climbing ***repays*** tenfold the *toil* it exacts. 登山はそれに伴う骨折に対し十倍も報いる. ¶He lamented the death of the companion who had ***shared*** his *toil* but not his triumph. 彼は自己の成功に先だって世を去ったその苦難をともにした妻の死を嘆いた. ¶without ***sparing*** *toil* 骨身を惜しまずに.

Q by ***hard*** and ***unremitting*** *toil* 間断なく懸命に骨折って. ¶years of ***honest*** *toil* 多年の正直な労働. ¶after years of ***incessant*** *toil* 多年苦労の後. ¶***irksome*** *toil* あきあきする骨折. ¶***onerous*** *toil* 骨の折れる労苦. ¶His past represents years of ***tedious*** *toil* and groping after light. 彼の過去は多年の面倒な骨折と光明の模索とを示している. ¶a life of ***unbroken*** *toil* 絶えず骨の折れる生活.

P ***by*** unremitting *toil* 間断ない労苦によって. ¶return ***from*** the day's *toil* 一日の仕事から帰る. ¶be caught ***in*** the *toils* of the law 法網にかかる. ¶***through*** *toil* 辛苦の結果. ¶obtained ***with*** *toil* 骨を折って得た ‖ exhausted ***with*** *toil* 辛労のため疲労し切って ‖ learn ***with*** great *toil* 骨を折って覚える.【類】He gained it ***with*** such *toil*.

toil, *v*. 骨折る, 辛苦する.

M He began *toiling* ***away*** at his herculean task. 彼はそのすこぶる困難な仕事に身を入れ始めた. ¶*toil* ***early*** and ***late*** 朝早くから夜おそくまで勤労する. ¶*toil* ***strenuously*** 奮闘努力する. ¶*toil* ***upward*** (***onward***) 辛苦して向上(前進)する. ¶*toil* ***valiantly*** and ***strenuously*** 勇敢に奮闘的に努力する.

M^{2} *toil* ***along*** 骨折り続ける.

P *toil* ***after*** the art of … …の技術を身につけようと. ¶*toil* ***at*** one's task 課せられた仕事に骨を折る. ¶*toil* ***for*** bread パンのために働く ‖ Gold groweth not; it must be *toiled* ***for***. 金はひとりでには生えない, これを得るためには骨を折らねばならない. ¶Children *toil* ***over*** the spelling-book. 子供たちはつづり方の本で苦しむ. ¶*toil* ***up*** the hill (=uphill) 骨折って坂を登る.

toiler, *n*. 労役者.

Q the ***busy*** *toilers* of Japan's big cities 日本の大都市における忙しい労役者. ¶the city's ***four-footed*** *toilers* [牛・馬など]都会で働く四足獣. ¶a ***patient*** *toiler* 我慢強い勤労者.

Q^{2} ***home*** *toilers* 家庭に働く人.

toilet, *n*. (**1**) 化粧, 身仕度.

V Wearing of stockings ***completed*** her *toilet*. [最後に]くつ下をはいてそれで彼女の身仕度ができた. ¶He ***made*** a hasty *toilet* for dinner. 彼は急いで食卓に出る仕度をした. ‖ She retired to ***make*** her *toilet*. 彼女は身仕舞をするために引下った.【類】***make*** one's *toilet* and smarten oneself up. ¶***perform*** one's *toilet* 化粧をする.

Q an ***elaborate*** *toilet* 念入りな化粧. ¶make a ***grand*** *toilet*, as if for a ball 舞踏会へでも行くように盛装する. ¶make a ***meticulous*** *toilet* 念入りすぎる化粧をする.

P a young girl ***at*** her *toilet* 化粧にかかっている少女. ¶***from*** a *toilet* of two hours 二時間の化粧ができ上って.

(**2**) 便所.

Q go to a ***regular*** *toilet* 毎日定って便通がある.

Q^{2} a ***flush*** *toilet* 水洗便所.

toilette, *n. F.* 化粧.

V ***make*** an elaborate *toilette* 念入りにおつくりをする.

token, *n*. 記念物, 形見, 印し.

V ***give*** her more tangible *tokens* of his friendship 彼女に彼の友情を一層具体的に表わす記念の品を与える. ¶All these are *tokens* ***showing*** in what direction further progress is to be expected. これらはすべて将来いかなる方面に一段の進歩を予期すべきかを示す標識である.

Q a ***feeble*** *token* of our warm friendship われらの最も深じんな友情を示すささやかな記念物. ¶as a ***mere*** *token* ほんのお印しとして. ¶as an ***outward*** *token* of … …を具体的に表わす記念物として. ¶a ***short-lived*** *token* 束の間の記念物. ¶as a ***slight*** *token* of gratitude ほんの感謝の印しに, 気は心で. ¶I hope you will accept it as a ***small*** *token* of my love and affection. いささか私の愛情の印しとしてそれをお受け下さい. ¶as a ***trifling*** *token* of my congratulation 私の祝意のお印しに.

Q^{2} receive many ***birthday*** *tokens* 誕生日の記念品をたくさんもらう. ¶a ***love*** *token* [指輪など]愛情の印し. ¶a ***pass***

token in a theater 劇場のパス(特殊の入場券).
P ***as*** a *token* of appreciation for (=of) ... ...に対する感謝の印しに ‖ ***as*** a *token* of rememblance 記念に.【類】***as*** a *token* of my admiration and esteem / ***as*** a *token* of his love / ***as*** a *token* of the friendship which exists between ... and ... ¶***by*** the same *token* 同じ理由で. ¶bow ***in*** *token* of respect 敬意を表するため頭を下げる(敬礼).【類】ropes of straw and paper hung round trees ***in*** *token* of reverence (しめかざり) / ***in*** *token* of gratitude (condolence) / ***in*** *token* of defeat (負けた) / a kiss ***in*** *token* of love / This is ***in*** *token* of a New Year's present (お年玉) / ***in*** *token* of gratitude for a service the translator had done him.
P² a *token* ***of*** victory 戦勝記念品 ‖ He made a liberal distribution of the *tokens* ***of*** his grateful sense of the happiness he had met in his hotel. 彼はホテルの優遇に満足して総花をまいた.【類】This is a mere *token* ***of*** my thanks. / The white flag is a *token* ***of*** surrender.

tolerance, *n.* かん忍, 寛容;〖医〗耐薬力.
V ***has*** no *tolerance* for ... ...を大目に見ない ‖ ***have*** a *tolerance* for a drug 薬が強量でないときかない(始終用いるため).
Q regard it with ***gentle*** *tolerance* やさしく寛大な態度でそれを見る. ¶It was regarded at first with ***kindly*** *tolerance*. それは最初大目に見られていた. ¶***religious*** *tolerance* 宗教上の寛容.
P look ***with*** *tolerance* upon ... 寛容の心をもって...を見る.

tolerant, *a.* 寛大な.
P *tolerant* ***as to***…...について寛大な. ¶To be serenely *tolerant* ***of*** all things and of all men is the national character of the English. あらゆる物あらゆる人に対して心静かで寛大なのは英国人の国民性である. ‖ *tolerant* ***of*** failure 失敗に対して寛大な.

tolerate, *v.* かん忍する, 寛容する.
M ***amusedly*** *tolerate* it それを一笑に付して寛容する. ¶*tolerate* it ***patiently*** それを我慢強く寛容する.
P be *tolerated* ***without*** question 不問に付する.

toleration, *n.* かん忍, 默認.
V ***evince*** a furious *toleration* of ... ...の極端な默認を示す. ¶***show*** an easy *toleration* for the competition of ... ...の競争を気軽に默認する.
P² exhibit toward others the *toleration* ***of*** their beliefs 彼らの信仰を默認することを他人に示す.

toll, *n.* 通行税, 通行料金; 犠牲者.
V A *toll* is ***charged*** on some specially constructed mountain roads. ある特別に敷設された山道では通行料金を取る. ¶***collect*** *tolls* at the gateway 入口で通行料金をとる. ¶***demand*** *toll* from every passing vessel そこを通過するあらゆる船から通行税を取る. ¶***levy*** *tolls* on vessels using the Panama Canal パナマ運河通行船の通行税を課す.【類】*Toll* is ***levied*** on the traveller at the bridge for construction and upkeep (維持). ¶a *toll* ***paid*** on a bridge 橋の通行税. ¶The railway is convenient, but ***takes*** its *toll* of human lives. 鉄道は便利だが死者を出す.【類】The accident ***took*** a heavy *toll* of lives.
Q The disease takes a ***heavy*** *toll* of infant life. その病気の幼児の死亡率は高い. ‖ The predatory cat takes ***heavy*** *toll* of young sparrows. 食肉のねこはすずめの子をたくさん取る.【類】War claims a ***heavy*** *toll* of youngsters. ¶The accident counted a ***high*** *toll*. その事故は多数の死者を出した. ¶Consumption takes so ***terrible*** a *toll* among overstrained and under-nourished bodies. 肺病は過労や栄養不良な者の間に多大な犠牲者を出す.
Q² the rapidly rising number of ***accident*** *tolls* 事故による死者の急激な増加. ¶The ***death*** *toll* rose to twenty-eight. 死者は二十八人に増加した.【類】It is estimated that the ***death*** *toll* may reach 100 or higher. / The ***death*** *toll* from bombing raids on Dresden in 1945 was 25,000—30,000 persons. / The ***death*** *toll* was mounting day by day. / The ***death*** *toll* in the diver accident moved upward as divers searched the sunken hold. / cause a heavy ***death*** *toll* in livestock (家畜). ¶The ***telegraph*** *tolls* amount to quite a sum. 電報料もばかにはならない. ¶The first six months of this year took a ***traffic*** *toll* of 15,750 persons killed and 540,000 injured. 本年の上半期における交通事故による死者は 15,750 人, 負傷者 540,000 人に及んだ. ¶China's ***war*** *toll* 中国の戦争犠牲者.
P ***with*** a *toll* of ninety-two lives 九十二人の死者を出して.
P² *tolls* ***on*** the canal 運河通行税.

tolling, *n.* 鐘の音.
P ***at*** the *tolling* of a bell 鐘を鳴らすと.

tomato, *n.* トマト.
Q ***fresh*** *tomatoes* 新鮮なトマト.

tomb, *n.* 墓穴, 墓; 墓標(石).
V ***open*** a *tomb* 墓をあばく. ¶***visit*** a *tomb* 墓参りをする.
Q a ***simple*** and ***noble*** *tomb* 質素で上品な墓.
P bury one's remains ***in*** a *tomb* その遺がいを墓に葬る. ¶an inscription ***on*** a *tomb* 墓石の碑銘. ¶take the bones ***out of*** a *tomb* 墓から骨を取出す. ¶a horizontal slab ***over*** a *tomb* 墓所に建てた水平な板石.
P² A *tomb* ***on*** his grave bears an inscription recording his personal history. 彼の墓碑にはその伝記が記してある.

tombstone, *n.* 墓石, 墓標.
V ***consecrate*** a *tombstone* 墓石建立式を行う. ¶***erect*** (=***set up***) a *tombstone* over a grave 墓に墓石を建てる. ¶***put*** a *tombstone* over the remains of ... ...の遺がいの上に墓石を建てる.
P inscribe ***on*** a *tombstone* 墓石に銘を刻む.
P² a *tombstone* ***of*** marble 大理石の墓石.

tome, *n.* 冊, 巻; 大冊.
Q two ***bulky*** *tomes* 二冊の部厚の本. ¶***old*** and ***forgotten*** *tomes* 古い忘れられている書物. ¶***ponderous*** *tomes* 大冊 ‖ turn out ***ponderous*** *tomes* on ... 大部の書を公にする.

tomorrow, *n.* あす; 将来.
Q of ***England's*** *tomorrow* 英国の明日(将来)について.
P [the] day ***after*** *tomorrow* 明後日.

ton, *n.* トン.
V The ship ***measures*** ... *tons*. その船は...トンある.
Q a ***long*** *ton* 英トン (2,240 ポンド). ¶a ***metric*** *ton* メートル・トン (1,000 キログラム). ¶***per*** *ton* トン当り. ¶a ***short*** *ton* 米トン (2,000 ポンド).
P² 1,000 *tons* ***of*** coal 一千トンの石炭.

tone, *n.* 調子; 音色, 音調; 語気, 気風.
V His speech ***altered*** the *tone* of the meeting. 彼の演説で会の形勢が一変した. ¶***assume*** a threatening *tone* 脅迫的な語気を帯びる. ¶***avoiding*** all *tone* of reproach, I said to her, quietly, "..." 少しもとがめ立をするような気持でなく私は静かに彼女に「...」と言った. ¶***brace up*** the moral *tone* 道徳的気風を振作する. ¶***change*** its *tone* towards ... その...に対する調子を変える. ¶The market ***displays*** a healthy *tone*. 市場は健全な調子を示している. ¶The bell ***has*** a beautiful *tone*. その鐘は音色がよい. ¶***imitate*** (=***mimic***) one's *tones* その調子をまねる. ¶***impart*** to it a *tone* of great vulgarity それをはなはだ俗悪化する. ¶***improve*** the *tone* of the body 身体の調子をよくする. ¶Her mind has ***lost*** its *tone*. 彼女は気が狂った. ¶***lower*** the *tone* of the press 新聞の調子を低下する ‖ ***lower*** the *tone* of morality 道徳基準を下げる. ¶The market ***maintains*** a steady *tone*. 市場は手堅い調子を保持している. ¶***raise*** the *tone* of public morals 公衆道徳の調子を高める.【類】The University of Chicago has ***raised*** the scholarly *tone* (学風) of the whole group of Midwestern universities. ¶The school ***retains*** much of the old *tone* and tradition. その学校には昔の気品と伝統が大分残っている.
Q in ***acid*** *tones* 辛らつな語調で. ¶in an ***agitated*** *tone* いらいらした語調で. ¶speak in an ***angry*** *tone* 怒った調子で言う. ¶speaking with ***apologetic*** *tone* 申し分けのような口振りで. ¶a ***callous*** and coarsely ***frivolous*** *tone* 軽兆浮薄な調子. ¶in a ***changed*** *tone* of voice 話の調子を変えて. ¶in a ***coaxing*** *tone* すかすような口調で. ¶He spoke to me in a ***commanding*** *tone*. 彼は命令するような調子で僕に話した. ¶The article has a ***controversial*** *tone*. その文には議論がましい語気がある. ¶speak in a ***cool*** *tone* 落着いて話す. ¶speak in a ***deep*** *tone* 太い声で話す.【類】the ***deep*** *tone* of a big bell. ¶in a ***deep*** and ***impressive*** *tone* 力がこもって人を感動させるような調子で. ¶in a ***dismal*** and ***sepulchral*** *tone* 気味の悪い陰気な調子で. ¶say in a ***dogmatic*** *tone* in one's voice 独断的な口調で言う. ¶with a ***dramatic*** *tone* in one's voice 声色を使うように. ¶speak in a ***dry*** and ***monotonous*** *tone* 無味乾燥で千編一律の口調で話す. ¶in ***dulcet*** *tones* 美妙な調子で(音楽など). ¶On that day a ***dyspeptic*** (=***depressed***) *tone* pervaded the debates in Parliament. その日(英国)議会の討議は惰気

満々であった. ¶in most ***emphatic*** *tones* きわめて力強い語調で. ¶in an ***encouraging*** *tone* 激励的口調で. ¶in an ***excited*** *tone* 興奮した口調で. ¶A very ***firm*** *tone* prevailed on the Bourse today. きょうの株式市場はきわめて強気であった. ¶in a ***flat*** *tone* 抑揚のない調子で. ¶sing in ***flute-like*** *tones* フリュートのような音色で歌う. ¶in a more ***forceful*** *tone* 一層強硬な調子で(催促状など). ¶in a doubtfully ***hesitant*** *tone* of voice 疑ぐり深いためらった語調で. ¶change to a ***higher*** and ***shriller*** *tone* もっとかん高い声に変る. ¶in ***honeyed*** *tones* 甘ったるい語調で. ¶at an ***imperative*** *tone* 高圧的の調子で. ¶in ***injured*** *tones* 怒気を含んだ語調で. ¶raise the ***intellectual*** *tone* of society 社会の知的水準を高める. ¶in a ***kindly*** *tone* 親切な口調で. ¶sing in a ***low*** (***high***) *tone* 低い(高い)調子で歌う. ¶She begged him, in the most ***moving*** *tone*, not to do so. 彼女はいとも哀れな口調でそうしないようにと彼にこうた. ¶in a ***muffled*** *tone* [of voice] 声の調子をおとして. ¶read it aloud in a ***musical*** *tone* of voice 音楽的な語調で声高にそれを読む. ¶a ***nasal*** *tone* 鼻声. ¶speak in her ***natural*** *tones* 彼女の自然の調子で話す. ¶an ***oily*** *tone* of voice ねこなで声. ¶He repeated the question in a more ***peremptory*** *tone*. 彼は一層断固たる調子でその質問を繰返した. ¶a ***pessimistic*** *tone* 悲観的な調子. ¶in a ***pleading*** *tone* 訴えるような調子で. ¶The ***prevailing*** *tone* is one of satisfaction. まず一般に満足している様子である. ¶proclaim in ***resolute*** *tones* 断固たる語調で宣言する. ¶in a ***respectful*** *tone* うやうやしい口調で. ¶say in a ***sharp*** *tone* 鋭い句調で言う. ¶speak in a ***sleepy*** *tone* 眠たい調子で話す. ¶I like the ***soft green*** *tone* of that picture. 僕はその絵の柔かい緑の色調が好きだ. ¶assuming a ***sober*** *tone* 改まって. ¶in ***solemn*** *tones* 厳粛な調子で. ¶shout in ***stentorian*** *tones* 大音声に叫ぶ. ¶speak in a ***subdued*** *tone* 低い語調で話す ‖ a ***subdued*** *tone* of color じみな色. ¶in a ***sweet*** *tone* of voice 美しい声で ‖ The ***sweet*** *tones* of a flute floated through the window. 美しい笛の音が窓から流れた. ¶a ***well-modulated*** *tone* うまく加減した調子.

Q² ***color*** *tone* 色調.

P speak ***above*** an ordinary *tone* 普通の調子より高く話す. ¶***in*** a *tone* of reproach (inquiry, half apology, authority, horror) 非難(など)の口調で ‖ wholesome and agreeable ***in*** *tone* 音色が健全で気持のよい ‖ remarked ***in*** *tones* of deep satisfaction (wounded dignity) 深く満足した(憤慨した)口調で述べられた. 【類】good-humored and temperate ***in*** *tone* / ***in*** the *tone* of a mother. ¶read ***with*** a *tone* 調子をつけて読む. 【類】***with*** a *tone* of contempt.

P² the *tone* ***of*** the nation 国民の気品.

tone, *v.* 和げる; 調和する.

M *tone* ***down*** a color 色彩を和げる ‖ *tone* ***down*** one's religious austerities 宗教的厳格さを和げる. 【類】*tone* ***down*** attacks on ... / *tone* ***down*** one's criticism of ... ‖ *tone* ***down*** one's skill in a game 〖比ゆ〗調子をおろす. ¶*tone* ***in*** (=harmonize) with ... ...と調和する. ¶*tone* ***up*** 調子をあげる, 力をつける.

P this colour *tones* ***with*** ... その色は...と調和する.

tongs, *n. pl.* 火ばし.

P a pair ***of*** *tongs* 火ばし一組.

tongue, *n.* 舌; 言葉, 国語.

V ***acquire*** a foreign *tongue* 外国語を修得する. ¶***banish*** the mother *tongue* from the teaching of English 英語教授に母国語を使わないようにする. ¶I ***bit*** my *tongue* sorely. 僕はひどく舌をかんだ. ¶***bite out*** one's *tongue* 舌をかみ切る. ¶***bridle*** (=***restrain***) one's *tongue* 口を慎む. ¶***clack*** the *tongue* 舌を鳴らす. ¶***cut out*** one's *tongue* 舌を切り取る. ¶***dart out*** the *tongue* [へびなど]舌をちらっと出す. ¶***examine*** a patient's *tongue* 患者の舌を見る. ¶***find*** one's *tongue* また口がきけるようになる(びっくりした状態から). 【類】we finally ***found*** our *tongues*, and managed to tell ... ¶I would not ***foul*** my *tongue* with his nasty name. 彼の名は言うも汚らわしい. ¶***give*** one's *tongue* to=express ... ...を言い表わす. ¶***govern*** the *tongue* 言葉を慎む. ¶She ***has*** two *tongues*. 彼女は二枚舌を使う. ¶He wisely ***held*** his *tongue*. 彼は利口だからだまっていた. ‖ They bribed him by money to ***hold*** his *tongue*. 彼らは口留料を使って彼をだき込んだ. 【類】***Hold*** your *tongue*!=Shut up! ¶***keep*** one's *tongue* ***quiet*** 沈黙を守る ‖ ***keep*** a civil *tongue* おとなしくしている. ¶The dog is ***lolling*** (=***hanging***) [out] the *tongue*. 犬が舌をだらりとたらしている. ¶The champagne ***loosened*** my *tongue*. シャンパン酒で私の口が軽くなった. ‖ The spell was broken, their *tongues* were ***loosened***. 沈黙が破れ彼らの舌がほぐれてきた. ¶***lose*** one's *tongue* 口がきけなくなる. ¶The man who can ***manage*** his *tongue* is a perfect man. 口が慎めれば君子だ. ¶***protract*** one's *tongue* 舌を出す. ¶***put out*** one's *tongue* at ... ...に対し舌を出す. ¶***rein*** (=restrain) one's *tongue* 口を慎む. ¶***retract*** one's *tongue* 舌を引っ込める. ¶The fire ***sent up*** long *tongues* of flame. 火が高く紅れんの炎を上げた. ¶***set*** one's *tongue* in motion しゃべり出す ‖ It will ***set*** the *tongue* of Mrs. Grundy wagging. 世間の口がうるさかろう. 【類】She lets everything escape her (何でも隠さずに言ってしまう) when her *tongue* is ***set*** in motion. ¶***set*** *tongues* ***wagging*** about the question その問題について世論を引起させる. ¶***speak*** the English *tongue* 英語を話す. 【類】He ***speaks*** five *tongues* besides his own. ¶***stammer*** a *tongue* that is not one's own 外国語をどもって話す. ¶This ***started*** jealous *tongues* ***wagging***. これがもとでねたみ深い人たちがとやかや言い出した. ¶***stick out*** one's *tongue* 舌を出す. ¶***thrust out*** a venomous *tongue* 毒づく. ¶***use*** the English *tongue* in print 印刷する文章を英語で書く. ¶***wag*** one's *tongue* しゃべる. ¶***wrench*** *tongues* from ... ...の舌を抜く.

V² My *tongue* ***cleaves*** (=***sticks***) to my mouth. 口がよくきけない. ¶His *tongue* ***failed*** him. 言葉が出なくなった. ¶His *tongue* ***faltered*** 彼は(舌がつれて)口ごもった. ¶The *tongue* ***lolls*** (=***hangs***) ***out***. [犬など]舌をだらりとたれる. ¶the vast area of the civilized world where the English *tongue* ***prevails*** 英語の行われる広い地域にわたる文明世界. ‖ *tongues* ***wagged*** and said that ... ...と言うのがもっぱらの評判だった.

Q have an ***abusive*** *tongue* 口が悪い. ¶written in the ***beautiful Enghish*** *tongue* 美しい英語で書かれた. ¶in a ***borrowed*** *tongue* 外国語で. ¶have a ***candied*** *tongue* 口先がうまい. ¶a ***carping*** *tongue* 悪口. ¶have a ***coated*** (=***furred or furry***) *tongue* 舌が真白になっている. ¶German, Russian, and Italian are technically ***complex*** *tongues*. ドイツ語・ロシア語・イタリア語は文法的に複雑な国語である. ¶***contemporary*** *tongues* and pens were active in the denunciation of ... 当時の人々は口に筆に...を盛んに非難したものである. ¶a ***devilish*** *tongue* 毒舌. ¶a ***dirty*** *tongue* きたない舌. ¶an ***eloquent*** (=a ***silver***) *tongue* 能弁. ¶the ***English*** *tongue* on its home soil 本場の英語. ¶be on ***every*** (=***everybody's***) *tongue* 万人の口に上る. ¶a ***facile*** *tongue* 快弁. ¶a man with a ***flattering*** *tongue* おべっかを言う人. ¶No poem can be rendered in a ***foreign*** *tongue* without losing much of its beauty. どんな詩でもこれを外国語に移すとその美点は大いにそこなわれる. ¶have a ***foul*** *tongue* 口ぎたない. ¶a ***glib*** *tongue* おしゃべり. ¶Spanish is one of the easiest of the ***Latin*** *tongues* to acquire. スペイン語はラテン系の国語中最も修得しやすいものの一つである. ¶Latin was used as a ***learned*** *tongue*. ラテン語は学者の言葉として用いられた. ¶a ***living*** *tongue* [死語に対して]生きた国語. ¶a ***loose*** *tongue* よくしゃべる口. ¶He knows Cervantes in his ***native*** *tongue* (=the original). 彼はセルヴァンテス(ドン・キホーテの作者)をその母国語で読んで知っている. ¶He has an ***oily*** *tongue*. 彼はお世辞がうまい. ¶learn languages for the pleasure of reading books in the ***original*** *tongues* 原語で書物を読む楽しみのために外国語を学ぶ. ¶a ***plausible*** *tongue* まことしやかな口振り. ¶keep the commodity always in the public eye and always on the ***public*** *tongue* その商品をいつも公衆の目に止まり公衆の口に上るようにする. ¶have a ***quick*** *tongue* 早口である. ¶a ***ready*** *tongue* 達弁. ¶He has a ***sharp*** *tongue*. 彼の言葉には角(かど)がある(毒舌だ). ¶have a ***smooth*** *tongue* すらすらしゃべる. ¶have a ***stammering*** *tongue* どもる. ¶He has a ***vulgar*** *tongue*. 彼は言葉が下品だ. ¶a ***white*** *tongue* 白い舌. ¶Hold your ***wicked*** (=***evil***) *tongue*. 悪口を言うな. ¶He has a ***witty*** *tongue*. 彼はこっけいなことを言う.

Q² speak French as one's ***mother*** *tongue* フランス語を母国語として話す.

P She said so ***in*** her own *tongue*. 彼女は自分の口からそう言った. ‖ writing ***in*** a *tongue* not his own 外国語で書いて. ¶He has half a dozen languages at the tip ***of*** his *tongue*. 彼は六カ国語に熟達している. ¶I've got the word on the tip of my tongue. その言葉が口まで出かかっている. ‖ His name is on all tongues (＝on all lips). その名はだれもが口にする. ‖ a new phrase now on the tongues of men 今流行している新しい成句. ¶ lick up ... with the tongue ... を舌でなめる.

P^{2} tongues of flame [めらめら燃える]炎の舌.

tonic, *n.* 強壮剤.

V take one's tonic 強壮剤を服用する.

Q Sea air is Nature's best tonic for mind and body. 海気は心身に対して自然が与える最良の強壮剤である. ¶ a bracing and regenerating tonic 元気を出させ回復を助長する強壮剤. ¶ act as the finest tonic for ... ...に最も効験ある強壮剤になる. ¶ Praise is a mental tonic. 賞賛は精神的強壮剤だ.

P, P^{2} valuable as a tonic 強壮剤として貴重な. ¶ a tonic for the dyspeptic 消化不良の人の強壮剤.

tonic, *a.* 強壮の.

P Music is tonic to the mind. 音楽は精神の強壮剤だ. ‖ Mountain (Sea) air is tonic to the weary brain. 山(海)の空気はつかれた頭にとって強壮剤になる.

tonnage, *n.* トン数.

V The ship has a tonnage of about 10,000. その船は約一万トンだ.

Q ships of fair tonnage 相当トン数のある船. ¶ a gross tonnage 総トン数. ¶ secure the necessary tonnage 必要な船腹を確保する. ¶ registered tonnage 登録トン数. ¶ vessels of small tonnage トン数の少ない船.

Q^{2} dead weight tonnage 重量トン数. ¶ displacement tonnage 排水トン数. ¶ Petroleum (Lumber) tonnage is required. 石油(木材)積載の船腹が必要である. ¶ steam (sailing) tonnage 汽(帆)船の船腹.

tonsure, *n.* 剃(て)髪.

V take the tonsure 剃髪する.

tool, *n.* 道具.

V keep one's tools bright 道具をぴかぴかさしておく. ¶ make a tool of a person 人を手先に使う. ¶ sharpen the tools 道具をとぐ.

Q an edged tool 刃物. ¶ Statisics is an indispensable tool for research in the social sciences. 統計学は社会科学の研究に必要なものである. ¶ a ready and handy literary tool 便利調法な参考書. ¶ Books are a scholar's tools. 本は学者の商売道具だ.

Q^{2} a burglar tool 泥棒の使う道具. ¶ a farm tool (＝implement) 農具. ¶ fire-fighting tools and equipment 消防用具及び施設. ¶ garden[ing] tools 種々の園芸用具. ¶ a hand tool 手工道具. ¶ a kitchen tool 台所道具. ¶ a machine tool 機械工具. ¶ primitive peasant tools 原始的農具類. ¶ it will serve as a research tool in ... それは...研究手段として役に立つだろう(重水など).

P the value of story-telling as an educational tool 教育上の手段としての説話の価値. ¶ He was used as a tool. 彼はお先棒に使われた. ¶ a set of tools 一組の道具. ¶ cut with a tool 道具で切る.

P^{2} She simply uses him as a tool for her own purposes. 彼女は単に自分の目的を達する道具として彼を使っている. ¶ the tools of one's trade 商売道具 ‖ They are tools of the party boss. 彼らはボスの手先に使われている.

tooling, *n.* [製本の]型押し.

Q blind (gold) tooling [表紙の]渡金しない(した)型押し.

toot, *n.* 笛音, 自動車の警笛.

V The guard signalling for departure received an answering toot from the engineer. 出発の合図をした車掌は機関手から応答の汽笛を受けた.

toot, *v.* 汽笛が鳴る.

M The train whistle tooted three times. 列車は三回汽笛を鳴らした.

tooth, *n.* 歯.

V bare one's teeth in a grin にやっと笑って歯をむき出す. ¶ brush one's teeth with a tooth-brush 歯ブラシで歯をみがく. ¶ clean the teeth with ... ...で歯を掃除する. ¶ clench the teeth 歯を食いしばる. ¶ click one's teeth 歯をかちっと鳴らす. ¶ The baby is cutting (＝developing) his teeth. 赤ん坊は歯が生えかけている. ¶ Too much indulgence in sweets decays the teeth. 余り甘い物を食べると歯が悪くなる. ¶ extract the teeth of penurious sufferers gratis 貧困者の歯を無料で抜く. ¶ fasten one's teeth on ... ...に食いつく. ¶ A dentist fixes teeth. 歯科医が歯を直す. ¶ get a tooth pulled out 歯を抜いてもらう. ¶ gnash one's teeth at the thought that ... ...ということを考えて歯ぎしりする. ¶ grind one's teeth 切歯する. ¶ That made them grit their teeth. そのため彼らは切歯やくわんした. ¶ I must have this tooth drawn (＝extracted, pulled out or taken out). 私はこの歯を抜いてもらわねばならない. ‖ have one's tooth filled 歯に詰めものをしてもらう ‖ have one's teeth repaired 歯を治療してもらう. ¶ kick one's teeth down one's throat ひどく人を非難する. ¶ The cold made my teeth clatter. 寒さで私は歯ががたがたした. ¶ pick one's teeth 歯をほじくる. 【類】Never pick your teeth without holding your hand before your mouth. ¶ pull out an aching tooth 痛む歯を抜き取る. ¶ put in (＝insert) an artificial tooth 入歯をする. ¶ put teeth in a law 法を施行する. ¶ rinse the teeth with peppermint water 薄荷水で歯をすすぐ. ¶ scale teeth 歯くそを取る. ¶ scrape teeth 歯をこする. ¶ set (＝clench) one's teeth 歯を食いしばる ‖ set the teeth of a saw のこぎりの目立をする ‖ a diabolical noise that might well set even artificial teeth on edge きっと入歯さえ浮かせるようないやな音. ¶ shed one's [false] teeth 入歯を落す. ¶ show the teeth 歯をむき出す ‖ show one's teeth [比ゆ的に]怒りを見せる, 反抗する. ¶ stain the teeth black＝blacken the teeth お歯黒をつける. ¶ stop teeth 歯に詰めものをする. ¶ suck one's teeth [うらやましがって]よだれを吸いこむ. ¶ unclench one's teeth [食いしばった]歯を押し開く. ¶ He used his teeth to pick up a scimitar. 彼は歯で三カ月形の刀をくわえて上げた. ¶ whiten the teeth by a brush and tooth-powder 歯磨ようじと歯磨粉で歯を白くする.

V^{2} A hollow tooth aches. むし歯が痛む. ¶ Her teeth chattered with cold. 寒いので彼女の歯がかちかち鳴った. ¶ His teeth churned. 彼の歯ががたがたした. ¶ Which tooth pains you? どの歯が痛みますか. ¶ His teeth sank into my arm. 彼は私の腕に歯を立てた.

Q artificial (＝false) teeth 義歯. ¶ a bad tooth 悪い歯. ¶ a carious tooth むし歯. ¶ He is born with a dainty tooth. 彼は生れつき食物がぜいたくだ. ¶ decayed teeth むし歯. ¶ a diseased tooth 不健全な歯. ¶ a double tooth 八重歯. ¶ a dull, chalky tooth 鈍い白亜質の歯. ¶ a festering tooth うずく歯. ¶ natural teeth 自然の歯. ¶ cut a new tooth 新しく歯が生える. ¶ her pearly teeth 彼女の真珠のような歯. ¶ pink-tinted teeth 淡紅色の歯. ¶ a man with prominent teeth 出歯の男. ¶ protruding teeth そっ歯. ¶ a redundant tooth 八重歯. ¶ go at it with set teeth ふんどしを緊めて掛る. ¶ Most girls have a sweet tooth. 女は大抵甘いものが好きだ. ¶ the upper (lower) teeth 上(下)歯. ¶ white, well-arranged teeth 白い並びのいい歯.

Q^{2} a dog tooth 犬歯, 糸切歯. ¶ the eye tooth of the upper jaw 上あごの犬歯. ¶ an incisor tooth 門歯. ¶ a milk tooth 乳歯. ¶ a saw tooth のこぎりの目. ¶ the stomach tooth of the low jaw 下あごの犬歯. ¶ a wisdom tooth 知恵(親知らず)歯.

P break it up between one's teeth それを歯でかみ切る ‖ mutter between one's teeth 口の内でぶつぶつ言う ‖ hold a pipe between one's teeth パイプをくわえる. ¶ walk around, a cigar in his teeth 葉巻をくわえて散歩する ‖ He cast it in my teeth. 彼は私を前においてずばりと言ってのけた. 【類】With a yachting-cap on his head and a half-smoked cigar in his teeth, he goes all over the ground. ‖ He took his own way in the teeth of all advice. 彼は皆の忠告に逆って気ままを通した. ‖ in the teeth of the wind 風に逆って. 【類】in the teeth of difficulties ‖ have an ache in a tooth 歯が痛む. ¶ in spite of one's teeth あらゆる反対にもかかわらず. ¶ armed to the teeth 十分に武装して. ¶ bite with the teeth 歯でかむ. ¶ bite off with the teeth 歯でかみ切る.

toothache, *n.* 歯痛.

V ease toothache 歯痛を静める. ¶ have a toothache 歯が痛む. ¶ stop the toothache 歯痛を止める.

Q have a bad toothache 歯がひどく痛む. ¶ a very severe toothache 非常に激しい歯痛. ¶ a violent toothache 激しい歯痛.

P a remedy for toothache 歯痛の療法. ¶ suffer from toothache 歯痛に悩む. ¶ a martyr to toothache 歯痛に悩む人. ¶ with a toothache 歯痛で.

toothpaste, *n.* ねり歯みがき.

V I told him not to squeeze the toothpaste in the middle. 私は彼にねり歯みがきは真中から絞ってはいけないと教

えてやった. 「り歯みがき.
Q *tubed toothpaste*=*toothpaste* in tubes チューブ入りのね
P a tube *of toothpaste* チューブ入り歯みがき一個.

toothpick, *n.* 小ようじ.
Q a *wooden toothpick* 木製小ようじ.

top, *n.* こま.
V *spin* a *top* こまを回す. ¶Boys *whip* a *top* to make it spin. 少年たちはこまをむちで打って回す. ¶A *top sleeps*. こまが(早く回転して)澄んでいる.

top, *n.* 頂上, 上部; 首位.
V The Vicar, having said grace, *cut* the *top* off his egg. 牧師補は食前の祈りをしてから卵の上半分を切りとった. ¶*follow* the *top* of a dike 土手伝いに行く. ¶*hold* the *top* 首位を占める. ¶*lop off* the *top* of a tree 木のうら(先)を切る. ¶when the *top* was *reached* 頂上に達したとき. ¶*realize* the *top* of one's ambition 一生の大願を成就する.
Q a *folding top* [馬車などの]折畳みほろ. ¶a book with a *gilt top* 天金の本. ¶the *very top* of it てっぺん.
Q² yell it from the *house tops* 家の天辺からそれをわめく. ¶a *mountain* (*hill*) *top* 山(丘)の頂上. ¶a *roof top* 屋根の天辺. ¶in *tree tops* こずえで ‖ The sun began to catch the *tree tops*. 木ずえに日がさして来た.
P pile *above* the *top* 一番上に積み重ねる. ¶There is a tea house *at* the *top*. 頂上に茶屋がある. ‖ Wood in water floats *at* the *top*. 木を水に入れると上に浮く. 【類】The title of the painting is inscribed by the artist *at* the *top* (上部に). / roofed (屋根があって) *at top* to keep off sunshine and rain. / The mistress of the house sits *at* the *top* (=*top end*) of the table, and her husband at the bottom [end]. ‖ *at* the *top* of the page ページの上部に ‖ *at* the *top* of the platform 政綱の第一に ‖ His name stands *at* the *top* of the list. 彼の名は表の真先に出ている. 【類】The story (記事) was printed *at* the *top* of a column on the first page. / the bright ones *at* the *top* of a class / The samurai was *at* the *top* of the social scale. / *at* the *top* of one's speed / shout *at* the *top* of one's voice ‖ the guide-words *at* the *top* of the pages=running heads ページの一番上にある見出し ‖ He is *at* the *top* of his little tree and has no further ambition. 彼は小成に甘んじてそれ以上の野心はない. ‖ There is plenty of room *at* the *top*. 腕があがればいくらでも職はある. ¶survey a person *from top* to toe 頭の先からつま先までじろじろ見る ‖ *from top* to bottom 上から下まで. ¶be a little bit *off* the *top* 少しはげている. ¶*on top* of that (《米》)=besides, moreover *or* furthermore その上に ‖ come out *on top* 群を抜く ‖ pile one *on top* of the other 上へ上へと重ねる ‖ *on top* of all other misfortunes 数々の不幸につけ加えて(泣面にはちで) ‖ This is like Bon and New Year's Day coming *on top* of each other. 盆と正月が一緒に来たようだ. ☞英語の諺に "as busy as all quarterdays have come together" というのがある. ¶glance at ... *over* the *top* of my book 私の(見ている)書物越しに…をちらりと見る. ¶get *to* the *top* of a tree 木の一番高い所へ登る ‖ come *to* the *top* 先頭に立つ; 表面に出る ‖ If you throw a cork into the water, it will rise *to* the *top*. コルクを水に投込むと水面に浮ぶ. ¶a carriage *without* a *top* ほろなし馬車. ¶a sideboard *with top* of marble 大理石張りの食器だな. ¶rub the bald shiny *top of* his head 彼のはげてぴかぴかする頭のてっぺんをこする.
O *top* and bottom 上下.

top, *v.* 頂上に至る, 頂点に達する.
M There was bread, and tongue, and ham, and cakes, and, to *top off* with, a large form of icecream. パンや牛の舌やハムや菓子やそれから最後に大形のアイスクリームがあった. ¶*top up* one's dinner with ... …を最後のごちそうとして食事をおしまいにする.
P *top in* everything except in price 値段は安く品物はよい ‖ He *tops* the rest *in* scholarship. 学問では彼が一番だ.

topic, *n.* 話題, 題目.
V *broach* a *topic* in conversation 話の題目を持出す. ¶He answered rather incoherently and *changed* the *topic* of conversation. 彼はこの問に対して言葉をにごし話題を他に転じた. ‖ to *change* (=*changing*) the *topic* 話は飛ぶが. ¶*discuss* their favorite *topics* around the fireplace 炉を囲んで彼らの得意な問題を談論する. 【類】*discuss* the *topics* of the day (時事問題). ¶*form* the liveliest *topic* of discussion 最も活気ある議題をなす. ¶before *leaving* this *topic* 話を他の題目に移す前に. ¶it *made* a good *topic* of conversation for ... それは…にとって好話題となった.
Q the one *absorbing topic* in British athletic circles this year will be ... 今年英国の体育界における唯一の好話題は…であろう. ¶an *alluring topic* 人の心を引きつける話題. ¶the *chief topic* of conversation 主なる話題. ¶We have *common topics* to talk about. 私らは話が合う. ¶*commonplace topics* 平凡な話題. ¶*current topics* of the hour 時事問題. ¶his elucidation of *economic topics* 彼の経済談. ¶It gave (=furnished) New Yorkers their most *fascinating topic* of conversation. それはニューヨークの人人の最も興味をひく話題となった. ¶the *general topic* of the breakfast tables 朝の食ぜんの一般の話題. ¶His mind is a storehouse of *fruitful topics* of conversation. 彼は話題に富んでいる. ¶on some *given topic* ある一定の題目に関して. ¶a *knotty topic* 難論題. ¶a *large topic* 大きな論題. ¶the *main topic* of discussion 主な議題. ¶the *leading topics* of the hour 目下の主な話題. ¶become a *national topic* of conversation 全国の話題となる. ¶*personal topics* 個人に関する話題. ¶a *popular topic* 人気のある話題. ¶*preliminary topics* of conversation 一通りのあいさつ. ¶a *prosaic topic* 殺風景な話題. ¶*seasonable topics* 時宜を得た話題. ¶*social topics* 世間話. ¶The war was the *sole topic* of conversation. 戦争の話で持切りだった. ¶*stale* and *musty topics* 陳腐で古臭い話題. ¶It is a *stock topic* of conversation. それは一つ話になっている. ¶*timely topics* 機宜を得た話題.
Q² *everyday topics* 日常の語り草. ¶*golf* and kindred *topics* ゴルフやそれに関する話題. ¶the *key topic* 中心議題. ¶all *poultry topics* 養鶏に関する一切の題目. ¶be nothing more than a breakfast *table topic* 朝の食卓で話題になるだけである. 「いて人と話す.
P speak with a person *on* a serious *topic* 重大な題目につ
P² a *topic for* discussion (conversation) 議(話)題. ¶these foremost *topics in* the thought of the time 時代思潮の最前線にあるこれらの話題. ¶the lighter, as well as with the grave, *topics of* the day 大小の時事問題 ‖ *topics of* conversation 話題.

top-knot, *n.* ちょんまげ.
V *wear top-knots* on their heads and two swords at their sides 頭にちょんまげを結び腰に両刀をたばさむ.

topper, *n.* 〘服飾〙トッパー. 「トッパー.
Q² her *flannel* (*blue-serge*) *topper* 彼女のフラノ(など)の
P² *toppers for* spring wear 春着のトッパー.

topple, *v.* 落ちる, 転覆する.
M *topple down* to the ground 地上に倒れ落ちる.
P *topple into* a river (well) 川(など)の中に転落する. ¶an ad-tower *toppled onto* the roof. 広告塔が(折れて)屋根に落ちた. ¶The stove pipe *toppled over* the roof. ストーブの煙突が屋根に倒れた.

tops, *a.* (《米口》) 最上の.
P He is *tops as* a doctor (=*in* doctoring). 医者としては最高だ.

torch, *n.* たいまつ; 知識の灯.
V *apply* a *torch* to ... …にたいまつで火をつける. ¶*carry* a *torch along* たいまつを持って行く. ¶*hand on* the *torch* which he has handed to me 彼が私に授けた知識の灯を後世に伝える. ¶*keep alight* the *torch* of civilization 文明のたいまつの消えないようにする. ¶*Torches* are *lighted*. たいまつがともされた. ‖ The *torch* he had *lighted* passed into France. 彼が指を染めた研究がフランスに渡って行った. ¶*pass* the *torch* to ... 〘比ゆ〙たいまつを…に伝える.
V² *Torches died out*. たいまつが消えた.
Q bear a *flaming torch* 燃立つたいまつを手に持つ. ¶an *electric torch*=(《英》) a flashlight (《米》) 懐中電灯. ¶a *plumber's torch* 鉛管工の火吹きランプ.
Q² a *pine torch* 松のたいまつ. ¶a *pocket* (*handbag*) *torch* 懐中電灯. ¶an electric *pocket torch* 懐中電灯.
P² the *light of* a *torch*=a torchlight たいまつの火.

torment, *n.* 苦痛, か責.
V *stretch out* the *torment* of death=kill by inches 五分だめしにする. ¶*suffer torments* 苦痛を受ける.
Q an *everlasting torment* to ... …にとって永久の苦しみ. ¶The child is a *positive torment*. あの子のうるさいったらない.
P² the *torments of* jealousy しっとの悩み.

torment, *v.* 悩ます, さいなむ, 困らす.
P This disease of mine will *torment* me *for* life. 僕はこ

の病気で一生苦しむだろう. ¶*torment* a person ***to*** death 人をさいなみ殺す. ¶*torment* a person ***with*** questions 人を質疑で困らす ‖ *tormented* ***with*** the stings of conscience 良心のか責に悩まされて.

torpedo, *n.* 水雷, 地雷.

V ***explode*** a *torpedo* 水雷を爆発させる. ¶***fire*** (=***discharge or launch***) a *torpedo* at a transport 運送船に向って水雷を発射する. ¶***lay*** (=***place or sink***) *torpedoes* 水雷を敷設する. ¶***recover*** a *torpedo* by boat ボートで水雷を拾い上げる.

Q an ***aerial*** *torpedo* 空中魚雷. ¶strike a ***submerged*** *torpedo* 機雷を爆発させる.

P defense nets ***against*** *torpedoes* 水雷防御網. ¶The ship was struck ***by*** a *torpedo*. その船は水雷に触れた.

torpid, *a.* 潜伏している, まひした.

M Snakes are *torpid* ***all winter***. へびは冬眠する.

P *torpid* ***in*** winter 冬には潜伏(冬眠)して.

torpor, *n.* まひ, 無感覚, 遅鈍.

P awakening ***from*** *torpor* 人事不省からわれに返って. ¶pass the winter ***in*** *torpor* 冬眠する.

torrent, *n.* 急流, 早瀬, 激流.

V ***follow up*** a *torrent* to ... 急流をさかのぼって…に至る. ¶***stem*** the *torrent* of ... …の勢いを阻止する.

Q an ***angry*** *torrent* 激流. ¶be swept away in the ***general*** *torrent* of change 変化の大勢に押し流される. ¶a ***noisy*** *torrent* of talk やかましいおしゃべり. ¶***rushing*** *torrents* 奔流. ¶a ***tumbling, tumultuous*** *torrent* 猛然たる激流.

Q^{2} a ***mountain*** *torrent* 山間の急流.

P It rains ***in*** *torrents*. 滝なす雨が降る. 【類】The rain is coming down ***in*** *torrents*.

P^{2} *torrents* ***of*** rain しのつく雨 ‖ *Torrents* ***of*** water were rolling down the mountain. 水が奔流をなして山から落下していた. ‖ a *torrent* ***of*** eloquence とうとう懸河の弁.

tortoise, *n.* かめ.

V The *tortoise* ***jogs*** steadily ***on***. かめがこっくりこっくりと歩いて行く.

torture, *n.* 苦痛, 責苦.

V ***inflict*** *torture* 苦痛を加える. ¶***invent*** frightful *tortures* 恐ろしいごう問の方法を案出する. ¶Who of us does not ***know*** the *torture* of trying to read a book printed in a language which we know but slightly? ほんのちょっとしか知っていない外国語で印刷した本を読もうとするときの苦しさを知らないものはあるまい. ¶***suffer*** (=***undergo***) *torture* 苦痛をこうむる. ¶***use*** *torture* on ... …を苦しめる.

V^{2} No *torture* would ***make*** me speak. どんなにひどいごう問にかけられても私は口外はしない.

Q inflict ***atrocious*** *torture* 残忍な苦痛を与える. ¶inflict ***mental*** *torture* upon ... …に精神的苦痛を与える. ¶***physical*** *torture* ごう問.

Q^{2} ***water*** *torture* 水責め.

P put (=subject) one ***to*** *torture* 人をごう問にかける. ¶***under*** the double *torture* of fear and impatience 心配と焦燥との二重苦を受ける.

P^{2} *torture* ***by*** fire and water 水火の責苦.

torture, *v.* 苦しめる, ごう問に掛ける.

P a boat *tortured* ***by*** storms and rough seas 荒天と荒波にもまれた小舟. ¶*torture* a person ***to*** death 人をいじめ殺す. ¶*torture* the questioner ***with*** one's silence 返事をせずに質問者を悩ます ‖ *torture* one ***with*** tight shoes 小さいくつをはかして苦しめる(くつ責めに掛ける) ‖ *torture* ... ***with*** the koto …を琴責にする.

torturing, *n.* 苦しみ.

P^{2} *torturings* ***of*** the heart はんもん.

Tory, *n.* [英国]王党員; 保守党員.

Q ***stern, unbending*** *Tories* 不屈不とうの王党員たち.

O a *Tory* candidate 保守党候補者.

toss, *n.* 投げ上げ, 銭投げ.

V ***lose*** the *toss* 銭投げ勝負に負ける. ¶***win*** the *toss* 銭投げ勝負に勝つ.

Q with an ***indignant*** *toss* of one's head 憤然と頭を振り立てて. ¶a ***petulant*** *toss* of the head むっとして振り立てた頭.

toss, *v.* 投げ上げる; 振り揺かす; 銭投げする.

M *toss* ***aside*** うっちゃる. ¶*toss* ***away*** 捨てる. ¶*toss* ***out*** the window 窓外に投げ出す ‖ He *tossed* ***out*** the first ball during pre-game ceremonies. 彼は試合前の儀式で始球を行った.

M^{2} The ship *tossed* ***about*** in the waves. 船は波に揺れていた. 【類】be *tossed* ***about*** by angry waves. ¶*toss* ***down*** ほうる. ¶*toss* ***off*** a glass of wine ぶどう酒を一杯飲み干す ‖ *toss* ***off*** a suggestion 思い付を述べる. ¶Let us *toss* ***up***. 銭投げ勝負をやろう. ‖ *toss* ***up*** a coin 銭投げをする. 【類】Well, let's *toss* ***up*** for it. If she comes down heads (表) we drink, and if she comes down tails (裏) we take the baths. See (いいか)?

P *tossed* ***by*** a bull 雄牛に突かれて. ¶*toss* ***from*** side to side [寝苦しいので]寝返りを打つ. ¶*toss* a thing ***in*** the air 物を空中にほうる. ¶*toss* a dollar ***in*** the counter 勘定台の上に一ドルをほうる. ¶*tossed* ***out of*** sledge そりからほうり出されて. ¶I *tossed* a penny ***to*** the beggar. 私はこじきに一ペニーを投げてやった. ¶they *tossed* ***with*** a sixpence to see who should ... だれが…するかそれを決めるために銭投げをした.

total, *n.* 総計, 全体.

V ***add up*** the *total* of an account 勘定をしめる. ¶***aggregate*** the enormous *total* of ... …という驚くべき総計になる. ¶the *total* was ***brought up*** to ... 総計…になった ‖ this ***brings*** the *total* ***up*** to ... これで総計…に達する. ¶***enlarge*** the sum *total* of human happiness 人間総体の幸福を増す. ¶***involve*** a *total* of ... …の総計になる. ¶this ***makes*** a *total* of ... これで…の総計になる. ¶***raise*** the *total* to ... 総計が増して…になる. ¶subscriptions to the fund have ***reached*** a *total* of ... その資金の寄付は総計…に達した. ¶***represent*** a *total* of ... 合計…になる. ¶***swell*** the *total* to ... 総額が…にかさむ. ¶the *total* ***realized*** by the two days' sales of ... …二日間の売上高.

Q reach (=foot up to) an ***astounding*** *total* 驚くべき総計になる. 【類】New York supports 194 parks, 82 playgrounds, and 24 parkways—comprising the ***astounding*** *total* of 8,703 acres in its park system. ¶New York's hotels have a ***combined*** *total* of over 130,000 guest rooms. ニューヨーク市のホテルの客室数は全体で十三万以上になる. ¶reach the ***enormous*** *total* of ... …という巨額に達する. ¶a ***grand*** *total* 総計. ¶amount to the ***huge*** *total* of ... …という巨大な数に達する. ¶amount to the ***impressive*** *total* of ... …というぼう大な金額になる. ¶the ***last year's*** *total* of ... 昨年…の総計. ¶the ***sum*** *total* of ... …の総締高. ¶a ***tremendous*** *total* ばく大な総計.

P a building ***with*** a *total* of about 1,500 office rooms 総計約一千五百の事務室を有するビルディング.

P^{2} a *total* ***of*** 27 bottoms 総計二十七隻.

total, *v.* 締める, 合計する.

P *total* ***around*** $200,000 総計約二十万ドルになる. ¶*total* ***over*** £5,000 合計五千ポンド以上になる. ¶*total* ***up to*** thousands 総計数千に達する.

totalitarianism, *n.* 全体主義.

Q^{2} ***Communist*** *totalitalianism* 共産党全体主義. ¶***fascist*** *totalitarianism* イタリア国粋党の全体主義.

totality, *n.* 全体, 合計.

P a plan ***in*** its *totality* (=entirety) そっくりそのまま(修正しない)の計画 ‖ It cannot be negated ***in*** its *totality*. 頭から否定するわけにはいかない.

toto, *n.* 全体, 総体.

P accept them ***in*** *toto* 彼らを全部受入れる.

totter, *v.* よろよろする, ふらふらする.

P *totter* feebly ***through*** the gateway よろよろして門をはいる. ¶*totter* ***to*** one's feet よろよろ立上る ‖ The Empire is *tottering* ***to*** its fall. その帝国はまさに倒れようとしている. ¶*totter* ***toward*** a person ひょろついて人の方へ寄る. ¶*totter* ***with*** age (weakness) 老齢(など)でよぼよぼする.

touch, *n.* 触感, 気味.

V The deer ***adds*** a *touch* of grace and spirit to the landscape. しかがいるのでその風景に優雅にして活気ある趣を添えている. ‖ ***add*** a *touch* of brightness and beauty to otherwise somber scenes さもないと地味になる風景にぱっとした美しい風致を添える. ¶The harp ***answers*** the *touch* of the master's hand. たて琴は名手の触れる手に応じて妙音を発する. ¶***convey*** a *touch* of individuality to one's works それらの作品に一種の個性を添える. ¶I ***felt*** a *touch* on my arm. 私の腕に何か触れるのを感じた. ¶He ***has*** a *touch* of inherited insanity. 彼にはちょっと精神病の遺伝がある. ‖ I ***have*** a *touch* of fever (influenza). 私はちょっと熱がある(流感の気味がある). 【類】I ***have*** a *touch* of the piles (じ). ¶***keep touch*** with ... …と接触を保つ. ¶***lend*** a picturesque *touch* of coloring to the sordid mass 万緑草中紅一点の趣を呈する ‖ The cherry blossoms ***lend*** pretty *touches* of color with their pinkish petals. 桜の淡紅色の花弁が美しい色彩を添える. ¶He completely ***lost touch*** with his family and friends. 彼はその家族や友人と全く音信不通となった. ‖ The vessel ***lost touch*** of her bearings in dense fog. その船は濃霧の中で方向を失った. ¶***maintain*** constant *touch* with the latest developments 絶えず最近発展の消息を知るようにしている. ¶The work ***shows*** evidently the *touch* of an artistic hand. その作にはたしかに芸術のにおいが出ている. ¶It ***wants*** a *touch* of salt. それはちょっと塩気が足りない.

Q act in the ***closest touch*** with ... ...と緊密な連絡を取って行動する. 【類】keep in ***close touch*** with ... ‖ in ***close touch*** with reality 現実に即して. ¶in ***constant touch*** with ... ...と絶えず接触して. ¶give life to a picture with a ***deft touch*** of the brush 巧妙な一と筆を揮って絵を生かす. ¶a ***delicate touch*** 微妙な筆致. ¶give a ***dramatic touch*** to ... ...に劇作的情趣を添える. ¶put the ***final*** (=finishing) *touches* to ... ...に最後の仕上げを施す. ¶make ***finishing*** *touches* on ... ...に最後の仕上げをする. ¶The transmitter he invented gave the telephone its ***finishing touch*** of utility. 彼が発明した送話器が電話機の実用性を完備させた. 【類】She was putting the ***finishing touches*** to her toilet (身支度). / give (=add) the ***finishing touches***. ¶have a ***firm touch*** with ... ...と十分接触を保っている. ¶The snow was the ***first touch*** of winter. その雪で始めて冬らしくなった. ¶bring them into ***harmonious touch*** with one another 彼らを互に調和させる. ¶a book full of ***human*** *touches* 人間味の満ちあふれている本. ¶His habit of reading in English keeps him in ***intellectual touch*** with the West. 彼は平常英文を読んでいるので西洋と知的に接触している. ¶Reading foreign newspapers and magazines keeps us in ***intelligent touch*** with the world. 外国の新聞雑誌を読んでいると世界情勢にうとくならずにいられる. ¶keep in fairly ***intimate touch*** with ... ...とかなり親しい接触を保つ. ¶There was a ***light touch*** on the shoulder. 肩に軽く触れたものがあった. ‖ a biography with a ***lighter touch*** くだけた書き方の伝記. ¶give ***literary touch*** to one's writing by introducing subjunctives 仮定法をそう入して文に文学的色彩を添える. ¶These French words have a ***magic touch***. これらのフランス語には魅力がある. ‖ as if by the ***magic touch*** of a fairy wand [せん女が]魔法のつえで触れでもしたように(こつ然と). 【類】The ***magic touch*** took instant effect. ¶I have a ***mild touch*** of influenza 私は軽い流感にかかっている. ¶Boy Scouts lined up lent a ***military touch*** to the animated scene. 勢ぞろいをした少年団がその活気のある場面に軍隊的な気分を添えた. ¶an ***Oriental touch*** 一まつの東洋的情調. ¶the close ***personal touch*** of the student with the master 生徒と先生との親密な個人的接触. ¶***pleasant*** *touches* of humor 気持のよいこっけい味. ¶give a ***romantic touch*** to ... ...に浪漫的な情趣を添える. ¶a ***slight touch*** of dreariness (depression) 少しさびしい(憂うつな)気分 ‖ It was not without a ***slight touch*** of irony in it. それはちょっと皮肉に感ぜられないこともなかった. ¶a ***soft touch*** 《俗》楽な役(俳優などの) ‖ It is the ***softest touch***. それはぬれ手であわのつかみどりだ. ¶a typewriter (piano) with a ***stiff*** (***soft***) *touch* 手触りの堅い(柔らかい)タイプライター(ピアノ).

Q[2] Garbo with a ***vagabond touch*** 浮浪性がかったガルボ. ¶the ***World-of-Tomorrow*** *touches* 新時代の趣き.

P The sharp knife cut it ***at*** a *touch*. そのよくきれるナイフがちょっと触るとそれは切れてしまった. 【類】burst ***at*** a *touch*. ¶keep ***in touch*** with ... ...と常に接触する ‖ bring the colonies closer ***in touch*** and sympathy with the Motherland 植民地と母国とを一層接触させ一層関心を持たせる. 【類】criticism ***in touch*** with the realities of life / get ***in touch*** with ... / keep ***in touch*** with the scientific activity of the world. ¶get ***in*** (=***into***) *touch* with the world 世界と接触する. 【類】try to get ***in touch*** with them. ¶***out of*** *touch* of the times (=age) 新時代と没交渉の ‖ be ***out of*** *touch* with the world 世情にうとい. ¶put ... ***to*** the *touch* ...を試験にかける ‖ It is cold ***to*** the *touch*. それを触って見ると冷たい. ¶an object ***with*** a slimy *touch* ねばねばした手ざわりのもの ‖ eyes ***with*** a *touch* of witchery in them 魔術師めいたまなざし. ¶***within touch*** of ... ...に手が触れるところに. ¶He was not ***without*** a *touch* of vanity. 彼は虚栄心が幾分ないでもなかった.

P[2] a *touch* ***of*** humor こっけいの気味 ‖ a *touch* ***of*** the sun 日射病の気味 ‖ a *touch* ***of*** Spain in Hollywood ハリウッドのスペイン的色彩 ‖ a *touch* ***of*** color is imparted to the assembly by ... ...のために万緑草中紅一点の概がある. 【類】There was a *touch* ***of*** irony in his speech. / There is a *touch* ***of*** Lincoln (リンカンのおもかげ) about him. / There was a *touch* ***of*** something alien and intrusive about him. ¶put the finishing *touches* ***upon*** a manuscript 原稿に最後の加筆をする. ¶in close *touch* ***with*** ... ...と密接な連絡を取って.

touch, *v.* 触れる; 怒らす; 寄航する.

M It is ***briefly*** *touched* upon. それが簡単に述べてある. ¶I was ***deeply*** *touched*. 私は深く感動した. ¶It *touched* her ***keenly***. それは激しく彼女の心を動かした. ¶It is very ***lightly*** *touched* upon. そのことはほんのちょっとしか述べてない. ¶Of that which *touches* us most ***nearly*** we know least. われわれに最も関係の深いものに対するわれわれの知識は最も浅いものだ. ¶He was ***slightly*** *touched*. 彼はちょっと感動した. ‖ I have not done more than *touch* very ***slightly*** upon it here. 私はここにはほんのちょっとその点に触れたにすぎない. ¶***so far as*** they *touch*, immediately or remotely, on ... 直接あるいは間接に...に関する限りでは.

M[2] *touch* ***down*** at the airport その空港に着陸する. ¶*touch* it ***off*** in a breath 一気に書(描)きあげる ‖ what *touched* it ***off***, apparently, was ... 見た所その誘因は...であった ‖ *touch* ***off*** fire-works 花火を打上げる ‖ *touch* ***off*** a riot 騒動を触発させる ‖ *touch* ***off*** a heated controversy 激論を挑発する. 【類】*touch* ***off*** a political debate in Parliament / If that measure is carried out, there may be *touched* ***off*** a new wave of terrorism. ‖ the drive (dispute) was *touched* ***off*** by ... その運動(紛争)は......が起したものであった ‖ *touch* ***off*** her face 手早く化粧をする ‖ *touch* it ***off*** to perfection (to a nicety) 申し分なく(きちんと)やる. ¶*touch* ***up*** a picture (book, poem) 絵(など)に修飾の筆を入れる ‖ *touch* ***up*** a horse with a whip むちで馬を軽く打つ. ¶the problems *touched* ***upon*** 論及した問題. ¶Only a few general considerations can be *touched* ***upon***. ほんの二三の点を概説することしかできない.

P The ship will *touch* ***at*** Japan. その船は日本に寄港する. ‖ *touch* ***at*** a port to take in coal 石炭積込のため寄港する. ¶*touched* ***by*** one's kindness (sympathy, enthusiasm) その親切(など)に動かされて ‖ *touched* ***by*** modern thought 近代思想に触れて. ¶*touch* a person ***on*** the shoulder 人の肩にちょっとさわる ‖ The ship *touched* ***on*** the bar when leaving. その船が出帆した時座洲(す)した. ‖ *touch* ***on*** the subject その問題に触れる ‖ He is reading all the current publications *touching* ***on*** his field of research. 彼は自分の研究方面に関する現代の本をことごとく読んでいる. 【類】We can *touch* ***on*** it only briefly here. / *touch* ***on*** one of the major problems facing the nation / while we are *touching* ***on***..., we may allude to ... / *touch* ***on*** the woman question in a wise, large spirit / *touch* ***on*** the fringe of the question / the collection of materials *touching* ***on*** the Far East. ¶If we knew the reason, we might be *touched* ***to*** tenderness instead of feeling like to blame. われわれがその理由を知っていれば非難する気にならずにかえって気の毒に感じるだろう. ‖ *touch* strawberries ***to*** pulverized sugar いちごに粉砂糖をちょっとつける ‖ They *touched* their hats ***to*** him. 彼らは帽子に手を触れて彼にあいさつをした. ‖ *touch* a person ***to*** the heart 人の心を動かす. ¶*touch* ***upon*** the coast 海岸に着船する ‖ *touch* ***upon*** a subject 問題に触れる ‖ They have been *touched* ***upon*** very briefly. それらのことはほんの簡単に述べておいた. 【類】It is an extremely complex subject, and it is not my present purpose to do more than *touch* ***upon*** it. / The most that can be done here is to *touch* ***upon*** the more salient features (顕著な点). / matters *touched* ***upon*** in the book / *touch* ***upon*** the finer issues of life / This will be *touched* ***upon*** again in another chapter. ¶*touch* ... ***with*** the hand ...を手でさわる ‖ *touched* ***with*** remorse 後悔して ‖ His scattered locks are scarcely *touched* ***with*** gray. 彼の乱れた髪にはまだ白髪が交っていない. ‖ He was *touched* ***with*** pity for the poor. 彼は貧者に対してあわれみの情が動いた. ¶No one can *touch* rouge ***without*** staining his fingers. 朱に交われば赤くなる.

touch-and-go, *a.* 不安な, あやふやな.

M *touch-and-go* ***all the time*** いつも不安な.

P It was *touch-and-go* ***with*** the sick man. 病人はいつど

うなるか分からなかった.

touchstone, *n.* 試金石.

P² the *touchstone* **by** which to test one's ability (its value). 実力(など)をためす試金石.

tough, *n.* 《米》ならず者, 乱暴者.

P a gang **of** *toughs* ぐれん隊.

tough, *a.* 堅い; つらい.

M² **as** *tough* as leather 皮のように堅く.

P Things are getting *tough* **with** us. 世の中がわれわれにとってやりにくくなってきた.

O have a *tough* time [of it] ひどい目に合う.

toughen, *v.* 強くなる.

M² *toughen* **up** すっかり強くなる.

tour, *n.* 漫遊, 遊歴, 旅行.

V **arrange** a *tour* to ... ...への漫遊を計画する. ¶He found it necessary to **cancel** his *tour* through illness. 彼は病気で旅行を中止しなければならないことになった. ¶**commence** a *tour* of the city 市の見物を始める ‖ He has just **completed** a *tour* of the world. 彼は丁度世界一週を終えた所だ. 【類】**complete** a *tour* of the India and the South Asian countries. ¶**finish** a *tour* of the Orient. ¶He **made** a *tour* of the United States. 彼は合衆国を漫遊した. 【類】**make** a *tour* of (=through) Japan / **make** a *tour* of the world on foot (徒歩で) ‖ **make** a *tour* of the damaged areas ‖ **make** a *tour* of these apartments (a ship's kitchens) アパート(など)を一覧する. ¶**organize** a *tour* to visit ... ...遊覧旅行を計画する. ¶**outline** a *tour* of ... at a pound-a-day rate 一日一ポンドの割で...巡遊の計画を立てる. ¶assist the traveller in **planning** his *tour* and disposing of his time to the best advantage 旅行家のために時間を最も有利に使用させる. ¶**take** a *tour* through (=around) ... ...の自転車旅行をやる.

V² This American *tour* **opened** at Boston, U.S.A., on Monday, 5th October, 1931, and **concluded** at Toronto, Canada, on Saturday, 19th March 1932. このアメリカ漫遊は一九三一年十月五日月曜日合衆国のボストンに始まり一九三二年三月十九日土曜日カナダのトロントに終った.

Q go on a **bridal** *tour* 新婚旅行に立つ. ¶We sent Mr. Yano to Europe and America on a **commercial** *tour*. 矢野氏を欧米へ商業視察に派遣しました. ¶The Mint is a large place, and a personally **conducted** *tour* occupies an hour and a half. その造幣局は広いので案内してもらって一通り見物するには一時間半かかる. ¶a **grand** *tour* [英国貴族の子弟の欧州]漫遊旅行; 海外大旅行. 【類】a Congressmen's "**grand** *tour*." ¶an **educational** *tour* 修学旅行. ¶We sent him to Italy on an **eight months'** *tour* of inspection of Oriental manuscripts. 東洋の写本を視察する目的で八カ月の予定で彼をイタリアに派遣した. ¶an **electioneering** *tour* 選挙の遊説旅行. ¶I accompanied him on his **European** *tour*. 私は彼のヨーロッパ漫遊のお供をした. ¶an **extended** *tour* in America アメリカ大旅行 ‖ He has returned from an **extented** *tour* of the West. 彼は広く西洋諸国を旅行して帰って来た. ¶make an **extensive** *tour* of Japan. 日本を広く遊歴する. 【類】He has just returned from an **extensive** *tour* of investigation through Western Japan. ¶He has just returned from a **five months'** *tour* of the district. 彼はその地方の五カ月にわたる漫遊から丁度帰ったところだ. ¶He had a **lengthy** *tour* in India. 彼はインドの長期旅行をした. ¶He is on an **official** *tour*. 彼は公用で旅行中である. ¶a **pedestrian** *tour* in Wales ウェールスの徒歩旅行. ¶Between **sporadic** *tours* she sang at private recitals. 時たまの地方巡業の間に彼女は独唱会を催した. ¶a **sudden** *tour* 突然の旅行. ¶a brief but not **uneventful** *tour* 短いが色々のことのあった旅.

Q² They were scheduled for a **belt line** *tour* of speech-making last night. 彼らの巡回演説旅行の予定が昨夜きまった. ¶a **business** *tour* 商用の旅行. ¶now on a **campaign** *tour* of the west coast 目下西海岸の遊説旅行中の. ¶a **camping** *tour* テント旅行. ¶a **canvassing** *tour* 遊説. ¶make a **concert** *tour* 演奏旅行. ¶take a **cycling** (**biking**) *tour* 自転車(オートバイ)旅行をする. ¶start on a **flying** *tour* of Scandinavia スカンジナビアの飛行機旅行に立つ. ¶a **food fact-finding** *tour* of Europe 欧州における食糧事情視察旅行. ¶visit the countries on **good-will** *tours* 親善を図る目的で諸国を歴訪する. ¶a **horseback** *tour* through Siberia シベリア横断の騎馬旅行. ¶an **inspection** *tour* 視察旅行. ¶a **lecturing** *tour* 講演旅行. ¶a **microphone** *tour* of ... ...の放送旅行. ¶a **mountaineering** *tour* 登山旅行. ¶a **museum** *tour* 博物館内の指導者付見学. ¶conduct a **party** *tour* 団体旅行の案内をする. ¶a **road** *tour* [鉄道・飛行機などによらない]道路の旅行. ¶a **round** (=an **around**) the world *tour* 世界漫遊. 【類】a **round-the-world air** *tour*. ¶return from a **shopping** *tour* あっちこっちの買物から家へ帰る. ¶a **sightseeing** *tour* 遊覧旅行. ¶a transcontinental **speaking** *tour* 大陸横断演説旅行. 【類】be on **speaking** *tours*. ¶a **speech-making** *tour* 演説旅行. 【類】undertake a **speech-making** *tour* throughout America. ¶a **stump** *tour* 《米》遊説旅行. ¶make a **summer** (**winter**) *tour* 夏季(冬季)旅行する. ¶a **three-week** plane *tour* 三週間の空の旅. ¶a **vacation** *tour* 休暇中の旅行. ¶take a **walking** *tour* in the interior 内地を徒歩旅行する. ¶make a **world** *tour* 世界漫遊をする.

P go **for** a *tour* in America 米国旅行に立つ ‖ He has started **for** a week's *tour* in the North. 彼は一週間の北方旅行に立った. ¶start **on** a *tour* of Europe and America 欧米漫遊の途につく. 【類】go **on** a *tour* abroad.

P² a *tour* **in** Europe ヨーロッパの旅. ¶an excursion, including a *tour* **of** three of the colleges 大学三校の見学を含む修学旅行 ‖ now on a *tour* **of** (=**round**) the world 目下世界漫遊の途上にある. ¶a *tour* **through** a factory (studio) 工場(など)の見学.

tour, *v.* 漫遊する.

M He *toured* Europe **three times**. 彼は欧州旅行を三回やった.

P *tour* **about** the world 世界を漫遊する. ¶may be *toured* from ... **by** automobile 自動車で...から旅行ができる.

tourism, *n.* 観光; 観光事業.

V **develop** and **supervise** *tourism* 観光事業を発展させかつ監理する. ¶**foster** *tourism* 観光を奨励する.

tourist, *n.* 漫遊者, 観光者.

V **attract** *tourists* to this country この国へ観光客を引付ける. ¶**import** *tourists* 観光者を招来する. ¶**lure** *tourists* to Japan 日本へ観光者を誘致する. ¶The travel agency **routes** many a *tourist* to Europe. その旅行会社はヨーロッパ行の多数の漫遊客の世話をする. ¶**skin** a *tourist* 観光客の金をまきあげる.

Q a **blasé** *tourist* 遊び飽きた旅行家. ¶**circum-mundane** *tourists*=globe-trotters 世界一週旅行家. ¶**foreign** *tourists* 外国の観光者. ¶a **hurrying** *tourist* せわしい観光客.

Q² a **lady** (=fair) *tourist* 婦人観光客.

P² *tourists* **of** international (=world-wide) experience 世界をまたにかけた漫遊者.

tournament, *n.* 試合, 勝抜戦.

V The annual tennis *tournament* is being **played off**. 例年のテニス試合が行われている. ¶**win** a *tournament* 試合に勝つ.

Q² a **bridge** (**chess**, **wrestling**) *tournament* [トランプの]ブリッジ(など)の試合. ¶a **marbles** *tournament* はじき玉の試合. ¶an inter-collegiate **tennis** *tournament* 大学対抗テニス・トーナメント.

P² a great *tournament* **between** ... ...間の大試合.

tousle, *v.* [髪を]ばらばらにする.

M² have one's hair *tousled* **up** 髪が乱れる.

O with *tousled* hair みだれ髪で.

tout, *n.* 《口語》客引き.

Q² a **cab** (**hotel**) *tout* タクシー(など)の客引き.

tout, *v.* 《口語》[客・投票など]勧誘する.

P *tout* [**for**] votes (patrons, jobs) 投票(など)をうるさく勧める. 【類】*tout* **for** orders (注文).

tow, *n.* 引き綱, 引き船.

P take (=have) a vessel **in** *tow* 船を引き綱で引く(引いている) ‖ a tugboat and barges **in** *tow* 引き船とその引いているはしけ. ¶Japanese fishing boats **in** *tow* **of** a motorboat モーターボートに引かれた日本漁船 ‖ she left here **in** *tow* for ... [遭難した]船は...に向って引き船に引かれてこの地を立った.

tow, *v.* 引き綱で引く.

M *tow* **off** a ship 船を綱で引く.

P *tow* a ship **into** a harbor (river) 船を港(など)に引き入れる ‖ be *towed* **into** the harbor by a tug (引き綱で). ¶*tow* her **out of** the ice 氷の中からその船を引き出す. ¶*tow* a boat **with** a rope ボートを綱で引く.

towel, *n.* タオル.

V **rinse** the *towel* タオルをすすぐ. ¶**use** a public *towel*

一般用のタオルを使う. ¶***wring*** a *towel* タオルを絞る.

Q ***common towels*** 共同用タオル. ¶a ***damped*** *towel* ぬれたタオル.

Q^{2} a ***baby towel*** 赤ん坊用タオル. ¶***bath*** and ***face towels*** 浴用及び洗顔用タオル. ¶a ***roller towel*** 繰出しタオル.

P dry oneself ***on*** a *towel* タオルでからだをふく. ¶rub the arms vigorously ***with*** a coarse *towel* until they glow with warmth 目のあらいタオルでほてって赤くなるまで激しく両腕を摩擦する.

tower, *n.* 塔, やぐら.

V The *tower* ***commands*** a fine view. その塔は眺(ちょう)望がよい. ¶The *tower* ***stands*** 325 feet high. その塔は高さ三百二十五フィートある. ¶How boldly the *towers* ***stand out*** against the sky! それらの塔は何とくっきりと大空にそそり立っていることよ.

Q a ***battlemented*** *tower* 胸壁のある塔. ¶a ***hoary*** *tower* 古色そう然たる塔. ¶the ***Leaning Tower*** of Pisa ピザの斜塔. ¶a ***lofty*** *tower* on a Mohammedan mosque 回教寺院の高い塔.

Q^{2} a ***church tower*** 教会の塔. ¶a ***clock tower*** on a library building. 図書館屋上の時計塔 ¶a ***watch tower*** 監視塔. ¶The ***Eiffel*** *tower* was erected over half a century years ago at a cost of $1,800,000. エッフェル塔は半世紀以上前に$1,800,000ドルの経費で建設された. ¶descend from (keep to) the ***ivory*** *towers* 象げの塔から降りる(にこもる). ¶a ***look-out*** *tower* 監視塔. ¶a ***peace*** *tower*＝a tower in commemoration of world peace 平和塔. ¶a ***radio*** (***TV***) *tower* ラジオ(テレビ)放送塔. ¶a ***shaft tower*** たて坑のやぐら.

P^{2} a *tower* ***over*** the gateway of a temple 寺の山門の塔.

tower, *v.* そびえ立っている, そびえる.

M *tower* ***high*** above ... ...の上に高くそびえる.

M^{2} The mountains *tower* ***up*** grandly. その山々が泰然としてそびえる. 【類】a tall straight fir-tree (もみの木) stood *towering* ***up*** in the middle of a forest.

P The statue of Liberty *towers* ***above*** the harbor of New York. 自由の像はニューヨークの港の上にそびえ立つ. ‖ he *towers* ***above*** his fellows for excellence in ... 彼は...の優秀をもってはるかに同輩を抜いている. 【類】*tower* ***above*** all competitors. ¶mountain heights *towering* ***into*** perpetual snow 永久の雪の中にそそり立つ山々 ‖ The noble peaks *tower* ***into*** the clouds. 高峰が雲表にそびえる. ¶The castle *towers* ***over*** the town. 城は町の上にそびえ立っている. ¶*tower* ***to*** the clouds 雲にそびえる ‖ *tower* ***to*** 4,500 feet 四千五百フィートの高さに達する. 【類】*tower* ***to*** a height of 14,109 feet from the surrounding plains.

town, *n.* 町; 町の住民; [いなかに対し]都会; 《英》主要都市(特にロンドン); 《米》[都市の]一区画(街).

V ***besiege*** a *town* 都市を包囲する. ¶***bill*** a *town* 街中にビラを張る. ¶***devastate*** a *town* 町を荒らす. ¶***do*** a *town* 町を見物する. ¶***erect*** a model *town* 模範都市を建設する. ¶***leave*** the *town* for the summer 避暑のために都会を去る. ¶***municipalize*** a *town* 町に市制を布く. ¶***plot*** (＝***lay out***) a *town* 都会を設計する. ¶***rebuild*** a *town* 都会を再建する. ¶The enemy ***seized*** the *town*. 敵が町を占領した. ¶This ***set*** the whole *town* talking. これが町の大評判になった. ¶The earthquake ***swallowed up*** the *town*. 地震で町が陥落してしまった. ¶The fire ***swept*** (＝wiped) the *town*. その火事で町が全滅になった. ¶a play that has ***taken*** the *town* 町の評判になった劇. ¶The news ***upset*** the whole *town*. そのニュースで全町は混乱状態になった. ¶The *town* was ***visited*** by the plague. その町に疫病が発生した.

V^{2} The *town* ***lies*** on the shore. その町は海岸にある. ¶Many *towns* ***sprang up*** in that part of the country. その地方に多くの都市が盛んにできた. ¶The *town* ***stretches*** along the bay. その町は湾に沿うている.

Q a ***busy*** industrial *town* 繁華な産業都市. ¶the ***chief*** *town* of ... ...の首都. ¶a ***crowded*** *town* 人口ちゅう密の都会. ¶a ***dear, delightful*** *town* なつかしい愉快な都会. ¶a ***developing*** *town* 開ける町. ¶a ***God-forsaken*** *town* 神に見放された町. ¶a ***good sized*** *town* かなり大きな都会. ¶The ***great*** *town* is abed. この大都市は眠っている. ¶a ***growing*** and ***flourishing*** *town* 発達繁盛する都会. ¶both in the ***large*** *towns* and country 大都市にもいなかにも. ¶in the ***lesser*** *towns* of the kingdom 王国のその小都市に. ¶a ***local*** *town* 《米》大都市週辺の小都市. ¶London is a ***man's*** *town*. ロンドンは(自然の趣を欠く)人工の都市である. ¶a ***military*** *town* 兵隊町. ¶an ***overgrown*** *town*, half village and half city 半村半市の膨張し過ぎた町. ¶a ***provincial*** *town* 地方都市. ¶The daimyo was then in his ***residential*** *town*. その大名は当時(在府でなく)お国にいた. ¶***rival*** *towns* 互に競争している都会. ¶a ***rural*** *town* いなか町. ¶a ***secluded*** *town* 奥まった都市. ¶Oxford, England's most ***sedate*** University *town* 英国の最も静かな大学街オクスフォード. ¶a ***shabby*** little mining *town* 荒廃した小鉱山町. ¶a ***sleepy old*** *town*, without a spark of enterprise 企業など少しも見られない眠ったような古い町. ¶a ***straggling*** *town* 町並のまばらな貧弱な都会. ¶a ***thriving*** *town* 繁栄する町. ¶The ***whole*** *town* was out there. 町中の人が出かけていた. 【類】The ***whole*** *town* knows of it.

Q^{2} a ***backwood*** *town* 《米》辺びな町. ¶a ***boom*** *town* 《米》成金都市. ¶a ***capital*** *town* 首都. ¶a ***castle*** *town* 城下町. ¶a ***cathedral*** *town* 大寺院のある町. ¶a ***China*** *town* 中国人街. ¶a ***coal*** *town* 炭坑都市. ¶a ***county*** *town* 《英》州の首都. ¶a ***garrison*** *town* 守備兵の駐とんする都市. ¶a ***highway*** *town* 街道に沿う町. ¶Portland, Ore., is her ***home*** *town*. オレゴン州のポートランドは彼女の生れた町だ. ¶his ***home*** *town* 彼の生れた町(村). ¶one of the best "***hotel***" *towns* in the country その国でホテルの設備の最もよい都市の一つ. ¶go to ***London*** *town* ロンドンへ行く. ¶the soot and grime of a ***manufacturing*** *town* 工業都市のばい煙と汚染. 【類】a ***manufacturing*** *town* grown out of a ***farming*** *town*. ¶a ***mining*** *town* 鉱山都市. ¶a ***market*** *town* 市場. ¶a ***model*** *town* 模範都市. ¶a ***namesake*** *town* 同名の町. ¶a ***post-war ghost*** *town* 戦後の(疲弊した)幽霊町. ¶Sandwich, the "***sand*** *town*," was one of the ancient Cinque Ports in Kent. サンドウィッチすなわち「砂の町」はケント州の古代の(特権を賦与された)五港の一つだった. ¶a [***sea-***]***coast*** *town* 海岸の都市. ¶a ***seaport*** *town* 海港都市. ¶a [***sea-***]***resort*** *town* 海水浴場を控えた町. ¶a ***station*** *town* 駅のある町. ¶a ***steel*** *town* 鋼鉄生産都市. ¶a ***university*** (***college***) *town* 大学町. ¶a small ***up-country*** *town* 《俗》小さな内地の(海岸から遠く離れた)町.

P sensible young men ***about*** *town* 気のきいた都会の青年. ¶***at*** the *town* of Chiba 千葉の町に. ¶go ***down*** *town*＝go shopping 下町へ行く(買物に行く). ¶***in*** *town* 上京して; 都会で ‖ ***In*** *town*, horse railroads have given way to electric. 都会では鉄道馬車は電車に変った. 【類】There is so much sickness ***in*** *town* at present. / He lives ***in*** *town*. ¶go ***into*** the *town* in order to ... ...のために都会に行く. ¶go ***out of*** *town* 都会を立つ ‖ It is the talk ***of*** the *town*. 町の評判だ. ¶walk ***round*** the *town* 町のあたりを歩く. ¶go up ***to*** *town* 《英》ロンドンに行く, 上京する. ☞ go to town には米口語で成功する (achieve success); 能率的に働く (work efficiently) の意がある.

townspeople, townsfolk, *n.* 都会人.

Q ***smartly-clad*** *townspeople* スマートな格好をした都会人.

P an ideal winter resort ***for*** *townsfolk* 都会人にとっての冬期の理想郷.

toy, *n.* おもちゃ, なぶり物; つまらないもの.

V ***make*** a *toy* of ... ...をおもちゃにする. 【類】***make*** a *toy* of a woman.

Q an ***educative*** *toy* 教育おもちゃ. ¶***gaily-painted*** *toys* 目立った彩色のおもちゃ. ¶It is more than an ***interesting scientific*** *toy*. それは単に興味のある科学的おもちゃ以上の(価値のある)ものだ.

Q^{2} a ***clockwork*** *toy* 時計仕掛のおもちゃ. ¶a ***floor*** *toy* (バス, 電車など)床の上で遊ぶおもちゃ. ¶a ***penny*** *toy* 安物おもちゃ.

P ***play with*** a *toy* おもちゃを持って遊ぶ.

P^{2} a *toy* ***of*** a gun おもちゃみたいな(小さな)銃.

toy, *v.* 遊ぶ, 戯れる.

M *toy* ***nervously*** with one's fingers いらいらした気持で指をもてあそぶ.

P *toy* ***with*** paper and pencil 紙と鉛筆をもてあそぶ ‖ *toy* ***with*** a serious matter 重大事件をおもちゃ扱いにする ‖ *toy* ***with*** the illusion that ... ...という錯覚をもってあそぶ ‖ He *toyed* ***with*** the idea of buying a car. 彼は自動車を買いたいと空想していた. ‖ He *toys* ***with*** oils in spare hours. 彼は暇の時には道楽に油絵を描く.

trace, *n.* 跡, こん跡, 足跡.

V The room ***bore*** *traces* of a fierce struggle. そのへやには猛烈な闘争のあった証跡があった. 【類】The bed ***bore*** *traces* of having been slept in. ¶It was found on analysis to ***contain*** *traces* of soda. 分析して見たらそれにはソーダのこん跡を含んでいることが分かった. ¶***cover*** one's *traces* [犯人などが]跡をくらます. ¶***destroy*** all *traces* of ... ...のこん跡をことごとく消滅する. ¶The body ***exhibited*** no *traces* of violence. その体には暴行の跡が見えなかった. ¶We failed to ***find*** any *trace* of him. われわれは捜したが彼のゆくえが分からなかった. 【類】No *trace* of the missing person (ゆくえ不明の人) was ***found.*** ¶***follow up*** a *trace* 跡をつける. ¶we ***have*** many *traces* even to the present day, in French names like ... それは...のようなフランス名の中に今なお幾多の名ごりを留めている. ¶***hide*** the *traces* of one's guilt 犯罪の証拠を隠ぺいする. ¶***leaving*** no *trace* 跡形なしに. 【類】vanish without *leaving* a *trace* behind / He ***left*** no *trace* with his parents of his whereabouts (ありか). ¶all *traces* of it have been ***obliterated,*** the site being now occupied by ... その敷地は今では...が占めていてそのこん跡は全く消失してしまった. ¶A postmortem examination ***revealed*** *traces* of a virulent poison. 死体検査の結果劇毒のこん跡が認められた. ¶go to France to ***see*** the *traces* of the battles 戦闘の跡を見るためにフランスに行く. ¶***show*** a *trace* of leprosy らい病のこん跡を示す. 【類】***show*** no *trace* of fatigue / ***show*** a *trace* of fear. ¶***wash*** the *traces* of tears from one's eyes 目から涙の跡を洗い去る.

V² No *trace* ***remains.*** 何らのこん跡も残っていない.

Q There is not the ***slightest*** *trace* of bitterness in his character. 彼の性格には人から悪く言われるような所が少しもない. ¶an ***unmistakable*** *trace* 明白なこん跡.

P speak English ***without*** a *trace* of Japanese accent 少しも和臭なしに英語を話す.

P² come across *traces* ***of*** bears くまの足跡に出くわす ‖ The *traces* ***of*** the war fire were removed. その戦災のこん跡が取除けられた. 【類】*traces* ***of*** an ancient civilization.

trace, *v.* 跡をつける.

M *trace* ***back*** through a thousand phases of Japanese life by the study of legends 昔ばなしを研究して日本人の生活における多方面の変遷をたどる ‖ It may be *traced* ***back*** to a very early date. それは非常に遠い昔にさかのぼることができる. ‖ *trace* ***back*** to its origin その源流にさかのぼる ‖ *trace* the causes of it ***back*** to ... ...までさかのぼってその原因を調べる. 【類】The quotation (引用文) cannot readily be *traced* ***to*** their sources. / *trace* phrases ***back*** to their distant obscure sources / His fear of fire *traces* ***back*** to an experience in his boyhood.

P The thief was *traced* ***by*** stolen goods. その盗人は盗んだ品から足がついた. ¶The family *traces* its descent ***from*** a prince of the blood. その家の先祖は皇族である. ¶His resentment can be clearly *traced* ***in*** his letter. 彼の憤慨はその手紙の文面に歴然と現われている. ¶*trace* an outline ***on*** paper 紙でその概形を写し取る. ¶It may be *traced* ***to*** a Chinese origin. その起原は中国に帰しうる. ‖ *trace* rumors ***to*** earth うわさの出所を徹底的に調べる. 【類】The murder was *traced* ***to*** a youth. ‖ It is *traced* ***to*** various causes. / *Trace* it ***to*** European influence. ¶*trace* ***with*** one's finger a beeline across the African continent and the Bay of Biscay until he reached London アフリカ大陸とビスケー湾を通る直線をロンドンまで指でたどる(世界地図の上で).

traceable, *a.* 跡づけうる, 由来する.

M the success is ***directly*** *traceable* to ... その成功の原因は直接...に帰することができる.

P Many of our customs are *traceable* ***to*** Buddhism. わが国の習慣は仏教から来ているものが多い.

tracing, *n.* 引写し.

P² *tracings* ***of*** patterns on the primitive pottery of Japan 日本上代陶器の模様引写し.

track, *n.* 《米》鉄道線路, 軌道; 路; 跡.

V to ***cover up*** one's *tracks* その足跡をくらますために. ¶***double*** the *track* 軌道を複線にする. ¶***follow*** the *track* of ... ...の跡をつける. ¶***jump*** (=***leave***) the *track* 《米》[列車が]脱線する. ☞ 英語用法は jump the metal, run off the line. ¶***keep*** close *track* of ... ...と緊密なる接触を保つ. ¶***lay*** a *track* 線路を敷く. ¶***leave*** the beaten *track* 普通の人の行かない所に行く(新奇を求める). ¶I have been out of England so long that I have quite ***lost*** *track* of what is being read. 私は随分長い間英国を去っていたので人が何を読んでいるのか全く見当がつかなくなった. ‖ ***lose*** *track* of a person (criminal) 人(など)のゆくえが不明になる. ¶***tread*** the beaten *track* [比ゆ的]先人の跡をたどる. ¶***watch*** the *track* of a departing ship 出航する船の航跡を見守る.

Q try ***another*** *track* もう一つの路を行って見る. ¶off the ***beaten*** *track* [しばしば比ゆ的に]常道をはずれて. ¶***electric car*** *tracks* 電車線路. ¶an ***endless*** *track* 戦車の無限軌道. ¶His researches were remote from the ***ordinary beaten*** *tracks.* 彼の研究は普通世人のやっているものと方面が全然違っていた. ¶a journey in ***out-of-the-way*** *tracks* 辺境の旅. ¶a ***quadruple*** *track* 四足獣の足跡. ¶set him on the ***right*** *track* 彼を正道に戻す ‖ This induced me to believe that I was at length on the ***right*** *track.* これで私はたしかな手掛りにありついたと思った. ¶a ***single*** (***double***) *track* 単(複)軌道線. ¶follow the ***wrong*** *track* 誤った道を歩む. ¶a ***well-beaten*** *track* よく人の通る道.

Q² a ***caterpillar*** *track* 無限軌道車. ¶"***hen*** *tracks*" 悪筆(ひじきの行列). ¶a ***race*** *track* 競馬場. ¶a ***railroad*** *track* 鉄道線路. 【類】lay a mile of ***railroad*** *track* in twenty-four hours. ¶a ***running*** *track* 競走場.

P far ***from*** the beaten *tracks* of commerce 普通商業の取引のある市場から遠く離れて. ¶***off*** the *track* [会話など]脱線して; 常道を踏みはずして ‖ pitch ***off*** the *track* 脱線する ‖ The train ran (=got) ***off*** the *track* (=metals). 汽車が脱線した. 【類】a train ***off*** the *track.* ¶follow ***in*** a person's *track* 人にならう. ¶***on*** the *track* 論題からはずれないで; 正当に ‖ a train running ***on*** the *track* 線路上を走っている列車. ¶The police have been ***on*** his *track* since. 以来警官は彼を捜索している. ‖ The dogs are ***on*** the *track* of the game. 犬は獲物を追跡している. ‖ trace ***on*** (=follow) the beaten *track* ありふれた道筋を旅行する; 常道をたどる. ¶The place lies ***outside*** (=is out of) the beaten *track* of tourists. その土地は観光者が普通行かないところにある.

P² a *track* ***for*** a train 列車の通る線路. ¶the *track* ***of*** a comet すい星の軌道.

O sports of both *track* and field=track and field sports トラックとフィールドの諸競技. ¶You'll find your train at *track* 8. 《米》君の列車は八番ホームだ.

track, *v.* 跡を追う, 追跡する.

M The thief was ***closely*** *tracked* by the policeman. その盗人は警官に尾行された.

M² *track* ***down*** an escaped prisoner (a criminal) 脱走した囚人(など)を追跡する ‖ *track* ***down*** on a gang of international gamblers 国際的とばく団を追いつめる.

P *track* the snow ***through*** 雪原を横切る. ¶*tracked* ***to*** its lair もと(原因)をただせば.

tract, *n.* 土地, 地域.

V He ***bought*** a big *tract* of land. 彼は広い土地を買った. ¶The land ***covers*** a *tract* of ... tsubo. その土地は...坪の地域を占めている.

Q an ***immense*** *tract* of land 広大な土地. ¶a ***level*** *tract* along the river 川沿いの平たんな地域. ¶pass through a ***well-wooded*** *tract* 森林地帯を通過する.

P The site is ***on*** a large *tract.* その敷地は大きな土地を包容している.

P² a *tract* ***of*** country 一地方. 【類】a *tract* ***of*** farm land.

tract, *n.* 小冊子.

Q a ***little*** *tract* of eighty pages 八十ページの小冊子.

Q² a ***sales*** *tract* 販売宣伝用冊子. ¶a ***socialist*** *tract* 社会党宣伝冊子.

traction, *n.* けん引; 《米》[集合的]電車.

Q with the introduction of ***electric*** *traction* [電車など]電気けん引の利用に従って. ¶***mechanical*** *traction* 機械けん引.

Q² rolling stock for ***animal*** *traction* 動物輸送用鉄道車両. ¶***city*** *traction* 市電. ¶***motor*** *traction* 発動機によるけん引. ¶The underground trolley is the best form of ***street*** *traction* yet devised. 地下電車はこれまで案出されたものの中で一番すぐれた市街電車の形式である.

tractor, *n.* トラクター.

Q A bull dozer is a ***powerful*** *tractor* for grading, road building, etc. ブルドーザーはこう配をつけたり, 道路を作ったりする強力なトラクターである.

Q² a ***farm*** *tractor* 耕作用トラクター.

trade, *n.* 商売, 取引; 貿易; 職業.

V ***advance*** their *trade* in cotton 彼らの綿花取引を発展さ

せる. ¶The war is ***affecting*** *trade*. 戦争が貿易に影響している. ¶The word *trade* is properly ***applied*** to pursuits which are distinguished from unskilled labor, agricultural employments, commerce, the learned professions, and the fine arts. 商売という言葉は熟練を要しない仕事・農業・商業・知的な職業及び芸術以外の職業に用いられる. ¶The Japanese in Formosa are endeavoring, naturally enough, to ***attract*** the *trade* to their own ports. 台湾の日本人は当然同地の商売を自分たちの港に引き付けようと努力している. ¶Accidental advertising greatly ***benefited*** his *trade*. 思いがけないことが宣伝になって彼の商売は大いに得をした. ¶***build up*** a *trade* 商売を確立する. 【類】***build up*** a good *trade* / America ***built up*** her world *trade* in a phenomenally short time. ¶They ***captured*** our *trade* in those articles. 彼らはそれらの品物のわれわれの市場を奪った. 【類】***capture*** the *trade* of the world. ¶***carry on*** one's trade その商売を営む. 【類】***carry on*** an extensive *trade* in ... ¶***choose*** a *trade* 職を選ぶ. ¶***conduct*** a *trade* with a heavy balance in one's own favor 大いにもうけて商売をやる. ¶***cultivate*** a *trade* with that country その国と貿易を始める. ¶The Samurai class ***despised*** *trade*. 武士階級は商売を軽べつした. ¶***develop*** international *trade* 国際通商を発展させる. ¶***do*** a roaring *trade* in ... …の商売が大繁盛する. ¶the trio of Powers which ***dominate*** the *trade* of the world 世界貿易の牛耳をとる三国. ¶***draw off*** *trade* from the South Seas 南洋から取引の手をひく. ¶***drive*** a lucrative *trade* in ... 割のよい…の商売を営む. 【類】***drive*** a certain contraband (禁制品) *trade*. ¶***drum up*** *trade* 商売の景気をつける(チンドン屋式に). ¶***encourage*** tourist *trade* to Japan 日本への観光旅行を奨励する. ¶***enter*** the *trade* その職業につく. 【類】a scarcity of apprentices (徒弟) ***entering*** the *trade*. ¶***establish*** a direct *trade* with ... …と直接貿易を開く. ¶***exercise*** the *trade* of shoemaking 製くつ業をやる. ¶with a view to ***extending*** *trade* 商売拡張の目的で. ¶***facilitate*** *trade* 通商の便宜をはかる. ¶***follow*** a *trade* ある職業に従事する. 【類】***follow*** a *trade* of his father. ¶***foster*** *trade* and commerce 通商貿易を助成する. 【類】***foster*** American *trade* in the Orient. ¶***give up*** *trade* 廃業する. ¶***handle*** a *trade* 一つの商売をやる. ¶Birmingham ***has*** a very large *trade* in steel goods. バーミンガムは鋼鉄製品を非常に手広く取引している. 【類】it ***has*** a large export in ... ¶***increase*** foreign *trade* 外国貿易を増進する. ¶***jeopardize*** all future *trade* あらゆる将来の貿易を阻害する. ¶***learn*** a *trade* 職業を覚える. ¶***lose*** one's *trade* 商売に失敗する ‖ The exporters have ***lost*** *trade*. 輸出業者は取引がなくなった. ¶***make*** a *trade* of politics 政治を職業とする. ¶Three English ships came to ***open*** *trade* with Japan. 三せきの英国船が日本と通商を開始するために来た. ¶***open up*** *trade* with Japan 日本と通商を開始する. 【類】***open up*** the Eastern *trade*. ¶The plague ***paralysed*** our *trade*. その悪疫がわが国の通商を停とんさせた. ¶***ply*** a (one's) *trade* [その]商売を営む. 【類】The kitemaker ***plies*** a popular *trade* in India, since here the flying of kites has been developed into a game requiring considerable skill. ¶***practice*** a *trade* 商売を営む. ¶***promote*** foreign *trade* 外国貿易を助長する. 【類】***promote*** *trade* between the two nations. ¶These draftsmen are ***pursuing*** their *trade* with success. これらの図案工たちは仕事がいそがしい. ¶***push*** our *trade* into every quarter of the globe われわれの商売を世界中に進出させる. ¶***ruin*** the wine *trade* of ... …のぶどう酒業を衰微させる. ¶***seek*** increased world *trade* 世界貿易の発展に努める. ¶***solicit*** *trade* 愛顧を求める. 【類】send around cards ***soliciting*** *trade*. ¶***stimulate*** *trade* between ... …間の通商を助長する.

v² Japan's *trade* in canned provisions has ***achieved*** a wonderful development since the war began. 日本のかん詰業は戦争開始以来非常な発達を遂げた. ¶The *trade* continues to ***expand*** from year to year. その商売は年々拡張して行く. ¶Japanese *trade* with India has lately ***grown*** by leaps and bounds. 日本のインド貿易は近年躍進また躍進の状態だ. ¶The British export coal *trade* has ***languished*** since the war. 英国の石炭輸出業は戦争以来衰えた. ¶The *trade* is going to ***revive***. 商売は復活しつつある.

Q the ***allied*** *trades* それと類似の商売. ¶in ***bad*** *trade* 不景気の時は. ¶build up a ***big*** *trade* in South America 南米と盛んに取引をするようになる. ¶the "***black trade***" [葬儀屋の]暗い商売. ¶do a ***brisk*** *trade* in ... …の商売が繁盛する ‖ a ***brisk*** export *trade* 盛んな輸出貿易. ¶the development of ***British*** *trade* in China 中国における英国貿易の発展. ¶do a ***busy*** *trade* 景気よく商売をやる. ¶the ***carrying*** *trade* of the sea 海運業. ¶the ***coastwise*** *trade* 沿岸貿易. ¶There is keen competition in the ***colonial*** *trade*. 植民地貿易は競争が激しい. ¶do a ***considerable*** *trade* with ... …と相当大きな取引をする. ¶the ***cosmopolitan*** *trade* in "white slave" 国際的ないわゆる「白人どれい」(売色)業. ¶a ***dangerous*** *trade* 危険な商売. ¶this ***dishonest*** *trade* このいんちき商売. ¶The city has an ***extensive*** *trade* in cotton. 同市では綿花を手広く取引している. ¶The town has a ***flourishing*** *trade* in lumber. その市は木材などの取引が盛んである. ¶forcibly push ***fresh*** *trade* 新しい商業発展を大いに努める. ¶do a ***good*** *trade* in ... …の商売をやって成功している ‖ if *trade* is ***good*** 景気がよければ. ¶carry on an ***illicit*** *trade* with ... と不正の取引を行う. ¶There is a considerable ***import*** as well as ***export*** *trade* in this commodity. この商品は大分輸出入がある. ¶this ***infamous*** *trade* この不面目な商売. ¶***intercoastal*** *trade* 沿岸貿易. ¶***internal*** (***international***) *trade* 国内(国際)貿易. ¶***interstate*** *trades* 《米》各州間の貿易. ¶do a ***large*** *trade* with ... …と盛んに取引をする ‖ The city has a ***large*** *trade* in grain. その市は穀類の大きな取引をやっている. ‖ The port-city has a ***large foreign*** *trade*. 同港は海外貿易を手広く営んでいる. ¶All ***legitimate*** *trades* are equally honorable. 合法的取引はどれも皆りっぱなものだ. ¶do a ***lively*** *trade* 活発な商売をやる. ¶have ***much*** *trade* with ... …と大いに取引する. ¶The Government has paid lip service to a conception of ***multilateral*** *trade*. 政府は多角貿易の着想に口先だけの好意を示した. ¶ply their ***nefarious*** *trade* 彼らの裏道商売をする. ¶American's export *trade* in shoes is ***negligible***. アメリカ人の製くつ輸出業は大したものじゃない. ¶build up ***new*** *trade* 新しい商売を営む. ¶the ***odious*** *trade* of informing 密告というやな仕事. ¶***postwar*** *trade* 戦後の貿易. ¶They drive a ***profitable*** *trade* in charms. 守り札を出すのが結構彼らの商売になっている. ¶a ***prosaic*** *trade* おもしろ味のない商売. ¶one's ***regular*** *trade* 本業. ¶do a ***roaring*** *trade* 商売大繁盛である. ¶ply the ***same old*** *trade* 相も変らずの商売をやっている. ¶***sea-borne*** *trade* 海上貿易. ¶***skilled*** *trades* 熟練(しているものの)職業. ¶if *trade* is ***slack*** 商売がひまだと. ¶***stagnant*** *trade* 商売の不振. ¶He drives a ***thriving*** *trade*. 彼は商売が繁盛している. ¶Quack doctors still ply their ***vicious*** *trade*. やぶ医者どもは今なお不正な商売を営んでいる. ¶Japan's ***maritime*** *trade* 日本の海運業. ¶***What*** is that man's *trade?* あの男の職業は何か. ¶a young merchant in the ***wholesale*** *trade* 卸売業をやっている若い商人.

Q² ***barter*** *trade* 物々交換貿易. ¶There is a ***bootleg*** *trade* in food and clothes which is expanding rapidly at exorbitant prices. べら棒な値段で食糧及び衣料に関するやみ取引が急速に増大しつつある. ¶Sanitary engineering is a branch of the ***building*** *trade*. 衛生工事は建築業の一部だ. ¶***Christmas*** *trade* クリスマス当て込みの商売. ¶***coal***[***ing***] *trade* 石炭積込業. 【類】the outlook of British ***coal*** *trade* for 1958. ¶the ***construction*** *trades* 土建業. ¶***contraband*** *trade* in opium アヘンの密貿易. ¶the plumbing and hot water ***engineering*** *trades* 管工及び熱湯工事業. ¶The bulk of the ***export*** *trade* is to be in textiles. 輸出業の大部分は織物の予定である. ‖ Our ***export*** *trade* is very brisk (dull). わが国の輸出貿易ははなはだ活況を呈している(不振だ). 【類】there is a considerable ***export*** *trade* in ... ¶stores that have a ***fancy*** *trade* 小間物を売る店. ¶the ***film*** *trade* 映画フィルム貿易業. ¶the ***furniture*** *trade* 家具商. ¶the wholesale ***grocery*** *trade* 雑貨卸業. ¶***home*** (= ***domestic***) *trade* 内国商業. ¶the ***ice cream*** *trade* in the summer and the baked ***chestnut*** *trade* in the winter 夏はアイスクリーム屋冬は焼ぐり屋. ¶a pioneer of the local ***iron*** *trade* その地方の鉄商の先駆者. ¶stamp out the illicit ***liquor*** *trade* 違法の酒類販売を撲滅する. ¶***luxury*** *trades*—acting, writing, dancing, painting, interior decorating ぜいたく商売—演技, 著作, 舞踊, 絵画, 室内装飾. ¶The ***milk*** *trade* of London is to a great extent in the hands of the Welsh. ロンドンの牛乳業は大部分ウェールス

人の手中にある. ¶The Thai Government would not give up its flourishing ***narcotics trade***. タイ国政府は繁栄をきわめている麻薬商売をやめないだろう. ¶the ***newspaper trade*** 新聞業. ¶the ***ocean-carrying trade*** 海運業. ¶conduct ***overseas trade*** 海外貿易をやる. ¶the ***pottery trade*** 製陶業. ¶the ***publishing trade*** 出版業. ¶the ***resort trade*** 観光業. ¶the ***sending-out trade*** 出前業. ¶the ***shipping trade*** 船舶業. ¶the ***tourist trade*** 観光業. ¶***transit trade*** 通過貿易. ¶the ***travel trade*** 旅行案内業. ¶***two-way*** (***one-way***) ***trade*** between ... and ... …と…との間の双(片)方の貿易. ¶***watch*** (***jewelery***) ***trade*** 時計商(など). ¶domestic ***water trade*** 家庭水道工事業. ¶the ***white slave trade*** (=traffic) [白人の]売春業. ¶seventeen nations that carry on threequarters of ***world trade*** 世界貿易の四分の三を占める十七カ国. 【類】for the growth of ***world trade***.

P make a living ***at*** a ***trade*** 商売で暮しを立てる ‖ sit all day ***at*** one's ***trade*** 終日すわってその仕事にかかっている. ¶a compositor (blacksmith, tailor, carpenter) ***by trade*** 商売は植字工(など). ¶There is a lull ***in trade***. 商売には小休みがある. 【類】engage ***in trade*** ‖ it is known ***in*** the ***trade*** as "..." それを業者は「…」と言っている. ¶go ***into trade*** 商売をやる. ¶owing to the growth ***of trade*** 商売が発展したため ‖ a revival ***of trade*** 商売の復活. ¶a Jack ***of*** all ***trades*** 何でも屋 ‖ a harmless "trick ***of*** the ***trade***" 害にならない商売の秘けつ. ¶discount ***to*** the ***trade*** 業者仲間の割引.

P² foster ***trade between*** ... …間に取引を奨励する. ¶our foreign ***trade in*** tea and raw silk わが国の茶及び生糸の海外貿易 ‖ ***trade in*** human life 人身売買. 【類】British ***trade in*** Manchuria. / There is a ***trade in*** tobacco. ¶a ***trade of*** the kerbstone 大道商売. ¶conduct its foreign ***trade through*** the port その港を通じて外国貿易を行う. ¶Japanese ***trade with*** Australia 日本の対豪貿易.

O ***Trade*** is at a standstill. 商売がぱったり止まっている. ¶How is [your] ***trade?*** ご商売はいかがですか.

trade, *v.* 交換する; 売買する; 貿易する.

M ***trade extensively*** with America アメリカと手広く取引する. ¶***trade internally*** or ***internationally*** 国内または海外の取引をやる.

P² a firm ***trading as*** A. Lambert and Sons エー・ランバート父子商会という名義で商売をやっている商店. ¶***trade at*** a store in a municipal market 市営マーケットの店で商売をやる. ¶the ship ***trades between*** ... その船は…間を通う. ¶business not ***trading for*** profit 非営利的な仕事 ‖ Will you ***trade*** this ***for*** that? これとそれと交換してくれませんか. ¶***trade in*** matches (pottery, chestnuts, ice cream) マッチ(など)を商う ‖ municipal ***trading in*** gas, water, and electricity ガス・水道及び電気事業の市営. ¶***trade on*** the credulity of the public in order to make money 公衆の盲信を悪用して金もうけをやる ‖ ***trade on*** the better feelings of humanity 人の慈善心を食い物にする. ¶merchants (countries) ***trading to*** China 対華貿易に従事している商人(など). ¶We are accustomed to ***trade with*** the firm. 手前どもはその会社と取引をしています. 【類】***trade with*** the West Indies (South Asia).

trademark, *n.* 商標.

Q² the "***roaring lion***" ***trademark*** of the Metro-Goldwyn-Mayer Pictures Corporation メトローゴールドウィンメーヤー映画社の商標「ほえるライオン」. ¶the ***Victor dog trademark*** ビクター会社の犬の商標.

P register ... ***as*** a ***trademark*** …を商標として登録する.

trader, *n.* 貿易商; 取引人, 商人.

Q a ***foreign trader*** 外国貿易商. ¶***international traders*** 国際的貿易商. ¶***prudent*** and ***industrious traders*** 用心深くて勤勉な商人. ¶a ***retail trader***=a shopkeeper 小売商人. ¶***skilled traders*** 商売になれている商人. ¶***small traders*** 小商人. ¶a ***tricky trader*** いんちき商人. ¶a ***victimized trader*** だまされた商人. ¶a ***wholesale trader*** (=merchant) 卸売商人. ¶a ***wicked trader*** 悪徳業者.

Q² a ***street trader*** 露店商人.

tradesman, *n.* 商人, 小売商人.

Q a ***once-prosperous tradesman*** 盛大にやっていたこともある商人. ¶one's ***ordinary tradesman*** その取りつけの商人. ¶a ***petty tradesman*** 小商人(家庭に出入の). ¶a ***ruined tradesman*** 失敗した小売商人. ¶a ***traveling tradesman*** 行商人.

Q² a ***kerbstone tradesman*** 大道商人.

trading, *n.* 取引, 売買.

P² ***trading in*** futures 先物取引. ¶***trading on*** the exchange 取引所での取引.

tradition, *n.* (**1**) 口碑, 伝説.

V the villages ***have*** a ***tradition*** that ... その村々には…という伝説がある. ¶***hunt up*** and ***compile traditions*** 口碑を収集して編集する. ¶***preserve*** the ***traditions*** of the past 過去の伝説を保存する. 【類】an early Japanese ***tradition preserved*** in the Kojiki tells us that ... ¶***reproduce*** a ***tradition*** current in one's time その時代に伝わっていた口碑を採録する. ¶the ***traditions woven*** around it それにまつわる伝説.

V² a beautiful but not trustworthy ***tradition declares*** that ... 考えは美しいが事実とは思われない伝説に…とある. ¶***tradition records*** that ... 伝説に…とある. ¶***Tradition represents*** him as a handsome person. 伝説にはあの人は美男子としている. ¶the ***tradition runs*** that ... 伝説に…とある. ¶***tradition says*** (=***relates*** or ***has it***) that ... …という言い伝えがある. ¶The ***tradition*** still ***survives***. その伝説は今に残っている.

Q according to ***ancient traditions*** 昔の伝説によると. ¶his treatment of ***discrepant traditions*** 区々たる伝説をさばく彼の態度. ¶a product of ***distorted tradition*** 伝説が口から口へ伝えられ自然姿を変じたもの. ¶***hazy tradition*** おぼろげな伝説. ¶***legendary traditions*** 伝説. ¶according to ***local tradition*** 土地の伝説によると. ¶According to ***Oriental tradition***, Mahomet married Khadijah when five years of age. 東洋の伝説によるとマホメットは五歳のときカーディージャと結婚した. ¶a ***picturesque tradition*** 美しい伝説. ¶according to a ***popular tradition*** 俗説によると. ¶***tradition*** is ***silent*** concerning ... …については何もない.

Q² according to an ***old family tradition*** その家に伝わる口碑によると.

P ***according to*** [a] ***tradition*** 伝説によると. ¶it is ***by tradition*** the work of ... それは…の作という言い伝えになっている.

(**2**) 伝統.

V ***break tradition*** 型を破る. ¶***build up tradition*** 伝統を築き上げる. ¶***cherish*** their inherited ***tradition*** 彼らの伝統を大切にする. ¶***defy*** the ***tratitions*** of our high calling 名誉ある(弁護士などの)職業の伝統に逆行する. ¶***discard tradition*** 伝統を捨てる. ¶***follow*** no ***tradition*** 伝統を追わない. ¶jealously ***guard*** the ***traditions*** of the Japan Sea and Port Arthur 日本海および旅順口の伝統を大切に守る. ¶***keep*** the same ***traditions***, which we have kept unsullied. われわれがりっぱに守ってきた伝統を維持する. ¶The workmen of the present day have ***lost*** the ***traditions*** of the art. 今日の職人には昔のような技術の奥儀といったものが残っていない. ¶***maintain*** the ***traditions*** of the men who have gone before them 先人から受継いだ伝統を持続する. ¶***relinquish*** a proudly cherished ***tradition*** 誇りをもって守ってきた伝統を捨てる. ¶He worthily ***upheld*** the great ***traditions*** of the early pioneers. 彼は初期開拓者の偉大な伝統をりっぱに維持した. 【類】Mr. E.H. Dring worthily ***upheld*** the ***traditions*** of the great house of Quaritch (ロンドンの書店) until his death in 1928. / ***uphold*** the ***traditions*** of their race by fighting magnificently. ¶***value tradition*** 伝統を重んじる.

Q I trust that, at this critical period, Japan will behave so as to be worthy of the ***best traditions*** of her great past. 私は日本がこの非常時においてその偉大な過去の最もりっぱな伝統を辱しめないように行動するものと確信する. ¶the most ***cherished traditions*** of the past 最も大切にした昔の伝統. 【類】anciently ***established traditions***. ¶uphold its ***fine traditions*** そのりっぱな伝統を支持する. ¶***grand traditions*** すばらしい伝統. ¶***high traditions*** 高尚な伝統. ¶influenced by ***hoary tradition*** 古い伝統の感化を受けて. ¶inheritors of an ***immortal tradition*** 久遠の伝統を継承したもの. ¶***industrial tradition*** 産業上の伝統. ¶according to ***long tradition*** 古くからの伝統によれば. ¶uphold its ***old traditions*** その過去を辱かしめないようにする. ¶cherish ***old-fashioned traditions*** 古風な伝統を温存する. ¶a ***self-perpetuating tradition*** 永遠に伝わる伝統. ¶true to ***time-hallowed tradition*** 古来の伝統を辱しめずに. ¶***time-honored tradition*** 古くからの伝統. ¶treasure it as a ***venerable tradition*** それを光栄ある伝統として大切にする.

Q² perpetuate the *family tradition* 家の伝統を存続する ‖ Learning was a *family tradition*. 学問はその家に代々伝わっていた. ¶strictly governed by *iron tradition* 盤石の伝統にきびしく支配される(茶道などのように). ¶uphold the *Waseda tradition* 早稲田の伝統を支持する.

P unhampered ***by** tradition* 伝統にとらわれずに. ¶a philanthropic family ***of*** the old *tradition* 昔から慈善で名高い家. ¶stick ***to*** a *tradition*, good or bad よかれあしかれ伝統を固守する. ¶It is a break ***with*** *tradition*. それは型破りである.

traduce, *v.* 非難する, 中傷する.

P He was *traduced* ***by*** a newspaper. 彼はある新聞に中傷された.

traffic, *n.* (**1**) 交通, [人・馬・車の]往来; 運送.

V ***accommodate*** growing *traffic* 交通のひん繁化に対応する. ¶***attract*** tourist *traffic* to ... …へ観光客を吸収する. ¶***block*** the *traffic* 交通を止める. ¶***capture*** the evergrowing tourist *traffic* of the world 世界中の観光客をますます引き付ける. ¶when *traffic* is most ***congested*** 交通が最も多い時に. ¶policemen at work ***controlling*** the *traffic* 交通整理に当っている巡査. ¶Snow ***disorganized*** the *traffic*. 雪で交通に故障ができた.【類】The *traffic* is ***disorganized*** by fog (snowfall). ¶avenues, boulevards, and streets upon which commercial *traffic* is ***excluded*** [円タクなどの]商業交通の禁止されている並木街・広小路及び普通街路. ¶The street ***has*** the most congested *traffic*. その街路が交通が一番ひん繁である. ¶We ***hear*** the *traffic* in this room. このへやは往来の雑音が聞える. ¶***hinder*** (=***impede***) the *traffic* 交通を妨害する. ¶*Traffic* was ***held up*** (=***paralysed***) by the snowstorm. 吹雪のために交通が途絶した.【類】*Traffic* was ***held up*** for some minutes by the accident (事故). ¶***increase*** Japan's tourist *traffic* from the United States 日本への米国観光客の量を増す.【類】with a view to ***increasing*** the tourist *traffic* between their countries. ¶The *traffic* in the street was ***interfered with*** for several hours. その街路の交通に数時間の故障を生じた. ¶*Traffic* is ***interrupted***. 交通が止まっている. ¶***maintain*** *traffic* 交通を持続する. ¶A fallen horse ***obstructed*** the *traffic*. 馬が倒れて交通の妨害になった. ¶it has been decided to ***open*** *traffic* from ... [鉄道などを]...から開通することに決定した. ¶***regulate*** the *traffic* of motor-vehicles. 自動車の交通を整理する. ¶***shut off*** *traffic* 交通をしゃ断する. ¶The plague in London ***stopped*** all *traffic* between the metropolis and the outer world. そのロンドンの疫病は首都と外界との間のあらゆる交通を途絶させた. ¶***suspend*** *traffic* 交通を一時止める. ¶***tie up*** *traffic* 《米》交通を途絶する.

V² *Traffic* generally has ***dwindled*** on the pavement. 一般に歩道の人通りが少くなった. ¶*Traffic* ***moves*** slowly in rural Spain. スペインのいなかでは交通が緩慢だ. ¶The *traffic* is ***thickening*** (***thinning***). 交通がひん繁に(少く)なってくる.

Q The tourist *traffic* is remarkably ***brisk***. 観光客の往来が著しく活発である. ¶***busy*** (=***heavy***) *traffic* ひんぱんな交通. ¶***congested*** *traffic* of the thoroughfare 大通りのひん繁な交通. ¶***dense*** *traffic* ひん繁な交通. ¶According to advance reports this year, the American tourist *traffic* to France should be very ***heavy*** this summer. 本年の予定報告から察してフランスへの米国観光者の数はこの夏非常に多いものと見られている. ¶the diminution of ***horse-drawn*** *traffic* 馬車交通の減退. ¶a broad stream of ***human*** and ***vehicular*** *traffic* 人車の広い流れ. ¶There is ***much*** (***little***) *traffic* in this street. この通は往来がひん繁だ(あまりない). ¶***pedestrian*** and ***vehicular*** (=vehicle) *traffic* 徒歩及び乗車の交通. ¶a dislocation of ***railway*** *traffic* 鉄道運輸の混乱. ¶endanger ***safe*** *traffic* 交通の安全を脅かす. ¶***wheeled*** (=***vehicular***) *traffic* 諸車の交通.【類】No ***wheeled*** *traffic* is allowed in these streets.

Q² ***air passenger*** *traffic* 旅客空輸. ¶***automobile*** (=***motor***) *traffic* 自動車の交通. ¶a ***busy river*** *traffic* ひん繁な河上の交通. ¶***canal*** *traffic* 運河の交通. ¶***freight*** *traffic* 貨物運送. ¶increase the ***customer*** *traffic* of a store 店の客足を多くする. ¶The street has the heaviest ***foot-passenger*** *traffic*. その通りは人通りが一番多い. ¶***inter-city*** *traffic* 都市連絡交通. ¶the ***international*** (***home***) ***tourist*** *traffic* 国際(国内)観光客の往来. ¶***motor*** *traffic*. 自動車の交通. ¶***motor-vehicle*** *traffic* モーター付諸車の往来. ¶***one-way*** *traffic* 一方交通. ¶***overland*** *traffic* 陸上交通. ¶the ***passenger*** *traffic* on railways and in cabs 鉄道及びタクシーによる旅客輸送 ‖ ***passenger*** and ***goods*** *traffic* 客貨輸送. ¶***plane*** *traffic* 空輸. ¶***rail*** and ***highway*** *traffic* 鉄道及び道路交通. ¶suspend ***railway*** *traffic* 鉄道輸送を止める. ¶***rush-hour*** *traffic* 混雑時の交通. ¶***shipping*** *traffic* 船舶の運輸. ¶The Bell System handles about 90 per cent of the ***telephone*** *traffic* in the United States. ベル会社系統が米国の通話の約九十パーセントを占める. ¶This year's ***tourist*** *traffic* will be much heavier than the last year's. 今年の観光客の往来は昨年をはるかに上回るだろう. ‖ The ***tourist*** *traffic* has been 30 per cent greater this cherry-blossom season than [the] last. この観桜季節は観光客の数が前季に比して三割多かった. ¶***waterway*** *traffic* 水上交通.

P The railway is open (=opened) ***to*** *traffic*. その鉄道は開通した.

P² high-speed *traffic* ***by*** air 空中の高速度運輸. ¶The *traffic* ***in*** road and ***on*** pavement is momentarily thickening. 車道並びに人道の交通は見る見るひん繁になってくる. ¶The *traffic* ***of*** this street is heavy. この街路は交通がひん繁だ. ¶Railway *traffic* ***on*** the Sanyo Line was crippled all Sunday. 山陽線は日曜一日中不通だった. ¶The *traffic* ***to*** the Continent during the summer months has been greatly in excess of previous years. 夏期中(欧州)大陸への旅客は前数年に比して非常に増加した.

(**2**) [主として不正な]取引, 売買.

V The firm ***does*** a great *traffic* (=transact an extensive business) in raw silk. その店は生糸の取引を大きくやっている.

Q ***human*** *traffic* 人身売買. ¶stamp out an ***illegal*** *traffic* [密輸出入などの]違法の商行為を撲滅する. ¶the movement to abolish licensing of women for ***immoral*** *traffic* 廃娼運動. ¶the ***international*** *traffic* in arms 兵器の国際的売買.

Q² ***drug*** and ***white-slave*** *traffic* 麻薬兼売春業. ¶the ***liquor*** *traffic* in all its forms あらゆる酒類売買 ‖ control (=keep down) illicit ***liquor*** *traffic* 酒の不正取引を取締る.

P² *traffic* ***in*** rice (furs) 米(など)の取引 ‖ a *traffic* ***in*** shame and vice 売春業.【類】*traffic* ***in*** women (young girls). / *traffic* ***in*** human flesh (人肉) / *traffic* ***in*** votes.

traffic, *v.* 売買する.

M *traffic* ***away*** honor 名誉を売る.

P *traffic* ***with*** natives ***for*** bear skins (ivory) 土人とくまの皮(など)の取引をする.

trafficker, *n.* 商人.

Q² a ***blackmarket*** *trafficker* やみ商人. ¶a ***drug*** (***liquor***) *trafficker* 麻薬(など)商人.

traffic-signal, *n.* 交通信号.

P ***against*** (=disregarding) a *traffic-signal* 交通信号を無視して.

tragedy, *n.* 悲劇, 惨事.

V Some one has ***made*** a *tragedy* on this subject. この問題を悲劇に仕組んだ人がある. ¶Then the *tragedy* ***took place***. そこでその悲劇が起った.

Q the ***blackest*** *tragedy* 最もすさまじい悲劇. ¶a ***domestic*** *tragedy* 家庭悲劇. ¶a ***double*** *tragedy* (情死などの)二重の悲劇. ¶a ***hidden*** *tragedy* 隠れた悲劇. ¶***needless*** *tragedy* 無用の人命損失. ¶a ***sevenfold*** *tragedy* [六人殺して自殺したなどの]七重の悲劇.

Q² an ***air*** *tragedy* 航空惨事. ¶a ***celluloid*** *tragedy* セルロイドによる火事. ¶a young man touched by the shadow of ***family*** *tragedy* 家庭悲劇の暗い影の影響を受けた青年. ¶a ***love*** *tragedy* 恋愛悲劇. ¶a case of "***war*** *tragedy*" 戦争悲劇の一例. ¶a ***world*** *tragedy* 世界の悲劇(戦争のこと).

P knowledge gained ***through*** the *tragedy* of experience 悲惨な経験から得た知識.

P² be a *tragedy* ***to*** ...にとっては悲劇だ.

trail, *n.* 跡, 足跡.

V men who ***blazed*** the *trail* 光彩ある事跡を残した人々. ¶***follow*** the same *trail* in life as his father [教師の子が教師になるなど]父と同じ職業につく. ¶The train ***left*** a *trail* of smoke. 汽車が進行する跡に煙をたなびかした. ¶first ***strike*** one's *trail* 始めてその人に出会う.

Q a shooting star with its ***blazing*** *trail* of light こうこうたる光の尾を引いた流星. ¶the ***slimy*** *trail* of a slug なめくじの通ったぬらぬらした跡.

Q² a winding ***forest*** *trail* made by gum-gatherers ゴム採集者の造った曲りくねった森林中の小道. ¶More than 20 miles of ***ski*** *trails* have been laid out on the hill. 二十マ

イル以上のスキー場が丘の上にできた.

P follow ***in*** its ***trail*** その足跡をたどる. ¶be ***off*** the ***trail*** 足跡を失する. ¶The police is ***on*** the ***trail*** of the criminal. 警察はその犯人の跡をつけている.

trail, *v.* 跡を追う, 跡をつける.

M ***trail*** one's legs ***along*** 足を引ずって歩く

P The skirt ***trails along*** the ground (***in*** the mud). スカートが地上を引ずる(など). ¶***trail*** a person ***to*** a place 人をある場所まで跡をつけて行く.

train, *n.* (**1**) 汽車, 列車.

V ***attack*** (=***bombard***) a ***train*** with stones 汽車を目がけて石を投げる. ¶***avoid*** a ***train*** by an inch 危うく汽車を避ける. ¶***blow up*** a ***train*** 列車を爆破する. ¶***board*** a ***train*** for his home town《米》汽車に乗って故郷の町に向う. ¶I ***caught*** the 5 p.m. ***train*** bound for ... 私は午後五時発...行の汽車に間に合った. 【類】I hope to ***catch*** the five-thirty ***train.*** / I was in a hurry to ***catch*** the last ***train*** home. / I have only a few minutes to ***catch*** their ***train.*** / I was hurrying to ***catch*** a ***train.*** ¶***change trains*** (cars) at ... for ... ...で...に汽車を乗換える. ¶The ***train*** was ***derailed*** (=ran off the metal). その列車が脱線した. ¶***despatch*** a ***train*** 列車を出す. ¶***drive*** a royal ***train*** お召列車を運転する. ¶***enter*** a ***train*** 汽車に乗る. ¶***flag*** a ***train*** 汽車に手旗信号をする. ¶Robbers ***held up*** the ***train.*** 賊がその汽車を襲った. ¶***leave*** the ***train*** at ... ...で下車する. ¶There! we have ***lost*** the ***train.*** そら! 汽車に乗り遅れた. ¶We can just ***make*** the seven-o'clock ***train.*** 僕たちは七時の汽車にやっと間に合うだろう. 【類】He's just ***made*** the ***train.*** ¶The bus from the Hotel ***meets*** all the principal ***trains*** at the station. そのホテルのバスが停車場で主要列車を全部待合わせています. ¶I ***missed*** my ***train*** by three minutes. 私は三分違いで汽車に乗り遅れた. 【類】impatient with fears of ***missing*** the last ***train.*** ¶***mount*** the ***train*** for a ride to ... 汽車に乗って...に行く. ¶***operate trains*** over a line ある線に列車を運転する. ¶***place*** a special ***train*** at the disposal of ... 特別列車を...の乗用に供する. ¶***pull trains*** on a railroad 線路の上を列車を引っ張る. ¶***quit*** the ***train*** 汽車を降りる. ¶***run*** (=***operate***) a ***train*** 列車を運転する. ¶People ***stormed*** the ***train*** and packed themselves in their places. 人が汽車に押寄せてきてそれぞれ席に収まった. ¶The ***train*** was ***snowed up.*** 汽車は雪に閉じ込められた. ¶***start*** a ***train*** 列車を発車させる. ¶***take*** (=***get***) a ***train*** at 1.40 p.m. 午後一時四十分の汽車に乗る ‖ ***take*** [a] ***train*** for ... ...行の汽車に乗る ‖ ***take*** the ***train*** back home 汽車に乗って帰る. ¶***take*** a ***train north*** (***south***) 北(など)行き汽車に乗る. ¶What ***train*** do you ***take*** [***out***] tonight? 今晩何時の汽車でお出でですか. ¶I often ***use*** that ***train.*** 私は度々その汽車に乗る. ¶an attempt to ***wreck*** a ***train*** 汽車を破壊しようとする計画.

V² I think the ***train arrives*** at noon. その汽車は正午着だと思います. ¶The ***train corresponds*** with the steamer. その汽車はその汽船に連絡する. ¶The ***train departs*** (=***leaves***). 汽車が出る. ¶A ***train draws*** into a station. 汽車が停車場にはいって来る. ¶The ***train drew up*** at the station. 汽車はその停車場に着いた. ¶A ***train gets out*** for ... every hour. ...行の汽車は毎時間出る. ¶The ***train glides*** smoothly into the station. 汽車はすべるように停車場にはいって行く. 【類】Then the ***train glides*** slowly out of the terminus (終着駅). ¶The ***train*** is ***going*** at full speed. 汽車は全速力で走っている. ¶The ***train moves out.*** 汽車が出て行く. ¶The ***train*** from ... ***puffs up*** to the platform. ...からの汽車はぽっぽっと煙を吐きながらホームへはいって来る. ¶The ***train*** was ***pulling in*** (***out***). 列車が入ってきた(出て行った). 【類】The ***train pulled*** into the station. / The engineer opens the throttle and the ***train pulls*** out of the station. ‖ a ***train pulling*** out of the station on a hundred miles' journey 百マイルの行程を前にして駅を出発する列車. ¶A ***train rattles*** into the station. 汽車がごうっと停車場にはいって来る. 【類】Promptly at 2.45 the ***train rattles*** out of the station on its journey north. / A freight ***train*** was ***rattling*** (=***lumbering***) away. ¶The ***train rattled in*** and ***pulled up*** sharply. 汽車がごうっとはいってきて急に止まった. ¶This ***train*** does not ***run*** on Saturday nights. この汽車は土曜の晩はない. 【類】The ***train*** was ***running*** at its top speed. ¶A ***train rushes*** alongside a platform. 汽車がプラットホームに沿って突進する. ¶The ***train slowed down*** (=***up***) and ***stopped*** (=***pulled up***). 汽車が速力をゆるめて止まった. ¶The whistle sounds, and the ***train starts*** out of the station. 汽笛が鳴って汽車は停車場から出て行く. ¶The ***train started up*** again. [停車した]汽車が再び出て行った. ¶The ***train steamed*** into the station. 汽車が停車場へはいってきた. ¶A ***train*** was ***steaming up*** to an adjoining platform and dislodging a load of hot, flurried people. 汽車が隣りのプラットホームにはいってきて大勢のあわてふためく乗客を降ろしていた. ¶a ***train traveling*** at 60 miles per hour 一時間六十マイル疾走の汽車. ¶The ***train whistled*** at the crossing. 列車が踏切で汽笛を鳴らした.

Q a luxuriously ***appointed train*** 設備のぜいたくな汽車. ¶a ***train bound*** for ... ...行の汽車. ¶an elaborate ***bridal train*** 数奇をこらした新婚列車. ¶"The Empire Builder," ***crack train*** of the Great Northern Railways 大北鉄道の花形列車ジー・エムパイア・ビルダー. ¶travel on ***day trains*** 昼(区間)列車で旅行する. ¶a ***departing train*** 発車して行く列車. ¶***down*** (***up***) ***trains*** 下り(上り)列車; 《米》南(北)方行きの列車. ¶I took the ***early train*** to ... 私は...行の早い朝汽車に乗った. ¶an ***east-bound train*** 東行列車. ¶an ***electric train*** 電気列車. ¶take [an] ***elevated train*** to ... ...行の高架線列車に乗る ‖ travel down town on an ***elevated train*** 高架鉄道で下町に行く. ¶a comfortable ***express train*** bore us swiftly to ... 乗心地のよい急行列車でわれわれは...へ急いだ. 【類】He expected his wife to arrive on that ***evening's express train.*** ¶a ***fast through train*** 快速直通列車. ¶The ***train*** (railway carriage) was ***full.*** その汽車(車台)は満員であった. ¶a ***jam-packed train*** 大入満員の列車. ¶a ***luxurious train*** 豪華な列車. ¶an ***out-bound*** (=***out-going***) ***train*** 出発の列車. ¶a ***palatial train*** 豪華な列車. ¶a ***returning train*** leaves ... for ... at 6.10 p.m. 戻りの列車は午後六時十分に...に向けて...を出る. ¶a ***slow train*** of freight cars 低速度の貨物列車. ¶The ***special train*** bearing the Roosevelt party ローズベルト氏一行を乗せている特別列車. 【類】The party was taken to Kyoto on a ***special train.*** ¶***well-filled trains*** 満員の汽車. ¶a ***west-bound train*** 西行きの汽車. ¶The ***workmen's trains*** are spinning briskly along from half past four. 労働者専用の汽車が四時半から忙しく出ている.

Q² an ***accommodation train***《米》各駅停車列車. ¶a fine ***all-steel train*** りっぱな全部鋼鉄製の列車. ¶a ***boat train*** 汽船連絡列車 ‖ a special ***boat train*** 特別汽船連絡列車. ¶a ***corridor train***《英》通廊列車. ¶a ***demonstration train*** 宣伝のための列車. ¶a ***goods train***=《米》a ***freight*** train 貨物列車. ¶I am coming on the ***half-past-four train*** Monday. 月曜日の四時半の汽車で行きます. ¶a ***limited express train*** 特別急行列車. ¶a ***long-distance train*** 長距離列車. ¶forward it by ***luggage train*** それを荷物列車で送る. ¶a ***mail train*** from ... to ... ...から...の郵便列車. ¶take the ***morning*** (***night***) ***train*** 朝(夜)の汽車に乗る. ‖ I left the city as I had announced on the first ***morning train.*** 私は予告しておいた通りに朝の一番汽車でその町を去った. 【類】take a ***night train*** and hurry off to ... ¶an ***owl train***《口語》深夜運転汽車. ¶Newspapers are sold on ***railroad trains.*** 新聞が列車内で販売される. 【類】Obviously the bus for long hauls is a means of transportation much inferior to the ***railroad train:*** it has no diners, no lavatories, no smokers. ¶in a ***railway train*** 汽車で. 【類】Smoking is prohibited in English ***railway train,*** except in compartments marked "Smoking." ¶a ***runaway train*** 暴走列車. ¶take a ***steamer train*** for Liverpool リバープール行きの汽船連絡列車に乗る. ¶a ***steamline***[***d***] ***train*** 流線型列車. ¶a ***troop train*** 軍隊輸送列車. ¶a solid ***vestibule train*** がん丈な(ボギー)貫通式列車. ¶a ***way train***《米》区間列車.

P He was ***aboard*** the ***train.***《米》彼はその汽車に乗っていた. ‖ take ... ***aboard*** the ***train*** ...を車内に持込む. ¶Most of Hollywood was ***at*** the ***train*** to see me off. ハリウッドの大部分の人々が私を見送るために列車の側にいた. ¶come ***by train*** 汽車で来る. 【類】brought ***by*** an early ***train*** / Tokyo is eighteen miles from Yokohama—fifty-five minutes ***by*** electric ***train.*** ¶step down (=alight) ***from*** a ***train*** 汽車から降りる. 【類】view the river ***from*** the ***train.*** ¶It is an hour's journey ***in*** (=by) ***train*** and bus. そこは汽車とバスで一時間の旅だ. ‖ conversation ***in*** a *train* 列車中の談話 ‖ You missed your watch and chain ***in*** the *train*, I believe. あなたはきっと汽車の中に鎖付の時計をなくしたでしょう. ¶get ***off*** a *train* 《米》 汽車から降りる. ¶a journey ***on*** a *train*=a railway journey 汽車の旅 ‖ the *train* ***on*** which I expect to depart 私が乗って行こうと思う汽車. 【類】 go ***on*** the 5•30 a.m. *train* / I am looking for a friend from Kobe ***on*** the 11.40 *train*. / I rode through the United States ***on*** this *train*. / Kyoto is reached from Tokyo in ten hours ***on*** *trains*. / I met an Englishman ***on*** a *train*. / Seats can be reserved ***on*** *trains* at 1/- per seat (一座席一シリングで.) / There were many interesting people ***on*** the *train*. / Do you sleep well ***on*** a *train*? / One night had to be spent ***on*** the *train*. / take breakfast (one's meals) ***on*** the *train* ‖ labels ***on*** the *train* 汽車の(方向)標識. ¶a dining car coupled ***on*** an express *train* 急行列車に連結した食堂車 ‖ Our compartment ***on*** the *train* was very stuffy and smelly. われわれの乗った車室は非常に蒸暑くいやなにおいがした. ‖ ***on*** the *train* to Kamakura 鎌倉行の汽車で.

P^2 a *train* ***for*** Kobe 神戸行の汽車. ¶a *train* ***of*** ten coaches 十両編成の列車 ‖ a *train* ***of*** wagons 貨物列車.

(**2**) 行列; 連続; 従者.

V This will ***bring*** an unending *train* of misfortunes. そうすると後から後へと不幸が続出するだろう. ¶***follow*** a *train* of thought 次から次へと考えが続く. ¶***follow out*** a *train* of reasoning 次々と推理を続ける.

P Evils follow ***in*** the *train* of war. 色々な弊害が戦争の結果生じる. 【類】 A tiny mishap may bring all sorts of disagreeable consequences ***in*** its *train*. ‖ All is now ***in*** *train* (=ready to operate). 万端用意ができている.

P^2 It brings with it a *train* ***of*** evils. それとともに打続く弊害をもたらす. ‖ a *train* ***of*** followers 多数の従者.

train, *v*. ならす, 養成する, 教育する.

M ***adequately*** *trained* in business 十分実業の教育を受けて. ¶persons not ***carefully*** *trained* in the use of the language 言葉使いをよく仕込まれていない人々. ¶***highly*** *trained* officers りっぱに訓練された将校. ¶***professionally*** *trained* personnel 練達の職員. ¶those who are not ***technically*** *trained* 技術を仕込まれていない人々. ¶be ***well*** *trained* in indoor sports 室内競技に熟達している.

M^2 The shot *trained* ***off***. 弾丸がはずれた. ¶*train* ***up*** (=bring up) a person 人を薫陶する.

P *train* her ***as*** a nurse 彼女を看護婦に仕込む. ¶His father's desire was to *train* him ***for*** the diplomatic service. 彼の父の念願は彼を外交官に仕込むことであった. ‖ *train* youth ***for*** the right use of leisure 余暇の善用を青年に教える. ¶*trained* ***in*** law (psychology, scientific method) 法律(など)を学んだ ‖ men and women *trained* ***in*** universities 大学出身の男女. ¶He *trained* her ***into*** a charming woman. 彼は愛きょうのある女に彼女を育て上げた. ¶*train* a person ***to*** a trade or a profession 商売または知能職業に人を仕込む. 【類】 *trained* ***to*** the legal profession (法律家).

trainee, *n*. 練習生.

Q^2 an *on-job trainee* 現職の研習生. ¶a ***swimming*** *trainee* 水泳練習生.

O a coach and his *trainees* コーチとその訓練生徒(選手など).

trainer, *n*. 訓練士.

Q^2 a ***dog*** (***lion, tiger***) *trainer* 犬(など)の訓練士. ¶a ***horse*** *trainer* 調教師.

training, *n*. 訓練, 修業, 教育.

V ***conduct*** the *training* of... =train ... ...の訓練をする. ¶He has ***had*** no college *training*. 彼は大学出ではない. ¶***impart*** a sound moral *training* 健全な道徳教育を施す. ¶***possess*** a specialist *training* in the subject その問題に関して専門的な教育を受けている. ¶the fine *training* they have ***received*** in their native land 彼らが故国で受けたりっぱな訓練. ¶***require*** a special *training* 特別の訓練を要する. ¶***secure*** *training* in ... ...の訓練を受ける. ¶***take*** such *training* そうした訓練を受ける. ¶***undergo*** a special *training* for this purpose この目的で特別の訓練を受ける. 【類】 ***undergo*** a special *training* in English pronunciation.

Q have no ***academic*** *training* 学校教育を受けていない. ¶He has had ***American*** *training* 彼は米国仕込みの教育を受けている. ¶***athletic*** *training* 競技の訓練. ¶a man who has no ***classical*** *training* 古典の教育を受けていない人. ¶The school features ***domestic*** *training*. その学校は家庭的教育を特徴とする. ¶Language study is a ***fine*** *training* for the intellect. 語学研究はよい頭の訓練になる. ¶***foreign*** *training* 外国で受けた教育. ¶a ***full-fledged*** *training* 本格の修業. ¶it is ***good*** *training* to visit a mill 工場見学はよい参考になる ‖ persons of ***good*** *training* よく仕込まれた人々. ¶those who lack a ***grammatical*** *training* 文法教育を受けていない人々. ¶***intellectual*** *training* 知的教育. ¶***intensive*** *training* 猛教育. ¶his ***legal*** *training* 彼の法律教育. ¶***manual*** *training* 手工. ¶***mental*** *training* 頭脳訓練. ¶***military*** *training* in schools 学校における軍事教練. ¶a ***modern*** *training* for the Chinese artisan 中国の工人に対する近代教育. ¶persons with ***music[al]*** *training*. 音楽の素養のある人々. ¶His ***old journalistic*** *training* was called into play. 彼が昔新聞記者をやった経験が役に立った. ¶It is a physical straining: not ***physical*** *training*. それは身体の過労であって身体の鍛練ではない. ¶by reason of their ***poor*** *training* in the practical use of English 英語の実用的訓練が貧弱であるために. ¶***prenatal*** *training* 生れない前の教育; 胎教. ¶***professional*** *training* 職業教育. ¶a ***regular*** *training* 規則正しい訓練. ¶***specialized*** *training* 専門教育. ¶***theoretical*** *training* 理論上の教育. ¶have a ***thorough*** *training* in phonetics 発音学上の十分な訓練を受けている. ¶The study of grammar is a ***valuable mental*** *training*. 文法の研究はりっぱな頭の訓練になる. ¶***vocational*** *training* 職業教育. ¶go abroad for a ***wider*** *training* in the subject one hopes to teach 自分が教えようとする学科を一層拡充するために外国に留学する.

Q^2 ***anti-gas*** *training* 毒ガス処置演習. ¶***body*** *training* 身体の訓練. ¶***character*** *training* 人格陶冶(ﾔ). ¶***citizenship*** *training* 市民教育. ¶***cold-season*** *training* 寒げい古. ¶an engineer with ***college*** *training* 大学出の技術者. ¶***field*** *training* 野外教練. ¶***flight*** (=flying) *training* 飛行訓練. ¶***ground*** *training* 地上訓練. ¶the ***home*** *training* of children 子供の家庭教育. ¶***in-service*** *training* 現職教育, 研修制度. ¶a doctrine of ***language*** *training* 語学訓練の一学説. ¶persons with ***law*** *training* 法律教育を受けた人々. ¶***mind*** *training* 精神教育. ¶***on-job*** (=***intra-service***) *training* 現職教育. ¶his ***Oxford*** *training* 彼がオクスフォード大学で受けた教育. ¶***personality*** *training* 個性陶冶. ¶receive one's ***school*** *training* under ... ...のもとで学校教育を受ける ‖ have not much formal ***school*** *training* 正式の学校教育を余り受けていない. ¶the ***shipboard*** *training* of marines 海員の船上訓練. ¶***skill*** (=***talent***) *training* 技術育成. ¶***teacher*** *training* 教員教育. ¶***trade*** *training* 手職の訓練. ¶a man of ***university*** *training*=a university man 大学出身者.

P the study of language ***as*** a *training* for the mind 頭脳訓練としての言語の研究. ¶improved ***by*** *training* 訓練によって改善された. ¶The volunteers are ***in*** *training*. その志願兵たちは教練中である. ‖ the Oxford crew ***in*** *training* for the boat race ボート競そうのために練習中のオクスフォード乗組員. ¶go ***into*** *training* 練習する. ¶Reservists are at present ***under*** *training*. 予備兵は目下訓練を受けている. ¶***without*** college *training* 大学教育なしに.

P^2 *training* ***for*** homemaking 花嫁教育 ‖ *training* ***for*** the scholastic profession 教職教育. ¶a *training* ***in*** the use of reference books 参考書使用上の訓練 ‖ a *training* ***in*** diplomacy 外交上の訓練.

training-ground, *n*. 養成所.

P the university ***as*** a *training-ground* for businessmen 実業家の養成所としての大学.

P^2 a *training-ground* ***in*** crime 罪悪の温床.

trainman, *n*. 《米》 列車乗務員.

V Two *trainmen* were ***killed*** and six passengers more or less severely injured in the wreck. その事故で二人の乗務員が死に六人の旅客が重軽傷を負った.

traintime, *n*. 列車時刻.

P He stayed ***until*** almost *traintime*. 彼はほとんど列車出発の時間までいた.

trait, *n*. 特性, 特色.

V ***have*** so many *traits* in common with ... ...と国民性の似通った所が多々ある. ¶He has ***inherited*** this ancestral *trait*. 彼はこの祖先の特性を受継いでいる.

Q an ***acquired*** *trait* 獲得形質. ¶a ***British*** *trait* 英国人の特性 (haughty reserve など). ¶Enthusiasm is a ***conspicuous*** *trait* in him. 熱心は彼の目立った特性である. ¶***desirable*** *traits* 好もしい特性 (courage, love of fair play, common sense など). ¶a ***disagreeable*** *trait* of some people

ある人々の不愉快な特性. ¶have good traits [人柄に]いい所がある. ¶In the family runs a hereditary trait. その家には一つの遺伝的特性がある. ¶human traits in the monkey さるのもつ人間的特性. ¶marked traits in Mr. T as psychologist 心理学者としてのT氏の著しい特色. ¶a national trait 国民性の一つ. ¶a normal and universal trait of human nature 人性の正常にして普遍的な特色. ¶physical traits 形態上の特色. ¶The sense of beauty is one of the strongest racial traits of the Japanese. 美の鑑賞力が日本人の持つ最も強い人種的特色の一つである.

Q^2 democratic character traits 民主的性格の諸特性. ¶self-ratings of personality traits 個性の自己評価.

P longevity as a family trait 家族的特徴としての長寿.

P^2 The leading traits in the character of Dr. Webster were enterprise, self-reliance, and indomitable persistence. ウェブスター博士の品性における主な特色は進取・独力独歩・及び不屈不とうの忍耐であった.

traitor, *n.* 謀反人.

V We have a traitor among us. われわれの中に裏切り者がいる. ¶turn traitor 謀反人になる.

Q a rank traitor 大反逆者.

P^2 a traitor to his office of trust 自己の任務をはずかしめるもの ‖ a traitor to one's country (party) 国(など)を売るもの.

tram[car], *n.* 《英》市街電車.

V hail a tramcar 電車を呼び止める. ¶take a tramcar 電車に乗る.

Q an electric tramcar 市街電車. ☞ a tram[car]=《米》a streetcar, a trolley [car]. ¶municipal trams 市電. ¶a suburban tram 郊外電車.

P go by tram=tram it 電車で行く. ¶seats in the tramcar 電車の座席 ‖ go in a tram 電車で行く. ¶take a ride on a tramcar 電車に乗る.

trammel, *n. pl.* 束縛.

V cast off trammels 束縛を脱する.

tramp, *n.* 徒歩旅行; 浮浪者; 不定期船.

V make (take) a tramp 徒歩旅行をする.

V^2 The poor old tramp plods along. かわいそうにあの年とった放浪者がとぼとぼ歩いて行く.

Q take a long tramp to ... ...へ長い道を徒歩で行く. ¶a professional tramp 常習的ルンペン. ¶The policeman comes along with the slow, swinging tramp of the night patrol, his lantern in his belt. 巡査が腰にランプを下げてゆるやかに体をゆるがしながら夜回りにやって来る.

Q^2 a shop tramp ひやかしの客.

P a haunt of tramps 浮浪人の巣くつ. ¶go on a tramp 不定期船で行く.

tramp, *v.* 踏みつける; 放浪する, 《俗》てくる.

M tramp down 踏みつぶす. ¶tramp up and down あちこち歩き回る. ¶hear heavy steps tramping upward (downward) のぼってくる(など)重い足どりが聞える.

Q Let's tramp it. てくって行こう.

P tramp about ... ...のあたりをさまよう. ¶tramp from ... to ... ...から...までてくる.

tramping, *n.* 散歩.

V enjoy tramping 散歩がすきだ.

trample, *v.* 踏み付ける; 無視する.

M^2 trample down 踏みにじる. 【類】trample [down] one's feelings.

P trample on the right of personal liberty 個人の自由を踏みにじる ‖ Don't trample on the flowers. 花を踏付けるな. ¶trample over one another お互を侮る. ¶he was trampled to death by ... 彼は...に踏殺された ‖ trample under foot a portrait of Christ キリストの肖像を踏付ける ‖ trample under feet 足下に踏みにじる. ¶trample upon the rights of ... ...の権利を踏みにじる.

trampling, *n.* 踏むこと.

Q public trampling of the Christian cross 絵踏み.

tram-rider, *n.* 電車に乗る人.

Q a constant tram-rider 電車常用者.

tramway, *n.* 《英》軌道, 市街鉄道.

Q an electric tramway 電気軌道. ☞ tramway=《米》street railway.

Q^2 cable tramway 架線式電車. ¶a horse tramway 馬車鉄道. ¶wire tramway 架線式電車. ¶an aerial or wire-rope tramway 懸垂式あるいは架線式電車.

P it can be reached by a very short journey by steam tramway from ... それは...から汽車でごくわずかな時間で行ける.

trance, *n.* 夢幻, こん睡.

Q poetic trance 詩的夢幻.

P awaken from trance こん睡からさめて. ¶He is in a trance. 彼はこん睡状態にある. ¶fall into trance こん睡状態になる.

P^2 a trance of delight 夢中の歓喜(こうこつ).

tranquil[l]ity, *n.* 平安, 平和; 平静.

V disturb the tranquillity of the night 夜の静寂を破る. ¶establish tranquillity 平和を建設する. ¶mar international tranquillity 国際的平和を害する. ¶recover one's tranquility 平静をとり戻す. ¶restore tranquillity to Europe ヨーロッパに平和を回復する.

Q national tranquillity 国家安康. ¶a disturbance of social tranquillity and good order 社会の平和及び秩序の混乱.

P in perfect tranquillity (=calmness) 全く平穏に; 落ち着き払って.

transact, *v.* 取引する.

P transact [business] with a person 人と取引をする. 【類】transact with the enemy for truce.

transaction, *n.* 取引; 処理; *pl.* 報告.

V carry on transations 取引する. ¶carry out common transactions of life 日常の人事を行う. ¶close a transaction 取引を終結する. ¶complete the transaction 取引を完了する. ¶facilitate the transaction between ... ...間の商取引を容易にする. ¶finance transactions 取引に対して金を出す. ¶handle all commercial banking transactions あらゆる商業銀行事務を取扱う. ¶have transaction with ... ...と取引をしている. ¶perform business transaction 商取引をする. ¶stop further financial transactions with ... ...とこの上の財政上の取引を停止する.

Q "A bargain," says the dictionary, "is an advantageous transaction."「bargain とは有利の取引」と辞書にある. ¶a delicate transaction 微妙な処理. ¶enormous transactions 巨額の取引. ¶extensive transaction 広範囲にわたる取引. ¶stop all further financial transactions with ... 今後...との金銭上の取引を一切やめる. ¶handy transaction of business 事務の簡略. ¶an illegal transaction やみ取引. ¶There have been a few important transactions. 二三の重要な取引が行われた. ¶insignificant transactions わずかな取引. ¶a large transaction 大取引. ¶very limited transactions はなはだ小口な取引. ¶a maritime transaction 海上取引. ¶moderate transactions 相当の分量の取引. ¶have no (small, large) transactions with ... ...と全く取引をしない(少ししている, 大いにしている). 【類】No transactions whatever to report. / No transactions in coal have taken place. ¶be involved (=mixed up) in shady transactions やみ取引の巻添えを食う. ¶speculative transactions 投機取引.

Q^2 through a barter transaction 物々交換取引によって. ¶the ratio of black-market transactions to legal sales in commodities 物資のやみ取引と合法的販売との割合. ¶as part of a business transaction 商取引の一部として. ¶a cash transaction 現金取引. ¶a foreign trade transaction 外国貿易の取引. ¶a trade transaction 商業取引.

P He lost money by the transaction. 彼はその取引で損をした. ¶He lost over the transaction some £60. 彼はその取引で六十ポンドばかり損をした. ¶the parties to a transaction 取引の当事者.

P^2 the transactions of the society その協会の会報. ¶transactions on the exchange 株式取引所の取引. ¶do business transactions with a person 人との商取引をする.

transcendent, *a.* 超越した.

P be transcendent of all earthly (=worldly) fame 浮世の名声に超然としている. ¶be transcendent of (=transcend) all experience and imaginations あらゆる経験や想像を越えている.

transcribe, *v.* 写す, 謄写する.

M transcribe it entire[ly] それを全部写す.

transcript, *n.* 写し, 写本.

Q printed in phonetic transcript 発音記号で印刷した.

P^2 a transcript of a middle school record 中学校の成績写し.

transcription, *n.* 転写, 謄写.

Q in phonetic[al] transcription 発音記号で.

transfer, *n.* 乗換; 乗換券; 転任.

V advise her transfer to a hospital 彼女の入院を勧める. ¶there you can readily make the transfer to ... そこですぐに...へ乗換えができる. ¶This necessitated his immediate transfer to the hospital. このため彼が早速入院することが必要であった. ¶take a transfer 乗換券を受取る.

Q an ignominious transfer [栄転の反対]左遷. ¶tele-

graphic or cable *transfers* of money to or from ... ...へ, または...から電信または海外電報による金の振替.

Q² a ***streetcar*** *transfer* 市電乗換券.

P open the books ***for*** *transfer* [株の]名義書換えをする ‖ ask ***for*** a *transfer* 乗換券を請求する.

P² the *transfer* ***from*** sail ***to*** steam 帆船から蒸汽船への転換. ¶*transfer* ***of*** jurisdiction 〖法〗移管.

transfer, *v.* 乗換える, 移す, 譲渡する.

P *transfer* ***at*** ... to a car going south ...で南方行きの電車に乗換える. ¶*transfer* art treasures ***from*** one's keeping ***into*** the hands of the nation 貴重美術品を自己の所有から国家の保管に移す(政府に献納する). ¶*transferred* ***from*** one position (=place) ***to*** another ある地位から他の地位に移されて. 【類】The Shogunate was *transferred* ***to*** the Fujiwara in 1219. ‖ *transfer* ***from*** a streetcar ***to*** a bus 電車からバスに乗換える. ¶*transfer* the scenic spot ***to*** the canvas その景色を油絵に描く ‖ He was *transferred* ***to*** other teachers. 彼は他の先生の手に移された. ‖ *transfer* ***to*** surface cars 路面電車に乗換える. 【類】Here the traveller *transfers* ***to*** a motor boat which takes him to his hotel. / Second or third class passengers may *transfer* ***to*** first or second class on payment of 3s. 6d. each way. / Please have this trunk *transferred* (転送) ***to*** the Union Station. ‖ *transfer* it ***to*** the account of ... それを...の勘定に繰入れる ‖ be *transferred* ***to*** the credit of ... ...の貸方に

transfigure, *v.* 形を変える. └繰入れる.

P *transfigured* ***with*** delight うれしさのあまり相好をくず

transfix, *v.* 突き通す; 金縛りにする. └して.

P *transfix* a person ***to*** the ground 人を大地に突き刺す. ¶*transfixed* ***with*** a spear やりで突き通されて ‖ *transfixed* ***with*** amazement (wonder) 仰天(驚き)のあまり棒立になっ

transform, *v.* 変形する. └て.

M be ***completely*** *transformed* 面目を一新する. ¶*transform* oneself ***temporarily*** into ... 一時...に化ける.

M² *transform* ***up*** (***down***) 電圧量を上(下)げる.

P A beard *transformed* him ***beyond*** recognition. ひげが生えたので彼は見違えるように変った. ¶*transform* one ***from*** an opponent ***into*** an ally 敵を味方に引入れる. ¶He was *transformed* ***into*** another man. 彼は別人のように変った. ¶a barn *transformed* ***into*** a garage 自動車々庫に変造した納屋. ¶Grubs *transform* ***to*** beetles. 地虫は甲虫に化

transformation, *n.* 変化. └ける.

V ***undergo*** an economic and political *transformation* 経済的並びに政治的の変化を受ける ‖ Public opinion has ***undergone*** a complete *transformation*. 世論が一変した.

Q² a ***Jekyll-to-Hyde*** *transformation* ジーキルがハイドに変るような変化. ¶***thought*** *transformation* 思想の変化.

transformer, *n.* 変圧器(トランス).

Q a ***step-up*** *transformer* 逓(て)昇変圧器.

Q² a ***power*** *transformer* 《電》トランス(変圧器). ¶a ***single-phase*** *transformer* 単相変圧器.

transfusion, *n.* 輸血.

Q² an apparatus for ***blood*** *tranfusion* 輸血装置.

transgress, *v.* 破る, 犯す, そむく.

P *transgress* ***against*** the rules respecting ... ...に関する規則に違犯する ‖ *transgress* ***against*** the rules of order 規律

transgression, *n.* 違犯, 違背. └にそむく.

Q a ***bold*** *transgression* 大胆な違犯. ¶Adultery, in the husband a ***pardonable*** *trangression*, is in the wife an overwhelming sin committed against family life. 夫の場合では許さるべき不義も妻の場合では家庭生活を破壊する大

transient, *n.* 《米》[ホテルの]短期の客. └罪である.

P a hotel ***for*** *transients* (=transients guests) 短期の客用ホテル. 【類】The hotel offers different rates ***for*** transients and residents (長期の客).

transit, *n.* 通過, 通行; 運搬.

Q ***cheap*** and ***rapid*** *transit* 安価で迅速な輸送. ¶the application of steam to ***marine*** *transit* 蒸汽の海運への応用. ¶owing to the introduction of ***rapid*** *transit* 交通の便がよくなったので. ¶***speedy*** *transit* 迅速な交通.

Q² ***high-speed*** *transit* 高速度交通.

P theft ***in*** *transit* 運送途中の盗難(引き抜きなど) ‖ damage suffered ***in*** *transit* 輸送中に受けた破損 ‖ The letter was nearly a month ***in*** *transit*. その手紙は約一カ月もかかった.

transit, *v.* 運搬する.

P *transit* it ***to*** another vessel それを他の船に積み換える.

transition, *n.* 移動, 変遷; 過渡.

V It ***makes*** the *transition* from the old conception to the new. それは古い概念から新しい概念への過渡期を画している.

Q an ***abrupt*** *transition* 突然の転換. ¶From ... to ... is an ***easy*** *transition*. ...から...へは推移が容易である. ¶pass into the stage of ... by ***insensible*** *transitions* 気づかないほどに徐々として...時代に移って行く. ¶a ***sudden*** *transi-*

P Japan ***in*** *transition* 過渡期の日本. └*tion* 激しい変遷.

P² Japan's sudden *transition* ***from*** medievalism ***to*** modernity 日本の中世紀体制から現代への飛躍的変遷. ¶swift *transitions* ***to*** other phases 他の状態への迅速な変転. 【類】the *transition* ***to*** full autonomy (完全自治). ¶a *transition* ***toward*** a new outlook on the world 世界に対する新しい

translate, *v.* 翻訳する. └見方への進展.

M ***admirably*** *translated* りっぱに翻訳されて. ¶*translating* ***back*** literally into Japanese idiom we reach his meaning which is that ... 逆に日本の語法に訳して見ると彼の言わんと欲する所がつかめるが, それは...である. ¶*translate* ***closely*** 綿密に翻訳する. ¶Poetry does not *translate* ***easily***. 詩の翻訳はむずかしい. ¶*translated* ***easily*** and ***idiomatically*** やさしくくだけた訳の. ¶***faithfully*** *translate* 忠実に翻訳する. ¶*translate* ***freely*** 自由訳にする. ¶***incorrectly*** *translated* 誤訳した. ¶*translate* ***literally*** (=word for word), it would read "..." 逐語訳にするとそれは...となる. ¶might be ***loosely*** *translated* "..." 意訳すると「...」ということになろう. ¶*translate* ***mechanically*** (=literally) 直訳する.

P Man's happiness is *translated* ***as*** something of luck, wealth and vitality combined. 人間の幸福は運, 富及び精力の合成と解される. ¶it is customary to *translate* ... ***by*** ... ...は普通...と訳すことになっている. ¶*translate* it ***by*** the word ... ...という言葉でそれを翻訳する. ¶*translated* ***from*** the German of Goethe ***by*** ... ...によってゲーテのドイツ語から翻訳された. 【類】a poem *translated* ***from*** English ***into*** Japanese. ¶the Japanese expression "..." is *translated* ***in*** English ***by*** ... 日本語の「...」という言葉は英語に訳すと...となる ‖ Japanese poems *translated* ***in*** English verse 英語の韻文に訳された日本の歌. ‖ the same idea *translated* ***in*** terms of art 芸術で表現された同じ思想. ¶*translate* it ***into*** Japanese それを日本語に翻訳する. 【類】*translated* ***into*** modern terms, it means that ... / The Bible has been *translated* ***into*** all tongues. / be *translated* ***into*** popular and understandable terms / 【類】captains of commerce who have *translated* their ideas ***into*** gold ‖ Tolerance depends on a sense of brotherhood *translated* ***into*** fact. 寛容は実現された同胞観念から起る. ‖ This is another dream of man *translated* ***into*** reality. これはまた実現された人間の夢想の一つである. ‖ *translated* ***into*** the language of reason 筋を立てて述べると ‖ *translate* it ***into*** deeds (=action) それを実行に移す. ‖ possibility *translated* ***into*** reality 実現化された可能性. 【類】a maximum benefit which should, in time, be *translated* ***into*** practice for the welfare of the country. ¶*translated* ***out of*** French ***into*** English フランス語から英語に翻訳された.

translation, *n.* 翻訳, 訳文.

V ***banish*** *translation* in English teaching 英語教授に翻訳を廃する. ¶This poem does not ***bear*** *translation*. この詩は訳されない. ¶***compare*** the *translation* with the original 翻訳を原文と比較する. ¶Her brother is now ***doing*** *translations* for a New York department store. 彼女の兄(弟)は今ニューヨークのあるデパートのために翻訳をやっている. ¶***make*** *translations* of a military nature 軍事関係の翻訳をやる ‖ ***make*** a rough *translation* into English 大体を英訳する. ¶the *translation* of the book has been ***performed*** by... その本の翻訳は...の手に成った. ¶An English *translation* is now being ***prepared***. その英語訳を目下準備中である. ¶The book has ***received*** *translation* into both English and Spanish. その本は英語及びスペイン語に翻訳された. ¶***translate*** a *translation* 重訳する. ¶***write*** good *translation* 巧みに翻訳する. ¶***undertake*** *translations* 翻訳を引受ける.

V² *Translations* of the book ***appeared*** in the chief European languages. その本の翻訳は主なヨーロッパの国語でできた.

Q an ***abridged*** *translation* 抄訳. ¶an ***anonymous*** *translation* 無名の翻訳. ¶an ***authorized*** *translation* [著者などから承認された]標準訳. ¶a ***close*** *translation* 直訳. ¶a ***complete*** *translation* of Hamlet ハムレットの全訳. ¶a ***correct*** *translation* 正しい訳. ¶***crude*** *translation* 生硬な訳. ¶an English *translation* of the Old Testament 旧約聖書の英訳. ¶an ***excellent*** *translation*, faithful in sense and spirit 意義と精神を忠実に移した名訳. ¶a ***faithful*** *translation* 忠実な訳. ¶A ***free*** *translation* is always more easy than a ***close*** *translation*. 自由訳はいつも精密訳より容易である. ¶a ***happy*** *translation* 適訳. ¶an ***idiomatic*** *translation* こなれた訳. ¶***incorrect*** *translation* 正しくない訳. ¶the nearest ***intelligible*** *translation* of it is ... それをできるだけ分かりやすく訳すと…となる. ¶a ***liberal*** (=free) *translation* 自由訳. ¶the ***literal*** (=***verbal***) *translation* of the name is ... その名を直訳すると…である. ¶a ***literal***, if not very ***graceful***, *translation* 余り優美ではない直訳的な翻訳. ¶a ***lucid*** *translation* 明快な翻訳. ¶a ***metrical*** *translation* 韻文訳. ¶an ***official*** *translation* of ... …の公式翻訳. ¶a ***rough***, though ***literal***, *translation* 逐語的だが粗雑な訳. ¶***second-hand*** *translation* 重訳. ¶***textual*** *translation* phrase by phrase 一句一句を追う原文の翻訳. ¶***unidiomatic*** *translations* 生硬な翻訳. ¶***unseen*** *translation* [学校の課題の]即席翻訳. ¶a ***verbal*** *translation* 逐語訳.

Q^2 ***English-verse*** *translation*. 英詩の翻訳. ¶a ***French*** *translation* of ... …の仏訳. ¶***prose*** *translation* 散文訳. ¶***sight*** *translation* [試験などの場合初めて見る文の]一覧翻訳. ¶A ***word for word*** *translation* of an idiom into another language generally makes nonsense. 慣用句を一語一語他国語に訳すと大抵無意味なものになる.

P ***in*** a *translation* done by ... …のやった翻訳中に. 【類】It will soon appear ***in*** a Japanese *translation*. ‖ it reads in *translation*:... それを翻訳すれば…. ¶He learned something of Chinese poetry ***through*** *translation*. 彼は翻訳を通じて漢詩を幾分知った.

P^2 an English *translation* ***by***…. …の英語訳. ¶a *translation* ***from*** the French of ... …のフランス語からの翻訳. ¶a *translation* ***near*** the original 原文に近い翻訳. ¶a *translation* ***of*** an article written by ... …の書いた論文の翻訳. 【類】The *translation* ***of*** the name of Anna May Wong (霜黄楊), the well-known Chinese film actress, is "Frosted Yellow Willow." / The *translation* ***of*** words and phrases was incorrectly made in a great many instances.

translator, *n.* 翻訳者.

V It may well ***defy*** the cleverest *translator*. それはいかに達者な翻訳者でもさじを投げるだろう.

Q a ***competent*** and ***conscientious*** *translator* 腕があって良心的な翻訳家. ¶It might well have baffled the ***deftest*** *translator*. それは老練の翻訳者も当惑しそうなことだ.

Q^2 a ***French*** *translator* 仏文からの翻訳者.

P^2 *translators* ***from*** the French フランス語からの翻訳家. ¶a *translator* ***into*** English 英語に翻訳する人.

transliteration, *n.* 写音.

Q ***Romanized*** *transliteration* ローマ字書き.

transmigration, *n.* 輪廻(りんね).

Q the dead freed from ***further*** *transmigration* of souls 輪廻から解放された死者たち.

transmission, *n.* 転送, 伝送.

Q ***electric*** *transmission* 電送. ¶***slow*** *transmission* of cablegrams in war time 戦時における海外電報の延着.

P The letter took more than a month ***in*** *transmission*. その手紙は一カ月以上かかって届いた. ‖ delayed ***in*** *transmission* 延着して. ¶*transmission* ***of*** news (a message) ニュース(など)の通報. ¶I entrusted him ***with*** its *transmission*. 私はその送達を彼に委任した.

P^2 *transmission* ***from*** father ***to*** son 父子相伝. ¶for *transmission* ***to*** ... …への伝送のため.

transmit, *v.* 送る, 伝達する.

M The message was ***incorrectly*** *transmitted*. その伝言は正しく伝えられなかった.

P *transmit* ***by*** wire 電報で送達する ‖ *transmit* money ***by*** radio 金を電信為替で送る. ¶*transmitted* ***from*** generation ***to*** generation 代々伝わった ‖ be *transmitted* ***from*** mouth ***to*** mouth それからそれへと伝わる ‖ *transmit* ***to*** an after age 後代に残す ‖ *transmit* a report ***to*** ... 報告を…に伝達する.

transmitter, *n.* 送(受)信器.

Q^2 a ***radio*** *transmitter* and receiver 無電送信機及び受信機. ¶use a ***relay*** *transmitter* 中継無電送信機を使用する. ¶place a ***television*** *transmitter* テレビ放送機を据えつける.

transmutation, *n.* 変形, 変化.

P^2 the *transmutation* ***of*** heat rays ***into*** luminous rays 熱光線の発光線への変化.

transmute, *v.* 変化する.

P be *transmuted* ***by*** one's imagination その想像で変化される. ¶*transmute* baser metals ***into*** gold 卑金属を金に変える.

transparency, *n.* 透明.

Q She was just from the bath, and her complexion had a ***soft, dewy*** *transparency*. 彼女は入浴直後であってその血色はほんのりとして露のような透明さを持っていた.

transparent, *a.* 透明の.

M^2 ***as*** *transparent* as air 空気のように透明な.

O window glass, *transparent* and opaque 透明のまたは不透明の窓ガラス.

transplant, *v.* 移植する.

P *transplant* people ***into***... 人々を…に移植する ‖ be *transplanted* ***into*** new soil 新しい土に移植する. ¶flowers *transplanted* ***to*** the garden 庭に移植した花.

transplanting, *n.* 移植.

V The tree will not ***bear*** *transplanting*. その木は移植にたえないだろう.

transport, *n.* 《英》輸送, 運搬; 輸送船; 有頂天.

V ***make*** *transport* to ... …へ輸送する.

Q a ***crowded*** and ***noisy*** *transport* 込合った騒々しい輸送船. ¶***marine*** *transport* 海上輸送 ¶***mechanical*** *transport* 機械的輸送. ¶***rural*** *transport* いなかの運送.

Q^2 work ***air*** *transport* 空輸を経営する ‖ Pan American Airways, world pioneer in international ***air*** *transport* 国際空輸の世界的先駆者である汎(パン)米航空会社. ¶***city*** *transport* 市内運送. ¶automobiles employed for pleasure driving, for ***goods*** *transport*, and for passenger traffic 遊乗用, 貨物運送用, 及び旅客輸送用自動車. ¶***inland*** *transport* 国内運送. ¶***land*** *transport* 陸運. ¶have ***motor*** *transport* 自動車輸送の装備がある. ¶the wonder and magic of modern ***ocean*** *transport* 近代海運の驚異と魔力. ¶an ***oil*** *transport* (=tanker) 油輸送船. ¶***overland*** *transport* 陸路輸送. ¶paralyze the ***rail*** *transport* of the whole country 全国の鉄道輸送を途絶させる. ¶***road*** *transport*= transport by road 道路による輸送. ¶a ***troop*** *transport* 軍隊輸送船. ¶***water*** *transport* 水運. ¶a ***400-passenger model*** *transport* 四百人船客型輸送船.

P ***in*** a *transport* of joy 喜びのあまり有頂天になって. ¶cheap means ***of*** *transport* 安価な輸送法.

transport, *v.* 輸送する; 有頂天にする.

P *transport* goods ***from*** ... ***to*** ... 品物を…から…へ輸送する. ¶*transported* ***to*** an imaginary world 身は想像の世界に移されて. ¶He was *transported* ***with*** joy. 彼は有頂天であった.

transportation, *n.* 《米》輸送; 運搬.

V The fruit (fish) will not ***bear*** *transportation* to any great distance. その果実(など)は余り遠い所への輸送はできないだろう. ¶***give*** free *transportation* to ... …への無賃輸送を許す. ¶*Transportation* will be ***made difficult*** in this state of weather. この天候では輸送が困難だろう. ¶we ***pay*** *transportation* to ... 当方で…までの旅費を持つ(遠方から使用人を雇う場合など). ¶***speed up*** *transportation* 輸送を迅速にする.

Q a system of ***cheap*** and ***rapid*** *transportation* 安価にして迅速な輸送の方法.

Q^2 ***ground*** (=***land***) *transportation* 地上輸送. ¶***ocean*** *transportation* 海上輸送. ¶combined ***rail and boat*** *transportation* 船車連絡輸送. ¶***railroad*** *transportation*=《英》 railway transport《米》鉄道輸送. ¶***street-car*** and ***bus*** *transportation* is functioning as usual 市電とバスがいつもの通り運転している. ¶***tricar*** *transportation* 三輪トラックによる輸送. ¶***water*** and ***land*** *transportation* 水陸上輸送. 【類】can choose ***water*** or ***rail*** *transportation*.

P^2 No convenience exists for *transportation* ***by*** railway or steamship. 鉄道または汽船による輸送の便は一切ない.

transpose, *v.* 置きかえる, 位置を転倒する.

P *transpose* ***from*** one side ***to*** the other 一方から他方へ置き換える. ¶*transpose* Japanese dates ***into*** Western 日本年代を西洋年代に換える.

trap, *n.* わな; 策略.

V ***bail*** his *trap* well 彼の計略をうまく封じる. ¶***build*** a

trap わなをかける. ¶*lay traps* for the unwary わなをかけてうっかり者を落し入れる. ¶I *set* (=*placed*) a *trap* for the rat. 私はねずみのわなを掛けた. 「もの.
Q *a virtual trap* to get your money 銭取り主義のまやかし
Q² a *light trap* 誘が灯. ¶a *steel trap* 鉄わな(とらばさみ).
P The crafty villain was caught *in* his own *trap*. その悪知恵のある悪漢は自分のわなにひっかかった. 【類】catch mice *in* a *trap*. ¶fall *into* a *trap* わなに落ちる ‖ walk straight *into* a *trap* 真ともにわなにはまり込む. ¶get *out of* a *trap* わなからのがれる.
P² a *trap for* mice ねずみ落し.

trap, *v*. わなにかける.
P be *trapped in* a lie 化の皮をひんむかれる.

trap-door, *n*. はね板, 上げ戸.
P the *trap-door in* the ceiling 天井の揚げぶた.

trash, *n*. 《米》くず, ごみ; つまらぬ人(もの).
V *throw trash* on the street (floor) くずを通り(など)に投げる. ☞ごみの意の英語用法は rubbish.
Q Those books are *light trash*. それらの本は紙くず同然だ. ¶This novel is *mere trash*. この小説はまったくのだ作だ. ¶the *white trash* 白人のくず(やくざ).
P Broken bottles go with garbage and not *with trash*. びんのかけらは台所のごみの方に入れるべきで一般のごみに 「は入れない.

travail, *n*. 分べん.
P She is *in travail*. 彼女は産気づいている.

travel, *n*. 旅; *pl*. 旅行記.
V *advertise travel* in Japan 日本旅行を宣伝する. ¶*build up travel* to the Far East 極東への旅行を盛んにする. ¶*encourage* (=stimulate) tourist *travel* 観光旅行を奨励する. ¶*extend* one's *travels* to ... その旅行を…まで延長する. ¶*make* extensive *travels* 広く旅行する. ¶*promote travel* to Japan 日本への旅行を増進する. 【類】*promote travel* to the Pacific and to the Orient. ¶*publish* one's *travels* その旅行記を刊行する. ¶*stimulate travel* to Japan 日本への旅行を奨励する ‖ a useful means of *stimulating travel* 旅行奨励の効果的手段.
Q *care-free travel* のんきな旅. ¶*economical travel* 平民旅行. ¶May is one of the loveliest months of the year for *English travel*. 五月はイギリスの旅行には最も適した月の一つだ. ¶*foreign travel* 外国の旅. ¶a permit of *free travel* 無料乗車(船)の許可. ¶*Travel* is usually *heavy* between Paris and London. パリーロンドン間の旅行は通常ひん繁である. ¶*independent* and *associated travel* 個人並びに団体旅行, ¶*individual travel* 個人旅行. ¶taste for *rapid travel* 快速旅行の趣味. ¶in those days when *travel* was *slow* and *difficult* 旅行が緩慢で困難な時代において. ¶*vertical travel* by elevators and escalators エレベーターやエスカレーターによる上下の移動. ¶make *world-wide travels* 世界を遍歴する.
Q² time gained by *air travel* 空中旅行で節約し得た時間 ‖ luxurious *air travel* ぜいたくな空の旅. ¶*camel travel* らくだの旅. ¶*business travel* 商売上の旅行. ¶*ground travel* [空中に対する]地上旅行. ¶*holiday travel* 休日の旅行. ¶*horseback travel* 馬上旅行. ¶*inter-city bus travel* 都市連絡のバス旅行. ¶*luxury travel* ぜいたく旅行. ¶foreign *motor travel* 自動車による外国旅行. ¶*ocean travel* 大洋航行. ¶*overseas travel* 外国旅行. ¶*party travel* 団体旅行. ¶*passenger travel* across the Atlantic [乗客としての]大西洋横断旅行. ¶The storm made *plane travel* impossible. 暴風雨のため飛行機旅行ができなかった. ¶*railway* (=*train*) *travel* 汽車旅行. ¶*sea* and *air travel* 海と空の旅. ¶*space travel* 宇宙旅行. ¶arrange *study travel* for high school and college students 高等学校及び大学生のための修学旅行の準備をする. ¶encourage (=promote) *tourist travel* to Japan 日本への観光旅行を促進す る. ¶*water* (*land*) *travel* 水上(陸上)旅行. ¶*world travel* 世界旅行.
P *during* one's *travels* in ... その…旅行中. ¶be back *from* one's *travels* 旅行から帰っている. ¶the importance *of travel* abroad 海外旅行の重要性 ‖ a book *of travels* 旅行記. ¶go (=set out) *on* one's *travels* その旅行に出掛ける.
P² *travel for* pleasure (=culture) 遊覧(教養)のための旅行. ¶extensive *travel in* the East 東洋における大旅行 ‖ *travel in* Japan 日本旅行. ¶free *travel on* the railways 無賃汽車旅行. ¶during his *travels through* Japan 彼の日本旅行中. ¶the promotion of *travel to* Japan 日本旅行の奨励.

travel, *v*. 旅行する, 進行する.
M *travel abroad* 海外へ旅行する. ¶*travel afoot* 徒歩で旅行する. ¶*travel away* from home 郷里から旅に出る. ¶*travel express* 急ぎの旅をする. ¶*travel extensively* in Europe ヨーロッパを広く旅行する. ¶Your boy is too old to *travel free* by rail. あなたの男のお子さんは年が上ですから無賃では汽車に乗れません. ¶*travel home* 旅から帰る. ¶*travel horizontally* (*vertically*) 横の(縦すなわち登山)旅行をする. ¶*travel incognito* 匿名で旅を(微行)する. ¶*travel luxuriously* ぜいたくな旅をする. ¶*travel penniless* 一文なしで旅行する. ¶*travel safely, cheaply* and *easily* 安全に安直に気楽に旅をする. ¶News *travelled slowly* in those days. そのころはニュースの伝わるのはおそかった. ¶*travel south* (*west*) 南(など)方に旅行する. ¶*travel third-class* on steamers and trains 汽車・汽船は三等で旅行する. ¶He *traveled widely* in the eastern parts of the United States. 彼は合衆国の東部を広く旅行した. ¶He has *traveled widely* in Europe. 彼はヨーロッパを広く旅を 「した.
M² *travel along* 《俗》歩む(特に足早で).
P He spent some years *traveling about* France and Italy. 彼はフランス及びイタリアをあちこち数年旅をして暮した. ¶*travel across* the continent 大陸横断旅行をする. ¶*travel around* the world 世界一周の旅行をする. ¶light *travels at* the rate of ... 光線は…の速度で進む. ¶*travel by* land (water, train) 陸路(など)で旅行する. 【類】*travel by* railroad and steamer / *travel* [by] the Midland Railway / *travel by* rail (boat) / *travel by* water. ¶*travel for* one's pleasure (health, amusement, recreation) 気晴らし(など)のために旅行する. ¶*travel from* one's birth-place to one's new home 生れ故郷から新しく家庭を持った所へ移る. 【類】A salesman *travels from* place to place for his firm. ¶*travel in* Egypt エジプトを旅する ‖ *travel in* a first-class carriage (=travel 1st) 一等で旅行する. 【類】*travel in* the second class (=second) ‖ *travel in* the cars 電車で旅行する ‖ *travel in* state 公式の旅行をする ‖ *travel in* pilgrim garb 巡礼姿で旅をする. ¶*travel into* other countries 他国へ旅行する. ¶Nothing *travels like* light. 光ほど早く進行するものはない. ¶Other critics *traveled on* the same road. 他の批評家も同じことを言った. ‖ *travel on* a half ticket (pass) 半切符(など)で旅行する ‖ *travel on* business 用事で旅する ‖ *travel on* a railroad (=the train *or* by rail) 汽車で旅行する. 【類】I will do anything I can to influence my friends to *travel on* your line. / *travel on* the Great Central's system. ¶it might be said that I am *traveling out of* my province in making remarks on ... …についてとやかく言うのは脱線だと言う人もあろう ‖ *travel out of* a country 国外へ旅行する. ¶*travel over* many lands 諸国を旅行する. ¶*travel through* a country ある国を遍歴する. ¶He has *travelled throughout* France. 彼はフランスをくまなく旅行した. ¶*travel to* all part of the world 世界中を旅行する. 【類】*travel to* Europe (a foreign country) ‖ *travel to* eternity by the alcohol route 酒で死ぬ ‖ *travel under* our own power 自力(徒歩)で旅行する ‖ *travel under* an assumed name 変名で旅行する. ¶*travel upon* ice 氷上を進む. ¶*travel with* pack-horses だ馬に乗って旅をする ‖ *travel with* a person 人とともに旅をする ‖ *travel with* the sun (=from west to east, eastward) [西から東へ]太陽とともに行く ‖ You feel confident and secure when you *travel with* American Express Travelers Cheques. 米国特別旅行者小切手をもって旅行すると気丈夫で安心だ.

travel[l]er, *n*. 旅行者. 「す(引付ける).
V *bring travellers* to our shores 旅行者をわが国にもたら
Q a *commercial travellers* =《米》a traveling salesman 注文取り. ¶*continental travelers* 大陸旅行者. ¶an *extensive traveler* 大旅行家. ¶a *famous traveler* 有名な旅行家. ¶"*fireside travellers*" [家にいて旅行記などを読んでいる]「炉辺の旅行家」. ¶*habitual* (=experienced) *traveller* 旅慣れた人. ¶*home-returning travelers* 帰国途中の旅行者. ¶an *inexperienced traveler* 旅慣れない人. ¶*intending travelers* 旅行をもくろんでいる人々. ¶an *international traveler* 国際旅行者. ¶*leisurely travelers* ゆっくりした旅人. ¶a *pedestrian traveler* 徒歩旅行家. ¶a *prospective traveler* in Europe ヨーロッパ旅行を考えている人. ¶"The cheapest place in the world is Antiochus, in Syria,"

says a ***returned traveler***. 旅から帰った人が「世界中で一番物の安価な所はシリアのアンテオカスだ」と言っている. ¶***scientific*** *travelers* 科学研究の旅行者. ¶***sophisticated*** *travelers* 経験を積んだ旅行家. ¶a ***veteran*** *traveler* 旅行の経験家.

Q^2 an ***air*** *traveler* 空路旅行者. ¶an ***air line*** *traveler* 航空による旅行者. ¶a ***fellow*** *traveler* 仲間の旅行者; [共産党などの]シンパ. ¶a ***sight-seeing*** *traveler*=a traveler for sightseeing 観光旅行者. ¶a ***space*** *traveler* 宇宙旅行者. ¶a ***world*** [***circle***] *traveler* 世界漫遊者.

P^2 a *traveler* ***by*** sea 海の旅行者. ¶*travelers* ***from*** abroad 海外からの旅行者たち.

travel[l]ing, 旅行.

V ***do*** *traveling* in the East 東洋の旅行をする.

Q ***incognito*** *traveling* 微行. ¶***quick*** *traveling* 迅速な旅行.

Q^2 ***holiday*** *travelling*=《米》vacationing 休暇旅行.

P^2 *traveling* ***by*** rail (=train) 汽車旅行. ¶In years past he had much *traveling* ***in*** Europe. 彼は今まで随分ヨーロッパを旅行した. ¶*traveling* ***to*** or ***from*** work 勤めの往復.

traverse, *v*. 横切る, 横断する.

M He *traversed* ***alone*** the whole continent of Africa from east to west. 彼は単身アフリカ大陸を東から西へ横断した.

P The district is *traversed* ***by*** several railroads. その地方は数条の鉄路が横断している. …

O *traverse* the desert (ocean, mountains) さばく(など)を横断する.

tray, *n*. 盆.

Q^2 an ***ash*** *tray* 灰ざら. ¶a ***cigarette*** *tray* たばこ盆. ¶bring a person his dinner ***on*** a *tray* ごちそうを盆にのせて持って来る.

treacherous, *a*. 裏切る, 二心のある.

P *treacherous* ***to*** … …に対して二の心ある.

treachery, *n*. 反逆, 裏切り.

V ***scent out*** *treachery* 裏切りを感ずく. ¶little ***suspecting*** any *treachery* 裏切られたとは少しも気がつかずに.

Q fall a victim to one's ***base*** *treachery* その卑劣な変節の犠牲になる. ¶***cloven-footed*** *treachery* 邪悪な二心. ¶***lurking*** *treachery* ひそかに行動する反逆.

P ***by*** *treachery* 悪計によって.

P^2 *treachery* ***to*** the democratic cause 民主主義への反逆.

tread, *n*. 踏歩き, 歩きぶり; 足音.

V I ***recognized*** his heavy *tread*. 私には彼の重い足音が分かった.

Q approach with ***cautious*** *tread* 抜き足差し足で近寄る. ¶a ***firm*** *tread* しっかりした足どり. ¶***gingerly*** *tread* 抜き足差し足. ¶a ***heavy*** (***light***) *tread* 重(軽)い足どり. ¶a ***soft*** *tread* そっと歩く足どり. ¶with ***soundless*** (=***noiseless***) *tread* 音を立てずに歩いて.

Q^2 with ***velvet*** *tread* やわらかな足どりで.

P The ground shook ***under*** his heavy *tread*. 地面が彼の重い足どりのために揺れた.

tread, *v*. 踏む, 踏付ける.

M *tread* ***gingerly*** on the tips of their toes (=on tiptoe) 足のつま先でこわごわ歩く. ¶*tread* ***heavily*** 重い足どりで歩く. ¶*tread* ***lightly*** 浮き浮き歩く. ¶*tread* ***out*** a fire 火を踏み消す. ‖ *tread* ***out*** the gut of a frog かえるの内臓を踏んで出す. 【類】The plants were *trodden* ***out*** by wild *animals*. ¶*tread* ***warily*** on a slippery ground すべらないように気を付けて歩く.

P *tread* the room ***from*** end ***to*** end へやの端から端へ歩いて行く. ¶*tread* a nail ***into*** one's foot くぎを踏み抜く. ¶*tread* ***on*** one's food 人の足を踏む ‖ The snow had been *trodden* ***into*** a disgusting slush everywhere. 雪が踏みにじられて至る所いやなぬかるみになっていた. ¶*tread* ***on*** air 心うきうきする ‖ *tread* ***on*** thin ice 薄氷を踏む; [比ゆ的に]危険を冒す ‖ *tread* ***on*** dangerous ground 危険な場所に足を入れる ‖ for fear of *treading* ***on*** somebody's corns 差しさわりがあるといけないから ‖ *tread* ***on*** the neck of … …を圧制する ‖ *Tread* ***on*** a worm, and it will turn. 裸虫を踏むと向って来る(一寸の虫にも五分の魂). ¶*trodden* ***under*** foot ***by*** … …に踏付けられて. ¶*treading* close ***upon*** the heel of … …とかかとを接して. ¶*tread* … ***with*** the feet …を足で踏む.

treason, *n*. 謀叛(むほん), 反逆.

V ***plot*** *treason* 反乱を企てる.

Q ***heinous*** *treason* 大反逆.

P^2 guilty of high *treason* ***against*** the nation 国家に対し反逆罪を犯した.

treasure, *n*. 財宝, 宝物; 宝(のような人).

V ***amass*** great *treasures* 多大な財貨を積む. ¶The Kaizuka at Omori was the first shell mound in Japan to ***yield up*** its *treasures* to scientific research. 大森の貝塚はその貴重埋蔵物が科学的に研究された日本における最初のものであった.

Q ***buried*** *treasures* 埋没した宝. ¶one's ***cherished*** *treasure* 秘蔵する宝物. ¶***literary*** *treasures* 貴重な文献. ¶He is a ***living*** *treasure*. 貴重な人物だ. ¶***national*** *treasures* 国宝. ¶***precious historical*** *treasures* 歴史上貴重な宝物. ¶I count my knowledge of socialism as the most ***precious intellectual*** *treasure*.—Upton Sinclair. 私は私の社会主義の知識を最も貴重な知的財宝と思っている. ¶***printed*** *treasures* 印刷された貴重な文献. ¶***rare old*** *treasures* まれな古宝. ¶He is a ***real*** *treasure* to our company. 彼は真にわが社の宝だ. ¶The content of the library is the ***sifted*** *treasure* of the feeling and thinking of our race. その図書館の収蔵図書はわれわれの民族の感情や思想のよく吟味した宝である. ¶salvage ***sunken*** *treasures* [海底などに]沈んだ宝を引上げる. ¶***unsuspected*** *treasures* 気付かれない宝.

Q^2 irreplaceable ***art*** *treasures* 貴重な美術品. ¶***ceramic*** *treasures* 陶器の宝物. ¶***museum*** *treasures* 博物館所蔵の種々の宝物. ¶a ***nature*** *treasure* 自然界の宝.

P^2 *treasures* ***of*** the feeling and thinking of our race わが民族の感情と思考の宝(書物). ¶He is a *treasure* ***to*** our company. 彼はうちの会社の宝だ.

treasure, *v*. 貯蔵する; 珍重する.

M ***reverently*** *treasured* [神・仏など]大切に保存してたる. ¶*treasure* ***up*** gold and silver 金銀を貯蔵する.

O *treasure* a recollection of one's old days 懐旧の念にひたる.

treasure-house, *n*. 宝庫.

Q a ***closed*** *treasure-house* 閉ざされた宝庫. ¶a ***perfect*** *treasure-house* of information concerning … …に関する知識のりっぱな宝庫.

treasurer, *n*. 会計係.

V^2 A *treasurer* ***pays*** bills. 勘定は会計が支払う.

P^2 a *treasurer* ***of*** a business company 商事会社の会計係.

treasury, *n*. 宝蔵; 国庫.

V The domestic *treasury* of a salaried employee is usually ***exhausted*** near the payday. 俸給生活者の家庭の財政は大抵月給日に近くなると疲弊して来る. ¶***replenish*** one's exhausted *treasury* そのさびしくなったふところを補充する.

Q The *treasury* is as ***empty*** as before. その金庫は依然として空だ. ¶"The ***Golden*** *Treasury*"「黄金詩集」. ¶the ***Imperial*** *Treasury* of Nara 奈良の御庫(正倉院).

Q^2 a ***state*** *treasury* 国庫.

P The charges will be borne ***by*** the *Treasury*. その費用は国庫が負担するであろう. ‖ defrayment ***by*** the *Treasury* 国庫支弁. ¶The money was disbursed ***from*** the *Treasury* as subsidy. その金は補助金として国庫から支出した.

treat, *n*. ちそう; 行楽.

V ***afford*** a *treat* for … …を大いに満足させる. ¶I do not remember ever having ***enjoyed*** so great an intellectual *treat* as that of listening to his lecture. 私は彼の講演を聴いたときほどに大なる知的歓喜を味わったことはない. ¶***give*** oneself a great *treat* 大いに自分を楽しませる. ¶Theatregoers ***have*** therefore a great *treat* in store for them. だから好劇家は大いに楽しみにして待っていてよい訳である. ‖ ***have*** a picnic excursion *treat* to a seaside resort 海岸へ遠足に連れてってもらう. ¶***provide*** enjoyable *treat* おもしろい娯楽を供給する. ¶***stand*** *treat* for … …をおごる.

Q The concert was a ***great*** *treat*. その演奏会は非常におもしろかった. ¶It is always a ***pleasant*** *treat* to hear from you. あなたからお便りがあるといつもうれしく思う. ¶have a ***rare*** *treat* in the shape of … …という珍らしいきょう応を受ける. ¶Music is a ***real*** *treat* to me. 音楽は本当におもしろい物だ.

P^2 a *treat* ***for*** jaded ears ばかになった耳へ(音楽などの)ごちそう. ¶Fire is a great *treat* ***to*** me. 火は私には大のごちそうです. ‖ a *treat* (=feast) ***to*** the eye 目の正月.

treat, *v*. 取扱う; 講述する; 療治する; おごる.

M be *treated* ***accordingly*** その積りで(含みで)あしらわれる. ¶*treat* a person ***appropriately*** 人をしかるべく取扱う. ¶*treat* a person ***badly*** 人を虐待する. ¶*treat* a patient ***brusquely*** 病人をそっけなく取扱う. ¶*treat* the subject too

casually その題目をあまり不用意に扱う. ¶*treat* a person ***civilly*** 人を丁寧に扱う. ¶***coolly treated*** by ... ...に冷遇されて. ¶*treated* ***courteously*** 厚遇されて. ¶***Cruelly*** *treated* by time, the old picture is now a mass of cracks. その古画は長年月のためにひどくひび割れが入っている. ¶*treat* the subject ***exhaustively*** その問題を余す所なく論述する. ¶*treat* one ***fairly*** 人を公平に扱う. ¶*treat* his sweetheart ***generously*** 彼の愛人を寛大に遇する. ¶*treated* ***handsomely*** 好遇されて. ¶*treat* people ***hospitably*** and ***kindly*** 人々を手厚く親切に遇する. ¶*treat* more ***humanely*** もっと人情味をもって遇する. ¶*treat* ***ill***=abuse 虐待する. ¶*treat* the subject ***incidentally*** and ***slightly*** その問題を冷淡に軽々しく取扱う. ¶*treat* a person ***indulgently*** 人を甘やかす. ¶***inequitably*** *treated* 不公平に待遇されて. ¶My master *treats* me ***kindly***. 私の主人は私を親切に扱ってくれる. ¶*treat* ***leniently*** with ... ...を寛大に処理する. ¶A habit is something not to be ***lightly*** *treated*. 習慣は恐ろしいものである. ¶*treat* it ***lightly***, ***good-humoredly*** それを軽く気さくに扱う. ¶billiards ***mathematically*** *treated* 数学的に扱った玉突. ¶***medically*** *treated* 医療を受けて. ¶The subjects are ***obscenely*** *treated*. これらのことはみだらな書き方がしてある. ¶current events ***pictorially*** *treated* 写真や絵で報道した時事. ¶be ***poetically*** *treated* 詩的に扱われる. ¶strings ***previously*** *treated* with powdered glass [たこ合戦に使うため]前もって粉末ガラスを施した糸. ¶If he is ***properly*** *treated* he is perfectly easy to manage. 彼はうまく機げんをとればきわめて御しやすい人間だ. ¶*treat* all religious matter ***reverently*** あらゆる宗教上の事柄を敬けんな態度で取扱う. ¶He was *treated* ***surgically***. 彼は手術を受けた. ¶*treat* a person ***tactfully*** 人をほどよくあしらう. ¶be ***warmly*** *treated* by ... ...にもてる. ¶*treat* one's wife ***well*** 妻にやさしくする.

P *treat* ***about*** a question (matter) 問題(など)について論述する. ¶One will be *treated* ***according to*** one's deserts. その功罪に応じて扱われるだろう. ¶It will be *treated* as confidential. それは秘密として扱われるだろう. ‖ *treat* a person ***as*** a superior (an equal) 人を目上(同輩)として遇する ‖ *treat* her ***as*** one of the family 彼女を家族の一人と見なす(家族並に取扱う). 【類】 *treat* it ***as*** contraband (禁制品) / *treat* one ***as*** Shinnin official (親任官) / He *treated* my mistake ***as*** a joke. ¶I was *treated* ***by*** him to ... 私は彼に...をおごられた. ¶He was *treated* ***for*** the disease. 彼はその病気の治療を受けた. ‖ He is *treating* ***for*** a loan. 彼は借金の交渉をしている. ¶*treat* a person ***in*** a cold way 人を冷遇する. ¶*treat* a person ***like*** a child 人を子供扱いにする. ¶The book *treats* ***of*** the question entirely from the practical side. その本はその問題を全く実用的方面から扱っている. ‖ articles *treating* ***of*** military and naval problems 陸海軍の問題に関する論文. 【類】 the enormous literature (ばく大な文献) *treating* ***of*** evolution. / His lecture *treats* ***of*** the period between 1833 and 1839. ¶they should be *treated* ***on*** a footing of equality with ... 彼らは...と同等に待遇さるべきである. ¶*treat* a person ***to*** (=stand a person) a drink 一杯おごる. 【類】 I *treated* him ***to*** ice cream (movies). / I was *treated* ***to*** a tiffin (中食). ‖ *treat* oneself ***to*** a novel 小説を読みふける ‖ *treat* a person ***to*** abuse and scurrilous language 人に悪口雑言を浴びせる ‖ *treat* people ***to*** the voices of many birds 色々な鳥の声のまねをして人をおもしろがらせる. ¶*treat* a peron ***with*** contempt (severity) 人を軽べつして(手ひどく)扱う ‖ *treat* a person ***with*** mere disdain 人を歯牙(ｼｶﾞ)にも掛けない ‖ *treat* a person ***with*** great consideration 人を丁重に扱う. 【類】 *treat* ***with*** clemency (kindness, high honor, the kindest attention and courtesy) / be *treated* ***with*** unusual fullness (至れり尽せりの扱い) ‖ slightly *treat* it ***with*** oil それをちょっと油でいためる ‖ *treat* (=deal) ***with*** the Chinese Government for ... 中国政府と...を商議する.

treatise, *n.* 論文.

V These are subjects each of which ***requires*** a separate voluminous *treatise*. これらは各自大冊の論文を必要とする題目である. ¶***write*** a severe *treatise* against ... ...攻撃の手きびしい論文を書く.

Q a ***controversial*** *treatise* 議論を内容にした本. ¶a ***dry technical*** *treatise* 無味乾燥な専門の論文. ¶an ***elementary*** *treatise* with explanatory notes 注解つきの初歩の本. ¶an ***exhaustive*** *treatise* 至れり尽せりの論文. ¶a ***learned*** *treatise* on ... ...に関する学術論文. ¶a ***mathematical*** *treatise* 数学の論文. ¶a ***scientific*** *treatise* 科学書. ¶be used in ***serious*** *treatise* [ある専門語などが]まじめな論文に用いられる. ¶***theoretical*** *treatises* 理論を説いた著作. ¶his ***voluminous*** *treatises* 彼の著した数冊のぼう大な専門書.

P² a sensible *treatise* ***on*** the use of English 英語の使用に関する好著 ‖ classic *treatises* ***on*** the subject その題目に関する古典. ¶a *treatise* ***regarding*** ... ...に関する論文.

treatment, *n.* (**1**) 取扱い, 処理; 論述.

V ***accord*** him the *treatment* of a minister 彼に大臣の礼遇を賜う. ¶***counteract*** a *treatment* 治療の害になるようなことをする. ¶It ***deserves*** a fuller *treatment* than is accorded here. それはここに述べてあるよりも一層十分な論述をする価値がある. ¶in order to ***ensure*** consistent *treatment* 取扱いがまちまちにならないように. ¶I did not ***expect*** such *treatment* at your hands. 私はあなたからそんな待遇を受けようとは思わなかった. ¶I have tried to ***find*** due *treatment* for it so far as my narrow limits permit. 私は紙面の許す限りそのことを相当細かく論じようとした. ¶***give*** a slight *treatment* to ... ...にちょっとふれる. ¶***inculcate*** the humane *treatment* of the lower animals 下等動物を親切に取扱うことを教える. ¶similar *treatment* was ***meted out*** to ... ...も同様に取扱われた. ¶***receive*** courteous *treatment* 丁寧な取扱いを受ける. ¶The matter ***requires*** a more detailed *treatment*. そのことはもっと詳細に論述する必要がある. ¶***set up*** an exceptional *treatment* against (in favor of) ... =discriminate ... ...に対して悪(善)い方に差別待遇をする. ¶I cannot ***suffer*** (=***tolerate***) such *treatment*. 私はこうした取扱いは我慢できない.

Q receive ***bad*** *treatment* 悪い待遇を受ける. ¶***brutal*** *treatment* 残忍な取扱い. ¶the ***comic*** *treatment* of religious subjects 宗教的題目の滑けい化. ¶***considerate*** *treatment* 思慮ある取扱い. ¶***courteous*** *treatment* 丁重な取扱い. ¶***discouraging*** and ***shabby*** *treatment* がっかりさせる粗末な待遇. ¶***discriminative*** *treatmment* 差別的待遇. ¶situations capable of ***dramatic*** *treatment* 劇になる局面. ¶an ***emotional*** and ***whimsical*** *treatment* of a problem あの問題の感情的で気まぐれな取扱い. ¶***equal*** *treatment* 平等の待遇. ¶give ***equitable economic*** *treatment* to workers 従業員に公平な経済上の待遇を与える. ¶receive ***exhaustive*** *treatment* 残す所なく詳説される. 【類】 an ***exhaustive*** *treatment* of a problem. ¶***fair*** *treatment* 公平な取扱い. ¶***harsh*** *treatment* か酷な取扱い. ¶***humane*** *treatment* 人情味のある取扱い. ¶***illiberal*** *treatment* 狭量な取扱い. ¶***impartial*** *treatment* of a subject ある問題の公平な処理. ¶***indulgent*** *treatment* 寛大な取扱い. ¶***inhuman*** *treatment* 人情味のない取扱い. ¶the ***irreverent*** *treatment* of religious subjects 宗教的題目の当を得ない取扱い. ¶***just*** *treatment* 公平な取扱い. ¶give ***lenient*** *treatment* to ... ...を寛大に扱う. ¶***poetic[al]*** *treatment* 詩化. ¶a ***pictorial*** *treatment* of a subject ある問題を取扱った絵画. ¶***pleasant*** *treatment* 愉快な取扱い. ¶***preferential*** *treatment* 特別待遇. ¶a more ***rational*** *treatment* of the violaters of law 法律違犯者に対する一層合法的な取扱い. ¶a ***scientific*** *treatment* of ... ...の科学的論述. ¶I will give you a ***short*** *treatment* of the subject. 私はあなたにその問題を簡単に説明してあげよう. ¶give ***similar*** *treatment* to ... ...に同様な取扱いをする. ¶***supercilious*** *treatment* 横柄な態度. ¶receive ***sympathetic*** *treatment* at the hands of ... ...から同情的な取扱いを受ける. ¶***technical*** *treatment* 技術的な操作. ¶a ***thorough monographic*** *treatment* of a subject ある問題に対する徹底的で専門的な解説. ¶***uncourteous*** *treatment* 丁重でない取扱い. ¶protect innocent persons from ***unjust*** *treatment* 罪もない人々が不当な取扱いを受けないよう保護する.

Q ***Army*** *treatment* of the soldiers 軍隊における兵士の取扱い. ¶administer ***emergency*** *treatment* 非常時処理を行う. ¶***heat*** *treatment* 熱処理. ¶***sewage*** *treatment*, disposal and utilization 下水の取扱い, 処理及び利用.

P I will not submit ***to*** such *treatment*. 私はそんな待遇には忍従しない.

P² the *treatment* ***of*** Japanese names in English text 英文中における日本名の取扱い.

(**2**) 療治.

V ***adopt*** simple home *treatment* 簡単な家庭療法を採用す

る. ¶He was ***following treatment*** for stuttering, and was obliged to remain dumb for eight days. 彼はどもり矯正を受けているので八日間口をきかずにいなければならなかった. ¶***obtain treatment*** privately [一般患者並でなく] 自分だけ特別に治療を受ける. ¶***repeat*** the ***treatment*** as required 必要なだけその療法を繰返してやる. ¶gastro-intestinal troubles which have ***resisted*** all ***treatment*** for ten years 十年間あらゆる治療も効がなかった胃腸病 ‖ cases which have ***resisted*** all ***treatment*** 医者の手に余る病人. 【類】Sleeplessness is a scourge which often ***resists*** all known *treatments.* / The majority of such cases ***resist*** all *treatment.* ¶***take*** medical ***treatment*** 医療を受ける ‖ ***take*** a ***treatment*** of quiet rest 静養療法をやる. ¶***try*** home ***treatment*** 家庭療法を試みる. 【類】***try*** many ***treatments*** for a skin disease. ¶He had ***undergone*** various ***treatments*** without success. その時までに彼は色々療治を受けたが効がなかった. 【類】***undergo*** unsuccessfully medical and surgical ***treatment*** / He is ***undergoing treatment*** at the hands of skilled surgeons.

V² He believed that my ***treatment*** would ***avail*** in her case. 彼女の病気に私の治療がよいだろうと彼は信じた. ¶The ***treatment worked*** well. その治療は効目があった.

Q ***climatic treatment*** 気候療法(転地など). ¶a ***combined treatment*** 併用治療. ¶***curative treatment*** 療法. ¶***European treatment*** of diseases ヨーロッパ風の療法. ¶***expectant treatment*** 大体自然に任せる治療. ¶***medical treatment*** 医療 ‖ free ***medical treatment*** 施療. 【類】give ***medical treatment*** to a patient. ¶the ***modern facial treatments*** for women 近代式の女子美顔術. ¶***moral treatment*** 精神療法. ¶an ***operative treatment*** 手術. ¶a ***palliative treatment*** 一時(緩和)的療法. ¶purely ***psychic treatment,*** such as hypnotism, Christian science, and the like 催眠術・クリスチャンサイエンスなどの純然たる精神療法. ¶the ***psychoanalytic treatment*** of neurotics 神経病者の精神分析的療法. ¶***rough treatment*** 荒々しい取扱い; 荒療治. ¶***Successful treatment*** is difficult in those cases. そうした病気に対する治療の成功は困難だ. ¶undertake ***various treatments*** 色々療治を受ける.

Q² ***anti-gas treatment*** 毒ガス患者の治療. ¶corrective ***beauty treatment*** 矯正的美容術. ¶So far, no dependable ***drug treatment*** for T.B. has been dicsovered. 結核に確かにきく薬療法がまだ発見されていない. ¶the ***first aid treatment*** 応急手当. ¶take a ***flesh reducing treatment*** やせる治療を受ける. ¶a simple ***home treatment*** for ... ...の簡単な自宅治療. ¶The physician ordered ***hospital treatment.*** 医師は入院を命じた. ¶undergo ***isolation treatment*** 隔離療法を受ける. ¶the ***open-air treatment*** for consumption 肺病の戸外療法. ¶***out-patient treatment*** 外来患者の治療. ¶a ***shock treatment*** [精神病の]震とう療法. ¶***wound treatment*** 傷の手当.

P use radium ***in*** the ***treatment*** of cancer がんの治療にラジウムを用いる. ¶The patient is ***past treatment.*** その病人はもう手遅れだ. ¶He finally succumbed ***under*** the ***treatment.*** 結局彼は治療中途に落命した. ‖ The case at last came ***under*** his ***treatment.*** その病人は仕舞に彼の手に掛った. ‖ He is still ***under treatment.*** 彼はいまだに治療を受けている. ‖ the disease ***under treatment*** 医療中の病気 ‖ He claims that ***under*** this ***treatment*** he has not lost a single case. この療治をやって助からなかった者は一人もなかったと彼は公言している. ‖ ***under treatment*** for ... [患者は]...の治療中. ¶I put the patient ***upon*** ... ***treatment.*** 私はその病人に...式療法を施した.

P² He is now under ***treatment at*** the ... Hospital. 彼は今...病院に入院している. ¶Dr. Friedmann's ***treatment for*** tuberculosis フリードマン博士の結核療法. 【類】a new ***treatment for*** cancer (consumption, syphilis).

treaty, *n.* 条約; 盟約.

V ***annul*** a ***treaty*** 条約を廃棄する. ¶***break*** (=***violate***) a ***treaty*** 条約を破る. ¶***conclude*** a ***treaty*** of peace with ... ...と講和条約を結ぶ ‖ a ***treaty*** was ***concluded*** between ... ...間に条約が締結された. ¶***denounce*** (=give notice of termination of) a ***treaty*** 条約廃棄のむねを通知する. ¶***draft*** a ***treaty*** in English 英文で起草する. ¶***draw*** a ***treaty*** 条約を起草する. ¶***effect*** a ***treaty*** 条約を締結する. ¶***exchange*** a ***treaty*** 条約を交換する. ¶a ***treaty*** of commerce was ***formed*** between ... ...間に通商条約が成立した. ¶foreigners ***having treaties*** with Japan 日本と条約を結んでいる外国の国民. ¶***make*** a ***treaty*** with ... ...と条約を結ぶ. ¶***negotiate*** a ***treaty*** of commerce 通商条約を締結商議する. ¶***negotiate*** and ***sign*** a ***treaty*** with ... ...と条約を商議して署名する. ¶***observe*** a ***treaty*** 条約を守る. ¶***ratify*** a ***treaty*** 条約を批准する. ¶***sign*** a ***treaty*** 条約に調印する. ¶***terminate*** a ***treaty*** 条約を解除する. ¶***uphold*** the ***treaty*** against the State その国家に不利な条約を維持する. ¶***violate*** a ***treaty*** 条約を破棄する.

Q a ***broken treaty*** 侵害された条約. ¶negotiate a ***commercial treaty*** with ... ...と通商条約を協定する. ¶The bookseller is buying very largely both at public sales and by ***private treaty.*** その書店(古本屋)は公売及び個人取引で盛んに買入をやっている. ¶***secret treaties*** or hidden agreements 秘密条約または秘密協定.

Q² conclude a ***peace*** (***trade***) ***treaty*** 平和(通商)条約を結ぶ.

P ***by treaty*** with ... ...との条約により ‖ contracted ***by treaty*** 条約で契約された. ¶The Government is ***in treaty*** (=negotiation) with ... for ... 政府は...のため...と交渉中だ. ‖ provisions ***in*** the ***treaty*** その条約の条款. ¶enter ***into*** a ***treaty*** with ... ...と条約を結ぶ. ¶***Under*** the ***treaty*** of Washington the British Empire scrapped four battle-ships and four battle cruisers. ワシントン条約に基き英国は戦艦四隻及び戦闘巡洋艦四隻を廃棄した.

P² a ***treaty between*** ... ...間の条約. ¶a ***treaty of*** capitulation 降服条約.

treble, *v.* 三倍になる(する).

M The number has ***nearly trebled*** itself. その数がほとんどその三倍になった.

tree, *n.* 木; 木材.

V ***bark up*** a ***tree*** 木の皮をはぐ. ¶***blaze trees*** [道・境などを示すために]皮を切って木に印をつける. ¶The wind ***blew down*** large ***trees.*** 風が大きな木を吹き倒した. ¶***climb*** a ***tree*** 木に登る. ¶***cut down*** a ***tree*** 木を切り倒す. ¶***deck*** (=***trim***) the Christmas ***tree*** クリスマス・ツリーを飾る. ¶***graft*** a ***tree*** with new varieties 木に新種を接木する. ¶***hew down trees*** 木を切り倒す. ¶It is forbidden to ***injure*** the ***trees.*** 樹木を傷つけることは禁じられている. ¶The storm ***overthrew*** and ***tore up trees.*** 暴風が樹木を倒して引き裂いた. ¶***plant*** a ***tree*** to commemorate one's visit その来訪の記念に木を植える ‖ ***plant*** (=***set up***) a Christmas ***tree*** クリスマス・ツリーを立てる. ¶The wind ***prostrated*** many ***trees.*** 風で木がたくさん倒れた. ¶***prune*** (=***trim***) a ***tree*** 木を刈り込む. ¶***raise*** fruit ***trees*** 果樹を栽培する. ¶***root*** a ***tree*** 木を根づかせる. ¶The lightning ***splintered*** a ***tree.*** 落雷で木が裂けた. ¶The wind ***sways trees.*** 風が木々をゆり動かす. ¶***tap*** a ***tree*** 木に刻目をつけて液汁を取る. ¶***tear up*** a ***tree*** by the roots 木を根こそぎにする. ¶The ***trees*** are hardly ***tipped*** with bud and much less with green. 木々はまだ芽を吹かない, まして緑の葉などはまだまだだ. ¶***train trees*** 木を仕立てる. ¶***uproot trees*** 樹木を根こそぎにする.

V² These ***trees bear.*** これらの木は実がなる. ¶The ***trees*** are ***growing up.*** 木は生長している. ¶***Trees shoot*** (=put forth buds). 木々の芽が出る.

Q The masts of the shipping crowd like the ***bare-branched trees*** of a winter forest. 船の帆柱が冬の森の裸の木のように林立している. ¶a ***dead tree*** 枯れ木. ¶***Deciduous trees*** lose their leaves in the fall. 落葉樹は秋に葉が落ちる. ¶***deciduous, broad-leaved trees*** 落葉するかつ葉樹. ¶an ***evergreen tree*** 常緑樹. ¶be killed by a ***falling tree*** 倒れてきた木のために死ぬ. ¶a ***full-grown tree*** 十分生長した木. ¶a ***genealogical tree*** 系図. ¶a ***hollow tree*** うつろな木. ¶a ***lonely tree*** 一本だけ立った木. ¶an avenue of ***giant trees*** 巨木の並木. ¶a ***growing tree*** 生長している木. ¶a ***leafy tree*** 葉の茂った木. ¶a ***monumental tree*** 記念樹. ¶***moss-bearded*** (***moss-draped***) ***trees*** こけの下った木. ¶a ***naked tree*** 葉が落ちてしまった木. ¶a stately ***old tree*** 堂々たる老樹. ¶***old gnarled trees*** 節だらけの古木. ¶***Sakaki,*** the *Cleyera japonica,* the ***sacred tree*** of the Shintoists. 神道信者が神聖視するさかき. ¶a ***tall tree*** 高い木. ¶a ***withered tree*** 枯木.

Q² The ***bamboo tree*** does not blossom until it reaches its 30th year. 竹は三十年たたないと花をもたない. ¶a ***bark tree*** 〘植〙キナの木. ¶a ***Christmas tree*** クリスマス・ツリー. ¶***dogwood trees*** presented to the City of Troy in return for young cherry trees 桜の苗木の返礼にトロイ市に寄贈された花水木. ¶a ***dwarf tree*** 盆栽. ¶paulownia, the "***Empress tree***" きり. ¶a ***family tree*** 系図. ¶old, ***past-ma-***

turity trees 盛りをすぎた老木. ¶a *rubber tree* ゴムの木. ¶*sentinel trees* 玄関先に立列ぶ樹木. ¶a *shade tree* 日よけの木. ¶a *shoe* (=*boot*) *tree* くつの木型. ¶The *street trees* add to the beauty of the city. 街路樹は都市の美を増す. ¶a useful *timber tree* 有用の材木.

P *among* the *trees* 樹間に. ¶monkeys leaping *from tree to tree* 木から木へ飛び移るさる ‖ hang oneself *from* a *tree* 木からぶらさがる. ¶pearls that grow *in trees* 木に生じる真珠 ‖ Tom is up *in* the *tree*. トムは木に登っている. ¶See the blackbird *in* the *tree*. 木にとまっているつぐみをご覧. 【類】I found a baby squirrel up *in* a *tree*. ¶the shade *of* a *tree* 木陰. ¶shake fruit *off* a *tree* 木を揺って果実を落とす. ¶Fruits grow *on trees*. 果実は木になる. ‖ pears *on* the *tree* 木になっているなしの実 ‖ a creeping plant *on trees* 木にからまる植物 ‖ trimmings *on* a Christmas *tree* クリスマス·ツリーの飾りつけ ‖ hang oneself *on* a *tree* 木で首をくくる. ¶take one's siesta *under* a *tree* by the running water 小川の傍の木の下で昼寝をする. ¶*up* a *tree* 《口語》進退きわまって. ¶a cat running *up* a *tree* 木をかけ上がるねこ. 【類】The squirrel is *up* the *tree*. ¶a hillside growing *with trees* 木のはえている山腹.

P² a *tree of* this genus この種の木 ‖ under the Bo-tree, "the *tree of* enlightenment" 「悟りの木」ぼだい樹の下に.

trek, *v.* 牛車で旅行する.

M *trek back* to ... …へ牛車で戻る.

tremble, *n.* 身震い, 戦りつ.

P all *in* a *tremble* ぶるぶる震えて. ¶He was all *of* a *tremble*. 彼は震え上っていた.

tremble, *v.* 身震いする, 戦りつする.

P *tremble at* the thought of ... …を思って身震いする. ¶*tremble before* a king 王の前へ出て身震いする. ¶*tremble for* (=with) fear (horror) 恐ろしいので身震いする. ¶His hands *tremble from* over-smoking (over-drinking). 彼は過度の喫煙(など)で手が震える. ¶*tremble in* one's shoes くつはきのまま身震いする ‖ The leaves *tremble in* the breeze. 木の葉が微風にそよぐ. ‖ His fate was *trembling in* the balance. 彼の運命は危急の状態にあった. ¶*tremble like* a leaf 木の葉のように震える. ¶*tremble with* anger (excitement, cold) 怒り(など)のために身震いする.

O *tremble* to think ... …を思うと身震いがする.

tremor, *n.* 身震い; 微震.

V *have tremor* of the hands 手がふるえる.

Q There is a *nervous tremor* in his voice. 彼の声は神経質に震えている. ¶notice a *slight tremor* as of an earthquake 地震のような軽微な振動に気がつく.

Q² *earth tremor* 地響き. ¶a *earthquake tremor* 地震.

P *in* a *tremor* of excitement (anger, delight) 興奮(など)で震えて. ¶not *without* nervous *tremor* 幾分神経質にからだを震わして ‖ *without* a *tremor* of the lips くちびる一つふるわせずに.

trench, *n.* みぞ, ざんごう.

V *excavate* (=*dig*) a *trench* ざんごうを掘る. ¶*mount* the *trenches* ざんごうに入って警備する. ¶*throw up* (=*open*) *trenches* ざんごう作業を始める.

Q dig a *chest-high trench* 胸までの深さのざんごうを掘る. ¶a *deep trench* 深いざんごう.

Q² a *shelter trench* えんぺいごう.

trench, *v.* 侵す, 蚕食する.

P *trench on* the domain of ... …の領域を侵す ‖ these studies therefore *trench* inevitably *on* the larger question of ... 従ってこれらの研究は勢いさらに大なる…の問題にわたることになる. 【類】*trench on* one's rights (privacy). ¶I refrain from *trenching* here *upon* the subject, which is dealt with elsewhere in this work. そのことは本書の別章に説いてあるのでここで立入ることは差控える.

trencherman, *n.* 食い手.

Q a *good trencherman*=a great eater 大食家. ¶a *poor trencherman*=a small eater 小食家.

trend, *n.* 傾向, 形勢.

V *change* the *trend* of public opinion 世論のすう勢を変える. ¶*follow* the *trend* of world influence 世界勢力の動向に従う ‖ *follow* the *trend* of a story almost perfectly 聴いている物語の筋をほとんど間違わずに話す. ¶*gauge* the *trend* of British public opinion 英国の世論のすう勢を打診する. ¶This summary is enough to *indicate* the *trend* of his argument. この提要で彼の議論振りが分かる. ¶*observe* the *trend* of public opinion 世論のすう勢を観察する. ¶modern Japanese paintings, *showing* the newer *trends* among Oriental artists 東洋芸術家の新傾向を示す現代日本画. ¶*understand* today's *trends* 現時の動向を理解する.

Q the *current trend* of thoughts 現代の思想傾向. ¶*economic trends* in Soviet Russia ソ連における経済的すう勢. ¶the *general trend* of public opinion 世論の一般的傾向. ¶The *predominant trend* of English politics is towards Socialistic measures. 英国政治は主として社会主義的方策の傾向がある. ¶the *recent trend* of Japanese thought 日本思想最近の動向 ‖ *recent trends* in ... …における最近の動向. ¶an *undesirable trend* 好ましからぬ傾向. ¶the *upward trend* of prices 物価上向きの傾向. ¶a *welcome trend* 喜ぶべき傾向.

Q² the "*away-from-school*" *trend* 学校をさぼる傾向. ¶the *fascist trend* of the Japanese army 日本軍隊の国粋党的傾向. ¶the current rapid *inflation trends* 現在の急激なインフレ傾向. ¶a drop in *price trends* 物価下落の傾向.

P *in view of* the *trend* of public opinion 世論のすう勢にかんがみて. ¶Prices are *on* the upward (downward) *trend*. 物価は上(下)向である.

P² the *trend of* the present age 現代の風潮. 【類】the *trend of* events. ¶the *trend to* nationalism 国家主義への傾向.

trend, *v.* 傾く, 傾向がある.

P The coast *trends to* the north. 海岸線は北方に向っている. ¶*trend toward*[*s*] ... …の方へ傾く.

trespass, *n.* 違犯, 侵害.

V *commit trespass* by venturing into ... …に侵害を加える.

Q an *unwarrantable trespass* on Cupid's domain 無粋の干渉.

P² a *trespass on* its sacred domain その聖域の侵犯 ‖ a *trespass on* decorum 礼節の違反.

trespass, *v.* 侵害する, 違犯する.

M *trespass far* beyond ... …の範囲をはるか越して侵害する. ¶But I must not *trespass further* on your space. これで筆をおく(投書家が).

P *trespass against* the law 法律を侵す ‖ *trespass against* a person 人の邪魔をする. ¶*trespass in* some one's house 人の家に侵入する. ¶I hope I am not *trespassing on* your time. お邪魔じゃありませんか. ‖ *trespass on* one's kindness 人の親切につけ込む ‖ *trespass on* private property 私有財産を侵害する. 【類】*trespass on* private grounds (私有地) ‖ May I *trespass on* you *for* the mustard? からしを取って下さいませんか. 【類】*trespass upon* your valuable time.

tress, *n.* [通例 *pl.*] 一房の髪.

Q beautiful *golden tresses* 美しい金髪.

triad, *n.* 三つ組.

Q a *lucky triad* 縁起のよい三つ組(松竹梅など).

trial, *n.* 試み, 試練; 困難; 裁判, 審理.

V *bring* a *trial* against ... …を告訴する. ¶The *trial* is *concluded*. The verdict is guilty, but the sentence is deferred. 公判が終る, [陪審員の]評決は有罪だ, しかし宣告は延期される. ¶*conduct trials* with ... …を試験する. ¶*endure* all the severe *trials* of life あらゆる世の苦難に打勝つ. ¶*face* a *trial* 裁判を受ける. ¶*give* it a thorough *trial* それを十分に試験する ‖ Please *give* us a *trial* ためしに一回御用命下さい. ¶Every situation in life *has* its *trial*. 人生いずれの境地にも苦難がある. ‖ *have* a *trial* of strength with ... …と力比べをする. ¶*make* [a] *trial* of (=test) his intelligence 彼の知性をためす ‖ *make* some *trials* 少しためして見る. ¶*stand trial* for ... …の裁判を受ける. ¶*take* one's *trial* at a court 裁判所で審問される. ¶*undergo trial* for ... …の審問を受ける.

Q a *bitter trial* 苦しい試練. ¶*celebrated trials* 有名な諸裁判. ¶a *criminal trial* 刑事裁判. ¶after an *extended trial* 広範囲にわたって試験した後. ¶give it a *fair trial* それを公平に試験する. ¶a *famous trial* 有名な裁判. ¶at the *first trial* 第一審で. ¶a *judicial trial* 裁判. ¶I find the boy a *great trial*. その子は実に厄介だ. ¶hold a *mock* (=*sham*) *trial* 模擬裁判を催す. ¶in the midst of a great *national trial* 国家的大試練のさ中に. ¶make a *new trial* 新しくこころみる. ¶The *official trial* of the ship was run. その船の正式試運転は終った. ¶by *patient trial* 辛抱してやって見て. ¶under *preliminary trial* 予審中. ¶He was submitted to *public trial*. 彼は公判に付せられた. ¶a *public trial* 公判. ¶a *sore* (=*severe*) *trial* きびしい試練. ¶*speedy trial* 迅速裁判. ¶be subject to a very *unfair trial* はなは

だ不公平な裁判を受ける.

Q² a *court trial* 裁判. ¶a *flight trial* 飛行のこころみ. ¶a *purge trial* 追放の審問. ¶*state trial* 国事犯裁判記録. ¶the *war crime trials* at Nuremberg ニュールンベルヒにおける戦犯裁判 ‖ "Class A" *war crimes trial* A 級戦犯裁判. 【類】spectators' tickets (傍聴券) for the *war crimes trials*.

P *After* a hasty *trial* the criminal was sentenced to death. 尋問もそこそこで罪人は死刑の宣告を受けた. ¶*as* a *trial* こころみに. ¶Her speed was 16.3 knots *at trial*. その船の試運転の時速は 16.3 ノットであった. ‖ *at* one's *trial* その試験のとき. ¶*during* the *trial* 審問中に. ¶The case is now down *for trial*. その事件は目下裁判にかけられることになっている. ‖ commit a person *for trial* on a charge of ... ...のかどで人を審問に付する. ¶hire a man *on trial* 仮採用をする. 【類】I think I will take you *on trial*. ‖ be *on trial* for the murder (theft) of... ...の殺害の罪科で公判中. 【類】go *on trial* for ... ‖ the speed obtained *on trial* was ... 試運転のときの速度は...であった. ¶the accused *pending trial* 予審中の被告. ¶the case will come *to trial* on ... その訴訟は...日に公判になる ‖ put it *to trial* それをためす. ¶The case is now *under trial*. その訴訟は今公判中である. ¶It is unfair to condemn a man *without trial*. 審問もしないで人を有罪と決するのは公正を欠く.

P² Twelfth-century England was under a *trial by* battle. 十二世紀の英国は戦争の試練を受けていた. ‖ *trial by* ordeal [琴責などの]呵(ｶ)責による審判 ‖ *trial by* jury 陪審公判. ¶a *trial of* skill 技術の試験 ‖ *trial of* machinery 機械の試運転. ¶a *trial to* patience うるさいこと.

triangle, *n.* 三角形; 三角関係.

V it provides the third side *completing* the *triangle* of ... それが第三辺となって...の三角が完成される.

Q the *eternal triangle*=a triangular love affair 三角関係. ¶an *inverted triangle* [底辺を上にした]逆の三角. ¶the *old hackneyed triangle* of hero, heroine, and villain 昔からよくある英雄と乙女と悪漢(立役・相手女優・敵役)の三つどもえ. ¶a *right-angled triangle* 直角三角形.

Q² a *love triangle* 三角関係.

P² a *triangle of* land 三角地帯.

tribe, *n.* 種族; 連中.

Q incursions of the *barbarian tribes* 蛮族の侵入. ¶the native *Australian tribe* 豪州原住民. ¶the *feathered tribes* 鳥類. ¶a *nomadic tribe* 遊牧の民. ¶an *ostracised tribe* 追放種族. ¶the *scribbling tribe* 三文文士連. ¶*truculent native tribes* 野蛮な土族. ¶a *vagrant tribe* 浮浪者群.

P² the *tribe of* cheap politicians 安っぽい政治屋族.

tribulation, *n.* 苦難.

P *through* great *tribulation* 非常な苦難を経て.

tribunal, *n.* 裁判所, 法衙(ｶﾞ).

Q an *extraordinary tribunal* 特別裁判所. ¶the *Far Eastern Tribunal* 極東裁判所. ¶the *highest tribunal* in the land, the Supreme Court. その国の最高の法廷である最高裁判所. ¶constitute a *special tribunal* 特別裁判所を設置する. ¶the House of Lords as a *judicial tribunal* 司法の府としての(英国)上院.

P² before the *tribunal of* conscience 良心の裁きの前に.

tribune, *n.* 演壇.

Q the *speaker's tribune* 演壇.

tributary, *a.* 貢を納める; 支流たる, [...に]注ぐ.

P brooks *tributary to* large creeks 大きな入江に会流する小川 ‖ It has become *tributary to* the Dutch. それはオランダの属国になった.

tribute, *n.* 貢; 手向け.

V *collect tributes* 貢を集める. ¶*deserve* a high *tribute* of respect 大いに尊敬を受ける価値がある. ¶*earn* his *tribute* of respect 彼から敬意を受ける. ¶*form* a worthy *tribute* to ... ...に対してりっぱな貢献となる. ¶*levy* a *tribute* on ... ...に貢税を課す. ¶*make* him the following glowing *tribute* 彼に次の絶賛の辞を呈している. ¶*offer* our *tribute* of admiration to ... ...にわれわれの賛辞を呈する. ¶At the time of the Russian conquest, the Kuznetsk "Tartars" were *paying tribute* to China with iron implements of their own manufacture. ロシア人に征服された時にクーズネツクのダッタン人は自国で造った鉄器の貢を中国に納めていた. 【類】They *paid* a *tribute* of elephants to the Grand Khan (大汗国) every year. ‖ *pay* a *tribute* of respect to his memory 彼の霊に敬意を表す ‖ *pay* him a *tribute* of unfeigned sorrow 彼の死を心から哀悼する. 【類】*pay* a *tribute* to the loyalty of ... / Scholars everywhere have united in *paying tribute* to the marvellous richness and fullness of information set forth in the O.E.D. / Everywhere *tributes* were *paid* to the memory of the glorious dead (名誉の戦死者). ¶None can *refuse* a *tribute* of admiration to ... 何人も...に賛辞を呈さざるを得ない. ¶*send* floral *tributes* 弔花を贈る. ¶*withhold* one's *tribute* of praise その賛辞を撤回する.

Q pay an *annual tribute* of ... ...の年貢を納める. ¶pay *cheerful tribute* to ... 喜んで...に賛辞を呈する. ¶one of the *finest tributes* to the nation's fallen heroes 国家のために倒れた勇士へのりっぱな手向け物の一つ. ¶offer a *floral tribute* at the tomb of ... ...の墓に花を手向ける. ¶pay a *generous* (=*liberal*) *tribute* to ... ...を激賞する. ¶pay a *glowing tribute* to his work for the Empire (his successful career) 帝国への彼の功労(など)に対して熱誠な賛辞を呈する. 【類】*Glowing tributes* are paid to his triumph (成功). ¶the *greatest tribute* that can be paid to his memory is to say that ... 彼の霊に対する最大の賛辞は...ということである. ¶pay [a] *high tribute* to the excellence (administrative ability) of ... ...の美徳(行政手腕)に対して大いに賛辞を呈する. 【類】The newspapers pay *high tributes* to his memory. / pay the *highest tribute* to his greatness / pay a *high tribute* to the British working men as an example to be imitated by ... / Too *high tribute* cannot be paid (=We cannot pay him too *high* a *tribute*) for his tireless industry. ¶pay an *involuntary tribute* of respect to ... ...知らず知らず頭が下がる. ¶pay him the *last tribute* 彼に最後のはなむけをする. 【類】pay one's *last tribute* of respect to ... / pay the *last tribute* of homage to ... ¶a *memorial tribute* 追悼. ¶lay a *mere tribute* of gratitude at the feet of ... ...の足下に感謝のほんの印しをおく. ¶He paid a *pious* and *graceful tribute* to his memory. その霊に彼はうやうやしく敬礼をした. ¶a *respectful tribute* from ... ...から寄せた敬意. ¶dedicated to a person as a *slight tribute* to his genius その天才にいささか敬意を表するために人にささげられた. ¶pay a *small tribute* to the memory of a great friend 親友の霊に対しささやかな手向け物をする. ¶pay one's *unstinted tribute* of admiration to ... ...を言葉を惜しまず称賛する. ¶pay a *warm tribute* to ... ...を熱心に称賛する. 【類】he paid a *warm tribute* (哀悼の意) to the memory of ...

P *as* a *tribute of* (=in token of) respect to the Emperor 皇帝に対する敬意のしるしとして. 【類】*as* a *tribute* to her on her eighty-fifth birthday. ¶he was the recipient *of* a *tribute* of admiration from ... 彼は...からの賛辞を受けた. ¶lay them *under tribute* 彼らに貢物を納めさせる.

P² a *tribute of* respect and admiration from ... ...からの敬意と称賛のささげ物(花輪など) ‖ a *tribute of* respect and gratitude is due to ... 敬意と感謝の贈物を...に捧げるべきだ. 【類】a graceful *tribute to* the memory of the noble man.

trice, *n.* 瞬間, せつな.

P appear (disappear) *in* a *trice* 瞬間に現われ(消え)る.

trick, *n.* 悪戯; 芸当; 癖.

V to *conceal* the *trick* その悪計を隠すため. ¶*do* (=*turn*) the *trick* うまくやる ‖ The measure *did* the *trick*. その方策が奇功を奏した. ¶*evolve tricks* in photography 写真術における妙技を発揮する. ¶*find out* a *trick* 悪計を看破する. ¶He *has* a *trick* of repeating himself. 彼はくり返して言う癖がある. ¶An old dog cannot *learn* new *tricks*. 老犬には新しい芸は仕込めない. ¶*perform* a *trick* 手品をやる. ¶*play* a *trick* on ... ...に一杯食わせる. ¶*serve* a person a *trick* 人を手管に乗せる. ¶I *suspect* some *trick*. 計略に掛けるのだと私は思う. ¶*teach tricks* to ... ...に術を授ける.

Q a *cynical tricks* 皮肉ないたずら ‖ He played me a *dirty trick*. 彼は僕に卑劣なことをした. ¶play *droll tricks* like a monkey さるのような滑けいなまねをする. ¶The wearing of white clothes is a *favorite trick* of soldiers fighting in snowcovered country. 白衣を着ることは雪のある国で戦う兵士のよくやる計略だ. ¶His collection is a museum of *forgers' tricks*. 彼の収集はにせ物博物館である. ¶a *hazing trick* いやがらせのいたずら. ¶frustrate his *knavish tricks* 彼の卑劣な計略をざ折する. ¶play a *little trick* on

……にちょっとふざける. ¶*low tricks* 下品な小細工. ¶*magic tricks* revealed 手品の種あかし. ¶play a *mean trick* on … …に対し卑劣な手段をろうする. ¶a *nasty trick* 卑劣なやり方. ¶a *new trick* 新手の詐欺. ¶The use of military titles before the names of officials of bogus enterprises is an *old* trick. いんちき事業の役員の名前に軍職名を冠用することは例の古い手である. ¶the *same old trick* 例の古い手. ¶a *scurvy trick* 下劣な手段. ¶The *trick* was rather too *severe*. そのいたずらは少しきき過ぎた. ¶a *shabby* (=*dishonorable*) *trick* けしからぬいたずら. ¶a *shrewd trick* 巧妙な手口; 姦(かん)策. ¶That's an *unfair trick* to play on them. それは彼らに対して不正なやり方だ. ¶a *waggish trick* 茶目ないたずら.

Q² *advertising tricks* 広告上の技巧. ¶a *cat-and-monkey trick* 人をだしに使うやり方. ¶a *confidence trick* (=game) 信用詐欺, とりこみ詐欺. ¶one of the Indian *conjuring tricks* 一つのインド手品. ¶a Chinese *fire* (*water*) *trick* 中国人の火(水)芸. ¶a "*disappearing-rabbit*" *trick* うさぎ隠しの手品. ¶a *sleight-of-hand trick* 手品. ¶a *Yankee trick* アメリカ式のやり方.

P see *through* a *trick* トリックを見抜く.

P² a *trick by* sleight-of-hand 手品の一芸当. ¶a *trick of* the trade 商売の一手段 ‖ a *trick of* the mind 心の迷い ‖ a *trick of* long diving 長時潜水法.

trick, *v.* だます, 欺く.

M He *cleverly tricked* his captors. 彼は自分を捕えた人をうまくだました. ¶She was *tricked out* in jewels. 彼女は宝石で飾り立てていた.

P *trick* a person *into* doing something 人をだまして何かやらせる ‖ She was *tricked into* a marriage with him. 彼女はだまされて彼と結婚した. 【類】*trick* a person *into* consent (approval). ¶*trick* a person *out of* money 人から金を詐取する. ¶*trick with* cards カルタでごまかす.

trickery, *n.* いんちき.

Q entirely free from *clap-trap trickery* 場当りをねらうようなことは毛頭ない. ¶*legal trickery* 法網をくぐる詐欺.

trickle, *v.* したたる, 漏れ出る.

M² The order *trickled down* to the execution level. その命令は実行する方面に徐々に伝わった(やっと実施される段になった). 【類】*trickle down* in thick drops. ¶People began to *trickle in* through the gates. 人が門からぽつりぽつりはいって来た. ¶The information *trickled out*. その情報はちょいちょい漏れた.

P Rain-water *trickled from* the eaves (roof). 軒(など)から雨水がしたたり落ちた. ¶Crystalline water was *trickling through* a crevice. 水晶のような水が割れ目を通してしたたり落ちていた.

tricycle, *n.* 三輪車, オート三輪.

Q *tradesmen's tricycles* 商用のオート三輪.

trifle, *n.* 細事, 取るに足らない物; 小量.

V I want you to *accept* this *trifle*. この粗品をお受け下さい. ¶*give* a *trifle* 些(さ)少の品を呈する. ¶I *have* only a *trifle* of three yen left. 私にはたった三円しか残っていない. ¶*rake up* every *trifle* to find fault with … …を悪口の種にしようとしてあらゆるつまらぬことをほじくり出す. ¶*receive* a *trifle* 些(さ)少の金(品)をもらう. ¶*Spare* a *trifle* for the waiter. 給仕に少し(心付を)やり給え.

Q The expense is a *mere trifle*. この費用はほんのわずかだ. ¶an *unconsidered trifle* 取るに足らないわずかの品.

P take offense *at* a *trifle* 小事に腹を立てる. 【類】One should not get angry *about* (=*at*) such a *trifle*. ¶*above* such *trifle* こうした小事に超越する. ¶take offense *at trifles* 小さなことに立腹する.

trifle, *v.* ばかにして扱う, もてあそぶ.

M *trifle away* one's time (money, energy) in … …につまらなく時(など)を費す.

P *trifle with* a serious matter 重大事件を軽く見る ‖ *trifle with* one's health 自分の健康を軽んじる ‖ *trifle* (=toy) *with* a woman's feelings 女心をもてあそぶ. 【類】*trifle with* facts / a thing not to be *trifled with*.

trim, *n.* 整備.

Q in *good trim* よく整備して. ¶I found everything in *perfect trim*. 私が行って見たら万事よく整とんしていた.

Q² a war-vessel in *fighting trim* 戦闘準備をした軍艦. ¶get into *walking trim* 徒歩旅行の準備を整える.

P *in trim* for … …の準備を整えて. ¶The boat is *out of trim*. そのボートは調子が悪い.

trim, *v.* 装飾をつける; きちんと整える; 刈込む.

M The gardener *trimmed* the hedge *clean*. 園丁が生がきをきれいに刈った.

M² *trim down* 切り詰める. ¶*trim in* 切り組む(木材を). ¶*trim* dead leaves *off* 枯葉を刈って取る. ¶*trim off* the lower leaves 下の方の葉を切り取る. 【類】*trim* unnecessary parts *off*. ¶*trim* oneself *up* 身なりを整える. ¶The children *trimmed* [*up*] Christmas trees. 子供らがクリスマスの飾木を格好よくはさみを入れた.

P *trim* bushes *into* good shape かん木を刈って形をよくする. ¶*trimmed with* embroidery (lace) ししゅう(など)で飾って ‖ *trim* a hat *with* flowers 帽子を花で飾る. 【類】Mary's new dress is *trimmed with* buttons.

O *trim* a hedge (turf, beard) 生垣(など)を刈込む.

trimming, *n.* 飾り, 装飾; 整理; *pl.* [食物の]添物.

Q² *gingerbread trimming* of a house 家の見掛倒しの装飾. ¶*window trimming* 窓飾り.

P roast meat *with trimmings* 添物のついた焼肉. ¶words *without trimmings* 飾り気のない言葉.

P² *trimmings of* a bonnet 婦人帽の飾り. 【類】the trimmings of a Christmas tree ‖ the *trimming of* personnel 人員整理.

trinity, *n.* 三位一体.

V *form* a *trinity* 三位一体を成す.

Q the *unholy trinity:* Mammon, Bacchus, and Priapus 聖ならざる三位一体すなわち金と酒と色.

trio, *n.* 三重奏, トリオ.

Q the *scenic trio* of Japan 日本三景. ¶a *vocal trio* 三重唱.

trip, *n.* 旅行, 短い旅行; 遊覧.

V I can't *afford* a *trip* to Europe. 私にはヨーロッパへ旅行する余裕がない. ¶*Arrange* your *trip* to include a stopover of a few days at this enjoyable playground. この愉快な遊覧地に数日滞在するようにあなたの旅程をお作りなさい. ‖ prospective travellers who are *arranging trips* to … …への旅行を計画している(目前に旅行を控えた)人々. ¶*contemplating* a *trip* to … …へ旅行しようと考えている. ¶The *trip* can be *done* comfortably in five days allowing one day for travel by train. その旅行は汽車の旅に一日を当てて五日で楽にできる. ¶The *trip* may be *encompassed* in the space of half a day. その旅行は半日でやれる. ¶I *enjoyed* the *trip* very much. 私のその旅行は大変おもしろかった. ¶We can *fit* the *trip* to your budget. お都合(懐勘定)のよろしいように旅行計画をお作り致します. ¶*give up* one's *trip* その旅行をやめにする. ¶*make* a *trip* around the world 世界一周旅行をやる. 【類】We *made* a *trip* from … to … in … days and … hours. / The steamer *makes* the *trip* in 5 or 6 hours. / *make* the *trip* in reverse order (逆に) / *make* a *trip* into the mountains / *make* a *trip* through Japan. ¶*map out* one's *trip* 旅行の計画を立てる. ¶I am *meditating* a *trip* to North China. 私は北中国へ旅行を計画している. ¶No traveller should *miss* a *trip* to the place. 旅行者は是非ともそこへ行って見るべきである. ¶*organize* a vacation *trip* 休暇中の旅行を計画する. ¶help the intending tourists to *plan* their *trip* intelligently 遊覧希望者の相談相手となって旅行をうまく計画させる. ¶The return *trip* from Chicago to Seattle is *routed* via the Northern Pacific Railway. シカゴからシァトルへの帰りの旅は北太平洋鉄道経由にしてある. ¶The walking *trip* was *ruined* (=*spoiled*) by the rain. 雨で徒歩旅行が台なしになった. ¶The magazine *sponsors* the *trip*. その旅行はその雑誌社の主催である. ¶*take* a *trip* through a foreign country 外国を旅行する. 【類】*take* a *trip* to Atami (Formosa) / *take* a *trip* around the world / He is *taking* this *trip* for study and observation. ¶*undertake* a *trip* 旅行を計画する. ¶*wind up* one's *trip* with … 観光旅行は…でき りあげる.

Q He went to Atami on his *bridal trip*. 彼は新婚旅行で熱海へ行った. ¶travel on carefully *budgeted trips* with but little to spare 余裕の乏しい細かに予算を立てた旅をする. ¶make a *cheap trip* [汽車・汽船などの]割引で行く. ¶his *coveted trip* to Europe 彼のヨーロッパへのあこがれの旅. ¶a *delightful trip* 愉快な旅. ¶that alone is worth the *entire trip* from … to … それだけで…から…への全旅行をやる価値がある. ¶an *experimental trip* for a new vessel 新しい船の試運転. ¶take an *extended trip* through … …を広く旅行する. 【類】while upon an *extended trip* abroad. / He was there on an ***extended trip*** in Europe. ¶make a ***flying trip*** to ... ...へ飛脚(大急ぎの)旅行をする. ¶contemplate a ***foreign trip*** 外国漫遊を計画する. ¶a ***globe-encircling trip*** 世界一周旅行. ¶on one's ***going trip*** その行きの旅に. ¶on the ***going*** or ***return trip*** or both 行きまたはもどりの旅または往復に. ¶start on the ***homeward trip*** to ... ...に帰国すべく出発する. ¶make a ***hurried trip*** to America アメリカへ急ぎの旅をする. ¶a ***leisurely trip*** ゆっくりした旅行. ¶a ***maiden trip*** (= voyage) 処女航海. ¶a ***main*** (***side***) ***trip*** 本筋(横道)の旅行. ¶an ***organized trip*** 計画を立てた旅行. ¶The baseball team is on an ***out-of-town trip***. その野球団はいなか回りをしている. ¶a ***pleasant*** and ***successful trip***. 愉快で好成績の旅行. ¶The ***round trip*** from ... and back takes three days. 《米》...からの往復旅行は三日間を要する. 【類】In the course of a year the ship does about sixteen ***round trips*** between Southampton and New York. ¶take a ***short trip*** 小旅行をする. ¶make a ***side trip*** to ... 旅行中側道をして...へ寄る. ¶a ***three months' trip*** through China 三カ月の中国の旅. ¶a ***two*** or ***three days' trip*** 二三日の小旅行. ¶an ***upcountry trip*** 内地旅行.

Q² an ***auto***[***mobile***] ***trip*** 自動車旅行. ¶The wrestlers were out on a ***barn-storming trip***. 《口語》相撲は地方巡業中であった. ¶go on a ***camping trip*** キャンプ旅行に出掛ける. ¶make a long ***car*** and ***boat trip*** 車や船の長旅をする. ¶a ***class trip*** クラスの修学旅行. ¶a ***convalescence trip*** 病後静養旅行. ¶The steamer affords a ***daylight trip***. その汽船では昼間の旅ができる. ¶a ***down-stream trip*** 河を船で下る旅行. ¶a ***field*** [***observation***] ***trip*** 見学. ¶a ***health trip*** 保養旅行. ¶I am coming over to Japan for a ***holiday trip*** at the beginning of next month. 私は来月始めに日本へ休暇旅行で行きます. ¶while on a ***honeymoon trip*** around the world 世界一週のみつ月旅行中. ¶an ***inspection trip*** 視察旅行. ¶make a ***motor trip*** across the country 国内自動車横断旅行をする. ¶an ***ocean trip*** 大洋旅行. ¶go on a ***one-day trip*** 日帰りの旅. ¶leave London for a ***pleasure trip*** to Japan 日本への遊覧旅行にロンドンを立つ. ¶make a ***rail trip*** to ... ...へ汽車旅行をする. ¶a sort of ***recreation trip*** 一種の気晴らし旅行. ¶ships on ***repatriation trips*** 引き上げ者を乗せる諸船. ¶be on a ***return trip*** 旅行からの帰途にある. ¶a ***round-the-world trip*** 世界一週旅行. ¶be on a ***school*** [***-ing***] ***trip*** 修学旅行途上にある. ¶a ***sea trip*** 海上旅行. ¶Mother took me downtown on a ***shopping trip***. 母は買物に下町へ私を連れて行った. ¶on a ***sight-seeing trip*** 観光の旅に. ¶a slumming ***trip*** 貧民くつ訪問. ¶a delightful ***steamship trip*** 愉快な汽船旅行. ¶a ***summer trip*** in Alaska アラスカの夏期旅行. ¶a ***train trip*** 汽車旅行. ¶on her ***trial trip*** [船が]その試運転中である. 【類】On her ***trial trip***, she maintained for four hours a speed of 16.79 knots. ¶parties contemplating a ***vacation trip*** 休暇旅行を計画中の諸団体. ¶a pleasant ***walking trip*** 楽しい徒歩旅行. ¶a ***wedding trip***=a honeymoon 新婚旅行. ¶a ***week-end trip*** 週末旅行. ¶a ***zoological collection trip*** 動物学上の収集旅行.

P ***at*** one ***trip*** 一航海に. ¶He will sail on the Empress of Japan ***for*** a ***trip*** to Japan. 彼はエンプレス・オヴ・ジャパン号で日本に向け出帆するだろう. ‖ prepare ***for*** a ***trip*** abroad 海外旅行の準備をする. ¶He has just returned ***from*** his ***trip*** to Hokkaido. 彼は北海道の旅から帰ったばかりだ. ¶an itinerary ***of*** a ***trip*** 旅行日程 ‖ go ***on*** a walking ***trip***=go hiking 徒歩旅行に出る. 【類】He is away ***on*** a ***trip***. ¶***within*** a pleasant ***trip*** of a few hours' steaming 数時間の愉快な海路で行ける所に.

P² a ***trip for*** health 保養旅行. ¶the ***trip from*** ... ***to*** ... and return ...から...への往復旅行 ‖ a ***trip in*** a vessel 船の旅. ¶plan a pleasure ***trip on*** the Thames テムズ河上の遊覧旅行を計画する ‖ a ***trip on*** the continent 大陸の旅. ¶a ***trip through*** the New York Assay Office ニューヨーク金属試験所の見学. ¶a ***trip to*** the movies 映画見物 ‖ a ***trip to*** the seashore 海岸への旅. ¶a ***trip to*** and ***through*** Ireland アイルランドへ観光旅行. ¶a ***trip up*** Mt. Fuji 富士登山.

trip, *v*. 小またに歩む; つまずく; つまずかせる.

M ***trip lightly*** into a streetcar 軽く電車に飛び乗る ‖ be ***tripped*** [up] ***unwarily*** あげ足を取られる.

M² come ***tripping down*** to meet us [子供が]出迎えにちょこちょこ走ってやって来る. ¶I was ***tripped up*** by him. 彼は私につまずいた. ‖ ***trip*** a person ***up*** 人をつまずかせる ‖ ***trip up*** the unwary 人のあげ足を取る.

P ***trip against*** (=on *or* over) a rope なわにつまずく. ¶***trip on*** a stone 石につまずく ‖ ***trip on*** the rug 敷物の上をさっさと歩む ‖ I've ***tripped on*** that sill two or three times myself. 私もあのしきいに二三度つまずいた. ¶I ***tripped over*** something hard. 私は何かかたい物につまずいた.

triplicate, *n*. [書類など]三通の中一通.

P a document ***in triplicate*** 三通に作った文書.

P² a ***triplicate of*** the document 三通の文書の中一通.

tripod, *n*. 三脚器.

Q² a ***cooking tripod*** 料理用の三足器(五徳の類).

tripper, *n*. 《英口》旅行者, 行楽者.

Q English ***day trippers*** across the Channel 英国のイギリス海峡横断日帰り旅行者.

triumph, *n*. がい旋, 勝利.

V ***achieve*** (=***score***, ***secure*** *or* ***win***) a ***triumph*** 勝利を得る. ¶***consummate*** an entire ***triumph*** over ... ...に対し完全な勝利を占める. ¶a fact that ***marks*** the ***triumph*** of science and civilization 科学と文明の勝利を示す事実.

Q ***another triumph*** of science また一つの科学の飛躍. ¶a ***diplomatic triumph*** 外交上の勝利. ¶the ***final triumph*** of good over evil 悪に対する善の終局的勝利. 【類】It proved the ***final triumph*** in his career. ¶achieve a ***great triumph*** 大勝利を博する ‖ Suspended judgment is the ***greatest*** triumph of intellectual discipline. 速断を下さないことは知的訓練の大勝利である. ¶a ***linguistic triumph*** [外国語でりっぱな詩を作るなどの]言語上の勝利. ¶the ***momentary triumph*** of the lily over the rose ゆりのばらに対する一時的勝利(若い人が飲過ぎなどで顔が青ざめている有様などをいう). ¶collect ***new triumphs*** 新しい勝利を重ねる. ¶These illustrations are ***perfect triumphs*** of the block-cutter's art. これらのさし絵は木版術の傑作である. ¶a ***short-lived triumph*** 束の間の勝利. ¶the ***ultimate triumph*** of ... ...の終局的勝利.

Q² make a ***stage triumph*** 舞台(演技)であてる.

P return ***in triumph*** がい旋する. ¶with a smile ***of triumph*** 勝利の微笑をたたえて. ¶***with triumph***=triumphantly 勝ち誇って.

P² a ***triumph for*** democracy 民々主義の勝利. ¶a ***triumph of*** the histrionic art 演劇上の傑作 ‖ The defeat of the general strike is, as a Frenchman has said, a ***triumph of*** common sense ***over*** illusion. 総罷業の敗北はあるフランス人が言った通り錯覚に対する常識の勝利である ‖ the ***triumph of*** right ***over*** might 腕力に対する正義の勝利. 【類】the ***triumph of*** right ***over*** wrong, of virtue over vice / the ***triumph of*** good ***over*** evil / The P.O.D. is a ***triumph of*** condensation. / The dishes (料理) are ***triumphs of*** the culinary art (料理法). / The bridge is a ***triumph of*** engineering skill. / a ***triumph of*** the ship builders' craft / ***triumphs of*** man ***over*** nature. ¶our military ***triumphs on*** land and sea 陸海におけるわが軍の勝利.

triumph, *v*. 勝ち誇る; がい歌を奏する.

P ***triumph in*** his success 彼の成功に喜び勇む. ¶He ***triumphed over*** death at the call of duty. 彼は死をも恐れず義務遂行のため勇み立った. 【類】The sun ***triumphed over*** the mist (霧を消散させた) just as I reached the mountain top. / ***triumphed over*** all the other teams / ***triumph over*** pain (disease).

triumphant, *a*. 勝ち誇る.

P He felt ***triumphant over*** a little adventure. 彼は小冒険の克服に勇み立った. 【類】Right was ***triumphant over*** wrong.

triviality, *n*. 平凡, 些(さ)末.

Q ***domestic trivialities*** 家庭の些事.

trolley, *n*. 《米》市街電車.

V The whole block was on fire so that the ***trolleys*** could not ***run by***. 一郭全部燃えていたので電車がその側を通れなかった.

Q the ***slow***, ***old-fashioned trolley*** のろい古くさい市電. ¶the ***underground trolley*** 地下電車.

P ***in*** a ***trolley*** 電車で.

troop, *n*. 軍隊, 群集.

V ***detach troops*** 兵を分遣する. ¶***disband troops*** 除隊する. ¶***detach troops from*** ... ...から兵士を分遣する. ¶***disperse*** enemy ***troops*** 敵兵を敗走させる. ¶***draw up troops*** 兵を整列させる. ¶The general will ***lead*** his ***troops*** to victory.

その大将はその軍隊を率いて敵を破るだろう. ¶ ***mass troops*** on the frontier 国境に軍隊を集結する. ¶ ***move troops*** to … …へ出兵する. ¶ ***muster in*** (***out***) ***troops*** 軍隊を召集(解散)する. ¶ ***quarter*** *troops* 軍隊を宿営させる. ¶ ***raise*** fresh *troops* 新たに兵士を募る. ¶ ***review*** the *troops* 閲兵する. ¶ ***station*** *troops* 兵を駐在させる. ¶ ***withdraw*** *troops* 撤兵する.

v² The *troops* are ***assembling*** (***dispersing***). 兵隊は集合(分散)している. ¶ *troops* ***came*** to the relief of … 軍隊が…の救援におもむいた. ¶ The *troops* ***fell back***. 軍隊が退却した. ¶ The *troops* ***marched*** past. 軍隊が分列行進をした.

Q ***air-borne*** (=***sky-borne***) *troops* 空てい部隊. ¶ a ***battle-tested*** *troop* 戦苦をなめた兵士 ¶ ***carefully-picked*** *troops* 選り抜きの兵士. ¶ ***foreign-armed*** and ***drilled*** *troops* in China 中国の外国式に武装し訓練した軍隊. ¶ ***friendly*** *troop* 友軍. ¶ ***seasoned*** *troops* 精鋭. ¶ Chinese ***Soviet-influenced*** *troops* 中国共産軍. ¶ a ***veteran*** *troop* 老練兵. ¶ the ***whole*** *troop* round him were astonished 彼を取巻く連中全部あっ気に取られた.

Q² ***air*** (***ground***) *troops* 空(陸)の兵士. ¶ ***garrison*** *troops* 守備隊. ¶ ***land*** *troops* 陸上軍. ¶ ***M.P.*** *troops* 憲兵隊;《英》国会派軍隊. ¶ American ***occupation*** *troops* アメリカ占領軍.

P surrounded ***by*** a *troop* of friends 大勢の友人に取巻かれて. ¶ a handful ***of*** *troops* 少数の軍隊. ¶ ***with*** a *troop* of followers 一群の従者を連れて.

P² *troops* ***of*** cavalry 騎兵隊 ‖ a *troop* (=gang) ***of*** children 子供の群. ¶ the Imperial *troops* ***under*** … …の率いる皇軍.

troop, *v.* 集まる, 群る.

M ***troop back*** through thirteen cars to one's own sleeping car 彼らの寝台車へ十三両を通って列をなして戻る. ¶ ***troop together*** (=***up***) 群り集まる.

M² (M) ***troop in*** (***out***) 群り来る(出る). ¶ ***troop off*** (=***away***) to … 群を成して…に去る.

P ***troop into*** a house (room) 屋(室)内にぞろぞろはいる. ¶ slowly ***troop out of*** the ward 静かに病室から出る.

trooper, *n.* 騎兵.

Q a ***khaki-clad*** *trooper* カーキー服を着た騎兵.

trophy, *n.* 戦利品; 戦勝記念品, トロフィー.

Q carry away the head as an ***honorable*** *trophy* of victory その首を名誉ある戦利品として持去る. ¶ a ***permanent*** *trophy*, which takes the form of a handsome silver cup りっぱな銀カップという永久の戦勝記念物.

Q² a ***tennis*** (***golf***) *trophy* テニス(ゴルフ)の優勝トロフィー.

P They keep the bear's skin and skull ***as*** *trophies*. 彼らはそのくまの皮と頭がい骨を戦闘記念として持っている.

P² a *trophy* ***of*** war 戦利品.

tropic, *n. pl.* 熱帯, 熱帯地方.

P situated ***beyond*** the *tropics* 熱帯地方のかなたに位置して. ¶ ***in*** the *tropics* 熱帯地方に. ¶ plants native ***to*** the *tropics* 熱帯地方原産の植物.

trot, *n.* 早足; だく; 足早の散歩.

P The cavalry advanced ***at*** a trot. 騎兵は早足で進んだ. ‖ ride ***at*** a *trot* 早足で騎行する. ¶ go ***for*** a *trot* 早足の乗馬に出掛ける. ¶ keep a person ***on*** the *trot* 人を働き通しにさせる.

trot, *v.* 小走りする.

M ***trot away*** 小走りして去る. ¶ ***trot out*** a horse 馬を走らせて足並を見る ‖ ***trot out*** a curio for show 骨とう品を出してみせる.

M² The boy ***trotted along*** after his mother. 少年は母親のあとから小走りについて行った.

trouble, *n.* 厄介, 手数; 紛争; 病気.

V ***adjust*** a *trouble* ごたごたを片付ける. ¶ It only ***aggravated*** the *trouble*. それがかえってことを大きくした. ¶ ***allay*** a *trouble* ごたごたを静める. ¶ ***alleviate*** (=***lessen***) *troubles* 苦労を軽減する. ¶ ***anticipate*** *trouble* 困難を予想する. ¶ This ***aroused*** *troubles* in the country. それが原因になってその国に面倒な事件が起った. ¶ He that will ***avoid*** *trouble* must avoid the world. 厄介がいやな人はこの世を去らなければならない. ¶ ***bear*** all the *troubles* of one's life 人生のあらゆる困難を忍ぶ. ¶ However, that is ***borrowing*** *trouble*. しかしそれは取越苦労というものだ. ¶ You will ***bring*** *trouble* on yourself if you do so. そんなことをすると労苦の種になるよ. ¶ ***bury*** one's *troubles* 心配を水に流す. ¶ ***cause*** *trouble* to … …に手数をかける. 【類】 ***cause*** a person much *trouble*. ¶ ***complicate*** one's *troubles* その困難を複雑化する. ¶ ***correct*** a *trouble* 困難を除去する. ¶ The ship ***developed*** engine *trouble*. 船が機関の故障を起す. ¶ the *trouble* was ***diagnosed*** as "…" その病気は「…」という診断であった. ¶ drink to ***drown*** *trouble* うさ晴らしに酒を飲む. 【類】 ***drown*** one's *troubles* in drink. ¶ This led him to attempt to ***end*** his *troubles* by suicide. このために彼は自殺によってその心配を清算しようとするに至った. ¶ ***endure*** *trouble* 困難を忍ぶ. ¶ ***expect*** *trouble* ahead 前に困難を予期する. 【類】 ***expect*** much *trouble* in finding a job. ¶ ***expend*** much *trouble* on … …に多くの労力を費す. ¶ ***forget*** their *troubles* in a roar of laughter 大笑いをして彼らの心配を忘れる. ¶ I beg you will not ***give*** yourself any *trouble*. 少しも御心配なさらないようにお願いします. ‖ if you ***give*** further *trouble* by … 君が…によってこの上私に面倒をかけるなら. 【類】 Since then he has ***given*** very little *trouble* to the police and law courts. ¶ ***have*** *trouble* with one's teeth 歯で悩む ‖ ***have*** *trouble* in … …で困っている ‖ I ***have*** much *trouble* to keep out of debt. 私は借金しないようにするのに随分骨が折れる. ‖ ***have*** *trouble* with the bowels 腸で難儀する. ¶ It doesn't pay to ***invite*** *trouble*. 事前に手を打った. ¶ lay the *trouble* at the door of … その厄介の原因を…に帰する. ¶ ***locate*** a *trouble* 故障の個所をつき止める. ¶ ***magnify*** the *trouble* ことを面倒にする. ¶ When others interfere, it always ***makes*** *trouble*. 他人が干渉するといつも面倒になる. 【類】 She is always ***making*** *troubles* (問題を起して). ¶ ***obviate*** the *trouble* of … …の厄介を除く. ¶ ***occasion*** (=cause) a great deal of *trouble* 非常にことが面倒になる. 【類】 Hoping this will not ***occasion*** you a great deal of *trouble*. ¶ ***produce*** *trouble* inside and distrust outside 内には厄介外には不信を引き起す. ¶ ***remedy*** the *trouble* その禍を除く. ¶ amply ***repay*** the *trouble* 十分その手数をかけるかいがある. ¶ ***save*** a person the *trouble* of … 人に…の手数を省かせる ‖ To do so ***saves*** much *trouble*. そうすると大分手数が省ける. 【類】 A great deal of *trouble* is thus ***saved***. ¶ ***request*** the *trouble* of … 恐縮ながら…をやってもらう. ¶ ***scent*** *trouble* ことが面倒になると感付く. ¶ neither *trouble* nor expense is ***spared*** to … …するためには手数も費用も惜しまない. ¶ He is bent on ***stirring up*** *trouble* between the two countries 彼は両国間に紛争を起そうとして躍起となっている. ¶ ***start*** some *trouble* 何か事件を起す. ¶ ***stop*** the *trouble* at its source その禍根を絶つ. ¶ ***take*** the *trouble* of … …の労を取る ‖ ***take*** all *trouble* off my hands respecting … …に関して私から一切の手数を取り去る. 【類】 You need not ***take*** any *trouble* about it. ¶ ***throw away*** one's *trouble* その心配を一切やめる. ¶ she ***unfolded*** (=***confided***) her *troubles* to … 彼女はその心配ごとを…に打明けた.

V² *trouble* ***arose*** over … …のことで問題が起った. ¶ *Trouble* was ***brewing*** in the capital. 首都に事件がぼっ発しようとしていた. ¶ And there ***lies*** the *trouble!* でそいつが厄介なことなんだ. ¶ No *trouble* ***occurred***. 無事に済んだ. ¶ The *trouble* is still ***seething***. その紛争がまだおさまらない.

Q His *trouble* became ***acute***. 彼の病気は激化した. ¶ ***give additional*** (=***extra***) *trouble* 余計な手数がかかる. ¶ ***anticipated*** *trouble* 予想した心配ごと. ¶ He is ill with a suspicion of a ***bronchial*** *trouble*. 彼は病気だが肺が悪いらしい. ¶ take ***considerable*** *trouble* in … …に大分骨を折る. ¶ suffer from ***digestive*** *troubles* 胃病にかかっている. ¶ ***domestic*** *troubles* 家庭のごたごた. ¶ in these days of austerity and ***economic*** *troubles* 切詰めた生活をしている今日では. ¶ The concern is in ***financial*** *trouble*. その社は財政難に陥っている. ¶ ***gastro-intestinal*** *troubles* 胃腸病. ¶ think it a ***great*** *trouble* それを面倒くさがる. ¶ a ***gruesome*** *trouble* うす気味の悪い厄介. ¶ ***international*** *troubles* 国際的紛争. ¶ It causes ***little*** *trouble*. それはほとんど面倒なことはない. ¶ That will spare me ***much*** *trouble*. これで私はだいぶ助かる. 【類】 with comparatively ***little*** *trouble*. ¶ ***needless*** *trouble* 無用な手数. ¶ The whole *trouble* was ***nervous***. 病気は全く(客観性がなく)神経から来ていた. ¶ ***No*** *trouble* at all. お安いご用です. ¶ a ***personal*** *trouble* 個人の心配事. ¶ ***political*** *troubles* 政争. ¶ a ***serious*** *trouble* 一大難事. ¶ a ***respiratory*** *trouble* 胸の病気. ¶ ***social*** *troubles* 社会の問題. ¶ come to him with the cry of an ***unsolved*** *trouble* 苦悩の叫びを発し彼の所へ来る. ¶ ***unsparing*** *trouble* 骨身をおしまない努力. ¶ ***uterine*** *trouble* 子宮病. ¶ ***worldly*** *troubles* 現世のわずらい. ¶ It would not be *worth* the *trouble*. それは手数をかけるだけの価値はないだろう.

Q² develop ***engine trouble*** 機関の故障を起す. ¶***eye trouble*** 眼病. ¶***family trouble*** 家庭の不和. ¶a victim of ***heart trouble*** 心臓病患者. ¶cause ***kidney trouble*** じん臓病を起す. ¶There were fears that ***labor troubles*** might spread. 労働争議が広がるおそれがあった. ¶He had ***lung trouble*** as a boy. 彼が子供のときに肺病をやった. ¶a ***school trouble*** 学校争議. ¶***skin trouble*** 皮膚病. 【類】Acne (にきび) is a common ***skin trouble.*** ¶***stomach troubles*** 色々の胃病. ¶***telephone trouble*** 電話の故障. ¶***throat trouble*** いんこう障害. ¶***traffic trouble*** 交通事故.

P I found it ***after*** much *trouble*. 私はようようのことでそれを見付けた. ¶there is not enough profit to make it worth their while to be ***at*** the *trouble* of ... ...を手数をかけてやるだけの利益が上がらない ‖ Would you be ***at*** the *trouble* to write that to him? 御面倒でもそれを先方へ手紙で言ってやっていただけましょうか. 【類】Would you be ***at*** the *trouble* to ring the bell for me? / Gold is scarce and can only be mined ***at*** great *trouble*. ¶Thank you ***for*** the *trouble* you have taken in sending it to us. それを私どもにわざわざお送り下さいまして有難う存じます. ¶The establishment is ***in*** *trouble* with the police. その店は警察と面倒なことになっている. 【類】He is ***in*** deep *trouble*. ¶This will get you ***into*** *trouble*. 君面倒なことになるよ. ¶Life is full ***of*** *troubles*. 人生は苦労が多い. ¶get ***out of*** *trouble* 困難を切抜ける ‖ keep ***out of*** *trouble* with foreign countries 外国と紛争を起さないようにする. ¶***owing to*** unexpected electrical *troubles* 思いがけない電気の故障があって. ¶pass ***through*** *troubles* 困難を通抜ける. ¶I've put you ***to*** much *trouble*, I'm afraid. 御迷惑をおかけしたんじゃないですか. ¶***with*** the least *trouble* できるだけ手数を省いて. ¶***without*** further *trouble* この上の面倒なく. 【類】***without*** any *trouble* ‖ The ascent of the mountain is well ***worth*** the *trouble*. その登山は骨を折る価値がある.

P² he is in great *trouble* ***about*** ... 彼は...について大いに困難している. ¶The *trouble* ***at*** the university has come to an end. その大学の紛争は片が付いた. ¶a *trouble* ***between*** ... ...間の争乱 ‖ *troubles* ***of*** sight, throat, lungs, abdomen 目・のど・肺・腸の病気. ¶a *trouble* ***over*** a matter ある事件に関するごたごた. ¶It is a *trouble* ***to*** him. それは彼に取って厄介なことである. ¶What is the *trouble* ***with*** you? あなたは何でお困りですか. ‖ the *trouble* ***with*** us is that ... 困ったことには...である.

trouble, *v.* わずらわす, 困らす, 心配させる.

M He is ***dreadfully*** *troubled* with corns on both his feet. 彼は両足に豆ができて非常に困っている. ¶If you do not succeed, do not *trouble* ***further***. うまく行かなかったらそれでやめて下さい. ¶he is ***seriously*** *troubled* over ... 彼は...で非常に悩んでいる.

P Don't *trouble* yourself ***about*** the future. 将来を心配なさるな. ‖ I am much *troubled* ***about*** the affair. 私はその件で大いに困っている. ¶be *troubled* ***by*** heat 暑さに苦しむ. 【類】be *troubled* ***by*** (=with) a cough. ¶May I *trouble* you ***for*** some money? 金を少々お借りできませんか. ‖ May I *trouble* you ***for*** the salt? 塩を取ってくれませんか(食卓で). ¶*troubled* ***in*** mind 心配している. ¶He is much *troubled* ***over*** the matter. 彼はそのことで大分心配している. ¶*troubled* ***with*** a headache (stomachache, sore throat) 頭痛(など)で困って. 【類】be *troubled* ***with*** falling hair (抜け毛) ‖ He is *troubled* ***with*** stage-fright. 彼は舞台度胸がなくって困っている. ‖ *trouble* a person ***with*** questions (inquiries, complaints) 質問(など)で人を悩ます ‖ be *troubled* ***with*** regrets ***for*** things done やったことを後悔する.

O so I didn't *trouble* to ... だから私は...しようとはしなかった. 【類】Oh, don't *trouble*, thanks. ¶I had to *trouble* him to ... 私は彼をわずらわして...してもらわなければならなかった.

trouble-shooter, *n.* 《米》争議の調停官.

Q One day in 1944 a ***young*** *trouble-shooter* was trying to fix a big labor trouble. 千九百四十四年のある日若い調停委員が大きなストをしずめようとかかった.

troublesome, *a.* 面倒な, 困難な.

M It's ***quite*** *troublesome*. 全くやっかいだ. ¶it is ***too*** *troublesome* to ... の苦悩にたえない.

P I have been very *troublesome* ***to*** you. 大変御面倒をおかけしました. ¶The route up the mountain would be *troublesome* ***without*** a guide. その登山は案内者がないと困難だろう.

trough, *n.* [舟形の]おけ, はち; 細長いくぼみ.

Q² a ***dough*** *trough* [パン屋の]こねばち. ¶***drinking*** *troughs* for horses and dogs 馬や犬に水を飲ませるおけ. ¶an ***eaves*** *trough* 軒のとい.

P² a *trough* ***between*** waves 波間の谷. ¶the *trough* ***of*** the sea 波の合い間.

troupe, *n.* [俳優などの]一座; 一組.

V ***import*** a new theatrical *troupe* 新規に俳優の一座を輸入する.

Q an ***itinerant theatrical*** *troupe* 移動劇団. ¶a ***mixed*** *troupe* of actors and actresses 男女優の混合一座. ¶The *troupe* is now ***performing*** in the theatre. その一座は目下その劇場でやっている. ¶a ***theatrical*** *troupe* on the road 旅役者の一座.

P² a mixed *troupe* ***of*** actors and actresses 男女優の一座.

O John Allen and his *troupe* ジョン・アレンとその一座.

trouper, *n.* 《米》〖劇〗座員.

Q² a ***star*** *trouper* 花形座員(幹部).

trousers, *n. pl.* ズボン.

V ***brush*** one's *trousers* clean ズボンにブラシをかける. ¶***button up*** (***zip up***) one's *trousers* ズボンのボタン(チャック)をかける. ¶***have*** one's *trousers* ***cuffed*** 《米》ズボンの下を折るように仕立させる. ¶***pull*** (=***hitch***) ***up*** one's *trousers* ズボンをぐいと引上げる. ¶***take down*** one's *trousers* ズボンを下げる. ¶***tuck*** one's *trousers* into one's socks ズボンの端をくつ下に入れ込む. ¶***turn up*** one's *trousers* ズボンの端を折り上げる. ¶Your *trousers* are ***unbuttoned.*** 君のズボンのボタンがはずれている. ¶***wear*** *trousers* ズボンをはいている.

Q ***bagged*** *trousers* だんぶくろズボン. ¶***close-fitting*** *trousers* ぴったり合うズボン. ¶***fancy-colored*** *trousers* 色変りのズボン. ¶***fashion-tailored*** *trousers* 流行型仕立のズボン. ¶***patched*** *trousers* 継ぎはぎのあるズボン. ¶***thin-bottomed*** *trousers* 下の細いズボン. ¶***spare*** *trousers*=trousers to spare 替えズボン.

Q² ***bell bottom*** *trousers* ラッパ形ズボン. ¶***blue serge*** *trousers* こん色セルのズボン. ¶***full-dress*** *trousers* 式服のズボン. ¶***knee*** *trousers* (=pants) 短ズボン. ¶***plush*** *trousers* 綿綿ビロードのズボン. ¶a pair of ***white flannel tennis*** *trousers* 白フランネルのテニス用ズボン一着. ¶***work*** *trousers* 作業ズボン.

P turn up the legs ***of*** *trousers* ズボンの脚部をまくり上げる ‖ a pair ***of*** *trousers* ズボン一着.

P² *trousers* ***with*** turnups (=cuffs) すそに折返しのあるズボン ‖ *trousers* ***with*** plain bottoms (=without cuffs) 折返しのないズボン.

trousseau, *n.* 嫁入道具.

V a prospective bride ***collecting*** an elaborate *trousseau* りっぱな嫁入道具をそろえる近々結婚の娘.

Q a ***bridal*** *trousseau* 嫁入道具.

Q² The school is equipped with a complete "***kitchen*** *trousseau.*" 学校は完全なすい事用具が備えてある.

trout, *n.* 〖集団〗あめます; [一尾の]あめます.

V ***hook*** a *trout* あめますを釣る. ¶I ***had*** *trout* for breakfast. 私は朝食にますを食べた. ¶***play*** *trout* among the minnows 鳥なき里のこうもりを気取る.

Q ***delicious*** *trout* 美味なます. ¶a ***rainbow*** *trout* [米国産の]にじます.

truant, *n.* 怠け者, ずるけ者.

V ***play*** *truant* from school 《英》学校をずる休みする ‖ The miller's boys ***played*** *truant* one day by the river. 粉屋の男の子たちがある日学校を怠けて川のそばで遊んでいた.

truce, *n.* 休戦; 休戦条約; 休み.

V ***carry out*** a *truce* 休戦を実行する. ¶***conclude*** a *truce* with ... ...と休戦条約を締結する. ¶For a number of years he ***enjoyed*** a *truce* from persecution. 数年間彼は従来の迫害を受けずにいた. ¶***make*** a *truce* 休戦する. ¶A *truce* has been ***patched up***. 休戦条約が大急ぎで作られた. ¶***put*** a *truce* to this talk この論議を切上げる.

Q an ***armed*** *truce* 武装のままの休戦. ¶a ***general*** *truce* 一般休戦. ¶an ***industrial*** *truce* between labor and management 労使間の闘争の休戦.

Q² order a ***three-week*** *truce* in the operations against ... ...に対する戦事行動に三週間の休戦を命じる.

P a flag ***of*** *truce* 休戦旗.

P² a *truce* ***between*** ... ...間の休戦. ¶a *truce* ***to*** quarreling けんかの中止.

truck, *n.* 《米》貨物自動車(トラック); 《英》無蓋貨車.

Q ***over-age*** and ***battered*** *trucks* 使用年限が過ぎ破損した貨

車. ¶drive a ***stolen truck*** 盗んだトラックを運転する.

Q² a ***delivery truck*** 配達用トラック. ¶a ***diesel truck*** ディーゼルトラック. ¶a ***fire truck*** 消防車. ¶a ***goods truck*** 《英》貨車. ¶a ***library truck***＝a library on wheels 移動図書館車. ¶a ***multi-ton truck*** 大型貨車(トラック).

P carry goods ***on*** a ***truck*** トラックで荷物を運ぶ.

truck, *n.* 《米》[市場向け]野菜.

V ***produce*** twice as much ***truck*** as the market consumes 市場でさばく二倍の量の野菜を生産する.

Q² ***garden truck***＝《英》garden produce 売り野菜.

truck, *v.* 交換する, 交易する.

P ***truck*** one thing ***for*** another 甲を乙と交換する. ¶***truck with*** a person ***for*** something 人とある品を交換する.

truckling, *n.* 世辞.

Q ***servile truckling*** 卑しい世辞.

truckload, *n.* 《米》トラックに一杯.

P² three ***truckloads of*** goods トラックに三台の荷物.

trudge, *v.* 苦しそうに歩む.

P ***trudge along*** a rugged road でこぼこ道を骨折って歩む.

true, *a.* 真実の, 本当の, 正しい.

M it is ***broadly true*** that ... ...ということは大体において間違っていない. ¶be ***true enough*** たしかに事実である. ¶be ***generally true*** 概して事実である. ¶be only ***half true*** 半分だけ事実である. ¶***historically true*** 史実的な. ¶***irresistibly true*** 論争の余地がないほど真実性のある. ¶It is not intended to be accepted as ***literally true***. それは文字通りに受取られようとして言ったのではない. ¶***manifestly true*** 明かに本当な. ¶***obviously true*** 明らかに真実な. ¶be ***perfectly true*** 全く事実である. ¶***plainly true*** 明かに本当な. ¶This may ***possibly*** be ***true***. 恐らくこれは本当だろう. ¶It is ***probably true***. 大方そうであろう. ¶be ***profoundly true*** どこまでも事実である. ¶***quite true*** 全く真実な. ¶Everything he uttered was ***solidly true***. 彼の言ったことは何から何まで確かに本当であった. ¶not ***strictly true*** 厳密に本当とは言えない. ¶***undoubtedly true*** 疑いもなく本当な. ¶***unerringly true*** 間違いなく本当な. ¶What he said is ***unquestionably true***. 彼の言ったことはもちろん本当のことです.

M² His wife was ***as true*** as steel. 彼の妻は鋼鉄のような貞節堅固な女であった. ‖ this is ***as true*** for... as for ... これは...においてもまた...においても事実(その通り)である.

P This news is strange, but it is ***true for*** all that. この報道は変は変だが本当だ. ¶This has been ***true in*** all civilized countries. これは全文明諸国に共通したことである. ¶the reverse is ***true of*** ... ...においてはその反対である ‖ the same is ***true of*** ... ...においても同様である. 【類】the same thing is ***true of*** ... / And what is ***true of*** individuals is equally ***true of*** nations. / This is as ***true of*** a nation as of an individual. / It is ***true of*** France, ***of*** Germany, and ***of*** the United States. / This is particularly ***true of*** the upper classes (上流社会). ‖ There are certain facts which are ***true of*** all languages. すべての国語に共通な事実がある ‖ unfortunately this is not ***true of*** ... 不幸にしてこれは...にはあてはまらない. ¶I will be ***true to*** you. あなたに本当のことを申上げましょう. ‖ ***true to*** oneself 自己に忠実に ‖ The translation is ***true to*** the original. その訳は原文に忠実だ. ‖ ***true to*** his promise (＝word) 彼の約束通り. 【類】***true to*** his time / be ***true to*** one's own conviction ‖ ***true to*** his trust 彼の信頼をはずかしめずに. 【類】be ***true to*** the principles of ... ‖ ***true to*** her own traditions その国の伝統に従って ‖ This mayor wasn't ***true to*** type. He was more like a school-master. この市長は風変りな市長だった. どちらかというと学校の先生らしかった. ‖ be ***true to*** life ほんものそっくりだ ‖ It is ***true to*** life (nature). それは生き写しだ(真にせまる). ¶Substantially the novel is ***true to*** history. 実質的にその小説は実話である.

O His dream came ***true***. 正夢となった.

true, *n.* 真実.

V ***distinguish true*** from false 真偽を区別する. ¶***sift*** the ***true*** from the false 本物とにせ物をより分ける.

P I can vouch for it ***as true***. 私はそれが本物だという保証をする. ¶It is ***out of true***. それは的を失している.

truism, *n.* 自明の理.

V ***illustrate*** once more the old ***truism*** that ... これもまた...という古い真理の例証になる. ¶To say that ... is merely to ***repeat*** a familiar ***truism***. ...ということは分かり切った真理を繰返して言うにすぎない.

Q it is an ***accepted truism*** that ... ...ということは一般に真理である. ¶an ***epigrammatical truism*** 寸鉄的至言. ¶repeat a ***familiar truism*** 世人周知のことを繰返す. ¶an ***immutable truism*** 不変の真理. ¶***utter truism*** 全くの真理.

O it is almost a ***truism*** to say that ... ...ということはほとんど説明の要がない.

trump, *n.* 切札; 最後の策, 奥の手.

V He ***holds trumps***. 彼には奥の手がある. ¶***lead trumps*** [カードで]親になる. ¶***play*** a ***trump*** 切札を出す; 奥の手を出す. ¶***turn up trumps*** まぐれあたりをする. 「札.

Q ***high trumps*** 切札全部手持 ‖ the ***highest trump*** 最高の切

P put a person ***to*** his ***trumps*** 人に最後の手を出させる.

trump, *v.* ねつ造する.

M ***trump up*** a story 風説をねつ造する ‖ ***trump up*** excuses to ... ...するための口実を作る.

trump-card, *n.* 切札.

V ***play*** one's ***trump-card*** 奥の手を出す. ¶The presentation of the missing letter ***proved*** a ***trump-card***. 見失った手紙を出したのがきめ手になった.

trumpet, *n.* らっぱ.

V ***blow*** (＝***sound*** *or* ***blare***) a ***trumpet*** らっぱを吹く ‖ ***blow*** (＝sound) one's own ***trumpet*** 自慢話をする, 自己宣伝をやる. ¶***flourish*** a ***trumpet*** らっぱを花やかに吹く.

Q a ***clangorous*** and ***clear trumpet*** 高らかに鳴り響くらっぱ.

Q² an ***ear trumpet*** 補聴器. ¶toot (＝tootle) the ***horn trumpet*** らっぱを吹く.

P announce it ***by trumpet*** それをらっぱで知らせる. ¶after a flourish ***of trumpets*** らっぱで一節吹奏の後 ‖ amidst a geaat fanfare ***of trumpets*** らっぱの花やかな吹奏の内に. ¶a flourish ***on*** a ***trumpet*** らっぱの一吹奏. ¶give orders ***through*** the ***trumpet*** らっぱで号令する.

trumpet, *v.* ふい聴する. 「世間にふい聴する.

M ***trumpet*** one's fame (talent) ***abroad*** 自分の評判(など)を

P ***trumpet*** a book ***into*** notice ある本をふい聴して世人の注

trumpeter, *n.* らっぱ手. 目を引く.

Q² a ***sergeant trumpeter*** らっぱ長(英国宮内省の).

truncheon, *n.* 《英》警棒.

V ***carry*** a ***truncheon*** (＝baton) ***along*** 警棒を持って歩く.

Q² a ***stout*** box-wood ***truncheon*** がん丈なボックス材の警棒.

P a policeman ***with*** a ***truncheon*** on his side 警棒をぶらさげた警官.

trunk, *n.* 旅行かばん(トランク); 樹幹; 《米》幹線; *pl.* 《米》[運動選手の]パンツ.

V ***break open*** one's ***trunk*** 人のかばんをこじあける. ¶***check*** one's ***trunks*** [鉄道]そのトランクをチッキで出す. ¶***leave*** one's ***trunk*** at the station かばんを停車場にあずけておく. ¶***pack*** [***up***] one's ***trunk*** かばんに詰める. ¶***unpack*** a ***trunk*** かばんに詰めたものを出す.

Q The curiosity of the boy was piqued by the ***locked trunk***. 少年の好奇心が錠を下したトランクを見て高まった. ¶***old gnarled trunks*** 年老いて節だらけの幹.

Q² ***bathing*** (＝***swim***) ***trunks*** 水泳用のパンツ. ¶a ***drawer trunk*** 引出式トランク. ¶the ***Saratoga Trunk*** サラトガ本線. ¶a ***tree trunk*** 木の幹. ¶a ***wardrobe trunk*** たんす兼用トランク.

P a long ***trunk with*** short legs 胴長の脚短か.

truss, *v.* 束ねる.

M ***trussed up*** with ropes なわでしかと束ねて.

trust, *n.* 信頼, 信用; トラスト(企業組合); 預り物.

V ***abuse*** one's master's ***trust*** その主人の信任を悪用する[使い込み・帳簿の不正など]. ¶***accept*** a ***trust*** 委託を引受ける. ¶***betray*** a ***trust*** 信頼を裏切る. ¶***break trust*** 信用を破棄する. ¶***build up*** a great commercial ***trust*** 一大企業合同を組織する. ¶***carry out*** a ***trust*** 信任に負けない. ¶***desert*** one's ***trust*** その信任にそむく. ¶***fail*** one's ***trust*** 背信する. ¶***fulfil*** one's ***trust*** その信頼を果す. ¶It is a question whether the new Cabinet will ***justify*** the nation's ***trust*** in them. 新内閣が国民の信頼を果すか否かは疑問である. ¶***keep trust*** 信用を持続する. ¶You have always ***maintained*** your ***trust*** in me. 君は終始一貫して僕を信頼した. ¶***misuse*** our ***trust*** われわれの信任を濫用する. ¶***organize*** a ***trust*** トラストを組織する. ¶***place*** (＝***put***) no ***trust*** in ... ...を信用しない. 【類】***put*** one's ***trust*** in God. ¶***repose trust*** in a person 人を信用する.

Q a sad story of ***misplaced trust*** 空だのみの悲しい物語.

¶It is offered to the ***national trust*** by its owner. 所有者はその保管を国家に一任しようと申し出た. ¶a position of ***public trust*** 公衆の信頼を受ける地位. ¶by an infamous abuse of the ***reposed trust*** in him by ... 不都合にも彼は…の信用を濫用して. ¶He detailed to me in ***sacred trust*** all the important particulars. 彼は秘密として重要な点をこまかく私に打明けた. ¶***family trust*** 財閥.

Q² ***brain trusts*** 頭脳委員会, 専門委員会(顧問団). ¶a giant

P The lodging-house is owned ***by*** a *trust* composed of earnest and philanthropic gentlemen. その下宿屋は熱心で慈悲深い神士たちのトラストが所有している. ¶give it ***in*** *trust* それを預ける ‖ hold it ***in*** *trust* それを預かっておく. ¶a breach ***of*** *trust* 背任. ¶accept ***on*** *trust* 信用して応じる ‖ to sell (buy) ***on trust*** 掛で売る(買う) ‖ take it ***on trust*** 始めからそれを信じて掛かる. 【類】principles taken ***on*** (=***upon***) *trust*.

P² his unshaken *trust* ***in*** the atoning blood of the Redeemer 救世主キリストの流した血が世の罪を償うという彼の揺がぬ信仰 ‖ one's *trust* ***in*** truth その真理に対する信頼. ¶The estate is left in *trust* ***with*** the ... company その財産はその会社に信託してある.

trust, *v.* 信じる, 信任する, 委任する.

M *trust* ***implicitly*** in his wisdom and power 彼の賢明と実力とを(口にこそ出さないが)心の中で信頼する. ¶*trust* ***largely*** to memory 主として記憶に頼る. ¶***stolidly*** *trust* in ... 断固として…を信用する.

P *trust* a person ***for*** a meal 人に一回の食事代をつけにする. ¶*trust* ***in*** God (=divine favor) 神の恵みを信じる ‖ *trusting* ***in*** your continued sympathy and co-operation いつまでもご同情と御協力を賜わらんことを信じて [手紙の終句]. 【類】*trust* ***in*** a person. ¶While reading, never *trust* ***to*** your memory, but fill up your notebook. 読書に際し決して記憶力を当にすることなく手帳に書き記せ. 【類】It is not safe to *trust* ***to*** the memory. ‖ *trust* ***to*** commonsense 常識に頼る ‖ *trust* ***to*** chance 運を天に任せる. 【類】It is the nature of the slum dwellers (貧民くつに住む者の根性) to live only for today and to *trust* ***to*** luck ***for*** tomorrow. / I'll *trust* ***to*** you ***for*** the performance of the task. ‖ he may be *trusted* ***to*** the extent (=amount) of £... …ポンドまでは彼と取引しても安全だろう. ¶*trust* him ***with*** some of the secrets of her life 彼女の生活の秘密を幾分彼に打明ける. ‖ He *trusted* me ***with*** his money. 彼は私に金を預けた. ‖ *trusted* ***with*** every confidence あらゆる秘密を打明けられて.

trustee, *n.* 管財人.

P commit property to the care ***of*** a *trustee* 財産を管財人に委任する.

trusteeship, *n.* 信託; 信託(委任)統治.

V ***hold*** the *trusteeship* of one's nephew's property そのおいの財産の受信託権を保有する.

Q² place the former Japanese-mandated islands under a "***strategic area***" *trusteeship* 旧日本委任統治の諸島を軍略地域信託管理の下におく. ¶a ***United Nations*** *trusteeship* 国際連合の信託管理. ¶the ***4-Power*** *trusteeship* agreed upon by the Big-3 Foreign Ministers at Moscow モスコーで三大国外相が一致した四強国の信託統活.

truster, *n.* 信頼しうる人.

Q² a ***brain*** *truster* 頭脳委員会の一員.

trustworthiness, *n.* 信頼しうること.

V ***increase*** the *trustworthiness* and consequent value of the work 信頼性を高め随ってその本の価値を増す.

truth, *n.* 真理, 真実, 実体.

V He ***acknowledged*** the *truth* of what was said. 彼は言われたことの真実性を認めた. ¶***ascertain*** the *truth* 事実を確かめる. ¶***assert*** a great *truth* 一大真理を説く. ¶***avoid*** the *truth* 事実をごまかす. ¶***bring*** the *truth* ***home*** その真理をしみじみ感じさせる. ¶***caricature*** the *truth* 事実を曲げる. ¶I ***challenge*** the *truth* of this statement. 私はこの言の真実を疑う. ¶***clear up*** the *truth* 真実を明らかにする. ¶to ***confess*** the *truth* 実は. ¶It ***contains*** the whole *truth*. それは全面的の事実を包含している. ¶***demonstrate*** the *truth* 事実を証明する. ¶emphatically ***deny*** the *truth* of a report 報道の事実を力強く否定する ‖ ***deny*** the *truth* out of shame 自分の恥になるのでそのことを事実でないという. ¶***discriminate*** *truth* from error 真偽を識別する. ¶No sophistry of argument will ever be able to ***dim*** or ***eclipse*** its shining *truth*. いかにでたらめを言いふらしてもその偉大な真理を到底曇らしたり隠したりすることはできない. ¶***discover*** (=***find out***) the *truth* 実状を明らかにする. ¶***discriminate*** *truth* from error 真偽を弁別する. ¶***dispute*** the *truth* of the statement その声明の真実性を問題にする. ¶***disseminate*** the *truth* in regard to ... …に関する真相を世間に知らせる. ¶***distort*** *truth* and facts 真理や事実を曲げる. ¶I ***doubt*** the *truth* of that statement. その言明は真偽のほどは明らかでない. ‖ The *truth* of the story has often been ***doubted***. その物語の真実性はしばしば疑われた. ¶quotations ***embodying*** these *truths* これらの真理を含む引用句. ¶***embroider*** the *truth* 事実を修飾する. ¶the *truth* of this remark is ***emphasized*** by ... この説の正しいことが…によって強調されている. ¶it serves to ***enforce*** the *truth* that ... それは…という事実を有力ならしめる. ¶these facts go to ***establish*** the *truth* of ... これらの事実は総合的に…の真実を証明する. ¶***feel out*** the *truth* 事実をさぐる. ¶***follow*** *truth* wherever it leads one あくまで(自分はどうなろうと)真理に追随する. ¶The bitter *truth* was ***forced*** home to me. そのおもしろくない事実がつくづく私の胸にこたえた. ¶***grasp*** the whole *truth* of ... …の実相をつかむ. ¶It ***has*** a *truth*.=There is a truth in it. それは一面において的中している. ¶***hide*** the *truth* 真実を隠す. ¶it ***illustrates*** the *truth* of ... それは…が事実であるという例証になる. ¶***learn*** new *truths* 新しい事実を知る. ¶***love*** *truth* 真理を愛する. ¶***prove*** the *truth* of the adage その格言の真実性を証明する. ¶It is by passing through error that the *truth* is ***reached***. 誤びゅうを経過して初めて真実に達しうるのだ. ¶***reach*** and ***convey*** the exact *truth* 正しい真理に到達してこれを伝える. ¶***realise*** its literal *truth* その正確な事態を知る. ¶***reason out*** the *truth* 事実を弁明する. ¶***reveal*** the *truth* 事実を明かす. ¶***sacrifice*** *truth* to effect 効果を出そうとして真実を犠牲にする ‖ ***sacrifice*** *truth* for rhetoric 文を飾るために事実を曲げる. ¶to ***say*** the *truth* 実を言うと. ¶***see*** *truth* 真理がわかる. ¶***seek*** *truth* with an earnest mind 熱心に真理を探求する. ¶***seize*** a *truth* by intuition 直覚的に事実をつかむ. ¶***separate*** the *truth* from the error 真偽を弁別する. ¶***set*** the *truth* before everything 何よりも真実を重んじる. ¶***set forth*** a *truth* 事実を述べる. ¶***speak*** the *truth* 真実を話す. ¶***spread*** *truths* 事実を流布する. ¶***state*** the bold *truth* むき出しに事実を述べる. ¶***strain*** the *truth* 事実を曲げる. ¶***stretch*** the *truth* 事実を誇張する. ¶***talk*** the *truth* 事実を話す. ¶fearlessly ***tell*** the *truth* as he learned it from observation 彼が観察によって知り得たままの事実を大胆に言う ‖ if the *truth* must be ***told*** 実の所を言うと ‖ ***tell*** plain *truths* in pure language 飾らない言葉で真実そのままを語る ‖ It pays to ***tell*** the *truth*. 本当のことを言って損はない. 【類】***tell*** the *truth* bluntly (あけすけ) / He was burning (むずむず) to ***tell*** the *truth*. / the duty of ***telling*** the *truth* / To ***tell*** the *truth*, I do not like him. / to ***tell*** you the honest *truth*. ¶***test*** the *truth* of an evidence 証拠の真実性をためす. ¶***think, speak*** and ***live*** the *truth* 真理を考え話しかつ実践する. ¶***understand*** the *truths* which underlie facts 事実の根抵をなす真理を理解する. ¶***utter*** the *truth* 真実を言う. ¶if you ***want*** the *truth* 実を言うと. ¶***withold*** the *truth* from the public 事実を世間に知らせないでおく.

V² The *truth* has ***come out***. その真相が分かった. ‖ when the *truth* of things ***came out***, I was told that ... ことの真相が分かった時…だということであった. ¶The *truth* has ***leaked out***. 分からなかったその真相が明らかになった. ¶*Truth* will always ***prevail***. 本当のことには勝てない.

Q an ***absolute*** *truth* 絶対的真理. ¶an ***acknowledged*** *truth* 認められた事実. ¶an ***artistic*** *truth* 芸術上の真理. ¶the ***basic*** *truth* underlying ... …の基礎を成す真理. ¶It is a fact; there is no ***disguising*** the *truth*. それは事実でありその実状を偽装しようとしてもそれはできない. ¶speak the ***downright*** *truth* 赤裸々の事実を言う. ¶the ***essential*** *truth* of ... …の根本的な事実. ¶an ***established*** *truth* 確立した事実. ¶an ***eternal*** (=***everlasting***) *truth* 永遠の真理. ¶the ***exact*** *truth* 正確な事実 ¶It is no fable, but the ***fair*** and ***square*** *truth*. それは作りごとではなくて公明正大な事実である. ¶state the ***full*** *truth* with regard to ... …に関して事実の全ぼうを述べる. ¶the ***fundamental*** *truth* 根本的の真理. ¶a ***general*** *truth* 一般の真理. ¶a ***glorious*** *truth* りっぱな真理. ¶take it all for ***gospel*** *truth* それを全部真に受ける. ¶a ***great*** *truth* 大真理. ¶a ***half*** *truth* 半面の真

理. ¶the ***grim truth*** 厳然たる事実. ¶Believe it or not, but that's ***heaven's truth***. 信じる信じないは人の勝手だがそれは正真正銘の事実である. ¶a practical illustration of the ***homely truth*** that ... …という卑近な真理の実例. ¶a ***half-humorous, half-tragic truth*** 半ば滑けい半ば悲劇的な事実. ¶to tell you the ***honest truth*** 本当のことを言えば. ¶***humble truth*** はえない事実. ¶***indiscriminate truth*** ばか正直. ¶an ***imcomplete truth*** 不完全な真理. ¶it is only the ***literal truth*** to say that ... …とは全く文字通り(掛値なし)の真実を言っているのである ‖ This is merely the statement of a ***literal truth***. これは誤りのない真実だけを述べたのである. ¶the stark ***naked truth*** 全く赤裸々な事実. ¶an enthusiast teaching ***new truths*** 新しい真理を教える熱心家. ¶there is ***no truth*** in the statement that ... …という言明には真実性がない. ¶True, yet ***not all*** the ***truth***. 本当だ(その点は)しかし全部の真理ではない. ¶an ***obvious*** or ***axiomatic truth*** 明白なすなわち自明的真理. ¶new ways of putting ***old truths*** 昔ながらの真理を説く新しい表現. ¶a ***paradoxical truth*** 非に似て実は是な真理. ¶only a ***partial truth*** ほんの一面的真理. ¶***permanent truths*** 永遠の真理. ¶***plain sexual truths*** 平明な性的事実. ¶the ***plain, unvarnished truth*** 平明にして飾りのない事実. ¶***Truth*** is ***powerful***. 真実には力がある. ¶to tell you the ***precise truth*** うそのない所を言えば. ¶the ***profound truth*** 千古不滅の真理. ¶the ***real truth*** of the matter 事件の真相. ¶***rhetorical truth*** 修辞上の真理. ¶***scientific truth*** 科学上の真理. ¶a ***self-evident truth*** 自明の真理. ¶in ***sober truth*** 実際. ¶Probably there is ***some truth*** (=an element of truth) in this contention. この議論には恐らく理がある. ¶a ***terrible truth*** 恐ろしい事実. ¶an ***undeniable truth*** 否定し得ない事実. ¶an ***unflattering truth*** 聞いてうれしくない事実. ¶a ***universal truth*** 普遍的真理(1+1=2 などの). ¶prefer pleasant error to ***unpleasant truth*** 不愉快な真実より愉快なうその方を好む. ¶a search for ***unprejudiced historic truth*** 偏見のない歴史的事実の探求. ¶***unquestioned truths*** 問題になり得ない(明かな)事実. ¶the ***unvarnished truth*** 飾りのない事実. ¶speak ***unwelcome truths*** 人から喜ばれない事実を話す. ¶***useful truth*** 有益な事実. ¶if the ***whole truth*** must be told 有りのままを残らず話さねばならないというなら(実のところ). 【類】the truth, the ***whole truth*** and nothing but the truth.

P seek ***after*** the ***truth*** 真理を探求する. ¶try to get ***at*** the ***truth*** 真相をつかもうと努める. ¶The figures are probably ***below*** the ***truth***. この数字は恐らく実際以下であろう. ¶Never speak anything ***for truth*** which you know or believe to be false. うそだと知っておりまたは信じることを決して本当だと言ってはならない. ¶Less than a century ago Japan was ***in truth*** a "hermit nation" sealed against the whole world. 百年足らず以前日本は事実世界に知られない全くの「隠とん国」であった. ‖ ***in*** good ***truth*** 実際. ¶There is a considerable measure ***of truth*** in the remark. その言葉には多大の真理が含まれている. ‖ perversion ***of truth*** 真理のゆがめ ‖ This is ***of*** a ***truth*** (=in truth) one of life's tragedies. これは正に人生悲劇の一つである. ¶The wheel is ***out of truth***. その車ははずれている. ¶***with*** equal ***truth*** it may be said that ... 同じ筆法で…と言いうる.

P² the ***truth about*** woman 女性についての事実. ¶There is a grain of ***truth in*** what he says. 彼の言うことには幾分の真理がある. ‖ The popular fallacy has many grains of ***truth in*** it. その誤った民間信仰には幾多真理の断片が含まれている. ¶the ***truths of*** religion (science) 宗教(科学)の種々の真理. 【類】The ***truth of*** the proverb, "Nothing succeeds like success," has been abundantly verified by Mr. Israel Zangwill. ¶There is some ***truth on*** both sides. 双方に幾分の真理がある.

truthfulness, *n.* 正確, 正直.

V This ***established*** the ***truthfulness*** of his conjecture beyond question. これで彼の憶測の的確なことを疑う余地がなくなった.

Q ***fearless truthfulness*** and dauntless moral courage 大胆な率直と不屈の道徳的勇気.

try, *n.* 試み, ためし, 努力.

V ***do*** another ***try*** もう一遍やって見る. ¶Let's ***have*** a ***try*** at it. 一つやって見ようじゃないか. ‖ ***have*** a ***try*** at Chinese 中国語を一つ習って見る.

Q one's ***first try*** at ... その人の…の始めての試み. ¶It is ***worth*** a ***try***. それはやって見る価値がある.

P ***at*** one ***try*** 一挙に.

try, *v.* 試みる, 試験する; 悩ます.

M ***try again*** 再び試みる. ¶***try hard*** not to yawn あくびをかみ殺す. 【類】***try*** very ***hard*** to get orders from ... ¶***just try*** a little ちょっとやって見る. ¶***try out*** the material in the classroom 教室で教材を使用して見る. 【類】***try out*** each other's strength. ¶***sorely tried*** by his failure in ... 彼の…における失敗をひどく苦にして. ¶***vainly try*** やって見たが効果がない. ¶***try*** it ***on*** どこまでやれるかためして見る;自分の力をためす; かぶってみる, 着てみる.

P ***try*** one's strength ***against*** a person 人に向って自分の力をためして見る. ¶They are ***trying*** another gun ***at*** the fort today. お台場できょうもまた大砲の試験をしている. 【類】The machinery has been erected and is being ***tried at*** the works. ‖ ***try*** one's hand (=skill) ***at*** ... …腕だめしに…をやってみる. ¶Let the question be ***tried*** (=decided) ***by*** arbitration. 調停によってその問題を落着させよ. ¶***try for*** college 大学に入学しようと努める ‖ ***try for*** reduction 割引をさせようとする ‖ ***try for*** the first prize 一等賞を獲得しようと努める ‖ He was ***tried for*** perjury and convicted. 彼は偽証罪で審問され有罪の宣告をされた. 【類】He was publicly ***tried for*** the murder of ... in the District Court. ¶***try*** metal ***in*** the furnace 炉で金属を精錬する ‖ ***try in*** vain 試みたがむだになる. ¶***try*** to play ***off*** the other powers against ... 他国を…と争わせて漁夫の利を占めようとする. ¶he proposed to ***try*** this method of treatment ***on*** ... 彼は…に対してこの治療法の試用を提案した ‖ ***Try*** it ***on*** your fund of general information. 君がこの常識質問に答えられるかどうかためして御覧なさい. ‖ ***Try*** it ***on*** your friends. それを友人にためして御覧. ‖ ***try on*** one's new suit 新調の服を着て見る ‖ ***try*** one's sword ***on*** ... その刀で…のためし切りをする. ¶be ***trying to*** the eye (one's health) 目が疲れる(からだにこたえる). ¶***try*** one's eyes ***with*** the small print 小さな活字で目を疲らす ‖ ***try*** tea ***with*** a slice of lemon in it レモン一片をそれに入れて茶を飲んで見る.

O ***Try*** what you can do. どれだけできるかやって御覧なさい. ¶***try*** to grasp that ... …と悟れ ‖ ***Try*** and see what will come [out of it]. どんなことになるかやってみろ.

trying, *n.* 試み, 試験.

Q an experiment ***worth trying*** やって見る価値のある実験.

trying, *a.* たえられない, しのぎにくい.

P Bad air is ***trying to*** the health. 悪い空気は健康を害する. ‖ The smell is very ***trying to*** foriegn nostrils. そのにおいは外人の鼻にはとてもたまらないほどいやなものだ.

tub, *n.* おけ, たらい, ふろおけ; 《俗》入浴.

V ***have*** a ***tub***=take a bath 《俗》入浴する. ¶I never ***miss*** my morning ***tub***. 私は朝の入浴をやらないことはない.

Q a ***cold tub*** 冷水浴.

P take a bath ***in*** a ***tub*** たらいで一浴びする.

tube, *n.* 管, 筒; 《英俗》地下鉄道; 《米》真空管.

V The ***tube*** has again raised its fare. 地下鉄は料金を再値上げした. ☞ 米語の subway に当る.

Q² a brazed ***copper*** (***brass***) ***tube*** 溶接した銅(黄銅)の管. ¶an ***electron tube*** [電子]真空管. ¶an ***iron*** (a ***steel***) ***tube*** 鉄(鋼鉄)管. ¶the ***penny tube*** (料金)一ペニー地下鉄. ¶a ***radio tube*** ラジオの真空管. ¶a ***speaking tube*** 伝声管. ¶a ***test tube*** 試験管. ¶a ***vacuum tube*** 真空管. ☞ tube は英語用法の valve に当る: a five-valve wireless set=《米》a five-tube radio set. ¶Through the ***voice tube***, he called to the engineer to slow down. 彼は伝声管で速力を緩めるように機関手に呼びかけた. ¶a ***weighing tube*** 秤量管.

P suck soda water ***through*** a ***tube*** (straw) くだ(ストロー)でソーダ水を飲む.

P² a ***tube for*** the passage of ... …を通す管.

tuberculin, *n.* ツベルクリン液.

V ***inject tuberculin*** [into the skin] ツベルクリンの注射を「する.

Q ***avian tuberculin*** 鳥のツベルクリン液. ¶***bovine tuberculin*** 牛のツベルクリン液.

tuberculosis, *n.* 結核症.

Q lie in bed with ***advanced tuberculosis*** 進んだ(末期)結核で床についている. ¶a girl with ***incipient tuberculosis*** 初期の結核症にかかっている少女.

tubing, *n.* 配管.
Q² ***neon light*** *tubing* ネオン光の配管.

tuck, *n.* 〖服飾〗ひだ(タック).
V ***make*** a *tuck* in the sleeves そでにひだを作る.
P ***with*** a little *tuck* in her skirt スカートにちょっとタックをとって.

tuck, *v.* 突き込む, くるむ; 縫いひだをつける, タックをとる.
M He *tucked* it ***away*** in his pockets as a memento. 彼は記念としてそれをポケットに突っ込んだ. ‖ Proverbs are likely to have *tucked* ***away*** in them a certain amount of unwisdom or folly. 格言には幾分不合理なばかげた考えを含んでいる.
M² *Tuck* your shirt ***in***. ワイシャツのすそを中に入れ給え. ¶ They charged you a dollar a yard for flannel, did they? Well, they did *tuck* it ***on***. ネルを一ヤールードルで売ったって? そりゃふっかけたのだ. ¶ *tuck* ***up*** one's sleeves そでをまくり上げる(縫いあげる) ‖ *tuck* oneself ***up*** in bed 床の中にもぐり込む.
P *tucked* safely ***between*** sheets シーツの間にもぐり込んで. ¶ *tuck* oneself ***in*** bed 床の中に身をくるみ込む. ¶ *tuck* a handkerchief ***into*** a pocket ハンカチをポケットに押込む. ¶ *tuck* it ***under*** one's pillow それをまくらの下に押込む.

tuft, *n.* 総(ふさ), 房; 茂み.
V ***transplant*** the young rice-shoot *tufts* 稲の苗を移植する.
P grow ***in*** *tufts* 房になって生える.
P² a *tuft* ***of*** grass (feather, wool, beard) 一むらの青草(など). ¶ a hem ***with*** *tufts* on ふさのついたへり.

tug, *n.* けん引; 力争; 中々の骨折.
V I ***felt*** a great *tug* at parting. 私は別れが非常につらかった. ¶ ***give*** a *tug* at a cord 綱をぐいとひっぱる. ¶ I ***had*** a great *tug* to persuade him. 私は彼を説き伏せるのに大骨を折った.
Q fight a ***gruesome*** *tug* of war [綱引のように]奪われまいともがく. ¶ a ***hard*** *tug* 重い引きもの; 苦闘.
Q² a ***steam*** *tug* 蒸気引き船.
P² a *tug* ***of*** war 綱引き ‖ Then comes the *tug* ***of*** war (=deadlock). いよいよ行詰りとなる.

tug, *v.* 引く, 引張る.
P The dog *tugged* ***at*** his chain and broke it. 犬は鎖を引張って切った. 【類】A dozen of the lads *tugged* lustily ***at*** a gun carriage bearing a sword Nelson himself had carried, a Union Jack, and a wreath.

tuition, *n.* 教授; 授業料.
V The school does not ***charge*** its students *tuition*. その学校は授業料を取らない. ¶ the *tuition* is ***conducted*** by ... 教授は…がやっている. ¶ ***give*** *tuition* (=lessons) 教授する. ¶ ***have*** private *tuition* 個人教授を受ける. ¶ ***increase*** *tuitions* 授業料を増す. ¶ ***receive*** *tuition* in ... …(学科)について教えを受ける.
Q under the ***experienced*** *tuition* of ... …の経験ある教授の下に. ¶ ***free*** *tuition* 無月謝教授 ‖ *Tuition* ***free***. [掲示]月謝無料. ¶ ***individual*** *tuition* 個人教授. ¶ ***oral*** *tuition* 口頭教授. ¶ the advantage of ***personal*** *tuition* 個人教授の利益. ¶ ***postal*** *tuition*=tuition by post, instruction by correspondence 通信教授. ¶ These are addresses where ***private*** *tuition* can be had. これらの場所では個人教授をやっている. ¶ give ***rapid*** *tuition* on violin バイオリンの速成教授する.
P Of this amount $... comes ***from*** *tuitions*. この金額の中…ドルは授業料からはいる. ¶ increase ***in*** *tuitions* 授業の増加. ¶ I was ***under*** the *tuition* of ... 私は…の教えを受けていた. ‖ No fewer than 1,500 girls are ***under*** his *tuition*. 彼の教えを受けている少女たちは一千五百名を下らない.
P² give *tuition* ***in*** ... …の教授をする. ¶ give rapid *tuition* ***on*** the violin バイオリンの速成教授を施す.

tulip, *n.* チューリップ.
V² Most *tulips* ***bloom*** here in May. 当地ではチューリップは大抵五月に咲きます.
Q ***vari-colored*** *tulips* 色さまざまのチューリップ.

tumble, *n.* 転倒, 転ぷく; 混乱.
V ***have*** a slight *tumble* ちょっところぶ.
Q have a ***nasty*** *tumble* ひどくころぶ.
P Things are all ***in*** *tumble*. 何もかもごっちゃになっている.

tumble, *v.* ころぶ, 倒れる, くずれる.
M *tumble* ***out*** 《俗》一言二言だしぬけに言う.
M² *tumble* ***down*** ころげる. ¶ *tumble* ***over*** a chair on the floor 床の上にいすを倒す ‖ *Tumbling* it ***over*** and ***over*** in his mind, he lost all patience. 繰返し繰返し考えたあげく彼はもう辛抱ができなくなった. ¶ It *tumbled* ***up*** almost the moment it was thrown down. それが投げ出された瞬間に起き上った
P *tumble* ***down*** the stairs 階段をあたふた下りる. ¶ *tumble* ***from*** a horse 馬からころげ落ちる. ¶ *tumble* ***in*** bed 床にもぐる. ¶ *tumble* ***into*** bed 寝床の中にころがり込む. ¶ *tumble* ***out of*** bed 床からころがり出る ‖ Passengers were *tumbled* ***out of*** the bus. 乗客はバスから吐き出された. 【類】 *tumble* ***out of*** one's compartment with bag and baggage. ¶ her work *tumbled* ***to*** the floor 彼女の編物(など)が床へころがり落ちた(居眠りをしたので). ¶ *tumble* ***up*** the stairs 階段をあたふた上がる.

tumbler, *n.* コップ; おきゃがり小法師(の類).
V² This *tumbler* doesn't ***come up***. このだるまは(ころんだきり)起きない.
Q² a ***glass*** *tumbler* 大コップ(水・牛乳などをのむ).

tumo[u]r, *n.* はれ物, 瘤腫(りゅうしゅ).
V The *tumor* has ***burst***. 瘤腫(りゅうしゅ)が破れた.
Q an ***inflammatory*** *tumor* 炎症性のはれ物. ¶ an ***innocent*** (***malignant***) *tumor* 良(悪)性のはれ物.
P, P² rise ***in*** a *tumor* はれ物になって出る. ¶ a *tumor* ***on*** the head (chin) 頭(など)のはれ物.

tumult, *n.* 騒動, 動乱.
V ***make*** a *tumult* 騒動をやる. ¶ ***pacify*** a *tumult* 暴動を静める.
Q a ***great*** *tumult* 大動乱. ¶ make a ***merry*** *tumult* 快活な騒ぎをする. ¶ a ***popular*** *tumult* 民衆の騒動.
P The country is ***in*** a *tumult*. その国は今騒いでいる.

tumultuous, *a.* 騒々しい.
M become ***extremely*** *tumultuous* 非常に騒がしくなる.

tune, *n.* 調子; 整調, 調和.
V ***change*** one's *tune* 話の調子を変える. ¶ ***finger out*** a *tune* 指で一曲をかなでる. ¶ ***hum*** a *tune* under the breath to keep up one's spirits 元気がめげないように低い声で鼻歌を歌う. ¶ Her joyful heart ***kept*** *tune* with the music of nature. 彼女の喜びに満ちた胸は自然の音楽と調子を合わせた. ¶ ***play*** a *tune* on the violin バイオリンで一曲奏する. 【類】***play*** hymn *tunes* on bells. ¶ The band ***struck up*** a lively *tune*. 音楽隊は元気のよい曲を演奏し出した. ¶ ***whistle*** a *tune* 口笛で一節吹く.
Q It is a ***difficult*** *tune* to remember. それは覚えるのに困難な曲だ. ¶ What is your ***favorite*** *tune?* あなたのお好きな曲は何ですか. ¶ an organ playing a ***gay*** *tune* 愉快な曲を奏するオルガン. ¶ a ***well-known*** *tune* 有名な曲.
Q² a ***comic-opera*** *tune* played from a barrel-organ 携帯オルガンで奏している喜劇オペラ曲. ¶ a ***cowboy*** *tune* カウボーイの曲. ¶ a senseless ***novelty*** *tune* ばからしい新奇な曲.
P sing ***in*** *tune* 調子をそろえて歌う ‖ be ***in*** *tune* with ... …と調子が合う ‖ He is ***in*** *tune*. 彼は上気げんだ. ¶ The piano is ***out of*** *tune*. そのピアノは調子が狂っている. ‖ ***out of*** *tune* with the trend of the times 時代の風潮に逆行して. 【類】get ***out of*** *tune* / a piano ***out of*** *tune*. ¶ ***to*** the *tune* of "For he's a jolly good fellow" 「ほんとに好い人だから」の曲に合わせて ‖ ***to*** the *tune* of over £20,000,000 金高二千万ポンド以上まで.
P² a *tune* ***for*** the dance 舞踏用の曲. ¶ it was out of *tune* ***with*** the atmosphere of ... それは…のふん囲気と調和しなかった.

tune, *v.* 調子を合わす, 適合させる; 〖ラジオ〗波長を合わせる.
M *tune* ***out*** 〖ラジオ〗雑音の入らないように波長をを合わせる.
M² *tune* ***in*** on the radio ラジオの波長を合わせる ‖ *tune* ***in*** on masterful musicians of the age ラジオをかけて当代一流の音楽家の演奏を聞く ‖ *tune* ***in*** to the frequency of a transmitting station 放送局の波長にダイヤルを合わせる. ¶ *tune* ***up*** to a proper pitch [楽器を]正当な調子に合わせる ‖ The musicians were *tuning* ***up***. 楽士たちは(楽器の)調子を合わせていた.
P *tune* ***to*** the standard 標準に合わせる.

tunnel, *n.* トンネル.
V ***bore*** (=***cut, drive, excavate*** or ***pierce***) a *tunnel* through solid granite みかげ石の岩にトンネルを造る. ¶ Presently the train ***entered*** a *tunnel*. 間もなく汽車はトンネルにはいった. ¶ ***run*** a *tunnel* to ... …にトンネルを通す. ¶ ***shoot*** a

tunnel トンネルを疾過する.
V² The *tunnel caved in*. そのトンネルが墜落した.
Q² pass *railway tunnels* in sections [汽車が]所所トンネルを通る. ¶a *street tunnel* 地下道. ¶the *Tanna Tunnel* 丹那トンネル. ¶a *wind tunnel* 風どう.
P go (run) *through* a *tunnel* トンネルを通過する. 【類】a train passing *through* a *tunnel*.

tunnel, *v.* トンネルを造る.
P *tunnel into* ... …にトンネルを造る. ¶The road *tunnels through* the rock. 道は岩を抜いてトンネルになっている.

turbine, *n.* 〘機〙タービン.
Q² an *air* (*steam, gas, water*) *turbine* 〘機〙空気(など)タービン.

turf, *n.* 芝, 芝地; [the] 競馬場.
V *Turf* is *used* for fuel. 芝は燃料に用いられる. ¶Good *turf affords* the best surface for lawn-tennis. 良い芝地はテニスコートには一番よい.
Q the *green turf* 緑の芝生.
P Crickets were chirping *in* the *turf* at our feet. きりぎりすが足もとの芝の中で鳴いていた. ¶a stretch *of turf* 広広した芝生. ¶squander money *on* the *turf* 競馬で金を浪費する ‖ His name was well-known *on* the *turf*. 彼は競馬界で有名であった. ¶cover *with turf* 芝でおおう.

turgid, *a.* 充満する.
P become *turgid with* blood 充血する.

turkey, *n.* 七面鳥.
V *talk turkey* 《米口》あからさまに(ぶしつけに)話す.
V² A *turkey gobbles*. 七面鳥はほろほろと鳴く.
P a drove *of turkeys* 一群の七面鳥.

turmoil, *n.* 騒動, 混雑.
P China *in turmoil* 動乱の中国 ‖ He was *in* the *turmoil* of it from start to finish. 彼は終始その渦中にあった.

turn, *n.* (**1**) 回転; 変化; 順番; 散歩.
V *answer* one's *turn* 自分の番に応じる. ¶*awaiting* their *turn* 彼らの番を待って. ¶*disturb turns* 順番を狂わせる. ¶*do* an ill *turn* to ... …に不親切だ ‖ *do* three or four "*turns*" a night [寄席の芸人など]一晩に三四回自分の持番を勤める ‖ He *did* me a good *turn*. 彼は私に親切にしてくれた. ¶*give* a fresh *turn* 新生面を開く. ¶*give* a *turn* to a key in the lock 錠の中でかぎを一回まわす ‖ The bad news *gave* me quite a *turn*. 《俗》その凶報で私は全くびっくりした. ¶Let us *have* a *turn* at wrestling. 相撲を一勝負やろう. ‖ I want to *have* a *turn* or two in Kobe. 神戸で一二回出歩きをしたい. ‖ *have* another *turn* at fencing フェンシングをもう一勝負やる. ¶in the years just *preceding* and *following* the *turn* of the century その世紀の前後の年に. ¶It *served* me a good *turn*. それは十分私の役に立った. ¶*shift* its *turn* その方向を替える. ¶*take* a *turn* in the garden 庭をちょっと散歩する. 【類】*take* a *turn* (=drive) along the seashore in an auto ‖ *Take* the first *turn* to the right. 最初の角を右へお曲りなさい. ‖ His condition has *taken* a *turn* for the better. 彼は快方に向った. ‖ The patient suddenly *took* a *turn* for the worse. 病人が急に悪くなった. ‖ *take turns* with ... …と交替する ‖ *take turns* in standing watch 交替で立番する ‖ *take turns* of one-hour shifts 一時間交替にする ‖ *take* their *turn* in regular rotation (輪番で) / *take turns* at sleeping and watching / he now *took* his *turn* to ... ¶*wait* one's *turn* in the barber's chair 床屋で自分の順番を待つ. 【類】*waiting* their *turn*.
V² My *turn* has *come*. 私の番になった. 【類】when one's *turn comes round*. ¶His *turn* for duty is *drawing near*. その出番が近づいている.
Q The road is full of *abrupt turns* and is dangerous for motoring. 道路は突然な曲り角が多く自動車運転に危険である. ¶*another turn* of the head and ... さらに目を転じると. ¶at *any turn* 至る所. ¶Matters (His illness) took a *bad turn*. 事態(病気)が悪い方に向かった. ¶The patient took a *critical turn*. 病人は危篤に陥った. ¶The trade has taken a very *decided turn* for the better. 商売は断然好転した. ¶Affairs have taken a very *different turn*. 模様ががらりっと変った. ¶in *due turn* 順番通りに. ¶At *every turn* we meet with new beauties. 至る所に新しい美観が展開する. ¶Things had a *favorable turn*. 事態が好転した. ¶The negotiations now took a *favorable turn*. 交渉がそこで好転した. 【類】His disease has taken a *favorable turn*. ¶do one a *good* (*ill*) *turn* 人に(不)親切にする.

¶Relations between Russia and Great Britain were taking a *grave turn*. 英ソの国交は険悪になりつつあった. ¶the *latest turn* in ... …における最近の発展. ¶No *left*[*-hand*] *turns* allowed. 〘掲示〙左せん回を禁ず. ¶The conversation took a *new turn*. 話が別のことに移った. ¶The conversation took a *personal turn*. 話が個人のことになった. ¶give the handle a *quarter turn* to the left ハンドルを左方へ四分の一回す. ¶a *right-about turn* 右に向きを変えること. ¶begin to take a *sensational turn* 扇情的な傾向を帯びて来る. ¶a *sharp turn* in the road 道路の急な曲り. ¶by a *strange turn* of the wheel of fate 運命の不思議な回り合わせで. ¶The road takes a *sudden turn* to the right. その道路は急に右方へ曲る. ¶The affair took an *unexpected turn*. 事件は予期しない方向へ転換した. ¶I took the *wrong turn* in the road. 私は道を間違えて曲った.
Q² There are no waits and no *stop-gap turns*. 幕合の時もなくまた穴埋めの演出もない(寄席など). ¶No "*U*" *turns* allowed. 〘掲示〙U 字型回り禁止.
P It meets one *at* every *turn*. それは至る所で目に触れる. ‖ *at* the *turn* of a century (season) 世紀(など)の変り目に ‖ be down-cast *at* the *turn* of affairs 事態の推移で意気消沈している. ¶*before* the *turn* of the century その世紀が改まらないうちに. ¶flushing and becoming pallid *by turns* 赤くなったり青くなったりして. 【類】become pale and red *by turns* = turn all manner of colors ‖ keep watch *by turns* 順番に見張りをする. 【類】be afflicted *by turns* with ..., ..., and... ¶go *for* a *turn* 運動に出掛ける. ¶A written word is a sign of a certain sound, and that sound is *in turn* the sign of an idea. 書下した言葉はある音の記号でありそしてその音はまた思想の記号である. ‖ This *in turn* proved very successful. これがまた実にうまく行った. ‖ a strange mixture of coldness and flame, *in turn* icicle and firebrand 冷熱の不思議な入り混じり, 氷柱となったり燃木となったり. 【類】The name has since been assumed by most of his successors as they *in turn* became the representative of the house. ‖ He was *in turn* pit-boy, poet, lecturer, and Baptist minister. 彼は鉱山の手伝い・詩人・講演者及びバプテスト派の宣教師という経歴であった. ‖ serve *in turn* a month at a time 一月替りで務める. 【類】watch four hours at night, *in turn*. / keep a watch *in turn* / Korean architecture was not original; it was based on that of China, which *in* its *turn* came from Burma, and that again probably from India. / Nothing should be based upon belief which is not *in* its *turn* based upon truth. ‖ wash *in turns* 順番に洗面する ‖ Permit me to ask you a question *in* my *turn*. 今度は私に一つ質問さして下さい. 【類】They all spoke, each *in* his *turn*. ¶The tide is now *on* the *turn*. / The tide of bad fortune was (悪運) *on* the *turn*. ¶You must not speak *out of* your *turn*. 君は自分の順番以外に話してはならない. ¶The pie is done *to* a *turn*. パイは片側がよく焼けたから今度は裏返す番だ.
P² *turn about* = alternately 順番に. ¶one's *turn for* night duty その夜番の順番 ‖ ¶the cluster of the egglets awaiting their *turn for* development 発育を待つ卵の原生体の群. ¶a *turn in* the park 公園の散策 ‖ a *turn in* the road 道路の曲り ‖ A *turn of* the wheel of fortune may make him a millionaire to-morrow. 運が向いて来れば彼はあすにも百万長者になれないものでもない. ‖ the *turn of* life 更年期 ‖ the *turn of* the tide 潮の変り目. ¶a sharp *turn to* the left 左方への急カーブ. ¶He took several *turns up* and *down* the room. 彼はへやの中を数回行ったり来たりした.
O *turn* and turn about 順番に. ¶it is your *turn* to ... 今度は君が…する番だ ‖ It will serve your *turn*. それは君のためになる. ¶It was his *turn* to be nonplussed. 今度は彼が参った.
(**2**) 性向, 癖, 性質; 型; 表現, 言い回し.
V He *has* a *turn* (≐special aptitude) for language. 彼は語学の才がある.
Q being of a *candid turn* of mind 表裏のないたちなので. ¶He bought it second-hand being of an *economical turn* of mind. つましい質だ, だから彼はそれを中古で買った. ¶with a *happy turn* of thought and expression 巧みな思想と言葉で. ¶a man of *humorous turn* 道化た人. ¶*idiomatic turns* of speech ある国語特有の言回し. ¶men of an *inquiring* (=*investigating*) *turn* of mind 研究好き

な人々. ¶an ***inquisitive turn*** of mind 好奇心の強い性質. ¶of a ***liberal turn*** of mind さばけた. ¶men of a ***military turn*** of mind 軍人らしい人々. ¶a man of a ***philosophical turn*** of mind 哲学的傾向の人. ¶of a more ***phlegmatic turn*** もっとゆう長な. ¶a ***practical turn*** of mind 実用の才 (academic に対し). ¶a ***queer turn*** of speech 妙な言回し. ¶He was of a ***romantic turn*** of mind. 彼は空想家であった. ¶of a ***scholarly turn*** of mind 学者風の. ¶of a ***serious turn*** of mind まじめなたちの. ¶of a ***speculative turn*** of mind 山気がある. ¶Not being of a ***superstitious turn***, I soon dismissed it from my mind. 迷信的でない私はじきにそれを忘れてしまった. ¶The average Cockney is a hard-headed, practical person of an ***unromantic turn*** of mind. ロンドンっ子は概して無風流でがん固で実際的な人間である. ¶have a ***visionary turn*** of mind 空想にふける傾向がある. ¶a ***witty*** (***clever***) ***turn*** of thought とん知のある(器用な)考え.

Q[2] He is not of a ***business turn***. 彼は商人向きではない.

P[2] have a ***turn for*** letters (music) 文学(など)好きである. ¶a ***turn of*** expression 言い回し.

turn, *v*. 回す, 回る, 振向く.

M A copper disk rotating slowly can be cut by a steel cutting tool; but if rotated at high speed it will ***turn about*** and cut the tool. 徐々に回転する銅円盤は鋼切り工具で切ることができるが急速度で回転すると反対に工具の方を切る. ¶***turn*** a boy ***adrift*** 子供を勘当する. ¶His heart ***turned again*** to her. 彼の心は再び彼女の方に向いた. ¶***turn alternately*** pale and red 青くなったり赤くなったりする. ¶***turn angrily*** toward ... かっとなって...の方に向く. ¶***turn aside*** a blow (one's anger) 一撃(その怒り)をそらす. 【類】***turn aside*** to hide one's blushes. ¶***turn away*** one's anger 怒りを他に紛らす ‖ ***turn away*** from sin 善心に立返る. 【類】***turn*** one's face ***away*** from a person / that impulse to ***turn away*** from the beaten track of life (世の常道) ‖ be ***turned away*** at the doors 門前払いを食う. 【類】be ***turned away*** empty-handed / He gave the reporter an interview when others have been ***turned away***. / The music hall ***turned*** hundreds ***away*** from its doors. / He saluted and ***turned away***. ‖ ***turn away*** at the grindstone といしを回してとぐ. ¶***turn back*** from the frontier 国境から引返す ‖ It is still not too late to ***turn back*** into the right path. 正道に立返るのは今からでも遅くはない. ‖ ***turn back*** to page five 五ページへ戻る ‖ The life of the association ***turns back*** 300 years. その協会の歴史は三百年を数える. ‖ ***turn back*** the clock of civilization 文明の時計を前にもどす(文明の起源にさかのぼる). 【類】To do so would ***turn*** the clock ***back*** many years. / ***turn back*** in imagination to ... ‖ ***turn back*** a criticism by saying ... ...と言って批評を反ばくする. ¶his head ***completely turned*** when ... ...した時彼の頭が全く変になった. ¶maple leaves ***turning crimson*** 深紅色になりかけている紅葉. ¶Prices ***turn downward*** 物価が下向になる. ¶His hair is beginning to ***turn gray***. 彼の髪は白くなりかけている. ¶***half-left turn*** 半ば左に向く. ¶The gas-jets are ***turned*** only ***half way up***. ガスの灯が半分ほどにしてある. ¶***turn homeward*** 帰路につく. ¶***turn head over heels*** さかさまにひっくり返る. ¶***turn hopefully*** to ... 有望と見て...に取掛る. ¶***turn*** a glove ***inside out*** 手袋を裏返しにする. ¶Go two blocks ahead and ***turn left*** there. 二丁ほど行って左に曲りなさい. ¶The day ***turned out*** fine (=fair). [どうかと思ったら]その日はいい天気になった. ‖ as things have ***turned out*** 事実そういうことになったのであるが. 【類】It was cloudy this morning, but fortunately has ***turned out*** clear. / The marriage ***turned out*** a very happy one. / Silk has ***turned out*** well (うまく行った) this year. / The beggar ***turned out*** to be a thief. / It ***turned out*** as we wished. / It is most likely to ***turn out*** bad. / The marriage ***turned out*** most happily. / I hope the affair will ***turn out*** better than expected. / It ***turned out*** just the opposite. / It will ***turn out*** to be a futile attempt. / Her baby ***turned out*** to be a girl. / It ***turned out*** a good speculation (よい投機). / His son ***turned out*** a drunkard, so he ***turned*** him ***out***. / The suspicions ***turned out*** to be justified. ‖ The case ***turned out*** (=went) against him. その訴訟は彼の敗訴であった. ‖ ***turn out*** in the morning in good heart for the day 朝元気で(働きに)出かける. 【類】***turn out*** for a mass meeting ‖ people ***turned out*** in large numbers to vote against ... ...に反対の投票をするため多数の人が出向いた ‖ ***turn*** one's toes ***out*** (***in***) 足の先きを外(内)へ向ける ‖ ***turn out*** war weapons 兵器を製作する ‖ ***turn out*** products 物資を生産する. 【類】What sort of clocks do they ***turn out***? / ***turn out*** on a massproduction basis (大量生産方式で) / The factory ***turns out*** more than a hundred cars in a week. / lack the manpower and the materials to ***turn out*** the production ‖ ***turn out*** a profit 利潤を見る ‖ ***turn out*** graduates from colleges 大学から卒業生を出す. 【類】Colleges ***turn out*** men fit for living good lives. ‖ be ***turned out*** in the cold 排斥される, 追い出される. ¶***turn out*** the light (a lamp) あかり(ランプ)を消す ‖ All the soldiers ***turn out*** in full fig (=dress) in the morning. 朝兵士が全部ちゃんと正装して出る. ‖ As fast as they are ***turned out***, they are sold. それはでき次第そばから売れて行く. 【類】I have ***turned out*** (=done *or* accomplished) a good deal of work. 私は大分仕事をした. ‖ ***Turn*** him (the dog) ***out***! あの人(など)を追出せ. ‖ All the miners ***turned out*** on strike. 坑夫が残らず罷業した. ¶When I told him the news of his father's sudden death he ***turned pale***. お父さんが急死したことを彼に話したら青くなった. ¶***turn purple*** with rage 怒りで顔がむらさきになる. ¶uneasiness ***quickly turned*** to laughter when ... ...したとき不安はたちまち大笑いとなった. ¶***Right turn!*** まわれ右. ¶***turn right-about*** 右手を向く. ¶The room seemed to be ***turning round*** and ***round***. へやがぐるぐる回っているように思われた. ¶***turn sharp***[***ly***] to the left 急角度に左方へ曲る. ¶The feet of many pilgrims ***turn thither*** from distant lands. 幾多の巡礼者が遠国からそこへ足を向ける. ¶The boat ***turned topsyturvy*** (=***bottom upwards*** *or* ***upside down***). ボートがひっくり返った. ¶The aeroplane ***turned turtle***. その飛行機は逆転した. ¶The road ***turned west*** (***east***) at that place. 道路はそこで西(など)に曲った. ¶Leaves ***turn yellow*** in fall. 葉が秋には黄色になる. ‖ ***turn yellow*** with jealousy [顔色が]しっとで青くなる.

M[2] ***turn*** one's head ***about*** [首の]向きを変える, 振り向く. 【類】The earth worm (みみず) was ***turning about***. / He ***turned about*** (=***around***) and faced me. ¶***turn at*** the corner 角を回る. ☞ 英語用法は turn the corner. ¶***turn down*** a plea for ... ...の弁解を否定する. ¶***turn down*** (=refuse) a request to ... 《米》...という要請を断る. 【類】***turn down*** a scheme (proposal) / The petition (invitation) was ***turned down***. / be ***turned down*** flat[ly] / ***turn down*** a plan declaring it was not reasonable / He was ***turned down*** (=ignored) in political circles. ‖ A leaf was ***turned down*** about the middle of the book. 本の半ばごろで一枚折ってあった. ¶***turn in*** fingers one by one 指を一つ一つ折る ‖ ***turn in*** weapons 武器を渡す ‖ ***turn in*** one's resignation 辞表を出す ‖ I thought I would ***turn in*** and have a cup of tea. 私はちょっとはいって茶を一杯飲もうと思った. ‖ ***turn in*** an alarm 警報器をかける ‖ ***turn in*** the edge ***of*** a sheet of paper 紙の角を内側に折る ‖ They ***turned in*** for a well-earned sleep. 一同りっぱに働いた後の睡眠を取るべく床についた. 【類】I ***turned in*** at 8.30 and slept till 8.15. / before I ***turn in*** for the night. ¶***turn in*** one's home work=《英》bring in one's home task 宿題を持ってくる. ¶He ***turned*** the servant ***off*** for misconduct. 彼は召使が不都合をしたので暇をやった. ‖ I have ***turned off*** (=***away***) a great deal of work. 私はたくさんの仕事を断った. ‖ ***turn off*** the light 灯を消す. 【類】***turn off*** the water (gas) / ***turn off*** the faucet (水せん) / ***turn off*** a stopwatch / The conductor stopped the car by ***turning off*** the electricity. / ***turn off*** a flow of liquid ‖ The road is ***turning off*** to the right. 道路は右へ折れている ‖ ***turn off*** to the right 右へ曲る ‖ ***turn*** it ***off*** as a joke それを冗談として片付ける ‖ have to ***turn off*** my face from him その人を正視するに忍びない ‖ be ***turned off*** from one's employ その会社から解雇される. ¶The operator ***turned on*** the light from the switch in the camera room. 技手が暗室内のスイッチで灯をつけた. ‖ ***turn on*** a phonograph 蓄音機をかける. 【類】***turn on*** the gas under the kettle of water for tea. / ***turn on*** a water faucet ‖ the conversation ***turned on*** the subject of ... 話は...のことになった. ¶***turn over*** pages ページをめくる. 【類】***turn over*** the leaves of a book upon one's knee ‖ ***turn over*** on one's back in bed 寝床の中で上向に変わる ‖ turn (=go or look) over documents 書類を調べる ‖ turn a wounded person over to a surgeon けが人を外科医に引渡す ‖ turn gold over to the government 政府に金を引渡す ‖ He was turned over to the police. 彼は警察に引渡された. ‖ turn one's business over to … その店を…に譲り渡す ‖ turn over responsibility to … 責任を…に移す ‖ money turned over in business 商売で渡した金.【類】turn its functions over to … / be turned over to international management / evacuate and turn it over to … / The matter will then be turned over to … for decision (決定にゆだねる). ‖ turn it over in one's mind それを熟考する ‖ turn over all the old ideas concerning … …に関する従来の観念をすべて変更する. ¶He turned round and voted for the Democrats. 彼は思い直して民主党に投票した. ‖ The earth turns round from west to east. 地球は西から東へ回転する. ¶I turn to at the first light. 私は夜が明けると仕事を始める. ¶The carpet being too large, we had to turn the edge under. しきものが大きすぎたので, 端を下に折りまげねばならなかった. ¶He was the only person who turned up. 来たのは彼だけだった.【類】Employees failed to turn (=show) up. / Something unexpected may have turned up. ‖ turn up one's sleeves そでをまくり上げる ‖ The sight turned me up.《俗》そのようすを見て私ははき気を催した. ‖ wait for "something to turn up" なにか持上るのを待つ.【類】But some unavoidable business turned up, and prevented me from keeping my promise. ‖ turn up soil 土地を耕す.【類】turn up the ground with plows ‖ turn up the lamp a little 少しランプの心を出す ‖ turn up one's nose at … …を鼻であしらう ‖ turn (=look) up a word in a dictionary 辞書で語を引いて見る ‖ turn up (=consult) a text for a passage ある文句を捜し出すため本文を調べる ‖ turn up a card=place a card with the face upward カルタを返して表を向ける ‖ His nose turned up slightly. 彼の鼻は少し上を向いている.

P The tide is turning against me. 形勢が私には不利になりつつある. ‖ turn against a person 人にそむく ‖ The newspaper turned against the Ministry. その新聞は内閣に反対した. ¶be turned by a crank 取っ手で回す(蓄音機など) ‖ The food situation is turning for the better. 食料事情は良い方へ向っている. ‖ turn for it to … それに…することを求める. ¶He was turned from the door. 彼は戸口から追返された. ‖ turn them from their faith 彼らの信仰を捨てさせる ‖ turn from a direct (right) course 真っすぐの進路(正道)からそれる ‖ turn a person from his purpose その目的を転向させる.【類】It is not easy to turn him from a settled purpose ‖ turn from the particular to the general 細説から概論にわたる.【類】turn it from loss to profit. ¶cause them to turn in their vaults (=graves) その人たちの霊が浮ばれないようにする ‖ He will turn in his grave and laugh at the item. 彼はこの記事を草葉のかげで見て笑うことであろう. ‖ turn in a considerable number of store fish 非常に多数の養魚を放す. ¶The speech was turned into ridicule. その演説は一笑に付し去られた. ‖ turn one's earnest story into ridicule 人のまじめな話を茶化す ‖ turn into a by-street 横町にはいる ‖ turn English into Japanese 英語を日本語に訳す ‖ turn prose into verse 散文を韻文に作り替える.【類】turn into a novel a drama entitled "…" ‖ Night is turned into day by artificial light. 不夜城となる. ‖ It looks as if it would turn into a gale. 暴風になりそうだ.【類】He carried away everything he could turn into money. ‖ I do not know any in the pharmacopoeia which will turn a pessimist into an optimist. 私は悲観者を楽観者にする妙薬を知らない. ‖ Swords are turned into ploughshares and spears into pruning-hooks. 戦争から平和に復帰する. ‖ Grubs turn into butterflies. 地虫がちょうになる. ¶a handsome young lad, scarcely turned of nineteen, fresh as a rose 十九になるかならない紅顔の美少年.【類】He was barely (やっと) turned of fifteen. ¶turning on his adversary 彼の敵手に向直って ‖ turn … on the street …を表へたたき出す ‖ turn on its axis (hinges) 軸(ちょうつがい)で回転する(戸などが) ‖ He turned on his heels. 彼はぐるりと向き直った. ‖ The conversation turned on the merits of Napoleon as a general. 大将としてのナポレオンの価値に話題が転じた. ‖ He turned on me with sarcasm. 彼は僕に対して軽べつ的態度を取った. ‖ The hose was turned on the fire. ホースは火炎に向けられた. ‖ The decision turned on a single fact. その決定は一つの事実に係っていた. ‖ The Yayoi-shiki pottery of ancient Japan was not turned on the wheel. 古代日本のやよい式陶器にはろくろが使ってなかった. ‖ turn a dog on a person 犬を人にけしかける. ¶turn a person out of doors (room, house) 人を戸口(など)の外に追い出す ‖ he was turned out of his club for … 彼は…のためにクラブから除名された. ¶He turned to the east and to the west, to the north and to the south. 彼は東西南北へと振向いた. ‖ His heart turned again to me. あの人は私に対してもと通り心が打解けて来た. ‖ his thoughts ever turn to … 彼の考えはいつも…の方へ向く ‖ It is a place to turn to when you are in need of information. それは何か知りたいことがあったら頼る場所だ(図書館など). ‖ In the portrait he is turned to the right. その肖像画で彼は右を向いている. ‖ Turning now to our own country, what do we find? 顧みてわが国はどうだろう.【類】if you will turn to pages 12 and 13 of this month's issue, you will find … ‖ You had better turn to and finish the work. それをやってしまったらいいでしょう. ‖ He turned to his work again. 彼は再び彼の仕事に取りかかった.【類】turn to book-collecting ‖ women turning to prostitution 売春に身を落そうとしている女 ‖ a trunk of a tree turned to stone 化石した木の幹 ‖ turn one's hobby to profitable account 自分の道楽を商売に転用する ‖ turn it to account as a reason for … それを利用して…の理由とする.【類】turn it to immediate account / You should turn your opportunities to good account. ‖ His love turned to bitter hate. 彼の愛情は激しい憎悪に変った. ‖ My first advice to the beginner in the study of law has always been to buy a good law dictionary and turn to it constantly. 法律を勉強する初学生への私がいつも忠告することは良い法律辞書を買って絶えず使用することだ. ¶turn to its pages for guidance その本を参考する ‖ He turned to me for help. 彼は私に援助を求めた. ‖ turn to a year-book for guidance 年鑑を参考する.【類】turn to the police for protection / It was to teaching that he first turned himself for a livelihood (生活). / turn to literature for consolation (慰謝) / turn to a dictionary for a word / turn to it for reference / turn to … for information regarding (=as to) … / To him she turned for advice in critical situations (大事な場合). ¶He turned to us on his heels. ぐるっと回ってわれわれの方へ向き直った. ¶The world's gaze turns towards Japan. 世界の目が日本に向けられている. ‖ a disposition in flowers to turn towards the sun 花の向日性 ‖ Their thoughts are turning toward the Far East. 彼らの考えは段々極東の方に向きつつある. ¶whenever talk turns upon … …の話が出ると ‖ Everything turned upon the result of the battle. 万事戦争の勝敗いかんによって決定するのであった. ‖ He turned sharply upon his heel and strode majestically away. 彼はぐるっときびすを返して堂々と濶(かつ)歩し去った. ‖ turn upon one severely きっとなってその方を向く. ¶one turns with interest to … われわれは興味を感じて…に思いを致すのである ‖ turn with confidence to the task of … …自信をもって…に着手する.【類】you can turn to it always with confidence for authentic information on…

turner, *n.* 旋盤工.

Q a *master turner* 旋盤工の職長.

P² a *turner in* wood 木細工師, 木工.

turning, *n.* 転回, 屈曲, 遠回り.

V The road *makes* several abrupt *turnings*. その道は急に曲っている所が数個所ある. ¶This *marked* the *turning* of the tide. これを境に風潮が一変した. ¶*take* the first (second) *turning* to the left and follow the tram line as far as the post office 最初(など)の曲り角を左に折れて郵便局まで電車の線路に沿って行く.

Q A *narrow turning* leads off to the left. せまい横道が左「方へついている.

P² This *turning of* the tide of fortune carried him from obscurity to renown, from poverty to opulence. 幸運が向いてきて名もない彼は有名になり貧乏から富裕の身と変った. ¶the third *turning to* your right leaving the station 停車場を出てから右手へ三つ目の曲り角. ¶I missed my way by *turning to* the right instead of to the left 私は左でなく右へ曲ったので道に迷った.【類】About three hundred yards further on (先に) there's a *turning* ***to*** the left.

turning-over, *n.* 熟考.

Q with ***much*** *turning-over* of the dictionary 字引と首引きで.

turning-point, *n.* 転向点, 変り目.

V this event ***formed*** a *turning-point* in the activity of ... このできごとが...の活動の転機だった. ¶The invention of fire-making ***marked*** a *turning-point* in the history of human progress. 火を造ることの発明は人間進歩における一転換期を画した. 【類】This ***marked*** a *turning-point* in his career (=life). / it ***marked*** a *turning-point* in the attitude of ... towards ... ¶***reach*** a *turning-point* in the development of ... ...の発達において一つの転換期に達する.

Q The company has come to a most ***important*** *turning-point* in its history. その会社はその創設以来の非常に重大な転換期に達した.

P It is that day that he marks ***as*** the *turning-point* in his illness. その日こそ彼の病気の転換期であると彼は見ているのである. ¶We are ***at*** a *turning-point* in the history of the world. われわれは世界史の転換期にある. 【類】arrive ***at*** its *turning-point*.

P[2] This was the *turning-point* ***for*** him. これが彼に取っての転換期であった. ¶It proved to be the *turning-point* ***in*** his career. それが後になって彼の経歴における転換期となった. 【類】The discovery was the *turning-point* ***in*** the history of the science. ¶Indeed, it was the *turning-point* ***of*** his fortunes. 実にそれは彼の運命の転向点であった.

turnout, *n.* 出席者; 生産高.

Q There was quite a ***big*** *turnout* (=attendance) at the lecture. その講義に多数の出席者があった. ¶There was an ***enormous*** *turnout*. 非常に多数の出席者があった. ¶A ***good*** *turnout* was shown in the balloting. その投票は出足がよかった.

P[2] the *turnout* ***of*** finished goods 完成品の生産量.

turnover, *n.* 売上高, 取引高; 〖労〗配置, 転換.

V ***do*** a *turnover* of three times that amount その三倍の売上成績をあげる. ¶He ***has*** a personal *turnover* of £150,000 per annum, guaranteed by chartered accountant. 彼には公認計理士によって保証された年額十五万ポンドの個人売上高がある. ¶***insure*** a quick *turnover* 敏活な資金の回転を確保する. ¶The commercial undertaking ***involves*** a total *turnover* of £155,000,000 annually. その商売は年一億五千五百万ポンドの総取引高がある.

Q ***frequent*** *turnover* 薄利多売. ¶We are content with small profits and a ***large*** *turnover*. 弊店は薄利多売で満足しています. ¶The store reduced the prices to make a ***quick*** *turnover*. その商店は資金の回収を急いで価格を下げた. ¶The operating force needed a ***thorough*** *turnover*. その作業労働力は徹底的な人員の配置転換が必要だった.

Q[2] ***labor*** *turnover* 〖労〗労働力の配置転換.

turnstile, *n.* 回転木戸.

Q[2] a ***subway*** *turnstile*. 地下鉄の回転木戸.

P Let him pass ***through*** the *turnstile*. 彼を回転口から出してやれ.

turntable, *n.* 転車台.

Q[2] a ***locomotive*** *turntable* 機関車転車台.

turnup, *n.* [ズボンの]折返し.

P trousers ***with*** (***without***) *turnups* 折返しのある(ない)ズボン.

turpitude, *n.* 卑劣, 下劣.

Q steeped in vices and sins of the ***deepest*** *turpitude* 最も卑劣な悪徳や罪悪に浸潤して. ¶It was occasioned by ***moral*** *turpitude* それは道義の退廃に起因した.

turret, *n.* やぐら.

P[2] a *turret* ***on*** a roof for the escape of smoke 煙出し用の屋上小塔.

tutelage, *n.* 保護, 世話, 指導.

Q the four years of ***democratic*** *tutelage* 民主的指導の四年間.

P ***under*** the *tutelage* of the white race 白人監督の下で.

tutor, *n.* 教師, 家庭教師.

P study ... ***under*** a *tutor* 家庭教師の下に...を学ぶ.

P[2] *tutors* ***in*** noble families 貴族の家庭教師. ¶a French *tutor* ***to*** their Royal Highnesses the Duke and Dutchess of York ヨーク公御夫妻のフランス語家庭教師.

tutor, *v.* 《米》個人教授をやる; 家庭教師をやる.

P He was *tutored* ***by*** a private teacher. 彼は個人教授を受けた. ¶*tutor* ***for*** one's living 生活のため家庭教師をやる.

tutorage, *n.* 教授, 指導.

P ***under*** the *tutorage* of a Dutch engineer オランダの技師に指導されて.

tutorship, *n.* 教授; 保護; 教育.

P ***under*** the *tutorship* of ... ...の教授を受けて.

twain, *n.* 二つ, 対.

P the skull cloven ***into*** *twain* 二つに割れた頭がい骨.

twang, *n.* 鼻声, 鼻音.

P speak ***with*** a *twang*=twang (*v.*) 鼻声で話す.

twang, *v.* 鼻声で言う; ぶーんと鳴らす.

M He *twangs* ***disagreeably***. 彼は聞いて不快なほど鼻声で話す.

P *twang* [***on***] a banjo (shamisen, guitar) バンジョー(など)をぶーんと鳴らす.

tweeds, *n. pl.* ツイード(スコッチ織)の服・ズボン.

V ***wear*** light *tweeds* and brown boots 軽いスコッチ織のずぼんとかつ色のくつをつける.

O Get me my *tweeds*. 私のツイードをとってくれ.

tweezers, *n.* 毛抜.

P a pair ***of*** *tweezers* 一ちょうの毛抜.

twelvemonth, *n.* 十二カ月, 一年.

P ***in*** the next *twelvemonth* 次の一年に.

twenty, *n.* 二十.

P be ***in*** one's late (early) *twenties* 二十代の末(初)である.

twice, *ad.* 二度, 再び, 二倍に.

M He is ***about*** *twice* as old as I am. 彼は私の二倍も年を取っている. ¶*twice* ***as much*** 二倍も. ¶*twice* ***weekly*** (=a week) 毎週二度.

O The bamboo has grown *twice* as tall as it was last year. その竹は去年の二倍延びた.

twig, *n.* 小枝.

V[2] The *twigs* were ***cracking*** in the fire. 小枝が火の中でぱちぱち音を立てていた.

Q a ***slender*** *twig* 細い小枝. ¶***tender*** *twigs* か弱い小枝.

Q[2] ***Willow*** *twigs* are pliable. 柳の小枝はしなやかだ.

P birds ***on*** the *twigs* of trees 木の小枝にとまっている小鳥.

twilight, *n.* [日出・日没前の]薄明.

V[2] The *twilight* ***came on***. 薄暮が迫った. ¶The *twilight* ***waned*** swiftly. 夕やみがぐんぐん迫って行った.

Q the ***ghostly*** *twilight* 気味の悪い薄明時. ¶the ***rosy*** *twilight* of boyhood バラ色の曙(しょ)光である少年時代.

Q[2] ***evening*** *twilight* たそがれ. ¶***morning*** *twilight* あさぼらけ.

P ***at*** *twilight* 薄明時に. ¶Reading ***in*** the *twilight* will hurt your eyes. 薄暗がりでの読書は目に悪い.

twin, *n.* 双子, 似た人または物.

V He ***had*** *twins* by her. 彼と彼女との間に双生児ができた.

Q ***fraternal*** (***identical***) *twins* 二(一)卵性双生児. ¶a ***unioval*** *twin* 一卵生双生児. ¶***phonetic*** *twins* 発音上相似た語.

P give birth ***to*** *twins* 双生児を生む.

twine, *v.* まとう, 巻く, からみつく.

M *twine* [themselves] ***together*** まとい合う.

P The vine *twines* ***round*** the tree. つるは木にまきつく. ‖ the Aldine trade mark, a dolphin *twined* ***round*** an anchor いるかがいかりの周囲に巻付いたオールダイン版の商標. ¶*twine* itself ***round*** ... ...の回りにからみ付く.

twinge, *n.* ずきずきする痛み.

P ***with*** a *twinge* of conscience 気がとがめて.

twinkle, *n.* またたき, きらめき.

V He ***had*** a merry *twinkle* in his eyes. 彼の目に愉快なまたたきがあった.

Q with a ***mischievous*** *twinkle* in his eye いたずらそうな目付をして. ¶There is a ***smiling*** *twinkle* in his eye. 彼の目にはにこやかなきらめきがある.

P with a *twinkle* ***in*** his eyes 目をぱちぱちさして. ¶turn to a person ***with*** a *twinkle* in one's eye 人の方に向いてその目をぱちっとさせる.

P[2] a *twinkle* ***of*** merriment 愉快なまばたき.

twinkle, *v.* きらきらする, またたく.

P His eyes *twinkled* ***at*** the jest. その冗談を聞いて彼は目をぱちぱちさせた. ¶Stars *twinkle* ***through*** the azure blue. 青空に星がぴかぴかする.

twinkling, *n.* きらめき, 瞬間.

P ***In*** a *twinkling* the scene had changed. またたく間にその光景は変った. ‖ ***in*** the *twinkling* of an eye またたく間に.

P[2] the *twinkling* ***of*** stars 星のきらめき.

twirl, *v.* くるくる回る.

M[2] The ribbons tautened and snapped, the broken and raveled ends *twirling* ***off*** idly into the water. テープが緊張してぷつっと切れ, 切れてもつれた端は水の中に力なく巻きこまれて行った.

twist, *n.* 一ねじ, 一より.

V ***give*** a wrist a violent *twist* 手首を激しくひねる. ¶He ***has*** a mental *twist*. 彼は量見がねじれている.

Q His answer showed a ***mental twist***. 彼の答は心のもつれを見せた. ¶That looks an ***odd twist***. 妙にこんがらかったんだ(当てがはずれて不利な地位に立ったときなど).

P ***by*** a *twist* of the imagination 変に気を回して. ¶throw a ball ***with*** a *twist* 一ひねりして球を投げる‖sigh ***with*** a *twist* of a smile ちょっとゆがんだ微笑を見せてため息をつく.

P² a ***twist of*** paper ねじった紙.

twist, *v.* ねじる, ひねる.

M *twist* ***apart*** ... ...をねじ離す. ¶*twist* ***open*** ねじあける. ¶*twist* ***round*** まとう; ねじ回す. ¶*twist* wires ***together*** 針金をより合わせる.

M² The worm was *twisting* ***about*** in such a lively way. みみずがこんなに活発にうねりくねっていた. ¶*twist* ***in*** ねじ込む. ¶*twist* ***off*** ... ...をねじ切る.

P *twist* paper ***into*** a spill 紙をひねって小よりにする.【類】*twist* hemp (wire) ***into*** a rope‖*twist* one's face ***into*** contortions 顔をゆがめる. ¶*twist* one's way ***through*** a crowd 群集の中を曲りくねって行く. ¶His face was *twisted* ***with*** pain. 彼の顔は痛さでゆがんでいた.

twisting, *n.* ねじること.

P break off ***by*** *twisting* ねじってもぎ取る.

twit, *v.* とがめる, ののしる, ひやかす.

P Englishmen are constantly being *twitted* (=reproached) ***by*** foreigners ***with*** their unsociable ways. 英国人は社交的でないと言って始終外国人から冷笑される.

twitch, *n.* ひきつり.

Q² a ***muscle*** *twitch* 筋肉のひきつり.

two, *n.* 二, 二個.

V It ***takes*** *two* to quarrel. けんかは二人でなくてはできない.

P divided equally ***between*** the *two* 二人の間に平等に分配されて. ¶***by*** *twos* and threes 三々五々. ¶tear ... ***in*** *two* ... を二つに裂く‖The vessel was split ***in*** *two*. その器物は二つに割れた.‖Flowers came out ***in*** *twos* and threes 花がちらほら咲き出した.

P² *two* ***in*** number 二個.

two-thirds, *n.* 三分の二.

P ***by*** *two-thirds* of the votes 表決の三分の二の多数をもって.

type, *n.* **(1)** 印(しるし); 表徴; 型; 見本.

V ***constitute*** the best *type* 最良の型となる. ¶The great thinker ***develops*** a certain *type* of countenance. 偉大な思想家には一種典型的な容ぼうができる.‖rear domestic animals so as to ***develop*** a good *type* 良種を造り出すように家畜を飼育する. ¶The girl ***has*** a delicate *type* of beauty. その少女は繊細な美人型だ.

Q an ***acute*** *type* of a disease 急性の病気. ¶a busy crowd of men and women of ***alien*** *types* and un-English bearing 外人型で英人らしくない態度のせわしい男女の群. ¶prisoners of ***all*** *types* あらゆる種類の囚人. ¶people of the "***below par***" *type* コンマ以下の人間. ¶people of a purely ***commercial*** *type* 純然たる商人風の人々. ¶belong to the ***Caucasian*** *type* of mankind コーカサス人種に属する. ¶language of a highly ***colloquial*** *type* 非常にくだけた会話体の言葉. ¶He is of a ***crude*** *type*. 彼は粗野なたちだ. ¶a sophist of a ***dangerous*** *type* 危険な型のき弁家. ¶The girl has a ***delicate*** *type* of beauty. その少女はたおやめ型の美人だ. ¶A good shingle roof is a most ***durable*** *type* of roof. 良い板ぶき屋根は長持する. ¶Almost ***every human*** *type* is to be studied here. ここではほとんどありとあらゆる種類の人間の研究ができる. ¶of an ***exaggerated*** *type* 誇張した. ¶The ginkgo-tree is representative of an ***extinct*** *type* いちょうは廃絶種の名残りである. ¶Soroku Ebara, one of the ***fine*** *types* of Christian Japanese 日本人のキリスト教徒としてりっぱな典型の一人たる江原素六. ¶***higher*** *types* of woman 高級な女. ¶a very ***human*** *type* of mankind 人類中非常に人間的な人種. ¶of the most ***improved*** *type* 最も改良された型の. ¶an ***intellectual*** *type* of mind インテリ型の人. ¶battle cruisers of the ***Invincible*** *type* 無敵艦型の戦闘巡洋艦. ¶extremely dressed, cigarette-smoking, ***jazzy*** *types* of girls 極端な服装をして巻タバコをくゆらすジャズ式の少女. ¶a factory equipped with the ***latest*** *type* of electrically-driven machinery 最新式電気運転の機械を据付けた工場. ¶a disease of a ***malignant*** *type* 悪性の病気. ¶women of decidedly ***masculine*** *type* 断然男子型の女. ¶investigation of more or less ***mechanical*** and ***statistical*** *type* 多少機械的で統計的な調査. ¶of the most ***modern*** *type* 最も現代的様式の. ¶a wholly ***new*** *type* of language course 語学教授の全く新しい型.【類】the ***newer*** *type* of general education. ¶an ***old-fashioned*** *type* 古風な様式. ¶of the ***ordinary*** *type* 普通の型の. ¶of the ***orthodox*** *type* 旧式の. ¶of a ***plain*** *type* あっさりした種類の. ¶flint implements of a very ***primitive*** *type* きわめて原始的な火うち石製の器具. ¶***racial*** *types* in the Philippine Islands フィリッピン諸島の色々な人種. ¶if of the ***right*** *type* 適当な人物であれば. ¶successful businessmen of ***self-educated*** *type* 独学で成功した実業家. ¶a person of a more ***serious*** *type* もっとまじめな型の人. ¶writing in ***slant*** *type* 傾斜型の書体. ¶of a ***soldierly*** *type* 軍人型の. ¶She is of a very ***superior*** *type* of young womanhood. 彼女はきわめて優秀な少女である. ¶an officer of the ***ultra-conservative*** *type* 極端に保守的な役員. ¶newspapers of ***varied*** *types* 色々の種類の新聞紙. ¶suffragettes of a ***violent*** or "***militant***" *type* 猛烈なすなわち過激派の婦人選挙権獲得運動参加の女. ¶He is of the ***wiry*** *type*. 彼は細くって長い. ¶a reactionary of the ***worst*** *type* 最も悪質の反動主義者.

Q² a ***border-line*** *type* いずれとも区別のつきかねる型. ¶women of the ***Catherine Hepburn*** *type* キャスリン・ヘプバーン型の女. ¶A "he-man" is a stout guy of the ***cowboy*** *type*. M 型の男とはカーボーイタイプのがっちりした男だ. ¶a "***curmudgeon*** *type*" 因業な型. ¶An atomic bomb more powerful than the ***Nagasaki*** *type* is now possible. 長崎型よりも一層有力な原子爆弾の製造が今では可能である. ¶the ***old-school*** *type* of inventor 旧式な発明家. ¶a ***paste-pot-and-scissors*** *type* of composition 切抜継合わせの文. ¶The "sway" type of earthquake is less disastrous than the "***shock***" *type*. 横ゆれ型の地震は縦ゆれ型のものよりも災害が少ない. ¶persons of the ***so-and-so*** *type* 某々式の人々. ¶The present large steam locomotives, of the ***so-called*** "***R***" *type*, pull, as a rule, 28 wagons, each with a load of 30 tons. いわゆるR式の現時の大きな蒸気機関車は通常各車三十トンの荷を積んだ二十八両の貨車をけん引する. ¶The ***work*** *type* of reading which we use in study われわれが勉強に使う(文学鑑賞でなく)知識獲得のための読物.

P deviate ***from*** the *type* 型破りである. ¶women ***of*** a certain *type* ある型の女. ¶classed ***under*** four *types* 四種に分類した.

P² a *type* ***of*** crane つるの一種‖He is a fine *type* ***of*** his race. 彼は同民族中のりっぱな人物だ.‖water is the *type* ***of*** instability 水は不安定の象徴である‖*types* ***of*** the beautiful English girl 美しい英国少女の典型‖He is the *type* ***of*** man who is endeared among older women. 彼は年配婦人に好かれるたちの男だ.‖the present *type* ***of*** order in the world 世界の現状.

O I am not the *type*. 私はそんな人間じゃない.

(2) 活字.

V ***compose*** one's *type* 活字を組む. ¶The edition is a limited one and the *type* has been ***distributed***. それは限定版で活字はもう解版してしまった. ¶***found*** a *type* 活字を鋳造する. ¶The chief expense of a book is ***laying down*** the *type*. 本の主な掛りは(活字の)組版である. ¶***pick*** *types* 活字を拾う. ¶***set*** *type* by hand 植字する‖The *type* of the present issue has been ***set*** on linotype machines operated by Japanese. 本号の製版は日本人がライノタイプで組んだものである. ¶***set up*** the *type* 活字を組む. ¶The *type* is now almost ***stereotyped***. 今ではその型がほとんどきまってしまった.

Q ***big*** *type* used for headlines 見出しに使う大型活字. ¶in ***black*** *type* ゴシック活字で. ¶in ***bold*** *type* 肉太活字で. ¶books in ***embossed*** *types* for the blind 盲人用浮出し文字印刷の本. ¶***heavy(-faced)*** *type* 肉太活字. ¶the ***hygienic*** *type* [視力を害しない]衛生的な活字. ¶words in ***italic*** *type* イタリック斜体で印刷した語‖Underlining is equivalent to the use of ***italic*** *type* in printing. 下線を引くことは印刷でイタリック活字を使うのに相当する. ¶be printed in ***larger*** *type* 一層大きな活字で印刷される.【類】be reset in ***larger*** and ***bolder*** *type*. ¶shown in ***light[-faced]*** *type* 細文字活字‖printed in ***lighter*** *type* もっと細い文字の活字で印刷した. ¶printed in ***plain*** (***full-face***) *type* 普通(黒字)の活字で印刷した. ¶text in ***Roman*** *type* ローマ体活字で印刷した本文.【類】long heading (長い見出し) in ***Roman*** *type*. ¶printed with ***rubber*** *type* ゴム活字で印刷した.

¶*small* but *legible type* 小さいがはっきりした活字. ¶in *thick type* 太字で ‖ the judicious use of *thick type* 太活字をうまく使うこと.

Q^2 figures printed in *bold face* (=*dark*) *type* 太い活字で印刷した数字 ‖ *Bold face type* shows p.m. hours. 肉太活字は午後の時間を示す[時間表など]. ¶be set in *7-point type* 七ポイントの活字に組んである.

P printed *from* new *types* on extra fine paper 特別高級紙に新しい活字で印刷した. 【類】be printed *from type* specially cast (特鋳活字). ¶The book is already *in type*. その本の組ができている. ‖ put them *in type* それを組版にする.

P^2 the face *of* a *type* 活字の面.

type, *v.* タイプ[ライター]で打つ.

M can *type* 60 words a *minute* 一分間に六十語打てる. ¶*busily typing* a letter 忙しそうに手紙をタイプして. ¶*type out* thirty pages 三十ページをタイプで打つ.

P *type from* a copy 原稿からタイプで打つ ‖ *type from* one's own thought 考えをすぐタイプで打つ. ¶*type on* (=*from*) dictation 口授された通りタイプする. ¶*type* it *with* two carbons 二枚カーボン紙を入れてタイプする.

typewrite, *v.* タイプ[ライター]で打つ.

M a document *closely typewritten* ぎっしりタイプ印書した書類.

P She *typewrites for* me. 彼女が私の書いたものをタイプで打ってくれる.

typewriter, *n.* 印字器, タイプライター.

V a knowledge of how to *handle* (=*manipulate*) a *typewriter* dexterously タイプライターを器用に扱う方法の知識. ¶*operate* a *typewriter* by the one-finger, hunt-and-pick method of one key at a time (なれない人がやるように)一本指でかぎを拾い拾いタイプを打つ ‖ *operate* the *typewriter* by the touch-system タッチ式でタイプを打つ. ¶*pound* the *typewriter* タイプを打つ. ¶A typist is a person who *runs* (=*operates*) a *typewriter*. タイピストはタイプライターを扱う人である. ¶I can *use* a *typewriter*. 私はタイプライターが使える.

Q a *noiseless typewriter* 無音タイプライター. ¶My *wretched typewriter* will not take a carbon. 私のタイプライターはひどいのでカーボンの複写は取れない.

Q^2 an *office typewriter* 事務用タイプライター.

P work (=hammer away) *at* a *typewriter* タイプする. ¶written *in typewriter* タイプした. ¶write a letter *on* a *typewriter* タイプライターで手紙を書く ‖ rap it off *on* a *typewriter* それをタイプで打つ. 【類】Square brackets (角括弧) are not usually to be found *on* a *typewriter*. / For all general purposes use a black riband (=ribbon) *on* your *typewriter*, never a fancy (変り) color. / get started *on* the *typewriter* / These symbols (記号) cannot be written *on* a *typewriter*. ¶be printed *with* a *typewriter* タイプで印書してある.

typewriting, *n.* タイプ[ライター]を打つこと.

V *do typewriting* タイプを打つ. ¶*practice typewriting*, key touching, etc. キータッチなどタイプを練習するのる.

typhoon, *n.* 台風.

V The *typhoon* failed to *hit* the main land of Japan. 台風は日本の本州を襲わなかった. ¶A *typhoon* is now *raging* here 当地には今台風が猛威をふるっている. ¶A *typhoon struck* the factory. 台風がその工場を襲った.

V^2 Another *typhoon* is *brewing*. また新しい台風ができかかっている.

Q The weather experts did their very best to keep tab on the *elusive typhoon*. 気象技師たちは最善を尽してその捕そくしがたい台風の観測をした. ¶a *frightful typhoon* 恐ろしい台風.

typical, *a.* 模範的な, 代表的な.

P individuals *typical of* the nation その国民の代表的な人人 ‖ These students are *typical of* their class. これらはクラスの代表的学生である. ‖ one, *typical of* many 多数を代表する一つ ‖ He was most *typical of* the times in which he lived. 彼はその時代での最も代表的なものであった.

typify, *v.* 代表する.

P The autumn in Japan is *typified by* the chrysanthemum. 日本の秋は菊によって代表されている.

typing, *n.* タイプ[ライター]印刷.

V *stop* one's *typing* タイプを打つのをやめる.

Q^2 *double*(*single*)*-space typing* 二(一)行間隔のタイプ印刷.

P good *at typing* タイプが巧い.

typist, *n.* タイピスト.

Q a *rapid typist* 達者なタイピスト.

Q^2 a *champion speed typist* 第一級高速度タイピスト. ¶*women typists* 婦人タイピストたち. ☞ 単数は a woman typist.

P She served the Army *as* a *typist*. 彼女はタイピストとして軍隊に勤めた. ¶dictate letters *to* one's *typist* タイピストに手紙を口授して打たせる.

tyrannize, *v.* 暴虐を加える, 圧制する.

P *tyrannize over* the people (the weak) 人民(弱者)を圧制する.

tyranny, *n.* 暴政, 虐待.

V Women and children *exercise* the *tyranny* of tears. 女子供は泣いて相手を困らせる. ¶*repress tyranny* 暴虐を押える.

V^2 Its *tyranny* has *become intolerable*. その圧制はたえられないものになった.

P^2 the *tyranny of* wealthy and powerful subjects 富力あり権力ある臣下の暴虐 ‖ the *tyranny of* the part *over* the whole 一部の全体に対する圧制 ‖ a *tyranny of* the older generation *over* another generation 古い世代の人々の新しい世代の人々に対する暴虐. 【類】the *tyranny of* nipping winds and early frosts (寒風と早霜).

tyrant, *n.* 暴君, 圧制者.

Q a *bloody tyrant* 残忍な暴君.

P Innocent people were trodden under foot *by* the *tyrant*. 罪のない民がその暴君に踏みにじられた.

tyre, *n.* =tire.

Q^2 The front *off-side tyre* is flat. 右側のタイヤがパンクしている. ¶*steel* (*iron*) *railway tyres* 鋼鉄(鉄)の汽車の輪鉄.

tyro, tiro, *n.* 初学者, 初心者.

Q the *mere tyro* in the art of scribbling 文筆の方ではずぶのしろうと. ¶It is evident to the *veriest tyro*. それはどんな初心者にでもよく分かる.

P^2 a mere *tyro at* one's job その仕事にはほんの初心者. ¶a *tyro in* grammar 文法の初学者.

U

ugly, *a.* 醜い, 見苦しい.

M *hideously ugly* 恐ろしく醜い. ¶The situation is getting *more ugly*. 事態はいよいよ悪化して行く. ¶In personal appearance Socrates was *notoriously ugly*. ソクラテスの風さいは醜いので有名だ.

ulcer, *n.* かいよう.

Q *peptic ulcers* 胃かいよう.

Q^2 a *stomach ulcer* 胃かいよう.

P^2 an *ulcer of* the stomach 胃かいよう. ¶a small *ulcer on* the surface of … …の表面の小さなかいよう.

ultimatum, *n.* 最後通ちょう.

V *pronounce* an *ultimatum* 最後通ちょうを声明する. ¶*send* (=*dispatch*) an *ultimatum* to … …に最後通ちょうを送る.

V^2 The *ultimatum expires* at noon tomorrow. その最後通ちょうは明日の正午を期限とする.

P^2 an *ultimatum from* … …からの最後通ちょう.

ultra-conservative, *a.* 極右の.

P be *ultra-conservative in* … …では超保守的である.

umbrage, *n.* 憤怒, 不快, 恨み.

V His writings *gave umbrage* to the authorities. 彼の書いたものがその筋の忌諱(きい)に触れた. ¶*take umbrage* at another's advancement 他人の昇進を不快に思う. 【類】He *took umbrage* at what I said (some inoffensive jest). / *take umbrage* about …

umbrella, *n.* こうもりがさ.

V The wind *blew* my *umbrella wrong side out*. 風で私の

かさはおちょこになった. ¶*carry* an *umbrella along* かさを持って行く. ¶*close* (=*fold, furl or shut*) one's *umbrella* かさをつぼめる. ¶He *forgot* his *umbrella* and came back for it. 彼はかさを忘れそれを取りに戻った. ¶*hold* an *umbrella* over one's head かさをさしかけてやる. ¶*open* (=*unfurl, unfold or spread*) an *umbrella* かさを開く. ¶*put up* (=*raise*) an *umbrella* かさをさす. ¶He *took* an *umbrella* for fear of being caught in [the] rain. 彼は雨に会うかも知れないのでかさを持って行った. ‖ *Take* an *umbrella* with you. かさを持ってらっしゃい. ‖ *take* an *umbrella along* かさを持って行く. ¶The wind *turned* my *umbrella* inside out in no time. 風がたちまち僕のかさをおちょこにした. ¶*waving* his *umbrella* かさを振りながら.

Q a *shabby umbrella* 見すぼらしいかさ. ¶a *stout umbrella* がん丈な洋がさ.

P man and woman *under* an *umbrella* 相合がさの男女 ‖ There was a small group of people, waiting *under umbrellas* for a car to Shinjiku. かさをさした小さな一群の人が新宿行の電車を待っていた. ‖ Will you let me walk *under* your *umbrella?* かさに入れて下さいませんか. ¶He pointed at it *with* his *umbrella*. 彼はかさでそれを指した.

umpire, *n*. 審判官.

Q an *impartial umpire* 公平な審判者.

P act *as* [an] *umpire* 審判(アンパイヤ)の役を勤める.

unable, *a*. できない, 力のない.

M *altogether unable* to ... ...することが全くできない. ¶*quite unable* at present to ... 現在...することが全くできない. ¶*utterly unable* to ... ...することが全然できない. ¶*wholly unable* to ... ...することが全く不可能で.

O *unable* to buy at your limits あなたの指値では買うことができない ‖ I am sorry to be *unable* to come. 遺憾ながら私は来られない. ‖ I am *unable* to comply with your wishes. 私はあなたの願いをいれることはできない. 【類】 *unable* to do anything at present / If *unable* to do so, teleragph. / people *unable* to read or write.

unaccomplished, *a*. 未完成の.

P be *unaccomplished in* ... ...に未熟である.

unaccounted, *a*. 不明の.

P The list of persons *unaccounted for* stood at 13. 生死不明は十三名であった.

unaccustomed, *a*. 慣れない.

M I am *quite unaccustomed* to speaking in public. 私は人前で話すことに全く慣れていない.

P *unaccustomed to* hearing (wearing, eating) 聞き(など)つけない. 【類】 *unaccastomed to* speech-making (public speaking) / be *unaccastomed to* labor.

unacquainted, *a*. 知らない, 不案内の.

P *unacquainted with* a person (matter) 人(など)を知らない.

unadmirable, *n*. ほめるに足らないもの.

V *admire* the *unadmirable* ほめる価値のないものをほめる.

unaffected, *a*. 影響を受けない.

P The ground was *unaffected by* the recent downpour. 最近のどしゃ降りにも道路はいたまなかった.

unanimity, *n*. 同意, 一致; 協和.

Q with almost *monotonous unanimity* ほとんど単調なほど一様に.

P The proposal was adopted *with* striking *unanimity*. その提案は目に立つほどの満場一致で可決された. ‖ *with* the *unanimity* of applause 満場の拍手で.

P² a *unanimity of* consent 満場の賛成.

unanimous, *a*. 同意の, 異議のない.

M they are *practically unanimous* in declaring that ... 彼らはほとんど異口同音に...と言明している.

P The meeting was *unanimous as to* the policy to be pursued. 取るべき政策については満場一致していた. ¶*unanimous for* reform 改革に対して異議のない. ¶*unanimous in* their praise of ... 口をそろえて...をほめて ‖ People were *unanimous in* their wish for peace. 人々は平和を願う点において異議がなかった. 【類】 the meeting was *unanimous in* protesting against ...

unappreciative, *a*. 有難がられない.

P be *unappreciative of* one's kindness 親切を無にする.

unarmed, *a*. 無防備の.

P *unarmed from* head *to* foot 身に寸鉄を帯びず.

unartful, *a*. 単純な.

M She was *rather unartful* in her manner. 彼女は立居振舞はむしろ飾らな過ぎた.

unattended, *a*. 伴われない, 従者のない.

M It was *fortunately unattended* with any loss of life. 幸にも生命には別状がなかった.

P The efforts have not been *unattended with* some degree of success. その努力は幾分の成功を伴わないこともなかった.

unavoidable, *a*. 不可避の.

M except when *absolutely unavoidable* どうにもならない場合は別として. ¶The delay was *quite unavoidable*. その遅延は全くどうにもならなかった.

P That's *unavoidable in* social life. それは社会生活では避け難いことだ.

unaware, *a*. 知らない.

Q He was *entirely unaware* that he was walking a wrong way. 道が違っていたことは全然気がつかなかった. ¶he is *quite unaware* that ... 彼は...ということを全く知らない.

P be *unaware of* the mistake その誤りに気がつかない. 【類】 of course I am not *unaware of* the fact that ... / He seemed *unaware of* the disturbance.

unbalanced, *a*. 平均を失っている, 心が乱れている.

M *mentally unbalanced* 精神錯乱して.

unbearable, *a*. 耐えられない.

P Life became *unbearable to* her. 彼女は生きているのが耐えられなかった. ¶be *unbearable without* it それがなくては我慢ができない.

unbecoming, *a*. 不似合いの.

M *utterly unbecoming* to a woman of her birth 姫御前(ひめごぜ)のあられもない.

P *unbecoming for* persons of education 教育ある人には不似合な. ¶It is *unbecoming of* him to do such a thing. そんなことをやるのはあの人の柄にない.

unbosom, *v*. 意中を打明ける.

P *unbosom* oneself of it *to* ... これを...に打明ける ‖ *unbosom* one's feeling (secret) *to* another 感じ(秘密)を人に打あける.

unbred, *a*. 無知の, しつけを受けていない.

P She is *unbred to* sewing. 針仕事は仕込まれていない.

unburden, *v*. 荷を卸す; 打明ける.

P At last he *unburdened* himself *to* a confidant. 遂に彼は腹心の友に意中を打明けた. 【類】 *unburden* one's heart (=mind) *to* another.

unbusinesslike, *a*. だらだらした.

M be *emphatically unbusinesslike* 特にだらだらした(てきぱきとやらない).

uncalled-for, *a*. 不用の, 余計の.

M What he said was *utterly uncalled-for*. 彼の言葉は全く余計なことだった.

O It's an *uncalled-for* remark. いらざるさし出口だ.

uncertain, *a*. 不確実な.

M His aim is *somewhat uncertain*. 彼のねらいははっきりしないところがある. ¶I'm *still uncertain* of my future. 私は将来がまだ不安だ.

P be *uncertain of* the truth (success) その真実(成功)がはっきりしない.

uncertainty, *n*. 不定, 不明, 不確実.

V *bring out* strongly the *uncertainty* of ... ...の不確実性をはっきりさせる. ¶*clear up uncertainties* with regard to his real attitude on the question その問題に関する彼の態度の真相について不明な点を明りょうにする. ¶*dispel* many *uncertainties* 幾多の不安を除去する. ¶*realize* the *uncertainty* of life 人生の無常を悟る.

V² some *uncertainty attaches* to ... ...には幾分不明な点がある.

Q *economic uncertainty* 経済的不安. ¶There is "*glorious uncertainty*" in book publishing and film production. 出版にも映画製作にも何が当るか分からないところにおもしろ味がある. ¶*grave uncertainties* 由々しい不安. ¶*moral uncertainty* 道義的不安. ¶there is *no uncertainty* as to ... ...については不安がない. ¶a *political uncertainty* 政治的不安.

Q² continue *world uncertainty* 世界不安を続ける.

P It is *above* all *uncertainty*. それには全く不安がない. ¶It has an element *of uncertainty*. それには不安の点がある.

P² a little *uncertainty about* ... ...についてのわずかな不安. ¶the *uncertainty in* foreign exchange 外国為替の不安定. ¶the *uncertainty of* life 人生の無常.

unchangeable, *a*. 不変の.

P be *unchangeable of* purpose 目標を変えない.

unchanged, *a*. 変らない, 変化のない.

P The city is practically *unchanged from* former times. その市は大体以前と変っていない.

uncivil, *a*. 不作法な.

M Nobody was *so uncivil* as to leave the room. だれ一人

へやを去るような不行儀はしなかった.

uncle, *n.* 叔(伯)父.

Q his ***pet*** *uncle* 彼の好きなおじさん. ¶his ***Pickwickian*** *uncle* 彼のピックウィックのようなおじ ☞肥満でお人好し (ディケンズの小説にある). ⌈mine 私のおじさん.

P^{2} an *uncle* ***by*** marriage 親せきのおじさん. ¶an *uncle* ***of***

uncolo[u]red, *a.* 着色してない, 飾り気のない.

P information *uncolored* ***by*** personal opinions or prejudices 個人の意見や偏見の色彩を伴わない情報.

uncomfortable, *a.* 不愉快な, 不自由な.

M This is a place not ***quite*** *uncomfortable* to live in for the moment. 当分住むにはそれほど悪くもない. ¶You must have found it ***very*** *uncomfortable.* それは随分不自由でしたでしょう.

P feel *uncomfortable* ***with*** foreigners (strangers) 外人(未知の人)と交際するとき気持がぴったりしない.

uncommon, *a.* 非常な, 非凡な, まれな.

M It is ***not*** *uncommon* to find it so. そうなっていることは珍しくはない. ¶***very*** *uncommon* はなはだまれな.

uncommonly, *ad.* まれに.

M ***not*** *uncommonly* しばしば.

O *uncommonly* cold 珍しく寒い.

unconcern, *n.* 平気, 無とん着.

V ***show*** *unconcern* 平気でいる.

Q not suggestive of ***forced*** *unconcern* 無理に平気を装った様子のない. ⌈で見る.

P view the matter ***with*** *unconcern* そのことを無関心な目

unconcerned, *a.* 無とん着な, 平気な; 無関係の.

M be ***blithely*** *unconcerned* about … …に対して涼しい顔をしている.

P He is *unconcerned* ***about*** personal appearance. 彼は身なりには無とん着である. 【類】be *unconcerned* ***about*** future. ¶He was *unconcerned* ***at*** her loss. 彼女を失ったことに対して彼は平気であった. ¶be *unconcerned* ***in*** (=***with***) the conspiracy その陰謀に無関係である.

O pretend to be *unconcerned* 知らない顔をする.

uncongenial, *a.* 性の合わない.

P These people are very *uncongenial* ***to*** me. この連中は私にはどうも性に合わない.

O an *uncongenial* (=disagreeable) task 性に合わない仕事.

unconscious, *a.* 知らない, 無意識な.

M remain ***magnificently*** *unconscious* of … …を知らぬが仏でいる. ¶***sublimely*** *unconscious* of … …には超然として.

P *unconscious* ***as to*** (=***about***) … …については無意識な. ¶After that he was *unconscious* ***for*** several hours. 彼はそれから数時間意識不明だった. ¶I am *unconscious* ***of*** having said so. 私はそう言った覚えがない. ¶*unconscious* ***through*** intoxication 酔って前後不覚な.

unconsciousness, *n.* 無意識, 人事不省.

P lapse ***into*** *unconsciousness* again また人事不省に陥る.

unconventional, *a.* 慣例に従わない.

M he is *unconventional* ***enough*** to urge that … 彼は…を勧めるほどに頭が新しい.

unconverted, *a.* 改宗してない, 帰依していない.

M some minds ***still*** *unconverted* to communism まだ共産主義者になっていない人々.

unconvinced, *a.* 納得しない.

P He remained *unconvinced* ***of*** his error. 彼は依然自己の

uncouth, *a.* 見慣れない, 異様な. ⌊誤りを悟らなかった.

M ***physically*** *uncouth* 外観異様な.

uncritical, *a.* 無批評な.

M all the papers remained ***strangely*** *uncritical* about … …について新聞は不思議なほど無批判的であった.

unction, *n.* 熱情; 〖宗教〗塗油.

Q be given ***extreme*** *unction* 臨終の塗油式を施される.

P declaim ***with*** *unction* 熱弁を揮う ‖ a story told ***with*** *unction* 力のはいった話. 【類】listen to it ***with*** *unction.*

undealt, *a.* そのままにした.

P The movement has become too serious to remain *undealt* ***with.*** その運動はそのまま捨置けないほど由々しいこ

undeceive, *v.* 欺かれたことを悟らせる. ⌊とになった.

M He was ***painfully*** *undeceived.* 彼は欺かれていたことを知ってくやしがった. ¶But I was ***soon*** *undeceived.* しかし私はすぐ自分の間違いに気づいた.

undecided, *a.* 定まらない, 決しない.

M He is ***still*** *undecided.* 彼は未だ心が決っていない.

undemocratic, *a.* 非民主主義的な.

M ***positively*** *undemocratic* 明かに非民主主義的な.

underdone, *a.* 半煮えの.

M The rice is ***partly*** *underdone.* ご飯にしんがある.

underestimate, *v.* 少なく見積る.

M ***too much*** *underestimate* the value of adult education. 成人教育の価値を過少評価する.

undergraduate, *n.* 大学生.

P while still an *undergraduate* ***at*** Oxford まだオックスフォード在学当時.

Q^{2} The book should be in the hands of ***college*** *undergradutaes.* 同書は大学生必携のものである. ¶a ***Harvard*** *undergraduate* ハーバード大学生.

underlap, *v.* 重なり合う.

M One plank ***slightly*** *underlaps* another 板は少しずつ重

underlay, *v.* 下積みにする. ⌊なり合っている.

P a dead body *underlaid* ***with*** snow 雪の下になった死体.

underling, *n.* 下役, 小役人.

P Who cares ***about*** those *underlings?* こんな小役人を相手

underneath, *n.* 下, 下部. ⌊にするもんか.

P ***from*** *underneath* 下から.

underrate, *v.* 軽視する.

M be ***considerably*** *underrated* 大いに軽視されている.

undersecretary, *n.* 次官.

Q^{2} a ***parliamentary*** *undersecretary* 政務次官. ¶a ***permanent*** *undersecretary* 事務次官.

P an *Undersecretary* ***of*** State ***for*** the Navy《米》海軍次

undersell, *v.* …より低廉に売る. ⌊官.

P We can *undersell* them ***in*** the Chinese market. われわれは中国市場では彼らより安く品を売ることができる.

underside, *n.* 下側.

P A crutch is an iron fitting shaped like a capital "U" with a vertical pin ***on*** the *underside,* all cast in one piece. 橈(ﾀﾞ)架は"U"字形をなし下部に垂直の棒が付き全部一緒に鋳造した鉄の装具である.

understaff, *v.* 人員不足させる.

M The library is ***scandalously*** *understaffed,* underpaid, and cramped for room. その図書館はひどく人手が足らず, 給料は安く, その上場所が狭過ぎる.

understand, *v.* 了解する.

M if I *understand* him ***aright*** 私の彼を見る所にして誤りがないとすれば. ¶*understand* ***clearly*** 明りょうに理解する. 【類】it must be ***clearly*** *understood* and borne in mind that … / I have always failed to *understand* very ***clearly*** why … ¶I wish to be ***distinctly*** *understood* that … …ということをはっきり理解しておいてもらいたい. ¶***easily*** *understand* 容易に理解する. ¶we wish it ***explicitly*** *understood* that … …ということを篤と理解して欲しい. ¶Most of the students *understand* English ***fairly well.*** 大半の学生は英語がかなり分かっている. ¶*understand* ***fully*** the significance of … …の意義を十分に理解する. ¶it is ***generally*** *understood* that … 一般に…と思われている. ¶***Now*** I *understand!*=Eureka! はは\u3042読めた. ¶as may be ***readily*** *understood* 容易に理解されるように. 【類】You can ***readily*** *understand* the fact that … ¶Do I *understand* you ***rightly?*** [あなたの考えを]そう解釈して間違いではありませんか. ¶The patient is getting better, ***so*** I *understand.* 病人はだんだんよくなっているそうです. ¶It was ***tacitly*** *understood.* そのことは暗黙の内に理解されていた. ¶***thoroughly*** *understand* 十分に理解する. ¶it is only ***vaguely*** *understood* that … …ということが薄々分かっているに過ぎない. ¶I can ***well*** *understand* it. そうでしょうとも. ¶*understand* ***wrong*** =misunderstand 曲解する.

P What am I to *understand* ***by*** your conduct? あなたのやり口は一体どうしたというのですか. ¶We *understand* ***from*** a reliable source that … 信ずべき筋から…だと聞いている.

O in respect to it I wish to be *understood* that … それに関して…と私は断っておきたい. ¶it must be *understood* that … …とぜひ御承知おきを願いたい. ¶easy to *understand* 分かりやすい.

understandable, *a.* 理解できる.

M make it easier and ***more*** *understandable* それをもっとやさしく分かりやすくする. ¶a thing not ***quite*** *understandable* あまりはっきりしないことがら.

understanding, *n.* 理解, 理解力; 分別.

V ***afford*** a better *understanding* of … …を一層よく理解させる. ¶***arrange*** a harmonious *understanding* as to … …について協調を図る. ¶***baffle*** one's *understanding* 理解に苦しむ. ¶***bring about*** a greater *understanding* between the Orient and the Occident 東西両洋間相互の理解を一層深める. 【類】***bring about*** a better *understanding* in America and Europe of the conditions (事情) in the East. ¶***build up*** sympathetic *understanding* among … …の間の同情的理解を築き上げる. ¶***create*** a better *understanding* between the two countries 両国間の理解を深める. ¶***deepen*** *understanding* 理解を深める. 【類】***deepen*** one's sympathies and *understanding*. ¶The *understanding* may be ***defined*** as the faculty of judgment. 理解力は判断する力という定義が下される. ¶***develop*** a sympathetic *understanding* of the people of other nations その国民に他国民に対する同情的な理解を持たせるようにする. ¶***diffuse*** in every quarter a clear *understanding* of … 一般に…を明確に理解させる. ¶***elude*** our *understanding* われわれの理解力に余る. ¶***enlarge*** the *understanding* of our own language 自国語の理解を普及させる. ¶***facilitate*** the *understanding* of … …の理解を容易ならしめる. ¶***further*** mutual *understanding* 相互の理解を助長する. ¶***gain*** a better *understanding* of … …を一層よく理解する. ¶this will ***give*** you a clear *understanding* of … これによって…をはっきり理解することができるだろう. ¶***have*** an *understanding* of … …に対し理解を持つ ‖ It is usually desirable to ***have*** an *understanding* with the taxi man before commencing a journey. 多くの場合出掛ける前にタクシーと(料金などの)話をつけておくことが望ましいことだ. ¶***improve*** one's *understanding* and use of words 語の理解と用法を一層よくする. ¶***increase*** mutual *understanding* 相互の理解を増す. ¶***insure*** a better *understanding* among … …間に一層の理解を確保する. ¶***keep*** a good *understanding* with … …と意志がよく通じている; …と気脈を通じている. ¶***lack*** *understanding* 理解力を欠く. ¶***obtain*** a satisfactory *understanding* from … …から満足な了解を得る. ¶It ***passes*** *understanding*. それは解せない. ¶Love ***passeth*** all *understanding*. 恋は思案の外. ¶***promote*** a better *understanding* between East and West 東西両洋間における一層の理解を増進する. 【類】He has assisted in ***promoting*** a better *understanding* between this country and his own ‖ ***promote*** *understanding* of Japan's point of view abroad 海外に日本の立場をもっとよく理解させる. ¶***reach*** an *understanding* 話がつく. 【類】***reach*** a clear *understanding* and stronger sympathy with … ¶***seek*** an *understanding* with … …との和解を求める. ¶***sharpen*** the *understanding* 理解力を鋭敏にする. ¶***strengthen*** international *understanding* and goodwill 国際間の理解と好意を強固にする. ¶should this *understanding* be ***violated*** この規約を破ると.

V² Full *understanding* will ***come*** gradually. 段々に十分理解するようになるだろう.

Q ***accurate*** *understanding* 精確な理解. ¶promote a ***better*** *understanding* between … …間に一層の理解を深める. ¶on the ***clear*** *understanding* that … …ということをはっきり理解して. ¶By the ***common*** *understanding*, Chamberlain was held chiefly accountable for the Boer War. 一般に南ア戦争の主なる責任者はチェンバーレンということになっていた. 【類】the growth of ***common*** *understanding* between the two nations. ¶for a more ***complete*** *understanding* of … …をさらに完全な了解に達するために. ¶a ***cordial*** *understanding* between … …の間の心からの親善. ¶essential to a ***correct*** *understanding* of … …の正しい理解に重要な. ¶obtain a ***deeper*** *understanding* of … …のより深い理解を得る. ¶He has not even a ***dim*** *understanding* of this truth. 彼はこの事実がちっとも分かっていない. ¶with the ***distinct*** *understanding* that … …ということをはっきり理解して. ¶have an ***excellent*** *understanding* すぐれた理解力を持っている. ¶secure a ***factual*** *understanding* of … …の事実に基ずく理解を確保する. ¶a man with a ***fine*** *understanding* 物わかりのいい人. ¶promote a ***friendly*** *understanding* between the two nations 二国間の友情を促進させる. ¶come to a ***full*** *understanding* 十分に話合がつく. ¶a ***full*** *understanding* of international affairs 国際事情の十分な理解. ¶bring about ***good*** *understanding* between the two nations その二国民間に十分な理解をもたらす. 【類】show ***good*** *understanding* for … ‖ have ***good*** *understanding* of economics 経済学に通じている. ¶with but a ***hazy*** *understanding* of the subject その問題をほんのばく然と理解しているだけで. ¶***Human*** *understanding* is finite. 人間の理解力には限度がある. ¶preliminary knowledge necessary to any ***intelligent*** *understanding* of the subject その問題を本当に理解するために必要な予備知識. ¶promote better ***international*** *understanding* さらに一段の国際的理解を増進する. ¶promote ***mutual*** *understanding* between Japan and America 日米相互の理解を増進する. 【類】promote a better ***mutual*** *understanding* / by ***mutual*** *understanding*. ¶gain an ***objective*** *understanding* of what is going on in Russia ロシアの現状を客観的(実地)に理解する. ¶have a ***poor*** *understanding* of what one reads 自分の読んだものがよく分かっていない. ¶There is some ***private*** *understanding* between them. 彼らの間には何か内密な話合がついている. ¶have a ***proper*** *understanding* of … …を正当に理解している. ¶it is essential for a ***right*** *understanding* of … …を正しく理解するにはそれはぜひ必要である. 【類】the ***right*** *understanding* of the situation. ¶arrive at a ***sane*** *understanding* with regard to … …に関して健全な理解を得る. ¶have a ***secret*** *understanding* with … …と黙契がある ‖ There is fraudulent ***secret*** *understanding* between the ostensible opponents. それは八百長だ. ¶arrive at a ***similar*** *understanding* with … …と同様の折合いを遂げる. ¶read the original with ***some*** *understanding* 原文を幾分理解して読む. ¶These two had not one word of ***spoken*** *understanding* between them. これらの二人はいまだかつて一語たりとも言葉を交して理解し合っていたのではなかった. ¶***sympathetic*** *understanding* of American ideals and prejudices アメリカ人の理想偏見に対する同情的な理解. 【類】a ***sympathetic*** *understanding* of their lives, customs, and ideals / a ***sympathetic*** *understanding* between the two peoples. ¶there is a ***tacit*** *understanding* between … …間には黙契がある. ¶She lost her heart to the sailor and in course of a week or two there was a ***tender*** *understanding* between them. 彼女はそのマドロスに一目ぼれしたが一二週間たつ中に両人はわりない仲になった. ¶a ***thorough*** *understanding* 十分な理解. ¶a ***verbal*** *understanding* 申合わせ.

Q² foster ***world*** *understanding* and tolerance through education 教育によって世界の理解と寛容を助長する.

P That is [going] ***against*** our *understanding*. それでは話が違う. ¶arrive ***at*** an *understanding* concerning … …について折合がつく. ¶It is ***beyond*** *understanding*. それは理解し得ないことだ. ¶***by*** a tacit *understanding* that … …という黙契により. ¶quick ***of*** *understanding* 分かりが早い. ¶***on*** this *understanding* こういう話合で. 【類】***on*** that *understanding* / ***on*** the *understanding* that … / I consented it ***on*** this *understanding*. ¶***through*** some *understanding* 幾分分かって. ¶come ***to*** an *understanding* before parting 別れる前に話合がつく ‖ come ***to*** an *understanding* on … …に関して折合がつく. ¶***with*** the *understanding* that … …ということを含んで ‖ read it ***with*** *understanding* それを理解しつつ読む. ¶poke into others' business ***without*** *understanding* 知りもしないのに人の仕事に口を出す.

P² It is always best to have a clear *understanding* ***as to*** the price to be paid before starting. [円タクなど]出る前に支払うべき代をはっきりきめておくのが一番だ. ¶a better *understanding* ***between*** men and women 男女間のよりよき理解. ¶come to a mutual *understanding* ***for*** … …に関し折合がつく. ¶This is my *understanding* ***of*** the affair. その件で私の了解しているのはこうなんです. ¶promote a better *understanding* ***on*** the part of the Japanese ***of*** other peoples of the world 他国民に対する日本人の理解を一段と増進させる.

O That's not my *understanding*. そんなはずではなかった. ‖ my *understanding* has always been to … 私は…とばかり思っていた. ¶it is my *understanding* that … 私は…と了解している.

undertake, *v.* 引受ける, 着手する.

M ***solemnly*** *undertake* it そのことを誓約する. ¶***tentatively*** *undertake* the task その仕事を試験的に引受ける. ¶The Roman Catholics ***unobtrusively*** *undertake* works of benevolence amongst the poor. カトリック教徒は貧民に対する慈善事業を人目に立たないようにやっている.

P The work is *undertaken* ***by*** members of the committee. その仕事は委員が引受ける. ¶*undertake* the responsibility ***for*** another 人に代ってその責任をとる.

O I cannot *undertake* what you ask, but will do the best for your interests. あなたの御依頼には応じ兼ますがあなたのために最善を尽します. ¶Will you *undertake* to let him know what has happened? ことの次第を彼に知らせていただけませんか.

undertaking, *n.* 計画, 事業.

V The *undertaking* was ***attended*** with much difficulty. その事業には大なる困難がともなった. ¶This ***defeated*** the *undertaking*. このためにその事業は失敗に終った. ¶***discharge*** one's arduous *undertaking* その骨の折れる事業を果たす. ¶***finance*** an *undertaking* 事業に資本を出す. ¶The society ***fathered*** (=founded) this great *undertaking*. 同協会がこの大事業を起した. ¶A new *undertaking* has been ***set*** on foot. 新しい事業が計画された.

Q ***charitable*** *undertakings* 慈善事業. ¶a ***colossal*** *undertaking* 巨大な事業. ¶companies formed as ***commercial*** *undertakings* 商事会社 ‖ It is not a ***commercial*** *undertaking*. それは営利を目標とする事業ではない. ¶a ***daring*** *undertaking* 大胆な計画. ¶It seemed an ***endless*** *undertaking*. それは果しのない事業のように思われた. ¶a ***formidable*** *undertaking* [多大の努力を要する]一大事業. ¶a ***hopeless*** *undertaking* 望みのない事業. ¶Running an ocean liner is a ***huge*** *undertaking*. 大洋定期船を運転することは大事業である. ¶***industrial*** *undertakings* 産業上の事業. ¶The company is a ***joint Anglo-Chinese*** *undertaking*. その会社は英中合弁事業である. ¶a ***laborious*** *undertaking* 骨の折れる仕事. ¶a very ***large*** *undertaking* 非常に大きな事業. ¶a ***laudable***, ***praiseworthy***, and ***beneficial*** *undertaking* 結構な賞賛に値しかつ有益な事業. ¶a ***national*** *undertaking* 国家事業. ¶***no light*** *undertaking* 容易でない事業. ¶***no small*** *undertaking* 大仕事. ¶a ***serious*** *undertaking* 重大な仕事. ¶a ***social*** *undertaking* 社会的事業. ¶a sufficiently ***stiff*** *undertaking* かなり骨の折れる仕事. ¶a ***vast*** *undertaking* 大事業.

Q² It is a ***business*** *undertaking*, not a speculation. それは商売上の仕事で, 投機ではない. ¶an ***engineering*** *undertaking* of vast magnitude 大規模の土木工事. ¶a ***Government*** *undertaking* 政府の事業. ¶a ***nonprofit*** *undertaking* 非営利的事業. ¶a ***public utility*** *undertaking* 公益事業. ¶a ***trial*** *undertaking* 試験的の仕事. ¶a ***tramway*** *undertaking* 市内電鉄事業.

P take part ***in*** an *undertaking* 事業に参加する. ¶enter ***upon*** an *undertaking* 事業を始める.

P² This long journey is a great *undertaking* ***for*** so old a man. この長い旅はそんな老人には大仕事である.

undertone, *n.* 低調子.

P say ***in*** an *undertone* 低い調子で言う. 【類】speak ***in*** *undertones.*

underway, *ad.* 進行中で.

M The preparations are ***well*** *underway* for the conference. 会議の準備は着々進行中だ. ☞ under way と underway の二つの書き方がある. → way.

underworld, *n.* 暗黒街.

P Al Capone was the king ***of*** the *underworld*. アルカポネは暗黒街の顔役だった.

undeserving, *a.* 価値のない.

P be *undeserving* ***of*** their censure 彼らの非難を受ける理由がない.

undesirable, *a.* 好ましくない.

M a ***most*** *undesirable* person もっとも好ましからぬ人物.

undeterred, *a.* 抑えられない.

P *undeterred* ***by*** his previous failure 前の失敗にもひるまず ‖ *undeterred* ***by*** the wiser counsels of his friends 友人たちの適切な助言にもかかわず. 【類】*undeterred* ***by*** rough weather.

undisguised, *a.* 打明けた, 飾りのない.

M His alarm was ***quite*** *undisguised*. 彼の驚がくははっきりそれと見受けられた.

undistinguishable, *a.* 区別のつかない.

P *undistinguishable* ***from*** … …と区別がつかない.

undivided, *a.* 分かたれない.

P be *undivided* ***in*** one's attention 余念がない.

undress, *n.* 平常服.

P Everybody is expected to appear ***in*** an *undress*. 皆平常服で出席するはず.

undress, *v.* きものをぬぐ.

P *undress* oneself ***in*** a warm room 暖かいへやで裸体になる.

undressing, *n.* 脱衣.

V ***start*** *undressing* 着物を脱ぎ始める.

undulation, *n.* 波動, 起伏.

P Worms move ***by*** *undulation*. 虫は体をうねらして進む. ‖ country stretching ***in*** *undulation* 起伏が連続している土地. 【類】The hills are raised ***in*** *undulations*.

uneasiness, *n.* 不安, 心配, 懸念.

V It is ***causing*** *uneasiness* in the British mind. それは英国人の心に不安を生じせしめつつある. ¶Do not ***give*** yourself the least *uneasiness*. 決して御心配なさるな. ¶He is suffering from a trifling indisposition which ***occasions*** no *uneasiness*. 彼は心配するほどではないちょっとした病気にかかっている.

Q a ***wide-spread*** *uneasiness* 世人一般の不安.

uneasy, *a.* 不安な, 心配な.

M ***extremely*** *uneasy* about … …について非常に不安な.

P I feel *uneasy* ***about*** my friend's health. 私は友人の健康を不安に思う. ¶I grew *uneasy* ***at*** his long absence. 彼が(出て行って)長く帰らないので不安になった. ¶Do not be *uneasy* ***in*** mind about the consequences. その結果を心配し給うな ‖ feel *uneasy* ***in*** tight clothes (shoes) 衣服(くつ)が窮屈で着(はき)心地が悪い. ¶The young king was *uneasy* ***on*** the throne. 若い王の王座は不安定であった.

unemployed, *a.* 仕事のない, 失職の.

V ***mobilize*** the *unemployed* for war purposes 失業者を戦争目的に動員する.

P relief ***of*** the *unemployed* 失業者の救助.

unemployment, *n.* 失業.

V ***absorb*** *unemployment* 失業群を消化する. ¶Technological progress does not ***cause*** *unemployment*. 工業の進歩は失業を生みはしない. ¶***conquer*** *unemployment* 失業を征服する. ¶***create*** *unemployment* 失業者を出す.

V² *Unemployment* ***exists*** among mine workers. 鉱夫間に失業者がある.

Q bring ***mounting*** *unemployment* 一時失業の増加をきたす. ¶***seasonal*** *unemployment* 季節失業.

Q² ***large-scale*** *unemployment* 大量失業. ¶***rock bottom*** *unemployment*, a virtually irreducible percentage 事実それ以下に減少し得ないぎりぎりの失業.

P statistics ***of*** *unemployment* 失業統計. ¶the problem ***of*** *unemployment* 失業問題.

unequal, *a.* 一様でない, 不つり合いの.

M The contest was ***too*** *unequal* to last long. 競技は段違いで長くは続かなかった.

P *unequal* ***in*** training 訓練のそろわない. 【類】*unequal* ***in*** size (volume). ¶I find myself *unequal* ***to*** what I have undertaken. 私が企てた事業は私の力に余ることが分かった. ‖ feeling himself *unequal* ***to*** conversation, the patient wrote in pencil, "…" 患者は話をする力がないと感じて鉛筆で「…」と書いた. 【類】He felt that he was *unequal* ***to*** the task. / She proved *unequal* ***to*** the job.

unequal[l]ed, *a.* 無比の, 類のない.

P *unequaled* ***in*** merit (beauty, strength) 功績(など)の点で比類のない ‖ His collection is said to be *unequaled* ***in*** the world. 彼の収集は世界無比だと言われている.

unerring, *a.* 誤りのない.

P He is *unerring* ***in*** his judgment. 彼の判断は誤りがない.

unescapable, *a.* 避けがたい.

P the inference is *unescapable* ***from*** these facts that … これらの事実から見て…と推断せざるを得ない.

unexpected, *a.* 意外な.

M It was ***quite*** *unexpected*. 全く意外であった. ¶the ***wholly*** *unexpected* North Korean blitz invasion 北鮮の全く不意を突いた電撃進攻.

unfair, *a.* 不正な, 不正直な.

M it is ***grossly*** *unfair* to compare it with … それと…を比較するのははなはだしい不公平だ. ¶***ridiculously*** *unfair* ばかばかしく不公平な.

P be *unfair* ***in*** one's dealings その取扱いが不公平である. ¶She is *unfair* ***to*** us in class. 彼女(先生)はわれわれのクラスに無理を言う.

unfaithful, *a.* 不信実な.

P be *unfaithful* ***in*** one's love 浮気をする. 【類】He is *unfaithful* ***in*** every way ***to*** his friend. ‖ *unfaithful* ***to*** one's duty (principle) 自分の職務(など)に不忠実な.

unfamiliar, *a.* 慣れていない, 親しくない.

P *unfamiliar* ***to*** the eye (ear) 目(耳)慣れない. ¶He is totally *unfamiliar* ***with*** this neighborhood. 彼はこの土地には全く不慣れである.

unfamiliarity, *n.* 不案内.

P through his *unfamiliarity* ***with*** the route 彼がその経路を知らなかったので.

unfavo[u]rable, *a.* 都合の悪い, 不利な.

P The weather was *unfavorable* ***for*** shooting. 天気は猟にはよくなかった.

unfit, *n.* 不適者(物).

V ***preserve*** the *unfit* 不適者(物)を保存する. ¶***protect*** the *unfit* 不適者(物)を保護する. ¶***weed out*** (=***eliminate*** *or* ***remove***) the *unfit* 不適物(植物など)を除く.

unfit, *a.* 不適当な.

M ***physically*** *unfit* for ... 肉体的に…に不適任な. ¶He is ***totally*** *unfit* for duty. 彼は職務を執るには全く適しない.

P women *unfit* ***for*** motherhood 母たるに適しない女 / He was dismissed as *unfit* ***for*** military service. / be *unfit* ***for*** repairs / The fish is condemned as *unfit* ***for*** food. ‖ It is *unfit* ***for*** description here. それは(下がかったことなどで)ここには記されない. ¶He is quite *unfit* ***to*** the work. 彼はその仕事に全く向かない.

unfit, *v.* 不適当にする.

P To sit up all night *unfits* one ***for*** work next day. 徹夜をすると翌日の仕事にさわる. 【類】The weakness of his constitution (体質) *unfits* him ***for*** such an office (役).

unfold, *v.* 開く.

M The buds *unfold* ***late*** (***early***) in spring. 晩(早)春に開花する.

unforeseen, *a.* 予測しがたい.

M The event was ***quite*** (=***entirely***) *unforeseen.* その事件は全く意外だった.

unformed, *a.* 未熟な.

M a ***still*** *unformed* mind まだ固まっていない心(十代の始めの少年など).

unfortunate, *a.* 不運な, 不幸な.

P *unfortunate* ***for*** him 彼に取って不運にも. ¶*unfortunate* ***in*** one's marriage まずい結婚をして不仕合わせな ‖ She has been *unfortunate* ***in*** her choice of representatives at Peking for some time. その国は在北京代表者(大使など)の人選がしばらくうまく行っていなかった.

unfounded, *a.* 根拠のない.

M The accusation is ***utterly*** *unfounded.* その非難は全然根拠がない.

unfriendly, *a.* 友情のない; 不親切な.

M They are ***rather*** *unfriendly* to foreign visitors. 外人客にいささか冷淡である.

P *unfriendly* ***to*** each other お互に友情のない.

unfruitful, *a.* 成果のない.

P be *unfruitful* ***of*** result 成績があがらない.

unfurl, *v.* 開く.

M The parachute will *unfurl* itself as ***soon*** as it is thrown into the air. 落下さんは空中に投出されるとたんに自然に開く.

ungrateful, *a.* 忘恩の; 有難くない.

P It is *ungrateful* ***of*** you to behave in such a way towards your benefactor. 恩人に対してそんな行動をやるとは君も恩知らずだ. ¶I know that I must seem *ungrateful* ***to*** you. 私は君に対して恩知らずと見えるに違いないことは承知している. ‖ Nothing is *ungrateful* ***to*** the hungry. 空腹だと何をもらっても有難い.

unhampered, *a.* 妨げられない.

P Government business has not yet sufficiently unofficial *unhampered* ***by*** red tape. 官庁の仕事はお役所風が十分抜けないで形式ばかりという弊がまだ残っている.

unhandy, *a.* 不便利な.

P My home is *unhandy* ***to*** tramcars. 私の家は電車には便利がよくない.

unhappiness, *n.* 不幸, 不仕合わせ.

Q ***conjugal*** *unhappiness* 夫婦の不和. ¶***domestic*** *unhappiness* 家庭の不和.

unhappy, *a.* 不仕合わせな, 不幸な.

M His connection with the university was ***remarkably*** *unhappy.* 彼と大学との関係はどうもおもしろくなかった(生徒から排斥されるなど).

P And so don't be *unhappy* ***about*** it. だからあまりくよくよするな. ¶He is *unhappy* ***in*** his present position. 彼の今の地位に満足していない.

unheard, *a.* 聞いたことのない.

P an event *unheard* ***of*** in history 前代未聞の事件 ‖ Such is a thing *unheard* ***of*** regarding a foreigner. こうしたことは外国人に関しては前例のないことである.

unification, *n.* 統一.

Q the ***present economic*** *unification* of the world 今日見られる経済的世界統一(打って一団となっていること).

Q² ***armed forces*** *unification* 三軍の統合. ¶***service*** *unification* 《米》陸海空軍統合(一元化).

P² the *unification* ***of*** thought 思想の統一.

uniform, *n.* 制服, 軍服.

V ***don*** military *uniform* 軍服を着る. ¶***wear*** a *uniform* 制服を着る. 【類】***wear*** *uniform* / ***wear*** the *uniform* of a field-marshal (元帥) / ***wear*** the *uniform* of one's rank (官位).

Q wear ***admiral's*** *uniform* 海軍大将の制服を着る. ¶attired in a ***blue*** *uniform* 紺地の制服を着て. ¶fail to appear in ***correct*** *uniform* 正しい制服を着けて出ない. ¶wearing the ***distinctive*** *uniform* of ... …専用の制服を着て. ¶officers in ***full*** *uniform* 礼装した士官たち. ¶***full*** and ***undress*** *uniforms* 正式及び略式の制服. ¶the ***garish*** *uniform* of red and blue 赤と青のはでな制服. ¶a ***gold*** *uniform* 金ぴかの制服. ¶officials in ***gorgeous*** *uniform* 豪華な礼服を着た役人たち. ¶a ***grand gold-laced*** *uniform* 大礼服. ¶a Eurasian in a ***khaki*** *uniform* カーキー色の制服を着た欧亜雑種人. ¶in a French ***military*** (=Army) *uniform* フランスの軍服姿で. ¶a ***naval*** (=Navy) *uniform* 海軍の制服. ¶in ***nurse's*** *uniform* 看護婦の制服を着て. ¶don streamlined ***olive drab*** *uniform* 流線形の暗緑色の制服を着る. ¶attired in a ***resplendent*** *uniform,* cocked hat, and white gloves 金ぴかの大礼服・三角帽・白の手袋といういでたちで. ¶a ***rich*** (=***showy***) *uniform* 美々しい制服.

Q² a Tommy's "***battle-dress***" *uniform* 《英》歩兵の戦闘服. ¶in ***blue serge*** *uniform* 紺サージの制服で. ¶500 suits of ***cavalry*** *uniform* 騎兵の制服五百着. ¶a ***combat*** *uniform* 戦闘服. ¶a ***dress*** *uniform* 礼装の制服. ¶the ***regulation*** *uniform* of blue 青の制服. ¶We have a ***school*** *uniform* in our school. われわれは学校の制服がある. ¶a ***service*** *uniform* [軍人の]通常服. ¶a ***waitress*** *uniform* 女給仕の制服.

P soldiers and officers ***in*** *uniform* 制服を着た将兵. 【類】a policeman ***in*** *uniform* / ***in*** cap and *uniform* ‖ appear ***in*** a *uniform* prescribed by the university 大学規定の制服を着て出る. 【類】not ***in*** *uniform* / interpreters ***in*** the *uniform* of Thom. Cook & Son / The King was ***in*** the *uniform* of a Field-Marshal. / He looks handsome ***in*** *uniform.* ¶***in*** *uniform* or ***out of*** *uniform* 制服または私服で. ¶It's a disgrace ***to*** the *uniform.* 制服(軍人)に対して恥じょくである.

uniform, *a.* 一様の, 一定の, そろいの.

P Human bodies are *uniform* ***in*** their structure and functions. 人間の体は人を異にしてもその構造と機能はすべて同様である. ¶*uniform* ***in*** size and shape with each other 双方とも大きさ形とも等しい. ¶books *uniform* ***with*** this volume この本と(装ていなどの)そろいの本 ‖ volume *uniform* ***with*** ... …と同等の容積.

uniformity, *n.* 一様, 画一.

V ***break*** the *uniformity* of ... …の画一を打破する. ¶*Uniformity* is ***imposed*** from without and has always failed: unity springs from within and always succeeds. 画一は外部から加えられるものでいつも失敗に終った; 統一は内部から発生するもので常に成功する. ¶***lack*** *uniformity* 均斉を欠く. ¶***preserve*** *uniformity* 画一を保持する. ¶***secure*** *uniformity* in (=of) ... …を画一にする.

Q ***essential*** *uniformity* 大同小異.

P² There is lack of *uniformity* ***in*** the annual reports. その(数年にわたる)年報は統一が欠けている. ¶the *uniformity* ***of*** scholarship 学力の均等.

unimpaired, *a.* そこなわれない.

P His faculties were *unimpaired* ***to*** the last. 息を引取るまでしっかりしていた.

unimprovable, *a.* 改善し得ない.

V ***improve*** the *unimprovable* 改善し得ないものを改善する.

uninitiated, *a.* しろうと.

P to those *uninitiated* ***into*** the intricacies of ... …の複雑性を心得ていない人々には.

uninterested, *a.* 関係のない, 無とん着の.

M He seemed ***utterly*** *uninterested* in all these matters. 彼はこれらの事柄に全く無とん着のようであった.

uninteresting, *a.* 興味のない.

M It may not be found ***altogether*** *uninteresting.* それは全然興味のないことでもなかろう.

P It seems *uninteresting* ***to*** him. それは彼にとって興味がないらしい.

union, *n.* 一致; 同盟, 連合; 結婚; 《米》労働組合.

V The *union* has not been ***blessed*** with children. その夫婦は子宝に恵まれなかった. ¶***break up*** a *union* of parts 部

分品に分解する. ¶*bring out* a closer *union* of ... ...を一層和合させる. ¶*develop* a closer commercial *union* 一層親密な商業上の一致を図る. ¶*dissolve union* 合同を解く. ¶*effect* a *union* 合併を遂げる ‖ *effect* the difficult union between poetic beauty and dramatic passion 詩的な美と劇的な情熱という困難な結合を完成する. ¶*establish* a firm *union* 堅固な合同を樹立する. ¶*form* an international *union* 国際的合同を作る. 【類】The thirteen colonies *formed* a *union*. ¶*legalize* her *union* with him 彼女と彼との縁組を正式なものにする.

Q in various States of the *American Union* アメリカ合衆国の諸州で. ¶*childless unions* 子供のない結婚. ¶*conjugal union* 縁組. ¶a *consanguineous union* 親族結婚. ¶the *Cotton Spinners' Union* 紡績業者組合. ¶a *happy union* 幸福な結婚. ¶*ill-assorted unions* bound by convenience, and not by love 愛情からでなく便宜上結ばれたつり合わない結婚. ¶a pledge of an *indissoluble union* 切っても切れない縁(ﾆﾞ)の証(ｼﾞｮ)たる子供. ¶an *industrial union* 産業別組合. ¶an *international union* 国際組合. ¶In Nikko we find an *intimate union* of art and nature, of architecture and landscape 日光は人工と自然, 建築と風光の緊密な組合わせである. ¶a girl combined in *matrimonial union* with ... ...と縁組をした少女. ¶a *national union* 全国組合. ¶This is the *one* and *only union* of the type in the country. その型では国中でもこれが唯一の組合だ. ¶live together in *perfect union* [夫婦が]和合している. ¶Theirs has been a *prosperous union*. その二人の結婚はうまく行っている. ¶Printers with their *strong unions* would strike if there was a wage cut. 印刷工は強固な組合ができているからもし賃銀引下をしたら罷業をするだろう. ¶the Universal *Postal Union* 万国郵便連合. ¶the *Young Abstainers' Union* 青年禁酒同盟.

Q² a *branch union* 支部組合. ¶a *company union* 御用組合. ¶the *Copyright Union* [作家などの]著作権連合. ¶a *craft union* 職業別組合. ¶the *customs union* 関税同盟. ¶a *labor union* 《米》労働組合. ¶a federation of *labor unions* 総同盟. ¶an *autonomous labor union* 自治労働組合. 【類】a Communist-led *labor union*. ¶a *labor supply union* 労働供給組合. ¶a *marriage union* 結婚. ¶the *Soviet Union*＝the Union of Soviet Socialist Republics (USSR) ソ連. ☞ Soviet Russia は無冠詞. ¶a *temperance union* 禁酒同盟. ¶a *trade union* 《英》労働組合 ‖ the world Federation of *Trade Unions* 世界労働連盟. ¶the *Transport Workers Union* 通運労組.

P live *in union* 和合する. ¶All cheered *to union*. 一斉に歓声をあげた.

P² a *union between* frosty January and blooming May 老人と若い女との結婚 ‖ the *union between* the male spermatozoa and the feminine ovary or egg cells 男性精子と女性卵子との結合. ¶a *union by* treaty 条約による連盟. ¶the *union of* the Godhead and Manhood in Jesus Christ イエスキリストにおける神人の合一 ‖ create through sport a *union of* nations スポーツを通じて列国の結合を作る ‖ a *union of* power and gentleness 剛と柔の合同(握手). ¶She entered into a second *union with* a man of wealth. 彼女は金満家と再婚した.

unionist, *n.* 労組員.

Q *executive unionists* 労組幹部(執行役員).

unique, *a.* 無比の, 無類の.

M *absolutely unique* 絶対に類のない. ¶*quite unique* 全く無二の.

P Japan is *unique in* her nationality. 日本の国体は他にその類を見ない.

unison, *n.* 一致.

P move *in unison* 一致して動く ‖ Their voices were *in unison* with the music. 彼らの歌声は音楽と調子が取れていた ‖ Let the class repeat them *in unison*. 級にそれを一せいに繰返して言わせよ. 【類】The show girls are hopping *in unison*. / They are now banded together so closely by ties of mutual interest that they could act *in unison* at any time they might wish to do so. ‖ work *in unison* with ... ...と一致協力してやる. 【類】His opinions are not *in unison* with those of the majority of men.

unit, *n.* 一個, 一人; 単位; 〘数〙[単位としての]一.

V *mistake* the *unit* 単位を間違える. ¶*score* 13.2 *units* in a test テストで十三点二分を得る. ¶*turn out* three *units* per second 毎秒三台(自動車など)生産する.

Q set up an *administrative unit* 一つの行政機構を作る. ¶a *civic unit* [市町のような]行政単位. ¶The sentence is the *common unit* of thought and language. 文は思想と言語の普通の単位である. ¶The Americans turned the vast area into a *complete unit*. アメリカ人はその広大な地域を完全な統一体にした. ¶a smoothly *functioning unit* 滞りなくその機能を発揮している団体. ¶The clause is a *larger unit* than the phrase in the sentence. 〘文法〙文の中で, 節は句よりもさらに大きな単位である. ¶a *mechanized unit* 機械化部隊. ¶*mobile units* 機動部隊. ¶a *monetary unit* 金銭の単位. 【類】*Yen* is the *monetary unit* of Japan. ¶*popular units* separated by language barriers 国語の障壁で分離された人々の集団. ¶The student is the *primary unit* of all university work. 学生はすべての大学活動の本源的存在である. ¶a *self-governing unit* 自治団体. ¶a *truck-mounted unit* トラック部隊(移動映画など). ¶an *unnamed unit* ○○隊.

Q² an *advance unit* 先遣部隊. ¶an *air-condition[ing] unit* 空気調節設備一式. ¶supply, technical, and labor troops not employed as *combat units* 戦闘部隊でない補給, 技術及び労務部隊. ¶provide temporary *dwelling units* for veterans 老兵のために臨時に住宅を支給する. ¶*efficiency units* 簡易住宅. ¶a *police unit* 警察部隊. ¶a *requisition unit* [占領地の]徴発隊. ¶a *service unit* [ラジオ・水道などの]修理班.

P act *as a unit* in ... ...において一団となって働く.

P² a *unit for* regulating the proportions of parts 各部分の比例を調節する単位. ¶The family is the *unit of* society. 家族は社会を構成する一分子である. ‖ a *unit of* force 力の単位.

unite, *v.* 結合する, 合体する.

M be *closely united* 結束が堅い. ¶*indivisibly united* 不可分的に合体した. ¶All parties should *unite together* in foreign policies. 全政党は外交政策では結束すべきだ.

P All the opponents of the measure should be *united against* it. 該案の反対者は一致してそれに対抗すべきである. ¶*unite at* an angle of ... ...の角度で接する. ¶firmly *united by* mutual love 互の愛で堅く結ばれて ‖ *unite by* confederacy 同盟する ‖ *unite for* mutual interest 相互のために合体する. ¶*unite to* marriage 結婚する ‖ In Germany the reader of plays at a theatre and the stage-manager are often *united in* one person. ドイツでは劇場の脚本主任が舞台監督を兼ねている場合がよくある. ‖ *unite in* a body in ... 一体となって...をする. 【類】Youth *unite in* the fight for peace ... ¶*unite* minor parties *into* one 諸小派を連合して単一党にする. ¶They all *unite on* that subject. 彼らはその問題に関して一致している. ¶It was *united to* the kingdom of Italy. それはイタリア王国に合併された. ‖ The hearts of all his subjects were *united to* him as the heart of one man. 彼の臣下一同は心を一にして彼に仕えた. ¶grace *united with* strength 威あってたけからず. 【類】*unite* ability *with* valor ‖ My family *unites with* me in congratulating you on your success. あなたの成功に対し私及び家内一同お喜び申上げます. 【類】Their names will forever be *united with* the story of the construction and completion of the Panama Canal. / Railways *unite* Stamboul *with* Adrianople and Belgrade.

unity, *n.* 一致, 統一.

V They *achieved unity* on the question. その問題に対し意見の一致を見た. ¶*bring about* the *unity* of a country 一国の統一を実現する. ¶*disturb* the *unity* of an idea 一つの思想の統一を乱す. ¶*find unity* in the movements of heavenly bodies 天体の運行に統一を見出す. ¶*have unity* 統一がある. ¶*lack unity* in utterance 言を一二にする. 【類】His writing *lacks unity*. ¶*preserve* the *unity* of ... ...の統一を保持する. ¶*secure unity* of spirit and action 精神と行動を一にする. ¶*shatter* world *unity* 世界の統一を破壊する.

Q the *moral unity* of the world 世界の道徳的一致. ¶*national unity* 国家の統一. ¶a *perfect unity* of purpose and co-operation 目的と共同作業の完全な一致.

P a nation *as* a *unity* 統一体としての国家. ¶dwell *at unity* with ... ...と和合して住む. ¶live *in unity* 調和して生活する. 【類】work *in unity*. ¶a lack *of unity* among ... ...間における不一致. ¶sing *with unity* 一同唱和する. ¶*without unity* or continuity 統一も連続もなく.

P² *unity in* variety (＝diversity) 多様にしてしかも一様. ¶The Emperor is the symbol of the State and the *unity of* the people. 〘憲法〙天皇は国家及び国民統合の象徴であ

る.

universal, *a.* 一般の, 世界的な.

P The likening of stars and star-groups to animals and other objects is almost ***universal among*** mankind. 星や星座を動物その他になぞらえるのはほとんど世界至る所に見る習慣である.

O a *universal* practice among primitive peoples 原始人の間ではきわめて普通の慣習.

universe, *n.* 宇宙, 万有.

V behave as if one ***owned*** the *universe* 宇宙でも征服したかのように振舞う. ¶the laws which ***regulate*** the physical *universe* 物質的宇宙を支配する法則.

Q the ***mythological*** *universe* 神話の宇宙. ¶the ***stellar*** *universe* 星の世界.

P things non-existent except ***in*** the *universe* of the imagination 想像の世界にしか存在しないもの. ¶the riddle ***of*** the *universe* 宇宙のなぞ ‖ the evolution ***of*** the *universe* 宇宙の進化 ‖ study the law ***of*** the *universe* 宇宙の法則を研究する. ¶Materialism resolutely refuses to admit anything ***outside*** or ***beyond*** the five-sense *universe*. 物質主義は五官の感得する世界以外のものは断然これを認めない.

P² He was the *universe* ***to*** her. 彼は彼女に取って何よりも大事なものであった.

university, *n.* 大学.

V ***attend*** *university* 大学に通う. ¶*Universities*, it is said, ought to be ***dedicated*** not to education, but to research. 大学は教育ではなく研究をその本領とすべきであると言われている. ¶***enter*** a *university* 大学に入学する. ¶***feed*** *universities* with students 学生を大学に送り込む. ¶***open*** the *university* and its degrees to women 大学とその学位を婦人に開放する. ¶He was obliged to ***quit*** the *university* from his lack of funds. 彼は学資がないのでその大学を退学せねばならなかった.

Q an ***ancient*** *university* like Cambridge ケンブリッジのような古い歴史のある大学. ¶a privately ***endowed*** *university* 個人の寄付になる大学. 【類】a generously ***endowed*** *university*. ¶The ladies all wore favors and rosettes of their respective ***favorite*** *Universities*. 婦人たちはそれぞれひいきする大学のき章やばら飾りを着けていた.

¶one of the ***major*** *universities* in Tokyo 東京一流大学の一つ. ¶***younger*** *universities* それほど古い歴史のない大学.

Q² a tax-supported ***state*** *university* 税で支持された州(国)立大学.

P attend lectures ***at*** the *university* その大学の講義に出席する. 【類】The Columbia Encyclopedia compiled and edited ***at*** Columbia *University* / He was educated ***at*** a *university*. ¶a degree conferred ***by*** *universities* 大学の学位. ¶send one's son ***to*** [a] *university* その息子を大学にやる.

P² a *university* ***for*** women＝a women's university 女子大学.

unjust, *a.* 不正の; 不公平な.

M ***flagrantly*** (＝***grossly***) *unjust* はなはだしく不公平な.

P It was *unjust* ***of*** them not to hear my side. 私の言い分を聞かないとは彼らは片手落であった.

unjustified, *a.* 条理が立たない.

P These stories are *unjustified* ***by*** facts. これらの話は事実がこれを証明していない.

unkind, *a.* 不親切な, 不人情な.

M be *unkind* ***enough*** to ... 不親切にも...する.

P it was *unkind* ***of*** you to ... 君が...したとは不親切な話だ. ¶*unkind* ***to*** a person 人に対して不親切な.

unkindly, *a.* 不親切な.

P very *unkindly* ***to*** us われわれにとても不親切な.

unkindness, *n.* 不親切.

V He never ***did*** an *unkindness* to anyone. 彼はだれにも決して不親切なことをしなかった.

unknown, *a.* 知られない, 不案内の.

M He is ***personally*** *unknown* to me. その人を私は親しく知っていない. ¶items ***quite*** *unknown* to the bill-of-fare of ordinary mortals 普通人の食卓にのぼらない品々. ¶remain ***still*** *unknown* to outsiders 第三者にはいまだに分からない. ¶His whereabouts have been ***utterly*** *unkown* so far. 彼のゆくえは今日まで全然不明だ.

P Falsehood is *unknown* ***in*** Heaven. 偽りは天国にはない. ¶a bookseller *unknown* ***to*** fame 名もない本屋. 【類】some writer now *unknown* ***to*** fame, but whose name will then be on everybody's lips / *unknown* ***to*** him / Kissing is *unknown* ***to*** the Malays.

unlearned, *a.* 無学の.

P a man *unlearned* ***in*** book lore 本からの知識のない人.

unlike, *a.* 似ていない, 異っている.

M ***quite*** (＝***totally or utterly***) *unlike* 全く似ていない. 【類】The picture is ***quite*** *unlike* him.

P The two are *unlike* ***in*** disposition. その二人は気質が違う.

unlikely, *ad.* あり得ない.

M It is ***not*** *unlikely*. ありそうなことである. ¶it is ***very*** *unlikely* that ... よもや...

unlimited, *a.* 無限の.

M The scope of his genius is ***almost*** *unlimited*. 彼の才能はほとんど無限だ.

P *unlimited* ***in*** material resources 資源は無尽蔵な.

unload, *v.* 荷を卸す.

M The transport will ***soon*** be *unloaded*. その輸送機(船)はじき荷卸しするだろう.

P *unload* cargoes ***from*** ships 船から荷を卸す. 【類】*unload* goods ***from*** a truck.

unlucky, *a.* 不運な.

P be *unlucky* ***in*** money-getting 金に縁がない ‖ be *unlucky* ***in*** a lottery くじに弱い.

unmarked, *a.* 目立たない.

P His reign was *unmarked* ***by*** important events. 彼の治世中は別にこれという重要事件もなかった.

O People are apt to pass it *unmarked*. それはとかく見すごされやすい.

unmatched, *a.* 無類の, 敵のない.

P *unmatched* ***in*** valor 剛勇無双の.

unmindful, *a.* 無とん着の.

P *unmindful* ***of*** ... ...を心に留めない.

unnecessary, *a.* 不必要な, 無益な.

P This renders it *unnecessary* ***for*** me to do anything. このために私は何もする必要がなくなる.

unobserved, *a.* 気づかない.

O slip in *unobserved* そっとしのび込む. 【類】let it go *unobserved*.

unoccupied, *a.* 住む人のない.

P a villa left *unoccupied* ***for*** years 長年空家になっている別荘.

unopened, *a.* 開かない, 封じたままの.

M The letter is ***still*** *unopened*. まだその手紙は開封してない.

unopposed, *a.* 反対されない.

P He was *unopposed* ***for*** re-election. 彼は異議なく再選された.

unpalatable, *a.* 不快な.

M The truth must be told ***however*** *unpalatable* it may sound. どんなに不快なことでも真実は語られねばならない.

P The decision was *unpalatable* ***to*** them. その決定は彼にとっては有難くなかった.

unparalleled, *a.* 匹敵するもののない, 比類のない.

P *unparalleled* ***in*** bravery (patriotism, physical strength) 剛勇(愛国心, 体力)無比の ‖ It is *unparalleled* ***in*** any other country in the world. それは他国に比類がない. 【類】a provocation *unparalleled* ***in*** the annals of diplomacy / *unparalleled* ***in*** modern history.

unpleasant, *a.* 不愉快な, 気に入らない.

P *unpleasant* ***for*** a person 人にとって不愉快な ‖ *unpleasant* ***to*** taste (touch) 口当り(手触り)のよくない ‖ *unpleasant* ***to*** the eye (ear) 見て(聞いて)不愉快な.

unpleasantness, *n.* 不愉快.

V might ***involve*** an *unpleasantness* おもしろくない結果を生じるかも知れない.

P ***without*** any *unpleasantness* なんら気まずいことなく.

unpopular, *a.* 不人望の, 人気のない.

M He is ***justly*** *unpopular* with all. 彼が一向人気のないのももっともだ.

P *unpopular* ***with*** his associates 彼の仲間に評判の悪い.

unpopularity, *n.* 不人望, 不人気.

V he ***earned*** a deserved *unpopularity* in educational circles by ... 彼は...のために教育界において不評判を買ったも当然だ. ¶***risk*** *unpopularity* 人気を落すようなことをする.

P² the *unpopularity* ***of*** the epistolary form as a method of authorship 著作の手法としての書簡文体の不人気.

unprepared, *a.* 準備のない, 用意のない.

M Dinner is ***still*** *unprepared*. 食事はまだ用意ができていない.

P We were all *unprepared* ***for*** the news. われわれは皆その知らせを予期していなかった(びっくりした). 【類】I was quite *unprepared* ***for*** the journey.

unproductive, *a*. 不生産の, 成果のない.

M Red-tape is ***mostly*** *unproductive*. 繁雑な形式は大概無

unprofessional, *a*. 職業にふさわしくない. ⌊益だ.

P it is *unprofessional* ***for*** (=***of***) a physician to ... ...する とは医者にあるまじきことだ.

unpromising, *a*. 見込のない. 「たしかに悲観的だ.

M The state of affairs is ***distinctly*** *unpromising*. 事態は

unprovided, *a*. 備えられていない.

M He was ***quite*** *unprovided* with the materials necessary for his work. 彼は自分の仕事に必要な材料を全然持合わせていなかった.

P One of the passengers was found *unprovided* ***with*** a ticket. 乗客の一人が切符を持っていないことが分かった. ‖ a vessel *unprovided* ***with*** compass or rudder. ら針盤もかじも備え付けていない船. 【類】Fourth-class carriages in Germany are *unprovided* ***with*** seats.

unpublished, *a*. 公にされない.

M writings ***hitherto*** *unpublished* これまで公にされていな

unready, *a*. 遅い. ⌊い文献.

P painfully *unready* ***of*** speech 痛々しいほどに口不調法

unrecognized, *a*. 認識されない. ⌊な.

M though its value (merit) had ***long*** been *unrecognized* その価値(など)は長い間認められなかったが.

unrelated, *a*. 関係がない.

M ***altogether*** *unrelated* to ... ...とはおよそ縁の遠い.

unrelenting, *a*. 容赦のない.

P *unrelenting* ***toward*** others 他人に対して容赦のない.

unreserve, *n*. 露骨.

Q the ***nauseous*** *unreserve* of a society novel 社会小説のへどを催させる赤裸々.

unreserved, *a*. 遠慮しない.

P *unreserved* ***in*** manner 態度に遠慮のない.

unresponsive, *a*. 応答しない.

P quite *unresponsive* ***to*** stimulus (influence) 刺激(など)に

unrest, *n*. 不安, 不穏. ⌊全く感応しない.

V ***produce*** *unrest* 不安を産む.

V[2] The deepest *unrest* ***prevails*** among the masses. この上もない不安が大衆の間にみなぎっている.

Q ***industrial*** *unrest* 産業界の不穏. ¶a state of ***political*** *unrest* 政界不穏. ¶***social*** *unrest* 社会的不安.

Q[2] ***labor*** *unrest* 労働不安. ¶because of the ***world*** *unrest* 世界の動揺のため.

unrestrained, *a*. 抑制のない, 気ままの.

P *unrestrained* ***by*** law or morals 法律や道徳に制限されな

unripe, *a*. 未熟な. ⌊い.

M ***quite*** *unripe* 全く未熟な. ¶The scheme is ***still*** *unripe*. その計画はまだ機が熟しない.

unrival[l]ed, *a*. 無比の.

P *unrivalled* ***in*** eloquence (bravery, strength) 雄弁(など)

unsaid, *a*. 言わずにある. ⌊並ぶ者のない.

M It is ***better*** *unsaid*. それは言わぬが花でしょう.

unsectarian, *a*. 宗派的でない.

M be ***entirely*** *unsectarian* [大学などが]全然宗派的でない.

unsettled, *a*. 未定の, 未決の. 「い.

M His mind is ***still*** *unsettled*. 彼の腹はまだきまっていな

O The weather is *unsettled*. 天候が定まらない.

unskil[l]ful, *a*. へたな.

P *unskilful* ***at*** accounts 計算がへたな.

unsolved, *v*. 未解決の[ままの].

M My doubt is ***still*** *unsolved*. 私の疑問はまだ解けない.

unsophisticated, *a*. 純真な.

M She is ***very*** *unsophisticated*. 彼女はとても純真である.

unsoundness, *n*. 不健全性.

Q the ***fundamental*** *unsoundness* of their economic policy 彼らの経済政策の根本的不健全性. ¶suffer from ***mental*** *unsoundness* 精神に異状がある.

unsparing, *a*. 容赦しない.

P *unsparing* ***of*** oneself 骨身を惜しまず.

unsteady, *a*. 不安定の.

P be *unsteady* ***of*** purpose 目的がぐらついている. ¶be *unsteady* ***on*** one's feet 足がふらふらしている.

unstinted, *a*. 惜しまない.

P *unstinted* ***in*** one's praise of ... 言葉を尽して...をほめて.

unsuccessful, *a*. 不成功の.

P *unsuccessful* ***in*** one's attempt その試みには失敗して.

unsuitable, *a*. 不適当な.

P *unsuitable* ***for*** ... ...に不適当な.

unsuited, *a*. 不適当な. 「全然不適当な.

M ***wholly*** *unsuited* to conditions in Japan 日本の事情に

P be *unsuited* ***for*** the purpose その目的に添わない. 【類】water *unsuited* ***for*** drinking. ¶*unsuited* ***to*** the taste of the proletariate プロ階級の趣味に合致しない.

unsupplied, *a*. 供給されない.

P The suburbs are *unsupplied* ***with*** water. 郊外には水道

unsure, *a*. 不確かな. ⌊の設備がない.

P be *unsure* ***of*** pronunciation 発音に自信がない.

unsurpassed, *a*. 超越されない.

P It is *unsurpassed* ***by*** anything. それは天下一品である. ¶*unsurpassed* ***for*** ... ...では並ぶもののない. ¶*unsurpassed* ***in*** valor and patriotism 勇気と愛国心にかけては並ぶもの

unsuspected, *a*. 疑われない. ⌊のない.

M ***totally*** *unsuspected* by ... ...からは全然疑念を持たれな

unsympathetic, *a*. 同情がない. ⌊いで.

P *unsympathetic* ***with*** the necessities of other people 他人の必要に対して思いやりのない.

untaught, *a*. 無学の.

M a person ***altogether*** *untaught* 全く無教育の人.

untinged, *a*. 染っていない.

P be *untinged* ***with*** communism 共産主義に染まっていな

untiring, *a*. うまない. ⌊い.

P he has been *untiring* ***in*** his efforts to ... 彼は...しようと努力してうまなかった.

untold, *a*. 無数の.

M The number is ***almost*** *untold*. その数はほとんど無数

untouched, *a*. 手のつかない. ⌊である.

M The interior is as yet ***practically*** *untouched* by European commerce. その奥地はまだ事実上欧州貿易から言えば処女地である.

P the wild recesses of the remote mountains and forests, *untouched* ***by*** the conditions of modern life 現代生活とは交渉のない人跡至らざる遠い山林地区 ‖ It is *untouched* ***by*** ink or oil. それは筆にしたことも絵にしたこともない ‖ small towns and villages *untouched* ***by*** railways 鉄道の通じていない小さな町や村.

O You'd better leave it *untouched*. その件は手を触れない

untrained, *a*. 訓練されない. ⌊方がいい.

P an audience *untrained* ***in*** biology 生物学の知識のない

untranslatable, *a*. 翻訳できない. ⌊聴衆.

M *untranslatable* ***literally*** 文字通りには訳し得ない.

untroubled, *a*. わずらわされない.

P *untroubled* ***by*** the thought of death 死ということを苦

untrue, *a*. 真実でない. ⌊にせずに.

M ***absolutely*** *untrue* 全然真実でない.

P[2] be *untrue* ***to*** facts 事実に反している ‖ *untrue* ***to*** one's friends (party, principle) 友だち(など)に忠実でない.

untrustworthy, *a*. 信頼できない.

M be ***wholly*** *untrustworthy* 全然信用がおけない.

untruth, *n*. うそ, でたらめ.

V The *untruth* has been ***brought*** home to him. その虚偽たることがひしひしと彼の心に分かってきた. ¶***spread*** an *untruth* うそを広める. ¶***tell*** an *untruth* うそをつく.

Q ***time-dishonored*** *untruths* 昔から信じるもののないうそ

ununderstandable, *a*. 分からない. ⌊いつわり.

P Women are eternally *ununderstandable* ***to*** men. 女は永久に男には分からない.

unused, *a*. 慣れていない.

P I am *unused* ***to*** such a mode of life. 私はこうした生活には慣れていない. 【類】hands *unused* ***to*** labor / *unused*

unwary, *n*. うっかりもの. ⌊***to*** society.

V ***catch*** the *unwary* 揚足を取る.

unwelcome, *a*. うれしくない.

P Nothing is *unwelcome* ***to*** a hungry man. ひもじい時は何でもござれ. 【類】news *unwelcome* ***to*** ...

unwholesome, *a*. 健康に悪い.

M Bad water is ***very*** *unwholesome*. 悪い水は非常に不衛生

unwind, *v*. 巻き戻す, ほどける. ⌊だ.

P *unwind* it ***from*** ... ...からそれを巻き戻す.

unworthy, *a*. 価値のない.

P *unworthy* ***to*** attention (confidence) 注意を払う(信任するだけの)価値のない ‖ *unworthy* ***of*** the times in which we live 今日の時代にふさわしくない ‖ a behavior *unworthy* ***of*** a gentleman 紳士にあるまじき挙動 ‖ Such unfair practices are *unworthy of* reputable business men. そんな不正なことをするのはりっぱな実業家として恥ずべきことだ. 【類】be *unworthy of* its traditions.

up, *n.* 上昇.

V It has ***had*** their "*ups* and downs." それにはいわゆる浮き沈みがあった.

P² the *ups* and downs ***of*** life 人生の浮沈.

up, *ad.* 上に.

P be *up* ***against*** financial difficulties 財政上の困難にぶつかる. ¶The house is *up* ***for*** sale. その家は売物に出ている. ¶*up* ***in*** the sky 上空に. ¶It will prove to be *up* ***to*** expectations. それは期待に添うことになるだろう. ‖ it's *up* ***to*** you to see to it that ... ...するように監視するのは君の責任だ ‖ *up* ***to*** now (=date) 今日まで ‖ be well *up* ***to*** standards of ... ...の標準には十分達している.

M ***half-way*** *up* the hill 坂の中途に. ¶be *up* ***proportionately*** それに準じて騰貴している ‖ I am not *up* ***to*** the mark today. きょうはからだの調子が変だ. ‖ What are you *up* ***to***? 君は何をしようとしているのか. ¶*Up* ***with*** you! =Get to your feet! 起て. ‖ *up* ***with*** the anchor 抜びょうして.

O He is *up* and doing. 彼は忙しい(活動している).

upbraid, *v.* 責める, とがめる.

P *upbraid* a person ***with*** (=***for***) ingratitude 忘恩をもって人を責める.

upbringing, *n.* 教育.

Q ***domestic*** *upbringing* 家庭教育. ¶He owed his success to the ***good*** *upbringing* his parents had given him. 彼の成功は両親のよいしつけによるものだった.

Q² ***family*** *upbringing* 家庭の育児.

P² The *upbringing* ***of*** children is a source of pleasure as well as of anxiety. 子供を育てることは心配でもあるがまた喜びでもある.

upbuilding, *n.* 建設.

Q the ***industrial*** *upbuilding* of a nation 国民の産業的建設. ¶the ***physical*** *upbuilding* of a nation 国民の体育.

upcountry, *a., ad.* 奥地の(に), 内地の(に).

P travel *upcountry* ***for*** miles to find hidden treasures かくされた宝を求めて奥地に旅行する.

upgrade, *n.* 上りこう配.

P The car can go ***on*** an *upgrade* (=go upgrade). 上りこう配を行く. ‖ Prices are ***on*** the *upgrade*. 値段は上向きだ.

upheaval, *n.* 〘地質〙隆起; 急変, 動乱.

Q ***communistic*** *upheavals* 共産主義者の動乱. ¶The world is in the midst of a great ***economic*** *upheaval*. 世界は経済上一大動揺の渦中にある. ‖ the ***economic*** *upheaval* of the war and postwar period 戦時並びに戦後の経済的動揺. ¶a great ***real estate*** *upheaval* 不動産価格の一大動揺. ¶such a ***political*** *upheaval* as the Norman Conquest ノルマン征服のような政変. ¶***social*** *upheavals* such as war 戦争のごとき社会的動乱. ¶a ***violent political*** *upheaval* 急激な政変. ¶a ***volcanic*** *upheaval* 火山性の隆起.

Q² the ***communist*** *upheaval* in Russia in November, 1917. 一九一七年十一月のロシアにおける共産党の動乱.

P² the *upheaval* ***in*** Russia ロシアの動乱. ¶*upheavals* ***on*** the earth 地表の隆起.

uphold, *v.* 支持する.

P I *upheld* him ***in*** his policy of ... 私は彼の...政策を支持した.

upholder, *n.* 支持者.

P Taiko was a most strenuous *upholder* ***of*** the laws and customs of the empire. 太閤は帝国の法律慣習をあくまで支持した人だった.

upholster, *v.* いす張りをする.

P chairs and settees *upholstered* ***in*** leather (costly fabrics) 皮(など)で張ったいす及び長いす ‖ stools *upholstered* ***in*** plush フラシ天で張った腰掛. ¶a couch *upholstered* ***with*** tapestry つづれ織張りの長いす.

upkeep, *n.* 維持, 扶養.

Q expenses of ***annual*** *upkeep* 一年の経費. ¶The Club has no funds beyond those for a ***bare*** *upkeep*. そのクラブはほんの経常費しかない.

P² The *upkeep* ***of*** the motor-cycle is very cheap. 自動自転車の維持費ははなはだ安い. ¶*upkeep* and repairs ***on*** houses 住宅の維持と修理.

uplifting, *n.* 向上.

Q ***moral*** *uplifting* 道徳の向上. ¶***social*** *uplifting* 社会の向上.

uppermost, *a.* 最上の.

P what is *uppermost* ***in*** the mind 頭で第一に考えていること.

upright, *n.* [支柱など]真直なもの.

P a post ***out of*** the *upright* 真直でない柱.

uprising, *n.* 登り.

Q the ***steep*** *uprising* of a hill 険しい上り坂.

Q² a ***guerrilla*** *uprising* ゲリラ隊の反乱. ¶a ***peasant*** *uprising* 百姓一き.

uproar, *n.* 騒動.

V ***cause*** an *uproar* in literary circles 文学界に波紋を起す.

P ***amidst*** a frenzied *uproar* 狂暴のまっただ中に. ¶Instantly the whole place was ***in*** an *uproar*. たちまちその場は全く動乱のちまたと化した.

uproot, *v.* 根絶させる.

O Bad habits are hard to *uproot*. 悪癖は根絶しにくい.

upset, *n.* 動揺.

V The news ***gave*** them quite an *upset*. そのニュースで彼らはすっかり面くらった.

upset, *v.* ひっくり返す[返る]; ろうばいさせる.

M The news ***completely*** *upset* them. その知らせで彼らはすっかり面くらった. ¶A tall bottle *upsets* ***easily***. 高いびんはじきひっくりかえる. ¶become ***stupidly*** *upset* by trifles つまらないことにばかばかしく弱り込む.

P He was much *upset* ***by*** the news. 彼はその報道に接して大いにろうばいした.

upstart, *n.* 成上りもの.

Q a ***postwar*** *upstart* 戦後の成上りもの(成金).

P The word is regarded ***as*** "*upstart*" in English, relegated to the addenda. その語は英語では新語と見なされ補遺の方に回されている.

upsurge, *n.* 高潮.

P² the *upsurge* ***of*** national sentiment 愛国心の高揚.

upturn, *n.* 上昇.

Q a ***sharp*** *upturn* 急上昇カーブ.

upward, *ad.* 以上.

V ***total*** *upward* of ... 総計...以上になる.

P² I waited for *upward* ***of*** (=more than) an hour. 私は一時間以上待った. ‖ *upward* ***of*** thirty years ago 三十年余り前.

O from ten years of age *upward* 十歳以上.

uranium, *n.* 〘化〙ウラン, ウラニウム.

Q ***enriched*** *uranium* for the experimental atomic reactor 実験原子炉用の濃縮ウラン. ¶Only half a pound of ***fissioning*** *uranium* would be enough to enable a hundred-ton plane to cover a distance of 14,000 miles. 核分裂ウラン半ポンドもあれば百トンの飛行機を一万四千マイル飛ばすこともできよう.

urchin, *n.* がき.

Q ***pallid, grubby*** *urchins* 血色の悪い汚ならしい小供. ¶a ***rugged*** *urchin* むさくるしい小供. ¶a ***wild*** *urchin* 野育ちのがき. ¶a ***wilful*** *urchin* やんちゃ坊主(子供).

urge, *n.* 迫力, 衝動.

V begin to ***feel*** the *urge* of sex 色気がつく ‖ ***feel*** an *urge* to save the oppressed 圧迫されている者を救いたい強い衝動を感じる. ¶***have*** the *urge* to learn English 英語を学ぼうとする熱心さがある. ¶***satisfy*** man's natural *urge* 人間生来の衝動を満足させる(性欲など).

Q the ***burning*** *urge* to outdo each other in the matter of ... ...の点でお互に負けまいとする燃えるような熱心. ¶The ***creative*** *urge* in a research worker is an asset of great value. 創造欲は研究家に取って非常に貴重な資本だ.

Q² satisfy their ***sightseeing*** *urge* 彼らの観光欲を満足させる.

urge, *v.* 急がす; 促す.

M *urge* one's horse ***forward*** その馬を急がす ‖ *urge* one's study ***forward*** 人を激励して学力を付けさせる. ¶***strongly*** *urge* 強く主張する.

M² *urge* ***on*** a horse 馬を進める ‖ *urge* ***on*** a person with intense heat 非常な熱意で人を説く ‖ *urge* him ***on*** to go ahead 更に前進するように彼を促す. ¶*urge* ***upon*** a person 切実に人を説く.

P notwithstanding all the objection which can rightly be *urged* ***against*** it その非を強く説くもっともなあらゆる反対にもかかわらず. ¶*urged* ***by*** his friends 友人たちに勧められて. ¶it has been *urged* ***from*** many quarters to ... ...するように色々の方面から切に勧められた. ¶more persistently *urge* the argument ***in favor of*** ... ...賛成説を一層根強く唱える. ¶the causes that had *urged* German ***into*** war ドイツが戦争するまでになった原因. ¶*urge* the fact ***on*** one's attention その事実に対し彼の注意を促す. ¶I *urged* him ***to*** an explanation. 私は彼に迫って説明をさせた. ¶*urge* ***upon*** him the advisabilily of ... ...するのが得策だと彼に説く. 【類】I *urged* ***upon*** him the necessity of perseverance (忍耐の必要).

O I *urged* him to resign. 私は彼に辞職を勧告した.

urgency, *n.* 緊急.

V *recognize* (*visualize*) the *urgency* of the situation 時局の緊急性を認める(感知する).

Q *extreme urgency* 大至急.

P *according to* the *urgency* of the case 場合の緩急に応じて. ¶a matter *of* great *urgency* 大緊急を要する事柄.

urgent, *a.* せがんで.

P He was *urgent with* me for further particulars. 彼はぜひもっと詳しいことを聞かしてくれと私に迫った.

urging, *n.* 強請.

P Children use it *without urging*. 小供たちはそうせよといわないでもそれを用いる.

urinal, *n.* 便所.

Q² a *street urinal* 公衆便所. ¶a *trough urinal* とい状小便所.

urine, *n.* 尿.

V *discharge urine* 小便をする. ¶*have urine examined* for sugar 尿中の糖分の有無を検査してもらう. ¶rise at night to *pass* the *urine* 夜小便に起きる. ¶*retain* the *urine* as long as possible できるだけ小便をこらえる. ¶*emit urine* 放尿する. ¶*secrete urine* 尿を分泌する. ¶*take* one's *urine* for medical examination 検尿のため尿を取る. ¶the quantity of *urine voided* in twenty four hours 二十四時間に排せつする小便の量.

P a cloudy appearance *in* the *urine* 小便のにごり.

urn, *n.* つぼ.

Q a *cinerary urn* 遺骨つぼ.

usable, *a.* 使える.

M This is an old tool, but *still usable*. この道具は古いがまだ使える.

usage, *n.* 使用; 慣例; 待遇.

V deserve *better usage* than ... ...よりはもっとよく待遇すべきである. ¶*usage* is *wavering* as to ... ...の点で(語などの)慣用がまちまちだ. ¶*improve* English *usage* 英作文の力をつける. ¶The pronunciation *represents* sound American *usage*. その発音は米国の正しい慣用を表わす. ¶It *stands* [with] rough *usage*. それは荒っぽく取扱っても大丈夫だ. ¶*suit* the *usages* of polite society 上流社会の慣習に適する.

V² *Usage determines* what good English is. 英語の良否は慣例できまる. ¶*Usage differs* (=*varies*). 慣用がまちまちである. ¶In the pronunciation of the word "schedule" American *usage favors* (ske—), and English *usage* (she—). "schedule" の発音は米国の慣習は「スケ」で英国のは「シェ」である. ¶the best *usage requires* ... 最善の慣用によると...となる.

Q the *accepted usage* is ... 一般の慣習は...である. ¶an *ancient usage* 昔の慣習. ¶write or speak English according to *approved modern usage* 現代において可と認められている慣用に従って英語を書きかつ話す. ¶in *British usage* 英国語法では. ¶be sanctioned by *colloquial usage* 口語用法として認められている. ¶*commercial usage* 商業上の慣例. ¶a departure from *common usage* 一般慣習からの逸脱. ¶*contemporary usage* in punctuation 句読法における当代の慣用. ¶*continental usage* 大陸の慣習. ¶the *correct usage* of the preposition 前置詞の正しい用法. ¶the *current usage* of Americanism 現代アメリカ語法. ¶*divergent usage* まちまちの慣用. ¶*divided usage* [語などの]まちまちの慣用. ¶*erroneous usage* 間違った慣用. ¶a *foreign usage* 外国人の言語慣用. ¶an example of a *general usage* 一般用語法の一例. ¶From slang to *good usage* there is sometimes but a step. 俗語と正しい用法とはほんの一歩という場合がある. ¶the *idiomatic usage* of words 語の習慣に合った用法. ¶the most common forms of *incorrect usage* 誤った語法のごく普通の形. ¶*international usages* 色々の国際的慣習. ¶foreign *linguistic usages*, now more or less acclimatized in England 今では多少英国化された外国の語法. ¶*long-established usages* 昔からの慣習. ¶rural as opposed to *metropolitan usage* [言葉などの]都市の慣習に対する地方の慣習. ¶approved *modern usage* 一般に認められた現代語法 ‖ A Dictionary of *Modern American Usage* [書名]現代アメリカ語法辞典. ¶be sanctioned by *popular usage* 大衆の語法として認められている. ¶The *preferred usages* of England and the United States are at variance on many points. 英米間の慣習は多くの点において一致していない. ¶the *present usage* 現在の慣習. ¶know English in its *proper usage* 英語の正しい用法を知る. ¶be liable to be subjected to *rough usage* [道具品物が]荒く取扱われ勝である. ¶*reputable usage* [語句などの]りっぱな用法. ¶*rough usage* 荒っぽい取扱. ¶even after a *single usage* 一回使用した後でも. ¶totally ignorant of *social usage* 社交上の慣例というものを全然知らないで. ¶a *slovenly usage* 不注意な言葉使い. ¶in its *strict usage* 厳格な用法では. ¶*wlll-established usage* allows us to say ... りっぱな慣習に従ってわれわれは...と言いうる. ¶This method has *wide usage*. この方法は広く行われている. ¶national differences in *verbal usage* 国中の話し言葉の相違. ¶*vulgate usage* 卑語の用法.

Q² confusing differences between *literary* and *newspaper usage* in capitalization 頭文字の使用上文学書と新聞紙の間に見られる入りまじった不統一. ¶in *trade usage* 貿易語としては. ¶*majority usage* 多数の人の慣習. ¶*present-day usage* [語などの]現代の慣用.

P It is authorized (=sanctioned) *by usage*. それは慣習が認めている. ¶It is *in* good *usage*. それは(語句などの)りっぱな用法である. ¶contrary *to* the *usage* of ... ...の慣例に反して. ¶meet *with* harsh *usage* 冷遇を受ける.

P² *Usage among* writers is not uniform. 文士間の言葉の使用法は一様ではない. ¶the cultivated *usage in* the south of England 英国南部における上流社会の慣習.

use, *n.* 使用, 用法; 慣例, 習俗; 効用.

V *abandon* the *use* of opium アヘンの吸飲をやめる. ¶*acquire* the *use* of the English language 英語が使えるようになる. ¶*allow* one the *use* of ... 彼に...の使用を許す. ¶*ban* the *use* of firearms 火器の使用を禁じる. ¶*discountenance* the *use* of perfumes 香水使用に反対する. ¶In the United States a population of 105,708,771 persons *enjoys* the *use* of 13,411,379 telephones. 合衆国では一億五百七十万八千七百七十一人中電話を使用する者一千三百四十一万一千三百七十九人に及ぶ. ‖ *enjoy* the exclusive *use* of ... ...の専用権を有する. ¶phrases for which it is quite impossible that I can *find* any *use* 私が絶対に使うことのない成句 ‖ *find* new *uses* for old products 従来の生産品に対し新用途を見付ける ‖ If you can *find use* for it I would be very glad. それを御使用下さいますれば幸いに存じます. ¶*forbid* the *use* of ... ...の使用を禁じる. ¶*give* the *use* of one's name その名を使用させる. ¶Hotel visitors can *have* the *use* of the hotel boat for boating or fishing. ホテルの客は舟遊びや魚つりにホテルのボートを使用することができる. ‖ The advice *has* its *uses*. 助言は無用でない. 【類】Hobbies (道楽) undoubtedly *have* their *uses*. ‖ I *have* no *use* for it. 私はそれはいらない; 《米口》私はそれがきらいだ. ‖ You may *have* the *use* of it. それを使っていてもよい(貸してあげる). ¶*illustrate* their *uses* by demonstration [商品など]実演でその用途を示す. ¶*improve* one's *use* of the English language 英語の使い方が巧みになるようにする. ¶*limit* the *use* of ... ...の使用を制限する. ¶Little by little she *lost* the *use* of her lower limbs. 彼女は段々に腰が立たなくなった. ¶*make use* of this opportunity この機会を利用する ‖ *Make* whatever *use* of them you like. それを好きなようにお使い下さい. ‖ In writing an English letter, do not *make use* of Japanese conventional phrases translated literally into English. 英文の手紙を書くとき日本語の慣用句を文字通り英語に訳さないようにせよ. 【類】*make use* of a subterfuge (とん辞) / The Religious Tract Society (宗教冊子協会) has already *made use* of 250 languages. / *make* the *use* of language, both spoken and written, a fine art. ¶It is now seldom *made use* of. それは今では滅多に使われない. ¶*obtain* the *use* of... ...を借用する. ¶He *offered* the *use* of his office while I was there. 彼は私がそこにいる間彼の事務所を私に使えと言ってくれた. ¶*popularize* the *use* of Esperanto エスペラントの使用を民衆化する. ¶*propagate* the *use* of Esperanto エスペラントの使用を宣伝する. ¶*relinquish* its *use* その使用を廃する. ¶*secure* the exclusive *use* of ... ...を専用する. ¶*sell* the *use* of one's name to fraudulent purposes 報酬を得て不正な目的にその名前の使用を許す. ¶*subserve* no practical *use* 実用性がない.

V² the *use* of ... is *extending* steadily ...はますます広く用いられつつある.

Q *accurate use* 正確な用法. ¶the forms of speech in *actual use* 実際使われている言語の形式. ¶The speaker made *ample use* of notes. その演説者は色々控えを用意してきた. ¶according to the *ancient use* of it その古式にのっとり. ¶an *archaic use* [語の]古い用法. ¶be turned to ***base*** *use* 卑しい用途に向けられる. ¶make the ***best*** *use* of it それをできるだけ活用する. ‖ make the ***best possible*** *use* of ... ...をできる限り利用する. ¶its ***chief*** *use* is in the manufacture of ... その主なる用途は...の製造にある. ¶in ***colloquial*** *use* 口語用法では. ¶come into ***common*** *use* 一般化する. 【類】a saying in ***common*** *use* / words in ***common*** *use* at the present time / When did the word "television" come into ***common*** *use?* ¶words in ***constant*** *use* 常用語 ‖ make a ***constant*** *use* of ... ...を絶えず使用する. 【類】In studying geographical material ***constant*** *use* must be made of maps / improve one's English with ***constant*** *use.* ¶The ***correct*** *use* of prepositions gives coherence, firmness, and compactness to style. 前置詞を正しく使うと文体がしまって, しっかりして簡潔になる. ¶a ***critical*** *use* of old materials 古い材料を批判しての使用. ¶Both "per cent" and "percent." are forms in good ***current*** *use.* "per cent" も "percent." もともにりっぱに現在使われている形である. ¶foods and materials in ***daily*** *use* 日用の食品並びに材料 ‖ come into ***daily*** *use* 日常使われるようになる. ¶The word *clap* is not in ***decent*** *use.* クラップ(りん病)という語は上品な言葉ではない. ¶These quotations and sayings are in ***daily modern*** *use.* これらの引用句やことわざは現在常用されている. ¶a ***derogatory*** *use* of a word 言葉の悪い意味での使用. ¶with a ***dexterous*** *use* of his fingers 彼の指を器用に使って. ¶goods for ***domestic*** *use* 家庭用品. ¶Writers on economics make ***effective*** *use* of graphic methods in the presentation of statistical material. 経済学関係の著作家は統計上の材料を示すに図表式を利用している. ‖ acquire an ***effective*** *use* of a foreign language 一外国語をりっぱに修める. ¶the ***endemic*** *use* of "of sorts" "of sorts" という句の(一般的でない)地方的使用. ¶***erroneous*** *use* 誤用. ¶obtain the ***exclusive*** *use* of ... ...を専用しうるようになる. ¶an ***extravagant*** *use* of dashes ダッシュの乱用. ¶teach the ***finer*** *uses* of the language to English-speaking pupils 英語を話す(本国の)生徒にその国語をもっと美しく使用することを教える. ¶make a ***foolish*** (=***unwise***) *use* of ... ...をへたな使い方をする. ¶***fraudulent*** *use* of British trade-marks in China 中国における英国商標の詐欺的使用. ¶offer the ***free*** *use* of one's library その蔵書を自由に使用させる ‖ In its compilation ***free*** *use* has been made of all available sources. その編集において利用しうる材料はことごとくこれを利用した. ¶make ***frequent*** *use* of ... ...をひん繁に用いる. 【類】a word of very ***frequent*** *use* in America. ¶make a more ***fruitful*** *use* of ... ...を一層有効に用いる. ¶make ***full*** *use* of their short respite (opportunities, one's leisure time) その休息時間(など)を十分利用する. 【類】make ***full*** *use* of the facilities (利便) afforded (=offered) by ... ‖ make the ***fullest*** possible *use* of our time (the available knowledge) われわれの時間(得られるだけの知識)をできるだけ利用する. 【類】make ***full*** and ***free*** *use* of its facilities. ¶stand no ***further*** *use* これ以上使用にたえない ‖ have no ***further*** *use* for ... ...は不用になっている. ¶come into (be in) ***general*** *use* 一般に用いられるようになる(用いられている). ¶make ***generous*** *use* of words and phrases like the foregoing 前掲のような語句をふんだんに使う. ¶make ***good*** *use* of one's opportunities その機会を十分利用する. 【類】make ***good*** *use* of one's powers of observation (観察力) / He does not know how to make ***good*** *use* of life. ‖ People rarely make ***good*** *use* of wealth they have not earned. 自分が作った富でないと十分利用できないものだ. ‖ make ***good*** *use* of their heels 逃げおおせる ‖ make a ***good*** *use* of eyes われわれの目を活用する ‖ put it (him) to ***good*** *use* それ(彼)を利用する. ¶make ***great*** *use* of ... 盛んに...を用いる. 【類】Iron is of ***great*** *use.* ¶for ***human*** *use* 人間に使わせるために. ¶***idiomatic*** *uses* of English 英語の慣用法 ‖ The ***idiomatic*** *use* of prepositions is a matter that causes trouble. 前置詞の慣用は厄介な問題である. ‖ be ready for ***idiomatic*** *use* 直ぐ使える. ¶***illicit*** *use* 不正な使用. ¶be ready for ***instant*** *use* いつでも使えるようになっている. ¶an ***immoderate*** *use* of the mental powers 脳の酷使 ‖ ***immoderate*** *use* of alchohol 過度の飲酒. ¶He made an ***improper*** *use* of the information. 彼はその知識を悪用した. ¶the earliest ***known*** *use* of the word この語の知られている限りの古い使用例. ¶make a ***judicious*** *use* of ... ...を賢明に用いる. ¶***lavish*** *use* of capital letters 大文字の繁用 ‖ too ***lavish*** *use* of color 色のらん用. 【類】make a ***lavish*** *use* of money and presents of other kinds. ¶a ***literary*** or ***poetical*** *use* 文学的なまたは詩的な用法. ¶things of ***little present*** *use* 現在ほとんど役に立たないもの. ¶words that are actually in ***living*** *use* 現に使用されている語. ¶They grow tobacco for ***local*** *use.* 彼らはその土地で消費するタバコを栽培する. ¶***military*** *use* 軍用. ¶a ***moderate*** (=***temperate***) *use* of alcohol 適度の飲酒. ¶make the ***most*** *use* of ... ...を最大に利用する. ¶***new*** *uses* of old terms 古い言葉の新しい用法 ‖ a ***new*** *use* for electricity 電気の新用途. ¶There is ***no*** *use* in argument as to taste. 趣味は議論の外である. 【類】There is ***no*** *use* in crying. / Ah, well, it's ***no*** *use* going back now. / It is ***no*** *use* keeping it back. / We have ***no*** *use* for his services. / Then there is ***no*** *use* of your going. ¶put it to a ***novel*** *use* それを新奇なことに使う. ¶***occasional*** *use* 折々の使用. ¶***ordinary*** *use* 普通の使用. ¶make a ***playful*** *use* of life 浮世を楽にする. ¶the ***pointless*** *use* of ... ...の無意味な使用(生かさずに殺して使うこと). ¶a ***poor*** *use* for capital 資本の拙劣な用法. ¶watches for ***popular*** *use* 大衆向の懐中時計. ¶have no ***practical*** *use* 実用性がない ‖ turn (=put) it to ***practical*** *use* それを実用に向ける. 【類】be of good ***practical*** *use* / The first ***practical*** *use* of electricity dates back to the age of ancient Arabians. ¶***private*** *use* 個人用 ‖ hire for ***private*** *use*=charter (*v.*) [バスなど]借切る ‖ a car for one's ***private*** *use*=a private car 自家用車. ¶make ***proper*** *use* of ... ...を正当に使用する ‖ the ***proper*** *use* of it is ... それは...に使うのが本格である ‖ the ***proper*** *use* of English 英語の正しい用法. ¶a telephone for ***public*** *use*=a public telephone 公衆電話. ¶a ***ready*** and ***fluent*** *use* of a language 一国語を達者に流ちょうに話すこと. ¶be of little ***real*** *use* あまり実用にならない. ¶in ***recent*** *use* 最近の用法では. ¶The Lucania was the ship in which the Cunard Company first made ***regular*** *use* of wireless telegraphy. キューナード会社はリューカニア号で始めて無線電信を常用することになった. ¶make ***right*** (***good***) *use* of ... ...を正しく(生かして)使う. ¶make ***scant*** *use* of ... ...をあまり用いない. ¶a tool with ***several*** *uses* 七徳(万能)器具. ¶These chopsticks are discarded after a ***single*** *use.* これらの木ばしは一度使うと捨ててしまう. ¶***slangy*** *uses* of words 語の俗語的用法. ¶the ***slipshod*** *use* of participles 〖文法〗分詞のだらしない用法. ¶We might be of ***some*** *use.* われわれでも何かのお役に立つかも知れない. ¶a ***sparing*** *use* 経済的使用. ¶make ***splendid*** *use* of one's wealth その富をりっぱに使う. ¶***standard*** *use* 模範的用法. ¶make a ***temporary*** *use* of the money その金を臨時に使う. ¶the ***true*** *use* of ... ...の真の用途. ¶***undiscriminating*** *use* 無差別使用. ¶***universal*** *use* 広範囲な利用. ¶The holder of the card is entitled to ***unlimited free*** *use* of the street railways of the city. そのカード所持者は市内電車を無制限に使用することができる. ¶the ***unwise*** *use* of wealth 富のへたな使い方. ¶be fit for ***various*** *uses* 色々の用途に向いている. ¶in ***wide*** (***narrow***) *use* 広(狭)義では. ¶***wise*** *use* of leisure (wealth) 閑暇(など)の賢明な利用 ‖ make the ***wisest possible*** *use* of the time at one's disposal 自分の自由にできる時間をあくまで有利に用いる. ¶a ***wrong*** *use* 間違った用法, 誤用.

Q[2] ***adjective*** *uses* of substantives 〖文法〗実名詞の形容詞的用法. ¶for ***emergency*** *use* only 非常時専用. 【類】for ***emergency*** *use* in case of war. ¶word in ***everyday*** *use* 常用語 ‖ service terms and expressions in ***everyday*** *use* 常用軍用語. ¶for ***future*** *use* 他日の使用のために ‖ Keep this catalogue for ***future*** *use.* このカタログを将来の参考に取っておき給え. ¶allocations for ***home*** *use* 家庭用割当て. ¶a garment for ***indoor*** *use* 室内着. ¶a hydro-extractor for ***laundry*** *use* 洗たく用しぼり器. ¶atomic energy for ***peacetime*** *uses* 平時用原子力 ‖ the ***peacetime*** *use* of nuclear energy 原子力の平時用途. ¶vessels exclusively for ***river*** *use* 河専用船. ¶salt for ***table*** *use* 食塩. ¶It is said that the potentialities of rockets are infinite so far as ***war*** *uses* are concerned. ロケットの兵器としての将来性は無限だといわれる. ¶for ***winter*** *use* 冬季用(冬向き).

P It is strictly incorrect, but ***according to*** reputable *use.* それは厳格に言えば正しくはないがしかし一般的の用法にはなっている. ¶***after*** *use* 使用後. ¶***before*** *use* 使用前.

¶ ***by*** the *use* of ... ...の使用により. ¶ Books are ***for use*** not for ornament. 書物は使うもので飾りものではない. ‖ memory of facts ***for use*** in examinations 試験のための事実の記憶. 【類】 collect and arrange ***for*** one's own *use* phrases that you think useful and effective / fit ***for*** *use* / ***for use*** only in case of fire / This is ***for use***, not for show (飾りもの) ‖ Thank you ***for*** the *use* of your ladder. はしごをお借りしまして有難う. ¶ abstain ***from*** *use* of ... ...の使用を控える. ¶ The method has not been ***in use*** long enough as yet to judge of its merits by its results. その方法は結果によってその善悪を判断しうるほどには長く用いられていない. ‖ The line is ***in use***. = The line is busy. [電話]お話中です. 【類】 an old dictionary still ***in use*** / It is the dictionary most ***in use*** among Japanese students of English. ‖ His delight was ***in*** the *use* of the pen. 彼はペンを使う(物を書く)ことが好きであった. ¶ it was first brought ***into use*** by ... それは...が使い始めた ‖ it has come ***into use*** as a substitute for ... それは...の代用品として用いられるようになった. ¶ It would be ***of*** no *use* for you to try. 君がやって見てもむだだろう. ‖ It will be ***of*** some *use* in the future. それは将来何かの役に立つだろう. ¶ It had long been ***out of use*** それは(その時)長い間用いられてはいなかった. ‖ go (=get) ***out of use*** 役に立たなくなる. ¶ It is regarded as ***past use***. それは廃物と見なされている. ¶ You are welcome ***to*** the *use* of my library. どうぞ私の蔵書を御利用下さい. ‖ put it ***to*** some *use* それを何かに役立てる. ¶ His trousers were worn threadbare ***with*** hard *use*. 彼のズボンは荒っぽくはいたので大分弱っていた. 【類】 The machine is rather hard to handle at first, but will soon be easier ***with use*** (慣れる).

P² a *use* ***for*** volcanic ash 火山灰の一用途 ‖ a good *use* ***for*** a bad gain 良くない利得の良い使い方. ¶ the *use* ***of*** electricity for lighting and traction 電気の照明及び運搬動力への使用. 【類】 the *use* ***of*** galvanism (電気振動操作) for medical purposes ‖ new *uses* ***of*** old things 古くからある物の新用途 ‖ What's the *use* ***of*** it? = What's it intended for? それ何に使うのだ. 【類】 What's the *use* ***of*** being so proud? ‖ the *use* ***of*** life 世渡り ‖ *use* ***of*** ground 地形の利用. ¶ This ink is especially manufactured for *use* ***with*** the Roneo Duplicator. 〖広告〗 このインキはロネオ複写器用として特製したものである.

use, *v.* 用いる, 利用する; 扱う.

M An eminent author has ***actually*** *used* the word in literature. 著名の作家がその語をその作品に実際使っている. ¶ the term "..." is *used* ***advisedly***, for ... 「...」という句はわざと用いたのでその訳は... ¶ ***commonly*** *used* words 常用語. 【類】 as ***commonly*** *used*, the word means ... ¶ The word "placeman" is often *used* ***contemptuously***. 「小役人」という語はよく侮べつ的に使われる. ¶ be not ***correctly*** *used* 正しい使い方になっていない. ¶ ***customarily*** *used* 習慣的に用いられる. ¶ "Queer" is the word often *used* ***euphemistially*** for "mad." queer (「変った」) という語は mad (「狂った」) の遠曲な表現としてよく用いられる. ¶ words ***figuratively*** *used* 比ゆ的に用いられた語. ¶ *use* the telephone ***freely*** 電話を盛んに使う. ¶ The word "stagy" is ***generally*** *used* disparagingly. 「芝居じみた」という語は一般に侮べつの意味に使われる. ¶ Many recognized writers and speakers *use* the word ***habitually***. 多数の世に認められている作家や弁士がその語を普通用いている. ¶ The Londoner seems to be always ***hardly*** *used* by the atmosphere. ロンドン人はいつも天候にいじめつけられているようだ. ¶ He might *use* me ***ill***, let him. 彼が私を虐待するなら虐待せよ. ¶ be ***incorrectly*** *used* for ... ...として不当に使われている. ¶ it is *used* ***instead*** of ... それは...の代りに用いられる. ¶ The words are *used* ***interchangeably***. それらの語は区別なしに共用されている. ‖ be *used* ***interchangeably*** with ... ...とかわるがる用いる. ¶ The medicine is *used* ***internally*** and ***externally***. その薬は内服外用ともに用いられる. ¶ it is now ***largely*** *used* for making ... それは今盛んに...の製造に用いられる. ¶ ***lavishly*** *use* hyphens ハイフンをやたらに使う. ¶ The word is *used* ***loosely***. その語はばく然と用いられている. ¶ it is ***much*** *used* by ... それは...が盛んに用いている. ¶ be ***properly*** *used* 正しく使われている. ¶ Newspapers ***seldom*** *use* type which is smaller than 6-point. 新聞は六ポイント以下の小活字は滅多に使わない. ¶ *use* a person ***scurvily*** 人を無礼に遇する. ¶ *use* a person ***severely*** 人をきびしく扱う. ¶ a ***slightly*** *used* car 自動車の中古品. ¶ *use* commas ***sparingly*** コンマを控え目に使う. ¶ it is often ***synonymously*** *used* as the word ... それはよく...という語と同義に使われる. ¶ In ladies' boarding schools a century ago, the rod was ***unsparingly*** *used*. 寄宿女学校では百年前にはどしどしむちを使ったものである. ¶ *use* one ***well*** (***badly***) 人をいたわって(こき)使う ‖ The world has not been *using* him ***well***. 彼は不遇の身であった. ¶ It is ***widely*** *used* (=in wide use). 広く用いられている. ¶ *use* money ***wisely*** and advantageously 金銭を賢明にかつ有益に使う ‖ Saving is *using* ***wisely*** instead of recklessly. 節約はやたらでなく賢明に使用することである. ¶ The word is ***wrongly*** *used*. その語は誤用されている.

M² He was *used* ***up*** [by fatigue]. 《米》 彼は疲労でくたくたになった. ‖ You can never *use* it ***up***. それは使い切れない(無尽蔵である). ‖ *use* ***up*** savings 貯蓄を使い果す. 【類】 *use* ***up*** all the material and supplies / They will not be *used* ***up*** so soon (でがある) ‖ *use* ***up*** a whole roll of film (フィルムを一本).

P *use* a man ***after*** his deserts 人をその功過に応じて遇する. ¶ *use* German ***as*** a vernacular ドイツ語を国語として使う ‖ *use* newspapers ***as*** kindling 新聞をたき付けに使う ‖ be *used* ***as*** food 食料としている. 【類】 be *used* as a guide (参考) / be *used* ***as*** a substitute for ... ‖ His home was *used* ***as*** headquarters. 彼の家を本部にした. ¶ She was roughly *used* ***by*** her husband. 彼女は夫に虐待された. ¶ to *use* America ***for*** an example アメリカを例に取ると ‖ plants *used* ***for*** food 食用植物 ‖ Musk is *used* ***for*** perfumes and as stimulant. じゃこうは香料や刺激剤に使われる. ¶ Alcohol is *used* ***for*** the thinning of lacquer. アルコールはラックを薄めるために用いられる. 【類】 We *use* the seal's fur ***for*** coats. / Castor (ひまし油) oil is *used* ***for*** medicine. / A jeep is a car to be *used* ***for*** general purposes (一般用). / Gravel (砂利) is much *used* ***for*** road-making. ¶ It is *used* ***in*** the Government offices. それは諸官庁で使用している. ‖ *Use* "lend" and "borrow" ***in*** a sentence. 〖文法〗 lend と borrow を使って一文を作れ. ¶ The paste can be *used* ***on*** wood work. そののりは木細工に使われる. ‖ A beaver's fur is *used* ***on*** coats. 上衣にビーバーの毛皮を着けてある. ‖ Policeman's clubs were *used* ***on*** the crowd. 警官がこん棒でその群集を制した. ¶ be *used* synonymously ***with*** ... ...と同義に用いられる ‖ Extracts from the book may be *used* ***with*** or ***without*** credit. この本からの抜粋には出所を示しても示さないでもよい.

O when *using* it should be ... それを使用する時には...すべきである.

used, *a.* [...に]慣れて (to).

M the public is getting ***so*** *used* to being told that ... 世間の人はよく...と言われつけている.

P You will soon get *used* ***to*** the work. 君はじきにその仕事に慣れるだろう. ‖ I am *used* ***to*** it. 私はそれに慣れている.

used, *v.* [to-infinitive を伴い]常に...した.

M He *used* ***always*** to go there. 彼はいつもそこへ出かけた. ¶ I *used* ***often*** to see him. 彼とはよく会ったものだ.

O I *used* to drink when young. 若いころはよく飲んだものだ. ☞ What ***did*** he ***use*** to say? (=What used he to say?) / He ***didn't use*** to answer. (=He used not to answer.) は俗語であるが, 米口語にはしばしば現われる.

useful, *a.* 有用の, 役に立つ.

M ***extremely*** *useful* きわめて有益な. ¶ I was careful to make myself ***generally*** *useful*. 私は何かと役に立つように気くばりをした. ¶ This is ***more*** (***less***) *useful* for the purpose. これはそのためにはさらに役に立つ(立たない).

P an information *useful* ***for*** ... ...に必要な一切の情報. 【類】 probably it will be *useful* ***for*** them to acquire a practical knowledge of English. ¶ *useful* ***to*** a person 人に取って有益な.

O Our education is ornamental instead of being *useful*. われわれの教育は役に立つというよりはかざりだ.

usefulness, *n.* 有益, 有用, 効用.

V ***broaden*** the *usefulness* of the institution その団体を一層有益なものにする. ¶ ***enhance*** (=***increase*** *or* ***enlarge***) the *usefulness* of ... ...を一層有益なものにする. ¶ It has ***lost*** its *usefulness*. それは役に立たなくなった. ¶ ***outgrow*** its *usefulness* [小さ過ぎて]役に立たなくなる. ¶ ***outlive*** its *usefulness* = become useless 廃物になる. ¶ The alliance has *outrun* (=outlived) its *usefulness*. その同盟は効果がなくなった. ¶The *usefulness* of ... has been amply ***proven***. ...の効果は十分証明された. ¶eager to ***show*** his *usefulness* 彼は気をきかしたつもりで(何か用をしてやる). ¶This will ***spoil*** his *usefulness* as an English teacher. このため彼は英語教員として役に立たなくなるだろう.

Q The invention is of ***commercial*** *usefulness*. その発明品は商品価値がある. ¶if its ***full*** *usefulness* is to be attained これが十分利用されれば. ¶Its ***immediate*** *usefulness* may be less apparent. その直接の効用はそれほど明りょうでないかも知れない.

P It is ***of*** the greatest *usefulness*. それは一番役に立つ.

useless, *a.* むだな.

P It is a treasure *useless* ***to*** the possessor. それは宝の持ち腐れだ.

M be ***utterly*** *useless* てんで役に立たない. ¶it is ***quite*** *useless* troubling to ... ...しようと苦心するのは全くむだな話だ.

user, *n.* 使用者.

Q the speech of ***cultivated*** *users* of English 英語を巧みに使う者の言葉. ¶a ***habitual*** *user* of ... ...の常用者. ¶a ***large*** *user* 大口需要者.

Q^2 a ***dictionary*** *user* 辞書使用者. ¶a ***road*** *user* 道路使用者. ¶a ***tobacco*** *user* タバコ愛用者.

usher, *v.* 案内する, 取次ぐ.

M *usher* a visitor ***out*** (=***forth***) 訪問客を外まで見送る.

M^2 *usher* ***in*** a guest 客を案内する. ¶when June is *ushered* ***in*** 六月に入ると ‖ Independence Day was *ushered* ***in*** by a salute of thirteen guns at sunrise. 独立祭は早朝十三発の祝砲によって始まった.

P He was *ushered* ***into*** the drawing-room. 彼は応接間に通された. ‖ he was *ushered* ***into*** (=***to***) the presence of ... 彼は...の面前に案内された. 【類】She *ushered* me ***into*** a small lobby. / The artist was *ushered* ***into*** the British public.

usual, *a.* 平常の, 通例の.

M The business is ***as*** *usual*. 商売は相も変らずだ ‖ My mother is as healthy ***as*** *usual*. 母は相変らず達者です.

P It is not *usual* ***for*** young people to seek solitude. 青年が孤独を求めることは普通でない. ¶It is *usual* ***with*** him to be late. 彼は遅れるのが普通だ. ‖ as is *usual* ***with*** that sort of people あのような連中の常として.

O be out of the *usual* 風変りである.

usurer, *n.* 高利貸.

Q^2 a ***society*** *usurer* 上流社会の高利貸.

usury, *n.* 高利.

V ***practice*** *usury* 高利貸をやる.

P lend money ***at*** *usury* 高利で金を貸す. ¶He dabbled ***in*** *usury* at odd times. 彼はちょいちょい高利で金を貸した.

utensil, *n.* 台所道具, 器具.

Q ***agricultural*** (=farming) *utensils* 農具. ¶***sacred*** *utensils* 宗教の式具. ¶***culinary*** *utensils* 調理用諸器具.

Q^2 ***cooking*** and ***dining*** *utensils* 調理及び食卓用諸器具. ¶***food*** *utensils* 食器類. ¶***household*** *utensils* 家庭諸道具. ¶***kitchen*** *utensils* 台所諸道具. ¶***writing*** *utensils* (= material) 文房具類.

utilitarian, *a.* 実利的な.

M He is ***coldly*** *utilitarian*. 彼はいかにも現金だ.

utility, *n.* 実用, 効果.

V It has ceased to ***have*** practical *utility*. それは実用に適しなくなった. ¶***increase*** its *utility* その効用を増す. ¶***lose*** its *utility* その効用を失う. ¶In this automation age, the rising generation ought to ***reach*** its highest economic *utility* early in life. このオートメーション時代に青年は早くからフルに経済活動ができるようになるべきだ.

Q be of ***considerable*** *utility* 大いに役に立つ. ¶objects of ***domestic*** *utility* 家庭有用品. ¶an object of the ***greatest*** *utility* きわめて実益のある物品. ¶It is of ***doubtful*** *utility*. その実用性は怪しいものだ. ¶Its *utility* is ***incontestable***. その効用には異論があり得ない. ¶be of ***little*** *utility* あまり役に立たない. ¶for its ***practical*** *utility* それに実用価値があるので ‖ from the point of view of ***practical*** *utility* 実利という点からは ‖ a design of ***practical*** *utility* 実用新案. ¶a ***public*** *utility* 公共事業会社(ガス・水道・交通など) ‖ the ***public*** *utility* of museums 博物館の公益 ‖ a corporation of ***public*** *utility* 公益団体, 公団. 【類】the motion picture as a ***public*** *utility* / The cinema is great new ***public*** *utility*. / mail, the railroad, and other ***public*** *utilities*. ¶***social*** *utility* 社会的効用.

P It will be found ***of*** great *utility* by its users. それは非常に有益なことが使用者に分かるであろう. 【類】***of*** no *utility* to ... ...にとって役に立たない.

utilization, *n.* 利用.

Q in view of its ***possible*** *utilization* それが多分利用されるものと見て. ¶the ***significant*** *utilization* of leisure 閑暇の有意義な利用.

P ***for*** *utilization* in agriculture 農業に利用するために.

P^2 *utilization* ***of*** waste=wealth from waste 廃物利用. ¶open new aspects ***on*** the *utilization* of heavy crude oil 重油の利用に新生面を開く.

utilize, *v.* 利用する.

M be ***fully*** *utilized* by ... ...によって十分利用される.

P The straw is *utilized* ***as*** litter, and ***as*** food for horses. わらは下敷き用及び馬の食用に用いられる. ¶*utilized* water ***for*** producing electric power 水を電力発生に利用する.

utmost, *n.* 極力, 極限.

V ***do*** one's *utmost* (=best) to give satisfaction 満足を与えるべく最善を尽す. 【類】***do*** its *utmost* in this direction. ¶***endeavor*** (=***exert***) one's *utmost* to ... ...するためその全力を尽せ. ¶***try*** our *utmost* to ... ...すべくわれわれの全力を尽す.

P ***at*** the *utmost* せいぜい. 【類】This watch is worth ten yen ***at*** the *utmost*. ¶work ***to*** the *utmost* 力の及ぶ限り働く ‖ ***to*** the *utmost* of my ability 力の限り. 【類】***to*** the *utmost* of one's power / exert oneself ***to*** the *utmost* in order to ...

P^2 the *utmost* ***of*** one's power 精一杯.

utopia, *n.* 理想郷.

Q ***mundane*** *utopia* 現世の理想郷.

utter, *v.* 言う, 発言する.

M ***fearlessly*** *utter* what one thinks the highest truth 至高の真理と考える所を大胆に話す. ¶*utter* ***forcibly***=rap out 力強く語る. ¶words *uttered* ***inadvertently*** うっかり話した言葉. ¶I don't think these words were *uttered* ***unmeaningly***. この言葉は無意味に口にしたものではあるまいと思う.

P *utter* ***with*** a nasal sound 鼻にかかった言葉で話す ‖ *utter* a cry ***with*** joy 歓喜の叫びをあげる.

O *utter* a cry of pain (sigh) 痛いと叫ぶ(など). 【類】*utter* one's thoughts (feelings, mind, etc.).

utterance, *n.* 発言, 発語.

V His surprise was so great that it ***choked*** his *utterance*. 彼はびっくりして口がきけなかった. ¶He strongly ***criticized*** the *utterances* of somc of the Congress speakers. 彼は二三国会議員の発言を酷評した. ¶Some unwise suggestions ***found*** *utterance*. ばか気た話を持出したものもあった. ‖ the complaint ***found*** *utterance* in ... その不平は...となって現われた. ¶He has recently ***given*** *utterance* to his views as follows: 彼は先ごろ次のごとく彼の意見を述べた. 【類】***give*** *utterance* to one's feelings / ***give*** *utterance* to what lurked (潜在する) in the minds of the people / Queen Elizabeth ***gave*** *utterance* to a truism when she said "To wear a crown is a thing more glorious to them that see it than it is pleasant to those that bear (いただく) it." ¶***stammer*** inarticulate *utterances* はっきりしないことをどもりながら言う.

Q an ***authoritative*** *utterance* 権威ある陳述. ¶***delirious*** *utterances* うわ言. ¶He has a ***distinct*** *utterance*. 彼ははっきり話す. ¶in ***elaborate*** *utterance* 慎重な言葉使いで. ¶It finds ***emphatic*** *utterance* in ... それは...に力強く言い現わしてある. ¶***enigmatic*** *utterances* なぞのような言葉. ¶***ex-parte*** *utterances* 〖法〗一方だけの陳述. ¶make one's ***first*** *utterance* その第一声を発する. ¶***free*** *utterances* from men of the moment 時の人のあけすけ話. ¶give ***full*** *utterance* to one's innermost conviction 自己の心の奥底の信念を十分に披歴する. ¶a man of ***good*** (***poor***) *utterance* 物言いの巧みな(へたな)人. ¶***indiscreet*** *utterances* 無分別な言葉. ¶an ***inflated*** *utterance* 誇張した放言. ¶***injudicious*** *utterances* 浅慮な言辞. ¶***imprudent*** *utterances* 不謹慎な発言. ¶***inspired*** *utterances* 感激した言葉. ¶an ***irresponsible*** *utterance* でたらめの言分. ¶give ***noblest*** *utterance* 非常にりっぱなことを述べる. ¶It was observed in an ***official*** *utterance*. それを公式に述べた. ¶speak in ***ordinary*** easy *utterance* 普通の気軽な調子で話す. ¶***pedantic*** *utterance* 学者ぶった口のきき方. ¶***pithy*** *utterances* 含蓄のある言辞. ¶***poetic*** *utterances* 詩的な言葉. ¶the ***pompous*** *utterances* of the platform 演壇からの大げさな

意思発表. ¶notable *public utterances* 注目すべき公会の席での言説 ‖ his *public* and *private utterances* on the problems of ... ...の問題に関する彼の公私の言説. ¶judging from his *published utterances* 彼の公開した言辞から判断すれば. ¶pronunciation in *rapid utterance* 早口で言うときの発音. ¶a *remarkable utterance* 人の注意を引く言明. ¶*resonant, full-throated utterances* from the stage 音吐朗々としたせりふ. ¶a *rhetorical utterance* 修辞的な言回し. ¶*scanning utterance* つづりをはっきり切った発音(切り口上). ¶*sensible utterances* on the question その問題に関する賢明な言説. ¶*slovenly utterance* だらしない話し振り. ¶his *written* and *spoken utterances* 彼の文筆及び口頭による発表.

Q² oft-recurring *alarmist utterances* of the daily press 日刊新聞にしばしば繰返される杞(き)憂家の言辞.

P² *utterances of* public men 公人の言説. ¶*sensible utterances* on the question その問題に関するもっともな言葉. ¶*utterance in* hasty conversation 早口の対話の口調.

uttermost, *n.* 際限, 行詰り.

P² the *uttermost of* the earth 世界の果.

V

vacancy, *n.* 欠員.

V His transfer *causes* a *vacancy* in the office. 彼が転任するのでその勤務先に欠員ができる. ¶*create vacancies* for others pushing up 後進のために道を開く. ¶*fill* [*up*] the *vacancy* created by the death of ... ...死亡のためその後任となる ‖ the method of *filling vacancies* 欠員の補充方法. 【類】*fill* the *vacancy* caused by the expiration (満期) of the term of Mr.... / *fill* a *vacancy* caused by the resignation (辞職) of ... ¶*fill up* a *vacancy* 一人の欠員を補充する. ¶He *has* a *vacancy* on his staff. 彼の部員に欠員がある. ‖ The orphan asylum *has* five *vacancies*. その孤児院は収容人員が五人不足している. ¶His retirement will *make* a *vacancy* in the firm business. 彼の退職で社に空席ができる. ¶to fill the *vacancy occasioned* by the resignation of ... ...の辞職によって生じた欠員を補充するために.

V² A *vacancy* has *occurred* in my office. 私の勤め先に欠員ができた.

Q We have no *immediate vacancy*. 当社に差当り欠員はない.

P act *during* a *vacancy* 欠員の補充ができるまで代理をする. ¶He was elected *to* the *vacancy*. 彼はその欠員の後任に選ばれた.

P² The *vacancy in* the ministry has been filled up. 省の欠員は補充された.

vacate, *v.* 職を退く; 立ちのく.

P a post *vacated by* death (resignation) 死(など)によって出来た空席. 【類】a Diet seat *vacated by* his death. ¶They will *vacate* the house *for* a few weeks. 彼らは二三週間家を留守にするだろう. ¶*vacate* (=evacuate) [*from*] a city 都市から疎開する.

vacation, *n.* 休暇; (米) 一般の休暇.

V I never *get* a *vacation*. 私は決して休暇を取らない. ‖ *get* three months' *vacation* 三カ月の休暇を取る. ¶schools *give* a *vacation* from ... to ... 学校は...から...まで休暇になる. ¶Summer *vacation* will not be *granted* to the officials of the Department this year. その省では今年は暑中休暇がない. ¶*have* a fortnight's *vacation* 二週間の休暇を取る. ¶*spend* a *vacation* of several weeks at farmhouse 農家で数週間の休暇を送る ‖ *spend* a *vacation* wisely 休暇を活用する. ¶*take* a *vacation* 休暇を取る ‖ *take* a *vacation* from work 仕事を休む. 【類】*take* a *vacation* for a week / *take* a *vacation* this winter in Maine (メーン州で).

V² Three *vacations occur* in the course of the year, viz., two weeks at Christmas, ten days at Easter and the usual two months in summer. 一年の間に三度の休暇がある, すなわちクリスマスに二週間, 復活祭に十日, 夏に通常二カ月.

Q take a *day's vacation* on Labor Day (米) 労働祭に一日休暇をとる. 【類】take a *week's vacation*. ¶a *long* (*short*) *vacation* 長(短)期休暇. ¶a *paid vacation* 有給休暇. ¶a reminder of a *pleasant vacation* 楽しい休暇の思い出.

Q² the *Christmas vacation* (=holiday) クリスマス休暇. ¶The long *summer vacation* is over. 長い暑中休暇が終った. ¶a *two-month vacation* 二カ月間の休暇.

P *during* the *vacation* 休暇の間. ¶while away *for* the *vacation* 休暇旅行中に. 【類】He is away *for* the *vacation*. ¶He returned home *in* the *vacation*. 彼は休暇に帰省した. ¶get back to one's home *on* a *vacation* (=(英) on a holiday) 休暇を取って帰省する ‖ while journeying *on* my *vacation* 休暇で私が旅行中 ‖ He was away *on* a *vacation*. 彼は休暇で旅に出ていた. ‖ substitute for a driver *on vacation* 休暇を取っている運転士の代りをする. ¶I was then *upon* my *vacation*. 私は当時休暇で休んでいた.

P² a *vacation between* two terms 二学期間の休暇. ¶take a *vacation of* six days 六日の休暇をとる. ¶a *vacation with* pay=a paid vacation.

vacation, *v.* (米) 休暇旅行をする.

V *enjoy vacationing* 休暇旅行を楽しむ.

O be away *vacationing* at ... 休暇をとって...にいる.

vacationist, *n.* (米) 休暇旅行者.

Q² a *summer vacationist* 夏期休暇旅行者. ¶a *week-end vacationist* 週末旅行者.

P The island was crowded *with vacationists* (=holidaymakers). 同島は休暇旅行者で混雑していた.

P² *vacationists from* town (cities) 都会からの休暇旅行者.

vaccinate, *v.* 種痘する.

P *vaccinate for* smallpox 種痘を行う.

vaccination, *n.* 種痘, ワクチン接種.

V *adopt vaccination* ワクチン接種法を採用する. ¶*take* (=*undergo*) *vaccination* 種痘を受ける. ¶Those in whom the *vaccination takes* will be saved from danger. 種痘してつく者は危険を免れるだろう.

Q *compulsory vaccination* 強制種痘. ¶*preventive vaccination* 予防接種(ワクチン注射). ¶have *smallpox vaccinations* 種痘をする.

P a certificate *of vaccination* against smallpox 種痘証.

P² *vaccination against* typhoid チフスの予防注射.

vacillate, *v.* 迷う.

P *vacillate between* the two courses 二つの進路の取捨に迷う. ¶*vacillate in* one's opinions (purpose) 意見(など)を決しかねる.

vacuum, *n.* 真空.

V *cause* (=*create*) a political *vacuum* 政治的空白を生む. ¶Her death has *left* a *vacuum* in his life. 彼女の死によって彼の一生に空白ができた. ¶*produce* a *vacuum* 真空を生じる.

Q a *complete* (=*perfect*) *vacuum* 完全真空. ¶a *partial vacuum* 不完全真空.

vagary, *n.* 物ずき, 気まぐれ.

P² Every *vagary of* taste is anticipated. どんな趣味の人でも満足するように配慮してある. 【類】*vagaries of* the mind (fashion).

vagrancy, *n.* 放浪罪.

P The tramp was arrested *for vagrancy*. 放浪者はその浮浪罪でつかまった.

vagrant, *n.* 浮浪者.

Q a *juvenile vagrant* 浮浪児.

vague, *a.* ばく然とした.

V Your instructions are *too vague*. お指図はあまりにもばく然としている.

vagueness, *n.* あいまい.

Q *hazy vagueness* あいまいもこ.

P Everything is still *in vagueness*. 何もかもまだばく然としている.

vain, *n.* 空虚.

P labor *in vain* むだ骨を折る ‖ All reflection was *in vain*. いくら考えても思い出せなかった. 【類】It is *in vain* for me to ask her; she will not go. / My work has not been *in vain*. ‖ strive (seek, plead) *in vain* いたずらに努力する(求める, 弁護する) ‖ go *in vain* むだ足になる ‖ I tried but *in vain*. 私はやって見たがむだだった.

vain, *a.* むだな; 自慢する.
M Their hopes were ***but vain***. 彼らの希望はむだだった.
P He is *vain **of*** his learning. 彼は学問を鼻にかける.【類】She is *vain **of*** her beauty (talent).
vainglory, *n.* 自負.
V ***check*** one's *vainglory* そのうぬぼれを制する.
valence, *n.* 原子価.
V Carbon ***has*** a *valence* of four. 炭素は四の原子価を有する.
valid, *a.* 有効な.
P The ticket is *valid **for*** three months. その切符は三カ月間有効だ. ‖ a ticket *valid **for*** a stay not exceeding three days 三日を越えない滞在に有効の切符.
validation, *n.* 確認.
P² *validation **of*** experts 専門参考人による確認.
validity, *n.* 有効, 真価.
V do not ***affect*** its *validity* その効力に影響を及ぼさない. ¶ ***derive*** its *validity* from ... …によって効力を生じる.
P The journey may be commenced on any date ***within*** the *validity* of the ticket. その旅行は切符の通用期間内では何日からでも始められる.
P² the *validity **of*** an argument 議論の説得力.
valise *n.* 《米》手提げカバン.
V ***pack*** a *valise* and leave a hotel 旅行カバンに荷をつめてホテルから出る. ☞ a valise=《英》portmanteau.
Q² a ***dress-suit*** *valise* 衣服用旅行カバン.
valley, *n.* 溪谷; 流域.
Q a ***bleak*** *valley* 荒涼たる溪谷. ¶ a ***richly-wooded*** *valley* うっそうたる溪谷. ¶ There is a succession of ***well-wooded*** *valleys* on the left. 左手にうっそうたる溪谷が後から後へと見えて来る.
Q² the ***Mississippi*** *valley* ミシシッピー流域.
P, P² a rivulet ***in*** a *valley* 谷の小川. ¶ a *valley **between*** ... …(と…との)間の溪谷.
valo[u]r, *n.* 勇気.
Q ***civic*** *valor* as displayed by a hero of peace 平和の勇士が示した日常生活における勇気. ¶ ***loyal*** *valor* 忠勇. ¶ ***savage*** *valor* 蛮勇. ¶ an incentive to ***soldierly*** *valor* 士気を鼓舞する刺激.
P It was accomplished ***by*** *valor*. それは勇気で達成された. ¶ unsurpassed ***in*** *valor* 剛勇無比の. ¶ He fought in the war ***with*** conspicuous *valor*. 彼は抜群の武勲をたてた.
valuable, *n. pl.* 貴重品.
V a case ***containing*** *valuables* 貴重品入りの箱. ¶ ***keep*** one's *valuables* under lock and key (in a safe) 貴重品を錠のおりる所(金庫)にしまっておく. ¶ ***leave*** one's *valuables* in care of ... その貴重品を…に預ける. ¶ ***lock up*** one's *valuables* 貴重品を鍵をかけて仕舞い込む.
Q ***small*** *valuables*, such as a ring or a diamond stud 指輪・ダイヤの飾りボタンなどの細かい貴重品.
valuable, *a.* 貴重な, 価値のある.
M ***intrinsically*** *valuable* 真に貴重な.
P *valuable **as*** a febrifuge 解熱剤として実効ある. ¶ money and other *valuables* 金品 ‖ be *valuable **as*** scrap つぶしがきく. ¶ It is *valuable **for*** the light it throws on ... それはそのために…が明りょうになるので貴重である. ¶ a service not *valuable **in*** money 金銭では評価のできない功労. ¶ The book is *valuable **to*** the student of English. その本は英学生には大いに役に立つ.
valuation, *n.* 評価.
Q arrive at ***different*** *valuations* 評価が不一致に終る. ¶ purchase it at a ***fair*** *valuation* それを公正な評価で買う. ¶ the ***jeweler's*** *valuation* of the necklace is $ ... 宝石商のその首飾りに対する評価は…ドルである. ¶ be disposed of at a ***low*** *valuation* 低い評価で処分される.
Q² ***home*** *valuation* 内国相場による評価法(輸入品の).
value, *n.* 価値, 価格; 真意.
V China town ***affects*** the *value* of property around its borders. シナ街はその周囲に隣接する土地家屋の価値に影響する. ¶ The goods ***afford*** a wonderful *value* for the money asked for it. その商品は驚くほど廉価だ. ¶ ***appreciate*** the *value* of learning, art, and science 学問・芸術及び科学の価値を認める. ¶ ***assess*** the *value* of ... …を評価する. ¶ ***attach*** much *value* to ... …を大いに重んじる. ¶ ***belittle*** the *value* of ... …の価値を軽視する. ¶ a money order ***covering*** the *value* of goods and postage 品物の代価と郵税に相当する金額の為替. ¶ ***depreciate*** its *value* as ... …としてのその価値を減じる. ¶ Excess of quantity may ***depress*** *value* to zero. 数量が過剰になると価値は零まで下がる. ¶ ***destroy*** its *value* as ... その…としての価値をなくする. ¶ ***detract*** the *value* of ... …にけちをつける. ¶ ***diminish*** the *value* of ... …の価値を減じる. ¶ ***endanger*** the scenic *value* of ... …の風致を害するおそれがある. ¶ The work is fully indexed, which ***enhances*** its *value* considerably. その本には細かい索引が付いているので一段とその価値が高められている. ‖ ***enhance*** the *value* of the book as a work of reference 参考書としてその本の価値を高める. ¶ learn to ***estimate*** its *value* その価値が分かるようになる. ¶ it is difficult to ***exaggerate*** the *value* of ... …は絶賛に値する. ¶ The *value* of gold is ***fixed*** by law at £3.17s. 10 1/2 d. per ounce. 金の価は法律によって一オンスに付三ポンド十七シリング十ペンス半に定められている. ¶ ***force up*** land *values* 地価をせり上げる. ¶ ***gauge*** the *value* of ... …を値踏みする. ¶ If I charge them too cheaply, they are sure to think that they don't ***get*** good *value* for their money. 私が余りに安くすると彼らはきっと値段だけの品物を受取っていないと考えるだろう. ‖ ***get*** the best *value* out of ... …を十分に活用する. ¶ ***give*** (=attach) undue *value* to ... …に重きをおきすぎる. 【類】This examination paper ***has*** a *value* of 80 points (=a grade of 80). この答案は八十点である. ¶ ***heighten*** the *value* of ... …の価値を高める. ¶ This kind of china ***holds*** a considerable *value* among collectors. この種の陶器は収集家にはかなり重要なものだ. ¶ seriously ***impair*** (=detract) the *value* of the work その作品の価値をひどく落す. ¶ The *value* of a book is ***increased*** by a good index. 本に良い索引があるとその価値が高まる. ¶ ***judge*** the *value* of ... …の価値を判断する. ¶ ***learn*** the *value* of earning a living for oneself 自活の値打を悟る. ¶ ***lessen*** the *value* of=derogate …の価値を減じる. ¶ In him the language has ***lost*** its dynamic *value*. 彼においてはその国語が動的価値を喪失した(化石してしまった). ¶ Foreigners are generally apt to ***magnify*** the *value* of the good things they find in another country. 外国人は概して自国以外の国に見る長所の価値を誇張する傾向がある. ¶ ***make*** the *value* as low as possible 価格をできる限り低くする. ¶ greatly ***multiply*** its *value* その価値を大いに増大する. ¶ ***place*** a high *value* on ... …を重要視する ‖ Low *value* is ***placed*** on human life. 人命が軽んじられている. ¶ ***possess*** no literary *value* 少しも文学的価値がない. ¶ ***prove*** its *value* to ... …にその価値を証明する. ¶ ***put*** a proper *value* upon (=on) ... …を正しく評価する. ¶ ***question*** traditional moral *values* 伝統的道徳の価値を疑う. ¶ The external trade of Java ***reached*** a *value* in 1901 of $119,000,000 gold. ジャバの外国貿易は一九〇一年に価格一億一千九百万(金)ドルに達した. ¶ ***realize*** the *value* of education 教育の真価を悟る. ¶ They complained that they were not ***receiving*** full *value* for their money. 彼らは代金に十分相当するだけの物を受取っていないと苦情を言った. ¶ ***recognize*** the *value* of propaganda obtained 宣伝になったということを認める. ¶ To send by express is preferable, for in case of loss *value* will be ***refunded***. 速達で送る方がよい, 紛失したとき弁償してもらえるから. ¶ ***Remember*** the *value* of brevity. 簡潔の価値を忘れるな. ¶ ***represent*** a *value* of about $20,000 約二万ドルの価格を示す. ¶ ***respect*** the *value* of the businessman's time 商売人の時の貴重さを認識する ‖ actors ***respect*** the *value* of being heard and understood 俳優は聴衆によく分かるようにすべきだということを知っている(台詞をはっきり言って). ¶ ***set*** (=put) a proper *value* upon ... …を正当に評価する ‖ He ***set*** too great a *value* on the services that he had rendered us. 彼はわれわれのために尽したことを恩にきせた. ¶ the declared exports ***show*** a *value* of ... 公表された輸出額は…を示す. ¶ ***test*** the *value* of a claim 主張の当否を験する. ¶ without meaning in the slightest degree to ***underestimate*** the *value* of his researches, I am compelled to point out that ... 私は彼の研究にけちを付ける積りは毛頭ないが…ということを指摘せざるを得ない. ¶ ***want*** the full *value* for one's money 十分代価に相当する品を欲する. ¶ Its *value* cannot be ***weighed*** in the scale of dollars and cents. その価値は金銭では計算できない.
Q elements of ***abiding*** *value* 永久的価値のある要素. ¶ ***actual*** *value* 実価. ¶ give ***adequate*** *value* for the money 代価相当の品を渡す. ¶ of inestimable ***advertising*** *value* 絶大の宣伝価値がある. ¶ ***aesthetic*** (=***esthetic***) *value* 美学

的価値. ¶possess property of ***appraised value*** of ... 見積り価格...の財産がある. ¶objects of art of ***archaeological value*** 考古学的価値のある美術品. ¶of doubtful ***artistic value*** 芸術的価値のおぼつかない. ¶***assessed value*** [課税などの]査定価格. ¶***average value*** 平均価値. ¶***calorific value*** 熱量. ¶the ***commercial value*** of a historic building 歴史的建築の商業的価値. 【類】the ***commercial value*** of the degree of M.D. / Manners (態度) have an enormous ***commercial value*** in life. ¶***comparative values*** of ... ...の相対的価値. 【類】The invention has a high ***commercial value***. ¶the ***corrective value*** of public opinion and newspaper comment 世論及び新聞の評論の教正的価値. ¶the ***corroborative value*** of excerpts 抜粋の確証的価値. ¶The study of English possesses a ***cultural value***. 英語研究には教養的価値がある. ¶plants reputed for their ***curative values*** 薬草. ¶a revaluation of ***current values*** 現時価値の再評価. ¶the ***decorative values*** of living plants 生きた植物の装飾的価値. ¶the ***declared value*** 申告価格. ¶the ***defensive value*** of rivers 河川の防御的価値. ¶the ***didactic value*** of text books 教科書の教授上の価値. ¶it is of ***direct working value*** to ... それは...にはそのまま役に立つ. ¶have a ***distinct historical value*** はっきりした歴史的価値を持っている. ¶a novel of ***doubtful value*** 大して価値のありそうもない小説. ¶a redistribution of ***dramatic values*** 劇的価値の再検討. ¶have little ***dynamic value*** [劇などが]ほとんど迫力がない. ¶the ***economic value*** of a working knowledge of English 活きた英語の知識の経済的価値. ¶the ***educative value*** of ... ...の教育的価値. ¶stories (an investment) of ***enduring value*** 永久的価値ある物語(投資). ¶***estimated value*** 見積り価格. ¶***ethical values*** 道徳的諸価値. ¶give a ***fictitious value*** to ... (それだけの価値のないもの)を買かぶる. ¶pay ***full value*** for damaged goods 損害貨物の全価格を賠償する. ¶sell at a ***fixed value*** 定価で売る. ¶utilize the ***full value*** of sunlight for health 健康のため日光の全価値を利用する ‖ take it in its ***full value*** それを全面的に信じる. ¶the ***genuine value*** 真価. ¶be of ***great value*** 大いに価値がある ‖ He set too ***great*** a ***value*** on the services that he had rendered us. 彼はわれわれの面倒を見たことを大いに恩に着せた. ¶of ***high value*** 高価な. ¶***honorific value*** 名声的価値. ¶the ***humanistic value*** of these studies これら学科の人文的価値. ¶of ***immediate practical value*** 直接実際上の価値のある. ¶be of ***immense value*** to ... ...にとって非常に貴重である. ¶It proved of ***incalculable value***. それには計りようのない価値があることが分かった. ¶place an ***increased value*** on ... ...を一層高く評価する. ¶masterpieces of the most ***indisputable artistic value*** 少しも議論の余地のない美術的価値ある傑作. ¶of ***inestimable value*** 計り知られぬほど価値のある. ¶***informational*** or ***inspirational value*** of a foreign lanuage 外国語の知識的または鼓吹的価値. ¶of ***insignificant commercial value***. 大して商業価値のない. ¶what remains on board is considered of ***insufficient value*** to cover the cost of salvage. 船内にあるものは引揚作業費もカバーできない程度のものと考えられている. ¶The cinema has a high ***international value***. 映画は大なる国際的価値を持つ. ¶It is not the ***intrinsic value*** of the present, but the spirit that prompts the giving, that is appreciated. 有難く思われるのは贈物そのものの値打ではなくて贈物にこもった精神である. ¶***intrinsic*** and ***extrinsic value*** 本質的なまたは外部的な価値. ¶***landed value*** [財産としての]土地. ¶books of ***lasting value*** 永久に価値のある諸書物. ¶have no ***literary value*** 文学的価値がない. ¶of ***little*** (***much***) ***value*** ほとんど価値のない(大いに価値のある). ¶***Low social value*** is placed on scholarship in the United States as compared with European countries. アメリカでは欧州諸国に比べて学識が社会的に重んじられない. ¶place ***low*** (***high***, a ***higher***) ***value*** on human life 人生を軽(重, 一層重)んじる. ¶have a good ***marketable value*** 高く売買ができる. ¶Authorship has ***money-making value***. 著作は金もうけになる. ¶be of ***much value***大いに価値がある. ¶the ***musical value*** of words 語の音楽的価値. ¶things of ***no value*** 価値のないもの. ¶the ***nominal value*** of a bill 手形の名義だけの価格. ¶of high ***nutritive value*** 栄養価の高い. 【類】Unlike sugar saccharin has no ***nutritive value*** whatever. ¶All shares have a ***par value*** of $100. すべての株式は百ドルの額面価格を有する. ¶The books were not known to be of any ***particular value*** and were sold as rubbish. それらの書物は何か特別の値打のある物とは気付かれないでつぶし値で売却された. ¶of ***peculiar value*** 独特の価値のある. 【類】have a ***peculiar value***. ¶The book should have a ***permanent value*** as a contribution to the history of English architecture. その本は英国建築史の一有力文献に寄与するものとして永久的価値を持つべきだ. 【類】a work of ***permanent value***. ¶The venom of the rattlesnake has a ***pharmaceutical value***. がらがらへびの毒には調剤的価値がある. ¶The word is used with its all ***poetic value***. その語の詩的な効果が十分出ている. ¶of ***practical value*** to ... ...には実際的価値がある. ¶fossils of ***priceless scientific value*** 科学的にすこぶる貴重な化石. ¶Its ***value*** is ***problematical***. その価値は疑わしい. ¶In English the consonants, when they are not mute, have more or less a fixed ***pronunciative value***, but the vowels are all arbitrary. 英語において子音は無声でない時は多少一定した発音価値を持っているが母音の方はすべて勝手次第である. ¶have ***psychological value*** 心理的価値がある, 気やすめになる. ¶be of ***real value*** of life 人生の本当の価値がある. 【類】buy a house for less than its ***real value***. ¶***relative value*** 相対的価値. ¶set the ***same value*** on ... ...を同等に重んじる. ¶This greatly enhances the ***scientific value*** of the work. これがその著作の科学的価値を高めている. ¶it proved of ***signal value*** in the treatment of ... それは...の療治に特効のあることが分った. ¶obtain ***social values*** 社会的有用の性格を持つ. ¶place ***small value*** on life 生命を軽んじる. ¶of ***specious value*** 見掛け倒しの. ¶In our estimation it has acquired a ***spiritual value***. それはわれわれから見ると精神的価値がか生じているように思われる. ¶of ***standard value*** 標準的価値のある. ¶The height possesses great ***strategic value***. その高地には大きな戦略的価値がある. ¶acquire a ***symbolic value*** 象徴的価値を持つようになる. ¶The book has at least a ***temporary value***. その本はとに角一時的の価値はある. ¶the ***therapeutic value*** of radium ラジウムの療病的価値. ¶It has a ***threefold value***. それには三重の価値がある. ¶the ***tremendous value*** of the motion picture for propaganda 映画の持つすばらしい宣伝価値. ¶be appreciated at their ***true value*** それらの真価通りに認められる. ¶give ***undue value*** to ... ...に重きをおき過ぎる. ¶of ***untold value*** ばく大な価値の. ¶stamps of ***varying values*** 価額色々取交ぜた切手. ¶English and its ***vocational value*** 英語とその職業的価値.

Q[2] assessors of ***art values*** 芸術的価値の鑑定家たち. ¶Nails have a very real ***barter value*** with farmers. くぎは農家との物々交換にはもってこいである. ¶with a ***black-market value*** of ... やみ値は...で. ¶a film of ***box-office value*** 入りのよい映画 ‖ The actress has a high ***box-office value*** その女優はドル箱だ(非常に人気がある). ¶tuition for two years of a ***cash value*** of six hundred dollars 現金にして六百ドルになる二年間の授業. ¶the ***cash-surrender value*** of a life insurance policy 生命保険証の解約返還額. ¶the ***entertainment value*** of the film その映画の演芸価値. ¶***exchange value*** 交換価値. ¶take a statement at its ***face value*** 声明を額面通りに受取る. 【類】accept it at its ***face value***. ¶Poultry manure has a high ***fertilizing value***. 鶏ふんは大いに肥料価値がある. ¶the ***food value*** of beer ビールの栄養価. 【類】high ***food value***. ¶***frequency value*** of a word 語の使用度. ¶The diet represents a ***heat value*** of 2,013 to 2,076 calories. その食物は二千十三カロリーから二千七十六カロリーの熱量がある. ¶***insurance value*** of one's life かけた保険契約金から見たその生命価値. ¶the growth of ***land values*** 土地価格の値上り. ¶have a ***market value*** 市場価値がある ‖ below their ***market value*** 市価を下回って. ¶the ***mass entertainment value*** of cinema productions 映画の持つ大衆娯楽としての価値. ¶the ***money value*** of time 時の金銭的価値. ¶temporary ***news value*** 一時的の新聞価値(きわものなど). ¶It has little ***news value***. それはあまり報道価値がない. ¶His ***nuisance value*** is very high. 彼のうるさがりは大いに力がある. ¶of equal ***nutriment*** (=***nutrition***) ***value*** 同程度の栄養価値のある. ¶***octane value*** [ガソリンの]オクタン価. ¶***poster value*** ポスターバリュー, 宣伝価値. ¶***presentation value*** 上映(演)価値(映画など). ¶have considerable ***propaganda value*** 大いに宣伝価値がある. ¶note a steady, relative decline in real ***property values*** in central business districts, especially in land values 商店街中心地の土地家屋特に土地価格の相対的じりさがりを認める. 【類】The presence of those individuals is detrimental to the ***property values*** (財産価値) in the neighborhood. ¶lower its ***publicity value*** その宣伝効果を下げる(一度展覧会に出た絵など) ‖ have considerable ***publicity value*** 大分宣伝効果がある. ¶***purchase value*** 買収価格. ¶have a ***sale value*** of ... 売れば...になる. ¶no ***salvage value*** 引揚作業をやるだけの価値のないもの. ¶Antique furniture is an example of ***scarcity value***. 古物の家具(の高いの)は希少価値の一例である. ¶her "***see***" ("***hear***") ***value*** 女講演者の顔(声)の価値. ¶***surplus value*** [マルクスの]剰余価値. ¶***surrender value*** 〘保険〙解約返還額. 【類】the ***surrender value*** given by the company for the policy. ¶Children born of parents in the declining years of life have a low ***survival value***. 人生の下り坂(中年後)にある両親の間にできた子供は寿命が短い. ¶***utility value*** 実用価値.

P accept checks ***at*** face ***value*** 額面価格で小切手を受取る. ¶be ***beyond*** all money ***value*** 金銭以上の価値がある. ¶The waters became noted ***for value*** in skin complaints. その鉱泉は皮膚病にきくので有名になった. ‖ pay ***for value*** received 入手した品に対して支払う. 【類】a note given ***for value*** received (金銭受領証). ¶amount ***in value*** to about ... 総計約...の価格に達する ‖ increase ***in value*** 価値が増大する ‖ be higher ***in*** the ***value*** of civilization 文化価値において一層高位にある. ¶jewellery (=jewels) ***of value*** 貴重な宝石類 ‖ it may prove ***of value*** to ... それは...に取って値打があると見られるようになるかも知れない ‖ It is reputed to be ***of value*** in kidney-diseases. それはじん臓病にきくと言われている. ‖ remove everything ***of value*** from the vessel 同船から大事なものはすべて他へ移す. ¶at the rate of ten per cent ***on*** its ***value*** その価格の一割の率で. ¶produce gold ***to*** the ***value*** of ... 金額...の金を産出する ‖ prizes ***to*** the ***value*** of ... 価格...の賞品. ¶Foreign money is changed ***under value***. 外国貨幣は低率に両替えされる. ‖ for ***under*** half its ***value*** その価の半分以下で. ¶This is ***worth*** the ***value*** of what you paid for. これは君の買った値段だけの価値はある.

P² the ***value in*** dollars ドルでの価格. ¶a scholarship of the ***value of*** £50 a year 年五十ポンドの奨学資金 ‖ small change to the ***value of*** three hundred yen 金高三百円の小銭 ‖ The ***value of*** furs is astonishing, a single skin of silver fox having fetched as much as £500. 毛皮の高いのには驚く, 銀ぎつねの皮がただの一枚で五百ポンドもする. ‖ His death brought home to me the ***value of*** his friendship. 彼の死によって彼との親交がいかに貴重なものであったかはっきり分かった. ¶a document of some ***value to*** future historians 将来の歴史家には幾らか価値のある文書 ‖ Twenty-five million pounds was the ***value to*** Britain in tourist traffic during 1935. 一九三五年観光客が英国に落した金は二千五百万ポンドであった.

value, *v.* 評価する, 尊重する.

M This was the end of a friendship which I ***valued*** so ***highly***. 私が大いに重んじていた友情がこれで終りを告げた. ‖ a distinguished scholar whose judgment I ***value highly*** その識見を私が尊重している知名の学者. ¶It is not to be ***lightly valued***. それは軽視すべきでない. ¶***value*** oneself so ***much*** upon it それを大いに得意がる.

P I ***value*** this ***above*** everything else. 私は何物にもましてこれを重んじる. ‖ ***value*** birth ***above*** accomplishment 生れ(毛並)を業績より重く見る. ¶The bird is ***valued as*** food. その鳥は食物として珍重されている. ¶property ***valued at*** ... 価格...の財産 ‖ It was ***valued at*** around $5,000 それは五千ドルがらみという評価であった. ¶They are ***valued for*** their rarity. それは物が少ないので珍重される. ¶***value*** oneself ***on*** one's birth 門地を自慢する. ¶***value upon*** ... 《英》...に手形を組む.

valve, *n.* 弁.

Q² an ***air*** (***gas, oil***) ***valve*** 〘機〙空気(など)弁. ¶a ***check valve*** 閉止弁. ¶lock up a ***safety valve*** 安全弁を閉める ‖ a ***safety valve*** to her energy 彼女の精力の安全弁 ‖ The free speech allowed to Englishmen is a great ***safety valve***. 英国人に許されている言論の自由は大きな安全弁である. ¶a ***sluice valve*** 水門弁. ¶a ***steam*** (***gas***) ***valve*** 蒸気(ガス)弁. ¶a ***test valve*** 試弁.

P² the ***valves of*** the heart 心臓の弁膜. ¶a ***valve on*** a boiler 汽かんの弁.

vamp, *v.* 改作する.

Q² ***vamp up*** an old scheme 古い案を作り直す ‖ ***vamp up*** an excuse 口実をもうける ‖ ***vamp up*** old furniture 古家具を修理する.

van, *n.* (**1**) 先ぽう, 先陣.

V He ***leads*** the ***van*** in this great movement. 彼はこの大運動の先頭に立っている.

P people who march ***in*** the ***van*** of progress 進歩の先頭に立って行進する人々. 【類】Our country is ***in*** the ***van*** of that movement. / The Nouvelle Revue Française stands ***in*** the ***van*** of French literary criticism (文学批評). ‖ ***in*** the ***van*** of the attack on ... (=leading the attack on ...) ...攻撃の急先ぽうに立って.

(**2**) 《英》荷物車.

Q a ***guard's van*** 車掌車.

Q² a ***furniture van*** 家具運搬車. ¶a ***goods van*** 貨車. ¶a ***luggage van*** 手荷物車. ¶a ***removal van*** 引越荷物運搬車. ¶a ***mail van*** 郵便車. ¶a ***moving van*** 移転運搬車.

vandalism, *n.* 蛮行, 破壊行為.

V ***commit*** a ***vandalism*** 蛮行を犯す ¶These ancient pictures in this historic town are bits that have ***escaped*** the ***vandalism*** of man and the wreck of time. この歴史的都市におけるこれらの古画は人間の蛮行や時の破壊を免れた遺物である.

Q² ***fascist vandalism*** ファッショ的暴力主義.

vane, *n.* 風見.

V² The ***vane turns*** with the wind. 風見は風につれて回る.

Q² be ***weather vanes*** for ... ...の傾向を予知する手段となる.

vanguard, *n.* 先ぽう.

P ***in*** the ***vanguard*** of civilization 文明の先頭に立って. 【類】***in*** the ***vanguard*** of scientific activity.

vanish, *v.* 消える, 消滅する.

M ***vanish away*** in smoke 雲散霧消する. ¶Their prospects have ***sadly vanished***. 彼らの希望はあわれにも消えうせた.

P ***vanish behind*** the cloud 雲隠れする. ¶A large portion of classic literature has ***vanished from*** the sight of men. 古典文学の大部分は亡びてしまって今日見るべくもない. ‖ ***vanish from*** public life 公生活から隠退する. ¶They had ***vanished in*** the crowd. 彼らは群集の中に消えてしまっていた. ‖ ***vanish in*** a streak of white smoke 白い一すじの煙となって消える. ¶***vanish into*** nothing 消えてなくなる. ¶***vanish into*** air 空中に消散する ‖ ***vanish into*** a space a long way off 遠いかなたに消え去る. ¶***vanish like*** a bubble あぶくのように消える. ¶***vanish out of*** one's sight 消えうせる. ¶those species have ***vanished without*** leaving a trace. これらの種族はあとかたもなく消えうせた.

O Before a pleasant face and a courteous manner, all obstacles ***vanish***. 愉快な顔と丁寧な物ごしとで一切の障害は消えてしまう. ¶He ***vanished*** as ghost-like as he came. 彼はひょう然ときてひょう然と去った.

vanity, *n.* 虚栄心, 虚栄, 自慢; 空(くう).

V ***excite*** one's ***vanity*** 虚栄心をそそる. ¶***feel*** the ***vanity*** of the world 世をはかなむ. ¶***flatter*** one's ***vanity*** その虚栄心に迎合する. ¶***gratify*** one's ***vanity*** その虚栄心を満足させる. ¶***hamper*** a foolish ***vanity*** 愚かな虚栄心を抑えてしまう. ¶***hurt*** one's ***vanity*** 虚栄心を傷つける ‖ It ***hurts*** my ***vanity***. それはおもしろくない. ¶***inflate*** the ***vanity*** of ... ...の虚栄心をあおる. ¶***pique*** (=***stimulate***) one's ***vanity*** その虚栄心を刺激する. ¶***please*** one's ***vanity*** その虚栄心を喜ばせる. ¶***realize*** the ***vanity*** of life 世をはかなむ. ¶***satirize*** human ***vanity*** 人間のはかなさを風刺する. ¶show it to ***satisfy*** one's ***vanity*** これ見よがしにそれを見せる. ¶***see*** the ***vanity*** of human greatness 人間は偉いといってもつまらないものだと悟る. ¶***tickle*** one's ***vanity*** 虚栄心をそそる. ¶***wound*** one's ***vanity*** その虚栄心を傷つける.

Q ***harmless vanity*** 罪のない虚栄心. ¶Goldsmith's ***innocent vanity*** ゴールドスミスの子供らしい虚栄. ¶With ***pardonable feminine vanity*** the majority of the young ladies wear gloves while operating, to better maintain the contour and complexion of their busily worked fingers. 大多数の若い女が忙しく働く指の格好や色つやを損じまいとして仕事中手袋をはめるのは虚栄ではあるが女として許すべきことだ. ¶***social vanities*** of their wives 彼らの妻の社交的虚栄心. ¶***useless vanity*** 無益の虚栄心.

P ***for vanity*** 虚栄のために. ¶***from*** mere ***vanity*** 単なる虚

栄から. ¶I say this *without vanity*. 私はこう言ってもうぬぼれではない. ‖ *without vanity* I may say that ... 自慢するのではないが…である.
P² *vanity in* dress 着道楽. ¶the *vanity of* fame 盛名のはかなさ ‖ the *vanity of* the world 世のあじけなさ, 物の哀れ ‖ the *vanity of* all phenomena あらゆる現象の空虚性.

vanquish, *v.* 負かす.
P *vanquish* a person *in* argument 人を閉口させる.

vapo[u]r, *n.* 蒸気, 水蒸気.
V *emit* a slight *vapor* 少量の水蒸気を発する. ¶*give off* a highly inflammable *vapor* 高度の燃性蒸気を発する.
Q a constant burst of *mephitic vapors* 有毒蒸気の絶え間ない爆発.
Q² *water vapor* 水蒸気.
P fly off [vanish] *in vapor* 蒸気となって発散する(消える). ¶change (=convert) ... *into vapour* ...を蒸気に変える. ¶watery *vapor in* the atmosphere 空中の水蒸気. ¶vanish *in vapor* (smoke) 湯気(煙)となって消える.

vapo[u]r, *v.* 消失させる.
M *vapor away* one's patriotism 愛国心を知らず知らず失わせる. ¶*vapor waveringly* ゆらゆら湯気が上る.

vapo[u]ring, *n.* 自慢, ほら.
Q *idle vaporings* of dreamers 夢想家のから気炎.

variance, *n.* 相違, 不和.
V I have *had* a slight *variance* with him. 私は彼とちょっと意見の衝突をした.
Q at *direct variance* with ... ...とは正反対の.
P I am *at variance* with him on that matter. 私はそのことについてはあの人と意見が合わない. 【類】 his view of ... is widely *at variance* with that of ... ‖ The statement made is quite *at variance* with facts. 作成された声明書は事実と全く相違している. 【類】 Compulsory celibacy (強制的独身) is *at variance* with the principles of modern society. / even when their respective Governments are *at variance*.

variant, *n.* 変形.
Q a *clever variant* of "The Moonstone" 「月長石」(小説)の巧妙な換骨奪胎. ¶a *developmental variant* 進化(によって生じた)変種. ¶his life story is a *modern variant* (=edition) of the proverbial romance of ... 彼の伝記は広く世に知られている...の物語を現代化したものだという感を与える.
P² Lown is a *variant of* loon. Lown は loon の変形である.

variation, *n.* 変化, 変形, 不同.
V *show* a wide *variation* 種々の変態を示す.
Q a *clever variation* of an old saying 古いことわざの巧妙な作り変え. ¶There is *considerable variation* in the use of capital letters. 大文字の用法は大分まちまちである. ¶*great* (*little*) *variation* 大きな(わずかの)変化. ¶*regional variations* of pronunciation 発音の方言的相違. ¶a *humorous variation* of the old saw that ... ...という古いことわざのおどけた改作. ¶*individual variations* 個々の不同. ¶They are subject to *wide variations*. 千差万別である.
Q² physical and psychical *sex variations* 性における肉体的精神的の相違.
P be liable *to variation* 変化しやすい ‖ be subject *to variation* 変化を受ける. ¶a class consisting of students *with* wide *variation* in capacities 玉石混交の学級. ¶*without variation* 一律に.
P² typographical *variations for* securing attention 注意を引くための活字の様式変化. ¶the *variation from* ... ...に比べての違い. ¶*variation in* the compass ら針盤の偏差 ‖ There has been no *variation in* the price of cotton for some time. 綿花の価格には暫く変動がない. ¶the *variations of* opinion 意見の区々 ‖ *variation of* temperature (strength, pressure) 温度(力,圧力)の変動.

variety, *n.* 変化, 多種多様, 種類; 《英》よせ.
V *add variety* to the entertainment 娯楽の単調を避ける. ¶*afford variety* by alternations of oral and written work 口頭と筆記の授業を交互にやって目先を変える. ¶They *comprise* three *varieties*. それには三種類ある. ¶It *created* a pleasing *variety* from the surrounding white. 周囲が白い所へそれが色変りで見る目に気持がよかった. ¶to *give variety* to the program (同じものばかりではあきるから)プログラムに変化を添えるために ‖ The main stylistic use of synonym is to *give variety* and accuracy of diction. 文体上同意語を使用するのは主として言い回しの変化と正確を与えるためである. ¶It has a *variety* of uses. それには色々用途がある. ¶'*Variety*' is *known* as 'Vaudeville' in the U.S.A. バライエテー(ショー)はアメリカではボードビルで通っている. ¶*lack variety* 変化を欠く. ¶*lend* pleasant *variety* to the view 景色に気持のよい変化を添える. 【類】 *lend variety* to one's table. ¶*offer* a *variety* of attractions 色々人目につくものがある. ¶*pass through* a *variety* of fortunes 色々な目に会う. ¶a florist *producing* new *varieties* 新種を作る花き栽培者. ¶*show* more *variety* in life 生活様式は一層多様化している. ¶A great *variety* of different theories have been *started* and *abandoned*. 種々様々な異説が持出されたり放棄されたりした. ¶A *variety* of improvements are *suggested*. 色色な改良案が提出されている. ¶*take on* an infinite *variety* of form 形式において無数の変化を示す. ¶after *trying* a *variety* of occupations 様々な職業をやってから.
Q *ameliorated varieties* of cereals 穀類の改良種. ¶The presence of a pretty lake gives a *beautiful variety* to the landscape. きれいな湖水があるのでその風景に美しい変化がある. ¶a *cheap variety* of leather 皮の安価な種類. ¶the most *common variety* 最も普通な種類. ¶in *countless varieties* of ways 数限りなく異った方法で. ¶Lamaism, a *degenerate variety* of northern Buddhism, is the religious system of Tibet and Mongolia. 北方仏教の堕落した一派たるラマ教はチベット及びモーコの宗教制度である. ¶flowers of *double variety* 八重の花. ¶of almost *endless variety* ほとんど無数に種類のある ‖ in *endless variety* 種々様々の. ¶*every variety* of ... 各種の... ¶a *great variety* of ladies' superior gloves 種々様々の高級婦人手袋. 【類】 flowers in *great variety* ‖ have a *great variety* of accomplishments 多芸. ¶an *immense variety* of ... ...種類の限りない. ¶in *infinite variety* 千差万別で. ¶We demand *more variety* in our food. もっと食物の変化が必要である. ¶give a *pleasant variety* to ... ...に快い変化を与える. ¶all its *possible variety* それのありとあらゆる種類. ¶*rare varieties* of Jubilee stamps 珍らしい祝典記念の切手の色々. ¶Emerald is a *rare green variety* of corundum, akin to the sapphire. エメラルドはサファイヤに類する緑色鋼玉の珍種である. ¶There is to be enjoyed a *rich variety* of scenery. そこは風景の変化に富んでいる ‖ a *rich variety* of autumnal tints 秋色のうつくしさ ‖ There azaleas are found in greatest abundance and *richest variety*. そこには色々の種類のつつじがきわめてたくさんにある. ¶the famous *seedless variety* of orange みかんの名高い種子なしの種類. ¶*several varieties* of spaniel 色々のスパニエル種猟犬. ¶a *special variety* of birds 鳥の特別種. ¶a *wide variety* of uses 種々なる用途 ‖ have a *wide variety* of subjects to talk about 話題に富む. 【類】 A school teacher has a *wide variety* of duties.
Q² Mocha is a *choice variety* of coffee. モカはコーヒーの中でも特上である. ¶of a *late blooming variety* 遅咲きの種類の.
P *by* a *variety* of means 色々の手段で. ¶*for* a *variety* of reasons 種々の理由から. ¶fires *from* a *variety* of causes 色々の原因から起った火災. ¶They are made *in* a *variety* of sizes. それはいろんな寸法に作られる. ‖ *in* a *variety* of ways (circumstances) 様々の方法(事情)で. 【類】 The word "instinct" may be used *in* a *variety* of significations. ‖ be rich *in variety* 変化に富む. ¶He often appears *in variety*. 《英》彼はよくよせに出る. ¶for the sake *of variety* 目先を変えるために. ¶a talk *on* a *variety* of topics よも山の話し. ¶We cannot live *without variety*. われわれは変化なしではいられない.
P² a *variety of* uses 種々な用途 ‖ the *variety of* his learning 彼の学問の多様性.

various, *a.* 種々な.
M *infinitely various* 数限りなく多種多様な.
P *various in* kind 多種多様の ‖ mountains *various in* their aspects 山容の異なる山々.

varnish, *n.* ニス.
P cover it *with* a glossy, black *varnish* 光沢のある黒いニスでそれを塗る.

varnish, *v.* ニスを塗る.
M² *varnish up* ニスを塗る.
P *varnish with* lacquer うるしで塗る.

vary, *v.* 変る; 変える.
M *vary* very *greatly* 非常に種類が多い. ¶*vary widely* 大分隔りがある.
P Medical fees *vary* in England *according to* the pa-

tient's income. 英国では医師の料金は患者の収入によって違いがある. ¶with a rate of interest ***varying between*** four and six percent 四分から六分の利率で ‖ The temperature ***varies between*** ... and ... 温度は...から...の間を上下する. ¶*vary* a bit ***from*** the original 原文とは少し異う ‖ The prices ***vary from*** £250 upwards. その価は二百五十ポンドから色々ある. ¶amounts (=sums) ***varying from*** ... ***to*** ... ...から...までの金高 ‖ the charge ***varies from*** ... ***to*** ... その料金は...から...までである. ¶*vary* ***in*** price (size, form, opinion) 値段(など)に等差のある ‖ They *vary* ***in*** color from light grey to blue and almost black. それらは薄ねずから紺またはほとんど黒まで色々ある(米国人の皮膚の色). ¶Fashion ***varies with*** the time and place. 流行は時と場所で違う. ‖ The rent of lodgings ***varies with*** the locality. へや代は場所によって高い安いがある. ‖ ***vary with*** the individual 個人個人で差がある ‖ Apparent distance ***varies with*** the weather, background, etc. 目測距離は天気や背景などによって異る. ‖ Prices ***vary with*** the weight. 値段は目方次第.

vase, *n.* 花びん, つぼ.

V ***fill*** the *vase* with water 花びんに水を入れる. 【類】a *vase* ***filled*** with peach blossoms.

Q a priceless ***antique vase*** 宝物的な古代の花びん. ¶This will make a ***perfect vase*** for flowers. これはりっぱな花びんになる.

Q her pet ***flower vase*** 彼女が大事にしている花びん.

P flowers ***in*** a *vase* 生けた花 ‖ a crack ***in*** the *vase* その花びんのひび. ¶a pair ***of*** *vases* 一対の花びん.

P² a *vase* ***for*** holding flowers 花びん.

vassal, *n.* 家臣.

Q Honda-Masanobu, Iyeyasu's ***favorite vassal*** 家康のちょう臣本田正信. ¶***immediate vassals*** 譜代の諸臣.

P² a *vassal* ***of*** the crown 国王(皇帝)の臣下.

vassalage, *n.* 臣たること.

V ***demand*** *vassalage* from the Philippines フイリッピンの従属を要求する.

vast, *a.* 広い.

P *vast* ***in*** extent 広ばくたる.

vaudeville, *n.* よせ演芸.

P appear ***in*** *vaudeville* よせに出る.

vault, *n.* 丸天井; 地下室; ひと飛び.

Q a ***fireproof*** *vault* 防火装置のある地下室. ¶an ***underground*** *vault* 地下金庫.

Q² a ***bank*** *vault* 銀行の地下金庫. ¶a ***family*** *vault* 一家の地下納骨所. ¶put away in a ***safe-deposit*** *vault* 地下の金庫に収める. ¶the ***Treasury*** *vaults* in Washington ワシントンの国庫の金庫. ¶the ***wine*** *vault* ぶどう酒貯蔵室.

P clear a brook ***in*** one *vault* 小川をぴょんと飛越える.

P² the *vault* ***of*** heaven 天空.

vault, *v.* 飛ぶ.

P *vault* ***from*** the saddle くらから飛降りる. ¶*vault* ***into*** the saddle くらに飛乗る. ¶*vault* ***over*** the gate 門を飛越える. ¶*vault* ***upon*** a horse 馬に飛乗る.

vaunt, *v.* 誇る.

P The foe *vaunts* ***over*** his victory. 敵は勝利を誇っている.

veer, *v.* 進路を変える.

V Summer typhoons *veer* ***northwestward.*** 夏期の台風は北西に進路を変える. ¶*veer* ***round*** in opinion 意見が変って行く ‖ *veer* ***round*** to the opposite party 反対派に合流する.

M² *veer* ***off*** (=away) to ... ...の方に転向する.

vegetable, *n.* 野菜; 草木, 植物.

V We ***grow*** our own *vegetables* in the garden. 手前では野菜を畑に作ります. ¶***Hasn't*** the grocer any other *vegetable* now? あの食料品店には何か他の野菜はありませんか. ¶The Dutch ***raise*** the best *vegetables* in Europe. オランダはヨーロッパ中で一番野菜が良い. ¶*Vegetables* will ***thrive*** on almost any type of soil. 野菜はまずどんな土にもよくできるものだ.

Q The soil all round is generally favorable to the growth of most ***European*** *vegetables*. そのまわりの土は概してヨーロッパ種の野菜の生育に適している. ¶***exuberant*** *vegetables* 勢いのよい野菜. ¶***forced*** *vegetables* 促成野菜品. ¶***green*** *vegetables* 青もの類. ¶***pickled*** *vegetables* つけ物. ¶a ***succulent*** *vegetable* 多汁の野菜.

Q² ***field*** *vegetables* 畑の野菜類(芋・なす・かぼちゃなど). ¶a common ***garden*** *vegetable* 普通の畑にできる野菜.

P a dealer ***in*** *vegetables*=《米》a vegetable man, 《英》a greengrocer 青物商. ¶live ***on*** *vegetables* 野菜を常食とする.

vegetation, *n.* 草木, 植物; 繁茂.

V The plant has ***attained*** a luxuriant *vegetation.* その植物は繁茂した.

V² A luxuriant *vegetation* ***appears*** on all sides. あたりには繁茂した草木が見える. ¶all *vegetation* ***ceases*** above ... ...以上の高所では一切の植物が成長しない. ¶Without air and water no *vegetation* can ***exist.*** 空気と水がなければ植物は生存し得ない.

Q the ***luxuriant*** *vegetation* of tropical forests 熱帯のうっそうたる草木. ¶***rank*** *vegetation* おい茂った草木. ¶***rich*** *vegetation* 豊富な植物. ¶The *vegetation* is ***sparse*** in that district. その地方は植物がまばらだ. ¶a Buddhist temple lying amidst ***verdant*** *vegetation* 青々とした草木の中に立っている寺院.

P the growth ***of*** *vegetation* 植物の生長.

vehemence, *n.* 激烈.

Q work with ***noisy*** *vehemence* 荒々しく仕事をする.

P carried away ***by*** the *vehemence* of one's own eloquence (passions) 自分の熱弁に酔って(情熱にかられて). ¶complain ***with*** growing *vehemence* ますます激しく不平を鳴らす.

vehement, *a.* 激しい.

P *vehement* ***in*** feeling 感情の激しい.

vehicle, *n.* 車, 乗物; 手段.

Q an ***aerial*** *vehicle* 索道車(ケーブルカー). ¶***antiquated*** *vehicles* 時代後れの乗物. ¶***horse-drawn*** *vehicles* 馬車. ¶the ***horseless*** *vehicle*=the motor-car 馬を用いない乗物(すなわち自動車). ¶The art of writing is the ***main*** *vehicle* for the exchange of thought. 文字は思想交換の主な手段である. ¶***mechanically-propelled*** *vehicles* 機械力による乗物. ¶***motor*** *vehicles* モーターのついた車, 自動車. ¶an ***official*** *vehicle* 公用車. ¶individuals not owing ***personal*** *vehicles* 自家用車を持たない人々. ¶***petrol-driven*** (=***-propelled***) *vehicles* (普通の)ガソリン自動車. ¶property found in ***public*** *vehicles* 公共乗物中の遺失物. ¶Latin was once the ***quasi-universal*** *vehicle* of culture. ラテン語は以前はほとんど全世界の文化用語であった. ¶***steam-propelled*** *vehicles* 蒸気を動力とする車(汽車).

Q² recondition ***army*** *vehicles* 軍用車を修理する. ¶***business*** (***pleasure***) *vehicles* 営業(行楽)用の車. ¶***motor*** *vehicles* 動力のついた車(自動車・トラックなど) ‖ a thoroughly winterized ***motor*** *vehicle* 暖房設備の完備した(滑り止めなどのついた)自動車. ¶repair of ***out-of-service*** *vehicles* 廃(破損)車の修理. ¶a ***passenger*** *vehicle* 乗用車. 【類】a public ***passenger*** *vehicle* (バスなど). ¶***railway*** *vehicles* 鉄道車両. ¶***road*** *vehicles* 路上の乗物 (trams, omnibuses, etc.). 【類】transfer from the terminus on to ***road*** *vehicles.*

P use the novel ***as*** a *vehicle* for the advocacy of one's views 意見を唱道するための手段として小説を用いる. ¶travel ***by*** [a] *vehicle* 乗物で旅行する. ¶No thoroughfares ***for*** *vehicles.* 諸車通行禁止. ¶carry goods ***in*** a *vehicle* 車で荷を運ぶ. ¶the driver's seat ***on*** a *vehicle* 運転手台, 御者台.

P² a *vehicle* ***for*** divine communication 神のお告げを伝えるもの(お筆先き) ‖ make English the *vehicle* ***of*** instruction in schools 英語を学校での教授用語にする ‖ fiction as a *vehicle* ***of*** moral teaching 勧善懲悪を教える道具としての小説 ‖ a *vehicle* ***of*** malaria (infection) マラリヤ(伝染病)の媒介物. 【類】Language is the *vehicle* ***of*** thought.

veil, *n.* ベール, 被い, 幕; 口実.

V ***draw*** a *veil* over ... ...を隠ぺいする. ¶***lift*** the *veil* 真相を明らかにする. ¶***strip*** the *veil* from hidden vices 秘められた罪悪を暴露する. ¶***take*** the *veil*=become a nun 尼になる.

Q a treasured bit of the ***bridal*** *veil* 大切にした一放の花嫁のベール.

P ***beneath*** the protecting *veil* of darkness 暗黒という保護幕のもとに. ¶***beyond*** the *veil* あの世に. ¶facts hidden ***in*** a *veil* of mystery なぞに包まれた事実. ¶***under*** the *veil* of ... ...を口実にして.

P² a *veil* ***of*** mist over a town 町を包んだもやのとばり.

veil, *v.* おおう, 隠す.

P a fact *veiled* ***from*** public knowledge 世間に隠してある事実. ¶The hill was *veiled* ***in*** a mist. その小山は霧に包まれた. ‖ It is *veiled* ***in*** mystery. それは神秘に包まれている.

vein, *n.* 静脈, 血管; 気質, 気分; 鉱脈.

V ***bind*** (=***tie***) ***up*** a *vein* 血管をくくる. ¶***bleed*** a *vein* 血管から血を出す. ¶***strike*** gold *veins* 金の鉱脈に打当てる.

Q in ***gloomy*** *vein* 陰うつな気分で. ¶in ***humorous*** *vein*

滑けい気分で. ¶in ***lighter vein*** 一層くつろいだ気持で. ¶speak of ... in the most ***optimistic vein*** 非常に楽観的な気分で...のことを語る. ¶In this book the subject is treated in a ***popular vein***. この本にはその問題が通俗的に論じられている. ¶in less ***serious vein*** もっとくだけた気持で.

P declare ***in*** a prophetic ***vein*** 予言者気取りで言明する ‖ he assured me ***in*** a ***vein*** of sincerity that ... 彼はまじめに...のことを私に保証した ‖ I am not ***in*** the ***vein*** (=mood) for work. 私は働く気がしない. ‖ The heroic blood runs ***in*** his ***veins***. その勇ましい血が彼の血管の中を通っている. ¶He is ***of*** an imaginative ***vein***. 彼は想像力に富んでいる.

P² a ***vein of*** coal 炭鉱脈.

velocity, *n.* 速度.

Q² Wild winds were sweeping at ***break-neck velocity*** through the city. 強風が猛速度で市街を吹きまくっていた.

P fly ***with*** the ***velocity*** of a swallow つばめの速度で飛ぶ.

P² a ***velocity of*** 1,000 feet a second 毎秒千フィートの速度 ‖ the ***velocity of*** the earth's motion 地球運行の速度 ‖ the ***velocity of*** sound 音速. 【類】The ***velocity of*** light is about 186,000 miles per second.

velvet, *n.* ビロード.

V² ***Velvet feels*** soft. ビロードは手触りが柔かい.

Q² ***imitation velvet*** ビロードまがい.

P embroidery ***on velvet*** ビロード地の刺しゅう.

vendetta, *n.* 復しゅう.

V² A small ***vendetta grows*** sometimes out of this lost ball business. [隣家の子供が]ボール投げをやっていて誤って投げた球がなくなったので二軒がちょっとしたかたき同士にな ることがある.

Q² a ***mass vendetta*** 集団でのかたき討ち.

vending, *n.* 呼売り.

Q² ***push-cart vending*** 手押車での呼売り.

vendor, *n.* 行商人, 呼売人.

Q an ***itinerant vendor*** 行商人.

Q² a ***black-market vendor*** かつぎ屋. ¶a ***door-to-door vendor*** 戸別行商人. ¶a ***retail vendor*** 小売商人. ¶a ***roadside vendor*** 往来の商人. ¶costermongers and ***street vendors*** 呼売や街頭売をする商人.

veneer, *n.* [ベニア板の]上張り板; 外飾.

Q a ***thin veneer*** 薄い上張り板 ‖ a ***thin veneer*** of culture (education) 教養(教育)の付焼刃.

P barbarians ***with*** a ***veneer*** of culture 文化の付焼刃をした未開人 ‖ ***with*** a ***veneer*** of novelty ちょっと目新しい.

P² a ***veneer of*** Western civilization [比ゆ的に] 西洋文明の模ほう.

veneer, *v.* 上張りする.

M Her civilization is only ***veneered over*** with foreign polish. その国の文化は表面に外国式のみがきがかけてあるだけだ.

P a pine desk ***veneered with*** mahogany マホガニ材を張った松材の机.

veneering, *n.* ベニヤ張り.

P² a superficial polish, a ***veneering of*** mahogany ***over*** common wood 表面の化粧すなわち普通材の上にマホガニ板を張ったもの.

venerate, *v.* 尊ぶ.

P His memory is ***venerated throughout*** the land. 彼は死後国をあげて尊敬されている.

veneration, *n.* 尊敬.

V ***foster*** a ***veneration*** for antiquity 古いものの尊重を奨励する.

Q entertain a ***sincere veneration*** for ... ...に対し真に尊敬の念を抱く.

P hold ancestors ***in veneration*** 祖先を敬う. ¶look upon the Court ***with*** religious ***veneration*** 宗教的崇拝の心で宮廷に対する. 【類】be filled ***with veneration*** for ...

P² a superstitious ***veneration for*** the past 過去に対する迷信的崇拝.

vengeance, *n.* 復しゅう.

V in a voice that sounds as though she was ***calling down*** the ***vengeance*** of Heaven upon ... ...をのろうような口調で. ¶I intend that my ghost shall ***carry out*** my ***vengeance***. 幽霊となって恨みを晴らしてみせる. ¶***demand vengeance*** on ... ...に復しゅうすることを要求する. ¶***denounce*** (=***prophesy***) ***vengeance*** 復しゅうするとおどかす. ¶***exact*** a ***vengeance*** from a person for ... ある人に...の復しゅうをする. ¶***execute*** one's ***vengeance*** upon ... ...にそのあだを返す. ¶***expect*** a ***vengeance*** from ... ...からの復しゅうを予期する. ¶***imprecate*** Heaven's ***vengeance*** on ... ...に天罰が下るように切願する. ¶***inflict vengeance*** on ... ...に復しゅうする. ¶***seek vengeance*** upon ... ...に復しゅうしようとする. ¶***swear vengeance*** against a person 人に復しゅうすることを誓う. ¶***take vengeance*** on (=upon) ... for ... ...に...のあだを返す ‖ ***take vengeance*** for one's father's death 父のあだを討つ. ¶***vow vengeance*** on ... ...に復しゅうすることを誓う. ¶***wreak*** one's ***vengeance*** upon ... ...に恨みを晴らす. 【類】She at last determined to ***wreak*** her ***vengeance*** by setting fire to his house.

Q ***bloodthirsty vengeance*** 血を見なければやまない(執念深い)復しゅう. ¶take a ***bloody vedgeance*** on the murderer その殺害者に血の復しゅうをする. ¶exact a ***fearful vengeance*** on ... ...に恐るべき復しゅうをする. ¶take an ***imaginary vengeance*** on ... ...に対して心の中であだを打つ. ¶wreak ***summary vengeance*** upon ... 手っとり早く...に恨みを晴らす.

P resolve ***on vengeance*** 復しゅうしようと決心する. ¶***with*** a ***vengeance***=《俗》 overwhelmingly ***or*** with a startling effect 思い切って, 意地になって, 猛烈に ‖ When it does rain here, it rains ***with*** a ***vengeance***. ここでは雨が降るとなるととてもひどい. ‖ swoop down ***with*** a ***vengeance*** upon ... [わし・戦闘機などが] ...に猛烈に襲いかかる. 【類】The waves dashed against the rock ***with*** a ***vengeance***. / Your words have come true ***with*** a ***vengeance***—that I should be forestalled (だし抜かれるだろうという君の言葉).

P² his attempted ***vengeance on*** his personal enemy 彼自身の敵に対して彼の企てた復しゅう.

venom, *n.* 毒, 毒液; 〖比ゆ〗悪意, 恨み.

V ***inject*** a ***venom*** into a rabbit (guinea pig) うさぎ(モルモット)に毒液を注射する.

P with a look ***of venom*** 針をふくんだ顔つきで.

vent, *n.* 漏れ口, 出口.

V ***find vent*** in a bitter cry [感情が高潮して]わっと大声あげて泣き出す ‖ Their admiration ***found vent*** in deep-chested cheers. 彼らの称賛は満身の歓呼となって表われた. ‖ ***find*** [a] ***vent*** in orderly and legal ways 秩序正しい合法的な手段で不満を訴える ‖ ***find*** a ***vent*** for his surcharged heart 彼の胸中のうつ憤に対してそのはけ口を求める ‖ a batch of students whose spirits ***found*** a ***vent*** in song 元気あふれて歌い出した一組の学生. ¶***get vent*** [火山など]出口を得る. ¶He is apt to ***give vent*** to his feelings. 彼はとかく遠慮なく物を言うたちだ. ‖ ***give vent*** to righteous indignation (one's pent-up feelings) 義(うつ)憤を漏らす ‖ to ***give vent*** to his chagrin 憤満を漏らそうとして ‖ ***give vent*** to dissatisfaction 不平を鳴らす ‖ ***give vent*** to mild expletives 軽い悪口を言う. 【類】He ***gave vent*** to the following reflection. ¶Popular excitement then began to ***seek*** more violent ***vents***. 人々の激こうがさらに激しくなってきた. ¶***take vent*** 漏れる.

Q give ***free vent*** to one's feelings その感情を言いたいだけ言う. ¶She longed to be alone that she might give ***full vent*** to her sorrow and despair. 彼女は自分独りになって思う存分悲哀と失望を味わいたかったのであった.

P feel the need of a ***vent for*** their emotions 彼らの感動のはけ口を得る必要を感じる.

ventilate, *v.* 風を通す; 世間に発表する.

M The room is not ***well ventilated***. そのへやは通風がよくない.

P ***ventilate*** a room ***by*** opening windows まどを開けてへやの換気をする. ¶***ventilate*** it ***in*** the press それを新聞に発表する.

ventilation, *n.* 換気, 換気法.

V This hall ***has*** the most thorough ***ventilation***. この会館は最も完全な換気装置がしてある. ¶***Ventilation*** is ***maintained*** mechanically. 換気が機械的に行われている.

Q have ***bad*** (***good***) ***ventilation*** 換気が悪い(良い). ¶a ***full ventilation*** of a problem 問題の自由討議. ¶***insufficient ventilation*** 不十分な換気.

P² a ***ventilation of*** grievances 苦情の打明け.

ventilator, *n.* 通風機.

V ***fix*** (=***install***) ***ventilators*** 通風装置をとりつける.

ventriloquism, *n.* 腹話術.

P one who is expert ***in ventriloquism***=an expert ventriloquist 腹話術の大家.

venture, *n.* 冒険, 冒険的投機事業.

V ***abandon*** the ***venture*** その冒険的事業をやめる. ¶***decline*** the ***venture*** その事業を拒絶する. ¶***launch*** a new journalistic ***venture*** 新たに新聞雑誌の事業を起す. ¶a ***venture made*** blindly=a leap in the dark 無鉄砲な試み.

Q a ***commercial venture*** 商業上の企業 ‖ poultry keeping as a ***commercial venture*** 商売としての養鶏. ¶their ***co-***

operative venture 彼ら共同の仕事. ¶a ***daring venture*** 勇敢な冒険. ¶his ***first venture*** in business 彼の最初に手掛けた事業. ¶an ***ill-starred venture*** 不成功に終った事業. ¶One ***lucky venture*** made his fortune. 彼はやって見た事業が一度あたって財産をこしらえた. ¶It is her fourth ***matrimonial venture***. それは彼女の四度目の結婚だ. ¶the principal promoter of the ***new venture*** 新事業の主な発起人 ‖ a ***new venture*** in broadcasting 放送の新しい試み. ¶a ***profitable venture*** もうかる仕事. ¶a ***private venture*** 個人の事業. ¶***speculative industrial ventures*** 投機的な工業上の企業. ¶a ***tiny venture*** 小企業. ¶With less than 100 students registered the summer school was an ***unprofitable venture***. 登録学生(入学生)百名以下だったのでその夏期学校は採算の取れない仕事だった.

Q[2] a ***business venture*** 商売上の試み ‖ proposed ***business venture*** 計画中の企業. ¶turn it into a ***money-making venture*** それを射利的事業化する. ¶a ***mountaineering venture*** 危険な登山.

P a bow drawn ***at*** a *venture* ためしに引いた弓 ‖ buy ***at*** a *venture* やまで買う ‖ I said ***at*** a *venture*. 私は当てずっぽうに言った. ¶He failed ***in*** all his *ventures*. 彼はやって見た事業が皆失敗した.

venture, *v.* やってみる; 思い切ってやる.

M *venture* ***forward*** 危険を冒して進む. ¶*venture* ***out*** into the wide ocean 危険を冒して広い大海に乗り出す. 【類】*venture* ***out*** on the thin ice / *venture* ***out*** to sea. ¶He might ***well*** *venture* on a more elaborate work on the same subject. 同じ題目について一層の力作を試みるのもよかろう.

P *venture* ***at*** it それをのるかそるかやってみる. ¶*venture* one's money ***in*** a speculation 投機にその金をつぎ込む ‖ *venture* one's life ***in*** war 生命を戦争の危険にさらす. ¶*venture* ***into*** a room 思い切って室にはいる. ¶*venture* ***near*** the door 思い切って戸口に近づく. ¶I have *ventured* ***on*** the work of attempting it. 私はあえてそれをやろうとした. ‖ *venture* ***on*** a lion's den 思いきってししの巣に入る ‖ *venture* one's fortune ***on*** ... ...に財産を投じる ‖ *venture* ***on*** a single chance 一か八かやってみる. ¶He is too timid to *venture* ***upon*** an undertaking. 彼は小心だから思いきった事業はやれない. ‖ *venture* ***upon*** a translation [難しいが] 一つ翻訳を試みる.

O I *venture* to hope that ... 私はおぼつかなくは思うが...を希望している. ‖ I *venture* to say (advocate). 私はあえて言う(弁護する). ‖ I can't *venture* to excuse it. 何とも申訳がありません. ‖ I *venture* to commend the book. 私はあえてその本を推奨する. ‖ I *venture* to think that ... 私は努めて...と考える.

veranda, *n.* 縁側, ベランダ.

Q an ***open*** (***covered***) *veranda* 屋根のない(ある)ベランダ.

P I heard some one walking ***in*** the *veranda*. だれか縁側を歩く音を私は聞付けた. ¶***on*** the shaded *veranda* overlooking the garden 庭に面した日陰になっている縁側で.

verb, *n.* 〖文法〗動詞.

V ***conjugate*** a *verb* 動詞を変化させる.

Q a ***reflexive*** *verb* 再帰動詞.

verbiage, *n.* 多弁.

Q ***excessive*** *verbiage* 度の過ぎる冗弁. ¶He gave vent to what was his ***usual*** *verbiage* on such an occasion. このような場合かならずやる例のおしゃべりを始めた. ¶***flowery*** *verbiage* 修飾の多い冗弁.

verdict, *n.* [陪審員の]評決; 判断; 意見.

V ***accept*** a *verdict* 評決に服する ‖ ***accept*** the *verdict* of the majority 多数の意見に従う. ¶the jury ***brought in*** a *verdict* of manslaughter against ... 陪審員は...に故殺罪の評決を下した ‖ The coroner ***brought in*** a *verdict* of death by suicide while in a fit of temporary insanity. 検死官はその死が一時的精神錯乱の発作中における自殺によるものという断案を下した. ‖ ***bring in*** a *verdict* of "not proven" 「証拠不十分」の評決を下す. ¶***deliver*** a *verdict* 評決を下す. ¶The jury ***found*** a *verdict* of "Guilty" and sentence of death was passed. 陪審員は「有罪」の評決を下しそして死刑の宣告が申し渡された. ¶The *verdict* of his teacher was ***fulfilled*** (***reversed***) by his future career. 彼の教師の断案は彼の将来の経歴によって確証された(裏切られた). ¶a *verdict* of ... damages and costs was ***given*** against ... ...の賠償金と訴訟費用とを支払うべき評決が...に下された. 【類】The *verdict* of history was ***given*** in his favor. ¶***pass*** a very unfavorable *verdict* on Carlyle カーライルに対してきわめて不利な批判をする. ¶It would be the very extremity of rashness to ***pronounce*** any decided *verdict* on such a subject. かかる問題に対して断案を下すのは早計の極というべきであろう. ¶The jury has failed to ***reach*** a *verdict*. 陪審官は評決を下すことができなかった. ¶The jury ***rendered*** a *verdict* of death by suicide. 陪審員は自殺による死亡という評決を下した. ¶***return*** a *verdict* to the effect that ... ...という意味の判決を下す. 【類】the jury (陪審員) ***returned*** the *verdict* of paying ... in favor of ... / ***return*** a *verdict* of "guilty" on ... ‖ The posterity ***reversed*** the *verdict*. 後世がその断案をくつがえした. ¶***wait*** the *verdict* of time 後世の断案をまつ ‖ like a culprit ***waiting*** [***for***] the *verdict* 裁決を待つ罪人のように.

Q the ***deliberate*** *verdict* of the most distinguished scholar 最も著名な学者の慎重な判断. ¶A ***favorable*** *verdict* was given. 有利な裁決が下された. ¶the ***general*** *verdict* here 当地における一般の意見 ‖ the ***general*** *verdict* is that ... 一般の評は...である. ¶render an ***impartial*** *verdict* 公平な評決を下す. ¶abide by the ***majority*** *verdict* 多数決に従う. ¶a ***partial*** *verdict* 片手落の評決. ¶The ***popular*** *verdict* was that it served him right. 世評はそれは彼にとって当然の報いということだった. ¶a ***sealed*** *verdict* 密封評決書. ¶the ***ultimate*** *verdict* of the ages and the slow justice of time 時代の経過による最後的断案と時のもたらす緩慢な正義. ¶a *verdict* ***unfavorable*** to ... ...反対説.

P He was condemned ***by*** the *verdict* of the public. 彼は世人に論難された.

P[2] a *verdict* ***for*** the plaintiff 原告に有利な評決. ¶What is your *verdict* ***on*** the coffee? そのコーヒーはどうですか. ¶a *verdict* ***of*** conviction 有罪評決 ‖ A *verdict* ***of*** guilty was returned. 有罪の評決が下された. ‖ a *verdict* ***of*** "Not guilty" 無罪の評決.

verdure, *n.* 青葉の草木.

Q the ***fresh*** *verdure* of spring 春の新緑. ¶a clump of ***luxuriant*** *verdure* 一群の生い茂った草木.

P The mountains are clad (=robed) ***in*** *verdure*. 山が青青とした草木におおわれている. ¶The hills are covered ***with*** *verdure*. 小山には青葉が茂っている.

verge, *n.* 縁(ふち), きわ.

P live ***at*** the *verge* of starvation 飢餓にひんしている. ¶***beyond*** the *verge* of the city 市外に ‖ ***beyond*** the *verge* of human credence 人間の信じうる境を超越して. ¶We parked the car ***on*** the grass *verge* at the side of the road. 道路のかたわらの草の縁に自動車を止めた. ‖ stand ***on*** the *verge* of bankruptcy 破産にひんしている. 【類】The company is ***on*** the *verge* of insolvency (破産). ‖ stand ***on*** the *verge* of one's grave (=death) 死にひんする ‖ His hat was just ***on*** the *verge* of being disreputable. 彼の帽子は随分ひどくなっていた. 【類】Just then the country was ***on*** the *verge* of another revolution. / The country is ***on*** the *verge* of collapse (=ruin). ‖ He is ***on*** the *verge* of (=close to) sixty. 彼は六十に近い. ¶symmetrical ***to*** the *verge* of monotony 単調と思われるくらい均勢のとれた ‖ The animals were ruthlessly hunted ***to*** the *verge* of extinction. その猟は絶滅にひんするまでに濫猟された ‖ push a person ***to*** the *verge* of exhaustion 人をくたくたになるまで働かせる.

verge, *v.* 近づく, 接近する.

M I say such a man *verges* very ***closely*** upon being either an ignoramus or a blatherskite, or both. こんな人はほとんど文盲かほら吹かまたはその両方だと言える.

P He is a "grand old man" *verging* ***on*** fourscore. 氏は八十歳になんなんとするいわゆる「元老」だ. 【類】then *verging* ***on*** ninety years / *verge* ***on*** eighty millions ‖ a patriotism which *verges* ***on*** chauvinism 盲目的とまで言える愛国主義. 【類】courage *verging* ***on*** temerity (無鉄砲) / Their zeal *verges* ***on*** fanaticism (熱狂). ‖ *verge* ***on*** burlesque 道化じみる. ¶*verge* ***to*** a close 終りに近づく. ¶*verge* ***upon*** war [紛争などが]戦争の危機にひんする ‖ *verge* ***upon*** frenzy (insanity) 狂乱(狂気)に近い.

verify, *v.* 証明する.

P learning not *verified* ***by*** experience 経験によって確かめられない学問. 【類】The driver's report was *verified* ***by*** an eyewitness. ¶be *verified* ***in*** the actual literature 実際の文献によって確かめられている.

verity, *n.* 真理.

Q the ***eternal*** *verities* 永久不変の真理.

P ***in*** all *verity* 全く. ¶***of*** a *verity* 真に.

vermicelli, *n.* マカロニの一種.

Q^2 *Soba* is a sort of ***buckwheat vermicelli*** そばはそば粉で作ったマカロニの一種だ.

vermin, *n.* [単・複同形] 害虫, 害獣.

V The *vermin* must be ***kept under.*** 害虫は防がなければならない.

Q^2 ***street vermin*** 街のダニ.

P a temple infested ***by*** those *vermin* (rats) それらの害虫(ねずみ)に荒された寺. ¶a plague ***of*** *vermin* 虫害. ¶The house swarms ***with*** *vermin.* その家には虫がうようよいる.

vernacular, *n.* 自国語; 《米口》方言; 《米》特殊の用語.

Q say in ***broad vernacular*** 土地の言葉丸出しで言う.

P foreign classics translated ***into*** the *vernacular* 自国語に翻訳された外国の古典. ¶English is giving place ***to*** the *vernacular* in that part of Asia. アジアのその地方では英語は自国語によって, とって代られつつある.

P^2 the *vernacular* ***of*** the lawyers (traders) 法律家(など)の用語.

versatile, *a.* 変化のある.

P *versatile* ***in*** mind (feeling, purpose, talent, color) 考え方(など)に変化のある(融通のきく).

versatility, *n.* 多芸, 多才.

P^2 his *versatility* ***of*** talent 彼の多才.

verse, *n.* 詩; 詩句.

V ***chant*** *verse* 詩を吟じる. ¶***compose*** (=***make***) *verses* 詩を作る. ¶***read*** *verse* ***aloud*** 詩を朗読する. ¶***write*** *verse* in a person's praise 人を賞賛した詩を書く.

Q a ***capping*** *verse* しり取り文句の詩. ¶a poorly ***constructed*** *verse* まずい詩. ¶a ***devotional*** *verse* 信仰的な詩. ¶a ***doggerel*** *verse* 悪詩. ¶an ***extempore*** *verse* 即興詩. ¶***live*** and ***spontaneous*** *verses* begotten of an irresistible impulse or "urge" to set free the soul 霊魂を開放しようとのやみ難い感激から生れた生気ある自然な詩. ¶***patriotic*** *verses* 愛国的な詩. ¶a ***society*** *verse* 軽妙な詩.

Q^2 a Japanese ***seventeen syllable*** *verse* 俳句.

P He is good ***at*** *verse.* 彼は作詩が巧みだ. ¶celebrate national events ***in*** *verse* 国家的のできごとを賛美した詩を作る ‖ a composition ***in*** *verse* 韻文. ¶turn it ***into*** *verse* それ(散文など)を詩にする.

P^2 a *verse* ***of*** six feet 六韻脚の詩.

versed, *a.* 熟達した, 通暁している.

M ***deeply*** *versed* in Japanese literature (=the literature of Japan) 日本の文学に深く通じている ‖ ***deeply*** *versed* in English affairs 英国の事情に通じて. ¶***well*** *versed* in the Analects of Confucius 論語に通暁した ‖ ***well*** *versed* (=proficient) in the art of … …の技術に熟達した. 【類】***well*** *versed* in office routine (事務).

P those *versed* ***in*** the question of … …の問題に精通した人々. 【類】one *versed* ***in*** human physiognomy (観相術) / be *versed* ***in*** the ways of the world (世情). ¶He is well *versed* ***on*** things Japanese. 彼は日本の事情に通じている.

version, *n.* 訳文; 解釈, 所説, 見解.

V I then turned to her, to ***elicit*** her *version* of the affair. 私はその時彼女がそのことをどう言うか聞いてみようとその方を向いた. ¶Now let me ***have*** (=***hear***) your own *version* of the affair. ところでその件についてあなたのお考えをうかがいたい. ¶During the Tokugawa age about one hundred different *versions* of the tale of the Ako vendetta were ***published.*** 徳川時代を通じて赤穂義士あだ討物語を取扱った本が百種ぐらい刊行された.

Q an ***abridged*** *version* of the Pawnbroker's Act 質商法の抜書. ¶an ***authorized*** *version* of the Bible きん定訳聖書. ¶a ***condensed*** *version* 要約. ¶There are ***conflicting*** *versions* of her death. 彼女の死因については色々異説がある. ¶a ***dramatic*** *version* of a novel 小説の脚色. ¶an ***expurgated*** *version* [差しさわりの個所を削除した]削除版. ¶write the ***first*** *version* of the President's message 大統領教書の第一稿を書く. ¶a ***metrical*** *version* of the Psalms 詩編の韻律訳. ¶In the event of disputes arising as to … the English *version* alone shall be ***official.*** …について紛議の生じる場合は英語の正文だけに拠ること. ¶a New England port—***one*** *version* of the story says Boston, the other New Bedford あるニューイングランドの港―一説にはボストンまた一説にはニューベッドフォード. ¶an ***Oriental*** *version* of "Beauty and the Beast" 「美女と野獣」の東洋版. ¶Let me hear your ***own*** *version* of the affair. その件についてのお考えをうかがいたい. ¶a comparison of the two ***painters'*** *versions* of "The Agony in the Garden" 二人の画家の「花園の苦もん」の描写比較. ¶a ***rationalistic*** *version* of the story is that … その話を筋道を立てて言えば…となる.

Q^2 the ***committee*** *version* of a bill ある議案の委員会案. ¶Bill Hart was the first ***movie*** *version* of the Wild West hero. ビル (Wm.S.) ハートは西部荒野の英雄に扮した最初の映画俳優だ. ¶a ***screen*** (=***movie*** *or* ***film***) *version* of a novel 小説の映画化. 【類】excellent ***screen*** (=***film***) *version* of a famous play. ¶a ***stage*** *version* of a novel 劇化した小説.

P ***according to*** the current *version* 坊間伝える所によれば.

P^2 This is my *version* ***of*** the affair. その件の私の解釈はこうです. ‖ "Pikatili"—his *version* ***of*** Piccadilly "Pikatili"—これを彼は Piccadilly の積りで言っている.

vessel, *n.* (**1**) 船.

V The dock can ***accommodate*** the largest *vessel.* そのドックはいかなる大船でも収容ができる. ¶***anchor*** one's *vessel* その船を停泊させる. ¶***board*** a *vessel* 乗船する. ¶***build*** a *vessel* 造船する. ¶***charter*** a foreign *vessel* 外国船を契約する. ¶***coal*** a *vessel* 船に石炭を積込む. ¶the *vessel* was ***commanded*** by … その船(艦)は…が船(艦)長だった. ¶***conduct*** *vessels* in and out 船を港内または港外に導く. ¶***employ*** a *vessel* as a transport 船を輸送船として使う. ¶***enlist*** a *vessel* in the Standing Squadron 軍艦を常備艦隊に編入する. ¶***enter*** a *vessel* 船の入港を税関に届ける. ¶***launch*** a *vessel* 船を進水させる. ¶***load*** a *vessel* on the berth 停泊中の船に積荷する. ¶***man*** a war *vessel* with … 軍艦に…を乗込ませる. ¶***moor*** a *vessel* 船をけい留する. ¶***pilot*** a great *vessel* safely to her destination 大船を水先案内してその目指す所へ安着させる. ¶Several steamship companies have ***put,*** or are ***putting,*** larger and faster *vessels* on the route. 三四の汽船会社はさらに大きな, さらに快速の船をその航路につかせたかまたはつかせようとしている. ‖ ***put*** a *vessel* into the water 船を水に浮べる. ¶***refloat*** a sunken *vessel* 沈没船を浮揚させる. ¶***relet*** a *vessel* 船をまた貸しする. ¶***remodel*** an old-type *vessel* 旧式船を改造する. ¶***renovate*** a *vessel* 船を更新する. ¶***scrap*** *vessels* 船をつぶす(解体して材料をそれぞれ利用する). ¶***search*** *vessels* for smuggled goods 船の密輸品を捜す. ¶The *vessel* and cargo were ***seized.*** 船と積荷が捕獲された. ¶The natives have ***stripped*** the *vessel.* 土人たちはその船の付属品を持去った.

V^2 *Vessels* can ***ride*** securely in almost all sorts of weather. 船はどんな天候でも安全に停泊できる. ¶The *vessel* ***steamed*** into (out of) the harbor. その船は入港(出)した.

Q a ***British-built*** *vessel* 英国製の船. ¶a ***formidable*** *vessel* 恐るべき船. ¶that ***ill-fated*** *vessel* その不運な船(難破した船など). ¶to meet a passenger on board an ***incoming*** *vessel* 入港船の船客を出迎えるために. ¶an ***ocean-going*** *vessel* 外洋通いの船. ¶an ***outgoing*** *vessel* 出船. ¶a ***sailing*** *vessel* 帆船. ¶the ***smartest*** *vessel* of the flotila その小艦隊中一番快速な軍艦. ¶a ***stranded*** *vessel* 座礁した船.

Q^2 a ***cargo*** *vessel* 貨物船. ¶a ***coast[ing]*** *vessel* 沿岸貿易船. ¶a ***composite*** *vessel* 鉄骨木造船. ¶a ***deep draft*** *vessel* 深喫水船. ¶a ***deep-sea*** (=***deep-water***) *vessel* 深海船. ¶a ***deportation*** *vessel* [追放者などの]移送船. ¶a ***fishing*** *vessel* 漁船. ¶an ***iron*** (a ***steel***) *vessel* 鉄(鋼)船. ¶a ***light-draft*** *vessel* 浅喫水船. ¶a ***mail*** *vessel* 郵便船. ¶a ***merchant*** *vessel* 商船. ¶a ***paddle-wheel*** *vessel* 外輪船. ¶laws governing ***passenger*** *vessels* 客船に関する諸法令. ¶a ***repatriation*** *vessel* 帰還者輸送船. ¶a ***rescue*** *vessel* 救助船. ¶a ***screw*** *vessel* スクリュー船. ¶a ***steam*** *vessel*=a steamer 蒸気船. ¶a ***war*** *vessel* 軍艦. ¶a ***wood*** *vssel* 木造船.

P the river is navigable ***for*** *vessels* not drawing 10 feet up to … その川は喫水十フィート以下の船舶は…まで航行ができる. ¶a trip ***in*** a *vessel* 船の旅. ¶A case of smallpox was discovered ***on*** the *vessel.* 天然痘の患者が一名船中に発見された. ¶The scene ***on*** the stricken *vessel* was heartrending. その遭難船上の有様は悲惨極まるものであった.

P^2 a *vessel* ***of*** war=a warship 軍艦 ‖ *vessels* ***of*** all kinds and sizes 各種艦船.

(**2**) 器, 容器.

V ***turn*** the *vessel* bottom upward 器を伏せる.

Q^2 a leaky ***tin*** *vessel* 水漏りするブリキの器. ¶the ***weaker*** *vessel* 女.

P^2 a *vessel* ***for*** liquids 液体を容れる器.

(3)〖医〗管.

Q a *capillary vessel* 毛細管. ¶a *lymphatic vessel*〖解〗リンパ管. ¶*sacred vessels* of a temple 寺院の諸聖器.

vest, *n.*《米》チョッキ.

V *wear* a *vest* under a coat 上衣の下にチョッキを着る.

Q^2 a *bullet-proof vest* 防弾チョッキ. ¶a *fancy vest* 変りチョッキ.

P wear a suit *without* a *vest* チョッキなしで洋服を着る.

vest, *v.* 装う; 付与する, 委ねる.

M a Pope *fully vested* 盛装した教皇.

P the management of the Society's affairs shall be *vested in* a Council consisting of ... 本協会の会務処理は…からなる評議員会に委任する ‖ sovereignty *vested in* the people 主権在民. 【類】The Executive power (行政権) shall be *vested in* a President of the United States of America. ¶He is *vested with* authority. 彼は権力を与えられている. ‖ be *vested with* the administration of … …の管理をまかされる.

vestibule, *n.* 玄関, 入口;《米》〖鉄道〗乗務員室.

V^2 a *vestibule leading* to the outside 玄関口.

Q a *spacious mosaic-paved vestibule* 広いモザイク舗装の玄関. ¶one who has a *wide vestibule* of the nose 鼻の下が長い人.

Q^2 a *box-office vestibule* 入場券売場.

P a motorman (conductor) *in* the *vestibule* 乗務員室の運転手(車掌).

P^2 Open-mindedness toward the gospel is the *vestibule to* conversion. 福音に対する虚心たん懐が発心の入門である.

vestige, *n.* 形跡, 名残.

V I *found* no *vestige* of his presence. 彼が居合わせたような形跡は少しも見当らなかった. ¶*have* not a *vestige* of evidence for … …の証拠となるべきものは微じんもない. 【類】The room *has* not a *vestige* of ornamentation (装飾). ¶this will effectually *obliterate* the last *vestige* of a spot which has always been associated with … 必ず…を連想させていた地点の最後の名残がこれで全然消失することになるだろう.

V^2 Of its former glory not a *vestige remains.* その昔の栄華は微じんもその名残を留めていない.

Q She parted with the *last vestige* of clothing. 彼女は一糸まとわぬ身となった.

P *without* a *vestige* of clothing 身に一糸をまとわずに.

P^2 There is not a *vestige of* truth in the report. その報告にはみじんの真実もない.

vestment, *n.* 服.

Q^2 *burial vestments* 葬式の式服.

vet, *n.*《米口》=veteran.

Q^2 *home-coming vets* 帰国(復員)軍人.

veteran, *n.* 老練家;《米》軍人, 老兵.

Q a *disabled veteran* 戦傷した軍人. ¶a *farm-enlisted veteran* 農村出身の勇士. ¶a *war-worn veteran* 戦争で疲れた軍人(戦傷兵など). ¶a *60-year-old veteran* of both World Wars 二回の大戦に出征した六十歳の軍人.

Q^2 an *amputee veteran* 手(足)を切断した軍人. ¶a *combat veteran* who lost his left hand in France フランスで左手を失った歴戦の勇士. ¶a *high-point veteran* 勤務得点の多い兵士. ¶a *Negro war veteran.* 黒人の老兵. ¶an *overseas veteran* 海外勤務の古兵. ¶a *sea veteran* 海の古つわもの, 老練な水夫. ¶a *student war veteran* 学徒出征軍人. ¶a *World War II veteran* 第二次大戦の勇士.

P an organization *of veterans*=a veterans' association 老兵会.

P^2 a *veteran in* the service of education 教育事業の年功者. 【類】*veterans in* the streetcar service 市電に多年勤務した人々.

veto, *n.* 否認; 拒否権; 禁止.

V *cancel* a *veto* 否認を取消す. ¶*have* a *veto* on … …に関し否認権を有する. ¶*interpose* one's *veto* 拒否する. ¶*put* (=*place*) a *veto* on (=upon) the proposal その提案を否認する.

Q The *president's veto* kept the bill from becoming a law. 大統領の拒否権によって同案は法律化しなかった.

Q^2 a *pocket veto*《米》大統領の議案の握りつぶし(国会通過の議案に署名しないこと). ¶a *shadow veto* 影の拒否権(米国国会で, 議案や動議の通過を議員の脅迫などで阻止する行為).

P be rejected *by* a *veto* 拒否権で葬られる. ¶the right *of veto* 否認権.

P^2 the *veto of* the House of Lords 上院の否認権. ¶a *veto on* legislation 立法に関する拒否権.

vex, *v.* 怒らす, 困らす, 悩ます.

M He was *deeply vexed.* 彼は非常に困っていた.

P He was really *vexed about* it. 彼はそのことで本当に怒っていた. ¶I am *vexed at* his idleness. 私は彼の不勉強には業を煮やしている. 【類】He is *vexed at* his failure. ¶He felt very much *vexed with* his students. 彼はその担任の学生のことで大分手を焼いていた. ‖ be *vexed with* worldly cares 俗事にわずらわされる. 【類】*vex* a person *with* questions / feel *vexed with* another *for* … / be *vexed with* a person *for* his laziness.

O I am *vexed* to hear such bad news. 私はそんな凶報を手にして心を傷めている.

vexation, *n.* 立腹, 当惑.

V *cause* (=*occasion*) a person *vexation* 人に腹を立てさせる. ¶*show vexation* 腹を立てる.

Q *manifold vaxations* 様々な悩み.

P *in vexation* of spirit 苦悩して. ¶The matter is full *of vexations.* そのことには種々面倒な点がある. ¶He went mad *with vexation.* 彼は苦悩の結果発狂した.

vexatious, *a.* くやしい.

M *How vexatious* (to have missed the train)! [列車に乗り遅れて]しゃくにさわるったらない.

viable, *a.* 生活力がある.

M be *economically viable* 生活力がある.

vibrant, *a.* 震える.

P The drama is *vibrant with* life all through. その劇は全編生気躍動している. ‖ be *vibrant with* life and energy 生気と活力にあふれている ‖ be *vibrant with* ideas 才気かん発である.

vibrate, *v.* 震動する.

P Their hearts *vibrated to* the speaker's stirring appeal. 彼らの胸は弁士の心を揺るがす演説に沸き立った. ¶*vibrate with* passion (rage, excitement) 激情(など)で震える ‖ pictures *vibrating with* life 生気発らつたる絵.

vibration, *n.* 振動.

V *awake vibrations* in the hearts of his countrymen 彼の同胞の胸にひしひしと迫る.

P^2 20 *vibrations per* second 毎秒二十の振動.

vice, *n.* 罪悪; 不道徳; 悪習, 欠点.

V completely *abandon vice* as a livelihood 悪行(売色・詐欺などを)生活の手段とすることを全然やめる. ¶*contract* a *vice* 悪癖がつく. ¶*have* a *vice* of … …の悪習がある ‖ The horse *has* no *vice.* その馬には悪いくせがない. 【類】He recommended the horse as *having* no *vices.*

V^2 No *vice goes alone.*《格言》ぬれぬ先こそ露をもいとえ.

Q It is not an *American vice* or an American virtue. それは米国人の悪いところでも善いところでもない. ¶*commercialized vice* [売春などの]営利化された悪習. ¶Drunkenness is a *degrading vice.* 飲酒は堕落させる悪習だ. ¶Ingratitude is a *despicable vice.* 忘恩は卑しむべき悪徳だ. ¶Opium smoking is a *harmful vice.* アヘン喫用は有害な悪習である. ¶an *incurable vice* 矯正し難い悪徳. ¶prohibition of *legalized vice* 売春禁止. ¶a *national vice* 国民的悪習. ¶an *odious vice* いとうべき悪徳. ¶Extravagance is her *sole vice.* ぜいたくが彼女の唯一の欠点だ. ¶*sexual vices* 性的罪悪(売色).

P Drunkenness is not *among* his *vices.* 彼には酒癖はない. ¶He is free *from vice.* 彼は悪いことはしない. ¶He is steeped *in vice.* 彼は悪に浸っている. ‖ indulge *in* a *vice* 身を持ちくずす. ¶He is sunk in the depths *of vice.* 彼は悪のどん底に落ちている. ¶give oneself up (=abandon oneself) *to* a *vice* 悪習にふける.

P^2 the *vice of* intemperance 飲酒の悪習.

vice-minister, *n.* 次官.

Q a *parliamentary vice-minister* 政務次官.

P^2 the *Vice-Minister of* Foreign Affairs 外務次官.

vicinity, *n.* 近接, 近所.

Q the affairs of the *immediate vicinity* 隣接地の事情. 【類】live in the *immediate vicinity* of a city. ¶towns in *near vicinity* 近接都市.

Q^2 *Tokyo-Yokohama vicinities* 東京横浜方面.

P *in* his *vicinity* 彼の近所に ‖ the cost of … is *in* the *vicinity* of (=about) … …の費用は…かそこいらである. 【類】*in* Tokyo and [its] *vicinities.*

P^2 in close *vicinity to* … …に近接して.

vicissitude, *n.* 変遷, 盛衰.

V It has *experienced* many *vicissitudes* of fortune. それ

は幾多の消長を経てきた. ¶The city, like human beings, ***had*** its *vicissitudes*. その都市には人間のように盛衰があった. ¶***survive*** the *vicissitudes* of time (thousand of years) 歳月(など)の変遷にたえて残存する. 【類】***survive*** many *vicissitudes*. ¶after ***undergoing*** some *vicissitudes* いくらかの変遷を経てから.

Q undergo ***considerable*** *vicissitudes* 幾多の変遷を経る. ¶after ***many*** (=various) *vicissitudes* 幾多の変遷を経て, 回り回って. ¶pass through ***strange*** *vicissitudes* 数奇な運命をたどる. ¶after ***various*** *vicissitudes* 幾多の変遷を経て.

P ***after*** many *vicissitudes* 幾多の変遷の後. ¶a life marked ***by*** *vicissitudes* 波らんの多い一生. ¶***in spite of*** all *vicissitudes* あらゆる盛衰にかかわらず. ¶It has been ***through*** (=seen) many *vicissitudes*. それは幾多の変遷を経てきた. ‖ pass ***through*** many *vicissitudes* 幾多の変遷を経る.

P² the *vicissitudes* ***of*** life 人生の栄枯.

victim, *n.* 犠牲, 被害者.

V The disease will ***carry off*** its *victims* in a few hours. その病気にかかると二三時間で命を取られる. ¶***entrap*** *victims* 犠牲者をとりこにする. ¶The falcon ***held*** the *victim* in the talons. そのたかがつめで獲物をおさえた. ¶***make*** a *victim* of one 人を犠牲にする. 【類】be ***made*** *victims* of business depression. ¶***offer up*** human *victims* 人身御供をささげる. ¶The *victim* was ***placed*** beyond medical aid. 患者は手遅れになった. ¶Thousands of *victims* were ***sacrificed*** to this disease. 数千の犠牲者がこの病気で死んだ. ¶She was one of the fairest *victims* consumption ever ***seized***. 彼女は肺病で死んだ女性の中で最も美人の一人であった. ¶a robber ***waylaying*** his *victims* かもを待伏せする賊.

Q a ***delighted*** *victim* 喜んでなる犠牲者. ¶become an ***easy*** *victim* of ... 手もなく…の犠牲になる. ¶Thousands of ***innocent*** *victims* suffer. 数千の罪のない犠牲者が苦しむ. ¶this ***poor*** *victim* of starvation この哀れな餓死者. ¶an ***unwary*** *victim* うかうかして犠牲になった者.

Q² an ***amnesia*** *victim* 健忘症患者. ¶a ***crime wave*** *victim* 犯罪の波に乗った犠牲者(青少年の犯罪者など). ¶a ***disaster*** *victim* 災害犠牲者. ¶an ***earthquake*** [disaster] *victim* 地震被害者. ¶a ***frostbite*** *victim* 凍傷患者. ¶a [an ***air***] ***raid*** *victim* 空襲被害者. ¶a ***malaria*** *victim* マラリヤ患者. ¶a ***war*** *victim* 戦争犠牲者. ¶"***white slave***" *victims* 売春業者の犠牲者(売られた白人の女たち).

P² He was a *victim* ***of*** a severe accident. 彼は大惨事の被害者だった. 【類】*victims* ***of*** street accidents (交通事故) ‖ *victims* ***of*** the S.S. Titanic 汽船タイタニック号の遭難者 ‖ I used to be the *victim* ***of*** severe colds. 私は以前よくひどいかぜにかかったものだ. ‖ This left him penniless and a *victim* ***of*** nervous prostration. このために彼は無一文になってそして神経衰弱にかかった. ‖ a *vitim* ***of*** circumstances 環境の犠牲者(不良児など) ‖ You're the *victim* ***of*** your own imagination! それは神経のせいだ ‖ *victims* ***of*** his pen [批評家の]やり玉にあがった人々. 【類】a *victim* ***of*** an indecent assault (風俗壊乱) ‖ a *victim* ***of*** stage-fright 場おくれする人 ‖ *victims* ***of*** misplaced confidence 空頼みを嘆く人々 ‖ The celebrated Dutch East India Company fell the *victim* ***of*** its own maladministration. 有名なオランダ東インド会社はその会社自身の不始末から悲境に陥ったのだ. ¶fall a *victim* ***to*** the charms of a lady 一婦人の色香に迷う ‖ fall a *victim* ***to*** stage-fright 舞台負けがする ‖ fall a *victim* ***to*** one's foolhardiness (passion) 向うみず(など)のために失敗する. 【類】fall a *victim* ***to*** consumption (yellow fever).

victimize, *v.* 犠牲にさせる.

P be *victimized* ***by*** a swindler さぎにかかる. ¶those *victimized* ***into*** listening to his effusion 彼の気炎にあてられた人々.

victor, *n.* 勝利者.

V ***acclaim*** a peron *victor* その勝と軍配を揚げる.

P² the *victor* ***in*** the South African War—Lord Roberts 南アフリカ戦争の勝利者ロバーツ卿. 【類】a *victor* ***in*** a contest. 競技の勝利者.

victory, *n.* 勝, 勝利; 戦勝.

V ***achieve*** an easy *victory* やすやすと勝利を得る. ¶***bring*** *victory* or Westminster Abbey 戦勝かまたは名誉の戦死を遂げる(英人についていう). ¶***buy*** a *victory* cheaply たやすく勝利を得る. ¶to ***celebrate*** the *victory* 戦勝を祝するために. ¶Japan's army ***claims*** *victory* on land. 日本軍は陸上の勝利を期している. ¶***consolidate*** *victories* gained in fighting war 戦果を拡大する. ¶This ***constitutes*** *victory*. これで勝になる. ¶***create*** *victory* out of defeat 敗北を転じて勝利に導く. ¶The *victory* is not yet ***decided***. 勝敗はまだ明らかでない. ¶The team ***disputed*** the *victory* up to the last minute of play. そのチームは競技の終りまでがん張った. ¶It is adequate to ***ensure*** *victory*. それで十分勝利が得られる. ¶***follow up*** the *victory* その勝に乗じる. ¶***gain*** a *victory* by a slim margin きわどい所で勝利を得る. 【類】a *victory* ***gained*** by the Americans under General Washington over the British. ¶***magnify*** *victories* 勝利を誇張する. ¶***obtain*** (=***score***) a *victory* 勝利を得る ‖ He ***obtained*** his first *victory* at the horse show. 彼は馬匹展覧会で始めて受賞した. ¶***secure*** a sweeping *victory* 大勝利を得る. ¶***snatch*** a lucky *victory* 運よく辛勝する. 【類】***snatch*** *victory* from defeat. ¶***win*** an easy *victory* over ... …に対しやすやすと勝利をしめる.

V² the *victory* ***fell*** to ... 勝利は…の手に帰した. ¶a *victory* ***turned*** to defeat [勝利が勝利にならず]失敗に終った勝利.

Q a ***bloodless*** *victory* 血を流さない勝利. ¶a ***brilliant*** *victory* 花々しい勝利. ¶Fashion will never gain a ***complete*** *victory* over nature. 流行は自然に対して完全に勝利を得るものでは決してない. ¶a ***crowning*** *victory* 最大の勝利, 優勝. ¶a ***crushing*** *victory* 圧倒的勝利. ¶a ***decisive*** *victory* 決定的勝利. ¶an ***easy*** (=***easily-won***) *victory* 快勝. ¶a ***diplomatic*** *victory* for ... …に取っての外交上の勝利. ¶it resulted in a ***final*** *victory* for ... それは結局…の勝となった. ¶gain a ***full*** *victory* 完全に勝を得る. ¶a ***glorious*** *victory* 名誉の勝利. ¶to achieve a ***great*** *victory* 大勝利を得るために. ¶a ***hollow*** *victory* むなしい勝利. ¶an ***inglorious*** *victory* 不名誉な勝利. ¶a ***moral*** *victory* 精神的勝利(敗戦でも精神的に収獲が多い場合). ¶The British ***naval*** *victories* over the Dutch in 1653 一六五三年の英国海軍のオランダに対する勝利. ¶gain a ***notable*** *victory* 著しい勝利を得る. ¶a ***Pyrrhic*** *victory* 引合わない勝利. ¶gain a ***sensational*** *victory* over ... …対してすばらしい勝利を得る. ¶win a ***signal*** *victory* 大勝利を得る. 【類】It resulted in a ***signal*** *victory* for the Japanese. ¶a ***splendid*** *victory* 堂々たる勝利. ¶***successive*** *victories* 連勝. ¶a ***sweeping*** (=an ***overwhelming***) *victory* 圧倒的勝利. ¶the ***ultimate*** *victory* 最後の勝利. ¶meet the failure as if it were a ***veiled*** *victory* 失敗を仮面を被った勝利であるかのように考える.

Q² an ***Axis*** *victory* 枢軸側の勝利. ¶***Communist*** *victories* in China 中国における共産党の勝利. ¶a ***landslide*** (=crushing) *victory* 大勝利. ¶a ***leftist*** *victory* in the elections 選挙における左派の勝利. ¶a ***Nazi*** (***Soviet***) *victory* ナチス(ソビエト)の勝利. ¶a ***propaganda*** *victory* 宣伝戦の勝利. ¶a ***Truman*** *victory* トルーマンの勝利.

P puffed up ***by*** *victory* 勝誇って ‖ animated ***by*** *victory* 勝利に元気づいて. ¶Prayers were offered ***for*** our *victory* in the war. その戦争にわれわれが勝利を得るように祈願がかけられた. ‖ "V ***for*** *Victory*" was the motto of Allied powers. 「ビクトリのV」は連合国側の標語だった. ¶the general returned ***from*** his *victories* at ... その将軍は…から凱旋した. ¶There were rejoicings ***over*** the *victory*. 戦勝の祝賀があった. ‖ crow ***over*** the *victory* 勝どきをあげる. ¶crowned ***with*** *victory* 勝利の栄冠を得て.

P² *victory* ***after*** victory 勝利に次ぐ勝利. ¶another *victory* ***against*** malaria マラリヤ征服に対するまた一つの勝利. ¶a *victory* ***for*** Japan 日本の勝利 ‖ *victory* ***for*** Cambridge (Japan, our army) ケンブリッヂ(など)の勝. ¶the Empire's *victory* ***in*** war 帝国の戦勝. ¶Nelson's *victory* ***near*** Trafalgar トラファルガー付近でのネルソンの勝利. ¶These achievements are the *victories* ***of*** peace. これらの功績は平時の勝利である. ‖ the *victory* ***of*** the Allies ***over*** German militarism ドイツ軍国主義に対する連合国の勝利. ‖ win a series ***of*** *victories* 連戦連勝する. ¶the *victory* of right ***over*** might (truth over falsehood, mind over matter) 力に対する正義(など)の勝利. 【類】the Japanese *victory* ***over*** the Russians / *victories* ***over*** self and passion / the *victory* of man (=man's victory) ***over*** nature.

victual, *n.* [通例 *pl.*] 食物, 食料.

P have plenty ***of*** *victuals* 食料が豊富だ ‖ from lack ***of*** *victuals* 食料不足のため.

victual, *v.* 食料を補給す.

P a steamer *victualed* ***at*** Colombo コロンボで食料を補給

した汽船. ¶*victual before* sailing 出帆前に食料を積む.

victualler, *n.* 酒類飲食店主.

Q a *licensed victualler* 《英》 許可を受けた酒類飲食店主.

vie, *v.* 競う.

M *vie successfully* with ... ...と競争して勝つ.

P We all *vied in* paying her attentions. われわれは競って彼女に好意を寄せた. ‖ the town *vies in* opulence with ... その町は富において...に比肩する ‖ *vie in* the praises of ... 競って...を賞賛する. ¶The city *vies with* ... in importance as center of industry. その都市は産業の一中心として...に劣らず重きをなしている. ‖ *vying* one *with* the other (=one anotheer) 互に競争して. 【類】*vie* one *with* another *in* praising ... ‖ Mountains *vie with* one another in lifting themselves to the blue heavens above. 諸峰が相争って青空にそそり立っている. 【類】*vie with* each other trying to ... / *vie with* one another *for* the first place (trophy). ¶The persecutions *vied* in horrors *with* those of the Spanish Inquisition. その(宗教的)迫害はその恐ろしさではスペインの宗教裁判に劣らなかった.

O each one *vies* to see that ... 銘々競って...しようとする.

view, *n.* (**1**) 意見, 見解; 目的; 考察.

V *abandon* one's *views* その意見を捨てる. ¶I do not *accept* this *view* of the present state of affairs. 私は現状に関するこの意見には賛同しない. ‖ All authors have not *accepted* this *view*. この意見は関係著作者がすべて認めている訳ではない. ¶*adopt* another's *views* without reflection 他人の説に雷同する. ¶*advance* a *view* 意見を出す. ¶*advocate* somewhat similar *views* 似たりよったりの意見を唱える. ¶*air* one's *views* on ... ...に関してその意見を述べる. ¶Old *views* are being rapidly *altered* by the progress of science. 科学の進歩によって旧説がどしどし改められつつある. ¶*antagonize* the *views* of ... ...の説に反対する. ¶This *view*, plausible as it may appear, is not *borne out* by facts. この見解は一見もっともらしく思われるかもしれないが事実はこれを証明していない. ¶feed one's fancy and *broaden* one's *views* with new impressions of life 人生の新しい印象を得て想像力を養い知見を広める. ¶*champion* the *view* that ... ...という説を擁護する. ¶*change* one's *views* on a subject ある問題に関して意見を変える. ¶he *combated* the *view* ruling in his day that ... 彼は...という当時有力だった見解に対して抗争した ‖ their *views* are vigorously *combated* by ... 彼らの意見は...によって手強く攻撃されつつある. ¶freely *communicate* one's *views* 腹蔵なくその意見を述べる. ¶strongly *confirm* the *view* that ... ...という説を力強く確証する ‖ this *view* is *confirmed* by the fact that ... この説は...という事実によって確証されている. ¶This *view* he *controverts* with all his power. 彼はこの説を徹頭徹尾論難している. ¶*corroborate* one's *view* 見解を確証する. ¶*disprove* one's *views* その説を論破する. ¶*dispute* his *views* 彼の意見を反ばくする. ¶*disseminate* one's *views* on ... ...に関してその意見を宣伝する. ¶I do not *endorse* this *view*. 私はこの意見に賛同しない. ¶*enlarge* one's *views* 見解を広める. 【類】*enlarge* the *view* of life. ¶*entertain* hopeful *views* 楽観する. ¶*exchange views* on ... ...に関して意見を交換する. 【類】*exchange views* fully and frankly (腹蔵なく率直に) / *exchange views* with leading Japanese (一流の日本人と). ¶*exhibit* a true and correct *view* of the state of affairs of ... ...の事態についての真正な意見を示す. ¶*expound* one's *views* on the subject of ... ...に関する意見を述べる. ¶*express* one's *views* on ... ...に関して意見を開陳する. ¶I am inclined to *favor* the *view* that ... 私は...という説に傾いている. ¶*form* well-grounded *views* regarding ... ...について十分根拠のある説を立てる. ¶I will do all in my power to *forward* your *views*. 私は御意見の行われるように全力を尽しましょう. ¶*get* a distorted *view* of ... ...のゆがんだ見方をする. ¶*give* one's *view* on the subject その問題について意見を述べる. ¶He *has views* of his own. 彼は自分の説を持っている. ¶let me *hear* your *views* on ... ...について御意見を聞かせて下さい. ¶some investigators *hold* the *view* that ... 研究家の中には...という説の人もある ‖ those who may *hold* this *view* forget that ... この説を持っているとしたら...ということを忘れているのだ. ¶*impose* one's *views* on others 他人に自説を押付ける. ¶*keep* the antiquated *view* that ... ...という時代遅れの説を捨てずにいる. ¶*maintain* independent *views* 自分一個の意見を保持する. ¶Will this *meet* your *view?* あなたはこの説に御同意でしょうか. ¶*modify* one's *views* その見方を変える. ¶*obtain* one's *views* その意見をたたく. ¶*offer* one's *views* to the public その意見を公表する. ¶*oppose* one's *views* その説に反対する. ¶*place* one's *view* before ... ...にその意見を述べる. ¶*present* one's *views* to ... ...に献策する. ¶When I first *propounded* this *view* before the Philological Society, it met with opposition. 私が最初この説を言語学会に発表した時に反対された. ¶this *view* was *put* strongly by ... ...がこの意見を強硬に主張した. ¶*put forth* (*forward*) *views* as to the possibility of ... ...の可能性について意見を述べる. ¶The speech accurately *reflects* the *views* of the Government. その演説は政府の意見を正確に反映している. ¶Articles in The Listener do not necessarily *represent* the *views* of the B.B.C. リスナー誌の記事は B.B.C. (英国放送協会) の意見を代表するものとは限らない. ¶I am always ready to *revise* my *views*. 私は(誤りと知れば)いつでも自説を改める考えだ. ¶*set forth* one's *views* on ... ...についてその意見を述べる. ¶*share* his *views* and opinions 彼と意見を同じくする. 【類】I am pleased to find that the author *shares* the *view* which I have myself advocated (唱道してきた) for years. / *share* the *views* of ... on this point. ¶*sound* the *views* of ... ...の意見をたたく. ¶There is little ground in psychological investigation to *substantiate* such a *view*. 心理学者の研究から言うとこうした説にはほとんど根拠がない. ¶facts that *support* (=*back up*) one's *view* その説を支持する諸事実. 【類】this seems to *support* the *view* advocated by him that ... ¶*take* a *view* of ... ...を観察する ‖ *take* the same *view* 同じ意見をいだく ‖ It was decided after the *views* of various authorities had been duly *taken* into account. それは各方面の権威者の諸説を適当に考慮して後決定されたものである. 【類】*take* new *views* of men and things. ¶I'll *tell* you my *views*—some day. 私の意見をお話しましょう—いつか. ¶*tolerate* no other *views* but his own 自説以外は受付けない. ¶*ventilate* one's stalwart *views* その強硬な意見を吐く.

V² That *view* is rapidly *obtaining* here. その意見はここで急速に有力になりつつある. ¶This *view* will finally *prevail*. この説が結局一般に行われるだろう.

Q a man of *advanced* and *liberal views* 進歩的で自由主義の思想を持っている人. ¶have very *adverse views* about ... ...について正反対の意見をもつ. ¶get an *all-round view* of a subject ある問題について融通のきく見方をする. ¶favor the *ancient view* 古来の説に賛成する. ¶express *authoritative* or really *enlightening views* on ... ...に関して権威あるまたは真に進歩的な意見を述べる. ¶present a *biased* or *prejudiced view* 色眼鏡で見たまたは一方に偏した説を持出す. ¶take *bright views* 楽観する. 【類】take *brighter views* of humanity. ¶take a *broad view* of ... ...を大観する. ¶*Broad* and *intelligent views* should be taken of the meaning of education. 教育の意味を広くかつ理知的に解すべきである. ‖ take *broader views* than most people do ... 一般人よりもさらに高所から物を見る. ¶take a *cheerful, happy view* of life 人生を明朗に幸福に見る. ¶entertain *childish views* 子供くさい意見をいだく. ¶take a *chivalrous view* of ... ...を義きょう的に見る. ¶the absence of *clear views* on the nature of ... ...の性質に関する認識不足. ¶get a *closer view* of ... ...をもっと綿密に観察する. ¶take a *comfortable view* of life 楽天的な人生観を持つ. ¶take a *commercial view* of the subject その問題を商業上から見る. ¶hold a *contrary view* to this これと反対の意見を持つ. 【類】a *contrary view* is taken by ... ¶take a *critical view* of the situation 時局を批判的に考察する. ¶take a *cynical view* of humanity 皮肉に人生を見る(世をすねる). ¶take a *dark view* of ... ...を悲観する. ¶Some scholars hold a *different view*. 学者の中にはそれと違った見解を抱くものもある. ‖ men of *different views* 見解を異にする人々. 【類】take a *different view* of the question. ¶take a *distorted view* of religion 宗教に偏見を持つ. ¶widely *divergent views* of ... ...についてのきわめて多岐(ﾀｷ)にわたる諸説. ¶take a more *enlightened view* of the situation 時局に対してもっと進歩的な見方をする. ¶the *evolutionary view* of language 言語に対する進化論的見方. ¶an *exaggerated view* of the danger その危害の誇大視 ‖ a grossly *exaggerated view* はなはだしく誇

張した見方. ¶take an ***extreme*** *view* of ... ...について極端な意見を持つ. ¶a ***fallacious*** *view* 虚偽の説. ¶a ***false*** *view* 虚説. ¶a ***fatalistic*** *view* 運命論者的な説. ¶obtain a ***general*** *view* of the subject その問題を概観する. ¶those who take a ***gloomy*** *view* of affairs 悲観的な見方をする人々. ¶the ***Greek*** *view* of life ギリシア人の人生観. ¶take a ***higher*** and ***broader*** *view* of ... ...を高所大所から見る. ¶take a ***hopeful*** *view* on ... ...に対して有望視する. 【類】take a more ***hopeful*** *view* of ... ¶an ***inside*** *view* of new China 新中国の内幕. ¶take a ***lenient*** *view* of it それを寛大に見る. ¶hold ***liberal religious*** *views* 自由な宗教上の意見をいだく. ¶take the ***lightest*** *view* of ... ...を最も軽視する. ¶take ***long*** (=***long-sighted***) *views* of ... ...将来をどう察する. ¶a very ***low*** *view* of education きわめて低級な教育観. ¶the futility, the meaninglessness of a ***materialistic*** *view* of life 人生を物質的な見方をすることのむだすなわち無意味さ. ¶take a more ***merciful*** *view* もっと同情のある見方をする. ¶arise from a ***mistaken*** *view* as to ... ...についての誤った見解から生じる. ¶hold ***moderate*** *views* 穏かな意見をいだく. ¶According to the ***modern*** *view*, the capital was not very large. 今日の目から見ればそれは大資本ではなかった. 【類】take the ***modern*** *view* of ... ¶a ***morbid*** *view* of life 病的な人生観. ¶those who hold more ***narrow*** and ***conventional*** *views* 一層偏狭で月並な意見をいだく人々. ¶a ***narrow-minded*** *view* of politics and religion 政治・宗教に対する偏狭な見解. ¶the ***normal*** *view* that ... ...という正常な見方. ¶a ***novel*** *view* 目新しい見方. ¶an ***obtuse*** *view* 鈍い観察. ¶the ***old-fashioned*** *view* was that ... 旧式な見方は...であった. ¶in ***one*** *view* it may be considered ... 見方によってそれは...とも考えられる. ¶a ***one-side[d]*** *view* 一方に偏した意見. ¶***opposing*** *views* on the subject その問題に関して相対立する説. ¶hold an ***opposite*** *view* to those of the party in power 与党と反対の説をいだく ‖ take the ***opposite*** *view* of the matter その件について反対の見方をする. ¶take a very ***optimistic*** *view* of the future of ... ...の将来を大いに楽観する. ¶an ***original*** *view* of ... ...の独創的意見. ¶an ***orthodox*** *view* 正統派の説. ¶my ***own*** *view* is that ... 私個人の意見は...である. ¶a ***peculiar*** *view* of ... ...の独特な見方. ¶What I have written represents my own ***personal*** *views*, and is not to be associated in any way with my official position in a Government Department. 私の書いたものは私個人の意見を述べたもので一省の官吏としての私の職務とは少しも関係がないのである. 【類】Every article is signed, and represents simply the ***personal*** *views* of the writer. / to gain a ***personal*** *view* (実地視察のため) of American industries. ¶obtain a ***perverted*** *view* 偏見をいだく. 【類】a ***perverted*** *view* of sexual matters. ¶take a ***pessimistic*** *view* of the outlook (situation) 前途(時局)を悲観する. ¶take a ***philosophic*** *view* of things 万事哲学的な見方をする. ¶a ***plausible*** *view* もっともらしい見解. ¶one's ***political*** *views* その政見. ¶according to the ***popular*** *view* 一般大衆の見方によれば. ¶take a ***practical*** *view* of life 人生を実際的に見る. ¶***professional*** and ***non-professional*** *views* 専門的及び非専門的意見. ¶inculcate a ***profounder*** and a more ***correct*** *view* of ... ...に対し一層深く一層正しい見方を説く. ¶hold ***pronounced*** *views* on social, political, or religious matters 社会・政治・宗教の諸問題についてはっきりした意見をいだく. ¶***radical*** *views* 急進的な思想. ¶***ready-made*** *views* そのまま借りた意見. ¶very ***revolutionary*** *views* きわめて革命的な意見. ¶He seems to believe that his views are the only ***right*** *views*. 彼は自分の意見だけが正しいものだと信じているようだ. ¶one's ***ripest*** *view* その最も円熟した意見. ¶***romantic*** *views* 架空的見解. ¶take a ***roseate*** (=***rosy***) *view* of the situation 時局を楽観する. ¶hold the ***same*** *view* 同じ意見をいだく. ¶a ***sane*** *view* 妥当な意見. 【類】***saner*** *views* of ... ¶It is a very ***sensible*** and ***practical*** *view* to take. それはきわめて賢明な実際的な意見である. ¶***short*** *views* 短見. ¶***shortsighted*** and ***narrow*** *views* 近視眼的で偏狭な見方. ¶hold a somewhat ***similar*** *view* ややそれに類する見方をしている. ¶take a ***sound*** and ***sensible*** *view* of the position 形勢を健全にまた賢明に考察する. ¶take ***strong*** *views* as to ... ...について強硬な意見を持つ. ¶***subversive*** *views* on patriotism, religion, marriage, and the family 愛国主義・宗教・結婚・家庭に関する破壊的見解. ¶a ***superficial*** and ***commonplace*** *view* 浅薄で平凡な観察. ¶This *view* is merely ***tentative***. この説は単に暫定的なものである. ¶the ***traditional*** *view* of his character 彼(歴史的人物)の性格に対する従来の見方. ¶this *view* of the matter, however, is ***true*** only in respect of ... しかしこの考え方は...に関してのみ正しいものである. ¶His *views* are theoretically ***unsound***. 彼の意見には理論的欠陥がある. ¶an ***untenable*** and ***obsolete*** *view* とるに足らない時代遅れの説. ¶***various pessimistic*** *views* are being expressed regarding ... ...について種々悲観説が述べられている. ¶***whimsical*** *views* 気まぐれな意見. ¶take a ***wide*** *view* of the whole matter 全体の問題を大観する. ¶take a ***wider*** and a more ***conscientious*** *view* of its responsibilities to the country 国家に対するそれの責任をより広範的により良心的に考察する. ¶a ***widespread*** *view* 普遍化した説. ¶a ***wild*** *view* 暴論.

Q[2] an ***alarmist*** *view* き憂. ¶a ***cartoon*** *view* of the situation 現状の漫画的見方. ¶take a ***common-sense*** *view* of ... ...について常識的な見方をする ‖ put a British ***common-sense*** *view* on ... ...に関し英国流の常識的な見方をする. ¶according to an ***expert*** *view* 専門家によれば. ¶a ***long-range*** *view* 長期の見通し. ¶a ***middle-of-the-road*** *view* 中庸の意見. ¶one's ***side*** *view* of politics その政治側面観. ¶a ***surface*** *view* 皮相な観察.

P ***according to*** my *view* 私の意見では. ¶***in*** *view* of the fact that ... ...という事実にかんがみて ‖ ***in*** this *view* この見解から言って. 【類】***in*** *view* of what has preceded (前例にかんがみ) it is almost unnecessary to say that ... / ***in*** *view* of those indisputable facts / ***in*** *view* of what is said before. / ***in*** *view* of the gravity (重大性) of the situation / ***in*** *view* of the urgency of the case (事件の緊急性) ‖ I agree with you ***in*** your *views*. 私はあなたと同意見です. ¶from a public point ***of*** *view* 公共的見地から見ると. ¶***on*** this *view* この観察(見解)によって ‖ ***on*** the most hopeful *view*=at best どう楽観しても(精々). ¶***under*** this *view* この見解のもとに. ¶***with*** the *view* of increasing the output 生産増進の目的で ‖ She was educated ***with*** a *view* to becoming a governess. 彼女は家庭教師を目的に教育された ‖ exposition ***with*** a *view* to the subject (reader) 題目(読者)本位の解釈. 【類】receive instruction ***with*** a *view* to becoming ... / ***with*** a *view* to getting some insight (徹底した見方) into ... ‖ ***with*** a special *view* to ... 特に...を目指して ‖ I employed him more ***with*** a *view* to his caution than to his ability. 私は彼をその手腕よりも慎重さを買って採用した. ‖ ***with*** no *view* of success 成功を度外視して.

P[2] a *view* ***against*** the matter ...の問題に対する反対論. ¶hold the same *view* ***as to*** ... ...について同意見をいだく. ¶his *view* ***of*** life 彼の人生観. 【類】Tennyson's *views* ***of*** religion. / an English *view* ***of*** American education ‖ What is your *view* ***of*** the matter? その件について御意見はいかがですか. ¶There are some who hold directly opposite *views* ***on*** this question. この問題に関しては正反対の意見をいだいている者がいくらかある. ¶exchange *views* ***regarding*** ... ...に関して意見を交換する.

(**2**) 眼界; ちょう望, 風景; [視覚的]観察.

V The hill ***affords*** a fine *view* of the city. その丘からは市街のながめがよい. 【類】All the bridges over the Thames ***afford*** fine *views*. ¶***attend*** the private *view* at the Royal Academy 王立美術院展を招待日に観覧する. ¶The *view* was ***blotted out*** by mist (=fog). そのながめは霧でだめになっていた. ¶It ***commands*** an extensive *view* of the town and the seashore. そこは町や海岸をよく見晴らす. 【類】***command*** a *view* of the entire gardens / The *views* of mountain and lake scenery ***commanded*** from the windows of the Hotel are unsurpassed by any in the district. ¶***drink in*** the *view* that it commands そこからのちょう望に見とれる. ¶struggle to ***get*** a good *view* of ... 争って...をよく見ようとする ‖ go higher to ***get*** a better *view* もっとよく見ようとしてさらに高い所に登る. ¶a good *view* of ... and the surrounding country may be ***had*** (=obtained) from ... ...とその付近は...からよく見える. ¶***obstruct*** the *view* ちょう望をさえぎる. ¶A fine *view* of the city can be ***obtained*** from the tower of the City Hall. 同市の公会堂の塔から市中がよく見晴らせる. ¶Observation cars ***offer*** unobstructed *views* of passing landscape. 展

望車は目をさえぎるものなく過ぎゆく景色を見せてくれる. ¶The ships in the bay *present* a beautiful *view*. 湾内の船は美しいながめを見せている. ¶*see* the *view* of ... …の風景を見る. ¶Trees *shut off* (=*out*) *views*. 木がじゃまをして見通せない. ¶*snatch* a momentary *view* of ... …をちらと見る. ¶The gas works *spoil* our *view*. ガス工場があるので見晴らしが台なしだ.

Q an ***admirable*** *view* of ... …のすばらしいながめ. ¶an ***aerial*** *view* taken from high above ... …の高所から見おろしたながめ. ¶In order that we may have a ***better*** *view*, I'll cut down some trees. 見晴らしがよくなるように木を少し切りましょう. ¶representing in ***bird's-eye view*** ... …の鳥かん図をなして ‖ take a ***bird's-eye*** (=***birdman's***) *view* 全局を一目に見る.【類】give the reader a ***bird's-eye*** *view* / can obtain a splendid ***bird's-eye view*** / a charming ***bird's-eye view***. ¶a ***brief*** *view* べっ見; 寸評. ¶take a ***careful*** *view* of ... …を念入りに観察する. ¶a ***close-up*** *view* 大写し. ¶a ***commanding*** *view* ちょう望. ¶command a ***complete*** *view* of Fuji from base to summit (=peak) ふもとからいただきまで富士の全景が見られる. ¶a ***concise bird's-eye*** *view* of men and things 人物及び事物の概観. ¶a ***cross-sectional*** *view* 断面図. ¶a ***delightful*** *view* 楽しいながめ. ¶a ***distant*** *view* of a castle 城の遠景. ¶***entrancing*** *views* うっとりする風景. ¶you may get an ***excellent*** *view* of the city and surroundings, including ... その都市と…を含むその付近の勝景が見られる. ¶an ***exquisite*** *view* 絶景. ¶an ***exterior*** *view* 外観. ¶the ***famous mirrored*** *view* of Fujiyama 名高いさかさ富士の景. ¶A ***fine*** *view* can be obtained from the terrace. その高台からよく見晴らせる. ¶it seems, at ***first*** *view*, to ... それはちょっと見ると…のように思われる. ¶a ***front*** *view* of a house 家の正面図. ¶***front*** and ***back*** *views* 前からの景と後からの景. ¶it gave us a ***full*** *view* of ... それによってわれわれは…の全ぼうを見ることができた ‖ in ***full*** *view* of all the world 世界環視の中に. ¶a ***general*** *view* of the war 戦争の大局. ¶a ***glorious*** *view* 絶景. ¶have a ***good*** *view* of ... …がよく見える. ¶a ***grand*** *view* 壮観. ¶an ***inside*** *view* 内幕. ¶an ***inspiring*** *view* 胸を打つ景色. ¶a ***kaleidoscopic*** *view* of the busy street traffic にぎやかな街頭往来の走馬灯のような風景. ¶the ***lovely*** *view* that lay stretched out before him 彼の前に展開していた美しい景色 ‖ What a ***lovely*** *view* you have here! お宅は何といういい景色でしょう. ¶a ***magnificent*** *view* is obtainable from ... …にはすばらしいながめがある.【類】command ***magnificent*** *views* in every direction. ¶a ***magnificent marine*** *view* すばらしい海景. ¶have a ***momentary*** *view* of ... …をべっ見する. ¶***near*** *views* 近景. ¶an ***obverse*** *view* of the round fan そのうちわの表. ¶a diagram showing as ***one*** *view* ... …の一覧図表. ¶an ***opened-up*** *view* of a typical tea factory showing the interior 内部の構造を示した代表的製茶工場の透視図. ¶an ***overhead*** *view* ふかん図. ¶one will see spread out before one a ***panoramic*** *view* of ... …のパノラマのような景色が眼前に展開するのを見るだろう. ¶a ***perspective*** *view* 遠景. ¶a ***picturesque*** *view* 絵のような風景. ¶a ***pretty*** *view* 美景. ¶a ***private*** *view* 招待日の内見. ¶a ***profile*** *view* 横からのながめ. ¶a ***prospective*** *view* 予想. ¶bring it before the ***public*** *view* それを公衆の眼前に持出す. ¶a ***rear*** *view* 背面図. ¶a ***sectional*** *view* 部分図. ¶a ***side*** *view* 側面図. ¶take in at a ***single*** *view* 一目で見て取る. ¶It affords ***splendid*** *views* seaward. そこは海のちょう望がすばらしい. ¶a ***superb*** *view* of London 壮麗なロンドンの景観. ¶a ***superb marine*** *view* in a frame of bold hills 線の太い小山をわくにした美しい海景. ¶the ***sweetest*** *view* in the world 世界の絶景. ¶the ***three famous*** *views* of Japan 日本三景. ¶a ***top*** *view* ふかん図. ¶It commands an ***unbroken*** *view* of the harbor and bay. そこから港湾の全景を一望の内に収められる. ¶an ***unobstructed*** *view* of ... …のさえぎるもののないながめ. ¶look at a ***whole*** *view* of the town below 眼下に町の風景を見る. ¶a ***wide*** and ***uninterrupted*** *view* 広ばくとしてさえぎるもののない展望.【類】take a ***wider*** *view*.

Q² an ***air*** (=***aerial***) *view* 鳥かん図; 航空写真. ¶a ***close-range*** *view* 近景. ¶a ***close-up*** *view* [映画などの]大写し. ¶the ***end*** *view* of a car 車の縦背面図. ¶a ***lantern*** *view* 幻灯で見せた光景. ¶***moving picture*** (=***cinematograph***) *views* were taken of ... …を活動写真に撮った. ¶the spectacular ***night*** *view* of Niagara Falls めざましいナイヤガラの夜景. ¶***sea*** *views* 海げしき. ¶a ***stereopticon*** *view* 〖光学〗実体鏡による映像. ¶a ***street*** *view* 街頭風景.

P ***at*** one *view*=at a glance 一目で ‖ ***at*** first *view* this would seem to be ... 一見これは…と見えるだろう ‖ The position was the most favorable one ***for*** a good *view* of the procession. その場所はその行列を見るのに最も都合のよい場所であった. ¶disappear ***from*** *view* 見えなくなる. ¶***in*** near *view* 接近して見たら ‖ We came ***in*** *view* of church spire. 教会の尖塔が見えて来た. ¶bring it ***into*** *view* それが見えるようにする ‖ The car came ***into*** *view* round the bend. 自動車は角を曲って見えて来た. ¶the breadth ***of*** *view* 視野の広大(高所大所から物を見ること). ¶keep ***off*** *view* 見せないようにする. ¶The exhibition will be ***on*** *view* until September 30. その展覧会は九月三十日まで公開される. ‖ pictures now ***on*** *view* at the Gallery その美術館に目下陳列中の絵画 ‖ an exhibition now ***on*** *view* in London 目下ロンドンに開催中の博覧会 ‖ ***on*** a closer *view* し細に見ると. ¶***with*** a fine and commanding *view* over the harbor and open sea 美しい港や外洋のちょう望があって.【類】a hotel ***with*** a *view* of the sea ‖ a post card ***with*** the *view* of a town (temple, shrine) 町(など)の風景絵はがき. ¶***within*** *view* of Mt. Fuji 富士山の見える所に.

P² The *view* ***from*** the hill behind the city, across the harbour and over the mountains beyond, is superb. 同市の裏山からの港や遠くの山々のながめは壮大だ.【類】The *view* ***from*** the top extends many miles. / a *view* northward ***from*** London Bridge. ¶a *view* ***in*** the Botanical Gardens その植物園内の一景. ¶A magnificent *view* ***over*** the bay and the town is obtained. その湾内と町のすばらしい景観がながめられる.

view, *v.* 見る, ながめる; 考察する.

M *view* an island ***afar*** 遠い島をながめる. ¶*viewed* ***broadly*** 概観すると ‖ on *viewing* ***broadly*** all the preceding symptoms we observe that ... 前述のすべての徴候を考察してわれわれは…と知る. ¶*viewed* ***critically*** 批判的に見ると. ¶***hypercritically*** *viewed* 酷評すれば. ¶*viewed* ***historically*** 史的考察を下すと. ¶*view* movies ***intelligently*** 理知的な見方で映画を見る. ¶*view* it ***optimistically*** それを楽観する. ¶The proposal is *viewed* ***unfavorably*** by the authorities. その提案は当局から好意をもって迎えられていない.

P They are *viewed* ***as*** models. それらは模範的のものと見られている. ¶*viewed* ***at*** this angle (=in this light) この観点からすれば. ¶*view* the problem ***from*** all angles その問題をあらゆる角度から考究する.【類】The subject is *viewed* ***from*** a new angle. / *viewed* ***from*** a critical standpoint. ¶*view* the matter ***in*** a new light その事件に対して新しい見方をする. ¶*view* it ***through*** an opening 穴からそれを見る. ¶*view* it ***with*** greatest alarm 仰天してそれを見る.【類】*view* it ***with*** suspicion (indifference) ‖ *viewed* ***with*** an unprejudiced eye 公平な目で見て ‖ be *viewed* ***with*** disfavor 毛ぎらいされる ‖ *view* it ***with*** a partial eye 不公平な目で見る.

viewer, *n.* 見る人.

Q² a ***moving picture*** *viewer* 映画を見る人. ¶a ***television*** (=TV) *viewer*=a televiewer テレビ視聴者.

viewpoint, *n.* 見地, 見解.

Q from a ***critical*** *viewpoint* 批判的見地から. ¶an ***historical*** *viewpoint* 歴史的見地. ¶act from a ***localized*** *viewpoint* 地方的見地から行動する. ¶an ***idealistic*** *viewpoint* 理想的見地. ¶from the ***larger*** *viewpoint* さらに広範囲な見地から. ¶study (=investigate) it from the ***practical*** *viewpoint* of dollars and cents 金銭という実際的見地からそれを研究する.

Q² It represents the ***communist*** *viewpoint*. それは共産党の見解を示す. ¶the ***Soviet*** *viewpoint* ソ連の見解.

P ***from*** the (=a) *viewpoint* ***of*** ... …の見地から.

P² their *viewpoint* ***on*** life 彼らの人生観.

vigil, *n.* 徹夜; 寝ずの番.

V ***keep vigil*** 寝ずにいる ‖ ***keep vigil*** over a sick child 病児に徹宵付き添う ‖ Relays of friends and acquaintances ***kept up*** a *vigil* throughout the night. 友人や知人が交替でお通夜をした.

Q keep one's ***onerous*** *vigil* 骨の折れる夜警をする.

P^2 keep *vigil **against*** the thieves 盗難に対して夜警をする.

vigilance, *n.* 寝ずの番; 用心.

V ***elude*** the *vigilance* of the police (=constables) 警官監視の目をくぐる. ¶***excercise vigilance*** 警戒する. 【類】Vessels trading among them had to ***exercise*** extreme *vigilance* to protect both life and property. ¶***keep*** a strict *vigilance* over ... ...の厳重な見張りを続ける. ¶***relax*** one's *vigilance* just a little ちょっと警戒の手をゆるめる. ¶***remit*** one's *vigilance* 警戒をゆるめる.

Q by ***constant*** *vigilance* 絶えず警戒して. ¶It is to be guarded with ***special*** *vigilance.* それは特に警戒を要する. ¶***unceasing*** *vigilance* 不断の警戒.

P watch ***with*** *vigilance* 監視する.

vigo(u)r, *n.* 気力, 活気.

V ***display*** great *vigor* 大元気を示す. ¶***give*** *vigor* to a languid constitution だらけた体を元気づける. ¶***have*** great *vigor* 元気おう盛である. ¶Pruning ***increases*** the *vigor* of a plant. 枝をおろすと木は勢がつく. ¶***lack*** *vigor* 気力がない. ¶He seems never to ***lose*** his youthful *vigor.* 彼はいつも青年の元気を失っていないように見える. ¶***regain*** its *vigor* その元気を回復する. ¶Uutil the last year he ***retained*** a *vigour* of mind and physique that might have been the envy of young men. 最後まで心身ともに壮者をしのぐものがあった.

Q ***barbaric*** *vigor* 蛮勇. ¶***bodily*** *vigor* as yet unimpaired by age まだ年負けのしない体力. ¶***constitutional*** *vigor* 体力. ¶people as yet in the ***full*** *vigor* of youth まだ若盛りの人々. ¶He seems to be in ***full mental*** *vigor* and to enjoy the best of health. 彼は元気発らつとして無上の健康を享有しているように見える. ¶a ***graphic*** *vigor* in his description of ... 彼の...の描写に示す写実力(迫真性). ¶attack one with ***great*** *vigor* 人を盛んに攻撃する. ¶with ***incessant*** *vigor* がん張り通して. ¶a man of ***much*** *vigor* of mind and body 心身共に元気おう盛の人. ¶the ***incomparable*** *vigor* of Kipling's novels キップリングの小説の比類ない筆力. ¶the ***lusty*** *vigor* of youth 青年期のおう盛な元気. ¶of ***marvelous*** *vigor* 驚くほど元気おう盛な. ¶***physical*** *vigor* 体力. ¶a ***momentary*** *vigor* ちょっとの元気. ¶Some of his similes have ***picturesque*** *vigor.* 彼の直喩(ゆ)中には絵画的な力を持っているものがある. ¶***sexual*** *vigor* 性的な力. ¶with ***unabated*** *vigor* 勢力が衰えずに. ¶roughness and ***uncouth*** *vigor* 蛮カラ. ¶***youthful*** *vigor* 青年の元気.

Q^2 ***hair*** *vigor* (=tonic) 養毛剤.

P men ***in*** the full *vigor* of life 男盛りの人々. ¶full ***of*** *vigor* 元気のあふれた. ¶The war continues ***with*** increasing *vigor.* 戦争は破竹の勢いで続いている. ‖ British political life resists cleansing ***with*** all the *vigor* of a dirty little boy.—H.G. Wells. 英国の政界はきたない(腕白)子僧そっくりのがん強さで身を清めることに反抗する.

P^2 the *vigor **of*** youth=youthful vigor.

villa, *n.* 別荘, 別邸.

Q a ***pretentious*** *villa* 堂々たる別荘. ¶a ***suburban*** *villa* 郊外の別荘.

Q^2 a ***lakeside*** (***riverside***) *villa* 湖(河)畔の別荘.

P In the summer he comes often to see us ***at*** the *villa.* 夏になると彼はよく別荘にわれわれを訪ねる.

P^2 the Imperial *villa **at*** Numazu 沼津の御用邸. ¶*villas* ***by*** the seaside 海岸の別荘.

O a *villa* to let (=for rent) 貸別荘.

village, *n.* 村.

Q the ***entire*** *village* 全村. ¶a ***fair-sized*** *village* かなりの大きさの村. ¶his ***natal*** (=***native***) *village* 彼の生れた村. ¶the market in a ***neighboring*** *village* 隣村の市場. ¶an ***obscure little*** *village* 名も知れない小村. ¶a ***quaint old*** *village* 風変りな古い村. ¶a ***retired*** *village* へんぴな村. ¶***straggling*** *villages* 点在する村落. ¶***suburban*** *villages* 郊外の村々. ¶an ***upcountry*** *village* 高地の村.

Q^2 a ***farm*** (=farming) *village* 農村. ¶The region is uninhabited except for a few scattered ***fishing*** *villages.* その地方には二三の小漁村が点在するだけの無人地帯である. ¶a picturesque ***old-world*** *village* 絵のような古風の村. ¶He discovered a ***Stone Age*** *village* 5,000 years old. 彼は五千年の歴史を有する石器時代の村落を発見した.

P a case of plague appeared on July 11th ***at*** the *village* of ... 一疫病患者が七月十一日...村に発生した ‖ live ***at*** a *village* 村に住む. ¶a man ***from*** the same *village* 同じ村から来ている人. ¶There is not ***in*** the *village* a tree or a stone I don't know. 私はその村のことなら一木一草の末に至るまで知らないものはない.

P^2 a *village **near*** ... ...付近の村.

villain, *n.* 悪人, 悪党.

V ***unmask*** (=***expose***) a *villain* 悪人の化の皮をはぐ.

Q a ***consummate*** *villain* 大悪人.

villainous, *a.* 悪漢的な.

M ***mildly*** *villainous* 悪漢じみた.

vindicate, *v.* [非難に対し]弁明する, えん罪をそそぐ.

P *vindicate* a nation ***from*** the calumnies of prejudiced foreigners 偏見の強い外人の非難に対し国のために弁明する ‖ *vindicate* a person ***from*** a charge (crime).

vindication, *n.* 弁護, 擁護.

Q a ***clear*** *vindication* of ... ...の明りょうな弁護.

vine, *n.* つる.

Q a ***climbing*** *vine* 上に伸びるつる. ¶a ***trailing*** *vine* 横にはうつる.

Q^2 a ***squash*** (***melon***) *vine* かぼちゃ(など)のつる. ¶a ***wistaria*** *vine* ふじづる.

P fruits growing ***on*** *vines* つるになる果実.

vintage, *n.* ぶどうの収穫.

Q the output of ***last year's*** *vintage* 昨年度のぶどうの収獲高. ¶wines of ***superior*** *vintages* 最優良ぶどう酒.

violate, *v.* 犯す, 破る.

M ***flagrantly*** *violate* the right はなはだしくその権利を侵害する.

P The law was often *violated* ***by*** the mobs. その法律はよく暴民によって破られた.

O *violate* one's privacy (peace) 人の私的生活(など)を犯す.

violation, *n.* 違犯, 侵害.

Q a ***direct*** *violation* of the law of ... ...法の直接違犯. ¶a most ***flagrant*** *violation* of medical ethics 医師道徳の最もはなはだしい違犯. ¶a ***gross*** *violation* はなはだしい違犯.

Q^2 a ***border*** (=***frontier***) *violation* 国境侵犯. ¶be arrested on charges of ***election law*** *violation* 選挙法違犯のかどで逮捕される. ¶a ***liquor*** *violation* 酒類取締り法違犯. ¶a ***civil rights*** *violation* 人権侵害. ¶a ***safety-code*** *violation* 保安法違犯. ¶a flagrant ***traffic*** *violation* はなはだしい交通規則違反.

P ***in*** *violation* of ... ...に違犯して ‖ act ***in*** *violation* of laws and regulations 法令違犯の行動をとる ‖ ***in*** *violation* of their treaty rights 彼らの条約上の権利を侵害して. 【類】***in*** *violation* of the police ordinances.

P^2 a *violation **of*** an agreement (the regulations) 協定(条例)違反 ‖ Any *violation **of*** the law is to be punished with fines in varying sums. その法律の違反者は(場合により)それぞれの金額の罰金に処せられる.

violative, *a.* 犯している.

P *violative **of*** existing treaty provisions 現行条約の諸条項に違犯した.

violator, *n.* 違反者.

V *Violators* will be ***prosecuted.*** 違反者は処罰せられる.

Q^2 a ***law*** *violator* 違法者. ¶speeders and other ***traffic*** *violators* 速度その他交通違反者.

violence, *n.* 暴力, 暴行.

V ***assuage*** the *violence* of one's suffering その苦悩を緩和する. 【類】***assuage*** the *violence* of wind. ¶***brave*** the *violence* of ... ...の暴力に対抗する. ¶***break*** the *violence* of ... ...の力を殺ぐ. ¶***commit*** no *violence* towards ... ...に対し少しも暴行を働かない ‖ attempt to ***commit*** *violence* on one's person 人体に危害を加えようとする. ¶***do*** a person *violence*=do violence to a person 人に暴行を加える ‖ ***do*** *violence* to one's conscience はなはだしく自己の良心にそむく ‖ ***do*** *violence* to a text 本文に勝手に変更を加える. 【類】***do*** *violence* to the English idiom (the rules of grammar) / ***do*** *violence* to (=rape) a woman. ¶***employ*** *violence* against ... ...に暴行を加える. ¶***meet*** *violence* with violence 暴に報いるに暴をもってする. ¶***offer*** *violence* to ... ...に暴行を加えようとする. ¶***suffer*** personal *violence* 危害をこうむる. ¶***threaten*** *violence* 暴力を加えると言っておどす. ¶***use*** *violence* toward ... ...に暴行を加える.

Q acts of ***atrocious*** and ***brutal*** *violence* 極悪非道な暴行. ¶with ***exceptional*** *violence* 異常な激しさで. ¶by recourse to ***excessive*** *violence* 極端な暴力に訴えて. ¶rage with ***great*** and ***ever-increasing*** *violence* えらい勢いでますます猛り狂う(台風など). ¶by the application of ***a little gentle*** *violence* ちょっとした力を加えることによって. ¶threaten a person with ***physical*** *violence* 人を暴力に訴えるとおどす.

Q^{2} Communist violence flared anew today in Malaya. 現在マレーで新たに共産党の暴力行為がぼっ発した. ¶ large-scale violence 大規模の暴力. ¶ mass violence 集団暴力. ¶ mob violence 暴徒の暴力.

P take ... by violence ...を力づくで取る. 【類】be conquered by violence. ¶ increase in violence 暴威を増す. ¶ different forms of violence 色々の暴行. ¶ resort (=appeal) to violence 腕力に訴える. ¶ with violence 暴力をもって.

P^{2} violence under the influence of sake 酒の上の乱暴.

violin, *n.* バイオリン.

V play the violin バイオリンをひく ‖ play first violin [比ゆ的に]音頭をとる.

P a solo on the violin バイオリン独奏.

virgin, *n.* 処女, 童貞.

Q an immaculate virgin 生娘. ¶ a nubile (=marriageable) virgin 結婚適齢の処女.

virginity, *n.* 処女性, 童貞; 純潔.

V give her virginity to her husband 処女を夫にささげる(初夜を明かす). ¶ lose one's virginity 処女(童貞)を失う. ¶ respect her viginity 彼女の処女性を尊重する. ¶ women who have retained their virginity 処女を通してきた婦人たち.

Q moral virginity 精神的処女性. ¶ physical virginity 肉体的処女性.

P be deprived of her virginity 処女を奪われる.

virility, *n.* 気力, 男らしさ.

V destroy the virility of her people その国民の気力を殺ぐ. ¶ He wasted his youthful virility in purchased embraces. 彼は不品行で青春の精力を消耗した.

Q robust, clean virility たくましく品行方正な男盛り.

P^{2} virility of style 文体の力強さ.

virtue, *n.* 徳; 善行; 美点; 価値; [薬などの]効能.

V accomplish the virtue of making the end well 有終の美をなす. ¶ accumulate virtue 善行を積む. ¶ copy the virtues of ... ...の長所にならう. ¶ corrupt virtue 道徳心を腐らす. ¶ cultivate virtues 徳を修める. ¶ emulate the virtues of a great man 偉人の善行をまねる. ¶ extol the virtues of ... ...の長所を賛美する. ¶ What virtues has that medicine? その薬にどんな効能があるか. ¶ She lost her virtue (=made a false step). 彼女は道に外れたことをした. ¶ make a virtue of necessity やりたくないことを必要と見て進んでやる. ¶ mock virtue 道徳をあざける. ¶ He has perceived the virtue of necessity and bowed gracefully to the inevitable. 彼は必然性の力を認めてその不可避的運命におとなしく従った. ¶ interior views portraying the simple virtues of husbandry and housewifery 倹約や家政という単純な諸徳を叙述した内部的観察. ¶ practice virtue 善行をなす. ¶ promote virtue 徳を高める; 長所を増進する. ¶ retain one's virtue 操を保つ. ¶ reward virtue and punish vice 善行を表彰し悪行を罰する. ¶ secure virtue 美点を獲得する. ¶ spurn the homely virtue of economy 倹約という家庭美徳を軽べつする.

V^{2} In this tiny canvas, all his virtues meet. この小さな絵の中に彼の長所が遺憾なく発揮されている.

Q an artificial virtue 偽善, えせ善行. ¶ Simplicity is a cardinal virtue in writing. 簡潔は作文では基本的価値を持つ. ‖ the cardinal virtues 基本的(七)徳 (justice, faith, prudence, hope, temperance, charity, fortitude). ¶ Loving one's neighbor is a Christian virtue. 隣人愛はキリスト教の徳である. ¶ civic virtues 奉公心. ¶ curative virtues 薬の効能. ¶ cultivation of domestic virtues 家庭上の諸徳の修養. ¶ women of easy virtue 浮気な女. ¶ an old man of established virtue 道徳堅固な一老人. ¶ an estimable virtue 尊重すべき美点(趣味など). ¶ Every virtue is more fair when it appears in a beautiful person. どんな徳行もそれが美ぼうの人の場合はさらにはえて見える. ¶ a false virtue 偽りの善行. ¶ purity and safety of female virtue 婦徳の純潔と安全. ¶ gentler virtues of patience, steadfastness, and devotion 忍耐・着実及び献身という温和な諸徳. ¶ the grave and temperate virtue of a Puritan life 清教徒の生活に現われた厳粛と節制の美徳. ¶ medicine of great virtue 特効薬. ¶ high virtues 高徳. ¶ homespun virtue 日常の諸美徳. ¶ There is little virtue in that medicine. あの薬は余りきかない. ¶ lofty virtues 気高い徳. ¶ a woman of very loose virtue すこぶるふしだらな女. ¶ magical virtues 色々の魔力. ¶ a masculine virtue 男の徳, 剛勇の徳. ¶ medicinal virtues 薬効. ¶ Its holy water has miraculous virtues. その聖なる水は霊験あらたかだ. ¶ a national virtue 国民的美徳. ¶ Self-restraint is a negative virtue. 克己は消極的な徳である. ¶ noblest virtues 最も崇高な諸徳. ¶ He excelled in the private virtues of chastity and temperance. 彼は貞節とか抑制とかの私行上の徳に秀でていた. ¶ He was generally respected for his private and civic virtues. 彼は公私の徳行で一般から尊敬されていた. ¶ professional virtues 職業上の道徳(仁義). ¶ a rare virtue in a poet 詩人としてまれな長所. ¶ social virtues 社交上の徳義 ‖ Patriotism is a high social virtue. 愛国心は崇高な社会的美徳である. ¶ spotless virtue 無きずの徳. ¶ a woman of stern (=flawless) virtue 道徳堅固な女. ¶ The readiness to do that is superb virtue. それを進んでやることは美徳である. ¶ The supreme virtue of the historian is truthfulness. 歴史家の最上の価値は真実である. ¶ women of suspected virtue 品行のいかがわしい女. ¶ talismanic virtues 不思議な効験. ¶ traditional virtues 伝統的な徳. ¶ verbal and practical virtue 言葉の上のまたは実際上の徳.

P They won the day, but only by virtue of hard fighting. 彼らは勝ちはしたが悪戦苦闘によってであった. ‖ by virtue of his strength of will 彼の意志の力によって ‖ by virtue of his ability 彼の手腕で. 【類】by virtue of his authority, office, influence / by virtue of an arrangement between ... / bewitch men by virtue of his soularoma (心の魅力). ¶ fall from virtue 堕落する ‖ stray from virtue 身を誤る, 邪道に陥る. ¶ excel in virtue 徳の高い ‖ in virtue of one's office=ex officio その職権によって ‖ acquired in virtue of the treaty その条約によって取得した ‖ in virtue of the Act of 1870 一八七〇年の法令により. ¶ a man of established virtue 有徳の士 ‖ a woman of virtue 貞婦.

virus, *n.* 〘医〙病原体(ビールス); 害毒.

Q What might be called the attenuated virus of socialism 社会主義の希薄になった害悪とも言うべきもの.

Q^{2} The tiny paralysis virus has not been completely identified. 中風の微少病原体はまだつきとめられていない. ¶ Spanish flu virus スペインかぜのビールス.

P^{2} the virus of smallpox (scarlet fever, rabies) ほうそう(など)のビールス.

visa, *n.* [旅行免状の]査証, 裏書き.

M examine a visa 査証を調べる. ¶ grant a visa for passage between ... ...間の査証を出す.

Q^{2} allow them exit visas from ... ...から出国の査証を彼らに与える. 【類】grant a person an exit visa. ¶ a State Department entry visa (米国)国務省発行の入国査証.

visa, *v.* 裏書きする, 査証する.

M go with a passport properly visaed 正式に査証を受けた旅行免状を持って行く.

visage, *n.* 顔, 容ぼう.

V imposing whiskers that adorn his visage 彼の顔に光彩を添えているいかめしいひげ.

Q brown visages of lascars 東インド人水夫のかっ色の顔.

viscera, *n. pl.* 内臓.

V remove viscera 内臓を取出す. ¶ take the viscera out of ... ...から内臓を取出す.

visé, *n.* =visa.

V obtain visés to passports 旅行免状の裏書をしてもらう.

visé, *v.* =visa [旅券などに]裏書する.

P The passport is visé'd by the Consul. その旅行免状は領事の裏書がしてある.

visible, *a.* 目に見える, 明白な.

M easily visible 容易に見える. ¶ faintly visible かすかに見える. ¶ stars less visible to the naked eye 肉眼には見えにくい星. ¶ become plainly visible はっきり見えてくる. ¶ Some are so small as to be scarcely visible to the naked eye. あまり小さくて肉眼ではちょっと見えないものもある.

P visible for miles around 数マイル四方から見える. ¶ visible from ... ...から見える. ¶ visible to the naked eye 肉眼に見える.

vision, *n.* 視力, 視覚; 幻想; 幻影; 光景.

V Dancing London! What a vision the words call up of life, of movement, of riotous hilarity. 踊るロンドン! その言葉はいかに躍動する生活, 喜々としてさんざめく生活を喚起することか. ¶ The very name conjures up visions. その名を聞いただけで光景がありありと目に浮ぶ. 【類】conjure up in one's mind a vision of ... ¶ try to give one a clearer vision of life 人をして一層明りょうに人生の姿を認めさせる. ¶ have a vision, which revealed to him

… 幻影が現われそれが彼に…を示した. ¶*impair* one's *vision* 視力を弱める, 目を痛める. ¶*see visions* 幻を見る ‖ King David *saw* a *vision* of the Messiah. ダビデ王は救世主を幻に見た. ¶The devout saint *stamps* his inward *vision* of holiness on his outward features. その敬けんな聖者はその聖なる心の姿を外ぼうに現わしている. ¶*warp* one's *vision* 視力をゆがます.

V² A *vision came* to him in sleep. 彼は睡眠中にある幻影を見た. ¶A *vision* of his dead father *met* his gaze. じっと見る彼の目に父の亡霊が映じた. ¶the *vision told* him that … その亡霊が彼に…と告げた. ¶The *vision vanished.* その幻が消えた.

Q a *beatific vision* 幻に見る神のお姿. ¶a *clearer vision* and a deeper insight 一層明りょうな観察と一層深いどう察. ¶an *entrancing vision* うっとりさせる光景. ¶*forward-looking vision* 先見の明. ¶a *keen vision* 鋭敏な視力. ¶clear to his *mental vision* 彼の心眼にありありと見える. ¶a *narrow vision* 短見. ¶He has *normal vision.* 彼の視力は普通だ. ¶he observed with *prophetic vision* some seventy years ago … 彼は約七十年前にその将来をどう察して…と予言した. ¶the *romantic visions* of youth 青春の夢想. ¶a *sane vision* 健実な眼識. ¶have a *wider vision* 一層眼界が広い.

Q² aid *night vision* 夜間の視力を補強する.

P It presented itself *before* the mental *vision.* それが心眼に見えた. ¶*beyond* one's *vision* 視界を越えた. ¶haunted *by visions* 幻影(幽霊)に悩まされて. ¶see the Virgin and Child *in* a *vision* 幻の中にキリストを抱いたマリアを見る ‖ as *in* a *vision* 幻のように ‖ appeared to him *in* a *vision* 彼の前に幻となって現われた. ¶a test *of vision* 視力検定. ¶He sees thing *with* the *vision* of a dreamer. 彼は空想家らしい見方をする.

P² She was a *vision of* delight. 彼女は歓喜そのものであった(非常によろこんだ). ‖ the *vision of* a poet 詩人の空想. 【類】a *vision of* eternal beauty.

visionary, *n.* 夢想家.

Q a *mere visionary* 単なる空想家. ¶Mahomet and other *oriental visionaries* マホメットその他東洋の夢想家.

visit, *n.* 訪問; 参拝; 泊り.

V *cut short* one's *visit* そこそこに辞し去る[訪問の場合など]. ¶It *deserves* a lengthy *visit.* それはゆっく見物する値打がある. ¶*exchange visits* and views with many of the political leaders of Japan 多数の日本一流の政治家と往来して意見を交換する. ¶*expect* a *visit* 来訪を心待に待つ. ¶I *had* a *visit* from him. 私は彼の訪問を受けた. ¶*make* a *visit* to … …を訪問する. 【類】*make* a *visit* of ceremony (儀礼上の) upon … / You have not *made* us a *visit* for a long time. ¶plant a tree in the enclosure to *memorialize* one's *visit* to … その…訪問を記念するために構内に木を植える. ¶*merit* a *visit* 一回の訪問に値する. ¶I *missed* your *visit* very much. 君が来ないので大変さびしかった. ¶*pay* a *visit* to a shrine 神社に参拝する ‖ *pay* a *visit* of sympathy to … [病人など] …に見舞の訪問をする ‖ *pay* a *visit* to Kamakura 鎌倉に遊ぶ. 【類】contemplate (考を持つ) *paying* a *visit* to … / *pay* America a *visit* / I have two more *visits* to *pay.* ¶*postpone* (=*prolong*) one's *visit* 訪問を延ばす. 【類】*prolong* their *visit* until the early part of March. ¶*receive* a *visit* from … …から訪問を受ける. ¶The *visit* was many times *repeated* later. その訪問はその後度々繰返された. ¶*return* (=*repay*) a *visit* [訪問に対して] 答礼に訪問する. 【類】*return* one's *visit* by calling on … ¶It may be well to remember the season characteristics of the place, and *time* (=schedule) one's *visit* accordingly. その土地の季節的特徴を記憶しておいてそれを参考にして訪問の時日を定めることにしたらよかろう. 「ら…までだろう.

V² the *visit* will *extend* from … to … その訪問期間は…か

Q pay the first *after-marriage visit* to a friend 友人に結婚後最初の訪問をする. ¶pay *another visit* to … …をもう一度訪問する. ¶He is now on a *brief visit* to England. 彼は今ちょっと英国へ行っている. ¶pay a *complimentary visit* 儀礼的な訪問をする. ¶a *domiciliary visit* 〖法〗家宅捜査. 【類】receive (pay) a *domicialiary visit.* ¶an *extended visit* 長期にわたる訪問(旅行). ¶pay one's *first visit* to England 英国を初めて訪れる. ¶I spent last Christmas there on a *flying visit.* 急ぎの旅行中この前のクリスマスをそこで過した. ¶pay a *formal visit* to … …を正式に訪問する. ¶He received *frequent visits* from the ghost. 彼はしばしばその亡霊に襲われた. ¶the *ghostly visit* of … to his love …の幽霊のその愛人のもとへの訪問. ¶pay a *hurried* (=*hasty*) *visit* to a place ある場所へ大急ぎの訪問をする. ¶pay one a *long-due visit* とうに訪問しなければならない人を訪問する. ¶receive *many visits* from … …から度々訪問を受ける. ¶have a *nice visit* 気持のよい訪問をする. ¶make *occasional visits* to … …を時折尋ねる. ¶*official visits* 職務上(公式)の訪問. ¶I have *one more visit* to pay. もう一カ所訪問するところがある. ¶a *personal visit* 自らの訪問 ‖ No *personal visits* are allowed. 直接面会謝絶. ¶I've much enjoyed this *pleasant visit.* 《米》あなたとお話できてほんとにうれしい. ¶a *professional visit* [医者の病家回診などの]職務上の訪問. ¶a *protracted visit* 長時間の訪問. ¶He made *repeated visits* to England. 彼はしばしば英国に遊んだ. ¶make *several visits* to … …を数回訪問する. ¶a *short visit* 短期の訪問. ¶a *social visit* 交際上の訪問. ¶make a *spectacular visit* to a shrine [お宮参りなどで]美装して神社に参拝する. ¶pay a *threatening visit* to … …に示威的訪問をする. ¶make *three visits* to … …を三度訪問する. ¶make a *transient visit* to … …をちょっと訪問する.

Q² a *business visit* 用務上の訪問. ¶a mere *chance visit* ほんの気まぐれの訪問. ¶the government sent warships on "*courtesy visits*" to … 政府は儀礼的な訪問旅行に軍艦を…に派遣した. ¶by means of *exchange visit* between … …間でお互に訪問し合って. ¶a *farewell visit* 告別の訪問 ‖ a *farewell visit* of ceremony 儀礼的な告別訪問. ¶a *flying visit* 急ぎの旅行. ¶be on a *good-will visit* to … …への親善旅行[訪問]中である. 【類】go to … for a *good-will visit.* ¶a *group visit* to a museum 博物館の団体参観. ¶a *house-to-house visit* 戸別訪問. ¶an *inspection visit* 視察訪問. ¶a *return visit* 再遊 ‖ pay a *return visit* to … …答礼訪問をする ‖ during his *return visit* その帰省中. ¶pay a *state visit* to the Emperor [国賓として]皇帝を正式に訪問する. 【類】the *state visit* of a king to … / arrived in Tokyo for a two-week *state visit.* ¶make a *surprise visit* to … [予告なしに]…を突然訪問する. 【類】have a *surprise visit* from … ¶He arrived here for (=on) a *three-day visit.* 彼は三日間滞在の予定で当地に来た. ¶a "*trouble-shooting*" *visit*「争議仲裁」の訪れ.

P The bar denies a customer more than one drink *at* each *visit.* その酒場は毎回客に一杯以上の酒は飲ませない. ¶his experience of England *during* his *visit* of 1626–28 彼の一八二六年から二十八年にかけての英国訪問の経験. ¶He has gone *for* a visit of a few days to Ikaho. 彼は数日滞在の予定で伊香保へ出かけた. ‖ He arrived in … *for* a week's *visit.* 彼は一週間の滞在の予定で…に着いた. ¶return *from* a *visit* 外出から帰って来る. ¶pay a round *of visits* in South-Asian countries 南アジア諸国を歴訪する. ¶He left here *on* a *visit* to Tokyo. 彼は東京へ向け当地を出発した. ‖ He is gone *on* a *visit.* 彼は訪問に出掛けた. ‖ while *on* a *visit* to … …へ行く途次に. 【類】George was *on* a *visit* to a farm. / he was absent *on* a *visit* to … ¶Will you oblige me *with* a *visit?* 遊びにお出で下さい. ¶He happened to be in the city *upon* a *visit.* 彼はたまたまその市へ行っていた.

P² pay a short *visit at* one's house その家をちょっと訪問する. ¶The university has been honored by a *visit from* H.M. the Emperor when he was yet a Crown Prince. 同大学は天皇陛下がまだ東宮のころお出でをいただいた. 【類】a *visit from* abroad. ¶on a *visit in* Paris パリーに行っている時. ¶a *visit of* condolence after a fire 火事見舞の訪問. ‖ the *visit of* the King of Saudi Arabia *to* America サウジアラビヤ国王のアメリカ御訪問. ¶*visits to* theatres, balls and evening parties 劇場・舞踏会及び夜会へ行くこと ‖ a *visit to* her paternal home お里帰り ‖ his *visit to* our shores 彼の来朝. 【類】This is my first *visit to* Tokyo. / The Tower, St. Paul's and other resorts which any foreigner after a *visit to* London of even two days would blush (はずかしく思う) to say he had not seen. ¶I came here once for a *visit with* a friend. ここは友人と一度来たことがある. ‖ My *visit with* him lasted two hours. 《米》彼との会見は二時間に及んだ.

visit, *v.* 訪問する；見舞う.

M *visit* ***incognito*** 微行する. ¶The exhibition was ***largely visited.*** その展覧会に多数の来観者があった. ¶The place was ***recently visited*** by a serious volcanic eruption. そこには最近火山の大爆発があった. ¶It was ***severely visited*** last year by an epidemic (hurricane). そこでは去年疫病(など)の惨禍をこうむった. ¶The exhibition was but ***sparsely visited*** by foreigners. その展覧会を見に行った外人はごく少なかった. ¶The two familes *visited* ***together*** (=exchanged calls). 両家は互いに往来した.

P *visit* a person ***at*** his residence 人を自宅に訪問する. 【類】*visit* ***at*** the firm / He was *visiting* ***at*** Zushi. ¶To make matters worse, he was *visited* ***by*** a severe illness. あいにくと彼は重い病気にかかった. ¶*visit* a foreign country ***for*** pleasure or ***for*** study 観光または研究に外遊する. ¶Sins of fathers *visited* ***upon*** (=***on***) the children. 親の因果が子に報いた. ¶After the recital, I *visited* ***with*** the pianist. 《米》リサイタルが終ってからそのピアニストと会談した. ‖ He is *visited* ***with*** retribution. 彼は天罰を受けた. ‖ He threatened to *visit* ***with*** the most rigorous punishment all hostile demonstrations. 彼は一切反対の示威運動を厳罰に処するとおどかした.

visitation, *n.* 訪問；天の配剤.

V ***make*** a house-to-house *visitation* 戸別訪問をする.

Q The whole tragedy seems like one of those ***awful visitations*** which come from time to time to teach the lesson of man's helplessness. 世間には時々災禍が起って人のか弱さを悟らせるのであるがこの惨事もまたこうした恐ろしい災禍の一つかと思われた. ¶a ***dreadful*** *visitation* of famine 恐るべき飢きんの到来.

Q² a ***school*** *visitation* 学校参観.

visiting, *n.* 訪問.

Q² ***door-to-door*** *visiting* 戸別訪問.

visitor, *n.* 訪問者，来観者.

V I ***expect*** a *visitor.* 私の所に訪問者があるはずです. ¶***guide*** a *visitor* about the place 見物人にそこの案内をする. ¶***have*** a *visitor.* 私の所には来客がある. ¶***receive*** *visitors* 客に応接する. ¶***see*** *visitors* 来客に会う. ¶refuse to ***see*** a *visitor* 面会を謝絶する. ¶***show*** *visitors* over a factory 来た人を案内して工場を見せる. ¶***size up*** a *visitor* 訪問客の人物を判定する. ¶It ***strikes*** the Western *visitor* to these shores. それはこの海国を訪問する西洋人に奇異な感じを起させる. ¶It is a place where foreign *visitors* are ***taken*** to see something really Japanese. それは外人客に何かしら真に日本らしいものを見せようとする時に連れて行く所だ. ‖ ***Take*** the *visitor* up to the drawing-room. お客さんを応接間へお通し申せ. ¶*Visitors* are ***welcomed*** at all meetings. どの会にも会員外の方の来会を歓迎します.

V² *visitors* ***flock*** to ... 見物人は…に集まる. ¶*Visitors* ***stream in*** at its many doors. 来観者はその数ある入口から流れ込む.

Q be kindly even to a ***casual*** *visitor* 通り一ぺんの客にも親切である. ¶a ***frequent*** *visitor* at a library よく図書館に出入する人 ‖ a ***frequent*** *visitor* to the inn その旅館の常客. ¶a ***ghostly*** *visitor* 幽霊. ¶***honored*** *visitors* 知名の参観者. ¶***late-staying*** *visitors* 遅くまでいる客. ¶***much-wished-for*** *visitors* 待ちに待っていた来客. ¶***out-of-town*** *visitors* 市外からきた人. ¶a ***passing*** *visitor* 通りすがりの訪問者. ¶***royal*** *visitors* from Norway ノールエイからの高貴の訪問者. ¶some ***stray*** *visitor* ぶらりと訪問した人. ¶a ***tedious*** *visitor* あきあきする客. ¶a great rush of ***trans-Pacific*** *vistors* 太平洋横断客の殺到. ¶an ***unwanted*** (=***unwelcome***) *visitor* 来てもらいたくない来訪者. ¶an ***unwelcome*** *visitor* 喜ばれない来訪者.

Q² a ***business*** *visitor* 商売上の来客. ¶***Coronation*** *visitors* from abroad 戴冠式拝観外来者. ¶***country*** (=***provincial***) *visitors* いなかから来た人. ¶a ***first-time*** *visitor* 始めての訪問者. ¶a ***London*** *visitor* ロンドン訪問の旅行者. ¶meet (=see) ***office*** *visitors* 役所の訪客を引見する. ¶a ***pleasure*** *visitor* 遊覧客. ¶a ***seaside*** (***mountain***) *visitor* [避暑などの]海(山)の客. ¶frequent ***White House*** *visitors* ホワイトハウス(大統領)の常連. ¶a ***winter*** (***summer***) *visitor* 避寒(暑)客.

P² *visitors* ***at*** a garden party at ... …の園遊会の参会者 ‖ *visitors* (=guests) ***at*** the hotel そのホテルの客. ¶*visitors* ***from*** abroad 外国からの客 ‖ polite and courteous to the *visitors* ***from*** other lands 外来客に丁重な. 【類】a *visitor* ***from*** the country (いなか) / *visitors* ***from*** all over the country ¶*visitors* ***to,*** and residents in, London ロンドンの訪問者と在住者 ‖ *visitors* ***to*** the institution 同校参観人. 【類】the *visitors* ***to*** the Imperial Library at Uyeno during the past year numbered ...

visor, *n.* [帽子の]ひさし.

Q a ***curved*** *visor* 曲ったひさし. ¶a ***straight*** *visor* 真すぐなひさし.

vista, *n.* 通景，見通し；予想.

V a train trap ***affording*** an ever-changing *vista* 絶えず変化する展望が得られる汽車の引窓. 【類】The opening between the two rows of trees ***afforded*** a *vista* of the lake. ¶Nothing ***obstructs*** the *vista* of the broad and blue Pacific. 広ばくたる紺ぺきを彩る太平洋の展望をさえぎるものとては何もない. ¶This ***opens*** a new *vista* to the Japanese. これは日本人に新しい見方を教える. ¶***open out*** (=***up***) new *vistas* of the possibilities of ... …の可能性に対して新生面を開く. 【類】***open up*** a new *vista* in the sphere of ... ¶The corridor ***presents*** a long *vista* of open doors to right and left. その廊下は左右に開いたとびらから長い見通しを呈している. ¶Electric wires ***ruin*** the *vista* of a Japanese street. 電線が日本の街路の見通しを台なしにしている.

Q the ***dim*** *vista* of one's childhood 子供のころのおぼろげな追憶. ¶***New*** *vistas* of mountain scenery are being presented at every turn. ぐるぐる回るごとに山容の新しい見通しが現われて来る. ¶offer an ***unbroken*** *vista* ずっと見通しがつく. ¶a ***vague, blurred*** *vista* of the great river その大河のおぼろにかすんだ姿を見はるかす眺望.

P a *vista* ***into*** one of the finest streets in London—Whitehall ロンドンで最も美しい街の一つすなわちホワイトホールの見通し. ¶the *vistas* ***of*** by gone days 昔の思い出.

visualization, *n.* (ありありと)心に描くこと.

Q a ***delightful*** *visualization* of "Alice in Wonderland" in a revue レビューにおける「不思議の国のアリス」のおもしろい夢現化.

visualize, *v.* 心に描く.

M I can ***still*** *visualize* the scene. いまだにその場面が目に浮かぶ. ¶*visualize* it as ***clearly*** as it would actually present itself 実際姿を現わしたかのようにはっきり目にうつる.

vital, *n.* 急所.

P the *vitals* ***of*** the body 身体の急所.

vital, *a.* 死活の.

P It is *vital* ***to*** the success of the scheme. それはその計画のかぎである. 【類】*vital* ***to*** the interests of the society.

vitality, *n.* 活気，活力.

V He ***has*** an exuberant *vitality.* 彼は元気おう盛だ. ¶***lower*** the *vitality* of the whole body 全身の活動力を低下させる. ¶He ***possesses*** inexhaustible *vitality.* 彼は精力絶倫だ. ¶Wheat seldom ***preserves*** its *vitality* beyond the eighth or ninth year. 小麦の種子は八九年以上になると滅多に発芽しない. ¶***reduce*** *vitality* 精力を減退させる. ¶***show*** renewed *vitality* 元気を盛り返す.

Q chicks of ***good*** (***low***) *vitality* 生活力の盛んな(低い)ひよっこ. ¶He has communicated something of ***his own*** *vitality* to his work. 彼の作には生命が打込んである. ¶show ***indomitable*** *vitality* 当るべからざる元気を示す. ¶***splendid*** *vitality* in advanced life 老いてますます盛んなこと，大元気. ¶***tenacious*** *vitality* 粘り強い活力.

P full ***of*** vigor and *vitality* はち切れそうな元気で.

vivacity, *n.* 快活，はつらつさ.

V Though old he still ***retains*** the *vivacity* of a young man. 年を取っているがなお青年のようにはつらつとしている.

Q Her *vivacity* is almost ***boisterous.*** 彼女は快活ではしゃぎ過ぎる.

vivid, *a.* 生々した.

P *vivid* ***in*** one's memory 記憶になまなましい. ¶people *vivid* ***with*** life 生気はつらつとした人々.

vividness, *n.* 躍如；生動.

V The illustrations ***add*** *vividness* to the story. さし絵があるのでその話が生々して来る.

P memories recalled ***with*** the *vividness* of real life まざまざとよみがえる記憶.

P² the *vividness* ***of*** pleasure 生々した楽しみ.

vivisection, *n.* 生体解剖.

V ***practice*** *vivisection* on ... …の生体解剖をする.

vocabulary, *n.* 語い，用語数.

V *acquire* a *vocabulary* 語いを覚え込む. ¶how to *build* a *vocabulary* 語い増加の方法. 【類】*build up* one's *vocabulary*. ¶*denude* the *vocabulary* 語いにある限りの語を並べる. ¶*develop* a *vocabulary* 語いを豊富にする. ¶One's *vocabulary* is greatly *enlarged* by reading. 語いは読書によって大いに増大する. ¶*enrich* one's *vocabulary* 語いを豊富にする. ¶he appears to have *exhausted* his *vocabulary* of uncomplimentary epithets in ... 彼は...の中にその豊富に持つ無作法な言葉の限りを尽したように見える. ¶*extend* (=*increase*) one's *vocabulary* 語いを増す. ¶The *vocabulary* is carefully *graded*. その語いは注意周到に易より難へと順を追っている. ¶He *has* an extensive *vocabulary*. 彼は語いが豊富だ. ¶*improve* a deficient *vocabulary* 不十分な語いを補強する. ¶*introduce* quite a new *vocabulary* on the subject その題目に関する新語を造る. ¶*keep* one's *vocabulary* in ready command 自分の語いを自由に駆使できるようにしておく. ¶The use of slang *narrows* one's *vocabulary*. 俗語を使うとその語いが狭くなる(色々な場合を同じような slang で間に合わすから). ¶He *possesses* a wide *vocabulary* of English words. 彼は英語の豊富な語いを持っている. ¶*widen* one's *vocabulary* 語いを増加する.

Q an *abundant vocabulary* 豊富な語い. ¶a consciously and laboriously *acquired vocabulary* 意識的に苦心して覚え込んだ語い. ¶an *active* (a *passive*) *vocabulary* 活用(認識)しうる語い. ¶a *basal vocabulary* 基本語い. ¶He is possessed of a *copious vocabulary*. 彼は豊富な語いを有する. ¶the *ever-increasing scientific vocabulary* たえず増加している科学用語. ¶have a *fair vocabulary* 相当語を知っている. ¶Your *functional vocabulary* includes the words that you can recall readily and use when you speak or write. あなたの(使える)機能語いは話したり書いたりする時すぐ思い出せる語を含む. ¶a thoroughly *good vocabulary* of every-day words and expressions 日用語及び成句の十分豊富な語い. ¶a *huge English vocabulary* 非常に豊富な英語の語い. ¶an *insufficient vocabulary* 不十分な語い. ¶He has a *larger vocabulary* than you have. 彼は君より語いが広い. ¶have a *large* and *discriminating vocabulary* of adjectives おびただしく多数の形容語を知っている. ¶the *legitimate vocabulary* of a language ある国語の(国語化しない外来語を除いた)正統の語い. ¶He could not express himself fully with the *limited vocabulary* at his command. 彼はその駆使しうる限られた語いでは十分意を通じることができなかった. ¶a *meager vocabulary* 貧弱な語い. ¶a traveller's *minimum vocabulary* 旅行家の(ぜひ知らねばならない)最小限度の語い. ¶a *poetical vocabulary* 韻文の語い(詩語). ¶contribute to a more *powerful vocabulary* 一層強力な語い獲得に役立つ. ¶a scientifically *restricted vocabulary* 学問的に制限した語い. ¶a *rich* (*poor*) *vocabulary* 豊富(貧弱)な語い. ¶*sham-antique vocabulary* 擬古体語い. ¶have a *small vocabulary* 語いが少ない. 【類】a *small vocabulary* of commonly recurring (常用の) words and phrases. ¶a *wide vocabulary* 広い語い.

Q² his *reading* (*writing*) *vocabulary* 彼の読書(作文)に役立つ用語数. ¶Your *recognition vocabulary* is about three times as large as your functional vocabulary. あなたの認識語いは機能語いの約三倍である. ¶the *working vocabulary* of an educated person 教育を受けた(学問のある)人の使用語数.

P rich (poor) *in vocabulary* 語いの豊富(貧弱)な ‖ Pity is a word that has no place *in* his *vocabulary*. 彼はあわれみということを知らない. ¶The extent *of* your *vocabulary* indicates the degree of your intelligence. 君の用語数で君の知能の程度が分かる.

P² a *vocabulary of* terms relating to ... ...に関する語い.

vocalize, *v.* 声に出す.

P The dog *vocalized* his pain *in* a series of long howl. その犬は痛いので何べんも長いうめき声をあげた.

vocation, *n.* 天職; 職業.

V *choose* a *vocation* in life 生業を選ぶ. ¶*claim* a *vocation* of some sort 何かに使ってくれと言う. ¶*discover* one's *vocation* その天職を発見する. 【類】Strange to say, it was not until he was 48 years of age that he *discovered* his true *vocation*. ¶*feel* a *vocation* 天職と感じる ‖ *feel* no *vocation* for ... ...を天職と思わない. ¶find one's *vocation* in life 天職を見出す. ¶*follow* the *vocation* of ... ...の職業に従事する. 【類】*follow* various *vocations*. ¶he *had* little or no *vocation* to ... 彼は...を自分に適した職業とはほとんど考えていなかった. ¶*mistake* one's *vocation* そのつくべき職業を誤る. ¶*ply* their *vocation* (=business) それぞれの職に精を出す. ¶Coal miners *pursue* their dangerous *vocations* underground. 採炭夫は地下で危険な仕事に従事する. ¶*select* a *vocation* 職業を選択する. ¶*take up* the *vocation* of engineering 技術者の仕事を選ぶ.

Q clear signs of *Divine vocation* 天職の明白な証拠. ¶*mechanical vocations* 機械関係の職業. ¶a *paying vocation* 引合う職業. ¶one's *real vocation* その天職. ¶*regular vocations* 本職. ¶choose the *right vocation* 適業を選ぶ.

P Although a physician *by vocation*, he was a botanist by avocation. 彼は本職は医者だがかたわら植物の研究をやっていた. ¶He became famous *in* different *vocations*. 彼は種々の方面で有名になった.

vogue, *n.* 流行, 人気.

V The medicine *enjoys* a tremendous *vogue*. その薬はすごい人気を博している. ¶The Russian novel *has* now the *vogue*. そのロシア小説が今流行している. 【類】Private theatricals (しろうと劇) *have* not at present the *vogue* which they enjoyed at the end of the nineteenth century. 【類】It *had* much *vogue*. ¶*lose* its *vogue* すたれる. 【類】begin to *lose vogue* / *lose vogue* and disappear. ¶The book has *obtained* a great *vogue*. その本は大人気を博した. ¶The word *owes* its *vogue* to a play. その語がはやり出したのはある劇のためである. ‖ *predict* a short *vogue* for ... ...が一時的に流行すると予言する. ¶*regain* its *vogue* また流行し出す. ¶it has *retained* its *vogue* since ... それは...以来ずっと流行している. ¶It *started* a tremendous *vogue*. それはものすごく流行しだした.

Q have a *brief vogue* ちょっとの間はやる. ¶a *distinct* and *growing* "*vogue*" for all things Russian in England 英国におけるロシア物の目に見えてぐんぐん勢を増す流行. ¶The novelist had so *enormous* a *vogue*. その小説家は非常に受けた. 【類】The poems had one *enormous vogue*. ¶At present there is a *great vogue* for pearls. 今真珠が大流行だ. ‖ The novel had a *great vogue* in its day. その小説は当時大いに読まれたものだ. 【類】The custom that had a *great vogue*. ¶*increasing vogue* ますます盛んな流行. ¶a *mere passing vogue* ほんの一時的流行. ¶The theory has most *popular vogue*. その説が一番一般に受けがいい. ¶have a *short vogue* 一時はやる. ¶give a *temporary vogue* to ... ...を一時はやらせる. ¶the *waning vogue* of Byron's poems バイロンの詩の退潮.

P The necktie is one of the kinds most *in vogue*. そのネクタイは一番流行しているものの一つである. 【類】Cycling, motoring, rowing, and yachting are much *in vogue*. / *Jujitsu* is much *in vogue* in foreign countries. / a word now *in vogue* / a word greatly *in vogue* some years ago / it remained *in vogue* until ... / fashions successively *in vogue*. ¶come *into vogue*=be brought *into vogue* 流行し出す. ¶go *out of vogue* すたれる ‖ a style now *out of vogue* 今はすたれた型.

P² in *vogue among* ... ...間に流行している. ¶There is quite a *vogue for* things South American in this country. この国では南米物が大はやりだ. 【類】The *vogue for* Western music concerts is very great in Tokyo at present. ‖ There is a *vogue* at present *for* collectors of art object to sell them off. 美術品収集家の売立てが昨今流行している. ¶It is the *vogue of* the day. それは現代の流行である. ¶It is in *vogue with* fashionable people. それは流行を追う人々の間に人気がある.

voice, *n.* (**1**) 声; 声援.

V It is not so very long since the telepone came to *carry* our *voice* wherever we want to go. 電話ができてわれわれの声が思う所へ伝えられるようになったのはそう昔のことではない. ¶Tears *choked up* her *voice*. 彼女は涙で声が出なかった. ¶*classify voices* according to their timbre 音色に従って声を分類する. ¶*counterfeit* the *voice* of ... ...の声色を使う. ¶*cultivate* the *voice* 音声を鍛錬する. ¶*develop* one's *voice* 音声を発達させる. ¶he *dropped* his *voice* to murmur confidentially that ... 彼は声を落して内証で...とささやいた. ¶I *found* no *voice* to speak. 私は言おうとしたが声が出なかった. ‖ At last I *found* my *voice*. 私は(あっけに取られていた後で)ようやくものが言えるよう

になった. ‖ The prophecy ***found*** a *voice* in his masterpiece. その予言は彼の傑作中に現われた. 【類】It is perhaps natural that the patriotic muse should ***find*** her *voice* in times of war rather than in times of peace. ¶I tried to call out, but my *voice* was ***frozen*** with horror. 私は声を出そうとしたがこわくて出なかった. ¶have ***got*** a pretty good *voice* かなり声がよい. ¶***give voice*** to one's joy よろこびを口に出す. 【類】"...," said I, finally ***giving voice*** to my thoughts / ***give voice*** to one's indignation in saying ... ¶love to ***hear*** my own *voice* 話している自分の声を聞くのを好む ‖ he ***heard*** a *voice* call him "..." 彼はだれか自分に「...」と声をかけるのを聞きつけた. 【類】a *voice* was ***heard*** to say ... ¶All *voices* were ***hushed.*** 声はすべて静まった(あたりがシンとしていた). ¶***imitate*** the *voice* of ... ...の声をまねる. ¶The dog learned to ***know*** his *voice* and to come when he whistled for him. その犬は彼の声を聞き分けて口笛を吹くとやって来るようになった. ¶***lend*** one's *voice* in aid of a bill that closely concerns the welfare of the masses 大衆の厚生に密接な関係のある議案を声援する. ¶***lift up*** (=speak) our *voice* in prayer 声をあげて祈る ‖ ***lift up*** one's *voice* in protest against ... 声を大にして...に抗議する. 【類】***lift up*** (=raise) one's *voice* to be heard better ‖ no *voice* is ***lifted up*** in behalf of the unfortunates who ... ...した不幸な人々のために叫ぶ者がない. ¶***lose*** one's *voice* 声が出なくなる. ¶***lower*** one's *voice* 声を低める. ¶***make voice*** 声を出す. ¶"***make up***" one's *voice* つくり声をする. ¶***Pitch*** your *voice* so that all members of the class can hear you with ease. クラス全体の者が楽に聞けるように高い声で言いなさい. ¶She ***possesses*** a soprano *voice* of unusally fine quality and training. 彼女は並以上にすぐれて訓練されたソプラノののどを持っている. ¶He is so deaf that he cannot hear, however much you ***raise*** the *voice.* 彼は大分耳が遠いから君がいくら声を張り上げても聞えはしない. ‖ too weak to ***raise*** his *voice* 高い声が出せないほど衰弱した ‖ ***raise*** one's *voices* against ... ...排斥の声を揚げる ‖ ***raising*** his *voice* to a high pitch 一段と声を張り上げて. 【類】I could not ***raise*** my *voice* to call to my sister. / No *voice* is ***raised*** in protest (抗議の声). / *voices* ***raised*** in anger. ¶I did not ***recognize*** his *voice.* 私は彼の声と気が付かなかった. ¶***recover*** one's *voice* 口がきけるようになる. ¶***save up*** one's *voice* for an hour later 一時間後の用意に声を節約する. ¶***sink*** one's *voice* 声を落す. ¶***squeak*** a shrill, female *voice* 女のきいきいした声をたてる. ¶***strain*** one's *voice* 声を張上げる. ¶***transmit*** the *voice* by wireless 無線電話で声を伝える. ¶***unite voices*** 声をそろえる. ¶***utter*** a *voice* 声を立てる.

v² a stentorian *voice* ***bellowed*** to them to ... 彼らに向って ...せよとどら声でわめいた. ¶The boy's *voice* "***breaks***" and becomes deeper at puberty. 少年の声は思春期になるといわゆる声変りがして太くなる. 【類】*Voice* ***breaks*** (=***changes***) by emotion or at manhood. ¶His *voice* ***caught.*** 声がのどにつかえた. ¶a *voice* ***came*** from the far end of the room, saying, "..."「...」という声がへやのずっと向の端から聞えて来た. ¶His *voice* does not ***carry*** far. 彼の声はよく透らない. ¶My *voice* has ***come back.*** 声のかれたのがなおった. ¶The *voice* ***cracks*** (=is cracked) at the age of puberty. 思春期になると声変りがする. ¶several *voices* ***exclaimed*** that ... 四五人が...と叫んだ. ¶My eyes were filled with tears, and for a moment my *voice* ***failed*** me. 私は目には涙があふれちょっとの間のどが詰って言葉が出なかった. ¶His *voice* ***faltered.*** 彼の声は曇った. ¶a *voice* ***hailed*** us from ... ...からわれわれに声をかけるものがあった. ¶A harsh *voice* ***jars*** on one's nerves. ざらざらした声は聞いていていらいらする. ¶His *voice* ***rang*** with indignation. 彼の怒声ががんがんと響いていた. ¶The *voices* ***rose*** to a deafening pitch. その声が耳をつんざくほどに高まった. ¶His *voice* ***shook*** (=***quaked, quivered or quavered***) with emotion. 彼の声は興奮で震えていた. ¶His *voice* ***thundered*** in Parliament. 彼の声は議場に鳴り響いた.

Q have an ***agreeable*** *voice* 感じのよい声をもっている. ¶in an ***angry*** *voice* 怒った声で. ¶an ***articulate*** *voice* 明せきな音声. ¶A *voice* bacame ***audible.*** だれかの声が聞えてきた. ‖ Few can speak in *voices* ***audible*** to the back row of the gallery in mammoth auditoriums. 巨大な講堂で階上席の後方まで透る声で話せる人は少ないものだ. ¶an ***authoritative*** *voice* shouted, "..."「...」という命令的な声が叫ばれた. ¶a ***bass*** *voice* 低い太い声, バスの声. ¶She has a very ***beautiful*** singing *voice.* 彼女の歌う声が非常に美しい. ¶a ***cross*** and ***bossy*** *voice* 怒ったどなり声(馭れなどの). ¶say in a ***broken*** *voice* [情が迫って]とぎれとぎれに言う. ¶in a ***cheerful*** *voice* はしゃいだ声で. ¶a woman with a ***clear*** *voice* きれいな声の女. ¶a ***cheering*** and ***chaffing*** *voice* 明朗なからかい半分の声で. ¶the ***clamorous*** *voices* of the supporters of woman's rights 女權擁護者のけんけんごうごうたる叫び. ¶***Contending*** *voices* were heard on all sides. 議論紛糾をきわめた. ¶a ***coaxing*** *voice* ねこなで声. ¶speak in a ***confident, straightforward*** *voice* 自信をもって率直に話す. ¶a ***coarse*** *voice* 耳ざわりな声. ¶a ***croaking*** (=***rusty***) *voice* さびた声. ¶a ***deep bass*** *voice* 胴間声. ¶in a ***deep, gruff*** *voice* 太いあらい声で. ¶His *voice* was ***deep, rolling, resonant.*** 彼の声は太くて雷のようでよく響いた. ¶the ***deep raucous*** *voices* of the Americans アメリカ人の太くてしわがれた声. ¶a ***deep, sonorous*** *voice* 太くて朗々たる声. ¶There was not a ***dissenting*** *voice.* だれ一人反対するものはなかった. ‖ recognize it without a ***dissenting*** *voice* それを異議なく認める. ¶She replied in a ***faint*** *voice.* 女はかすかな声で答えた. ¶speak with a ***feigned*** *voice* 作り声で(声色を使って)話す. ¶a chorus of ***female*** (***male***) *voices* 女(男)声合唱. ¶have a ***fine*** *voice* りっぱな声を持っている. ¶say in a ***firm strong*** *voice* しっかりした強い声で言う. ¶a ***florid*** *voice* あでやかな声. ¶He is younger and his *voice* is ***fresher.*** 彼はもっと若くその声も一層生々している. ¶a ***full*** and ***melodious*** *voice* 豊かな美しい声. ¶the ***gay*** *voices* of young children 子供たちのにぎやかな話し声. ¶a ***gentle*** *voice* やさしい声. ¶The speech was in ***good*** *voice.* その演説は声がよかった. ¶The butler announced the gentleman's name in a ***gramophone*** *voice.* 給仕長がその紳士の名を紋切形の声で通した. ¶a ***gruff*** *voice* 荒い声. ¶in a ***half-suppressed*** *voice* 声を半分殺して. ¶a ***high-pitched*** *voice* 高いかんばしった声. ¶a ***harsh grating*** *voice* ざらざらした耳ざわりな声. ¶in a ***high*** *voice* 高い声で. ¶a ***high*** and ***strident*** *voice* かん高いきーきーした声. ¶a ***hoarse*** *voice* しわがれ声. ¶a ***huge*** *voice* 大声. ¶a ***husky*** *voice* しわがれ声. ¶an ***incisive*** *voice* 鋭い声. ¶a ***large*** *voice* 大声. ¶a ***loud, discordant*** *voice* 高い調子はずれの声. ¶in a ***low*** *voice* 低い声で. ¶He added in a ***lower*** *voice.* 彼は声を落して付け加えた. ¶speak with ***low*** and ***indistinct*** *voice*=mutter 不明りょうな声で言う(つぶやく). ¶a ***magnetic*** *voice* 魅力のある声. ¶a ***magnificent*** *voice* すばらしい声. ¶a ***malicious*** *voice* 意地の悪い声(敵意のある). ¶a ***mawkish*** *voice* むかむかする声. ¶appeal in a ***moving*** *voice* to ... ...に胸を打つ声で訴える. ¶in a ***muffled*** *voice* 声をひくめて(ハンケチなどでおうて). ¶She has a very ***musical*** *voice.* 彼女は非常に音楽的な声を持っている. ¶a ***natural*** (=chest) *voice* 自然の声(地声). ¶a ***penetrative*** *voice* よく透る声. ¶a ***piercing*** *voice* 鋭い声. ¶a ***pleasing*** *voice* 気持のよい声. ¶in a ***quaking*** (=***quavering or quivering***) *voice* 声を震わせて. ¶a ***querulous*** *voice* ぶつぶつ不平を言う声. ¶in a ***quiet*** *voice* 静かな声で. ¶in a ***ragged*** (=harsh) *voice* 荒々しい声で. ¶The ***raucous*** *voice* of the newsboy woke my morning slumber. 私は新聞売子のだみ声に朝目をさましました. ¶a ***resolute*** *voice* said ... ...ときっぱりと言う声がした. ¶a ***resonant*** *voice* よく響く声. ¶a ***rich, powerful*** *voice* 豊かな力のある声. ¶a ***rough*** and ***deep*** *voice* 荒っぽい太い声. ¶a ***sepulchral*** *voice* [うつろに響く]陰気な声. ¶a ***sharp, staccato*** *voice* 鋭くて, 語尾の短い声. ¶They speak with a ***single*** *voice* on matters of ... ...の件について彼らの語ることは意見が一致している. ¶with scarcely a ***single discordant*** *voice* ほとんど満場一致で. ¶a ***small*** *voice* 小さな声. ¶a ***soft, cultivated*** *voice* 柔かいみがきのかかった音声. ¶a ***soft modulated*** *voice* 穏和な声. ¶She speaks with ***soft, well-bred*** *voices.* 彼女は柔かい洗練された声で話す. ¶The possession of a ***sonorous*** *voice* is a very necessary qualification to a public speaker. よく響く声を持つことは演壇に立つ人にはきわめて必要なことだ. ¶a ***squeaky*** *voice* きーきー声. ¶utter a ***startling*** *voice* 突拍子もない声を出す. ¶a ***stentorian*** *voice* 太くて通る声. ¶say in a ***stern*** *voice* きっとした声で言う. ¶the ***still small voice*** 良心の声. ¶a ***strident*** *voice* きーきー声. ¶a ***subdued*** *voice* 調子を落した声. ¶a ***suppliant*** *voice* 哀願する声. ¶say bitter things in a *sweet voice* 美しい声でひどいことを言う. ¶a ***sweet purring voice*** 甘い, 鼻にかかった声. ¶in a ***tearful, trembling voice*** ふるえた泣声で. ¶say in a ***tired voice*** 疲れた声で言う. ¶with a ***trembling voice*** which interpreted her anger 彼女の怒りを示す震え声で. ¶a ***throaty, strained voice*** しわがれた緊張した声. ¶speak with an absolutely ***unanimous voice*** 全く異口同音に言う. ¶"Look out!" cried an ***unknown voice***.「ほらっ」とだれかの声があがった. ¶speak in an ***unsteady voice*** 落着きのない声で言う. ¶a ***veiled voice*** 含み声. ¶say in a ***withering voice*** 聞くものがめ入るような声で言う.

Q^2 a ***head*** (=***falsetto***) ***voice*** 作り声. ¶She possesses a delightful ***mezzo-soprano voice***. 彼女は心持のよいメゾ・ソプラノの声をもっている. ¶the preludings of the mighty ***organ voice*** 強く響くオルガンの序曲演奏. ¶the ***radio voice*** from Japan 日本から放送通信.

P talk ***below*** their *voices* 低い声で語る. ¶gentle ***in*** *voice* 声のやさしい ‖ ***in*** *a voice* that rose above all others 一際高い声で ‖ Are you ***in*** *voice* tonight? [歌手などに]今晩は声の調子はいいですか. ¶shout at the top ***of*** one's *voice* 声を限りに怒鳴る ‖ in a suppressed tone ***of*** *voice* 声を殺して. ¶count ***on*** one's *voice* その声援を当にする. ¶The speaker was ***out of*** *voice*. その弁士は声が十分出なかった. ¶speak ***under*** one's *voice* 低声で話す. ¶discuss the matter, ***with*** *voice* or pen 口や筆でその問題を論じる ‖ I called out ***with*** a loud *voice*. 私は声を大きくして呼掛けた. ‖ ***with*** his *voice* raised in pitch 高調子で ‖ exclaim ***with*** one *voice* 声を合わせて叫ぶ ‖ speak ***with*** one *voice* 異口同音に言う. ¶***without*** a single dissentient *voice* 満場一致で.

P^2 raise one's *voice* ***against*** what one regards as fallacies 誤りと考えることを痛撃する. ¶a *voice* ***at*** the back of the hall said: ... 会場の後の方から…と言う声が聞えた. ¶suddenly he was startled by a *voice* ***from*** behind, crying ... 彼は不意に後から…と叫び声を聞いて驚いた ‖ a *voice* ***from*** heaven commanded him to ... 天に声あり彼に…と命じた. ¶raise a *voice* ***in*** defense of ... …擁護の声を揚げる. ¶*voice* ***of*** authority つるの一声. ¶shout in a *voice* ***of*** thunder 雷のような声でどなる ‖ The journal is the *voice* (=organ) ***of*** the publishing industry. その新聞は出版業者の機関紙である. ‖ [the] *Voice* ***of*** America (=V.O.A.) アメリカの声.

(**2**) 発言権;〘音楽〙[声学の]声, 歌う声;〘文法〙態.

V ***claim*** a *voice* in the matter その件に対し発言権があると主張する. ¶All should ***have*** a *voice* in the matter. 何人もその件について発言権を有すべきだ. ‖ he is entitled to ***have*** a *voice* upon ... 彼は…に発言しうる資格がある ‖ ***have*** little *voice* in the management. その経営には余り発言権がない. 【類】We all ***have*** a *voice* in our government. / ***have*** no *voice* in the decision. ¶She has ***lost*** her *voice*. 彼女は声が出なくなった(声楽家など).

Q ***active*** (***passive***) *voice*〘文法〙能(受)動態. ¶The choice lies with you; yours is the ***determining*** *voice*. その選択は君にかかっている, 君の一言は決定的だ. ¶a ***male*** (***female***) *voice*〘音〙男(女)声. ¶a ***mixed*** *voice*〘音〙混声. ¶she is given a ***preponderant*** *voice* in ... その国は…に対して優越的発言権を与えられている. ¶give it a ***preponderating*** *voice* over others それに優先発言権を与える.

P we are not allowed to have any *voice* ***with respect to*** ... われわれは…については発言を許されていない.

voicing, *n.* 表現.

Q the ***aesthetic*** *voicing* of Japanese civilization 日本文化の美的表現.

void, *n.* 空所; 真空.

V This work is intended to ***fill*** a *void* which has hitherto existed in the philatelist's library. この著書は今日まで切手収集家の参考図書の欠陥を補うために出版したのである. 【類】***fill*** the (this) *void*. ¶His death has ***left*** the *void*. 彼が死んだので欠員ができた. ¶it is calculated to ***supply*** a *void* in ... それは…における欠陥を補うためのものである.

Q an ***aching*** *void* (in one's heart) [愛する人(子)を失って]胸中のせつない空虚. ¶His going away (departure) left a ***sensible*** *void*. 彼がいなくなってさびしい.

P vanish ***into*** the *void* 雲散霧消する. ¶There is still some *void* ***among*** works of this class which remains to be filled. その部門の著書はまだ多少不十分だからそれを補う必要がある.

void, *a.* 空の, 無効の.

P the pass is *void* ***after*** ... パスは…後は無効. ¶be *void* ***by*** reason of legal incapacity 法的には無効である. ¶The story is quite *void* ***of*** foundation. その話は全然根拠がない. ‖ His style is *void* ***of*** affectation. 彼の文体には気どった所がない. 【類】a story *void* ***of*** humanity.

O The contract was declared *void*. その契約は無効と判定された.

volcano, *n.* 火山.

V^2 The *volcano* ***burst*** into eruption. その火山が爆発した. ¶The *volcano* ***seemed*** sleeping for centuries. その火山は数世紀間活動を休止しているように思われた. ¶A *volcano* ***spouts*** flame and lava. 火山は火炎と溶岩を噴出する.

Q an ***active*** *volcano* 活火山. ¶an ***extinct*** *volcano* 死火山. ¶a ***quiescent*** (=***dormant or sleeping***) *volcano* 休火山. 【類】The *volcano* lies ***dormant*** (=***asleep***). ¶a ***submarine*** *volcano* 海底火山.

P^2 a *volcano* ***in*** eruption 爆発中の火山.

volition, *n.* 意志.

P do it ***of*** one's own *volition* それを自分の意志でする.

volley, *n.* 一斉射撃, 連発.

V ***discharge*** a *volley* of bad puns だじゃれを連発する. ¶***fire*** a *volley* 連射する. ¶***fire off*** several *volleys* of small arms 小銃を数回斉射する. ¶Suddenly a *volley* ***roared out***. 突然一斉射撃が始まった.

P fire ***by*** *volleys* 一斉射撃をする. ¶Bullets were poured ***in*** a deadly *volley*. 恐ろしい弾丸が雨あられと発射された.

P^2 a *volley* ***of*** applause われるようなかっさい ‖ a *volley* ***of*** wild cries があがあというわめき声. 【類】a *volley* ***of*** abuses (curses).

volley, *v.* 斉射する.

P *volley* ***at*** ... …に一斉射撃を加える.

volplane, *n.* 滑走.

Q make a ***splendid*** *volplane* from a height of 300 feet 三百フィートの高度からすばらしい滑走下降をやる.

volubility, *n.* 能弁, 喋々(ちょうちょう).

P ***with*** great *volubility* of tongue, he explained ... 彼は…を能弁に説明した.

volume, *n.* (**1**) 巻, 冊; 本.

V ***attain*** its twelfth *volume* with the present issue [雑誌など]今回の発行でその第十二巻に達する. ¶*volumes* ***autographed*** to the owner その持主にあてた著者の署名などのある本. ¶***bring out*** a *volume* on ... …に関する一巻を出す. ¶I ***closed*** the *volume* with regret. 私はその本を(おもしろいので)惜しみながら閉じた. ¶Years have been spent in ***compiling*** this *volume*. この書物の編集に数年を費した. ¶The library ***comprises*** about ... *volumes*. その蔵書は約…巻に上る. ¶***consult*** *volumes* of philosophy 数巻の哲学書を参考する. ¶The subject would ***demand*** a *volume*, not an article. その問題を取扱うとなると一小論文では足りなくて一巻の単行本を要するだろう. ¶A dictionary of proverbs ***deserves*** a *volume* to itself. ことわざの辞書は別に単行本として出せるだけの価値がある. ¶The report ***fills*** a fat *volume*. その報告は部厚な一冊になっている. ¶it might fitly ***form*** a companion *volume* to ... それは正しく…の姉妹編として適当であろう. ¶the portrait chosen to ***head*** this *volume* この巻頭を飾るために選ばれた肖像画. ¶***keep*** the *volume* at one's elbow as an indispensable reference in connection either with reading or with writing 読み書きの際の必要参考書として座右に備えておく. ¶***lay down*** a *volume* [読み終って]書物を下におく. ¶***loan*** a *volume* 本を貸す. ¶The dictionary will ***make*** two stout *volumes*. その辞書は部厚な二巻になる. ¶*volumes* would be ***needed*** to set forth in anything like detail the scope of ... …の範囲を少しく詳細に解説するとどうしても数巻の本になる. ¶***open*** the great *volume* of Nature 自然という大きな書物を開く. ¶***publish*** a slim *volume* of sonnets 薄いソネット集を出版する. 【類】***publish*** a *volume* on ... ¶***Reach*** me *volume* I, if you please. どうぞ第一巻をとって下さい. ¶it would ***require*** a *volume* to deal with ... …を論じるには一巻の本を要するだろう. 【類】It would ***require*** a *volume* to reply fully to this question. ¶***skim over*** a *volume* 書物を飛び読みする. ¶The development of this theme would ***take*** a thick *volume*. この論題を詳説すると大部の書物になることであろう. 【類】it would ***take*** a *volume* to ... ¶***take up*** a *volume* [読むために]書物を手に取る. ¶he ***wrote*** fourteen great *volumes* on ... 彼は…に関して十四巻の大著作をした. 【類】*Volumes* might be ***written*** upon it.

Q an *attractive volume* 人を引きつける書物. ¶*back volumes* of a journal 雑誌の旧号(の合本). ¶*bound volumes* of a magazine 雑誌の合本. ¶a *bright* and *cheery* little *volume* 明るくて楽しい小冊子. ¶a *bulky volume* かさばる本. ¶a *closely-printed volume* of more than seven hundred pages 七百ページ以上ある組のこまかい一巻. ¶in one *compact volume* ぎっしり詰った内容の単行本. ¶the *concluding volume* of his "System of Medicine" 彼の「医学系統」の最終編. ¶a *convenient volume* 手ごろの本. ¶a *dull volume* おもしろくない本. ¶this *elaborate* yet *lucid volume* 込入っているが分かりよいこの本. ¶an *enthralling volume* 人を魅了する本. ¶This is her *first published volume*. これは彼女の出した最初の単行本である. ¶*foregoing volumes* of the series 双書中の既刊書. ¶a *handsome de luxe volume* りっぱな豪華本. ¶a *handy volume* 手ごろな本. ¶two of the *heaviest volumes* which it has been our lot to handle われわれ(書評家)が取扱うことになった一番大部の本の中の二巻. ¶The catalogue is in three *large volumes*. その目録は大冊三巻から成っている. ¶publish it as an *independent volume* それを別冊として出版する. ¶a *massive volume* 大冊な本. ¶*meaty volumes* 内容の豊かな本. ¶a *memorial volume* 記念出版物. ¶*momentous volumes* 重要な本. ¶With the publication of its October issue the magazine begins a *new volume*. その雑誌は十月の発行の分が改巻第一号である. ¶two *odd volumes* of an encyclopaedia 百科全書中の端本二冊. ¶an *out-of-print little volume* 絶版の小著. ¶a more *portable volume* 一層携帯に便利な本. ¶a *portly volume* of 1,200 pages 千二百ページの堂々たる本. ¶a *posthumous volume* 遺著. ¶require a far more *pretentious volume* それよりずっと大きな本でなくては収録されない. ¶It is a *rare volume* suppressed before publication. それは出版前に発売禁止になった珍本である. ¶His magazine articles are now republished in a *separate volume* (=book form). 彼が雑誌に出した論文は現在単行本になっている. ¶The subject is too comprehensive to be treated fully within the compass of a *single volume*. その題目は広範にわたるので一冊の本では論じ尽されない. ¶a *sizable volume* かなり大きな本. ¶a *slender volume* 薄い本. ¶a *slim small volume* 薄くて小さい本. ¶a *stout volume* 部厚い本. ¶a *substantial-sized volume* 大型の本. ¶a *sumptuous volume* 豪華本. ¶a *supplementary volume* 続編. ¶a *tabooed volume* 禁書. ¶a *thick volume* 厚い本. ¶a *thin little volume* 薄っぺらな小本. ¶a *treasured volume* 秘蔵本. ¶an *unfinished volume* 読みさしの本. ¶a *vellum-bound volume* 牛皮紙装てい本. ¶In the dispute was made use of a *whole volume* of adjectival invective. その論争は非難悪態の限りを尽した.

Q² a *companion volume* to ... ...の姉妹編. ¶a *folio volume* 二つ折りの本. ¶its *sister volume* その姉妹編.

P It will be complete *in* four more *volumes*. それはあと四冊で完了するだろう. ‖ combine ... *in* a single *volume* ... を一冊の合本にする ‖ bind the work *in* one *volume* when complete 完成したときそれを製本して一冊の本にする ‖ an encyclopedia *in* many *volumes* 何巻にもなっている百科事典.

P² There were *volumes of* nonsense in the speech. その演説はたわごとだらけであった.

(**2**) 容量, 数量.

V *express* (=*tell or speak*) *volumes* for ... ...を雄弁に物語る, 意味深長である. ¶His anger was *gathering volume*. 彼の怒りは次第につのった. ¶A pipe organ *gives* much more *volume* than an ordinary one. パイプオルガンの方が普通のオルガンよりはずっと音量がある. ¶*increase* her *volume* of tourist travel その国への観光客を増す. ¶*pour out volumes* of abuse 悪口雑言を浴びせる.

Q sing out in *full volume* 力強く歌い出す. ¶rise to a *greater volume* of sound さらに大きな音響となる. ¶the *growing volume* of traffic 増大する交通量. ¶a markedly *increased volume* of tourist trade 観光業の著しい発展 ‖ export in steadily *increasing volume* 着々数量を増している輸出. ¶an *overwhelming volume* 圧倒的な量.

Q² *dollar volume* of retail trade 小売取引のドルでの量. ¶swell its *export volume* southward 南方向け輸出量を増大する. ¶increase the *sales volume* of a store 商店の販売量を増す.

P The imports and exports continue to grow *in volume*. 輸出品も輸入品も引続きその数量を増している. ‖ record-breaking *in volume* of travel 旅行者数における記録破り ‖ a further increase *in* the *volume* of business transacted 取引件数における一段の増加. ¶a voice *of* great *volume* 豊かな声量.

P² the *volume of* manufacture 生産額 ‖ the *volume of* travel on a railroad for a given period 一定時間内の鉄道の交通量(旅客輸送量) ‖ The *volume of* a body equals its mass divided by its density. 〚物理〛物体の容積はその質量を密度で除したものに等しい. 【類】*volumes of* smoke.

volunteer, *n.* 志願兵, 義勇兵.

V *join* the *volunteers* 義勇兵の仲間にはいる. ¶*send out volunteers* to ... ...へ志願兵を派遣する.

Q *one-year volunteers* 一年志願兵.

P² a *volunteer in* a contest [競技の]飛入り.

volunteer, *v.* 進んでことに当る, 志願する.

P² He *volunteered as* special correspondent for the Austro-Italian War. 彼はオーストリア・イタリア戦争の特別通信員を志願した. ¶*volunteer in* the undertaking 進んでその事業に参画する. ¶*volunteer for* service 兵役を志願する.

vomit, *v.* 吐く.

M A chimney *vomits forth* smoke. 煙突から煙が出る. 【類】An active volcano *vomits forth* smoke and lava (溶岩). ¶trains *vomit [out]* crowds of passengers at a terminus 列車が終着駅で乗客の大群を吐き出す.

P *vomit* curses (abuses, insults) *at* ... ...に悪口(など)を浴びせる.

vomiting, *n.* 嘔(おう)吐.

V *cause* (=*induce*) *vomiting* 嘔吐を催させる. ¶*stimulate vomiting* 嘔吐を催させる.

P² a *vomiting of* blood 吐血.

vortex, *n.* 渦.

P He was drawn *into* the *vortex*. 彼はその渦中に巻込まれた. 【類】be drawn *into* the *vortex* of war.

P² the *vortex of* revolution (religious controversies) 革命(宗教の論争)の渦巻.

votary, *n.* 崇拝者, 愛好家.

V the pastime *counts votaries* among ... その遊戯の愛好家の中には...がある. ¶Moving pictures and Western sports *number* their *votaries* by the hundreds of thousands. 映画と西洋風のスポーツの愛好家は数十万を算する.

Q *ardent votaries* of a temple 寺院の熱心な参拝者. ¶an *enthusiastic votary* of ... ...の熱心家. ¶The game of chess has many *keen votaries* in the Metropolis 将棋を熱心にやる人は首都に多数ある.

P² a *votary of* Bacchus 上戸(左きき) ‖ a *votary of* abstinence (vegetarianism) 禁酒(菜食)主義者 ‖ a *votary of* science 科学者.

vote, *n.* 投票, 得票; 選挙権; 表決.

V He was *awarded* an illuminated *vote* of thanks. 彼は装飾文字の感謝状をもらった. ¶*buy* a *vote* 投票を買収する. ¶*call for* a rising *vote* 起立採決を要求する. ¶*cast* one's *vote* for ... ...に投票する ‖ *cast votes* in an election 選挙で投票する ‖ the total number of *votes cast* 投票総数 ‖ The *vote cast* for his opponents was as follows. 彼の反対者の得票数次の通り. ¶*count* the *votes* 投票総数を計算する. ¶*dodge* the *vote* 棄権する. ¶*exercise* one's casting *vote* 決裁投票を行う. ¶*garner* over 1,000 *votes* 千票以上獲得する. ¶*give* (=poll) one's *vote* to ... ...に投票する. ¶*have* the *vote* 表決権を有する ‖ She seems to believe that when women *have* the *vote*, there will be no more war. 彼女は婦人が選挙権を持てば戦争はなくなると信じているようだ. ¶*influence* a great many *votes* in his favor 多数の投票者に働きかけて自分に投票させる. ¶He will *lose* the farmers' *vote*. 彼は農民の投票を失うだろう. ¶*move* the *vote* of thanks from ... to ... ...から...に感謝の意を表する動議を提出する ‖ *move* a *vote* for no confidence 不信任案の動議を提出する. ¶He *obtained* more than 100,000 *votes* over his nearest competitor. 彼の得票は次点者より十万票以上多かった. ‖ He *obtained* a *vote* to non-confidence. 彼は不信任決議を受けた. ¶*pass* a *vote* of thanks on him for ... ...に対し彼に感謝の意を表する動議を提出する ‖ *pass* a *vote* of want (=lack) of confidence against the Government 政府不信任案を可決する. 【類】*pass* a *vote* of confidence in favor of the ministry (内閣). ¶He *polled* (=obtained *or* received) 276 *votes*. 彼は二百七十六票を得た. 【類】Nearly 80,000 *votes* were *polled* for him for mayor. ¶He was the candidate that *received* the greatest number of *votes*. 彼が最高点を得た候補者だ.【類】He ***received*** 45,121 *votes* to 14,601 for Mr. ..., Republican (民主党候補...氏). ¶***reconsider*** a *vote* 投票を再考する. ¶A larger number of the delegates refrained from ***recording*** their *votes*. 多数の委員は投票しなかった. ¶***secure*** 211 *votes* 二百十一票を得る. ¶***sell*** a *vote* 投票を売る. ¶***solicit*** *votes* [選挙で]投票を懇請する. ¶His speeches will ***sway*** *votes*. 彼の演説は投票を左右するだろう. ¶***take*** a *vote* on a motion (the issue, the question) 動議(など)に対して採決を行う ‖ when the judges ***took*** a *vote*, it was found that ... 審査員が決を採って見たら...だということが分かった.【類】a *vote* was ***taken*** by secret ballot (無記名投票) as to ... ¶***use*** one's *vote* intelligently 慎重に投票権を行使する. ¶***win*** a great many *votes* 非常に多数の票を得る.

V² my own *vote* ***goes*** to ... 私は...に賛成する.

Q on the ***affirmative*** *vote* of ... ...を可とする票決によって. ¶a ***cordial*** *vote* of thanks 懇篤な感謝の表決. ¶without a ***dissenting*** *vote* 反対投票もなく(満場一致で). ¶elected by ***direct*** *vote* of the people 国民の直接投票で選ばれた. ¶put it to a ***direct popular*** *vote* それを直接国民投票に訴える. ¶a ***fair*** *vote* 清き一票. ¶when ***important*** *votes* are taken 重要表決を行うとき. ¶cast a ***negative*** *vote* 反対投票をする. ¶the conference decided unanimously, less ***one*** *vote*, to ... その会議は一票を除き満場一致で...を議決した. ¶the meeting passed with a unanimity marred by only ***one dissentient*** *vote* a resolution urging ... その会は...勧告の決議案をわずか一票の反対があっただけで満場一致をもって通過させた. ¶***open*** (***secret***) *vote* 記名(無記名)投票. ¶a ***parliamentary*** *vote* by a woman 婦人の国会議員選挙投票. ¶a ***null*** and ***void*** vote 無効投票. ¶be elected by ***popular*** *vote* 国民投票で選ばれる. ¶***secret*** *vote* with plural entry 無記名連記投票. ¶a ***preliminary*** *vote* 予備投票. ¶***spoilt*** *votes* 無効投票. ¶by the ***unanimous*** *vote* of the assembly その会の満場一致の表決をもって.

Q² The chairman has a ***casting*** *vote*. 議長は決裁投票権を有する. ¶take a ***confidence*** *vote* 信任を表決に付する. ¶***floating*** *votes* 浮動票. ¶seek for the ***labor*** *vote* in the factory section 工場街の労働者の票を求める. ¶draw ***left-wing*** *votes* away from ... ...から左翼の票を引抜く. ¶pass a resolution by a ***majority*** *vote* 多数で決議案を通す.【類】by an overwhelmingly ***majority*** *vote* (圧倒的多数) ‖ result in a ***majority*** *vote* for ... 結局...側の多数得票(票勝ち)となる. ¶poll the ***maximum*** *vote* 最高得票を得る. ¶a ***minority*** *vote* 少数者投票. ¶force a "***no confidence***" *vote* to the floor 不信任案を無理に表決にもって行く. ¶a ***referendum*** *vote* 一般(総員)投票. ¶take a ***referendum*** *vote* on prohibition 禁酒令に関して国民投票を行う. ¶a ***roll-call*** *vote* 指名投票. ¶a ***secret written ballot*** *vote* 記名秘密投票. ¶the ***Socialist*** *vote* against the measure その議案反対の社会党の投票. ¶***standing*** *vote* 起立投票. ¶take a ***strike*** *vote* スト突入を表決する. ¶a ***two-thirds*** *vote* 三分の二の投票[結果]. ¶approval by a ***voice*** *vote* 口頭投票による賛成.【類】pass a bill by a ***voice*** *vote*. ¶fail by a ***tie*** *vote* 同数得票で破れる.【類】The proposal lost by a ***tie*** *vote*. ¶Decisions will be taken by ***two-thirds*** *vote*. 決議案は三分の二の多数得票で決まるだろう.【類】A ***two-thirds*** *vote* is required on important issues (重要問題). ¶The motion was defeated by a ***two-thirds majority*** *vote* 動議は三分の二の多数で票決された. ¶by a ***31 to 11*** *vote* 三十一票対十一票で.

P He was beaten ***by*** one *vote*. 彼は一票の差で敗れた ‖ referendum was defeated ***by*** a *vote* of ... to ... ...その一般投票は...対...で否決された ‖ ***by*** a five-to-four *vote* 五対四の票決によって.【類】He was re-elected (再選された) ***by*** a *vote* of 251 against 150. / The bill was passed (可決) ***by*** a *vote* of 276 to 54. ‖ ***by*** a *vote* concurred in by ... ...の一致の表決をもって ‖ determine a matter ***by*** *vote* (yeas and nays) 表決で賛否を決める. ¶canvass ***for*** *votes* 得票運動をする. ¶***on*** the final *vote* for the adoption of ... ...を可決確定の場合において. ¶put the matter ***to*** *vote* その件を票決に付する. ¶***with*** one dissentient *vote* 一票の反対をもって. ¶***without*** a single dissenting *vote* 一票の反対もなく.

P² cast a *vote* ***against*** ... ...に反対の投票をする. ¶take a *vote* ***by*** ballot 無記名投票で採決する. ¶I cast a *vote* ***for*** a man whom I respected. 私は尊敬している人に投票した. ¶have *votes* ***in*** the election of members of Parliament 国会議員の選挙権を有する. ¶pass a *vote* ***of*** censure on ... ...に関する懲罰決議を可決する ‖ a *vote* ***of*** assent (dissent) 承認(否認)投票 ‖ A *vote* ***of*** thanks was passed to the chair. 議長に対し感謝の決議がなされた. ¶by thirty-three *votes* ***to*** thirty 三十票対三十三票をもって. ¶a *vote* ***upon*** a measure 議案についての表決.

vote, *v.* 投票する, 選挙する.

M *vote* ***intelligently*** and ***conscientiously*** 賢明に良心的に投票する. ¶*vote* ***out*** a measure 議案を否決する ‖ be *voted* ***out*** 落選する. ¶*vote* ***unanimously*** that ... ...ということを異議なく決議する.

M² The suggestion was *voted* ***down*** by a large majority. その提案は大多数をもって否決された.【類】The measure (議案) was *voted* ***down***, six to one. / *vote* ***down*** a resolution. ¶He was *voted* ***in*** by a handsome majority. 彼は相当大きな多数で選出された.

P *vote* it ***above*** the average それを並以上と判定する. ¶*vote* ***against*** him 彼に反対の投票をする ‖ *vote* ***against*** the bill その議案に反対投票をする. ¶*vote* ***at*** an election 選挙投票をする. ¶*vote* ***by*** ballot 無記名投票で票決する ‖ *vote* ***by*** show of hands 挙手をもって表決する ‖ *vote* ***by*** standing (=rising) 起立で表決する. ¶*vote* ***for*** the man of one's choice 好きな人に投票する ‖ urge all whom it may concern to *vote* ***for*** ... 関係者に...に投票することを勧める ‖ *vote* ***for*** a candidate (bill) 候補者(など)に賛成投票をする ‖ I *vote* ***for*** hiking. 《口語》私はハイキングには賛成だ. ¶*vote* ***in favor of*** it それに賛成して投票する ‖ *vote* ***in*** the election ***for*** ... その選挙で...に投票する. ¶*vote* one ***into*** the chair 人を議長に選挙する. ¶*vote* ***on*** a proposal (question) 提案(など)について採決する. ¶*vote* ***upon*** whether or not it should ... それが...することの可否について決を採る. ¶*vote* ***with*** the opposition 反対党と同じ投票をする.

voter, *n.* 選挙人, 投票者.

V ***swing*** *voters* 投票者を動かす.

Q ***in-between*** *voters* どっちつかずの投票者. ¶a ***qualified*** *voter* 有権者.

Q² an ***absentee*** *voter* 不在投票者. ¶a ***pluralist*** *voter* 《英》二つ以上の兼職を有する選挙人(各職ごとに一票を有する). ¶the ***white-collar*** and ***middle*** and ***upper income*** *voters* 勤め人, 中及び上流階層の投票者. ¶bring out ***women*** *voters* 婦人投票者を狩り出す.

P a roll ***of*** *voters* 選挙人名簿.

voting, *n.* 投票.

Q ***hasty*** *voting* 急速の投票. ¶***intelligent*** *voting* よく考えた上での投票. ¶***plural*** *voting* 連記投票. ¶***secret*** *voting* 無記名投票. ¶***single*** *voting* 単記投票.

Q² ***proxy*** *voting* 委任投票.

P elect officials ***by*** *voting* 役員を投票で選挙する.

P² *voting* ***by*** ballot (mail, voice, roll-call) 投票紙(郵便, 発言, 指名)投票. ¶*voting* ***by*** rising (show of hands) 起立(挙手)採決.

vouch, *v.* 証明する.

P I don't *vouch* ***for*** the truth of the report. 私はその報告が事実だという保証はしない. ‖ *vouch* ***for*** the reliability of ... の確実性を保証する ‖ *vouch* ***for*** him 彼の保証人になる.

voucher, *n.* 証票.

Q² a ***cash*** *voucher* 金券. ¶a ***purchase*** *voucher* 商品券.

vouchsafe, *v.* [喜んで]与える, 許す.

P *vouchsafe* a glance ***at*** her 彼女の方をちらと見る.

vow, *n.* 誓, 誓約.

V ***abrogate*** one's *vow* その誓を捨てる. ¶***break*** one's *vow* その誓を破る. ¶***carry*** one's *vow* into execution 誓を決行する. ¶***discharge*** (=***fulfil***) a grateful *vow* 謝恩の誓を果す. ¶***keep*** one's *vow* その誓を守る. ¶***make*** a *vow* that ... ...という誓を立てる.【類】***make*** a *vow* not again to ... ¶***pronounce*** one's solemn *vows* おごそかにその誓を立てる ‖ ***pronounce*** *vows* to God 神に誓願を立てる. ¶***register*** a *vow* of vengeance against ... ...に復しゅうの誓を立てる ‖ ***register*** a *vow* never again to ... これからは決して...しないと心に誓う. ¶***renew*** their *vows* of fidelity to the countess 伯爵夫人に忠誠を尽すという誓を新たに立てる. ¶***take*** a *vow* of chastity 貞節を通すという誓を立てる ‖ ***take*** a *vow*, saying ... ...と言って誓う ‖ He ***took*** the *vows* of the Augustinian order. 彼はオーガスティン派の僧となった. ¶***vow*** a *vow* to be better in the future 将来は慎むと誓を立てる.

Q a ***rash*** *vow* 軽卒な誓. ¶he made a ***solemn*** *vow* that ...

彼は…とおごそかに誓った. 【類】take one's ***solemn vows*** in the following words.

Q^2 take the ***Buddhist vows*** 仏教徒たる誓を立てる. ¶***wedding vows*** [結婚式の]新郎新婦の誓い.

P faithful ***to*** one's *vow* 誓約通りに. ¶***under*** [a] ***vow*** of poverty (virginity, celibacy) [僧など]貧乏(など)を誓って.

vow, *v.* 誓う.

P *vow* vengeance ***against*** the oppressor 圧制者への報復を誓う. ¶he ***vowed to*** God that … 彼は…しようと神に誓った ‖ ***vow to*** oneself 自分に誓う ‖ women ***vowed to*** celibacy [尼など]独身を誓った女.

vowel, *n.* 母音.

Q a ***round vowel*** [o 音のように]口を丸くする母音.

voyage, *n.* 航海, 船の旅; 空の旅.

V ***abandon*** a *voyage* [船が]出航をやめる. ¶***accomplish*** the *voyage* in three days 三日でその航海を終る. ¶***continue*** one's *voyage* to … …へ向けその航海を続ける. ¶***effect*** a *voyage* by steamer from … …から汽船で航海する. ¶The Portuguese ***extended*** their *voyages* beyond it. ポルトガル人はその先まで航行した. ¶We ***had*** a rough *voyage*. われわれは難航であった. ¶***make*** a *voyage* in the ship その船で行く. ¶The ship ***pursued*** her *voyage*. その船は航海を続けた. ¶She will not ***stand*** a long *voyage*. 同船は長い航海にはたえ得ないだろう. 【類】can ***stand*** the *voyage*. ¶Only a few men ***survived*** the *voyage*. その航海で生き残ったものはほんのわずかであった.

Q an ***adventurous*** *voyage* 冒険的な航海. ¶an ***arctic*** *voyage* 北極への航海. ¶I wished him ***bon*** *voyage*. 私は彼に(航海中)御機げんようといった. ¶a ***brief*** *voyage* 短かい航海. ¶have a ***comfortable*** *voyage* 気持ちよい航海をする. ¶an ***eventful*** *voyage* 色々事件のあった航海. ¶on her ***first*** *voyage* その船の処女航海に. ¶He had a ***good*** *voyage*. 彼は好い航海をした. ¶She left here on her ***homeward*** [***bound***] *voyage*. その船は当地を出帆して帰航の途についた. ¶she sailed on her ***initial*** (＝maiden) *voyage* from … その船は処女航海で…を出帆した. ¶***inward*** *voyage* 帰航. ¶a ***lengthy*** *voyage* 長い航海. ¶She arrived at … on her ***maiden*** *voyage*. その船は処女航海で…に着いた. 【類】She is due to make her ***maiden voyage*** on September 26. / … made a ***maiden voyage*** across the Pacific. ¶***out*** and ***home*** *voyages* 往復の航海. ¶a steamer on the ***outward*** *voyage* 往航の汽船. ¶I wish you a ***pleasant*** (***happy***) *voyage*. [航海中]御気げんよう. ¶a ***record-breaking*** *voyage* 新記録を造った航海. ¶a ***rough*** *voyage* 難航海. ¶wish one a ***safe*** *voyage* 人に安全な航海を祈るむねを述べる. ¶make a ***short*** *voyage* 短い航海をする. ¶He received as much as £40 in tips on a ***single*** *voyage*. 彼は一航海でチップを四十ポンドももらった. ¶The boat had a ***smooth*** *voyage*, with only two days of rough sea. その汽船は荒れたのは二日だけで平穏な航海をした. ¶a ***trans-atlantic*** *voyage* 大西洋横断航海.

Q^2 passengers on an ***ocean*** *voyage* 大洋航海中の船客. ¶during the ***return*** *voyage* 帰路の航海中. ¶a ***Stateside*** *voyage* [米人が]米本国行の航海. ¶set out on a ***training*** *voyage* 練習航海の途につく. ¶be sent on a ***trial*** *voyage* to … まで…試運航で派遣される. ¶a ***whaling*** *voyage* 捕鯨航海.

P She was lost off … ***during*** a tempestuous *voyage*. その船は難航中…沖でゆくえ不明になった. ¶***in*** the *voyage* of life 人生の行路で. ¶***on*** her *voyage* out その船の往航で ‖ "Wanted ***on*** the *voyage*." [手荷物のはり札]航海中入用. 【類】"Not wanted ***on voyage***." ‖ he was drowned ***on*** a *voyage* from … to … 彼は…から…への航行中にでき死した. 【類】start ***on*** a *voyage* to … / set out ***on*** (＝***upon***) a *voyage* 航海に出発する ‖ be lost ***on*** the *voyage* 航海中ゆくえ不明となる.

P^2 make a ***voyage across*** an ocean 大洋横断航海をする. ¶***voyage at*** sea 航海. ¶whilst on a ***voyage from*** Hongkong ***to*** Japan 香港から日本への航海中に. ¶my first ***voyage over*** the Pacific 私の最初の太平洋横断航海. ¶the ***voyage of*** life 人生航路. ¶one's ***voyage to*** America アメリカへの渡航.

voyager, *n.* 航行者.

Q^2 an ***air voyager*** 航空旅客. ¶one's ***fellow voyagers*** その同じ航行者など(空路も含む).

vulgar, *a.* 卑俗な.

M ***grossly*** *vulgar* きわめて卑俗な.

P ***vulgar in*** one's speech (posture) 話し振り(姿勢)の野卑な.

vulgarism, *n.* 卑語.

Q an ***English*** *vulgarism* 英語の卑語. ¶a ***fashionable*** (an ***unfashionable***) *vulgarism* 社交場裡(ﾘ)で使える(使えない)卑語. ¶"Dark-complected" for "dark-complexioned" is a ***national*** *vulgarism*. dark-complexioned を dark-complected というのはその国(米国)の卑語だ.

P "Leetle" is ***vulgarism for*** "little." leetle は little の俗語だ.

vulgarity, *n.* 下品, 野卑.

V ***excuse*** my *vulgarity*, but … びろうな話ですが…

Q The ***uneducated*** *vulgarity* of expression. 無教育者の卑俗な言い回し. ¶highly ***tinted*** *vulgarity* はなはだしい俗悪さ.

Q^2 the height of ***bourgeois*** *vulgarity* ブルジョアの俗悪さの骨頂.

vulgarize, *v.* 俗悪にする.

M The scenic beauty has been ***greatly*** *vulgarized* by adbills and posters. 広告ビラやポスターでその景色の美観は大いにそがれた.

vulnerability, *n.* 弱性.

Q ***military*** *vulnerability* 軍事上の弱点.

vulnerable, *a.* [傷を]受けやすい.

P be ***vulnerable to*** temptation 誘惑にかかりやすい. 【類】be ***vulnerable*** (＝open) ***to*** public criticism.

O The Maginot Line proved to be ***vulnerable***. マジノ[要塞]線は結局不落ではなかった.

W

wad, *n.* 柔らかで小さな詰め物; 束; 《米》一束の札.

P He added a few bills ***to*** the *wad*. 彼はその札束に二三枚札を加えた. ¶He plugged his ears ***with*** *wads* of cotton. 耳に綿の詰めものをした. 【類】stuff a hole ***with*** a *wad*.

P^2 a ***wad of*** paper (cloth) 紙(布)の丸めたもの ‖ a ***wad of*** bills 《米》札束 ‖ make ***wads of*** money 《米口》大金をもうける.

wadded, *a.* 詰め物をした.

P He is well ***wadded with*** conceit. 彼は慢心しきっている.

wadding, *n.* 詰めもの.

Q^2 a ***cotton*** (***floss-silk***) *wadding* 綿(真綿)の詰め物.

waddle, *v.* よたよた歩く.

M ***waddle up*** the steps (＝upstairs) [ふとっちょが]よたよた階段をのぼる.

wade, *n.* 徒渉.

P^2 a ***wade in*** a brook 小川の徒渉.

wade, *v.* 徒渉する.

P ***wade across*** a river 川を歩いて渡る. ¶***wade through*** water (snow, sand) 川(など)を歩いて渡る ‖ ***wade through*** slaughter to … 殺りくを行いつつ…に進む ‖ ***wade through*** all that fine print その細字の印刷物に目を通す. 【類】The judge had to ***wade through*** all the documents. / ***wade through*** difficulties.

waft, *n.* 漂い.

P^2 the ***waft of*** incense 芳香の漂い.

waft, *v.* 漂う.

P Falling leaves ***wafted across*** the river ***by*** the breeze. 落葉が風に吹かれて川向うへ飛んできた. ¶songs of birds ***wafted on*** the breezes ***from*** … 鳥の声が微風で…から吹き送られて来た. 【類】a fragrance ***wafted from*** the meadow. ¶The murmurs of voices were ***wafted to*** me on the slight breeze. ささやく声が微風に運ばれて私の耳に聞えて来た.

wag, *v.* 振る; 動かす; 移りかわる.

M Her tongue *wags* a bit too ***freely***. 彼女はちょっと口が軽すぎる. ¶The dog is *wagging* his tail ***slowly***. 犬がゆっくり尾を振っている.

M^2 This is how the world ***wags on***. 世の中とはこんなものだ.

wage, *n.* 賃金, 給料.

V *affect wages* 賃金に影響する. ¶He finds it difficult to properly *apportion* his weekly *wage.* 彼にはその週給の支出を適当に割り当てることがむずかしい. ¶*command* a good *wage* いい給料が得られる. ¶*cut down wages* 賃金を下げる. ¶*dock* men's *wages* [遅刻などの場合]賃金から差引く. ¶*earn wages* 給金を取る. ¶*get* good *wages* 十分な賃金を取る. ¶*have* good *wages* いい賃金をもらっている. ¶*make* (=*obtain*) good *wages* いい給料を取る. ¶*pay* reasonable *wages* 相当な賃金を払う. ¶*raise* one's *wage* その賃金を上げる. ¶*receive* one's weekly *wage* その週給を受取る ‖ Girls do not in many cases *receive* a *wage* that support themselves. 女子は自活もできないほどしか給料を受けていない場合が多い. ¶*seek* higher *wages* もっと高い給料を求める. ¶*set* the 12,000-yen "standard *wage*" 一万二千円標準賃金を決める. ¶*supplement* a *wage* on which one may not be able to live in comfort 余裕ある生活のできないような給料の補いをする.

Q an *adequate* living *wage* 相応の生活を支えるに足る賃金. ¶*annual wage* guaranteed 年額賃金制の保証. ¶*daily wages* 日給. ¶A first-class hand, she can earn, for a woman, a *decent wage.* 彼女は一流の女工だから女にしてはかなりの給料を取る. ¶earn a *fair wage* かなりの給料を取る. ¶*fine wage* 結構な給料. ¶at *good wages* いい給料で. ¶for *half wages* 半額の給料で. ¶have *high wages* 高給を受けている. ¶at *low wages* 安い賃金で. ¶a *lucrative wage* 割りのよい賃金. ¶supplement one's *meager wage* その薄給を補う. ¶a *minimum wage* 最低賃金. ¶*monthly wages* 月給. ¶a *nominal wage* 名目賃金. 【類】only *nominal wages* attached to their posts. ¶*overboosted wages* 釣り上げた賃金. ¶the *prevailing wage* 一般職種別賃金 (P.W. と略す). ¶the *real wage* 実質賃金. ¶artisans earning a *regular* and *decent wage* 相当な定給を得ている職工. ¶a *weekly wage* of $50 週給五十ドル.

Q^2 *board wages* 食費・宿泊手当; 食費・宿泊がやっとできる程度の賃金. ¶a *living wage* 生活賃金. 【類】content with a *living wage* / hardly receive a *living wage* / a job that would pay a *living wage* / adequate *living wages.* ¶the *starvation wages* he receives from the sweater 強欲な雇主からもらう食うや食わずの低賃金. ¶a *subsistence wage* 生活給. ¶"*take home*" *wages* 手取り賃金. ¶*war wages* 戦時特別賃金.

P work *at* a *wage* of ... …の給料で働く. ¶strike *for* higher *wages* 賃金値上を要求してストをやる. 【類】one who works *for wages*=a wageworker. ¶a sudden rise *in wages* 突然の給料引上げ. ¶The scale *of wages* (=The wage scale) is not high. 賃金率は高くない ‖ demand a higher rate *of wages* もっと高率の給料を要求する. ¶Can you get along *on* your *wages*? 君は今の給料でやって行けるか.

P^2 a *wage by* the hour 時間給. ¶a *wage for* living 生活賃金. ¶*wages on* efficiency 能率賃金.

wage-earner, *n.* 賃金を受ける人.

Q the *chief* wage-earner of a family 一家の主たる賃金労働者. ¶*ill-paid wage-earners* 給料の低い使用人. ¶*struggling wage-earners* 苦闘する賃金労働者.

wager, *n.* かけ.

V *have* a *wager* on ... …に対してかけをする. ¶*lay* a *wager* (=bet) with a person that ... 人と…のかけをする. ¶*lose* one's *wager* かけをして負ける. 【類】I've *lost* the *wager.* ¶*make* a *wager* that ... …というかけをする. ¶I will *match* you a *wager* on that. 僕もそれに君と同じ金額をかける. ¶*Name* your *wager.* 君いくらかける. ¶*offer* a *wager* いくらかけると言い出す. ¶*settle* a *wager* かけのきまりをつける. ¶*take up* a *wager* かけに乗る. ¶*win* a *wager* かけをして勝つ.

Q a *foolish wager* ばかなかけ. ¶a *queer* (=*curious*) *wager* 変ったかけ. ¶a *small wager* 少額のかけ.

P walk round the world *for* a *wager* かけで徒歩世界一周をする ‖ eating *for* a *wager*=an eating bout ものを食うかけ. 【類】undertake *for* a *wager* of $... to eat ... ¶the condition *of* a *wager* かけの条件.

P^2 there have been *wagers* in the city *as to* ... 従来その町では…のかけが行われている. ¶a *wager on* a horse race 競馬のかけ.

wager, *v.* かけをする; かける.

P I will *wager* my crown *against* your flute *upon* the issue! 貴公とその問題についてかけをしよう, わしが負けたら王冠を渡そう, 貴公が負けたらその笛を申し受けよう. ¶*wager on* ... …に対してかけをする. ¶I will *wager* a hundred to one *for* ... 私は…に対して負けたら相手のかけ高の百倍出そう.

O I will *wager* you a new hat that you will ... 君が…したら新しい帽子を買ってやろう.

wag[g]on, *n.* 荷馬車, トラック; 《英》貨車.

V *hitch* the *wagon* to the stars 高い望みを持つ. 【類】*Hitch* your *wagon* to a star. ¶*keep* one's *wagon* in a shed 車を車庫に入れておく. ¶*pull in* (*out*) a *wagon* 馬車を中に入れる(引っぱり出す).

V^2 The *wagon labored* in the mud. その荷馬車は泥道で進むのに骨を折った. ¶The *wagon lurched* to the sides. その荷馬車は左右に片かしぎがした. ¶a *wagon* was slowly *toiling on* toward ... 一台の荷馬車が…の方へ徐行していた.

Q a *covered wagon* 有がい車; 《米》[ほろ馬車から]ほろのついたトラック. ¶*high-loaded wagons* 荷を高く積んだ荷馬車. ¶an *open wagon* 無がい車.

Q^2 a *bogie wagon* ボギー車. ¶a *bull wagon* 牛車. ¶a *coal wagon* 石炭専用車. ¶a *gipsy wagon* [移動する人などの]住宅車. ¶a *goods wagon* 《英》貨車 (=a freight car). ¶a *grain wagon* 穀物運搬車. ¶a *honey wagon* 肥車. ¶a *hook-and-ladder wagon* [救助用の]引っかけはしご付消防自動車. ¶the "*living wagons*" of gipsies ジプシーの住宅兼用の馬車. ¶a *meat wagon* 食肉専用車. ¶a *milk wagon* 牛乳運搬車. ¶an *ox wagon* 牛車. ¶a *railway wagon* 《英》貨車. ¶a *road wagon* [一頭立ての]軽装馬車. ¶a *station wagon* 《米》[客・貨兼用の]木造車体の自動車. ¶a *timber wagon* 木材専用貨車. ¶a *top wagon* [積載物をおろすための]傾斜装置のついた貨車. ¶an *ore wagon* 鉱石専用車.

P *on* a [water] *wagon* 《米》禁酒して. 【類】He has gone *on* the *wagon.* ¶load *upon* a *wagon* 馬車に荷を積む.

waif, *n.* 浮浪者(児).

Q^2 a *London waif* ロンドンの浮浪児. ¶*street waifs* 街の浮浪者たち.

wail, *v.* 泣き悲しむ; ぴゅうと鳴る.

M Sirens *wailed out.* サイレンが鳴った.

M^2 *wail over* one's death その死を泣き悲しむ ‖ She *wailed over* her father's remains. 父の死がいにすがって泣き悲しんだ.

waist, *n.* 腰(ウエスト).

V She *has* a slender *waist.* 彼女はウエストが細い. ‖ She *has* no *waist.* 彼女は胴も腰も同じだ. ¶*measure* one's *waist* 腰まわりを計る. ¶*slim* the *waist* and flatten the abdomen 腰を細くし腹を平にする ‖ *slim* one's *waist* and hips 細腰にする. ¶*wriggle* the *waist* 腰をもじもじさせる.

V^2 Her *waist measures* 20 inches around (=round). 彼女の腰まわりは二十インチだ.

Q have a *slim waist* ウエストがほっそりしている.

P People buy "extras" from paper boys who dash through the streets with bells jingling *at* their *waists.* 人人は腰に鈴をじゃらじゃら鳴らして街路を飛んで行く新聞売子の号外を買う. ¶*round* one's *waist* その腰のまわりに.

P^2 She has the *waist of* a wasp's. 彼女のウエストははちのように細い. 【類】the *waist of* a shirt (trousers). ¶The water was *up to waist.* 水が深くて私の腰まで来た.

waistband, *n.* バンド.

V *tighten* (*loosen*) one's *waistband* バンドをし(ゆる)める. ¶*wear* a *waistband* バンドをつける.

waistcoat, *n.* 《英》男子用チョッキ.

V *leave off* one's *waistcoat* チョッキを脱ぐ.

wait, *n.* 待ち.

V *No wait* allowed in a game. 待ったなし ¶*have* a long *wait* at ... …で長く待たされる. 【類】We *had* a long *wait* for the train. ¶*take* the *wait* as a matter of course 待つのをあたりまえだと思う.

Q I don't like these *long waits.* こんなに待たされちゃたまらない. ¶after a further *tiresome wait* その上あきあきするほど待った後で.

P *after* a long *wait* 長らく待ってから. ¶lie *in wait* for ... 「…を待伏せする.

P^2 There was a *wait of* twenty minutes. 二十分間待った.

wait, *v.* (**1**) 待つ.

M *wait a bit* ちょっと待つ. ¶*wait a moment* (*an hour, all day*) ちょっと(など)待つ. ¶*anxiously wait* for a reply (your proposal) 返事(など)を今か今かと待っている. 【類】I am *anxiously waiting* to hear from you with reference to ...

¶*wait **awhile*** しばらく待つ. ¶*wait **confidently*** for ... ...を確信をもって待つ. ¶*wait **expectantly*** 首を長くして待つ. ¶I shall not *wait **here*** any longer. 私はもうこれ以上ここで待たない. ¶*wait **impatiently*** for ... ...をいらいらして待つ. ¶*wait **long*** for an answer 返事をいつまでも待つ. ¶*wait **patiently*** 気長く待つ. ¶*wait **ruefully*** for ... 心細そうに...を待つ.

P *wait* one's turn ***at*** a barber's 床屋で番を待つ. ¶*wait **for*** a better chance チャンスをねらう, 選球する ‖ *wait **for*** a fall in the rate of exchange 為替レートの下落を待つ ‖ *wait **for*** a favorable move in the developments of the situation 時をかせぐ ‖ *wait **for*** a streetcar 電車を待つ ‖ *wait **for*** hire 客待ちをする ‖ *wait **for*** the turning of the tide 潮待ちする ‖ a sailing vessel *waiting **for*** a wind 風をねらう帆船 ‖ without *waiting **for*** an answer 返事の先を越して ‖ those who *wait **for*** dead men's shoes 遺産をねらっている人々 ‖ I *wait **for*** your answer by return of post. 折返し御返事を下さるようお待ち致します. ‖ runners *waiting **for*** the sign [スタートの]号令を待つランナーたち. 【類】 *wait **for*** a person's return / I wanted to telephone and *waited **for*** the conversation to end. / Automobiles were in *waiting **for*** the party at the landing. / anglers patiently *waiting **for*** a bite (魚の食い) / *wait **for*** further instructions ‖ Don't *wait* dinner ***for*** me. 待たないで食事をしてくれ. 【類】 *wait* one's opportunity ***for*** another attempt. ¶*wait **till*** later (next week) もっと後(来週)まで待つ ‖ *wait **till*** the rising of the tide 潮待ちをする.

O *Wait* till you receive my instructions. こちらから指図するまで待て. ‖ *Wait* till getting off is through. 降りる方がすんでからお乗り下さい. 【類】 *wait* until one's name is called. ¶players *waiting* to go on 幕明を待つ登場者群.

(2) 給仕する.

M He is too ***much waited*** upon. 彼は余りちやほやされ過ぎている.

P *wait* well ***at*** table 手際よく食事の給仕をする. ¶*wait **on*** table 食事の給仕をする ‖ A waiter *waits **on*** us. [食事に]ボーイがついている. ‖ Are you *waited **on***? 御用をお伺いしましたか(店などで念のため客に尋ねる言葉). ‖ *wait **on*** her like a slave どれいのように彼女の気げんをとる ‖ being *waited **on*** by many servants 多数の召使いにかしずかれて ‖ She has a maid to *wait **upon*** her. 彼女は小間使を使っている. 【類】 He *waited **on*** His Majesty the Emperor. ‖ *wait **on*** (=***upon***) oneself 自分で給仕して食べる. ‖ I will *wait **upon*** your convenience. 御都合のよいようにお取り計らいしましょう. ‖ May success *wait **upon*** your efforts! 御成功を祈る.

waiter, *n.* 給仕人, ボーイ; 《米》 [家庭の]小間使; 盆.

V ***fee*** a *waiter* ボーイにチップをやる. ¶***remember*** (=***consider or tip***) the *waiter* ボーイにチップをやる.

Q a ***colored waiter*** wearing a white apron 白のエプロンをかけた黒人の給仕. ¶a bottle of Burgundy set on a ***dumb waiter*** 盆にのせたぶどう酒一びん. ¶a ***full-fledged waiter*** 一人前になった給仕人. ¶How hard it is to bear the disapproving frown of an ***undertipped waiter***! 少ししかチップをやらないボーイの渋面を見るのは実につらい.

Q^2 a ***minority waiter*** 職を失った給仕人(在野の政党をもじった言い回し).

waiting, *n.* 待つこと.

V ***have*** tedious *waiting* 待ちあぐむ ‖ ***have*** long *waiting* at a station 駅で長時間待つ.

Q with ***anxious waiting*** on the part of ... ...に今か今かと待たせて. ¶***watchful waiting*** 注意深い待機, 潮待ち.

P a lord (lady) ***in*** *waiting* 《英》 侍従(女王付侍女).

P^2 be accustomed to *waiting **at*** table 食卓の給仕に慣れている.

waitress, *n.* 給仕女.

Q^2 a ***tearoom*** (***coffee shop***) *waitress* 喫茶(など)店ガール.

O **She** is a Johnsons' *waitress.* 彼女はジョンソンさんの女中だ.

waiver, *n.* 〘法〙 [権利の]故意(または任意放)棄権.

P^2 *waiver **of*** recourse 〘法〙 上訴権の放棄.

wake, *n.* 通夜; 跡.

V ***hold*** [a] *wake* over a corpse 新仏のお通夜をする.

Q follow in the ***same wake*** 同じ轍(てつ)を踏む.

P follow ***in*** one's *wake* その轍(てつ)を踏む ‖ ***in*** the *wake* of ... came vice ...に付随して弊害が生じた 【類】 follow ***in*** the *wake* of one's predecessors (先輩).

P^2 the *wake **of*** a typhoon (boat) 台風(など)の通った跡.

wake, *v.* 起す, 目ざます; 目がさめる.

M I wish you'd *wake* me up ***earlier*** than usual. いつもより朝早く起してもらいたい. ¶***suddenly*** *wake* up to a realization of the fact that ... 突然...の事実を実感する.

M^2 *Wake **up***, England! 起て, 英国. ‖ The city is *waking **up***. 市民は自覚しだした. ‖ *Wake* me ***up*** at five-thirty. 明朝五時半に起してくれ. ‖ *wake* him ***up*** from his nap 昼寝している彼を起す ‖ he will *wake **up*** some day and find out that ... その中目がさめて...に気がつくだろう ‖ *wake **up*** fit for the duties of the day 今の自己の職責を自覚する ‖ *wake **up*** with a start はっと目をさます ‖ *wake **up*** to the danger of ... ...の危険を悟る. 【類】 *wake **up*** out of its long slumber in regard to ...

P *wake **at*** dawn あけがたに目がさめる. ¶*wake **from*** sleep 眠りからさめる ‖ She *woke **from*** her trance of two hundred years. その国は二百年のこん睡状態から目ざめた. ¶The scene suddenly *woke **into*** life. その場面が突如として眼前に見えてきた. ¶*wake **out of*** a dream 夢からさめる. 【類】 The noise *waked* us all ***out of*** a sound sleep. ¶A collector sometimes *wakes **to*** new interest in a subject. 収集家はある種の題目に新しい興味をもちだすことがある. ‖ *wake **to*** the consciousness that another day has arrived to be killed 目がさめるとまた退屈な一日が来たということを意識する. ¶*wake **with*** the dawn 夜の引き明けと同時に目をさます.

wakefulness, *n.* 目ざめ.

V ***increase*** the *wakefulness* 目がますますさえる.

waken, *v.* 目ざめさせる; 目ざめる.

P Weren't you *wakened **by*** the earthquake last night? ゆうべの地震で目がさめませんでしたか. ¶Nature seems to be newly *wakened **from*** a dead sleep. 自然が熟睡から新たにさめたように思われる. 【類】 *waken **from*** sleep. ¶Sometimes archaic words are *wakened **to*** new life by a poet. 詩人はよく古語を生かして使う.

wakening, *n.* 目ざめ.

P^2 a *wakening **from*** torpor 無感覚からわれに返ること.

walk, *n.* **(1)** 徒歩, 散歩; 歩き方; 〘野球〙 四球.

V ***do*** a brisk two-mile *walk* 元気よく二マイル徒歩する. ¶***get*** a *walk* from a pitcher 〘野球〙 投手から四球を奪う. ¶***give*** a batter a *walk* 〘野球〙 打者に敬遠の四球を与える. ¶***have*** (=***make or take***) a *walk* 散歩する. ¶***take*** a long *walk* home 長い道を歩いて家に帰る. 【類】 ***take*** a *walk* down the street / The meal over, all of us ***took*** a *walk* in the garden. / I think I'd better ***take*** a *walk* around the block and shake dinner down (腹っこなしに).

Q an ***awkward walk*** ぶざまな歩き方. ¶take a ***brisk walk*** 活発に歩く. 【類】 ten minutes' ***brisk walk*** took us to ... ¶a ***clumsy walk*** 不格好な歩き方. ¶take a ***constitutional walk*** 健康のための散歩をする. ¶one's ***customary walk*** その人の習慣になっている散歩. ¶a ***dignified walk*** 大ものらしい歩き方. ¶a ***dragging*** and ***despondent walk*** 足を引きずる力のない歩き方. ¶It's within an ***easy walk*** of the town. 町から楽に歩いて行ける所だ. ¶a ***full day's walk*** 歩いて一日たっぷりの行程. ¶He has a ***graceful walk***. 彼は上品な歩き方をする. ¶a ***hopeful, springy walk*** 希望に満ちた足の軽やかな歩き振り. ¶a ***leisured walk*** そぞろ歩き. ¶I have been for a ***little walk***. 私は少し散歩して来た. ¶go for a ***long walk*** ハイキングに出かける. ¶the ***measured walk*** of policemen 警官の歩調のそろった歩き方. ¶It would be a ***muddy walk***. 道がぬかるんでいるだろう. ¶a ***nimble walk*** 足早の徒歩. ¶an ***outdoor walk*** 屋外散歩. ¶a ***pretty walk*** of 1/2 hr. over the pine-clad beach 気持のよい三十分の松原海岸の散歩. ¶take a ***romantic walk*** by moonlight with the lady of one's love 意中の女と月夜にロマンチックな散歩をする. ¶a ***sauntering walk*** 漫歩. ¶take a ***sharp walk*** ぐんぐん歩く. ¶within a ***short walk*** of ... ...からちょっと歩いて行かれる所に. ¶purchases made in the course of a ***single walk*** through the streets 一ぺん町へ出掛けたついでの買物. ¶go a ***solitary walk*** 独りで散歩する. ¶He has an ***ungainly walk***. 彼は不様な歩きつきをする. ¶a ***vigorous walk*** 活発な足どり. ¶Her *walk* is ***waddling***, like that of a duck. 彼女の歩きつきはよたよたしてあひるのようだ. ¶a ***wandering walk*** 漫歩. ¶a ***weary walk*** 疲れた歩き振り.

Q^2 an ***autumn walk*** 秋の散歩. ¶go out for a long ***cross-country walk*** 郊外ハイキングに出かける. ¶take a ***Christmas walk*** [晩さん後など]クリスマスの散歩をする. ¶an ***early morning walk*** 早朝の散歩.

P go ***at*** a *walk* 並足で歩いて行く ‖ make for ... ***at*** a brisk *walk* 足早に…に向う ‖ The horse proceeded ***at*** a *walk* (trot, gallop). 馬は並足で(早足で, かけ足で)進んだ. ¶I know him ***by*** his *walk*. 歩きつきであの人と私には分かる. ¶go ***for*** a *walk* 散歩に行く. ¶accompany a friend ***on*** a *walk* 友だちのお伴をして散歩する. ¶I got tired ***with*** my *walk*. 私は歩き疲れた. ¶It is ***within*** an easy *walk* of three hours. それは三時間で楽に歩いて行ける所だ.

P^2 a *walk* ***by*** moonlight 月下の散歩. ¶a *walk* ***for*** exercise (pleasure) 運動(など)のための散歩. ¶It is only about five minutes' *walk* ***from*** our place. それは私たちの所からほんの五分位で行ける所です. ¶a *walk* ***in*** a garden (the country) 庭園(いなか)の散歩 ‖ a *walk* ***in*** the moonlight 月下の散歩. ¶a *walk* ***under*** the shade of trees 木陰の散歩.

(2) 道, 歩道; 方面; 職業.

Q contemporary characters of real interest and importance in ***all*** *walks* of life 現代各方面の名士 ‖ in ***all different*** *walks* of life 社会のあらゆる(色々の)方面で. ¶his ***chosen*** *walk* of life 彼の選んだ職業. ¶the men in the ***common*** *walks* of life 普通の生業についている人たち. ¶in ***different*** *walks* of life 社会の色々変った方面で. ¶pepole in ***every*** *walk* of life 社会各方面の人々 ‖ notable men and women in ***every*** *walk* of life 各方面の有名な紳士淑女. ¶one's ***favorite*** *walk* 好んで歩く歩道. ¶people from the ***humbler*** *walks* of life [もっと]下積みの連中 ‖ The majority must toil in the ***humbler*** *walks* of the profession. 多数はその職業の下っぱとして骨を折らなければならない. ¶an ***icy*** *walk* 氷の張った(すべりやすい)道. ¶It would be a ***muddy*** *walk*. 道路がぬかるんでいるだろう. ¶pedestrians' ***underground*** *walks* 通行人用の地下道. ¶***lovely flower-bordered*** *walks* 花でふち取られた美しい道. ¶a ***public*** *walk* 公道. ¶a ***shady*** *walk* beneath the leafy trees 葉の茂った木陰の薄暗い道. ¶a ***wooden*** *walk* 木製の歩み板.

Q^2 ***business*** *walks* (＝circles) 実務界. ¶a ***city*** *walk* 市内の歩道. ¶a ***gravel*** *walk* [庭園・公園内の]砂利歩道. ¶a ***side*** *walk* 《米》 歩道.

P choose it ***as*** one's *walk* of life それを定職として選ぶ. ¶persons who have really achieved anything worth while ***in*** any *walk* of life いずれかの方面で何か有益なことを実際成し遂げた人々. ¶play catch ***on*** the *walk* 歩道でボール投げをする ‖ signs which we see ***on*** a *walk* or ride 歩道であるいは車上で見る広告.

P^2 a *walk* ***in*** the country いなか道. ¶become acquainted with men of eminence in every *walk* ***of*** life 各方面の名士と知り合いになる.

walk, *v.* 歩く, 散歩する.

M *walk* two or three ***abreast*** 二三人並んで歩く. ¶*walk* ***alone*** down the street 通りを一人で歩く. ¶*walk* ***arm in arm*** 腕をくんで歩く. ¶*walk* ***away*** from … …から立ち去る ‖ *walk* ***away*** sick at heart 不快に思って立ち去る ‖ He *walked* ***away*** with his master's money. 彼は主人の金を持逃げした. ¶*walk* ***back*** 歩いて帰る. ¶*walk* ***barefoot*** はだしで歩く. ¶an earnest desire to *walk* ***close*** with God どこまでも神の道を歩もうとする切なる願い. ¶*walk* on ***briskly*** ずんずん歩いて行く. ¶*walk* ***delicately*** 遠慮がちに歩く. ¶the faculty of *walking* ***erect*** [人間のように]直立して歩くという能力. ¶*walk* ***far*** into the woods 森の中深く入り込む. ¶I can't *walk* any ***farther***. もうこれ以上一歩も歩けません. ¶*walk* ***fast*** 早足で歩く. ¶*walk* ***forth*** 歩いて進む. ¶Chaplin *walks* ***funny*** on the screen. チャップリンは映画で妙な歩きつきをする. ¶*walk* ***gingerly*** 用心してく. ¶*walk* ***gracefully*** しとやかに歩く. ¶*walk* ***hand in hand*** 手に手を取って歩く. ¶*walk* ***heavily*** up and down the stairs 大儀そうに階段を昇ったり降りたりする. ¶*walk* ***home*** 帰宅する. ¶I cancelled the rest of my order and warmly *walked* ***out***. [料理屋などで]私は注文の残りを取消して憤然と立ち去った. ‖ *walk* ***out*** [on strike] 《米》 ストで職場を放棄する ‖ Railroad workers are *walking* ***out***. 鉄道従業員は目下スト中. ‖ *walk* ***out*** en masse in protest against … (会議などで)…に反対して集団退場をやる. ¶*walk* ***pigeon-toed*** 内またに歩く. ¶*walk* ***quickly*** (＝***rapidly***) on ぐんぐん歩いて行く. ¶*walk* ***side by side*** 並んで歩く. ¶*walk* ***slow***[***ly***] ゆっくり歩く. ¶*walk* ***softly*** (***gently***) そっと歩く. ¶*walk* ***sullenly away*** すねてその場を去る. ¶*walk* ***sure foot***[***edly***] しっかり足を踏みしめて歩く. ¶One can easily *walk* ***upright*** in it. 容易にその中を真すぐ立ったままで歩くことができる. ¶*walk* ***upstairs*** (***downstairs***) 二階へ上る(階下へ降りる). ¶*walk* ***wearily*** [くたびれて]だるそうに歩く. ¶*walk* ***worthily*** in his footsteps りっぱに彼の後を継ぐ. ¶*walk* ***zigzag*** ジグザグ(千鳥足)に歩く.

M^2 *walk* ***about*** here and there 歩き回る. ¶*walk* ***along*** with dragging feet 足を棒にして歩く. ¶He came *walking* ***along***. てくでやってきた. ¶Pray *walk* ***in***. どうぞおはいり下さい. ‖ *walk* ***in*** God's way 神の道を歩む. ¶The policeman *walked* the man ***off***. 警官がその男を引立てて行った. ‖ *walk* ***off*** the headache 散歩をして頭痛をなおす ‖ *walk* ***off*** from their jobs 〖労〗 職場を放棄する ‖ *walk* ***off*** with slow steps ゆうゆうと歩いてその場を去る ‖ *walk* ***off*** with a trunk トランクを持ち去る; 持ち逃げする ‖ A boarding-house servant *walked* ***off*** with the property of a guest. 下宿屋の召使が宿泊人の品を持逃げした. ‖ The shoplifter *walked* coolly ***off***. その万引は何食わぬ顔をして去って行った. ¶*walk* ***on*** the sidewalk 歩道を歩く. ¶*walk* ***over*** to one's desk [用事で]人のデスクへ行く. ¶*walk* ***to and fro*** 行ったり来たりする. ¶*Walk* ***up***. いらっしゃい(見世物などでの呼声) ‖ *walk* ***up*** to the table テーブルに歩み寄る. 【類】 He had never been in to see the printings (印刷物), but after *walking* ***up*** to the broad steps [広い階段まで] he decided to leave it until another time.

P *walk* ***about*** the city all day 終日市中を歩き回る. ¶*walk* ***across*** a street 通りを横切る. 【類】 *walk* ***across*** a meadow. ¶*walk* ***against*** time 大急ぎで歩く. ¶*walk* ***along*** the road (a country path) (いなか)道を歩く ‖ *walk* ***along*** the beach 浜伝いに歩く. ¶*walk* the horse ***at*** a slow pace 馬をゆっくり歩かせる. ¶He *walked* ***before*** me in the street. 彼は通りで私の先に歩いて行った. ¶Please go first, I'll *walk* ***behind*** [you]. どうぞお先に, 私はお後に続いて参ります. ¶*walk* ***beside*** a person 人と並んで歩く. ¶*walk* ***by*** faith 信仰生活をする. ¶*walk* ***down*** a street 通りを歩いて行く. ¶*walk* ***down*** a street in the sun 日の当る通りを歩いて行く. 【類】 *walk* ***down*** the street toward City Hall (市役所). ¶*walk* ***for*** amusement (exercise) 楽しみ(など)に散歩する. ¶*walk* ***in*** the country (park) いなか(など)を歩く ‖ *walk* ***in*** the sand 砂の中を歩く ‖ *walk* ***in*** one's sleep 夢中歩行する ‖ *walk* rightly ***in*** the path of Christianity 正しいキリスト教徒の信仰生活をする. ¶*walk* ***into*** a shop 店に立寄る ‖ *walk* ***into*** a trap わなにかかる ‖ *walk* ***into*** the center of a room へやのまん中に進み出る. 【類】 *walk* ***into*** police headquarters (警察本部). ¶*walk* ***on*** the sidewalk 歩道を歩く ‖ *walk* ***on*** the seashore 海岸を散歩する ‖ *walk* ***on*** air 有頂天になる, [うれしさに]われを忘れる. 【類】 You have made me so happy that I feel as if I could *walk* ***on*** air. ‖ The dog's foot had been hurt, and the poor fellow could not *walk* ***on*** it. 犬が足をけがしていたのでかわいそうにその足を地につけては歩けなかった. ‖ *walk* ***on*** the sole of the foot 足の裏をつけて歩く. ¶*walk* ***out of*** the room へやから出る. ¶*walk* ***over*** the lawn (carpet) 芝生(など)の上を歩く ‖ *walk* ***over*** a person ***into*** a superior post 人を乗越して昇進する. ¶*walk* ***past*** a person 人を追い越す. ¶*walk* ***through*** the streets of London ロンドンの街道を歩く. 【類】 *walk* ***through*** the streets of Rome / *walk* ***through*** a lane of frenzied worshipers (熱狂したファン) ‖ *walk* ***through*** the pouring rain (slush and mud) どしゃ降り(など)を突いて歩く. ¶*walk* ***to*** school every morning with a chum 毎朝仲よしと学校へ行く. ¶*walk* ***up*** a moderate incline こう配のゆるやかな坂を上る ‖ *walk* ***up*** the street 通りを向うの方に歩いて行く. ¶*walk* ***up*** and ***down*** one's room [考えごとなどして]へや中をあちこち歩き回る ‖ I *walk* ***up*** and ***down*** these steps a hundred times a day. 僕はこの階段を一日百回は上り下りする. ¶*walk* ***upon*** one's hands 逆立をして歩く. ‖ *walk* ***with*** a cane ステッキをついて歩く ‖ *walk* ***with*** big strides 大またで歩く ‖ *walk* ***with*** measured steps 足並をそろえて歩く ‖ *walk* ***with*** a quick step 足早やに歩く ‖ *walk* ***with*** God 神の道を歩む. 【類】 *walk* ***with*** a slight limp (少しびっこを引いて).

walker, *n.* 徒歩者.

Q a ***good*** *walker* 健脚家. ¶a ***slow*** *walker* 足ののろい人. ¶a fairly ***strong*** *walker* かなりの健脚家.

Q^2 the ***champion long-distance*** *walker* of the world 長距離強歩世界選手権保持者. ¶a ***floor*** *walker*＝a floorwalker 《米》 [デパートなどの]売場監督. ¶a ***jay*** *walker* (＝jaywalker) 《米》 信号を無視して通路を横切る人. ¶a ***sleep*** *walker* = sleepwalker 夢遊病者, 夢中歩行者. ¶a ***street*** *walker*=a streetwalker 街頭売春婦. ¶a ***tight-rope walker*** [サーカスの]綱渡りの芸人. ¶a ***track walker*** 鉄道の保線係.

walking, *n.* 徒歩.

V The journey ***involves*** some *walking.* その旅行では幾分歩く必要がある. ¶I ***prefer walking*** to driving. 私は車より徒歩の方がよい. ¶***try walking*** for one's health 健康のために散歩をやって見る.

Q ***brisk walking*** 活発な歩行. ¶***easy walking*** 漫歩. ¶one will reach there in less than an ***hour's walking*** from ... ...から歩いて一時間足らずでそこに行けるでしょう. ¶There is ***no walking*** in the snow. 雪の中は歩かれない. ¶***rough walking*** 難路の歩行.

Q^2 ***sleep walking*** 夢中歩行. ¶an emergency net for ***tight-rope walking*** [サーカスの]綱渡りショーに使う救助網.

P It's an hour's distance ***by walking.*** 歩いて一時間の距離だ. ¶I am fond ***of walking.*** 私は歩くのが好きだ.

walkout, *n.* 〖労〗同盟罷業(スト).

Q^2 stage a ***one-day walkout*** 一日ストを決行する. ¶a ***protest walkout*** 〖労〗不服スト. ¶a "***sympathy***" ***walkout*** 〖労〗同情スト. ¶a "***wildcat***" ***walkout*** 〖労〗山ねこ争議. ¶stage a ***24-hour walkout*** 二十四時間ストを決行する.

wall, *n.* 壁, へい; [通例 *pl.*] 城壁.

V The *walls* are ***broken*** by well-proportioned niches containing blue vases with colorful flowers. 四壁にはほどよい大きさのくぼみがあってそこに花やかな花をさした青い花びんがおいてある. ¶***break down*** this almost unscalable *wall* of seclusion このほとんど侵すべからざる隔壁を打破する. ¶***build*** a *wall* several feet thick 数フィートの厚さにへいを築く. ¶Pictures ***enliven*** the *walls.* 絵は壁をにぎやかにする. ¶The *walls* of the restaurant were wonderfully ***festooned*** and balloons of every size and color hung from the ceiling. その料理屋の四壁は美しくかけ飾りが施してあり色々様々の大小風船が天井からつるしてあった. ¶***flatten out*** *walls* 壁を取りくずす. ¶The *walls* of this room are ***lined*** with hundreds of books. このへやの壁に沿って幾百冊という本が並んでいる. ¶The *walls* were ***paneled*** with mahogany. 壁にはマホガニー材の鏡板が張ってあった. ¶the city is enclosed within a high *wall,* ***pierced*** by four gates—the ... gate on the west, the ... gate on the east その市には高い城壁がめぐらしてあり, 西には...門・東には...門...と四つの門がついている. ¶***scale*** the *walls* of ... ...の城壁をよじ上る. ¶***throw up*** a *wall* へいを急造する. ¶Its *walls* are ***wainscoted*** with oak paneling of fine color and quality. その四壁には色の美しい良質のかしの羽目板が張ってある. ¶***whitewash*** a *wall* へいを白塗にする.

V^2 The hall was so full that the *walls* seemed to ***bulge.*** その会館ははちきれるほどの満員であった. ¶*Walls* ***have*** ears. 〖諺〗壁に耳あり.

Q a ***blank wall*** 窓のない平壁. ¶a ***crenellated wall*** 銃眼状に装飾した壁. ¶***crumbling walls*** ぼろぼろとくずれるへい. ¶a ***dead wall*** 出入口のないへい. ¶the ***Great Wall*** of China 万里の長城. ¶The rocks presented a high ***impenetrable wall,*** over which the water tumbled in a sheet of featherly foam. 岩は高くびようぶのように立っていて, そこからふわふわした水あわが一枚の羽根のようになって落下していた. ¶***lofty walls*** of rock 高い岩壁. ¶a ***moldering wall*** くずれかかったへい ‖ Bits of ivy were seen clinging to the ***moldering wall.*** つたが少しくずれかかった壁にはっていた. ¶a ***smoke-covered*** (=***smoke-stained***) *wall* ばい煙で黒ずんだ壁. ¶a ***smoky wall*** 煙ですすけた壁. ¶The stump-orator was surrounded by a ***solid wall*** of humanity. その大道演説家の回りに人のかきねを築いた. ¶***sound-insulated walls*** 防音壁.

Q^2 a ***brick wall*** れんがべい. ¶a ***castle wall*** 城壁. ¶a ***fire wall*** 防火壁. ¶a ***partition wall*** [建物の]仕切り壁. ¶break down the ***prison wall*** 刑務所のへいをぶちこわす. ¶a ***quay wall*** [波止場の]岩壁. ¶a ***retaining wall*** 防砂壁. ¶a ***sea wall*** which keeps high waves out of a harbor breakwater 防波堤. ¶increase the height of its ***tariff wall*** その国の関税障壁を強化する. ¶***town walls*** 都市の周囲の城壁.

P bump ***against*** the *wall* 壁にごつんとぶっつかる ‖ lean ***against*** a *wall* 壁にもたれかかる ‖ with one's back ***against*** the *wall* 窮地に陥って. ¶separated ***by*** a *wall* 壁で隔てられて. ¶the nails ***in*** the *walls* 壁に打込んだくぎ ‖ His framed portrait was hung upon hooks ***in*** the *wall.* 彼の肖像は額になって壁に下げてあった. ¶doodles ***on*** the *wall* へいに書いてあるらく書き(似顔などの) ‖ His work has often appeared ***on*** the *walls* of the Royal Academy. 彼の作品は英国の文展に幾度か入選した. ‖ writing ***on*** (=***upon***) the *walls* 壁に書いてある文字; 〖聖書〗差迫った災難のしるし. ¶***outside*** the *walls* of ... ...の城外に ‖ be ***outside*** the city *walls* その市を囲む城壁の外にある. ¶get (=climb) ***over*** the *walls* 壁をよじ上って越える. ¶The shot passed ***through*** a *wall.* 弾丸が壁を突き通した. ¶a lamp fixed ***to*** the *wall* 壁に取付けたランプ ‖ go ***to*** the *wall* 窮地に陥る, 負ける. ¶***under*** the *walls* of Peiping 北京城下. ¶a map ***upon*** the *wall* 壁にかけた地図. ¶surrounded ***with*** a wall へいをめぐらした ‖ do away ***with*** a *wall* へいを取りこわす. 【類】an old *wall* has been done away ***with.*** ¶confined ***within*** *walls* 室内に閉込められて ‖ ***within*** the *walls* of a school 校内で.

wall, *v.* 壁を回らす.

M^2 The pond was ***walled in*** by the thick growth of trees. その池はまわりの木の茂みに囲まれていた. ¶***wall up*** 壁でふさぐ.

wallet, *n.* 札入れ, 紙入れ.

V I've ***lost*** a *wallet* while on a train. 列車で財布をなくした.

Q^2 a black ***leather wallet*** 黒かわの紙入れ.

wallow, *v.* ころげまわる; ふける.

P *wallow* (=revel) ***in*** pleasure (sensuality) 快楽(など)にふける ‖ *wallow* ***in*** money 金がふんだんにある. 【類】*wallow* ***in*** beastly pleasures (獣欲) / *wallow* ***in*** mud (=mire) / *wallow* ***in*** a pool of blood.

waltz, *n.* ワルツ.

V ***dance*** a *waltz* ワルツを踊る.

wand, *n.* 棒, つえ.

Q The fairy waved her ***magic wand.*** よう精は魔法のつえを振った.

P a world of crystal created ***by*** the *wand* of Jack Frost 寒さ小僧のいたずらでできた水晶の世界.

wander, *v.* さまよう.

M *wander* ***away*** to ... ...の方へさまよい行く. ¶one's thoughts *wander* ***back*** to one's home 思いはやがてわが家のことに及ぶ. ¶*wander* ***deep*** into the woods 森の中深くふみこむ. ¶*wander* too ***far*** from one's subject 話が大脱線をする.

M^2 *wander* ***about*** ほっつき歩く. ¶The dog *wandered* ***off*** and got lost. 犬はほっつき歩いて道に迷った.

P *wander* ***about*** the streets 街路を歩き回る ‖ the man who has *wandered* a great deal ***about*** the world, the cosmopolitan 世界を放浪した天下浪人. ¶*wander* ***from*** the course (=road, right path) 進路を踏み迷う, わき道に入る. ¶*wander* ***from*** the point 話の筋から脱線する ‖ *wander* ***from*** a subject 話が脱線する. ¶*wander* ***in*** a strange land 他国を放浪する ‖ His wife *wandered* ***in*** strange pastures. 彼の妻が他に男をこしらえた. ¶*wander* ***into*** a by-path 横道へ入り込む ‖ My eye *wanders* ***into*** the little sunlit court outside. 目は外の日の当っている中庭に落ちる. ¶*wander* ***on*** the Alps アルプス山中をぶらつく. ¶*wander* ***over*** the fields 野原をさまよう. ¶*wander* ***through*** the jungle 密林をさまよう.

wanderer, *n.* 放浪者.

Q some ***poor homeless wanderer*** ある哀れな家なしの放浪者.

P a *wanderer* ***about*** the streets 街頭を放浪する人.

wandering, *n.* 放浪.

Q ***aimless*** *wanderings* あてのない放浪.

Q^2 After long "***marriage wanderings,***" she at last attained the goal for which she had longed and sought in ***labyrinthine*** *wanderings.* 長い間結婚の相手に迷ったが迷路の中で久しく求めて来た目的の人物にいよいよ出会った.

P in the course ***of*** one's *wanderings* そのさすらい中に ‖ be fond ***of*** *wanderings* さまよい歩くのが好きである.

P^2 a *wandering* ***from*** the main subject (=right path) 本題(など)からの脱線. ¶the *wandering* ***of*** the thoughts 思想の錯乱.

wane, *n.* 衰退.

P The moon is ***on*** the *wane.* 月はかけつつある. ‖ The day was ***on*** the *wane.* 日盛りが過ぎていた. 【類】Their influence was ***on*** the *wane.* / His popularity has long been ***on*** the *wane.* / His star (運勢) is ***on*** the *wane.*

wane, *v.* かける; 衰える.

M Summer is *waning* ***fast.*** 夏も終りに近づいてきた.

P *wane* (=pale) ***into*** insignificance compared with ... ...に比して顔色なしである. ¶The interest *waned* ***to*** extinction. その関心は薄らいで消えてしまった.

want, *n.* 不足, 欠乏; 心要, 入用.

V *cover* urgent *wants* 緊急の用に応じる. ¶one *feels* a *want* of words to enable the pen to give an adequate description of the beauty of ... ...の美は筆に尽せない. ¶The book will *fill* a long-felt *want*. その本は年来感じていた欠陥を満たしてくれるであろう. ¶*keep want* at bay 生活にことかかぬようにする. ¶*meet* the *wants* of the public 公衆の要求に応じる. 【類】 to *meet* this *want* is the aim of ... ¶*realize* the *want* of ... ...の必要を痛感する. ¶*relieve* their *wants* 彼らの窮乏を緩和する. ¶*satisfy* a *want* of society 社会の一つの要求を満足させる ‖ *satisfy* a *want* of nature 用を足す(便通など). ¶This *shows want* of care. これは不注意ということになる. ¶*study* the *want* of the English market 英国市場の要求を研究する. ¶Her parents *supplied* all her *wants*. 彼女の両親が何不自由なくしてくれた. 【類】 *supply* a long-felt *want*.

Q I am in no *absolute want* of the thing at present. 今のところその品が私になくてならぬというのではない. ¶It has long been an *acknowledged want*. それは長い間人が認めてきた必要物である. ¶*bodily wants* 肉体上の欲望. ¶a *curious want* of proportion 妙な不釣り合い. ¶*daily wants* 日用品. ¶*dire want* 大欠乏. ¶satisfy an *existing want* 現存している欠陥を満たす ‖ Purchases are being made merely for *existing wants*. 当座に必要なものだけを買っている. ¶He is in *extreme want*. 彼は(財政的に)非常に困っている. ¶It is in *immediate want* of repairs. それは修繕の必要に差迫られている. ¶Commerce is an *indestructible want* of humanity. 商業は人類にとって永久に必要なものである. ¶I cared for his *material wants*. 私は彼の生活の方の世話をしてやった. ¶satisfy a great *public want* 公衆の大きな不足を満たしてやる. ¶*sharply felt wants* 切実に感じられる欠陥. ¶We suffered from *utter want* of any common topic of conversation. われわれは共通の話題が全然ないので弱った. ‖ the *utter want* of seriousness 全くの不まじめ. ¶minister to *various wants* 種々の必要を満たす.

P He found himself *above want*. 彼は不足を感じなかった. ‖ the people who are *above want* 食うに困らない人(たち). ¶The famine was caused *by* the *want* of seasonable rains. その凶作は季節順当の雨が降らないために起った. ‖ Good matter is often spoiled *by want* of art. 技術不足のため折角のよい材料がだめになることがよくある. ¶The venture died *for want* of support. その事業は援助がなかったために不成功に終った. ‖ which, *for want* of a better word (=designation), I will call ... 私は他に適当の語がないからそれを仮に...と言うことにしよう ‖ hair tangled *for want* of combing くしを使わないため乱れた髪 ‖ many intelligences stunted *for want* of opportunity 機会がないために発展を阻止された幾多賢明な人たち ‖ *for want* of business 商売不振のため ‖ *for want* of funds to pay ... ...を支払う資金がないため ‖ *for want* of space 紙面に限りがあるから ‖ *for want* of any other alternative しようことなしに ‖ *for want* of employment 仕事がないから. 【類】 *for want* of a better course / I have been refused admittance *for want* of room. / *For want* of something to do I thought I would take a bath. / *for* one's own *want* of prudence. ¶*from want* of ability (experience, food, means, skill) 才能(など)が足らないために ‖ The plants died *from want* of water. それらの植物は水が切れて枯れてしまった. 【類】 Many people are suffering *from want* of the mere necessaries of life. / *from want* of knowledge of the law. ¶The widow is *in want*. 未亡人は(財政上)困っている. ‖ He is *in want* of work. 彼は仕事を求めている. ‖ They are often *in want* of food. 彼らはしばしば食物がなくて困る. 【類】 the costermonger *in want* of ready money to replenish his stock / The house is *in want* of repair. / be much in *want* of ... / Do you know of any one who is *in want* of a maid? ¶*through want* of heirs (funds) 相続人(金)がないために. ¶reduced *to want* 貧乏に陥って ‖ minister *to* one's *want* その必要に応じる. ¶He often argues *with* delightful *want* of logic. 彼は論理を超越した痛快な議論をすることが往々ある.

P² a *want of* due respect toward a superior 先輩に対する然るべき尊敬の欠乏 ‖ *want of* nutrition 栄養の不足 ‖ *want of* offspring 子のないこと ‖ *want of* confidence 信頼の欠如 ‖ *want of* application 不勉強 ‖ *want of* unity 支離滅裂. 【類】 *want of* etiquette / *want of* experience (practice) / *want of* method.

want, *v.* 必要とする; 欠乏する.

M I *want* it *back* right soon. それをすぐ返して欲しい. ‖ Boss *wants* you *back* to work. 主人が君に帰って働いてくれと言っている. ¶I *want* it *badly* (=*sadly*). 私は是非それが必要だ. ¶It may be *wanted elsewhere*. それは他の方で欲しいと言うかも知れない. ¶He is *lamentably wanting* in common sense. 彼は気の毒な位常識を欠いている. ¶I *wanted* very *much* to teach him a lesson, but desisted. よっぽどとっちめてやろうと思ったがやめた. ¶I may *want* you *suddenly*. 僕は君に急に用事ができるかもしれない. ¶It is *urgently wanted*. それは至急入用だ.

P You are *wanted at* the president's office. 社長がお呼びです. ¶a person *wanted by* law (the government) お尋ね者. ¶He was kind enough to see that I *wanted for* nothing. 彼は私が何不自由ないように十分心尽しをしてくれた. ‖ What do you *want* me *for*, Sir? 何の御用ですか ‖ We *want* Bob *for* our captain. ボブをわれわれの主将にしたい. ‖ He is *wanted for* murder (highway robbery). 彼は殺人(追はぎ)のけん疑でお尋ね者になっている. ¶It *wants* a minute *of* the hour. その時間の一分前. ‖ It *wants* an inch *of* the regulation measurement. それは規定の寸法より一インチ足らない. ‖ I *want* some months *of* eighteen. 私は二三カ月で満十八歳になる. ¶He's *wanted on* the phone (=by phone). 彼に電話がかかってきている. ¶What do you *want with* me? 私に何の御用がおありなのですか.

O *Wanted*—the truth about Japan. 日本の実相に対する知識の欠乏. ‖ *Wanted*: a cook for a small family. 〖広告〗コック入用当方小家庭. ¶I want you to see what this watch *wants*. この時計はどこが悪いのか見て下さい. ¶I *want* these shoes resoled. このくつの底を張りかえてくれ. ‖ I *want* a shave (hair-cut). ひげ(など)をやってくれ.

wanting, *a.* 欠けている.

M He is *a bit* (=*a little*) *wanting*. あいつは少し足りない. ¶be *so wanting* in liberality as to think that ... ...と考えるほど雅量がない. ¶One volume is *still wanting* to complete the set. そのセットはまだ一冊足りない.

P *wanting in* lucidity 明りょうを欠いている ‖ *wanting in* consideration (perseverance, politeness, judgment, common sense) 熟慮(など)の欠けている ‖ You are *wanted in* the office. 君事務所まで来てくれ. ‖ German sounds *wanting in* Engligh 英語にないドイツ語の音. ¶*wanting to* the occasion (one's duty, oneself) その場合(など)に必要な.

wanton, *v.* もてあそぶ.

P his swimming, or rather *wantoning with* the water 彼の水泳—と言うよりむしろ水遊び. ¶The wind wontoned *with* the leaves. 風は木の葉にたわむれた.

war, *n.* 戦争.

V *anticipate* a third *war* 第三次大戦を予想する. ¶*war* was *averted* by ... ...によって戦争が避けられた. ¶The best way to *avoid war* is to be prepared for it. 戦争を回避する最善の方法は戦争に備えることである. ¶*begin* a *war* of extermination upon the "tipping" evil チップの悪習廃止運動を起す. ¶*bring on war* 戦争を起す. ¶boldly *carry* the *war* into the enemy's country 勇敢に敵国に攻入る. ¶*carry on war* against ... ...との戦争を続ける. ¶We are prepared to *confront* a long *war*. われわれは長期抗戦の覚悟をしている. ¶*continue war* to the better end あくまで戦争を継続する. ¶*declare war* against (=on) ... ...に宣戦を布告する ‖ The Reds *declare war* on organized society. 共産主義者は組織社会に対し宣戦している. ‖ in the event of *war* being *declared* 宣戦の暁には. 【類】 they expect *war* will soon be *declared* with ... / *War* was formally (公式に) *declared* on Spain by the United States on the 25th day of April, 1898. ¶strongly *denounce war* 強硬に戦争を非難する. ¶the work of the League of Nations in the direction of *eliminating war* 戦争排除の方面における国際連盟の仕事. ¶America *entered* the *war* against Germany to make the world safe for democracy. 米国は民主主義が世界において無事に行われることを目的に対独戦争に参加した. ‖ on the day we *entered* the *war* われわれが戦争を開始した日に. ¶*fight* the *war* to the finish 勝負のつくまで戦う. ¶*finance* a *war* 戦争の費用をまかなう. ¶*follow* a *war* 戦争を続ける. ¶Newspapers *fomented war*. 新聞が戦争を醸成した. ¶*force war* on ... ...に挑戦する. ¶*foresee war*

戦争を予想する. ¶if we ever ***have*** another *war* with ... 再び…と開戦することがあるとしたら. ¶***humanize war*** 戦争を人道化する. ¶***lose*** a ***war*** 戦争に負ける. ¶***levy war*** against ... …と戦端を開く. ¶The chief has power to ***make war*** and peace. 元首は開戦講和の権を握っている. ‖ ***make war*** that she may acquire a neighbor's territory 隣国の領土を得んがために戦争をする ‖ ***make war*** successfully with ... …と戦争して勝利を得る ‖ ***make war*** on (=upon) a person in behalf of ... …のために人に戦いをいどむ. ¶***open war*** with ... …と戦端を開く. ¶***prevent war*** 戦争を防止する. ¶***outlaw war*** 戦争を不法とする. ¶***prosecute*** a civil ***war*** 内乱を起す. ¶This has ***provoked*** the present *war*. このために今次の戦争が起った. ¶***pursue*** the ***war*** to a complete victory 完全に勝利を得るまでこの戦争を続ける. ¶***renew*** a ***war*** 戦争を再開する. ¶***spark*** the second World *War* 第二次世界大戦の口火を切る. ¶***start*** a ***war*** on ... …に対し戦争を始める. ¶it ***took*** a ***war*** to ... 戦争の結果始めて…ということがわかった. ¶***undertake*** a prolonged *war* against ... …に対して長期戦を起す. ¶***wage war*** against ... …に対して戦争をする ‖ ***wage*** a ***war*** of nerves 神経戦争をやる ‖ ***wage*** a ***war*** of extermination against ... …撲滅の手段を取る ‖ ***wage war*** with the pen on the government 筆で政府と戦う. 【類】Japan ***waged*** two ***wars*** successfully against enemies presumed at the time to be greater in power. ¶***win*** a ***war*** 戦争に勝つ.

V² ***war broke out*** between ... …間に戦争が起った. ¶***War burst forth.*** 戦争がぼっ発した. ¶the ***war*** that has just ***closed*** 丁度今終った戦争. ¶Will ***war come*** in Europe? ヨーロッパに戦争があるだろうか. ¶should ***war come about*** between ... 万一…間に戦端が開かれると. ¶The ***war dragged*** miserably ***on***. その悲惨な戦争がだらだらと続いた. ¶The ***war*** is virtually ***ended***. その戦争は終ったも同然だ. ‖ "This is the war," he declared, "to ***end war***." 「この戦争は戦争を永久に廃止するための戦争だ」と彼は公言した. ¶while the ***war*** was ***raging*** in Spain スペインで戦がたけなわだった時 ‖ For five years the ***war raged*** without any signal success for either side. 五年間双方に大した勝利もなく激戦が続けられた. ¶The ***war runs*** riot. 戦争が猛烈に進行する. ¶The ***war spread***. 戦火が拡大した.

Q an ***abhorrent war*** いむべき戦争. ¶an ***aggressive war*** 侵略戦争. ¶when ***air war*** comes 一たん空中戦争となれば. ¶a ***bloody war*** 血戦. ¶the ***Chino-Japanese War*** 日シ戦争. ¶the ***Civil War*** 南北戦争. ¶an all-out ***civil war*** 全面的内戦. ¶a ***cold*** (***hot***) ***war*** 冷(熱)戦 ‖ a "***cold war***" against communism 反共冷戦. ¶when this ***cursed war*** is over このうべき戦争が終ったら. ¶a ***defensive war*** 防御戦. ¶a ***devastating war*** 大戦争. ¶the then ***existing war*** 当時行われていた戦争. ¶a most ***expensive war*** 多大な出費を要する戦争. ¶wage ***fierce*** and ***interminable wars*** with their rivals 彼らの敵と激烈なしかも際限のない戦争をする. ¶a ***full-fledged*** civil ***war*** 本格の国内戦. ¶a ***gigantic war*** 大戦争. ¶a ***good war*** 正義の戦争. ¶the ***great war*** of 1914—1918 一九一四年から一九一八年までの大戦 ‖ the ***greatest war*** in history 歴史上最大の戦争. ¶an ***ideological war*** 理論(イデオロギー)闘争. ¶***War*** is very ***imminent***. 戦争が目前に切迫している. ¶when ***war*** is ***impending*** 戦争が差迫っている時. ¶make ***incessant war*** on their neighbors 隣国と絶えず戦争をする. ¶an ***inky war*** 筆による論戦. ¶an ***intestine war*** 内乱. ¶the ***late war*** この前の戦争. ¶a ***lost war*** 敗戦. ¶the Russo-Japanese ***maritime war*** 日露海戦. ¶an ***offensive war*** of conquest 攻略戦. ¶an ***old-fashioned colonial war*** 昔流の植民地戦争, 相も変らぬ搾取戦争. ¶wage ***perpetual war*** with ... …と絶えず戦う. ¶the ***present war*** 今次の戦争. ¶a ***protracted war*** 長期戦. ¶a ***recent war*** 近時の戦争. ¶a ***racial war*** 異民族間の戦争. ¶***Real war*** is yet to come. 戦はこれからだ. ¶wage a ***relentless war*** against flies, mosquitoes, rats, and vermin はえ・蚊・ねずみ及び害虫を容赦なく退治する. ¶a ***religious war*** 宗教戦. ¶a ***severe war*** 激戦. ¶wage a ***systematic war*** against a disease 病気を組織的に征服する. ¶***unproductive*** and necessarily ***sterile war*** 不生産的な従って当然無益な戦争. ¶A ***threatened war*** with Japan was avoided by Chinese diplomacy. 正にぼっ発しようとした対日戦は中国の外交手段によって回避された. ¶an ***unjustified war*** 戦う理由のない戦争. ¶an ***unpopular war*** 不人気な戦争. ¶The Health Department is waging ***vigorous war*** on dirty alleys, foul water and open vaults. 保健省ではきたない横町や汚水や開放どぶなどの清掃工作をやっきとなって進めている. ¶have a ***wordy war*** 舌戦をする.

Q² a ***class war*** 階級闘争. ¶a ***color war*** 人種戦. ¶a ***full-scale war*** 本格的な戦争. ¶wage a ***gang war*** on ... ギャング一党が…になぐりこみをかける. ¶***guerilla war*** 遊撃戦. ¶a ***hit-and-run war*** 〘野球〙一打一点の戦い. ¶a ***labor war*** 労働戦争. ¶a combined ***land, sea*** and ***air war*** 海・陸・空の総合戦(立体戦). ¶a ***large-scale civil war*** 大規模な内戦. ¶a ***lightning war*** 電撃戦. ¶Two rival stores carried on a ***price war***. 二軒の商売がたきの店が物価(引下げ)戦をやった. ¶wage a ***propaganda war*** on ... …に対し宣伝戦をやる. ¶a ***push-button war*** 押しボタン式(電撃)戦争. ¶a ***showdown war*** 最後の決戦. ¶a ***small-scale war*** 小規模な戦争. ¶a ***tariff war*** 関税戦争. ¶the ***Thirty-years War*** 〘史〙三十年戦争. ¶be engaged in a "***trade war***" 「貿易戦」をやっている. ¶a ***two-front war*** [戦線が二つある]二面戦争. 【類】in both ***World Wars*** / a veteran (老兵) of two ***world wars*** / the prevention of a third ***world war***.

P ***after war*** 終戦後 ‖ ***after*** long ***wars*** with ... …との長期にわたる戦争の後. ¶a nation ***at war*** 交戦国. 【類】Our nation is ***at war***. / be ***at war*** with one's environment (環境と). ¶as ***before*** the ***war*** 戦前同様に. ¶***during*** the late ***war*** in Korea 最近朝鮮における戦争中に. ¶desire ***for war*** 戦争を欲する ‖ prepare ***for war*** 戦に備える. ¶***In war*** prepare for peace. 戦時において平時に備えよ. ‖ erect statues to heroes who fell ***in war*** 戦死した勇士たちの像を建てる ‖ He has been ***in*** the ***wars***. 彼は数回実戦に参加した. ¶go ***into*** (=enter) ***war*** 戦争をする ‖ France will not be drawn ***into war*** on Russia's behalf. フランスがロシアのために戦争に巻きこまれるようなことはないだろう. ¶is there any prospect ***of war*** with ...? …と戦争が始まるような形勢が見えますか. ‖ in the arena ***of war*** 戦場において. ¶***owing to*** the ***war*** 戦争のために. ¶she has too much common sense to go ***to war*** with ... その国は常識があるから…と戦争するようなことはしない. ¶at a time when philosophy was ***at war*** with faith 哲学が(宗教の)信仰と戦っていた当時は. ¶***since*** the ***war*** 終戦以来.

P² a ***war between*** a pigmy and a giant 小人と大男の戦い ‖ a ***war between*** ideas 思想戦. ¶a ***war for*** a great cause 大義のための戦争. ¶***wars of*** 1894—5 and 1904—5 一八九四年から一八九五年までと一九〇四年から一九〇五年までの間の戦争 ‖ ***war of*** the government (people) 政府(人民)の戦争 ‖ a ***war of*** extermination of rats ねずみ全滅戦 ‖ a ***war of*** nerves 神経戦 ‖ a ***war of*** attrition 持久戦 ‖ a ***war of*** ideologies=an ideological war ‖ The ***war of*** words between ... and ... is still waging fiercely. …と…との舌戦はいぜん激烈に続けられている. ‖ the ***war of*** Japan with Russia=the Ruso-Japanese war. ¶***war on*** consumption 肺病撲滅戦 ‖ Japan's participation in the ***war on*** Germany 対ドイツ戦における日本の参加. ¶a ***war to*** the death 背水の陣. ¶***war upon*** the brothel 廃娼(しょう)運動. ¶a ***war without*** battle 戦闘なき戦争(冷戦).

war, *v*. 闘争する, 戦う.

M ***war valiantly*** against misused words 語の誤用に対し敢然として反対を唱える.

P ***war against*** evil 悪と戦う. ¶***war for*** the control of the Pacific 太平洋の制海権のために戦う. ¶***war on*** the white slave trade 人身売買に対して戦う. ¶***war with*** some principle ある主義と戦う.

warbling, *n*. さえずり; 響き.

P² the ***warbling of*** the lark ひばりのさえずり ‖ the ***warbling of*** an air-raid siren 空襲警報の響き.

war-cloud, *n*. 戦雲.

V the ***war-clouds hung*** over ... …に戦雲がみなぎった.

war-cry, *n*. ときの声.

V ***raise*** a ***war-cry*** ときの声を揚げる.

Q a regular ***journatlstic war-cry*** 新聞の常套(とう)の標語.

ward, *n*. 病室; 後見, 監督.

Q a ***surgical ward*** 外科施療室.

Q² a ***casualty ward*** 事故患者室(病院の). ¶a ***city ward*** 市巡回人(単称括称とも). ¶a ***hospital ward*** 病棟. ¶an ***isolating ward*** 隔離病室.

P put one ***in ward*** 人に後見を付ける. ¶The boy is ***under ward***. その少年は監督を受けている.

ward, *v*. 避ける.

M *ward off* danger (disease) 危険(など)を避ける ‖ *ward off* an attack (evil, a blow) 攻撃(など)を回避する ‖ *ward off* extensive questioning about … …に関する広範な質問を切抜ける. 【類】*ward off* the spread of a false doctrine / *ward off* any aggressive invasion (侵略戦).

warden, *n.* 監理者.

Q^{2} an *air-raid warden* 防空監視人. ¶a *port warden* 港知事. ¶a *prison warden* 刑務所長.

wardrobe, *n.* [団]衣装;洋服ダンス(など).

V My mother *had* a *wardrobe* which was the envy of all the neighborhood. 私の母は近所中の者からうらやまれるほどの衣装持ちであった. ¶a very slender *wardrobe packed up* in a very portable box きわめて携帯に便利な箱に詰込んだほんのわずかな衣類.

Q an *extensive wardrobe* たくさんの着物. ¶He has a *large* (*small*) *wardrobe*. 彼は衣装持だ(でない). ¶a *limited wardrobe*. わずかな衣装. ¶We were travellers and our *wardrobes* were necessarily *small*. われわれは旅をしていたので銘々の衣類といってはもちろんわずかなものであった.

Q^{2} a *shoe wardrobe* (=box) くつ箱.

P a bride *with* a large *wardrobe* 衣類をたくさん持った花嫁.

wardship, *n.* 後見.

V *have* the *wardship* of … …がその後見をしている.

P He is *under wardship*. 彼は後見を受けている.

ware, *n.* [通例 *pl.*] 器物, 品物.

V Peddlers *cry* their *wares* aloud. 行商人は大声で商品を呼売する. ¶*display wares* 商品を陳列する. ¶Butchers, fishermen, and fruit and vegetable venders *exposed* their *wares* for sale. 肉屋や魚屋や八百屋が商品を陳列して売っていた. ¶*foist* spurious *wares* on the market まやかしの品を市場に送り出す. ¶The people who *had wares* to sell huddled together under the roofs. 器物を売る商人どもは屋根の下に一緒に集まった. ¶*hawk* their *wares* in streets 街頭で商品を呼売する. ¶to *market* one's *wares* その品を市で売るために. ¶*mend* broken *ware* こわれた器物を修繕する. ¶hawkers *roaring out* their *wares* 大きな声で品を呼売する行商. ¶*praise* one's own *wares* 自画自賛する. ¶The pedlers all *shouted* their *wares* and motioned me to buy. 行商は盛んに品を呼上げ私に買えと手まねですすめた. ¶These patent-medicine peddlers *sang* quaintly their *wares*. これら売薬行商の売声は歌を歌うような妙な調子だった. ¶*take* one's *wares* to a market 商品を市場に持って行く.

Q *ceramic wares* 陶磁器. ¶a piece of *cloisonné ware* 七宝焼一個. ¶*coarse* and *meretricious ware* 粗造の毒々しく飾った製品. ¶*hand-made ceramic ware* 手造りの焼物. ¶*shoddy wares* 見かけ倒しの品. ¶*vile wares* だもの.

Q^{2} *luxury wares* [宝石などの]ぜいたく品類. ¶*marquetry ware* 象眼細工品. ¶*table ware*=tableware 食器 ‖ modern *table ware* 文化食器. ¶*willow wares* 柳条製品.

P^{2} The *wares in* that store are dear. あの店の品は高い. ¶*wares of* all kinds ありとあらゆる品物.

warehouse, *n.* 倉庫.

V *hire* a *warehouse* for the occasion 臨時に倉庫を借りる.

Q a *gaunt*, *unlovely warehouse* 物すごい殺風景な倉庫. ¶a *pawnbroker's warehouse* 質屋の蔵. ¶a *universal supply warehouse* よろず屋, なんでも屋.

Q^{2} a *freight warehouse* 貨物置場(倉庫).

P deposit *in* a *warehouse* 倉庫に預け入れる.

warfare, *n.* 闘争; 戦争.

V *have* a wordy *warfare* 口論をする. ¶*heal* class *warfare* 階級闘争が起らないようにする. ¶*Warfare* is *mechanized*. 戦争は機械化した. ¶*wage warfare* against … …に戦争を仕かける.

Q be used *in* actual *warfare* 実戦に用いられる. ¶*aggressive warfare* 侵略戦. ¶*chemical warfare*, *offensive* and *defensive* 攻勢守勢の化学戦. ¶breaches of the customs of *civilized warfare* by a belligerent 交戦国の一方の戦時国際法の慣例違反. ¶*economic warfare* 経済戦争. ¶in those days of *endless warfare* 戦争の絶えない当時. ¶*fierce* and *bitter warfare* 猛烈で苛酷な戦争. ¶a *full-fledged warfare* 本格的戦争. ¶*hand-to-hand warfare* 白兵戦. ¶*incessant domestic warfare* in the house 絶えまない一家の風波. ¶resort to *industrial warfare* 産業ストをやる. ¶A mere incident may cause *international warfare*. ちょっとした事件でも国際戦争の原因になる. ¶*journalistic warfare* 新聞紙上の争い. ¶in *maritime warfare* 海上戦で. ¶*mimic warfare* 擬戦. ¶*modern warfare* 近代戦争. ¶*naval warfare* 海戦. ¶*open warfare* 公然と戦端を開いた戦争. ¶*strenuous warfare* 熱烈な戦争. ¶*wordy warfare* 舌戦.

Q^{2} *air warfare* 空中戦. ¶*class warfare* 階級闘争. ¶*germ warfare* 細菌戦. ¶There has been frequent *guerrilla warfare* by both sides. 双方にゲリラ戦が行われた. 【類】wage *guerrilla warfare*. ¶*land warfare* 陸上戦. ¶the excitement of *party warfare* 党派争いの激こう. ¶*race warfare* 民族戦争. ¶conduct *submarine* and *air warfare* against … …に対し水中・空中戦を行う.

P *after* long *warfare* 長期にわたる戦争の後に. ¶Smokeless steam coal is very invaluable *in* marine *warfare*. 汽かん用無煙炭は海上戦には非常に大切である. ¶the science *of warfare* 戦術.

P^{2} *warfare by* land 陸上戦. ¶the *warefare of* science with theology 科学と神学の戦い.

warm, *n.* 《口語》暖まり.

V *have* a *warm* by the fire 火に暖まる.

warm, *a.* 暖い.

M The day was *oppressively warm*. その日は暑苦しかった. ¶It's a little *too warm* for the season. この季節にしては少し暖か過ぎる. ¶I was scarcely *well warm* in my new abode when … …した当時は新住宅で席いまだ暖ならずというところだった.

P a seat still *warm from* another's occupation 前の人が立ったばかりでまだ暖かい席. ¶*warm in* one's office 職務に慣れた ‖ I was scarce well *warm in* the very new abode, when … その家に引越早々… ‖ He was *warm in* his praise of her. 彼は彼女を熱心にほめた. ‖ be very *warm in* reception 接待に大変愛想がいい. ¶*warm with* wine 酒で興奮して(一杯気げんで).

O With a good stove I was as *warm* as a toast. いいストーブはあるし私はほんとに暖かだった.

warm, *v.* 熱する.

M^{2} *warm up* 《米》[試合前]軽い練習(ウォームアップ)する ‖ The speaker gradually *warmed up* to his subject. 弁士は段々その演説に熱が出てきた. ‖ The club is only really *warming up* to its work when the midnight hour has chimed. そのクラブの仕事は真夜中の時を打つと始めて本格的になって来る ‖ *warm up* machinery 機械運転の用意をする ‖ The weather has *warmed up*. 陽気が暖かになってきた. ‖ *warm up* sake in a bottle 酒のかんをする.

P *warm* oneself *at* the fire 火にあたる. ¶*warm* one's feet *before* the fire 足を火で暖める. ¶get *warmed into* work 仕事に油がのる. ¶*warm* one's hands *over* the fire (brazier) 手を火(など)にかざして暖める. ¶*warm to* one's work その仕事に熱して来る ‖ He was very frank, yet I did not *warm to* him. 彼は非常にあけっぴろげであったが私は彼としたしくならなかった. ‖ be *warmed to* 100 degrees 百度の暑さになる. ¶*warming with* subject その問題に油が乗ってきて.

warmer, *n.* 暖めるもの.

Q^{2} a *bench warmer* 『野球』補欠選手. ¶a *foot warmer* ゆたんぽ(など).

warmth, *n.* あたたかみ; 熱意.

V *apply warmth* to a swelling はれ物を暖める. ¶He *has* no *warmth* of heart. あの人は親切気がない. ¶*take warmth* by fire 火にあたる.

Q advocate it with *astonishing warmth* 驚くほどの熱心さでそれを唱道する. ¶*genial warmth* 気持ちよい暖かさ.

Q^{2} *body warmth* 体温.

P a heart wanting *in warmth* 暖みのない. ¶wear a heavy winter coat *for warmth* 防寒のため厚い冬オーバーを着る. ¶for the sake *of warmth* 温度を高めるために. ¶speak *with warmth* やっきとなって語る ‖ He snapped back at me *with* much *warmth*. 大いに気色ばんで私に逆襲した.

P^{2} the *warmth of* the sun (body, a fire) 太陽(など)の熱.

warm-up, *n.* 《米》[試合前の]軽い練習(ウォーミングアップ).

V *have* a light *warm-up* 軽いウォーミングアップをする.

☞日本語のウォーミングアップは warm-up, warming-up excercise など.

warn, *v.* 警告する.

P *warn* him *against* … 彼に…をしないように用心させる ‖ all persons are *warned against* … …しないように一般の人に警告する ‖ I was *warned against* him. 私は彼を用心するように注意された. ¶he must be *warned* in time *against* ... ...に対してぜひ未然に彼の目をさまさせる必要がある. ¶be *warned* ***by*** the example of ... ...のお手本で戒められる. ¶*warn* sailors ***from*** rocks (shoals) 岩(など)のあることを船員に警告する. ¶He was *warned* ***of*** danger. 彼は危険を警告された. 【類】 *warn* a person ***of*** the consequences of his action. ¶*warn* a tenant ***out of*** a house 借家人に家あけ渡しを通告する. ¶*warn* a person ***to*** silence 沈黙を守れと人に注意する.

O I must *warn* the student that ... 私はその学生に...と訓戒せねばならない. ¶I *warn* you if you do not pay by tomorrow, I will prosecute you. 前もって申し上げておきますがもし明日までにお支払い下さらなければあなたを告訴しします.

warning, *n.* 警告.

V ***carry out*** one's *warnings* その警告通りにする. ¶***circulate*** a *warning* 警告を回す. ¶***display*** storm *warnings* 暴風の警告を掲示する. ¶***extend*** a *warning* to ... ...に対し警告をする. ¶***give*** *warning* of ... ...の警告を与える ‖ ***give*** *warning* against ... ...に対して用心させる ‖ I ***give*** you a week's *warning* (=notice) to go out of these lodgings. 私はあなたにこの下宿を一週間後に出てもらいたい. ¶His example ***has*** its *warnings* for us. 彼の例はわれわれの戒めとなる. ¶He refused to ***heed*** the *warning*. 彼はがんとしてその警告を顧みなかった. ‖ He cried "wolf" so often that we had ceased to ***heed*** the *warning*. 彼はしばしば「危機」呼ばわりをするのでわれわれはその警告にとん着しなくなっていた. ¶The police ***issued*** a *warning*. 警察では警告を発した. ‖ ***issue*** a *warning* against a storm あらしが来るぞと警報を発する. ¶***make*** a *warning* of ... ...の警告をする. ¶***reiterate*** the *warning*: "..."「...」という警報を繰り返す. ¶***send out*** a *warning* to ... ...に警告を発する. ¶***serve*** a *warning* on ... ...に関して警告を発する. ¶***sound*** a *warning* against ... ...に対して警報を鳴らす. ¶***take*** *warning* by another's failure 人の失敗にかんがみる ‖ we may well ***take*** *warning* from ... われわれは...にかんがみる所があるべきだ ‖ ***take*** another's *warning* in good part 人の警告を心よく受ける ‖ Trespassers ***take*** *warning!* 〖掲示〗私有地侵入無用. ¶***utter*** a *warning* against hasty conclusions founded upon premature investigations 不十分な調査に基き軽々に結論を下さないよう忠告する.

Q give ***disciplinary*** *warnings* to students 学生に訓育上の注意を与える. ¶an ***earnest*** *warning* 切なる警告. ¶give an ***exemplary*** *warning* to ... ...の見せしめになる. ¶***grave*** *warnings* 重大な警告. ¶a ***kindly*** *warning* 親切な注意. ¶turn a maid servant away at a ***minute's*** *warning* 予告を与えないで下女に暇を出す. ¶at a ***moment's*** *warning* 予告を与えないで. ¶issue a ***needful*** *warning* to ... ...に必要な警告を発する. ¶a ***personal*** *warning* 本人への警告. ¶a ***practical*** *warning* 実際的な警告. ¶without ***previous*** *warning* 予告なしに. ¶give a person ***proper*** *warning* of ... 人に...の然るべき警告を与える. ¶a ***salutary*** *warning* 健実な訓戒. ¶a ***serious*** *warning* 真剣なる訓戒. ¶utter a ***strong*** *warning* きびしく訓戒する. ¶a ***timely*** *warning* 時宜を得た戒告. ¶If *warning* is ***unavailing***, arrest follows. 改めない場合は逮捕される. ¶a ***weighty*** *warning* 重大な警告.

Q^2 have little ***advance*** *warning* ほとんどだし抜けだった. ¶an ***air raid*** *warning* 空襲警報. ¶a ***gale*** (***storm***) warning to ships and fishermen 船舶や漁民に対する大風(あらし)の警報.

P ***after*** due *warning* 適当に注意をした後で. ¶the example of ... stood ***as*** a *warning* to ... ...の例が...への警告となった. ¶She turned the servant away ***at*** a minute's *warning*. 彼女は即座に女中に暇をやった. ¶***notwithstanding*** the *warnings* of the police 警察の警告も聞かないで. ¶sound a note ***of*** *warning* 警報を発する. ¶attack ***without*** *warning* 突然襲撃する ‖ ***without*** any *warning* 突然.

P^2 a *warning* ***against*** ... ...に対する警告. ¶a *warning* ***for*** the future 将来の戒め. ¶a *warning* ***on*** the matter そのことについての注意. ¶as a *warning* ***to*** other youths 他の若い者への見せしめに ‖ He is a *warning* ***to*** idle students. 彼は怠け者の学生にとっての戒めになる.

warp, *v.* ゆがむ, 反る; ゆがめる, 反らせる.

P a plank *warped* ***by*** heat 熱で曲った板 ‖ judgment *warped* ***by*** self-interest 利己心でかたよった判断. ¶Some words are *warped* ***from*** their primary meanings. ある言葉はその原義から曲げて使われている. ¶be *warped* ***into*** a foreign meaning 曲解される. ¶Some of Japanese sounds cannot be *warped* ***to*** English ones. 日本語の中には英語の音に合わせられないものがある.

warpath, *n.* 征戦の途.

P^2 be ***on*** the *warpath* for the country 国のために征戦の途にある.

warrant, *n.* 逮捕状; 保証.

V ***execute*** a *warrant* of arrest 逮捕状によって執行する. ¶You ***have*** no *warrant* for what you do. 君がそんなことをしては言訳が立たない. ¶***issue*** a *warrant* for the arrest of ... on a charge of murder 殺人罪で...に対し逮捕状を出す. ¶***procure*** a *warrant* from ... for ... ...から...の認許を得る. ¶***produce*** a *warrant* issued by ... authorizing ... ...が出した...の権限委任状を提出する. ¶***serve*** a *warrant* 令状を送達する.

Q^2 an ***arrest*** *warrant* 逮捕状. ¶a ***county*** (***town***) *warrant* 県費(町費)支払命令書. ¶a ***death*** *warrant* 死亡証明書. ¶a ***distress*** *warrant* 困窮証明書. ¶a ***search*** *warrant* 〖法〗捜索状.

P The station master carries a truncheon ***as*** a *warrant* of his authority. 駅長は彼の権限の証明として笏杖(しゃくじょう)を携帯している. ¶enter a house ***on*** a *warrant* 逮捕状によって家にはいる. ¶He is ***under*** a *warrant* of apprehension. 彼に対して逮捕命令が発せられている. ¶I can do it ***with*** the *warrant* of a good conscience. 私はそうしても良心に恥じない.

P^2 a *warrant* ***for*** one's arrest ある人に対する逮捕状 ‖ a *warrant* ***for*** a domiciliary visit 家宅捜索状. ¶There is a *warrant* ***of*** arrest out against ... ...に対する逮捕状が出ている. ¶a *warrant* ***of*** production 拘引状.

warrant, *v.* 保証する.

O This material is *warranted* [to be] real silk. この布地は本物の絹という保証がある.

P I will *warrant* it ***for*** ten years. 私はそれに十年間の保証を付けます. ¶You are not *warranted* ***in*** making such a statement. 君がこのような陳述をするという法はない.

warranty, *n.* 保証.

V With every watch we ***issue*** a *warranty* guaranteeing that it is in sound going order. 時計には一々合格品である旨の保証書を添えます.

P ***under*** the *warranty* of ... ...の保証の下に.

warrior, *n.* 武人, 勇士.

Q a ***brave*** *warrior* 勇敢な軍人. ¶a ***doughty*** *warrior* 勇ましい武士. ¶an ***experienced*** *warrior* 歴戦の勇士. ¶a ***loyal*** *warrior* [国王・政府に対して]忠義な戦士. ¶a ***mighty*** *warrior* 大戦士, 英雄. ¶a ***professional*** *warrior* 戦士. ¶a ***winged*** *warrior* 空軍の将兵, 荒わし.

war-service, *n.* 戦役服務.

P He has received a medal from a foreign government ***for*** *war-service*. 彼は外国政府から従軍記章をもらった.

warship, *n.* 軍艦.

V ***dispatch*** *warships* 軍艦を急派する. ¶***strike*** a *warship* out of the active list 軍艦を非役に編入する.

Q Suddenly a fleet of ***Russian*** *warships* was seen in the offing. 突然ロシアの艦隊が沖に見えた.

P^2 an ***overage*** *warship* 艦齢超過の軍艦, 老朽艦. ¶submarines and ***surface*** *warships* 潜水艦及び海上諸艦.

wary, *a.* 注意深い.

P *wary* ***in*** one's scheme 計画の用意周到な. ¶He is *wary* ***of*** telling secrets. 彼は用心深くて秘密を明かさない.

wash, *n.* 洗浄; 洗たく(物); [液体]洗剤; 漂流場.

V ***get*** a *wash* at a fountain 泉水で一浴する. ¶***give*** it a good *wash* それをよく洗う. ¶***hang*** *wash* over the stove (on the clothesline) ストーブの上(物干しづな)に洗たくものをぶら下げる. ¶***have*** a good *wash* in cold water 冷水でよく洗う. ¶***take*** a *wash* down with cold water 冷水を浴びる.

Q ***dry*** *wash* [アイロンをかけない]洗い干し. ¶This claret (tea, soup) is ***mere*** *wash*. この赤ぶどう酒(など)はてんで水っぽい. ¶***wet*** *wash* 水洗い.

Q^2 Formerly nearly everything you wore could go safely into the ***family*** *wash*. 昔は大抵の衣類は家庭で差支えなく洗たくができた. ¶a ***hair*** *wash* 頭髪洗液. ¶***land*** *wash* [海浜の]高潮線に集まる漂流物. ¶a ***mouth*** *wash* 液体歯みがき.

P It is ***at*** the *wash*. それは洗たくに出してある. ¶It is not yet back ***from*** the *wash*. それはまだ洗たく屋から戻っていない. ¶The shirts are ***in*** the *wash*. ワイシャツは洗たくし

である. ¶send underwear *to* the *wash* (=laundry) 下着を洗たくに出す ‖ ... go *to* the *wash* ...は洗たくに出す.

wash, *v.* 洗う; [ニス・絵具などで]薄く塗る(上塗する).

M His body was *washed* ***ashore.*** 彼の死体は海岸へ打上げられた. ¶The bridge was *washed* ***away*** by the swollen river. 橋は川の増水で洗い流された. ‖ *wash* ***away*** one's sins 罪を洗い清める. ¶*wash* ***out*** a spot (paint) しみ(など)を洗い落す ‖ She looked *washed* ***out*** after reading. 彼女は読書のあとつかれてぐったりしていた. ¶*wash* ***out*** (=***off***) stains 汚れを洗い落す. ¶The blankets are strong, *wash* ***well,*** and moth-proof. その毛布は丈夫で洗たくがきき, しみが食わない.

M² *wash* one's anger ***down*** with a glass of wine ぶどう酒を一杯飲んで腹の立つのを水に流す. ¶*wash* ***over*** with gold 金でめっきする. ¶be *washed* ***overboard*** [波浪で]甲板からさらわれる. ¶*wash* ***thoroughly*** よく洗う. ¶*wash* ***up*** dishes after a meal 食後に食器などを洗う. ¶a corpse *washed* ***up*** by the waves 波で打上げられた死体. 【類】A whale was *washed* ***up*** on shore.

P a district *washed* ***by*** the Mediterranean [Sea]地中海に沿う一地方. ¶*wash* ***for*** a living 洗たくをして生活を立てる. ¶*wash* one's soul ***from*** sins 罪を洗い落して魂を清める. ¶*wash* one's face ***in*** hot water 湯で顔を洗う. ¶It was *washed* ***to*** the beach. それは波で浜辺へ打ち寄せられた. ¶*wash* it ***with*** soap [and water] 石けんでそれを洗う ‖ walls *washed* ***with*** blue (yellow) 青(など)に塗りかえた壁 ⌊(ニスなどで).

washday, *n.* 洗たく日.

O Friday is our *washday.* 《米》金曜日は私たちの洗たく日です. ☞ 英語は washing-day.

washer, *n.* 洗たく機; 洗たくする人.

V She is a ***good*** *washer* 彼女は洗たくがうまい. ¶***install*** a *washer* in a kitchen 台所に洗たく機を備えつける. ¶***keep*** a *washer* in motion 洗たく機を動かしておく.

washing, *n.* 洗たく; 洗たく物.

V The goods do not ***bear*** (=***stand***) *washing.* その品は洗たくがきかない. ¶Mother is ***doing*** her *washing.* 母は洗たくをしている. 【類】a woman ***doing*** the family *washing* in the stream (canal). ¶I have ***got*** my *washing* to do. 私には洗たく物がある. ¶***give*** them a final *washing* in water それらを最後に水洗いをする. ¶***hang*** the *washing* ***out*** to dry 洗たくものをつるして干す. ¶Mother ***has*** *washing* of dresses to do. 母は着物の洗たく仕事がある.

Q He gave his face a ***perfunctory*** *washing.* 彼はほんの申しわけに顔を洗っただけだった.

Q² do the ***family*** *washing* 家庭で洗たくをする.

P Garments shrunk ***in*** *washing* are replaced. 着物が洗たくで縮んだ場合は品物のお引替えします.

washroom, *n.* 便所.

Q an ***immaculately tidy*** *washroom* ちっとも汚れていない ⌊きれいな便所.

wasp, *n.* はち.

P He was stung ***by*** a *wasp.* 彼ははちに刺された. ¶a girl ***like*** a *wasp*=a wasp-waisted girl, 《俗》a wasp [はちのように]ウエストの細い女の子.

wastage, *n.* 残物.

Q² ***food*** *wastage* [捨てた]残飯, さらの残り.

waste, *n.* 徒費; 廃物; 広々した原.

V ***avoid*** *waste* むだをはぶく ‖ ***avoid*** prodigal *waste* 浪費を避ける. ¶It ***involves*** *waste.* それではむだができる. ‖ It ***involves*** a wicked *waste* of precious time. それでは貴重な時間を徒費することになってよくない. ¶It simply ***means*** a *waste* of labor and postage. それでは全くむだ骨を折り郵税を浪費することになる. ¶***reduce*** *waste* むだをはぶく. ¶***stop*** *waste* on ... ...のむだをやめる.

Q an utterly ***barren*** *waste* 全く不毛の荒地. ¶a ***depopulated*** *waste* 住民の絶えた荒野. ¶it seems rather a ***foolish*** *waste* of time for him to ... 彼が...するのはむしろ愚かな時間の空費らしく思われる. ¶a ***frighful*** *waste* of time はなはだしい時間の空費. ¶a ***hideous*** *waste* はなはだしいむだ. ¶an ***intolerable*** *waste* of time はなはだしい時間の空費. ¶a ***mere*** (***sheer***=***utter***) *waste* of labor 全くのむだ骨. ¶a ***prodigal*** *waste* of time 非常な時間の空費. ¶a ***prodigious*** *waste* of money おびただしい金銭の浪費. ¶a very ***silly*** *waste* of time ばかばかしい時間の浪費. ¶the ***trackless*** *waste* of ocean 広ばくたる大洋.

Q² ***kitchen*** *waste*=《米》garbage 台所のくず. ¶***city*** *waste* (=refuse) 都市のごみ. ¶the great expanses of the ***ocean*** *wastes* 広ばくたる大洋. ¶***table*** *waste* 食いのこし.

P wealth ***from*** *waste* 廃物利用. ¶The city was burned ***into*** a desolate *waste.* その市は焼けて荒涼たる廃所と化した. ¶go ***to*** *waste* むだになる.

P² the *waste* ***from*** a factory 工場から出る廃物. ¶It is simply *waste* ***of*** time. それは全くひまつぶしだ. ‖ it is a *waste* ***of*** valuable time to ... ...することは貴重な時間の空費だ. ¶a *waste* ***of*** words しゃべり損 ‖ It is *waste* ***of*** money. 金がもったいない. ‖ a *waste* ***of*** waters (snow) 大海原 ⌊(雪原).

waste, *v.* 徒費する.

M *waste* ***away*** to a skeleton やせ衰えて骨と皮ばかりになる ‖ *waste* ***away*** 浪費する. ¶Our schoolboys' time is ***criminally*** *wasted* by our stupidly old-fashioned system of teaching foreign languages. ばかげたほど旧式な外国語教授法がわが国に行われているために学童の時間を徒費させているのは罪なことだ. ¶a stone *wasted* ***off*** 表面を平にしてある石. ¶*waste* ***prodigally*** 途方もなく濫費する.

P He is *wasted* ***into*** a shadow. 彼はやせて骨と皮ばかりになった. ¶*waste* ***on*** middlemen ブローカー(仲買人)のためむだに金を使う ‖ I will not *waste* words ***on*** such a fool. 僕はこんなばかに口をきいたってむだだから言わない. ‖ *waste* money ***on*** luxuries ぜいたく品に金を浪費する. ¶Many a day does he *waste* ***over*** those useless schemes. 彼はあんな無益な計画に多くの日を費す. 【類】Don't *waste* any more time ***over*** it. ¶dead bodies *wasting* ***to*** clay 腐敗して土となる死体. ¶*waste* one's time and money ***upon*** useless things 役にもたたないことに時間と金を徒費する. ¶countries *wasted* ***with*** (=***by***) war-fire 戦火で荒れ果てた ⌊国々.

wasteful, *a.* 浪費的な.

M ***stupidly*** *wasteful* ばかげて浪費的な.

P *wasteful* ***of*** life むだな殺生をする.

watch, *n.* (**1**) 懐中(腕)時計.

V ***carry*** a *watch* 時計を持つ. ¶***consult*** one's *watch* to learn the time 時刻を知ろうと時計を見る. ¶***draw out*** one's *watch* 懐中時計を取出す. ¶***fix*** a *watch* 時計を修理する. ¶***Have*** you a *watch* with you? 時計をお持ちですか. ¶***hock*** (=pawn) a *watch* 《米》時計を入質する. ¶***mend*** a *watch* 時計を直す. 【類】have one's *watch* ***mended*** (***oiled***). ¶***pledge*** one's *watch* at the nearest pawnbroker's shop すぐ近くの質屋に時計を質入れする. ¶***pull out*** (=***produce***) one's *watch* 懐中時計を取出す. ¶The time changes here, and *watches* must be ***put forward*** an hour. ここで時間が変るから時計を一時間進めなければならない. ¶***regulate*** a *watch* 時計を調整する. ¶I have ***sent*** my *watch* to be mended. 時計を直しにやってある. ¶***set*** one's *watch* by (=with)... 時計を...に合わせる, ¶***set*** (=***put***) one's *watch* ***back*** (***ahead***) an hour 時計を一時間戻す(進める) ‖ I ***set*** my *watch* by guess at half past two. 二時半ごろだろうと見当をつけて時計を合わせた. ¶***steal*** a *watch* from ... ...から時計を盗む. ¶It is fashionable to ***wear*** small *watches* now. 時計は小型が今の流行です. ¶***wind*** [***up***] a *watch* 時計を巻く.

V² My *watch* ***gains*** (***loses***) a little. 私の時計は少し進む(遅れる). ¶My *watch* has ***gone*** to be cleaned. 私の時計は掃除にやってある. ¶" Click, click, click " ***went*** my *watch.* 私の時計はかちかち動いていた. ‖ My *watch* ***goes*** (=***moves***) ***a little too fast.*** 私の時計は少し進む. ¶The *watch* has ***run down.*** 時計が(巻かないために)止まった. ¶My *watch* has ***stopped.*** 私の時計が止まった. ¶The *watch* ***ticks.*** 時計はかちかちいっている.

Q a ***cute little*** *watch* かわいらしい小型の時計. ¶My *watch* is ***fast*** (***slow***). 僕の時計は進んで(遅れて)いる. ¶wear a ***gold*** *watch* 金時計を持つ. ¶a ***nickel*** *watch* ニッケルの時計. ¶***radium*** (=" ***glowworm*** ") *watch* ラジウム文字時計. ¶a ***Swiss*** *watch* スイス製の時計.

Q² a ***clock*** *watch* [昔あった]時を告げる懐中時計. ¶I've picked a smart Lord Elgin for my ***graduation*** *watch.* 私の卒業記念として素敵なエルジン製の時計を手に入れた. ¶a ***one-dollar*** *watch* 一ドル懐中時計. ¶a ***self-winding*** *watch* ぜんまいが自動的に巻ける時計. ¶a ***stop*** *watch* ストップ・ウォッチ. ¶a ***thin-model*** *watch* 薄型の時計. ¶a ***wrist*** *watch* 腕時計.

P What time is it ***by*** your *watch?* あなたの時計で今何時 ⌊ですか.

(**2**) 見張, 番.

V In ***handing over*** his *watch* to his relieving colleagues an engineer has to satisfy himself that everything is working satisfactorily. 見張りの引継ぎをする時機関士は事故の心配のないことを確認しなければならない. ¶*keep watch* 監視する, お通夜をする. 【類】*keep watch* for the enemy / *keep watch* against a thief / *keep watch* during the night ‖ *keep* a careful *watch* on one's movements その行動を注意深く見張っている ‖ The shepherds *keep* their *watch* over their flocks by night. 羊飼いはその(羊)群の夜番をする. ¶*maintain* a vigilant *watch* 油断なく見張っている. ¶*place* a *watch* 番人をおく. ¶*relieve* the *watch* 当直の交代をする. ¶*set* a *watch* on ... ...に番人をつける.

Q keep *close watch* upon the pennies 小銭(きん少の出費など)決しておろそかにしない. ¶keep a *close* and *constant watch* on the work 絶えず厳重に仕事を監視する. ¶keep a *sharp watch* 抜目なく警戒する. ¶a *sleepless watch* 不寝番. ¶keep a *strict watch* on ... ...を厳重に見張る.

Q² a *standing watch* 立番. ¶a *town watch* 町の見張番.

P *during* a *watch* 見張り中. ¶*in* the *watches* of the night 夜眠らずにいる時. ¶He is *off watch*. 彼は非番だ. ¶men *on watch* 当番の人々. 【類】the engineer *on watch* ‖ he is constantly *on* the *watch* (=lookout) for ... 彼は絶えず...を見張っている. 【類】*on* the *watch* for an opportunity of ... ¶*under* close *watch* 厳重監視の下に.

watch, *v.* 見詰める, 見張る.

M *anxiously watch* 熱心に見つめる. ¶*breathlessly watch* 息を殺してうかがう. ¶*watch* the market *closely* 市況を細かに観察する ‖ *watch* events *closely* 事件の経過を精察する. 【類】*watch* him *closely* / the situation is being *closely watched*. ¶*eagerly watch* for a chance 熱心に機会をねらう. ¶very *jealously watched* いささかの油断なく監視されて. ¶*watch keenly* the development of the situation 時局の発展を注意して見守る. 【類】Its progress will be *keenly watched* by us. ¶*watch* him *narrowly* 彼をじっと見つめる. ¶*Watch out*, all the same! それでも気をつけろ. ‖ *Watch out* for these pictures. 〖広告〗これらの映画をお見逃しないように. ☞ 英語用法では look out が普通. ¶*watch sharply* for ... ...をきびしく監視する.

P affectionate disciples *watching around* his bed 彼の寝床を取巻く師匠思いの弟子たち. ¶*watch at* one's bedside 人のまくらべを見守る. ¶*watch by* his bed 床に付添う ‖ The parade was *watched by* thousands of spectators. その観兵式は数千の人が見物していた. ¶*watch for* a chance (=an opportunity) 機会を待構える ‖ *watch for* fires 火事を警戒する. ¶*watch off* the harbor mouth 港外で監視する. ¶*watch* a person *out of* sight 姿が見えなくなるまで人を目送する. ¶My guardian angel will *watch over* me. 私の守本尊が私を守って下さるでしょう. ‖ *watch over* the land 国を守護する ‖ *watch over* the dictionary in its progress through the press 辞書の印刷過程を監視する. ¶*watch with* the sick 寝ずに病人を看護する. ¶*watch* ... *through* the window 窓越しに...を注視する ‖ *watch* it *with* much interest 多大の興味を持ってそれを見守る.

O *Watch* your step, please. 足下御用心, 気をつけて下さい.

watcher, *n.* 熱心な観察者.

V *corrupt* the *watchers* 監視人を買収する.

Q a *thoughtful watcher* of events at the present time 現時のできごとに思慮深く注意する人.

Q² a *poll watcher* 投票監理人.

watchful, *a.* 注意して.

M *constantly watchful* 絶えず注意して. ¶be *ever watchful* 絶えず目を光らしている.

P Be *watchful against* temptations. 誘惑に陥らないよう用心せよ. ¶be *watchful of* the times 天下の形勢をうかがう ‖ be *watchful of* one's own interests 自分の利益には抜け目がない.

watching, *n.* 監視.

Q *anxious watching* はらはらしながら見守ること. ¶keep *strict watching* 厳重に見張る.

watchmaker, *n.* 時計製造者.

P² *watchmakers to* the Admiralty [英国]海軍省御用時計師.

watchman, *n.* 警備員.

Q² a *hotel watchman* ホテルの守衛. ¶a *night watchman* on his rounds 巡回している夜警.

watchword, *n.* 合言葉, 標語.

Q efficiency, the *modern watchword* 現代の合言葉「能率」. ¶"Excelsior" is *our watchword*. 「より高く」ということがわれらの標語である.

P² During the seventeenth century monopoly became the *watchword of* the Dutch. 十七世紀に独占ということがオランダ人の標語となった.

water, *n.* (**1**) 水; 水道.

V A sponge *absorbs water*. 海綿は水を吸収する. ¶*add* a little very hot *water* 熱い湯を少し加える. ¶*bail water* out of the boat 船のあかをくみ出す. ¶*boil water* in a tea kettle for tea やかんにお茶の湯をわかす. ¶Swimmers in winter *brave* the icy *water* of the River Sumida. 寒中水泳者は隅田川の氷のような水をものともしない. ¶It *brings* the *water* to one's mouth. それを見ると口によだれが出て来る. ‖ consecrated *water brought* from the Jordan ヨルダン川から持ってきた聖なる流れ. ¶*calm* the *waters* of that stormy sea 荒れた海の波を静める. ¶A steamer's screw *churns* the *water*. 汽船の推進機が水をかき回す. ¶*conserve water* 水を節約する. ¶*cut* (=*shut*) *off water* [水道など]断水する. ¶*dash* cold *water* in one's face その顔へ冷水をぶっかける. ¶*discharge water* 放水する. ¶They *disturb* the placid *water* of the lake with their early plunge. 彼らは朝っぱらから水浴びをやってその静かな湖水をかき乱す. ¶*drain* off *water* 水を切る. ¶*draw water* from a well 井戸から水をくむ ‖ *draw* the *water* off a pond 池の水さらいをする. ¶*dump* the hot *water* on ... ...に湯をどっとあける. ¶Sometimes divers *enter* the *water* feet first. 飛込みをやる時(直立のまま)足を先にして水にはいることがある. ¶"*find*" *water* [水の出そうな場所を選定して]井戸を掘る. ¶*flip water* from ... ...から水を[ぱたぱた]はたいて切る. ¶Oxygen and hydrogen combine to *form water*. 酸素と水素が合して水となる. ¶*harness* the *waters* of the river 河水を水力電気に利用する. ¶An island *has water* all around it. 島は回りが水である. ¶I think I *hear water* running. 水が出しっぱなしになっているらしい. ¶Sponges *hold water*. 海綿は水を含む. ‖ The theory *holds* every *water* and is essentially unassailable. その学説は全くすきがなく本質的に論ばくを許さない. ‖ *hold* the *water back* 水をせき止める. ¶*keep down* the *water* from overflowing その水のはんらんを防ぐ. ¶The *water* is *laid on* direct to the stables. 水が直接うまやへ引いてある. ‖ In the winter hot *water* is *laid on*. 冬は湯が出るようになっている. ¶*let water run* 水を出す ‖ *let water through* 水が浸透する. ¶The recent rains had *raised* the *water* very much. この前の雨でひどく水かさが増していた. ¶*obtain* drinking *water* 飲料水を得る. ¶*pipe water* from the well パイプで井戸から水を引く. ¶fountains *playing water* 噴水. ¶*pour water* over burning coals 燃えている石炭に水をかける. ¶*pump water* from a deep well 深い井戸からポンプで水を揚げる. ¶Don't *put* too much *water* on these plants. これらの植木には余り水をやるな. ¶*put in water* 水をさす. ¶*quaff water* 水をぐいと飲む. ¶The wind *ruffled* the *water*. 風で水面にちりめんじわが寄った. ¶Baths *run* hot and cold *water*. ふろには湯も水も出るようになっている. ¶*souse* (=dash) *water* on the head 頭に水をぶっかける. ¶*spill water* 水をこぼす. ¶*splash water* 水をはねかす. ¶*spout water* [くじらが]水を噴出する. ¶*spray water* on to ... ...に霧を吹きかける. ¶*sprinkle water* on ... 水を...にかける ‖ *sprinkle water about* 水をまき散らす. ¶*spurt water* 水を噴出させる. ¶*squeeze out* the *water* from a towel タオルをしぼる. ¶*squirt* the *water* into the ear 耳の中に水をふきかける. ¶*sterilize water* 水を殺菌する. ¶*store water* 貯水する. ¶*swash water* on a floor 床にばちゃばちゃ水をまく. ¶*swish water* from a broom [水にぬらした]ほうきの水をしゅっと切る. ¶*take* the *waters* at Hamburg ハンブルグへ湯治に行く ‖ The ship *took* the *water*. 船が進水した. ¶*take in water* 浸水する. ¶He *threw* cold *water* upon the scheme. 彼はその計画にけちをつけた. ¶*tread water* 立ち泳ぎをする. ¶*turn on* (*off*) *water* 出口をひねって水を出す(止める). ¶I *want* some hot *water* to drink. 私は湯が飲みたい.

V² The *water churns* among the rocks. 水が岩間に逆巻いている. ¶The *water comes* above the knees. 水がひざの上までつく. ¶The *water* is *coming in*. 水が侵入して来る. ¶The *waters* of the lake *descend* in some places to the extraordinary depth of 93 fathoms. 湖水には九十三ひろという驚くべき深さの所がある. ¶*Water drips* from the eaves. ひさしから水がしたたる. ¶*Waters foam* and *sparkle* in the river. 川では水があわ立ちきらめいている.

¶The *water* is ***going out***. 水が引いている. ¶this wonderful *water* ***issues*** from the springs of ... この驚くべき水は...の泉から出る. ¶*Water* is ***rising*** fast. ずんずん増水している. ¶The *water* is now ***runnig high***. もうそろそろあげ潮だ. ¶The *water* ***sinks*** into the earth. 水が地面にしみ込む. ¶The *water* ***springs*** from the rock. その水は岩からわき出る. ¶The river *water* ***stood*** 30 feet above normal level. 河水が平常水準より三十フィート高かった. ¶*Water* is ***subsiding*** fast. 水がずんずん退いて引く. ¶The *waters* are ***swelling***. 水かさが増している.

Q ***aerated*** *waters* ***natural*** or ***artificial*** 天然または人造の炭酸水. ¶the ***black*** *waters* of the mighty river—the Thames 大テムズ川の黒ずんだ水. ¶***blood-tinged*** *waters* 血で色のついた水 ‖ leave ***boiled*** *water* to cool 湯をさます. ¶***boiling*** *water* 熱湯. ¶***clear, hot*** *water* 白湯(さゆ). ¶soak it in ***cold*** *water* overnight 一晩中冷水につけておく. ¶***contaminated*** *water* 汚水. ¶***crystal-clear*** *water* 水晶のように澄んだ水. ¶***dead*** *water* たまり水. ¶He was picked up on ***deep*** *water* in a boat. 彼はボートに乗って水の深い所に出ているのを拾い上げられた. ¶***drinkable*** *water*=water fit to drink 飲用水. ¶the ***eddying*** *water* 渦巻く水. ¶The *water's* ***fine*** in Canada. カナダは水遊びにはよい. ¶a Yedoite of the ***first*** *water* きっすいの江戸っ子. ¶make ***foul*** *water* [船が]水をにごらす. ¶***fragrant*** (=***perfumed***) *waters* 香水. ¶***free*** *water* [水せんなどから]漏れている水. ¶***fresh*** *water* 淡水. ¶***hard*** (***soft***) *water* 硬(軟)水. ¶***heavy*** *water* 〘化〙重水. ¶at ***high*** (***low***) *water* 満(干)潮時に. ¶He seems to be usually in ***hot*** *water* about something or other. 彼は大抵何かしら心配ごとがあるようだ. ¶All rooms are fitted with electric heaters, electric fans, ***hot*** and ***cold running*** *water*. どの室にも電熱器や扇風機やひねれば出る湯や水の設備がある. ¶***juvenile*** *water* 若水. ¶a spring of ***limpid*** *water* すき透った水. ¶***muddy*** *water* 泥水. ¶drink ***plain*** *water* 真水を飲む. ¶It is a land of beautiful mountains and valleys with fine trees and much ***running*** *water*. そこには美しい山や谷もありまたすてきな樹木がありそして流水も多い. 【類】within the perpetual sound of the ***running*** *water*. ¶***salty*** *water* しょっぱい水. ¶***slack*** *water* よどんだ水. ¶Thus the scheme may now be deemed to have got into ***smooth*** *water*. かくしてその計画は今や軌道に乗ったものと思ってよい. ¶***soapy*** *water* 石けん水. ¶***stagnant*** *water* よどんだ水. ¶***still*** *water* 静止した水. ¶There is ***sufficient*** (=***ample***) *water* for vessels of any size. どんな喫水の船でも差支えない. ¶***strong*** *waters* 火酒; 硝酸 (=aqua fortis). ¶***tepid*** (=***lukewarm***) *water* 微温湯. ¶provide plenty of ***troubled*** *water* in which the Communists can fish 共産主義者に漁夫の利を与えるに十分な紛争を作る. ¶***turbid*** *water* 濁った水. ¶***untreated*** *water* from the river 処理してないそのままの河水.

Q² ***ammonia*** *water* アンモニア水. ¶***city*** *water* [都市の]水道. ¶***drinking*** *water* (=water fit to drink) 飲料水. ¶***feed*** *water* [ボイラーなどへの]給水用の水 ‖ an apparatus for injecting ***feed*** *water* into a steam boiler 蒸気がまに給水する装置. ¶melted ***snow*** *water* とけた雪水. ¶sparkling ***soda*** *water* あわ立つソーダ水 ‖ stale ***soda*** *water* 気の抜けたソーダ水. ¶***street*** *water* 街路の雨水. ¶***surface*** *water* 地表水. ¶***toilet*** *water* 化粧水.

P keep oneself ***above*** *water* 頭を水から出している ‖ manage to keep one's head ***above*** *water* どうやらこうやら借金しないで生活する. ¶***across*** the *water* 水をへだてて向う岸の. ¶spend the summer ***among*** the mountains and the *waters* 山水の間に夏を過ごす. ¶a rock four feet below the surface ***at*** low *water* 干潮の時に水深四フィートの所にある岩. ¶hold one's head ***below*** the *water* 頭を水の中に入れている. ¶sink ***beneath*** the *water* 水中に沈む. ¶go ***by*** *water* 水路で行く. ¶live ***in*** *water* 水中に住む ‖ soak a towel ***in*** cold *water* 冷水にタオルを浸す. ¶fall ***into*** *water* 水中に落ち込む. ¶shed blood ***like*** *water* とめどもなく血を流す ‖ waste money ***like*** *water* 金を湯水のように使う. ¶a dearth ***of*** *water*=a water famine 水ききん. ¶a vast expanse (=stretch) ***of*** *water* 広々とした水面 ‖ Yet none could check the rise ***of*** the *waters*. しかもだれ一人この大勢を阻止することはできなかった. ¶small bubbles ***on*** the *water* 水上に浮ぶ小さなあわ ‖ keep oneself afloat ***on*** the *water* 体が沈まないようにする ‖ Boats sail ***on*** *water*. ボートは水上を走る. ‖ an excursion ***on*** the *water*=a boat excursion 船遊び. ¶A dense fog lies ***over*** the *water*. 濃霧が水上にたれこめている. ¶move ***through*** the *water* 水を押しわけて行く. ¶The town is five feet ***under*** *water*. その町は五フィート水に浸っている. ‖ spear fish ***under*** *water* 水中の魚を突く ‖ remain ***under*** *water* 水中に留まる ‖ The village was twice ***under*** *water* in the last twenty years from the overflow of the river. 村はこの川のはんらんで過去二十年間に二回浸水した. ¶fill it ***with*** *water* それに水を一杯入れる. ¶*water* ***on*** the brain 脳水腫(しゅ).

「水, 洪水; *pl.* 鉱泉.

(2) [しばしば *pl.*] [流動する水の意から] 海面, 近海, 河(湖)

V Her razor-edged bows ***cleave*** the *waters*. その船のかみそりの刃のような船首が波を切って進む. ¶***cross*** the *waters* 海(など)を越える. ¶go to ***drink*** the *waters* [保養に]温泉に行く. ¶These vessels ***frequent*** the *waters* of the Pacific Ocean. これらの船はしばしば太平洋上を航行する. ¶***navigate*** narrow *waters* 狭い海面を航行する. ¶***plow*** (英 ***plough***) the *waters* of the ocean [船が]大洋の波をける. ¶Here the river ***pours*** its *waters* into the sea. 川はここで海に入る. ¶***regulate*** the *waters* [of a river] 治水する.

V² Still *waters* ***run*** deep. 〘諺〙浅瀬にあだ波.

Q in "***blue*** *water*" 深海で. ¶The tunny fish, weight 731 pounds, length $9^1/_2$ feet, is the second largest ever caught in ***British*** *waters*. 重量七百三十一ポンド長さ九フィート二分の一のまぐろが英国近海でとれたものでは第二位の大きさのものである. ¶the ***coastal*** *waters* of the United States アメリカの沿海. ¶the ***curative*** *waters* of the White Sulphur Springs ホワイト・サルファー温泉の治病水. ¶***defensive*** *waters* 防衛水域. ¶She now maintains a considerable naval force in ***Far Eastern*** *waters*. その国は今や極東の海域でかなりの海軍力を保持している. ¶the ***gray*** *waters* of the Seine River セーヌ川の灰色の水. ¶It was the first steamer beheld in ***Japanese*** *waters*. それは最初に日本近海に姿を現わした汽船であった. ¶trouble ***legal*** *waters* 法曹界を荒す. ¶the ***murky*** *waters* of the Thames テムズの濁水. ¶***mineral*** *waters* 鉱泉水; 《英口》ラムネ(ソーダ水). ¶***moving*** *waters* 流水. ¶***ornamental*** *waters* in a park 公園の(装飾用の)池. ¶***pellucid*** *waters* [川・湖水などの]すき透った水. ¶***pirate infested*** *waters* 海賊が出没する海. ¶***salt*** *water* 塩水. ¶the ***shallow*** *waters* near the shore 海岸近くの浅瀬. ¶***seething*** (=***turbulent***) *waters* 立ち騒ぐ波浪. ¶be sailing in ***smooth*** *waters* 〘比ゆ〙平穏無事に過ぎている. ¶Never dive in ***strange*** *waters*. [川や海で]なれない水に飛込んではいけない. ¶***territorial*** *waters* 領海. ¶***thermal*** *waters* 温泉. ¶in ***these*** *waters* この近海に. ¶its ***tributary*** *waters* その支流. ¶the ***tumbling*** (=***gushing***) *water* 奔流. ¶***upper*** *waters* (=reaches) 上流.

Q² ***angling*** *waters* 釣場. ¶in ***China*** *waters* シナ海に(で). ¶***coast*** *waters* 沿海. ¶be rich in ***fishing*** *waters* 釣場が多い. ¶The ***flood*** *waters* receded. はんらんした水が引いた. ¶***trout*** *waters* ますのとれる湖川など. ¶the fleet wandering in ***home*** *waters*. 自国の近海を回遊している艦隊.

P A ten percent revenue on all fish taken ***from*** Portuguese *waters* is Portugal's oldest tax. ポルトガル近海からとれる魚類全部の十パーセントを国庫の収入にするというのがポルトガルの一番古い税である. ¶close of day ***on*** Hawaiian *waters* ハワイ近海の日の入り. ¶the visit of the French fleet ***to*** British *waters* フランス艦隊の英国近海訪

(3) 小便. └問.

V Much pain is felt in ***making*** *water*. 小便する時にひどく痛む. ¶On no account must the patient be allowed to get up, either to ***pass*** *water* or to have the bowels removed. どんなことがあっても病人に起きて小便・大便の用をたさせてはいけない. 【類】He had a full bladder (ぼうこう) which is bursting to ***pass*** *water*. ¶He desired to urinate and was in fear of being unable to ***retain*** his *water*. 彼は尿意を催しあやうく漏らしそうになった.

(4) 純度.

Q an aristocrat of the ***first*** *water* れっきとした貴族 ‖ a volume which may be described, without exaggeration, as a literary gem of the ***first*** *water* まさに文学上の宝石と評しても誇張でない著作 ‖ a humorist of the ***first*** *water* 第一流のユーモア小説家.

water, *v.* かんがいする.

M *water* [***out***] plants 植物に水をやる. ¶The country is

well watered. その地方は給水が十分だ.

M² *water down* a bill 議案を骨抜きにする ‖ *water down* the original stiff demand to a demand that ...強硬な要求を...という要求に緩和する.

P the region ***watered by*** the stream その小川の流れている土地.

water-closet, *n.* 便所.

Q² a high ***cistern*** *water-closet* 高置水そう式便所.

water-colo[u]r, *n.* 水彩画.

V "***do***" him in *water-colors* 彼の(肖像を)水彩画にかく.

P a painting ***in*** *water-color*=a water-color 水彩画.

water-crane, *n.* 給水せん.

Q a ***fixed*** *water-crane* [鉄道などの]固定給水せん.

waterfall, *a.* 滝.

Q A ***tiny*** *waterfall* was gushing over the edge of a precipice. 小滝ががけぷちから流れ落ちていた.

watering, *n.* 注水.

V give a ***good*** *watering* [植木など]水を十分にやる.

watering-cart, *n.* 散水車.

Q² a ***street*** *watering-cart* (=water wagon) 街路散水車.

watering-place, *n.* 《英》海水浴場, 湯治場.

Q ***English*** *watering-places,* inland and at the seaside 英国の内地及び海岸の湯治場. ¶a ***pretty*** and ***fashionable*** *watering-place* on the southern coast 上流社会の集まる南部海岸の美しい海水浴場. ¶a ***rising*** *watering-place* 新興の海浜避暑地.

watermark, *n.* 最高水準.

V ***reach*** the high *watermark* of her culture その文化の最盛期に達する.【類】England ***reached*** high *watermark* in the matter of (において) naval expenditures in 1904.

watermark, *v.* すかし模様を入れる.

P The words "..." are *watermarked* ***on*** the paper.「...」の言葉がすかしにして紙に入れてある.

water-power, *n.* 水力.

V ***utilize*** the *water-power* of Niagara Falls for economic purposes ナイアガラばく布の水力を経済的用途に利用する.

P The machines are driven ***by*** *water-power.* その機械は水力を使う.

water-rate, *n.* 水道使用料.

V ***pay*** the *water-rate* 水道使用料を払う.

water-ring, *n.* 波紋.

V ***start*** the *water-rings* 水に環形波紋を起す.

watershed, *n.* 分水界, 分水線.

V it ***forms*** the *watershed* between the rivers flowing into ... and those ... それは...に流れる川と...に流れる川との分水線をなす.

water-supply, *n.* 給水.

V The city of Hamburg ***draws*** the *water-supply* from the River Elbe. ハムブルグ市の給水はエルベ川から引いてある.

Q the inadequacy of the ***existing*** *water-supply* 現在の水道の不十分.

waterway, *n.* 水路.

Q the hourly perils of collision on the ***crowded*** *waterway* その混雑する水路で毎時間起る衝突の危険. ¶***navigable*** *waterways* 航行しうる水路.

P ***by*** *waterways* 水路で.

water-wheel, *n.* 水車.

Q an ***overshot*** *water-wheel* 上射式水車. ¶an ***undershot*** *water-wheel* 下射式水車.

Q² a ***wood*** *water-wheel* 木製水車.

waterworks, *n.* 水道.

V Modern *waterworks* have been ***installed,*** the supply being furnished by the ... River. 給水を...川から得て現代式水道を敷設している. ‖ ***install*** home *waterworks* and lights 専用の水道と電灯を取りつける.

wave, *n.* 波; 波長; 揺れ動き; 《口語》毛髪のウエーブ.

V The crime has ***aroused*** a *wave* of popular indignation. その犯罪に対して世人は一般に憤慨した. ¶***calm*** the *waves* 波浪を静める. ¶She ***has*** a *wave* in her hair. 彼女の髪の毛は縮んでいる. ¶***raise*** the *waves* (billows) 波浪(大波)を起す. ¶***rule*** the *waves* 海洋を支配する. ¶***start*** a *wave* of buying 買手が急にふえる. ¶***stem*** the *waves* 波に逆らって進む. ¶***watch*** the *waves* in the water 波を見守る.

V² The *waves* ***beat*** upon the seashore. 波が海岸に打ち寄せる. ¶*Waves* ***break.*** 波が砕ける. ¶The *waves* ***flag up*** against the walls. 波が岩壁に広がる. ¶*Waves* ***howl*** in the distance. 遠くにうねりが聞える. ¶The *waves* ***ran*** high. 波が高かった. ¶*Waves* ***rise.*** 波が立つ. ¶*Waves* ***surge.*** 波がうねる. ¶The *waves* ***swash*** against the bulkhead. 波が隔壁に打当る. ¶The *waves* ***swept*** (=***washed or dashed***) over the deck. 波が甲板を洗った.【類】A cold *wave* ***swept*** (=hit) the coast area.

Q a ***cold*** *wave* 寒波; [毛髪の]コールド・パーマ ‖ A ***cold*** *wave* passed over the country. はなはだしい寒波が全国を襲った.【類】A sub-zero (零度以下の) ***cold*** *wave* bore down on the northeastern States. ¶***electric[al]*** *waves* 電波. ¶***great*** *waves* 大波. ¶The *waves* were too ***high*** to bathe. 波が高いので海水浴ができなかった. ¶***medium*** *wave* 〖ラジオ〗[百メートルないし八百メートルの長さの]中波長. ¶***monstrous*** *waves* 巨大な波. ¶***mountainous*** *waves* 山なす波. ¶Her hair has ***natural*** *waves.* 彼女の髪は天然パーマ(ちちれ毛)だ. ¶***short*** (***long***) *waves* 短(長)波. ¶***permanent*** *waves* パーマネント・ウエーブ. ¶watering-places on the sea-coast where the *waves* are ***powerful*** 波の強い海水浴場. ¶***surging*** *waves* うねり. ¶a ***tidal*** *wave* 津波. ¶***violent*** *waves* 怒とう. ¶As far as the eye could reach, ***white-crested*** *waves* were to be seen rolling in all directions. 目のとどく限り四方八方に白波がのたくっていた.

Q² A ***crime*** *wave* sweeps Manila. マニラでは犯罪のあらしが吹きまくっている.【類】***Crime*** *waves* generally follow wars. / the mounting ***crime*** *wave.* ¶a ***heat*** *wave* 熱波, 輻射熱(かげろうなど) ‖ the toll of a ***heat*** *wave* 炎熱の犠牲(死者数).【類】a 96-degree ***heat*** *wave* / during a summer ***heat*** *wave* (熱波) / It is during a ***heat*** *wave* that the ice-cream soda-fountain establishment (アイスクリーム, ソーダ水屋) does a roaring trade (商売繁盛する). ¶a ***juvenile crime*** *wave* 青少年の犯罪ひん発. ¶He was born, bred, and nurtured within sound and sight of the ***ocean*** *wave.* 彼は海岸に生れ大海の波の音を聞き波を見て育った. ¶***radar*** *waves* [高周波数をもつ]レーダー電波. ¶***radio*** *waves* [無線周波数をもつ]ラジオ電波. ¶The European ***snow*** *waves* have extended from end to end of the Continent. 欧州の降雪をもたらす寒波は大陸のすみずみまで広がった. ¶***sound*** *waves* 音波. ¶inspire a ***suicide*** *wave* 自殺の流行を起させる.

P The tiny craft was soon out ***among*** the big *waves.* 小船は間もなく大波の間に現われた. ¶The ship dropped out of sight ***behind*** big *waves.* その船は大波にさえぎられて見えなくなった. ¶those who sleep ***beneath*** the *waves* 波の下(海底)に眠る人々. ¶The ship was tossed about ***by*** the *waves.* その船は波に翻ろうされた. ‖ transformed as if ***by*** the *wave* of a magic wand 魔法使いがつえを一振りしたように外観が変って. ¶rise ***in*** *waves* 波のように次ぎ次ぎ起る ‖ toss about ***in*** the *waves* 波にもてあそばれる. ¶at the mercy ***of*** the *waves* 波のまにまに ‖ hear the long roll ***of*** the *waves* 長い波のうねりが聞える. ¶The light glimmers ***on*** the *waves.* 光が波の上にちらちらと光る. ¶The ship labored ***over*** the *waves* 船が波にもまれた. ¶tear ahead ***through*** mountainous *waves* 山なす波を分けて突進する. ¶float ***upon*** the *waves* 波の上に浮ぶ. ¶go to a summer (winter) resort ***with*** the first *wave* of heat (cold) 熱(寒)波が襲来するとすぐに避暑(寒)する.

P² a tidal *wave* ***from*** the Atlantic 大西洋から押し寄せて来る津波. ¶with a *wave* ***of*** his hand 手を一度振って ‖ as the *waves* ***of*** popularity or unpopularity pass over them 人気の消長によって(役員などの変動があるなど).

wave, *v.* 手を振る.

M *wave* ***aside*** 手まねで排斥する. ¶*wave* ***away*** (***off***) 手を振って去らせる; 手を振ってことわる.【類】*wave* a child ***away.*** ¶People were looking down, *waving* from their window. I *waved* ***back.*** 人々は窓から見て手を振っていた. 私も手を振ってそれに答えた. ¶I *waved* him ***nearer.*** 私は手まねをして彼をそばへ寄せた. ¶Branches *waved* ***wildly*** to and fro. 枝があちこちと激しく揺れた.

M² *wave* us ***on*** [交通警官など]手を振って進めと合図する.

P Flags are *waving* ***in*** the air (breeze) 旗が空中(風)に翻っている. ‖ Her hair *waves* ***in*** beautiful curves. 髪が美しい曲線の波を見せている. ¶A sun-flag *waves* ***over*** his house. 日の丸が彼の家の上に翻っている.【類】The British flag *waves* ***over*** a considerable part of South Africa. ¶I *waved* ***to*** him to do it. 私は手を振って彼にそれをしろと合図した. ‖ She *waved* ***to*** me in a farewell.=She waved me a farewell. 私の方に手を振ってさようならをした. ¶*wave* goodby ***toward*** ... ...の方にさよならと手を振る.

wave-length, *n.* 波長.

V private wireless stations ***using*** *wave-lengths* below those allotted to the public and commercial services —

般公衆用または商業用に規定したものより短い波長を使用する個人の無線局.

P transmit *on* a *wave-length* of 1,000 meters 千メートルの波長で伝送する.

waver, *v.* ためらう.

P *waver between* … …の間に立ってためらう. ¶I found that they had not *wavered in* their attachment to each other. お互いの愛情は決して変らないことを私は知った. ‖ This caused them to *waver in* their faith. このために彼らの信仰がぐらつき出した. 【類】He never *wavered in* his conviction that his mission in life was to be a poet.

waving, *n.* 振ること.

P² There was cheering and *waving of* handkerchiefs. 歓呼する者やハンカチを振る者があった. ‖ the *waving of* the grass 草原の波動.

wax, *n.* ろう(ワックス).

Q² *animal wax* 動物性ワックス. ¶*paraffin wax* パラフィン・ワックス. ¶*sealing wax* 封ろう. ¶*vegetable wax* 木ろう.

P form figures *in wax* ろうで色々な像を作る. ¶coat it *with wax* ろうでその上塗りする.

wax, *v.* 段々大きくなる, 段々盛んになる.

M *wax eloquent* over … …の話に油が乗る. ¶*wax* very *enthusiastic* about … …の気炎をあげる.

O The moon *waxes* and wanes. 月は円くなったりかけたりする.

way, *n.* (**1**) 道, 進路.

V *ask* one's *way* 道をたずねる ‖ *ask* a person the *way* to … 人に…への道を聞く. ¶*bar* one's *way* その通行を妨げる. ¶*beg* one's *way* from door to door 門付の物もらいをして旅をする. ¶*block* the *way* of youth 青年の進路をふさぐ. ¶*break* one's *way* at a place for the night 旅行の途中である場所へ一泊する ‖ The chick *breaks* its *way out* into the world. ひよっ子は(からを破って)世の中に出て来る. ¶*carve* one's *way* to fortune by the sword 剣道で身を立てる. ¶*clear* the *way* [通れるように]道を明ける ‖ *clear* the *way* at a procession 行列の先頭に立つ ‖ *clear* the *way* for … …のために道を開く ‖ to *clear* the *way*, let me remark that … 順序として…を申し上げる. ¶*cleave* one's *way* through many difficulties to prosperity 万難を排して進路を切り開き繁栄の域に達する. ¶*climb* one's way [*up*] よじ登る. ¶The policeman *clubbed* his *way* to the scene of fight. その巡査はこん棒を振回して群集を制しけんかをしている場所に突進した. ¶*conquer* one's *way* to the higher happiness 進路に横たわる苦難を克服してさらに大きな幸福に到達する. ¶*corkscrew* one's *way* through a crowd 群集の中を縫って行く. ¶The street *cuts* its *way* through the city. その町は市の一方から一方に抜けている. ‖ *cut* one's *way* through the enemy's ranks [敵陣に切り込んで]血路を切開く ‖ Great men are those who *cut* their *way* to success through difficulties, 偉人というのは幾多の困難を排して成功に達する人々のことである. ‖ The argument *cuts* both *ways*. その議論は両方に通じる. ‖ His silence appears to me to *cut* both *ways*. 彼が口をつぐんでいるのはよくも悪くも取れる. ¶*cut out* one's own *way* in life 独立独歩する. ¶*develop ways* to … …する方法を案出する. ¶sleepy burros and ox-carts *dispute* the *way* with high-powered motorcars. のろのろしたろばや牛車も通れば高速度の自動車も通る. ¶*dodge* one's *way* through the mass of vehicles 多数の乗物をよけて進む. ¶The case is now *dragging* its *way* through the courts. その事件は今裁判所の審理中で遅々として一向はかどらない. ¶He *earns* his *way* and spends on outside work the time he should devote to his studies. 彼は勉強の時間をアルバイトに使っている. 【類】*earn* one's *way* through college. ¶*edge* (*elbow*) one's *way* through a crowd 群集を肩で切って(ひじで押しのけて)進む. ¶*facing* two *ways*=at the crossroads 岐路に立って. ¶*feel* one's *way* up the stairs 手探りで階段を上る ‖ The blind *feel* the *way* with the cane. 盲人はつえで道を探る. ‖ *feel* one's *way* in the dark / Bugs *feel* their *way* on the ground with their feelers (触角). ¶*fiddle* one's *way* バイオリンをひいて旅かせぎをする. ¶*fight* one's *way* bravely 雄々しく奮闘しつつ進む ‖ *fight* one's *way* to the front of crowds, led by curiosity 好奇心に駆られてぐいぐい群集の前へ押し出る ‖ *fight* one's *way* out of the seething swaying mob ごった返すやじの群からようよう抜け出る ‖ *fight* one's *way* to eminence in one's profession. 奮闘努力してその方面で名を揚げる. 【類】*fight* one's *way* in life / *fight* her own *way* in the world / *fight* one's *way* through the enemy. ¶In those days many precious art objects *found* their *way* across the Atlantic. 当時貴重の美術品がたくさん大西洋を横切って(アメリカに)送られた. ‖ they *found* their own *way* from … to … 彼らは…から…まで自由行動を取った(団体旅行などで). 【類】A young man must *find* his own *way* in the world, without props and safeguards (支持や保護). ‖ His articles often *find* their *way* into print (type in newspapers). 彼の文章はよく活字になる(新聞に出る). 【類】These expressions never *found* their *way* into books. / Many spurious imitations have *found* their *way* into famous collections. / *find* one's *way* through a forest / We hope this book may *find* its *way* into the studies (書斎) of our teachers. / Like many another fetching girl (美女), Alice Adair *found* her *way* into films by the dancing route. / Those slang expressions will *find* their *way* into good English. / Not a penny of American money *found* its *way* into the enterprise. ‖ *find* its *way* into legal channels 正規ルートにのせられる ‖ *find* its *way* into print (=the press) [その本が]印刷の運びになる ‖ The word has *found* its *way* into some diplomatic documents. この語は外交文書などに使われるようになった. ‖ somehow *find* one's *way* out of the woods 何とかして森から抜け出す ‖ *find* one's *way* to another's heart 人に取り入る ‖ Rivers *find* their *way* to the sea. 川は海へ流れて行く. ‖ The songs of the poet *found* their *way* to him. その詩人の歌が彼の目についた. ‖ at the appointed hour I *found* my *way* to … 指定された時間に私は…に行った. ¶I had some difficulty in *finding* my *way back*. 私は帰り道が分からなくってちょっと困った. ‖ He has *found* his *way back* into the screen. 彼は映画に返り咲きをした. ¶We *find* our *ways home* by moonlight if the moon is at the full. われわれは満月だと月の光で家に帰る. ¶*find* one's *way out* 外へ出る; [問題などを]解決する ‖ We tried in vain to *find* our *way out*. われわれは出口を見つけようとしたがどうしても見つからなかった. ‖ It is by no means easy to *find* one's *way out*. 出口を見つけるのは決して容易ではない. ¶*force* one's *way* from a humble origin to an exalted position 身を微せんに起して高位に押し進む ‖ *force* its own *way* in spite of all obstacles 万難を排して勇進する. 【類】*force* one's *way* through the crowds. ¶*force* one's *way out* 無理に外へ出る ‖ *force* one's *way* through a big crowd しゃにむに群集の中に入て行っく ‖ The question has been *forcing* its *way* to the front in a very decided manner. その問題ははっきり表面に浮び上って来ている. ¶*forge* one's own *way* to success 成功への道を切り開く. ¶*freshen* the *way* [船が]速力を増す. ¶*get* (=*gain*) one's *way*=attain one's object 目的を達する. ¶*give way* くずれる, こわれる; 負ける; 譲歩する ‖ The bridge *gave way*. 橋が落ちた. ‖ one's health *gives way* 健康が衰える ‖ Sellers are *giving way*. 売手は譲歩している. 【類】His health *gave way* completely. ‖ She felt hysterical, and was afraid to *give way*. ‖ *give way* before … …に恐れて退く ‖ *give way* under the strain 押されて腰くだけする ‖ Stand back! Make room! *Give way* for the firemen! どいた! あけろ! 消防だ! ‖ *give way* to anger (=one's temper) かんしゃくを起す ‖ He will not *give way* to vexation. 彼は怒りはしないだろう. ‖ He never *gave way* to temptation. 彼は決して誘惑にかからなかった. ‖ *give way* to a state of despondency 悲観する ‖ *give way* to tears 涙にくれる ‖ *give way* to drink again [一度禁酒などして]また酒を飲み出す ‖ his mind *gave way* under the strain of …の圧迫に耐えず彼の心がくじけた. ¶*grease* the *ways* for … …に有利な情勢を作る. ¶*go* the *way* of … …と同じ道をたどる(運命に落つく) ‖ *go* one's *way* その場を去る. 【類】We parted and *went* our *ways*. ‖ I know your opinion *goes* a great *way* with him. 君のいうことは先方に大分ききめがある. ‖ *go* the *way* of all flesh 死ぬ ‖ They have *gone* the *way* of the waste-paper basket. 結局かみくずかご行きとなった(投稿など). ¶*grope* one's *way along* 手探りをして行く. 【類】*grope* their *way* blindly (盲人のように) *along* ‖ dimly *grope* one's *way* to the conception that … おぼろげながら…ということを知るようになる. 【類】*grope* one's *way* through the darkness of the street / *grope* one's *way* to the door. ¶clerks who *have* yet their *way* to make in the world これから出世しようという店員たち ‖ You cannot ***have*** your own *way* in everything. 君は何でも我を通すということはできない. ‖ If I ***had*** my *way*, I would abolish all this nonsense. 私の勝手になるものならこんなばからしいことはやめてしまう. 【類】He was obdurate (強情) and succeeded in ***having*** his own *way*. / ***have*** one's *way* by fair means or foul (是が非でも). ¶***impede*** the *way* to one's motorcar その自動車の通行妨害をする. ¶***jimmy*** one's *way* into a locked house てこでこじあけて鍵の下りた家にはいる. ¶***labor*** one's *way* with great difficulty 大骨を折って道を歩く. ¶***lead*** the *way* 先に立って案内をする ‖ ***lead*** the *way* in ... 率先して...する ‖ ***Lead*** the *way*, please. どうぞお先へ. ‖ He ***led*** the *way* in drinking the health of the newlyweds (=newlywedded couple). 彼は新郎新婦への乾杯の音頭取りをやった. ‖ The hostess ***leads*** the *way* to the table (drawing-room). 主人の妻が先に立って食卓(など)へ案内する. ‖ ***lead*** the *way* ***upstairs*** 二階へ案内する ‖ He ***led*** her *way*. 彼は彼女の先に立った. ¶***lose*** one's *way* 道に迷う. ¶***make*** one's *way* to ... ...に進んで行く ‖ When really attractive, popular games may be adopted from one people to another till they ***make*** their *way* round the world. 本当におもしろいと民衆の遊戯は国から国へと伝わって行って仕舞には世界を一周する. ‖ a carp ***making*** its *way* up a waterfall こいの滝上り ‖ The slang expression has ***made*** its *way* into the language of literature. その卑語が文学にも用いられるようになった. ‖ It rapidly ***made*** its *way* into universal favor. それは人気をさらった. ‖ Be active! That's the way to ***make*** your *way* [*up*] in the world. 活発にやり給え, そうすれば立身する ‖ ***make*** ***way*** (=***room***) for the younger 後進に道を譲る. ‖ It took the French Revolution to sweep away the relics of the Middle Ages and ***make*** ***way*** for the new era of industry, as in politics. フランス革命が起って中世紀の遺物を一掃し去り政治並びに産業において一新紀元を画する道を開いた. ¶Snails are ***making*** their *way* as an article of food. かたつむりは段々食料品となりつつある. ¶***make*** one's *way* on foot along the track 線路ずたいに歩く ‖ They ***made*** ***way*** for us. われわれが通る道をあけてくれた. ‖ The book hâs ***made*** its *way* into a new language. その本は新しく別の国語に翻訳された. ‖ The word is a provincialism, but has ***made*** its *way* into standard speech. この語は(元来)方言であるが, 次第に標準語になった. ‖ ***make*** one's way through a forest 森林の中にはいって行く. ¶***make*** one's *way* ***home*** 家路をたどる ‖ ***make*** one's *way* ***out*** 外に出る. ¶***mistake*** one's *way* 道を間違える. ¶The permanent *way* was ***obstructed*** by derailed wagons and debris. 鉄道の線路が脱線した貨車や破損物でふさがっていた. ¶They resolved to ***obtain*** their *way* by force, regardless of consequences. 彼らは結果がどうあろうと力づくでその目的を達しようと決心した. ¶His great work ***opened*** the *way* anew for much fruitful investigation. 彼の大功績によって色々効果的に研究できるよう新方面を開拓した. ‖ ***open*** the *way* for promotion of their juniors 後進のために途を開く. ¶The precipice ***overhangs*** the *way*. その絶壁が道にかぶさっている. ¶I shall only ***pass*** this *way* once. 私はこの道を二度と通ることはないだろう. ‖ I happened to ***pass*** that *way*. 私は偶然そこを通った. ¶in order to ***pave*** the *way* for the accomplishment of my scheme 私の計画遂行準備のために ‖ Untold matrimonial misery, ***paving*** the *way* to separation and divorce, arises from the ignorance of the young wife. やがては別居となり離婚とまでなる数知れない結婚生活の悲惨が若い妻の無知から起る. 【類】***pave*** the *way* for future efforts / ***pave*** the *way* to success. ¶The school ***pays*** its *way* (=is self-supporting). その学校は自力でやっている. ‖ Even with a ten cent tariff, the system wouldn't completely ***pay*** its own *way*. 関税は一割でもこのやり方じゃ収支償わない. ¶***pay*** his *way* as he goes 金のことでは人の厄介にならないようにする ‖ The company does not even ***pay*** its *way*. その会社は収支さえ償わないという始末だ. ‖ provide money to ***pay*** the children's *way* through college 子供などを大学にやる金を支給する ‖ endow promising students unable to ***pay*** their own *way* 学費が払えない有為な学生に金を支給する. ¶***pick*** one's *way* through a muddy road 泥道の拾い歩きをする. ¶***pick*** one's *way* across a street 気をつけて通路を横切る. ¶Proudly the giant liner ***plowed*** its way down the bay. 誇らしげにその巨大な定期船は水を切って湾を下って行った. ¶***point*** the other *way* 反対の側を指さす ‖ ***point*** the *way* to ... ...への道を指示する. ¶***point out*** the right *way* 正しい道を指示する. ¶***prefer*** the *way* of intrigue and disruption 陰謀と崩壊への道を選ぶ. ¶Each step ***prepares*** the *way* for the next. 一歩一歩が役に立って行く. ‖ all these things ***prepared*** the *way* for ... すべてこれらのことが...の準備になった ‖ The Catholic missionaries were ***preparing*** the *way* for Portugal's conquest of the islands. カトリックの宣教師たちはポルトガルがその島島を征服する準備工作を施していた. ‖ Luxury ***prepares*** the *way* to poverty. ぜいたくは貧乏のもと. ¶***provide*** a *way* of retreat 退却のために備える. ¶He bowed and ***pursued*** his *way*. 彼はお辞儀をして行ってしまった. ¶***push*** one's *way* through the seething crowd わきかえる群集を押分けて行く ‖ ***push*** one's *way* to a good front place 前列の見よい場所へ押し進む. 【類】***push*** one's *way* into the interior of China. ¶***realize*** the *way* things are going in the world 世界の動きを見てとる. ¶The criminal was set free only to ***resume*** the *way* of life that led to his ruin. 犯人は解放されたがまた罪の道に逆戻りした. ¶I cannot ***see*** my *way* to comply with your request. 私はお申し出を承諾し兼ねます. ‖ I trust you may ***see*** your *way* clear to ... あなたが...して下さることと私は信じている. ‖ ***seeing*** the *way* almost clear 大体見通しがついたので ‖ We have not ***seen*** our *way* to doing otherwise. われわれには他に取るべき道がなかった. ‖ ***see*** one's *way* out of a difficulty 困難を切り抜ける ‖ It was very difficult to ***see*** my *way* through the streets because of the fog. 霧のため通りの見通しがきかなかった. ‖ the Government has not ***seen*** its *way* to making ... 政府としてはまだ...する段になっていない. ¶***seek*** the middle *way* between ... [一方に偏せず]...と...との中を取るようにする. ¶***shorten*** the *way* from ... to ... ...から...に至る行程を短縮する. ¶***shovel*** a *way* through the snow 雪かきをする. ¶Please ***show*** me the *way* to the station. 停車場へ行く道を教えて下さい. 【類】This boy will ***show*** you the *way*. ¶He ***smiled*** his *way* into millions. 彼は愛きょうで百万長者になった. ¶***smooth*** one's *way* 行く先の困難を除く. ¶***soak*** its *way* into ... ...にしみこむ. ¶The message is ***speeding*** its *way* along thousands of miles of the ocean bed. 幾千マイルの海底に沿ってその音信が急行している. ¶***squeeze*** one's *way* through a crowd 人込みの中を押して行く. ¶***steer*** our *way* through the busy throngs of businessmen and workers 多忙な実務家や労働者の群を突切って進んで行く ‖ ***steer*** one's *way* in the voyage of life 世の中を渡る. ¶***take*** one's *way* toward the door ドアの方へ行く ‖ ***take*** one's *way* ***out*** 外へ出る. ¶***thread*** their *way* through the traffic 車馬や人通りの間を縫って行く ‖ ***thread*** one's *way* through the tables 食卓の間を縫って行く(宴会などで). 【類】try to ***thread*** one's *way* through the intricacies (錯雑) of ... / The gigantic C.P.R. liner Empress of Britain ***threaded*** her *way* up the muddy waters of the Yangtse. ¶***toil*** one's *way* through life (university) 刻苦して人生(など)を進む. ¶***trudge*** all the *way* to ... わざわざ...まで歩く. ¶The thing is ***turned*** the other *way* ***round***. それは逆さだ. ¶***water*** the carriage *ways* 車道に水をまく. ¶Aluminium is slowly ***wedging*** its *way* in the metal market. 金属界でアルミニウムは徐々に台頭しつつある. 【類】***wedge*** one's *way* through the crowded bus. ¶Whither shall we first ***wend*** our *way?* 最初にどこへ行こうか ‖ Let us ***wend*** our *way* ***east***. [方向を転じて]東に行こう. ‖ as we ***wended*** our *way* ***out*** われわれが退出した時(参観者など). 【類】a shrine to which thousands of pilgrims annually ***wend*** their *way* / ***wend*** one's *way* along the banks of the river / Silently they ***wended*** their *way* through the darkness. ¶***win*** one's *way* in the world 立身する ‖ ***win*** one's *way* to fame 有名人になる ‖ those who have ***won*** their *way* from obscurity to renown 低い地位から起って出世した人々 ‖ He ***won*** his *way* ***up*** from a private in the ranks. 彼は一兵卒から身を起した. ‖ The custom has ***won*** its *way* today among all classes. その習慣は今日あらゆる階級に行われている. ‖ Americanism is ***winning*** its *way* in the British Isles. 米語は英本国にはいり込みつつある. 【類】The law ***won*** its *way* into other countries. / ***win*** its *way* slowly into public favour / The new invention *won* its *way* more and more into favor. / The idea is *winning* its *way* throughout the world. ‖ *win* its *way* to the front 群を抜く ‖ fairly *win* their *way* to fame りっぱに評判を取る. 【類】*win* its *way* to general popularity ‖ The monthly will undoubtedly *win* its *way* to rapid popularity. その月刊雑誌はきっとたちまち一般から持てはやされるだろう. ¶The brook *winds* its *way*. 小川がうねうね流れて行く. ‖ *wind* one's *way* into another's affections (favor) 人の愛(好意)に巧みに取り入る. ¶The birds *winged* their *way* to the south. 鳥の群が南に飛んだ. ¶With no further formal education, he had *worked* his *way* to a major position. それ以上には正式な教育を受けずして彼は重要な位置にこぎ付けたのであった. 【類】*work* one's *way* through college / He *worked* his *way* through preparatory school and through Yale. / He *worked* his *way* through college as a waiter. ¶*work* one's *way up* 段々出世する. 【類】After *working* his *way up* as third, second, and first officer in the ship, he was appointed chief officer. / *work* one's *way up* till he is ... / I believe it is a good thing for anybody to *work* his *way up* from the bottom. / he *worked* his *way up* from being a poor and unknown country boy in New York, to a position of ... / *work up* one's *way* from obscurity to renown (from poverty to affluence) / *work* his *way up* to a position of importance (重要な). ¶*worm* one's *way* through the press of people 虫がはうようにして人込の中を通り抜ける ‖ hose lines *worming* their *way* all over the place [火事場で]一面にはっているホース.

Q *all* the *way* from ... to ... ...から...までずっと ‖ sing *all* the *way* back ずっと歌を歌いながら帰る ‖ walk *all* the *way* to work 職場に行くまでの道を歩く. ¶an *alternative way* of reaching ... ...に達するもう一つの道. ¶go *another way* 別の道を行く. ¶an *arterial way* 大通り. ¶go round by the *back way* to the kitchen 裏を通って台所へ回る. ¶*both ways* 往復. ¶a *convenient way* to go to ... is ... ...へ行くに便利な道は...である. ¶They departed on their *different ways*. 銘々別れて違った道に去った. ¶one yen *each way* 片道一円. ¶a public *fair way* 公道. ¶we are *half way* to ... now 今...半分来た所だ. ¶keep out of *harm's way* 害を避ける. ¶on his *homeward way* 彼の帰国(宅)の途中で. ¶The ship made *little way*. 船脚がはかどらなかった. ¶Dr. Murray's Dictionary is a *long way* first. マレー博士の辞書は優に第一だ. ‖ It's only a *little way*. じきそこです ‖ One feels like a traveller, who, the sun having set, has a *long way* to go. 日暮れて道遠しの感がある. ‖ A mile is a *long way* to go. 一マイルというとちと歩きでがある. ‖ It's a *long way* off. 遠距離だ. ‖ A flying machine with a safe non-stop range of 1,500 miles was still a *long way* off. 千五百マイルの無着陸飛行を無事に決行しうる飛行機の完成はまだ前途りょう遠であった. ‖ A feminine smile goes a *long way* in business. 女の微笑は商売には大分ききめがある. ‖ it will be going a *long way* toward ... それは大いに...の役に立つだろう. 【類】She was an heiress (家付き娘) with whom, as with royal personages, a little beauty goes a *long way*. ‖ go a *long way* to meet ... ...を迎えに遠くまで行く ‖ It's a *long way* from saying to doing. 言うはやすく行うは難し. ¶We were in *luck's way*. われわれは運がよかった. ‖ Another pigeon! Egad, I'm in *luck's way* this morning. またはとだ! ああけさは運がいいぞ. ¶the *Milky Way*=the Galaxy 銀河. ¶The plan has made *no way* (=progress). その計画ははかどらない. ¶In an *off and on way*, I've known him a long time. 続けて交際はしていないがあの人は随分前から知っています. ¶take the train *one way* and walk back 行きは汽車で帰りは徒歩にする. ¶the *only way* from ... to ... ...から...までの一本道 ‖ the *only way* out is to ... 唯一の解決法は...である. ¶the *way out* (*in*) 出(入)口. ¶find one's *own way* home どうかこうか宅へ戻る. ¶the *permanent way* 《英》『鉄道』線路. ☞米語用法は the right of the way. ‖ The train was late owing to work on the *permanent way*. 線路工事のために汽車が遅れた. ¶go by a *round-about way* 回り路をする. ¶We went our *separate ways*. われわれはそれぞれ別れ別れに行った. ‖ We must go *separate ways*. われわれは意見が合わない. ¶They went their *several ways*. 彼らはそれぞれの行く先へ行った. ¶take the *shortest way* 一番近い道を行く. ¶New York's Great *White Way* ニューヨーク市の不夜街 (Broadway 盛り場の一部). ¶the river threads its *winding way* through ... その川は...を曲りくねり縫って行く. ¶go the *wrong way* 道を間違える. 「道.

Q^2 the *flower way* 花道. ¶a *wagon way* [炭山の]地下馬車

P He lives just *across* the *way* from our house. 彼はわれわれの家の真向いに住んでいる. ¶help *along* the *way* 手を貸して道を通してやる. ¶go *by way* of the air 空路で行く. 【類】His voyage back to England will be made *by way* of (経由で) Suez. ‖ halt *by* the *way* at ... 途中...へ留る ‖ go home *by* that *way* あの道を通って家へ帰る. ¶go *down* Ginza *way* 銀座通りを行く. ¶wander *from* the *way* 道を踏み迷う. ¶Aw, go away, you're always *in* the *way*. えい, あっちへ行け, お前はいつも邪魔をする. ‖ it is the only difficulty *in* the *way* of ... それが...の邪魔になる唯一の障害である ‖ Great difficulties stand *in* the *way* of its achievement. その完成には幾多の大困難がある. ‖ An accident threw it *in* his *way*. 彼は偶然それに出会った. ‖ Strange circumstances threw her *in* my *way*. 私は妙な事情で彼女に出あった. ‖ Am I *in* your *way*? お邪魔ではないですか. ‖ It never fell *in* my *way* to hear what became of her. 彼女の消息はとんと私の方では分からなかった. ¶fall *into* the *way* of being drunk all the time いつも酒に酔っている. ¶She went a mile *of* the *way* with me. 彼女は一マイルだけは私と一緒に行った. ¶The train proceeded *on* its *way*. その汽車は進行した. ‖ The remittance is now *on* the *way*. 金はもう送ってしまった. ‖ tarry *on* the way 道草を食う ‖ Dial home and tell them I'm *on* the *way*. もう出かけたと家のものに電話してくれ. ‖ *on* the *way* down (up) the river 川しも(かみ)に行く途中で(こぎ下(上)って) ‖ *on* the *way* over to ... ...への行きに ‖ the vessel is now *on* her *way* to ... 同船は...へ航海中だ ‖ *on* the *way* to work 出勤の途中で ‖ The tide is turning again and recovery is *on* the *way*. 景気が段々直ってくる. ‖ A child is already *on* the *way*. もう子ができている. ‖ That will not advance him much *on* his *way*. それは大して彼の役に立たないだろう. ‖ *on* the *way* back 帰り道で ‖ *on* our *way* back from ... ...へ帰る途中. 【類】*on* the *way* out to work / *on* one's *way* to business in the morning / I passed through Korea from Peking *on* the *way* to Japan. ‖ a "school" of logs *on* their *way* to the mills. 川を通って工場へ運搬中の丸太の群 ‖ He is already well advanced *on* the *way* to cure. 彼はすでに大分快方に向っている. ¶be *out of* one's *way* 回り道になる ‖ get *out of* one's *way* to visit a person わざわざ遠回りして人を訪問する ‖ He has gone *out of* his *way* to offer suggestions. 彼は進んで注意をしてくれた. 【類】He went *out of* his *way* to assist me in every way he could. ‖ Nobody went *out of* his or her *way* to make me feel at home. 男でも女でもだれ一人私の居心地がいいようにさせてはくれなかった. ‖ I went (=got) *out of* my *way* to visit him. 私はわざわざ彼を訪ねて行った. 【類】Don't go *out of* your *way* for me. ‖ he is something *out of* the *way* in ... 彼は...では変りものだ ‖ There is no *way out of* it. どうしようもない. ‖ Get *out of* the *way*! どけ. ‖ Keep *out of* the *way*! 近寄るな. ‖ keep it *out of* harm's *way* それを安全な所におく. ¶a neighbor *over* the *way* 道の向側の家の人. 【類】His house is *over* the *way*. ¶We passed the school *upon* our *way*. われわれは途中その学校の前を通った.

P^2 loiter on the *way from* school 学校の帰りに道草をくう. ¶a little *way off* the road 道路から少し離れて. ¶the *way through* a gate 門をくぐって行く道. ¶Which is the *way to* the station? 駅へはどう行くのですか. ‖ rolls of paper on the *way to* a newspaper office 新聞社へ運ばれて行くロール紙.

O Please step this *way*. どうぞこちらへお出で下さい. ‖ Will you walk this *way*? どうぞこちらへ. 【類】He is coming this *way*. / Are you going that *way*? ‖ Going My *Way* [映画の題名]わが道を行く.

(**2**) 方法; 様式; 行状.

V *adopt* European *ways* and methods 欧風にならう ‖ *adopt* the *ways* and garments of men 男の風をする. ¶*affect* foreign *ways* ハイカラがる. ¶*amend* one's *ways* 行いを改める. ¶*appreciate* "foreign *ways*" いわゆる西洋風を賞美する. ¶It is no disgrace to marry a fallen girl provided she has *changed* her *way* of living. 転落の女で

あろうとすでにその生活法を変えた以上これと結婚しても一向恥辱ではない. ‖ ***change*** the *way* of thinking 頭の切替えをする. ¶***devise*** some *way* to raise money for the purpose そのための基金調達の方法を案出する. ¶***figure out*** a *way* to get it away from him それを彼から巻上げる工夫を凝らす. ¶Pupils trained on this system would be able to ***find*** their *way* about France without difficulty, and hold their own in general conversation. この方法で教授された生徒はフランスに行っても不自由なく一通りの話は結構用がたせる. ‖ I hope that some *way* may be ***found*** out of the difficulties. どうにかしてこの難問題の解決ができようと思う. 【類】***find*** a *way* of overcoming the difficulty ‖ How shall we be able to ***find*** the *way?* どうしたらその方法が見つかりましようか. ‖ I will ***find*** a *way*. 方法を考えて見よう. ‖ He knows how to ***find*** his *way* to success. 彼は成功の秘けつを心得ている. ¶***give up*** one's bad *ways* その悪い癖を捨てる. ¶he ***has*** the *way* of saying ... 彼には...という口癖がある ‖ if they ***have*** their *way* (彼らが)自分の思い通りになれば ‖ allow a person to ***have*** his own *way* その人を勝手にさせておく ‖ He ***has*** a *way* of interspersing his conversation with fragments of bad French. へたなフランス語の単語なんかを会話にまぜる癖がある. ‖ He ***has*** the *way* of exaggerating things. あの人はことを大げさ(大業)にいう癖がある. ¶let him ***have*** his *way* 彼を気ままにさせる. ¶***hew*** one's *way* to one's fortune 成功への道を切り開く. ¶I don't ***know*** the *way*. 私はやり方を知らない. ¶***know*** the *way* to ... ...の方法を知っている ‖ Rats ***know*** their *way* into the warehouse. ねずみはその倉庫にはいる方法を知っている. ‖ The wicked ***know*** the *ways* of their own kind. じゃの道はへび. ¶***master*** the *way* of Western civilization 西洋文明を会得する. ¶***mend*** the *ways* of the careless 不注意な人の癖を直す ‖ ***mend*** one's *ways* under the frank criticisms of another 他人の遠慮のない批評を受けて癖を直す. ¶***observe*** their *ways* of doing things 彼らのやり方を見守る. ¶persuade the girl to ***renounce*** her vicious *ways* その少女に正業に立返るように説き勧める. ¶Old-fashioned people ***spurn*** newfangled *ways*. 頭の古い人たちは新奇の事を排斥する. ¶***suggest*** a *way* out of the difficulty 難局打破の方法を説く. ¶***understand*** women's *ways* 女のくせを心得る ‖ He is a foreigner and does not ***understand*** our *ways*. 彼は外人だからわれわれの慣習は分からない.

Q in an ***abrupt*** *way* 不意に. ¶in the ***accustomed*** *way* 例によって例のごとく. ¶knowledge of ***American*** *ways* 米国の習慣についての知識 ‖ the ***American*** *way* of life アメリカ式の生活様式 ‖ That is the ***American*** *way*. それはアメリカ流だ. ¶an ***amiable*** *way* of declining a request 要求をやさしくこばむ方法. ¶put in ***another*** *way*=put it another way=stated in another way 別言すれば ‖ That's ***another*** *way* of looking at the matter. それも一つの見解だ, そうも見られる. ¶a ***backhanded*** *way* of saying 遠回しな言い方. ¶His business is in a ***bad*** *way* (=condition). あの人の商売は振わない. ‖ the trade is in a ***bad*** *way* in consequence of ... その商売は...の結果振わない ‖ The firm is in a ***bad*** *way* financially. その店の経済状態は悪い ‖ ***bad*** *ways* 不行跡. ¶the ***best*** *way* is to ... ...するに限る ‖ the ***best*** *way* out of the difficulty 困難を切り抜ける最善の方法 ‖ one of the ***best*** *ways* to ... ...する最善の方法の一つは... ‖ Endeavor to settle in the ***best*** *way* you can. 最善と思われるやり方で取りきめをするように努力せよ. ‖ about the ***best*** *way* would be ... まず一番いい方法は...だろう. ¶He answered in his ***blunt*** *way*. 例のそっけない調子で答えた. ¶His business is in a very ***big*** *way*. あの人は商売を非常に手広くやっている. ¶state in a ***brief*** *way* 簡単に述べる ‖ in the ***briefest possible*** *way* できるだけ簡単な方法で. ¶in a ***business-like*** *way* てきぱきと, 事務的に. ¶She must have fallen into those ***careless*** *ways*. 彼女はそうしたふしだらなやり方をするようになったに相違ない. ¶in a ***casual*** *way* 偶然. ¶in a ***certain*** *way* 一面から考えて見れば, 見方によっては. ¶a ***cheap*** *way* to kill time 手軽な退屈しのぎの方法. ¶This is the ***common*** *way* of trade. これが商売では通例だ. ¶act in a ***condescending*** *way* へりくだった態度をする. ¶***conventional*** *ways* 従来のやり方. ¶***crooked*** *ways* 不正手段. ¶It is too late to do anything in a ***curative*** *way*. もう療治は手遅れだ. ¶He has a ***curious*** *way* about him. 彼には妙な癖がある. ¶in the ***customary*** *way* 従来の仕方で. ¶Wishes not fulfilled is the ***customary*** *way* of the world. ままにならぬは浮世の常. ¶***democratic*** *way* of talking 砕けた物の言い方. ¶reading in a ***desultory*** *way* 漫読. ¶to put the matter in a ***different*** *way* 言葉を変えて言えば. ¶That's not a ***diplomatic*** *way* of saying it. そう言うと角が立つ. ¶in a ***dirty, sneaky*** *way* きたないこうかつなやり口で. ¶They were disposed of in ***diverse*** *ways*. それらは様々の方法で処分された. ¶The distribution of tracts is an ***easy*** *way* of doing good, and also a cheap way. [宗教上などの]小冊子を配布するのは善事をなす容易な方法でありまた安価な方法でもある. ¶in a most ***effective*** *way* きわめて効果的に. ¶It can be read ***either*** *way*. それは二通りの意味に取れる. ¶He has an ***elaborate*** *way* of acting. 彼の芸は細かい. ¶an ***elementary*** *way* 初歩的な方法. ¶an ***emphatic*** *way* of saying 強勢的な言い方. ¶assimilate oneself to ***European*** *ways* 欧風に同化する. ¶The illustrations are in ***every*** *way* worthy of the letterpress (=text). そのさし絵はどの点から見ても本文と同様の値打がある. ‖ be satisfactory in ***every*** *way* どんな点から見ても申分がない. 【類】It is an excellent novel in ***every*** *way*. ¶He was gradually reclaimed from his ***evil*** *ways* and led gently into the way of righteousness. 彼は次第にその悪習が改まり徐々に正道へ導かれて行った. ¶bow in an ***exaggerated*** *way* 仰々しく頭を下げる. ¶an ***excellent*** *way* to do it is to ... それをする絶好の方法は...することである. ¶in an ***extraordinary*** *way* 突飛な方法で. ¶The possibility of such a danger as this had never, in the ***faintest*** *way*, occurred to me. 私はこんな危険があろうとは少しも考えていなかった. ¶The scheme is on a ***fair*** *way* to realisation. その計画は着々進展している. ‖ Christianity is in a very ***fair*** *way* here. ここはキリスト教が非常に盛んである. ‖ It is in a ***fair*** *way* to be ruined. それはたしかに滅びかけている. ‖ be in a ***fair*** *way* to disappear [おもしろくない流行など]だんだん姿を消しつつある ‖ be on the ***fair*** *way* toward the goal 着々目標に向って進んでいる ‖ The business is in a ***fair*** *way*. 商売は盛んである. ‖ I'm now on a ***fair*** *way* to success. こうなればもうしめたものだ. ‖ be in a ***fair*** *way* 順境に立っている. ¶***familiar*** *ways* 常用の手段. ¶in a ***far-fetched*** *way* こじつけて. ¶The ***farthest*** *way* round is sometimes the nearest way home. 急がば回れということがある. ¶***foolish*** *ways* of foolish women 愚かな女の愚かな仕方. ¶He is quite at home in ***foreign*** *ways*. 彼は西洋風に慣れ切っている. ¶in a ***formal*** *way* 表立って, 改まって. 【類】in a ***formal*** *way* of speaking. ¶compete in a ***friendly*** *way* 敵意なく競争する. ¶The idea spread in a ***friend-to-friend*** *way*. その思想が友だちから友だちへと伝わった. ¶live in a ***frugal*** *way* つましく暮す. ¶in a ***general*** *way* (=sense) 一般的に. ¶A ***good*** *way* to test a passage for variety is to read it aloud. 文章の一節が単調であるかないかを試験するには音読して見るのがよい. ‖ a ***good*** *way* of learning to write well 作文上達のよい方法. ¶in a ***good-natured*** *way* 悪気なく. ¶a return to the ***good old*** *ways* 昔の良風に帰ること. ¶distinctively impressive in their ***grim*** *way* 物すごく印象が際立って深い. ¶I formed a partnership with him in the ***grocery*** *way* (=line). 私はあの人と仲間で乾物の店を出した. ¶teach English composition in too ***haphazard*** a *way* 全くでたらめな方法で英作文を教える. ¶He had a ***happy*** *way* of ridding himself of applicants for office. 彼は就職志望者を追い払う妙案を心得ていた. ¶a ***happy-go-lucky*** *way* of ... ...の行き当りばったりの方法. ¶welcome a person in a ***hearty*** *way* 人を心から歓迎する. ¶his ***high-handed*** *ways* 彼の高飛車なやり口. ¶do it in an ***honest*** *way* それを地道にやって行く ‖ get one's bread in an ***honest*** *way* 正直に暮しを立てる. ¶be called "..." in a ***homely*** *way* 俗称...で呼ばれている. ¶Is suicide an ***honorable*** or a ***cowardly*** *way* of settling difficulties? 自殺は困難を解決するりっぱな方法か. ¶The present writer belongs, in his ***humble*** *way*, to the second school. 筆者は端くれではあるが第二の派の方に属するものである. ‖ express one's congratulations in a ***humble*** *way* いささか祝意を表する. ¶in an ***illegal*** *way* 非合法的に. ¶make money in an ***improper*** *way* 不正な方法で金もうけをする. ¶***inexpensive*** and ***enjoyable*** *ways* of using leisure 金を掛けず愉快に暇を利用する方法. ¶in some ***inexplicable*** *way* ある合点の行かない方法で. ¶He had a peculiarly ***ingratiating way*** with women. 彼は女に対して特にとり入るようにした. ¶The book is written in an ***interesting, non-technical way***. その本は通俗的におもしろく書いてある. ¶in a half ***joking*** (=***jesting***) ***way*** おもしろ半分に. ¶speak in a ***kind*** and ***considerate way*** 親切な思いやりのある口振りで話す. ¶a ***laconic way*** of putting pregnant and telling facts 意味深長な事実を簡潔に述べる方法. ¶spend money in a ***lavish way*** 盛んに金を使う. ¶by a ***lawful way*** 合法的に. ¶live in a ***leisurely way*** ゆうゆうと暮す. ¶treat a person in a ***liberal way*** 人を寛大に取扱う. ¶He is a linguist in a very ***limited way***. 彼はあれでも語学者だ. ‖ He is in ***limited way*** a poet. 彼は一個の小詩人である. ¶He is very busy in a ***literary way***. 彼は文学方面の仕事が大分忙しい. ¶lively stories told in a ***lively way*** 話し方も中味も生き生きとした話. ¶explain why in a ***lucid*** and ***interesting way*** 明りょうにかつおもしろくその理由を説明する. ¶in a ***manful*** (=***manly***) ***way*** 男らしく. ¶in ***manifold ways*** 種々様々に. ¶It is of use in ***many ways***. それは色々役に立つ. ‖ befriend a person in ***many ways*** 人と何くれとなく親しくする ‖ find ***many ways*** of dodging 色々回避する方法を知る. ¶in a ***material way*** 物質的に. ¶say in a ***matter-of-fact way*** 平気で言う. ¶his ***methodical way*** of doing things 彼の秩序正しい物事のやり方. ¶in the ***middle way*** どっちつかずに ‖ a policy of the "***middle way***" 中道を行く方針. ¶in a ***minor way*** 小さいながらに. ¶in a ***moderate way*** 適度に. ¶teach medicine in the ***modern way*** 現代式に医学の教授をする. ¶Work began in 1899 in a ***modest way***. 仕事は一八九九年に小さく始められた. ¶He has been kind to me in ***more ways*** than one. 私はこれまで一方ならずあの人のお世話になった. ¶God moves in a ***mysterious way***. 神の動きは不思議なものだ. ¶***naive ways*** 無邪気な態度. ¶maltreat her in a ***nameless way*** 何とも言いようのないように彼女を虐待する. ¶This seems to be ***nature's way*** of doing things. これが天の常法らしい. ¶in a ***new, forceful***, and ***convincing way*** 新しくて力強いしかも成るほどと思わせるやり方で. ¶***98 ways*** to prepare oysters かきの料理法九十八種. ¶There is absolutely ***no way*** out of it. どうしても抜き差しができない. ‖ This is ***no way*** inferior to that. この品は決してそれより劣っていない. ‖ Such a thing is in ***no way*** to be permitted. もっての外だ. ‖ I can in ***no way*** equal him. あの人には及びもつかない. ‖ can in ***no way*** be made light of (=slighted) どうして仲々ばかにならない. 【類】This is in ***no way*** an exaggeration. ‖ ***No*** better ***way*** could be found of doing it. そうするのにこれ以上よい方法はない. ¶There is ***no way*** of curing the disease. その病気を直す方法はない. ‖ I can in ***no way*** make myself to think like that. どうしてもそういう気持になれない. ¶speak in a very ***offhand way*** 全然用意なく話す. ¶the ***old way*** 昔流. ¶The ***old way*** that. 例の手(やり口)だよ. ‖ It is much easier to continue in the ***old ways***. 従来通りやって行く方がよっぽど楽だ. ‖ in the ***old time-honored way*** 昔からやって来たように. ¶The workaday world turns from playing to its ***old humdrum workaday ways*** again. 仕事日になると世人は遊びから再び元の平々凡々な仕事日の常務に向き直る. ¶settle ***one way*** or another (=the other) どうにかまとまりをつける. ¶the ***one best way*** 唯一の最善の方法. ¶the ***only way*** out of the difficulty その困難から脱却する唯一の方法. 【類】That's the ***only*** [wise] ***way*** of doing it. ¶an ***optimistic way*** of thinking 甘い考え方. ¶be arranged in an ***orderly way*** きちんと配列してある. ¶the ***ordinary way*** of constitutional government 憲政の常道 ‖ in the ***ordinary way*** of business 普通の商売のやり方では. ¶by his own ***original way*** 彼一流の独自の方法で. ¶He is a remarkable man in ***other ways*** [その点は感心しないが] 他の点では彼は非凡な人だ ‖ the ***other way*** about 全く反対に ‖ find some ***other way*** out of it 何か別の解決手段を考える ‖ It is just the ***other way*** about with me. 丁度私と反対です. ‖ turn it the ***other way*** round ぐるっと反対の方へ向ける. ¶in his ***own way*** 自己流で ‖ He is a genius in his ***own way***. 彼は一種の天才だ. ‖ China has learned to do things in her ***own way***. 中国は段々に物事を自己流でやるようになった. ‖ They are useful in their ***own ways***. それらもそれぞれ有用のものだ. ‖ They acted each in his ***own way***. 彼らはそれぞれ単独の行動を取った. ‖ If you will please people, you must please them in their ***own way***. 人の気げんをとるにはその人の身になってその喜ぶようにやるべきだ. ‖ Have your ***own way*** then. それならいいようになさい. ¶In conclusion, I should like to thank you for the ***patient way*** in which you have listened to my lecture. この講演の終りに臨んで御静聴をわずらわしたことを感謝致します. ¶in a ***patronizing way*** 恩着せ顔に. ¶set forth the principles in a ***plain, fresh*** and ***interesting way*** その原理を平明に新鮮味を持たせ興味深く述べる. ¶He likes her in a ***Platonic way***. 彼は友として彼女を愛している. ¶put a thing in a ***plausible way*** もっともらしく物を言う. ¶talk in a ***ponderous way*** 重々しい調子で話す. ¶The business is in a ***poor way***. その商売が振わない. ‖ a ***poor way*** of ... ...のまずいやり方. ¶explain, in a ***popular way***, a problem ... 問題を通俗的に説明する. ¶a ***possible way*** out for ... ...の打開策. ¶show one's sympathy in a ***practical way*** [口先だけでなく]行為をもって情を示す. ¶He meets me often in a ***professional way***. あの人は仕事の方の用でよく僕に会う. ¶in the ***proper way*** 適切に. ¶earn money in a ***proper honest way*** 正しい方法で金をもうける. ¶in a ***public way*** 公然と. ¶***quarrelsome ways*** けんかをする癖. ¶a ***queer way*** of showing kindness 妙な親切振り. ¶He smiled in his ***quiet way***. 彼は静かに微笑した. ¶render help in a ***quiet*** and ***unostentatious way*** 穏かに人目に立たないように手助けをする. ¶in a ***rational way*** 合理的方法で. ¶"The ***real way*** to learn is to teach"—so runs an old saying. 古いことわざに「真に学ぶ道は教えることである」とある. ¶a ***refined*** and ***artistic way*** of arranging flowers 優美で芸術的な生花の方法. ¶the ***regular way*** 〖株〗正規の取引. ¶in his incorrigibly ***reticent*** and ***offish way*** 彼の手の下しようのないほど無口で打解けない態度で. ¶learn one's history in the ***right way*** 歴史を正しく学ぶ ‖ There is a ***right*** and a ***wrong way*** to handle a broom. ほうきの扱い方にうまい, まずいがある. ¶in a ***rough way*** 大体から見て. ¶Indirect taxation is a very ***rough-and-ready way*** of making the rich pay in due proportion to their wealth. 間接税は富者をしてその富の中から相当額を支払わせるごく手取り早い方法である. ¶a very ***round-about way*** of saying ... ...のごく遠回しな言い方 ‖ I heard it in a ***round-about way***. 私はそれをまた聞きした. ¶The only ***safe way*** to follow is the rule, "Hands off." 君子は危きに近よらずさ. ¶in precisely the ***same way*** 全く同筆法で ‖ in much the ***same way*** 大体同じように. ¶arrange the matter in a ***satisfactory way*** そのことを満足できるように処理する. ¶a spot very attractive in a ***scenic way*** 風景のよい所. ¶consider the matter in a ***scientific way*** その事柄を科学的に考える. ¶The word spells in ***several ways***. その語には色々のつづり方がある. ‖ in ***several ways*** 色々な点で. ¶The mark "c/o" is a ***short way*** of writing "care of." c/o という記号は care of の省略である. ‖ it is a ***short way*** of saying (=shortened form of) ... それは...の簡単な言い方である. ¶in a ***similar way*** 同筆法で. ¶He has a ***sluggish way*** of carrying out things. 彼は物事をてきぱきと実行しない. ¶The firm began business in a very ***small way***. その店は始めは小規模であった. ‖ start a business in a ***small way*** 小規模に商売を始める ‖ He must be poet and artist in a ***small way***. その人はいくらか詩人でもあり芸術家でもあるに相違ない. ‖ live in a ***small way*** 細く暮す. 【類】hold a wedding in a ***small way***. ¶acquaintances made in a ***social way*** 交際場裏で知り合になった人人. ¶Language is always changing, in ***some way*** or other. 言語はいつも何らかの変化をなしつつある. ‖ find ***some way*** in ... どうにかして...する ‖ There's always ***some way*** out you know. 君どうにかなるものだよ. ‖ I will help you in ***some way*** or other. 何とかして御助力しましょう. ‖ in ***some ways*** ある点では. 【類】He was an eccentric in ***some ways*** as he was brilliant in others. / ***Some way*** must be found to help him. ¶behave in a ***stepmotherly way*** to ... ...に対して継母のような素振りをする. ¶act in a ***subtle way*** 微妙に働く. ¶in ***such*** a ***way*** that ... ...という具合に. ¶describe it in a ***summarizing way*** それを概説する. ¶the ***surest way*** to ... is to ... ...の最も確実な方法は...である. ¶***swash buckler ways*** 空いばり屋式. ¶leave them alone to go their own ***sweet way*** 彼らを勝手に楽しませておく. ¶in a ***stealthy way*** こっそりと. ¶a ***superficial way*** of thinking 浅はかな考え方. ¶do things in a ***systematic***, instead of a ***haphazard***, *way* 物事を出たらめにやらず組織的にやる. ¶convey ideas in a ***telling way*** 思想を胸に答えるように伝える. ¶in a ***thousand different ways*** 千差万別に. ¶Young students and university graduates find an Atlantic trip a ***topping way*** of spending their holiday. 青年学徒や大学卒業生は大西洋の旅行が休暇を過すすばらしい方法であることを知る. ¶***traditional ways*** of thinking (doing things) 従来の考え方(やり方). ¶He claims to have found a ***true way*** to get well and keep well. 彼は健康回復及び保健の真の方法を発見したと言っている. ‖ in a ***tricky way*** ずるいやり方で. ¶The child was accustomed at home to having her own ***undisputed way***. その女の子は家庭でわがまま一杯で通すことに慣れていた. ¶in some ***unexplained way*** 何という訳とも知れずに. ¶***un-Japanese ways*** 非日本的の習慣. ¶do kind things in an ***unkind way*** [外観は]不親切に(内実は)親切を尽す. ¶in the most ***unmistakable way*** てっきり. ¶***unsociable ways*** 無愛想な態度. ¶I realized, in an ***unthinking way***, that I was doing wrong. 私は何となく間違ったことをしていたと悟った. ¶Things are going on in the ***usual way***. 万事平常と変りがない. ¶in a ***vague way*** it was felt that ... ばく然と…と感じた. 【類】In a ***vague way*** he seems to suggest the old Japanese drawings of learned men. ¶He entertained me in ***various ways***. 彼は種々私をもてなしてくれた. ¶in ***varying ways*** 色々な方法で. ¶undue introduction of ***Western ways*** 西洋風の輸入超過. ¶Well, gossip is busy with his name.—In ***what way?*** さて, 世間では大分あの人のうわさが高い.-どんな風に. ‖ It doesn't look Japan-made in ***what way*** you may look at it. どう見ても和製とは見えない. ¶in his ***whimsical way*** 彼一流の気紛れなやり口で. ¶She has a ***winning way*** with her. 彼女には人を引きつける魅力がある. ¶It is ***women's way***. それが女の行き方だ. ¶in a ***wrong way*** 間違ったやり方で ‖ To do so is going the ***wrong way*** to work. そうするのはやり方が間違っている. ¶adjust the saddle ***wrong way*** ronnd=put the wrong end of a saddle foremost くらをうしろ前におく.

Q[2] ***boy ways*** 男の子の常習. ¶***building ways*** 建築様式. ¶be ignorant of ***city ways*** 市の様子にくらい. ¶in a ***family way*** くつろいで ‖ be in the ***family way*** 《英口》妊娠している. ¶the ***Harvard way*** of doing things ハーバード(大学)流のやり方. ¶the ***home-country way*** 本国風. ¶the ***London ways*** ロンドン様式. ¶in a ***makeshift way*** 間に合わせに. ¶the ***Nazi way*** of life ナチス式生活様式. ¶a ***saving way*** 救う道. ¶his essentially ***twentieth-century way*** of looking at things 彼の主として二十世紀的なものの見方.

P ***according to*** the *way* of thinking=in a sense 考えようによっては. ¶help ***along*** the *way* ちょっと役に立つ(廃物利用など). ¶***by way*** of a change we will visit ... われわれは方面を変えて…へ行こう ‖ Let us go to ... ***by way*** of a start. まず…に行こう. ‖ ***by way*** of a luxury ぜいたく品として ‖ just ***by way*** of a joke ちょっと座興に ‖ ***by way*** of abbreviation=for short 略して ‖ ***by way*** of a new experience 話の種に ‖ ***by way*** of bidding farewell 別れを惜しんで ‖ ***by way*** of precaution against a bad year 凶年の用心に ‖ nod ***by way*** of recognition わかったしるしにうなずく ‖ ***by way*** of a side-show 相の手に ‖ merely ***by way*** of suggestion ほんの御参考までに ‖ ***by way*** of exception いつになく ‖ ***by way*** of consolation 気休めに ‖ ***by way*** of a parentheses it may be mentioned that ... ちなみに記す ‖ ***by way*** of a makeshift 間に合わせに ‖ ***by way*** of trial (=experiment) 試しに. 【類】***By way*** of conclusion to my speech let me emphasize (力説する) one point ‖ I now take, ***by way*** of contrast, a glimpse of ... その対照としてちょっと…のことを述べる ‖ ***by way*** of compensation (experiment) 埋合わせ(試し)に. 【類】say a few words ***by way*** of apology / ***by way*** of compensation / they call it ... ***by way*** of pseudonym (異名) / He remarked this ***by way*** of introduction / I called on him ***by way*** of returning compliments. / So much ***by way*** of apology. / ***By way*** of conclusion, several facts deserve mention. / ***by way*** of commentary (注釈として) I may note that ... / ***by way*** of showing an example ‖ Mrs. ... and her husband, ***by*** the *way*, are cousins. 因みに…夫妻はいとこ同志です ‖ ***By*** the *way* I have something to tell you. それはそうと君にお話したいことがある. ‖ ***By*** the *way*, what time is it? ときに今何時ですか. ‖ Why, ***by*** the *way*, does no one ever ...? ところでどうしてだれも…しないんですか. ‖ provide for the widows and orphans of comrades who have fallen ***by*** the *way* 倒れた戦友の未亡人と孤児の扶養に備える. ¶Yes, ***in*** a *way*. さよう, 見ようによっては(そうとも考えられる) ‖ I really like it, ***in*** a *way*. ほんとに私はちょっとそれが好きなのだ. ‖ What you say is right ***in*** a *way*. 君の言うことにも一応もっともだ. ‖ ***In*** his *way* he was great. 彼もまた一種の豪傑であった. ‖ ***in*** a *way* (manner) of thinking 考えようによっては ‖ That is all right ***in*** a *way*. それはまたそれで結構なことだ. ‖ ***In*** a *way* (=sense), this statement is true. 考えようによってはこの言葉は真理だ. ‖ Well, once ***in*** a *way* it won't hurt me. まあ, たまにこうしたことをやっても大したことはなかろう. ‖ Mister is often used colloquially, or vulgarly, ***in*** a *way* similar to the French Monsieur and German Herr in addressing a man whose name is unknown. ミスターはくだけたまたは俗っぽい使い方でフランス語の Monsieur ドイツ語の Herr 同様に知らない人に話しかけるときに用いられる. ‖ grin ***in*** a *way* peculiar to him 彼一流の歯を出した笑い方をする ‖ Once ***in*** a *way* I don't mind, but you are late every day. たまになら構わないが君は毎日遅刻している. ‖ He can not be justified ***in*** the *way* he acts. あのやり方じゃ人が納得しまい. ‖ We now travel ***in*** *ways* hardly imagined before. 今日われわれは以前ほとんど想像したこともないような風な旅行をする. ‖ He thumped her ***in*** the *way* of play. 彼はふざけて彼女を打った. ‖ The motor-man demanded something so grotesque ***in*** the *way* of fare. 運転手は目の玉の飛び出るような賃銀を要求した. ‖ do this ***in*** the *way* of business これを商売にやる ‖ A new departure ***in*** the *way* of steam engines has been invented by an Australian engineer. 新案の蒸気機関が豪州の一技師によって発明された. ¶Don't stand ***in*** my *way!* 私の邪魔をするな(そこどけ). ‖ get ***in*** the *way* of ... …の邪魔をする ‖ be wise ***in*** the *ways* of the world 世故にたけている ‖ It offers nothing very great ***in*** the *way* of financial compensation. それは経済的には大した報酬は出さない. 【類】Hollywood fashions ***in*** the *way* of clothing are servilely imitated by the Japanese. / The first part of the descent is uninteresting, with nothing much ***in*** the *way* of scenery. / For over 120 years the house of Spalding and Hodge has been the great centre for the supply of everything ***in*** the *way* of paper (紙業一切). / Japan offers a great deal ***in*** the *way* of the picturesque for tourists. / Here we have plenty ***in*** the *way* of green vegetables. ¶the proverb is good ***in*** its *way*, but ... ことわざはよいこともあるが… ¶He is a good boy to her ***in*** his *way*. 彼はあれでも彼女によくしている積りなのだ. 【類】I assure you that there is not a more clever man, ***in*** his *way*, in England. ¶A child is already ***on*** the *way*. [お腹に]子ができている. ¶***to*** my *way* of thinking 私に言わせると, 私から見ると. ¶Negotiations for ... are ***under way***. …の交渉が進行中である. ‖ Talks are now ***under way***. 今会談が行われている. ¶go ***out of*** his *way* to ... わざわざ…するために行く ‖ You needn't go ***out of*** your *way* on my account. わざわざ私のためにそうなさらないで下さい. ‖ keep ***out of*** the *way* 邪魔にならないようにする ‖ He kept [himself] ***out of*** harm's *way*. 彼は害を避けるようにしていた. ¶be fairly ***under way*** 軌道に乗っている ‖ preparations are already well ***under way*** for ... すでに…の準備が十分できている. 【類】Preparations are ***under way*** for a wedding. ‖ The scheme is now well ***under way*** to become a reality at any time. その計画はいつでも実現しうるように今や着々進行中である. 【類】negotiations are ***under way*** between ... and ... which are expected to result soon in ... / It is understood that negotiations are now ***under way*** for the placing of the contracts. / The plan is now well ***under way***. / The campaign of publicity is now ***under way***. ‖ plans are ***under way*** for the construction of ... / The project is fairly ***under way***. ‖ whilst the ship was ***under way*** その船の進行中 ‖ The vessel struck a reef whilst ***under way***. 同船は進行中暗礁に乗りあげた. 【類】when the train was well ***under way***. ☞ underway ともつづる.

P[2] her ***way of*** life 彼女の生活の仕方 ‖ men of all ***ways of*** thinking in politics それぞれ政見を異にした人々 ‖ their *ways of* thought 彼らの考え方 ‖ It depends on one's *way of* thinking. 気の持方一つだ. ‖ the *way of* reasoning 論法 ‖ a *way of* life 一つの生き方 ‖ a *way of* thought 一つの考え方 ‖ The *ways of* life among the Esquimaux. エスキモー族の生活様式 ‖ be acquainted with the people's *way of* living 下情に通じる ‖ her *way of* saying 彼女の口ぐせ ‖ the *way of* Gods 神ながらの道 ‖ Mutual aid is the *way of* a *samurai*. 武士は相見互い ‖ Such is the *way of* the world. 世の中ってそうしたもんなんだ. ‖ Inscrutable are the *ways of* Heaven. 人間万事塞翁が馬(天の摂理ははかり得ないものがある). ‖ You will soon get used to the *way of* ours. じきわれわれの習慣におなれになりますよ. ‖ Such is the *way of* human nature. 人間性というものはこうしたものだ. ‖ to some of you my *way of* thinking may seem odd or perverse when I tell you that ... ...と言ったら諸君の中には私の考え方を変だとかねじけているとか思う方があるかも知れない. 【類】 his *way of* doing things (=method) / but this is merely another *way of* saying that ... ¶It was suggested as a *way out of* the tangle of difficulties. それが乱麻を断つ方法として暗示された. ‖ A *way out of* the difficulty has yet to be found. まだ解決の道がつかない. ‖ the *way out of* depression 不景気を打破する方法. ¶That's not the *way to* success. それではうまく行きようはない. ‖ the *way to* beauty 美しくなる方法. ¶That's the *way with* servants, all the world over. 世界中のどこへ行っても召使という者はそうしたものだ.

O That's the *way* to talk in America. アメリカではその調子で話さなくってはいけない. ‖ That is not the *way* to spell his name. それでは彼の名のつづりが違う. ‖ That's his *way*. 例の手さ. ¶May be there is a *way* out. 何か打開策があるかも知れん. ¶I ain't given that *way*. 私はそうゆうようにはできていない.

wayside, *n.* 路傍.

P the wild flowers ***by*** the *wayside* 路傍に咲いた野の花 ‖ linger ***by*** the *wayside* 道草を食う. ¶Coming years are like milestones ***on*** the *wayside* of life. 来る年は人生の行路の一里塚のようなものだ.

weak, *a.* 弱い.

M The market is ***decidedly*** *weaker* (stronger). 市場は断然弱(強)気だ. ¶***notoriously*** *weak* in geography ばかばかしく地理の知識に欠けている. ¶be not ***so*** *weak* as she looks [その女が]見かけほどには弱くない. ¶be ***too*** *weak* to walk 歩けないほど弱い.

P He is still *weak* ***after*** (=***from***) his illness. 彼は病後でまだ体が衰弱している. ¶*weak* ***by*** nature 生れつき虚弱な. ¶those *weak* ***in*** mathematics 数学が不得手な人たち ‖ *weak* ***in*** mind and body 心身虚弱な ‖ be *weak* ***in*** the head (=upper story) うすばかである ‖ *weak* ***in*** hearing 耳の遠い ‖ *weak* ***in*** spelling (Latin) つづり(など)が弱い. 【類】 a baseball team *weak* ***in*** fielding (pitchers). ¶*weak* ***of*** brain (heart, understanding) 頭(など)の悪い. ¶*weak* ***on*** the classics 古典の知識に乏しい ‖ I am *weak* ***on*** names. 私は名が覚えられない.

weak, *n.* [the を付けて] 弱者.

P ***bully*** the *weak* 弱者をいじめる. ¶***champion*** the *weak* against the strong 強者に対して弱者を擁護する. ¶***oppress*** the *weak* 弱者を圧迫する. ¶Laws exist to ***protect*** the *weak* from the strong, the just from the unjust, the person of good intent from the swindler. 法律は強者に対して弱者を, 不正に対して正義を, 詐欺者に対して善意の人々を保護するために存在する. ¶***support*** the *weak* 弱者を助ける.

P Today the patient is ***at*** his *weakest*. 今日は病人が今までになく衰弱している. ¶The *weak* ***in*** courage are strong in cunning. 小胆者は大胆な謀略を策する.

weaken, *v.* 弱める.

M *weaken* it ***considerably*** それをよほど弱らす. 【類】 The storm has ***considerably*** *weakened* the sea-wall. ¶The illness has ***permanently*** *weakened* him. 病気で彼はすっかり体が弱ってしまった.

P *weaken* it ***by*** mixing まぜものをしてそれを弱める.

weakness *n.* 弱味.

V ***admit*** one's *weakness* 自分の弱さを自認する. ¶***betray*** *weakness* 弱味を見せる. ¶***correct*** this *weakness* この短所を改める. ¶He ***has*** a *weakness* for figures. 彼は算数にうとい. ‖ he ***has*** a special *weakness* (=passion) for ... 彼は...が至って好きだ. ‖ She ***has*** a *weakness* for tall, thin men 彼女は背の高いやせぎすの男が好きだ. ‖ ***have*** a *weakness* for women 女に甘い(のろい). ¶It is possible through environment largely to ***overcome*** hereditary *weakness*, and greatly to strengthen hereditary advantages. 環境によって大いに遺伝的短所を征服し大いに遺伝的長所を強化することができる. ¶***reveal*** one's *weakness* 弱点を暴露する. ¶He used his talent to ***satirize*** the political and social *weaknesses* and follies of his time. 彼はその才を使ってその時代の政治上並びに社会上の弱点や幣害を風刺した. ¶***show*** *weakness* in ... ...の点で弱味があることを示す.

Q Cases of drunkeness are now severely dealt with which would have been looked upon as ***amiable*** *weaknesses* a generation ago. 三十年程前には愛きょうと見られていた大酔も今日では容赦なく取扱われる. ¶a ***chronic*** *weakness* 慢性的病弱. ¶show ***constitutional*** *weakness* 身体の虚弱を示す. ¶This is our ***Japanese*** *weakness*. これがわれわれ日本人の短所だ. ¶a ***lingering*** *weakness* はかばかしくない健康. ¶***logical*** *weakness* 論理の弱味. ¶***mental*** *weakness* 精神薄弱, 低能. ¶***moral*** *weakness* 道徳上の弱味. ¶***national*** *weakness* 国民の短所. ¶A treacle pudding is a ***particular*** *weakness* of mine. 糖みつをかけたプディングは私の大好物だ. ¶***physical*** *weakness* 身体の虚弱. ¶a ***reprehensible*** *weakness* 捨てておかれない欠点. ¶***senile*** *weakness* 老衰. ¶a ***serious*** *weakness* 深刻な弱点. ¶***vacillating*** *weakness* [果断のない]弱腰.

Q² ***heart*** *weakness* 心臓薄弱. ¶the ***leg*** *weakness* of young chicks ひよっこの脚の弱さ.

P die ***from*** *weakness* 病弱で死ぬ. ¶take advantage ***of*** one's *weakness* その短所に乗じる. ¶personally I must confess ***to*** a *weakness* for ... 実は私は...が好きだ ‖ tender ***to*** *weakness* やさし過ぎる. ¶totter ***with*** *weakness* 体に力がなくってよろめく.

P² his *weakness* ***for*** wine (cards, women) 彼の酒(など)好き ‖ have a *weakness* ***for*** detective stories 探偵ものが大好きだ. ¶Candy is a *weakness* ***of*** mine. あまい物には目がない.

wealth, *n.* 富; 豊富.

V Popularity generally ***accompanies*** *wealth*. 人望は概して富に伴うものだ. ¶Carnegie ***accumulated*** his *wealth* in the course of his life-time at the rate of about a million a year. カーネギーはその生がいに一年およそ百万(ドル)の割合で金を作った. ¶***achieve*** great *wealth* 巨大の富を作る. ¶rapidly or suddenly ***acquire*** (=***procure***) great *wealth* 急速にまたは突然に巨財を得る ‖ ***acquire*** *wealth* and position 富と地位を得る. ¶***amass*** (=***gather or pile up***) one's *wealth* dishonestly 不正手段をもって財産を作る. ¶***attain*** *wealth* 富を得る. ¶the great traffic by which nations ***build*** their *wealth* 諸国民がその富を作り上げる大貿易. ¶These people ***count*** their *wealth* in a score of millions and more. これらの人たちは何千万という富を有している. ¶***court*** *wealth* 富を求める. ¶***covet*** more *wealth* いよいよ富を欲する. ¶***employ*** one's *wealth* その財産を使用する. ¶***enjoy*** an untold *wealth* ばく大なる財産を享有する. ¶***equalize*** *wealth* 富を平等にする. ¶***exhaust*** the national *wealth* 国富を消耗する. ¶***exploit*** natural *wealth* 自然の資源を利用する. ¶***flatter*** *wealth* 富める人にへつらう. ¶The few rich ***flaunt*** their *wealth* in the faces of the many poor. 小数の金持ちがこれ見よがしに多数の貧民に富を誇示する. ¶***gauge*** one's *wealth* その富の程度を計る. ¶***get*** *wealth* honestly 正直に働いて富を得る. ¶***govern*** *wealth* discreetly 富を善用する. ¶***have*** a *wealth* of ideas いい考えがあとからあとから出る ‖ ***have*** a *wealth* of rich hair ふさふさした毛をしている ‖ ***have*** a *wealth* of information about ... ...に関する豊富な知識を持っている. ¶***increase*** the *wealth* of the nation 国の富を増す. ¶***invest*** one's *wealth* in ... ...に投資する. ¶***lavish*** one's *wealth* on ... その財産を...に浪費する. ¶The interior of the house is as perfect as *wealth* and art can ***make*** it. 家の中は金にあかして善美をつくしてある. ¶***mobilize*** *wealth* [戦争などのため]富を動員する. ¶He has ***obtained*** his *wealth* by hard labor. 彼は労苦して富を得た. ¶***possess*** enormous *wealth* ばく大な財産を有する. ¶trade, our system of ***producing*** and ***distributing*** *wealth* 商業すなわちわれわれの富を作り富を分配する手段. ¶***use*** *wealth* generously 惜しげなく財産を使用する ‖ ***use*** one's *wealth* unselfishly 社会のために自分の財を費す. ¶Mongolian women ***wear*** their *wealth* on their hair. モーコの女は頭の飾りに金を掛ける.

Q justly *acquired wealth* 正当に得た富. ¶*colossal* (=*vast or immense*) *wealth* 巨大な富. ¶a man of *fabulous wealth* 途方もない財産の持主. ¶The invention brought him *fabulous wealth*. その発明で彼はばく大な富を得た. ¶*hereditary wealth* 祖父伝来の富. ¶*illgotten wealth* 不正手段で得た富. ¶*inherited wealth* 相続した財産. ¶*intangible wealth* in the form of … …という無形の財産. ¶a man of *large wealth* 巨富を有する人. ¶His poems have *luxuriant wealth* of imagery. 彼の詩は空想に富んでいる. ¶*mineral wealth* 鉱物資源. ¶homes of *moderate wealth* 中産階級の家庭. ¶He accumulated *sufficient wealth* to retire from the screen. 彼は銀幕から引退しても十分暮して行けるだけの富を蓄積した. ¶the *natural wealth* of a country 一国の資源. ¶earn *undreamed wealth* 夢にも思わない富を手に入れる. ¶a man of *untold wealth* 大財産家. ¶gain a *vast wealth* ばく大な富を得る.

Q² the *per capita wealth* of a country 一国の一人当りの富. ¶a levy on *war wealth* 戦時利得に対する課税.

P Health is *above wealth*. 健康は富貴にまさる. ¶seek *after wealth* 富を求める. ¶the thirst *for wealth* 富の渇望. 【類】be thirsty *for wealth* ‖ Some go in *for wealth*, and others go in for fame. 金を欲しがる者もあれば名誉を欲しがる者もある. ¶grow largely *in wealth* and influence 大いに富と勢力を増す ‖ decline *in wealth* 身代が左前になる ‖ live *in wealth* 裕福に暮す ‖ die *in wealth* 富んで死ぬ. ¶a man *of wealth* 裕福な人 ‖ the pursuit *of wealth* 富の追求. ¶come *to* (=acquire) one's *wealth* 富を得る ‖ add *to* (=increase) one's *wealth* その富を増す ‖ He was born *to wealth*. 彼は富貴の家に生れた. ¶The story is told *with* a *wealth* of details. その話は事細かに語られている. ‖ a book *with* a *wealth* of colored illustrations 彩色のさし絵がたくさん入っている本 ‖ a dictionary *with* a *wealth* of illustrative examples and pictures 用例やさし絵のたくさんある辞典 ‖ retire *with wealth* and honor 金と名誉を得て引退する ‖ *With* all his *wealth* he is unhappy. あんなに財産があっても彼は不幸だ.

P² *wealth from* waste 廃物利用. ¶Japan is famed for its *wealth of* flowers and flowering trees. 日本は草花や花の咲く木が豊富なので有名だ. ‖ A special feature of the Oxford Dictionary is its *wealth of* illustrative quotations. オクスフォード辞典の特色の一つは引用による説明が豊富なことだ. ‖ a *wealth of* learning 豊富な学識 ‖ the *wealth of* material 材料の豊富 ‖ There is a *wealth of* ornamentation. おびただしい装飾がある. ‖ The tourist left Japan with a *wealth of* delightful memories. その観光客は幾多の愉快な記憶をもって日本を去った. ‖ There is a *wealth of* meaning in this brief utterance. この簡単な言葉には豊富な意味が含まれている.

wealthy, *a.* 富んだ.

P *wealthy in* knowledge 知識が豊富な.

wean, *v.* 離乳させる.

M you must be *weaned away* from the idea that … …という考えを捨てなければいけない.

P *wean* oneself *from* liquor 酒を断つ.

weapon, *n.* 武器.

V *add* another *weapon* to armory of one's opponent 敵の武器にさらに一個の武器を加える. ¶*brandish weapons* 武器を振り回す. ¶*carry weapons along* 武器を携帯する. ¶The enemy never ventured to *cross weapons* with us in close fight. 敵はわれわれと接戦しようとは決してしなかった. ¶*forge weapons* for the fighters 戦士のために武器を作る. ¶*load* a *weapon* [けん銃など]武器に弾丸を込める. ¶It would be *placing* (=*putting*) *weapons* in the hands of the competitors. それでは競争者の手に武器を渡すようなものだ. ¶*poise* a *weapon* [投やりなど]武器のねらいをつける. ¶*sheathe* the *weapon* 武器をさやに納める; 和ぼくする. ¶He *used* his sharpened *weapon* of satire with considerable effect. 彼はその鋭い風刺という武器をすこぶる効果的に使用した. ¶*wield* a *weapon* 武器を揮う.

Q a *bacteriological weapon* 細菌兵器. ¶be armed with modern *chemical weapons* 新化学兵器で武装している. ¶carry a *concealed weapon* 凶器をかくして持っている. ¶a *dangerous weapon* 凶器. ¶The torpedo is the *deadliest weapon* of naval warfare. 水雷は海戦の武器として最も恐るべきものである. ¶a *defensive weapon* 防御的武器. ¶Money is a *double-edged weapon*. 金はよくも悪くも使える道具だ. ¶Irony is a very *effective weapon* of attack. 反語は非常に効果的な攻撃の武器である. ¶an *explosive weapon* 爆発武器(飛道具). ¶a *flying weapon* とび道具. ¶a *formidable weapon* 恐るべき武器. ¶a *genocidal weapon* 大量殺りく兵器. ¶an *ideological weapon* イデオロギー(思想)という兵器. ¶an *incisive weapon* 鋭利な武器. ¶a *lethal weapon* 凶器. ¶the air force as the *main national weapon* 国家主要の武器としての空軍. ¶a *missile* [*weapon*] とび道具; ミサイル兵器. ¶*murderous weapons* 凶器. ¶*nuclear weapons* 核兵器. ¶an *offensive weapon* of war 戦争の攻撃武器. ¶a *powerful weapon* 有力な武器. ¶our *trusty weapons* われわれの頼みにする武器. ¶a *two-edged weapon* 両刃の武器. ¶*warlike weapons* 兵器. ¶a *working weapon* for peace 平和に役立つ兵器.

Q² *atomic* and other *mass-destruction* (=genocidal) *weapons* 原子及びその他の大量殺人兵器. ¶a *key weapon* 主要兵器. ¶a *new-type weapon* 新型兵器. ¶a powerful *propaganda weapon* 強力な宣伝武器. ¶the use of atomic energy as a *war weapon* 兵器としての原子力利用.

P the use of education *as* a political *weapon* 政治上の武器としての教育の利用. ¶hurt *with* a *weapon* 武器で傷ついて.

P² a *weapon against* a person 人を攻撃する武器. ¶new *weapons for* fighting disease 闘病の新武器. ¶a *weapon of* precision 精鋭な武器(新発明の薬品・治療法など) ‖ a *weapon of* defense (offense) 防護(攻撃)兵器.

wear, *n.* 着用; 持ち(耐久); 消耗.

V It is fitted to *endure* constant, everyday *wear*. それは不断着に適している. ¶The shoes *give* double *wear*. そのくつは二足分もつ. ‖ They *give* excellent *wear*. それは実によくもつ. ¶The rug *shows wear*. その敷物は使い古してある. ¶*prolong* the *wear* of … …を長くもたせる. ¶The shoes will not *withstand* rough *wear*. そのくつはやたらに着用したらだめになる.

Q suitable for *between-season's wear* あい着に適した. ¶The hat is now in *general wear*. その帽子は目下流行している. ¶clothes for *informal wear* 平服. ¶Its *wear* is *short*. それはもちが悪い. ¶The stuff gives *long wear*. その生地は丈夫だ. ¶a collar of *yesterday's wear* 前日着けたカラ.

Q² be suited for *all-purpose wear* [いつどこにでも着て行かれる]万能着に適している. ¶the latest in *bathing wear* 海水着の最新型. ¶*beach wear* 海水着. ¶clothes for *everyday wear* 不断着 ‖ It's too good for *everyday wear*. ふだん着にはもったいない. 【類】a light pair of brown shoes for *everyday wear*. ¶*home wear* 家庭着. ¶I was well supplied with pretty frocks of all sorts, for *morning* and *evening wear*. 私は朝から夜までの色々な型のきれいなドレスを沢山買ってもらった. ¶*next-to-skin wear* はだ着. ¶*road depreciation* and *wear* 道路の陥没と破損. ¶*sports wear* スポーツ(運動)着. ¶for *street wear* 外出用の. ¶a light suit for *summer wear* 軽い夏服. ¶get a new suit for *Sunday wear*. ¶*town wear* 外出着. ¶*visiting wear* 訪問着. ¶heavy cloths for *winter wear* 厚い冬着. 【類】They are all for *winter wear*.

P a woman's dress *for wear* in the forenoon 婦人が午前に着る服. ¶scuffs (skirts, socks, shoes) *for* children's *wear* 子供用のスリッパー(など). ¶the coat I have *in wear* 私が今着ている上衣. ¶It will have twenty years *of wear*. それは二十年は持つだろう.

wear, *v.* 着る; すりへらす; 保つ.

M That is a bit too colorful to *wear around here*. ここ(室内)で着るにはちとはで過ぎる. ¶Time *wore away*. 時がたって行った. ‖ The long winter night was *wearing away*. 長い冬の夜が静かにふけて行った. ‖ *wear away* one's health 健康がじりじりと悪くなる ‖ The inscription has *worn away*. 銘は消えて読めなくなっている. ¶Stockings soon *wear badly*. [女の]長ぐつ下はじき悪くなる. ¶The grooves have *worn deep*. [敷居などの]みぞがすれて深くなった. ¶This stuff *wears long*. この布地は長もちする. ¶His patience *wore out*. 彼の堪忍袋の緒が切れた. ‖ The machinery is *wearing out*. その機械は廃物になりつつある. ‖ *wear out* life in idle projects むだなことを企んであたら一生をむだにする ‖ *wear out* the knees of one's trousers ずぼんのひざがすり切れる ‖ be *worn out* with toil 力業で疲れ果てる ‖ be *worn out* with fatigue 疲れで弱っている ‖ He is utterly *worn out* with age. 彼は取る年波ですっかり弱った. ‖ *wear out* one's youth and strength あたら若さと精力をすり減らす ‖ I am afraid it will soon *wear out*. それは間もなく使い古しで役に立たなくなるかも知れない. 【類】The machine *wore out* rapidly. ¶ *wear **quickly*** すぐにいたむ. ¶ rails *worn **smooth*** with use ま滅してなめらかになった軌道. ¶ This cloth will *wear **thin***. この布はすれて薄くなるだろう. ¶ My patience is *wearing **thin***. がまんがしきれない. ‖ Coins *wear **thinner*** with use. 硬貨は使ううちに薄くなる. ¶ be ***thoroughly** worn* out 疲れ果てる ‖ clothes ***thoroughly** worn* to rags ぼろぼろになった着物. ¶ trousers *worn **threadbare*** by much use 着古してぼろぼろになったズボン ‖ theories of philosophy *worn **threadbare*** with hard use よく持出されるので陳腐になった哲学説. ¶ Members' badges must be *worn **visibly***. 会員章は見える所に着けていなければならない. ¶ *wearing **well*** and looking well 持ちもよく見かけもよい.

M² The heels of my shoes are *wearing **down***. 私のくつのかかとが減ってきている. ¶ *worn **down*** with fatigue ひどく疲労して. ¶ The rusticity of her gait, manners, and deportment began to *wear **off*** sensibly. 彼女のいなか者らしい歩きつきや態度や身のこなしが目に見えて取れていった. ¶ Its novelty has *worn **off***. もうそれは珍らしくない. ‖ Its novelty rapidly *wears **off***. それはじきに珍しくなくなる. ‖ The nap *wore **off***. けばがすり切れた. ‖ The follies of youth *wear **off*** with age. 若気の道楽は年をとると直る. ‖ *wear **off*** the fat [運動などして]ぜい肉をとる ‖ Enthusiasm *wears **off***. 熱がさめる. 【類】take rest till the fever *wears* itself ***off*** ‖ The necessary contact with people of both sexes gradually *wore **off*** some of the rougher corners. [共学などで]男女が必然的に接触していると段々お互いの角がとれてくる. ‖ The color has *worn **off***. 色がさめた. ¶ as the day (night) *wears **on*** 日がたけて(夜がふけて)来るにつれて ‖ as the summer *wore **on*** 夏が終りに近づくにつれ. 【類】as the evening (week) *wore **on*** ‖ Jewels are *worn **in*** pins and other ornaments. 宝石はピンやその他の飾りにはめて身に着ける. ¶ The rope is *wearing **through***. なわがすれて切れかかっている.

P *wear **about*** one 身に着ける. ¶ a watch-chain *worn **across*** the breast 胸に掛けた時計のくさり. ¶ *wear* it ***as*** a badge それを記章として着ける. ¶ Inros were *worn **at*** the girdle. 印ろうは腰に着けた. ¶ The floor is *worn **by*** many feet. 床は大勢の人に踏まれてすり減っている. ‖ It is *worn **by*** それは時代がたって損じている. ¶ *wear **for*** years 数年もつ. ¶ A wakizashi, short sword, is *worn **in*** the belt along with the katana, or sword properly so called. 脇(わき)差すなわち短かい方の刀は本式の刀とともに腰に差すものである. ¶ *wear **in*** bed 寝巻に着る ‖ a rubber shoe *worn **over*** another shoe 他のくつの上にはくオーバーシューズ ‖ She *wears* a diamond pin ***in*** her hair. 彼女は髪にダイヤ入りのピンをさしている. ¶ We *wear* shoes ***on*** our feet. くつは足にはく. 【類】*wear* gloves ***on*** one's hands / *wear* a red band ***on*** one's coat-sleeve ‖ An engagement ring should be *worn **on*** the right hand. 婚約の指輪は右の手にはめるのが本当だ. 【類】The wedding ring is *worn **on*** the third finger of the left hand. ¶ big felt slippers to *wear **over*** our shoes くつの上にはく大きなフェルトのスリッパー. ¶ *wear* a ribbon ***round*** one's hat 帽子の回りにリボンを巻いている. ¶ The tuxedo coat is often *worn **to*** the theatre with ladies. タキシードはよく婦人と一緒に劇場へ行く時に着用される. 【類】Englishmen do not *wear* gloves ***to*** dinner parties, to the theater, or to concerts. ‖ *worn **to*** bits (=ribbons, rags *or* tatters) [きものが]ずたずたに切れた. ¶ books *worn **with*** too frequent handling ひんぱんに使用するのでいたんだ本 ‖ They *wear **with*** superior resistance. それらは一層耐久力がある.

weariness, *n.* 退屈.

V ***endure*** the *weariness* of a long railway journey 長い汽車旅行の退屈を忍ぶ. ¶ ***while away*** the *weariness* of ... ... の退屈をしのぐ.

Q² There is ***war** weariness* among the peoples of the world. 世界の人々は戦争にあきあきしている.

P we have pointed out ***to** weariness* that ... われわれは口がすっぱくなるほど...と注意した. ¶ weighed down ***with** weariness* 退屈の余り.

P² *weariness **from*** labor 働き疲れ. ¶ go to death out of *weariness **with*** the world 世の中がいやになって死ぬ.

wearing, *n.* 着用.

Q the ***first** wearing* of clothes きものの初着. ¶ This dinner-coat (=tuxedo) was but its ***third** wearing*. そのタキシードは出来てから着たのが三度目であった.

P They will stretch ***by** wearing*. 着(はい)ていればのびるだろう. ¶ old shoes that are ***past** wearing* はけなくなった古ぐつ.

weary, *a.* あきた.

M become *weary* (=wearied) ***of*** the monotony その単調にあきる ‖ a prince *weary **of*** his magnificence 高貴な身分にあきた王子 ‖ He is *weary **of*** life (living) 彼は人生(生きているの)がいやになっている. 【類】be *weary **of*** reading it. ¶ *weary **with*** walking (waiting) 歩き(待ち)くたびれて ‖ be *weary **with*** toil 肉体労働で疲れる.

weary, *v.* あきさせる.

M *weary **out*** one's days in woe 苦悩の月日を送る. ¶ The old man, *wearied **by*** his long journey, retired early. その老人は長い旅行で疲れていたので早く床についた.

P We were *wearied **of*** waiting. われわれは待ちあぐんだ. ‖ He will soon *weary **of*** the task. 彼はじきに仕事にあきるだろう. ¶ He *wearies* (=bores) me ***to*** death. 私はあの人にはうんざりする. ¶ be *wearied **to*** death 疲れてくたくたになって. ¶ But it is not our purpose to *weary **with*** statistics. しかし統計を並べ立てていたずらに読者をあかすのがわれわれの本意でない. ‖ He *wearied* himself ***with*** labor. 彼は働き疲れがしていた.

weather, *n.* 天気, 天候.

V We ***encountered*** stormy *weather* all the way across. われわれは航海中ずっとしけを食った. ¶ ***escape*** the bitter *weather* 避寒する. ¶ Bad *weather* was ***expected*** before us. 間もなく天気が変る模様であった. ¶ the worst *weather* I have ***experienced*** 私がこれまでに経験した最悪の天候. 【類】We ***experienced*** heavy *weather* during the voyage. ¶ ***forecast*** (=***foretell** or **predict***) [the] *weather* 天気を予報する. ¶ We ***had*** fine *weather* on that day. その日は上天気であった. ¶ Incoming vessels ***report*** heavy *weather* at sea. 入港の船は海が荒れていることを報告している. ¶ We must ***take** weather* as it comes. 天候はどうにもならない. ¶ Wet *weather* is much ***wanted***. 雨天をしきりに望んでいる.

V² This *weather **agrees*** with you. この気候は君の体に適している. ¶ The *weather* has ***broken***. 天気がゆるんだ. ¶ The *weather **changed***. 天気が変った. ¶ The *weather* is ***clearing*** gradually. 天気が次第に快晴に向う. 【類】The *weather **cleared*** and the sun shone. ¶ I am glad the *weather* has ***cleared off*** (=***up***). 天気になってうれしい. ¶ should the *weather **continue** bad* (***fine***) 悪い(良い)天気が続いたら. ¶ The *weather* is ***growing warm***. 陽気が段々暖かになってきた. ¶ I hope the *weather* will ***hold***. 私は天気がもてばいいと思っている. ¶ The *weather* has ***improved***. 天気がよくなった. ¶ *weather **permitting***=if weather permits もし天気なら ‖ as soon as *weather **permits*** 天気がよくなり次第に. ¶ Very bad *weather* is ***prevailing*** here. 当地は非常に悪い天気が続いている. ¶ when hot *weather **sets in*** 陽気が暑くなると. ¶ I hope the *weather* will ***stay fine***. 《米》天気が続くだろう. ¶ when the *weather **turned cold*** 陽気が寒くなった時.

Q rather ***agreeable** weather* やや気持のよい天気. ¶ in ***all** weathers*=rain or shine どんな天気でも. ¶ ***bad** weather* at sea 海上の荒れ. 【類】owing to ***bad** weather* ‖ ***Bad** weather* was to be expected before us. 今にも天候が悪化する模様であった. ‖ He experienced ***bad*** (***fine, variable***) *weather* during the voyage. 彼の航海中は悪天候(上天気, 変りやすい天気)だった. ¶ ***beastly** weather* 実にいやな天気. ¶ ***beautiful*** (=***exhilarating, glorious***) *weather* うららかな天気. ¶ ***boisterous** weather* 荒れ日より. ¶ ***bracing** weather* さわやかな天気. ¶ in this ***broiling** weather* この炎天に ‖ ***broiling*** summer *weather* 夏の焼けつくような暑さ. ¶ It was ***charming** weather* yesterday. きのうは実に気持のよい天気でした. ¶ In ***clear** weather* we can see Mt. Fuji on the right hand. 晴れた日には右手に富士山が見える. ¶ ***clear*** and ***fine** weather* 快晴の日より. ¶ ***close** weather* うっとうしい天気. ¶ ***cloudy** weather* 曇天 ‖ The *weather* is ***cloudy*** with snow (showers). 雪(夕立)で曇っている. ¶ ***cold** weather* 寒い陽気 ‖ ***cold*** and ***warm** weather* alternate 寒くなったり暖かになったり. ¶ ***comfortable*** (=***agreeable***) *wheather* しのぎよい気候. ¶wonderfully ***cool, pleasant*** *weather* 非常に涼しく心地よい天気. ¶***damp*** *weather* じめじめした陽気. ¶***delicious*** *weather* 結構な天気. ¶owing to the ***deplorable*** *weather* いやな天気のために. ¶***doubtful*** *weather* おぼつかない天気. ¶***dry*** *weather* 乾燥した陽気. ¶The *weather* is ***dull*** with rain. 雨が降って天気がうっとうしい. ‖ a spell of ***dull*** (=***gloomy***) *weather* うっとうしい天気続き. ¶***dull*** and ***overcast*** *weather* 空が曇ってどんよりした天気. ¶in ***dusty*** *weather* ほこりのひどい日に. ¶in ***fair*** or ***foul*** *weather* 天気はよくても悪くても. ¶It is useless to think about going out in this ***fearful*** *weather*. こんないやな天気に外出しようと思ってもだめだ. ¶***fine*** *weather* 絶好な天気. ¶***fresh*** *weather* さわやかな天気. ¶***frightful*** *weather* 恐ろしい日より. ¶***frosty*** *weather* 寒空. ¶***depressing*** *weather* うっとうしい天気. ¶***exhilarating*** *weather* うららかな天気. ¶***foul*** *weather* 悪天候. ¶Few people like ***gray*** *weather* and rain. 曇った天気や雨降りが好きな人は滅多にない. ¶***hazy*** *weather* かすんだ空. ¶***heavy*** *weather* 悪天候. ¶Incoming vessels report ***heavy*** *weather* at sea 入港船によると海上は荒れている. ¶the prolonged spell of ***hot*** *weather* 長期にわたる暑気. ¶a ***hot*** and ***humid*** *weather* 暑くてじめじめした天気. ¶***ice-cold December*** *weather* 極寒の十二月の陽気. ¶***ideal*** *weather* 理想的な天候. ¶in the most ***inclement*** *weather* 険悪をきわめた天候に. ¶***invigorating*** *weather* 生きかえるような天気. ¶***just*** the *weather* for angling 釣にはもってこいの天気. ¶***Magnicent*** *weather* favored the athletic meet. その運動会はすばらしい上天気に恵まれた. ¶***mild*** *weather* 暖かい陽気. ¶***nasty*** *weather* いやな天気. ¶***perfect*** *weather* 絶好の天候. ¶if ***pleasant*** *weather* continues 気持のよい天気が続けば. ¶when the *weather* is ***propitious*** 天気が好都合の時に. ¶The ***rainy*** *weather* has come. 梅雨になった. ¶***real*** "***Queen's*** *weather*" 本当の女王(日本)晴れ. ¶***Rotten*** *weather!* くさくさする. ¶***rough*** *weather* 荒(ㇵ)天. ¶It was altogether ***royal*** *weather* for the fete. 全くその祝典には申分のない天気であった. ¶***seasonable*** *weather* 順当の陽気. ¶***sloppy*** *weather* じめじめした天気. ¶in ***snowy*** *weather* 雪降りの日に. ¶***splendid*** *weather* 好天気. ¶***squally*** (=***stormy***) *weather* 荒天 ‖ braving (=facing *or* defying) ***stormy*** *weather* 荒天を突いて. ¶***sunshining*** *weather* 照る日. ¶***superb*** *weather* 絶好の天候. ¶encounter ***terrible*** *weather* 恐ろしい暴風雨に出会う. ¶encounter ***terrific*** *weather* 恐ろしい悪天候に出あう. ¶The *weather* is ***thick*** with rain. 雨で天気がどんよりしている. ¶***thick*** and ***foggy*** *weather* 曇った霧の深い天気. ¶***threatening*** *weather* 険悪を予想させる天候. ¶be grounded at ... through ***trying*** *weather* 悪天候をついて...に着陸する. ¶despite of the ***unfavorable*** *weather* 天気が悪いにもかかわらず ‖ be forced back by ***unfavorable*** *weather* [船が]悪天候のため止むなく引返す. ¶***unpleasant*** *weather* 不愉快な天気. ¶***unpromising*** *weather* 心細い天気. ¶Unfortunately the *weather* was ***unpropitious*** during the whole of our brief sojourn. 不幸にして私たちの短い滞在中ずっと天気具合が悪かった. ¶very ***unsettled*** *weather* 非常に変りやすい天気. ¶The *weather* was unspeakably ***vile*** on the first two days out. 出発して当初の二日というものは何とも言えないいやな天気続きだった. ¶***voluptuous*** *weather* すてきな天気. ¶in the ***warm*** *weather* of summer 夏の暑い時に. ¶***warm*** and ***genial*** *weather* 暖かでのどかな日より. ¶Cheese molds in ***warm, wet*** *weather*. むし暑い日にはチーズがかびる. ¶This ***wet*** *weather* is gloomy. この雨天は非常にうっとうしい. ‖ The road is muddy in ***wet*** *weather* 道路は雨でどろんこだ. ‖ in ***wet*** *weather* as well as fine 降っても照っても. 【類】I do not care to go to any place in such ***wet*** *weather* as this. ¶***wild*** and ***stormy*** *weather* 険悪な荒れ日より. ¶***wretched*** *weather* ひどい天気.

Q[2] A season of fine crisp ***December*** *weather* arrived. 身の引きしまる好天の十二月の季節になった. ¶glorious ***spring*** *weather* うららかな春の陽気. ¶during dreary ***winter*** *weather* 荒涼たる冬の天候の間.

P ***during*** foggy *weather* 霧が立ちこめている間. ¶We cannot go out ***in*** such *weather*. われわれはこんな天気では外出はできない. ‖ ***in spite of*** rainy *weather* 雨天にもかかわらず. ¶owing to the severity ***of*** the *weather* 天候険悪のため ‖ regardless ***of*** the *weather*=rain or shine 晴雨にかかわらず ‖ in all sorts ***of*** *weather* どんな天気でも ‖ stress ***of*** *weather* 天候険悪 ‖ change ***of*** *weather* 天気の変り ‖ All depends on the state ***of*** the *weather*. すべては天候いかんによる. ¶It depends ***on*** the *weather*. それは天気次第である. ¶***on account of*** the bad *weather* today 今日は天気が悪いので. ¶***owing to*** bad *weather* at sea 海が荒れているので. ¶march ***through*** bad *weather* 悪天候の中を行進する. ¶***under*** foul *weather* 悪天候の下に ‖ ***under*** all *weathers* 天候がどうあろうと ‖ ***under*** the *weather* 《米口》時候あたりがして, 気分のすぐれない; 少し酔っぱらって. 【類】If I look a little ***under*** the *weather* it is probably attributable to having retired so late.

P[2] the *weather* ***during*** the voyage 航海中の天候.

weather, *v.* 風化する; [風雨を]冒す; [困難を]切り抜ける.

M *weather out* a storm that beats upon one 吹きつけるあらしをしのぎおおせる.

P The rocks are *weathered* ***into*** fantastic forms. 岩が風化して奇異な形になっている. ¶*weather* [***through***] financial difficulties 財政の困難を切り抜ける.

O *weathering* a storm あらしを冒して.

weathercock, *n.* 風見.

V[2] The *weathercock* ***points*** to the east. 風見が東を指している. ¶The *weathercock* ***turns*** with the wind. 風見は風で回る.

weave, *v.* 織る; くねりながら進む.

M *weave* history and fiction ***carefully together*** in a story 歴史をまとめて架空を念入りに一つの物語をつづる. ¶The story is ***skilfully*** *woven* into a connected narrative. その話は手際よくまとめてある. ¶*weave* one's way ***uphill*** 山をうねうね登る.

M[2] the narrative is *woven* ***round*** ... その話は...を骨子としてできている.

P The book contains incidents *woven* ***about*** the life and adventures of a remarkable young lady. その本には一人の珍らしい若い女の一生とその波らん重畳のいきさつがつづってある. ¶The fabric was *weaving* ***at*** her loom. その布を彼女は機で織っていた. ¶cloths *woven* ***by*** hand 手織りの布. ¶*woven* ***from*** long wool 長い羊毛で織った. ¶patterns *woven* ***in*** fabrics 織出し模様. ¶*weave* the incidents together ***into*** one continuous narrative それらのできごとをつづりあわせて一つの物語にまとめる ‖ Thread is *woven* ***into*** cloth. 糸を織って布にする ‖ The blankets have the hotel crest *woven* ***into*** them at the top and bottom. 毛布にはそのホテルの紋章が上下に織出してある. ¶It is *woven* ***of*** silk. それは絹物である. ¶*woven* ***on*** looms• 機で織った. ¶*weave* cloth ***out of*** thread 糸で布を織る. ¶*weave* one's way ***through*** a forest 森の中をくねりながら進む. ¶*weave* ***with*** the twill あや織にする.

weaver, *n.* 織工.

Q[2] a ***silk*** *weaver* 絹織工.

weaving, *n.* 織仕事.

V ***do*** one's *weaving* 機(ﾊﾀ)を織る.

Q[2] ***basket*** *weaving* かご作り. ¶***canvas*** *weaving* ズック織り. ¶***sail-cloth*** *weaving* 帆布織り.

web, *n.* 織物; くもの巣.

V a spider ***spinning*** a *web* 巣をかけているくも. ¶***weave*** a *web* 織物を織る.

Q a ***shameless*** and ***transparent*** *web* of falsehoods うそ八百. ¶the ***spider's*** *web* くもの巣.

P The spider catches flies ***in*** his *web*. くもは網ではえを捕る.

P[2] a *web* ***of*** lies うそで固めた話.

wed, *v.* 結婚する; 結び付く.

M They are ***happily*** *wedded*. 彼らは幸福な結婚をした.

P They are so *wedded* ***to*** old customs. 彼らは非常に旧習に執着している. ‖ He is *wedded* ***to*** old ideas. 彼は旧思想にとらわれている. ‖ A society *weds* ***to*** ceremonies whence the soul has fled. 社会は精神が抜けてしまうと形式的に流れる.

wedding, *n.* 結婚.

V ***attend*** a *wedding* 結婚式へ出る. ¶***celebrate*** a *wedding* of ... and ... ...と...の結婚式をあげる. ¶We shall soon ***have*** a *wedding* in the family. 間もなく私たちの家に婚礼があります. ¶Only one out of every thousand married couples live to ***keep*** their golden wedding. 千組の夫婦の中で金婚式をあげるまで生きる者はわずかに一組しかない. ‖ Here will the *wedding* be ***kept*** (=***solemnized***). ここでその結婚式が行われる.

V When does the *wedding* ***come off*** (=***take place***)? 結婚式はいつ行われますか? ¶How did the *wedding* ***go off*** at the cottage? そのいなか家の結婚式はどんなぐあいでしたか.

Q a *fashionable wedding* りっぱな結婚式. ¶a "*quiet*" *wedding*, to which only the immediate family and very close friends are invited 近親者とごく親密な友だちだけを招いてあげる質素な結婚式.

Q^2 the ***Anderson-Palmer*** *wedding* アンダーソン・パーマー両家の結婚. ¶***church*** *weddings* 教会結婚. ¶***home*** (=***house***) *wedding* 自宅結婚. ¶a ***penny*** *wedding* 招待客の寄付金婚礼. ¶***proxy*** *wedding* 代理結婚(戦争などで本人がいない時の). ¶celebrate their ***silver*** *wedding* その銀婚式をあげる. ☞ crystal wedding (十五年), china wedding (二十年), gold wedding (五十年), diamond wedding (六十またはは七十五年).

P I was present ***at*** the *wedding*. 私はその結婚式に列席した ‖ a white rosette worn ***at*** a *wedding* 結婚式につける白ばらの花飾り. ¶on the occasion ***of*** the *wedding* その結婚式の折に.

P^2 *wedding* ***before*** the altar 神前結婚. ¶her *wedding* ***to*** ... 彼女の…との結婚. ¶He has passed the "golden" anniversary of his *wedding* ***with*** literature. 彼が文筆生活にはいってから五十年たった.

wedge, *n.* くさび.

V the first *wedge* was ***driven*** into the concert of the powers when ... …の時に列強協力における決裂の端を開いた. ¶***drive in*** a *wedge* くさびを打込む.

Q a ***fatal entering*** *wedge* 決定的なくさび. ¶the ***original entering*** *wedge* 最初に打込むくさび.

P insert (=drive in) the thin end ***of*** the *wedge* 気のつかない内にくさびを打込んで動かしがたい既製事実を作りあげようとする. ¶cleave (fasten) ***with*** a *wedge* くさびを差して割る(締める). 【類】 force apart ***with*** a *wedge*.

wedge, *v.* 押込む.

M^2 I was *wedged* ***in*** between ... 私は…の間に押し込まれた ‖ *wedge* oneself ***in*** むりに割り込む. ¶*wedge* ***up*** くさびでしめる.

P be *wedged* ***between*** ... and ... …と…の板ばさみになる. ¶*wedge* ***into*** the middle of an electric car 電車の真ん中にわり込む. ¶*wedging* ***of*** a little domestic teaching into the mass of the ordinary school work たくさんの普通の授業の中に幾分家庭向きの授業をわり込ませること. ¶*wedge* a rail ***on*** sleepers ... …レールをまくら木にくさびでとめる. ¶*wedge* oneself ***through*** a narrow opening せまい出口(通路など)に無理に入る.

wedlock, *n.* 結婚.

Q a child born in ***lawful*** *wedlock* 嫡出の子. ¶They lived in ***sterile*** *wedlock* for three years. 結婚して三年たったが子がなかった.

P born ***in*** *wedlock* 嫡出の. ¶bear a child ***out of*** *wedlock* 私生児を生む ‖ Many more girls than boys were born ***out of*** *wedlock*. 新生児は男子よりも女子の方が多かった.

Wednesday, *n.* 水曜日.

Q^2 ***Spy*** *Wednesday* 間ちょう水曜日(復活祭前々の水曜日をいう).

weed, *n.* 雑草; 《俗》タバコ; 喪章; *pl.* 喪服.

V ***dig up*** the *weeds* 雑草を掘取る. ¶***extirpate*** *weeds* 雑草を根だやしする. ¶The *weed* must be ***kept under***. 雑草をはびこらしてはいけない. ¶***pull up*** *weeds* 雑草を抜取る. ¶***root up*** (=***uproot***) *weeds* 雑草を根こぎにする. ¶***smoke*** a penny *weed* 安タバコをのむ. ¶***wear*** a *weed* on one's hat 帽子に喪章をつける.

V^2 The *weed* ***grow*** apace. 雑草は生長が早い. ¶The *weeds* ***run*** riot in my garden. 雑草が私の家の庭にやたらはびこっている. ¶*Weeds* ***spring up***. 雑草が生える.

Q a ***common*** *weed* 普通の雑草. ¶the [***fragrant***] *weed* タバコ. ¶a ***troublesome*** *weed* 厄介な雑草. ¶***widow's*** *weeds* [婦人の]喪服. 【類】 a wan woman in rusty ***widow's*** *weeds* leading a child in one hand and carrying her frugal marketings in the other.

P a plot overgrown ***with*** *weeds* 雑草が一面に生えた地面 ‖ An uncultivated garden will be overrun ***with*** *weeds*. 畑は耕さないと雑草がはびこる.

weed, *v.* 抜取る.

M *weed* ***out*** root and all 雑草を根ごと抜き取る ‖ The worthless books in a library should be *weeded* ***out***. 図書館のくだらない書物は取除いてしまうべきだ. 【類】 *weed* ***out*** incompetent ones (hopeless pupils) / *weed* ***out*** the drones / *weed* ***out*** the weaker institutions / The police officers are *weeding* ***out*** the unlicensed liquor sellers (不正酒屋).

weeding, *n.* [不用物の]整理.

Q ***judicious*** *weeding* in one's collection その収集のおろぬき(整理).

week, *n.* 週, 週間.

V ***appoint*** a "*week*" of effort against (for) ... …に反対(助成)の「週間」を指定する. ¶***establish*** a five-day *week* (労働日・授業日など)五日一週の制を設ける. ¶***spend*** a very busy *week* 多忙な一週間を送る. ¶not a *week* ***goes by*** in which the newspapers do not report some such case as this: 次のような事件が新聞に出ない週間はない.

Q spend many a ***dreary*** *week* おもしろくない幾週間かを送る. ¶twice in ***every*** *week* 毎週二回. ¶at the end of a ***hectic*** *week* or so 一週間ばかり大多忙をきわめた後で. ¶an ***idle*** *week* 仕事をしない一週間. ¶***last*** (***next***) *week* 先(来)週 ‖ some time during ***next*** *week* 来週中に. ¶In Moscow ***last*** *week* was an anniversary *week*. モスコーでは先週は記念週間だった. ¶the ***past*** *week* or so 先週あたり. ¶during the ***rush*** *week* of Christmas いそがしいクリスマス週間中. ¶in the ***second*** *week* of September 九月へはいって第二週目に.

Q^2 an ***accentuation*** *week* 強調週間. ¶***Boy Scout Week*** ボイスカウト週間. ¶***Christian Youth Week*** キリスト教青年週間. ¶during ***Christmas*** *week* クリスマス週間中. ¶a ***clean-up*** *week* 清掃週間. ¶the ***Commencement*** *Week* 《米》卒業式週間. ¶the ***ember*** *week*. 四季斎日週間. ¶The ***exhortation*** *week*. 勧話週間(四旬斎前第三日曜日の前週). ¶the ***expectation*** *week* ヤソ昇天節と聖霊降臨祭日との間の週. ¶a ***five-day*** *week* of forty-four hours 〖労〗一週五日四十四時間労働. ¶a ***forty-eight hours*** *week* (=48-hour) 〖労〗一週四十八時間労働. ¶work a ***full work*** *week* 一週間休日なしに働く. ¶***Good Speech*** *Week* よい言葉(言葉の改善)の週間. ¶launch a "***Human Rights*** *Week*" 「人権週間」を始める. ¶He'll be back ***Monday*** *week*. 来週の月曜日に戻ります. ¶observe ***National Laugh*** *week* 全国笑おう週間を行う. ¶***Old Home*** *Week* [離れている家族友人などが集まる里帰り的な]帰郷週間. ¶observe ***Self-Denial*** *Week* [救世軍の]自制週間を挙行する. ¶The Mayor proclaimed May 5 to 17 as ***Spring*** Cleaning *Week*. 市長は五月五日から十七日まで春期大掃除週間と告示した. ¶***today*** (=this day) *week* 《英》来週(先週)の今日. ☞ 米語用法は today last (next) week. ¶limit the ***work*** *week* to forty-eight hours 一週の労働時間を四十八時間に制限する. ¶***World Youth*** *Week* 世界青少年週間.

P ***above*** a *week* 一週間以上. ¶***after*** a *week* 一週間後に. ¶***At*** the fifth *week* thrifty Leghorn chicks are beautifully fledged. 五週間目に発育良好なレグホンひなは美しく羽根が生える. ¶board ***by*** the *week* 一週幾らで下宿する ‖ hire a boat ***by*** the *week* 一週いくらでボートを賃借りする ‖ We pay the wages ***by*** the *week*. 賃金は毎週払だ. ¶***during*** a *week* 一週間中(に) ‖ ***during*** the next *week* or two 次の一二週間中に. ¶***for*** a *week* 一週(七日)間 ‖ I shall be away from home ***for*** a *week* or so. 私は一週間かそこいら家を留守にする. ‖ ***for*** a few *weeks* ahead ここ数週間は. ¶***in*** a *week* or so 一週間位たって ‖ ***in*** a *week* from the present time 今から一週間たって ‖ She has been sick in bed ***in*** the past *week*. この一週間病気でふせっている. ‖ I shall finish it ***in*** a *week*. 一週間でこしらえ上げます. ¶***within*** a *week* 一週間以内に ‖ ***Within*** the past *weeks* a rush of such cases has broken out. この数週間こんな事件が盛んに起っている.

P^2 *week* ***after*** week=*week* ***by*** week. ¶a *week* ***from*** today 今日から一週間. ¶a *week* ***of*** alternating snow and frost 交互に雪が降り寒気が増した一週.

O *week* in *week* out 毎週毎週. ¶before the *week's* out その週間が終らない内に. ¶A British Labor Women's *Week* is to be held from June 6 to June 14. 英国婦人労働者週間が六月六日から六月十四日まで催されるはず.

weekday, *n.* 日曜以外の日.

P ***on*** ordinary *weekdays* [日曜日以外の]平日に.

weekend, *n.* 週末; 週末旅行.

V ***spend*** a *weekend* with a friend 友人と週末を送る.

Q a ***gloomy*** *weekend* [懐の暖くない]憂うつな週末. ¶have a ***long*** *weekend* 週末に休日がかさなる, 連休になる.

Q^2 a carefree ***seaside*** *weekend* うさ晴しの(楽しい)海岸の週末行楽.

P ***at*** *weekend* 週末に. ¶go away ***for*** the *weekend* 週末旅

行に出かける. ¶go ***on*** a *weekend* [trip] 週末旅行に出かける. ¶stay at ... ***over*** the *weekend* 週末を…で過ごす.

weekend, *v.* 週末を送る.

P He's *weekending* down ***at*** Atami. 彼は熱海で週末保養をやっている.

weekender, *n.* 週末旅行者.

P The beach was unusually crowded ***with weekenders*** from neighboring towns. 海水浴場は近くの都市からの週末旅行者でいつになくにぎわっていた.

weep, *v.* 泣く.

M ***weep afresh*** at the thought そのことを思い出してまた涙を流す. ¶*weep* ***aloud*** 声を出して泣く. ¶*weep* ***away*** one's time 泣き暮す. ¶*weep* ***bitterly*** おいおい泣く. ¶They *wept* their eyes ***blind***. 彼らは目を泣きつぶした. ¶*weep* ***copiously*** おいおい泣く. ¶*weep* ***noisily*** 声を立てて泣く. ¶*weep* oneself ***out*** 思う存分泣く. 【類】*weep* one's eyes (heart) ***out***. ¶*weep* ***sorely*** ひどく泣く.

P *weep* ***at*** the pain inflicted 苦痛を受けて泣く ‖ *weep* ***at*** the sad news その悲報に接して泣く. ¶*weep* ***for*** joy at the sight of ... …を見てうれし泣をする ‖ *weep* ***for*** the deceased 故人のために泣く. ¶*weep* ***in*** sympathy もらい泣きする. ¶She was *weeping* ***into*** her handkerchief. 彼女はハンケチに顔を埋めて泣いていた. ¶She *wept* ***over*** its pages. 彼女はその本を読んで泣いた. ‖ She *wept* ***over*** her lost happiness. 彼女は身の不幸を悲しんで泣いた. 【類】*weep* ***over*** the death of ... ¶She *wept* partly ***through*** sorrow and partly ***through*** anger. 彼女は悲しさと腹だたしさで泣いた. ¶I *wept* ***with*** her ***for*** company. 私は彼女のもらい泣をした. 【類】*weep* ***with*** pain (vexation).

weeping, *n.* 泣き.

Q ***suppressed*** (=***subdued***) *weeping* 忍び泣き.

weigh, *v.* 考量する, 計る; 目方がある; 重視される, 重きをなす.

M The goods were ***carefully*** *weighed* at the time of shipment. 品物は船積み(送り出し)のとき目方を厳重に検査された. ¶This point deserves to be ***carefully*** *weighed*. この点は慎重に考慮すべきだ. ¶be considered and ***duly*** *weighed* 十分勘考される. ¶His words *weigh* ***heavily*** with me (=upon my mind). 彼の言葉がとても気がかりだ. ‖ The matter *weighed* ***heavily*** on the mind. そのことがひどく気がかりであった. ¶How ***heavy*** does it *weigh?* その目方はどの位あるか. 【類】It *weighed* ***heavily*** upon his conscience. ¶*weigh* ***light*** 目方が軽い. ¶*weigh* ***little*** 目方がほとんどかからないよ; 重要でない. ¶How ***much*** do you *weigh?* 体重はどれだけあります. ¶The baker *weighs* ***out*** bread. パン屋はパンの目方を計って売る. ‖ *weigh* ***out*** to the customers on a pair of scales 天びん計りで計って客に売る. ¶*weigh* the matter ***patiently*** その件を熟慮する.

M² be *weighed* ***down*** 抑制される ‖ *weighed* ***down*** with age 年のせいで弱って ‖ When a sandman comes the child's eyelids *weigh* ***down***. 眠りの精がやって来る(眠気がさす)と子供のまぶたがたるむ. ‖ The fruit *weighs* ***down*** the branches. 枝もたわわに実がなっている. ‖ The slender stalks are *weighed* ***down*** with flowers. 細い茎が花でしな垂れている.

P He *weighs* ***above*** ... pounds. 彼は体重が…ポンド以上ある. ¶If a man applies for a position, his personal appearance will *weigh* greatly ***for*** or ***against*** him. 就職志願の場合には風さいのよしあしが大いにものを言う. ‖ *weigh* one thing ***against*** another. 甲と乙を比較考量する. ¶It is *weighed* ***in*** the balance and accepted and rejected as the case may be. それを考量してあるいは取りあるいは捨てる. ‖ He was *weighed* ***in*** the balance and found wanting. 彼は考査の結果不合格になった. ‖ *weigh* her culture ***in*** the scales of Western civilization 西洋文化の規準でその国の文化を考査する. ¶*weigh* it ***on*** a scale それを計量する ‖ The error *weighed* ***on*** (=upon) his mind. 彼はその過失を気に病んだ. ‖ Fatigue *weighed* ***on*** him. 疲れが出た. ¶It *weighs* ***under*** ... tons. その目方は…トン以下である. ¶This argument *weighs* ***with*** me. 私はこの議論を重要視する.

weighing, *n.* 計量; 考量.

P ***through*** an impartial *weighing* of facts 事実を公平に考量して.

weight, *n.* 重さ; 重要性.

V This fact ***adds*** great *weight* to his conclusions. この事実が大いに彼の結論に重みを加えている. ¶this ***adds*** another *weight* of proof adverse to the opinion that ... これは…という意見に対しまた一つの反証になる. ¶***ascertain*** its *weight* その目方を確かめる. ¶***attach*** *weight* (=importance) to ... …に重きをおく. ¶***attain*** a *weight* of ... …の重さになる. ¶***bring*** the *weight* of his official position to bear upon ... 彼の職権を…に発動する. ¶another consideration which will ***carry*** *weight* is this, that ... もう一つ軽々に付することのできない点は…である ‖ His opinion ***carries*** *weight*, since he is an acknowledged authority on that subject. 彼はその方の押しも押されもしない権威であるからその意見は大いに重きをなしている. 【類】His opinion ***carries*** *weight* in Europe and America. / ***carry*** great *weight* with parents / the argument (議論) that ***carries*** most *weight*. ¶***check*** *weight* 目方を計る. ¶the rumor ***derives*** additional *weight* from the fact that ... そのうわさは…の事実に徴して一層確実性を増す ‖ The book ***derives*** *weight* from its author's high repuptation. その本は著者の名声で重く見られている. ¶The opinion will ***exercise*** considerable *weight* in the long run. その意見は結局相当重きをなすようになるであろう. ¶***feel*** the *weight* of this solemn obligation この重大な義務に対する責任を感じる. ¶They ***fetch*** more than their *weight* in gold. それらは金以上の価に(非常に高価に)売れる. ¶***gain*** *weight* 目方が増す ‖ opinions that rather ***gain*** their *weight* from their wisdom than from their sources その出所よりはむしろその知性によって重きをなす意見. ¶The public opinion is ***gathering*** *weight*. その世論が勢力を得つつある. ¶***give*** special *weight* to ... 特に…を重要視する ‖ ***give*** *weight* to the statement その声明に重きをおく. 【類】***give*** due *weight* to another's opinion / His great continental repute ***gave*** *weight* to his pronouncements in favor of contraception. / he ***gave*** the *weight* of his authority to the condemnation (非難) of ... / in the selection of candidates for employment *weight* is ***given*** to ... ¶***have*** *weight* 重きをなす ‖ It ***has*** some (no) *weight* with me. 私にとっては相当大事だ(問題にならない). ‖ The expression ***has*** the *weight* of usage. その言い回しには慣用されているという強味がある. ‖ this point ***has*** such *weight* that ... この点は非常に重要であるから… 【類】the opinion of persons whose judgment ***has*** *weight* with him / He ***has*** great *weight* in the world of letters. ¶we cannot ***lay*** very much *weight* on ... われわれは…には余り重きをおくことはできない. ¶***lend*** one's *weight* to ... …に力添えをする. ¶***lessen*** *weight* 重量を少くする. ¶The crane is capable of ***lifting*** *weights* up to five tons. その起重機は重量五トンまでの物をあげることができる. ¶He has ***lost*** much *weight*. 彼は大分目方が減った. ¶The association has ***made*** the *weight* of its judgment ***felt*** in the opposite scale. 同協会の判定はかえって反対側を利する結果となった. ¶***pick up*** *weight* 体重が増す. ¶He has ***put on*** much *weight*(=flesh). 彼は大分目方がふえた. ¶***raise*** a *weight* ある重量の物をあげる. ¶He has ***restored*** *weight*. 彼は元通りの体重になった. ¶***take*** one's *weight* その体重を計る. ¶***throw*** the *weight* of responsibility upon ... …に責任を負わせる ‖ ***throw*** one's *weight* behind him 後援する. 【類】***throw*** the *weight* of one's power on the side of ... ‖ I ***threw*** the whole *weight* of my influence and active exertions in his favor. 私は自己の勢力と努力とをあげて彼のために尽した. ¶sit on the edge of a chair as if afraid to ***trust*** one's *weight* to it いすが重量にたえ得ないかのようにその端に腰を下す. ¶The merchant should ***use*** correct *weights* and measures. 商人は度量衡を正確に使用しなければならない.

V² The patient's *weight* ***fell*** from 94 pounds to 74 pounds. その病人の体重は九十四ポンドから七十四ポンドに減じた. 【類】His *weight* ***fell*** considerably. / The *weight* ***fell*** to one hundred and thirty-three pounds.

Q attach some ***additional*** *weight* to the fact that ... …という事実をさらに重要視させることになる. ¶the ***big*** *weight* of tradition 伝統の偉大な力. ¶an increase of ***bodily*** *weight* 体重の増加. ¶As the narrator of the story is well known as a scientist, his words carry ***considerable*** *weight*. その話をする人は科学者として有名なので彼の言葉は相当の威力を持つ. ¶***dead*** *weight* [貨車などの]死重 ‖ carry about ... tons ***dead*** *weight* 約…トンの死重がある ‖ fall like a ***dead*** *weight* どっと倒れる ‖ The goods remained a ***dead*** *weight* on the store shelves. その品は売残り(店ざらし)になっていた. ¶As the letter was ***double*** *weight* I put another stamp on it. その手紙の目方が倍量だったから私は

もう一枚切手をはった. ¶give ***due weight*** to differences 相違した諸点について然るべく考量する. ¶light ***feather's weight*** 鳥の毛の軽さ. ¶give ***good weight*** 量(ｸﾞｲ)をよくする. ¶an opinion that carries ***great weight*** 非常に重きをなす意見. ¶***gross weight*** 全重量, 総トン数 ‖ Freight is payable on ***gross weight***. 運賃は総重量で支払うことになっている. ¶lift a ***heavy weight*** 重量品を持ち上げる. ¶***honest weight*** 正しい目方. ¶the ***light weight*** of the purses of most students 大抵の学生のポケット・マネーの不足. ¶attach (=add) ***little weight*** to ... …に余り重きをおかない. ¶people of ***medium weight*** and medium height 中肉中背の人々. ¶attach ***most weight*** to ... …を大いに重視する. ¶***net weight*** 正味の重量. ¶it is of ***no weight*** to argue that ... …という議論は力がない. ¶They give ***short weight*** and short measure in that store. あの店は量(ｸﾞｲ)や尺が足りない. ¶***total weight*** 全重量. ¶of ***uniform weight*** 重量均一の. ¶the ***vast numeric weight*** ばく大な数の力. ¶tales that are ***worth*** their ***weight*** in gold 非常に値打ちのある話 ‖ she is ***worth*** her ***weight*** in gold to ... 彼女は…にとって非常に大切な人である. 【類】His work (作品) is often ***worth*** its ***weight*** in gold.

P sell goods ***at*** full ***weight*** 品を目方たっぷりに売る. ¶Down upon him with a crash came a heavy bale, crushing his limbs ***beneath*** its ***weight***. 彼の上に重い箱がどかと落ちて来て手足がその重荷に押しつぶされた. ¶***by*** the sheer ***weight*** of its merit 全くそれに値打ちがあるために ‖ It is sold ***by weight***. それは目方で売る. ¶It is ... pounds ***in weight***. その重量は…ポンドある. ‖ heavy (light) ***in weight*** 目方が重(軽)い ‖ vary (=differ) ***in weight*** 重さが不同である. ¶fall ***of*** its own ***weight*** それ自体の重みで倒れる ‖ opinions ***of weight*** 重きをなす意見 ‖ He is a politician and diplomat ***of weight***. 彼は勢力のある政治家であり外交官である. ‖ a medical man ***of*** considerable ***weight*** かなり勢力のある医師. ¶a narrow wooden plank that bends ***under*** one's ***weight*** 人が来るとその重みで曲る狭い木の板 ‖ The table groans ***under*** the ***weight*** of delicacies. その食卓には山海の珍味がどっさり並べてあった. ‖ ***under*** the ***weight*** of such crushing disadvantages こうしたぐうの音も出ない不利な立場に押えつけられて ‖ ***under*** the ***weight*** of cumulative evidence 次々と証拠を持ち出されて ‖ fail ***under*** the ***weight*** of years 年のせいで失敗する ‖ The whole edifice broke down ***under*** its own ***weight***, so to speak. いわばその大建築は自分の重みで崩解してしまったのであった. ¶He was loaded down ***with*** a ***weight*** of discouragement. 彼は落胆の結果意気消沈していた.

P² ***weight in*** lbs ポンド計算の重量. ¶the ***weight of*** authority (learning, influence) 権威(など)の力 ‖ the ***weight of*** authority appears to be on the side of ... …の方にしっかりした根拠があるようだ ‖ The ***weight of*** evidence is against him. 証拠[の結果]は彼に不利である.

weight, *v.* 負わせる.

P He was ***weighted with*** great responsibility (care, secret). 彼は重大な責任(など)を負わされていた.

welcome, *n.* 歓迎.

V ***accord*** a most hearty ***welcome*** to ... …を心から歓迎する. ¶He ***addressed*** the audience a hearty ***welcome***. 彼は聴衆に向って心から歓迎の辞を述べた. ¶***bid*** them a hearty ***welcome*** 彼らに心から歓迎の辞を述べる ‖ ***bid welcome*** to ... …を歓迎する. ¶***deserve*** a cordial ***welcome*** 心からの歓迎を受ける資格がある. ¶***earn*** one's ***welcome*** その歓迎を受ける. ¶Japan ***extends*** a ***welome*** to visitors from every land. 日本は各国からの来客を歓迎する. 【類】The whole Japanese nation will ***extend*** a hearty ***welcome*** to those attending the Olympics in Tokyo. ‖ ***Welcome*** is ***extended*** to visitors by the secretary of the meeting. その会に会員以外の方の来会を歓迎する. ¶You are sure to ***find*** a ***welcome***. あなたが行けばきっと歓迎されます. ‖ The translation should ***find*** a ***welcome*** with (=from) those who find the original French a difficulty. フランス語の原文が楽に読めない人々からこの翻訳は当然歓迎されるであろう. ¶***give*** a hearty ***welcome*** to ... …を心から歓迎する. ¶***guarantee*** a royal ***welcome*** to ... …にきわめて手厚い歓迎を保証する. ¶A gay display of flying colors ***made*** a cheery ***welcome***. 歓迎のために美々しく国旗が翻っていたのでにぎやかであった. ¶We ***offer*** you a cordial ***welcome*** to join the 126,000 members already enrolled in our Union. すでに登録済のわが組合員十二万六千名の中にあなたが加わって下さるよう心からお勧めします. ¶The bore had ***overstayed*** (=***outstayed***) his ***welcome***. 彼は長居で迷惑がられていた. ¶***prepare*** a ***welcome*** for ... …のために歓迎の準備をする. ¶***procure*** his ***welcome*** 彼の歓迎を受ける. 【類】Her sunny (晴々した) face and the water lilies that she brought to the poor children ***procured*** for her a double ***welcome*** (なお一層の歓迎). ¶we ***received*** a great ***welcome*** from ... われわれは…から大いに歓迎された. ¶***smile*** a timid ***welcome*** to ... …に対し微笑を浮べておずおずと歓迎の意を表する. ¶The ship ***tooted*** her noisy ***welcome***. その船はやかましく汽笛を鳴らして歓迎した. ¶***wear out*** one's ***welcome*** 余り度々訪問(または余り長居)して愛想をつかされる. ¶***wish*** ... a hearty ***welcome*** …に心から歓迎の辞を述べる.

Q A glowing fire offered a ***cheerful welcome***. へやにはいると盛んに火が燃えてるのでうれしかった. ¶He is sure of a ***cold welcome***. 彼は冷遇されるにきまっている. 【類】receive a ***cold welcome***. ¶extend a ***cordial welcome*** to ... …を衷心から歓迎する ‖ you will always find a ***cordial welcome*** awaiting you at ... …ではいつも君を衷心から歓迎してくれるだろう. ¶extend an ***eager welcome*** to ... …を熱心に歓待する. ¶receive an ***enthusiastic welcome*** 熱烈な歓迎を受ける. ¶a ***genial welcome*** 心からの歓迎. ¶give the ***heartiest welcome*** to ... …を衷心から歓迎する. ¶The mistress and an attendant bevy of maids knelt down and touched their foreheads to the polished floor in ***hospitable welcome***. 女主人とそれにかしずく一群の侍女はようこそお越し下されましたとばかりひざまずいてとぎ出しの床に頭をすりつけた. ¶give a ***joyous welcome*** to ... …を喜んで歓迎する. ¶a ***kindly*** and ***hospitable welcome*** 親切な手厚い歓待. ¶be given a ***lavish welcome*** at ... …でやたらとちやほやされる. ¶the idea will find a ***ready welcome*** in the hearts of ... その案は…などから喜んで迎えられるだろう. ¶be given a ***riotous welcome*** 熱狂的に歓迎される. ¶a ***royal welcome*** [王侯のような]りっぱな歓迎. ¶a ***spontaneous*** and ***hearty welcome*** わざとらしい所のない心からの歓待. ¶a ***tumultuous*** (=violent) ***welcome*** 猛烈な歓迎. ¶He will find his ***warmest welcome***. 彼はそこで熱誠の限りをもって歓迎されるだろう. ‖ deserve a ***warm welcome*** from ... …からの厚い歓迎に価する. 【類】words of ***warm welcome***. ¶The book cannot fail to receive a ***warm*** and ***appreciative welcome***. その本は必ず熱誠と相当の評価をもって歓迎される. ¶a ***warm*** and ***hearty welcome*** 熱誠こめた歓迎. ¶a ***wide welcome*** 一般の歓迎.

P receive a great demonstration ***of welcome*** 大歓迎を受ける. ¶The party was received ***with*** a ***welcome*** everywhere. 一行は至る所で歓迎された. ¶enter ***without welcome*** 歓迎を受けずにはいって行く.

P² a ***welcome in*** Tokyo ***to*** ... 東京における…の歓迎.

welcome, *a.* 歓迎される; 喜ばしい.

M You are ***perfectly welcome*** to keep it as long as you please. いつまででも御遠慮なくそれをお留め置きになっても一向構いません. ‖ He is ***perfectly welcome*** to do so. 彼はそうしたって少しも差支えない(私に異存はない). ¶You are ***quite welcome*** to all my books. この私の本はどれでも御随意に御覧になってください. ‖ You are ***welcome to*** any service I can do. 私にできることなら御遠慮なくおおせつけ下さい. ¶You are ***very welcome*** to come to my home. 御遠慮なく私の家へお出でください.

P You are ***welcome to*** it. それをお持ち(または御使用)下さい. ‖ We are very poor, but what we have you are ***welcome to***. 貧乏世帯ですがありますものはどうぞ御遠慮なく. ‖ The money is ***welcome to*** me. その金が私の手に入ったのはうれしい.

O You are ***welcome*** to use my library. 御遠慮なく私の図書室をお使用下さい. ‖ Much obliged.—You're ***welcome***. お世話になりました.—どう致しまして.

welcome, *v.* 歓迎する.

M The Prime Minister was ***welcomed back*** to England by Mrs. Asquith. 総理大臣アスキスは帰英してその妻に迎えられた. ‖ ***welcome back*** one of their number [帰還者の]仲間の一人を喜んで迎える ‖ ***welcome*** a person ***back*** 帰宅を喜んで迎える ‖ ***Welcome back*** your vacation from Honolulu. ホノルルからの休暇旅行からの安着をお祝いします. ¶He was ***cordially welcomed***. 彼は心から歓待された. ¶be eagerly welcomed by the Poultry Press as contributors 養鶏新聞から寄稿家として大いに歓迎される. ¶He was enthusiastically welcomed. 彼は熱誠わくがごとき歓迎を受けた. ¶America graciously welcomes you. アメリカは賓客として諸君を歓迎する. ¶welcome gladly 快く歓迎する. ¶I gratefully welcome corrections. 誤りの個所を御指摘下さいますれば有難く存じます. ¶be heartily to be welcomed 心から歓迎すべきである. ¶He was welcomed home to Japan by his friends. 彼は友人たちから帰朝の歓迎を受けた. ¶He was hospitably welcomed. 彼は丁重な歓迎を受けた. ¶The suggestion was warmly welcomed. その注意は大いに喜ばれた.

M^2 welcome in the first of May 喜んで五月一日を迎える. 【類】welcome in a new year.

P He was warmly welcomed by the press and public. 彼は新聞雑誌や社会一般から熱心に歓迎された. ¶welcome criticism from all quarters どの方面の御批判も歓迎します. ¶welcome a baby into the world 子供の出生を喜ぶ. ¶The audience welcomed her with applause. 聴衆は拍手かっさいして彼女を迎えた. ‖ welcome him with a banquet 宴会を開いて彼を歓迎する ‖ welcome with open arms 大手を広げて歓迎する.

welcome, *int.* ようこそ.

M Welcome home! お帰んなさい(長途の旅行などから); 帰国歓迎. 【類】Welcome home, gentlemen! / welcome soldiers home from the war.

P^2 Welcome to England! [外国人の]英国来訪歓迎. ‖ Welcome to you all! みなさんようこそ.

weld, *v.* 合わせる.

P weld the scattered material into a coherent narrative 諸方から材料を集めて一つのまとまった記事にまとめる ‖ weld written and spoken English into an identity 言文の英語を一致させる ‖ weld materials into a consistent whole 種種の材料をつづり合わせて一つにまとめる ‖ weld them into a nation それらの人々を打って一丸とし, 一国民に造り上げる.

welding, *n.* 溶接.

Q^2 arc welding 〖電〗アーク溶接. ¶fusion welding 溶接.

welfare, *n.* [個人または社会の]幸福, 福利, 厚生.

V advance the physical, social, intellectual, moral, and spiritual welfare of young men and women 青年男女の体位的・社会的・知的・道徳的並びに精神的幸福を増進する. ¶affect the welfare of society 社会の福利に影響する. 【類】affect the future welfare of this country. ¶benefit the social welfare 社会の福利に資する. ¶It concerns his welfare. それは彼一身の幸不幸に関する. ¶may endanger their welfare 彼らの幸福をおびやかすことになるかも知れない. ¶have deeply at heart the social welfare of ... ...の社会的福利を深く念頭におく ‖ those who have the welfare of the country at heart その母国の前途を憂える人々. ¶He was indefatigable in all kinds of good works designed to improve the welfare of the people. 彼は国民の厚生を目的としたありとあらゆる善事をこつこつ行った. ¶menace public welfare 公益を害する恐れがある. ¶promote the welfare of ... ...の福利を増進する.

Q economic welfare 経済的福利(向上). ¶be interested in the educational welfare of the public 一般の教育的向上に関心を持つ. ¶the eternal welfare of souls 霊魂の永遠の幸福. ¶advance the general welfare of ... ...の一般的福利を増進する. ¶promote human welfare 人類の幸福を増進する. ¶material and spiritual welfare 物質的及び精神的幸福. ¶high moral welfare 高い道徳的幸福. ¶National welfare is the end of politics. 国民の幸福が政治の目的である. ‖ He had national welfare at heart all through his life. 彼は終生国民の幸福を念願した. ¶promote the public welfare 公衆の福利を増進する.

Q^2 child welfare 児童厚生. ¶community welfare 社会の厚生. ¶infant welfare 保育. ¶public welfare 民生. ¶student welfare 学生の厚生.

P for public welfare 公益上. ¶for the welfare of one's nation 国民幸福のために.

P^2 the welfare of mankind 人類の幸福.

well, *n.* 井戸.

V clean a well 井戸をさらう. ¶dig a well 井戸を掘る. ¶The well was drilled in solid rock. その井戸は堅い岩板を掘り抜いたものだった. ¶drill an oil well 油井をうがつ. ¶preserve the pure well of English undefiled 英語の純粋性を保存する. ¶put down (=sink) a well in search of petroleum 石油を求めて掘る.

Q an abandoned well 廃井. ¶an artesian well 掘井戸. ¶that inexhaustible well of "Volkspoesie" Grimm's Fairy Tales かのグリムの童話の尽きない興味.

P Wives are chatting at the well. 細君連が井戸端会議をしている. ¶Water is drawn from a well in buckets. 水はバケツで井戸からくむ. ¶She drowned herself in a well. 彼女は井戸へ身を投げて死んだ.

well, *ad., a.* よく; よい.

M That's well enough as it is. それで結構いいんだ. ‖ You are not well enough to get out yet. まだすっかりなおっていない. ¶He speaks English and Japanese equally well. 彼は英語も日本語も同じようによく話す. ¶exceedingly well 非常によく. ¶This serves me excellently well. これは結構私の役に立つ. ¶He writes English fairly well. 彼はかなりよく英文を書く. ¶I full well know that ... 私は...を十分承知している. ¶passably well どうにかよく. ¶The season is now pretty well ended. もう季節はずれになった. ¶quite well 実によく ‖ be not quite well again まだ本当に治っていない. ¶really well ほんとうによく. ¶remarkably well 非常によく. ¶He speaks English tolerably well. どうにか英語が話せる. ¶do it unusually well それを際立ってよくやる. ¶I am not very well yet. まだ(健康が)ほんとじゃない.

M^2 He is well on in years. 彼はよほど年を取っている. ‖ until well on into the evening (nineteenth centrury) 相当夕刻(など)になるまで. ¶He is well up in Latin. 彼はかなりラテン語ができる.

P it is well for you that ... ...は君のために結構なことだ. ¶All is well with me. 私は無事です. ‖ It is a sign that all is not well with the nation's economy. それは国家経済がうまく行っていない証拠だ.

well, *v.* わき出る.

M well up from the depths 深みからわき出る ‖ joy welling up in one's heart 油然として心にわく喜び ‖ Chagrin welled up once in a while. 時々くやしさがこみあげた. 【類】Tears welled up in her eyes.

P Tears welled from my eyes. 涙が私の目からあふれ出た. ¶well into the modern period ずっと近代期まで.

well-being, *n.* 幸福, 安寧.

V threaten the well-being of society 社会の安寧をおびやかす.

Q Animal well-being is induced by physical exercise. 身体の健全は運動によって得られる. ¶the physical and moral well-being 肉体的及び精神的幸福. ¶the physical and mental well-being of ... ...の肉体的及び精神的幸福. ¶the ultimate well-being of humanity 人類究極の幸福.

welling-up, *n.* 湧(ゆう)出.

Q a sudden welling-up of enthusiasm 突然わいた熱意.

well-known, *a.* 有名な.

M when he was less well-known 彼がさほど有名でなかった時分.

P well-known as an authority of economics 経済学の権威として名のある. ¶The hotel is well-known for its excellent cuisine and cellar. そのホテルは料理と酒がよいので有名である. ¶well-known in the fields of entertainment, literature and art 演芸・文学・芸術の方面で有名な.

well-wisher, *n.* 好意を持つ人.

Q real well-wishers of China 真に中国のためを思う人々. ¶a sincere well-wisher 誠意ある同情者.

P well-wishers to the laboring classes 労働者階級に好意を持つ人たち.

welter, *v.* ころがる.

P They found him weltering in a pool of blood. 彼らは彼が血潮の海にころがっているのを見つけた. 【類】welter in sin (idleness, pleasures).

west, *n.* 西; [W-] 西洋; 《米》[the W-] 西部.

Q the civilized West 文明の高い西洋. ¶the Far West 《米》極西部(主に太平洋岸の三州). ¶the Middle West 《米》中西部(シカゴを中心としロッキー山脈に及ぶ広大な地域).

P The sun is downing at the west. 太陽は西に沈みつつある. ¶from west to east 西から東へ. ¶as the sun was in the low west 太陽が西に傾いたころ. ¶I say, how very black the sky is on the west. おや西の方の空が真暗になった. ‖ The country is bounded on the west by a sea. その国は西の方は海で限界されている. ¶6 miles to the west 西方六マイル ‖ it lies to the west of ... それは...の西に位する.

westerly, *n.* 西風.

Q the *pevailing westerlies* of the temperate zones 温帯地方で主に吹く西風.

western, *n.* 《米》西部劇.

Q a *rough-and-tumble western* 荒々しい西部劇.

wet, *n.* しめり.

V *get* a *wet* 一杯やる.

P The servant went outside *in* the *wet* to hire an automobile. 召使は外の雨の降る中をハイヤーを頼みに出て行った. ¶He was just coming in *out of* the *wet*. 彼は丁度雨の降る表からはいって来る所だった. ¶I went *through* the *wet* to the exhibition. 私は雨の降る中をその展覧会を見に行った.

wet, *a.* ぬれた.

M 《米》You're *all wet*. 君は全然見当がちがっている. ¶I got *wet all over* (=*alright*). びしょぬれだ. ¶I am *wet through*. びしょぬれだ. ¶*dripping wet* 水がしたたるほどぬれた.

P a newspaper *wet from* the press 印刷したての新聞. ¶*wet from* top *to* toe 頭のてっぺんから足のつま先までぬれて. ¶*wet to* the skin びしょぬれになって. ¶Her soft little face was *wet with* tears. 彼女のもやもやした小さな顔が涙でぬれていた. ‖ *wet with* perspiration (dew) 汗(など)でぬれて.

O *wet* or fine 晴雨にかかわらず.

wet, *v.* ぬらす.

P her sleeves *wetted with* tears 涙でぬれた彼女のそで.

whack, *n.* 《米俗》冒険.

V *take* a *whack* at the enterprise. その事業を一か八かやってみる.

whack, *v.* びしゃりびしゃり打つ.

M *whack away* at a dog 《俗》犬をびしりびしり打つ.

whale, *n.* 鯨.

V throw a sprat to *catch* a *whale* えびでたいを釣る. ¶The *whale blows*. 鯨が潮を吹く. ¶He is a *regular whale* (guy) for work. 《米》あいつはよく働く.

Q a *right whale* 真鯨.

P a school *of whales* 鯨の群.

P² He is a *whale at* business. 彼は商売の鬼だ.

wharf, *n.* 波止場.

Q² a *sufferance wharf* 《英》[私設の]公許波止場.

P The ship lies *alongside* the *wharf*. その船は波止場に横付になっている. ‖ unload *alongside* a *wharf* 波止場で荷を陸上げする. ¶moor *at* a *wharf* [船が]はとばに停泊する. ¶I met him *on* the *wharf* at Kobe. 私は神戸の波止場であの人に会った. ‖ deliver fur *on* (=*alongside*) *wharf* 毛皮を桟橋渡しにする.

P² a *wharf for* the loading or unloading of vessels 船舶の貨物を積卸しする波止場.

wharfage, *n.* 波止場の施設.

V New York City *furnishes* the excellent *wharfage*. ニューヨーク市にはりっぱな波止場がある.

what, *pron.* 何.

V *What* I have *done*, I have done. [私が]やったことはやったことだ. ¶I can't *get what* you *mean*. 何のことか分かりません(もっと分かるように言って下さい). ‖ *What* did you *do* with yourself? 君はどうしたか. ¶You never *know what* you may catch. どんな病気が君にうつるか分かりはしない. ¶*What* did you *say*? え?(何と言ったんですか). ‖ If you do this, I'll pay you ten dollars. *What* do you *say*? これをやってくれれば十ドルやる. やるかね. ‖ *What* will people *say*? 世間で何と言うだろう. ‖ He means *what* he *says*. 彼が言ってることは本気だ. ‖ *What* I *say* is all true. 私の言うことは皆ほんとだ. ‖ *What* did I *say*? そらみろ(言わないこっちゃない).

P You don't know *what* you're talking *about*. 君は自分がしゃべっていることが自分にわかっていない. ¶*What* are you driving *at*? 君何を言っているのか. ¶*What for*? 何のために. ¶*What's* that *for*? それ何に使うの. ‖ *What* do you want me *for*? 何か御用ですか. ‖ *What* are you back *for*? 何で戻って来たのです. ‖ *What* do you meet here *for*? 何でここに集ってるの. ‖ I want you to meet him. Yes, but *what for*? 彼に会ってくれ—何のために. ‖ *What* do you learn English *for*? 英語を何のために習うのか. ‖ *What* are you looking *for*? 何をさがしてるの. ‖ *What* is the City of Denver famous *for*? デンバーという市は何で有名ですか. ‖ We give the report *for what* it is worth. [真偽のほどは分らないが]そのまま報告をします. ¶*From what* I hear, he seems to be a responsible man. 私の聞いたところでは彼は責任ある人らしい. ¶*What of* it? それがどうしたと言うんだ. ¶*What with* drink and [*what with*] fright I don't know much about it. 酔ってたしこわかったのでそのことはよく覚えていません.

O *What* is more, he was awarded a grand prize. それどころか彼は特賞までもらった. ¶*What* though we are poor? われわれが貧乏だってそれがどうしたと言うの. ‖ *What* if he doesn't come? もし(彼が)来なかったら? ¶Not a day but *what* I hear her sing. からすの鳴かぬ日はあっても, 彼女の歌を聞かぬ日はない. ¶and *what* not=and all kinds of other things その他何やかや.

whatever, *pron.* 何でも.

V *Do whatever* you like. どうでもいいようになさい. ¶*Whatever* I *have* is yours. 私のものは皆な君のものだ. ¶*Whatever* I *say* in this case, I mean it. この場合私の言うことは一切真剣なのだ.

V² *Whatever happens*, I will go. どんなことがあっても私は行く.

wheat, *n.* 小麦.

V *grind wheat* into flour 小麦をひく. ¶*raise wheat* 小麦を作る. ¶*separate* the *wheat* from the chaff 小麦を脱穀する. ¶*whip wheat* with a flail 小麦を連枷(ｶﾞ)で打つ.

Q *bearded wheat* のぎのある小麦. ¶*beardless wheat* のぎのない小麦. ¶*cracked wheat* ひき割小麦.

Q² *kaoliang wheat* こうりゃん. ¶seed *winter wheat* 耐寒性の小麦をまく.

P a fine crop *of wheat* 小麦の豊作.

wheedle, *v.* おだてる, 口車に乗せる.

P *wheedle* a person *into* good temper 人をうまくとりなして上気げんにさせる ‖ *wheedle* a person *into* doing it 人を口車に乗せてそうさせる. ¶*wheedle* a person *out of* one's money 人をだまして金を取る.

wheel, *n.* 車; 自転車; 《俗》大物.

V *buckle* a *wheel* 一生けん命に自転車を踏む. ¶*clog* the *wheel* 車に制動器を付ける ‖ *clog* the *wheels* of efficiency 能率の向上を妨げる. ¶*oil* the *wheels* of society 社会の車に油をさす(社会諸機関の運行を円滑にする). ¶hear the *wheels* of a carriage 車輪の音が聞える. ¶*ride* a *wheel* 自転車に乗る. ¶These elder statesmen *set* the *wheels* within wheels in motion. これらの元老政治家は黒幕の内で策動する. ¶He "*takes* the *wheel*", and steers the great ship of his business through the boisterous ocean of modern competition. 彼はその大会社の船長格でかじを取り現代の競争という荒海を乗切って行く. ¶*tire* a *wheel* 車輪にタイヤを付ける. ¶*turn* a *wheel* 車輪を回す.

V² The *wheel* has *come off*. 車輪がはずれた. ¶The *wheel goes round*. 車輪が回転する. ¶A *wheel rolls along*. 車輪がころがって行く. ¶the *wheels splashing* through small rivers of muddy water 小さな濁流の中をばしゃばしゃ行く車.

Q a *big wheel* in political circles (the party) 政界(党)の大もの. ¶the *potter's wheel* ろくろ. ¶*rubber-tired wheels* ゴム輪の車. ¶a *toothed wheel* 歯車.

Q² a *balance wheel* in world affairs 世界問題についてのバランスの歯車. ¶a *Ferris wheel* メリーゴーラウンドの一種. ¶a *steel wheel* 鋼鉄車輪. ¶The national emergency forced the *steering wheel* again into his hands. 非常時に際し彼は再び国家を背負って立つことになった(宰相など). ¶a *warning wheel* 予報輪(時計が時を知らせる前に鳴響く車輪).

P with ... *at* the *wheel* (=helm) ...がその衝に当って ‖ be alert *at* the *wheel* [自動車など]操縦に注意する. ¶He put a spoke *in* my *wheel* 彼は私の行動の邪魔をした. ¶a machine *on* six *wheels* 六つの車輪の上に据えてある機械 ‖ a library *on wheels* 巡回図書館 ‖ skating *on wheels* ローラースケート ‖ a post office *on wheels* 移動郵便車. 【類】a house *on wheels* / The cars are veritable hotels *on wheels*. / The dining cars on the line are in the true sense of the word "restaurants *on wheels*." ‖ go round the world *on* a *wheel* (=bicycle) 自転車で世界を一周する ‖ a short evening spin *on* the *wheel* 夕方少時の自転車散歩 ‖ pottery shaped (=fashioned) *on* the *wheel*=wheel-shaped pottery ろくろで造った陶器. ¶There is a wheel *within wheels*. 裏には裏がある.

P² He is a very important *wheel in* the machinery of the world's progress. 彼は世界の進歩という機械で非常に重要な役割を持っている車輪だ.

wheel, *v.* 回る.

M *wheel right* (*left*) [車が]右(左)に向きを変える.

M² *wheel* one's horse *about* 乗っている馬の向きを変える ‖ *wheel about* to the other extreme 反対の方向に向を変え

る. ¶*wheel* suddenly ***around*** 急カーブを切る, 突然方向を転じる. ¶The patient was then *wheeled* ***off*** on a trolley. それからその病人を運搬車で運んで行った. ¶*wheel* ***round*** ぐるっと向を変える.

wheeling, *n.* 車の通行; 《口語》自転車で乗り回すこと.

Q It is ***bad*** (***good***) *wheeling.* その道は車の通行には悪い(良い). 「転車で走るのによい.

P The road is good ***for*** *wheeling* (cycling). その道路は自

wheeze, *v.* ぜいぜい息をする.

M *wheeze* ***out*** ぜいぜいしながら言う. 【類】The old man *wheezed* ***out*** a few words.

whereabouts, *n.* 所在.

Q His ***present*** *whereabouts* is unknown. 彼の現住所は不明である. ☞ whereabouts は通例単数で受ける.

V ***conceal*** one's *whereabouts* その居所を秘密にする. ¶try to ***locate*** the *whereabouts* of ... …のゆくえを捜す.

wherewithal, *n.* 資金.

V ***give*** him *wherewithal* to live 彼に生活費を当てがう. ¶***have*** not *wherewithal* to pay my bill 勘定を払う金がない. ¶***obtain*** the *wherewithal* to erect two bungalows 二むねの軽便平屋を建てるに必要な金を得る. ¶I ***raised*** the *wherewithal* from my banker, pledging with him marketable securities. 私は有価証券を抵当にして取引銀行にその金を融通してもらった.

whet, *v.* とぐ.

P *whet* a knife ***on*** the stone ナイフをと石でとぐ.

O *whet* one's curiosity 人の好奇心をそそる.

whiff, *n.* 一吹き.

V ***have*** a *whiff* 一服やる. ¶I ***want*** a *whiff* of fresh air. いい風が一息欲しい.

P blow smoke ***in*** *whiffs* 煙をぷっぷっと吹く.

P² a *whiff* ***of*** sea breeze 一陣の海風.

while, *n.* 時.

V I called on him and ***spent*** a pleasant *while.* 私は彼を訪問してしばらくおもしろく遊んで来た. ¶It ***takes*** a great *while* to make it. それを造るには大分時間を要する.

Q rest ***every little*** *while* ちょいちょい休息する. ¶for a ***good*** *while* しばらくの間 ‖ He has been a ***good*** *while* in France. 大分長いことフランスに滞在している. ‖ I was lost in admiration for a ***good*** *while.* 私はしばらくの間ただ感嘆するのほかはなかった. ‖ I called on him a ***good*** *while* ago. 彼を訪問してからもう大分になる. ¶once in a ***great*** *while* ごくまれに, どうかすると. ¶I am off for a ***little*** *while.* じき帰って来るよ. ‖ in a ***little*** *while* 間もなく, そのうち ‖ just for a ***little*** *while* 今しばし ‖ the matter you mentioned a ***little*** *while* ago さっきの話 ‖ He hasn't shown up in a ***long*** *while.* しばらく姿を見せない. 【類】once in a ***long*** *while* / I haven't seen him for this ***long*** *while.* ¶in the ***mean*** *while* ‖ in the meanwhile とかくする内に.

P ***after*** a *while* しばらくして ‖ There will be no more inconvenience ***after*** a *while.* しばらくの御辛抱, もう少しの辛抱. ‖ ***after*** a short *while* ほどなく. ¶***at*** *whiles* 時々. ¶when off duty, or ***between*** *whiles* 明け番の時かまたはあい間あい間に. ¶***for*** a *while* 暫時の間. ¶once ***in*** a *while* たまに.

O It is (not) worth the *while.* それはやりがいがある(ない). ‖ It was not worth *while* to go. 行きがいがなかった. ‖ accomplish something worth *while* in life 一生の内にやりがいのあることをやり遂げる. ¶be waiting all the *while* その間ずっと待っている.

while, *v.* 時を過ごす.

M *while* ***away*** days on the beach 海岸で日を送る ‖ *while* ***away*** the day with music 音楽を聞いて楽しく一日を過ごす ‖ *while* ***away*** the time 暇つぶしをする. 【類】*while* ***away*** rainy days / I didn't know how to *while* ***away*** my tedium.

whim, *n.* 気まぐれ.

V ***follow*** one's own *whim* and one's selfish pleasure 気まぐれに自分勝手な道楽をやる ‖ permit them to ***follow*** their own *whims* 彼らの気の向くままにさせる. ¶***please*** the *whim* of a stupid person ばか者の御気げんを取る. ¶to ***suit*** one's *whims* 御気げんをとろうと.

V² He took up a job as *whim* or opportunity ***came*** to him. 気が変って職を持つようになった.

Q in an ***idle*** *whim* 浮いた心で. ¶This is a ***mere*** *whim* of his. これはあの男のほんの気まぐれだ.

P ***at*** the *whim* of the moment そのときのでき心で.

P² Her *whim* ***for*** gardening didn't last long. 気まぐれの庭いじりも長くは続かなかった.

whine, *v.* くんくんいう; くよくよする, こぼす.

M *whine* ***out*** 鼻声で言う. ¶My poor Fido has been *whining* ***piteously*** for want of a companion. 私の所のファイドーはかわいそうに相手がないのでくんくんないている. ¶the dog *whined* ***softly*** 犬はくんくんないた.

P *whine* ***about*** being unlucky 不運をかこつ.

whip, *n.* むち; 《英》〖政治〗総務.

V The *whip* was lustily ***applied*** to his bare body. むちが強く彼の素はだに当てられた. ‖ ***apply*** a *whip* gently to ... …に軽くむちを当てる. ¶I heard the driver ***cracking*** his *whip.* 私は御者がむちをぴしりといわせる音を聞いた. ¶The horse, ***feeling*** the *whip,* started off at a gallop. 馬はむちを当てられてかけ足で走り始めた. ¶***flick*** a *whip* 軽くむちで打つ. ¶***flip*** a *whip* むちをぴしぴしいわせる. ¶***use*** *whip* on ... = scourge ... …にむちを当てる.

Q² a heavy ***dog*** *whip* 太い犬むち ‖ the ***government*** (***opposition***) *whip* 与(野)党院内総務 ‖ the ***minority*** *whip* 少数党院内総務. ¶a ***party*** *whip* 政党院内総務. ☞ 英議会内で党出身議員の出席などを督励する役. 米の floor leader に当る.

P a flick ***of*** the *whip* むちの軽打. ¶strike one ***with*** a *whip* むちで人を打つ.

whip, *v.* むちうつ.

M *whip* ***smartly*** 激しくむちで打つ.

M² *whip* ***in*** while others are talking 話に割り込む. ¶*whip* ***off*** one's coat 上衣をぬぐ ‖ *whip* ***off*** hounds [呼んで]猟犬のねらいをそらす. ¶*whip* ***up*** a donkey ろばにむちを当てる ‖ *whip* ***up*** one's enthusiasm 気を励ます ‖ a propaganda to *whip* ***up*** war feelings among the people 国民に戦時意識をかきたてる宣伝.

P *whip* hogs ***to*** death [焼豚用に]豚をむち打って殺す.

whip-hand, *n.* むちを持つ方の手.

V ***get*** the *whip-hand* of one 人よりも優位に立つ, 人を制する. ¶***have*** the *whip-hand* 統御の能力を有する.

whipping, *n.* むち打ち.

Q get a ***good*** *whipping* したたかなぐられる; 敗北する. 【類】You shall have a ***good*** *whipping* later.

whir, *n.* ぶんぶん, びゅー.

P² the *whir* ***of*** a plane propeller プロペラーのぶんぶんいう音.

whirl, *n.* 旋回.

P The snow fell ***in*** a *whirl.* 雪はまんじどもえに降りしきっていた. ‖ My brain seems to be ***in*** a *whirl.* 私は頭がぐらぐらしている.

P² the *whirl* ***of*** the brain めまい.

whirl, *v.* 渦を巻く.

M be *whirled* ***along*** in an airplane すっと飛行機で持って行かれる. ¶The leaves *whirled* ***around*** in a circle. 木の葉が風で渦を巻いた. ¶The car *whirled* ***down*** the street. 車は通りを疾走した.

P With a hearty "Good-bye" my country cousin was *whirled* ***into*** the darkness. 心からの「さようなら」をした後で私のいなかからきたいとこ(を乗せた汽車)はたちまちやみの中に姿を消してしまった. ¶*whirl* ***round*** a ballroom [ダンサーが]ダンスホールをぐるぐる回る.

whirlpool, *n.* 渦.

P The boat was drawn ***into*** a *whirlpool.* そのボートは渦の中へ引込まれた.

whisk, *n.* ひと振り.

P² The horse brushed off flies with a *whisk* ***of*** its tail. 馬はその尾を振ってはえを追った.

whisk, *v.* 切り落す; 急に去る.

M *whisk* flies ***away*** はえをうちわなどで払う.

M² *whisk* (=chop) ***off*** one's head in a twinkling またたくまにその頭をちょんぎる ‖ *whisk* ***off*** to ... …に急いで行く ‖ Catching the purse between thumb and forefinger, he *whisked* it ***into*** his inside pocket. 財布をつまんで自分のかくしにさっと入れた(すりなど).

whisker, *n.* ほおひげ.

V ***cultivate*** (***grow or raise***) *whiskers* ほおひげを生やす. ¶***shave off*** *whiskers* ほおひげをそり落す. ¶***singe*** one's *whiskers* ほおひげの端を焼く. ¶***wear*** false *whiskers* ほおにつけひげをする ‖ He ***wears*** *whiskers* on his cheeks. 彼はほおにひげを生やしている.

V² The *whiskers* ***grow*** on the cheeks. ほおひげはほおに生える.

Q ***bushy*** *whiskers* もしゃもしゃのひげ. ¶with a ***dashing*** *whisker* しゃれたほおひげを生やして. ¶in ***false*** *whiskers*

ほおにつけひげをして. ¶*gray whiskers* ごま塩のほおひげ. ¶a man with ***voluminous*** *whiskers* 豊かなほおひげをたくわえた人.

Q^2 ***chin*** *whiskers* あごひげ.

whisk[e]y, *n.* ウイスキー.

V We ***distill*** *whisky* out of rye or corn. ウイスキーはライ麦かまたは小麦で造る. ¶***drink*** *whisky* ***straight*** ウイスキーをストレートで飲む. ☞英語は neat という.

Q^2 ***straight*** *whisky* 生一本のウイスキー.

whisper, *n.* ささやき.

Q an ***audible*** *whisper* 聞えるささやき. ¶in ***awe-struck*** *whispers* おどおどした小声で. ¶speak in a ***confidential*** and ***thrilling*** *whisper* 内密に心をそそるような声でささやく. ¶Everywhere you hear ***dark*** *whispers* of rising prices. 至る所で物価が上がるといういやな話がこそこそされている. ¶in a ***loud*** *whisper* 声高に内証話をして. ¶They were talking the scheme over in ***muffled*** *whispers.* 彼らは低いささやき声でその計画の相談をしていた. ¶say in a ***sepulchral*** *whisper* 陰気な小声で話す. ¶***sibilant*** *whisper* かすれた低い声.

Q^2 talk in ***stage*** *whispers* 人に聞えよがしの声で私語する ‖ frequently consent one's attorney in ***stage*** *whispers* 自分の弁護人に何べんも声を出して「そうだそうだ」と返事する. ¶***Washington*** *whispers* [新閣僚などの](米首都)ワシントン下馬評.

P He is so weak that he cannot speak ***above*** *a whisper.* 彼は衰弱しているので低い声でなくては話ができない. ¶say ***in*** a *whisper* ささやく. 【類】 talk ***in*** *whisper* / They spoke ***in*** *whispers.*

whisper, *v.* ささやく.

M It is *whispered* ***about*** that one of the Cabinet ministers will resign next month. 来月閣僚が一人辞任するというわさが立っている. ¶*whisper* ***audibly*** 他の人に聞えるようにささやく. ¶*whisper* ***hoarsely*** しゃがれ声でささやく. ¶*whisper* ***slyly*** to ... こっそり…にささやく. ¶The trees *whispered* ***soft*** and ***low.*** 木が静かに低い声でささやいた.

P *whisper* ***against*** ... 陰で…の悪口を言う ‖ *whisper* ***against*** a person ある人に対して陰謀を企てる. ¶*whisper* ***at*** his ear 彼の耳にささやく. ¶*whisper* ***in*** one's ear 人に耳打ちをする. ¶*whisper* a word or two ***into*** another's ear 人の耳に一言二言ささやく. ¶*whisper* ***to*** a person 人にささやく. ¶be it *whispered* ***with*** abated breath 大きな声では言えないが.

whistle, *n.* 口笛, 汽笛; のど(笛).

V ***blow*** a *whistle* 汽笛を鳴らす. ¶***give*** a warning *whistle* 警笛を鳴らす. ¶***sound*** a steam *whistle* サイレンを鳴らす. ¶***wet*** the *whistle* 《俗》一杯(酒を)やる. ¶The *whistle* ***blew*** and the train began to move. 汽笛が鳴って列車が動き出した. ¶The *whistle* ***sounds,*** and the train starts out of the station. 汽笛が鳴って列車は駅から出発する.

Q a ***shrill*** *whistle* ぴゅーという気笛(サイレン).

Q^2 a ***factory*** *whistle* 工場のサイレン. ¶a ***fire*** *whistle* 火事のサイレン. ¶a ***locomotive*** *whistle* 機関車の汽笛. ¶a ***steam*** *whistle* 汽笛. ¶A ***warning*** *whistle* blew. 警笛が一声鳴った.

P ***At*** the conductor's *whistle* the engine-driver starts his locomotive-engine 車掌が笛を鳴らすと機関手は機関車の運転を始める. ¶call ***by*** a *whistle* 口笛(または呼子)を吹いて呼ぶ.

whistle, *v.* 口笛を吹く, 汽笛を鳴らす; ひゅーと飛ぶ.

M *whistle* life ***away*** 一生をのんきに過す ‖ *whistle* ***away*** gently to oneself 静かに独り口笛を吹く. ¶*whistle* a dog ***back*** 犬を口笛で呼びもどす. ¶*whistle* a tune ***merrily*** 楽しげに口笛を吹く. ¶The wind *whistled* ***mournfully*** among the roof tops. 風は屋根にぴゅーぴゅーと吹きつけた. ¶*wistle* ***down*** the wind 〚比ゆ〛むだ話をする, むだな議論をする. ¶*whistle* ***shrilly*** 鋭く口笛を吹く.

P *whistle* ***for*** a taxi 口笛を吹いてタクシーを呼ぶ ‖ You may *whistle* ***for*** it. むだ骨だろう. ¶The bullet *whistled* ***past*** our ears. 弾丸がわれわれの耳をかすめて通った. ¶The wind *whistled* ***through*** the branches of the grove. 風がその森の木の間をひゅーひゅー吹いた.

white, *n.* 白; 白人; 白衣.

V ***turn up*** the *whites* of the eyes 白目を出す.

Q A pearl is usually ***creamy*** or ***silvery*** *white* in color. 真珠は大抵クリーム色か銀白色である. ¶be ***chalky*** *white* 白墨のように白い. ¶an ***opaque*** *white* 不透明な白. ¶Everything was dressed in ***silvery*** *white* with snow. 雪であらゆる物が真白に雪化粧した. ¶cooks attired in ***spotless*** *white* 汚点一つない白服を着けたコック. ¶***virgin*** *white* 純白.

P pass off ***as*** (=***for***) a *white* [混血黒人が]白人として通る. ¶be dressed ***in*** *white* 白衣をまとう ‖ a woman ***in*** *white* 白衣の天使(看護婦) ‖ wounded soldiers attired (=clad) ***in*** *white* 白衣の勇士.

P^2 the *white* ***of*** an egg 卵の白味. 【類】 the *white* ***of*** an eye.

white, *a.* 白い, [顔が, 恐怖などで]青い.

M Her face was ***marbly*** *white.* 彼女の顔は大理石のように白かった. ¶***pearly*** *white* [teeth] 真珠のような白い[歯]. ¶***spotlessly*** *white* (汚点一つない)真白な. ¶He is ***very*** *white.* 顔が真青だ.

M^2 a face ***as*** *white* as that of a corpse 死人の形相を呈した顔 ‖ a face ***as*** *white* as milk (chalk) ミルク(など)のように白い顔. 【類】 Her face turned ***as*** *white* as a sheet.

P *white* ***like*** silver 銀のように白い. ¶a desert *white* ***with*** the bones of the war dead 戦死者の遺骨で白くなっている砂原 ‖ The daisy is *white* ***with*** a yellow center. ひな菊は花が白く, 中心が黄色い.

whiteness, *n.* 白.

V ***give*** a pearly *whiteness* to the skin 皮膚を(真珠のように)光沢のある純白にする.

Q Ill health showed in the ***transparent*** *whiteness* of her skin. はだが透通って白いので彼女が健康を害していることがわかった.

whitewash, *n.* 胡粉(ごふん).

V ***put*** *whitewash* on ... …に胡粉を塗る.

V^2 The *whitewash* ***came off.*** 胡粉がはげた.

whitewash, *v.* ごま化す; 《米》ゼロ敗させる.

O *whitewash* one's fault (defect, error) あやまり(など)をごま化す ‖ *whitewash* an opponent team 相手チームをゼロ敗させる.

whittle, *v.* 削る, 削りとる.

M *whittle* ***away*** a fortune 財産を(少しずつ)減らす.

M^2 *whittle* ***down*** [小刀などで]けずりとる, 減じる ‖ *whittle* ***down*** the figure to less than ... 数字を…以下に削減する. 【類】 *whittle* ***down*** the price to ... / *whittle* ***down*** expenses for ... / The physical resistance of the people has been *whittled* ***down*** by the combination of hardships.

P *whittle* ***at*** a timber 材木を削り取ろうとする.

whiz, *v.* ひゅーという.

P We heard a shot *whiz* ***over*** our vessel. われわれの船の上を弾丸がひゅーと飛んで行った. ¶An arrow *whizzed* ***past.*** 矢がぴゅーとそばを飛んだ.

who, *pron.* だれ.

V^2 Possibly he is still alive. *Who* ***knows?*** 彼はまだ生きているかも知れないがはっきり分からない.

P *Who* ***from?*** 《口語》だれから(電話など). ‖ *Who* is the letter (phone) ***from?*** 《口語》手紙(などは)だれから. ¶*Who* were you talking ***to?*** だれに話しかけたんだ ‖ *Who* shall I say ***to*** Mr. M.? Mさんにどなたと言いましょうか(来訪者に対して). ¶*Who* was she talking ***with?*** 彼女の話している相手はだれですか. ☞口語ではしばしば whom に代用される.

whole, *n.* 全体.

V ***constitute*** (=***form***) a harmonious *whole* 渾(こん)然一体となる ‖ It ***forms*** a complete *whole* in itself. それはそれだけで完全だ. ¶We shall never ***know*** the *whole* of anything—Pascal. われらは何物もその全部を知ることはない. ‖ ***know*** the *whole* of one's trade 商売の全般を知る. ¶***recover*** the *whole* 全部を取り戻す. ¶***resolve*** a *whole* into its elements 完全の組織体をその成分に分析する. ¶***swallow*** ... *whole* …を丸のみにする. ¶He ***threw*** the *whole* of himself into the work. 彼は仕事に全力を注いだ.

Q a ***coherent*** *whole* 渾然たる一体. ¶Two-halves make a ***complete*** *whole.* 半分を二つ合わせれば完全な一になる. ¶a part of a ***comprehensive, coordinated*** *whole* 概括的で調整された全体の一部. ¶produce a ***harmonious*** *whole* 調和を得た一体を成す. ¶elements (=parts) of an ***organic*** *whole* 一個に組織された構成要素. ¶He desires to sell the collection as an ***undivided*** *whole.* 彼はその収集を分売せず全体として売りたいという希望を持っている. ¶form a ***united*** *whole* 合成して完全体を成す.

P The resolution was finally adopted by the conference ***as*** a *whole.* その決議はやがて会議全体の決議として可決された. ‖ London ***as*** a *whole,* is never called the "City." ロンドン全体を「市部」ということは決してない. 【類】 The book, ***as*** a *whole,* is one of the most successful of the recent publishing season. ¶abstain from food ***in*** *whole* or part 絶食または減食する. ¶English men of science, *on* the *whole*, are better literary men than Americans. 概して英国の科学者は米国の科学者より文学の素養がある.【類】My opinion is *on* the *whole* the same as yours. ¶He was an active participant ***throughout*** the *whole* of that affair. 彼はその事件の始めから終りまで直接そのことにあずかっていた.

P² the *whole of* the day その日一日.

wholesale, *n.* 卸し.

P They are worth ... yen ***at*** *wholesale*. それは卸売で…円する. ¶sell (buy) ***by*** *wholesale* 《英》卸しで売る(買う). ☞ sell *at* wholesale (retail) は米語用法.

whoop, *n.* ときの声.

V The whistle ***emits*** an exultant war *whoop*, and the vessel glides away amidst a cloud of black smoke. 汽笛が勇ましく鳴って船は黒煙の中をなめらかに進む. ¶***give*** a *whoop* of rage 怒りの叫びをあげる. ¶***raise*** war *whoops* ときの声をあげる.

P banzai uttered ***with*** a jubilant *whoop* 歓呼の声で叫んだ万歳.

whoop, *v.* わっと叫ぶ.

M *whoop* dogs ***on*** 犬をけしかける. ¶*whoop* it ***up*** 《米俗》大騒ぎする.

whooping-cough, *n.* 百日ぜき.

V ***have*** *whooping-cough* 百日ぜきにかかっている.

whorehouse, *n.* 娼(しょう)家.

V ***enter*** the *whorehouse* 売春婦になる.

why, *n.* 理由.

V I don't ***see*** *why*. 私にはなぜか分からない.

P I hate questions ***of*** *whys* and hows. なぜとかどうしてとかいう質問はきらいだ.【類】None ***of*** your *whys!*

wick, *n.* ランプの心.

V ***clip*** a *wick* 心をちょきんと切る. ¶cut the ***burnt*** *wick* from a candle ろうそくの心を切る. ¶***lower*** the *wick* 心を引込ませる. ¶***trim*** the *wick* 心を切る. ¶***turn*** the *wick* too high 心を出し過ぎる. ¶***turn up*** the *wick* 心を出す.

wickedness, *n.* 邪悪.

Q the ***manifold*** *wickedness* of the human heart 人心にやどる様々な邪悪.

wide, *a.* 広い.

M ***How*** *wide* is it? 幅はいくらあるか. ¶an organization ***nation-wide*** in its scope 全国的な規模の団体. ¶say a thing ***so*** *wide* of the mark てんで見当違いなことを言う.

P a net *wide* ***at*** the mouth and narrow at the other end 入口が広くて末端がせまくなっている網. ¶*wide* ***from*** the purpose その目的と大いに反した. ¶This is *wide* ***of*** the truth. これは大分事実と違っている. ‖ The statement is not very *wide* ***of*** the mark. その陳述は当らずといえども遠からずである.【類】one would probably not be very far *wide* ***of*** the mark if one conjectured that ... / If we estimate it at ... we shall probably not be *wide* ***of*** the mark.

widening, *n.* 拡大.

Q² ***street*** *widening* 市街道路幅の拡大.

P ***with*** the *widening* of human knowledge 人間の知識が拡大するにつれて.

widow, *n.* 未亡人, 後家.

V The deceased ***leaves*** a *widow*, three daughters, and two sons. 故人は未亡人と三人の娘と二人の息子を後に残している. ¶***marry*** a wealthy *widow* 裕福な後家と結婚する.

Q ***destitute*** *widows* and orphans 貧しい後家と孤児たち. ¶a ***disconsolate*** *widow* 夫に死に別れて憂いに沈んだ妻. ¶an ***inconsolable*** *widow* 夫に死なれ慰めてもあきらめかねている未亡人. ¶a ***rich*** (=***wealthy***) *widow* 金持ちの未亡人.

Q² a ***grass*** *widow* 離婚または別居生活の妻. ¶a ***war*** *widow* 戦争未亡人.

P² Eurenie, [the] *widow* ***of*** Napoleon III ナポレオン三世の未亡人ユーレニー.

O She remained a *widow* until death. 彼女は死ぬまで後家で通した.

widow, *v.* 未亡人にさせる.

P be *widowed* ***by*** a war 戦争で未亡人になる.

widowhood, *n.* 後家暮し.

Q live in ***chaste*** *widowhood* 貞節な後家暮しをする. ¶women who have lived for many years in ***continent*** *widowhood* 多年貞節に後家を立てて来た婦人たち.

P live ***in*** *widowhood* 後家で暮す.

width, *n.* 幅.

V ***measure*** the *width* of a cloth 布の幅を計る.

Q² a ***standard*** *width* and gauge [軌道の]標準軌間. ¶a film in ***16mm*** or ***35mm*** *width* 十六ミリまたは三十五ミリの映画.

P It is five feet ***in*** *width*. その幅は五フィートある.

P² *width* ***of*** clothing stuff 布地の幅.

wield, *v.* 振り回す.

P *wield* ... ***with*** a hand 片手で…を振り回す.

wife, *n.* 妻.

V ***abandon*** a *wife* 妻を捨てる. ¶The prudent youth waits till he can ***afford*** a *wife*. 思慮ある青年は妻を養って行くことができるまで結婚を延ばす. ¶***Bring*** your *wife* with you when you com next. 今度お出での時は奥様をお連れ下さい. ¶he ***bundled*** his *wife* and small family ***together*** and set out for ... 彼は子供の少ない一家をたたんで…に向った. ¶***divorce*** (=***repudiate***) one's *wife* 妻を離縁する. ¶***forsake*** (=***desert***) one's *wife* 妻を見捨てる. ¶***get*** a *wife* 妻を持つ. ¶He ***has*** a *wife* and family depending upon him. 彼には扶養すべき妻子がある. ¶***impregnate*** one's *wife* 妻をはらませる. ¶***keep*** a *wife* on one's paltry salary 薄給で妻を養う. ¶***leave*** one's *wife* and live with ... 妻を捨てて…と同せいする ‖ ***leave*** a *wife* and four children 妻子五人を残して死ぬ. ¶He ***lost*** his beloved *wife* through death. 彼は愛妻に死に別れた. ¶She is a good girl, and will ***make*** a hard-working, devoted *wife*. あの娘はよい子だから一生懸命に働く忠実な妻になるだろう. ¶He ***married*** a *wife* by whom he had two daughters. 彼は妻を迎えて二人の娘をもうけた.【類】He ***married*** (=took) a Japanese *wife*.=He was married to a Japanese woman. ¶***play*** the *wife* 女房役をつとめる. ¶***put away*** one's *wife* and live in open adultery with another woman 妻を離縁して他の女と公然不義な生活をする. ¶***remarry*** one's divorced *wife* 一たん離縁した妻を再び迎える. ¶***take*** one's *wife* 妻をめとる ‖ He has not ***taken*** a *wife*. 彼はこれまで妻を持たなかった. ‖ Many of the officers of the fur companies ***took*** to (=unto) themselves *wives* from the women of the Columbia River tribes. 毛皮会社の役員でコロンビア河畔のインディアンの娘を妻にしたものが多数あった. ‖ ***take*** a *wife* from the stage 女優を妻にする. ¶***tame*** a *wife* 妻を手なずける. ¶He ***thrashed*** his *wife* to death. 彼はその妻をむち打って死に至らしめた. ¶He ***uses*** his *wife* very ***ill***. 彼は妻を虐待する.

Q an ***abused*** and ***neglected*** *wife* 虐待され冷遇された妻. ¶an ***adorable*** *wife* 愛慕すべき妻. ¶an ***ailing*** *wife* 病弱の妻. ¶an ***amiable*** *wife* 愛想(あいそ)のよい細君. ¶***British-born*** *wives* of Germans ドイツ人の英国生れの妻. ¶a ***chaste*** and ***beautiful*** *wife* 貞節にして美しい妻. ¶a ***cold*** *wife* 冷淡な妻. ¶a ***devoted*** *wife* 夫思いの妻. ¶***docile*** *wives* すなおな妻. ¶a ***drunkard's*** *wife* 飲酒家の妻. ¶a ***faithful and devoted*** *wife* 忠実な夫思いの妻. ¶It is not ***every*** *wife* who is worth her weight in gold. [黄金相当の価値がある]理想の妻なんてそうざらにはいない. ¶a ***faithless*** (=***unfaithful***) *wife* 不貞な妻. ¶a ***forsaken*** *wife* 見捨てられた妻. ¶a ***hard-up*** *wife* 生活の苦しい妻. ¶a ***good*** *wife* 良妻. ¶an ***immoral*** *wife* 不倫な妻. ¶***intemperate*** *wives* 放らつな妻. ¶recognize a woman as one's ***lawful*** *wife* 女性を正式の妻として認める. ¶a ***left-handed*** *wife* 二号. ¶Mandokoro, the Taiko's ***legitimate*** *wife* 太閤の正妻政所. ¶a ***loving*** *wife* 愛妻. ¶a ***lustful*** *wife* 好色な妻. ¶a ***matchless*** *wife* またとない良妻. ¶a ***morganatic*** *wife* (貴人がめとった)賤(いや)しい妻(遺産相続権がない). ¶a ***nagging*** *wife* 口やかましい妻. ¶a ***plural*** *wife* [一夫多妻制度で]一人の男の妻の一人. ¶He married ***seven*** *wives*. 彼は妻を七人かえた. ¶a ***sickly*** *wife* 病身の妻. ¶a ***suitable*** *wife* 似合いの妻. ¶a ***termagant*** *wife* 口やかましい妻. ¶She was the "***unmarried*** (=***unwedded***) *wife*" of a Communist organizer. 彼女はある共産党オルグのいわゆる内縁の妻であった. ¶a most ***virtuous*** *wife* きわめて貞淑な妻. ¶a ***war-bereaved*** *wife* 戦争未亡人. ¶a ***wedded, lawful*** *wife* 正式に結婚した妻. ¶a ***working*** *wife* かせぎに出る妻.

Q² an "***Army*** *wife*" [慰問婦など]「兵隊妻」. ¶a ***common-law*** *wife* 内縁の妻. ¶a ***daytime*** *wife* [女秘書など]昼間妻. ¶a ***Dutch*** *wife* 竹夫人. ¶a ***model*** *wife* 模範的な妻. ¶an ***office*** *wife* [女秘書など]オフィス・ワイフ. ¶She is an absolutely ***one-man*** *wife*. 彼女はあくまで一人の夫を守る女である. ¶a ***war*** (=***GI***) *wife* 戦争でできた妻.

P he married ***as*** his second *wife* ... 彼は…と二度目の結婚をした. ¶the children they had ***by*** (=that were born of) their Japanese *wives* 彼らの日本人の妻にできた子供たち.

P² have (=get) ... ***for*** one's wife …を妻にする. ¶a *wife* ***for*** a night (life) 一夜(一生の)妻. ¶take ... ***to*** *wife* …をめとる. ¶a married man ***with*** a *wife* to support 妻帯の人.

P[2] *wife to* ... ...の妻.

wild, *a.* 野趣のある；狂奔して，夢中で.

M It is ***wild enough*** to have monkeys in its trees. その土地は林にさるがいるくらいでまだ開けていない. ¶be ***nobly wild*** 気高くて荒削り，行いは荒っぽいが考えはりっぱである(青年の理想).

P He is *wild* (=crazy *or* mad) ***about*** music. 彼は音楽に熱中している. ¶The weeds are running *wild* ***over*** the garden. 庭園は雑草がはびこっている. ¶He was *wild* ***with*** delight. 彼は狂喜していた. 【類】*wild* ***with*** emotion (enthusiasm, anxiety) / He was *wild* ***with*** excitement at the news. / make a person *wild* ***with*** joy (=glee) / get *wild* ***with*** rage / grow *wild* ***with*** wine.

wild, *n.* 荒野.

Q[2] a ***desert*** *wild* さばくの荒野.

P ***in*** the *wilds* of Siberia シベリアの荒野に.

wilderness, *n.* 荒地.

V ***make*** the *wilderness* ***blossom*** like rose 荒地を開拓する. ¶***subdue*** the *wilderness* 荒野を征服(開墾)する. ¶***tame*** the *wilderness* 荒地を開墾する.

Q London after midnight was once a ***desolate*** *wilderness*. 真夜中過ぎのロンドンはせきばくたる荒野といった時代もあった. ¶a ***Godforsaken*** *wilderness* 神も見捨てた荒野. ¶an ***untamed*** *wilderness* 荒涼たる原野. ¶a ***watery*** *wilderness*=a wilderness of waters 大海原.

wildfire, *n.* 野火.

V spread ***like*** *wildfire* [うわさなど]野火のようにひろがる.

wile, *n.* 手管.

V ***use*** her *wiles* to ... ...しようと術策を用いる. ¶He is able to ***withstand*** the *wiles* of women. 彼は女にはだまされない. 「だまして...させた.

P He persuaded her to ... ***by*** his *wiles*. 彼は彼女をうまく

will, *n.* (**1**) 意志.

V ***bear*** no good *will* to ... ...に好意はいささかも持たない. ¶It gives me great pleasure to ***carry out*** their *will*. あの方々の所存を実行するのは私のよろこびとする所です. ¶***cause*** ill *will* 反感を起させる. ¶***change*** one's will その意志を変える. ¶***convey*** the *will* and ideas of those who govern to those who are governed 上意を下達する. ¶the actions of a spoiled child when his *will* is ***crossed*** 気にさからった時あまやかした子供のする行為. ¶***cultivate*** a good *will* and harmony between ... ...間の好意と融和を計る. ¶***develop*** one's *will* 意志をのばす. ¶***discover*** the *will* of the goods 神々の意志を知る. ¶***do*** one's own *will* その意志通りにする. ¶Heat ***enervates*** the *will*. 暑さは意志を弱める. ¶***execute*** the *will* of the majority of the people 多数者の意志を実行する. ¶***exercise*** one's *will* 意志を働かせる. ¶Law lacks its essential elements if it does not properly ***express*** the State's collected *will*. 国家の総意を適当に表示しない法律はその根本的要素を欠いていることになる. ¶He must always ***have*** his *will*. 彼はいつも我を通さなければやまない. ‖ ***have*** his *will* of her 彼女をなびかせる ‖ He ***has*** a *will* of his own. 彼には意地がある. ¶***impose*** one's *will* upon others その考え通りに他人にやらせる. ¶***maintain*** a firm *will* 堅い意志を捨てない. ¶***obey*** the *will* of one's master その主人の意に従う. ¶***reveal*** His *will* to man 神のみむねを人間に告げる. ¶***serve*** the *will* of others without independent volition 付和雷同する. ¶***show*** a *will* that can conquer all difficulties 万難に打ち勝つ気概を示す. ¶I ***took*** his *will* for the deed. 私は彼がそうしようとする志を買ってやった(人が自分に恩返しをしようと心がけている場合など). ¶***train*** the *will* 意志をきたえる. ¶***withstand*** a person's *will* 人の意にさからう. ¶***work*** one's *will* その志を遂げる.

Q even with the ***best*** *will* in the world いかに最善の意志をもってしても. ¶the correct interpretation of the ***deliberate, intelligent, dependable, popular*** *will* of Japan 思慮があり賢明でたしかな日本民衆の意志に対する正しい解釈. ¶through the power of ***determined*** *will* 確固たる意志の力で. ¶Japan's course is being regarded with ever-increasing ***good*** *will*. 日本のやり方は日に増し好意をもって見られるようになっている. ‖ break down ***good*** *will* 善意をくじく ‖ take it in ***good*** *will* それを善意に解釈する ‖ Democracy is based on ***good*** *will* and mutual understanding. 民主々義は善意と相互の理解に基づく. ¶a declaration of ***heaven's*** *will* 天命. ¶he has never manifested the slightest ***ill*** *will* toward ... 彼は...に対し少しもいやな様子を見せなかった. ¶an ***imperial*** *will* 陛下の御意向. ¶He is endowed with ***indomitable*** *will*. 彼には天与の不とう不屈の意志がある. ‖ a man of almost ***indomitable*** *will* ほとんど抜くべからざる堅固な意志の人. ¶He has ***no*** *will* of his own. 彼は自分の意志というものを持っていない. ¶***obstinate*** *will* 執ような意志. ¶the ***sovereign*** *will* of the people 国民至高の総意. ¶a man of ***strong*** (***weak***) *will* 意志の強(弱)い人. ¶at your own ***sweet*** *will* あなたの思召通りに. ¶realization of the ***true*** *will* of the people 民衆の真意の実現.

Q[2] ***iron*** *will* 鉄の意志.

P He did it ***against*** his *will*. 彼は不本意ながらそうした ‖. It was much ***against*** her *will*. それは決して彼女の意志ではなかった. ‖ though it is ***against*** one's *will* 心ならずも. 【類】He married her ***against*** the *will* of her parents. / consent ***against*** one's *will*. ¶The vocal cords can be opened or shut ***at*** *will*. 声帯は自由自在に開閉ができる. ‖ ***at*** the *will* of ... ...の意志で. ¶dismissal ***by*** the *will* of the Government 諭旨免官 ‖ become a married couple ***by*** the *will* of Heaven 縁があって夫婦になる. ¶strength ***of*** *will* 意思の力 ‖ ***of*** one's own *will* 自分から進んで ‖ ***of*** one's own free *will* その自由意志で(勝手に) ‖ the freedom ***of*** the *will* 意志の自由. ¶bend ***to*** another's *will* 他人の意志に屈する. ¶We set to work ***with*** a *will*. われわれは身を入れて仕事に取りかかった. ‖ rub and rinse ***with*** a *will* せっせと洗たく物をする.

P[2] do the ***will of*** God 神の意志を実行する ‖ the ***will of*** the people 民意.

(**2**) 遺言；遺言状.

V ***administer*** one's *will* その遺言を実行する. ¶***destroy*** a *will* 遺言状を破棄する. ¶***draw up*** (=***make***) a *will* 遺言状を作成する ‖ He ***drew*** [***up***] a *will* in which he bequeathed all he possessed to his wife. 彼は所有財産を全部妻に譲るむねの遺言書を作成した. ¶***leave*** a *will* 遺言をする.

Q one's ***last*** *will* and testament その遺言書(法律上の成句).

P property left ***by*** his *will* 彼の遺言で残された財産 ‖ ***by*** the *will* of ... ...の遺言で. ¶leave something to one's cousin ***in*** one's *will* 遺言でいとこに何か残す. ¶some precious stones left to her ***under*** a *will* 遺言で彼女に残された宝石. 【類】***Under*** the *will* of Cecil Rhodes, scholarships were founded at Oxford, his old University, for students from ... / The foundation (財団) was established in 1912 with a bequest (遺産) of $25,000 ***under*** the *will* of Louis Clark Vanuxem.

will, *v.* 意図する；遺言状で残す.

M But Heaven *willed* ***otherwise***. しかし天はそうはさせなかった. 「に譲る.

P *will* one's property ***to*** one's son 遺言状でその財産を子

O they are superstitious, if you *will*, but ... 彼らは迷信的だと言えないこともないがしかし... ‖ As a means of improving your conversational power I advise you to read dialogues—or modern plays, if you *will*. 会話熟達の一つの方法として対話でもまた近代劇でも読むことを君にお勧めする. ¶He *wills* to do it. 彼はそれをやる気だ.

willing, *a.* 進んでやる気のある.

M I'm ***quite*** *willing* to do it. 私は喜んでそれをやります.

O They are *willing* to learn English. 彼らは英語を学びたがっている.

willingly, *ad.* 喜んで.

M ***very*** *willingly* 二つ返事で.

willingness, *n.* 快諾.

V ***express*** one's *willingness* その快諾を表示する. ¶***show*** a *willingness* 喜んでやることを示す. ¶***signify*** one's *willingness* to support the movement その運動を進んで援助するむねを示す.

Q a ***gracious*** *willingness* 丁重な快諾.

O *willingness* to work 喜んで働く気持.

willow, *n.* 柳.

V ***wear*** the *willow* 失恋する，恋人の死をいたむ(柳の葉で作った花輪をつけたことから).

Q[2] a ***pussy*** *willow* ねこやなぎ. ¶a ***weeping*** *willow* しだれ柳.

will-power, *n.* 意志の力.

Q ***indomitable*** *will-power* 不屈の意志の力.

win, *n.* 勝利.

Q the ***first*** *win* since 1923 一九二三年以来始めての勝利.

win, *v.* 勝つ.

M *win* ***back*** the trophy 勝って勝杯を取り戻す ‖ *win* ***back*** world respect 世界の尊敬を取り戻す(敗戦国などが) ‖ *win* her **back** [自分を捨てた]愛人を取り戻す. ¶***win easily*** 楽々と勝つ ‖ He can ***easily win*** the love of any woman he comes to deal with. あの男にかかってはどんな女でもころっとまいってしまう. ¶***fairly win*** one's honors りっぱに名誉を得る. ¶*win* ***out*** 勝つ, 乗り切る. ¶*win* him ***over*** to our side 彼をわれわれの味方に取入れる. ¶will ***probably win*** the prize おそらく賞を獲得するだろう.

M^2 be easy to ***win over*** 組しやすい ‖ ***win over*** an opponent team 相手のチームを破る ‖ ***win*** a person ***over*** by foul means 人をろう絡する ‖ ***win*** a person ***over*** to one's side 人をうまく自分の方に取入れる. 【類】***win*** a person ***over*** to do what one wants / ***win*** them ***over*** to one's views (= way of thinking).

P ***win against*** all obstacles あらゆる障害に打勝つ ‖ On 40 occasions Oxford has *won* the Boat Race ***against*** 46 by Cambridge. ボートレースにおいてこれまでケンブリッジの四十六回に対しオクスフォードは四十回勝っている. 【類】In the basketball game the Philippines ***won against*** China by the heavy score of 38 to 17. ¶how to ***win at*** racing 徒歩競争に勝つ方法. ¶In the football game we ***won by*** 8 points to 3. そのしゅう球試合でわれわれは八対三で勝った. ‖ ***win by*** more than two minutes 二分強の差で勝つ ‖ ***win*** a game ***by*** a (=the) score of 5 to 4 五対四で勝つ ‖ ***win by*** a neck [競馬で]首だけの差で勝つ ‖ ***win by*** four lengths over … …に四艇身勝つ. 【類】***win by*** a margin of six lengths / ***win by*** … after eight consecutive defeats / ***win*** a game ***by*** a lopsided score (一方的なスコア) of 14—3 ‖ ***win by*** tenderness (kindness) やさしく(親切に)して取入る ‖ ***win by*** chance 偶然に勝つ. ¶This *won* ***for*** him the first prize of $15,000. これで彼は一等賞一万五千ドルを得た. ¶***win*** the race ***from*** … …と競艇して勝つ. 【類】General Andrew Jackson *won* the battle of New Orleans ***from*** the British in 1815 at the close of the War of 1812. ¶***win in*** a lottery 富くじを当てる. ¶***win*** a victory ***over*** … …を破って勝利を得る. ¶***win through*** difficulties 困難を切り抜ける. ¶***win*** the natives ***to*** Christianity 土人をキリスト教にはいらせる. ¶Her beauty and amiability ***won upon*** everybody. 彼女は美しくて愛きょうがあるのでだれからも愛された. ¶***win with*** a score of 6—5 六対五の得点で勝つ ‖ ***win with*** toil 骨折って勝つ.

wince, *v.* [痛さ・こわさなどに]たじろぐ.

P ***wince at*** allusion (sarcasm) あてつけ(など)にへきえきする. ¶***wince from*** (***under***) blows. ¶***wince under*** the flails of his reviewers 批評家連の酷評にたじろぐ. 【類】***wince under*** bitter criticism.

winch, *n.* 『機』ウインチ.

Q^2 a ***cargo winch*** 船荷ウインチ. ¶a ***crab winch*** かにウインチ. ¶a ***hand winch*** 手動ウインチ. ¶a ***steam winch*** スチーム・ウインチ.

wind, *n.* (**1**) 風.

V ***brave*** the *winds* and waves 風波をしのぐ. ¶***break*** (= ***emit or discharge***) *wind* from (=through) the anus 放ひする. ¶***face*** a biting *wind* 身を切るような風に向う. ¶The rumor has ***got wind***. そのうわさが世間に広まった. ‖ He ***got wind*** and ran way. 彼は風をくらって逐電した. ‖ ***get wind*** of what is going on 様子が変だと感付く. ¶***raise*** the *wind* 資金を才覚する. ¶***Sowing*** the *wind* is reaping the whirlwind. [旧約聖書から]一つの悪事をすれば幾十倍もひどい罰を受ける. ¶That fence will never ***stand*** a strong *wind*. あのかきねは強い風にはとてももつまい. ¶***take*** the *wind* off (=out of) one's sails 話の腰を折る. ¶God ***tempers*** the *wind* to the shorn lamb. 神は弱者に味方する.

V^2 The *wind* has ***abated***. 風がないだ. ¶The *wind* was ***blowing*** northerly. 北風が吹いていた. ¶The *wind* seems to have ***changed*** to the south. 風が南に回ったらしい. ¶The *wind* ***died away***. 風が静まった. ¶The *wind* has ***fallen*** (=***dropped***). 風がやんだ. ¶***Wind goes down***. 風が静まる. ¶The *wind* ***hissed*** and ***raged***. 風がひゅーひゅー吹きすさんだ. ¶The *wind* ***howled*** frightfully. 風が恐ろしく怒号した. ¶The *wind* has ***lulled***. 風が一時ないだ. ¶The *wind* ***moaned*** dismally over the empty fields. 空ばくたる原野を風が陰うつなうなりをあげて吹いた. ¶The *wind* ***raved*** through the trees. 風が樹間を吹き荒れた. ¶The *wind* ***rises***. 風が出る. ¶The *wind* ***roared*** among the pine forests. 風が松林の中をごうごうと吹いた. ¶***Wind shrieks*** in the rigging. 風が帆綱に当ってびゅーびゅーうなった. ¶The *wind* ***sits*** in that quarter. 風はその方面で止まっている. ¶The *wind* ***soughed*** (=***moaned***) through trees. 風が樹間をひゅーひゅーと吹いた. ¶A freezing *wind* ***sprang up***. 凍えるような寒風が吹き出した. ¶The *wind* has ***subsided*** into a soft, warm breeze. 風がないできて暖かな軟風になった. ¶The *wind* was ***whirling*** snowflakes in eddies. 風で雪片がくるくる舞っていた. ¶The ***wind whistles*** in the chimney. 風が煙突の中でひゅーひゅーいう. 【類】The *wind* ***whistled*** through the streets.

Q in spite of an ***adverse wind*** 逆風をも構わず. ¶in ***all winds*** and weathers どんな天候でも. ¶a ***big wind*** 大風. ¶a ***biting north wind*** はだを刺すような北風. ¶a ***bleak wind*** はだ寒い風. ¶a ***blinding wind*** 目をあけていられない風. ¶a ***boisterous wind*** 騒々しい風. ¶a ***choppy wind*** 変りやすい風. ¶a ***contrary wind*** 向い風. ¶a ***cutting wind*** はだを切る風. ¶a ***fair wind*** 順風. ¶A ***favorable wind*** sprang up. 順風が出た. ¶a ***fitful wind*** 気まぐれな風. ¶***freezing wind*** 氷のような風. ¶The *wind* is ***fresh***. 風が強い. ¶a ***gentle wind*** そよ吹く風. ¶a ***heavy wind*** ひどい風. ¶The *wind* is ***high***. 風が強い. ¶the ***icy wind*** of a northern winter 北国の冬の氷のように冷たい風. ‖ The ***icy wind*** cut me to the bone. 氷のように冷たい風が骨までしみた. ¶It is an ***ill wind*** [that] blows nobody good. 風が吹けばおけ屋がもうかる. ¶a ***light wind*** 微風. ¶a ***local wind*** 一地方の風. ¶The night was still with only the sound of a ***low wind*** in the trees. 木の間にかすかに風の吹く声がするだけで夜はしんとしていた. ¶a ***merry wind*** さわやかな風. ¶a ***misty wind*** 霧を含んだ風. ¶a ***moderate wind*** 弱い風. ¶a ***nasty wind*** いやな風. ¶a ***northerly*** (***southerly***) ***wind*** 北(南)風. ¶a ***piercing wind*** はだを刺すような風. ¶The ***prevailing winds*** are southerly and southwesterly. 主に吹いているのは南風と南西の風です. ¶a ***rain-bearing wind*** 雨を含む風. ¶a ***rustling wind*** さわさわする風. ¶kimono-clad girls annoyed by a ***searching wind*** しつっこい風に悩むきもの姿の少女. ¶a ***severe wind*** 烈風. ¶a ***sharp wind*** はだを切る風. ¶a ***shifting wind*** 方向の変わる風. ¶a ***slight wind*** 微風. ¶a ***small wind*** 微風. ¶The ***soft wind*** wafts the smell of roses. 軟風がばらの香をふうわりと吹き送る. ‖ A ***soft wind*** kissed the treetops. そよ風がこずえをひゅーひゅーと吹いた. ‖ the murmur of ***soft winds*** in the tree-tops こずえを吹く軟風. ¶The *wind* is ***steady***. 風がむらなく吹く. ¶A ***stinging wind*** swept the woods. 刺すような寒風が森を吹きまくった. ¶a ***stormy wind*** 暴風. ¶a ***strong wind*** 強風. ¶a ***strongish wind*** かなりの強風. ¶an ***unfavorable wind*** 逆風. ¶a ***vehement wind*** 烈風.

Q^2 in the teeth of an ***eighteen-mile wind*** 時速十八マイルの強風をおかして. ¶a ***gale wind*** 暴風. ¶a ***head wind*** 向い風. ¶an ***inshore wind*** 海岸に吹きつける風. ¶The ***night wind*** blew in cold against her bare breast. 彼女のむき出しの胸には夜風がしみた. 【類】a chill ***night wind***. ¶a ***north*** (***south***) ***wind*** 北(南)風. ¶an ***off-shore wind*** 沖から吹く風. ¶The skin becomes rough or chapped by the harsh, ***spring winds***. 荒い春風で皮膚がかさかさになってあかぎれができる. ¶***trade wind*** 貿易風. ¶a ***whirl wind*** 旋風.

P sail (steam) ***against*** the wind 風に向って帆(蒸気)で航行する. ¶The ship ran ***before*** the *wind*. 船は順風を受けて快走した. ¶***between wind*** and water 喫水線の辺に; [比ゆ的] 急所に. ¶a sand bank piled up ***by*** the *wind* 風でできた砂堤. ¶go ***down*** the *wind* 風下に行く; 衰える, 左前になる. ¶The vane turns ***in*** the *wind*. 風見は風で回る. ‖ Pines sing ***in*** the *wind*. 松風が立つ. ‖ There was a lull ***in*** the *wind*. 風がちょっと静まった. ‖ bamboos ***in*** the *wind* 風にそよぐ竹 ‖ straws ***in*** the *wind* 風にそよぐ芦, 『比ゆ』それと察知されるもの ‖ The flag is fluttering ***in*** the *wind*. 旗は風でぱたぱたしている. ¶a gust ***of*** *wind* 一陣の風 ‖ He is fat, and scant ***of*** *wind*. 彼は肥えているので息切れがする. ¶the fragrance of the plum-blossom carried ***on*** the *wind* 風が運んで来る梅が香. ¶Branches swayed about ***to*** the *wind*. 枝は風に揺れた. ¶go ***up*** the *wind* 風上に行く. ¶The boat drifted ***with*** the *wind*. そのボートは風のまにまに漂った. ‖ sail ***with*** the *wind* 追風を受けて進む ‖ The weathercock turning ***with*** the *wind* 風でくるくる回る風見.

P^2 the ***wind among*** the reeds 芦原を吹く風. ¶A cutting ***wind from*** the north fills the air with dust and dirt. 身を切るような北風が吹いて砂塵りが立つ. ‖ a ***wind from*** the

sea 海風.
(2) おなら.
P² *wind from* the stomach (bowels) 胃(腸)から出るガス.
V *break wind* at … …にへをひっかける.

wind, *v.* 巻く; 閉鎖する.
M The sleepy little river *wound slowly* through green meadows or beneath dark pines. 眠そうな静かな小川が緑の牧場や松の茂みの下を曲りくねって流れていた.
M² The company was *wound up* voluntarily. その会社は自発的に解散した. ¶*wind up* a company (one's business) 会社を解散する(店を閉鎖する) ‖ *wind up* one's talk 話をむすぶ. 【類】He *wound up* his speech with the remark. ‖ *wind up* a branch 支店を閉じる ‖ *wind up* its career as … …としての経歴を終える. 【類】*wind up* a conference / *wind up* a debate ‖ *wind up* an estate [死者・破産者などの]財産を処理する ‖ *wind up* one's home 家をたたむ. ¶*wind up* lend-lease 武器貸与法を廃止する ‖ *wind* oneself *up* for further effort 今一息とがんばる ‖ *winding up* the proceedings, he proposed the health of … 議事終了を告げて彼は…のために乾杯の音頭をとった ‖ *wind* [*up*] a watch [懐中]時計を巻く ‖ *winding up* a 2,530-mile flight from Hawaii … ハワイから二千五百三十マイルの飛行を終えて ‖ *wind up* in liquidation 会社を解散して清算にはいる ‖ he *wound up* [his remarks] by saying that … …と言って話を切り上げた.
P *wind* flowers *around* a pillar 花を柱にからませる. ¶*wind* a person *in* one's arms 人を両手で抱きかかえる. ¶*wind* oneself *into* some one's favor 巧みに人に取り入る ‖ *wind* woolen yarn *into* a ball 毛糸を巻いて玉にする. ¶*wind* thread *on* a reel (spool) 糸を糸巻(など)に巻く. ¶The stream *winds through* the valley. 谷間をその川がえんえんと流れている.

wind-break, *n.* 防風.
P² a *wind-break of* trees 防風林.

winding, *n.* 曲り角.
P *at* the *winding* of the road 道の曲り角で.

windlass, *n.* 〖機〗ウインチ.
Q² a *hand* (*steam*) *windlass* 手動(蒸気)ウインチ.

windmill, *n.* 風車.
V *fight windmills* ひとり角力をとる(ドン・キホーテの故事から出た句).
Q a *Dutch windmill* オランダ型風車.

window, *n.* 窓; 窓ガラス; 飾り窓(ショーウィンドー).
V *break* a *window* 窓をこわす. ¶*clean windows* 窓の掃除をする. ¶*close* a *window* 窓を締める. ¶The Somerset House is said to *contain* 3,600 *windows*. サマーセット・ハウスには三千六百の窓があるということだ. ¶*crack* a *window* ガラスにひびを入らす. ¶*dress up* a store *window* 店の窓を装飾する. ¶*glaze* a *window* 窓ガラスを入れる. ¶*leave open* the *window* at the top 窓の上の方を開ける. ¶*let* (=*keep*) the *window down* from the top for ventilation 換気のために窓の上部を開けておく. ¶*lower* a *window* 窓を下ろす. ¶*make* a *window* 窓をあける. ¶*open* a *window* 窓を開ける ‖ *open* the *window* to admit air 窓を開けて風を入れる. ¶*place windows* in the east and west walls 東と西の壁に窓をつける. ¶*putty* the *window* 窓のガラスにパテをつける. ¶*raise* a *window* 窓を上に開ける. ¶*shut* the *window half-way down* (*a little further, altogether*) 窓を半分(など)締める. ¶*smash* a *window* 窓を打ちこわす. ¶*throw open windows* 窓を開け放す. ¶*unlatch* the *window* 窓の締りをはずす. ¶I *want* the *window up* (*down*). [汽車などの]窓を締めて(あけて)おいてもらいたい.
V² The *window looks out* toward the sea (on the street). その窓から海が見える(通りに面する).
Q a *curtained window* カーテンのある窓. ¶a *double window* 二重窓. ¶a *French window* 観音開きの窓. ¶an *iron-framed window* 鉄わくの窓. ¶a *steel-barred window* [刑務所の]鉄窓. ¶a *strongly-lighted window* 灯がこうこうとともっている家の窓. ¶A woman appeared, with agonizing gestures, at an *upper window* of a burning house. 焼けている家の二階の窓に一人の女が苦もんする風情で姿を見せた.
Q² from one's *bedroom window* その寝室の窓から. ¶the *car window* of a train 汽車の窓. ¶look out of the *carriage window* 車窓から外を見る. ¶a *clerestory window* (教会などの)高窓. ¶a *display window* [商店の]陳列窓. ¶a *plateglass window* 板ガラスの入った窓. ¶a *shop* (=*store*) *window* 商店の陳列窓. ¶a *show window* 飾り窓. ¶a *stained-glass window* 着色ガラス窓. ¶a *ticket window* [駅の]切符売場. ¶a panoramic *train window* 刻々に風景の変る汽車の窓. ¶an *upstairs window* 二階の窓.
P sit *at* one's *window* 自分のへやの窓際にすわる ‖ He was *at* the *window*. 彼は窓際にいた. ‖ lean out *at* the *window* 乗り出して窓から顔を出す. ¶The thief entered *by* the *window*. 賊は窓からはいった. ‖ break in *by* the *window* 窓から押入る. ¶*From* the *window* is a view of the lake and woods in the park. 窓から公園の湖水や木立が見渡される. ¶A sign *in* the *window* said: Sale of Men's Shirts. ショーウィンドーに「男物シャツ販売」と出ていた. ‖ display goods *in* the *windows* 商品を窓に陳列する ‖ exhibit them *in* its *window* それらの品をその店の飾り窓に陳列する. 【類】The pieces (品) have been on display *in* the *windows* of Arthur & Bond at Yokohama. ¶We have curtains *on* the *windows*. 宅では窓にカーテンが掛けてあります. ¶The rain froze *on* the *window*. 雨が窓について凍った. ¶look *out of* a *window* 窓から外をながめる. ¶lean *over* the *window* 窓からからだを乗り出す ‖ be draped down *over* the *window* 窓掛けを引いてある. ¶A whiff of chloroform came *through* an open *window*. 開いた窓からクロロホルムの臭がぷんとして来た. ‖ look out *through* the *window* 窓越しに外を見る. ¶*under* the *window* 窓下に.
P² A *window on* the world: recent happenings in pictures. 世界展望の窓時事画報.
O The *window* is up (down). [汽車などの]窓が締めて(あけて)ある.

windowpane, *n.* 窓ガラス.
V *crack* (=*break*) a *windowpane* 窓ガラスをこわす.
Q a *frosted windowpane* 霜模様の窓ガラス.

window-shield, *n.* 破風(はふ)窓.
Q a *glass window-shield* [自動車などの]ガラス製破風窓.

window-shopper, *n.* 《米》飾り窓をのぞく人.
P an endless stream *of* saunterers and *window-shoppers* つきない散歩人とひやかし客の流れ.

windward, *n.* 風上.
P cast anchor *to windward* 風上へいかりを投げる.

wine, *n.* ぶどう酒; 酒.
V *cut out wine* 酒をやめる. ¶*decant wine* ぶどう酒をおりの立たないように器から器へ静かに移す. ¶*drink wine* 酒を飲む. ¶We *have wine* enough to go round. 全体に行渡るだけの酒がある. ‖ *have* a *wine* 小宴を張る. ¶*heat* (*warm*) *wine* かんをする. ¶a *wine imported* from … …から輸入したぶどう酒. ¶a white *wine made* from grapes ぶどうで造った白ぶどう酒. ¶*mull wine* 酒を暖める. ¶after the *wine* has been *passed round* 酒が全体に行渡ってから. ¶*pour* (=*fill*) *out wine* 酒を注ぐ. ¶Do you *prefer* tea or *wine*? 茶と酒とどちらがよろしいですか. ¶*Save* this *wine* for tomorrow. この酒をあすの分に取っておけ. ¶No *wines* will be *served* at the dinner. その晩さん会に酒は出ません. ¶*serve out wine* [宴会などに]酒を出す. ¶*strain wine* ぶどう酒をこす. ¶*take wine* 酒を飲む ‖ *take wine* with … …と乾杯をする. ¶*taste wine* 酒の味を鑑定する. ¶Good *wine* is *thrown away* upon me. 僕はよいぶどう酒を飲んでも分からない. ¶*try wine* before buying 買う前にぶどう酒を飲んで見る. ¶*water wine* 酒に水を割る. ¶*work* a *wine* ぶどう酒の素を発酵させる.
V² This *wine* does not *agree* with me. この酒は私の口に合わない. ¶Our *wine* is *running short*. 家のぶどう酒が残り少なになった.
Q *adulterated wines* 混ぜ物をしたぶどう酒. ¶*dry* (*sweet*) *wine* 甘くない(甘い)ぶどう酒. ¶*Good wine* needs no bush. 品が良ければ広告はいらない. ¶*light wine* of claret type 赤ぶどう酒系のさっぱりしたぶどう酒. ¶*medicated wines* 薬用ぶどう酒. ¶*rough wine* 渋いぶどう酒. ¶*strong wine* 強い酒.
P call *for wine* first まず酒を命じる. ¶indulge *in wine* 酒にふける ‖ when *in wine* 酒がはいると, 酔うと. ¶a glass *of wine* 一杯のぶどう酒. ¶under the influence *of wine* 酒の勢で. ¶May I help you *to* some *wine*? 少しぶどう酒をお注ぎしましょうか. ¶serve a guest *with wine* 客に酒を出す.

winebowl, *n.* 酒杯.
P drown worldly cares *in* the *winebowl* 一杯やって浮世の苦労を忘れる.

wing, *n.* 翼.
V *add* a new *wing* to the building 建物に新しい翼を付け

る. ¶a dove ***beating*** its *wings* 羽ばたきするはと. ¶The bird ***broke*** its *wing*. その鳥はつばさをくじいた. ¶A cock ***clapped*** his *wings* and crowed. おんどりが羽ばたきして時をつくった. ¶the ***east*** *wing* of a hospital 病院の東そで. ¶***flap*** the *wings* 羽ばたきする. ¶***fold*** its *wings* 羽をおさめる. ¶***furl*** (***unfurl***) the *wings* 羽をすぼめる(ひろげる). ¶It is ten years since he produced the first speed wagon and ***gave*** *wings* to deliveries. 彼が最初の快速運搬車を造って配達が迅速にできるようになってから十年になる. ¶***spread*** *wings* 翼を広げる. ¶***take*** *wing* 翼で飛ぶ ‖ Money ***takes*** *wing*. 金がどんどんなくなる.

Q the leader of the disruptive ***left*** *wing* 破壊的左翼の首領 ‖ the vociferous ***left*** *wing* (=leftists) 騒がしい左翼. ¶The ***healing*** *wings* of sleep descended on the patient. 病人は回復の眠りに落ちた. ¶***untried*** *wings* まだ飛んだ経験のないつばさ.

Q^2 ***butterfly*** *wings* ちょうの羽根. ¶***theater*** *wings* 舞台の両そで.

P a sparrow wounded ***in*** the *wing* 羽を傷めたすずめ. ¶birds (insects) ***on*** (=***upon***) the *wing* 飛ぶ鳥(など) ‖ fly ***on*** the *wings* of the wind 風の翼に乗って飛ぶ ‖ But time is ***on*** the *wing* and so must we be. しかし時がぐんぐん立って行くからわれわれは急がなければならない(話などの場合). ‖ wafted ***on*** the *wings* of the wind 風の翼にはこばれて. ¶The hen gathers her chickens ***under*** her *wings*. めんどりがひなを羽の下に集める. ¶move ***through*** the air ***with*** *wings*. [鳥が]空を飛ぶ.

wing, *v.* 飛ぶ.

M *wing* ***homeward*** [鳥が]ねぐらに帰る; [飛行機が]基地に帰る.

winger, *n.* [左右]翼の人.

Q the ***Left*** *Wingers* 左翼の連中.

wingspread, *n.* 翼長.

Q^2 The plane has a ***200-foot*** *wingspread*. 同機は翼長二百フィートある.

wink, *n.* 一まばたき, 目くばせ(ウインク).

V I ***got*** hardly a *wink* of sleep. 私はほとんどまんじりともしなかった. ¶He ***gave*** me a *wink*. 彼は私に目くばせをした. ¶I have not ***slept*** one *wink*. 私はまんじりともしなかった. ¶***tip*** the *wink* 目くばせをする.

Q a ***deliberate*** *wink* 念入りな目くばせ. ¶a wonderfully ***emphasizing*** *wink* はっとするような強いウインク. ¶return with a ***knowing*** *wink* 心得たとウインクで応答する. 【類】She gave me a ***knowing*** *wink*. ¶with a ***sly*** *wink* ずるそうに目くばせして.

P ***with*** a *wink* at ... …に目くばせして.

wink, *v.* 目くばせ(ウインク)する.

M *wink* ***impudently*** at ... 図々しく…にウインクする. ¶*wink* ***knowingly*** at ... 心得顔に…に目くばせする. ¶*wink* ***sardonically*** at... あざ笑うように…に目くばせする. ¶*wink* ***significantly*** ...に意味深のウインクをする. ¶*wink* ***slyly*** at ... …にずるそうに目くばせする.

P He *winked* ***at*** me. 彼は私に目くばせをした. ‖ *wink* (= connive) ***at*** one's fault (wrong, carelessness) その落度(など)を大目に見る. 【類】The police *winked* ***at*** the offenders (犯人).

winner, *n.* 勝利者.

V ***pronounce*** (=***declare***) ... the *winner* …を受賞者として発表する.

Q a ***probable*** *winner* 勝ちそうな人.

Q^2 become ***bread*** *winners* and home makers 自活して世帯を持つ. ¶an ***essay contest*** *winner* 懸賞論文の入選者. ¶a ***many-times*** *winner* 度重なる受賞者. ¶a ***medal*** *winner* ≒a medalist メダル受賞者(ゴルフなどの) ‖ a ***Medal Honor*** *winner* 《米》名誉勲章受領者. ¶***Nobel Prize*** *winners* in literature ノーベル文学賞受賞者 ‖ a ***1937 Nobel Prize*** *winner* 一九三七年度ノーベル賞受賞者. ¶a ***prize*** *winner* twice in succession 二回連続受賞者 ‖ a ***prize*** *winner* in a Better Babies Contest 赤ちゃんコンクールで入賞した赤ん坊. ¶the ***second*** (***third, fourth***) ***place*** *winners* 第二(三, 四)席の入賞者. ¶individual and ***team*** *winners* 個人賞受賞者及び団体賞受賞者. ¶a ***three-time*** *winner* of the Pulitzer Prize for drama ピューリツアー戯曲賞三回受賞者.

P^2 *winners* ***in*** a lottery くじに当った人たち ‖ the *winner* ***in*** a debating competition for the ... prize 討論会で…賞を受けた人. ¶he is declared the *winner* ***of*** the Gold Medal offered by ... 彼は…の提供にかかる金杯受賞者たるむねが発表された ‖ The *winner* ***of*** the Nobel prize for literature for 1953 一九五三年度のノーベル文学賞(など)受賞者.

O He was pronounced the *winner*. 彼の勝と発表された.

winnow, *v.* [穀物の]もみがらをとる.

Q *winnow* the chaff ***from*** the grain 穀類をひにかけてもみがらを取る.

winter, *n.* 冬.

V He ***numbers*** eighty *winters*. 彼は八十の高齢である. ¶***pass*** the *winter* on the south coast 南海岸で冬を過す.

V^2 The *winter* is ***coming on***. 冬が近づいている. ¶*Winter* ***creeps on***. 冬が知らない間に来る. ¶The *winter* has ***set in***. 冬になった.

Q a ***bleak*** *winter* 荒涼たる冬. ¶the rigors of ***blizzardy*** *winters* ふぶき立つ寒い冬のきびしさ. ¶a ***chilly*** *winter* 冷たい冬. ¶a ***cold*** *winter* 厳冬. ¶a rather ***cool*** *winter* わりかた寒くない(暖い)冬. ¶***crisp*** *winter* 乾燥してぴりぴりする冬. ¶***early*** *winter* 初冬. ¶a ***fresh*** *winter* きびきびした冬. ¶a ***frigid*** *winter* 酷寒の冬. ¶a ***frosty*** *winter* 霜の降る冬. ¶***General Winter*** [戦争の運命を支配する]冬将軍. ¶a ***green*** (=***mild*** *or* an ***open***) *winter* しのぎいい冬. ¶a ***hard*** (=***rigorous*** *or* ***severe***) *winter* 寒さのきびしい冬. ¶the ***hoary*** *winter* 白色(降雪)の冬. ¶an ***icy*** *winter* 結氷の多い冬. ¶a ***mild*** and ***open*** *winter* 暖く雪が積らない冬. ¶a ***raw*** *winter* しめっぽく寒い冬.

P provide ***against*** *winter* 冬の用意をする. ¶***During*** the *winter*, that part of the rice-fields which lie low is left fallow, while the terraces are sown with wheat. 冬の間低地のたんぼには何も作らないでそのままにしておくが山田には小麦をまく. ¶prepare ***for*** the *winter* 冬の支度をする. ¶***in*** *winter* 冬は ‖ ***in*** the *winter* of 1877-78 一八七七年から七八年へかけての冬に. ¶in the depth (=dead) ***of*** *winter* 真冬に. ¶a man ***of*** eighty *winters* 八十の老人. ¶It will keep ***over*** the *winter*. それは冬中保つ. ¶***through*** (= ***throughout***) the *winter* 冬中.

winter, *v.* 冬を過す, 避寒する.

P *winter* ***at*** a coast town 海岸町で越年する. ¶The *winter* is over (=is gone). 冬が過ぎた.

winterize, *v.* 《米》[車など]冬季用の施設をする.

P *winterize* a motor-vehicle ***for*** snow and ice 自動車に冬季用の設備をする.

wipe, *v.* ぬぐう.

M *wipe* ***away*** a reproach 悪評を一掃する ‖ *wiped* her tears ***away*** [女が]その涙をふいた. 【類】The rain then falling *wiped* ***away*** all the footprints (足跡). ¶The blackboard has been *wiped* ***clean***. 黒板はきれいにふきとられた. ¶*wipe* dishes ***dry*** さらの水をふき取る. ¶It was *wiped* ***out*** from his memory. それは彼の頭から抜けた. ‖ *wipe* ***out*** human lives 全滅させる ‖ *wipe* ***out*** enemy remnants 残敵を掃とうする ‖ *wipe* ***out*** injustice 不正を一掃する ‖ It threatens to *wipe* ***out*** the industry. それはその産業をつぶす恐れがある. ‖ *wipe* ***out*** these difficulties これらの困難を除去する ‖ *wipe* ***out*** the economic sore spots that breed war 戦争を醸成する経済の痛手を除去する ‖ *wipe* ***out*** old traditions 古い伝統をたち切る ‖ *wipe* ***out*** all traces of militarism 軍国主義の傷跡をぬぐいとる ‖ *wipe* ***out*** one's chances 切角の好機を逸する ‖ *wipe* ***out*** the bureaucracy of the Education Ministry 文部省の官僚主義を一掃する ‖ *wipe* ***out*** black markets やみ市を一掃する ‖ Properties of the well-to-do have been *wiped* ***out***. 金持どもは財産を失った. ‖ Airplanes have almost *wiped* ***out*** distances. 航空機で距離というものがほとんどなくなった. ‖ *wipe* ***out*** wrongs by reconciliation 話合いで苦情の種を除く ‖ Their savings were nearly all *wiped* ***out*** by a bad investment. 彼らの貯金はまずい投資でほとんどなくなってしまった. ‖ completely *wipe* it ***out*** それを完全にぬぐい取る ‖ *wipe* ***out*** deficits 赤字をなくする ‖ *wipe* ***out*** losses 損失を埋める. ¶It cannot be ***summarily*** *wiped* out of existence. それは容易に撲滅されるものではない.

P *wipe* tears ***from*** the eyes 目から涙をぬぐう. ¶It will be *wiped* ***off*** the face of the earth. それは地球上から姿を消すであろう. ‖ *wipe* ***off*** (=settle) old scores 旧債を済ませる; 古い恨みをはらす. ¶The wicked must be *wiped* ***out of*** existence. 悪人は撲滅せねばならない. ¶*wipe* it ***with*** a handkerchief (sponge, one's sleeve) それをハンカチ(など)でぬぐう.

wire, *n.* 針金; 電線; 電報.

V The telephone *wires* were ***kept busy*** with inquiries. [名士の病気などで]見舞の電話が引っ切りなしにかかった. ¶***lay on*** electric *wire* 電線を引く. ¶***pull*** [the] *wires* かげで操る. ¶***reel*** *wire* 針金を巻く. ¶***send*** a *wire* 電報を打つ. ¶***tap*** electric *wires* 盗電する ‖ ***tap*** a telephone *wire* [電工

が修理のため]電線を調べる. ¶The gale ***tore down*** telegraph *wires.* 烈風で電線が切断した. ¶***twist together wires*** ワイヤをよりあわせる.

v² a London *wire* to the Asahi, under date [of] the 21st inst., ***runs*** ... 今月二十一日付朝日へのロンドン電報に…とある. ¶a *wire* from Osaka ***says*** that ... 大阪からの電報によれば…

Q the ***aerial wire*** 〖無電〗空中線. ¶***barbed wire*** 有刺鉄線. ¶***coarser wire*** より粗製のワイヤ. ¶lay an ***electric wire*** 電線を張る(敷設する). ¶a ***high-tension wire***=《米》a high-voltage cable 高圧線. ¶***hot*** (=***live***) ***wire*** 電流の通っている線. ¶***fine wire*** 細い針金. ¶awful death by a "***live wire***" 電線に触れての惨死 ‖ He is a ***live wire.*** 《米俗》彼は活動家だ.

Q² ***copper wire*** 銅線. ¶***earth*** (=***ground***) ***wire*** 地線(漏電を地中に導くもの). ¶***fence wire*** かき根用針金. ¶***iron*** (***steel***) ***wire*** 鉄(鋼)線. ¶galvanized ***iron wire*** めっきした鉄線. ¶a ***party wire*** (=line) [電話]共同加入線. ¶by ***return wire*** 打返し電報で. ¶***Telegraph wires*** were broken down in many places. 電線があちこち切れた. ¶***1-inch mesh wire*** 一インチ網線. ¶***overhead*** (***underground***) ***wires*** 地上(下)線. ¶***trolley wires*** 電車の架空線.

P ***by wire*** 電報で. ¶give marching order ***by wire*** 行進の電命を下す ‖ report immediately ***by wire*** 直ちに電報で報告する. 【類】As soon as I hear from him, I will let you know ***by wire.*** ¶in accordance with the instruction ***in*** your *wire* 御電命通りに. ¶draw out gold ***into*** *wire* 金を引延ばして針金にする. ¶colored balls mounted ***on wires*** in countingframes 計算器のかまちにはめられた針金に取り付けた着色珠. ¶send photographs ***over wires*** 写真を電送する. ¶communication either ***with wire*** or ***without*** (=either with or without wire) 有線または無線での通信.

wire, *v.* 打電する.

M ***wire back*** 返電する. ¶***wire immediately*** to ... 直ちに…へ電報で知らせる.

P ***Wire*** me ***at*** Kobe. 私にあてて神戸へ電報を打って下さい. ¶***wire for*** a person 電報を打って人を呼ぶ. ¶***wire to*** ... ...に電報を打つ.

wireless, *n.* 無線; 《英》ラジオ.

V I ***received*** a *wireless* from 私は…から無線電信を受けた.

P send a message ***by wireless*** (=radio) 無線電報を打つ ‖ news transmitted ***by wireless*** 無線によるニュース. ¶hear baseball ***on*** the *wireless* (=radio) ラジオで野球の試合を聞く. ¶He is to be heard occasionally in lecture halls or ***over*** the *wireless.* 彼は折々講堂やラジオで講演をする.

wire-web, *n.* 電線網.

Q ***aerial*** and ***subteranean*** ***wire-webs*** 空中及び地中の電線網.

wiring, *n.* 配線.

Q ***Defective wiring*** is one of the causes of fire. 不完全な配線は火災の一原因をなしている. ¶***electric wiring*** 電力配線. ¶***indoor wiring*** 内線.

wisdom, *n.* 知恵; 賢明; 知識.

V ***appreciate*** the *wisdom* of the suggestion その賢明な提言の真価を認める. ¶We generally ***attach*** *wisdom* to those who guess right. われわれは一般に正しい推察をする者を知者だとする. ¶Let us ***consider*** the *wisdom* of following his advice. 彼の助言に従うのが賢明であるかどうか審議しよう. ¶I venture to ***dispute*** the *wisdom* of the policy. 私はそれは策を得たものでないと断言したい. ¶I ***doubt*** the *wisdom* of the course on which they are embarking. 私は彼らが現に採っている方針の妥当性を疑う. ¶***endorse*** the *wisdom* of such an expedient こうした便法を取るのが得策だと裏書する. ¶***get*** *wisdom* 知恵がつく. ¶we have yet to ***learn*** the *wisdom* of ... …することがいいかどうかまだ分からない. ‖ ***learn*** *wisdom* at a very bitter school にがい経験をして悟る ‖ He had ***learned*** the *wisdom* of going early. [良い席を取るには]早く行くのに限るということを知っていた. ¶The case would ***overtax*** the *wisdom* of Solon. その事件はソロンのような名裁判官の手にも余る. ¶***pour forth*** *wisdom* 名言を吐く. ¶I ***question*** the *wisdom* of his methods. 私は彼のやり口はどうかと思う. ¶it is to be hoped that Congress can be made to ***see*** the *wisdom* of ... 議会が…するのが得策だということを知るようにしたいものだ. ¶***seek*** *wisdom* from a priest 牧師から知恵を借りる. ¶He ***showed*** his *wisdom* in refraining from it. 彼がそうしなかったのは賢い.

v² It represents the best that human *wisdom* could ***devise.*** それは人知の企図しうる最善である.

Q Teachers hand on their ***acquired*** *wisdom* to their pupils and so extend individual life. 教師はその獲得した知恵をその弟子に伝えかくして個人的生活を拡大する. ¶***borrowed*** *wisdom* 入れ知恵. ¶***calm*** *wisdom* 落ちついた賢明さ. ¶***collective*** *wisdom* 衆知. ¶the ***combined*** *wisdom* of ... …が持寄った知恵. ¶He is laden with ***commercial*** *wisdom.* 彼は商売のこつを心得ている. ¶It is of ***doubtful*** *wisdom.* それはどうかと思う. ¶***far-seeing*** *wisdom* 先見の明. ¶***learned*** *wisdom* 学んだ知識, 学識. ¶***political*** *wisdom* 政治上の知恵. ¶rich in ***practical*** (=worldly) *wisdom* 世故にたけた. ¶show ***profound*** *wisdom* 英知のあることを示す. ¶***refulgent*** *wisdom* 光彩を放つ知性. ¶***ripe*** *wisdom* 円熟した賢明さ. ¶that mine of ***scientific*** *wisdom,* Chamber's Technical Dictionary あの科学知識の宝庫, すなわちチェンバーの技術用語辞典. ¶Sincerity is ***true*** *wisdom.* 誠実は真の知恵である. ¶the ***ultimate*** *wisdom* of adopting the broad gauge [鉄道の]広軌を採用することの究極の利益. ¶***worldly*** *wisdom* 世才.

Q² a repository of ***housekeeping*** *wisdom* 家政の知識の泉.

P advance (=increase *or* grow) ***in*** *wisdom* 知恵が進む. ¶a man ***of*** *wisdom,* truth, and goodness 知・真・徳を具えた人. ¶people ***with*** profound *wisdom* 非常に賢明な人々.

P² There is great *wisdom* ***in*** the saying "Seek to have less rather than more." 「足るを知れ」ということは誠に知言である. ¶the *wisdom* ***of*** the creator 造化の妙 ‖ He has the *wisdom* ***of*** Solomon. ソロモンのような大賢人だ.

wise, *n.* 方法, 風(ふう).

Q in ***any*** *wise*=at all どうしても. ¶He is in ***no*** *wise* a gentleman. 彼はどう見ても紳士ではない.

P labelled respectively ***in*** this *wise*: それぞれ次のようにレッテルが張ってある ‖ A conversation is often commenced ***in*** this *wise* (=manner). 会話の口切りはよくこんな風なことがある.

wise, *a.* 賢い, 賢明な, 利口な; 知っている.

M he was *wise* ***enough*** to ... 彼は賢明にも…した. ¶be ***worldly*** *wise* 世なれている.

P He is *wise* ***beyond*** his years. 彼は年に似合わず利口だ. ¶be none the *wiser* ***for*** ... …でも一向に分からない. 【類】I was none the *wiser* ***for*** his explanation. ¶He is *wise* ***in*** money matters. 彼は金銭上のことにかけては利口だ. ‖ *wise* ***in*** council, brave in war 善謀善戦 ‖ *wise* ***in*** the ways of the world 世故にたけた. ¶It was *wise* ***of*** you to keep out of debt. 君が借金をしないのは利口だ. ¶get *wise* ***to*** ..., =become aware of ... 《米》…が分かってくる ‖ Everybody who is *wise* ***to*** flying will be an idol among women. 《米》[飛行機] 操縦士はみんな女性の偶像である. ‖ I am *wise* ***to*** your game. その手は食わない.

O He was *wiser* than his generation in this respect. 彼はこの点では同時代の人々より賢かった.

wish, *n.* 願い; *pl.* 願望, 好意.

V Please ***accept*** my hearty *wishes* as well as my word of appreciation. 私の賛辞とともに心からなる好意を受けて頂きたい. ¶Every *wish* was ***anticipated.*** かゆい所に手が届くといった工合だった. ¶***anticipate*** and ***gratify*** every *wish* あらゆる願望を察して満足させる. ‖ She always ***anticipates*** my *wishes.* 彼女はいつも私が言わない先に気をきかしてやってくれる. ¶***ascertain*** their *wishes* in the matter この問題についての彼らの希望を確める. ¶***attain*** one's *wishes* その希望を達成する. ¶***carry*** one's *wishes* into effect その希望を実現させる. ¶***carry out*** our *wishes* われわれの希望通りにする. ¶***consult*** her *wishes* 彼女の希望をたずねる. ¶kindly ***convey*** the best *wishes* of Mrs. ... to ... …へ…夫人からくれぐれもよろしくとお伝え下さい. ¶I have never ***denied*** him a *wish.* 彼の望むことは一度も私はこばんだことはない. ¶***dictate*** one's *wishes* to ... …の希望の達成を命じる. ¶It ***echoes*** the universal *wish.* それは一般の希望を言表わしたものだ. ¶***exchange*** mutual good *wishes* 互にあいさつを交す. ¶***express*** a *wish* that ... …という希望を述べる ‖ ***express*** a *wish* for good luck 御成功を祈ると言う ‖ ***express*** one's *wish* against ...=deprecate (*v.*) ... …を排斥する. ¶***extend*** one's best *wishes* to ... その厚意を…に述べる ‖ I ***extend*** my best *wishes* for the success of your venture. お仕事が成功することを心から祈っています. ¶***follow*** the *wishes* of the donors 寄贈者の希望通りにする.

¶*form* (=*make*) a *wish* 希望を起す. ¶*fulfill* one's *wish* その希望をとげる ‖ The god is reputed for his ability to *fulfill* the *wishes* of worshippers. その神様は霊験あらたかであるという評判だ. ¶I am sorry I cannot *further* your *wishes*. お気の毒ですが御希望には添いかねます. ¶*gain* a *wish* 希望を達する. ¶She *got* her *wish*. 彼女の願い通りになった. ¶*give* their good *wishes* to Japan 日本に彼らの好意を寄せる. ¶He never *gives up* a *wish* once made. 彼は一度思い立ったことは決して捨てない. ¶*grant* a *wish* 願いを一つかなえてやる. 【類】I will *grant* you three *wishes*. ¶*gratify* her *wishes* 彼女の希望を満足させる. ¶*have* a *wish* to ... ...したい気がある ‖ He *has* a great *wish* to go abroad. 彼は非常に洋行したがっている. ‖ I *have* no *wish* to find fault with him, but ... 彼のあら捜しをしたくはないが... ‖ *have* every *wish* anticipated かゆい所に手が届くようにされる ‖ You *have* our best *wishes*. われわれは心から御健康(成功など)を祈っています. ¶*indicate* one's *wish* to ... ...したいという自分の希望を示す. ¶*intimate* one's *wish* その希望を告げる. ¶*lay* one's *wishes* before ... ...に希望を述べる. ¶he *left* a written *wish* that ... 彼は...という願いを書残して行った. ¶*make* one's *wishes known* その希望を発表する. ¶*meet* one's *wishes* その希望に添う. 【類】*meet* every *wish* of his. ¶*obtain* (=*realize*) one's *wish* その願いがかなう. ¶*offer* good *wishes* for the New Year to ... ...に新年の祝辞を述べる ‖ *offer* the team my best *wishes* for success in its fight against ... ...との試合での勝利のお祝をそのティームに述べる. ¶*receive* the good *wishes* of ... ...の祝辞を受ける. ¶I heartily *reciprocate* your good *wishes*. 御好意に対して厚くお礼を申上げます. ¶heartily *re-echo* the *wishes* expressed by ... ...の述べた希望を心から賛成する. ¶*resist* one's *wishes* その念願を制する. ¶*respect* the *wishes* of ... ...の意志を尊重する. 【類】She ought to *respect* her husband's *wishes*. ¶*satisfy* one's every *wish* その言いなり放題にさせる. 【類】an obsequious shopman (おついしょうのうまい店員) anxious to *satisfy* her every expressed or unexpressed *wish*. ¶He did not live to *see* his *wish* become an actual fact. 彼は自分の希望が実現するのを見るまで生きていなかった. ¶*send* one's *wishes* for the success of ... ...の成功を切に希望するむねを申し送る. ¶*signify* one's *wishes* to ... ...にその希望を開陳する. ¶*specify* the *wish* 希望を明示する. ¶*tender* our warmest *wishes* to ... ...にわれわれの切なる希望を申し出る. ¶*voice* the *wishes* of ... ...の希望を声明する.

V^2 To you all *go* my best *wishes*. 私は諸君一同に対して私の好意を表明する.

Q one's *constant wish* 宿願. ¶the *dearest wish* of his heart 彼が心に持つ最も切なる念願. ¶vaguely *defined wishes* ばく然とした念願. ¶an *earnest wish* 切ない望み. ¶carry out his *father's wishes* 父の希望通りやる. ¶express a *fervent wish* that ... ...という切なる希望を述べる. ¶With the *heartiest good wishes* for 1958—and all time! 一九五八年並びに将来に対しあなたの御清福をお祈りして(年賀状など). ¶carry out the lady's *last wishes* その婦人の臨終の願いをかなえてやる. ¶realize one's *long-cherished wish* 宿願がかなう. ¶the fulfilment of a *long-fostered wish* 宿願成就. ¶by *mutual wish* 相方の希望で. ¶Their *several wishes* shall be met. 彼らのそれぞれの願望をかなえさせてやる. ¶a *sincere* and *heart-felt wish* 誠心誠意の願望. ¶That he will soon recover and be once again hard at work is the *warm wish* of all who know him. 彼が早く回復して再び張り切って働くようになることを彼の知人は皆熱望している. ¶a *widespread wish* was expressed that he should continue in office. 彼が引続きその職にあるようにとの希望を持っている人が多数あった.

P The offer is far *above* my *wish*. 私にとってはその申出はうま過ぎる. ¶much *against* her *wish* 彼女の希望とは大分違って. ¶*at* the *wish* of his parents 彼の両親の希望によって ‖ *at* his own *wish* 彼自身の希望で. ¶*by* his *wish* 彼の希望で. ¶Many thanks for your kind letter *of* New Year's *wishes*. 新年の御祝詞を頂きまして誠に有難う. ¶contrary *to* the expressed *wishes* of the dead 故人の希望に反して ‖ in obedience *to* the express[ed] *wish* of ... ...のたっての希望により. ¶in accordance *with* his *wish* 彼の希望によって ‖ *With* all best *wishes*, in which my sisters join me. 御気げんよう, 妹たちもよろしく申上げてくれということです. 【類】*with* every good *wish*.

P^2 with the best *wishes for* the happy New Year 新年をお祝いして. 【類】with my kindest *wishes for* your wife and family as well as yourself. ¶It is the earnest *wish of* every one in this country. それはわが国においてだれしも切望している所である.

wish, *v*. 欲する.

M he is *always wishing* to ... 彼は絶えず...したがっている. ¶I *confidently wish* him success in ... 確信して私は彼の...における成功を祈る. ¶*cordially wish* it a success 心からその成功を祈る. ¶By succeeding I would *dearly wish* to pay back even an infinitesimal part of your kindness to me. 成功したらぜひ万分の一の御恩返しをいたしたいと念願しています. ¶I *earnestly wish* I could have been present. 私はほんとうに出席ができたらよかったと思う. ¶We *fervently wish* all our patrons a happy and prosperous New Year. われわれはお得意各位につつしんで新年のお祝いを申上げます. ¶I *heartily* (=*sincerely*) *wish* you every success. 私は心から御成功をお祈りします. 【類】We *heartily wish* success to him in his praiseworthy enterprise. ‖ I *heartily wish* him "Many happy returns of the day" 心から彼の誕生日をお重ねになることを願う. ¶*much* as I *wish* to go 行きたいのは山々だが. ¶We *wish particularly* for our readers a happy and prosperous New Year. われわれは特に読者諸君の幸福にして栄ある新年を迎えられんことをお祈りします. ¶if I am allowed to *wish so much* 欲を言えば. ¶I *wish* you *well* at the Coronation. 私はあなたに戴冠式の祝意を述べる. ‖ *wish* a person *well* (*ill*) 人の幸(不)運を祈る. 【類】He never ceases to *wish* me *well*.

P I do not *wish for* charcoal; we have plenty. 炭はいらない, たくさんあるから. ‖ I do not *wish for* the business. 私はその取引を希望しない. ‖ this is devoutly to be *wished for* as ... ...であるからこのことは切望にたえない ‖ Do you *wish for* any particular brand. 何か特別のレッテルの品[種]が御入用なのですか. 【類】*wish for* something better / If you *wish for* peace, prepare for war. / Those who *wish for* a day's leisurely enjoyment are advised to trust entirely to their legs after reaching the station. / I *wish for* the volume the most signal success. / I *wish for* it all the success it so richly deserves. ¶I *wish to* Heaven I were now in London. 今僕がロンドンにいたら実によいのだが.

O I *wish* to take this opportunity to ... この機会に私は...したい. ¶I *wish* it might prove true. ほんとになればよいが. 【類】Little girls *wish* they might have a dozen birthdays in one year; big girls wish they might have one birthday in a dozen years.

wishful, *a*. 念願とする.

P be *wishful for* happy days 幸福の日を待ち望んでいる. ¶He is *wishful in* prompt aid. 彼は急援を望んでいる.

wit, *n*. 知恵; 機知, しゃれ; 機知に富んだ人.

V *exercise* one's *wits* 頭を働かせる. ¶*fillip* (=*stimulate*) one's *wits* 知恵をしぼる. ¶*gather* one's scattered *wits* 乱れた気を落着ける. ¶a woman who *has* her *wits* about her 抜目のない女. ¶He *keeps* his *wits* about him. 彼は抜かりがない. ¶*lose* one's *wit* 発狂する. ¶He is interested in *matching wits* with trout. 彼はます釣りが好きだ. ¶*perpetrate* a *wit* しゃれを飛ばす. ¶*set* one's *wits* to work 気転をきかせる. ¶a mode of *sharpening* one's *wits* 知恵をみがく方法. ¶*strain* one's *wits* その知恵袋をしぼる. ¶*use* one's *wits* 頭を使う. ¶*work* one's *wits* 頭を働かせる.

Q a *cheap wit* だじゃれ. ¶He is not the *comic wit* that explodes the reader into a huge guffaw of laughter and vanishes. 彼には読者を爆笑させて姿を消すといったしゃれたことはできない. ¶the *delicate wit*, the ease, the gaiety of his style その文に見られる軽いかいぎゃく, 気軽さ, 陽気さ. ¶*incisive* (=*keen or trenchant*) *wit* 鋭い才知. ¶*innate wit* 生得の機知. ¶*lambent wit* 軽妙な才気. ¶He has a *pretty wit*. 彼には相当の機知がある. ¶have *quick* (=*nimble*) *wits* 気転がきく. ¶*ready wit* とん知. ¶a man of *slow wits* とんまな人.

Q^2 a conversation full of *mother* (=native) *wit* and good sense 生得の機知と良識に満ちた会話.

P live *by* one's *wits* 一定の生業なくやりくりでその日を送る ‖ the most wonderful thing ever invented *by* the *wit* of man これまでの人知による発明の中で最も驚異に値するもの. ¶a flash *of wit* 機知のひらめき. ¶frightened *out of* one's *wits* あわてて ‖ A proverb is the wisdom of men and the *wit* ***of*** one. ことわざは衆人の知恵を個人の機知でまとめたものである.

wit, *v*. 知る.

O to *wit*=that's to say, namely 即ち ‖ one of the most popular romances ever written, to *wit*, "Don Quixote" 古来最も好評を博した伝奇小説の一つすなわちドン・キホーテ.

with, *prep*. と共に.

M I am ***entirely with*** him when he says ... 彼の…という意見は大いにわが意を得たものだ. ¶ ***Simultaneously with*** ... …と同時に. ¶ ***so with*** this case この場合も同様である.

withdraw, *v*. 撤回する, 引下がる.

M The troops are being ***gradually*** *withdrawn*. 軍隊は徐徐に撤退している. ¶ *withdraw* oneself ***entirely*** from society and the world 全く世を捨てる.

P He has *withdrawn* ***from*** his office. 彼は役所をやめた. ‖ *withdraw* ***from*** engagement 約束を取消す ‖ *withdraw* ***from*** membership 脱会する. 【類】His name is *withdrawn* ***from*** the list. / *withdraw* ***from*** the presence of the Emperor. ¶ *withdraw* ***into*** a corner すみへ引込む. ¶ *withdraw* ***to*** one's den その居間へ引下がる.

withdrawal, *n*. 脱退.

Q² restrict ***bank withdrawals*** 銀行の預金引出しを制限する. 【類】the limit in ***bank withdrawals*** to ¥300 per month per household head and ¥100 per month for each additional number of the family (家族一人増すごとに). ¶ the limitation of ***deposit withdrawals*** 預金引出しの制限. ¶ a ***mass withdrawal*** from the party その会からの大挙脱退.

P² *withdrawal* ***from*** membership 脱会 ‖ *withdrawal* ***from*** consideration 不問に付すること ‖ *withdrawal* ***from*** ordinary life 遁世. ¶ *withdrawal* ***of*** recourse 上訴の取下げ.

wither, *v*. しぼむ.

M The flowers have *withered* ***away*** (=***up***). 花がしぼんでしまった.

P it *withers* ***into*** insignificance when placed alongside ... それは…と比べると顔色なしである.

within, *n*. 内部.

P by spontaneous movement ***from within*** 内部からの自発的行動によって ‖ The door opens ***from within***. 戸は内側から開く.

without, *prep*. なく.

M The rumor is ***entirely without*** the foundation. その風説は全く事実無根である. ‖ ***entirely without*** reason ただ訳もなく. ¶ ***well-nigh without*** number ほとんど無数に.

witness, *n*. 証明; 証人.

V Your compassion ***bears witness*** to your noble spirit. あなたの御同情はあなたが高潔な精神の持主である証拠です. ‖ I can ***bear witness*** from my own observation. 私はその目撃者として証明を与えることができる. ¶ ***interrogate*** a *witness* 証人を審問する. ¶ A *witness* was ***summoned*** to appear in court. 一証人が法廷に出頭するよう召喚された. ¶ ***swear*** a *witness* 証人に宣誓させる.

Q bear ***ample*** *witness* to ... …を十分証明する. ¶ ***auricular*** *witness* 聞いた事実を立証する証人. ¶ bear ***conclusive*** *witness* against ... 徹底的に…を反証する. ¶ a ***credible*** *witness* 信頼できる証人. ¶ ***disinterested*** *witnesses* 私利私情にとらわれない証人. ¶ bear ***eloquent*** *witness* to the truth of ... …の真実性を雄弁に立証する. ¶ bear ***false*** *witness* against ... …に不利な偽証をする. ¶ an ***invisible*** *witness* of the scene その場を物の陰から見た人. ¶ a ***living*** *witness* 生き証人. ¶ a ***lying*** *witness* 偽証する証人. ¶ a ***perjured*** *witness* 偽証した証人. ¶ bear ***remarkable*** *witness* to ... …に対し注目すべき立証をする. ¶ an important ***relevant*** *witness* その事件の有力な参考人. ¶ bear ***silent*** *witness* to ... …を暗默の内に証明する. ¶ a ***trustworthy*** *witness* 信頼するに足る証人.

Q² a ***defense*** *witness* 被告の証人 ‖ be called as a ***defense*** *witness* at a trial 裁判に被告側証人として召喚される. ¶ an ***eye*** *witness* of the scene その光景の目撃者 ‖ one ***eye*** *witness* is worth more than ten ***ear*** *witness[es]*. 一人の見証人は十人の伝聞者よりも確かである(法律格言). ¶ an ***expert*** *witness* 鑑定人. ¶ a ***non-expert*** *witness* 一般証人. ¶ a ***prosecution*** *witness* 検事側の証人. ¶ a ***reference*** *witness* 参考人. ¶ a ***subpoena*** *witness* 召喚された証人.

P attend a court of law ***as*** a *witness* 証人として法廷に出頭する. ¶ attested ***by*** a *witness* 証人の証明した. ¶ ***in*** *witness* whereof, I have hereunder set my hand and seal this ... day of ... その証として私は下に署名押印をする, 年月日. ¶ call (=take) ... ***to*** *witness* …を証明してもらう; …を証人に立てる.

P² a *witness* ***against*** the accused 被告に不利な証人. ¶ The earthquake was believed to be a *witness* ***to*** the wrath of God. その地震は神の怒りの証拠であると信じられた. ‖ He is a *witness* ***to*** my personality. あの人が私の人格を保証してくれます. ¶ a *witness* ***under*** subpoena 喚問を受けている証人.

witness, *v*. 証言する.

P *witness* ***against*** (***for***) the accused 被告に不(有)利な証言をする.

O He was also a playwright, as *witness* theatrical bills in my possession. 彼がまた劇作家であったことは私の所蔵している芝居のびらで証明ができる.

witticism, *n*. 機知.

Q ***cheap*** *witticism* 安っぽいしゃれ ‖ a ***shallow*** *witticism* 浅薄なかいぎゃく.

wizard, *n*. 魔法使い.

Q a ***financial*** *wizard* 金融界の鬼. ¶ a ***white*** *wizard* 白魔, 善魔.

woe, *n*. 災禍.

V ***denounce*** (=***prophesy***) *woe* upon (=against) ... …の災禍を予言する. ¶ A hasty man never wants *woe*. 性急の人はよく災難にあう. ¶ ***Woe betide*** you if you break your word. なんじ違約せば禍来るべし(約束を破ったらただではすまないぞ).

Q ***common*** *woes* to ... …に共通の悩み. 【類】Sickness and poverty are ***common*** *woes*. ¶ *Woe* ***to*** him that strives with the Maker. 神と争う者こそみじめである.

P He was faithful to me ***in*** weal and *woe*. 彼はよきにつけあしきにつけ私に誠実を尽してくれた. ¶ the weight ***of*** *woe* 押えつけられるようなつらい思い.

P² *woe* [be] ***to*** ... …は禍なるかな, …に禍あれ[のろいの言葉].

wolf, *n*. おおかみ; 飢え.

V ***cry*** *wolf* 虚報を伝える. ¶ The young man sends home monthly fractions of his surplus wealth to ***keep*** the *wolf* from the paternal door. 青年は毎月少しの使い残りを郷里に送って父の一家に飢渇をしのがせている. 【類】Hard work and thrift ***kept*** the *wolf* from the hearth if not from the door. ¶ *Wolves* ***howl***. おおかみがほえる.

P a pack ***of*** *wolves* 一群のおおかみ.

woman, *n*. 女.

V All the universities in the British Isles ***admit*** *women* to membership and degrees. 英国本土の大学はすべて女子の入学を許可しかつこれに学位を授ける. ¶ ***deliver*** a parturient *woman* 助産をする, 赤ん坊をとり上げてやる. ¶ ***enfranchise*** *women* 婦人選挙権を付与する. ¶ Like many of his contemporaries he ***espoused*** a *woman* from the Columbia River tribes. その時代の人にはそうした人が多かったが彼もまたコロンビア河畔のインディアンの娘を妻にした. ¶ ***fish*** a *woman* 女をなびかせようとする. ¶ ***keep*** *women* of ill-fame 売春婦をおく. ¶ ***make*** an honest *woman* of ... [二号など]…を正妻に直す. ¶ ***marry*** a *woman* 妻をめとる; 牧師が女の結婚式を行う. ¶ ***matriculate*** *women* in a university 女子の大学入学を許す. ¶ ***play*** the *woman* めめしく振舞う. ¶ ***rape*** (=***violate or ravish***) a *woman* 強かんする. ¶ *women* ***reclaimed*** from a life of sin 罪の生活から足を洗った女. ¶ ***seduce*** a *woman* 女を誘かいする. ¶ ***shield*** a *woman* 女をかばう. ¶ ***treat*** *women* as mere ministers to one's pleasure=make playthings of women 女をもてあそぶ. ¶ I never will ***understand*** *women*. 女ってわからないものだ.

Q an ***accomplished*** *woman* 多芸な女. ¶ a rather ***agreeable*** *woman* ちょっと感じのいい女. ¶ an ***attractive, witty,*** absolutely "***unmoral***" *woman* of the world 魅力がありとん知がきいているが全くだらしのない世間ずれした女. ¶ an ***awful*** *woman* with the spectacles めがねをかけた恐ろしい女. ¶ a ***barren*** *woman* うまずめ(石女). ¶ I prefer intellectual to physically ***beautiful*** *women*. 私は肉体美よりも理知的な女の方が好きだ. ¶ a ravishingly ***beautiful young*** *woman* 若くてほれぼれする美女. ¶ a ***benevolent*** (***generous, kind, merciful***) *woman* 慈善心のある(大ような, 親切な, なさけ深い)女. ¶ She has established a reputation as one of the ***best-dressed*** *women* in America. 彼女はアメリカ第一流の服装をした女という定評がある. ¶ a ***bony*** *woman* 骨ばった女. ¶ a ***bright modern*** *woman* 明朗な近代的女性. ¶ a ***caged*** *woman* かごの鳥になっている女. ¶ a ***careworn*** *woman* of five and thirty 三十五の心配でやつれた女. ¶ a ***chic*** elderly *woman* 意気なとしま. ¶ a ***childless*** *wom-*

an 子供のない女. ¶She passes herself off as a ***Christian*** *woman*. 彼女はキリスト教徒(白人)と見せかけている. ¶an eminently ***clubbable*** *woman* 大層交際好きの女. ¶a ***comely young*** *woman* かわいらしい若い女. ¶a ***cultured*** *woman* 教養のある女. ¶a ***dark*** (***fair***) *woman* 色の黒い(白い)女. ¶a ***decent*** *woman* 堅気の婦人. ¶a ***delicate*** *woman* きゃしゃな女. ¶a ***demure little*** *woman* 目立って内気な小柄の女. ¶a ***disreputable*** *woman* 評判の悪い女. ¶a ***dissolute*** *woman* 身持の悪い女. ¶a ***domestic*** *woman* 家庭向の婦人. ¶an ***elderly*** *woman* 中年女. ¶confessions of a ***fallen*** *woman* 堕落の女の告白. 【類】***rescue*** a fallen *woman*. ¶a ***fast*** *woman* 男ぐせの悪い女. ¶a ***frail-looking*** *woman* か弱そうな女. ¶a ***fertile*** *woman* 多産の女. ¶a ***fussy*** *woman* 気むずかしい女. ¶***go-ahead*** *woman* 気の勝った女. ¶a rather ***good-looking*** *woman* of forty-odd 四十を越えた水々しい年増女. ¶a ***healthy*** and ***able-bodied*** *woman* 丈夫な体格のよい女. ¶a ***high-bred*** *woman* 育ちのよい女. ¶a ***high-minded*** *woman* 気品の高い女. ¶A very ***homely*** *woman* is often referred to in Japan as having "a face like a sneezing chin." よく日本ではごくきりょうの悪い女を「ちんがくしゃみをしたような顔」をしているという. ¶***humble self-effacing Japanese*** *women* 謙譲の徳を持つ日本の婦人. ¶the ***ideal*** *woman* for whom he yearns 多年あこがれの理想の女. ¶***idle, rich*** *women* 金があって暇のある女(有閑マダム). ¶an ***ill-conditioned*** *woman* 意地の悪い女. ¶***illiterate*** *women* of the slums 長屋の字の読めないおかみさんたち. ¶a ***keen, brisk, little*** *woman* 鋭敏なはきはきした少女. ¶a ***kept*** *woman* かこいもの. ¶***kimono-garbed*** (=***clad***) *women* きものを着た女たち. ¶a ***kindly*** *woman* of the world 世間慣れした親切な婦人. ¶a ***leading*** *woman* 〚映画〛主演する女. ¶a ***leisured*** *woman* 有閑婦人. ¶a ***light*** *woman* しりの軽い女. ¶a ***literary*** *woman* 女流作家. ¶a ***loose*** *woman* だらしない女 ‖ the evils of liquor and ***loose*** *women* 酒と悪い女の害. ¶***lost*** *women* 堕落女. ¶a ***loud*** *woman* 《俗》けばけばしい服装の女. ¶a "***mannish***" *woman* 「Mがかった」女. ¶a ***married*** *woman* 人妻. ¶a ***menstruating*** *woman* 月経期中の婦人. ¶for a ***mere*** *woman* 女のくせに. ¶a religiously ***minded*** *woman* 信仰心のある女. ¶a ***modern-minded young Chinese*** *woman* 新しい型の若い中国女. ¶a ***new*** *woman* 新しい女. ¶a ***noble-faced*** *woman* 上品な顔をした婦人. ¶one of the ***most-talked-of*** *women* of her day 当時評判になった女. ¶an ***older*** *woman* 中年の女. ¶an ***old-young*** *woman* 早くから老こんだ若い女. ¶an ***oversexed*** *woman* 色気たっぷりの女. ¶a very ***passionate*** *woman* きわめて熱情的な女. ¶a ***phlegmatic*** *woman* 冷淡な女. ¶a ***plump*** *woman* 丸々肥えた女. ¶a ***pretty*** *woman* 美人. ¶***professional*** *women* 職業婦人. ¶a ***public*** *woman* 遊女. ¶a ***respectable*** *woman* かたぎの女. ¶a ***sharp, clever*** *woman* 利口ですきのない女. ¶an American "***smart***" *woman* すごい米国女. ¶a ***strong, robust*** peasant *women* がん丈な百姓女. ¶a ***stout old*** *woman* でっぷりした老年の女. ¶a ***sweet-faced*** *woman* 愛くるしい顔の女. ¶a ***sweet-mouthed*** *woman* 口先のうまい女. ¶a ***tall*** *woman* with a pale, oval face おもながな顔をした背の高い女. ¶a ***tall, willowy*** *woman* 高くてすらっとした女. ¶a ***tall, hard-featured*** *woman* のっぽで, 固い表情の女. ¶a ***town-bred*** *woman* 都会育ちの女. ¶An ***ugly old*** *woman* serves as a foil to a pretty girl. 醜い老女は美女の引立て役になる. ‖ She was the ***ugliest*** *woman* I ever beheld. 始めてあんな醜い女に出会った. ¶an ***unmarried*** *woman* 未婚婦人. ¶a ***vicious*** *woman* 素行の修まらない女. ¶a ***virtuous*** *woman* 貞節な婦人. ¶a ***wanton*** *woman* 移り気な女. ¶a ***winsome*** *woman* ほれぼれする女. ¶a ***withered old*** *woman* しわくちゃ(梅干)婆さん. ¶a ***womanly*** *woman* 女らしい女. ¶a ***working*** *woman* 勤労婦人 [→ a career woman]. ¶a ***worldly-minded*** *woman* 俗気たっぷりの女.

Q² an ***apple*** *woman* りんご売りの女. ¶a ***Bible*** *woman* 女伝道師. ¶a ***business*** *women* 職業婦人. ¶a sort of ***butterfly*** *woman* who is never really in love with any one 本当の恋愛の味を知らない浮気女. ¶a ***career*** *woman* 職業婦人. ¶a ***club*** *woman* 《米》クラブに出入りする婦人; 社交界の婦人. ¶a ***Diet*** *woman* (=a Dietwoman) 婦人代議士. ¶a ***fireside*** *woman* 家庭的な女. ¶a ***gipsy*** *woman* [放浪民族]ジプシー女. ¶a ***newspaper-woman*** [新聞の]婦人記者. ¶a ***sales*** *woman*=a salesgirl 女店員. ¶a ***sewing*** *woman* 縫い子. ¶a ***society*** *woman* 社交界の婦人. ¶a ***university*** *woman* 女子の大学生または大学出身者.

P talk ***about*** *women* 女の話をする. ¶government ***by*** *women* 女の政治.

P² a *woman* ***among*** ten thousand 万人中にたった一人というような女. ¶a *woman* ***in*** industry 産業婦人. ¶a *woman* ***of*** intellect and culture 教養のある婦人 ‖ a *woman* ***of*** remarkable personality りっぱな人格を具えた婦人 ‖ the *woman* ***of*** one's heart 意中の女 ‖ a *woman* ***of*** the gutter どん底の女 ‖ a *woman* ***of*** pleasure 遊女 ‖ a *woman* ***of*** quality 貴婦人 ‖ a *woman* ***of*** easy virtue みだらな女 ‖ a *woman* ***of*** the world 世間ずれした女. ‖ a *woman* ***of*** the town 街頭の女 ‖ a *woman* ***of*** (=***with***) aristocratic features 貴族的な顔立ちの女.

womanhood, *n.* 女たること; 成女期; [集合的に] 女性.

V on ***reaching*** *womanhood* 一人前の女になって.

Q ***budding*** *womanhood* つぼみの少女期. ¶***early*** *womanhood* 女の若盛り. ¶***Japanese*** *womanhood* 日本の女性. ¶***late*** *womanhood* 女の晩年期. ¶***unfolding*** *womanhood* 女の発育期. ¶wholesome and beautiful ideals of ***useful*** *womanhood* 有用な女性たらんとする健全にしてかつ美しい理想. ¶when she was in ***young*** *womanhood* 彼女の若い時に.

P grow ***to*** *womanhood* 女に成る ‖ She is an honor ***to*** *womanhood*. 彼女は女性の誇りだ.

womanliness, *n.* 女らしさ.

V ***cultivate*** (***lose***) *womanliness* 女らしさを養(失)う.

wonder, *n.* 驚異.

V It ***created*** a nine-days' *wonder*. それはほんの一時の評判に過ぎなかった. ¶***do*** (=perform) *wonders* 人をあっと言わせることをやる ‖ The editor has ***done*** *wonders* of compression. 編集者は文を驚くほどに簡潔にしている. ¶***excite*** our *wonder* 私たちの驚異をあおる. ¶***feel*** *wonder* 驚異を感じる. ¶the strange case of ... ***formed*** a nine days' *wonder* to the people of ... ...の変った事件はほんの一時だけ...の人々のうわさに上った. ¶***inspire*** *wonder* and admiration 深く嘆賞させる. ¶***perform*** *wonders* in the management of ... ...の経営で奇跡を演じる. ¶Co-operation is a giant that can ***work*** *wonders*. 協力は不思議な大事をなしうる巨人である. ‖ It ***works*** *wonders* as a mental tonic. それは不思議に精神的強壮剤になる. 【類】A change of medicine sometimes ***works*** *wonders*. / A vocation like that will ***work*** *wonders* for your nerves.

Q I was seized with ***admiring*** *wonder*. 私は嘆賞おく能わずであった. ¶Is it ***any*** *wonder* that ...? ...に何の不思議があろう. ¶be lost in a ***delirious*** *wonder* われを忘れて驚嘆している. ¶a ***linguistic*** *wonder* 語学の天才. ¶a ***mechanical*** *wonder* 驚くべき機械. ¶The Niagara Falls is one of the ***natural*** *wonders* of the world. ナイアガラばく布は世界の天然奇観の一つである. ‖ It may be a ***nine-day's*** *wonder* among them. それは彼らの間の一時的評判に過ぎぬかも知れない. ¶It is ***no*** *wonder* that he should have succeeded. 彼が成功したのは何も驚くに足らないことだ. ‖ ***No*** *wonder* you didn't go. 君が行かなかったのも無理はない. ‖ He refused the offer and ***no*** *wonder* (=not without reason). 彼はその申し出を断わったがそれは当然だ. ‖ ***No*** *wonder!* 道理で. ¶the ***only*** *wonder* is that ... ただ一つ不思議は...だ. ¶in ***open-eyed*** *wonder* 驚異の目をみはって. ¶***scenic*** *wonders* 勝景. ¶She is a ***real*** *wonder* in grade-school teaching. 彼女は小学教育にかけては実に驚くべき女性である. ¶one of the ***seven*** *wonders* of the world 世界の七不思議の一つ. ¶He gazed at it in ***silent*** *wonder*. 口あんぐりでそれをながめていた. ¶***small*** *wonder* if ... ...としてもさして驚くに足らない ‖ ***Small*** *wonder* [that] disease and filth and wretchedness are domesticated there. そこに病気やきたならしさやむさくるしさが巣を食っているのはむしろ当然と言えよう. 【類】it is ***small*** *wonder* to learn that ... ¶It is a ***technical*** *wonder* to the potters of the present day. それは今日の陶工から見ると驚嘆すべき技術である. ¶an event of ***three days'*** *wonder* 三日もたてばうわさも消えるような事件. ¶***What*** a *wonder!* 驚いたね!

Q² a ***boy*** *wonder* of the classroom クラスの天才児童. ¶a ***child*** *wonder* of golf ゴルフの天才児. ¶a ***college*** *wonder* 天才の大学生. ¶a ***world*** *wonder* 世界の不思議.

P He answered the question correctly yesterday.—Yes, ***for*** a *wonder!* きのう彼は問題を間違えずに答えた.—へーえ, そりゃ驚いた. ‖ gape ***from*** *wonder* あきれて口あんぐり.

¶ gaping *from wonder* びっくりしてあっけにとられて. ¶ he was lost *in wonder* at ... 彼は...にわれを忘れて驚嘆した ‖ All looked on *in wonder*. みんなは驚きあきれてながめていた. ¶ He did it alone *to* a *wonder*. 彼は独力でやったんだ, 驚いたね. ¶ you will see *with wonder* that ... 君は...を見て驚くことだろう.
P² *Wonder of* wonders! 驚くなかれ.
O It is a *wonder* that it did not break. それが破れなかったのが不思議だ.

wonder, *v.* 驚く.
M you may ***well wonder*** that ... ...ことを驚くのも当然だ.
P I *wonder* ***at*** his learning. 私は彼の学識に驚く. ‖ nor is this to be *wondered* ***at*** when it is borne in mind that ... を思えばこれまた驚くに足らないことだ ‖ it is hardly to be *wondered* ***at*** that ... ...だとてさして驚くに足らない.
O I *wonder* whether it will rain tomorrow. あした雨が降るか知ら. ¶ I *wonder* if he will come. 彼は来るか知ら.

wonderful, *a.* 驚くべき.
P His health is *wonderful* ***for*** a man of his age. 彼は年にしては驚いた元気だ. ¶ It is *wonderful* ***in*** the extreme. それは実に驚くべきことだ.
O *wonderful* to say 不思議なことには.

wonderland, *n.* 仙境.
Q a ***scenic*** *wonderland* 風景絶佳の地.

wont, *n.* 習慣.
Q as was his ***frequent*** *wont* 彼がいつもやるように.
Q² as is his ***everyday*** *wont* 彼が毎日のおきまり通り.

woo, *v.* 口説く.
P Soft breezes *wooed* them (=the trees) ***to*** blossoms. 軟風に誘われて木が花を咲かした.

wood, *n.* 森; 木; 材木; *pl.* 《米》森林.
V ***bundle*** *wood* まきを束ねる. ¶ ***burn*** *wood* into charcoal 木を焼いて炭にする. ¶ ***chop*** *wood* with an ax おので木を切る. ¶ ***collect*** *wood* for one's fire 火をたくためにまきを集める. ¶ ***cut*** *wood* 木を切る. ¶ the chief *woods* ***employed*** in building houses are ... 家屋の建築に用いる主な木材は...である. ¶ ***gather*** *wood* for fuel まきを集める. ¶ ***get*** *wood* for a fire たき火のまきをとる. ¶ ***have*** a *wood* before one's dwelling その家の前に森がある. ¶ ***put*** [***in***] (=***lay***) more *wood* on the fire 火にもっとまきをくべる. ¶ ***split*** *wood* まきを割る. ¶ ***thread*** the *wood* 森を縫って行く. ¶ ***tie*** *woods* ***up*** in faggots まきを束ねる. ¶ The honoki ***yields*** a soft whitish *wood*, strong and flexible, used in various manufactures. ほうの木材はやわらかく白く丈夫でしなやかで色々な細工に使用される. ¶ The *wood* is ***rotting***. その材木は腐りかけている.
Q ***choice*** *woods* 名木(材). ¶ ***dead*** *wood* 枯木; 冗語(むだな語). ¶ in the ***deep*** *woods* 奥深い森で. ¶ The town is now situated in the center of a ***dense*** *wood*. 現在その町は密林の真ん中に位置を占めている. ¶ ***fragrant*** *wood* 香木. ¶ ***hard*** (***soft***) *wood* 堅(軟)材. ¶ ***kindling*** *wood* 燃えているまき. ¶ *Woods* are ***pretty*** in the fall. 秋は木々が美しい. ☞ 米語用法では woods を単数に扱うことがある: a thick (=dense) woods. ¶ ***rotten*** *wood* 腐った木材. ¶ ***seasoned*** *wood* 乾燥した材木. ¶ ***shadowy*** *woods* 木陰で薄暗い森. ¶ ***unseasoned*** *wood* 生木. ¶ This is ***virgin*** *woods*. 《米》これは原始林だ.
P Sherries are much fresher and more delicious if drunk ***from*** the *wood* than they are when bottled. シェリーはびん詰よりたるから出して飲む方が余ほど新鮮味が豊かでまたおいしくもある. ¶ beer ***in*** (=***from***) the *wood* [たる入りの]生ビール. ¶ ***out of*** the *woods* 危険(困難)から(脱する) ‖ You are not ***out of*** the *wood* yet. 君はまだ危険だ(用心すべきだ). ¶ wine aged ***in*** *wood* for over fifteen years 十五年以上たる詰になって熟したぶどう酒 ‖ a figure of Daikoku cut in the round ***in*** *wood* 木彫の大黒. ¶ walk ***in*** the *woods* 森林の中を歩く. ¶ an armful ***of*** *wood* 一かかえのまき. ¶ an engraving ***on*** *wood* 木材の彫刻. ¶ walk ***through*** the *wood* 森林を通って行く. ¶ a road paved ***with*** *wood* 木材舗装の道路.
P² *wood* ***for*** fuel まき.

wooded, *a.* 樹木を植えた.
M ***densely*** (=***thickly***) *wooded* hills 樹木の茂った小山. ¶ ***heavily*** *wooded* 樹木の茂った. ¶ ***luxuriantly*** *wooded* 樹木のこんもりした.

woof, *n.* 横糸.
V ***interlace*** silk *woof* with cotton warp 絹のよこ糸に綿のたて糸を混紡する.

wooing, *n.* 求愛.
Q ***unsuccessfull*** *wooing* 不成功に終った求愛.

wool, *n.* 羊毛.
V We ***get*** *wool* from sheep. 羊毛は羊から取る.
V ***shear*** the *wool* from sheep ... 羊から羊毛を刈り取る. ¶ ***wear*** *wool* in winter 冬季には毛ものを着る.
Q ***all*** *wool* 純毛. ¶ Much cry, ***little*** *wool*. 骨折損のくたびれもうけ. ¶ ***reworked*** *wool* 再製羊毛. ¶ ***synthetic*** *wool* 合成毛.
Q² ***cotton*** *wool* 綿毛. ¶ ***part*** *wool* 混紡毛. ¶ ***steel*** *wool* [研ま用の]鋼毛. ¶ a ball of ***knitting*** *wool* 毛糸の玉. ¶ ***virgin*** *wool* 新製羊毛(再製に対し).
P dyed ***in*** the *wool* 糸染めの, トップ染めの; きっすいの. 【類】 a Communist dyed ***in*** the *wool*=a dyed-in-the-wool Communist. ¶ cloth made ***of*** *wool* 羊毛で織った布.

wool[l]en, *n.* 毛製品.
Q² ***baby*** *woolens* 赤ん坊用毛製品類.

word, *n.* 語; [通例無冠詞]ことづて, 音信.
V ***accept*** one's *word* for it その言葉を信じる. ¶ in conclusion we would ***add*** a *word* of grateful acknowledgment to him for ... 最後に...に対し彼に一言感謝の意を付記したい. ¶ ***address*** a few *words* to ... ...に向って一言を申述べる. ¶ ***await*** *word* from ... ...からのさた(たより)を待つ. ¶ ***back up*** one's *words* by one's deeds その言葉を行為によって裏書する. ¶ ***bandy*** *words* with ... ...と言争いをする. ¶ A new slang *word* has been ***born***. 新しい一つの俗語ができた. ¶ I don't ***believe*** a *word* of it. 私はそれを全然信じない. ¶ ***boil down*** several thousand *words* to a couple of pages 数千語を二三ページに縮める. ¶ to ***borrow*** his own *words* 彼自身の言葉を借りて言えば. 【類】 to ***borrow*** the writer's *words*. ¶ A gentleman never ***breaks*** his *word*. 紳士は決して約束を破らない. ¶ Don't ***breathe*** a *word* of this to anyone. このことは一切だれにも漏らすな. 【類】 I will not ***breathe*** a *word* about (=of) it. ¶ a messenger ***brought*** *word* that ... 使いで...ということを言ってよこした ‖ It will ***bring*** a *word* of approval from the lips of the most exacting gourmet. それはいかに口のおごった人でもうまいと言うだろう. ‖ This ***brings*** to mind Victor Hugo's *words*. これでヴイクトル・ユーゴーの言葉が思い出される. ¶ ***capitalize*** a *word* 語を頭文字で始める. ¶ They were uttered in tones so low that he could scarcely ***catch*** the *words*. その言葉は彼にはほとんど聞きとれないほど低かった. ¶ The *words* were ***caught up*** by someone near him. その言葉をだれか彼の近くにいた人が聞付けた. ¶ ***change*** *words* with ... ...と言葉を交わす. ¶ ***Choose*** *words* for the following blanks: 次の空所に適語を入れよ. ¶ ***click away*** one thousand *words* an hour on the typewriter 一時間一千語をタイプライターで打つ. ¶ ***coin*** (=***concoct or cook up***) *words* 新語を造る. ¶ ***cross*** *words* with ... ...とわたり合う. ¶ the *word* "..." shall be ***construed*** as ... 「...」の語は...の意味に解釈してもらいたい. ¶ The book ***contains*** the last *word* in electric science. その本は電気学の権威だ. ¶ ***copy*** *words* on to separate slips 語を別々の紙片に写す. ¶ Unfortunately it is easier to ***criticize*** a *word* than to replace it by a better one. 困ったことには語を不適当だということは容易だが何という語に替えたらよいかを決定するのはむずかしい. ¶ ***cross out*** (=***delete***) a *word* 一語削る. ¶ the *word* is ***derived*** from the name of ... その語は...という名から来た. ¶ ***deserve*** a *word* of mention on account of ... ...であるから一言述べる必要がある. 【類】 ***deserve*** a few *words* in passing (ついでに). ¶ a *word* or two may be ***devoted*** to ... ...について一言述べておくがよかろう. ¶ ***divide*** a *word* correctly 語を正しく分節する(シラブルによって). ¶ I do not ***doubt*** your *word*. 私は君の言葉を疑わない. ¶ ***Drop*** me a *word*. ちょっとたよりを下さい. ‖ let ***drop*** a *word* of praise 一言賞賛の言葉を漏らす. ¶ ***echo*** his *words* 彼の語をそのまま繰返す; その所信に賛成する. ¶ "***edit***" a speaker's *words* [演説を報道する場合など]多少弁士の言葉に手を入れる. ¶ ***enclose*** a *word* in brackets かっこ内へ一語を入れる. ¶ ***enfranchise*** foreign *words* 外国語をその国語に採り入れる. ¶ ***enunciate*** a *word* distinctly 語を明ょりうに発音する. ¶ ***exchange*** a *word* or two of tender greeting with ... ...と一言二言やさしいあいさつの言葉を交わす. ¶ ***expunge*** (=***erase***) *words* of a sentence written on the blackboard 黒板に書いた文から数語を消す. ¶ He ***fathered*** the *word*. 彼がその語の生みの親である. ¶ I cannot ***find*** *words* to thank you. あなたにお礼の申上げようもありません. 【類】 I cannot ***find*** *words* to express my thanks to ... for ... / He was almost

unable to ***find*** any *words* in which to express his gratitude. / It seemed to me then that I should say more, but ***found*** no *words* ready on my tongue. ¶He ***flung*** the *words* in my teeth. 彼は私に向ってその言葉を吐き出すように言った. ¶***follow*** one's *words* closely その言うことを拝聴する. ¶Their initials ***form*** the *words* "Anzacs". それらの頭字をとると Anzacs (=*A*ustralian and *N*ew *Z*ealand *A*rmy *C*orps) という語ができる. ‖ He has a happy capacity for ***forming*** *words*. 彼は新語を造ることが上手だ. ¶This took her breath away and ***froze*** the *words* on her lips. これを見て彼女はびっくりして言葉がのどにつかえてしまった. ¶***fulfil*** the prophetic *words* 予言を実現させる. ¶***gain*** the good *word* of ... ...の賞賛を博する. ¶***get*** a *word* in edgewise 横合から一言口を出す ‖ I just ***got word*** from ... 丁度...から伝言を得た. ¶***give*** the *word* of command 号令をかける ‖ My ***word*** was ***given***, and I was determined to fulfil my engagements. 私は約束したからにはそれを守る決心をしていた. ‖ he ***gave*** his *word* of honor that he would not ... 彼は名誉にかけて...しないと約束した ‖ You ***gave*** us your *word!* 約束はどうした. 【類】 ***Give*** me your *word*. / I ***give*** my ***word*** for it. ‖ against one thing a *word* of caution may be ***given***, and that is, never to ... 一言御注意申し上げておきたいことは決して...なさるなということである. ‖ ***give*** a *word* of approval to ... 承諾の意を...に伝える. ¶properly ***group*** *words* 語を適当に配列する. ¶I ***have*** his *word* for it that she is "very clever," 彼は彼女が「非常に利口だ」と明言している. ‖ For three years his mother ***had*** no *word* from him. 三年間彼の母の所に彼から便りがなかった. ‖ ***have*** a *word* with ... ...とちょっと話をする ‖ I think I'll ***have*** a *word* with him in private. 内々で彼に話したい. ‖ ***have*** *words* with one's wife 妻と口争いをする ‖ ***have*** *words* (=quarrel) together 言い争う. 【類】 ***have*** *words* with another from mutual misunderstanding ‖ I ***have*** a *word* to say against ... 私は...に反対だ. ‖ I ***have*** no *words* to thank you enough. 何ともお礼の申しようもありません. 【類】 I ***have*** no *word* to express my gratitude. / ***have*** no *word* of apology to make. ¶***hear*** the last *words* 臨終の言葉を聞く. ¶We ***hear*** the *word* often ***spoken***. その言葉はよくきく. ¶How often one ***hears*** and ***reads*** *words* like these today. こうした語を今日実によく耳にする. ¶***hunt up*** a *word* in a dictionary 辞書で語を捜す. ¶***hurl*** *words* of thunder at ... ...をどなりつける. ¶***insert*** a *word* between two words 二語の間に一語をはさむ. ¶They failed to ***keep*** their *word*. 彼らは約束を違えた. ¶He does not ***know*** a *word* of German. 彼はドイツ語のドの字も知らない. ¶***lavish*** *words* on ... いたずらに...を喋々(ちょうちょう)論じる. ¶***leave word*** with ... for ... ...あてに伝言を...に頼む ‖ He vanished, ***leaving*** not a *word* behind him. 彼は一言の言いおきもなく姿を消した. ‖ ***leaving word*** that ... ...と言いおいて. 【類】 He ***left*** no *word* as to the object of his call. ‖ ***leave out*** a *word* 一語を抜かす. ¶***look up*** a *word* in a dictionary 語を辞書で引く. ¶***lisp*** a few *words* [幼児・酔っぱらいなど]二言三言むにゃむにゃ言う. ¶***love*** *words* 語を愛する. ¶***make*** a *word* (=converse briefly) with ... ...とちょっと話をする ‖ ***make words*** with ... about ... ...のことで...と言い合いをする. ¶***Mark*** these *words*. この言葉に注意したまえ(いいかね). ‖ ***Mark*** my *words!* よく聞け. ¶speak without carefully ***measuring*** one's *words* 深く考えずに言う. ¶***merit*** a special *word* of commendation 特別の賛辞を受けるに足りる. ¶He is not a man to ***mince*** his *words*. 彼は物を露骨に言うたちだ. ‖ not to ***mince*** *words* 忌たんなく言うと. ¶***mind*** the *word* その命令を守る. ¶***mispronounce*** the *word* その語の発音を誤る. ¶***misread*** a *word* 語を読み誤る. ¶***miss*** [***out***] a *word* 一語を落す. ¶***misspell*** a *word* 語のつづりを誤る. ¶***mouth*** (=***pronounce***) one's *words* correctly その語を正しく発音する. ¶***muffle*** *words* 言葉を不明りょうに発音する. ¶***mumble*** a few confused *words* もぐもぐ二言三言不明りょうなことをいう. ¶***mutter*** some unintelligible *words* 何か不明りょうな語をつぶやく. ¶***nasalize*** *words* 言葉が鼻にかかる. ¶It is too manifest to ***need*** a *word* of argument. それは弁明する必要のないほど明らかなことだ. ¶He did not ***offer*** a single *word* in reply. 彼は一言も返答しなかった. ¶***pass*** the *word* ***on*** to ... ...にその言葉を伝える ‖ We should not ***pass*** the *words* without protest. われわれはその言を不問に付してはならない. ¶***pen*** a few *words* 二言三言書く. ¶To the truth of it I ***pledge*** my *word* of honor. そのことのたしかなことは僕が名誉にかけて誓う. ¶***pluralize*** *words* 単語を複数にする. ¶The typist ***pounded*** over a hundred and fifty *words* in sixty seconds. そのタイピストは一分間に百五十語以上を打った. ¶volubly ***pour forth*** senseless *words* 愚にもつかぬことをぺらぺらしゃべる. ¶***preach*** the *word* 神の道を説く. ¶Nobody ***proffered*** a *word*. 一言も提言するものがなかった. ¶***pronounce*** the *word* with accent on the first syllable 第一つづりに強勢をおいてその語を発音する ‖ ***Pronounce*** the magic *words*, "You will get well!" 「お前は直るよ」という神秘な語を口にせよ(信仰によって病気が直る). ¶***put*** the *words* into her mouth 彼女にそう言わせる. ¶when she got done, I ***put in*** my *word*, and said that ... 彼女が語り終ると私は言葉をはさんで...といった. ¶***put words together*** in sentences 語をつづって文章にする. ¶to ***quote*** his own *words* 彼の言葉を引用すると. ¶***recall*** his *words* 彼の言葉を思い出す. ¶I have ***received*** no *word* from him. 彼から音さたがありません. ‖ *word* was ***received*** at headquaters that ... 本部に...との通知が来た. 【類】 I ***received word*** that ... ¶***record*** 118 *words* a minute on a typewriter タイプで一分間に百十八語を打つ. ¶***reject*** the *word* "..." as suggesting, if it does not actually mean ... 事実...を意味していないにしてもそれを暗示しているという所から「...」なる語を使わないことにする. ¶Parrots ***repeat words*** and phrases. おおむは語句をまねて言う. ¶The book ***represents*** the last *word* in dictionary making. その本は辞書として最も完備したものである. 【類】 The new building ***represented*** the last *word* in department store design and construction. / Some of the Great Western Expresses ***represent*** undoubtedly the last *word* (最高) in modern travel comfort. ¶He ***said*** not a *word*. 彼は一言も言わなかった. ‖ He ***said*** every good *word* for it and left unsaid every bad one that he possibly could. 彼はそれに対してあらゆる賞賛の辞を呈したが悪いことは一言も言わずにおいた. ¶He has ***sent word*** to excuse himself. 彼は(招待などを)断ってやった. ¶***send back*** *word* that ... ...といって返信してやる. ¶***send word home*** to our parents that ... 故郷の両親に...と言ってやる. ¶*word* was ***sent out*** to ... that ... ...に...と言づてをしてやった. ¶the *words* were ***set*** to music by ... その歌詞を...が作曲した. ¶***skip*** a *word* 一語飛ばす. ¶***slur words*** in reading 語の発音を不明りょうに読む. ¶***space out*** one's *words* 語間にあいまをおいて話す. ¶He can scarcely ***speak*** a *word* of Japanese. 彼は日本語を一言もしゃべれない. ‖ ***speak*** a *word* in season 時宜に適したことを一言いう. 【類】 ***speak*** *words* of kindness and encouragement to all. ¶***stamp*** these *words* upon one's brain これらの数語を銘記する. ¶He ***stints*** no *words* in praising it. 彼はそれを激賞してやまない. ¶***strike out*** (=***whittle off***) *words* 語を削除する. ¶He did not ***suffer*** one *word* to fall in vain from the mouth of his teacher. 彼はその教師の言うことを一言一句聞き取ろうとした. ¶***swallow*** one's *words* 食言する. ¶***Swallow*** the *words*. その言葉を取り消せ. ¶***take*** the *words* from a person's mouth 言葉の先取をする ‖ I ***took*** his *word* for it. 私は彼の言葉を真にうけた. ‖ When one is believed to be untruthful, no one will ***take*** one's *word*. うそつきだと思われたが最後だれもその人の言うことは信じなくなる. 【類】 You should never ***take*** his *words* just as they are. ¶***take back*** one's *words* 前言を撤回する. ¶after ***talking*** a few *words* with ... ...と二言三言話してから. ¶***think over*** the pregnant *words* of ... ...の意味深長な言葉を熟考する. ¶***throw out*** a *word* of counsel to ... 一言...に助言する. ¶***torture*** *words* 語を無理な意味に使う. ¶***toss*** a *word* to ... ...に一言吐き出すように言う. ¶***trace*** a *word* to its origin 語の語原を探る ‖ He ***traced*** the *words* with a shaking hand. 彼は震える手でようよう字を書いた. ¶***turn*** (=look) ***up*** a *word* in the dictionary 辞書で語を引く. ¶How many *words* can you ***type*** a minute? 一分間何語ぐらいタイプが打てますか. 【類】 ***type*** [***out***] 75 words a minute. ¶***underline*** (=***underscore, dash***) a *word*= put a dash under a word 語の下に線を引く. ¶There are no roads as we ***understand*** the *word*. 道路らしい道路はない. ¶to ***use*** the *words* of Tennyson テニソンの言葉を引用すれば ‖ he ***used*** these *words* in his letter to ... 彼は

…への彼の手紙にこう言っている ‖ ***use*** a ***word*** properly 語を正しく用いる. 【類】 ***use words*** accurately, forcibly, exactly. ¶***utter*** broken and meaningless ***words*** 切れ切れな無意味なことを言う. ¶***venture*** a ***word*** 思い切って言う. ¶a woman who ***wants*** the last ***word*** 何とか口返答をしなければ気のすまない女. ¶I need not ***waste*** any more ***words*** upon the importance of … …の重要性については私はもうこれ以上言う必要はない. ¶***weigh*** these ***words*** thoughtfully これらの言葉を熟考する. ¶***whisper*** honeyed ***words*** in the ear of … …の耳に甘い言葉をささやく. 【類】 ***whisper*** a few ***words*** into his ear. ¶Do not ***write*** the ***words*** too close or too far apart. 語と語を余り詰め過ぎたり離し過ぎたりしてはいけない. ¶***write down*** the ***words*** その語を書きつける.

v² ***words accompanying*** a gift 贈物に添えてある言葉. ¶The ***word came*** that he could not come. 彼から来られないといってよこした. ¶***word came back*** that … …という返事が来た. ¶a thrill that ***words*** cannot ***describe*** 言葉では言い表わせない感激. ¶Half-formed ***words died*** on her lips. 彼女は何か言おうとしたが途切れてしまった. ¶***Words dropped*** from his lips. 言葉が彼の口から漏れた. ¶***Words*** cannot ***express*** how disappointed I was. 私の失望は言い表わすに言葉がなかった. ¶***Words fail*** in one's attempt of description. 述べようとしても言葉がない. ‖ ***words fail*** to give a distinct or adequate idea of … 言葉では…の明白なまたは十分な観念を与えることはできない ‖ How dirty the prisons were, ***words fail*** to describe. 刑務所のきたなかったことと言ったらお話にならない. ‖ ***words fail*** us to express our joy at … 言葉では私たちは…の喜びを言い現わすことはできない. ¶His ***words*** are apt to ***fall unheeded.*** 彼の言葉はおろそかにされやすい. ¶***Words flow*** easily. 言葉がすらすらと出る. ¶***word*** soon ***went around*** that … たちまち…とのうわさがたった. ¶soon ***word went out*** over the campus that … たちまち…という評判が学生間にたった ‖ ***word went out*** to the world that …という評判が世間にたった. ¶there ***happened*** some ***words*** between them about … …について二人の間に言い争いがあった. ¶The ***word rose*** to his lips. その語が彼の口に出て来た. ¶***Words ran high.*** 激論があった. ¶His ***words*** are still ***vibrating*** in my ear. 彼の言葉がまだ私の耳に響いている.

Q ***acrostic words*** 文字遊戯(数語の始めまたは終りの letter をつづると一語になる). ¶You must pay five cents for each ***additional word.*** 一語増すごとに五セントずつとられる. ¶To bring two vowels sound together in ***adjacent words*** produces an unpleasant sound. 続いている二語の二つの母音が一緒に響くのは感じが悪いものだ. ¶A few ***words*** may not be ***amiss*** in this connection. これについて一言述べるのもむだではなかろう. ¶fully ***Anglicized words*** 十分英語化した語. ¶without so much as the interchange of ***angry words*** けんか一つせずに. ¶we parted without ***another word*** それ以上一言も言わずに別れた. ¶***antiquated words*** 廃語. ¶***appropriate words*** 適切な言葉. ¶***ardent words*** of admiration 熱誠な賞賛の言葉. ¶***beautiful words*** 美しい言葉. ¶The word "revolution" is hardly too ***big*** a ***word*** for the occasion. その場合を革命と言ってもほとんど誇張したことにはならない. ‖ use ***big words*** 大げさな語を使う. ¶in ***blunt words*** ぶっきら棒に. ¶***borrowed words*** 借用語. ¶He did not bear out these ***brave words.*** 彼は口ではこんなりっぱなことを言ったものの実行ができなかった. ¶utter ***broken*** and ***meaningless words*** 切れ切れな意味の取れないことを言う. ¶the ***burning words*** of Dante ダンテの熱烈な言葉. ¶a ***careless word*** 不注意な言葉. ¶a few ***cheering words*** of comfort 二三慰めの言葉. ¶his ***classic words*** on … 彼の…に関するりっぱな著作. ¶"Esteem" is rather a ***cold word.***「尊敬」という語はむしろ冷ややかな感じのする言葉である. ¶***colorful words*** 多彩な言葉. ¶***common words*** of speech and literature 話や文に普通用いる語. ¶***common*** and ***indispensable words*** なくてならない普通の語. ¶a ***composite word***〖文法〗合成語. ¶a ***comprehensive word*** 意義の広い語. ¶write an apology in ***contrite words*** いかにも申しわけないといった謝罪状を書く. ¶a ***croaking word*** 泣言. ¶have ***cross words*** with … …とけんかをする. ¶one of our most ***current words*** われわれが最も多く使う語の一つ. ¶a ***customary word*** 慣用語. ¶a ***deep word*** 意味の深い語. ¶a ***depreciatory word*** 軽べつの語. ¶if I may use a ***disagreeable word*** いやな言葉ではあるが. ¶Though Art's ***earlier word*** is cleverness, its ***later word*** is repose. 芸術のもとの意味は器用だが今は静寂の意となっている. ¶She had some ***earnest words*** to say to the mothers of this land. 彼女はこの国のお母さんたちに向って二三誠意ある言葉を送った. ¶'Tiffin' is an ***Eastern English word*** for dinner. tiffin は東部英語で昼食の意である. ¶too ***elaborate*** and ***bookish words*** 凝りすぎた文章語. ¶have an ***encouraging word*** for … …は将来有望である. ¶an ***epidemic word*** 流行語. ¶ ***Every word*** tells. 一言一句急所を突く. ¶in the ***exact words*** of the speaker その言葉を引用すれば. ¶an ***exotic word*** 外来語. ¶by ***express words*** 明文によって ‖ the law has ***experss words*** for … …に対する明文がある. ¶He gave me ***fair words.*** 彼は私にお世辞を言った. ¶***famous words*** 有名な言葉. ¶a ***fashionable word*** 流行語. ¶I let the ***fatal word*** fall from my lips. 私はうっかりその言葉を口に出してしまった. ¶to use one of his ***favorite words*** 彼の好んで使った言葉で言えば. ¶***feeble words*** 力のない言葉. ¶in ***felicitous words*** 適切な言葉で. ¶It may be told in a ***few words.*** それは二三語で述べられる. ‖ a man of ***few words*** 口数の少ない人 ‖ in as ***few words*** as possible できるだけ手短かに ‖ The explanation can be given in a ***few words.*** それは簡短に説明できる. ‖ convey in the ***fewest words*** the maximum of information 最少の語数で最大の情報を伝える. ¶say in the ***fewest possible words*** consistent with clearness of statement できるだけ簡単明りょうに言う. ¶Those are ***fighting words,*** man! おい, 口論なら負けないぞ. ¶as a ***final word*** of warning, I should like to say that … 最後の御注意として…と申し上げたい. ¶bring the ***fitting word*** to mind 適語を思い出す. ¶in the cable he used the ***following words***: 一海外電報で彼はこう言っている. ¶a ***forbidden word*** 忌み言葉. ¶in ***forcible words*** 力のある言葉で. ¶***golden words*** uttered by the wisest men of antiquity 先哲の金言. ¶That was not a ***good word*** to choose. 言いようが悪かった. ‖ It is customary to say a ***good word*** for the departed. 故人のことはよく言うのが常法だ. ‖ He has a ***good word*** for every one. 彼はだれでもほめる. ‖ Few Londoners have a ***good word*** for the Underground. ロンドン人で地下鉄をよく言うものはほとんどない. ‖ he has a very ***good word*** to say for … 彼は…を激賞している. ‖ put in a ***good word*** on one's behalf その人のために有利なことを言ってよしなにとりなす. ¶for want of a ***better word,*** we call it "…" 他に適当な言葉がないからわれわれは仮にそれを「…」と言う. ¶a ***grim word*** すご味のある言葉. ¶in ***half-a-dozen words*** わずか六語で. ¶These are ***hard words*** but honest. これは苦言ではあるが真情がこもっている. ¶speak ***harsh words*** ひどいことを言う. ¶describe it in a few ***hasty words*** それを二三の語でそこそこに記述する. ¶This often leads to ***high words,*** and frequently hard blows. こうしたことからよく口論となりまた往々なぐりあいにもなる. ‖ ***High words*** were passed between them. 激語が二人の間に交わされた. ‖ They had ***high words*** upon the subject. 彼らはその問題で激論を戦わした. ¶***high-sounding*** (=***high-flown***) ***words*** 仰々しい言葉. ¶***homely words*** 平凡な言葉 ‖ The poet makes the ***homeliest words*** dance to his tunes. その詩人は平凡な語を踊らして詩の調子を出す. ¶***honied*** (=sweet) ***words*** 甘い言葉. ¶***hot words*** 激語. ¶speak ***idle words*** むだ口をきく ‖ Our ***idle words*** are much more genuine than our studied and deliberate utterances. 考えずに言ったことの方が深く考えて言ったことよりも却って純真味がある. ‖ ***idle words*** of diplomacy 外交上のお座なりの言葉. ¶an ***ill-favored word*** 人の喜ばない言葉. ¶a great historian who has recorded the event with ***imperishable words*** その事件を不朽の文字をもって記録した偉大な歴史家. ¶***imprudent words*** 無分別な言葉. ¶an ***indelicate*** or ***immodest word*** さしさわりがあるかつつましくない言葉. ¶***inspiring words*** 人を感激させる言葉. ¶an ***italicized word*** イタリックスの語. ¶***jocular words*** 滑けい語. ¶say to a person more ***kind words*** than ever before いつになくやさしい言葉をかける ‖ say some ***kind words*** to … …にやさしい言葉の一つもかける ‖ ***kind words*** of counsel 慈訓. ¶a few ***kindly words*** of congratulation and good wishes 短い懇切な祝辞. ¶he has the ***last word*** to say about … 彼の説は…については最も重きをなしている ‖ He must always have the ***last word,*** whether right or wrong. 彼はいつも善かれ悪しかれ最後に何とか言わずにはいられないたちだ. ‖ During seasons of solitude here dull is the ***last word*** to describe my state of mind. ここで幾季節もさびしく暮す私の心情は「つまらない」という一語に尽きている. ‖ It should be accepted as the ***last word*** in dictionary making. それは辞書として理想的のものであると言わなければならない. ‖ The book is the ***last word*** on the subject. 同書はその題目に関する決定版(最も権威のある本)だ. ‖ the ***last word*** in attractiveness きわめて美しいもの ‖ the ***last word*** in pipes パイプの最高級品.【類】The new car is the ***last word*** in comfort and beauty. / the ***last word*** in modern hotel construction. / The Panama-Pacific Universal Exposition will be the "***last word***" in expositions. ‖ have the ***last word*** 言い負かす. ¶supply the ***last*** and ***definite word*** upon the argument 論議にとどめを刺すもの ‖ a poet about whose work the ***last word*** has not yet been spoken まだ評価の確定しない詩人. ¶one's ***lightest words*** 意味もないような言葉 ‖ His ***lightest word*** was listened to with attention. 彼の口から出たちょっとした言葉まで(聴衆が)傾聴した. ¶***living words*** 現代語. ¶I told him in so ***many words*** that he was a liar. 私は彼に向ってあから様に彼がうそつきだといってやった. ‖ ***Many words*** will not fill a bushel 口約だけでは人は助からない ‖ say in so ***many words*** そうとはっきり言う. ¶a ***meaningful word*** 意味深長な言葉. ¶it is utterly impossible to give, in ***mere words***, even when assisted by pictures, an adequate idea of ... よしんば絵の力を借りても言葉では…を十分に伝えることはとうてい不可能である. ¶a ***misspelled words*** つづりの間違った語. ¶***mouth-filling words*** 口はばったい語. ¶He pronounced several ***mysterious words***. 彼は何とも意味の分からない言葉を数語もらした. ¶a ***nasty word*** [わいせつがかった]いやな言葉. ¶a pure ***native word*** (外来でない)純国語. ¶***naughty words*** いやな言葉. ¶look ***new words*** in a dictionary 辞書で新語を調べる. ¶a ***new-coined word*** 新造語. ¶a ***new-fangled word*** 新流行語. ¶He said ***no word*** of reproach. 彼は何ともとがめ立てはしなかった. ‖ Pray, make ***no words*** about it. そのことはどうぞ何もおっしゃらないで. ¶a ***nonce word*** その場だけの造語. ¶***numeral words*** 数語. ¶the revival of ***obsolete words*** 廃語の復活. ¶an ***offensive word*** いやな感じの言葉. ¶say in ***one word*** 一語で言う ‖ just ***one*** more ***word*** もう一言だけ(付け加える) ‖ Just ***one word*** with you. ちょっと申し上げたいことがある. ¶It is my pleasant task to speak the ***opening words***. 開会の辞を述べることは私の愉快に思う所であります. ¶an ***opprobrious word*** 侮べつの意味を含む言葉. ¶or in ***other words*** 換言すれば. ¶an ***outright word*** むきだしの言葉. ¶***overworked words*** 余りひん繁に用いられる語. ¶we have his ***own word*** for it, that ... 彼はその件について…と自分で言っている ‖ give it in his ***own words*** それを彼自身の口から出た言葉で述べる. ‖ state the author's ideas in ***our own words*** 著者の考えをわれわれの言葉で述べる. ¶***passionate words*** 熱烈なる言葉. ¶Now a ***personal word***. さて一言私のことに関して申し上げる. ¶in ***plain words*** 平たく言えば ‖ be written in the ***plainest words*** possible できるだけ分かりやすく書かれてある. ¶a ***plaintive word*** 泣き言. ¶a ***powerful*** and ***dignified word*** 力のこもった威厳のある言葉. ¶Nerve is a ***prettier word*** than cheek. [心臓が強いという意味の]ナーヴ(心臓)はチーク(鉄面皮)よりはましな語である. ¶a ***pregnant word*** 含蓄のある語. ¶the power of the ***printed word*** 印刷した語の偉力 ‖ It is by means of the ***printed word*** that the modern world is controlled. 印刷した言葉こそ今日の世界を統制するものだ. ¶***private words*** for women 女だけへの言葉. ¶***prophetic words*** 予言. ¶His store of ***quaint words*** and phrases was inexhaustible. 彼の持つ奇抜な語句は無尽蔵であった. ¶Composition consists in putting the ***right words*** together in the right way. 作文とは適当な語を適当に結び合わせることである. ‖ command the ***right word*** at the right time 適当な時に適当な言葉が出る.【類】I wished to say something, but could not find the ***right words***. ¶A ***royal word*** cannot be broken. 勅令は取り消し得ない. ¶a ***sanguinary word*** 殺伐な言葉. ¶most of ***scientific words*** are monosemantic. 科学用語の多くは単一の語義をもっている. ¶***secret word*** has it that ... 秘密情報によれば… ¶in ***seasoned words*** 思慮ある言い方で. ¶deft mingling of exquisitely ***selected words*** into variegated tints of meaning うまく選択した語を巧みに取交ぜて文のあやを織出すこと. ¶a ***sensible word*** 分別ある言葉. ¶***sesquipedalian*** (=long and pedantic) ***words*** 長くってむずかしい語. ¶A ***sharp word*** of command rings out again and again. 激しい号令が幾度もかけられる. ‖ Her ***sharp words*** stung him to the quick. 彼女の鋭い言葉がぐさっと彼の胸にささった. ¶a ***short word*** for... …の略語. ‖ a ***short, plain word*** 簡易な語. ¶in ***sincere*** and ***comforting words*** 真心のある慰安になる言葉で. ¶to sum up in a ***single word*** 一言で言えば. ¶a '***smutty***' and ***offensive word*** 卑わいないやらしい言葉. ¶tell in ***soft words*** おだやかに言う. ¶a ***solid word*** without a hyphen ハイフンをつけないで一語にした語. ¶a ***sonorous mouthfilling word*** 調子の好いどっしりした言葉. ¶give a ***special word*** of mention to ... …を特記する.【類】give a ***special word*** of commendation to ... ¶use the ***spoken word*** 口語を使う. ¶wound one in a few ***stinging words*** 刺すような言葉で人の心を傷つける. ¶***sublime words*** 崇高な語. ¶***sweet-sounding words*** 聞いて美しい言葉. ¶break one's ***sworn word*** 誓言を破る. ¶a ***synonymous word*** 同意語. ¶a ***tabooed word*** 忌(い)言葉. ¶in a few ***tearful words*** 涙ながらの二言三言で. ¶a highly ***technical word*** きわめて専門的な語. ¶speak ***tender words*** to ... …にやさしい言葉をかける. ¶***threatening words*** おどし文句. ¶a ***timely word*** about ... …について時宜を得た意見. ¶He spoke softly in her ear the ***trembling words*** of love. 彼は彼女の耳にふるえる恋の言葉をささやいた. ¶a tangle of ***ugly words*** 悪口のやりとり. ¶***uncleanly words*** 下劣な語. ¶an ***undignified word*** 品の悪い語. ¶***untranslatable English words*** 翻訳不可能の英単語. ¶No ***unnecessary word*** is included, and no ***necessary word*** is omitted. 不要語は省き必要語はすべて網らしてある. ¶an ***unnative word*** 他国(外来)言葉. ¶***well-chosen words*** 選択よろしきを得た言葉. ¶a ***well-put-in word*** ぴったりあてはまった語. ¶***whispered words*** ささやいた言葉. ¶***written words*** 書いた語. ¶use the ***wrong word*** 間違った言葉を用いる.

Q² A verb is an ***action word***. 活動を示す語である. ¶***Book words*** are words more often written than spoken. 文語は話すよりも書かれる語である. ¶a ***brimstone word*** [畜生! といった]のろいの言葉. ¶mutter ***charm words*** じゅもんを唱える. ¶a ***code word*** 暗号用語. ¶a ***devil word*** [畜生といった]激語. ¶a ***dialect word*** 方言. ¶a mere ***dictionary word*** 辞書だけに見る(実用性のない)語. ¶an ***everyday word*** 常用語. ¶the principal's ***farewell words*** to the graduating class 卒業生のクラスに対する校長の送別の辞. ¶a ***four-letter word*** 四字つづりの語. ¶a ***frequency word*** 繁用語. ¶a ***ghost word*** 幽霊語(実際には存在しないで誤って辞書に採入れられた語). ¶It can be expressed in ***half-a-dozen words*** それは五六語で言い表わせる. ¶names of ships familiar in our mouths as ***household words*** よくわれわれの口に上る船名 ‖ He became a ***household word***. 彼は有名になった.【類】We all know their names; they are ***household words***. / His name is a ***household word*** in the literature and journalism of today. ¶a ***key word*** 重要語. ¶a ***law word*** 法律語. ¶a ***loan word*** 外来語. ¶a ***newspaper word*** 新聞語. ¶a ***parting word*** 告別の辞. ¶a ¶speak ***parting words*** to ... …に別れのあいさつをする. ¶a ***refrain word*** in songs 歌の折返し ‖ a meaningless ***refrain word*** in old songs 古い歌にある意味のない折返し. ¶a ***root word*** 基礎語. ¶a ***slang word*** 卑語. ¶***soldier*** and ***sailor words*** and phrases [陸海の]兵隊言葉. ¶Inflation is a ***swear word***. 皆んながインフレに業をにやしている. ¶a ***test word*** of a secret society 秘密クラブの合言葉. ¶a ***title word*** 見出し語. ¶a ***transition word***〚修辞〛転換語. ¶The ***watch word*** of this century is "Excelsior". 今世紀の標語は「さらに高く」ということである. ‖ The ***watch word*** of today is efficiency 今日の標語は能率だ.

P contention ***about words*** 語についての論争. ¶***according to word*** brought to Japan by ... …が日本へもたらした報道によれば. ¶***at*** a ***word*** from ... …から一言かけられると ‖ ***At*** the ***word*** "prison!" every drop of his blood was chilled.「刑務所」という言葉に彼はぞっとした. ‖ Up rose the men ***at*** the ***word*** of command. 号令一下人々は起立した. ‖ ***At*** these ***words***, he felt full of joy. 彼は大喜びであった. ‖ I'll take you ***at*** your ***word***. 君の言を信じよう. ¶It is ***beyond words*** beautiful. それは言葉に言い尽せない

ほど美しい. ‖ She was haughty ***beyond*** all *words*, but generous to her inferiors. 彼女は言いようもないほどごう慢であったがしかし目下の者には寛大であった. ¶teach ***by*** *word* and deed 言行の両方から教える ‖ Report must be given either ***by*** *word* of mouth (=speech) or in writing. 報告は口頭または書面ですべきである. ¶repeat a poem word ***for*** *word* 詩を一語一語間違えずに暗誦する ‖ translate word ***for*** *word* 逐語訳をする. ¶***in*** *a word*, it is not too much to say that ... 要するに...と言っても過言ではない ‖ ***In*** *a word*, he tires of everything. つまり彼は何にでもあきるのだ. ‖ love ***in*** *word* 口先だけの愛 ‖ He is faithful ***in*** *word* and deed. 彼は言行ともに誠意がある. ‖ describe it ***in*** *words* それを言葉で述べる ‖ ***in*** the *words* of Shakespeare (the English proverb) シェークスピア(など)の言葉で言えば ‖ an artist ***in*** *words* 言葉の芸術家(文の巧みな人など) ‖ a puzzle ***in*** *words* 言葉のなぞ(語ろ合わせなど). ¶put ***into*** *words* 言葉に移す. ¶I am a man ***of*** my *word*. 私は約束はほごにしません. ¶***On*** my *word* of honor. 私の言葉にかけて, 誓って. ‖ ***On*** his *word* an accident may be avoided or incurred. 彼(交通巡査など)の言葉次第で事故が避けられもするし起りもする ‖ a play ***on*** (=***upon***) *words* しゃれ. ¶***pending*** *word* from ... ...から何分のさたがあるまで. ¶say it ***through*** *words* それを口に出して言う. ¶***Upon*** my *word*, I do not understand you. 君の言うことがどうしても分からない. ¶***With*** these *words* (=So saying) he left the room. そう言って彼はへやを出ていった. ‖ a badge ***with*** the *words* "Safety First" on it「安全第一」という語句の付いている記章 ‖ He looked pleased ***with*** those *words*. 彼はその言葉を聞いて満足げに見えた. ¶I left him ***without*** a *word*. 私は一言も言わず彼と別れた. ‖ speech ***without*** *words* 言葉のない言葉 ‖ We sped towards our goal ***without*** more *words*. それからは口もきかずにわれわれは行先に急いだ. ‖ The matter has touched us so keenly that we are ***without*** *words* to express the sentiments within us. その事件は私たちの心には痛切に感じられ何とも心情の言い現わしようがない. ‖ ***without*** a *word* (=notice) of warning 前ぶれもなく(いきなり). 【類】***without*** a *word* of apology / He left the room ***without*** another *word*. ‖ We parted ***without*** a *word* on either side. どちらも無言で別れた.

P² a scientific gathering in which learned men use big ***words about*** something they do not understand 学者が自分にも分からない偉いことを言う科学者の会合. ¶a ***word as to*** ... ...について一言. ¶***words by*** ... music by ... 歌詞は...作曲は... ¶Fearful is no ***word for*** it. 恐ろしいどころの騒ぎじゃない. ‖ Rich is not the ***word for*** me. 私を金持などいうのは当らない. ‖ No, that is not the *word* ***for*** it. いや, その言葉は当らない. ¶***words from*** a foreign language 外来語. ¶a ***word in*** season 時宜を得た言葉 ‖ A ***word in*** your ear. ちょっとお耳を拝借. ‖ a ***word in*** the nominative of address 呼びかけの主語(君とかあなたたち, など). ¶I give you my ***word of*** honor. 私の名誉にかけて誓う. ‖ a ***word of*** six letters=a six-letter word 六字からなる語 ‖ *Word* ***of*** honor, I never saw such a beauty, alive and breathing, in my life. 全くこんな生きた美人は今までに見たことがない. ‖ There is no ***word of*** excuse for such a reproach. そう言われては一言もない. ‖ a ***word of*** command 命令の一語 ‖ the *Word* ***of*** God=the Bible 聖書 ‖ Freedom is a ***word of*** wide application. 自由という語は応用の広い言葉だ. 【類】A ***word of*** explanation here will not be amiss. / ***words of*** gratitude must be extended to ... ¶The work represents the "last ***word***" ***on*** the entomology of the Far East. その著作は極東におけるこん虫学の最高権威である. ‖ ***words*** (=an inscription) ***on*** a tombstone 墓碑銘. ¶a ***word to*** women 婦人への一言. ¶Just a ***word with*** you. ちょっと君にお話したいことがある.

O it is hardly the *word*—... would be a better one, for ... それはちょっと不適当な語で...には...の方がよかろう.

word, *v.* 言葉で述べる.

M The magazine articles are ***plainly*** *worded*. その雑誌に採録してある文はやさしく書いてある. ¶The letter is ***poorly*** *worded*. その手紙の文句はまずい. ¶***prettily*** *worded* 言葉使いが美しい.

wording, *n.* 言葉使い.

Q A ***different*** *wording* might make the meaning clearer. 別の言い方をした方がもっとはっきりするかも知れない. ¶an ***excellent*** *wording* すばらしい言い回し. ¶a ***new*** *wording* 新しい言い回し. 【類】The modern demand for "moral and social justice" is but a ***new*** *wording* of the Golden Rule: "Do unto others as you would have others do unto you."

word-play, *n.* しゃれ.

Q an ***unintentional*** *word-play* 思わず口から出たしゃれ.

word-sketch, *n.* 写実文.

Q a ***graphic*** *word-sketch* 写実的な文.

work, *n.* (**1**) 仕事; 事業.

V ***accomplish*** one's *work* 仕事を仕上げる ‖ ***accomplish*** a *work* of international importance 国際的重要性のある仕事を成し遂げる. ¶***achieve*** a really good *work* in ... ...の方面で真にりっぱな事業をなし遂げる. ¶in ***advancing*** *work* 仕事を発展させる上において. ¶***aid*** the campaign *work* その運動を助ける. ¶The work of the Society is being ***appreciated*** as time goes by. 同協会の事業は日に増し認められつつある. ¶***arrange*** the *work* of one's past years 従来やって来た仕事のしめくくりをする. ¶***begin*** one's *work* afresh その仕事を新規に始める ‖ ***begin*** one's *work* in the world 世の中に出る ‖ ***begin*** *work* with the year 1927-28 一九二七年度に仕事を始める. ¶***bring*** a *work* to a close 仕事の片をつける. ¶***carry*** a *work* to its conclusion 事業を完成する. ¶***carry on*** the *work* as a side line その仕事を副業としてやる ‖ Many of the poorer Italians ***carry on*** some kind of *work* in their homes (=at home). 比較的貧乏なイタリア人は大概家庭で何らかの内職をしている. ‖ ***carry on*** the *work* with great energy and effectiveness 非常に熱心に, また有効に仕事を続行する ‖ Funds to ***carry on*** this national *work* are urgently needed. その国家的事業を遂行するための資金がぜひ必要である. 【類】The school ***carries on*** a very useful *work*. / ***carry on*** the *work* of rescue. ¶***carry out*** *work* 仕事をする. ¶The employees ***ceased*** *work*, demanding an increase of pay. 従業員は増給を要求してストをやった. ¶at the period when they are ***choosing*** their *work* for life 一生の仕事を物色しつつある. ¶***close*** *work* 仕事を仕舞う. ¶The examiner ***collected*** the *work* (=papers) of the students. 試験官は学生の答案を集めた. ¶We have ***commenced*** the *work*, but it proceeds slowly. われわれはその仕事を始めたが遅々としてはかどらない. 【類】*Work* will be ***commenced*** at once and pushed forward with the utmost despatch. / ***commence*** *work* without delay 早速仕事を始める. ¶***complete*** the *work* of destruction 完全に破壊する. ¶***conduct*** *work* in a businesslike manner てきぱきことを運ぶ. ¶Catherine II. of Russia ***consolidated*** the *work* begun by Peter the Great. ロシアのキャザリン二世はピーター大帝の始めた事業を確立した. ¶Under the new system forty-eight hours ***constitute*** a week's *work*. 新制度では四十八時間が一週間の仕事ということになる. ¶***continue*** one's *work* in lexicography その辞書編集の仕事を続ける ‖ ***continue*** the *work* of conquest 征服の事業を続ける ‖ I have to ***continue*** the *work* on hand. 私は今手があけられない. ¶***contract*** a *work* to foreign contractors 第三国人の請負師に請負わせる. ¶laboriously ***correct*** the *work* of each pupil 生徒の作文を一人一人丹念に添削してやる. ¶the professors who ***cover*** this *work* at the colleges この学科担当の諸教授. ¶***cripple*** the *work* of ... ...の事業を挫折させる. ¶devices that ***cut*** homemaker's *work* 家庭の労力節約になる道具. ¶***cut*** the *work* ***short*** その仕事を早く切り上げる. ¶stubbornly ***demand*** *work* from students 強硬に学生の勉強を要求する. ¶***desire*** extra private *work* 内職を望む. ¶***discontinue*** the *work* その仕事を中止する. ¶***distribute*** the *work* その仕事を分担させる. ¶She has servants to ***do*** all her *work*. 彼女には自分の仕事を一切してくれる召使いがある. ‖ ***do*** the *work* without drawing the emoluments 無報酬でその仕事をやる ‖ He ***did*** all his *work* of translation single-handed. 彼は独力でその翻訳を全部やった. ‖ An adverb-phrase is a group of words which ***does*** the *work* of an adverb. 〘文法〙副詞句は副詞の役をする語群である. 【類】***do*** no *work* / ***do*** the *work* of laborers / We are eager to ***do*** the *work* of the world. / ***do*** one's *work* reverently / ***do*** one's *work* conscientiously / He has ***done*** his *work* very well. / I'd rather ***do*** my own *work* myself than have someone do it for me. / Mother ***does*** the *work* about the house. / At what age do literary men ***do*** their best *work*? / ***do*** brain *work* / The *work* is ***done*** perfunctorily (お役目的に). / It was he that ***did*** the *work*. / ***do*** a great *work* in the world / ***do*** a *work* one enjoys / ***do*** the *work* of six (六人分の仕事) / ***do*** one's *work* efficiently. ¶***effect*** a great *work* 大事業をなし遂げる. ¶***enjoy*** *work* 仕事を楽しむ. ¶***enter*** newspaper *work* 新聞の仕事に従事する. ¶***execute*** clerical *work* 書記の仕事をやる. ¶***expedite*** *work* 仕事をはかどらせる. ¶***extend*** one's *work* その事業を拡張する. ¶greatly ***facilitate*** the *work* of ... 大いに...の仕事をはかどらせる. 【類】Inventions ***facilitate*** the *work* of the world. ¶***find*** some *work* for him to do 何か彼のやる仕事を見つけてやる. ¶a meeting to ***further*** the charitable *work* in aid of ... ...救済の慈善事業を促進するための会合. ¶He has as yet failed to ***find*** *work*. 彼はまだ仕事が見つからない. 【類】At last she ***found*** *work* as a dancer at a theatre in Piccadilly. ¶***finish*** (=***get through***) a hard day's *work* 骨の折れる一日の仕事を終る ‖ ***finish*** the day's *work* その日の仕事を終る. 【類】*Work* on the building is ***finished***. ¶***forward*** the noble *work* of ... ...というりっぱな仕事を進める. ¶unable to ***get*** *work* 仕事が得られないで. ¶***give*** *work* to ... ...に仕事を与える. ¶In arithmetic his *work* was ***graded*** twenty per cent. 彼の算術の成績は百点満点で二十点に採点された. ¶It only ***hinders*** the natural *work* of healing. そんなことをしたら自然に直る妨害になるだけだ. ¶attempt to ***identify*** unsigned *works* with individual artists. 無落款の作品をそれぞれの画家の作と鑑定しようと試みる. ¶***institute*** research *work* 研究作業を始める. ¶***knock off*** *work* an hour earlier 一時間早く仕事を打ち切る. 【類】Charles Darwin always ***knocked off*** his day's *work* at noon. ¶***lay*** one's *work* ***aside*** その仕事を中止する. ¶As they ***left*** *work* without notice they forfeited their pay. 彼らは無断で仕事をよしたので給料をもらえなかった. ‖ He ***left*** the *work* to me. [故人となった]彼はその仕事を私にまかせた. ‖ She ***leaves*** her *work* at six for good. 彼女は六時に最後の仕事をきりあげて家へ帰る. ¶***leave off*** *work* 仕事を中止する. ¶He was anxious to ***lighten*** my *work* in little way. 彼は少しでも私の仕事を楽にさせようと苦心した. ¶The craftsmen used to ***love*** their *work*. [当時は]職人たちは自分の仕事を楽しんでいたものだ. ¶It ***makes*** short *work* of cleaning clothes and dishes. そうすると衣類の洗たくやさら洗いの仕事が手っとり早くすむ. ‖ He ***made*** short *work* of my arguments. 彼は私の議論をあっさり片づけてしまった. ‖ ***make*** short *work* of a rival purchaser 競争して買おうとする人を出し抜く. ¶***mar*** the *work* of ... ...の仕事をだいなしにする. ¶***mark*** one's pupils' *work* 受持ち生徒の答案に採点する. ¶I ***miss*** my *work*. 私は仕事がなくなったのでさびしい. ¶***necessitate*** little *work* あまり労力を要しない. ¶***overlap*** the *work* of other institutions 他の協会の仕事と重複する. ¶***perfect*** the good *work* one has begun すでに着手したりっぱな仕事を完成する. ¶***perform*** a great *work* for the poor 貧困者のために大きな仕事をする. 【類】***perform*** effective *work*. ¶***plan*** one's life *work* 一生の仕事を計画する. ¶***practice*** good *works* りっぱな仕事をする. ¶***press*** the *work* vigorously その仕事をぐんぐん進行させる. ¶vigorously ***prosecute*** one's missionary *work* 元気よく伝道の仕事をやる. ¶The manufacture ***provides*** *work* (=employment) for more than 10,000 males and females. その製造業は一万余の男女に仕事を与えている. ¶***pursue*** the *work* one commenced 着手した仕事を続ける. ¶***push*** the *work* ***along*** その仕事を急ぐ. ¶***push*** the *work* ***forward*** with unwavering devotion 不退転の決意でその仕事を進める. ¶The *work* is being ***pushed on*** as quickly as possible. その仕事は大至急進行されている. ¶he decided to ***put*** in hand the *work* of ... 彼は...の仕事に着手しようと決心した ‖ ***put*** the *work* in final shape 最後の仕上げをする. ¶his fatal inclination to ***put off*** *work* to the last moment せっぱつまるまで仕事を延ばすという彼の悪い癖. ¶***quit*** *work* 仕事をやめる ‖ ***quit*** *work* in a body=go on strike, 《米》walk out ストをする. ¶She was compelled by illness to ***relinquish*** her useful *work*. 彼女は病気のために有益な仕事をやめねばならなかった. ¶***re-open*** *works* 仕事を再開する. ¶The collection ***represents*** the *work* of a life-time. その収集は一生かかってやったものだ. ¶Heavy *work* is ***required*** in mathematics in that school. その学校では数学はなかなか勉強しなければ追いつかない. ¶The strikers gave in and ***resumed*** (=***returned to***) *work*. ストライキは折れて復業した. ‖ He ***resumed*** his class *work* at the university in January. 彼は(一時休学していたが)一月にまた大学に出席し出した. ¶*work* is much ***retarded*** by political excitement 仕事が政界の動揺で大分妨げられた. ¶***rush*** the *work* 仕事を大急ぎでやる. ¶***rush*** the *work* ***through*** 仕事を大急ぎで片づける. ¶"***scamp***" one's *work* 仕事を怠る ‖ The *work* has been shamefully ***scamped***. その仕事は思い切り手を抜いてある. ¶***seek*** *work* 仕事を求める. ¶***set*** *work* 仕事を課する. ¶I am glad to find he doesn't ***shirk*** *work*. 彼は骨惜みをしないのがうれしい. ¶I will ***show*** him his *work*. 彼に仕事のやり方を教えてやろう. ¶***shun*** *work* 仕事をいやがる. ¶***slouch*** one's *work* 《口語》仕事をぞんざいにやる. ¶***stand*** hard *work* 骨の折れる仕事に耐える. ¶***start*** (=set to) *work* 仕事を始める. ¶***stop*** *work* and protest for ... 仕事を休んで...を主張する. ¶***strike*** *work* for an advance of wages 給料の値上を要求してストをやる. ¶The church has ***survived*** the rough iconoclastic *work* of the Reformation. その教会は宗教改革という荒っぽい偶像破壊の難を免れて今日まで存続した. ¶*Work* is ***suspended*** in wet weather. 雨天の際は仕事は中止される. ¶Teachers should ***take*** their *work* seriously. 教師はその仕事をまじめにやるべきだ. ‖ ***take*** the *work* in hand その仕事に着手する. ¶***take up*** honest *work* 正業につく ‖ The strikers have ***taken*** their *work* ***up*** again スト工員たちが復業した. ¶He has ***undertaken*** a useful *work* in editing the book. 彼はその本の編集という有益な仕事をやった. ‖ I ***undertook*** the *work* though against my will. いやいやその仕事を引受けた. ¶***upset*** the *work* of the digestive apparatus 腹をこわす. ¶a young woman who ***wants*** *work* 職業を求めている一人の若い女 ‖ ***want*** *work* at home 内職を求めている. ¶He ***wrought*** a marvelous *work*. 彼は驚嘆すべき仕事をやった.

v² The *work* of Rodin ***extends*** over half a century. The first works which are known to us can be dated from about the year 1860, and the last are dated 1916. ロダンの労作は半世紀にわたっている. その世に知れている最初の作は一八六〇年ごろで最後の作は一九一六年である.

Q causes of success and failure in ***academic*** *work* 学業成否の諸原因 ‖ their performance in ***academic*** *work* 彼ら(生徒)の学課成績 ‖ be exceedingly poor in ***academic*** *work* 学業成績が著しく劣等である. ¶do ***active*** *work* 活躍する ‖ do ***active*** *work* in the industrial *work* 産業方面で活躍する. ¶***administrative*** *work* 行政事務, 監理事務. ¶[an] ***admirable*** *work* りっぱな仕事. ¶go through the grades to ***advanced*** *work* 小学校を卒業して中学校に進む. ¶do ***all*** the *work* single-handed すべて単独で仕事をする. ¶My *work* is very ***amateurish***. 僕の仕事ははなはだしろうとくさい(写真など). ¶one's divinely ***appointed*** *work* in life=one's mission その天職. ¶at the end of an ***arduous day's*** *work* 骨の折れる一日の仕事を終えて. ¶above the ***average*** *work* 並以上の(成績など). ¶It was a ***bad night's*** *work*. それは一晩かかってやった仕事としては成績があがらなかった. ¶carry on a ***beneficent*** *work* 慈善事業を行う. 【類】do ***beneficent*** *work* of some kind or other with our wealth. ¶one's ***careful*** *work* その念入りな仕事. ¶***ceaseless*** and ***indomitable*** *work* うまずたゆまぬ作業. ¶do ***certain*** *work* ある仕事をやる. ¶engage in ***charitable*** and ***religious*** *work* 慈善と宗教の事業に従事する. ¶the ***Christianizing*** and ***educative*** *work* of Spain in the Philippines フィリッピン島におけるスペインのキリスト教化と教育事業. ¶***civilian*** *work* 軍事外の仕事. ¶***clean*** *work* 鮮かな手際 ¶***clerical*** *work* in the office 事務系の仕事. ¶***contracted*** *work* 請負仕事. ¶***cooperative*** *work* with ... ...との協力. ¶***counter-subversive*** *work* 破壊活動防止工作. ¶***creative*** *work* 創作. ¶do ***creditable*** and ***careful*** *work* りっぱな行届いた仕事をする. ¶It stands as the ***crowning*** *work* of his great life. それは彼の偉大なる一生の最大な業績である. ¶His *work* is as yet ***crude***. 彼の仕事は未熟だ. ¶do ***cruel*** *work* 残酷なことをする. ¶come back to one's ***daily*** *work* その日々の仕事に立ち返る. ¶do a ***day's*** *work* 一日の仕事をする. ¶do some ***detective*** *work* 何か探偵の仕事をやる. ¶***disagreeable*** *work* 不愉快な仕事. ¶***domestic*** *work* 家事. ¶It represents fruit of nearly thirty years' ***earnest, conscientious*** *work*. それは約三十年間熱心にまじめに働いた成果である. ¶***delicate*** *work* in metal 金属のこまかい仕事. ¶is not ***easy*** *work* 楽な仕事ではない.

¶***educational*** *work* 教育事業. ¶The objects of the Mission were ***educational*** and ***evangelic*** *work*. その伝道会の目的は教育と布教とであった. ¶facilities for ***effective*** *work* 仕事の能率を上げる施設. ¶be of ***elaborate*** *work* 手が込んでいる. ¶an ***epochal*** *work* 画期的事業. ¶The society is doing much ***excellent*** *work*. その協会は非常に好成績をあげている. ¶***excessive*** *work* 過労. ¶do ***experimental*** *work* 実験をやる ‖ begin ***experimental*** *work* with … …の実験に取掛かる. ¶it is most ***fascinating*** *work* to … …することには実に魅力がある. ¶That's ***fast*** *work*. 早い成功でしたね(探偵など). ¶after a hard day's ***fatiguing*** *work* 一生懸命に一日働いてから. ¶Overcome with the ***fatiguing*** *work* of the day, she fell asleep. 彼女は一日骨を折ったので疲れて眠ってしまった. ¶The Y.M.C.A. is doing ***fine*** *work*. キリスト青年会はりっぱな事業をやっている. ‖ do ***fine*** *work* 好成績をあげる ‖ While at college he did particularly ***fine*** *work* in English. 大学で英語が優秀であった. ¶the very ***first*** *work* at the piano 全く最初のピアノ演奏. ¶He can do ***first-class*** *work*. 彼にはりっぱな腕がある. ¶***first-rate*** *work* 高級な仕事. ¶a factory at ***full*** *work* on the production of … …の製作に全力を尽している工場 ‖ The mine is now in ***full*** *work*. その鉱山は目下盛んに活動している. ¶He has done ***good*** *work* in this direction. 彼はこの方面にりっぱな成績をあげた. ‖ The school is doing ***good*** *work* in its own way. その学校はその独自の方面でりっぱな仕事をしている. 【類】He is a boy of ***good*** *works* (操行のよい). / do ***good*** *work* for … / To him the pride of ***good*** *work* accomplished is the sufficient reward. / the ability to do ***good*** *work* / expect ***good*** *work* from … / It is by his ***best*** *work* that a man should be judged. ¶It was a ***good day's*** *work*. その日は大いに仕事のはかが行った. ¶do a ***great*** *work* for the world 世界のために偉大な仕事をする. ¶In his case about 2 per cent is genius and the rest is ***hard*** *work*. 彼について言えば約二パーセントが天才で他は勤勉努力の結果だ. ‖ It is ***hard*** *work* (=difficult) to tell them apart. 離すとどっちがどっちだか分からない. 【類】earn eighteen shillings a week by ***hard*** *work* / it is ***hard*** *work* to … ‖ put in ***hard*** *work* 勉強する ‖ require ***hard*** *work* 骨が折れる. ¶after a ***hard day's*** *work* 一日せっせと働いた後で. ¶by dint of ***hard honest*** *work* 正直に一所懸命働いたために. ¶***heavy*** *work* 重労働. ¶do ***heavy*** *work* 骨の折れる仕事をやる. ¶find her ***honest*** *work* [売春婦など]正業につかせる. ¶I was too feeble to do an ***honest day's*** *work*. 私には実直に一日の仕事をやるだけの元気がなかった. 【類】do ***honest*** *work*. ¶a ***hot*** *work* 苦しい仕事. ¶at the end of a ***hot, tiring day's*** *work* 一日の劇務を終えてから. ¶***hungry*** *work* 腹の減る仕事. ¶do ***ignominious*** *work* いやしい仕事をする. ¶a more ***important*** *work* もっと大事な仕事. ¶***independent*** *work* on the part of students 学生の自主的勉強. ¶do ***indoor*** (***outdoor***) *work* 屋内(外)で仕事をする. ¶***industrial*** *work* 製作作業. ¶***instructional*** *work* 授業. ¶Severe ***intellectual*** *work* require intense mental concentration. むずかしい頭の仕事は精神の集結を必要とする. ¶be engaged in ***journalistic*** *work* 新聞編集の仕事をやっている. ¶***junior*** *work* 初年級の学業. ¶He has bestowed many years of ***laborious*** *work* on the solution of this problem. 彼はこの問題の解決に多年の労苦をささげた. ¶men returning from ***late***, or going to ***early***, *work* 遅く仕事から帰るかまたは仕事に早出をする人々. ¶***manual*** *work* 筋肉労働. ¶***mean*** and ***crooked*** *work* 卑劣で邪悪なやり口. ¶accomplish a ***memorable*** *work* 記念すべき仕事を完成する. ¶***mental*** *work* 精神労働. ¶***methodical*** *work* 組織立った仕事. ¶a ***national*** *work* 国家事業. ¶take up one's ***new*** *work* 新しい仕事につく, 就任する. ¶a ***noble*** *work* [恥かしくない]りっぱな仕事. ¶He thought teaching a ***noble, honorable*** *work* at which to spend a life-time. 彼は一生の仕事として教師は気高くりっぱな職業であると思った. ¶the ***noble*** and ***pioneering*** *work* of … …のあっぱれな草分けの仕事. ¶he has done a ***notable*** *work* in … 彼は…の方面で仕事をした. 【類】He did ***notable*** *work* as an observer (実地研究家) in natural history. ¶allot two men and a boy to ***one man's*** *work* 一人前の仕事に二人の大人と少年一人を振り当てる. ¶***organizational*** *work* 組織の仕事. ¶a real ability for ***original*** *work* 独創的な仕事をやる真の能力. ¶***outdoor*** *work* 戸外の仕事. ¶do ***outstanding*** *work* 抜群の成績をあげる ‖ clear up all ***outstanding*** *work* 主な仕事を残らず片付ける. ¶***painstaking*** *work* 骨の折れる仕事. ¶representation and jurisdiction over ***particular*** *work* 特殊作業代表及び管轄. ¶after much ***patient*** *work* he found that … 努力の結果…ということが分かった. ¶Afforestation is a ***patriotic*** *work*. 造林は一つの愛国的事業である. ¶***persistent hard*** *work* 不とう不屈の勉励. ¶***physical*** *work* 筋肉労働. ¶It is not ***pleasant*** *work*. それは愉快な仕事ではない. ¶make ***poor*** *work* of it へまをやる ‖ his ***poor*** *work* in school 彼の学業の不成績 ‖ This is ***poor*** *work* beside yours. これは君のに比べるとなってない. ¶As he grew older and kept on painting, and refused to prepare for ***practical*** bread-winning *work*, his parents grew impatient. 相当大きくなってもなお彼が絵を続けていて実際的な生業につかぬので彼の両親はやきもきした. ¶***productive*** *work* 生産的な事業. ¶After years of ***professional*** *work* he settled down as landlord of a public house in England. 彼は多年芸人商売をやっていたがやがて英国で居酒屋の主人におさまった. ¶one's ***public*** *work* その公的な仕事 ‖ ***public*** *works* [道路・水利など] 公共事業. ¶have no ***regular*** *work* 定職がない. ¶***routine*** *work* きまり切った(毎日の)仕事. ¶***sanitary*** *work* 衛生事業. ¶***secretarial*** *work* 秘書の仕事(事務). ¶***sedentary*** *work* 座業. ¶The skill can be acquired by ***sheer hard*** *work* and nothing else. それに熟達するにはただただ一所懸命にやるより他に途はない. ¶***shoddy*** *work* 堅実味のない仕事. ¶I made ***short*** *work* of him. 彼(訪問客など)をあっさり切上げてしまった. ¶***slipshod*** *work* だらしのない仕事. ¶do ***sloppy*** *work* 仕事をぞんざいにする. ¶It is ***slow*** *work*. まどろっこい. ‖ make ***slow*** *work* of… …をぐずぐずやる, …で油を売る. ¶***smart*** *work* 気のきいた仕事. ¶***solid*** and ***honest*** *work* どっしりした着実な仕事. ¶the ***specific*** *work* for which He brought you into the world 君の使命(天職). ¶he is doing a ***splendid*** *work* in connection with … 彼は…に関連したすばらしい仕事をしている ‖ accomplish ***splendid*** *work* すばらしい成績を上げる. ¶They have some sort of ***steady*** *work* to occupy their minds. 彼らには何か屈託がある. ‖ have some ***steady*** *work* あるきまった仕事を持っている. ¶***steady, persistent*** *work* うまずたゆまぬ努力. ¶***strenuous*** *work* たゆまぬ努力. ¶give a ***super-abundant*** *work* for a single pair of hands ただの二本の手にはあり余るほどの仕事を与える. ¶***tabular*** *work* 図表作成. ¶Some very ***thorough*** *work* is done. 何かしっかりした仕事をやる. ¶***topiary*** *work* 樹木の整形. ¶***tough, laborious*** *work* 困難な(骨の折れる)仕事. ¶The bower is canopied on with a ***trellis*** *work* of vines. 涼亭の上にぶどうだながある. ¶No work is ***trivial*** to him. 彼は小事にも誠実である. ¶after twelve years of ***unremitting hard*** *work* 十二年間せっせと働いて. ¶***uphill*** *work* 骨の折れる仕事. ¶do [a] ***useful*** *work* [一つの]有益な仕事をする. 【類】He has done a ***useful*** *work* for college students of that college. ¶he has done much ***valuable*** *work* for … 彼は…にとって非常に貴重な仕事をした. ¶***whole-hearted*** *work* 力一杯の仕事. ¶***women's*** *work* for women 女のための女の仕事. ¶accomplish a ***wonderful*** *work* 驚くべき事業をなし遂げる. ¶***world-wide*** *work* 世界的な事業. ¶a ***60-year-old*** *work* 創立以来六十年の事業.

Q[2] ***after-hours*** *work* 残業. ¶***art metal*** *work* 金属工芸. ¶***brain*** (=head) *work* 頭脳(精神)労働. ¶The ***building*** *work* was carried out by … 建築工事は…がやった. ¶***charity*** (=***chritable***) *work* 慈善事業. ¶***child welfare*** *work* 児童福祉事業. ¶It is not meant for ***class*** *work* (=classwork) in school. それは教室内の作業のためのものではない(本など). ¶be poor in his ***classroom*** *work* (=classwork) [運動の選手など]学課は不成績である. ¶Everything went like ***clock*** *work*. 万事順調に行った. ¶do ***collegiate-level*** *work* 大学程度の研究をする. ¶***composition*** *work* 作文の練習. ¶reinforced ***concrete*** *work* 鉄筋コンクリート工事. ¶speedy ***construction*** *work* 突貫工事. ¶a ***contract*** *work* (=job) 請負仕事. ¶do ***copying*** *work* 写しものをする. ¶***desk*** *work* 事務(系統)の仕事. ¶***detail*** *work* 細かい仕事. ¶do ***engineering*** *work* 土木(など)の仕事をやる. ¶***ensemble*** *work* 組立作業. ¶***excavation*** *work* for a projected skyscraper 高層建築基礎工事. ¶***farm*** *work* 農園の仕事. ¶***field*** *work* 野良仕事; [理科などの] 野外作業(研究). ¶a Japanese ***film*** *work* 日本の映画事業. ¶***foundation*** *work* 基礎工事. ¶***free-lance*** *work* 自由契約の仕事. ¶***ginger-***

bread work on a house 家の外部の俗っぽい装飾. ¶take ***graduate work*** 専攻科(大学院など)にはいる. 【類】He is now doing ***graduate work*** at Columbia University. ¶***grand-scale engineering*** *work* 大仕かけな土木工事. ¶It looks much like ***guess*** *work*. それは全くあて推量に過ぎないようだ. ¶All men, old as well as young, enjoy ***gymnasium*** *work*. 若いも若きも(室内)体操を喜ぶ. ¶***hand*** *work* 手工. ¶***home*** *work* 宿題; 居宅作業 ‖ do one's ***home*** *work* 宿題をやる; 内職をやる ‖ long-continuing ***home*** *work* 永続性のある内職. ¶do ***household*** *work* 家事をやる. ¶***iron*** *work* 鉄工事. ☞ iron works は「鉄工所」. ¶do ***kitchen*** *work* 勝手仕事をする. ¶***laboratory*** (***field***) *work* 研究室(実地)の仕事. ¶do the ***laundry*** *work* 洗たく仕事をする. ¶make it one's ***life*** *work* それをその一生の仕事にする ‖ determine upon a ***life*** *work* 終生の仕事を定める ‖ He does not know where his ***life*** *work* lies. 彼は自分の一生の仕事が何であるか分かっていない. ‖ pursue astronomy for one's ***life*** *work* 天文学を終生の仕事としてやる. 【類】choose one's ***life*** *work* / the ***life*** *work* that lies before one / as a ***life*** *work*. ¶***lump*** *work* 請負仕事. ¶***machine*** *work* 機械製. ¶***muscle*** *work* 筋肉労働. ¶inlaid ***mosaic*** *work* 象眼のモザイク細工. ¶***millinery*** *work* 婦人帽子製作. ¶do ***newspaper*** *work* 新聞記者の仕事をやる; 新聞事業を経営する. ¶He started his ***newspaper*** *work* as a club reporter on the Seattle Times. 氏が新聞界に入ったのはシャトルのクラブ詰記者が振り出しだった. ¶***night*** *work* 夜業. ¶***number*** *work* 数の学課. ¶handle ***office*** *work* 事務を取扱う. ¶***out-of-door*** *work* 戸外の仕事. ¶***overseas information*** *work* 海外情報の仕事. ¶***overtime*** *work* 時間外労働. ¶a mass of ***paper*** *work* 山積する書類の仕事. ¶the voluminous ***paper*** *work* that has been imposed on them by the state 国家から命ぜられた山のような書類. ¶***parrot*** *work* [個性のない]模造品. ¶***part-time*** (***full-time***) *work* パートタイムの(固定した)仕事 ‖ take up ***part-time*** extra *work* to augment one's income 収入の足しに時間給で定時外の仕事をする. ¶a ***patch*** work of quotations woven as deftly as possible into a new fabric 引用句を巧みにつなぎ合わせて作った新しい文章. ¶The plant had to turn from ***peace*** *work* to war work. その工場は平和産業から戦時産業に切り換えなければならなかった. ¶***personnel*** *work* in a department store 百貨店の人事. ¶***picket*** *work* [ストなどの]見張り(ピケ). ¶***pioneer*** *work* 創業的事業 ‖ do ***pioneer*** *work* 草分けの仕事をする. 【類】He did a good ***pioneer*** *work* with lasting results. ¶do ***pioneering*** *work* 新分野を切り開く. ¶***platform*** *work* 演壇の仕事(講演などの). ¶***police*** *work* 警察事務. ¶***post-graduate*** *work* in anthropology and psychology 人類学及び心理学の専攻科目. ¶***post-war reconstruction*** *work* 戦後の復興事業. ¶***practice*** *work* 実習. ¶***piece*** *work* でき高払い. ¶***prison*** *work* 刑務所(囚人)の作業. ¶conduct ***propaganda*** *work* among … …の中に宣伝をやる. ¶***propagandist*** *work* 宣伝事業. ¶***quality*** *work* [大学などの]質をよくする仕事. ¶the ***reclamation*** *work* 埋立工事. ¶take up active ***Red Cross*** *work* in the war zone 戦場で活発に赤十字事業をやる. ¶***rehabilitation*** *work* 更生事業. ¶the League of the Judicial ***Rehabilitation*** *Work* 司法保護事業連盟. ¶***Reisner*** *work* 寄木細工. ¶international ***relations*** *work* 国際関係の仕事. ¶medical ***relief*** *work* 医療救護. ¶conduct ***repair*** *work* on … …を修理する. ¶***rescue*** *work* 救護事業. ¶complete ***research*** *work* 研究(調査)を完成する ‖ through first-hand ***research*** *work* 研究を自分の手でやってみて. 【類】do ***research*** *work* at Rockefeller Institute. ¶do one's ***school*** *work* 学校の勉強をする. ¶do ***scout*** *work* for the M-G-M 〖映〗M-G-M 会社のために新人さがしをやる. ¶***seat*** *work*=seatwork [生徒の]机上でやる課業. ¶internal ***security*** *work* 国防(安全保障)の仕事. ¶***space*** *work* 一行いくらで書く文筆の仕事. ¶***steel*** *work* [ビルなどの]鉄骨工事. ¶I want ***summer*** *work*. 夏期の仕事が欲しい. ¶one's ***teaching*** *work* at Harvard ハーバード大学でのその先生の仕事. ¶***Team*** *work* is essential for success. 団体協力が成功に必要だ. ¶do ***team*** *work* with … …と共同作業をやる ‖ the spirit of ***team*** *work* 協力(チームワーク)精神. 【類】have fine (perfect) ***team*** *work*. ¶***trade-promotion*** *work* 貿易振興工作. ¶the leader of German ***undercover*** *work* in Argentina アルゼンチンにおけるドイツの潜行運動主動者. ¶He has done his ***undergraduate*** *work* at Yale. 彼はエール大学で修業をした. ¶***undergraduate*** and ***graduate*** *work* 大学課程及び修士課程の履修. ¶students who could do standard ***university*** *work* 本式の大学課程をやればやれる学生. ¶***unemployment relief*** *work* 失業救済事業. ¶***uphill*** *work* 骨折仕事. ¶women's ***war*** *work* 婦人の戦時勤労. ¶***welfare*** *work* 厚生事業.

P　Though a peer he is not ***above*** *work*. 彼は貴族であるが仕事をすればその威厳にかかわるとは考えていない. ¶tired, ***after*** a day's *work* 一日働いて疲れて. ¶building of a pagoda ***as*** a *work* of merit 功徳のための塔の建築. ¶see the University ***at*** *work* 大学の授業を参観する ‖ There may be other factors ***at*** *work*. 他の原因も介在しているのかも知れない. ‖ The machinery is ***at*** *work* (=on the job). その機械は運転中. ‖ It seemed to the audience that some supernatural power was ***at*** *work* 聴衆には何か超自然的な力が作用しているように思えた. 【類】He is ***at*** *work* at (=on) fossils (化石の研究). / ***at*** *work* independently on … / He is hard ***at*** *work* on a novel ‖ die ***at*** one's *work* 殉職する ‖ You can make money ***at*** this *work*. この仕事で金もうけができる. ‖ be ***at*** *work* early in the morning 早朝から就業している ‖ be an artist ***at*** the *work* その仕事に妙を得ている. ¶He is noted ***for*** his *work* in synthetic chemistry. 彼は合成化学の研究家として知られている. ¶rest ***from*** one's *work* 仕事を休む ‖ He came home ***from*** his *work* in the evening. 彼は夕方仕事から家に帰って来た. ¶He is ***in*** *work*. 彼は職についている. ‖ ***in*** a *work* of this character この種の仕事では. ¶The conjuring is a wonderfully clever piece ***of*** *work*. その手品は実にうまくできている. ‖ the successful accomplishment ***of*** a great *work* 偉大な事業の達成. ¶The factory people are ***on*** night *work*. 工場では夜業をしている. ‖ get started ***on*** one's literary *work* 文筆の仕事にとりかかる. ¶be ***out of*** *work* 失業している. 【類】About 300 men have been thrown ***out of*** *work*. ¶huddle ***over*** one's *work* 仕事をぞんざいにやる. ¶***through*** hard *work* 骨を折って. ¶go ***to*** *work* 出勤する ‖ Hey, boys! Get down ***to*** *work*. おいみんな仕事にかかれ. ‖ go ***to*** *work* upon … …に取りかかる. 【類】go back ***to*** *work*. ¶***Under*** the unaccustomed *work* I broke down. 慣れない仕事なので私はへたばった. ¶Help me ***with*** my *work*. この仕事を手伝ってくれ. ‖ I am not through ***with*** my *work* yet. 私はまだ仕事が済まない. ‖ How's he getting on ***with*** his *work*? 彼の仕事はどうですか.

P²　Paul Binner and his noble *work* ***among*** the deaf ポール・ビナーと耳の不自由な者のための彼の崇高な事業. ¶his *work* ***for*** the encouragement of Oriental studies 東洋学奨励のための彼の事業 ‖ *Work* ***for*** them is only an interval in play. あの連中の仕事は遊びの合の手みたいなものだ. ¶It is not the *work* ***of*** a day or a month or a year. それは一日や一月や一年やでできる仕事ではない. ‖ That seemed to be the *work* ***of*** a magician. それは魔術師のやったことのように思えた. ‖ It's the *work* ***of*** thieves. それは泥棒のしわざだ. ‖ This was the *work* ***of*** life to which his nature fits him. これが彼の本性に適した終生の仕事であった. ‖ The fire is thought to be the *work* ***of*** an incendiary. その火事の原因は放火ということだ. ‖ a *work* ***of*** the greatest difficulty 困難きわまる仕事 ‖ the *work* ***of*** reform 改革事業. ‖ That's the *work* ***of*** your imagination. そりゃ神経のせいだ. ¶The story proved to be nothing but a *work* ***of*** imagination. その話は結局根のないものだった. ¶*work* ***on*** the construction of … …の建築工事 ‖ The *work* ***on*** the railway has been energetically proceeded with. その鉄道工事は大いに進行を急いだ. ‖ women's *work* ***on*** newspapers and magazines 新聞雑誌編集における婦人の仕事 ‖ the artist is at *work* ***on*** … その画家は…を制作中である. 【類】His story is often a *work* ***of*** imagination. / my *work* ***on*** Lesson 16. ¶He is at present at *work* ***upon*** a revised edition of his dictionary. 彼は今彼の辞書の改訂をやっている. ¶undertake systematic research *work* ***with regard to*** (=concerning) … …に関する組織的研究を試みる. ¶*work* ***without*** pay 無給労働.

(**2**) 作品, 著作; 工芸(作)品.

V　To ***analyze*** the *works* of the best painters requires very subtle discriminations. 一流画家の作品を解剖するにはきわめて鋭敏な眼識を要する. ¶***annotate*** the *works* of Bacon ベイコンの著作に注釈を施す. ¶the *work* is questionably ***assigned*** to … それは…の作ということだが疑わし

い. ¶***bring*** the *work* into line with recent researches その本に最近の研究をとり入れる. ¶he ***brought out*** a small *work* entitled ... 彼は…という題名の小著を出版した. ¶***compile*** a superfluous *work* むだな本を編集する. ¶His aim was to ***compose*** a *work* which has a reason for its existence. 存在理由のある著述を作るというのが彼の目的であった. ¶a *work* ***conceived*** and executed ***con amore*** 道楽に考え作り上げたもの. ¶a *work* that may still be ***consulted*** with profit 今日でもなお参考書として有益な著作. ¶***copy*** *or* ***photograph*** *works* of art 美術品を複写または写真にとる. ¶"***crib***" (=copy) one's *work* [絵など]その作を模写する. ¶***eulogize*** one's *work* その作を称賛する. ¶The *work* was ***executed*** by a well-known artist. それは有名な画家の作品だ. ‖ *work* ***executed*** by students 学生の製作品. ¶***form*** an invaluable *work* of reference 非常に貴重な参考書となっている. ¶***inscribe*** a *work* to ... 著書を…に献題する. ¶He has ***left*** behind Titanic *work*. 彼は偉大な作品を残して死んだ. ¶***pirate*** *works* of English authors 英国の著者の作を盗み取る. ¶I rarely fail to ***place*** my *work*. 私の原稿は滅多に没書にはならない. ¶***prepare*** a *work* for press 著作を印刷に付する準備をする. ¶***produce*** a *work* of art 美術品を制作する ‖ I do not pretend to have ***produced*** a *work* without mistakes. 私は誤りがない本を作ったなどと思い上ってはいない. ¶He has ***published*** several *works* of great scientific importance. 彼はすこぶる科学的に重要性のある著書を数種出した. ¶***reprint*** the *works* of the dead 故人の著作を復刻する. ¶It has long been the wish of our scholars to ***see*** a *work* of this kind. この種の著作を見たいというのがわが国の学徒たちの長い間の望みだった. ¶***send*** the *work* ***forth*** with every desire to ... …ことを切に祈りつつ本書を世に送る. ¶***sign*** one's *works* その作品に銘を打つ. 【類】***sign*** one's *work* with one's name.

V[2] the *work* that ***follows*** is ... 本書は…(序文などの言葉).

Q an ***all-one-hand*** *work* [何もかも一人でやる]一元的作品. ¶The *work* is now ***antiquated***. その本はもう古い. ¶***authoritative*** *works* of reference 権威ある参考書. ¶a ***botanical*** *work* 植物学の本. ¶***choice*** *works* in lacquer 精選した(極上等の)漆器. ¶a ***clandestine*** *work* 秘密出版書. ¶a ***colossal*** *work* 一大巨作. ¶a ***composite*** *work* 合作. ¶a ***contemporary*** *work* 現代の作品. ¶prizes offered for ***creditable*** *works* 優秀作品にかけた懸賞. ¶the ***crowning*** *work* of his great life 輝やかしい彼の一生の作品中の傑作. ¶an ***epoch-making*** *work* 画期的著作. ¶an ***erudite*** *work* うん蓄を傾けた著書. ¶several ***excellent*** *works* already exist on this subject. この問題に関してはすぐれた著書が幾つかある. 【類】an ***excellent*** *work* of its kind. ¶It is merely the refashioning of a previously ***existing*** *work*. それは前からあった本の焼直しに過ぎない. ¶his ***extant*** *works* 現存する彼の著作. ¶an ***extinct*** *work* 逸書. ¶It has long been recognized as one of the ***fairest*** and most ***lucid*** *works* on socialism. それは多年社会主義に関する著作の中でも最も公平で簡明なものと認められている. ¶a ***forgotten*** *work* 世間から忘れられた著作. ¶a ***great*** *work* of art 偉大な芸術品. ¶a ***great*** and ***permanent*** *work* of art 永久性のある名画. ¶a ***hand-written*** *work* 写本. ¶a ***handy*** and ***compendious*** *work* of reference 手ごろで要を得た参考書. ¶a ***handy little*** *work* 手ごろなポケット型の本. ¶***historical*** *works* 歴史に関する著作. ¶***important*** and ***authoritative*** *works* 重要な権威ある著述. ¶an ***indispensable*** *work* of reference for ... …に不可欠な参考書. ¶a deeply ***interesting*** *work* 非常に興味深い著作. ¶The Atlas forms an ***invaluable*** *work* of reference. その世界地図は非常に貴重な参考書である. ¶***Japanese*** *works* of art in porcelain, bronze, and lacquer 磁器・青銅製品及び漆器の日本工芸品. ¶his most ***labored*** *work* 彼の最大力作. ¶***learned*** *works* of sociology 高級な社会学の著書. ¶The NED is the greatest ***lexicographical*** *work* on the English language ever undertaken. NED は英語辞書編集における空前の偉業である. ¶a ***literary*** *work* of seven volumes 七巻ものの文学作品 ‖ do one's ***literary*** *work* 著作をやる. 【類】***Literary*** *work* does not pay (割に合わない) in Spain. ‖ dabble in ***literary*** *work* 著述に手を出す. ¶one's ***main*** *work* その主な著作. ¶The Dictionary of National Biography is a ***massive*** *work* consisting of 66 volumes. 英国人名辞典は六十六巻からなる巨大の著作である. ¶a ***monumental*** *work* on the history of Japan 日本史に関する画期的な著作. 【類】accomplish a ***monumental*** *work* on Buddhism. ¶Publishing is the business of ***multiplying*** literary *works*. 出版は著作を複製する仕事である. ¶the ***outstanding*** *work* of the year その年の最も傑出した著作. 【類】***outstanding*** *work* in Italian fiction (小説) of its period. ¶a ***pleasant*** and ***engaging*** *work* [見て]気持ちのよい魅力的な作品. ¶a ***ponderous*** *work* 大部の著作. ¶the author's most ***popular*** *work* その著者の一番評判の好い作. ¶the ***present*** *work* 本書(序文などで). ¶the proud acquisition of an oil painter's ***priceless*** *work* of art 自慢の種となるような貴重な油絵の入手. ¶a ***primary*** (***secondary***) *work* 根本的(根本的著作を基本にした)著作. ¶a ***pure*** and ***chaste*** *work* 純潔高雅な著作. ¶***rare*** and ***valuable*** *works* 珍貴な作品. ¶It is quite a ***recent*** *work*. それはごく新しい著作だ. ¶a ***scholarly*** *work* 学術的著作. ¶a ***second-rate*** *work* 二流の作品. ¶a ***serious*** *work* of great value 大いに価値のある(まじめな)著作. ¶a ***small*** *work* 小著. ¶a ***special*** (=specialized) *work* 専門書. ¶a ***sumptuous*** *work*, beautifully printed and profusely illustrated 美麗に印刷され多数さし絵がはいった豪華本. ¶a purely ***technical*** *work* 技術専門書. ¶a ***tough*** *work* 堅い書物. ¶a ***trashy*** *work* 取るに足らない作. ¶a ***type-written*** *work* タイプライターで打った著作. ¶an ***unserviceable*** *work* 役に立たない本. ¶a ***valuable*** *work* of (=for) reference 貴重な参考書. ¶***various*** *works* 色々な作品. ¶read the ***whole*** *work* in proof その本全体を校正で読む. ¶a ***youthful*** *work* 若い時の著作.

Q[2] an ***art*** *work* 美術書. ¶a separate and ***companion*** *work* to ... …の別冊姉妹編. ¶***cinematograph*** *works* of the Paramount パ社の映画作品. ¶an ***early*** (a ***middle***, ***late***) ***period*** *work* 初(中・後)期の作. ¶a ***four-volume*** *work* on logics 論理学に関する四巻もの. ¶a ***handicraft*** *work* 手芸書. ¶a handy ***one-volume*** *work* of ready reference 軽便な一巻ものの参考書. ¶The OED is the ***parent*** *work* of the POD, the COD and the SOD. OED は POD, COD 及び SOD の親本である. ¶Breal's ***pioneer*** *work* on semantics ブレアルの意味論に関する独創的著作. ¶Milton's ***prose*** *works* ミルトンの散文作品. ¶a ***reference*** *work* 参考書 ‖ an old-line ***reference*** *work* 旧式の参考書. ¶a ***seven-volume*** *work* 七巻もの. ¶a ***standard*** *work* of its class 類書中の定本 ‖ a ***standard*** *work* of English literature 定評のある英文学の作品 ‖ The book is generally recognized as a ***standard*** *work* on the subject. 同書はその問題に関する定本として一般に認められている. ¶an exhibit of ***student*** *works* 生徒作品の展示. ¶a ***tapestry*** *work* つづれ織の製品(どんちょうなど).

P ***among*** his *works* in sculpture are a bust of ..., a statue of ... 彼の彫刻品の中には…の胸像, …の立像などがある. ¶regard a speech ***as*** a *work* of art 演説を芸術品と見なす.

P[2] Here is another welcome *work* ***from*** his pen. 彼がまた好著書を公にした. ¶a *work* ***in*** silver 銀製品. ¶the *works* ***of*** modern historians concerning the past, produced after a study of the original sources 根本史料によって作った近代史家の歴史に関する著作 ‖ *works* ***of*** the same kind 同種類の作品 ‖ *works* ***of*** ceramic art 陶磁器製品 ‖ a *work* ***of*** art executed by ... …の製作に係る芸術品 ‖ the statue is the *work* ***of*** ... その像は…の作だ ‖ *works* ***of*** moral purpose 道徳的目標を有する作品 ‖ The story is a *work* ***of*** imagination. その話は作ったものだ. ‖ these are the *work* ***of*** ... これらは…の作である ‖ To analyze and trace the cause of this would be the *work* ***of*** a long essay, or perhaps of a volume. この理由を分析し研究しようとしたら大論文否恐らく一巻の著作を書かなければなるまい. ‖ the *work* ***of*** his hands 彼の手製品. ¶*works* ***upon*** history 歴史上の著作.

(**3**) *pl.* 工場; *pl.* 施設; *pl.* [機械の]動く部分.

V The employers have ***closed*** their *works*. 経営者は工場を閉鎖した. 【類】The *works* are ***closed***. ¶***construct*** harbor *works* 築港する. ¶***re-organize*** a *works* 工場を改組する. ¶***shut down*** a *works* 工場を[一時]閉鎖する.

Q The average life of any machine constantly running, for example, in a ***large*** *works*, is accurately known. 例えば大工場のそれのごとく絶えず運転している機械の平均寿命は正確に分かっている. ¶the ***upper*** *works* of a ship 船の乾げん.

Q[2] ***defense*** *works* 防衛施設; 築城, とりで ‖ set up ***defense*** *works* 防塁を設ける. ¶a ***gas*** *works* ガス工場. ¶The ***glass*** (***brick***) *works* is near the station. ガラス(など)工場は駅の近くだ. ¶an ***ice*** *works* 製氷所. ¶an ***iron*** *works* 鉄工所. ¶a ***lithography*** *works* 石版工場. ¶a ***munitions*** *works* 軍需工場. ¶an ***ordnance*** *works* 兵器工場. ¶a ***printing*** *works* 印刷所(工場). ¶a ***salt*** *works* 製塩所. ¶the Anshan ***steel*** *works* 安山鉄鋼場.

P² the *works* ***of*** a watch 時計の機械.

work, *v*. 働く, 動く; 働かす, 動かす; 運行する.

M *work* most ***arduously*** upon the manuscript of a book 全力を尽して書物の原稿を書く. ¶*work* ***assiduously*** 精出して働く. ¶*work* ***away*** industriously at ... せっせと...をやって行く. ¶The arrangement has not *worked* ***badly***. そのやり方は成績が悪くなかった. ¶It seems that my plan is *working* ***beautifully***. 私の案は誠にうまく行っているらしい. ¶Sesshu, Masanobu, and Motonobu *worked* ***chiefly*** in monochrome, using color sparingly. 雪舟•正信及び元信は余り色絵具を使わないで主として単色画を描いた. ¶*work* ***confidently*** and ***cheerfully*** 安心して愉快に働く. ¶*work* ***conscientiously*** 良心的(まじめ)に働く. ¶The vessel is *working* ***deeper*** into the sand (mud). その船は次第に砂(泥)深くはまり込んで行く. ¶*work* ***diligently*** かいがいしく働く. ¶*work* ***double tides*** (=day and night) 昼夜兼行で働く. ¶*work* ***far*** into the night 夜遅くまで働く. ¶*work* ***faithfully*** 誠実に働く. ¶*work* ***frantically*** 血まなこになってやる. ¶*work* ***freely*** (***stiffly***) [機械など]なめらかに動く(ぎすぎすする). ¶*work* ***full time*** 全部の時間を提供して働く. ¶*work* ***hand in hand*** with ... ...と提携して働く. ¶The carpenter *works* ***handily***. その大工は仕事が器用だ. ¶He *worked* ***hard*** at school and was always the first in his class. 彼は学校で大勉強をしいつも一番であった. ‖ *work* ***hard*** at one's studies (lessons, profession) その学業(など)に精を出す. 【類】*work* ***hard*** at arithmetic problems (算術の問題) ‖ He *works* his men very ***hard***. 彼は非常に人使いが荒い. ¶He is so weak that he can ***hardly*** *work*. 衰弱していて仕事はほとんどやれない. ¶*work* together ***harmoniously*** for their common interests. 共同の利益のために一致協力して働く. ¶*work* ***heartily*** 身を入れて働く. ¶*work* ***joylessly*** いやいや働く. ¶*work* ***laboriously*** 刻苦勉強する. ¶*work* ***late*** into the night 夜遅くまで働く ‖ avoid *working* ***late*** at night 勉強(仕事)で夜ふかしをしないようにする. ¶*work* ***late*** and ***early*** 朝から夜遅くまで働く. ¶*work* onc's fingers ***nervously*** 指を神経質に動かす. ¶*work* ***nimbly*** 敏活に働く. ¶*work* ***out*** detailed arrangements 細かい準備をする ‖ *work* ***out*** a compromise 妥協を成立させる ‖ *work* ***out*** one's own destiny 自己の運命を開拓する ‖ *work* ***out*** a mine 鉱山を開発する ‖ *work* ***out*** at ... yen [計算してみると]...円になる ‖ It *works* ***out*** at the rate of ... それは...の割合になる ‖ *work* ***out*** a further development of the plan その計画の前進を計る ‖ *work* ***out*** in detail 細かに記述する ‖ *work* ***out*** a formula 一つの方式を考え出す ‖ *work* ***out*** practical means for ... ...の実行できうる方法を考え出す ‖ *work* ***out*** sums 算術の問題を解く. 【類】*work* ***out*** theories in one's own chosen field ‖ *work* ***out*** wrong 間違ったやり方をする. 【類】*work* ***out*** methods of ... / *work* ***out*** one's *ideas* / *work* ***out*** improvements on ... / *work* ***out*** one's invention / *work* ***out*** a merger (併合) / *work* ***out*** a plan / *work* ***out*** a policy / try to *work* ***out*** a program for ... / *work* ***out*** a long-range recovery program / *work* ***out*** one's own salvation / The system has been *worked* ***out*** with much thought and labor. / The puzzle won't *work* ***out***. / It does not *work* ***out*** in practice. / *work* ***out*** its solution / *work* ***out*** a just settlement / *work* ***out*** the question whether ... / *work* ***out*** difficult problems that confront them / *work* ***out*** the problem of life by himself / *work* ***out*** the problem for themselves / The market value of radium in Europe at the present moment *works* ***out*** (=is calculated) at somewhere about $2,500,000 per ounce. / *work* ***out*** at an average of ... / The fare charged *worked* ***out*** at a penny a mile. / Second-class fares (二等乗車賃) *work* ***out*** at about three-fifths of the first and the charge for third-class amounts to about one-fifth of the first-class fare. / These statistics *work* ***out*** to 1.24 passenger deaths for every 100,000,000 passenger miles flown. / The travelling expenses *work* ***out*** at ... per day each. ‖ It will *work* ***out*** to our mutual advantage. それは結局われわれ双方の利益になるだろう. ¶The men are *working* ***overtime*** (=till after usual hours). 職工が残業をしている. ¶failure to report to *work* ***punctually*** 出勤時刻の不正確. ¶*work* ***quickly*** and ***earnestly*** 敏活かつ熱心に働く. ¶The engine *works* ***satisfactorily***. その機関は具合よく運転する. ¶We *work* ***shorthanded***. われわれは手不足だ. ¶*work* ***single-handed*** 人手を借りずにやる. ¶Everything is *working* ***smoothly***. 万事滞りなく行っている. ‖ The typewriter *works* ***smoothly***. このタイプライターは調子がいい. ¶The Carnegie Institution *works* ***specially*** for the promotion of science. カーネギー研究所は科学の進歩をその主眼としている. ¶*work* ***steadily*** むらなく働く. ¶***strenuously*** *work* for one's own interests 自身の利益のために奮闘努力する. ¶It *worked* so ***strongly*** on my soul. 私はそのために非常に胸を打たれた. ¶It does not always *work* ***successfully***. それはいつもうまく行くという訳には行かない. ¶*work* ***tirelessly*** うまずに働く. ¶*work* ***together*** amicably 折合よく働く ‖ *work* ***together*** for their common good 共同の利益のため協力する. ¶*work* ***vigorously*** in this direction 鋭意この方面に尽力する ‖ The mine is being *worked* ***vigorously***. 鉱山は目下盛んに採掘中. ¶The plan has not *worked* ***well*** in practice. その案は実地にやってうまく行かなかった. ‖ The student *worked* ***well*** enough not to be dismissed and poorly enough not to excel. その学生は退学をされるまでの不成績にはならなかったがそれかといって優秀な成績を取るほどの勉強もしなかった. ‖ The engines are *working* very ***well*** (***badly***). それらの機械はとても調子がよい(悪い). ¶*work* ***zealously*** 熱心に働く. ¶The plan is *working* ***smoothly***. その案はうまく行っている.

M² *work* the good yarn ***in*** with bad 良い糸に悪い糸を混ぜて織る ‖ slowly *work* ***in*** a wire 徐々に鉄線を通す ‖ My plan did not *work* ***in*** with theirs. 私の案は彼らの案と合わなかった. ¶*work* ***in*** an incident in a novel ある出来事を小説に織り込む. ¶It *worked* ***off*** in about an hour. それ(感など)は一時間ばかりで消えてしまった. ‖ *work* ***off*** (=get rid of) the cold かぜを抜く ‖ *work* ***off*** one's debt to... 仕事をして...に対する負債を片づける ‖ *work* ***off*** impurities 不純物を除く ‖ About 1,000 copies of the book were *worked* ***off***. その本が千部ばかりでき上った. ‖ *work* ***off*** surplus fat [肥えた人が体操などをして]ぜい肉をとる ‖ *work* ***off*** shopworn goods 店ざらし品を整理する ‖ He *works* ***off*** his bad temper on his servants. 彼は腹が立つと召使いに当りちらす. ‖ *work* ***off*** one's vexation 悩み(くやしさ)を忘れる. ¶To be *worked* ***on***. 工事所要個所. ‖ *work* ***on*** till late at night 遅くまで働き続ける ‖ *work* ***on*** bravely to the end 最後まで勇敢に努力を続ける. ¶Things are *working* ***round*** in my favor. 形勢がだんだん私に有利になってきた. ‖ He began by ... and *worked* ***round*** to the main theme. 彼は...から筆を起しやがて本題に入った. ¶*work* ***up*** an appetite 働いて腹を減らす ‖ *work* ***up*** a business 商売を築き上げる ‖ *work* ***up*** a collection of data into a book form 集めた材料を整理して本にする ‖ *work* ***up*** from the bottom 根底から築き上げる ‖ There is an impression that a man may *work* ***up*** faster in a smaller company than in a large one. 大きな会社よりも小さな会社の方が昇進が早いように思われる. ‖ *work* ***up*** the excitement of the mob 群集を興奮させる ‖ *work* ***up*** materials into finished goods 材料を加工して製品にする ‖ *worked* ***up*** all the money he had 手持ちの金を全部使い果した ‖ *work* ***up*** a reputation for oneself 自分の名声をあげる ‖ *work* ***up*** a trade in coal 石炭の商売を始める ‖ *work* oneself ***up*** into a passion 自分で興奮する ‖ *work* oneself ***up*** to imaginary misfortune [実際はそうでないのに]自分は不幸の身だと思い込む ‖ a young fighter who has *worked* his way ***up*** 自己の進路を切り開いた勇敢な青年 ‖ *work* one's way ***up*** to a position of trust and responsibility 努力して信用と責任ある地位に進出する ‖ Things were *working* ***up*** to a climax. 事態は次第に頂点に近づいていた. ‖ *work* ***up iron*** into tools 鉄から器具を作る.

P learn to *work* ***against*** the clock 急速度で仕事がやれるようになる ‖ in the long run it will *work* ***against*** ... それは結局は...の不利になるであろう. ¶men who *work* ***about*** machinery 機械に近接して働く男たち. ‖ It is *working* ***against*** the collar for that boy to study. その少年には勉強はにが手である. ¶This aroused the usual hostility in minds *working* ***along*** the older grooves. これは例によって頭の古い連中の反感を買った. ‖ *work* ***against*** a deadline 期限を前に大童で活動する. ¶*work* ***as*** a clerk 書記として働

く. ¶a man who *works **at*** a desk 机に向って仕事をする人 ‖ A compositer *works **at*** the case. 植字工は活字箱に向って仕事をする. ‖ earn money by *working **at*** home 自宅で働いて金もうけをする ‖ *work **at*** exercises 練習問題をやる ‖ *work **at*** one's writing その原稿を書く ‖ These engines *work **at*** 2,500 h.p. これらの機関は二千五百馬力で運転する. ‖ The factory is *working **at*** top capacity. その工場は全能力をあげて仕事をやっている. ‖ *work **at*** one's trade (vocation) その家業(業務)を営む ‖ He has *worked **at*** the topic (=subject) for many years. 彼は多年その問題を研究してきた. ‖ *work **at*** a difficult problem in mathematics 数学の難問題を解こうとする ‖ *work **at*** a social reform 社会改良に従事する ‖ The author is still *working **at*** the dictionary. 著者が今もその辞書の編集に従事している. ‖ *work **at*** some trade or other 何かの商売をやる ‖ a railway train *worked **by*** locomotive 機関車がけん引する列車. ¶*worked **by*** electricity (spring) 電気(など)仕掛けの ‖ *work **by*** [the] day 日ぎめで働く ‖ *work **by*** night 夜間働く. ¶A man earns what he *works **for***. 人は目的を持って働いて始めてそれを自分のものにできるのだ. 【類】When a man *works* only ***for*** himself, he gets neither rest here, nor reward hereafter.—R. Collyer. ‖ *work **for*** about an hour on urgent papers 至急を要する書類に一時間ばかり目を通す ‖ He never had to *work **for*** a living. 彼は決して食うために働く必要はなかった. ‖ The student was compelled to *work **for*** self-support. その学生は苦学をしなければならなかった. ‖ I have been *working **for*** a salary all my life. 私は一生俸給生活をして来た. 【類】those who *work **for*** small pay ‖ teachers who are *working **for*** a higher certificate さらに上級の免許状を得ようと勉強している教師 ‖ *Work **for*** the world—Marx's favorite slogan. マルクスの好んで用いた標語一世界のために働け ‖ *work **for*** the good of humanity (a great cause) 人類(大義)のために働く. 【類】those *working **for*** common ends / institutions *working **for*** public good ‖ *work* more ***for*** the injury than for the good of ... ...の利益となるよりもむしろ害になる ‖ I *work **for*** Mr. ... 私は...氏の所で働いている. ‖ *work **for*** the company as a clerk-typist 事務兼タイピストとしてその会社に勤める. ¶*work **from*** hunger 空腹なので(パンのために)働く. ¶A blacksmith *works **in*** iron and a carpenter in timber. かじ屋は鉄, 木工は材木を取扱って仕事をする. ‖ *work **in*** oil and water-color 油絵や水彩画を描く. 【類】*work **in*** the interest of humanity (人類) / *work **in*** one's study till late ‖ *work **in*** the city and live in the suburbs 職場は都市で住居は郊外である ‖ *work **in*** a feeble manner うわついて仕事をする ‖ *work **in*** literature 文学方面で働く ‖ *working **in*** shift 交替作業 ‖ *work **in*** full swing フルに動く(運転する). ¶*work **into*** one's favor 人に取り入る ‖ women's hair *worked **into*** a rope なわのように編んだ女の頭髪 ‖ *work* far ***into*** the night 夜遅くまで働く(勉強する). ¶*work **like*** a nigger 真黒になって働く ‖ It *works **like*** a charm. [薬など] それは不思議にきく. ‖ The treatment (medicine) *works **like*** magic. その療法(薬)は不思議にきく. ¶I set to *work **on*** the proof soon after breakfast. 私は朝食を済ませるとすぐに校正の仕事に取掛った. ‖ A man was *working **on*** a tombstone in the churchyard, engraving an epitaph. 一人の男が教会の境内で石碑に銘を刻んでいた. 【類】The painter *worked **on*** the portrait for four years and then left it unfinished. / *work **on*** a tapestry (つづれにしき) / At present I am *working **on*** a 5 ft. canvas—a picture of sheep. ‖ He has been *working **on*** the problem these four years. 彼はこの四年間その問題の解決に努めてきた. ‖ The police are *working **on*** the case. 警察はその事件を取扱っている. ‖ *work **on*** a railway 鉄道に勤める ‖ He formerly *worked **on*** a magazine (newspaper). 彼はもとある雑誌(など)に関係していた. ‖ people *working **on*** the post but residing off the post 職場はそこにあるが別の所に住んでいる人々. ¶*working **on*** this suggestion これに暗示を得て(研究など) ‖ *work **on*** the mystery of cancer がんのなぞを解くことに努める ‖ He had been *working **on*** the idea for years. 彼は多年にわたってその着想を物にしようと努力していた. ‖ *work **on*** pictures 映画の仕事をする(映画俳優など) ‖ *work **on*** the curiosity of the young 青年の好奇心に働きかける. 【類】*work **on*** a problem of ... ‖ *work* damaged goods ***on*** customers 客にいたんだ品をはめこむ ‖ Oil engines *work **on*** refined or crude petroleum. 石油発動機は精製石油または重油で運転する. 【類】*work **on*** the same plan with a difference (趣きを変えて). ¶*work* one ***out of*** one's errors その過ちを改めさせる. ¶*work **through*** a third party 第三者を通じて働きかける ‖ *work **through*** the literature bearing on the subject その題目に関する文献をあさる ‖ *work* one's way ***through*** college 苦学(アルバイト)して大学を出る. ¶*work **to*** the same end 同じ目的で働く ‖ The storm *wrought* great mischief ***to*** fruit-trees. その暴風で果樹に大被害があった. ‖ It has not yet been *worked **to*** the limit. まだ行き詰りにはなっていない. ¶*work **towards*** such a result こうした結果をもたらすように仕向ける ‖ It *works **toward*** the same end. それは同じ目的達成を助長する. ‖ *work **toward*** peace 平和に向って努力する. ¶*work **under*** the capitalist for a wage 給料を得るために資本家の下で働く ‖ The factories are *worked **under*** forced draught. 諸工場は大車輪で仕事をやっている. ¶*work **upon*** (=appeal to) man's desire for the betterment of his condition さらに良い地位を得ようとする欲望に訴える ‖ accept it as a basis to *work **upon*** それを労働(研究)の基礎条件にすることに同意する ‖ *Working **upon*** this hypothesis inquiries were made. この仮説を基礎にして研究が進められた ‖ *work **upon*** another's feelings 人の感情に働きかける(訴える). ¶*work **with*** hand (head) 筋肉(精神)労働をする ‖ the old American passion for *working **with*** their hands 肉体労働をいとわないという昔からのアメリカ人の情熱 ‖ The painter *works **with*** his brush and paint. 画家は絵筆と絵具を使って製作をする. ‖ *work **with*** the group and class グループやクラスで教授する ‖ all who *works **with*** poultry 養鶏の仕事をやるすべての人々. 【類】One who *works **with*** wood is called a carpenter. ‖ An idiot cannot *work **with*** figures. 白痴は数の計算ができない. ‖ *work **with*** a retail florist for fourteen dollars a week 一週十四ドルで花屋に奉公する ‖ His talk on how he *works **with*** his English classes was full of valuable hints. 彼の英語教授経験談は貴重な示唆に富んでいた. ‖ This man is going to *work **with*** us in the advertising department. この人は今度宣伝部で一緒に仕事をすることになりました(新入社の人の紹介). ‖ *work **with*** a will 身を入れて働く ‖ The methods that *work **with*** one will not necessarily work with another. 甲の人がやってうまく行く方法必ずしも乙の人にもそうであるとは限らない. 【類】A laborer is one who *works **with*** his hands; an artisan is one who *works **with*** his hands and his head; an artist is one who *works **with*** his hands, his head, and his heart. ‖ He *worked* (=operated) his farm ***with*** success. 彼は農園経営に成功した. ‖ His face *worked **with*** emotion. 興奮して顔の筋肉がぴくぴく動いた. ¶*work **without*** cessation のべつ幕なしに働く.

worker, *n.* 働き手, 労務員.

v Missionary labors ***invest*** the humblest *worker* in the vineyard with a nobility that kings might envy. 伝道に従事する人にはいかに下っぱのものでも王侯がうらやむような尊さが備わる. ¶***underpay*** and ***sweat*** *workers* 職工を安い賃金でこき使う.

Q an ***accurate*** and ***speedy*** *worker* 仕事が正確で早い人. ¶an ***active*** *worker* for the reform その改革運動に実際に働いている人(行動隊員). ¶an ***ardent*** *worker* in the movement その運動の熱心な参加者. ¶***busy social*** *workers* 忙しい社会事業家. ¶***casual*** *workers* 臨時の労働者. ¶a ***ceaseless*** *worker* 間断なく働く人. ¶a ***clerical*** *worker* 事務員. 【類】a high-class ***clerical*** *worker*. ¶a most ***conscientious*** *worker* もっとも良心的な働き手. ¶a ***deliberate*** *worker* 念入りに仕事をする人. ¶a ***diligent*** and ***indefatigable*** *worker* うまずたゆまぬ働き手. ¶a ***domestic*** *worker* 家庭生活者. ¶an ***earlier*** *worker* in the field その方面の開拓者の一人. ¶an ***earnest*** (a ***faithful***) *worker* まじめ(忠実)に働く人. ¶an ***energetic*** *worker* 精力家. ¶a ***fast*** *worker* 仕事が早い人. ¶a ***fitful*** *worker* 気分で働く人. ¶Some students are very ***hard*** *workers*. 学生の中には非常な勉強家もある. ¶a ***hard conscientious*** *worker* 非常にまじめな努力家. ¶a ***heavy*** *worker* 重労働者. ¶an ***honest*** *worker* with poultry 実直(地道)な養鶏家. ¶***industrial*** *workers* 産業労働者. ¶an ***industrious*** and ***conscientious*** *worker* まじめな勤勉家. ¶***intellectual*** (=***brain***) *workers* 精神労働者. ¶***internal*** and ***external*** *workers* 内勤外勤者. ¶a ***literary*** *worker* 文士. ¶a ***loyal*** *worker* 忠実に働く人. ¶a ***manual*** *worker* 筋肉労働者. ¶a ***mental*** (=brain) *worker* 精神労働者.

¶ ***meritorious*** and ***persevering*** *workers* 力量があってよく勉励する人. ¶ a ***migrant*** *worker* 出かせぎ人. ¶ an ***outdoor*** *worker* 現業労働者. ¶ an ***overly talkative*** *worker* 不まじめで口数の多い働き手. ¶ a ***patient*** *worker* 辛棒強い働き手. ¶ ***political*** *workers* 政治関係者. ¶ the efforts of ***previous*** *workers* in the same field 同じ方面に活動した先輩の努力. ¶ a ***prolific*** *worker* 多作家. ¶ a ***quick*** *worker* 敏腕家. ¶ ***regular*** *worker* 定業者. ¶ a ***reliable*** *worker* 信頼のできる働き手. ¶ ***religious*** *workers* 宗教家. ¶ ***scholarly*** *workers* 学者. ¶ a ***scientific*** *worker* 科学者. ¶ a ***sedulous*** *worker* 勤勉家. ¶ a ***skilled*** (***semi-skilled***) *worker* [半]熟練工. ¶ ***social*** *workers* 社会事業にたずさわる人. ¶ ***subsequent*** *workers* in the same field 同じ方面で活動する後輩. ¶ a ***serious*** *worker* まじめな働き手. ¶ a ***tireless*** *worker* 辛抱強い勉強家. ¶ ***unorganized*** *workers* 未組織労働者たち. ¶ an ***unskilled*** *worker* 不熟練工. ¶ He is an ***unsteady*** *worker*. あの人は仕事がむらである. ¶ a ***versatile*** (=an all-round) *worker* 何の仕事でもできる人. ¶ Japan's ***veteran*** reform *workers* 日本社会改革家中の元老. ¶ a ***zealous*** and ***indefatigable*** *worker* 熱心でうまない働き手.

Q² an ***auto*** *worker* 自動車工場労働者(従業員). ¶ an ***arsenal*** *worker* 兵器所労務者. ¶ a ***brain*** *worker* 頭脳(精神)労働者. ¶ a ***building*** *worker* 土建従業者, 土建労務者. ¶ a ***child*** *worker* 未成年労務者. ¶ a ***city*** *worker* 市で勤める人. ¶ a ***civil service*** *worker* 文官, 公務員. ¶ a ***clothing*** *worker* =clothworker 織物職工. ¶ a ***coal-mine*** *worker* 炭鉱労務者. ¶ a ***communications*** *worker* 通信事業従業員. ¶ a ***construction*** *worker* 建設労働者. ¶ a ***day*** *worker* 日雇労務者. ¶ a ***dock*** *worker* [船の]ドック従業員. ¶ an ***earth*** *worker* 土方. ¶ an ***electric industry*** *worker* 電機事業労務者. ¶ a ***factory*** *worker* 工員. ¶ a ***famine relief*** *worker* 飢餓救済事業従事員. ¶ ***fellow*** *workers* in the same workshop 同じ職場で働く同僚たち. ¶ a ***fixed-salary*** *worker* 固定給従業員. ¶ a ***full-time*** (***part-time***) *worker* 専任(嘱託)職員. ¶ a ***government*** *worker* 政府職員 ‖ a surplus ***government*** *worker* 過剰公務員. ¶ the ***head*** *worker* of the University settlement 大学セットルメントの首脳者. ¶ ***home*** *workers* 自宅で仕事をする人. ¶ a ***hotel*** *worker* ホテル従業員. ¶ an ***indoor*** *worker* 室内労働者. ¶ an ***iron*** *worker* 鉄工所の工員. ¶ a ***kitchen*** *worker* 料理労務者. ¶ a ***metal*** *worker* 金属工. ¶ a ***middle-class white-collar*** *worker* 中流どころの勤め人. ¶ a pure ***muscle*** *worker* 純筋肉労働者. ¶ The ***newspaper*** *workers* are necessary late birds. 新聞記者は(夜ふかしをするから)朝寝坊だ. ¶ a ***non-Government*** *worker* 公務員外の労務者(会社員など). ¶ a ***non-union*** *worker* 非組合員. ¶ an ***office*** *worker* 事務員. ¶ ***peace-industry*** *workers* 平和産業従業者. ¶ a ***pipe fitting*** *worker*=a pipe fitter 鉛管工. ¶ a ***post-office*** *worker* 郵便局従業員. ¶ a ***power plant*** *worker* 発電所従業員. ¶ a ***production*** *worker* 生産工場の従業員. ¶ a ***public health*** *worker* 保健所員. ¶ a ***public office*** (service) *worker* 公務員. ¶ revival of collective bargaining rights for ***public service*** *workers* 公職労務者の団体交渉権の復活. ¶ ***railroad*** *workers*=《米》 railroaders, railroad men 鉄道従業員 ‖ ***Railroad*** *workers* walked out. 鉄道屋がストに突入した. ¶ a ***rank-and-file*** *worker* 平社員, 平の勤労者. ¶ a ***Red*** *worker* 共産党員(共産主義者)の労働者. ¶ a ***Red Cross*** *worker* 赤十字社職員. ¶ a ***rehabilitation*** *worker* 更生事業従業員. ¶ a ***research*** *worker* 研究(調査)員. ¶ study rooms for ***research*** *workers* in a library 図書館の研究者専用室. ¶ a ***routine*** *worker* 常務勤労者. ¶ ***screen*** and ***stage*** *workers* 映画・舞台方面の従業員たち. ¶ a ***student personnel*** *worker* 学生厚生関係者. ¶ a ***textile*** *worker* 織物工. ¶ a ***traffic*** *worker* 交通従業員. ¶ a trained ***relief*** *worker* 訓練された救護員. ¶ a ***transit*** *worker* [運輸の]交通労務者. ¶ a ***wage*** *worker* 賃金労務者. ¶ a ***war*** *worker* 戦時産業工員. ¶ the Chinese coolies brought to Japan as ***war*** *workers* 工場の産業工員として日本に連れてきた中国の苦力. 【類】 Paris was crowded just then with English and American soldiers and ***war*** *workers*. ¶ a ***war-industry*** *worker* 戦時産業の工員. ¶ a ***welfare*** *worker* 厚生職員. ¶ a ***white-collar*** [*worker*] 《米俗》 サラリーマン, お勤め人. ☞ 英の black-coat [worker] に当る. ¶ a ***whole-time*** *worker* 定時勤務者. ¶ a ***widow*** *worker* 勤労未亡人. ¶ ***women*** *workers* 婦人労務者たち. ☞ 単数は a woman worker 例: *a* woman student—women students. ¶ ***women office*** *workers* 勤労女性. ¶ a ***wonder*** *worker* すばらしい業績をあげる人(物). ¶ a ***word*** *worker* もっぱら言葉を使う仕事をする人. ¶ Dr. Nitobe was Japan's great ***world peace*** *worker*. 新渡戸博士は世界平和のために働いた日本の偉人であった. ¶ a ***$20-a-week*** *worker* 週給二十ドルの勤労者.

P² *workers* ***for*** international peace 国際平和のために尽力する人々. ¶ *workers* ***in*** the cause その主義のために活動する人たち ‖ other *workers* ***in*** the same field その方面の仕事をする他の人たち ‖ a *worker* ***in*** education (charity) 教育(慈善)家 ‖ *workers* ***in*** ivory 象げ工. ¶ an energetic *worker* ***of*** the Salvation Army 精力おう盛な救世軍軍人. ¶ a successful *worker* ***with*** the pen 成功した文士 ‖ a *worker* ***with*** poultry 養鶏家.

working, *n.* 作業, 運転; 経営; *pl.* [鉱山などの]坑道, 現場.

V ***compare*** the *working* of two types of motor omnibuses 二種の乗合自動車の運転ぶりを比較する. ¶ the *workings* ***extended*** for miles under ground 地下数マイルに延びている坑道. ¶ ***make*** a trial *working* 試運転をする. ¶ The good-fellowship of the members of the staff ***promotes*** the easy *working* of the administrative machine in their hands. その部員の親ぼくが事務の円滑を助けている. ¶ ***quicken*** the *working* of the brain 頭脳の活動を敏活にする. ¶ ***recommence*** (=***resume***) *working* 仕事を再開する. ¶ ***set*** a machine *working* 機械の運転を開始させる. ¶ ***understand*** the *working* of the machine その機械の具合をのみ込んでいる.

Q ***gradual*** *working* up to perfection 漸次完成への接近. ¶ The *senryu* enables us to get a subtle insight into the ***inner*** *workings* of the human heart. 川柳は人情の機微に触れている. ‖ the ***inner*** *working* of the Oriental mind 東洋人の精神活動 ‖ the ***inner*** *working* of a movement 運動の内幕 ‖ He is thoroughly acquainted with the ***inner*** *workings* of the business. 彼はその商売の内幕をよく知っている. ‖ attempt to explore the ***inner*** *workings* of his mind 彼の心がどう動くかを探ろうとする. ¶ the ***old*** (***new***) *workings* 廃(新)坑. ¶ the ***unpredictable*** *workings* of the human mind 予想できない人の心.

Q² ***farm*** *working* 農場作業. ¶ ***saw mill*** *working* 製材. ¶ ***construction*** *working* 土木作業.

P² the *workings* ***of*** an agency 団体の事業内容 ‖ the *working* ***of*** a business 商売の経営 ‖ the *working* ***of*** a democratic system of government 民主政治の機能.

workman, *n.* 工員, 職人.

V The industry ***employs*** about 270,000 *workmen*. その工業に従事する工員は約二十七万人ある. ¶ The *workmen* have been ***paid off***. 工員たちは給料をもらって解雇された. ¶ The *workmen* must be carefully ***picked***. 工員はよく注意して選ばねばならない.

V² An ill *workman* ***quarrels*** with his tools. へたな職人は道具に難くせをつける. ¶ The *workmen* ***struck*** for higher wages. 工員は賃銀値上を要求してストをした.

Q ***all-round*** *workmen* 万能職工, 熟練工. ¶ a ***capital*** *workman* りっぱな工員. ¶ ***down-trodden*** *workmen* 酷使されている工員. ¶ an ***efficient*** *workman* 優良な工員. ¶ a ***good*** (***bad***) *workman* 腕のある(ない)工員. ¶ a ***masterly*** *workman* 腕のある職人.

Q² The ***lower-bracket*** *workman* spends 25 percent of his income by buying one packet of cigarettes daily. 下積みの労働者は毎日一箱のシガレットを買うのに収入の二十五パーセント費している.

P² *workmen* ***in*** one's employment 人に雇われている職工. ¶ *workmen* ***on*** a railway=railway men, 《米》 railroad men 鉄道従業員.

workmanship, *n.* でき栄え, 製作.

Q ***conscientious*** *workmanship* 良心的な仕事(ぶり). ¶ ***defective*** *workmanship* 不完全な製作. ¶ ***delicate*** *workmanship* 細かい細工. ¶ be of ***elaborate*** *workmanship* 手がこんでいる. ¶ a machine of ***excellent*** *workmanship* 優秀な製作の機械. ¶ a jewel of ***exquisite*** *workmanship* みごとなでき栄えの宝石細工. ¶ articles of ***good*** (***bad***) *workmanship* できの良(悪)い品 ‖ The firm has a name for ***good*** *workmanship*. 同社の品は仕事がいいので有名だ. ¶ be of ***inferior*** *workmanship* 細工がまずい. ¶ of ***rare*** and ***costly*** *workmanship* できが非常に良くて高価な. ¶ ***rude*** but ***elegant old*** *workmanship* of style and execution 稚拙ではあるが様式やできに雅致のある昔の製作振り. ¶ of ***sound*** *workmanship* 製作のしっかりした.

P ***of*** Indian *workmanship* インド製の ‖ This is ***of*** his *workmanship*. これは彼の作品である.

workshop, *n.* 仕事場.

V ***tidy up*** (=put in order) a *workshop* 仕事場をきちんと片付ける.

Q a ***mechanical workshop*** 機械工場.

Q^2 a "***dwelling***" *workshop* 住宅を兼ねた工場. ¶a ***radio*** *workshop* ラジオのテスト放送スタジオ.

workout, *n.* 《米》〖競技〗練習.

P Players are out in the playgrounds ***for*** a light *workout*. 選手は競技場に出て軽い練習をやっている.

world, *n.* 世界; 世間; 社会, ...界.

V ***abjure*** the *world* and become a monk 世を捨てて出家する. ¶prevent the misery which ***afflicts*** the *world* 世の中の悲惨を予防する. ¶***astonish*** the *world* 世界を驚がくさせる. ¶***astound*** the *world* 世人を仰天させる. ¶***beat*** the *world* in ... ...では世界第一. ¶I think he is qualified enough to ***begin*** the *world* for himself. 私は彼には独力で世渡りを始めるだけの資格が十分にあると思う. ¶Hope will ***bring*** a new *world* before one. 人は希望をいだくことにより新生面を開きうる. ¶***build*** tomorrow's *world* 明日の世界を築き上げる. ¶Manners ***carry*** the *world* for the moment, character for all time.—A.B. Alcott. 世界を動かすという点において態度は一時的であるが品性は永久である. ‖ He ***carries*** the *world* before him. 彼は行くところ成功せざるはない. ¶***command*** the *world* 天下をへいげいする. ¶***conquer*** the *world* 世界を征服する. ¶***convulse*** the *world* 世界を震がいさせる. ¶have no face to ***countenance*** the *world* 世間に顔向けができない. ¶***dazzle*** the *world* 世界をあっと言わせる. ¶***defy*** the whole *world* 全世界に反抗する. ¶***dominate*** the *world* 世界を支配する. ¶***electrify*** the *world* 世界を震がいさせる. ¶***encircle*** the *world* 世界を一周する. ¶another international conflict such as ***engulfed*** the *world* from 1914 to 1918 千九百十四年から十八年にかけて世界をその渦中に巻き込んだ例のような第二次の国際的争闘. ¶***enjoy*** the *world* 世の中をおもしろく思う. ¶Reading books ***enlarges*** one's *world*. 読書は人の心の世界を拡大する. ¶***enlighten*** the *world* on ... ...に関し世を啓発する. ¶***enrich*** the *world* by one's efforts and learning その努力と学問によって世界を豊かにする. ¶The pelvis is the gate by which the children ***enter*** the *world*. 骨盤は子供の世に出る門である. 【類】God ***entered*** the *world* through the womb of the Blessed Virgin Mary (聖母マリア). ¶***face*** the *world* with a philosophy unborrowed from books 書物からの借りものでない哲学をもって世に対する ‖ It is not good for a man to ***face*** the *world* alone. 男は妻がなくてはいけない. ‖ young men who are about to ***face*** the *world* 実社会に出ようとする青年たち. ¶***feed*** the *world* 世界[の人民]に食糧を供給する. ¶***fight*** all the *world* 全世界を相手に戦う. ¶He ***found*** a limitless *world* in his books. 彼は書籍の中に無限の世界を発見した. ¶***forsake*** the *world* 世を捨てる; 出家する. ¶English is a language that is fast ***girdling*** the *world*. 英語は急速に世界に普及しつつある国語である. ¶I would ***give*** the *world* to ... ...することができれば何を与えても惜しくない. ¶the economic crisis ***gripping*** the entire *world* 全世界を捕えている経済危機. ¶He ***has*** the *world* before him. 彼には前途洋々だ. ‖ Thus he ***had*** now the *world* to begin again on a new account. かくして彼は世の中に出直すことになった. ¶***hold*** the animal *world* in subjection 動物界を支配する. ¶Charlie Chaplin has helped to ***internationalize*** the *world* by laughter. チャーリー・チャップリンは笑いによる世界の国際化に役立った. ¶The event has ***kept*** the *world* ***astir*** for the last ten months. その事件が過去十カ月間世界を騒がせて来た. ¶***know*** the *world* 世間を知る. 【類】You ought to ***know*** the *world* a lot more. ¶By the white man's burden is meant the task of ***leading*** the *world*. 白人の責務とは世界の進歩を指導する任務を指す. ‖ America undoubtedly ***leads*** the *world* (=all other nations) in motion pictures. 米国は映画においてたしかに世界一である. 【類】***lead*** the *world* in originality (civilization) / The United States now ***leads*** the *world* in the export of manufactures. / ***lead*** the *world* in the production of ... / Hawaii ***leads*** the *world* in the excellence and quantity of its canned pineapples. ‖ In Noah Webster's time, the U.S. ***led*** the *world* in lexicography. ノア・ウエブスター時代には辞書ではアメリカが世界をリードしていた. ¶It is our duty to ***leave*** the *world* better than we found it. 生れた時よりもさらに一層世界をよくして世を去るのがわれわれの義務である. ¶the only nation capable of ***licking*** the *world* in stagnation 不景気という点ではどの国にもひけを取らない唯一の国. ¶***lift*** the *world* = elevate humanity 人類を向上させる. ¶***make*** the *world* an agreeable place to live in 世界を愉快に住める所にする ‖ They have ***made*** the *world* ***better*** for their having lived in it. 彼らが世に出たがために世界は一層向上したのである. ¶***mend*** the *world* 世界を改善する. ¶ideas that ***moved*** the *world* 世界を動かした思想. 【類】men who are ***moving*** the *world*. ¶Books ***open up*** a new *world* of delight to juveniles. 書物は少年少女に歓喜の新天地を展開する. ¶***paralyze*** the business *world* in general 一般に実業界を麻ひさせる. ¶This great work has ***placed*** the intellectual *world* under a debt of deep gratitude. 学術界はこの偉大な著作に負う所が大である. ¶***redeem*** the *world* 世を救う. ¶***reduce*** the whole *world* to a den of wild beasts 全世界を野獣の巣窟に堕落させる. ¶***renounce*** the *world* and live in great austerity 世を捨てて厳正無欲の生活を送る. 【類】***renounce*** the *world* and lead a cloistered life (=shut oneself up in a monastery). ¶***revolutionize*** the *world* 世界を根本的に変革する. ¶money ***rules*** the *world* 万事金の世の中 ‖ It is often said that love and hunger ***rule*** the *world*. 愛と飢えが世界を支配するとはよく言われる. ¶It will ***save*** a *world* of time. そうすると大いに時間の節約ができる. ¶She ***searched*** the *world* for her father. 彼女は父を世界中さがし回った. 【類】***search*** the *world* for markets. ¶set out to ***see*** the *world* 世界を見物に出掛ける. ¶***shake*** (=***startle***) the *world* 天下を震がいさせる. 【類】***startle*** the scientific *world*. ¶***strike*** the *world* with wonder 世界を驚倒させる. ¶***Take*** the *world* as it is. 世の中をこうしたものだとあきらめなさい. ¶***tell*** the *world* about ... 世界に向って...を宣伝する. 【類】It will not be wise to ***tell*** the *world* in future the exact number of the flying machines a country possesses. ¶The news ***thrilled*** the *world*. その報道は世界の胸を躍らせた. ¶***tour*** the *world* on a cruise (in a yacht) 遊船(など)で世界を漫遊する. ¶He ***traveled*** the *world* ***over*** to exhibit his marvellous talents. 彼はその不思議な技術をみせに世界を漫遊した. ¶He has ***traveled***, and ***seen*** the *world*. 彼は旅行をして世界を見ている. ¶***walk*** the *world* with dignity 世の中を堂々と渡る.

V^2 since the *world* ***began*** 開びゃく以来. ¶The *world* has ***changed*** since then. それから世界は変っている. ¶it was only when he died that an astonished *world* ***discovered*** that ... 世間が...ということを発見して驚いたのは彼が死んだ時が初めてであった. ¶as the *world* ***goes*** 世間並にいうと ‖ How ***goes*** the *world* with you? 景気はいかがです. ¶The *world* ***goes forward***. 世が進む. ¶as the *world* ***goes on*** and intelligence spreads 世の中が進んで知識が普及するにつれて. ¶The *world* ***goes*** pretty ***well*** with him. 彼は(生活などが)かなりうまく行っている. ‖ a man with whom the *world* has not ***gone well*** 逆境の人. ¶as the *world* ***knows*** 世間周知の通り. ¶A new *world* ***opend up*** for him. 新しい世界が彼に開けてきた. ¶What will the *world* ***say***? 世間が何と言うだろう. ¶—and so the *world* ***wags*** always! 一世の中のことはすべてこういったぐあいだが(そう入句).

Q the *world* ***above*** 天上界. ¶one of the most distinguished names of the ***academic*** *world* 学界で最も著名な一人. ¶For ***all*** the *world* the sea looked like a beautiful lake. その海はどう見ても湖水にしか見えなかった. ‖ with only $50 in ***all*** the *world* 天にも地にもたった五十ドルしか持たないで. ¶It is found ***all*** the *world* over. それは世間至る所にある. ¶the ***ancient*** *world* 古代. ¶preferring death and union in ***another*** *world* to life and separation in this この世で離れて生きているよりはいっそ死んであの世で一緒になる方がましだと考えて ‖ It is like entering ***another world***. 別世界にはいるような感じがする. ¶the ***athletic world*** 運動競技界. ¶in a ***busy world*** such as this 今のようなせわしい世の中では. ¶be submitted to a ***candid*** *world* 世の識者に問う. ¶this ***changing*** *world* この変り行く世界. ¶all the denominations known in the ***Christian*** *world* (=Christendom) キリスト教界で知られている全部の分派. ¶She is almost a generation behind the rest of the ***civilized*** *world*. その国は自余の文明諸国に遅れること約三十年である. ‖ the principal countries of the ***civilized*** *world* 世界の主な文明国. ¶this ***cold, heartless, cruel*** *world* この冷たい無情なむごたらしい世の中. ¶the ***commercial** world* 商業界. ¶We are living in a ***confused*** and ***divided** world.* 今日の世界は混乱と分裂の世界である. ¶a closely ***co-operating** world* 緊密に協力している世界. ¶It is recognized by a ***discerning** world.* それは具眼の人士から認められている. ¶the ***economic** world* 経済界. ¶impressions of the ***external** world* 外界の印象. ¶the ***external, sensible** world* 知覚しうる外界. ¶take part in the social life and gaieties of the ***fashionable** world* of London ロンドン上流社会の派手な社交界に仲間入りする. ¶in this ***fast-moving** world* このテンポの早い世の中で. ¶the ***feathered** world* 鳥の世界. ¶It is a real boon to the ***feminine** world.* それは女性に真に喜ばれるものだ. ¶the ***financial** world* 財界. ¶It has been dug out of the ruins of a ***former** world.* それは上代の遺跡の中から発掘されたものである. ¶one of the greatest influences working toward the creation of a ***friendly** world* 世界の親和を築き上げるにあずかって大いに力ある勢力の一つ. ¶the ***gay** world* はなやかな社会. ¶the ***Greco-Roman** world* ギリシア及びローマの世. ¶the ***hard, stormy** world* つれないあらし吹く世の中. ¶our ***hustling** world* この忙しい世の中. ¶the ***industrial*** and ***commercial** world* 産業界及び商業界. ¶the ***inner** world* 精神界. ¶the ***journalistic** world* 新聞界. ¶the ***learned** world* 学界. ¶he startled the ***literary** world* with his ... 彼の作...で文壇をあっと言わせた. ¶the ***lower** world* 地獄. ¶Europe has been a ***man's** world,*—managed by men and largely for men. ヨーロッパは男の世界であった, 男が支配しまたそれが主として男のためにである. ¶the ***material** world* 物質界. ¶the ***medical** world* 医学界. ¶astonish the ***military** world* 軍人社会を驚かす. ¶the needs of the busy men in the ***modern** world* 多忙な現代人の必需品. ¶the ***moral** world* 道徳(精神)の世界. ¶the ***moving** world* of waters 流れる水の世界. ¶those most eminent in the ***musical** world* 音楽界で最も有名な人々. ¶the ***natural** world* 自然界. ¶the ***next** world* 来世. ¶she is known to the ***novel-reading** world* as ... 彼女は小説愛読者仲間には...で知られている. ¶His rapid elevation in the ***official** world* has been due to other causes than merit or ability. 彼が官界でとんとん拍子に昇進したのは功績や才幹以外のものがその原因となったのである. ¶the ***operatic** world* 歌劇界. ¶the ***Oriental** world* 東洋の世界. ¶the ***outer** world* 外界. ¶draw the attention of the ***outside** world* 諸外国の注意を引く ‖ the ***outside** world* 実世界(学校などから見て). ¶the ***outside practical** world* [学校に対し]外部の実社会. ¶the ***phenomenal** world* 現象界. ¶the ***physical** world* 物質界. ¶in the ***polite** world* 上流社会では. ¶the ***postwar** world* 戦後の世界. ¶the ***present** world* 現世. ¶This is a ***rough** world* of ours. 世の中はせちがらい. ¶Ours is a ***shrinking** world.* 世界が段々小さくなる. ¶It's a ***small** world* after all. 世間は広いようで狭い. ¶success in the ***social** world* 社交界での成功. ¶the ***theatrical*** (=theater) *world* 劇界. ¶These giants of the ***tree** world* reach up far above the lesser forest growth. これら樹木界の巨人は断然群を抜いている. ¶the ***under** world* 下界. ¶an ***unknown** world* 未知の世界. ¶the ***visible** world* [霊界に対し] 現世. ¶8,000 miles across the ***watery** world* 八千マイルの波とうを越えて. ¶In the nineteenth century the western world—the ***western aesthetic** world*—discovered the Orient. 十九世紀に西洋—西洋の美術界—が東洋を発見した. ¶plod on through the ***wet** world* 雨の中をとぼとぼと歩く. ¶a hero whose fame resounded throughout the ***whole** world* 名声世界に鳴り渡った英雄. ¶in this ***wicked** world* この邪悪の世に. ¶the happiest woman in the ***wide** world* この広い世界で最も幸福な女. ¶in the ***wild** world* 未開の土地では. ¶the *world* ***within*** 内界. ¶the *world* ***without*** 外界. ¶the ***workaday** world* 実社会. ¶a ***work-driven** world* 仕事に追われる世界.

Q² the ***amusement** world* 興業界. ¶the ***animal*** (***vegetable, mineral***) *world* 動(植・鉱)物界. ¶the ***Arab** world* アラビア人社会. ¶a treasure of the ***art** world* 芸術界の至宝. ¶the ***artist** world* 芸能界. ¶The helicopter is a jack-of-all-trades of the ***aviation** world.* ヘリコプターは航空界の万能機である. ¶the ***bourgeois** world* ブルジョア社会. ¶this ***bubble** world* このうたかたの世. ¶the ***capitalist** world* 資本主義社会. ¶in the ***club** world* クラブ界で. ¶the ***Communist** word* 共産党の社会. ¶the ***dancing** world* 舞踊界. ¶the ***English-speaking** world* 英語を話す世界. ¶far from the ***every day** world* 日常生活とは遠く離れて. ¶the ***fish** world* 魚の世界. ¶Materialism resolutely refuses to admit anything outside or beyond the ***five-sense** world.* 唯物主義は五感で識別できるもの以外は断じて認めない. ¶a veteran in the ***gambling** world* とばく界の古顔. ¶the ***gas*** (***coal, rubber***) *world* ガス(石炭・ゴム)界. ¶in the ***grocery** world* 食糧品界で. ¶the ***horse** world* of London ロンドンの馬事. ¶the ***insect** world* こん虫界. ¶within the ***Iron Curtain** world* 鉄のカーテンの内側で. ¶the American ***labor** world* 米国労働界. ¶the ***newspaper*** (***magazine***) *world* 新聞(雑誌)界. ¶a great revolution in the ***novel** world* 小説界の一大革命. ¶the ***novel-reading** world* 小説読者層. ¶the ***outdoor sports** world* 戸外運動界. ¶the ***overseas** world* 海外の諸国. ¶plant life of the ***Pacific** world* 太平洋の生物. ¶sex in the ***plant** world* 植物界における性. ¶the ***play-house** world* 劇界. ¶the conditions of the ***publishing** world* 出版界の状況. ¶the ***reading** world* 読書界. 【類】well-known to the ***reading** world* of Paris. ¶the ***thinking** world* 思想界. ¶the ***water** world* 水界. ¶the ***wonder** world* 驚異の世界.

P knock (=roam) ***about*** the *world* 世界を放浪する. ¶He is ***above*** the *world.* 彼は俗世間を超越している. ¶dare to fight ***against*** the *world* single-handed 一国で世界を相手に戦おうとする. ¶travel ***around*** the *world* 世界を一周する. ¶I wouldn't offend him ***for*** the *world.* 私は絶対に彼を怒らすまい. ‖ Not ***for** worlds,* Sir, not for worlds! 絶対に, はい, 絶対にそうではありません. ‖ They look ***for*** all the *world* like the real articles. どう見ても本物としか見えない. ¶withdaw ***from*** the *world* 隠とんする. ¶***in*** this *world* of ours われわれの住むこの世界では, この現世では. ‖ ***in*** this *world* and in that to come 現世及び来世で. ¶How ***in*** the *world* did you do it? 一体それはどうしてやったんです. ‖ Where ***in*** the *world* can it be? [物を捜すときなど]どこへ行ってしまったのだろう. 【類】Who ***in*** the *world* are you? ‖ rise ***in*** the *world* 出世する ‖ ***in*** the *world* forty years ago 四十年前の世に ‖ the leading men ***in*** the *world* of thought and action 思想及び実践方面における一流の人物 ‖ ***in*** this *world* of shams このいつわりの多い世に ‖ serve her husband ***in*** the *world* of the dead あの世で夫の世話をする ‖ He was yet comparatively unknown ***in*** the *world* of scholarship. 氏はまだ学界にあまり知られていなかった. ‖ even with the best will ***in*** the *world* いかに好意を持っていても ‖ suffer more ***in*** the *world* to come 来世でもっと苦しむ. ¶He was then not yet born ***into*** this *world.* 彼はその時まだ生れていなかった. ‖ go out ***into*** the *world* 世間へ出る. ¶a man ***of*** the *world* 世慣れた人 ‖ ignorant ***of*** the *world* 世間知らずの ‖ a citizen ***of*** the *world*=a world citizen 世界市民 ‖ There are worlds ***of** worlds* in London. ロンドンにはいろいろさまざまな社会がある. ¶live ***out of*** the *world* 隠とんしている. ¶live ***outside*** one's own little *world* 自己の小さな世界を越えて生きる. ¶travel all ***over*** the *world* 世界をまたにかける. ¶the peoples ***throughout*** the *world*=world peoples 世界中の諸民族. ¶get ***through*** the *world* respectably 恥ずかしくなく世を渡る. ¶Darwin's works are studied ***throughout*** the civilized *world.* ダーウィンの著書はすべての文明国で研究されている. ¶well-known ***to*** the *world* of travel 旅行界には有名な. ¶keep in touch ***with*** the *world* 世間に遅れないようにする.

P² in a *world* ***like*** ours われわれが住んでいるような世界では. ¶the *world* ***of*** ideas and ideals 観念と理想との世界 ‖ the *world* ***of*** wealth and fashion 富と流行の社会 ‖ in the *world* ***of*** change 変り行く世の中で ‖ the *world* ***of*** arts and letters 美術と文芸の世界 ‖ the *worlds* ***of*** sense and of spirit=the material and spiritual world 物質界と精神界 ‖ In a *world* ***of*** uncertainties like this, it is well to be prepared for any emergency. こんな不安の世の中ではまさかの折の用意をしておく方がよい. ‖ a *world* ***of*** streetcars and automobiles 無数の電車や自動車. 【類】a *world* ***of*** vices (troubles). ¶*world* ***without*** end=forever 永遠に.

world-conflict, *n.* 世界戦争.

V the *world-conflict* which was then ***devastating*** Europe 当時欧州を荒らしていた世界戦争.

world-fame, *n.* 世界的名声.

V ***acquire** world-fame* (=world-wide fame) 世界的名声を博する.

world-order, *n.* 世界体制.

Q a *new* (*old*) *world-order* 世界新(旧)体制. ¶a ***totalitarian world-order*** 全体主義的世界秩序.

world-struggle, *n.* 世界的闘争.

P the coming *world-struggle* ***for*** industrial supremacy 来るべき世界産業支配戦.

worm, *n.* 虫.

V ***tread*** the *worm* to death 虫を踏み殺す.

V² The *worm* has ***turned*** at last. 仏の顔も三度であった. ¶A *worm* ***wriggles***. 虫がもくもくはう.

Q² a ***wire*** *worm* こめつき虫の幼虫; やすで.

P become food ***for*** *worms* 死ぬ.

P² the *worm* ***of*** conscience 良心のかしゃく.

worm, *v.* [虫のように]徐々にはい込む.

M *worm* ***out*** a secret 色々手を尽くして秘密を探り出す.

M² *worm* one's way ***in*** (***out***) 徐々に入り込む(出る).

P *worm* oneself ***into*** another's favor たくみに取り入る. ‖ *worm* oneself (=one's way) ***into*** society 次第に社交界に入り込む. ¶*worm* one's hands ***through*** (***into***) … 手をそっと…に入れる.

worry, *n.* 心配.

V ***end*** money *worries* 金の心配をなくす. ¶***endure*** a *worry* uncomplainingly 不平を鳴らさず苦悩にたえる. ¶he is constantly ***finding*** a *worry* in … 彼は…にはいつも閉口している. ¶***have*** many *worries* 心配ごとが多い.

Q big *worries* 大心配. ¶***Financial*** *worries* have arisen. 金の心配ができた. ¶He wears an expression of ***great*** *worry*. 彼は大分心配そうな顔つきをしている. ¶***household*** *worries* 家庭の悩み. ¶life's ***little*** *worries*=small worries of life. 人生のちょっとした悩み. ¶***mental*** *worry* 精神上の心配. ¶free from ***pecuniary*** *worries* 金の心配のない. ¶let ***unreasonable*** *worries* get the upperhand つまらない心配でくよくよする.

Q² with no ***money*** *worries* in his head 金銭上の心配はなく.

P² do away with all the *worries* ***concerning*** the future 将来のことについて一切心配しない. ¶the *worry* ***of*** household cares 家事上の心配.

O What's your (=the) *worry?* 何を心配してるんだい.

worry, *v.* 苦しめる; 心配する(させる).

M He was ***constantly*** ***worried*** by creditors. 彼は借金取に始終苦しめられた. ¶He *worried* ***much*** about his failure to find work. 彼は就職ができないので大いに閉口した.

M² *worry* ***along*** 苦労しながら暮す.

P He was *worried* ***about*** his health. 彼は健康のことを心配していた. ‖ *worry* ***about*** examination (unemployment) 試験(失業)を気にする ‖ *worry* ***about*** dying 死ぬのを苦にする. 【類】so that such people never have to *worry* ***about*** their future / I have nothing to *worry* ***about*** in this life. / A chronic invalid *worries* ***about*** his health. ¶*worry* a person ***by*** jest 冗談言って困らせる ‖ One cannot afford to be *worried* ***by*** such a thing. そんなことを気にしたら切りがない. ¶If you are late your mother will *worry* ***for*** you. 君帰りが遅いとお母さんが心配するよ. ¶*worry* oneself ***into*** illness 心配のあまり病気になる. ¶*worry* ***over*** trifles つまらないことにくよくよする ‖ *worry* ***over*** the situation 時局を心配する. ¶*worrying* me ***to*** death 私に死ぬほど(ひどい)苦労をかけて. ¶*worry* oneself ***with*** over-anxiety 取越し苦労をする.

O No one will be *worried* to buy. だれも買おうなどとは思わないだろう.

worrying, *n.* 心配.

V ***give up*** useless *worrying* 下らない心配をやめる. ¶***Stop*** *worrying!* くよくよするな.

worse, *n.* 一層悪いもの.

V ***get*** the *worse* of it. [議論などで]負ける.

V² if the *worst* ***comes*** (=happens) 万一のことがあったら. ¶But *worse* ***followed***. 所がさらに悪いことが続いた.

worse, *a.* さらに悪い.

P He was *worse* ***for*** the liquor. 彼は酔っていた. ‖ He assured us that we would not be the *worse* ***for*** it, if we comply with his request. 彼の要求に応じたからとて決して損はないと彼は保証した. ‖ He was the *worse* ***for*** drink. 彼は酔っていた. ¶change (=turn) ***for*** the *worse* 一層悪化する.

O *worse* than all, … 何より悪いことには… ¶Money so spent is *worse* than wasted. そんな風に金を使うのは浪費するよりまだ悪い. 【類】it is *worse* than useless for purposes of … ¶He is 180 pounds *worse* than nothing. 彼は百八十ポンドの体重を持っているがそれが何の役にも立たない.

worsening, *n.* 悪化.

Q the ***gradual*** *worsening* of international relations 国際関係が次第に悪化すること.

P² *worsening* ***of*** the condition of coal supply 石炭事情の悪化.

worship, *n.* 礼拝.

V The *worship* of … is ***celebrated***. …の礼拝が行われる. ¶***offer*** *worship* to … = worship (*vt.*) … …を礼拝する. ¶***shift*** one's *worship* in favor of … …に転向(くら替え)する.

Q ***ancestral*** (=ancestor) *worship* 祖先崇拝. ¶a ***blind*** *worship* 盲目的尊敬. ¶His cult became the ***dominant*** *worship* of the whole country. 彼の教が全国の主な宗教となった. ¶***religious*** *worship* 宗教上の礼拝. ¶***social*** *worship* [教会などで]集団礼拝.

Q² ***church*** *worship* 教会での礼拝. ¶***devil*** *worship* 魔鬼礼拝. ¶***family*** and ***ancestral tablet*** *worship* 家族及び先祖の位はい礼拝. ¶***fire*** *worship* 拝火. ¶***group*** *worship* 集団拝礼. ¶***hero*** *worship* 英雄崇拝.

P bend one's knee ***in*** *worship* 片ひざついて礼拝する ‖ ***in*** the *worship* of money 金を崇拝して. ¶the center ***of*** *worship* 崇拝の中心.

P² the *worship* ***of*** heroes=hero-worship.

worship, *v.* 拝む.

M ***devoutly*** *worship* the rising sun うやうやしく日の出を拝む. ¶***Where*** does he *worship?* 彼はどこの教会に行くのか.

P *worship* ***as*** a deity 神として祭る. ¶*worship* ***at*** the tomb of … …の墓に参拝する ‖ Many pilgrims *worship* ***at*** the shrine. 多くの巡礼者がその神社へ参拝する. ‖ the modern tendency to *worship* ***at*** the shrine of reason 理性を尊崇するという近代的傾向. ¶*worship* ***before*** the shrines 神前に拝する. ¶*worship* ***by*** hymns 賛美歌を唱えて礼拝する. ¶*worship* ***from*** a distance よう拝する. ¶*worship* ***in*** a temple 寺参りをする.

worship[p]er, *n.* 礼拝者.

Q ***enthusiastic*** *worshippers* at Bacon's shrine 熱心なベーコン崇拝者. ¶Ruskin was a ***puritan*** *worshiper* of beauty. ラスキンは心からの美の賛美者であった.

Q² I am not a ***hero*** *worshiper* of criminals and bad men. 私は罪人や悪人を英雄視しない.

P² a *worshipper* ***at*** the Shrine of Free Trade 自由貿易礼賛者.

worship[p]ing, *n.* 礼拝.

P change their garments previous ***to*** *worshiping* in the temple 寺参りに先だって更衣する.

worst, *n.* 最悪.

V ***avert*** the *worst* ほどのよい所で切り上げる. ¶***brave*** the *worst* 最悪を物ともしない. ¶***get*** (=***have***) the *worst* of a quarrel (dispute) けんかに負ける ‖ ***get*** the *worst* of a deal 貧乏くじを引く. ¶***give*** a person the *worst* of it 負かす, 圧倒する. ¶***make*** the *worst* of … …を悲観する, …の悪い面だけを見る.

V² The *worst* of ills ***befell*** her. 彼女に最大の不幸がふりかかった. ¶if [the] *worst* ***comes*** to [the] worst 万一の場合には, せっぱ詰まれば. ¶The *worst* has ***happened***. 大変なことになった. ‖ if the *worst* ***happens*** 悪くすると.

P The storm was ***at*** its *worst*. あらしの絶頂であった. ‖ The American language ***at*** its *worst*. 米語の最も悪い面. ‖ ***at*** [the] *worst* 最悪の場合にも, どう間違っても. ‖ ***At*** [the] *worst*, our lives are safe. どうころんでもわれわれの命だけは大丈夫だ. ¶be prepared ***for*** the *worst* 最悪に備えている.

P² the *worst* ***of*** it is that … 一番困ったことは… ‖ The *worst* ***of*** you is that you will never admit when you are in the wrong. 間違っていてもそうと言わないのが君の一番悪い癖だ.

worth, *n.* 価値.

V ***applaud*** its *worth* その価値をほめそやす. ¶***appraise*** the *worth* of … …の価値を評価する. ¶***appreciate*** one's moral *worth* その道徳的真価を認める. ¶***buy*** a shilling's *worth* of … …を一シリングだけ買う. ¶***get*** one's money's *worth* 金相当の品を得る. ¶***Give*** me a dollar's *worth* of this tea. このお茶を一ドルください. ¶***prove*** its *worth* as … …としてのその真価を示す. ¶***purchase*** about 100 yen *worth* of … …を約百円買う. ¶the lowest estimate would ***put*** the *worth* of … 最低に見積っても…の値打があるだろう.

Q glass vessels of ***artistic*** *worth* 美術的価値のあるガラス器. ¶It is of ***great*** *worth*. それは非常に値うちがある. ‖ a person of ***great worth*** 重要人物. ¶***net worth*** 正味の価値. ¶old books stored away as things of ***no worth*** つまらない物として仕舞い込んであった古書. ¶highly advertise new books of ***passing worth*** 際物的新刊書を大々的に広告する. ¶a treasure of ***priceless worth*** 無価の至宝. ¶of ***solid*** *worth* 真に価値のある. ¶show one's ***true*** *worth* 真価を示す.

Q² a novel of ***penny*** *worth* 三文小説. ¶Indeed any man with ***twopence*** *worth* of sense must have done so. 実際少しでも常識のある人ならそうしたに違いない. ¶Please give me ***100-yen*** *worth* of stamps. 切手を百円だけ下さい.

P What knowledge is ***of*** most *worth?* 何の知識が最も価値のあるものだろうか. ¶showy ***without*** real *worth* 見かけ倒しの. ¶It is worth many times its *worth* ***in*** gold. それはそれを黄金にした幾倍もの(非常に)値打がある. ¶millions of pounds' *worth* ***of*** goods 数百万ポンドの商品.

worth, *a.* 価値がある.

M It is ***easily*** *worth* four dollars a pound in the market. それは市場では一ポンド四ドルの値打がたっぷりある. ¶Pigs are now ***hardly*** *worth* their keep. 当今は豚を飼っても割に合わない. ¶It is *worth* as ***much.*** それだけの値打はある. 【類】He had something very ***much*** *worth* saying. ¶It is *worth* ***noticing.*** それは注意に値する. ¶It is well *worth* ***perusal.*** それは熟読の価値が十分ある. ¶He is *worth* three hundred and sixty thousand ***pounds*** per annum. 彼には三十六万ポンドの年収がある. ¶He is now *worth* ***ten millions***; he began life without a penny in his pocket. 今では彼は千万長者だがしかしもとをただせば裸一貫からやり上げたものだ. ¶This book is ***really*** *worth* reading. この本は全く一読の価値がある. ¶It is ***well*** *worth* the sacrifice. 犠牲を払うだけの価値が十分ある. ¶It is *worth* ***while*** to read (=reading) the book.=The book is *worth* reading. その本は読むだけの価値がある. ‖ The work is *worth* your ***while.*** その仕事はあなたがやる値打がある. ¶The book is *worth* its ***weight*** in gold. その本は同量の黄金と同じ価値がある.

O for all one is *worth*=to the utmost 力の限り ‖ For what it is *worth* we offer this suggestion. 善し悪しは別として私はこの提案をします.

worthless, *a.* 無価値な.

M be ***simply*** (=***utterly***) *worthless* 全然価値がない.

worthy, *a.* 値打のある.

M ***distinctly*** *worthy* of praise たしかに賞賛する値打のある. ¶a subject ***eminently*** *worthy* of careful study 大いに周到な研究に値する問題. ¶It is ***hardly*** *worthy* of serious consideration. それはちょっとまじめに考えるだけの値打がない. ¶Nothing ***particularly*** *worthy* of notice occurred during the two following days. その後二日間はとりたてて注意するほどのことが起らなかった. ¶The book is ***well*** *worthy* of his reputation. その本はさすがに大家の作だ. ‖ It is an occasion ***well*** *worthy* of the most elaborate celebration. そのことは大々的に祝賀するだけの値打が十分ある. ‖ It is ***well*** *worthy* of the brush of the masters. それは画伯が題材として取扱うだけの価値が十分ある.

P be not *worthy* ***of*** one's age 年がいもなく ‖ They have no homes *worthy* ***of*** the name of houses. 彼らは家と名のつくほどの家を持っていない. ‖ a scene *worthy* ***of*** transfer to an artist canvas 画布に移して見たい光景 ‖ those who do nothing *worthy* ***of*** existence 何一つこれぞということをやらない人々 ‖ a hero whose example is *worthy* ***of*** emulation その流れをくむに足る勇士 ‖ It is a thing *worthy* ***of*** seeing. 見ものだ. ‖ Those *worthy* ***of*** assistance, except in rare cases, seldom require assistance.—Carnegie. 助力する価値のある人たちは滅多に援助を要しない. 【類】This shows that he is *worthy* ***of*** respect. / a person *worthy* ***of*** trust / There is nothing *worthy* ***of*** special mention. / He has merits *worthy* ***of*** note. / a matter *worthy* ***of*** attention / abuse and rancor *worthy* ***of*** a fishwife / sustain no damage *worthy* ***of*** remark (=mention ***or*** the name) / There is no change *worthy* ***of*** mention. / The city has no park *worthy* ***of*** notice. / try to be *worthy* ***of*** one's patronage / be well *worthy* ***of*** a long pilgrimage (長い巡礼) / be *worthy* ***of*** the reputation / life *worthy* ***of*** a human being / charities *worthy* ***of*** our support. / It is *worthy* ***of*** all admiration. / *worthy* ***of*** particular attention / *worthy* ***of*** respect as opinions / I do not know how far these suggestions are *worthy* ***of*** credence (信用) / These are questions *worthy* ***of*** the best thought, the best ability, and the highest patriotism of the Japanese people.

O Wyatt had written odes, but probably the first poem *worthy* that name is Spenser's Epithalamion. ワイアットは賦を作ったがおそらく本格的な賦はスペンサーのエピサレーミオンを端緒とすべきであろう. ¶I regret that a short notice, and the pressure of official duties have rendered it impossible to prepare an address *worthy* this great occasion. 私は時間が十分ないのと公務多端のためこの晴れの席にふさわしい式辞を用意することができなかったことを残念に思います.

worthy, *n.* 名士.

Q ***famous English*** *worthies* 英国の名士. ¶***local*** *worthies* 地方の名士. ¶***scientific*** *worthies* 知名の科学者.

P our country's *worthies* ***in*** the past 過去におけるわが国の名士.

wound, *n.* 負傷, 傷.

V ***aggravate*** a *wound* 傷を悪化させる. ¶***bind up*** a *wound* 傷に包帯をする. ¶The blow ***caused*** a *wound.* そのパンチでけがをした. ¶***cicatrize*** a *wound* 傷を直す. ¶***close*** a *wound* with stitches 傷を縫う. ¶***dress*** a *wound* 傷に包帯をする. ¶***fester*** a *wound* 傷をとがめる. ¶Seven *wounds* were ***found*** upon her head. 彼女は頭に七カ所傷を受けた. ¶The woman ***had*** two bullet *wounds*, one in the neck and the other in the head. その婦人は二個所の銃創を受けた, 一つはくびに, も一つは頭に. ¶***heal*** a *wound* 傷をいやす. ¶***inflict*** a *wound* 傷を負わせる ‖ ***inflict*** *wounds* on (=upon) one's face その顔に傷を負わせる. ¶***irritate*** a *wound* 傷を刺激する. ¶***mortify*** a *wound* 傷をとがめる. ¶***receive*** a *wound* in one's foot 足をけがする. ¶***scar*** a *wound* 傷跡を残す. ¶***sew up*** (=***suture***) a *wound* 傷を縫う. ¶***skin over*** a *wound* 傷口がふさがるようにする. ¶***stitch*** a *wound* 傷口を縫う. ¶***tend*** a *wound* by disinfecting and bandaging 消毒や包帯をして傷の手当をする. ¶***tie up*** *wounds* 傷口を固くくくる. ¶***undress*** a *wound* 傷の包帯を取る. ¶The *wound* ***festered*** (=***gathered or suppurated***) 傷がうんだ.

Q an ***angry*** (=red and painful) *wound* 炎症を起している傷. ¶a ***bleeding*** *wound* 出血する傷. ¶a ***contused*** *wound* 打撲傷. ¶receive a ***fatal*** *wound* 致命傷を受ける. ¶a ***festering*** *wound* のう傷. ¶a ***fresh*** (=***green***) *wound* 生傷. ¶a ***gaping*** *wound* 口のあいた傷. ¶a ***grievous*** *wound* to Russian honor ロシアの名誉にとっての大痛手. ¶sew together (=suture) the lips of an ***incised*** *wound* 切り傷の口を縫い合わす. ¶a ***lacerated*** *wound* 裂傷. ¶a ***light*** *wound* 軽傷. ¶a ***mortal*** *wound* 致命傷. ¶a ***punctured*** *wound* 刺傷. ¶a ***ragged*** *wound* ざくろ傷. ¶a ***serious*** *wound* 痛手. ¶inflict ***severe*** *wounds* on ... …に重傷を負わせる. ¶a ***shot*** (=***gunshot***) *wound* 銃創. ¶a ***slight*** *wound* 軽傷. ¶an ***ugly*** *wound* 醜い傷.

Q² a ***bullet*** *wound* in the head 頭の銃創 ‖ dress a ***bullet*** *wound* in one's arm その腕にうけた銃創を包帯する. 【類】receive a ***bullet*** *wound* in the leg / He has a ***bullet*** *wound* in the left breast. ¶a ***gunshot*** *wound* 銃創. ¶a ***head*** *wound* 頭の傷. ¶an ***operation*** *wound* 手術の傷. ¶a ***sword*** *wound* 刀傷. ¶a ***stab*** *wound* 刺し傷. ¶a ***war*** *wound* 戦傷.

P² He died ***of*** (=***from***) his *wounds.* 彼は負傷して死んだ. ¶the *wounds* ***in*** the forehead and face 額と顔の傷.

wound, *v.* 傷つける.

M ***deeply*** *wounded* by ... …から深手を負って. ¶He was ***mortally*** *wounded.* 彼は致命傷を受けた. ¶He was ***seriously*** *wounded* in the head. 彼は頭に重傷を受けた.

P He was *wounded* ***by*** a stray bullet. 彼は流弾に当って負傷した. ¶He was *wounded* (=got hurt) ***in*** the arm. 彼は腕をいためた. ‖ He felt that he was *wounded* ***in*** his self-esteem. 彼は自尊心を傷つけられたように感じた. ¶*wound* a person ***to*** the quick 人の急所を突く ‖ *wound* a person ***to*** death 人に致命的な深手を負わす.

wrangle, *n.* 論争.

Q² a bitter ***two-day*** *wrangle* 二日間にわたる猛烈な論争.

wrangle, *v.* 論争する.

P *wrangle* ***with*** a person ***about*** a matter ある問題について人と論争する.

wrangling, *n.* 論争.

Q promote ***unseemly*** *wrangling* 不体裁な論争を起させる.

wrap, *v.* 巻く, 包む.

M *wrap* it ***air-tight*** 寸分のすき間なくそれを包む.

M² *wrap* ***up*** one's lunch 弁当を包む ‖ *wrap* it ***up*** in paper and tie it with a string 紙で包んでひもでしばる ‖ *wrap* ***up*** warmly 厚着をする ‖ be *wrapped* ***up*** in the study of ... …の勉強に没頭する ‖ It is very disagreeable to see a person *wrapped* ***up*** in himself. 自分のことしか考えないような人を見るのは実にいやなものだ. ‖ he is *wrapped* ***up*** in ... 彼は…に凝っている.

P *wrap* a blanket ***about*** one 毛布に体をくるむ. ¶*wrap* it ***around*** one それを身に巻く. ¶*wrap* it ***in*** a newspaper それを新聞紙に包む ‖ He is *wrapped* ***in*** furs from top to toe. 彼は頭からつま先まで毛皮にくるまっている. ‖ All the people in the hotels were *wrapped* ***in*** deep slumber. ホテルでは皆深い眠りに落ちていた. 【類】*wrapped* ***in*** silence / The whole matter is *wrapped* ***in*** mystery.

wrapper, *n.* 包紙；へや着.

Q a ***transparent*** *wrapper* [セロハンのような]透明包装紙.

Q^2 a ***cellophane*** *wrapper* セロハンの包装紙. ¶a ***package*** *wrapper* 包装係. ¶a ***paper*** *wrapper* for packing 包装紙 ‖ books in ***paper*** *wrappers* 包紙を掛けた本.

P a woman ***in*** *wrapper* へや着をつけた婦人.

wrath, *n.* 憤怒.

V ***allay*** the exuberant editorial *wrath* 編集者の物すごい激昂を和らげる. ¶He ***called down*** (=***drew***) upon himself the *wrath* of God (those in authority). 彼は自身の上に神(当局者)の怒りを招いた. ¶***dare*** the *wrath* of ... …から怒られるのを承知でやる. ¶***excite*** the *wrath* of ... …を怒らせる. ¶***incur*** the Divine *wrath* 神の怒りを招く ‖ ***incur*** the *wrath* of Mrs. Grundy 世人の怒りを招く. ¶***invoke*** God's *wrath* upon ... 神罰が…にあたるようにと祈る. ¶***master*** one's *wrath* 怒りを抑える. ¶***nurse*** one's *wrath* 怒りをいだく. ¶***raise*** (=***rouse***) the *wrath* of ... …を激憤させる. ¶***repress*** one's *wrath* 自分の怒りを抑制する. ¶***restrain*** (=***keep down***) one's *wrath* 怒りをおさえる. ¶***soothe*** the *wrath* of ... …の怒りを静める. ¶popular *wrath* was ***stirred*** up by ... …によって世人の憤怒を買った. ¶***turn away*** the divine *wrath* 神の怒りを和らげる. 【類】A soft answer ***turned away*** *wrath*. ¶***wreak*** one's *wrath* upon ... …に怒りを漏らす.

Q manifestations of ***Divine*** *wrath* 神の怒りの顕示. ¶***just*** *wrath* 義憤. ¶at the risk of rousing much ***patriotic*** *wrath*, I must admit that ... 国士連は大いに憤慨するであろうがそれでもなお私は…を容認しなければならない. ¶scourge them with the lash of ***righteous*** *wrath* 彼らに破邪顕正の剣を揮う. ¶seething with ***suppressed*** *wrath* こみ上げる怒りを抑えて.

P ***in*** *wrath* 怒って ‖ ***in*** one's *wrath* 腹立ちまぎれに. ¶slow (quick) ***to*** *wrath* 容易に怒らない(怒りっぽい). ¶burn ***with*** ⌊*wrath* かんかんに怒る.

wreak, *v.* 漏らす.

M *wreak* ***out*** one's vengeance うっ憤を晴らす.

wreath, *n.* 花輪.

V ***bestow*** a magnificent *wreath* upon his grave 彼の墓に見事な花輪をささげる. ¶***lay*** (=***place***) a *wreath* on the tomb of George Washington ワシントンの墓に花輪をささげる. 【類】very gently, very respectfully, do I ***lay*** my *wreath* on the grave of ... / ***lay*** *wreaths* at the foot of a monument.

Q "***natural***" (***artificial***) *wreaths* 天然花(作り花)の花輪.

P^2 a *wreath* ***for*** the head 花の冠. ¶a *wreath* ***of*** smoke (vapor, cloud) 巻き上がる煙(など).

wreathe, *v.* 花輪を掛ける.

P^2 a pretty face *wreathed* ***in*** smiles 微笑を浮かべた美しい顔. ¶*wreathe* flowers ***into*** a garland 花を花輪にする. ¶a column *wreathed* ***with*** vines (flowers) ぶどうのつる(など) ⌊の巻きついた円柱.

wreck, *n.* 難船；残がい；敗残の身.

V The gale ***caused*** many *wrecks*. その暴風で多数難船があった. 「が起った.

V^2 A disastrous *wreck* has ***happened***. 難破船の一大悲惨事

Q ***abject*** *wrecks* of humanity 絶望のふちに沈む人たち. ¶a ***complete*** *wreck* 完全な破滅. ¶***ghastly*** *wrecks* of an air-plane 物すごい飛行機の残がい. ¶He is a ***hopeless*** *wreck*. 彼はもうだめだ(過労などで体を損じた人). ¶the salvage of ***human*** *wrecks* 悲境にある人々の救済. ¶a ***mental*** as well as a ***physical*** *wreck* 肉体的並びに精神的な破滅(した人). ¶He was a ***mere*** *wreck* of his former self. 彼は敗残の身だった. ¶***scattered*** *wrecks* on a stormbeaten shore あらしに吹き寄せられた破船の残がい. ¶She has now become a ***total*** *wreck*. その船は全くの破船となった. ¶a ***world-weary*** *wreck* 世をはかなむ人.

Q^2 a ***train*** *wreck* [衝突・転覆した]列車の残がい.

P He was killed ***in*** the *wreck*. 彼はその海難で死んだ. ¶The shore is strewn ***with*** *wrecks*. その海岸一面に難破船の破片が散らばっている.

P^2 the *wreck* ***of*** hopes 希望の消滅.

wreck, *v.* 破壊する(させる). 「こわれた.

M The bridge was ***completely*** *wrecked*. その橋はすっかり

P The ship was *wrecked* ***at*** sea. その船は航海中難破した. ¶ships *wrecked* ***in*** the late gale この間の強風で難破した船. ¶The ship *wrecked* ***on*** a sunken rock. その船は暗礁に乗り ⌊上げて大破した.

wreckage, *n.* 破損物.

V ***clear*** (=***remove***) the *wreckage* 破壊物を取り片付ける.

Q ***Various*** *wreckage* recognized as belonging to her has been found. その船に所属の物と確認された色々な残がいが見つかった.

P^2 *wreckage* ***of*** a ship (plane) 船(など)の残がい.

wrecker, *n.* 破壊者.

Q^2 a ***house*** *wrecker* 家庭を破壊する人.

wrench, *n.* ねじり；回螺(ら)器.

V ***give*** a *wrench* to one's ankle 足くびをくじく ‖ ***give*** a *wrench* at the door-handle 戸口のハンドルをぐっとねじる.

Q^2 a ***box*** (=pipe) *wrench* つぼ回螺(ら)器.

wrench, *n.* こじつけ.

P^2 the *wrench* ***of*** a meaning 意味のこじつけ.

wrench, *v.* ねじる.

M *wrench* ***open*** ねじあける. 「ple) ***off***.

M^2 *wrench* ***off*** ねじり取る. 【類】*wrench* a button (an ap-

P *wrench* ***at*** the door-knob 戸口のとっ手をねじる. ¶*wrench* the dagger ***from*** his grasp 彼からその短刀をもぎとる. ¶The lid of the box has been *wrenched* ***out of*** place. その箱のふたが(ちょうつがいなどをはずして)無理にこじ明け ⌊られている.

wrest, *v.* ねじり取る；曲げる.

P *wrest* it ***from*** the hands of ... …の手からそれをねじり取る ‖ He had *wrested* ***from*** books most of the knowledge he acquired. 彼はその持っていた知識の大部分を書籍から得た. ‖ The word is so badly *wrested* ***from*** its simple meaning. その語の単純な意味をはなはだしく曲解している. ‖ I tried to *wrest* the gun ***from*** his hands. 私は彼の手から銃をもぎ取ろうとした. ‖ *wrest* ***from*** her the supremacy of the world その国から世界支配権を奪取する. 【類】Many foreign phrases, in actual English quotation, have been *wrested* (ゆがめられてある) more or less ***from*** their proper original meaning. ¶*wrest* (=grasp) ***with*** a problem ⌊問題と取組む.

wrestle, *n.* 闘争.

Q a ***long, tough*** *wrestle* 長期の力争.

Q^2 a ***life-and-death*** *wrestle* with ... …と死にもの狂いの闘 ⌊争.

wrestle, *v.* 争う.

M *wrestle* ***each other*** 互に争う.

P *wrestle* ***for*** precedence in ... われ先に争って…する. ¶The English *wrestled* ***from*** the Dutch the carrying trade of the seas and command of the water. 英国はオランダから海運業と制海権を奪取した. ‖ *wrestle* ***from*** the grasp of ... …の手からもぎ取る. ¶*wrestle* ***with*** difficult problems 難問題と取組む ‖ a new woman (wife) *wrestling* ***with*** cookery-books 料理の本と首っ引きをする新しい型の女(など). 【類】problems ***with*** which the world has been *wrestling* / *wrestle* ***with*** the problems of choosing a profession / It *wrestled* ***with*** its environment and put its enemies under foot.

wrestler, *n.* 力士, レスラー.

V The *wrestler* ***won*** two falls out of three. そのレスラーは三本の中二本フォール勝ちした.

Q a ***well-known*** Lancashire *wrestler* 有名なランカシャのレスラー；ランカシャ(ホールド)の巧みな一流レスラー. ¶a graded name-list of ***professional*** *wrestlers* すもうの番付.

Q^2 a high-ranking ***judo*** *wrestler* 柔道高段者. ¶a ***sumo*** ⌊*wrestler* 力士.

wrestling, *n.* すもう, レスリング.

V We ***enjoyed*** *wrestling* on television. テレビですもう(レスリング)を見た. ¶***practice*** *wrestling* すもう(レスリング)の練習をする.

Q ***Greco-Roman*** *wrestling* グレコ・ローマン型レスリング (fall を決め手とする型). ¶after much ***inward*** *wrestling* 大いに苦悩した後で. ¶***professional*** *wrestling*=prowrestling プロレス.

Q^2 ***amateur*** *wrestling* アマチュアレス ‖ ***amateur free style*** *wrestling* アマ自由型レスリング. ¶*Lancashire wrestling* ランカシャ型のレスリング (hold を主にした型で catch-as-catch-can style ともいう).

P He held the ring *at wrestling* against all comers. 彼はすもうでだれが出て来ても土俵を譲らなかった. ¶antagonists *in wrestling* すもうの相手.

wretch, *n.* やつ, 野郎.

Q a ***contemptible*** *wretch* 情ないやつ, 卑劣なやつ. ¶an ***impudent*** *wretch* ずぶとい(生意気な)やつ. ¶a ***poor*** *wretch* かわいそうなやつ.

wretched, *a.* 不成績の.

P I am so *wretched* ***on*** names. 私は人の名を覚えるのが大の不得手だ.

wriggle, *v.* うごめく.

M² *wriggle* ***up*** to the ridge 山の背までよじ登る.

P *wriggle* ***out of*** a difficulty どうにかこうにか困難を切り抜ける.

wring, *v.* しぼる.

M *wring* the clothes ***dry*** 着物を固くしぼる. ¶dip a cloth into the water and *wring* it ***out*** 布を水に入れてしぼる.

M² *wring* ***off*** the head of a bird 鳥のくびをねじりとる.

P *wring* a consent ***from*** a person 無理矢理承諾させる. ¶His soul *wrang* ***with*** agony. 彼は大いに苦しんだ.

wrinkle, *n.* しわ; 心得; 手.

V ***acquire*** *wrinkles* しわがよる. ¶***have*** *wrinkles* しわがよっている. ¶***iron out*** *wrinkles* アイロンでしわをのばす. ¶***leave*** disfiguring *wrinkles* in the face 顔に醜いしわを残す. ¶***press out*** *wrinkles* in a dress ドレスのしわをプレスしてのばす. ¶***remove*** *wrinkles* しわを取る. ¶***smooth*** a *wrinkle* しわをのばす.

Q a ***new*** *wrinkle* in holdup 追いはぎの新(あら)手.

P full ***of*** *wrinkles* しわだらけの. ¶His face is seamed ***with*** *wrinkles.* 彼の顔にはしわがよっている. ¶His morning-coat fits him ***without*** a *wrinkle.* 彼のモーニングはぴったり合っている.

P² "*wrinkles*" ***in*** practical navigation 実地航海の心得.

wrist, *n.* 手首.

V I ***caught*** (=***took***) him by the *wrist.* 私は彼の手首をつかまえた. ¶***handcuff*** a person's *wrists* behind [him] うしろ手に手錠をはめる. ¶***sprain*** (=***strain***) one's *wrist* 手首をくじく. ¶***twist*** one's *wrist* その手をねじる.

writ, *n.* 令状.

V ***issue*** a *writ* against … …の逮捕状を発する. ¶***serve*** a *writ* on … …に令状を発する.

Q ***Holy*** (=***Sacred***) *Writ* 聖書.

Q² An ***Admiralty*** *writ* has been placed on board. 海軍省案は委員会の議に付せられた.

P² a *writ* ***of*** attachment 逮捕令状 ‖ a *writ* ***of*** ease 解雇状; 離縁状 ‖ a *writ* ***of*** summons 〖法〗呼出状 ‖ by a *writ* or order ***of*** court 裁判所の令状または命令によって. ¶a *writ* ***to*** a jailer to … …すべしとの看守の令状.

writ, *v.* [write の古体の過去または過去分詞].

M those whose names are *writ* ***large*** across the pages of the history of Europe and of the world 欧州史及び世界史のページに名前を特筆大書されている人々 ‖ It is *writ* ***large*** in today's men of taste. それが現代の趣味人にはっきり現われている.

P Their names are *writ* ***in*** gold. 彼らの名前はさんとして輝いている.

write, *v.* 書く; 手紙を書く.

M *write* ***artistically*** 美辞をつづる. ¶*write* ***back*** 返事を出す. ¶He thinks that the English language is generally ***better*** *written* in England than in America. 彼は一般に米国人の書く英語よりも英国人の書く英語の方が上等だと思っている. ¶*write* ***bodly*** 悪筆である. ¶a story ***brightly*** *written* りっぱに描かれた物語. ¶The story is ***briskly*** *written.* その物語は生々と描かれている. ¶*write* ***calmly*** and ***sensibly*** on the question その問題について冷静にしかも巧みに記述する. ¶*write* ***charmingly*** of … …について美文をもって書く. ¶*write* ***clearly*** and ***forcibly*** 明白に力強く書く. ¶*write* ***copiously*** in verse 韻文で長たらしく書く. ¶*write* ***crooked*** 字をねじけて書く. ¶It is the best way to *write* ***direectly*** to his father. 直接に彼の父に知らせるのが一番好い. ¶*write* ***distinctly*** はっきり字を書く. ¶He has the gift of *writing* ***entertainingly*** for young folk. 彼は子供がおもしろがるような書き方をする文才を持っている. ¶an article *written* ***expressly*** for the use of the paper 特にその新聞のために書かれた文. ¶an article *written* ***freshly, informingly,*** and ***entertainingly*** 新鮮味を出して教訓的にかつおもしろく書かれた文. ¶*write* a letter ***hurriedly*** 急いで手紙をしたためる. ¶It is *written* ***indelibly*** in my soul. それは私の心に深く刻み込まれている. ¶*write* ***industriously*** in one's notebook 自分の手帳に丹念に書き留める. ¶*write* ***learnedly*** on a subject ある問題についてうん蓄を傾けて書く. ¶*write* too ***much*** on the subject その件をくどく書き過ぎる. ¶*write* ***neatly*** and ***legibly*** きれいにはっきりと書く. ¶*write* one "***on the level***" 人を公平に書く. ¶*write* ***out*** 清書する; くわしく書き記す ‖ *write* ***out*** a check 小切手を切る ‖ *write* ***out*** fair 清書する ‖ *write* ***out*** a report (document) 報告(文書)を書き上げる ‖ *write* ***out*** a speech 演説の草稿を書く. ¶*write* ***over again*** 書き直す. ¶He reads and *writes* ***passably.*** 彼はどうにか読み書きができる. ¶*write* very ***pessimistically*** concerning … …に関してははなはだしく悲観的な口調で書く. ¶He cannot *write* even a letter ***satisfactorily.*** 満足に手紙も書けない. ¶a ***sensibly*** *written* book 良識をもって書かれた本. ¶The name is *written* ***underneath.*** その名は下に書いてある. ¶*write* ***uphill*** しり上りに書く. ¶*write* English ***well*** 英文が達者だ. ¶*write* ***wrong*** 書き誤る.

M² *write* ***down*** 書きつける; 記録する; 酷評する ‖ *write* ***down*** in one's notebook … …を手帳に記す. 【類】*write* ***down*** from her lips (口述を) that … ‖ *write* ***down*** all opposition 敵側をこきおろす ‖ "*write* ***down***" to a magazine audience 雑誌読者向きに調子を下げて書く. 【類】Authors ought to avoid "*writing* ***down.***" ¶*write* ***off*** [こげつきなど]棒引きにする; だめだと決めてしまう ‖ *write* ***off*** a bad debt [こげつき負債など]棒引きにする, [請求権など]取消す ‖ *write* ***off*** the meeting as a failure その会議は失敗ときめつける ‖ *write* ***off*** partially the infamy of … …の汚名を幾分そそぐ ‖ *write* ***off*** 1947 as a bad financial year 一九四七年を金融不況の年と批判する. ¶*write* ***up*** 掲示する; 記録する; 書き立てる ‖ *write* (=play) it ***up*** それを書きたてる. 【類】The resort was greatly *written* ***up.***

P I am not fitted to *write* ***about*** *it.* 私はそのことを書くに適していない. ‖ I will *write* you ***about*** the details later on. 詳細は後から手紙で申し上げます. ‖ There are always plenty of topics to *write* ***about.*** 取上げて記すべき問題がいつでもたくさんある. ¶*write* ***against*** a person (book) 人(など)を非難して書く. ¶the matter ***around*** which these chapters were *written* 本書の主題として取扱った事柄. ¶*write* ***at*** full length 詳細に書く. ¶*written* ***by*** hand 手記の(タイプでなく) ‖ *write* ***by*** shorthand 速記する ‖ It is said of Marquis Okuma that all his books have been *written* ***by*** his tongue. 大隈侯の著書はいずれも口述されたものだということだ. ‖ Butane is *written* ***by*** the chemist C_4H_{10}, which means that it has four atoms of carbon and ten of hydrogen in every molecule. [人造ゴム]ブタンの分子式は C_4H_{10} である, それは炭素が四と水素が十の分子からできているという意味である. ¶*write* ***for*** the masses 大衆のために執筆する ‖ *write* ***for*** profit (print) 報酬(印刷)を目的に執筆する ‖ *write* ***for*** press 出版するために書く ‖ *write* ***for*** a newspaper (magazine) 新聞(など)に寄稿する ‖ a dissertation *written* ***for*** the degree of B.D. 神学学士号請求の論文 ‖ I will *write* ***for*** a copy. 一部注文しよう. ‖ *write* or call ***for*** a prospectus [学校などの]規則書を取り寄せるかまたはもらいに行く. ¶*write* ***from*** dictation 口述を書き取る ‖ *write* ***from*** … …から手紙を出す ‖ *write* ***from*** the shoulder 懸腕直筆で書く. ¶*write* ***in*** haste 筆を走らせる ‖ *write* ***in*** a letter 手紙に書いてやる ‖ *write* ***in*** pen (pencil, chalk) ペン(など)で書く. 【類】a note *written* ***in*** pen [and ink] ‖ *write* ***in*** pencil (chalk) 鉛筆(など)で書く ‖ *write* ***in*** a thick hand 肉太に書く ‖ *write* ***in*** the hotel register ホテルの宿帳に記入する(投宿する) ‖ *write* ***in*** answer 返事として書く ‖ Thus he *writes* ***in*** his recent book. 彼の最近の著作にこう書いてある. ‖ a letter *written* ***in*** French フランス語の手紙 ‖ Refinement is *written* ***in*** every line of his face. その教養の深さは顔にありありと見えている. ¶be *written* ***into*** law 法文化してある ‖ be *written* ***into*** a treaty 条約に成文されている. ¶Virgil *wrote* ***of*** the founding of Rome; her dissolution is as grand a subject. ヴァージルはローマの創建について書いたがその崩壊もこれに劣らぬ大きな題目である. ¶*write* ***on*** Japan 日本に関することを書く ‖ *write* ***on*** mathematics 数学書を著わす ‖ *write* it ***on*** the chalk board それを黒板に書く ‖ *write* articles ***on*** topics about which they really know very little 彼らのよく知らない色々な問題について文を書く ‖ *write* ***on*** the blackboard ***with*** chalk チョー

クで黒板に書く ‖ *write* ***on*** but one side of the paper 紙の片面だけに書く ‖ It is *written* ***on*** my heart. それは私の心に銘せられている. ¶ I will *write* ***to*** you soon. じきにお便り致します. ‖ he wrote [*to*] us saying that ... ...と彼から便りが来た ‖ I will inform him of the matter by *writing* ***to*** him a long letter. 私は細かく手紙で書いてそのことを先方へ知らせます ¶ *write* ***to*** a person ***about*** a matter ある件について手紙を出す. ¶ a newspaperman *writing* ***under*** his own name 署名記事を書いている新聞記者 ‖ *write* ***under*** a pen name 書いたものに雅号を使う. ¶ He says so with hope still *written* ***upon*** his face. 彼は相変らずその顔に希望の色を見せてそう言っている. ¶ *write* ***with*** a pen (pencil, ball-point pen) ペン(など)で書く ‖ *write* ***with*** pen and ink ペンとインキで書く ‖ *write* ***with*** the left hand 左手で書く ‖ *write* ***with*** a typewriter タイプライターで書く. 【類】 *write* ***with*** a lead pencil / *write* ***with*** ink (chalk) / I want something to *write* ***with*** ‖ *write* ***with*** a small initial 小文字で書始める ‖ *written* ***with*** the reformed alphabet 改正字母で書かれた ‖ an inscription *written* ***with*** Chinese characters 漢字で書いた碑文 ‖ Though phonetically alike, they are *written* ***with*** different ideographs. 音は同じであるが字が違っている. 【類】 *write* ***with*** ease / *write* ***with*** artistic skill 技巧的に書く.

O he *writes* me to say that ... 彼は手紙で...と私の所に言ってきた. ¶ *write* a good (bad) hand 筆蹟がうまい(下手だ). ☞ 文章の方は *write* [in] good (bad) style.

writer, *n.* 執筆家, 文士, 作家.

V ***discover*** the *writer* in his writings 著作を読んでその作家の人物を知る. ¶ he ***quotes*** a *writer* in an English paper as saying that ... 彼は英国の新聞のある筆者の言葉として...を引用している. ¶ ***select*** reputable *writers* as one's models 文のお手本として有名な作者を選ぶ.

Q ***ancient*** *writers* 古代の著作家. ¶ Kipling and other ***Anglo-Indian*** *writers* キプリング及びその他の英系インド作家. ¶ an ***arid*** *writer* 無味乾燥な作家. ¶ ***careless slipshod*** *writers* 大ざっぱな締りのない文章を書く作家. ¶ a ***comic*** *writer* 喜劇作家. ¶ a ***coming*** *writer* 新進文士. ¶ a ***dull*** *writer* 興味の乏しい文を書く作家. ¶ ***earliar*** *writers* 昔の作者たち. ¶ ***editorial*** *writers* 〖新聞〗 論説委員 ‖ He rose from copy boy to chief ***editorial*** *writer* on a leading New York newspaper. 氏は原稿はこびを振り出しにニューヨーク一流新聞の主要論説委員となった. ¶ ***eloquent*** *writers* 文体の流麗な文士. ¶ one of our most ***enduring*** *writers* わが国の不朽の作者の一人. ¶ a ***fair*** *writer* 能文家. ¶ ***English*** *writers* and their products 英国作家及びその作品. ¶ a ***feeble*** *writer* 貧弱な作家. ¶ the ***foremost authoritative*** *writer* on aviation in this country 航空術に関するこの国の最高権威の著述家. ¶ a ***full-fledged*** *writer* 一家をなす作家. ¶ a ***gifted*** *writer* 天才作家. ¶ a ***good*** *writer* 筆が立つ人. ¶ a ***humorous*** *writer* = a humorist ユーモア作家. ¶ the most ***illuminating*** *writer* 最も参考になるように書く人. ¶ an ***illustrious*** *writer* 著名な作家. ¶ an ***industrious*** and ***abundant*** *writer* 熱心な多作家. ¶ an ***inexperienced*** *writer* 未熟の作家(著者). ¶ an ***inferior*** *writer* 三等作者. ¶ the greatest ***living*** *writer* of English prose 現に生きている英国散文作家として最も偉大な人. ¶ Maeterlinck and other ***mystical*** *writers* of the day メーテルリンクやその他当時の神秘小説の作家. ¶ a ***nationally known*** *writer* 国内に知れ渡った作家. ¶ the relief of ***needy*** *writers* 貧困文士の救済. ¶ ***new*** and ***unknown*** *writers* 新進の無名作家. ¶ ***newspaper-trained*** *writers* 新聞社で鍛え上げた文士連. ¶ an ***obscure*** *writer* 名もない作家. ¶ an ***optimistic*** *writer* 楽天的な作家. ¶ a very ***picturesque*** and ***interesting*** writer 描写が美しく興味のある作家. ¶ a prominent ***popular*** *writer* 著名な大衆作家. ¶ a ***practiced*** (= *trained*) *writer* 老練な作家. ¶ as the ***present*** *writer* ventures to think 筆者が考えるように. ¶ a ***productive*** *writer* 多作家. ¶ a ***prolific*** *writer* of fiction 著作に富む小説家. 【類】 a ***prolific*** *writer* on social questions. ¶ a representative ***professional*** *writer* 代表的職業著述家. ¶ three most ***prominent*** *writers* on the subject その問題について最も著名な三人の執筆家 【類】 a ***prominent*** *writer* on economic subjects. ¶ ***refreshing*** and ***clear-sighted*** *writer* 読んで清々する文を書く頭脳明敏な作家. ¶ a ***slow*** *writer* 遅筆家. ¶ ***standard*** *writers* 第一流の作家. ¶ a ***talented*** *writer* 手腕のある作家. ¶ a ***thrilling*** *writer* 血わき肉踊る文を書く人. ¶ ***ultrapatriotic*** and ***jingoistic*** *writers* 超愛国的で対外硬派の執筆家. ¶ an ***unthinking*** *writer* 考えの浅い作家. ¶ an ***untrained*** *writer* 未熟な記者. ¶ a ***verbose*** *writer* 文の冗漫な作家. ¶ a ***versatile*** *writer* 行くとして可ならざるなき作家. ¶ a ***voluminous*** *writer* on the subject of Japan 日本に関して多数の著作をした人. ¶ a ***wellknown naval*** *writer* 海軍のことを書くので有名な人.

Q² an "***ad***" (= advertisement) *writer* 広告文案家. ¶ an advertising ***copy*** *writer* 宣伝用(ビラなど)文案家. ¶ ***beginning*** *writers* of fiction 小説の初心者. ¶ a ***Big Name*** *writer* 一流作家. ¶ a ***book*** *writer* 著作家. ¶ an ***entertainment*** *writer* 娯楽をねらう作家. ¶ a ***feature*** *writer* 特別記事専門の寄稿家. ¶ a ***fiction*** *writer* 創作家. ¶ a ***film script*** *writer* 映画の台本作家. ¶ a ***free-lance*** *writer* [社または部専属でない]記者, 寄稿家. ¶ a ***ghost*** *writer* 代作者. ¶ ***highbrow*** *writers* of today 《米》 現代の知識人ぶる文筆家たち. ¶ a ***law*** *writer* 法律関係のものを書く人. ¶ a great ***imagination*** *writer* 構想力に富む大作家. ¶ a ***letter*** *writer* 手紙を書く人; 書簡文範 ‖ a rotten ***letter*** *writer* 手紙のへたな人. ¶ a ***magazine story*** *writer* 雑誌小説の作家. ¶ a ***news*** *writer* 報道記者. ¶ a ***newspaper*** *writer* 新聞記者及び寄稿家. ¶ Great ***nonsense*** *writers*, such as Lewis Carroll, Edward Lear, etc. ¶ tell it so concisely as to defy the ***precis*** *writer* それは要約文の筆者そっちのけの簡潔さで書いてある. ¶ a ***radio script*** *writer* ラジオの台本作家. ¶ a ***scenario*** *writer* 《映》 シナリオ・ライター. ¶ a ***screen*** *writer* 映画台本(脚本)家. ¶ a typist and ***shorthand*** *writer* タイピスト兼速記者. ¶ a ***socialist*** *writer* 社会主義の作家. ¶ a ***song*** *writer* 歌詞専門の作家. ¶ a ***textbook*** *writer* 教科書の著者. ¶ the leading ***travel*** *writers* of the day 現代の一流旅行記作家. ¶ a ***woman*** *writer* (*pl.* ***women*** *writers*) 女流作家. ¶ a ***wrapper*** *writer* 帯封書き.

P² a *writer* ***about*** baseball 野球記者. ¶ a *writer* ***for*** newspapers (magazines) 新聞(など)に執筆する人 ‖ a *writer* ***for*** pay 報酬を得るために書く人. ¶ He is well known as a *writer* ***in*** magazines. 彼は雑誌執筆者として有名だ. ¶ a *writer* ***of*** authority 権威ある筆者. ¶ a *writer* ***of*** novels 小説家 ‖ *writers* ***of*** the first class 第一流の執筆者 ‖ the *writer* ***of*** this magazine article この文の筆者. ¶ a *writer* ***on*** Japan (= Japanese subjects) 日本のことを書く人 ‖ a *writer* ***of*** distinction 著名作家 ‖ a *writer* ***of*** English 英文家 ‖ the *writer* ***of*** a letter 手紙の主(書いた本人) ‖ a *writer* ***of*** a weekly review 週刊評論の担当者. ¶ a *writer* ***on*** grammar 文法書の著者. ¶ a *writer* ***without*** style (= who lacks style) 文体に特徴のない(平凡な)作家.

writhe, *v.* もだえる.

P *writhe* ***in*** pain 苦痛にもだえる. 【類】 *writhe* ***in*** agony. ¶ The snake *writhes* ***along*** the branch (***through*** the bush). へびが木の枝(など)をぬたくる. ¶ *writhe* ***with*** shame 恥辱にもだえる.

writing, *n.* **(1)** 書くこと; 文; *pl.* 著述, 著作.

V ***adopt*** *writing* as a profession 文筆を業とする. ¶ ***begin*** *writing* 文筆をとるようになる. ¶ ***decipher*** ancient *writing* 古文を判読する. ¶ He ***does*** much *writing*. 彼は盛んに書く. ¶ I ***have*** some *writing* to do. 私は少し書きものがある. ¶ ***place*** *writings* of Copernicus on the Index of prohibited books コペルニクスの著作を禁書とする. ¶ ***practice*** *writing* 作文の練習をする. ¶ Mr. Balfour's *writings* have been ***produced*** in the intervals of a busy life. バルフォア氏の著作は多忙な生活の余暇に書いたものである. ¶ ***publish*** his collected *writings* 彼の著作集を出版する. ¶ ***spice*** one's *writing* with concrete cases and amusing examples 具体的な事実と興味ある事例をあげて文章に味をつける.

Q ***anonymous*** *writing* 匿名の執筆. ¶ ***argumentative*** *writing* 論争的な文. ¶ ***biographical*** *writing* 伝記文. ¶ ***commercial*** *writing* 稿料かせぎの執筆. ¶ He has done ***considerable*** *writing* for books and periodicals. 彼は著作に雑誌寄稿に大分文筆活動をやった. ¶ ***controversial*** *writings* 議論文. ¶ ***correct*** *writing* 正しい文. ¶ ***creative*** *writing* 創作. ¶ the art of ***descriptive*** *writing* 写生文の書き方. ¶ ***elegant*** *writing* 雅文をつづること. ¶ ***faulty*** *writing* 間違っている文. ¶ No attempt is made for ***fine*** *writing*. [この文は]美文的に書こうとしたのではない. ¶ ***forcible*** *writing* 雄健な筆致. ¶ The word should be avoided in ***formal*** (= serious) *writing* その語は正式の文には避けた方がよい. ¶ ***formal*** and ***informal*** *writing* 正式と略式な書き方. ¶ ***Good*** *writing* is a by-product of one's general reading. 文章の巧みなことは読書の副産物である. ¶the ***historical*** *writing* of our time 歴史に関する現代の文章. ¶***inspired*** and ***patriotic*** *writings* 感激した愛国的著作. ¶***journalistic*** or ***other ephemeral literary*** *writings* 新聞または他の一時的の文章. ¶***lucid*** *writing* 明折な文章. ¶***master*** *writings* of great historians of all nations 世界一流歴史家の大文字. ¶***microscopic*** *writing* 細字書き. ¶***political*** *writings* 政治上の論文. ¶***popular*** *writings* 大衆向の作品. ¶his ***posthumous*** *writings* 氏の遺稿. ¶at the ***present*** (=***this***) *writing* 本文を草するに当って. ¶Smithson was a greater man than is indicated by his ***published*** *writings* alone. スミスソンは単にその出版された著述だけに表われているよりはさらに偉大な人物であった. ¶***ready*** *writing* 速筆(遅筆に対して). ¶***religious*** *writings* 宗教に関する文. ¶***slanderous*** *writings* of their enemies and persecutors 彼らの敵や迫害者の非難的な文字. ¶***Slipshod*** *writing* is the sin of the age. 粗雑な文章は現代の弊である. ¶***tasteful*** *writing* 味わい深い文. ¶It may not be fine *writing*, but it is ***vivid*** *writing*. それは美文ではないかも知れないがしかし生き生きした文章だ.

Q² ***backhand***[***ed***] *writing* 左傾斜の書き方. ¶***composiiton*** *writing* 作文. ¶improve one's ***English*** *writing* and speaking 英語の書き方話し方がうまくなる ‖ foreign quotations likely to be met with in ***English*** *writing* 英文中によくある外国語の引用. ¶The age of ***letter*** *writing* is past. 手紙で用を足す時代は過ぎた. ¶***looking-glass*** *writing* [鏡で見ると読める]逆書き. ¶***maunscript*** *writing* [活字のような print-script に対し]筆記体の書. ¶lecturing and ***magazine*** *writing* 講演並びに雑誌寄稿. ¶a ***master*** *writing* 大文章. ¶a style of ***newspaper*** *writing* 新聞の文体. ¶***precise*** *writing* [長い文を縮める]簡約書き. ¶***prose*** *writings* 散文の文献. ¶a bit of "***Rule Britannia***" *writing* 愛国歌調の片影. ¶***stencil-paper*** *writing* 謄写版体の書きもの. ¶***student*** *writing* 学生の文. ¶Lawrence was a ***working-class*** *writer* ローレンスは労働者出身の作家であった.

P ***at*** this *writing* この文を草する時に. ¶a few days ***before*** this *writing* この記事(手紙)を書く数日前. ¶***by*** *writing* 文書による. ¶quotations ***from*** English *writings* 英文からの引用句. ¶***in*** *writing* or orally 書面または口頭で ‖ an answer ***in*** *writing* 文書による返事〘法〙答弁書 ‖ It must be ***in*** *writing* それは文書でなくてはならない. ‖ be communicated ***in*** *writing* 文書によって通知される. ‖ be remiss ***in*** *writing* to a person 人にごぶさたをしている ‖ have a reply ***in*** *writing* 文書による返事をもらう ‖ prove that the instrument forged is ***in*** his *writing* その偽造文書は彼が書いたものであることを証明する. ¶***up to*** the present *writing* この文を書くときまでに ‖ We have not had any response to it ***up to*** this *writing*. この文を草するまでその返事は受取っていません. ¶go on ***with*** *writing* 書き続ける.

P² *writings* ***about*** an author ある著者に関する文献. ¶*writing* ***for*** a living 生活のための執筆. ¶Some of the best *writing* ***in*** the English language today is to be found in the better-class journals. 今日英語の最も優秀な文章の例は一流の新聞・雑誌にこれを見ることができる. ¶a *writing* ***on*** ... ...に関する著作. 【類】*writings* ***on*** nuclear fission (核分裂). ¶*writing* ***to*** dictation 書き取り.

(**2**) 書くこと; 字体, 文字.

V ***learn*** *writing* 習字をする. ¶I cannot ***make out*** his *writing*. あの人の書いた文字は私には読めない. ¶if you do not ***mind*** my bad *writing* 私の悪筆でも構わなければ. ¶At a glance she ***recognized*** the *writing* of her son. 彼女は一見してむすこの筆跡だと分かった.

Q It was written in ***bold, clear*** *writing* upon the blackboard. それは太いはっきりした字体で黒板に書かれていた. ¶correspondence in ***clear*** and ***legible*** *writing* はっきりと読みやすく書いてある手紙. ¶a ***crabbed*** *writing* 分かりにくい書体の書きもの. ¶in ***deliberate*** *writing* 丁寧な書体で. ¶***fair*** *writing* 能書. ¶***legible*** and ***neat*** *writing* 明白できれいな筆跡. ¶in ***loose*** *writing* 締りのない書体で. ¶a habit of ***slovenly*** *writing* だらしのない字を書く習慣. ¶***supposititious*** *writings* 偽筆.

P a poor hand ***at*** *writing* 字のへたな人. ¶the great dim ages ***before*** *writing* in Europe ヨーロッパに文字ができる前のおぼろげにしか分からない時代. ¶apply ***in*** *writing* 文書で出願する ‖ The letter was undoubtedly ***in*** his *writing*. その手紙は確かに彼の手筆であった.

wrong, *n*. 非行.

V ***abrogate*** the *wrongs* 不正を取除く. ¶repentantly ***admit*** one's *wrongs* 自分の非を後悔する. ¶***avenge*** one's *wrongs* on some one 人に復しゅうをする. ¶You would ***do*** *wrong* not to thank him. 君は彼にお礼を言わなくては悪い. ‖ ***do*** a person *wrong* 人に間違ったことをする ‖ Owen, what has ***done*** *wrong* with you? オーウエン, どうかしたのか. ‖ The police can ***do*** no *wrong*. 警官のすることは失行にならない. ‖ The King can ***do*** no *wrong*. 王は神聖である. ¶***mend*** one's *wrongs* その非行を改める. ¶***redress*** *wrongs* 不法を正す. ¶***remedy*** the *wrongs* 不正を改める. ¶***repair*** *wrongs* 失行に対する埋合わせをする. ¶***right*** (=***correct***) one's *wrongs* 非を正す.【類】***right*** this *wrong* to the gentler sex (女性) ‖ He felt confident that his *wrongs* would be ***righted***. 彼は自分の失行が正される(埋合わせができる)ものと信じていた. ¶***suffer*** *wrongs* 不当な取扱いを受ける.

V² Two *wrongs* do not ***make*** a right. 二つの非行は一つの善行にならない. ☞ Two negatives do not make an affirmative.

Q a ***clamorous*** *wrong* やかましく言われる失態. ¶a ***grievous national*** *wrong* 由々しき国家的失態. ¶do a person an ***irreparable*** *wrong* 人に取り返しのつかない不法を行う. ¶commit a ***legal*** *wrong* 法律に触れる. ¶right an ***old*** *wrong* 旧悪を改める. ¶do them a ***positive*** *wrong* 彼らに明かに害になる. ¶the redress of ***social*** *wrongs* 社会弊害の矯正. ¶suffer an ***unmerited*** *wrong* ぬれぎぬを着る.

Q² ***fancy*** *writing* 曲書き(広告など).

P abstain ***from*** all *wrongs* 決して曲ったことをしない ‖ be free ***from*** all *wrongs* 非行は全然ない. ¶He is entirely ***in*** the *wrong*. 彼が全く間違っている. ‖ He acknowledged himself ***in*** the *wrong*. 自分の非を認めた. ¶brood ***over*** one's *wrongs* 自分の非行を反省する.

P² a *wrong* ***against*** ... ...に対する非行.

wrong, *a*. 間違っている.

M It is ***admittedly*** *wrong*. それはたしかに間違っている. ¶We were ***entirely*** *wrong*. われわれは全然間違っていた. ¶we shall probably not be ***far*** *wrong* if we suppose that ... われらが...と想像しても左ほど間違ではあるまい. ¶Such things are *wrong* ***morally*** and ***spiritually***. こうしたことは道徳的にも精神的にも間違っている. ¶Surely something is ***radically*** *wrong* in ... ...には確かに何か根本的の間違いがある. ¶Something is ***seriously*** *wrong* with the engine. 発動機に大分狂っている所がある. ¶It is ***simply*** *wrong*. それは全然間違いだ. ¶***utterly*** *wrong* 全然間違って. ¶I would not be ***very*** *wrong* to say that ... 私が...と言っても大して間違いはあるまい.

P They must have been *wrong* ***about*** my age. 彼らは私の年を思い違いをしていたに違いない. ¶His accounts are *wrong* ***by*** some £40,000. 彼の計算は約四万ポンド間違っている. ¶He was *wrong* ***in*** his conjecture. 彼の推察は間違っていた. ‖ be *wrong* ***in*** the garret 気が狂っている. ¶it was *wrong* ***of*** you to ... 君が...したのは悪かった. ¶Nothing is *wrong* ***with*** me. 僕は無事だ. ‖ Something seems *wrong* ***with*** the last line. 最後の句に何か間違いがあるらしい(引用句など). ‖ Something is *wrong* ***with*** the machinery. どこか機械に故障がある.【類】There is something very *wrong* ***with*** its economy. / Everything went *wrong* ***with*** us.

O reject it as *wrong* 誤りとしてそれを拒否する. ¶This doorknob doesn't work. What's *wrong*, I wonder? このドアのとっ手はきかない. どうしたんだろう.

wrong-doer, *n*. 失行者.

V ***lead*** the *wrong-doer* ***back*** into (=to) the right way 失行者を正道に立ち戻らせる.

P complain ***against*** the *wrong-doer* 犯罪者の非を鳴らす.

wrongful *a*. 不正な.

P *wrongful* ***to*** others 他人に対して不正な.

wrought, *a*. 造った.

P figures *wrought* ***in*** gold 金製の像.

X

X-ray, *n.* エックス線.

P put him ***under*** the *X-ray* 彼にエックス線をかける.

xylophone, *n.* 木琴.

V ***play*** the *xylophone* 木琴を奏する.

P performance ***on*** the *xylophone* 木琴演奏.

Y

yacht, *n.* ヨット.

V ***keep*** a *yacht* ヨットを持っている.

Q² a ***steam*** *yacht* 蒸気ヨット.

P sail ***in*** (=***on***) a *yacht* ヨットに乗って行く. ¶a race ***of*** *yachts*=a yacht race ヨット競走.

yachting, *n.* ヨット遊び.

V ***enjoy*** *yachting* ヨット遊びをする.

yank, *v.* 《口語》ぐいと引く.

M *yank* ***out*** a loose tooth ゆるんだ歯を引き抜く.

P He *yanked* me ***out of*** the water. 彼は私を水中から引上げた.

Yankee, *n.* 米人.

Q² the ***go-ahead*** (=go-getting) *Yankee* 進取的な米人.

yard, *n.* ヤード(ヤール); 帆げた.

V ***man*** the *yards* (船が)登げん礼を行う.

P measure ***by*** the *yard* ヤールで計る. ¶***within*** a few *yards* of this place この場所から数ヤードの所に.

P² a *yard* ***in*** width 幅一ヤール. ¶six *yards* ***of*** cloth 六ヤールの布. ¶I saw him standing a few *yards* ***off*** the car. 彼が車から二三ヤード離れて立っているのが見えた.

yap, *n.* 叫び(犬の).

Q give three loud ***sharp*** *yaps* of warning [犬が]三度警戒の意味で高く鋭くほえる.

yard, *n.* 庭; 場.

V He ***keeps*** a small poultry *yard* which includes three young cocks. 彼の所には三羽の雄のひよっ子のいる小さな鶏舎がある.

Q a ***covered*** *yard* 屋根のある置場. ¶a ***front*** (***back***) *yard* 前(裏)庭.

Q² a ***chicken*** *yard* 養鶏場. ¶a ***junk*** *yard* くず物置場. ¶a ***lumber*** *yard* 《米》木材置場. ¶a ***marshaling*** *yard* 〚鉄道〛操車場. ☞ 車両入換場所の意では《米》a switchyard, 《英》a shunting-yard. ¶a ***play*** *yard* for babies 赤ん坊の遊び場(芝生の). ¶a ***railroad*** (=《英》***railway***) *yard* 鉄道駅構内. ¶a ***school*** *yard* 校庭. ¶a ***stock*** *yard* 〚鉄道〛[臨時の]家畜置場. ¶an open ***storage*** *yard* for coal 屋根のない石炭貯蔵場. ¶a ***timber*** *yard* 材木置場. ¶a ***waste disposal*** *yard* at the water front 水際にあるごみ捨場.

P ***at*** Scotland *Yard* ロンドン警視庁で. ¶enclose poultry ***in*** a *yard* 家きんを鶏舎に閉込める.

yardstick, *n.* 物指, ヤード尺.

V It is impossible to ***apply*** the same *yardstick* to poets and artists as to other people. 詩人や美術家をその他の人たちに対すると同じような尺度ではかることはできない.

Q an ***accurate*** *yardstick* for measuring ... ...を測定する正確な尺度(標準).

yarn, *n.* 糸; 《口語》物語.

V He was induced to ***spin*** a *yarn* for the benefit of his friend. 彼は友人のために長話をさせられた. ¶***tell*** (=spin) a long *yarn* 長話をする.

Q a ***big*** *yarn*=a large story 大げさな話. ¶an ***entertaining little*** "*yarn*" おもしろい小話. ¶a ***spicy*** *yarn* わい談.

P spin cotton ***into*** *yarn* 綿を紡いで糸にする. ¶a skein ***of*** *yarn* 糸のかせ.

yarn, *n.* 毛糸.

Q ***woolen*** *yarn* 毛糸.

Q² ***knitting*** *yarn* [メリヤス・セーターの]編み糸. ¶***wooly-nylon*** *yarn* ウーリナイロンの編み糸.

yaw, *v.* 抜け出る.

P *yaw* ***out of*** the line [軍艦が]戦列から逸出する.

yawn, *n.* あくび.

V He rubbed his eyes, and, ***giving*** a heavy *yawn*, looked sleepily about him. 彼は目をこすり大きなあくびをしながらねむたそうに辺りを見回した. 【類】***give*** the first *yawn* of the approaching wakefulness (だんだん目がさめて来る). ¶***hide*** a *yawn* behind one's hand 手であくびを隠す. ¶***stifle*** (=***suppress***) a *yawn* あくびをかみ殺す.

Q with a ***hideous*** *yawn* 恐ろしく大きなあくびをしながら.

P stretch oneself ***with*** a *yawn* あくびをして背伸びをする.

yawn, *v.* あくびをする.

M *yawn* ***heavily*** 大あくびをする. ¶*yawn* ***out*** ... あくびをしながら...という. ¶*yawn* ***publicly*** 人の前であくびをする.

P Hell *yawns* ***for*** him. 地獄が口を開けて彼を待っている. ¶*yawn* ***over*** the evening papers 夕刊を見ながらあくびをする.

year, *n.* (**1**) 年.

V Mr. Unwin has ***begun*** the *year* with ... [英国の出版者]アンウイン氏が本年になって最初に出版したのは...であった. ¶Japanese ***celebrate*** the New *Year* more elaborately than Europeans or Americans. 日本人は欧米人よりも一層念入りに正月を祝う. ¶The society has just ***closed*** the first *year* of its activities. 協会は今その活動の第一年を終った. ¶He has just ***completed*** his first *year* of office as American Ambassador in London. 彼はロンドン駐在米国大使として在任満一カ年になった. ¶It ***costs*** him three *years* of toil to win. 彼はそれを得るまでには三年の労苦を要する. 【類】an undertaking that has ***cost*** three *years* of unremitting (不断の) labor. ¶The investigation ***covered*** nearly two *years*. その調査はかれこれ二カ年にわたった. 【類】The course of study (修業年限) ***covers*** three *years*. ¶he has ***devoted*** fifty *years* of his diligent life to the study of ... 彼は五十年の間黙々として...を研究した. ¶***enter*** a new *year* 新年にはいる. ¶The company has ***experienced*** a most unremunerative *years*. その会社はこの一年ははなはだ不成績であった. ¶Pessimists ***forecast*** a bad *year*. 凶年だと悲観をしている者もある. ¶He ***got*** 25 *years* for robbery. 彼は強盗犯で二十五年(の刑務)を食った. ¶He has ***given*** many *years* to the study of this problem. 彼はこの問題の研究に多年従事していた. ¶***hail*** the new *year* 新年を迎える. ¶we ***had*** a record *year* in regard to ... ...の点において画期的な年であった ‖ He ***has*** many *years* to live. 彼は春秋に富む. ¶to ***mark*** the tenth *year* of its successful history of enterprise and development その創業十年を記念するために. ¶It has ***occupied*** ten *years* in course of construction. その建築は十年かかった. ‖ The course ***occupies*** three *years* 修業年限は三年である. ¶***put on*** *years* 歳を取る ‖ One has not ***put on*** *years* in vain. かめの甲より年の劫. ¶It has now ***reached*** the 30th *year* of its existence. それは創立以来三十年となった. ¶The book ***represents*** *years* of patient toil, far-reaching investigation, and untiring research. その著作は多年にわたる堅忍不抜の労苦と広範な調査とうまざる研究との成果である. ¶The work will ***require*** ten *years* to complete. その仕事は完成するまでに十年はかかろう. ¶He ***rounds out*** twenty *years* as head of the university this week. 彼は学長となってから今週で二十周年になる. ¶Fifty-one *years* have I ***scratched off*** from my calendar. 私も五十一を越した. ¶He ***served*** twenty-seven *years* in jail for murder. 彼は殺人罪で二十七年の刑期を勤めた. ¶They ***spent*** *years* in these experiments all of which proved fruitless. 彼らはこれらの実験に数年を費したが それは みな不成績に終った. ‖ He has ***spent*** *years* on shorthand. 彼は多年速記をやってきた.【類】I have ***spent*** thirty *years* with Waseda. ¶***take*** several more *years* to complete 完成するまでになお数年を要する ‖ ***take*** a *year* ***off*** 一年の休暇を取る. ¶***usher*** in the New *Year* 新年を迎える. ¶He received the visits of those friends who had come to ***wish*** him many more *years* of happy life. 彼はその万歳を祝いにやって来た友人たちの訪問を受けた.

v² Several *years* have ***drifted by*** since Rudolph Valentino crossed the Great Divide. ルドルフ・バレンチノが幽明境を異にしてから数年が流れた. ¶The *year* will ***expire*** tomorrow. 年はあしたで暮れる. ¶The *years* ***flowed on***. 歳月が流れた. ¶The *years* ***went on***. 歳月がたって行った. ¶in the *years* that ***lie*** ahead これから先の年月に. ¶The exhibition *year* ***opened*** with Cruft's Dog Show. その年の展覧会はクラフト犬の展覧会が最初だった. ¶The goods have increased in popularity as the *years* have ***passed*** [***by***] (＝progressed). その品は年がたつにつれてますます評判がよくなった. ¶as the *years* ***roll by*** (＝***on***) 年が進むにつれて. ¶The *years* ***ran on***. 年がぐんぐんたって行った.

Q ***academic*** (＝school) *year* 学年. ¶in ***after*** *years* 後年に. ¶***all*** the *year* round (＝around) 年中. ¶***Another*** *year* or two slipped by. また一二年たった. ¶The crop will be better this year than in an ***average*** *year*. 今年の作柄は平年より良いだろう. ¶a ***bad*** *year* for the rice crop 米作の凶年. ¶the ***banner*** *year* for trade 商業大発展の年 ‖ a ***banner*** *year* for crops 豊年 ‖ the ***banner*** *year* for men-hours lost [争議のため]最も多く労働時間をむだにした年. ¶a man's ***best*** *years* 人の働き盛り. ¶Yes, 1925 was a ***bitter*** *year* for the phonograph, and for Victor. そうです, 千九百二十五年は蓄音機にとってまたビクター(会社)にとって苦しい年でした. ¶three ***blissful*** *years* of married life 結婚生活の楽しい三年. ¶a ***bumper*** *year* of foreign trade 外国貿易の当り年. ¶in ***bygone*** *years* 以前は. ¶in the ***closing*** *years* of the last century and the opening of the new 前世紀の末葉から今世紀の初頭にかけて ‖ in his ***closing*** *years* 彼の晩年に. ¶the ***coming*** *year* 来年. ¶a ***common*** *year* 平年(うるう年に対し). ¶the ***concluding*** *years* of his life 彼の晩年. ¶the ***critical*** *years* of a woman's life 女一生の危期. ¶a ***crowded*** *year* 波らんの多い年. ¶a ***crowning*** *year* of training 訓練には絶好の年. ¶in this ***crucial*** *year* 今年のような困難な年に. ¶fresh cases admitted during this ***current*** *year* 本年度の新収容者(感化院など). ¶spend one's ***declining*** *years* [of life] in the country その晩年をいなかで送る. ¶the ***dying*** *year* 去り行く年. ¶since ***early*** *years* 幼少のころから ‖ in his ***early*** *years* 彼の若いころは ‖ in the ***early*** *years* of adulthood (manhood) 壮年時代に. ¶in their ***elder*** *years* 彼らの中年時代に. ¶He was reelected president for the ***ensuing*** *year*. 彼は翌年の会長に再選された. ¶the least ***eventful*** *years* of his life 彼の一生中で最も波らんの少なかった時代. ¶once ***every*** *year* 毎年一回. ¶with ***every passing*** *year* 年ごとに. ¶one ***fat*** *year* 成績のあがった年. ¶a ***favorable*** *year* [農作など]当り年. ¶for a ***few*** *years* ahead (＝to come) ここ二三年は. ¶in the ***fifth*** *year* of pregnancy 妊娠(分べん)後五年目に. ¶the ***first*** *year* of life 生れた年 ‖ the ***first*** two *years* of peace 戦後最初の二年間. ¶the ***fiscal*** *year* ended June 30, 1950 [米国の]一九五〇年六月三十日終った会計年度.【類】enter a new ***fiscal*** (＝***financial***) *year*. ¶This year has been a "***fisherman's*** *year*" in the north. 今年は北国の漁師の当り年だった. ¶in a few ***fleeting*** *years* じきに立ってしまう二三年の内に. ¶the ***following*** *year* 翌年. ¶in ***formative*** *years* of life 人生の成長期間において. ¶in ***former*** *years* 以前は. ¶a ***full*** *year* まる一年 ‖ ten ***full*** *years* 丸十年. ¶a ***golden*** *year* for dealers in war supplies 軍需品業者の当り年. ¶a ***good*** *year* for ... ...の豊年. ¶a champagne of a ***good*** *year* and brand 年代も商標も良いシャンパン酒. ¶a ***good many*** *years* ago 幾年も前に. ¶I wish you a ***happy*** and ***prosperous*** New *Year*. 新年に当り幸福と繁栄を祈ります(謹賀新年). ¶*year* ***in*** and *year* ***out*** 一年中.【類】The business man goes about (に取掛る) his business, the leisured man goes about his pleasure, in much the same way *year* ***in*** and *year* ***out***. ¶the *year* ***incorporated*** [会社など]設立の年. ¶be a mere piling up of ***insignificant*** *years* 馬齢を加えるに過ぎない. ¶during the one hundred and thirty-four ***intervening*** *years* その間の百三十四年間. ¶the ***judicial*** *year* 司法年度. ¶all ***last*** *year* 昨年一ぱい ‖ for the ***last*** [one] *year* or two 過去一二年の間に ‖ Things have changed in the ***last*** fifteen *years*. 過去十五年の間に事態が変ってしまった. ¶of (＝in) ***late*** *years* 近年 ‖ in these ***later*** *years* 近年 ‖ in the ***later*** (***earlier***) *years* of the 19th century 十九世紀の末葉ごろ(初期)に. ¶in his ***latter*** *years* 彼の晩年に. ¶a ***lean*** *year* 凶年 ‖ ten ***lean*** *years* 不景気の十年. ¶for ten ***long*** *years* 十年以上にわたって ‖ skill obtained by ***long*** *years* of practice 多年の練習によって得た熟練. ¶the result of ***many*** *years* of careful study and research 多年の綿密な調査研究の結果 ‖ It is the only new unabridged dictionary in ***many*** *years*. 近年出版された大辞典と言えばこれをおいて他にない. ¶in his ***maturer*** *years* もっと大人になってから. ¶The year 1929 is a ***memorable*** *year* in the annals of the German film. 一九二九年はドイツの映画史上記憶すべき年である. ¶her ***natal*** *year* 彼女の出生の年. ¶Houses are decorated at ***New*** *Year* in the branches of pine-trees and bamboos. 正月には家々に松の枝や竹が飾り付けられる.【類】street scenes at the ***New*** *Year*. ¶An extension of the company's operations is contemplated for ***next*** *year*. その会社は来年度に事業拡張を決行しようとしている. ¶forty ***odd*** *years* ago 四十何年前. ¶hear the ***old*** *year* rung out and the new year rung in 旧年を送り新年を迎える鐘の音を聞く. ¶the ***Olympic*** *Year* オリンピック競技のある年. ¶The river is closed to navigation by ice about ***one-half*** the *year*. その川は氷のために約半年は航行が途絶される. ¶***one and one-half*** *years* 一年半. ☞ one and a half year[s], one year and a half ともいう. ¶In the year 1936 there were three kings in the British Empire—almost the ***only*** *year* in British history that has known three kings. 一九三六年には英帝国内に三人の王様が[入れ替り立ち替り]あった, これは英国史においてほとんど他に類例のないことである. ¶in the ***opening*** *years* of the 19th century 十九世紀の初めごろに. ¶in ***passed*** *years*＝in years past 過ぎし数年に. ¶during the ***passing*** (＝current) *year* この一年間に. ¶He has been sick in the ***past*** *year*. 彼はこの一年間病気だ. ¶the *year* just ***past*** つい去年. ¶in ***postwar*** *years* 戦後に. ¶the ***previous*** *year* その前年. ¶in ***prewar*** *years* 戦前に.【類】since ***prewar*** *years*. ¶From 1879 to 1883 inclusive were Edison's most ***productive*** *years*. 一八七九年から一八八三年の終りまでがエジソンが最も多くの発明を公にした年であった. ¶Of ***recent*** *years* there has been a flood of books about China. 近年中国に関する著書がおびただしく出た.【類】exhibitions held of ***recent*** *years* ‖ The method has come more and more into vogue within ***recent*** *years*. その方法は近年ますます行われてきた.【類】Of ***recent*** *years* Harvard has come to great eminence (著名) for its activity in matters of the theatre. / a custom of but ***recent*** *years*. ¶***regnal*** *year* 17 即位第十七年. ¶He occupied the ***remaining*** *years* of his life in authorship. 彼は余生をもっぱら著作に費した.【類】He gave the ***remaining*** twenty-six *years* of his life to Princeton (大学). ¶the ***reproductive*** *years* of woman 女子の妊娠可能期間. ¶The prospects of the crop for the ***running*** (＝***current***) *year* are good. 今年の作柄は良好だ. ¶a ***sad*** *year* 悲惨な年. ¶in ***scant*** ten *years* わずか十年間に. ¶last for ***several*** *years* 数年続く. ¶eight ***short*** *years* before ほんの八年前. ¶enter one's ***seventy-second*** *year* 満七十一歳になる. ¶the ***standard*** *year* 平年. ¶***stormy*** *years* 多難な年. ¶for ***ten consecutive*** (＝***successive***) *years* 引続き十年間. ¶of our ***tender*** *years* 幼い時分の. ¶a ***terrible*** famine *year* 大ききんの年. ¶The cold ***this*** *year* is quite unprecedented. 今年の寒さは全く空前のことだ. ‖ in ***this*** *year* of our Lord 1939 本年すなわち西暦一九三九年に ‖ if he came in ***these*** *years* of grace もし彼が(生き返って)われわれの時代に来て見たら ‖ in ***these*** *years* 近年 ‖ ***these*** five *years* この五年間. ¶in ***those long ago*** *years* of our undergraduate experience at Waseda われわれの随分昔の早稲田の学生時代に. ¶This is the ***tercentenary year*** of its existence. 今年はその創立三百年にあたる. ¶the ***twentieth year*** of life 二十歳. ¶through ***untold years*** 数えきれないほどの年数にわたって. ¶***What year*** is this? 今年は紀元何年ですか. 【類】In ***what year*** were you born? ¶the ***whole year*** round＝during the whole year 一年中 ‖ He is a ***whole year*** older than I am. 彼は丸一つ僕より年上だ. ‖ They have flowers the ***whole year*** in the open air. そこでは一年中戸外に花が咲いている. ‖ We have to wait another ***whole year***. あと一年待たねばならない. ¶snow of ***yester years*** 残雪.

Q² in the ***anniversary year*** of ... ...の記念祭の年に. ¶in the "***boom***" ***year*** of 1929 一九二九年の好景気に ‖ in the ***boom year*** of 1929 一九二九年の好景気の年に. ¶the peak ***building year*** [住宅など]建築の成績が最もあがった年 ‖ the calendar *year* 暦年. 【類】A ***calendar year*** (暦年) is from January 1 to December 31 inclusive. / extending over three ***calendar years***. ¶the 1949 ***cereal year*** 一九四九収穫年度. ¶the ***college year*** 大学の学年. ¶1940—the ***centenary year*** of the Cunard Company 一九四〇年すなわち(英国)キューナード汽船会社の百年祭に当る年. 【類】in the ***centenary year*** of the poet's birth. ¶the ***Coronation year*** 戴冠式のある年. ¶in the previous ***crop year*** (1946–47) 前収穫年度(一九四六—四七)に. ¶in the ***depression years*** of the early thirties 一九三〇年代始めの不況時代に. ¶the ***Diamond Jubilee year*** 六十年記念の年. ¶in the ***election year*** of 1948 一九四八年の選挙に ‖ a Presidential ***election year*** 大統領選挙の年. ¶an ***exhibition year*** 《英》博覧会のある(あった)年. ¶a terrible ***famine year*** 恐ろしいききんの年. ¶the ***freshman year*** 《米》[大学]一年生の学年. ¶in ***future years*** 今後多年にわたって. ¶a ***horse-power year*** 延年馬力. ¶This is the ***jubilee year*** of the college. 今年はその大学の記念祭がある. ¶her first ***laying year*** [鶏など]最初の卵を産む年. ¶the ***leap year*** うるう年. ¶in my ***little-girl years*** 私の少女時代に. ¶her eleven ***movie years*** 彼女の映画生活十一年. ¶***non-war years*** 戦争のなかった数年. ¶in ***peace-time years*** 平和時代に. ¶The year 1956 promised to be a ***peak year*** for foreign trade. 一九五六年度は外国貿易にとって最高の年となる見込みであった. ¶The year 1939 was the ***peak production year*** (最高生産高の年) for the industry. ¶the ***predepression years*** 不況前の時代. ¶***prosperity years*** 景気のよい時代. ¶a "***record year***" [最高]記録の年. ¶a bad ***rice year*** 米不作の年 ‖ the 1950 ***rice year*** (Nov. 1, 1949, to Oct. 31, 1950) 一九五〇年米穀年度. ¶the ***school year*** 学年. ¶the ***sophomore year*** 《米》[大学]第二学年. ¶during the ***war years*** 戦時中 ‖ the former (latter) part of the ***war years*** 戦争の前(後)半. ¶in ***wartime years*** 戦時中に.

P ***after years*** of preparation 数年間準備をしてから ‖ ***after*** all these *years* いまだに. ¶***at*** forty *years* of age 四十歳で ‖ The *year* ***at*** which he returned to his home country is not known, nor the period of his death. 彼が本国へ帰った年も不明だし死んだ年も分からない. ¶an index ***by year*** 年別索引 ‖ be measured ***by years*** 年数で計算する. ¶be wise ***beyond*** one's *years* 年のわりに利口である. ¶***during*** the *years* 1865–1868 一八六五年から一八六八年までに ‖ ***during*** this last *year* ここ一年の内に. ¶***during*** the *year* after next 明後年中. ¶***for*** some two or three *years* past 過去二三年の間 ‖ ***for*** *years* ahead (＝to come) [これからの]数年間 ‖ He has been my master's loyal chauffeur ***for*** 20 *years*. 彼は二十年来私の主人の忠実な自動車運転手をやっている. ‖ best wishes ***for*** the New *Year* 新年の祝詞 ‖ ***for*** many and many *years* to come 末長く ‖ The fishing is over ***for*** the *year*. 釣も今年はもうお仕舞だ. 【類】He has been ***for*** many *years* in the service. ¶children ***from*** two *years* old and under 二歳以下の子. ¶a hen laying 150 eggs ***in*** a *year* 一カ年に百五十個卵を生むめんどり ‖ The magazine is now ***in*** its 30th *year* of publication. その雑誌は初号以来三十年になる. ‖ ***in*** the *year* of the Tiger (Sheep, Ox) とら(など)の年に ‖ ***in*** the *years* that followed それから多年にわたって ‖ America was discovered ***in*** the *year* 1492. アメリカは一四九二年に発見された. ‖ ***in*** this *year* of grace 1932 西暦一九三二年の今年 ‖ ***in*** the *years* that are just ahead of us ここ数年に ‖ ***in*** *years* gone by 過去において ‖ ***in*** the *years* ahead 今後は ‖ ***in*** *years* to come 今後多年にわたって ‖ ***in*** the *years* that followed それに続く数年間に ‖ once ***in*** four *years* 四年に一度 ‖ the most valuable contribution to the subject ***in*** *years* 近年におけるその問題への最も貴重な貢献 ‖ He is paying his first visit to New York ***in*** three *years*. 彼は三年振りでニューヨーク市に来る. ¶***Inside of*** (＝***Within***) a *year*, the company was no more. 一年以内にその会社はつぶれてしまった. ¶after a couple ***of*** *years* およそ二年の後に. ¶***on*** the third *year* 第三年目に. ¶***through*** [***out***] the *year* 一年を通して. ¶French and American interests are reckoned 360 days ***to*** the *year*. 仏米では利息を一年を三百六十日で計算する. ¶***up to*** last *year* 去年まで. ¶She has grown more beautiful ***with*** the *years*. 彼女は年々美しくなる. ¶***within*** the *year* その年の内に＝***within*** four and a half *years* 四年半の内に ‖ ***within*** a *year* and a day 〘法〙満一年以内に.

P² *year* ***after*** year 来る年も来る年も. ¶the *year* ***before*** last 一昨年. ¶the next *year* ***but*** one 再来年 ‖ the last *year* ***but*** two＝three years ago 一昨々年. ¶*Year* ***by*** *year*, century by century English has grown and changed. 年を重ね世紀を重ね英語は発達し変化した. ¶in five *years* ***from*** the death of his father 彼の父の死後五年たってから. ¶the *year* ***in*** books 本年の出版界(書物から見た今年). ¶the tenth *year* ***of*** issue 発行後十年目 ‖ the *year* ***of*** the completion of the Tokyo-Yokohama railway 京浜鉄道が完成された年 ‖ Many *years* ***of*** patient waiting 辛抱強く待った数年 ‖ *years* ***of*** prosperity 繁栄の年 ‖ the *years* ***of*** silence between ... and ... ...と...の間の無音信の数年. 【類】a *year* ***of*** travel in America / a *year* ***of*** woe (＝disaster).

O a *year* and a half 一年半. ¶a *year* and a day. たっぷり一カ年. ¶*year* in and *year* out 来る年も来る年も. ¶Before the *year* was ***out***, the work was well under way. その年の内に仕事は大分進行していた.

(2) 年齢.

V Purple, though beautiful, ***adds years*** to the age. 紫は美しいが年をふけて見せる. ¶She ***attained*** her 101st *year*. 彼女は百一歳になった. ‖ ***attain*** *years* of maturity 成年に達する. ¶He ***bears*** his *years* lightly. 彼は気が若い. ¶He ***carries*** his *years* nobly. 彼はしっかりして年にめげない. ‖ He ***completed*** his 100th *year* on the 15th inst. 彼は本月十五日に満百歳になった. ¶***count*** one's *years* 年を数える. ¶He has not yet ***finished*** his seventeenth *year*. 彼はまだ満十七歳になっていない. ¶***look*** one's *years* 年相応に見える. ¶They are still vigorous and do not ***show*** their *years*. 彼らはいまだに元気で年を取っていない. ¶***take*** ten *years* off one's age 十歳年を若返らせる. ¶***touch*** one's sixtieth *year* 六十歳になる. ¶Though he ***turned*** seventy *years* of age, he was still full of vigor. 七十を越したが彼はまだ大元気だった. ¶He ***wears*** his four score *years* lightly. 彼は八十歳でなおかくしゃくとしている.

Q owing to his ***advancing years*** 老齢のために. ¶despite his ***fifty-odd years*** 五十幾歳になっているにもかかわらず. ¶during their most ***impressionable years*** 彼らの最も感激的な時代に. ¶It is mere piling up of ***insignificant years***. 馬齢を加えるだけのことである. ¶in his ***later years***＝in the later years of his life 彼の晩年において. 【類】There were in 1936 still many people in the neighbourhood of Yasnaya Polyana who remembered the Tolstoy of the ***last years*** (晩年の). ¶a man of ***mature years*** 円熟した人. 【類】a scholar of ***mature years***, who has made his name by important contributions to learning. ¶his ***oncoming years*** 彼の寄る年波. ¶people of ***riper years*** 一層年輩の人々. ¶innocent girls of ***tender years*** 年端も行かない無邪気な少女 ‖ in ***tender years*** うら若い時分に.

P Tennyson was a great poet ***at*** 24 *years* of age. テニスンは二十四歳で大詩人であった. ¶He is wise ***beyond*** his *years*. 彼は年に似合わず利口だ. ¶He is older ***by*** three *years*. 彼は三つだけ年上だ. ¶tall ***for*** his *years* 年にしては背が高い. ¶The list is arranged ***in*** *years*. その表は年齢順になっている. 【類】a man young ***in*** *years*＝a young man / He is old ***in*** *years*, but young in experience (spirit). ¶a boy ***of*** ten *years* 十歳の少年. ¶I'm sure he is ***over*** forty *years* of age. あの人はきっと四十以上だ. ¶***past*** seventy *years* of age 七十歳を過ぎて. ¶He cannot be ***under*** fifty *years* of age. 彼は五十以下ということはない.

year-end, *n*. 年末.

P *at* the *year-end* 年末に. ¶*toward* the *year-end* 年末近くに.

yearn, *v.* あこがれる.

P *yearn after* ... ...にあこがれる. ¶The soul *yearns for* some one to love. 魂は愛人を求める. ¶*yearn for* a sight of ... ...を一目見たいと思う ‖ the peace *for* which the human heart *yearns* 人間の心があこがれる平和. ¶*yearn toward* (=*to*) a person 人にあこがれる.

yearning, *n.* あこがれ.

V *feel* a *yearning* toward ... ...にあこがれを感じる. ¶in his heart *surged* the *yearning* for ... 彼の胸中には...へのあこがれが波打っていた.

Q perfect love as typifying the *inner yearning* of two beings to become one 二人の人間が一人になろうとする心のあこがれを象徴する完全の愛. ¶*strong yearnings* 強いあこがれ. ¶*tormenting yearnings* 悩ましいあこがれ.

P the *yearning for* children and the joy in their possession 子供を熱望する情とそれを持つ喜び.

yell, *n.* 叫び; [応援の]エール.

V They *gave* loud *yells* like the red men of the woods. 彼らは森のインディアンのように大声に叫んだ. ‖ Let's *give* him a big *yell*. あいつを大声で応援してやろう. ¶*utter* a wild *yell* of agony 激しく苦しみの叫びを発する.

Q a *blood-curdling yell* 血も凍るような(すごい)叫び. ¶The coal man indulges in a *demoniacal yell*, which is doubtless his professional rendering of "Coal! Coal!" 「ロンドンの」石炭売りは「石炭」「石炭」という呼声の積りだろうが何ともえたいの知れない叫声を出す. ¶A *savage yell* went up. 物すごい蛮声が響いた. ¶shout with *soul-maddening yell* 聞いていると気が変になりそうな声を出す.

Q² a *college yell* 大学の応援の叫び. ¶a vociferous exchange of *university yells* 大学エールの猛烈な交換. ☞ エール大学のは Bre-ke-ke-kex Co-ax Co-ax.

yell, *v.* 叫ぶ.

M *yell loud* enough to wake Lazarus ラザロでも目をさますような大声で叫ぶ. ¶*yell out* orders 大声を張り上げて命令する.

P *yell at* ... ...にどなりつける. ¶*yell for* help 叫んで助けを求める. ¶*yell like* demons わめき狂う. ¶*yell with* pain 苦しみわめく.

yellow, *n.* 黄色.

Q *golden yellow* 黄金色. ¶Dandelions are of a *vivid yellow*. たんぽぽはあざやかな黄である.

yellow, *a.* 黄色い.

P be *yellow with* age 年月を経て黄色っぽくなっている. ¶be *yellow with* jealousy (envy) しっと(ねたみ)で顔が黄色くなる. ☞ green with envy (jealousy) ともいう. ‖ The fields were *yellow with* wheat. 畑は小麦で黄金色だった.

yelp, *n.* 激しくほえる声.

V The dog *gave* a *yelp* when his tail was stepped on. 犬はしっぽを踏まれてきゃんとないた.

P The dog, *with* a joyous *yelp*, ran to his master. 犬はうれしそうにわんわんほえながら飼主の方へ走っていった.

yelp, *v.* 激しくほえる.

P The dog *yelped out of* the house into the garden. その犬はほえながら家から庭に飛び出した.

yen, *n.* 円[貨幣].

Q the *depreciated yen* 下落した円価 ‖ war with the *depreciated yen* 円価下落に対する対策.

P It cost me *above* (=*over*) 20 *yen*. 私はそれに二十円以上出した. ¶I cannot go *beyond* fifty *yen*. 私は五十円以上は出せない. ¶I cannot sell it *under* 3000 *yen*. 私はそれを三千円以下では手放したくない.

yen, *n.* 熱望.

V *have yen* for drinking (gambling) 一杯(など)やりたい.

yes, *n.* うん, 諾.

V *Say yes*. うんと言え.

P I've come *for yes* or no. 僕は諾否を聞きに来た.

O On the whole, *yes!* 大体はそうだ.

yesterday, *n.* きのう; 過去.

Q *cheerful yesterdays* 楽しかった過去.

P the day *before yesterday* おととい. ¶men *of* today and *yesterday* 現在並びに過去の人 ‖ While science is *of yesterday*, religion is almost as old as the human race. 科学は比較的新しいものであるが宗教はほとんど人類同様古いものである. ¶I have been here *since* (=*from*) *yesterday*. 僕はきのうからここに来ている.

yield, *n.* 利得, 利回り; 産出高.

V *compute* the *yield* on investments 投資の利回りを計算する. ¶*give* varying *yields* 大小種々の利益を生む. ¶This method of culture materially *increases* the *yield* of fruit. その栽培法は著しく果実を増産する. 【類】*increase* the *yield* (収穫) of the soil.

Q about an *average yield* 大体平作. ¶*enormous yield* ばく大な産高. ¶*gross yield* 大収穫. ¶the estimated *total yield* of a fief 大名の領地の概算総収穫高. ¶the *yearly yield* of books 書籍の年間発行量.

Q² the actual *barn yield* of a crop 農作物の実収高(納屋に収めた). ¶the *egg yield* 鶏卵の生産高. 【類】a low (不成績な) *egg yield*. ¶*harvest yield* [農作物]収穫高. ¶As a result of drought, *wheat yields* will be lower than last year. ひでりのため小麦作は去年より下回るだろう. ¶the *1947 yield* of corn 《米》一九四七年のとうもろこしの収穫高.

P² the *yield from* fruit trees 果樹の収穫. ¶the *yield of* a farm 農場の収穫 ‖ a *yield of* 201 eggs per fowl 一羽当り二百一個の産卵. ¶*yield on* investments 投資の利回り.

yield, *v.* 産出する; 従う.

M *yield abundantly* 豊富に産出する. ¶*freely yield* to the sensations of thirst 盛に(水などを)飲む. ¶*gracefully yield* to necessity いさぎよくやる. ¶*Yield* oneself *instinctively* to the deep emotions of religious awe. 宗教の尊厳に対し本能的に深く感動する. ¶*yield meekly* to one's suggestion おとなしくその忠言を容れる. ¶*yield peacefully* おとなしく屈服する. ¶*yield poorly* (=*scantily*) 少ししか収穫がない. ¶*yield unresistingly* ころりとまいる. ¶*yield well* 生産が多い.

M² *yield up* one's life to ... 生命を...にささげる ‖ *yield up* a secret 秘密を漏らす ‖ When a fountain-pen does not *yield up* its contents in a proper flow, we stimulate it by jerks. 万年筆のインキの出が悪い時は振って出す.

P He *yields to* all her wishes. 彼は彼女の希望をことごとくいれる. ‖ *yielding to* his ardent wishes 彼の切なる願いをいれて ‖ *yield to* the desire of drink 飲酒欲に負ける ‖ I *yield to* no man in my admiration for Nikko. 日光の美を賞賛することにおいて僕はだれにも譲らない. ‖ a stubborn hip gout, which he found would *yield to* no remedy どう治療しようが治らないと知れたがんこな座骨神経痛 ‖ a branch of knowledge, which *yields to* none in importance 他のいずれにも譲らず重要な学科. 【類】*yield to* none in one's knowledge of ... ‖ I cannot *yield to* the request (wish) of ... 私は...の申出(など)に応じることはできない. 【類】They believe that China *yields* nothing *to* reason, but everything to force. ‖ even though it may seem a digression, I *yield to* the temptation to ... それは脱線と思われるかも知れないが私はつい...をしたくなる ‖ The dye will not *yield to* soap or soda. その染料は石けんやソーダでは落ちないでしょう. 【類】A writer is warned not to *yield to* the temptation to sprinkle his pages with obsolete expressions. ‖ *yield to* a wave of pity 同情の念に駆られる. 【類】never *yield to* misfortunes. ¶*yield under* protest 不承不承に服する.

yielding, *n.* 譲歩.

P *by* a *yielding* on both sides 双方折れ合って.

yoke, *n.* 束縛; きずな.

V *bear* the *yoke* cheerfully 喜んでその束縛を忍ぶ. ¶*cast off* (=break away from) the *yoke* of ... ...の束縛を脱する. ¶*endure* the *yoke* その束縛を忍ぶ. ¶The Dutch *flung* (=*shook*) *off* the *yoke* of Spanish oppression. オランダは圧制なスペインの支配を振り捨てた. ¶In 1783 the American Colonies *threw off* the *yoke* of England. 一七八三年にアメリカの植民地は英国の支配を脱した.

Q be under a *foreign yoke* 外国の支配下にある ‖ the *heavy yoke* of opinion 世論の圧迫.

P *beneath* the *yoke* その支配を受けて. ¶submit *to* one's *yoke* その支配に屈する. ¶carry two buckets *on* a *yoke*, one at each end 天びん棒のあと先にバケツをぶらさげて運ぶ. ¶come *under* the *yoke* of ... ...の支配を受ける ‖ By small indulgences he fell *under* the *yoke* of irresistible habit. 彼はちょっと気を許したのがくせとなって今更どうにもならなかった(喫煙など). 【類】bring (send) them *under* the *yoke* of tradition. ¶Thine irresolute will must prove a *yoke upon* thy fortune. なんじの優柔不断は必ず

なんじの幸運の障害となりてつきまとうべし.
P² the *yoke of* love 愛情のきずな.

yolk, *n.* [卵の]黄身.
V ***beat*** the *yolk* of an egg with a table spoonful of flour 卵の黄身を大さじ一杯の小麦粉にかきまぜる.

yore, *n.* 昔.
P The building, although greatly dilapidated, still stands as ***of*** *yore*. その建物は大分破損はしているが昔のままである. ‖ Japan in the days ***of*** *yore*. 往時の日本. 【類】 Health is better attended to today than ***of*** *yore*.

you, *pron.* [人称代名詞第二人称].
P The rest are ***for*** *you* to infer. 他は推して知るべしだ. ¶Shame ***on*** *you!* 恥ずかしくないか. ¶Good wishes ***to*** *you* and your family. 皆さんにもよろしく. ‖ Good luck ***to*** *you* all. みなさん御気げんよう. ☞米南部では you all を複数及び単数に用いる, 単数の場合はその group (主に family) を暗示する. How's *y'all?*=How are you [and your people]?

young, *n.* 子.
V Animals ***bring forth*** (=***bear, beget*** *or* ***throw***) their *young*. 動物は子を産む. ¶The kangaroo ***carries*** its *young* in a pouch. カンガルーはその子を腹袋に入れて持ち運ぶ. ¶***desert*** its *young* その子を捨てる. ¶***feed*** its *young* with milk その子に乳を飲ませる. ¶The giraffe seems never to ***have*** more than one *young* at a time. キリンは決して一度に一匹以上は子を産まないようだ. ¶***produce*** *young* 子を産む. ¶***raise*** its *young* その子を育てる.
P The mare is ***with*** *young*. その雌馬ははらんでいる. ¶the *young* ***of*** a sheep 羊の子.

young *a.* 若い.
M An old man will be *young* ***again***. 老人は若返るだろう. ¶Respectability is a word that is ***comparatively*** *young* in the English language. リスペクタビリテイ(品位)という語は比較的新しい英語である. ¶He is ***perennially*** *young* in spirit, though white with age. 彼は頭は年のせいで白髪になっているが気はいつまでも若い. ¶She appears ***quite*** *young*, but in reality she is over thirty. 彼女は見たところとても若いが本当は三十を越えている.
P Men are *young* ***at*** fifty. 男は五十になっても若い. ‖ *young* ***at*** the game その仕事に不なれな. ¶look *young* ***for*** one's age 年の割に若く見える. ¶*young* ***in*** year but old in experience 年は若いが経験の積んだ ‖ Though old in years, he is *young* ***in*** spirit. 年は取っても気は若い. ‖ She looks *young* ***in*** that blue suit. [彼女は]あの青いスーツを着ると若く見える.

youngster, *n.* 青年, 若者.
Q "A ***fine*** *youngster*," said he to the young mother. 「良いお子さんです」と彼はその子のまだ若い母親に言った. ¶those ***postwar*** *youngsters* これら戦後の若者たち.

youth, *n.* (**1**) 青年; [集合的に]若者.
V ***equip*** *youth* for the struggle of life 青年を人生の苦闘にたえるように仕込む. ¶***pilot*** modern *youth* 現代の青年を指導する.
Q her ***adored*** *youth* 彼女のあこがれの若者. ¶an ***ambitious*** *youth* 向上心のある青年. ¶an ***attractive*** *youth*, well schooled, well bred, well groomed 教養が高くて育ちがよく身なりのきちんとした人好きのする青年. ¶***beardless*** *youth* ひげのない青年. ¶a ***beauteous*** *youth* 美少年. ¶a ***brave*** *youth* 勇敢な若者. ¶***callow swaggering*** *youths* 生意気な青年. ¶***carefree*** (=easy-going) *youth* のんきな若者たち. ¶a ***comely*** *youth* 美ぼうの青年. ¶a ***consumptive, neurotic*** *youth* 胸の悪い神経質な若者. ¶***decent*** and ***respectable*** *youths* 上品で卑しからぬ青年. ¶***feminine*** *youth* 若い女たち. ¶***flannel-troursered*** *youths* in nautical peaked caps 山高な水兵帽をかぶったフラノズボンの青年. ¶a ***fresh-faced*** *youth* 紅顔の少年. ¶***gilded*** *youth* 貴公子たち. ¶a ***handsome, rosy-cheeked*** (=***peach-faced***) *youth* 紅顔の美少年. ¶an ***immature*** *youth* 黄口の青年. ¶an ***impressionable*** *youth* 敏感な青年. ¶an ***improvident*** *youth* 思慮のない青年. ¶an ***industrious*** *youth* 勤勉な若者. ¶a ***peach-faced*** *youth* 紅顔の少年. ¶an ***inexperienced*** *youth* 初心な青年. ¶a ***love-lorn***(=***-sick***) *youth* 恋に悩む青年. ¶a knot of ***lusty*** *youths* 一群の元気おう盛な青年たち. ¶our ***modern*** *youths* わが国のこのごろの青年たち. ¶a ***promising*** *youth* 前途有望な青年. ¶Paris has a great attraction for French ***provincial*** *youth* of both sexes. パリはフランスの地方青年男女にとって大きな魅力を持っている. ¶a ***raw*** *youth* 無経験な青年. ¶a ***romantic*** *youth* 空想に走る若者. ¶a ***rowdy*** *youth* 壮士. ¶***scanty-attired*** *youths* [競技練習などで]手足がむき出しの若者たち. ¶a ***smart*** *youth* 抜目のない(利口な)若者. ¶the ***sporting*** *youth* of the world 世界のスポーツ青年. ¶her ***sweet*** *youth* (=lover) 彼女の若いつばめ. ¶a ***talented*** *youth* 才幹のある青年. ¶a ***thoughtless*** *youth* 思慮の浅い青年. ¶an ***unconventional*** *youth* 慣例にとらわれない(自由奔放な)青年. ¶an ***unspoiled*** (=unsophisticated) *youth* 純真な青年. ¶***verdant*** *youth* 未熟な青年たち. ¶a ***witful*** *youth* 機知に富んだ青年.
Q² ***college*** *youth* 大学生たち. ¶***farm*** *youths* 農村青年たち. ¶a ***greenhorn*** *youth* 青二才. ¶***teen-age*** *youths*=teenagers 十代の少年少女. ¶a handful of ***village*** *youths* 一団の村の青年.
P ***As*** *a youth* he studied law at the University of Prusbury, but not practiced his profession. 青年時代彼はプラスベリー大学で法律を学んだがその職業にはつかなかった. ¶Life in a London bank offers great attractions ***to*** *youth*. ロンドンの銀行生活は若い者には非常に魅力がある.
P² a *youth* ***of*** eighteen 十八歳の青年 ‖ a *youth* ***of*** promise in painting circles 画壇のホープ. ¶decent-looking *youths* ***with*** intelligent faces and respectable appearance 理知的な顔と卑しからぬ風さいをしている上品な青年たち ‖ ¶a *youth* ***with*** hoary hair 白髪の青年(老書生).

(**2**) 若さ; 青年期.
V ***challenge*** *youth* in vitality 壮者をしのぐ. ¶***destroy*** *youth* 若さを台なしにする. ¶He has ***kept*** his *youth* extraordinarily well. 彼は実に若い. ¶the secret of ***keeping*** one's *youth* 若さを保つ秘けつ. ¶***renew*** *youth* 若返らせる. ¶the art of ***retaining*** *youth* 年を取らない法. ¶Her sorrow ***sucked*** the *youth* completely out of her heart. 彼女は悲嘆に暮れてすっかり年を取ってしまった. ¶***take*** his *youth* into consideration 彼が若いことを考慮に入れる. ¶***waste*** one's *youth* 青春期を空費する. ¶***wear out*** one's *youth* and strength 青春と元気とを消耗する.
Q She was a beauty in her ***distant*** *youth*. 彼女は昔は美しかった. ¶from ***early*** *youth* onward 若い時代から. 【類】 in ***early*** *youth*. ¶the capital sin of his ***hot*** *youth* 彼が血気盛んな青年時代に犯した重い罪 ‖ He was wild in his ***hot*** *youth*. 血気盛んな頃は乱暴(放とう)だった. ¶in ***my own*** *youth*, far away in the dark backward and abysm of time 過去の暗いどん底生活の私の若い時分に. ¶his ***perennial*** *youth* and vigor 彼のいつまでも衰えない若さと元気. ¶from his ***tender*** *youth* 彼のうら若い時代から. 【類】 in his ***tender*** *youth*. ¶a key to ***perpetual*** *youth* 不老の秘けつ. ¶***undying*** *youth* 不老. ¶***verdant*** *youth* 青春期.
P ***from*** [one's] *youth* onward (=upward) 青年時代からずっと ‖ men and women who have shared each other's joys and sorrows ***from*** *youth* to old age 若いころから年を取るまで苦楽を共にしてきた男女. ¶Good or bad habits, formed ***in*** *youth*, often go with us through the rest of our lives. 良いにせよ悪いにせよわれわれが青年時代に作った習慣はしばしば一生付きまとうものだ. 【類】 For some reason or other (何かの理由で), he was unable to attend school ***in*** *youth*.
P² after *youth* ***of*** dissipation 放とう三まいの青年期を過ぎて ‖ the *youth* ***of*** a nation 一国家の初期の時代.

youthful, *a.* 若々しい.
P The clothes are a bit too loud and *youthful* ***for*** a woman of her age. そのきものは彼女ぐらいの年ばいの女には少しはでで若すぎる.
O a *youthful* figure 若々しい姿. 【類】 *youthful* ambitions (appearance).

Z

zeal, *n.* 熱心, 熱意.

V *appreciate* one's *zeal* その熱心さを認識する. ¶*awaken* one's *zeal* 熱意を呼び起す. ¶*bring zeal* to one's work 仕事に精を出す. ¶his *zeal* was *chilled* (=*damped*) by ... 彼の熱意が...のためにさめた. ¶the noble *zeal displayed* by ... ...が示した尊い熱意. ¶*fire* the *zeal* of ... ...の熱意を高める. ¶You *lack zeal.* 君は熱意が足りない. ¶*manifest zeal* 熱心さを示す. ¶Your *zeal* is *misapplied.* 君の熱意は見当はずれだ. ¶*show* indefatigable *zeal* in advancing its interests その利益の増進に心血を注ぐ.

Q *fiery zeal* 燃ゆる熱意. ¶*indiscreet zeal* 無分別な熱意. ¶*misplaced zeal* せん気筋(見当違い)の熱心. ¶actuated by *religious zeal* 宗教的熱情に鼓舞されて. 【類】with *religious zeal.* ¶with *untiring zeal* うむことを知らない熱心さで.

P inspired *by* a mistaken *zeal* of patriotism for the Fatherland 誤った愛国心に鼓舞されて. ¶work *with zeal* 熱心に働く.

P^{2} *zeal for* science 科学に対する熱心 ‖ the missionary's *zeal for* the soul of the heathen 異教徒の魂を救おうとする宣教師の熱意. ¶in their *zeal without* knowledge 彼らは熱心ではあるが知識を欠いているので.

zealous, *a.* 熱望する.

P *zealous for* liberty (welfare, success) 自由(など)を熱望せる. ¶*zealous in* one's task (work, undertaking) 仕事(など)に熱心な.

zenith, *n.* 頂点.

V *attain* its *zenith* その頂点に達する. ¶*pass* its *zenith* その絶頂点を過ぎる. ¶It *reached* the *zenith* of its fame (=glory) towards the end of the eighteenth century. それは十八世紀の末ごろになってその名声の絶頂に達した. 【類】*reach* the *zenith* of one's power / Shanghai had not yet *reachd* the *zenith* of her prosperity. / She has not yet *reached* the *zenith* of her possibilities (発展性). ¶hats that have *seen* their *zenith* 大分古くなっている帽子.

P His fame was then *at* its *zenith.* 当時彼の名声は絶頂に達していた. 【類】If a girl is twenty-one years old, she is *at* the *zenith* of her matrimonial chances (結婚の機会)./ even *at* the *zenith* of his powers as a novelist. ¶It was *in* the *zenith* of its prosperity (splendor). それは繁栄(など)をきわめていた. 【類】*in* the *zenith* of their powers and celebrity (名声) / *in* the *zenith* (=at the height) of his fame.

zephyr, *n.* 軟風.

V^{2} when the evening *zephyrs murmur* among the trees 夕風が木々の間にそよぐころ.

zero, *n.* 零.

V *enter* a *zero* 零と採点をする. ¶*put* a *zero* on one's paper その答案にゼロをつける. ¶The thermometer *registers zero.* 寒暖計は氷点を示している.

Q reach the lowest possible temperature or *absolute zero* (−273°C) 最低温度すなわち絶対零度(摂氏零下二七三度)に達する.

Q^{2} the *ground zero* [爆弾の空中爆発]直下地点.

P During the recent cold snap of January, 1913, the lowest recorded temperature in San Francisco was 31 degrees *above zero.* 最近一九一三年一月のにわかの寒気襲来の時サンフランシスコにおける最低気温は三十一度だった. ¶with the temperature *at zero* 温度は零度であって ‖ My knowledge on the subject stands *at zero.* その方面の私の知識は皆無である. ¶The mercury stands at 20 [degrees] *below zero.* 寒暖計が零下二十度である. ¶The temperature is down *to zero.* 温度は零度に下っている. ‖ Our hopes were reduced *to zero.* われわれの希望はゼロになった.

zest, *n.* 興味.

V *add zest* to ... ...に興味を添える. ¶*give zest* to appetite 食欲を進める ‖ Study *gives zest* to play. 勉強は遊戯の興味を増進する. ¶*lose zest* in reading 読書に対する興味を失う.

Q The *full zest* of life was his till the end. 彼は死ぬまで人生を十分に楽んでいた. ¶throw oneself into its affairs with the *keenest zest* 最大の興味をもってその事件の渦中に投じる. 【類】devour (読みふける) novels with the *keenest zest.* ¶re-read the Bible with *renewed zest* 新たなる興味をもって聖書を再読する. ¶*youthful zest* 青年の熱情.

P eat *with zest* (=relish) うまいと思って食べる ‖ work *with zest* 興味をもって働く.

P^{2} *zest for* enjoyment (pleasure) 快楽に対する興味. ¶loss of *zest in* life 生きる意欲の喪失.

zigzag, *n.* 山形; Z 字形(ジグザグ).

Q We went up a *long zigzag* before we came to the top of the mountain. われわれは長い Z 字型の道を登って山頂に着いた. ¶a *tedious zigzag* あきあきする Z 字形路.

P walk (sail) *in zigzag* 千鳥足をふむ(ジグザグに進航する).

zigzag, *v.* ジグザグに進む.

M *zigzag slowly* toward ... ...の方向へゆっくりジグザグに進む.

zigzag, *ad.* ジグザグに.

P a road running *zigzag across* a hill 丘に Z 字型についている道.

zinc, *n.* 亜鉛.

Q^{2} *scrap zinc* くず亜鉛. ¶*sheet zinc* 圧延トタン.

Zionism, *n.* シオン主義.

Q^{2} *world Zionism* 世界シオン(民族故国復帰)主義.

zip, *v.* チャックをかける(つける).

M^{2} *zip off*=unzip チャックをはずす. ¶*zip on* (=*up*) チャックをかける(はずす) ‖ *zip up* a bag (jacket) バッグ(ジャケツ)のチャックを閉める.

zip-liner, *n.* 裏がチャックづきのコート.

P a *zip-liner* (=ziplined coat) *for* three seasons 三季節用オーバー(チャックづき裏地の). ☞ zipliner は zip out すれば春・秋着に, zip in すると冬着となる.

zipper, *n.* チャック.

P a bag (vest, slacks) *with* a *zipper* チャックづきのバグ(など).

zone, *n.* 地帯, 界.

Q the merged *American* and *British zones* [西ドイツの]米英併合地帯. ¶an *erogenous zone* 性欲(に関係ある肉体の域)帯. ¶the *floral zone* 植物地帯. ¶a *neutral zone* 中立地帯. ¶the *temperate* (*torrid, frigid*) *zone* 温(熱・寒)帯.

Q^{2} the Fair's *amusement zone* 博覧会の歓楽地帯. ¶a *buffer zone* 緩衝地帯. ¶a *combat zone* 交戦地帯. ¶the *cotton zone* (=belt) in America アメリカの綿花地帯. ¶a *danger zone* 危険地帯. ¶a *delivery zone* 〘郵便〙配達区域. ¶The Nihonbashi district is the capital's *downtown zone.* 日本橋地区は首都の下町(商業)地帯である. ¶the *fire zone* 〘軍〙火線区域. ¶a *fire-prevention zone* 防火地帯. ¶an alpine *flower zone* お花ばたけ. ¶a *fun zone* at an exhibition 博覧会の娯楽地帯. ¶a *holiday zone* 行楽地域. ¶a *loading zone* 積込み区域. ¶a *malaria zone* マラリヤ流行地帯. ¶a "*No parking*" *zone* 駐車禁止地域. ¶a "*no passing*" *zone* 通行止め地域. ¶the American *occupation zone* in Germany ドイツの米占領地帯. 【類】The United States and Great Britain fused their *occupation zones* economically. / The 38 parallel separates the American and Russian *occupation zones* of Korea ¶a *parking zone* [自動車の]駐車地域. ¶a *residence zone* 住宅区域. ¶a *safety zone* 安全地帯. ¶a *school* (*business*) *zone* 文教(商店街)地区. ¶the *Suez Canal zone* スエズ運河地帯. ¶withdraw her troops to the *treaty zone* 軍隊を条約地帯まで撤退させる. ¶a *twilight zone*=a border line 薄明地帯, いずれとも区別の付けにくい点. ¶a *war zone* 交戦地帯. ¶a fact-finding tour of *world hunger zones* 世界ききん地方の実情調査旅行.

P^{2} a *zone of* operations 作戦地区.

zoo, *n.* 《俗》動物園; [Z-] ロンドンの動物園.

P There can be little doubt that feeding-time *at* the *Zoo* is the hour that appeals quite as irresistibly to the inmates as to the onlooker. その動物園の給食時間はたしかに見物人に取ってもまた動物に取ってもきわめて興味ある時間である.

zoom, *v.* ぶーんと音を立てる.

M^{2} *zoom down* (*up*) [飛行機が]ぶーんと急降下(上昇)する.

A LIST OF COMPOUND WORDS, SOLID AND HYPHENED

A

able-bodied *a.* 頑健な: an *able-bodied* young man.
A-bomb *n.* [<atom bomb, atomic bomb] 原子爆弾.
about-face *n.*, *v.* 回れ右(をする); 百八十度の転回(をする).
aboveboard *a.*, *ad.* 公明正大の(に): do business *aboveboard*.
above-mentioned *a.* 前述の: as *above-mentioned*.
absent-minded *a.* うっかりした.
ad-lib *n.*, *v.*, *a.* [<ad libitum] 台本にないせりふ(を言う).
aforementioned *a.* 前記の.
aforesaid *a.* 前述の.
aforethought *n.*, *a.* 予めの考え(予め考えた).
aforetime *ad.* さきに, 以前に.
afterbirth *n.* 後産(あとざん).
afterdeck *n.* 後甲板.
after-dinner *a.* 正(晩)さん後の.
aftereffect *n.* 余波; 副作用.
afterglow *n.* 夕焼け.
afterimage *n.* 『心理』残像.
afterlife *n.* あの世; 晩年.
aftermath *n.* [事件の]余波.
aftershock *n.* 余震.
aftertaste *n.* あと味.
afterthought *n.* 後知恵.
aftertime *n.* 今後, 未来.
afterworld *n.* あの世.
aid[e]-de-camp *n.* 副官; 武官.
air-borne *a.* 空輸の: an *air-borne* troop. 「つまった.
air-bound *a.* [パイプなど]空気の
air-conditioned *a.* 空気調節装置のある. *cf.* air conditioning.
air-cool *v.* 冷房装置をする. *cf.* air cooler.
aircraft *n.* 航空機.
aircraft[s]man *n.* 航空兵.
air-dry *v.*, *a.* 空気乾燥する(した).
airfield *n.* 飛行場.
air-line *a.* [<air line] 一直線の.
airmail *n.*, *v.* 航空郵便(で出す).
airman *n.* 飛行士.
airplane *n.* 飛行機.
airport *n.* 空港.
airproof *a.* 耐気性の.
air-raid *a.* [<air raid] 空襲の: an *air-raid* shelter (warning).
airship *n.* 飛行船.
airsick *a.* 飛行機に酔った.
airtight *a.* 気密の: an *airtight* container.
airway *n.* 航空路; 放送区域.
alehouse *n.* ビヤホール.
all-American *a.* 全米(代表)の.
all-around *a.* 万能の: an *all-around* athlete.
all-out *a.* 総力をあげた: an *all-out* effort.
all-round *a.* =all-around.
all-time *a.* 未曾有の, 最高記録の: an *all-time* high 最高額.
alongshore *ad.* 岸に沿うて.
alongside *ad.* [船が]横付けに.
apple-polisher *n.* 《米俗》ごますり 「apple pie.
applesauce *n.* アップルソース. *cf.*
areaway *n.* [建物間の]通路, 中庭.
armorbearer *n.* 騎士の従者.
armor-clad *a.* 装甲した: an *armor-clad* ship. 「装甲した.
armor-plated *a.* [<armor plate]
around-the-clock *a.* 二十四時間連続の: an *around-the-clock* air- 「raid.
arrowhead *n.* やじり.
ash-colored *a.* 灰白色の.
ash-pale *a.* 青白い.
assembly-lined *a.* 流れ作業の: an *assembly-lined* plant. *cf.* the assembly line. 「議員.
assemblyman *n.* [州議会の]下院
atom -bomb *v.* 原爆攻撃する. **—atom-bombing.** 「て.
awe-struck(-stricken) *a.* 畏怖し

B

baby-sit *v.* るす番子守をする. *cf.* a baby sitter. **—baby-sitting.**
backbone *n.* 背骨; 中堅: the *backbone* of Japan.
backdoor *a.* 裏口の.
backdown *n.* 後退, 降服.
backdrop *n.* 背景の幕.
backfield *n.* 『フットボール』後衛.
backfire *n.* 迎え火.
background *n.* 背景.
backhand *n.* 『庭球』バックハンド. **—backhander.** 「の部屋の.
back-room *a.* [<back room] 奥
backside *n.* 後部.
backslide *v.* 悪に逆戻りする. **—backslider.**
backstage *a.*, *ad.* 舞台裏の(に): *backstage* activities (maneuvering).
backstair *a.* 裏手階段の; 秘密の: a *backstair* intrigue.
backstitch *n.*, *v.* 返し針縫い(をする). 「ローク.
backstroke *n.* 『庭球』バックスト
backtrack *v.* 《米》引返す; 手を引 「く.
backwash *n.* 引潮.
backwater *n.* 逆流した水; 沈滞.
backwoods *n. pl.* 《米》辺境地帯. **—backwoodsman.**
bakehouse *n.* パン屋.
barbershop *n.* 理髪店. *cf.* 《英》a barber's. 「刺線.
barbwire *n.* [<barbed wire] 有
bareback *a.*, *ad.* 裸馬の(に): ride *bareback*.
barefaced *a.* あつかましい: a *barefaced* lie.
barefoot[ed] *a.*, *ad.* はだしの(に): walk *barefoot*.
barehanded *a.*, *ad.* 素手の(で).
bareheaded *a.*, *ad.* 無帽の(で).
barelegged *a.* くつ下なしの, 脚がむき出しの.
barkeep[er] *n.* バーテン.
barleycorn *n.* 大麦のつぶ.
barmaid *n.* バーの女.
barman *n.* =bartender.
barnyard *n.* 《米》家畜小屋の庭.
bartender *n.* バーテン.
baseball *n.* 野球. *cf.* a base hit, base running.
baseborn *a.* 生れの卑しい.
basebred *a.* 育ちの悪い.
basketball *n.* 『競技』バスケット. **—basketballer.**
bat-blind *a.* 目のよく見えない.
bat-eyed *a.* 目のよく見えない.
bathhouse *n.* 浴場.
bathrobe *n.* 《米》ねまき.
bathroom *n.* 浴室.
bathtub *n.* 浴槽.
battle-ax[e] *n.* 戦闘用おの.
battledore *a.* 羽子板.
battleplane *n.* 戦闘機.
battleship *n.* 戦艦.
beachcomber *n.* はとばごろ; うちよせる大波.
beachhead *n.* 『軍』海浜頭.
bearskin *n.* 熊の皮.
bedbug *n.* なんきん虫.
bedchamber *n.* 寝室.
bedclothes *n. pl.* 寝具類.
bedcover *n.* ベッドカバー.
bedgown *n.* 寝室着.
bedridden *a.* 寝たきりの.
bedrock *n.* 『鉱』床岩; [物事の]真相: get down to *bedrock*.
bedroom *n.* 寝室.
bedsick *a.* 病床の. 「*bedside*.
bedside *n.* まくらべ: stand at her
bedsore *n.* [病人の]とこずれ.
bedspread *n.* 《米》寝台かけ.
bedtime *n.* 就寝時.
beehive *n.* はちの巣.
beefsteak *n.* ビフテキ.
beekeeping *n.* 養蜂.
beeline *n.* 《米》直線.
beerhouse *n.* ビヤホール. *cf.* alehouse.
beeswax *n.*, *v.* みつろう(をぬる).

bellboy *n.* 《米》ホテルのボーイ.
belles-lettres *n.* 純文学.
bellflower *n.* 〘植〙ほたるぶくろ.
bellhop *n.* =bellboy.
bellyache *n.* 腹痛: complain of one's *bellyache*.
big-hearted *a.* 寛大な.
big-time *a.* [<big time] 一流の: a *big-time* operator.
bigwig *n.* 《口語》大物.
billboard *n.* 《米》掲示板.
billet-doux *n.* ラブレター.
bindweed *n.* 野生のひるがお(類).
birdman *n.* 飛行家. *cf.* birdwoman. 「view.
bird's-eye *a.* 鳥瞰の: a *bird's-eye*
birthday *n.* 誕生日.
birthplace *n.* 生れ故郷.
birthright *n.* 生得権(貴族などの).
blackball *v.* 反対投票する. **—blackballer.**
blackberry *n.* 黒いちご.
blackbird *n.* [米国産] くろどり.
blackboard *n.* 黒板.
blackcoat *n.* 黒服; 《英》サラリーマン. *cf.* whitecollar.
black-eyed *a.* [<black eye] 打たれて目のふちにあざのできた.
blackface *n.* 《米》黒人に扮した芸
black-hearted *a.* 腹黒い. ⌊人.
blackjack *n.* こん棒; ジョッキ.
black-list *v.* ブラックリストにのせる. **—black-listed.**
blackmail *n.*, *v.* 恐かつ(する).
blackout *n.* [<black out] 灯火管
blacksmith *n.* かじ屋. ⌊制; 停電.
bladesmith *n.* 刀かじ.
blameworthy *a.* 責めてよい.
blear-eyed *a.* [<blear eyes] 目のくもった, かすみ目の. 「る.
blink-eyed *a.* 目をぱちくりさせ
blindfold *n.*, *v.* 目かくし(をする).
blindman's holiday たそがれ時.
blockbuster *n.* 《口語》大型爆弾.
blockhead *n.* のろま, 低能.
bloodcurdling *a.* ぞっとさせる: a *bloodcurdling* murder case.
bloodhorse *n.* 《米》サラブレッド(種の馬).
bloodhound *n.* 《英》警察犬.
blood-red *a.* 血のように赤い; 血染めの.
bloodshed *n.* 流血(の惨事).
bloodshot *a.* 充血した, 血走った: *bloodshot* eyes.
bloodstained *a.* 血まみれの: a *bloodstained* flag (shirt, coat).
bloodsucker *n.* 吸血鬼; いそうろ
bloodthirsty *a.* 血に飢えた. ⌊う.
bloody-eyed *a.* 目の血走った.
bloody-minded *a.* 殺伐な.
blowgun *n.* 吹矢筒.
blowhole *n.* [鯨の]噴水孔.
blowout *n.* [タイヤの]パンク.
blowpipe *n.* 火吹き竹.
blowtorch *n.* 《米》[鉛管工の]衝風灯. 「破産.
blowup *n.* [<blow up] 爆発; 《米》
Bluebeard *n.* 青ひげ男 (六度も妻を殺したという男). 「き鳥).
bluebird *n.* 《米》ブルーバード (鳴
blue-black *a.* 濃紺色の.
blue-blooded *a.* 貴族出の.
bluecoat *n.* 紺色制服.
blue-eyed *a.* 青目の.
bluejacket *n.* 水兵.
bluepencil *v.* 〘新聞〙編集する.
blueprint *n.* 青写真; 原案: the *blueprint* for the new policy.
blue-sky law 〘法〙青空法.
bluestocking *n.* 文学かぶれの女.
boardwalk *n.* 《米》[海岸の]遊歩
boathouse *n.* ボート小屋. ⌊場.
boatload *n.* ボートに一杯(の荷): a *boatload* of....
boatman *n.* 船頭, 船子.
bobbysocks *n.* 少女のソックス **—bobbysoxer.**
bobtail *n.*, *a.* ボッブ刈(した).
body-building *n.* ボディビル.
bodyguard *n.* 護衛.
boilerman *n.* ボイラー係り.
bold-faced *a.* [活字]肉太の. **—boldface.**
bombproof *a.* 防弾の.
bombsight *n.* 爆撃照準器.
bondholder *n.* 公債所有者.
bondmaid *n.* 女の奴隷.
bond[s]man *n.* 男の奴隷.
bond[s]woman *n.* =bondmaid.
bonehead *n.* のろま.
bonfire *n.* かがり火.
boogie-woogie *n.* ブギウギ.
bookbinder *n.* 製本屋(人). **—bookbindery.**
bookcase *n.* 本箱. 「keeper.
bookkeeping *n.* 簿記. **—book-**
bookmaker *n.* 編さん者.
bookmark[er] *n.* 本のしおり.
bookmobile *n.* 《米》移動図書館.
bookrack *n.* 本たて. 「selling.
bookseller *n.* 本屋(人). **—book-**
bookstack *n.* [図書館の]書架.
bookstall *n.* 書籍売店.
bookstand *n.* 《米》書籍売店.
bookstore, bookshop *n.* 本屋.
bookworm *n.* [本の]しみ; 読書狂.
bootblack *n.* くつみがき(人).
bootlegging *n.* 《米》酒などの密造, 密売. **—bootlegger.**
bootlick *n.* 《米》おべっか.
borderland *n.* 国境地方.
borderline *a.* 不明確な, どっちつかずの: a *borderline* case.
bottleneck *n.* 隘路: the *bottleneck* of manufacturing industry.
bottlebrush *n.* びんを洗うブラシ.
bowknot *n.* ちょう結び.
bowlegged *a.* がに股の.
bowstring *n.* 弓のつる.
boxcar *n.* 〘鉄道〙有蓋車.
box-office *a.* [<box office] [切符売場から]人気のある, 興行成績上の: a *box-office* film (star).
brainsick *a.* 気の変な.
brakeman *n.* 〘鉄道〙制動手. ☞ 《英》brakesman.
brand-new *a.* 《米》真新しい: a *brand-new* hat.
brassware *n.* 真ちゅう製器具.
breadboard *n.* パン切り台.
breadstuff *n.* パンの原料; パン.
breadwinner *n.* [一家の]かせぎ手.
breakdown *n.* [<break down] 故障; 崩壊.
breakneck *a.* 危険極まる: at *breakneck* speed.
breakthrough *n.* [<break through] 〘軍〙敵陣突破.
breakup *n.* [<break up] 崩壊; 解
breakwater, *n.* 防波堤. ⌊散.
breastbone *n.* 胸骨.
breastpin *n.* 《米》ネクタイピン; ブローチ.
breastplate *n.* 胸当て.
breastwork *n.* 〘軍〙胸壁. 「な.
breath-taking *a.* はっとするよう
brickbat *n.* れんがのかけら; 《口語》憎まれ口.
bricklayer *n.* れんが工.
brickwork *n.* れんが工事.
brickyard *n.* れんが工場.
bridegroom *n.* 花むこ, 新夫.
bridesmaid *n.* 花嫁付添いの処女.
bridgehead *n.* 〘軍〙橋頭堡(ᵖ).
bridgework *n.* 架橋工事.
broadcast *n.*, *v.* 放送(する). **—broadcasting.**
broadcloth *n.* ブロード地.
broadgauge[d] *a.* [<broad gauge] 〘鉄道〙広軌の: a *broad-gauge* track.
broad-minded *a.* 寛大な.
broadside *n.* 〘海〙船の横正面.
broken-down *a.* めちゃめちゃにこわれた.
broken-hearted *a.* 悲嘆にくれた.
broomstick *n.* ほうきの柄.
brother-in-law *n.* 義理の兄(弟).
browbeat *v.* 威かくする.
brown-eyed *a.* とび色をした目の.
buckhorn *n.* しかのつの.
buckskin *n.* しか皮.
bucktooth *n.* 出っ歯.
buckwheat *n.* そば.
built-in *a.* つくりつけの: a *built-in* locker.
bulldog *n.* ブルドッグ.
bulldozer *n.* ブルドーザー.
bulletproof *a.* 防弾の: a *bullet-proof* waistcoat.
bullfighter *n.* 闘牛士.
bullfrog *n.* 食用がえる.
bullheaded *a.* がんこな.
bullnecked *a.* 首のずんぐりした.
bull's-eye *n.* 的の中心点. 「屋.
bunkhouse *n.* 《米》労働者用の小
burglarproof *a.* 泥棒よけの.
businesslike *a.* 事務的な.
businessman *n.* 実業家. *cf.* businesswoman.
busman *n.* バス乗務員.
busybody *n.* おせっかい屋.
buttercup *n.* 〘植〙うまのあしがた.
butterfat *n.* 乳脂.
butterfly *n.* ちょう; 気まぐれもの.
bye-bye *interj.* 〘幼児語〙はいちゃい. 「*election* campaign.
by[e]-election *n.* 補欠選挙: a *by-*
bygone *a.* 過去の: *bygone* days.
bylaw *n.* [会社などの]内規.
by-line *n.* 《米》〘新聞〙[寄稿論文

の]署名欄. **—by-liner.**
by-name *n.* ペンネーム; あだ名.
by-pass *n.* 間道, 抜道: *by-pass* tactics (桂馬とび作戦).
bypath *n.* [本道に添うた]側道.
by-player *n.* わき役.
bystander *n.* 見物, 第三者.
by-street *n.* 裏通り.

C

cabinetmaker *n.* 家具師; 組閣する人(首班).
cabinetwork *n.* 指物細工.
cableway *n.* 索道: an aerial *cableway*. 「手.
cabman *n.* 御者; タクシーの運転
cabstand *n.* タクシーの駐車場.
cakewalk *n.* 《米》ケーキウォーク(ダンス).
callboy *n.* 呼び出し係. 「員.
cameraman *n.* [新聞社の]写真部
camerawork *n.* 『映』写真技術.
campfire *n.* キャンプ・ファイア.
campground *n.* キャンプ地.
campstool *n.* 折畳み式のいす.
candlelight *n.* ろうそくの明り.
candle-shaped *a.* [西洋ろうそくのように] 先き細の.
candlestick *n.* しょく台.
cardboard *n.* ボール紙.
cardplaying *n.* トランプ遊び. **—cardplayer.**
cardsharp[er] *n.* トランプさぎ師.
carefree *a.* 苦労のない.
care-laden *a.* 苦労性の.
caretaker *n.* 世話人, 管理人.
careworn *a.* 苦労やつれした.
carfare *n.* 車賃.
carpetbag *n.* 旅行かばん.
carpetbagger *n.* 渡り者.
carryall *n.* 《米》一頭立の軽装馬車; 大型自動車.
carry-over *n.* 繰越し部分.
car-sick *a.* 自動車に酔った.
castaway *a., n.* 脱ぎ捨てられた(もの); 社会から見捨てられた(人).
castoff *a., n.* 捨てられた(物, 人).
castor-oil *a.* [<castor oil] ひまし油の.
catchall *n.* がらくた入れ, 合財袋: a *catchall* bag / the *catchall* department (総務部).
catchpenny *a.* 安ぴかの. 「標語.
catchword *n.* 見出し語; [政治の]
cat's-paw *n.* 手さき, かいらい.
cattleman *n.* 牛飼い; 牧場主.
causeway *n.* 土手道.
cave-in *n.* [土地・鉱山の]陥没.
centerpiece *n.* [レースの]テーブル・センター.
chairman *n.* 議長, 座長. *cf.* chairwoman.
chambermaid *n.* 寝室係の女中.
chatterbox *n.* おしゃべり.
checkbook *n.* 小切手帳.
checkerboard *n.* チェッカー盤.
checkoff *n.* 《米》『労』組合費の天引き.
checkup *n.* 《米》照合, 引合せ.
cheekbone *n.* ほお骨.
chessboard *n.* チェッス盤.
chessman *n.* [チェッスの]こま.
chestnut *n.* くりの木(実).
chicken-hearted *a.* 気の小さい.
childbearing *n.* 出産, 分べん.
childbirth *n.* 出産.
childlike *a.* 子供のような, 無邪気
Chinaman *n.* 中国人. 「な.
Chinatown *n.* ナンキン街.
chinaware *n.* せと物.
chit-chat *n.* おしゃべり.
chophouse *n.* 食堂; ちゃぶ屋.
chopsticks *n. pl.* はし. 「節.
Christmastide *n.* クリスマス季
churchman *n.* 聖職者; 教会員. *cf.* churchwoman.
churchyard *n.* 教会の境内; 墓地.
citybuster *n.* 《口語》原(水)爆.
clansman *n.* 一門の人.
clapboard *n.* 羽目板.
claptrap *n., a.* むだ話(の); 人気と
classmate *n.* 級友. 「り(の).
classroom *n.* 教室.
clay-built *a.* 粘土作りの.
clean-cut *a.* 輪郭のはっきりした.
clean-fingered (-handed) *n.* 潔白な. 「そった.
clean-shaved *a.* ひげをきれいに
cleanup *n.* 掃除; 『口語』もうけ.
clear-cut *a.* 輪郭のはっきりした.
clear-headed *a.* 頭のさえた.
clear-sighted *a.* よく目のきく; 明敏な.
cloakroom *n.* 携帯品一時預り所.
clockwise, clockways *a., ad.* 右回りの(に).
clockwork *n.* ぜんまい仕かけ; 規則正しいこと: like *clockwork*.
close-fisted *a.* けちな.
close-mouthed (-lipped) *a.* 口の堅い, 無口な. 「ズアップ.
close-up *n.* 『映画』大写し, クロー
clothesbag *n.* 洗たく物袋.
clotheshorse *n.* 衣類かけ.
clothespeg *n.* 洗たくばさみ.
clothespin *n.* 洗たくばさみ.
cloudburst *n.* 《米》突然の豪雨: an evening *cloudburst*.
cloud-capped *a.* 雲をいただいた: a *cloud-capped* mountain.
cloven-footed (-hoofed) *a.* ひずめのわれた; 悪魔のような.
clubhouse *n.* クラブ会館.
coal-black *a.* まっ黒な.
coarse-grained *a.* きめのあらい, がさつな.
coastland *n.* 海岸地帯.
coastline *n.* 海岸線.
coastways, coastwise *ad.* 海岸に沿って.
cobblestone *n.* 玉石, 丸石.
cockcrow[ing] *n.* 鶏鳴, あかつき.
cockeyed *a.* 斜視の; ゆがんだ.
cockfight *n.* 闘鶏. 「馬.
cockhorse *n.* [おもちゃの]揺れ木
cockpit *n.* [飛行機などの]操縦士室.
cockscomb *n.* [鳥の]とさか.
cocktail *n.* カクテル.
coco[a]nut *n.* ここやしの実.
cod-liver *a.* 肝油の: *cod-liver* oil.
coffee-brown *a.* チョコレート色
coffeepot *n.* コーヒー沸かし. 「の.
cogwheel *n.* はめば歯車.
cold-blooded *a.* 冷血の, 冷酷な: a *cold-blooded* landowner.
cold-hearted *a.* 冷淡な.
coldproof *a.* 耐寒の.
cold-shoulder *v.* [<cold shoulder] [人を]冷遇する.
color-blind *a.* [<color blind] 色盲の. 「る.
color-wash *v.* [...に] 泥絵具を塗
comeback *n.* 返り咲き(カムバック): have a fine *comeback*.
comedown *n.* 落ぶれ; [地位・名声の]失墜.
come-on *n.* 《米俗》お人よし.
commonwealth *n.* 国家, 国民.
congressman *n.* 《米》下院議員. *cf.* congresswoman.
cookbook *n.* 料理の本.
copperplate *n.* 銅板.
coppersmith *n.* 銅細工人.
copybook *n.* 習字帳.
copyholder *n.* [印刷] 校正助手.
copyright *n.* 版権.
corkscrew *n.* せん抜き.
corncob *n.* 《米》とうもろこしのパイプ.
cornerstone *n.* 土台石.
cornerwise, cornerways, *ad.* 斜めに, すじ違いに.
cornfield *n.* 《米》とうもろこし畑; 《英》麦畑.
cornflour *n.* とうもろこし粉.
cornhusk *n.* とうもろこしの皮.
cornstalk *n.* とうもろこしの茎.
cornstarch *n.* とうもろこし粉.
cottonseed *n.* 綿の種子.
counterclockwise *a., ad.* 時計の針と反対の(に), 左回りに.
counterespionage *n.* スパイ対抗組織.
counterevidence *n.* 反証.
counterintelligence *n.* 《米》対敵ちょう報活動. 「返しの.
counteroffensive *a.* 反抗の, 捲
counterplot *n.* 対抗策.
counterreformation *n.* 反対改革.
countersign *n.* 『軍』合言葉.
counterstroke *n.* 反撃.
counterword *n.* 転用語.
count-out *n.* 『拳闘』打倒宣告.
country-dance *n.* 地方踊り. ☞ countrydance ともつづる.
countryfolk *n.* いなかの人々.
countryman *n.* いなかの人. *cf.* countrywoman.
countryseat *n.* 別邸.
countryside *n.* いなか(の住民).
courthouse *n.* 裁判所; 《米》郡役所. *cf.* courtroom.
court-martial *n., v.* 軍法会議(に
courtroom *n.* 法廷. 「付する).
courtyard *n.* 中庭.
cousin-german *n.* いとこ.
cowboy *n.* 《米》牛飼い, カウボイ. *cf.* cowgirl.
cowherd *n.* 牛飼い.
cowhide *n.* 皮のむち.
cowpox *n.* 牛痘.

coxcomb *n.* きざなだて男.
crackbrained *a.* 気のふれた.
crackdown *n.* [ギャングなどの]弾圧.
crackerjack *n.*《米口》すばらしい人(もの), ぴかー.
crackjaw *a.*《口語》発音しにくい. *cf.* jaw-breaking.
crack-up *n.* 大破損, めちゃめちゃ.
craftsman *n.* 工員, 職人.
cream-colored *a.* クリーム色の.
crossbar *n.* 横木, かんぬき.
crossbeam *n.*『建』大ばり.
crossbill *n.* いすか.
crossbred *n., a.* 雑種(の).
crossbreed *v.* 異種交配する.
cross-country *a.*《米》田野横断の: a *cross-country* drive. 「た).
crosscut *n., a.* 横引き(の), 横断(し
cross-examine *v.* 反対尋問をする. **—cross-examination.**
cross-eyed a. 斜視の. 「る.
cross-fertilize *v.* 異花受精させ
cross-grained *a.* 木目の不規則な; 心のねじけた.
cross-legged *a.* 脚をくんで.
crosspatch《口語》気むずかし屋.
cross-purpose *n.* 矛盾した目的.
cross-question *n., v.* 反対尋問(する).
crossroads *n. pl.* 十字路: stand at the *crossroads.* 「する).
cross-stitch *n., v.* ちどりがけ(に
cross-town *a.*《米》市内横断の: a *cross-town* bus.
crosswise, crossways *ad.* ぶっ違いに. 「パズル.
crossword puzzle クロスワード・
crowbar *n.* かなてこ.
crow's-foot *n.* 目じりのしわ.
cupbearer *n.* [宴席での]しゃくと
cupboard *n.* 食器だな. 」り.
cupcake *n.* カップケーキ.
curbstone *n.* [歩道の]ふち石.
curbstone broker『株』場外取引
cureall *n.* 万能薬. 」人.
custom-built *a.* 注文製の.
custom-made *a.*《米》あつらえの: a *custom-made* suit.
cut-and-dry *a.* 陳腐な, 新味のない: a *cut-and-dry* speech.
cutaway *n.* モーニングコート.
cutlet *n.* カツレツ.
cutoff *n.* 近道; しゃ断.
cutout *n.* [雑誌などの]切り抜き.
cutthroat *n., a.* 人殺し(の).
cuttlefish *n.* いか. 「ざける人.
cutup *n.*《米俗》みえを張る人, ふ
cutwater *n.* [船首の]水切り.
cutworm *n.* 根切り虫.

D

daddy-long-legs *n.*《米》あしながぐも; ががんぼ.
dairyman *n.* 牛乳屋; 酪農場主. *cf.* dairymaid.
daredevil *a., n.* 向うみずの(人).
darkroom *n.* 暗室.
datemark *n.* 日付印.
daybook *n.* 日記帳.
daybreak *n.* 夜明け: at *daybreak.*
daydream *n.* 白日夢. **—daydreamer.**
daylight *n.* 日光, 昼. 「間.
daylight-saving time《米》夏時
daytime *n.* 昼間: in the *daytime.*
deadhead *n.*《米口》無賃乗客, 無料入場者.
deadline *n.* 死線; 締切時間.
deadlock *n.* 行きずまり.
dead-pan *a.* [<dead pan]《米》無表情な.
deadwood *n.* 枯木; 冗員.
deaf-mute *n.* ろうあ者.
deathbed *n.* 臨終: on one's *deathbed.*
deathblow *n.* 致命的な打撃: It was a *deathblow* to the business.
deathlike *a.* 死のような: *deathlike* silence.
deathmask *n.* デスマスク.
deathtrap *n.* [火災などに]危険な
deathwatch *n.* 通夜. 」建物.
deep-freeze *n.,v.* 冷蔵(する).
deep-seated (-rooted) *a.* 根深い: *deep-seated* prejudice (enmity). 「*set* eyes.
deep-set *a.* 深くくぼんだ: *deep-*
deep-voiced *a.* 太い声の.
deerskin *n.* しか皮.
dirt-cheap *a.* 二束三文の.
dockyard *n.* 造船所.
dogcart *n.* 犬馬車; 一種の馬車.
dog-cheap *a.* ばか安い.
dog-ear *n.* 折れたページのすみ.
dogfight *n.*《口語》激しい空中戦.
doghouse *n.* 犬小屋.
do-gooder *n.* [空想的な]社会改良
dog's-ear *n.* =dog-ear. 」家.
dog-tired *a.* 疲れ切った.
dog-tooth *n.* 犬歯.
dogtrot *n.* [馬術の]軽いだく.
dogwood *n.* [北米産の]花みずき.
do-nothing *a.* 怠惰な: a *do-nothing* fellow.
doorbell *n.* ドアのベル.
doorcase *n.* ドアわく.
doorframe *n.* =doorcase.
doorkeeper *n.* 門衛, ドアマン.
doorknob *n.* ドアの握り.
doorman *n.* ドアマン.
doornail *n.* びょうくぎ.
doorplate *n.* [金属製の]標札.
doorpost *n.* 門柱.
doorsill *n.* しきい.
doorstep *n.* 入口の上り段.
doorway *n.* 戸口, 出入口.
dooryard *n.*《米》入口の前庭.
double-barreled *a.* 二連銃の.
double-breasted *a.* ダブルの: a *double-breasted* coat.
double-chinned *a.* 二重あごの: a *double-chinned* matron.
double-cross *v.* 裏切る.
double-dealing *a.* 裏表のある.
double-decker *n.* 二階付きバス; 二重座席の旅客機.
double-edged *a.* 両刃の.
double-faced *a.* 二重人格の.
double-header *n.*『野球』ダブルヘッダー.
double-park *v.*《米》自動車を他人の車と列べて駐車する.
double-quick *a., ad.*《軍》かけ足の(で). 「quick.
double-time *a., ad.* =double-
double-tongued *a.* 二枚舌の.
doughboy *n.*《米口》歩兵.
doughnut *n.* ドーナッツ.
downcast *a.* うつ向きの, しおれた. **—n.** 破滅, 滅亡.
down-Easter *n.*《米》東部の人. *cf.* He lives down East.
downfall *n.* 転落; [雨・雪など]大降り. **—downfallen.**
downgrade *a., ad.* 下り坂の(で). *v.* [階級など]降等させる.
downhearted *a.* がっかりした.
downhill *a.* 下り坂の.
downpour *n.* どしゃぶり.
downright *a., ad.* 徹底的の(に), 全くの: a *downright* lie.
downstairs *ad.* 階下へ(に).
downstream *a., ad.* 川しもの(に).
downtown *a., ad.* 下町の(に): go *downtown* shopping / in *downtown* Tokyo.
downtrodden *a.* ふみにじられた.
draftsman *n.* 製図工.
dragnet *n.* 引き網.
dragonfly *n.* とんぼ.
drainpipe *n.*『機』ドレンパイプ.
dramshop *n.*《英》酒場.
draughtsman *n.* =draftsman.
drawback *n.* ひけ目, 不利.
drawbridge *n.* はね橋.
drawknife *n.* 曲り柄のナイフ.
drawshave *n.* =drawknife.
dreadnaught, dreadnought *n.* ド級戦艦. 「むち打ち.
dressing-down *n.*《口語》大目玉;
dressmaker *n.* 洋裁師. **—dressmaking.**
driftwood *n.* 流木. 「練]教官.
drillmaster *n.* 調練師;『軍』[教
drive-in *n.*《米》ドライブ・イン: a *drive-in* theater.
driveway *n.* ドライブウェー; [邸宅への]私道. 「プキック(する).
drop-kick *n.,v.*『ラグビー』ドロッ
drugstore *n.*《米》薬局(喫茶店などを兼ねるもの).
drumbeat *n.* 太鼓の音.
drumfire *n.* 猛砲火.
drumstick *n.* 太鼓のばち.
dry-as-dust *a.* 無味乾燥な.
dry-clean *v.* ドライクリーニングをする. *cf.* dry cleaning.
dry-cure *v.* 干(ひ)物にする.
dry-dock *v.* [<dry dock] ドックに入れる. 「りをする.
dry-nurse *v.* [<dry nurse] 子守
drysalter *n.*《英》乾物屋(人).
dugout *n.*『野球』ダグアウト;『軍』待避ごう.
dumbbell *n.* あれい.
dumbwaiter *n.*《米》[食器, 料理などの]運搬車.
dumpcart *n.* ごみ運搬車.
dunghill *n.* こやしの山.
dustman *n.*《英》ごみ運搬人夫.
dustpan, dustbin *n.* ごみとり.

Dutchman *n.* オランダ人;《米口》ドイツ人. *cf.* Dutchwoman.
articles.
duty-free *a.* 免税の: *duty-free*
dyed-in-the-wool *a.* トップ染めの; きっすいの: a *dyed-in-the-wool* Communist＝a Communist dyed in the wool.
dyestuff *n.* 染料.

E

eagle-eyed *a.* 目の鋭い.
earache *n.* 耳の痛み.
ear-deafening *a.* 耳をろうする
eardrop *n.* 耳飾り. ⌊ばかりの.
eardrum *n.* 中耳.
earflap *n.* [防寒用]耳おおい.
earlap *n.* 耳たぶ. 「(する).
earmark *n., v.*〖経〗イヤマーク
earmuffs *n. pl.*《米》耳おおい.
earphone *n.* [頭にかける]受話器, イヤホーン.
earpick *n.* 耳かき.
earpiece *n.* 受話器; 耳おおい.
earplug *n.* 耳のせん.
earshot *n.* [呼べば]聞えるところ: out of (within) *earshot* of....
earthborn *a.* 地上に生れた: *earthborn* creatures.
earthnut *n.* ピーナッツ, 落花生.
earthenware *n.* 土器, 陶器.
earthly-minded *a.* 俗世間的な.
earthquake *n.* 地震.
earthwork *n.* 土工; 土塁.
earthworm *n.* みみず.
earwax *n.* 耳あか.
earwig *n.* はさみ虫.
Eastertide *n.* 復活祭季節.
easygoing *a.* のんきな.
eavesdrop *v.* 立聞きする. **—eavesdropper.** 「向けて.
edgeways, edgewise *ad.* 刃を
eggplant *n.* なす.
egg-shaped *a.* 卵形の.
eggshell *n.* 卵のから.
elbowroom *n.*《米》十分の余地, 十分の運動範囲.
empty-handed *a.* から手で, 徒手の. 「な.
empty-headed *a.* 頭のからっぽ
enamelware *n.* ほうろう引き器.
endways, endwise *ad.* 端を前に向けて; 立てて. 「driver).
engineman *n.* 機関士 (engine
Englishman *n.* 英国人. *cf.* Englishwoman.
even-handed *a.* 公平な, 正しい.
even-minded *a.* 落着いた.
even-tempered *a.* 心の平静を失わない.
eventide *n.*〖詩〗夕まぐれ. 「る.
ever-changing *a.* 絶えず変化す
evergreen *a.* 常緑の. **—*n.*** 常緑
everlasting *a.* 永久の. ⌊樹.
evermore *ad.* 常に, 永久に.
everybody *pron.* だれでも.
everyday *a.* 毎日の. 「one).
everyone *pron.* だれでも (＝every
everything *pron.* 何でも.
everyway *ad.* どうみても, 全く.
everywhere *ad.* 何処でも.
evildoer *n.* 悪人.
evil-affected *a.* 運の悪い. 「けた.
evil-minded *a.* 腹黒い, 心のねじ
evil-starred *a.* 星回り(運)の悪い.
eyeball *n.* 眼球.
eyebrow *n.* まゆ.
eyeglasses *n. pl.* 鼻目がね.
eyelash *n.* まつげ.
eyeful *n.*《米俗》美しい女.
eyelid *n.* まぶた.
eye-opening *a.* [<eye opener] 目を見ひらくような(珍事など).
eyepiece *n.* 接眼レンズ.
eyeshot *n.* 視野, 眼界: beyond (within) *eyeshot* of....
eyesight *n.* 視力.
eyesore *n.* 目ざわり.
eyestrain *n.* 目のつかれ.
eyetooth *n.* 糸切り歯.
eyewash *n.* 洗眼, 目ぐすり.
eyewater *n.* 目ぐすり.
eyewink *n.* またたき, 一目.
eyewitness *n.* 目撃者, 証人.

F

fact-finding *a.* 実情調査の: a *fact-finding* committee.
fade-in *n.*〖映画〗溶明.
fade-out *n.*〖映画〗溶暗.
faint-hearted *a.* おく病な, 気の弱い. 「の.
faint-voiced *a.* 消え入るような声
fair-haired *a.* 金髪の (blond).
fair-minded *a.* 公平な.
fair-skinned *a.* 色白の. 「寧な.
fair-spoken *a.* 口先のうまい; 丁
fair-weather *a.* 好天の時だけの (まさかの時の役に立たない).
fairyland *n.* おとぎの国.
fallout *n.* 落下物: atomic (radioactive) *fallout* (原子灰).
false-hearted *a.* 不信の.
fancy-free *a.* 恋を知らない.
fancywork *n.* 手芸.
fan-shaped *a.* 扇形の.
farewell *n.* 告別: a *farewell*
far-famed *a.* 知名の. ⌊party.
far-fetched *a.* 持って回った, こじ
far-flung *a.* 広範囲の. ⌊つけの.
farmhouse *n.* 農場付属の住宅; 農
farmyard *n.* 農家の庭. ⌊家.
far-off *a.* 遠く離れた: a *far-off* country.
far-reaching *a.* 広範囲にわたる.
far-seeing *a.* 先見の明のある.
far-sighted *a* ＝far-seeing.
far-western *a.*《米》極西部の.
fashionmonger *n.* 流行を追う人, おしゃれ.
fat-brained *a.* うすのろの.
fathead *n.* のろま.
father-in-law *n.* 義父.
fatherland *n.* 祖国.
faultfinder *n.* 口やかましい人. *cf.* find fault with....
faultfinding *a.* あらさがしの, 口やかましい. 「雇用制度.
feather-bedding *n.*《米》水増し
featherbrain *n.* のろま. **—feather-brained.**
featheredge *n.*〖木工〗薄刃べり. **—featheredged.**
feather-headed *a.* ＝featherbrained.
featherweight *n.*〖拳闘〗フェザー級(のボクサー).
feeble-minded *a.* 低能の.
feedbag *n.* [馬の]かいば袋.
feed-water *a.* [<feed water] 給水の.
fence-rider *n.* 日よりみ主義の人. **—fence-riding.**
ferryboat *n.* 渡し舟, 連絡船.
ferryman *n.* 渡し守, 渡船業者.
fiberboard *n.*〖建築〗せんい板.
Fiberglas *n.*〖商標〗せんいガラス. *cf.* fiber glass.
fiddle-de-dee *int.* ばかな, へえだ.
fiddle-faddle *n.* ばかげたこと.
fiddlestick *n.* バイオリンの弓. *cf.* Fiddlesticks! (ばかばかしい).
fieldpiece *n.* 野砲.
fieldwork *n.* 土塁.
fifty-fifty *a., ad.* 五分五分の(に).
figurehead *n.* かいらい.
filmgoer *n.* 映画ファン. *cf.* a theatergoer. 「せん細な.
fine-drawn *a.* 細く引延ばされた;
fingernail *n.* 指のつめ.
fingerprint *n.* 指紋.
finger-shaped *a.* 指形の.
firearms *n. pl.* 火器(銃・砲など).
fireball *n.* 火の玉.
firebox *n.*〖機〗火室. 「る人.
firebrand *n.* たいまつ; たきつけ
firebreak *n.*《米》防火帯(線).
firebrick *n.* 耐火れんが.
firebug *n.*《米口》放火狂.
firecracker *n.* かんしゃく玉.
fire-eater *n.*《俗》けんか早い人.
firefly *n.* ほたる.
fireguard *n.* 炉の囲い; 防火地帯.
firehouse *n.* 消防署.
fireman *n.* 消防手; 火夫.
fireplace *n.* 炉.
fireplug *n.* 消火せん.
fireproof *a.* 耐火性の. 「chat.
fireside *n., a.* 炉辺(の): a *fireside*
firetrap *n.* 燃えやすい建物; 火災の際逃げ口のない建物.
firewater *n.*《米》火酒.
fireweed *n.* 焼けあとに生える雑
firewood *n.* たきぎ. ⌊草.
fireworks *n.* 花火; のろし.
firm-rooted *a.* 根の生えた. 「の.
first-born *a.* 最初に生れた, 長子
first-class *a., ad.* 第一級の(で); すばらしい(く).
firstcomer *n.* 先着者.
first-hand *a., ad.* 直接の(に): *first-hand* information.
first-rate *a., ad.* 第一級の(で); すばらしい(く).
first-rater *n.* 第一級の人物.
firstrunner *n.*〖映画〗第一封切館. *cf.* firstrun theater.
fishbone *n.* 魚の骨.
fisherman *n.* 漁夫.
fishhook *n.* 釣ばり.
fishmonger *n.*《英》魚屋; 魚売り.

fishwife *n.* 魚売りの女.
flagpole, flagstaff *n.* 旗ざお.
flagship *n.* 旗艦.
flagstone *n.* 敷石.
flap-doodle *n.* 《俗》でたらめ.
flap-eared *a.* たれ耳の.
flare-up *n.* [<flare up] ぱっとあがる火炎; 激怒.
flashlight *n.* 閃光; 《米》懐中電灯.
flatboat *n.* 平底船.
flat-bottomed *a.* 平底の.
flatcar *n.* 《米》〖鉄道〗無蓋車.
flatfish *n.* 〖魚〗ひらめ. 「ed.
flatfoot *n.* 偏平足. **—flatfoot-**
flat-nosed *a.* ししっ鼻の.
flat-roofed *a.* 平屋根の.
flattop *n.* 《米》空母.
flaxen-haired *a.* 亜麻色の髪の.
flaxseed *n.* 麻種 (linseed)
flea-bitten *a.* のみに食われた.
flesh-and-blood *a.* 骨肉の, 血のつながった.
flesh-colored はだ色の: *flesh-colored* hose.
fleshpot *n.* 肉なべ.
flinthead *n.* 矢じり.
flip-flap *n.* ぱたぱた鳴る音.
floodlight *n.* 投光照明 (フラッド
floodgate *n.* 水門. 　　　└ライト).
floodwater *n.* 洪水.
floorcloth *n.* ぞうきん; 床の敷物.
floorwalker *n.* 《米》売場監督.
flophouse *n.* 《米》[労働者の]簡易
flowerpot *n.* 植木ばち. 　└宿泊所.
flyblown *a.* [あおばえなど]卵を産みつけた.
fly-by-night *a., n.* 頼りにならない(人), 無責任な(人).
flycatcher *n.* はえとり.
fly-fish *v.* 蚊ばりで釣りをする. **—fly-fishing.**
flying-off *n.* 〖空〗離陸.
flyleaf *n.* [本の]見返し(白紙の).
flypaper *n.* はえ取り紙.
flyspeck *n., v.* [はえの]しみ(をつける). **—fly-specked.**
flytrap *n.* はえとり器. 「クサー).
flyweight *n.* 〖拳闘〗フライ級(のボ
fogbound *a.* 濃霧に閉込められた.
foghorn *n.* 霧笛.
folklore *n.* 民俗学.
folksong *n.* 民謡, 俗曲. ☞ folk song ともつづる.
folkways *n.* [社会の]習性.
foodstuff *n.* 食料.
foolhardy *a.* 向こうみずの.
foolproof *a.* 《米口》[ばかにも出来るほど]簡単な.
foolscap *n.* フルールスカップ判の
football *n.* 蹴球. 　　└洋紙.
footboard *n.* 踏み板.
footboy *n.* 小間使いの少年.
footbridge *n.* 歩行者専用の橋.
footfall *n.* 足音.
footgear *n.* はきもの(くつ, くつ下など). 「中の小山.
foothill *n.* 山のふもとの小山, 山脈
foothold *n.* 足がかり, 足場.
footlights *n. pl.* 脚光, フットライト: appear before the *footlights*.
footman *n.* 従ぼく.
footmark *n.* 足跡.
footnote *n.* 脚注: an English text furnished with appropriate
footpace *n.* 歩幅. 　└*footnotes*.
footpad *n.* 追いはぎ.
footpath *n.* 小道.
footprint *n.* 足跡.
footrest *n.* 足台.
footsore *n.* くつずれ, 緒(ᵒ)ずれ.
footstep *n.* 足音; 足どり; ふみ段.
footstool *n.* 足台.
footwear *n.* はきもの (footgear).
footwork *n.* [スポーツ・ダンスなどの]足さばき.
footworn *a.* 歩きつかれた, 踏みへらされた: a *footworn* traveler (path).
foreign-born *a.* 外国生れの.
forest-belted *a.* [<forest belt] 森林地帯の.
forest-born *a.* 森林生れの.
forever *ad.* 永久に. ☞ 英語つづりは for ever.
forthcoming *a.* 来るべき.
forthright *a., ad.* 率直な(に).
forthwith *ad.* たちどころに.
fortnight *n.* 二週間.
fortnightly *a., ad.* 隔週の(に). **—** *n.* 隔週刊行物.
fortuneteller *n.* 占い者.
forty-niner *n.* 《米》1849 年当時のゴールドラッシュに加わった人.
foul-minded *a.* 精神のいやしい.
foul-mouthed *a.* 口ぎたない, みだらな言葉を使う.
fountainhead *n.* 源泉; 本源. ☞《英》つづりは fountain-head.
fountain-pen *n.* 万年筆. ☞《米》つづりは fountain pen. 「屋.
four-flusher *n.* 《米俗》はったり
four-footed *a.* 四つ足の.
Four-H club [米国の] 4H クラブ (head, hand, heart, health).
four-in-hand *n.* [普通の]ネクタイ; 四頭立ての馬車.
fourpenny *n.* 四ペンス銀貨.
fourposter *n.* 四柱式寝台.
fourscore *n., a.* 八十(の).
foursquare *a.* 四辺形の; 率直な.
foxhole *n.* 〖軍〗たこつぼ.
foxhound *n.* 猟犬.
fox-trot *v.* [<fox trot)〖ダンス〗フォックス・トロットを踊る. *cf.* dance a fox trot.
frame-up *n.* 《米》陰謀, たくらみ.
framework *n.* わく; 組織, 機構: the *framework* of society.
free-and-easy *n.* 喫煙自由の音楽会 (smoking concert).
freeboard *n.* 〖海〗乾舷.
freebooter *n.* 海賊 (buccaneer).
freeborn *v.* 自由の身に生れた, 自由民の.
freedman *n.* 奴隷から解放された人. *cf.* freedwoman.
free-for-all *a.* 乱闘の: a *free-for-all* fight.
freehand *a.* 自在画の: a *freehand* drawing.
freehanded *a.* 大まかな, 出し惜しみしない.
free-lance *v.* [<free lance] 自由業に従事する.
freeman *n.* 自由人. *cf.* free-woman. 「密結社).
freemason *n.* フリーメーソン(秘
free-soil *a.* 《米》[奴隷制を許さない]自由地区の. **—free-soiler.**
free-spoken *a.* あけすけな.
freethinker *n.* 自由思想家. *cf.* free thought. 「free will.
freewill *a.* 自由意志の. *cf.* one's
Frenchman *n.* フランス人. *cf.* *Frenchwoman.* 「鮮明な.
fresh-colored *a.* 色の生々した,
freshman *n.* 《米》[大学の]一年生.
fresh-water *a.* 淡水の: *fresh-water* fish.
friedcake *n.* あげたケーキ(ドーナッツなど).
frontiersman *n.* 《米》辺境開拓者.
front-page *a.* 第一面向きの, 重要な: *front-page* news トップニュース.
frostbite *n., v.* しもやけ(にする); 霜害(を与える).
frostbitten *a.* 霜害をうけた, しもやけの: *frostbitten* fingers (toes).
frostwork *n.* 霜の花.
frosty-haired *a.* ごましお頭の.
fruitbearer *n.* 実のなる木.
full-back *n.* 〖蹴球〗フルバック.
full-blooded *a.* 純血の.
full-bodied *a.* [ぶどう酒など]こくのある.
full-faced *a.* まともに向って;〖活字〗肉太の.
full-fashioned *a.* [靴下] フルファションの. 「分な.
full-fledged *a.* 一人前の, 資格十
full-grown *a.* 十分成長した.
full-hearted *a.* 一心を打ちこんだ.
full-length *n., a.* 全身大(の), 全身像(の).
full-mouthed *a.* 大声の.
full-rigged *a.* 全装備の.
full-scale *a.* 全面的の.
full-time *a.* 全時間の, 専任の: a *full-time* worker.
fund-raising *a.* 募金の.
furthermore *ad.* なおその上に.
furthermost *a.* 最も遠い.

G

gadabout *n.* 《口語》遊び歩く人. *cf.* gad about.
gadfly *n.* [馬などにつく]あぶ.
gainsay *v.* 反対する, 否認する.
gallstone *n.* 胆石.
galvanometer *n.* 〖電〗検流計.
gamebag *n.* 獲物袋.
gamecock *n.* 闘鶏. *cf.* game bird. 猟鳥. 「bler).
gamester *n.* ばくち打ち (gam-
gangboard *n.* ＝gangplank.
gangplank *n.* [船の]歩み板.
gangsman *n.* 《米》ギャング (gangster).
gangway *n.* 通路, 歩み板.
garbageman *n.* 《米》ごみ屋.
gasbag *n.* 気嚢(ᵒ); 《俗》ほら吹き.

gaslight *n.* ガス灯.
gatehouse *n.* 門番小屋.
gateway *n.* 門口, 出入口.
gearshift *n.* 変速てこ(レーバー).
gearwheel *n.* 歯車.
general-purpose *a.* 一般向きの.
genocidal *a.* 大量殺害の: *genocidal* weapons.
gentlefolk[s] *n.* 良家の人々.
gentleman *n.* 紳士.
gentle-mannered *a.* ふるまいの上品な, しとやかな. 「女.
gentlewoman *n.* 上流の婦人, 淑
germicide *n.* 殺菌剤. **—germicidal.** 「逃亡
getaway *n.* [＜get away]《口語》
get-together *n.*《米》会合.
ghost-haunted *a.* 幽霊の出る.
ghost-write *v.*《米》代作をする.
giddy-brained *a.* 軽卒な.
gilt-edged *a.* [本など]金ぶちの; 最上の.
gimlet-eyed *a.* 鋭い目の.
gingerbread *n.* しょうが入りのケーキ. 「交渉.
give-and-take *n.* 互譲; 友好的な
giveaway *n.*《米口》[ラジオ·テレビの]賞品: a *giveaway* show (program).
glassman *n.* ガラス屋.
glass-eyed *a.* 義眼の.
glasshouse *n.* 温室. ☞ 英語つづりは glass-house.
glassware *n.* ガラス製品.
globetrotter *n.* 世界観光旅行家.
G-man *n.*《米口》連邦検察庁員.
go-ahead *n., a.* [＜go ahead] 積極(的な), 進歩(的な).
goalkeeper *n.*『スポーツ』ゴールキーパー. 「ったりの.
go-as-you-please *a.* 行き当りば
goatherd *n.* やぎ飼い.
goatskin *n.* やぎ皮.
gobbledygook *n.*《米》やたらに専門語のとび出す表現(官庁語など).
go-between *n.* 仲人, 媒介人.
go-by *n.*《口語》見て見ぬふりをして通りすぎること: give a person
gocart *n.* あんよ車. └a *go-by*.
godchild *n.* 名づけ子. *cf.* goddanghter, godson. -mother.
god-forsaken *a.* 神に見捨てられた.
godgiven, *a.* 神より与えられた.
godparent *n.* 名づけ親. *cf.* godfather, godmother.
godsend *n.* 天からのさずかり.
Godspeed *n.* [別れの際などの]祝福.
go-getter *n.*《口語》活動家, やり
goggle-eyed *a.* 目のぎょろぎょろした.
gold-brick *n., v.*《米口》ぺてん(にかける). *cf.* gold-bricker ぺてん
gold-filld *a.* 金張りの. └師.
goldfish *n.* 金魚.
gold-rimmed *a.* 金ぶちの: *gold-rimmed* spectacles.
good-by, good-bye *n.* さよなら. ☞ 口語では goodby, goodbye ともつづる.
good-for-nothing *a., n.* 役に立たない(人). 「りのある.
good-hearted *a.* 親切な, 思いや
good-humored *a.* 愉快な, 上気げんの.
good-looking *a.* きりょうのよい.
good-natured *a.* 性質のよい, 人のよい. 「柄のよい.
good-tempered *a.* やさしい, 人
goodwife *n.* [一家の]主婦.
goodwill, good-will *n.* 好意; [店の]のれん. ☞ good will ともつづる.
goody-goody *a., n.*《口語》善人
go-off *n.* 出発. └ぶる(人).
gooseberry *n.* グスベリー.
goose-fleshed(-skinned) *a.* 鳥はだの. 「がん首.
gooseneck *n.* [がちょうの首から]
gownsman *n.* ガウンをまとう人(法官, 僧侶, 大学教授など).
granddad[dy] *n.*『幼児語』おじいちゃん. *cf.* grandma.
grandchild *n.* 孫. *cf.* grandson, granddaughter.
grandnephew *n.* おい(めい)の子. *cf.* grandniece.
grandparent *n.* 祖父(母). *cf.* grandfather, grandmother.
grandstand *n.* 特別観覧席: a *grandstand* play.
granduncle *n.* 大おじ. *cf.* grandaunt. 「金.
grant-in-aid *n.* [政府からの]補助
grapefruit *n.* グレープフルーツ.
grapevine *n.* ぶどうづる.
grass-blade *n.* 草の葉.
grass-carpeted *a.* 芝生の.
grass-green *a.* もえぎ色の.
grasshopper *n.* ばった, きりぎりすの類.
grassland *n.* 草原, 牧場.
graveclothes *n.* きょうかたびら.
gravestone *n.* 墓石.
graveyard *n.* 墓地.
graybeard *n.* 老翁. *cf.* gray-bearded. 「の.
gray-haired(-headed) *a.* 白髪
great-hearted *a.* 腹の大きい.
great-uncle *n.* 大おじ. *cf.* great-aunt. 「称.
greenback *n.*《米》米国紙幣の異
green-belt *a.* 緑地帯の: a *green-belt* town.
green-blind *a.* 緑色盲の. *cf.* green blindness.
green-eyed *a.* 緑色の目の.
greengrocer *n.*《英》やお屋(人).
greenhorn *n.*《口語》新米, かけ出し.
greenhouse *n.* 温室 (hothouse).
greenroom *n.*『劇』楽屋.
greensand *n.* 緑砂.
greenwood *n.* 緑の森.
greyhound, grayhound *n.* 「犬]グレーハウンド. 「種.
griddlecake *n.* ホットケーキの一
gridiron *n.*《米》蹴球場.
grillroom *n.* 料理店.
gripsack *n.*《米》手さげかばん.
grogshop *n.*《英》居酒屋.
groomsman *n.* 新郎の付添人.
groundhog *n.* [米国産]もぐら. ☞ ground hog ともつづる.
groundnut *n.* なんきん豆.
groundsill *n.* 土台(材木).
groundwork *n.* 土台, 基礎(工作).
grown-up *a.* 成人した, おとなの. ☞ 名詞は通例 grownup.
guardhouse *n.* 衛兵(番人)詰所.
guardsman *n.* 番人;《米》州民兵.
guesswork *n.* あてごと; 推量.
guidebook *n.* 旅行案内.
guided-missile *n.* 誘導弾.
guidepost *n.* 道標.
gunboat *n.* 砲艦. 「つ;《俗》刑事.
gumshoes *n. pl.*《米》ゴム(底)ぐ
guncotton 綿火薬.
gunfire *n.* 銃(砲)火.
gunman《米》ピストル強盗.
gunpowder *n.* 火薬.
gunrunning *n.* 銃器密輸入. **—gunrunner.**
gunshot *n.* 射撃; 射程.
gunsmith *n.* 銃(砲)工.
gunstock *n.* 銃床.

H

hackman *n* 貸馬車屋の御者.
hacksaw *n.* かねのこ.
hail-fellow[-well-met] *a* 極めて
hailstone *n.* あられ. └親切な.
hailstorm *n.* ひょうの大降り.
hairbreadth, hair's-breadth *n., a.* 極めてわずか(の), きわどい: a *hairbreadth* escape.
hairbrush *n.* ヘアブラシ.
haircut *n.* 散髪: I want a *haircut*.
hair-do *n.* 髪のかた.
hairdresser *n.* 理髪師.
hairdressing *n.* 理髪.
hairline *n.* 毛すじ; 細線.
hairpin *n.* ヘアピン.
hair-raising *a.* 身の毛もよだつ.
hairsplitting *a.* [区別など] こまかすぎる, 小事にこだわる.
hairspring *n.* [時計]ひげぜんまい.
hairy-chested *a.* 胸毛のこい. *cf.* hairy-armed.
half-and-half *a., ad.* 半々の(に); どっちつかずの(に).
halfback *n.*『フットボール』中衛.
half-baked *a.* なま焼けの; 不完全な.
half-boiled *a.* なま煮えの, 半熟の.
half-bred *a.* 混血の.
half-breed *n., a.* 混血児(の).
half-blood *n.* 腹(たね)ちがいの兄弟, 混血児. **—half-blooded.**
half-caste *n.* 混血児(欧州人とアジア人との).
half-hearted *a.* 気乗りうすの.
half-hour *n.* 半時間.
half-length *n., a.* 半身像(の).
half-mast *n., a.* 半旗(の).
halfpenny *n.* 半ペニ銅貨.
half-sole *v.* [くつを]半ばりにする.
half-track, halftrack *n.* [後半だけ]無限軌道式の軍用自動車.
halfway *a., ad.* 中途の(で).

half-witted *a.* 低能の.
hallway *n.* 《米》玄関先, 廊下.
hammerhead *n.* しゅもくざめ. *cf.* hammer head (ハンマーの頭).
handbag *n.* ハンドバッグ, 手さげ.
handbaggage *n.* 《米》手荷物.
handball *n.* 手まり.
handbell *n.* 振り鈴.
handbill *n.* ちらし, ビラ.
handbook *n.* 手引き, 旅行案内.
handbreadth, hand's-breadth *n.* 手のはば.
handcart *n.* 手押し車.
handcuffs *n.*, *v.* 手錠(をかける).
handicraft *n.* 手工, 手芸.
handicuff *n.* なぐり合い.
hand-in-hand *ad.* 手に手をとって: walk *hand-in-hand* with...
handiwork *n.* 工作; 手工品.
hand-knit[ted] *a.* 手編みの: a *hand-knit* sweater.
handmade *a.* 手製の.
handmaid *n.* 女中, 小間使い.
hand-me-down *n.* 《米口》既製品. 「物.
handout *n.* 《米俗》[食物など]施し
hand-picked *a.* 手でつんだ.
handrail *n.* 手すり.
handsaw *n.* 手のこ(ぎり).
handset *n.* [電話の]送受話器.
hand-sewn *a.* 手縫いの.
handshake *n.* 握手. 「んぼ返り.
handspring *n.* [手をつけてやる]と
hand-to-hand *n.*, *a.* 接戦(の): a *hand-to-hand* fight.
hand-to-mouth *a.* その日ぐらし
handwork *n.* 手細工. 手工. 「の.
handwriting *n.* 手蹟, 筆写物. — **handwritten.**
hangdog *n.* げすな男.
hanger-on *n.* 《口語》いそうろう.
hangman *n.* 絞首刑執行人.
hangnail *n.* ささくれ. 「ろ.
hangout *n.* 《俗》[悪漢どもの] ねじ
hangover *n.* 《米口》残りもの; 《俗》二日酔. 「たりの.
happy-go-lucky *a.* 行き当りばっ
hard-baked *a.* 堅く焼いた.
hard-bitter *a.* 手ごわい, がんこな, しつような.
hard-boiled *a.* 堅くゆでた; 無情な, がっちりした.
hard-dried *a.* [魚など]乾物にした. 「た.
hard-earned *a.* 骨折ってもうけ
hard-faced, *a.* こわい顔の, こわおもての: a *fard-faced* landlady. 「*fisted* man.
hard-fisted *a.* けちな: a *hard-*
hard-grained *a.* [材木など]目のつんだ. 「こな.
hard-headed *a.* 頭のかたい, がん
hard-hearted *a.* 無情な, 薄情な.
hardpan *n.* [地層の]硬盤; 《米》しっかりした土台.
hard-pressed *a.* 窮地に落入った.
hard-shell[ed] *a.* からの堅い.
hardware *n.* 金物.
hardwood *n.* 堅木.
hardwood[ed] *a.* 堅木の.
hard-worked *a.* 働き疲れた: a *hard-worked* laborer.
hard-working *a.* 勤勉な. 「な.
harebrained *a.* 低能な; 向うみず
harvestman *n.* 刈入れする農夫.
has-been *n.* 《米口》盛りをすぎた人(もの).
hatband *n.* 帽子のリボン.
hatchway *n.* [甲板の]ハッチ.
hatrack *n.* 帽子かけ.
have-not *n.*, *a.* 無資力の(人, 国): *have-not* countries＝have-nots.
hawk-eyed *a.* 目の鋭い; すきのな
hawknose *n.* かぎ鼻. 「い.
hayfork *n.* 干し草用くまで.
hayloft, haymow *n.* 干し草置場.
haymaker *n.* 乾し草を作る人, 干草機.
hayseed *n.* 《米俗》いなかもの.
haystack *n.* 干し草の山. 「(の).
haywire *n.*,*a.* 《米俗》てんやわんや
H-bomb *n.* [<hydrogen bomb] 水爆.
headache *n.* 頭痛; 悩み. 「た.
headdress *n.* かむりもの; 髪のか
headfirst *ad.* まっさかさまに.
headforemost *ad.*＝headfirst.
headgear *n.* かぶりもの.
head-hunter *n.* 首狩り土人. — **head-hunting.**
headland *n.* みさき.
headlight *n.* 《米》[自動車の]ヘッドライト. 「ing).
headline *n.* [新聞の]見出し (head-
headlong *a.*, *ad.* まっさかさまの(に), あわてた(て): fall *headlong* into the water.
headmaster *n.* 小学校の校長. *cf.* headmistress.
head-on *a.* はち合せの: a *head-on* collision.
headphone *n.* 頭にかける受話器.
headpiece *n.* かぶりもの; 頭にかぶる受話器.
headquarters *n.* 本部, 司令部.
headrest *n.* [いすの]頭かけ.
headsman *n.* 首切り役人.
headspring *n.* 水源.
headstone *n.* かなめ石; 墓石.
headstream *n.* 源流.
headstrong *a.* 強情な: a passionate, *headstrong* boy.
headwaiter *n.* 給仕頭.
headwaters, *n. pl.* 水源, 源流.
headway *n.* 前進, 進歩: make *headway* in electronics.
headwork *n.* 頭の働き; 思想.
hearsay *n.* うわさ, ゴシップ.
heartache *n.* 心痛, なやみ.
heartbeat *n.* 心臓の鼓動.
heartbreaking *a.* 悲痛な, 断腸の.
heartbroken *a.* 悲嘆にくれた.
heartburn *n.* 胸やけ; ねたみ.
heart-burning *a.* むしゃくしゃした. 「たみ.
heartburnings *n. pl.* うらみ. ね
heartfelt *a.* 感銘した: *heartfelt* sympathy.
heart-free *a.* 恋をしていない.
hearthrug *n.* 炉ばたの敷物.
hearthstone *n.* 炉石; 炉辺. 「ing.
heart-rending *a.* ＝heartbreak-
heart-shaped *a.* ハート形の.
heartsick *a.* やるせない: *heartsick* groans.
heartsore *n.*, *a.* 心痛(した).
heartstricken *a.* 悲嘆に胸もつぶれる, 身も世もあらぬ.
heart-to-heart *a.* 『米』腹をわって: a *heart-to-heart* talk.
heart-warming *a.* 心のあたたまる. 「からの.
heart-whole *a.* 恋を知らない; 心
heatstroke *n.* 日射病.
heavy-armed *a.* 重装甲の. 「な.
heavy-hearted *a.* 心の重い, 悲痛
heavy-laden *a.* 重圧下にある.
heavyweight *n.* 『拳闘』ヘビー級選手.
hedgehog *n.* 《米》やまあらし.
hedge-hopping *n.*, *a.* 低空飛行(の).
heir-at-law *n.* 法延相続人.
heirloom *n.* 家宝.
hell-bent *a.* 《米》極度に熱中して, 夢中の: be *hell-bent* for war (peace).
hellcat *n.* 意地悪女; 魔女.
hellfire *n.* 地獄の火; 地獄の責め
helmsman *n.* 舵(かじ)手. 「苦.
helpmate, helpmeet *n.* 協力者; つれあい(妻または夫).
helter-skelter *a.*, *ad.* あわてふためいた(て), てんやわんやの(で).
he-man *n.* 《口語》男らしい男.
hemstitch *n.* 糸抜きかがり.
henpecked *a.* かかあ天下の: a *henpecked* husband.
henchman *n.* [ボスに対し]子分.
henhouse *n.* 鶏舎.
herdsman *n.* 牧羊者.
hereby *ad.* これによって.
herefrom *ad.* これから.
hereinafter *ad* [書類などで]下記に. 「記に.
hereinbefore *ad.* [書類などで]上
heretofore *ad.* 今まで, 従来.
hereupon *ad.* これによって; 直ちに.
herewith *ad.* これによって.
heyday *n.* 全盛, 真盛り.
hide-and-seek *n.* かくれんぼ.
hide-out *n.* [悪人などの]かくれ家.
higgledy-piggledy *ad.* ひどい乱雑で, ごたごたして.
high-aimed *a.* 望みの高い.
high-colored *a.* 色彩の強い.
highball *n.* 《米》ハイボール.
highborn *a.* 高貴の生れの, 名門の.
highboy *n.* 《米》高脚のたんす.
highbred *a.* 純血の; 生れ(育ち)のよい. 「テリ.
highbrow *n.* 《米口》知識人, イン
higher-up *n.* 《米》上役, おえら方.
high-fidelity *a.* 『電』感度の正確で高い (hi-fi と略す).
highflier *n.* 高く飛ぶもの(人, 鳥); とてつもない野心家.
high-flown *a.* 大げさな, 誇張した: *high-flown* language. 「な.
highflying *a.* 高度飛行の; 大げさ
high-frequency *a.* [＜high frequency] 『電』 高周波の.

high-grade *a.* 高級の, 上等の.
high-handed *a.* 高圧的な.
high-hat *v., a.* 《米口》尊大ぶる(尊大ぶった). **—high-hatted.**
high-heeled *a.* ハイヒールをはいた. 「した.
high-keyed *a.* 調子の高い; 緊張
highland *n.* 高地.
highlight *n., v.* 呼びもの(にする): radio *highlights; highlighted* programs (news)
high-mettled *a.* 血気盛んな.
high-minded *a.* 高潔な.
high-octane *a.* 高オクタン価の: *high-octane* gasoline.
high-pitched *a.* 調子の高い, かん高い. a *high-pitched* voice.
high-pressure *a.* 高圧の, 無理強いの: *highpressure* salesman-
high-priced *a.* 高価の. ⌊ship.
high-ranking *a.* 高位(官)の: a *high-ranking* officer.
highroad *n.* 本道, 公道.
high-school *a.* [< high school] 高校の: a *high-school* student.
high-sounding *a.* 大げさな: *high-sounding* remarks.
high-speed *a.* [<high speed] 高速力の.
high-spirited *a.* 意気盛んな.
high-strung *a.* 鋭敏な; 興奮しやすい.
high-tension *a.* 『電』高圧(の).
high-toned *a.* 調子の高い; いやにとりすました.
high-water mark 高水標, 高潮線のあと. *cf.* high water.
highwayman *n.* 追いはぎ.
hijacker *n.* 《米》[輸送中の貨物を]横取りする人. ☞ highjacker ともつづる. **—hijacking.**
hillman *n.* 山国の人.
hillside *n.* 山腹.
hilltop *n.* 山頂.
hinterland *n.* 奥(内)地.
history-maker *n.* 歴史を作る人. **—history-making.**
hit-and-run *a.* 『野球』ヒットアンドランの; ひき逃げの: a *hit-and-run* driver.
hitchhike *v.* 《米口》自動車に便乗して無賃旅行する. **—hitch-hiker.**
hit-or-miss *a.* 行き当りばったりの. *cf.* happy-go-lucky.
hoarfrost *n.* 白霜.
hoary-headed *a.* 白髪(頭)の.
hobbyhorse *n.* 木馬.
hocus-pocus *n.* 魔術師のじゅもん; 手品; ごまかし. 「や.
hodgepodge *n.* 混乱, てんやわん
hog-maned *a.* [馬の]たて髪を刈り込んだ.
holdback *n.* [<hold back] 抑制.
holdup *n., a.* 《米口》追いはぎ(の): a *holdup* man. 「た.
hollow-cheeked *a.* ほおのこけ
hollow-eyed *a.* 目のくぼんだ.
hollow-hearted *a.* 不実な.
hollow-toned *a.* 空ひびきの.
homeborn *a.* 本国生れの.
homebound *a.* 本国行きの.
homebred *a.* 本国育ちの; 粗野な, うぶな. 「など).
home-brew *n.* 自家製飲料(ビール
home-brewed *a.* 自家醸造の: *home-brewed* ale.
homecoming *n.* 帰省(郷). 「ど).
home-cooked *a.* 手製の(料理な
homefelt *a.* しみじみ胸をうつ.
homeland *n.* 故国.
homemade *a.* 手製の, 国産の.
homeroom *n.* 『教育』ホームルーム. ☞ home room ともつづる.
homesick *a.* ホーシックの.
homespun *n., a.* ホームスパン(の): *homespun* cloth.
homestead *n.* 《米》家屋敷.
homestretch *n.* 『競技』ホームストレッチ.
homework *n.* 宿題; 家庭の仕事.
honeybee *n.* みつばち.
honeycomb *n.* みつばちの巣.
honeydew *n.* [植物の]甘い汁; [あぶら虫の出す]甘いみつ: a *honey-dew* melon.
honeymoon *n.* みつ月(旅行): spend a *honeymoon* at...
honeysuckle *n.* すいかずら.
honeysweet *a.* みつのように甘い.
honey-tongued *a.* 口先のうまい.
hoodwink *v.* [馬の目おおいから]人の目をごまかす.
hookup *n.* 『ラジオ』中継; 接続: a nation-wide *hookup*.
hookworm *n.* 十二指腸虫. 「プ.
hornpipe *n.* 『ダンス』ホーンパイ
horn-rimmed *a.* [目がね]角ぶちの: thick *horn-rimmed* glasses (ロイドの目がね).
hornswoggle *v.* 《米俗》だます, ぺてんにかける.
hornwork *n.* つの細工. 「した.
horny-fingered *a.* 指のごつごつ
horror-stricken (-struck) *a.* 恐怖におそわれた.
horseback *n., ad.* 馬上(で). 「の.
horse-faced *a.* 顔の長い, 馬づら
horseflesh *n.* 馬肉; [集合的に]馬.
horsefly *n.* あぶ.
horsehair *n.* 馬の毛.
horsehide *n.* 馬の皮.
horseman *n.* 騎手; 乗馬家. *cf.* horsewoman.
horseplay *n.* ばか騒ぎ.
horsepower *n.* 馬力.
horseradish *n.* 西洋わさび.
horseshoe *n.* 馬てい(形).
horsetail *n.* 馬の尾. 「つ).
horsewhip, *n., v.* 馬のむち(で打
hoseman *n.* [消防の]ホース係.
hotbed *n.* 温床; [悪の]温床: the *hotbed* of social evils.
hot-blooded *a.* 血気にはやる, 向う見ずの.
hot-brained *a.* 激しやすい.
hotelkeeper *n.* ホテル経営者.
hotfoot *ad.* 《口語》大急ぎで.
hothead *n.* 激しやすい人, せっかち.
hot-headed(-brained) *a.* 激しや
hothouse *n.* 温室. ⌊すい.
hot-tempered *a.* 短気な, かんしゃく持ちの.
hot-water *a.* 熱湯の: a *hot-water* bottle.
hourglass *n.* 砂時計.
houseboat *n.* 屋形船.
housebreaker *n.* 押しこみ強盗. **—housebreaking.**
housebroken *a.* [犬など]屋内に住むように訓練された.
houseboy *n.* 下男, 小使い.
housebug *n.* なんきん虫.
housecoat *n.* [婦人の]ゆったりした部屋着. ☞ house coat ともつ
householder *n.* 世帯主. ⌊づる.
housekeeper *n.* ハウスキーパー. **—housekeeping.**
housemaid *n.* 女中.
houseman *n.* 下僕, 下男.
houseroom *n.* 住家の部屋.
house-to-house *a.* 戸ごとの.
housetop *n.* 屋根.
housewarming *n.* 新宅祝のパー
housewife *n.* 主婦. ⌊ティ.
housewifery *n.* 家政, 家事.
housework *n.* 家事. 「た.
hugger-mugger *n.* 混乱, ごたご
hula-hula *n.* ハワイの踊り
humankind *n.* 人類. 「り.
hummingbird *n.* [米国産]はちど
humpback *n.* =hunchback. 「い.
humble-looking *a.* みすぼらし
hunchback *n.* せむし. **—hunch-backed.**
hundredfold *a., ad.* 百倍の(に).
hunky-dory *a.* 《米俗》ちゃんとした, きちんとした.
huntsman *n.* 《英》狩猟家; きつね狩の猟犬係.
hurdy-gurdy *n.* 手回し風琴.
hurly-burly *n.* 大さわぎ, 混乱.
hurry-scurry *a., ad.* あわてた(て).
husbandman *n.* 農夫, 百姓.
hush-hush *a.* 《俗》ごく内密の.

I

iceberg *n.* 氷山, 流氷.
iceboat *n.* 水上ヨット.
icebound *a.* 氷に閉ざされた.
icebox *n.* 冷蔵庫.
icebreaker *n.* 砕氷船; 砕氷器.
icecap *n.* 万年雪.
ice-cream cone アイスクリームコーン. *cf.* ice cream.
icefall *n.* 凍結したたき.
ice-free *a.* 氷の張らない.
icehouse *n.* 氷室.
ice-locked *a.* =icebound.
iceman *n.* 氷屋(人).
ice-skate *v.* 氷すべりをする. *cf.* ice states (スケートぐつ).
ill-advised *a.* 無分別な.
ill-affected *a.* 不満な, 不服な.
ill-boding *a.* 不吉の.
ill-bred *a.* 育ちの悪い. *cf.* ill breeding.
ill-conditioned *a.* たちの悪い.
ill-considered *a.* 浅はかな.
ill-disposed *a.* 意地の悪い.

ill-fated *a.* 不運な.
ill-favored *a.* ぶきりょうな.
ill-founded *a.* 根拠のない.
ill-gotten *a.* 不正手段で得た: *ill-gotten* money.
ill-humored *a* [<ill humor] 不きげんな.
ill-informed *a.* 消息に通じない.
ill-judged *a.* 浅はかな.
ill-mannered *a.* 不作法な.
ill-matched *a.* 不つり合いの.
ill-natured *a.* [<ill nature] いじ悪な, ひねくれた.
ill-sorted *a.* =ill-matched.
ill-spent *a.* 使い方の悪い.
ill-starred *a.* 不運な.
ill-suited *a.* しっくりしない.
ill-tempered *a.* [<ill temper] 不きげんな, いじの悪い.
ill-timed *a.* 折のわるい.
ill-treat *v.* 冷遇する. **ill-treatment.**
ill-usage *n.* ぎゃく待, 酷使.
ill-use *v.* ぎゃく待(酷使)する.
ill-willed *a.* [<ill will] 不親切な, きらいな.
income *n.* 収入.
incoming *a.* 来るべき, 新任(着)の.
incomings *n. pl.* 収入. *cf.* outgoings.
Indo-China *n.* インドシナ. —**Indo-Chinese.**
Indo-European *a.* インド・ヨーロッパ語族の, 印欧語族の.
ingoing *a.* 入り来る, 新来の.
ingrowing *a.* 内部に成長する.
ink-blurred *a.* インキの散った.
inkpot *n.* インキつぼ. *cf.* ink bottle.
ink-stained *a.* インキのしみのついた: an *ink-stained* duster.
inkstand *n.* インキスタンド.
inkholder *n.* インキ入れ.
inkhorn *n.* インキ入れ(つぼ).
inkwell *n.* インキつぼ.
in-law *n.* 《口語》姻戚.
inlay *v.* はめ込む.
innkeeper *n.* 宿屋の主人.
inset *n.*, *v.* さし込み(さし込む).
in-shoot *n.* 『野球』インシュート.
inshore, *n.*, *a.* 近海(の): *inshore* fishing (fisheries).
instep *n.* 足の甲.
interact *v.* 相互に作用する.
inter-Allied *a.* 連合国間の.
inter-American *a.* 米大陸間の.
interclass *a.* クラス間(対抗)の: an *interclass* basketball tournament.
intercollege *a.* =intercollegiate 大学間(対抗)の: an *intercollege* regatta.
intermarriage *n.* 雑婚; 近親結婚.
internal-combustion 内燃機関の: an *internal combustion* engine.
interphone *n.* [電話の]内線.
interplay *n.* 相互作用.
interstate *a.* 『米』各州間の: *interstate* trade.
Irish-American *n.* アイルランド系のアメリカ人.
Irishman *n.* アイルランド人. *cf.* Irishwoman.
ironbound *a.* 鉄張りの, 鉄のように堅い: *ironbound* rules.
ironclad *a.* 鉄甲の: *ironclad* ships.
iron-fisted *a.* 鉄拳の.
iron-gray *a.* 鉄灰色の.
iron-handed *a.* 圧制的な.
iron-hearted *a.* 冷酷無情な.
ironmonger *n.* 金物屋(人).
ironsides *n. pl.* 鉄甲艦.
ironstone *n.* 鉄鉱石.
ironware *n.* 金物.
iron-willed *a.* [<iron will] 鉄の意志の.
ironwork *n.* 鉄製(部分).
ironworks *n.* 鉄工所.

J

jackboot *n.* 長ぐつ.
jack-in-office *n.* 横柄な小役人.
jack-in-the(a)-box *n.* びっくり箱.
jack-in-the-pulpit *n.* [北米の]まむしぐさ.
jackknife *n.* ジャックナイフ.
jack-of-all-trades *n.* 何でも屋.
jack-o'-lantern *n.* 鬼火, きつね火.
jackstraw *n.* わら人形.
jailbird *n.* 《口語》囚人.
jailbreak *n.* 脱獄者.
Jayhawker *n.* [南北戦当時の]ゲリラ隊員.
jaywalk *v.* 《米口》交通規則を無視する. —**jaywalker.**
jellyfish *n.* くらげ.
jerkwater *n.* 《米口》支線専用の列車.
jerry-build *v.* 安ぶしんをする.
jerry-builder *n.* たたき大工.
jet-black *a.* 真黒な, 漆黒の.
jet-propelled *a.* 噴射推進の: a *jet*[*-propelled*] plane.
jewel-studded *a.* 宝石をちりばめた.
jigsaw puzzle 切抜きはめ絵.
jitterbug *n.*, *v.* ジルバ(をおどる). —**jitterbugging.**
jobholder *n.* 定職のある人; 《米》官吏.
job-seeker *n.* 求職者.
Johnny-jump-up *n.* 《米》野生のすみれ.
joint-stock company 株式会社.
journeyman *n.* [年期奉公を終えた]一人前の職人.
journeywork *n.* 手間仕事.
joy-ride *v.* [<joy ride] 面白半分に(自動車を)乗り回す. —**joy-riding, a joy-rider.**
jumpmaster *n.* 落下さん部隊の降下指揮官.
juryman *n.* 陪審員.

K

keepsake *n.* 記念品, 形見.
keyboard *n.* [ピヤノ・タイプなどの]鍵(けん)盤.
keyhole *n.* かぎ穴.
keyman *n.* 中心になる人, 要人. ☞ key man ともつづる.
keynote *n.* 『音楽』主音; 基調.
keystone *n.* かなめ石; 中枢.
kickback *n.* 《米口》盗品の送り返し; ぴんはね.
kickoff *n.* 『フットボール』キックオフ; 発端.
kill-joy *n.* 他人の興をそぐ人.
kind-hearted *a.* 親切心のある, 情深い.
kinfolk *n.* =kinsfolk.
king-size[d] *a.* 特大の.
kinsfolk *n.* 親類.
kinsman *n.* [男の]親類. *cf.* kinswoman.
kiss-off *n.* 《米俗》お払い箱.
kiss-me-quick *n.* 三色すみれ.
kitchenmaid *n.* 下働き.
kitchenware *n.* 台所道具.
Klansman *n.* 《米》KKK 団の団員.
knapsack *n.* 背のう, ランドセル.
kneecap *n.* ひざのさら.
knee-deep *a.* ひざの深さの: The snow lay *knee-deep.*
knee-high *a.* ひざの高さの.
kneehole desk 両そで机.
knee-length *a.* ひざの長さの.
kneepad *n.* ひざ当て.
knickerbockers *n. pl.* ゆるい半ずぼん. ☞ knickers と略す.
knickknack, nicknack *n.* 小さい装身具.
knight-errant *n.* 武者修業者. —**knight-errantry.**
knockabout *n.* 《米》小型のヨット.
knockdown *n.*, *a.* 打倒(する); 折りたたみ式(の).
knock-kneed *a.* [脚部が]内またの.
knockout *n.* 《米》『拳闘』ノックアウト; 《米俗》大へんな美人.
knothole *n.* [木の]ふし穴.
know-how *n.* 《米口》知識, こつ: the *know-how* of atomic energy.
know-it-all *n.*, *a.* 知ったかぶりする(人).
know-nothing *n.* 無知の人.
K-ration *n.* 《米軍》K 号携行食.

L

labor-saving *a.* 労力節約の.
lacework *n.* レース編み.
ladybug *n.* てんとう虫.
ladyfinger *n.* 指がたのスポンジケーキ.
ladykiller *n.* 《俗》女殺し(美男子)
ladylove *n.* 女の愛人, 恋人.
lambskin *n.* 子羊の毛皮.
lamplight *n.* ランプの光り. —**lamplighter.**
lamppost *n.* 街灯柱: as tall as a *lamppost.*
landfall *n.* 『海』陸地近接.
landlady *n.* [下宿屋の]おかみ.
landholder *n.* 地主.
landlocked *a.* 陸地に囲まれた.
landlord *n.* [下宿屋の]亭主; 地主.
landlubber *n.* 『海』おか者.
landmark *n.* 『海』陸標; 顕著な事件.
landowner *n.* 地主.
landscape *n.* 風景(画).
landslide *n.* 山くずれ; 《米》[選挙など]圧倒的な勝利.
landslip *n.* 《英》山くずれ.
landsman *n.* 『海』新しい船員; 陸上の人.
lapboard *n.* [裁縫師の]ひざ板.
large-handed *a.* 気前のよい.
large-minded, large-hearted *a.* 度量の大きい, 寛大な.

large-scale *a.* 大規模の: *large-scale* business operations.
latchkey *n.* [ドアの]かけ金のかぎ.
latchstring *n.* かけ金のひも.
latticework *n.* 格子作り(細工).
laughingstock *n.* 笑いの種, 物笑い.
laundryman *n.* 洗たく屋. *cf.* landrywoman.
law-abiding *a.* 法を守る: *law-abiding* people.
lawbreaker *n.* 法律違反者.
lawgiver *n.* 立法者.
lawmaker *n.* 立法者.
layman *n.* 俗人; [専門家に対し]しろうと. 「雇.
layoff *n.* 《米》休業, [一時的な]解
layout *n.* 設計; [雑誌の]編集(レーアウト): the *layout* of an illustrated magazine.
layover *n.* 途中下車. *cf.* stopover.
leaden-hearted *a.* 無気力な.
leadwork *n.* 鉛細工.
leafstalk *n.* 葉柄.
lean-to *n., a.* さしかけ(の).
leapfrog *n.* かえるとび, 馬とび.
lease-lend *a.* =lend-lease.
leastways, leastwise *ad.* 少くとも, とにかく.
leatherneck *n.* 《米俗》船員.
leave-taking *n.* いとまごい. *cf.* take leave of...
left-hand *a.* 左手の, 左側の.
left-handed *a* 左ききの, 不器用
leftover *n.* 残りもの, 残飯. しな.
left-wing *a.* 左翼の. *cf.* leftwinger.
lend-lease *a.* 《米》武器貸与法による: the *Lend-Lease* Act.
lengthways, lengthwise *ad.* 長く, 縦に. 「《口語》失望.
letdown *n.* [<let down] 減少;
letterhead *n.* 便せんなどの頭部の印刷文字.
letter-perfect *a.* [文書など]一字一句正確な, 完全な.
letterpress *n.* 印刷物. *cf.* letter press (複写印刷器). 「止.
letup *n.* [<let up] 《口語》終止, 中
level-headed *a.* 《米》分別のある, 常識のある.
life-and-death *a.* 生死の.
lifeblood *n.* 生き血; 活力.
lifeboat *n.* 救助艇.
life-giving *a.* 生気を与える.
lifeguard *n.* 《米》水泳場監視人.
lifelike *a.* 生き写しの: a *life-like* portrait. 「friendship.
lifelong *a.* 一生の: *lifelong*
lifesaver *n.* 《米》水難救助者; 水泳場監視人; 救いの神. **—life-saving.** 「*size* statue.
life-size[d] *a.* 実物大の: a *life-*
lifespring *n.* 生命の泉, 命の綱.
lifetime *n., a.* 一生がい(の).
lifework *n.* 一生の仕事. 「ーイ.
liftman *n.* 《英》エレベーター・ボ
light-armed *a.* 〘軍〙軽装備の.
lightface *n.* 〘印刷〙細字活字.
light-fingered *n.* 手の早い: *light-fingered* gentry (すり連中).
light-footed(-heeled) *a.* 足どりの軽い.
light-headed *a.* 無思慮な.
light-hearted *a.* 苦労のない.
lighthouse *n.* 灯台: a *lighthouse* keeper.
light-minded *a.* 頭のからっぽな, 浅はかな.
lightweight *n.* 〘拳闘〙ライト級選
light-year *n.* 〘天文〙光年. し手.
lily-lived *a.* おく病な.
limekiln *n.* 石灰焼がら.
limelight *n.* 石灰光; 人目をひくもの: in the *limelight*.
limestone *n.* 石灰岩.
limewater *n.* 石灰水.
line[s]man *n.* 電信(線路)工夫.
line-up, lineup *n.* 〘野球〙ラインナップ.
lion-hearted *a.* 勇猛な.
lip-deep *a.* 口先だけの. *cf.* lip
lipstick *n.* 棒べに. しservice.
livelong *a.* 長期の, 長い.
lively-looking *a.* 元気のよい.
liveryman *n.* [ロンドンの]同業組合員; 貸馬車屋.
livestock *n.* 家畜類.
liverwort *n.* ぜにごけ. 「ジ.
liverwurst *n.* 《米》肝臓ソーセー
lockjaw *n.* 〘病〙破傷風.
lockout *n.* 〘労〙工場閉鎖.
locksmith *n.* 錠前屋.
lockup *n.* 留置場.
logbook *n.* 航海日誌.
loggerhead *n.* まぬけ, のろま.
logrolling *n.* 丸太ころがし; 《米》協力, 助け合い.
logwood *n.* ロッグウッド(材).
long-awaited *a.* 待ちくたびれた.
longboat *n.* [船載の]長艇, 最大艇.
longbow *n.* 大弓.
longcloth *n.* 上質綿布.
long-distance *a.* [電話など]長距離の: a *long-distance* call.
long-drawn[out] *a.* 長引いた, 長
long-eared *a.* 長耳の. し期の.
long-faced *a.* 長い顔の.
longhand *n.* [shorthand に対し]普通の書き方. 「る.
long-headed *a.* 長頭の; 先の見え
long-legged *a.* 足長の.
long-limbed *a.* 手足の長い.
long-lived *a.* 長寿の: a *long-lived* tortoise. 「のある.
long-sighted *a.* 遠視の; 先見の明
long-standing *a.* 長年の.
long-suffering *a., n.* しん棒強い(こと).
long-winded *a.* 息の長続きする, 長ったらしい: a *long-winded* description (explanation).
longshoreman *n.* はとば人足.
long-tongued *a.* おしゃべりの.
looker-on *n.* 傍観者, 見物人.
look-in *n.* ひとのぞき; 短かい訪問.
loophole *n.* 銃眼; 抜け道.
loose-fitting *a.* よく合わない, だぶだぶの.
loose-jointed *a.* つぎ目のゆるい; 自由に動く. 「式の.
loose-leaf *a.* [帳簿]ルースリーフ
loose-tongued *a.* おしゃべりな.
lop-eared *a.* たれ耳の.
lopsided *a.* 一方に傾いた.
loud-speaker *n.* 拡声器(ラウドスピーカー). 「り暮す人.
lotus-eater *n.* 快楽主義者, のんび
love-child *n.* 私生児.
lovelock *n.* あいきょう巻毛.
lovelorn *a.* 失恋した, 恋にやつれ
love-making *n.* 求愛. した.
lovesick *a.* 恋わずらいの.
lowborn *a* 生れの卑しい.
lowboy *n.* 《米》脚の短いたんす *cf.* highboy.
lowbred *a.* 育ちのいやしい.
lowbrow *n., a.* 《米俗》知性の低い(人): films (magazines) for the *lowbrow*.
low-down *a.* 《米口》身分の低い, 卑しい. *n.* 実情.
lowermost *a.* 最低の.
lowland *n.* 低地. 「もしい.
low-lived *a.* 生活程度の低い; さ
low-minded *a.* 心の卑しい.
low-necked *a.* [婦人服で]えりぐりの深い: a *low-necked* suit (dress).
low-pitched *a.* 調子の低い.
low-pressure *a.* 低圧の.
low-spirited *a.* 意気消沈の.
low-water mark *n.* 干潮線. *cf.* low water.
lumberjack, lunberman. *n.* 《米》木材切出し人夫.
lumbermill *n.* 製材場.
lumberyard *n.* 《米》木材置場.
lying-in *n.* 産の床につくこと.
lynx-eyed *a.* 目の鋭い.

M

machine-gun *v.* [<machine gun] 機銃掃射する: *machine-gunning* an enemy position.
machine-made *a.* 機械作りの.
machineman *n.* 機械工, 印刷工.
machine-sewed *a.* ミシン縫いの.
mad-brained *a.* 熱狂しやすい.
madcap *a.* 向こう見ずの: a *mad-cap* girl.
made-up *a.* でっちあげた: a *made-up* story.
madhouse *n.* 精神病院.
madman *n.* 気ちがい.
maidenhair *n.* 一種のしだ: a *maidenhair* tree (いちょう).
maidenhead *n.* 処女膜.
maidservant *n.* 女中.
mailbox *n.* 《米》郵便ポスト.
mailclad *a.* 鎖かたびらを着た.
mailman *n.* 《米》郵便集配人.
mailplane *n.* 郵便飛行機.
mainland *n.* 本土, 大陸.
mainmast *n.* 〘海〙メーンマスト.
mainsail *n.* 主帆.
mainstay *n.* 〘海〙メーンマストの支索; 頼みの綱.
make-believe *n., a.* かこつけ(の), みせかけ(の): a *make-believe* sleep.

makeshift *n.* 間にあわせもの: use... as a *makeshift* for...
make-up *n.* 化粧(メーキャップ); 組立, 構造.
mail-order house 《米》通信販売店. *cf.* mail order
man-hater *n.* 社交ぎらいの人.
manhole *n.* マンホール.
man-hour *n.* 人時(一人一時間の仕事の量).
man-made *a.* 人間の作った, 人工の: a *man-made* moon.
man-of-war *n.* 軍艦.
manpower *n.* 人力; 人的資源. ☞ man power ともつづる.
manservant *n.* 下男, しもべ.
manslaughter *n.* 殺人.
mantleshelf *n.* 炉だな.
mare's-nest *n.* つまらない大発見(あけてびっくり玉手箱).
marksman *n.* 射手.
markup *n.* 《米口》値上げ.
mastermind *n.* 《米》かげであやつる黒幕.
masterpiece *n.* 傑作.
masterwork *n.* 傑作.
masthead *n.* 〖海〗マストの先端.
matchbox *n.* マッチ箱.
matchmaker *n.* マッチ製造人; なこうど. 「料).
matchwood *n.* マッチの軸木(材
matter-of-course *a.* もちろんの, 当然の. *cf.* a matter of course.
matter-of-fact *a.* 事実に則した. *cf.* a matter of fact.
mayflower *n.* 《英》さんざし.
Maypole, maypole *n.* 五月柱.
mealy-mouthed *a.* 遠回しの, 口先のうまい
mean-spirited *a.* 心のさもしい.
merchantman *n.* 商艦.
merry-andrew *n.* 道化師.
merry-go-round *n.* メリーゴーランド.
merrymaking *n., a.* 大浮かれ(の). *cf.* merrymaker.
metalwork *n.* 金属細工. **—metalworker.** 「ルム.
microfilm *n.* 〖写真〗マイクロフィ
microwave *n.* 〖通信〗超短波.
middle-aged *a.* 中年の.
middle-class *a.* 中流の.
middleman *n.* 仲買人; なこうど.
middlemost *a.* 真中の.
middle-size[d] *a.* 中型の.
middleweight *n.* 〖拳闘〗ミドルウェート級選手.
midshipman *n.* 〖海〗少尉候補生.
milepost *n.* マイル標.
milestone *n.* マイル標石.
milk-and-water *a.* 水っぽい; 気力のない.
milkmaid *n.* 乳しぼりの女.
milkman *n.* 牛乳屋.
milksop *n.* 腰抜け, 弱虫.
milk-white *a.* 乳白色の.
millhand *n.* 製粉工, 職工.
millpond *n.* 水車用貯水池.
millstone *n.* 石うす, ひきうす.
millwork *n.* 製粉工場の作業.
mincemeat *n.* メンチミート(パイなどの材料). 「乱闘.
mix-up *n.* 《口語》混乱, ごたごた;
mock-heroic *a.* 英雄を気どった.
mockingbird *n.* [米国産]ものまね鳥. 「行機など).
mock-up *n.* 実物大の模型(器具·飛
moldboard *n.* 〖農〗すきのへら, *cf.* molding board.
mollycoddle *n.* あまやかされていた男(少年), 弱虫. 「ち.
moneybag *n.* 財布; *pl.* 富, 金持
money-changer *n.* 両替商.
moneygrubber *n.* 守銭奴.
moneylender *n.* 金貸し.
money-making *a.* 金もうけの.
moneymonger *n.* =moneylender. 「ふざけ.
monkeyshine *n.* 《米》いたずら,
moonbeam *n.* 月の光.
moonflower *n.* よるがお.
moonlight *n.* 月光: in the *moon-*
moonrise *n.* 月の出. ⌊*light.*
moonset *n.* 月の入り.
moonshine *n.* 月光; 《米》密造(密輸入)酒. **—moonshiner.**
moon-struck(-stricken) *a.* 気の狂った.
moorland *n.* 荒野. 「人).
mophead *n.* むしゃくしゃ頭(の
morning-glory *n.* あさがお.
mortarboard *n.* [大学の]角帽.
mossback *n.* 《米俗》頭の古い人.
moss-covered *a.* こけの一面に生えた.
moss-grown *a.* こけの生えた: 古くさい: a *moss-grown* idea.
moth-eaten *a.* 虫の食った.
mother-in-law *n.* 義理の母, 《口語》まま母.
motherland *n.* 母国.
motorboat *n.* モーターボート.
motorbus *n.* バス.
motorcade *n.* 《米》自動車の流れ.
motorcar *n.* 自動車.
motorcycle *n.* オートバイ. 「士.
motorman *n.* [電車·列車の]運転
mountain-high *a.* 山のように高い: *mountain-high* ocean waves.
mountaintop *n.* 山頂.
muzzleloader *n.* さきごめ銃.

N

namesake *n.* 同名者(特に人の名にちなんだ).
narrow-gauge *a.* 狭軌の: a *narrow-gauge* track.
narrow-minded *a.* 心の狭い.
nation-wide *a.* 全国にわたる.
native-born *a.* その土地生れの.
nearby *a., ad.* 近くの(で).
near-sighted *a.* 近視の.
neat-handed *a.* 手の器用な.
neckband *n.* [服·シャツの]えり.
neckcloth *n.* ネクタイ.
neckerchief *n.* ネッカチーフ.
necklace *n.* 首飾り.
neckpiece *n.* 毛皮のえりまき.
necktie *n.* ネクタイ.
neckwear *n.* ネクタイ·カラー類.
needlewoman *n.* お針の女.
needlework *n.* 針仕事, ししゅう.
ne'er-do-well *n.* やくざ.
network *n.* 網状組織; 〖ラジオ〗放送網: railway (radio) *network.*
nevermore *ad.* 二度と...しない.
newcomer *n.* 新参者, 新社員.
newfangled *a.* 新奇な, 新流行の: the *newfangled* low hemline.
new-fashioned *a.* 新流行の.
newly-weds *n.* 《米》新婚夫婦.
new-mown *a.* 刈りたての(芝な
newsboy *n.* 新聞売子. 「ど).
newscast *n., v.* ニュース放送(する). **—newscaster.**
newsdealer *n.* 新聞·雑誌販売人.
newsletter 秘密(私的な)情報.
newsman *n.* 新聞記者.
newsmonger *n.* 金棒引き.
newspaperman *n.* 新聞記者.
newsprint *n.* 新聞印刷用紙.
newsreel *n.* ニュース映画. *cf.* a news film.
newsstand *n.* 《米》新聞·雑誌売場.
newswriter *n.* 新聞記者.
new-world *a.* 新世界の. *cf.* the New World.
next-door *a.* 隣家の: a *next-door* neighbor. 「る.
nickel-plate *v.* ニッケルメッキす
nickname *n.* あだ名. 「寝酒.
nightcap *n.* ナイトキャップ; 《俗》
nightdress, nightgown *n.* ねま
nightfall *n.* 日暮れ. ⌊き.
nighthawk *n.* よたか; 《口語》夜ふかしする人.
nightlong *ad., a.* 終夜(の).
nightman *n.* おわい屋.
nightmare *n.* 悪夢.
nightshift *n.* 夜勤; 夜勤の工員たち: workers on the *nightshift* = nightshifts.
nightshirt *n.* [男子用]ねまき.
nighttime *n.* 夜間.
nightwalker *n.* 夢遊病者; 売春婦.
nimble-fingered *a.* [すりなど]手の早い.
nimble-footed *a.* 足の早い.
nimble-witted *a.* 機転のきく.
no-account *a.* 《米俗》無能な.
nobleman *n.* 貴人, 貴族. *cf.* noblewoman.
noble-minded *a.* 高潔な, 寛大な.
nohow *ad.* 《口語》決して...でない.
nonappearance *n.* 姿を現わさぬこと, 欠席.
noncom *n.* [<non-commissioned officer] 《口語》下士官.
nonconductor *n.* 不導体, 絶縁体.
nonfiction *n.* 散文文学(ノンフィクション).
nonpayment *n.* 不払い.
nonplused *a.* ぽかんとした.
nonproductive *a.* 非生産的な.
nonprofessional *a.* ノンプロの.
nonprofit *a.* 非営利的な: *nonprofit* business. 「(人).
nonresident *a., n.* 定住しない
nonresistance *n.* 無抵抗.
nonsmoker *n.* 禁煙者.
nonstop *a.* 無停車の, 無着港の: a *nonstop* train (flight).

nonunion *a.* 組合に加入しない: *nonunion* plant (shop).
nonvoter *n.* [投票]棄権者.
noonday *n.* 正午.
noontime, noontide *n.* 昼.
northeast *n., a.* 北東(の). — **northeastern, northeasterly.**
northwest *n., a.* 北西(の). — **northwestern, northwesterly.**
noseband *n.* 馬の鼻皮.
nosebleed *n.* 鼻血. —**nosebleeding.**
nose-dive *v.* [<nose dive] 急降下する; 暴落する.
nosegay *n.* 花束.
nose-led *a.* 自由に引き回される.
nosepiece *n.* [よろいの]鼻当て.
notebook *n.* ノートブック.
noteworthy *a.* 注目すべき.
noway[s] *ad.* 決して…でない.
nutcracker *n.* くるみわり器.
nutbrown *a.* くり色の.
nursemaid *n.* 子守り女.
nurseryman *n.* 苗木屋.

O

oarsman *n.* [ボートの]こぎ手.
oatcake *n.* オートミールの堅焼きビスケット.
oatmeal *n.* オートミール.
ocean-going *a.* 遠洋航海の. — **ocean-goer.**
octogenarian *n., a.* 八十歳代(の).
odd-looking *a.* 風変りの.
odd-mannered *a.* [態度の]変った.
odd-numbered *a.* 奇数の.
off-color *a.* 色の悪い; 《米》いかがわしい.
offhand, *ad., a.* 即座に(の). *offhand* remarks.
officeholder *n.* 公務員.
offprint *n.* 抜刷り.
offset *n., v.* バランス(をとる); 〘印刷〙オフセット(にする).
offshore *a., ad.* 沖の(に), 海の(に). *offshore* fisheries.
offshoot *n.* [樹幹から出た]枝.
offside, off-side *a.* 反対側の.
offspring *n.* 子女, 子孫.
off-stage *a.* 舞台裏の.
off-the-record *a.* 記録にとめない, 非公開の.
oftentimes *ad.* しばしば.
oilman *n.* 油商人.
oilskin *n.* 油布(防水用). *cf.* oil-paper, oilcloth.
oilstove *n.* 石油ストーブ.
old-age *a.* 老人の: the *old-age* pension.
old-clothesman *n.* 古着屋.
old-fashioned *a.* 古風の, 流行おくれの: an *old-fashioned* piano.
old-hat *a.* 時代おくれの.
old-line *a.* 旧式の.
old-school *a.* 旧派(式)の.
old-timer *n.* [<old-time] 先輩, 古顔.
old-womanish *a.* 小やかましい.
old-world *a.* 太古の. *cf.* the Old World.

olive-colored *a.* オリーブ色の.
oncoming *n., a.* 近接(した).
one-eyed *a.* 一眼の; 不正な.
one-horse *a.* 一頭立の: a *one-horse* sleigh.
one-night stand 《米》一夜限りの興行.
one-sided *a.* 一方的な: a *one-sided* game.
one-step *n., v.* 〘ダンス〙ワンステップ(を踏む).
one-time *a.* かつての, 之の: a *one-time* State Minister.
one-track *a.* 〘鉄道〙単線の.
one-way *a.* 一方だけの, 片道の: a *one-way* ticket.
one-worlder *n.* [<one world] [世界は一なりという]国際主義者.
open-air *a.* 戸外の: an *open-air* school (market)
open-armed *a.* 両手を広げた: an *open-armed* welcome.
open-door *a.* 門戸開放の, 機会均等の: the *open-door* policy.
open-eared *a.* 傾聴した: *open-eared* attention.
open-eyed *a.* びっくりした: *open-eyed* astonishment.
open-handed *a.* 気前のよい.
open-hearted *a.* あけっぱなしの, 打とけた.
open-minded *a.* 虚心の, 偏見のない.
open-mouthed *a.* 口あんぐりの; 口広の: an *open-mouthed* pitcher.
open-topped *a.* 上部のあいた, ふたのない.
openwork *n.* すかし細工.
orangeade *n.* オレンジエード.
orange-colored *a.* オレンジ色の.
orchardman *n.* 果樹栽培者.
out-and-out *a.* 完全な, 徹底的な: an *out-and-out* fool.
outboard *ad., a.* 船外に(の).
outbreak *n.* [<break out] [事件などの]突発.
outbuilding *n.* 離れ家.
outburst *n.* 突発, 爆発: an *outburst* rage (laughter).
outcast *n.* [世の中から]見すてられた人: the *outcast* of society.
outclass *v.* …より高級の, …にまさる.
outcome *n.* 結果.
outfield 〘野球〙外野. —**outfielder.**
outgo *n.* 出費, 支出.
outgoing *a.* 出て行く. —**outgoings** (出費).
outgrow *v.* …より大きくなりすぎる: He has *outgrown* all his clothes.
outgrowth *n.* 自然的な発展, 結果.
outguess *v.* …を出し抜く.
outhouse *n.* はなれ; 《米》屋外の便所.
outlander *n.* 外人; 局外者.
outlandish *a.* 異国風の; 奇怪な.
outlast *v.* …より長持ちする.
outlaw *n.* 無法者.
outlay *n., v.* 支出(する), 出費(する).
outlet *n.* 出口, はけ口.
outline *n.* 輪かく, 大要.
outlive *v.* …より長生きする.
outlook *n.* ながめ; 外観.

outlying *a.* 辺ぴな.
outmatch *v.* …よりまさる.
outmoded *a.* 流行おくれの.
outnumber *v.* 数で…にまさる.
out-of-date *a.* 時代おくれの. ☞ out of date ともつづる.
out-of-door[s] *a.* 戸外の. ☞ out of doors ともつづる.
out-of-the-way *a.* 辺ぴな; 風変りの.
outpatient *n.* 外来患者.
outplay *v.* 競技で…を圧倒する.
outpoint *v.* 点数で…をまかす.
outport *n.* 外港.
outpost *n.* 〘軍〙前哨点(隊).
outpour *n.* [<pour out] 流出(物). —**outpouring.**
output *n.* 生産高.
outrank *v.* 《米》…より高位にある.
outreach *v.* 手をさしのばす; …を越す.
outride *v.* [馬で]…より早く進む; [あらしなどを]乗り切る.
outright *a., ad.* 徹底的な(に); 直ちに.
outrun *v.* …より早く走る; …の範囲を越える.
outsell *v.* …より多く売る.
outset *n.* 手始め.
outshine *v.* …より明るく光る; 顔色なからしめる.
outside *n., a., ad.* 外部(の, に).
outsider *n.* 局外者, しろうと.
outsit …より長居する.
outsize *n., a.* 特大(の): an *outsize* hat.
outskirts *n. pl.* 町はずれ, 外辺.
outsmart *v.* 《米口》だます, 出し抜く.
outspoken *a.* 率直な, あけすけな.
outspread *v., a.* 広げる(がる): with *outspread* arms.
outstanding *a.* 目立つ, 顕著な.
outstay *v.* 長居する: *outstay* one's welcome.
outstep *v.* …の度を越す: *outstep* the truth.
outstretched *a.* 張り広げて: *outstretched* arms.
outstrip *v.* …より速く行く; にまさる.
outwear *v.* [<wear out] …より持ちがよい; 着古す, すり切らす.
outweigh *v.* …より重い; …より重要だ(価値がある).
outwit *v.* …を出し抜く, …の裏をかく.
outwork *v*, 〘築城〙外塁.
outworn *a.* [<wear out] つかれ切った.
oval-faced *a.* おもながの.
oval-shaped *a.* 卵形の.
overact *v.* やりすぎる; [役割など]誇張して演じる.
overactive *a*, 活躍しすぎる.
overall *a.* 全般にわたる. *cf.* overalls.
overawe *v* おどしつける.
overbalance *v.* 重要さでまさる.
overbearing *a.* 横柄な: assume an *overbearing* air.
overbid *v.* …より高値をつける.
overblown *a.* [花が]盛りをすぎた; 吹きとばされた: *overblown* flowers (leaves).
overboard *ad.* 船外へ, 《米》外へ(列車・飛行機の): fall *overboard.*

overbold *a.* 大胆すぎる, 無鉄砲の.
overbuild *v.* 建物の上に建てる; 建物を建てすぎる.
overcast *a., v.* 空が一面にくもった(くもる).
overcloud *v.* 一面かきくもる(くもらす): The sky is *overclouding.*
overcharge *v.* 法外な値を吹っかける; 荷をつみすぎる.
overcoat *n.* オーバー.
overcome *v.* 負かす; 圧倒する: *overcome* difficulties (temptation).
overcrowd *v.* [人が]込みすぎる.
overdevelop *v.* 〚写真〛現象を過度にする.
overdo *v.* 度を越してやる; 煮(焼き)すぎる: *overdo* one's part / beef *overdone.*
overdose *n., v.* 薬の盛りすぎ(薬を盛りすぎる).
overdraw *v.* [預金など]超過引出しをやる. 「る.
overdrive *v.* [人・動物を]酷使す
overdue *a.* [支払い]期間切れの; 延着した: an *overdue* check / The train was in *overdue.*
overeat *v.* 食い過ぎる: *overeat* oneself. *cf.* overdrink.
overestimate *v.* 過大に見積る: *overestimate* one's abilities.
overexert *v.* 努力しすぎる: *overexert* oneself.
overexpose *n.* 〚写真〛露出しすぎる. **—overexposure.**
overflow *v.* [水が]あふれる, はんらんする: a glass filled to *overflowing.*
overgrow *v.* [雑草など]はびこる; 成長しすぎる. **—overgrowth.**
overhand *a., ad.* うわて投げの(で), オーバハンドの(で).
overhang *v.* …の上にさしかかる. *n.* 突き出したもの. **—overhanging.**
overhaul *v.* 分解して精査する: *overhaul* an engine. **—overhauling.**
overhead *ad., a.* 頭上に(の): an *overhead* railway / stars *overhead.*
overhear *v.* 立聞きする.
overhours *n. pl.* 残業時間.
overjoy *v.* 大喜びさせる: be *overjoyed* at (with)… **—overjoyed.**
overladen *a.* =overloaded.
overland *ad., a.* 陸上で(の): an *overland* route / go *overland* to ….
overlap *v.* 重なる(ねる), 一部がかちあう: tiles that *overlap* each other. 「する.
overlay *v.* …の上におく, うわ塗
overloaded *a.* 荷を積みすぎた.
overlook *v.* 見降ろす, …の見晴らしがきく; 大目に見る, 目を通す. **—overlooking.**
overnight *ad., a.* 夜通し(の).
overpass *n.* 《米》高架道路.
overpay *v.* 払いすぎる: The joy *overpays* the toil.
overpeopled *a.* 人口過剰の: *overpeopled* areas (districts).
overplay *v.* =overact.
overpopulation *n.* 人口過剰.
overpower *v.* 打ち勝つ, 圧倒する. **—overpowering.**
overpraise *n., v.* ほめすぎ(る).
overproduction *n.* 生産過剰.
overrate *v.* 過大評価する.
overreach *v.* 広がる, …に及ぶ; 出し抜く.
override *v.* 踏みにじる; [規則など]無効にする: rules that *override* the previous.
overrun *v.* 侵略する, 荒らす, はびこる: be *overrun* with weeds.
oversea[s] *ad., a.* 海外で(の): an *overseas* edition.
overseer *v.* 監督.
overshadow *v.* くもらせる; 顔色なからしめる. 「ズ.
overshoes *n., pl.* オーバーシュー
overshoot *v.* 射越す; やりすぎる: *overshoot* the mark.
oversight *n.* 見落し, 手抜かり.
oversize *a.* 特大の.
oversleep *v.* 寝すごす. 「ろがる).
overspread *v.* 一面にひろげる(ひ
overstate *v.* 大げさに言う.
overstay *v.* 長居しすぎる: *overstay* one's welcome.
overstep *v.* 行き過ぎる, 越権する: *overstep* one's authority.
overstrain *v.* 緊張しすぎる: *overstrain* one's nerves.
overstuffed *a.* 過度に詰込む: an *overstuffed* chair. 「る).
oversupply *n., v.* 供給過多(にな
overtake *v.* …に追いつく: be *overtaken* with terror (fear).
over-the-counter *a.* [取引が]店先の: *over-the-counter* sales (transaction).
overthrow *v.* ひっくりかえす, てんぷくする.
overtime *n., a., ad.* 時間外労働(の, で): work *overtime.*
overtop *v.* …より高い; にまさる.
overture *n.* 正式の申し込み.
overturn *v.* ひっくりかえす(る).
overwhelming *a.* 圧倒的な: an *overwhelming* majority.
overwork *n., v.* 過労(におちいらせる): *overwork* oneself.
overwrought *a.* 過労の, つかれ切った, 興奮した: *overwrought* nerves.
oxcart *n.* 牛車. 「ンス菊.
oxeye *n.* ひな菊類; [米国産]フラ
ox-eyed *a.* [牛のような]大きな目
oxhide *n.* 牛皮. 」の.
oysterhouse *n.* かき料理屋.

P

pacemaker *n.* [競走・競馬で]先頭に立ってペースを整える人[馬]. **—pacemaking.**
pace-setter *n.* =pace-maker: the *pace-setter* for communism.
packman *n.* 行商人.
packsack *n.* 旅行者の荷物の袋(ふり分け荷物など).
packsaddle *n.* 荷ぐら.
paddy-field *n.* 水田.
paddywhack *v.* 《米》平手打ち.
paid-in *a.* [会費など]支払済みの: a *paid-in* member.
paid-up *a.,* 払い込み済みの: a *paid-up* bill.
painstaking *a.* [<take pains] 骨を折る: one's *painstaking* work.
paintbox *n.* 絵具箱.
paintbrush *n.* 絵筆.
paleface *n.* 《米》[インデアンから見た]白人.
pale-hearted *a.* おく病な.
pancake *n.* パンケーキ; 円形の薄氷; 〚空〛平落ち.
panic-stricken(-struck) *a.* 恐慌にとりつかれた, あわてふためいた.
paper-bound *a.* 〚製本〛仮とじの.
parent-teacher *a.* 両親・教師の: a *parent-teacher* association.
part-time *a.* 非常勤の: a *part-time* worker. **—part-timer.**
party-and-party *a.* 当事者間の: *party-and-party* negotiations.
party-spirited *a.* 党派心の強い.
passageway *n.* 廊下; 通路.
passbook *n.* 《英》銀行通帳(bank-
passer-by *n.* 通行人. 」book).
passkey *n.* あいかぎ.
password *n.* あい言葉.
pasteboard *n.* ボール紙.
patchwork *n.* つぎはぎ細工.
pathfinder *n.* 開拓者.
pathway *n.* 道, 歩道.
patrolman *n.* 《米》巡査.
patternmaker *n.* 模型製作者, [織物の]がら・模様の図案家. ☞ pattern maker ともつづる.
pawnbroker *n.* 質屋(人): a *pawnbroker's* shop.
pawnshop *n.* 質屋. 「税制.
pay-as-you-earn *n.* 《英》源泉課
pay-as-you-go *n.* 現金引換: on the *pay-as-you-go* plan.
paybox *o.* 《英》[劇場の]切符売場. 《米》box office.
paycheck *n.* 後援者, スポンサー.
payday *n.* 給料日.
paymaster *n.* 会計主任.
pay-off *n.* [<pay off] 給料支払(日); 解雇.
peace-loving *a.* 平和愛好の: a *peace loving* nation.
peacemaker *n.* 調停者.
peacetime *a.* 平時の: *peace-time* industry.
peacock *n.* 雄のくじゃく. *cf.* peahen, peafowl.
pea-green *a.* [<pea green] 黄色味がかった緑色の.
peanut *n.* 南京豆.
pear-shaped *a.* 西洋なし形の.
pea-souper *n.* [<pea soup] 《英》濃霧(特にロンドンの).
peephole *n.* のぞき穴.

penholder *n.* ペン軸.
penknife *n.* ペンナイフ.
penman *n.* 筆者；字のうまい人. **—penmanship.**
penny-a-line *a.* 一行一ペニの,安原稿書きの. **—penny-a-liner.**
penny-wise *a.* 一文惜しみの: *penny-wise* and pound-foolish.
penrack *n.* ペン軸かけ.
pent-house *n.* さしかけ小屋.
pent-up *a.* 閉じこめられた: *pent-up* fury (rage, emotion).
penwork *n.* 文筆業. **—penworker.**
pepper-and-salt *a.* [服地]霜降りの: a *pepper-and-salt* overcoat.
pepperbox *n.* こしょう入れ.
permanent-waved *a.* パーマをかけた.
photo-offset *n.* 〖印刷〗写真オフセット.
photoprint *n.* 写真印刷.
pickaback *ad.* 肩車にのせて: carry a child *pickaback.*
pickax[e] *n.* つるはし.
pick-me-up *n.* 《口語》興奮剤.
piecemeal *n., a., ad.* 断片的(の,に): spend money [by] *piecemeal.*
piecework *n.* でき高仕事.
pigeon-breasted *a.* [<pigeon breast] はと胸の.
pigeon-hearted *a.* おく病な.
pigeonhole *n.* はとの巣；整理だな.
pigeon-toed *a.* 内またの.
pig-eyed *a.* 小さなくぼんだ目をした.
pigheaded *a.* 強情な.
pignut *n.* 南京豆.
pigpen *n.* 豚小屋.
pigtail *n.* 弁髪, おさげ. **—pigtailed.**
pillowcase, pillowslip *n.* まくらカバー.
pinball *n.* ピンボール(ぱちんこ): a *pinball* game (machine).
pinch-hit *v.* 〖野球〗代打に出る. *cf.* pinch hitter.
ping-pong *n.* ピンポン.
pinhead *n.* ピンの頭.
pinhole *n.* [針で突いたような]小穴.
pinpoint *n.* 針の先き.
pin-prick *n.* 針でさすこと.
pin-up *n., a.* 《米》[ピンでとめた]美人写真(の)；同美人(の): a *pin-up* girl / This is my *pin-up.*
pipeline *n.* [ガソリン・ガスなどの]輸送管.
pitch-dark(-black) *a.* 真っくらな.
pitchfork *n.* [農具]くま手.
pitchstone *n.* れきせい岩.
pitter-patter *n., ad.* ぱたぱた(と): She came *pitter-pattering* on the floor.
place-hit *v.* [<place hit] 〖野球〗ねらい打ちをやる.
placeman *n.* 《英》官吏.
plain-clothes *a.* 平服の: a *plain-clothes* man.
plain-spoken *a.* 露骨な.
plasterboard *n.* プラスボード(一種の板紙).
platelayer *n.* 《英》線路工手(track-layer.).
playback *n.* 録音再生.
playbill *n.* 芝居のビラ(番付).
playbook *n.* 脚本.
playboy *n.* 道楽息子: a Hollywood *playboy.*
play-by-play *a.* ゲーム毎に: a *play-by-play* description of a game.
playday *n.* 休日.
playfellow *n.* =playmate.
playgoer *n.* 芝居の常連.
playground *n.* 運動場.
playhouse *n.* 劇場；おもちゃの家.
playmate *n.* 遊び友だち.
play-off *n.* [引きわけの]決勝試合.
plaything *n.* おもちゃ.
playtime *n.* 遊び時間.
playwrite *n.* 劇作家.
pocketbook *n.* 紙入れ.
pocketknife *n.* 小形のナイフ.
point-blank *a., ad.* 率直な(に): a *point-blank* refusal / refuse the request *pointblank.*
pointsman *n.* 〖鉄道〗転てつ手.
policeman *n.* 巡査. *cf.* policewoman.
poorbox *n.* 慈善箱.
poorhouse *n.* 貧民院.
popeyed *a.* 出目の.
popshop *n.* 《英》質屋.
portal-to-portal *a.* [工場の]入門から出門までの: the *portal-to-portal* pay.
portfire *n.* のろし打上げ(点火)装置.
porthole *n.* 砲門；銃眼.
post-free *a.* 郵税無料の.
postman *n.* 《英》郵便集配人.
postmark *n.* [郵便の]消印.
post-office *a.* [<post office] 郵便局の: a *post-office* order.
postpaid *a.* 郵税先払いの.
potboy *n.* 居酒屋のボーイ.
pothole *n.* おとし穴.
pothook *n.* 自在かぎ.
pothouse *n.* 《英》下等なビヤホール.
pothunter *n.* 賞品目あての競技者.
powerboat *n.* 発動機船.
praiseworthy *a.* ほめるべき,感心な.
pressman *n.* 印刷工；《英》新聞記者.
pressroom *n.* 印刷室.
presswork *n.* 印刷作業.
pretty-pretty *a.* 飾りすぎた,きざな.
prick-eared *n.* [犬の]立耳の.
printseller *n.* 版画商.
printworks *n.* プリントもの(さらさ)工場.
prizeman *n.* 受賞者. *cf.* prize winner.
profit-and-loss *a.* 損益の: a *profit-and-loss* account.
profit-sharing *a.* [<profit sharing] 利益分配制の: *cf.* share the proft.
proofread *v.* 校正を読む. **—proofreader, proofreading.**
propeller-driven *a.* プロペラー推進の. *cf.* jet-propelled.
proud-hearted *a.* 高慢ちきな.
psalmbook *n.* 讃美歌集.
public-minded (-spirited) *a.* 公共心のある.
public-school *a.* [<public school] 《米》公立学校の: a *public-school* children.
public-utility *a.* [<public utility] 公共事業の: a *public-utility* corporation.
puddinghead *n.* のろま, ばか.
puff-puff *n.* 《英》汽車ぽっぽ.
pug-nosed *a.* ししっ鼻の.
pullback *n.* 《口語》障害；不利.
pull-over *n.* 頭からかぶるもの(セーターなど). *cf.* pull a sweater over the head.
pull-up *n.* 停止,〖飛〗水平飛行からの急上昇.
punyfoot *v., n.* しのび足する(人).
pulpwood *n.* パルプ材.
pureblood *n.* 純血. **—pure-blooded.**
purebred *a.* 純血の.
purple-colored *a.* むらさき色の.
purseproud *a.* 金(富)が自慢の.
pushball *n.* プッシュボール.
push-button *a.* [<push button] 押しボタン式の: *push-button* warfare.
pushcart *n.* [行商人の]手押し車.
push-over *n.* やさしい仕事；弱いチーム(相手).
pussycat *n.* こねこ.
pussyfoot *v.* 盗み足する, こっそり歩く.
put-off *n.* 言いのがれ；延期.
put-out *n.* [<put off] 〖野球〗刺殺.
put-up *a.* 八百長の: a *put-up* game.
puzzle-headed *a.* 頭の混乱した.

Q

quarryman *n.* 石切工.
quarterback *n.* 〖フットボール〗クォーターバック.
quarter-bound *a.* 背皮装ていの. *cf.* quarter binding.
quarter-hour *n.* 15分間.
queer-looking *a.* 格好の変った.
quick-eyed *a.* 目の早い.
quick-firer *n.* 速射砲.
quick-freeze *v.* 《米》[食料品など]急速冷凍する.
quicklime *n.* 生石灰.
quicksand *n.* 流砂.
quick-scented *a.* きゅう覚の鋭敏な.
quick-sighted *a.* 目の早い.
quicksilver *n.* 水銀.
quickstep *n.* 速歩(曲)；〖ダンス〗クィックステップ.
quick-tempered *a.* 怒りっぽい.
quick-witted *a.* とんちのきく.

R

rabbit-hearted *a.* びくびくした.
raceabout *n.* 競走用ヨット(自動車).
racecourse *n.* 競技場の走路, 競馬場.
raceway *n.* 水路.
rack-rent *v.* [<rack rent] 法外な地代をとる.
radioactive *a.* 〖理〗放射性の: a *radioactive* isotope (fallout). **—radioactivity**
radio-control *a.* 無電操作の: a *radio-control,* pilotless plane.
radiophone *n.* 無線電話.

radiotelegram *n.* 無線電報. **—radiotelegraph.**

radiotelephone, radiophone *n.* 無線電話. **—radiotelephony.**

ragman *n.* くず屋, ぼろ屋.

ragpicker *n.* ばたや. ⌊bobtail.

ragtag 下層民: *ragtag* and

ragtime *n.* 〚音楽〛ラッグタイム: *ragtime* music.

railhead *n.* レールの終端.

railroad *n.* 《米》鉄道: a *railroad* accident (crossing, carriage, fare, company).

railroader *n.* 《米》鉄道員 (railroad man).

railroading *n.* 鉄道敷設作業.

railway *n.* 《英》鉄道; 《米》軽便鉄道, 市内電車: street *railway.*

rainbow *n.* にじ.

raincoat *n.* レーンコート.

raindrop *n.* 雨だれ.

rainfall *n.* 降雨: have a light (heavy) *rainfall.*

rainmaker *n.* 雨男. 「コート.

rainproof *a.* 防水の. **—***n.* レーン

rain-soaked *a.* 雨でびしょぬれの.

rain-sodden *a.* =rain-soaked.

rainstorm *n.* 暴風雨.

raintight *a.* =raincoat.

rainwear *n.* 雨衣類. 「ト.

rake-off *n.* 《米俗》分け前, リベー

rapeseed *n.* なたねのたね.

ratepayer *n.* 《英》=taxpayer.

rattlesnake *n.* がらがらへび.

rattletrap *n.* がた馬車(など).

rattrap *n.* ねずみとり器.

rawboned *a.* やせこけた.

razorback *n.* らくだなどの背; 《米》半野生の豚.

razoredge *n.* かみそりの刃, 鋭い刃; 危機: be on a *razoredge.* **—razoredged.**

r-colored *a.* 〚音声〛r の音質を有する (ar, or, er など).

reach-me-down *n., a.* 《口語》[洋服など]でき合い(の), 既製品(の): We have no *reach-me-downs* to sell.

ready-made *a.* 既製の, 借りものの: *ready-made* suits (opinions).

rear-end *a.* [列車など]後尾の: a *rear-end* collision.

rearmost *a.* 最後尾の.

record-breaking *a.* 記録破りの. *cf.* a record breaker / break the record.

redbait *v.* 赤だといって弾圧する: *redbait* journalism. 「nal).

redbird *n.* [北米産の]うそ (cardi-

red-blind *a.* 赤色盲の.

red-blooded *a.* 元気一杯の, 張り切った. 「ぎ.

redbreast *n.* こまどり; [米国産]し

redcap *n.* 《米》[鉄道の]赤帽.

redcoat *n.* 英兵(アメリカ独立戦争当時の).

red-eyed *v.* 目の赤い.

red-handed *a.* 手の赤い; 現行犯の: be caught *red-handed.*

redhead *n.* 《米》赤毛の人. **—redheaded.**

red-hot *a.* 赤熱した; 興奮した; 最新の: *a red-hot* argument / *red-hot* news. 「district.

red-light *a.* 紅灯の: a *red-light*

red-necked *a.* 首の赤い(鳥など).

redskin *n., a.* アメリカンインデアン(の).

red-tape *v.* [<red tape] お役所風の. **—red-tapism.**

resthouse *n.* 休泊所.

rice-grower *n.* 米造りの農夫.

rich-breasted *a.* 胸のふっくりし

rich-voiced *a.* 声量のある. した.

ridgepole *n.* 〚建築〛むな木.

rifleman *n.* ライフル銃兵, ライフル銃の名手. 「銃の名手.

rifleshot *n.* ライフル弾, ライフル

right-handed *a.* 右ききの; 右ねじの: a *right-handed* screw. **—right-hander.**

right-minded *a.* 心の正しい.

right-wing *a.* 右翼の. **—right-winger.**

ringbolt *n.* 環付きボールト.

ringleader *n.* 主導者, 首領.

ringman *n.* [競馬の]かけ屋.

ringmaster *n.* [サーカスの]団長.

ringside *n.* [拳闘などの]リングサ

ringworm *n.* たむし. ⌊イド.

rip-roaring (-roarious) *a.* 騒々しい. have a *rip-roarious* time.

risk-money *n.* [出納係などへの]不足金補償手当.

riverbed *n.* 河床.

river-god *n.* 川の神.

riverhead *n.* 水源.

riverside *n., a.* 河岸(の): a *river-*

roadbed *n.* 路床. ⌊*side* inn.

roadblock *n.* 〚軍〛道路上の防さい.

roadbook *n.* 旅行案内.

roadhouse *n.* ロードハウス(キャバレなどもある).

roadman *n.* 道路工夫.

roadshow *n.* 〚映画〛ロードショー.

roadside *n.* 街道の: a *roadside*

roadstead *n.* 〚海〛投錨地. ⌊inn.

road-test *n.* 《米口》[才能を]実地

roadway *n.* 道路. ⌊にためす.

rock-bottom *a.* [<rock bottom] 最低の: *rock-bottom* prices.

rock-bound *a.* 岩石に囲まれた, 岩だらけの: *a rock-bound* pond (island).

rock-climbing *n.* ロック・クライミング. **—rock-climber.**

rocket-launcher *n.* ロケット発射台. **—rocket-launching.**

rock-ribbed *a.* 岩層のある; 頑固

rockwork *n.* 岩壁工事. ⌊な.

rollback *a.* [統制による]物価引下げの; 捲き返しの: the *rollback* tactics. 「る.

roll-call *v.* [<roll call] 点呼をと

roller-skate *v.* [<roller skate] ローラースケートをやる.

roll-top *a.* [上部が畳み込み式の]: a *roll-top* desk.

roommate *v.* 同室者.

rootstock *n.* 〚植〛根茎.

rope-dancer *n.* 綱渡りの芸人. **—rope-dancing.**

ropewalker *n.* =rope-dancer. **—ropewalking.**

ropeway *v.* =cableway.

rosebush *n.* ばらのかん木.

rose-colored *a.* [<rose color] ばら色の; 有望な.

roseleaf *n.* ばらの花弁(葉).

rosepink *a.* =rose-colored.

rosered *a.* =rose-colored.

rosewood *n.* したん.

rosy-cheeked *a.* ばら色のほおの.

rough-and-ready *a.* 間にあわせの: *rough-and-ready* methods.

rough-and-tumble *a.* 乱戦の: a *rough-and-tumble* fight.

rough-dry *a., v.* アイロンがけしない(で干す).

rough-hew *v.* 荒けずりする.

rough-hewn *a.* 荒けずりの: a *rough-hewn* city plan.

rough-mannered *a.* 態度のあらあらしい.

roughneck *n.* 《米》乱暴者.

roughrider *n.* 荒馬を乗りこなす人, 調馬師.

roughshod *a.* 滑り止めの金具のついた: a *roughshod* horse.

rough-spoken *a.* 乱暴な口を利く.

rough-wrought *a.* 荒造りの.

roundabout *a.* 遠回りの, 回り道の: a *roundabout* journey.

round-edged *a.* かどのまるい.

Roundhead *n.* 〚英史〛議会党員.

roundhouse *n.* 《米》円形の機関車庫.

round-shouldered *a.* ねこ背の: a *round-shouldered* old woman.

roundsman *n.* 《米》巡査部長.

round-table *a.* [<round table] 円卓の: a *round-table* conference.

round-the-clock *a.* 二十四時間連続の: a *round-the-clock* strafe.

round-trip *a.* 《米》往復の: a *round-trip* ticket.

roundup *n.* [<round up] 《米》家畜の狩り集め(人); 一斉検挙.

roundworm *n.* 回虫.

rowboat *n.* こぎ舟, ボート.

rubberneck *n., a.* やじ馬(の). **—** *v.* 首を長くしてのぞく: *rubberneck* for a sight.

rubber-stamp *a.* [<rubber stamp] 目くら判を押す.

rubdown *n.* [<rub down] からだをこすること, マッサージ.

rubstone *n.* と石. 「がたびし.

rumble-tumble *n.* がたがた車;

rumrunner *n.* 《米口》酒類密輸入者(船). **—rumrunning.**

runabout *v.* 走り回る人; 浮浪人; 小型車. 「ごまかし.

runaround *n.* 《米俗》言いのがれ,

runaway *n., a.* 逃亡(の), かけ落ち(の): a *runaway* horse (marriage) / a *runaway* mob (暴民).

run-down *a.* [<run down] つかれきった, 病気の; こわれた.

runner-up *n.* 〚競技〛第二着(次点)者: be reduced to the *runner-*

run-off *n.* 決勝戦; 雨水. ⌊*up.*

run-of-the-mill *a.* 並行の.
runway *n.* [飛行機の]滑走路; [動物の]通り路.
rustproof *a.* さびない: a *rust-proof* table spoon (knife).

S

sabercut *n.* サーベルの傷(あと).
sackcloth *n.* ズック.
sack-lined *a.* [<sack line] サック形の(ドレスなど).
saddleback *n., a.* くら形(の).
saddlebag *n.* くら袋.
saddlecloth *n.* くら敷き.
safeblower *n.* [火薬を使う]金庫破り(人).
safebreaker *n.* 金庫破り(人).
safe-deposit *n.* 貸金庫. *a.* 貴重品保管の: a *safe-deposit* company.
safeguard *v.* 保護する, 保管する: *safeguard* one's life (health).
sailboat *n.* 帆船. *cf.* sailing boat.
sailcloth *n.* 帆布, カンバス.
sailorman *n.* 船員 (sailor).
saleroom *n.* 売場.
salesclerk *n.*《米》店員.
salesgirl *n.*《米》女店員.
saleslady *n.* =saleswoman.
salesman *n.* 店員;《米》外交員.
saleswoman *n.* 女店員.
salespeople *n., pl.* [*sing.* salesperson]《米》販売人, 外交員.
saloonkeeper *n.*《米》酒場の主人, ーバーテン.
saltpan *n.* 塩がま; *pl.* 製塩所.
salt-water *a.* [<salt water] 塩水の: *salt-water* fish.
sandbag *n.* 砂袋.
sandbank *n.* 砂丘 (dune).
sandblast *n.* 砂吹き(器).
sandbox *n.* [機関車の]サンドボックス.
sandfly *n.* 砂ばえ.
sandglass *n.* 砂時計.
sandman *n.* [おとぎ話の]睡魔: *Sandman* comes! (ねんねだよ).
sandpaper *n.* サンドペーパー.
sandstone *n* 砂岩.
sandstorm *n.* 砂あらし.
saphead *n.*《米口》のろま.
satinwood *n.* マホガニー類の樹木.
sauceboat *n.* 船形のソース入れ.
saucebox *n.* なまいきな青二才.
saucepan *n.* シチューなべ.
save-all *n.* むだを省く装置.
sawbones *n.*《俗》外科医.
sawbuck *n.*《米俗》10ドル紙幣.
sawdust *n.* おがくず.
sawed-off gun 銃身の短かい銃.
sawhorse *n.* 木びき台.
sawmill *n.* 製材所.
saw-tooth[ed] *a.* [<saw tooth] ぎざぎざの.
saxhorn *n.*〖楽器〗サクスホーン.
say-so *n.*《米口》独断.
scaleboard *n.* [画・鏡などの]裏板.
scapegoat *n.* 人の罪を背負うもの, 身代り.
scarecrow *n.* かかし; こけおどし; 骨と皮.
scarehead *n.*《米俗》[新聞の]こけおどしの大見出し.
scaremonger *n.* [戦争・災害などの]デマをとばす人.
scar-faced *a.* 傷あとのある顔の.
scarfpin *n.* ネクタイピン. *cf.* scarf ring.
scatterbrain[s] *n.* そわそわと落着かぬ人. **—scatter-brained.**
sceneshifter *n.* [芝居の]道具方.
schoolbook *n.* 教科書.
schoolboy *n.* 男生徒. **—schoolgirl.**
schoolfellow *n.* 同期生.
schoolma'am, schoolmarm *n.*《米》女教師. 「校の先生.
schoolman *n.* スカラ哲学者; 学校の先生.
schoolmaster *n.* 男教師, 校長. *cf.* schoolmistress.
schoolmate *n.* 学友.
schoolmiss *n.* 女学生(特になまいきな女学生).
schoolhouse *n.* 校舎. ☞ school house ともつづる.
schoolroom *n.* 教室.
schoolship *n.* [船員の]練習船.
schoolteacher *n.* [小・中学校の]教師.
schooltime *n.* 授業時間.
schoolwork *n.* 学業(成績).
schoolyard *n.* 校庭.
scoreboard *n.* [競技の]得点板.
scorebook *n.* スコアブック. *cf.* score card.
Scotchman *n.* スコットランド人. *cf.* Scotchwoman.
scrapbook *n.* スクラップブック.
scratchcat *n.* 意地わる女.
scratch-pad *n.* 走り書きメモ.
screenplay *n.* [映画の]脚本, 台本.
screenwriter *v.* [映画の]脚(台)本書き.
screwball *n.*《米》変り者, 奇人.
scewdriver *n.* ねじ回し. ☞ screw driver ともつづる.
scrollwork *n.* 唐草模様.
scuttlebutt *n.* [甲板上の]飲水用だる.
Seabees *n. pl.*〖米海〗[the] 軍設営部隊.
seaboard *n.* 海岸.
sea-born *a.* 海から生れた, 海の: the *sea-born* goddess / the *sea-born* city =Venice.
sea-borne *n.* 船で運ばれた: *sea-borne* articles (fire weapons).
seacoast *n.* 海岸.
seafaring *n.* 海上旅行の: a *seafaring* life. **—seafarer.**
seafowl *n.* 海鳥. *cf.* sea bird.
sea-front *a.* [<sea front] 海に面した: a *sea-front* hotel.
seagirt *a.* 海に囲まれた: a *seagirt* country.
sea-god *n.* 海神. *cf.* sea-goddess.
seagoing a. 遠洋航海に適する: a *seagoing* vessel. 「色の.
sea-green *a.* [<sea green] 青緑
seaman *v.* 水夫, 船員. **—seamanship.**
seamark *n.* 上潮線; 航路目標.
sea-minded *a.* 海にあこがれる, 船員志望の.
seamstress *n.* お針の女.
seapiece *n.* 海景画.
seaplane *n.* 水上機.
seaport *n.* 海港.
searchlight *n.* サーチライト.
seascape *n.* 海景. *cf.* landscape.
seashore *n.* 海岸.
seasick *a.* 船酔いの. **—seasickness.**
seat-mile *n.*〖空〗シートマイル.
seaway *n.* 海路.
seaweed *n.* 海草.
seaworthy *a.* 航海に適する.
second-best *a.* 次善の: be content with the *second-best*.
second-hand *a.* [<second hand] 古の; 古手の: a *second-hand* knowledge.
seedbed *n.* 苗床; [悪の]温床.
seedcake *n.* 種入れケーキ.
seedsman *n.* 種まき人; 種子商.
seedtime *n.* 種まき時.
seesaw *n., a.* シーソー(の): a *seesaw* game.
sellout, sell-out *n.* 売払い; 売切れ; 大入れ. 「party.
send-off *n.* 送別; give a *send-off*
serviceman *n.* 軍人. *cf.* service man (修理員).
setback *n.* 妨害; 逆転, 逆流.
set-down *n.* 罵倒: give a person a *set-down*.
set-in *n.* [<set in] [潮など]さし込み; 開始. 「装飾.
set-off *n.* [<set off] 引立てるもの,
setout *n.* [食器など]一式; 飾り立て; 開始: at the first *setout*.
set-to *n.*《口語》なぐり合い. 「し.
setup *n.* 機構;《米》態度, 身のこな
sewerman *n.* 下水夫. *cf.* sewer gas (pipe).
sewn-up *a.*《俗》疲れ切って, へべれけに酔って.
shabby-genteel *a.* [落ちぶれた貴人が]見えを張る.
shabby-looking *a.* みすぼらしい.
shadowboxing *n.* [けん闘]シャドー・ボクシング.
shake-down *n.* 仮の寝どこ; 振り落し;《米俗》頭はね, わいろ.
shake-up *n.*《米》大騒ぎ; 大移動: the *shake-up* of government personnel.
shamefaced *a.* 内気な, つつましやかな; 恥かしそうな: a *shame-faced* country girl. 「broker.
sharebroker *n.* 《英》=stock-
sharecropper *n.*《米》[分わけ]小作人. 「holder.
shareholder *n.* 《英》=stock-
share-out *n.* [組合などの]配給物.
sharkskin *n.* さめ皮;〖織物〗シャークスキン地.
sharp-angled *a.* 鋭角の. 「な.
sharp-cut *a.* はっきりした, 鮮明
sharp-eared *a.* 耳の先のとがった; 耳のさとい.
sharp-edged *a.* [<sharp edge] 切り口のすっきりした. 「目の.
sharp-eyed *a.* [<sharp eye] 鋭い
sharp-nosed *a.* [<sharp nose] 鼻先のとがった; 嗅覚の鋭い.
sharp-pointed *a.* 尖端の鋭い.
sharp-set *a.* 空腹な, 飢えた; 熱望する.
sharpshooter *n.* 射撃の名手.

sharp-witted *a.* 抜け目のない, すばしこい.
shavetail *n.* 《米俗》新任の少尉さ
sheepcot[e] *n.* 羊小屋. ⌊ん.
sheepfold *n.* 《米》羊のおり.
sheepherder *n.* =shepherd.
sheepman *n.* 羊飼い.
sheeppen *n.* =sheepfold.
sheep's-eye *v.* [<sheep's eye] 色目を使う.
sheepshead *n.* [料理用の]羊の頭.
sheepshearing *n.* 羊毛刈り. —**sheepshearer.**
sheepskin *n.* 羊皮; 《米口》大学の卒業証書.
sheepwalk *n.* 《英》牧羊場.
shellback *n.* 《俗》老水夫.
shellfire *n.* 砲火.
shellfish *n.* 貝類; 甲殻類(かにえび
shellproof *a.* 防弾の. ⌊の類).
shell-shocked *a.* [<shell shock] 弾丸衝撃を起した.
shellwork *n.* 貝細工.
shepherd's-purse *n.* なずな.
she-woman *n.* 女らしい女. *cf.* he-man. 「るこう薬.
shinplaster *n.* むこうずねにつけ
shindig, shin-dig *n.* 《米俗》ダンス, パーティ.
shipboard *n.* 船側; 船.
shipbuilder *n.* 造船家, 造船技師. —**shipbuilding.**
shipload *n.* 船一杯分の荷: a *shipload* of coal (oil).
shipman *n.* 水夫; 船長.
shipmate *n.* 船員仲間.
shipowner *n.* 船主.
ship-rigged *a.* [帆船が]儀装した.
shipshape *a.* きちんとした: keep everything *shipshape.*
shipworm *n.* ふなくい虫.
shipwreck *n., v.* 難船(する); 破滅
shipyard *n.* 造船所. ⌊(する).
shirtband *n.* シャツのえり.
shirt-sleeve *a.* [shirt sleeve] くつろいだ; 露骨な: *shirt-sleeve* philosophy.
shirtwaist *n.* シャツ形ブラウス.
shockheaded *n.* 乱髪の: a *shock-headed* artist.
shoeblack *n.* くつみがき(人). *cf.* *bootblack.*
shoehorn *n.* くつべら.
shoelace *n.* くつひも.
shoemaker *n.* くつ屋. —**shoemaking.**
shoeshine *n.* 《米》くつみがき(行為); くつみがき(人): I want a *shoeshine.*
shoestring *n.* くつひも; 《米口》僅少なもとで: start a business on a *shoestring.*
shopgirl *n.* 女店員.
shophours *n. pl.* 営業時間: *shophours:* 9:00 A.M.—4:00 P.M.
shopkeeper *n.* 店主, 小売商人. —**shopkeeping.**
shoplifter *n.* 万引き(人). —**shoplifting.**
shopman *n.* 店員.
shop-soiled *a.* =shopworn.

shoptalk *n.* [<talk shop] 商売用語; 商売の話.
shopwalker *n.* 売場主任(監督).
shopwindow *n.* 陳列窓. *cf.* window-shopping.
shopworn *a.* たなざらしの: *shopworn* articles.
shore-based *a.* [軍用機の]陸上基地の(空母に対して).
shoreline *n.* 海岸線.
shoresman *n.* [海上勤務に対して]陸上勤務の人.
shortbread *n.* バタクッキー.
shortcake *n.* ショートケーキ.
short-change *v.* 《米口》釣り銭を少く渡す; ごまかす.
shortcoming *n.* 欠点.
short-dated *a.* 短期の: a *short-dated* note. 「*band* writer.
shorthand *n.* 速記(術): a *short-*
short-handed *a.* 手不足の.
short-headed *a.* [<short head]
shorthorn *n.* 短角牛. ⌊短頭の.
short-legged *a.* 片ちんばの.
short-lived *a.* [<short life] 短命の: *short-lived* memory.
short-range *a.* 射程の短かい: a *short-range* revolver.
short-sighted *a.* 近視の; 短見の: a *short-sighted* policy.
short-spoken *a.* そっけない, ぶっきらぼうな.
shortstop *n.* 〖野球〗遊撃手.
short-tempered *a.* 短気な.
short-term *a.* 短期の: a *short-term* loan.
short-time *a.* [<short time] 操短の: *short-time* operations.
short-waisted *a.* [衣服が]胴の短かい.
short-wave *a.* [<short wave] 短波の: a *short-wave* radio outfit.
short-winded *a.* 息切れのする.
shotgun *n.* 散弾銃(猟銃など).
shot-put[ting] *n.* 〖競技〗砲丸投げ.
shoulderpiece *n.* 肩あて.
shovel-nosed *a.* 平ぺたい鼻の: a *shovel-nosed* shark.
showboat *n.* 演芸船(ショーボート).
showcase *n.* 陳列箱. *cf.* show window.
showdown *n.* [<show down] 《米口》真相暴露; 対決: the Berlin *showdown.*
showman *n.* 見世物師, ショーマン. —**shomanship.**
show-off *n.* [<show off] 見せびらかし; 見せびらかす人.
showroom *n.* 陳列室.
showup *n.* 《米口》すっぱ抜き.
shrewd-brained *a.* 抜け目のない.
shrewd-headed *a.* =shrewd-headed. 「顔付の.
shrewd-looking *a.* 抜け目のない
shrill-toned *a.* きーという調子の.
shrill-voiced *a.* きーきー声の.
shutdown *n.* [<shut down] [工場などの]閉鎖, 操業休止.
shut-in *a., n.* [室などに]ひきこもった(人). 「の]しゃ断.
shutoff *n.* [<shut off] [水流など

shutout *n.* [<shut out] 締め出し; 工場閉鎖; 〖野球〗シャットアウト.
shuttlecock *n.* 羽子(はね). *cf.* bat-
sickbed *n.* 病床. ⌊tledore.
sickroom *n.* 病室.
sideboard *n.* [かべにつけておく]食器だな. 「ひげ.
sideburns *n., pl.* 《米》短かいほお
sidecar *n.* オートバイのサイドカ
sidehill *n.* 《米》山腹. ⌊ー.
side-kick *n.* 《俗》相棒, 仲間.
sideline *n.* 側線; 内職.
sidelong *a.* 斜めの: cast a *sidelong* glance on...
sidepiece *n.* お添えもの, 付属物.
sidesaddle *n.* 婦人用くら.
sideslip *n., v.* 横すべり(する); 〖空〗横転(する). —**side-slipped, side-slipping.**
side-splitting *a.* 腹をよじるような: *side-splitting* story.
side-step *v.* [<side step] 横へそれる; 問題などさける: *side-step* the main point.
sideswipe *v.* 《米》横突する.
sidetrack *n.* 〖鉄道〗側線, 待避線.
sidewalk *n.* 《米》歩道, 人道.
sideway *n.* 横道; 人道.
sideway[s], sidewise *a., ad.* 横の(に): look *sideways* at...
side-wheel *a.* [船の両側に]外車のある: a *side-wheel* ship. —**sidewheeler.**
sightseeing *n., a.* 観光(の): a *sightseeing* bus (party). —**sightseer.**
signalman *n.* 信号係.
signboard *n.* 看板.
signpost *n.* 道標.
silk-lined *a.* 絹地裏の(ついた).
silkman, silk-man *n.* 養蚕業者.
silk-stocking *a.* [<silk stocking] 絹くつ下をはいた; ぜいたくな.
silkworm *n.* かいこ.
silverberry *n.* [北米産]ぐみ.
silverfish *n.* 銀色の魚.
silver-gilt *a.* 銀めっきの.
silver-gray *a.* 銀灰色の: *silver-gray* hair.
silver-haired *a.* 銀髪の.
silver-plated *a.* [<silver plate] 銀ぎせの.
silverpoint *n.* 銀筆.
silversmith *n.* 銀細工屋. 「な.
silver-tongued *a.* 弁説さわやか
silverware *n.* 銀器; 銀食器.
simple-hearted *a.* 無邪気な, お人よしの.
single-breasted *a.* [上衣など]シングルの: a *single-breated* sack-coat. *cf.* double-breasted.
single-entry *a.* [<sigle entry] 〖簿記〗単記式の. 「誠実な.
single-eyed *a.* 片目の; 二心ない,
single-flowored *a.* 単花弁の.
single-foot *n., v.* [馬など]かるがけ(で走る).
single-handed *a.* 片手の; 独力の: by one's *single-handed* effort. 「な.
single-hearted *a.* 純真な, 献心的

single-minded *a.* ＝single-hearted.
single-stick *n.* 片手で持つ木刀.
single-track *a.* 〖鉄道〗単線の: a *single-track* trolley.
singsong *a.* 抑揚のない: in a *singsong* voice (tone). 「の温床.
sinkhole *n.* 流しの穴, 排水孔; 悪
sister-in-law *n.* 義姉妹(よめ小じゅうと). 「スト.
sit-down [strike] 〖労〗すわり込み
sixpenny *a.* 《英》6ペンスの: a *sixpenny* bit (銀貨).
six-shooter *n.* 6連発ピストル.
sketchbook *n.* スケッチ[写生]帳. ☞ sketch book ともつづる.
skidproof *a.* 滑り止めの: a *skidproof* tire.
skin-deep *a.* 皮一重の, 皮相の: Beauty is but *skin-deep*.
skinflint *n.* 非常なけちんぼう.
skintight *a.* 肌にぴったり合う.
skirunner *n.* スキーヤー (skier).
sky-blue *a.* 空色の.
sky-high *a., ad.* 空までとどくほどの(に): Trees grew *sky-high*.
skylark *n.* ひばり.
skylight *n.* 天窓(あかりとり).
skyline *n.* [山・建物など]空に映った輪かく: the *skyline* of lower Manhattan.
skyman *n.* 《口語》飛行士.
skyrocket *n.* 流星花火, のろし. *v.* [値が]急騰する: The prices are *skyrocketing*. 「scape.
skyscape *n.* 空景色. *cf.* land-
skyscraper *n.* 摩天楼.
skysign *n.* 空中広告.
skywriting *n.* [ジェット機など]空に描いた広告文字.
slantways, slantwise *ad., a.* 斜めに(の).
slap-bang *a.* ＝slapdash.
slapdash *a.* 無鉄砲な, ぞんざいな: *slapdash* work (methods).
slap-happy *a.* 《俗》[なぐられて]ふらふらした; 間の抜けた.
slapstick *n.* ちゃんばら(どたばた)劇: a *slapstick* comedy.
slap-up *a.* 最新流行の, すばらしい: a *slap-up* costume.
slate-roofed *a.* [屋根など]スレートぶきの.
slaughterhouse *n.* と殺場.
slaveholder *n.* 奴隷所有者. —**slaveholding.**
sledge-hammer *v., a.* [<sledge hammer] 大ハンマー(のような強力な).
sleepwalker *n.* 夢遊病者. —**sleepwalking.**
sleepy-eyed *a.* ねむそうな目の.
sleepyhead *n.* おねぼう; ぼんやり者. 「い.
slim-waisted *a.* ウエストのほそ
slingshot *n.* ぱちんこ(石投器).
slip-on *a., n.* [<slip on] [シャツ・ブラウスなど]引っかけて着る(も
slipover *n., a.* ＝slip-on. ⌊の).
slipshod *a.* だらしのない, いいかげんな.
slipslop *a., n.* 水っぽい(飲み物); 安っぽい(作品).
slipstick *n.* 《米》計算尺. 「誤り.
slip-up *n.* 《口語》[うっかりした]
slopshop *n.* 既製の安服を売る店.
slopwork *n.* 安服仕立て; 安服.
slowdown *n.* 〖労働〗能率低下, サボ.
slow-motion *a.* [高速度写真]スローモーションの: a *slow-motion* picture.
slow-moving *a.* スローモーの; [商品など]足のおそい: *slow-moving* merchandise. 「coach.
slowpoke *n.* のろま. *cf.* slow
slow-up *n.* 遅速, ぐずぐずすること. 「まの.
slow-witted *a.* 頭のにぶい, のろ
small-minded *a.* けちくさい.
smallpox *n.* ほうそう. 「剣.
smallsword *n.* [フェシング]突き
small-time *a.* 《米》三流の: a *small-time* businessman. *cf.* bigtime.
smallwares *n., pl.* 《英》小間物類.
smashup *n.* 《米》大衝突; 大損害; 完敗, ぺちゃんこ.
smoke-dried *a.* くん製にした: *smoke-dried* salmon (meat).
smokehouse *n.* くん製所.
smokejack *n.* [煙突に取りつけた]焼ぐし回し.
smoke-screened *a.* [<smoke screen] 煙幕を張った.
smokestack *n.* [汽船・工場の]煙突.
smoking-room *a.* [<smoking room] 喫煙室の.
smooth-faced *a.* ひげのない; きれいにそった.
smooth-shaven *a.* きれいにそった (close-shaven.)
smooth-spoken *a.* 相手を納得させるように話す. 「よい.
smooth-tongued *a.* [話の]調子の
snakeskin *n.* 蛇皮. 「とる).
snapshot *n., v.* 〖写真〗スナップ(を
sneak-raid *a.* [空軍の]奇襲攻撃の.
snowball *n., v.* 雪つぶて(を投げあう): throw a *snowball* / have a *snowball* battle.
snowbank *n.* 雪の吹きだまり.
snowblink *n.* 雪原の照り返し.
snow-blind *a.* 雪めくらの. —**sow-blindness.**
snow-bound *a.* 雪に閉ざされた.
snowcap *n.* 山頂の雪.
snow-capped *a.* 山頂に雪をいただいた: a *snow-capped* mountain.
snowdrift *n.* 雪の吹きだまり.
snowdrop *n.* 〖植〗スノードロップ.
snowfall *n.* 降雪(量): have a heavy *snowfall*.
snowflake *n.* 雪片.
snowman *n.* 雪だるま.
snowplow, 《英》**snowplough** *n.* 除雪器; 除雪車.
snowshed *n.* 〖鉄道〗雪おおい.
snowshoe *n., v.* 雪ぐつ(で歩く), かんじき(で歩く).
snowslide, snowslip *n.* [小型の]雪なだれ.
snow-white *a.* 雪白の.
so-and-so *n.* だれそれ, 何某: Mr. So-and-so.
soapbox *n.* 石けん箱. *a.* 《米》街頭演説の: a *soapbox* orator.
soapsuds *n., pl.* 石けんのあわ.
soapstone *n.* 石けん石. 「な.
sober-minded *a.* 落着いた, 冷静
so-called *a.* いわゆる: their *so-called* education.
Social-Democratic *a.* [<Social Demoracy] 社会民主主義の: a *Social-Democratic* Party. —**Social-Democrat.**
softball *n.* 《米》ソフトボール; ソフトボールの野球.
soft-boiled *a.* [卵など]半熟の.
soft-headed *a.* ばかな, 抜けている.
soft-hearted *a.* 心のやさしい, 同情深い. 「い.
soft-shell[ed] *a.* からのやわらか
soft-shoe *a.* バレー用ぐつの.
soft-soap *v.* [<soft soap] ソフト石けんを用いる; へつらう. —**soft-soaper.**
soft-spoken *a.* 話のものやわらか
somebody *pron.* だれか. ⌊な.
someday *ad.* いつか. 「く.
somehow *ad.* 何とかして, ともか
someone *pron.* ある人, だれか.
something *pron.* あるもの, 何か.
sometime *ad., a.* いつか(の): a *sometime* Mayor of Berlin.
sometimes *ad.* 時々, 時折.
someway[s] *ad.* 何とかして, どうにか.
somewhat *ad.* やや, いく分.
somewhere *ad.* どこかに, いつか.
somewhile *ad.* いつか, その中.
songbird *n.* 鳴き鳥; 歌姫.
songbook *n.* 唱歌集.
son-in-law *n.* むこ, 養子.
soot-black *a.* 真黒の.
soothsayer *n.* うらない者. —**soothsaying.**
sore-eyed *a.* ただれ目の.
sorehead *n.* 《米口》くやしがる人, 不平家. 「た.
sorrow-stricken *a.* 悲嘆にくれ
soundboard *n.* 反響板. *cf.* sounding board. 「ボックス.
soundbox *n.* [蓄音器の]サウンド
soundproof *a.* 防音の.
southeaster *n.* [<southeast] 南東の強風. —**southeasterly.**
southpaw *n.* 〖野球〗左腕投手.
southwester *n.* [<southwest] 西南の強風. —**southwesterly.**
sourdough *n.* 《米俗》山師(金鉱などの). 「草.
space-filler *n.* [雑誌などの]うめ
space-saving *a., n.* 紙面省略(のための).
spaceship *n.* 宇宙旅客機.
space-writer *a.* 〖新聞〗一行いくらで書く寄稿家. 「作.
spadework *n.* [研究などの]基礎工
speakeasy *n.* 《米俗》もぐり酒場.

spearhead *n.* やりの穂先；〘軍〙最前線.
spear[s]man *n.* やり使い, やり兵.
speckle-faced *a.* そばかすだらけ
speechmaker *n.* 演説家. ⌊の.
speedboat *n.* 快速艇(モーターボート). 「りの巡査.
speedcop *n.* 《米俗》速度違犯取締
speed-up *n.* [<speed up] スピードアップ.
speedway *n.* 高速度自動車道路, 自動車競走場. 「**bound.**
spellbinder *n.* 雄弁家. **—spell-**
spelldown *n.* つづり字競技(何回かミスするとアウトになる).
spendthrift *n.* 金使いの荒い人, 放とう息子(など).
spick-and-span *a.* ま新しい: *spick-and-span* new. 「ロ.
spillway *n.* [ダムなどの]余水出し
spindrift *n.* 波しぶき. 「ぽ.
spindlelegs *n., pl.* 長い足; のっ
spitball *n.* 《口語》[紙をかんで作った]紙つぶて; 〘野球〙スピットボール(反則になる).
spitchcock *n.* うなぎのかばやき.
spitfire *n.* 短気者, がみがみ女.
splashboard *n.* [車の]どろよけ; [小舟の]波よけ.
spoilsman *n.* 《米》猟官者(官職につく目的で党のため又は選挙運動などにたずさわる人).
spoondrift *n.* =spindrift. 「の.
spoon-fashioned *a.* スプーン型
spoon-fed *a.* [子供病人など]さじで食べさせられて; あまやかされて: a *spoon-fed* child.
sportsman *n.* スポーツマン. *cf.* sportswoman. **—sportsmanship.** 「注目.
spotlight *n.* スポットライト, 世の
spread-eagle *a., v.* [<spread eagle] [手足を]わしのように広げた(広げる).
spreadhead *n.* [新聞の]大見出し.
springboard *n.* 〘水泳〙飛込み台(diving board); 〘スキー〙跳躍台.
springhead *n.* 源流, 水源.
springhouse *n.* 泉水のある小屋.
springtime, springtide *n.* 春; 青春.
spyglass *n.* 小形の望遠鏡.
spymaster *n.* スパイ団の親分.
square-built *a.* 肩幅のある, がっしりした: a *square-built* young man.
square-faced *n.* 角ばった顔の.
square-shouldered *a.* 肩の張った.
square-toed *a.* [くつなど]先の広い; きちょうめんな, 旧式な.
squint-eyed *a.* 斜視の; 横目の, 流し目の. 「boy.
stableman *n.* 馬丁. *cf.* stable-
stagecoach *n.* 駅馬車.
stagecraft *n.* 演出法.
stagehand *n.* 舞台係(道具方照明係など). 「れた.
stage-struck *a.* 舞台生活にあこが
staghorn *n.* 鹿の角. 「hound.
staghound *n.* しか狩猟犬. *cf.* fox-

stained-glass *a.* [<stained glass] 着色ガラスの.
stainless-steel *a.* [<stainless steel] ステンレス製の.
staircase, stairway *n.* 階段.
stairhead *n.* 階段の頂上.
stakeholder *n.* [ばくちなどの]かけ金を預る人. 「した目の.
stalk-eyed *a.* [かにのような]突出
stalking-horse *n.* [選挙候補者の]あて馬. 「首領.
standard-bearer *n.* 旗手; 政党の
standard-gauge *a.* [<standard gauge] 〘鉄道〙標準軌道の: *standard-gauge* tracks.
stand-by *n.* 頼りになる人, 支持者.
stander-by *n.* 傍観者, 見物人.
standfast *n.* しっかりした人.
stand-in *n.* 〘映画〙身代り俳優, ふき替え. 「引分け.
stand-off *n.* 隔離; 〘ゲーム〙同点,
standpat *a.* 現状維持の. **—standpatter.**
standpipe *n.* 配水塔(水槽).
standpoint *n.* 観点, 立場: from the *standpoint* of commercialism.
standstill *n.* [<stand still] 停止, 休止, 行きずまり.
stand-up *a.* 直立した, 立ちながらの. a *stand-up* collar / *stand-up* drinks.
starboard *n., a.* 〘海〙右げん(の).
starfish *n.* ひとで.
stargaze *v.* 星を眺める; ぼんやり眺める. **—stargazer, stargazing.**
starlight *n., a.* 星あかり(の).
starlike *a.* 星形の; ぴかぴかする.
star-spangled *a.* 星をちりばめた: the *Star-Spangled* Banner.
star-studded *a.* 星をちりばめた: the *star-studded* sky.
state-aided *a.* 国庫補助の.
statecraft *n.* 国政, 政治的手腕.
Statehouse *n.* 《米》州会議事堂.
stateroom *n.* [<state room] 〘海〙特別室; 《米》[列車の]特別寝台.
statesman *n.* 政治家. *cf.* stateswoman. **—statesmanship.**
state-wide *a.* 《米》全州にわたって.
stationmaster, station-master *n.* 《英》駅長. ☞《米》station agent. 「(人).
stay-at-home *a., n.* 出ぶしょうの
stay-in *a.* 《英》坐り込みの: a *stay-in* (=sit-down) strike.
steadfast *a.* しっかりした, 不動の: a *steadfast* gaze.
steady-going *a.* 着実な, まじめの. *opp.* easy-going.
steamboat 蒸気船.
steam-roller *a., v.* [<steam roller] 蒸気ローラーの(でならす); 圧倒的な(圧倒する): The Red Army *steam-rollered* the Hungarian rebellions. / He *steam-rollered* the opposition.
steamtight *a.* 蒸気のもらない: a *steamtight* pipe.

steel-blue *a.* [<steel blue] 鋼青
steel-clad *a.* 鉄甲を着た. ⌊色の.
steel-gray *a.* [<steel gray] 鉄灰色の: *steel-gray* stockings.
steel-plated *a.* 鋼板を張った, 装甲の. 「**worker.**
steelworks *n.* 製鋼所. **—sheel-**
steelyard *n.* さおばかり.
steeplechase *n.* 野外横断競走.
steepletop *n.* 尖(せん)頭の頂き.
steersman *n.* 舵(だ)手. 「時計.
stem-winder *n.* 《米》りゅうず巻
stencil-cutter *n.* 原紙切り. **—stencil-cutting.** 「sister.
stepbrother *n.* まま娘. *cf.* step-
step-down *v.* 電圧を下げる. a *step-down* transformer.
step-in *a.* [<step in] 足を突っこんではく(着る): *step-in* boots (pants).
stepladder *n.* 段ばしご, きゃたつ.
stepmother *n.* まま母. *cf.* stepdaughter. 「child.
stepparent *n.* まま親. *cf.* step-
step-up *n.* 電圧を上げる.
stern-fared *a.* いかつい顔の.
stick-in-the-mud *n.* 頑張り屋: 頑固もの: Hey, Mr. *Stick-in-the-mud!*
stickpin *n.* ネクタイピン. 「ばり.
stick-to-itiveness *n.* 《米口》がん
stick-up *n.* [<stick up] 強盗, 追いはぎ: a *stick-up* man.
stiff-necked *a.* [<stiff neck] 頑
stillbirth *n.* 死産. ⌊固な.
stillborn *n.* 死産の.
still-hunt *v.* こっそりねらう.
still-life *a.* [<still life] 〘画〙静物
stinkbomb *n.* 悪臭弾. ⌊の.
stinkbug *n.* 悪臭を発する虫.
stinkpot *n.* 悪臭を放つものを入れ
stinkwood *n.* 臭木(材). ⌊る容器.
stitchwork *n.* かがり[の仕事].
stockbreeder *n.* 収畜業者. **—stockbreeding.**
stockbroker *n.* 《米》株式仲買人. **—stockbroking.**
stockholder *n.* 《米》株主; 《英》公債所有者.
stockjobber *n.* 《米》株式仲買人.
stockman *n.* 《米》牧畜業者.
stockpile *n.* 補給品の山: *stockpiles* of atomic weapons (warplanes).
stockroom *n.* [物資の]貯蔵所; 商品陳列室. ☞stock room ともつ
stockstill *a.* 不動の. ⌊づる.
stocktaking *n.* 商品のたなおろし.
stokehold *n.* [汽船の]ボイラー室.
stokehole *n.* ボイラーの口; ボイラー室.
stomach-ache *n.* 腹痛: have a *stomach-ache.*
stone-blind *a.* 全然めくらの.
stone-broke, stony-broke *a.* 《英俗》一文なしの.
stonecutter *n.* 石工; 石切り器.
stone-deaf *a.* 金つんぼの.
stonemason *n.* 石工.
stonework *n.* 石細工. **—stoneworker.**

stony-hearted *a.* 無情な.
stopcock *n.* コックのせん.
stopgap *n.* 穴ふさぎ；間にあわせ.
stopover *n., a.* [<stop over] 途中下車(の)：a *stopover* ticket / make a *stopover* at...
storehouse *n.* 倉庫；宝庫：a *storehouse* of information. 「主.
storekeeper *n.* 《米》小売商人，店
storeroom *n.* 貯蔵所，物置き.
storm-beaten *a.* 暴風雨に荒された：a *storm-beaten* area.
stormbound *a.* [汽船が]出港不能の. *cf.* snowbound.
stormproof *a.* 暴風雨除けのしてある：a *stormproof* hold.
storm-stayed *a.* 暴風雨で出港不可能の. 「まくる.
storm-swept *a.* のあらしの吹き
storm-tossed *a.* [船が]暴風で揺れ
stormwind *n.* 暴風しけ. 」た.
storybook *n.* 物語本. 「そつき.
storyteller *n.* 話し家；《口語》う
stout-hearted *a.* 雄々しい，勇敢な. 「た.
stove-heated *a.* ストーブで熱し
stovepipe *n.* ストーブの煙とつ：a *stovepipe* hat (シルクハット).
stowaway *n.* [<stow away] 密航者.
straightaway *n., a.* 直線(の)；〚競馬〛直線コース(の).
straightedge *n.* 直じょうぎ.
straight-faced *a.* 感情を表面に出さない.
straightforward *a., ad.* まっすぐの(に)：a *straightforward* offer (answer).
straight-out *a.* 《米口》徹底した：a *straight-out* Communist.
straightway *ad.* すぐ，直ちに.
strawboard *n.* ボール紙. 「の.
straw-colored *a.* 青みがかった黄
streamline *n., v.* 流線形(にする).
streamlined *a.* 流線形の：a *streamlined* car (train).
streetcar *n.* 市内電車.
streetwalker *n.* 売春婦. —**streetwalking.**
stretch-out *n.* 〚労〛労働強化.
strikebreaker *n.* ストを破る人. —**strikebreaking.**
strong-arm *a., v.* [<strong arm] 《米》腕ずくの(腕力を用いる)，暴力の(暴力をふるう).
strong-bodied *a.* 体の頑丈な.
strongbox *v.* 金庫.
strong-hearted *a.* =strong-minded.
stronghold *n.* とりで，要さい.
strong-minded *a.* 心のしっかりした；勝気な.
strongroom *n.* 金庫べや.
strong-willed *a.* 意志の強固な.
stuck-up *a.* 《口語》そっくり返って，つんとすました.
studbook *v.* 馬の血統台帳.
studhorse *n.* 種馬.
stylebook *n.* 文章便覧；〚服飾〛スタイルブック.
submarine-chaser *n.* 駆潜艇.

sugar-coated *a.* 糖衣の：*sugar-coated* cold tablets (かぜ薬の錠
sugarhouse *n.* 砂糖工場. 」剤).
sugar-loaf *a.* [<sugar loaf] 棒状の：a *sugar-loaf* hat.
sugarworks *n.* 砂糖工場.
sulky-looking *a.* ぶっちょうずら
summertime *n.* 夏期. 」の.
sundew *n.* もうせんこけ.
sun-bathe *v.* 日光浴をする. —**sun-bathed.**
sunbeam *n.* 光線.
sunbonnet *n.* [婦人用]日よけ帽.
sunburn *n., v.* 日やけ(する).
sunburnt *a.* 日やけした：*sunburnt* arms.
sunburst *n.* 急にさす強烈な日光.
sun-cured *a.* [魚など]日干しにした.
sundown *n.* 日没：get home before *sundown.* 「**dried.**
sun-dry *v.* 日でかわかす. —**sun-**
sunfast *a.* [色など]あせない：*sunfast* cloth.
sunflower *n.* 日まわり.
sunglasses *n. pl.* サングラス.
sunlight *v.* 日光. —**sunlit.**
sunproof *a.* 日光を通さない；色の
sunrise *n.* 日の出. 」さめない.
sunroom *n.* 日光浴室(サンルーム).
sunset *n.* 日没.
sunshade *n.* 日よけ；日がさ.
sunshine *n.* 日の輝き，日なた.
sunspot *n.* 太陽黒点.
sunstroke *n.* 日射病.
sunup *n.* 日の出.
sunwise *ad.* 右回りに(clockwise).
sure-enough *a.* [<sure enough] 確実な：a *sure-enough* program.
sure-fire *a.* 《米口》確実な.
sure-footed *a.* 足が地についた，
surfboard *n.* 波乗り板. 」確実な.
surfboat *n.* [寄せ波を切る]軽舟.
swallowtail *n.* 燕尾服.
swallow-tailed *a.* [<swallow-tail] 燕尾形の：*a swallow-tailed* coat.
swashbuckler *n.* からいばりする人. —**swashbuckling.**
sweatshop *n.* 労働さく取工場.
sweepstakes *n., pl.* [競馬の]大穴.
sweetheart *n.* 恋人.
sweet-scented *a.* 芳香のある.
sweetmeats *n., pl.* 菓子類.
sweet-tempered *a.* 気立てのや
swellfish *n.* ふぐ. 」さしい.
swell-headed *a.* うぬぼれの強い.
swift-footed *a.* 足の早い.
swift-handed *a.* 手の早い，動きの早い.
switchback *n.* 〚鉄道〛スイッチバック；〚映〛切り返し.
switch-blade *a.* バネ仕かけの：a *switch-blade* knife.
switchboard *n.* 配電盤；《米》交換台. 「手.
switchman *n.* 《米》〚鉄道〛転てつ
switchyard *n.* 〚鉄道〛操車場.
swollen-bodied *a.* からだのむくんだ. *cf.* swollen-eyed, swollen-faced, swollen-footed.

swordfish *n.* めかじき.
swordplay *n.* 剣術.
sword[s]man *n.* 剣士. —**swordsmanship.**

T

tablecloth *n.* テーブル掛け. *cf.* table clothing.
tableland *n.* 台地，高原.
tablespoon *n.* 食卓用大さじ.
tablespoonful *n.* 大さじ一杯：a *tablespoonful* of sugar (flour).
tableware *n.* 食卓用器.
tailboard *n.* [トラックの]尾板.
tail-down *a., ad.* 〚空〛尾部を下げて.
tailfin *n.* 尾びれ；〚空〛尾部垂直板.
tailgate *n.* =tailboard.
taillight *n.* 尾灯. *cf.* tail lamp.
tailor-made *a.* 〚服飾〛テーラーメード：a *tailor-made* blouse (suit).
tailpiece *n.* 尾片；楽器の緒(ᵒ)じめ.
tailrace *n.* [発電所の]放水路.
tailspin *n.* 〚空〛きりもみ.
take-down *a.* 取りはずし式の：a *take-down* shack (bookshelf).
take-home pay 手どりの給料.
take-in 《口語》[<take in] ぺてん，さぎ.
take-off *n.* [<take off]〚空〛離陸；〚競技〛跳躍の踏切り.
take-up *n.* [<take up] ぴんと張ること；締め道具. 「き.
talebearer *n.* ゴシップ屋，金棒引
talecarrier *n.* =talebearer.
talesman *n.* 補欠陪審員.
taleteller *n.* [物語の]話し手. 「言.
talking-to *n.* 《口語》お目玉，お小
tallboy *n.* 《英》高脚のたんす. *cf.* highboy.
tankman *n.* 戦車兵.
tap-dance *v.* [<tap dance] タップダンスを踊る. —**tap-dancer.**
tape-record *v.* [<tape recorder] 録音する. —**tape-recorded.**
tape-tied *a.* テープで結んだ.
taproom *n.* 《英》酒場.
taproot *n.* 〚植〛直根.
tar-dipped *a.* コールターに浸した：*tar-dipped* timber.
tar-paved *a.* 仮舗装の：a *tar-paved* street.
tariff-protected *a.* 保護関税の.
tariff-raised *a.* 関税引上の.
taskmaster *n.* 仕事を割り当てる人，現場監督.
taskwork *n.* 割り当て仕事.
tax-exempt *a.* 免税の：*tax-exempt* items.
tax-free *a.* 免(無)税の.
taxicab *n.* タキシー.
taximan *n.* タキシーの運転手 (taxi driver).
taxiplane *n.* 乗合飛行機
taximeter *n.* [タキシーの]料金自動表示器.
taxpayer *n.* 納税者.
teacup *n.* 茶わん. —**teacupful,**
teagown *n.* 茶会服.

teammate *n.* チーム仲間.
teamwork *n.* チームワーク.
teapot *n.* 茶びん, きゅうす.
teardrop *n.* 涙(の一しずく).
tearoom *n.* 茶室.
tear-stained *a.* 涙でぬれた(くもった): a *tear-stained* tune of music. 「**spoonful.**
teaspoon *n.* 茶さじ. **—tea-**
tea-table *a.* [<tea table] 茶会の: a *tea-table* talk.
teataster *n.* 茶の格付をする人.
teatime *n.* お茶の時間.
teethridge *n.* 歯ぐき. 「**ager.**
teen-age[d] *a.* 十代の. **—teen-**
tender-eyed *a.* 目のやさしい.
tenderfoot *n.* 新参者.
tender-hearted *a.* 心のやさしい.
terror-stricken(-struck) *a.* 恐怖におびえた. 「edition.
textbook *n.* 教科書: the *textbook*
thanksgiver *n.* 感謝する人.
thanksgiving *n.* 感謝の表示; [T-] 感謝祭; *Thanksgiving* [Day].
Thailand *n.* タイ国. **—Thailander.**
thankworthy *a.* 感謝に値する.
thenceforth *ad.* それ以来.
thereabout[s] *ad.* その辺に; おおよそ: from the 1660 or *thereabouts.*
therefrom *ad.* そこから, それか
therein *ad.* そこに. 「ら.
thereupon *ad.* そこで, さっそく.
therewith *ad.* それをもって.
thick-brained *a.* 頭の悪い.
thickhead *a.* のろま. **—thick-headed.** 「首の太い.
thick-necked *a.* [<thick neck]
thick-set *a.* 生え茂った; でっぷりした: a *thick-set* chauffeur.
thick-skinned *a.* 鈍感な.
thick-skulled *a.* =thick-headed.
thick-witted *a.* =thick-headed.
thing-in-itself *n.* [カントの哲学の]物自体.
thin-skinned *a.* 鋭敏な.
third-class *a., ad.* 三等の[で]: a *third-class* ticket / travel to Berlin *third-class.*
third-rate *a.* 三流の.
thistledown *n.* あざみの冠毛.
thorn-pricked *a.* ちかちかする.
thoroughbred *a.* 純血種の(サラブレッドの). 「*oughfare.*
thoroughfare *n.* 交通: No *thor-*
thoroughgoing *a.* 徹底した: a *thoroughgoing* reform / a *thoroughgoing* scoundrel (rascal).
thoroughpaced *a.* [馬が]よく調練された: a *thoroughpaced* racer.
thought-inspiring *a.* =thought-provoking.
thought-out *a.* 考え抜いた: a *thought-out* plan. 「富んだ.
thought-provoking *a.* 示唆(しさ)に
thought-worn *a.* 考えつかれた.
threadbare *a.* [衣服の]すれきれた; 陳腐な: a *threadbare* excuse (argument).
threadneedle *n.* [子供の]くぐり抜け遊戯.
threadworm *n.* ぎょう虫.
three-bagger *n.* 〖野球〗三塁打 (three-base hit).
three-color *a.* 三(原)色の: *three-color* printing.
three-D, 3-D *a.* 三次元の, 立体の: a *three-D* picture (film).
three-decker *n.* 三層甲板船 (three-deck vessel).
three-legged *n.* 三脚の: a *three-legged* stool.
three-piece *a.* [衣服]三つぞろいの: a *three-piece* suit.
three-piled *a.* 三重の, 三層の.
three-ply *a.* 三枚合わせの.
three-quarter 四分の三の: a *three-quarter* portrait.
throwaway *n.* ビラ, ちらし.
throwback *v.* 投げ返し; 〖映画〗切り返し.
throwoff *n.* 開始: at the *throwoff.*
thumbmark *n.* 指のあと.
thumbnail *n.* 親指のつめ; 極小の: a *thumbnail* sketch.
thumbprint *n.* [親指の]指紋.
thumbstall *n.* 親指のサック.
thumbtack *n.* 《米》画びょう.
thunderbolt *n.* 雷電: It came upon us like a *thunderbolt.*
thunderclap *n.* 雷鳴; 寝耳に水.
thundercloud *n.* [あらしの]雷雲.
thunderhead *n.* 入道雲.
thundershower *n.* 雷雨.
thunderstorm *n.* 雷雨.
thundersquall *n.* 雷雨
thunderstricken, thunderstruck *n.* 雷に打たれた; びっくり仰天した.
ticket-of-leave *n.* 仮出獄の: a *ticket-of-leave* man.
tidbit, titbit *n.* おもしろい豆ニュース; 《米》うまいものの一口.
tidewater *n.* 潮水; 海岸.
tideway *n.* 潮路.
tie-in *a.* だき合せの: *tie-in* sale.
tight-fisted *a.* けちな.
tight-laced *a.* きついコルセットをつけた.
tight-lipped *a.* 口の堅い.
tightrope *n.* [サーカスなどの]張り綱: a *tightrope* dancer.
timberland *n.* 《米》森林地.
timberwork *n.* 木組み.
timberyard *n.* 《英》材木置場.
timecard *n.* [就業時間を示す]タイムカード.
time-expired *a.* [勤務など]満期の: a *time-expired* soldier.
time-honored *a.* 昔ながらの, 由緒ある.
timekeeper *n.* 時計; 作業時間係.
timepiece *n.* 時計 (timekeeper).
timesaving *a.* 時間節約の.
timeserver *n.* ひより見主義者.
timetable *n.* 時刻表.
timework *n.* 時間仕事.
timeworn *a.* 使い古した.
tinman *n.* =tinsmith.
tin-plate *v.* [<tin plate] ブリキめっきにする.
tinsmith *n.* ブリキ職, トタン屋.
tinware *n.* ブリキ細工品.
tinwork *n.* ブリキ細工. **—tinworks** (工場).
tip-off *n.* [競馬などの]内報, 秘密の情報: They got a *tip-off* on the raid. 「pectation.
tiptoe *n.* つま先: on *tiptoe of* ex-
tiptop *n., a.* 絶頂(の); とびきり上等(の). 「seat.
tip-up *a.* 上げ起し式の: a *tip-up*
tired-out *a.* つかれ切った.
titmouse *n.* しじゅうがらの一種.
tittle-tattle *n.* うわさ, ゴシップ.
toadeater *n.* おべっか(人). **—toadeating.**
toadfish *n.* ふぐ.
toadstone *n.* がま石.
toadstool *v.* きのこ, 毒たけ.
to-and-fro *a.* 前後(左右)の: *to-and-fro* motion. 「司会者.
toastmaster *n.* 乾杯を提議する人;
toecap *n.* くつのつま革.
toe-dance *v.* [<toe dance] トーダンスをやる.
toenail *n.* 足指のつめ.
toeshoe *n.* トーダンス用のくつ.
toilworn *a.* つかれ切った. 「所.
tollbooth *n.* 監獄; 道銭取り立て番
tollgate *n.* 道銭取り立て門. *cf.* toll bridge, toll road.
tollhouse *n.* [有料道路の]料金取りたて番所.
tollkeeper *n.* 道銭取り立て人.
tomboy *n.* おてんば娘.
tomcat *n.* 雄ねこ.
tombstone *n.* 墓石.
tomfool *a.* ばか者, とんま. 「倒.
tongue-lashing *n.* 口ぎたない罵
tongue-tie *n., v.* 舌足らず(舌がもつれる). **—tongue-tied.**
tongue-twisted *a.* 舌をかむような(発音).
tongue-wagging *n.* 口のよく回ること. *cf.* wag one's tongue.
toolbox *n.* 道具箱.
toolmaker *n.* 工具製作者.
toolsmith *n.* =toolmaker.
toothache *n.* 歯痛.
toothbrush *n.* 歯ブラシ.
toothcomb *n.* 歯の細かいくし.
toothpaste *n.* ねりはみがき.
toothpick *n.* 小ようじ.
tooth-shaped *a.* 歯型の.
toothwash *n.* 水歯みがき.
topcoat *n.* オーバー. 「な.
top-drawer *a.* 第一位の, 最も重要
top-dress *v.* 敷肥(しきごえ)する; [道路に]砂礫をしく. **—top-dressing.**
top-flight *a.* 一流の: a *top-flight* buriness man.
top-heavy *a.* 頭でっかちの, 不安定な: a *top-heavy* vessel.
top-hole *a.* 《英》飛切り上等の.
topknot *n.* [鳥の]冠毛; [人の]まげ.
toplofty *a.* 《口語》おたかくとまった, 高慢な.
topmast *n.* 〖海〗トップマスト.
topmost *a.* 最高の. 「の.
topnotch *a.* 《米口》一流の, 最高

top-ranking *a.* 最高階級の: *top-ranking* officers.

top-secret *a.* 極秘の: *top-secret* information.

topside *n.* 上側.

topsoil *n., v.* 表土(を除く).

topsy-turvy *ad.* あべこべの, めちゃめちゃの.

torchbearer *n.* たいまつ持ち; 光をかがげる人.

torchlight *n.* たいまつの明り: a *torchlight* procession.

toss-up *n.* [<toss up] [勝負を決める]投げ銭; 五分五分: It's a *toss-up* whether...

touch-and-go *a.* 一触即発の, 不安な: a *touch-and-go* enterprise.

touchback *n.* 〘フートボール〙タッチバック.

touchdown *n.* 〘フートボール〙タッチダウン; 〘空〙短時間の着陸.

touch-last *n.* 鬼ごっこ.

touch-me-not *n.* 〘植〙ほうせん

touchstone *n.* 試金石. └か.

tough-faced *a.* こわおもての.

tough-mascled(-sinewed) *a.* 筋肉隆々とした.

tourist-crammed *a.* 観光客で一

townet *n.* 引き網. └杯の.

towboat *n.* 引き船 (tugboat).

towheaded *n.* [<towhead] うす茶色の髪の. 「rope).

towline *n.* [船の]引き綱 (towing

townhouse *n.* 《英》市庁舎, 市会議事堂 (town hall). ☞ town house ともつづる.

townsfolk, townspeople *n.* 市民, 都会人. ☞ 単数は townsman, townswoman.

towpath *n.* 引き船水路.

towrope *n.* =towline.

toyhouse *n.* おもちゃの家.

toyland *n.* おもちゃの国. *cf.* toytown.

toyshop *n.* おもちゃ屋.

tracklayer *n.* 《米》線路工手. *cf.* 《英》platelayer. 「保線係.

trackman, trackwalker *n.* 《米》

trade-in *n.* [<trade in] 新品購入一部の代金として提供する品物(自動車など).

trade-mark, trademark *n.* 商標. *cf.* trade name.

tradespeople, tradesfolk *n.* 《英》商人. ☞ 単数は tradesman, tradeswoman. 「混み合う.

traffic-congested *a.* 交通頻繁の,

trainboy *n.* 列車の売り子.

train-giddy *a.* 汽車に酔った.

trainload *n.* 一列車分(の貨物).

trainman *n.* 《米》列車の乗務員.

tramcar *n.* 《英》市(都)電.

tramline *n.* 《英》市電の軌道. *cf.* 《米》street railway.

tramroad, tramway *n.* 《米》[鉱山の]トロッコ用軌道.

travel-bent *a.* 旅行好きの.

travel-soiled(-stained) *a.* 旅でよごれた. 「かれた.

travel-tired(-weary) *a.* 旅行でつ

travel-worn *a.* 旅やつれした.

trawlboat *n.* トロール船.

trawlnet *n.* トロール網.

treadboard *n.* 踏板.

treadmill *n.* [奴隷の]踏み車.

treadwheel *n.* 踏み車.

treasure-trove *n.* [地中から]掘り出した宝物. 「茂った.

tree-clad(-covered) *a.* 木の生え

tree-dotted *a.* 立木の点在した: the *tree-dotted* beach.

tree-fringed *a.* 木々のふちどった: a *tree-fringed* lake.

treenail *n.* 木くぎ.

treetop *n.* こずえ.

trencherman *n.* 大食家.

trestlework *n.* 〘土木〙トレスル.

tribesman *n.* 部落民, 蕃民.

trim-edged *n.* ふちを刈った, すそ刈りした. 「の行きとどいた.

trim-hedged *a.* いけがきの手入れ

trolleyman *n.* 《米》市電の乗務員.

troublemaker *n.* ごたごたを起す人.

trouble-shooter *n.* 故障を見つけて修理する人, 修理員; [けんかの]火消し役.

truckload *n.* トラック一台分: a *truckload* of furniture (coal, timber).

truckman *n.* トラックの運転手. *cf.* truck driver. 「忠実な.

true-blue *a.* [<true blue] 誠実な,

trueborn *a.* 生れの正しい; きっ粋の: a *trueborn* New Yorker (Tokyoite).

truebred *a.* 血統の正しい, 育ちの

true-hearted *a.* 忠実な. └よい.

truelove *n.* [<true love] 意中の人, 恋人: a *true-love* knot.

trueman *n.* 忠実な人.

trustworthy *a.* 頼みにする: a *trustworthy* friend.

try-on *n.* [<try on] 《口語》やってみること; 仮縫い. 「興行.

tryout *n.* 《米口》予選; 〘劇〙試験

T-shirt *a.* [<T shirt] 丸首シャツの: the *T-shirt* look.

tube-shaped *a.* 管状の.

tub-thumping *a.* 熱弁を振う.

tuck-in *n.* 《英俗》ごちそう.

tuckshop *n.* 《英俗》売店.

tugboat *n.* 引き船.

tufthunter *n.* おべっか使い. —**tufthunting.**

tumble-down *n.* 今にも倒れそうな, あれはてた: a *tumble-down* shanty.

turfman *n.* 競馬ファン.

turnabout *n.* 方向転換, 転向; 《米》回転木馬. 「所.

turnaround *n.* 転換; [車の]回転場

turnback *n.* 折り返し; ひきょう

turnbuckle *n.* 引締めねじ. └者.

turncoat *n.* 変節者.

turndown *a.* 折りえりの: a *turndown* collar. *opp.* turnup.

turnkey *n.* 看守. 「《英》スト.

turnout *n.* 人出; 出席者; 生産高;

turnover *n.* 転ぷく; [仕事など]転換: the *turnover* of war industry.

turnpike *n.* [有料道路の]料金取立門 (tollgate): a *turnpike* road.

turn-round *n.* [汽船の]寄港.

turnscrew *n.* =screwdriver.

turnstile *n.* 回転木戸.

turntable *n.* 転車台; レコードの回転盤: a phonograph *turntable.*

turnup *n.* 《英》ずぼんの折返し.

turtledove *n.* きじばと.

turtle-neck *a.* [<turtle neck] とっくり首の: a *turtle-neck* sweat-

twice-married *a.* 再婚の. └er.

twice-reviewed *a.* 再検討した.

twice-revised *a.* 改訂した.

twice-told *a.* 二度話された, 陳腐な: a *twice-told* story.

twin-born *a.* 双生の.

twin-screw *a.* 〘海〙双推進機の.

two-bagger *n.* 〘野球〙二塁打 (two-base hit).

twodecker *n.* 二階付きバス(電車). *cf.* double-decker.

two-edged *a.* もろ刃の.

two-faced *a.* 二心ある: a *two-faced* woman.

two-fisted *a.* 《米》強力な: make *two-fisted* effort.

two-handed *a.* 両手(用)の: a *two-handed* saw (sword).

two-master *n.* 二本マストの船.

two-party *a.* 二大政党の: the *two-party* system.

two-piece *a.* 〘服飾〙ツーピースの: *a two-piece* suit.

two-step *n.* 二拍子の曲(ダンス).

two-tongued *a.* 二枚舌の.

two-way *a.* 二路の, 往復の: a *two-way* radio.

typescript *n.* タイプ印書. 「**ting.**

typesetter *n.* 植字工. —**typeset-**

typewriter *n.* タイプライター. —**typewrite, typewritten.**

U

U-boat *n.* [ドイツの] Uボート.

U-bolt *n.* U 字型ボールト.

umbrella-shaped *a.* 雨傘形の, きのこ形の.

underage *a.* [<under age] 未成年の, 未成熟の.

underbred *a.* しつけ(育ち)の悪い.

underbrush *n.* 《米》下ばえ.

underclassman 《米》下級生.

underclothes, underclothing *n.* 下着(類). 「秘密な.

undercover *a.* [<under cover]

undercurrent *n.* 底流, 暗流.

undercut *v.* 下を切取る, [価格を]切下げる: *undercut* prices. 「者.

underdog *v.* 《口語》[人生の]敗残

underdone *a.* 《英》なま焼けの. *opp.* overdone. 「くびる.

underestimate *v.* 安く見積る, 見

underfed *a.* [<underfeed] 食(燃)料不足の: *underfed* children.

undergarment *n.* 下着.

undergo *v.* 経験する, こうむる: *undergo* trials (damages, danger, death). 「生.

undergraduate *n.* [大学の]在学

underground *a.* 地下の: *underground* activities (movement).

undergrowth *n.* 下ばえ. **—undergrown.**

underhand *a.* 下手投げの.

underhanded *a.* 人手の足りない; 不正な.

underlay *v.* …の下に敷く.

underline *v.* 下線を引く; 強調する.

underlying *a.* 下層にある: *the underlying* strata.

undermentioned *a.* 下記の.

undermine *a., v,* [転覆の目的で]…の下を掘る; ひそかに害する: *undermine* one's health.

undernourished *a.* 栄養下良の. **—undernourishment.**

underpaid *a.* [<underpay] 給料の安い.

underpants *n., pl.*《米》下ズボン.

underpass *n.* 地下道.

underproduction *n.* 生産不足. *opp.* overpopulation.

underrate *v.* =underestimate.

undersea *a.* [<under the sea] 海中(底)の. **—underseas.**

undersecretary *n.* [各省の]次官.

undersell *v.* …より安値で売る: *undersell* one's rivals in trade.

undershirt《米》シャツ, はだ着.

underside *n.* 下面, 内面.

undersigned *a.* 下名の: we, the *undersigned,* …

undersized *a.* 小形の.

understaffed *a.* 人員の足りない.

understate *v.* ひかえ目に述べる. **—understatement.**

understudy *n., v.* 代役(のけいこをする), をつとめる.

undertaker *n.* 葬儀屋; 請負人.

undertenant *n.* また借り人.

under-the-counter *a.* 内々の, 不正の.

undertone *n.* 低音; 小声: speak in *undertones.*

undervalue *v.* 安くふむ, みくびる.

underwaist *n.* 胴着下.

underwater *a.* [<under the water] 水中の.

underway *ad.* 進行して: The program is *underway.* ☞ under way ともつづる.

underwear *n.* 下着, シャツ類.

underweight *a.* 重量不足の: an *underweight* boxer.

underwork *v.* 十分働かない(働かせない).

underworld *n.* 下層社会, 暗黒界: *underworld* slang.

underwriter *n.* 保険業者; 株式引受人.

undreamed-of *a.* 信じられない.

unheard-of *a.* 未曾有の.

union-managed *a.* 労組管理の.

unlooked-for *a.* 意外な, 無用の: an *unlooked-for* visiter / *unlooked-for* remarks.

up-and-coming *a.*《米口》進取的な, 見込みのある: *up-and-coming* youngsters (writers).

up-and-down *a.* [<up and down] 高低のある: an *up-and-down* motion.

upborne *a.* [<upbear] 持ち上げた. 支持した.

upbraid *v.* しかる, とがめる.

upbringing *n.* [<bringing up] 教育, しつけ.

upbraid *v.* とがめる, 叱る.

upbuild *v.* [<build up] 建設する.

upcast *a.* [<cast up] 上に向けた: with *upcast* eyes (looks).

upcountry *n., a.*《口語》内地(の), 奥地(の): travel *upcountry* in China.

upend *v.* [<end up] さかさまにする(おく).

upgrade *n.* 登りこう配. *a., ad.* 登りこう配の(になって).

upgrowth *n.* [<grow up] 成長, 発達.

upheaval *n.* [<upheave] 持ちあげ;『地質』隆起.

uphill *a.* 登り坂の; 骨のおれる: go *uphill.*

uphold *v.* 持上げる; 支持する; 元気づける: *uphold* the morale of soldiers.

upholster *v.* [いすを]修繕する: an *upholstered* chair. **—upholsterer, upholstery.**

upkeep *n.* [<keep up] [土地·家屋などの]維持 (maintenance).

upland *n., a.* 高地(の): an *upland* country.

uplift *v.* 持上げる, 高揚する: *uplift* spirits (morale).

upper-bracket *a.* [番付など]上位にある: *upper-bracket* taxpayers.

upper-class *a.* 上流階級の: *upper-class* people.

uppercut *n.*『拳闘』アッパーカット.

uppermost *a., ad.* まっ先の(に), 最上の(に).

up-point *v.* [配給品の]点数を増す. *opp.* down-point.

uprear *v.* 起す; 育てる.

upright *a.* 直立した, まっすぐな, まっ正直な: an *upright* man.

uprise *v.* [太陽が]昇る; 出現する; [暴動を]起す. **—uprising.**

uproar *v.* 大騒ぎ. **—uproarious.**

uproot *v.* 根こぎにする: *uproot* a tree (bad habits).

uprouse *v.* 目を覚まさせる.

upset [<set up] *v.* くつがえす. **—***a.* 混乱した: *upset* a plan (schedule) / The whole town was *upset.*

upshot *n.* 結果, 結局: the *upshot* of the matter is this:…

upside-down *a.* [<upside down] さかさまの.

upstage *ad., a.* 舞台のかみてで(の).

upstairs *ad.* 二階へ.

upstanding *a.* 直立した.

upstart *n.* 成り上り者, 成金.

upstate *n., a.*《米》北部(の): an *upstate* college / *upstate* people.

upstream *ad., a.* 上流に(の): row *upstream. opp.* downstream.

upstroke *n.* 上へ向けて引いた線.

upsurge *n., v.* [感情の]高まり(ること).

upswing *v.* 向上する, 前進する.

uptake *n.* [<take up] 取上げること; 理解力: be quick in the *uptake.*

upthrow *n.* [<throw up] 投上げ.

upthrust *n.* 押上げ, 突き上げ.

up-to-date *a.* [<up to date] 最新の.

uptown *ad., n.* 山手(に). *opp.* downtown.

upturn *v.* [turn up] 上に向ける, 上向になる. **—upturned.**

U-shaped *a.* U字型をした.

U-turn *n.* U字型曲線: make a *U-turn.*

V

vainglory *n.* 強い虚栄心, 虚飾. **—vainglorious.**

vanguard *n.* 前衛. *opp.* rearguard.

vaper-filled *a.* 水蒸気のみちた.

vaper-tight *a.* 水蒸気のもらない.

vase-shaped *a.* 花びん形の.

V-Day *n.* [<Victory Day] 大戦紀念日. ☞ V-E Day と V-J Day がある.

velvet-footed *a.* なめらかな足の; 足音のしない.

velvet-lined *a.* ビロード製の.

vermillion-red *a.* 明るい朱色の.

verse-writer *n.* 詩人, 作詞家.

vest-pocket *a.* 小形の: a *vest-pocket* camera (edition).

veteran-student *n.*《米》除隊兵学生. ☞ vet student ともいう.

viewpoint *n.* 見解: from my *viewpoint.*

vine-covered(-clad) *a.* つるの生えしげった: *vine-covered* walls.

vineyard *n.* ぶどう園.

violet-blue *a.* 紫紺色の.

violet-colored *a.* 紫色の.

voice-valve *n.* 声帯.

vote-getting *a.* 得票の.

V-shaped *a.* V字型をした.

V-sign *n.* [<victory sign] [第二次大戦中の] 勝利の印 (人さし指と中指でV字の形をとった).

W

wage-control *a.* 賃金統制の: the *wage-control* bill.

wage-fund *n.*『労』労銀資本: the *wage-fund* theory.

wageworker *n.* 賃金労働者. *cf.* wage earner.

wagonload *n.* 馬車(トラック)一台分の荷.

waistband *n.*『服飾』ウェーストバンド. *cf.* waist belt.

waistbelt *n.*『服飾』ベルト, バンド.

waistcloth *n.* 腰巻(ふんどしなど).

waistcoat *n.*《英》チョッキ(vest).

waist-deep *a., ad.* 腰まで深い(く).

waistline *n.*『服飾』ウェーストライン.

walkaway *n.* 楽勝.

walkie-talkie *n.* 携帯用無線電話.

walk-on *n.* せりふのない端役.

walkout *n.* [<walk out]《米》スト.

walkover *n.* 無競争の勝利, 楽勝.

walk-up *n.* エレベーターのない安アパート.

wallflower *n.* 《口語》[舞踏会で]相手のないダンサー(女).
wall-newspaper *n.* かべ新聞.
wall-painting *n.* かべ画.
wallpaper *n.* かべ紙.
want-ad *n.* 求職(人)広告.
wardroom *n.* [軍艦の]士官室.
warehouse *n.* 倉庫. **—warehouseman.** 「列室.
wareroom *n.* 商品貯蔵室, 商品陳
warlike *a.* 軍事の, 好戦的な: a *warlike* tribe.
warm-blooded *a.* [<warm blood] 温血の; 熱血の.
warm-hearted *a.* 思いやりのある. *cf.* heart-warming.
warmonger *n.* 戦争挑発者.
warpath *n.* 出征路. 「plane.
warplane *n.* 軍用機. *cf.* battle-
warship *n.* 軍艦. 「try.
wartime *n.* 戦時: *wartime* indus-
warworn *a.* 戦いにつかれた, 戦争であらされた. 「い.
washbasin *n.* 《英》せんたくたら
washboard *n.* せんたく板.
washbowl *n.* 《米》＝washbasin.
washcloth *n.* 手ぬぐい, ふきん.
washday *n.* せんたく日.
washed-out *n.* 色のあせた; 《口語》つかれ切った. 「れた.
washed-up *a.* しくじった, すてら
washerman *n.* せんたく屋(人). *cf.* washerwoman.
washhand *a.* 《英》洗顔用の: a *washhand* basin.
washhouse *n.* せんたく屋.
washout *n.* [<wash out] [土砂などの]流失, 破壊.
washtub *n.* 洗たくおけ.
washwoman *n.*＝washerwoman.
washrag *n.* ＝washcloth.
washroom *n.* 便所.
washstand *n.* 洗面台. 「い.
wasp-waisted *a.* ウェーストの細
wastebasket *n.* くずかご. ☞ wastepaper basket ともいう.
wasteland *n.* 不耕作地, 荒地.
wastepaper *n.* 紙くず: a *wastepaper* basket.
watchboat *n.* 巡ら船.
watchcase *n.* 小型時計のケース.
watchdog *n.* 番犬.
watchmaker *n.* 時計屋(人). **—watchmaking.**
watchman *n.* 番人. 「tower.
watchtower *n.* 望楼. *cf.* clock
watchword *v.* 合い言葉; 標語.
water-borne *a.* 水上輸送の: *water-borne* traffic.
waterbuck *n.* 大かもしか.
water-color[ed] *a.* [<water color] 水彩の.
water-cooled *a.* [<water cooler] 水冷式の.
watercourse *n.* 水流, 水路.
watercraft *n.* 水泳(など); 船.
water-drinker *n.* 鉱泉を飲む人; 禁酒家.
waterfall *n.* 滝. 「る人(器).
waterfinder *n.* 地下水脈を見つけ
waterfowl *n.* 水鳥.
watergate *n.* 水門. ☞ water gate ともつづる. 「sea-girt.
water-girt *a.* 水に囲まれた. *cf.*
waterglass *n.* ガラス; *pl.* 水中をのぞく水めがね. ☞ water glass ともつづる. 「位の.
water-level *a.* [<water level] 水
water-locked(-walled) *a.* 水に閉ざされた, 四面水の.
water-logged *n.* 水びたしの.
waterman *n.* 船頭. 「し模様.
watermark *n.* 水位標; [紙の]すか
watermelon *n.* すいか.
water-power *a.* [<water power] 水力の: *water-power* electricity.
waterproof *a.* 防水の. *n.* 防水服(レーンコートなど).
water-repellent *a.* 水をはじく式の. 「scape.
waterscape *n.* 水景. *cf.* land-
watershed *n.* 川の流域.
watershoot *n.* 排水どい(管); ウオーターシュート.
water-short *a.* 水不足の.
waterside *n., a.* 水辺(の).
water-skiing *n.* 水上スキー. **—water-skier.**
water-soak *v.* 水につける. **—water-soaked.**
watersoluble *a.* 水溶性の.
watertight *a.* 水を通さない: a *watertight* container.
waterway *n.* 水路. *cf.* watercourse.
waterweed *n.* 水草.
waterworks *n.* 上水道.
waterworn *a.* 水の作用で磨滅した: *waterworn* rocks.
watt-hour *n.* 〚電〛ワット時(watt-hr. と略す).
wattmeter *v.* 〚電〛ワット計.
wave-beaten *a.* 波の打ちよせる.
wave-dashed *a.* 波のぶっつかる.
wavemeter *n.* 電波計.
wave-tossed *a.* 波にもまれる: a *wave-tossed* boat.
wave-washed *a.* 波の洗う.
waxwork *n.* ろう細工.
waybill *n.* 乗客名簿; 貨物運送状.
wayfarer *n.* 旅人.
waylay *v.* 待伏せする.
wayside *n., a.* 道ばた(の).
waywise *a.* 道のくわしい.
weak-headed *a.* 低能の.
weak-kneed *a.* 優柔不断の: *weak-kneed* diplomacy. 「ed.
weak-minded *a.* ＝weak-head-
weak-sighted *a.* 視力の弱い.
weather-beaten *a.* 風雨にさらされた: a *weather-beaten* face.
weatherboard *n.* 雨よけ板.
weather-bound *a.* 悪天候のため出港できない.
weathercock *n.* 風見.
weathereye *n.* 天候[観測]眼.
weatherglass *n.* 晴雨計.
weatherman *n.* 気象関係の人.
weatherproof *a., v.* 風雨に耐える(建物など). 「のできた.
weather-stained *a.* 風雨でしみ
weather-strip *v.* [<weather strip] [ドア・窓など]すき間ふさぎをする. 「い.
weather-wise *a.* 天候観測のうま
weatherworn *a.* 風雨でいたんだ.
webfoot *n.* 水かき足. **—webfooted.**
webtoed *a.* 水かき足の.
wedge-shaped *a.* くさび形(V)の.
wedgewise *ad.* くさび形に.
weekday *n.* 平日.
week-end *a.* [<week end] 週末の. ☞ weekend ともつづる. **—week-ender.**
weighbridge *n.* 橋ばかり.
weighhouse *n.* 貨物計量所.
well-advised *a.* 思慮のある.
well-appointed *a.* 十分準備の整った.
well-armed *a.* 十分武装した.
well-balanced *a.* 均整のとれた; 常識のある: a *well-balanced* mind.
well-behaved *a.* 行儀のよい.
well-being *n.* 安寧, 福利.
wellborn *a.* 生れ(しつけ)のよい.
well-bred *a.* 育ち(しつけ)のよい.
well-chosen *a.* 適切な.
well-conducted *a.* 品行のよい.
well-connected *a.* 親戚のよい.
well-content[ed] *a.* 十分満足した.
well-cooked *a.* 料理の上手な.
well-defined *a.* 輪かくのはっきりした.
well-disposed *a.* 気立てのよい.
well-doer *n.* 徳行家. **—well-doing.**
well-done *a.* 《英》[肉が]よく焼けた. *cf.* underdone.
well-dressed *a.* 身なりのよい: a *well-dressed* gentleman.
well-earned *a.* 自力でかち得た.
well-educated *a.* 十分教育を受けた.
well-favored *a.* きりょうのよい.
well-fed *a.* 栄養の十分な, よく肥った.
well-fixed *a.* ＝well-to-do.
well-founded *a.* 事実に立脚した.
well-furnished *a.* 給与の十分な; 設備のない.
well-groomed *a.* [馬・髪など]よく手入れの行きとどいた; りゅうとした身なりの.
well-grounded *a.* 基本訓練を受けた; 正当な理由のある.
well-handled *a.* 能率的な: *well-handled* business work.
wellhead *n.* 水源.
well-informed *a.* 博識の: a *well-informed* man.
well-intentioned *a.* 善意の.
well-judged *a.* 判断の正確な, 機定を得た.
well-kept *a.* 手入れのよい: *well-kept* furniture (clothing).
well-knit *a.* [体格の]がっちりし
well-known *a.* 周知の. 　した.
well-looking *a.* 美ぼうの. *cf.* good-looking.
well-made *a.* できのよい, 釣合い

のよくとれた.
well-mannered *a.* 行儀のよい.
well-meaning *a.* =well-intentioned. **—well-meant.**
well-nigh *ad.* ほとんど全く: *well-nigh* impossible.
well-off *a.* [<well off] 裕福な. *opp.* badly-off.
well-ordered *a.* 秩序のある: a *well-ordered* nation (troop).
well-pleasing *a.* 満足な.
well-preserved *a.* 保存のよい: a *well-preserved* suit (coat).
well-proportioned *a.* 均衡のとれた.
well-read *a.* 博識の: a *well-read* scholar.
well-set *a.* [体格が]がっちりした.
well-spoken *a.* 上品な言葉使いの: She is wise and *well-spoken*.
wellspring *n.* 源泉.
well-suited *a.* ぴったりした.
well-thought-of *a.* 評判のよい.
well-timbered *a.* 樹木の茂った; [体格の]がん丈な.
well-timed *a.* 好機の.
well-to-do *a.* 裕福な: a *well-to-do* farmer.
well-wisher *n.* 人の幸福を祈る人.
well-worn *a.* 使い古した: a *well-worn* quotation (phrase).
Welshman *n.* ウェールス人. *cf.* Welshwoman.
welterweight *n.* 〖拳闘〗ウェルター級の選手.
West-Indian *a.* 西インドの.
wet-blanket v. [<wet blanket] 興をさます, けちをつける.
wet-eared *a.* 乳くさい, 青二才の: a *wet-eared* boy.
whaleboat *n.* [捕鯨の]キャッチャーボート. *cf.* whaler.
whalebone *n.* 鯨のひげ.
whalefin *n.* 〖商〗鯨のひげ.
whaleman *n.* 捕鯨者.
whatnot *n.* [<what not] *n.* 本だな; 《口語》いろんなもの, 何やかや.
wheelbarrow *n.* 手押し車.
wheelhouse *n.* 操舵(だ)室.
wheelman *n.* 自転車乗り(cyclist).
whereabouts *ad.* どの辺に. **—*n.*** 居所, ありか.
whereas *conj.* してみると, ところが.
whereupon *ad.* そこで.
whetstone *n.* と石; 刺激物.
whipcord *n.* むちなわ.
whiplash *n.* むち打ち: He wants a good *whiplash* (うんとなぐってやらなくちゃ).
whippersnapper *n.* つまらない人間, 若僧.
whirlabout *n.*, *a.* 旋回(する).
whirligig *n.* 回転木馬.
whirlpool *n.* うずまき.
whirlwind *n.* 旋風.
whistle-stop *n.* 《米口》中間の小駅.
whitebait *n.* 〖魚〗しらす.
whitebeard *n.* 白ひげの老翁.
whitecap *n.* 白波.
white-collar *a.* 《米口》サラリーマンの: a *white-collar* job.
whitefish *v.* 《米》白ます.
white-handed *a.* [サラリーマンなど]白い手をした; 潔白な.
white-headed *a.* 白髪の.
white-livered *a.* おく病な.
white-slave *a.* [<white slave] 白人醜業婦の: *white slave* traffic.
whitesmith *n.* ブリキ屋(人), トタン屋(人).
whitewash *n.*, *v.* 水しっくい(をぬる); 〖スポーツ〗完敗(させる).
whitewood *n.* 白色の木材; しなの木.
whizz-bang *n.* [砲丸が]ぴゅーずどん.
whodunit *n.* [<who done it] 《米俗》推理小説.
whole-bound *a.* 総革とじの.
whole-hearted *a.* 心をこめた, 心から. **—whole-heartedly.**
whole-hoofed *a.* 〖動〗単蹄の.
whole-length *a.* 全身の: a *whole-length* portrait (statue).
whole-meal *a.* [ふすまを取去らない]粗麦製の: *whole-meal* bread.
wholesale *a.* 卸し売りの. *opp.* retail. **—wholesaler.**
whole-wheat *a.* [ふすまを取去らない]粗麦の: *whole-wheat* flour.
whorehouse *n.* 売春宿, 女郎屋.
whoremaster *n.* 売春婦の客.
wide-awake *n.* 油断(抜け目)のない.
wide-eyed *a.* 目を見開いた, びっくりした.
wide-spread *a.* 普及した, 一般的な.
wildcat *n.* 山猫; 非合法の: a *wildcat* strike.
wild-eyed *a.* 目が怒りにもえた.
wildfire *n.* 鬼火, 野火: spread like *wildfire*.
wildflower *n.* 野花. ☞ wild flower ともつづる.
wildfowl *n.* 野鳥. ☞ wild fowl ともつづる.
wild-goose chase とほうもない企図. *cf.* wild goose.
wildwood *n.* 自然林.
wet-nurse *v.* [<wet nurse] うばとなる, 乳を与える. **—wet-nursing.**
windbag *n.* 《俗》空論をまくしたてる人, 大ぶろしき.
wind-blown *a.* 風に吹きとばされた, 吹きさらしの.
wind-borne *a.* 風で運ばれた.
wind-bound *a.* [船など]風にとじこめられた.
windbreak *n.* 防風林.
windfall *n.* 風で落ちた果物; 思わぬ授かりもの(幸運).
windgauge *n.* 風速(力)計.
winding-up *n.* 結末; 清算.
windmill *n.* 風車.
windowpane *n.* 窓ガラス. *cf.* window glass.
window-shopping *n.* ショーウィンドーを覗いて歩くこと, ひやかし. **—window-shopper.**
windpipe *n.* のどぶえ.
windscreen *n.* =windshield.
wind-shaken *a.* [<wind shake] 風でゆれている(いたんだ).
windshield *n.* [自動車の]風よけガラス.
windstorm 暴風. *cf.* rainstorm.
wind-swept *a.* 吹きさらしの: a *wind-swept* hill.
windtight *a.* 風(空気)の入らない.
windup *n.* 終末, 仕上げ; 〖野球〗[投手の]ワインドアップ.
winebag *n.* 酒袋; 《俗》大酒家.
winebibber *n.* 大酒家. **—winebibbing.**
winebottle *n.* ぶどう酒びん.
winebowl *n.* 飲酒用大杯.
winecup *n.* さかずき.
wineglass *n.* [ぶどう酒用の]グラス.
winegrower *n.* ぶどう園主(醸造家).
wineskin *n.* =winebag.
wing-footed *a.* 足に翼のある, 高速の.
wingspread *n.* [飛行機の]翼長.
winter-beaten *a.* 寒気にあてられた: *winter-beaten* vegetable.
wintertime *n.* 冬季.
wiredancer *n.* ワイヤ渡り芸人.
wiredraw *v.* [金属を延ばして]針金にする; 引延ばす. **—wire-drawing.**
wirehair *n.* ワイヤヘア(小犬の名).
wire-haired *a.* 毛のこわい.
wireman *n.* 架線工夫.
wirephoto *n.* 有線電送写真.
wirepuller *n.* あやつり人形師; 黒幕.
wireworks *n.* 針金工場.
wireworm *n.* 盗聴者; 情報屋.
wire-wove *a.* 金網の; [用紙など]光沢のある.
wisecrack *n.* ぴりっとした冗談, 警句.
wiseman *n.* 賢人. *cf.* wise-woman.
wish-wash *n.* 水っぽい酒(など). **—wish-washy.**
witchcraft *n.* 魔法; 魅力.
withhold *v.* さし控える, 許さない.
withstand *v.* 抗する, たえる.
wolf-call *n.* 《米俗》[女の子への]口笛.
wolfhound *n.* 一種の猟犬.
womenfolk[s] *n.* 婦人たち.
womanhater *n.* 女ぎらい(の男).
womankind *n.* 女性. *cf.* mankind.
womanlike *a.* 女らしい. *cf.* womanish.
woman-suffrage *a.* [<woman suffrage] 婦人参政権の. **—woman-suffragist.**
wonderland *n.* おとぎの国.
wonder-stricken (-struck) *a.* あっけにとられた.
wonderwork *n.* 奇跡. **—wonderworker.**
woodbin *n.* まき入れ.
woodbox *n.* 木箱.
woodchopper *n.* 木こり. ☞ wood chopper ともつづる.
woodchuck *n.* [米国産]モルモット.
woodcraft *n.* 木細工. **—woodcraftsman.**
woodcut *n.* 木版画. *cf.* wood block. **—woodcutter, woodcutting.**

woodenhead *n.* 《口語》間抜け. **—woodenheaded.**
wooden-shoed *a.* [<wooden shoe] 木ぐつをはいた.
woodenware *n.* 木製器具.
woodhouse *n.* まき小屋.
woodjobber *n.* =woodpecker.
woodland *n.*, *v.* 森林地帯(の): *woodland* scenery. **—woodlander.**
woodman *n.* きこり. 「歌.
wood-notes *n.* 鳥の鳴声; 単調な
woodpecker *n.* きつつき.
woodpile *n.* まきの山.
woodprint *n.* =woodcut.
woodshed *n.* まき小屋.
woodsman *n.* 森の住人; 木材切出人夫 (lumberman).
wood-wind *a.* [<wood wind] 木管楽器の.
woodwork *n.* 木細工物. **—woodworker, woodworking.**
woodworm *n.* 木くい虫.
wool-dyed *a.* トップ染めの.
woolgathering *n.*, *a.* 羊毛集め(の); ぼんやり(した), 放心(の).
woolgrower *n.* 牧羊者.
wool-lined *a.* 毛裏の.
woolman *n.* 羊毛商人.
woolpack *n.* 羊毛の俵.
woolsack *n.* 羊毛製の袋.
woolwork *n.* 毛糸のししゅう.
wordbook *n.* 単語集.
wordbuilding *n.* 『文法』造語法 (word formation).
word-finder *n.* 単語集, 辞書.
word-for-word *a.* [<word for word] 逐語の: a *word-for-word* translation.
word-of-mouth *a.* 口頭の. *cf.* by word of mouth.
word-perfect *a.* 『劇』せりふの完全な. 「地口.
wordplay *n.* 語句の争い; しゃれ,
word-stress *n.* 語の強意.
workability *n.* 実行(耕作)可能性.
workaday *a.* 仕事日の, つまらない: in this *workaday* world.
workbag *n.* 仕事袋.
workbasket *n.* 針仕事のかご.
workbench *n.* 仕事台.
workbox *n.* 道具箱, お針の箱.
workday *n.* 平日. *opp.* holiday.
workhand *n.* 働き手, 従業員.
workhouse *n.* 《米》少年感化院; 《英》貧民院.
working-class *a.* 労働階級の.
working-day *a.* =workaday.
workingman *n.* 労働者. *cf.* workingwoman.
workman *n.* 労働者, 職人. *cf.* workwoman. **—workmanship.**
workout *n.* 《米》[競技前の]練習: have a light *workout*.
workpeople *n.* 労働者, 職工. ☞ 単数は workman(-woman).
workplace *n.* 職場.
workroom *n.* 仕事部屋.
workshop *n.* 作業場; 実験室: a radio *workshop*.
work-shy *a.* 仕事ぎらいの.
worktable *n.* 作業台.
work-up *n.* 『印刷』[こめ物が浮き上ってできた]かす.
world-beater *n.* すばらしい人(考え, もの). **—world-beating.**
world-conscious *a.* 世界(の出来事)に関心のある.
worldly-minded *a.* 世俗的な.
worldly-wise *a.* 世故にたけた.
world-weary *a.* 世の中がいやになった.
world-wide *a.* 全世界の: a statesman of *world-wide* fame.
world-wise *a.* =worldly-wise.
world-without-end *a.* 永遠の.
worm-eaten *a.* 虫の食った, 古くさい: *worm-eaten* customs (practices).
wormhole *n.* 虫の害.
worn-out *n.* 使い古した, すれ切れた; つかれきった.
worth-while *n.* 骨折りがいのある: a *worth-while* experiment.
would-be *a.* ひとりよがりの; [いつかは]なるつもりの: a *would-be* poet (novelist).
wound-dressing *n.* 外傷用手当品, ほうたい.
wrinkled-browed *a.* まゆをひそめた. *cf.* wrinkled-cheeked.
wristband *n.* そで口のカフス.
wristwork *n.* 『野球』[打球の]リストワーク.
write-up *n.* [<write up] [新聞などの]書き立て.
wrong-directed *a.* 誤導の.
wrongdoer *n.* 悪事をする人, 加害者. **—wrongdoing.** 「意地の.
wrong-headed *a.* 考え違いの; 片
wrong-minded *a.* 心のねじけた.
wrong-timed *a.* 時期を失した.
wrought-up *a.* 神経が興奮した.
wry-faced *a.* しかめっつらの.
wry-mouthed *a.* 口のゆがんだ.
wryneck *n.* 鳥の名(きつつきの一種).

X

X-ray *v.*, *a.* [<X ray] X 線で調べる: *X-ray* the chest. / *X-ra*[illegible] photograph. / *X-ray* tube. **X-rayed, X-raying.**
X-shaped *a.* X 字型をした.
X-type *a.* X 型の.

Y

yachtsman *n.* ヨット乗り(所有[illegible] *cf.* yachtswoman.
yardman *n.* 『鉄道』構内係.
yardstick *n.* ヤードさお尺.
yarn-dyed *a.* 糸染めの.
yearbook *n.* 年鑑.
yearlong *a.* 年中続いて.
yellowback *n.* 黄表紙本. **—**[illegible] **low-backed** *a.*
yellowbird *n.* 黄鳥.
yellow-breasted *a.* 黄色い胸の. *cf.* yellow-eyed, yellow-legged, yellow-tailed, yellow-throated, etc. 「犬契約.
yellow-dog contract 『労』のら
yellow-green *a.* 黄緑色の.
yesterday *n.* 昨日. *cf.* yestereve, yestermorn.
yo-heave-yo *int.* よいとまけ, えんやらや.
yokefellow *n.* 共働者.
young-manlike *a.* [<young-man] 青年のような. *cf.* young-womanlike.
young-manly *a.* [青年のように] 若々しい. *cf.* young-womanly.
young-looking *a.* 若そうな.
youth-training *n.* 青年訓練: a *youth-training* school. **—youth-trainer.**
Y-shaped *a.* Y 字型をした.
Yuletide *n.* クリスマス季節.

Z

zebrawood *n.* しま材(ニューギニア産).
zero-zero weather 『空』視程ゼロの悪天候(飛行不能の状態).
zigzag *n.*, *a.* Z 字型(の). **—***v.* Z 字型に進む(なる): The path r[illegible] *zigzag*[*ging*] up the hill.
zinc-coated *a.* 亜鉛引きの.
zoneplate *n.* 『光学』同心円回[illegible]